Abréviations utilisées dans ce dictionnaire

GW00547157

weather, meteorology	METEOR	
military, armaments	MIL	
music	MUS	
mythology	MYTH(C	
noun	n	
nautical, maritime	NAUT	
feminine noun	nf	
masculine noun	nm	
masculine or feminine noun	nm ou	
masculine noun, feminine noun	nm, f	
masculine and feminine noun	nmf	
proper noun	npr	nom propre
numeral	num	numéral
offensive	offens	injurieux
officially recognized term	offic	terme officiellement recommandé par l'Académie
oneself	o.s.	
pejorative	pej / péj	péjoratif
personal	pers	personnel
philosophy	PHILO	philosophie
photography	PHOT(O)	photographie
phrase(s)	phr	locution(s)
physics	PHYS	physique
plural	pl	pluriel
politics	POL(IT)	politique
possessive	poss	possessif
past participle	pp	participe passé
prefix	prefix / préf	préfixe
preposition	prep / prép	préposition
present participle	p prés	participe présent
pronoun	pron	pronom
proverb	prov	proverbe
psychology, psychiatry	PSYCH(OL)	psychologie
past tense	pt	passé
something	qqch	quelque chose
someone	qqn	quelqu'un
railways	RAIL	rail
relative	rel	relatif
religion	RELIG	religion
someone, somebody	sb	quelqu'un
school	SCH / SCOL	domaine scolaire, éducation
Scottish English	Scot	anglais écossais
separable	sep	séparable
singular	sg / sing	singulier
slang	sl	argot
sociology	SOCIOL	sociologie
formal	sout	soutenu
something	sthg	quelque chose
subject	subj / suj	sujet
superlative	superl	superlatif
technology, technical	TECH(NOL)	technique, technologie
telecommunications	TELEC / TÉLÉCOM	télécommunications
theatre	THEAT / THÉÂTRE	théâtre
very informal	tfam	très familier
television	TV	télévision
printing, typography	TYPO	typographie
uncountable noun	U	substantif non comptable
British English	UK	anglais britannique
university	UNIV	université
American English	US	anglais américain
usually	usu	habituellement
link verb followed by a predicative adjective or noun	v att	verbe attributif
verb	vb / v	verbe
intransitive verb	vi	verbe intransitif
impersonal verb	v impers	verbe impersonnel
very informal	v inf	très familier
pronominal verb	vp	verbe pronominal
transitive verb	vt	verbe transitif
vulgar, offensive	vulg	vulgaire, susceptible de choquer
zoology	ZOOL	zoologie

COMPACT PLUS DICTIONARY

FRENCH – ENGLISH

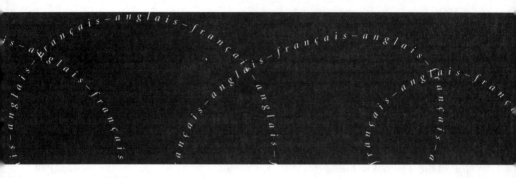

ENGLISH – FRENCH

Hodder Murray
www.hoddereducation.co.uk

LAROUSSE

Orders: please contact Bookpoint Ltd, 130 Milton Park, Abingdon, Oxon OX14 4SB.
Telephone: (44) 01235 827720. Fax: (44) 01235 400454. Lines are open 9.00–5.00, Monday to Saturday, with a 24-hour message answering service. Visit our website at www.hoddereducation.co.uk

© Larousse 2006

First published in 2005 by Larousse

Hodder Murray, an imprint of Hodder Education,
a member of the Hodder Headline Group
338 Euston Road
London NW1 3BH

Larousse
21, rue du Montparnasse
75283 Paris Cedex 06

Impression number 10 9 8 7 6 5 4 3 2 1
Year 2010 2009 2008 2007 2006

All rights reserved. Apart from any use permitted under UK copyright law, no part of this publication may be reproduced or transmitted in any form or by any means, electronic or mechanical, including photocopying and recording, or held within any information storage and retrieval system, without permission in writing from the publisher or under licence from the Copyright Licensing Agency Limited. Further details of such licences (for reprographic reproduction) may be obtained from the Copyright Licensing Agency Limited, 90 Tottenham Court Road, London W1T 4LP.

A catalogue record for this title is available from the British Library

ISBN-10: 0340 915 196
ISBN-13: 978 0340 915 196
Imprimé en Italie par «La Tipografica Varese S.p.A.» Varese en Mars 2006

DICTIONNAIRE COMPACT PLUS

FRANÇAIS – ANGLAIS

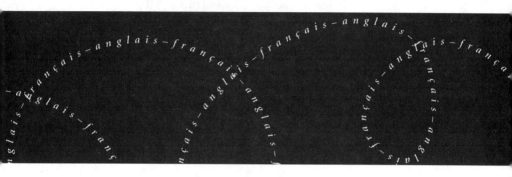

ANGLAIS – FRANÇAIS

Hodder Murray

www.hoddereducation.co.uk

LAROUSSE

Direction éditoriale / Publishing Managers
Ralf Brockmeier, Janice McNeillie

◆

Coordination éditoriale / Project Management
Marc Chabrier, Sinda López

◆

Rédaction / Editors
Sylvain Blanche, Pat Bulhosen, Marie Chochon, Rosalind Combley, Christy Johnson, Sandra Koch, Marie Ollivier-Caudray, Donald Watt

◆

Sécretariat d'édition / Copy preparation
Marie Chochon, Xavier Truchet

◆

Remerciements à / With thanks to
Aurélie Prissette

◆

Informatique éditoriale / Data Management
Dalila Abdelkader, Ivo Kulev

◆

Conception graphique / Layout
Laurence Lebot

◆

Fabrication / Production
Nicolas Perrier

◆

Marketing
Agathe Morel

◆

Composition / Typesetting
APS-Chromostyle

Guide de communication / Communication guide

◆

Protocole typographique / Layout
Jacqueline Bloch

◆

Composition / Typesetting
IGS

Sommaire

Contents

To our readers

This new French dictionary in the *Larousse* range is designed specifically to meet the needs of the intermediate-level user.

Our aim is to meet the criteria that make for quality in dictionaries: comprehensive and up-to-date coverage as well as ease of use and reliability.

Entries have been carefully chosen to provide an accurate and idiomatic reflection of French and English as they are written and spoken today. Special attention has been given to new words and phrases, especially in essential fields such as business, information technology, politics and culture.

Learning a language involves not only learning grammar and vocabulary, but also how to use a word correctly in context. This new dictionary covers thousands of set phrases and examples to help the user recognise the most representative contexts in which a word is used.

As you would expect from a *Larousse* dictionary, the layout is clear and well-structured, making it easy to distinguish between the two languages and find what you're looking for.

The text also reflects the international nature of the two languages: many Swiss, Belgian and Canadian terms are included and American English has been given generous treatment throughout.

Sometimes a translation alone is not enough to render the full meaning of certain words and expressions, many of which have a cultural resonance for which there is no equivalent in the other language. Special emphasis is placed on such 'culture-bound' items, using explanatory glosses and, where possible, giving approximate cultural equivalents in order to make the significance of the term clearer to the non-native speaker. In addition, certain entries are accompanied by boxed cultural notes which provide even fuller information about the significance of a particular institution or concept.

False friends and confusables are highlighted in the text to help the user avoid common translation errors which result from misleading similarities between words in the two languages. For example, "eventually" is not a translation of the French word *eventuellement*. "Day" isn't only translated by *jour*, but also by *journée* when emphasising duration.

In order to help the user when speaking or writing in the foreign language, the dictionary includes a number of usage notes at the foot of the page. These show typical expressions and structures used in everyday situations, such as expressing opinions, giving advice, or making a complaint, and also in more specific contexts, such as during a job interview, or when chairing a meeting.

The emphasis on communication is developed further in a 64-page communication guide. Here you'll find clear and practical help with communicating in French by letter, e-mail, telephone and even text-messaging.

Our aim with this new *College* dictionary is to offer you a new educational and communication tool that goes beyond the traditional bilingual dictionary. We're sure that this dictionary will be invaluable to you in your dealings with the French-speaking world, and will help you on your way to mastering the French language.

The Publisher

Au lecteur

Ce nouveau dictionnaire appartenant à la gamme *Larousse* des dictionnaires d'anglais s'adresse à vous, lycéen ou angliciste, qui souhaitez progresser dans la maîtrise de l'anglais.

Conçu de manière à répondre au mieux aux critères de qualité d'un dictionnaire utilisé pour les études, le *Compact Plus* allie richesse et actualité, convivialité de la présentation et pédagogie.

Les mots et expressions qui y figurent offrent une image fidèle de l'anglais contemporain tel qu'il est étudié en classe. Un soin tout particulier a été accordé à la sélection des nouveaux mots, notamment dans les domaines essentiels de l'informatique, de la politique et de la société.

La maîtrise de l'anglais passe bien sûr par l'apprentissage des mots, mais aussi par leur utilisation correcte en contexte. Ainsi, ce nouveau dictionnaire présente des milliers et des milliers de constructions lexicales et d'exemples pour vous familiariser avec les contextes les plus représentatifs des mots.

Une typographie claire et contrastée, et non dépourvue d'une certaine élégance, vous permet, à chaque instant, de distinguer les deux langues en vous offrant ainsi le confort de lecture que vous êtes en droit d'exiger d'un dictionnaire *Larousse*.

L'anglais américain a fait l'objet d'un traitement privilégié non seulement dans les mots, sens et expressions retenus du côté anglais, mais également du côté français, puisque nous vous proposons pour chaque terme une traduction britannique et américaine lorsque c'est nécessaire.

Partant du principe qu'un dictionnaire est aussi un pont entre les cultures et les sociétés, nous avons voulu privilégier cette dimension en vous aidant à mieux comprendre les civilisations anglo-saxonnes. De nombreuses gloses et notes culturelles interviennent pour expliquer le terme lorsque sa traduction est impossible ou insuffisante, lorsqu'il faut aller au-delà des mots.

Un traitement particulier des faux amis et des paronymes vous permettra de contourner les écueils qui résultent de l'identité ou de la parenté graphique des mots : « lecture » n'est pas la traduction du mot anglais *lecture*. « Étranger » ne se traduit pas seulement par *stranger* mais également, et même plus souvent par *foreigner*. Le texte que nous vous présentons est très riche en conseils de ce type afin de vous permettre de mieux saisir les subtilités de la langue de Shakespeare.

Pour répondre à vos besoins spécifiques, notamment en ce qui concerne la communication à l'écrit comme à l'oral, le dictionnaire *Compact Plus* propose des fenêtres regroupant autour d'un certain nombre de thèmes tels que l'approbation, le remerciement, la comparaison, etc. des phrases adaptées à des situations typiques. Celles-ci viennent ainsi enrichir l'information lexicale contenue dans les entrées correspondantes et vous permettent de varier et de rendre plus idiomatique votre expression en anglais.

L'axe de communication déjà bien présent dans les colonnes du dictionnaire est prolongé et amplifié par un véritable guide de communication de 64 pages en supplément. Vous y trouverez des réponses claires et pratiques aux problèmes de communication rencontrés dans vos échanges avec des personnes anglophones. Des conseils supplémentaires vous aident à déjouer les pièges de la langue anglaise.

Vous offrir un nouvel outil pédagogique et de communication qui va au-delà d'un simple dictionnaire bilingue, tel est le but que nous nous sommes fixé avec le nouveau *Compact Plus*. Nous sommes convaincus que cet ouvrage vous accompagnera fidèlement dans vos échanges avec le monde anglo-saxon et vous aidera à avancer très vite dans la maîtrise de l'anglais.

L'Éditeur

Comment utiliser ce dictionnaire

mot d'entrée
headword

transcription phonétique dans l'alphabet phonétique international
pronunciation shown in International Phonetic Alphabet

signalisation précise des sens et du contexte
meaning and context clearly labelled

cuire [98] [kɥir] ■ **vt 1.** [viande, œuf] to cook ▸ **cuire à feu doux** *ou* **petit feu** to simmer ▸ **cuire à gros bouillons** to boil hard **2.** [tarte, gâteau] to bake **3.** [briques, poterie] to fire.
■ **vi 1.** [viande, œuf] to cook / [tarte, gâteau] to bake ▸ **faire cuire qqch** to cook/bake sthg **2.** *fig* [personne] to roast, to be boiling ▸ **il vous en cuira!** *fig* you'll suffer (for it)!, you'll regret it!
◆ ***à cuire*** **loc adj : chocolat à cuire** cooking chocolate ▸ **pommes à cuire** cooking apples.

numéros d'homographes
homograph numbers

indicateurs de domaine
specialist field labels

corner[1] [3] [kɔrne] ■ **vi** [sirène] to blare (out).
■ **vt** [page] to turn down the corner of.
corner[2] [kɔrnɛr] **nm** FOOTBALL corner (kick).

introduit une phrase d'exemple, une construction ou une expression figée
introduces an illustrative example, construction or fixed phrase

niveau de langue familier
informal register

gâteau, x [gato] **nm** cake ▸ **gâteau d'anniversaire** birthday cake ▸ **gâteau de miel** honeycomb ▸ **gâteau sec** biscuit *UK*, cookie *US* ▸ **c'est du gâteau** *fam* it's a piece of cake.

les *faux-amis* indiquent au lecteur les erreurs à éviter
false friends warn the user of common translation problems

éventuellement [evɑ̃tɥɛlmɑ̃] **adv** possibly.

FALSE FRIENDS / FAUX AMIS
éventuellement

Eventually is not a translation of the French word *éventuellement*. Eventually is translated by *finalement*.
▸ **Eventually, I decided to give up / *J'ai finalement décidé d'abandonner***

numéro qui renvoie aux tables de conjugaison
cross-reference number to French verb tables

introduit une sous-entrée
introduces a sub-entry

restaurer [3] [restɔre] **vt** to restore.
◆ ***se restaurer*** **vp** to have something to eat.

forme féminine
feminine form

niveau de langue
register labels

radin, e [radɛ̃, in] *fam péj* ■ **adj** stingy.
■ **nm, f** skinflint.

Comment utiliser ce dictionnaire

numéros indiquant les divisions sémantiques à l'intérieur d'une catégorie grammaticale

numbered sense divisions within a grammatical category

les *paronymes* indiquent au lecteur les erreurs à éviter

confusables warn the user of common translation problems

expérience [ɛksperjɑ̃s] **nf** **1.** [pratique] experience ▸ **avoir de l'expérience** to have experience, to be experienced **2.** [essai] experiment ▸ **faire l'expérience de qqch** to experience *ou* try sthg ▸ **tenter l'expérience** to try.

CONFUSABLE / PARONYME

expérience

Ce mot se traduit de deux façons différentes selon que l'on parle d'une expérience de type scientifique : *experiment*, ou bien d'un ensemble de connaissances, de la pratique d'une activité : *experience*

constructions grammaticales

grammatical constructions

édredon [edrədɔ̃] **nm** eiderdown *UK*, comforter *US*.

variantes britanniques et américaines

British and American variants given

explication donnée sous forme de glose lorsqu'il n'y a pas de traduction directe

explanatory gloss provided where there is no direct translation

ASSEDIC, ***Assedic*** [asedik] (abr de ***Association pour l'emploi dans l'industrie et le commerce***) **nfpl** *French unemployment insurance scheme* ▸ **toucher les ASSEDIC** to get unemployment benefit *UK ou* welfare *US*.

sigles et abréviations

abbreviations and acronyms

renvoi de la forme irrégulière au verbe à l'infinitif

cross-reference from irregular verb forms to main verb

sois ➤ ***être***.

RTT [ɛrtete] (abr de ***réduction du temps de travail***) ■ **nf** (statutory) reduction in working hours.
■ **nm** (extra) day off *(as a result of shorter working hours)* ▸ **poser/prendre un RTT** to book *ou* claim a day's holiday, to take a day off *US*.

CULTURE

RTT

Meant to combat relatively high unemployment, the law mandating a 35-hour working week – commonly called **les trente-cinq heures** – has not exactly met its goal, but it does give salaried workers more leisure time. Most now have **journées de RTT** (short for **réduction du temps de travail**) once or twice a month. Some companies have kept the 39-hour working week, however, and the **Medef**, France's main employers' organization, is trying to get the law abolished.

précisions sur la traduction

extra information that clarifies the translation

introduit une nouvelle catégorie grammaticale

introduces a new grammatical category

information de nature culturelle ou encyclopédique

information of a cultural or encylopedic nature

How to use the dictionary

headword

mot d'entrée

pronunciation shown in International Phonetic Alphabet

transcription phonétique dans l'alphabet phonétique international

introduces a new grammatical category

introduit une nouvelle catégorie grammaticale

ask [ɑːsk] ■ **vt 1.** [gen] demander ▸ **to ask sb sthg** demander qqch à qqn ▸ **he asked me my name** il m'a demandé mon nom ▸ **she asked him about his job** elle lui a posé des questions sur son travail ▸ **to ask sb for sthg** demander qqch à qqn ▸ **to ask sb to do sthg** demander à qqn de faire qqch ▸ **he asked them a favour** il leur a demandé un service ▸ **if you ask me...** si tu veux mon avis... **2.** [put - question] poser **3.** COMM **: to ask a price** demander un prix ▸ **what are you asking for it?** combien en voulez-vous *OR* demandez-vous? **4.** [invite] inviter.
■ **vi** demander.
◆ ***ask after*** **vt insep** demander des nouvelles de.
◆ ***ask for*** **vt insep 1.** [person] demander à voir **2.** [thing] demander.

introduces an illustrative example, construction or fixed phrase

introduit une phrase d'exemple, une construction ou une expression figée

specialist field labels

indicateurs de domaine

introduces a sub-entry

introduit une sous-entrée

homograph numbers

numéros d'homographes

bass [1] [beɪs] ■ **adj** bas (basse).
■ **n 1.** [singer] basse *f* **2.** [double bass] contrebasse *f* **3.** = ***bass guitar***.
bass [2] [bæs] (pl **bass** *OR* **-es** [-iːz]) **n** [fish] perche *f*.

register labels

niveau de langue

feminine form

forme féminine

false friends warn the user of common translation problems

les *faux-amis* indiquent au lecteur les erreurs à éviter

patron ['peɪtrən] **n 1.** [of arts] mécène *m*, protecteur *m*, -trice *f* **2.** *fml* [customer] client *m*, -e *f*.

FALSE FRIENDS / FAUX AMIS

patron

Patron n'est pas la traduction du mot anglais *patron*. Patron se traduit par *owner*.
▸ Il connaît bien le patron du bar / *He knows the owner of the bar well*

British and American variants given

variantes britanniques et américaines

elasticated *UK* [ɪ'læstɪkeɪtɪd], ***elasticized*** *US* [ɪ'læstɪsaɪzd] **adj** élastique.

hyphenated compound words and compound words that have their own distinct meaning treated as headwords

les mots composés s'écrivant avec un trait d'union ou considérés comme des unités de sens autonomes font l'objet d'entrées indépendantes

computer-aided, computer-assisted **adj** assisté(e) par ordinateur.
computer-aided design **n** conception *f* assistée par ordinateur.
computer crime **n** fraude *f* informatique.

How to use the dictionary

meaning and context clearly labelled

signalisation précise des sens et du contexte

poisonous ['pɔɪznəs] **adj 1.** [fumes] toxique **2.** [plant] vénéneux(euse) **3.** [snake] venimeux(euse) **4.** *fig* [rumours, influence] pernicieux(euse).

CONFUSABLE / PARONYME

poisonous

When translating **poisonous**, note that ***vénéneux*** and ***venimeux*** are not interchangeable. ***Vénéneux*** applies to plants, whereas ***venimeux*** applies to animals.

numbered sense divisions within a grammatical category

numéros indiquant les divisions sémantiques à l'intérieur d'une catégorie grammaticale

confusables warn the user of common translation problems

les *paronymes* indiquent au lecteur les erreurs à éviter

abbreviations and acronyms

sigles et abréviations

explanatory gloss provided where there is no direct translation

explication donnée sous forme de glose lorsqu'il n'y a pas de traduction directe

DEA (abbr of ***Drug Enforcement Administration***) **n** *agence américaine de lutte contre la drogue*.

cross-reference from irregular verb forms to main verb

renvoi des formes irrégulières des verbes à l'infinitif

had (*weak form* [həd], *strong form* [hæd]) **pt & pp** ➤ ***have***.

extra information on pronunciation

information supplémentaire sur la prononciation

shadow cabinet **n** *UK* cabinet *m* fantôme.

CULTURE

Shadow Cabinet

Au Royaume-Uni, le « Cabinet fantôme » est une sorte de « contre-gouvernement » de rechange, formé à l'avance par le principal parti d'opposition en cas de chute du pouvoir en place. Il est constitué de politiciens qui occupent les mêmes fonctions et qui bénéficient des mêmes privilèges que leurs homologues du « Cabinet » réel, c'est à dire les ministres entourant le Premier ministre : il y a ainsi des ministres des Finances, de la Défense ou des Affaires étrangères « fantômes ». Au Parlement, ils occupent une aile à la Chambre des communes qui fait face aux membres du parti majoritaire au pouvoir.

information of a cultural or encylopedic nature

information de nature culturelle ou encyclopédique

irregular comparatives and superlatives given

comparatifs et superlatifs des adjectifs donnés

contracted verb forms given with cross-references to full forms

renvoi des formes contractées des verbes aux formes complètes

good [gʊd] **adj** (comp **better**, superl **best**).

she's [ʃi:z] = ***she is***, ***she has***.

TRADEMARKS

Words considered to be trademarks have been designated in this dictionary by the symbol ®. However, neither the presence nor the absence of this symbol should be regarded as affecting the legal status of any trademark.

LES NOMS DE MARQUE

Les noms de marque sont désignés dans ce dictionnaire par le symbole ®. Néanmoins, ni ce symbole ni son absence éventuelle ne peuvent être considérés comme susceptibles d'avoir une incidence quelconque sur le statut légal d'une marque.

A NOTE ON ENGLISH COMPOUNDS

As in most modern dictionaries, we give lexicalized compounds (i.e. nouns consisting of more than one word) the same prominence as simplex headwords. This means that compounds that are considered as independent units of meaning appear as entries in their own right.

LES MOTS COMPOSÉS ANGLAIS

À l'instar de la plupart des dictionnaires actuels, nous accordons aux mots composés lexicalisés (c'est-à-dire aux substantifs composés de plus d'un mot) la même importance qu'aux mots simples. Ainsi, les composés anglais considérés comme des unités de sens autonomes font l'objet d'une entrée à part entière.

FRENCH VERBS

French verbs have a number (from [1] to [116]) which refers to the conjugation table given at the back of the dictionary. This number is not repeated for reflexive verbs when these appear as sub-entries.

LES VERBES FRANÇAIS

Les verbes français sont suivis d'une numérotation (de [1] à [116]) qui renvoie aux tableaux de conjugaison présentés à la fin de l'ouvrage. Ce chiffre n'est pas répété après les verbes pronominaux lorsque ceux-ci sont présentés en sous-entrées.

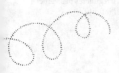

Liste des encadrés / List of boxes

LES NOTES CULTURELLES

La liste ci-dessous donne les titres des notes culturelles figurant dans la partie anglais-français du dictionnaire. Celles-ci apparaissent dans des encadrés à la fin des entrées auxquelles elles sont rattachées.

Auld Alliance
Backbencher
Bank of England
Bank Holiday
Caucus
Checks and Balances
Chequebook Journalism (UK), Checkbook Journalism (US)
Congress
Constitution
Credit Rating
Devolution
Downing Street
Entente Cordiale
Federal Reserve
Financial Year (UK), Fiscal Year (US)
Fleet Street
Fort Knox
Fourth of July
-gate
Green Card
Holidays
House of Commons
House of Lords
House of Representatives
Impeachment
International Trade Administration
Ivy League
Labor Day
Lawyer
Medicare/Medicaid
Minimum Wage
NAFTA
New Deal
NHS
NI (National Insurance)
Outsourcing
Oxbridge
Pension
Pentagon
Pledge of Allegiance
Primaries
Private Education
Retirement Age
SAT
Senate
September 11 & Ground Zero
Shadow Cabinet
Special Relationship
Spin
State Education
Super Bowl
Thanksgiving
United Kingdom
US Open
Wasp
White House
Wimbledon
Working Hours
World Series
Yankee

CULTURAL NOTES

Below is a list of the cultural notes about France and French-speaking countries in this dictionary. They appear immediately after the entry to which they belong.

L'Académie française
Année fiscale/ Année budgétaire
Arrondissement
L'Assemblée nationale
Bac +
Bande dessinée
Banlieue
La Banque centrale européenne
La Bastille
Belgicisme
La Bibliothèque nationale de France
Charges
Chômage
Classes préparatoires
Collège
Comité d'entreprise
Conseil général et conseil régional
Cotisations
Département
DOM-TOM
L'Élysée
Plan d'épargne
Fête
La Fête de la musique
La fonction publique
Francophonie
Grande école
Helvétisme
Île-de-France
Impôts
Le Journal officiel
Lois
Lycée
Mai 68
Matignon
Mutuelle
Plan
Pot
Préavis de licenciement
Presse régionale/ nationale
Quai
Quatorze juillet
Le Québec
Région
La rentrée
Retraite
La Révolution française
Rive droite, Rive gauche
RMI
Tirer les rois
Roland-Garros
RTT
Sécurité sociale
Le seizième
Le Sénat
Taxe foncière/Taxe d'habitation
Le Tour de France
TVA
Verlan
Vouvoyer

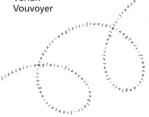

LES MODULES « USAGE »

Les modules « usage » offrent des exemples de tournures à employer lorsque l'on veut s'exprimer en anglais dans une situation donnée. Ils apparaissent au bas de la page comprenant l'entrée à laquelle ils sont rattachés et commencent par « Comment exprimer . . . » :

Comment exprimer ...

l'accord
que l'on n'aime pas quelqu'un
la réponse à une annonce
la certitude
la comparaison
la compassion
que l'on a compris/que l'on n'a pas compris
la condition
une demande de confirmation
les conseils
le début d'une conversation
ses craintes
que l'on n'aime pas quelque chose [« dégoûts »]
les demandes
le désaccord
la désapprobation

Comment exprimer ...

ses encouragements à quelqu'un
lors d'un entretien d'embauche
les excuses
l'explication
les félicitations
l'incertitude
l'indifférence
l'indignation
l'interdiction
les invitations
les menaces
l'obligation
l'opinion
les ordres
la permission
la persuasion
les plaintes

Comment exprimer ...

la préférence
les présentations
les propositions
que l'on donne raison à quelqu'un
le refus
des regrets
les remerciements
la prise de rendez-vous
un résumé de ses idées
que l'on dirige une réunion
au revoir
les souhaits
un changement de sujet
la supposition
la surprise
que l'on donne tort à quelqu'un
les vœux

◆

USAGE NOTES

The usage notes give typical examples of ways in which you can express yourself in French in a particular situation or context. They appear at the bottom of the page containing the entry to which they belong and are entitled "How to . . .":

How to ...

reply to an advertisement
ask for and give advice
express agreement
apologize
express certainty
express comparison
complain
concede a point
confirm
congratulate someone
make conversation
correct somebody
express disagreement
express disapproval
express dislikes
express encouragement
ask for and give explanations
express fear

How to ...

say goodbye
express greetings
express indifference
express indignation
express oneself in a job interview
introduce oneself and other people
invite somebody to do something
express likes
arrange to meet somebody
chair a meeting
express obligation
offer to do something
express opinions
give orders
ask for permission

How to ...

express persuasion
express preferences
express prohibition
express refusal
express regret
make a request
change the subject
make a suggestion
summarize
express supposition
express surprise
express sympathy
express thanks
make threats
express uncertainty
say you have or haven't understood
express wishes

LES FAUX-AMIS

Les encadrés sur les faux amis de la partie anglais-français du dictionnaire sont présentés sous forme d'avertissement. Ils expliquent au lecteur francophone les erreurs de traduction à éviter et donnent des exemples d'emploi en contexte ainsi que la traduction correcte.

achievement	comprehensive	formidable	lecture	regard
actual	consistent	genial	library	resume
actually	demand	genteel	patron	sensible
advertisement	entertain	hazard	pretend	stage
agenda	eventually	jolly	proper	surname
appeal	fabric	journey	recipient	sympathetic

◆

FALSE FRIENDS

The false friends boxes on the French side of the dictionary offer a warning to the English user on how to avoid common translation mistakes when translating into English. They also give contextualisation of the false friend as well as its translation into French.

achever	course	hasard	location	regarder
actuel	décevoir	inhabité	misère	résumer
actuellement	décidé	injure	mondain	sensible
comédien	délai	journée	photographe	stage
compréhensive	demande	lecture	prétendre	surnom
couramment	éventuellement	librairie	propre	sympathique

◆

LES PARONYMES

Les encadrés sur les paronymes de la partie français-anglais du dictionnaire indiquent au lecteur francophone les erreurs à éviter lorsqu'il doit s'exprimer en anglais ou traduire vers l'anglais.

alternatif	compréhensible	fatigant	maison	relations
campagne	économique	féminin	ombre	satisfaisant
certitude	électrique	histoire	particulier	sécurité
civil	endormi	historique	politique	sensuel
classique	étranger	humain	prix	seul
comique	expérience	magique	se rappeler	vivant

◆

CONFUSABLES

The "confusables" boxes on the English side of the dictionary offer a warning to the English user on how to avoid common translation mistakes when translating into or speaking in French.

attentive	cold	fork	original	rock
ball	confidence	interrogation	partial	romantic
before	consume	know	poisonous	shell
bench	day	land	preparation	take
brain	devotion	language	reconcile	towards
bring	evening	material	replace	year

Transcription phonétique

Voyelles anglaises

[ɪ] pit, big, rid
[e] pet, tend
[æ] pat, bag, mad
[ʌ] putt, cut
[ɒ] pot, log
[ʊ] put, full
[ə] mother, suppose
[iː] bean, weed
[ɑː] barn, car, laugh
[ɔː] born, lawn
[uː] loop, loose
[ɜː] burn, learn, bird

Diphtongues

[eɪ] bay, late, great
[aɪ] buy, light, aisle
[ɔɪ] boy, foil
[əʊ] no, road, blow
[aʊ] now, shout, town
[ɪə] peer, fierce
[eə] pair, bear, share
[ʊə] poor, sure, tour

Semi-voyelles

[j] you, spaniel
[w] wet, why, twin

Consonnes

[p] pop, people
[b] bottle, bib
[t] train, tip
[d] dog, did
[k] come, kitchen
[g] gag, great
[tʃ] chain, wretched
[dʒ] jig, fridge
[f] fib, physical
[v] vine, livid
[θ] think, fifth
[ð] this, with
[s] seal, peace
[z] zip, his
[ʃ] sheep, machine
[ʒ] usual, measure
[h] how, perhaps
[m] metal, comb
[n] night, dinner
[ŋ] sung, parking
[l] little, help
[r] right, carry

◆

NOTES SUR LA TRANSCRIPTION PHONÉTIQUE

Anglais-Français

1. Accents primaire et secondaire
Les symboles [ˈ] et [ˌ] indiquent respectivement un accent primaire et un accent secondaire sur la syllabe suivante.

2. Prononciation du 'r' final
Le symbole [ʳ] indique que le 'r' final d'un mot anglais ne se prononce que lorsqu'il forme une liaison avec la voyelle du mot suivant ; le 'r' final est presque toujours prononcé en anglais américain.

3. Anglais britannique et américain
Les différences de prononciation entre l'anglais britannique et l'anglais américain ne sont signalées que lorsqu'elles sortent du cadre de règles générales préétablies. Le 'o' de **dog**, par exemple, est généralement plus allongé en anglais américain, et ne bénéficie pas d'une seconde transcription phonétique. En revanche, des mots comme **schedule**, **clerk**, **cliché**, etc. dont la prononciation est moins évidente, font l'objet de deux transcriptions phonétiques.

4. Mots ayant deux prononciations
Nous avons choisi de ne donner que la prononciation la plus courante du mot, sauf dans les cas où une variante est particulièrement fréquente, comme par exemple le mot **kilometre** [ˈkɪləmiːtəʳ, kɪˈlɒmɪtəʳ].

5. Les formes accentuées et atones
La prononciation de certains mots monosyllabiques anglais varie selon le degré d'emphase qu'ils ont dans la phrase ; **the**, par exemple, se prononce [ðiː] en position accentuée, [ðə] en position atone, et [ðɪ] devant une voyelle. Ces informations sont présentées de la manière suivante dans le dictionnaire : **the** [weak form [ðə], before vowel [ðɪ], strong form [ðiː].

Français-Anglais

1. Le symbole ['] représente le 'h aspiré' français, par exemple **hachis** ['aʃi].

2. Comme le veut la tendance actuelle, nous ne faisons pas de distinction entre le 'a' de **pâte** et celui de **patte,** tous deux transcrits [a].

3. Prononciation du 'e' muet
Lorsque le 'e' peut ne pas être prononcé dans le discours continu, il a été mis entre parenthèses, comme par exemple pour le mot **cheval** [ʃ(ə)val].

Phonetic transcription

French vowels

[i]	fille, île
[e]	pays, année
[ɛ]	bec, aime
[a]	lac, papillon
[o]	drôle, aube
[ɔ]	hotte, automne
[u]	outil, goût
[y]	usage, lune
[ø]	aveu, jeu
[œ]	peuple, bœuf
[ə]	le, je

Nasal vowels

[ɛ̃]	limbe, main
[ɑ̃]	champ, ennui
[ɔ̃]	ongle, mon
[œ̃]	parfum, brun

Semi-vowels

[j]	yeux, lieu
[w]	ouest, oui
[ɥ]	lui, nuit

Consonants

[p]	prendre, grippe
[b]	bateau, rosbif
[t]	théâtre, temps
[d]	dalle, ronde
[k]	coq, quatre
[g]	garder, épilogue
[f]	physique, fort
[v]	voir, rive
[s]	cela, savant
[z]	fraise, zéro
[ʃ]	charrue, schéma
[ʒ]	rouge, jabot
[m]	mât, drame
[n]	nager, trône
[ɲ]	agneau, peigner
[l]	halle, lit
[r]	arracher, sabre

◆

NOTES ON PHONETIC TRANSCRIPTION

French-English

1. The symbol ['] has been used to represent the French 'h aspiré', e.g. **hachis** ['aʃi].

2. We have followed the modern tendency not to distinguish between the 'a' in **pâte** and the 'a' in **patte**. Both are represented in the text by the phonetic symbol [a].

3. Internal schwa
In cases where the schwa [ə] is likely to be ignored in connected speech but retained in the citation form, the [ə] has been shown in brackets, e.g. **cheval** [ʃ(ə)val].

English-French

1. Primary and secondary stress
The symbol [ˈ] indicates that the following syllable carries primary stress and the symbol [ˌ] that the following syllable carries secondary stress.

2. Pronunciation of final 'r'
The symbol [ʳ] in English phonetics indicates that the final 'r' is pronounced only when followed by a word beginning with a vowel. Note that it is nearly always pronounced in American English.

3. British and American English
Differences between British and American pronunciation have not been shown where the pronunciation can be predicted by a standard set of rules, for example where the 'o' in **dog** is lengthened in American English. However, phonetics have been shown for the more unpredictable cases of **schedule, clerk, cliché** etc.

4. Alternative pronunciations
Our approach being primarily functional rather than descriptive, we have avoided giving variant pronunciations unless both variants are met with equal frequency, e.g. **kilometre** [ˈkɪləmiːtəʳ, kɪləmɪːtəʳ].

5. Strong and weak forms
The pronunciation of certain monosyllabic words varies according to their prominence in a sentence, e.g. **the** when stressed is pronounced [ðiː]; when unstressed, [ðə] and before a vowel [ðɪ]. This information is presented in the text as follows: **the** [weak form [ðə], before vowel [ðɪ], strong form [ðiː]].

a [1], ***A*** [a] **nm inv** a, A ▸ **prouver par a + b** to prove conclusively ▸ **de A à Z** from A to Z.
◆ ***A*** **1.** abr de ***anticyclone*** **2.** (abr écrite de ***ampère***) A, amp **3.** (abr écrite de ***autoroute***) M *UK*.

a [2] **1.** [conjugaison] ➤ ***avoir*** **2.** [unité de mesure] (abr écrite de ***are***) a.

à [a] *(contraction de "à + le" =* **au***, contraction de à + les =* **aux***)* **prép 1.** [introduisant un complément d'objet indirect] to ▸ **parler à qqn** to speak to sb ▸ **donner qqch à qqn** to give sthg to sb, to give sb sthg ▸ **penser à qqch** to think about sthg ▸ **l'appartenance à un parti** membership of *UK* ***ou*** in *US* a party
2. [introduisant un complément de lieu - situation] at, in, on / [- direction] to ▸ **être à la maison/au bureau** to be at home/at the office ▸ **il habite à Paris/à la campagne** he lives in Paris/in the country ▸ **il vit au Pérou** he lives in Peru ▸ **aller à Paris/à la campagne/au Pérou** to go to Paris/to the country/to Peru ▸ **un voyage à Londres/aux Seychelles** a journey to London/to the Seychelles ▸ **c'est au rez-de-chaussée** it's on the ground floor ▸ **à ma droite** on ***ou*** to my right
3. [introduisant un complément de temps] **: à onze heures** at eleven o'clock ▸ **au mois de février** in the month of February ▸ **à lundi!** see you (on) Monday! ▸ **à plus tard!** see you later! ▸ **de huit à dix heures** from eight to ten o'clock ▸ **se situer à une heure/à 10 kilomètres de l'aéroport** to be situated an hour/10 kilometres (away) from the airport ▸ **à ma naissance** when I was born ▸ **au XVIIe siècle** in the 17th century
4. [introduisant un complément de manière, de moyen] **: à haute voix** out loud, aloud ▸ **rire aux éclats** to roar with laughter ▸ **agir à son gré** to do as one pleases ▸ **acheter à crédit** to buy on credit ▸ **à pied/cheval** on foot/horseback
5. [indiquant une caractéristique] with ▸ **une fille aux cheveux longs** a girl with long hair ▸ **l'homme à l'imperméable** the man with the raincoat
6. [introduisant un chiffre] **: ils sont venus à dix** ten of them came ▸ **un livre à 10 euros** a 10-euro book, a book costing 10 euros ▸ **la vitesse est limitée à 50 km à l'heure** the speed limit is 50 km per ***ou*** an hour ▸ **un groupe de 10 à 12 personnes** a group of 10 to 12 people, a group of between 10 and 12 people ▸ **nous travaillons à sept dans la même pièce** there are seven of us working in the same room ▸ **deux à deux** two by two
7. [marquant l'appartenance] **: c'est à moi/toi/lui/elle** it's mine/yours/his/hers ▸ **ce vélo est à ma soeur** this bike is my sister's ***ou*** belongs to my sister ▸ **une amie à moi** a friend of mine
8. [introduisant le but] **: coupe à champagne** champagne goblet ▸ **le courrier à poster** the mail to be posted ▸ **appartement à vendre/louer** flat for sale/to let
9. [introduisant l'attribution] **: je suis à vous dans une minute** I'll be with you in a minute
10. [indiquant la cause ou la conséquence] **: on l'a distribué à sa demande** it was given out at his request ▸ **je l'ai reconnu à sa voix/démarche** I recognized him by his voice/walk
11. [suivi de l'infinitif] **: la somme est à régler avant le 10** the full amount has to ***ou*** must be paid by the 10th.

AB [1] (abr écrite de ***assez bien***) fair grade (as assessment of schoolwork), ≃ B-.

AB [2] (abr écrite de ***agriculture biologique***) *food label guaranteeing that a product is made from at least 95% organic ingredients (100% in the case of a single ingredient).*

abaisser [4] [abese] **vt 1.** [rideau, voile] to lower / [levier, manette] to push ***ou*** pull down **2.** [diminuer] to reduce, to lower **3.** *sout* [avilir] to debase.
◆ ***s'abaisser*** **vp 1.** [descendre - rideau] to fall, to come down / [- terrain] to fall away **2.** [s'humilier] to demean o.s. ▸ **s'abaisser à faire qqch** to lower o.s. to do sthg.

abandon [abɑ̃dɔ̃] **nm 1.** [désertion, délaissement] desertion ▸ **à l'abandon** [jardin, maison] neglected, in a state of neglect **2.** [renonciation] abandoning, giving up **3.** [cession] renunciation, giving up ▸ **faire abandon de qqch (au profit de qqn)** to make sthg over (to sb) **4.** [nonchalance, confiance] abandon.

abandonné, e [abɑ̃dɔne] **adj** [mine, exploitation] disused / [village] deserted / [maison, voiture, enfant, animal] abandoned.

abandonner [3] [abɑ̃dɔne] **vt 1.** [quitter - femme, enfants] to abandon, to desert / [- voiture, propriété] to abandon ▸ **abandonner son poste** to desert one's post **2.** [renoncer à] to give up, to abandon **3.** [se retirer de - course,

concours] to withdraw from **4.** [céder] **: abandonner qqch à qqn** to leave sthg to sb, to leave sb sthg.
◆ ***s'abandonner*** **vp 1.** [se laisser aller] **: s'abandonner à qqch** to give o.s. up to sthg **2.** [s'épancher] to pour out one's feelings.

abasourdi, ***e*** [abazurdi] **adj** stunned.

abasourdir [32] [abazurdir] **vt** to stun.

abat-jour [abaʒur] **nm inv** lampshade.

abats [aba] **nmpl** [d'animal] offal *(U)* / [de volaille] giblets.

abattage [abataʒ] **nm** [d'arbre] felling.

abattement [abatmɑ̃] **nm 1.** [faiblesse physique] weakness **2.** [désespoir] dejection **3.** [déduction] reduction ▸ **abattement fiscal** tax allowance *UK*, tax exemption *US*.

abattis [abati] **nmpl** giblets.

abattoir [abatwar] **nm** abattoir *UK*, slaughterhouse.

abattre [83] [abatr] **vt 1.** [faire tomber - mur] to knock down / [- arbre] to cut down, to fell / [- avion] to bring down **2.** [tuer - gén] to kill / [- dans un abattoir] to slaughter **3.** [épuiser] to wear out / [démoraliser] to demoralize.
◆ ***s'abattre*** **vp : s'abattre (sur)** [toit, arbre] to crash down (on) / [pluie] to beat down (on) / [avion, rapaces] to swoop down (on) / [insectes, maladie, fléau] to descend (on).

abattu, ***e*** [abaty] ■ **pp** ➤ ***abattre***.
■ **adj 1.** [déprimé] demoralized, dejected **2.** [affaibli] very weak.

abbaye [abei] **nf** abbey.

abbé [abe] **nm 1.** [prêtre] priest **2.** [de couvent] abbot.

abc [abese] **nm** basics *pl*.

abcès [apsɛ] **nm** abscess ▸ **crever l'abcès** *fig* to make a clean breast of things.

abdication [abdikasjɔ̃] **nf** abdication.

abdiquer [3] [abdike] ■ **vt 1.** [renoncer à] to renounce **2.** [suj: roi] to abdicate.
■ **vi 1.** [roi] to abdicate **2.** [renoncer] to give up.

abdomen [abdɔmɛn] **nm** abdomen.

abdominal, ***e***, ***aux*** [abdɔminal, o] **adj** abdominal.
◆ ***abdominaux*** **nmpl 1.** [muscles] abdominal *ou* stomach muscles **2.** [exercices] **: faire des abdominaux** to do stomach exercises.

abdos [abdo] **nmpl 1.** [muscles] abs, stomach muscles **2.** [exercices] stomach exercises, abs (exercises) ▸ **faire des abdos** to do abs *ou* stomach exercises.

abécédaire [abesedɛr] **nm** ABC *(book)*.

abeille [abɛj] **nf** bee.

aberrant, ***e*** [abɛrɑ̃, ɑ̃t] **adj** absurd.

aberration [abɛrasjɔ̃] **nf** aberration.

abhorrer [3] [abɔre] **vt** *sout* to abhor.

abîme [abim] **nm** abyss, gulf.

abîmer [3] [abime] **vt** [détériorer - objet] to damage / [- partie du corps, vue] to ruin.
◆ ***s'abîmer*** **vp 1.** [gén] to be damaged / [fruits] to go bad **2.** *fig* [personne] **: s'abîmer dans** [lecture] to bury o.s. in / [pensées] to lose o.s. in.

abject, ***e*** [abʒɛkt] **adj** despicable, contemptible.

abjurer [3] [abʒyre] **vt** RELIG to renounce.

ablatif [ablatif] **nm** ablative.

ablation [ablasjɔ̃] **nf** MÉD removal.

ablutions [ablysjɔ̃] **nfpl : faire ses ablutions** to perform one's ablutions.

abnégation [abnegasjɔ̃] **nf** selflessness.

aboie, ***aboies*** ➤ ***aboyer***.

aboiement [abwamɑ̃] **nm** bark, barking *(U)*.

abois [abwa] **nmpl : être aux abois** *fig* to be in dire straits.

abolir [32] [abɔlir] **vt** to abolish.

abolition [abɔlisjɔ̃] **nf** abolition.

abominable [abɔminabl] **adj** appalling, awful.

abominablement [abɔminabləmɑ̃] **adv 1.** [très mal] abominably **2.** [extrêmement] awfully.

abomination [abɔminasjɔ̃] **nf** abomination.

abondamment [abɔ̃damɑ̃] **adv 1.** [beaucoup] plentifully **2.** [largement] extensively.

abondance [abɔ̃dɑ̃s] **nf 1.** [profusion] abundance ▸ **en abondance** in abundance **2.** [opulence] affluence ▸ **vivre dans l'abondance** to live in affluence.

abondant, ***e*** [abɔ̃dɑ̃, ɑ̃t] **adj** [gén] plentiful / [végétation, chevelure] luxuriant / [pluie] heavy.

abonder [3] [abɔ̃de] **vi** to abound, to be abundant ▸ **abonder en qqch** to be rich in sthg ▸ **abonder dans le sens de qqn** to be entirely of sb's opinion.

abonné, ***e*** [abɔne] **nm, f 1.** [à un journal, à une chaîne de télé] subscriber / [à un théâtre] season-ticket holder **2.** [à un service public] consumer.

abonnement [abɔnmɑ̃] **nm 1.** [à un journal, à une chaîne de télé] subscription / [à un théâtre] season ticket **2.** [au téléphone] rental / [au gaz, à l'électricité] standing charge.

abonner [3] [abɔne] ◆ ***s'abonner*** **vp : s'abonner à qqch** [journal, chaîne de télé] to subscribe to sthg, to take out a subscription to sthg / [service public] to get connected to sthg / [théâtre] to buy a season ticket for sthg.

abord [abɔr] **nm : être d'un abord facile/difficile** to be very/not very approachable ▸ **au premier abord, de prime abord** at first sight ▸ **dès l'abord** from the outset.
◆ ***abords*** **nmpl** [gén] surrounding area *sg* / [de ville] outskirts.
◆ ***d'abord*** **loc adv 1.** [en premier lieu] first **2.** [avant tout] **: (tout) d'abord** first (of all), in the first place.

abordable [abɔrdabl] **adj** [lieu] accessible / [personne] approachable / [de prix modéré] affordable.

abordage [abɔrdaʒ] **nm** boarding.

aborder [3] [abɔrde] ■ **vi** to land.
■ **vt 1.** [personne, lieu] to approach **2.** [question] to tackle.

aborigène [abɔriʒɛn] **adj** aboriginal.
◆ ***Aborigène*** **nmf** (Australian) aborigine.

abouti, ***e*** [abuti] **adj 1.** [projet, démarche] successful **2.** [œuvre] accomplished.

aboutir [32] [abutir] **vi 1.** [chemin] **: aboutir à/dans** to end at/in **2.** [négociation] to be successful ▸ **aboutir à qqch** to result in sthg.

aboutissement [abutismɑ̃] **nm** outcome.

aboyer [13] [abwaje] **vi** to bark.

abracadabrant, e [abrakadabrɑ̃, ɑ̃t] **adj** preposterous.

abrasif, ive [abrazif, iv] **adj** abrasive.
◆ ***abrasif*** **nm** abrasive.

abrégé, e [abreʒe] **adj** abridged.
◆ ***abrégé*** **nm** résumé, summary ▸ **faire un abrégé de qqch** [texte] to summarize sthg ▸ **en abrégé** [mot, phrase] in abbreviated form / [écrire] in brief.

abréger [22] [abreʒe] **vt** [visite, réunion] to cut short / [discours] to shorten / [mot] to abbreviate.

abreuver [5] [abrœve] **vt** [animal] to water ▸ **abreuver qqn de** *fig* to shower sb with.
◆ ***s'abreuver*** **vp** to drink.

abreuvoir [abrœvwar] **nm** [lieu] watering place / [installation] drinking trough.

abréviation [abrevjasjɔ̃] **nf** abbreviation.

abri [abri] **nm** shelter ▸ **être à l'abri** to be sheltered ▸ **mettre sa fortune à l'abri dans le pétrole** to invest one's money safely in oil ▸ **se mettre à l'abri** to shelter, to take shelter ▸ **abri antiatomique** nuclear fallout shelter ▸ **abri de jardin** garden shed ▸ **abri à vélos** bicycle stand.
◆ ***à l'abri de*** **loc prép 1.** [pluie] sheltered from / [chaleur, obus] shielded from / [regards] hidden from **2.** *fig* safe from ▸ **à l'abri des contrôles** safe from checks ▸ **nos économies nous mettront à l'abri de la misère** our savings will shield us against poverty *ou* will protect us from hardship ▸ **personne n'est à l'abri d'une erreur** anyone can make a mistake.

Abribus® [abribys] **nm** bus shelter.

abricot [abriko] **nm & adj inv** apricot.

abricotier [abrikɔtje] **nm** apricot tree.

abriter [3] [abrite] **vt 1.** [protéger] **: abriter qqn/qqch (de)** to shelter sb/sthg (from) **2.** [héberger] to accommodate.
◆ ***s'abriter*** **v + prep : s'abriter (de)** to shelter (from).

abroger [17] [abrɔʒe] **vt** to repeal.

abrupt, e [abrypt] **adj 1.** [raide] steep **2.** [rude] abrupt, brusque.

abruti, e [abryti] *fam* ■ **adj** moronic.
■ **nm, f** moron.

abrutir [32] [abrytir] **vt 1.** [abêtir] **: abrutir qqn** to deaden sb's mind **2.** [accabler] **: abrutir qqn de travail** to work sb into the ground **3.** [étourdir] to daze.
◆ ***s'abrutir*** **vp 1.** [s'épuiser] **: s'abrutir de travail** to work o.s. into the ground **2.** [s'abêtir] to become moronic.

abrutissant, e [abrytisɑ̃, ɑ̃t] **adj 1.** [bruit, travail] stupefying **2.** [jeu, feuilleton] moronic.

abrutissement [abrytismɑ̃] **nm 1.** [épuisement] exhaustion **2.** [intellectuel] mindless state.

ABS (abr de ***Antiblockiersystem***) **nm** ABS.

abscisse [apsis] **nf** abscissa.

absence [apsɑ̃s] **nf 1.** [de personne] absence ▸ **en l'absence de** in the absence of **2.** [carence] lack.

absent, e [apsɑ̃, ɑ̃t] ■ **adj 1.** [personne] **: absent (de)** [gén] away (from) / [pour maladie] absent (from) **2.** [regard, air] vacant, absent **3.** [manquant] lacking.
■ **nm, f** absentee.

absentéisme [apsɑ̃teism] **nm** absenteeism.

absenter [3] [apsɑ̃te] ◆ ***s'absenter*** **vp : s'absenter (de la pièce)** to leave (the room).

abside [apsid] **nf** apse.

absinthe [apsɛ̃t] **nf** [plante] wormwood / [boisson] absinth.

absolu, e [apsɔly] **adj** [gén] absolute / [décision, jugement] uncompromising.
◆ ***absolu*** **nm : l'absolu** the Absolute ▸ **dans l'absolu** out of context.

absolument [apsɔlymɑ̃] **adv** absolutely.

absolution [apsɔlysjɔ̃] **nf** absolution.

absolutisme [apsɔlytism] **nm** absolutism.

absorbant, e [apsɔrbɑ̃, ɑ̃t] **adj 1.** [matière] absorbent **2.** [occupation] absorbing.

absorber [3] [apsɔrbe] **vt 1.** [gén] to absorb **2.** [manger] to take **3.** [entreprise] to take over.
◆ ***s'absorber*** **vp : s'absorber dans qqch** to get *ou* become absorbed in sthg.

absorption [apsɔrpsjɔ̃] **nf 1.** [gén] absorption **2.** ÉCON takeover.

abstenir [40] [apstənir] ◆ ***s'abstenir*** **vp 1.** [ne rien faire] **: s'abstenir (de qqch/de faire qqch)** to refrain (from sthg/from doing sthg) **2.** [ne pas voter] to abstain.

abstention [apstɑ̃sjɔ̃] **nf** abstention.

abstentionnisme [apstɑ̃sjɔnism] **nm** abstaining.

abstenu, e [apstəny] **pp** ➤ ***abstenir***.

abstiendrai, abstiendras ➤ ***abstenir***.

abstinence [apstinɑ̃s] **nf** abstinence ▸ **faire abstinence** to refrain from eating meat.

abstraction [apstraksjɔ̃] **nf** abstraction ▸ **faire abstraction de** to disregard.

abstrait, e [apstrɛ, ɛt] **adj** abstract.
◆ ***abstrait*** **nm : l'abstrait** the abstract.

absurde [apsyrd] ■ **adj** absurd.
■ **nm : l'absurde** the absurd ▸ **raisonnement par l'absurde** reductio ad absurdum.

absurdité [apsyrdite] **nf** absurdity ▸ **dire des absurdités** to talk nonsense *(U)*.

abus [aby] **nm** abuse ▸ **abus de confiance** breach of trust ▸ **abus de droit** POLIT abuse of privilege ▸ **abus de pouvoir** abuse of power.

abuser [3] [abyze] ■ **vi 1.** [dépasser les bornes] to go too far **2.** [user] **: abuser de** [autorité, pouvoir] to overstep the bounds of / [femme] to take advantage of / [temps] to take up too much of ▸ **abuser de ses forces** to overexert o.s.
■ **vt** *sout* to mislead.
◆ ***s'abuser*** **vp : s'abuser sur** to delude o.s. about.

abusif, ive [abyzif, iv] **adj 1.** [excessif] excessive **2.** [fautif] improper.

AC (abr de ***appellation contrôlée***) **nf** *government certification guaranteeing the quality of a French wine.*

acabit [akabi] **nm : du même acabit** *péj* of the same type.

acacia [akasja] **nm** acacia.

académicien, enne [akademisjɛ̃, ɛn] **nm, f** academician / [de l'Académie française] member of the French Academy.

académie [akademi] **nf 1.** SCOL & UNIV ≃ regional education authority *UK*, ≃ school district *US* **2.** [institut] academy ▸ **l'Académie française** the French Academy *(learned society of leading men and women of letters)* ▸ **l'Académie Goncourt** *literary society whose members choose the winner of the Prix Goncourt.*

CULTURE

L'Académie française

Founded in 1635 by Cardinal Richelieu, this learned society, consisting mostly of writers, is considered the highest authority on the French language. Its 40 members, often called **les Immortels** or simply **les Quarante**, are chosen for life. Appointment to the **Académie** is often considered a supreme honour – in fact, elections are subject to the French president's approval. The **Académie** awards numerous literary prizes, but its main task is an authoritative dictionary covering definitions, proper and improper word usage, and common grammar problems. The latest complete edition, published in 1992, is accessible online; so is part of the ninth edition, the first volume of which appeared in 1994.

académique [akademik] **adj 1.** UNIV academic **2.** [conventionnel] conventional.

acadien, enne [akadjɛ̃, ɛn] **adj** Acadian.
◆ ***Acadien, enne*** **nm, f** Acadian.
◆ ***acadien*** **nm** LING Acadian.

acajou [akaʒu] **nm & adj inv** mahogany.

acariâtre [akarjatr] **adj** bad-tempered, cantankerous.

acarien [akarjɛ̃] **nm** [gén] acarid / [de poussière] dust mite.

accablant, e [akablɑ̃, ɑ̃t] **adj 1.** [soleil, chaleur] oppressive **2.** [preuve, témoignage] overwhelming.

accabler [3] [akable] **vt 1.** [surcharger] **: accabler qqn de** [travail] to overwhelm sb with ▸ **accabler qqn d'injures** to shower sb with abuse **2.** [accuser] to condemn.

accalmie [akalmi] **nf** *litt & fig* lull.

accaparer [3] [akapare] **vt** to monopolize ▸ **son travail l'accapare** his work takes up all his time.
◆ ***s'accaparer*** **vp : s'accaparer qqch** to seize sthg.

accédant, e [aksedɑ̃, ɑ̃t] **nm, f : un accédant à la propriété** a new homeowner.

accéder [18] [aksede] ◆ ***accéder à*** **vt 1.** [pénétrer dans] to reach, to get to **2.** [parvenir à] to attain **3.** [consentir à] to comply with.

accélérateur [akseleratœr] **nm** accelerator.

accélération [akselerasjɔ̃] **nf** [de voiture, machine] acceleration / [de projet] speeding up.

accéléré [akselere] **nm** CINÉ accelerated motion.
◆ ***en accéléré*** **loc adj** CINÉ [TV] speeded-up, accelerated.

accélérer [18] [akselere] ■ **vt** to accelerate, to speed up ▸ **accélérer le pas** to quicken one's pace ▸ **accélérer le mouvement** *fam* to get things moving.
■ **vi** AUTO to accelerate.
◆ ***s'accélérer*** **vpi** [pouls, cœur] to beat faster ▸ **son débit s'accélère** he's talking faster and faster.

accent [aksɑ̃] **nm 1.** [prononciation] accent ▸ **avoir un accent** to speak with *ou* to have an accent ▸ **elle a un très bon accent** her accent is very good **2.** [signe graphique] accent ▸ **accent aigu/grave/circonflexe** acute/grave/circumflex (accent) **3.** [intonation] tone ▸ **accent tonique** stress ▸ **mettre l'accent sur** *litt* to stress / *fig* to stress, to emphasize.

accentuation [aksɑ̃tɥasjɔ̃] **nf 1.** [à l'écrit] accenting / [en parlant] stress **2.** [intensification] intensification.

accentuer [7] [aksɑ̃tɥe] **vt 1.** [insister sur, souligner] to emphasize, to accentuate **2.** [intensifier] to intensify **3.** [à l'écrit] to put the accents on / [en parlant] to stress.
◆ ***s'accentuer*** **vp** to become more pronounced.

acceptable [aksɛptabl] **adj** acceptable.

acceptation [aksɛptasjɔ̃] **nf** acceptance.

accepter [4] [aksɛpte] **vt** to accept ▸ **acceptez-vous les cartes de crédit?** do you take credit cards? ▸ **accepter de faire qqch** to agree to do sthg ▸ **accepter que** *(+ subjonctif)* **: accepter que qqn fasse qqch** to agree to sb doing sthg ▸ **j'accepte qu'il vienne** I agree to him coming ▸ **elle accepte qu'il lui parle** she puts up with him talking to her ▸ **je n'accepte pas qu'il me parle ainsi** I won't have him talking to me like that.
◆ ***s'accepter*** **vp** *(emploi réfléchi)* to accept o.s. ▸ **je me trouvais trop grosse, maintenant je m'accepte telle que je suis** I used to think of myself as too fat; now I've learned to live with the way I am.

acception [aksɛpsjɔ̃] **nf** sense.

accès [aksɛ] **nm 1.** [entrée] entry ▸ **avoir/donner accès à** to have/to give access to ▸ **'accès interdit'** 'no entry' ▸ **'accès réservé aux riverains'** 'residents only'
2. [voie d'entrée] entrance
3. [abord] **: être d'un accès facile/difficile** [personne] to be approachable/unapproachable / [livre] to be easy/difficult (to read)
4. [crise] bout ▸ **accès de colère** fit of anger
5. INFORM **: accès à distance** remote access ▸ **accès commuté** dial-up access ▸ **accès non autorisé** unauthorized access
6. FIN **: à accès immédiat** instant-access ; **compte à accès immédiat** instant-access account.

accessible [aksesibl] **adj 1.** [lieu, livre] accessible / [personne] approachable / [prix, équipement] affordable **2.** [sensible] **: accessible à** susceptible to.

accession [aksɛsjɔ̃] **nf : accession à** [trône, présidence] accession to / [indépendance] attainment of.

accessit [aksesit] **nm** ≃ certificate of merit *UK*, ≃ Honourable Mention *US*.

accessoire [akseswar] ■ **nm** **1.** [gén] accessory **2.** [de théâtre, cinéma] prop.
■ **adj** secondary.

accessoirement [akseswarmɑ̃] **adv** if need be.

accident [aksidɑ̃] **nm** accident ▸ **par accident** by chance, by accident ▸ **accident de parcours** hiccup ▸ **accident de la route/de voiture/du travail** road/car/industrial accident ▸ **accident de terrain** bump.

accidenté, e [aksidɑ̃te] ■ **adj** **1.** [terrain, surface] uneven **2.** [voiture] damaged **3.** [vie] eventful.
■ **nm, f** *(gén pl)* **: accidenté de la route** accident victim.

accidentel, elle [aksidɑ̃tɛl] **adj** accidental.

accidentellement [aksidɑ̃tɛlmɑ̃] **adv** [rencontrer] by chance, accidentally / [mourir] in an accident.

acclamation [aklamasjɔ̃] **nf** *(gén pl)* cheers *pl*, cheering *(U)*.

acclamer [3] [aklame] **vt** to cheer.

acclimatation [aklimatasjɔ̃] **nf** acclimatization, acclimation *US*.

acclimater [3] [aklimate] **vt** to acclimatize, to acclimate *US* / *fig* to introduce.
◆ ***s'acclimater*** **vp : s'acclimater à** to become acclimatized *ou* acclimated *US* to.

accointances [akwɛ̃tɑ̃s] **nfpl : avoir des accointances dans/avec** *péj* to have contacts in/with.

accolade [akɔlad] **nf** **1.** TYPO brace **2.** [embrassade] embrace ▸ **donner l'accolade à qqn** to embrace sb.

accoler [3] [akɔle] **vt** **1.** [par accolade] to bracket together **2.** [adjoindre] **: accoler qqch à** to add sthg to.

accommodant, e [akɔmɔdɑ̃, ɑ̃t] **adj** obliging.

accommodement [akɔmɔdmɑ̃] **nm** compromise.

accommoder [3] [akɔmɔde] **vt** **1.** CULIN to prepare **2.** [mettre en accord] **: accommoder qqch à** to adapt sthg to.
◆ ***s'accommoder*** **vp : s'accommoder de** to put up with ▸ **s'accommoder à** to adapt to.

accompagnateur, trice [akɔ̃paɲatœr, tris] **nm, f** **1.** MUS accompanist **2.** [guide] guide.

accompagnement [akɔ̃paɲmɑ̃] **nm** **1.** MUS accompaniment **2.** CULIN side dish.

accompagner [3] [akɔ̃paɲe] **vt** **1.** [personne] to go with, to accompany ▸ **accompagner qqn à l'aéroport** [gén] to go to the airport with sb / [en voiture] to take sb to the airport **2.** [agrémenter] **: accompagner qqch de** to accompany sthg with ▸ **elle accompagna sa réponse d'un sourire** she answered with a smile **3.** [compléter] to go with ▸ **un échantillon de parfum accompagne tout achat** a sample of perfume comes with every purchase ▸ **un plat accompagné de vin blanc** a dish served with white wine **4.** MUS to accompany ▸ **accompagner qqn au piano/à la guitare** to accompany sb on the piano/guitar.

accompli, e [akɔ̃pli] **adj** accomplished.

accomplir [32] [akɔ̃plir] **vt** to carry out.
◆ ***s'accomplir*** **vp** to come about.

accomplissement [akɔ̃plismɑ̃] **nm** [d'apprentissage] completion / [de travail] fulfilment *UK*, fulfillment *US*.

accord [akɔr] **nm** **1.** [gén] agreement ▸ **conclure un accord avec** to come to an agreement with ▸ **en accord avec** in harmony with ▸ **d'un commun accord** with one accord ▸ **accord salarial** wage settlement
2. COMM & ÉCON **: accord à l'amiable** out-of-court settlement, mutual agreement ▸ **accord commercial** trade agreement ▸ **accord de crédit** credit agreement ▸ **accord d'entreprise** *ou* **d'établissement** collective agreement ▸ **accord de licence** licensing agreement ▸ **en accord avec notre politique commerciale** in line with *ou* in keeping with our business policy ▸ **en accord avec le chef de service, nous avons décidé que...** together with the head of department, we have decided that
3. [harmonie] harmony ▸ **vivre en parfait accord** to live in perfect harmony
4. LING agreement, concord ▸ **accord en genre/nombre** gender/number agreement
5. MUS chord ▸ **accord parfait** triad *ou* common chord
6. [acceptation] approval ▸ **donner son accord à qqch** to approve sthg
7. POLIT **: accord bilatéral** bilateral agreement ▸ **accord de libre-échange** free-trade agreement ▸ **accord de paix** peace agreement.
◆ ***d'accord*** ■ **loc adv** OK, all right.
■ **loc adj : être d'accord (avec)** to agree (with) ▸ **(je ne suis) pas d'accord !** [je refuse] no (way)! / [c'est faux] I disagree! ▸ **tomber** *ou* **se mettre d'accord** to come to an agreement, to agree.

accordéon [akɔrdeɔ̃] **nm** accordion ▸ **avoir les chaussettes en accordéon** to have one's socks down around one's ankles.

accorder [3] [akɔrde] **vt** **1.** [donner] **: accorder qqch à qqn** to grant sb sthg ▸ **accorder toute sa confiance à qqn** to give sb one's complete trust **2.** [attribuer] **: accorder qqch à qqch** to accord sthg to sthg ▸ **accorder de l'importance à** to attach importance to **3.** [harmoniser] to match **4.** GRAMM **: accorder qqch avec qqch** to make sthg agree with sthg ▸ **accorder le verbe avec le sujet** to

COMMENT EXPRIMER...
l'accord

I quite agree / Je suis tout à fait d'accord
It's true / C'est vrai
You're right / Vous avez raison
I couldn't agree (with you) more / Je suis entièrement de votre avis
Absolutely / Absolument !
I think so too / C'est aussi mon avis
That's just what I was thinking / C'est exactement ce que je pensais
That's fine *OR* OK by me / Pas de problème
That sounds like a good idea / Ça semble être une bonne idée
I don't see why not / Pourquoi pas ?

make the verb agree with the subject **5.** MUS to tune ▸ **les musiciens accordent leurs instruments** [avant un concert] the players are tuning up.
◆ ***s'accorder*** ■ vp **1.** [gén] : **s'accorder (pour faire qqch)** to agree (to do sthg) ▸ **ils se sont accordés pour baisser leurs prix** they agreed among themselves that they would drop their prices ▸ **s'accorder à faire qqch** to be unanimous in doing sthg ▸ **tous s'accordent à dire que...** they all agree *ou* concur that... **2.** [être assorti] to match ▸ **ce qu'il dit ne s'accorde pas avec sa personnalité** he's saying things which are out of character **3.** GRAMM to agree ▸ **s'accorder en genre avec** to agree in gender with.
■ **vpt : s'accorder quelques jours de repos** to take a few days off.

accordeur [akɔrdœr] **nm** tuner.

accoster [3] [akɔste] ■ **vt 1.** NAUT to come alongside **2.** [personne] to accost.
■ **vi** NAUT to dock.

accotement [akɔtmɑ̃] **nm** [de route] shoulder ▸ **accotement stabilisé** hard shoulder *UK*, shoulder *US* ▸ **accotement non stabilisé** soft verge *UK*, soft shoulder *US*.

accouchement [akuʃmɑ̃] **nm** childbirth ▸ **accouchement sans douleur** natural childbirth ▸ **accouchement sous X** *a woman's right to anonymity in childbirth.*

accoucher [3] [akuʃe] **vi : accoucher (de)** to give birth (to).

accouder [3] [akude] ◆ ***s'accouder*** **vp** to lean on one's elbows ▸ **s'accouder à** to lean one's elbows on.

accoudoir [akudwar] **nm** armrest.

accouplement [akupləmɑ̃] **nm** mating, coupling.

accoupler [3] [akuple] **vt 1.** AGRIC [pour le trait] to yoke *ou* to couple together **2.** ZOOL to mate.
◆ ***s'accoupler*** **vpi** [animaux] to mate.

accourir [45] [akurir] **vi** to run up, to rush up.

accours, ***accourt*** ➤ ***accourir***.

accouru, ***e*** [akury] **pp** ➤ ***accourir***.

accoutré, ***e*** [akutre] **adj** *péj* : **être bizarrement accoutré** to be strangely got up.

accoutrement [akutrəmɑ̃] **nm** *péj* getup.

accoutrer [3] [akutre] ◆ ***s'accoutrer*** **vp** *péj* : **s'accoutrer bizarrement** to get o.s. up very strangely.

accoutumance [akutymɑ̃s] **nf** [adaptation] adaptation / MÉD addiction.

accoutumé, ***e*** [akutyme] **adj** usual.
◆ ***comme à l'accoutumée*** **loc adv** *sout* as usual.

accoutumer [3] [akutyme] **vt : accoutumer qqn à qqn/qqch** to get sb used to sb/sthg ▸ **accoutumer qqn à faire qqch** to get sb used to doing sthg.
◆ ***s'accoutumer*** **vp : s'accoutumer à qqn/qqch** to get used to sb/sthg ▸ **s'accoutumer à faire qqch** to get used to doing sthg.

accréditation [akreditasjɔ̃] **nf** FIN accreditation.

accréditer [3] [akredite] **vt** [rumeur] to substantiate ▸ **accréditer qqn auprès de** to accredit sb to.
◆ ***s'accréditer*** **vp** to gain substance.

accro [akro] *fam* ■ **adj : accro à** hooked on.
■ **nmf : c'est une accro de la planche** she's a windsurfing freak.

accroc [akro] **nm 1.** [déchirure] tear ▸ **faire un accroc à** to tear **2.** [incident] hitch ▸ **sans accroc** without a hitch.

accrochage [akrɔʃaʒ] **nm 1.** [accident] collision **2.** *fam* [dispute] row **3.** [de tableaux] hanging.

accroche [akrɔʃ] **nf** COMM catch line.

accrocher [3] [akrɔʃe] **vt 1.** [suspendre] : **accrocher qqch (à)** to hang sthg up (on) **2.** [déchirer] : **accrocher qqch (à)** to catch sthg (on) **3.** [attacher] : **accrocher qqch (à)** to hitch sthg (to) ▸ **accrocher un pendentif à une chaîne** to attach a pendant to a chain **4.** [heurter] to bump into ▸ **il a accroché l'aile de ma voiture** he caught *ou* scraped my wing **5.** [retenir l'attention de] to attract ▸ **qui accroche le regard** eye-catching ▸ **un slogan qui accroche** a catchy slogan.
◆ ***s'accrocher*** **vp 1.** [s'agripper] : **s'accrocher (à)** to hang on (to) ▸ **accroche-toi à la poignée!** hang on (tight) to the handle! ▸ **s'accrocher à qqn** *fig* to cling to sb **2.** *fam* [se disputer] to row, to have a row ▸ **ils ne peuvent pas se supporter, ils vont s'accrocher tout de suite** they can't stand each other so they're bound to start arguing straight away **3.** *fam* [persévérer] to stick at it ▸ **avec lui, il faut s'accrocher!** he's hard work!

accrocheur, ***euse*** [akrɔʃœr, øz] **adj 1.** [qui retient l'attention] eye-catching **2.** [opiniâtre] tenacious.

accroire [akrwar] **vt** *sout* : **en faire accroire à qqn** to take sb in.

accroissement [akrwasmɑ̃] **nm** increase, growth.

accroître [94] [akrwatr] **vt** to increase.
◆ ***s'accroître*** **vp** to increase, to grow.

accroupir [32] [akrupir] ◆ ***s'accroupir*** **vp** to squat.

accru, ***e*** [akry] **pp** ➤ ***accroître***.

accu [aky] **nm : recharger ses accus** *fam fig* to recharge one's batteries.

accueil [akœj] **nm 1.** [lieu] reception **2.** [action] welcome, reception.

accueillant, ***e*** [akœjɑ̃, ɑ̃t] **adj** welcoming, friendly.

accueillir [41] [akœjir] **vt 1.** [gén] to welcome **2.** [loger] to accommodate.

acculer [3] [akyle] **vt 1.** [repousser] : **acculer qqn contre/à** to drive sb up against/into **2.** *fig* : **acculer qqn à** [ruine, désespoir] to drive sb to / [faute] to force sb into.

accumulateur [akymylatœr] **nm 1.** BANQUE & INFORM accumulator **2.** ÉLECTR (storage) battery.

accumulation [akymylasjɔ̃] **nf** accumulation.

accumuler [3] [akymyle] **vt** to accumulate / *fig* to store up.
◆ ***s'accumuler*** **vp** to pile up.

accusateur, ***trice*** [akyzatœr, tris] ■ **adj** accusing.
■ **nm, f** accuser.

accusation [akyzasjɔ̃] **nf 1.** [reproche] accusation **2.** DR charge ▸ **mettre en accusation** to indict ▸ **l'accusation** the prosecution.

accusé**, **e [akyze] **nm, f** accused, defendant.
◆ ***accusé de réception*** **nm** acknowledgement (of receipt).

accuser [3] [akyze] **vt 1.** [porter une accusation contre] **: accuser qqn (de qqch)** to accuse sb (of sthg) ▸ **on m'accuse d'avoir menti** I'm being accused of lying **2.** DR **: accuser qqn de qqch** to charge sb with sthg ▸ **de quoi l'accuse-t-on?** what's the charge against him? **3.** [mettre en relief] to emphasize ▸ **la lumière accuse les reliefs** sunlight emphasizes the outlines
▸▸ **accuser réception de** to acknowledge receipt of ▸ **accuser le coup** [en boxe] to reel with the punch / [fatigue] to show the strain / [moralement] to take it badly.

ace [ɛs] **nm** SPORT ace.

acerbe [asɛrb] **adj** acerbic.

acéré**, **e [asere] **adj** sharp.

acériculture [aserikyltyr] **nf** maple sugar production.

acétate [asetat] **nm** acetate.

acétone [asetɔn] **nf** acetone.

achalandé**, **e [aʃalɑ̃de] **adj** [en marchandises] **: bien achalandé** well-stocked.

acharné**, **e [aʃarne] **adj** [combat] fierce / [travail] unremitting.

acharnement [aʃarnəmɑ̃] **nm** relentlessness.

acharner [3] [aʃarne] ◆ ***s'acharner*** **vp 1.** [combattre] **: s'acharner contre** *ou* **après** *ou* **sur qqn** [ennemi, victime] to hound sb / [suj: malheur] to dog sb **2.** [s'obstiner] **: s'acharner (à faire qqch)** to persist (in doing sthg).

achat [aʃa] **nm 1.** [objet, marchandise] purchase ▸ **faire des achats** to go shopping **2.** [acte] **: achat d'émotion** emotional purchase ▸ **achats par Internet** *ou* **en ligne** online shopping ▸ **achat spontané** *ou* **d'impulsion** *ou* **impulsif** impulse buy **3.** ÉCON **: achat au comptant** *ou* **contre espèces** cash purchase ▸ **achat à crédit** credit purchase ▸ **achat d'espace** buying of (advertising) space ▸ **achat JAT** JIT purchasing ▸ **achat juste à temps** just-in-time purchasing ▸ **achats regroupés** one-stop shopping *ou* buying.

acheminer [3] [aʃmine] **vt** to dispatch.
◆ ***s'acheminer*** **vp : s'acheminer vers** [lieu, désastre] to head for / [solution, paix] to move towards *UK* *ou* toward *US*.

acheter [28] [aʃte] **vt 1.** *litt* & *fig* [cadeau, objet, produit] to buy ▸ **acheter qqch au kilo** to buy sthg by the kilo ▸ **acheter qqch comptant/en gros/d'occasion/à crédit** to buy sthg cash/wholesale/second-hand/on credit ▸ **acheter des actions** *ou* **une part d'une entreprise** to buy into a business ▸ **acheter qqch à qqn** [pour soi] to buy sthg from sb / [pour le lui offrir] to buy sb sthg, to buy sthg for sb ▸ **acheter qqch pour qqn** to buy sthg for sb, to buy sb sthg **2.** [soudoyer - témoin, juge] to bribe, to buy (off) / [- électeurs] to buy ▸ **le juré s'est fait acheter par la Mafia** the juror was bought by the Mafia.

acheteur**, **euse [aʃtœr, øz] **nm, f** buyer, purchaser ▸ **acheteur impulsif** impulse buyer.

achevé**, **e [aʃve] **adj** *sout* **: d'un ridicule achevé** utterly ridiculous.

achèvement [aʃɛvmɑ̃] **nm** completion.

achever [19] [aʃve] **vt 1.** [terminer] to complete, to finish (off) **2.** [tuer, accabler] to finish off.
◆ ***s'achever*** **vp** to end, to come to an end.

FAUX AMIS / FALSE FRIENDS
achever
Achieve is not a translation of the French word *achever*. Achieve is translated by *accomplir*.
▸ We've achieved nothing today / *Nous n'avons rien accompli aujourd'hui*

achoppement [aʃɔpmɑ̃] ➤ ***pierre***.

achopper [3] [aʃɔpe] **vi : achopper sur** *litt* & *vieilli* to stumble on *ou* over / *fig* to come up against, to meet with.

acide [asid] ■ **adj 1.** [saveur] sour **2.** [propos] sharp, acid **3.** CHIM acid.
■ **nm 1.** CHIM acid ▸ **acide acétique/chlorhydrique/sulfurique** acetic/hydrochloric/sulphuric *ou* sulfuric *US* acid ▸ **acide aminé** amino acid **2.** *arg* acid.

acidité [asidite] **nf 1.** CHIM acidity **2.** [saveur] sourness **3.** [de propos] sharpness.

acid jazz [asiddʒaz] **nm** acid jazz.

acidulé**, **e [asidyle] **adj** slightly acid, ➤ ***bonbon***.

acier [asje] **nm** steel ▸ **acier inoxydable** stainless steel.

aciérie [asjeri] **nf** steelworks *sg*.

acné [akne] **nf** acne ▸ **acné juvénile** teenage acne.

acolyte [akɔlit] **nm** *péj* henchman.

acompte [akɔ̃t] **nm** deposit ▸ **verser un acompte** to put down *ou* pay a deposit ▸ **acompte minimum** minimum deposit.

acoquiner [3] [akɔkine] ◆ ***s'acoquiner*** **vp : s'acoquiner avec qqn** to gang up with sb.

à-côté [akote] (**pl à-côtés**) **nm 1.** [point accessoire] side issue **2.** [gain d'appoint] extra.

à-coup [aku] (**pl à-coups**) **nm** jerk ▸ **par à-coups** in fits and starts.

acoustique [akustik] ■ **nf 1.** [science] acoustics *(U)* **2.** [d'une salle] acoustics *pl*.
■ **adj** acoustic.

acquéreur [akerœr] **nm** buyer.

acquérir [39] [akerir] **vt 1.** [gén] to acquire **2.** [conquérir] to win.
◆ ***s'acquérir*** **vp : s'acquérir qqch** to win sthg, to gain sthg.

acquiers**, **acquiert ➤ ***acquérir***.

acquiescement [akjɛsmɑ̃] **nm** approval.

acquiescer [21] [akjese] **vi** to acquiesce ▸ **acquiescer à** to agree to.

acquis**, **e [aki, iz] ■ **pp** ➤ ***acquérir***.
■ **adj 1.** [caractère] acquired **2.** [droit, avantage] established.
◆ ***acquis*** **nmpl** [connaissances] knowledge *(U)*.

acquisition [akizisjɔ̃] **nf** acquisition.

acquit [aki] **nm** receipt ▸ **pour acquit** COMM received ▸ **faire qqch par acquit de conscience** *fig* to do sthg to set one's mind at rest.

acquittement [akitmɑ̃] **nm 1.** [d'obligation] settlement **2.** DR acquittal.

acquitter [3] [akite] **vt 1.** DR to acquit **2.** [régler] to pay **3.** [libérer] **: acquitter qqn de** to release sb from.
◆ ***s'acquitter*** **vp : s'acquitter de qqch** [payer] to settle sthg / *fig* to carry sthg out.

acra [akra] **nm** *Creole fried fish or vegetable ball.*

âcre [akr] **adj 1.** [saveur] bitter **2.** [fumée] acrid.

acrimonie [akrimɔni] **nf** acrimony.

acrobate [akrɔbat] **nmf** acrobat.

acrobatie [akrɔbasi] **nf** acrobatics *(U)* ▸ **acrobaties aériennes** aerobatics *pl.*

acrobatique [akrɔbatik] **adj** acrobatic.

acronyme [akrɔnim] **nm** acronym.

acrylique [akrilik] **adj & nm** acrylic.

acte [akt] **nm 1.** [action] act, action ▸ **faire acte d'autorité** to exercise one's authority ▸ **faire acte de bonne volonté** to make a gesture of goodwill ▸ **faire acte de candidature** to submit an application
2. THÉÂTRE act ▸ **une pièce en un seul acte** a one-act play
3. DR deed ▸ **acte d'accusation** charge ▸ **acte administratif** administrative act ▸ **acte d'association** partnership agreement *ou* deed, articles of partnership ▸ **acte d'huissier** writ ▸ **acte juridique** legal transaction ▸ **acte de naissance/de mariage/de décès** birth/marriage/death certificate ▸ **acte notarié** deed executed by a notary ▸ **acte de succession** attestation of inheritance *ou* will ▸ **acte de vente** bill of sale
4. RELIG certificate ▸ **acte de baptême** baptismal certificate
5. MÉD **: acte (médical)** [consultation] (medical) consultation / [traitement] (medical) treatment
6. PSYCHO **: passer à l'acte** [gén] to act / [névrosé, psychopathe] to act out
▸▸ **faire acte de présence** to put in an appearance ▸ **prendre acte de** to note, to take note of ▸ **demander acte de qqch** to ask for formal acknowledgment of sthg.
◆ ***actes*** **nmpl** [de colloque] proceedings.

acteur, trice [aktœr, tris] **nm, f** actor (f actress).

actif, ive [aktif, iv] **adj** [gén] active ▸ **la population active** the working population.
◆ ***actif*** **nm** FIN assets *pl* ▸ **actif corporel** tangible assets ▸ **actif imposable sur les plus-values** chargeable assets ▸▸ **avoir qqch à son actif** to have sthg to one's credit.

action [aksjɔ̃] **nf 1.** [gén] action ▸ **dans le feu de l'action, en pleine action** right in the middle *ou* at the heart of the action ▸ **entrer en action** [pompiers, police] to go into action / [loi, règlement] to become effective, to take effect ▸ **passer à l'action** to go into action / MIL to go into battle ▸ **sous l'action de** under the effect of
2. [acte] action, act ▸ **bonne/mauvaise action** good/bad deed ▸ **une action syndicale est à prévoir** some industrial action is expected
3. DR action, lawsuit ▸ **intenter une action contre *ou* à qqn** to bring an action against sb, to take legal action against sb, to take sb to court
4. FIN share ▸ **ses actions ont baissé/monté** *fig & hum* his stock has fallen/risen *fig* ▸ **action au porteur** transferable *ou* bearer share ▸ **actions cotées en Bourse** common stock
5. RELIG **: action de grâces** thanksgiving.
◆ ***d'action*** **loc adj 1.** [mouvementé - roman] action-packed ▸ **film d'action** action film
2. [qui aime agir] **: homme/femme d'action** man/woman of action
3. POLIT **: journée/semaine d'action** day/week of action.

actionnaire [aksjɔnɛr] **nmf** FIN shareholder *UK*, stockholder *US* ▸ **actionnaire minoritaire** minority shareholder *UK*, minority stockholder *US*.

actionner [3] [aksjɔne] **vt** to work, to activate.

activement [aktivmɑ̃] **adv** actively.

activer [3] [aktive] **vt** to speed up.
◆ ***s'activer*** **vp** to bustle about.

activisme [aktivism] **nm** activism.

activiste [aktivist] **adj & nmf** activist.

activité [aktivite] **nf 1.** [gén] activity ▸ **en activité** [volcan] active ▸ **activité d'éveil** early learning experience
2. ÉCON **: activité centrale** core business ▸ **activité professionnelle** job, profession ▸ **rester en activité** ADMIN to remain in gainful employment.

actuaire [aktɥɛr] **nmf** actuary.

actualisation [aktɥalizasjɔ̃] **nf** [d'un texte] updating.

actualiser [3] [aktɥalize] **vt** to update, to bring up to date.

actualité [aktɥalite] **nf 1.** [d'un sujet] topicality ▸ **être d'actualité** to be topical **2.** [événements] **: l'actualité sportive/politique/littéraire** the current sports/political/literary scene.
◆ ***actualités*** **nfpl : les actualités** the news *sg.*

actuel, elle [aktɥɛl] **adj 1.** [contemporain, présent] current, present ▸ **à l'heure actuelle** at the present time **2.** [d'actualité] topical.

> FAUX AMIS / FALSE FRIENDS
> **actuel**
>
> Actual is not a translation of the French word *actuel.* Actual is translated by *réel or exact.*
> ▸ The actual cost was more than £1000 / *Le coût réel était de plus de 1 000 livres*
> ▸ What were her actual words? / *Quels ont été ses mots exacts ?*

actuellement [aktɥɛlmɑ̃] **adv** at present, currently.

> FAUX AMIS / FALSE FRIENDS
> **actuellement**
>
> Actually is not a translation of the French word *actuellement.* Actually is translated by *vraiment or au fait.*
> ▸ What did he actually say? / *Qu'est-ce qu'il a dit vraiment ?*
> ▸ She's actually working on a new novel / *En fait, elle travaille à un nouveau roman*

acuité [akɥite] **nf** acuteness ▸ **acuité visuelle** keenness of sight.

acuponcteur**, **trice**, **acupuncteur**, **trice [akypɔ̃ktœr, tris] **nm, f** acupuncturist.

acupuncture**, **acuponcture [akypɔ̃ktyr] **nf** acupuncture.

adage [adaʒ] **nm** adage, saying.

adaptabilité [adaptabilite] **nf** adaptability.

adaptable [adaptabl] **adj** adaptable.

adaptateur**, **trice [adaptatœr, tris] **nm, f** adapter.
◆ ***adaptateur*** **nm** ÉLECTR adapter.

adaptation [adaptasjɔ̃] **nf** adaptation.

adapter [3] [adapte] **vt 1.** [gén] to adapt ▸ **adapté aux circonstances** appropriate ▸ **adapté d'une nouvelle de...** adapted from a short story by... ▸ **la méthode n'est pas vraiment adaptée à la situation** the method isn't very appropriate for this situation **2.** [fixer] to fit ▸ **adapter qqch à qqch** to fit sthg to sthg ▸ **adapter un embout à un tuyau** to fit a nozzle onto a pipe.
◆ ***s'adapter*** **vp : s'adapter (à)** to adapt (to) ▸ **il s'est bien adapté à sa nouvelle école** he has settled down well in his new school.

ADD (abr de ***analogique/digital/digital***) ADD.

additif [aditif] **nm 1.** [supplément] rider, additional clause **2.** [substance] additive.

addition [adisjɔ̃] **nf 1.** [ajout, calcul] addition **2.** [note] bill, check *US*.

additionnel**, **elle [adisjɔnɛl] **adj** extra, additional.

additionner [3] [adisjɔne] **vt 1.** [mélanger] **: additionner une poudre d'eau** to add water to a powder **2.** [chiffres] to add up.
◆ ***s'additionner*** **vp** to add up.

adduction [adyksjɔ̃] **nf** [des eaux, du gaz] supply.

adénome [adenom] **nm** adenoma.

adepte [adɛpt] **nmf** follower.

adéquat**, **e [adekwa, at] **adj** suitable, appropriate.

adéquation [adekwasjɔ̃] **nf** appropriateness.

adhérence [aderɑ̃s] **nf** [de pneu] grip.

adhérent**, **e [aderɑ̃, ɑ̃t] ■ **adj : adhérent à** adhering *ou* sticking to.
■ **nm, f : adhérent (de)** member (of).

adhérer [18] [adere] **vi 1.** [coller] to stick, to adhere ▸ **adhérer à** [se fixer sur] to stick *ou* adhere to / *fig* [être d'accord avec] to support, to adhere to **2.** [être membre] **: adhérer à** to become a member of, to join.

adhésif**, **ive [adezif, iv] **adj** sticky, adhesive.
◆ ***adhésif*** **nm** adhesive.

adhésion [adezjɔ̃] **nf 1.** [à une idée] **: adhésion (à)** support (for) **2.** [de pneu] **: une bonne adhésion à la route** good road-holding *(U)* **3.** [à un parti] **: adhésion (à)** membership (of).

adieu [adjø] ■ **interj** goodbye!, farewell! ▸ **dire adieu à qqch** *fig* to say goodbye to sthg.
■ **nm** *(gén pl)* farewell ▸ **faire ses adieux à qqn** to say one's farewells to sb.

adipeux**, **euse [adipø, øz] **adj** [tissu] adipose / [personne] fat.

adjacent**, **e [adʒasɑ̃, ɑ̃t] **adj** adjoining, adjacent.

adjectif [adʒɛktif] **nm** GRAMM adjective ▸ **adjectif attribut** predicative adjective ▸ **adjectif épithète** attributive adjective.

adjoindre [82] [adʒwɛ̃dr] **vt : adjoindre qqch à qqch** to add sthg to sthg.
◆ ***s'adjoindre*** **vp** to appoint, to take on.

adjoint**, **e [adʒwɛ̃, ɛ̃t] ■ **adj** deputy *(avant n)*, assistant *(avant n)*.
■ **nm, f** deputy, assistant ▸ **adjoint au maire** deputy mayor.

adjonction [adʒɔ̃ksjɔ̃] **nf** addition ▸ **sans adjonction de sel/sucre/conservateurs** with no added salt/sugar/preservatives.

adjudant [adʒydɑ̃] **nm** [dans la marine] warrant officer / [dans l'armée] company sergeant major ▸ **adjudant chef** [dans la marine] warrant officer 1st class *UK*, chief warrant officer *US* / [dans l'armée] regimental sergeant major.

adjudicataire [adʒydikatɛr] **nmf** successful bidder.

adjudication [adʒydikasjɔ̃] **nf 1.** [vente aux enchères] sale by auction **2.** ADMIN awarding.

adjuger [17] [adʒyʒe] **vt : adjuger qqch (à qqn)** [aux enchères] to auction sthg (to sb) / [décerner] to award sthg (to sb) ▸ **adjugé!** sold!
◆ ***s'adjuger*** **vp : s'adjuger qqch** to give o.s. sthg.

adjurer [3] [adʒyre] **vt** *sout* to implore, to beg.

adjuvant [adʒyvɑ̃] **nm 1.** [médicament] adjuvant **2.** [stimulant] stimulant.

admets ➤ *admettre*.

admettre [84] [admɛtr] **vt 1.** [tolérer, accepter] to allow, to accept ▸ **je n'admets pas qu'on me parle sur ce ton!** I won't tolerate *ou* stand being talked to like that! **2.** [supposer] to suppose, to assume ▸ **admettons que** *(+ subjonctif)* supposing *ou* assuming (that) **3.** [autoriser] to allow ▸ **il ne sera pas admis en classe supérieure** he won't be admitted to *ou* allowed into the next year *UK ou* class *US* ▸ **être admis à faire qqch** to be allowed to do sthg ▸ **les enfants de moins de 10 ans ne sont pas admis** children under the age of 10 are not admitted **4.** [accueillir, reconnaître] to admit ▸ **admettre qqn dans un club** to admit sb as a member of a club ▸ **j'admets mon erreur/mon incertitude** I admit I was wrong/I am unsure.

administrateur**, **trice [administratœr, tris] **nm, f 1.** [gérant] administrator ▸ **administrateur de biens** administrator of an estate ▸ **administrateur judiciaire** receiver **2.** [de conseil d'administration] director **3.** INFORM **: administrateur de site (Web)** webmaster.

administratif**, **ive [administratif, iv] **adj** administrative.

administration [administrasjɔ̃] **nf 1.** [service public] **: l'Administration** ≃ the Civil Service **2.** [gestion] administration.

administrer [3] [administre] **vt 1.** [gérer] to manage, to administer **2.** [médicament, sacrement] to administer.

admirable [admirabl] **adj 1.** [personne, comportement] admirable **2.** [paysage, spectacle] wonderful.

admirablement [admirabləmɑ̃] **adv** admirably.

admirateur**, **trice [admiratœr, tris] **nm, f** admirer.

admiratif**, **ive [admiratif, iv] **adj** admiring.

admiration [admirasjɔ̃] **nf** admiration ▸ **être en admiration devant qqn/qqch** to be filled with admiration for sb/sthg.

admirer [3] [admire] **vt** to admire.

admis, e [admi, iz] **pp** ➤ ***admettre***.

admissible [admisibl] ■ **adj 1.** [attitude] acceptable **2.** SCOL eligible.
■ **nmf** SCOL eligible candidate.

admission [admisjɔ̃] **nf** admission.

admonester [3] [admɔnɛste] **vt** *sout* to admonish.

ADN (abr de ***acide désoxyribonucléique***) **nm** DNA.

ado [ado] (abr de ***adolescent***) **nmf** *fam* teen, teenager.

adolescence [adɔlesɑ̃s] **nf** adolescence.

adolescent, e [adɔlesɑ̃, ɑ̃t] ■ **adj** adolescent.
■ **nm, f** adolescent, teenager.

adonis [adɔnis] **nm** Adonis.

adonner [3] [adɔne] ◆ ***s'adonner*** **vp : s'adonner à** [sport, activité] to devote o.s. to / [vice] to take to.

adopter [3] [adɔpte] **vt 1.** [gén] to adopt **2.** [loi] to pass.

adoptif, ive [adɔptif, iv] **adj** [famille] adoptive / [pays, enfant] adopted.

adoption [adɔpsjɔ̃] **nf** adoption ▸ **d'adoption** [pays, ville] adopted / [famille] adoptive.

adorable [adɔrabl] **adj** adorable, delightful.

adorateur, trice [adɔratœr, tris] ■ **adj** adoring, worshipping *UK*, worshiping *US*.
■ **nm, f 1.** [de personne] admirer **2.** RELIG worshipper *UK*, worshiper *US*.

adoration [adɔrasjɔ̃] **nf 1.** [amour] adoration ▸ **être en adoration devant qqn** to worship sb **2.** RELIG worship.

adorer [3] [adɔre] **vt 1.** [personne, chose] to adore **2.** RELIG to worship.

adosser [3] [adose] **vt : adosser qqch à qqch** to place sthg against sthg.
◆ ***s'adosser*** **vp : s'adosser à** *ou* **contre qqch** to lean against sthg.

adoucir [32] [adusir] **vt 1.** [gén] to soften **2.** [chagrin, peine] to ease, to soothe.
◆ ***s'adoucir*** **vp 1.** [temps] to become *ou* get milder **2.** [personne] to mellow.

adoucissant, e [adusisɑ̃, ɑ̃t] **adj** soothing.
◆ ***adoucissant*** **nm** softener.

adoucissement [adusismɑ̃] **nm 1.** [de température] **: il y a eu un adoucissement de la température** the weather has become milder **2.** [de peine] soothing, easing **3.** [de l'eau] softening.

adoucisseur [adusisœr] **nm : adoucisseur d'eau** water softener.

adrénaline [adrenalin] **nf** adrenalin.

adresse [adrɛs] **nf 1.** [gén & INFORM] address ▸ **ce restaurant est une bonne adresse** this restaurant is a good place to go ▸ **à l'adresse de** *fig* for the benefit of ▸ **adresse électronique** e-mail address ▸ **adresse Internet** Internet address ▸ **adresse IP** IP adress **2.** [habileté] skill **3.** [subtilité] cleverness, adroitness ▸ **répondre avec adresse** to give a tactful answer **4.** [mot] headword.

adresser [4] [adrese] **vt 1.** [faire parvenir] **: adresser qqch à qqn** to address sthg to sb ▸ **cette lettre vous est adressée** this letter is addressed to you *ou* has your name on the envelope **2.** [envoyer] **: adresser qqn à qqn** to refer sb to sb ▸ **adresser un malade à un spécialiste** to refer a patient to a specialist **3.** [destiner] **: adresser la parole à qqn** to speak to sb ▸ **adresser un compliment à qqn** to pay sb a compliment ▸ **adresser un reproche à qqn** to level a reproach at sb ▸ **adresser un sourire à qqn** to smile at sb.
◆ ***s'adresser*** **vp : s'adresser à** [parler à] to speak to / [être destiné à] to be aimed at, to be intended for ▸ **à qui s'adresse cette remarque?** who's this remark aimed at? ▸ **il faut vous adresser au syndicat d'initiative** you should apply to the tourist office ▸ **le ministre s'adressera d'abord aux élus locaux** the minister will first address the local councillors.

Adriatique [adriatik] **nf : l'Adriatique** the Adriatic.

adroit, e [adrwa, at] **adj** skilful *US*, skillful *US*.

adroitement [adrwatmɑ̃] **adv** skilfully *UK*, skillfully *US*.

ADSL (abr de ***asymmetric digital subscriber line***) **nm** ADSL ▸ **passer à l'ADSL** to switch *ou* upgrade *ou* go over to ADSL.

aduler [3] [adyle] **vt** to adulate.

adulescent, e [adylesɑ̃, ɑ̃t] **nm, f** overgrown teenager, kidult.

adulte [adylt] **nmf & adj** adult.

adultère [adyltɛr] ■ **nm** [acte] adultery.
■ **adj** adulterous.

adultérin, e [adylterɛ̃, in] **adj** illegitimate.

advenir [40] [advənir] **v impers** to happen ▸ **qu'advient-il de...?** what is happening to...? ▸ **qu'est-il advenu de...?** what has happened to *ou* become of...? ▸ **advienne que pourra** come what may.

advenu [advəny] **pp** ➤ ***advenir***.

adverbe [advɛrb] **nm** adverb.

adversaire [advɛrsɛr] **nmf** adversary, opponent.

adverse [advɛrs] **adj** [opposé] opposing, ➤ ***parti***.

adversité [advɛrsite] **nf** adversity.

advient ➤ ***advenir***.

advint ➤ ***advenir***.

AE (abr de ***adjoint d'enseignement***) **nm** *non-certified teacher*.

AELE (abr de ***Association européenne de libre-échange***) **nf** EFTA.

AEN (abr de ***Agence pour l'énergie nucléaire***) **nf** *French nuclear energy agency*, ≃ AEA *UK*, ≃ AEC *US*.

aération [aerasjɔ̃] **nf** [circulation d'air] ventilation / [action] airing.

aéré, e [aere] **adj 1.** [pièce] well-ventilated ▸ **mal aéré** stuffy **2.** *fig* [présentation] well-spaced.

aérer [18] [aere] **vt 1.** [pièce, chose] to air **2.** *fig* [présentation, mise en page] to improve.
◆ ***s'aérer*** **vp** [sortir] to get some fresh air.

aérien**, **enne [aerjɛ̃, ɛn] **adj** **1.** [grâce] ethereal / [démarche] light **2.** [câble] overhead *(avant n)* **3.** [transports, attaque] air *(avant n)* ▸ **compagnie aérienne** airline (company).

aérobic [aerɔbik] **nm** aerobics *(U)*.

aérodrome [aerɔdrom] **nm** airfield.

aérodynamique [aerɔdinamik] ■ **nf** aerodynamics *(U)*.
■ **adj** streamlined, aerodynamic.

aérogare [aerɔgar] **nf** **1.** [aéroport] airport **2.** [gare] air terminal.

aéroglisseur [aerɔglisœr] **nm** hovercraft.

aérogramme [aerɔgram] **nm** aerogramme *UK*, aerogram *US*, air letter.

aéromodélisme [aerɔmɔdelism] **nm** model aircraft making.

aéronautique [aerɔnotik] ■ **nf** aeronautics *(U)*.
■ **adj** aeronautical.

aéronaval**, **e**, **als [aerɔnaval] **adj** air and sea *(avant n)*.
◆ ***aéronavale*** **nf : l'aéronavale** ≃ the Fleet Air Arm *UK*, ≃ Naval Air Command *US*.

aérophagie [aerɔfaʒi] **nf** abdominal wind.

aéroport [aerɔpɔr] **nm** airport.

aéroporté**, **e [aerɔpɔrte] **adj** airborne.

aérosol [aerɔsɔl] **nm** & **adj inv** aerosol.

aérospatial**, **e**, **aux [aerɔspasjal, o] **adj** aerospace *(avant n)*.
◆ ***aérospatiale*** **nf** aerospace industry.

AF ■ **nfpl** (abr écrite de ***allocations familiales***), abr écrite de ***allocation***.
■ **nf** (abr de ***Assemblée fédérale***) (Swiss) Federal Assembly.

affabilité [afabilite] **nf** affability.

affable [afabl] **adj** **1.** [personne] affable, agreeable **2.** [parole] kind.

affabulateur**, **trice [afabylatœr, tris] **nm, f** inveterate liar.

affabulation [afabylasjɔ̃] **nf** fabrication.

affacturage [afaktyraʒ] **m** FIN factoring.

affaiblir [32] [afeblir] **vt** *litt* & *fig* to weaken.
◆ ***s'affaiblir*** **vp** *litt* & *fig* to weaken, to become weaker.

affaiblissement [afeblismɑ̃] **nm** weakening.

affaire [afɛr] **nf** **1.** [question] matter **2.** [situation, polémique] affair ▸ **ce n'est pas une mince affaire, c'est tout une affaire** it's quite a business **3.** [marché] deal ▸ **conclure une affaire avec qqn** to clinch a deal with sb ▸ **faire affaire avec qqn** to have dealings with sb ▸ **faire une affaire** to get a bargain *ou* a good deal ▸ **une affaire en or** a real bargain **4.** [entreprise] business ▸ **monter une affaire** to set up a business **5.** [procès] case ▸ **l'affaire est jugée demain** the trial concludes tomorrow ▸ **affaire civile/correctionnelle** civil/criminal action
▸▸ **avoir affaire à qqn** to deal with sb ▸ **vous aurez affaire à moi!** you'll have me to deal with! ▸ **c'est l'affaire d'une minute** it will only take a minute ▸ **faire l'affaire** to do nicely ▸ **j'en fais mon affaire** leave it to me ▸ **fais ce que tu veux, c'est ton affaire** do what you like: it's your business *ou* problem ▸ **tirer qqn d'affaire** to get sb out of trouble ▸ **être sorti** *ou* **tiré d'affaire** [après une aventure, une faillite] to be out of trouble *ou* in the clear / [après une maladie] to be off the danger list *UK* *ou* critical list *US*.
◆ ***affaires*** **nfpl** **1.** COMM business *(U)* ▸ **être dans les affaires** to be a businessman (f businesswoman) ▸ **pour affaires** [voyager, rencontrer] for business purposes, on business ▸ **voyage/repas d'affaires** business trip/lunch **2.** [objets personnels] things, belongings **3.** [activités] affairs ▸ **se mêler** *ou* **s'occuper de ses affaires** to mind one's own business ▸ **toutes affaires cessantes** forthwith ▸ **toutes affaires cessantes, ils sont allés chez le maire** they dropped everything and went to see the mayor **4.** POLIT affairs ▸ **être aux affaires** to run the country, to be the head of state ▸ **les affaires de l'État** affairs of state ▸ **les Affaires étrangères** ≃ the Foreign Office *(sg)* *UK*, ≃ the State Department *(sg)* *US* ▸ **affaires intérieures** internal affairs.

affairé**, **e [afere] **adj** busy.

affairer [4] [afere] ◆ ***s'affairer*** **vp** to bustle about.

affairisme [aferism] **nm** racketeering.

affaissement [afɛsmɑ̃] **nm** GÉOGR subsidence.

affaisser [4] [afese] ◆ ***s'affaisser*** **vp** **1.** [se creuser] to subside, to sink **2.** [tomber] to collapse.

affaler [3] [afale] ◆ ***s'affaler*** **vp** to collapse.

affamé**, **e [afame] **adj** starving.

affect [afɛkt] **nm** affect.

affectation [afɛktasjɔ̃] **nf** **1.** [attribution] **: affectation de qqch à** allocation of sthg to **2.** [nomination] appointment, posting **3.** [manque de naturel] affectation.

affecté**, **e [afɛkte] **adj** [personne] affected, mannered ▸ **parler d'une manière affectée** to speak affectedly.

affecter [4] [afɛkte] **vt** **1.** [consacrer] **: affecter qqch à** to allocate sthg to **2.** [nommer] **: affecter qqn à** to appoint sb to **3.** [feindre] to feign **4.** [émouvoir] to affect, to move.

affectif**, **ive [afɛktif, iv] **adj** emotional.

affection [afɛksjɔ̃] **nf** **1.** [sentiment] affection ▸ **avoir de l'affection pour** to be fond of **2.** [maladie] complaint.

affectionner [3] [afɛksjɔne] **vt** to be fond of.

affectivité [afɛktivite] **nf** emotions *pl*.

affectueusement [afɛktɥøzmɑ̃] **adv** affectionately.

affectueux**, **euse [afɛktɥø, øz] **adj** affectionate.

afférent**, **e [aferɑ̃, ɑ̃t] **adj** **1.** DR **: afférent à qqch** pertaining *ou* relating to sthg **2.** ANAT afferent.

affermir [32] [afɛrmir] **vt** [gén] to strengthen / [chairs] to tone up.
◆ ***s'affermir*** **vp** **1.** [matière] to be strengthened / [chairs] to be toned up **2.** [pouvoir] to be consolidated.

affichage [afiʃaʒ] **nm** **1.** [d'un poster, d'un avis] putting up, displaying **2.** ÉLECTRON **: affichage à cristaux liquides** LCD, liquid crystal display ▸ **affichage numérique** digital display.

affiche [afiʃ] **nf** [gén] poster / [officielle] notice ▸ **affiche publicitaire** (advertising) poster ▸ **être à l'affiche** *fig* to be on.

afficher [3] [afiʃe] **vt 1.** [liste, poster] to put up / [vente, réglementation] to put up a notice about **2.** [laisser transparaître] to display, to exhibit.
◆ ***s'afficher*** **vp : s'afficher avec qqn** to flaunt o.s. with sb.

affichette [afiʃɛt] **nf** small poster.

afficheur [afiʃœr] **nm 1.** [entreprise] billposter **2.** ÉLECTRON display.

affilée [afile] ◆ ***d'affilée*** **loc adv : trois jours d'affilée** three days running.

affiler [3] [afile] **vt** to sharpen.

affilié, e [afilje] **adj : affilié à** affiliated to.

affiner [3] [afine] **vt** *litt* & *fig* to refine.
◆ ***s'affiner*** **vp** [silhouette] to become thinner / [devenir plus raffiné] to become more refined.

affinité [afinite] **nf** affinity ▸ **avoir des affinités avec** to have an affinity with.

affirmatif, ive [afirmatif, iv] **adj 1.** [réponse] affirmative **2.** [personne] positive.
◆ ***affirmatif*** **adv** affirmative.
◆ ***affirmative*** **nf : nous aimerions savoir si vous serez libre mecredi; dans l'affirmative, nous vous prions de...** we'd like to know if you are free on Wednesday; if you are *ou* if so, please... ▸ **répondre par l'affirmative** to reply in the affirmative.

affirmation [afirmasjɔ̃] **nf** assertion.

affirmativement [afirmativmɑ̃] **adv : répondre affirmativement** to answer in the affirmative.

affirmer [3] [afirme] **vt 1.** [certifier] to maintain, to claim **2.** [exprimer] to assert.
◆ ***s'affirmer*** **vp** to assert o.s.

affixe [afiks] **nm** affix.

affleurer [5] [aflœre] **vi** *fig* to rise to the surface.

affliction [afliksjɔ̃] **nf** affliction.

affligé, e [afliʒe] **adj** afflicted.

affligeant, e [afliʒɑ̃, ɑ̃t] **adj 1.** [désolant] saddening, distressing **2.** [lamentable] appalling.

affliger [17] [afliʒe] **vt** *sout* **1.** [attrister] to sadden, to distress **2.** [de défaut, de maladie] **: être affligé de** to be afflicted with.
◆ ***s'affliger*** **vp** *sout* **: s'affliger de** to be distressed at *ou* about.

affluence [aflyɑ̃s] **nf** crowd, crowds *pl*.

affluent [aflyɑ̃] **nm** tributary.

affluer [3] [aflye] **vi 1.** [choses] to pour in, to flood in **2.** [personnes] to flock **3.** [sang] **: affluer (à)** to rush (to).

afflux [afly] **nm 1.** [de liquide, dons, capitaux] flow **2.** [de personnes] flood.

affolant, e [afɔlɑ̃, ɑ̃t] **adj 1.** [inquiétant] frightening **2.** [troublant] disturbing.

affolé, e [afɔle] **adj** horrified.

affolement [afɔlmɑ̃] **nm** panic.

affoler [3] [afɔle] **vt 1.** [inquiéter] to terrify **2.** [émouvoir] to drive mad.
◆ ***s'affoler*** **vp** [paniquer] to panic.

affranchi, e [afrɑ̃ʃi] **adj 1.** [lettre - avec timbre] stamped / [- à la machine] franked **2.** [personne, esclave] liberated.

affranchir [32] [afrɑ̃ʃir] **vt 1.** [lettre - avec timbre] to stamp / [- à la machine] to frank **2.** *arg crime* [renseigner] to put in the picture, to fill in **3.** [libérer] **: affranchir qqn de qqch** to liberate *ou* free sb from sthg **4.** [esclave] to set free, to liberate.
◆ ***s'affranchir*** **vp : s'affranchir de qqch** [se libérer de] to free o.s. from sthg.

affranchissement [afrɑ̃ʃismɑ̃] **nm 1.** [de lettre - avec timbre] stamping / [- à la machine] franking **2.** [libération] liberation, emancipation.

affres [afr] **nfpl** *littéraire* throes.

affréter [18] [afrete] **vt** to charter.

affreusement [afrøzmɑ̃] **adv 1.** [horriblement] horribly **2.** [énormément] awfully.

affreux, euse [afrø, øz] **adj 1.** [repoussant] horrible **2.** [effrayant] terrifying **3.** [détestable] awful, dreadful.

affriolant, e [afrijɔlɑ̃, ɑ̃t] **adj** enticing.

affront [afrɔ̃] **nm** insult, affront ▸ **faire un affront à qqn** to insult sb.

affrontement [afrɔ̃tmɑ̃] **nm** confrontation.

affronter [3] [afrɔ̃te] **vt** to confront.
◆ ***s'affronter*** **vp** to confront each other.

affubler [3] [afyble] **vt** *péj* **: être affublé de** to be got up in.
◆ ***s'affubler*** **vp : s'affubler de qqch** *péj* to get o.s. up in sthg.

affût [afy] **nm : être à l'affût (de)** to be lying in wait (for) / *fig* to be on the lookout (for).

affûter [3] [afyte] **vt** to sharpen.

afghan, e [afgɑ̃, an] **adj** Afghan.
◆ ***afghan*** **nm** [langue] Afghan, Pashto.
◆ ***Afghan, e*** **nm, f** Afghan.

Afghanistan [afganistɑ̃] **nm : l'Afghanistan** Afghanistan.

afin [afɛ̃] ◆ ***afin de*** **loc prép** in order to. ◆ ***afin que*** **loc conj** *(+ subjonctif)* so that.

AFNOR, Afnor [afnɔr] (abr de ***Association française de normalisation***) **nf** *French industrial standards authority*, ≃ BSI *UK*, ≃ ASA *US*.

a fortiori [afɔrsjɔri] **adv** all the more.

AFP (abr de ***Agence France-Presse***) **nf** *French press agency*.

africain, e [afrikɛ̃, ɛn] **adj** African.
◆ ***Africain, e*** **nm, f** African.

afrikaner [afrikanɛr], ***afrikaander*** [afrikɑ̃dɛr] **adj** Afrikaner.
◆ ***Afrikaner, Afrikaander*** **nmf** Afrikaner.

Afrique [afrik] **nf : l'Afrique** Africa ▸ **l'Afrique australe** Southern Africa ▸ **l'Afrique noire** sub-Saharan Africa ▸ **l'Afrique du Nord** North Africa ▸ **l'Afrique du Sud** South Africa.

afro [afro] **adj inv** afro.

after-shave [aftœrʃɛv] **nm inv** & **adj inv** aftershave.

ag. abr de ***agence***.

AG (abr de ***assemblée générale***) **nf** ≃ AGM *UK*, ≃ annual meeting *US*.

agaçant, ***e*** [agasɑ̃, ɑ̃t] **adj** irritating.

agacement [agasmɑ̃] **nm** irritation.

agacer [16] [agase] **vt** to irritate.

agate [agat] **nf** agate.

âge [aʒ] **nm** age ▸ **à l'âge de** at the age of ▸ **en âge de faire qqch** old enough to do sthg ▸ **en bas âge** very young ▸ **quel âge as-tu?** how old are you? ▸ **ce n'est pas de ton âge!** [tu es trop jeune] you're not old enough! / [tu es trop vieux] you're too old (for it)! ▸ **d'un certain âge** middle-aged ▸ **prendre de l'âge** to age ▸ **l'âge adulte** adulthood ▸ **l'âge ingrat** the awkward *ou* difficult age ▸ **d'un âge avancé** elderly ▸ **âge de fer/de bronze** Iron/Bronze Age ▸ **avoir l'âge légal (pour voter)** to be old enough to vote, to be of age ▸ **âge mental** mental age ▸ **d'âge mûr** of mature years ▸ **âge d'or** golden age ▸ **le premier âge** infancy ▸ **le quatrième âge** [période] advanced old age / [groupe social] very old people ▸ **âge de raison** age of reason ▸ **le troisième âge** [personnes] the over-sixties, senior citizens.

âgé, ***e*** [aʒe] **adj** **1.** [vieux] old ▸ **elle est plus âgée de moi** she's older than I am **2.** [de tel âge] **: être âgé de 20 ans** to be 20 years old *ou* of age ▸ **un enfant âgé de 3 ans** a 3-year-old child.

agence [aʒɑ̃s] **nf** agency ▸ **agence immobilière** estate agent's *UK*, real estate agency *US* ▸ **agence matrimoniale** marriage bureau ▸ **Agence nationale pour l'emploi** ≃ Jobcentre *UK* ▸ **agence de presse** press *ou* news agency ▸ **agence de publicité** advertising agency ▸ **agence de voyages** travel agency, travel agent's *UK*.

agencement [aʒɑ̃smɑ̃] **nm** arrangement.

agencer [16] [aʒɑ̃se] **vt** to arrange / *fig* to put together.
◆ ***s'agencer*** **vp** to fit together.

agenda [aʒɛ̃da] **nm** diary.

agenouiller [3] [aʒnuje] ◆ ***s'agenouiller*** **vp** to kneel ▸ **s'agenouiller devant** *fig* to bow down before.

agent [aʒɑ̃] **nm** agent ▸ **agent d'affacturage** factoring agent ▸ **agent artistique** agent ▸ **agent d'assurances** insurance agent ▸ **agent atmosphérique/économique** atmospheric/economic factor ▸ **agent de change** stockbroker ▸ **agent commercial** sales representative ▸ **agent double** double agent ▸ **agent immobilier** estate agent *UK*, real estate agent *US* ▸ **agents de maîtrise** lower management ▸ **agent de police** police officer ▸ **agent de publicité** advertising agent ▸ **agent secret** secret agent.

agglomérat [aglɔmera] **nm** *fig* & GÉOL agglomerate.

agglomération [aglɔmerasjɔ̃] **nf** **1.** [amas] conglomeration **2.** [ville] conurbation ▸ **l'agglomération parisienne** the Parisian urban area.

aggloméré [aglɔmere] **nm** chipboard.

agglomérer [18] [aglɔmere] **vt** to mix together.
◆ ***s'agglomérer*** **vp** **1.** [surface] to bind **2.** [foule] to gather.

agglutiner [3] [aglytine] **vt** to stick together.
◆ ***s'agglutiner*** **vp** [foule] to gather, to congregate.

aggravation [agravasjɔ̃] **nf** worsening, aggravation.

aggraver [3] [agrave] **vt** to make worse.
◆ ***s'aggraver*** **vp** to get worse, to worsen.

agile [aʒil] **adj** agile, nimble.

agilement [aʒilmɑ̃] **adv** agilely.

agilité [aʒilite] **nf** *litt* & *fig* agility.

agios [aʒjo] **nmpl** FIN bank charges.

agir [32] [aʒir] **vi** **1.** [faire, être efficace] to act ▸ **en cas d'incendie, il faut agir vite** in the event of a fire, it is important to act quickly ▸ **assez parlé, maintenant il faut agir!** enough talk, let's have some action! **2.** [se comporter] to behave ▸ **agir selon sa conscience** to act according to one's conscience, to let one's conscience be one's guide **3.** [influer] **: agir sur** to have an effect on ▸ **laisser agir la justice** to let justice take its course **4.** DR **: agir contre qqn** [en droit pénal] to prosecute sb / [en droit civil] to sue sb.
◆ ***s'agir*** **v impers : il s'agit de...** it's a matter of... ▸ **il s'agit de faire qqch** we/you must do sthg ▸ **de quoi s'agit-il?** what's it about? ▸ **de qui s'agit-il?** who is it? ▸ **de quoi s'agit-il dans ce film/cette lettre ?** what is this film/letter about? ▸ **mais enfin, il s'agit de sa santé!** but her health is at stake (here)! ▸ **quand il s'agit de râler, tu es toujours là!** you can always be relied upon to moan! ▸ **il s'agirait d'une grande première scientifique** it is said to be an important first for science ▸ **il s'agit de savoir si...** the question is whether...

agissements [aʒismɑ̃] **nmpl** *péj* schemes, intrigues.

agitateur, ***trice*** [aʒitatœr, tris] **nm, f** POLIT agitator.

agitation [aʒitasjɔ̃] **nf** agitation / [politique, sociale] unrest.

agité, ***e*** [aʒite] **adj** **1.** [gén] restless / [enfant, classe] restless, fidgety / [journée, atmosphère] hectic **2.** [mer] rough.

agiter [3] [aʒite] **vt** **1.** [remuer - flacon, objet] to shake / [- drapeau, bras] to wave ▸ **'agiter avant l'emploi'** 'shake well before use' **2.** [énerver] to perturb.
◆ ***s'agiter*** **vp** [personne] to move about, to fidget / [mer] to stir / [population] to get restless.

agit-prop [aʒitprɔp] **nf** POLIT agitprop.

agneau [aɲo] **nm** **1.** [animal, viande] lamb ▸ **doux comme un agneau** gentle as a lamb **2.** [cuir] lambskin.

agonie [agɔni] **nf** [de personne] mortal agony / *fig* death throes *pl* ▸ **être à l'agonie** to be at death's door.

agoniser [3] [agɔnize] **vi** [personne] to be dying / *fig* to be on its last legs.

agoraphobie [agɔrafɔbi] **nf** agoraphobia.

agrafe [agraf] **nf** **1.** [de bureau] staple **2.** MÉD clip.

agrafer [3] [agrafe] **vt** **1.** [attacher] to fasten **2.** *fam fig* [attraper] to nab.

agrafeuse [agraføz] **nf** stapler.

agraire [agrɛr] **adj** agrarian.

agrandir [32] [agrɑ̃dir] **vt** **1.** [élargir - gén & PHOTO] to enlarge / [- rue, écart] to widen **2.** *fig* [développer] to expand **3.** [faire paraître plus grand] **: agrandir qqch** to make sthg look bigger.
◆ ***s'agrandir*** **vp** **1.** [s'étendre] to grow **2.** *fig* [se développer] to expand.

agrandissement [agrɑ̃dismɑ̃] **nm 1.** [gén & PHOTO] enlargement **2.** *fig* [développement] expansion.

agréable [agreabl] **adj** pleasant, nice.

agréablement [agreabləmɑ̃] **adv** pleasantly.

agréé, e [agree] **adj** [concessionnaire, appareil] authorized.

agréer [15] [agree] **vt** *sout* **1.** [accepter] **: faire agréer qqch** to have sthg accepted ▸ **veuillez agréer mes salutations distinguées** *ou* **l'expression de mes sentiments distingués** yours faithfully **2.** [convenir] **: agréer à qqn** to suit *ou* please sb.

agrégat [agrega] **nm 1.** [agglomérat] aggregate **2.** *fig* & *péj* [amas] hotchpotch *UK*, hodgepodge *US*.

agrégation [agregasjɔ̃] **nf** *competitive examination for secondary school and university teachers.*

agrégé, e [agreʒe] **nm, f** *holder of the agrégation.*

agrément [agremɑ̃] **nm 1.** [caractère agréable] attractiveness ▸ **d'agrément** [jardin] ornamental / [voyage] pleasure *(avant n)* **2.** [approbation] consent, approval.

agrémenter [3] [agremɑ̃te] **vt : agrémenter qqch (de qqch)** to embellish sthg (with sthg).
◆ ***s'agrémenter*** **vp : s'agrémenter de qqch** [vêtement] to be trimmed *ou* adorned with sthg.

agrès [agrɛ] **nmpl** SPORT gym apparatus *(U)*.

agresser [4] [agrɛse] **vt 1.** [suj: personne] to attack **2.** *fig* [suj: bruit, pollution] to assault.

agresseur [agrɛsœr] **nm** attacker.

agressif, ive [agrɛsif, iv] **adj** aggressive.

agression [agrɛsjɔ̃] **nf** attack / MIL & PSYCHO aggression.

agressivement [agrɛsivmɑ̃] **adv** aggressively.

agressivité [agrɛsivite] **nf** aggressiveness.

agricole [agrikɔl] **adj** agricultural.

agriculteur, trice [agrikyltœr, tris] **nm, f** farmer.

agriculture [agrikyltyr] **nf** agriculture, farming.

agripper [3] [agripe] **vt 1.** [personne] to cling *ou* hang on to **2.** [objet] to grip, to clutch.
◆ ***s'agripper*** **vp : s'agripper à qqn** to cling *ou* hang on to sb ▸ **s'agripper à qqch** to grip *ou* clutch sthg.

agroalimentaire [agroalimɑ̃tɛr] ■ **adj : industrie agroalimentaire** food-processing industry ▸ **les produits agroalimentaires** processed foods *ou* foodstuffs.
■ **nm : l'agroalimentaire** the food-processing industry.

agronome [agrɔnɔm] **nmf** agronomist.

agronomie [agrɔnɔmi] **nf** agronomy.

agronomique [agrɔnɔmik] **adj** agronomic.

agrume [agrym] **nm** citrus fruit.

aguerrir [32] [agerir] **vt** to harden.
◆ ***s'aguerrir*** **vp : s'aguerrir (contre)** to become hardened (to).

aguets [agɛ] ◆ ***aux aguets*** **loc adv : être/rester aux aguets** to be *ou* keep on the lookout.

aguichant, e [agiʃɑ̃, ɑ̃t] **adj** enticing.

aguicher [3] [agiʃe] **vt** to entice, to allure.

ah [a] **interj** oh!, ah! ▸ **ah bon?** really? ▸ **ah, quelle bonne surprise!** what a nice surprise!

Ah (abr écrite de ***ampère-heure***) ah.

ahuri, e [ayri] **adj : être ahuri (par qqch)** to be taken aback (by sthg).

ahurir [32] [ayrir] **vt** [étonner] to astound.

ahurissant, e [ayrisɑ̃, ɑ̃t] **adj** astounding.

ahurissement [ayrismɑ̃] **nm** astonishment.

ai [ɛ] ➤ ***avoir***.

aide [ɛd] ■ **nf 1.** [gén] help ▸ **à l'aide!** help! ▸ **appeler (qqn) à l'aide** to call (to sb) for help ▸ **venir en aide à qqn** to come to sb's aid, to help sb ▸ **aide ménagère** home help *UK*, home helper *US* **2.** [secours financier] aid ▸ **aide fiscale** tax credit ▸ **aide gouvernementale** *ou* **de l'État** government aid ▸ **aide sociale** social security *UK*, welfare *US*.
■ **nmf** [adjoint] assistant ▸ **aide de camp** MIL aide-de-camp.
◆ ***à l'aide de*** **loc prép** with the help *ou* aid of.

aide-éducateur, trice [ɛdedykatœr, tris] **nm, f** SCOL teaching assistant.

aide-mémoire [ɛdmemwar] **nm inv** aide-mémoire / [pour examen] revision notes *pl UK*.

aider [4] [ede] **vt** to help ▸ **aider qqn à faire qqch** to help sb to do sthg ▸ **aider à faire qqch** to help to do sthg ▸ **aider qqn dans qqch** to help sb with sthg ▸ **se faire aider par** *ou* **de qqn** to be helped by sb, to get help from sb.
◆ ***s'aider*** **vp 1.** [s'assister mutuellement] to help each other **2.** [avoir recours] **: s'aider de** to use, to make use of.

aide-soignant, e [ɛdswaɲɑ̃, ɑ̃t] (**mpl aides-soignants, fpl aides-soignantes**) **nm, f** nursing auxiliary *UK*, nurse's aide *US*.

aie, aies ➤ ***avoir***.

aïe [aj] **interj 1.** [exprime la douleur] ow!, ouch! **2.** [exprime le désagrément] oh dear!, oh no!

AIEA (abr de ***Agence internationale de l'énergie atomique***) **nf** IAEA.

aïeul, e [ajœl] **nm, f** *sout* grandparent, grandfather (f grandmother).

aïeux [ajø] **nmpl** ancestors.

aigle [ɛgl] **nm** eagle.

aiglon [ɛglɔ̃] **nm** eaglet.

aigre [ɛgr] **adj 1.** [gén] sour **2.** [propos] harsh.

aigre-doux, aigre-douce [ɛgrədu, ɛgrədus] **adj 1.** CULIN sweet-and-sour **2.** [propos] bittersweet.

aigrelet, ette [ɛgrəlɛ, ɛt] **adj 1.** [vin] vinegary **2.** [voix] sharpish.

aigrement [ɛgrəmɑ̃] **adv** bitterly.

aigrette [ɛgrɛt] **nf** egret.

aigreur [ɛgrœr] **nf 1.** [d'un aliment] sourness **2.** [d'un propos] harshness.
◆ ***aigreurs d'estomac*** **nfpl** heartburn *(U)*.

aigri, e [egri] **adj** embittered.

aigrir [32] [egrir] **vt** **1.** [aliment] to make sour **2.** [personne] to embitter.
◆ ***s'aigrir*** **vp** **1.** [aliment] to turn sour **2.** [personne] to become bitter.

aigu, uë [egy] **adj** **1.** [son] high-pitched **2.** [objet, lame] sharp / [angle] acute **3.** [douleur] sharp, acute **4.** [conflit, grève] bitter **5.** [intelligence, sens] acute, keen.
◆ ***aigu*** **nm** high note.

aiguillage [egɥijaʒ] **nm** [RAIL - manœuvre] shunting, switching *US* / [- dispositif] points *pl UK*, switch *US*.

aiguille [egɥij] **nf** **1.** [gén] needle ▸ **aiguille à tricoter** knitting needle ▸ **aiguille de pin** pine needle ▸ **chercher une aiguille dans une botte de foin** *fig* to look for a needle in a haystack **2.** [de pendule] hand **3.** GÉOGR peak.

aiguiller [3] [egɥije] **vt** **1.** RAIL to shunt, to switch *US* **2.** [personne, conversation] to steer, to direct.

aiguillette [egɣɥijɛt] **nf** : **aiguillettes de canard** strips of duck breast.

aiguilleur [egɥijœr] **nm** **1.** RAIL pointsman *UK*, switchman *US* **2.** AÉRON : **aiguilleur du ciel** air-traffic controller.

aiguillon [egɥijɔ̃] **nm** **1.** [dard] sting **2.** [stimulant] spur, incentive.

aiguiser [3] [egize] **vt** *litt* & *fig* to sharpen ▸ **aiguiser l'appétit** to whet the appetite.

aïkido, aikido [ajkido] **nm** aikido.

ail [aj] (pl **ails** *ou* **aulx** [o]) **nm** garlic *(U)* / : **ail des bois** *Québec* wild leek.

aile [ɛl] **nf** **1.** [gén] wing ▸ **battre de l'aile** to be in a bad way ▸ **donner des ailes à qqn** to lend sb wings ▸ **voler de ses propres ailes** to stand on one's own two feet **2.** [de moulin] sail.

aileron [ɛlrɔ̃] **nm** **1.** [de requin] fin **2.** [d'avion] aileron.

ailier [elje] **nm** winger.

aille, ailles ➤ ***aller.***

ailleurs [ajœr] **adv** elsewhere, somewhere *ou* someplace *US* else ▸ **elle avait l'esprit ailleurs** *fig* her mind was on other things ▸ **nulle part ailleurs** nowhere *ou* noplace *US* else ▸ **partout ailleurs** everywhere *ou* everyplace *US* else.
◆ ***d'ailleurs*** **loc adv** moreover, besides.
◆ ***par ailleurs*** **loc adv** moreover, furthermore.

ailloli, aïoli [ajɔli] **nm** garlic mayonnaise.

aimable [ɛmabl] **adj** kind, nice.

aimablement [ɛmabləmɑ̃] **adv** kindly.

aimant[1], e [ɛmɑ̃, ɑ̃t] **adj** loving.

aimant[2] [ɛmɑ̃] **nm** magnet.

aimanter [3] [ɛmɑ̃te] **vt** to magnetize.

aimer [4] [eme] **vt** **1.** [gén] to like ▸ **aimer bien qqn/qqch** to like sb/sthg, to be fond of sb/sthg ▸ **aimer bien faire qqch** to (really) like doing sthg ▸ **aimer (à) faire qqch** to like to do sthg, to like doing sthg ▸ **j'aime à croire que...** I like to think that... ▸ **elle aime qu'on l'appelle par son surnom** she likes being called by her nickname ▸ **je n'aime pas que tu rentres seule le soir** I don't like you coming home alone at night ▸ **j'aimerais (bien) que tu viennes avec moi** I'd like you to come with me ▸ **j'aimerais bien une autre tasse de café** I wouldn't mind another cup of coffee ▸ **aimer mieux qqch** to prefer sthg ▸ **aimer mieux faire qqch** to prefer doing *ou* to do sthg **2.** [d'amour] to love.
◆ ***s'aimer*** **vp** **1.** *(emploi réfléchi)* to like o.s. **2.** *(emploi réciproque)* to love each other ▸ **s'aimer bien** to like each other.

aine [ɛn] **nf** groin.

aîné, e [ene] ■ **adj** [plus âgé] elder, older / [le plus âgé] eldest, oldest.
■ **nm, f** [plus âgé] older *ou* elder child, older *ou* eldest son/daughter / [le plus âgé] oldest *ou* eldest child, oldest *ou* eldest son/daughter ▸ **elle est mon aînée de deux ans** she is two years older than me.

aînesse [ɛnɛs] ➤ ***droit.***

ainsi [ɛ̃si] **adv** **1.** [manière] in this way, like this **2.** [valeur conclusive] thus ▸ **ainsi donc** so ▸ **et ainsi de suite** and so on, and so forth ▸ **pour ainsi dire** so to speak ▸ **ainsi soit-il** RELIG so be it, amen.
◆ ***ainsi que*** **loc conj** **1.** [comme, de même que] as **2.** [et] as well as.

aïoli = ***ailloli.***

air [ɛr] **nm** **1.** [gén] air ▸ **le grand air** the fresh air ▸ **à l'air libre** in the open air ▸ **dans l'air** *ou* **les airs** (up) in the air *ou* sky *ou* skies *littéraire* ▸ **il y a de l'orage dans l'air** *litt* & *fig* there's a storm brewing ▸ **en plein air** (out) in the open air, outside ▸ **prendre l'air** to get some (fresh) air ▸ **en l'air** [projet] (up) in the air / *fig* [paroles] empty ▸ **les mains en l'air!** hands up! ▸ **encore des paroles en l'air!** more empty words! ▸ **air comprimé** compressed air ▸ **air conditionné** air-conditioning ▸ **s'envoyer en l'air** *vulg* to get laid **2.** [apparence, mine] air, look ▸ **il a l'air triste** he looks sad ▸ **il a l'air de bouder** it looks as if he's sulking ▸ **il a l'air de faire beau** it looks like being a nice day ▸ **sans en avoir l'air** without showing it ▸ **sans en avoir l'air, elle a tout rangé en une heure** she tidied up everything in an hour without even looking busy ▸ **d'un air dégagé** in a casual manner ▸ **n'avoir l'air de rien** to look *ou* seem unremarkable, to look *ou* seem insignificant ▸ **ça n'a l'air de rien comme ça, mais c'est une lourde tâche** it doesn't look much but it's quite a big job ▸ **un air de famille** a family resemblance ▸ **prendre de grands airs** to put on airs (and graces *UK*) **3.** MUS tune / [à l'opéra] aria.

Airbag® [ɛrbag] **nm** airbag.

aire [ɛr] **nf** **1.** [gén] area ▸ **aire d'atterrissage** landing strip ▸ **aire d'embarquement** boarding area ▸ **aire de jeu** playground ▸ **aire de lancement** launching site ▸ **aire de repos** lay-by *UK*, rest area *US* ▸ **aire de stationnement** parking area **2.** [nid] eyrie.

airelle [ɛrɛl] **nf** bilberry.

aisance [ɛzɑ̃s] **nf** **1.** [facilité] ease **2.** [richesse] : **il vit dans l'aisance** he has an affluent lifestyle.

aise [ɛz] ■ **nf** *sout* pleasure ▸ **être à l'aise** *ou* **à son aise** [confortable] to feel comfortable / [financièrement] to be comfortably off ▸ **mettez-vous à l'aise** make yourself comfortable ▸ **mettre qqn mal à l'aise** to make sb feel ill at ease *ou* uneasy ▸ **en prendre à son aise** to do as one likes ▸ **à votre aise** please yourself, as you wish.

■ **adj : être bien aise (de faire qqch)** to be delighted (to do sthg).
◆ ***aises*** **nfpl : aimer ses aises** to like one's (home) comforts ▸ **prendre ses aises** to make o.s. comfortable.

aisé, e [eze] **adj 1.** [facile] easy **2.** [riche] well-off.

aisément [ezemɑ̃] **adv** easily.

aisselle [ɛsɛl] **nf** armpit.

ajonc [aʒɔ̃] **nm** gorse *(U)*.

ajournement [aʒurnəmɑ̃] **nm** adjournment, postponement.

ajourner [3] [aʒurne] **vt 1.** [reporter - décision] to postpone / [- réunion, procès] to adjourn **2.** [candidat] to refer.

ajout [aʒu] **nm** addition.

ajouter [3] [aʒute] **vt** to add ▸ **ajouter que** to add that ▸ **ajouter foi à qqch** *sout* to give credence to sthg.
◆ ***s'ajouter*** **vp : s'ajouter à qqch** to be in addition to sthg.

ajustage [aʒystaʒ] **nm** fitting.

ajusté, e [aʒyste] **adj** [coupé] fitted, tailored.

ajuster [3] [aʒyste] **vt 1.** [monter] **: ajuster qqch (à)** to fit sthg (to) **2.** [régler] to adjust **3.** [vêtement] to alter **4.** [tir, coup] to aim **5.** [arranger - coiffure, cravate] to adjust.
◆ ***s'ajuster*** **vp** to be adaptable.

ajusteur [aʒystœr] **nm** fitter.

alaise, alèse [alɛz] **nf** undersheet.

alambiqué, e [alɑ̃bike] **adj** convoluted.

alarmant, e [alarmɑ̃, ɑ̃t] **adj** alarming.

alarme [alarm] **nf** alarm ▸ **donner l'alarme** to give *ou* raise the alarm.

alarmer [3] [alarme] **vt** to alarm.
◆ ***s'alarmer*** **vp** to get *ou* become alarmed.

alarmiste [alarmist] ■ **nmf** scaremonger.
■ **adj** alarmist.

albanais, e [albanɛ, ɛz] **adj** Albanian.
◆ ***albanais*** **nm** [langue] Albanian.
◆ ***Albanais, e*** **nm, f** Albanian.

Albanie [albani] **nf : l'Albanie** Albania.

albâtre [albatr] **nm** alabaster.

albatros [albatros] **nm** albatross.

albinos [albinos] **nmf & adj inv** albino.

album [albɔm] **nm** album ▸ **album (de) photo** photo album.

albumine [albymin] **nf** albumin.

alcalin, e [alkalɛ̃, in] **adj** alkaline.

alchimiste [alʃimist] **nmf** alchemist.

alcool [alkɔl] **nm** alcohol ▸ **alcool à brûler** methylated spirits *pl* ▸ **alcool à 90 degrés** surgical spirit ▸ **alcool de prune/poire** plum/pear brandy.

alcoolémie [alkɔlemi] **nf : taux d'alcoolémie** blood alcohol level.

alcoolique [alkɔlik] **nmf & adj** alcoholic.

alcoolisé, e [alkɔlize] **adj** alcoholic.

alcoolisme [alkɔlism] **nm** alcoholism.

Alc(o)otest® [alkɔtɛst] **nm** ≃ Breathalyser® *UK*, ≃ Breathalyzer® *US* ▸ **passer un Alcootest** to be breathalysed *UK ou* breathalyzed *US*.

alcôve [alkov] **nf** recess ▸ **secret d'alcôve** intimate secret.

aléa [alea] **nm** *(gén pl) sout* hazard.

aléatoire [aleatwar] **adj 1.** [avenir] uncertain **2.** [choix] random.

alémanique [alemanik] **adj : Suisse alémanique** German-speaking (part of) Switzerland.

ALENA (abr de ***Accord de libre-échange nord-américain***) **nm** NAFTA *(North American Free Trade Agreement)*.

alentour [alɑ̃tur] **adv** around, around about.
◆ ***alentours*** **nmpl** surroundings ▸ **les alentours de la ville** the outskirts of the city ▸ **aux alentours de** [spatial] in the vicinity of / [temporel] around.

alerte [alɛrt] ■ **adj 1.** [personne, esprit] agile, alert **2.** [style, pas] lively.
■ **nf** alarm, alert ▸ **donner l'alerte** to sound *ou* give the alert ▸ **alerte à la bombe** bomb scare ▸ **fausse alerte** false alarm.

alerter [3] [alɛrte] **vt** to warn, to alert.

alèse = ***alaise***.

alexandrin [alɛksɑ̃drɛ̃] **nm** alexandrine.

algèbre [alʒɛbr] **nf** algebra.

Alger [alʒe] **npr** Algiers.

Algérie [alʒeri] **nf : l'Algérie** Algeria.

algérien, enne [alʒerjɛ̃, ɛn] **adj** Algerian.
◆ ***Algérien, enne*** **nm, f** Algerian.

algérois, e [alʒerwa, az] **adj** of/from Algiers.
◆ ***Algérois, e*** **nm, f** person from Algiers.

algue [alg] **nf** seaweed *(U)*.

alias [aljas] ■ **adv** alias.
■ **nm** INFORM [dans un mail, sur le bureau] alias.

aliassage [aljasaʒ] **m** INFORM aliasing.

alibi [alibi] **nm** alibi.

alicament [alikamɑ̃] **nm** [avec additifs] nutraceutical, dietary supplement / [biologique] organic food *(consumed for its health benefits)*.

aliénation [aljenasjɔ̃] **nf** alienation ▸ **aliénation mentale** insanity.

aliéné, e [aljene] ■ **adj 1.** MÉD insane **2.** DR alienated.
■ **nm, f** MÉD insane person.

aliéner [18] [aljene] **vt** [abandonner - indépendance, liberté, droit] to give up / DR to alienate.
◆ ***s'aliéner*** **vpt : s'aliéner qqn** to alienate sb.

alignement [aliɲmɑ̃] **nm** alignment, lining up ▸ **alignement sur** alignment with ▸ **être dans l'alignement de** to be in line with.

aligner [3] [aliɲe] **vt 1.** [disposer en ligne] to line up, to align **2.** [présenter] to set out **3.** [adapter] **: aligner qqch sur** to align sthg with, to bring sthg into line with.
◆ ***s'aligner*** **vp** to line up ▸ **s'aligner sur** POLIT to align o.s. with.

aliment [alimɑ̃] **nm** [nourriture] food *(U)*.

alimentaire [alimɑ̃tɛr] **adj 1.** [gén] food *(avant n)* ▸ **c'est juste un travail alimentaire** I'm doing this job just for the money **2.** DR maintenance *(avant n)*.

alimentation [alimɑ̃tasjɔ̃] **nf 1.** [nourriture] diet ▸ **magasin d'alimentation** grocer's *UK*, food store *US* **2.** [approvisionnement] **: alimentation (en)** supply *ou* supplying *(U)* (of).

alimenter [3] [alimɑ̃te] **vt 1.** [nourrir] to feed **2.** [approvisionner] **: alimenter qqch en** to supply sthg with **3.** *fig* [entretenir] to keep going.
◆ ***s'alimenter*** **vp** to eat.

alinéa [alinea] **nm 1.** [retrait de ligne] indent **2.** [dans un document officiel] paragraph.

aliter [3] [alite] **vt : être alité** to be bedridden.
◆ ***s'aliter*** **vp** to take to one's bed.

Allah [ala] **nm** Allah.

allaitement [alɛtmɑ̃] **nm** [d'enfant] breast-feeding / [d'animal] suckling.

allaiter [4] [alete] **vt** [enfant] to breast-feed / [animal] to suckle.

allant [alɑ̃] **nm : plein d'allant** dynamic.

allé, e [ale] **pp** ➤ ***aller***.

alléchant, e [aleʃɑ̃, ɑ̃t] **adj** mouth-watering, tempting.

allécher [18] [aleʃe] **vt : il a été alléché par l'odeur/la perspective** the smell/prospect made his mouth water.

allée [ale] **nf 1.** [dans un jardin] path / [dans une ville] avenue **2.** [passage] aisle / [devant une maison, une villa] drive, driveway ▸ **les allées du pouvoir** the corridors of power **3.** [trajet] **: allées et venues** comings and goings ▸ **toutes ces allées et venues pour rien** all this running around for nothing **4.** *Québec* [golf] fairway.

allégation [alegasjɔ̃] **nf** allegation.

allégé, e [aleʒe] **adj** [régime, produit] low-fat.

allégeance [aleʒɑ̃s] **nf** allegiance.

allègement [alɛʒmɑ̃] **nm 1.** [diminution - d'un fardeau] lightening / [- d'une douleur] relief **2.** ÉCON & FIN reduction ▸ **allègement fiscal** tax reduction.

alléger [22] [aleʒe] **vt 1.** [fardeau] to lighten **2.** [douleur] to relieve.

allégorie [alegɔri] **nf** allegory.

allègre [alɛgr] **adj 1.** [ton] cheerful **2.** [démarche] jaunty.

allégresse [alegrɛs] **nf** elation.

alléguer [18] [alege] **vt : alléguer une excuse** to put forward an excuse ▸ **alléguer que** to plead (that).

Allemagne [almaɲ] **nf : l'Allemagne** Germany ▸ **l'(ex-)Allemagne de l'Est** (the former) East Germany ▸ **l'(ex-)Allemagne de l'Ouest** (the former) West Germany.

allemand, e [almɑ̃, ɑ̃d] **adj** German.
◆ ***allemand*** **nm** [langue] German.
◆ ***Allemand, e*** **nm, f** German ▸ **un Allemand de l'Est/l'Ouest** an East/a West German.

aller [31] [ale] ■ **nm 1.** [trajet] outward journey **2.** [billet] single ticket *UK*, one-way ticket *US* ▸ **aller (et) retour** return *UK ou* round-trip *US* (ticket).

■ **vi 1.** [gén] to go ▸ **allez!** come on! ▸ **allez, au revoir!** bye then! ▸ **vas-y!** go on! ▸ **allons-y!, on y va!** let's go!, off we go! ▸ **aller (et) venir** [de long en large] to pace up and down / [entre deux destinations] to come and go, to go to and fro ▸ **comment y va-t-on?** how do you get there?
2. *(+ infinitif)* **: aller faire qqch** to go and do sthg ▸ **aller chercher les enfants à l'école** to go and pick up the children from school ▸ **aller travailler/se promener** to go to work/for a walk ▸ **ne va pas croire/penser que...** don't go and believe/think that...
3. [indiquant un état] **: comment vas-tu?** how are you? ▸ **je vais bien** I'm very well, I'm fine ▸ **aller mal : il va mal** he's not at all well, he's very poorly ▸ **comment ça va? ça va** [santé] how are you? fine *ou* all right / [situation] how are things? fine *ou* all right ▸ **aller mieux** to be better
4. [convenir] **: ce type de clou ne va pas pour ce travail** this kind of nail won't do *ou* isn't suitable for this job ▸ **aller avec** to go with ▸ **aller à qqn** to suit sb / [suj: vêtement, taille] to fit sb ▸ **le bleu lui va** blue suits her, she looks good in blue ▸ **ces couleurs ne vont pas ensemble** these colours don't go well together
5. [mener - véhicule, chemin] to go ▸ **cette rue va vers le centre** this street leads towards the city centre
6. [fonctionner - machine] to go, to run / [- moteur] to run / [- voiture, train] to go
▸▸ **cela va de soi, cela va sans dire** that goes without saying ▸ **il y va de votre vie!** your life is at stake!, your life depends on it! ▸ **il en va de... comme...** the same goes for... as... ▸ **il en va de même pour lui** the same goes for him ▸ **aller à la faillite/l'échec** to be heading for bankruptcy/failure ▸ **allons bon, j'ai perdu ma clef maintenant!** oh no, now I've lost my key! ▸ **y aller** [le faire] **: vas-y doucement, c'est fragile** gently *ou* easy does it: it's fragile.
■ **v aux** *(+ infinitif)* [exprime le futur proche] to be going to, will ▸ **je vais arriver en retard** I'm going to arrive late, I'll arrive late ▸ **nous allons bientôt avoir fini** we'll soon have finished.
◆ ***s'en aller*** **vp 1.** [partir] to go (away), to be off ▸ **allez-vous-en!** go away!
2. [disparaître] to go away ▸ **ça s'en ira au lavage/avec du savon** it'll come out in the wash/with soap.

allergie [alɛrʒi] **nf** allergy.

allergique [alɛrʒik] **adj : allergique (à)** allergic (to).

aller-retour [alerətur] **nm** return *UK ou* round-trip *US* (ticket).

alliage [aljaʒ] **nm** alloy.

alliance [aljɑ̃s] **nf 1.** [union - stratégique] alliance / [- par le mariage] union, marriage ▸ **cousin par alliance** cousin by marriage **2.** [bague] wedding ring **3.** [organisation] **: l'Alliance française** *organization promoting French language and culture abroad* **4.** [marketing] **: alliance de marque** co-branding.

allié, e [alje] ■ **adj : allié (à)** allied (to).
■ **nm, f** ally.
◆ ***Alliés*** **nmpl : les Alliés** the Allies.

allier [9] [alje] **vt 1.** [métaux] to alloy **2.** [associer] to combine.
◆ ***s'allier*** **vp** to become allies ▸ **s'allier qqn** to win sb over as an ally ▸ **s'allier à qqn** to ally with sb.

alligator [aligatɔr] **nm** alligator.

allitération [aliterasjɔ̃] **nf** alliteration.

allô [alo] **interj** hello!

allocataire [alɔkatɛr] **nmf** beneficiary.

allocation [alɔkasjɔ̃] **nf 1.** [attribution] allocation **2.** [aide financière] **: allocation chômage** unemployment benefit *(U) UK ou* compensation *(U) US* ▸ **allocation logement** housing benefit *(U) UK*, rent subsidy *(U) US* ▸ **allocations familiales** family credit *(U) UK*, welfare *(U) US*.

allocs [alɔk] (abr de ***allocations familiales***) *fam* **nfpl : les allocs** family credit *(U) UK*, welfare *(U) US*.

allocution [alɔkysjɔ̃] **nf** short speech.

allongé, ***e*** [alɔ̃ʒe] **adj 1.** [position] **: être allongé** to be lying down *ou* stretched out **2.** [forme] elongated.

allongement [alɔ̃ʒmɑ̃] **nm** lengthening.

allonger [17] [alɔ̃ʒe] ■ **vt 1.** [gén] to lengthen, to make longer ▸ **la coupe vous allonge la silhouette** the cut of the garment makes you look slimmer **2.** [jambe, bras] to stretch (out) ▸ **allonger le cou** to stretch one's neck **3.** [personne] to lay down **4.** *fam* [argent] to dish out ▸ **cette fois-ci, il a fallu qu'il les allonge** this time he had to cough up *ou* to fork out **5.** *fam* [coup] to aim ▸ **allonger une taloche à qqn** to give sb a slap.
■ **vi** [jours] to grow longer.
◆ ***s'allonger*** **vp 1.** [gén] to get longer **2.** [se coucher] to lie down ▸ **allonge-toi un peu** have a little lie-down **3.** [se déployer] to stretch (out) ▸ **il/le chien s'allongea sur le tapis** he/the dog stretched out on the rug.

allopathique [alɔpatik] **adj** allopathic.

allouer [6] [alwe] **vt : allouer qqch à qqn** to allocate sthg to sb.

allumage [alymaʒ] **nm 1.** [de feu] lighting **2.** [d'appareil électrique] switching *ou* turning on **3.** [de moteur] ignition.

allume-cigares [alymsigar] **nm inv** cigar lighter.

allume-gaz [alymgaz] **nm inv** gas lighter.

allumer [3] [alyme] **vt 1.** [lampe, radio, télévision] to turn *ou* switch on ▸ **allume dans la cuisine** turn the kitchen light on **2.** [gaz] to light / [cigarette] to light (up) **3.** *fam* [personne] to turn on.
◆ ***s'allumer*** **vp 1.** [gén] to light up ▸ **s'allumer de** *fig* [de joie, curiosité] to light up with **2.** ÉLECTR to come *ou* go on.

allumette [alymɛt] **nf** match ▸ **craquer une allumette** to strike a match.

allumeuse [alymøz] **nf** *fam péj* tease.

allure [alyr] **nf 1.** [vitesse] speed ▸ **à toute allure** at top *ou* full speed **2.** [prestance] presence ▸ **avoir de l'allure** to have style **3.** [apparence générale] appearance ▸ **avoir une drôle d'allure** to look odd ▸ **avoir fière allure** to cut a striking figure.

allusion [alyzjɔ̃] **nf** allusion ▸ **faire allusion à** to refer *ou* allude to.

alluvions [alyvjɔ̃] **nmpl** alluvion *(U)*.

almanach [almana] **nm** almanac.

aloès [alɔɛs] **nm** aloe.

aloi [alwa] **nm : de bon aloi** [mesure] of real worth ▸ **de mauvais aloi** [gaîté] not genuine / [plaisanterie] in bad taste.

alors [alɔr] **adv 1.** [jadis] then, at that time **2.** [à ce moment-là] then ▸ **je préfère renoncer tout de suite, alors!** in that case I'd just as soon give up straight away!
3. [exprimant la conséquence] then, so ▸ **il s'est mis à pleuvoir, alors nous sommes rentrés** it started to rain, so we came back in ▸ **et alors, qu'est-ce qui s'est passé?** so what happened? ▸ **il va se mettre en colère – et alors?** he'll be angry – so what?
4. [emploi expressif] well (then) ▸ **alors, qu'est-ce qu'on fait?** well, what are we doing? ▸ **alors là, il exagère!** he's going a bit far there! ▸ **ça alors!** well fancy that!
◆ ***d'alors*** **loc adv** at that time ▸ **le cinéma d'alors était encore muet** films were still silent in those days.
◆ ***jusqu'alors*** **loc adv** (up) until then.
◆ ***alors que*** **loc conj 1.** [exprimant le temps] while, when ▸ **l'orage éclata alors que nous étions encore loin de la maison** the storm broke while *ou* when we were still a long way from the house
2. [exprimant l'opposition] even though ▸ **elle est sortie alors que c'était interdit** she went out even though it was forbidden ▸ **ils aiment le café alors que nous, nous buvons du thé** they like coffee, whereas we drink tea.

alouette [alwet] **nf** lark.

alourdir [32] [alurdir] **vt 1.** [gén] to weigh down, to make heavy **2.** *fig* [impôts] to increase.
◆ ***s'alourdir*** **vp 1.** [taille] to get bigger **2.** [paupières] to grow heavy.

aloyau [alwajo] **nm** sirloin.

alpage [alpaʒ] **nm** high mountain pasture.

Alpes [alp] **nfpl : les Alpes** the Alps.

alpestre [alpɛstr] **adj** alpine.

alpha [alfa] **nm** alpha ▸ **l'alpha et l'oméga de** *fig* the beginning and the end of.

alphabet [alfabɛ] **nm** alphabet.

alphabétique [alfabetik] **adj** alphabetical.

alphabétisation [alfabetizasjɔ̃] **nf** teaching of literacy.

alphabétiser [3] [alfabetize] **vt : alphabétiser qqn** to teach sb (how) to read and write ▸ **alphabétiser un pays** to eliminate illiteracy from a country.

alpin, ***e*** [alpɛ̃, in] **adj** alpine.

alpinisme [alpinism] **nm** mountaineering.

alpiniste [alpinist] **nmf** mountaineer.

Alsace [alzas] **nf : l'Alsace** Alsace.

alsacien, ***enne*** [alzasjɛ̃, ɛn] **adj** Alsatian.
◆ ***alsacien*** **nm** [dialecte] Alsatian.
◆ ***Alsacien***, ***enne*** **nm, f** Alsatian.

altération [alterasjɔ̃] **nf 1.** [dégradation - gén] alteration, distortion / [- de santé] deterioration **2.** MUS inflection.

altercation [alterkasjɔ̃] **nf** altercation.

alter ego [alterego] **nm inv** alter ego.

altérer [18] [altere] **vt 1.** [détériorer] to spoil **2.** [santé] to harm, to affect / [vérité, récit] to distort.
◆ ***s'altérer*** **vp 1.** [matière - métal] to deteriorate / [- aliment] to go off, to spoil **2.** [santé] to deteriorate.

alternance [altɛrnɑ̃s] **nf 1.** [succession] alternation ▸ **en alternance** alternately **2.** POLIT change of government party.

alternatif, ive [altɛrnatif, iv] **adj 1.** [périodique] alternating **2.** [parallèle] alternative.
◆ ***alternative*** **nf** alternative.

PARONYME / CONFUSABLE
alternatif

Quand vous traduisez **alternatif**, attention à utiliser le bon mot : ***alternative*** signifie parallèle et désigne un fonctionnement autre, non traditionnel, tandis que *alternate* signifie intermittent.

alternativement [altɛrnativmɑ̃] **adv** alternately.

alterner [3] [altɛrne] ■ **vt : (faire) alterner qqch et qqch** to alternate sthg with sthg.
■ **vi** [se succéder] **: alterner (avec)** to alternate (with).

altesse [altɛs] **nf : Son Altesse** His/Her Highness.

altier, ère [altje, ɛr] **adj** haughty.

altimètre [altimɛtr] **nm** altimeter.

altiport [altipɔr] **nm** *airport at high altitude, used especially to serve ski resorts.*

altitude [altityd] **nf** altitude, height ▸ **en altitude** at (high) altitude ▸ **monter en altitude** to climb to altitude ▸ **prendre de l'altitude** AÉRON to gain height *ou* altitude.

alto [alto] **nm** [MUS - voix] alto / [- instrument] viola.

alu [aly] *fam* ■ **nm** [métal] aluminium *UK*, aluminum *US* / [papier] aluminium *UK ou* aluminum *US* foil, tinfoil.
■ **adj : papier alu** aluminium *UK ou* aluminum *US* foil, tinfoil.

aluminium [alyminjɔm] **nm** aluminium *UK*, aluminum *US*.

alunir [32] [alynir] **vi** to land on the moon.

alunissage [alynisaʒ] **nm** moon landing.

alvéole [alveɔl] **nf 1.** [cavité] cavity ▸ **alvéole dentaire** tooth socket **2.** [de ruche, poumon] alveolus.

amabilité [amabilite] **nf** kindness ▸ **avoir l'amabilité de faire qqch** to be so kind as to do sthg.

amadou [amadu] **nm** touchwood, tinder.

amadouer [6] [amadwe] **vt** [adoucir] to tame, to pacify / [persuader] to coax.
◆ ***s'amadouer*** **vp** to relent.

amaigri, e [amegri] **adj** [visage] gaunt / [trait] (more) pinched ▸ **je le trouve très amaigri** he looks a lot thinner *ou* as if he's lost a lot of weight.

amaigrir [32] [amegrir] **vt** to make thin *ou* thinner.
◆ ***s'amaigrir*** **vp** to get thin *ou* thinner.

amaigrissant, e [amegrisɑ̃, ɑ̃t] **adj** slimming *(avant n) UK*, reducing *(avant n) US*.

amaigrissement [amegrismɑ̃] **nm** loss of weight.

amalgame [amalgam] **nm 1.** TECHNOL amalgam **2.** [de styles] mixture **3.** [d'idées, de notions] **: il ne faut pas faire l'amalgame entre ces deux questions** the two issues must not be confused.

amalgamer [3] [amalgame] **vt** to combine.
◆ ***s'amalgamer*** **vp : s'amalgamer avec *ou* à** to be combined *ou* mixed with.

amande [amɑ̃d] **nf** almond ▸ **en amande** *fig* almond-shaped.

amandier [amɑ̃dje] **nm** almond tree.

amanite [amanit] **nf : amanite phalloïde** death-cap (mushroom).

amant [amɑ̃] **nm** (male) lover.
◆ ***amants*** **nmpl** lovers.

amarre [amar] **nf** rope, cable ▸ **larguer les amarres** [bateau] to cast off / *fam fig* [partir] to hit the road.

amarrer [3] [amare] **vt 1.** NAUT to moor **2.** [fixer] to tie down **3.** [navette spatiale] to dock.
◆ ***s'amarrer*** **vpi 1.** NAUT [à une berge] to moor / [dans un port] to dock, to berth **2.** [navette spatiale] to dock.

amaryllis [amarilis] **nf** amaryllis.

amas [ama] **nm** pile.

amasser [3] [amase] **vt 1.** [objets] to pile up **2.** [argent] to accumulate.
◆ ***s'amasser*** **vp 1.** [gén] to pile up **2.** [foule] to gather.

amateur [amatœr] **nm 1.** [connaisseur - d'art, de bon café] **: amateur de** lover of **2.** [non-professionnel] amateur ▸ **faire qqch en amateur** to do sthg as a hobby **3.** *péj* [dilettante] amateur.

amateurisme [amatœrism] **nm 1.** SPORT amateurism **2.** *péj* [dilettantisme] amateurishness.

amazone [amazon] **nf** horsewoman ▸ **monter en amazone** to ride sidesaddle.

Amazone [amazon] **nf : l'Amazone** the Amazon (River).

Amazonie [amazoni] **nf : l'Amazonie** the Amazon (Basin).

amazonien, enne [amazonjɛ̃, ɛn] **adj** Amazonian ▸ **la forêt amazonienne** the Amazon rain forest.

ambages [ɑ̃baʒ] ◆ ***sans ambages*** **loc adv** *sout* without beating about the bush.

ambassade [ɑ̃basad] **nf** embassy.

ambassadeur, drice [ɑ̃basadœr, dris] **nm, f** ambassador.

ambiance [ɑ̃bjɑ̃s] **nf** atmosphere ▸ **il y a de l'ambiance!** there's a good atmosphere!

ambiant, e [ɑ̃bjɑ̃, ɑ̃t] **adj : température ambiante** room temperature.

ambidextre [ɑ̃bidɛkstr] ■ **nmf** ambidextrous person.
■ **adj** ambidextrous.

ambigu, uë [ɑ̃bigy] **adj** ambiguous.

ambiguïté [ɑ̃bigɥite] **nf** ambiguity ▸ **sans ambiguïté** [parler, répondre] unambiguously / [réponse, attitude] unambiguous.

ambitieux, euse [ɑ̃bisjø, øz] ■ **nm, f** ambitious person.
■ **adj** ambitious.

ambition [ɑ̃bisjɔ̃] **nf 1.** *péj* [arrivisme] ambitiousness **2.** [désir] ambition ▸ **avoir l'ambition de faire qqch** to have an ambition to do sthg.

ambitionner [3] [ɑ̃bisjɔne] **vt : ambitionner qqch/ de faire qqch** to seek sthg/to do sthg.

ambivalent**, **e [ɑ̃bivalɑ̃, ɑ̃t] **adj** ambivalent.

ambre [ɑ̃br] **nm 1.** [couleur] amber **2.** [matière] **: ambre (gris)** ambergris.

ambré**, **e [ɑ̃bre] **adj** [couleur] amber.

ambulance [ɑ̃bylɑ̃s] **nf** ambulance.

ambulancier**, **ère [ɑ̃bylɑ̃sje, ɛr] **nm, f** ambulanceman (f ambulancewoman).

ambulant**, **e [ɑ̃bylɑ̃, ɑ̃t] **adj** travelling *UK*, traveling *US (avant n)*.

AME (abr de ***Accord monétaire européen***) m EMA *(European Monetary Agreement)*.

âme [ɑm] **nf 1.** [esprit] soul ▸ **de toute mon âme** with all my heart *ou* soul ▸ **dans l'âme** [par goût] at heart / [accompli] through and through ▸ **c'est un artiste dans l'âme** he's a born artist ▸ **avoir une âme de comédien** to be a born actor ▸ **une bonne âme** *hum* a kind soul **2.** [personne] **: âme sœur** soulmate ▸ **être l'âme de qqch** to be the heart and soul of sthg ▸ **c'était elle, l'âme du groupe** *fig* she was the inspiration of the group ▸ **un village de 500 âmes** a village of 500 souls **3.** [caractère] spirit, soul ▸ **avoir *ou* être une âme généreuse** to have great generosity of spirit

▸▸ **aller *ou* errer comme une âme en peine** to wander around like a lost soul ▸ **en mon âme et conscience** in all honesty ▸ **sans rencontrer âme qui vive** without seeing a living soul ▸ **rendre l'âme** to breathe one's last.

amélioration [ameljɔrasjɔ̃] **nf** improvement.

améliorer [3] [ameljɔre] **vt** to improve.

◆ ***s'améliorer*** **vp** to improve.

amen [amɛn] **adv** amen.

aménagé**, **e [amenaʒe] **adj** [cuisine, camping] fully-equipped.

aménagement [amenaʒmɑ̃] **nm 1.** [de lieu] fitting out ▸ **aménagement du territoire** town and country planning, regional development **2.** [de programme] planning, organizing.

aménager [17] [amenaʒe] **vt 1.** [pièce] to fit out **2.** [programme] to plan, to organize.

amende [amɑ̃d] **nf** fine ▸ **mettre qqn à l'amende** to penalize sb ▸ **faire amende honorable** to admit one's mistake.

amendement [amɑ̃dmɑ̃] **nm** POLIT amendment.

amender [3] [amɑ̃de] **vt 1.** POLIT to amend **2.** AGRIC to enrich.

◆ ***s'amender*** **vp** to mend one's ways.

amène [amɛn] **adj** *sout* amiable, affable.

amener [19] [amne] **vt 1.** [mener] to bring **2.** [inciter] **: amener qqn à faire qqch** [suj: circonstances] to lead sb to do sthg / [suj: personne] to get sb to do sthg **3.** [occasionner, préparer] to bring about.

◆ ***s'amener*** **vp** *fam* **1.** [arriver] to turn up, to show up **2.** [venir] to come.

aménorrhée [amenɔre] **nf** MÉD amenorrhoea, amenorrhea *US*.

amenuiser [3] [amənɥize] **vt 1.** [rendre plus petit] **: ses cheveux amenuisent son visage** her hair makes her face look thinner **2.** [réduire] to diminish, to reduce.

◆ ***s'amenuiser*** **vp** to dwindle, to diminish.

amer**, **ère [amɛr] **adj** bitter.

amèrement [amɛrmɑ̃] **adv** bitterly.

américain**, **e [amerikɛ̃, ɛn] **adj** American.

◆ ***américain*** **nm** [langue] American English.

◆ ***Américain**, **e*** **nm, f** American.

américanisme [amerikanism] **nm** Americanism.

amérindien**, **enne [amerɛdjɛ̃, ɛn] **adj** Native American.

◆ ***Amérindien**, **enne*** **nm, f** Native American.

Amérique [amerik] **nf : l'Amérique** America ▸ **l'Amérique centrale** Central America ▸ **l'Amérique du Nord** North America ▸ **l'Amérique du Sud** South America ▸ **l'Amérique latine** Latin America.

amerrir [32] [amerir] **vi** [hydravion] to land (on the sea) / [cabine spatiale] to splash down.

amertume [amɛrtym] **nf** bitterness.

améthyste [ametist] **nf** amethyst.

ameublement [amœbləmɑ̃] **nm** [meubles] furniture / [action de meubler] furnishing.

ameublir [32] [amœblir] **vt** [sol] to break up.

ameuter [3] [amœte] **vt** [curieux] to draw a crowd of / [quartier, voisins] to bring out.

ami**, **e [ami] ■ **adj** friendly ▸ **dans une maison amie** in the house of friends.

■ **nm, f 1.** [camarade] friend ▸ **c'est un de mes amis/ une de mes amies** he's/she's a friend of mine ▸ **je m'en suis fait une amie** she became my friend *ou* a friend (of mine) ▸ **ami d'enfance** childhood friend ▸ **petit ami** boyfriend ▸ **petite amie** girlfriend **2.** [partisan] supporter, friend ▸ **club des amis de Shakespeare** Shakespeare club *ou* society.

◆ ***en ami*** **loc adv** [par amitié] as a friend ▸ **je te le dis en ami** I'm telling you as a friend *ou* because I'm your friend.

◆ ***faux ami*** **nm** LING false friend.

amiable [amjabl] **adj** [accord] friendly, informal.

◆ ***à l'amiable*** **loc adv & loc adj** out of court.

amiante [amjɑ̃t] **nm** asbestos.

amibe [amib] **nf** amoeba, ameba *US*.

amibien**, **enne [amibjɛ̃, ɛn] **adj** amoebic, amebic *US*.

◆ ***amibien*** **nm** amoeba, ameba *US*.

amical**, **e**, **aux [amikal, o] **adj** friendly.

◆ ***amicale*** **nf** association, club *(for people with a shared interest)*.

amicalement [amikalmɑ̃] **adv 1.** [de façon amicale] amicably, in a friendly way **2.** [dans une lettre] yours (ever), (with) best wishes.

amidon [amidɔ̃] **nm** starch.

amidonner [3] [amidɔne] **vt** to starch.

amincir [32] [amɛ̃sir] ■ **vt : amincir qqn** to make sb look slimmer.

■ **vi** to get slimmer *ou* thinner.

◆ ***s'amincir*** **vp** *fig* [diminuer] to dwindle, to diminish.

amincissant**, **e [amɛ̃sisɑ̃, ɑ̃t] **adj** slimming.

amiral, aux [amiral, o] **nm** admiral.

amitié [amitje] **nf 1.** [affection] affection ▸ **prendre qqn en amitié** to befriend sb ▸ **avoir de l'amitié pour qqn** to be fond of sb **2.** [rapports amicaux] friendship ▸ **faire qqch par amitié** to do sthg out of friendship ▸ **faire ses amitiés à qqn** to give sb one's good *ou* best wishes **3.** [courrier] **: (toutes) mes amitiés** best regards *ou* wishes ▸ **amitiés, Marie** love *ou* yours, Marie.

AMM (abr de ***Autorisation de mise sur le marché***) **nf** *official authorization for marketing a pharmaceutical product.*

ammoniac, aque [amɔnjak] **adj** CHIM ammoniac.
◆ ***ammoniac*** **nm** ammonia.
◆ ***ammoniaque*** **nf** ammonia (water).

amnésie [amnezi] **nf** amnesia.

amnésique [amnezik] ■ **adj** amnesic.
■ **nmf** amnesic, amnesiac.

amniocentèse [amnjɔsɛ̃tɛz] **nf** amniocentesis.

amnistie [amnisti] **nf** amnesty.

amnistier [9] [amnistje] **vt** to amnesty.

amocher [3] [amɔʃe] **vt** *fam* to mess up.
◆ ***s'amocher*** **vp** *fam* to mess o.s. up.

amoindrir [32] [amwɛ̃drir] **vt** to diminish.
◆ ***s'amoindrir*** **vp** to dwindle, to diminish.

amollir [32] [amɔlir] **vt** [personne] to make soft.
◆ ***s'amollir*** **vp** [personne] to go soft.

amonceler [24] [amɔ̃sle] **vt** to accumulate.
◆ ***s'amonceler*** **vp** to pile up, to accumulate.

amoncelle, amoncelles ➤ ***amonceler.***

amont [amɔ̃] **nm** upstream (water) ▸ **en amont de** [rivière] upriver *ou* upstream from / *fig* prior to.

amoral, e, aux [amɔral, o] **adj 1.** [qui ignore la morale] amoral **2.** *fam* [débauché] immoral.

amorce [amɔrs] **nf 1.** [d'explosif] priming / [de cartouche, d'obus] cap **2.** [à la pêche] bait **3.** *fig* [commencement] beginnings *pl*, germ.

amorcer [16] [amɔrse] **vt 1.** [explosif] to prime **2.** [à la pêche] to bait **3.** *fig* [commencer] to begin, to initiate.
◆ ***s'amorcer*** **vp** to begin.

amorphe [amɔrf] **adj 1.** [personne] lifeless **2.** [matériau] amorphous.

amorti [amɔrti] **nm 1.** FOOTBALL **: faire un amorti** to trap the ball **2.** TENNIS drop shot.

amortir [32] [amɔrtir] **vt 1.** [atténuer - choc] to absorb / [- bruit] to deaden, to muffle **2.** [dette] to pay off **3.** [achat] to write off.

amortissement [amɔrtismɑ̃] **nm 1.** [de choc] absorption / [de bruit] deadening, muffling **2.** [de dette] payment, paying off **3.** [d'achat] writing off ▸ **amortissement dégressif** *ou* **accéléré** accelerated depreciation.

amortisseur [amɔrtisœr] **nm** AUTO shock absorber.

amour [amur] **nm 1.** [gén] love ▸ **amour maternel/filial** maternal/filial love ▸ **pour l'amour de** for the love of ▸ **pour l'amour du ciel** for heaven's sake ▸ **éprouver de l'amour pour qqn** to feel love for sb ▸ **faire l'amour** to make love ▸ **faire qqch avec amour** to do sthg with loving care *ou* love ▸ **faire qqch par amour pour qqn** to do sthg for the love of *ou* out of love for sb ▸ **filer le parfait amour** to live out love's dream **2.** [liaison] (love) affair, romance **3.** [jolie chose] **: un amour de** a darling (little) **4.** [personne] **: un amour** an angel, a dear ▸ **apporte les glaçons, tu seras un amour** be a dear *ou* darling and bring the ice cubes ▸ **un amour de petite fille** a delightful little girl.
◆ ***amours*** **nfpl** [vie sentimentale] love-life ▸ **à tes amours!** [toast] here's to you! / [quand on éternue] bless you!

amouracher [3] [amuraʃe] ◆ ***s'amouracher*** **vp : s'amouracher de** to become infatuated with.

amourette [amurɛt] **nf** passing fancy, brief love affair.

amoureusement [amurøzmɑ̃] **adv** amorously.

amoureux, euse [amurø, øz] ■ **adj 1.** [personne] in love ▸ **être/tomber amoureux (de)** to be/fall in love (with) **2.** [regard, geste] loving.
■ **nm, f 1.** [prétendant] suitor **2.** [passionné] **: amoureux de** lover of ▸ **un amoureux de la nature** a nature lover.

amour-propre [amurprɔpr] **nm** pride, self-respect.

amovible [amɔvibl] **adj 1.** [déplaçable] detachable, removable **2.** [fonctionnaire] removable.

ampère [ɑ̃pɛr] **nm** amp, ampere.

amphétamine [ɑ̃fetamin] **nf** amphetamine.

amphi [ɑ̃fi] **nm** *fam* lecture hall *ou* theatre *UK* ▸ **cours en amphi** lecture.

amphibie [ɑ̃fibi] ■ **nm** amphibian.
■ **adj** amphibious.

amphithéâtre [ɑ̃fiteatr] **nm 1.** HIST amphitheatre *UK*, amphitheater *US* **2.** [d'université] lecture hall *ou* theatre *UK*.

ample [ɑ̃pl] **adj 1.** [vêtement - gén] loose-fitting / [- jupe] full **2.** [projet] extensive ▸ **pour de plus amples informations** for further details **3.** [geste] broad, sweeping.

amplement [ɑ̃pləmɑ̃] **adv** [largement] fully, amply.

ampleur [ɑ̃plœr] **nf 1.** [de vêtement] fullness **2.** [d'événement, de dégâts] extent
▸▸ **prendre toute son ampleur** to reach its height.

ampli [ɑ̃pli] (abr de ***amplificateur***) **nm** *fam* amp.

amplificateur, trice [ɑ̃plifikatœr, tris] **adj** ÉLECTR amplifying ▸ **un phénomène amplificateur de la croissance** *fig* a phenomenon which increases growth.
◆ ***amplificateur*** **nm 1.** [gén] amplifier **2.** PHOTO enlarger.

amplifier [9] [ɑ̃plifje] **vt 1.** [mouvement, son] to amplify / [image] to magnify, to enlarge **2.** [scandale] to increase / [événement, problème] to highlight.
◆ ***s'amplifier*** **vp** [son] to grow *ou* get louder / *fig* [revendications, phénomène] to grow.

amplitude [ɑ̃plityd] **nf 1.** [de geste] fullness **2.** [d'onde] amplitude **3.** [de température] range.

ampoule [ɑ̃pul] **nf 1.** [de lampe] bulb **2.** [sur la peau] blister **3.** [médicament] ampoule, vial, phial *UK*.

ampoulé, e [ɑ̃pule] **adj** *péj* pompous.

amputation [ɑ̃pytasjɔ̃] **nf** MÉD amputation.

amputer [3] [ɑ̃pyte] **vt** MÉD to amputate / *fig* [couper] to cut (back *ou* down) ▸ **son article a été amputé d'un tiers** his article was cut by a third.

Amsterdam [amstɛrdam] **npr** Amsterdam.

amulette [amylɛt] **nf** amulet.

amusant, e [amyzɑ̃, ɑ̃t] **adj** [drôle] funny / [distrayant] amusing ▸ **c'est très amusant** it's great fun.

amuse-gueule [amyzgœl] **nm inv** *fam* cocktail snack, (party) nibble.

amusement [amyzmɑ̃] **nm** amusement *(U)*.

amuser [3] [amyze] **vt** to amuse, to entertain ▸ **cela ne m'amuse pas du tout** I don't find that in the least bit funny ▸ **elle m'amuse** she makes me laugh ▸ **tu crois que ça m'amuse d'être pris pour un imbécile?** do you think I enjoy being taken for a fool?

◆ ***s'amuser*** **vp** to have fun, to have a good time ▸ **amusez-vous bien!** enjoy yourselves!, have a good time! ▸ **elles ont construit une hutte pour s'amuser** they built a hut, just for fun ▸ **s'amuser à faire qqch** to amuse o.s. (by) doing sthg ▸ **il s'amuse à faire des avions en papier en cours** he spends his time making paper planes in class.

amygdale [amidal] **nf** tonsil.

an [ɑ̃] **nm** year ▸ **avoir sept ans** to be seven (years old) ▸ **l'an dernier/prochain** last/next year ▸ **en l'an 2000** in the year 2000 ▸ **le premier** *ou* **le jour de l'an** New Year's Day ▸ **le nouvel an** the New Year ▸ **bon an mal an** taking the good years with the bad.

anabolisant [anabɔlizɑ̃] **nm** anabolic steroid.

anachronique [anakrɔnik] **adj** anachronistic.

anachronisme [anakrɔnism] **nm** anachronism.

anagramme [anagram] **nf** anagram.

ANAH (abr de ***Agence nationale pour l'amélioration de l'habitat***) [ana] **nf** *national agency responsible for housing projects and restoration grants.*

anal, e, aux [anal, o] **adj** anal ▸ **stade anal** PSYCHO anal phase.

analgésique [analʒezik] **nm & adj** analgesic.

anallergique [analɛrʒik] **adj** hypoallergenic.

analogie [analɔʒi] **nf** analogy.

analogique [analɔʒik] **adj** analog, analogue *UK*.

analogue [analɔg] ■ **nm** equivalent, analog, analogue *UK*.

■ **adj** analogous, comparable.

analphabète [analfabɛt] **nmf & adj** illiterate.

analphabétisme [analfabetism] **nm** illiteracy.

analyse [analiz] **nf 1.** [étude] analysis ▸ **analyse des résultats** processing of results ▸ **analyse de texte** textual analysis ▸ **en dernière analyse** in the final analysis

2. ÉCON **: analyse des concurrents** competitive analysis ▸ **analyse des coûts** *ou* **du prix de revient** cost analysis ▸ **analyse de faisabilité** feasibility study ▸ **analyse de marché** market survey *ou* research

3. CHIM & MÉD test, analysis ▸ **analyse de sang** blood analysis *ou* test

4. [psychanalyse] analysis *(U)* ▸ **être en analyse** to be in analysis

5. INFORM analysis ▸ **analyse numérique** numerical analysis ▸ **analyse des performances du système** system evaluation.

analyser [3] [analize] **vt 1.** [étudier, psychanalyser] to analyse *UK*, to analyze *US* **2.** CHIM & MÉD to test, to analyse *UK*, to analyze *US*.

◆ ***s'analyser*** **vp** to be analysed *UK ou* analyzed *US* ▸ **un tel comportement ne s'analyse pas facilement** such behaviour is not easy to understand.

analyste [analist] **nmf** analyst.

analyste-programmeur, euse [analistprɔgramœr, øz] (mpl **analystes-programmeurs**) (fpl **analystes-programmeuses**) **nm, f** systems analyst.

analytique [analitik] **adj** analytical.

ananas [anana(s)] **nm** pineapple.

anar [anar] **nmf & adj** *fam* anarchist.

anarchie [anarʃi] **nf 1.** POLIT anarchy **2.** [désordre] chaos, anarchy.

anarchique [anarʃik] **adj** anarchic.

anarchiste [anarʃist] **nmf & adj** anarchist.

anathème [anatɛm] **nm** anathema ▸ **jeter l'anathème sur** *fig* & *sout* to curse.

anatomie [anatɔmi] **nf** anatomy.

anatomique [anatɔmik] **adj** anatomical.

ANC (abr de ***African National Congress***) **nm** POLIT ANC.

ancestral, e, aux [ɑ̃sɛstral, o] **adj** ancestral.

ancêtre [ɑ̃sɛtr] **nmf** [aïeul] ancestor / *fig* [forme première] forerunner, ancestor / *fig* [initiateur] father (f mother).

anchois [ɑ̃ʃwa] **nm** anchovy.

ancien, enne [ɑ̃sjɛ̃, ɛn] **adj 1.** [gén] old ▸ **un meuble ancien** an antique **2.** *(avant n)* [précédent] former, old ▸ **l'ancien franc** the old franc ▸ **mon ancienne école** my old school ▸ **un ancien combattant** a (war) veteran, an ex-serviceman **3.** [qui a de l'ancienneté] senior ▸ **vous n'êtes pas assez ancien dans la profession** you've not been in the job long enough **4.** [du passé] ancient ▸ **l'Ancien Régime** the Ancien Régime.

◆ ***ancien*** **nm** [mobilier] **: l'ancien** antiques *pl* ▸ **meublé entièrement en ancien** entirely furnished with antiques.

◆ ***anciens*** **nmpl** elders.

anciennement [ɑ̃sjɛnmɑ̃] **adv** formerly, previously.

ancienneté [ɑ̃sjɛnte] **nf 1.** [d'une tradition] oldness **2.** [d'un employé] seniority.

ancrage [ɑ̃kraʒ] **nm 1.** NAUT anchorage **2.** [enracinement] **: l'ancrage d'un parti dans l'électorat** a party's electoral base.

ancre [ɑ̃kr] **nf** NAUT anchor ▸ **jeter l'ancre** to drop anchor ▸ **lever l'ancre** to weigh anchor / *fam* [partir] to make tracks.

ancrer [3] [ɑ̃kre] **vt** [bateau] to anchor / *fig* [idée, habitude] to root ▸ **une idée bien ancrée** a firmly-rooted idea.

Andes [ɑ̃d] **nfpl : les Andes** the Andes ▸ **la cordillère des Andes** the Andes Mountain Ranges.

Andorre [ɑ̃dɔr] **nf : (la principauté d')Andorre** (the principality of) Andorra.

andouille [ɑ̃duj] **nf 1.** [charcuterie] *type of sausage made of pig's intestines, eaten cold)* **2.** *fam* [imbécile] dummy.

andouillette [ɑ̃dujɛt] **nf** *type of sausage made of pig's intestines, eaten hot.*

androgyne [ɑ̃drɔʒin] ■ **nmf** androgynous person.
■ **adj** androgynous.

âne [an] **nm 1.** ZOOL ass, donkey **2.** *fam* [imbécile] ass.

anéantir [32] [aneɑ̃tir] **vt 1.** [détruire] to annihilate / *fig* to ruin, to wreck **2.** [démoraliser] to crush, to overwhelm.
◆ ***s'anéantir*** **vp** [disparaître] to vanish.

anéantissement [aneɑ̃tismɑ̃] **nm 1.** [destruction] annihilation / *fig* wrecking, ruin **2.** [abattement] dejection.

anecdote [anɛkdɔt] **nf** anecdote.

anecdotique [anɛkdɔtik] **adj** anecdotal.

anémie [anemi] **nf** MÉD anaemia *UK*, anemia *US* / *fig* enfeeblement.

anémié, e [anemje] **adj** anaemic *UK*, anemic *US*.

anémier [9] [anemje] **vt** MÉD to make anaemic *UK* *ou* anemic *US* / *fig* to weaken.
◆ ***s'anémier*** **vp** MÉD to become anaemic *UK* *ou* anemic *US* / *fig* to weaken.

anémique [anemik] **adj** anaemic *UK*, anemic *US*.

anémone [anemɔn] **nf** anemone.

ânerie [anri] **nf** *fam* **1.** [caractère] stupidity *(U)* **2.** [parole, acte] **: dire/faire une ânerie** to say/do something stupid.

ânesse [anɛs] **nf** she-ass, she-donkey.

anesthésie [anɛstezi] **nf** anaesthesia, anesthesia *US* ▸ **sous anesthésie** under (the) anaesthetic *ou* anesthetic *US*, under anaesthesia ▸ **anesthésie locale** local anaesthetic *ou* anesthetic *US* ▸ **anesthésie générale** general anaesthetic *ou* anesthetic *US*.

anesthésier [9] [anɛstezje] **vt** to anaesthetize, to anesthetize *US*.

anesthésique [anɛstezik] **nm & adj** anaesthetic, anesthetic *US*.

anesthésiste [anɛstezist] **nmf** anaesthetist, anesthetist *US*, anesthesiologist *US*.

aneth [anɛt] **nm** dill.

anfractuosité [ɑ̃fraktɥozite] **nf** crevice.

ange [ɑ̃ʒ] **nm** angel ▸ **ange gardien** guardian angel ▸ **être aux anges** *fig* to be in seventh heaven.

angélique [ɑ̃ʒelik] ■ **nf** angelica.
■ **adj** angelic.

angélus [ɑ̃ʒelys] **nm** [sonnerie] angelus (bell).

angevin, e [ɑ̃ʒvɛ̃, in] **adj 1.** [de l'Anjou] of/from Anjou **2.** [d'Angers] of/from Angers.
◆ ***Angevin, e*** **nm, f 1.** [de l'Anjou] person from Anjou **2.** [d'Angers] person from Angers.

angine [ɑ̃ʒin] **nf** [pharyngite] pharyngitis / [amygdalite] tonsillitis ▸ **angine de poitrine** angina (pectoris).

anglais, e [ɑ̃glɛ, ɛz] **adj** English.
◆ ***anglais*** **nm** [langue] English.
◆ ***Anglais, e*** **nm, f** Englishman (f Englishwoman) ▸ **les Anglais** the English.
◆ ***anglaises*** **nfpl** ringlets.
◆ ***à l'anglaise*** **loc adv** CULIN boiled ▸ **filer à l'anglaise** *fig* to make *ou* sneak off.

angle [ɑ̃gl] **nm 1.** [coin] corner ▸ **angle mort** [zone invisible] blind spot ▸ **arrondir les angles** *fig* to smooth things over ▸ **la maison qui est à** *ou* **qui fait l'angle** the house on the corner ▸ **meuble d'angle** corner unit **2.** MATH angle ▸ **angle droit/aigu/obtus** right/acute/obtuse angle ▸ **la rue fait un angle droit avec l'avenue** the street is at right angles to the avenue **3.** [aspect] angle, point of view ▸ **voir les choses sous un certain angle** to see things from a certain point of view ▸ **vu sous l'angle économique/du rendement, cette décision se comprend** from an economic/a productivity point of view, the decision makes sense.

Angleterre [ɑ̃glətɛr] **nf : l'Angleterre** England.

anglican, e [ɑ̃glikɑ̃, an] **adj & nm, f** Anglican.

anglo-normand [ɑ̃glɔnɔrmɑ̃, ɑ̃d] (mpl **anglo-normands**, fpl **anglo-normandes**) **adj** GÉOGR of the Channel islands ▸ **les îles anglo-normandes** the Channel Islands.

anglophone [ɑ̃glɔfɔn] ■ **nmf** English-speaker.
■ **adj** English-speaking, anglophone.

anglo-saxon, onne [ɑ̃glosaksɔ̃, ɔn] **adj** Anglo-Saxon.
◆ ***anglo-saxon*** **nm** [langue] Anglo-Saxon, Old English.
◆ ***Anglo-Saxon, onne*** **nm, f** Anglo-Saxon.

angoissant, e [ɑ̃gwasɑ̃, ɑ̃t] **adj** agonizing, harrowing / [sens affaibli] **: j'ai trouvé l'attente très angoissante** the wait was a strain on my nerves.

angoisse [ɑ̃gwas] **nf** anguish.

angoissé, e [ɑ̃gwase] ■ **adj** anguished.
■ **nmf** neurotic.

angoisser [3] [ɑ̃gwase] **vt** [effrayer] to cause anxiety to.
◆ ***s'angoisser*** **vp 1.** [être anxieux] to be overcome with anxiety **2.** *fam* [s'inquiéter] to fret.

Angola [ɑ̃gola] **nm : l'Angola** Angola.

angolais, e [ɑ̃gɔlɛ, ɛz] **adj** Angolan.
◆ ***Angolais, e*** **nm, f** Angolan.

angora [ɑ̃gɔra] **nm & adj** angora.

anguille [ɑ̃gij] **nf** eel ▸ **il y a anguille sous roche** *fig* something's up, something's going on.

anguleux, euse [ɑ̃gylø, øz] **adj** angular.

anicroche [anikrɔʃ] **nf** hitch.

animal**, **e**, **aux [animal, o] **adj** **1.** [propre à l'animal] animal *(avant n)* **2.** [instinctif] instinctive.
◆ ***animal*** **nm** **1.** [bête] animal ▸ **animal en peluche** stuffed animal ▸ **animal sauvage/domestique** wild/domestic animal **2.** *péj* [personne] lout, oaf.

animalerie [animalri] **nf** pet shop.

animalier**, **ère [animalje, ɛr] **adj** [peintre, sculpteur] animal *(modif)* ▸ **parc animalier** wildlife park.

animateur**, **trice [animatœr, tris] **nm, f** **1.** RADIO & TV host, presenter *UK* **2.** [socioculturel, sportif] activities organizer **3.** [de manifestation] organizer.

animation [animasjɔ̃] **nf** **1.** [de rue] activity, life / [de conversation, visage] animation **2.** [publicitaire] demonstration, promotion **3.** [activités] activities *pl* **4.** CINÉ animation.

animé**, **e [anime] **adj** [rue] lively / [conversation, visage] animated / [objet] animate.

animer [3] [anime] **vt** **1.** [mettre de l'entrain dans] to animate, to liven up **2.** [présenter] to host, to present *UK* **3.** [organiser des activités pour] to organize activities for.
◆ ***s'animer*** **vp** **1.** [visage] to light up **2.** [rue] to come to life, to liven up.

animisme [animism] **nm** animism.

animiste [animist] **nmf** & **adj** animist.

animosité [animozite] **nf** animosity.

anis [ani(s)] **nm** BOT anise / CULIN aniseed.

anisette [anizɛt] **nf** anisette.

ankylosé**, **e [ɑ̃kiloze] **adj** [paralysé] stiff / [engourdi] numb.

ankyloser [3] [ɑ̃kiloze] ◆ ***s'ankyloser*** **vpi** **1.** MÉD to ankylose **2.** [devenir raide - bras, jambe] to become numb / [- personne] to go stiff.

annales [anal] **nfpl** **1.** [revue] review *sg*, journal *sg* **2.** [d'examen] past papers *UK* ▸ **les annales du bac** ≃ A-level past papers **3.** [chronique annuelle] chronicle *sg*, annals ▸ **rester dans les annales** *fig* to go down in history.

anneau**, **x [ano] **nm** **1.** [gén] ring **2.** [maillon] link **3.** [de reptile] coil.
◆ ***anneaux*** **nmpl** SPORT rings.

année [ane] **nf** year ▸ **d'année en année** from year to year ▸ **d'une année à l'autre** [croissance, déclin] year-on-year ▸ **elle est en troisième année de médecine** she's in her third year at medical school ▸ **souhaiter la bonne année à qqn** to wish sb a Happy New Year ▸ **tout au long de l'année, toute l'année** all year long *ou* round ▸ **année bissextile** leap year ▸ **année civile** calendar *ou* civil year ▸ **année fiscale** fiscal *ou* tax *ou* financial *UK* year ▸ **une année sabbatique** a sabbatical (year) ▸ **année scolaire** school year.
◆ ***à l'année*** **loc adv** [louer, payer] annually, on a yearly basis.

CULTURE

Année fiscale/Année budgétaire

In France, the fiscal year is the year for which taxes are due. For private individuals, the fiscal and calendar years are one and the same. There is always a year's gap – for example, income tax due in 2004 is calculated on the basis of income earned in 2003. The French budgetary year also coincides with the calendar year. All government budgets are revised annually, and Parliament passes the new federal budget every December.

année-lumière [anelymjɛr] (pl **années-lumière**) **nf** light year ▸ **à des années-lumière de** *fig* light years away from.

annexe [anɛks] ■ **nf** **1.** [de dossier] appendix, annexe *UK*, annex *US* **2.** [de bâtiment] annexe *UK*, annex *US*.
■ **adj** related, associated.

annexer [4] [anɛkse] **vt** **1.** [incorporer] **: annexer qqch (à qqch)** to append *ou* annex sthg (to sthg) **2.** [pays] to annex.
◆ ***s'annexer*** **vp** **1.** [s'attribuer] to grab **2.** [s'ajouter] **: s'annexer à qqch** to be associated with sthg.

annexion [anɛksjɔ̃] **nf** annexation.

annihiler [3] [aniile] **vt** [réduire à néant] to destroy, to wreck.
◆ ***s'annihiler*** **vp** to be destroyed, to be wrecked.

anniversaire [anivɛrsɛr] ■ **nm** [de mariage, mort, événement] anniversary / [de naissance] birthday ▸ **bon** *ou* **joyeux anniversaire!** happy birthday!
■ **adj** anniversary *(avant n)*.

annonce [anɔ̃s] **nf** **1.** [déclaration] announcement / *fig* sign, indication **2.** [texte] advertisement ▸ **annonce commerciale** display ad ▸ **passer une annonce** to place an advert *UK ou* advertisement ▸ **petite annonce** classified advertisement, small ad *UK*, want ad *US*.

COMMENT EXPRIMER...

la réponse à une annonce

I saw your ad in today's paper / J'ai vu votre annonce dans le journal d'aujourd'hui
I'm calling about the flat advertised in yesterday's paper / J'appelle au sujet de l'appartement qui était dans le journal hier
Is the flat still available? / Est-ce que l'appartement est encore libre ?
I'm phoning to enquire about office cleaning services / Pouvez-vous me renseigner sur les services de nettoyage de bureaux ?
I was very interested to see your advertisement for the post of translator / Votre annonce concernant un poste de traducteur m'a vivement intéressé
I decided to apply for the advertised post because I want to work abroad / J'ai décidé de poser ma candidature pour le poste de la petite annonce parce que je veux travailler à l'étranger

annoncer [16] [anɔ̃se] **vt 1.** [faire savoir] to announce ▸ **je vous annonce que je me marie** I'd like to inform you that I'm getting married ▸ **on annonce des réductions d'impôts** tax reductions have been announced **2.** [indiquer] to herald ▸ **ça n'annonce rien de bon** it doesn't bode well, it isn't a very good sign **3.** [prédire] to predict ▸ **ils annoncent du soleil pour demain** sunshine is forecast for tomorrow, the forecast for tomorrow is sunny **4.** [présenter] to announce ▸ **qui dois-je annoncer?** what name shall I say? **5.** [jeux de cartes] to declare ▸ **annoncer la couleur** *fam fig* **: j'ai annoncé la couleur, ils savent que je démissionnerai s'il le faut** I've laid my cards on the table *ou* made no secret of it: they know I'll resign if I have to.

◆ ***s'annoncer*** **vp : s'annoncer bien/mal** to look/not to look promising ▸ **la crise s'annonce** there is a crisis looming.

annonceur, euse [anɔ̃sœr, øz] **nm, f** advertiser.

annonciateur, trice [anɔ̃sjatœr, tris] **adj : annonciateur de qqch** heralding sthg.

Annonciation [anɔ̃sjasjɔ̃] **nf** [événement] Annunciation / [jour] Annunciation (Day).

annotation [anɔtasjɔ̃] **nf 1.** [note explicative] annotation **2.** [note personnelle] note.

annoter [3] [anɔte] **vt** to annotate.

annuaire [anɥɛr] **nm** annual, yearbook ▸ **annuaire téléphonique** telephone directory, phone book.

annualisation [anɥalizasjɔ̃] **nf** calculation on a yearly basis.

annualiser [3] [anɥalize] **vt** to calculate on a yearly basis, to annualize ▸ **annualiser la durée du temps de travail** to annualize the work time.

annuel, elle [anɥɛl] **adj 1.** [tous les ans] annual, yearly **2.** [d'une année] annual.

annuellement [anɥɛlmɑ̃] **adv** annually, yearly.

annuité [anɥite] **nf 1.** [paiement] annual payment, annual instalment *UK ou* installment *US* **2.** [année de service] year (of service).

annulaire [anylɛr] ■ **nm** ring finger.
■ **adj** ring-shaped, annular.

annulation [anylasjɔ̃] **nf 1.** [de rendez-vous, réservation] cancellation **2.** [de mariage] annulment.

annuler [3] [anyle] **vt 1.** [rendez-vous, réservation] to cancel **2.** [mariage] to annul **3.** [procédure] to declare invalid **4.** INFORM to undo.

◆ ***s'annuler*** **vp** to cancel each other out.

anoblir [32] [anɔblir] **vt** to ennoble.

anode [anɔd] **nf** anode.

anodin, e [anɔdɛ̃, in] **adj 1.** [blessure] minor **2.** [propos] harmless **3.** [détail, personne] insignificant.

anomalie [anɔmali] **nf** anomaly.

ânon [anɔ̃] **nm** young donkey *ou* ass.

ânonner [3] [anɔne] **vt & vi** to recite in a drone.

anonymat [anɔnima] **nm** anonymity ▸ **garder l'anonymat** to remain anonymous.

anonyme [anɔnim] ■ **nm** [écrivain] anonymous author.
■ **adj** anonymous.

anorak [anɔrak] **nm** anorak.

anorexie [anɔrɛksi] **nf** anorexia.

anorexique [anɔrɛksik] **adj & nmf** anorexic.

anormal, e, aux [anɔrmal, o] ■ **adj 1.** [inhabituel] abnormal, not normal **2.** [intolérable, injuste] wrong, not right **3.** [handicapé] mentally handicapped.
■ **nm, f** mentally handicapped person.

anormalement [anɔrmalmɑ̃] **adv** abnormally.

ANPE (abr de ***Agence nationale pour l'emploi***) **nf** *French national employment agency*, ≃ Jobcentre *UK* ▸ **s'inscrire à l'ANPE** to register as unemployed.

anse [ɑ̃s] **nf 1.** [d'ustensile] handle **2.** GÉOGR cove.

antagonisme [ɑ̃tagɔnism] **nm** antagonism.

antagoniste [ɑ̃tagɔnist] ■ **nmf** antagonist.
■ **adj** antagonistic.

antan [ɑ̃tɑ̃] ◆ ***d'antan*** **loc adj** *littéraire* of old, of yesteryear.

antarctique [ɑ̃tarktik] **adj** Antarctic ▸ **le cercle polaire antarctique** the Antarctic Circle.

◆ ***Antarctique*** **nm 1.** [continent] **: l'Antarctique** Antarctica **2.** [océan] **: l'Antarctique** the Antarctic (Ocean).

antécédent [ɑ̃tesedɑ̃] **nm 1.** *(gén pl)* [passé] history *sg* **2.** GRAMM antecedent.

◆ ***antécédents*** **nmpl** MÉD case history.

antédiluvien, enne [ɑ̃tedilyvjɛ̃, ɛn] **adj** antediluvian, ancient.

antenne [ɑ̃tɛn] **nf 1.** [d'insecte] antenna, feeler ▸ **avoir des antennes** *fam fig* to have a sixth sense **2.** [de télévision, de radio] aerial *UK*, antenna *US* ▸ **antenne parabolique** dish aerial *ou* antenna *US*, satellite dish ▸ **être à l'antenne** to be on the air ▸ **hors antenne** off the air **3.** [bâtiment] unit **4.** [succursale] branch, office.

antenne-relais (pl **antennes-relais**) [ɑ̃tɛnrəlɛ] **nf** TÉLÉCOM mobile phone mast *UK*.

antépénultième [ɑ̃tepenyltjɛm] ■ **nf** LING antepenultimate (syllable).
■ **adj** antepenultimate.

antérieur, e [ɑ̃terjœr] **adj 1.** [dans le temps] earlier, previous ▸ **antérieur à** previous *ou* prior to **2.** [dans l'espace] front *(avant n)*.

antérieurement [ɑ̃terjœrmɑ̃] **adv** earlier, previously ▸ **antérieurement à** prior to.

anthologie [ɑ̃tɔlɔʒi] **nf** anthology.

anthracite [ɑ̃trasit] ■ **nm** anthracite.
■ **adj inv** charcoal grey *UK ou* gray *US*.

anthrax® [ɑ̃traks] **nm** *fam* MÉD anthrax.

anthropologie [ɑ̃trɔpɔlɔʒi] **nf** anthropology.

anthropométrie [ɑ̃trɔpɔmetri] **nf** anthropometry.

anthropophage [ɑ̃trɔpɔfaʒ] ■ **nmf** cannibal.
■ **adj** cannibalistic.

antiacarien, enne [ɑ̃tiakarjɛ̃, ɛn] ■ **adj** antimite ▸ **traitement *ou* shampooing antiacarien** antimite treatment *ou* shampoo.
■ **nm** antimite treatment.

antiaérien, enne [ɑ̃tiaerjɛ̃, ɛn] **adj** antiaircraft.

anti-âge [ɑ̃tiaʒ] **adj : crème anti-âge** antiageing *UK ou* antiaging *US* cream.

antialcoolique [ɑ̃tialkɔlik] **adj : ligue antialcoolique** temperance league.

anti-aliassage [ɑ̃tialjasaʒ] **nm** INFORM anti-aliasing.

antiaméricanisme [ɑ̃tiamerikanism] **nm** anti-Americanism.

antibactérien, enne [ɑ̃tibakterjɛ̃, ɛn] **adj** antibacterial.

antibiotique [ɑ̃tibjɔtik] **nm & adj** antibiotic.

antibrouillard [ɑ̃tibrujar] **nm & adj inv : (phare** *ou* **feu) antibrouillard** fog light, fog lamp *UK*.

antibruit [ɑ̃tibrɥi] **adj inv** antinoise ▸ **mur antibruit** noise reduction barrier.

antibuée [ɑ̃tibɥe] ➤ ***dispositif***.

anticalcaire [ɑ̃tikalkɛr] **adj** antiliming *(avant n)*, antiscale *(avant n)*.

anticancéreux, euse [ɑ̃tikɑ̃serø, øz] **adj 1.** [centre, laboratoire] cancer *(avant n)* **2.** [médicament] anticancer *(avant n)*.

antichambre [ɑ̃tiʃɑ̃br] **nf** antechamber ▸ **faire antichambre** *fig* to wait patiently *(to see somebody)*.

anticipation [ɑ̃tisipasjɔ̃] **nf 1.** FIN advance ▸ **paiement par anticipation** advance payment, payment in advance **2.** LITTÉR **: roman d'anticipation** science fiction novel.

anticipé, e [ɑ̃tisipe] **adj** early.

anticiper [3] [ɑ̃tisipe] ■ **vt** to anticipate.
■ **vi : anticiper (sur qqch)** to anticipate (sthg).

anticléricalisme [ɑ̃tiklerikalism] **nm** anticlericalism.

anticolonialisme [ɑ̃tikɔlɔnjalism] **nm** anticolonialism.

anticolonialiste [ɑ̃tikɔlɔnjalist] **nmf & adj** anticolonialist.

anticommunisme [ɑ̃tikɔmynism] **nm** anticommunism.

anticoncurrentiel [ɑ̃tikɔ̃kyrɑ̃sjɛl] **adj** ÉCON anticompetitive.

anticonformiste [ɑ̃tikɔ̃fɔrmist] **adj & nmf** [gen] nonconformist / POLIT anti-Establishment.

anticonstitutionnel, elle [ɑ̃tikɔ̃stitysjɔnɛl] **adj** [gen] unconstitutional / POLIT anticonstitutional.

anticorps [ɑ̃tikɔr] **nm** antibody.

anticorrosion [ɑ̃tikɔrozjɔ̃] **adj inv** anticorrosive.

anti-crénelage [ɑ̃tikrenlaʒ] **nm** INFORM anti-aliasing.

anticyclone [ɑ̃tisiklon] **nm** anticyclone.

antidater [3] [ɑ̃tidate] **vt** to backdate.

antidémarrage [ɑ̃tidemaraʒ] **adj inv : système antidémarrage** immobilizer.

antidémocratique [ɑ̃tidemɔkratik] **adj** POLIT antidemocratic.

antidépresseur [ɑ̃tidepresœr] **nm & adj m** antidepressant.

antidérapant, e [ɑ̃tiderapɑ̃, ɑ̃t] **adj** [pneu] non-skid / [semelle, surface] non-slip.
◆ ***antidérapant*** **nm** [pneu] anti-skid tyre *UK ou* tire *US*.

antidopage [ɑ̃tidɔpaʒ], ***antidoping*** [ɑ̃tidɔpiŋ] **adj inv : contrôle antidopage** drugs test.

antidote [ɑ̃tidɔt] **nm** antidote.

antidumping [ɑ̃tidœmpiŋ] **adj** [loi, législation] antidumping.

anti-effraction [ɑ̃tiefraksjɔ̃] **adj inv** [dispositif] antitheft.

antifascisme [ɑ̃tifaʃism] **nm** POLIT antifascism.

antifasciste [ɑ̃tifaʃist] **adj & nmf** POLIT antifascist.

antigang [ɑ̃tigɑ̃g] ■ **adj** ➤ ***brigade***.
■ **nf** organized crime division.

antigel [ɑ̃tiʒɛl] **nm inv & adj inv** antifreeze.

antillais, e [ɑ̃tijɛ, ɛz] **adj** West Indian.
◆ ***Antillais, e*** **nm, f** West Indian.

Antilles [ɑ̃tij] **nfpl : les Antilles** the West Indies ▸ **aux Antilles** in the West Indies.

antilope [ɑ̃tilɔp] **nf** antelope.

antimilitarisme [ɑ̃timilitarism] **nm** antimilitarism.

antimilitariste [ɑ̃timilitarist] **nmf & adj** antimilitarist.

antimite [ɑ̃timit] **adj inv : boule antimite** mothball.

antimondialisation [ɑ̃timɔ̃djalizasjɔ̃] **nf & adj inv** POLIT antiglobalization.

antimondialiste [ɑ̃timɔ̃djalist] **adj** antiglobalization.

antinucléaire [ɑ̃tinykleɛr] **adj** antinuclear.

Antiope [ɑ̃tjɔp] **npr** *information system available via the French television network,* ≃ Teletext *UK*.

antiparasite [ɑ̃tiparazit] ■ **nm** suppressor.
■ **adj inv** anti-interference.

antipathie [ɑ̃tipati] **nf** antipathy, hostility.

antipathique [ɑ̃tipatik] **adj** unpleasant ▸ **elle m'est antipathique** I dislike her, I don't like her.

antipelliculaire [ɑ̃tipelikylɛr] **adj : shampooing antipelliculaire** antidandruff shampoo.

antiphrase [ɑ̃tifraz] **nf** antiphrasis.

COMMENT EXPRIMER...

qu'on n'aime pas quelqu'un

I don't really like him/her / Je ne l'aime pas trop
I hate him / Je le déteste
I can't stand him / Je ne peux pas le voir
He gets on my nerves / Il me tape sur les nerfs
I find him really unpleasant / Je le trouve vraiment antipathique
I'm not very keen on my boss / Je n'aime pas trop mon chef

antipode [ɑ̃tipɔd] **nm : être à l'antipode** *ou* **aux antipodes (de)** [lieu] to be on the other side of the world (from) / *fig* to be diametrically opposed (to).

antipoison [ɑ̃tipwazɔ̃] ➤ ***centre***.

antiquaire [ɑ̃tikɛr] **nmf** antique dealer.

antique [ɑ̃tik] **adj 1.** [de l'antiquité - civilisation] ancient / [- vase, objet] antique **2.** [vieux] antiquated, ancient.

antiquité [ɑ̃tikite] **nf 1.** [époque] **: l'Antiquité** antiquity **2.** [ancienneté] great age, antiquity **3.** [objet] antique.

antirabique [ɑ̃tirabik] **adj : vaccin antirabique** rabies vaccine.

antiraciste [ɑ̃tirasist] **adj & nmf** antiracist.

antireflet [ɑ̃tirəflɛ] **adj inv** [surface] non-reflecting.

antirides [ɑ̃tirid] **adj inv** antiwrinkle.

antirouille [ɑ̃tiruj] **adj inv** [traitement] rust *(avant n)* / [revêtement, peinture] rustproof.

antisèche [ɑ̃tisɛʃ] **nf** *arg scol* crib (sheet), cheat sheet *US*, pony *US*.

antisémite [ɑ̃tisemit] ■ **nmf** anti-Semite.
■ **adj** anti-Semitic.

antisémitisme [ɑ̃tisemitism] **nm** anti-Semitism.

antiseptique [ɑ̃tisɛptik] **nm & adj** antiseptic.

antisismique [ɑ̃tisismik] **adj** earthquake-proof.

antislash [ɑ̃tislaʃ] **nm** INFORM backslash.

antisyndicalisme **nm** union bashing *fam UK*.

antiterroriste [ɑ̃titɛrɔrist] **adj** antiterrorist.

antithèse [ɑ̃titɛz] **nf** antithesis.

antitranspirant, e [ɑ̃titrɑ̃spirɑ̃, ɑ̃t] **adj** antiperspirant.

antitrust [ɑ̃titrœst] **adj** ÉCON [loi, législation] antimonopoly *UK*, antitrust *US*.

antitussif, ive [ɑ̃titysif, iv] **adj** cough *(avant n)*.
◆ ***antitussif*** **nm** cough mixture *UK ou* syrup *US*.

antiviral, aux [ɑ̃tiviral, o] **nm** antivirus.

antivirus [ɑ̃tivirys] **nm** INFORM antivirus software.

antivol [ɑ̃tivɔl] ■ **nm inv** antitheft device.
■ **adj inv** antitheft.

antre [ɑ̃tr] **nm** den, lair.

anus [anys] **nm** anus.

anxiété [ɑ̃ksjete] **nf** anxiety ▸ **être dans l'anxiété** to be very worried *ou* anxious.

anxieusement [ɑ̃ksjøzmɑ̃] **adv** anxiously.

anxieux, euse [ɑ̃ksjø, øz] ■ **adj** anxious, worried ▸ **être anxieux de qqch** to be worried *ou* anxious about sthg ▸ **être anxieux de faire qqch** to be anxious to do sthg.
■ **nm, f** worrier.

anxiolytique [ɑ̃ksjɔlitik] ■ **adj** anxiolytic.
■ **nm** tranquillizer *UK*, tranquilizer *US*.

AOC (abr de ***appellation d'origine contrôlée***) **nf** *label guaranteeing origin of French wine*.

aorte [aɔrt] **nf** aorta.

août [u(t)] **nm** August ▸ **le quinze août** Assumption Day ; voir aussi ***septembre***.

aoûtat [auta] **nm** harvest tick.

aoûtien, enne [ausjɛ̃, ɛn] **nm, f** August holidaymaker *UK ou* vacationer *US*.

apaisement [apɛzmɑ̃] **nm 1.** [moral] comfort **2.** [de douleur] alleviation **3.** [de tension, de crise] calming.

apaiser [4] [apeze] **vt 1.** [personne] to calm down, to pacify **2.** [conscience] to salve / [douleur] to soothe / [soif] to slake, to quench / [faim] to assuage.
◆ ***s'apaiser*** **vp 1.** [personne] to calm down **2.** [besoin] to be assuaged / [tempête] to subside, to abate / [douleur] to die down / [scrupules] to be allayed.

apanage [apanaʒ] **nm** *sout* privilege ▸ **être l'apanage de qqn/qqch** to be the prerogative of sb/sthg.

aparté [aparte] **nm 1.** THÉÂTRE aside **2.** [conversation] private conversation ▸ **prendre qqn en aparté** to take sb aside.

apartheid [apartɛd] **nm** apartheid.

apathie [apati] **nf** apathy.

apathique [apatik] **adj** apathetic.

apatride [apatrid] ■ **nmf** stateless person.
■ **adj** stateless.

APEC [apɛk] (abr de ***association pour l'emploi des cadres***) **nf** *employment agency for professionals and managers*.

apercevoir [52] [apɛrsəvwar] **vt 1.** [voir] to see, to catch sight of **2.** [comprendre] to see, to perceive.
◆ ***s'apercevoir*** **vp : s'apercevoir de qqch** to notice sthg ▸ **s'apercevoir que** to notice (that).

aperçois, aperçoit ➤ ***apercevoir***.

aperçu, e [apɛrsy] **pp** ➤ ***apercevoir***.
◆ ***aperçu*** **nm** general idea ▸ **donner un aperçu de qqch** to give a general idea of sthg.

apéritif, ive [aperitif, iv] **adj** whetting the appetite.
◆ ***apéritif*** **nm** aperitif ▸ **prendre l'apéritif** to have an aperitif, to have drinks *(before a meal)*.

apesanteur [apəzɑ̃tœr] **nf** weightlessness.

à-peu-près [apøprɛ] **nm inv** approximation.

aphasie [afazi] **nf** aphasia.

aphone [afɔn] **adj** voiceless.

aphorisme [afɔrism] **nm** aphorism.

aphrodisiaque [afrɔdizjak] **nm & adj** aphrodisiac.

aphte [aft] **nm** mouth ulcer.

API (abr de ***alphabet phonétique international***) **nm** IPA.

apiculteur, trice [apikyltœr, tris] **nm, f** beekeeper.

apiculture [apikyltyr] **nf** beekeeping.

apitoie, apitoies ➤ ***apitoyer***.

apitoiement [apitwamɑ̃] **nm** pity.

apitoyer [13] [apitwaje] **vt** to move to pity.
◆ ***s'apitoyer*** **vp** to feel pity ▸ **s'apitoyer sur** to feel sorry for.

ap. J.-C. (abr écrite de ***après Jésus-Christ***) AD.

APL (abr de ***aide personnalisée au logement***) **nf** housing benefit *UK*, rent subsidy *US*.

aplanir [32] [aplanir] **vt 1.** [aplatir] to level **2.** *fig* [difficulté, obstacle] to smooth away, to iron out.
◆ ***s'aplanir*** **vp** *fig* [se résoudre] to be ironed out.

aplati, e [aplati] **adj** flattened ▸ **la Terre est aplatie aux pôles** the Earth is oblate.

aplatir [32] [aplatir] **vt** [gén] to flatten / [couture] to press flat / [cheveux] to smooth down.
◆ ***s'aplatir*** **vp 1.** [s'écraser] to be flattened **2.** [s'étaler] to lie flat ▸ **s'aplatir devant qqn** *fig* to grovel before sb.

aplomb [aplɔ̃] **nm 1.** [stabilité] balance **2.** [audace] nerve, cheek *UK* ▸ **garder/perdre son aplomb** to keep/lose one's nerve.
◆ ***d'aplomb*** **loc adv** steady ▸ **se tenir d'aplomb** to be steady ▸ **ne pas se sentir d'aplomb** to feel out of sorts.

APN **nm abr écrite de *appareil photo numérique*.**

apnée [apne] **nf : plonger en apnée** to dive without breathing apparatus.

apocalypse [apɔkalips] **nf** apocalypse.

apocalyptique [apɔkaliptik] **adj** apocalyptic.

apogée [apɔʒe] **nm** ASTRON apogee / *fig* peak.

apolitique [apɔlitik] **adj** apolitical, unpolitical.

apologie [apɔlɔʒi] **nf** justification, apology ▸ **faire l'apologie de qqn/qqch** to praise sb/sthg.

apoplexie [apɔplɛksi] **nf** apoplexy.

apostrophe [apɔstrɔf] **nf 1.** [signe graphique] apostrophe **2.** [interpellation] rude remark.

apostropher [3] [apɔstrɔfe] **vt : apostropher qqn** to speak rudely to sb.

apothéose [apɔteoz] **nf 1.** [consécration] great honour *UK* ***ou*** honor *US* **2.** [point culminant - d'un spectacle] grand finale / [- d'une carrière] crowning glory.

apôtre [apotr] **nm** apostle, disciple ▸ **se faire l'apôtre de qqch** *fig* to be the ***ou*** an advocate of sthg.

Appalaches [apalaʃ] **nmpl : les Appalaches** the Appalachians.

apparaissais, apparaissions ➤ ***apparaître***.

apparaître [91] [aparɛtr] ■ **vi 1.** [gén] to appear ▸ **apparaître à qqn en songe *ou* rêve** to appear ***ou*** to come to sb in a dream ▸ **après le bosquet, on voit apparaître le village** after you pass the copse, the village comes into view ▸ **cette histoire m'apparaît bien dérisoire aujourd'hui** the whole thing strikes me as being ridiculous now ▸ **faire apparaître** to reveal **2.** [se dévoiler] to come to light ▸ **la voir dans un contexte professionnel la fait apparaître sous un jour complètement nouveau** seeing her in a professional context shows her in a completely new light.
■ **v impers : il apparaît que** it seems ***ou*** appears that.

apparat [apara] **nm** pomp ▸ **d'apparat** [dîner, habit] ceremonial ▸ **en grand apparat** with great pomp and ceremony.

appareil [aparɛj] **nm 1.** [gén] device / [électrique] appliance ▸ **porter un appareil (auditif)/(dentaire)** to wear a hearing aid/a brace *UK* ***ou*** braces *US* ▸ **appareil de contrôle** tester ▸ **appareil ménager** household appliance **2.** [téléphone] phone, telephone ▸ **qui est à l'appareil?** who's speaking? **3.** [avion] aircraft **4.** [structure] apparatus ▸ **l'appareil législatif** the machinery of the law ▸ **l'appareil du parti** the party apparatus ***ou*** machinery
▸▸ **dans le plus simple appareil** in one's birthday suit.
◆ ***appareil digestif*** **nm** digestive system.
◆ ***appareil photo*** **nm** camera ▸ **appareil photo jetable** disposable camera ▸ **appareil photo numérique** digital camera ▸ **appareil reflex** reflex camera.

appareillage [aparɛjaʒ] **nm 1.** [équipement] equipment **2.** NAUT getting under way.

appareiller [4] [apareje] ■ **vt** [assortir] to match up.
■ **vi** NAUT to get under way.

apparemment [aparamɑ̃] **adv** apparently.

apparence [aparɑ̃s] **nf** appearance ▸ **malgré les *ou* en dépit des apparences** in spite of appearances ▸ **sauver les apparences** to keep up appearances.
◆ ***en apparence*** **loc adv** seemingly, apparently.

apparent, e [aparɑ̃, ɑ̃t] **adj 1.** [superficiel, illusoire] apparent **2.** [visible] visible ▸ **coutures apparentes** topstitched seams **3.** [évident] obvious.

apparenté, e [aparɑ̃te] **adj : apparenté à** [personne] related to / *fig* [ressemblant] similar to / [affilié] affiliated to.

apparenter [3] [aparɑ̃te] ◆ ***s'apparenter à*** **v + prep** [ressembler à] to be like.

appariteur [aparitœr] **nm** porter *UK*, campus policeman *US*.

apparition [aparisjɔ̃] **nf 1.** [gén] appearance ▸ **faire son apparition** to make one's appearance **2.** [vision - RELIG] vision / [- de fantôme] apparition.

appart [apart] (abr de ***appartement***) **nm** *fam* flat *UK*, apartment *US*.

appartement [apartəmɑ̃] **nm** flat *UK*, apartment *US*.

appartenance [apartənɑ̃s] **nf : appartenance à** [famille] belonging to / [parti] membership of *UK* ***ou*** in *US*.

appartenir [40] [apartənir] **vi 1.** [être la propriété de] **: appartenir à qqn** to belong to sb **2.** [faire partie de] **: appartenir à qqch** to belong to sthg, to be a member of sthg **3.** *fig* [dépendre de] **: il ne m'appartient pas de faire...** *sout* it's not up to me to do... ▸ **pour des raisons qui m'appartiennent** for my own reasons / *(tournure impersonnelle)* **: il ne vous appartient pas d'en décider** it's not for you to decide, the decision is not yours (to make).

appartenu [apartəny] **pp inv** ➤ ***appartenir***.

appartiendrai, appartiendrais ➤ ***appartenir***.

apparu, e [apary] **pp** ➤ ***apparaître***.

appât [apa] **nm** [à la pêche] bait, lure.

appâter [3] [apate] **vt** *litt* & *fig* to lure.

appauvrir [32] [apovrir] **vt** to impoverish.
◆ ***s'appauvrir*** **vp** to grow poorer, to become impoverished.

appel [apɛl] **nm 1.** [gén] call ▸ **faire appel à qqn** to appeal to sb ▸ **faire appel à qqch** [nécessiter] to call for sthg / [avoir recours à] to call on sthg ▸ **un appel au secours *ou* à l'aide** *litt* a call for help / *fig* a cry for help ▸ **appel de détresse** NAUT distress call / [d'une personne] call for help

▸ **l'appel du large** the call of the sea ▸ **appel au peuple** appeal to the people ▸ **appel (téléphonique)** (phone) call ▸ **appel en PCV** reverse-charge call *UK*, collect call *US*
2. DR appeal ▸ **appel à témoins** appeal for witnesses (to come forward) ▸ **faire appel** to appeal ▸ **sans appel** final ▸ **sa décision est sans appel** his decision is final
3. [pour vérifier - gén] roll-call / SCOL registration ▸ **manquer à l'appel** to be absent ▸ **répondre à l'appel** to be present
4. COMM **: appel de fonds** call for funds ▸ **appel d'offres** invitation to tender ▸ **répondre à un appel d'offres** to make a bid
5. [signe] **: faire un appel de phares** to flash *ou* blink *US* one's headlights
6. INFORM call ▸ **appel par référence/valeur** call by reference/value ▸ **programme/séquence d'appel** call routine/sequence.

appelant [aplɑ̃] **nm** [leurre] decoy / *Québec* [sifflet] birdcall.

appelé [aple] **nm** conscript, draftee *US*.

appeler [24] [aple] ▪ **vt 1.** [gén] to call ▸ **appeler au secours** *ou* **à l'aide** to call for help ▸ **appeler qqn par la fenêtre** to call out to sb from the window **2.** [téléphoner] to ring *UK*, to call ▸ **appelez ce numéro en cas d'urgence** dial this number in an emergency **3.** [faire venir] to call for ▸ **appeler un taxi** [dans la rue] to hail a taxi / [par téléphone] to phone for *ou* to call a taxi **4.** [entraîner] to lead to ▸ **un coup en appelle un autre** one blow leads to another **5.** [nommer] **: être appelé à un poste** to be appointed to a post **6.** [amener] **: appeler qqn à faire qqch** to call on sb to do sthg ▸ **il faut appeler les gens à voter** *ou* **aux urnes** people must be urged to vote.
▪ **vi** [solliciter] **: en appeler à qqch** to appeal to sthg ▸ **j'en appelle à vous en dernier recours** I'm coming to you as a last resort.
◆ ***s'appeler*** **vp 1.** [se nommer] to be called ▸ **comment cela s'appelle?** what is it called? ▸ **il s'appelle Patrick** his name is Patrick, he's called Patrick **2.** [se téléphoner] **: on s'appelle demain?** shall we talk tomorrow?

appelette [aplɛt] **nf** INFORM applet.

appellation [apɛlasjɔ̃] **nf** designation, name ▸ **appellation contrôlée** *government certification guaranteeing the quality of a French wine* ▸ **appellation d'origine** DR label of origin.

appelle, appelles ➤ ***appeler***.

appendice [apɛ̃dis] **nm** appendix.

appendicite [apɛ̃disit] **nf** appendicitis.

appentis [apɑ̃ti] **nm** lean-to.

appesantir [32] [apəzɑ̃tir] **vt** [démarche] to slow down.
◆ ***s'appesantir*** **vp 1.** [s'alourdir] to become heavy **2.** [insister] **: s'appesantir sur qqch** to dwell on sthg.

appétissant, e [apetisɑ̃, ɑ̃t] **adj** [nourriture] appetizing.

appétit [apeti] **nm** appetite ▸ **appétit de qqch/de faire qqch** *fig* appetite for sthg/for doing sthg ▸ **bon appétit!** enjoy your meal! ▸ **couper/ouvrir l'appétit à qqn** to spoil/whet sb's appetite ▸ **manger de bon appétit** to eat heartily.

applaudir [32] [aplodir] ▪ **vt** to applaud.
▪ **vi** to clap, to applaud ▸ **applaudir à qqch** *fig* to applaud sthg ▸ **les gens applaudissaient à tout rompre** there was thunderous applause.

applaudissements [aplodismɑ̃] **nmpl** applause *(U)*, clapping *(U)*.

applicable [aplikabl] **adj : applicable (à)** applicable (to).

application [aplikasjɔ̃] **nf** [gén & INFORM] application ▸ **mettre qqch en application** to apply sthg.

applique [aplik] **nf** wall lamp.

appliqué, e [aplike] **adj 1.** [élève] hardworking **2.** [écriture] careful.

appliquer [3] [aplike] **vt** [gén] to apply / [loi] to enforce.
◆ ***s'appliquer*** **vp 1.** [s'étaler, se poser] **: cette peinture s'applique facilement** this paint goes on easily **2.** [concerner] **: s'appliquer à qqn/qqch** to apply to sb/sthg **3.** [se concentrer] **: s'appliquer (à faire qqch)** to apply o.s. (to doing sthg).

appliquette [aplikɛt] **nf** INFORM applet.

appoint [apwɛ̃] **nm 1.** [monnaie] change ▸ **faire l'appoint** to give the right money **2.** [aide] help, support ▸ **d'appoint** [salaire, chauffage] extra ▸ **lit d'appoint** spare bed.

appointements [apwɛ̃tmɑ̃] **nmpl** salary *sg*.

apport [apɔr] **nm 1.** [gén & FIN] contribution ▸ **apport de gestion** management buy-in **2.** [de chaleur] input.

apporter [3] [apɔrte] **vt 1.** [gén] to bring ▸ **ça m'a beaucoup apporté** *fig* I got a lot from it **2.** [raison, preuve] to provide, to give **3.** [contribuer à] to give, to bring / [provoquer] to bring about **4.** [mettre - soin] to exercise / [- attention] to give.

apposer [3] [apoze] **vt 1.** [affiche] to put up **2.** [signature] to append.

apposition [apozisjɔ̃] **nf** GRAMM apposition ▸ **en apposition** in apposition.

appréciable [apresjabl] **adj 1.** [notable] appreciable **2.** [précieux] **: un grand jardin, c'est appréciable!** I/we really appreciate having a big garden.

appréciation [apresjasjɔ̃] **nf 1.** [de valeur] valuation / [de distance, poids] estimation **2.** [jugement] judgment **3.** SCOL assessment.

apprécier [9] [apresje] **vt 1.** [gén] to appreciate **2.** [évaluer] to estimate, to assess.
◆ ***s'apprécier*** **vp** to like one other.

appréhender [3] [apreɑ̃de] **vt 1.** [arrêter] to arrest **2.** [craindre] **: appréhender qqch/de faire qqch** to dread sthg/doing sthg.

appréhension [apreɑ̃sjɔ̃] **nf** apprehension.

apprenais ➤ ***apprendre***.

apprendre [79] [aprɑ̃dr] **vt 1.** [étudier] to learn ▸ **apprendre à faire qqch** to learn (how) to do sthg **2.** [enseigner] to teach ▸ **apprendre qqch à qqn** to teach sb sthg ▸ **apprendre à qqn à faire qqch** to teach sb (how) to do sthg **3.** [nouvelle] to hear of, to learn of ▸ **apprendre que** to hear that, to learn that ▸ **apprendre qqch à qqn** to tell sb of sthg.

apprenne ➤ ***apprendre***.

apprenti, e [aprɑ̃ti] nm, f [élève] apprentice / *fig* beginner ▸ **apprenti sorcier** *fig* sorcerer's apprentice.

apprentissage [aprɑ̃tisaʒ] nm **1.** [de métier] apprenticeship **2.** [formation] learning ▸ **apprentissage de la vie** learning about life ▸ **apprentissage par le jeu** edutainment.

apprêter [4] [aprete] vt to prepare.
◆ ***s'apprêter*** vp **1.** [être sur le point] **: s'apprêter à faire qqch** to get ready to do sthg **2.** [s'habiller] **: s'apprêter pour qqch** to dress up for sthg.

appris, e [apri, iz] pp ➤ ***apprendre***.

apprivoiser [3] [aprivwaze] vt to tame.
◆ ***s'apprivoiser*** vp **1.** [animal] to become tame **2.** [personne] to become more sociable.

approbateur, trice [aprɔbatœr, tris] adj approving.

approbation [aprɔbasjɔ̃] nf approval.

approchant, e [aprɔʃɑ̃, ɑ̃t] adj similar ▸ **quelque chose d'approchant** something similar.

approche [aprɔʃ] nf [arrivée] approach ▸ **à l'approche des fêtes** as the Christmas holidays draw near ▸ **il a pressé le pas à l'approche de la maison** he quickened his step as he approached the house.
◆ ***approches*** nfpl [abords] surrounding area *sg*.

approcher [3] [aprɔʃe] ■ vt **1.** [mettre plus près] to move near, to bring near ▸ **approcher qqch de qqn/qqch** to move sthg near (to) sb/sthg ▸ **approche la table du mur** move *ou* draw the table closer to the wall ▸ **n'approche pas ta main de la flamme** don't put your hand near the flame **2.** [aborder] to go up to, to approach.
■ vi to approach, to go/come near ▸ **approchez!** come nearer! ▸ **n'approchez pas!** keep *ou* stay away! ▸ **approcher de** [moment, fin] to approach ▸ **on approche de Paris** we're getting near to *ou* we're nearing Paris ▸ **approcher de la perfection** to be *ou* to come close to perfection.
◆ ***s'approcher*** vp to come/go near, to approach ▸ **s'approcher de qqn/qqch** to approach sb/sthg ▸ **s'approcher d'une ville** to approach *ou* to near a town.

approfondi, e [aprɔfɔ̃di] adj thorough, detailed ▸ **traiter qqch de façon approfondie** to go into sthg thoroughly.

approfondir [32] [aprɔfɔ̃dir] vt **1.** [creuser] to make deeper **2.** [développer] to go further into.
◆ ***s'approfondir*** vp **1.** [se creuser] to become deeper **2.** [se compliquer] to deepen.

approprié, e [aprɔprije] adj **: approprié (à)** appropriate (to).

approprier [10] [aprɔprije] vt **1.** [adapter] to adapt **2.** *Belgique* to clean.
◆ ***s'approprier*** vp [s'adjuger] to appropriate.

approuver [3] [apruve] vt **1.** [gén] to approve of ▸ **approuver qqn de faire qqch** to commend sb for doing sthg **2.** DR to approve.

approvisionnement [aprɔvizjɔnmɑ̃] nm supplies *pl*, stocks *pl*.

approvisionner [3] [aprɔvizjɔne] vt **1.** [compte en banque] to pay money into **2.** [magasin, pays] to supply.
◆ ***s'approvisionner*** vp **: s'approvisionner chez/à** [suj: particulier] to shop at/in / [suj: commerçant] to get one's stock from.

approximatif, ive [aprɔksimatif, iv] adj approximate, rough.

approximation [aprɔksimasjɔ̃] nf approximation.

approximativement [aprɔksimativmɑ̃] adv approximately, roughly.

appt abr de ***appartement***.

appui [apɥi] nm **1.** [soutien] support ▸ **à l'appui de** in support of **2.** [de fenêtre] sill.

appuie, appuies ➤ ***appuyer***.

appui-tête [apɥitɛt] (pl **appuis-tête**) nm headrest.

appuyé, e [apɥije] adj [allusion] heavy / [regard] insistent.

appuyer [14] [apɥije] ■ vt **1.** [poser] **: appuyer qqch sur/contre qqch** to lean sthg on/against sthg, to rest sthg on/against sthg ▸ **le vélo était appuyé contre la grille** the bicycle was resting *ou* leaning against the railings **2.** [presser] **: appuyer qqch sur/contre** to press sthg on/against ▸ **appuyer sur l'endroit sensible** to press on the sore spot **3.** *fig* [soutenir] to support ▸ **la police, appuyée par l'armée** the police, backed up *ou* supported by the army.
■ vi **1.** [reposer] **: appuyer sur** to lean *ou* rest on **2.** [presser] to push ▸ **il faut appuyer de toutes ses forces** you have to press as hard as you can ▸ **appuyer sur** [bouton] to press ▸ **appuyer sur la gâchette** to pull the trigger **3.** *fig* [insister] **: appuyer sur** to stress **4.** [se diriger] **: appuyer sur la** *ou* **à droite** to bear right.
◆ ***s'appuyer*** vp **1.** [se tenir] **: s'appuyer contre/sur** to lean against/on, to rest against/on ▸ **s'appuyer contre la rampe** to lean against the banister **2.** [se baser] **: s'appuyer sur** to rely on ▸ **ce récit s'appuie sur une expérience vécue** this story is based on a real-life experience **3.** [compter] **: s'appuyer sur** to rely on, to count on **4.** *fam* [supporter, prendre en charge] **: s'appuyer qqn** to put up with sb ▸ **s'appuyer qqch** to take sthg on.

apr. abr de ***après***.

âpre [apr] adj **1.** [goût, discussion, combat] bitter **2.** [ton, épreuve, critique] harsh **3.** [concurrence] fierce.

âprement [aprəmɑ̃] adv bitterly, fiercely.

après [aprɛ] ■ prép **1.** [gén] after ▸ **après avoir mangé, ils...** after having eaten *ou* after they had eaten, they... ▸ **après cela** after that ▸ **après le départ de Paul** after Paul left ▸ **après quoi** after which ▸ **il était juste après moi dans la file** he was just behind me in the queue ▸ **la gare est après le parc** the station is past *ou* after the park **2.** [indiquant l'attirance, l'attachement, l'hostilité] **: soupirer après qqn** to yearn for sb ▸ **aboyer après qqn** to bark at sb ▸ **se fâcher après qqn** to get angry at *ou* with sb.
■ adv **1.** [temps] afterwards *UK*, afterward *US* ▸ **après, je rentrerai à la maison** I'll go home afterwards ▸ **un mois après** one month later ▸ **le mois d'après** the following *ou* next month ▸ **bien après** a long *ou* good while after, much later ▸ **peu après** shortly after *ou* afterwards

2. [lieu, dans un ordre, dans un rang] **: la rue d'après** the next street ▸ **c'est ma sœur qui vient après** my sister's next.

◆ ***après coup*** loc adv afterwards *UK*, afterward *US*, after the event ▸ **il n'a réagi qu'après coup** it wasn't until afterwards *ou* later that he reacted.

◆ ***après que*** loc conj *(+ indicatif)* after ▸ **je le verrai après qu'il aura fini** I'll see him after *ou* when he's finished ▸ **après qu'ils eurent dîné,...** after dinner *ou* after they had dined,...

◆ ***après tout*** loc adv after all ▸ **après tout, ça n'a pas beaucoup d'importance** after all, it's not particularly important.

◆ ***d'après*** loc prép according to ▸ **d'après ce qu'elle dit** from what she says ▸ **d'après moi** in my opinion ▸ **d'après lui** according to him.

◆ ***et après*** loc adv *(employée interrogativement)* **1.** [questionnement sur la suite] and then what? ▸ **et après? qu'a-t-il fait?** and then what did he do?
2. [exprime l'indifférence] so what? ▸ **et après? qu'est-ce que ça peut faire?** *fam* so what? who cares?

après-demain [apredmɛ̃] adv the day after tomorrow.

après-guerre [aprɛgɛr] nm post-war years *pl* ▸ **d'après-guerre** post-war.

après-midi [apremidi] nm inv & nf inv afternoon.

après-rasage [apreraza3] (pl **après-rasages**) nm & adj inv aftershave.

après-ski [apreski] (pl **après-skis**) nm [chaussure] snowboot.

après-soleil [apresɔlɛj] adj inv after-sun *(avant n)*.

après-vente [aprevɑ̃t] ➤ ***service***.

âpreté [aprəte] nf **1.** [de goût, discussion, combat] bitterness **2.** [de voix, épreuve, critique] harshness **3.** [de concurrence] ferocity.

à-propos [aprɔpo] nm inv [de remarque] aptness ▸ **faire preuve d'à-propos** to show presence of mind.

APS (abr de ***Advanced Photo System***) nm APS.

apte [apt] adj **: apte à qqch/à faire qqch** capable of sthg/of doing sthg ▸ **apte (au service)** MIL fit (for service).

aptitude [aptityd] nf **: aptitude (à *ou* pour qqch)** aptitude (for sthg) ▸ **aptitude à *ou* pour faire qqch** ability to do *ou* for doing sthg.

aquagym [akwa3im] nf aquarobics *(U)*.

aquarelle [akwarɛl] nf watercolour *UK*, watercolor *US*.

aquarium [akwarjɔm] nm aquarium.

aquatique [akwatik] adj [plante, animal] aquatic / [milieu, paysage] watery, marshy.

aqueduc [akdyk] nm aqueduct.

aqueux, euse [akø, øz] adj watery.

aquilin [akilɛ̃] ➤ ***nez***.

Aquitaine [akitɛn] nf **: l'Aquitaine** Aquitaine.

AR nm **1.** abr écrite de ***accusé de réception*** **2.** abr écrite de ***aller-retour*** **3.** abr de ***arrière***.

arabe [arab] ■ adj [peuple] Arab / [désert] Arabian.
■ nm [langue] Arabic.
◆ ***Arabe*** nmf Arab.

arabesque [arabɛsk] nf **1.** [ornement] arabesque **2.** [ligne sinueuse] flourish.

Arabie [arabi] nf **: l'Arabie** Arabia ▸ **l'Arabie Saoudite** Saudi Arabia.

arabophone [arabɔfɔn] ■ adj Arabic-speaking.
■ nmf Arabic speaker.

arachide [araʃid] nf peanut, groundnut.

araignée [areɲe] nf spider ▸ **avoir une araignée dans le *ou* au plafond** *fam fig* to have a screw loose.
◆ ***araignée de mer*** nf spider crab.

araser [3] [araze] vt GÉOL to erode.

arbalète [arbalɛt] nf crossbow.

arbitrage [arbitra3] nm **1.** [SPORT - gén] refereeing / [- au tennis, cricket] umpiring **2.** DR arbitration.

arbitraire [arbitrɛr] adj arbitrary.

arbitrairement [arbitrɛrmɑ̃] adv arbitrarily.

arbitre [arbitr] nm **1.** [SPORT - gén] referee / [- au tennis, cricket] umpire **2.** [conciliateur] arbitrator.
◆ ***libre arbitre*** nm free will.

arbitrer [3] [arbitre] vt **1.** [SPORT - gén] to referee / [- au tennis, cricket] to umpire **2.** [conflit] to arbitrate.

arborer [3] [arbɔre] vt **1.** [exhiber] to display, to sport **2.** [expression] to wear.

arborescence [arbɔresɑ̃s] nf INFORM tree.

arboriculteur, trice [arbɔrikyltœr, tris] nm, f tree grower.

arboriculture [arbɔrikyltyr] nf tree growing.

arbouse [arbuz] nf arbutus berry.

arbre [arbr] nm **1.** *fig* & BOT tree ▸ **arbre fruitier** fruit tree ▸ **arbre généalogique** family tree ▸ **arbre de Noël** Christmas tree **2.** [axe] shaft ▸ **arbre de transmission** AUTO drive shaft, propeller shaft.

arbrisseau, x [arbriso] nm shrub.

arbuste [arbyst] nm shrub.

ARC [ark] (abr de ***Association de Recherche sur le Cancer***) nf *French national cancer research charity*.

arc [ark] nm **1.** [arme] bow **2.** [courbe] arc ▸ **arc de cercle** arc of a circle **3.** ARCHIT arch.

arcade [arkad] nf **1.** ARCHIT arch ▸ **arcades** arcade *sg* **2.** ANAT **: arcade sourcilière** arch of the eyebrows.

arc-bouter [3] [arkbute] ◆ ***s'arc-bouter*** vp to brace o.s.

arceau, x [arso] nm **1.** ARCHIT arch **2.** [objet métallique] hoop.

arc-en-ciel [arkɑ̃sjɛl] (pl **arcs-en-ciel**) nm rainbow.

archaïque [arkaik] adj archaic.

arche [arʃ] nf ARCHIT arch.

archéologie [arkeɔlɔ3i] nf archaeology.

archéologique [arkeɔlɔ3ik] adj archaeological.

archéologue [arkeɔlɔg] nmf archaeologist.

archer [arʃe] nm archer.

archet [arʃɛ] nm MUS bow.

archétype [arketip] nm archetype.

archevêché [arʃəveʃe] **nm** [charge] archbishopric / [logement] archbishop's palace.

archevêque [arʃəvɛk] **nm** archbishop.

archi [arʃi] *fam* ■ **nf** abr écrite de ***architecture***.
■ **nm ou nf** abr écrite de ***architecte***.
■ **préf** extremely ▸ **archiconnu** extremely well-known ▸ **archiplein** jam-packed.

archipel [arʃipɛl] **nm** archipelago.

architecte [arʃitɛkt] **nmf** architect ▸ **architecte d'intérieur** interior designer.

architectural**, **e**, **aux [arʃitɛktyral, o] **adj** architectural.

architecture [arʃitɛktyr] **nf** architecture / *fig* structure.

archiver [3] [arʃive] **vt** to archive.

archives [arʃiv] **nfpl** [de bureau] records / [de musée] archives.

archiviste [arʃivist] **nmf** archivist.

arctique [arktik] **adj** Arctic ▸ **le cercle polaire arctique** the Arctic Circle.
◆ ***Arctique*** **nm : l'Arctique** the Arctic.

ardemment [ardamɑ̃] **adv** fervently, passionately.

ardent**, **e [ardɑ̃, ɑ̃t] **adj** **1.** [soleil] blazing **2.** [soif, fièvre] raging / [passion] burning **3.** [yeux, couleur] blazing.

ardeur [ardœr] **nf** **1.** [vigueur] fervour *UK*, fervor *US*, enthusiasm **2.** [chaleur] blazing heat.

ardoise [ardwaz] **nf** slate.

ardu**, **e [ardy] **adj** **1.** [travail] arduous / [problème] difficult **2.** [pente] steep.

are [ar] **nm** *100 square metres*.

aréna [arena] **nm** *Québec sports centre with skating rink*, arena *US*.

arène [arɛn] **nf** arena ▸ **l'arène politique** the political arena.
◆ ***arènes*** **nfpl** [romaines] amphitheatre *sg UK*, amphitheater *sg US* / [pour corridas] bullring *sg*.

arête [arɛt] **nf** **1.** [de poisson] bone **2.** [d'un toit, d'une montagne] ridge **3.** [du nez] bridge.

arg. abr de ***argus***.

argent [arʒɑ̃] **nm** **1.** [métal, couleur] silver **2.** [monnaie] money ▸ **argent comptant** cash ▸ **argent liquide** (ready) cash ▸ **argent mal acquis** *ou* **sale** dirty money ▸ **argent de poche** pocket money *UK*, allowance *US* ▸ **en avoir pour son argent** to get one's money's worth.

argenté**, **e [arʒɑ̃te] **adj** silvery, silver.

argenterie [arʒɑ̃tri] **nf** silverware.

argentin**, **e [arʒɑ̃tɛ̃, in] **adj** **1.** [son] silvery **2.** [d'Argentine] Argentinian.
◆ ***Argentin**, **e*** **nm, f** Argentinian.

Argentine [arʒɑ̃tin] **nf : l'Argentine** Argentina.

argile [arʒil] **nf** clay.

argileux**, **euse [arʒilø, øz] **adj** clayey.

argot [argo] **nm** slang.

argotique [argɔtik] **adj** slang, slangy.

arguer [8] [argɥe] **vi** *sout* [prétexter] **: arguer de qqch (pour)** to put sthg forward as a reason (for).

argument [argymɑ̃] **nm** argument ▸ **tirer argument de qqch** to use sthg as an argument ▸ **argument de vente** COMM selling point.

argumentaire [argymɑ̃tɛr] **nm** COMM promotion leaflet.

argumentation [argymɑ̃tasjɔ̃] **nf** argumentation.

argumenter [3] [argymɑ̃te] **vi** to argue ▸ **argumenter en faveur de/contre qqch** to argue for/against sthg.

argus [argys] **nm : coté à l'argus** *rated in the guide to secondhand car prices*.

aride [arid] **adj** *litt* & *fig* arid / [travail] thankless.

aridité [aridite] **nf** *litt* & *fig* aridity.

aristocrate [aristɔkrat] **nmf** aristocrat.

aristocratie [aristɔkrasi] **nf** aristocracy.

aristocratique [aristɔkratik] **adj** aristocratic.

arithmétique [aritmetik] ■ **nf** arithmetic.
■ **adj** arithmetical.

armagnac [armaɲak] **nm** armagnac.

armateur [armatœr] **nm** ship owner.

armature [armatyr] **nf** **1.** *fig* & CONSTR framework **2.** [de parapluie] frame / [de soutien-gorge] underwiring **3.** MUS key signature.

arme [arm] **nf** *litt* & *fig* weapon ▸ **arme blanche** blade ▸ **l'arme chimique/nucléaire** chemical/nuclear weapons ▸ **arme à feu** firearm ▸ **une bonne arme psychologique** a good psychological weapon ▸ **le pouvoir est une arme à double tranchant** power is a double-edged sword ▸ **passer l'arme à gauche** *fam fig* to snuff it.
◆ ***armes*** **nfpl** **1.** [armée] **: les armes** the army **2.** [blason] coat of arms *sg* ▸ **aux armes de** bearing the arms of ▸▸| **faire ses premières armes** [apprendre] to learn the ropes ▸ **passer qqn par les armes** to send sb to the firing squad ▸ **partir avec armes et bagages** to leave taking everything ▸ **prendre les armes** to take up arms.

armé**, **e [arme] **adj** armed ▸ **être armé de** to be armed with.

armée [arme] **nf** army ▸ **l'armée de l'air** the air force ▸ **l'armée de terre** the army.
◆ ***Armée du salut*** **nf : l'Armée du salut** the Salvation Army.

armement [arməmɑ̃] **nm** **1.** [MIL - de personne] arming / [- de pays] armament / [- ensemble d'armes] arms *pl* ▸ **la course aux armements** the arms race **2.** [de fusil] cocking **3.** [d'appareil photo] winding-on **4.** [de navire] fitting-out.

Arménie [armeni] **nf : l'Arménie** Armenia.

arménien**, **enne [armenjɛ̃, ɛn] **adj** Armenian.
◆ ***arménien*** **nm** [langue] Armenian.
◆ ***Arménien**, **enne*** **nm, f** Armenian.

armer [3] [arme] **vt** **1.** [pourvoir en armes] to arm ▸ **être armé pour qqch/pour faire qqch** *fig* [préparé] to be equipped for sthg/to do sthg **2.** [fusil] to cock **3.** [appareil photo] to wind on **4.** [navire] to fit out.
◆ ***s'armer*** **vp** *litt* & *fig* **: s'armer (de)** to arm o.s. (with).

armistice [armistis] **nm** armistice.

armoire [armwar] **nf** [gén] cupboard *UK*, closet *US* / [garde-robe] wardrobe ▸ **armoire à glace** wardrobe with a mirror ▸ **c'est une armoire à glace!** *fam fig* he's built like the side of a house! ▸ **armoire à pharmacie** medicine cabinet.

armoiries [armwari] **nfpl** coat of arms *sg*.

armure [armyr] **nf** armour *UK*, armor *US*.

armurerie [armyrri] **nf** [magasin] gunsmith's (shop).

armurier [armyrje] **nm** [d'armes à feu] gunsmith / [d'armes blanches] armourer *UK*, armorer *US*.

ARN (abr de ***acide ribonucléique***) **nm** RNA.

arnaque [arnak] **nf** *fam* rip-off.

arnaquer [3] [arnake] **vt** *fam* to rip off ▸ **se faire arnaquer** to be had.

arobase [arɔbaz] **nm** INFORM 'at', @ ▸ **l'arobase** the 'at' symbol *ou* sign.

aromate [arɔmat] **nm** [épice] spice / [fine herbe] herb.

aromathérapie [arɔmaterapi] **nf** aromatherapy.

aromatique [arɔmatik] **adj** aromatic.

aromatisé, e [arɔmatize] **adj** flavoured *UK*, flavored *US* ▸ **aromatisé à la vanille** vanilla-flavoured.

aromatiser [3] [arɔmatize] **vt** to flavour *UK*, to flavor *US*.

arôme [arom] **nm 1.** [gén] aroma / [de fleur, parfum] fragrance **2.** [goût] flavour *UK*, flavor *US*.

arpège [arpɛʒ] **nm** arpeggio.

arpenter [3] [arpɑ̃te] **vt 1.** [marcher] to pace up and down **2.** [terrain] to survey.

arpenteur [arpɑ̃tœr] **nm** surveyor.

arqué, e [arke] **adj 1.** [objet] curved **2.** [jambe] bow *(avant n)*, bandy / [nez] hooked / [sourcil] arched.

arr. abr de ***arrondissement***.

arraché [araʃe] ◆ ***à l'arraché*** **loc adv : gagner** *ou* **emporter la victoire à l'arraché** to snatch victory.

arrachement [araʃmɑ̃] **nm** *fig* wrench.

arrache-pied [araʃpje] ◆ ***d'arrache-pied*** **loc adv : travailler d'arrache-pied** to work away furiously.

arracher [3] [araʃe] **vt 1.** [extraire - plante] to pull up *ou* out / [- dent] to extract
2. [déchirer - page] to tear off *ou* out / [- chemise, bras] to tear off ▸ **se faire arracher une dent** to have a tooth out ▸ **il a eu un bras arraché dans l'explosion** he had an arm blown off in the explosion
3. [prendre] **: arracher qqch à qqn** to snatch sthg from sb / *fig* [extorquer] to extract sthg from sb / [susciter] to wring sthg from sb ▸ **arracher des aveux/une signature à qqn** to wring a confession/signature out of sb ▸ **j'ai réussi à lui arracher le pistolet des mains** [très vite] I managed to snatch the gun away *ou* to grab the gun from him / [après une lutte] I managed to wrest the gun from his grip ▸ **pas moyen de lui arracher le moindre commentaire** it's impossible to get him to say anything
4. [soustraire] **: arracher qqn à** [milieu, lieu] to drag sb away from / [lit, sommeil] to drag sb from / [habitude, torpeur] to force sb out of / [mort, danger] to snatch sb from ▸ **arracher un bébé à sa mère** to take a child from its mother ▸ **arracher qqn au sommeil** to force sb to wake up ▸ **comment l'arracher à son ordinateur?** how can we get *ou* drag him away from his computer?
◆ ***s'arracher*** **vp 1.** [se détacher] **: s'arracher de** *ou* **à** [milieu, lieu] to drag o.s. away from / [lit, sommeil] to drag o.s. from ▸ **s'arracher à son travail/à son ordinateur/de son fauteuil** to tear o.s. away from one's work/computer/armchair
2. [se disputer] **: s'arracher qqn/qqch** to fight over sb/sthg ▸ **c'est à s'arracher les cheveux** *fam* it's enough to drive you crazy
3. *fam* [partir] to split, to beat it ▸ **allez, on s'arrache!** come on, let's be off!

arraisonner [3] [arɛzɔne] **vt** [navire] to stop and inspect.

arrangeant, e [arɑ̃ʒɑ̃, ɑ̃t] **adj** obliging.

arrangement [arɑ̃ʒmɑ̃] **nm 1.** [gén] arrangement **2.** [accord] agreement, arrangement.

arranger [17] [arɑ̃ʒe] **vt 1.** [gén] to arrange ▸ **il a bien arrangé son appartement** his appartment is nicely laid out ▸ **c'est Paul qui a arrangé la cérémonie/l'exposition** Paul organized the ceremony/put the exhibition together **2.** [convenir à] to suit ▸ **ce soir ou demain, comme ça t'arrange** tonight or tomorrow, as it suits you *ou* as is convenient for you ▸ **mardi? non, ça ne m'arrange pas** Tuesday? no, that's no good for me **3.** [régler] to settle ▸ **c'est arrangé, tu peux partir** it's all settled, you're free to leave now **4.** [améliorer] to sort out **5.** [réparer] to fix.
◆ ***s'arranger*** **vp** to come to an agreement ▸ **s'arranger pour faire qqch** to manage to do sthg ▸ **arrangez-vous pour être là à cinq heures** make sure you're there at five o'clock ▸ **il s'arrange toujours pour partir plus tôt** he always manages to leave early ▸ **cela va s'arranger** things will work out ▸ **les choses s'arrangeront d'elles-mêmes** things'll sort themselves out *ou* take care of themselves ▸ **s'arranger avec : je m'arrangerai avec lui pour qu'il garde les enfants** I'll arrange for him to look after the children.

arrdt. abr écrite de ***arrondissement***.

arrérages [areraʒ] **nmpl** arrears.

arrestation [arɛstasjɔ̃] **nf** arrest ▸ **être en état d'arrestation** to be under arrest.

arrêt [arɛ] **nm 1.** [d'un mouvement] stopping ▸ **à l'arrêt** [véhicule] stationary / [machine] (switched) off ▸ **marquer un temps d'arrêt** to stop *ou* to pause for a moment ▸ **tomber en arrêt devant qqch** to stop dead in front of sthg ▸ **je suis tombé en arrêt devant un magnifique vaisselier** I stopped short in front of a splendid dresser
2. [interruption] interruption ▸ **sans arrêt** [sans interruption] non-stop / [sans relâche] constantly, continually ▸ **ce train est sans arrêt jusqu'à Arcueil** this train is non-stop *ou* goes straight through to Arcueil ▸ **arrêt maladie** *ou* **de travail** [congé] sick leave / [certificat] doctor's *ou* medical certificate ▸ **être en arrêt maladie** to be on sick leave ▸ **arrêt du travail** stoppage
3. [station] **: arrêt (d'autobus)** (bus) stop ▸ **'arrêt demandé'** 'stop requested' ▸ **arrêt facultatif** request stop *UK*, flag stop *US* ▸ **je descends au prochain arrêt** I'm getting off at the next stop
4. [livraison] **: 'arrêts fréquents'** 'slow deliveries'

5. DR decision, judgment ▸ **rendre un arrêt** to deliver *ou* to pronounce a judgment ▸ **signer son arrêt de mort** *fig* to sign one's own death warrant.

arrêté [arete] **nm 1.** FIN settlement **2.** ADMIN order, decree ▸ **par arrêté préfectoral** by order of the prefect.

arrêter [4] [arete] ■ **vt 1.** [gén] to stop ▸ **la circulation est arrêtée sur la N7** traffic is held up *ou* has come to a standstill on the N7 **2.** INFORM [ordinateur] to shut down **3.** [cesser] **: arrêter de faire qqch** to stop doing sthg ▸ **arrête, tu me fais mal!** stop it: you're hurting me! ▸ **arrêter de fumer** to stop smoking ▸ **il a arrêté de travailler l'an dernier** he retired last year **4.** [abandonner - gén] to give up / [- école] to leave **5.** [voleur] to arrest ▸ **se faire arrêter** to get *ou* be arrested **6.** [fixer] to decide on ▸ **arrêter son choix** to make one's choice **7.** [suj: médecin] **: arrêter qqn** to put sb on sick leave ▸ **arrêter un patient** to put a patient on sick leave.
■ **vi** to stop.
◆ ***s'arrêter*** **vp** to stop ▸ **s'arrêter net** to stop dead *ou* short ▸ **s'arrêter à qqch : il ne s'arrête pas à ces détails** he's not going to dwell on these details ▸ **s'arrêter de faire** to stop doing ▸ **elle s'est arrêtée de jouer en me voyant** she stopped playing when she saw me ▸ **s'arrêter chez qqn** to stay with sb ▸ **tu peux t'arrêter chez l'épicier en venant?** could you stop off at the grocer's on your way here? ▸ **nous nous étions arrêtés à la page 56** we'd left off at page 56.

arrhes [ar] **nfpl** deposit *sg*.

arrière [arjɛr] ■ **adj inv** back, rear ▸ **roue arrière** rear *ou* back wheel ▸ **marche arrière** reverse gear.
■ **nm 1.** [partie postérieure] back ▸ **à l'arrière** at the back *UK*, in back *US* ▸ **assurer ses arrières** *fig* to play safe **2.** SPORT back.
◆ ***en arrière*** **loc adv 1.** [dans la direction opposée] back, backwards ▸ **faire un pas en arrière** to take a step back *ou* backwards **2.** [derrière, à la traîne] behind ▸ **rester en arrière** to lag behind.
◆ ***en arrière de*** **loc prép** behind.

arriéré, e [arjere] **adj 1.** [mentalité, pays] backward **2.** [dette] outstanding, overdue.
◆ ***arriéré*** **nm** arrears *pl*.

arrière-boutique [arjɛrbutik] (pl **arrière-boutiques**) **nf** back shop.

arrière-garde [arjɛrgard] (pl **arrière-gardes**) **nf** rearguard ▸ **combat d'arrière-garde** *litt* & *fig* rearguard action.

arrière-goût [arjɛrgu] (pl **arrière-goûts**) **nm** aftertaste.

arrière-grand-mère [arjɛrgrɑ̃mɛr] (pl **arrière-grands-mères**) **nf** great-grandmother.

arrière-grand-père [arjɛrgrɑ̃pɛr] (pl **arrière-grands-pères**) **nm** great-grandfather.

arrière-grands-parents [arjɛrgrɑ̃parɑ̃] **nmpl** great-grandparents.

arrière-pays [arjɛrpei] **nm inv** hinterland.

arrière-pensée [arjɛrpɑ̃se] (pl **arrière-pensées**) **nf 1.** [raison intéressée] ulterior motive **2.** [réserve] **: sans arrière-pensée** without reservation.

arrière-plan [arjɛrplɑ̃] (pl **arrière-plans**) **nm** background.

arrière-saison [arjɛrsɛzɔ̃] (pl **arrière-saisons**) **nf** late autumn.

arrière-train [arjɛrtrɛ̃] (pl **arrière-trains**) **nm** hindquarters *pl*.

arrimer [3] [arime] **vt 1.** [attacher] to secure **2.** NAUT to stow.

arrivage [arivaʒ] **nm 1.** [de marchandises] consignment, delivery **2.** [de touristes] influx.

arrivant, e [arivɑ̃, ɑ̃t] **nm, f** [personne] arrival.

arrivée [arive] **nf 1.** [venue] arrival **2.** TECHNOL inlet.

arriver [3] [arive] ■ **vi 1.** [venir] to arrive ▸ **en arriver à faire qqch** *fig* to begin to do sthg ▸ **j'arrive!** (I'm) coming! ▸ **arriver à Paris** to arrive in *ou* reach Paris ▸ **on arrive à quelle heure?** what time do we get there? ▸ **être bien arrivé** [personne, colis] to have arrived safely ▸ **l'eau m'arrivait aux genoux** the water came up to my knees ▸ **j'arrive tout juste de vacances** I'm just back from my holidays ▸ **la soixantaine/retraite est vite arrivée** sixty/retirement is soon here
2. [réussir dans la vie] to succeed, to get on
3. [parvenir] **: arriver à faire qqch** to manage to do sthg, to succeed in doing sthg ▸ **il n'arrive pas à faire ses devoirs** he can't do his homework ▸ **je parie que tu n'y arriveras pas!** I bet you won't be able to do it! ▸ **tu n'arriveras jamais à rien** you'll never get anywhere
4. [se produire] to happen ▸ **ce sont des choses qui arrivent** these things happen ▸ **tu ne te décourages jamais? – si, ça m'arrive** don't you ever get discouraged? – yes, from time to time
▸▸ **j'en arrive parfois à me demander si...** sometimes I (even) wonder if... ▸ **en arriver là : depuis, je ne lui parle plus – c'est malheureux d'en arriver là** since then, I haven't spoken to him – it's a shame it has come to that.
■ **v impers** to happen ▸ **il arrive que** *(+ subjonctif)* **: il arrive qu'il soit en retard** he is sometimes late ▸ **il arrive à tout le monde de se décourager** we all get fed up sometimes ▸ **il arrive à tout le monde de se tromper** anyone can make a mistake ▸ **il lui arrive d'oublier quel jour on est** he sometimes forgets what day it is ▸ **quoi qu'il arrive** whatever happens.

arrivisme [arivism] **nm** *péj* ambition.

arriviste [arivist] ■ **adj** self-seeking, careerist.
■ **nmf** careerist.

arrobas, arobas [arɔbas] **nf** = ***arobase***.

arrogance [arɔgɑ̃s] **nf** arrogance.

arrogant, e [arɔgɑ̃, ɑ̃t] ■ **adj** arrogant.
■ **nm, f** arrogant person.

arroger [17] [arɔʒe] ◆ ***s'arroger*** **vp : s'arroger le droit de faire qqch** to take it upon o.s. to do sthg.

arrondi [arɔ̃di] **nm** [de jupe] hemline.

arrondir [32] [arɔ̃dir] **vt 1.** [forme] to make round **2.** [capital] to increase **3.** [chiffre - au-dessus] to round up / [- en dessous] to round down.
◆ ***s'arrondir*** **vp** [corps, visage] to fill out.

arrondissement [arɔ̃dismɑ̃] **nm 1.** ADMIN arrondissement *(administrative division of a département or city)* **2.** [de somme - au-dessus] rounding up / [- en dessous] rounding down.

CULTURE

Arrondissement

This word is most often used in reference to the purely geographical divisions of France's three largest cities: Paris, Marseilles, and Lyons. Paris's 20 **arrondissements** are arranged in a spiral around the **Île de la Cité** and do not always correspond to neighbourhood boundaries; **le Marais**, for example, straddles the third and fourth **arrondissements**. The divisions are given in ordinal numbers: **Paris 15ème, le sixième**. Such expressions are often used to evoke a defining characteristic of the neighbourhood in question. **Le sixième**, for example, is associated with the city's intellectual life. **Arrondissements** are also administrative divisions of France's **départements**.

arrosage [arozaʒ] **nm** [de jardin] watering / [de rue] spraying.

arroser [3] [aroze] **vt 1.** [jardin] to water / [rue] to spray **2.** [couler à travers] to flow through **3.** *fam* [café] **: arroser son café (avec)** to lace one's coffee (with) **4.** *fam* [repas] to wash down **5.** *fam* [célébrer] to celebrate **6.** *fam* [soudoyer] **: arroser qqn** to grease sb's palm.

arrosoir [arozwar] **nm** watering can.

arsenal, aux [arsənal, o] **nm 1.** [de navires] naval dockyard **2.** [d'armes] arsenal ▸ **arsenal de pêcheur** fishing gear.

arsenic [arsənik] **nm** arsenic.

art [ar] **nm** art ▸ **l'art de faire qqch** the art of doing sthg ▸ **art culinaire** art of cooking ▸ **art dramatique/graphique** dramatic/graphic art ▸ **le septième art** cinema.
◆ ***arts*** **nmpl : arts appliqués** applied arts ▸ **les arts et métiers** *college for the advanced education of those working in commerce, manufacturing, construction and design* ▸ **Salon des Arts ménagers** ≃ Ideal Home Exhibition *UK*, home crafts exhibition *ou* show *US* ▸ **arts martiaux** martial arts.

art. abr de ***article***.

Arte [arte] **npr** *Franco-German cultural television channel*.

artère [artɛr] **nf 1.** ANAT artery ▸ **artère coronaire** coronary artery **2.** [rue] arterial road *UK*, main road *US*.

artériel, elle [arterjɛl] **adj** arterial.

artériosclérose [arterjɔskleroz] **nf** arteriosclerosis.

arthrite [artrit] **nf** arthritis.

arthrose [artroz] **nf** osteoarthritis.

artichaut [artiʃo] **nm** artichoke.

article [artikl] **nm 1.** [gén] article ▸ **article défini/indéfini** definite/indefinite article ▸ **article de fond** feature ▸ **articles de bureau** office supplies ▸ **articles de luxe** luxury goods ▸ **articles de mode** fashion accessories ▸ **'articles en promotion'** 'special offers' **2.** INFORM record **3.** [sujet] point ▸ **elle dit qu'on lui doit trois millions, et sur cet article, tu peux lui faire confiance!** she says she's owed three millions, and on that score *ou* point, you can believe what she says! **4.** [paragraphe] article, clause ▸ **article de loi** article of law ▸ **l'article 10 du contrat** point *ou* paragraph *ou* clause 10 of the contract
⏭ **faire l'article** to make a sales pitch ▸ **à l'article de la mort** at death's door.

articulation [artikylasjɔ̃] **nf 1.** ANAT & TECHNOL joint **2.** [prononciation] articulation **3.** [d'une démonstration] structure.

articulé, e [artikyle] **adj** jointed.

articuler [3] [artikyle] **vt 1.** [prononcer] to articulate **2.** ANAT & TECHNOL to articulate, to joint **3.** DR to set out.
◆ ***s'articuler*** **vp** to hang together ▸ **s'articuler sur/autour de qqch** [réflexion] to be based *ou* centred on sthg.

artifice [artifis] **nm 1.** [moyen astucieux] clever device *ou* trick **2.** [tromperie] trick.

artificiel, elle [artifisjɛl] **adj** artificial.

artificiellement [artifisjɛlmɑ̃] **adv** artificially.

artificier [artifisje] **nm 1.** [en pyrotechnie] fireworks expert **2.** MIL [soldat] blaster / [spécialiste] bomb disposal expert.

artillerie [artijri] **nf** MIL artillery.

artilleur [artijœr] **nm** artilleryman.

artisan, e [artizɑ̃, an] **nm, f** craftsman (f craftswoman).
◆ ***artisan*** **nm** [responsable] **: être l'artisan de** *fig* to be the architect of.

artisanal, e, aux [artizanal, o] **adj** craft *(avant n)* ▸ **fabrication artisanale** cottage industry.

artisanat [artizana] **nm** [métier] craft / [classe] craftsmen.

artiste [artist] **nmf 1.** [créateur] artist ▸ **artiste peintre** painter **2.** [interprète] performer.

artistique [artistik] **adj** artistic.

ARVA [arva] (abr de ***appareil de recherche de victimes d'avalanches***) **nm** *equipment for searching for avalanche victims*.

as[1] [a] ➤ ***avoir***.

as[2] [as] **nm 1.** [carte] ace **2.** [premier] number one **3.** [champion] star, ace
⏭ **être fringué comme l'as de pique** *fam* to look like a scarecrow ▸ **passer à l'as** *fam* to go by the board ▸ **être plein aux as** *fam* to be rolling in it.

a/s (abr écrite de ***aux soins de***) c/o.

AS (abr de ***association sportive***) **nf** sports association.

ASA, Asa [aza] (abr de ***American Standards Association***) **nf** ASA.

asc. abr de ***ascenseur***.

ascendant, e [asɑ̃dɑ̃, ɑ̃t] **adj** rising.
◆ ***ascendant*** **nm 1.** [influence] influence, power ▸ **avoir de l'ascendant sur qqn** to have influence over sb **2.** ASTROL ascendant.

ascenseur [asɑ̃sœr] **nm 1.** [in a building] lift *UK*, elevator *US* **2.** INFORM scroll bar.

ascension [asɑ̃sjɔ̃] **nf 1.** [de montagne] ascent **2.** [d'avion] climb **3.** [progression] rise.
◆ ***Ascension*** **nf : l'Ascension** Ascension (Day).

ascensionnel, elle [asɑ̃sjɔnɛl] **adj** upward.

ascèse [asɛz] **nf** asceticism.

ascète [asɛt] **nmf** ascetic.

ASCII [aski] (abr de ***American Standard Code for Information Interchange***) **adj** ASCII.

ASE (abr de ***Agence spatiale européenne***) **nf** ESA.

aseptique [asɛptik] **adj** aseptic.

aseptisé, e [asɛptize] **adj** MÉD sterilized / *fig* [ambiance] impersonal / [discours, roman, univers] sanitized.

aseptiser [3] [asɛptize] **vt** to asepticize.

ashkénase [aʃkenaz] **adj & nmf : (juif) ashkénase** Ashkenazi ▸ **les ashkénases** the Ashkenazim.

asiatique [azjatik] **adj 1.** [de l'Asie en général] Asian **2.** [d'Extrême-Orient] oriental.
◆ ***Asiatique*** **nmf** Asian.

Asie [azi] **nf : l'Asie** Asia ▸ **l'Asie centrale** Central Asia ▸ **l'Asie du Sud-Est** Southeast Asia.

asile [azil] **nm 1.** [refuge] refuge ▸ **asile de nuit** night shelter **2.** POLIT **: demander/accorder l'asile politique** to seek/to grant political asylum **3.** *vieilli* [psychiatrique] asylum.

asocial, e, aux [asɔsjal, o] ■ **adj** antisocial.
■ **nm, f** social misfit.

aspect [aspɛ] **nm 1.** [apparence] appearance ▸ **d'aspect agréable** nice-looking ▸ **un bâtiment d'aspect imposant** an imposing-looking building ▸ **la viande a un aspect bizarre** the meat looks odd ▸ **donner l'aspect de qqch à qqn** to give sb the appearance of sthg, to make sb look like sthg ▸ **cette couleur donne à la pièce un aspect terne** this colour makes the room look dull
2. [point de vue] aspect, facet ▸ **envisager *ou* examiner une question sous tous ses aspects** to consider a question from all angles ▸ **vu sous cet aspect** seen from this angle *ou* point of view ▸ **sous un aspect nouveau** in a new light
3. LING aspect
4. [vue] **: à l'aspect de** *sout* at the sight of.

asperge [aspɛrʒ] **nf** [légume] asparagus.

asperger [17] [aspɛrʒe] **vt : asperger qqch de qqch** to spray sthg with sthg ▸ **asperger qqn de qqch** [arroser] to spray sb with sthg / [éclabousser] to splash sb with sthg.
◆ ***s'asperger*** **vp : s'asperger de qqch** to spray o.s. with sthg.

aspérité [asperite] **nf** [du sol] bump.

aspersion [aspɛrsjɔ̃] **nf 1.** [d'eau] sprinkling, spraying **2.** RELIG sprinkling, aspersion.

asphalte [asfalt] **nm** asphalt.

asphyxie [asfiksi] **nf 1.** MÉD asphyxia, suffocation **2.** *fig* [de l'économie] paralysis.

asphyxier [9] [asfiksje] **vt 1.** MÉD to asphyxiate, to suffocate ▸ **mourir asphyxié** to die of asphyxiation **2.** *fig* [économie] to paralyse *UK*, to paralyze *US*.
◆ ***s'asphyxier*** **vp** to suffocate.

aspic [aspik] **nm** [vipère] asp.

aspirant, e [aspirɑ̃, ɑ̃t] **adj : hotte aspirante** cooker hood *UK*, extractor hood ▸ **pompe aspirante** suction pump.
◆ ***aspirant*** **nm** [armée] ≃ officer cadet / [marine] ≃ midshipman.

aspirateur [aspiratœr] **nm** Hoover® *UK*, vacuum cleaner ▸ **passer l'aspirateur** to do the vacuuming *ou* hoovering *UK*.

aspiration [aspirasjɔ̃] **nf 1.** [souffle] inhalation **2.** TECHNOL suction **3.** LING aspiration.
◆ ***aspirations*** **nfpl** aspirations.

aspirer [3] [aspire] ■ **vt 1.** [air] to inhale / [liquide] to suck up **2.** TECHNOL to suck up, to draw up.
■ **vi** [désirer] **: aspirer à qqch/à faire qqch** to aspire to sthg/to do sthg.

aspirine [aspirin] **nf** aspirin.

assagir [32] [asaʒir] **vt** to quieten down.
◆ ***s'assagir*** **vp** to quieten down.

assaillant, e [asajɑ̃, ɑ̃t] ■ **adj** attacking.
■ **nm, f** assailant, attacker.

assaillir [47] [asajir] **vt** to attack, to assault ▸ **assaillir qqn de qqch** *fig* to assail *ou* bombard sb with sthg.

assainir [32] [asenir] **vt 1.** [logement] to clean up **2.** [eau] to purify **3.** ÉCON to rectify, to stabilize.

assainissement [asenismɑ̃] **nm 1.** [de quartier] cleaning up **2.** [d'eau] purification **3.** ÉCON stabilization.

assaisonnement [asɛzɔnmɑ̃] **nm** [sauce] dressing / [condiments] seasoning.

assaisonner [3] [asɛzɔne] **vt 1.** [salade] to dress / [viande, plat] to season **2.** [propos] to season **3.** *fam* [gronder] to tell off ▸ **se faire assaisonner par qqn** to get a (good) telling-off from sb.

assassin, e [asasɛ̃, in] **adj** provocative.
◆ ***assassin*** **nm** [gén] murderer / POLIT assassin.

assassinat [asasina] **nm** [gén] murder / POLIT assassination.

assassiner [3] [asasine] **vt** [tuer - gén] to murder / POLIT to assassinate.

assaut [aso] **nm 1.** [attaque] assault, attack ▸ **prendre d'assaut** [lieu] to storm / [personne] to attack **2.** SPORT bout
▸▸ **faire assaut de** to vie with each other in.

assécher [18] [aseʃe] **vt** to drain.
◆ ***s'assécher*** **vp** to become dry, to dry up.

ASSEDIC, Assedic [asedik] (abr de ***Association pour l'emploi dans l'industrie et le commerce***) **nfpl** *French unemployment insurance scheme* ▸ **toucher les ASSEDIC** to get unemployment benefit *UK ou* welfare *US*.

assemblage [asɑ̃blaʒ] **nm 1.** [gén] assembly **2.** INFORM **: langage d'assemblage** assembler *ou* assembly language.

assemblée [asɑ̃ble] **nf 1.** [réunion] meeting **2.** [public] gathering **3.** ADMIN & POLIT assembly ▸ **assemblée constituante** constituent assembly ▸ **assemblée consultative** advisory body ▸ **Assemblée galloise *ou* du pays de Galles**

Welsh Assembly ▸ **Assemblée générale** General Assembly ▸ **l'Assemblée nationale** *lower house of the French parliament.*

CULTURE

L'Assemblée nationale

The National Assembly is the lower house of the French parliament. Its members, the **députés**, are chosen in the **élections législatives** held every five years. The president or his government can dissolve the assembly to hold a special election and possibly obtain a greater majority in the current government's favour. This can also be done in an effort to resolve a conflict between parliament and government by means of an election. But the government is not immune to the assembly's own power: **députés** can topple the government by formally censuring it or by rejecting its platform.

assembler [asɑ̃ble] **vt 1.** [monter] to put together **2.** [réunir - objets] to gather (together) **3.** [associer] to connect **4.** [personnes - gén] to bring together, to assemble / [- députés] to convene.
◆ ***s'assembler*** **vp** to gather.

assener [19] [asəne], ***asséner*** [18] [asene] **vt : assener un coup à qqn** [frapper] to strike sb, to deal sb a blow.

assentiment [asɑ̃timɑ̃] **nm** assent ▸ **donner son assentiment à qqch** to give one's assent to sthg.

asseoir [65] [aswar] ■ **vt 1.** [sur un siège] to put ▸ **asseoir qqn** [le mettre sur un siège] to sit sb down / [le redresser dans son lit] to sit sb up ▸ **être assis : j'étais assise sur un tabouret** I was sitting on a stool ▸ **nous étions assis au premier rang** we were seated in the first row
2. [fondations] to lay
3. *fig* [réputation] to establish ▸ **asseoir qqch sur qqch** to base sthg on sthg ▸ **asseoir l'impôt sur le revenu** to base taxation on income ▸ **asseoir sa réputation sur qqch** to base one's reputation on sthg.
■ **vi : faire asseoir qqn** to seat sb, to ask sb to take a seat.
◆ ***s'asseoir*** **vp** to sit (down) ▸ **asseyez-vous donc** please, do sit down ▸ **venez vous asseoir à table avec nous** come and sit at the table with us.

assermenté, e [asɛrmɑ̃te] **adj 1.** [fonctionnaire, expert] sworn **2.** [témoin] under oath.

assertion [asɛrsjɔ̃] **nf** assertion.

asservir [32] [asɛrvir] **vt** [assujettir] to enslave ▸ **être asservi à une cause** to be in thrall to a cause.

asservissement [asɛʀvismɑ̃] **nm 1.** [personne] enslavement **2.** TECHNOL remote control.

assesseur [asesœr] **nm** assessor.

asseyais, asseyions ➤ ***asseoir***.

asseyez, asseyons ➤ ***asseoir***.

assez [ase] **adv 1.** [suffisamment] enough ▸ **assez grand pour qqch/pour faire qqch** big enough for sthg/to do sthg ▸ **assez de** enough ▸ **assez de lait/chaises** enough milk/chairs ▸ **il en reste juste assez** there is/are just enough left ▸ **en avoir assez de qqn/qqch** to have had enough of sb/sthg, to be fed up with sb/sthg **2.** [plutôt] quite, rather.

assidu, e [asidy] **adj 1.** [élève] diligent **2.** [travail] painstaking **3.** [empressé] **: assidu (auprès de qqn)** attentive (to sb).

assiduité [asidɥite] **nf 1.** [zèle] diligence **2.** [fréquence] **: avec assiduité** regularly.
◆ ***assiduités*** **nfpl** *péj* & *sout* attentions ▸ **poursuivre qqn de ses assiduités** to press one's attentions on sb.

assidûment [asidymɑ̃] **adv 1.** [avec zèle] assiduously, diligently **2.** [fréquemment] regularly.

assiégeant, e [asjeʒɑ̃, ɑ̃t] **adj** besieging *(avant n).*
◆ ***assiégeant*** **nm** besieger.

assiéger [22] [asjeʒe] **vt** *litt* & *fig* to besiege.

assiette [asjɛt] **nf 1.** [vaisselle] plate ▸ **assiette creuse** *ou* **à soupe** soup plate ▸ **assiette à dessert** dessert plate ▸ **assiette plate** dinner plate **2.** [de cavalier] seat **3.** [d'impôt] base ▸ **assiette fiscale** *ou* **de l'impôt** taxable income **4.** CULIN **: assiette anglaise** assorted cold meats *pl UK*, cold cuts *pl US* ▸ **assiette de crudités** *raw vegetables served as an hors-d'œuvre*
▸▸ **ne pas être dans son assiette** to feel off colour *UK ou* color *US*.

assiettée [asjete] **nf** plate, plateful.

assignation [asiɲasjɔ̃] **nf 1.** [attribution] **: assignation de qqch à qqn** allocation of sthg to sb **2.** DR summons.

assigner [3] [asiɲe] **vt 1.** [fonds, tâche] **: assigner qqch à qqn** to allocate *ou* assign sthg to sb **2.** [personne] **: assigner qqn à qqch** to assign sb to sthg **3.** DR **: assigner qqn en justice** to issue a writ against sb.

assimilation [asimilasjɔ̃] **nf** assimilation ▸ **assimilation de qqch à qqch** assimilation of sthg to sthg ▸ **assimilation de qqn à qqn** comparison of sb to sb.

assimiler [3] [asimile] **vt 1.** [aliment, connaissances] to assimilate **2.** [confondre] **: assimiler qqch (à qqch)** to liken sthg (to sthg) ▸ **assimiler qqn à qqn** to compare sb to sb.
◆ ***s'assimiler*** **vp 1.** [se comparer] **: s'assimiler à qqn** to be (able to be) compared to sb **2.** [s'intégrer] to integrate.

assis, e [asi, iz] ■ **pp** ➤ ***asseoir***.
■ **adj** sitting, seated ▸ **place assise** seat.
◆ ***assise*** **nf 1.** [base] seat, seating **2.** BIOL & GÉOL stratum.
◆ ***assises*** **nfpl 1.** DR **: (cour d')assises** crown court *UK*, circuit court *US* **2.** [congrès] conference *sg*.

assistance [asistɑ̃s] **nf 1.** [aide] assistance ▸ **prêter assistance à qqn** to lend assistance to sb ▸ **l'Assistance publique** *French authority which manages the social services and state-owned hospitals* ▸ **être à l'Assistance (publique)** to be in care *UK* ▸ **assistance technique** technical aid **2.** [auditoire] audience.

assistant, e [asistɑ̃, ɑ̃t] **nm, f 1.** [auxiliaire] assistant ▸ **assistante sociale** social worker **2.** UNIV assistant lecturer.

assister [3] [asiste] ■ **vi : assister à qqch** to be at sthg, to attend sthg.
■ **vt** to assist.

associatif, ive [asɔsjatif, iv] **adj 1.** [mémoire] associative **2.** [vie] community *(avant n).*

association [asɔsjasjɔ̃] **nf 1.** [gén] association ▸ **association d'idées** association of ideas **2.** [union] society association ▸ **association à but non lucratif** DR non-profit *ou* non-profit-making *UK* organization ▸ **association humanitaire** charity organization ▸ **association sportive** sports club **3.** COMM partnership ▸ **association de libre-échange** free-trade agreement.

associé**, **e [asɔsje] ■ **adj** associated.
■ **nm, f 1.** [collaborateur] associate **2.** [actionnaire] partner.

associer [9] [asɔsje] **vt 1.** [personnes] to bring together **2.** [idées] to associate **3.** [faire participer] **: associer qqn à qqch** [inclure] to bring sb in on sthg / [prendre pour partenaire] to make sb a partner in sthg.
◆ ***s'associer*** **vp 1.** [prendre part] **: s'associer à qqch** [participer] to join *ou* participate in sthg / [partager] to share sthg **2.** [collaborer] **: s'associer à *ou* avec qqn** to join forces with sb **3.** [se combiner] **: s'associer à qqch** to be combined with sthg.

assoiffé**, **e [aswafe] **adj** thirsty / **: assoiffé de pouvoir** *fig* power-hungry.

assois ➤ *asseoir*.

assombrir [32] [asɔ̃brir] **vt 1.** [plonger dans l'obscurité] to darken **2.** *fig* [attrister] to cast a shadow over.
◆ ***s'assombrir*** **vp 1.** [devenir sombre] to grow dark **2.** *fig* [s'attrister] to darken.

assommant**, **e [asɔmɑ̃, ɑ̃t] **adj** *péj* deadly boring.

assommer [3] [asɔme] **vt 1.** [frapper] to knock out **2.** [ennuyer] to bore stiff **3.** [de reproches] to overwhelm.

Assomption [asɔ̃psjɔ̃] **nf : l'Assomption** the Assumption.

assorti**, **e [asɔrti] **adj 1.** [accordé] **: bien assorti** well-matched ▸ **mal assorti** ill-matched ▸ **une cravate assortie au costume** a tie which matches the suit **2.** [varié] assorted.

assortiment [asɔrtimɑ̃] **nm** assortment, selection ▸ **assortiment de produits** product mix.

assortir [32] [asɔrtir] **vt 1.** [objets] **: assortir qqch à qqch** to match sthg to *ou* with sthg **2.** [magasin] to stock.
◆ ***s'assortir*** **vp** to match ▸ **s'assortir de qqch** to be accompanied by *ou* with sthg.

assoupi**, **e [asupi] **adj 1.** [endormi] dozing **2.** *fig* & *littéraire* [sens, intérêt] dulled / [passion, haine] spent / [querelle] dormant.

assoupir [32] [asupir] **vt 1.** *sout* [enfant] to send to sleep **2.** *fig* & *littéraire* [douleur] to soothe.
◆ ***s'assoupir*** **vp 1.** [s'endormir] to doze off **2.** *fig* & *littéraire* [douleur] to die down.

assoupissement [asupismɑ̃] **nm 1.** [sommeil] doze **2.** *fig* & *sout* **: l'assoupissement culturel** cultural apathy.

assouplir [32] [asuplir] **vt 1.** [corps] to make supple **2.** [matière] to soften **3.** [règlement] to relax ▸ **assouplir ses positions** to take a softer line **4.** [caractère] to mellow.
◆ ***s'assouplir*** **vp 1.** [physiquement] to become supple **2.** [moralement] to mellow.

assouplissant [asuplisɑ̃] **nm** (fabric) softener.

assouplissement [asuplismɑ̃] **nm 1.** [de corps] limbering up **2.** [de matière] softening **3.** [de règlement] easing, relaxation **4.** [de caractère] mellowing.

assourdir [32] [asurdir] **vt 1.** [rendre sourd] to deafen **2.** [abrutir] to exhaust, to wear out **3.** [amortir] to deaden, to muffle.

assouvir [32] [asuvir] **vt** *littéraire* to satisfy.
◆ ***s'assouvir*** **vp** *littéraire* to be satisfied.

ASSU**, **Assu [asy] (abr de ***Association du sport scolaire et universitaire***) **nf** *former schools and university sports association.*

assujetti**, **e [asyʒeti] **adj : assujetti à l'impôt** subject to tax *ou* taxation.

assujettir [32] [asyʒetir] **vt 1.** [peuple] to subjugate **2.** [soumettre] **: assujettir qqn à qqch** to subject sb to sthg **3.** [fixer] to secure.
◆ ***s'assujettir*** **vp : s'assujettir à qqch** to submit to sthg.

assumer [3] [asyme] **vt 1.** [fonction - exercer] to carry out / [- prendre] to take on **2.** [risque, responsabilité] to accept **3.** [condition] to come to terms with **4.** [frais] to meet.
◆ ***s'assumer*** **vp** to come to terms with o.s.

assurance [asyrɑ̃s] **nf 1.** [gén] assurance ▸ **avoir l'assurance que** to feel certain *ou* assured that ▸ **manquer d'assurance** to be insecure, to have no self-confidence ▸ **s'exprimer avec assurance** to speak with assurance *ou* confidently **2.** [contrat] insurance ▸ **contracter *ou* prendre une assurance** to take out insurance ▸ **assurance auto *ou* automobile** car *ou* automobile *US* insurance ▸ **assurance chômage** unemployment insurance ▸ **assurance contre le vol** insurance against theft ▸ **assurance maladie** health insurance ▸ **assurance personnelle *ou* volontaire** private health insurance ▸ **assurance responsabilité civile *ou* au tiers** third party insurance ▸ **assurance tous risques** AUTO comprehensive insurance ▸ **assurance-vie** life assurance *UK*, life insurance *US* ▸ **assurance vieillesse** retirement pension.

assuré**, **e [asyre] **nm, f** policy holder ▸ **assuré social** National Insurance contributor *UK*, Social Security contributor *US*.

assurément [asyremɑ̃] **adv** *sout* certainly.

assurer [3] [asyre] ■ **vt 1.** [promettre] **: assurer à qqn que** to assure sb (that) ▸ **il m'a assuré qu'il viendrait** he assured me he'd come ▸ **assurer qqn de qqch** to assure sb of sthg **2.** [permanence, liaison] to provide ▸ **assurer le ravitaillement des populations sinistrées** to provide disaster victims with supplies ▸ **une permanence est assurée le samedi après-midi** there is someone on duty on Saturday afternoons **3.** COMM to insure ▸ **j'ai fait assurer mes bijoux** I had my jewels insured **4.** [paix] to ensure ▸ **pour mieux assurer la sécurité de tous** to ensure greater safety for all **5.** [échelle] to secure, to fix.
■ **vi** *fam* **: il assure en physique/anglais** he's good at physics/English ▸ **elle a beau être nouvelle au bureau, elle assure bien** she may be new to the job but she certainly copes (well).
◆ ***s'assurer*** **vp 1.** [vérifier] **: s'assurer que** to make sure (that) ▸ **assure-toi que tout va bien** make sure everything's OK ▸ **s'assurer de qqch** to ensure sthg, to make sure of sthg ▸ **assurez-vous de la validité de votre passeport** make sure your passport is valid **2.** COMM **: s'assurer (contre qqch)** to insure o.s. (against sthg) ▸ **s'assurer**

contre le vol/l'incendie to insure o.s. against theft/fire **3.** [obtenir] **: s'assurer qqch** to secure sthg **4.** [se stabiliser] to steady o.s.

Assyrie [asiri] **npr f : (l')Assyrie** Assyria.

assyrien, enne [asirjɛ̃, ɛn] **adj** Assyrian.
◆ ***Assyrien, enne*** **nm, f** Assyrian.

astérisque [asterisk] **nm** asterisk.

asthmatique [asmatik] **nmf & adj** asthmatic.

asthme [asm] **nm** MÉD asthma.

asticot [astiko] **nm** maggot.

astigmate [astigmat] **nmf & adj** astigmatic.

astiquer [3] [astike] **vt** to polish.

astrakan [astrakɑ̃] **nm** astrakhan.

astral, e, aux [astral, o] **adj** astral, star *(avant n)*.

astre [astr] **nm** star.

astreignant, e [astrɛɲɑ̃, ɑ̃t] **adj** demanding.

astreindre [81] [astrɛ̃dr] **vt : astreindre qqn à qqch** to subject sb to sthg ▸ **astreindre qqn à faire qqch** to compel sb to do sthg.
◆ ***s'astreindre*** **vp : s'astreindre à qqch** to subject o.s. to sthg ▸ **s'astreindre à faire qqch** to compel o.s. to do sthg.

astreint, e [astrɛ̃, ɛ̃t] **pp** ➤ ***astreindre***.

astringent, e [astrɛ̃ʒɑ̃, ɑ̃t] **adj** astringent.
◆ ***astringent*** **nm** astringent.

astrologie [astrɔlɔʒi] **nf** astrology.

astrologique [astrɔlɔʒik] **adj** astrological.

astrologue [astrɔlɔg] **nm** astrologer.

astronaute [astrɔnot] **nmf** astronaut.

astronautique [astrɔnotik] **nf** astronautics *(U)*.

astronome [astrɔnɔm] **nmf** astronomer.

astronomie [astrɔnɔmi] **nf** astronomy.

astronomique [astrɔnɔmik] **adj** astronomical.

astrophysicien, enne [astrɔfisisjɛ̃, ɛn] **adj** astrophysicist.

astrophysique [astrɔfisik] **nf** astrophysics *(U)*.

astuce [astys] **nf 1.** [ruse] (clever) trick **2.** [ingéniosité] shrewdness *(U)* **3.** [plaisanterie] wisecrack.

astucieux, euse [astysjø, øz] **adj 1.** [idée] clever **2.** [personne] shrewd.

asymétrique [asimetrik] **adj** asymmetric, asymmetrical.

atavisme [atavism] **nm** atavism.

atelier [atəlje] **nm 1.** [d'artisan] workshop **2.** [de peintre] studio.

atermoiement [atɛrmwamɑ̃] **nm 1.** [tergiversation] procrastination **2.** DR postponement.

athée [ate] ■ **nmf** atheist.
■ **adj** atheistic.

athéisme [ateism] **nm** atheism.

athénée [atene] **nm** *Belgique* secondary school.

Athènes [atɛn] **npr** Athens.

athénien, enne [atenjɛ̃, ɛn] **adj** Athenian.
◆ ***Athénien, enne*** **nm, f** Athenian.

athlète [atlɛt] **nmf** athlete.

athlétique [atletik] **adj** athletic.

athlétisme [atletism] **nm** athletics *(U)* *UK*, track and fields *US*.

Atlantide [atlɑ̃tid] **nf : l'Atlantide** Atlantis.

atlantique [atlɑ̃tik] **adj** Atlantic.
◆ ***Atlantique*** **nm : l'Atlantique** the Atlantic (Ocean).

atlas [atlas] **nm** atlas.

Atlas [atlas] ■ **npr** MYTHOL Atlas.
■ **npr m** GÉOGR **: l'Atlas** the Atlas Mountains.

atmosphère [atmɔsfɛr] **nf** atmosphere.

atmosphérique [atmɔsferik] **adj** atmospheric.

atoca [atɔka] **nm** *Québec large cranberry*.

atoll [atɔl] **nm** atoll.

atome [atom] **nm** atom ▸ **avoir des atomes crochus avec qqn** to be on the same wavelength as sb.

atomique [atɔmik] **adj 1.** [gén] nuclear **2.** CHIM & PHYS atomic.

atomiseur [atɔmizœr] **nm** spray.

atone [atɔn] **adj 1.** [inexpressif] lifeless **2.** MÉD atonic **3.** [voyelle] unstressed.

atours [atur] **nmpl** *littéraire* **: paré de** *ou* **dans ses plus beaux atours** in all one's finery.

atout [atu] **nm 1.** [carte] trump ▸ **l'atout est à piques** spades are trumps **2.** *fig* [ressource] asset, advantage.

ATP ■ **nf** (abr de ***Association des tennismen professionnels***) ATP.
■ **nfpl** (abr de ***arts et traditions populaires***) arts and crafts ▸ **musée des ATP** arts and crafts museum.

âtre [atr] **nm** *littéraire* hearth.

atroce [atrɔs] **adj 1.** [crime] atrocious, dreadful **2.** [souffrance] horrific, atrocious **3.** [temps] terrible.

atrocement [atrɔsmɑ̃] **adv 1.** [horriblement] horribly, terribly **2.** [exagérément] terribly.

atrocité [atrɔsite] **nf 1.** [horreur] atrocity **2.** [calomnie] insult.

atrophie [atrɔfi] **nf** atrophy.

atrophier [9] [atrɔfje] ◆ ***s'atrophier*** **vp** to atrophy.

attabler [3] [atable] ◆ ***s'attabler*** **vp** to sit down (at the table) ▸ **s'attabler devant qqch** to sit down to sthg.

attachant, e [ataʃɑ̃, ɑ̃t] **adj** lovable.

attache [ataʃ] **nf** [lien] fastening.
◆ ***attaches*** **nfpl** links, connections.

attaché, e [ataʃe] **nm, f** attaché ▸ **attaché d'ambassade** attaché ▸ **attaché commercial/culturel/militaire** commercial/cultural/military attaché ▸ **attaché de presse** [diplomatique] press attaché / [d'organisme, d'entreprise] press officer.

attaché-case [ataʃekɛz] (pl **attachés-cases**) **nm** attaché case.

attachement [ataʃmɑ̃] **nm** attachment.

attacher [3] [ataʃe] ■ **vt 1.** [lier] **: attacher qqch (à)** to fasten *ou* tie sthg (to) / *fig* [associer] to attach sthg (to) ▸ **attacher un chien à une corde/à sa niche** to tie a dog to a rope/to his kennel **2.** [paquet] to tie up ▸ **attacher un colis avec une ficelle** to tie up a parcel **3.** [lacet] to do up / [ceinture de sécurité] to fasten ▸ **peux-tu m'aider à attacher ma robe?** can you help me do up my dress? **4.** [associer] to link, to connect ▸ **le scandale auquel son nom est/reste attaché** the scandal with which his name is/remains linked **5.** *fig* [émotionnellement] **: attacher qqn à** to bind sb to.

■ **vi** CULIN **: attacher (à)** to stick (to) ▸ **poêle/casserole qui n'attache pas** nonstick pan/saucepan.

◆ ***s'attacher*** **vp 1.** [émotionnellement] **: s'attacher à qqn/qqch** to become attached to sb/sthg **2.** [se fermer] to fasten ▸ **s'attacher avec *ou* par qqch** to do up *ou* fasten with sthg ▸ **s'attacher avec une fermeture Éclair®/des boutons** to zip/to button up **3.** [s'appliquer] **: s'attacher à qqch/à faire qqch** to devote o.s. to sthg/to doing sthg, to apply o.s. to sthg/to doing sthg ▸ **je m'attache à le rendre heureux** I try (my best) to make him happy.

attaquant, e [atakɑ̃, ɑ̃t] ■ **adj** attacking.

■ **nm, f** attacker.

attaque [atak] **nf 1.** [gén & MÉD] attack ▸ **attaque à main armée** holdup / *fig* **: attaque contre qqn/qqch** attack on sb/sthg **2.** MUS [de note] attack

▸▸ **être d'attaque** to be on *UK ou* in *US* form ▸ **être/se sentir d'attaque pour faire qqch** to be/feel up to doing sthg.

attaquer [3] [atake] **vt 1.** [gén] to attack ▸ **il s'est fait attaquer par deux hommes** he was attacked *ou* assaulted by two men **2.** [DR - personne] to take to court ▸ **attaquer qqn en justice** to bring an action against sb, to take sb to court ▸ **attaquer qqn en diffamation** to bring a libel action against sb / [- jugement] to contest **3.** *fam* [plat] to tuck into ▸ **on attaque le beaujolais?** *fam* shall we have a go at that Beaujolais? **4.** [tâche] to tackle ▸ **prêt à attaquer le travail?** ready to get *ou* to settle down to work?

◆ ***s'attaquer*** **vp 1.** [combattre] **: s'attaquer à qqn** to attack sb ▸ **s'attaquer à qqch : s'attaquer aux préjugés** to attack *ou* to fight *ou* to tackle prejudice **2.** *fig* **: s'attaquer à qqch** [tâche] to tackle sthg ▸ **il s'est tout de suite attaqué au problème** he tackled the problem right away **3.** [agir sur] to attack ▸ **les bactéries s'attaquent à vos gencives** bacteria attack your gums.

attardé, e [atarde] ■ **adj 1.** [idées] outdated **2.** [passants] late **3.** *vieilli* [enfant] backward.

■ **nm, f** *vieilli* [enfant] backward child.

attarder [3] [atarde] ◆ ***s'attarder*** **vp : s'attarder sur qqch** to dwell on sthg ▸ **s'attarder à faire qqch** to stay on to do sthg, to stay behind to do sthg.

atteignais, atteignions ➤ ***atteindre***.

atteindre [8] [atɛ̃dr] **vt 1.** [situation, objectif] to reach ▸ **il a atteint son but** he's reached his goal *ou* achieved his aim ▸ **je n'arrive pas à atteindre le dictionnaire qui est là-haut** I can't reach the dictionary up there ▸ **les taux d'intérêt ont atteint un nouveau record** interest rates have reached a record high ▸ **atteindre des objectifs de vente** to reach *ou* fulfil *UK ou* fulfill *US* sales targets ▸ **atteindre la gloire** to attain glory **2.** [toucher] to hit ▸ **atteindre la cible** to hit the target ▸ **la balle/le policier l'a atteint en pleine tête** the bullet hit/the policeman shot him in the head ▸ **leur politique n'atteint pas son but** their policy misses its target **3.** [affecter] to affect ▸ **rien ne l'atteint** nothing affects *ou* can reach him **4.** [maladie, fléau] to affect ▸ **la tumeur a déjà atteint le poumon** the tumour has already spread to the lung ▸ **être atteint d'un mal incurable** to be suffering from an incurable disease **5.** [communiquer avec] to contact, to reach ▸ **impossible d'atteindre ceux qui sont à l'intérieur (du bâtiment)** the people inside are incommunicado.

atteint, e [atɛ̃, ɛ̃t] ■ **pp** ➤ ***atteindre***.

■ **adj 1.** [malade] **: être atteint de** to be suffering from **2.** *fam* [fou] touched.

◆ ***atteinte*** **nf 1.** [préjudice] **: atteinte à** attack on ▸ **porter atteinte à** to undermine ▸ **hors d'atteinte** [hors de portée] out of reach / [inattaquable] beyond reach **2.** [effet] effect.

attelage [atlaʒ] **nm 1.** [chevaux] team **2.** [harnachement] harnessing *(U)*.

atteler [24] [atle] **vt 1.** [animaux, véhicules] to hitch up / [wagons] to couple **2.** [à une tâche] **: atteler qqn à** to assign sb to.

◆ ***s'atteler*** **vp : s'atteler à** to get down to.

attelle [atɛl] **nf** splint.

attenant, e [atnɑ̃, ɑ̃t] **adj : attenant (à qqch)** adjoining (sthg).

attendre [73] [atɑ̃dr] ■ **vt 1.** [gén] to wait for ▸ **le déjeuner nous attend** lunch is ready ▸ **attendre qqn à *ou* pour dîner** to expect sb for dinner ▸ **attendre son tour** to wait one's turn ▸ **attendre que** *(+ subjonctif)* **: attendre que la pluie s'arrête** to wait for the rain to stop ▸ **attendre de : attends d'être grand** wait till *ou* until you're older ▸ **faire attendre qqn** [personne] to keep sb waiting ▸ **les résultats se font attendre** we're all waiting for the results ▸ **désolé de m'être fait attendre** sorry to have kept you waiting **2.** [espérer] **: attendre qqch (de qqn/qqch)** to expect sthg (from sb/sthg) ▸ **nous attendons beaucoup de la réunion** we expect a lot (to come out) of the meeting **3.** [suj: surprise, épreuve] to be in store for ▸ **une mauvaise surprise l'attendait** there was a nasty surprise in store for her **4.** [suj: femme enceinte] **: attendre un bébé *ou* un enfant** to be expecting (a child),to be pregnant.

■ **vi** to wait ▸ **attends!** hang on!

◆ ***s'attendre*** **vp : s'attendre à** to expect ▸ **il faut s'attendre à tout** we should be prepared for anything.

◆ ***en attendant*** **loc adv 1.** [pendant ce temps] meanwhile, in the meantime ▸ **finis ton dessert, en attendant, je vais faire le café** finish your dessert, and in the meantime I'll make the coffee **2.** [quand même] all the same ▸ **oui mais, en attendant, je n'ai toujours pas mon argent** that's as may be, but I still don't have my money.

attendrir [32] [atɑ̃drir] **vt 1.** [viande] to tenderize **2.** [personne] to move.

◆ ***s'attendrir*** **vp : s'attendrir (sur qqn/qqch)** to be moved (by sb/sthg).

attendrissant, e [atɑ̃drisɑ̃, ɑ̃t] **adj** moving, touching.

attendrissement [atɑ̃drismɑ̃] **nm** pity.

attendrisseur [atɑ̃drisœr] **nm** meat tenderizer.

attendu, e [atɑ̃dy] **pp** ➤ ***attendre***.
◆ ***attendu*** ■ **nm** DR reasoning *(U)*.
■ **prép** considering.
◆ ***attendu que*** **loc conj** since, considering that.

attentat [atɑ̃ta] **nm** attack ▸ **attentat à la bombe** bomb attack, bombing ▸ **attentat à la pudeur** DR indecent assault.

attentat-suicide [atɑ̃tasɥisid] (pl **attentats-suicides**) **nm** suicide attack / [à la bombe] suicide bombing.

attente [atɑ̃t] **nf 1.** [station] wait ▸ **en attente** in abeyance **2.** [espoir] expectation ▸ **contre toute attente** contrary to all expectations ▸ **répondre aux attentes de qqn** to live up to sb's expectations.

attenter [3] [atɑ̃te] **vi : attenter à** [liberté, droit] to violate ▸ **attenter à l'honneur/à la réputation de qqn** to undermine sb's honour/reputation ▸ **attenter à ses jours** to attempt suicide ▸ **attenter à la vie de qqn** to make an attempt on sb's life.

attentif, ive [atɑ̃tif, iv] **adj 1.** [auditoire] **: attentif (à qqch)** attentive (to sthg) **2.** [soin] careful, scrupulous.

attention [atɑ̃sjɔ̃] ■ **nf 1.** [concentration] attention ▸ **écouter qqn avec attention** to listen to sb attentively, to listen hard to what sb's saying ▸ **faire attention à** to pay attention to
2. [éveiller l'intérêt] **: attirer l'attention de qqn** to catch *ou* to attract sb's attention ▸ **appeler *ou* attirer l'attention de qqn sur qqch** to call sb's attention to sthg, to point sthg out to sb ▸ **porter qqch à l'attention de qqn** to bring sthg to sb's attention
3. [prudence] attention ▸ **à l'attention de** for the attention of ▸ **faire attention à** to be careful of ▸ **fais bien attention en descendant de l'escabeau** do be careful coming down the stepladder ▸ **fais particulièrement attention au dernier paragraphe** pay special attention to the last paragraph ▸ **faire attention à sa ligne** to watch one's weight ▸ **faire attention à sa santé** to take care of *ou* to look after one's health
4. [égard] attention *(U)*, attentiveness *(U)* ▸ **avoir une petite attention pour qqn** to do nice things for sb ▸ **être plein d'attentions pour qqn** to lavish attention on sb.
■ **interj** watch out!, be careful! ▸ **'attention chien méchant'** 'beware of the dog' ▸ **attention au départ!** stand clear of the doors! ▸ **'attention fragile'** 'handle with care' ▸ **attention à la marche** mind the step ▸ **'attention peinture fraîche'** 'wet paint' ▸ **'attention travaux'** 'men at work'.

attentionné, e [atɑ̃sjɔne] **adj** thoughtful ▸ **attentionné auprès de** attentive to.

attentisme [atɑ̃tism] **nm** [gén] waiting game / POLIT wait-and-see policy.

attentivement [atɑ̃tivmɑ̃] **adv** attentively, carefully.

atténuante [atenɥɑ̃t] ➤ ***circonstance***.

atténuation [atenɥasjɔ̃] **nf** [de lumière] dimming / [de propos] toning down / [de douleur] easing ▸ **atténuation de peine** DR reduction in sentence.

atténuer [7] [atenɥe] **vt** [douleur] to ease / [propos, ton] to tone down / [lumière] to dim, to subdue / [bruit] to quieten.
◆ ***s'atténuer*** **vp** [lumière] to dim, to fade / [bruit] to fade / [douleur] to ease.

atterrer [4] [atere] **vt** to stagger.

atterrir [32] [aterir] **vi** to land ▸ **atterrir dans qqch** *fig* to land up in sthg.

atterrissage [aterisaʒ] **nm** landing ▸ **atterrissage sans visibilité** blind landing ▸ **atterrissage forcé** emergency landing.

attestation [atɛstasjɔ̃] **nf 1.** [certificat] certificate **2.** [action] attestation **3.** [preuve] proof.

attester [3] [atɛste] **vt 1.** [confirmer] to vouch for, to testify to **2.** [certifier] to attest.

attifer [3] [atife] *fam péj* **vt** to get up.
◆ ***s'attifer*** **vp** to get *ou* doll o.s. up.

attique [atik] **nm** ARCHIT attic.

attirail [atiraj] **nm** *fam* [équipement] gear.

attirance [atirɑ̃s] **nf** attraction ▸ **avoir/éprouver de l'attirance pour** to be/to feel attracted to.

attirant, e [atirɑ̃, ɑ̃t] **adj** attractive.

attirer [3] [atire] **vt 1.** [gén] to attract ▸ **couvre ce melon, il attire les guêpes** cover that melon up: it's attracting wasps ▸ **attirer l'attention de qqn sur qqch** to call sb's attention to sthg, to point sthg out to sb **2.** [amener vers soi] **: attirer qqn à/vers soi** to draw sb to/towards one ▸ **il m'a attiré vers le balcon pour me montrer le paysage** he drew me towards the balcony to show me the view **3.** [provoquer] **: attirer des ennuis à qqn** to cause trouble for sb ▸ **sa démission lui a attiré des sympathies** her resignation won *ou* earned her some sympathy.
◆ ***s'attirer*** **vp : s'attirer qqch** to bring sthg on o.s. ▸ **s'attirer la colère de qqn** to incur sb's anger ▸ **s'attirer des ennuis** to get o.s. into trouble, to bring trouble upon o.s..

attiser [3] [atize] **vt 1.** [feu] to poke **2.** *fig* [haine] to stir up.

attitré, e [atitre] **adj 1.** [habituel] usual **2.** [titulaire - fournisseur] by appointment / [- représentant] accredited.

attitude [atityd] **nf 1.** [comportement, approche] attitude **2.** [posture] posture.

attouchement [atuʃmɑ̃] **nm** caress.

attractif, ive [atraktif, iv] **adj 1.** [force] magnetic **2.** [prix] attractive.

attraction [atraksjɔ̃] **nf 1.** [gén] attraction **2.** [force] **: attraction magnétique** magnetic force ▸ **l'attraction terrestre** the earth's gravitational force.
◆ ***attractions*** **nfpl 1.** [jeux] amusements **2.** [spectacle] attractions.

attrait [atrɛ] **nm 1.** [séduction] appeal **2.** [intérêt] attraction.
◆ ***attraits*** **nmpl** attractions.

attrape [atrap] **nf** trick.

attrape-nigaud [atrapnigo] (pl **attrape-nigauds**) **nm** con.

attraper [3] [atrape] **vt 1.** [gén] to catch ▸ **attraper qqn par le bras** to grab sb by the arm ▸ **attrape Rex, attrape!** come on Rex, get it! ▸ **que je ne t'attrape plus à écouter aux portes!** don't let me catch you listening at the door again! **2.** *fam* [gronder] to tell off ▸ **se faire attraper (par qqn)** to get a telling-off (from sb) **3.** [habitude, accent] to pick up **4.** *fam* [avoir] to get ▸ **attraper un coup de soleil** to get sunburnt ▸ **attraper froid** *ou* **un rhume** to catch *ou* to get a cold.

attrayant, e [atrɛjɑ̃, ɑ̃t] **adj** attractive.

attribuer [7] [atribɥe] **vt 1.** [tâche, part] **: attribuer qqch à qqn** to assign *ou* allocate sthg to sb, to assign *ou* allocate sb sthg / [privilège] to grant sthg to sb, to grant sb sthg / [récompense] to award sthg to sb, to award sb sthg **2.** [faute] **: attribuer qqch à qqn** to attribute sthg to sb, to put sthg down to sb.
◆ ***s'attribuer*** **vp 1.** [s'approprier] to appropriate (for o.s.) **2.** [revendiquer] to claim (for o.s.)

attribut [atriby] **nm 1.** [gén] attribute **2.** GRAMM complement.

attribution [atribysjɔ̃] **nf 1.** [de prix] awarding, award **2.** [de part, tâche] allocation, assignment **3.** [d'avantage] bestowal.
◆ ***attributions*** **nfpl** [fonctions] duties.

attrister [3] [atriste] **vt** to sadden.
◆ ***s'attrister*** **vp** to be saddened.

attroupement [atrupmɑ̃] **nm** crowd.

attrouper [3] [atrupe] ◆ ***s'attrouper*** **vp** to form a crowd, to gather.

au [o] ➤ *à*.

aubade [obad] **nf** dawn serenade.

aubaine [obɛn] **nf** piece of good fortune.

aube [ob] **nf 1.** [aurore] dawn, daybreak ▸ **à l'aube** at dawn ▸ **à l'aube de** *fig* at the dawn of **2.** RELIG alb.

aubépine [obepin] **nf** hawthorn.

auberge [obɛrʒ] **nf** [hôtel] inn ▸ **auberge de jeunesse** youth hostel ▸ **on n'est pas sorti de l'auberge** *fam fig* we're not out of the woods yet.

aubergine [obɛrʒin] ■ **nf 1.** BOT aubergine *UK*, eggplant *US* **2.** *péj* [contractuelle] traffic warden *UK*, meter maid *US*.
■ **adj inv** [couleur] aubergine.

aubergiste [obɛrʒist] **nmf** innkeeper.

auburn [obœrn] **adj inv** auburn.

aucun, e [okœ, yn] ■ **adj indéf 1.** [sens négatif] **: ne... aucun** no ▸ **il n'y a aucune voiture dans la rue** there aren't any cars in the street, there are no cars in the street ▸ **sans faire aucun bruit** without making a sound **2.** [sens positif] any ▸ **il lit plus qu'aucun autre enfant** he reads more than any other child.
■ **pron indéf 1.** [sens négatif] none ▸ **aucun des enfants** none of the children ▸ **aucun d'entre nous** none of us ▸ **aucun (des deux)** neither (of them) **2.** [sens positif] **: plus qu'aucun de nous** more than any of us ▸ **d'aucuns** *sout* some (people).

aucunement [okynmɑ̃] **adv** not at all, in no way.

audace [odas] **nf 1.** [hardiesse] daring, boldness **2.** [insolence] audacity ▸ **avoir l'audace de faire qqch** to have the audacity *ou* cheek *UK* to do sthg **3.** [innovation] daring innovation.

audacieux, euse [odasjø, øz] ■ **adj 1.** [projet] daring, bold **2.** [personne, geste] bold.
■ **nm, f** daring person.

au-dedans [odədɑ̃] **loc adv** inside.
◆ ***au-dedans de*** **loc prép** inside.

au-dehors [odəɔr] **loc adv** outside.
◆ ***au-dehors de*** **loc prép** outside.

au-delà [odəla] ■ **loc adv 1.** [plus loin] beyond **2.** [davantage, plus] more.
■ **nm : l'au-delà** the hereafter, the afterlife.
◆ ***au-delà de*** **loc prép** beyond.

au-dessous [odəsu] **loc adv** below, underneath.
◆ ***au-dessous de*** **loc prép** below, under(neath).

au-dessus [odəsy] **loc adv** above.
◆ ***au-dessus de*** **loc prép** above, over.

au-devant [odəvɑ̃] **loc adv** ahead.
◆ ***au-devant de*** **loc prép : aller au-devant de** to go to meet ▸ **aller au-devant du danger** to court danger.

audible [odibl] **adj** audible.

audience [odjɑ̃s] **nf 1.** [public, entretien] audience **2.** DR hearing **3.** [marketing] **: audience captive** captive audience ▸ **audience cible** target audience.

Audimat [odimat] **nm** audience rating, ≃ Nielsen® ratings *US* ▸ **course à l'Audimat®** ratings war.

audionumérique [odjɔnymerik] **adj** digital audio.

audiovisuel, elle [odjɔvizɥɛl] **adj** audiovisual.
◆ ***audiovisuel*** **nm** TV and radio.

audit [odit] **nm** audit ▸ **audit marketing** COMM marketing audit.

auditeur, trice [oditœr, tris] **nm, f** listener.
◆ ***auditeur*** **nm 1.** UNIV **: auditeur libre** *person allowed to attend lectures without being registered,* auditor *US* **2.** FIN auditor.

auditif, ive [oditif, iv] **adj 1.** [appareil] hearing *(avant n)* **2.** [mémoire] auditory.

audition [odisjɔ̃] **nf 1.** [fait d'entendre] hearing **2.** DR examination **3.** THÉÂTRE audition **4.** MUS recital.

auditionner [3] [odisjɔne] **vt & vi** to audition.

auditoire [oditwar] **nm** [public] audience ▸ **auditoire cible** COMM target audience.

auditorium [oditɔrjɔm] **nm** [de concert] auditorium / [d'enregistrement] studio.

auge [oʒ] **nf** [pour animaux] trough.

augmentatif, ive [ogmɑ̃tatif, iv] **adj** augmentative.

augmentation [ogmɑ̃tasjɔ̃] **nf : augmentation (de)** increase (in) ▸ **augmentation (de salaire)** rise *UK ou* raise *US* (in salary) ▸ **augmentation des prix** price increase.

augmenter [3] [ogmɑ̃te] ■ **vt** to increase / [prix, salaire] to raise / [personne] to give a rise *UK* ***ou*** raise *US* to ▸ **la crise a fait augmenter le prix du pétrole** the crisis has pushed up the price of oil ▸ **elle a été augmentée** *fam* she got a (pay) rise *UK* ***ou*** a raise *US* ▸ **augmenter qqch de : augmenter les impôts de 5 %** to put up ***ou*** to raise ***ou*** to increase taxes by 5%.
■ **vi** to increase, to rise ▸ **achetez maintenant, ça va augmenter!** buy now: prices are on the increase ***ou*** going up! ▸ **le froid augmente** it's getting colder ▸ **la douleur augmente** the pain is getting worse ▸ **la violence augmente dans les villes** urban violence is on the increase.

augure [ogyr] **nm** [présage] omen ▸ **être de bon/mauvais augure** to be a good/bad sign.

augurer [3] [ogyre] **vt : augurer bien/mal de qqch** to augur well/ill for sthg.

auguste [ogyst] **adj** august.

aujourd'hui [oʒurdɥi] **adv** today.

aulx ➤ ***ail***.

aumône [omon] **nf : faire l'aumône à qqn** to give alms to sb ▸ **faire l'aumône de qqch à qqn** *fig* to favour *UK* ***ou*** favor *US* sb with sthg.

aumônier [omonje] **nm** RELIG chaplain.

auparavant [oparavɑ̃] **adv 1.** [tout d'abord] first (of all) **2.** [avant] before, previously.

auprès [oprɛ] ◆ ***auprès de*** **loc prép 1.** [à côté de] beside, next to **2.** [dans l'opinion de] in the eyes of **3.** [comparé à] compared with **4.** [en s'adressant à] to.

auquel [okɛl] ➤ ***lequel***.

aurai, ***auras*** ➤ ***avoir***.

auréole [oreɔl] **nf 1.** ASTRON & RELIG halo **2.** [trace] ring.

auréoler [3] [oreɔle] **vt : être auréolé de** to be crowned with.

auriculaire [orikylɛr] **nm** little finger.

aurore [orɔr] **nf** dawn ▸ **aurore boréale** northern lights *pl*, aurora borealis ▸ **à l'aurore de** *fig* at the dawn of.

ausculter [3] [oskylte] **vt** MÉD to sound.

auspice [ospis] **nm** *(gén pl)* sign, auspice ▸ **sous d'heureux auspices** promisingly ▸ **sous les auspices de qqn** under the auspices of sb.

aussi [osi] **adv 1.** [pareillement, en plus] also, too ▸ **moi aussi** me too ▸ **j'y vais aussi** I'm going too ***ou*** as well ▸ **elle aussi travaille à Rome** she too works in Rome, she works in Rome as well ▸ **il parle anglais et aussi espagnol** he speaks English as well as Spanish ▸ **aussi sec** *fam* right away **2.** [dans une comparaison] **: aussi... que** as... as ▸ **il n'est pas aussi intelligent que son frère** he's not as clever as his brother ▸ **je n'ai jamais rien vu d'aussi beau** I've never seen anything so beautiful ▸ **aussi léger qu'il soit, je ne pourrai pas le porter** even though it's light ***ou*** light though it is, I won't be able to carry it ▸ **aussi incroyable que cela paraisse** incredible though ***ou*** as it may seem ▸ **aussi doucement que possible** as quietly as possible **3.** *sout* [introduisant une explication] so ▸ **il était très timide, aussi n'osa-t-il rien répondre** he was very shy, and so he didn't dare reply.
◆ ***(tout) aussi bien*** **loc adv** just as easily, just as well ▸ **je ferais aussi bien de partir** I might as well leave ▸ **j'aurais pu (tout) aussi bien refuser** I could just as easily have said no.
◆ ***aussi bien... que*** **loc conj** as well... as ▸ **tu le sais aussi bien que moi** you know as well as I do ▸ **il ne s'est jamais senti aussi bien que depuis qu'il a arrêté de fumer** he's never felt so well since he stopped smoking.

aussitôt [osito] **adv** immediately.
◆ ***aussitôt que*** **loc conj** as soon as.

austère [ostɛr] **adj 1.** [personne, vie] austere **2.** [vêtement] severe / [paysage] harsh.

austérité [osterite] **nf 1.** [de personne, vie] austerity **2.** [de vêtement] severeness / [de paysage] harshness.

austral, ***e*** [ostral] (pl **australs** ***ou*** **austraux** [ostro]) **adj** southern.

Australie [ostrali] **nf : l'Australie** Australia ▸ **l'Australie-Méridionale** South Australia ▸ **l'Australie-Occidentale** Western Australia.

australien, ***enne*** [ostraljɛ̃, ɛn] **adj** Australian.
◆ ***Australien***, ***-enne*** **nm, f** Australian.

autant [otɑ̃] **adv 1.** [comparatif] **: autant que** as much as ▸ **ce livre coûte autant que l'autre** this book costs as much as the other one ▸ **autant de (... que)** [quantité] as much (... as) / [nombre] as many (... as) ▸ **il a dépensé autant d'argent que moi** he spent as much money as I did ▸ **il y a autant de femmes que d'hommes** there are as many women as men ▸ **autant il est gentil avec moi, autant il est désagréable avec elle** he is as kind to me as he is unpleasant to her **2.** [à un tel point, en si grande quantité] so much / [en si grand nombre] so many ▸ **autant de patience** so much patience ▸ **autant de gens** so many people ▸ **elle boit toujours autant** she still drinks just as much (as she used to) ▸ **il ne peut pas en dire autant** he can't say the same ▸ **en faire autant** to do likewise ▸ **tu devrais en faire autant** you should do the same **3.** [il vaut mieux] **: autant dire la vérité** we/you *etc* may as well tell the truth ▸ **autant revenir demain** I/you *etc* might as well come back tomorrow.
◆ ***autant que*** **loc conj : (pour) autant que je sache** as far as I know ▸ **pour autant qu'on puisse faire la comparaison** inasmuch as a comparison can be made.
◆ ***d'autant*** **loc adv** accordingly, in proportion ▸ **si le coût de la vie augmente de 2 %, les salaires seront augmentés d'autant** if the cost of living goes up by 2%, salaries will be raised accordingly.
◆ ***d'autant mieux*** **loc adv** all the better ▸ **d'autant mieux que** all the better since ▸ **il a travaillé d'autant mieux qu'il se sentait encouragé** he worked all the better for feeling encouraged.
◆ ***d'autant que*** **loc conj : d'autant (plus) que** all the more so since ▸ **il vous écoutera d'autant plus qu'il vous connaît** he'll listen to you, especially as ***ou*** particularly as he knows you ▸ **d'autant moins que** all the less so since

▸ **elle est d'autant moins excusable qu'on l'avait prévenue** what she did is all the less forgivable as she'd been warned.
◆ ***pour autant*** loc adv for all that ▸ **la situation n'est pas perdue pour autant** the situation isn't hopeless for all that, it doesn't necessarily mean all is lost.

autarcie [otarsi] nf autarky.

autel [otɛl] nm altar.

auteur [otœr] nm **1.** [d'œuvre] author **2.** [inventeur] originator **3.** [responsable] perpetrator.

authenticité [otɑ̃tisite] nf authenticity, genuineness.

authentifier [9] [otɑ̃tifje] vt to authenticate.

authentique [otɑ̃tik] adj authentic, genuine.

autisme [otism] nm autism.

autiste [otist] ■ nmf autistic person.
■ adj autistic.

autistique [otistik] adj autistic.

auto [oto] nf car ▸ **auto tamponneuse** bumper car, Dodgem® *UK*.

autobiographie [otɔbjɔgrafi] nf autobiography.

autobiographique [otɔbjɔgrafik] adj autobiographical.

autobronzant**, **e [otɔbrɔ̃zɑ̃, ɑ̃t] adj self-tanning ▸ **lotion autobronzante** self-tanning lotion.
◆ ***autobronzant*** nm self-tanning product.

autobus [otɔbys] nm bus ▸ **autobus à impériale** ≃ double-decker bus.

autocar [otɔkar] nm coach *UK*, bus *US*.

autocassable [otɔkasabl] adj break-open ▸ **ampoule autocassable** break-open vial.

autocensure [otɔsɑ̃syr] nf self-censorship, self-regulation ▸ **pratiquer l'autocensure** to censor o.s.

autocensurer [3] [otɔsɑ̃syre] ◆ ***s'autocensurer*** vp *(emploi réfléchi)* to censor o.s..

autochtone [otɔktɔn] nmf & adj native.

autocollant**, **e [otɔkɔlɑ̃, ɑ̃t] adj self-adhesive, sticky.
◆ ***autocollant*** nm sticker.

autocouchettes [otɔkuʃɛt] adj inv : **train autocouchettes** car-sleeper train.

autocritique [otɔkritik] nf self-criticism.

autocuiseur [otɔkɥizœr] nm pressure cooker.

autodéfense [otɔdefɑ̃s] nf self-defence *UK*, self-defense *US*.

autodérision [otɔderizjɔ̃] nf self-mockery.

autodétermination [otɔdetɛrminasjɔ̃] nf self-determination.

autodétruire [98] [otɔdetrɥir] ◆ ***s'autodétruire*** vp [machine, person] to self-destruct.

autodidacte [otɔdidakt] ■ nmf self-taught person.
■ adj self-taught.

autodiscipline [otɔdisiplin] nf self-discipline.

auto-école [otɔekɔl] (pl **auto-écoles**) nf driving school.

autofinancement [otɔfinɑ̃smɑ̃] nm self-financing.

autofocus [otɔfɔkys] nm & adj inv autofocus.

autogène [otɔʒɛn] adj : **training autogène** autogenic training.

autogéré**, **e [otɔʒere] adj self-managed.

autogestion [otɔʒɛstjɔ̃] nf (workers') self-management.

autographe [otɔgraf] ■ nm autograph.
■ adj autograph *(avant n)*.

autoguidé**, **e [otɔgide] adj [missile] guided.

automate [otɔmat] nm [robot] automaton.

automatique [otɔmatik] ■ nm **1.** [pistolet] automatic **2.** TÉLÉCOM ≃ direct dialling *UK ou* dialing *US*.
■ adj automatic.

automatiquement [otɔmatikmɑ̃] adv automatically.

automatisation [otɔmatizasjɔ̃] nf automation.

automatiser [3] [otɔmatize] vt to automate.
◆ ***s'automatiser*** vpi to become automated.

automatisme [otɔmatism] nm **1.** [de machine] automatic operation **2.** [réflexe] automatic reaction, automatism.

automédication [otɔmedikasjɔ̃] nf self-medication.

automitrailleuse [otɔmitrajøz] nf armoured *UK ou* armored *US* vehicle.

automnal**, **e**, **aux [otɔnal, o] adj autumnal, autumn *(avant n)*.

automne [otɔn] nm autumn, fall *US* ▸ **en automne** in the autumn, in the fall *US* ▸ **être à l'automne de sa vie** *fig* to be in the autumn of one's life.

automobile [otɔmɔbil] ■ nf car, automobile *US*.
■ adj [industrie, accessoires] car *(avant n)*, automobile *(avant n) US* / [véhicule] motor *(avant n)*.

automobiliste [otɔmɔbilist] nmf driver, motorist.

automoteur**, **trice [otɔmɔtœr, tris] adj self-propelled.
◆ ***automoteur*** nm *large self-propelled river barge*.
◆ ***automotrice*** nf railcar.

autonettoyant**, **e [otɔnɛtwajɑ̃, ɑ̃t] adj self-cleaning.

autonome [otɔnɔm] adj **1.** [gén] autonomous, independent **2.** INFORM off-line **3.** [appareil] self-contained.

autonomie [otɔnɔmi] nf **1.** [indépendance] autonomy, independence **2.** AUTO [aviation] range ▸ **autonomie de vol** [aviation] flight range **3.** POLIT autonomy, self-government.

autonomiste [otɔnɔmist] nmf & adj separatist.

autoportrait [otɔpɔrtrɛ] nm self-portrait.

autopropulsé**, **e [otɔprɔpylse] adj self-propelled.

autopsie [otɔpsi] nf post-mortem, autopsy.

autoradio [otɔradjo] nm car radio.

autorail [otɔraj] nm railcar.

auto-reverse [otɔrivɛrs] **adj inv** auto-reverse.

autorisation [otɔrizasjɔ̃] **nf 1.** [permission] permission, authorization ▸ **avoir l'autorisation de faire qqch** to be allowed to do sthg ▸ **demander/accorder l'autorisation de faire qqch** to request/grant permission to do sthg ▸ **autorisation de découvert** BANQUE overdraft facility **2.** [attestation] pass, permit.

autorisé, e [otɔrize] **adj** [personne] in authority ▸ **milieux autorisés** official circles.

autoriser [3] [otɔrize] **vt** to authorize, to permit ▸ **autoriser qqn à faire qqch** [permission] to give sb permission to do sthg / [possibilité] to permit *ou* allow sb to do sthg.

autoritaire [otɔritɛr] **adj** authoritarian.

autoritarisme [otɔritarism] **nm** authoritarianism.

autorité [otɔrite] **nf** authority ▸ **faire autorité** [ouvrage] to be authoritative / [personne] to be an authority ▸ **faire qqch d'autorité** to do sthg out of hand.

autoroute [otɔrut] **nf** motorway *UK*, freeway *US* / : **autoroute de l'information** INFORM information highway *ou* superhighway.

autoroutier, ère [otɔrutje, ɛr] **adj** motorway *(avant n) UK*, freeway *(avant n) US*.

auto-stop [otɔstɔp] **nm** hitchhiking, hitching ▸ **faire de l'auto-stop** to hitchhike, to hitch ▸ **prendre quelqu'un en auto-stop** to pick up a hitchhiker.

auto-stoppeur, euse [otɔstɔpœr, øz] (mpl **auto-stoppeurs**, fpl **auto-stoppeuses**) **nm, f** hitchhiker, hitcher.

autosuggestion [otɔsygʒɛstjɔ̃] **nf** autosuggestion.

autour [otur] **adv** around, round *UK*.
◆ ***autour de*** **loc prép 1.** [sens spatial] around, round *UK* **2.** [sens temporel] about, around.

autre [otr] ■ **adj indéf 1.** [distinct, différent] other, different ▸ **dans d'autres circonstances...** in other circumstances..., had the circumstances been different... ▸ **je préfère une autre marque de café** I prefer another *ou* a different brand of coffee ▸ **l'un et l'autre projets** both projects ▸ **nous autres consommateurs...** we consumers... ▸ **un autre jour** some other day ▸ **autre chose** something else **2.** [supplémentaire] other ▸ **il nous faut une autre chaise** we need one more *ou* an extra *ou* another chair ▸ **tu veux une autre tasse de café?** would you like another cup of coffee?
3. [qui est différent par une certaine supériorité] **: c'est un (tout) autre homme que son père** he's not at all like his father, he's a different man from his father ▸ **leur ancien appartement avait un autre cachet!** their old flat had far more character!
4. [qui reste] other, remaining ▸ **les autres passagers ont été rapatriés en autobus** the other *ou* remaining passengers were bussed home.
■ **pron indéf : l'autre** the other (one) ▸ **un autre** another (one) ▸ **les autres** [personnes] the others / [objets] the others, the other ones ▸ **l'un à côté de l'autre** side by side ▸ **d'une semaine à l'autre** from one week to the next ▸ **aucun autre, nul autre, personne d'autre** no one else, nobody else ▸ **quelqu'un d'autre** somebody else, someone else ▸ **rien d'autre** nothing else ▸ **l'une chante, l'autre danse** one sings and the other dances ▸ **l'un et l'autre sont venus** they both came, both of them came ▸ **l'un ou l'autre ira** one or other (of them) will go ▸ **ni l'un ni l'autre n'est venu** neither (of them) came ▸ **ni l'une ni l'autre de ces raisons** neither of these reasons ▸ **l'un dans l'autre** all in all, at the end of the day.

autrefois [otrəfwa] **adv** in the past, formerly.

autrement [otrəmɑ̃] **adv 1.** [différemment] otherwise, differently ▸ **je n'ai pas pu faire autrement que d'y aller** I had no choice but to go ▸ **autrement dit** in other words **2.** [sinon] otherwise **3.** *sout* [beaucoup plus] far more ▸ **je n'en suis pas autrement étonné** it doesn't particularly surprise me.

Autriche [otriʃ] **nf : l'Autriche** Austria.

autrichien, enne [otriʃjɛ̃, ɛn] **adj** Austrian.
◆ ***Autrichien, enne*** **nm, f** Austrian.

autruche [otryʃ] **nf** ostrich ▸ **avoir un estomac d'autruche** *fig* to have a cast-iron stomach ▸ **pratiquer la politique de l'autruche** *fig* to bury one's head in the sand.

autrui [otrɥi] **pron indéf inv** others, other people.

auvent [ovɑ̃] **nm** canopy.

Auvergne [ovɛrɲ] **npr f : (l')Auvergne** the Auvergne.

aux [o] ➤ ***à***.

auxiliaire [oksiljɛr] ■ **nmf** [assistant] assistant ▸ **auxiliaire médical** medical auxiliary.
■ **nm** GRAMM auxiliary (verb).
■ **adj 1.** [secondaire] auxiliary **2.** ADMIN assistant *(avant n)*.

auxquels, **auxquelles** [okɛl] ➤ ***lequel***.

av. abr de ***avenue***.

AV **nm 1.** (abr de ***avis de virement***) *notification of bank transfer* **2.** abr de ***avant***.

avachi, e [avaʃi] **adj 1.** [gén] misshapen **2.** [personne] listless ▸ **il était avachi dans un fauteuil** he was slumped in an armchair.

aval, als [aval] **nm** backing *(U)*, endorsement.
◆ ***en aval*** **loc adv** *litt & fig* downstream.
◆ ***en aval de*** **loc prép** *litt & fig* downstream of.

avalanche [avalɑ̃ʃ] **nf** *litt & fig* avalanche.

avaler [3] [avale] **vt 1.** [gén] to swallow ▸ **avaler qqch de travers : j'ai dû avaler quelque chose de travers** something went down the wrong way ▸ **je n'ai rien avalé depuis deux jours** I haven't had a thing to eat for two days **2.** *fig* [supporter] to take ▸ **avaler la pilule** to swallow a bitter pill ▸ **avaler des couleuvres** [insultes] to swallow insults / [mensonges] to be taken in ▸ **dur à avaler** difficult to swallow **3.** *fam fig* [croire - mensonge] to swallow, to buy ▸ **elle lui ferait avaler n'importe quoi** he believes anything she says.

avaliser [3] [avalize] **vt 1.** [traite] to endorse **2.** [décision, projet] to back.

avance [avɑ̃s] **nf 1.** [progression, somme d'argent] advance ▸ **donner à qqn une avance sur son salaire** to give sb an advance on his/her salary ▸ **avance bancaire** (bank) overdraft ▸ **avance de fonds** loan **2.** [distance, temps] lead ▸ **avoir 10 points d'avance sur qqn** to have a 10 point lead over sb ▸ **le train a dix minutes d'avance** the train is ten minutes early ▸ **le train a une avance de dix minutes**

sur l'horaire the train is running ten minutes ahead of schedule ▸ **prendre de l'avance (dans qqch)** to get ahead (in sthg) ▸ **prendre de l'avance dans ses études** to get ahead in one's studies.

◆ ***avances*** **nfpl : faire des avances à qqn** to make advances towards sb.

◆ ***à l'avance*** loc adv in advance ▸ **réservez longtemps à l'avance** book early.

◆ ***d'avance*** loc adv in advance ▸ **savourant d'avance sa revanche** already savouring his revenge.

◆ ***en avance*** loc adv **: être en avance** to be early ▸ **être en avance sur qqch** to be ahead of sthg ▸ **être en avance sur son temps** *ou* **époque** to be ahead of one's time.

◆ ***par avance*** loc adv in advance.

avancé, ***e*** [avɑ̃se] adj **1.** [dans le temps - heure] late ▸ **à une heure avancée** late at night ▸ **la saison est avancée** it's very late in the season ▸ **arriver à un âge avancé** to be getting on in years **2.** [développé - intelligence, économie] advanced ▸ **un enfant avancé pour son âge** a child who's mature for his years ▸ **à un stade peu avancé** at an early stage ▸ **te voilà bien avancé!** *iron* a (fat) lot of good that's done you!

◆ ***avancée*** nf **1.** [progression] progress **2.** [d'un toit] overhang.

avancement [avɑ̃smɑ̃] nm **1.** [développement] progress **2.** [promotion] promotion.

avancer [16] [avɑ̃se] ■ vt **1.** [objet, tête] to move forward / [date, départ] to bring forward / [main] to hold out ▸ **tu es trop loin, avance ta chaise** you're too far away: move *ou* bring your chair forward ▸ **l'heure du départ a été avancée de 10 minutes** the starting time was put forward 10 minutes **2.** [projet, travail] to advance **3.** [montre, horloge] to put forward ▸ **avancer sa montre (d'une heure)** to put one's watch forward (an hour) **4.** [argent] **: avancer qqch à qqn** to advance sb sthg.

■ vi **1.** [approcher] to move forward ▸ **avoir du mal à avancer** to make slow progress **2.** [progresser] to advance ▸ **au fur et à mesure que la nuit avançait** as the night wore on ▸ **avancer dans qqch** to make progress in sthg ▸ **avancer dans une enquête/son travail** to make progress in an investigation/one's work ▸ **faire avancer les choses** [accélérer une action] to speed things up / [améliorer la situation] to improve matters **3.** [faire saillie] **: avancer (dans/sur)** to jut out (into/over), to project (into/over) **4.** [montre, horloge] **: ma montre avance de dix minutes** my watch is ten minutes fast **5.** [servir] **: ça n'avance à rien** that won't get us/you anywhere ▸ **ça t'avance à quoi de mentir?** *fam* what do you gain by lying?

◆ ***s'avancer*** vp **1.** [s'approcher] to move forward ▸ **s'avancer vers qqn/qqch** to move towards sb/sthg ▸ **il s'avança vers moi** he came towards me **2.** [prendre de l'avance] **: s'avancer (dans qqch)** to get ahead (in sthg) ▸ **s'avancer dans son travail** to make progress *ou* some headway in one's work **3.** [s'engager] to commit o.s. ▸ **je m'avance peut-être un peu trop en affirmant cela** it might be a bit rash of me to say this.

avant [avɑ̃] ■ prép before ▸ **je ne serai pas prêt avant une demi-heure** I won't be ready for another half an hour ▸ **peu avant les élections** a short while *ou* time before the elections ▸ **ta santé passe avant ta carrière** your health is more important than *ou* comes before your career ▸ **vous tournez à droite juste avant le feu** you turn right just before the lights.

■ adv before ▸ **quelques jours avant** a few days earlier *ou* before ▸ **tu connais le cinéma? ma maison se situe un peu avant** do you know the cinema? my house is just this side of it ▸ **bien avant** [spatial] well before / [temporel] well before *ou* beforehand.

■ adj inv front ▸ **les roues avant** the front wheels.

■ nm **1.** [partie antérieure] front ▸ **montez à l'avant** sit in the front

2. SPORT forward ▸ **jouer avant droit/gauche** to play right/left forward.

◆ ***avant de*** loc prép **: avant de faire qqch** before doing sthg ▸ **avant de partir** before leaving ▸ **je ne signerai rien avant d'avoir vu les locaux** I won't sign anything until *ou* before I see the premises.

◆ ***avant que*** loc conj *(+ subjonctif)* **: je dois te parler avant que tu partes** I must speak to you before you leave ▸ **ne dites rien avant qu'il n'arrive** don't say anything until he arrives.

◆ ***avant tout*** loc adv above all ▸ **sa carrière passe avant tout** his career comes first ▸ **avant tout, je voudrais vous dire ceci** first (and foremost), I'd like to tell you this.

◆ ***en avant*** loc adv forward, forwards ▸ **en avant, marche!** MIL forward march!

◆ ***en avant de*** loc prép in front of ▸ **le barrage routier a été installé en avant de Dijon** the roadblock was set up just before Dijon.

avantage [avɑ̃taʒ] nm **1.** [gén & TENNIS] advantage ▸ **avoir un avantage sur qqn/qqch** to have an advantage over sb/sthg ▸ **c'est (tout) à ton avantage** it's in your (best) interest ▸ **les avantages et les inconvénients d'une solution** the advantages and disadvantages *ou* pros and cons of a solution ▸ **tu as tout avantage à l'acheter ici** you'd be much better off buying it here ▸ **se montrer à son avantage** to look one's best ▸ **tirer avantage de la situation** to turn the situation to (one's) advantage **2.** ÉCON advantage ▸ **avantage concurrentiel** competitive advantage ▸ **avantages financiers** financial benefits ▸ **avantage fiscal** tax benefit ▸ **avantages en nature** fringe benefits, perks ▸ **avantages sociaux** welfare benefits.

avantager [17] [avɑ̃taʒe] vt **1.** [favoriser] to favour *UK*, to favor *US* **2.** [mettre en valeur] to flatter.

avantageusement [avɑ̃taʒøzmɑ̃] adv favourably *UK*, favorably *US*.

avantageux, ***euse*** [avɑ̃taʒø, øz] adj **1.** [attrayant] attractive **2.** [profitable] profitable, lucrative **3.** [économique - prix] reasonable **4.** [flatteur] flattering **5.** *sout* [présomptueux] **: prendre l'air avantageux** to look superior.

avant-bras [avɑ̃bra] nm inv forearm.

avant-centre [avɑ̃sɑ̃tr] (pl **avants-centres**) nm centre *UK ou* center *US* forward.

avant-coureur [avɑ̃kurœr] ➤ ***signe***.

avant-dernier, ***ère*** [avɑ̃dɛrnje, ɛr] (mpl **avant-derniers**, fpl **avant-dernières**) adj second to last, penultimate.

avant-garde [avɑ̃gard] (pl **avant-gardes**) nf **1.** MIL vanguard **2.** [idées] avant-garde ▸ **d'avant-garde** avant-garde.

avant-goût [avɑ̃gu] (pl **avant-goûts**) nm foretaste.

avant-hier [avɑ̃tjɛr] **adv** the day before yesterday.

avant-première [avɑ̃prəmjɛr] (pl **avant-premières**) **nf** preview ▸ **présenté en avant-première** [film, pièce] previewed.

avant-projet [avɑ̃prɔʒɛ] (pl **avant-projets**) **nm** pilot study.

avant-propos [avɑ̃prɔpo] **nm inv** foreword.

avant-veille [avɑ̃vɛj] (pl **avant-veilles**) **nf : l'avant-veille** two days earlier.

avare [avar] ■ **nmf** miser.
■ **adj** miserly ▸ **être avare de qqch** *fig* to be sparing with sthg.

avarice [avaris] **nf** avarice.

avarie [avari] **nf** damage *(U)*.

avarié, e [avarje] **adj 1.** [aliment] rotting, bad ▸ **de la viande avariée** tainted meat ▸ **cette viande est avariée** this meat has gone off *UK ou* bad **2.** [marchandise] spoilt, damaged **3.** NAUT **: navire avarié** damaged ship.

avarier [avarje] ◆ ***s'avarier*** **vpi** [denrée alimentaire] to go off *UK ou* bad.

avatar [avatar] **nm** [transformation] metamorphosis.
◆ ***avatars*** **nmpl** *fam* [mésaventures] misfortunes.

avec [avɛk] ■ **prép 1.** [gén] with ▸ **avec respect** with respect, respectfully ▸ **avec ce nouveau scandale, le ministre va tomber** this new scandal will mean the end of the minister's career ▸ **c'est fait avec du cuir** it's made from leather ▸ **et avec ça?, et avec ceci?** *fam* [dans un magasin] anything else? ▸ **tous les résidents sont avec moi** all the residents support me *ou* are behind me *ou* are on my side ▸ **une maison avec jardin** a house with a garden **2.** [vis-à-vis de] to, towards *UK*, toward *US* ▸ **être gentil avec qqn** to be kind *ou* nice to sb ▸ **se comporter bien/mal avec qqn** to behave well/badly towards sb.
■ **adv** *fam* with it/him *etc* ▸ **je vous mets les os avec?** shall I put the bones in for you? ▸ **tiens mon sac, je ne peux pas courir avec!** hold my bag: I can't run with it!

Ave (Maria) [ave(marja)] **nm inv** Hail Mary.

avenant, e [avnɑ̃, ɑ̃t] **adj** pleasant.
◆ ***avenant*** **nm** DR additional clause.
◆ ***à l'avenant*** **loc adv** in the same vein.

avènement [avɛnmɑ̃] **nm 1.** [d'un roi] accession **2.** *fig* [début] advent.

avenir [avnir] **nm** future ▸ **avoir de l'avenir** to have a future ▸ **d'avenir** [profession, concept] with a future, with prospects.
◆ ***à l'avenir*** **loc adv** in future.

Avent [avɑ̃] **nm : l'Avent** Advent.

aventure [avɑ̃tyr] **nf 1.** [gén] adventure **2.** [liaison amoureuse] affair
▸▸ **dire la bonne aventure à qqn** to tell sb's fortune.
◆ ***à l'aventure*** **loc adv** at random, haphazardly ▸ **marcher/rouler à l'aventure** to walk/to drive aimlessly ▸ **partir à l'aventure** to go off in search of adventure.
◆ ***d'aventure*** **loc adv 1.** [roman, film] adventure *(avant n)* **2.** by (any) chance ▸ **si d'aventure tu le vois** if by any chance you see him.

aventurer [3] [avɑ̃tyre] **vt 1.** [risquer] to risk **2.** *sout* [remarque] to venture.
◆ ***s'aventurer*** **vp** to venture (out) ▸ **s'aventurer à faire qqch** *fig* to venture to do sthg.

aventureux, euse [avɑ̃tyrø, øz] **adj 1.** [personne, vie] adventurous **2.** [projet] risky.

aventurier, ère [avɑ̃tyrje, ɛr] **nm, f** adventurer.

avenu, e [avny] **adj : nul et non avenu** DR null and void.

avenue [avny] **nf** avenue.

avéré, e [avere] **adj** [fait, information] known, established ▸ **c'est un fait avéré que...** it is a known fact that...

avérer [18] [avere] ◆ ***s'avérer*** **vp : il s'est avéré (être) à la hauteur** he proved (to be) up to it ▸ **il s'est avéré (être) un musicien accompli** he proved to be an accomplished musician.

averse [avɛrs] **nf** downpour ▸ **averse de neige** snow-flurry.

aversion [avɛrsjɔ̃] **nf : aversion pour** aversion to, loathing for ▸ **prendre qqn/qqch en aversion** to take an intense dislike to sb/sthg ▸ **avoir qqn/qqch en aversion** to have an aversion to sb/sthg.

averti, e [avɛrti] **adj 1.** [expérimenté] experienced **2.** [initié] **: averti (de)** (well-)informed (about).

avertir [32] [avɛrtir] **vt 1.** [mettre en garde] to warn **2.** [prévenir] to inform ▸ **avertissez-moi dès que possible** let me know as soon as possible.

avertissement [avɛrtismɑ̃] **nm 1.** [gén] warning **2.** [avis] notice, notification.

avertisseur, euse [avɛrtisœr, øz] ■ **adj** warning *(avant n)*.
■ **nm 1.** [Klaxon] horn **2.** [d'incendie] alarm.

aveu, x [avø] **nm** confession ▸ **de l'aveu de tout le monde, c'est lui le responsable** everyone agrees that he is responsible ▸ **passer aux aveux** to make a confession.

aveuglant, e [avœglɑ̃, ɑ̃t] **adj 1.** [lumière] blinding **2.** *fig* [vérité] blindingly obvious.

aveugle [avœgl] ■ **nmf** blind person ▸ **les aveugles** the blind.
■ **adj** *litt & fig* blind.

aveuglement [avœgləmɑ̃] **nm** blindness.

aveuglément [avœglemɑ̃] **adv** blindly.

aveugler [5] [avœgle] **vt 1.** *litt & fig* [priver de la vue] to blind **2.** [fenêtre] to board up.
◆ ***s'aveugler*** **vp : s'aveugler sur qqn** to be blind to sb's faults.

aveuglette [avœglɛt] ◆ ***à l'aveuglette*** **loc adv : marcher à l'aveuglette** to grope one's way ▸ **avancer à l'aveuglette** *fig* to be in the dark.

aviateur, trice [avjatœr, tris] **nm, f** aviator.

aviation [avjasjɔ̃] **nf 1.** [transport aérien] aviation **2.** MIL airforce.

aviculture [avikyltyr] **nf** [gén] bird-breeding / [de volailles] poultry farming.

avide [avid] **adj 1.** [vorace, cupide] greedy **2.** [désireux] **: avide (de qqch/de faire qqch)** eager (for sthg/to do sthg).

avidement [avidmɑ̃] **adv** **1.** [avec appétit, convoitise] greedily **2.** [avec intérêt] avidly **3.** [avec passion] eagerly.

avidité [avidite] **nf** **1.** [voracité, cupidité] greed **2.** [passion] eagerness.

Avignon [aviɲɔ̃] **npr** Avignon ▸ **en Avignon** in Avignon ▸ **le festival d'Avignon** the Avignon Festival.

avilir [32] [avilir] **vt** **1.** [personne] to degrade **2.** [monnaie, marchandise] to devalue.
◆ ***s'avilir*** **vp** **1.** [personne] to demean o.s. **2.** [monnaie, marchandise] to depreciate.

aviné, e [avine] **adj** **1.** [personne] inebriated **2.** [haleine] smelling of alcohol.

avion [avjɔ̃] **nm** plane, aeroplane *UK*, airplane *US* ▸ **en avion** by plane, by air ▸ **par avion** [courrier] airmail ▸ **avion de ligne** airliner ▸ **avion à réaction** jet (plane).

aviron [avirɔ̃] **nm** **1.** [rame] oar **2.** SPORT **: l'aviron** rowing.

avis [avi] **nm** **1.** [opinion] opinion ▸ **changer d'avis** to change one's mind ▸ **être d'avis que** to think that, to be of the opinion that ▸ **à mon avis** in my opinion ▸ **les avis sont partagés** opinion is divided **2.** [conseil] advice *(U)* **3.** [notification] notification, notice ▸ **sauf avis contraire** unless otherwise informed ▸ **jusqu'à nouvel avis** until further notice ▸ **avis de débit/crédit** debit/credit advice ▸ **avis de recherche** [d'un criminel] wanted poster / [d'un disparu] missing person poster.

avisé, e [avize] **adj** [sensé] sensible ▸ **être bien/mal avisé de faire qqch** to be well-advised/ill-advised to do sthg.

aviser [3] [avize] ■ **vt** **1.** [informer] **: aviser qqn de qqch** to inform sb of sthg **2.** *sout* [apercevoir] to notice.
■ **vi** to reassess the situation.
◆ ***s'aviser*** **vp** **1.** *sout* [s'apercevoir] **: s'aviser de qqch** to notice sthg ▸ **s'aviser que** to notice (that) **2.** [oser] **: s'aviser de faire qqch** to take it into one's head to do sthg ▸ **ne t'avise pas de répondre!** don't you dare answer me back!

aviver [3] [avive] **vt** **1.** [intensifier - feu] to revive, to rekindle / [- couleur] to brighten / [- désir] to excite / [- blessure] to irritate / [- querelle] to stir up / [- crainte] to heighten **2.** [menuiserie] to square off.

av. J.-C. (abr écrite de ***avant Jésus-Christ***) BC.

avocat, e [avɔka, at] **nm, f** **1.** DR barrister *UK*, attorney-at-law *US* ▸ **avocat d'affaires** commercial lawyer ▸ **avocat de la défense** counsel for the defence *UK*, defense counsel *US* ▸ **avocat général** ≃ counsel for the prosecution *UK*, ≃ prosecuting attorney *US* **2.** [défenseur] **: se faire l'avocat de qqch** to champion sthg ▸ **se faire l'avocat du diable** *fig* to play devil's advocate.
◆ ***avocat*** **nm** [fruit] avocado.

avoine [avwan] **nf** oats *pl*.

avoir[1] [avwar] **nm** **1.** [biens] assets *pl* **2.** COMM & FIN credit note ▸ **j'ai un avoir de 150 euros à la boucherie** I've got 150 euros credit at the butcher's / [en comptabilité] credit (side) ▸ **avoir fiscal** tax credit.
◆ ***avoirs*** **nmpl** ÉCON & FIN assets *pl*, holdings *pl* ▸ **avoirs numéraires** *ou* **en caisse** cash holdings.

avoir[2] [1] [avwar] ■ **v aux** to have ▸ **j'ai fini** I have finished ▸ **il a attendu pendant deux heures** he waited for two hours.
■ **vt** **1.** [posséder] to have (got) ▸ **il a deux enfants/les cheveux bruns** he has (got) two children/brown hair ▸ **la maison a un grand jardin** the house has (got) a large garden ▸ **nous avons plus grand si vous préférez** we have it in a larger size if you prefer
2. [être âgé de] **: il a 20 ans** he is 20 (years old) ▸ **il a deux ans de plus que son frère** he is two years older than his brother ▸ **quel âge as-tu?** how old are you?
3. [obtenir] to get ▸ **je pourrais vous avoir des places gratuites** I could get you free tickets ▸ **je l'ai eu au téléphone** I got him on the phone
4. [éprouver] to have ▸ **avoir du chagrin** to feel sorrowful ▸ **avoir de la sympathie pour qqn** to have a liking for sb
5. [porter sur soi] to have on, to wear ▸ **tu vois la dame qui a le foulard?** do you see the lady with the scarf?
▸▸| **se faire avoir** *fam* to be had *ou* conned ▸ **en avoir assez (de qqch/de faire qqch)** to have had enough (of sthg/of doing sthg) ▸ **j'en ai pour cinq minutes** it'll take me five minutes ▸ **en avoir après qqn** to have (got) it in for sb ▸ **en avoir après** *ou* **contre qqch** to be angry about sthg ; ➤ ***faim, peur, soif***
◆ ***avoir à*** **v + prep** [devoir] **: avoir à faire qqch** to have to do sthg ▸ **tu n'avais pas à lui parler sur ce ton** you had no need to speak to him like that, you shouldn't have spoken to him like that ▸ **tu n'avais qu'à me demander** you only had to ask me ▸ **tu n'as qu'à y aller toi-même** just go (there) yourself, why don't you just go (there) yourself?
◆ ***il y a*** **v impers** **1.** [présentatif] there is/are ▸ **il y a un problème** there's a problem ▸ **il y a des problèmes** there are (some) problems ▸ **qu'est-ce qu'il y a?** what's the matter?, what is it? ▸ **il n'y a qu'à en finir** we'll/you'll *etc* just have to have done (with it)
2. [temporel] **: il y a trois ans** three years ago ▸ **il y a longtemps de cela** that was a long time ago ▸ **il y a longtemps qu'il est parti** he left a long time ago
3. (à *l'infinitif*) **: il va y avoir de la pluie** there's going to be some rain.

avoisinant, e [avwazinɑ̃, ɑ̃t] **adj** **1.** [lieu, maison] neighbouring *UK*, neighboring *US* **2.** [sens, couleur] similar.

Avoriaz [avɔrjaz] **npr : le festival d'Avoriaz** *festival of science fiction and horror films held annually at Avoriaz in the French Alps.*

avortement [avɔrtəmɑ̃] **nm** **1.** MÉD abortion **2.** *fig* [d'un projet] abandonment.

avorter [3] [avɔrte] **vi** **1.** MÉD **: (se faire) avorter** to have an abortion **2.** [échouer] to fail.

avorton [avɔrtɔ̃] **nm** *péj* [nabot] runt.

avouer [6] [avwe] **vt** **1.** [confesser] to confess (to) **2.** [reconnaître] to admit **3.** [déclarer] to avow.
◆ ***s'avouer*** **vp** to admit (to being) ▸ **s'avouer vaincu** to admit defeat.

avril [avril] **nm** April ; voir aussi ***septembre***.

AVS (abr de ***assurance vieillesse et survivants***) **nf** *Swiss pension scheme.*

axe [aks] **nm** **1.** GÉOM & PHYS axis ▸ **axe des abscisses/des ordonnées** x-/y-axis **2.** [de roue] axle **3.** [route] **: les grands axes** the major roads ▸ **axe rouge** *section of the Paris road system where parking is prohibited to avoid congestion* **4.** [prolongement] **: dans l'axe de** directly in line with ▸ **la perspective s'ouvre dans l'axe du palais** the view opens out from the palace **5.** [de politique, de parti] line ▸ **développer de nouveaux axes de recherche** to open up new areas of research ▸ **il est dans l'axe du parti** [membre] he's in the mainstream of the party ▸ **sa politique s'articule autour de deux axes principaux** her policy revolves around two main themes *ou* issues.

axer [3] [akse] **vt : axer qqch sur qqch** to centre *UK ou* center *US* sthg on sthg ▸ **axer qqch autour de qqch** to centre *UK ou* center *US* sthg around sthg.

axial**, e, **aux [aksjal, o] **adj** axial.

axiome [aksjom] **nm** axiom.

ayant [ɛjɑ̃] **p prés** ➤ ***avoir***.

ayant droit [ɛjɑ̃drwa] (pl **ayants droit**) **nm** beneficiary.

ayatollah [ajatɔla] **nm** ayatollah.

azalée [azale] **nf** azalea.

azimut [azimyt] ◆ ***tous azimuts*** **loc adj** [défense, offensive] all-out.

azote [azɔt] **nm** nitrogen.

AZT (abr de ***azothymidine***) **nm** AZT.

aztèque [aztɛk] **adj** Aztec.
◆ ***Aztèque*** **nmf** Aztec.

azur [azyr] **nm** *littéraire* **1.** [couleur] azure **2.** [ciel] skies *pl*.

azyme [azim] ➤ ***pain***.

b

b, ***B*** [be] **nm inv** b, B.
◆ ***B*** (abr écrite de ***bien***) *good grade (as assessment on schoolwork)*, ≃ B+.

BA (abr de ***bonne action***) **nf** *fam* good deed.

baba [baba] ■ **nm 1.** CULIN **: baba (au rhum)** rum baba **2.** [hippie] *person practising hippie lifestyle and values.*
■ **adj inv** *fam* **: en rester baba** to be flabbergasted.

babeurre [babœr] **nm** buttermilk.

babil [babil] **nm** [d'enfant] babble, babbling.

babiller [3] [babije] **vi** to babble.

babines [babin] **nfpl** chops ▸ **se lécher les babines** *fig* to lick one's lips.

babiole [babjɔl] **nf 1.** [objet] knick-knack **2.** [broutille] trifling matter.

bâbord [babɔr] **nm** port ▸ **à bâbord** to port, on the port side.

babouche [babuʃ] **nf** (oriental) slipper.

babouin [babwɛ̃] **nm** baboon.

baby-foot [babifut] **nm inv** table football *UK*, foosball *US*.

baby-sitter [bebisitœr] (pl **baby-sitters**) **nmf** baby-sitter.

baby-sitting [bebisitiŋ] (pl **baby-sittings**) **nm** baby-sitting ▸ **faire du baby-sitting** to baby-sit.

bac [bak] **nm 1.** *fam* SCOL *school-leaving examinations leading to university entrance qualification* ▸ **bac +** *level of studies after the bac* **2.** [bateau] ferry **3.** [de réfrigérateur] **: bac à glace** ice-cube tray ▸ **bac à légumes** vegetable drawer / [d'imprimante, de photocopieuse] **: bac à papier** paper tray **4.** [d'évier] sink.

CULTURE
Bac +

In France, the expression Bac + designates the years of study corresponding to different university diplomas: Bac + 2 for the DEUG (**diplôme d'études universitaires générales**), Bac + 3 for the **licence**, Bac + 4 for the **maîtrise**, and Bac + 5 for a DEA (**diplôme d'études approfondies**) or a DESS (**diplôme d'études supérieures spécialisées**). The term is used on CVs to show one's level of education, and in job advertisements to indicate the level required (eg **niveau Bac + 5 exigé**). It is also useful when introducing oneself: **J'ai un Bac + 5 en Anglais.**

BAC [bak] (abr de ***brigade anticriminalité***) **nf** *police squad specializing in patrols to combat crime.*

baccalauréat [bakalɔrea] **nm** *school-leaving examinations leading to university entrance qualification.*

bâche [baʃ] **nf** [toile] tarpaulin.

bachelier, ***ère*** [baʃəlje, ɛr] **nm, f** *holder of the baccalauréat.*

bachot [baʃo] *vieilli* = ***baccalauréat***.

bachotage [baʃɔtaʒ] **nm** *fam* cramming *UK*.

bacille [basil] **nm** bacillus.

bâcler [3] [bakle] **vt** to botch.

bacon [bekɔn] **nm** bacon.

bactéricide [bakterisid] **adj** bactericidal.

bactérie [bakteri] **nf** bacterium.

badaud, ***e*** [bado, od] **nm, f** [curieux] curious onlooker / [promeneur] stroller.

badge [badʒ] **nm 1.** [insigne] badge **2.** [document d'identité] swipe card.

badger [badʒe] **vi** [en arrivant] to clock in ***ou*** on / [en sortant] to clock out ***ou*** off.

badgeuse [badʒøz] **nf** swipe card reader.

badigeon [badiʒɔ̃] **nm** whitewash.

badigeonner [3] [badiʒɔne] **vt 1.** [mur] to whitewash **2.** [plaie] to paint **3.** [tarte, pain] to brush.

badin, ***e*** [badɛ̃, in] **adj** playful.

badinage [badinaʒ] **nm** *sout* joking.

badiner [3] [badine] **vi** *sout* to joke ▸ **ne pas badiner avec qqch** not to treat sthg lightly.

badminton [badmintɔn] **nm** badminton.

BAFA, ***Bafa*** [bafa] (abr de ***brevet d'aptitude aux fonctions d'animation***) **nm** *diploma for youth leaders and workers.*

baffe [baf] **nf** *fam* slap.

baffle [bafl] **nm** speaker.

bafouer [6] [bafwe] **vt 1.** [principe] to trample upon **2.** [personne] to ridicule.

bafouille [bafuj] **nf** *fam* letter.

bafouiller [3] [bafuje] **vi & vt** to mumble.

bâfrer [3] [bafre] *fam* ■ **vi** to guzzle.
■ **vt** to wolf down.

bagage [bagaʒ] **nm 1.** *(gén pl)* [valises, sacs] luggage *(U)*, baggage *(U)* ▸ **faire ses bagages** to pack ▸ **bagages à main** hand luggage ▸ **plier bagage** to pack one's bags (and leave) **2.** [connaissances] (fund of) knowledge ▸ **bagage intellectuel/culturel** intellectual/cultural baggage.

bagagiste [bagaʒist] **nmf** [chargement des avions] baggage handler / [à l'hôtel] porter / [fabricant] travel goods manufacturer.

bagarre [bagar] **nf** brawl, fight ▸ **chercher la bagarre** *fam* to look for a fight.

bagarrer [3] [bagare] **vi** to fight.
◆ ***se bagarrer*** **vp** to fight.

bagarreur, ***euse*** [bagarœr, øz] ■ **adj** aggressive.
■ **nm, f** *fig* fighter.

bagatelle [bagatɛl] **nf 1.** [objet] trinket **2.** [somme d'argent] **: acheter qqch pour une bagatelle** to buy sthg for next to nothing ▸ **la bagatelle de X euros** *iron* a mere X euros **3.** [chose futile] trifle **4.** [sexe] **: être porté sur la bagatelle** to be quite a one for the ladies.

Bagdad [bagdad] **npr** Baghdad.

bagnard [baɲar] **nm** convict.

bagne [baɲ] **nm 1.** [prison] labour *UK* **ou** labor *US* camp **2.** [sentence] hard labour *UK* **ou** labor *US* ▸ **c'est le bagne ici** *fig* it's slave labour *UK* **ou** labor *US* here.

bagnole [baɲɔl] **nf** *fam* car.

bagou(t) [bagu] **nm** patter ▸ **avoir du bagout** to have the gift of the gab.

bague [bag] **nf 1.** [bijou, anneau] ring ▸ **bague de fiançailles** engagement ring **2.** [de cigare] band **3.** TECHNOL **: bague de serrage** clip.

baguer [3] [bage] **vt** [oiseau, arbre] to ring.

baguette [bagɛt] **nf 1.** [pain] baguette, French stick *UK* **2.** [petit bâton] stick ▸ **baguette de coudrier** hazel stick **ou** switch ▸ **baguette magique** magic wand ▸ **d'un coup de baguette magique** as if by magic ▸ **baguette de sourcier** divining rod ▸ **baguette de tambour** drumstick ▸ **mener qqn à la baguette** to rule sb with a rod of iron **3.** [pour manger] chopstick ▸ **manger avec des baguettes** to eat with chopsticks **4.** [de chef d'orchestre] baton ▸ **sous la baguette du jeune chef** under the baton of the young conductor.

Bahamas [baamas] **nfpl : les Bahamas** the Bahamas ▸ **aux Bahamas** in the Bahamas.

bahut [bay] **nm 1.** [buffet] sideboard **2.** [coffre] chest **3.** *arg scol* [lycée] secondary school **4.** *fam péj* [voiture] old banger.

baie [bɛ] **nf 1.** [fruit] berry **2.** GÉOGR bay **3.** [fenêtre] **: baie vitrée** picture **ou** bay window.

baignade [bɛɲad] **nf** [action] swimming *(U)*, bathing *(U)* ▸ **'baignade interdite'** 'no swimming/bathing'.

baigner [4] [beɲe] ■ **vt 1.** [donner un bain à] to bath *UK*, to bathe *US* **2.** [tremper, remplir] to bathe ▸ **baigné de soleil** bathed in sunlight.
■ **vi : baigner dans le luxe** to be surrounded by wealth ▸ **baigner dans son sang** to lie in a pool of blood ▸ **les tomates baignaient dans l'huile** the tomatoes were swimming in oil ▸ **tout/ça baigne** *fam* everything's/it's great.
◆ ***se baigner*** **vp 1.** [dans la mer] to go swimming, to swim **2.** [dans une baignoire] to have *UK* **ou** take a bath.

baigneur, ***euse*** [bɛɲœr, øz] **nm, f** swimmer, bather.
◆ ***baigneur*** **nm** [poupée] baby doll.

baignoire [bɛɲwar] **nf** bath *UK*, bathtub *US*.

bail [baj] (pl **baux** [bo]) **nm** DR lease ▸ **renouveler un bail** to renew a lease ▸ **bail à loyer** residential lease ▸ **bail reconductible** renewable lease
▸▸ **ça fait un bail que** *fam* it's ages since.

bâillement [bajmɑ̃] **nm** yawning *(U)*, yawn.

bâiller [3] [baje] **vi 1.** [personne] to yawn **2.** [vêtement] to gape.

bailleur, ***eresse*** [bajœr, bajrɛs] **nm, f** lessor ▸ **bailleur de fonds** backer.

bâillon [bajɔ̃] **nm** gag.

bâillonner [3] [bajɔne] **vt** to gag.

bain [bɛ̃] **nm 1.** [gén] bath ▸ **faire couler un bain** to run a bath ▸ **prendre un bain** to have *UK* **ou** take a bath ▸ **bain de boue** mudbath ▸ **bain moussant** foaming bath oil ▸ **bain à remous** spa bath, whirlpool bath ▸ **bain révélateur ou de développement** developing bath, developer ▸ **bain de vapeur** steam bath ▸ **bains-douches** public baths **2.** [dans mer, piscine] swim ▸ **bain de mer** swimming **ou** bathing in the sea ▸ **bain de minuit** midnight swim **ou** dip **3.** [de partie du corps] **: bain de bouche** mouthwash ▸ **bain de pieds** foot-bath **4.** [bassin] **: grand bain** [bassin] big pool / [côté] deep end ▸ **petit bain** [bassin] children's pool / [côté] shallow end
▸▸ **être dans le bain** [s'y connaître] to be in the swing of things / [être compromis] to be in it up to one's neck ▸ **se mettre dans le bain** to get the hang of things ▸ **prendre un bain de foule** to go on a walkabout *UK* ▸ **prendre un bain de soleil** to sunbathe ▸ **la manifestation s'est terminée dans un bain de sang** the demonstration ended in a bloodbath.

bain-marie [bɛ̃mari] (pl **bains-marie**) **nm : au bain-marie** in a bain-marie.

baïonnette [bajɔnɛt] **nf 1.** [arme] bayonet **2.** ÉLECTR bayonet fitting.

baise [bɛz] **nf** *vulg* fucking.

baisemain [bɛzmɛ̃] **nm : faire le baisemain à qqn** to kiss sb's hand.

baiser [4] [beze] ■ **nm** kiss.
■ **vt & vi** *vulg* to fuck.

baisse [bɛs] **nf 1.** [gén] **: baisse (de)** drop (in), fall (in) ▸ **en baisse** falling / ÉCON falling off ▸ **la tendance est à la baisse** there is a downward trend ▸ **les ventes ont accusé une baisse ces derniers temps** there has been a recent falling off in sales **2.** INFORM **: baisse de tension** brownout.

baisser [4] [bese] ■ **vt** [gén] to lower / [radio] to turn down ▸ **le rideau est baissé** THÉÂTRE the curtain's down / [boutique] the shutters are down ▸ **baisser les bras** to throw in the sponge *ou* towel *fig* ▸ **baisser le ton** to modify one's tone ▸ **baisser les yeux** to look down ▸ **en baissant la tête** [posture] with one's head down *ou* bent / [de tristesse] head bowed (with sorrow).
■ **vi 1.** [descendre] to go down ▸ **le jour baisse** it's getting dark **2.** [santé, vue] to fail ▸ **sa vue baisse** his eyesight's fading *ou* getting weaker *ou* failing **3.** [prix] to fall ▸ **ces mesures visent à faire baisser les prix du mètre carré** these measures are intended to bring down the price per square metre **4.** [s'affaiblir - malade] to grow weaker / [- talent] to decline ▸ **la qualité baisse** the quality's deteriorating.
◆ ***se baisser*** **vp** to bend down ▸ **se baisser pour éviter un coup** to duck in order to avoid a blow.

bajoues [baʒu] **nfpl** jowls.

bakchich [bakʃiʃ] **nm** baksheesh.

bal [bal] **nm** ball ▸ **bal masqué/costumé** masked/fancy-dress ball ▸ **bal musette** dance with accordion music ▸ **bal populaire** *(local) dance open to the public.*

BAL, Bal (abr de ***boîte aux lettres (électronique)***) [bal] **nf** E-mail.

balade [balad] **nf** *fam* stroll ▸ **faire une balade** to go for a stroll.

balader [3] [balade] ■ **vt 1.** *fam* [traîner avec soi] to trail around **2.** [emmener en promenade] to take for a walk.
■ **vi : envoyer balader qqn** to send sb packing.
◆ ***se balader*** **vp** *fam* **1.** [se promener - à pied] to go for a walk / [- en voiture] to go for a drive **2.** [traîner] to be kicking around.

baladeur, euse [baladœr, øz] **adj** wandering.
◆ ***baladeur*** **nm** personal stereo.
◆ ***baladeuse*** **nf** inspection lamp.

balafre [balafr] **nf 1.** [blessure] gash **2.** [cicatrice] scar.

balafré, e [balafre] **adj** scarred.

balai [balɛ] **nm 1.** [de nettoyage] broom, brush ▸ **balai mécanique** carpet sweeper **2.** [d'essuie-glace] wiper blade **3.** *fam* [an] **: il a 50 balais** he's 50 years old.

balai-brosse [balɛbrɔs] (pl **balais-brosses**) **nm** (long-handled) scrubbing *UK ou* scrub *US* brush.

balaie, balaies ➤ ***balayer.***

balance [balɑ̃s] **nf 1.** [instrument] scales *pl* ▸ **balance de ménage** kitchen scales ▸ **faire pencher la balance** *fig* to tip the balance ▸ **mettre tout son poids** *ou* **tout mettre dans la balance** *fig* to use (all of) one's influence to tip the scales ▸ **mettre deux arguments en balance** to balance two arguments **2.** COMM & POLIT balance ▸ **balance de caisse** cash balance ▸ **balance des comptes** balance of payments ▸ **balance des paiements/commerciale** balance of payments/of trade ▸ **balance des pouvoirs** balance of power **3.** *arg crime* [dénonciateur] rat, grass *UK.*
◆ ***Balance*** **nf** ASTROL Libra ▸ **être Balance** to be (a) Libra.

balancement [balɑ̃smɑ̃] **nm** [mouvement - d'objet, de hanches] swaying / [- de bras, de jambe] swinging / [- de navire] motion.

balancer [16] [balɑ̃se] ■ **vt 1.** [bouger] to swing **2.** *fam* [lancer] to chuck **3.** *fam* [jeter] to chuck out.
■ **vi 1.** *sout* [hésiter] to waver **2.** [osciller] to swing.
◆ ***se balancer*** **vp 1.** [sur une chaise] to rock backwards and forwards **2.** [sur une balançoire] to swing **3.** *fam* **: se balancer de qqch** not to give a damn about sthg.

balancier [balɑ̃sje] **nm 1.** [de pendule] pendulum **2.** [de funambule] pole.

balançoire [balɑ̃swar] **nf** [suspendue] swing / [bascule] seesaw.

balayage [balɛjaʒ] **nm** [gén] sweeping / TECHNOL scanning.

balayer [11] [baleje] **vt 1.** [nettoyer] to sweep **2.** [chasser] to sweep away **3.** *fig* [écarter] to brush aside **4.** [suj: radar] to scan / [suj: projecteurs] to sweep (across).

balayette [balɛjɛt] **nf** small brush.

balayeur, euse [balɛjœr, øz] **nm, f** roadsweeper *UK*, street cleaner.
◆ ***balayeuse*** **nf** [machine] roadsweeper *UK*, street cleaner.

balayures [balejyr] **nfpl** sweepings.

balbutiement [balbysimɑ̃] **nm 1.** [bredouillement] stammering **2.** [discours confus] **: balbutiements** [d'un ivrogne] slurred speech *(U)* / [d'un bébé] babbling *(U).*
◆ ***balbutiements*** **nmpl** [d'une technique, d'un art] early stages, beginnings / [débuts] infancy *(U).*

balbutier [9] [balbysje] ■ **vi 1.** [bafouiller] to stammer **2.** *fig* [débuter] to be in its infancy.
■ **vt** [bafouiller] to stammer (out).

balcon [balkɔ̃] **nm 1.** [de maison - terrasse] balcony / [- balustrade] parapet **2.** [de théâtre, de cinéma] circle.

balconnet [balkɔnɛ] **nm : soutien-gorge à balconnet** half-cup bra.

baldaquin [baldakɛ̃] **nm 1.** ARCHIT canopy **2.** ➤ ***lit.***

Bâle [bal] **npr** Basel.

Baléares [balear] **nfpl : les Baléares** the Balearic Islands ▸ **aux Baléares** in the Balearic Islands.

baleine [balɛn] **nf 1.** [mammifère] whale **2.** [de corset] whalebone **3.** [de parapluie] rib.

baleinier, ère [balɛnje, ɛr] **adj** whaling *(avant n).*
◆ ***baleinier*** **nm** whaler.
◆ ***baleinière*** **nf** [bateau] whaler.

Bali [bali] **npr** Bali ▸ **à Bali** in Bali.

balinais, e [balinɛ, ɛz] **adj** Balinese.
◆ ***Balinais, e*** **nm, f** Balinese *(inv).*

balisage [balizaʒ] **nm 1.** [action] marking out **2.** [signaux - NAUT] markers *pl*, marker buoys *pl* / AÉRON runway lights *pl* / AUTO road signs *pl* **3.** INFORM tagging, mark-up.

balise [baliz] **nf 1.** NAUT marker (buoy) **2.** AÉRON runway light **3.** AUTO road sign **4.** INFORM tag.

baliser [3] [balize] ■ **vt** to mark out.
■ **vi** *fam* to be scared stiff.

balistique [balistik] ■ **nf** ballistics *(U)*.
■ **adj** ballistic.

balivernes [balivɛrn] **nfpl** nonsense *(U)*.

Balkans [balkɑ̃] **nmpl : les Balkans** the Balkans.

ballade [balad] **nf** ballad.

ballant, e [balɑ̃, ɑ̃t] **adj : les bras ballants** arms dangling.
◆ ***ballant*** **nm** [mouvement] **: avoir du ballant** to sway.

ballast [balast] **nm 1.** [chemin de fer] ballast **2.** NAUT ballast tank.

balle [bal] **nf 1.** [d'arme à feu] bullet ▸ **balle à blanc** blank ▸ **balle perdue** stray bullet ▸ **se tirer une balle dans la bouche/tête** to shoot o.s. in the mouth/head ▸ **tué par balles** shot dead
2. [de jeu] ball ▸ **balle de golf** golfball ▸ **balle de ping-pong/tennis** table-tennis/tennis ball ▸ **balle de jeu/match** TENNIS game/match point
3. [de marchandises] bale
4. *fam* [argent] franc ▸ **t'as pas cent balles?** have you got a hundred francs? / [monnaie] can you spare some change?
▸▸ **la balle est dans son camp** *fig* the ball's in his court ▸ **se renvoyer la balle** to pass the buck ▸ **saisir la balle au bond** to jump at the chance.

ballerine [balrin] **nf 1.** [danseuse] ballerina **2.** [chaussure] ballet shoe.

ballet [balɛ] **nm** [gén] ballet / *fig* [activité intense] to-ing and fro-ing.

ballon [balɔ̃] **nm 1.** [jeux & SPORT] ball ▸ **jouer au ballon** to play with a ball ▸ **ballon de football** football *UK*, soccer ball *US* ▸ **le ballon ovale** rugby ▸ **le ballon rond** football *UK*, soccer *US* **2.** [montgolfière, de fête] balloon ▸ **ballon (de baudruche)** (party) balloon **3.** [verre de vin] **: ballon de rouge** glass of red (wine) **4.** AÉRON (hot-air) balloon ▸ **ballon d'essai** *litt* pilot balloon / *fig* test ▸ **lancer un ballon d'essai** [se renseigner] to put out feelers / [faire un essai] to do a trial run, to run a test **5.** CHIM round-bottomed flask / **: souffler dans le ballon** to be breathalysed *UK* *ou* breathalyzed *US*.

ballonné, e [balɔne] **adj : avoir le ventre ballonné, être ballonné** to be bloated.

ballot [balo] **nm 1.** [de marchandises] bundle **2.** *vieilli* [imbécile] twit.

ballottage [balɔtaʒ] **nm** POLIT second ballot ▸ **en ballottage** standing for a second ballot *UK*, running in the second round *US*.

ballotter [3] [balɔte] ■ **vt** to toss about ▸ **être ballotté entre** *fig* to be torn between.
■ **vi** [chose] to roll around.

ballottine [balɔtin] **nf : ballottine de foie gras** *meat roll made with foie gras*.

ball-trap [baltrap] **nm** clay pigeon shooting.

balluchon = ***baluchon***.

balnéaire [balneɛr] **adj : station balnéaire** seaside resort.

balourd, e [balur, urd] ■ **adj** clumsy.
■ **nm, f** clumsy idiot.

balte [balt] **adj** Baltic.
◆ ***Balte*** **nmf** person from the Baltic states.

Baltique [baltik] **nf : la Baltique** the Baltic (Sea).

baluchon, balluchon [balyʃɔ̃] **nm** bundle ▸ **faire son baluchon** *fam* to pack one's bags (and leave).

balustrade [balystrad] **nf 1.** [de terrasse] balustrade **2.** [rambarde] guardrail.

bambin [bɑ̃bɛ̃] **nm** kiddie.

bambou [bɑ̃bu] **nm 1.** [plante] bamboo ▸ **pousse de bambou** bamboo shoot **2.** [matériau] **: en bambou** bamboo.

bamboula [bɑ̃bula] **nf : faire la bamboula** *fam* to have a wild time.

ban [bɑ̃] **nm 1.** [de mariage] **: publier** *ou* **afficher les bans** to publish *ou* display the banns **2.** [applaudissements] round of applause
▸▸ **être/mettre qqn au ban de la société** to be outlawed/to outlaw sb (from society) ▸ **le ban et l'arrière-ban** the whole lot of them.

banal, e, als [banal] **adj** commonplace, banal ▸ **pas** *ou* **peu banal** unusual.

banalisé, e [banalize] **adj 1.** [véhicule] unmarked **2.** INFORM general-purpose.

banaliser [3] [banalize] **vt** [véhicule] to remove the markings from.
◆ ***se banaliser*** **vp** to become commonplace.

banalité [banalite] **nf 1.** [caractère banal] banality **2.** [cliché] commonplace ▸ **échanger des banalités** to make smalltalk.

banane [banan] **nf 1.** [fruit] banana **2.** [sac] bum-bag *UK*, fanny pack *US* **3.** [coiffure] quiff *UK*.

bananier, ère [bananje, ɛr] **adj** banana *(avant n)* ▸ **république bananière** banana republic.
◆ ***bananier*** **nm 1.** [arbre] banana tree **2.** [cargo] banana boat.

banc [bɑ̃] **nm** [siège] bench ▸ **le banc des accusés** DR the dock ▸ **(au) banc des témoins** (in the) witness box *UK*, (on the) stand *US* ▸ **sur les bancs de l'école** in one's schooldays ▸ **banc public** park bench ▸ **banc d'essai** test-bed ▸ **être au banc d'essai** *fig* to be at the test stage ▸ **faire un banc d'essai** *litt* to test (an engine) / *fig* to have a trial run ▸ **banc des joueurs** [hockey] players' bench ▸ **banc de neige** *Québec* snowbank ▸ **banc des pénalités** *ou* **des punitions** [hockey] penalty box ▸ **banc de poissons** shoal of fish ▸ **banc d'huîtres** [dans la mer] oyster bed / [dans un restaurant] display of oysters ▸ **banc de sable** sandbank.

bancaire [bɑ̃kɛr] **adj** bank *(avant n)*, banking *(avant n)*.

bancal, e, als [bɑ̃kal] **adj 1.** [personne] lame **2.** [meuble] wobbly **3.** [théorie, idée] unsound.

bancassurance [bɑ̃kasyrɑ̃s] **nf** bancassurance.

bandage [bɑ̃daʒ] **nm** [de blessé] bandage.

bande [bɑ̃d] **nf 1.** [de tissu, de papier] strip ▸ **bande dessinée** comic strip ▸ **la bande dessinée** [genre] comic strips **2.** [bandage] bandage ▸ **bande Velpeau**® crepe bandage

3. [de billard] cushion ▸ **par la bande** *fig* by a roundabout route
4. [groupe] band ▸ **bande de...!** *fam* bunch of...! ▸ **une bande de menteurs/voleurs** a bunch of liars/crooks ▸ **en bande** in a group ▸ **ils ne se déplacent qu'en bande** they always go around in a gang ▸ **faire bande à part** to keep to o.s. ▸ **il a encore décidé de faire bande à part** he's decided yet again to go it alone
5. [pellicule de film] film
6. [d'enregistrement] tape ▸ **bande audionumérique** DAT tape ▸ **bande magnétique** (magnetic) tape ▸ **bande originale** CINÉ original soundtrack ▸ **bande vidéo** video(tape)
7. [voie] **: bande d'arrêt d'urgence** hard shoulder *UK*, shoulder *US*
8. RADIO **: bande de fréquence** waveband ▸ **sur la bande FM** on FM
9. NAUT **: donner de la bande** to list.

CULTURE

Bande dessinée

La bande dessinée, or BD, is very popular both in France and Belgium. Comics are considered the 'ninth art' and judged on both literary and artistic quality; they have come a long way from the newspaper strips that made them popular. Bookshops have sections devoted to BD, and some have even been made into films. Beginning in the 1970s, the art form saw an explosion of styles and considerable creative development that lasted until the end of the 20th century. The **Festival international de la bande dessinée** is held in Angoulême every summer.

bande-annonce [bɑ̃danɔ̃s] (pl **bandes-annonces**) **nf** trailer.

bandeau [bɑ̃do] **nm** **1.** [sur les yeux] blindfold **2.** [dans les cheveux] headband.

bandelette [bɑ̃dlɛt] **nf** strip (of cloth).

bander [3] [bɑ̃de] ■ **vt** **1.** MÉD to bandage ▸ **bander les yeux de qqn** to blindfold sb **2.** [arc] to draw back **3.** [muscle] to flex.
■ **vi** *vulg* to have a hard-on.

banderole [bɑ̃drɔl] **nf** streamer.

bande-son [bɑ̃dsɔ̃] (pl **bandes-son**) **nf** soundtrack.

bandit [bɑ̃di] **nm** **1.** [voleur] bandit **2.** [personne sans scrupules] crook.

banditisme [bɑ̃ditism] **nm** serious crime.

bandoulière [bɑ̃duljɛr] **nf** bandolier ▸ **en bandoulière** across the shoulder.

bangladais, e [bɑ̃gladɛ, ɛz] **adj** Bangladeshi.
◆ ***Bangladais, e*** **nm, f** Bangladeshi.

Bangladesh [bɑ̃gladɛʃ] **nm : le Bangladesh** Bangladesh ▸ **au Bangladesh** in Bangladesh.

banjo [bɑ̃(d)ʒo] **nm** banjo.

banlieue [bɑ̃ljø] **nf** suburbs *pl* ▸ **en banlieue** in the suburbs ▸ **la grande banlieue** the outer suburbs ▸ **la banlieue parisienne** the Paris suburbs ▸ **réseau de banlieue** commuter *ou* suburban network.

CULTURE

Banlieue

In France, this word is often associated with crime, poverty, unemployment and other social problems. For historical reasons connected with the construction of large low-income housing units, the immediate suburbs of large cities are low-rent areas offering little in the way of job opportunities and cultural events. Therefore, residents of these areas must often cope with long commutes to the city centre. An even more pejorative term for the suburbs is **la Zone**, once used to describe the areas surrounding Paris itself. They, too, had an unsavoury reputation.

banlieusard, e [bɑ̃ljøzar, ard] **nm, f** *person living in the suburbs.*

bannière [banjɛr] **nf** [étendard] banner.

bannir [32] [banir] **vt : bannir qqn/qqch (de)** to banish sb/sthg (from).

banque [bɑ̃k] **nf** **1.** [activité] banking ▸ **banque d'entreprise** corporate banking **2.** [établissement, au jeu] bank ▸ **banque d'affaires/commerciale/de dépôt** merchant/commercial/deposit bank ▸ **Banque centrale européenne** European Central Bank ▸ **banque d'émission** issuing bank, issuing house ▸ **Banque d'Angleterre** Bank of England ▸ **Banque de France** Bank of France **3.** INFORM **: banque de données** data bank **4.** MÉD **: banque d'organes/du sang/du sperme** organ/blood/sperm bank.

CULTURE

La Banque centrale européenne

The European Central Bank – provided for in the Maastricht Treaty that established the European Union (1991) – sets and enforces monetary policy in the euro zone, along with the national banks of the zone's member nations. It is also charged with maintaining price stability. The euro zone, with an economy second only to that of the United States, includes 12 of the 25 European Union members: France, Belgium, Germany, Austria, Greece, Ireland, Italy, Luxembourg, Finland, the Netherlands, Portugal, and Spain. The other EU member countries must satisfy strict economic criteria before adopting the euro as their currency.

banqueroute [bɑ̃krut] **nf** bankruptcy ▸ **faire banqueroute** to go bankrupt.

banquet [bɑ̃kɛ] **nm** (celebration) dinner / [de gala] banquet.

banquette [bɑ̃kɛt] **nf** seat ▸ **banquette arrière** back seat.

banquier, ère [bɑ̃kje, ɛr] **nm, f** banker.

banquise [bɑ̃kiz] **nf** ice field.

baobab [baɔbab] **nm** baobab.

baptême [batɛm] **nm 1.** RELIG baptism, christening **2.** [première fois] **: baptême de l'air** maiden flight ▸ **baptême du feu** baptism of fire.

baptiser [3] [batize] **vt** to baptize, to christen.

baptismal, e, aux [batismal, o] **adj** baptismal, ➤ ***fonts***.

baquet [bakɛ] **nm 1.** [cuve] tub **2.** [siège] bucket seat.

bar [bar] **nm 1.** [café, unité de pression] bar ▸ **bar à café** *Suisse* coffee bar ▸ **bar à vin** wine bar **2.** [poisson] bass.

baragouiner [3] [baragwine] **vt** *fam* **1.** [langue] **: il baragouine le français** he speaks broken French **2.** [bredouiller] to gabble.

baraka [baraka] **nf** *fam* **: avoir la baraka** to be lucky.

baraque [barak] **nf 1.** [cabane] hut **2.** *fam* [maison] house **3.** [de forain] stall, stand.

baraqué, e [barake] **adj** *fam* well-built.

baraquement [barakmɑ̃] **nm** camp *(of huts for refugees, workers etc)*.

baratin [baratɛ̃] **nm** *fam* smooth talk ▸ **faire du baratin à qqn** to sweet-talk sb.

baratiner [3] [baratine] *fam* ■ **vt** [femme] to chat up *UK*, to sweet-talk / [client] to give one's sales pitch to.
■ **vi** to be a smooth talker.

Barbade [barbad] **npr f : la Barbade** Barbados.

barbant, e [barbɑ̃, ɑ̃t] **adj** *fam* deadly dull *ou* boring.

barbare [barbar] ■ **nm** barbarian.
■ **adj 1.** *péj* [non civilisé] barbarous **2.** [cruel] barbaric.

barbarisme [barbarism] **nm** GRAMM barbarism.

barbe [1] [barb] **nm** [cheval] barb.

barbe [2] [barb] **nf** beard ▸ **se laisser pousser la barbe** to grow a beard ▸ **sans barbe** [rasé] beardless, clean-shaven / [imberbe] beardless, smooth-chinned ▸ **fausse barbe** false beard ▸ **barbe à papa** candyfloss *UK*, cotton candy *US* ▸ **faire qqch (au nez et) à la barbe de qqn** *fig* to do sthg right under sb's nose ▸ **quelle** *ou* **la barbe!** *fam* what a drag! ▸ **rire dans sa barbe** to laugh up one's sleeve.
◆ ***barbes*** **nfpl** [de papier] ragged edge / [d'encre] smudge.

barbecue [barbəkju] **nm** barbecue.

barbelé, e [barbəle] **adj** barbed ▸ **fil de fer barbelé** barbed wire.
◆ ***barbelé*** **nm** barbed wire *(U)*.

barber [3] [barbe] **vt** *fam* to bore stiff.
◆ ***se barber*** **vp** *fam* to be bored stiff.

barbiche [barbiʃ] **nf** goatee (beard).

barbiturique [barbityrik] **nm** barbiturate.

barboter [3] [barbɔte] ■ **vi** to paddle.
■ **vt** *fam* to nick *UK*, to pinch.

barboteuse [barbɔtøz] **nf** rompers *pl*, romper suit *UK*.

barbouillé, e [barbuje] **adj : être barbouillé, avoir l'estomac barbouillé** to feel sick *UK ou* nauseous *US*.

barbouiller [3] [barbuje] **vt 1.** [salir] **: barbouiller qqch (de)** to smear sthg (with) **2.** *péj* [peindre] to daub **3.** *fam* [écrire sur] to scribble on.

barbu, e [barby] **adj** bearded.
◆ ***barbu*** **nm** bearded man.
◆ ***barbue*** **nf** [poisson] brill.

barda [barda] **nm 1.** *arg mil* kit **2.** *fam* [attirail] gear ▸ **avec tout son barda** with all his/her gear.

barde [bard] ■ **nm** [poète] bard.
■ **nf** CULIN bacon, bard.

bardé, e [barde] **adj : il est bardé de diplômes** he's got heaps of diplomas.

barder [3] [barde] ■ **vt** CULIN to bard.
■ **vi** *fam* **: ça va barder** there'll be trouble.

barème [barɛm] **nm** [de référence] table / [de salaires] scale.

barge [barʒ] **nf** [bateau] barge.

baril [baril] **nm** barrel ▸ **un baril de pétrole** a barrel of oil.

barillet [barijɛ] **nm 1.** [petit baril] cask **2.** [de revolver, de serrure] cylinder.

bariolé, e [barjɔle] **adj** multicoloured *UK*, multicolored *US*.

barjo(t) [barʒo] **adj inv** *fam* nuts.

barmaid [barmɛd] **nf** barmaid.

barman [barman] (pl **barmans** *ou* **barmen** [barmɛn]) **nm** barman *UK*, bartender *US*.

baromètre [barɔmɛtr] **nm** barometer.

baron, onne [barɔ̃, ɔn] **nm, f** baron (f baroness).
◆ ***baron*** **nm** [magnat] baron.

baroque [barɔk] ■ **nm** ART **: le baroque** the Baroque style.
■ **adj 1.** [style] baroque **2.** [bizarre] weird.

baroud [barud] **nm : baroud d'honneur** last stand.

barque [bark] **nf** small boat ▸ **savoir mener sa barque** *fig* to be well-organized.

barquette [barkɛt] **nf 1.** [tartelette] pastry boat **2.** [récipient - de fruits] basket, punnet *UK* / [- de frites] carton / [- de crème glacée] tub.

barrage [baraʒ] **nm 1.** [de rue] roadblock **2.** CONSTR dam.

barre [bar] **nf 1.** [gén & DR] bar ▸ **barres asymétriques/parallèles** asymmetric/parallel bars ▸ **barre fixe** [gymnastique] high bar ▸ **barre de chocolat** chocolate bar ▸ **barre des témoins** DR witness box *UK*, stand *US* ▸ **appeler qqn à la barre** to call sb to the witness box *UK ou* stand *US* ▸ **c'est le coup de barre** *fig* it's a rip-off ▸ **avoir un coup de barre** *fig* to be shattered *UK ou* pooped *US* ▸ **mettre** *ou* **placer la barre trop haut** to set too high a standard
2. NAUT helm ▸ **être à la barre** *fig* & NAUT to be at the helm ▸ **prendre la barre** *litt* to take the helm / *fig* to take charge
3. [trait] stroke ▸ **barre oblique** slash
4. INFORM **: barre d'espacement** space bar ▸ **barre de défilement** scroll bar ▸ **barre d'état** status bar ▸ **barre de menu** menu bar ▸ **barre d'outils** tool bar.

barré, e [bare] **adj** [chèque] crossed ▸ **chèque non barré** open cheque

▸▸ **c'est mal barré** *fam* it's got off to a bad start ▸ **on est mal barré pour y être à 8 h** we haven't got a hope in hell of being there at 8.
◆ ***barré*** **nm** barré.

barreau [baro] **nm** bar ▸ **le barreau** DR the Bar.

barrer [3] [bare] **vt 1.** [rue, route] to block ▸ **barrer la route à qqn** *litt* & *fig* to stand in sb's way **2.** [mot, phrase] to cross out **3.** [bateau] to steer.
◆ ***se barrer*** **vp** *fam* to clear off.

barrette [barɛt] **nf** [pince à cheveux] (hair) slide *UK*, barrette *US*.

barreur, ***euse*** [barœr, øz] **nm, f** NAUT helmsman / [à l'aviron] cox.

barricade [barikad] **nf** barricade ▸ **monter sur les barricades** *fig* to man the barricades.

barricader [3] [barikade] **vt** to barricade.
◆ ***se barricader*** **vp** to barricade o.s. ▸ **se barricader chez soi** to shut o.s. away (at home).

barrière [barjɛr] **nf** *litt* & *fig* barrier ▸ **barrière de dégel** *ban on heavy lorries on certain roads during a thaw*.

barrique [barik] **nf** barrel.

barrir [32] [barir] **vi** to trumpet.

bar-tabac [bartaba] (pl **bars-tabacs**) **nm** *bar also selling cigarettes and tobacco*.

baryton [baritɔ̃] **nm** baritone.

bas[1] [ba] **nm** [vêtement] stocking ▸ **des bas avec/sans couture** seamed/seamless stockings ▸ **bas fins** sheer stockings ▸ **bas de laine** *litt* woollen *UK* *ou* woolen *US* stocking / *fig* savings, nest egg ▸ **bas (de) Nylon**® nylon stockings ▸ **bas résille** fishnet stockings ▸ **bas de soie** silk stockings ▸ **bas à varices** support stockings.

bas[2], ***basse*** [ba, baz] *(prononcé* [bas] *devant un nm commençant par voyelle ou 'h' muet)* **adj 1.** [gén] low ▸ **attrape les branches basses** grasp the lower *ou* bottom branches ▸ **à bas prix** cheap, for a low price ▸ **le niveau de la classe est très bas** the (achievement) level of the class is very low **2.** *péj* [vil] base, low ▸ **les basses besognes** the dirty work ▸ **les bas morceaux** [en boucherie] the cheap cuts **3.** [peu fort] low, quiet ▸ **parler à voix basse** to speak in a low *ou* quiet voice **4.** [inférieur] low, lowly *littéraire* ▸ **de basse condition** from a poor family ▸ **le bas clergé** the minor clergy **5.** [incliné vers le sol] **: marcher la tête basse** to hang one's head as one walks ▸ **un chien avec la queue basse** a dog with its tail between its legs **6.** MUS bass.
◆ ***bas*** ■ **nm** [partie inférieure] bottom, lower part ▸ **le bas du dos** the small of the back
▸▸ **avoir/connaître des hauts et des bas** to have/go through ups and downs.
■ **adv** low ▸ **les prix ne descendront pas plus bas** prices won't come down any further ▸ **voir plus bas** see below ▸ **à bas...!** down with...! ▸ **bas les pattes!** *fam* hands off! ▸ **parler bas** to speak in a low voice, to speak softly ▸ **mettre le son plus bas** to turn the sound down ▸ **mettre bas** [animal] to give birth.
◆ ***de bas en haut*** **loc adv** from bottom to top, from the bottom up ▸ **regarder qqn de bas en haut** to look sb up and down.
◆ ***d'en bas*** **loc adj : les voisins d'en bas** the people downstairs ▸ **la porte d'en bas est fermée** the downstairs door is shut.
◆ ***en bas*** **loc adv** at the bottom ▸ **le village semblait si petit, tout en bas** the village looked so small, down there *ou* below / [dans une maison] downstairs.
◆ ***en bas de*** **loc prép** at the bottom of ▸ **attendre qqn en bas de chez lui** to wait for sb downstairs ▸ **en bas de la côte** at the bottom *ou* foot of the hill ▸ **signez en bas du contrat** sign at the bottom of the contract.
◆ ***bas de gamme*** ■ **adj** downmarket.
■ **nm** bottom of the range.

basalte [bazalt] **nm** basalt.

basané, ***e*** [bazane] **adj** tanned *UK*, tan *US*.

bas-bleu [bablø] (pl **bas-bleus**) **nm** *péj* bluestocking.

bas-côté [bakote] (pl **bas-côtés**) **nm** [de route] verge *UK*, shoulder *US*.

bascule [baskyl] **nf 1.** [balance] weighing machine **2.** [balançoire] seesaw.

basculer [3] [baskyle] ■ **vi** to fall over, to overbalance / [benne] to tip up ▸ **basculer dans qqch** *fig* to tip over into sthg.
■ **vt** to tip up, to tilt.

base [baz] **nf 1.** [partie inférieure] base ▸ **à la base du cou** at the base of the neck ▸ **la base** [d'entreprise, de syndicat] the rank and file
2. [principe fondamental] basis ▸ **à base de** based on ; **une boisson à base d'orange** an orange-based drink ▸ **sur la base de** on the basis of ▸ **établir qqch/reposer sur une base solide** to set sthg up/to rest on a sound basis
3. MIL **: base (aérienne/militaire/navale)** (air/army/naval) base ▸ **base d'opérations/de ravitaillement** operations/supply base ▸ **rentrer à la base** to go back to base
4. [astronautique] **: base de lancement** launching site
5. MATH **: système de base cinq/huit** base five/eight system
6. INFORM **: base de données** database ▸ **base de données relationnelles** relational database / ÉCON **: base de clientèle** *ou* **base (de données) de consommateurs** customer base
7. [cosmétique] **: base de maquillage** make-up base
8. SPORT [détente] **: base de loisirs** (outdoor) leisure *ou* sports complex
9. *Québec* **: base de plein air** outdoor recreation area.
◆ ***bases*** **nfpl** [fondations] foundations, basis *sg* / [acquis] basic knowledge *sg* ▸ **avoir de bonnes bases en arabe/musique** to have a good grounding in Arabic/in music.
◆ ***à la base*** **loc adv 1.** [en son fondement] **: le raisonnement est faux à la base** the basis of the argument is false
2. [au début] at the beginning.
◆ ***de base*** **loc adj 1.** [fondamental - vocabulaire, industrie] basic / [- principe] basic, fundamental ▸ **militant de base** grassroots militant
2. [salaire, traitement] basic.

base-ball [bɛzbol] (pl **base-balls**) **nm** baseball.

base line [bɛzlajn] **nf** strapline.

baser [3] [baze] **vt** to base ▸ **baser qqch sur** *fig* to base sthg on.
◆ ***se baser*** **vp : sur quoi vous basez-vous pour affirmer cela?** what are you basing this statement on?

bas-fond [bafɔ̃] (pl **bas-fonds**) **nm** [de l'océan] shallow.
◆ ***bas-fonds*** **nmpl** *fig* **1.** [de la société] dregs **2.** [quartiers pauvres] slums.

basilic [bazilik] **nm** [plante] basil.

basilique [bazilik] **nf** basilica.

basique [bazik] **adj** basic.

basket [baskɛt] ■ **nm** = ***basket-ball***.
■ **nf** [chaussure] trainer *UK*, sneaker *US* ▸ **lâche-moi les baskets!** *fam fig* get off my back!

basket-ball [baskɛtbol] **nm** basketball.

basmati [basmati] **nm** basmati (rice).

basque [bask] ■ **adj** Basque ▸ **le Pays basque** the Basque country.
■ **nm** [langue] Basque.
■ **nf** [vêtement] tail *(of coat)* ▸ **être toujours pendu aux basques de qqn** *fam fig* to be always tagging along after sb.
◆ ***Basque*** **nmf** Basque.

bas-relief [barəljɛf] (pl **bas-reliefs**) **nm** bas-relief.

basse [bas] ■ **adj** ➤ ***bas***.
■ **nf** MUS bass.

basse-cour [baskur] (pl **basses-cours**) **nf 1.** [volaille] poultry **2.** [partie de ferme] farmyard.

bassement [basmɑ̃] **adv** despicably ▸ **être bassement intéressé** to be motivated by petty self-interest.

bassesse [basɛs] **nf 1.** [mesquinerie] baseness, meanness **2.** [action vile] despicable act.

basset [basɛ] **nm** basset hound.

bassin [basɛ̃] **nm 1.** [cuvette] bowl **2.** [pièce d'eau] (ornamental) pond **3.** [de piscine] **: petit/grand bassin** children's/main pool **4.** ANAT pelvis **5.** GÉOL basin ▸ **bassin houiller** coalfield ▸ **le Bassin parisien** the Paris basin.

bassine [basin] **nf** bowl, basin.

bassiner [3] [basine] **vt 1.** [humecter] to bathe **2.** *fam* [importuner] to bore.

bassiste [basist] **nmf** bass player.

basson [basɔ̃] **nm** [instrument] bassoon / [personne] bassoonist.

bastide [bastid] **nf 1.** [maison] *traditional farmhouse or country house in southern France* **2.** HIST *walled town (in south-west France)*.

Bastille [bastij] **nf : la Bastille** [forteresse] the Bastille / [quartier] Bastille, the Bastille area ▸ **la prise de la Bastille** the storming of the Bastille.

CULTURE

La Bastille

The Bastille was a prison whose takeover and destruction by angry Parisians on the 14th of July 1789 marked the symbolic beginning of the French Revolution. Stones from the prison's foundation can still be seen in the train station beneath the square. Today, the **colonne de Juillet** (which actually commemorates the Revolution of 1830) takes its place. The **Opéra Bastille**, erected in 1989, boasts more seats than the venerable **Opéra Garnier**, but its architectural style and acoustics have not impressed everyone. The Bastille has not lost its symbolic power as many political demonstrations conclude at the square.

bastingage [bastɛ̃gaʒ] **nm** (ship's) rail.

bastion [bastjɔ̃] **nm** *litt* & *fig* bastion.

baston [bastɔ̃] **nf** *tfam* punch-up *UK*, brawl.

bas-ventre [bavɑ̃tr] (pl **bas-ventres**) **nm** lower abdomen.

bât [ba] **nm** packsaddle ▸ **c'est là que le bât blesse** *fig* that's his/her *etc* weak point.

bataille [bataj] **nf 1.** MIL battle ▸ **bataille aérienne** [à grande échelle] air battle / [isolée] dogfight ▸ **bataille aéronavale** sea-air battle ▸ **bataille rangée** pitched battle **2.** [bagarre] fight ▸ **bataille de polochons** pillow fight ▸ **bataille de rue** street fight *ou* brawl **3.** [jeu] **: la bataille** ≃ beggar-my-neighbour *UK* ▸ **bataille navale** battleships *(U)*
▸▸ **en bataille** [cheveux] dishevelled *UK*, disheveled *US*.

batailler [3] [bataje] **vi : batailler pour qqch/pour faire qqch** to fight for sthg/to do sthg.

bataillon [batajɔ̃] **nm** MIL battalion / *fig* horde.

bâtard, e [batar, ard] ■ **adj 1.** [enfant] illegitimate **2.** *péj* [style, solution] hybrid.
■ **nm, f** illegitimate child.
◆ ***bâtard*** **nm 1.** [pain] *short loaf of bread* **2.** [chien] mongrel.

batavia [batavja] **nf** Webb lettuce *UK*, iceberg lettuce.

bateau [bato] **nm 1.** [embarcation - gén] boat / [- plus grand] ship ▸ **bateau à moteur** motor boat ▸ **bateau à voile** sailing boat *UK*, sailboat *US* ▸ **bateau de pêche** fishing boat ▸ **mener qqn en bateau** *fig* to take sb for a ride **2.** [de trottoir] driveway entrance *(low kerb)* **3.** *(en apposition inv)* **: encolure bateau** boat neck **4.** *(en apposition inv)* [sujet, thème] well-worn ▸ **c'est bateau!** it's the same old stuff!

bateau-bus [batobys] (pl **bateaux-bus**) **nm** riverbus ▸ **prendre le bateau-bus** to take the riverbus.

bateau-mouche [batomuʃ] (pl **bateaux-mouches**) **nm** riverboat *(on the Seine)*.

bateleur, euse [batlœr, øz] **nm, f** street acrobat.

bath [bat] **adj inv** *fam vieilli* super, super-duper.

bâti, e [bati] **adj 1.** [terrain] developed **2.** [personne] **: bien bâti** well-built.
◆ ***bâti*** **nm 1.** COUT tacking **2.** CONSTR frame, framework.

batifoler [3] [batifɔle] **vi** to frolic.

bâtiment [batimɑ̃] **nm 1.** [édifice] building **2.** [dans l'industrie] **: le bâtiment** the building trade **3.** NAUT ship, vessel.

bâtir [32] [batir] **vt 1.** CONSTR to build **2.** *fig* [réputation, fortune] to build (up) / [théorie, phrase] to construct **3.** COUT to tack.
◆ ***se bâtir*** **vp** to be built.

bâtisse [batis] **nf** house.

bâton [batɔ̃] **nm 1.** [gén] stick ▸ **bâton de réglisse** liquorice *UK ou* licorice *US* stick ▸ **bâton de ski** ski pole **2.** *fam fig* 10,000 francs
⏭ **mettre des bâtons dans les roues à qqn** to put a spoke in sb's wheel ▸ **à bâtons rompus** [conversation] rambling ▸ **parler à bâtons rompus** to talk of this and that.

bâtonnet [batɔnɛ] **nm** rod.

bâtonnier [batɔnje] **nm** DR ≃ President of the Bar.

batracien [batrasjɛ̃] **nm** amphibian.

battage [bataʒ] **nm : battage (publicitaire** *ou* **médiatique)** (media) hype.

battant, e [batɑ̃, ɑ̃t] ■ **adj : sous une pluie battante** in the pouring *ou* driving rain ▸ **le cœur battant** with beating heart.
■ **nm, f** fighter.
◆ ***battant*** **nm 1.** [de porte] door *(of double doors)* / [de fenêtre] half *(of double window)* **2.** [de cloche] clapper.

batte [bat] **nf** SPORT bat.

battement [batmɑ̃] **nm 1.** [mouvement - d'ailes] flap, beating *(U)* / [- de cœur, pouls] beat, beating *(U)* / [- de cils, paupières] flutter, fluttering *(U)* **2.** [bruit - de porte] banging *(U)* / [- de la pluie] beating *(U)* **3.** [intervalle de temps] break ▸ **une heure de battement** an hour free.

batterie [batri] **nf 1.** ÉLECTR & MIL battery ▸ **batterie antichars** antitank battery ▸ **batterie d'accumulateurs** battery of accumulators ▸ **recharger ses batteries** *fig* to recharge one's batteries **2.** [attirail] **: batterie de cuisine** kitchen utensils *pl* **3.** MUS drums *pl* ▸ **Harvey Barton à la batterie** Harvey Barton on drums **4.** [série] **: une batterie de** a string of ▸ **batterie de tests/mesures** battery of tests/of measures.

batteur [batœr] **nm 1.** MUS drummer **2.** CULIN beater, whisk **3.** [SPORT - de cricket] batsman / [- de base-ball] batter.

batteuse [batøz] **nf** AGRIC thresher.

battoir [batwar] **nm 1.** [à tapis] carpet beater **2.** *fig* [main] great mitt *ou* paw.

battre [83] [batr] ■ **vt 1.** [gén] to beat ▸ **battre en neige** [blancs d'œufs] to beat until stiff ▸ **battre la campagne** *ou* **le pays** *litt* to comb the countryside / *fig* to be in one's own little world ▸ **battre la semelle** to stamp one's feet *(to keep warm)* ▸ **battre qqn à mort** to batter sb to death ▸ **battre qqn à plate couture** *ou* **plates coutures** to beat sb hollow ▸ **battre tous les records** *litt & fig* to set a new record **2.** [parcourir] to scour **3.** [cartes] to shuffle.
■ **vi** [gén] to beat ▸ **l'émotion faisait battre mon cœur** my heart was beating *ou* racing with emotion ▸ **battre des cils** to blink ▸ **battre de l'aile** to be in a bad way ▸ **battre des mains** to clap (one's hands).
◆ ***se battre*** **vp** to fight ▸ **se battre contre qqn** to fight sb ▸ **nous nous battons pour la paix/contre l'injustice** we're fighting for peace/against injustice.

battu, e [baty] ■ **pp** ➤ ***battre***.
■ **adj 1.** [tassé] hard-packed ▸ **jouer sur terre battue** TENNIS to play on clay **2.** [fatigué] **: avoir les yeux battus** to have shadows under one's eyes.
◆ ***battue*** **nf 1.** [chasse] beat **2.** [chasse à l'homme] manhunt.

baud [bo] **nm** baud.

baudroie [bodrwa] **nf** monkfish.

baudruche [bodryʃ] **nf 1.** [ballon] balloon **2.** *fig* [personne] front man.

baume [bom] **nm** *litt & fig* balm ▸ **mettre du baume au cœur de qqn** to comfort sb.

baux ➤ ***bail***.

bauxite [boksit] **nf** bauxite.

bavard, e [bavar, ard] ■ **adj** talkative.
■ **nm, f** chatterbox / *péj* gossip.

bavardage [bavardaʒ] **nm 1.** [papotage] chattering **2.** *(gén pl)* [racontar] gossip *(U)*.

bavarder [3] [bavarde] **vi** to chatter / *péj* to gossip.

bavarois, e [bavarwa, waz] **adj** Bavarian.
◆ ***bavarois*** **nm** *fam* [gâteau] ≃ mousse.
◆ ***Bavarois, e*** **nm, f** Bavarian.

bave [bav] **nf 1.** [salive] dribble **2.** [d'animal] slaver **3.** [de limace] slime.

baver [3] [bave] **vi 1.** [personne] to dribble **2.** [animal] to slaver **3.** [limace] to leave a slime trail **4.** [stylo] to leak
⏭ **en baver** *fam* to have a hard *ou* rough time of it.

bavette [bavɛt] **nf 1.** [bavoir, de tablier] bib **2.** [viande] flank
⏭ **tailler une bavette (avec qqn)** *fam* to have a chat (with sb).

baveux, euse [bavø, øz] **adj 1.** [bébé] dribbling **2.** [lettre] blurred **3.** [omelette] runny.

Bavière [bavjɛr] **npr f : (la) Bavière** Bavaria.

bavoir [bavwar] **nm** bib.

bavure [bavyr] **nf 1.** [tache] smudge **2.** [erreur] blunder.

bayer [3] [baje] **vi : bayer aux corneilles** to stand gazing into space.

bazar [bazar] **nm 1.** [boutique] general store **2.** *fam* [désordre] jumble, clutter.

bazarder [3] [bazarde] **vt** *fam* to chuck out, to get rid of.

BCBG (abr de ***bon chic bon genre***) ■ **nmf** ≃ Sloane (Ranger) *UK*, ≃ preppie *US*.
■ **adj** ≃ Sloaney *UK*, ≃ preppie *US*.

BCE (abr de ***Banque centrale européenne***) **nf** ECB.

BCG (abr de ***bacille Calmette-Guérin***) **nm** BCG.

bcp abr de ***beaucoup***.

bd abr de ***boulevard***.

BD, ***bédé*** [bede] (abr de ***bande dessinée***) **nf : une BD** a comic strip ▸ **la BD** comic strips *pl*.

beach-volley [bitʃvolɛ] (pl **beach-volleys**) **nm** beach volleyball ▸ **jouer au beach-volley** to play beach volleyball.

béant, ***e*** [beɑ̃, ɑ̃t] **adj** [plaie, gouffre] gaping / [yeux] wide open.

béarnais, ***e*** [bearnɛ, ɛz] **adj** of/from the Béarn.
◆ ***Béarnais***, ***e*** **nm, f** person from the Béarn.
◆ ***béarnaise*** **nf : (sauce) béarnaise** Béarnaise sauce.

béat, ***e*** [bea, at] **adj 1.** [content de soi] smug **2.** [heureux] blissful.

béatement [beatmɑ̃] **adv** blissfully.

béatitude [beatityd] **nf 1.** RELIG beatitude **2.** [bonheur] bliss.

beau, ***belle***, ***beaux*** [bo, bɛl] **adj** (**bel** [bɛl] *devant voyelle ou 'h' muet*) **1.** [joli - femme] beautiful, good-looking / [- homme] handsome, good-looking / [- chose] beautiful ▸ **se faire beau/belle** to get dressed up, to do o.s. up ▸ **ce n'était pas beau à voir** *fam* it wasn't a pretty sight ▸ **de beaux vêtements** fine clothes
2. [temps] fine, good ▸ **la mer sera belle** the sea will be calm
3. *(toujours avant le n)* [important] fine, excellent ▸ **une belle somme** a tidy sum (of money) ▸ **un beau coup en Bourse** a spectacular deal on the Stock Exchange
4. *iron* [mauvais] **: une belle grippe** a nasty dose of the flu ▸ **c'est du beau travail!** a fine mess this is! ▸ **garde tes belles promesses *ou* tes beaux serments!** you can keep your promises! ▸ **j'en ai appris *ou* entendu de belles sur toi!** I heard some right things about you!
5. *(sens intensif)* **: un beau jour** one fine day
6. [noble] fine, noble ▸ **une belle âme** a noble nature
▸▸ **elle a beau jeu de dire ça** it's easy *ou* all very well for her to say that.
◆ ***beau*** ■ **adv : il fait beau** the weather is good *ou* fine ▸ **j'ai beau essayer...** however hard I try..., try as I may... ▸ **j'ai beau dire...** whatever I say...
■ **nm : être au beau fixe** to be set fair ▸ **avoir le moral au beau fixe** *fig* to have a sunny disposition ▸ **faire le beau** [chien] to sit up and beg.
◆ ***belle*** **nf 1.** [femme] lady friend
2. [dans un jeu] decider
▸▸ **(se) faire la belle** *fam* to escape.
◆ ***bel et bien*** **loc adv** well and truly, actually ▸ **elle s'est bel et bien échappée** she got away and no mistake.
◆ ***de plus belle*** **loc adv** more than ever ▸ **il s'est mis à travailler de plus belle** he went back to work with renewed energy.

Beaubourg [bobur] **npr** *name commonly used to refer to the Pompidou Centre.*

beaucoup [boku] ■ **adv 1.** [un grand nombre] **: beaucoup de** a lot of, many ▸ **beaucoup de monde** a lot of people ▸ **il y en a beaucoup** there are many *ou* a lot (of them)
2. [une grande quantité] **: beaucoup de** a lot of ▸ **beaucoup d'énergie** a lot of energy ▸ **elle a beaucoup de goût** she has a lot of *ou* a great deal of taste ▸ **il n'a pas beaucoup de temps** he hasn't a lot of *ou* much time ▸ **il n'en a pas beaucoup** he doesn't have much *ou* a lot (of it) ▸ **il est pour beaucoup dans son succès** he played a large part in *ou* he had a great deal to do with her success
3. *(modifiant un verbe)* a lot ▸ **il boit beaucoup** he drinks a lot ▸ **c'est beaucoup dire** that's saying a lot ▸ **je vous remercie beaucoup** thank you very much (indeed)
4. *(modifiant un adjectif comparatif)* much, a lot ▸ **c'est beaucoup mieux** it's much *ou* a lot better ▸ **beaucoup trop vite** much too quickly.
■ **pron inv** many ▸ **nous sommes beaucoup à penser que...** many of us think that...
◆ ***de beaucoup*** **loc adv** by far ▸ **elle est de beaucoup la plus douée** she's the most talented by far, she is by far the most talented ▸ **je la préfère, et de beaucoup** I much prefer her.

beauf [bof] **nm 1.** *péj archetypal lower-middle-class French man* **2.** *fam* [beau-frère] brother-in-law.

beau-fils [bofis] (pl **beaux-fils**) **nm 1.** [gendre] son-in-law **2.** [de remariage] stepson.

beau-frère [bofrɛr] (pl **beaux-frères**) **nm** brother-in-law.

beaujolais [boʒɔlɛ] **nm** beaujolais (wine).

Beaujolais [boʒɔlɛ] **npr m : le Beaujolais** (the) Beaujolais (region).

beau-père [bopɛr] (pl **beaux-pères**) **nm 1.** [père du conjoint] father-in-law **2.** [de remariage] stepfather.

beauté [bote] **nf** beauty ▸ **de toute beauté** absolutely beautiful ▸ **en beauté** [magnifiquement] in great style / *sout* [femme] ravishing ▸ **être en beauté** to look stunning
▸▸ **finir en beauté** to end with a flourish *ou* on a high note ▸ **pour la beauté du geste** for the beauty of it.
◆ ***beautés*** **nfpl** [d'un paysage] beauties, beauty spots / [d'une œuvre] beauties.

beaux-arts [bozar] **nmpl** fine art *(U)*.
◆ ***Beaux-Arts*** **nmpl : les Beaux-Arts** *French national art school.*

beaux-parents [boparɑ̃] **nmpl 1.** [de l'homme] husband's parents, in-laws **2.** [de la femme] wife's parents, in-laws.

bébé [bebe] ■ **nm** baby ▸ **bébé phoque** seal pup, baby seal.
■ **adj inv** babyish.

bébé-bulle [bebebyl] (pl **bébés-bulles**) **nm** bubble baby.

bébé-éprouvette [bebeepruvɛt] (pl **bébés-éprouvette**) **nm** test-tube baby.

bébête [bebɛt] **adj** silly.

bec [bɛk] **nm 1.** [d'oiseau] beak ▸ **donner des coups de bec à** to peck (at)
2. [d'instrument de musique] mouthpiece

3. [de casserole] lip ▸ **bec à gaz** gas burner ▸ **bec de gaz** [réverbère] gaslamp *(in street)* ▸ **bec verseur** spout
4. *fam* [bouche] mouth ▸ **avoir toujours la cigarette/pipe au bec** to have a cigarette/pipe always stuck in one's mouth ▸ **être** *ou* **rester le bec dans l'eau** to be left high and dry ▸ **ouvrir le bec** to open one's mouth ▸ **clouer le bec à qqn** to shut sb up ▸ **bec fin** gourmet
▸▸ **avoir bec et ongles** to be well-equipped and ready to fight ▸ **tomber sur un bec** to run into *ou* to hit a snag.

bécane [bekan] **nf** *fam* **1.** [moto, vélo] bike **2.** [machine, ordinateur] machine.

bécasse [bekas] **nf 1.** [oiseau] woodcock **2.** *fam* [femme sotte] silly goose.

bécassine [bekasin] **nf 1.** [oiseau] snipe **2.** *fam* [jeune fille naïve] silly little goose.

bec-de-lièvre [bɛkdəljɛvr] (pl **becs-de-lièvre**) **nm** harelip.

béchamel [beʃamɛl] **nf : (sauce) béchamel** béchamel sauce.

bêche [bɛʃ] **nf** spade.

bêcher [4] [beʃe] **vt** to dig.

bêcheur, ***euse*** [beʃœr, øz] **nm, f** *fam* stuck-up person.

bécoter [3] [bekɔte] **vt** *fam* to snog *UK ou* smooch with.
◆ ***se bécoter*** **vp** to snog *UK*, to smooch.

becquée [beke] **nf : donner la becquée à** to feed.

becqueter, ***béqueter*** [27] [bɛkte] **vt** to peck at.

becter [4] [bɛkte] **vi** *fam* to eat.

bedaine [bədɛn] **nf** potbelly.

bédé = ***BD***.

bedeau, ***x*** [bədo] **nm** verger.

bedonnant, ***e*** [bədɔnɑ̃, ɑ̃t] **adj** potbellied.

bédouin, ***e*** [bedwɛ̃, in] **adj** Bedouin.
◆ ***Bédouin***, ***e*** **nm, f** Bedouin.

bée [be] **adj : bouche bée** open-mouthed.

bégaiement [begɛmɑ̃] **nm** stammering.

bégayer [11] [begeje] ■ **vi** to have a stutter *ou* stammer.
■ **vt** to stammer (out).

bégonia [begɔnja] **nm** begonia.

bègue [bɛg] ■ **adj : être bègue** to have a stutter *ou* stammer.
■ **nmf** stutterer, stammerer.

bégueule [begœl] *fam péj* ■ **adj** prudish.
■ **nf** prude.

béguin [begɛ̃] **nm** *fam* **: avoir le béguin pour qqn** to have a crush on sb ▸ **avoir le béguin pour qqch** to be mad keen on sthg.

beige [bɛʒ] **adj & nm** beige.

beigne [bɛɲ] **nf** *fam* slap.

beignet [bɛɲɛ] **nm** fritter.

bel [bɛl] ➤ ***beau***.

bêler [4] [bele] **vi** to bleat.

belette [bəlɛt] **nf** weasel.

belge [bɛlʒ] **adj** Belgian.
◆ ***Belge*** **nmf** Belgian.

belgicisme [bɛlʒisism] **nm** [mot] Belgian word / [tournure] Belgian expression.

CULTURE

Belgicisme

Belgium's **Conseil supérieur de la langue française**, formed in 1985, provides guidance on the usage and diffusion of the French language. The Council's 41 members issue formal opinions, conduct sociolinguistic research, and work to promote the language among the general public, government authorities and other groups. The Council collaborates with similar bodies in France, Switzerland and Quebec.

Belgique [bɛlʒik] **nf : la Belgique** Belgium.

Belgrade [bɛlgrad] **npr** Belgrade.

bélier [belje] **nm 1.** [animal] ram **2.** [poutre] battering ram.
◆ ***Bélier*** **nm** ASTROL Aries ▸ **être Bélier** to be (an) Aries.

Belize [beliz] **npr m : le Belize** Belize ▸ **au Belize** in Belize.

belladone [beladɔn] **nf** deadly nightshade.

bellâtre [bɛlatr] **nm** *péj* smoothie.

belle [bɛl] **adj & nf** ➤ ***beau***.

belle-famille [bɛlfamij] (pl **belles-familles**) **nf 1.** [de l'homme] husband's family, in-laws *pl* **2.** [de la femme] wife's family, in-laws *pl*.

belle-fille [bɛlfij] (pl **belles-filles**) **nf 1.** [épouse du fils] daughter-in-law **2.** [de remariage] stepdaughter.

belle-mère [bɛlmɛr] (pl **belles-mères**) **nf 1.** [mère du conjoint] mother-in-law **2.** [de remariage] stepmother.

belles-lettres [bɛllɛtr] **nfpl** (great) literature *(U)*.

belle-sœur [bɛlsœr] (pl **belles-sœurs**) **nf** sister-in-law.

belligérant, ***e*** [beliʒerɑ̃, ɑ̃t] **adj & nm, f** belligerent.

belliqueux, ***euse*** [belikø, øz] **adj** [peuple] warlike / [humeur, tempérament] aggressive.

belote [bəlɔt] **nf** *French card game*.

belvédère [bɛlvedɛr] **nm 1.** [construction] belvedere **2.** [terrasse] viewpoint.

bémol [bemɔl] **adj & nm** MUS flat.

bénédictin, ***e*** [benediktɛ̃, in] ■ **adj** Benedictine.
■ **nm, f** Benedictine ▸ **travail de bénédictin** *fig* painstaking task.
◆ ***Bénédictine*** **nf** [liqueur] Benedictine.

bénédiction [benediksjɔ̃] **nf** blessing ▸ **donner sa bénédiction à** *fig* to give one's blessing to.

bénéfice [benefis] **nm 1.** [avantage] advantage, benefit ▸ **au bénéfice de** in aid of ▸ **accorder à qqn le bénéfice du doute** to give sb the benefit of the doubt ▸ **c'est tout bénéfice** *fam* **: à ce prix-là, c'est tout bénéfice** at that price, you make a 100% profit on it ▸ **sous bénéfice d'inventaire** *without liability to debts beyond inherited assets*

▸ **tirer (un) bénéfice de qqch** to derive some benefit *ou* an advantage from sthg ▸ **c'est le bénéfice que l'on peut tirer de cette conduite** that's the reward for such behaviour **2.** [profit] profit ▸ **bénéfices de fin d'exercice** year-end profits ▸ **bénéfice imposable** taxable profit ▸ **bénéfice net/brut** net/gross profit ▸ **faire *ou* enregistrer un bénéfice brut/net de 5 000 euros** to gross/to net 5,000 euros ▸ **bénéfices réinvestis** ploughback *(U) UK*, plowback *(U) US* ▸ **intéressement aux bénéfices** profit-sharing ▸ **rapport cours-bénéfice** price-earnings ratio ▸ **bénéfices commerciaux** trading profit *sg*.

bénéficiaire [benefisjɛr] ■ **nmf** [gén] beneficiary / [de chèque] payee.
■ **adj** [marge] profit *(avant n)* / [résultat, société] profit-making.

bénéficier [9] [benefisje] **vi : bénéficier de** [profiter de] to benefit from / [jouir de] to have, to enjoy / [obtenir] to have, to get ▸ **bénéficier de circonstances atténuantes** to have the benefit of *ou* to be granted extenuating circumstances ▸ **bénéficier d'une forte remise** to get a big reduction.

bénéfique [benefik] **adj** beneficial.

Bénélux, Benelux [benelyks] **nm : le Bénélux** Benelux ▸ **les pays du Bénélux** the Benelux countries.

benêt [bənɛ] ■ **nm** clod.
■ **adj** *(seulement masculin)* silly, simple.

bénévolat [benevɔla] **nm** voluntary work.

bénévole [benevɔl] ■ **adj** voluntary.
■ **nmf** volunteer, voluntary worker.

bénévolement [benevɔlmɑ̃] **adv** voluntarily, for nothing.

Bengale [bɛ̃gal] **nm : le Bengale** Bengal ▸ **au Bengale** in Bengal.

bénin, igne [benɛ̃, iɲ] **adj** [maladie, accident] minor ▸ **une forme bénigne de rougeole** a mild form of measles / [cancer] benign ▸ **une tumeur bénigne** benign tumour.

Bénin [benɛ̃] **nm : le Bénin** Benin ▸ **au Bénin** in Benin.

béninois, e [beninwa, waz] **adj** Beninese.
◆ ***Béninois, e*** **nm, f** Beninese *(inv)*.

bénir [32] [benir] **vt 1.** [gén] to bless **2.** [se réjouir de] to thank God for.

bénit, e [beni, it] **adj** consecrated ▸ **eau bénite** holy water.

bénitier [benitje] **nm** holy water font.

benjamin, e [bɛ̃ʒamɛ̃, in] **nm, f** [de famille] youngest child / [de groupe] youngest member.

benne [bɛn] **nf 1.** [de camion] tipper **2.** [de téléphérique] car **3.** [pour déchets] skip *UK*, Dumpster® *US*.

benzine [bɛ̃zin] **nf** benzine.

béotien, enne [beɔsjɛ̃, ɛn] **nm, f** philistine.

BEP, Bep (abr de ***brevet d'études professionnelles***) **nm** *school-leaver's diploma (taken at age 18)*.

BEPC, Bepc (abr de ***brevet d'études du premier cycle***) **nm** *former school certificate (taken at age 16)*.

béqueter = **becqueter**.

béquille [bekij] **nf 1.** [pour marcher] crutch **2.** [d'un deux-roues] stand.

berbère [bɛrbɛr] **adj & nm** Berber.
◆ ***Berbère*** **nmf** Berber.

bercail [bɛrkaj] **nm** fold ▸ **rentrer au bercail** *fig* to return to the fold.

berceau, x [bɛrso] **nm** cradle.

bercer [16] [bɛrse] **vt 1.** [bébé, bateau] to rock ▸ **son enfance a été bercée de cette musique** he was brought up on this kind of music **2.** *fig* [tromper] **: bercer qqn de** to delude sb with.
◆ ***se bercer*** **vp** *fig* **: se bercer de** to delude o.s. with ▸ **se bercer d'illusions** to delude o.s.

berceuse [bɛrsøz] **nf 1.** [chanson] lullaby **2.** *Québec* [fauteuil] rocking chair.

Bercy [bɛrsi] **npr 1.** [ministère] *the French Ministry of Finance* **2.** [stade] *large sports and concert hall in Paris*.

BERD, Berd [bɛrd] (abr de ***Banque européenne pour la reconstruction et le développement***) **nf** EBRD.

béret [berɛ] **nm** beret ▸ **béret basque** (French) beret.

bergamote [bɛrgamɔt] **nf** bergamot orange.

berge [bɛrʒ] **nf 1.** [bord] bank **2.** *fam* [an] **: il a plus de 50 berges** he's over 50.

berger, ère [bɛrʒe, ɛr] **nm, f** shepherd (f shepherdess).
◆ ***bergère*** **nf** [canapé] wing chair.
◆ ***berger allemand*** **nm** German shepherd, Alsatian *UK*.

bergerie [bɛrʒəri] **nf** sheepfold.

bergeronnette [bɛrʒərɔnɛt] **nf** wagtail.

berk [bɛrk] **interj** *fam* ugh, yuk.

Berlin [bɛrlɛ̃] **npr** Berlin ▸ **Berlin-Est** East Berlin ▸ **Berlin-Ouest** West Berlin ▸ **le mur de Berlin** the Berlin Wall.

berline [bɛrlin] **nf** saloon (car) *UK*, sedan *US*.

berlingot [bɛrlɛ̃go] **nm 1.** [de lait] carton **2.** [bonbon] boiled sweet.

berlue [bɛrly] **nf : j'ai la berlue!** I must be seeing things!

bermuda [bɛrmyda] **nm** bermuda shorts *pl*.

Bermudes [bɛrmyd] **nfpl : les Bermudes** Bermuda *sg* ▸ **aux Bermudes** in Bermuda ▸ **le triangle des Bermudes** the Bermuda Triangle.

bernard-l'ermite [bɛrnarlɛrmit] **nm inv** hermit crab.

berne [bɛrn] **nf : en berne** ≃ at half-mast ▸ **mettre les drapeaux en berne** to fly the flags at half-mast.

berner [3] [bɛrne] **vt** to fool.

berrichon, onne [beriʃɔ̃, ɔn] **adj** of/from the Berry.
◆ ***Berrichon, onne*** **nm, f** person from the Berry.

besace [bəzas] **nf** pouch.

bésicles, besicles [bezikl] **nfpl** *hum* specs.

besogne [bəzɔɲ] **nf** job, work *(U)* ▸ **aller vite en besogne** *fig* to be a fast worker ▸ **se mettre à la besogne** to get down to work.

besoin [bəzwɛ̃] **nm** need ▸ **avoir besoin de qqch/de faire qqch** to need sthg/to do sthg ▸ **au besoin** if necessary, if need *ou* needs be ▸ **être dans le besoin** to be in need.
◆ ***besoins*** **nmpl** [exigences] needs
▸▸ **faire ses besoins** to relieve o.s. ▸ **pour les besoins de la cause** for the purpose in hand.

bestiaire [bɛstjɛr] **nm** [recueil] bestiary.

bestial**, e, **aux [bɛstjal, o] **adj** bestial, brutish.

bestiole [bɛstjɔl] **nf** (little) creature.

best-seller [bɛstselɛr] (pl **best-sellers**) **nm** best-seller.

bétail [betaj] **nm** cattle *pl* ▸ **vingt têtes de bétail** twenty head of cattle.

bête [bɛt] ■ **nf** [animal] animal / [insecte] insect ▸ **bête à bon Dieu** ladybird *UK*, ladybug *US* ▸ **bête féroce** wild animal ▸ **bête de somme** beast of burden
▸▸ **bête à concours** *fam* swot *UK ou* grind *US (who does well at competitive exams)* ▸ **chercher la petite bête** to nitpick ▸ **c'est sa bête noire** that's his/her pet hate ▸ **ils nous regardaient comme des bêtes curieuses** they were staring at us as if we'd come from Mars ▸ **travailler comme une bête** to work like a slave *ou* dog.
■ **adj 1.** [stupide] stupid ▸ **être bête comme ses pieds** to be as thick as two short planks *UK*,to be as dumb as the day is long *US* ▸ **il est plus bête que méchant** he's not wicked, just (plain) stupid **2.** [simple] **: c'est tout bête** there's nothing to it ▸ **c'est tout bête, il suffisait d'y penser!** it's so simple, we should have thought of it before! **3.** [regrettable] **: c'est bête de ne pas y avoir pensé** it's silly *ou* stupid not to have thought of it.

bêtement [bɛtmɑ̃] **adv 1.** [de façon bête] stupidly **2.** [simplement] **: tout bêtement** just, quite simply.

***bêtifiant**, e* [betifjɑ̃, ɑ̃t] **adj** idiotic.

bêtise [betiz] **nf 1.** [stupidité] stupidity **2.** [action, remarque] stupid thing ▸ **faire/dire une bêtise** to do/say something stupid ▸ **faire des bêtises** to be stupid *ou* silly.

bêtisier [betizje] **nm** collection of howlers ▸ **le bêtisier de la semaine** PRESSE gaffes of the week.

béton [betɔ̃] **nm 1.** [matériau] concrete ▸ **béton armé** reinforced concrete ▸ **béton précontraint** prestressed concrete **2.** *fig* **: en béton** [argument] cast-iron.

bétonner [3] [betɔne] ■ **vt** to concrete.
■ **vi** FOOTBALL to play defensively.

bétonnière [betɔnjɛr] **nf** cement mixer.

bette [bɛt], ***blette*** [blɛt] **nf** Swiss chard.

betterave [betrav] **nf** beetroot *UK*, beet *US* ▸ **betterave fourragère** mangel-wurzel ▸ **betterave sucrière** *ou* **à sucre** sugar beet.

beuglement [bøgləmɑ̃] **nm 1.** [de bovin] mooing *(U)*, lowing *(U)* **2.** [de radio] blaring *(U)*.

beugler [5] [bøgle] **vi 1.** [bovin] to moo, to low **2.** *fam* [personne] to bellow / [radio] to blare out.

beur [bœr] **nmf** *person born in France of North African immigrant parents.*

beurk [bœrk] *fam* = ***berk***.

beurre [bœr] **nm** [aliment] butter ▸ **beurre de cacahuètes** peanut butter ▸ **beurre de cacao** cocoa butter ▸ **beurre demi-sel** slightly-salted butter ▸ **beurre noir** brown butter sauce
▸▸ **compter pour du beurre** to count for nothing ▸ **faire son beurre** to make one's pile ▸ **mettre du beurre dans les épinards** to make life a little more comfortable.

***beurré**, e* [bœre] **adj 1.** [couvert de beurre] buttered **2.** *fam* [ivre] plastered.

beurrer [5] [bœre] **vt** to butter.

beurrier**, **ère [bœrje, ɛr] **adj** [industrie] butter *(avant n)* / [région] butter-producing.

beurrier [bœrje] **nm** butter dish.

beuverie [bœvri] **nf** drinking session.

bévue [bevy] **nf** blunder ▸ **faire** *ou* **commettre une bévue** to slip up.

Beyrouth [berut] **npr** Beirut ▸ **Beyrouth-Est** East Beirut ▸ **Beyrouth-Ouest** West Beirut.

BHV (abr de ***Bazar de l'Hôtel de Ville***) **nm** *large department store in central Paris.*

biais [bjɛ] **nm 1.** [ligne oblique] slant ▸ **en** *ou* **de biais** [de travers] at an angle / *fig* indirectly ▸ **regarder qqn en** *ou* **de biais** to give sb a sidelong glance ▸ **traverser la rue en biais** to cross the street diagonally **2.** COUT bias ▸ **tailler un tissu dans le biais** to cut a piece of cloth on the bias **3.** [aspect] angle ▸ **je ne sais pas par quel biais le prendre** I don't know how *ou* from what angle to approach him **4.** [moyen détourné] expedient ▸ **par le biais de** by means of **5.** [dans des statistiques] bias.

biaiser [4] [bjeze] **vi** *fig* to dodge the issue.

bibande [bibɑ̃d] **adj** dual-band.

bibelot [biblo] **nm** trinket, curio.

biberon [bibrɔ̃] **nm** baby's bottle ▸ **nourrir au biberon** to bottle-feed.

bible [bibl] **nf** bible.

bibliobus [biblijɔbys] **nm** mobile library.

bibliographie [biblijɔgrafi] **nf** bibliography.

bibliographique [biblijɔgrafik] **adj** bibliographical.

bibliophile [biblijɔfil] **nmf** book lover.

bibliothécaire [biblijɔtekɛr] **nmf** librarian.

bibliothèque [biblijɔtɛk] **nf** **1.** [meuble] bookcase **2.** [édifice, collection] library ▸ **bibliothèque municipale** public library ▸ **la Bibliothèque nationale de France** *the French national library*.

CULTURE

La Bibliothèque nationale de France

The **Bibliothèque nationale** and the **Bibliothèque de France** (also called **Bibliothèque François Mitterrand**), both in Paris, are the centrepieces of the French library system. The **BN** is home to an extensive collection of manuscripts, etchings, photographs, maps, medals and coins. The **BDF**, opened in 1996, holds 10 million printed volumes and offers audiovisual materials. Mitterrand pushed for its construction to alleviate a lack of space at the BN. Its four ultramodern towers are constructed to resemble open books and have been the object of some controversy: the towers are made of glass and steel, so that the collection is exposed to the sun. The BDF is also the world's largest virtual library, with 50,000 works accessible online.

biblique [biblik] **adj** biblical.

Bic® [bik] **nm** ball-point pen.

bicarbonate [bikarbɔnat] **nm : bicarbonate (de soude)** bicarbonate of soda.

bicentenaire [bisɑ̃tnɛr] ■ **adj** two-hundred-year-old *(avant n)*.
■ **nm** bicentenary *UK*, bicentennial *US*.

biceps [bisɛps] **nm** biceps.

biche [biʃ] **nf** ZOOL hind, doe.

bichonner [3] [biʃɔne] **vt** [choyer] to cosset, to pamper.
◆ ***se bichonner*** **vp** to spruce o.s. up / [femme] to doll o.s. up.

bicolore [bikɔlɔr] **adj** two-coloured *UK*, two-colored *US*.

bicoque [bikɔk] **nf** *péj* house.

bicorne [bikɔrn] **nm** cocked hat.

bicyclette [bisiklɛt] **nf** bicycle ▸ **rouler à bicyclette** to cycle.

bidasse [bidas] **nm** *fam* squaddie *UK*, grunt *US*.

bide [bid] **nm** *fam* **1.** [ventre] belly **2.** [échec] flop.

bidet [bidɛ] **nm** **1.** [sanitaire] bidet **2.** *hum* [cheval] nag.

bidon [bidɔ̃] ■ **adj inv** *fam* [faux] phony, phoney *UK*.
■ **nm** **1.** [récipient] can **2.** *fam* [ventre] belly **3.** *fam* [simulation] **: c'est du bidon** it's (a load of) rubbish.

bidonner [3] [bidɔne] ◆ ***se bidonner*** **vp** *fam* to laugh one's head off.

bidonville [bidɔ̃vil] **nm** shantytown.

bidouiller [3] [biduje] **vt** [serrure, logiciel] to fiddle around with, to tamper with / [appareil] to fix.

bidouilleur [bidujœr] **nm** INFORM do-it-yourselfer.

bidule [bidyl] **nm** *fam* thing, thingy.

bielle [bjɛl] **nf** connecting rod.

biélorusse [bjelɔrys] **adj** Belorussian, Byelorussian.
◆ ***Biélorusse*** **nmf** Belorussian, Byelorussian.

Biélorussie [bjelɔrysi] **nf : la Biélorussie** Belorussia, Byelorussia.

bien [bjɛ̃] ■ **adj inv** (**mieux** *est le comparatif et le superlatif de* **bien**) **1.** [satisfaisant] good ▸ **il est bien comme prof** he's a good teacher ▸ **il est bien, ce bureau** this is a good office ▸ **c'est bien de s'amuser mais il faut aussi travailler** it's all right to have fun but you have to work too
2. [en bonne santé] well ▸ **je ne me sens pas bien** I don't feel well
3. [joli] good-looking ▸ **tu ne trouves pas qu'elle est bien comme ça?** don't you think she looks good *ou* nice like that? ▸ **tu es très bien en jupe** [cela te sied] you look very nice in a skirt / [c'est acceptable pour l'occasion] a skirt is perfectly all right ▸ **il est bien de sa personne** he's a good-looking man
4. [à l'aise] comfortable ▸ **on est bien ici** it's nice here
5. [convenable] respectable ▸ **ce n'est pas bien de tirer la langue** it's naughty *ou* it's not nice to stick out your tongue.
■ **nm** **1.** [sens moral] **: le bien** good ▸ **le bien et le mal** good and evil
2. [intérêt] good ▸ **je te dis ça pour ton bien** I'm telling you this for your own good ▸ **pour le bien public** in the public interest ▸ **grand bien te/lui fasse!** *iron* much good may it do you/him!
3. [richesse, propriété] property, possession ▸ **avoir du bien au soleil** *fam* to be well-off *ou* rich
▸▸ **faire du bien à qqn** to do sb good ▸ **dire du bien de qqn/qqch** to speak well of sb/sthg ▸ **mener à bien** to bring to fruition, to complete ▸ **en tout bien tout honneur** with the best of intentions.
■ **adv** **1.** [de manière satisfaisante] well ▸ **aller** *ou* **se porter bien** to feel well *ou* fine ▸ **on mange bien ici** the food's good here ▸ **il ne s'est pas bien conduit** he didn't behave well ▸ **tu as bien fait** you did the right thing ▸ **tu ferais bien d'y aller** you would be wise to go ▸ **tu tombes bien!** you've come at (just) the right time! ▸ **c'est bien fait!** it serves him/her *etc* right!
2. [avec soin] **: écoute-moi bien** listen (to me) carefully ▸ **as-tu bien vérifié?** did you check properly? ▸ **fais bien ce que l'on te dit** do exactly *ou* just as you're told ▸ **mélangez bien** stir well ▸ **soigne-toi bien** take good care of yourself
3. [sens intensif] quite, really ▸ **bien souvent** quite often ▸ **en es-tu bien sûr?** are you quite sure (about it)? ▸ **j'espère bien que...** I do hope that... ▸ **on a bien ri** we had a good laugh ▸ **il y a bien trois heures que j'attends** I've been waiting for at least three hours ▸ **c'est bien aimable à vous** it's very kind *ou* good of you
4. [renforçant un comparatif] **: il est parti bien plus tard** he left much later ▸ **on était bien moins riches** we were a lot worse off *ou* poorer
5. [servant à conclure ou à introduire] **: bien, c'est fini pour aujourd'hui** well, that's it for today ▸ **bien, je t'écoute** well, I'm listening ▸ **très bien, je vais avec toi** all right then, I'll go with you
6. [en effet] **: c'est bien lui** it really is him ▸ **c'est bien ce que je disais** that's just what I said
7. [dans la correspondance] **: bien à toi** love ▸ **bien à vous** yours.

■ interj : **eh bien!** oh well! ▸ **eh bien, qu'en penses-tu?** well, what do you think? ▸ **je n'irai pas! – bien, n'en parlons plus!** I won't go! – very well *ou* all right (then), let's drop the subject!
◆ ***biens*** **nmpl** property *(U)* ▸ **tous mes biens** all my worldly goods, all I'm worth ▸ **biens (de consommation) durables** durable goods, durables ▸ **biens de consommation** consumer goods ▸ **biens d'équipement** capital equipment *ou* goods ▸ **biens sociaux** corporate assets.
◆ ***bien de, bien des*** **loc adj : bien des gens sont venus** quite a lot of people came ▸ **bien des fois** many times ▸ **il a bien de la chance** he's very *ou* really lucky ▸ **il a eu bien de la peine à me convaincre** he had quite a lot of trouble convincing me.
◆ ***bien entendu*** **loc adv** of course.
◆ ***bien entendu que*** **loc conj** of course ▸ **bien entendu que j'aimerais y aller** of course I'd like to go.
◆ ***bien que*** **loc conj** *(+ subjonctif)* although, though ▸ **bien que malade, il a tenu à y aller** although he was ill, he insisted on going.
◆ ***bien sûr*** **loc adv** of course, certainly.
◆ ***bien sûr que*** **loc conj** of course ▸ **bien sûr qu'elle n'avait rien compris!** of course she hadn't understood a thing!

bien-aimé**, **e [bjɛ̃neme] (**mpl bien-aimés**, **fpl bien-aimées**) **adj & nm, f** beloved.

bien-être [bjɛ̃nɛtr] **nm inv 1.** [physique] wellbeing **2.** [matériel] wellbeing, comfort.

bienfaisance [bjɛ̃fəzɑ̃s] **nf** charity.

bienfaisant**, **e [bjɛ̃fəzɑ̃, ɑ̃t] **adj** beneficial.

bienfait [bjɛ̃fɛ] **nm 1.** [effet bénéfique] benefit **2.** [faveur] kindness.

bienfaiteur**, **trice [bjɛ̃fɛtœr, tris] **nm, f** benefactor.

bien-fondé [bjɛ̃fɔ̃de] (**pl bien-fondés**) **nm** validity.

bienheureux**, **euse [bjɛ̃nørø, øz] **adj 1.** RELIG blessed **2.** [heureux] happy.

biennal**, **e**, **aux [bjenal, o] **adj** biennial.
◆ ***biennale*** **nf** biennial festival.

bien-pensant**, **e [bjɛ̃pɑ̃sɑ̃, ɑ̃t] (**mpl bien-pensants**, **fpl bien-pensantes**) **adj & nm, f** *péj* conformist.

bienséance [bjɛ̃seɑ̃s] **nf** decorum.
◆ ***bienséances*** **nfpl** conventions.

bientôt [bjɛ̃to] **adv** soon ▸ **à bientôt!** see you soon!

bienveillance [bjɛ̃vejɑ̃s] **nf** kindness.

bienveillant**, **e [bjɛ̃vejɑ̃, ɑ̃t] **adj** kindly.

bienvenu**, **e [bjɛ̃vny] ■ **adj** [qui arrive à propos] welcome.
■ **nm, f : être le bienvenu/la bienvenue** to be welcome ▸ **soyez le bienvenu!** welcome!
◆ ***bienvenue*** **nf** welcome ▸ **souhaiter la bienvenue à qqn** to welcome sb.

bière [bjɛr] **nf 1.** [boisson] beer ▸ **bière blonde** lager ▸ **bière brune** brown ale ▸ **bière pression** draught *UK ou* draft *US* beer **2.** [cercueil] coffin ▸ **mettre quelqu'un en bière** to put someone in his/her coffin.

biffer [3] [bife] **vt** *sout* to cross out.

bifidus [bifidys] **nm** bifidus ▸ **yaourt au bifidus** bio *ou* bifidus yoghurt.

bifteck [biftɛk] **nm** steak ▸ **du bifteck haché** (best) mince *UK*, lean ground beef *US*.

bifurcation [bifyrkasjɔ̃] **nf** [embranchement] fork / *fig* new direction.

bifurquer [3] [bifyrke] **vi 1.** [route, voie ferrée] to fork **2.** [voiture] to turn off **3.** *fig* [personne] to branch off.

bigame [bigam] ■ **adj** bigamous.
■ **nmf** bigamist.

bigamie [bigami] **nf** bigamy.

bigarré**, **e [bigare] **adj** [vêtement, fleur] variegated, multicoloured *UK*, multicolored *US* / [foule] colourful *UK*, colorful *US*.

bigarreau**, **x [bigaro] **nm** cherry.

bigophone [bigɔfɔn] **nm** *fam vieilli* [téléphone] blower *UK*, horn *US*.

bigorneau**, **x [bigɔrno] **nm** winkle.

bigot**, **e [bigo, ɔt] *péj* ■ **adj** bigoted.
■ **nm, f** bigot.

bigoudi [bigudi] **nm** curler.

bigrement [bigrəmɑ̃] **adv** *fam vieilli* [beaucoup] a lot / [très] very.

bijou**, **x [biʒu] **nm 1.** [joyau] jewel **2.** *fig* [chef-d'œuvre] gem.

bijouterie [biʒutri] **nf 1.** [magasin] jeweller's *UK ou* jeweler's *US* (shop) **2.** [activité] jewellery-making *UK*, jewelry-making *US* **3.** [commerce] jewellery *UK ou* jewelry *US* trade.

bijoutier**, **ère [biʒutje, ɛr] **nm, f** jeweller *UK*, jeweler *US*.

Bikini® [bikini] **nm** bikini.

bilan [bilɑ̃] **nm 1.** FIN balance sheet ▸ **bilan de l'exercice** end-of-year balance sheet ▸ **déposer son bilan** to declare bankruptcy **2.** [état d'une situation] state of affairs ▸ **faire le bilan (de)** to take stock (of) ▸ **bilan de santé** checkup.

bilatéral**, **e**, **aux [bilateral, o] **adj 1.** [stationnement] on both sides (of the road) **2.** [contrat, accord] bilateral.

bile [bil] **nf** bile ▸ **déverser sa bile** to vent one's spleen ▸ **se faire de la bile** *fam* to worry.

biliaire [biljɛr] **adj** biliary ▸ **calcul biliaire** gallstone ▸ **vésicule biliaire** gall bladder.

bilieux**, **euse [biljø, øz] **adj 1.** [teint] bilious **2.** [tempérament] irascible.

bilingue [bilɛ̃g] ■ **adj** bilingual.
■ **nmf** [personne] bilingual person.
■ **nm** [dictionnaire] bilingual dictionary.

bilinguisme [bilɛ̃gɥism] **nm** bilingualism.

billard [bijar] **nm 1.** [jeu] billiards *(U)* **2.** [table de jeu] billiard table
▸▸ **passer *ou* monter sur le billard** *fam* to go under the knife.

bille [bij] **nf 1.** [d'enfant] marble **2.** [de billard] ball **3.** *fam* [tête] face **4.** [de bois] block of wood.

billet [bijɛ] **nm 1.** [lettre] note ▸ **billet doux** love letter **2.** [argent] : **billet (de banque)** (bank) note, bill *US* ▸ **un billet de 100 euros** a 100-euro note ▸ **billet à ordre**

promissory note, note of hand ▸ **billet au porteur** bearer bill ▸ **faux billet** forged bank note ▸ **le billet vert** the dollar **3.** [ticket] ticket ▸ **billet aller *ou* simple** single (ticket) *UK*, one-way ticket *US* ▸ **billet aller-retour** return (ticket) *UK*, round-trip ticket *US* ▸ **billet de train/d'avion** train/plane ticket ▸ **voyageurs munis de billets** ticket holders ▸ **billet de loterie** lottery ticket.

billetterie [bijɛtri] **nf 1.** [à l'aéroport] ticket desk / [à la gare] booking office *ou* hall **2.** [bureau, service] ticket office **3.** BANQUE ATM, cash dispenser *UK*.

billion [biljɔ̃] **nm** billion *UK*, trillion *US*.

bimensuel, elle [bimɑ̃sɥɛl] **adj** fortnightly *UK*, twice monthly.
◆ ***bimensuel*** **nm** fortnightly review *UK*, semimonthly *US*.

bimestriel, elle [bimɛstrijɛl] **adj** two-monthly.

bi-monétaire [bimɔnetɛr] **adj** [système] dual-currency.

bimoteur [bimɔtœr] ■ **adj** twin-engined.
■ **nm** twin-engined plane.

binaire [binɛr] **adj** binary.

biner [3] [bine] **vt** to hoe.

biniou [binju] **nm** (Breton) bagpipes *pl*.

binocle [binɔkl] **nm** pince-nez.
◆ ***binocles*** **nmpl** *fam vieilli* specs.

binôme [binom] **nm** binomial.

bio [bjo] **adj inv** organic ▸ **aliments bio** organic food.

biocarburant [bjɔkarbyrɑ̃] **nm** biofuel.

biochimie [bjɔʃimi] **nf** biochemistry.

biodégradable [bjɔdegradabl] **adj** biodegradable.

biodiversité [bjɔdiversite] **nf** biodiversity.

bioéthique [bjɔetik] **nf** bioethics *(U)*.

biographie [bjɔgrafi] **nf** biography.

biographique [bjɔgrafik] **adj** biographical.

biologie [bjɔlɔʒi] **nf** biology.

biologique [bjɔlɔʒik] **adj 1.** [sciences] biological **2.** [naturel] organic.

biopsie [bjɔpsi] **nf** biopsy.

biorythme [bjɔritm] **nm** biorhythm.

biosphère [bjɔsfɛr] **nf** biosphere.

biotechnologie [bjɔtɛknɔlɔʒi] **nf** biotechnology.

bioterrorisme [bjɔtɛrorism] **nm** bioterrorism.

bip [bip] **nm 1.** [signal] tone, beep ▸ **parlez après le bip (sonore)** please speak after the beep *ou* tone **2.** [appareil] beeper, bleeper *UK*.

bipède [bipɛd] **nm & adj** biped.

biper [3] [bipe] **vt** to page.

bique [bik] **nf 1.** *fam* [chèvre] (nanny) goat **2.** *péj* [femme] **: vieille bique** old bag.

BIRD [bœrd] (abr de ***Banque internationale pour la reconstruction et le développement***) **nf** IBRD.

biréacteur [bireaktœr] **nm** twin-engined jet.

birman, e [birmɑ̃, an] **adj** Burmese.
◆ ***birman*** **nm** [langue] Burmese.
◆ ***Birman, e*** **nm, f** Burmese.

Birmanie [birmani] **nf : la Birmanie** Burma.

bis[1]***, e*** [bi, biz] **adj** greyish-brown *UK*, grayish-brown *US* ▸ **pain bis** brown bread.

bis[2] [bis] ■ **adv 1.** [dans adresse] **: 5 bis** 5a **2.** [à la fin d'un spectacle] encore.
■ **nm** encore.

bisannuel, elle [bizanɥɛl] **adj** biennial.

bisbille [bizbij] **nf** squabble, tiff ▸ **être en bisbille (avec)** to be on bad terms (with).

biscornu, e [biskɔrny] **adj 1.** [difforme] irregularly shaped **2.** [bizarre] weird.

biscotte [biskɔt] **nf** *toasted bread sold in packets and often eaten for breakfast.*

biscuit [biskɥi] **nm 1.** [sec] biscuit *UK*, cookie *US* / [salé] cracker **2.** [gâteau] sponge.

bise [biz] **nf 1.** [vent] north wind **2.** *fam* [baiser] kiss ▸ **grosses bises** love and kisses.

biseau, x [bizo] **nm** bevel ▸ **en biseau** bevelled *UK*, beveled *US*.

bisexuel, elle [bisɛksɥɛl] **adj** bisexual.

bison [bizɔ̃] **nm** bison.

bisou [bizu] **nm** *fam* kiss.

bisque [bisk] **nf** *thick soup, the ingredients of which have been pureed* ▸ **bisque de homard** lobster bisque.

bissextile [bisɛkstil] ➤ ***année***.

bistouri [bisturi] **nm** lancet.

bistrot, bistro [bistro] **nm** *fam* cafe, bar.

bit [bit] **nm** INFORM bit.

BIT (abr de ***Bureau international du travail***) **nm** ILO.

bit(t)e [bit] **nf** *vulg* cock.

bitume [bitym] **nm 1.** [revêtement] asphalt **2.** CHIM bitumen.

bivouac [bivwak] **nm** bivouac.

bivouaquer [3] [bivwake] **vi** to bivouac.

bizarre [bizar] **adj** strange, odd.

bizarrement [bizarmɑ̃] **adv** strangely, oddly.

bizarrerie [bizarri] **nf** strangeness.

bizutage [bizytaʒ] **nm** *practical jokes played on new arrivals in a school or college*, ≃ ragging *UK*, ≃ hazing *US*.

blabla, bla-bla [blabla] **nm inv** *fam* waffle *UK*.

blackbouler [3] [blakbule] **vt 1.** [à une élection] to blackball **2.** *fam* [à un examen] to fail.

black-out [blakawt] **nm** blackout.

blafard, e [blafar, ard] **adj** pale.

blague [blag] **nf 1.** [plaisanterie] joke ▸ **blague à part** joking apart ▸ **sans blague!** no!, really? ▸ **c'est une blague?** are you kidding? **2.** [sac] **: blague à tabac** tobacco pouch.

blaguer [3] [blage] *fam* **vi** to joke.

blagueur, euse [blagœr, øz] *fam* ■ **adj** jokey.
■ **nm, f** joker.

blaireau**, **x [blɛro] **nm 1.** [animal] badger **2.** [de rasage] shaving brush **3.** *fam péj* [homme] ≃ Essex man *UK*, ≃ Joe Sixpack *US* / [femme] ≃ Essex girl *UK*.

blairer [4] [blɛre] **vt** *fam* **: je ne peux pas la blairer** I can't stand her.

blâme [blam] **nm 1.** [désapprobation] disapproval **2.** [sanction] reprimand.

blâmer [3] [blame] **vt 1.** [désapprouver] to blame **2.** [sanctionner] to reprimand.

blanc**, **blanche [blɑ̃, blɑ̃ʃ] **adj 1.** [gén] white ▸ **avoir les cheveux blancs** to be white-haired *ou* snowy-haired *littéraire* **2.** [non écrit] blank ▸ **elle a remis (une) copie blanche** she handed in a blank sheet of paper ▸ **vote blanc** blank vote **3.** [pâle] pale ▸ **être blanc comme un cachet d'aspirine** *fam hum* [non bronzé] to be completely white ▸ **blanc comme un linge** white as a sheet **4.** [monotone] **: d'une voix blanche** in a monotone **5.** [examen] mock.

◆ ***blanc*** ■ **nm 1.** [couleur] white ▸ **blanc cassé** off-white ▸ **le blanc lui va bien** she looks good in white **2.** [personne] white (man) **3.** [linge de maison] **: le blanc** the (household) linen ▸ **faire une machine de blanc** to do a machine-load of whites **4.** [sur page] blank (space) **5.** [dans conversation] blank **6.** [de volaille] white meat **7.** [vin] white (wine) ▸ **blanc de blancs** *white wine from white grapes* ▸ **un blanc sec** a dry white wine **8.** [cornée] **: blanc de l'œil** white of the eye ▸ **regarder qqn dans le blanc des yeux** to look sb straight in the eye.

■ **adv : voter blanc** to return a blank vote.

◆ ***blanche*** **nf 1.** [personne] white (woman) ▸ **il a épousé une Blanche** he married a white woman **2.** MUS minim *UK*, half note *US*.

◆ ***blanc d'œuf*** **nm** egg white.

◆ ***à blanc*** ■ **loc adj** [cartouche] blank ▸ **une balle à blanc** a blank.

■ **loc adv 1.** [armement] **: tirer à blanc** to shoot *ou* fire blanks **2.** [à un point extrême] **: chauffer à blanc** to make white-hot.

◆ ***en blanc*** ■ **loc adj 1.** [chèque, procuration] blank ▸ **laisser une ligne/page en blanc** to leave a line/page blank **2.** [personne] **: une mariée en blanc** a bride wearing white.

■ **loc adv** [peindre, colorer] white / [s'habiller, sortir] in white.

blanc-bec [blɑ̃bɛk] (pl **blancs-becs**) **nm** *péj* & *vieilli* greenhorn.

blanchâtre [blɑ̃ʃatr] **adj** whitish.

blanche ➤ ***blanc.***

blancheur [blɑ̃ʃœr] **nf** whiteness.

blanchiment [blɑ̃ʃimɑ̃] **nm 1.** [décoloration] bleaching **2.** [coloration en blanc] whitewashing ▸ **blanchiment d'argent** *fig* money laundering.

blanchir [32] [blɑ̃ʃir] ■ **vt 1.** [mur] to whitewash **2.** [linge, argent] to launder ▸ **blanchir l'argent de la drogue** to launder money from drug trafficking **3.** [légumes] to blanch **4.** [sucre] to refine / [décolorer] to bleach ▸ **le temps a blanchi ses cheveux** time has turned his hair white **5.** *fig* [accusé] **: blanchir qqn de qqch** to clear sb of sthg.

■ **vi 1.** [d'émotion] **: blanchir (de)** to go white (with) **2.** [barbe, cheveux] **: elle a blanchi** her hair has turned white.

blanchissage [blɑ̃ʃisaʒ] **nm 1.** [de linge] laundering **2.** [de sucre] refining.

blanchisserie [blɑ̃ʃisri] **nf** laundry.

blanchisseur**, **euse [blɑ̃ʃisœr, øz] **nm, f** launderer, laundryman (f laundrywoman).

blanchon [blɑ̃ʃɔ̃] **nm** *Québec* whitecoat *(baby seal)*.

blanquette [blɑ̃kɛt] **nf 1.** CULIN *stew of veal, lamb or chicken served in a white sauce* ▸ **blanquette de veau** veal blanquette **2.** [vin] **: blanquette de Limoux** *sparkling wine from Limoux*.

blasé**, **e [blaze] ■ **adj** blasé.

■ **nm, f** blasé person.

blason [blazɔ̃] **nm** coat of arms.

blasphémateur**, **trice [blasfematœr, tris] ■ **adj** blasphemous.

■ **nm, f** blasphemer.

blasphématoire [blasfematwar] **adj** blasphemous.

blasphème [blasfɛm] **nm** blasphemy.

blasphémer [18] [blasfeme] **vt** & **vi** to blaspheme.

blatte [blat] **nf** cockroach.

blazer [blazɛr] **nm** blazer.

blé [ble] **nm 1.** [céréale] wheat, corn *UK* ▸ **blé en herbe** unripe wheat *ou* corn *UK* ▸ **blé noir** buckwheat ▸ **blond comme les blés** with corn-coloured hair **2.** *fam* [argent] dough.

bled [blɛd] **nm 1.** [brousse] *North African interior* **2.** *fam péj* [village isolé] godforsaken place.

blême [blɛm] **adj : blême (de)** pale (with).

blêmir [32] [blemir] **vi** to go *ou* turn pale.

blennorragie [blenɔraʒi] **nf** gonorrhoea *UK*, gonorrhea *US*.

blessant**, **e [blɛsɑ̃, ɑ̃t] **adj** hurtful.

blessé**, **e [blese] **nm, f** wounded *ou* injured person ▸ **un grand blessé** a badly wounded *ou* injured person.

blesser [4] [blese] **vt 1.** [physiquement - accidentellement] to injure, to hurt / [- par arme] to wound ▸ **ses chaussures lui blessent les pieds** his shoes make his feet sore **2.** [moralement] to hurt.

◆ ***se blesser*** **vp** to injure o.s., to hurt o.s. ▸ **elle s'est blessée au bras** she injured *ou* hurt her arm.

blessure [blesyr] **nf** *litt* & *fig* wound.

blet**, **blette [blɛ, blɛt] **adj** overripe.

blette = ***bette.***

bleu**, **e [blø] ■ **adj 1.** [couleur] blue ▸ **avoir les yeux bleus** to have blue eyes, to be blue-eyed ▸ **avoir une peur bleue** to have the fright of one's life, to be terrified ▸ **il a les lèvres bleues** his lips are blue ▸ **bleu de froid** blue with cold ▸ **bleu ciel** sky blue ▸ **bleu clair** light blue **2.** [viande] very rare.

■ **nm, f** *fam fam* [novice - généralement] newcomer / [- à l'armée] raw recruit / [- à l'université] fresher *UK*, freshman *US*.

◆ ***bleu*** **nm 1.** [couleur] blue ▸ **bleu foncé** dark blue ▸ **bleu marine** navy blue ▸ **bleu outremer** ultramarine ▸ **bleu pâle/pétrole/roi** pale/petrol/royal blue ▸ **admirer le bleu du ciel/de la mer** to admire the blueness of the sky/sea **2. : le**

grand bleu the blue depths of the sea **3.** [meurtrissure] bruise ▸ **être couvert de bleus** to be black and blue, to be covered in bruises ▸ **se faire un bleu à la cuisse** to bruise one's thigh **4.** [fromage] blue cheese **5.** [antiseptique] **: bleu de méthylène** methylene blue **6.** [vêtement] **: bleu de travail** overalls *pl UK*, coveralls *pl US*.

◆ ***bleue*** **nf** [mer] **: la grande bleue** the Mediterranean (sea).

◆ ***au bleu*** **loc adj** CULIN **: truite au bleu** trout au bleu.

◆ ***les Bleus*** **nmpl** SPORT *the French national team*.

bleuet [bløɛ] **nm** cornflower / *Québec* [fruit] blueberry.

bleuetière [bløtjɛr] **nf** *Québec* blueberry field.

bleuir [32] [bløir] **vt & vi** to turn blue.

bleuté, e [bløte] **adj** bluish.

blindé, e [blɛ̃de] **adj 1.** [véhicule] armoured *UK*, armored *US* / [porte, coffre] armour-plated *UK*, armor-plated *US* **2.** *fam fig* [personne] hardened **3.** *fam* [être ivre] **: être blindé** to be plastered.

◆ ***blindé*** **nm** armoured *UK* *ou* armored *US* car.

blinder [3] [blɛ̃de] **vt 1.** [véhicule] to armour *UK*, to armor *US* / [porte, coffre] to armour-plate *UK*, to armor-plate *US* **2.** *fam* [endurcir] to harden.

◆ ***se blinder*** **vp** *fam fig* to harden o.s.

blini [blini] **nm** blini.

blizzard [blizar] **nm** blizzard.

bloc [blɔk] **nm 1.** [gén] block ▸ **être tout d'un bloc** [en un seul morceau] to be made of a single block / [trapu] to be stockily built / [direct] to be simple and straightforward / [inflexible] to be unyielding ▸ **former un bloc** [sociétés] to form a group / [amis, alliés] to stand together / [composants] to form a single whole ▸ **faire bloc** to form a block ▸ **faire bloc avec/contre qqn** to stand (together) with/against sb ▸ **le bloc des pays de l'Est** *ou* **soviétique** HIST the Eastern *ou* Soviet bloc ▸ **le bloc des pays de l'Ouest** *ou* **occidental** the Western Alliance
2. [assemblage] unit ▸ **bloc frigorifique** refrigeration unit ▸ **bloc opératoire** [salle] operating theatre *UK* *ou* room *US* / [locaux] surgical unit ▸ **bloc sanitaire** toilet block
3. [de papier] pad ▸ **bloc de bureau/papier** desk/writing pad ▸ **bloc à en-tête** headed notepad
4. INFORM **: bloc d'alimentation** power pack ▸ **bloc de calcul** arithmetic unit ▸ **bloc de mémoire** memory bank.

◆ ***à bloc*** **loc adv : visser une vis à bloc** to screw a screw down hard ▸ **gonfler un pneu à bloc** to blow a tyre right up *UK* *ou* all the way *US* up, to blow a tire all the way up *US*
▸▸ **il est gonflé** *ou* **remonté à bloc** *fam* he's on top form *ou* full of beans.

◆ ***en bloc*** **loc adv** as a whole ▸ **j'ai tout rejeté en bloc** I rejected it lock, stock and barrel ▸ **condamner une politique en bloc** to condemn a policy outright.

blocage [blɔkaʒ] **nm 1.** ÉCON freeze, freezing *(U)* **2.** [de roue] locking **3.** PSYCHO (mental) block **4.** CONSTR rubble.

blockhaus [blɔkos] **nm** blockhouse.

bloc-moteur [blɔkmɔtœr] (pl **blocs-moteurs**) **nm** engine block.

bloc-notes [blɔknɔt] (pl **blocs-notes**) **nm** notepad, scratchpad *US*.

blocus [blɔkys] **nm** blockade.

blond, e [blɔ̃, blɔ̃d] ■ **adj** fair, blond.
■ **nm, f** fair-haired *ou* blond man, fair-haired *ou* blonde woman.

◆ ***blond*** **nm : blond cendré/vénitien/platine** ash/strawberry/platinum blond.

◆ ***blonde*** **nf 1.** [cigarette] Virginia cigarette **2.** [bière] lager.

blondeur [blɔ̃dœr] **nf** blondness, fairness.

blondir [32] [blɔ̃dir] **vi** to go *ou* turn blond ▸ **faire blondir** CULIN to fry gently without browning.

bloquer [3] [blɔke] **vt 1.** [porte, freins] to jam / [roues] to lock ▸ **c'est le tapis qui bloque la porte** the carpet's jamming the door **2.** [route, chemin] to block / [personne] **: être bloqué** to be stuck ▸ **je suis bloqué à la maison avec un gros rhume** I'm stuck at home with a bad cold ▸ **bloqué par la neige** snowbound **3.** [prix, salaires, crédit] to freeze ▸ **les pourparlers sont bloqués** the negotiations are at a standstill *ou* have reached an impasse **4.** [regrouper] to combine ▸ **on va bloquer les activités sportives le matin** we'll have all sports events in the morning **5.** PSYCHO **: être bloqué** to have a (mental) block ▸ **ça la bloque** she has a mental block about it.

◆ ***se bloquer*** **vp 1.** [se coincer] to jam **2.** PSYCHO **: se bloquer contre** to have a (mental) block about ▸ **je me bloque quand on me parle sur ce ton** my mind goes blank *ou* I freeze when somebody speaks to me like that.

blottir [32] [blɔtir] ◆ ***se blottir*** **vp : se blottir (contre)** to snuggle up (to).

blouse [bluz] **nf 1.** [de travail, d'écolier] smock **2.** [chemisier] blouse.

blouser [3] [bluze] ■ **vi** to be full.
■ **vt** *fam* **: blouser qqn** to pull a fast one on sb.

blouson [bluzɔ̃] **nm** bomber jacket, blouson ▸ **blouson noir** ≃ teddy boy *UK*.

blue-jean [bludʒin] (pl **blue-jeans** [bludʒins]) **nm** jeans *pl*.

blues [bluz] **nm inv** blues.

bluff [blœf] **nm** bluff.

bluffer [3] [blœfe] *fam* **vi & vt** to bluff.

blush [blœʃ] **nm** blusher.

BN **nf abr écrite de *Bibliothèque nationale*.**

BNF **nf abr écrite de *Bibliothèque nationale de France*.**

boa [bɔa] **nm** boa.

boat people [botpipəl] **nmpl** boat people.

bob [bɔb] **nm** SPORT bob.

bobard [bɔbar] **nm** *fam* fib.

bobine [bɔbin] **nf 1.** [cylindre] reel, spool **2.** ÉLECTR coil **3.** *fam vieilli* [visage] face.

bobo[1] [bɔbo] **nm** *(langage enfantin)* **: se faire bobo** to hurt o.s. ▸ **j'ai bobo à la tête** my head hurts.

bobo[2] [bobo] (abr de ***Bourgeois bohème***) *fam* **nmf** *left-leaning yuppie*.

bobsleigh [bɔbslɛg] **nm** bobsleigh *UK*, bobsled *US*.

bocage [bɔkaʒ] **nm 1.** [bois] grove **2.** GÉOGR bocage.

bocal, aux [bɔkal, o] **nm** jar.

bock [bɔk] nm beer mug.

body-building [bɔdibildiŋ] nm : **le body-building** body building *(U)*.

bœuf [bœf] (pl -s [bø]) nm **1.** [animal] ox **2.** [viande] beef ▸ **bœuf bourguignon** *beef stew in a red-wine sauce* ▸ **bœuf en daube** *beef braised in wine and stock* ▸ **bœuf miroton** *slices of beef reheated in stock*.

bof [bɔf] interj *fam* [exprime le mépris] so what? / [exprime la lassitude] I don't really care.

bogue [bɔg], **bug** [bʌg] nm INFORM bug ▸ **le bogue de l'an 2000** the millennium bug.

bohème [bɔɛm] ■ adj bohemian.
■ nf : **la bohème** bohemia.

Bohême [boɛm] nf : **la Bohême** Bohemia.

bohémien, enne [bɔemjɛ̃, ɛn] ■ adj **1.** [tsigane] gipsy *(avant n)* **2.** [non-conformiste] bohemian.
■ nm, f **1.** [tsigane] gipsy **2.** [non-conformiste] bohemian.
◆ ***Bohémien, enne*** nm, f Bohemian.

boire [108] [bwar] ■ vt **1.** [s'abreuver] to drink ▸ **boire un coup** *fam* ou **pot** *fam* ou **verre** to have a drink ou jar *UK* ▸ **boire un coup de trop** *fam* to have one too many ▸ **commander** ou **demander quelque chose à boire** to order a drink ▸ **boire les paroles de qqn : il buvait ses paroles** he was lapping up everything she said ▸ **boire la tasse** *fam* [en nageant] to swallow water / [perdre de l'argent] to lose a lot of money / [faire faillite] to go under **2.** [absorber] to soak up, to absorb.
■ vi to drink ▸ **boire comme un trou** *fam* to drink like a fish ▸ **fais-le boire** [malade, enfant, animal] give him a drink ou something to drink ▸ **il boit trop** he has a drink problem ▸ **nous buvons à ta santé** we're drinking to ou toasting your health.

bois [bwa] ■ nm wood ▸ **un bois de pins** a pine grove ▸ **en bois** wooden ▸ **chèque en bois** *fig* bad ou rubber cheque *UK*, bad ou rubber check *US* ▸ **bois mort** dead wood *UK*, deadwood *US* ▸ **bois vert** green wood ▸ **petit bois** kindling ▸ **toucher du bois** *fam fig* to touch wood *UK*, to knock on wood *US*.
■ nmpl **1.** MUS woodwind *(U)* **2.** [cornes] antlers.
◆ ***de bois*** loc adj **1.** [charpente, jouet, meuble] wooden **2.** [impassible] : **je ne suis pas de bois** I'm only human.

boisé, e [bwaze] adj wooded.

boiser [3] [bwaze] vt to afforest.

boiserie [bwazri] nf panelling *(U) UK*, paneling *(U) US*.

boisson [bwasɔ̃] nf **1.** [breuvage] drink ▸ **boisson chaude/froide** hot/cold drink ▸ **être pris de boisson** to be intoxicated **2.** [habitude] drink *(U)*, drinking *(U)*.

boîte [bwat] nf **1.** [récipient] box ▸ **boîte d'allumettes** [pleine] box of matches / [vide] matchbox ▸ **boîte de conserve** can, tin *UK* ▸ **boîte aux lettres** [pour la réception] letterbox / [pour l'envoi] postbox *UK*, mailbox *US* ▸ **mettre qqch à la boîte** to post *UK* ou to mail *US* sthg ▸ **boîte à musique** musical box *UK*, music box *US* ▸ **boîte noire** black box ▸ **boîte à ordures** dustbin *UK*, trash can *US* ▸ **boîte de Pandore** Pandora's box ▸ **boîte postale** post office box ▸ **en boîte** canned, tinned *UK* ▸ **mettre qqn en boîte** *fig* to pull sb's leg
2. AUTO : **boîte à gants** glove compartment, glove box ▸ **boîte de vitesses** gearbox *UK*, transmission *US*
3. INFORM : **boîte d'arrivée** ou **de départ** in ou out box ▸ **boîte de dialogue** dialog box ▸ **boîte aux lettres électronique** electronic mailbox ▸ **boîte vocale** voice mail
4. *fam* [entreprise] company, firm / [lycée] school ▸ **boîte à bac** *péj* crammer *UK* ▸ **boîte d'intérim** temping agency ▸ **j'ai changé de boîte** I got a job with a new firm
5. *fam* [discothèque] : **boîte (de nuit)** nightclub, club ▸ **aller en boîte** to go to a nightclub.

boiter [3] [bwate] vi **1.** [personne] to limp **2.** [meuble] to wobble.

boiteux, euse [bwatø, øz] ■ adj **1.** [personne] lame **2.** [meuble] wobbly **3.** *fig* [raisonnement] shaky.
■ nm, f lame person.

boîtier [bwatje] nm **1.** [boîte] case **2.** TECHNOL casing.

boitiller [3] [bwatije] vi to limp slightly.

bol [bɔl] nm **1.** [récipient] bowl **2.** [contenu] bowl, bowlful ▸▸ **avoir du bol** *fam* to be lucky ▸ **prendre un bol d'air** to get some fresh air.
◆ ***au bol*** loc adj [coupe de cheveux] pudding-bowl *(avant n) UK*, bowl *(avant n) US*.
◆ ***bol alimentaire*** nm bolus.

bolet [bɔlɛ] nm boletus.

bolide [bɔlid] nm **1.** [véhicule] racing *UK* ou race *US* car ▸ **comme un bolide** like a rocket **2.** ASTRON meteor.

Bolivie [bɔlivi] nf : **la Bolivie** Bolivia.

bolivien, enne [bɔlivjɛ̃, ɛn] adj Bolivian.
◆ ***Bolivien, enne*** nm, f Bolivian.

bombance [bɔ̃bɑ̃s] nf : **faire bombance** *fam* to have a feast.

bombardement [bɔ̃bardəmɑ̃] nm bombardment, bombing *(U)*.

bombarder [3] [bɔ̃barde] vt **1.** MIL to bomb **2.** [assaillir] : **bombarder qqn/qqch de** to bombard sb/sthg with **3.** *fam fig* [nommer] : **bombarder qqn chef de personnel** to pitchfork sb into the job of personnel manager.

bombardier [bɔ̃bardje] nm **1.** [avion] bomber **2.** [aviateur] bombardier.

bombe [bɔ̃b] nf **1.** [projectile] bomb / *fig* bombshell ▸ **bombe atomique** atom ou atomic bomb ▸ **bombe incendiaire** incendiary ou fire bomb ▸ **bombe à retardement** time bomb **2.** [casquette] riding hat **3.** [atomiseur] spray, aerosol **4.** CULIN : **bombe glacée** (ice-cream) bombe ▸▸ **faire la bombe** to live it up.

bombé, e [bɔ̃be] adj bulging, rounded.

bomber[1] [3] [bɔ̃be] ■ vt **1.** [torse] to stick out **2.** *fam* [dessiner à la bombe] to spray.
■ vi **1.** [devenir convexe] to bulge **2.** *fam* [aller vite] to bomb along.

bomber[2] [bɔ̃bœr] nm bomber jacket.

bôme [bom] nf NAUT boom.

bon, bonne [bɔ̃, bɔn] adj (**meilleur** *est le comparatif et le superlatif de bon*) **1.** [gén] good ▸ **de bonnes notes** SCOL good ou high marks *UK* ou grades *US* ▸ **il a une bonne santé** he's in good health, his health is good ▸ **viens te baigner, l'eau est bonne!** come for a swim: the water's lovely and warm!
2. [généreux] good, kind ▸ **bon cœur : avoir bon cœur** to be kind-hearted

3. [utilisable - billet, carte] valid
4. [correct] right ▸ **c'est la bonne rue** it's the right street ▸ **c'est bon!** [c'est juste] that's right! / [ça suffit] that'll do! / [c'est d'accord] OK!
5. [dans l'expression d'un souhait] **: bonne année!** Happy New Year! ▸ **bonne chance!** good luck! ▸ **bonnes vacances!** have a nice holiday *UK* *ou* vacation *US*!
6. [en intensif] **: une bonne tranche** a thick slice ▸ **une bonne fois pour toutes** once and for all
▸▸ **être bon pour qqch/pour faire qqch** *fam* to be fit for sthg/for doing sthg ▸ **tu es bon pour une contravention** you'll end up with *ou* you'll get a parking ticket ▸ **bon à** *(+ infinitif)* fit to ▸ **c'est bon à savoir** that's worth knowing.
◆ ***bon*** ■ **adv : à quoi bon...?** what's the use...? ▸ **il fait bon** the weather's fine, it's fine ▸ **sentir bon** to smell good ▸ **tenir bon** to stand firm.
■ **interj 1.** [marque de satisfaction] good!
2. [marque une transition] right, so, well now ▸ **bon, où en étais-je?** well now *ou* right *ou* so, where was I?
3. [marque de surprise] **: ah bon!** really?
■ **nm 1.** [constatant un droit] voucher ▸ **bon d'achat** gift token *ou* voucher *UK*, gift certificate *US* ▸ **bon de caisse** cash voucher ▸ **bon de commande** order form ▸ **bon de livraison** delivery note ▸ **bon de réduction** discount coupon
2. FIN **: bon d'épargne** savings bond *ou* certificate ▸ **bon du Trésor** FIN treasury bill *ou* bond
3. *(gén pl)* [personne] **: les bons et les méchants** good people and wicked people
4. [éléments valables] good *(U)*.
◆ ***bon à tirer*** **nm** final corrected proof ▸ **donner le bon à tirer** to pass for press.
◆ ***pour de bon*** **loc adv** seriously, really.

bonbon [bɔ̃bɔ̃] **nm 1.** [friandise] sweet *UK*, piece of candy *US* ▸ **bonbon acidulé** acid drop **2.** *Belgique* [gâteau] biscuit.

bonbonne [bɔ̃bɔn] **nf** demijohn.

bonbonnière [bɔ̃bɔnjɛr] **nf 1.** [boîte] sweet-box *UK*, candy box *US* **2.** *fig* [appartement] bijou flat *UK* *ou* apartment *US*.

bond [bɔ̃] **nm** [d'animal, de personne] leap, bound / [de balle] bounce ▸ **faire un bond** to leap (forward) ▸ **faire faux bond à qqn** to let sb down.

bonde [bɔ̃d] **nf 1.** [d'évier] plug **2.** [trou] bunghole **3.** [bouchon] bung.

bondé, e [bɔ̃de] **adj** packed.

bondieuserie [bɔ̃djøzri] **nf** *péj* **1.** [bigoterie] religiosity **2.** [objet] religious trinket.

bondir [32] [bɔ̃dir] **vi 1.** [sauter] to leap, to bound ▸ **bondir sur qqn/qqch** to pounce on sb/sthg **2.** [s'élancer] to leap forward **3.** *fig* [réagir violemment] **: bondir (de)** to jump (with).

bonheur [bɔnœr] **nm 1.** [félicité] happiness **2.** [chance] (good) luck, good fortune ▸ **par bonheur** happily, fortunately ▸ **au petit bonheur** haphazardly ▸ **porter bonheur** to be lucky, to bring good luck.

bonhomie [bɔnɔmi] **nf** good-naturedness, good nature.

bonhomme [bɔnɔm] (pl **bonshommes** [bɔ̃zɔm]) **nm 1.** *fam péj* [homme] fellow **2.** [petit garçon] fellow **3.** [représentation] man ▸ **bonhomme de neige** snowman
▸▸ **aller son petit bonhomme de chemin** *fig* to go at one's own pace.

boniche [bɔniʃ] **nf** *péj* servant, skivvy *UK*.

bonification [bɔnifikasjɔ̃] **nf 1.** [de terre, de vin] improvement **2.** SPORT bonus points *pl*.

bonifier [9] [bɔnifje] **vt** to improve.
◆ ***se bonifier*** **vp** to improve.

boniment [bɔnimɑ̃] **nm 1.** [baratin] sales talk *(U)* **2.** [mensonge] (tall) story.

bonjour [bɔ̃ʒur] **nm** hello / [avant midi] good morning / [après midi] good afternoon ▸ **c'est simple comme bonjour** it's (as) easy as ABC.

bonne [bɔn] ■ **nf** maid.
■ **adj** ➤ ***bon***.

bonne-maman [bɔnmamɑ̃] (pl **bonnes-mamans**) **nf** granny, grandma.

bonnement [bɔnmɑ̃] **adv : tout bonnement** just, simply.

bonnet [bɔnɛ] **nm 1.** [coiffure] (woolly) hat *UK*, (wooly) hat *US* ▸ **bonnet d'âne** ≃ dunce's cap ▸ **bonnet de bain** swimming cap ▸ **bonnet de nuit** *fig* [personne] misery ▸ **gros bonnet** *fig* [personne] big cheese ▸ **bonnet phrygien** Phrygian cap *(worn by the sans-culottes during the French Revolution)* **2.** [de soutien-gorge] cup
▸▸ **bonnet blanc et blanc bonnet** six of one and half a dozen of the other.

bonneterie [bɔnɛtri] **nf 1.** [magasin] hosier's (shop) **2.** [marchandise] hosiery *(U)* **3.** [commerce] hosiery (business *ou* trade).

bon-papa [bɔ̃papa] (pl **bons-papas**) **nm** grandad, grandpa.

bonsoir [bɔ̃swar] **nm** [en arrivant] hello, good evening / [en partant] goodbye, good evening / [en se couchant] good night.

bonté [bɔ̃te] **nf 1.** [qualité] goodness, kindness ▸ **ayez la bonté de...** please be so kind as to... ▸ **avoir la bonté de faire qqch** *sout* to be so good *ou* kind as to do sthg **2.** *(gén pl) littéraire* [acte] act of kindness.

bonus [bɔnys] **nm** [prime d'assurance] no-claims bonus.

booléen, enne [buleɛ̃, ɛn] **adj** Boolean.

boom [bum] **nm** boom.

boomerang [bumrɑ̃g] **nm** boomerang.

booster [3] [buste] **vt** to boost.

borborygme [bɔrbɔrigm] **nm** rumbling *(U)*.

bord [bɔr] **nm 1.** [de table, de vêtement] edge / [de verre, de chapeau] rim ▸ **à ras bords** to the brim ▸ **chapeau à larges bords** wide-brimmed *ou* broad-brimmed hat **2.** [de rivière] bank / [de lac] edge, shore ▸ **au bord de la mer** at the seaside ▸ **sur les bords de Seine** on the embankment (in Paris), on the banks of the Seine **3.** [de bois, jardin] edge / [de route] edge, side ▸ **le bord du trottoir** the kerb *UK* *ou* curb *US* ▸ **sur le bord de la route** by the roadside **4.** [d'un moyen de transport] **: jeter** *ou* **balancer** *fam* **qqch**

par-dessus bord to throw *ou* to chuck sthg overboard ▸ **passer par-dessus bord** to fall overboard ▸ **virer de bord** NAUT to tack
▸▸ **être du même bord** *fig* to be on the same side.
◆ ***à bord de*** loc prép : **à bord de qqch** on board sthg ▸ **à bord d'un navire/d'une voiture** on board a ship/car ▸ **monter à bord d'un bateau/avion** to board a boat/plane.
◆ ***au bord de*** loc prép **1.** *litt* at the edge of ▸ **s'arrêter au bord de la route** to stop by the roadside ▸ **se promener au bord de l'eau/la mer** to walk at the water's edge/the seaside **2.** *fig* on the verge of ▸ **au bord des larmes/de la dépression** on the verge of tears/a nervous breakdown.
◆ ***sur les bords*** loc adv slightly, a touch ▸ **il est un peu radin sur les bords** he's a bit tight-fisted.

bordeaux [bɔrdo] ■ **nm 1.** [vin] Bordeaux **2.** [couleur] claret.
■ **adj inv** claret.

bordée [bɔrde] **nf** broadside ▸ **bordée d'injures** *fig* torrent of abuse ▸ **bordée de neige** *Québec* heavy snowfall.

bordel [bɔrdɛl] **nm** *vulg* **1.** [maison close] brothel **2.** [désordre] shambles *sg*.

border [3] [bɔrde] **vt 1.** [vêtement] **: border qqch de** to edge sthg with **2.** [être en bordure de] to line **3.** [voile] to haul on **4.** [couverture, personne] to tuck in.

bordereau, x [bɔrdəro] **nm 1.** [liste] schedule **2.** [facture] invoice **3.** [relevé] slip ▸ **bordereau de salaire** pay slip.

bordure [bɔrdyr] **nf 1.** [bord] edge ▸ **en bordure de** on the edge of **2.** [de fleurs] border **3.** [de vêtement] edge, edging.

boréal, e, aux [bɔreal, o] **adj** northern.

borgne [bɔrɲ] ■ **nmf** [personne] one-eyed person.
■ **adj 1.** [personne] one-eyed **2.** [fenêtre] with an obstructed view **3.** *fig* [sordide] disreputable.

borne [bɔrn] **nf 1.** [marque] boundary marker ▸ **borne kilométrique** ≃ milestone **2.** [limite] limit, bounds *pl* ▸ **dépasser les bornes** to go too far ▸ **sans bornes** boundless **3.** *fam* [kilomètre] kilometre *UK*, kilometer *US* **4.** INFORM **: borne interactive** interactive terminal **5.** ÉLECTR terminal.

borné, e [bɔrne] **adj 1.** [horizon] limited **2.** [personne] narrow-minded / [esprit] narrow.

Bornéo [bɔrneo] **npr** Borneo ▸ **à Bornéo** in Borneo.

borner [3] [bɔrne] **vt** [terrain] to limit / [projet, ambition] to limit, to restrict.
◆ ***se borner*** **vp : se borner à qqch/à faire qqch** [suj: personne] to confine o.s. to sthg/to doing sthg.

bosniaque [bɔsnjak] **adj** Bosnian.
◆ ***Bosniaque*** **nmf** Bosnian.

Bosnie [bɔsni] **nf : la Bosnie** Bosnia.

bosquet [bɔskɛ] **nm** copse.

bosse [bɔs] **nf 1.** [sur tête, sur route] bump ▸ **se faire une bosse** to get a bump ▸ **un terrain plein de bosses** a bumpy piece of ground **2.** [de bossu, chameau] hump
▸▸ **avoir la bosse des maths** *fam* to have a good head for maths *UK* *ou* math *US* ▸ **rouler sa bosse** *fam* to knock around *ou* about *UK*.

bosseler [24] [bɔsle] **vt 1.** [cabosser] to dent **2.** [travailler] to emboss.

bosser [3] [bɔse] **vi** *fam* to work hard.

bosseur, euse [bɔsœr, øz] *fam* ■ **adj** hard-working.
■ **nm, f** hard worker.

bossu, e [bɔsy] ■ **adj** hunchbacked.
■ **nm, f** hunchback.

bot [bo] ➤ ***pied***.

botanique [bɔtanik] ■ **adj** botanical.
■ **nf : la botanique** botany.

botte [bɔt] **nf 1.** [chaussure] boot ▸ **botte de caoutchouc** wellington (boot) *UK*, rubber boot *US* ▸ **lécher les bottes de qqn** *fam fig* to lick sb's boots ▸ **en avoir plein les bottes** *fam fig* to have had a bellyful **2.** [de légumes] bunch **3.** [en escrime] thrust, lunge.

botter [3] [bɔte] **vt 1.** [chausser] **: être botté de cuir** to be wearing leather boots **2.** *fam* [donner un coup de pied à] to boot **3.** *fam vieilli* [plaire à] **: ça me botte** I dig it.

bottier [bɔtje] **nm** [de bottes] bootmaker / [de chaussures] shoemaker.

bottillon [bɔtijɔ̃] **nm** (ankle) boot.

Bottin® [bɔtɛ̃] **nm** phone book.

bottine [bɔtin] **nf** (ankle) boot.

bouc [buk] **nm 1.** [animal] (billy) goat ▸ **bouc émissaire** *fig* scapegoat **2.** [barbe] goatee.

boucan [bukɑ̃] **nm** *fam* row, racket.

bouche [buʃ] **nf 1.** ANAT mouth ▸ **j'ai la bouche sèche** my mouth feels dry ▸ **avoir la bouche pleine** to have one's mouth full ▸ **bouche à oreille** grapevine ▸ **de bouche à oreille** through the grapevine, by word of mouth ▸ **rester bouche cousue** to keep one's lips sealed **2.** [orifice] **: bouche d'aération** air vent ▸ **bouche d'arrosage** water pipe, standpipe ▸ **bouche d'égout** manhole, inspection chamber ▸ **bouche d'incendie** fire hydrant ▸ **bouche de métro** metro entrance *ou* exit
▸▸ **garder qqch pour la bonne bouche** to save sthg till last *ou* the end ▸ **faire la fine bouche** to be awkward, to make difficulties.

bouché, e [buʃe] **adj 1.** [en bouteille] bottled **2.** *fam* [personne] dumb, thick.

bouche-à-bouche [buʃabuʃ] **nm inv : faire du bouche-à-bouche à qqn** to give sb mouth-to-mouth resuscitation.

bouche-à-oreille [buʃalɔrɛj] **nm inv : par le bouche-à-oreille** through the grapevine, by word of mouth.

bouchée [buʃe] **nf** mouthful ▸ **bouchée à la reine** CULIN chicken vol-au-vent ▸ **pour une bouchée de pain** *fig* for a song.

boucher[1] [3] [buʃe] **vt 1.** [fermer - bouteille] to cork / [- trou] to fill (in *ou* up) **2.** [passage, vue] to block.
◆ ***se boucher*** **vp** to get blocked (up) ▸ **se boucher le nez** to hold one's nose.

boucher[2]***, ère*** [buʃe, ɛr] **nm, f** butcher.

boucherie [buʃri] **nf 1.** [magasin] butcher's (shop) ▸ **boucherie chevaline** horse butcher's (shop) **2.** [commerce] butchery (trade) **3.** *fig* [carnage] slaughter.

boucherie-charcuterie [buʃriʃarkytri] (pl **boucheries-charcuteries**) **nf** butcher's (shop).

bouche-trou [buʃtru] (pl **bouche-trous**) **nm 1.** [personne] **: servir de bouche-trou** to make up (the) numbers **2.** [objet] stopgap.

bouchon [buʃɔ̃] **nm 1.** [pour obturer - gén] top / [- de réservoir] cap / [- de bouteille] cork ▸ **bouchon de cire** buildup of wax in the ear **2.** [de canne à pêche] float **3.** [embouteillage] traffic jam.

bouchonner [3] [buʃɔne] ■ **vt 1.** [cheval] to rub down **2.** [enfant] to pamper.
■ **vi : ça bouchonne sur l'autoroute** there is a traffic jam on the motorway.

boucle [bukl] **nf 1.** [de ceinture, soulier] buckle **2.** [bijou] **: boucle d'oreille** earring **3.** [de cheveux] curl **4.** [de fleuve, d'avion & INFORM] loop.

bouclé, e [bukle] **adj** [cheveux] curly / [personne] curly-haired.

boucler [3] [bukle] **vt 1.** [attacher] to buckle / [ceinture de sécurité] to fasten **2.** [fermer] to shut **3.** *fam* [enfermer - voleur] to lock up / [- malade] to shut away **4.** [encercler] to seal off **5.** [terminer] to finish.

bouclier [buklije] **nm** *litt & fig* shield.

bouddha [buda] **nm** [statuette] buddha.
◆ ***Bouddha*** **nm** Buddha.

bouddhisme [budism] **nm** Buddhism.

bouddhiste [budist] **nmf & adj** Buddhist.

bouder [3] [bude] ■ **vi** to sulk.
■ **vt** [chose] to dislike / [personne] to shun ▸ **elle me boude depuis que je lui ai fait faux bond** she has cold-shouldered me ever since I let her down.

boudeur, euse [budœr, øz] ■ **adj** sulky.
■ **nm, f** sulky person.

boudin [budɛ̃] **nm 1.** CULIN blood pudding *UK ou* sausage *US* ▸ **boudin blanc/noir** white/black pudding *UK* **2.** *fam péj* [personne] podge *UK*.

boudiné, e [budine] **adj 1.** [gros] pudgy, podgy *UK* **2.** [serré] **: être boudiné dans ses vêtements** to be squeezed into one's clothes.

boudoir [budwar] **nm 1.** [salon] boudoir **2.** [biscuit] sponge finger *UK*, ladyfinger *US*.

boue [bu] **nf** mud ▸ **traîner qqn dans la boue, couvrir qqn de boue** *fig* to drag sb *ou* sb's name through the mud.

bouée [bwe] **nf 1.** [balise] buoy **2.** [pour flotter] rubber ring ▸ **bouée de sauvetage** lifebelt.

boueux, euse [buø, øz] **adj** muddy.
◆ ***boueux*** **nm** *fam* dustman *UK*, garbage collector *US*.

bouffant, e [bufɑ̃, ɑ̃t] **adj** [manche, jupe] full / [cheveux] bouffant.

bouffe [buf] **nf** *fam* grub.

bouffée [bufe] **nf 1.** [de fumée] puff / [de parfum] whiff / [d'air] breath ▸ **bouffées de chaleur** hot flushes *UK ou* flashes *US* **2.** [accès] surge ▸ **bouffées délirantes** mad fits.

bouffer [3] [bufe] ■ **vi** [manches] to puff out.
■ **vt 1.** *fam* [manger] to eat ▸ **on a bien/mal bouffé** the food was great/terrible **2.** [gaspiller] to be heavy on, to soak up ▸ **bouffer de l'essence** to be heavy on petrol *UK ou* gas *US*
▸▸| **bouffer du curé** to be a priest-hater ▸ **bouffer du communiste** to be a commie-basher.
◆ ***se bouffer*** **vp** *(emploi réciproque) fam* **: se bouffer le nez** [une fois] to have a go at one another / [constamment] to be at daggers drawn.

bouffi, e [bufi] **adj : bouffi (de)** swollen (with).

bouffon, onne [bufɔ̃, ɔn] **adj** farcical.
◆ ***bouffon*** **nm 1.** HIST jester **2.** [pitre] clown.

bouge [buʒ] **nm** *péj* **1.** [taudis] hovel **2.** [café] dive.

bougeoir [buʒwar] **nm** candlestick.

bougeotte [buʒɔt] **nf : avoir la bougeotte** to have itchy feet.

bouger [17] [buʒe] ■ **vt** [déplacer] to move.
■ **vi 1.** [remuer] to move ▸ **je ne bouge pas (de chez moi) aujourd'hui** I'm staying at home today **2.** [vêtement] to shrink **3.** [changer] to change **4.** [s'agiter] **: ça bouge partout dans le monde** there is unrest all over the world.
◆ ***se bouger*** **vp** *fam* **1.** [faire des efforts] to move *ou* shift o.s. **2.** [se déplacer] to move (over).

bougie [buʒi] **nf 1.** [chandelle] candle **2.** [de moteur] spark plug, sparking plug *UK*.

bougon, onne [bugɔ̃, ɔn] ■ **adj** grumpy.
■ **nm, f** grumbler.

bougonner [3] [bugɔne] **vt & vi** to grumble.

bougre, esse [bugr, ɛs] **nm, f** *fam* [homme] guy, bloke *UK* / [femme] (old) girl.
◆ ***bougre*** **nm** *fam* **: bougre d'andouille!** you damned idiot!, you bloody fool! *UK*

boui-boui [bwibwi] (pl **bouis-bouis**) **nm** *fam péj* dive, (cheap) caff *UK*.

bouillabaisse [bujabɛs] **nf** bouillabaisse *(Provençal fish soup)*.

bouillant, e [bujɑ̃, ɑ̃t] **adj 1.** [qui bout] boiling **2.** [très chaud] boiling hot **3.** *fig* [ardent] fiery.

bouille [buj] **nf** *fam* [visage] face.

bouilleur [bujœr] **nm : bouilleur de cru** *small-scale distiller*.

bouilli, e [buji] **adj** [eau, lait, viande] boiled.
◆ ***bouilli*** **nm** [viande] boiled meat / [bœuf] boiled beef.

bouillie [buji] **nf** baby's cereal ▸ **réduire en bouillie** [légumes] to puree ▸ **c'est de la bouillie pour les chats** it's a dog's breakfast ▸ **réduire en bouillie** [personne] to reduce to a pulp ▸ **mettre qqn en bouillie** to beat sb to a pulp.

bouillir [48] [bujir] **vi 1.** [aliments] to boil ▸ **faire bouillir** to boil **2.** *fig* [personne] **: bouillir (de)** to seethe (with).

bouilloire [bujwar] **nf** kettle.

bouillon [bujɔ̃] **nm 1.** [soupe] stock ▸ **bouillon cube** stock cube ▸ **bouillon de légumes** vegetable stock ▸ **boire** *ou* **prendre un bouillon** *fam* [en nageant] to swallow water / *fig* to suffer heavy losses, to take a bath **2.** [bouillonnement] bubble ▸ **éteindre le feu dès le premier**

bouillon turn off the heat as soon as it boils ▸ **faire bouillir à gros bouillons** to bring to a rolling boil **3.** [bactériologique] **: bouillon de culture** culture medium.

bouillonner [3] [bujɔne] **vi 1.** [liquide] to bubble **2.** [torrent] to foam **3.** *fig* [personne] to seethe.

bouillotte [bujɔt] **nf** hot-water bottle.

boul. abr de ***boulevard***.

boulanger, ***ère*** [bulɑ̃ʒe, ɛr] ■ **adj** bakery *(avant n)*, baking *(avant n)*.

■ **nm, f** baker.

boulangerie [bulɑ̃ʒri] **nf 1.** [magasin] bakery, baker's (shop) *UK* **2.** [commerce] bakery trade.

boulangerie-pâtisserie [bulɑ̃ʒripatisri] (pl **boulangeries-pâtisseries**) **nf** ≃ bakery, ≃ baker's (shop) *UK*.

boule [bul] **nf** [gén] ball / [de loto] counter / [de pétanque] bowl ▸ **boule de commande** INFORM trackball ▸ **boule de neige** snowball ▸ **faire boule de neige** to snowball

▸▸ **se mettre en boule** *fam* to blow one's top ▸ **perdre la boule** *fam* to lose one's marbles.

◆ ***boules*** **nfpl 1.** [jeux] boules *(game played on bare ground with steel bowls)* **2.** *tfam* **: avoir les boules** [être effrayé] to be scared stiff / [être furieux] to be pissed off *tfam* / [être déprimé] to be feeling down.

◆ ***boules Quiès***® **nfpl** wax earplugs.

bouleau, ***x*** [bulo] **nm** silver birch.

bouledogue [buldɔg] **nm** bulldog.

boulet [bulɛ] **nm 1.** [munition] **: boulet de canon** cannonball ▸ **tirer à boulets rouges sur qqn** *fig* to let fly at sb **2.** [de forçat] ball and chain **3.** *fig* [fardeau] millstone (around one's neck).

boulette [bulɛt] **nf 1.** [petite boule] pellet **2.** [de viande] meatball.

boulevard [bulvar] **nm 1.** [rue] boulevard ▸ **les grands boulevards** *Paris boulevards running from the Place de la République to la Madeleine* **2.** THÉÂTRE light comedy *(U)*.

bouleversant, ***e*** [bulvɛrsɑ̃, ɑ̃t] **adj** distressing.

bouleversement [bulvɛrsəmɑ̃] **nm** disruption.

bouleverser [3] [bulvɛrse] **vt 1.** [objets] to turn upside down **2.** [modifier] to disrupt **3.** [émouvoir] to distress.

boulgour [bulgur] **nm** bulgar *ou* bulgur wheat.

boulier [bulje] **nm** abacus.

boulimie [bulimi] **nf** bulimia.

bouliste [bulist] **nmf** boules player.

Boulle [bul] **npr : l'école Boulle** *prestigious school training cabinetmakers.*

boulon [bulɔ̃] **nm** bolt.

boulonner [3] [bulɔne] ■ **vt** to bolt.

■ **vi** *fam* to slog (away).

boulot[1], ***otte*** [bulo, ɔt] **adj** dumpy.

boulot[2] [bulo] **nm** *fam* **1.** [travail] work **2.** [emploi] job.

boum [bum] ■ **interj** bang!

■ **nm 1.** [bruit] bang ▸ **faire boum** to go bang **2.** *fig* & ÉCON boom.

■ **nf** *fam vieilli* party.

bouquet [bukɛ] **nm 1.** [de fleurs - gén] bunch (of flowers) / [- formel] bouquet **2.** [crevette] prawn **3.** [de vin] bouquet **4.** [de feu d'artifice] crowning piece **5.** CULIN **: bouquet garni** bouquet garni **6.** TV **: bouquet de programmes** multi-channel package ▸ **bouquet numérique** channel package, channel bouquet

▸▸ **ça c'est le bouquet!** *fam* that takes the biscuit *UK ou* cake *US*!

bouquetin [buktɛ̃] **nm** ibex.

bouquin [bukɛ̃] **nm** *fam* book.

bouquiner [3] [bukine] **vi** & **vt** *fam* to read.

bouquiniste [bukinist] **nmf** secondhand bookseller.

bourbeux, ***euse*** [burbø, øz] **adj** muddy.

bourbier [burbje] **nm** [lieu] quagmire, mire / *fig* mess.

bourbon [burbɔ̃] **nm** [whisky] bourbon.

bourde [burd] **nf 1.** [baliverne] rubbish *(U)* **2.** *fam* [erreur] blunder.

bourdon [burdɔ̃] **nm 1.** [insecte] bumblebee **2.** [cloche] (large) bell **3.** [ton grave] drone

▸▸ **avoir le bourdon** *fam* to be (feeling) down.

bourdonnement [burdɔnmɑ̃] **nm** [d'insecte, de voix, de moteur] buzz *(U)*

▸▸ **avoir des bourdonnements d'oreilles** to have a ringing in one's ears.

bourdonner [3] [burdɔne] **vi 1.** [insecte, machine, voix] to buzz **2.** [oreille] to ring.

bourg [bur] **nm** market town.

bourgade [burgad] **nf** village.

bourgeois, ***e*** [burʒwa, az] ■ **adj 1.** [valeur] middle-class **2.** [cuisine] plain **3.** *péj* [personne] bourgeois.

■ **nm, f** bourgeois.

bourgeoisie [burʒwazi] **nf** ≃ middle classes *pl*.

bourgeon [burʒɔ̃] **nm** bud.

bourgeonner [3] [burʒɔne] **vi** to bud.

bourgmestre [burgmɛstr] **nm** ***Belgique*** & ***Suisse*** burgomaster.

bourgogne [burgɔɲ] **nm** Burgundy *(wine)*.

Bourgogne [burgɔɲ] **nf : la Bourgogne** Burgundy.

bourguignon, ***onne*** [burgiɲɔ̃, ɔn] **adj** [de Bourgogne] Burgundian.

◆ ***Bourguignon***, ***onne*** **nm, f** Burgundian.

bourlinguer [3] [burlɛ̃ge] **vi** *fam* [voyager] to bum around the world.

bourrade [burad] **nf** thump.

bourrage [buraʒ] **nm** [de coussin] stuffing.

◆ ***bourrage de crâne*** **nm** *fam* **1.** [bachotage] cramming *UK* **2.** [propagande] brainwashing.

bourrasque [burask] **nf** gust of wind.

bourratif, ***ive*** [buratif, iv] **adj** stodgy.

bourre [bur] **nf 1.** [de coussin] stuffing **2.** [de laine] flock **3.** [de bourgeon] down

▸▸ **être à la bourre** *fam* [dans travail] to be behind / [dans activité] to be running late.

bourré, ***e*** [bure] **adj** *fam* **1.** [plein] **: bourré (de)** [salle] packed (with) / *fig* chock-full (of) **2.** [ivre] plastered.

bourreau, ***x*** [buro] **nm 1.** HIST executioner **2.** [personne cruelle] torturer ▸ **bourreau de travail** workaholic.

bourrelé [burle] ➤ ***remords***.

bourrelet [burlɛ] **nm** **1.** [de graisse] roll of fat **2.** [de porte] draught *UK* *ou* draft *US* excluder.

bourrer [3] [bure] **vt** **1.** [remplir - coussin] to stuff / [- pipe] to fill / [- sac, armoire] **: bourrer qqch (de)** to cram sthg full (of) **2.** *fam* [gaver] **: bourrer qqn (de)** to stuff sb (with) **3.** *fam* [estomac] **: ça bourre!** it's really filling!

◆ ***se bourrer*** **vp** *fam* **1.** [se gaver] **: se bourrer (de qqch)** to stuff o.s. (with sthg) **2.** [se soûler] **: se bourrer la gueule** to get plastered.

bourricot [buriko] **nm** (small) donkey.

bourrique [burik] **nf** **1.** [ânesse] she-ass ▸ **faire tourner qqn en bourrique** *fam fig* to drive sb up the wall **2.** *fam* [personne] pigheaded person.

bourru, e [bury] **adj** [peu aimable] surly.

bourse [burs] **nf** **1.** [porte-monnaie] purse ▸ **sans bourse délier** without spending anything **2.** [d'études] grant / [au mérite] scholarship ▸ **avoir une bourse** to have a grant *ou* scholarship.

◆ ***Bourse*** **nf** [marché] stock exchange, stock market ▸ **la Bourse de Paris** the Paris Stock Exchange ▸ **jouer en Bourse** to speculate on the stock exchange *ou* stock market ▸ **Bourse de commerce** commodity market.

◆ ***bourses*** **nfpl** scrotum.

boursicoter [3] [bursikɔte] **vi** to dabble (on the stock market).

boursier, ère [bursje, ɛr] ■ **adj** **1.** [élève] on a grant *ou* scholarship **2.** FIN stock-exchange *(avant n)*, stock-market *(avant n)*.

■ **nm, f** **1.** [étudiant] student on a grant/scholarship **2.** FIN stockbroker.

boursouflé, e [bursufle] **adj** **1.** [enflé] swollen **2.** [emphatique] overblown.

boursoufler [3] [bursufle] **vt** to puff up, to swell.

◆ ***se boursoufler*** **vp** [peinture] to blister.

bous, bout ➤ ***bouillir***.

bousculade [buskylad] **nf** **1.** [cohue] crush **2.** [agitation] rush.

bousculer [3] [buskyle] **vt** **1.** [pousser] to shove **2.** [faire tomber] to knock over **3.** [presser] to rush **4.** [modifier] to overturn.

◆ ***se bousculer*** **vp** to jostle each other.

bouse [buz] **nf : bouse de vache** cow dung.

bousiller [3] [buzije] **vt** *fam* **1.** [abîmer] to ruin, to knacker *UK* **2.** [bâcler] to botch.

boussole [busɔl] **nf** compass.

bout [bu] **nm** **1.** [extrémité, fin] end ▸ **bout à bout** end to end ▸ **au bout de** [temps] after / [espace] at the end of ▸ **d'un bout à l'autre** [de ville] from one end to the other / [de livre] from beginning to end ▸ **bout du nez** tip of the nose ▸ **bout filtre** filter tip **2.** [morceau] bit ▸ **un bout de ciel bleu** a patch of blue sky ▸ **donne-m'en un bout** give me some *ou* a piece *ou* a bit ▸ **bout d'essai** screen test ▸ **faire un bout de chemin avec qqn** to go part of the way with sb

▸▸| **au bout du compte** all things considered ▸ **au bout d'un moment** after a while ▸ **à bout de bras : porter un paquet à bout de bras** to carry a parcel (in one's outstretched arms) ▸ **à tout bout de champ** every five minutes ▸ **être à bout** to be exhausted ▸ **il n'est pas au bout de ses peines** his troubles are not over yet ▸ **à bout de souffle** out of breath, breathless ▸ **en bout de course** at the end of the race ▸ **être à bout de forces** to have no strength left ▸ **être à bout de nerfs** to be on the verge of a breakdown ▸ **en voir le bout : enfin, on en voit le bout** at last, we're beginning to see the light at the end of the tunnel ▸ **mener qqn par le bout du nez** to lead sb by the nose ▸ **à bout portant** at point-blank range ▸ **pousser qqn à bout** to drive sb to distraction ▸ **être au bout du rouleau** to have come to the end of the road ▸ **venir à bout de** [personne] to get the better of / [difficulté] to overcome.

◆ ***bout de chou*** **nm** *fam* poppet *UK*, sweetie.

boutade [butad] **nf** [plaisanterie] jest.

boute-en-train [butɑ̃trɛ̃] **nm inv** live wire ▸ **il était le boute-en-train de la soirée** he was the life and soul of the party.

bouteille [butɛj] **nf** bottle ▸ **mettre en bouteille** *ou* **bouteilles** to bottle ▸ **prendre de la bouteille** *fam fig* to be getting on a bit.

boutique [butik] **nf** [gén] shop / [de mode] boutique ▸ **boutique hors-taxe** duty-free shop ▸ **fermer boutique** to shut up shop ▸ **parler boutique** to talk shop.

bouton [butɔ̃] **nm** **1.** COUT button ▸ **bouton de manchette** cuff link **2.** [sur la peau] pimple, spot *UK* **3.** [de porte] knob **4.** [commutateur] switch **5.** [bourgeon] bud **6.** INFORM **: bouton de réinitialisation** reset button.

bouton-d'or [butɔ̃dɔr] (pl **boutons-d'or**) **nm** buttercup.

boutonner [3] [butɔne] **vt** to button (up).

◆ ***se boutonner*** **vp** [vêtement] to button.

boutonneux, euse [butɔnø, øz] **adj** pimply, spotty *UK*.

boutonnière [butɔnjɛr] **nf** [de vêtement] buttonhole.

bouton-pression [butɔ̃presjɔ̃] (pl **boutons-pression**) **nm** press-stud *UK*, snap fastener *US*.

bouture [butyr] **nf** cutting.

bouvier [buvje] **nm** **1.** [personne] herdsman **2.** [chien] sheepdog.

bouvreuil [buvrœj] **nm** bullfinch.

bovidé [bɔvide] **nm** bovine.

bovin, e [bɔvɛ̃, in] **adj** bovine.

◆ ***bovins*** **nmpl** cattle.

bowling [buliŋ] **nm** **1.** [jeu] bowling **2.** [lieu] bowling alley.

box [bɔks] (pl **boxes**) **nm** **1.** [d'écurie] loose box **2.** [compartiment] cubicle ▸ **le box des accusés** the dock **3.** [parking] lockup garage *UK*.

boxe [bɔks] **nf** boxing.

boxer[1] [3] [bɔkse] ■ **vi** to box.

■ **vt** *fam* to thump.

boxer[2] [bɔksɛr] **nm** [chien] boxer.

boxeur [bɔksœr] **nm** SPORT boxer.

boyau [bwajo] **nm 1.** [chambre à air] inner tube **2.** [corde] catgut **3.** [galerie] narrow gallery.
◆ ***boyaux*** **nmpl** [intestins] guts.

boycott [bɔjkɔt] **nm** boycott.

boycotter [3] [bɔjkɔte] **vt** to boycott.

boy-scout [bɔjskut] (pl **boy-scouts**) **nm** *vieilli* boy scout.

BP (abr de ***boîte postale***) **nf** PO Box.

BPF (abr écrite de ***bon pour francs***) *printed on cheques before space for amount to be inserted.*

bracelet [braslɛ] **nm 1.** [bijou] bracelet **2.** [de montre] strap.

bracelet-montre [braslɛmɔ̃tr] (pl **bracelets-montres**) **nm** wristwatch.

braconnage [brakɔnaʒ] **nm** poaching.

braconner [3] [brakɔne] **vi** to go poaching, to poach.

braconnier [brakɔnje] **nm** poacher.

brader [3] [brade] **vt** [solder] to sell off / [vendre à bas prix] to sell for next to nothing.

braderie [bradri] **nf** clearance sale.

braguette [bragɛt] **nf** fly, flies *pl UK*.

braille [braj] **nm** Braille.

braillement [brajmɑ̃] **nm** bawl, howl ▸ **les braillements d'un bébé** the crying *ou* howling of a baby.

brailler [3] [braje] ■ **vi** to bawl.
■ **vt** to bawl (out).

braire [112] [brɛr] **vi 1.** [âne] to bray **2.** *fam* [personne] to bellow.

braise [brɛz] **nf** embers *pl* ▸ **cuire sous la braise** to cook in the embers of a fire ▸ **de braise** *fig* fiery.

braiser [4] [breze] **vt** to braise.

bramer [3] [brame] **vi** [cerf] to bell.

brancard [brɑ̃kar] **nm 1.** [civière] stretcher **2.** [de charrette] shaft ▸ **ruer dans les brancards** *fig* to rebel, to protest.

brancardier, ère [brɑ̃kardje, ɛr] **nm, f** stretcher-bearer.

branchage [brɑ̃ʃaʒ] **nm** branches *pl*.

branche [brɑ̃ʃ] **nf 1.** [gén] branch **2.** [de lunettes] arm **3.** [de compas] leg.

branché, e [brɑ̃ʃe] **adj 1.** ÉLECTR plugged in, connected **2.** *fam* [à la mode] trendy.

branchement [brɑ̃ʃmɑ̃] **nm 1.** [raccordement] connection, plugging in **2.** [bifurcation] branch.

brancher [3] [brɑ̃ʃe] **vt 1.** [raccorder & INFORM] to connect ▸ **brancher qqch sur** ÉLECTR to plug sthg into **2.** *fam* [orienter] to steer ▸ **brancher qqn sur qqch** to start sb off on sthg ▸ **brancher la conversation sur** to steer the conversation towards **3.** *fam* [plaire] to appeal to.

branchies [brɑ̃ʃi] **nfpl** [de poisson] gills.

brandade [brɑ̃dad] **nf : brandade de morue** *creamed salt cod.*

brandir [32] [brɑ̃dir] **vt** to wave.

branlant, e [brɑ̃lɑ̃, ɑ̃t] **adj** [escalier, mur] shaky / [meuble, dent] wobbly.

branle [brɑ̃l] **nm : mettre en branle** to set in motion.

branle-bas [brɑ̃lba] **nm inv** pandemonium *(U)* ▸ **branle-bas de combat** action stations *pl*.

branler [3] [brɑ̃le] ■ **vt 1.** [hocher] **: branler la tête** to shake one's head **2.** *tfam* [faire] **: qu'est-ce qu'il branle?** what is he playing at?
■ **vi** [escalier, chaise] to be shaky / [dent, meuble] to be wobbly.
◆ ***se branler*** **vp** *vulg* to wank *UK*, to jerk off *US*.

braquage [brakaʒ] **nm 1.** AUTO lock **2.** [attaque] holdup.

braquer [3] [brake] ■ **vt 1.** [diriger] **: braquer qqch sur** [arme] to aim sthg at / [télescope] to train sthg on / [regard] to fix sthg on **2.** [contrarier] to antagonize **3.** *fam* [attaquer] to hold up.
■ **vi** to turn (the wheel).
◆ ***se braquer*** **vp** [personne] to take a stand.

braqueur, euse [brakœr, øz] **nm, f** holdup man *m* (holdup woman *f*) *(in bank)*.

bras [bra] **nm 1.** [gén] arm ▸ **bras dessus bras dessous** arm in arm ▸ **le bras en écharpe** with one's arm in a sling ▸ **bras droit** right-hand man *ou* woman ▸ **bras de fer** [jeu] arm wrestling / *fig* trial of strength ▸ **baisser les bras** to throw in the towel ▸ **en bras de chemise** in one's shirt-sleeves ▸ **se croiser les bras** just to sit there ▸ **avoir le bras long** [avoir de l'influence] to have pull **2.** [main-d'œuvre] hand, worker **3.** [de cours d'eau] branch ▸ **bras de mer** arm of the sea.

brasier [brazje] **nm** [incendie] blaze, inferno.

Brasilia [brazilja] **npr** Brasilia.

bras-le-corps [bralkɔr] ◆ ***à bras-le-corps*** **loc adv** bodily.

brassage [brasaʒ] **nm 1.** [de bière] brewing **2.** *fig* [mélange] mixing.

brassard [brasar] **nm** armband.

brasse [bras] **nf** [nage] breaststroke ▸ **brasse coulée** breaststroke ▸ **brasse papillon** butterfly (stroke).

brassée [brase] **nf** armful.

brasser [3] [brase] **vt 1.** [bière] to brew **2.** [mélanger] to mix **3.** *fig* [manier] to handle.

brasserie [brasri] **nf 1.** [usine] brewery **2.** [industrie] brewing (industry) **3.** [café-restaurant] brasserie.

brasseur, euse [brasœr, øz] **nm, f 1.** [de bière] brewer **2.** *fig* **: brasseur d'affaires** wheeler-dealer **3.** [nageur] breaststroke swimmer.

brassière [brasjɛr] **nf 1.** [de bébé] (baby's) vest *UK ou* undershirt *US* **2.** [gilet de sauvetage] life jacket **3.** *Québec* [soutien-gorge] bra.

bravade [bravad] **nf** bravado ▸ **par bravade** out of bravado.

brave [brav] ■ **adj 1.** *(après n)* [courageux] brave **2.** *(avant n)* [honnête] decent **3.** [naïf et gentil] nice.
■ **nmf : mon brave** my good man.

bravement [bravmɑ̃] **adv 1.** [courageusement] bravely **2.** [résolument] determinedly.

braver [3] [brave] **vt 1.** [parents, règlement] to defy **2.** [mépriser] to brave.

bravo [bravo] **interj** bravo!
◆ ***bravos*** **nmpl** cheers.

bravoure [bravur] **nf** bravery.

BRB (abr de ***Brigade de répression du banditisme***) **nf** *French serious crime squad.*

break [brɛk] **nm 1.** [voiture] estate (car) *UK*, station wagon *US* **2.** [jazz] break **3.** *fam* [pause] break ▸ **faire un break** to take a break **4.** SPORT **: faire le break** [tennis] to break service / *fig* to pull away.

brebis [brəbi] **nf** ewe ▸ **brebis galeuse** black sheep.

brèche [brɛʃ] **nf 1.** [de mur] gap **2.** MIL breach
▸▸ **battre qqn en brèche** [attaquer] to knock sb down ▸ **battre qqch en brèche** *fig* to demolish sthg ▸ **être sur la brèche** to be hard at work.

bredouille [brəduj] **adj : être/rentrer bredouille** to be/to return empty-handed.

bredouillement [brədujmɑ̃] **nm** stammering.

bredouiller [3] [brəduje] ■ **vi** to stammer.
■ **vt** to stammer (out).

bref, ***brève*** [brɛf, brɛv] **adj 1.** [gén] short, brief ▸ **soyez bref!** make it brief! **2.** LING short.
◆ ***bref*** **adv** in short, in a word ▸ **en bref** briefly.
◆ ***brève*** **nf** PRESSE brief news item.

brelan [brəlɑ̃] **nm : un brelan** three of a kind ▸ **un brelan de valets** three jacks.

breloque [brəlɔk] **nf** charm.

brème [brɛm] **nf** [poisson] bream.

Brésil [brezil] **nm : le Brésil** Brazil ▸ **au Brésil** in Brazil.

brésilien, ***enne*** [breziljɛ̃, ɛn] **adj** Brazilian.
◆ ***Brésilien***, ***enne*** **nm, f** Brazilian.

Bretagne [brətaɲ] **nf : la Bretagne** Brittany.

bretelle [brətɛl] **nf 1.** [d'autoroute] access road, slip road *UK* ▸ **bretelle d'accès** access road **2.** [de fusil] sling ▸ **porter l'arme à la bretelle** to carry one's weapon slung over one's shoulder **3.** [de pantalon] **: bretelles** braces *UK*, suspenders *US* ▸ **se faire remonter les bretelles** *fig* to be told to pull one's socks up **4.** [de bustier] strap.

breton, ***onne*** [brətɔ̃, ɔn] **adj** Breton.
◆ ***breton*** **nm** [langue] Breton.
◆ ***Breton***, ***onne*** **nm, f** Breton.

breuvage [brœvaʒ] **nm** [boisson] beverage.

brève ➤ ***bref***.

brevet [brəvɛ] **nm 1.** [certificat] certificate ▸ **brevet de secouriste** first-aid certificate **2.** [diplôme] diploma ▸ **brevet des collèges** *school certificate taken after four years of secondary education* **3.** [d'invention] patent ▸ **déposer un brevet** to file a patent **4.** *fig* [assurance] guarantee.

breveter [27] [brəvte] **vt** to patent ▸ **faire breveter qqch** to take out a patent on sthg, to patent sthg.

bréviaire [brevjɛr] **nm** breviary.

bribe [brib] **nf** [fragment] scrap, bit / *fig* snippet ▸ **bribes de conversation** snatches of conversation.

bric [brik] ◆ ***de bric et de broc*** **loc adv** any old how ▸ **meublé de bric et de broc** furnished with bits and pieces.

bric-à-brac [brikabrak] **nm inv** bric-a-brac.

bricolage [brikɔlaʒ] **nm 1.** [travaux] do-it-yourself, DIY *UK* **2.** [réparation provisoire] patching up.

bricole [brikɔl] **nf 1.** [babiole] trinket **2.** [chose insignifiante] trivial matter.

bricoler [3] [brikɔle] ■ **vi** to do odd jobs (around the house).
■ **vt 1.** [réparer] to fix, to mend *UK* **2.** [fabriquer] to make, to knock up *UK*.

bricoleur, ***euse*** [brikɔlœr, øz] ■ **adj** handy (about the house).
■ **nm, f** do-it-yourselfer, home handyman (f handywoman).

bride [brid] **nf 1.** [de cheval] bridle ▸ **à bride abattue** at full tilt ▸ **lâcher la bride à qqn** to give sb his/her head **2.** [de chapeau] string **3.** COUT bride, bar **4.** TECHNOL flange.

bridé [bride] ➤ ***œil***.

brider [3] [bride] **vt** [cheval] to bridle / *fig* to rein (in).

bridge [bridʒ] **nm** [jeu & MÉD] bridge.

brie [bri] **nm** [fromage] Brie.

briefer [3] [brife] **vt** to brief.

briefing [brifiŋ] **nm** briefing.

brièvement [brijɛvmɑ̃] **adv** briefly.

brièveté [brijɛvte] **nf** brevity, briefness.

brigade [brigad] **nf 1.** [d'ouvriers, de soldats] brigade **2.** [détachement] squad ▸ **brigade antigang** organized crime diivision ▸ **brigade des mœurs/des stups** vice/drugs squad ▸ **brigade volante** flying squad *UK*.

brigadier [brigadje] **nm 1.** MIL corporal **2.** [de police] sergeant.

brigand [brigɑ̃] **nm 1.** [bandit] bandit **2.** [homme malhonnête] crook.

brigandage [brigɑ̃daʒ] **nm 1.** [vol à main armée] armed robbery **2.** [action malhonnête] robbery.

briguer [3] [brige] **vt** *sout* to aspire to ▸ **briguer un second mandat** to seek re-election.

brillamment [brijamɑ̃] **adv** [gén] brilliantly / [réussir un examen] with flying colours *UK* *ou* colors *US*.

brillant, ***e*** [brijɑ̃, ɑ̃t] **adj 1.** [qui brille - gén] sparkling / [- cheveux] glossy / [- yeux] bright ▸ **brillant de : yeux brillants de malice** eyes sparkling with mischief ▸ **yeux brillants de fièvre** eyes bright with fever **2.** [remarquable] brilliant ▸ **pas brillant** not brilliant ▸ **sa santé n'est pas brillante** he's not well, his health is not too good ▸ **les résultats ne sont pas brillants** the results aren't too good *ou* aren't all they should be.
◆ ***brillant*** **nm 1.** [diamant] brilliant **2.** [éclat] shine.
◆ ***brillant à lèvres*** **nm** [cosmétique] lip gloss.

brillantine [brijɑ̃tin] **nf** brilliantine.

briller [3] [brije] **vi** to shine.

brimade [brimad] **nf 1.** [vexation] victimization *(U)*, bullying *(U)* **2.** *arg scol* ragging *(U)* *UK*, hazing *(U)* *US*.

brimer [3] [brime] **vt 1.** [tracasser] to victimize, to bully **2.** *arg scol* to rag *UK*, to haze *US*.

brin [brɛ̃] **nm 1.** [tige] twig ▸ **brin d'herbe** blade of grass ▸ **un beau brin de fille** a fine figure of a girl **2.** [fil] strand **3.** [petite quantité] **: un brin (de)** a bit (of) ▸ **faire un brin de toilette** to have a quick wash.

brindille [brɛ̃dij] **nf** twig.

bringue [brɛ̃g] **nf** *fam* binge ▸ **faire la bringue** to go on a binge.

bringuebaler, ***brinquebaler*** [3] [brɛ̃gbale] **vi** [voiture] to jolt along.

brio [brijo] **nm 1.** MUS brio **2.** [talent] **: avec brio** brilliantly.

brioche [brijɔʃ] **nf 1.** [pâtisserie] brioche **2.** *fam* [ventre] paunch.

brioché, ***e*** [brijɔʃe] **adj** [pain] brioche-style.

brique [brik] ■ **nf 1.** [pierre] brick **2.** [emballage] carton **3.** *fam* [argent] *10,000 francs.*

■ **adj inv** brick red.

briquer [3] [brike] **vt** to scrub.

briquet [brikɛ] **nm** (cigarette) lighter.

briqueterie [brikɛtri] **nf** brickworks *sg*.

briquette [brikɛt] **nf** [conditionnement] carton.

bris [bri] **nm** [destruction] breaking ▸ **bris de glace** broken windows.

brisant [brizɑ̃] **nm** [écueil] reef.

◆ ***brisants*** **nmpl** [récif] breakers.

brise [briz] **nf** breeze.

brisé, ***e*** [brize] **adj** *fig* broken ▸ **brisé de chagrin** overwhelmed by sorrow ▸ **brisé de fatigue** exhausted.

brise-glace(s) [brizglas] **nm inv** [navire] icebreaker.

brise-jet [brizʒɛ] **nm inv** nozzle *(for tap).*

brise-lames [brizlam] **nm inv** breakwater.

brise-mottes [brizmɔt] **nm inv** harrow.

briser [3] [brize] **vt 1.** [gén] to break **2.** *fig* [carrière] to ruin / [conversation] to break off / [espérances] to shatter.

◆ ***se briser*** **vp 1.** [gén] to break **2.** *fig* [espoir] to be dashed / [efforts] to be thwarted.

briseur, ***euse*** [brizœr, øz] **nm, f : briseur de grève** strike-breaker.

bristol [bristɔl] **nm 1.** [papier] Bristol board **2.** *vieilli* [carte de visite] visiting *UK* *ou* calling *US* card.

britannique [britanik] **adj** British.

◆ ***Britannique*** **nmf** British person, Briton ▸ **les Britanniques** the British.

broc [bro] **nm** jug.

brocante [brɔkɑ̃t] **nf 1.** [commerce] secondhand trade **2.** [objets] secondhand goods *pl.*

brocanteur, ***euse*** [brɔkɑ̃tœr, øz] **nm, f** dealer in secondhand goods.

brocart [brɔkar] **nm** brocade.

broche [brɔʃ] **nf 1.** [bijou] brooch **2.** CULIN spit ▸ **cuire à la broche** to spit-roast **3.** ÉLECTR & MÉD pin **4.** [de métier à filer] spindle.

broché, ***e*** [brɔʃe] **adj 1.** [tissu] brocade *(avant n)*, brocaded **2.** TYPO **: livre broché** paperback (book).

brochet [brɔʃɛ] **nm** pike.

brochette [brɔʃɛt] **nf 1.** [ustensile] skewer **2.** [plat] kebab **3.** *fam fig* [groupe] string, row.

brochure [brɔʃyr] **nf 1.** [imprimé] brochure, booklet **2.** [de livre] binding **3.** [de tissu] brocaded pattern.

brocoli [brɔkɔli] **nm** broccoli *(U).*

brodequin [brɔdkɛ̃] **nm** boot.

broder [3] [brɔde] **vt & vi** to embroider.

broderie [brɔdri] **nf 1.** [art] embroidery **2.** [ouvrage] (piece of) embroidery.

broie, ***broies*** ➤ ***broyer***.

Brogniart [brɔɲar] **npr : le palais Brogniart** *name by which the Paris Stock Exchange is sometimes known.*

bromure [brɔmyr] **nm** bromide.

bronche [brɔ̃ʃ] **nf** bronchus ▸ **j'ai des problèmes de bronches** I've got chest problems.

broncher [3] [brɔ̃ʃe] **vi** to stumble ▸ **sans broncher** without complaining, uncomplainingly.

bronchiolite [brɔ̃kjɔlit] **nf** bronchiolitis.

bronchite [brɔ̃ʃit] **nf** bronchitis *(U).*

bronzage [brɔ̃zaʒ] **nm 1.** [de peau] tan, suntan **2.** [de métal] bronzing.

bronzant, ***e*** [brɔ̃zɑ̃, ɑ̃t] **adj** suntan *(avant n).*

bronze [brɔ̃z] **nm** bronze.

bronzé, ***e*** [brɔ̃ze] **adj** tanned *UK*, tan *US*, suntanned.

bronzer [3] [brɔ̃ze] **vi** [peau] to tan / [personne] to get a tan.

brosse [brɔs] **nf** brush ▸ **brosse à cheveux** hairbrush ▸ **brosse à dents** toothbrush ▸ **brosse à habits** clothes brush ▸ **avoir les cheveux en brosse** to have a crew cut.

brosser [3] [brɔse] **vt 1.** [habits, cheveux] to brush **2.** [paysage, portrait] to paint.

◆ ***se brosser*** **vp** to brush one's clothes, to brush o.s. down ▸ **se brosser les cheveux/les dents** to brush one's hair/teeth.

brou ◆ ***brou de noix*** **nm 1.** [liqueur] walnut liqueur **2.** [teinture] walnut stain.

brouet [bruɛ] **nm** gruel.

brouette [bruɛt] **nf** wheelbarrow.

brouhaha [bruaa] **nm** hubbub.

brouillard [brujar] **nm** [léger] mist / [dense] fog ▸ **brouillard givrant** freezing fog ▸ **être dans le brouillard** *fig* to be lost.

brouille [bruj] **nf** quarrel.

brouillé, ***e*** [bruje] **adj 1.** [fâché] **: être brouillé avec qqn** to be on bad terms with sb ▸ **être brouillé avec qqch** *fig* to be hopeless *ou* useless at sthg **2.** [teint] muddy **3.** ➤ ***œuf***.

brouiller [3] [bruje] **vt 1.** [désunir] to set at odds, to put on bad terms **2.** [vue] to blur **3.** [RADIO - accidentellement] to cause interference to / [- délibérément] to jam **4.** [rendre confus] to muddle (up).

◆ ***se brouiller*** **vp 1.** [se fâcher] to fall out ▸ **se brouiller avec qqn (pour qqch)** to fall out with sb (over sthg) **2.** [se troubler] to become blurred **3.** [devenir confus] to get muddled (up), to become confused **4.** MÉTÉOR to cloud over.

brouilleur [brujœr] **nm** INFORM scrambler.

brouillon, onne [brujɔ̃, ɔn] **adj** careless, untidy.
◆ ***brouillon*** **nm** rough copy, draft.

broussaille [brusaj] **nf : les broussailles** the undergrowth ▸ **en broussaille** *fig* [cheveux] untidy / [sourcils] bushy.

broussailleux, euse [brusajø, øz] **adj 1.** [région] scrubby **2.** [sourcils] bushy.

brousse [brus] **nf** GÉOGR scrubland, bush.

brouter [3] [brute] ■ **vt** to graze on.
■ **vi 1.** [animal] to graze **2.** TECHNOL to judder, to shudder.

broutille [brutij] **nf** trifle.

broyer [13] [brwaje] **vt** to grind, to crush.

broyeur [brwajœr] **nm : évier à broyeur** sink with waste *UK* ***ou*** garbage *US* disposal unit.

bru [bry] **nf** *sout* daughter-in-law.

brucelles [brysɛl] **nfpl 1.** [pince] (pair of) tweezers **2.** *Suisse* [pince à épiler] (pair of) eyebrow tweezers.

brugnon [bryɲɔ̃] **nm** nectarine.

bruine [brɥin] **nf** drizzle.

bruire [105] [brɥir] **vi** [feuilles, étoffe] to rustle / [eau] to murmur.

bruissement [brɥismɑ̃] **nm** [de feuilles, d'étoffe] rustle, rustling *(U)* / [d'eau] murmur, murmuring *(U)*.

bruit [brɥi] **nm 1.** [son] noise, sound ▸ **bruit de fond** background noise ▸ **des bruits de pas** the sound of footsteps ▸ **un bruit sec** a snap ▸ **un bruit sourd** a thud
2. [vacarme & TECHNOL] noise ▸ **un bruit d'enfer** a huge racket ▸ **faire du bruit** to make a noise ▸ **sans bruit** silently, noiselessly ▸ **il s'avance sans bruit** he moves forward without a sound
3. [rumeur] rumour *UK*, rumor *US* ▸ **le bruit court que...** rumour has it ***ou*** it is rumoured that... ▸ **faire circuler des faux bruits** to spread false rumours
4. [retentissement] fuss ▸ **faire du bruit** to cause a stir ▸ **on a fait beaucoup de bruit autour de cet enlèvement** the kidnapping caused a furore *UK* ***ou*** furor *US*.

bruitage [brɥitaʒ] **nm** sound effects *pl*.

brûlant, e [brylɑ̃, ɑ̃t] **adj 1.** [gén] burning (hot) / [liquide] boiling (hot) / [plat] piping hot **2.** *fig* [amour, question] burning.

brûlé, e [bryle] ■ **adj** [calciné] burnt.
■ **nm, f** badly burnt person ▸ **un grand brûlé** a patient suffering from third-degree burns ▸ **service pour les grands brûlés** burns unit.
◆ ***brûlé*** **nm** burnt part ▸ **un goût de brûlé** a burnt taste ▸▸ **ça sent le brûlé** [odeur] there's a smell of burning / *fam fig* there's trouble brewing.

brûle-pourpoint [brylpurpwɛ̃] ◆ ***à brûle-pourpoint*** **loc adv** point-blank, straight out.

brûler [3] [bryle] ■ **vt 1.** [gén] to burn / [suj: eau bouillante] to scald ▸ **la fumée me brûle les yeux** the smoke is making my eyes sting ▸ **le piment me brûle la langue** the chilli is burning my tongue ▸ **brûler la chandelle par les deux bouts** to burn the candle at both ends ▸ **brûler les planches** to give an outstanding performance ▸ **brûler ses dernières cartouches** to shoot one's bolt
2. [café] to roast
3. [feu rouge] to drive through / [étape] to miss out, to skip ▸ **brûler un stop** to fail to stop at a stop sign ▸ **brûler les étapes** [progresser rapidement] to advance by leaps and bounds / *péj* to cut corners, to take short cuts.
■ **vi 1.** [gén] to burn / [maison, forêt] to be on fire ▸ **avoir le front/la gorge qui brûle** to have a burning forehead/a burning sensation in the throat ▸ **la forêt a brûlé** the forest was burnt down ***ou*** to the ground
2. [être brûlant] to be burning (hot) ▸ **brûler de** *fig* to be consumed with ▸ **brûler de faire qqch** to be longing ***ou*** dying to do sthg ▸ **brûler de parler à qqn** to be dying to talk to sb ▸ **brûler de fièvre** to be running a high temperature ▸ **brûler d'impatience/de désir** to be burning with impatience/desire.
◆ ***se brûler*** **vp** to burn o.s. ▸ **se brûler la main** to burn one's hand.

brûlis [bryli] **nm** burn-off.

brûlure [brylyr] **nf 1.** [lésion] burn ▸ **brûlure au premier/second/troisième degré** first-degree/second-degree/third-degree burn **2.** [sensation] burning (sensation) ▸ **avoir des brûlures d'estomac** to have heartburn.

brume [brym] **nf** mist.

brumeux, euse [brymø, øz] **adj** misty / *fig* hazy.

brun, e [brœ̃, bryn] ■ **adj** brown / [cheveux] dark.
■ **nm, f** dark-haired man (f woman).
◆ ***brun*** **nm** [couleur] brown.
◆ ***brune*** **nf 1.** [cigarette] *cigarette made of dark tobacco* **2.** [bière] brown ale.

brunâtre [brynatr] **adj** brownish.

brunir [32] [brynir] ■ **vt 1.** [peau] to tan **2.** [métal] to polish, to burnish.
■ **vi** [personne] to get a tan / [peau] to tan.

Brushing® [brœʃiŋ] **nm : faire un Brushing à qqn** to give sb a blow-dry, to blow-dry sb's hair.

brusque [brysk] **adj** abrupt.

brusquement [bryskəmɑ̃] **adv** abruptly.

brusquer [3] [bryske] **vt** to rush / [élève] to push.

brusquerie [bryskəri] **nf** abruptness.

brut, e [bryt] **adj 1.** [pierre précieuse, bois] rough / [sucre] unrefined / [métal, soie] raw / [champagne] extra dry ▸ **(pétrole) brut** crude (oil) **2.** *fig* [fait, idées] crude, raw **3.** ÉCON gross.
◆ ***brute*** **nf** brute.

brutal, e, aux [brytal, o] **adj 1.** [violent] violent, brutal ▸ **être brutal avec qqn** to be brutal to sb **2.** [soudain] sudden **3.** [manière] blunt.

brutalement [brytalmɑ̃] **adv 1.** [violemment] brutally **2.** [soudainement] suddenly **3.** [sèchement] bluntly.

brutaliser [3] [brytalize] **vt** to mistreat.

brutalité [brytalite] **nf 1.** [violence] violence, brutality **2.** [caractère soudain] suddenness.
◆ ***brutalités*** **nfpl** brutality *(U)*.

Bruxelles [bry(k)sɛl] **npr** Brussels.

bruxellois, e [brysɛlwa, az] **adj** of/from Brussels.
◆ ***Bruxellois, e*** **nm, f** person from Brussels.

bruyamment [brɥijamɑ̃] **adv** noisily.

bruyant**, **e [brɥijɑ̃, ɑ̃t] **adj** noisy.

bruyère [bryjɛr] **nf 1.** [plante] heather **2.** [lande] heathland.

BT ■ **nm** (abr de ***brevet de technicien***) *vocational training certificate (taken at age 18).*
■ **nf** (abr de ***basse tension***) LT.

BTA (abr de ***brevet de technicien agricole***) **nm** *agricultural training certificate (taken at age 18).*

BTP (abr de ***bâtiment et travaux publics***) **nmpl** *building and public works sector.*

BTS (abr de ***brevet de technicien supérieur***) **nm** *advanced vocational training certificate (taken at the end of a 2-year higher-education course).*

bu**, **e [by] **pp** ➤ ***boire***.

BU (abr de ***bibliothèque universitaire***) **nf** *university library.*

buanderie [byɑ̃dri] **nf** laundry.

Bucarest [bykarɛst] **npr** Bucharest.

buccal**, **e**, **aux [bykal, o] **adj** buccal ▸ **par voie buccale** orally.

bûche [byʃ] **nf 1.** [bois] log ▸ **bûche de Noël** Yule log ▸ **prendre *ou* ramasser une bûche** *fam* to fall flat on one's face **2.** *fam* [personne] lump.

bûcher [1] [byʃe] **nm 1.** [supplice] **: le bûcher** the stake **2.** [funéraire] pyre.

bûcher [2] [3] [byʃe] *fam* ■ **vi** to swot *UK*, to grind *US*.
■ **vt** to swot up *UK*, to grind *US*.

bûcheron**, **onne [byʃrɔ̃, ɔn] **nm, f** forestry worker.

bûcheur**, **euse [byʃœr, øz] *fam* ■ **adj** hard-working.
■ **nm, f** swot *UK*, grind *US*.

bucolique [bykɔlik] **adj** pastoral.

Budapest [bydapɛst] **npr** Budapest.

budget [bydʒɛ] **nm 1.** [personne, entreprise] budget ▸ **avoir un petit budget** to be on a (tight) budget ▸ **boucler son budget** to make ends meet ▸ **se fixer un budget** to decide on a budget ▸ **un budget de deux millions** a two million budget **2.** FIN & POLIT **: le Budget** ≃ the Budget ▸ **amputer le budget** to cut the budget ▸ **budget économique** economic budget.

budgétaire [bydʒetɛr] **adj** budgetary ▸ **année budgétaire** fiscal *ou* financial *UK* year.

budgétisation [bydʒetizasjɔ̃] **nf** budgeting.

budgétiser [3] [bydʒetize] **vt** to budget for.

buée [bɥe] **nf** [sur vitre] condensation.

Buenos Aires [bɥenozɛr] **npr** Buenos Aires.

buffet [byfɛ] **nm 1.** [meuble] sideboard **2.** [repas] buffet **3.** [café-restaurant] **: buffet de gare** station buffet.

buffle [byfl] **nm** [animal] buffalo.

bug [bʌg] **nm** = ***bogue***.

buis [bɥi] **nm** box(wood).

buisson [bɥisɔ̃] **nm** bush.

buissonnière [bɥisɔnjɛr] ➤ ***école***.

bulbe [bylb] **nm** bulb.

bulgare [bylgar] **adj** Bulgarian.
◆ ***bulgare*** **nm** [langue] Bulgarian.
◆ ***Bulgare*** **nmf** Bulgarian.

Bulgarie [bylgari] **nf : la Bulgarie** Bulgaria.

bulldozer [byldozɛr] **nm** bulldozer.

bulle [byl] **nf 1.** [gén] bubble ▸ **bulle de savon** soap bubble **2.** [de bande dessinée] speech balloon **3.** INFORM **: bulle d'aide** pop-up text, tooltip **4.** RELIG (papal) bull.

bulletin [byltɛ̃] **nm 1.** [communiqué] bulletin ▸ **bulletin d'informations** news bulletin ▸ **bulletin (de la) météo** weather forecast ▸ **bulletin de santé** medical bulletin **2.** [imprimé] form ▸ **bulletin de consigne** left luggage ticket *UK*, luggage room *ou* checkroom ticket *US* ▸ **bulletin de participation** entry form ▸ **bulletin de vote** ballot paper ▸ **bulletin blanc** blank ballot paper **3.** SCOL report *UK*, report card *US* ▸ **bulletin mensuel/trimestriel** monthly/end-of-term report **4.** [certificat] certificate ▸ **bulletin de naissance** birth certificate ▸ **bulletin de salaire *ou* de paye** pay slip.

bulletin-réponse [byltɛ̃repɔ̃s] (pl **bulletins-réponse**) **nm** reply form.

bungalow [bœ̃galo] **nm** [maison] bungalow / [de vacances] chalet.

bunker [bunkœr] **nm** bunker.

buraliste [byralist] **nmf 1.** [d'un bureau de tabac] tobacconist **2.** [préposé] clerk.

bure [byr] **nf 1.** [étoffe] *coarse brown woollen cloth* **2.** [de moine] frock.

bureau [byro] **nm 1.** [gén] office ▸ **aller au bureau** to go to the office ▸ **travailler dans un bureau** to work in an office, to have an office job *ou* a desk job ▸ **bureau d'aide sociale** social security *UK ou* welfare *US* office ▸ **bureau de change** [banque] bureau de change, foreign exchange office / [comptoir] bureau de change, foreign exchange counter ▸ **bureau d'études** design office ▸ **bureau paysager** open-plan office *(with plants)* ▸ **bureau de poste** post office ▸ **bureau de tabac** tobacconist's ▸ **bureau de vote** polling station **2.** [meuble] desk ▸ **bureau à cylindre** roll-top desk **3.** [comité] committee ▸ **le syndicat réuni en bureau confédéral** the union meeting at federal committee level **4.** INFORM desktop.

bureaucrate [byrokrat] **nmf** bureaucrat.

bureaucratie [byrokrasi] **nf** bureaucracy.

bureaucratique [byrokratik] **adj** *péj* bureaucratic.

bureautique [byrotik] **nf** office automation.

burette [byrɛt] **nf 1.** [flacon] cruet **2.** [de chimiste] burette **3.** [de mécanicien] oilcan.

burin [byrɛ̃] **nm 1.** [outil] chisel **2.** [gravure] engraving.

buriné**, **e [byrine] **adj** engraved / [visage, traits] lined.

Burkina [byrkina] **nm : le Burkina** Burkina Faso ▸ **au Burkina** in Burkina Faso.

burkinabé [byrkinabe] **adj** of/from Burkina Faso.
◆ ***Burkinabé*** **nmf** person from Burkina Faso.

burlesque [byrlɛsk] ■ **adj 1.** [comique] funny **2.** [ridicule] ludicrous, absurd **3.** THÉÂTRE burlesque.
■ **nm : le burlesque** the burlesque.

burnous [byrnu] **nm** **1.** [manteau] burnous **2.** [de bébé] hooded cape.

burundais, e [burundɛ, ɛz] **adj** Burundian.
◆ ***Burundais, e*** **nm, f** Burundian.

Burundi [burundi] **nm : le Burundi** Burundi ▸ **au Burundi** in Burundi.

bus [bys] **nm** bus.

buse [byz] **nf** **1.** [oiseau] buzzard **2.** [tuyau] pipe, duct **3.** *fam fig* idiot.

busqué [byske] ➤ ***nez***.

buste [byst] **nm** [torse] chest / [poitrine de femme, sculpture] bust.

bustier [bystje] **nm** [corsage] bustier / [soutien-gorge] strapless bra.

but [byt] **nm** **1.** [point visé] target **2.** [objectif] goal, aim, purpose ▸ **avoir pour but de** to aim to ▸ **errer sans but** to wander aimlessly ▸ **il touche au but** he's nearly there ▸ **à but non lucratif** DR non-profit, non-profit-making *UK* ▸ **aller droit au but** to go straight to the point ▸ **dans le but de faire qqch** with the aim *ou* intention of doing sthg **3.** GRAMM purpose **4.** SPORT goal ▸ **gagner/perdre par 5 buts à 2** to win/to lose by 5 goals to 2 ▸ **marquer un but** to score a goal
⏭ **de but en blanc** point-blank, straight out ▸ **...demanda-t-elle de but en blanc...** she suddenly asked.

butane [bytan] **nm : (gaz) butane** butane / [domestique] butane, Calor gas® *UK*.

buté, e [byte] **adj** stubborn.
◆ ***butée*** **nf** **1.** ARCHIT abutment **2.** TECHNOL stop.

buter [3] [byte] ■ **vi** **1.** [se heurter] **: buter sur/contre qqch** to stumble on/over sthg, to trip on/over sthg / *fig* to run into/come up against sthg **2.** SPORT to score a goal.
■ **vt** **1.** [étayer] to support **2.** *tfam* [tuer] to do in, to bump off.
◆ ***se buter*** **vp** to dig one's heels in ▸ **se buter contre** *fig* to refuse to listen to.

butin [bytɛ̃] **nm** [de guerre] booty / [de vol] loot / [de recherche] finds *pl*.

butiner [3] [bytine] ■ **vi** to collect nectar.
■ **vt** [suj: abeille] to collect nectar from / *fig* to gather.

butoir [bytwar] **nm** **1.** [de porte] doorstop **2.** [de chemin de fer] buffer *UK*.

butte [byt] **nf** [colline] mound, rise ▸ **butte de tir** MIL butts *pl* ▸ **être en butte à** *fig* to be exposed to.

buvable [byvabl] **adj** [boisson] drinkable / [ampoule] (to be) taken orally.

buvard [byvar] **nm** [papier] blotting-paper / [sous-main] blotter.

buvette [byvɛt] **nf** **1.** [café] refreshment room, buffet **2.** [de station thermale] pump room.

buveur, euse [byvœr, øz] **nm, f** drinker.

buvez, buvons ➤ ***boire***.

BVA (abr de ***Brulé Ville Associés***) **npr** *French market research company*.

BVP (abr de ***Bureau de vérification de la publicité***) **nm** *French advertising standards authority*, ≃ ASA *UK*.

Byzance [bizɑ̃s] **npr** HIST Byzantium
⏭ **c'est Byzance!** it's fantastic!

BZH (abr écrite de ***Breizh***) Brittany *(as nationality sticker on a car)*.

c[1], ***C*** [se] **nm inv** c, C.

◆ ***C*** **1.** (abr écrite de ***celsius, centigrade***) C **2.** (abr écrite de ***coulomb***) C **3.** abr de ***code***.

c[2] abr écrite de ***centime***.

c' ➤ *ce*.

ca abr de ***centiare***.

CA ■ **nm 1.** abr écrite de ***chiffre d'affaires*** **2.** abr écrite de ***conseil d'administration*** **3.** abr écrite de ***corps d'armée***.

■ **nf** (abr de ***chambre d'agriculture***) *local government body responsible for agricultural matters*.

ça [sa] **pron dém 1.** [désignant un objet - éloigné] that / [- proche] this **2.** [sujet indéterminé] it, that ▸ **comment ça va?** how are you?, how are things? ▸ **ça ira comme ça** that will be fine ▸ **ça y est** that's it ▸ **c'est ça** that's right **3.** [renforcement expressif] **: où ça?** where? ▸ **qui ça?** who?

çà [sa] **adv : çà et là** here and there.

cabale [kabal] **nf 1.** [personnes] cabal / [intrigue] cabal, intrigue ▸ **monter une cabale contre qqn** to plot against sb **2.** HIST cabala, cabbala, kabbala.

caban [kabɑ̃] **nm** [] reefer jacket *UK*, reefer *US* / [d'officier] pea jacket.

cabane [kaban] **nf 1.** [abri] cabin, hut / [remise] shed ▸ **cabane à lapins** hutch **2.** *fam* [prison] **: en cabane** in the clink.

cabanon [kabanɔ̃] **nm 1.** [à la campagne] cottage **2.** [sur la plage] chalet **3.** [cellule] padded cell **4.** [de rangement] shed.

cabaret [kabarɛ] **nm** cabaret.

cabas [kaba] **nm** shopping bag.

cabillaud [kabijo] **nm** (fresh) cod.

cabine [kabin] **nf 1.** [de navire, d'avion, de véhicule] cabin **2.** [compartiment, petit local] cubicle ▸ **cabine d'essayage** fitting room ▸ **cabine téléphonique** phone booth, phone box *UK*.

cabinet [kabinɛ] **nm 1.** [pièce] **: cabinet particulier** [de restaurant] private dining room ▸ **cabinet de toilette** ≃ bathroom ▸ **cabinet de travail** study
2. [toilettes] toilet
3. [local professionnel] office ▸ **cabinet d'affaires** business consultancy ▸ **cabinet d'assurances** insurance firm *ou* agency ▸ **cabinet dentaire/médical** dentist's/doctor's surgery *UK*, dentist's/doctor's office *US* ▸ **monter un cabinet** to set up a practice
4. [gouvernement] cabinet / [de ministre] advisers *pl* ▸ **cabinet du Premier ministre** Prime Minister's departmental staff ▸ **cabinet fantôme** shadow cabinet ▸ **faire partie du cabinet** to be in *ou* a member of the Cabinet.

◆ ***cabinets*** **nmpl** toilet *sg*.

câble [kabl] **nm** cable ▸ **(télévision par) câble** cable television.

câblé, ***e*** [kable] **adj** TV equipped with cable TV.

câbler [3] [kable] **vt 1.** TV [ville, région] to link to a cable television network, to wire for cable / [émission] to cable **2.** ÉLECTR to cable **3.** [fils] to twist together (into a cable), to cable **4.** TÉLÉCOM [message] to cable(cast).

cabosser [3] [kabɔse] **vt** to dent.

cabot [kabo] ■ **adj** theatrical.

■ **nm 1.** [personne] poser **2.** *fam* [chien] mutt.

cabotage [kabɔtaʒ] **nm** coastal navigation.

caboteur [kabɔtœr] **nm** [navire] coaster.

cabotin, ***e*** [kabɔtɛ̃, in] *péj* ■ **adj** theatrical.

■ **nm, f 1.** *fam* [acteur] ham (actor) **2.** [frimeur] poser.

cabrer [3] [kabre] ◆ ***se cabrer*** **vp 1.** [cheval] to rear (up) / [avion] to climb steeply **2.** *fig* [personne] to take offence *UK ou* offense *US*.

cabri [kabri] **nm** kid.

cabriole [kabrijɔl] **nf** [bond] caper / [pirouette] somersault.

cabriolet [kabrijɔlɛ] **nm** convertible.

CAC, ***Cac*** [kak] (abr de ***Compagnie des agents de change***) **nf : l'indice CAC-40** *the French stock exchange shares index*.

caca [kaka] **nm** *fam* pooh *UK*, poop *US* ▸ **faire caca** to do a pooh *UK ou* poop *US* ▸ **caca d'oie** greeny-yellow.

cacahouète, ***cacahuète*** [kakawɛt] **nf** peanut.

cacao [kakao] **nm 1.** [poudre] cocoa (powder) **2.** [boisson] cocoa **3.** [graine] cocoa bean.

cachalot [kaʃalo] **nm** sperm whale.

cache [kaʃ] ■ **nf** [cachette] hiding place.
■ **nm 1.** [masque] card *(for masking text)* **2.** CINÉ & PHOTO mask.

cache-cache [kaʃkaʃ] **nm inv : jouer à cache-cache** to play hide-and-seek.

cache-col [kaʃkɔl] **nm inv** scarf.

cachemire [kaʃmir] **nm 1.** [laine] cashmere **2.** [dessin] paisley.

cache-nez [kaʃne] **nm inv** scarf.

cache-oreilles [kaʃɔrɛj] **nm inv** earmuffs.

cache-pot [kaʃpo] **nm inv** pot holder.

cacher [3] [kaʃe] **vt 1.** [gén] to hide ▸ **je ne vous cache pas que...** to be honest,... **2.** [vue] to mask.
◆ ***se cacher*** **vp : se cacher (de qqn)** to hide (from sb).

cache-sexe [kaʃsɛks] **nm inv** G-string.

cachet [kaʃɛ] **nm 1.** [comprimé] tablet, pill **2.** [marque] postmark **3.** [style] style, character ▸ **avoir du cachet** to have character **4.** [rétribution] fee **5.** [sceau] seal.

cacheter [27] [kaʃte] **vt** to seal.

cachette [kaʃɛt] **nf** hiding place ▸ **en cachette** secretly.

cachot [kaʃo] **nm 1.** [cellule] cell **2.** [punition] solitary confinement.

cachotterie [kaʃɔtri] **nf** little secret ▸ **faire des cachotteries (à qqn)** to hide things (from sb).

cachottier, ère [kaʃɔtje, ɛr] ■ **adj** secretive.
■ **nm, f** secretive person.

cachou [kaʃu] **nm** *sweet taken to freshen the breath.*

cacophonie [kakɔfɔni] **nf** din.

cactus [kaktys] **nm** cactus.

c.-à-d. (abr écrite de ***c'est-à-dire***) i.e.

cadastre [kadastr] **nm** [registre] ≃ land register / [service] ≃ land registry *UK*, ≃ land office *US*.

cadavérique [kadaverik] **adj** deathly.

cadavre [kadavr] **nm** corpse, (dead) body ▸ **un cadavre ambulant** a walking skeleton.

caddie [kadi] **nm** [golf] caddie.

Caddie® [kadi] **nm** [chariot] (shopping) trolley *UK*, shopping cart *US*.

cadeau, x [kado] ■ **nm** present, gift ▸ **faire cadeau de qqch à qqn** to give sthg to sb (as a present) ▸ **cadeau d'anniversaire** birthday present ▸ **il ne nous a pas fait de cadeau** *fam* he didn't do us any favours.
■ **adj inv : idée cadeau** gift idea ▸ **paquet cadeau** gift-wrapped parcel *UK* *ou* package *US*.

cadenas [kadna] **nm** padlock.

cadenasser [3] [kadnase] **vt** to padlock.
◆ ***se cadenasser*** **vp** to padlock.

cadence [kadɑ̃s] **nf 1.** [rythme musical] rhythm ▸ **en cadence** in time **2.** [de travail] rate.

cadencé, e [kadɑ̃se] **adj** rhythmical.

cadet, ette [kadɛ, ɛt] ■ **adj** younger.
■ **nm, f 1.** [de deux enfants] younger / [de plusieurs enfants] youngest ▸ **il est mon cadet de deux ans** he's two years younger than me ▸ **c'est le cadet de mes soucis** *fig* that's the least of my worries **2.** SPORT junior.

cadran [kadrɑ̃] **nm** dial ▸ **cadran solaire** sundial.

cadre [kadr] **nm 1.** [de tableau, de porte] frame ▸ **cadre de bicyclette** bicycle frame
2. [contexte] context ▸ **cadre de vie** (living) environment ▸ **dans le cadre de** as part of / [limite] within the limits *ou* scope of ▸ **cela n'entre pas dans le cadre de mes fonctions** it falls outside the scope of my responsibilities ▸ **sortir du cadre de** to go beyond (the scope of)
3. [décor, milieu] surroundings *pl*
4. [responsable] **: cadre moyen/supérieur** middle/senior manager ▸ **jeune cadre dynamique** *iron* dynamic young executive ▸ **un poste de cadre** an executive *ou* a managerial post ▸ **être rayé des cadres** to be dismissed
5. [sur formulaire] box ▸ **'cadre réservé à l'administration'** 'for official use only'
6. DR **: loi cadre** outline law ▸ **plan cadre** blueprint (project) ▸ **réforme cadre** general outline of reform
7. INFORM [page Internet] frame / [PAO] box.

cadrer [3] [kadre] ■ **vi** to agree, to tally.
■ **vt** CINÉ, PHOTO & TV to frame.

cadreur, se [kadrœr, øz] **nm, f** cameraman (f camerawoman).

caduc, caduque [kadyk] **adj 1.** [feuille] deciduous **2.** [qui n'est plus valide] obsolete.

CAF [kaf] ■ **nf** (abr de ***Caisse d'allocations familiales***) Child Benefit office *UK*, Aid to Dependent Children office *US*.
■ (abr de ***coût, assurance, fret***) cif.

cafard [kafar] **nm 1.** *fam* SCOL sneak / [à la police] rat, grass *UK* **2.** [insecte] cockroach **3.** *fig* [mélancolie] **: avoir le cafard** to feel low *ou* down.

cafarder [3] [kafarde] **vi 1.** [dénoncer - SCOL] to sneak / [- à la police] to snitch, to grass *UK* **2.** [déprimer] to feel low *ou* down.

cafardeux, euse [kafardø, øz] **adj** low, down.

café [kafe] ■ **nm 1.** [plante, boisson] coffee ▸ **café crème** *coffee with frothy milk* ▸ **café glacé** iced coffee ▸ **café en grains** coffee beans ▸ **café au lait** white coffee *UK*, coffee with milk *US (with hot milk)* ▸ **café liégeois** *coffee ice cream with whipped cream poured over* ▸ **café moulu** ground coffee ▸ **café noir** black coffee ▸ **café en poudre** *ou* **soluble** instant coffee **2.** [lieu] bar, café.
■ **adj inv** coffee-coloured *UK*, coffee-colored *US*.

caféine [kafein] **nf** caffeine ▸ **sans caféine** caffeine-free.

cafétéria [kafeterja] **nf** cafeteria.

café-théâtre [kafeteatr] (pl **cafés-théâtres**) **nm** ≃ cabaret.

cafetier [kaftje] **nm** café owner.

cafetière [kaftjɛr] **nf 1.** [récipient] coffeepot **2.** [électrique] coffeemaker / [italienne] percolator.

cafouiller [3] [kafuje] **vi** *fam* **1.** [s'embrouiller] to get into a mess **2.** [moteur] to misfire / TV to be on the blink.

cafter [3] [kafte] **vi** *fam* to sneak, to snitch.

cafteur, euse [kaftœr, øz] **nm, f** *fam* sneak, snitch.

cage [kaʒ] **nf 1.** [pour animaux] cage **2.** [dans une maison] **: cage d'escalier** stairwell **3.** ANAT **: cage thoracique** rib cage.

cageot [kaʒo] **nm** [caisse] crate.

cagibi [kaʒibi] **nm** boxroom *UK*, storage room *US*.

cagneux, ***euse*** [kaɲø, øz] **adj : avoir les genoux cagneux** to be knock-kneed.

cagnotte [kaɲɔt] **nf 1.** [caisse commune] kitty **2.** [économies] savings *pl*.

cagoule [kagul] **nf 1.** [passe-montagne] balaclava **2.** [de moine] cowl **3.** [de voleur, de pénitent] hood.

cahier [kaje] **nm 1.** [de notes] exercise book *UK*, notebook ▸ **cahier de brouillon** rough book *UK*, notebook *US* ▸ **cahier de textes** homework book **2.** COMM **: cahier des charges** specification.

cahin-caha [kaɛ̃kaa] **adv : aller cahin-caha** to be jogging along.

cahot [kao] **nm** bump, jolt.

cahoter [3] [kaɔte] ■ **vi** to jolt around.
■ **vt 1.** [secouer] to jolt **2.** *fig* [malmener] to knock around.

cahute [kayt] **nf** shack.

caïd [kaid] **nm 1.** [chef de bande] leader **2.** *fam* [homme fort] big shot.

caillasse [kajas] **nf** *fam* loose stones *pl*.

caille [kaj] **nf** quail.

caillé, ***e*** [kaje] **adj** [lait] curdled / [sang] clotted.
◆ ***caillé*** **nm** CULIN curds *pl*.

cailler [3] [kaje] **vi 1.** [lait] to curdle / [sang] to clot **2.** *fam* [avoir froid] to be freezing.
◆ ***se cailler*** **vp 1.** [lait] to curdle / [sang] to clot **2.** *fam* [avoir froid] **: on se caille** it's freezing.

caillot [kajo] **nm** clot.

caillou, ***x*** [kaju] **nm 1.** [pierre] stone, pebble **2.** *fam* [pierre précieuse] rock **3.** *fam* [crâne] head.

caillouteux, ***euse*** [kajutø, øz] **adj** stony.

caïman [kaimɑ̃] **nm** cayman.

Caire [kɛr] **npr : Le Caire** Cairo.

caisse [kɛs] **nf 1.** [boîte] crate, box ▸ **caisse à outils** toolbox
2. TECHNOL case
3. MUS **: grosse caisse** bass drum
4. [guichet] cash desk, till / [de supermarché] checkout, till ▸ **caisse enregistreuse** cash register ▸ **caisse rapide** [dans un supermarché] quick-service till, express checkout ▸ **passer à la caisse** [magasin] to go to the cash desk / [supermarché] to go through the checkout / [banque] to go to the cashier's desk / [recevoir son salaire] to collect one's wages ▸ **avoir 3 000 euros en caisse** to have 3,000 euros in the till
5. [recette] takings *pl* ▸ **les caisses de l'État** the coffers of the State ▸ **tenir la caisse** *fig* to hold the purse strings ▸ **caisse noire** slush fund
6. [organisme] **: caisse d'allocation** ≃ social security *UK* *ou* welfare *US* office ▸ **caisse d'Allocations familiales** Child Benefit office *UK*, Aid to Dependent Children office *US* ▸ **caisse primaire d'Assurance maladie** *French Social Security office in charge of medical insurance* ▸ **caisse d'épargne** [fonds] savings fund / [établissement] savings bank ▸ **caisse de prévoyance** contingency fund ▸ **caisse de retraite** pension fund.

caissette [kɛsɛt] **nf** small box.

caissier, ***ère*** [kesje, ɛr] **nm, f** cashier.

caisson [kɛsɔ̃] **nm 1.** MIL & TECHNOL caisson **2.** ARCHIT coffer.

cajoler [3] [kaʒɔle] **vt** to cuddle.

cajolerie [kaʒɔlri] **nf** cuddle.

cajou [kaʒu] ➤ ***noix***.

cake [kɛk] **nm** fruitcake.

cal[1] [kal] **nm** callus.

cal[2] (abr écrite de ***calorie***) cal.

calamar [kalamar], ***calmar*** [kalmar] **nm** squid.

calaminé, ***e*** [kalamine] **adj** coked up.

calamité [kalamite] **nf** disaster.

calandre [kalɑ̃dr] **nf 1.** [de voiture] radiator grill **2.** [machine] calender.

calanque [kalɑ̃k] **nf** rocky inlet.

calcaire [kalkɛr] ■ **adj** [eau] hard / [sol] chalky / [roche] limestone.
■ **nm** limestone.

calciner [3] [kalsine] **vt** to burn to a cinder.

calcium [kalsjɔm] **nm** calcium.

calcul [kalkyl] **nm 1.** [opération] **: le calcul** arithmetic ▸ **calcul mental** mental arithmetic ▸ **calcul algébrique** calculus **2.** [compte] calculation ▸ **ça reviendra moins cher, fais le calcul!** it'll be cheaper: just work it out! ▸ **le raisonnement est correct, mais le calcul est faux** the method's right, but the calculations are wrong **3.** *fig* [plan] plan ▸ **un mauvais** *ou* **faux calcul** a bad move ▸ **agir par calcul** to act out of self-interest **4.** MÉD **: calcul (rénal)** kidney stone ▸ **calcul biliaire** gall stone.

calculateur, ***trice*** [kalkylatœr, tris] **adj** *péj* calculating.
◆ ***calculateur*** **nm** computer.
◆ ***calculatrice*** **nf** calculator ▸ **calculatrice de poche** pocket calculator.

calculer [3] [kalkyle] ■ **vt 1.** [déterminer] to calculate, to work out ▸ **calculer le montant de la facture** to calculate the bill ▸ **calculer qqch de tête** to work out sthg in one's head **2.** [prévoir] to plan ▸ **mal/bien calculer qqch** to judge sthg badly/well.
■ **vi 1.** [faire des calculs] to calculate **2.** [dépenses] [dépenser avec parcimonie] to budget carefully, to count the pennies *péj*.

calculette [kalkylɛt] **nf** pocket calculator.

Calcutta [kalkyta] **npr** Calcutta.

cale [kal] **nf 1.** [de navire] hold ▸ **cale sèche** dry dock ▸ **être en cale sèche** to be in dry dock ▸ **cale de construction** *ou* **de lancement** slip, slipway **2.** [pour immobiliser] wedge ▸ **mettre une voiture sur cales** to put a car on blocks **3.** [d'ébéniste] **: cale à poncer** sanding block.

calé, ***e*** [kale] **adj** *fam* **1.** [personne] clever, brainy ▸ **être calé en** to be good at **2.** [problème] tough.

calebasse [kalbas] **nf** gourd.

calèche [kalɛʃ] **nf** (horse-drawn) carriage.

caleçon [kalsɔ̃] **nm 1.** [sous-vêtement masculin] boxer shorts *pl*, pair of boxer shorts ▸ **caleçon long** longjohns *pl*, pair of longjohns **2.** [vêtement féminin] leggings *pl*, pair of leggings.

Calédonie [kaledɔni] **nf : la Calédonie** Caledonia.

calembour [kalɑ̃bur] **nm** pun, play on words.

calendes [kalɑ̃d] **nfpl : renvoyer qqch aux calendes grecques** to postpone sthg indefinitely.

calendrier [kalɑ̃drije] **nm 1.** [système, agenda, d'un festival] calendar **2.** [emploi du temps] timetable *UK*, schedule *US* **3.** [d'un voyage] schedule.

cale-pied [kalpje] (pl **cale-pieds**) **nm** toe-clip.

calepin [kalpɛ̃] **nm** notebook.

caler [3] [kale] ■ **vt 1.** [avec cale] to wedge **2.** [stabiliser, appuyer] to prop up **3.** *fam* [remplir] **: ça cale (l'estomac)** it's filling.

■ **vi 1.** [moteur, véhicule] to stall **2.** *fam* [personne] to give up.

calfeutrer [3] [kalføtre] **vt** to draughtproof *UK*.

◆ ***se calfeutrer*** **vp** to shut o.s. up *ou* away.

calibre [kalibr] **nm 1.** [de tuyau] diameter, bore / [de fusil] calibre *UK*, caliber *US* / [de fruit, d'œuf] size ▸ **de gros calibre** large-calibre **2.** *fam fig* [envergure] calibre *UK*, caliber *US* ▸ **du même calibre** of the same calibre.

calibrer [3] [kalibre] **vt 1.** [machine, fusil] to calibrate **2.** [fruit, œuf] to grade.

calice [kalis] **nm 1.** RELIG chalice **2.** BOT calyx.

calicot [kaliko] **nm 1.** [tissu] calico **2.** [banderole] banner.

Californie [kalifɔrni] **nf : la Californie** California ▸ **la Basse Californie** Lower California.

californien, ***enne*** [kalifɔrnjɛ̃, ɛn] **adj** Californian.

◆ ***Californien***, ***enne*** **nm, f** Californian.

califourchon [kalifurʃɔ̃] ◆ ***à califourchon*** **loc adv** astride ▸ **être (assis) à califourchon sur qqch** to sit astride sthg.

câlin, ***e*** [kalɛ̃, in] **adj** affectionate.

◆ ***câlin*** **nm** cuddle ▸ **faire un câlin à qqn** to give sb a cuddle.

câliner [3] [kaline] **vt** to cuddle.

calisson [kalisɔ̃] **nm** *small iced cake made with almond paste*.

calleux, ***euse*** [kalø, øz] **adj** calloused.

call-girl [kɔlgœrl] (pl **call-girls**) **nf** call girl.

calligraphie [kaligrafi] **nf** calligraphy.

callosité [kalozite] **nf** callus.

calmant, ***e*** [kalmɑ̃, ɑ̃t] **adj** soothing.

◆ ***calmant*** **nm** [pour la douleur] painkiller / [pour l'anxiété] tranquillizer *UK*, tranquilizer *US*, sedative.

calmar ➤ ***calamar***.

calme [kalm] ■ **adj** quiet, calm ▸ **par temps calme** when there's no wind.

■ **nm 1.** [gén] calm, calmness ▸ **dans le calme** quietly, calmly ▸ **du calme!** calm down! ▸ **être au calme** to have *ou* to enjoy peace and quiet ▸ **garder son calme** to keep calm ▸ **perdre son calme** to lose one's composure ▸ **retrouver son calme** to calm down, to regain one's composure ▸ **rétablir le calme** to restore order ▸ **le calme plat** [de la mer] dead calm ▸ **c'est le calme plat en ce moment** *fig* things are very quiet at the moment ▸ **c'est le calme avant la tempête** it's is the calm before the storm **2.** [absence de bruit] peace (and quiet).

calmer [3] [kalme] **vt 1.** [apaiser] to calm (down) **2.** [réduire - douleur] to soothe / [- inquiétude] to allay.

◆ ***se calmer*** **vp 1.** [s'apaiser - personne, discussion] to calm down / [- tempête] to abate / [- mer] to become calm **2.** [diminuer - douleur] to ease / [- fièvre, inquiétude, désir] to subside.

calomnie [kalɔmni] **nf** [écrits] libel / [paroles] slander.

calomnier [9] [kalɔmnje] **vt** [par écrit] to libel / [verbalement] to slander.

calomnieux, ***euse*** [kalɔmnjø, øz] **adj** [écrits] libellous *UK*, libelous *US* / [propos] slanderous.

calorie [kalɔri] **nf** calorie.

calorifère [kalɔrifɛr] ■ **nm** stove.

■ **adj** heat-giving.

calorifique [kalɔrifik] **adj** calorific.

calorifuge [kalɔrifyʒ] ■ **adj** insulating.

■ **nm** insulation.

calorique [kalɔrik] **adj** calorific.

calot [kalo] **nm 1.** [de militaire] ≃ beret **2.** [bille] (large) marble.

calotte [kalɔt] **nf 1.** [bonnet] skullcap **2.** *fam* [gifle] slap **3.** GÉOGR **: calotte glaciaire** ice cap.

calque [kalk] **nm 1.** [dessin] tracing **2.** [papier] **: (papier) calque** tracing paper **3.** *fig* [imitation] (exact) copy ▸ **il est le calque de son père** he's the spitting image of his father **4.** [traduction] calque, loan translation.

calquer [3] [kalke] **vt 1.** [carte] to trace **2.** [imiter] to copy exactly ▸ **calquer qqch sur qqch** to model sthg on sthg **3.** [traduire littéralement] to translate literally.

calvados [kalvados] **nm** Calvados.

calvaire [kalvɛr] **nm 1.** [croix] wayside cross **2.** *fig* [épreuve] ordeal.

◆ ***Calvaire*** **nm : le Calvaire** Calvary.

calviniste [kalvinist] **adj** & **nmf** Calvinist.

calvitie [kalvisi] **nf** baldness ▸ **calvitie précoce** premature baldness.

camaïeu [kamajø] **nm** monochrome ▸ **en camaïeu** monochrome, in monochrome.

camarade [kamarad] **nmf 1.** [compagnon, ami] friend ▸ **camarade de classe** classmate ▸ **camarade d'école** schoolfriend **2.** POLIT comrade.

camaraderie [kamaradri] **nf 1.** [familiarité, entente] friendship **2.** [solidarité] comradeship, camaraderie.

cambiste [kɑ̃bist] ■ **adj** FIN foreign exchange *(avant n)*.

■ **nmf** FIN foreign exchange dealer.

Cambodge [kɑ̃bɔdʒ] **nm : le Cambodge** Cambodia ▸ **au Cambodge** in Cambodia.

cambodgien, ***enne*** [kɑ̃bɔdʒjɛ̃, ɛn] **adj** Cambodian.

◆ ***Cambodgien***, ***enne*** **nm, f** Cambodian.

cambouis [kɑ̃bwi] **nm** dirty grease.

cambré, ***e*** [kɑ̃bre] **adj** arched.

cambrer [3] [kɑ̃bre] **vt : cambrer les reins** *ou* **la taille** to arch one's back.
◆ ***se cambrer*** **vp** [se redresser] to arch one's back.

cambriolage [kɑ̃brijɔlaʒ] **nm** burglary.

cambrioler [3] [kɑ̃brijɔle] **vt** to burgle *UK*, to burglarize *US*.

cambrioleur, ***euse*** [kɑ̃brijɔlœr, øz] **nm, f** burglar.

cambrousse [kɑ̃brus] **nf** *fam* **: en pleine cambrousse** out in the sticks.

cambrure [kɑ̃bryr] **nf 1.** [de pied] instep ▸ **cambrure des reins** *ou* **du dos** small of the back **2.** [de poutre] curve / [de chaussure] arch.

came [kam] **nf 1.** TECHNOL cam **2.** *tfam* [drogue] stuff.

camé, ***e*** [kame] *tfam* ■ **adj** [drogué] stoned.
■ **nm, f** junkie.

camée [kame] **nm** cameo.

caméléon [kameleɔ̃] **nm** *litt* & *fig* chameleon.

camélia [kamelja] **nm** camellia.

camelote [kamlɔt] **nf** [marchandise de mauvaise qualité] junk, rubbish *UK*.

camembert [kamɑ̃bɛr] **nm 1.** [fromage] Camembert **2.** [graphique] pie chart.

camer [3] [kame] ◆ ***se camer*** *tfam* **vpi** to be a junkie ▸ **se camer à la cocaïne** to be on coke.

caméra [kamera] **nf 1.** CINÉ & TV camera ▸ **caméra cachée** *ou* **invisible** hidden camera **2.** [d'amateur] cinecamera.

cameraman [kameraman] (pl **cameramen** [kameramɛn] *ou* **cameramans**) **nm** cameraman.

Cameroun [kamrun] **nm : le Cameroun** Cameroon ▸ **au Cameroun** in Cameroon.

camerounais, ***e*** [kamrunɛ, ɛz] **adj** Cameroonian.
◆ ***Camerounais***, ***e*** **nm, f** Cameroonian.

Caméscope® [kameskɔp] **nm** camcorder ▸ **Caméscope® numérique** digital camcorder.

camion [kamjɔ̃] **nm** truck, lorry *UK* ▸ **camion de déménagement** removal van *UK*, moving van *US*.

camion-citerne [kamjɔ̃sitɛrn] (pl **camions-citernes**) **nm** tanker *UK*, tanker truck *US*.

camionnage [kamjɔnaʒ] **nm** road haulage *UK*, trucking *US*.

camionnette [kamjɔnɛt] **nf** van.

camionneur [kamjɔnœr] **nm 1.** [conducteur] lorry-driver *UK*, truckdriver *US* **2.** [entrepreneur] road haulier *UK*, trucker *US*.

camion-poubelle (pl **camions-poubelles** [kamjɔ̃pubɛl]) **nm** dustcart *UK*, (dust)bin lorry *UK*, garbage truck *US*.

camisole [kamizɔl] ◆ ***camisole de force*** **nf** straitjacket.

camomille [kamɔmij] **nf 1.** [plante] camomile **2.** [tisane] camomile tea.

camouflage [kamuflaʒ] **nm** [déguisement] camouflage / *fig* [dissimulation] concealment.

camoufler [3] [kamufle] **vt** [déguiser] to camouflage / *fig* [dissimuler] to conceal, to cover up ▸ **camoufler qqch en qqch** to camouflage sthg as sthg.
◆ ***se camoufler*** **vp** [se cacher] to hide.

camouflet [kamuflɛ] **nm** *littéraire* [affront] snub ▸ **infliger un camouflet à qqn** to snub sb.

camp [kɑ̃] **nm 1.** [gén] camp ▸ **camp de concentration** concentration camp ▸ **camp de prisonniers** prisoner of war camp ▸ **camp de réfugiés** refugee camp ▸ **camp retranché** fortified camp, fortress ▸ **camp de scouts** scout camp ▸ **camp de travail (forcé)** forced labour *UK ou* labor *US* camp ▸ **camp de vacances** holiday *UK ou* vacation *US* camp ▸ **camp volant** temporary camp ▸ **ficher le camp** *fam* to get lost, to clear off ▸ **lever le camp** to break camp / *fig* to clear off *ou* out ▸ **foutre le camp** *tfam* [personne] to bugger off *UK*, to take off *US* **2.** SPORT half (of the field) **3.** [parti] side ▸ **il faut choisir son camp** you must decide which side you're on ▸ **changer de camp** to change sides ▸ **passer dans l'autre camp** to go over to the other side.

campagnard, ***e*** [kɑ̃paɲar, ard] ■ **adj 1.** [de la campagne] country *(avant n)* **2.** [rustique] rustic.
■ **nm, f** countryman (f countrywoman).

campagne [kɑ̃paɲ] **nf 1.** [habitat] country / [paysage] countryside ▸ **à la campagne** in the country ▸ **en rase campagne** in open country ▸ **battre la campagne** [police] to comb the countryside / [divaguer] to wander **2.** MIL campaign ▸ **partir en campagne** to start campaigning **3.** [publicité & POLIT] campaign ▸ **faire campagne** to campaign ▸ **campagne d'affichage** poster campaign ▸ **campagne commerciale** marketing campaign ▸ **campagne de diffamation** whispering campaign ▸ **campagne électorale** election campaign ▸ **campagne de presse** press campaign ▸ **campagne publicitaire** *ou* **de publicité** advertising campaign, publicity campaign ▸ **campagne teasing** teaser campaign ▸ **campagne télévisuelle** television campaign ▸ **campagne de vente** sales campaign.

PARONYME / CONFUSABLE
campagne
Pour traduire le mot campagne, il vaut mieux utiliser *countryside* plutôt que *country* qui signifie d'abord pays.

campanule [kɑ̃panyl] **nf** bellflower, campanula.

campé, ***e*** [kɑ̃pe] **adj : bien campé** [personnage] well-rounded / [récit] well-constructed ▸ **être bien campé (sur ses jambes)** to stand firmly on one's feet.

campement [kɑ̃pmɑ̃] **nm** camp, encampment.

camper [3] [kɑ̃pe] ■ **vi** to camp.
■ **vt 1.** [poser solidement] to place firmly **2.** *fig* [esquisser] to portray.
◆ ***se camper*** **vp : se camper devant qqn/qqch** to plant o.s. in front of sb/sthg.

campeur, ***euse*** [kɑ̃pœr, øz] **nm, f** camper.

camphre [kɑ̃fr] **nm** camphor.

camphré, ***e*** [kɑ̃fre] **adj** camphorated.

camping [kɑ̃piŋ] **nm** **1.** [activité] camping ▸ **faire du camping** to go camping ▸ **camping sauvage** camping in the wild, wilderness camping *US* **2.** [terrain] campsite.

camping-car [kɑ̃piŋkar] (pl **camping-cars**) **nm** camper, camper-van *UK*, Dormobile® *UK*.

Camping-Gaz® [kɑ̃piŋgaz] **nm inv** butane gas-stove, ≃ Primus® stove *UK*.

campus [kɑ̃pys] **nm** campus.

camus [kamy] ➤ ***nez***.

Canada [kanada] **nm : le Canada** Canada ▸ **au Canada** in Canada.

Canadair® [kanadɛr] **nm** fire-fighting plane, tanker plane *US*.

canadianisme [kanadjanism] **nm** Canadianism.

canadien, ***enne*** [kanadjɛ̃, ɛn] **adj** Canadian.
◆ ***canadienne*** **nf** [veste] sheepskin jacket.
◆ ***Canadien***, ***enne*** **nm, f** Canadian.

canaille [kanaj] ■ **adj** **1.** [coquin] roguish **2.** [vulgaire] crude.
■ **nf** **1.** [scélérat] scoundrel **2.** *hum* [coquin] little devil.

canal, ***aux*** [kanal, o] **nm** **1.** [gén] channel ▸ **par le canal de qqn** *fig* [par l'entremise de] through sb ▸ **canal de distribution** distribution channel, channel of distribution **2.** [voie d'eau] canal ▸ **canal maritime** *ou* **de navigation** ship canal **3.** ANAT canal, duct ▸ **canal auditif** auditory canal ▸ **canal lacrymal** tear duct, lacrymal canal *(terme spécialisé)* **4.** AGRIC canal ▸ **canal de drainage/d'irrigation** drainage/irrigation canal **5.** INFORM **: canal IRC** *ou* **de dialogue en direct** IRC channel.
◆ ***Canal*** **nm : Canal+** *French pay-TV channel*.

canalisation [kanalizasjɔ̃] **nf** **1.** [conduit] pipe **2.** *litt & fig* [action de canaliser] channelling.

canaliser [3] [kanalize] **vt** **1.** [cours d'eau] to canalize **2.** *fig* [orienter] to channel.

canapé [kanape] **nm** **1.** [siège] sofa ▸ **canapé convertible** sofa bed **2.** CULIN canapé.

canapé-lit [kanapeli] (pl **canapés-lits**) **nm** sofa bed.

canaque, ***kanak*** [kanak] **adj** Kanak.
◆ ***Canaque*** **nmf** Kanak.

canard [kanar] **nm** **1.** [oiseau] duck **2.** [fausse note] wrong note **3.** *fam* [journal] rag.

canari [kanari] ■ **nm** canary.
■ **adj inv : jaune canari** canary yellow.

Canaries [kanari] **nfpl : les Canaries** the Canaries ▸ **aux Canaries** in the Canaries.

Canberra [kɑ̃bera] **npr** Canberra.

cancan [kɑ̃kɑ̃] **nm** **1.** [ragot] piece of gossip ▸ **dire des cancans sur qqn** to spread gossip about sb **2.** [danse] cancan.

cancaner [3] [kɑ̃kane] **vi** **1.** [canard] to quack **2.** [médire] to spread gossip ▸ **cancaner sur qqn** to spread gossip about sb.

cancanier, ***ère*** [kɑ̃kanje, ɛr] ■ **adj** gossipy.
■ **nm, f** gossip.

cancer [kɑ̃sɛr] **nm** MÉD cancer.
◆ ***Cancer*** **nm** **1.** ASTROL Cancer ▸ **être Cancer** to be (a) Cancer **2.** GÉOGR **: le tropique du Cancer** the tropic of Cancer.

cancéreux, ***euse*** [kɑ̃serø, øz] ■ **adj** **1.** [personne] suffering from cancer **2.** [tumeur] cancerous.
■ **nm, f** [personne] cancer sufferer.

cancérigène [kɑ̃seriʒɛn] **adj** carcinogenic.

cancérologue [kɑ̃serɔlɔg] **nmf** cancerologist.

cancre [kɑ̃kr] **nm** *fam* dunce.

cancrelat [kɑ̃krəla] **nm** cockroach.

candélabre [kɑ̃delabr] **nm** candelabra.

candeur [kɑ̃dœr] **nf** ingenuousness.

candi [kɑ̃di] **adj : sucre candi** (sugar) candy.

candidat, ***e*** [kɑ̃dida, at] **nm, f : candidat (à)** candidate (for).

candidature [kɑ̃didatyr] **nf** **1.** [à un poste] application ▸ **poser sa candidature pour qqch** to apply for sthg **2.** [à une élection] candidacy, candidature *UK*.

candide [kɑ̃did] **adj** ingenuous.

cane [kan] **nf** (female) duck.

caneton [kantɔ̃] **nm** (male) duckling.

canette [kanɛt] **nf** **1.** [de fil] spool **2.** [petite cane] (female) duckling **3.** [de boisson - bouteille] bottle / [- boîte] can.

canevas [kanva] **nm** **1.** COUT canvas **2.** [plan] structure.

caniche [kaniʃ] **nm** poodle.

canicule [kanikyl] **nf** heatwave.

canif [kanif] **nm** penknife.

canin, ***e*** [kanɛ̃, in] **adj** canine ▸ **exposition canine** dog show.
◆ ***canine*** **nf** canine (tooth).

caniveau, ***x*** [kanivo] **nm** gutter.

cannabis [kanabis] **nm** cannabis.

canne [kan] **nf** **1.** [bâton] walking stick ▸ **canne à pêche** fishing rod **2.** *fam* [jambe] pin.
◆ ***canne à sucre*** **nf** sugar cane.

canné, ***e*** [kane] **adj** cane.

canneberge [kanbɛrʒ] **nf** cranberry.

cannelé, ***e*** [kanle] **adj** fluted.

cannelle [kanɛl] ■ **nf** **1.** [aromate] cinnamon **2.** [robinet] tap *UK*, faucet *US*.
■ **adj inv** [couleur] cinnamon.

cannelloni [kanelɔni] (pl **cannelloni** *ou* **cannellonis**) **nm** cannelloni.

cannelure [kanlyr] **nf** **1.** [de colonne] flute **2.** BOT & GÉOL striation.

Cannes [kan] **npr** Cannes ▸ **le festival de Cannes** the Cannes Film Festival.

cannibale [kanibal] **nmf & adj** cannibal.

cannibalisme [kanibalism] **nm** cannibalism / [sociologie & ÉCON] cannibalization.

canoë [kanɔe] **nm** canoe.

canoë-kayak [kanɔekajak] (pl **canoës-kayaks**) **nm** kayak.

canon [kanɔ̃] ■ **nm** **1.** [arme] gun / HIST cannon **2.** [tube d'arme] barrel **3.** *fam* [verre de vin] glass (of wine) **4.** MUS : **chanter en canon** to sing in canon **5.** [norme & RELIG] canon.
■ **adj** ➤ ***droit***.

canonique [kanɔnik] **adj** canonical ▸ **d'un âge canonique** *fig* of a venerable age.

canoniser [3] [kanɔnize] **vt** to canonize.

canopée [kanɔpe] **nf** [écologie] canopy.

canot [kano] **nm** dinghy ▸ **canot pneumatique** inflatable dinghy ▸ **canot de sauvetage** lifeboat.

canotage [kanɔtaʒ] **nm** rowing, boating ▸ **faire du canotage** to go rowing *ou* boating.

canotier [kanɔtje] **nm** **1.** [rameur] rower **2.** [chapeau] boater.

cantal [kɑ̃tal] **nm** *semi-hard cheese from the Auvergne.*

cantate [kɑ̃tat] **nf** cantata.

cantatrice [kɑ̃tatris] **nf** [d'opéra] (opera) singer / [de concert] (concert) singer.

cantine [kɑ̃tin] **nf** **1.** [réfectoire] cafeteria, canteen *UK* **2.** [malle] trunk.

cantique [kɑ̃tik] **nm** hymn.

canton [kɑ̃tɔ̃] **nm** **1.** [en France] ≃ district **2.** [en Suisse] canton.

cantonade [kɑ̃tɔnad] ◆ ***à la cantonade*** **loc adv** : **parler à la cantonade** to speak to everyone (in general).

cantonais, e [kɑ̃tɔnɛ, ɛz] **adj** Cantonese ▸ **riz cantonais** egg fried rice.
◆ ***cantonais*** **nm** [langue] Cantonese.
◆ ***Cantonais, e*** **nm, f** native *ou* inhabitant of Canton.

cantonal, e, aux [kɑ̃tɔnal, o] **adj** **1.** [en France] ≃ district *(avant n)* **2.** [en Suisse] cantonal.

cantonnement [kɑ̃tɔnmɑ̃] **nm** [MIL - action] billeting / [- lieu] billet.

cantonner [3] [kɑ̃tɔne] **vt** **1.** MIL to quarter, to billet **2.** [maintenir] to confine ▸ **cantonner qqn à** *ou* **dans** to confine sb to.
◆ ***se cantonner*** **vp** : **se cantonner dans** to confine o.s. to.

cantonnier [kɑ̃tɔnje] **nm** roadman.

canular [kanylar] **nm** *fam* hoax.

canyon [kanjɔn, kanjɔ̃] **nm** canyon.

canyoning [kaɲɔniŋ] **nm** canyoning.

CAO (abr de ***conception assistée par ordinateur***) **nf** CAD.

caoutchouc [kautʃu] **nm** **1.** [substance] rubber ▸ **en caoutchouc** rubber ▸ **caoutchouc mousse** foam rubber **2.** [plante] rubber plant **3.** [élastique] rubber *ou* elastic *UK* band.

caoutchouteux, euse [kautʃutø, øz] **adj** rubbery.

cap [kap] **nm** **1.** GÉOGR cape ▸ **le cap de Bonne-Espérance** the Cape of Good Hope ▸ **le cap Horn** Cape Horn ▸ **passer le cap de qqch** *fig* to get through sthg ▸ **passer le cap de la quarantaine** *fig* to turn forty **2.** [direction] course ▸ **changer de cap** to change course ▸ **mettre le cap sur** to head for.
◆ ***Cap*** **nm** : **Le Cap** Cape Town.

CAP (abr de ***certificat d'aptitude professionnelle***) **nm** *vocational training certificate (taken at secondary school).*

capable [kapabl] **adj** **1.** [apte] : **capable (de qqch/de faire qqch)** capable (of sthg/of doing sthg) **2.** [à même] : **capable de faire qqch** likely to do sthg ▸ **capable de réussir** likely to succeed **3.** DR competent.

capacité [kapasite] **nf** **1.** [de récipient] capacity **2.** [de personne] ability **3.** DR [mentale] capacity **4.** UNIV : **capacité en droit** [diplôme] *qualifying certificate in law gained by examination after 2 years' study.*

cape [kap] **nf** [vêtement] cloak ▸ **rire sous cape** *fig* to laugh up one's sleeve.

CAPES, Capes [kapɛs] (abr de ***certificat d'aptitude au professorat de l'enseignement du second degré***) **nm** *secondary school teaching certificate,* ≃ PGCE *UK*.

capésien, enne [kapesjɛ̃, ɛn] **nm, f** *person holding a secondary school teaching qualification.*

CAPET, Capet [kapɛt] (abr de ***certificat d'aptitude au professorat de l'enseignement technique***) **nm** *specialized teaching certificate.*

capharnaüm [kafarnaɔm] **nm** mess.

capillaire [kapilɛr] ■ **adj** **1.** [lotion] hair *(avant n)* **2.** ANAT & BOT capillary.
■ **nm** **1.** BOT maidenhair fern **2.** ANAT capillary.

capillarité [kapilarite] **nf** PHYS capillarity.

capitaine [kapitɛn] **nm** captain ▸ **capitaine au long cours** NAUT master mariner.

capitainerie [kapitɛnri] **nf** harbour *UK ou* harbor *US* master's office.

capital, e, aux [kapital, o] **adj** **1.** [décision, événement] major **2.** DR capital.
◆ ***capital*** **nm** FIN capital ▸ **capital d'exploitation** working capital ▸ **capital santé** *fig* reserves *pl* of health ▸ **capital social** authorized *ou* share capital.
◆ ***capitale*** **nf** [ville, lettre] capital.
◆ ***capitaux*** **nmpl** capital *(U)* ▸ **capitaux gelés** frozen assets.

capitalisation [kapitalizasjɔ̃] **nf** capitalization ▸ **capitalisation boursière** capital stock.

capitaliser [3] [kapitalize] ■ **vt** FIN to capitalize / *fig* to accumulate.
■ **vi** to save.
◆ ***capitaliser sur*** **v + prep** to cash in on, to capitalize on.

capitalisme [kapitalism] **nm** capitalism.

capitaliste [kapitalist] **nmf & adj** capitalist.

capital-risque [kapitalrisk] **nm** venture *ou* risk capital.

capital-risqueur [kapitalriskœr] (pl **capital-risqueurs**) **nm** venture capitalist.

capiteux, euse [kapitø, øz] **adj** **1.** [vin] intoxicating / [parfum] heady **2.** [charme] alluring.

capitonné*, *e [kapitɔne] **adj** padded ▸ **capitonné de cuir** with leather upholstery.

capitonner [3] [kapitɔne] **vt** to pad.

capituler [3] [kapityle] **vi** to surrender ▸ **capituler devant qqn/qqch** to surrender to sb/sthg.

caporal*, *aux [kapɔral, o] **nm 1.** MIL lance corporal **2.** [tabac] Caporal tobacco.

caporal-chef [kaporalʃɛf] (pl **caporaux-chefs** [kaporoʃɛf]) **nm** corporal.

capot [kapo] ■ **adj inv** [aux jeux de cartes] **: mettre qqn capot** to take all the tricks from sb.
■ **nm 1.** [de voiture] bonnet *UK*, hood *US* **2.** [de machine] (protective) cover.

capote [kapɔt] **nf 1.** [de voiture] hood *UK*, top *US* **2.** [manteau] greatcoat, overcoat **3.** [chapeau] bonnet **4.** *fam* [préservatif] condom ▸ **capote anglaise** *vieilli* condom, French letter *UK*.

capoter [3] [kapɔte] **vi 1.** [se retourner] to overturn **2.** *Québec* [perdre la tête] to lose one's head **3.** [échouer] to come to nothing.

câpre [kapr] **nf** caper.

caprice [kapris] **nm** whim ▸ **les caprices de la météo** the vagaries of the weather ▸ **faire des caprices** to be temperamental.

capricieux*, *euse [kaprisjø, øz] ■ **adj** [changeant] capricious ⁄ [coléreux] temperamental.
■ **nm, f** temperamental person.

capricorne [kaprikɔrn] **nm** ZOOL capricorn beetle.
◆ ***Capricorne*** **nm 1.** ASTROL Capricorn ▸ **être Capricorne** to be (a) Capricorn **2.** GÉOGR **: le tropique du Capricorne** the tropic of Capricorn.

capsule [kapsyl] **nf 1.** [de bouteille] cap **2.** ASTRON, BOT & MÉD capsule.

capter [3] [kapte] **vt 1.** [recevoir sur émetteur] to pick up **2.** [source, rivière] to harness **3.** *fig* [attention, confiance] to gain, to win.

capteur [kaptœr] **nm** PHYS sensor ▸ **capteur solaire** solar panel.

captieux*, *euse [kapsjø, øz] **adj** specious.

captif*, *ive [kaptif, iv] ■ **adj** captive ▸ **être captif de qqch** *fig* to be a slave to sthg.
■ **nm, f** prisoner.

captivant*, *e [kaptivɑ̃, ɑ̃t] **adj** [livre, film] enthralling ⁄ [personne] captivating.

captiver [3] [kaptive] **vt** to captivate.

captivité [kaptivite] **nf** captivity ▸ **en captivité** in captivity.

capture [kaptyr] **nf 1.** [action] capture **2.** [prise] catch **3.** INFORM **: capture d'écran** [image] screenshot ⁄ [action] screen capture.

capturer [3] [kaptyre] **vt** to catch, to capture.

capuche [kapyʃ] **nf** (detachable) hood.

capuchon [kapyʃɔ̃] **nm 1.** [bonnet - d'imperméable] hood ⁄ [- de religieux] cowl **2.** [bouchon] cap, top.

capucin [kapysɛ̃] **nm** RELIG Capuchin.

capucine [kapysin] **nf** [fleur] nasturtium.

Cap-Vert [kapvɛr] **nm** Cape Verde.

caquelon [kaklɔ̃] **nm** fondue dish.

caquet [kakɛ] **nm 1.** [de poule] cackling *(U)* **2.** *péj* [bavardage] chatter *(U)* ▸ **rabattre le caquet à** *ou* **de qqn** to shut sb up.

caqueter [27] [kakte] **vi 1.** [poule] to cackle **2.** *péj* [personne] to chatter.

car [1] [kar] **nm** bus, coach *UK*.

car [2] [kar] **conj** because, for.

carabine [karabin] **nf** rifle.

carabiné*, *e [karabine] **adj** *fam* [tempête] violent ⁄ [rhume] stinking ⁄ [amende] heavy.

Caracas [karakas] **npr** Caracas.

caraco [karako] **nm** loose blouse.

caracoler [3] [karakɔle] **vi 1.** [cheval] to prance ⁄ [cavalier] to caracole **2.** *fig* [sautiller] to prance around.

caractère [karaktɛr] **nm 1.** [gén] character ▸ **avoir du caractère** to have character ▸ **avoir bon caractère** to be good-natured ▸ **avoir mauvais caractère** to be bad-tempered ▸ **ce n'est pas dans son caractère d'être agressif** it's not in his character *ou* it's not in his nature to be aggressive ▸ **en petits/gros caractères** in small/large print ▸ **en caractères gras** in bold (type) ▸ **caractères d'imprimerie** block capitals ▸ **appartement/maison de caractère** flat/house with character **2.** [caractéristique] feature, characteristic ▸ **à caractère officiel** of an official nature ▸ **tous les caractères d'une crise économique** all the hallmarks of an economic crisis **3.** BIOL characteristic ▸ **caractère acquis/héréditaire** acquired/hereditary characteristic *ou* trait.

caractériel*, *elle [karakterjɛl] ■ **adj** [troubles] emotional ⁄ [personne] emotionally disturbed.
■ **nm, f** emotionally disturbed person.

caractérisé*, *e [karakterize] **adj** [net] clear ▸ **être d'une grossièreté caractérisée** to be downright rude.

caractériser [3] [karakterize] **vt** to be characteristic of.
◆ ***se caractériser*** **vp : se caractériser par qqch** to be characterized by sthg.

caractéristique [karakteristik] ■ **nf** characteristic, feature.
■ **adj : caractéristique (de)** characteristic (of).

carafe [karaf] **nf** [pour vin, eau] carafe ⁄ [pour alcool] decanter ▸ **rester en carafe** *fam* to be left stranded.

carafon [karafɔ̃] **nm** small carafe.

caraïbe [karaib] **adj** Caribbean.
◆ ***Caraïbe*** **nmf** Carib.
◆ ***Caraïbes*** [karaib] **nfpl : les caraïbes** the Caribbean ▸ **dans les Caraïbes** in the Caribbean.

carambolage [karɑ̃bɔlaʒ] **nm** pileup.

caramel [karamɛl] ■ **nm 1.** CULIN caramel **2.** [bonbon - dur] caramel, toffee, taffy *US* ⁄ [- mou] fudge.
■ **adj inv** [couleur] caramel.

caraméliser [3] [karamelize] **vt** [sucre] to caramelize ⁄ [gâteau] to coat with caramel.
◆ ***se caraméliser*** **vp** to caramelize.

carapace [karapas] **nf** shell ⁄ *fig* protection, shield.

carapater [3] [karapate] ◆ ***se carapater*** **vp** *fam* to hop it, to skedaddle, to scarper *UK*.

carat [kara] **nm** carat, karat *US* ▸ **or à 9 carats** 9-carat gold.

caravane [karavan] **nf 1.** [de camping, de désert] caravan **2.** [groupe de personnes] procession.

caravaning [karavaniŋ] **nm** caravanning *UK*.

caravelle [karavɛl] **nf** NAUT caravel.

carbone [karbɔn] **nm** carbon ▸ **(papier) carbone** carbon paper.

carbonique [karbɔnik] **adj : gaz carbonique** carbon dioxide ▸ **neige carbonique** dry ice.

carboniser [3] [karbɔnize] **vt** to burn to a cinder.

carbonnade [karbɔnad] **nf** CULIN *type of stew*.

carburant [karbyrɑ̃] ■ **adj m : mélange carburant** (fuel) mixture.
■ **nm** fuel.

carburateur [karbyratœr] **nm** carburettor *UK*, carburetor *US*.

carbure [karbyr] **nm** carbide.

carburer [3] [karbure] **vi 1.** [moteur] **: carburer bien/mal** to be well/badly tuned **2.** *fam* [être en forme] to be fine.

carcajou [karkaʒu] **nm** wolverine.

carcan [karkɑ̃] **nm** HIST iron collar / *fig* yoke.

carcasse [karkas] **nf 1.** [d'animal] carcass **2.** [de bâtiment, navire] framework **3.** [de véhicule] shell.

carcéral**, e, **aux [karseral, o] **adj** prison *(avant n)*.

carcinome [karsinɔm] **nm** carcinoma.

cardan [kardɑ̃] **nm** universal joint.

carder [3] [karde] **vt** to card.

cardiaque [kardjak] ■ **adj** cardiac ▸ **être cardiaque** to have a heart condition ▸ **crise cardiaque** heart attack.
■ **nmf** heart patient.

cardigan [kardigɑ̃] **nm** cardigan.

cardinal**, e, **aux [kardinal, o] **adj** cardinal.
◆ ***cardinal*** **nm 1.** RELIG cardinal **2.** [nombre] cardinal number.

cardiologue [kardjɔlɔg] **nmf** heart specialist, cardiologist.

cardio-vasculaire [kardjɔvaskylɛr] (pl **cardio-vasculaires**) **adj** cardiovascular.

cardon [kardɔ̃] **nm** cardoon.

Carême [karɛm] **nm : le Carême** Lent ▸ **faire Carême** to fast for *ou* to observe Lent.

carence [karɑ̃s] **nf 1.** [de personne, gouvernement] inadequacy, incompetence **2.** [manque] **: carence (en)** deficiency (in).

carène [karɛn] **nf** NAUT hull.

caréner [18] [karene] **vt 1.** [navire] to careen **2.** [carrosserie] to streamline.

***caressant**, e* [karɛsɑ̃, ɑ̃t] **adj** affectionate.

caresse [karɛs] **nf** caress ▸ **faire une caresse à qqn** to caress sb.

caresser [4] [karese] **vt 1.** [personne] to caress / [animal, objet] to stroke **2.** *fig* [espoir] to cherish.

car-ferry [karferi] (pl **car-ferries**) **nm** car ferry.

cargaison [kargezɔ̃] **nf 1.** [transports] cargo **2.** *fam* [grande quantité] load, pile.

cargo [kargo] **nm 1.** [navire] freighter **2.** [avion] cargo plane.

cari = *curry*.

caribou [karibu] **nm** caribou.

caricatural**, e, **aux [karikatyral, o] **adj** [récit] exaggerated.

caricature [karikatyr] **nf 1.** [gén] caricature **2.** *péj* [personne] sight.

carie [kari] **nf 1.** MÉD caries *(U)* **2.** BOT blight.

***carié**, e* [karje] **adj 1.** MÉD [dent] decayed, bad / [os] carious **2.** [blé] smutty / [arbre] blighted.

carillon [karijɔ̃] **nm 1.** [cloches] bells *pl* **2.** [d'horloge, de porte] chime.

carillonner [3] [karijɔne] ■ **vi** to ring.
■ **vt 1.** [heure] to strike, to chime **2.** *fig* [nouvelle] to announce.

caritatif**, **ive [karitatif, iv] **adj** charitable.

carlingue [karlɛ̃g] **nf 1.** [d'avion] cabin **2.** [de navire] keelson.

carmélite [karmelit] **nf** Carmelite (nun).

carmin [karmɛ̃] ■ **adj inv** crimson.
■ **nm** [couleur] crimson / [colorant] cochineal.

carnage [karnaʒ] **nm** slaughter, carnage.

carnassier**, **ère [karnasje, ɛr] **adj** carnivorous.

carnassier [karnasje] **nm** carnivore.

carnaval [karnaval] **nm** carnival.

carnet [karnɛ] **nm 1.** [petit cahier] notebook ▸ **carnet d'adresses** address book ▸ **carnet de bord** logbook ▸ **carnet de commandes** ÉCON order book ▸ **carnet de notes** SCOL report *UK*, report card *US* ▸ **elle a eu un bon carnet (de notes)** she got a good report *UK ou* good grades *US* ▸ **carnet de route** logbook ▸ **carnet de santé** child's health record **2.** [bloc de feuilles] book ▸ **carnet de chèques** chequebook *UK*, checkbook *US* ▸ **carnet de tickets** book of tickets ▸ **carnet de timbres** book of stamps.

carnivore [karnivɔr] ■ **adj** carnivorous.
■ **nm** carnivore.

carotide [karɔtid] ■ **adj** ANAT carotid.
■ **nf** ANAT carotid artery.

carotte [karɔt] ■ **nf** carrot ▸ **carottes râpées** grated carrots ▸ **carottes Vichy** glazed carrots ▸ **les carottes sont cuites** *fam* they've/we've *etc* had it.
■ **adj inv** [couleur] carroty.

carpe [karp] ■ **nf** carp ▸ **être muet comme une carpe** *fig* not to say a word.
■ **nm** ANAT carpus.

carpette [karpɛt] **nf 1.** [petit tapis] rug **2.** *fam péj* [personne] doormat.

carquois [karkwa] **nm** quiver.

carré, e [kare] **adj** 1. [gén] square ▸ **20 mètres carrés** 20 square metres 2. [franc] straightforward.
◆ ***carré*** **nm** 1. [quadrilatère] square ▸ **élever un nombre au carré** MATH to square a number ▸ **carré blanc** TV *white square in the corner of the screen indicating that a television programme is not recommended for children* ▸ **carré de soie** [foulard] silk square 2. [sur un navire] wardroom 3. [jeux de cartes] **: un carré d'as** four aces 4. CULIN **: carré d'agneau** rack of lamb 5. [petit terrain] patch, plot.

carreau (pl -x) [karo] **nm** 1. [carrelage] tile 2. [sol] tiled floor ▸ **rester sur le carreau** *fig* to be knocked out 3. [vitre] window pane 4. [motif carré] check ▸ **à carreaux** [tissu] checked / [papier] squared 5. [cartes à jouer] diamond ▸ **l'atout est carreau** diamonds are trumps
▸▸ **se tenir à carreau** to watch one's step.

carrefour [karfur] **nm** 1. [de routes, de la vie] crossroads *sg* 2. [forum] forum, conference.

carrelage [karlaʒ] **nm** 1. [action] tiling 2. [surface] tiles *pl*.

carreler [24] [karle] **vt** to tile.

carrelet [karlɛ] **nm** 1. [poisson] plaice 2. [filet de pêche] net.

carreleur [karlœr] **nm** tiler.

carrément [karemɑ̃] **adv** 1. [franchement] bluntly 2. [complètement] completely, quite 3. [sans hésiter] straight.

carrer [3] [kare] ◆ ***se carrer*** **vp : se carrer dans** to settle o.s. in.

carrière [karjɛr] **nf** 1. [profession] career ▸ **embrasser une carrière** to take up a career ▸ **faire carrière dans qqch** to make a career (for o.s.) in sthg 2. [gisement] quarry.

carriériste [karjerist] **nmf** *péj* careerist.

carriole [karjɔl] **nf** 1. [petite charrette] cart 2. *Québec* [traîneau] sleigh.

carrossable [karɔsabl] **adj** suitable for vehicles.

carrosse [karɔs] **nm** (horse-drawn) coach.

carrosserie [karɔsri] **nf** 1. [de voiture] bodywork, body 2. [industrie] coachbuilding *UK*.

carrossier [karɔsje] **nm** coachbuilder *UK*.

carrousel [karuzɛl] **nm** [équitation] carousel ▸ **carrousel d'avions** *fig* aerial display.

carrure [karyr] **nf** 1. [de personne] build / *fig* stature 2. [de vêtement] width across the shoulders.

cartable [kartabl] **nm** schoolbag.

carte [kart] **nf** 1. [gén] card ▸ **carte d'abonnement** season ticket ▸ **carte d'adhérent** *ou* **de membre** membership card ▸ **carte d'anniversaire** birthday card ▸ **carte d'électeur** polling card *UK*, voter registration card *US* ▸ **carte d'embarquement** boarding card ▸ **carte d'étudiant** student card ▸ **carte de fidélité** loyalty card, frequent user card ▸ **carte à gratter** scratch card ▸ **carte grise** ≃ logbook *UK*, ≃ car registration papers *US* ▸ **carte d'identité** identity card ▸ **carte d'invitation** invitation card ▸ **Carte Orange** season ticket *(for use on public transport in Paris)* ▸ **carte postale** postcard ▸ **carte à puce** smart card ▸ **carte de séjour** residence permit ▸ **Carte Vermeil** *card entitling senior citizens to reduced rates in cinemas, on public transport etc* ▸ **carte de vœux** New Year greetings card ▸ **carte de visite** visiting card *UK*, calling card *US* ▸ **à la carte** TV pay-per-view ▸ **donner carte blanche à qqn** *fig* to give sb a free hand
2. BANQUE & COMM **: carte bancaire** bank card, cash card *UK* ▸ **Carte Bleue®** Visa Card® *(with which purchases are debited directly from the holder's current account)* ▸ **carte de crédit** credit card ▸ **carte de crédit illimitée** gold card
3. INFORM & TÉLÉCOM card ▸ **carte magnétique** swipe card ▸ **carte d'extension (mémoire)** add-in card ▸ **carte graphique** graphics card ▸ **carte à mémoire** memory card ▸ **carte mère** motherboard ▸ **carte réseau** network card ▸ **carte son** soundcard ▸ **carte téléphonique** phonecard
4. [de jeu] **: carte (à jouer)** (playing) card ▸ **abattre ses cartes** to lay down one's cards / *fig* to show one's hand ▸ **battre les cartes** to shuffle the cards ▸ **brouiller les cartes** *fig* to cloud *ou* obscure the issue ▸ **tirer les cartes à qqn** to read sb's cards
5. GÉOGR map ▸ **carte d'état-major** ≃ Ordnance Survey map *UK*, ≃ US Geological Survey map *US* ▸ **carte routière** road map ▸ **carte marine** nautical chart
6. [au restaurant] menu ▸ **à la carte** [menu] à la carte / [horaires] flexible ▸ **manger à la carte** to eat à la carte ▸ **carte des vins** wine list.

cartel [kartɛl] **nm** 1. ÉCON cartel 2. POLIT coalition.

carter [kartɛr] **nm** 1. [de bicyclette] chain guard 2. [de moteur] crankcase, sump *UK*.

carte-réponse [kartrepɔ̃s] (pl **cartes-réponses**) **nf** reply card.

cartésien, enne [kartezjɛ̃, ɛn] ■ **adj** 1. [rationnel] logical, rational 2. [relatif à Descartes] Cartesian.
■ **nm, f** Cartesian.

cartilage [kartilaʒ] **nm** cartilage.

cartilagineux, euse [kartilaʒinø, øz] **adj** 1. [tissu] cartilaginous 2. [viande] gristly.

cartographie [kartɔgrafi] **nf** cartography.

cartomancien, enne [kartɔmɑ̃sjɛ̃, ɛn] **nm, f** fortune-teller *(using cards)*.

carton [kartɔ̃] **nm** 1. [matière] cardboard ▸ **en carton** cardboard ▸ **carton ondulé** corrugated cardboard 2. [emballage] cardboard box ▸ **carton à dessin** portfolio 3. [cible] target ▸ **faire un carton** *fam* to target-shoot / *fig* to take potshots 4. [carte] **: carton d'invitation** formal invitation 5. FOOTBALL **: carton jaune** yellow card ▸ **carton rouge** red card.

cartonné, e [kartɔne] **adj** [livre] hardback.

carton-pâte [kartɔ̃pat] (pl **cartons-pâtes**) **nm** pasteboard ▸ **de** *ou* **en carton-pâte** cardboard.

cartouche [kartuʃ] **nf** 1. [gén & INFORM] cartridge 2. [de cigarettes] carton.

cas [ka] **nm** case ▸ **au cas où** in case ▸ **au cas où il ne viendrait pas** in case he doesn't come ▸ **auquel cas** in which case ▸ **dans** *ou* **en ce cas** in that case ▸ **dans certains cas, en certains cas** in some *ou* certain cases ▸ **dans le meilleur des cas** at best ▸ **dans le pire des cas** at worst ▸ **dans le premier cas** in the first instance ▸ **en aucun cas** under no circumstances ▸ **en tout cas** in any case, anyway ▸ **en cas de** in case of ▸ **en cas d'urgence** in an emergency ▸ **en cas de besoin** if need be ▸ **ce n'est pas le cas** that's not the case ▸ **c'est le cas de le dire** you've hit the nail on the head ▸ **le cas échéant** if the need arises, if need be ▸ **cas de conscience** matter of conscience ▸ **cas de force majeure** emergency ▸ **cas limite** borderline case ▸ **cas social** person with social problems ▸ **envisageons ce cas de figure** let us consider that possibility ▸ **faire grand cas de** to set great store by ▸ **faire peu de cas de** [argument, raison] to pay scant attention to / [invité, ami] to ignore.

casanier, ***ère*** [kazanje, ɛr] **adj & nm, f** stay-at-home.

casaque [kazak] **nf 1.** [veste] overblouse ▸ **tourner casaque** *fig* to change sides **2.** [équitation] blouse.

cascade [kaskad] **nf 1.** [chute d'eau] waterfall / *fig* stream, torrent ▸ **en cascade** *fig* one after the other **2.** CINÉ stunt.

cascadeur, ***euse*** [kaskadœr, øz] **nm, f 1.** [au cirque] acrobat **2.** CINÉ stuntman (f stuntwoman).

cascher = ***kas(c)her***.

case [kaz] **nf 1.** [habitation] hut **2.** [de boîte, tiroir] compartment / [d'échiquier] square / [sur un formulaire] box.

casemate [kazmat] **nf** bunker.

caser [3] [kaze] **vt 1.** *fam* [trouver un emploi pour] to get a job for **2.** *fam* [loger] to put up **3.** *fam* [marier] to marry off **4.** [placer] to put.

◆ ***se caser*** **vp** *fam* **1.** [trouver un emploi] to get (o.s.) a job **2.** [se marier] to get hitched **3.** [se loger] to find a place to live.

caserne [kazɛrn] **nf** barracks *sg*.

cash [kaʃ] **nm** cash ▸ **payer cash** to pay (in) cash.

casher = ***kas(c)her***.

casier [kazje] **nm 1.** [compartiment] compartment / [pour le courrier] pigeonhole **2.** [meuble - à bouteilles] rack / [- à courrier] set of pigeonholes **3.** [à la pêche] lobster pot.

◆ ***casier judiciaire*** **nm** (police) record ▸ **casier judiciaire vierge** clean (police) record.

casino [kazino] **nm** casino.

Caspienne [kaspjɛn] **npr : la Caspienne** the Caspian Sea.

casque [kask] **nm 1.** [de protection] helmet ▸ **casque intégral** crash helmet **2.** [séchoir] hairdryer **3.** [à écouteurs] headphones *pl*.

◆ ***Casques bleus*** **nmpl : les Casques bleus** the UN peace-keeping force, the Blue Berets.

casqué, ***e*** [kaske] **adj** wearing a helmet.

casquer [3] [kaske] **vi** *fam* to cough up.

casquette [kaskɛt] **nf** cap.

cassant, ***e*** [kasɑ̃, ɑ̃t] **adj 1.** [fragile - verre] fragile / [- cheveux] brittle **2.** [dur] brusque.

cassation [kasasjɔ̃] ➤ ***cour***.

casse [kas] ■ **nf 1.** [action] breakage **2.** *fam* [violence] aggro *UK* **3.** [de voitures] scrapyard **4.** TYPO **: haut/bas de casse** upper/lower case.

■ **nm** *fam* [cambriolage] break-in.

cassé, ***e*** [kase] **adj 1.** [voûté, courbé] stooped **2.** [voix] trembling, breaking.

casse-cou [kasku] **nmf** [personne] daredevil.

casse-croûte [kaskrut] **nm inv** snack.

casse-noisettes [kasnwazɛt], ***casse-noix*** [kasnwa] **nm inv** nutcracker.

casse-pieds [kaspje] *fam* ■ **adj inv** annoying.

■ **nmf** pain (in the neck).

casser [3] [kase] ■ **vt 1.** [briser] to break ▸ **à tout casser** *fam fig* [extraordinaire] fabulous, fantastic / [tout au plus] at (the) most ▸ **une soirée à tout casser** one hell of a party ▸ **casser la baraque** *fam* THÉÂTRE to bring the house down / [faire échouer un plan] to ruin it all ▸ **casser la croûte** *fam* to have a bite to eat ▸ **casser sa pipe** *fam* to kick the bucket ▸ **casser qqch en mille morceaux** to smash sthg to bits *ou* smithereens ▸ **casser la figure** *fam* *ou* **gueule** *tfam* **à qqn** to smash sb's face in ▸ **casser les oreilles à qqn** *fam* [avec de la musique] to deafen sb / [en le harcelant] to give sb a lot of hassle ▸ **casser les pieds à qqn** *fam* to get on sb's nerves **2.** DR to quash **3.** COMM **: casser les prix** to slash prices.

■ **vi** to break.

◆ ***se casser*** **vp 1.** [se briser] to break **2.** [membre] **: se casser un bras** to break one's arm **3.** *fam* [se fatiguer] to strain o.s. **4.** *fam* [s'en aller] to hop it, to push off ▸ **casse-toi!** get lost!, push off!

⏭ **se casser la figure** *fam* *ou* **gueule** *tfam* [personne] to take a tumble, to come a cropper *UK* / [livre, carafe] to crash to the ground / [projet] to bite the dust, to take a dive ▸ **ne te casse pas la tête, fais une omelette** don't put yourself out: just make an omelette.

casserole [kasrɔl] **nf 1.** [ustensile] saucepan ▸ **à la casserole** CULIN braised **2.** [voiture] heap, (old) banger *UK* **3.** *fam* [instrument] **: être une vraie casserole** to sound tinny

⏭ **passer à la casserole** *fam* to be bumped off / [sexuellement] to get laid.

casse-tête [kastɛt] **nm inv 1.** *fig* [problème] headache **2.** [jeu] puzzle.

cassette [kasɛt] **nf 1.** [coffret] casket **2.** [de musique, vidéo] cassette **3.** INFORM **: cassette audionumérique** DAT tape.

casseur [kasœr] **nm 1.** [cambrioleur] burglar **2.** [manifestant] rioting demonstrator.

cassis [kasis] **nm 1.** [fruit] blackcurrant / [arbuste] blackcurrant bush / [liqueur] blackcurrant liqueur **2.** [sur la route] dip.

cassolette [kasɔlɛt] **nf 1.** CULIN small baking dish **2.** [brûle-parfum] incense-burner.

cassonade [kasɔnad] **nf** brown sugar.

cassoulet [kasulɛ] **nm** *stew of haricot beans and meat.*

cassure [kasyr] **nf** break.

castagnettes [kastaɲɛt] **nfpl** castanets.

caste [kast] **nf** caste.

casting [kastiŋ] **nm** [acteurs] cast / [sélection] casting ▸ **aller à un casting** to go to an audition.

castor [kastɔr] **nm** beaver.

castration [kastrasjɔ̃] **nf** castration.

castrer [3] [kastre] **vt** to castrate / [chat] to neuter / [chatte] to spay.

cataclysme [kataklism] **nm** cataclysm.

catacombes [katakɔ̃b] **nfpl** catacombs.

catadioptre [katadjɔptr], **Cataphote**® [katafɔt] **nm 1.** [sur la route] Catseye® *UK*, highway reflector *US* **2.** [de véhicule] reflector.

catalan, e [katalɑ̃, an] **adj** Catalan, Catalonian.
◆ **catalan nm** [langue] Catalan.
◆ **Catalan, e nm, f** Catalan, Catalonian.

Catalogne [katalɔɲ] **nf : la Catalogne** Catalonia.

catalogue [katalɔg] **nm** catalogue, catalog *US*.

cataloguer [3] [katalɔge] **vt 1.** [classer] to catalogue, to catalog *US* **2.** *péj* [juger] to label.

catalyseur [katalizœr] **nm** *fig* & CHIM catalyst.

catalytique [katalitik] ➤ ***pot***.

catamaran [katamarɑ̃] **nm 1.** [voilier] catamaran **2.** [d'hydravion] floats *pl*.

Cataphote® = ***catadioptre***.

cataplasme [kataplasm] **nm** poultice.

catapulter [3] [katapylte] **vt** to catapult.

cataracte [katarakt] **nf** cataract.

catarrhe [katar] **nm** catarrh.

catastrophe [katastrɔf] **nf** disaster, catastrophe ▸ **catastrophe naturelle** natural disaster / [assurances] act of God ▸ **atterrir en catastrophe** to crash-land ▸ **partir en catastrophe** to leave in a mad rush.

catastrophé, e [katastrɔʃe] **adj** shocked, upset.

catastrophique [katastrɔfik] **adj** disastrous, catastrophic.

catch [katʃ] **nm** wrestling.

catéchèse [kateʃɛz] **nf** catechesis.

catéchisme [kateʃism] **nm** catechism.

catégorie [kategɔri] **nf 1.** [gén] category **2.** [de personnel] grade **3.** [de viande, fruits] quality **4.** ÉCON : **catégorie sociale** social class ▸ **catégorie socio-économique** socio-economic class ▸ **catégorie socio-professionnelle** socioprofessional group **5.** SPORT class ▸ **toutes catégories** for all comers.

catégoriel, elle [kategɔrjɛl] **adj 1.** [d'une catégorie] category *(avant n)* ▸ **classement catégoriel** classification by category **2.** ÉCON : **revendications catégorielles** sectional claims *(claims relating to one category of workers only)* **3.** LING & PHILO category *(avant n)*.

catégorique [kategɔrik] **adj** categorical.

catégoriquement [kategɔrikmɑ̃] **adv** categorically.

caténaire [katenɛr] **adj** & **nf** catenary.

cathédrale [katedral] **nf** cathedral.

cathode [katɔd] **nf** cathode.

cathodique [katɔdik] ➤ ***tube***.

catholicisme [katɔlisism] **nm** Catholicism.

catholique [katɔlik] **adj** Catholic ▸ **pas (très) catholique** *fig* dubious, dodgy *UK*.

catimini [katimini] ◆ ***en catimini*** **loc adv** secretly.

catogan [katɔgɑ̃] **nm** ribbon *(securing hair at the back of the neck)*.

cauchemar [koʃmar] **nm** *litt* & *fig* nightmare.

cauchemardesque [koʃmardɛsk] **adj** nightmarish.

caudal, e, aux [kodal, o] **adj** caudal, tail *(avant n)*.

causal, e, als *ou* **aux** [kozal, o] **adj** causal.

causalité [kozalite] **nf** causality.

causant, e [kozɑ̃, ɑ̃t] **adj : peu causant** not very chatty.

cause [koz] **nf 1.** [gén] cause ▸ **gagner qqn à sa cause** to win sb over (to one's cause) ▸ **je suis tout acquis à sa cause** I support him wholeheartedly ▸ **à cause de** because of ▸ **pour cause de** on account of, because of ▸ **pour la bonne cause** [pour un bon motif] for a good cause / *hum* [en vue du mariage] with honourable intentions ▸ **et pour cause!** and for good reason! ▸ **être (la) cause de qqch** to cause sthg ▸ **faire cause commune avec qqn** to make common cause with sb ▸ **une cause perdue** a lost cause **2.** DR case ▸ **plaider la cause de qqn** *litt* & *fig* to plead sb's case
▸▸ **être en cause** [intérêts] to be at stake / [honnêteté] to be in doubt *ou* in question ▸ **être hors de cause** to be beyond suspicion ▸ **mettre qqn en cause** to implicate sb ▸ **mettre qqch en cause** to call sthg into question ▸ **remettre en cause** to challenge, to question ▸ **son départ remet tout en cause** her departure reopens the whole question *ou* debate.

causer [3] [koze] ■ **vt : causer qqch à qqn** to cause sb sthg.
■ **vi 1.** [bavarder] : **causer (de)** to chat (about) **2.** [jaser] : **causer (sur)** to gossip (about).

causerie [kozri] **nf** talk ▸ **causerie télévisée** talk show, chat show *UK*.

causette [kozɛt] **nf** *fam* chat ▸ **faire la causette avec qqn** to have a chat with sb.

causticité [kostisite] **nf** causticness, causticity.

caustique [kostik] **adj** & **nm** caustic.

cauteleux, euse [kotlø, øz] **adj** sly.

cautériser [3] [koterize] **vt** to cauterize.

caution [kosjɔ̃] **nf 1.** [somme d'argent] guarantee ▸ **libérer qqn sous caution** DR to free sb on bail ▸ **payer la caution de qqn** to stand bail for sb **2.** [personne] guarantor ▸ **se porter caution pour qqn** to act as guarantor for sb **3.** [soutien] support, backing.

cautionner [3] [kosjɔne] **vt 1.** [se porter garant de] to guarantee **2.** *fig* [appuyer] to support, to back.

cavalcade [kavalkad] **nf 1.** [de cavaliers] cavalcade **2.** [d'enfants] stampede.

cavale [kaval] **nf** *fam* : **être en cavale** to be on the run.

cavaler [3] [kavale] **vi** *fam* [courir] to run *ou* rush around ▸ **cavaler après qqn/qqch** to chase (after) sb/sthg.
◆ ***se cavaler*** **vpi** *fam* to clear off.

cavalerie [kavalri] **nf 1.** MIL cavalry **2.** [de cirque] horses *pl*.

cavalier, ère [kavalje, ɛr] ■ **adj 1.** [destiné aux cavaliers] : **allée cavalière** bridle path **2.** *sout* [impertinent] offhand.
■ **nm, f 1.** [à cheval] rider **2.** [partenaire] partner ▸ **faire cavalier seul** *fig* to go it alone.
◆ ***cavalier*** **nm** [aux échecs] knight.

cavalièrement [kavaljɛrmɑ̃] **adv** in an offhand manner.

cave [kav] ■ **nf 1.** [sous-sol] cellar **2.** [de vins] (wine) cellar **3.** [cabaret] cellar *UK ou* basement *US* nightclub.
■ **nm** *arg crime* outsider.
■ **adj** [joues] hollow / [yeux] sunken.

caveau (pl -x) [kavo] **nm 1.** [petite cave] small cellar **2.** [cabaret] nightclub **3.** [sépulture] vault.

caverne [kavɛrn] **nf** cave.

caverneux, euse [kavɛrnø, øz] ➤ ***voix***.

caviar [kavjar] **nm** caviar.

caviarder [3] [kavjarde] **vt** to blue-pencil, to censor.

caviste [kavist] **nm** cellarman.

cavité [kavite] **nf** cavity.

CB (abr de ***citizen's band, canaux banalisés***) **nf** CB.

cc **1.** (abr écrite de ***cuillère à café***) tsp **2.** (abr écrite de ***charges comprises***) inclusive.

CC (abr de ***corps consulaire***) CC.

CCE (abr de ***Commission des communautés européennes***) **nf** ECC.

CCI (abr de ***Chambre de commerce et d'industrie***) **nf** CCI.

CCP (abr de ***compte chèque postal, compte courant postal***) **nm** *post office account*, ≃ giro account *UK*, ≃ Post Office checking account *US*.

CD **nm 1.** (abr de ***chemin départemental***) minor road **2.** (abr de ***compact disc***) CD **3.** (abr de ***comité directeur***) steering committee **4.** (abr de ***corps diplomatique***) CD.

CDD **nm** (abr écrite de ***contrat à durée déterminée***) fixed-term contract ▸ **elle est en CDD** she's on a fixed-term contract.

CdF (abr de ***Charbonnages de France***) **nmpl** *French national coal board*.

CDI **nm 1.** (abr de ***centre de documentation et d'information***) *school library* **2.** (abr de ***contrat à durée indéterminée***) permanent contract ▸ **elle est en CDI** she's got a permanent contract.

CD-Rom [sederɔm] (abr de ***compact disc read only memory***) **nm** CD-Rom.

CDS (abr de ***Centre des démocrates sociaux***) **nm** *French political party*.

CDU (abr de ***Classification décimale universelle***) **nf** DDS.

ce, cette [sə, sɛt] (pl **ces** [se]) *(le masculin* ce *devient* **cet** [sɛt] *devant une voyelle ou un 'h' muet)* ■ **adj dém** [proche] this, these *pl* / [éloigné] that, those *pl* ▸ **ce mois, ce mois-ci** this month ▸ **cette année, cette année-là** that year ▸ **regarde de ce côté-ci et pas de ce côté-là** look on this side, not that side ▸ **ces jours-ci** these days ▸ **et pour ces messieurs, ce sera?** now what will the *ou* you gentlemen have?
■ **pron dém inv** *(c' devant le verbe être 3ieme personne singulier)* **: c'est** it is, it's ▸ **ce sont** they are, they're ▸ **c'est à lui/à toi de décider** it's up to him/up to you to decide ▸ **c'est mon bureau** this is my office, it's my office ▸ **ce sont mes enfants** these are my children, they're my children ▸ **c'est à Paris** it's in Paris ▸ **c'était hier** it was yesterday ▸ **qui est-ce?** who is it? ▸ **ce qui, ce que** what ▸ **ce que tu es naïf!** you're so naive!, how naive you are! ▸ **ils ont eu ce qui leur revenait** they got what they deserved ▸**..., ce qui est étonnant**..., which is surprising ▸ **elle n'achète même pas ce dont elle a besoin** she doesn't even buy what she needs ▸ **vous savez bien ce à quoi je pense** you know exactly what I'm thinking about ▸ **faites donc ce pour quoi on vous paie** do what you're paid to do ▸ **pour ce faire** *sout* to this end ▸ **sur ce, elle se leva** with that, she got up.

CE ■ **nm 1.** abr écrite de ***comité d'entreprise*** **2.** (abr de ***cours élémentaire***) ▸ **CE1** *second year of primary school* ▸ **CE2** *third year of primary school*.
■ **nf** (abr de ***Communauté européenne***) EC.

CEA (abr de ***Commissariat à l'énergie atomique***) **nm** *French atomic energy commission*, ≃ AEA *UK*, ≃ AEC *US*.

CECA, Ceca [seka] (abr de ***Communauté européenne du charbon et de l'acier***) **nf** ECSC.

ceci [səsi] **pron dém inv** this ▸ **ceci pour vous dire que...** this is just to say (that)... ▸ **ceci n'explique pas cela** this doesn't explain that ▸ **ceci (étant) dit** having said that ▸ **à ceci près que** with the exception that, except that.

cécité [sesite] **nf** blindness.

céder [18] [sede] ■ **vt 1.** [donner] to give up ▸ **'cédez le passage'** 'give way *UK*', 'yield *US*' ▸ **céder le passage à qqn** to let sb through, to make way for sb **2.** [revendre] to sell.
■ **vi 1.** [personne] **: céder (à)** to give in (to), to yield (to) **2.** [chaise, plancher] to give way.

cédérom [sederɔm] **nm** INFORM CD-ROM.

CEDEX, Cedex [sedɛks] (abr de ***courrier d'entreprise à distribution exceptionnelle***) **nm** *accelerated postal service for bulk users*.

cédille [sedij] **nf** cedilla ▸ **c cédille** c cedilla.

cèdre [sɛdr] **nm** cedar.

CEI (abr de ***Communauté d'États Indépendants***) **nf** CIS.

ceindre [81] [sɛ̃dr] **vt 1.** [entourer] **: ceindre qqch de qqch** to put sthg around sthg **2.** [mettre] to put on.

ceinture [sɛ̃tyr] **nf 1.** [gén] belt ▸ **attachez vos ceintures** fasten your seat *ou* safety belts ▸ **ceinture de chasteté** chastity belt ▸ **ceinture à enrouleur** inertia-reel seat belt ▸ **ceinture noire** [judo] black belt ▸ **elle est ceinture blanche/noire** she is a white/black belt ▸ **ceinture orthopédique** surgical corset ▸ **ceinture de sauvetage** life belt ▸ **ceinture de sécurité** seat *ou* safety belt ▸ **ceinture verte** green belt ▸ **se serrer la ceinture** *fig* to tighten one's belt **2.** ANAT waist ▸ **frapper au-dessous de la ceinture** *litt & fig* to hit below the belt ▸ **nu jusqu'à la ceinture** naked from the waist up **3.** COUT waistband **4.** [d'une ville] **: petite/grande ceinture** inner/outer circle.

ceinturer [3] [sɛ̃tyre] **vt 1.** [porter avec une ceinture] **: vous pouvez la ceinturer** [robe] you can wear it with a belt **2.** [saisir par la taille] to grab around the waist / SPORT to tackle **3.** [lieu] to surround, to encircle ▸ **les remparts ceinturent la ville** the town is surrounded by ramparts **4.** BOT to girdle.

ceinturon [sɛ̃tyrɔ̃] **nm** belt.

cela [səla] **pron dém inv** that ▸ **cela ne vous regarde pas** it's *ou* that's none of your business ▸ **il y a des années de cela** that was many years ago ▸ **c'est cela** that's right ▸ **cela dit...** having said that... ▸ **malgré cela** in spite of that, nevertheless.

célébration [selebrasjɔ̃] **nf** celebration.

célèbre [selɛbr] **adj** famous.

célébrer [18] [selebre] **vt** **1.** [gén] to celebrate **2.** [faire la louange de] to praise.

célébrité [selebrite] **nf** **1.** [renommée] fame **2.** [personne] celebrity.

céleri [sɛlri] **nm** celery ▸ **céleri rémoulade** CULIN *grated celeriac in mustard dressing.*
◆ ***céleri rave***, ***céleri-rave*** **nm** celeriac.

célérité [selerite] **nf** *littéraire* speed.

céleste [selɛst] **adj** heavenly.

célibat [seliba] **nm** celibacy.

célibataire [selibatɛr] ■ **adj** single, unmarried ▸ **père** *ou* **mère célibataire** single parent.
■ **nmf** single person, single man (f woman) ▸ **célibataire endurci** confirmed bachelor.

celle ➤ ***celui***.

celle-ci ➤ ***celui-ci***.

celle-là ➤ ***celui-là***.

celles ➤ ***celui***.

celles-ci ➤ ***celui-ci***.

celles-là ➤ ***celui-là***.

cellier [selje] **nm** storeroom.

Cellophane® [selɔfan] **nf** Cellophane® ▸ **sous Cellophane** (wrapped) in Cellophane.

cellulaire [selylɛr] **adj** **1.** BIOL & TÉLÉCOM cellular **2.** [destiné aux prisonniers] **: régime cellulaire** solitary confinement ▸ **voiture cellulaire** prison van.

cellule [selyl] **nf** **1.** [gén & INFORM] cell ▸ **cellule photoélectrique** photoelectric cell **2.** [groupe] unit ▸ **cellule de crise** [groupe] emergency committee / [réunion] emergency committee meeting.

cellulite [selylit] **nf** cellulite.

celluloïd [selylɔid] **nm** celluloid.

cellulose [selyloz] **nf** cellulose.

celte [sɛlt] **adj** Celtic.
◆ ***Celte*** **nmf** Celt.

celtique [sɛltik] ■ **adj** Celtic.
■ **nm** [langue] Celtic.

celui, ***celle*** [səlɥi, sɛl] (mpl **ceux** [sø], fpl **celles** [sɛl]) **pron dém** **1.** [suivi d'un complément prépositionnel] the one ▸ **celle de devant** the one in front ▸ **ceux d'entre vous qui...** those of you who... **2.** [suivi d'un pronom relatif] **: celui qui** [personne] the one who / [objet] the one which *ou* that ▸ **c'est celle qui te va le mieux** that's the one which *ou* that suits you best ▸ **celui que vous voyez** the one (which *ou* that) you can see, the one (whom) you can see ▸ **ceux que je connais** those I know **3.** [suivi d'un adjectif, d'un participe] the one ▸ **achetez celle conforme aux normes** buy the one that complies with the standard ▸ **tous ceux désirant participer à l'émission** all those wishing *ou* who wish to take part in the show.

celui-ci, ***celle-ci*** [səlɥisi, sɛlsi] (mpl **ceux-ci** [søsi], fpl **celles-ci** [sɛlsi]) **pron dém** this one, these ones *pl* ▸ **c'est celui-ci que je veux** this is the one I want, I want this one ▸ **ah celui-ci, il me fera toujours rire!** now he always makes me laugh!

celui-là, ***celle-là*** [səlɥila, sɛlla] (mpl **ceux-là** [søla], fpl **celles-là** [sɛlla]) **pron dém** that one, those ones *pl* ▸ **celui-là... celui-ci** the former... the latter ▸ **c'est celui-là que je veux** that's the one I want, I want that one ▸ **il a toujours une bonne excuse, celui-là!** he's always got a good excuse, that one!

cénacle [senakl] **nm** [coterie] circle.

cendre [sɑ̃dr] **nf** ash ▸ **réduire qqch en cendres** to reduce sthg to ashes.
◆ ***cendres*** **nfpl** [restes des morts] ashes ▸ **renaître de ses cendres** *fig* to rise from the ashes.
◆ ***Cendres*** **nfpl : le mercredi des Cendres** Ash Wednesday.

cendré, ***e*** [sɑ̃dre] **adj** [chevelure] **: blond cendré** ash blond.

cendrier [sɑ̃drije] **nm** **1.** [de fumeur] ashtray **2.** [de poêle] ashpan.

cène [sɛn] **nf** (Holy) Communion.
◆ ***Cène*** **nf : la Cène** the Last Supper.

censé, ***e*** [sɑ̃se] **adj : être censé faire qqch** to be supposed to do sthg.

censément [sɑ̃semɑ̃] **adv** *sout* supposedly.

censeur [sɑ̃sœr] **nm** **1.** SCOL ≃ deputy head *UK*, ≃ vice-principal *US* **2.** CINÉ & PRESSE censor **3.** *fig* [juge] critic.

censure [sɑ̃syr] **nf** **1.** [presse & CINÉ] [- contrôle] censorship / [- censeurs] censors *pl* **2.** POLIT censure **3.** PSYCHO censor.

censurer [3] [sɑ̃syre] **vt** **1.** CINÉ, PRESSE & PSYCHO to censor **2.** [juger] to censure.

cent [sɑ̃] ■ **adj num inv** one hundred, a hundred ▸ **deux cents filles** two hundred girls ▸ **elle est aux cent coups** [affolée] she's frantic ▸ **faire les cent pas** to pace up and down ▸ **je ne vais pas attendre cent sept ans** *fam* I'm not going to wait forever (and a day) ▸ **le quatre cent mètres haies** the four hundred metres hurdle *ou* hurdles.
■ **nm** **1.** [nombre] a hundred ▸ **j'habite au cent** I live at number one hundred **2.** [mesure de proportion] **: pour cent** percent ▸ **cent pour cent** a hundred percent **3.** [sɛnt] [monnaie] cent ; voir aussi ***six***.

centaine [sɑ̃tɛn] **nf** **1.** [cent unités] hundred **2.** [un grand nombre] **: une centaine de** about a hundred ▸ **des centaines (de)** hundreds (of) ▸ **plusieurs centaines de** several hundred ▸ **par centaines** in hundreds.

centenaire [sɑ̃tnɛr] ■ **adj** hundred-year-old *(avant n)* ▸ **être centenaire** to be a hundred years old.
■ **nmf** centenarian.
■ **nm** [anniversaire] centenary *UK*, centennial *US*.

centiare [sɑ̃tjar] **nm** square metre *UK ou* meter *US*.

centième [sɑ̃tjɛm] ■ **adj num inv, nm & nmf** hundredth.
■ **nf** THÉÂTRE hundredth performance ; voir aussi ***sixième***.

centigrade [sɑ̃tigrad] ➤ ***degré***.

centigramme [sɑ̃tigram] **nm** centigram.

centilitre [sɑ̃tilitr] **nm** centilitre *UK*, centiliter *US*.

centime [sɑ̃tim] **nm** cent.

centimètre [sɑ̃timɛtr] **nm 1.** [mesure] centimetre *UK*, centimeter *US* ▸ **centimètre cube** cubic centimetre *UK ou* centimeter *US* **2.** [ruban, règle] tape measure.

central, ***e***, ***aux*** [sɑ̃tral, o] **adj** central.
◆ ***central*** **nm 1.** TENNIS centre *UK ou* center *US* court **2.** [de réseau] **: central téléphonique** telephone exchange.
◆ ***centrale*** **nf 1.** [usine] power plant *ou* station *UK* ▸ **centrale hydroélectrique** hydroelectric power plant *ou* station *UK* ▸ **centrale nucléaire** nuclear power plant *ou* station *UK* **2.** [syndicale] *group of affiliated trade unions* **3.** ÉCON **: centrale d'achat** COMM buying group / [dans une entreprise] central purchasing department.
◆ ***Centrale*** **nf** *grande école training highly-qualified engineers.*

centralien, ***enne*** [sɑ̃traljɛ̃, ɛn] **nm, f** engineering student.

centralisation [sɑ̃tralizasjɔ̃] **nf** centralization.

centraliser [3] [sɑ̃tralize] **vt** to centralize.

centre [sɑ̃tr] **nm** [gén] centre *UK*, center *US* ▸ **le centre** [d'une ville] the centre ▸ **centre d'accueil** reception centre *UK ou* center *US* ▸ **centre aéré** outdoor centre *UK ou* center *US* ▸ **centre antipoison** poison centre *UK ou* center *US* ▸ **centre d'appels** call centre *UK ou* center *US* ▸ **centre commercial** shopping centre *UK ou* mall *US* ▸ **centre de coût** cost centre *UK ou* center *US* ▸ **centre culturel** arts centre *UK ou* center *US* ▸ **centre de documentation** reference library ▸ **centre droit/gauche** moderate right/left ▸ **il est (de) centre gauche** he's left-of-centre *UK ou* left-of-center *US* ▸ **centre équestre** riding school ▸ **centre de gravité** centre *UK ou* center *US* of gravity ▸ **centre hospitalier** hospital (complex) ▸ **centre industriel** industrial area ▸ **centre nerveux** nerve centre *UK ou* center *US* ▸ **centre de rééducation** rehabilitation centre *UK ou* center *US* ▸ **centre social** social services *UK ou* welfare *US* office ▸ **centre de tri** sorting office.

centrer [3] [sɑ̃tre] **vt** to centre *UK*, to center *US*.

centre-ville [sɑ̃trəvil] (pl **centres-villes**) **nm** city centre *UK ou* center *US*, town centre *UK ou* downtown *US*.

centrifuge [sɑ̃trifyʒ] ➤ ***force***.

centrifugeuse [sɑ̃trifyʒøz] **nf 1.** TECHNOL centrifuge **2.** CULIN juice extractor.

centriste [sɑ̃trist] ■ **adj** POLIT centre *(avant n) UK*, center *(avant n) US*.
■ **nmf** centrist.

centuple [sɑ̃typl] **nm : être le centuple de qqch** to be a hundred times sthg ▸ **au centuple** a hundredfold.

centupler [3] [sɑ̃typle] **vt & vi** to increase a hundredfold.

cep [sɛp] **nm** stock.

CEP (abr de ***certificat d'études primaires***) **nm** *school-leaving certificate formerly taken at end of primary education.*

cépage [sepaʒ] **nm** (type of) vine.

cèpe [sɛp] **nm** cep.

cependant [səpɑ̃dɑ̃] **conj** however, yet.
◆ ***cependant que*** **loc conj** *littéraire* while.

céramique [seramik] **nf 1.** [matière, objet] ceramic **2.** [art] ceramics *(U)*, pottery.

cerbère [sɛrbɛr] **nm** ill-tempered doorkeeper.

cerceau (pl -x) [sɛrso] **nm** hoop.

cercle [sɛrkl] **nm** circle ▸ **décrire des cercles dans le ciel** [avion, oiseau] to fly around in circles, to wheel round, to circle ▸ **en cercle** in a circle ▸ **cercle d'amis** circle of friends ▸ **le cercle de ses conseillers (les plus proches)** her (inner) circle of advisers ▸ **cercle de famille** family circle ▸ **cercle littéraire** literary circle ▸ **cercle polaire** polar circle ▸ **cercle de qualité** ÉCON quality circle ▸ **cercle vicieux** vicious circle.

cerclé, ***e*** [sɛrkle] **adj** ringed ▸ **des lunettes cerclées d'écaille** horn-rimmed glasses.

cercueil [sɛrkœj] **nm** coffin.

céréale [sereal] **nf** cereal.

cérébral, ***e***, ***aux*** [serebral, o] ■ **adj 1.** [du cerveau] cerebral **2.** [personne, activité] intellectual.
■ **nm, f** intellectual.

cérémonial, ***als*** [seremɔnjal] **nm** ceremonial.

cérémonie [seremɔni] **nf** ceremony ▸ **cérémonie d'ouverture/de clôture** opening/closing ceremony ▸ **sans cérémonie** without ceremony, informally ▸ **faire des cérémonies** to make a fuss.

cérémonieux, ***euse*** [seremɔnjø, øz] **adj** ceremonious.

CERES [serɛs] (abr de ***Centre d'études, de recherches et d'éducation socialiste***) **nm** *formerly, the intellectual section of the French socialist party.*

cerf [sɛr] **nm** stag.

cerfeuil [sɛrfœj] **nm** chervil.

cerf-volant [sɛrvɔlɑ̃] (pl **cerfs-volants**) **nm 1.** [jouet] kite **2.** [insecte] stag beetle.

cerise [səriz] ■ **nf** cherry ▸ **cerise à grappes** choke berry ▸ **la cerise sur le gâteau** *fig* the icing *ou* cherry on the cake.
■ **adj inv** cherry.

cerisier [sərizje] **nm** [arbre] cherry (tree) / [bois] cherry (wood).

CERN, ***Cern*** [sɛrn] (abr de ***Conseil européen pour la recherche nucléaire***) **nm** CERN.

cerne [sɛrn] **nm** ring.

cerné [sɛrne] ➤ ***œil***.

cerner [3] [sɛrne] **vt 1.** [encercler] to surround **2.** [entourer d'un trait] to ring **3.** *fig* [sujet] to define.

certain, ***e*** [sɛrtɛ̃, ɛn] ■ **adj** certain ▸ **c'est une chose certaine** there's no doubt about it ▸ **être certain de qqch** to be certain *ou* sure of sthg ▸ **être certain que** to be certain *ou* sure (that) ▸ **je suis pourtant certain d'avoir mis mes clés là** but I'm certain *ou* sure I left my keys there.
■ **adj indéf** *(avant n)* certain ▸ **il a un certain talent** he has some talent *ou* a certain talent ▸ **à un certain moment** at some point ▸ **certains jours** some days ▸ **un certain temps** for a while ▸ **dans une certaine mesure** to a certain

extent ▸ **avoir un certain âge** to be getting on, to be past one's prime ▸ **c'est un monsieur d'un certain âge** he's getting on a bit ▸ **un certain M. Lebrun** a Mr Lebrun.
◆ ***certains*** (fpl certaines) **pron indéf pl** some.

certainement [sɛrtɛnmɑ̃] **adv** [probablement] most probably, most likely / [bien sûr] certainly.

certes [sɛrt] **adv** of course.

certificat [sɛrtifika] **nm 1.** [attestation, diplôme] certificate ▸ **certificat d'aptitude professionnelle** vocational training certificate ▸ **certificat d'études** *primary school-leaving certificate* ▸ **certificat médical** medical certificate ▸ **certificat de scolarité** *certificate of regular attendance at school or university* **2.** [référence] reference.

certifié, e [sɛrtifje] **adj : professeur certifié** qualified teacher.

certifier [9] [sɛrtifje] **vt 1.** [assurer] **: certifier qqch à qqn** to assure sb of sthg **2.** [authentifier] to certify.

certitude [sɛrtityd] **nf** certainty, certitude.

PARONYME / CONFUSABLE

certitude

Quand vous voulez traduire **certitude**, employez *certitude* pour exprimer le fait ou l'idée dont on est sûr, et *certainty* pour parler de l'attitude.

cérumen [serymɛn] **nm** wax, earwax.

cerveau [sɛrvo] **nm** brain.

cervelas [sɛrvəla] **nm** saveloy.

cervelle [sɛrvɛl] **nf 1.** ANAT brain **2.** [facultés mentales, aliment] brains *pl*
▸▸ **se brûler la cervelle** to blow one's brains out ▸ **se creuser la cervelle** to rack one's brains.

cervical, e, aux [sɛrvikal, o] **adj** cervical ▸ **(vertèbre) cervicale** cervical vertebra.

ces [sɛ] ➤ ***ce***.

CES **nm 1.** (abr de ***collège d'enseignement secondaire***) *former secondary school* **2.** abr écrite de ***Contrat emploi-solidarité***.

César [sezar] **nm : les Césars** *French cinema awards.*

césarienne [sezarjɛn] **nf** caesarean *UK* **ou** cesarean *US* (section).

cessante [sɛsɑ̃t] ➤ ***affaire***.

cessation [sɛsasjɔ̃] **nf** suspension.

cesse [sɛs] **nf : n'avoir de cesse que** *(+ subjonctif)* ***sout*** not to rest until.
◆ ***sans cesse*** **loc adv** continually, constantly.

cesser [4] [sese] ■ **vi** to stop, to cease.
■ **vt** to stop ▸ **cesser de faire qqch** to stop doing sthg.

cessez-le-feu [seselfø] **nm inv** cease-fire.

cession [sɛsjɔ̃] **nf** transfer.

c'est-à-dire [setadir] **conj 1.** [en d'autres termes] **: c'est-à-dire (que)** that is (to say) **2.** [introduit une restriction, précision, réponse] **: c'est-à-dire que** well..., actually...

cet ➤ ***ce***.

cétacé [setase] **nm** cetacean.

cette ➤ ***ce***.

ceux ➤ ***celui***.

ceux-ci ➤ ***celui-ci***.

ceux-là ➤ ***celui-là***.

cévenol, e [sevnɔl] **adj** of/from the Cévennes region.

Ceylan [selɑ̃] **nm** Ceylon.

cf. (abr écrite de ***confer***) cf.

CFA ■ **nf** (abr de ***Communauté financière africaine***) ▸ **franc CFA** *currency used in former French African colonies.*
■ **nm** (abr de ***centre de formation des apprentis***) *centre for apprenticeship training.*

CFAO (abr de ***conception de fabrication assistée par ordinateur***) **nf** CAM.

CFC (abr de ***chlorofluorocarbone***) **nm** CFC.

CFDT (abr de ***Confédération française démocratique du travail***) **nf** *French trade union.*

CFES (abr de ***certificat de fin d'études secondaires***) **nm** *school-leaving certificate.*

CFF (abr de ***Chemins de fer fédéraux***) **nmpl** *Swiss railways.*

CFL (abr de ***Chemins de fer luxembourgeois***) **nmpl** *Luxembourg railways.*

CFP (abr de ***Compagnie française des pétroles***) **nf** *French oil company.*

CFTC (abr de ***Confédération française des travailleurs chrétiens***) **nf** *French trade union.*

COMMENT EXPRIMER...

la certitude

I'm sure it'll work / Je suis sûr que ça va marcher
I'm totally convinced this is the right way to do things / Je suis tout à fait convaincu que c'est comme ça qu'il faut agir
We are certain that you will be completely satisfied with the service / Nous sommes certains que le service vous donnera entière satisfaction
There's no doubt in my mind that his suggestion is the best / Je ne doute pas un instant que son idée soit la meilleure
I know for a fact that he couldn't have done it / Je sais pertinemment que ça ne peut pas être lui
Take it from me: we will never get them to agree to this / Je vous assure que nous n'obtiendrons jamais leur accord
Believe me. I know what I'm talking about / Croyez-moi. Je sais de quoi je parle
I bet he changes his mind! / Je parie qu'il va changer d'avis !

CGC (abr de ***Confédération générale des cadres***) **nf** *French management union.*

CGI (abr de ***common gateway interface***) **npr f** INFORM CGI.

CGT (abr de ***Confédération générale du travail***) **nf** *major association of French trade unions (affiliated to the Communist party).*

ch. **1.** (abr écrite de ***charges***), ➤ ***charge*** **2.** abr de ***chauffage*** **3.** (abr écrite de ***cherche***), ➤ ***chercher***.

CH (abr écrite de ***Confédération helvétique***) *Switzerland (as nationality sticker on a car).*

chablis [ʃabli] **nm** [vin] Chablis.

chacal [ʃakal] **nm** jackal.

chacun, e [ʃakœ̃, yn] **pron indéf** each (one) / [tout le monde] everyone, everybody ▸ **chacun de nous/de vous/d'eux** each of us/you/them ▸ **chacun pour soi** every man for himself ▸ **tout un chacun** every one of us/them.

chagrin, e [ʃagrɛ̃, in] **adj** [personne] grieving / [caractère, humeur] morose.
◆ ***chagrin*** **nm** grief ▸ **avoir du chagrin** to grieve.

chagriner [3] [ʃagrine] **vt 1.** [peiner] to grieve, to distress **2.** [contrarier] to upset.

chahut [ʃay] **nm** uproar.

chahuter [3] [ʃayte] ■ **vi** to cause an uproar.
■ **vt 1.** [importuner - professeur] to rag, to tease / [- orateur] to heckle **2.** [bousculer] to jostle.

chahuteur, euse [ʃaytœr, øz] ■ **adj** disruptive, rowdy.
■ **nm, f 1.** [enfant] disruptive child **2.** [manifestant] heckler.

chai [ʃɛ] **nm** wine and spirits store *ou* storehouse.

chaîne [ʃɛn] **nf 1.** [gén] chain ▸ **des catastrophes en chaîne** a whole catalogue of disasters ▸ **chaîne de bicyclette** bicycle chain ▸ **chaîne de montagnes** mountain range ▸ **chaîne de sûreté** [sur un bijou] safety chain / [sur une porte] (door) chain ▸ **la chaîne alimentaire** the food chain
2. [dans l'industrie] **: chaîne de fabrication/de montage** production/assembly line ▸ **travail à la chaîne** production-line work ▸ **produire qqch à la chaîne** to mass-produce sthg
3. [magasins] chain ▸ **chaîne de détail** retail chain ▸ **chaîne de distribution** distribution chain
4. TV channel ▸ **chaîne câblée** cable channel ▸ **chaîne à la carte** pay-per-view channel ▸ **chaîne cryptée** pay channel *(for which one needs a special decoding unit)* ▸ **une chaîne payante** a subscription TV channel ▸ **chaîne à péage** *ou* **à la séance** pay-TV channel ▸ **chaîne publique** publicly-owned channel, public service channel *US* ▸ **chaîne de télévision** television channel, TV channel ▸ **chaîne thématique** specialized channel
5. [appareil] stereo (system) ▸ **chaîne compacte** compact system ▸ **chaîne hi-fi** hi-fi system ▸ **chaîne laser** CD system
6. INFORM string ▸ **chaîne vide/de caractères** nul/character string.
◆ ***chaînes*** **nfpl** *fig* chains, bonds.

chaînette [ʃɛnɛt] **nf** small chain.

chaînon [ʃɛnɔ̃] **nm** *litt* & *fig* link.

chair [ʃɛr] ■ **nf** flesh ▸ **bien en chair** plump ▸ **en chair et en os** in the flesh ▸ **chair à saucisse** sausage meat ▸ **avoir la chair de poule** to have goose pimples *ou* gooseflesh, to have goosebumps *US*.
■ **adj inv** flesh-coloured *UK*, flesh-colored *US*.

chaire [ʃɛr] **nf 1.** [estrade - de prédicateur] pulpit / [- de professeur] rostrum **2.** UNIV chair.

chaise [ʃɛz] **nf** chair ▸ **chaise électrique** electric chair ▸ **chaise haute** high chair ▸ **chaise longue** [d'extérieur] deckchair / [d'intérieur] chaise longue ▸ **être assis entre deux chaises** *fig* to be in an awkward situation.

chaland [ʃalɑ̃] **nm** [bateau] barge.

châle [ʃal] **nm** shawl.

chalet [ʃalɛ] **nm 1.** [de montagne] chalet **2.** *Québec* [maison de campagne] (holiday) cottage *UK*, (vacation) cottage *US*.

chaleur [ʃalœr] **nf** heat ▸ **'ne pas exposer à la chaleur'** 'store in a cool place' ▸ **quelle chaleur!** what a scorcher! / [agréable] warmth ▸ **les grandes chaleurs** the hottest days of the summer ▸ **chaleur humaine** human warmth ▸ **avec chaleur** [accueillir] warmly ▸ **plaider une cause avec chaleur** to plead a case fervently *ou* with fervour *UK ou* fervor *US* ▸ **en chaleur** [animal] on *UK ou* in *US* heat ▸ **la jument a ses chaleurs** the mare's on *UK ou* in *US* heat.

chaleureusement [ʃalœrøzmɑ̃] **adv** warmly.

chaleureux, euse [ʃalœrø, øz] **adj** warm.

challenge [ʃalɑ̃ʒ] **nm 1.** SPORT tournament **2.** *fig* [défi] challenge.

challenger [tʃalɛndʒœr] **nm** *fig* & SPORT challenger.

chaloupe [ʃalup] **nf** rowing boat *UK*, rowboat *US*.

chalumeau [ʃalymo] **nm 1.** TECHNOL blowtorch, blowlamp *UK* **2.** [paille] (drinking) straw.

chalut [ʃaly] **nm** trawl ▸ **pêcher au chalut** to trawl.

chalutier [ʃalytje] **nm 1.** [bateau] trawler **2.** [pêcheur] trawlerman.

chamade [ʃamad] **nf : battre la chamade** [cœur] to pound.

chamailler [3] [ʃamaje] ◆ ***se chamailler*** **vp** *fam* to squabble.

chaman [ʃaman] **nm** shaman.

chamanisme [ʃamanism] **nm** shamanism.

chambardement [ʃɑ̃bardəmɑ̃] **nm** *fam* [bouleversement] upheaval.

chambarder [3] [ʃɑ̃barde] **vt** *fam* **1.** [pièce] to turn upside down **2.** [projet] to upset.

chambouler [3] [ʃɑ̃bule] **vt** *fam* to make a mess of, to turn upside down.

chambranle [ʃɑ̃brɑ̃l] **nm** [de porte, fenêtre] frame / [de cheminée] mantelpiece.

chambre [ʃɑ̃br] **nf 1.** [où l'on dort] **: chambre (à coucher)** bedroom ▸ **garder la chambre** to stay in one's room ▸ **faire chambre à part** to sleep in separate rooms ▸ **réserver une chambre d'hôtel** to book a hotel room ▸ **chambre à un lit, chambre pour une personne** single room ▸ **chambre pour deux personnes** double room ▸ **chambre à deux lits** twin-bedded room ▸ **chambre**

d'amis spare room ▸ **chambre de bonne** maid's room / [louée à un particulier] attic room *(often rented to a student)* ▸ **chambre d'hôte** bed and breakfast
2. [local] room ▸ **chambre forte** strongroom ▸ **chambre froide** cold store ▸ **chambre à gaz** gas chamber ▸ **chambre noire** darkroom
3. DR division ▸ **chambre d'accusation** court of criminal appeal ▸ **Chambre des appels correctionnels** District Court
4. POLIT chamber, house ▸ **la Chambre des communes** the House of Commons *UK* ▸ **Chambre des députés** ≃ House of Commons *UK*, ≃ House of Representatives *US* ▸ **la Chambre haute/basse** the Upper/Lower Chamber ▸ **la Chambre des lords** *ou* **des pairs** the House of Lords *UK*
5. COMM **: chambre de commerce** chamber of commerce ▸ **chambre de compensation** clearing house ▸ **chambre des métiers** guild chamber
6. TECHNOL chamber ▸ **chambre à air** [de pneu] inner tube ▸ **chambre de combustion** combustion chamber.

chambrée [ʃɑ̃bre] **nf** room, roomful / [de soldats] barrack room.

chambrer [3] [ʃɑ̃bre] **vt 1.** [vin] to bring to room temperature **2.** *fam* [se moquer] **: chambrer qqn** to pull sb's leg, to wind sb up *UK*.

chameau, x [ʃamo] **nm 1.** [mammifère] camel **2.** *fam injur* [homme] pig / [femme] cow.

chamois [ʃamwa] ■ **nm** chamois / [peau] chamois (leather).
■ **adj inv** [couleur] fawn.

champ [ʃɑ̃] **nm 1.** [gén] field ▸ **champ de bataille** battlefield ▸ **il est mort au champ d'honneur** he died for his country ▸ **champ de blé** field of wheat ▸ **champ de maïs** cornfield ▸ **champ de courses** racecourse ▸ **champ magnétique** magnetic field ▸ **fleurs des champs** wild flowers ▸ **champ de tir** MIL [terrain] rifle range / [portée d'une arme] field of fire ▸ **champ visuel** field of vision *ou* view ▸ **laisser le champ libre à qqn** *fig* to leave the field open *ou* clear for sb ▸ **avoir le champ libre** to have a free hand ▸ **être dans le champ** to be in shot ▸ **sortir du champ** to go out of shot **2.** [étendue] area ▸ **champ d'action** sphere of activity **3.** INFORM field ▸ **champ d'action** sensitivity ▸ **champ variable** variable field.
◆ ***sur le champ*** **loc adv** immediately, at once, right away.

champagne [ʃɑ̃paɲ] **nm** champagne ▸ **champagne rosé** pink champagne.

champagnisé [ʃɑ̃aŋize] ➤ ***vin***.

champenois, e [ʃɑ̃pənwa, az] **adj : méthode champenoise** champagne-style.

champêtre [ʃɑ̃pɛtr] **adj** rural.

champignon [ʃɑ̃piɲɔ̃] **nm 1.** BOT & MÉD fungus ▸ **pousser comme des champignons** *fig* to mushroom **2.** [comestible] mushroom ▸ **champignon de Paris** button mushroom ▸ **champignon vénéneux** toadstool **3.** *fam* [accélérateur] accelerator ▸ **appuyer sur le champignon** to put one's foot down *UK*, to step on the gas *US*.

champion, onne [ʃɑ̃pjɔ̃, ɔn] ■ **nm, f** champion ▸ **champion du monde** world champion.
■ **adj** *fam* brilliant.

championnat [ʃɑ̃pjɔna] **nm** championship ▸ **championnat du monde** world championship.

chance [ʃɑ̃s] **nf 1.** [bonheur] luck *(U)* ▸ **avoir de la chance** to be lucky ▸ **ne pas avoir de chance** to be unlucky ▸ **bonne chance!** good luck! ▸ **quelle chance!** what luck!, how lucky! ▸ **porter chance** to bring good luck ▸ **souhaiter bonne chance à qqn** to wish sb good luck **2.** [probabilité, possibilité] chance, opportunity ▸ **avoir des chances de faire qqch** to have a chance of doing sthg ▸ **avoir une chance sur dix de réussir** to get a one-in-ten chance of succeeding ▸ **donner sa chance à qqn** to give sb a chance ▸ **tenter sa chance** to try one's luck ▸ **il y a peu de chances que...** there's not much chance that... ▸ **négociations de la dernière chance** last-ditch negotiations.

chancelant, e [ʃɑ̃slɑ̃, ɑ̃t] **adj 1.** [titubant, bancal] unsteady **2.** *fig* [mémoire, santé] shaky.

chanceler [24] [ʃɑ̃sle] **vi** [personne, gouvernement] to totter / [meuble] to wobble.

chancelier [ʃɑ̃səlje] **nm 1.** [premier ministre] chancellor **2.** [de consulat, d'ambassade] secretary.
◆ ***Chancelier*** **nm : le Chancelier de l'Échiquier** the Chancellor of the Exchequer.

chancellerie [ʃɑ̃sɛlri] **nf 1.** [ministère de la justice] chancery *UK*, Department of Justice *US* **2.** [en Allemagne] chancellor's office **3.** [de consulat, d'ambassade] chancery.

chanceux, euse [ʃɑ̃sø, øz] **adj** lucky.

chancre [ʃɑ̃kr] **nm 1.** MÉD chancre **2.** BOT canker.

chandail [ʃɑ̃daj] **nm** (thick) sweater.

Chandeleur [ʃɑ̃dlœr] **nf** Candlemas.

chandelier [ʃɑ̃dəlje] **nm** [pour une bougie] candlestick / [à plusieurs branches] candelabra.

chandelle [ʃɑ̃dɛl] **nf** [bougie] candle ▸ **dîner aux chandelles** candlelit dinner ▸ **brûler la chandelle par les deux bouts** *fig* to burn the candle at both ends ▸ **devoir une fière chandelle à qqn** *fig* to owe sb a big favour *UK ou* favor *US* ▸ **tenir la chandelle** to play gooseberry *UK* ▸ **voir trente-six chandelles** *fam fig* to see stars.

change [ʃɑ̃ʒ] **nm 1.** [troc & FIN] exchange ▸ **donner le change à qqn** to pull the wool over sb's eyes ▸ **gagner au change** to be better off ▸ **perdre au change** to lose out **2.** [couche de bébé] disposable nappy *UK ou* diaper *US*.

changeant, e [ʃɑ̃ʒɑ̃, ɑ̃t] **adj 1.** [temps, humeur] changeable **2.** [reflet] shimmering.

changement [ʃɑ̃ʒmɑ̃] **nm** change ▸ **je voudrais bien un peu de changement** I'd like things to change a little ▸ **j'ai trois changements/je n'ai pas de changement pour aller chez elle** I have to change three times/I don't have to change to get to her place ▸ **changement d'adresse** change of address ▸ **changement de cap** *ou* **de direction** change of course ▸ **changement de ligne** line feed ▸ **changement de marque** COMM rebranding / [marketing] brand switching ▸ **changement de page** page break ▸ **changement de programme** change of plan ▸ **'changement de propriétaire'** 'under new ownership' ▸ **changement de température/temps** change in temperature/(the) weather ▸ **changement de vitesse** gear lever *UK*, gear stick *UK*, gearshift *US*.

changer [17] [ʃɑ̃ʒe] ■ vt **1.** [gén] to change ▸ **changer qqch contre** to change *ou* exchange sthg for ▸ **changer qqch de place** to move sthg ▸ **changer qqn en** to change sb into ▸ **changer un malade** to put fresh clothes on a sick person ▸ **j'ai fait changer les freins** I had new brakes put in
2. [modifier] to change, to alter ▸ **changer l'ordre du jour de la réunion** to change the agenda of the meeting ▸ **mais ça change tout!** ah, that makes a big difference! ▸ **ne rien changer à qqch** not to make any changes to sthg ▸ **il ne veut rien changer à ses habitudes** he won't alter his ways one jot *ou* iota ▸ **ça me/te changera** that will be a (nice) change for me/you ▸ **viens, ça te changera les idées** come along, it'll take your mind off things
3. ÉCON : **changer un billet pour avoir de la monnaie** to change a note in order to get small change ▸ **changer des euros en dollars** to change euros into dollars, to exchange euros for dollars
▸▸ **changer son fusil d'épaule** to have a change of heart.
■ **vi 1.** [gén] to change ▸ **changer d'adresse** [personne] to move to a new address / [commerce] to move to new premises ▸ **changer d'air** to have a break ▸ **changer d'avis** to change one's mind ▸ **ça changera!** that'll make a change! ▸ **changer de chaîne** [une fois] to change channels / [constamment] to zap ▸ **changer de coiffure** to get a new hairstyle ▸ **changer de décor** THÉÂTRE to change the set ▸ **changer de direction** to change direction ▸ **changer de place (avec qqn)** to change places (with sb) ▸ **changer de train (à)** to change trains (at) ▸ **changer de vitesse** AUTO to change gear ▸ **changer de voiture** to change one's car ▸ **pour changer** for a change
2. [modifier] to change, to alter ▸ **changer de comportement** to alter one's behaviour *UK ou* behavior *US*.
◆ ***se changer*** **vp 1.** [se rhabiller] to change, to get changed
2. [se transformer] **: se changer en** to change into ▸ **la grenouille se changea en prince** the frog turned into a prince.

changeur [ʃɑ̃ʒœr] **nm 1.** [personne] moneychanger **2.** [appareil] **: changeur de monnaie** change machine.

chanoine [ʃanwan] **nm** canon.

chanson [ʃɑ̃sɔ̃] **nf** song ▸ **c'est toujours la même chanson** *fig* it's the same old story.

chansonnette [ʃɑ̃sɔnɛt] **nf** ditty.

chansonnier, ère [ʃɑ̃sɔnje, ɛr] **nm, f** cabaret singer-songwriter.

chant [ʃɑ̃] **nm 1.** [chanson] song, singing *(U)* / [sacré] hymn ▸ **chant du cygne** *fig* swansong ▸ **chant grégorien** Gregorian chant **2.** [art] singing *(U)* ▸ **prendre des leçons de chant** to take singing lessons.
◆ ***au chant du coq*** **loc adv** at cockcrow.

chantage [ʃɑ̃taʒ] **nm** *litt* & *fig* blackmail ▸ **faire du chantage** to use *ou* resort to blackmail ▸ **faire du chantage à qqn** to blackmail sb.

chantant, e [ʃɑ̃tɑ̃, ɑ̃t] **adj 1.** [accent, voix] lilting **2.** [musique, air] catchy.

chanter [3] [ʃɑ̃te] ■ **vt 1.** [chanson] to sing **2.** *fam* [raconter] to tell **3.** *littéraire* [célébrer] to sing *ou* tell of ▸ **chanter les louanges de qqn** to sing sb's praises.
■ **vi** [gén] to sing ▸ **chanter juste** to sing in tune ▸ **chanter faux** to sing off key
▸▸ **faire chanter qqn** to blackmail sb ▸ **si ça vous chante!** *fam* if you feel like *ou* fancy it *UK*!

chanterelle [ʃɑ̃trɛl] **nf** [champignon] chanterelle.

chanteur, euse [ʃɑ̃tœr, øz] **nm, f** singer.

chantier [ʃɑ̃tje] **nm 1.** CONSTR (building) site ▸ **sur le chantier** on the site / [sur la route] roadworks *pl UK*, roadwork *(U) US* ▸ **chantier de démolition** demolition site *ou* area ▸ **chantier naval** shipyard, dockyard **2.** *fig* [désordre] shambles *sg*, mess.
◆ ***en chantier*** **loc adv** in progress ▸ **mettre un ouvrage en chantier** to get a project started.

Chantilly [ʃɑ̃tiji] **nf : (crème) Chantilly** Chantilly cream.

chantonner [3] [ʃɑ̃tɔne] **vt & vi** to hum.

chanvre [ʃɑ̃vr] **nm** hemp.

chaos [kao] **nm** chaos.

chaotique [kaɔtik] **adj** chaotic.

chap. (abr écrite de ***chapitre***) ch.

chaparder [3] [ʃaparde] **vt** *fam* to steal.

chapeau, x [ʃapo] **nm 1.** [coiffure] hat ▸ **chapeau melon** bowler hat ▸ **tirer son chapeau à qqn** to take one's hat off to sb **2.** PRESSE introductory paragraph
▸▸ **chapeau!** *fam* nice one! ▸ **démarrer sur les chapeaux de roues** *fam* to take off like a bat out of hell.

chapeauter [3] [ʃapote] **vt** [service] to head / [personnes] to supervise.

chapelain [ʃaplɛ̃] **nm** chaplain.

chapelet [ʃaplɛ] **nm 1.** RELIG rosary ▸ **dire son chapelet** to say one's rosary, to tell one's beads **2.** [de saucisses, d'oignons] string **3.** *fig* [d'injures] string, torrent.

chapelier, ère [ʃapəlje, ɛr] ■ **adj** hat *(avant n)*.
■ **nm, f** [pour hommes] hatter / [pour femmes] milliner.

chapelle [ʃapɛl] **nf 1.** [petite église] chapel / [partie d'église] choir ▸ **chapelle ardente** chapel of rest **2.** [coterie] clique.

chapelure [ʃaplyr] **nf** (dried) breadcrumbs *pl*.

chaperon [ʃaprɔ̃] **nm 1.** LITTÉR **: le Petit chaperon Rouge** Little Red Riding Hood **2.** [personne] chaperone.

chapiteau [ʃapito] **nm 1.** [de colonne] capital **2.** [de cirque] big top.

chapitre [ʃapitr] **nm 1.** [de livre & RELIG] chapter **2.** [de budget] head, item **3.** *fig* [sujet] subject.

chapitrer [3] [ʃapitre] **vt** *sout* to reprimand.

chapon [ʃapɔ̃] **nm 1.** [volaille] capon **2.** [en-cas] *piece of bread rubbed with garlic and oil.*

chaque [ʃak] **adj indéf** each, every ▸ **chaque personne** each person, everyone ▸ **j'ai payé ces livres 100 euros chaque** I paid 100 euros each for these books.

char [ʃar] **nm 1.** MIL **: char (d'assaut)** tank **2.** [charrette] cart, waggon *UK*, wagon **3.** [de carnaval] float **4.** *Québec* [voiture] car **5.** HIST chariot.

charabia [ʃarabja] **nm** gibberish.

charade [ʃarad] **nf** charade.

charbon [ʃarbɔ̃] **nm 1.** [combustible] coal ▸ **charbon de bois** charcoal ▸ **être sur des charbons ardents** *fig* to be like a cat on hot bricks *UK ou* on a hot tin roof *US* **2.** [maladie] anthrax.

charbonnage [ʃarbɔnaʒ] **nm** coalmining ▸ **les charbonnages** collieries, coalmines.

charbonnier, ère [ʃarbɔnje, ɛr] **adj** coal *(avant n).*
◆ ***charbonnier*** **nm 1.** [cargo] collier **2.** [vendeur] coal merchant / [livreur] coalman.

charcuter [3] [ʃarkyte] **vt** *fam péj* to butcher ▸ **se faire charcuter** to be hacked about.

charcuterie [ʃarkytri] **nf 1.** [magasin] pork butcher's **2.** [produits] pork meat products **3.** [commerce] pork meat trade.

charcutier, ère [ʃarkytje, ɛr] **nm, f** [commerçant] pork butcher.

chardon [ʃardɔ̃] **nm 1.** [plante] thistle **2.** [sur un mur] spikes *pl*.

chardonneret [ʃardɔnrɛ] **nm** goldfinch.

charentais, e [ʃarɑ̃tɛ, ɛz] **adj** of/from Charente.
◆ ***charentaise*** **nf** (bedroom) slipper.

charge [ʃarʒ] **nf 1.** [fardeau] load ▸ **charge maximum** maximum load ▸ **charge utile** capacity load ▸ **charge à vide** empty weight
2. [fonction] office ▸ **charge élective** elective office ▸ **charge de notaire** notary's office
3. [responsabilité] responsibility ▸ **être à la charge de** [personne] to be dependent on ▸ **ses enfants sont encore à sa charge** his children are still his dependants ▸ **les travaux sont à la charge du propriétaire** the owner is liable for the cost of the work ▸ **prendre qqch en charge** [payer] to pay (for) sthg / [s'occuper de] to take charge of sthg ▸ **prendre qqn en charge** to take charge of sb
4. ÉLECTR & MIL charge ▸ **charge d'explosifs** explosive charge ▸ **charge négative/positive** negative/positive charge ▸ **donner la charge** to charge ▸ **revenir à la charge** *litt* to mount a fresh attack / *fig* to go back onto the offensive
5. DR charge, accusation ▸ **de très lourdes charges pèsent contre lui** there are very serious charges hanging over him ▸ **témoin à charge** witness for the prosecution
▸▸ **j'accepte, à charge de revanche** I accept, provided that you'll let me do the same for you some time.
◆ ***charges*** **nfpl 1.** [d'appartement] service charge
2. ÉCON expenses, costs ▸ **charges courantes** current expenses ▸ **charges directes** direct costs ▸ **charges d'exploitation** running costs ▸ **charges fiscales** tax (burden) ▸ **charges incompressibles** necessary expenses ▸ **charges opérationnelles** FIN operating costs ▸ **charges patronales** employer's contributions ▸ **charges salariales** wage costs ▸ **charges sociales** ≃ employer's contributions.

CULTURE

Charges

Also called **charges locatives** or **charges d'habitation**, these are the maintenance and daily operation costs of an apartment block. They are divided up among owners and tenants, though tenants pay monthly sums while proprietors pay only every three months. **Charges** generally include water and sometimes also electricity. In classified ads, **charges comprises** or **CC** means the fees are included in the advertised rent; **hors charges, HC** and **charges en sus** mean they are extra.

chargé, e [ʃarʒe] ■ **adj 1.** [véhicule, personne] **: chargé (de)** loaded (with) **2.** [responsable] **: chargé (de)** responsible (for) **3.** [occupé] full, busy.
■ **nm, f : chargé d'affaires** chargé d'affaires ▸ **chargé de cours** ≃ lecturer ▸ **chargé de mission** head of mission.

chargement [ʃarʒəmɑ̃] **nm 1.** [action] loading **2.** [marchandises] load ▸ **un chargement de gravier** a load of gravel.

charger [17] [ʃarʒe] **vt 1.** [gén & INFORM] to load ▸ **être chargé** to be loaded **2.** [remplir] to fill **3.** ÉLECTR, DR & MIL to charge **4.** [donner une mission à] **: charger qqn de faire qqch** to put sb in charge of doing sthg.
◆ ***se charger*** **vp : se charger de qqn/qqch** to take care of sb/sthg, to take charge of sb/sthg ▸ **se charger de faire qqch** to undertake to do sthg.

chargeur [ʃarʒœr] **nm 1.** ÉLECTR charger **2.** [d'arme] magazine **3.** [d'appareil photo] cartridge, cassette **4.** [personne - qui expédie une charge] shipper / [- qui charge] docker *UK*, longshoreman *US*, stevedore *US*.

chariot [ʃarjo] **nm 1.** [charrette] handcart **2.** [à bagages, dans un hôpital] trolley *UK*, cart *US* ▸ **chariot élévateur** forklift truck **3.** [de machine à écrire] carriage.

charismatique [karismatik] **adj** charismatic.

charisme [karism] **nm** charisma.

charitable [ʃaritabl] **adj** charitable / [conseil] friendly.

charité [ʃarite] **nf 1.** [aumône & RELIG] charity ▸ **demander la charité** to beg (for charity) ▸ **faire la charité à qqn** to give sb charity **2.** [bonté] kindness.

charivari [ʃarivari] **nm** hullabaloo.

charlatan [ʃarlatɑ̃] **nm** *péj* charlatan.

charlotte [ʃarlɔt] **nf** CULIN charlotte.

charmant, e [ʃarmɑ̃, ɑ̃t] **adj** charming.

charme [ʃarm] **nm 1.** [séduction] charm ▸ **faire du charme (à qqn)** to turn on the charm (for sb) **2.** [enchantement] spell ▸ **tenir sous le charme** to hold spellbound ▸ **rompre le charme** to break the spell **3.** [arbre] ironwood, hornbeam **4.** [tourisme] **: hôtel de charme** hotel
▸▸ **se porter comme un charme** *fam* to be as fit as a fiddle.

charmer [3] [ʃarme] vt to charm ▸ **être charmé de faire qqch** to be delighted to do sthg.

charmeur, ***euse*** [ʃarmœr, øz] ■ **adj** charming.
■ **nm, f** charmer ▸ **charmeur de serpents** snake charmer.

charnel, ***elle*** [ʃarnɛl] **adj** carnal.

charnier [ʃarnje] **nm** mass grave.

charnière [ʃarnjɛr] ■ **nf** hinge / *fig* turning point.
■ **adj** [période] transitional.

charnu, ***e*** [ʃarny] **adj** fleshy.

charognard [ʃarɔɲar] **nm** *litt* & *fig* vulture.

charogne [ʃarɔɲ] **nf** **1.** [d'animal] carrion *(U)* **2.** *tfam* [crapule - homme] bastard / [- femme] bitch.

charpente [ʃarpɑ̃t] **nf** **1.** [de bâtiment, de roman] framework **2.** [ossature] frame.

charpenté, ***e*** [ʃarpɑ̃te] **adj : être bien charpenté** [personne] to be well-built / [roman] to be well-constructed.

charpentier [ʃarpɑ̃tje] **nm** carpenter.

charpie [ʃarpi] **nf** [pansement] lint, shredded linen.
◆ ***en charpie*** **loc adv : mettre** *ou* **réduire qqch en charpie** to tear sthg to shreds ▸ **je vais le mettre** *ou* **réduire en charpie** *fig* I'll make mincemeat (out) of him.

charretier, ***ère*** [ʃartje, ɛr] ■ **adj** cart *(avant n)*.
■ **nm, f** carter ▸ **jurer comme un charretier** to swear like a trooper.

charrette [ʃarɛt] **nf** cart.

charrier [9] [ʃarje] ■ **vt** **1.** [personne, fleuve] to carry **2.** *fam* [se moquer de] **: charrier qqn** to take sb for a ride.
■ **vi** *fam* [exagérer] to go too far.

charrue [ʃary] **nf** plough *UK*, plow *US* ▸ **mettre la charrue avant les bœufs** *fam fig* to put the cart before the horse.

charte [ʃart] **nf** charter ▸ **l'École nationale des chartes** *grande école for archivists and librarians.*

charter [ʃartɛr] ■ **nm** chartered plane.
■ **adj inv** *(en apposition)* charter *(avant n)*.

chartreuse [ʃartrøz] **nf** **1.** RELIG Carthusian monastery **2.** [liqueur] Chartreuse.

chas [ʃa] **nm** eye *(of needle)*.

chasse [ʃas] **nf** **1.** [action] hunting ▸ **aller à la chasse** to go hunting ▸ **chasse à courre** hunting *(on horseback with hounds)* ▸ **chasse au daim/renard/tigre** deer/fox/tiger hunt
2. [période] **: la chasse est ouverte/fermée** it's the open/close season
3. [domaine] **: chasse gardée** private hunting *ou* shooting preserve / *fig* preserve
4. [poursuite] chase ▸ **faire la chasse à qqn/qqch** *fig* to hunt (for) sb/sthg, to hunt sb/sthg down ▸ **se mettre en chasse pour trouver un emploi/une maison** to go job-hunting/house-hunting ▸ **prendre qqn/qqch en chasse** to give chase to sb/sthg ▸ **prendre en chasse une voiture** to chase a car ▸ **chasse à l'homme** manhunt ▸ **chasse aux sorcières** witch hunt
5. [des cabinets] **: chasse (d'eau)** flush ▸ **tirer la chasse** to flush the toilet.
◆ ***chasse au trésor*** **nf** treasure hunt.

chassé-croisé [ʃasekrwaze] (pl **chassés-croisés**) **nm** toing and froing.

chasse-neige [ʃasnɛʒ] **nm inv** snowplough *UK*, snowplow *US*.

chasser [3] [ʃase] ■ **vt** **1.** [animal] to hunt **2.** [faire partir - personne] to drive *ou* chase away / [- odeur, souci] to dispel.
■ **vi** **1.** [aller à la chasse] to go hunting, to hunt **2.** [roues] to skid.

chasseur, ***euse*** [ʃasœr, øz] **nm, f** hunter.
◆ ***chasseur*** **nm** **1.** [d'hôtel] page, messenger, bellhop *US* **2.** MIL **: chasseur alpin** *soldier specially trained for operations in mountainous terrain* **3.** [avion] fighter.
◆ ***chasseur de têtes*** **nm** headhunter.

châssis [ʃasi] **nm** **1.** [de fenêtre, de porte, de machine] frame **2.** [de véhicule] chassis **3.** [de tableau] stretcher.

chaste [ʃast] **adj** chaste.

chasteté [ʃastəte] **nf** chastity.

chasuble [ʃazybl] ■ **nf** chasuble.
■ **adj** ➤ ***robe***.

chat[1], ***chatte*** [ʃa, ʃat] **nm, f** cat ▸ **un petit chat** a kitten ▸ **chat de gouttière** ordinary cat, alley cat *US* ▸ **chat persan/siamois** Persian/Siamese cat ▸ **chat sauvage** wildcat / *Québec* [raton laveur] raccoon ▸ **il n'y a pas un chat** *fam* there's not a soul ▸ **il n'y a pas de quoi fouetter un chat** it's nothing to make a fuss about ▸ **appeler un chat un chat** to call a spade a spade ▸ **avoir d'autres chats à fouetter** to have other fish to fry ▸ **avoir un chat dans la gorge** to have a frog in one's throat ▸ **jouer à chat** to play tag ▸ **jouer à chat perché** to play off-ground tag ▸ **jouer au chat et à la souris avec qqn** *fig* to play cat-and-mouse with sb.

chat[2] [tʃat] **nm** INFORM chat.

châtaigne [ʃatɛɲ] **nf** **1.** [fruit] chestnut **2.** *fam* [coup] clout.

châtaignier [ʃateɲe] **nm** [arbre] chestnut (tree) / [bois] chestnut.

châtain [ʃatɛ̃] **adj** & **nm** chestnut, chestnut-brown.

château, ***x*** [ʃato] **nm** **1.** [forteresse] **: château (fort)** castle **2.** [résidence - seigneuriale] mansion / [- de monarque, d'évêque] palace ▸ **château de cartes** *litt* & *fig* house of cards ▸ **château gonflable** [jeu de plage, attraction] bouncy castle *UK* ▸ **château de sable** sandcastle ▸ **les châteaux de la Loire** the Châteaux of the Loire ▸ **bâtir des châteaux en Espagne** *fig* to build castles in the air **3.** [vignoble] château, vineyard **4.** [réservoir] **: château d'eau** water tower.

chateaubriand, ***châteaubriant*** [ʃatobrijɑ̃] **nm** Chateaubriand steak.

châtelain, ***e*** [ʃatlɛ̃, ɛn] **nm, f** lord (f lady) of the manor.

châtier [9] [ʃatje] **vt** *sout* **1.** [punir] to punish **2.** [polir] to refine, to hone.

chatière [ʃatjɛr] **nf** **1.** [pour chat] cat-flap **2.** [d'aération] air vent.

châtiment [ʃatimɑ̃] **nm** punishment.

chaton [ʃatɔ̃] **nm** **1.** [petit chat] kitten **2.** BOT catkin **3.** [de bague] setting **4.** [pierre] stone.

chatouiller [3] [ʃatuje] **vt 1.** [faire des chatouilles à] to tickle **2.** *fig* [titiller] to titillate.

chatouilles [ʃatuj] **nfpl** tickling *(U)*.

chatouilleux, euse [ʃatujø, øz] **adj 1.** [sensible aux chatouilles] ticklish **2.** *fig* [susceptible] touchy.

chatoyant, e [ʃatwajɑ̃, ɑ̃t] **adj** [reflet, étoffe] shimmering / [bijou] sparkling.

chatoyer [13] [ʃatwaje] **vi** [reflet, étoffe] to shimmer / [bijou] to sparkle.

châtrer [3] [ʃatre] **vt** to castrate / [chat] to neuter / [chatte] to spay.

chatte ➤ ***chat***.

chatterton [ʃatɛrtɔn] **nm** ÉLECTR insulating tape *UK*, friction tape *US*.

chaud, e [ʃo, ʃod] **adj 1.** [gén] warm / [de température très élevée, sensuel] hot ▸ **une boisson chaude** a hot drink ▸ **marrons chauds** roast chestnuts ▸ **chaud lapin** randy devil **2.** *fig* [enthousiaste] **: être chaud pour qqch/pour faire qqch** to be keen on sthg/on doing sthg ▸ **je ne suis pas très chaud pour le faire** *fam* I'm not really eager to do it **3.** [animé] tense ▸ **avoir une chaude discussion sur qqch** to debate sthg heatedly.

◆ ***chaud*** ■ **adv : avoir chaud** to be warm *ou* hot ▸ **il fait chaud** it's warm *ou* hot ▸ **manger chaud** to have something hot (to eat) ▸ **servir chaud** serve hot ▸ **tenir chaud** to keep warm ▸ **j'ai eu chaud** [l'échapper belle] I had a narrow *ou* lucky escape / [avoir peur] I had a nasty shock *ou* fright ▸ **ne lui pose pas la question à chaud** don't just spring the question on him in the midst of it all.

■ **nm** heat ▸ **rester au chaud** to stay in the warm ▸ **un chaud et froid** a chill.

chaudement [ʃodmɑ̃] **adv** warmly.

chaud-froid [ʃofrwa] (pl **chauds-froids**) **nm** *poultry or game served cold in a thick white sauce glazed with jelly.*

chaudière [ʃodjɛr] **nf** boiler.

chaudron [ʃodrɔ̃] **nm** cauldron.

chauffage [ʃofaʒ] **nm 1.** [action] heating **2.** [appareil] heating (system) ▸ **chauffage central** central heating.

chauffant, e [ʃofɑ̃, ɑ̃t] **adj** heating ▸ **couverture chauffante** electric blanket ▸ **plaque chauffante** hotplate.

chauffard [ʃofar] **nm** *péj* reckless driver.

chauffe-biberon [ʃofbibrɔ̃] (pl **chauffe-biberons**) **nm** bottle-warmer.

chauffe-eau [ʃofo] **nm inv** waterheater.

chauffe-plats [ʃofpla] **nm inv** hotplate, chafing dish.

chauffer [3] [ʃofe] ■ **vt** [rendre chaud] to heat (up) ▸ **chauffer à blanc** to heat until white-hot.

■ **vi 1.** [devenir chaud] to heat up **2.** [moteur] to overheat **3.** *fam* [barder] **: ça va chauffer** there's going to be trouble.

◆ ***se chauffer*** **vp : se chauffer à qqch** to heat one's house with sthg.

chaufferette [ʃofrɛt] **nf 1.** [réchaud] hotplate, chafing dish **2.** [pour les pieds] foot-warmer.

chaufferie [ʃofri] **nf** boiler room.

chauffeur [ʃofœr] **nm 1.** AUTO driver ▸ **chauffeur du dimanche** Sunday driver ▸ **chauffeur de taxi** taxi driver **2.** [de chaudière] stoker.

chaume [ʃom] **nm 1.** [paille] thatch **2.** [de céréales] stubble.

chaumière [ʃomjɛr] **nf** cottage.

chaussée [ʃose] **nf** road, roadway ▸ **'chaussée déformée'** 'uneven road surface'.

chausse-pied [ʃospje] (pl **chausse-pieds**) **nm** shoehorn.

chausser [3] [ʃose] ■ **vt 1.** [chaussures, lunettes, skis] to put on ▸ **chausser qqn** to put sb's shoes on **2.** [fournir] to supply shoes to **3.** [suj: chaussures] to fit.

■ **vi : chausser du 39** to take size 39 (shoes).

◆ ***se chausser*** **vp** to put one's shoes on.

chausse-trape (pl **chausse-trapes**), ***chausse-trappe*** (pl **chausse-trappes**) [ʃostrəp] **nf** trap.

chaussette [ʃosɛt] **nf** sock.

chausseur [ʃosœr] **nm** shoemaker.

chausson [ʃosɔ̃] **nm 1.** [pantoufle] slipper **2.** [de danse] ballet shoe **3.** [de bébé] bootee **4.** CULIN turnover ▸ **chausson aux pommes** apple turnover.

chaussure [ʃosyr] **nf 1.** [soulier] shoe ▸ **chaussure basse** low-heeled shoe, flat shoe ▸ **chaussure à crampons** [pour football, rugby] studded boot / [pour athlétisme] spiked shoe ▸ **chaussure de marche** [de randonnée] hiking *ou* walking boot / [confortable] walking shoe ▸ **chaussure montante** (ankle) boot ▸ **chaussure à scratch** shoe with Velcro® fastenings ▸ **chaussure de ski** ski boot ▸ **chaussures à talon** (shoes with) heels ▸ **trouver chaussure à son pied** *fam fig* to find Mr/Miss Right **2.** [industrie] footwear industry.

chauve [ʃov] ■ **adj** [sans cheveux] bald.

■ **nm** bald man.

chauve-souris [ʃovsuri] (pl **chauves-souris**) **nf** bat.

chauvin, e [ʃovɛ̃, in] ■ **adj** chauvinistic.

■ **nm, f** chauvinist.

chauvinisme [ʃovinism] **nm** chauvinism.

chaux [ʃo] **nf** lime ▸ **blanchi à la chaux** whitewashed.

chavirer [3] [ʃavire] ■ **vi 1.** [bateau] to capsize **2.** *fig* [tourner] to spin **3.** *fig* [échouer] to founder.

■ **vt 1.** [bateau] to capsize **2.** [meuble] to tip over.

chéchia [ʃeʃja] **nf** fez.

check-up [tʃɛkœp] **nm inv** checkup.

chef [ʃɛf] **nm 1.** [d'un groupe] head, leader / [au travail] boss ▸ **en chef** in chief ▸ **chef de cabinet** principal private secretary *UK* ▸ **chef de chantier** foreman ▸ **chef d'entreprise** company head ▸ **chef d'établissement** SCOL headteacher *UK*, headmaster (f headmistress) *UK*, principal *US* ▸ **chef d'État** head of state ▸ **chef d'état-major** chief of staff ▸ **chef de fabrication** production manager ▸ **chef de famille** head of the family ▸ **chef de file** POLIT (party) leader / [catégorie, produit] category leader ▸ **chef de gare** stationmaster ▸ **chef de marque** brand manager ▸ **chef d'orchestre** conductor ▸ **chef du personnel** personnel manager ▸ **chef de produit** product manager ▸ **chef de projet** project manager ▸ **chef de rayon** departmental manager *ou* supervisor ▸ **chef de service** ADMIN departmental manager ▸ **une mentalité de petit chef** a petty-minded attitude to one's subordinates **2.** [cuisinier] chef ▸ **la spécialité du chef aujourd'hui** the chef's special today

▸▸ **de son propre chef** on one's own initiative ▸ **j'ai agi de mon propre chef** I acted on my own initiative ▸ **leur décision me concerne au premier chef** their decision has immediate implications for me ▸ **opiner du chef** to nod agreement.

◆ ***chef d'accusation*** **nm** charge, count.

chef-d'œuvre [ʃɛdœvr] (pl **chefs-d'œuvre**) **nm** masterpiece.

chef-lieu [ʃɛfljø] (pl **chefs-lieux**) **nm** ≃ county town *UK*, ≃ county seat *US*.

cheik [ʃɛk] **nm** sheikh.

chelem [ʃlɛm] **nm** SPORT slam ▸ **grand chelem** grand slam ▸ **petit chelem** small *ou* little slam.

chemin [ʃəmɛ̃] **nm 1.** [voie] path ▸ **chemin d'accès** path ▸ **chemin de terre** dirt track ▸ **chemin de traverse** *litt* path across the fields / *fig* short cut ▸ **chemin vicinal** byroad, minor road **2.** [parcours] way / *fig* road ▸ **on s'est retrouvé à mi-chemin** we met halfway ▸ **en chemin** on the way ▸ **nous en avons parlé en chemin** we talked about it on the way *ou* on our way ▸ **faire du chemin** to cover a lot of ground / *fig* to gain ground ▸ **se frayer un chemin dans la foule** to force one's way through the crowd ▸ **rebrousser chemin** to turn back ▸ **le chemin de croix** the way of the cross ▸ **prendre le chemin des écoliers** *fig* to go the long way around ▸ **prendre le chemin de l'exil** to go into exile ▸ **être/rester sur le droit chemin** *fig* to be on/to keep to the straight and narrow ▸ **détourner qqn du droit chemin** to lead sb astray.

◆ ***chemin de fer*** **nm** railway *UK*, railroad *US* ▸ **employé des chemins de fer** railman, rail worker *UK*.

cheminée [ʃəmine] **nf 1.** [foyer] fireplace **2.** [conduit d'usine] chimney **3.** [encadrement] mantelpiece **4.** [de paquebot, locomotive] funnel.

cheminement [ʃəminmɑ̃] **nm** [progression] advance / *fig* [d'idée] development.

cheminer [3] [ʃəmine] **vi** [avancer] to make one's way / *fig* [idée] to develop.

cheminot [ʃəmino] **nm** railwayman *UK*, railroad man *US*.

chemise [ʃəmiz] **nf 1.** [d'homme] shirt ▸ **chemise de nuit** [de femme] nightdress, nightgown **2.** [dossier] folder.

chemiserie [ʃəmizri] **nf** [magasin] shirtmaker's / [industrie] shirtmaking.

chemisette [ʃəmizɛt] **nf** [d'homme] short-sleeved shirt / [de femme] short-sleeved blouse.

chemisier [ʃəmizje] **nm 1.** [vêtement] blouse **2.** [marchand, fabricant] shirtmaker.

chenal, aux [ʃənal, o] **nm** [canal] channel.

chenapan [ʃnapɑ̃] **nm** *hum* rascal.

chêne [ʃɛn] **nm** [arbre] oak (tree) / [bois] oak.

chenet [ʃənɛ] **nm** firedog.

chenil [ʃənil] **nm** [pour chiens] kennel.

chenille [ʃənij] **nf 1.** [insecte] caterpillar **2.** [courroie] caterpillar track.

chenu, e [ʃəny] **adj** *littéraire* [tête, barbe] hoary.

cheptel [ʃɛptɛl] **nm** [bétail] livestock *(U)*.

chèque [ʃɛk] **nm** cheque *UK*, check *US* ▸ **faire un chèque** to write a cheque *UK ou* check *US* ▸ **toucher un chèque** to cash a cheque *UK ou* check *US* ▸ **chèque (bancaire)** (bank) cheque *UK ou* check *US* ▸ **chèque barré** crossed cheque *UK ou* check *US* ▸ **chèque en blanc** blank cheque *UK ou* check *US* ▸ **chèque en bois** *fam* bad *ou* rubber cheque *UK ou* check *US* ▸ **chèque de caisse** credit voucher ▸ **chèque postal** post office cheque *UK ou* check *US* ▸ **chèque sans provision** bad cheque *UK ou* check *US* ▸ **chèque de voyage** traveller's cheque *UK*, traveler's check *US*.

chèque-cadeau [ʃɛkkado] (pl **chèques-cadeaux**) **nm** gift token *UK*, gift voucher *UK*, gift certificate *US*.

chèque-repas [ʃɛkrəpa] (pl **chèques-repas**), ***chèque-restaurant*** [ʃɛkrɛstɔrɑ̃] (pl **chèques-restaurant**) **nm** luncheon voucher.

chèque-vacances (pl **chèques-vacances**) [sɛkvakɑ̃s] **nm** *voucher that can be used to pay for holiday accommodation, activities, meals, etc.*

chéquier [ʃekje] **nm** chequebook *UK*, checkbook *US*.

cher, chère [ʃɛr] ■ **adj 1.** [aimé] **: cher (à qqn)** dear (to sb) ▸ **un être cher** a loved one ▸ **mon souhait le plus cher** my dearest devout wish ▸ **Cher Monsieur** [au début d'une lettre] Dear Sir ▸ **Chère Madame** [au début d'une lettre] Dear Madam **2.** [produit, vie, commerçant] expensive ▸ **voilà un dîner pas cher!** now this is a cheap dinner!

■ **nm, f** *hum* **: mon cher** dear.

◆ ***cher*** **adv : valoir cher, coûter cher** to be expensive, to cost a lot ▸ **donner cher : je donnerais cher pour le savoir** I'd give anything to know ▸ **payer cher** to pay a lot ▸ **je l'ai payé cher** *litt* & *fig* it cost me a lot ▸ **je l'ai eu pour pas cher** *fam* I didn't pay much for it.

◆ ***chère*** **nf : aimer la bonne chère** *sout* to like to eat well.

chercher [3] [ʃɛrʃe] ■ **vt 1.** [gén] to look for ▸ **chercher qqn du regard** *ou* **des yeux** to look around for sb ▸ **chercher qqn/qqch à tâtons** to fumble *ou* to grope for sb/sthg ▸ **chercher refuge auprès de qqn** to seek refuge with sb ▸ **il faut vite chercher du secours** you must get help quickly ▸ **vous l'aurez cherché!** you're asking for it! ▸ **chercher midi à quatorze heures** *fam* to look for complications (where there are none) **2.** [prendre] **: aller/venir chercher qqn** [à un rendez-vous] to (go/come and) meet sb / [en voiture] to (go/come and) pick sb up ▸ **aller/venir chercher qqch** to (go/come and) get sthg **3.** *fam* [atteindre] **: ça va chercher dans les 15 euros** it will come to about 15 euros.

■ **vi : chercher à faire qqch** to try to do sthg ▸ **cherche pas à comprendre** *fam* don't bother to try to *ou* and understand.

◆ ***se chercher*** **vp** to try to find o.s. ▸ **ils se sont cherchés pendant longtemps** they spent a long time looking for each other.

chercheur, euse [ʃɛrʃœr, øz] ■ **adj 1.** [esprit] inquiring **2.** ➤ ***tête***.

■ **nm, f** [scientifique] researcher.

chèrement [ʃɛrmɑ̃] **adv** dearly.

chéri, e [ʃeri] ■ **adj** dear.

■ **nm, f** darling.

chérir [32] [ʃerir] **vt** [personne] to love dearly / [chose, idée] to cherish.

cherté [ʃɛrte] **nf** high cost.

chétif, ive [ʃetif, iv] **adj 1.** [malingre] sickly, weak **2.** [rabougri] stunted, puny **3.** *littéraire* [insuffisant] meagre *UK*, meager *US*.

cheval, aux [ʃəval, o] **nm 1.** [animal] horse ▸ **à cheval** on horseback ▸ **traverser une rivière à cheval** to ride across a river ▸ **être à cheval sur qqch** [être assis] to be sitting astride sthg / *fig* [siècles] to straddle sthg / *fig* [tenir à] to be a stickler for sthg ▸ **l'étang est à cheval sur deux propriétés** the pond straddles two properties ▸ **il est très à cheval sur les principes** he is a stickler for principles ▸ **cheval d'arçons** horse *(in gymnastics)* ▸ **cheval de bataille** *fig* hobby horse ▸ **cheval de course** racehorse ▸ **cheval de labour** plough *UK* *ou* plow *US* horse ▸ **cheval de manège** school horse ▸ **cheval de trait** draught *UK* *ou* draft *US* horse ▸ **chevaux de bois** merry-go-round *sg* ▸ **monter sur ses grands chevaux** to get on one's high horse ▸ **remède de cheval** drastic remedy **2.** [équitation] riding, horse-riding ▸ **faire du cheval** to ride **3.** AUTO & FIN **: cheval fiscal** horsepower.

chevaleresque [ʃəvalrɛsk] **adj** chivalrous.

chevalerie [ʃəvalri] **nf 1.** [qualité] chivalry **2.** HIST knighthood.

chevalet [ʃəvalɛ] **nm** [de peintre] easel.

chevalier [ʃəvalje] **nm** knight ▸ **chevalier servant** (faithful) admirer.

chevalière [ʃəvaljɛr] **nf** [bague] signet ring.

chevalin, e [ʃəvalɛ̃, in] **adj** [de cheval] horse *(avant n)* / *fig* horsey.

chevauchée [ʃəvoʃe] **nf 1.** [course] ride, horse-ride **2.** [cavalcade] cavalcade.

chevaucher [3] [ʃevoʃe] **vt** [être assis] to sit *ou* be astride.

◆ ***se chevaucher*** **vp** to overlap.

chevelu, e [ʃəvly] **adj** hairy.

chevelure [ʃəvlyr] **nf** [cheveux] hair.

chevet [ʃəvɛ] **nm** head *(of bed)* ▸ **être au chevet de qqn** to be at sb's bedside.

cheveu, x [ʃəvø] **nm** [chevelure] hair ▸ **avoir les cheveux taillés en brosse** to have a crew cut ▸ **se faire couper les cheveux** to have one's hair cut ▸ **s'arracher les cheveux** to tear one's hair out ▸ **avoir un cheveu sur la langue** to have a lisp ▸ **arriver comme un cheveu sur la soupe** to come at an awkward moment ▸ **couper les cheveux en quatre** to split hairs ▸ **tiré par les cheveux** farfetched, contrived.

cheville [ʃəvij] **nf 1.** ANAT ankle ▸ **il ne t'arrive pas à la cheville** *fam fig* he can't hold a candle to you **2.** [pour fixer une vis] Rawlplug® *UK*, (wall) anchor *US* ▸ **cheville ouvrière** *fig* & AUTO kingpin.

chèvre [ʃɛvr] ■ **nf** [animal] goat ▸ **ménager la chèvre et le chou** to run with the hare and hunt with the hounds.

■ **nm** [fromage] goat's cheese.

chevreau, x [ʃəvro] **nm** kid.

chèvrefeuille [ʃɛvrəfœj] **nm** honeysuckle.

chevreuil [ʃəvrœj] **nm 1.** [animal] roe deer **2.** CULIN venison.

chevron [ʃəvrɔ̃] **nm 1.** CONSTR rafter **2.** [motif décoratif] chevron.

chevronné, e [ʃəvrɔne] **adj** [expérimenté] experienced.

chevrotant, e [ʃəvrɔtɑ̃, ɑ̃t] **adj** tremulous.

chevrotine [ʃəvrɔtin] **nf** buckshot.

chewing-gum [ʃwiŋgɔm] (pl **chewing-gums**) **nm** chewing gum *(U)*.

chez [ʃe] **prép 1.** [dans la maison de] **: il est chez lui** he's at home ▸ **il rentre chez lui** he's going home ▸ **c'est une coutume/un accent bien de chez nous** it's a typical local custom/accent ▸ **il va venir chez nous** he is going to come to our place *ou* house ▸ **il habite chez nous** he lives with us ▸ **elle l'a raccompagné chez lui** [à pied] she walked him home / [en voiture] she gave him a lift home

2. [dans un magasin, une société] **: être chez le coiffeur/médecin** to be at the hairdresser's/doctor's ▸ **aller chez le coiffeur/le médecin** to go to the hairdresser's/the doctor's ▸ **il a travaillé chez IBM** he worked at *ou* for IBM ▸ **une robe de chez Dior** a Dior dress, a dress designed by Dior

3. [en ce qui concerne] **: chez les jeunes** among young people ▸ **chez les Anglais** in England

4. [dans les œuvres de] **: chez Proust** in (the works of) Proust

5. [dans le caractère de] **: cette réaction est normale chez lui** this reaction is normal for *ou* with him ▸ **ce que j'apprécie chez lui, c'est sa gentillesse** what I like about him is his kindness.

chez-soi [ʃeswa] **nm inv** home, place of one's own.

chialer [3] [ʃjale] **vi** *fam* to blubber.

chiant, e [ʃjɑ̃, ɑ̃t] **adj** *tfam* **1.** [très ennuyeux] damned *ou* bloody *UK* boring **2.** [contrariant] damned *ou* bloody *UK* annoying ▸ **c'est chiant** it's a damned *ou* bloody *UK* pain.

chic [ʃik] ■ **adj** *(inv en genre)* **1.** [élégant] smart, chic **2.** *vieilli* [serviable] nice.

■ **nm** style ▸ **bon chic bon genre** ≃ Sloaney *UK*, ≃ preppie *US* ▸ **avoir le chic pour faire qqch** to have the knack of doing sthg.

■ **interj : chic (alors)!** great!

chicane [ʃikan] **nf** [querelle] squabble.

chicaner [3] [ʃikane] ■ **vt : chicaner qqn sur qqch** to quibble with sb over sthg.

■ **vi** [contester] **: chicaner (sur qqch)** to quibble (over *ou* about sthg).

◆ ***se chicaner*** **vp** to squabble, to bicker.

chiche [ʃiʃ] ■ **adj 1.** [avare] mean ▸ **être chiche de** to be sparing with **2.** [peu abondant] meagre *UK*, meager *US*, scanty **3.** *fam* [capable] **: il n'est pas chiche de le faire!** he wouldn't dare (do it)!

■ **interj : chiche!** (you) want a bet?

chichement [ʃiʃmɑ̃] **adv** [pauvrement] meagrely *UK*, meagerly *US*.

chichi [ʃiʃi] **nm : faire des chichis** *fam* to make a fuss.

chicorée [ʃikɔre] **nf** [salade] endive *UK*, chicory *US* / [à café] chicory ▸ **chicorée frisée** curly endive.

chien [ʃjɛ̃] **nm 1.** [animal] dog ▸ **chien d'aveugle** guide dog ▸ **chien de chasse** [d'arrêt] gundog ▸ **chien esquimau**

husky ▸ **chien de garde** guard dog ▸ **chien policier** police dog ▸ **chien savant** performing dog ▸ **entre chien et loup** at dusk *ou* twilight ▸ **se regarder en chiens de faïence** to stare grimly at each other **2.** [d'arme] hammer
▸▸ **avoir un mal de chien à faire qqch** to have a lot of trouble doing sthg ▸ **en chien de fusil** curled up ▸ **avoir du chien** to have class *ou* style.

chiendent [ʃjɛ̃dɑ̃] **nm** couch grass.

chien-loup [ʃjɛ̃lu] (pl **chiens-loups**) **nm** German shepherd, Alsatian (dog) *UK*.

chienne [ʃjɛn] **nf** (female) dog, bitch.

chier [9] [ʃje] **vi** *vulg* to shit ▸ **faire chier qqn** to bug sb, to get on sb's tits *UK* ▸ **se faire chier** to be bored shitless.

chiffe [ʃif] **nf : c'est une chiffe molle** he's spineless.

chiffon [ʃifɔ̃] **nm** [linge] rag ▸ **parler chiffons** to talk clothes.

chiffonné, e [ʃifɔne] **adj** [visage, mine] worn.

chiffonner [3] [ʃifɔne] **vt 1.** [vêtement] to crumple, to crease / [papier] to crumple **2.** *fam fig* [contrarier] to bother.

chiffonnier, ère [ʃifɔnje, ɛr] **nm, f** rag-and-bone man (f woman) *UK*.
◆ ***chiffonnier*** **nm** [meuble] chiffonier.

chiffre [ʃifr] **nm 1.** [caractère] figure, number ▸ **chiffre arabe/romain** Arabic/Roman numeral **2.** [montant] sum ▸ **chiffre d'affaires** COMM turnover, sales revenue, volume of sales ▸ **chiffre d'affaires annuel** annual turnover ▸ **chiffre rond** round number ▸ **chiffre de ventes** sales figures *pl* **3.** [code secret] code.

chiffrer [3] [ʃifre] ■ **vt 1.** [numéroter] to number **2.** [évaluer] to calculate, to assess **3.** [coder] to encode.
■ **vi** *fam* to mount up.
◆ ***se chiffrer*** **vp : se chiffrer à** to add up to.

chignole [ʃiɲɔl] **nf** drill.

chignon [ʃiɲɔ̃] **nm** bun *(in hair)* ▸ **se crêper le chignon** *fig* to scratch each other's eyes out.

chiisme [ʃiism] **nm** Shiism.

Chili [ʃili] **nm : le Chili** Chile ▸ **au Chili** in Chile.

chilien, enne [ʃiljɛ̃, ɛn] **adj** Chilean.
◆ ***Chilien, enne*** **nm, f** Chilean.

chimère [ʃimɛr] **nf 1.** MYTHOL chimera **2.** [illusion] illusion, dream.

chimérique [ʃimerik] **adj 1.** [illusoire] illusory **2.** [rêveur] fanciful.

chimie [ʃimi] **nf** chemistry.

chimiothérapie [ʃimjɔterapi] **nf** chemotherapy.

chimique [ʃimik] **adj** chemical.

chimiquement [ʃimikmɑ̃] **adv** chemically.

chimiquier [ʃimikje] **nm** chemical tanker.

chimiste [ʃimist] **nmf** chemist.

chimpanzé [ʃɛ̃pɑ̃ze] **nm** chimpanzee.

chinchilla [ʃɛ̃ʃila] **nm** chinchilla.

Chine [ʃin] **nf : la Chine** China.

chiné, e [ʃine] **adj** mottled.

chiner [3] [ʃine] **vi** to look for bargains.

chinois, e [ʃinwa, az] **adj** Chinese.
◆ ***chinois*** **nm 1.** [langue] Chinese ▸ **c'est du chinois** *fig* it's all Greek to me **2.** [passoire] conical sieve.
◆ ***Chinois, e*** **nm, f** Chinese person ▸ **les Chinois** the Chinese.

chinoiserie [ʃinwazri] **nf** [objet] Chinese curio, piece of chinoiserie / *fig* unnecessary complication.
◆ ***chinoiseries*** **nfpl** unnecessary complications, red tape *sg*.

chiot [ʃjo] **nm** puppy.

chiottes [ʃjɔt] **nfpl** *vulg* shithouse *sg*.

chiper [3] [ʃipe] **vt** *fam* [voler] to pinch, to nick *UK*.

chipie [ʃipi] **nf** vixen *péj*.

chipolata [ʃipɔlata] **nf** chipolata.

chipoter [3] [ʃipɔte] *fam* **vi : chipoter (sur)** [nourriture] to pick (at) / [contester] to quibble (over *ou* about).

chips [ʃips] **nfpl : (pommes) chips** (potato) crisps *UK*, (potato) chips *US*.

chiqué [ʃike] **nm : c'est du chiqué** it's all sham.

chiquenaude [ʃiknod] **nf** flick.

chiquer [3] [ʃike] ■ **vt** to chew.
■ **vi** to chew tobacco.

chiromancien, enne [kirɔmɑ̃sjɛ̃, ɛn] **nm, f** palmist.

chiropracteur [kirɔpraktœr] **nm** = ***chiropraticien***.

chiropraticien, enne [kirɔpratisjɛ̃, ɛn] **nm, f** chiropractor.

chirurgical, e, aux [ʃiryrʒikal, o] **adj** surgical.

chirurgie [ʃiryrʒi] **nf** surgery ▸ **chirurgie esthétique** plastic surgery.

chirurgien [ʃiryrʒjɛ̃] **nm** surgeon.

chirurgien-dentiste [ʃiryrʒjɛ̃dɑ̃tist] (pl **chirurgiens-dentistes**) **nm** dental surgeon.

chiure [ʃjyr] **nf : chiure (de mouche)** flyspecks *pl*.

ch.-l. abr de ***chef-lieu***.

chlinguer = ***schlinguer***.

chlore [klɔr] **nm** chlorine.

chloroforme [klɔrɔfɔrm] **nm** chloroform.

chlorophylle [klɔrɔfil] **nf** chlorophyll.

chlorure [klɔryr] **nm** chloride.

chnoque = ***schnock***.

choc [ʃɔk] **nm 1.** [heurt, coup] impact ▸ **de choc** *fig* shock *(avant n)* **2.** [conflit] clash **3.** [émotion] shock ▸ **choc opératoire** post-operative shock **4.** *(en apposition)* **: images-chocs** shock pictures ▸ **prix-choc** amazing bargain.

chocolat [ʃɔkɔla] ■ **nm** chocolate ▸ **chocolat au lait/noir** milk/plain chocolate ▸ **chocolat à cuire/à croquer** cooking/eating chocolate ▸ **chocolat Liégeois** *chocolate ice cream with Chantilly cream*.
■ **adj inv** chocolate (brown).

chocolaté, e [ʃɔkɔlate] **adj** chocolate (flavoured) *UK*, chocolate (flavored) *US*.

chocolatier, ère [ʃɔkɔlatje, ɛr] ■ **adj** chocolate *(avant n)*.
■ **nm, f** [fabricant] chocolate manufacturer / [commerçant] confectioner.
◆ ***chocolatière*** **nf** [récipient] chocolate pot.

chœur [kœr] **nm 1.** [chorale] choir / *fig* [d'opéra] chorus ▸ **chanter en chœur** to sing in chorus ▸ **en chœur** *fig* all together **2.** [d'église] choir, chancel.

choir [72] [ʃwar] **vt** *littéraire* **: laisser choir qqch** to let sthg fall ▸ **laisser choir qqn** *fig & litt* to let sb down ▸ **se laisser choir dans qqch** to drop *ou* fall into sthg.

choisi, e [ʃwazi] **adj** selected / [termes, langage] carefully chosen.

choisir [32] [ʃwazir] ■ **vt : choisir (de faire qqch)** to choose (to do sthg).
■ **vi** to choose.

choix [ʃwa] **nm 1.** [gén] choice ▸ **le livre de ton choix** any book you like ▸ **au choix** as you prefer ▸ **répondre au choix à l'une des trois questions** answer any one of the three questions ▸ **vous avez fromage ou dessert au choix** you have a choice of either cheeses or a dessert ▸ **avoir le choix** to have the choice ▸ **donner le choix à qqn** to give sb a *ou* the choice ▸ **faire un choix** to make a choice ▸ **ils ne nous ont pas laissé le choix** they left us no alternative *ou* other option **2.** [qualité] **: de premier choix** grade *ou* class one ▸ **articles de second choix** seconds **3.** [gamme] **: un choix de** a choice *ou* range *ou* selection of.

choléra [kɔlera] **nm** cholera.

cholestérol [kɔlɛsterɔl] **nm** cholesterol.

chômage [ʃomaʒ] **nm** unemployment ▸ **au chômage** unemployed ▸ **chômage de longue durée** long-term unemployment ▸ **chômage de masse/massif/à grande échelle** mass unemployment ▸ **chômage partiel** part-time *ou* short-time *UK* (working) ▸ **chômage structurel** long-term unemployment ▸ **être mis au chômage technique** to be laid off.

CULTURE

Chômage

In France, unemployment benefits are administered by the **ASSEDIC**, or **Associations pour l'emploi dans l'industrie et le commerce**. Eligible jobseekers receive **allocations chômage**, or **ARE** (**aide au retour à l'emploi**) based on their previous salary. Workers who resign are not eligible, and people wishing to receive benefits must register with the **ANPE**, or **Agence nationale pour l'emploi**. Both employees and employers finance the system through monthly contributions. All French employers, with the exception of the state, participate.

chômé, e [ʃome] **adj : jour chômé** public holiday.

chômer [3] [ʃome] ■ **vt** to keep.
■ **vi** to be unemployed / *fig* to be idle.

chômeur, euse [ʃomœr, øz] **nm, f** unemployed person ▸ **les chômeurs** the unemployed.

chope [ʃɔp] **nf** tankard.

choper [3] [ʃɔpe] **vt** *fam* **1.** [voler, arrêter] to pinch, to nick *UK* **2.** [attraper] to catch.

choquant, e [ʃɔkɑ̃, ɑ̃t] **adj** shocking.

choquer [3] [ʃɔke] **vt 1.** [scandaliser] to shock **2.** [traumatiser] to shake (up).

choral, e, als *ou* ***aux*** [kɔral, o] **adj** choral.
◆ ***choral, als*** **nm** [chant] chorale.
◆ ***chorale*** **nf** [groupe] choir.

chorégraphie [kɔregrafi] **nf** choreography.

choriste [kɔrist] **nmf** chorister.

chose [ʃoz] ■ **nf** thing ▸ **ce n'est pas la même chose** [cela change tout] it's a different matter ▸ **ce sont des choses qui arrivent** it's just one of those things ▸ **c'est (bien) peu de chose** it's nothing really ▸ **c'est la moindre des choses** it's the least I/we can do ▸ **chaque chose en son temps** everything in good time ▸ **chose promise chose due** a promise is a promise ▸ **de deux choses l'une** (it's got to be) one thing or the other ▸ **dire bien des choses à qqn** to give sb one's regards ▸ **il n'avait acheté que des bonnes choses** he had only bought good things to eat ▸ **la chose publique** POLIT the state ▸ **les choses de la vie** the things that go to make up life ▸ **ne pas faire les choses à moitié** not to do things by halves ▸ **parler de choses et d'autres** to talk of this and that ▸ **regarder les choses en face** to face up to things ▸ **une chose est sûre, il perdra** one thing's (for) sure, he'll lose.
■ **nm** *fam* **1.** [truc] thingy, whatsit **2.** [personne] thingy, what's-his-name (f what's-her-name).
■ **adj inv : se sentir (tout) chose** to feel a bit peculiar.

chou, x [ʃu] ■ **nm 1.** [légume] cabbage ▸ **chou de Bruxelles** Brussels sprout ▸ **faire chou blanc** *fam fig* to draw a blank **2.** [pâtisserie] choux bun ▸ **chou à la crème** cream puff **3.** [personne] **: mon chou** darling.
■ **adj inv** sweet, cute.

choucas [ʃuka] **nm** jackdaw.

chouchou, oute [ʃuʃu, ut] **nm, f** favourite *UK*, favorite *US* / [élève] teacher's pet.
◆ ***chouchou*** **nm** [pour les cheveux] scrunchy, scrunchie.

chouchouter [3] [ʃuʃute] *fam* **vt** to pet.

choucroute [ʃukrut] **nf** sauerkraut ▸ **choucroute garnie** *sauerkraut with meat and potatoes.*

chouette [ʃwɛt] ■ **nf** [oiseau] owl.
■ **adj** *fam* great.
■ **interj : chouette (alors)!** great!

chou-fleur [ʃuflœr] (pl **choux-fleurs**) **nm** cauliflower.

choyer [13] [ʃwaje] **vt** *sout* to pamper.

CHR (abr de ***centre hospitalier régional***) **nm** regional hospital.

chrétien, enne [kretjɛ̃, ɛn] **adj & nm, f** Christian.

chrétienté [kretjɛ̃te] **nf** Christendom.

Christ [krist] **nm** Christ.

christianiser [3] [kristjanize] **vt 1.** [personne] to convert (to Christianity) **2.** [pays] to christianize.

christianisme [kristjanism] **nm** Christianity.

chromatique [krɔmatik] **adj 1.** MUS [en optique] chromatic **2.** BIOL chromosomal.

chrome [krom] **nm** **1.** [de voiture] chrome **2.** CHIM chromium.

chromé, e [krome] **adj** chrome-plated ▸ **acier chromé** chrome steel.

chromosome [krɔmɔzom] **nm** chromosome.

chronique [krɔnik] ■ **nf** **1.** [annales] chronicle ▸ **défrayer la chronique** to be the talk of the town **2.** PRESSE : **chronique sportive** sports section.
■ **adj** chronic.

chrono [krɔno] = ***chronomètre***.

chronobiologie [kronobjolɔʒi] **nf** chronobiology.

chronologie [krɔnɔlɔʒi] **nf** chronology.

chronologique [krɔnɔlɔʒik] **adj** chronological.

chronomètre [krɔnɔmɛtr] **nm** SPORT stopwatch.

chronométrer [18] [krɔnɔmetre] **vt** to time.

chronométreur [krɔnɔmetrœr] **nm** SPORT timekeeper.

chrysalide [krizalid] **nf** chrysalis.

chrysanthème [krizɑ̃tɛm] **nm** chrysanthemum.

CHS (abr de ***Comité d'hygiène et de sécurité***) **nm** health and safety committee.

chu, e [ʃy] **pp** ➤ ***choir***.

CHU (abr de ***centre hospitalo-universitaire***) **nm** *teaching hospital*.

chuchotement [ʃyʃɔtmɑ̃] **nm** whisper.
◆ ***chuchotements*** **nmpl** whispering *(U)*.

chuchoter [3] [ʃyʃɔte] **vt & vi** to whisper.

chuinter [3] [ʃyɛ̃te] **vi** [siffler] to hiss.

chut [ʃyt] **interj** sh!, hush!

chute [ʃyt] **nf** **1.** [gén] fall ▸ **faire une chute** to (have *ou* take a) fall ▸ **faire une chute de cheval** to come off a horse ▸ **chute de cheveux** hair loss ▸ **chute d'eau** waterfall ▸ **chute libre** free fall ▸ **chute de neige** snowfall ▸ **chute de pierres** falling rocks ▸ **chute de reins** small of the back ▸ **chute de tension** MÉD drop in blood pressure / ÉLECTR & PHYS voltage drop ▸ **chute des ventes** COMM fall-off in sales ▸ **la chute du mur de Berlin** the fall of the Berlin Wall ▸ **entraîner qqn dans sa chute** to drag sb down with one **2.** [de tissu] scrap / CINÉ : **chutes de pellicule** film trims.

chuter [3] [ʃyte] **vi** **1.** [baisser] to fall, to drop **2.** [tomber] to fall.

Chypre [ʃipr] **nf** Cyprus ▸ **à Chypre** in Cyprus.

chypriote [ʃipriɔt], ***cypriote*** [sipriɔt] **adj** Cypriot.
◆ ***Chypriote, Cypriote*** **nmf** Cypriot.

ci [si] **adv** *(après n)* **: à cette heure-ci il n'y a plus personne** there's nobody there at this time of day ▸ **ce livre-ci** this book ▸ **cette fois-ci j'ai compris! NOW** I've got it! ▸ **ces jours-ci** these days.

Ci (abr écrite de ***curie***) Ci.

CIA (abr de ***Central Intelligence Agency***) **nf** CIA.

ci-après [siaprɛ] **adv** below.

cibiste [sibist] **nmf** CB enthusiast.

cible [sibl] **nf** *litt & fig* target ▸ **groupe cible** target group.

ciblé [sible] **adj** COMM targeted.

cibler [3] [sible] **vt** to target.

ciboire [sibwar] **nm** ciborium.

ciboulette [sibulɛt] **nf** chives *pl*.

cicatrice [sikatris] **nf** scar.

cicatriser [3] [sikatrize] *litt & fig* **vt** to heal.
◆ ***se cicatriser*** **vp** to heal.

ci-contre [sikɔ̃tr] **adv** opposite.

CICR (abr de ***Comité international de la Croix-Rouge***) **nm** ICRC.

ci-dessous [sidəsu] **adv** below.

ci-dessus [sidəsy] **adv** above.

CIDEX, Cidex [sidɛks] (abr de ***courrier individuel à distribution exceptionnelle***) **nm** *system grouping letter boxes in country areas*.

CIDJ (abr de ***centre d'information et de documentation de la jeunesse***) **nm** *careers advisory service*.

cidre [sidr] **nm** cider *UK*, hard cider *US* ▸ **cidre bouché** *superior bottled cider* ▸ **cidre doux/brut** sweet/dry cider.

CIDUNaTI [sidynati] (abr de ***Comité interprofessionnel d'information et de défense de l'union nationale des travailleurs indépendants***) **nm** *union of self-employed craftsmen*.

Cie (abr écrite de ***compagnie***) Co.

ciel ■ **nm** **1.** (pl **ciels** [sjɛl]) [firmament] sky ▸ **ciel clair/nuageux** clear/cloudy sky ▸ **ciel de plomb** leaden sky ▸ **à ciel ouvert** open-air ▸ **lever les bras au ciel** to throw up one's hands *(in exasperation, despair)* **2.** (pl **cieux** [sjø]) [paradis, providence] heaven ▸ **c'est le ciel qui l'envoie!** he's heaven-sent! ▸ **que le ciel vous entende!** may heaven help you! ▸ **être au septième ciel** to be in seventh heaven ▸ **remuer ciel et terre (pour faire qqch)** to move heaven and earth (to do sthg) ▸ **tomber du ciel** *fam* to be heaven-sent *ou* a godsend.
■ **interj** *hum & sout* good heavens!
◆ ***cieux*** **nmpl** heaven *sg* ▸ **partir vers d'autres cieux** to be off to distant parts.

CIEP (abr de ***Centre international d'études pédagogiques***) **nm** *French centre for educational research*.

cierge [sjɛrʒ] **nm** RELIG (votive) candle.

cigale [sigal] **nf** cicada.

cigare [sigar] **nm** cigar.

cigarette [sigarɛt] **nf** cigarette ▸ **cigarette blonde/brune** cigarette made from Virginia/dark tobacco.

cigarillo [sigarijo] **nm** cigarillo.

ci-gît [siʒi] **adv** here lies.

cigogne [sigɔɲ] **nf** stork.

ci-inclus, e [siɛ̃kly, yz] **adj** enclosed.
◆ ***ci-inclus*** **adv** enclosed.

ci-joint, e [siʒwɛ̃, ɛ̃t] **adj** enclosed.
◆ ***ci-joint*** **adv : veuillez trouver ci-joint...** please find enclosed...

cil [sil] **nm** ANAT eyelash, lash.

ciller [3] [sije] **vi** to blink (one's eyes) ▸ **sans ciller** *fig* without blinking.

cimaise [simɛz] **nf** [de salle d'exposition] gallery wall.

cime [sim] **nf** [d'arbre, de montagne] top / *fig* height.

ciment [simɑ̃] **nm** cement.

cimenter [3] [simɑ̃te] **vt** to cement.

cimetière [simtjɛr] **nm** cemetery.

ciné [sine] **nm** *fam* cinema *UK*, movies *pl US*.

cinéaste [sineast] **nmf** film-maker.

ciné-club [sineklœb] (pl **ciné-clubs**) **nm** film club.

cinéma [sinema] **nm** **1.** [salle, industrie] cinema *UK*, movies *pl US* ▸ **aller au cinéma** to go to the cinema *UK* *ou* the movies *US* ▸ **cinéma d'art et d'essai** art house ▸ **cinéma en plein air** [dans les pays chauds] open-air cinema / [aux U.S.A.] drive-in (movie-theater) **2.** [art] cinema *UK*, film *UK*, movies *pl US* ▸ **un acteur de cinéma** a film star ▸ **cinéma publicitaire** COMM screen advertising *UK* ▸ **école de cinéma** film *ou* film-making school *UK*, movie-making school *US* ▸ **faire du cinéma** to be in film *UK* *ou* movies *US* / *fig* to put on an act ▸ **le cinéma muet** silent films *UK* *ou* movies *US* ▸ **arrête (de faire) ton cinéma!** [de mentir] stop putting us on! / [de bluffer] stop shooting your mouth off!

cinémathèque [sinematɛk] **nf** film *UK* *ou* movie *US* library ▸ **la Cinémathèque française** *the French film institute*.

cinématographique [sinematɔgrafik] **adj** cinematographic.

cinéphile [sinefil] **nmf** film *UK* *ou* movie *US* buff.

cinétique [sinetik] ■ **nf** kinetics *(U)*.
■ **adj** kinetic.

cinglant, e [sɛ̃glɑ̃, ɑ̃t] **adj** *litt* & *fig* biting / [pluie] driving.

cinglé, e [sɛ̃gle] *fam* ■ **adj** nuts, nutty.
■ **nm, f** nutcase.

cingler [3] [sɛ̃gle] ■ **vt** to lash.
■ **vi** *littéraire* [naviguer] to sail.

cinq [sɛ̃k] ■ **adj num inv** five ▸ **à la page cinq** on page five ▸ **il arrive le cinq novembre** he's arriving on November (the) fifth *ou* the fifth of November ▸ **cinq minutes** [d'horloge] five minutes / [un moment] a short while ▸ **j'en ai pour cinq minutes** it'll only take me five minutes.
■ **nm** five ▸ **il était moins cinq** *fam* it was a near thing ; voir aussi ***six***.
◆ ***cinq sur cinq*** loc adv : **je te reçois cinq sur cinq** *litt* & *fig* I'm reading *ou* receiving you loud and clear.
◆ ***en cinq sec*** **loc adv** *fam* in no time at all, in the twinkling of an eye ▸ **en cinq sec, c'était fait** it was done before you could say "Jack Robinson".

cinquantaine [sɛ̃kɑ̃tɛn] **nf** **1.** [nombre] **: une cinquantaine de** about fifty **2.** [âge] **: avoir la cinquantaine** to be in one's fifties.

cinquante [sɛ̃kɑ̃t] **adj num inv** & **nm** fifty ; voir aussi ***six***.

cinquantenaire [sɛ̃kɑ̃tnɛr] ■ **nmf** *person in his/her fifties*.
■ **nm** [de personne] fiftieth birthday / [d'événement] fiftieth anniversary / [d'institution] golden jubilee.
■ **adj** fifty-year-old.

cinquantième [sɛ̃kɑ̃tjɛm] **adj num inv, nm** & **nmf** fiftieth ; voir aussi ***sixième***.

cinquième [sɛ̃kjɛm] ■ **adj num inv, nm** & **nmf** fifth.
■ **nf** SCOL ≃ Year 2 *UK*, ≃ seventh grade *US* ; voir aussi ***sixième***.

cinquièmement [sɛ̃kjɛmmɑ̃] **adv** fifthly, in the fifth place.

cintre [sɛ̃tr] **nm** **1.** [pour vêtements] coat hanger **2.** ARCHIT arch, curve.

cintré, e [sɛ̃tre] **adj** **1.** COUT waisted **2.** ARCHIT arched, vaulted.

CIO (abr de ***Comité international olympique***) **nm** IOC.

cirage [siraʒ] **nm** **1.** [action] polishing **2.** [produit] shoe polish
▸▸ **être dans le cirage** *fam* to be in a daze.

circoncis [sirkɔ̃si] **adj** circumcised.

circoncision [sirkɔ̃sizjɔ̃] **nf** circumcision.

circonférence [sirkɔ̃ferɑ̃s] **nf** **1.** GÉOM circumference **2.** [pourtour] boundary.

circonflexe [sirkɔ̃flɛks] ➤ ***accent***.

circonscription [sirkɔ̃skripsjɔ̃] **nf** district ▸ **circonscription électorale** [nationale] constituency *UK*, district *US* / [locale] ward *UK*.

circonscrire [99] [sirkɔ̃skrir] **vt** **1.** GÉOM to circumscribe **2.** [incendie, épidémie] to contain **3.** *fig* [sujet] to define.
◆ ***se circonscrire*** **vp : se circonscrire autour de** to be centred *UK* *ou* centered *US* on *ou* around.

circonspect, e [sirkɔ̃spɛ, ɛkt] **adj** cautious.

circonspection [sirkɔ̃spɛksjɔ̃] **nf** caution, wariness.

circonstance [sirkɔ̃stɑ̃s] **nf** **1.** [occasion] occasion **2.** *(gén pl)* [contexte, conjoncture] circumstance ▸ **circonstances atténuantes** DR mitigating circumstances ▸ **de circonstance** appropriate ▸ **étant donné les circonstances** given the circumstances *ou* situation.
◆ ***pour la circonstance*** **loc adv** for the occasion.

circonstancié, e [sirkɔ̃stɑ̃sje] **adj** detailed.

circonstanciel, elle [sirkɔ̃stɑ̃sjɛl] **adj** GRAMM adverbial.

circuit [sirkɥi] **nm** **1.** [chemin] route
2. [parcours touristique] tour ▸ **circuit touristique** tourist route
3. SPORT & TECHNOL circuit ▸ **en circuit fermé** [en boucle] closed-circuit *(avant n)* / *fig* within a limited circle ▸ **circuit automobile** racing circuit ▸ **circuit imprimé/intégré** printed/integrated circuit ▸ **couper le circuit** to switch off ▸ **mettre en circuit** to connect ▸ **rétablir le circuit** to switch on
4. ÉCON network ▸ **circuit commercial** commercial channel ▸ **le film est fait pour le circuit commercial** it's a mainstream film ▸ **circuit de distribution** distribution channel, channel of distribution ▸ **le circuit de distribution du pain** the distribution channels for bread ▸ **circuits de vente** commercial channels
5. [tuyaux] (pipe) system ▸ **circuit de refroidissement** cooling system.

circulaire [sirkylɛr] **nf** & **adj** circular.

circulation [sirkylasjɔ̃] **nf** **1.** [mouvement] circulation ▸ **mettre en circulation** to circulate ▸ **retirer de la circulation** to withdraw from circulation ▸ **circulation (du**

sang) circulation **2.** [trafic] traffic ▸ **route à grande circulation** main road, trunk road *UK* ▸ **'circulation alternée'** 'traffic control ahead' ▸ **disparaître de la circulation** *fig* to disappear from the scene.

circulatoire [sirkylatwar] **adj** circulatory.

circuler [3] [sirkyle] **vi 1.** [sang, air, argent] to circulate ▸ **faire circuler qqch** to circulate sthg **2.** [aller et venir] to move (along) ▸ **circulez!** move along! ▸ **on circule mal en ville** the traffic is bad in town **3.** [train, bus] to run **4.** *fig* [rumeur, nouvelle] to spread.

cire [sir] **nf 1.** [matière] wax ▸ **cire d'abeilles** beeswax ▸ **cire à cacheter** sealing wax ▸ **musée de cire, cabinet de cire** *vieilli* waxworks *sg* **2.** [encaustique] polish.

ciré, ***e*** [sire] **adj 1.** [parquet] polished **2.** ➤ ***toile***.
◆ ***ciré*** **nm** oilskin.

cirer [3] [sire] **vt** [chaussures] to polish
▸▸ **(n')en avoir rien à cirer (de qqch)** *fam* not to give a damn (about sthg) ▸ **j'en ai rien à cirer** *fam* I don't give a damn.

cireux, ***euse*** [sirø, øz] **adj 1.** [pâle] waxen **2.** [matière] waxy.
◆ ***cireuse*** **nf** floor polisher.

cirque [sirk] **nm 1.** [gén] circus **2.** GÉOL cirque **3.** *fam fig* [désordre, chahut] chaos *(U)* / [TV, radio] **: cirque médiatique** media circus.

cirrhose [siroz] **nf** cirrhosis *(U)*.

cisaille [sizaj] **nf** shears *pl*.

cisaillement [sizajmɑ̃] **nm** [de métal] cutting / [de branches] pruning.

cisailler [3] [sizaje] **vt** [métal] to cut / [branches] to prune.

ciseau, ***x*** [sizo] **nm** chisel.
◆ ***ciseaux*** **nmpl** scissors.

ciseler [25] [sizle] **vt 1.** [pierre, métal] to chisel **2.** [bijou] to engrave **3.** *fig* [parfaire] to polish (up).

ciselure [sizlyr] **nf** [bois] carving / [objet précieux] engraving.

Cisjordanie [sizʒɔrdani] **nf : la Cisjordanie** the West Bank.

cisjordanien, ***enne*** [sizʒɔrdanjɛ̃, ɛn] **adj** of/from the West Bank.
◆ ***Cisjordanien***, ***enne*** **nm, f** person from the West Bank.

cistercien, ***enne*** [sistersjɛ̃, ɛn] **adj** Cistercian.
◆ ***cistercien*** **nm** Cistercian.

citadelle [sitadɛl] **nf** *litt* & *fig* citadel.

citadin, ***e*** [sitadɛ̃, in] ■ **adj** city *(avant n)*, urban.
■ **nm, f** city dweller.

citation [sitasjɔ̃] **nf 1.** DR summons *sg* **2.** [extrait] quote, quotation.

cité [site] **nf 1.** [ville] city **2.** [lotissement] housing estate *UK ou* project *US* ▸ **cité ouvrière** council estate *UK*, housing project *US* ▸ **cité universitaire** halls *pl* of residence *UK*, dormitory *US*.

cité-dortoir [sitedɔrtwar] (pl **cités-dortoirs**) **nf** dormitory town, bedroom community *US*.

citer [3] [site] **vt 1.** [exemple, propos, auteur] to quote **2.** DR [convoquer] to summon **3.** MIL **: être cité à l'ordre du jour** to be mentioned in dispatches.

citerne [sitɛrn] **nf 1.** [d'eau] water tank **2.** [cuve] tank ▸ **citerne à mazout** oil tank.

cité U [sitey] **nf** *fam* abr écrite de ***cité universitaire***.

citoyen, ***enne*** [sitwajɛ̃, ɛn] **nm, f** citizen.

citoyenneté [sitwajɛnte] **nf** citizenship.

citron [sitrɔ̃] ■ **nm** lemon ▸ **citron pressé** fresh lemon juice ▸ **citron vert** lime.
■ **adj inv** lemon yellow.

citronnade [sitrɔnad] **nf** (still) lemonade.

citronnelle [sitrɔnɛl] **nf** [plante] lemon balm.

citronnier [sitrɔnje] **nm** lemon tree.

citrouille [sitruj] **nf** pumpkin.

civet [sivɛ] **nm** stew ▸ **civet de lièvre** jugged hare.

civière [sivjɛr] **nf** stretcher.

civil, ***e*** [sivil] ■ **adj 1.** [gén] civil **2.** [non militaire] civilian.
■ **nm, f** civilian ▸ **dans le civil** in civilian life ▸ **policier en civil** plain-clothes policeman (f policewoman) ▸ **soldat en civil** soldier in civilian clothes.

PARONYME / CONFUSABLE
civil

Le mot français **civil** peut se traduire de deux façons : *civil* s'utilise pour parler du comportement, tandis que *civilian* désigne ce qui n'est pas militaire.

civilement [sivilmɑ̃] **adv : se marier civilement** to get married at a registry office *UK ou* in a civil ceremony *US*.

civilisation [sivilizasjɔ̃] **nf** civilization.

civilisé, ***e*** [sivilize] **adj** civilized.

civiliser [3] [sivilize] **vt** to civilize.
◆ ***se civiliser*** **vp** to become civilized.

civilité [sivilite] **nf** civility.
◆ ***civilités*** **nfpl** *sout* compliments.

civique [sivik] **adj** civic ▸ **instruction civique** civics *(U)*.

civisme [sivism] **nm** sense of civic responsibility.

cl (abr écrite de ***centilitre***) cl.

clac [klak] **interj** [porte] slam! / [taquets] click!

clafoutis [klafuti] **nm** [gâteau] *cake made from a batter poured over fruit.*

claie [klɛ] **nf 1.** [treillis] rack **2.** [clôture] hurdle.

clair, ***e*** [klɛr] **adj 1.** [précis, évident] clear ▸ **c'est clair et net** there's no two ways about it ▸ **cette affaire n'est pas très claire** there's something fishy about all this ▸ **il est clair que c'est impossible** it's clear that it's impossible, clearly it's impossible **2.** [lumineux] bright ▸ **la pièce est très claire le matin** the room gets a lot of light in the morning ▸ **une nuit claire** a clear night ▸ **par temps clair** in clear weather **3.** [pâle - couleur, teint] light ▸ **il a le regard clair** he's got bright eyes / [- tissu, cheveux] light-coloured *UK*, light-colored *US* ▸ **porter des vêtements clairs** to wear light *ou* light-coloured clothes.

◆ ***clair*** ■ **adv : voir clair (dans qqch)** *fig* to have a clear understanding (of sthg).

■ **nm : passer le plus clair de son temps à faire qqch** to spend most *ou* the bulk of one's time doing sthg ▸ **mettre *ou* tirer qqch au clair** to shed light upon sthg.

◆ ***clair de lune*** (pl **clairs de lune**) **nm** moonlight *(U)* ▸ **au clair de lune** in the moonlight.

◆ ***en clair*** **loc adv** TV unscrambled *(esp of a private TV channel)* ▸ **diffuser en clair** TV to broadcast unscrambled programmes ▸ **'en clair jusqu'à 20h'** 'can be watched by non-subscribers until 8 o'clock'.

◆ ***claire*** **nf 1.** [bassin] oyster bed **2.** [huître] fattened oyster.

clairement [klɛrmɑ̃] **adv** clearly.

claire-voie [klɛrvwa] ◆ ***à claire-voie*** **loc adv** openwork *(avant n)*.

clairière [klɛrjɛr] **nf** clearing.

clairon [klɛrɔ̃] **nm** bugle.

claironner [3] [klɛrɔne] ■ **vi** to play the bugle.

■ **vt** *fig* [crier] **: claironner qqch** to shout sthg from the rooftops.

clairsemé, e [klɛrsəme] **adj** [cheveux] thin / [arbres] scattered / [population] sparse.

clairvoyant, e [klɛrvwajɑ̃, ɑ̃t] **adj** perceptive.

clamer [3] [klame] **vt** to proclaim.

clameur [klamœr] **nf** clamour *UK*, clamor *US*.

clamser [3] [klamse] **vi** *tfam* to kick the bucket, to snuff it *UK*.

clan [klɑ̃] **nm** clan.

clandestin, e [klɑ̃dɛstɛ̃, in] ■ **adj** [journal, commerce] clandestine / [activité] covert.

■ **nm, f** [étranger] illegal immigrant *ou* alien / [voyageur] stowaway.

clandestinité [klɑ̃destinite] **nf** clandestine nature ▸ **dans la clandestinité** [travailler] clandestinely / [vivre] underground.

clapet [klapɛ] **nm 1.** TECHNOL valve **2.** *fam fig* [bouche] trap.

clapier [klapje] **nm** [à lapins] hutch.

clapotement [klapɔtmɑ̃], ***clapotis*** [klapɔti] **nm** [de vagues] lapping *(U)*.

clapoter [3] [klapɔte] **vi** [vagues] to lap.

clapotis = ***clapotement***.

claquage [klakaʒ] **nm** MÉD strain ▸ **se faire un claquage** to pull *ou* to strain a muscle.

claque [klak] **nf 1.** [gifle] slap ▸ **donner une claque à qqn** to slap sb **2.** THÉÂTRE claque **3.** *Québec* [pour chaussures] galosh, rubber *US*

▸▸ **en avoir sa claque (de)** *fam* to be fed up (with), to be fed up to the back teeth (with) *UK*.

claqué, e [klake] **adj** *fam* [éreinté] bushed, whacked *UK*.

claquement [klakmɑ̃] **nm 1.** [de porte - qui se ferme] slam, slamming *(U)* / [- mal fermée] banging *(U)* **2.** [de doigts] snap, snapping *(U)*.

claquemurer [3] [klakmyre] ◆ ***se claquemurer*** **vp** to shut o.s up *ou* away.

claquer [3] [klake] ■ **vt 1.** [fermer] to slam **2. : faire claquer** [langue] to click / [doigts] to snap / [fouet] to crack **3.** *fam* [gifler] to slap **4.** *fam* [dépenser] to blow **5.** *fam* [fatiguer] to wear out.

■ **vi 1.** [porte, volet] to bang **2.** *fam* [personne] to kick the bucket, to snuff it *UK* **3.** *fam* [machine] to conk out **4.** [ampoule] to burn out, to go.

◆ ***se claquer*** **vp 1.** [se fatiguer] to wear o.s. out **2.** [se déchirer] **: se claquer un muscle** to pull *ou* tear a muscle.

claquettes [klakɛt] **nfpl** [danse] tap dancing *(U)* ▸ **faire des claquettes** to tap dance.

clarification [klarifikasjɔ̃] **nf** *litt & fig* clarification.

clarifier [9] [klarifje] **vt** *litt & fig* to clarify.

◆ ***se clarifier*** **vp** *fig* to become clear.

clarinette [klarinɛt] **nf** [instrument] clarinet.

clarté [klarte] **nf 1.** [lumière] brightness **2.** [transparence] clearness **3.** [netteté] clarity.

classe [klas] **nf 1.** [gén] class ▸ **billet de première/deuxième classe** first-/second-class ticket ▸ **de grande classe** first-class, high-class ▸ **classe d'âge** age group ▸ **les classes moyennes/dirigeantes** the middle/ruling classes ▸ **classe ouvrière** working class ▸ **l'ensemble de la classe politique** the whole of the political establishment *ou* class ▸ **classe touriste** economy class, coach *US*

2. SCOL **: aller en classe** to go to school ▸ **camarade de classe** classmate ▸ **classe de neige** skiing trip *(with school)* ▸ **classes préparatoires** *school preparing students for Grandes Écoles entrance exams* ▸ **classe de rattrapage** remedial class ▸ **classe verte** field trip *(with school)* ▸ **faire la classe** [être enseignant] to teach / [donner un cours] to teach *ou* to take a class

3. [catégorie] category, type

4. MIL rank ▸ **la classe 70** the 1970 levy

▸▸ **la *ou* quelle classe!** *fam* first class!, fantastic! ▸ **faire ses classes** MIL to do one's training.

CULTURE

Classes préparatoires

After taking the **baccalauréat**, especially motivated students can go on to the **classes préparatoires**, two years of intensive coursework focussing on literature (**hypokhâgne** and **khâgne**), the sciences (**maths sup** and **maths spé**), economics (**prépa HEC**), biology (**maths sup bio**), or veterinary medicine (**véto**). The **classes prépas** are much more difficult and competitive than university courses: admission is stricter, the academic year lasts longer, and students have about twice as many hours of classes. At the end of these courses, students take extremely difficult exams in the hope of gaining admission to one of the prestigious **grandes écoles** (**École normale supérieure, Polytechnique, HEC** *etc.*).

classé, e [klase] **adj** [monument] listed *UK*.

classement [klasmɑ̃] **nm 1.** [rangement] filing **2.** [classification] classification **3.** [rang - SCOL] position / SPORT placing **4.** [liste - SCOL] class list / SPORT final placings *pl* ▸ **classement général** overall placings *pl*.

classer [3] [klase] **vt 1.** [ranger] to file **2.** [plantes, animaux] to classify **3.** [cataloguer] **: classer qqn (parmi)** to label sb (as) **4.** [attribuer un rang à] to rank.
◆ ***se classer*** **vp** to be classed, to rank ▸ **se classer troisième** to come third.

classeur [klasœr] **nm 1.** [meuble] filing cabinet **2.** [portefeuille] file, folder **3.** [d'écolier] ring binder.

classification [klasifikasjɔ̃] **nf** classification ▸ **classification périodique des éléments** CHIM periodic table.

classique [klasik] ■ **nm 1.** [auteur] classical author ▸ **les grands classiques** the great classical authors **2.** [œuvre] classic **3.** ART & MUS **: le classique** [musique] classical (music) / [architecture] classical architecture / [beaux-arts] classical art.
■ **adj 1.** ART & MUS classical **2.** [sobre] classic **3.** [habituel] classic ▸ **ça, c'est l'histoire classique!** it's the usual story!

PARONYME / CONFUSABLE
classique
Attention lorsque vous traduisez ce mot : *classic* signifie typique, standard, alors que *classical* renvoie à la tradition, aux références culturelles admises.

claudication [klodikasjɔ̃] **nf** limp / MÉD claudication.

clause [kloz] **nf** clause ▸ **clause d'exemption** POLIT opt-out clause.

claustrer [3] [klostre] ◆ ***se claustrer*** **vp** *sout* to shut o.s. away *ou* up.

claustrophobie [klostrɔfɔbi] **nf** claustrophobia.

clavecin [klavsɛ̃] **nm** harpsichord.

clavicule [klavikyl] **nf** collarbone.

clavier [klavje] **nm** keyboard ▸ **clavier AZERTY/QWERTY** AZERTY/QWERTY keyboard.

clé, ***clef*** [kle] ■ **nf 1.** [gén] key ▸ **la clé du mystère** the key to the mystery ▸ **fermer qqch à clé** to lock sthg ▸ **clés en main** [usine] turnkey / [logement] ready for immediate entry ▸ **acheter une maison clé** *ou* **clés en main** to buy a house with vacant *ou* immediate possession ▸ **mettre qqn/qqch sous clé** to lock sb/sthg up ▸ **clé de contact** AUTO ignition key ▸ **mettre la clé sous la porte** to clear out ▸ **prendre la clé des champs** to get away **2.** [outil] **: clé anglaise** *ou* **à molette** adjustable spanner *UK ou* wrench *US*, monkey wrench ▸ **clé universelle** adjustable spanner *UK ou* wrench *US* **3.** MUS [signe] clef ▸ **clé de sol/fa** treble/bass clef ▸ **à la clé** *fig* at the end (of it all) **4.** INFORM **: clé d'accès** enter key ▸ **clé de protection** data protection.
■ **adj : industrie/rôle clé** key industry/role ▸ **mot/position clé** key word/post.
◆ ***clé de voûte*** **nf** *litt* & *fig* keystone.

clean [klin] **adj** *fam* [chose, lieu] neat / [personne] clean-living.

clef = ***clé***.

clématite [klematit] **nf** clematis.

clémence [klemɑ̃s] **nf 1.** *sout* [indulgence] clemency **2.** *fig* [douceur] mildness.

clément, e [klemɑ̃, ɑ̃t] **adj 1.** [indulgent] lenient **2.** *fig* [température] mild.

clémentine [klemɑ̃tin] **nf** clementine.

cleptomane = ***kleptomane***.

clerc [klɛr] **nm** [assistant] clerk ▸ **clerc de notaire** lawyer's clerk.

clergé [klɛrʒe] **nm** clergy.

clérical, e, aux [klerikal, o] ■ **adj** clerical.
■ **nm, f** clericalist.

CLES, ***Cles*** [klɛs] (abr de ***contrat local emploi-solidarité***) **nm** *community work scheme for young unemployed people*.

clic [klik] **nm** INFORM click ▸ **clic droit** right-click ▸ **clic gauche** left-click.

Clic-Clac® [klikklac] **nm** pull-out sofa bed.

cliché [kliʃe] **nm 1.** PHOTO negative **2.** [banalité] cliché.

client, e [kliɑ̃, ɑ̃t] **nm, f 1.** [de notaire, d'agence] client / [de médecin] patient **2.** [acheteur] customer **3.** [habitué] regular (customer).

clientèle [kliɑ̃tɛl] **nf 1.** [ensemble des clients] customers *pl* ▸ **clientèle captive** captive market / [de profession libérale] clientele **2.** [fait d'être client] **: accorder sa clientèle à** to give one's custom to.

clientélisme [klijɑ̃telism] **nm** *péj* populism.

cligner [3] [kliɲe] ■ **vt : cligner les yeux** to blink.
■ **vi : cligner de l'œil** to wink ▸ **cligner des yeux** to blink.

clignotant, e [kliɲɔtɑ̃, ɑ̃t] **adj** [lumière] flickering.
◆ ***clignotant*** **nm 1.** AUTO indicator *UK*, turn signal *US* ▸ **mettre son clignotant** to indicate *UK* **2.** *fig* & ÉCON warning sign.

clignoter [3] [kliɲɔte] **vi 1.** [yeux] to blink **2.** [lumière] to flicker.

climat [klima] **nm** *litt* & *fig* climate ▸ **climat économique** economic climate.

climatique [klimatik] **adj** climatic.

climatisation [klimatizasjɔ̃] **nf** air-conditioning.

climatisé, e [klimatize] **adj** air-conditioned.

clin [klɛ̃] ◆ ***clin d'œil*** **nm : faire un clin d'œil (à)** to wink (at) ▸ **en un clin d'œil** in a flash.

clinique [klinik] ■ **nf** clinic.
■ **adj** clinical.

clinquant, e [klɛ̃kɑ̃, ɑ̃t] **adj** *litt* & *fig* flashy.
◆ ***clinquant*** **nm 1.** [faux bijou] imitation jewellery *(U) UK ou* jewelry *(U) US* **2.** *fig* [éclat] gloss.

clip [klip] **nm 1.** [vidéo] pop video **2.** [boucle d'oreilles] clip-on earring.

cliquable [klikabl] **adj** clickable ▸ **plan cliquable** sensitive map.

clique [klik] **nf** *péj* clique.
◆ ***cliques*** **nfpl : prendre ses cliques et ses claques** *fam* to pack one's bags (and go).

cliquer [3] [klike] **vi** INFORM to click / [bouton gauche] to left-click / [bouton droit] to right-click.

cliqueter [27] [klikte] **vi 1.** [pièces, clés, chaînes] to jingle, to jangle **2.** [verres] to clink.

cliquetis [klikti] **nm 1.** [de pièces, clés, chaînes] jingling *(U)*, jangling *(U)* **2.** [de verres] clinking *(U)*.

clitoris [klitɔris] **nm** clitoris.

clivage [klivaʒ] **nm 1.** GÉOL cleavage **2.** *fig* [division] division.

cloaque [klɔak] **nm** [lieu] cesspit.

clochard, e [klɔʃar, ard] **nm, f** tramp.

cloche [klɔʃ] ■ **nf 1.** [d'église] bell **2.** [couvercle] **: cloche à fromage** glass cover for cheese **3.** *fam* [idiot] idiot **4.** *(en apposition)* [jupe] flared.
■ **adj** *fam* **: ce qu'elle peut être cloche, celle-là!** she can be such an idiot!

cloche-pied [klɔʃpje] ◆ ***à cloche-pied*** **loc adv** hopping ▸ **sauter à cloche-pied** to hop.

clocher[1] [klɔʃe] **nm** [d'église] church tower ▸ **esprit de clocher** parochialism, parish-pump mentality.

clocher[2] [3] [klɔʃe] **vi : il y a quelque chose qui cloche** there's something wrong here ▸ **qu'est-ce qui cloche?** what's wrong *ou* up?

clochette [klɔʃɛt] **nf 1.** [petite cloche] (little) bell **2.** [de fleur] bell.

clodo [klɔdo] **nmf** *fam* tramp.

cloison [klwazɔ̃] **nf** [mur] partition.

cloisonner [3] [klwazɔne] **vt** [pièce, maison] to partition (off) / *fig* to compartmentalize.

cloître [klwatr] **nm** cloister.

cloîtrer [3] [klwatre] **vt 1.** RELIG to cloister **2.** [enfermer] to shut away (from the outside world).
◆ ***se cloîtrer*** **vp 1.** [s'enfermer] to shut o.s. away ▸ **se cloîtrer dans** *fig* to retreat into **2.** [RELIG - sœur] to enter a convent / [- moine] to enter a monastery.

clonage [klonaʒ] **nm** cloning ▸ **clonage thérapeutique** therapeutic cloning.

clone [klɔn] **nm** clone.

cloner [3] [klone] **vt** to clone.

clope [klɔp] **nm & nf** *fam* cigarette, fag *UK*.

clopin-clopant [klɔpɛ̃klɔpɑ̃] **adv : aller clopin-clopant** [person] to hobble along / *fig* to struggle along.

clopiner [3] [klɔpine] **vi** to hobble along.

clopinettes [klɔpinɛt] **nfpl** *fam* **: gagner des clopinettes** to earn peanuts.

cloporte [klɔpɔrt] **nm** woodlouse.

cloque [klɔk] **nf** blister.

cloquer [3] [klɔke] **vi** to blister.

clore [113] [klɔr] **vt** to close / [négociations] to conclude ▸ **clore une session** INFORM to log out.

clos, e [klo, kloz] ■ **pp** ➤ ***clore***.
■ **adj** closed.
◆ ***clos*** **nm 1.** [terrain] enclosed field **2.** [vignoble] vineyard.

clôture [klotyr] **nf 1.** [haie] hedge / [de fil de fer] fence ▸ **clôture électrifiée** *ou* **électrique** electric fence **2.** [fermeture] closing, closure **3.** [fin] end, conclusion ▸ **clôture des inscriptions le 20 décembre** UNIV the closing date for enrolment is December 20th **4.** FIN close ▸ **à la clôture** at the close ▸ **en clôture** at closing ▸ **combien valait l'euro en clôture ?** what did the euro close at?

clôturer [3] [klotyre] **vt 1.** [terrain] to enclose **2.** [négociation] to close, to conclude.

clou [klu] **nm 1.** [pointe] nail ▸ **clou de girofle** CULIN clove ▸ **clou sans tête** brad ▸ **clou (de) tapissier** (carpet) tack ▸ **des clous!** *fam* no chance! ▸ **maigre comme un clou** as thin as a rake ▸ **mettre au clou** [en gage] to pawn / [en prison] to put in the clink ▸ **pas un clou : ça ne vaut pas un clou** it's not worth a bean ▸ **pour des clous** for nothing **2.** [attraction] highlight ▸ **le clou de** the climax *ou* highlight of.
◆ ***clous*** **nmpl** *vieilli* pedestrian crossing *(sg) UK*, crosswalk *US*.

clouer [3] [klue] **vt** [fixer - couvercle, planche] to nail (down) / [- tableau, caisse] to nail (up) / *fig* [immobiliser] **: rester cloué sur place** to be rooted to the spot ▸ **être cloué au lit (par)** *fam* to be laid up in bed (with).

clouté, e [klute] **adj** [vêtement] studded.

clown [klun] **nm** clown ▸ **faire le clown** to clown around, to act the fool.

CLT (abr de ***Compagnie luxembourgeoise de télévision***) **nf** *Luxembourg TV company*.

club [klœb] **nm** club.

cm (abr écrite de ***centimètre***) cm.

CM ■ **nf** (abr de ***Chambre des métiers***) *chamber of commerce for trades*.
■ **nm** (abr de ***cours moyen***) ▸ **CM1** *fourth year of primary school* ▸ **CM2** *fifth year of primary school*.

CMU (abr de ***Couverture maladie universelle***) [seɛmy] **nf** *health insurance system for the less well-off*, ≃ Medicaid *US*.

CNAC [knak] (abr de ***Centre national d'art et de culture***) **nm** *official name of the Pompidou Centre*.

CNAM [knam] (abr de ***Conservatoire national des arts et métiers***) **nm** *science and technology school in Paris*.

CNC **nm 1.** (abr de ***Conseil national de la consommation***) *official consumer protection organization* **2.** (abr de ***Centre national de la cinématographie***) *national cinematographic organization*.

CNDP (abr de ***Centre national de documentation pédagogique***) **nm** *national organization for educational resources*.

CNE (abr de ***Caisse nationale d'épargne***) **nf** *national savings bank*.

CNEC [knɛk] (abr de ***Centre national de l'enseignement par correspondance***) **nm** *national education body organizing correspondence courses*, ≃ Open University *UK*.

CNES, Cnes [knɛs] (abr de ***Centre national d'études spatiales***) **nm** *French national space research centre*.

CNIL [knil] (abr de ***Commission nationale de l'informatique et des libertés***) **nf** *watchdog committee supervising the application of data protection legislation*.

CNIT, Cnit [knit] (abr de ***Centre national des industries et des techniques***) **nm** *exhibition centre at la Défense near Paris*.

CNJA (abr de ***Centre national des jeunes agriculteurs***) **nm** *young farmers' union.*

CNPF (abr de ***Conseil national du patronat français***) **nm** *national council of French employers,* ≃ CBI *UK*.

CNRS (abr de ***Centre national de la recherche scientifique***) **nm** *national scientific research organization.*

CNTS (abr de ***Centre national de transfusion sanguine***) **nm** *national blood transfusion centre.*

CNUCED, **Cnuced** [knysɛd] (abr de ***Conférence des Nations unies pour le commerce et l'industrie***) **nf** UNCTAD.

coach [kotʃ] (pl **coachs** *ou* **coaches**) **nm** SPORT coach, trainer.

coaguler [3] [kɔagyle] ■ **vt 1.** [sang] to clot **2.** [lait] to curdle.
■ **vi 1.** [sang] to clot **2.** [lait] to curdle.
◆ ***se coaguler*** **vp 1.** [sang] to clot **2.** [lait] to curdle.

coaliser [3] [kɔalize] **vt** to group together, to unite.
◆ ***se coaliser*** **vp 1.** [s'allier] to form a coalition *ou* an alliance **2.** [s'unir] to unite.

coalition [kɔalisjɔ̃] **nf** coalition.

coasser [3] [kɔase] **vi** [grenouille] to croak.

COB, **Cob** [kɔb] (abr de ***Commission des opérations de Bourse***) **nf** *commission for supervision of stock exchange operations,* ≃ SIB *UK*, ≃ SEC *US*.

cobalt [kɔbalt] **nm** cobalt.

cobaye [kɔbaj] **nm** *litt* & *fig* guinea pig.

cobra [kɔbra] **nm** cobra.

co-branding [kobrɑ̃diŋ] **nm** co-branding.

coca [kɔka] ■ **nm** BOT coca.
■ **nf** coca extract.

Coca® [kɔka] **nm** [boisson] Coke®.

cocagne [kɔkaɲ] ➤ ***mât, pays.***

cocaïne [kɔkain] **nf** cocaine.

cocaïnomane [kokainɔman] **nmf** cocaine addict.

cocarde [kɔkard] **nf 1.** [insigne] roundel **2.** [distinction] rosette.

cocardier, **ère** [kɔkardje, ɛr] ■ **adj** [chauvin] jingoistic.
■ **nm, f** jingoist.

cocasse [kɔkas] **adj** funny.

coccinelle [kɔksinɛl] **nf 1.** [insecte] ladybird *UK*, ladybug *US* **2.** [voiture] Beetle.

coccyx [kɔksis] **nm** coccyx.

coche [kɔʃ] **nm : manquer le coche** *fam fig* to miss the boat.

cocher¹ [kɔʃe] **nm** coachman.

cocher² [3] [kɔʃe] **vt** to tick (off) *UK*, to check (off) *US*.

cochère [kɔʃɛr] ➤ ***porte.***

cocheur [kɔʃœr] **nm** *Québec* [golf] **: cocheur d'allée** pitching wedge ▸ **cocheur de sable** sand wedge.

cochon, **onne** [kɔʃɔ̃, ɔn] ■ **adj** dirty, smutty.
■ **nm, f** *fam péj* pig ▸ **un tour de cochon** a dirty trick.
◆ ***cochon*** **nm** pig ▸ **cochon d'Inde** guinea pig ▸ **cochon de lait** sucking pig.

cochonnaille [kɔʃɔnaj] **nf** *fam* [charcuterie] pork.

cochonner [3] [kɔʃɔne] **vt** *fam* to mess up.

cochonnerie [kɔʃɔnri] **nf** *fam* **1.** [nourriture] muck *(U)* **2.** [chose] rubbish *(U) UK*, trash *(U) US* **3.** [saleté] mess *(U)* **4.** [obscénité] dirty joke, smut *(U)*.

cochonnet [kɔʃɔnɛ] **nm 1.** [petit cochon] piglet **2.** [jeux] jack.

cocker [kɔkɛr] **nm** cocker spaniel.

cockpit [kɔkpit] **nm** cockpit.

cocktail [kɔktɛl] **nm 1.** [réception] cocktail party **2.** [boisson] cocktail **3.** *fig* [mélange] mixture ▸ **cocktail Molotov** Molotov cocktail.

coco [kɔko] **nm 1.** ➤ ***noix*** **2.** *fam péj* [individu] guy, bloke *UK* **3.** *péj* [communiste] commie.

cocon [kɔkɔ̃] **nm** *fig* & ZOOL cocoon.

cocooning [kɔkuniŋ] **nm : faire du cocooning** to cocoon o.s.

cocorico [kɔkɔriko] **nm** [du coq] cock-a-doodle-doo.

cocotier [kɔkɔtje] **nm** coconut tree.

cocotte [kɔkɔt] **nf 1.** [marmite] casserole (dish) **2.** [poule] hen ▸ **cocotte en papier** paper shape **3.** *péj* [courtisane] tart.

Cocotte-Minute® [kɔkɔtminyt] **nf** pressure cooker.

cocu, **e** [kɔky] **nm, f** & **adj** *fam* cuckold.

code [kɔd] **nm 1.** [gén] code ▸ **code d'accès** INFORM access code ▸ **code source** *ou* **natif** source code ▸ **code ASCII** ASCII code ▸ **code–barres** bar code ▸ **code de caractères** INFORM character code ▸ **code d'entrée** [sur une porte] door code ▸ **code génétique** genetic code ▸ **code international de signaux** NAUT International Code ▸ **code postal** postcode *UK*, zip code *US*
2. BANQUE & ÉCON **: code banque** bank code ▸ **code confidentiel** [carte de crédit] personal identification number, PIN ▸ **code guichet** sort code ▸ **code secret** PIN number
3. [phares] dipped headlights *pl UK*, dimmed headlights *pl US* ▸ **se mettre en codes** to dip *UK ou* dim *US* one's headlights
4. DR **: code civil** *ou* **Napoléon** civil code ▸ **code de commerce** commercial law ▸ **Code général des impôts** general tax code ▸ **code maritime** navigation laws ▸ **code pénal** penal code ▸ **code de la route** highway code *UK*, motor vehicle laws *US* ▸ **code du travail** labour *UK ou* labor *US* legislation.
◆ ***codes*** **nmpl** [phares] dipped headlights *pl UK*, low beams *pl US* ▸ **se mettre en codes** to dip one's headlights *UK*, to put on low beams *US*.

codé, **e** [kɔde] **adj** encoded, coded ▸ **message codé** cryptogram ▸ **langage codé** secret language.

codéine [kɔdein] **nf** codeine.

coder [3] [kɔde] **vt** to code.

codétenu, **e** [kɔdetny] **nm, f** (fellow) prisoner.

Codévi [kɔdevi] (abr de ***compte pour le développement industriel***) **nm** *savings account, money from which is invested in industrial development.*

codifier [9] [kɔdifje] **vt** to codify.

coefficient [kɔefisjɑ̃] **nm** coefficient ▸ **affecter qqch d'un coefficient** to weight sthg ▸ **coefficient d'activité** activity ratio ▸ **coefficient de capital** output ratio ▸ **coefficient d'erreur** margin of error ▸ **coefficient d'exploitation** operating ratio ▸ **coefficient multiplicateur** multiplying factor ▸ **coefficient de rendement** coefficient of efficiency ▸ **coefficient statistique** statistical weight ▸ **coefficient de trésorerie** cash ratio.

coéquipier, ***ère*** [kɔekipje, ɛr] **nm, f** teammate.

cœur [kœr] **nm** heart ▸ **au cœur de l'hiver** in the depths of winter ▸ **au cœur de l'été** at the height of summer ▸ **au cœur du conflit** at the height of the conflict ▸ **beau** *ou* **joli** *ou* **mignon comme un cœur** as pretty as a picture ▸ **de bon cœur** willingly ▸ **de tout son cœur** with all one's heart ▸ **à cœur ouvert** MÉD open-heart ▸ **parler à cœur ouvert à qqn** to have a heart-to-heart with sb ▸ **aller droit au cœur : vos paroles me sont allées droit au cœur** your words went straight to my heart ▸ **apprendre par cœur** to learn by heart ▸ **avoir qqch à cœur** to have one's heart set on sthg ▸ **avoir bon cœur** to be kind-hearted ▸ **avoir le cœur à faire qqch** to be in the mood to do *ou* to feel like doing sthg ▸ **avoir le cœur dur** *ou* **sec, avoir un cœur de pierre** to have a heart of stone ▸ **avoir le cœur sur la main** to be big-hearted ▸ **avoir mal au cœur** to feel sick ▸ **avoir un cœur d'artichaut** to fall in love very easily ▸ **en avoir le cœur net** to be clear in one's (own) mind ▸ **avoir le cœur serré** *ou* **gros** to have a heavy heart ▸ **briser** *ou* **fendre le cœur de qqn** to break sb's heart ▸ **des mots venus du (fond du) cœur** heartfelt words ▸ **s'en donner à cœur joie** [prendre beaucoup de plaisir] to have a whale of a time ▸ **je ne le porte pas dans mon cœur** *fam* I'm not particularly fond of him ▸ **manquer de cœur, ne pas avoir de cœur** to be heartless ▸ **ne pas avoir le cœur de faire qqch** not to have the heart to do sthg ▸ **prendre les choses à cœur** to take things to heart ▸ **serrer qqn contre son cœur** to clasp sb to one's breast ▸ **soulever le cœur à qqn** to make sb feel sick ▸ **tenir à cœur** to be close to one's heart.

◆ ***cœur de pierre*** **nm** heart of stone.

coexistence [kɔɛgzistɑ̃s] **nf** coexistence.

coexister [3] [kɔɛgziste] **vi** to coexist.

COFACE [kɔfas] (abr de ***Compagnie française d'assurance pour le commerce extérieur***) **nf** *export insurance company*, ≃ ECGD *UK*.

coffrage [kɔfraʒ] **nm** [pour le béton] formwork *(U)* / [charpente] coffering.

coffre [kɔfr] **nm 1.** [meuble] chest **2.** [de voiture] boot *UK*, trunk *US* **3.** [coffre-fort] safe

▸▸| **avoir du coffre** *fam fig* to have a lot of puff *UK*.

coffre-fort [kɔfrəfɔr] (pl **coffres-forts**) **nm** safe.

coffrer [3] [kɔfre] **vt 1.** *fam* [emprisonner] to put behind bars, to bang up *UK* **2.** TECHNOL to put up shuttering for.

coffret [kɔfrɛ] **nm 1.** [petit coffre] casket ▸ **coffret à bijoux** jewellery *UK ou* jewelry *US* box **2.** [de disques] boxed set.

cogestion [kɔʒɛstjɔ̃] **nf** joint management.

cogitation [kɔʒitasjɔ̃] **nf** *hum* cogitation.

cogiter [3] [kɔʒite] **vi** *hum* to cogitate.

cognac [kɔɲak] **nm** cognac, brandy.

cogner [3] [kɔɲe] ■ **vt** *fam* to beat up.

■ **vi 1.** [heurter] to bang **2.** *fam* [donner des coups] to hit **3.** [soleil] to beat down.

◆ ***se cogner*** **vp 1.** [se heurter] to bump o.s. ▸ **se cogner à** *ou* **contre qqch** to bump into sthg ▸ **se cogner la tête/le genou** to hit one's head/knee **2.** *fam* [se battre] to have a fight *ou* punch-up *UK*.

cognitif, ***ive*** [kɔgnitif, iv] **adj** cognitive.

cohabitation [kɔabitasjɔ̃] **nf 1.** [de personnes] living together, cohabitation **2.** POLIT cohabitation.

cohabiter [3] [kɔabite] **vi 1.** [habiter ensemble] to live together **2.** POLIT to cohabit.

cohérence [kɔerɑ̃s] **nf** consistency, coherence.

cohérent, ***e*** [kɔerɑ̃, ɑ̃t] **adj 1.** [logique] consistent, coherent **2.** [unifié] coherent.

cohéritier, ***ère*** [kɔeritje, ɛr] **nm, f** joint heir (f heiress).

cohésion [kɔezjɔ̃] **nf** cohesion.

cohorte [kɔɔrt] **nf** [groupe] troop.

cohue [kɔy] **nf 1.** [foule] crowd **2.** [bousculade] crush.

coi, ***coite*** [kwa, kwat] **adj : rester coi** *sout* to remain silent.

coiffe [kwaf] **nf** headdress.

coiffé, ***e*** [kwafe] **adj : être bien/mal coiffé** to have tidy/untidy hair ▸ **être coiffé d'une casquette** to be wearing a cap.

coiffer [3] [kwafe] **vt 1.** [mettre sur la tête] **: coiffer qqn de qqch** to put sthg on sb's head **2.** [les cheveux] **: coiffer qqn** to do sb's hair **3.** [recouvrir] to top, to cover **4.** [diriger] to head.

◆ ***se coiffer*** **vp 1.** [les cheveux] to do one's hair **2.** [mettre sur sa tête] **: se coiffer de** to wear, to put on.

coiffeur, ***euse*** [kwafœr, øz] **nm, f** hairdresser.

◆ ***coiffeuse*** **nf** [meuble] dressing table.

coiffure [kwafyr] **nf 1.** [chapeau] hat **2.** [cheveux] hairstyle **3.** [profession] hairdressing.

coin [kwɛ̃] **nm 1.** [angle] corner ▸ **au coin du feu** by the fireside ▸ **envoyer qqn au coin** [à l'école] to make sb stand in the corner ▸ **à tous les coins de rue** on every street corner ▸ **manger sur un coin de table** to eat a hasty meal ▸ **regarder qqn du coin de l'œil** [à la dérobée] to look at sb out of the corner of one's eye

2. [parcelle, endroit] place, spot ▸ **du coin** local ▸ **les gens du coin** [ici] the people who live around here, the locals / [là-bas] the people who live there, the locals ▸ **dans le coin** in the area ▸ **je passais dans le coin et j'ai eu envie de venir te voir** I was in the area and I felt like dropping in (on you) ▸ **dans un coin de la maison** somewhere in the house ▸ **rester dans son coin** to keep oneself to oneself ▸ **un coin de ciel bleu** a patch of blue sky ▸ **dans un coin de ma mémoire** *fig* in a corner of my memory ▸ **un coin perdu** [isolé] an isolated spot / [arriéré] a godforsaken place *péj* ▸ **coin cuisine** kitchen area ▸ **le petit coin** *fam* the little boys'/girls' room

3. [outil] wedge

4. [matrice] die.

coincé, ***e*** [kwɛ̃se] **adj** *fam* [personne] hung up.

coincer [16] [kwɛ̃se] **vt 1.** [bloquer] to jam **2.** *fam* [prendre] to nab / *fig* to catch out *UK* **3.** [acculer] to corner, to trap.

◆ ***se coincer*** **vp** to get stuck.

coïncidence [kɔɛ̃sidɑ̃s] **nf** coincidence.

coïncider [3] [kɔɛ̃side] **vi** to coincide.

coing [kwɛ̃] **nm** [fruit] quince.

coït [kɔit] **nm** coitus.

coite [kwat] **f** ➤ ***coi***.

coke [kɔk] ■ **nf** [cocaïne] coke.

■ **nm** [combustible] coke.

col [kɔl] **nm 1.** [de vêtement] collar ▸ **faux col** detachable collar ▸ **col roulé** polo neck *UK*, turtleneck *US* **2.** [partie étroite] neck **3.** ANAT **: col du fémur** neck of the thighbone *ou* femur ▸ **col de l'utérus** cervix, neck of the womb **4.** GÉOGR pass.

col. abr de ***colonne***.

colchique [kɔlʃik] **nm** [plante] autumn crocus.

coléoptère [kɔleɔptɛr] **nm** beetle.

colère [kɔlɛr] **nf 1.** [irritation] anger ▸ **être/se mettre en colère** to be/get angry ▸ **ravaler sa colère** to keep one's temper **2.** [accès d'humeur] fit of anger *ou* rage ▸ **piquer une colère** to fly into a rage.

coléreux, euse [kɔlerø, øz], ***colérique*** [kɔlerik] **adj** [tempérament] fiery / [personne] quick-tempered.

colifichet [kɔlifiʃɛ] **nm** [bijou] trinket.

colimaçon [kɔlimasɔ̃] ◆ ***en colimaçon*** **loc adv** spiral.

colin [kɔlɛ̃] **nm** [merlu] hake.

colin-maillard [kɔlɛ̃majar] (pl **colin-maillards**) **nm** blind man's buff.

colique [kɔlik] **nf 1.** *(gén pl)* [douleur] colic *(U)* **2.** [diarrhée] diarrhoea *UK*, diarrhea *US*.

colis [kɔli] **nm** parcel *UK*, package *US*.

colistier, ère [kɔlistje, ɛr] **nm, f** fellow candidate.

coll. **1.** abr de ***collection*** **2.** (abr de ***collaborateurs***) ▸ **et coll.** et al.

collabo [kɔlabo] **nmf** *péj* & HIST collaborator.

collaborateur, trice [kɔlabɔratœr, tris] **nm, f 1.** [employé] colleague **2.** [de journal] contributor **3.** HIST collaborator.

collaboration [kɔlabɔrasjɔ̃] **nf** collaboration.

collaborer [3] [kɔlabɔre] **vi 1.** [coopérer, sous l'Occupation] to collaborate **2.** [participer] **: collaborer à** to contribute to.

collage [kɔlaʒ] **nm 1.** [action] sticking, gluing **2.** ART collage.

collant, e [kɔlɑ̃, ɑ̃t] **adj 1.** [substance] sticky **2.** [vêtement] close-fitting, tight-fitting **3.** *fam* [personne] clinging, clingy.

◆ ***collant*** **nm** tights *pl UK*, panty hose *pl US*.

collatéral, e, aux [kɔlateral, o] ■ **adj 1.** ANAT collateral **2.** ARCHIT side *(avant n)* **3.** DR collateral.

■ **nm, f** DR collateral.

collation [kɔlasjɔ̃] **nf** [repas] snack.

colle [kɔl] **nf 1.** [substance] glue **2.** [question] poser ▸ **poser une colle à qqn** to set sb a (real) poser **3.** [SCOL - interrogation] test / [- retenue] detention ▸ **avoir une heure de colle** to get an hour's detention.

collecte [kɔlɛkt] **nf** collection.

collecteur, trice [kɔlɛktœr, tris] ■ **adj : égout collecteur** main sewer.

■ **nm, f : collecteur de fonds** fundraiser ▸ **collecteur d'impôts** tax collector.

collectif, ive [kɔlɛktif, iv] **adj 1.** [responsabilité, travail] collective **2.** [billet, voyage] group *(avant n)*.

◆ ***collectif*** **nm 1.** [équipe] team **2.** LING collective noun **3.** FIN **: collectif budgétaire** collection of budgetary measures.

collection [kɔlɛksjɔ̃] **nf 1.** [d'objets, de livres, de vêtements] collection ▸ **faire la collection de** to collect **2.** COMM line.

collectionner [3] [kɔlɛksjɔne] **vt** *litt* & *fig* to collect.

collectionneur, euse [kɔlɛksjɔnœr, øz] **nm, f** collector.

collectivité [kɔlɛktivite] **nf** community ▸ **les collectivités locales** ADMIN the local communities ▸ **collectivité territoriale** ADMIN (partially) autonomous region.

collège [kɔlɛʒ] **nm 1.** SCOL ≃ secondary school ▸ **le Collège de France** the Collège de France **2.** [de personnes] college ▸ **collège électoral** electoral college.

CULTURE

Collège

In France, the **collège** is a state secondary school for children aged 11 to 15. Students begin in **sixième** and finish in **troisième**. At the end of **troisième** they take an exam known as the **brevet des collèges**, which can also be passed simply on the basis of grades achieved throughout the year. Successful students may then go on to study for the **baccalauréat** at a **lycée**. In 1975 the Ministry of Education instituted the **collège unique**, an initiative to offer all students in this age range the same programme of study to widen access to education. But accomplishing this has proved difficult and there have already been several reforms.

collégial, e, aux [kɔleʒjal, o] **adj** collegial, collegiate.

◆ ***collégiale*** **nf** collegiate church.

collégien, enne [kɔleʒjɛ̃, ɛn] **nm, f** schoolboy (schoolgirl).

collègue [kɔlɛg] **nmf** colleague.

coller [3] [kɔle] ■ **vt 1.** [fixer - affiche] to stick (up) [- timbre] to stick **2.** [appuyer] to press ▸ **coller son nez à la vitre** to press one's face to the window **3.** INFORM to paste **4.** *fam* [mettre] to stick, to dump **5.** SCOL to give (a) detention to, to keep behind **6.** [embarrasser] to catch out *UK* **7.** *fam* [suivre] to cling to ▸ **la voiture nous colle de trop près** the car's keeping too close to us **8.** *fa*

[donner] : **coller qqch à qqn** to give sthg to sb, to give sb sthg ▸ **je vais lui coller mon poing sur la figure!** I'm going to thump him on the nose!
■ vi **1.** [adhérer] to stick ▸ **avoir les doigts qui collent** to have sticky fingers **2.** [être adapté] : **coller à qqch** [vêtement] to cling to sthg / *fig* to fit in with sthg, to adhere to sthg ▸ **coller à la peau de qqn** *litt* to cling to sb / *fig* to be inherent to *ou* innate in sb ▸ **une émission qui colle à l'actualité** a programme that keeps up with current events **3.** *fam* [bien se passer] to be *ou* go OK ▸ **ça colle!** it's OK! ▸ **ça ne colle pas entre eux** they're not hitting it off very well **4.** [suivre] : **coller à** to stick close to.
◆ ***se coller*** vp **1.** *fam* [subir] to get landed with ▸ **s'y coller** *fam* [s'atteler à un problème, une tâche] to set about it, to get stuck in *UK* **2.** [se plaquer] : **se coller contre qqn/qqch** to press o.s. against sb/sthg ▸ **se coller à *ou* contre un mur pour ne pas être vu** to press o.s. up against a wall in order not to be seen.

collerette [kɔlrɛt] **nf** **1.** [de vêtement] ruff **2.** [de tuyau] flange.

collet [kɔlɛ] **nm** **1.** [de vêtement] collar ▸ **mettre la main au collet de qqn** to grab sb by the collar *ou* the scruff of the neck ▸ **être collet monté** [affecté, guindé] to be strait-laced **2.** [piège] snare.

colleur, euse [kɔlœr, øz] **nm, f : colleur d'affiches** bill-sticker, bill poster.
◆ ***colleuse*** **nf** **1.** CINÉ splicer, splicing unit **2.** [imprimerie] pasting machine **3.** PHOTO mounting press.

collier [kɔlje] **nm** **1.** [bijou] necklace ▸ **collier de perles** pearl necklace **2.** [d'animal] collar **3.** [barbe] *fringe of beard along the jawline.*

collimateur [kɔlimatœr] **nm : avoir qqn dans le collimateur** *fam* to have sb in one's sights.

colline [kɔlin] **nf** hill.

collision [kɔlizjɔ̃] **nf** [choc] collision, crash ▸ **entrer en collision avec** to collide with.

colloque [kɔlɔk] **nm** colloquium.

collusion [kɔlyzjɔ̃] **nf** collusion.

collyre [kɔlir] **nm** eye lotion.

colmater [3] [kɔlmate] **vt** **1.** [fuite] to plug, to seal off **2.** [brèche] to fill, to seal.

colo [kɔlo] **nf** *fam* children's holiday camp *UK*, summer camp *US*.

colocataire [kɔlɔkatɛr] **nmf** ADMIN co-tenant / [gen] flatmate *UK*, roommate.

colombage [kɔlɔ̃baʒ] **nm** half-timbering ▸ **à colombages** half-timbered.

colombe [kɔlɔ̃b] **nf** dove.

Colombie [kɔlɔ̃bi] **nf : la Colombie** Colombia.

colombien, enne [kɔlɔ̃bjɛ̃, ɛn] **adj** Colombian.
◆ ***Colombien, enne*** **nm, f** Colombian.

Colombo [kɔlɔ̃bo] **npr** Colombo.

colon [kɔlɔ̃] **nm** settler.

côlon [kolɔ̃] **nm** colon.

colonel [kɔlɔnɛl] **nm** colonel.

colonelle [kɔlɔnɛl] **nf** colonel's wife.

colonial, e, aux [kɔlɔnjal, o] **adj** colonial.

colonialisme [kɔlɔnjalism] **nm** colonialism.

colonialiste [kɔlɔnjalist] **nmf & adj** colonialist.

colonie [kɔlɔni] **nf** **1.** [territoire] colony **2.** [d'expatriés] community ▸ **colonie de vacances** children's holiday *UK ou* summer camp *US*.

colonisation [kɔlɔnizasjɔ̃] **nf** colonization.

coloniser [3] [kɔlɔnize] **vt** *litt & fig* to colonize.

colonne [kɔlɔn] **nf** column ▸ **en colonne** in a line *ou* column.
◆ ***colonne vertébrale*** **nf** spine, spinal column.

colorant, e [kɔlɔrɑ̃, ɑ̃t] **adj** colouring *UK*, coloring *US*.
◆ ***colorant*** **nm** colouring *UK*, coloring *US* ▸ **colorant alimentaire** food colouring *UK ou* coloring *US*.

coloration [kɔlɔrasjɔ̃] **nf** colour *UK*, color *US*, colouring *UK*, coloring *US*.

coloré, e [kɔlɔre] **adj** **1.** [de couleur] coloured *UK*, colored *US* **2.** *fig* [diversifié, imagé] colourful *UK*, colorful *US*.

colorer [3] [kɔlɔre] **vt** [teindre] to colour *UK*, to color *US* ▸ **colorer qqch de** *fig* to colour *UK ou* color *US* sthg with.
◆ ***se colorer*** **vp** [les cheveux] to colour *UK*, to color *US*, to dye ▸ **se colorer de** *fig* to be coloured *UK ou* colored *US* with.

coloriage [kɔlɔrjaʒ] **nm** **1.** [action] colouring *UK*, coloring *US* **2.** [dessin] drawing.

colorié, e [kɔlɔrje] **adj** colourful *UK*, colorful *US*, coloured *UK*, colored *US*.

colorier [9] [kɔlɔrje] **vt** to colour in *UK*, to color in *US*.

coloris [kɔlɔri] **nm** shade.

colorisation [kɔlɔrizasjɔ̃] **nf** CINÉ colourization *UK*, colorization *US*.

coloriser [3] [kɔlɔrize] **vt** CINÉ to colourize *UK*, to colorize *US*.

colossal, e, aux [kɔlɔsal, o] **adj** colossal, huge.

colosse [kɔlɔs] **nm** **1.** [homme] giant **2.** [statue] colossus.

colportage [kɔlpɔrtaʒ] **nm** hawking.

colporter [3] [kɔlpɔrte] **vt** [marchandise] to hawk / [information] to spread.
◆ ***se colporter*** **vp** [information] to spread.

colporteur, euse [kɔlpɔrtœr, øz] **nm, f** **1.** [de marchandises] hawker **2.** [de ragots] gossip.

coltiner [3] [kɔltine] ◆ ***se coltiner*** **vp** *fam* to be landed with.

colza [kɔlza] **nm** rape(seed).

coma [kɔma] **nm** coma ▸ **être dans le coma** to be in a coma.

comateux, euse [kɔmatø, øz] ■ **adj** comatose.
■ **nm, f** person in a coma.

combat [kɔ̃ba] **nm** **1.** [bataille] battle, fight ▸ **mettre/être hors de combat** to put/be out of the fight / *fig* to put/be out of the game ▸ **combat aérien/naval** air/sea battle ▸ **combat rapproché** close combat ▸ **des combats de rue** street fighting ▸ **avion de combat** warplane, fighter plane ▸ **tenue de combat** battledress **2.** *fig* [lutte] struggle ▸ **son long combat contre le cancer** his long struggle against cancer **3.** SPORT fight ▸ **combat de boxe** boxing match.

combatif, ive [kɔ̃batif, iv] **adj** [humeur] fighting *(avant n)* / [troupes] willing to fight.

combativité [kɔ̃bativite] **nf** fighting spirit.

combattant, e [kɔ̃batɑ̃, ɑ̃t] ■ **adj** fighting *(avant n).*
■ **nm, f** [en guerre] combatant / [dans bagarre] fighter ▸ **ancien combattant** veteran.

combattre [83] [kɔ̃batr] ■ **vt** *litt* & *fig* to fight (against).
■ **vi** to fight.

combattu, e [kɔ̃baty] **pp** ➤ ***combattre***.

combien [kɔ̃bjɛ̃] ■ **conj** how much ▸ **combien de** [nombre] how many / [quantité] how much ▸ **combien de temps?** how long? ▸ **combien de fois?** how many times?, how often? ▸ **ça fait combien?** [prix] how much is that? / [longueur, hauteur *etc*] how long/high *etc* is it? ▸ **combien coûte ce livre?** how much is this book?, how much does this book cost? ▸ **l'indice a augmenté de combien?** how much has the rate gone up by? ▸ **de combien est le déficit?** how large is the deficit? ▸ **combien sont-ils?** how many of them are there? ▸ **combien tu pèses?** how much do you weigh? ▸ **combien tu mesures?** how tall are you?
■ **adv** how (much).
■ **nm inv : le combien sommes-nous?** what date is it? ▸ **tous les combien?** how often?

combientième [kɔ̃bjɛ̃tjɛm] ■ **nmf : il est le combientième?** where did he come?
■ **adj : c'est le combientième examen qu'on passe?** that makes how many exams we've taken?

combinaison [kɔ̃binɛzɔ̃] **nf** **1.** [d'éléments] combination **2.** [de femme] slip **3.** [vêtement - de mécanicien] boiler suit *UK*, overalls *pl UK*, overall *US* / [- de ski] ski suit **4.** [de coffre] combination **5.** [manœuvre] scheme.

combine [kɔ̃bin] **nf** *fam* trick.

combiné [kɔ̃bine] **nm** receiver.

combiner [3] [kɔ̃bine] **vt** **1.** [arranger] to combine **2.** [organiser] to devise.
◆ ***se combiner*** **vp** to turn out.

comble [kɔ̃bl] ■ **nm** height ▸ **le comble de** the height of ▸ **c'est un** *ou* **le comble!** that beats everything! ▸ **être au comble du désespoir** to be in the depths of despair ▸ **être au comble du bonheur** to be overjoyed.
■ **adj** packed.
◆ ***combles*** **nmpl** attic *sg*, loft *sg* ▸ **loger sous les combles** to live in an attic.

combler [3] [kɔ̃ble] **vt** **1.** [gâter] to spoil ▸ **combler qqn de** to shower sb with **2.** [boucher] to fill in ▸ **combler un trou** to fill a hole **3.** [déficit] to make good / [lacune] to fill.

combustible [kɔ̃bystibl] ■ **nm** fuel.
■ **adj** combustible.

combustion [kɔ̃bystjɔ̃] **nf** combustion.

COMECON, Comecon [kɔmɛkɔn] (abr de ***Council for Mutual Economic Assistance***) **nm** COMECON.

comédie [kɔmedi] **nf** **1.** CINÉ & THÉÂTRE comedy ▸ **la Comédie-Française** the Comédie Française ▸ **comédie musicale** musical ▸ **jouer la comédie** *fig* to put on an act **2.** [complication] palaver.

comédien, enne [kɔmedjɛ̃, ɛn] ■ **nm, f** [acteur] actor (f actress) / *fig* & *péj* phony, phoney *UK*.
■ **adj** *fig* & *péj* **: être comédien** to be a phony *ou* phoney *UK*.

> FAUX AMIS / FALSE FRIENDS
> **comédien**
> Comedian is not a translation of the French word *comédien*. Comedian is translated by *comique*.
> ▸ He's one of Britain's finest comedians / *C'est un des meilleurs comiques de Grande-Bretagne*

COMES, Comes [kɔmɛs] (abr de ***Commissariat à l'énergie solaire***) **nm** *solar energy commission*.

comestible [kɔmɛstibl] **adj** edible.
◆ ***comestibles*** **nmpl** food *(U)*.

comète [kɔmɛt] **nf** comet ▸ **tirer des plans sur la comète** *fig* to count one's chickens (before they are hatched).

comice [kɔmis] **nm : comice agricole** *local farmers' meeting*.

comique [kɔmik] ■ **nm** **1.** THÉÂTRE comic, comedian (f comedienne) ▸ **c'est un grand comique** he's a great comic actor **2.** [genre] **: le comique** comedy.
■ **adj** **1.** [style] comic **2.** [drôle] comical, funny.

> PARONYME / CONFUSABLE
> **comique**
> Quand vous traduisez **comique**, utilisez *comic* pour parler du genre théâtral, et *comical* pour désigner ce qui est drôle.

comité [kɔmite] **nm** committee ▸ **en petit comité** *fig* with a few close friends ▸ **Comité européen de normalisation** European Standards Commission ▸ **comité d'entreprise** works council *UK (also organizing leisure activities).*

CULTURE

Comité d'entreprise

Every French company with 50 or more employees must have a **comité d'entreprise**, or CE. Made up of members of the company's different unions and presided over by the firm's CEO, this group keeps a close eye on the company's day-to-day functioning and defends employees' interests when called upon. It can also help employees in financial difficulty by offering them help with accommodation or other assistance, sometimes even extending its aid to the worker's family. The CE organizes leisure activities and offers cinema tickets, trips, and the like at reduced prices.

commandant [kɔmɑ̃dɑ̃] **nm** commander ▸ **commandant de bord** AÉRON captain.

commande [kɔmɑ̃d] **nf 1.** [de marchandises] order ▸ **passer une commande** to place an order ▸ **passer commande de 10 véhicules** to order 10 vehicles ▸ **sur commande** to order ▸ **disponible sur commande** available on request ▸ **le garçon a pris la commande** the waiter took the order ▸ **payer à la commande** to pay while ordering ▸ **commande renouvelée** repeat order **2.** TECHNOL control ▸ **être aux commandes (de), tenir les commandes (de)** [d'avion, de machine] to be at the controls (of) / *fig* & NAUT to be at the helm (of) ▸ **commande à distance** remote control **3.** INFORM command ▸ **commande de contact** contact operate ▸ **commande d'interruption** break feature ▸ **commande numérique** digital control ▸ **commande vocale** voice-operated.

commandement [kɔmɑ̃dmɑ̃] **nm** command ▸ **les dix commandements** RELIG the Ten Commandments.

commander [3] [kɔmɑ̃de] ■ **vt 1.** [ordonner] to order, to command **2.** MIL to command **3.** [contrôler] to operate, to control **4.** COMM to order.

■ **vi** to be in charge ▸ **commander à qqn de faire qqch** to order sb to do sthg.

◆ ***se commander*** **vp : ça ne se commande pas** *fig* it is uncontrollable.

commanditaire [kɔmɑ̃ditɛr] ■ **nm** DR backer.

■ **adj** DR **: (associé) commanditaire** sleeping partner *UK*, silent partner *US*.

commandite [kɔmɑ̃dit] **nf** share (of limited partners) ▸ **commandite par actions** partnership limited by shares.

commanditer [3] [kɔmɑ̃dite] **vt 1.** [entreprise] to finance **2.** [meurtre] to put up the money for **3.** [tournoi] to sponsor.

commando [kɔmɑ̃do] **nm** commando (unit).

comme [kɔm] ■ **conj 1.** [introduisant une comparaison] like ▸ **il sera médecin comme son père** he'll become a doctor (just) like his father ▸ **nous nagerons comme quand nous étions en Sicile** we'll go swimming as *ou* like we did when we were in Sicily ▸ **il se mit à pleurer comme pour m'émouvoir** he started to cry as though to move me ▸ **il ne m'a pas injurié, mais c'était tout comme** he didn't actually insult me, but it was close *ou* as good as **2.** [exprimant la manière] as ▸ **fais comme il te plaira** do as you wish ▸ **comme tu le dis** as you say ▸ **il était comme fou** he was like a madman ▸ **comme prévu/convenu** as planned/agreed ▸ **comme bon vous semble** as you think best ▸ **il est comme ça, on ne le changera pas!** that's the way he is; you won't change him! ▸ **comme ci comme ça** *fam* so-so ▸ **tu t'entends bien avec lui? – comme ci comme ça** do you get on with him? – sort of *ou* so-so **3.** [tel que] like, such as ▸ **les arbres comme le marronnier** trees such as *ou* like the chestnut ▸ **D comme Denise** D for Denise

4. [en tant que] as ▸ **comme professeur, il est nul** as a teacher he's hopeless ▸ **qu'est-ce que vous avez comme vin?** what (kind of) wine do you have?

5. [ainsi que] **: les filles comme les garçons iront jouer au foot** both girls and boys will play football ▸ **l'un comme l'autre sont très gentils** the one is as kind as the other, they are equally kind

6. [introduisant une cause] as, since ▸ **comme il pleuvait, nous sommes rentrés** as it was raining, we went back.

■ **adv excl** [marquant l'intensité] how ▸ **comme tu as grandi!** how you've grown! ▸ **comme c'est difficile!** it's so difficult! ▸ **regarde comme il nage bien!** (just) look what a good swimmer he is!, (just) look how well he swims!

◆ ***comme si*** **loc conj** as if ▸ **elle faisait comme si de rien n'était** she pretended (that) there was nothing wrong, she pretended (that) nothing had happened ▸ **il se conduit comme s'il était encore étudiant** he behaves as if he was still a student.

◆ ***comme quoi*** **loc adv** to the effect that ▸ **comme quoi, on ne peut pas tout prévoir** which just goes to show you can't think of everything.

◆ ***quelque chose comme*** **loc adv** [à peu près] something like ▸ **cela fait quelque chose comme 2 000 euros** that comes to something like 2,000 euros.

commémoration [kɔmemɔrasjɔ̃] **nf** commemoration.

commémorer [3] [kɔmemɔre] **vt** to commemorate.

commencement [kɔmɑ̃smɑ̃] **nm** beginning, start ▸ **au commencement** at first, in the beginning.

commencer [16] [kɔmɑ̃se] ■ **vt 1.** [entreprendre] to begin, to start ▸ **vous commencez le travail demain** you start (work) tomorrow ▸ **nous allons commencer notre descente vers Milan** we are beginning our descent towards Milan **2.** [être au début de] to begin ▸ **c'est son numéro qui commence le spectacle** her routine begins the show, the show begins with her routine.

■ **vi** to start, to begin ▸ **ça commence bien!** *litt* & *iron* things are off to a good start! ▸ **tu commences à m'énerver!** you're getting on my nerves! ▸ **commencer à faire qqch** to begin *ou* start to do sthg, to begin *ou* start doing sthg ▸ **il commence à pleuvoir/neiger** it's started to rain/to snow ▸ **commencer par faire qqch** to begin *ou* start by doing sthg ▸ **commence par enlever les couvertures** first, take the blankets off ▸ **commencer mal/bien** to start badly/well ▸ **pour commencer, du saumon** to start the meal *ou* as a first course, salmon ▸ **que tout le monde contribue, à commencer par toi!** let everyone give something, starting with you!

comment [kɔmɑ̃] ■ **adv interr** how ▸ **comment?** what? ▸ **comment ça va?** how are you? ▸ **comment cela?** how come?
■ **adv excl : comment donc!** of course!, sure thing! *US* ▸ **et comment!** *fam* and how!, absolutely!
■ **nm inv** ➤ ***pourquoi***.

commentaire [kɔmɑ̃tɛr] **nm 1.** [explication] commentary ▸ **commentaire de la rencontre, Pierre Pastriot** with live commentary from the stadium, Pierre Pastriot ▸ **commentaire de texte : faire un commentaire de texte** to comment on a text **2.** [observation] comment ▸ **avez-vous des commentaires?** any comments *ou* remarks? ▸ **faire un commentaire** to make a remark *ou* a comment ▸ **je te dispense** *ou* **je me passe de tes commentaires** I can do without your remarks ▸ **sans commentaire!** enough said!

commentateur, ***trice*** [kɔmɑ̃tatœr, tris] **nm, f** RADIO & TV commentator ▸ **commentateur sportif** sports commentator.

commenter [3] [kɔmɑ̃te] **vt** to comment on.

commérage [kɔmeraʒ] **nm** *péj* gossip *(U)*.

commerçant, ***e*** [kɔmɛrsɑ̃, ɑ̃t] ■ **adj 1.** [rue] shopping *(avant n)* / [quartier] commercial ▸ **un quartier très commerçant** a good shopping area **2.** [personne] business-minded ▸ **il a l'esprit commerçant** he's a born salesman.
■ **nm, f** shopkeeper *UK*, storekeeper *US* ▸ **commerçant de détail** retail trader ▸ **commerçant en gros** wholesale trader ▸ **petit commerçant** small trader.

commerce [kɔmɛrs] **nm 1.** [achat et vente] commerce, trade ▸ **cela fait marcher le commerce** it's good for business ▸ **faire du commerce avec qqn/un pays** to trade with sb/a country ▸ **commerce bilatéral** bilateral trade ▸ **dans le commerce** in the shops *UK ou* stores *US* ▸ **cela ne se trouve plus dans le commerce** this item is no longer sold ▸ **commerce de gros/détail** wholesale/retail trade ▸ **commerce électronique** electronic commerce, e-commerce ▸ **commerce équitable** fair trade ▸ **commerce extérieur** foreign trade **2.** [magasin] business ▸ **le petit commerce** small shopkeepers *pl* ▸ **tenir un commerce** to run a business
▸▸ **être d'un commerce agréable** *sout* to be easy to get on with.

commercial, ***e***, ***aux*** [kɔmɛrsjal, o] ■ **adj** [entreprise, valeur] commercial / [politique] trade *(avant n)*.
■ **nm, f** marketing man (f woman).

commercialisable [kɔmɛʀsjalizabl] **adj** [objet, produit] marketable.

commercialisation [kɔmɛrsjalizasjɔ̃] **nf** marketing.

commercialiser [3] [kɔmɛrsjalize] **vt** to market.

commère [kɔmɛr] **nf** *péj* gossip.

commets ➤ ***commettre***.

commettre [84] [kɔmɛtr] **vt** to commit.
◆ ***se commettre*** **vp** *sout* **: se commettre avec** to become involved with.

commis, ***e*** [kɔmi, iz] **pp** ➤ ***commettre***.
◆ ***commis*** **nm** assistant ▸ **commis voyageur** commercial traveller *UK ou* traveler *US*.

commisération [kɔmizerasjɔ̃] **nf** *sout* commiseration.

commissaire [kɔmisɛr] **nm** commissioner ▸ **commissaire aux comptes** auditor ▸ **commissaire de police** (police) superintendent *UK*, (police) captain *US*.

commissaire-priseur [kɔmisɛrprizœr] (pl **commissaires-priseurs**) **nm** auctioneer.

commissariat [kɔmisarja] **nm : commissariat de police** police station.

commission [kɔmisjɔ̃] **nf 1.** [délégation] commission, committee ▸ **commission du budget** budget committee ▸ **commission d'enquête** commission of inquiry *UK*, fact-finding committee *US* ▸ **la Commission nationale de l'informatique et des libertés** *watchdog committee supervising the application of data protection legislation* ▸ **commission paritaire** joint commission ▸ **commission parlementaire** parliamentary committee **2.** [message] message ▸ **n'oublie pas de lui faire la commission** don't forget to give him the message **3.** [rémunération] commission ▸ **commission d'affacturage** FIN factoring charges ▸ **commission de compte** account fee.
◆ ***commissions*** **nfpl** shopping *(U)* ▸ **faire les commissions** to do the shopping.

commissionnaire [kɔmisjɔnɛr] **nm** [intermédiaire] agent ▸ **commissionnaire en douane** customs agent *ou* broker ▸ **commissionnaire de transport** forwarding agent ▸ **commissionnaire en gros** factor / [d'un message] messenger / [d'un objet] delivery boy *ou* man.

commissure [kɔmisyr] **nf : la commissure des lèvres** the corner of the mouth.

commode [kɔmɔd] ■ **nf** chest of drawers.
■ **adj 1.** [pratique - système] convenient / [- outil] handy **2.** [aimable] **: pas commode** awkward **3.** [facile] easy.

commodité [kɔmɔdite] **nf** convenience.
◆ ***commodités*** **nfpl** [conforts] comforts.

commotion [kɔmosjɔ̃] **nf** MÉD shock ▸ **commotion cérébrale** concussion.

commuer [7] [kɔmɥe] **vt : commuer qqch en** to commute sthg to.

commun, ***e*** [kɔmœ̃, yn] **adj 1.** [gén] common / [décision, effort] joint / [salle, jardin] shared ▸ **tous d'un commun accord ont décidé que...** they decided unanimously that... ▸ **commun à** common to ▸ **le court de tennis est commun à tous les propriétaires** the tennis court is the common property of all the residents ▸ **avoir qqch en commun** to have sthg in common ▸ **faire qqch en commun** to do sthg together ▸ **c'est sans commune mesure avec...** there's no comparison with... ▸ **la vie commune** [conjugale] conjugal life, the life of a couple **2.** [courant] usual, common ▸ **il est d'un courage peu commun** he's uncommonly *ou* exceptionally brave ▸ **un nom peu commun** a very unusual name.
◆ ***commun*** **nm : le commun** the ordinary ▸ **hors du commun** out of the ordinary ▸ **le commun des mortels** ordinary people.
◆ ***commune*** **nf** town ▸ **la commune et ses alentours** [en ville] ≃ the urban district / [à la campagne] ≃ the rura

district ▸ **c'est la commune qui paie** the local authority *OU* the council *UK* is paying.
◆ ***Commune*** **nf** HIST Paris Commune.
◆ ***communs*** **nmpl** outhouses.

communal, e, aux [kɔmynal, o] **adj** [école] local / [bâtiments] council *(avant n).*

communautaire [kɔmynotɛr] **adj** community *(avant n).*

communauté [kɔmynote] **nf 1.** [groupe] community ▸ **vivre en communauté** to live communally **2.** [de sentiments, d'idées] identity **3.** POLIT : **la Communauté européenne** the European Community ▸ **la Communauté d'États indépendants** the Commonwealth of Independent States.

commune ➤ ***commun.***

communément [kɔmynemɑ̃] **adv** commonly.

communiant, e [kɔmynjɑ̃, ɑ̃t] **nm, f** communicant ▸ **premier communiant** *child taking first communion.*

communicatif, ive [kɔmynikatif, iv] **adj 1.** [rire, éternuement] infectious **2.** [personne] communicative.

communication [kɔmynikasjɔ̃] **nf 1.** [gén] communication ▸ **communication en entreprise** communication ▸ **communication de masse** mass media ▸ **faire une communication sur l'atome** to deliver a lecture on the atom ▸ **il a des problèmes de communication (avec les autres)** he has problems communicating with *OU* relating to people ▸ **moyens de communication** means of communication **2.** TÉLÉCOM : **communication (téléphonique)** (phone) call ▸ **être en communication avec qqn** to be talking to sb ▸ **obtenir la communication** to get through ▸ **recevoir/prendre une communication** to receive/take a (phone) call ▸ **je vous passe la communication** I'll put you through ▸ **communication interurbaine** long-distance (phone) call ▸ **communication en PCV** reverse-charge call *UK*, collect call *US*.

communier [9] [kɔmynje] **vi** RELIG to take communion ▸ **communier (dans)** *fig* to be united (in).

communion [kɔmynjɔ̃] **nf** RELIG communion ▸ **être en communion avec** *fig* & *littéraire* to commune with.

communiqué [kɔmynike] **nm** communiqué ▸ **communiqué de presse** press release.

communiquer [3] [kɔmynike] ▪ **vt : communiquer qqch à** [information, sentiment] to pass on *OU* communicate sthg to / [chaleur] to transmit sthg to / [maladie] to pass sthg on to.
▪ **vi : communiquer avec** to communicate with.
◆ ***se communiquer*** **vp** [se propager] to spread.

communisme [kɔmynism] **nm** communism.

communiste [kɔmynist] **nmf** & **adj** communist.

commutateur [kɔmytatœr] **nm** switch.

commutation [kɔmytasjɔ̃] **nf 1.** DR : **commutation de peine** commutation of sentence **2.** TECHNOL switching.

Comores [kɔmɔr] **nfpl : les Comores** the Comoro Islands, the Comoros ▸ **aux Comores** in the Comoro Islands.

comorien, enne [kɔmɔrjɛ̃, ɛn] **adj** Comoran, Comorian.
◆ ***Comorien, enne*** **nm, f** Comoran, Comorian.

compact, e [kɔ̃pakt] **adj 1.** [épais, dense] dense **2.** [petit] compact.
◆ ***compact*** **nm** [disque laser] compact disc, CD.

compagne ➤ ***compagnon.***

compagnie [kɔ̃paɲi] **nf 1.** [gén & COMM] company ▸ **être en bonne/mauvaise compagnie** to be in good/bad company ▸ **fausser compagnie à qqn** to slip away from sb ▸ **tenir compagnie à qqn** to keep sb company ▸ **elle avait un chien pour toute compagnie** her dog was her only companion ▸ **et compagnie** and company / *iron* and the rest ▸ **tout ça, c'est mensonge/arnaque et compagnie** *fam fig* that's nothing but a pack of lies/a swindle ▸ **compagnie aérienne** airline (company) ▸ **compagnie d'assurances** insurance company ▸ **compagnie de navigation** shipping company ▸ **en compagnie de** in the company of ▸ **compagnie (théâtrale)** (theatre) group *OU* company *OU* troupe **2.** [assemblée] gathering.

compagnon [kɔ̃paɲɔ̃], ***compagne*** [kɔ̃paɲ] **nm, f** companion.
◆ ***compagnon*** **nm** HIST journeyman.

comparable [kɔ̃parabl] **adj** comparable.

comparaison [kɔ̃parɛzɔ̃] **nf** [parallèle] comparison ▸ **en comparaison de, par comparaison avec** compared with, in *OU* by comparison with.

comparaître [91] [kɔ̃parɛtr] **vi** DR : **comparaître (devant)** to appear (before).

comparatif, ive [kɔ̃paratif, iv] **adj** comparative.
◆ ***comparatif*** **nm** GRAMM comparative.

comparativement [kɔ̃parativmɑ̃] **adv** comparatively.

comparé, e [kɔ̃pare] **adj** comparative / [mérites] relative.

comparer [3] [kɔ̃pare] **vt 1.** [confronter] : **comparer (avec)** to compare (with) ▸ **comparer (à)** to compare to *OU* with **2.** [assimiler] : **comparer qqch à** to compare *OU* liken sthg to.

COMMENT EXPRIMER...

la comparaison

She is more intelligent than her sister / Elle est plus intelligente que sa sœur
I think the first suggestion was better / Je crois que la première idée était meilleure
This book is not as good as his last one / Son dernier livre n'est pas aussi bon que le précédent
They're (both) as lazy as each other / Ils sont aussi paresseux l'un que l'autre
It's like this one, only smaller / Il est comme celui-ci, mais en plus petit
This year's results are pretty good compared with last year's / Les résultats de cette année sont plutôt bons comparés à ceux de l'année dernière

comparse [kɔ̃pars] **nmf** *péj* stooge.

compartiment [kɔ̃partimɑ̃] **nm** compartment.

compartimenter [3] [kɔ̃partimɑ̃te] **vt** [meuble] to partition / *fig* [administration] to compartmentalize.

comparu, e [kɔ̃pary] **pp** ➤ ***comparaître***.

comparution [kɔ̃parysjɔ̃] **nf** DR appearance.

compas [kɔ̃pa] **nm 1.** [de dessin] pair of compasses, compasses *pl* **2.** NAUT compass.

compassé, e [kɔ̃pase] **adj** *sout* staid, stuffy.

compassion [kɔ̃pasjɔ̃] **nf** *sout* compassion.

compatibilité [kɔ̃patibilite] **nf** compatibility ▸ **compatibilité sanguine** blood-group compatibility *ou* matching.

compatible [kɔ̃patibl] **adj** INFORM **: compatible (avec)** compatible (with) ▸ **compatible PC** PC-compatible ▸ **compatible Mac** Mac-compatible ▸ **compatible vers le haut/le bas** upward-/downward-compatible.

compatir [32] [kɔ̃patir] **vi : compatir (à)** to sympathize (with).

compatissant, e [kɔ̃patisɑ̃, ɑ̃t] **adj** sympathetic.

compatriote [kɔ̃patrijɔt] **nmf** compatriot, fellow countryman (f countrywoman).

compensation [kɔ̃pɑ̃sasjɔ̃] **nf 1.** [dédommagement] compensation ▸ **en compensation** in compensation **2.** [équilibrage] balance.

compensé, e [kɔ̃pɑ̃se] **adj** built-up.

compenser [3] [kɔ̃pɑ̃se] ■ **vt** [perte] to compensate *ou* make up for / [chèque] to clear.
■ **vi** to compensate, to make up.

compère [kɔ̃pɛr] **nm 1.** [complice - d'un camelot] accomplice / [- d'un artiste] stooge **2.** LITTÉR **: (mon) compère le lapin** Mister Rabbit.

compétence [kɔ̃petɑ̃s] **nf 1.** [qualification] skill, ability **2.** DR competence ▸ **cela n'entre pas dans mes compétences** that's outside my scope.

compétent, e [kɔ̃petɑ̃, ɑ̃t] **adj 1.** [capable] capable, competent **2.** ADMIN & DR competent ▸ **les autorités compétentes** the relevant authorities.

compétitif, ive [kɔ̃petitif, iv] **adj** competitive.

compétition [kɔ̃petisjɔ̃] **nf** competition ▸ **faire de la compétition** to go in for competitive sport ▸ **compétition automobile** car race.

compétitivité [kɔ̃petitivite] **nf** competitiveness.

compil [kɔ̃pil] **nf** *fam* compilation album.

compilation [kɔ̃pilasjɔ̃] **nf** compilation.

complainte [kɔ̃plɛ̃t] **nf** lament.

complaire [110] [kɔ̃plɛr] **vi : complaire à qqn** *sout* to please sb.
◆ ***se complaire*** **vp : se complaire dans qqch/à faire qqch** to revel in sthg/in doing sthg.

complaisance [kɔ̃plɛzɑ̃s] **nf 1.** [obligeance] kindness **2.** [indulgence] indulgence **3.** [autosatisfaction] **: avec complaisance** indulgently.

complaisant, e [kɔ̃plɛzɑ̃, ɑ̃t] **adj 1.** [aimable] obliging, kind **2.** [indulgent] indulgent.

complément [kɔ̃plemɑ̃] **nm 1.** [gén & GRAMM] complement ▸ **complément d'information** additional *ou* further information ▸ **complément du nom** possessive phrase ▸ **complément d'objet direct** direct object ▸ **complément d'objet indirect** indirect object **2.** [reste] remainder.

complémentaire [kɔ̃plemɑ̃tɛr] **adj 1.** [supplémentaire] supplementary **2.** [caractères, couleurs] complementary.

complet, ète [kɔ̃plɛ, ɛt] **adj 1.** [gén] complete ▸ **c'est complet!** *fam* that's all I/we need ▸ **la famille au (grand) complet** the whole family **2.** [plein] full.
◆ ***complet(-veston)*** **nm** suit.

complètement [kɔ̃plɛtmɑ̃] **adv 1.** [vraiment] absolutely, totally **2.** [entièrement] completely.

compléter [18] [kɔ̃plete] **vt** [gén] to complete, to complement / [somme d'argent] to make up.
◆ ***se compléter*** **vp** to complement one another.

complexe [kɔ̃plɛks] ■ **nm 1.** PSYCHO complex ▸ **avoir des complexes** to have hang-ups, to be hung up ▸ **sans complexe** *ou* **complexes** well-adjusted ▸ **complexe d'infériorité/de supériorité** inferiority/superiority complex **2.** [ensemble] complex ▸ **complexe hospitalier/scolaire/sportif** hospital/school/sports complex ▸ **complexe multisalle** multiplex (cinema).
■ **adj** complex, complicated.

complexé, e [kɔ̃plɛkse] **adj** hung up, mixed up.

complexifier [kɔ̃plɛksifje] **vt** to make (more) complex.

complexité [kɔ̃plɛksite] **nf** complexity.

complication [kɔ̃plikasjɔ̃] **nf** intricacy, complexity.
◆ ***complications*** **nfpl** complications.

complice [kɔ̃plis] ■ **nmf** accomplice.
■ **adj** [sourire, regard, air] knowing.

complicité [kɔ̃plisite] **nf** complicity.

compliment [kɔ̃plimɑ̃] **nm** compliment.

COMMENT EXPRIMER...

la compassion

I'm so sorry / Je suis vraiment désolé
I was so sorry to hear about (the death of) your father / J'ai été vraiment désolé d'apprendre le décès de ton père
Please accept my condolences / Toutes mes condoléances
Our thoughts are with you / Nous sommes de tout cœur avec vous
How awful for you! / Ça doit être terrible pour toi !
You know where I am if you need me / Tu sais où me trouver si tu as besoin de moi
If there's anything I can do / Si je peux faire quoi que ce soit
I sympathize / Je compatis
You poor thing! / Mon/Ma pauvre !
Poor Bill! / Le pauvre Bill !
Get well soon! / Remets-toi vite !

complimenter [3] [kɔ̃plimɑ̃te] **vt** to compliment.

compliqué, e [kɔ̃plike] **adj** [problème] complex, complicated / [personne] complicated.

compliquer [3] [kɔ̃plike] **vt** to complicate.
◆ ***se compliquer*** **vp** to get complicated.

complot [kɔ̃plo] **nm** plot.

comploter [3] [kɔ̃plɔte] **vt & vi** *litt & fig* to plot.

comportement [kɔ̃pɔrtəmɑ̃] **nm** behaviour *UK*, behavior *US* ▸ **comportement d'achat** purchasing behaviour ▸ **comportement du consommateur** consumer behaviour.

comportemental, e, aux [kɔ̃pɔrtəmɑ̃tal, o] **adj** behavioural *UK*, behavioral *US*.

comporter [3] [kɔ̃pɔrte] **vt 1.** [contenir] to include, to contain **2.** [être composé de] to consist of, to be made up of.
◆ ***se comporter*** **vp** to behave.

composant, e [kɔ̃pozɑ̃, ɑ̃t] **adj** constituent, component.
◆ ***composant*** **nm** component.
◆ ***composante*** **nf** component.

composé, e [kɔ̃poze] **adj** compound.
◆ ***composé*** **nm 1.** [mélange] combination **2.** CHIM & LING compound.

composer [3] [kɔ̃poze] ■ **vt 1.** [constituer] to make up, to form ▸ **être composé de** to be made up of **2.** [créer - roman, lettre, poème] to write / [- musique] to compose, to write **3.** [numéro de téléphone] to dial / [code] to key in.
■ **vi** to compromise.
◆ ***se composer*** **vp** [être constitué] **: se composer de** to be composed of, to be made up of.

composite [kɔ̃pozit] ■ **nm** composite.
■ **adj 1.** [disparate - mobilier] assorted, of various types / [- foule] heterogeneous **2.** [matériau] composite.

compositeur, trice [kɔ̃pozitœr, tris] **nm, f 1.** MUS composer **2.** TYPO typesetter.

composition [kɔ̃pozisjɔ̃] **nf 1.** [gén] composition / [de roman] writing, composition **2.** TYPO typesetting **3.** SCOL test ▸ **composition française** French composition **4.** [caractère] **: être de bonne composition** to be good-natured.

compost [kɔ̃pɔst] **nm** compost.

composter [3] [kɔ̃pɔste] **vt** [ticket, billet] to date-stamp.

compote [kɔ̃pɔt] **nf** compote ▸ **compote de pommes** stewed apples, apple sauce ▸ **j'ai les jambes en compote** *fam fig* my legs feel like jelly.

compotier [kɔ̃pɔtje] **nm** fruit bowl.

compréhensible [kɔ̃preɑ̃sibl] **adj** [texte, parole] comprehensible / *fig* [réaction] understandable.

PARONYME / CONFUSABLE
compréhensible

Attention à ce mot, qui peut se traduire par ***comprehensible*** pour désigner le caractère intelligible (d'un texte...), ou par ***understandable*** si l'on veut parler d'une attitude concevable, qui se comprend.

compréhensif, ive [kɔ̃preɑ̃sif, iv] **adj** understanding.

FAUX AMIS / FALSE FRIENDS
compréhensive

Comprehensive is not a translation of the French word *compréhensive.* Comprehensive is translated by *complet* or *exhaustif.*
▸ We need to draw up a comprehensive list of all members / *Il faut que nous dressions la liste complète de tous les membres*

compréhension [kɔ̃preɑ̃sjɔ̃] **nf 1.** [de texte] comprehension, understanding **2.** [indulgence] understanding.

comprenais, comprenions ➤ ***comprendre.***

comprendre [79] [kɔ̃prɑ̃dr] ■ **vt 1.** [gén] to understand ▸ **c'est à n'y rien comprendre** it's just baffling ▸ **(c'est) compris?** [vous avez suivi] is it clear?, do you understand? / [c'est un ordre] do you hear me! ▸ **comprends-tu l'importance d'une telle décision?** do you realize how important such a decision it is? ▸ **je comprends!** I see! ▸ **je vous comprends, cela a dû être terrible** I know how you feel; it must have been awful ▸ **faire comprendre qqch à qqn** [le lui prouver] to make sthg clear to sb / [l'en informer] to give sb to understand sthg ▸ **se faire comprendre** to make o.s. understood ▸ **mal comprendre** to misunderstand **2.** [comporter] to comprise, to consist of ▸ **l'équipe comprend trois joueurs étrangers** there are three foreign players in the team **3.** [inclure] to include **4.** *(au passif)* [se situer] **: l'inflation sera comprise entre 5 % et 8 %** inflation will be (somewhere) between 5% and 8%.
■ **vi** to understand.
◆ ***se comprendre*** **vp** to understand one another ▸ **ça se comprend** that's understandable.

comprenne, comprennes ➤ ***comprendre.***

compresse [kɔ̃prɛs] **nf** compress.

COMMENT EXPRIMER...
qu'on a compris/qu'on n'a pas compris

I see (what you mean) / Je vois (ce que vous voulez dire)
I understand / Je comprends
I think I've got it now / Ça y est, je crois que j'ai compris
I'm afraid I don't understand / Désolé, je ne comprends pas
I'm sorry, I don't follow you / Pardon, mais je ne vous suis pas
I'm sorry I didn't catch what you said / Pardon, je n'ai pas saisi ce que vous avez dit
Sorry. Would you mind repeating that? / Excusez-moi, pourriez-vous répéter, s'il vous plaît ?

compresser [4] [kɔ̃prese] **vt** [gén] to pack (tightly) in, to pack in tight / INFORM to compress.

compresseur [kɔ̃presœr] ➤ ***rouleau***.

compression [kɔ̃presjɔ̃] **nf** [de gaz] compression / *fig* cutback, reduction.

comprimé, e [kɔ̃prime] **adj** compressed.
◆ ***comprimé*** **nm** tablet ▸ **comprimé effervescent** effervescent tablet.

comprimer [3] [kɔ̃prime] **vt 1.** [gaz, vapeur] to compress **2.** [personnes] **: être comprimés dans** to be packed into.

compris, e [kɔ̃pri, iz] ■ **pp** ➤ ***comprendre***.
■ **adj 1.** [situé] lying, contained **2.** [inclus] **: service (non) compris** (not) including service, service (not) included ▸ **tout compris** all inclusive, all in ▸ **y compris** including.

compromets ➤ ***compromettre***.

compromettant, e [kɔ̃prɔmetɑ̃, ɑ̃t] **adj** compromising.

compromettre [84] [kɔ̃prɔmɛtr] **vt** to compromise.
◆ ***se compromettre*** **vp : se compromettre (avec qqn/dans qqch)** to compromise o.s. (with sb/in sthg).

compromis, e [kɔ̃prɔmi, iz] **pp** ➤ ***compromettre***.
◆ ***compromis*** **nm** compromise.

compromission [kɔ̃prɔmisjɔ̃] **nf** *péj* base action.

comptabiliser [3] [kɔ̃tabilize] **vt** to enter in an account.

comptabilité [kɔ̃tabilite] **nf** [comptes] accounts *pl* ▸ **comptabilité informatisée** computerized accounts / [service] **: la comptabilité** accounts, the accounts department.

comptable [kɔ̃tabl] ■ **nmf** accountant.
■ **adj** accounting *(avant n)*.

comptant [kɔ̃tɑ̃] ■ **adj inv** cash, in cash.
■ **adv : payer** *ou* **régler comptant** to pay cash.
◆ ***au comptant*** **loc adv : payer au comptant** to pay cash.

compte [kɔ̃t] **nm 1.** [action] count, counting *(U)* / [total] number ▸ **faire le compte (de)** [personnes] to count (up) / [dépenses] to add up ▸ **il n'y a pas le compte** [personnes] they're not all here *ou* there, some are missing / [dépenses] it doesn't add up ▸ **compte à rebours** countdown ▸ **compte rond** round number **2.** BANQUE & COMM account ▸ **ouvrir un compte** to open an account ▸ **régler un compte** to settle an account ▸ **compte bancaire** *ou* **en banque** bank account ▸ **compte client** client account ▸ **compte courant** current account *UK*, checking account *US* ▸ **compte de courrier électronique** INFORM e-mail account ▸ **compte créditeur** account in credit ▸ **compte débiteur** overdrawn account, debit account ▸ **compte de dépôt** deposit account ▸ **compte d'épargne** savings account ▸ **compte épargne logement** savings account *(for purchasing a property)* ▸ **compte d'exploitation** operating account ▸ **compte joint** joint account ▸ **compte numéroté** numbered account ▸ **compte postal** post office account ▸ **compte professionnel** *ou* **commercial** business account ▸ **compte de profits et pertes** profit and loss account
▸▸ **avoir son compte** to have had enough ▸ **être/se mettre à son compte** to be/become self-employed ▸ **mettre qqch sur le compte de qqn** to put sthg on sb's bill ▸ **prendre qqch en compte, tenir compte de qqch** to take sthg into account ▸ **elle n'a pas tenu compte de mes conseils** she took no notice of *ou* ignored my advice ▸ **recevoir son compte** *litt* to get one's (final) wages / *fam fig* to get one's marching orders *ou* the sack *UK* ▸ **régler son compte à qqn** *fam fig* to give sb a piece of one's mind ▸ **rendre compte de** to account for ▸ **se rendre compte de qqch** to realize sthg ▸ **se rendre compte que** to realize (that) ▸ **s'en tirer à bon compte** to get off lightly ▸ **y trouver son compte** to do well out of it ▸ **tout compte fait** all things considered.
◆ ***comptes*** **nmpl** accounts ▸ **comptes clients** accounts payable ▸ **comptes consolidés** *ou* **intégrés** consolidated accounts ▸ **comptes fournisseurs** accounts receivable ▸ **comptes de résultats** year-end accounts ▸ **comptes de résultats courants** above-the-line accounts ▸ **comptes de résultats exceptionnels** below-the-line accounts ▸ **demander des comptes à qqn** to ask sb for an explanation of sthg, to ask sb to account for sthg ▸ **devoir des comptes à** to be accountable to ▸ **faire les comptes** to do the accounts ▸ **faire ses comptes** to do one's accounts ▸ **faire des comptes d'apothicaire** to account for every last penny ▸ **régler ses comptes avec qqch** to come to terms with sthg ▸ **régler ses comptes avec qqn** to have it out with sb ▸ **rendre des comptes (à qqn)** to give *ou* to offer (sb) an explanation.
◆ ***pour le compte de*** **loc prép** for ▸ **elle travaille pour le compte d'une grande société** she works for a large firm, she freelances for a large firm.

compte-chèques (**pl compte-chèques**), ***compte chèques*** (**pl compte chèques**) [kɔ̃tʃɛk] **nm** current account *UK*, checking account *US*.

compte-gouttes [kɔ̃tgut] **nm inv** dropper ▸ **au compte-gouttes** *fig* sparingly.

compter [3] [kɔ̃te] ■ **vt 1.** [dénombrer] to count ▸ **j'ai compté qu'il restait 200 euros dans la caisse** according to my reckoning there are 200 euros left in the till ▸ **on peut les compter sur les doigts de la main** you can count them on the fingers of one hand **2.** [avoir l'intention de] **: compter faire qqch** to intend to do sthg, to plan to do sthg.
■ **vi 1.** [calculer] to count ▸ **compter jusqu'à 10** to count (up) to 10 ▸ **tu as dû mal compter** you must have got your calculations wrong, you must have miscalculated **2.** [être important] to count, to matter ▸ **ce qui compte, c'est ta santé/le résultat** the important thing is your health/the end result ▸ **tu comptes beaucoup pour moi** you mean a lot to me ▸ **compter parmi** [faire partie de] to be included amongst, to rank amongst ▸ **elle compte parmi les plus grands pianistes de sa génération** she is one of the greatest pianists of her generation ▸ **compter pour** to count for ▸ **compter pour quelque chose/rien** to count for something/nothing ▸ **compter avec** [tenir compte de] to reckon with, to take account of ▸ **compter sur** [se fier à] to rely *ou* count on ▸ **ne compte pas trop sur la chance** don't count *ou* rely too much on luck.
◆ ***à compter de*** **loc prép** as from, starting from ▸ **à compter de ce jour, nous ne nous sommes plus revu** from that day on, we never saw each other again.
◆ ***sans compter*** ■ **loc prép** [excepté] not including.

■ **loc adv : se dépenser sans compter** *fig* to give unsparingly of o.s.
◆ ***sans compter que*** **loc conj** besides which ▸ **il est trop tôt pour aller dormir, sans compter que je n'ai pas du tout sommeil** it's too early to go to bed, quite apart from the fact that I'm not at all sleepy.

compte rendu (pl **comptes rendus**), ***compte-rendu*** (pl **comptes-rendus**) [kɔ̃trɑ̃dy] **nm** report, account.

compte-tours [kɔ̃ttur] **nm inv** rev counter, tachometer.

compteur [kɔ̃tœr] **nm** meter ▸ **remettre les compteurs à zéro** *fig* to go back to square one, to start all over again.

comptine [kɔ̃tin] **nf** nursery rhyme.

comptoir [kɔ̃twar] **nm 1.** [de bar] bar / [de magasin] counter **2.** HIST trading post **3.** *Suisse* [foire] trade fair.

compulser [3] [kɔ̃pylse] **vt** to consult.

compulsif, ive [kɔ̃pylsif, iv] **adj** PSYCHO compulsive.

comte [kɔ̃t] **nm** count.

comté [kɔ̃te] **nm 1.** [fromage] *type of cheese similar to Gruyère* **2.** ADMIN [au Canada] county **3.** HIST earldom.

comtesse [kɔ̃tɛs] **nf** countess.

con, conne [kɔ̃, kɔn] *tfam* ■ **adj** damned *ou* bloody *UK* stupid.
■ **nm, f** stupid bastard (f bitch).

concassé, e [kɔ̃kase] **adj** [poivre] coarse-ground ▸ **blé concassé** cracked wheat.

concasser [3] [kɔ̃kase] **vt** to crush / [poivre] to grind.

concaténation [kɔ̃katenasjɔ̃] **nf** concatenation.

concaténer [3] [kɔ̃katene] **vt** to concatenate ▸ **concaténer des fichiers** to concatenate files.

concave [kɔ̃kav] **adj** concave.

concéder [18] [kɔ̃sede] **vt : concéder qqch à** [droit, terrain] to grant sthg to / [point, victoire] to concede sthg to ▸ **concéder que** to admit (that), to concede (that).

concentration [kɔ̃sɑ̃trasjɔ̃] **nf** concentration.

concentré, e [kɔ̃sɑ̃tre] **adj 1.** [gén] concentrated **2.** [personne] **: elle était très concentrée** she was concentrating hard **3.** ➤ ***lait***.
◆ ***concentré*** **nm** concentrate ▸ **concentré de tomates** CULIN tomato purée.

concentrer [3] [kɔ̃sɑ̃tre] **vt** to concentrate.
◆ ***se concentrer*** **vp 1.** [se rassembler] to be concentrated **2.** [personne] to concentrate.

concentrique [kɔ̃sɑ̃trik] **adj** concentric.

concept [kɔ̃sɛpt] **nm** concept ▸ **concept de marketing** marketing concept.

concepteur, trice [kɔ̃sɛptœr, tris] **nm, f** designer.

conception [kɔ̃sɛpsjɔ̃] **nf 1.** [gén] conception **2.** [d'un produit, d'une campagne] design, designing *(U)* **3.** INFORM **: conception assistée par ordinateur** computer-aided design ▸ **conception et fabrication assistées par ordinateur** computer-aided manufacturing.

concernant [kɔ̃sɛrnɑ̃] **prép** regarding, concerning.

concerner [3] [kɔ̃sɛrne] **vt** to concern ▸ **être/se sentir concerné par qqch** to be/feel concerned by sthg ▸ **en ce qui me concerne** as far as I'm concerned.

concert [kɔ̃sɛr] **nm 1.** MUS concert **2.** [entente] accord ▸ **de concert avec qqn** together with sb.

concertation [kɔ̃sɛrtasjɔ̃] **nf** consultation.

concerter [3] [kɔ̃sɛrte] **vt** [organiser] to devise (jointly).
◆ ***se concerter*** **vp** to consult (each other).

concerto [kɔ̃sɛrto] **nm** concerto.

concession [kɔ̃sesjɔ̃] **nf 1.** [compromis & GRAMM] concession ▸ **faire des concessions (à qqn)** to make concessions (to sb) **2.** [autorisation] rights *pl*, concession.

concessionnaire [kɔ̃sesjɔnɛr] ■ **nmf 1.** [automobile] (car) dealer ▸ **concessionnaire agréé** authorized dealer **2.** [qui possède une franchise] franchise holder.
■ **adj** concessionary.

concevable [kɔ̃səvabl] **adj** conceivable.

concevoir [52] [kɔ̃səvwar] **vt 1.** [enfant, projet] to conceive **2.** [comprendre] to conceive of ▸ **je ne peux pas concevoir comment/pourquoi** I cannot conceive how/why **3.** *sout* [éprouver] to feel.
◆ ***se concevoir*** **vp** to be imagined.

concierge [kɔ̃sjɛrʒ] **nmf** caretaker *UK*, superintendent *US*, concierge.

concile [kɔ̃sil] **nm** council.

conciliabule [kɔ̃siljabyl] **nm** [discussion] consultation.

conciliant, e [kɔ̃siljɑ̃, ɑ̃t] **adj** conciliating.

conciliateur, trice [kɔ̃siljatœr, tris] ■ **adj** conciliatory, placatory.
■ **nm, f** conciliator, arbitrator.

conciliation [kɔ̃siljasjɔ̃] **nf 1.** [règlement d'un conflit] reconciliation, reconciling **2.** [accord & DR] conciliation ▸ **geste de conciliation** conciliatory gesture.

concilier [9] [kɔ̃silje] **vt 1.** [mettre d'accord, allier] to reconcile ▸ **concilier qqch et *ou* avec qqch** to reconcile sthg with sthg **2.** [gagner à sa cause] **: concilier qqn à** to win sb over to.
◆ ***se concilier*** **vp : se concilier qqn** to win sb over ▸ **se concilier qqch** to gain sthg.

concis, e [kɔ̃si, iz] **adj** [style, discours] concise / [personne] terse ▸ **soyez plus concis** come to the point.

concision [kɔ̃sizjɔ̃] **nf** conciseness, concision.

concitoyen, enne [kɔ̃sitwajɛ̃, ɛn] **nm, f** fellow citizen.

conclu, e [kɔ̃kly] **pp** ➤ ***conclure***.

concluant, e [kɔ̃klyɑ̃, ɑ̃t] **adj** [convaincant] conclusive.

conclure [96] [kɔ̃klyr] ■ **vt** to conclude ▸ **conclure de qqch que** to conclude from sthg that ▸ **en conclure que** to deduce (that).
■ **vi : les experts ont conclu à la folie** the experts concluded he/she was mad ▸ **le tribunal a conclu au suicide** the court returned a verdict of suicide.

conclusion [kɔ̃klyzjɔ̃] **nf 1.** [gén] conclusion ▸ **en arriver à la conclusion que** to come to the conclusion that ▸ **conclusion, la voiture est fichue** *fam* the result is that the car is a write-off *UK* *ou* is totaled *US* **2.** [partie finale] close.

◆ ***conclusions*** **nfpl** [d'un rapport] conclusions, findings / DR submissions ▸ **déposer** *OU* **signifier des conclusions** to file submissions with a court.

◆ ***en conclusion*** **loc adv** as a *OU* in conclusion, to conclude.

concocter [3] [kɔ̃kɔkte] **vt** to concoct.

concombre [kɔ̃kɔ̃br] **nm** cucumber.

concomitant, e [kɔ̃kɔmitɑ̃, ɑ̃t] **adj** concomitant.

concordance [kɔ̃kɔrdɑ̃s] **nf** [conformité] agreement ▸ **concordance des temps** GRAMM sequence of tenses.

concorde [kɔ̃kɔrd] **nf** concord.

Concorde® [kɔ̃kɔrd] **nm** Concorde®.

concorder [3] [kɔ̃kɔrde] **vi 1.** [coïncider] to agree, to coincide **2.** [être en accord] **: concorder (avec)** to be in accordance (with) **3.** [avoir un même but] to coincide.

concourir [45] [kɔ̃kurir] **vi 1.** [contribuer] **: concourir à** to work towards *UK* *ou* toward *US* **2.** [participer à un concours] to compete.

concours [kɔ̃kur] **nm 1.** [examen] competitive examination ▸ **concours de recrutement** competitive entry examination **2.** [compétition] competition, contest ▸ **hors concours** [dans une compétition] ineligible / *fig* exceptional ▸ **concours hippique** horse show **3.** [collaboration] help ▸ **avec le concours de qqn** with sb's help *ou* assistance **4.** [coïncidence] **: concours de circonstances** combination of circumstances.

concret, ète [kɔ̃krɛ, ɛt] **adj** concrete.

concrètement [kɔ̃krɛtmɑ̃] **adv** [en réalité] in real *ou* practical terms.

concrétiser [3] [kɔ̃kretize] **vt** [projet] to give shape to / [rêve, espoir] to give solid form to.

◆ ***se concrétiser*** **vp** [projet] to take shape / [rêve, espoir] to materialize.

conçu, e [kɔ̃sy] **pp** ➤ ***concevoir.***

concubin, e [kɔ̃kybɛ̃, in] **nm, f** partner, common-law husband (f wife).

concubinage [kɔ̃kybinaʒ] **nm** living together, cohabitation.

concupiscent, e [kɔ̃kypisɑ̃, ɑ̃t] **adj** lustful.

concurremment [kɔ̃kyramɑ̃] **adv** jointly.

concurrence [kɔ̃kyrɑ̃s] **nf 1.** [rivalité] rivalry **2.** ÉCON competition ▸ **concurrence déloyale** unfair competition ▸ **des prix défiant toute concurrence** unbeatable prices ▸ **faire (de la) concurrence à** to be in competition with ▸ **vous pouvez être en découvert à concurrence de 5000 euros** your overdraft limit is 5000 euros **3.** [montant] **: jusqu'à concurrence de** to the amount of, not exceeding ▸ **vous pouvez être en découvert à concurrence de 5000 euros** your overdraft limit is 5000 euros.

concurrencer [3] [kɔ̃kyrɑ̃se] **vt** to compete *ou* to be in competition with ▸ **ils nous concurrencent dangereusement** they are very serious *OR* dangerous competitors for us.

concurrent, e [kɔ̃kyrɑ̃, ɑ̃t] ■ **adj** rival, competing.
■ **nm, f** competitor.

concurrentiel, elle [kɔ̃kyrɑ̃sjɛl] **adj** competitive ▸ **marchandises vendues à des prix concurrentiels** competitive-priced goods.

condamnable [kɔ̃danabl] **adj** reprehensible.

condamnation [kɔ̃danasjɔ̃] **nf 1.** DR sentence **2.** [dénonciation] condemnation.

condamné, e [kɔ̃dane] **nm, f** convict, prisoner.

condamner [3] [kɔ̃dane] **vt 1.** DR **: condamner qqn (à)** to sentence sb (to) ▸ **condamner qqn à une amende** to fine sb **2.** *fig* [obliger] **: condamner qqn à qqch** to condemn sb to sthg **3.** [malade] **: être condamné** to be terminally ill **4.** [interdire] to forbid **5.** [blâmer] to condemn **6.** [fermer] to fill in, to block up.

condensateur [kɔ̃dɑ̃satœr] **nm** condenser.

condensation [kɔ̃dɑ̃sasjɔ̃] **nf** condensation.

condensé [kɔ̃dɑ̃se] ■ **nm** summary.
■ **adj** ➤ ***lait.***

condenser [3] [kɔ̃dɑ̃se] **vt** to condense.

◆ ***se condenser*** **vp** to condense.

condescendance [kɔ̃desɑ̃dɑ̃s] **nf** condescension ▸ **avec condescendance** condescendingly ▸ **traiter qqn avec condescendance** to patronize sb.

condescendant, e [kɔ̃desɑ̃dɑ̃, ɑ̃t] **adj** condescending.

condescendre [73] [kɔ̃desɑ̃dr] **vi** *sout* **: condescendre à qqch/à faire qqch** to condescend to sthg/to do sthg.

condescendu [kɔ̃desɑ̃dy] **pp inv** ➤ ***condescendre.***

condiment [kɔ̃dimɑ̃] **nm** condiment.

condisciple [kɔ̃disipl] **nm** fellow student.

condition [kɔ̃disjɔ̃] **nf 1.** [gén] condition ▸ **condition préalable** prerequisite ▸ **condition requise** requirement ▸ **condition sine qua non** essential condition ▸ **être en bonne condition physique** to be in condition, to be fit ▸ **j'accepte, mais à une condition** I accept but on one condition ▸ **remplir une condition** to fulfil a condition ▸ **se mettre en condition** [physiquement] to get into shape **2.** [place sociale] station ▸ **la condition féminine** the lives

COMMENT EXPRIMER...

la condition

If we get cut off, I'll call you back / Si on est coupé, je te rappelle

Let me know if you need any more information / Si vous avez besoin d'autres renseignements, n'hésitez pas à me contacter

You won't win unless you practise / Vous ne gagnerez pas si vous ne vous entraînez pas

He'll do it on condition that he's well paid / Il le fera à condition d'être bien payé

I'll need more convincing before I give it the go-ahead / Il faudra me convaincre davantage pour que je donne le feu vert

They wouldn't have come if they'd known / S'ils avaient su, ils ne seraient pas venus

of women, the female condition ▸ **la condition des ouvriers** the workers' lot ▸ **une femme de condition modeste** a woman from a modest background.
◆ ***conditions*** **nfpl 1.** [circonstances] conditions ▸ **conditions de vie** living conditions ▸ **conditions atmosphériques** atmospheric conditions ▸ **conditions climatiques/économiques** weather/economic conditions ▸ **conditions du marché** market conditions **2.** [de paiement] terms ▸ **conditions de vente/d'achat** terms of sale/purchase.
◆ ***à condition de*** **loc prép** providing *ou* provided (that).
◆ ***à condition que*** **loc conj** *(+ subjonctif)* providing *ou* provided (that).
◆ ***sans conditions*** ■ **loc adj** unconditional.
■ **loc adv** unconditionally.

conditionné, e [kɔ̃disjɔne] **adj 1.** [emballé] **: conditionné sous vide** vacuum-packed / [marchandises] packaged **2.** ➤ ***air***.

conditionnel, elle [kɔ̃disjɔnɛl] **adj** conditional.
◆ ***conditionnel*** **nm** GRAMM conditional.

conditionnement [kɔ̃disjɔnmɑ̃] **nm 1.** [action d'emballer] packaging, packing **2.** [emballage] package **3.** PSYCHO & TECHNOL conditioning.

conditionner [3] [kɔ̃disjɔne] **vt 1.** [déterminer] to govern **2.** PSYCHO & TECHNOL to condition ▸ **la publicité conditionne nos choix** advertising influences our choices **3.** [emballer] to pack.

condoléances [kɔ̃dɔleɑ̃s] **nfpl** condolences.

conducteur, trice [kɔ̃dyktœr, tris] ■ **adj** conductive.
■ **nm, f** [de véhicule] driver.
◆ ***conducteur*** **nm** ÉLECTR conductor.

conduire [98] [kɔ̃dɥir] ■ **vt 1.** [voiture, personne] to drive ▸ **conduire les enfants à l'école** to take *ou* to drive the children to school **2.** PHYS [transmettre] to conduct **3.** *fig* [diriger] to manage **4.** *fig* [à la ruine, au désespoir] **: conduire qqn à qqch** to drive sb to sthg ▸ **ce qui nous conduit à la conclusion suivante** which leads *ou* brings us to the following conclusion.
■ **vi 1.** AUTO to drive ▸ **conduire à droite/gauche** to drive on the right-hand/left-hand side of the road **2.** [mener] **: conduire à** to lead to ▸ **cet escalier ne conduit nulle part** this staircase doesn't lead anywhere.
◆ ***se conduire*** **vp** to behave ▸ **se conduire bien** to behave (o.s.) well ▸ **se conduire mal** to behave badly, to misbehave.

conduisais, conduisions ➤ ***conduire***.

conduit, e [kɔ̃dɥi, it] **pp** ➤ ***conduire***.
◆ ***conduit*** **nm 1.** [tuyau] conduit, pipe ▸ **conduit d'aération** air duct ▸ **conduit de ventilation** ventilation shaft **2.** ANAT duct, canal ▸ **conduit auditif** auditory canal ▸ **conduit lacrymal** tear duct, lachrymal duct *(terme spécialisé)*.
◆ ***conduite*** **nf 1.** [pilotage d'un véhicule] driving ▸ **la conduite à droite/gauche** driving on the right-hand/left-hand side of the road ▸ **avec conduite à droite/gauche** right-hand/left-hand drive ▸ **conduite en état d'ébriété** drink-driving *UK*, drunk-driving *US* **2.** [direction] running **3.** [comportement] behaviour *(U) UK*, behavior *(U) US* ▸ **pour bonne conduite** [libéré, gracié] for good behaviour ▸ **mauvaise conduite** misbehaviour *UK*, misbehavior *US*, misconduct **4.** [canalisation] **: conduite de gaz/d'eau** gas/water main, gas/water pipe.

cône [kon] **nm** GÉOM cone.

confection [kɔ̃fɛksjɔ̃] **nf 1.** [réalisation] making **2.** [industrie] clothing industry.

confectionner [3] [kɔ̃fɛksjɔne] **vt** to make.

confédéral, e, aux [kɔ̃federal, o] **adj** confederal.

confédération [kɔ̃federasjɔ̃] **nf 1.** [d'états] confederacy **2.** [d'associations] confederation.

conférence [kɔ̃ferɑ̃s] **nf 1.** [exposé] lecture **2.** [réunion] conference ▸ **conférence de presse** press conference ▸ **conférence au sommet** summit conference.

conférencier, ère [kɔ̃ferɑ̃sje, ɛr] **nm, f** lecturer.

conférer [18] [kɔ̃fere] **vt** [accorder] **: conférer qqch à qqn** to confer sthg on sb.

confesse [kɔ̃fɛs] **nf : aller à confesse** to go to confession.

confesser [4] [kɔ̃fese] **vt 1.** [avouer] to confess **2.** RELIG **: confesser qqn** to hear sb's confession.
◆ ***se confesser*** **vp** to go to confession.

confession [kɔ̃fesjɔ̃] **nf** confession.

confessionnal, aux [kɔ̃fesjɔnal, o] **nm** confessional.

confessionnel, elle [kɔ̃fesjɔnɛl] **adj** RELIG denominational.

confetti [kɔ̃feti] **nm** confetti *(U)*.

confiance [kɔ̃fjɑ̃s] **nf 1.** [foi] confidence ▸ **avec confiance** confidently ▸ **confiance excessive** overconfidence ▸ **avoir confiance en** to have confidence *ou* faith in ▸ **avoir confiance en soi** to be self-confident ▸ **confiance de la clientèle** *ou* **du client** client confidence ▸ **en toute confiance** with complete confidence ▸ **de confiance** trustworthy ▸ **faire confiance à qqn/qqch** to trust sb/sthg ▸ **manquer de confiance en soi** to lack self confidence ▸ **placer sa confiance en qqn** to put one's trust *ou* to place one's confidence in sb ▸ **reprendre confiance en soi** to regain one's self-confidence **2.** POLIT **: voter la confiance au gouvernement** to pass a vote of confidence in the government ▸ **vote de confiance** vote of confidence ▸ **les hommes de confiance du gouvernement** the Government's advisers.

confiant, e [kɔ̃fjɑ̃, ɑ̃t] **adj 1.** [sans méfiance] trusting **2.** [assuré] **: confiant (en qqch)** confident (of sthg).

confidence [kɔ̃fidɑ̃s] **nf** confidence ▸ **en confidence** in confidence ▸ **faire des confidences à qqn** to confide in sb ▸ **être dans la confidence** to be in the know.

confident, e [kɔ̃fidɑ̃, ɑ̃t] **nm, f** confidant (f confidante).

confidentiel, elle [kɔ̃fidɑ̃sjɛl] **adj** confidential.

confier [9] [kɔ̃fje] **vt 1.** [donner] **: confier qqn/qqch à qqn** to entrust sb/sthg to sb **2.** [dire] **: confier qqch à qqn** to confide sthg to sb.
◆ ***se confier*** **vp : se confier à qqn** to confide in sb.

configuration [kɔ̃figyrasjɔ̃] **nf** TECHNOL configuration / INFORM **: configuration par défaut** default setting / [conception] layout.

confiné, e [kɔ̃fine] **adj 1.** [air] stale / [atmosphère] enclosed **2.** [enfermé] shut away.

confins [kɔ̃fɛ̃] **nmpl : aux confins de** on the borders of ▸ **les confins de l'Europe et de l'Asie** the borders of Europe and Asia.

confirmation [kɔ̃firmasjɔ̃] **nf** confirmation.

confirmer [3] [kɔ̃firme] **vt** [certifier] to confirm ▸ **confirmer qqn dans qqch** to confirm sb in sthg ▸ **il n'a pas été confirmé dans ses fonctions** he was not retained in the post.
◆ ***se confirmer*** **vp** to be confirmed.

confiscation [kɔ̃fiskasjɔ̃] **nf** confiscation.

confiserie [kɔ̃fizri] **nf 1.** [magasin] sweet shop *UK*, candy store *US*, confectioner's **2.** [sucreries] sweets *pl UK*, candy *(U) US*, confectionery *(U)*.

confiseur, euse [kɔ̃fizœr, øz] **nm, f** confectioner.

confisquer [3] [kɔ̃fiske] **vt** to confiscate.

confit, e [kɔ̃fi, it] **adj** ➤ ***fruit***.
◆ ***confit*** **nm** conserve.

confiture [kɔ̃fityr] **nf** jam.

conflagration [kɔ̃flagrasjɔ̃] **nf** [bouleversement] cataclysm.

conflictuel, elle [kɔ̃fliktyɛl] **adj** conflicting.

conflit [kɔ̃fli] **nm 1.** [situation tendue] clash, conflict **2.** [entre États] conflict **3.** ÉCON & POLIT **: conflit d'intérêts** conflict of interests ▸ **conflit du travail** industrial dispute.

confluent [kɔ̃flyɑ̃] **nm** confluence ▸ **au confluent de** at the confluence of.

confondre [75] [kɔ̃fɔ̃dr] **vt 1.** [ne pas distinguer] to confuse **2.** [accusé] to confound **3.** [stupéfier] to astound.
◆ ***se confondre*** **vp 1.** [se mêler] to merge **2.** *fig* **: se confondre en excuses** to apologize profusely ▸ **il s'est confondu en remerciements** he thanked me/him *etc* profusely.

confondu, e [kɔ̃fɔ̃dy] **pp** ➤ ***confondre***.

conformation [kɔ̃fɔrmasjɔ̃] **nf** structure.

conforme [kɔ̃fɔrm] **adj : conforme à** in accordance with.

conformé, e [kɔ̃fɔrme] **adj : bien conformé** well-formed ▸ **mal conformé** ill-formed.

conformément [kɔ̃fɔrmemɑ̃] ◆ ***conformément à*** **loc prép** in accordance with.

conformer [3] [kɔ̃fɔrme] **vt : conformer qqch à** to shape sthg according to.
◆ ***se conformer*** **vp : se conformer à** [s'adapter] to conform to / [obéir] to comply with.

conformiste [kɔ̃fɔrmist] ■ **nmf** conformist.
■ **adj 1.** [traditionaliste] conformist **2.** [Anglican] Anglican.

conformité [kɔ̃fɔrmite] **nf 1.** [ressemblance] **: conformité (à)** conformity (to) **2.** [accord] **: être en conformité avec** to be in accordance with.

confort [kɔ̃fɔr] **nm** comfort ▸ **tout confort** with all mod cons *UK*, with all modern conveniences *US*.

confortable [kɔ̃fɔrtabl] **adj** comfortable.

confortablement [kɔ̃fɔrtabləmɑ̃] **adv** comfortably ▸ **confortablement payé** well-paid.

conforter [3] [kɔ̃fɔrte] **vt : conforter qqn (dans qqch)** to strengthen sb (in sthg).

confrère, consœur [kɔ̃frɛr, kɔ̃sœr] **nm, f** colleague.

confrérie [kɔ̃freri] **nf** brotherhood.

confrontation [kɔ̃frɔ̃tasjɔ̃] **nf 1.** [face à face] confrontation **2.** [comparaison] comparison.

confronter [3] [kɔ̃frɔ̃te] **vt 1.** [mettre face à face] to confront / *fig* **: être confronté à** to be confronted *ou* faced with **2.** [comparer] to compare.

confus, e [kɔ̃fy, yz] **adj 1.** [indistinct, embrouillé] confused **2.** [gêné] embarrassed ▸ **je suis vraiment confus** I'm really very sorry.

confusément [kɔ̃fyzemɑ̃] **adj 1.** [pêle-mêle] in confusion **2.** [indistinctement] indistinctly **3.** [vaguement] vaguely.

confusion [kɔ̃fyzjɔ̃] **nf 1.** [gén] confusion **2.** [embarras] confusion, embarrassment.

congé [kɔ̃ʒe] **nm 1.** [arrêt de travail] leave *(U)* ▸ **congé (de) maladie** sick leave ▸ **congé de maternité** maternity leave **2.** [vacances] holiday *UK*, vacation *US* ▸ **en congé** on holiday *UK* ***ou*** vacation *US* ▸ **congé annuel** annual leave ▸ **congés payés** paid holiday *(U)* ***ou*** holidays ***ou*** leave *(U) UK*, paid vacation *US* ▸ **une journée/semaine de congé** a day/week off **3.** [renvoi] notice ▸ **donner son congé à qqn** to give sb his/her notice ▸ **prendre congé (de qqn)** *sout* to take one's leave (of sb).

congédier [9] [kɔ̃ʒedje] **vt** to dismiss.

congé-formation [kɔ̃ʒefɔrmasjɔ̃] (pl **congés-formation**) **nm** training leave.

congélateur [kɔ̃ʒelatœr] **nm** freezer.

congélation [kɔ̃ʒelasjɔ̃] **nf** [technique] freezing / [durée] freezing time ▸ **sac de congélation** freezer bag.

COMMENT EXPRIMER...

une demande de confirmation

I am writing to confirm the arrangements for our visit / Je vous écris pour confirmer les modalités de notre visite

Dear John, this is just to confirm our meeting on Monday at 10 / Cher John, juste un mot pour confirmer notre rendez-vous de lundi à 10 h

I assume these figures have been checked? / Ces chiffres ont été vérifiés, je suppose ?

Are you sure of your facts? / Êtes-vous sûr de ce que vous affirmez ?

So you think I should take the job, do you? / Alors comme ça, tu penses que je devrais accepter le travail ?

I owe you $5, right? / Je te dois 5 dollars, c'est (bien) ça ?

congeler [25] [kɔ̃ʒle] **vt** to freeze ▸ **tarte/viande congelée** frozen pie/meat.
◆ ***se congeler*** **vp** *(emploi passif)* [dans un congélateur] to freeze ▸ **la mayonnaise ne se congèle pas** you can't freeze mayonnaise.

congénital, e, aux [kɔ̃ʒenital, o] **adj** congenital.

congère [kɔ̃ʒɛr] **nf** snowdrift.

congestion [kɔ̃ʒɛstjɔ̃] **nf** congestion ▸ **congestion pulmonaire** pulmonary congestion.

conglomérat [kɔ̃glɔmera] **nm** conglomerate.

Congo [kɔ̃go] **nm** [pays] **: le Congo** the Congo ▸ **au Congo** in the Congo ▸ **la République démocratique du Congo** the Democratic Republic of Congo / [fleuve] **: le Congo** the Congo.

congolais, e [kɔ̃gɔlɛ, ɛz] **adj** Congolese.
◆ ***congolais*** **nm** CULIN coconut cake.
◆ ***Congolais, e*** **nm, f** Congolese person.

congratuler [3] [kɔ̃gratyle] **vt** to congratulate.

congre [kɔ̃gr] **nm** conger eel.

congrégation [kɔ̃gregasjɔ̃] **nf** congregation.

congrès [kɔ̃grɛ] **nm 1.** [colloque] assembly **2.** HIST [réunion] congress.
◆ ***Congrès*** **nm** [parlement américain] **: le Congrès** Congress / [en Afrique du Sud] **: Congrès national africain** African National Congress.

congressiste [kɔ̃gresist] **nmf** congress participant.

congrue [kɔ̃gry] ➤ ***portion***.

conifère [kɔnifɛr] **nm** conifer.

conique [kɔnik] **adj** conical.

conjecture [kɔ̃ʒɛktyr] **nf** conjecture ▸ **se perdre en conjectures** to lose o.s. in conjecture.

conjecturer [3] [kɔ̃ʒɛktyre] **vt & vi** to conjecture.

conjoint, e [kɔ̃ʒwɛ̃, ɛ̃t] ■ **adj** joint.
■ **nm, f** spouse.

conjointement [kɔ̃ʒwɛ̃tmɑ̃] **adv : conjointement (avec qqn)** jointly (with sb).

conjonctif, ive [kɔ̃ʒɔ̃ktif, iv] **adj 1.** ➤ ***tissu*** **2.** GRAMM conjunctive.

conjonction [kɔ̃ʒɔ̃ksjɔ̃] **nf** conjunction ▸ **conjonction de coordination/de subordination** GRAMM coordinating/subordinating conjunction.

conjonctivite [kɔ̃ʒɔ̃ktivit] **nf** conjunctivitis *(U)*.

conjoncture [kɔ̃ʒɔ̃ktyr] **nf** ÉCON situation, circumstances *pl* ▸ **conjoncture économique mondiale** world economy.

conjoncturel, elle [kɔ̃ʒɔ̃ktyrɛl] **adj** [situation, tendance] economic.

conjugaison [kɔ̃ʒygɛzɔ̃] **nf 1.** [union] uniting **2.** GRAMM conjugation.

conjugal, e, aux [kɔ̃ʒygal, o] **adj** conjugal.

conjuguer [3] [kɔ̃ʒyge] **vt 1.** [unir] to combine **2.** GRAMM to conjugate ▸ **conjuguer au futur** to conjugate in the future tense.
◆ ***se conjuguer*** ■ **vp** *(emploi passif)* GRAMM to conjugate, to be conjugated.
■ **vpi** [s'unir] to work together, to combine.

conjuration [kɔ̃ʒyrasjɔ̃] **nf 1.** [conspiration] conspiracy **2.** [exorcisme] exorcism.

conjurer [3] [kɔ̃ʒyre] **vt 1.** [supplier] to beg ▸ **je vous en conjure!** *sout* I beg (of) you! **2.** [exorciser] to exorcize **3.** [écarter] to avert.
◆ ***se conjurer*** **vp** to plot, to conspire.

connaissais, connaissions ➤ ***connaître***.

connaissance [kɔnɛsɑ̃s] **nf 1.** [savoir] knowledge *(U)* ▸ **à ma connaissance** to (the best of) my knowledge ▸ **la connaissance de la marque** brand familiarity ▸ **une connaissance approfondie de l'espagnol** a thorough knowledge *ou* good command of Spanish ▸ **en connaissance de cause** with full knowledge of the facts ▸ **et j'en parle en connaissance de cause** and I know what I'm talking about ▸ **être en pays de connaissance** [dans un domaine] to be on familiar ground / [dans un milieu] to be among familiar faces ▸ **prendre connaissance de qqch** to study sthg, to examine sthg ▸ **prendre connaissance des faits** to learn about *ou* to hear of the facts ▸ **prendre connaissance d'un texte** to read *ou* to peruse a text **2.** [personne] acquaintance ▸ **une vieille connaissance** an old acquaintance ▸ **faire connaissance (avec qqn)** to become acquainted (with sb) ▸ **une fois que vous aurez mieux fait connaissance** once you've got to know each other better ▸ **faire la connaissance de** to meet **3.** [conscience] **: perdre/reprendre connaissance** to lose/regain consciousness ▸ **sans connaissance** unconscious.
◆ ***connaissances*** **nfpl** knowledge ▸ **avoir des connaissances** to be knowledgeable ▸ **avoir de solides connaissances en** to have a thorough knowledge of *ou* a good grounding in ▸ **avoir des connaissances sommaires en** to have a basic knowledge of, to know the rudiments of.

connaisseur, euse [kɔnɛsœr, øz] ■ **adj** expert *(avant n)*.
■ **nm, f** connoisseur.

connaître [91] [kɔnɛtr] **vt 1.** [gén] to know ▸ **connaître qqn de nom/de vue** to know sb by name/sight ▸ **faire connaître** [avis, sentiment] to make known / [décision, jugement] to make known, to announce ▸ **je suis impatient de connaître les résultats** I'm anxious to know *ou* to hear the results ▸ **la connaissant, ça ne me surprend pas** knowing her, I'm not surprised ▸ **y connaître quelque chose en** to have some idea *ou* to know something about ▸ **ne rien y connaître : je n'y connais rien en biologie** I don't know a thing about biology **2.** [éprouver] to experience ▸ **il a connu bien des déboires** he has had *ou* suffered plenty of setbacks ▸ **la tour avait connu des jours meilleurs** the tower had seen better days.
◆ ***se connaître*** **vp 1. : s'y connaître en** [être expert] to know about ▸ **je m'y connais peu en informatique** I don't know much about computers ▸ **il s'y connaît** he knows what he's talking about/doing ▸ **pour les gaffes, tu t'y connais!** *fam* when it comes to blunders, you take

some beating! **2.** [soi-même] to know o.s. **3.** [se rencontrer] to meet (each other) ▸ **ils se connaissent** they've met each other.

connecter [4] [kɔnɛkte] vt to connect.
◆ ***se connecter*** vp to log on, to log in ▸ **se connecter sur Internet** to log on to the Internet.

connecteur [kɔnɛktœr] nm : **connecteur à broche** INFORM pin connector.

connerie [kɔnri] nf *tfam* stupidity *(U)* ▸ **faire/dire des conneries** to do/to say something damned *ou* bloody *UK* stupid.

connexe [kɔnɛks] adj related.

connexion [kɔnɛksjɔ̃] nf connection ▸ **connexion à (l')Internet** Internet connection.

connivence [kɔnivɑ̃s] nf connivance ▸ **être de connivence (avec qqn)** to be in league (with sb).

connotation [kɔnɔtasjɔ̃] nf connotation.

connu, e [kɔny] ■ pp ➤ ***connaître***.
■ adj **1.** [célèbre] well-known, famous **2.** [su] : **connu de qqn** known to sb.

conquérant, e [kɔ̃kerɑ̃, ɑ̃t] ■ adj conquering.
■ nm, f conqueror.

conquérir [39] [kɔ̃kerir] vt to conquer.

conquête [kɔ̃kɛt] nf conquest ▸ **faire la conquête de qqch** to conquer sthg ▸ **faire la conquête de qqn** to win sb over.

conquiers, conquiert ➤ ***conquérir***.

conquis, e [kɔ̃ki, iz] pp ➤ ***conquérir***.

consacré, e [kɔ̃sakre] adj **1.** [habituel] established, accepted **2.** RELIG consecrated.

consacrer [3] [kɔ̃sakre] vt **1.** RELIG to consecrate **2.** [employer] : **consacrer qqch à** to devote sthg to ▸ **as-tu dix minutes à me consacrer?** can you spare me ten minutes? **3.** [couronner] to crown ▸ **le jury l'a consacré meilleur acteur** the jury voted him best actor.
◆ ***se consacrer*** vp : **se consacrer à** to dedicate o.s. to, to devote o.s. to.

consanguin, e [kɔ̃sɑ̃gɛ̃, in] adj : **frère consanguin** half-brother ▸ **sœur consanguine** half-sister ; voir aussi ***mariage***.

consciemment [kɔ̃sjamɑ̃] adv knowingly, consciously.

conscience [kɔ̃sjɑ̃s] nf **1.** [connaissance & PSYCHO] consciousness ▸ **avoir conscience de qqch** to be aware of sthg **2.** [morale] conscience ▸ **agir selon sa conscience** to follow one's conscience ▸ **avoir qqch sur la conscience** to have sthg on one's conscience ▸ **bonne/mauvaise conscience** clear/guilty conscience ▸ **conscience professionnelle** professional integrity, conscientiousness.

consciencieusement [kɔ̃sjɑ̃sjøzmɑ̃] adv conscientiously.

consciencieux, euse [kɔ̃sjɑ̃sjø, øz] adj conscientious.

conscient, e [kɔ̃sjɑ̃, ɑ̃t] adj conscious ▸ **être conscient de qqch** [connaître] to be conscious of sthg.

conscription [kɔ̃skripsjɔ̃] nf conscription, draft *US*.

conscrit [kɔ̃skri] nm conscript, recruit, draftee *US*.

consécration [kɔ̃sekrasjɔ̃] nf **1.** [reconnaissance] recognition / [de droit, coutume] establishment **2.** RELIG consecration.

consécutif, ive [kɔ̃sekytif, iv] adj **1.** [successif & GRAMM] consecutive **2.** [résultant] : **consécutif à** resulting from.

conseil [kɔ̃sɛj] nm **1.** [avis] piece of advice, advice *(U)* ▸ **donner un conseil** *ou* **des conseils (à qqn)** to give (sb) advice ▸ **suivre le conseil de qqn** to take somebody's advice **2.** [personne] : **conseil (en)** consultant (in) **3.** [assemblée] council ▸ **conseil d'administration** board of directors ▸ **conseil de classe** staff meeting ▸ **le Conseil constitutionnel** *French government body ensuring that laws, elections and referenda are constitutional* ▸ **conseil de discipline** disciplinary committee ▸ **le Conseil d'État** the (French) Council of State ▸ **conseil général** ≃ county council ▸ **le Conseil des ministres** ≃ the Cabinet

COMMENT EXPRIMER...

les conseils

Demander conseil

What should I do? / Qu'est-ce que je dois faire ?
What would you do, if you were me? / Qu'est-ce que tu ferais, à ma place ?
What do you think? / Qu'est-ce que tu en penses ?
Do you think I should tell him? / Tu crois que je devrais le lui dire ?
Would you kindly let me know what I need to do to book / Ayez l'obligeance de me dire ce que je dois faire pour réserver

Donner un conseil

You'd better take an aspirin / Vous devriez prendre une aspirine
You really should tell her / Tu devrais le lui dire
If I were you, I'd go home / À votre place, je rentrerais à la maison
I think you should have a rest / Je pense que vous devriez vous reposer
Why don't you talk to her about it? / Et si tu lui en parlais ?
I'd think twice about going / J'y réfléchirais à deux fois avant d'y aller
It might be better to do it yourself / Ce serait peut-être mieux de le faire toi-même
You could always try writing to him / Ce serait peut-être pas mal de lui écrire
My advice would be to close the account immediately / Je vous conseille de clôturer immédiatement votre compte

▸ **conseil municipal** town council *UK*, city council *US* ▸ **conseil régional** regional council ▸ **le Conseil supérieur de la magistrature** *French state body that appoints members of the judiciary.*

CULTURE

Conseil général et conseil régional

These bodies were established in a 1982 law calling for the decentralization of power in France. Each region has its own **conseil régional** whose members are chosen in national elections held every six years. They oversee **lycées** and further education programmes, as well as programmes for regional development. In turn, each **département** except Paris has a **conseil général** whose members serve six-year terms. Every three years, half the members' terms expire. They are responsible for **collèges**, development and planning within the **département** and social services. Abstention rates in **Conseil** elections are usually quite high.

conseiller[1] [4] [kɔ̃seje] ■ **vt 1.** [recommander] to advise ▸ **conseiller qqch à qqn** to recommend sthg to sb **2.** [guider] to advise, to counsel.
■ **vi** [donner un conseil] **: conseiller à qqn de faire qqch** to advise sb to do sthg.

conseiller[2], ***ère*** [kɔ̃seje, ɛr] **nm, f 1.** [guide] counsellor *UK*, counselor *US* ▸ **conseiller financier indépendant** independent financial adviser ▸ **conseiller matrimonial** marriage guidance counsellor *UK*, marriage counselor *US* **2.** [d'un conseil] councillor *UK*, councilor *US* ▸ **conseiller municipal** town councillor *UK*, city councilman (f councilwoman) *US*.

consensuel, ***elle*** [kɔ̃sɑ̃sɥɛl] **adj : politique consensuelle** consensus politics.

consensus [kɔ̃sɛ̃sys] **nm** consensus.

consentement [kɔ̃sɑ̃tmɑ̃] **nm** consent.

consentir [37] [kɔ̃sɑ̃tir] ■ **vt 1.** [accorder] **: consentir qqch à qqn** to grant sb sthg **2.** [accepter] **: consentir que** *(+ subjonctif)* **: je consens qu'il vienne** I consent to his coming.
■ **vi : consentir à qqch** to consent to sthg.

conséquence [kɔ̃sekɑ̃s] **nf** consequence, result ▸ **avoir des conséquences (sur qqch)** to have consequences (for sthg) ▸ **sans conséquence** [sans importance] of no importance ▸ **ne pas tirer à conséquence** to be of no consequence.

conséquent, ***e*** [kɔ̃sekɑ̃, ɑ̃t] **adj 1.** [cohérent] consistent **2.** *fam* [important] sizeable, considerable.
◆ ***par conséquent*** **loc adv** therefore, consequently.

conservateur, ***trice*** [kɔ̃sɛrvatœr, tris] ■ **adj** conservative.
■ **nm, f 1.** POLIT conservative **2.** [administrateur] curator.
◆ ***conservateur*** **nm** preservative.

conservation [kɔ̃sɛrvasjɔ̃] **nf 1.** [état, entretien] preservation **2.** [d'aliment] preserving.

conservatoire [kɔ̃sɛrvatwar] **nm** academy ▸ **conservatoire de musique** music college ▸ **le Conservatoire (national supérieur d'art dramatique)** *national drama school in Paris.*

conserve [kɔ̃sɛrv] **nf** canned *ou* tinned *UK* food ▸ **en conserve** [en boîte] canned, tinned *UK* / [en bocal] preserved, bottled.
◆ ***de conserve*** **loc adv** together.

conserver [3] [kɔ̃sɛrve] **vt 1.** [garder, entretenir] to keep ▸ **conserver qqch précieusement** to treasure sthg ▸ **'conserver au frais'** 'keep in a cool place' **2.** [entreposer - en boîte] to can / [- en bocal] to bottle **3.** [personne] **: être bien conservé** to be well-preserved ▸ **le sport, ça conserve** *fam* sport keeps you young.
◆ ***se conserver*** **vp** to keep ▸ **les pommes doivent se conserver sur des clayettes** apples must be stored on racks ▸ **les truffes au chocolat ne se conservent pas longtemps** (chocolate) truffles don't keep long.

considérable [kɔ̃siderabl] **adj** considerable.

considération [kɔ̃siderasjɔ̃] **nf 1.** [réflexion, motivation] consideration ▸ **en considération de qqch** in consideration of sthg ▸ **prendre qqch en considération** to take sthg into consideration ▸ **la question mérite considération** the question is worth considering ▸ **sans considération du coût** regardless *ou* without considering (the) cost **2.** [estime] respect ▸ **par considération pour** out of respect *ou* regard for ▸ **jouir d'une grande considération** to be highly considered *ou* regarded, to be held in great esteem **3.** [correspondance] **: veuillez agréer l'assurance de ma considération distinguée** yours faithfully *UK*, yours sincerely *US*.

considérer [18] [kɔ̃sidere] **vt** to consider ▸ **tout bien considéré** all things considered.

consigne [kɔ̃siɲ] **nf 1.** [ordre] orders *pl* **2.** *(gén pl)* [instruction] instructions *pl* **3.** [entrepôt de bagages] left-luggage office *UK*, checkroom *US*, baggage room *US* ▸ **consigne automatique** lockers *pl*, left-luggage lockers *pl UK* **4.** [somme d'argent] deposit.

consigné, ***e*** [kɔ̃siɲe] **adj** returnable.

consigner [3] [kɔ̃siɲe] **vt 1.** [bagages] to leave in the left-luggage office *UK* *ou* checkroom *US* *ou* baggage room *US* **2.** *sout* [relater] to record, to set down **3.** MIL to confine to barracks **4.** *vieilli* & SCOL **: consigner qqn** to give sb detention.

consistance [kɔ̃sistɑ̃s] **nf** [solidité] consistency / *fig* substance ▸ **sans consistance** [fade] colourless *UK*, colorless *US*.

consistant, ***e*** [kɔ̃sistɑ̃, ɑ̃t] **adj 1.** [épais] thick **2.** [nourrissant] substantial **3.** [fondé] sound.

consister [3] [kɔ̃siste] **vi : consister en** to consist of ▸ **consister à faire qqch** to consist in doing sthg.

consœur ➤ ***confrère***.

consolation [kɔ̃sɔlasjɔ̃] **nf** consolation.

console [kɔ̃sɔl] **nf 1.** [table] console (table) **2.** INFORM **: console de jeux** games console ▸ **console de visualisation** VDU, visual display unit.

consoler [3] [kɔ̃sɔle] **vt 1.** [réconforter] **: consoler qqn (de qqch)** to comfort sb (in sthg) **2.** [apaiser] to soothe.
◆ ***se consoler* vp : se consoler de qqch** to get over sthg.

consolider [3] [kɔ̃sɔlide] **vt** *litt* & *fig* to strengthen.

consommateur*, *trice [kɔ̃sɔmatœr, tris] **nm, f** [acheteur] consumer / [d'un bar] customer.

consommation [kɔ̃sɔmasjɔ̃] **nf 1.** [utilisation] consumption ▸ **faire une grande *ou* grosse consommation de** to use (up) a lot of / ÉCON **: consommation ostentatoire** conspicuous consumption **2.** [boisson] drink.

consommé*, *e [kɔ̃sɔme] **adj** *sout* consummate.
◆ ***consommé* nm** consommé.

consommer [3] [kɔ̃sɔme] ■ **vt 1.** [utiliser] to use (up) **2.** [manger] to eat ▸ **'à consommer avant 05/2005'** 'best before *ou* use by 5/05' **3.** [énergie] to consume, to use.
■ **vi 1.** [boire] to drink **2.** [voiture] **: cette voiture consomme beaucoup** this car uses a lot of fuel.

consonance [kɔ̃sɔnɑ̃s] **nf** consonance ▸ **un nom aux consonances harmonieuses** a beautiful name.

consonne [kɔ̃sɔn] **nf** consonant.

consort [kɔ̃sɔr] **adj m** ➤ ***prince***.
◆ ***consorts* nmpl : Paul et consorts** *péj* Paul and his sort, Paul and those like him.

consortium [kɔ̃sɔrsjɔm] **nm** consortium.

conspirateur*, *trice [kɔ̃spiratœr, tris] **nm, f** conspirator.

conspiration [kɔ̃spirasjɔ̃] **nf** conspiracy.

conspirer [3] [kɔ̃spire] ■ **vt** [comploter] to plot.
■ **vi** to plot, to conspire ▸ **conspirer contre qqn** to conspire against sb.
◆ ***conspirer à* v + prep** *sout* to conspire to ▸ **tout conspire à la réussite de ce projet** everything conspires *ou* combines to make this project a success.

conspuer [7] [kɔ̃spɥe] **vt** to boo.

constamment [kɔ̃stamɑ̃] **adv** constantly.

constance [kɔ̃stɑ̃s] **nf 1.** [persévérance] perseverance ▸ **avoir de la constance** to be indefatigable **2.** [permanence, fidélité] constancy.

constant*, *e [kɔ̃stɑ̃, ɑ̃t] **adj** constant ▸ **constant dans ses amitiés** faithful to one's friends *ou* in friendship ▸ **en euros constants** FIN in constant euros.

constat [kɔ̃sta] **nm 1.** [procès-verbal] report ▸ **constat à l'amiable** *joint insurance statement made by drivers after an accident* ▸ **constat d'huissier** *affidavit made before a bailiff* **2.** [constatation] established fact ▸ **faire le constat de qqch** to note sthg ▸ **constat d'échec** acknowledgement of failure.

constatation [kɔ̃statasjɔ̃] **nf 1.** [révélation] observation **2.** [fait retenu] finding.

constater [3] [kɔ̃state] **vt 1.** [se rendre compte de] to see, to note **2.** [consigner - fait, infraction] to record / [- décès, authenticité] to certify.

constellation [kɔ̃stelasjɔ̃] **nf** ASTRON constellation.

consternation [kɔ̃stɛrnasjɔ̃] **nf** dismay.

consterner [3] [kɔ̃stɛrne] **vt** to dismay.

constipation [kɔ̃stipasjɔ̃] **nf** constipation.

constipé*, *e [kɔ̃stipe] **adj 1.** MÉD constipated **2.** *fam fig* [manière, air] ill at ease.

constituant*, *e [kɔ̃stitɥɑ̃, ɑ̃t] **adj** constituent ; voir aussi ***assemblée***.

constitué*, *e [kɔ̃stitɥe] **adj 1.** [personne] **: normalement/bien constitué** of normal/sound constitution **2.** [composé] **: constitué de** consisting of, composed of **3.** [établi par la loi] constituted.

constituer [7] [kɔ̃stitɥe] **vt 1.** [élaborer] to set up **2.** [composer] to make up **3.** [représenter] to constitute **4.** [établir] to agree, to settle (on).
◆ ***se constituer* vp : se constituer de** to be made up of, to consist of ▸ **se constituer en** to form ▸ **se constituer prisonnier** to give o.s. up ▸ **se constituer partie civile** DR to sue privately for damages.

constitution [kɔ̃stitysjɔ̃] **nf 1.** [création] setting up **2.** [de pays, de corps] constitution **3.** [composition] composition **4.** [établissement] establishment.

constitutionnel*, *elle [kɔ̃stitysjɔnɛl] **adj** constitutional.

constructeur [kɔ̃stryktœr] **nm 1.** [fabricant] manufacturer / [de navire] shipbuilder **2.** [bâtisseur] builder.

constructif*, *ive [kɔ̃stryktif, iv] **adj 1.** [créateur] creative **2.** [positif] constructive.

construction [kɔ̃stryksjɔ̃] **nf 1.** [dans l'industrie] building, construction ▸ **construction navale** shipbuilding **2.** [édifice] structure, building **3.** *fig* & GRAMM construction.

construire [98] [kɔ̃strɥir] **vt 1.** [bâtir, fabriquer] to build ▸ **se faire construire une maison** to have a house built **2.** [roman] to structure **3.** [théorie, phrase] to construct **4.** GRAMM to construe ▸ **on construit "vouloir" avec le subjonctif** "vouloir" is construed with *ou* takes the subjunctive.

construisais*, *construisions ➤ ***construire***.

construit*, *e [kɔ̃strɥi, it] **pp** ➤ ***construire***.

consul [kɔ̃syl] **nm** consul ▸ **consul honoraire** honorary consul.

consulat [kɔ̃syla] **nm 1.** [charge] consulship **2.** [résidence] consulate.

consultant*, *e [kɔ̃syltɑ̃, ɑ̃t] ■ **adj : médecin consultant** consultant.
■ **nm, f** consultant ▸ **consultant en gestion** management consultant.

consultatif*, *ive [kɔ̃syltatif, iv] **adj** consultative, advisory.

consultation [kɔ̃syltasjɔ̃] **nf 1.** [d'ouvrage] **: de consultation aisée** easy to use **2.** MÉD & POLIT consultation **3.** [d'expert] (professional) advice.

consulter [3] [kɔ̃sylte] ■ **vt 1.** [compulser] to consult ▸ **consulter ses notes** to go over one's notes **2.** [interroger, demander conseil à] to consult, to ask ▸ **consulter qqn du regard** to look questioningly at sb **3.** [spécialiste] to consult, to see.
■ **vi** [médecin] to see patients, to take *ou* hold surgery *UK* / [avocat] to be available for consultation.
◆ ***se consulter* vp** to confer.

consumer [3] [kɔ̃syme] **vt 1.** *sout* [brûler] to burn, to destroy **2.** *fig & littéraire* [épuiser] to consume, to eat up.
◆ ***se consumer*** **vp** to waste away ▸ **se consumer de qqch** *littéraire* to be eaten up *ou* consumed with sthg.

consumérisme [kɔ̃symerism] **nm** consumerism.

contact [kɔ̃takt] **nm 1.** [gén] contact ▸ **le contact du marbre est froid** marble is cold to the touch ▸ **au contact de** on contact with ▸ **au contact de l'air** in contact with *ou* when exposed to the air ▸ **au contact des jeunes** through mixing *ou* associating with young people
2. [relations] contact ▸ **avoir des contacts avec** to have contact with ▸ **entrer en contact avec qqn** to contact sb, to get in touch with sb ▸ **mettre qqn et qqn en contact, mettre qqn en contact avec qqn** to put sb in touch with sb ▸ **prendre contact avec** to make contact with ▸ **prendre des contacts** to establish some contacts ▸ **rester en contact (avec)** to stay in touch (with)
3. AUTO ignition ▸ **mettre/couper le contact** to switch on/off the ignition
4. ÉLECTR contact, switch ▸ **il y a un mauvais contact** there's a loose connection somewhere ▸ **nous avons perdu le contact radio avec eux** we're no longer in radio contact with them
5. AÉRON & MIL contact ▸ **entrer en contact avec qqn** to make contact with sb.

contacter [3] [kɔ̃takte] **vt** to contact.

contagieux, euse [kɔ̃taʒjø, øz] ■ **adj** MÉD contagious / *fig* infectious.
■ **nm, f** contagious patient.

contagion [kɔ̃taʒjɔ̃] **nf** MÉD contagion ▸ **pour éviter tout risque de contagion** to avoid any risk of infection *ou* contagion / *fig* infectiousness.

container ➤ ***conteneur***.

contamination [kɔ̃taminasjɔ̃] **nf 1.** MÉD contamination ▸ **pour éviter la contamination** to avoid contamination **2.** [de l'environnement, des aliments] contamination ▸ **contamination radioactive** radioactive contamination **3.** LING contamination.

contaminer [3] [kɔ̃tamine] **vt** [infecter] to contaminate / *fig* to contaminate, to infect.

conte [kɔ̃t] **nm** story ▸ **conte de fées** fairy tale *ou* story.

contemplation [kɔ̃tɑ̃plasjɔ̃] **nf** contemplation ▸ **rester en contemplation devant** to gaze in contemplation at.

contempler [3] [kɔ̃tɑ̃ple] **vt** to contemplate.

contemporain, e [kɔ̃tɑ̃pɔrɛ̃, ɛn] ■ **adj : contemporain (de)** contemporary (with).
■ **nm, f** contemporary.

contenance [kɔ̃tnɑ̃s] **nf 1.** [capacité volumique] capacity **2.** [attitude] **: se donner une contenance** to give an impression of composure ▸ **perdre contenance** to lose one's composure.

conteneur [kɔ̃tənœr], ***container*** [kɔ̃tɛnɛr] **nm** (freight) container.

contenir [40] [kɔ̃tnir] **vt** to contain, to hold, to take.
◆ ***se contenir*** **vp** to contain o.s., to control o.s.

content, e [kɔ̃tɑ̃, ɑ̃t] **adj 1.** [joyeux] happy **2.** [satisfait] **: content (de qqn/qqch)** happy (with sb/sthg), content (with sb/sthg) ▸ **content de faire qqch** happy to do sthg.
◆ ***content*** **nm : avoir son content de** to have one's fill of.

contentement [kɔ̃tɑ̃tmɑ̃] **nm** satisfaction.

contenter [3] [kɔ̃tɑ̃te] **vt** to satisfy ▸ **voilà qui devrait contenter tout le monde** this should satisfy *ou* please everybody.
◆ ***se contenter*** **vp : se contenter de qqch/de faire qqch** to content o.s. with sthg/with doing sthg ▸ **se contenter de peu** to be content with little ▸ **elle s'est contentée de sourire** she merely smiled.

contentieux [kɔ̃tɑ̃sjø] **nm** [litige] dispute / [service] legal department.

contenu, e [kɔ̃tny] **pp** ➤ ***contenir***.
◆ ***contenu*** **nm 1.** [de récipient] contents *pl* **2.** [de texte, discours] content.

conter [3] [kɔ̃te] **vt** to tell.

contestable [kɔ̃tɛstabl] **adj** questionable.

contestataire [kɔ̃tɛstatɛr] ■ **nmf** anti-establishment figure.
■ **adj** anti-establishment.

contestation [kɔ̃tɛstasjɔ̃] **nf 1.** [protestation] protest, dispute **2.** POLIT **: la contestation** anti-establishment activity.

conteste [kɔ̃tɛst] ◆ ***sans conteste*** **loc adv** unquestionably.

contester [3] [kɔ̃tɛste] ■ **vt** to dispute, to contest.
■ **vi** to protest.

conteur, euse [kɔ̃tœr, øz] **nm, f** storyteller.

contexte [kɔ̃tɛkst] **nm** context.

contextualiser [kɔ̃tɛkstyalize] **vt** to contextualize.

contiens, contient ➤ ***contenir***.

contigu, uë [kɔ̃tigy] **adj : contigu (à)** adjacent (to).

continent [kɔ̃tinɑ̃] **nm** continent.

continental, e, aux [kɔ̃tinɑ̃tal, o] **adj** continental.

contingence [kɔ̃tɛ̃ʒɑ̃s] **nf** MATH & PHILO contingency.
◆ ***contingences*** **nfpl** contingencies, eventualities ▸ **les contingences de la vie quotidienne** everyday happenings *ou* events ▸ **prévoir toutes les contingences** to take unforeseen circumstances into consideration.

contingent [kɔ̃tɛ̃ʒɑ̃] **nm 1.** MIL national service conscripts *pl UK*, draft *US* **2.** COMM quota.

contingenter [3] [kɔ̃tɛ̃ʒɑ̃te] **vt** to put a quota on.

continu, e [kɔ̃tiny] **adj 1.** [ininterrompu] continuous **2.** ÉLECTR [courant] direct.
◆ ***continu*** **nm** MATH & PHILO continuum.
◆ ***en continu*** **loc adv** continuously, uninterruptedly.

continuation [kɔ̃tinɥasjɔ̃] **nf** continuation.

continuel, elle [kɔ̃tinɥɛl] **adj 1.** [continu] continuous **2.** [répété] continual.

continuellement [kɔ̃tinɥɛlmɑ̃] adv continually.

continuer [7] [kɔ̃tinɥe] ■ vt 1. [poursuivre] to carry on with, to continue (with) ▸ **continuez le repas sans moi** go on with the meal without me **2.** [prolonger] to continue ▸ **continuer son chemin** [voyageur] to keep going / [idée] to keep gaining momentum.
■ vi to continue, to go on ▸ **arrête-toi ici, moi je continue** you can stop right here; I'm going on ▸ **la route continue jusqu'au village** the road runs straight on to the village ▸ **si tu continues, ça va mal aller!** if you keep this up, you'll be sorry! ▸ **continuer à** *ou* **de faire qqch** to continue to do *ou* doing sthg ▸ **il continue à** *ou* **de pleuvoir** it keeps on raining ▸ **ma plante continue de grandir** my plant keeps getting bigger.
◆ ***se continuer*** vp to continue, to carry on.

continuité [kɔ̃tinɥite] nf continuity.

contondant, e [kɔ̃tɔ̃dɑ̃, ɑ̃t] adj blunt.

contorsionner [3] [kɔ̃tɔrsjɔne] ◆ ***se contorsionner*** vp to contort (o.s.), to writhe.

contour [kɔ̃tur] nm 1. [limite] outline **2.** *(gén pl)* [courbe] bend.

contourner [3] [kɔ̃turne] vt *litt* & *fig* to bypass, to get around.

contraceptif, ive [kɔ̃trasɛptif, iv] adj contraceptive.
◆ ***contraceptif*** nm contraceptive.

contraception [kɔ̃trasɛpsjɔ̃] nf contraception.

contracter [3] [kɔ̃trakte] vt **1.** [muscle] to contract, to tense / [visage] to contort **2.** [maladie] to contract, to catch **3.** [engagement] to contract ▸ **contracter une alliance** to enter into an alliance / [assurance] to take out **4.** [moralement] to make tense *ou* nervous **5.** [habitude] to pick up, to acquire **6.** [rendre anxieux] to make tense **7.** LING to contract.

contraction [kɔ̃traksjɔ̃] nf contraction / [état de muscle] tenseness ▸ **avoir des contractions** to have contractions.

contractuel, elle [kɔ̃traktɥɛl] ■ adj contractual.
■ nm, f traffic warden *UK*, traffic policeman (f policewoman) *US*.

contradiction [kɔ̃tradiksjɔ̃] nf contradiction.

contradictoire [kɔ̃tradiktwar] adj contradictory ▸ **débat contradictoire** open debate.

contragestion [kɔ̃traʒɛstjɔ̃] nf emergency contraception.

contraignais, contraignions ➤ ***contraindre.***

contraignant, e [kɔ̃trɛɲɑ̃, ɑ̃t] adj restricting.

contraindre [80] [kɔ̃trɛ̃dr] vt : **contraindre qqn à faire qqch** to compel *ou* force sb to do sthg ▸ **être contraint de faire qqch** to be compelled *ou* forced to do sthg.
◆ ***se contraindre*** vp **1.** *sout* [se maîtriser] to contain o.s., to control o.s. **2.** [s'obliger] **: se contraindre à faire qqch** to make o.s. do sthg, to force o.s. to do sthg.

contraint, e [kɔ̃trɛ̃, ɛ̃t] ■ pp ➤ ***contraindre.***
■ adj forced ▸ **contraint et forcé** under duress.
◆ ***contrainte*** nf constraint ▸ **contrainte budgétaire** budget constraint ▸ **sans contrainte** freely.

contraire [kɔ̃trɛr] ■ nm : **le contraire** the opposite ▸ **je n'ai jamais dit le contraire** I have never denied it.
■ adj opposite ▸ **contraire à** [non conforme à] contrary to / [nuisible à] harmful to, damaging to.
◆ ***au contraire*** loc adv on the contrary.
◆ ***au contraire de*** loc prép unlike.

contrairement [kɔ̃trɛrmɑ̃] ◆ ***contrairement à*** loc prép contrary to.

contrariant, e [kɔ̃trarjɑ̃, ɑ̃t] adj **1.** [personne] contrary, perverse **2.** [événement] annoying, tiresome.

contrarier [9] [kɔ̃trarje] vt **1.** [contrecarrer] to thwart, to frustrate **2.** [irriter] to annoy.
◆ ***se contrarier*** vp to contrast.

contrariété [kɔ̃trarjete] nf annoyance.

contraste [kɔ̃trast] nm contrast ▸ **faire contraste avec** to contrast with.

contraster [3] [kɔ̃traste] vt & vi to contrast.

contrat [kɔ̃tra] nm contract, agreement ▸ **remplir son contrat** *fig* to keep *ou* fulfil one's promise ▸ **contrat d'apprentissage** apprenticeship contract ▸ **contrat collectif** collective agreement ▸ **contrat à durée déterminée/indéterminée** fixed-term/permanent contract ▸ **Contrat emploi-solidarité** *government-sponsored contract for the unemployed involving professional training* ▸ **contrat reconductible** renewable agreement ▸ **contrat de sponsoring** sponsorship deal.

contravention [kɔ̃travɑ̃sjɔ̃] nf [amende] fine ▸ **contravention pour stationnement interdit** parking ticket ▸ **dresser une contravention à qqn** to fine sb.

contre [kɔ̃tr] ■ prép **1.** [juxtaposition, opposition] against ▸ **se blottir contre qqn** to cuddle up to sb ▸ **mettez-vous contre le mur** stand (right) by the wall ▸ **contre toute attente** contrary to *ou* against all expectations **2.** [proportion, comparaison] **: élu à 15 voix contre 9** elected by 15 votes to 9 ▸ **parier à 10 contre 1** to bet 10 to 1 **3.** [échange] (in exchange) for ▸ **j'ai échangé mon livre contre le sien** I swapped my book for hers **4.** [pour protéger de] against ▸ **pastilles contre la toux** cough lozenges ▸ **s'assurer contre le vol** to take out insurance against theft.
■ adv **1.** [juxtaposition] **: prends la rampe et appuie-toi contre** take hold of the rail and lean against it **2.** [opposition] **: vous êtes pour ou contre?** are you for or against?
■ nm **1.** ➤ ***pour*** **2.** SPORT **: marquer sur un contre** FOOTBALL to score on a counter attack ▸ **faire un contre** [au rugby] to intercept the ball.
◆ ***par contre*** loc adv on the other hand ▸ **il est très compétent, par contre il n'est pas toujours très aimable** he's very competent, but on the other hand he's not always very pleasant.

contre-attaque [kɔ̃tratak] (pl **contre-attaques**) nf counterattack.

contrebalancer [16] [kɔ̃trəbalɑ̃se] vt to counterbalance, to offset.
◆ ***se contrebalancer*** vp : **se contrebalancer de** *fam* not to give a damn about.

contrebande [kɔ̃trəbɑ̃d] nf [activité] smuggling / [marchandises] contraband ▸ **passer qqch en contrebande** to smuggle sthg.

contrebandier, ère [kɔ̃trəbɑ̃dje, ɛr] nm, f smuggler

contrebas [kɔ̃trəba] ◆ ***en contrebas*** loc adv (down) below. ◆ ***en contrebas de*** loc prép below.

contrebasse [kɔ̃trəbas] nf **1.** [instrument] (double) bass **2.** [musicien] (double) bass player.

contrecarrer [3] [kɔ̃trəkare] vt to thwart, to frustrate.

contrecœur [kɔ̃trəkœr] ◆ ***à contrecœur*** loc adv grudgingly.

contrecoup [kɔ̃trəku] nm consequence.

contre-courant [kɔ̃trəkurɑ̃] ◆ ***à contre-courant*** loc adv **1.** [d'un cours d'eau] against the current, upstream **2.** [à rebours] : **aller à contre-courant** to go against the grain **3.** [s'opposer] : **aller à contre-courant de la mode** to go against the trend ▸ **cela va à contre-courant de ce que je voulais faire** that is the (exact) opposite of what I wanted to do.

contredire [103] [kɔ̃trədir] vt to contradict.
◆ ***se contredire*** vp **1.** *(emploi réciproque)* to contradict (each other) **2.** *(emploi réfléchi)* to contradict o.s.

contredit, e [kɔ̃trədi, it] pp ➤ ***contredire***.

contrée [kɔ̃tre] nf [pays] land / [région] region.

contre-écrou [kɔ̃trekru] (pl **contre-écrous**) nm lock-nut.

contre-espionnage [kɔ̃trɛspjɔnaʒ] nm counter-espionage.

contre-exemple [kɔ̃trɛgzɑ̃pl] (pl **contre-exemples**) nm example to the contrary.

contre-expertise [kɔ̃trɛkspɛrtiz] (pl **contre-expertises**) nf second (expert) opinion.

contrefaçon [kɔ̃trəfasɔ̃] nf [activité] counterfeiting / [produit] forgery.

contrefaire [109] [kɔ̃trəfɛr] vt **1.** [signature, monnaie] to counterfeit, to forge **2.** [voix] to disguise.

contrefait, e [kɔ̃trəfɛ, ɛt] adj **1.** [frauduleux] forged **2.** *sout* [difforme] deformed.

contreficher [3] [kɔ̃trəfiʃe] ◆ ***se contreficher*** vp : **se contreficher de** *fam* not to give a damn about.

contre-filet [kɔ̃trəfilɛ] (pl **contre-filets**) nm sirloin.

contrefort [kɔ̃trəfɔr] nm **1.** [pilier] buttress **2.** [de chaussure] back.
◆ ***contreforts*** nmpl foothills.

contre-indication [kɔ̃trɛ̃dikasjɔ̃] (pl **contre-indications**) nf contraindication.

contre-interrogatoire [kɔ̃trɛ̃terɔgatwar] (pl **contre-interrogatoires**) nm cross-examination.

contre-jour [kɔ̃trəʒur] ◆ ***à contre-jour*** loc adv against the light.

contremaître, esse [kɔ̃trəmɛtr, ɛs] nm, f foreman (f forewoman).

contremarque [kɔ̃trəmark] nf [pour sortir d'un spectacle] pass-out ticket *UK*.

contre-offensive [kɔ̃trɔfɑ̃siv] (pl **contre-offensives**) nf counteroffensive.

contre-OPA [kɔ̃trɔpea] nf inv counterbid.

contre-ordre = ***contrordre***.

contrepartie [kɔ̃trəparti] nf **1.** [compensation] compensation **2.** [contraire] opposing view.
◆ ***en contrepartie*** loc adv in return.
◆ ***en contrepartie de*** loc prép (as a *ou* in compensation) for ▸ **service en contrepartie duquel...** for which services...

contre-performance [kɔ̃trəpɛrfɔrmɑ̃s] (pl **contre-performances**) nf disappointing performance.

contrepèterie [kɔ̃trəpɛtri] nf spoonerism.

contre-pied [kɔ̃trəpje] nm : **prendre le contre-pied de** to do the opposite of.

contreplaqué, contre-plaqué [kɔ̃trəplake] nm plywood.

contre-plongée [kɔ̃trəplɔ̃ʒe] (pl **contre-plongées**) nf low-angle shot.
◆ ***en contre-plongée*** loc adv from below ▸ **prends-la en contre-plongée** get a low-angle shot of her, shoot her from below.

contrepoids [kɔ̃trəpwa] nm *litt* & *fig* counterbalance, counterweight.

contrepoint [kɔ̃trəpwɛ̃] nm counterpoint.

contrepoison [kɔ̃trəpwazɔ̃] nm antidote.

contre-pouvoir [kɔ̃trəpuvwar] (pl **contre-pouvoirs**) nm counterbalance.

contre-publicité [kɔ̃trəpyblisite] (pl **contre-publicités**) nf **1.** [mauvaise publicité] adverse *ou* bad publicity *(U)* **2.** [publicité offensive] negative advertising *(U)*.

contrer [3] [kɔ̃tre] vt **1.** [s'opposer à] to counter **2.** [jeux de cartes] to double.

contresens [kɔ̃trəsɑ̃s] nm **1.** [erreur - de traduction] mistranslation / [- d'interprétation] misinterpretation **2.** [absurdité] nonsense *(U)*.
◆ ***à contresens*** loc adv [traduire, comprendre, marcher] the wrong way.

contresigner [3] [kɔ̃trəsiɲe] vt to countersign.

contretemps [kɔ̃trətɑ̃] nm hitch, mishap.
◆ ***à contretemps*** loc adv MUS out of time / *fig* at the wrong moment.

contrevenant, e [kɔ̃trəvnɑ̃, ɑ̃t] nm, f offender.

contrevenir [40] [kɔ̃trəvnir] vi : **contrevenir à** to contravene, to infringe.

contrevenu [kɔ̃trəvny] pp inv ➤ ***contrevenir***.

contribuable [kɔ̃tribɥabl] nmf taxpayer.

contribuer [7] [kɔ̃tribɥe] vi : **contribuer à** to contribute to *ou* towards ▸ **contribuer au succès de** to contribute to *ou* to have a part in the success of ▸ **il n'a pas contribué à la discussion** he took no part in the discussion ▸ **contribuer à faire qqch** to go towards doing sthg.

contribution [kɔ̃tribysjɔ̃] nf : **contribution (à)** contribution (to) ▸ **mettre qqn à contribution** to call on sb's services.
◆ ***contributions*** nfpl taxes ▸ **contributions directes/indirectes** direct/indirect taxation.

contrit, e [kɔ̃tri, it] adj contrite.

contrôle [kɔ̃trol] nm **1.** [vérification - de déclaration] check, checking *(U)* / [- de documents, billets] inspection ▸ **contrôle aérien** flight control ▸ **contrôle des comptes**

ou **fiscal** audit ▸ **il a un contrôle fiscal** ≃ the Inland Revenue *UK ou* IRS *US* is checking his tax return ▸ **contrôle de gestion** management control ▸ **contrôle d'identité** identity check ▸ **contrôle judiciaire** ≃ probation ▸ **placé sous contrôle judiciaire** ≃ put on probation ▸ **contrôle parental** parental control ▸ **contrôle de qualité** quality control ▸ **contrôle radar** AUTO radar speed-trap ▸ **contrôle de routine** routine inspection ▸ **contrôle technique** AUTO test of roadworthiness, MOT (test) *UK*, inspection *US*
2. [maîtrise, commande] control ▸ **contrôle des armements** arms control ▸ **perdre le contrôle de qqch** to lose control of sthg ▸ **contrôle des naissances** birth control ▸ **contrôle des prix** price control
3. [salle] control room
4. SCOL test ▸ **avoir un contrôle en chimie** to have a chemistry test ▸ **contrôle continu** UNIV continuous assessment
5. [direction] running, supervision ▸ **avoir le contrôle de** [d'un secteur, de compagnies] to have control of / [d'un pays, d'un territoire, d'un match] to be in control of.

contrôler [3] [kɔ̃trole] **vt 1.** [vérifier - documents, billets] to inspect / [- déclaration] to check / [- connaissances] to test **2.** [maîtriser, diriger] to control **3.** TECHNOL to monitor, to control **4.** [superviser] to supervise.
◆ ***se contrôler*** **vp** to control o.s.

contrôleur, euse [kɔ̃trolœr, øz] **nm, f** [de train] ticket inspector / [d'autobus] (bus) conductor ▸ **contrôleur aérien** air traffic controller / COMM [au service des achats] gatekeeper.

contrordre, contre-ordre (pl **contre-ordres**) [kɔ̃trɔrdr] **nm** countermand ▸ **sauf contrordre** unless otherwise instructed.

controverse [kɔ̃trɔvɛrs] **nf** controversy.

controversé, e [kɔ̃trɔvɛrse] **adj** [personne, décision] controversial.

contumace [kɔ̃tymas] **nf** DR **: condamné par contumace** sentenced in absentia.

contusion [kɔ̃tyzjɔ̃] **nf** bruise, contusion.

conurbation [kɔnyrbasjɔ̃] **nf** conurbation.

convaincant, e [kɔ̃vɛ̃kɑ̃, ɑ̃t] **adj** convincing.

convaincre [114] [kɔ̃vɛ̃kr] **vt 1.** [persuader] **: convaincre qqn (de qqch)** to convince sb (of sthg) ▸ **votre dernier argument m'a convaincu** your last argument has won me over ▸ **convaincre qqn (de faire qqch)** to persuade sb (to do sthg) **2.** DR **: convaincre qqn de** to find sb guilty of, to convict sb of ▸ **convaincre qqn de vol** to convict sb of theft, to find sb guilty of theft.

convaincu, e [kɔ̃vɛ̃ky] ■ **pp** ➤ ***convaincre***.
■ **adj** [partisan] committed ▸ **d'un ton convaincu, d'un air convaincu** with conviction.

convainquais, convainquions ➤ *convaincre*.

convainquant [kɔ̃vɛ̃kɑ̃] **p prés** ➤ *convaincre*.

convalescence [kɔ̃valesɑ̃s] **nf** convalescence ▸ **être en convalescence** to be convalescing *ou* recovering.

convalescent, e [kɔ̃valesɑ̃, ɑ̃t] **adj & nm, f** convalescent.

convenable [kɔ̃vnabl] **adj 1.** [manières, comportement] polite / [tenue, personne] decent, respectable **2.** [approprié] suitable **3.** [acceptable] adequate, acceptable.

convenablement [kɔ̃vnabləmɑ̃] **adv 1.** [s'habiller, se tenir] properly **2.** [être payé] decently **3.** [travailler] adequately.

convenance [kɔ̃vnɑ̃s] **nf : à ma/votre convenance** as suits me/you best.
◆ ***convenances*** **nfpl** proprieties.

convenir [40] [kɔ̃vnir] **vi 1.** [décider] **: convenir de qqch/de faire qqch** to agree on sthg/to do sthg ▸ **nous avions convenu de nous retrouver à midi** we had agreed to meet at noon
2. [plaire] **: convenir à qqn** to suit sb, to be convenient for sb ▸ **ce travail ne lui convient pas du tout** this job's not right for him at all ▸ **la vie que je mène me convient parfaitement** the life I lead suits me perfectly
3. [être approprié] **: convenir à** *ou* **pour** to be suitable for ▸ **10 h, cela vous convient-il?** does 10 o'clock suit you? ▸ **il convient de...** it is advisable to... ▸ **il voudrait savoir ce qu'il convient de faire** he would like to know the right thing to do
4. *sout* [admettre] **: convenir de qqch** to admit to sthg ▸ **je conviens d'avoir dit cela** I admit to having said that ▸ **convenir que** to admit (that) ▸ **j'en conviens** *sout* I admit it.

convention [kɔ̃vɑ̃sjɔ̃] **nf 1.** [règle, assemblée] convention **2.** [accord] agreement ▸ **convention collective** collective agreement.
◆ ***conventions*** **nfpl : les conventions** convention *(U)*.
◆ ***de convention*** **loc adj** conventional.

conventionné, e [kɔ̃vɑ̃sjɔne] **adj** subsidized, ≃ National Health *(avant n)* *UK*.

conventionnel, elle [kɔ̃vɑ̃sjɔnɛl] **adj** conventional.

convenu, e [kɔ̃vny] ■ **pp** ➤ ***convenir***.
■ **adj 1.** [décidé] **: comme convenu** as agreed **2.** *péj* [stéréotypé] conventional.

COMMENT EXPRIMER...

le début d'une conversation

Let me introduce myself: I'm John / Je me présente : John
Hi. It's Ann, isn't it? / Bonjour. Tu t'appelles Ann, c'est ça ?
So, how do you know David? / Alors, comment avez-vous connu David ?
Haven't we met before? / Est-ce que nous ne nous sommes pas déjà rencontrés ?
Is this your first time here? / C'est la première fois que vous venez ici ?
Have you been waiting long? / Ça fait longtemps que vous attendez ?
It's hot today, isn't it? / Il fait chaud aujourd'hui, hein ?

convergent, e [kɔ̃vɛrʒɑ̃, ɑ̃t] **adj** convergent.

converger [17] [kɔ̃vɛrʒe] **vi : converger (vers)** to converge (on).

conversation [kɔ̃vɛrsasjɔ̃] **nf** conversation ▸ **détourner la conversation** to change the subject ▸ **être en grande conversation avec** to be deep in conversation with.

converser [3] [kɔ̃vɛrse] **vi** *sout* **: converser (avec)** to converse (with).

conversion [kɔ̃vɛrsjɔ̃] **nf 1.** [gén] **: conversion (à/en)** conversion (to/into) **2.** SKI kick turn.

converti, e [kɔ̃vɛrti] **nm, f : prêcher un converti** *fig* to preach to the converted.

convertible [kɔ̃vɛrtibl] ■ **nm** [canapé-lit] sofa bed.
■ **adj** convertible.

convertir [32] [kɔ̃vɛrtir] **vt : convertir qqn (à)** to convert sb (to) ▸ **convertir qqch (en)** to convert sthg (into).
◆ ***se convertir*** **vp : se convertir (à)** to be converted (to).

convertisseur [kɔ̃vɛrtisœr] **nm 1.** [métallurgie, électricité] converter ▸ **convertisseur d'images** TV image converter **2.** INFORM **: convertisseur numérique** digitizer ▸ **convertisseur série-parallèle** staticizer.

convexe [kɔ̃vɛks] **adj** convex.

conviction [kɔ̃viksjɔ̃] **nf** conviction ▸ **avoir la conviction que** to be convinced (that) ▸ **avec/sans conviction** with/without conviction.
◆ ***convictions*** **nfpl** [credo] fundamental beliefs ▸ **avoir des convictions politiques** to have political convictions.

conviendrai, conviendrons ➤ ***convenir***.

convier [9] [kɔ̃vje] **vt : convier qqn à** to invite sb to.

convive [kɔ̃viv] **nmf** guest *(at a meal)*.

convivial, e, aux [kɔ̃vivjal, o] **adj 1.** [réunion] convivial **2.** INFORM user-friendly.

convocation [kɔ̃vɔkasjɔ̃] **nf** [avis écrit] summons *sg*, notification to attend.

convoi [kɔ̃vwa] **nm 1.** [de véhicules] convoy ▸ **convoi exceptionnel** wide load **2.** [train] train.

convoiter [3] [kɔ̃vwate] **vt** to covet.

convoitise [kɔ̃vwatiz] **nf** covetousness.

convoler [3] [kɔ̃vɔle] ➤ ***noces***.

convoquer [3] [kɔ̃vɔke] **vt 1.** [assemblée] to convene **2.** [pour un entretien] to invite **3.** [subalterne, témoin] to summon **4.** [à un examen] **: convoquer qqn** to ask sb to attend.

convoyer [13] [kɔ̃vwaje] **vt** to escort.

convoyeur, euse [kɔ̃vwajœr, øz] ■ **adj** escort *(avant n)*.
■ **nm, f** escort ▸ **convoyeur de fonds** security guard.

convulser [3] [kɔ̃vylse] **vt** to convulse.
◆ ***se convulser*** **vp** to convulse.

convulsif, ive [kɔ̃vylsif, iv] **adj** convulsive.

convulsion [kɔ̃vylsjɔ̃] **nf** convulsion.

cookie [kuki] **nm 1.** [petit gâteau] biscuit *UK*, cookie *US* **2.** INFORM cookie.

cool [kul] **adj inv** *fam* [décontracté] laid-back, cool.

coopérant [kɔɔperɑ̃] **nm 1.** MIL *person engaged in voluntary work abroad as an alternative to military service* **2.** ÉCON *foreign expert working in developing country*.

coopératif, ive [kɔɔperatif, iv] **adj** cooperative.
◆ ***coopérative*** **nf** [groupement] cooperative ▸ **coopérative de consommation** consumers' cooperative.

coopération [kɔɔperasjɔ̃] **nf 1.** [collaboration] cooperation ▸ **en coopération avec qqn** in collaboration with sb **2.** [aide] **: la coopération** ≃ overseas development.

coopérer [18] [kɔɔpere] **vi : coopérer (à)** to cooperate (in).

cooptation [kɔɔptasjɔ̃] **nf** co-opting.

coordinateur, trice [kɔɔrdinatœr, tris] ■ **adj** coordinating.
■ **nm, f** coordinator.

coordination [kɔɔrdinasjɔ̃] **nf** coordination ; voir aussi ***conjonction***.

coordonnée [kɔɔrdɔne] ■ **adj** LING **: propositions coordonnées** coordinate clauses.
■ **nf** LING coordinate clause.
◆ ***coordonnées*** **nfpl 1.** GÉOGR & MATH coordinates **2.** [adresse] address and phone number, details ▸ **laissez-moi vos coordonnées** leave me your name, address and phone number.

coordonner [3] [kɔɔrdɔne] **vt** to coordinate.

copain, ine [kɔpɛ̃, in] ■ **adj** friendly, matey *UK* ▸ **être très copains** to be great friends.
■ **nm, f** [ami] friend, mate *UK* / [petit ami] boyfriend (f girlfriend).

copeau, x [kɔpo] **nm** [de bois] (wood) shaving.

Copenhague [kɔpɛnag] **npr** Copenhagen.

copie [kɔpi] **nf 1.** [double, reproduction] copy ▸ **copie (certifiée) conforme** certified copy **2.** [SCOL - de devoir] clean *ou* fair *UK* copy / [- d'examen] paper, script **3.** INFORM **: copie d'écran** screenshot ▸ **copie de sauvegarde** backup copy.

copier [9] [kɔpje] ■ **vt** [gén & INFORM] to copy.
■ **vi : copier sur qqn** to copy from sb.

copier-coller [kɔpjekɔle] **nm inv** INFORM copy and paste.

copieur, euse [kɔpjœr, øz] **nm, f** [étudiant] copier.
◆ ***copieur*** **nm** [photocopieur] copier, photocopier.

copieusement [kɔpjøzmɑ̃] **adv** copiously.

copieux, euse [kɔpjø, øz] **adj** copious.

copilote [kɔpilɔt] **nmf** copilot.

copine ➤ ***copain***.

coprocesseur [kɔprɔsɛsœr] **nm : coprocesseur mathématique** INFORM maths *UK ou* math *US* coprocessor.

coproducteur, trice [kɔprɔdyktœr, tris] **nm, f** [pour spectacle] coproducer.

coproduction [kɔprɔdyksjɔ̃] **nf** coproduction ▸ **en coproduction** coproduced.

coproduire [kɔprɔdɥir] **vt** CINÉ & TV to coproduce.

copropriétaire [kɔprɔprijetɛr] **nmf** co-owner, joint owner.

copropriété [kɔprɔprijete] **nf** co-ownership, joint ownership, condominium *US*.

copulation [kɔpylasjɔ̃] **nf** copulation.

copuler [3] [kɔpyle] **vi** to copulate.

copyright [kɔpirajt] **nm** copyright.

coq [kɔk] **nm** cock *UK*, rooster *US* ▸ **coq de bruyère** grouse ▸ **coq de combat** gamecock ▸ **le coq gaulois** the French cockerel ▸ **coq au vin** *chicken cooked with red wine, bacon, mushrooms and shallots* ▸ **fier comme un coq** *fig* as proud as a peacock ▸ **être comme un coq en pâte** *fig* to be in clover ▸ **sauter** *ou* **passer du coq à l'âne** to jump from one subject to another.

coq-à-l'âne [kɔkalan] **nm inv** [dans la conversation] sudden change of subject ▸ **faire un coq-à-l'âne** to go on to something completely different.

coque [kɔk] **nf 1.** [de noix] shell **2.** [de navire] hull.

coquelet [kɔklɛ] **nm** cockerel.

coquelicot [kɔkliko] **nm** poppy.

coqueluche [kɔklyʃ] **nf** whooping cough ▸ **être la coqueluche de** *fig* to be the idol *ou* darling of.

coquet, ette [kɔkɛ, ɛt] **adj 1.** [vêtements] smart, stylish / [ville, jeune fille] pretty **2.** *(avant n) hum* [important] **: la coquette somme de 100 livres** the tidy sum of £100.
◆ ***coquette*** **nf** flirt.

coquetier [kɔktje] **nm** eggcup.

coquetterie [kɔkɛtri] **nf 1.** [désir de plaire] coquettishness **2.** [élégance] smartness, stylishness.

coquillage [kɔkijaʒ] **nm 1.** [mollusque] shellfish **2.** [coquille] shell.

coquille [kɔkij] **nf 1.** [de mollusque, noix, œuf] shell ▸ **coquille de noix** [embarcation] cockleshell ▸ **coquille Saint-Jacques** scallop ▸ **rentrer dans sa coquille** *fig* to go back into one's shell **2.** TYPO misprint.

coquillettes [kɔkijɛt] **nfpl** pasta shells.

coquin, e [kɔkɛ̃, in] ■ **adj** [sous-vêtement] sexy, naughty / [regard, histoire] saucy.
■ **nm, f** rascal.

cor [kɔr] **nm 1.** [instrument] horn ▸ **cor de chasse** hunting horn **2.** [au pied] corn.
◆ ***à cor et à cri*** **loc adv : réclamer qqch à cor et à cri** to clamour *UK ou* clamor *US* for sthg.

corail, aux [kɔraj, o] **nm 1.** [gén] coral **2.** RAIL **: train corail** ≃ express train.
◆ ***corail*** **adj inv** coral (pink).

Coran [kɔrɑ̃] **nm : le Coran** the Koran.

coranique [kɔranik] **adj** Koranic.

corbeau, x [kɔrbo] **nm 1.** [oiseau] crow **2.** [délateur] writer of poison-pen letters.

corbeille [kɔrbɛj] **nf 1.** [panier] basket ▸ **corbeille à papier** wastepaper basket, waste basket *US* **2.** INFORM trash (can) / [d'une messagerie électronique Mac] **: corbeille d'arrivée/de départ** in/out box **3.** THÉÂTRE (dress) circle **4.** [de Bourse] stockbrokers' enclosure *(at Paris Stock Exchange)*.

corbillard [kɔrbijar] **nm** hearse.

cordage [kɔrdaʒ] **nm 1.** [de bateau] rigging *(U)* **2.** [de raquette] strings *pl*.

corde [kɔrd] **nf 1.** [filin] rope ▸ **corde à linge** clothesline, washing line *UK* ▸ **corde lisse** climbing rope ▸ **corde à nœuds** knotted climbing rope ▸ **corde raide** high wire, tightrope ▸ **être sur la corde raide** *litt* to be on *ou* to walk the tightrope / *fig* to walk a tightrope, to do a (difficult) balancing act ▸ **corde à sauter** skipping rope *UK*, jump rope *US* ▸ **sauter à la corde** to skip *UK*, to jump rope *US* **2.** [d'instrument, arc] string ▸ **avoir plus d'une corde à son arc** *fig* to have more than one string to one's bow **3.** ANAT **: cordes vocales** vocal cords **4.** [équitation] rails *pl* ▸ **être à la corde** to be on the inside ▸ **prendre un virage à la corde** to hug a bend **5.** [athlétisme] inside (lane)
▸▸ **usé jusqu'à la corde** [vêtement] threadbare / [histoire] well-worn, hackneyed ▸ **faire vibrer la corde sensible** to strike the right chord.
◆ ***cordes*** **nfpl 1.** MUS strings ▸ **instruments à cordes** stringed instruments **2.** [d'un ring] **: les cordes** the ropes ▸▸ **être dans les cordes de qqn** to be (in) sb's line ▸ **il tombe** *ou* **pleut des cordes** it's raining cats and dogs.

cordeau [kɔrdo] **nm** [de jardinier] line ▸ **tracé au cordeau** *fig* [route] dead straight.

cordée [kɔrde] **nf** roped party *(of mountaineers)*.

cordelette [kɔrdəlɛt] **nf** string.

cordial, e, aux [kɔrdjal, o] **adj** warm, cordial.
◆ ***cordial, aux*** **nm** *vieilli* tonic, pick-me-up.

cordialement [kɔrdjalmɑ̃] **adv** [saluer] warmly, cordially / [en fin de lettre] kind regards.

cordialité [kɔrdjalite] **nf** warmth.

cordillère [kɔrdijɛr] **nf** mountain range / GÉOGR cordillera ▸ **la cordillère des Andes** the Andes (cordillera).

cordon [kɔrdɔ̃] **nm** string, cord ▸ **cordon ombilical** umbilical cord ▸ **cordon de police** police cordon.

cordon-bleu [kɔrdɔ̃blø] (pl **cordons-bleus**) **nm** cordon bleu cook.

cordonnerie [kɔrdɔnri] **nf 1.** [magasin] shoe repairer's, cobbler's *vieilli* **2.** [activité, commerce] shoe repairing.

cordonnier, ère [kɔrdɔnje, ɛr] **nm, f** shoe repairer, cobbler *vieilli*.

Cordoue [kɔrdu] **npr** Cordoba.

Corée [kɔre] **nf** Korea ▸ **la Corée du Nord/du Sud** North/South Korea.

coréen, enne [kɔreɛ̃, ɛn] **adj** Korean.
◆ ***Coréen, enne*** **nm, f** Korean.

coreligionnaire [kɔrəliʒjɔnɛr] **nmf** fellow Christian/Jew *etc*.

coriace [kɔrjas] **adj** *litt* & *fig* tough.

coriandre [kɔrjɑ̃dr] **nf** coriander.

cormoran [kɔrmɔrɑ̃] **nm** cormorant.

corne [kɔrn] **nf 1.** [gén] horn / [de cerf] antler ▸ **corne d'abondance** *fig* horn of plenty ▸ **corne de brume** foghorn **2.** [callosité] hard skin *(U)*, callus.

cornée [kɔrne] **nf** cornea.

corneille [kɔrnɛj] **nf** crow.

cornélien, enne [kɔrneljɛ̃, ɛn] **adj** *involving the conflict between love and duty*.

cornemuse [kɔrnəmyz] **nf** bagpipes *pl*.

corner [1] [3] [kɔrne] ■ **vi** [sirène] to blare (out).
■ **vt** [page] to turn down the corner of.

corner [2] [kɔrnɛr] **nm** FOOTBALL corner (kick).

cornet [kɔrnɛ] **nm** **1.** [d'aliment] cone, cornet *UK vieilli* **2.** [de jeu] (dice) shaker.

corniaud, ***corniot*** [kɔrnjo] **nm** **1.** [chien] mongrel **2.** *fam* [imbécile] idiot.

corniche [kɔrniʃ] **nf** **1.** [route] cliff road **2.** [moulure] cornice.

cornichon [kɔrniʃɔ̃] **nm** **1.** [condiment] gherkin, pickle *US* **2.** *fam* [imbécile] idiot.

corniot = ***corniaud***.

Cornouailles [kɔrnwaj] **nf : la Cornouailles** Cornwall.

corollaire [kɔrɔlɛr] **nm** corollary.

corolle [kɔrɔl] **nf** corolla.

coron [kɔrɔ̃] **nm** [village] mining village.

coronaire [kɔrɔnɛr] ➤ ***artère***.

corporation [kɔrpɔrasjɔ̃] **nf** corporate body.

corporel, ***elle*** [kɔrpɔrɛl] **adj** **1.** [physique - besoin] bodily / [- châtiment] corporal **2.** DR tangible.

corps [kɔr] **nm** **1.** [gén] body ▸ **être au corps à corps** to fight hand-to-hand ▸ **tremblant de tout son corps** trembling all over ▸ **le corps du délit** DR corpus delicti ▸ **corps étranger** foreign body ▸ **corps gras** fat **2.** [groupe] **: corps d'armée** (army) corps ▸ **corps céleste** celestial *ou* heavenly body ▸ **corps diplomatique** diplomatic corps ▸ **le corps électoral** the electorate ▸ **corps enseignant** [profession] teaching profession / [d'école] teaching staff ▸ **le corps exécutif** the executive ▸ **corps expéditionnaire** task force ▸ **corps de garde** [soldats] guards / [local] guardroom ▸ **le corps législatif** the legislative body ▸ **le corps médical** the medical profession **3.** [partie principale] **: corps de bâtiment** main body of a building
▸▸ **à mon corps défendant** against my will ▸ **donner corps à une idée/un plan** to give substance to an idea/a scheme ▸ **faire corps avec** to form (an integral) part of ▸ **se dévouer corps et âme à** to commit o.s. body and soul to ▸ **se jeter** *ou* **se lancer à corps perdu dans qqch** to throw o.s. (headlong) into sthg ▸ **prendre corps** to take shape ▸ **sombrer corps et biens** to go down with all hands ▸ **il s'est perdu corps et biens** *fig* he's disappeared without trace.

corpulent, ***e*** [kɔrpylɑ̃, ɑ̃t] **adj** corpulent, stout.

corpus [kɔrpys] **nm** corpus.

corpuscule [kɔrpyskyl] **nm** corpuscle.

correct, ***e*** [kɔrɛkt] **adj** **1.** [exact] correct, right **2.** [honnête] correct, proper **3.** [acceptable] decent / [travail] fair.

correctement [kɔ̃rɛktəmɑ̃] **adv** **1.** [sans faute] accurately **2.** [décemment] properly.

correcteur, ***trice*** [kɔrɛktœr, tris] ■ **adj** corrective.
■ **nm, f** **1.** [d'examen] examiner, marker *UK*, grader *US* **2.** TYPO proofreader.
◆ ***correcteur orthographique*** **nm** spell-checker.

correctif, ***ive*** [kɔrɛktif, iv] **adj** corrective.
◆ ***correctif*** **nm** rider ▸ **apporter un correctif à qqch** to qualify sthg.

correction [kɔrɛksjɔ̃] **nf** **1.** [d'erreur] correction **2.** [punition] punishment ▸ **donner une correction à qqn** to give sb a good hiding **3.** [modification] correction **4.** TYPO proofreading **5.** [notation] marking **6.** [qualité] correctness **7.** [bienséance] propriety **8.** ÉCON **: correction des variations saisonnières** seasonal adjustment.

correctionnel, ***elle*** [kɔrɛksjɔnɛl] **adj** DR **: tribunal correctionnel** ≃ magistrates' *UK ou* criminal *US* court ▸ **peine correctionnelle** *sentence of up to five years' imprisonment.*
◆ ***correctionnelle*** **nf** DR ≃ magistrates' *UK ou* criminal *US* court ▸ **passer en correctionnelle** to appear before the magistrate *UK ou* judge *US*.

corrélation [kɔrelasjɔ̃] **nf** correlation.

correspondance [kɔrɛspɔ̃dɑ̃s] **nf** **1.** [gén] correspondence ▸ **cours par correspondance** correspondence course **2.** [transports] connection ▸ **assurer la correspondance avec** to connect with.

correspondant, ***e*** [kɔrɛspɔ̃dɑ̃, ɑ̃t] ■ **adj** corresponding.
■ **nm, f** **1.** [par lettres] correspondent, pen pal, penfriend *UK* **2.** [par téléphone] **: je vous passe votre correspondant** I'll put you through **3.** PRESSE correspondent ▸ **de notre correspondant à New York** from our New York correspondent ▸ **correspondant de guerre/de presse** war/newspaper correspondent.

correspondre [75] [kɔrɛspɔ̃dr] **vi** **1.** [être conforme] **: correspondre à** to correspond to **2.** [communiquer] to communicate **3.** [par lettres] **: correspondre avec** to correspond with.
◆ ***se correspondre*** **vp** [s'accorder] to correspond.

correspondu, ***e*** [kɔrɛspɔ̃dy] **pp** ➤ ***correspondre***.

corrida [kɔrida] **nf** bullfight.

corridor [kɔridɔr] **nm** corridor.

corrigé [kɔriʒe] **nm** correct version.

corriger [17] [kɔriʒe] **vt** **1.** TYPO to correct, to proofread **2.** [noter] to mark **3.** [modifier] to correct **4.** [guérir] **: corriger qqn de** to cure sb of **5.** [punir] to give a good hiding to.
◆ ***se corriger*** **vp** **1.** [d'un défaut] **: se corriger de** to cure o.s. of **2.** [devenir raisonnable] to mend one's ways.

corroborer [3] [kɔrɔbɔre] **vt** to corroborate.

corroder [3] [kɔrɔde] **vt** [ronger] to corrode / *fig* to erode.

corrompre [78] [kɔrɔ̃pr] **vt** **1.** [soudoyer] to bribe **2.** [dépraver] to corrupt **3.** *fig* [gâter] to spoil.

corrompu, ***e*** [kɔrɔ̃py] ■ **pp** ➤ ***corrompre***.
■ **adj** [fonctionnaire, âme] corrupt.

corrosif, ***ive*** [kɔrozif, iv] **adj** **1.** [acide] corrosive **2.** *fig* [ironie] biting.
◆ ***corrosif*** **nm** corrosive.

corrosion [kɔrozjɔ̃] **nf** corrosion.

corruption [kɔrypsjɔ̃] **nf** **1.** [subornation] bribery ▸ **corruption de fonctionnaire** bribery of a public official **2.** [dépravation] corruption **3.** [décomposition] decomposition **4.** [altération] debasing.

corsage [kɔrsaʒ] **nm** **1.** [chemisier] blouse **2.** [de robe] bodice.

corsaire [kɔrsɛr] **nm 1.** [navire, marin] corsair, privateer **2.** [pantalon] pedal-pushers *pl.*

corse [kɔrs] ■ **adj** Corsican.
■ **nm** [langue] Corsican.
◆ ***Corse*** ■ **nmf** Corsican.
■ **nf : la Corse** Corsica ▸ **en Corse** in Corsica.

corsé, e [kɔrse] **adj** [café] strong / [vin] full-bodied / [plat, histoire] spicy.

corser [3] [kɔrse] **vt 1.** [plat, sauce] to spice up **2.** [histoire] to liven up **3.** [vin] to strengthen.
◆ ***se corser*** **vp** [se compliquer] to get complicated ▸ **ça se corse** things are getting serious.

corset [kɔrsɛ] **nm** corset ▸ **corset orthopédique** MÉD surgical corset.

cortège [kɔrtɛʒ] **nm** procession ▸ **cortège funèbre** funeral procession, cortege.

cortisone [kɔrtizɔn] **nf** cortisone.

corvée [kɔrve] **nf 1.** MIL fatigue (duty) **2.** [activité pénible] chore.

cosignataire [kosiɲatɛr] **nmf** DR cosignatory.

cosinus [kosinys] **nm** cosine.

cosmétique [kɔsmetik] **nm & adj** cosmetic.

cosmique [kɔsmik] **adj** cosmic.

cosmonaute [kɔsmɔnot] **nmf** cosmonaut.

cosmopolite [kɔsmɔpɔlit] **adj** cosmopolitan.

cosmos [kɔsmos] **nm 1.** [univers] cosmos **2.** [espace] outer space.

cosse [kɔs] **nf 1.** [de légume] pod **2.** *fam vieilli* [paresse] : **avoir la cosse** to feel lazy.

cossu, e [kɔsy] **adj 1.** [personne] wealthy, moneyed **2.** [maison] opulent.

costard [kɔstar] **nm** *fam* suit.

Costa Rica [kɔstarika] **nm : le Costa Rica** Costa Rica ▸ **au Costa Rica** in Costa Rica.

costaricien, enne [kɔstarisjɛ̃, ɛn] **adj** Costa Rican.
◆ ***Costaricien, enne*** **nm, f** Costa Rican.

costaud, e [kɔsto, od] **adj** sturdily built.
◆ ***costaud*** **nm** strapping man.

costume [kɔstym] **nm 1.** [folklorique, de théâtre] costume **2.** [vêtement d'homme] suit ▸ **costume trois-pièces** three-piece suit.

costumé, e [kɔstyme] **adj** fancy-dress *(avant n).*

costumier, ère [kɔstymje, ɛr] **nm, f** THÉÂTRE wardrobe master (f mistress).

cotation [kɔtasjɔ̃] **nf** FIN quotation ▸ **cotation en Bourse** quoting on the stock exchange.

cote [kɔt] **nf 1.** [marque de classement] classification mark / [marque numérale] serial number **2.** FIN [valeur] quotation / [liste] share (price) index ▸ **inscrit à la cote** [valeurs] listed ▸ **hors-cote** unlisted **3.** [de cheval] odds *pl* **4.** [popularité] rating ▸ **avoir la cote (auprès de qqn)** *fam* to be popular (with sb) / [d'un homme politique] **: cote de popularité** approval rating **5.** [niveau] level ▸ **cote d'alerte** [de cours d'eau] danger level / *fig* crisis point.

côte [kot] **nf 1.** ANAT & BOT [de bœuf] rib / [de porc, mouton, agneau] chop ▸ **côte à côte** side by side **2.** [pente] hill **3.** [littoral] coast ▸ **la Côte d'Azur** the French Riviera **4.** [tissu] **: velours à côtes** corduroy.

coté, e [kɔte] **adj** [estimé] popular ▸ **être coté** to be well thought of ▸ **être bien/mal coté** to be highly/poorly rated / FIN listed ▸ **non coté** unlisted ▸ **valeurs cotées en Bourse** listed securities.

côté [kote] **nm 1.** [gén] side ▸ **côté sous le vent** NAUT leeward side ▸ **être couché sur le côté** to be lying on one's side ▸ **être aux côtés de qqn** *fig* to be by sb's side ▸ **d'un côté..., de l'autre côté...** on the one hand..., on the other hand... ▸ **et côté finances, ça va?** *fam* how are things moneywise? ▸ **elle a un côté naïf** there's a naive side to her ▸ **prendre qqch du bon/mauvais côté** to take sthg in good/bad part **2.** [endroit, direction] direction, way ▸ **de quel côté est-il parti?** which way did he go? ▸ **de l'autre côté de** on the other side of ▸ **de tous côtés** from all directions ▸ **du côté de** [près de] near / [direction] towards *UK*, toward *US* / [provenance] from ▸ **elle est partie du côté du village** she went towards the village ▸ **cherchons du côté des auteurs classiques** let's look amongst classical authors.
◆ ***à côté*** **loc adv 1.** [lieu - gén] nearby / [- dans la maison adjacente] next door ▸ **les voisins d'à côté** the nextdoor neighbours **2.** [cible] **: tirer à côté** to shoot wide (of the target).
◆ ***à côté de*** **loc prép 1.** [proximité] beside, next to **2.** [en comparaison avec] beside, compared to **3.** [en dehors de] **: passer à côté de** [chemin, difficulté, porte] to miss / [occasion] to miss out on ▸ **être à côté du sujet** to be off the point ▸ **être à côté de la plaque** *fam* to have (got hold of) the wrong end of the stick.
◆ ***de côté*** **loc adv 1.** [se placer, marcher] sideways **2.** [en réserve] aside ▸ **mettre/laisser qqch de côté** to put/leave sthg aside.

coteau [kɔto] **nm 1.** [colline] hill **2.** [versant] slope.

Côte-d'Ivoire [kotdivwar] **nf : la Côte-d'Ivoire** the Ivory Coast.

côtelé, e [kotle] **adj** ribbed ▸ **velours côtelé** corduroy.

côtelette [kotlɛt] **nf** [de porc, mouton, d'agneau] chop / [de veau] cutlet.

coter [3] [kɔte] **vt 1.** [marquer, noter] to mark **2.** FIN to quote **3.** [carte, plan] to mark the heights on.

coterie [kɔtri] **nf** *péj & vieilli* set, clique.

côtier, ère [kotje, ɛr] **adj** coastal.

cotisation [kɔtizasjɔ̃] **nf** [à club, parti] subscription / [à la Sécurité sociale] contribution.
◆ ***cotisations*** [kɔtizasjɔ̃] **nfpl : cotisations patronales** employer's contributions ▸ **cotisations salariales** employee's contributions.

CULTURE
Cotisations

These are the contributions, similar to National Insurance Contributions in the UK, that every French employer and employee must make monthly to Social Security programmes (health insurance, maternity benefits, disability and life insurance, family benefits, retirement pensions, and housing subsidies). Employee contributions are based on salary. Companies pay about twice as much per month as their employees.

cotiser [3] [kɔtize] **vi** [à un club, un parti] to subscribe / [à la Sécurité sociale] to contribute.
◆ ***se cotiser*** **vp** to club together.

coton [kɔtɔ̃] **nm** cotton ▸ **coton (hydrophile)** (absorbent) cotton, cotton wool *UK* ▸ **filer un mauvais coton** *fig* to be in a bad way.

cotonnade [kɔtɔnad] **nf** cotton fabric.

Coton-Tige® [kɔtɔ̃tiʒ] (pl **Cotons-Tiges**) **nm** cotton bud *UK*, Q-tip® *US*.

côtoyer [13] [kotwaje] **vt 1.** [longer] to run alongside **2.** *fig* [frôler] to verge on **3.** *fig* [fréquenter] to mix with.

cotte [kɔt] **nf** HIST tunic ▸ **cotte de mailles** coat of mail.

cou [ku] **nm** [de personne, bouteille] neck ▸ **se jeter au cou de qqn, sauter au cou de qqn** to throw one's arms around sb's neck ▸ **jusqu'au cou** *fig* up to one's eyes ▸ **se pendre au cou de qqn** to hang around sb's neck.

couac [kwak] **nm** false *ou* wrong note.

couard, e [kwar, ard] *sout* ■ **adj** cowardly.
■ **nm, f** coward.

couchage [kuʃaʒ] **nm** sleeping arrangements *pl*, ➤ ***sac***.

couchant [kuʃɑ̃] ■ **adj** ➤ ***soleil***.
■ **nm** west.

couche [kuʃ] **nf 1.** [de peinture, de vernis] coat, layer / [de poussière] film, layer **2.** [épaisseur] layer ▸ **couche d'ozone** ozone layer ▸ **en avoir *ou* en tenir une couche** *fam* to be as dumb as they come, to be (as) thick as two short planks *UK* **3.** [de bébé] nappy *UK*, diaper *US* **4.** [classe sociale] stratum.
◆ ***couches*** **nfpl** *vieilli* confinement *(U)*, labour *(U)* *UK*, labor *(U)* *US*.
◆ ***fausse couche*** **nf** miscarriage.

couché, e [kuʃe] **adj : être couché** [étendu] to be lying down / [au lit] to be in bed.

couche-culotte [kuʃkylɔt] (pl **couches-culottes**) **nf** disposable nappy *UK* *ou* diaper *US*.

coucher[1] [3] [kuʃe] ■ **vt 1.** [enfant] to put to bed **2.** [objet, blessé] to lay down ▸ **coucher une bouteille/moto** to lay a bottle/motorbike on its side ▸ **la pluie a couché les herbes** the rain flattened the grasses **3.** *sout* [inscrire] to mention ▸ **coucher qqn sur son testament** to name sb in one's will.
■ **vi 1.** [dormir] to sleep ▸ **cela va te faire coucher tard** that will keep you up late **2.** [passer la nuit] to spend the night ▸ **on couchera à l'hôtel** [une nuit] we'll spend the night *ou* we'll sleep in a hotel / [plusieurs nuits] we'll stay in a hotel ▸ **un nom à coucher dehors** *fam* an impossible name **3.** *fam* [avoir des rapports sexuels] **: coucher avec** to sleep with.
◆ ***se coucher*** **vp 1.** [s'allonger] to lie down ▸ **se coucher à plat ventre** to lie face down **2.** [se mettre au lit] to go to bed ▸ **je vous empêche de vous coucher?** am I keeping you up? **3.** [se courber] to bend over **4.** [astre] to set.

coucher[2] [kuʃe] **nm 1.** [d'astre] setting ▸ **au coucher du soleil** at sunset **2.** [de personne] going to bed ▸ **le coucher du roi** the king's going-to-bed ceremony.

couchette [kuʃɛt] **nf 1.** [de train] couchette **2.** [de navire] berth.

coucheur [kuʃœr] **nm : mauvais coucheur** *fig* awkward customer.

couci-couça [kusikusa] **adv** *fam* so-so.

coucou [kuku] ■ **nm 1.** [oiseau] cuckoo **2.** [pendule] cuckoo clock **3.** *péj* [avion] crate.
■ **interj** peekaboo!

coude [kud] **nm 1.** [de personne, de vêtement] elbow ▸ **être au coude à coude** to be shoulder to shoulder ▸ **jouer des coudes** to elbow people aside ▸ **se serrer les coudes** to stick together **2.** [courbe] bend.

coudée [kude] **nf : avoir les coudées franches** to have room to move *ou* elbow room.

cou-de-pied [kudpje] (pl **cous-de-pied**) **nm** instep.

coudoyer [13] [kudwaje] **vt** to rub shoulders with.

coudre [86] [kudr] ■ **vt 1.** [bouton] to sew on **2.** MÉD to sew up, to stitch.
■ **vi** to sew.

coudrier [kudrije] **nm** hazel tree.

couenne [kwan] **nf** [de lard] rind.

couette [kwɛt] **nf 1.** [édredon] duvet *UK*, comforter *US* **2.** [coiffure] bunches *pl* *UK*, pigtails *pl* *UK*.

couffin [kufɛ̃] **nm 1.** [berceau] Moses basket *UK*, bassinet *US* **2.** [cabas] basket.

couille [kuj] **nf** *(gén pl)* *vulg* ball.

couiner [3] [kwine] **vi 1.** [animal] to squeal **2.** [pleurnicher] to whine.

coulant, e [kulɑ̃, ɑ̃t] **adj 1.** [fluide] runny **2.** [style] fluent **3.** *fam* [indulgent] easy-going, laid-back.

coulée [kule] **nf** **1.** [de matière liquide] **: coulée de lave** lava flow ▸ **coulée de boue** mudslide **2.** [de métal] casting.

couler [3] [kule] ■ **vi** **1.** [liquide] to flow ▸ **la sueur coulait sur son visage** [abondamment] sweat was pouring down his face / [goutte à goutte] sweat was trickling down his face ▸ **faire couler un bain** to run a bath ▸ **fais couler l'eau** turn on the water ▸ **fais couler un peu d'eau dessus** pour a little water over it **2.** [beurre, fromage, nez] to run ▸ **avoir le nez qui coule** to have a runny nose **3.** [robinet] to drip / [tonneau, stylo] to leak **4.** [temps] to slip by **5.** [navire, entreprise] to sink ▸ **couler à pic** to sink straight to the bottom

▸▸ **cela coule de source** it's obvious ▸ **faire couler beaucoup d'encre** *fig* to cause a lot of ink to flow.

■ **vt** **1.** [navire] to sink **2.** [métal, bronze] to cast **3.** *fam* [personne, entreprise] to ruin.

◆ ***se couler*** **vp** [se glisser] to slip ▸ **se la couler douce** *fam* to have an easy life.

couleur [kulœr] ■ **nf** **1.** [teinte, caractère] colour *UK*, color *US* ▸ **de couleur vive** brightly-coloured *UK*, brightly-colored *US* ▸ **aux couleurs du parti** in party colours ▸ **la couleur de la peau** skin colour ▸ **prendre des couleurs** to get a tan *ou* a bit of colour in one's cheeks ▸ **une personne de couleur** a person of colour ▸ **couleurs primaires** *ou* **fondamentales** primary colours ▸ **couleurs complémentaires** complementary colours ▸ **télévision en couleurs** colour television ▸ **haut en couleur** [personne] high-coloured *UK*, high-colored *US* / [quartier, récit] colourful *UK*, colorful *US* **2.** [linge] coloureds *pl UK*, coloreds *(pl) US* **3.** [jeux de cartes] suit **4.** [d'opinion] leaning

▸▸ **annoncer la couleur** to state one's intentions ▸ **en faire voir de toutes les couleurs à qqn** to give sb a hard time ▸ **on en a vu de toutes les couleurs** *fam* we've been through some hard times ▸ **sous couleur de qqch/de faire qqch** under the guise of sthg/of doing sthg.

■ **adj inv** [télévision, pellicule] colour *(avant n) UK*, color *(avant n) US*.

couleuvre [kulœvr] **nf** grass snake ▸ **avaler des couleuvres** *fam fig* [être impassible] to swallow insults.

coulis [kuli] **nm** CULIN puree.

coulissant, e [kulisɑ̃, ɑ̃t] **adj** sliding *(avant n)*.

coulisse [kulis] **nf** **1.** [glissière] **: fenêtre/porte à coulisse** sliding window/door **2.** COUT hem.

◆ ***coulisses*** **nfpl** THÉÂTRE wings ▸ **dans les coulisses** *fig* behind the scenes.

coulisser [3] [kulise] **vi** to slide.

couloir [kulwar] **nm** **1.** [corridor] corridor **2.** GÉOGR gully **3.** SPORT [transports] lane ▸ **couloir aérien** air lane ▸ **couloir d'autobus** bus lane.

coulommiers [kulɔmje] **nm** *soft cheese made from cow's milk*.

coulpe [kulp] **nf : battre sa coulpe** to repent one's sins openly.

coup [ku] **nm** **1.** [choc - physique, moral] blow ▸ **donner un coup de coude à qqn** to nudge sb ▸ **rouer qqn de coups** to give sb a beating ▸ **coup bas** *litt* blow *ou* punch below the belt / *fig* blow below the belt ▸ **c'est un coup bas!** *fig* that's below the belt! ▸ **coup de couteau** stab *(with a knife)* ▸ **un coup dur** *fig* a heavy blow ▸ **donner un coup de fouet à qqn** *fig* to give sb a shot in the arm ▸ **coups et blessures** DR grievous bodily harm ▸ **coup de grâce** *litt* & *fig* coup de grâce, death blow ▸ **coup de pied** kick ▸ **coup de poing** punch ▸ **compter les coups** *litt* & *fig* to keep score ▸ **prendre des coups** to get knocked about ▸ **recevoir un coup** to get hit

2. [action nuisible] trick ▸ **faire un sale coup à qqn** *fam* to play a dirty trick on sb ▸ **coup fourré** stab in the back ▸ **il prépare un coup** he's up to something

3. [SPORT - au tennis] stroke ▸ **coup droit** (forehand) drive / [- en boxe] blow, punch / [- au football] kick ▸ **coup franc** free kick

4. [d'éponge, de chiffon] wipe ▸ **passe un coup d'éponge sur la table** give the table a wipe (with the sponge) ▸ **un coup de crayon** a pencil stroke ▸ **donner un coup de balai** to give the floor a sweep

5. [bruit] noise ▸ **coup de feu** shot, gunshot ▸ **coup de sonnette** ring ▸ **coup de tonnerre** thunderclap

6. [action spectaculaire] **: coup d'éclat** feat ▸ **coup d'État** coup (d'état) ▸ **coup de théâtre** *fig* dramatic turn of events

7. *fam* [fois] time ▸ **du premier coup** first time, at the first attempt ▸ **ce coup-ci, on s'en va** this time, we're off

8. [armement] shot, blast ▸ **un coup de revolver** a shot, a gunshot ▸ **le coup est parti** [revolver] the gun went off / [fusil] the rifle went off ▸ **(revolver à) six coups** six-shooter ▸ **tirer un coup de canon** to fire *ou* to blast a cannon

9. *vulg* [éjaculation] **: tirer un** *ou* **son coup** to shoot one's load *vulg*

▸▸ **avoir un coup de barre/de pompe** *fam* to feel shattered *UK ou* pooped *US* ▸ **boire un coup** to have a drink ▸ **être dans le coup** [être à la mode] to be up to date / [être au courant] to be in the know ▸ **faire les quatre cents coups** to lead a wild life ▸ **frapper un grand coup** to strike a decisive blow ▸ **marquer le coup** to mark the occasion ▸ **en prendre un coup** to take a knock ▸ **rattraper le coup** to sort things out ▸ **tenir le coup** to hold out ▸ **tenter le coup** to have a go ▸ **tous les coups sont permis** *litt* & *fig* (there are) no holds barred ▸ **valoir le coup** to be well worth it.

◆ ***à coups de*** **loc prép : démoli à coups de marteau** smashed to pieces with a hammer ▸ **à coups de primes** through *ou* by dint of special bonuses.

◆ ***au coup par coup*** **loc adv** *fam* bit by bit ▸ **négocier au coup par coup** to have piecemeal negotiations.

◆ ***coup de fil*** **nm** phone call.

◆ ***coup de foudre*** **nm** love at first sight.

◆ ***coup du lapin*** **nm** AUTO whiplash *(U)*.

◆ ***coup de main*** **nm** **1.** [raid] smash-and-grab (attack) / MIL coup de main

2. [aide] **: donner un coup de main à qqn** to give *ou* to lend sb a hand

3. [savoir-faire] **: avoir le coup de main** to have the knack *ou* the touch.

◆ ***coup d'œil*** **nm** **1.** [regard] look, glance ▸ **au premier coup d'œil** straight away *ou* immediately *ou* at a glance ▸ **d'un coup d'œil, il embrassa le tableau** he took in the situation at a glance ▸ **jeter un petit coup d'œil à** to have a quick look *ou* glance at

2. [appréciation] **: avoir le coup d'œil** to have a good eye ▸ **valoir le coup d'œil** to be worth seeing
3. [panorama] view.
◆ ***coup de soleil*** **nm** sunburn *(U)* ▸ **prendre** *ou* **attraper un coup de soleil** to get sunburnt.
◆ ***coup de téléphone*** **nm** telephone *ou* phone call ▸ **donner** *ou* **passer un coup de téléphone à qqn** to telephone *ou* phone sb ▸ **recevoir un coup de téléphone** to receive *ou* to get a phone call.
◆ ***coup de vent*** **nm** gust of wind ▸ **partir en coup de vent** to rush off.
◆ ***à coup sûr*** **loc adv** definitely.
◆ ***du coup*** **loc adv** as a result ▸ **elle ne pouvait pas venir, du coup j'ai reporté le dîner** as she couldn't come, I put the dinner off, she couldn't come so I put the dinner off.
◆ ***coup sur coup*** **loc adv** one after the other.
◆ ***sur le coup*** **loc adv 1.** [mourir] instantly
2. [à ce moment-là] straightaway, there and then ▸ **je n'ai pas compris sur le coup** I didn't understand immediately *ou* straightaway.
◆ ***sous le coup de*** **loc prép 1.** [sous l'action de] **: tomber sous le coup de la loi** to be a statutory offence *UK ou* offense *US*
2. [sous l'effet de] in the grip of.
◆ ***tout à coup*** **loc adv** suddenly.

coupable [kupabl] ■ **adj 1.** [personne, pensée] guilty ▸ **plaider coupable/non coupable** DR to plead guilty/not guilty **2.** [action, dessein] culpable, reprehensible / [négligence, oubli] sinful.
■ **nmf** guilty person *ou* party.

coupant, e [kupɑ̃, ɑ̃t] **adj 1.** [tranchant] cutting **2.** *fig* [sec] sharp.

coupe [kup] **nf 1.** [verre] glass ▸ **coupe de champagne** glass of champagne **2.** [à fruits] dish **3.** SPORT cup ▸ **Coupe du monde** World Cup **4.** [d'arbres] felling **5.** [de vêtement, aux cartes] cut ▸ **coupe (de cheveux)** haircut **6.** [plan, surface] (cross) section **7.** [de phrase] break **8.** [réduction] cut, cutback ▸ **coupes budgétaires** budget cuts.

coupé, e [kupe] **adj : bien/mal coupé** well/badly cut.
◆ ***coupé*** **nm** coupé.

coupe-circuit [kupsirkɥi] (pl **coupe-circuit** *ou* **coupe-circuits**) **nm** circuit breaker.

coupe-faim [kupfɛ̃] **nm inv** appetite suppressant.

coupe-feu [kupfø] ■ **nm inv** firebreak.
■ **adj inv** fire *(avant n)* ▸ **porte coupe-feu** fire door.

coupe-gorge [kupgɔrʒ] **nm inv** dangerous place.

coupelle [kupɛl] **nf** dish.

coupe-ongles [kupɔ̃gl] **nm inv** nail clippers *pl*.

coupe-papier [kuppapje] (pl **coupe-papier** *ou* **coupe-papiers**) **nm** paper knife.

couper [3] [kupe] ■ **vt 1.** [gén & INFORM] to cut ▸ **se faire couper les cheveux** to have one's hair cut **2.** [arbre] to cut down **3.** [pain] to slice ▸ **couper qqch en tranches fines/épaisses** to slice sthg thinly/thickly, to cut sthg into thin/thick slices / [rôti] to carve **4.** [envie, appétit] to take away ▸ **couper le souffle** *ou* **la respiration à qqn** to take sb's breath away **5.** [vin] to dilute **6.** [jeux de cartes - avec atout] to trump / [- paquet] to cut **7.** [découper] to cut out **8.** [interrompre, trancher] to cut off ▸ **couper qqn** *fam* to interrupt sb **9.** [traverser] to cut across.
■ **vi 1.** [gén] to cut ▸ **attention, ça coupe!** careful, it's sharp! ▸ **couper à travers champs** to cut across country *ou* the fields ▸ **couper par une petite route** to cut through by a minor road **2.** *fam* [échapper] **: couper à** to get out of ▸ **tu dois y aller, tu ne peux pas y couper!** you've got to go: there's no way you can get out of it!
▸▸ **couper court à qqch** to cut sthg short.
◆ ***se couper*** **vp 1.** [se blesser] to cut o.s. ▸ **se couper le** *ou* **au front** to cut one's forehead **2.** [se croiser] to cross **3.** [s'isoler] **: se couper de** to cut o.s. off from.

couper-coller [kupekɔle] **nm inv** INFORM **: faire un couper-coller** to cut and paste.

couperet [kuprɛ] **nm 1.** [de boucher] cleaver **2.** [de guillotine] blade.

couperose [kuproz] **nf** [sur le visage] blotchiness.

couperosé, e [kuproze] **adj** blotchy.

coupe-vent [kupvɑ̃] **nm inv** [vêtement] windcheater, windbreaker *US*.

couple [kupl] **nm** [de personnes] couple / [d'animaux] pair.

couplé, e [kuple] **adj** [équitation] doubled.
◆ ***couplé*** **nm** [équitation] double.

coupler [3] [kuple] **vt** [objets] to couple.

couplet [kuplɛ] **nm** verse.

coupole [kupɔl] **nf** ARCHIT dome, cupola.

coupon [kupɔ̃] **nm 1.** [d'étoffe] remnant **2.** FIN coupon **3.** [billet] ticket.

coupon-réponse [kupɔ̃repɔ̃s] (pl **coupons-réponse**) **nm** reply coupon.

coupure [kupyr] **nf 1.** [gén] cut / [billet de banque] note *UK*, bill *US* ▸ **grosses coupures** large denominations *ou* bills *US* ▸ **petite coupure** small denomination note *UK ou* bill *US* ▸ **coupure de courant** ÉLECTR power cut / INFORM blackout ▸ **coupure de presse** (press) cutting *UK ou* clipping *US* ▸ **coupure publicitaire** commercial break **2.** *fig* [rupture] break.

cour [kur] **nf 1.** [espace] courtyard, yard ▸ **avec vue sur (la) cour** looking onto the inside of the building *ou* onto the courtyard ▸ **cour d'honneur** main courtyard ▸ **cour de récréation** playground *UK*, schoolyard *US* **2.** [du roi, tribunal] court / *fig* & *hum* following ▸ **Messieurs, la Cour!** all rise!, be upstanding in court! *UK* ▸ **cour d'appel** Court of Appeal *UK ou* Appeals *US*, appellate court *US* ▸ **cour d'assises** ≃ Crown Court *UK*, ≃ Circuit court *US* ▸ **Cour de cassation** final Court of Appeal *UK ou* Appeals *US* ▸ **la Cour des comptes** *the French audit office* ▸ **Haute cour (de justice)** High Court *(for impeachment of president or ministers)* ▸ **cour martiale** court-martial
▸▸ **faire la cour à** [femme] to court / *fig* to charm, to woo ▸ **jouer dans la cour des grands** *fig* to be up there with the leaders.

courage [kuraʒ] **nm** courage ▸ **bon courage!** good luck! ▸ **prendre son courage à deux mains** to pluck up courage ▸ **je n'ai pas le courage de faire mes devoirs** I can't bring myself to do my homework ▸ **perdre courage** to loose heart.

courageusement [kuraʒøzmɑ̃] **adv** courageously.

courageux, euse [kuraʒø, øz] **adj** **1.** [brave] brave **2.** [qui a de l'énergie] energetic **3.** [audacieux] bold.

couramment [kuramɑ̃] **adv** **1.** [parler une langue] fluently ▸ **il parle l'anglais couramment** he speaks English fluently **2.** [communément] commonly ▸ **ça se dit couramment** it's a common *ou* an everyday expression.

FAUX AMIS / FALSE FRIENDS

couramment

Currently is not a translation of the French word *couramment*. Currently is translated by *actuellement*.

▸ He's currently living in Italy / *Actuellement, il habite en Italie*

courant, e [kurɑ̃, ɑ̃t] **adj** **1.** [habituel] everyday *(avant n)* ▸ **en anglais courant** in everyday *ou* conversational English **2.** [normal] standard **3.** [en cours] present ▸ **votre lettre du 17 courant** your letter of the 17th of this month *ou* the 17th instant *UK*.

◆ ***courant*** **nm** **1.** [marin, atmosphérique, électrique] current ▸ **branché sur le courant** plugged into the mains ▸ **couper le courant** to cut off the power ▸ **mettre le courant** to switch the power on ▸ **nager contre** *ou* **remonter le courant** *litt* to swim against the current / *fig* to go against the tide ▸ **il y a trop de courant** the current is too strong ▸ **courant d'air** draught *UK*, draft *US* ▸ **courant alternatif** alternating current ▸ **le courant passe bien entre nous** *fig* we're on the same wavelength **2.** [d'idées] current ▸ **les courants de l'opinion** currents *ou* trends in public opinion **3.** [laps de temps] **: dans le courant du mois/de l'année** in the course of the month/the year ▸ **courant décembre** in the course of December.

◆ ***au courant*** **loc adv : être au courant** to know (about it) ▸ **tu es au courant de la panne?** do you know about the breakdown? ▸ **mettre qqn au courant (de)** to tell sb (about) ▸ **tenir qqn au courant (de)** to keep sb informed (about) ▸ **se mettre/se tenir au courant (de)** to get/keep up to date (with).

courbatu, e [kurbaty] **adj** aching.

courbature [kurbatyr] **nf** ache.

courbaturé, e [kurbatyre] **adj** aching.

courbe [kurb] ■ **nf** curve ▸ **courbe de niveau** [sur une carte] contour (line) ▸ **courbe de température** MÉD temperature curve.

■ **adj** curved.

courber [3] [kurbe] ■ **vt** **1.** [tige] to bend **2.** [tête] to bow.

■ **vi** to bow.

◆ ***se courber*** **vp** **1.** [chose] to bend **2.** [personne] to bow, to bend down.

courbette [kurbɛt] **nf** [révérence] bow ▸ **faire des courbettes** *fig* to bow and scrape.

coureur, euse [kurœr, øz] **nm, f** **1.** SPORT runner ▸ **coureur cycliste** racing cyclist **2.** *fam fig* [amateur] **: coureur (de jupons)** womanizer.

courge [kurʒ] **nf** **1.** [légume] marrow *UK*, squash *US* **2.** *fam* [imbécile] dimwit.

courgette [kurʒɛt] **nf** courgette *UK*, zucchini *US*.

courir [45] [kurir] ■ **vi** **1.** [aller rapidement] to run ▸ **courir après qqn/qqch** *fig* to chase after sb/sthg, to run after sb/sthg ▸ **courir après la célébrité** to strive for recognition ▸ **elle ne court pas après l'argent** she's not after money ▸ **laisse courir!** *fig* let it go! ▸ **faire courir qqn** *fig* to pull sb's leg ▸ **partir en courant** to run off **2.** SPORT to race **3.** [se précipiter, rivière] to rush ▸ **j'y cours** I'll rush over **4.** [se propager] **: le bruit court que...** rumour *UK ou* rumor *US* has it that... ▸ **faire courir un bruit** to spread a rumour *UK ou* rumor *US*.

■ **vt** **1.** SPORT to run in **2.** [parcourir] to roam (through) ▸ **quelqu'un comme ça, ça ne court pas les rues** people like that are hard to come by **3.** [faire le tour de] to go around **4.** [fréquenter : bals, musées] to do the rounds of ▸ **elle court les musées** she's an inveterate museum-goer **5.** [encourir] **: courir un risque** to run a risk ▸ **faire courir un risque** *ou* **danger à qqn** to put sb at risk.

couronne [kurɔn] **nf** **1.** [ornement, autorité] crown **2.** [de fleurs] wreath ▸ **couronne mortuaire** *ou* **funéraire** funeral wreath **3.** [monnaie - de Suède, d'Islande] krona / [- du Danemark, de Norvège] krone / [- de la République tchèque] crown.

couronnement [kurɔnmɑ̃] **nm** **1.** [de monarque] coronation **2.** [d'édifice] crown **3.** *fig* [apogée] crowning achievement.

couronner [3] [kurɔne] **vt** **1.** [monarque] to crown **2.** [récompenser] to give a prize to ▸ **être couronné de succès** *fig* to be crowned with success **3.** [conclure] **: cette nomination vient couronner sa carrière** *fig* this nomination is the crowning achievement of his carreer.

courrai, courras ➤ ***courir***.

courre [kur] ➤ ***chasse***.

courriel [kurjɛl] *Québec* **nm** INFORM e-mail.

courrier [kurje] **nm** mail, letters *pl*, post *UK* ▸ **courrier du cœur** agony *UK ou* advice *US* column *UK* ▸ **courrier direct** COMM direct mailing *ou* mailshot *UK* ▸ **courrier électronique** INFORM electronic mail, e-mail ▸ **courrier des lecteurs** [rubrique] letters to the editor.

courroie [kurwa] **nf** TECHNOL belt / [attache] strap ▸ **courroie de transmission** driving belt ▸ **courroie de ventilateur** fanbelt.

courroucé, e [kuruse] **adj** *littéraire* wrathful.

courroucer [16] [kuruse] **vt** *littéraire* to anger.

courroux [kuru] **nm** *littéraire* wrath, rage.

cours [kur] ■ ➤ ***courir***.

■ **nm** **1.** [écoulement] flow ▸ **cours d'eau** waterway ▸ **donner** *ou* **laisser libre cours à** *fig* to give free rein to ▸ **reprendre son cours : la vie reprend son cours** life goes on

2. [déroulement] course ▸ **au cours de** during, in the course of ▸ **au cours de notre dernier entretien** when we last spoke ▸ **en cours** [année, dossier] current / [affaires] in hand ▸ **en cours de route** on the way ▸ **entraver le cours de la justice** to hinder the course of justice ▸ **suivre son cours** to take its course

3. FIN [de devises] rate ▸ **cours du change** exchange rate ▸ **cours des devises** foreign exchange rate ▸ **cours du dollar** dollar rate ▸ **avoir cours** [monnaie] to be legal tender ▸ **ne plus avoir cours** [monnaie] to be out of circulation, to be no longer legal tender *ou* currency / [pratique, théorie] to be obsolete / [expression, terme] to be obsolete *ou* no longer in use ▸ **au cours du marché** at the market *ou* trading price
4. FIN [d'actions] price, trading rate ▸ **cours des actions** share prices ▸ **cours acheteur** bidding price ▸ **premier cours, cours d'ouverture** opening price ▸ **dernier cours, cours de clotûre** closing price ▸ **le cours d'ouverture de ces actions était de 10 euros** those shares opened at 10 euros
5. [leçon] class, lesson ▸ **aller en cours** to go to one's class ▸ **donner des cours (à qqn)** to teach (sb) ▸ **être en cours** to be in class ▸ **faire cours : c'est moi qui vous ferai cours cette année** I'll be teaching you this year ▸ **j'ai cours tous les jours** [élève, professeur] I have classes every day ▸ **suivre un cours *ou* des cours d'espagnol** to go to *ou* to attend a Spanish class ▸ **cours intensifs** crash course *sg* ▸ **cours magistral** lecture ▸ **cours particuliers** private lessons ▸ **cours de rattrapage/du soir** remedial/evening class
6. [classe] **: cours élémentaire** ≃ second-year infants *UK*, ≃ first grade *US* ▸ **cours moyen** ≃ third-year infants *UK*, ≃ second grade *US* ▸ **cours préparatoire** ≃ first-year infants *UK*, ≃ nursery school *US*
7. [avenue] avenue.

course [kurs] **nf 1.** [action] running *(U)* ▸ **au pas de course** at a run ▸ **être dans la course** *fig* to be in touch *ou* in the know ▸ **faire la course avec qqn** to race (with) sb ▸ **la course au pouvoir/à la présidence** the race for power/ the presidency ▸ **course aux armements** arms race
2. [compétition] race ▸ **jouer aux courses** to bet on the races *ou* on the horses ▸ **course attelée *ou* sous harnais** harness race ▸ **course automobile/cycliste** car/cycle race ▸ **course contre la montre** *litt* race against the clock, time-trial / *fig* race against time ▸ **course de fond *ou* d'endurance** long-distance race ▸ **course d'obstacles** [en équitation] steeplechase ▸ **course à pied** (foot) race ▸ **je fais de la course à pied tous les jours** I run every day
3. [excursion] trip ▸ **faire une course en montagne** to go for a trek in the mountains
4. [en taxi] journey
5. [mouvement] flight, course
6. [commission] errand ▸ **faire des courses** to go shopping ▸ **j'ai une course à faire** I've got to buy something *ou* to get something from the shops.

FAUX AMIS / FALSE FRIENDS
course

Course is not a translation of the French word *course*. Course is translated by *cours* or *série*.
▸ I'm doing a computer course / *Je suis des cours d'informatique*
▸ She had a course of injections / *Elle a reçu une série de piqûres*

courser [3] [kurse] **vt** *fam* to chase, to run after ▸ **elle s'est fait courser par des voyous** she was chased by some thugs.

coursier, ère [kursje, ɛr] **nm, f** messenger.

coursive [kursiv] **nf** gangway.

court, e [kur, kurt] **adj 1.** [dans l'espace] short ▸ **la jupe est trop courte de trois centimètres** the skirt is three centimetres too short **2.** [dans le temps] short, brief ▸ **pendant un court instant** for a brief *ou* fleeting moment ▸ **à court terme** short-term **3.** [faible, insuffisant] small, slender ▸ **avoir la respiration courte *ou* le souffle court** to be short of breath *ou* wind ▸ **avoir la mémoire courte** to have a short memory.
◆ ***court*** ■ **v** ➤ ***courir***.
■ **adv : être à court d'argent/d'idées/d'arguments** to be short of money/ideas/arguments ▸ **nous étions presque à court d'eau** we were low on *ou* running short of water ▸ **prendre qqn de court** to catch sb unawares ▸ **tourner court** to stop suddenly ▸ **appelez-moi Jeanne, tout court** just call me Jeanne.
■ **nm : court de tennis** tennis court.

courtage [kurtaʒ] **m 1.** [profession] brokerage, broking ▸ **courtage électronique** e-broking, online broking **2.** [commission] brokerage, commission ▸ **vente par courtage** selling on commission.

court-bouillon [kurbujɔ̃] (pl **courts-bouillons**) **nm** court-bouillon.

court-circuit [kursirkɥi] (pl **courts-circuits**) **nm** short circuit.

court-circuiter [3] [kursirkɥite] **vt** ÉLECTR to short-circuit / *fig* to bypass.

courtier, ère [kurtje, ɛr] **nm, f** broker ▸ **courtier d'assurances** insurance broker ▸ **courtier de Bourse** stockbroker ▸ **courtier de change** bill broker ▸ **courtier électronique** e-broker, online broker.

courtisan, e [kurtizɑ̃, an] **nm, f 1.** HIST courtier **2.** [flatteur] sycophant.
◆ ***courtisane*** **nf** courtesan.

courtiser [3] [kurtize] **vt 1.** [femme] to woo, to court **2.** *péj* [flatter] to flatter.

court-jus [kurʒy] (pl **courts-jus**) **nm** *fam* ÉLECTR short.

court-métrage [kurmetraʒ] (pl **courts-métrages**) **nm** short (film).

courtois, e [kurtwa, az] **adj** courteous.

courtoisie [kurtwazi] **nf** courtesy.

couru, e [kury] ■ **pp** ➤ ***courir***.
■ **adj** popular ▸ **c'est couru (d'avance)** *fam fig* it's a foregone conclusion.

cousais, cousions ➤ ***coudre***.

couscous [kuskus] **nm** couscous *(traditional North African dish of semolina served with a spicy stew of meat and vegetables)*.

cousin, e [kuzɛ̃, in] **nm, f** cousin ▸ **cousin germain** first cousin.

coussin [kusɛ̃] **nm 1.** [de siège] cushion ▸ **coussin d'air** air cushion **2.** *Québec* [baseball] base.

coussinet [kusinɛ] **nm 1.** [coussin] small cushion **2.** [de patte d'animal] pad.

cousu, ***e*** [kuzy] ■ pp ➤ ***coudre***.
■ adj : **c'est du cousu main** *fam fig* it's top-quality stuff ▸ **cousu de fil blanc** *fig* obvious.

coût [ku] nm cost ▸ **coût du crédit** credit charges *ou* costs ▸ **coût de production** production cost ▸ **le coût de la vie** the cost of living.
◆ ***coûts*** [ku] nmpl COMM : **coûts constants** fixed costs ▸ **coûts directs** direct costs ▸ **coûts de distribution** distribution costs ▸ **coûts engagés** committed costs ▸ **coûts évitables** avoidable costs ▸ **coûts indirects** indirect costs ▸ **coûts induits** unavoidable costs ▸ **coûts maîtrisables** controllable costs ▸ **coût récurrents** recurrent *ou* running costs ▸ **coût de revient des produits vendus** cost of sales ▸ **coûts variables** variable costs.

coûtant [kutɑ̃] ➤ ***prix***.

couteau, ***x*** [kuto] nm **1.** [gén] knife ▸ **couteau à cran d'arrêt** flick knife *UK*, switchblade *US* ▸ **couteau de cuisine** kitchen knife ▸ **à couper au couteau** *fig* that you could cut with a knife ▸ **avoir le couteau sous la gorge** *fig* to have a gun to one's head ▸ **être à couteaux tirés (avec qqn)** *fig* to be at daggers drawn (with sb) **2.** [coquillage] razor shell *UK*, razor clam *US*.

coutelas [kutla] nm [de cuisine] large knife.

coutellerie [kutɛlri] nf [produits] cutlery *UK*, silverware *US* / [industrie] cutlery industry / [atelier] cutlery factory / [magasin] cutler's (shop).

coûter [3] [kute] ■ vi **1.** [valoir] to cost ▸ **ça coûte combien?** how much is it? ▸ **coûter cher** to be expensive, to cost a lot / *fig* to be costly ▸ **coûter cher à qqn** to cost sb a lot / *fig* to cost sb dear *ou* dearly **2.** *fig* [être pénible] to be difficult.
■ vt *fig* to cost.
◆ ***coûte que coûte*** loc adv at all costs.

coûteux, ***euse*** [kutø, øz] adj costly, expensive.

coutume [kutym] nf [gén & DR] custom ▸ **avoir coutume de faire qqch** to be in the habit of doing sthg ▸ **la coutume veut que...** tradition dictates that...

coutumier, ***ère*** [kutymje, ɛr] adj customary ▸ **il est coutumier du fait** he's always doing that.

couture [kutyr] nf **1.** [action] sewing ▸ **faire de la couture** to sew **2.** [points] seam ▸ **couture apparente** topstitching, overstitching **3.** [activité] dressmaking ▸ **haute couture** (haute) couture, designer fashion.

couturier, ***ère*** [kutyrje, ɛr] nm, f couturier ▸ **grand couturier** fashion designer, couturier.

couvée [kuve] nf [d'œufs] clutch / [de poussins] brood.

couvent [kuvɑ̃] nm [de sœurs] convent / [de moines] monastery.

couver [3] [kuve] ■ vt **1.** [œufs] to sit on **2.** [dorloter] to mollycoddle **3.** [maladie] to be coming down with, to be sickening for *UK*.
■ vi [poule] to brood / *fig* [complot] to hatch.

couvercle [kuvɛrkl] nm [de casserole, boîte] lid, cover / [de flacon, bombe, aérosol] top, cap.

couvert, ***e*** [kuvɛr, ɛrt] ■ pp ➤ ***couvrir***.
■ adj **1.** [submergé] covered ▸ **couvert de** covered with **2.** [habillé] dressed ▸ **être bien couvert** to be well wrapped up **3.** [nuageux] overcast.
◆ ***couvert*** nm **1.** [abri] : **se mettre à couvert** to take shelter ▸ **sous le couvert de l'amitié** *fig* under a cloak of friendship **2.** [place à table] place (setting) ▸ **mettre *ou* dresser le couvert** to set *ou* lay *UK*the table.
◆ ***couverts*** nmpl cutlery *(U) UK*, silverware *(U) US*.

couverture [kuvɛrtyr] nf **1.** [gén] cover ▸ **couverture sociale** social security cover **2.** [de lit] blanket ▸ **couverture chauffante** electric blanket ▸ **tirer la couverture à soi** *fam fig* to take (all) the credit (for o.s.) **3.** [toit] roofing *(U)* **4.** PRESSE coverage ▸ **assurer la couverture** to give coverage ▸ **couverture (de) presse *ou* médiatique** media *OR* press coverage.

couveuse [kuvøz] nf **1.** [poule] sitting hen **2.** [machine] incubator.

couvre-chef [kuvrəʃɛf] (pl **couvre-chefs**) nm *hum* hat.

couvre-feu [kuvrəfø] (pl **couvre-feux**) nm curfew.

couvre-lit [kuvrəli] (pl **couvre-lits**) nm bedspread.

couvre-pied (pl **couvre-pieds**) [kuvrəpje] nm quilt, eiderdown *UK*.

couvre-pieds [kuvrəpje] nm inv = ***couvre-pied***.

couvreur [kuvrœr] nm roofer.

couvrir [34] [kuvrir] vt **1.** [gén] to cover ▸ **couvrir qqn/qqch de** *litt* & *fig* to cover sb/sthg with **2.** [protéger] to shield **3.** [son] to drown (out) **4.** PRESSE [événement] to cover, to give coverage to.
◆ ***se couvrir*** vp **1.** [se vêtir] to wrap up **2.** [se recouvrir] : **se couvrir de feuilles/de fleurs** to come into leaf/blossom **3.** [ciel] to cloud over **4.** [se protéger] to cover o.s.

cover-girl [kɔvœrgœrl] (pl **cover-girls**) nf cover girl.

covoiturage [kɔvwatyraʒ] nm car sharing, car pooling ▸ **pratiquer le covoiturage** to belong to a car pool.

cow-boy [kɔbɔj] (pl **cow-boys**) nm cowboy.

coyote [kɔjɔt] nm coyote.

CP nm abr écrite de ***cours préparatoire***.

CPAM (abr de ***caisse primaire d'assurances maladie***) nf *national health insurance office*.

cps (abr écrite de ***caractères par seconde***) cps.

cpt abr de ***comptant***.

CQFD (abr de ***ce qu'il fallait démontrer***) QED.

crabe [krab] nm crab.

crac [krak] interj crack!

crachat [kraʃa] nm spit *(U)*.

craché, ***e*** [kraʃe] adj : **c'est son père tout craché** he's the spitting image of his father.

cracher [3] [kraʃe] ■ vi **1.** [personne] to spit **2.** [crépiter] to crackle **3.** *fam fig* [dénigrer] : **cracher sur qqn** to run sb down **4.** *fam* [dédaigner] : **ne pas cracher sur qqch** not to turn one's nose up at sthg.
■ vt [sang] to spit (up) / [lave, injures] to spit (out).

crachin [kraʃɛ̃] nm drizzle.

crachoir [kraʃwar] nm spittoon ▸ **tenir le crachoir** *fam fig* to monopolize the conversation.

crack [krak] **nm 1.** [cheval] top horse **2.** *fam* [as] star (performer) ▸ **c'est un crack en mathématiques** he's a whiz at maths *UK ou* math *US* **3.** [drogue] crack.

crado [krado] **adj** *fam* filthy.

craie [krɛ] **nf** chalk.

craignais, craignions ➤ *craindre*.

craindre [80] [krɛ̃dr] **vt 1.** [redouter] to fear, to be afraid of ▸ **craindre le pire** to fear the worst ▸ **craindre de faire qqch** to be afraid of doing sthg ▸ **je crains d'avoir oublié mes papiers** I'm afraid I've forgotten my papers ▸ **craindre que** *(+ subjonctif)* to be afraid (that) ▸ **je crains que oui/non** I'm afraid so/not ▸ **je crains qu'il oublie** *ou* **n'oublie** I'm afraid he may forget ▸ **il n'y a rien à craindre** there's no cause for alarm, there's nothing to fear **2.** [être sensible à] to be susceptible to ▸ **ça craint le froid** [plante] it's sensitive to cold, it doesn't like the cold.

craint, e [krɛ̃, ɛ̃t] **pp** ➤ *craindre*.

crainte [krɛ̃t] **nf** fear ▸ **de crainte de faire qqch** for fear of doing sthg ▸ **de crainte que** *(+ subjonctif)* for fear that ▸ **il a fui de crainte qu'on ne le voie** he fled for fear that he might be seen *ou* for fear of being seen ▸ **éveiller** *ou* **susciter les craintes de qqn** to alarm sb.

craintif, ive [krɛ̃tif, iv] **adj** timid.

cramer [3] [krame] **vt & vi** *fam* to burn.
◆ ***se cramer*** **vp** *fam* to burn o.s. ▸ **se cramer le doigt** to burn one's finger.

cramoisi, e [kramwazi] **adj** crimson.

crampe [krɑ̃p] **nf** cramp.

crampon [krɑ̃pɔ̃] **nm 1.** [crochet - gén] clamp / [- pour alpinisme] crampon **2.** *fam* [personne] (persistent) bore.

cramponner [3] [krɑ̃pɔne] ◆ ***se cramponner*** **vp** [s'agripper] to hang on ▸ **se cramponner à qqn/qqch** *litt & fig* to cling to sb/sthg.

cran [krɑ̃] **nm 1.** [entaille, degré] notch, cut **2.** *(U)* [audace] guts *pl* ▸ **avoir du cran** to have guts.

crâne [kran] **nm** skull ▸ **se mettre qqch dans le crâne** *fig* to get sthg into one's head.

crâner [3] [krane] **vi** *fam* to show off.

crâneur, euse [kranœr, øz] *fam* ■ **adj** boastful.
■ **nm, f** show-off.

crânien, enne [kranjɛ̃, ɛn] **adj : boîte crânienne** skull ▸ **traumatisme crânien** head injury.

crapaud [krapo] **nm** toad.

crapule [krapyl] **nf** scum *(U)*.

crapuleux, euse [krapylø, øz] **adj** sordid.

craqueler [24] [krakle] **vt** to crack.
◆ ***se craqueler*** **vp** to crack.

craquelure [kraklyr] **nf** crack.

craquement [krakmɑ̃] **nm** crack, cracking *(U)*.

craquer [3] [krake] ■ **vi 1.** [produire un bruit] to crack / [plancher, chaussure] to creak **2.** [se déchirer] to split **3.** [s'effondrer - personne] to crack up / [- régime, projet] to be falling apart **4.** *fam* [être séduit par] **: craquer pour** to fall for.
■ **vt** [allumette] to strike.

crash [kraʃ] (pl **crashs** *ou* **crashes**) **nm** crash landing.

crasse [kras] ■ **nf 1.** [saleté] dirt, filth **2.** *fam* [mauvais tour] dirty trick.
■ **adj** crass.

crasseux, euse [krasø, øz] **adj** filthy.

cratère [kratɛr] **nm** crater.

cravache [kravaʃ] **nf** riding crop.

cravacher [3] [kravaʃe] ■ **vt** to whip.
■ **vi** *fam fig* to pull out all the stops.

cravate [kravat] **nf** tie, necktie *US*.

crawl [krol] **nm** crawl.

crayon [krɛjɔ̃] **nm 1.** [gén] pencil ▸ **crayon à bille** ball-point (pen) ▸ **crayon de couleur** crayon ▸ **crayon noir** pencil **2.** TECHNOL pen ▸ **crayon optique** light pen.

crayon-feutre [krɛjɔ̃føtr] (pl **crayons-feutres**) **nm** felt-tip (pen).

crayonner [3] [krɛjɔne] **vt** [dessin] to sketch.

CRDP (abr de ***centre régional de documentation pédagogique***) **nm** *local centre for educational resources*.

créance [kreɑ̃s] **nf** COMM debt ▸ **créance douteuse** doubtful debt ▸ **créance exigible** debt due ▸ **créance hypothécaire** debt secured by a mortagage ▸ **créance irrécouvrable** bad debt.

créancier, ère [kreɑ̃sje, ɛr] **nm, f** creditor.

créateur, trice [kreatœr, tris] ■ **adj** creative.
■ **nm, f** creator.
◆ ***Créateur*** **nm : le Créateur** the Creator.

créatif, ive [kreatif, iv] **adj** creative.
◆ ***créatif*** **nm** ideas man, designer.

création [kreasjɔ̃] **nf 1.** creation ▸ **la création (du monde)** RELIG the Creation **2.** COMM **: création de marque** brand building.

créativité [kreativite] **nf** creativity ▸ **créativité commerciale** creative marketing.

créature [kreatyr] **nf** creature.

crécelle [kresɛl] **nf** rattle.

crèche [krɛʃ] **nf 1.** [de Noël] crib *UK*, crèche *US* **2.** [garderie] crèche *UK*, day-care center *US*.

crécher [18] [kreʃe] **vi** *fam* to crash.

crédibiliser [3] [kredibilize] **vt** to make credible.

COMMENT EXPRIMER...
ses craintes

I'm frightened of spiders / J'ai peur des araignées
I was terrified / J'étais mort de peur
I'm afraid I might lose my job / J'ai peur de perdre mon emploi
I'm worried about him / Je suis inquiète pour lui
I'm dreading telling her / J'appréhende de le lui dire
I'm dreading the meeting / J'appréhende la réunion

crédibilité [kredibilite] **nf** credibility.

crédible [kredibl] **adj** credible.

CREDIF, ***Crédif*** [kredif] (abr de ***Centre de recherche et d'étude pour la diffusion du français***) **nm** *former official body promoting use of the French language.*

crédit [kredi] **nm 1.** COMM credit ▸ **crédit à la consommation** consumer credit ▸ **crédit à court/long terme** long-term/short-term credit ▸ **crédit à l'exportation** export credit ▸ **crédit fournisseur** supplier credit ▸ **crédit gratuit** interest-free credit ▸ **crédit illimité** unlimited credit ▸ **crédit d'impôt** tax rebate *ou* credit *(for bondholders)* ▸ **crédit municipal** pawnshop ▸ **crédit personnalisé** individual *ou* personal credit arrangement *ou* facility ▸ **crédit relais** bridging loan ▸ **crédit renouvelable** *ou* **revolving** revolving credit *UK*, revolver credit *US* ▸ **crédit sur six mois** six months' credit ▸ **crédit de TVA** VAT credit ▸ **faire crédit à qqn** to give sb credit ▸ **accorder/obtenir un crédit** to grant/to obtain credit ▸ **acheter/vendre qqch à crédit** to buy/sell sthg on credit **2.** BANQUE & FIN [actif, en comptabilité] credit ▸ **crédit bancaire** bank credit ▸ **faire créditer un compte de 1000 euros** to pay 1000 euros into one's account **3.** *fig* & *sout* influence.

crédit-bail [kredibaj] (pl **crédits-bails**) **nm** leasing.

créditer [3] [kredite] **vt** [compte] to credit / *fig* : **créditer qqn de qqch** to credit sb with sthg.

créditeur, ***trice*** [kreditœr, tris] ■ **adj** in credit.
■ **nm, f** creditor.

credo [kredo] **nm** creed, credo.

crédule [kredyl] **adj** credulous.

crédulité [kredylite] **nf** credulity.

créer [15] [kree] **vt 1.** RELIG [inventer] to create **2.** [fonder] to found, to start up **3.** [causer] : **créer des problèmes à qqn** to create trouble for sb.

crémaillère [kremajɛr] **nf 1.** [de cheminée] trammel ▸ **pendre la crémaillère** *fig* to have a housewarming (party) **2.** TECHNOL rack.

crémation [kremasjɔ̃] **nf** cremation.

crématoire [krematwar] ➤ ***four***.

crématorium [krematɔrjɔm] **nm** crematorium, crematory *US*.

crème [krɛm] ■ **nf 1.** [produit de beauté] cream ▸ **crème antirides** anti-wrinkle cream ▸ **crème autobronzante** self-tanning cream ▸ **crème dépilatoire** depilatory cream ▸ **crème hydratante** moisturizer ▸ **crème à raser** shaving cream
2. CULIN cream ▸ **crème anglaise** custard *UK* ▸ **crème brûlée** crème brûlée ▸ **crème (au) caramel** crème caramel ▸ **crème Chantilly** Chantilly cream ▸ **crème de cassis** blackcurrant liqueur ▸ **crème fouettée** whipped cream ▸ **crème fraîche** crème fraîche ▸ **crème fraîche liquide** single cream *UK*, light cream *US* ▸ **crème glacée** ice cream ▸ **crème pâtissière** confectioner's custard ▸ **crème renversée** custard cream *UK*, cup custard *US* ▸ **escalopes à la crème** escalopes with cream sauce ▸ **framboises à la crème** raspberries and cream
3. [personne] : **la crème des maris/des hommes** the best of husbands/of men.
■ **adj inv** cream.

crémerie [krɛmri] **nf** dairy.

crémeux, ***euse*** [kremø, øz] **adj** creamy.

crémier, ***ère*** [kremje, ɛr] **nm, f** dairyman (f dairywoman).

créneau, ***x*** [kreno] **nm 1.** [de fortification] crenel **2.** [pour se garer] : **faire un créneau** to reverse into a parking space **3.** [de marché] niche **4.** [horaire] window, gap.

crénelage [krenlaʒ] **m** INFORM aliasing.

crénelé, ***e*** [krenle] **adj** crenelated.

créole [kreɔl] **adj** & **nm** creole.
◆ ***créoles*** **nfpl** dangly earrings.

crêpe [krɛp] ■ **nf** CULIN pancake.
■ **nm** [tissu] crepe.

crêper [4] [krepe] **vt** to backcomb *UK*, to tease *US*.

crêperie [krɛpri] **nf** pancake restaurant.

crépi [krepi] **nm** roughcast.

crépinette [krepinɛt] **nf** *flat sausage.*

crépir [32] [krepir] **vt** to roughcast.

crépiter [3] [krepite] **vi** [feu, flammes] to crackle / [pluie] to patter.

crépon [krepɔ̃] ■ **adj** ➤ ***papier***.
■ **nm** seersucker.

CREPS, ***Creps*** [krɛps] (abr de ***centre régional d'éducation physique et sportive***) **nm** *regional sports centre.*

crépu, ***e*** [krepy] **adj** frizzy.

crépuscule [krepyskyl] **nm** [du jour] dusk, twilight / *fig* twilight ▸ **au crépuscule** at dusk, at twilight.

crescendo [kreʃendo, kreʃɛ̃do] ■ **adv** crescendo ▸ **aller crescendo** *fig* [bruit] to get *ou* grow louder and louder / [dépenses, émotion] to grow apace.
■ **nm inv** *fig* & MUS crescendo.

cresson [kresɔ̃] **nm** watercress.

Crète [krɛt] **nf** : **la Crète** Crete.

crête [krɛt] **nf 1.** [de coq] comb **2.** [de montagne, vague, oiseau] crest.

crétin, ***e*** [kretɛ̃, in] *fam* ■ **adj** cretinous, idiotic.
■ **nm, f** cretin, idiot.

crétois, ***e*** [kretwa, az] **adj** Cretan.
◆ ***Crétois***, ***e*** **nm, f** Cretan.

cretonne [krətɔn] **nf** cretonne.

creuser [3] [krøze] **vt 1.** [trou] to dig **2.** [objet] to hollow out **3.** [taille, reins] to arch **4.** *fig* [approfondir] to go into deeply
▸▸ **ça creuse!** *fam* that gives you an appetite!
◆ ***se creuser*** **vp 1.** [devenir creux] to become hollow **2.** *fam fig* [réfléchir] to rack one's brains **3.** *fig* [s'élargir] to deepen, to widen.

creuset [krøzɛ] **nm** crucible / *fig* melting pot.

creux, ***creuse*** [krø, krøz] **adj 1.** [vide, concave] hollow **2.** [période - d'activité réduite] slack / [- à tarif réduit] off-peak **3.** [paroles] empty.
◆ ***creux*** **nm 1.** [concavité] hollow ▸ **le creux de la main** the hollow of one's hand **2.** [période] lull
▸▸ **être au creux de la vague** *fig* to be at a low point.

crevaison [krəvɛzɔ̃] **nf** puncture *UK*, flat tyre *UK*, flat (tire) *US*.

crevant, ***e*** [krəvɑ̃, ɑ̃t] **adj** *fam* **1.** [fatigant] exhausting, knackering *UK* **2.** [amusant] hilarious.

crevasse [krəvas] **nf** [de mur] crevice, crack / [de glacier] crevasse / [sur la main] crack.

crève [krɛv] **nf** *fam* bad *ou* stinking cold ▸ **attraper la crève** to catch one's death (of cold).

crevé, ***e*** [krəve] **adj 1.** [pneu] burst, punctured, flat **2.** *fam* [fatigué] dead, shattered *UK*.

crève-cœur [krɛvkœr] **nm inv** heartbreak.

crever [19] [krəve] ■ **vi 1.** [éclater] to burst ▸ **on a crevé sur la rocade** *fam* we had a puncture *UK* *ou* a flat *US* on the bypass
2. *tfam* [mourir] to die ▸ **crever de** *fig* [jalousie, orgueil] to be bursting with ▸ **crever de faim** [par pauvreté] to be starving / [être en appétit] to be starving *ou* famished ▸ **crever d'envie de faire qqch** to be dying to do sthg ▸ **je crève de chaud!** I'm baking *ou* boiling!
■ **vt 1.** [percer] to burst ▸ **crever un œil à qqn** [agression] to gouge *ou* to put out sb's eye / [accident] to blind sb in one eye ▸ **cela crève le cœur** it's heartbreaking *ou* heartrending ▸ **ça crève les yeux** *fam* [c'est évident] it's as plain as the nose on your face, it sticks out a mile / [c'est visible] it's staring you in the face, it's plain for all to see ▸ **crever le plafond** [prix] to go through the roof
2. *fam* [épuiser] to wear out.
◆ ***se crever*** **vp** *fam* to wear o.s. out ▸ **se crever au boulot** *ou* **à la tâche** to work o.s. to death.

crevette [krəvɛt] **nf : crevette (grise)** shrimp ▸ **crevette (rose)** prawn.

CRF (abr de ***Croix-Rouge française***) **nf** French Red Cross.

cri [kri] **nm 1.** [de personne] cry, shout / [perçant] scream / [d'animal] cry ▸ **pousser un cri** to cry (out), to shout ▸ **pousser des cris de joie** to shout for *ou* with joy ▸ **pousser un cri de douleur** to cry out in pain ▸ **à grands cris** *fig* loudly **2.** [appel] cry ▸ **demander qqch à grands cris** to cry out for sthg ▸ **le dernier cri** *fig* the latest thing ▸ **cri du cœur** cri de cœur ▸ **jeter** *ou* **lancer un cri d'alarme** to warn against the danger.

criailler [3] [kriaje] **vi** to scream, to squawk.

criant, ***e*** [krijɑ̃, ɑ̃t] **adj** [injustice] blatant.

criard, ***e*** [krijar, ard] **adj 1.** [voix] strident, piercing **2.** [couleur] loud.

crible [kribl] **nm** [instrument] sieve ▸ **passer qqch au crible** *fig* to examine sthg closely.

criblé, ***e*** [krible] **adj** riddled ▸ **être criblé de dettes** to be up to one's eyes in debt.

cric [krik] **nm** jack.

cricket [krikɛt] **nm** cricket.

criée [krije] ➤ ***vente***.

crier [10] [krije] ■ **vi 1.** [pousser un cri] to shout (out), to yell ▸ **crier à l'aide** *ou* **au secours** to shout for help, to cry for help ▸ **crier de douleur** to scream with *ou* to cry out in pain ▸ **crier de joie** to shout for joy **2.** [parler fort] to shout **3.** [protester] **: crier contre** *ou* **après qqn** to nag sb, to go on at sb ▸ **crier au scandale** to call it a scandal, to cry shame **4.** *sout* [grincer] to creak.
■ **vt** to shout (out) ▸ **crier famine** to complain of hunger ▸ **elle nous cria de partir** she shouted at us to go.

crime [krim] **nm 1.** [délit] crime ▸ **crime de lèse-majesté** *fig* treason *(U)* **2.** [meurtre] murder ▸ **crime passionnel** crime of passion ▸ **crimes contre l'humanité** crime against humanity.

Crimée [krime] **nf : la Crimée** the Crimea ▸ **la guerre de Crimée** the Crimean War.

criminalité [kriminalite] **nf** crime.

criminel, ***elle*** [kriminɛl] ■ **adj** criminal.
■ **nm, f** criminal ▸ **criminel de guerre** war criminal.

crin [krɛ̃] **nm** [d'animal] hair ▸ **à tout crin** *fig* dyed-in-the-wool.

crinière [krinjɛr] **nf** mane.

crique [krik] **nf** creek.

criquet [krikɛ] **nm** locust / [sauterelle] grasshopper.

crise [kriz] **nf 1.** MÉD attack ▸ **crise cardiaque** heart attack ▸ **crise de foie** bilious attack ▸ **crise de tétanie** muscle spasm
2. [accès] fit ▸ **crise de larmes** fit of tears ▸ **crise de nerfs** attack of nerves ▸ **piquer une crise** *fam* to have a fit, to fly off the handle
3. [élan] (sudden) urge
4. [phase critique] crisis ▸ **en crise** in crisis.

crispant, ***e*** [krispɑ̃, ɑ̃t] **adj** irritating, frustrating.

crispation [krispasjɔ̃] **nf 1.** [contraction] contraction **2.** [agacement] irritation.

crispé, ***e*** [krispe] **adj** tense, on edge.

crisper [3] [krispe] **vt 1.** [contracter - visage] to tense / [- poing] to clench **2.** [agacer] to irritate.
◆ ***se crisper*** **vp 1.** [se contracter] to tense (up) **2.** [s'irriter] to get irritated.

criss [kris] **nm** kris.

crisser [3] [krise] **vi** [pneu] to screech / [étoffe] to rustle.

cristal, ***aux*** [kristal, o] **nm** crystal ▸ **en cristal** crystal ▸ **cristal de roche** quartz.

cristallin, ***e*** [kristalɛ̃, in] **adj 1.** [limpide] crystal clear, crystalline **2.** [roche] crystalline.
◆ ***cristallin*** **nm** crystalline lens.

cristalliser [3] [kristalize] **vt** *litt* & *fig* to crystallize.
◆ ***se cristalliser*** **vp** to crystallize.

critère [kritɛr] **nm** criterion.

critérium [kriterjɔm] **nm** qualifier.

critiquable [kritikabl] adj [décision] debatable / [personne] open to criticism.

critique [kritik] ■ adj critical ▸ **avoir l'esprit** *ou* **le sens critique** to have good judgement, to be discerning ▸ **se montrer très critique envers** *ou* **à l'égard de** to be very critical towards.
■ nmf critic ▸ **critique d'art** art critic ▸ **critique de cinéma** film *UK ou* movie *US* critic *ou* reviewer ▸ **critique littéraire** literary critic ▸ **critique musical** music critic ▸ **critique de théâtre** drama critic.
■ nf criticism ▸ **adresser** *ou* **faire une critique à un auteur** to level criticism at an author ▸ **la critique** the critics *pl* ▸ **la critique littéraire** literary criticism ▸ **très bien/mal accueilli par la critique** acclaimed/panned by the critics.

critiquer [3] [kritike] vt to criticize.

croasser [3] [krɔase] vi to croak, to caw.

croate [krɔat] adj Croat, Croatian.
◆ ***Croate*** nmf Croat, Croatian.

Croatie [krɔasi] nf : **la Croatie** Croatia.

croc [kro] nm **1.** [de chien] fang ▸ **montrer les crocs** *fig* to bare one's teeth **2.** [crochet] hook.

croc-en-jambe [krɔkɑ̃ʒɑ̃b] (pl **crocs-en-jambe**) nm : **faire un croc-en-jambe à qqn** to trip sb up.

croche [krɔʃ] nf quaver *UK*, eighth (note) *US*.

croche-pied [krɔʃpje] (pl **croche-pieds**) nm : **faire un croche-pied à qqn** to trip sb up.

crochet [krɔʃɛ] nm **1.** [de métal] hook ▸ **vivre aux crochets de qqn** to live off sb **2.** [tricot] crochet hook **3.** TYPO square bracket **4.** [détour] : **faire un crochet** to make a detour **5.** [boxe] : **crochet du gauche/du droit** left/right hook.

crocheter [28] [krɔʃte] vt to pick.

crochu, ***e*** [krɔʃy] adj [doigts] claw-like / [nez] hooked.

croco [krɔko] nm *fam* crocodile (skin).

crocodile [krɔkɔdil] nm crocodile.

crocus [krɔkys] nm crocus.

croire [107] [krwar] ■ vt **1.** [chose, personne] to believe ▸ **à l'en croire, on n'y arrivera jamais** to hear him talk, you'd think we'd never manage it ▸ **je n'en crois pas un mot** I don't believe a word of it ▸ **je te crois sur parole** I'll take your word for it ▸ **on lui a fait croire que la réunion était annulée** they led him to believe that the meeting had been cancelled **2.** [penser] to think ▸ **à la voir, on croirait sa sœur** to look at her, you'd think she was her sister ▸ **tu crois?** do you think so? ▸ **il te croyait parti** he thought you'd left ▸ **croire que** to think (that).
■ vi : **croire à** to believe in ▸ **croire à la vie éternelle** to believe in eternal life ▸ **croire en** to believe in, to have faith in ▸ **croire en Dieu** to believe in God.
◆ ***se croire*** vp **1.** [prétendre être] : **il se croit plus fort que moi** he thinks he's stronger than me ▸ **se croire tout permis** to think one can get away with anything ▸ **s'y croire** *fam* to think one is it ▸ **il s'y croit!** he really thinks a lot of himself! ▸ **tu te crois malin?** think you're clever, do you? **2.** [penser se trouver] : **on se croirait au Japon** you'd think you were in Japan.

croisade [krwazad] nf *fig* & HIST crusade.

croisé, ***e*** [krwaze] adj [veste] double-breasted.
◆ ***croisé*** nm HIST crusader.
◆ ***croisée*** nf **1.** [fenêtre] casement, window **2.** [croisement] : **à la croisée des chemins** *litt* & *fig* at a crossroads.

croisement [krwazmɑ̃] nm **1.** [intersection] junction, intersection **2.** BIOL crossbreeding.

croiser [3] [krwaze] ■ vt **1.** [jambes] to cross / [bras] to fold **2.** [passer à côté de] to pass **3.** [chemin] to cross, to cut across **4.** [métisser] to interbreed.
■ vi NAUT to cruise.
◆ ***se croiser*** vp [chemins] to cross, to intersect / [personnes] to pass / [lettres] to cross / [regards] to meet.

croisière [krwazjɛr] nf cruise.

croisillon [krwazijɔ̃] nm : **à croisillons** lattice *(avant n)*.

croissais, ***croissions*** ➤ ***croître***.

croissance [krwasɑ̃s] nf growth, development ▸ **croissance démographique** population growth ▸ **croissance économique** economic growth *ou* development ▸ **croissance du marché** market growth ▸ **croissance zéro** zero growth.

croissant, ***e*** [krwasɑ̃, ɑ̃t] adj increasing, growing.
◆ ***croissant*** nm **1.** [de lune] crescent **2.** CULIN croissant.

croître [93] [krwatr] vi **1.** [grandir] to grow **2.** [augmenter] to increase.

croix [krwa] nf cross ▸ **en croix** in the shape of a cross ▸ **croix gammée** swastika ▸ **la croix de guerre** the Military Cross ▸ **croix de Malte/St André** Maltese/St Andrew's cross ▸ **faire une croix sur qqch** *fig* to write sthg off ▸ **c'est un jour à marquer d'une croix blanche** it's a red-letter day ▸ **porter sa croix** to have one's cross to bear ▸ **la croix et la bannière** *fig* the devil's own job ▸ **c'est la croix et la bannière pour le faire manger** it's an uphill struggle to get him to eat.
◆ ***en croix*** loc adv : **placer** *ou* **mettre deux choses en croix** to lay two things crosswise.

Croix-Rouge [krwaruʒ] nf : **la Croix-Rouge** the Red Cross.

croquant, ***e*** [krɔkɑ̃, ɑ̃t] adj crisp, crunchy.
◆ ***croquant*** nm *vieilli* yokel.

croque-madame [krɔkmadam] nm inv *toasted cheese-and-ham sandwich with a fried egg.*

croque-mitaine [krɔkmitɛn] (pl **croque-mitaines**) nm bogeyman.

croque-monsieur [krɔkməsjø] nm inv *toasted cheese-and-ham sandwich.*

croque-mort [krɔkmɔr] (pl **croque-morts**) nm *fam* undertaker's assistant.

croquer [3] [krɔke] ■ vt **1.** [manger] to crunch **2.** [dessiner] to sketch ▸ **(jolie) à croquer** *fig* pretty as a picture.
■ vi to be crunchy.

croquette [krɔkɛt] nf croquette.

croquis [krɔki] nm sketch ▸ **faire un croquis** to make a sketch.

cross [krɔs] **nm** [exercice] cross-country (running) / [course] cross-country race.

crosse [krɔs] **nf 1.** [d'évêque] crozier **2.** [de fusil] butt **3.** [hockey] hockey stick.

crotale [krɔtal] **nm** rattlesnake.

crotte [krɔt] **nf** [de lapin etc] droppings *pl* / [de chien] dirt ▸ **crotte!** *fam* damn!

crottin [krɔtɛ̃] **nm** [de cheval] (horse) manure.

croulant, ***e*** [krulɑ̃, ɑ̃t] ■ **adj** crumbling.
■ **nm, f** *fam* old fogey, wrinkly *UK*.

crouler [3] [krule] **vi** to crumble ▸ **crouler sous** *litt* & *fig* to collapse under.

croupe [krup] **nf** rump ▸ **monter en croupe** to ride pillion.

croupier [krupje] **nm** croupier.

croupion [krupjɔ̃] **nm** ZOOL rump / CULIN parson's nose *UK*, pope's nose *US*.

croupir [32] [krupir] **vi** *litt* & *fig* to stagnate.

CROUS, ***Crous*** [krus] (abr de ***centre régional des œuvres universitaires et scolaires***) **nm** *student representative body dealing with accommodation, catering etc.*

croustade [krustad] **nf** croustade.

croustillant, ***e*** [krustijɑ̃, ɑ̃t] **adj 1.** [croquant - pain] crusty / [- biscuit] crunchy **2.** [grivois] spicy, juicy.

croustiller [3] [krustije] **vi** to be crusty.

croûte [krut] **nf 1.** [du pain, terrestre] crust ▸ **casser la croûte** *fam fig* to have a bite to eat ▸ **gagner sa croûte** *fam fig* to earn a liiving *ou* crust *UK* **2.** CULIN **: en croûte** in piecrust *ou* pastry **3.** [de fromage] rind **4.** [de plaie] scab **5.** *fam péj* [tableau] daub.

croûton [krutɔ̃] **nm 1.** [bout du pain] crust **2.** [pain frit] crouton **3.** *fam péj* [personne] fuddy-duddy.

croyable [krwajabl] **adj** believable ▸ **c'est pas croyable!** it's unbelievable *ou* incredible!

croyais, ***croyions*** ➤ ***croire***.

croyance [krwajɑ̃s] **nf** belief.

croyant, ***e*** [krwajɑ̃, ɑ̃t] ■ **p prés** ➤ ***croire***.
■ **adj : être croyant** to be a believer.
■ **nm, f** believer.

CRS (abr de ***Compagnie républicaine de sécurité***) **nm** *member of the French riot police* ▸ **on a fait appel aux CRS** the riot police were called in.

cru, ***e*** [kry] ■ **pp** ➤ ***croire***.
■ **adj 1.** [non cuit] raw ▸ **manger qqch cru** to eat sthg raw ▸ **avaler** *ou* **manger qqn tout cru** to make mincemeat out of *ou* to wipe the floor with sb **2.** [violent] harsh **3.** [direct] blunt **4.** [grivois] crude.
◆ ***cru*** **nm** [vin] vintage, wine / [vignoble] vineyard ▸ **du cru** *fig* local ▸ **un grand cru** a fine wine ▸ **de son propre cru** *fig* of one's own devising.

crû [kry] **pp** ➤ ***croître***.

cruauté [kryote] **nf** cruelty.

cruche [kryʃ] **nf 1.** [objet] jug *UK*, pitcher *US* **2.** *fam péj* [personne niaise] idiot.

crucial, ***e***, ***aux*** [krysjal, o] **adj** crucial.

crucifix [krysifi] **nm** crucifix.

crucifixion [krysifiksjɔ̃] **nf** crucifixion.

cruciverbiste [krysivɛrbist] **nmf** crossword enthusiast.

crudité [krydite] **nf** crudeness.
◆ ***crudités*** **nfpl** crudités.

crue [kry] **nf** rise in the water level ▸ **en crue** in spate.

cruel, ***elle*** [kryɛl] **adj** cruel.

cruellement [kryɛlmɑ̃] **adv** cruelly.

crûment [krymɑ̃] **adv 1.** [sans ménagement] bluntly **2.** [avec grossièreté] crudely.

crustacé [krystase] **nm** shellfish, crustacean ▸ **crustacés** shellfish *(U)*.

cryoconservation [krijɔkɔ̃sɛrvasjɔ̃] **nf** cryonics *(U)*, cryopreservation *f*.

cryptage [kriptaʒ] **nm** encryption.

crypte [kript] **nf** crypt.

crypter [kripte] **vt** to encrypt ▸ **chaîne cryptée** encrypted channel.

cs (abr écrite de ***cuillère à soupe***) tbs, tbsp.

CSA (abr de ***Conseil supérieur de l'audiovisuel***) **nm** *French broadcasting supervisory body.*

CSCE (abr de ***Conférence sur la sécurité et la coopération en Europe***) **nf** CSCE.

CSEN (abr de ***Confédération des syndicats de l'Éducation nationale***) **nf** *confederation of teachers' unions.*

CSG (abr de ***contribution sociale généralisée***) **nf** *income-related tax contribution.*

CSP (abr de ***catégorie socio-professionnelle***) **nf** *socio-professional group.*

Cuba [kyba] **npr** Cuba ▸ **à Cuba** in Cuba.

cubain, ***aine*** [kybɛ̃, ɛn] **adj** Cuban.
◆ ***Cubain***, ***aine*** **nm, f** Cuban.

cube [kyb] **nm** cube ▸ **4 au cube = 64** 4 cubed is 64 ▸ **élever au cube** MATH to cube ▸ **mètre cube** cubic metre *UK* *ou* meter *US*.
◆ ***gros cube*** **nm** big motorbike *UK* *ou* motorcycle *US*, hog *US*.

cubique [kybik] **adj** cubic.

cubisme [kybism] **nm** cubism.

cubitus [kybitys] **nm** ulna.

cucu(l) [kyky] **adj inv** *fam* silly.

cueille, ***cueilles*** ➤ ***cueillir***.

cueillette [kœjɛt] **nf** picking, harvesting.

cueilli, ***e*** [kœji] **pp** ➤ ***cueillir***.

cueillir [41] [kœjir] **vt 1.** [fruits, fleurs] to pick **2.** *fam* [personne] to catch, to nab.

cuillère**, **cuiller [kɥijɛr] **nf** [instrument] spoon ▸ **cuillère à café** coffee spoon / CULIN teaspoon ▸ **cuillère à dessert** dessertspoon ▸ **cuillère à soupe** soup spoon / CULIN tablespoon ▸ **petite cuillère** [contenu] teaspoon.

cuillerée [kɥijere] **nf** spoonful ▸ **cuillerée à café** CULIN teaspoonful ▸ **cuillerée à soupe** CULIN tablespoonful.

cuir [kɥir] **nm** leather / [non tanné] hide ▸ **en cuir** leather ▸ **cuir chevelu** ANAT scalp.

cuirasse [kɥiras] **nf** [de chevalier] breastplate / *fig* armour *UK*, armor *US*.

cuirassé [kɥirase] **nm** battleship.

cuire [98] [kɥir] ■ **vt 1.** [viande, œuf] to cook ▸ **cuire à feu doux** *ou* **petit feu** to simmer ▸ **cuire à gros bouillons** to boil hard **2.** [tarte, gâteau] to bake **3.** [briques, poterie] to fire.
■ **vi 1.** [viande, œuf] to cook / [tarte, gâteau] to bake ▸ **faire cuire qqch** to cook/bake sthg **2.** *fig* [personne] to roast, to be boiling ▸ **il vous en cuira!** *fig* you'll suffer (for it)!, you'll regret it!
◆ ***à cuire*** **loc adj : chocolat à cuire** cooking chocolate ▸ **pommes à cuire** cooking apples.

cuisais**, **cuisions ➤ ***cuire***.

cuisant**, **e [kɥizɑ̃, ɑ̃t] **adj** [douloureux] stinging, smarting / *fig* bitter.

cuisine [kɥizin] **nf 1.** [pièce] kitchen ▸ **cuisine intégrée** fitted kitchen **2.** [art] cooking, cookery *UK* ▸ **faire la cuisine** to do the cooking, to cook ▸ **elle fait très bien la cuisine** she's an excellent cook ▸ **la cuisine au beurre/à l'huile** cooking with butter/oil ▸ **cuisine bourgeoise** home cooking **3.** [ensemble de mets] cuisine, food, dishes *pl* ▸ **apprécier la cuisine chinoise** to enjoy Chinese food **4.** *fam* [combine] scheming *(U)*, schemes *pl* ▸ **cuisine électorale** electoral hanky-panky *(U)*.

cuisiné**, **e [kɥizine] **adj : plat cuisiné** ready-cooked meal.

cuisiner [3] [kɥizine] ■ **vt 1.** [aliment] to cook **2.** *fam* [personne] to grill.
■ **vi** to cook ▸ **bien/mal cuisiner** to be a good/bad cook.

cuisinier**, **ère [kɥizinje, ɛr] **nm, f** cook.
◆ ***cuisinière*** **nf** cooker *UK*, stove *US* ▸ **cuisinière électrique/à gaz** electric/gas cooker *UK* *ou* stove *US*.

cuissardes [kɥisard] **nfpl** [de pêcheur] waders / [de femme] thigh boots.

cuisse [kɥis] **nf 1.** ANAT thigh **2.** CULIN leg ▸ **cuisses de grenouille** frog's legs.

cuisson [kɥisɔ̃] **nf** cooking.

cuissot [kɥiso] **nm** haunch ▸ **cuissot de chevreuil** haunch of venison.

cuistot [kɥisto] **nm** *fam* cook.

cuistre [kɥistr] *littéraire* ■ **nm** prig.
■ **adj** priggish.

cuit**, **e [kɥi, kɥit] ■ **pp** ➤ ***cuire***.
■ **adj : bien cuit** [steak] well-done ▸ **trop cuit** overcooked, overdone ▸ **jambon cuit** cooked ham ▸ **attendre que ça tombe tout cuit (dans le bec)** to wait for things to fall into one's lap ▸ **être cuit** *fam fig* to have had it ▸ **notre sortie de dimanche, c'est cuit!** we can kiss our Sunday excursion goodbye!
◆ ***cuite*** **nf** *fam* **: prendre une cuite** to get plastered *ou* smashed.

cuiter [3] [kɥite] ◆ ***se cuiter*** **vp** *fam* to get plastered *ou* smashed.

cuivre [kɥivr] **nm 1.** [métal] **: cuivre (rouge)** copper ▸ **cuivre jaune** brass **2.** *(gén pl)* [objet] brass (object).
◆ ***cuivres*** **nmpl : les cuivres** MUS the brass.

cuivré**, **e [kɥivre] **adj** [couleur, reflet] coppery / [teint] bronzed.

cul [ky] **nm 1.** *tfam* [postérieur] bum *UK*, ass *US* ▸ **avoir le cul entre deux chaises** to be in an awkward position ▸ **en avoir plein le cul de qqch** *tfam* to be sick and tired of sthg ▸ **être comme cul et chemise** to be as thick as thieves **2.** [de bouteille] bottom ▸ **faire cul sec** *fam* to down one's drink in one.

culasse [kylas] **nf 1.** [d'arme à feu] breech **2.** AUTO cylinder head.

culbute [kylbyt] **nf 1.** [saut] somersault **2.** [chute] tumble, fall.

culbuter [3] [kylbyte] ■ **vt** [objet] to knock over.
■ **vi 1.** [faire une chute] to (take a) tumble **2.** [se renverser] to (do a) somersault.

cul-de-jatte [kydʒat] (pl **culs-de-jatte**) **nm** legless person.

cul-de-sac [kydsak] (pl **culs-de-sac**) **nm** dead end.

culinaire [kylinɛr] **adj** culinary.

culminant [kylminɑ̃] ➤ ***point***.

culminer [3] [kylmine] **vi** [surplomber] to tower ▸ **culminer à** [s'élever à] to reach its highest point at / *fig* to peak at.

culot [kylo] **nm 1.** *fam* [toupet] nerve, cheek *UK* ▸ **avoir le culot de** to have the nerve *ou* cheek *UK* to ▸ **avoir du culot** to have a lot of nerve **2.** [de cartouche, ampoule] cap.

culotte [kylɔt] **nf 1.** [sous-vêtement féminin] panties *pl*, knickers *pl UK*, pair of panties *ou* of knickers *UK* **2.** [vêtement] **: culottes courtes/longues** short/long trousers *UK* *ou* pants *US* ▸ **porter la culotte** *fam fig* to wear the trousers *UK* *ou* pants *US*.

culotté**, **e [kylɔte] **adj** [effronté] **: elle est culottée** she's got a nerve.

culpabiliser [3] [kylpabilize] ■ **vt : culpabiliser qqn** to make sb feel guilty.
■ **vi** to feel guilty.

culpabilité [kylpabilite] **nf** guilt.

culte [kylt] **nm 1.** [vénération, amour] worship **2.** [religion] religion.

cultivateur**, **trice [kyltivatœr, tris] **nm, f** farmer.

cultivé**, **e [kyltive] **adj** [personne] educated, cultured.

cultiver [3] [kyltive] **vt 1.** [terre, goût, relation] to cultivate **2.** [plante] to grow.
◆ ***se cultiver*** **vp** to cultivate *ou* improve one's mind.

culture [kyltyr] **nf 1.** AGRIC cultivation, farming ▸ **culture biologique** organic farming ▸ **culture intensive/extensive** intensive/extensive farming ▸ **les cultures** cultivated land
2. [savoir] culture, knowledge ▸ **culture d'entreprise** corporate culture ▸ **culture générale** [connaissances] general knowledge / [éducation] general education ▸ **avoir une bonne culture générale** [candidat] to be well up on general knowledge / [étudiant] to have had a broadly-based education ▸ **culture physique** physical training
3. [civilisation] culture
4. BIOL culture ▸ **faire une culture de cellules** to grow cells.

culturel, elle [kyltyrɛl] **adj** cultural.

culturisme [kyltyrism] **nm** bodybuilding.

cumin [kymɛ̃] **nm** cumin.

cumul [kymyl] **nm** [de fonctions, titres] concurrent holding / [de salaires] concurrent drawing.

cumulé, e [kymyle] **adj : intérêts cumulés** accrued interest.

cumuler [3] [kymyle] **vt** [fonctions, titres] to hold simultaneously / [salaires] to draw simultaneously / [intérêts] to accrue.

cumulus [kymylys] **nm** cumulus.

cupide [kypid] **adj** greedy.

cupidité [kypidite] **nf** greed, cupidity.

curaçao [kyraso] **nm** curaçao.

curatif, ive [kyratif, iv] **adj** curative.

cure [kyr] **nf** (course of) treatment ▸ **faire une cure de fruits** to go on a fruit-based diet ▸ **cure d'amaigrissement** slimming course *UK*, reducing treatment *US* ▸ **cure de désintoxication** [d'alcool] drying-out treatment / [de drogue] detoxification treatment ▸ **cure de sommeil** sleep therapy ▸ **faire une cure thermale** to undergo treatment at a spa.

curé [kyre] **nm** parish priest.

cure-dents [kyrdɑ̃] **nm inv** toothpick.

cure-pipe (pl -s) [kyrpip] **nm** = ***cure-pipes***.

cure-pipes [kyrpip] **nm inv** pipe cleaner.

curer [3] [kyre] **vt** to clean out.
◆ ***se curer*** **vp : se curer les ongles** to clean one's nails.

curetage [kyrtaʒ] **nm** curettage.

curie [kyri] **nf** curia.

curieusement [kyrjøzmɑ̃] **adv** curiously, strangely.

curieux, euse [kyrjø, øz] ■ **adj 1.** [intéressé] curious ▸ **curieux de qqch/de faire qqch** curious about sthg/to do sthg **2.** [indiscret] inquisitive **3.** [étrange] strange, curious.
■ **nm, f** busybody.

curiosité [kyrjozite] **nf** curiosity.
◆ ***curiosités*** **nfpl** interesting sights.

curiste [kyrist] **nmf** *person undergoing treatment at a spa.*

curling [kœrliŋ] **nm** curling.

curriculum vitae [kyrikylɔmvite] **nm inv** curriculum vitae *UK*, résumé *US*.

curry [kyri], ***carry*** [kari], ***cari*** [kari] **nm 1.** [épice] curry powder **2.** [plat] curry.

curseur [kyrsœr] **nm** cursor.

cursus [kyrsys] **nm** degree course.

cutané, e [kytane] **adj** cutaneous, skin *(avant n)*.

cuti [kyti] **nf : virer sa cuti** *fam fig* to throw off one's shackles.

cutiréaction, cuti-réaction (pl **cuti-réactions**) [kytireaksjɔ̃] **nf** skin test.

cutter [kœtɛr] **nm** Stanley knife®.

cuve [kyv] **nf 1.** [citerne] tank **2.** [à vin] vat.

cuvée [kyve] **nf 1.** [récolte] vintage **2.** [contenu de cuve] vatful.

cuver [3] [kyve] **vt 1.** [faire séjourner en cuve] to put in a vat to ferment **2.** [alcool, déception] **: cuver qqch** to sleep sthg off.

cuvette [kyvɛt] **nf 1.** [récipient] basin, bowl **2.** [de lavabo] basin / [de W.-C.] bowl **3.** GÉOGR basin.

cv (abr écrite de ***cheval-vapeur***) [puissance] HP.

CV **nm 1.** (abr de ***curriculum vitae***) CV *UK*, résumé *US* ▸ **ça fera bien dans ton CV** it'll look good on your CV *UK ou* résumé *US* **2.** (abr écrite de ***cheval-vapeur***) hp / [puissance fiscale] *classification of former car tax.*

CVS (abr de ***corrigées des variations saisonnières***) **adj** seasonally adjusted.

cx **nm** [coefficient de pénétration dans l'air] drag coefficient.

cyanure [sjanyr] **nm** cyanide.

cybercafé [sibɛrkafe] **nm** cybercafé, Internet café.

cybercommerce [sibɛrkɔmɛrs] **nm** e-commerce.

cybercrime [sibɛrkrim] **nm** INFORM e-crime.

cyberespace [sibɛrɛspas], ***cybermonde*** [sibɛrmɔ̃d] **nm** cyberspace.

cyberjargon [sibɛrʒargɔ̃] **m** INFORM netspeak.

cybermonde [sibɛrmɔ̃d] **nm** = ***cyberspace***.

cybernaute [sibɛrnot] **nm** (net) surfer, cybersurfer, cybernaut.

cybernovice [sibɛrnɔvis] **nmf** *fam* INFORM newbie.

cybersquatting [sibɛrskwatiŋ] **m** INFORM cybersquatting.

cyclable [siklabl] ➤ ***piste***.

cyclamen [siklamɛn] **nm** cyclamen.

cycle [sikl] **nm 1.** [série] cycle ▸ **cycle alimentaire** food cycle ▸ **cycle menstruel** menstrual cycle ▸ **cycle de négociations** round of negotiations **2.** [formation] cycle ▸ **premier cycle** UNIV first and second years *UK*, freshman and sophomore years *US* / SCOL lower secondary school years *UK*, junior high school *US* ▸ **second cycle** UNIV ≃ final year

UK ≃ senior year *US* / SCOL upper school *UK*, high school *US* ▸ **troisième cycle** UNIV ≃ postgraduate year *ou* years **3.** ÉCON cycle ▸ **cycle des affaires** business cycle ▸ **cycle conjoncturel** business cycle ▸ **cycle expansion-récession** boom and bust (cycle) ▸ **cycle de vie du produit** product lifecycle.

cyclique [siklik] **adj** cyclic, cyclical.

cyclisme [siklism] **nm** cycling.

cycliste [siklist] ■ **nmf** cyclist.
■ **adj** cycle *(avant n)*.

cyclo-cross [siklɔkrɔs] **nm inv** cyclo-cross.

cyclomoteur [siklɔmɔtœr] **nm** moped.

cyclone [siklon] **nm** cyclone.

cyclothymique [siklɔtimik] **nmf** & **adj** manic-depressive.

cyclotourisme [siklɔturism] **nm** cycle touring.

cygne [siɲ] **nm** swan.

cylindre [silɛ̃dr] **nm** **1.** AUTO & GÉOM cylinder **2.** [rouleau] roller.

cylindrée [silɛ̃dre] **nf** engine capacity.

cylindrique [silɛ̃drik] **adj** cylindrical.

cymbale [sɛ̃bal] **nf** cymbal.

cynique [sinik] ■ **nmf** cynic.
■ **adj** cynical.

cynisme [sinism] **nm** cynicism.

cyprès [siprɛ] **nm** cypress.

cypriote, ***Cypriote*** ➤ ***chypriote***.

cyrillique [sirilik] **adj** Cyrillic.

cystite [sistit] **nf** cystitis *(U)*.

cytise [sitiz] **nm** laburnum.

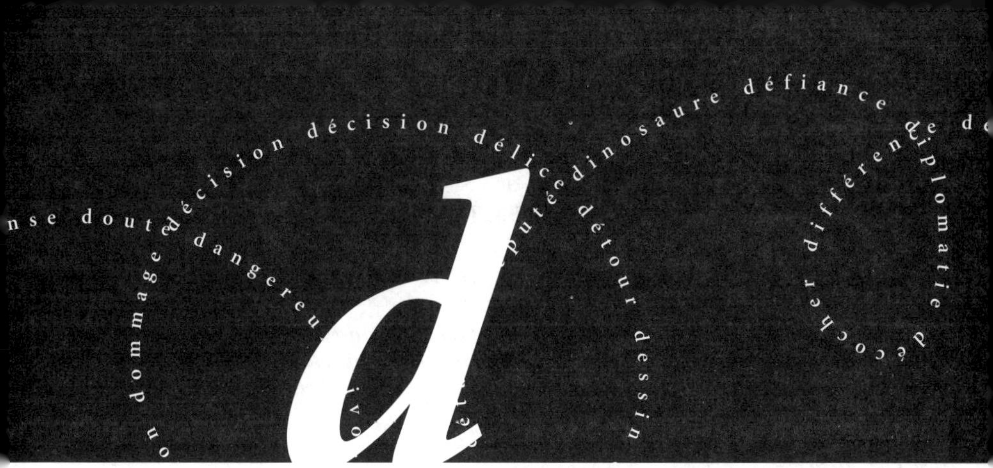

d, ***D*** [de] **nm inv** d, D.

d' ➤ ***de***.

da (abr écrite de ***déca***) da.

DAB [deabe, dab] (abr de ***distributeur automatique de billets***) **nm** ATM.

d'abord [dabɔr] ➤ ***abord***.

d'accord [dakɔr] **loc adv : d'accord!** all right!, OK! ▸ **être d'accord avec** to agree with.

dactylo [daktilo] **nf** [personne] typist / [procédé] typing.

dactylographier [9] [daktilɔgrafje] **vt** to type.

dada [dada] **nm 1.** [cheval] horsie, gee-gee *UK* **2.** *fam* [occupation] hobby **3.** *fam* [idée] hobbyhorse **4.** ART Dadaism.

dadais [dadɛ] **nm** fool ▸ **un grand dadais** a big *ou* great lump.

dahlia [dalja] **nm** dahlia.

daigner [4] [deɲe] **vi** to deign.

daim [dɛ̃] **nm 1.** [animal] fallow deer **2.** [peau] suede.

dais [dɛ] **nm** canopy.

Dakar [dakar] **npr** Dakar.

dal (abr écrite de ***décalitre***) dal.

dallage [dalaʒ] **nm** [action] paving / [dalles] pavement.

dalle [dal] **nf** [de pierre] slab / [de lino] tile ▸ **avoir la dalle** *fam fig* to be famished *ou* starving ▸ **que dalle!** *fam fig* zilch!, not a (damn) thing!, damn all! *UK*

dalmatien, ***enne*** [dalmasjɛ̃, ɛn] **nm, f** dalmatian.

daltonien, ***enne*** [daltɔnjɛ̃, ɛn] ■ **adj** colour-blind *UK*, color-blind *US*.
■ **nm, f** colour-blind *UK ou* color-blind *US* person.

dam[1] [dam] **nm : au grand dam de** [déplaisir] to the great displeasure of.

dam[2] (abr écrite de ***décamètre***) dam.

Damas [damas] **npr** Damascus.

dame [dam] **nf 1.** [femme] lady ▸ **dame de compagnie** lady's companion ▸ **dame d'honneur** lady-in-waiting ▸ **la première dame de France** France's First Lady ▸ **faire** *ou* **jouer les grandes dames** *péj* to put on airs **2.** [cartes à jouer] queen ▸ **la dame de cœur** the queen of hearts.
◆ ***dames*** **nfpl** draughts *UK*, checkers *US*.

dame-jeanne [damʒan] (pl **dames-jeannes**) **nf** demijohn.

damer [3] [dame] **vt** to pack down.

damier [damje] **nm 1.** [de jeu] draughtboard *UK*, checkerboard *US* **2.** [motif] **: à damier** checked.

damnation [danasjɔ̃] **nf** damnation.

damné, ***e*** [dane] ■ **adj** *fam* damned.
■ **nm, f** damned person.

damner [3] [dane] **vt** to damn.
◆ ***se damner*** **vp** to be damned ▸ **se damner pour** *fig* to risk damnation for.

dancing [dɑ̃siŋ] **nm** dance hall.

dandiner [3] [dɑ̃dine] ◆ ***se dandiner*** **vp** to waddle.

dandy [dɑ̃di] **nm** dandy.

Danemark [danmark] **nm : le Danemark** Denmark ▸ **au Danemark** in Denmark.

danger [dɑ̃ʒe] **nm** danger ▸ **en danger** in danger ▸ **hors de danger** out of danger ▸ **courir un danger** to run a risk ▸ **narguer le danger** to flout danger ▸ **danger public** public menace.

dangereusement [dɑ̃ʒrøzmɑ̃] **adv** dangerously.

dangereux, ***euse*** [dɑ̃ʒrø, øz] **adj** dangerous.

danois, ***e*** [danwa, az] **adj** Danish.
◆ ***danois*** **nm 1.** [langue] Danish **2.** [chien] Great Dane.
◆ ***Danois***, ***e*** **nm, f** Dane.

dans [dɑ̃] **prép 1.** [dans le temps] in ▸ **je reviens dans un mois** I'll be back in a month *ou* in a month's time ▸ **vous serez livré dans la semaine** you'll get the delivery within the week *ou* some time this week
2. [dans l'espace] in ▸ **dans une boîte** in *ou* inside a box ▸ **c'est dans ma chambre/mon sac** it's in my room/my bag ▸ **dans le train/l'avion** on the train/the plane
3. [avec mouvement] into ▸ **entrer dans une chambre** to come into a room, to enter a room

4. [indiquant un état, une manière] in ▸ **dans nos rangs** within our ranks ▸ **vivre dans la misère** to live in poverty ▸ **il est dans le commerce** he's in business ▸ **je l'ai fait dans ce but** I did it with this aim in mind
5. [environ] : **dans les...** about... ▸ **ça coûte dans les 30 euros** it costs about 30 euros ▸ **il était dans les cinq heures du soir** it was around five pm.

dansant, e [dɑ̃sɑ̃, ɑ̃t] **adj** *litt & fig* dancing ▸ **soirée dansante** dance ▸ **thé dansant** tea dance.

danse [dɑ̃s] **nf 1.** [art] dancing ▸ **danse classique/folklorique/moderne** ballet/folk/modern dancing ▸ **danse du ventre** belly dancing **2.** [musique] dance.

danser [3] [dɑ̃se] ■ **vi 1.** [personne] to dance **2.** [bateau] to bob / [flammes] to flicker.
■ **vt** to dance.

danseur, euse [dɑ̃sœr, øz] **nm, f** dancer ▸ **en danseuse** [cyclisme] standing on the pedals ▸ **danseur étoile** principal dancer.

dantesque [dɑ̃tɛsk] **adj** Dantesque, Dantean.

DAO (abr de ***dessin assisté par ordinateur***) **nm** CAD.

dard [dar] **nm** [d'animal] sting.

darder [3] [darde] **vt** to beat down ▸ **darder un regard sur** *fig* to shoot a glance at.

dare-dare [dardar] **adv** *fam* on the double.

darne [darn] **nf** [de poisson] steak.

dartre [dartr] **nf** sore.

DAT (abr de ***digital audio tape***) DAT.

DATAR, Datar [datar] (abr de ***Délégation à l'aménagement du territoire et à l'action régionale***) **nf** *regional land development agency.*

datation [datasjɔ̃] **nf** dating.

date [dat] **nf 1.** [jour+mois+année] date ▸ **date d'émission** date of issue ▸ **date limite de consommation** use-by date ▸ **date limite de vente** sell-by *UK ou* pull *US* date ▸ **de longue date** long-standing ▸ **date de naissance** date of birth **2.** [moment] event ▸ **une réalisation qui fera date** an achievement which will stand out.

dater [3] [date] ■ **vt** to date.
■ **vi 1.** [marquer] to be *ou* mark a milestone **2.** *fam* [être démodé] to be dated.
◆ ***à dater de*** **loc prép** as of *ou* from.

dateur, euse [datœr, øz] **adj** date *(avant n).*
◆ ***dateur*** **nm** [timbre] datestamp / [de montre] date indicator.

datif [datif] **nm** GRAMM dative.

datte [dat] **nf** date.

dattier [datje] **nm** date palm.

daube [dob] **nf** CULIN ≃ stew.

dauphin [dofɛ̃] **nm 1.** [mammifère] dolphin **2.** HIST : **le dauphin** the dauphin **3.** [successeur] heir apparent.

dauphine [dofin] **nf** HIST : **la dauphine** the dauphine.

daurade [dɔrad] **nf** sea bream.

davantage [davɑ̃taʒ] **adv 1.** [plus] more ▸ **davantage de** more **2.** [plus longtemps] (any) longer.

dB (abr écrite de ***décibel***) dB.

DB (abr de ***division blindée***) **nf** armoured *UK ou* armored *US* division.

DCA (abr de ***défense contre aéronefs***) **nf** AA *(anti-aircraft).*

DCT (abr de ***diphtérie coqueluche tétanos***) **nm** *vaccine against diphtheria, tetanus and whooping cough.*

DDA (abr de ***Direction départementale de l'agriculture***) **nf** *local offices of the Ministry of Agriculture.*

DDASS, Ddass [das] (abr de ***Direction départementale d'action sanitaire et sociale***) **nf** *department of health and social security* ▸ **un enfant de la DDASS** a state orphan.

DDD (abr de ***digital digital digital***) DDD.

DDE (abr de ***Direction départementale de l'Équipement***) **nf** *local offices of the Ministry of the Environment.*

DDT (abr de ***dichloro-dyphényl-trichloréthane***) **nm** DDT.

DDTAB (abr de ***diphtérie, tétanos, typhoïde, paratyphoïde A***) **nm** *vaccine against diphtheria, tetanus, typhoid and paratyphoid.*

de [də] *(formes contractées de : 'de + le' =* **du**, *'de + les' =* **des***)*
■ **prép 1.** [provenance] from ▸ **revenir de Paris** to come back *ou* return from Paris ▸ **il est sorti de la maison** he left the house, he went out of the house
2. [avec à] : **de... à** from... to ▸ **de Paris à Tokyo** from Paris to Tokyo ▸ **de dix heures à midi** from ten o'clock to *ou* till midday ▸ **il y avait de quinze à vingt mille spectateurs** there were between fifteen and twenty thousand spectators
3. [indique le moment] : **de jour** during the *ou* by day ▸ **travailler de nuit** to work nights
4. [indique la cause] : **mourir de peur/de faim** to die of fright/of hunger
5. [indique le moyen] : **faire signe de la main** to wave
6. [indique la manière] : **de toutes ses forces** with all one's strength
7. [appartenance] of ▸ **la porte du salon** the door of the sitting room, the sitting room door ▸ **le frère de Pierre** Pierre's brother ▸ **la maison de mes parents** my parents' house
8. [indique la détermination, la qualité] : **le plus jeune de la classe** the youngest pupil in the class ▸ **un verre d'eau** a glass of water ▸ **un peignoir de soie** a silk dressing gown ▸ **un appartement de 60 m²** a flat 60 metres square ▸ **un bébé de trois jours** a three-day-old baby ▸ **une ville de 500 000 habitants** a town with *ou* of 500,000 inhabitants ▸ **le train de 9 h 30** the 9.30 train
9. [servant de lien syntaxique] : **se séparer de qqn** to leave sb ▸ **sûr de soi** sure of o.s..
■ **art partitif 1.** [dans une phrase affirmative] some ▸ **je voudrais du vin/du lait** I'd like (some) wine/(some) milk ▸ **boire de l'eau** to drink (some) water ▸ **acheter des légumes** to buy some vegetables
2. [dans une interrogation ou une négation] any ▸ **ils n'ont pas d'enfants** they don't have any children, they have no children ▸ **avez-vous du pain?** do you have any bread?, have you got any bread? ▸ **voulez-vous du thé?** would you like some tea?

■ **art déf** [dans une affirmation] **: il a de bonnes idées** he has *ou* he's got (some) good ideas / [dans une négation] **: nous ne faisons pas de projets pour cet été** we are not making any plans for this summer.

DE (abr de ***diplômé d'État***) **adj** qualified ▸ **infirmière DE** qualified nurse, ≃ RN.

dé [de] **nm 1.** [à jouer] dice, die **2.** [morceau] dice, cube ▸ **couper en dés** CULIN to dice **3.** COUT **: dé (à coudre)** thimble.

DEA (abr de ***diplôme d'études approfondies***) **nm** postgraduate diploma.

dealer[1] [dile] **vt** to deal.

dealer[2] [dilœr] **nm** *fam* dealer.

déambuler [3] [deɑ̃byle] **vi** to stroll (around).

débâcle [debakl] **nf** [débandade] rout / *fig* collapse.

déballage [debalaʒ] **nm** [des bagages] unpacking.

déballer [3] [debale] **vt** to unpack / *fam fig* to pour out.

débandade [debɑ̃dad] **nf** dispersal.

débaptiser [3] [debatize] **vt** to rename.

débarbouiller [3] [debarbuje] **vt : débarbouiller qqn** to wash sb's face.
◆ ***se débarbouiller*** **vp** to wash one's face.

débarcadère [debarkadɛr] **nm** landing stage.

débardeur [debardœr] **nm 1.** [ouvrier] docker **2.** [vêtement] slipover.

débarquement [debarkəmɑ̃] **nm** [de marchandises] unloading ▸ **le Débarquement** HIST the D-Day landings.

débarquer [3] [debarke] ■ **vt** [marchandises] to unload / [passagers & MIL] to land.
■ **vi 1.** [d'un bateau] to disembark **2.** MIL to land **3.** *fam* [arriver à l'improviste] to turn up / *fig* to know nothing.

débarras [debara] **nm** junk room ▸ **bon débarras!** *fig* good riddance!

débarrasser [3] [debarase] **vt 1.** [pièce] to clear up / [table] to clear **2.** [ôter] **: débarrasser qqn de qqch** to take sthg from sb.
◆ ***se débarrasser*** **vp : se débarrasser de** to get rid of.

débat [deba] **nm** debate ▸ **élargir le débat** to broaden *ou* widen the debate.
◆ ***débats*** **nmpl** proceedings.

débattre [83] [debatr] ■ **vt** to debate, to discuss.
■ **vi : débattre de qqch** to debate *ou* discuss sthg.
◆ ***se débattre*** **vp** to struggle ▸ **se débattre avec** *ou* **contre** *fig* to struggle with *ou* against.

débattu, e [debaty] **pp** ➤ ***débattre***.

débauche [deboʃ] **nf** debauchery ▸ **une débauche de** *fig* a profusion of.

débauché, e [deboʃe] ■ **adj** debauched.
■ **nm, f** debauched person.

débaucher [3] [deboʃe] **vt 1.** [corrompre] to debauch, to corrupt **2.** [licencier] to make redundant *UK*, to lay off *US*.

débile [debil] ■ **nmf 1.** [attardé] retarded person ▸ **débile mental** mentally retarded person ▸ **débile profond** profoundly retarded person **2.** *fam* [idiot] moron.
■ **adj** *fam* stupid.

débilitant, e [debilitɑ̃, ɑ̃t] **adj** debilitating.

débilité [debilite] **nf 1.** [stupidité] stupidity **2.** [maladie] debility, deficiency.

débiner [3] [debine] ◆ ***se débiner*** **vp** *fam* to clear off.

débit [debi] **nm 1.** [de marchandises] (retail) sale **2.** [magasin] **: débit de boissons** bar ▸ **débit de tabac** tobacconist's, tobacco shop *US* **3.** [coupe] sawing up, cutting up **4.** [de liquide] (rate of) flow **5.** [élocution] delivery **6.** FIN debit ▸ **avoir un débit de 100 euros** to be 100 euros overdrawn **7.** INFORM rate ▸ **débit de traitement** data though put.

débitant, e [debitɑ̃, ɑ̃t] **nm, f 1.** [de boissons] publican *UK*, bar owner *US* **2.** [de tabac] tobacconist, tobacco dealer *US*.

débiter [3] [debite] **vt 1.** [marchandises] to sell **2.** [arbre] to saw up / [viande] to cut up **3.** [suj: robinet] to have a flow of **4.** *fam fig* [prononcer] to spout **5.** FIN to debit ▸ **débiter qqn d'une somme** to debit sb with an amount.

débiteur, trice [debitœr, tris] ■ **adj 1.** [personne] debtor *(avant n)* **2.** FIN debit *(avant n)*, in the red.
■ **nm, f** debtor.

déblaiement [deblɛmɑ̃], ***déblayage*** [deblɛjaʒ] **nm** clearing.

déblatérer [18] [deblatere] **vi** *fam péj* [médire] **: déblatérer contre** to rant on about.

déblayage = ***déblaiement***.

déblayer [11] [debleje] **vt** [dégager] to clear ▸ **déblayer le terrain** *fig* to clear the ground.

déblocage [deblɔkaʒ] **nm 1.** TECHNOL [d'un écrou, d'un dispositif] unblocking, releasing / [de freins] unjamming **2.** [réouverture - d'un tuyau] clearing, freeing, unblocking / [- d'une route] clearing **3.** ÉCON [des salaires, des prix] unfreezing / BANQUE [d'un compte] freeing **4.** [dans une mine] haulage.

débloquer [3] [deblɔke] ■ **vt 1.** [machine] to get going again **2.** [crédit] to release **3.** [compte, salaires, prix] to unfreeze.
■ **vi** *fam* to talk nonsense *ou* rubbish *UK*.

déboguer [debɔge] **vt** to debug.

déboires [debwar] **nmpl 1.** [déceptions] disappointments **2.** [échecs] setbacks **3.** [ennuis] trouble *(U)*, problems.

déboisement [debwazmɑ̃] **nm** deforestation.

déboiser [3] [debwaze] **vt** [région] to deforest / [terrain] to clear (of trees).
◆ ***se déboiser*** **vp** to become deforested.

déboîter [3] [debwate] ■ **vt 1.** [objet] to dislodge ▸ **déboîter une porte** to take a door off its hinges **2.** [membre] to dislocate.
■ **vi** AUTO to pull out.
◆ ***se déboîter*** **vp 1.** [se démonter] to come apart / [porte] to come off its hinges **2.** [membre] to dislocate.

débonnaire [debɔnɛr] **adj** good-natured, easy-going.

débordant, e [debɔrdɑ̃, ɑ̃t] **adj 1.** [activité] bustling **2.** [personne] **: débordant de** [joie, vie] overflowing with / [santé, énergie] bursting with.

débordement **[debɔrdəmɑ̃] nm 1.** [de fleuve, récipient] overflowing **2.** [de joie, tendresse] outburst.
◆ ***débordements*** **nmpl** excesses.

déborder [3] **[debɔrde]** ■ **vi** [fleuve, liquide] to overflow / *fig* to flood ▶ **laisser déborder la baignoire** to let the bath overflow ▶ **l'eau a débordé du lavabo** the sink has overflowed ▶ **les pluies ont fait déborder la rivière** the rain made the river burst its banks ▶ **déborder de** [vie, joie] to be bubbling with.
■ **vt** [limite] to go beyond ▶ **vous débordez le sujet** you've gone beyond the scope of the topic ▶ **être débordé de travail** to be up to one's eyes in *ou* snowed under with work.

débouché **[debuʃe] nm 1.** [issue] end **2.** *(gén pl)* COMM outlet **3.** [de carrière] prospect, opening.

déboucher [3] **[debuʃe]** ■ **vt 1.** [bouteille] to open **2.** [conduite, nez] to unblock.
■ **vi : déboucher sur** [arriver] to open out into / *fig* to lead to, to achieve.

débouler [3] **[debule]** ■ **vi** [personne - arriver] to charge up / [animal] to bolt.
■ **vt** to hurtle down.

déboulonner [3] **[debulɔne] vt** [statue] to dismantle.

débourser [3] **[deburse] vt** to pay out.

déboussoler [3] **[debusɔle] vt** *fam* to throw, to disorient, to disorientate *UK*.

debout **[dəbu] adv** [gén] **: être debout** [sur ses pieds] to be standing (up) / [réveillé] to be up / [objet] to be standing up *ou* upright ▶ **être debout à 5 h** to be up at 5 o'clock ▶ **les murs sont encore debout** the walls are still standing ▶ **mettre qqch debout** to stand sthg up ▶ **se mettre debout** to stand up ▶ **debout!** get up!, on your feet! ▶ **je préfère rester debout** I'd rather stand ▶ **ne restez pas debout** (please) sit down
▶▶ **tenir debout** [bâtiment] to remain standing / [argument] to stand up ▶ **il ne tient pas debout** he's asleep on his feet ▶ **le raisonnement ne tient pas debout** the argument doesn't hold water *ou* hold up.

débouter [3] **[debute] vt** DR to dismiss.

déboutonner [3] **[debutɔne] vt** to unbutton, to undo.
◆ ***se déboutonner*** **vp** [défaire ses boutons] to undo one's buttons/one's jacket *etc*.

débraillé, e **[debraje] adj** dishevelled *UK*, disheveled *US*.

débrancher [3] **[debrɑ̃ʃe] vt 1.** [appareil] to unplug **2.** [téléphone] to disconnect.

débrayage **[debrɛjaʒ] nm 1.** [AUTO - pièce] clutch / [- action] disengagement of the clutch **2.** [arrêt de travail] stoppage.

débrayer [11] **[debreje] vi 1.** AUTO to disengage the clutch, to declutch *UK* **2.** [cesser le travail] to stop work.

débridé, e **[debride] adj** *fig* & *sout* [imagination, sensualité] unbridled.

débris **[debri]** ■ **nm** piece, fragment.
■ **nmpl 1.** [restes] leftovers **2.** *fig* & *littéraire* [d'armée, fortune] remains / [d'un état] ruins.

débrouillard, e **[debrujar, ard]** *fam* ■ **adj** resourceful.
■ **nm, f** resourceful person.

débrouillardise **[debrujardiz] nf** *fam* resourcefulness.

débrouiller [3] **[debruje] vt 1.** [démêler] to untangle **2.** *fig* [résoudre] to unravel, to solve.
◆ ***se débrouiller*** **vp : se débrouiller (pour faire qqch)** to manage (to do sthg) ▶ **se débrouiller en anglais/math** to get by in English/maths ▶ **débrouille-toi!** you'll have to sort it out (by) yourself!

débroussailler [3] **[debrusaje] vt** [terrain] to clear / *fig* to do the groundwork for.

débuguer [3] **[debyge] vt** = ***déboguer***.

débusquer [3] **[debyske] vt 1.** [gibier] to drive out **2.** [personne] to flush out.

début **[deby] nm** beginning, start ▶ **au début** at the start *ou* beginning ▶ **au début de** at the beginning of ▶ **dès le début** (right) from the start.
◆ ***débuts*** **nmpl** debut *sg* ▶ **faire ses débuts** to make one's debut.

débutant, e **[debytɑ̃, ɑ̃t] nm, f** beginner.

débuter [3] **[debyte] vi 1.** [commencer] **: débuter (par)** to begin (with), to start (with) **2.** [faire ses débuts] to start out.

déca **[deka] nm** *fam* decaff.

deçà **[dəsa]** ◆ ***deçà delà*** **loc adv** here and there. ◆ ***en deçà de*** **loc prép 1.** [de ce côté-ci de] on this side of **2.** [en dessous de] short of.

décacheter [27] **[dekaʃte] vt** to open.

décade **[dekad] nf** period of ten days.

décadence **[dekadɑ̃s] nf 1.** [déclin] decline **2.** [débauche] decadence.

décadent, e **[dekadɑ̃, ɑ̃t] adj** decadent.

décaféiné, e **[dekafeine] adj** decaffeinated.
◆ ***décaféiné*** **nm** decaffeinated coffee.

décaissement **[dekesɛmɑ̃] nm 1.** FIN payment, disbursement *(terme spécialisé)* **2.** [déballage] unpacking **3.** BOT planting out.

décaisser [4] **[dekese] vt 1.** FIN to pay, to disburse *(terme spécialisé)* **2.** [déballer] to unpack, to take out of its container.

décalage **[dekalaʒ] nm** gap / *fig* gulf, discrepancy ▶ **décalage horaire** [entre zones] time difference / [après un vol] jet lag.

décalcification **[dekalsifikasjɔ̃] nf** decalcification.

décalcomanie **[dekalkɔmani] nf** transfer *(adhesive) UK*, decal *US*.

décaler [3] [dekale] **vt 1.** [dans le temps - avancer] to bring forward / [- retarder] to put back **2.** [dans l'espace] to move, to shift.
◆ ***se décaler*** **vp** to move.

décalquer [3] [dekalke] **vt** to trace.

décamper [3] [dekɑ̃pe] **vi** *fam* to clear off.

décan [dekɑ̃] **nm** ASTROL decan.

décanter [3] [dekɑ̃te] ■ **vt : laisser décanter** [liquide] to allow to settle / *fig* [idée] to allow to settle down ***ou*** become clearer.
■ **vi** [liquide] to settle / *fig* [idées] to become clear.
◆ ***se décanter*** **vp** [idées] to become clear.

décapant, ***e*** [dekapɑ̃, ɑ̃t] **adj 1.** [nettoyant] stripping **2.** *fig* [incisif] cutting, caustic.
◆ ***décapant*** **nm** (paint) stripper.

décaper [3] [dekape] **vt** [en grattant] to sand / [avec un produit chimique] to strip.

décapiter [3] [dekapite] **vt 1.** [personne - volontairement] to behead / [- accidentellement] to decapitate **2.** [arbre] to cut the top off **3.** *fig* [organisation, parti] to remove the leader ***ou*** leaders of.

décapotable [dekapɔtabl] **nf & adj** convertible.

décapsuler [3] [dekapsyle] **vt** to take the top off, to open.

décapsuleur [dekapsylœr] **nm** bottle opener.

décarcasser [3] [dekarkase] ◆ ***se décarcasser*** **vp** *fam* **: se décarcasser (à faire qqch)** to slog away (at doing sthg).

décédé, ***e*** [desede] **adj** deceased.

décéder [18] [desede] **vi** to die.

déceler [25] [desle] **vt 1.** [révéler] to reveal **2.** [repérer] to detect.

décélération [deselerasjɔ̃] **nf** deceleration.

décembre [desɑ̃br] **nm** December ; voir aussi ***septembre***.

décemment [desamɑ̃] **adv 1.** [convenablement] properly **2.** [raisonnablement] reasonably.

décence [desɑ̃s] **nf** decency.

décennie [deseni] **nf** decade.

décent, ***e*** [desɑ̃, ɑ̃t] **adj** decent.

décentralisation [desɑ̃tralizasjɔ̃] **nf** decentralization.

décentraliser [3] [desɑ̃tralize] **vt** to decentralize.

décentrer [3] [desɑ̃tre] **vt** to move off-centre *UK* ***ou*** off-center *US*.

déception [desɛpsjɔ̃] **nf** disappointment.

décerner [3] [desɛrne] **vt : décerner qqch à** to award sthg to.

décès [desɛ] **nm** death.

décevant, ***e*** [desəvɑ̃, ɑ̃t] **adj** disappointing.

décevoir [52] [desəvwar] **vt** to disappoint.

> FAUX AMIS / FALSE FRIENDS
> **décevoir**
> Deceive is not a translation of the French word *décevoir*. Deceive is translated by *tromper*.
> ▸ He's been deceiving them all along / *Il les a trompés depuis le début*

déchaîné, ***e*** [deʃene] **adj 1.** [vent, mer] stormy, wild **2.** [passion] unrestrained / [opinion publique] raging **3.** [personne] wild.

déchaîner [4] [deʃene] **vt** [passion] to unleash / [rires] to cause an outburst of.
◆ ***se déchaîner*** **vp 1.** [éléments naturels] to erupt **2.** [personne] to fly into a rage.

déchanter [3] [deʃɑ̃te] **vi** to become disillusioned.

décharge [deʃarʒ] **nf 1.** DR discharge **2.** ÉLECTR discharge ▸ **décharge électrique** electric *UK* ***ou*** electrical *US* shock **3.** [reçu] receipt **4.** [dépotoir] rubbish tip *UK*, rubbish dump *UK*, garbage dump *US* ▸ **décharge municipale** city/town dump.

déchargement [deʃarʒəmɑ̃] **nm** unloading.

décharger [17] [deʃarʒe] **vt 1.** [véhicule, marchandises] to unload ▸ **décharger des bananes d'un navire** to unload bananas from ***ou*** to take bananas off a ship **2.** [arme - tirer] to fire, to discharge ▸ **décharger son arme sur qqn** to fire one's gun at sb / [- enlever la charge de] to unload **3.** [soulager - cœur] to unburden / [- conscience] to salve / [- colère] to vent ▸ **décharger sa mauvaise humeur sur qqn** to vent one's temper on sb **4.** [libérer] **: décharger qqn de** to release sb from.
◆ ***se décharger*** **vp 1.** ÉLECTR to go flat **2.** [se libérer] **: se décharger de qqch sur** to offload sthg onto **3.** [rivière] **: se décharger dans** to flow into.

décharné, ***e*** [deʃarne] **adj** [maigre] emaciated.

déchausser [3] [deʃose] **vt : déchausser qqn** to take sb's shoes off.
◆ ***se déchausser*** **vp 1.** [personne] to take one's shoes off **2.** [dent] to come loose.

dèche [dɛʃ] **nf** *fam* **: être dans la dèche** to be broke.

déchéance [deʃeɑ̃s] **nf 1.** [déclin] degeneration, decline **2.** [d'un souverain] dethronement **3.** DR loss.

déchet [deʃɛ] **nm** [de matériau] scrap.
◆ ***déchets*** **nmpl** refuse *(U)*, waste *(U)* ▸ **déchets radioactifs** radioactive waste.

déchetterie® [deʃɛtri] **nf** recycling centre *UK* ***ou*** center *US*.

déchiffrer [3] [deʃifre] **vt 1.** [inscription, hiéroglyphes] to decipher / [énigme] to unravel **2.** MUS to sight-read.

déchiqueter [27] [deʃikte] **vt** to tear to shreds.

déchirant, e [deʃirɑ̃, ɑ̃t] **adj** heartrending.

déchirement [deʃirmɑ̃] **nm 1.** [division] rift, split **2.** [souffrance morale] heartbreak, distress.

déchirer [3] [deʃire] **vt 1.** [papier, tissu] to tear up, to rip up ▸ **attention, tu vas déchirer ton collant** mind not to rip your tights ▸ **déchirer une page en deux** to tear a page in two **2.** [blesser] to tear (the skin *ou* flesh of), to gash ▸ **un bruit qui déchire les tympans** an earpiercing *ou* earsplitting noise **3.** *fig* [diviser] to tear apart ▸ **le pays est déchiré par la guerre depuis 10 ans** the country has been torn apart by war for 10 years.
◆ ***se déchirer*** **vp 1.** [personnes] to tear each other apart **2.** [matériau, muscle] to tear ▸ **ce tissu se déchire facilement** this material tears easily ▸ **se déchirer un muscle/tendon/ligament** to tear a muscle/tendon/ligament.

déchirure [deʃiryr] **nf** tear / *fig* wrench ▸ **déchirure musculaire** MÉD torn muscle.

déchoir [71] [deʃwar] **vi** *sout* [s'abaisser] to demean o.s.

déchu, e [deʃy] ■ **pp** ➤ ***déchoir.***
■ **adj 1.** [homme, ange] fallen / [souverain] deposed **2.** DR : **être déchu de** to be deprived of.

décibel [desibɛl] **nm** decibel.

décidé, e [deside] **adj 1.** [résolu] determined **2.** [arrêté] settled.

FAUX AMIS / FALSE FRIENDS
décidé
Decided is not a translation of the French word *décidé*. Decided is translated by *net*.
▸ His work was a decided improvement / *Son travail était une nette amélioration*

deci-delà [dəsi] **adv** *sout* here and there.

décidément [desidemɑ̃] **adv** really.

décider [3] [deside] ■ **vt 1.** [prendre une décision] : **décider (de faire qqch)** to decide (to do sthg) ▸ **décider que** to decide (that) **2.** [convaincre] **: décider qqn à faire qqch** to persuade sb to do sthg.
■ **vi** [déterminer] **: décider de qqch** to decide on sthg.
◆ ***se décider*** **vp 1.** [personne] **: se décider (à faire qqch)** to make up one's mind (to do sthg) **2.** [affaire] to be decided, to be settled **3.** [choisir] **: se décider pour** to decide on, to settle on.

décideur [desidœr] **nm** decision-maker.

décilitre [desilitr] **nm** decilitre *UK,* deciliter *US.*

décimal, e, aux [desimal, o] **adj** decimal.
◆ ***décimale*** **nf** decimal.

décimer [3] [desime] **vt** to decimate.

décimètre [desimɛtr] **nm 1.** [dixième de mètre] decimetre *UK,* decimeter *US* **2.** [règle] ruler ▸ **double décimètre** ≃ foot rule.

décisif, ive [desizif, iv] **adj** decisive.

décision [desizjɔ̃] **nf** decision ▸ **décision d'achat** purchasing decision ▸ **prendre une décision** to take *ou* make a decision.

décisionnaire [desizjɔnɛr] **nmf** decision-maker.

déclamer [3] [deklame] **vt** to declaim.

déclaration [deklarasjɔ̃] **nf 1.** [orale] declaration, announcement ▸ **faire une déclaration** to make a statement ▸ **je ne ferai aucune déclaration!** no comment! ▸ **déclaration de guerre/d'amour** declaration of war/of love ▸ **faire une déclaration d'amour (à qqn)** to declare one's love (to sb) ▸ **selon les déclarations du témoin** according to the witness's statement **2.** [écrite] report, declaration / [d'assurance] claim ▸ **faire une déclaration de perte de passeport à la police** to report the loss of one's passport to the police ▸ **déclaration de naissance/de décès** registration of birth/death ▸ **déclaration d'impôts** tax return ▸ **déclaration de revenus** statement of income ▸ **déclaration de sinistre** damage claim.

déclarer [3] [deklare] **vt 1.** [annoncer] to declare ▸ **déclarer que** to declare (that) **2.** [signaler] to report ▸ **rien à déclarer** nothing to declare ▸ **déclarer une naissance** to register a birth.
◆ ***se déclarer*** **vp 1.** [se prononcer] **: se déclarer pour/contre qqch** to come out in favour *UK ou* favor *US* of/against sthg **2.** [se manifester] to break out.

déclasser [3] [deklase] **vt 1.** [personne - gén] to downgrade / SPORT to relegate **2.** [objets] to get out of order.

déclenchement [deklɑ̃ʃmɑ̃] **nm** [de mécanisme] activating, setting off / *fig* launching.

déclencher [3] [deklɑ̃ʃe] **vt** [mécanisme] to activate, to set off / *fig* to launch.
◆ ***se déclencher*** **vp** [mécanisme] to go off, to be activated / *fig* to be triggered off.

déclic [deklik] **nm 1.** [mécanisme] trigger **2.** [bruit] click.

déclin [deklɛ̃] **nm 1.** [de civilisation, population, santé] decline ▸ **une personnalité sur son déclin** *fig* a celebrity on the wane **2.** [fin] close.

déclinaison [deklinɛzɔ̃] **nf** GRAMM declension.

décliner [3] [dekline] ■ **vi 1.** [santé, population, popularité] to decline **2.** [jour] to draw to a close.
■ **vt 1.** [offre, honneur] to decline ▸ **décliner une invitation** to decline an invitation ▸ **décliner toute responsabilité** to accept no responsibility **2.** GRAMM to decline / *fig* [gamme de produits] to develop **3.** [énoncer] to state.
◆ ***se décliner*** **vp** GRAMM to decline.

déclivité [deklivite] **nf** slope, incline.

décloisonner [3] [deklwazɔne] **vt** *fig* to decompartmentalize.

déclouer [3] [deklue] **vt** to take the nails out of.

décocher [3] [dekɔʃe] **vt** *litt* & *fig* to let fly ▸ **décocher un regard** to shoot a glance.

décoction [dekɔksjɔ̃] **nf** decoction.

décodage [dekɔdaʒ] **nm** decoding.

décoder [3] [dekɔde] **vt** to decode.

décodeur [dekɔdœr] **nm** decoder.

décoiffer [3] [dekwafe] **vt** [cheveux] to mess up.
◆ ***se décoiffer*** **vp** **1.** [cheveux] to be messed up **2.** [enlever son chapeau] to take off one's hat.

décoincer [16] [dekwɛ̃se] **vt** **1.** [chose] to loosen / [mécanisme] to unjam **2.** *fam* [personne] to loosen up.
◆ ***se décoincer*** **vp** **1.** [mécanisme] to loosen **2.** *fam fig* [personne] to loosen up.

déçois, ***déçoit*** ➤ ***décevoir***.

décolérer [18] [dekɔlere] **vi : il n'a pas décoléré** he hasn't calmed down.

décollage [dekɔlaʒ] **nm** *litt & fig* takeoff.

décollé, ***e*** [dekɔle] **adj : il a les oreilles décollées** his ears stick out.

décollement [dekɔlmɑ̃] **nm : décollement de la rétine** MÉD detachment of the retina.

décoller [3] [dekɔle] ■ **vt** [étiquette, timbre] to unstick / [papier peint] to strip (off).
■ **vi** *litt & fig* to take off.
◆ ***se décoller*** **vp** [étiquette, timbre] to come unstuck / [papier peint] to peel off.

décolleté, ***e*** [dekɔlte] **adj** [vêtement] low-cut.
◆ ***décolleté*** **nm** **1.** [de personne] neck and shoulders *pl* **2.** [de vêtement] neckline, neck.

décolonisation [dekɔlɔnizasjɔ̃] **nf** decolonization.

décolorant, ***e*** [dekɔlɔrɑ̃, ɑ̃t] **adj** bleaching *(avant n)*.
◆ ***décolorant*** **nm** bleach.

décoloration [dekɔlɔrasjɔ̃] **nf** bleaching.

décolorer [3] [dekɔlɔre] **vt** [par décolorant] to bleach, to lighten / [par usure] to fade.
◆ ***se décolorer*** **vp** **1.** [se ternir] to fade **2.** [cheveux] to bleach.

décombres [dekɔ̃br] **nmpl** debris *(U)*.

décommander [3] [dekɔmɑ̃de] **vt** to cancel.
◆ ***se décommander*** **vp** to cancel (one's appointment).

décomposé, ***e*** [dekɔ̃poze] **adj** **1.** [pourri] decomposed **2.** [visage] haggard / [personne] in shock.

décomposer [3] [dekɔ̃poze] **vt** **1.** [gén] **: décomposer (en)** to break down (into) **2.** *fig* [troubler] to distort.
◆ ***se décomposer*** **vp** **1.** [se putréfier] to rot, to decompose **2.** [se diviser] **: se décomposer en** to be broken down into **3.** *fig* [s'altérer] to be distorted.

décomposition [dekɔ̃pozisjɔ̃] **nf** **1.** [putréfaction] decomposition **2.** *fig* [analyse] breakdown, analysis.

décompresser [4] [dekɔ̃prese] ■ **vt** TECHNOL to decompress, to uncompress / INFORM [fichier] to unzip.
■ **vi** to unwind.

décompression [dekɔ̃presjɔ̃] **nf** decompression.

décompte [dekɔ̃t] **nm** **1.** [calcul] breakdown (of an amount) **2.** [réduction] deduction ▸ **j'ai fait le décompte de ce que tu me dois** I've deducted *ou* taken off what you owe me.

décompter [3] [dekɔ̃te] **vt** to deduct.

déconcentrer [3] [dekɔ̃sɑ̃tre] **vt** **1.** [disséminer] to decentralize **2.** [distraire] to distract.
◆ ***se déconcentrer*** **vp** to be distracted.

déconcertant, ***e*** [dekɔ̃sɛrtɑ̃, ɑ̃t] **adj** disconcerting.

déconcerter [3] [dekɔ̃sɛrte] **vt** to disconcert.

déconfit, ***e*** [dekɔ̃fi, it] **adj** crestfallen.

déconfiture [dekɔ̃fityr] **nf** collapse, ruin.

décongeler [25] [dekɔ̃ʒle] **vt** to defrost.

décongestionner [3] [dekɔ̃ʒɛstjɔne] **vt** to relieve congestion in ▸ **décongestionner la circulation** to reduce traffic.

déconnecter [4] [dekɔnɛkte] **vt** to disconnect ▸ **être déconnecté** *fam* to be out of touch.
◆ ***se déconnecter*** **vp** INFORM to disconnect, to log off.

déconner [3] [dekɔne] **vi** *tfam* [dire] to talk crap ***ou*** rubbish *UK* / [faire] to mess ***ou*** muck *UK* around.

déconseillé, ***e*** [dekɔ̃seje] **adj : c'est fortement déconseillé** it's extremely inadvisable.

déconseiller [4] [dekɔ̃seje] **vt : déconseiller qqch à qqn** to advise sb against sthg ▸ **déconseiller à qqn de faire qqch** to advise sb against doing sthg.

déconsidérer [18] [dekɔ̃sidere] **vt** to discredit.
◆ ***se déconsidérer*** **vp** to be discredited.

décontaminer [3] [dekɔ̃tamine] **vt** to decontaminate.

décontenancer [16] [dekɔ̃tnɑ̃se] **vt** to put out.
◆ ***se décontenancer*** **vp** to be put out.

décontracté, ***e*** [dekɔ̃trakte] **adj** **1.** [muscle] relaxed **2.** [détendu] casual, laid-back.

décontracter [3] [dekɔ̃trakte] **vt** to relax.
◆ ***se décontracter*** **vp** to relax.

déconvenue [dekɔ̃vny] **nf** disappointment.

décor [dekɔr] **nm** **1.** [environs] setting **2.** [décoration] interior decoration, décor **3.** THÉÂTRE scenery *(U)* / CINÉ sets *pl*.

décorateur, ***trice*** [dekɔratœr, tris] **nm, f** CINÉ & THÉÂTRE designer ▸ **décorateur d'intérieur** interior decorator.

décoratif, ***ive*** [dekɔratif, iv] **adj** decorative.

décoration [dekɔrasjɔ̃] **nf** decoration.

décorer [3] [dekɔre] **vt** to decorate.

décortiquer [3] [dekɔrtike] **vt** [noix] to shell / [graine] to husk / *fig* to analyse *UK* ***ou*** analyze *US* in minute detail.

décorum [dekɔrɔm] **nm** decorum.

décote [dekɔt] **nf** **1.** [réduction d'impôt] tax relief **2.** FIN below-par rating.

découcher [3] [dekuʃe] **vi** to stay out all night ▸ **elle a découché** she stayed out all night, she didn't sleep at home last night.

découdre [86] [dekudr] **vt** COUT to unpick ▸ **en découdre** to come to blows.
◆ ***se découdre*** **vp** to come unstitched.

découler [3] [dekule] **vi : découler de** to follow from.

découpage [dekupaʒ] **nm 1.** [action] cutting out / [résultat] paper cutout **2.** CINÉ preparation of screenplay **3.** ADMIN **: découpage (électoral)** division into constituencies *UK ou* districts *US* **4.** *fig* [de texte] cutting, editing.

découper [3] [dekupe] **vt 1.** [couper] to cut up **2.** *fig* [diviser] to cut out.
◆ ***se découper*** **vp** *fig* **: se découper sur** to stand out against.

découplé, e [dekuple] **adj : bien découplé** well-proportioned.

découpure [dekupyr] **nf** [bord] indentations *pl*, jagged outline.

décourageant, e [dekuraʒɑ̃, ɑ̃t] **adj** discouraging.

découragement [dekuraʒmɑ̃] **nm** discouragement.

décourager [17] [dekuraʒe] **vt** to discourage ▸ **décourager qqn de qqch** to put sb off sthg ▸ **décourager qqn de faire qqch** to discourage sb from doing sthg.
◆ ***se décourager*** **vp** to lose heart.

décousu, e [dekuzy] ■ **pp** ➤ ***découdre***.
■ **adj** *fig* [conversation] disjointed.

découvert, e [dekuvɛr, ɛrt] ■ **pp** ➤ ***découvrir***.
■ **adj** [tête] bare / [terrain] exposed.
◆ ***découvert*** **nm** BANQUE overdraft ▸ **être à découvert (de 1 000 euros)** to be (1,000 euros) overdrawn.
◆ ***découverte*** **nf** discovery ▸ **aller à la découverte de** to explore.

découvrir [34] [dekuvrir] **vt 1.** [trouver, surprendre] to discover ▸ **découvrir du pétrole/de l'or** to strike oil/gold ▸ **on a découvert l'arme du crime** the murder weapon has been found **2.** [ôter ce qui couvre, mettre à jour] to uncover ▸ **il fait chaud dans la chambre; va découvrir le bébé** it's hot in the bedroom, take the covers off the baby **3.** [laisser voir] to reveal ▸ **sa robe lui découvrait le dos** her dress revealed her back.
◆ ***se découvrir*** **vp 1.** [se dévêtir] to take off one's clothes, to undress **2.** [ôter son chapeau] to take off one's hat **3.** [ciel] to clear ▸ **ça se découvre** it's clearing up **4.** [se trouver - cousin, penchant] to discover ▸ **elle s'est découvert des amis partout** she discovered she had friends everywhere ▸ **il s'est découvert un don pour la cuisine** he found he had a gift for cooking.

décrasser [3] [dekrase] **vt** to scrub.

décrépit, e [dekrepi, it] **adj** decrepit.

décrépitude [dekrepityd] **nf 1.** [de personne] decrepitude **2.** [d'objet] dilapidation.

decrescendo [dekreʃendo] ■ **nm inv** decrescendo.
■ **adv** MUS decrescendo ▸ **aller decrescendo** *fig* to wane.

décret [dekrɛ] **nm** decree ▸ **décret ministériel** *order to carry out legislation given by the Prime Minister*.

décréter [18] [dekrete] **vt 1.** ADMIN to decree **2.** [décider] **: décréter que** to decide that.

décrier [10] [dekrije] **vt** *sout* to decry.

décrire [99] [dekrir] **vt** to describe.

décrisper [3] [dekrispe] **vt 1.** [personne] to put at ease **2.** [atmosphère] to ease.
◆ ***se décrisper*** **vp** to relax.

décrit, e [dekri, it] **pp** ➤ ***décrire***.

décrochement [dekrɔʃmɑ̃] **nm 1.** GÉOL thrust fault **2.** [action] unhooking **3.** [partie en retrait] recess.

décrocher [3] [dekrɔʃe] ■ **vt 1.** [enlever] to take down **2.** [téléphone] to pick up **3.** *fam* [obtenir] to land.
■ **vi** *fam* [abandonner] to drop out.
◆ ***se décrocher*** **vp** to fall down.

décroiser [3] [dekrwaze] **vt** to unfold, to uncross.

décroissant, e [dekrwasɑ̃, ɑ̃t] **adj** [courbe] decreasing / [influence] diminishing ▸ **par ordre décroissant** in descending order.

décroître [94] [dekrwatr] **vi** to decrease, to diminish / [jours] to get shorter.

décrotter [3] [dekrɔte] **vt** to clean the mud off.

décru, e [dekry] **pp** ➤ ***décroître***.
◆ ***décrue*** **nf** drop in the water level.

décrypter [3] [dekripte] **vt** to decipher.

déçu, e [desy] ■ **pp** ➤ ***décevoir***.
■ **adj** disappointed.

déculotter [3] [dekylɔte] **vt : déculotter qqn** to take sb's trousers *UK ou* pants *US* off.
◆ ***se déculotter*** **vp** to take off one's trousers *UK ou* pants *US*.

déculpabiliser [3] [dekylpabilize] **vt : déculpabiliser qqn** to free sb from guilt.
◆ ***se déculpabiliser*** **vp** to free o.s. from guilt.

décupler [3] [dekyple] **vt & vi** to increase tenfold.

dédaigner [4] [dedeɲe] **vt 1.** [mépriser - personne] to despise / [- conseils, injures] to scorn **2.** [refuser] **: dédaigner de faire qqch** *sout* to disdain to do sthg ▸ **ne pas dédaigner qqch/de faire qqch** not to be above sthg/above doing sthg.

dédaigneusement [dedɛɲøzmɑ̃] **adv** disdainfully.

dédaigneux, euse [dedɛɲø, øz] **adj** disdainful.

dédain [dedɛ̃] **nm** disdain, contempt.

dédale [dedal] **nm** *litt & fig* maze.

dedans [dədɑ̃] **adv & nm** inside.
◆ ***de dedans*** **loc adv** from inside, from within.
◆ ***en dedans*** **loc adv** inside, within.
◆ ***en dedans de*** **loc prép** inside, within ; voir aussi ***là-dedans***.

dédicace [dedikas] **nf** dedication.

dédicacer [16] [dedikase] **vt : dédicacer qqch (à qqn)** to sign *ou* autograph sthg (for sb).

dédié, e [dedje] **adj** INFORM dedicated.

dédier [9] [dedje] **vt : dédier qqch (à qqn/à qqch)** to dedicate sthg (to sb/to sthg).

dédire [103] [dedir] ◆ ***se dédire*** **vp** *sout* to go back on one's word.

dédit [dedi] **nm** DR penalty (clause).

dédommagement [dedɔmaʒmɑ̃] **nm** compensation.

dédommager [17] [dedɔmaʒe] **vt** **1.** [indemniser] to compensate **2.** *fig* [remercier] to repay.

dédouanement [dedwanmɑ̃], ***dédouanage*** [dedwanaʒ] **nm** customs clearance.

dédouaner [3] [dedwane] **vt** [marchandises] to clear through customs.

dédoublement [dedubləmɑ̃] **nm** halving, splitting (in two) ▸ **dédoublement de la personnalité** *fig* & PSYCHO split personality.

dédoubler [3] [deduble] **vt** to halve, to split / [fil] to separate.
◆ ***se dédoubler*** **vp** **1.** *fig* & PSYCHO to have a split personality **2.** *fig* & *hum* [être partout] to be in two places at once.

dédramatiser [3] [dedramatize] **vt** [événement] to play down / [situation] to defuse.

déductible [dedyktibl] **adj** deductible.

déduction [dedyksjɔ̃] **nf** deduction.

déduire [98] [dedɥir] **vt : déduire qqch (de)** [ôter] to deduct sthg (from) / [conclure] to deduce sthg (from).

déduisais, ***déduisait*** ➤ ***déduire***.

déduit, ***e*** [dedɥi, it] **pp** ➤ ***déduire***.

déesse [deɛs] **nf** goddess.

DEFA, ***Defa*** [defa] (abr de ***diplôme d'État relatif aux fonctions d'animation***) **nm** *diploma for senior youth leaders*.

défaillance [defajɑ̃s] **nf** **1.** [incapacité - de machine] failure / [- de personne, organisation] weakness **2.** [malaise] blackout, fainting fit ▸ **défaillance cardiaque** MÉD heart failure.

défaillant, ***e*** [defajɑ̃, ɑ̃t] **adj** [faible] failing.

défaillir [47] [defajir] **vi** **1.** [s'évanouir] to faint **2.** [faire défaut] to fail.

défaire [109] [defɛr] **vt** **1.** [détacher] to undo ▸ **défaire ses cheveux** to let one's hair down *litt* ▸ **défaire les lacets d'une botte** to unlace a boot / [valise] to unpack / [lit] to strip ▸ **le lit défait** [pas encore fait] the unmade bed **2.** *sout* [vaincre] to defeat.
◆ ***se défaire*** **vp** **1.** [ne pas tenir] to come undone **2.** *sout* [se séparer] **: se défaire de** to get rid of ▸ **il ne veut pas se défaire de son vieux chien** he won't get rid of his old dog.

défaisais, ***défaisions*** ➤ ***défaire***.

défait, ***e*** [defɛ, ɛt] ■ **pp** ➤ ***défaire***.
■ **adj** *fig* [épuisé] haggard.
◆ ***défaite*** **nf** defeat.

défaitisme [defetism] **nm** defeatism.

défaitiste [defetist] **nmf** & **adj** defeatist.

défalcation [defalkasjɔ̃] **nf** deduction ▸ **défalcation faite des frais** after deduction of expense.

défalquer [3] [defalke] **vt** to deduct.

défasse, ***défasses*** ➤ ***défaire***.

défaut [defo] **nm** **1.** [imperfection] flaw ▸ **défaut d'élocution** *ou* **de prononciation** speech defect *ou* impediment ▸ **défaut de fabrication** manufacturing fault **2.** [de personne] fault, shortcoming **3.** [manque] lack ▸ **des roses ou, à défaut, des tulipes** roses or, failing that, tulips ▸ **à défaut de** for lack *ou* want of ▸ **un voyage reposant à défaut d'être intéressant** a restful if not interesting trip ▸ **faire défaut** to be lacking ▸ **l'eau fait (cruellement) défaut** there is a serious water shortage ▸ **notre fournisseur nous a fait défaut** our supplier let us down ▸ **par défaut** [être jugé] in one's absence / [calculer] to the nearest decimal point **4.** DR default ▸ **défaut de paiement** default in payment, non-payment.

défaveur [defavœr] **nf** disfavour *UK*, disfavor *US* ▸ **être en défaveur** to be out of favour *UK ou* favor *US* ▸ **tomber en défaveur** to fall out of favour *UK ou* favor *US*.

défavorable [defavɔrabl] **adj** unfavourable *UK*, unfavorable *US*.

défavorisé, ***e*** [defavɔrize] **adj** disadvantaged, underprivileged.

défavoriser [3] [defavɔrize] **vt** to handicap, to penalize.

défectif, ***ive*** [defɛktiv, iv] **adj** GRAMM defective.

défection [defɛksjɔ̃] **nf** **1.** [absence] absence **2.** [abandon] defection.

défectueux, ***euse*** [defɛktɥø, øz] **adj** faulty, defective.

défendable [defɑ̃dabl] **adj** *litt* & *fig* defensible.

défendais, ***défendions*** ➤ ***défendre***.

défendeur, ***eresse*** [defɑ̃dœr, rɛs] **nm, f** defendant.

défendre [73] [defɑ̃dr] **vt** **1.** [personne, opinion, client] to defend **2.** [interdire] to forbid ▸ **défendre qqch à qqn** to forbid sb sthg ▸ **défendre à qqn de faire qqch** to forbid sb to do sthg ▸ **défendre que qqn fasse qqch** to forbid sb to do sthg.
◆ ***se défendre*** **vp** **1.** [se battre, se justifier] to defend o.s. **2.** *fam* [se débrouiller] **: se défendre (en)** to get by (in) **3.** [nier] **: se défendre de faire qqch** to deny doing sthg **4.** [thèse] to stand up.

défendu, ***e*** [defɑ̃dy] ■ **pp** ➤ ***défendre***.
■ **adj : 'il est défendu de jouer au ballon'** 'no ball games'.

défense [defɑ̃s] **nf** **1.** [d'éléphant] tusk **2.** [interdiction] prohibition, ban ▸ **'défense de fumer/de stationner/d'entrer'** 'no smoking/parking/entry' ▸ **'défense d'afficher'** 'stick *UK ou* post no bills' ▸ **mais défense expresse d'en parler!** but you're strictly forbidden to talk about it! **3.** [protection] defence *UK*, defense *US* ▸ **pour la défense des institutions** in order to defend *ou* to safeguard the institutions ▸ **prendre la défense de** to stand up for ▸ **défense antiaérienne** MIL anti-aircraft defence *UK ou* defense *US* ▸ **défense des consommateurs** consumer protection ▸ **la défense nationale** MIL national defence *UK ou* defense *US* ▸ **un secret Défense** a military secret ▸ **défense passive** civil defence *UK ou* defense *US* ▸ **légitime**

défense DR self-defence *UK*, self-defense *US* ▸ **je dirai pour ma défense que...** I will say in my (own) defence *UK ou* defense *US* that...

défenseur [defɑ̃sœr] **nm 1.** DR counsel for the defence *UK*, defense attorney *US* **2.** [partisan] champion **3.** [hockey] **: défenseur droit** right defence *UK ou* defense *US* ▸ **défenseur gauche** left defence *UK ou* defense *US*.

défensif, ***ive*** [defɑ̃sif, iv] **adj** defensive.
◆ ***défensive*** **nf : être sur la défensive** to be on the defensive.

déféquer [18] [defeke] **vi** to defecate.

déférence [deferɑ̃s] **nf** deference.

déférer [18] [defere] ■ **vt** DR to refer.
■ **vi** *sout* [céder] **: déférer à** to defer to.

déferlement [defɛrləmɑ̃] **nm** [de vagues] breaking / *fig* surge, upsurge.

déferler [3] [defɛrle] **vi** [vagues] to break / *fig* to surge.

défi [defi] **nm** challenge ▸ **mettre qqn au défi de faire qqch** to challenge sb to do sthg ▸ **relever le défi** to take up the challenge.

défiance [defjɑ̃s] **nf** distrust, mistrust.

défiant, ***e*** [defjɑ̃, ɑ̃t] **adj** distrustful, mistrustful.

déficeler [24] [defisle] **vt** to untie.

déficience [defisjɑ̃s] **nf** deficiency.

déficient, ***e*** [defisjɑ̃, ɑ̃t] **adj** deficient.

déficit [defisit] **nm 1.** FIN deficit ▸ **être en déficit** to be in deficit ▸ **déficit budgétaire** budget deficit ▸ **déficit commercial** trade deficit *ou* gap ▸ **société en déficit** company in deficit **2.** [manque & MÉD] deficiency.

déficitaire [defisitɛr] **adj 1.** in deficit ▸ **être déficitaire** to be in deficit **2.** [production, récolte] poor.

défier [9] [defje] **vt 1.** [braver] **: défier qqn de faire qqch** to defy sb to do sthg **2.** *vieilli* [provoquer] **: défier qqn (à)** to challenge sb (to).
◆ ***se défier*** **vp** *littéraire* **: se défier de qqn/qqch** to mistrust sb/sthg.

défigurer [3] [defigyre] **vt 1.** [blesser] to disfigure **2.** [enlaidir] to deface.

défilé [defile] **nm 1.** [parade] parade ▸ **défilé de mode** fashion parade **2.** [couloir] defile, narrow pass.

défiler [3] [defile] **vi 1.** [dans une parade] to march past **2.** [se succéder] to pass.
◆ ***se défiler*** **vp** *fam* to back out.

défini, ***e*** [defini] **adj 1.** [précis] clear, precise **2.** GRAMM definite.

définir [32] [definir] **vt** to define.

définitif, ***ive*** [definitif, iv] **adj** definitive, final.
◆ ***en définitive*** **loc adv** in the end.

définition [definisjɔ̃] **nf** definition ▸ **par définition** by definition ▸ **à haute définition** high-definition.

définitivement [definitivmɑ̃] **adv** for good, permanently.

défiscaliser [3] [defiskalize] **vt** to exempt from taxation.

déflagration [deflagrasjɔ̃] **nf** explosion.

déflation [deflasjɔ̃] **nf** deflation ▸ **cette mesure est destinée à faire de la déflation** this measure is intended to deflate the economy.

déflationniste [deflasjɔnist] **adj** deflationary, deflationist ▸ **pratiquer une politique déflationniste** to deflate the economy.

déflecteur [deflɛktœr] **nm** quarterlight *UK*, vent *US*.

déflorer [3] [deflɔre] **vt** [jeune fille] to deflower / *fig* to taint.

défonce [defɔ̃s] **nf** *fam* high.

défoncé, ***e*** [defɔ̃se] **adj 1.** [abîmé - route] with large potholes / [- chaise] broken, broken-down **2.** *fam* [drogué] high, stoned.

défoncer [16] [defɔ̃se] **vt** [caisse, porte] to smash in / [route] to break up / [mur] to smash down / [chaise] to break.
◆ ***se défoncer*** **vp** *fam* **1.** to trip, to get high **2.** [se surpasser] to go all out, to work flat out.

déformant, ***e*** [defɔrmɑ̃, ɑ̃t] **adj** distorting.

déformation [defɔrmasjɔ̃] **nf 1.** [d'objet, de théorie] distortion **2.** MÉD deformity ▸ **déformation professionnelle** *mental conditioning caused by one's job.*

déformer [3] [defɔrme] **vt** to distort.
◆ ***se déformer*** **vp** [changer de forme] to be distorted, to be deformed / [se courber] to bend.

défoulement [defulmɑ̃] **nm** unwinding, letting off of steam.

défouler [3] [defule] *fam* **vt** to unwind.
◆ ***se défouler*** **vp** to let off steam, to unwind.

défrayer [11] [defreje] **vt** [payer] **: défrayer qqn** to pay sb's expenses *ou* costs.

défricher [3] [defriʃe] **vt** [terrain] to clear / *fig* [question] to do the groundwork for.

défriser [3] [defrize] **vt 1.** [cheveux] to straighten **2.** *fam fig* [déplaire] to bother.

défroisser [3] [defrwase] **vt** to smooth out.

défunt, ***e*** [defœ̃, œ̃t] ■ **adj** [décédé] late.
■ **nm, f** deceased.

dégagé, ***e*** [degaʒe] **adj 1.** [ciel, vue] clear / [partie du corps] bare **2.** [désinvolte] casual, airy **3.** [libre] **: dégagé de** free from.

dégagement [degaʒmɑ̃] **nm 1.** [passage] passage **2.** [émanation] emission **3.** [évacuation] freeing, extricating.

dégager [17] [degaʒe] ■ **vt 1.** [odeur] to produce, to give off **2.** [délivrer - blessé] to free, to extricate **3.** [idée] to bring out **4.** [bénéfice] to show **5.** [budget] to release **6.** [pièce] to clear ▸ **dégager les branches de la route** to clear the branches off the road, to clear the road of branches

7. [libérer] : **dégager qqn de** to release sb from ▸ **dégager qqn de ses dettes** to cancel sb's debt ▸ **dégager qqn de sa promesse** to release *ou* to free sb from their promise.
■ vi *fam* [partir] to clear off ▸ **dégage!** clear off!, get lost!
◆ ***se dégager*** vp **1.** [se délivrer] : **se dégager de qqch** to free o.s. from sthg / *fig* to get out of sthg ▸ **se dégager d'une étreinte** to extricate o.s. from an embrace ▸ **se dégager d'une obligation** to free o.s. from an obligation **2.** [se désencombrer] to clear **3.** [émaner] to be given off **4.** [émerger] to emerge ▸ **il se dégage du rapport que les torts sont partagés** it appears from the report that both sides are to blame.

dégaine [degɛn] nf *fam* gawkiness *(U)*.

dégainer [4] [degene] vt [épée, revolver] to draw.

dégarnir [32] [degarnir] vt to strip, to clear.
◆ ***se dégarnir*** vp [vitrine] to be cleared / [arbre] to lose its leaves ▸ **sa tête se dégarnit, il se dégarnit** he's going bald.

dégât [dega] nm *litt* & *fig* damage *(U)* ▸ **dégâts matériels** structural damage ▸ **faire des dégâts** to cause damage ▸ **limiter les dégâts** *fig* to call a halt before things get any worse.

dégel [deʒɛl] nm **1.** [fonte des glaces] thaw **2.** FIN unfreezing.

dégeler [25] [deʒle] ■ vt **1.** [produit surgelé] to thaw **2.** FIN to unfreeze **3.** *fig* [dérider] to warm up.
■ vi to thaw.
◆ ***se dégeler*** vp *fig* to thaw, to warm up.

dégénéré, e [deʒenere] adj & nm, f degenerate.

dégénérer [18] [deʒenere] vi to degenerate ▸ **dégénérer en** to degenerate into.

dégénérescence [deʒeneresɑ̃s] nf degeneration, degeneracy.

dégingandé, e [deʒɛ̃gɑ̃de] adj *fam* gangling.

dégivrer [3] [deʒivre] vt [pare-brise] to de-ice / [réfrigérateur] to defrost.

dégivreur [deʒivrœr] nm [de voiture, avion] de-icer / [de réfrigérateur] defroster.

déglinguer [3] [deglɛ̃ge] vt *fam* to smash (to pieces).
◆ ***se déglinguer*** vp *fam* to fall to pieces.

déglutition [deglytisjɔ̃] nf swallowing.

dégonflé, e [degɔ̃fle] ■ adj [pneu, roue] flat.
■ nm, f *fam* [personne] chicken, yellow-belly.

dégonfler [3] [degɔ̃fle] ■ vt to deflate, to let down *UK*.
■ vi to go down ▸ **faire dégonfler** to reduce the swelling of.
◆ ***se dégonfler*** vp **1.** [objet] to go down **2.** *fam* [personne] to chicken out.

dégorger [17] [degɔrʒe] ■ vt **1.** [tuyau] to clear (out) **2.** [eau] to discharge **3.** [soie, laine] to purify.
■ vi **1.** [tissu] to run **2.** CULIN : **faire dégorger** to soak.

dégot(t)er [3] [degɔte] vt *fam* to dig up.
◆ ***se dégot(t)er*** vp *fam* to dig up for o.s.

dégouliner [3] [deguline] vi to trickle.

dégourdi, e [degurdi] ■ adj clever.
■ nm, f clever person.

dégourdir [32] [degurdir] vt **1.** [membres - ankylosés] to restore the circulation to / [- gelés] to warm up **2.** *fig* [déniaiser] : **dégourdir qqn** to teach sb a thing or two.
◆ ***se dégourdir*** vp **1.** [membres] : **se dégourdir les jambes** to stretch one's legs **2.** *fig* [acquérir de l'aisance] to learn a thing or two.

dégoût [degu] nm disgust, distaste ▸ **le dégoût de la vie** world-weariness ▸ **ravaler son dégoût** to swallow one's distaste.

dégoûtant, e [degutɑ̃, ɑ̃t] ■ adj **1.** [sale] filthy, disgusting **2.** [révoltant, grossier] disgusting.
■ nm, f disgusting person.

dégoûté, e [degute] ■ adj [écœuré] disgusted ▸ **elle m'a regardé d'un air dégoûté** she gave me a look of disgust ▸ **dégoûté de** sick of.
■ nm, f : **faire le dégoûté** to be fussy.

dégoûter [3] [degute] vt to disgust ▸ **dégoûter qqn de qqch/de faire qqch** to put sb off sthg/off doing sthg ▸ **c'est à vous dégoûter d'être serviable** it's enough to put you (right) off being helpful.

dégoutter [3] [degute] vi : **dégoutter (de qqch)** to drip (with sthg).

dégradant, e [degradɑ̃, ɑ̃t] adj degrading.

dégradation [degradasjɔ̃] nf **1.** [de bâtiment] damage / [du sol] erosion **2.** [de moral] decline **3.** [de personne] degradation **4.** [de situation] deterioration.

dégradé, e [degrade] nm [technique] shading off / [résultat] gradation ▸ **un dégradé de bleu** a blue shading.
◆ ***en dégradé*** loc adv [cheveux] layered ▸ **tons en dégradé** colours *US ou* colors *US*shading off (into one another).

COMMENT EXPRIMER...

qu'on n'aime pas quelque chose

I don't like flying / Je n'aime pas prendre l'avion
I hate driving at night / Je déteste conduire la nuit
I can't stand lies / Je ne supporte pas le mensonge
I'm not really into sport / Je ne suis pas très branché sport
I'm not crazy about the idea / L'idée ne m'emballe pas vraiment
I don't like being told what to do / Je n'aime pas qu'on me dise ce que je dois faire

dégrader [3] [degrade] **vt 1.** [officier] to degrade **2.** [abîmer - bâtiment] to damage / [- sol] to erode **3.** *fig* [avilir] to degrade, to debase.
◆ ***se dégrader*** **vp 1.** [bâtiment, santé] to deteriorate **2.** *fig* [personne] to degrade o.s.

dégrafer [3] [degrafe] **vt** to undo, to unfasten.
◆ ***se dégrafer*** **vp** to come undone.

dégraissage [degrɛsaʒ] **nm 1.** [de vêtement] dry-cleaning **2.** [de personnel] trimming, cutting back.

dégraisser [4] [degrese] **vt 1.** [vêtement] to dry-clean **2.** [personnel] to trim, to cut back.

degré [dəgre] **nm 1.** [gén] degree ▸ **à un degré avancé de** at an advanced stage of ▸ **compréhensif jusqu'à un certain degré** understanding to a degree *ou* up to a point ▸ **degrés centigrades** *ou* **Celsius** degrees centigrade *ou* Celsius ▸ **degré de parenté** degree of kinship ▸ **cousin au premier degré** first cousin ▸ **équation du premier/second degré** equation of the first/second degree ▸ **prendre qqn/qqch au premier degré** to take sb/sthg at face value **2.** *sout* [marche] step.

dégressif, ***ive*** [degresif, iv] **adj : tarif dégressif** decreasing price scale.

dégrèvement [degrɛvmɑ̃] **nm** tax relief.

dégriffé, ***e*** [degrife] **adj** ex-designer label *(avant n)*.
◆ ***dégriffé*** **nm** ex-designer label garment.

dégringolade [degrɛ̃gɔlad] **nf** *litt* & *fig* tumble.

dégringoler [3] [degrɛ̃gɔle] ■ **vt** to tumble down.
■ **vi** [tomber] to tumble / *fig* to crash.

dégriser [3] [degrize] **vt** *sout* [désenivrer] to sober up ▸ **dégriser qqn** *fig* to bring sb to his/her senses.

dégrossir [32] [degrosir] **vt 1.** [matériau] to rough-hew **2.** *fig* [affaire, question] to rough out **3.** *fig* [personne] to polish.
◆ ***se dégrossir*** **vp** [personne] to become more polished.

déguenillé, ***e*** [degənije] **adj** ragged.

déguerpir [32] [degɛrpir] **vi** to clear off.

dégueulasse [degœlas] *tfam* ■ **adj 1.** [très sale, grossier] filthy ▸ **blague dégueulasse** dirty joke **2.** [très mauvais - plat] disgusting / [- temps] lousy.
■ **nmf** scum *(U)*.

dégueuler [5] [degœle] **vi** *fam* to throw up.

déguisé, ***e*** [degize] **adj** disguised / [pour s'amuser] in fancy dress.

déguisement [degizmɑ̃] **nm** disguise / [pour bal masqué] fancy dress.

déguiser [3] [degize] **vt** to disguise.
◆ ***se déguiser*** **vp : se déguiser en** [pour tromper] to disguise o.s. as / [pour s'amuser] to dress up as.

dégustation [degystasjɔ̃] **nf** tasting, sampling ▸ **dégustation de vin** wine tasting.

déguster [3] [degyste] ■ **vt** [savourer] to taste, to sample.
■ **vi** *fam* [subir] **: il va déguster!** he'll be in for it!

déhancher [3] [deɑ̃ʃe] ◆ ***se déhancher*** **vp** [en marchant] to swing one's hips / [en restant immobile] to put all one's weight on one leg.

dehors [dəɔr] ■ **adv** outside ▸ **aller dehors** to go outside ▸ **dormir dehors** to sleep out of doors, to sleep out ▸ **jeter** *ou* **mettre qqn dehors** to throw sb out.
■ **nm** outside.
■ **nmpl : les dehors** [les apparences] appearances.
◆ ***en dehors*** **loc adv 1.** [à l'extérieur] outside **2.** [vers l'extérieur] outwards *UK*, outward *US*.
◆ ***en dehors de*** **loc prép** [excepté] apart from.

déjà [deʒa] **adv 1.** [dès cet instant] already **2.** [précédemment] already, before **3.** [au fait] **: quel est ton nom déjà?** what did you say your name was? **4.** [renforce une affirmation] **: ce n'est déjà pas si mal** that's not bad at all.

déjanter [3] [deʒɑ̃te] **vt : déjanter un pneu** to take a tyre *UK ou* tire *US* off the rim.

déjà-vu [deʒavy] **nm inv : c'est du déjà-vu** it's old hat.

déjection [deʒɛksjɔ̃] **nf** [action] evacuation.
◆ ***déjections*** **nfpl** excrement *(U)*.

déjeuner [5] [deʒœne] ■ **vi 1.** [le matin] to have breakfast **2.** [à midi] to have lunch.
■ **nm 1.** [repas de midi] lunch ▸ **déjeuner d'affaires** business lunch **2.** *Québec* [dîner] dinner.

déjouer [6] [deʒwe] **vt** to frustrate ▸ **déjouer la surveillance de qqn** to elude sb's surveillance.

delà [dəla] ➤ ***au-delà***.

délabré, ***e*** [delabre] **adj** ruined.

délabrement [delabrəmɑ̃] **nm 1.** [de bâtiment] dilapidation, ruining **2.** [de personne] ruin.

délacer [16] [delase] **vt** to unlace, to undo.

délai [delɛ] **nm 1.** [temps accordé] period ▸ **dans un délai de** within (a period of) ▸ **dans les délais impartis** by the deadline ▸ **sans délai** immediately ▸ **délai de livraison** delivery time, lead time ▸ **délai de paiement** repayment period **2.** [sursis] extension (of deadline) **3.** DR **: délai de carence** *period during which benefit is not paid*.

FAUX AMIS / FALSE FRIENDS

délai

Delay is not a translation of the French word *délai*. Delay is translated by *retard*.
▸ There's a three-hour delay on all international flights / *Il y a trois heures de retard sur tous les vols internationaux*

délaissé, ***e*** [delese] **adj** abandoned.

délaisser [4] [delese] **vt 1.** [abandonner] to leave **2.** [négliger] to neglect.

délassement [delasmɑ̃] **nm** relaxation.

délasser [3] [delase] **vt** to refresh.
◆ ***se délasser*** **vp** to relax.

délateur, ***trice*** [delatœr, tris] **nm, f** informer.

délation [delasjɔ̃] **nf** informing.

délavé, e [delave] **adj** faded.

délayage [delɛjaʒ] **nm** verbiage, waffle *UK*.

délayer [11] [deleje] **vt 1.** [diluer] **: délayer qqch dans qqch** to mix sthg with sthg **2.** *fig* [exposer longuement] to pad out.

Delco® [dɛlko] **nm** AUTO distributor.

délectable [delɛktabl] **adj** *sout* delectable.

délectation [delɛktasjɔ̃] **nf** [plaisir] delight ▸ **avec délectation** in delight.

délecter [4] [delɛkte] ◆ ***se délecter*** **vp : se délecter de qqch/à faire qqch** to delight in sthg/in doing sthg.

délégation [delegasjɔ̃] **nf** delegation ▸ **agir par délégation** to be delegated to act.

délégué, e [delege] ■ **adj** [personne] delegated.
■ **nm, f** [représentant] **: délégué (à)** delegate (to) ▸ **délégué de classe/du personnel/syndical** class/staff/trade union representative.

déléguer [18] [delege] **vt : déléguer qqn (à qqch)** to delegate sb (to sthg).

délestage [delɛstaʒ] **nm 1.** [de ballon, de navire] removal of ballast **2.** [de circulation] (temporary) diversion, detour.

délester [3] [delɛste] **vt 1.** [ballon, navire] to remove ballast from **2.** [circulation routière] to set up a diversion on, to divert, to detour *US* **3.** *fig & hum* [voler] **: délester qqn de qqch** to relieve sb of sthg.

délibératif, ive [deliberatif, iv] **adj : avoir voix délibérative** to have voting rights.

délibération [deliberasjɔ̃] **nf** deliberation ▸ **le projet sera mis en délibération** the project will be debated ▸ **après délibération du jury** after due deliberation by the jury.
◆ ***délibérations*** **nfpl** [décisions] resolutions, decisions.

délibéré, e [delibere] **adj 1.** [intentionnel] deliberate **2.** [résolu] determined.
◆ ***délibéré*** **nm** DR judge's deliberations *pl*.

délibérément [deliberemɑ̃] **adv 1.** [en connaissance de cause] after deliberation *ou* due consideration **2.** [intentionnellement] deliberately, on purpose.

délibérer [18] [delibere] **vi : délibérer (de *ou* sur)** to deliberate (on *ou* over).

délicat, e [delika, at] **adj 1.** [gén] delicate **2.** [aimable] thoughtful, sensitive **3.** [exigeant] fussy, difficult ▸ **faire le délicat** to be fussy.

délicatement [delikatmɑ̃] **adv** delicately.

délicatesse [delikatɛs] **nf 1.** [gén] delicacy **2.** [tact] delicacy, tact.

délice [delis] **nm** delight.
◆ ***délices*** **nfpl** [plaisirs] delights, pleasures ▸ **faire les délices de qqn** to delight sb, to give sb great pleasure ▸ **faire ses délices de qqch** to take delight in sthg, to enjoy sthg greatly.

délicieusement [delisjøzmɑ̃] **adv** [agréablement] delightfully.

délicieux, euse [delisjø, øz] **adj 1.** [savoureux] delicious **2.** [agréable] delightful.

délictueux, euse [deliktɥø, øz] **adj** criminal.

délié, e [delje] **adj** [doigts] nimble.

délier [9] [delje] **vt** to untie ▸ **délier qqn de** *fig & sout* to release sb from.
◆ ***se délier*** ■ **vpi** [langue] to loosen ▸ **après quelques verres, les langues se délient** a few drinks help to loosen people's tongues.
■ **vpt** [s'exercer] **: se délier les jambes/les doigts** to relax one's leg muscles/one's fingers.
◆ ***se délier de*** **v + prep** to release o.s. from ▸ **se délier d'une obligation** to free o.s. from an obligation.

délimitation [delimitasjɔ̃] **nf 1.** [de territoire] fixing of the boundaries **2.** [de fonction] demarcation **3.** *fig* [de sujet] definition.

délimiter [3] [delimite] **vt** [frontière] to fix / *fig* [question, domaine] to define, to demarcate.

délinquance [delɛ̃kɑ̃s] **nf** delinquency ▸ **délinquance informatique** cybercrime ▸ **délinquance juvénile** juvenile delinquency.

délinquant, e [delɛ̃kɑ̃, ɑ̃t] ■ **adj** delinquent.
■ **nm, f** delinquent ▸ **petit délinquant** petty criminal.

déliquescent, e [delikɛsɑ̃, ɑ̃t] **adj** *fam* [personne] feeble / *vieilli* [mœurs] decaying.

délirant, e [delirɑ̃, ɑ̃t] **adj 1.** MÉD delirious **2.** [extravagant] frenzied **3.** *fam* [extraordinaire] crazy.

délire [delir] **nm** MÉD delirium ▸ **en délire** *fig* frenzied.

délirer [3] [delire] **vi** MÉD to be *ou* become delirious / *fam fig* to rave.

délit [deli] **nm** crime, offence *UK*, offense *US* ▸ **en flagrant délit** red-handed, in the act ▸ **délit de fuite** failure to stop *(after an accident)* ▸ **délits d'initiés** FIN insider trading *(U)*.

délivrance [delivrɑ̃s] **nf 1.** [libération] freeing, release **2.** [soulagement] relief **3.** [accouchement] delivery.

délivrer [3] [delivre] **vt 1.** [prisonnier] to free, to release **2.** [pays] to deliver, to free ▸ **délivrer de** to free from / *fig* to relieve from **3.** [remettre] **: délivrer qqch (à qqn)** to issue sthg (to sb) **4.** [marchandise] to deliver.
◆ ***se délivrer*** **vp 1.** [se libérer] **: se délivrer (de)** to free o.s. (from) **2.** [passeport] to be issued.

déloger [17] [delɔʒe] **vt : déloger (de)** to dislodge (from).

déloyal, e, aux [delwajal, o] **adj 1.** [infidèle] disloyal **2.** [malhonnête] unfair.

Delphes [dɛlf] **npr** Delphi.

delta [dɛlta] **nm** delta.

deltaplane, delta-plane (pl **delta-planes**) [dɛltaplan] **nm** hang glider.

déluge [delyʒ] **nm 1.** RELIG **: le Déluge** the Flood ▸ **ça remonte au Déluge** *fig* it's ancient history **2.** [pluie] downpour, deluge ▸ **un déluge de** *fig* a flood of.

déluré, e [delyre] **adj** [malin] quick-witted / *péj* [dévergondé] saucy.

démagogie [demagɔʒi] **nf** demagogy, demagoguery.

démagogique [demagɔʒik] **adj** demagogic.

démagogue [demagɔg] **nmf** demagogue.

demain [dəmɛ̃] ■ **adv 1.** [le jour suivant] tomorrow ▸ **demain matin** tomorrow morning **2.** *fig* [plus tard] in the future.
■ **nm** tomorrow ▸ **à demain!** see you tomorrow!

demande [dəmɑ̃d] **nf 1.** [souhait] request ▸ **à la demande générale** by popular demand ▸ **accéder à une demande** to accede to a demand ▸ **demande d'argent** request for money
2. [démarche] proposal ▸ **demande en mariage** proposal of marriage ▸ **faire sa demande en mariage (auprès de qqn)** to propose (to sb)
3. [candidature] application ▸ **demande d'emploi** job application ▸ **'demandes d'emploi'** 'situations wanted' ▸ **faire une demande de bourse/visa** to apply for a scholarship/visa
4. [commande] order
5. ÉCON demand ▸ **la demande des consommateurs** consumer demand ▸ **demande du marché** market demand
6. DR petition ▸ **demande en renvoi** request for transfer of a case (to another court).

FAUX AMIS / FALSE FRIENDS
demande
Demand is not the usual translation of the French word *demande*. Demand is generally translated by *exigence* or *revendication*.
▸ His demands were too absurd to accept / *Ses exigences étaient trop absurdes pour être prises en compte*
▸ The union's wage demands cannot be accepted / *Les revendications salariales du syndicat ne peuvent être acceptées*

demandé**, **e [dəmɑ̃de] **adj** in demand.

demander [3] [dəmɑ̃de] ■ **vt 1.** [réclamer, s'enquérir] to ask for ▸ **demander qqch à qqn** to ask sb for sthg ▸ **je lui ai demandé la raison de son départ** I asked her why she (had) left ▸ **je te demande pardon** I'm sorry
2. [appeler] to call ▸ **on vous demande à la réception/au téléphone** you're wanted at reception/on the telephone ▸ **qui demandez-vous?** who do you want?
3. [désirer] to ask, to want ▸ **je ne demande pas mieux** I'd be only too pleased (to), I'd love to
4. [exiger] **: tu m'en demandes trop** you're asking too much of me ▸ **demander l'impossible** to ask for the impossible
5. [nécessiter] to require ▸ **ça demande réflexion** it needs thinking about, it needs some thought
6. [chercher] to look for, to require ▸ **'on demande un livreur'** 'delivery boy wanted *ou* required'.
■ **vi 1.** [réclamer] **: demander à qqn de faire qqch** to ask sb to do sthg ▸ **il m'a demandé de lui prêter ma voiture** he asked me to lend him my car ▸ **ne demander qu'à...** to be ready to... ▸ **je ne demande qu'à vous embaucher/aider** I'm more than willing to hire/help you
2. [nécessiter] **: ce projet demande à être étudié** this project requires investigation *ou* needs investigating.
◆ ***se demander*** **vp : se demander (si)** to wonder (if *ou* whether) ▸ **cela ne se demande pas!** need you ask! *iron*

demandeur [1], ***euse*** [dəmɑ̃dœr, øz] **nm, f** [solliciteur] **: demandeur d'asile** asylum-seeker ▸ **demandeur d'emploi** job-seeker.

demandeur [2], ***eresse*** [dəmɑ̃dœr, drɛs] **nm, f** DR plaintiff.

démangeaison [demɑ̃ʒɛzɔ̃] **nf** [irritation] itch, itching *(U)* / *fam fig* urge.

démanger [17] [demɑ̃ʒe] **vi** [gratter] to itch ▸ **ça me démange de...** *fig* I'm itching *ou* dying to...

démanteler [25] [demɑ̃tle] **vt** [construction] to demolish / *fig* to break up.

démaquillant**, **e [demakijɑ̃, ɑ̃t] **adj** make-up-removing *(avant n)*.
◆ ***démaquillant*** **nm** make-up remover.

démaquiller [3] [demakije] **vt** to remove make-up from.
◆ ***se démaquiller*** **vp** to remove one's make-up.

démarcation [demarkasjɔ̃] **nf** [frontière] demarcation / *fig* separation.

démarchage [demarʃaʒ] **nm : démarchage à domicile** door-to-door selling ▸ **démarchage électoral** canvassing.

démarche [demarʃ] **nf 1.** [manière de marcher] gait, walk **2.** [raisonnement] approach, method **3.** [requête] step ▸ **faire les démarches pour faire qqch** to take the necessary steps to do sthg.

démarcheur**, **euse [demarʃœr, øz] **nm, f 1.** [représentant] door-to-door salesman (f saleswoman) **2.** [prospecteur] canvasser.

démarque [demark] **nf** [solde] markdown.

démarquer [3] [demarke] **vt 1.** [solder] to mark down **2.** SPORT not to mark.
◆ ***se démarquer*** **vp 1.** SPORT to shake off one's marker **2.** *fig* [se distinguer] **: se démarquer (de)** to distinguish o.s. (from).

démarrage [demaraʒ] **nm** starting, start ▸ **démarrage en côte** hill start.

démarrer [3] [demare] ■ **vi 1.** [véhicule] to start (up) / [conducteur] to drive off **2.** SPORT to break away **3.** *fig* [affaire, projet] to get off the ground.
■ **vt 1.** [véhicule] to start (up) ▸ **faire démarrer** to start **2.** *fam fig* [commencer] **: démarrer qqch** to get sthg going.

démarreur [demarœr] **nm** starter.

démasquer [3] [demaske] **vt 1.** [personne] to unmask **2.** *fig* [complot, plan] to unveil.
◆ ***se démasquer*** **vp** to show one's true colours *UK ou* colors *US*.

démêlant**, **e [demɛlɑ̃, ɑ̃t] **adj** conditioning *(avant n)*.
◆ ***démêlant*** **nm** conditioner.

démêlé [demɛle] **nm** quarrel ▸ **avoir des démêlés avec la justice** to get into trouble with the law.

démêler [4] [demɛle] **vt** [cheveux, fil] to untangle / *fig* to unravel.
◆ ***se démêler*** **vp : se démêler les cheveux** to comb out one's hair ▸ **se démêler de** *fig* to extricate o.s. from.

démembrer [3] [demɑ̃bre] **vt** [animal] to dismember / *fig* [réseau] to break up.

déménagement [demenaʒmɑ̃] **nm** removal.

déménager [17] [demenaʒe] ■ **vt** to move.
■ **vi** to move, to move house.

déménageur [demenaʒœr] **nm** removal man *UK*, mover *US*.

démence [demɑ̃s] **nf** MÉD dementia / [bêtise] madness.

démener [19] [demne] ◆ ***se démener*** **vp** *litt* & *fig* to struggle.

dément, ***e*** [demɑ̃, ɑ̃t] ■ **adj** MÉD demented / *fam* [extraordinaire, extravagant] crazy.
■ **nm, f** demented person.

démenti [demɑ̃ti] **nm** denial ▸ **apporter un démenti à qqch** to deny sthg (formally).

démentiel, ***elle*** [demɑ̃sjɛl] **adj** MÉD demented / *fam* [incroyable] crazy.

démentir [37] [demɑ̃tir] **vt** **1.** [réfuter] to deny **2.** [contredire] to contradict.
◆ ***se démentir*** **vp : ne pas se démentir** *sout* to remain unchanged.

démerder [3] [demɛrde] ◆ ***se démerder*** **vp** *tfam* [se débrouiller] to (know how to) look after o.s.

démériter [3] [demerite] **vi** **1.** [être indigne] **: démériter de** to show o.s. (to be) unworthy of **2.** [être dévalorisé] **: en quoi a-t-il démérité?** what has he done wrong? ▸ **démériter auprès de qqn** to come down in sb's estimation.

démesure [deməzyr] **nf** excess, immoderation.

démesurément [deməzyremɑ̃] **adv** excessively.

démets ➤ ***démettre***.

démettre [84] [demɛtr] **vt** **1.** MÉD to put out (of joint) **2.** [congédier] **: démettre qqn de** to dismiss sb from.
◆ ***se démettre*** **vp** **1.** MÉD **: se démettre l'épaule** to put one's shoulder out (of joint) **2.** [démissionner] **: se démettre de ses fonctions** to resign.

demeurant [dəmœrɑ̃] ◆ ***au demeurant*** **loc adv** all things considered.

demeure [dəmœr] **nf** **1.** *sout* [domicile, habitation] residence **2.** DR **: mettre qqn en demeure (de faire qqch)** to order sb (to do sthg).
◆ ***à demeure*** ■ **loc adj** permanent.
■ **loc adv** permanently.

demeuré, ***e*** [dəmœre] ■ **adj** simple, half-witted.
■ **nm, f** half-wit.

demeurer [5] [dəmœre] **vi** **1.** *(v aux : être)* [habiter] to live **2.** *(v aux : être)* [rester] to remain.

demi, ***e*** [dəmi] **adj** half ▸ **cela n'a été qu'un demi-succès** it wasn't a complete ***ou*** it was only a partial success ▸ **une demi-pomme** half an apple ▸ **un kilo et demi** one and a half kilos ▸ **il est une heure et demie** it's half past one ▸ **à demi** half ▸ **dormir à demi** to be half-asleep ▸ **ouvrir à demi** to half-open ▸ **faire les choses à demi** to do things by halves.
◆ ***demi*** **nm** **1.** [bière] beer, ≃ half-pint *UK* **2.** FOOTBALL midfielder **3.** [rugby] **: demi de mêlée** scrumhalf ▸ **demi d'ouverture** fly half, standoff (half).
◆ ***demie*** **nf : à la demie** on the half-hour ▸ **je te rappelle à la demie** I'll call you back at half past.

demi-bouteille [dəmibutɛj] (pl **demi-bouteilles**) **nf** half-bottle.

demi-cercle [dəmisɛrkl] (pl **demi-cercles**) **nm** semicircle ▸ **en demi-cercle** semicircular.

COMMENT EXPRIMER...

les demandes

Demander quelque chose

Could you give me a hand? / Tu peux me donner un coup de main ?
Could you help me please? I'm looking for Mr Rover / Pardon, j'ai besoin d'un service. Je cherche M. Rover
Could you possibly come back later? / Vous serait-il possible de revenir plus tard ?
Can you tell him I'll call back? / Peux-tu lui dire que je le rappellerai ?
Could I have some more paper, please? / Vous pourriez me donner encore du papier, s'il vous plaît ?
Do you mind if I phone home? / Est-ce que je peux téléphoner chez moi ?
Please let me know if you're coming / Préviens-moi si tu viens
I would be grateful if you would send me some samples / Je vous remercie de bien vouloir m'envoyer des échantillons
I would appreciate it if you could give me a hand with these figures / Je vous serais reconnaissant de m'aider à faire ces calculs
Would you please send me your latest catalogue? / Veuillez me faire parvenir votre dernier catalogue

Accepter de rendre service

With pleasure / Avec plaisir
Yes, of course / Oui, bien sûr
Yes, I'll tell him / Oui, je le lui dirai
Not at all / Pas du tout
No trouble at all / Aucun problème
I'd be delighted to help / Je serais ravi de rendre service

Refuser

No, I'm sorry, I can't / Non, je suis désolé. Je ne peux pas
Not just now / Pas maintenant
I'm afraid it's just not possible / Je regrette, mais c'est tout à fait impossible
Sorry, you're asking the wrong person / Désolé, ce n'est pas moi qui peux vous répondre

demi-douzaine [dəmiduzɛn] (pl **demi-douzaines**) **nf** half-dozen ▸ **une demi-douzaine (de)** half a dozen.

demi-fin, e [dəmifɛ̃, in] (mpl **demi-fins**, fpl **demi-fines**) **adj** [haricots] medium.

demi-finale [dəmifinal] (pl **demi-finales**) **nf** semifinal.

demi-frère [dəmifrɛr] (pl **demi-frères**) **nm** half-brother.

demi-gros [dəmigro] **nm : (commerce de) demi-gros** cash and carry.

demi-heure [dəmijœr] (pl **demi-heures**) **nf** half an hour, half-hour.

demi-jour [dəmiʒur] **nm** half-light.

demi-journée [dəmiʒurne] (pl **demi-journées**) **nf** half a day, half-day.

démilitariser [3] [demilitarize] **vt** to demilitarize.

demi-litre [dəmilitr] (pl **demi-litres**) **nm** half a litre *UK* *ou* liter *US*, half-litre *UK*, half-liter *US*.

demi-mal [dəmimal] (pl **demi-maux**) **nm : ce n'est que demi-mal** things *ou* it could have been worse.

demi-mesure [dəmiməzyr] (pl **demi-mesures**) **nf** **1.** [quantité] half a measure **2.** [compromis] half-measure.

demi-mot [dəmimo] ◆ ***à demi-mot*** **loc adv : comprendre à demi-mot** to understand without things having to be spelled out.

déminage [deminaʒ] **nm** [de sol] mine clearance / [d'eau] minesweeping.

déminer [3] [demine] **vt** to clear of mines.

demi-pension [dəmipɑ̃sjɔ̃] (pl **demi-pensions**) **nf** **1.** [d'hôtel] half-board *UK*, modified American plan *US* **2.** [d'école] **: être en demi-pension** to take school lunches *ou* dinners *UK*.

demi-pensionnaire [dəmipɑ̃sjɔnɛr] (pl **demi-pensionnaires**) **nmf** *child who has school lunches*.

demi-place [dəmiplas] (pl **demi-places**) **nf** **1.** [pour spectacle] half-price ticket **2.** [dans transports publics] half-fare.

démis, e [demi, iz] **pp** ➤ ***démettre***.

demi-saison [dəmisɛzɔ̃] **nf : une veste de demi-saison** a spring/autumn jacket.

demi-sel [dəmisɛl] **adj inv** slightly salted.

demi-sœur [dəmisœr] (pl **demi-sœurs**) **nf** half-sister.

demi-soupir [dəmisupir] (pl **demi-soupirs**) **nm** quaver rest *UK*, eighth note rest *US*.

démission [demisjɔ̃] **nf** resignation ▸ **remettre sa démission** to hand in one's notice.

démissionnaire [demisjɔnɛr] ■ **nmf** person resigning.
■ **adj** resigning *(avant n)* / [ministre] outgoing *(avant n)*.

démissionner [3] [demisjɔne] ■ **vi** [d'un emploi] to resign / *fig* to give up.
■ **vt** *hum* **: démissionner qqn** to talk sb into resigning.

demi-tarif [dəmitarif] (pl **demi-tarifs**) ■ **adj** half-price.
■ **nm 1.** [tarification] half-fare **2.** [billet] half-price ticket.

demi-teinte [dəmitɛ̃t] (pl **demi-teintes**) **nf** halftone ▸ **en demi-teinte, en demi-teintes** *fig* subtle.

demi-ton [dəmitɔ̃] (pl **demi-tons**) **nm** semitone *UK*, halftone *US*.

demi-tour [dəmitur] (pl **demi-tours**) **nm** [gén] half-turn / MIL about-turn ▸ **faire demi-tour** to turn back.

démo [demo] **nf** *fam* demo ▸ **faire une démo à qqn** to give s.o. a demo.

démobiliser [3] [demɔbilize] **vt** MIL to demobilize ▸ **être démobilisé** *fig* to be demotivated.

démocrate [demɔkrat] ■ **nmf** democrat.
■ **adj** democratic.

démocrate-chrétien, enne [demɔkratkretjɛ̃, ɛn] (mpl **démocrates-chrétiens**, fpl **démocrates-chrétiennes**) ■ **adj** Christian-Democratic.
■ **nm, f** Christian Democrat.

démocratie [demɔkrasi] **nf** democracy ▸ **les démocraties occidentales** the Western democracies.

démocratique [demɔkratik] **adj** democratic.

démocratisation [demɔkratizasjɔ̃] **nf** democratization.

démocratiser [3] [demɔkratize] **vt** to democratize ▸ **démocratiser les voyages à l'étranger** to put foreign travel within everyone's reach.
◆ ***se démocratiser*** **vpi 1.** POLIT to become more democratic **2.** [devenir accessible] to become available to anyone.

démodé, e [demɔde] **adj** old-fashioned.

démographie [demɔgrafi] **nf** demography.

démographique [demɔgrafik] **adj** demographic.

demoiselle [dəmwazɛl] **nf 1.** [jeune fille] maid ▸ **demoiselle d'honneur** bridesmaid **2.** [libellule] dragonfly.

démolir [32] [demɔlir] **vt 1.** [gén] to demolish ▸ **l'alcool lui a démoli la santé** alcohol ruined *ou* wrecked his health **2.** *fam* [frapper] **: démolir qqn** to smash sb's face in ▸ **se faire démolir** to get one's face smashed in.
◆ ***se démolir*** **vpt : se démolir la santé** to ruin one's health ▸ **se démolir la santé à faire qqch** *fam* to kill o.s. *ou* to bust a gut doing sthg.

démolisseur [demɔlisœr] **nm** demolition worker.

démolition [demɔlisjɔ̃] **nf** demolition ▸ **en démolition** in the course of being demolished.

démon [demɔ̃] **nm 1.** [diable, personne] devil, demon ▸ **le démon** RELIG the Devil **2.** *fig* **: le démon de l'alcool/de la curiosité** the demon drink/curiosity ▸ **le démon de midi** middle-aged lust.

démoniaque [demɔnjak] **adj 1.** [diabolique] diabolical **2.** [possédé du démon] possessed.

démonstrateur, trice [demɔ̃stratœr, tris] **nm, f** demonstrator.

démonstratif, ive [demɔ̃stratif, iv] **adj 1.** [argument] convincing **2.** [personne & GRAMM] demonstrative.
◆ ***démonstratif*** **nm** GRAMM demonstrative.

démonstration [demɔ̃strasjɔ̃] **nf 1.** [gén] demonstration **2.** MIL show, demonstration.

démontable [demɔ̃tabl] **adj** able to be dismantled *ou* taken to pieces.

démontage [demɔ̃taʒ] **nm** dismantling, taking to pieces / [de moteur] stripping down.

démonté, e [demɔ̃te] **adj** [océan] raging.

démonte-pneu [demɔ̃tpnø] (pl **démonte-pneus**) **nm** tyre lever *UK*, tire iron *US*.

démonter [3] [demɔ̃te] **vt 1.** [appareil] to dismantle, to take apart **2.** [troubler] **: démonter qqn** to put sb out.
◆ ***se démonter*** **vp** *fam* to be put out.

démontrer [3] [demɔ̃tre] **vt 1.** [prouver] to prove, to demonstrate **2.** [témoigner de] to show, to demonstrate.

démoralisant, e [demɔralizɑ̃, ɑ̃t] **adj** demoralizing.

démoraliser [3] [demɔralize] **vt** to demoralize.
◆ ***se démoraliser*** **vp** to lose heart.

démordre [76] [demɔrdr] **vt : ne pas démordre de** to stick to.

démordu [demɔrdy] **pp inv** ➤ ***démordre***.

démotiver [3] [demɔtive] **vt** to demotivate.

démouler [3] [demule] **vt** to turn out of *ou* remove from a mould *UK ou* mold *US*.

démultiplication [demyltiplikasjɔ̃] **nf** TECHNOL reduction in gear ratio.

démunir [32] [demynir] **vt** to deprive.
◆ ***se démunir*** **vp : se démunir de** to part with.

démystifier [9] [demistifje] **vt 1.** [concept] to demystify **2.** [personne] to disabuse.

dénatalité [denatalite] **nf** fall in the birthrate.

dénationaliser [3] [denasjɔnalize] **vt** to denationalize.

dénaturé, e [denatyre] **adj 1.** [parents] unfit **2.** [goût] unnatural **3.** TECHNOL denatured.

dénaturer [3] [denatyre] **vt 1.** [goût] to impair, to mar **2.** TECHNOL to denature **3.** [déformer] to distort.

dénégation [denegasjɔ̃] **nf** denial.

déneigement [denɛʒmɑ̃] **nm** snow clearance.

déneiger [23] [deneʒe] **vt** to clear snow from.

déneigeuse [deneʒøz] **nf** *Québec* snowblower.

déni [deni] **nm** denial ▸ **déni de justice** DR denial of justice.

déniaiser [4] [denjeze] **vt** *hum* & *vieilli* **: déniaiser qqn** to teach sb a thing or two.

dénicher [3] [deniʃe] **vt** *fig* **1.** [personne] to flush out **2.** *fam* [objet] to unearth.

denier [dənje] **nm** denier *(coin)*.
◆ ***deniers*** **nmpl : les deniers publics** the public purse *sg* ▸ **les deniers de l'État** the State coffers.

dénigrer [3] [denigre] **vt** to denigrate, to run down.

dénivelé [denivle] **nm** difference in level *ou* height.

dénivellation [denivɛlasjɔ̃] **nf 1.** [différence de niveau] difference in level *ou* height **2.** [de route] bumps *pl*, unevenness *(U)* **3.** [pente] slope.

dénombrer [3] [denɔ̃bre] **vt** [compter] to count / [énumérer] to enumerate.

dénominateur [denɔminatœr] **nm** denominator ▸ **dénominateur commun** *fig* & MATH common denominator.

dénomination [denɔminasjɔ̃] **nf** name.

dénommé, e [denɔme] **adj : un dénommé Robert** someone by the name of Robert.

dénoncer [16] [denɔ̃se] **vt 1.** [gén] to denounce ▸ **dénoncer qqn à qqn** to denounce sb to sb, to inform on sb ▸ **dénoncer qqn aux autorités** to denounce sb *ou* to give sb away to the authorities **2.** *fig* [trahir] to betray.
◆ ***se dénoncer*** **vp** *(emploi réfléchi)* to give o.s. up.

dénonciation [denɔ̃sjasjɔ̃] **nf** denunciation.

dénoter [3] [denɔte] **vt** to show, to indicate.

dénouement [denumɑ̃] **nm 1.** [issue] outcome **2.** [d'un film, d'un livre] denouement.

dénouer [6] [denwe] **vt** [nœud] to untie, to undo / *fig* to unravel.
◆ ***se dénouer*** ■ **vpi 1.** [cheveux] to come loose *ou* undone / [lacet] to come undone *ou* untied **2.** [crise] to end, to be resolved.
■ **vpt : se dénouer les cheveux** to let down one's hair *litt*.

dénoyauter [3] [denwajote] **vt** [fruit] to stone *UK*, to pit *US*.

denrée [dɑ̃re] **nf** [produit] produce *(U)* ▸ **denrées alimentaires** foodstuffs ▸ **denrée de base** basic commodity ▸ **denrée rare** *fig* rare commodity.

dense [dɑ̃s] **adj 1.** [gén] dense **2.** [style] condensed.

densité [dɑ̃site] **nf** density ▸ **densité de population** population density ▸ **double/haute densité** INFORM double/high density.

dent [dɑ̃] **nf 1.** [de personne, d'objet] tooth ▸ **il claquait des dents** his teeth were chattering ▸ **faire ses dents** to cut one's teeth, to teethe ▸ **mordre à belles dents dans** to get one's teeth into ▸ **dent de lait** baby *ou* milk *UK* tooth ▸ **dent de sagesse** wisdom tooth ▸ **en dents de scie** jagged, serrated ▸ **avoir les dents longues** to have high hopes ▸ **avoir une dent contre qqn** to have it in for sb ▸ **ne rien avoir à se mettre sous la dent** to have nothing left to eat ▸ **ne pas desserrer les dents** not to open one's mouth ▸ **grincer des dents** to gnash one's teeth **2.** GÉOGR peak.

dentaire [dɑ̃tɛr] **adj** dental.

dental, e, aux [dɑ̃tal, o] **adj** LING dental.

denté, e [dɑ̃te] **adj 1.** TECHNOL toothed ▸ **roue dentée** cogwheel **2.** [feuille] dentate.

dentelé, e [dɑ̃tle] **adj** serrated, jagged.

dentelle [dɑ̃tɛl] **nf** lace *(U)*.

dentier [dɑ̃tje] **nm 1.** [dents] dentures *pl* **2.** TECHNOL set of teeth, teeth *pl*.

dentifrice [dɑ̃tifris] **nm** toothpaste.

dentiste [dɑ̃tist] **nmf** dentist.

dentition [dɑ̃tisjɔ̃] **nf** teeth *pl*, dentition.

dénuder [3] [denyde] **vt** to leave bare / [fil électrique] to strip.
◆ ***se dénuder*** **vp** to strip (off).

dénué, e [denɥe] **adj** *sout* **: dénué de** devoid of.

dénuement [denymɑ̃] **nm** destitution *(U)*.

dénutrition [denytrisjɔ̃] **nf** malnutrition.

déodorant, e [deɔdɔrɑ̃, ɑ̃t] **adj** deodorant.
◆ ***déodorant*** **nm** deodorant.

déontologie [deɔ̃tɔlɔʒi] nf professional ethics *pl*.

dép. abr de *départ*, *département*.

dépannage [depanaʒ] nm repair ▸ **service de dépannage** AUTO breakdown service.

dépanner [3] [depane] vt **1.** [réparer] to repair, to fix **2.** *fam* [aider] to bail out.

dépanneur, euse [depanœr, øz] nm, f repairman (f repairwoman).

◆ **dépanneuse** nf [véhicule] breakdown truck *UK*, breakdown lorry *UK*, tow truck *US*, wrecker *US*.

dépareillé, e [depareje] adj [ensemble] non-matching / [paire] odd.

déparer [3] [depare] vt to spoil.

départ [depar] nm **1.** [de personne] departure, leaving ▸ **être sur le départ** to be ready to go ▸ **on en a parlé après son départ** we discussed it after he went ▸ **départ en préretraite** early retirement ▸ **les grands départs** the holiday exodus **2.** [de véhicule] departure ▸ **le départ du train est à 7 h** the train leaves at 7a.m **3.** *fig* & SPORT start ▸ **faux départ** false start ▸ **douze chevaux ont pris le départ (de la course)** there were twelve starters.

◆ **au départ** loc adv to start with.

◆ **au départ de** loc prép : **visites au départ des Tuileries** tours departing from the Tuileries.

◆ **de départ** loc adj **1.** [gare, quai, heure] departure *(avant n)* **2.** [initial] : **l'idée de départ** the initial *ou* original idea ▸ **salaire de départ** starting salary.

départager [17] [departaʒe] vt **1.** [concurrents, opinions] to decide between **2.** [lors d'une élection] to choose between **3.** [séparer] to separate.

département [departəmɑ̃] nm **1.** [territoire] département, department *territorial and administrative division of France* **2.** [service] department.

CULTURE

Département

This is the second-largest administrative division in France (the biggest being the **région**). There are 96 **départements** in France itself (including Corsica); the other four are the overseas **départements d'outre-mer**. Each one has a number based on its alphabetical order, except for the five that surround Paris: they were added after all the others and so are numbered from 91 to 95. **Département** numbers are engraved on number plates to show where vehicles are registered. They are also used in conversation instead of **département** names: **Il a déménagé dans le 78** (the **Yvelines**).

départemental, e, aux [departəmɑ̃tal, o] adj *of a French département*.

◆ **départementale** nf secondary road, ≃ B road *UK*.

départir [32] [departir] ◆ **se départir** vp : **ne pas se départir de** to retain.

dépassé, e [depase] adj **1.** [périmé] old-fashioned **2.** *fam* [déconcerté] : **dépassé par** overwhelmed by.

dépassement [depasmɑ̃] nm **1.** [en voiture] overtaking *UK*, passing *US* ▸ **dépassement sans visibilité** overtaking blind *UK* **2.** FIN overspending ▸ **dépassement de coûts** cost overrun.

dépasser [3] [depase] ■ vt **1.** [doubler] to pass, to overtake *UK* ▸ **se faire dépasser** [en voiture] to be passed, to be overtaken *UK* **2.** [être plus grand que] to be taller than ▸ **elle me dépasse d'une tête** she's a head taller than me **3.** [être plus long que] to be longer than **4.** [excéder] to exceed, to be more than ▸ **ça dépasse mes moyens** it's beyond my means, it's more than I can afford ▸ **'ne pas dépasser la dose prescrite'** 'do not exceed the stated dose' **5.** [durer plus longtemps que] : **dépasser une heure** to go on for more than an hour **6.** [surpasser] to outshine ▸ **dépasser l'attente de qqn** to surpass *ou* to exceed sb's expectations **7.** [aller au-delà de] to exceed ▸ **la tâche dépasse mes forces** the task is beyond me **8.** [franchir] to pass ▸▸ **ça me dépasse** *fam* it's beyond me ▸ **les échecs, ça me dépasse!** chess is (quite) beyond me!

■ vi : **dépasser (de)** to stick out (from) ▸ **pas une mèche ne dépassait de son chignon** her chignon was impeccable *ou* hadn't a hair out of place.

◆ **se dépasser** ■ vp *(emploi réciproque)* to pass one another ▸ **les voitures cherchent toutes à se dépasser** the cars are all jostling for position.

■ vpi to excel o.s.

dépassionner [3] [depasjɔne] vt to take the heat out of.

dépaysement [depeizmɑ̃] nm change of scene, disorientation.

dépayser [3] [depeize] vt **1.** [désorienter] to disorient, to disorientate *UK* **2.** [changer agréablement] to make a change of scene for.

dépecer [29] [depəse] vt **1.** [découper] to chop up **2.** [déchiqueter] to tear apart.

dépêche [depɛʃ] nf dispatch.

dépêcher [4] [depeʃe] vt *sout* [envoyer] to dispatch.

◆ **se dépêcher** vp to hurry up ▸ **se dépêcher de faire qqch** to hurry to do sthg.

dépeignais, dépeignions ➤ ***dépeindre***.

dépeindre [81] [depɛ̃dr] vt to depict, to describe.

dépeint, e [depɛ̃, ɛ̃t] pp ➤ ***dépeindre***.

dépénalisation [depenalizasjɔ̃] nf decriminalization.

dépénaliser [3] [depenalize] vt to decriminalize.

dépendance [depɑ̃dɑ̃s] nf **1.** [de personne] dependence ▸ **être sous la dépendance de** to be dependent on **2.** [à la drogue] dependency **3.** [de bâtiment] outbuilding.

dépendant, e [depɑ̃dɑ̃, ɑ̃t] adj : **dépendant (de)** dependent (on).

dépendre [73] [depɑ̃dr] vt **1.** [être soumis] : **dépendre de** to depend on ▸ **ça dépend** it depends **2.** [appartenir] : **dépendre de** to belong to **3.** [décrocher] to take down.

dépendu [depɑ̃dy] pp inv ➤ ***dépendre***.

dépens [depɑ̃] nmpl DR costs ▸ **aux dépens de qqn** at sb's expense ▸ **je l'ai appris à mes dépens** I learned that to my cost.

dépense [depɑ̃s] nf **1.** [frais] expense ▸ **dépenses de marketing** marketing spend **2.** *fig* & FIN expenditure *(U)*

▸ **dépenses engagées** incurred expenditure *ou* expenses ▸ **dépenses et recettes** incomings and outgoings ▸ **les dépenses publiques** public spending *(U)* **3.** [consommation] consumption.

dépenser [3] [depɑ̃se] **vt 1.** [argent] to spend ▸ **dépenser sans compter** to spend lavishly **2.** *fig* [énergie] to expend.
◆ ***se dépenser*** **vp** *litt* & *fig* to exert o.s.

dépensier, ère [depɑ̃sje, ɛr] **adj** extravagant.

déperdition [depɛrdisjɔ̃] **nf** loss ▸ **déperdition de chaleur** heat loss.

dépérir [32] [deperir] **vi 1.** [personne] to waste away **2.** [santé, affaire] to decline **3.** [plante] to wither.

dépêtrer [4] [depetre] ◆ ***se dépêtrer*** **vp : se dépêtrer de** *fam* [se dégager de] to get out of / *fig* [se sortir de] to extricate o.s. from / *fig* [se débarrasser de] to get rid of.

dépeuplement [depœpləmɑ̃] **nm 1.** [de pays] depopulation **2.** [d'étang, de rivière, de forêt] emptying of wildlife.

dépeupler [5] [depœple] **vt 1.** [pays] to depopulate **2.** [étang, rivière, forêt] to drive the wildlife from.
◆ ***se dépeupler*** **vp 1.** [pays] to become depopulated **2.** [rivière, étang] to have a diminishing *ou* disappearing wildlife population.

déphasé, e [defaze] **adj** ÉLECTR out of phase / *fam fig* out of touch.

dépiauter [3] [depjote] **vt** *fam* [animal] to skin / *fig* [texte] to pull to pieces.

dépilatoire [depilatwar] **adj : crème dépilatoire** depilatory cream.

dépistage [depistaʒ] **nm 1.** [de gibier, de voleur] tracking down **2.** [de maladie] screening ▸ **dépistage du SIDA** AIDS testing.

dépister [3] [depiste] **vt 1.** [gibier, voleur] to track down **2.** [maladie] to screen for **3.** [déjouer] to throw off the scent **4.** *fig* [découvrir] to detect.

dépit [depi] **nm** pique, spite ▸ **par dépit** out of pique *ou* spite.
◆ ***en dépit de*** **loc prép** in spite of.

dépité, e [depite] **adj** cross, annoyed.

déplacé, e [deplase] **adj 1.** [propos, attitude, présence] out of place **2.** [personne] displaced.

déplacement [deplasmɑ̃] **nm 1.** [d'objet] moving ▸ **déplacement de vertèbre** MÉD slipped disc *UK ou* disk *US* **2.** [voyage] travelling *(U) UK*, traveling *(U) US* ▸ **en déplacement** away on business ▸ **valoir le déplacement** *fig* to be worth going.

déplacer [16] [deplase] **vt 1.** [objet] to move, to shift / *fig* [problème] to shift the emphasis of **2.** [muter] to transfer.
◆ ***se déplacer*** **vp 1.** [se mouvoir - animal] to move (around) / [- personne] to walk **2.** [voyager] to travel **3.** MÉD **: se déplacer une vertèbre** to slip a disc *UK ou* disk *US*.

déplaire [110] [deplɛr] **vt 1.** [ne pas plaire] **: cela me déplaît** I don't like it ▸ **il m'a tout de suite déplu** I took an instant dislike to him **2.** [irriter] to displease ▸ **n'en déplaise à mon patron** *hum* whether my boss likes it or not.

déplaisant, e [deplɛzɑ̃, ɑ̃t] **adj** *sout* unpleasant.

déplaisir [deplezir] **nm** *sout* displeasure.

dépliant [deplijɑ̃] **nm** leaflet ▸ **dépliant touristique** tourist brochure.

déplier [10] [deplije] **vt** to unfold.
◆ ***se déplier*** **vp** to unfold.

déploiement [deplwamɑ̃] **nm 1.** MIL deployment **2.** [d'ailes] spreading **3.** [de voile] unfurling, opening **4.** *fig* [d'efforts] display ▸ **un grand déploiement de** a major display of.

déplorable [deplɔrabl] **adj** deplorable.

déplorer [3] [deplɔre] **vt 1.** [regretter] to deplore **2.** [pleurer] to mourn.

déployer [13] [deplwaje] **vt 1.** [déplier - gén] to unfold / [- plan, journal] to open / [ailes] to spread **2.** MIL to deploy **3.** [mettre en œuvre] to expend **4.** [manifester] to display ▸ **elle a déployé toute son éloquence** she brought all her eloquence to bear.

déplu, e [deply] **pp** ➤ ***déplaire***.

dépoitraillé, e [depwatraje] **adj** *fam péj* with one's shirt wide open.

dépoli, e [depɔli] **adj** [métal] tarnished / [verre] frosted.

dépolitiser [3] [depɔlitize] **vt** to depoliticize.

déportation [depɔrtasjɔ̃] **nf 1.** [exil] deportation **2.** [internement] transportation to a concentration camp.

déporté, e [depɔrte] **nm, f 1.** [exilé] deportee **2.** [interné] prisoner *(in a concentration camp)*.

déporter [3] [depɔrte] **vt 1.** [dévier] to carry off course ▸ **la voiture a été déportée sur la gauche** the car swerved to the left **2.** [exiler] to deport **3.** [interner] to send to a concentration camp.
◆ ***se déporter*** **vpi** [doucement] to move aside / [brusquement] to swerve ▸ **se déporter vers la droite/gauche** to veer (off) to the right/left.

déposant, e [depozɑ̃, ɑ̃t] **nm, f 1.** FIN depositor **2.** DR deponent.

déposé, e [depoze] **adj : marque déposée** registered trademark ▸ **modèle déposé** patented design.

déposer [3] [depoze] ■ **vt 1.** [poser] to put down **2.** [personne, paquet] to drop ▸ **je te dépose?** can I drop you off?, can I give you a lift? **3.** [argent, sédiment] to deposit ▸ **déposer de l'argent sur son compte** to pay money into one's account, to deposit money in one's account **4.** ADMIN to register ▸ **déposer sa candidature** to apply ▸ **déposer une plainte** to lodge a complaint **5.** DR to file ▸ **déposer son bilan** FIN to go into liquidation ▸ **déposer un brevet** to file a patent application, to apply for a patent **6.** [monarque] to depose **7.** [moteur] to take out.
■ **vi 1.** DR to testify, to give evidence **2.** [sédiment] to form a deposit.
◆ ***se déposer*** **vp** to settle.

dépositaire [depozitɛr] **nmf 1.** COMM agent **2.** [d'objet] bailee ▸ **dépositaire de** *fig* person entrusted with.

déposition [depozisjɔ̃] **nf** deposition.

déposséder [18] [depɔsede] **vt : déposséder qqn de** to dispossess sb of.

dépôt [depo] **nm 1.** [d'objet, d'argent, de sédiment] deposit, depositing *(U)* ▸ **verser un dépôt (de garantie)** to put

down a deposit ▸ **dépôt à terme/à vue** open-access/restricted access deposit ▸ **dépôt calcaire *ou* de tartre** layer of scale *ou* fur ▸ **dépôt d'ordures** rubbish dump *UK*, garbage dump *US*
2. ADMIN registration ▸ **dépôt de bilan** petition in bankruptcy ▸ **dépôt de brevet** patent registration ▸ **dépôt légal** copyright registration ▸ **dépôt d'une liste électorale** presentation of a list of candidates ▸ **dépôt d'une marque** registration of a trademark
3. [garage] depot
4. [entrepôt] store, warehouse ▸ **dépôt de munitions** ammunition dump
5. [prison] ≃ police cells *pl* ▸ **au dépôt** in the cells.
◆ ***en dépôt*** **loc adv** FIN in trust, in safe custody ▸ **avoir en dépôt** to have on bond ▸ **mettre en dépôt** to bond.

dépoter [3] [depɔte] **vt** [plante] to remove from the pot.

dépotoir [depɔtwar] **nm** **1.** [décharge] rubbish dump *UK*, garbage dump *US* ⁄ *fam fig* dump, tip *UK* **2.** [usine] sewage works *sg UK*, sewage plant *US*.

dépouille [depuj] **nf** **1.** [peau] hide, skin **2.** [humaine] remains *pl* ▸ **dépouille mortelle** mortal remains.
◆ ***dépouilles*** **nfpl** spoils.

dépouillement [depujmɑ̃] **nm** **1.** [sobriété] austerity, sobriety **2.** [examen] perusal ▸ **dépouillement de scrutin** counting of the votes.

dépouiller [3] [depuje] **vt** **1.** [priver] **: dépouiller qqn (de)** to strip sb (of) **2.** [examiner] to peruse ▸ **dépouiller le scrutin** to count the votes.
◆ ***se dépouiller*** **vp : se dépouiller de** to divest o.s. of.

dépourvu, ***e*** [depurvy] **adj : dépourvu de** without, lacking in ▸ **dépourvu de virus** INFORM virus-free.
◆ ***au dépourvu*** **loc adv : prendre qqn au dépourvu** to catch sb unawares.

dépoussiérer [18] [depusjere] **vt** to dust (off).

dépravation [depravasjɔ̃] **nf** depravity.

dépravé, ***e*** [deprave] ■ **adj** depraved.
■ **nm, f** degenerate.

dépraver [3] [deprave] **vt** to deprave.
◆ ***se dépraver*** **vp** to become depraved.

dépréciation [depresjasjɔ̃] **nf** FIN depreciation.

déprécier [9] [depresje] **vt** **1.** [marchandise] to reduce the value of **2.** [œuvre] to disparage.
◆ ***se déprécier*** **vp** **1.** [marchandise] to depreciate **2.** [personne] to put o.s. down.

dépressif, ***ive*** [depresif, iv] ■ **adj** depressive.
■ **nm, f** depressive (person).

dépression [depresjɔ̃] **nf** depression ▸ **faire de la dépression** to be depressed ▸ **dépression nerveuse** nervous breakdown.

déprimant, ***e*** [deprimɑ̃, ɑ̃t] **adj** depressing.

déprime [deprim] **nf** *fam* **: faire une déprime** to be (feeling) down.

déprimé, ***e*** [deprime] **adj** depressed.

déprimer [3] [deprime] ■ **vt** to depress.
■ **vi** *fam* to be (feeling) down.

déprogrammer [3] [deprɔgrame] **vt** to remove from the schedule ⁄ TV to take off the air.

dépuceler [24] [depysle] **vt** *fam* **: dépuceler qqn** to take sb's virginity.

depuis [dəpɥi] ■ **prép** **1.** [à partir d'une date ou d'un moment précis] since ▸ **je ne l'ai pas vu depuis son mariage** I haven't seen him since he got married ▸ **il est parti depuis hier** he's been away since yesterday ▸ **depuis le début jusqu'à la fin** from beginning to end ▸ **depuis 12 h jusqu'à 20 h** from 12 to *ou* till 8 p.m ▸ **depuis quand est-ce que tu me donnes des ordres?** since when do you give me orders?
2. [exprimant une durée] for ▸ **il est malade depuis une semaine** he has been ill for a week ▸ **depuis 10 ans/longtemps** for 10 years/a long time ▸ **depuis le temps que tu le connais, tu pourrais lui demander** considering how long you've known him you could easily ask him ▸ **depuis peu** recently, not long ago ▸ **depuis toujours** always ▸ **depuis combien de temps le connais-tu?** how long have you known him for?
3. [dans l'espace] from ▸ **depuis la route, on pouvait voir la mer** you could see the sea from the road ▸ **depuis le premier jusqu'au dernier** from the first to the last.
■ **adv** since (then) ▸ **depuis, nous ne l'avons pas revu** we haven't seen him since (then).
◆ ***depuis lors*** **loc adv** since then ▸ **il n'est pas retourné au village depuis lors** he hasn't been back to the village since then.
◆ ***depuis que*** **loc conj** since ▸ **je ne l'ai pas revu depuis qu'il s'est marié** I haven't seen him since he got married.

dépuratif, ***ive*** [depyratif, iv] **adj** cleansing, eliminating.
◆ ***dépuratif*** **nm** depurative.

députation [depytasjɔ̃] **nf** **1.** [délégation] deputation **2.** [fonction] **: candidat à la députation** parliamentary candidate *UK*.

député [depyte] **nm** **1.** [délégué] representative **2.** POLIT [au parlement] member of parliament *UK*, representative *US* ▸ **député européen** Euro-MP, MEP ⁄ [en France] deputy ⁄ [en Grande-Bretagne] member of parliament ⁄ [aux États-Unis] Congressman (f Congresswoman) ▸ **député-maire** *deputy who is also a mayor.*

députer [3] [depyte] **vt** to send as representative.

déraciner [3] [derasine] **vt** *litt* & *fig* to uproot.

déraillement [derajmɑ̃] **nm** derailment.

dérailler [3] [deraje] **vi** **1.** [train] to leave the rails, to be derailed **2.** *fam fig* [mécanisme] to go on the blink **3.** *fam fig* [personne] to go to pieces.

dérailleur [derajœr] **nm** [de bicyclette] derailleur.

déraison [derɛzɔ̃] **nf** lack of reason.

déraisonnable [derɛzɔnabl] **adj** unreasonable.

déraisonner [3] [derɛzɔne] **vi** *sout* to talk nonsense.

dérangement [derɑ̃ʒmɑ̃] **nm** trouble ▸ **en dérangement** out of order.

déranger [17] [derɑ̃ʒe] ■ **vt** **1.** [personne] to disturb, to bother ▸ **ça vous dérange si je fume?** do you mind if I smoke? ▸ **désolé de vous déranger** sorry to disturb you ▸ **'ne pas déranger'** 'do not disturb' **2.** [plan] to disrupt

▸ **ça lui a dérangé l'esprit** she was badly shaken up by it **3.** [maison, pièce] to make untidy ▸ **ne dérange pas mes papiers!** don't get my papers mixed up *ou* in a muddle!
■ **vi** to be disturbing.
◆ ***se déranger*** **vp 1.** [se déplacer] to move ▸ **ce coup de fil m'a évité de me déranger** that phone call saved me a trip ▸ **il a refusé de se déranger** he wouldn't come (out) **2.** [se gêner] to put o.s. out ▸ **ne vous dérangez pas, je reviendrai** please don't go to any trouble; I'll come back later.

dérapage [derapaʒ] **nm 1.** [glissement] skid ▸ **dérapage contrôlé** controlled skid **2.** *fig* excess.

déraper [3] [derape] **vi** [glisser] to skid / *fig* to get out of hand.

dératé, e [derate] **nm, f** *fam* **: courir comme un dératé** to run flat out.

dératisation [deratizasjɔ̃] **nf** extermination of rats.

derechef [dərəʃɛf] **adv** *sout* once again.

dérèglement [derɛgləmɑ̃] **nm** [de machine] malfunction / [de fonction corporelle] upset.

déréglementation [dereglәmɑ̃tasjɔ̃] **nf** deregulation.

déréglementer [3] [dereglәmɑ̃te] **vt** to deregulate.

dérégler [18] [deregle] **vt** [mécanisme] to put out of order / *fig* to upset.
◆ ***se dérégler*** **vp** [mécanisme] to go wrong / *fig* to be upset *ou* unsettled.

dérider [3] [deride] **vt** *fig* **: dérider qqn** to cheer sb up.
◆ ***se dérider*** **vp** to cheer up.

dérision [derizjɔ̃] **nf** derision ▸ **tourner qqch en dérision** to hold sthg up to ridicule.

dérisoire [derizwar] **adj** derisory.

dérivatif, ive [derivatif, iv] **adj** derivative.
◆ ***dérivatif*** **nm** distraction.

dérivation [derivasjɔ̃] **nf 1.** [de cours d'eau, circulation] diversion, detour **2.** LING & MATH derivation.

dérive [deriv] **nf 1.** [aileron] centreboard *UK*, centerboard *US* **2.** [mouvement] drift, drifting *(U)* ▸ **aller** *ou* **partir à la dérive** *fig* to fall apart.

dérivé [derive] **nm** CHIM & LING derivative.

dérivée [derive] **nf** MATH derivative.

dériver [3] [derive] ■ **vt 1.** [détourner] to divert *UK*, to detour *US* **2.** LING to derive.
■ **vi 1.** [aller à la dérive] to drift **2.** *fig* [découler] **: dériver de** to derive from.

dériveur [derivœr] **nm** sailing dinghy *(with centreboard)*.

dermato [dɛrmato] **nmf** *fam* dermatologist.

dermatologie [dɛrmatɔlɔʒi] **nf** dermatology.

dermatologue [dɛrmatɔlɔg] **nmf** dermatologist.

dernier, ère [dɛrnje, ɛr] ■ **adj 1.** [gén] last ▸ **samedi dernier** last Saturday ▸ **l'année dernière** last year ▸ **un dernier mot/point!** one final word/point! ▸ **avoir le dernier mot : il faut toujours qu'il ait le dernier mot** he always has to have the last word **2.** [ultime] last, final ▸ **jusqu'à son dernier jour** to his dying day, until the day he died ▸ **c'est mon dernier prix** [vendeur] it's the lowest I'll go / [acheteur] that's my final offer
3. [plus récent] latest ▸ **je ferai mes valises au dernier moment** I'll pack at the last minute *ou* possible moment ▸ **une nouvelle de dernière minute** a late newsflash
4. [du bas] bottom ▸ **les chaussettes sont dans le dernier tiroir** the socks are in the bottom drawer / [du haut] top ▸ **au dernier étage** on the top floor / [du bout] last ▸ **un siège au dernier rang** a seat in the back (row)
5. [extrême, sens négatif] **: c'est la dernière chose à faire** it's the last thing one should do.
■ **nm, f** last ▸ **ce dernier** the latter ▸ **petit dernier** baby of the family ▸ **son dossier est le dernier de la pile** her file is at the bottom of the pile ▸ **j'étais toujours le dernier en classe** I was always (at the) bottom of the class.
◆ ***en dernier*** **loc adv** last ▸ **entrer en dernier** to go in last, to be the last one to go in.

dernièrement [dɛrnjɛrmɑ̃] **adv** recently, lately.

dernier-né, dernière-née [dɛrnjene, dɛrnjɛrne] (**mpl derniers-nés, fpl dernières-nées**) **nm, f** [bébé] youngest (child) ▸ **la dernière-née de Fiat®** *fig* the new Fiat®.

dérobade [derɔbad] **nf** evasion, shirking *(U)*.

dérobé, e [derɔbe] **adj 1.** [volé] stolen **2.** [caché] hidden.
◆ ***à la dérobée*** **loc adv** surreptitiously.

dérober [3] [derɔbe] **vt** *sout* to steal.
◆ ***se dérober*** **vp 1.** [se soustraire] **: se dérober à qqch** to shirk sthg **2.** [s'effondrer] to give way.

dérogation [derɔgasjɔ̃] **nf** [action] dispensation / [résultat] exception.

déroger [17] [derɔʒe] **vi : déroger à** to depart from.

dérouiller [3] [deruje] **vt 1.** [nettoyer] to remove the rust from **2.** *fam* [frapper] **: dérouiller qqn** to give sb a belting.
◆ ***se dérouiller*** **vp** *fig* to stretch (o.s.)

déroulement [derulmɑ̃] **nm 1.** [de bobine] unwinding **2.** *fig* [d'événement] development.

dérouler [3] [derule] **vt** [fil] to unwind / [papier, tissu] to unroll.
◆ ***se dérouler*** **vp** to take place.

déroutant, e [derutɑ̃, ɑ̃t] **adj** disconcerting, bewildering.

déroute [derut] **nf** MIL rout / *fig* collapse ▸ **mettre en déroute** to rout.

dérouter [3] [derute] **vt 1.** [déconcerter] to disconcert, to put out **2.** [dévier] to divert *UK*, to detour *US*.

derrick [derik] **nm** derrick.

derrière [dɛrjɛr] ■ **prép** behind ▸ **ça s'est passé derrière chez moi** it happened behind my house ▸ **derrière son indifférence apparente** beneath his apparent indifference ▸ **je sais bien ce qu'elle dit derrière mon dos** I'm quite aware of what she says behind my back.
■ **adv 1.** [en arrière] behind, the other side ▸ **tu vois le bureau de poste? la bibliothèque est juste derrière** do you see the post office? the library's just behind it **2.** [dans le fond] at the rear *ou* back ▸ **installe-toi derrière** [dans une voiture] sit in the back.

■ nm **1.** [partie arrière] back ▸ **la porte de derrière** the back door **2.** [partie du corps] bottom, behind ▸ **coup de pied au derrière** kick up the backside *ou* in the pants.
◆ ***par derrière*** loc adv from behind ▸ **il est passé par derrière** [la maison] he went round the back ▸ **dire du mal de qqn par derrière** to criticize sb behind his/her back.

des [de] ■ **art indéf** ➤ ***un.***
■ **prép** ➤ ***de.***

dès [dɛ] **prép** from ▸ **dès son arrivée** the minute he arrives/arrived, as soon as he arrives/arrived ▸ **dès le deuxième verre, il ne savait plus ce qu'il disait** after his second glass he started talking nonsense ▸ **dès l'enfance** since childhood ▸ **dès la frontière** on reaching the border ▸ **dès 1900** as far back as 1900, as early as 1900 ▸ **dès maintenant** from now on ▸ **je vais le faire dès aujourd'hui** I'm going to do it this very day ▸ **dès demain** starting *ou* from tomorrow.
◆ ***dès lors*** loc adv from then on ▸ **il a quitté la ville; dès lors, on n'a plus entendu parler de lui** he left the town and he's never been heard of since.
◆ ***dès lors que*** loc conj [puisque] since ▸ **dès lors qu'il a renoncé à ce poste, il ne peut prétendre à une augmentation** given that *ou* since *ou* as he refused that job, he can't expect a rise ▸ **dès lors que la loi entre en vigueur, il faut s'y conformer** as soon as the law comes into force, it must be respected.
◆ ***dès que*** loc conj as soon as ▸ **dès qu'il peut, il part en vacances** whenever he can, he goes off on holiday ▸ **dès que tu pourras** as soon as you can.

désabusé, e [dezabyze] **adj** disillusioned.

désaccord [dezakɔr] **nm** disagreement.

désaccordé, e [dezakɔrde] **adj** out of tune.

désaccoutumer [3] [dezakutyme] **vt : désaccoutumer qqn de** to get sb out of the habit of.
◆ ***se désaccoutumer*** **vp : se désaccoutumer de qqch/de faire qqch** to become unaccustomed to sthg/to doing sthg.

désaffecté, e [dezafɛkte] **adj** disused.

désaffection [dezafɛksjɔ̃] **nf** disaffection.

désagréable [dezagreabl] **adj** unpleasant.

désagréablement [dezagreabləmɑ̃] **adv** unpleasantly.

désagréger [22] [dezagreʒe] **vt** to break up.
◆ ***se désagréger*** **vp** to break up.

désagrément [dezagremɑ̃] **nm** annoyance.

désaltérant, e [dezalterɑ̃, ɑ̃t] **adj** thirst-quenching.

désaltérer [18] [dezaltere] ■ **vt** to quench the thirst of.
■ **vi** to be thirst-quenching.
◆ ***se désaltérer*** **vp** to quench one's thirst.

désamorcer [16] [dezamɔrse] **vt** [arme] to remove the primer from / [bombe] to defuse / *fig* [complot] to nip in the bud.

désappointer [3] [dezapwɛ̃te] **vt** to disappoint.

désapprendre [79] [dezaprɑ̃dr] **vt** to forget.

désapprobateur, trice [dezaprɔbatœr, tris] **adj** disapproving.

désapprobation [dezaprɔbasjɔ̃] **nf** disapproval.

désapprouver [3] [dezapruve] ■ **vt** to disapprove of.
■ **vi** to disapprove.

désarçonner [3] [dezarsɔne] **vt** *litt & fig* to throw.

désargenté, e [dezarʒɑ̃te] **adj** short (of money).

désarmant, e [dezarmɑ̃, ɑ̃t] **adj** disarming.

désarmement [dezarməmɑ̃] **nm** disarmament ▸ **désarmement unilatéral** unilateral disarmament.

désarmer [3] [dezarme] ■ **vt** to disarm / [fusil] to unload.
■ **vi 1.** [pays] to disarm **2.** *fig* [personne] to give up / [haine] to cease.

désarroi [dezarwa] **nm** confusion.

désassorti, e [dezasɔrti] **adj** [dépareillé] non-matching.

désastre [dezastr] **nm** disaster.

désastreux, euse [dezastrø, øz] **adj** disastrous.

désavantage [dezavɑ̃taʒ] **nm** disadvantage.

désavantager [17] [dezavɑ̃taʒe] **vt** to disadvantage.

désavantageux, euse [dezavɑ̃taʒø, øz] **adj** unfavourable *UK*, unfavorable *US*.

désaveu, x [dezavø] **nm 1.** [reniement] denial **2.** [désapprobation] disapproval.

COMMENT EXPRIMER...

le désaccord

I'm afraid I don't agree / Je regrette, mais je ne suis pas d'accord
I can't agree with you on that, I'm afraid / Désolé, mais là, je ne suis pas d'accord avec toi
I think you're wrong / Je crois que vous vous trompez
I don't think that's true / Je ne crois pas que ça soit vrai
I totally disagree / Je ne suis absolument pas d'accord
You couldn't be more wrong / Tu te trompes complètement
With respect, I think you're forgetting one important point / Si je peux me permettre, je pense que vous oubliez un point important
I take your point, but... / Je comprends votre point de vue, mais...
That's all very well, but... / Tout ça, c'est très bien, mais...
You can't be serious! / Tu plaisantes !
Nonsense!/ Rubbish! / N'importe quoi !

désavouer [6] [dezavwe] **vt** to disown.
◆ ***se désavouer*** **vp** to go back on one's word.

désaxé, e [dezakse] ■ **adj** [mentalement] disordered, unhinged.
■ **nm, f** unhinged person.

descendance [desɑ̃dɑ̃s] **nf 1.** [origine] descent **2.** [progéniture] descendants *pl.*

descendant, e [desɑ̃dɑ̃, ɑ̃t] **nm, f** [héritier] descendant.

descendre [73] [desɑ̃dr] ■ **vt** *(v aux : être)* **1.** [escalier, pente] to go/come down ▸ **descendre la rue en courant** to run down the street ▸ **descendre un fleuve** [en nageant] to swim downstream / [en bateau] to sail down a river **2.** [rideau, tableau] to lower ▸ **il faudrait descendre le cadre de deux centimètres** the frame should be taken down two centimetres **3.** [apporter] to bring/take down **4.** *fam* [personne, avion] to shoot down ▸ **se faire descendre** to get shot **5.** *fam* [critiquer] to pan, to slate ▸ **il s'est fait descendre par le jury** he was slated by the jury.
■ **vi** *(v aux : être)* **1.** [gén] to go/come down ▸ **j'ai rencontré la concierge en descendant** I met the caretaker on my way down **2.** [température, niveau] to fall ▸ **la température est descendue au-dessous de zéro** the temperature has dropped *ou* fallen below zero **3.** [passager] to get off ▸ **descendre de bateau** to get off a boat, to land ▸ **descendre d'un bus** to get off a bus ▸ **descendre de vélo** to get off one's bike ▸ **descendre d'une voiture** to get out of a car **4.** [loger] **: descendre chez** to stay with ▸ **descendre à l'hôtel** to stay in a hotel **5.** [être issu] **: descendre de** to be descended from ▸ **le prince descendait des Habsbourg** the prince was descended from the Habsburgs **6.** [marée] to go out **7.** [se rendre] to go down ▸ **descendre en ville** to go into town, to go downtown *US* **8.** [suivre une pente] to go down *ou* downwards *UK ou* downward *US* ▸ **le jardin descend en pente douce jusqu'à la plage** the garden slopes gently down to the beach.

descendu, e [desɑ̃dy] **pp** ➤ ***descendre***.

descente [desɑ̃t] **nf 1.** [action] descent ▸ **à sa descente d'avion** as he disembarked *ou* got off the aircraft ▸ **descente en piqué** dive ▸ **descente en vol plané** glide, gliding fall **2.** [pente] downhill slope *ou* stretch ▸ **courir/déraper dans la descente** to run/to skid down **3.** *fam fig* [capacité à boire] **: il a une bonne descente** he can certainly put it away **4.** [irruption] raid ▸ **faire une descente** ADMIN to carry out a (surprise) inspection / MIL to mount a raid / *fam* to make an unexpected visit ▸ **descente de police** police raid **5.** [tapis] **: descente de lit** bedside rug.

descriptif, ive [dɛskriptif, iv] **adj** descriptive.
◆ ***descriptif*** **nm** [de lieu] particulars *pl* / [d'appareil] specification.

description [dɛskripsjɔ̃] **nf** description.

désemparé, e [dezɑ̃pare] **adj** [personne] helpless / [avion, navire] disabled.

désemplir [32] [dezɑ̃plir] **vi : ce restaurant ne désemplit pas** this restaurant is always packed.

désencombrer [3] [dezɑ̃kɔ̃bre] **vt** to clear.

désendettement [dezɑ̃dɛtmɑ̃] **nm** degearing *UK*, debt reduction.

désenfler [3] [dezɑ̃fle] **vi** to go down, to become less swollen.

désengagement [dezɑ̃gaʒmɑ̃] **nm** disengagement.

désensibiliser [3] [desɑ̃sibilize] **vt** to desensitize.

déséquilibre [dezekilibr] **nm** imbalance.

déséquilibré, e [dezekilibre] **nm, f** unbalanced person.

déséquilibrer [3] [dezekilibre] **vt 1.** [physiquement] **: déséquilibrer qqn** to throw sb off balance **2.** [perturber] to unbalance.

désert, e [dezɛr, ɛrt] **adj** [désertique - île] desert *(avant n)* / [peu fréquenté] deserted.
◆ ***désert*** **nm** desert.

déserter [3] [dezɛrte] **vt & vi** to desert.

déserteur [dezɛrtœr] **nm** MIL deserter / *fig & péj* traitor.

désertification, [dezɛrtifikasjɔ̃], ***désertisation*** [desɛrtizasjɔ̃] **nf** desertification / [de région] depopulation.

désertion [dezɛrsjɔ̃] **nf** desertion.

désertique [dezɛrtik] **adj** desert *(avant n)*.

désertisation = ***désertification***.

désespérant, e [dezɛsperɑ̃, ɑ̃t] **adj 1.** [déprimant] depressing **2.** [affligeant] hopeless.

désespéré, e [dezɛspere] **adj 1.** [regard] desperate **2.** [situation] hopeless.

désespérément [dezɛsperemɑ̃] **adv 1.** [sans espoir] hopelessly **2.** [avec acharnement] desperately.

désespérer [18] [dezɛspere] ■ **vt 1.** [décourager] **: désespérer qqn** to drive sb to despair **2.** [perdre espoir] **: désespérer que qqch arrive** to give up hope of sthg happening.
■ **vi : désespérer (de)** to despair (of).
◆ ***se désespérer*** **vp** to despair.

désespoir [dezɛspwar] **nm** despair ▸ **en désespoir de cause** as a last resort ▸ **faire le désespoir de qqn** to be the despair of sb.

déshabillé [dezabije] **nm** negligee.

déshabiller [3] [dezabije] **vt** to undress.
◆ ***se déshabiller*** **vp** to undress, to get undressed.

COMMENT EXPRIMER...

la désapprobation

I don't approve of smoking / Je suis contre le tabac
I'm totally against it / Je m'y oppose complètement
In my opinion, it's an absolute disgrace / À mon avis, c'est une honte
As far as I'm concerned, it's too bureaucratic / À mon avis, il y a trop de paperasserie
I don't think it's right to smack children / Je pense qu'il ne faut pas frapper les enfants
I'm not happy about you staying out late / Ça ne me plaît pas que tu rentres tard
It's just not on! / C'est inacceptable !

déshabituer [7] [dezabitɥe] **vt : déshabituer qqn de faire qqch** to get sb out of the habit of doing sthg.
◆ ***se déshabituer*** **vp : se déshabituer de qqch** to become unaccustomed to sthg.

désherbant**, **e [dezɛrbɑ̃, ɑ̃t] **adj** weed-killing.
◆ ***désherbant*** **nm** weedkiller.

désherber [3] [dezɛrbe] **vt & vi** to weed.

déshérité**, **e [dezerite] ■ **adj 1.** [privé d'héritage] disinherited **2.** [pauvre] deprived.
■ **nm, f** [pauvre] deprived person.

déshériter [3] [dezerite] **vt** to disinherit.

déshonneur [dezɔnœr] **nm** disgrace.

déshonorant**, **e [dezɔnɔrɑ̃, ɑ̃t] **adj** dishonourable *UK*, dishonorable *US*.

déshonorer [3] [dezɔnɔre] **vt** to disgrace, to bring disgrace on.
◆ ***se déshonorer*** **vp** to disgrace o.s.

déshumaniser [3] [dezymanize] **vt** to dehumanize.

déshydratation [dezidratasjɔ̃] **nf** dehydration.

déshydrater [3] [dezidrate] **vt** to dehydrate.
◆ ***se déshydrater*** **vp** to become dehydrated.

desiderata [deziderata] **nmpl** requirements.

design [dizajn] ■ **adj inv** modern.
■ **nm inv** modernism.

désignation [deziɲasjɔ̃] **nf 1.** [appellation] designation, name **2.** [nomination] appointment.

désigner [3] [deziɲe] **vt 1.** [choisir] to appoint **2.** [signaler] to point out **3.** [nommer] to designate.
◆ ***se désigner*** **vp : se désigner (volontaire) pour qqch/pour faire qqch** to volunteer for sthg/to do sthg.

désillusion [dezilyzjɔ̃] **nf** disillusion.

désillusionner [3] [dezilyzjɔne] **vt** to disillusion.

désincarné**, **e [dezɛ̃karne] **adj 1.** RELIG disembodied **2.** [éthéré] unearthly.

désindustrialisation [dezɛ̃dystrijalizasjɔ̃] **nf** deindustrialization.

désinence [dezinɑ̃s] **nf** LING ending.

désinfectant**, **e [dezɛ̃fɛktɑ̃, ɑ̃t] **adj** disinfectant.
◆ ***désinfectant*** **nm** disinfectant.

désinfecter [4] [dezɛ̃fɛkte] **vt** to disinfect.

désinflation [dezɛ̃flasjɔ̃] **nf** disinflation.

désinformation [dezɛ̃fɔrmasjɔ̃] **nf** disinformation.

désinstaller [3] [dezɛ̃stale] **vt** INFORM to uninstall.

désintégration [dezɛ̃tegrasjɔ̃] **nf** [désagrégation] disintegration / *fig* break-up.

désintégrer [18] [dezɛ̃tegre] **vt** to break up.
◆ ***se désintégrer*** **vp** to disintegrate, to break up.

désintéressé**, **e [dezɛ̃terese] **adj** disinterested.

désintéresser [4] [dezɛ̃terese] ◆ ***se désintéresser*** **vp : se désintéresser de** to lose interest in.

désintérêt [dezɛ̃terɛ] **nm** lack of interest.

désintoxication [dezɛ̃tɔksikasjɔ̃] **nf** detoxification.

désinvolte [dezɛ̃vɔlt] **adj 1.** [à l'aise] casual **2.** *péj* [sans-gêne] offhand.

désinvolture [dezɛ̃vɔltyr] **nf 1.** [légèreté] casualness **2.** *péj* [sans-gêne] offhandedness ▸ **avec désinvolture** in an offhand manner.

désir [dezir] **nm 1.** [souhait] desire, wish **2.** [charnel] desire.

désirable [dezirabl] **adj** desirable.

désirer [3] [dezire] **vt 1.** *sout* [chose] **: désirer faire qqch** to wish to do sthg ▸ **vous désirez?** [dans un magasin] can I help you? / [dans un café] what can I get you? **2.** [sexuellement] to desire
▸▸ **laisser à désirer** to leave a lot to be desired.

désireux**, **euse [dezirø, øz] **adj** *sout* **: désireux de faire qqch** anxious to do sthg.

désistement [dezistəmɑ̃] **nm : désistement (de)** withdrawal (from).

désister [3] [deziste] ◆ ***se désister*** **vp 1.** DR **: se désister de qqch** to withdraw sthg **2.** [se retirer] to withdraw, to stand down.

désobéir [32] [dezɔbeir] **vi : désobéir (à qqn)** to disobey (sb).

désobéissance [dezɔbeisɑ̃s] **nf** disobedience.

désobéissant**, **e [dezɔbeisɑ̃, ɑ̃t] **adj** disobedient.

désobligeant**, **e [dezɔbliʒɑ̃, ɑ̃t] **adj** *sout* offensive.

désodorisant**, **e [dezɔdɔrizɑ̃, ɑ̃t] **adj** deodorizing.
◆ ***désodorisant*** **nm** deodorizer, air freshener.

désodoriser [3] [dezɔdɔrize] **vt** to deodorize.

désœuvré**, **e [dezœvre] **adj** idle.

désœuvrement [dezœvrəmɑ̃] **nm** idleness.

désolant**, **e [dezɔlɑ̃, ɑ̃t] **adj** disappointing.

désolation [dezɔlasjɔ̃] **nf 1.** [destruction] desolation **2.** *sout* [affliction] distress.

désolé**, **e [dezɔle] **adj 1.** [ravagé] desolate **2.** [très affligé] distressed **3.** [contrarié] very sorry.

désoler [3] [dezɔle] **vt 1.** [affliger] to sadden **2.** [contrarier] to upset, to make sorry.
◆ ***se désoler*** **vp** [être contrarié] to be upset.

désolidariser [3] [desɔlidarize] **vt 1.** [choses] **: désolidariser qqch (de)** to disengage *ou* disconnect sthg (from) **2.** [personnes] to estrange.
◆ ***se désolidariser*** **vp : se désolidariser de** to dissociate o.s. from.

désopilant**, **e [dezɔpilɑ̃, ɑ̃t] **adj** hilarious.

désordonné**, **e [dezɔrdɔne] **adj** [maison, personne] untidy / *fig* [vie] disorganized.

désordre [dezɔrdr] **nm 1.** [fouillis] untidiness ▸ **en désordre** untidy ▸ **dans le désordre** in random order **2.** *fig* [confusion] disorder **3.** [agitation] disturbances *pl*, disorder *(U)*.

désorganiser [3] [dezɔrganize] **vt** to disrupt.
◆ ***se désorganiser*** **vp** to become disorganized.

désorienté**, **e [dezɔrjɑ̃te] **adj** disoriented, disorientated *UK*.

désorienter [3] [dezɔrjɑ̃te] **vt** [égarer] to disorient, to disorientate *UK* / *fig* [déconcerter] to bewilder.

désormais [dezɔrmɛ] **adv** from now on, in future.

désosser [3] [dezɔse] **vt** to bone.

despote [dɛspɔt] ■ **nm** [chef d'État] despot / *fig* & *péj* tyrant.
■ **adj** despotic.

despotique [dɛspɔtik] **adj** despotic.

despotisme [dɛspɔtism] **nm** [gouvernement] despotism / *fig* & *péj* tyranny.

desquels, **desquelles** [dekɛl] ➤ ***lequel***.

DESS (abr de ***diplôme d'études supérieures spécialisées***) **nm** *postgraduate diploma*.

dessaisir [32] [desezir] **vt** DR **: dessaisir qqn d'une affaire** to withdraw a case from sb.
◆ ***se dessaisir*** **vp** *sout* **: se dessaisir de qqch** to relinquish sthg.

dessaler [3] [desale] ■ **vt** [poisson] **: faire dessaler** to soak.
■ **vi** NAUT to capsize.

dessaouler, ***dessoûler*** [3] [desule] ■ **vt** to sober up.
■ **vi** to sober up ▸ **ne pas dessaouler** *fam* to be permanently plastered.

dessécher [18] [deseʃe] **vt** [peau] to dry (out) / *fig* [cœur] to harden.
◆ ***se dessécher*** **vp** [peau, terre] to dry out / [plante] to wither / *fig* to harden.

dessein [desɛ̃] **nm** *sout* intention.
◆ ***à dessein*** **loc adv** intentionally, on purpose.

desserrer [4] [desere] **vt** to loosen / [poing, dents] to unclench / [frein] to release.

dessert [desɛr] **nm** dessert.

desserte [desɛrt] **nf 1.** [transports] (transport) service *UK*, (transportation) service *US* **2.** [meuble] sideboard.

desservir [38] [desɛrvir] **vt 1.** [transports] to serve **2.** [table] to clear **3.** [désavantager] to do a disservice to.

dessin [desɛ̃] **nm 1.** [graphique] drawing ▸ **dessin animé** cartoon *(film)* ▸ **dessin humoristique** cartoon *(drawing)* ▸ **dessin industriel** draughtsmanship *UK*, draftsmanship *US* **2.** *fig* [contour] outline.

dessinateur, ***trice*** [desinatœr, tris] **nm, f** artist, draughtsman (f draughtswoman) *UK*, draftsman (f draftswoman) *US* ▸ **dessinateur industriel** draughtsman *UK*, draftsman *US*.

dessiner [3] [desine] ■ **vt** [représenter] to draw / *fig* to outline.
■ **vi** to draw.
◆ ***se dessiner*** **vp** [se former] to take shape / *fig* to stand out.

dessoûler = ***dessaouler***.

dessous [dəsu] ■ **adv** underneath.
■ **prép** underneath, under.
■ **nm** [partie inférieure - gén] underside / [- d'un tissu] wrong side
▸▸ **avoir le dessous** to come off worst ▸ **être au trente-sixième dessous** to be in dire straits ▸ **connaître le dessous des cartes (de)** to have inside information (on) ▸ **les dessous de la politique/la finance** the hidden side of politics/the financial world.
■ **nmpl** [sous-vêtements féminins] underwear *(U)*.
◆ ***en dessous*** **loc adv** underneath / [plus bas] below ▸ **ils habitent l'appartement d'en dessous** they live in the flat below *ou* downstairs ▸ **agir par en dessous** to act in an underhand way.
◆ ***en dessous de*** **loc prép** below.

dessous-de-plat [dəsudpla] **nm inv** tablemat.

dessous-de-table [dəsudtabl] **nm inv** bribe, backhander *UK*.

dessus [dəsy] ■ **adv** on top ▸ **n'oubliez pas d'inscrire l'adresse dessus** don't forget to write the address on it ▸ **faites attention à ne pas marcher dessus** be careful not to walk on it.
■ **nm 1.** [partie supérieure] top **2.** [étage supérieur] upstairs ▸ **les voisins du dessus** the upstairs neighbours
▸▸ **avoir le dessus** to have the upper hand ▸ **reprendre le dessus** to get over it ▸ **sens dessus dessous** upside down.
◆ ***en dessus*** **loc adv** on top.

dessus-de-lit [dəsydli] **nm inv** bedspread.

déstabilisateur, ***trice*** [destabilizatœr, tris] **adj** destabilizing.

déstabilisation [destabilizasjɔ̃] **nf** destabilization.

déstabiliser [3] [destabilize] **vt** to destabilize.

destin [dɛstɛ̃] **nm** fate, destiny.

destinataire [dɛstinatɛr] **nmf** addressee.

destination [dɛstinasjɔ̃] **nf 1.** [direction] destination ▸ **arriver à destination** to reach one's destination ▸ **un avion à destination de Paris** a plane to *ou* for Paris **2.** [rôle] purpose.

destinée [dɛstine] **nf** destiny.

destiner [3] [dɛstine] **vt 1.** [consacrer] **: destiner qqch à** to intend sthg for, to mean sthg for **2.** [vouer] **: destiner qqn à qqch/à faire qqch** [à un métier] to destine sb for sthg/to do sthg / [sort] to mark sb out for sthg/to do sthg.
◆ ***se destiner*** **vp : se destiner à** to intend to go into.

destituer [7] [dɛstitɥe] **vt** to dismiss.

destitution [dɛstitysjɔ̃] **nf** dismissal.

destructeur, ***trice*** [dɛstryktœr, tris] ■ **adj** destructive.
■ **nm, f** destroyer.

destruction [dɛstryksjɔ̃] **nf** destruction.

déstructuration [destryktyrasjɔ̃] **nf** breaking down.

déstructurer [3] [destryktyre] **vt** to break down.

désuet, ***ète*** [dezɥɛ, ɛt] **adj** [expression, coutume] obsolete / [style, tableau] outmoded.

désuétude [dezɥetyd] **nf : tomber en désuétude** [expression, coutume] to become obsolete / [style, tableau] to become outmoded.

désuni, ***e*** [dezyni] **adj** divided.

désunion [dezynjɔ̃] **nf** division, dissension.

désunir [32] [dezynir] **vt** [scinder] to divide, to separate / *fig* to divide.
◆ ***se désunir*** **vp** [athlète] to lose one's stride.

détachable [detaʃabl] **adj** detachable, removable.

détachage [detaʃaʒ] **nm** stain removal.

détachant, ***e*** [detaʃɑ̃, ɑ̃t] **adj** stain-removing.
◆ ***détachant*** **nm** stain remover.

détaché, ***e*** [detaʃe] **adj** detached ▸ **détaché à** *ou* **auprès de** on temporary assignment to, seconded to *UK*.

détachement [detaʃmɑ̃] **nm** **1.** [d'esprit] detachment **2.** [de fonctionnaire] temporary assignment, secondment *UK* **3.** MIL detachment.

détacher [3] [detaʃe] **vt** **1.** [enlever] **: détacher qqch (de)** [objet] to detach sthg (from) / *fig* to free sthg (from) ▸ **détacher une guirlande** to take down a garland ▸ **détacher une recette d'un magazine/un timbre d'un carnet** to tear a recipe out of a magazine/a stamp out of a book ▸ **coupon à détacher** tear-off coupon **2.** [nettoyer] to remove stains from, to clean ▸ **j'ai donné ton costume à détacher** I took your suit to the cleaner's **3.** [délier] to undo / [cheveux] to untie **4.** ADMIN **: détacher qqn auprès de** to send sb on temporary assignment to, to second sb to *UK* ▸ **je vais être détaché auprès du ministre** I will be sent on temporary assignment *ou* on secondment to the Ministry.
◆ ***se détacher*** **vp** **1.** [tomber] **: se détacher (de)** to come off **2.** [se défaire] to come undone **3.** [ressortir] **: se détacher sur** to stand out on **4.** [s'éloigner] **: se détacher de qqn** to drift apart from sb ▸ **je me suis détachée de ma famille/de l'art figuratif** I grew away from my family/from figurative art ▸ **il a eu du mal à se détacher d'elle** he found it hard to leave her behind.

détail [detaj] **nm** **1.** [précision] detail ▸ **faire quelques remarques de détail** to make a few minor comments ▸ **jusque dans les moindres détails** down to the smallest detail ▸ **pour plus de détails, écrivez à...** for further details, write to... **2.** [description] **: faire le détail de** to give a detailed breakdown *ou* description of **3.** COMM **: le détail** retail.
◆ ***au détail*** **loc adj & loc adv** retail ▸ **vendre qqch au détail** to sell sthg retail, to retail sthg ▸ **vous vendez le œufs au détail?** do you sell eggs separately?
◆ ***en détail*** **loc adv** in detail ▸ **raconter une histoire en détail** to tell a story in detail.

détaillant, ***e*** [detajɑ̃, ɑ̃t] ■ **adj** retail.
■ **nm, f** retailer.

détaillé, ***e*** [detaje] **adj** detailed.

détailler [3] [detaje] **vt** **1.** [expliquer] to give details of **2.** [vendre] to retail.

détaler [3] [detale] **vi** **1.** [personne] to clear out **2.** [animal] to bolt.

détartrant, ***e*** [detartrɑ̃, ɑ̃t] **adj** descaling.
◆ ***détartrant*** **nm** descaling agent.

détartrer [3] [detartre] **vt** to scale, to descale.

détaxe [detaks] **nf : détaxe (sur)** [suppression] removal of tax (from) / [réduction] reduction in tax (on).

détecter [4] [detɛkte] **vt** to detect.

détecteur, ***trice*** [detɛktœr, tris] **adj** detecting *(avant n)*, detector *(avant n)*.
◆ ***détecteur*** **nm** detector ▸ **détecteur de fumée** smoke detector.

détection [detɛksjɔ̃] **nf** detection / INFORM **: détection de virus** virus check.

détective [detɛktiv] **nm** detective ▸ **détective privé** private detective.

déteindre [81] [detɛ̃dr] ■ **vt** to fade.
■ **vi** to fade ▸ **déteindre sur** *fig* to rub off on ▸ **déteindre au lavage** to run (in the wash).

déteint, ***e*** [detɛ̃, ɛ̃t] **pp** ➤ ***déteindre***.

dételer [24] [detle] ■ **vt** **1.** [cheval] to unharness **2.** [wagon] to unhitch.
■ **vi** *fam fig* **: sans dételer** at a stretch.

détendre [73] [detɑ̃dr] **vt** **1.** [corde] to loosen, to slacken / *fig* to ease **2.** [personne] to relax.
◆ ***se détendre*** **vp** **1.** [se relâcher] to slacken / *fig* [situation] to ease / [atmosphère] to become more relaxed **2.** [se reposer] to relax.

détendu, ***e*** [detɑ̃dy] ■ **pp** ➤ ***détendre***.
■ **adj** **1.** [corde] loose, slack **2.** [personne] relaxed.

détenir [40] [detnir] **vt** **1.** [objet] to have, to hold **2.** [personne] to detain, to hold.

détente [detɑ̃t] **nf** **1.** [de ressort] release **2.** [d'une arme] trigger **3.** [repos] relaxation **4.** POLIT détente **5.** [d'athlète] thrust
▸▸ **être dur à la détente** to be slow on the uptake.

détenteur, ***trice*** [detɑ̃tœr, tris] **nm, f** [d'objet, de secret] possessor / [de prix, record] holder.

détention [detɑ̃sjɔ̃] **nf** **1.** [possession] possession **2.** [emprisonnement] detention ▸ **détention préventive** remand (in custody).

détenu, ***e*** [detny] ■ **pp** ➤ ***détenir***.
■ **adj** detained.
■ **nm, f** prisoner.

détergent, ***e*** [detɛrʒɑ̃, ɑ̃t] **adj** detergent *(avant n)*.
◆ ***détergent*** **nm** detergent.

détérioration [deterjɔrasjɔ̃] **nf** [de bâtiment] deterioration / [de situation] worsening.

détériorer [3] [deterjɔre] **vt** **1.** [abîmer] to damage **2.** [altérer] to ruin.
◆ ***se détériorer*** **vp** **1.** [bâtiment] to deteriorate / [situation] to worsen **2.** [s'altérer] to be spoiled.

déterminant, ***e*** [detɛrminɑ̃, ɑ̃t] **adj** decisive, determining.
◆ ***déterminant*** **nm** **1.** LING determiner **2.** MATH determinant.

détermination [detɛrminasjɔ̃] **nf** **1.** [définition] determining *(U)* **2.** [fixation] determination **3.** [résolution] determination, decision.

déterminé, ***e*** [detɛrmine] **adj** **1.** [quantité] given *(avant n)* **2.** [expression] determined.

déterminer [3] [detɛrmine] **vt** **1.** [préciser] to determine, to specify **2.** [provoquer] to bring about ▸ **déterminer qqn à faire qqch** to cause sb to do sthg.
◆ ***se déterminer*** **vp : se déterminer à faire qqch** to decide to do sthg.

déterminisme [determinism] **nm** determinism.

déterré, e [detere] **adj : avoir une mine de déterré** to look like death warmed up.

déterrer [4] [detere] **vt** to dig up.

détersif, ive [detersif, iv] **adj** detergent *(avant n)*.
◆ ***détersif*** **nm** detergent.

détestable [detestabl] **adj** dreadful.

détester [3] [deteste] **vt** to detest.

détiendrai, détiendras ➤ ***détenir***.

détonant, e [detɔnɑ̃, ɑ̃t] **adj** explosive.

détonateur [detɔnatœr] **nm** TECHNOL detonator / *fig* trigger.

détonation [detɔnasjɔ̃] **nf** detonation.

détoner [3] [detɔne] **vi** to detonate.

détonner [3] [detɔne] **vi** MUS to be out of tune / [couleur] to clash / [personne] to be out of place.

détour [detur] **nm 1.** [crochet] detour ▶ **faire un détour (par)** to make a detour (through) **2.** [méandre] bend ▶ **au détour du chemin** at the bend in the road ▶ **sans détour** *fig* directly.

détourné, e [deturne] **adj** [dévié] indirect / *fig* roundabout *(avant n)*.

détournement [deturnəmɑ̃] **nm** diversion, detour ▶ **détournement d'avion** hijacking ▶ **détournement de fonds** embezzlement ▶ **détournement de mineur** corruption of a minor.

détourner [3] [deturne] **vt 1.** [dévier - gén] to divert, to detour *US* / [- avion] to hijack **2.** [écarter] **: détourner qqn de** to distract sb from, to divert sb from **3.** [la tête, les yeux] to turn away **4.** [argent] to embezzle.
◆ ***se détourner*** **vp** to turn away ▶ **se détourner de** *fig* to move away from.

détracteur, trice [detraktœr, tris] **nm, f** detractor.

détraqué, e [detrake] *fam* ■ **adj 1.** [déréglé] on the blink **2.** [fou] nutty, loopy.
■ **nm, f** nutcase, nutter *UK*.

détraquer [3] [detrake] **vt** *fam* [dérégler] to break / *fig* to upset.
◆ ***se détraquer*** **vp** *fam* [se dérégler] to go wrong / *fig* to become unsettled.

détrempe [detrɑ̃p] **nf** ART tempera.

détremper [3] [detrɑ̃pe] **vt 1.** [sol] to soften **2.** [peinture] to thin.

détresse [detres] **nf** distress ▶ **en détresse** in distress.

détriment [detrimɑ̃] ◆ ***au détriment de*** **loc prép** to the detriment of.

détritus [detrity(s)] **nm** detritus.

détroit [detrwa] **nm** strait ▶ **le détroit de Bering** the Bering Strait ▶ **le détroit de Gibraltar** the Strait of Gibraltar.

détromper [3] [detrɔ̃pe] **vt** to disabuse.
◆ ***se détromper*** **vp** to disabuse o.s. ▶ **détrompez-vous!** think again!

détrôner [3] [detrone] **vt** [souverain] to dethrone / *fig* to oust.

détrousser [3] [detruse] **vt** *vieilli* to rob.

détruire [98] [detrɥir] **vt 1.** [démolir, éliminer] to destroy **2.** [massacrer] to wipe out **3.** *fig* [anéantir] to ruin.
◆ ***se détruire*** **vp** to destroy o.s.

détruisais, détruise ➤ ***détruire***.

détruit, e [detrɥi, it] **pp** ➤ ***détruire***.

dette [dɛt] **nf** debt ▶ **avoir des dettes** to have debts ▶ **dette extérieure** foreign *ou* external debt ▶ **dette publique** *ou* **de l'État** public debt ▶ **être criblé de dettes** to be up to your ears *ou* eyes in debt.

DEUG, Deug [dœg] (abr de ***diplôme d'études universitaires générales***) **nm** *university diploma taken after two years of humanities-oriented courses* ; voir aussi ***DEUST***.

deuil [dœj] **nm** [douleur, mort] bereavement / [vêtements, période] mourning *(U)* ▶ **en deuil** in mourning ▶ **porter le deuil** to be in *ou* wear mourning ▶ **faire son deuil de qqch** *fig* to wave sthg goodbye.

DEUST, Deust [dœst] (abr de ***diplôme d'études universitaires scientifiques et techniques***) **nm** *university diploma taken after two years of science courses* ; voir aussi ***DEUG***.

deux [dø] ■ **adj num inv** two ▶ **ses deux fils** his two sons, both his sons ▶ **tous les deux jours** every two days, every second day, every other day ▶ **en moins de deux** *fam fig* in no time at all, in two ticks *UK*.
■ **nm** two ▶ **les deux** both ▶ **par deux** in pairs ; voir aussi ***six***.

deuxième [døzjɛm] **adj num inv, nm & nmf** second ; voir aussi ***sixième***.

deuxièmement [døzjɛmmɑ̃] **adv** secondly.

deux-pièces [døpjɛs] **nm inv 1.** [appartement] two-room flat *UK* *ou* apartment *US* **2.** [bikini] two-piece (swimsuit).

deux-points [døpwɛ̃] **nm inv** colon.

deux-roues [døru] **nm inv** two-wheeled vehicle.

deux-temps [døtɑ̃] **nm inv** [mécanique] two-stroke (engine).

dévaler [3] [devale] ■ **vt** to run down.
■ **vi** to hurtle down.

dévaliser [3] [devalize] **vt** [cambrioler - maison] to ransack / [- personne] to rob / *fig* to strip bare.

dévalorisant, e [devalɔrizɑ̃, ɑ̃t] **adj** demeaning.

dévalorisation [devalɔrizasjɔ̃] **nf** depreciation.

dévaloriser [3] [devalɔrize] **vt 1.** [monnaie] to devalue **2.** [personne] to run *ou* put down.
◆ ***se dévaloriser*** **vp 1.** [monnaie] to fall in value **2.** *fig* [personne] to run *ou* put o.s. down.

dévaluation [devalɥasjɔ̃] **nf** devaluation.

dévaluer [7] [devalɥe] ■ **vt** to devalue.
■ **vi** to devalue.
◆ ***se dévaluer*** **vp** to devalue.

devancer [16] [dəvɑ̃se] **vt 1.** [précéder] to arrive before **2.** [surpasser] to be in front of **3.** [anticiper] to anticipate.

devant [dəvɑ̃] ■ **prép 1.** [en face de] in front of ▶ **il a déposé le paquet devant la porte** he left the parcel outside the door **2.** [en avant de] ahead of, in front of ▶ **aller**

droit devant soi to go straight ahead *ou* on ▶ **nous passerons devant lui pour lui montrer le chemin** we'll go ahead of him to show him the way **3.** [en présence de, face à] in the face of ▶ **pleurer devant tout le monde** [devant les gens présents] to cry in front of everyone / [en public] to cry in public ▶ **son attitude devant le malheur** his attitude in the face of *ou* to disaster.
■ **adv 1.** [en face] in front ▶ **tu peux te garer juste devant** you can park (right) in front **2.** [en avant] in front, ahead ▶ **elle est loin devant** she's a long way ahead ▶ **mettez les plus petits de la classe devant** put the shortest pupils at the *ou* in front.
■ **nm** front ▶ **prendre les devants** to make the first move, to take the initiative ▶ **sur le devant de la scène** *fig* in the limelight.
◆ ***de devant*** **loc adj** [pattes, roues] front *(avant n).*

devanture [dəvɑ̃tyr] **nf** shop *UK ou* store *US* window ▶ **à la devanture de** on display in.

dévastateur, trice [devastatœr, tris] **adj** devastating.

dévastation [devastasjɔ̃] **nf** devastation.

dévaster [3] [devaste] **vt** to devastate.

déveine [devɛn] **nf** *fam* bad luck.

développement [devlɔpmɑ̃] **nm 1.** [gén & ÉCON] development ▶ **développement durable** sustainable development ▶ **développement de nouveaux produits** new product development ▶ **une stratégie de développement de nouveaux produits** a new–product development strategy **2.** PHOTO developing **3.** [exposé] exposition.
◆ ***développements*** **nmpl** developments.

développer [3] [devlɔpe] **vt** to develop / [industrie, commerce] to expand / PHOTO to develop ▶ **faire développer des photos** to have some photos developed.
◆ ***se développer*** **vp 1.** [s'épanouir] to spread **2.** ÉCON to grow, to expand.

développeur [devlɔpœr] **nm** [INFORM - entreprise] software development *ou* design company / [- personne] software developer *ou* designer.

devenir [40] [dəvnir] **vi** to become ▶ **que devenez-vous?** *fig* how are you doing?

devenu, e [dəvny] **pp** ➤ ***devenir***.

dévergondé, e [devɛrgɔ̃de] ■ **adj** shameless, wild.
■ **nm, f** shameless person.

dévergonder [3] [devɛrgɔ̃de] ◆ ***se dévergonder*** **vp** to go to the bad, to get into bad ways.

déverrouiller [3] [devɛruje] **vt 1.** [porte] to unbolt **2.** [arme] to release the catch of.

déverser [3] [devɛrse] **vt 1.** [liquide] to pour out **2.** [ordures] to tip (out) **3.** [bombes] to unload, to drop **4.** *fig* [injures] to pour out.
◆ ***se déverser*** **vp : se déverser dans** to flow into.

déversoir [devɛrswar] **nm** overflow.

dévêtir [44] [devetir] **vt** *sout* to undress.
◆ ***se dévêtir*** **vp** *sout* to undress, to get undressed.

dévêtu, e [devety] **pp** ➤ ***dévêtir***.

déviant, e [devjɑ̃, ɑ̃t] **adj** deviant.

déviation [devjasjɔ̃] **nf 1.** [gén] deviation **2.** [d'itinéraire] diversion, detour.

dévider [3] [devide] **vt** [fil] to unwind.

deviendrai, deviendras ➤ ***devenir***.

devienne, devient ➤ ***devenir***.

dévier [9] [devje] ■ **vi : dévier de** to deviate from.
■ **vt** to divert, to detour *US*.

devin, devineresse [dəvɛ̃, dəvinrɛs] **nm, f** soothsayer ▶ **je ne suis pas devin!** I'm not psychic *ou* a mindreader!

deviner [3] [dəvine] **vt** to guess.
◆ ***se deviner*** **vp 1.** [aller de soi] to just come naturally **2.** [se voir] **: ça se devine facilement** that's easy to see.

devinette [dəvinɛt] **nf** riddle.

devis [dəvi] **nm** estimate ▶ **faire un devis** to (give an) estimate.

dévisager [17] [devizaʒe] **vt** to stare at.

devise [dəviz] **nf 1.** [formule] motto **2.** [monnaie] currency ▶ **devise forte/faible** hard/soft currency ▶ **devise flottante** floating currency.
◆ ***devises*** **nfpl** [argent] currency *(U)* ▶ **acheter des devises** to buy foreign currency.

deviser [3] [dəvize] **vi 1.** *sout* [parler] **: deviser de** *ou* **sur** to converse about **2.** *Suisse* [faire un devis] to estimate.

dévisser [3] [devise] ■ **vt** to unscrew.
■ **vi** [alpinisme] to fall (off).

de visu [devizy] **adv : constater qqch de visu** to see sthg with one's own eyes.

dévoiler [3] [devwale] **vt** to unveil / *fig* to reveal ▶ **dévoiler ses charmes** *euphém* to reveal all.

devoir [53] [dəvwar] ■ **nm 1.** [obligation] duty ▶ **faire son devoir** to do one's duty ▶ **je ne l'ai prévenu que par devoir** I warned him only because I thought it was my duty **2.** SCOL homework *(U)* ▶ **faire ses devoirs** to do one's homework ▶ **devoir de français** French essay ▶ **devoir sur table** (written) class test.
■ **vt 1.** [argent, respect] **: devoir qqch (à qqn)** to owe (sb) sthg ▶ **je ne demande que ce qui m'est dû** I'm only asking for what's due me
2. [être redevable de] **: devoir qqch à qqn** to owe sthg to sb ▶ **je lui dois d'être ici** it's thanks to him that I'm here ▶ **je te dois bien ça** that's the least I can do for you
3. [marque l'obligation] **: devoir faire qqch** to have to do sthg ▶ **je dois partir à l'heure ce soir** I have to *ou* must leave on time tonight ▶ **on ne doit pas fumer** smoking i[s] forbidden *ou* is not allowed ▶ **tu devrais faire attentio[n]** you should be *ou* ought to be careful ▶ **il n'aurait pas d[û] mentir** he shouldn't have lied, he ought not to have lied
4. [marque la probabilité] **: il doit faire chaud là-bas** [it] must be hot over there ▶ **il a dû oublier** he must hav[e] forgotten ▶ **une offre qui devrait les intéresser** an offe[r] which should interest them
5. [marque le futur, l'intention] **: devoir faire qqch** to b[e] (due) to do sthg, to be going to do sthg ▶ **elle doit arrive[r] à 6 heures** she's due to arrive at 6 o'clock ▶ **je dois voi[r] mes parents ce week-end** I'm seeing *ou* going to see m[y] parents this weekend
6. [être destiné à] **: il devait mourir trois ans plus ta[rd]** he was to die three years later ▶ **cela devait arriver** it ha[d] to happen, it was bound to happen.
◆ ***se devoir*** **vp : se devoir de faire qqch** to be dut[y] bound to do sthg ▶ **tu es grand, tu te dois de donn[er] l'exemple** you're a big boy now; it's your duty to set

good example ▸ **comme il se doit** as is proper ▸ **les époux se doivent fidélité** spouses *ou* husbands and wives must be faithful to each other.

dévolu**, **e [devɔly] **adj** *sout* **: dévolu à** allotted to.
◆ ***dévolu*** **nm : jeter son dévolu sur** to set one's sights on.

dévorer [3] [devɔre] **vt** to devour ▸ **être dévoré de** *fig* to be eaten up by *ou* with / [manger] **: être dévoré par les moustiques** to be eaten alive *ou* bitten to death by mosquitoes ▸ **dévorer qqn du regard** to stare hungrily at sb / [tenailler] to devour ▸ **être dévoré par la faim** to be ravenously hungry ▸ **être dévoré par l'envie** to be eaten up with envy.

dévot**, **e [devo, ɔt] ■ **adj** devout.
■ **nm, f** devout person.

dévotion [devɔsjɔ̃] **nf** devotion ▸ **avec dévotion** [prier] devoutly / [soigner, aimer] devotedly ▸ **faire ses dévotions** to perform one's devotions.

dévoué**, **e [devwe] **adj** devoted.

dévouement [devumɑ̃] **nm** devotion.

dévouer [6] [devwe] ◆ ***se dévouer*** **vp 1.** [se consacrer] **: se dévouer à** to devote o.s. to **2.** *fig* [se sacrifier] **: se dévouer pour qqch/pour faire qqch** to sacrifice o.s. for sthg/to do sthg.

dévoyé**, **e [devwaje] **adj & nm, f** delinquent.

dévoyer [13] [devwaje] *littéraire* **vt** to lead astray.
◆ ***se dévoyer*** **vp** to go astray.

devrai**, **devras ➤ ***devoir***.

dextérité [dɛksterite] **nf** dexterity, skill ▸ **avec dextérité** skilfully *UK*, skillfully *US*.

dézipper [3] [dezipe] **vt** INFORM [fichier] to unzip.

dg (abr écrite de ***décigramme***) dg.

DG (abr de ***directeur général***) **nm** GM.

DGE (abr de ***dotation globale d'équipement***) **nf** *state contribution to local government capital budget.*

DGF (abr de ***dotation globale de fonctionnement***) **nf** *state contribution to local government revenue budget.*

DGI (abr de ***Direction générale des impôts***) **nf** *central tax office.*

DGSE (abr de ***Direction générale de la sécurité extérieure***) **nf** *French intelligence and espionage service*, ≃ MI6 *UK*, ≃ CIA *US*.

diabète [djabɛt] **nm** diabetes *(U)*.

diabétique [djabetik] **nmf & adj** diabetic.

diable [djabl] **nm** devil ▸ **au diable** [loin] miles from anywhere ▸ **habiter au diable vauvert** to live miles away ▸ **avoir le diable au corps** to be a real handful ▸ **c'est bien le diable si je ne récupère pas mon argent!** I'll be damned if I don't get my money back! ▸ **envoyer qqn au diable** to send sb packing ▸ **(que) le diable m'emporte si je mens!** the devil take me if I'm lying! ▸ **tirer le diable par la queue** to live from hand to mouth ▸ **un mauvais diable** a bad sort ▸ **un pauvre diable** a wretched man, a poor wretch.
◆ ***du diable**, **de tous les diables*** **loc adj : faire un boucan de tous les diables** *fam* to kick up a hell of a racket ▸ **il a eu un mal de tous les diables pour finir à temps** he had a devil of a job to finish in time.

diablement [djabləmɑ̃] **adv** *vieilli* horribly.

diablesse [djablɛs] **nf** she-devil / [femme turbulente] shrew, vixen.

diablotin [djablɔtɛ̃] **nm** imp.

diabolique [djabɔlik] **adj** diabolical.

diabolo [djabɔlo] **nm 1.** [jouet] diabolo **2.** [boisson] fruit cordial and lemonade ▸ **diabolo menthe** mint (cordial) and lemonade.

diacre [djakr] **nm** RELIG deacon.

diadème [djadɛm] **nm** diadem.

diagnostic [djagnɔstik] **nm 1.** MÉD diagnosis ▸ **diagnostic prenatal** antenatal diagnosis **2.** FIN **: diagnostic financier** financial healthcheck, diagnostic audit.

diagnostiquer [3] [djagnɔstike] **vt** *fig* & MÉD to diagnose.

diagonale [djagɔnal] **nf** diagonal ▸ **en diagonale** diagonally ▸ **lire en diagonale** *fig* to skim.

diagramme [djagram] **nm** graph ▸ **diagramme à bâtons** bar graph *ou* chart *UK*.

dialecte [djalɛkt] **nm** dialect.

dialectique [djalɛktik] **nf & adj** dialectic.

dialogue [djalɔg] **nm** discussion ▸ **c'est un dialogue de sourds** they're/you're *etc* never going to agree ▸ **dialogue en direct** Internet Relay Chat, IRC.
◆ ***dialogues*** **nmpl** dialogue *(U)*, dialog *(U)* *US*.

dialoguer [3] [djalɔge] **vi 1.** [converser] to converse **2.** INFORM to interact.

dialyse [djaliz] **nf** dialysis.

diamant [djamɑ̃] **nm** [pierre] diamond.

diamétralement [diametralmɑ̃] **adv : diamétralement opposé** diametrically opposed.

diamètre [djamɛtr] **nm** diameter.

diantre [djɑ̃tr] **interj** *littéraire* & *vieilli* by Jove!

diapason [djapazɔ̃] **nm** [instrument] tuning fork ▸ **se mettre au diapason** *fig* to get on the same wavelength.

diaphane [djafan] **adj** [peau, teint] translucent / [tissu] diaphanous.

diaphragme [djafragm] **nm** diaphragm.

diapositive [djapozitiv] **nf** slide.

diarrhée [djare] **nf** diarrhoea *UK*, diarrhea *US*.

diatribe [djatrib] **nf** *sout* diatribe.

dichotomie [dikɔtɔmi] **nf** dichotomy.

dico [diko] **nm** *fam* dictionary.

Dictaphone® [diktafɔn] **nm** Dictaphone®.

dictateur [diktatœr] **nm** dictator.

dictatorial, e, aux [diktatɔrjal, o] **adj** dictatorial.

dictature [diktatyr] **nf** dictatorship.

dictée [dikte] **nf** dictation.

dicter [3] [dikte] **vt** to dictate.

diction [diksjɔ̃] **nf** diction.

dictionnaire [diksjɔnɛr] **nm** dictionary ▸ **dictionnaire bilingue/encyclopédique** bilingual/encyclopedic dictionary.

dicton [diktɔ̃] **nm** saying, dictum.

didactique [didaktik] **adj** didactic.

dièse [djɛz] ■ **adj** sharp ▸ **do/fa dièse** C/F sharp.
■ **nm** sharp / [symbole] hash *UK*, pound sign *US* ▸ **appuyez sur la touche dièse** press the hash key *UK ou* pound key *US*.

diesel [djezel] **adj inv** diesel ▸ **moteur diesel** diesel engine.

diète [djɛt] **nf** diet ▸ **être à la diète** [régime] to be on a diet / [jeûne] to be fasting.

diététicien, enne [djetetisjɛ̃, ɛn] **nm, f** dietician.

diététique [djetetik] ■ **nf** dietetics *(U)*.
■ **adj** [considération, raison] dietary / [produit, magasin] health *(avant n)*.

dieu, x [djø] **nm** god ▸ **comme un dieu** *fig* & *hum* divinely ▸ **jurer ses grands dieux** to swear to God.
◆ ***Dieu*** **nm** God ▸ **bon Dieu!** *fam* for God's sake!, for Pete's sake! ▸ **mon Dieu!** my God! ▸ **Dieu sait où/comment** God knows where/how ▸ **Dieu sait combien il l'a aimée!** God knows he loved her! ▸ **Dieu vous bénisse/entende!** may God bless/hear you! ▸ **Dieu merci!** thank God! ▸ **le bon Dieu** the good Lord ▸ **on lui donnerait le bon Dieu sans confession** he looks as if butter wouldn't melt in his mouth.

diffamation [difamasjɔ̃] **nf** [écrite] libel / [orale] slander ▸ **attaquer qqn en diffamation** to sue sb for slander/libel.

diffamatoire [difamatwar] **adj** defamatory ▸ **parler/agir de façon diffamatoire** to speak/act slanderously.

différant [diferɑ̃] **pp** ➤ ***différer***.

différé, e [difere] **adj** recorded.
◆ ***différé*** **nm : en différé** TV recorded / INFORM off-line.

différemment [diferamɑ̃] **adv** differently.

différence [diferɑ̃s] **nf 1.** [distinction] difference, dissimilarity ▸ **faire la différence entre** to make the distinction between, to distinguish between ▸ **faire des différences entre ses enfants** to treat one's children differently from each other ▸ **j'ai accepté son offre à cette différence près que, cette fois, je sais ce qui m'attend** I accepted his offer but this time I know what to expect **2.** [écart] difference ▸ **différence d'âge** age difference *ou* gap **3.** [particularité] **: revendiquer sa différence** to be proud to be different.

différencier [9] [diferɑ̃sje] **vt : différencier qqch de qqch** to differentiate sthg from sthg.
◆ ***se différencier*** **vp : se différencier de** to be different from.

différend [diferɑ̃] **nm** [désaccord] difference of opinion ▸ **avoir un différend avec** to have a difference of opinion with.

différent, e [diferɑ̃, ɑ̃t] **adj : différent (de)** different (from).

différentiel, elle [diferɑ̃sjɛl] **adj** differential.

différer [18] [difere] ■ **vt** [retarder] to postpone.
■ **vi : différer de** to differ from, to be different from ▸ **différer (selon)** to vary (according to).

difficile [difisil] ■ **adj** difficult.
■ **nm : faire le/la difficile** to be hard to please.

difficilement [difisilmɑ̃] **adv** with difficulty.

difficulté [difikylte] **nf 1.** [complexité, peine] difficulty **2.** [obstacle] problem ▸ **en difficulté** in difficulty.

difforme [difɔrm] **adj** deformed.

difformité [difɔrmite] **nf** deformity.

diffraction [difraksjɔ̃] **nf** diffraction.

diffus, e [dify, yz] **adj** diffused / *fig* vague.

diffuser [3] [difyze] **vt 1.** [lumière] to diffuse **2.** [émission] to broadcast **3.** [livres] to distribute **4.** INFORM **: diffuser sur (l')Internet** to webcast.

diffuseur [difyzœr] **nm 1.** [appareil] diffuser **2.** [de livres] distributor.

diffusion [difyzjɔ̃] **nf 1.** [d'émission, d'onde] broadcast ▸ **diffusion hertzienne** *ou* **terrestre** terrestrial television ▸ **diffusion numérique** digital broadcasting **2.** [de livres] distribution.

digérer [18] [diʒere] ■ **vi** to digest.
■ **vt 1.** [repas, connaissance] to digest **2.** *fam fig* [désagrément] to put up with.

digeste [diʒɛst] **adj** (easily) digestible.

digestible [diʒɛstibl] **adj** digestible.

digestif, ive [diʒɛstif, iv] **adj** digestive.
◆ ***digestif*** **nm** liqueur.

digestion [diʒɛstjɔ̃] **nf** digestion.

digital, e, aux [diʒital, o] **adj 1.** *fam* TECHNOL digital **2.** ➤ ***empreinte***.
◆ ***digitale*** **nf** digitalis.

digne [diɲ] **adj 1.** [honorable] dignified **2.** [méritant] **: digne de** worthy of ▸ **digne de foi** trustworthy.

dignement [diɲmɑ̃] **adv** with dignity.

dignitaire [diɲitɛr] **nm** dignitary ▸ **haut dignitaire** mandarin.

dignité [diɲite] **nf** dignity ▸ **se draper dans sa dignité** to stand on one's dignity.

digression [digresjɔ̃] **nf** digression.

digue [dig] **nf** dike.

diktat [diktat] **nm** diktat.

dilapider [3] [dilapide] **vt** to squander.

dilatation [dilatasjɔ̃] **nf** dilation.

dilater [3] [dilate] **vt** to dilate.
◆ ***se dilater*** **vp** to expand, to dilate.

dilatoire [dilatwar] **adj** delaying *(avant n)*.

dilemme [dilɛm] **nm** **1.** [gén] dilemma **2.** COMM [entreprise, produit] problem child.

dilettante [diletɑ̃t] **nmf** dilettante ▸ **faire qqch en dilettante** to dabble in sthg.

diligence [diliʒɑ̃s] **nf** *sout* & HIST diligence.

diligent, e [diliʒɑ̃, ɑ̃t] **adj** *vieilli* diligent.

diluant [dilɥɑ̃] **nm** thinner.

diluer [7] [dilɥe] **vt** to dilute.

diluvien, enne [dilyvjɛ̃, ɛn] **adj** torrential.

dimanche [dimɑ̃ʃ] **nm** Sunday ▸ **dimanche des Rameaux** Palm Sunday ; voir aussi ***samedi***.

dimension [dimɑ̃sjɔ̃] **nf** **1.** [mesure] dimension **2.** [taille] dimensions *pl*, size **3.** *fig* [importance] magnitude ▸ **à la dimension de** equal to.
◆ ***à deux dimensions*** **loc adj** two-dimensional.
◆ ***à trois dimensions*** **loc adj** three-dimensional.

diminué, e [diminɥe] **adj** diminished.

diminuer [7] [diminɥe] ■ **vt** [réduire] to diminish, to reduce.
■ **vi** [intensité] to diminish, to decrease.
◆ ***se diminuer*** **vp** to put o.s. down.

diminutif, ive [diminytif, iv] **adj** diminutive.
◆ ***diminutif*** **nm** diminutive.

diminution [diminysjɔ̃] **nf** diminution.

DIN, Din [din] (abr écrite de ***Deutsche Industrie Norm***) DIN.

dinde [dɛ̃d] **nf** **1.** [animal] turkey **2.** *péj* [femme] stupid woman.

dindon [dɛ̃dɔ̃] **nm** turkey ▸ **être le dindon de la farce** *fig* to be made a fool of.

dîner [3] [dine] ■ **vi** to dine.
■ **nm** dinner ▸ **dîner d'affaires/aux chandelles** business/candlelit dinner.

dînette [dinɛt] **nf** doll's tea party ▸ **faire la dînette** to have a snack ▸ **jouer à la dînette** to have a doll's tea party.

dingue [dɛ̃g] *fam* ■ **adj** **1.** [personne] crazy **2.** [histoire] incredible.
■ **nmf** loony.

dinosaure [dinozɔr] **nm** dinosaur.

diocèse [djɔsɛz] **nm** diocese.

diode [djɔd] **nf** diode.

dioptrie [djɔptri] **nf** dioptre *UK*, diopter *US*.

dioxine [diɔksin] **nf** dioxin.

diphasé, e [difaze] **adj** two-phase.

diphtérie [difteri] **nf** diphtheria.

diphtongue [diftɔ̃g] **nf** diphthong.

diplomate [diplɔmat] ■ **nmf** [ambassadeur] diplomat.
■ **nm** CULIN diplomat pudding.
■ **adj** diplomatic.

diplomatie [diplɔmasi] **nf** diplomacy.

diplomatique [diplɔmatik] **adj** diplomatic.

diplôme [diplom] **nm** diploma.

diplômé, e [diplome] ■ **adj : être diplômé de/en** to be a graduate of/in.
■ **nm, f** graduate.

dire [102] [dir] **vt : dire qqch (à qqn)** [parole] to say sthg (to sb) / [vérité, mensonge, secret] to tell (sb) sthg ▸ **dire quelque chose : son visage me dit quelque chose** I've seen her face before, her face seems familiar ▸ **dire à qqn de faire qqch** to tell sb to do sthg ▸ **il m'a dit d'arrêter** he told me to stop ▸ **il m'a dit que...** he told me (that)... ▸ **cela va sans dire** that goes without saying ▸ **c'est vite dit** *fam* that's easy (for you/him *etc*) to say ▸ **c'est beaucoup dire** that's saying a lot ▸ **elle est vraiment difficile, et ce n'est pas peu dire** she's very difficult - and I mean difficult ▸ **comment dire** *ou* **dirais-je?** how shall I put it *ou* say? ▸ **en dire long** *fig* to speak volumes ▸ **entre nous soit dit** between you and me ▸ **il n'a rien trouvé à dire sur la qualité** he had no criticisms to make about the quality ▸ **je ne te/vous le fais pas dire** how right you are, I couldn't have put it better myself ▸ **je te l'avais bien dit** I told you so ▸ **la ville proprement dite** the actual town ▸ **dire du bien/du mal (de)** to speak well/ill (of) ▸ **que dirais-tu de...?** what would you say to...? ▸ **dire de : que dis-tu de ma perruque?** what do you think of *ou* how do you like my wig? ▸ **qu'en dis-tu?** what do you think (of it)? ▸ **on dit que...** they say (that)... ▸ **on dirait que...** it looks as if... ▸ **on dirait de la soie** it looks like silk, you'd think it was silk ▸ **et dire que je n'étais pas là!** and to think I wasn't there! ▸ **ça ne me dit rien** [pas envie] I don't feel like it, I don't fancy that *UK* / [jamais entendu] I've never heard of it ▸ **si (l')on peut dire** in a way, so to speak.
◆ ***se dire*** ■ **vp** **1.** [penser] to think (to o.s.) **2.** [s'employer] **: ça ne se dit pas** [par décence] you mustn't say that / [par usage] people don't say that, nobody says that ▸ **nous nous disions tout** we had no secrets from each other **3.** [se traduire] **: 'chat' se dit 'gato' en espagnol** the Spanish for 'cat' is 'gato'.
■ **vpt** [penser] to think (to o.s.), to say to o.s. ▸ **maintenant, je me dis que j'aurais dû accepter** now I think I should have accepted.
◆ ***au dire de*** **loc prép** according to.
◆ ***cela dit*** **loc adv** having said that.
◆ ***dis donc*** **loc adv** *fam* so / [au fait] by the way / [à qqn qui exagère] look here!
◆ ***pour ainsi dire*** **loc adv** so to speak.
◆ ***à vrai dire*** **loc adv** to tell the truth.

direct, e [dirɛkt] **adj** direct.
◆ ***direct*** **nm** **1.** [boxe] jab ▸ **un direct du gauche** a straight left **2.** [train] nonstop train / [avion] non stop plane ▸ **un vol direct Paris-New York** a direct *ou* non stop flight from Paris to New York **3.** RADIO & TV **: le direct** live transmission *(U)* ▸ **en direct** live.

directement [dirɛktəmɑ̃] **adv** **1.** [tout droit] straight **2.** [franchement] **: entrer directement dans le sujet** to broach a subject immediately **3.** [sans intermédiaire] direct ▸ **adresse-toi directement au patron** go straight to the boss **4.** [personnellement] **: cela ne vous concerne pas directement** this doesn't affect you personally *ou* directly ▸ **je me sens directement visé** I feel singled out *ou* personally targeted.

directeur, trice [dirɛktœr, tris] ■ **adj** **1.** [dirigeant] leading *(avant n)* ▸ **comité directeur** steering committee **2.** [central] guiding *(avant n)*.
■ **nm, f** director, manager ▸ **directeur d'agence** [dans une banque] bank manager ▸ **directeur artistique** artistic director ▸ **directeur commercial** sales director *ou* manager ▸ **directeur de la communication** director of communications ▸ **directeur d'école** headteacher *UK*, headmaster (f headmistress) *UK*, principal *US* ▸ **directeur général** general manager, managing director *UK*, chief executive officer *US* ▸ **directeur du marketing** marketing director *ou* manager ▸ **directeur du personnel** personnel manager ▸ **directeur de produit** product manager ▸ **directeur de prison** prison governor *UK ou* warden *US* ▸ **directeur des ressources humaines** human resources manager ▸ **directeur de thèse** UNIV thesis supervisor ▸ **directeur des ventes** sales manager.

direction [dirɛksjɔ̃] **nf** **1.** [gestion, ensemble des cadres] management ▸ **prendre la direction de** [société, usine] to take over the running *ou* management of / [journal] to take over the editorship of ▸ **sous la direction de** under the management of ▸ **orchestre (placé) sous la direction de** orchestra conducted by
2. [orientation] direction ▸ **en *ou* dans la direction de** in the direction of ▸ **'toutes directions'** 'all routes' ▸ **jeter un regard en direction de qqn** to cast a glance at *ou* towards sb ▸ **prenez la direction Nation** [dans le métro] take the Nation line ▸ **vous allez dans quelle direction?** which way are you going?, where are you heading for?
3. AUTO steering ▸ **direction assistée** power steering
4. CINÉ, THÉÂTRE & TV **: direction (d'acteurs)** directing, direction.

directive [dirɛktiv] **nf** directive.

directorial, e, aux [dirɛktɔrjal, o] **adj** managerial.

directrice ➤ ***directeur***.

dirigeable [diriʒabl] **nm : (ballon) dirigeable** airship.

dirigeant, e [diriʒɑ̃, ɑ̃t] ■ **adj** ruling *(avant n)*.
■ **nm, f** [de pays] leader / [d'entreprise] manager.

diriger [17] [diriʒe] **vt** **1.** [mener - entreprise] to run, to manage / [- orchestre] to conduct / [- film, acteurs] to direct / [- recherches, projet] to supervise ▸ **mal diriger une société** to mismanage a company **2.** [conduire orienter] to steer ▸ **diriger qqn vers la sortie** to direct sb to the exit ▸ **diriger un élève vers un cursus littéraire** to guide *ou* to steer a student towards an arts course **3.** [pointer] **: diriger qqch sur** to aim sthg at ▸ **diriger un canon vers *ou* sur une cible** to aim *ou* to level *ou* to point a cannon at a target ▸ **diriger qqch vers** to aim sthg towards *UK ou* toward *US* ▸ **diriger ses pas vers** *litt* & *fig* to head for ▸ **diriger son regard vers qqn** to look in the direction of sb.
◆ ***se diriger*** **vp : se diriger vers** to go towards *UK ou* toward *US*, to head towards *UK ou* toward *US* ▸ **se diriger vers la sortie** to make one's way to the exit ▸ **nous nous dirigeons vers le conflit armé** *fig* we're headed for armed conflict.

dirigisme [diriʒism] **nm** interventionism.

disais, disions ➤ ***dire***.

discal, e, aux [diskal, o] ➤ ***hernie***.

discernement [disɛrnəmɑ̃] **nm** **1.** [jugement] discernment ▸ **il a agi avec discernement** he showed (good) judgement in what he did **2.** *sout* [distinction] distinction.

discerner [3] [disɛrne] **vt** **1.** [distinguer] **: discerner qqch de** to distinguish sthg from **2.** [deviner] to discern.

disciple [disipl] **nmf** disciple.

disciplinaire [disiplinɛr] **adj** disciplinary ▸ **mesure disciplinaire** disciplinary measure.

discipline [disiplin] **nf** discipline ▸ **discipline de fer** iron rule.

discipliné, e [disipline] **adj** disciplined.

discipliner [3] [discipline] **vt** [personne] to discipline / [cheveux] to control.

disc-jockey [diskʒɔkɛ] (**pl disc-jockeys**) **nm** disc jockey.

disco [disko] ■ **adj inv** disco *(avant n)*.
■ **nm** disco (music).

discographie [diskɔgrafi] **nf** discography.

discontinu, e [diskɔ̃tiny] **adj** [ligne] broken / [bruit, effort] intermittent.

discontinuer [7] [diskɔ̃tinɥe] **vi : sans discontinuer** without interruption.

discordance [diskɔrdɑ̃s] **nf** discrepancy.

discordant, e [diskɔrdɑ̃, ɑ̃t] **adj** discordant.

discorde [diskɔrd] **nf** discord.

discothèque [diskɔtɛk] **nf** **1.** [boîte de nuit] night club **2.** [de prêt] record library.

discount [disk(a)unt] **nm** discount.

discourir [45] [diskurir] **vi** to talk at length ▸ **discourir sur** to hold forth on.

discours [diskur] **nm** **1.** [allocution] speech ▸ **faire un discours** to make a speech ▸ **discours inaugural** POLIT inaugural address *ou* speech *US* **2.** LING **: discours direct/indirect** direct/indirect speech *UK ou* discourse *US*.

discouru, e [diskury] **pp** ➤ ***discourir***.

discrédit [diskredi] **nm** discredit, disrepute ▸ **jeter le discrédit sur** to bring disgrace on.

discréditer [3] [diskredite] **vt** to discredit.
◆ ***se discréditer*** **vp** to discredit o.s.

discret, ète [diskrɛ, ɛt] **adj** [gén] discreet / [réservé] reserved.

discrètement [diskrɛtmɑ̃] **adv** discreetly.

discrétion [diskresjɔ̃] **nf** **1.** [réserve, tact, silence] discretion **2.** [sobriété] sobriety, simplicity ▸ **avec discrétion** discreetly.
◆ ***à discrétion*** ■ **loc adj** unlimited.
■ **loc adv** as much as you want.

discrétionnaire [diskresjɔnɛr] **adj** discretionary.

discrimination [diskriminasjɔ̃] **nf** discriminatio ▸ **sans discrimination** indiscriminately.

discriminatoire [diskriminatwar] **adj** discriminatory

disculper [3] [diskylpe] **vt** to exonerate.
◆ ***se disculper*** **vp** to exonerate o.s.

discussion [diskysjɔ̃] **nf** **1.** [conversation, examen] discussion **2.** [contestation, altercation] argument ▸ **sans discussion** without argument.

discutable [diskytabl] **adj** **1.** [contestable] questionable **2.** [douteux] doubtful, questionable.

discutailler [3] [diskytaje] **vi** *fam péj* to argue over trivialities *ou* details.

discuter [3] [diskyte] ■ **vt** **1.** [débattre] **: discuter (de) qqch** to discuss sthg **2.** [contester] to dispute.
■ **vi** **1.** [parlementer] to discuss **2.** [converser] to talk **3.** [contester] to argue.
◆ ***se discuter*** **vp** to be questionable *ou* debatable.

disert, e [dizɛr, ɛrt] **adj** *littéraire* articulate.

disette [dizɛt] **nf** *sout* [famine] famine / *fig* [manque] shortage.

diseur, euse [dizœr, øz] **nm, f : diseur de bonne aventure** fortune-teller.

disgrâce [disgras] **nf** disgrace.

disgracieux, euse [disgrasjø, øz] **adj** **1.** [sans grâce] awkward, graceless **2.** [laid] plain.

disjoindre [82] [disʒwɛ̃dr] **vt** [planches, tuiles] to take apart / *fig* to separate, to distinguish.
◆ ***se disjoindre*** **vp** to come apart.

disjoint, e [disʒwɛ̃, ɛ̃t] **pp** ➤ ***disjoindre***.

disjoncter [disʒɔ̃kte] **vi** **1.** ÉLECTR to short-circuit **2.** *fam* [perdre la tête] to flip, to crack up.

disjoncteur [disʒɔ̃ktœr] **nm** trip switch, circuit breaker.

dislocation [dislɔkasjɔ̃] **nf** MÉD dislocation.

disloquer [3] [dislɔke] **vt** **1.** MÉD to dislocate **2.** [machine, empire] to dismantle.
◆ ***se disloquer*** **vp** [machine] to fall apart *ou* to pieces / *fig* [empire] to break up.

disparaissais, disparaissions ➤ ***disparaître***.

disparaître [91] [disparɛtr] **vi** **1.** [gén] to disappear, to vanish ▸ **disparais!** get lost! ▸ **faire disparaître** [personne] to get rid of / [obstacle] to remove **2.** [mourir] to die.

disparate [disparat] **adj** [éléments] disparate / [couleurs, mobilier] badly matched.

disparité [disparite] **nf** **1.** [écart] disparity **2.** [différence - d'éléments] disparity / [- de couleurs] mismatch.

disparition [disparisjɔ̃] **nf** **1.** [gén] disappearance / [d'espèce] extinction ▸ **en voie de disparition** endangered **2.** [mort] passing.

disparu, e [dispary] ■ **pp** ➤ ***disparaître***.
■ **nm, f** dead person, deceased.

dispatcher [3] [dispatʃe] **vt** to dispatch, to despatch.

dispendieux, euse [dispɑ̃djø, øz] **adj** *sout* expensive.

dispensaire [dispɑ̃sɛr] **nm** community clinic *UK*, free clinic *US*.

dispense [dispɑ̃s] **nf** **1.** [exemption] exemption ▸ **dispense d'âge** special dispensation *(for people under or over the age limit)* **2.** [certificat] certificate of exemption.

dispenser [3] [dispɑ̃se] **vt** **1.** [distribuer] to dispense **2.** [exempter] **: dispenser qqn de qqch** [corvée] to excuse sb sthg, to let sb off sthg ▸ **je te dispense de tes réflexions!** *fig* spare us the comments!, keep your comments to yourself!
◆ ***se dispenser*** **vp : se dispenser de qqch/de faire qqch** to get out of sthg/of doing sthg.

disperser [3] [dispɛrse] **vt** to scatter (around) / [collection, brume, foule] to break up / *fig* [efforts, forces] to dissipate, to waste.
◆ ***se disperser*** **vp** **1.** [feuilles, cendres] to scatter / [brume] to break up, to clear / [foule] to break up, to disperse **2.** [personne] to take on too much at once, to spread o.s. too thin.

dispersion [dispɛrsjɔ̃] **nf** scattering / [de collection, brume, foule] breaking up / *fig* [d'efforts, de forces] waste, squandering.

disponibilité [disponibilite] **nf** **1.** [de choses] availability **2.** [de fonctionnaire] leave of absence ▸ **en disponibilité** on leave of absence **3.** [d'esprit] alertness, receptiveness.
◆ ***disponibilités*** **nfpl** available funds, liquid assets.

disponible [disponibl] **adj** **1.** [place, personne] available, free **2.** [fonctionnaire] on leave of absence.

dispos, e [dispo, oz] **adj** fresh, full of energy.

disposé, e [dispoze] **adj : être disposé à faire qqch** to be prepared *ou* willing to do sthg ▸ **être bien disposé envers qqn** to be well-disposed towards *UK* *ou* toward *US* sb.

disposer [3] [dispoze] ■ **vt** **1.** [arranger] to arrange **2.** [inciter] **: disposer qqn à faire qqch** to lead *ou* move sb to do sthg.
■ **vi : disposer de** [moyens, argent] to have available (to one), to have at one's disposal / [chose] to have the use of / [temps] to have free *ou* available ▸ **vous pouvez disposer** you may leave *ou* go.
◆ ***se disposer*** **vp : se disposer à qqch/à faire qqch** *sout* to prepare for sthg/to do sthg.

dispositif [dispozitif] **nm** [mécanisme] device, mechanism ▸ **dispositif antibuée** demister *UK*, defogger *US* ▸ **dispositif antiparasite** suppressor ▸ **dispositif de sûreté** safety device.

disposition [dispozisjɔ̃] **nf** **1.** [arrangement] arrangement **2.** [disponibilité] **: à la disposition de** at the disposal of, available to.
◆ ***dispositions*** **nfpl** **1.** [mesures] arrangements, measures **2.** DR provisions **3.** [dons] **: avoir des dispositions pour** to have a gift for.

disproportion [disprɔpɔrsjɔ̃] **nf** disproportion.

disproportionné, e [disprɔpɔrsjɔne] **adj** out of proportion.

dispute [dispyt] **nf** argument, quarrel.

disputer [3] [dispyte] **vt 1.** [SPORT - course] to run / [- match] to play **2.** [lutter pour] to fight for.
◆ ***se disputer*** **vp 1.** [se quereller] to quarrel, to fight **2.** SPORT to be played **3.** [lutter pour] to fight over *ou* for.

disquaire [diskɛr] **nm** record dealer.

disqualification [diskalifikasjɔ̃] **nf** disqualification.

disqualifier [9] [diskalifje] **vt** to disqualify.

disque [disk] **nm 1.** MUS record / [vidéo] videodisc *UK ou* videodisk *US* ▸ **disque compact** *ou* **laser** compact disc **2.** ANAT disc *UK*, disk *US* **3.** INFORM disk ▸ **disque dur** hard disk **4.** SPORT discus.
◆ ***disque de stationnement*** **nm** parking disc *UK ou* permit *US*.

disquette [diskɛt] **nf** diskette, floppy disk ▸ **disquette haute/double densité** high/double density disk ▸ **disquette système** system diskette.

dissection [disɛksjɔ̃] **nf** dissection.

dissemblable [disɑ̃blabl] **adj** dissimilar.

dissémination [diseminasjɔ̃] **nf 1.** [dispersion] scattering, spreading (out) / *fig* dissemination, spreading **2.** [répartition] scattering.

disséminer [3] [disemine] **vt** [graines, maisons] to scatter, to spread (out) / *fig* [idées] to disseminate, to spread.

dissension [disɑ̃sjɔ̃] **nf** dissent.

disséquer [18] [diseke] **vt** *litt* & *fig* to dissect.

dissertation [disɛrtasjɔ̃] **nf** essay.

disserter [3] [disɛrte] **vi : disserter sur** [à l'écrit] to write on / [à l'oral] to speak on.

dissidence [disidɑ̃s] **nf** dissent, dissidence.

dissident, e [disidɑ̃, ɑ̃t] **adj** & **nm, f** dissident.

dissimulateur, trice [disimylatœr, tris] ■ **adj** dissembling.
■ **nm, f** dissembler.

dissimulation [disimylasjɔ̃] **nf 1.** [hypocrisie] duplicity **2.** [de la vérité] concealment.

dissimulé, e [disimyle] **adj** [hypocrite] dissembling, duplicitous.

dissimuler [3] [disimyle] **vt** to conceal.
◆ ***se dissimuler*** **vp 1.** [se cacher] to conceal o.s., to hide **2.** [refuser de voir] **: se dissimuler qqch** to close one's eyes to sthg.

dissipation [disipasjɔ̃] **nf 1.** [dispersion] dispersal, breaking up / *fig* [de malentendu] clearing up / [de craintes] dispelling **2.** [indiscipline] indiscipline, misbehaviour *UK*, misbehavior *US* **3.** [dilapidation] squandering **4.** [débauche] dissipation.

dissipé, e [disipe] **adj 1.** [turbulent] unruly, badly behaved **2.** [frivole] dissipated, dissolute.

dissiper [3] [disipe] **vt 1.** [chasser] to break up, to clear / *fig* to dispel **2.** [dilapider, gâcher] to squander **3.** [distraire] to lead astray.
◆ ***se dissiper*** **vp 1.** [brouillard, fumée] to clear **2.** [élève] to misbehave **3.** *fig* [malaise, fatigue] to go away / [doute] to be dispelled.

dissocier [9] [disɔsje] **vt 1.** [séparer] to separate, to distinguish **2.** CHIM to dissociate.

dissolu, e [disɔly] **adj** dissolute.

dissolution [disɔlysjɔ̃] **nf 1.** DR dissolution **2.** [mélange] dissolving **3.** *sout* [débauche] dissipation.

dissolvais, dissolvions ➤ ***dissoudre***.

dissolvant, e [disɔlvɑ̃, ɑ̃t] **adj** solvent.
◆ ***dissolvant*** **nm** [solvant] solvent / [pour vernis à ongles] nail polish *ou* varnish *UK* remover.

dissonance [disɔnɑ̃s] **nf** dissonance / *fig* clash, discord.

dissoudre [87] [disudr] **vt : (faire) dissoudre** to dissolve.
◆ ***se dissoudre*** **vp 1.** [substance] to dissolve **2.** DR to be dissolved.

dissous, oute [disu, ut] **pp** ➤ ***dissoudre***.

dissuader [3] [disɥade] **vt** to dissuade.

dissuasif, ive [disɥazif, iv] **adj** deterrent.

dissuasion [disɥazjɔ̃] **nf** dissuasion ▸ **force de dissuasion** deterrent (effect).

dissymétrique [disimetrik] **adj** dissymmetrical.

distance [distɑ̃s] **nf 1.** [éloignement] distance ▸ **à distance** at a distance / [télécommander] by remote control ▸ **à une distance de 300 mètres** 300 metres away ▸ **se tenir à distance** to keep one's distance ▸ **tenir qqn à distance** to keep sb at a distance *ou* at arm's length ▸ **garder ses distances** to keep one's distance ▸ **prendre ses distances** *fig* to stand back *ou* aloof ▸ **tenir la distance** *litt* & *fig* to go the distance, to stay the course **2.** [intervalle] interval ▸ **il l'a revue à deux mois de distance** he saw her again two months later ▸ **ils sont nés à deux mois de distance** they were born within two months of each other **3.** [écart] gap ▸ **ce malentendu a mis une certaine distance entre nous** we've become rather distant from each other since that misunderstanding.

distancer [16] [distɑ̃se] **vt** to outstrip.

distanciation [distɑ̃sjasjɔ̃] **nf** distance.

distancier [9] [distɑ̃sje] ◆ ***se distancier*** **vp : se distancier de** to distance o.s. from.

distant, e [distɑ̃, ɑ̃t] **adj 1.** [éloigné] **: une ville distante de 10 km** a town 10 km away ▸ **des villes distantes de 10 km** towns 10 km apart **2.** [froid] distant.

distendre [73] [distɑ̃dr] **vt** [ressort, corde] to stretch / [abdomen] to distend.
◆ ***se distendre*** **vp** to distend.

distendu, e [distɑ̃dy] **pp** ➤ ***distendre***.

distillation [distilasjɔ̃] **nf** distilling, distillation.

distiller [3] [distile] **vt** [alcool] to distil *UK*, to distill *US* / [pétrole] to refine / [miel] to secrete / *fig* & *littéraire* to exude.

distillerie [distilri] **nf** [industrie] distilling / [lieu] distillery.

distinct, e [distɛ̃, ɛ̃kt] **adj** distinct.

distinctement [distɛ̃ktəmɑ̃] **adv** distinctly, clearly.

distinctif, ive [distɛ̃ktif, iv] **adj** distinctive.

distinction [distɛ̃ksjɔ̃] **nf** distinction.

distingué, e [distɛ̃ge] **adj** distinguished.

distinguer [3] [distɛ̃ge] **vt 1.** [différencier] to tell apart, to distinguish **2.** [percevoir] to make out, to distinguish **3.** [rendre différent] **: distinguer de** to distinguish from, to set apart from.
◆ ***se distinguer*** **vp 1.** [se différencier] **: se distinguer (de)** to stand out (from) **2.** [s'illustrer] to distinguish o.s. **3.** [être perçu] **: au loin se distinguait la côte** you could make out the coast in the distance.

distraction [distraksjɔ̃] **nf 1.** [inattention] inattention, absent-mindedness ▸ **par distraction** absent-mindedly **2.** [passe-temps] leisure activity.

distraire [112] [distrɛr] **vt 1.** [déranger] to distract **2.** [divertir] to amuse, to entertain.
◆ ***se distraire*** **vp** to amuse o.s.

distrait, e [distrɛ, ɛt] ■ **pp** ➤ ***distraire***.
■ **adj** absent-minded.

distraitement [distrɛtmɑ̃] **adv** absent-mindedly, absently.

distrayais, distrayons ➤ ***distraire***.

distrayant, e [distrɛjɑ̃, ɑ̃t] **adj** entertaining.

distribanque [distribɑ̃k] **nm** ATM, cash dispenser *UK*.

distribuer [7] [distribɥe] **vt** to distribute / [courrier] to deliver / [ordres] to give out / [cartes] to deal / [coups, sourires] to dispense.

distributeur, trice [distribytœr, tris] **nm, f** distributor.
◆ ***distributeur*** **nm 1.** AUTO & COMM distributor ▸ **distributeur agréé** authorized dealer **2.** [machine] **: distributeur (automatique) de billets** BANQUE ATM, cash machine, cash dispenser *UK* / [transports] ticket machine ▸ **distributeur de boissons** drinks machine.

distribution [distribysjɔ̃] **nf 1.** [répartition, diffusion, disposition] distribution ▸ **distribution du courrier** postal *ou* mail delivery ▸ **distribution des prix** SCOL prize-giving *UK* ▸ **distribution à domicile** door drop ▸ **distribution JAT** JIT distribution ▸ **distribution juste à temps** just-in-time distribution ▸ **la grande distribution** large volume distribution **2.** [approvisionnement] supply ▸ **distribution d'eau/de gaz** water/gas supply **3.** CINÉ & THÉÂTRE cast.

district [distrikt] **nm** district.

dit, dite [di, dit] ■ **pp** ➤ ***dire***.
■ **adj 1.** [appelé] known as **2.** DR said, above **3.** [fixé] **: à l'heure dite** at the appointed time.

dites, dîtes ➤ ***dire***.

dithyrambique [ditirɑ̃bik] **adj** eulogistic.

DIU (abr de ***dispositif intra-utérin***) **nm** MÉD IUD.

diurétique [djyretik] **nm & adj** diuretic.

diurne [djyrn] **adj** diurnal.

diva [diva] **nf** prima donna, diva.

divagation [divagasjɔ̃] **nf** wandering.
◆ ***divagations*** **nfpl** ramblings.

divaguer [3] [divage] **vi** to ramble.

divan [divɑ̃] **nm** divan *(seat)*.

divergeant [divɛrʒɑ̃] **p prés** ➤ ***diverger***.

divergence [divɛrʒɑ̃s] **nf** divergence, difference / [d'opinions] difference.

divergent, e [divɛrʒɑ̃, ɑ̃t] **adj** divergent.

diverger [17] [divɛrʒe] **vi** to diverge / [opinions] to differ.

divers, e [divɛr, ɛrs] ■ **adj 1.** [différent] different, various ▸ **à usages divers** multipurpose *(avant n)* **2.** [disparate] diverse **3.** *(avant n)* [plusieurs] several, various ▸ **en diverses occasions** on several *ou* various occasions **4.** PRESSE **: 'divers'** 'miscellaneous'.
■ **adj indéf pl** POLIT others ▸ **les divers droite/gauche** other right/left-wing parties.

diversement [divɛrsəmɑ̃] **adv** variously, in different ways.

diversification [divɛrsifikasjɔ̃] **nf** diversification.

diversifier [9] [divɛrsifje] **vt** to vary, to diversify.
◆ ***se diversifier*** **vp** to diversify.

diversion [divɛrsjɔ̃] **nf** diversion ▸ **créer une diversion, faire diversion** to create a diversion.

diversité [divɛrsite] **nf** diversity.

divertir [32] [divɛrtir] **vt** [distraire] to entertain, to amuse.
◆ ***se divertir*** **vp** to amuse o.s., to entertain o.s.

divertissant, e [divɛrtisɑ̃, ɑ̃t] **adj** entertaining, amusing.

divertissement [divɛrtismɑ̃] **nm 1.** [passe-temps] form of relaxation **2.** MUS divertimento.

dividende [dividɑ̃d] **nm** dividend.

divin, e [divɛ̃, in] **adj** divine.

divination [divinasjɔ̃] **nf** divination.

divinement [divinmɑ̃] **adv** divinely.

divinité [divinite] **nf** divinity.

diviser [3] [divize] **vt 1.** [gén] to divide, to split up ▸ **diviser pour régner** *fig* to divide and rule **2.** MATH to divide ▸ **diviser 8 par 4** to divide 8 by 4.
◆ ***se diviser*** **vp 1.** [se séparer] to divide **2.** [diverger] to be divided.

divisible [divizibl] **adj** divisible.

division [divizjɔ̃] **nf 1.** MATH division ▸ **faire une division** to do a division **2.** [fragmentation] splitting, division, partition ▸ **la division du travail** ÉCON the division of labour *UK ou* labor *US* ▸ **division cellulaire** BIOL cell division **3.** [désaccord] division, rift **4.** FOOTBALL division ▸ **un club de première/deuxième/troisième division** a first/second/third division club **5.** MIL division ▸ **division aéroportée** MIL airborne division ▸ **division blindée** armoured *UK ou* armored *US* division.

divisionnaire [divizjɔnɛr] **adj** divisional.

divorce [divɔrs] **nm 1.** DR divorce ▸ **demander le divorce** to ask for a divorce, to sue for divorce **2.** *fig* [divergence] gulf, separation.

divorcé, ***e*** [divɔrse] ■ **adj** divorced.
■ **nm, f** divorcee, divorced person.

divorcer [16] [divɔrse] **vi** to divorce.

divulgation [divylgasjɔ̃] **nf** disclosure.

divulguer [3] [divylge] **vt** to divulge.

dix [dis] **adj num inv & nm** ten ; voir aussi ***six***.

dix-huit [dizɥit] **adj num inv & nm** eighteen ; voir aussi ***six***.

dix-huitième [dizɥitjɛm] **adj num inv, nm & nmf** eighteenth ; voir aussi ***sixième***.

dixième [dizjɛm] ■ **nf** SCOL ≃ Year 3 *(at primary school) UK*, ≃ second grade *US*.
■ **adj num inv, nm & nmf** tenth ; voir aussi ***sixième***.

dix-neuf [diznœf] **adj num inv & nm** nineteen ; voir aussi ***six***.

dix-neuvième [diznœvjɛm] **adj num inv, nm & nmf** nineteenth ; voir aussi ***sixième***.

dix-sept [disɛt] **adj num inv & nm** seventeen ; voir aussi ***six***.

dix-septième [disɛtjɛm] **adj num inv, nm & nmf** seventeenth ; voir aussi ***sixième***.

dizaine [dizɛn] **nf 1.** MATH ten **2.** [environ dix] **: une dizaine de** about ten ▸ **par dizaines** [en grand nombre] in their dozens.

DJ [didʒi, didʒe] (abr de ***disc-jockey***) **nm** DJ.

Djakarta [dʒakarta] **npr** Jakarta.

djellaba [dʒelaba] **nf** jellaba.

Djibouti [dʒibuti] **npr** Djibouti.

djiboutien, ***enne*** [dʒibutjɛ̃, ɛn] **adj** of/from Djibouti.
◆ ***Djiboutien***, ***enne*** **nm, f** person from Djibouti.

dm (abr écrite de ***décimètre***) dm.

DM (abr écrite de ***deutsche Mark***) DM.

DNS (abr de ***Domain Name System***) **m** INFORM DNS.

do[1] [do] **nm inv** MUS C / [chanté] doh *UK*, do *US*.

do[2] (abr écrite de ***dito***) do.

doberman [dobɛrman] **nm** Doberman (pinscher).

doc [dɔk] (abr de ***documentation***) **nf** literature, brochures *pl* ▸ **pouvez-vous me donner de la doc sur cet ordinateur?** could you give me some literature about this computer?

doc. (abr écrite de ***document***) doc.

docile [dɔsil] **adj 1.** [obéissant] docile **2.** [cheveux] manageable.

docilement [dɔsilmɑ̃] **adv** meekly, obediently.

docilité [dɔsilite] **nf** obedience.

dock [dɔk] **nm 1.** [bassin] dock **2.** [hangar] warehouse.

docker [dɔkɛr] **nm** docker *UK*, longshoreman *US*, stevedore *US*.

docte [dɔkt] **adj** *iron* professorial.

doctement [dɔktəmɑ̃] **adv** [savamment] learnedly.

docteur [dɔktœr] **nm 1.** [médecin] doctor ▸ **docteur en médecine** doctor of medicine **2.** UNIV **: docteur ès lettres/sciences** ≃ PhD ▸ **docteur honoris causa** ≃ Hon. PhD.

doctoral, ***e***, ***aux*** [dɔktɔral, o] **adj** *péj* pompous, professorial.

doctorat [dɔktɔra] **nm 1.** [grade] doctorate, PhD ▸ **doctorat d'État** doctorate *(leading to high-level research)* ▸ **doctorat du troisième cycle** doctorate *(awarded by a specific university)*, PhD **2.** [épreuve] doctoral exam.

doctoresse [dɔktɔrɛs] **nf** *vieilli* woman *ou* lady doctor.

doctrinaire [dɔktrinɛr] **adj 1.** [dogmatique] doctrinaire **2.** [sentencieux] sententious.

doctrine [dɔktrin] **nf** doctrine.

docudrame [dɔkydram] **m** TV docudrama.

document [dɔkymɑ̃] **nm** document.

documentaire [dɔkymɑ̃tɛr] **nm & adj** documentary.

documentaliste [dɔkymɑ̃talist] **nmf** [d'archives] archivist / PRESSE & TV researcher.

documentation [dɔkymɑ̃tasjɔ̃] **nf 1.** [travail] research **2.** [documents] paperwork, papers *pl* **3.** [brochures] documentation.

documenté, ***e*** [dɔkymɑ̃te] **adj 1.** [personne] well-informed **2.** [étude] well-documented.

documenter [3] [dɔkymɑ̃te] **vt** to document.
◆ ***se documenter*** **vp** to do some research.

dodeliner [3] [dɔdəline] **vi : dodeliner de la tête** to nod gently.

dodo [dodo] **nm** *fam* beddy-byes *(U)* ▸ **faire dodo** to sleep.

dodu, ***e*** [dɔdy] **adj** *fam* [enfant, joue, bras] chubby / [animal] plump.

dogmatique [dɔgmatik] **adj** dogmatic.

dogme [dɔgm] **nm** dogma.

dogue [dɔg] **nm** mastiff.

doigt [dwa] **nm** finger ▸ **un doigt de** (just) a drop ou finger of ▸ **montrer qqch du doigt** to point at sthg ▸ **doigt de pied** toe ▸ **être à deux doigts de faire qqch** to be within an ace of doing sthg ▸ **mettre le doigt dans l'engrenage** to get involved ▸ **se mettre le doigt dans l'œil** *fam* to be kidding o.s. ▸ **je m'en mords les doigts** I could kick myself (for it) ▸ **obéir à qqn au doigt et à l'œil** to obey sb's every whim, to be at sb's beck and call.

doigté [dwate] **nm** delicacy, tact.

dois ➤ ***devoir***.

doive ➤ ***devoir***.

doléances [doleɑ̃s] **nfpl** *sout* grievances.

dollar [dɔlar] **nm** dollar.

dolmen [dɔlmɛn] **nm** dolmen.

DOM [dɔm] (abr de ***département d'outre-mer***) **nm** *French overseas département.*

domaine [dɔmɛn] **nm 1.** [propriété] estate ▸ **mis en bouteille au domaine** [dans le Bordelais] chateau-bottled ▸ **domaine skiable** area developed for skiing *(within a commune or across several communes)* **2.** [secteur, champ d'activité] field, domain ▸ **dans tous les domaines** in every field *ou* domain ▸ **l'art oriental, c'est son domaine** she's a specialist in oriental art ▸ **tomber dans le domaine public** to come out of copyright.

domanial, e, aux [dɔmanjal, o] **adj** national, state *(avant n).*

dôme [dom] **nm 1.** ARCHIT dome **2.** GÉOGR rounded peak.

domestication [dɔmɛstikasjɔ̃] **nf** domestication.

domestique [dɔmɛstik] ■ **nmf** (domestic) servant.
■ **adj** family *(avant n)* / [travaux] household *(avant n).*

domestiquer [3] [dɔmɛstike] **vt 1.** [animal] to domesticate **2.** [éléments naturels] to harness.

domicile [dɔmisil] **nm 1.** [gén] (place of) residence ▸ **travailler à domicile** to work from *ou* at home ▸ **ils livrent à domicile** they do deliveries ▸ **sans domicile fixe** of no fixed abode ▸ **élire domicile** to take up residence ▸ **domicile conjugal** DR marital home **2.** [d'entreprise] (registered) address.

domiciliation [dɔmisiljasjɔ̃] **nf : domiciliation bancaire** domiciliation.

domicilié, e [dɔmisilje] **adj : domicilié à** (officially) resident in *ou* at.

domicilier [9] [dɔmisilje] **vt 1.** ADMIN to domicile ▸ **je me suis fait domicilier chez mon frère** I gave my brother's place as an accommodation address **2.** BANQUE & COMM to domicile.

dominant, e [dɔminɑ̃, ɑ̃t] **adj 1.** [qui prévaut] dominant **2.** [qui surplombe] dominating.
◆ ***dominante*** **nf 1.** [caractéristique] dominant feature *ou* characteristic **2.** [couleur] dominant colour *UK ou* color *US* **3.** MUS dominant.

domination [dɔminasjɔ̃] **nf 1.** [autorité] domination, dominion **2.** [influence] influence.

dominer [3] [dɔmine] ■ **vt 1.** [surplomber, avoir de l'autorité sur] to dominate **2.** [surpasser] to outclass **3.** [maîtriser] to control, to master **4.** *fig* [connaître] to master.
■ **vi 1.** [régner] to dominate, to be dominant **2.** [prédominer] to predominate **3.** [triompher] to be on top, to hold sway.
◆ ***se dominer*** **vp** to control o.s.

dominicain, e [dɔminikɛ̃, ɛn] **adj** Dominican.
◆ ***Dominicain, e*** **nm, f** Dominican.

dominical, e, aux [dɔminikal, o] **adj** Sunday *(avant n).*

Dominique [dɔminik] **nf : la Dominique** Dominica.

domino [dɔmino] **nm** domino.

dommage [dɔmaʒ] **nm 1.** [préjudice] harm *(U)* ▸ **dommages et intérêts, dommages-intérêts** damages ▸ **quel dommage!** what a shame! ▸ **c'est dommage que** *(+ subjonctif)* it's a pity *ou* shame (that) **2.** [dégâts] damage *(U).*

domotique [dɔmɔtik] **nf** home automation.

dompter [3] [dɔ̃te] **vt 1.** [animal, fauve] to tame **2.** [rebelles, enfants] to subdue **3.** *fig* [maîtriser] to overcome, to control.

dompteur, euse [dɔ̃tœr, øz] **nm, f** [de fauves] tamer.

DOM-TOM [dɔmtɔm] (abr de ***départements d'outre-mer/territoires d'outre-mer***) **nmpl** *French overseas départements and territories.*

CULTURE

DOM-TOM

The **départements d'outre-mer** (DOM) and **territoires d'outre-mer** (TOM) are France's non-European territories. **La métropole** includes mainland France and Corsica. The four **DOM** – Martinique, French Guiana, Guadeloupe and Réunion – have been monodepartmental **régions** since 1982. As such, they each have a **conseil regional** and a **conseil général** that oversee economic, social, cultural, and scientific development. The **TOM** – Wallis and Futuna, French Polynesia, New Caledonia and TAAF – enjoy a high degree of autonomy; some even have their own legislative assemblies. The partially autonomous island territories of Mayotte and Saint-Pierre-et-Miquelon are each governed by a prefect.

don [dɔ̃] **nm 1.** [cadeau] gift ▸ **faire don de** to make a gift *ou* present of ▸ **faire don d'un bien à qqn** to donate a piece of property to sb ▸ **ceux qui ont fait don de leur vie pour leur pays** those who have laid down *ou* sacrificed their lives for their country ▸ **don du sang** blood donation ▸ **encourager les dons d'organes** to promote organ donation **2.** [aptitude] knack ▸ **elle a un don pour la danse** she has a talent for dancing, she's a gifted dancer ▸ **elle a le don de trouver des vêtements pas chers** she has a flair for finding cheap clothes.

DON [dɔn] (abr de ***disque optique numérique***) **nm** *digital optical disk.*

donateur, trice [dɔnatœr, tris] **nm, f** donor.

donation [dɔnasjɔ̃] **nf** settlement.

donc [dɔ̃k] **conj** so ▸ **je disais donc...** so as I was saying... ▸ **allons donc!** come on! ▸ **tais-toi donc!** will you be quiet!

donjon [dɔ̃ʒɔ̃] **nm** keep.

donjuanisme [dɔ̃ʒyanism] **nm** womanizing.

donnant [dɔnɑ̃] ◆ ***donnant donnant*** **loc adv** fair's fair.

donne [dɔn] **nf** [jeux] deal.

donné, e [dɔne] **adj** given ▸ **à cet instant donné** at this (very) moment ▸ **à un moment donné** at one point ▸ **c'est donné** it's a gift ▸ **c'est pas donné** it's not exactly cheap ▸ **étant donné que** given that, considering (that).
◆ ***donnée*** **nf 1.** INFORM & MATH datum, piece of data ▸ **données numériques** numerical data ▸ **fichier/saisie/transmission de données** data file/capture/transmission **2.** [élément] fact, particular ▸ **je ne connais pas toutes les données du problème** I don't have all the information about this question.

donner [3] [dɔne] ■ vt **1.** [gén] to give / [se débarrasser de] to give away ▸ **donner à manger aux enfants/chevaux** to feed the children/horses ▸ **donner de la voix** to raise one's voice ▸ **donner des nouvelles à qqn** to give sb news ▸ **donner qqch à qqn** to give sb sthg, to give sthg to sb ▸ **donner qqch à faire à qqn** to give sb sthg to do, to give sthg to sb to do ▸ **donner rendez-vous à qqn** ADMIN to make an appointment with sb / [ami, amant] to make a date with sb ▸ **donner sa voiture à réparer** to leave one's car to be repaired ▸ **donner une fessée à qqn** to smack sb's bottom, to spank sb ▸ **quel âge lui donnes-tu?** how old do you think he is? **2.** *fam* [dénoncer] to rat on, to shop *UK* **3.** [occasionner] to give, to cause ▸ **ne rien donner** to be no use *ou* good, to be unproductive ▸ **en ajoutant les impôts, cela donne la somme suivante** when you add (in) *ou* on the tax, it comes to the following amount.
■ vi **1.** [tomber] **: donner dans** to fall into / *fig* to have a tendency towards *US ou* toward *US* ▸ **sans donner dans le mélodrame** without becoming too melodramatic **2.** [s'ouvrir] **: donner sur** to look (out) onto ▸ **la chambre donne sur le jardin/la mer** the room overlooks the garden/the sea **3.** [produire] to produce, to yield ▸ **la vigne a bien/mal donné cette année** the vineyard had a good/bad yield this year **4.** [amener] **: donner à penser/entendre que** to lead sb to think/understand that.
◆ ***se donner*** vp **1.** [se consacrer] **: se donner à qqch** to give *ou* devote o.s. to sthg ▸ **se donner à une cause** to devote o.s. *ou* one's life to a cause **2.** [s'abandonner] **: se donner à qqn** to give o.s. to sb.

donneur, euse [dɔnœr, øz] nm, f **1.** MÉD donor ▸ **donneur de sang** blood donor **2.** [jeux de cartes] dealer.

dont [dɔ̃] pron rel **1.** [complément de verbe ou d'adjectif] **: la personne dont tu parles** the person you're speaking about, the person about whom you are speaking ▸ **l'accident dont il est responsable** the accident for which he is responsible ▸ **c'est quelqu'un dont on dit le plus grand bien** he's someone about whom people speak highly *(la traduction varie selon la préposition anglaise utilisée avec le verbe ou l'adjectif)* **2.** [complément de nom ou de pronom - relatif à l'objet] of which, whose / [- relatif à personne] whose ▸ **un meuble dont le bois est vermoulu** a piece of furniture with woodworm ▸ **la boîte dont le couvercle est jaune** the box whose lid is yellow, the box with the yellow lid ▸ **c'est quelqu'un dont j'apprécie l'honnêteté** he's someone whose honesty I appreciate ▸ **celui dont les parents sont divorcés** the one whose parents are divorced **3.** [indiquant la partie d'un tout] **: plusieurs personnes ont téléphoné, dont ton frère** several people phoned, one of whom was your brother *ou* and among them was your brother ▸ **j'ai vu plusieurs films dont deux étaient particulièrement intéressants** I saw several films, two of which were particularly interesting.

dopage [dɔpaʒ] nm doping.

dopant, e [dɔpɑ̃, ɑ̃t] adj stimulant.
◆ ***dopant*** nm dope *(U)*.

dope [dɔp] nf *fam* dope.

doper [3] [dɔpe] vt to dope.
◆ ***se doper*** vp to take stimulants.

dorade [dɔrad] = ***daurade***.

doré, e [dɔre] adj **1.** [couvert de dorure] gilded, gilt ▸ **doré sur tranche** gilt-edged **2.** [couleur] golden.

dorénavant [dɔrenavɑ̃] adv from now on, in future.

dorer [3] [dɔre] ■ vt **1.** [couvrir d'or] to gild **2.** [peau] to tan **3.** CULIN to glaze.
■ vi CULIN **: faire dorer** to brown.
◆ ***se dorer*** vp to tan.

dorloter [3] [dɔrlɔte] vt to pamper, to cosset.

dormant, e [dɔrmɑ̃, ɑ̃t] adj [eau] still.

dormeur, euse [dɔrmœr, øz] nm, f sleeper.

dormir [36] [dɔrmir] vi **1.** [sommeiller] to sleep ▸ **dormir debout** to be asleep on one's feet ▸ **à dormir debout** unbelievable, implausible **2.** [rester inactif - personne] to slack, to stand around (doing nothing) / [- capitaux] to lie idle.

dorsal, e, aux [dɔrsal, o] adj dorsal.

dortoir [dɔrtwar] nm dormitory.

dorure [dɔryr] nf **1.** [couche d'or] gilt **2.** [ce qui est doré] golden *ou* gilt decoration.

doryphore [dɔrifɔr] nm colorado beetle.

dos [do] nm back ▸ **dos à dos** back to back ▸ **de dos** from behind ▸ **sur le dos** on one's back ▸ **'voir au dos'** 'see over' ▸ **à dos d'âne** (riding) on a mule ▸ **ne rien avoir à se mettre sur le dos** to have nothing to wear ▸ **tourner le dos à** [être tourné] to have one's back to / *litt* & *fig* [se tourner] to turn one's back on ▸ **dos crawlé** backstroke ▸ **avoir bon dos** to be the one who always gets the blame ▸ **en avoir plein le dos** *fam* to have had it up to here, to be fed up to the back teeth *UK* ▸ **se mettre qqn à dos** to put sb's back up.

DOS, Dos [dɔs] (abr de ***Disk Operating System***) nm DOS.

dosage [dozaʒ] nm [de médicament] dose / [d'ingrédient] amount.

dos-d'âne [dodan] nm inv bump.

dose [doz] nf **1.** [quantité de médicament] dose ▸ **'ne pas dépasser la dose prescrite'** 'do not exceed the prescribed dose' **2.** [quantité] share ▸ **forcer la dose** *fam fig* to overdo it ▸ **une (bonne) dose de bêtise** *fam fig* a lot of silliness ▸ **j'en ai eu ma dose** *fam fig* I've had enough.

doser [3] [doze] vt [médicament, ingrédient] to measure out / *fig* to weigh, to weigh up *UK*.

doseur [dozœr] nm [appareil] measure / [de cuisine] measuring jug *UK ou* cup *US*.

dossard [dosar] nm number *(on competitor's back)*.

dossier [dosje] nm **1.** [de fauteuil] back **2.** [documents] file, dossier ▸ **dossier suspendu** suspension file **3.** [classeur] file, folder **4.** INFORM folder **5.** UNIV **: dossier d'inscription** registration forms *pl* **6.** *fig* [question] question.

dot [dɔt] nf dowry.

dotation [dɔtasjɔ̃] nf **1.** DR endowment **2.** ADMIN grant

doter [3] [dɔte] vt [pourvoir] **: doter de** [talent] to endow with / [machine] to equip with.

douairière [dwɛrjɛr] nf [veuve] dowager.

douane [dwan] nf **1.** [service, lieu] customs *pl* ▸ **passer la douane** to go through customs **2.** [taxe] (import) duty.

douanier, ère [dwanje, ɛr] ■ adj customs *(avant n)*.
■ nm, f customs officer.

doublage [dublaʒ] **nm** **1.** [renforcement] lining **2.** [de film] dubbing **3.** [d'acteur] understudying.

double [dubl] ■ **adj** double ▸ **chambre/lit double** double room/bed ▸ **contrat en double exemplaire** contract in duplicate ▸ **double menton** double chin ▸ **double vitrage** double glazing ▸ **avoir la double nationalité** to have dual nationality ▸ **c'est un argument à double tranchant** the argument cuts both ways ▸ **fermer à double tour** to double lock ▸ **une phrase à double sens** a double-entendre.
■ **adv** double ▸ **voir double** to see double, to have double vision.
■ **nm** **1.** [quantité] **: le double** double ▸ **coûter le double de** to cost twice as much as
2. [copie] copy ▸ **tu as un double de la clé?** have you got a spare *ou* duplicate key? ▸ **en double** in duplicate ▸ **j'ai une photo en double** I've got two of the same photograph
3. [d'une personne] double
4. TENNIS doubles *sg* ▸ **jouer un double** to play (a) doubles (match).

doublé [duble] **nm** **1.** [en orfèvrerie] rolled gold *UK* **2.** [réussite double] double.

double-clic, ***doubles-clics*** [dublklik] **nm** INFORM double-click.

double-cliquer [3] [dublklike] **vt** INFORM to double-click on ▸ **double-cliquer sur l'image** to double-click on the picture.

doublement [dubləmɑ̃] ■ **adv** doubly.
■ **nm** [de lettre] doubling.

doubler [3] [duble] ■ **vt** **1.** [multiplier] to double **2.** [plier] to (fold) double **3.** [renforcer] **: doubler (de)** to line (with) **4.** [dépasser] to pass, to overtake *UK* **5.** [film, acteur] to dub **6.** *fam* [trahir] to con, to double-cross **7.** [augmenter] to double.
■ **vi** **1.** [véhicule] to pass, to overtake *UK* **2.** [augmenter] to double.
◆ ***se doubler*** **vp : se doubler de** to be coupled with.

doublure [dublyr] **nf** **1.** [renforcement] lining **2.** CINÉ stand-in.

douce ➤ ***doux***.

douceâtre [dusatr] **adj** sickly (sweet), cloying.

doucement [dusmɑ̃] **adv** **1.** [descendre] carefully / [frapper] gently ▸ **doucement!** gently *ou* easy (does it)! **2.** [traiter] gently / [parler] softly **3.** [médiocrement] (only) so-so.

doucereux, ***euse*** [dusrø, øz] **adj** **1.** [saveur] sickly (sweet), cloying **2.** [mielleux] smooth, suave.

doucette [dusɛt] **nf** BOT lamb's lettuce.

douceur [dusœr] **nf** **1.** [de saveur, parfum] sweetness **2.** [d'éclairage, de peau, de musique] softness **3.** [de climat] mildness **4.** [de caractère] gentleness **5.** [plaisir] pleasure.
◆ ***douceurs*** **nfpl** [friandises] sweets *UK*, candy *(U)* *US*.
◆ ***en douceur*** ■ **loc adv** smoothly.
■ **loc adj** smooth.

douche [duʃ] **nf** **1.** [appareil, action] shower ▸ **prendre une douche** to take *ou* have *UK* a shower **2.** *fam fig* [déception] letdown ▸ **douche écossaise** shock to the system.

doucher [3] [duʃe] **vt** **1.** [donner une douche à] **: doucher qqn** to give sb a shower **2.** *fam fig* [décevoir] to let down.
◆ ***se doucher*** **vp** to take *ou* have *UK* a shower, to shower.

douchette [duʃɛt] **nf** bar-code reader *ou* scanner *(for bulky items)*.

doudou [dudu] **nm** *fam* [langage enfantin] security blanket.

doudoune [dudun] **nf** quilted jacket.

doué, ***e*** [dwe] **adj** talented ▸ **être doué pour** to have a gift for.

douer [6] [due] **vt : douer qqn de** to endow sb with.

douille [duj] **nf** **1.** [d'ampoule] socket **2.** [de cartouche] cartridge.

douillet, ***ette*** [dujɛ, ɛt] ■ **adj** **1.** [confortable] snug, cosy *UK*, cozy *US* **2.** [sensible] soft.
■ **nm, f** wimp.

douillettement [dujɛtmɑ̃] **adv** snugly.

douleur [dulœr] **nf** *litt* & *fig* pain ▸ **se tordre de douleur** to writhe in pain ▸ **nous avons la douleur de vous annoncer...** it is with great sorrow that we announce...

douloureux, ***euse*** [dulurø, øz] **adj** **1.** [physiquement] painful **2.** [moralement] distressing **3.** [regard, air] sorrowful.

doute [dut] **nm** doubt ▸ **avoir des doutes sur** to have misgivings about ▸ **mettre qqch en doute** to cast doubt on sthg.
◆ ***sans doute*** **loc adv** no doubt ▸ **sans aucun doute** without (a) doubt.

douter [3] [dute] ■ **vt** [ne pas croire] **: douter que** *(+ subjonctif)* to doubt (that).
■ **vi** [ne pas avoir confiance] **: douter de qqn/de qqch** to doubt sb/sthg, to have doubts about sb/sthg ▸ **j'en doute** I doubt it.
◆ ***se douter*** **vp : se douter de qqch** to suspect sthg ▸ **je m'en doutais** I thought so ▸ **je m'en doute** I'm not surprised.

douteux, ***euse*** [dutø, øz] **adj** **1.** [incertain] doubtful **2.** [contestable] questionable **3.** *péj* [mœurs] dubious / [vêtements, personne] dubious-looking.

douve [duv] **nf** **1.** [en équitation] water jump **2.** [d'un fût] stave **3.** ZOOL fluke.

douves [duv] **nfpl** [de château] moat *sg*.

Douvres [duvr] **npr** Dover.

doux, ***douce*** [du, dus] **adj** **1.** [éclairage, peau, musique] soft **2.** [saveur, parfum] sweet **3.** [climat, condiment] mild **4.** *sout* [agréable] pleasant **5.** [pente, regard, caractère] gentle.
◆ ***doux*** **loc adv : il fait doux** the weather is mild.
◆ ***en douce*** **loc adv** secretly.

douzaine [duzɛn] **nf** **1.** [douze] dozen **2.** [environ douze] **: une douzaine de** about twelve.

douze [duz] **adj num inv** & **nm** twelve ; voir aussi ***six***.

douzième [duzjɛm] **adj num inv, nm** & **nmf** twelfth ; voir aussi ***sixième***.

doyen**, **enne [dwajɛ̃, ɛn] **nm, f** [le plus ancien] most senior member.

DP (abr de ***délégué du personnel***) **nm** *staff representative.*

DPLG (abr de ***diplômé par le gouvernement***) **adj** *holder of official certificate for architects, engineers etc.*

dr. (abr écrite de ***droite***) R, r.

Dr (abr écrite de ***Docteur***) Dr.

draconien**, **enne [drakɔnjɛ̃, ɛn] **adj** draconian.

dragage [dragaʒ] **nm** dredging.

dragée [draʒe] **nf 1.** [confiserie] sugared almond ▸ **tenir la dragée haute à qqn** to hold out against sb **2.** [comprimé] pill.

dragon [dragɔ̃] **nm 1.** [monstre, personne autoritaire] dragon **2.** [soldat] dragoon **3.** [Corée du Sud, Taiwan, Chine, Indonésie, Singapour...] **: les dragons (asiatiques)** the (Asian) tiger economies.

drague [drag] **nf 1.** TECHNOL dredger **2.** *fam fig* [flirt] picking up.

draguer [3] [drage] **vt 1.** [nettoyer] to dredge **2.** *fam* [personne] to try to pick up, to chat up *UK*, to get off with *UK*.

dragueur**, **euse [dragœr, øz] **nm, f** *fam* **: c'est un dragueur** he's always on the pull *UK* ***ou*** on the make *US* ▸ **quelle dragueuse!** she's always chasing after men!

◆ ***dragueur*** **nm** [bateau] dredger.

drainage [drɛnaʒ] **nm** draining.

drainer [4] [drene] **vt 1.** [terrain, plaie] to drain **2.** *fig* [attirer] to drain off.

dramatique [dramatik] ■ **nf** play.

■ **adj 1.** THÉÂTRE dramatic **2.** [grave] tragic.

dramatisation [dramatizasjɔ̃] **nf** dramatization.

dramatiser [3] [dramatize] **vt** [exagérer] to dramatize.

dramaturge [dramatyrʒ] **nm** playwright, dramatist.

drame [dram] **nm 1.** [catastrophe] tragedy ▸ **faire un drame de qqch** *fig* to make a drama of sthg **2.** LITTÉR drama.

drap [dra] **nm 1.** [de lit] sheet **2.** [tissu] woollen *UK* ***ou*** woolen *US* cloth ▸ **être dans de beaux draps** *fig* to be in a real mess.

drapeau**, **x [drapo] **nm** flag ▸ **drapeau blanc** white flag ▸ **le drapeau tricolore** the tricolour *UK*, the tricolor *US*, the French flag ▸ **être sous les drapeaux** *fig* to be doing military service.

draper [3] [drape] **vt** to drape.

◆ ***se draper*** **vp : se draper dans** to drape o.s. in.

draperie [drapri] **nf 1.** [tenture] drapery **2.** [industrie] cloth industry.

drap-housse [draus] (pl **draps-housses**) **nm** fitted sheet.

drapier**, **ère [drapje, ɛr] ■ **adj** clothing *(avant n).*

■ **nm, f 1.** [fabricant] cloth manufacturer **2.** [marchand] draper *UK vieilli.*

drastique [drastik] **adj** drastic.

drave [drav] **nf** *Québec* drive (of floating logs).

dressage [drɛsaʒ] **nm** [d'animal] training, taming.

dresser [4] [drese] **vt 1.** [lever] to raise **2.** [faire tenir] to put up **3.** *sout* [construire] to erect **4.** [acte, liste, carte] to draw up / [procès-verbal] to make out **5.** [dompter] to train **6.** *fig* [opposer] **: dresser qqn contre qqn** to set sb against sb.

◆ ***se dresser*** **vp 1.** [se lever] to stand up **2.** [s'élever] to rise (up) / *fig* to stand ▸ **se dresser contre qqch** to rise up against sthg.

dresseur**, **euse [drɛsœr, øz] **nm, f** trainer.

dressing [drɛsiŋ] **nm** dressing room *(near a bedroom).*

dressoir [drɛswar] **nm** dresser.

DRH ■ **nf** (abr de ***direction des ressources humaines***) personnel department.

■ **nm** (abr de ***directeur des ressources humaines***) personnel manager.

dribbler [3] [drible] ■ **vi** SPORT to dribble.

■ **vt** SPORT **: dribbler qqn** to dribble past sb.

drille [drij] **nm : un joyeux drille** a cheery person.

driver [3] ■ **nm** [drajvœr] [golf] driver.

■ **vi** [drajve] [golf] to drive.

drogue [drɔg] **nf 1.** [stupéfiant] drug ▸ **la drogue** drugs *pl* ▸ **drogue dure** hard drug **2.** [médicament] medicine.

drogué**, **e [drɔge] ■ **adj** drugged.

■ **nm, f** drug addict.

droguer [3] [drɔge] **vt** [victime] to drug.

◆ ***se droguer*** **vp** [de stupéfiants] to take drugs.

droguerie [drɔgri] **nf** hardware shop *UK* ***ou*** store *US*.

droguiste [drɔgist] **nmf : chez le droguiste** at the hardware shop *UK* ***ou*** store *US*.

droit**, **e [drwa, drwat] **adj 1.** [du côté droit] right ▸ **le côté droit** the right-hand side **2.** [rectiligne, vertical, honnête] straight ▸ **droit comme un i** straight as a ramrod, bolt upright ▸ **jupe droite** straight skirt ▸ **rester dans le droit chemin** to keep to the straight and narrow.

◆ ***droit*** ■ **adv** straight ▸ **tout droit** straight ahead ▸ **aller droit au but** *fig* to go straight to the point ▸ **ça m'est allé droit au cœur** it went straight to my heart ▸ **il est allé droit à l'essentiel** he went straight to the point.

■ **nm 1.** DR law ▸ **étudiant en droit** law student ▸ **faire son droit** to study law ▸ **droit canon** canon law ▸ **droit civil/commercial/constitutionnel** civil/commercial/constitutional law ▸ **droit coutumier** common law ▸ **droit écrit** statute law ▸ **droit international** international law ▸ **droit pénal** criminal law ▸ **droit privé/public** private/public law ▸ **capacité en droit** ≃ law degree ▸ **point de droit** point of law ▸ **de droit commun** common-law *(avant n)* **2.** [prérogative] right ▸ **avoir droit à** to be entitled to ▸ **avoir le droit de faire qqch** to be allowed to do sthg ▸ **être dans son droit** to be within one's rights ▸ **être en droit de faire qqch** to have a right to do sthg ▸ **je suis en droit d'obtenir des explications** I'm entitled to an explanation ▸ **de quel droit?** by what right? ▸ **droit d'aînesse** birthright ▸ **droit d'asile** right of asylum ▸ **droit de cuissage** HIST droit de seigneur ▸ **droit de grâce** power of pardon ▸ **droit de grève** right to strike ▸ **droit de regard** right of access ▸ **droit de réponse** right of reply ▸ **droit de visite** visiting rights *pl*, access ▸ **droit de vote** right to vote ▸ **droits d'auteur** royalties ▸ **droits cinématographiques** film *UK* ***ou*** movie *US* rights ▸ **droits de douane** customs duty ▸ **droit**

exclusifs exclusive rights ▸ **droits de l'homme** human rights ▸ **droits d'inscription** registration fees ▸ **tous droits (de reproduction) réservés** copyright, all rights reserved ▸ **à qui de droit** to the proper authority.
◆ ***droite*** **nf 1.** [gén] right, right-hand side ▸ **à droite** on the right ▸ **à droite de** to the right of ▸ **garder/serrer sa droite** to keep to the right ▸ **la porte de droite** the door on the right, the right-hand door **2.** POLIT **: la droite** the right (wing) ▸ **de droite** right-wing.

droitier, ère [drwatje, ɛr] ■ **adj** right-handed.
■ **nm, f** right-handed person, right-hander.

droiture [drwatyr] **nf** straightforwardness.

drôle [drol] **adj 1.** [amusant] funny **2. : drôle de** [bizarre] funny / *fam* [remarquable] amazing.

drôlement [drolmɑ̃] **adv 1.** *fam* [très] tremendously **2.** [bizarrement] in a strange way **3.** [de façon amusante] in a funny way.

drôlerie [drolri] **nf** humour *UK*, humor *US*.

dromadaire [drɔmadɛr] **nm** dromedary.

dru, e [dry] **adj** thick.
◆ ***dru*** **adv : tomber dru** to fall heavily.

drugstore [drœgstɔr] **nm** drugstore.

druide [drɥid] **nm** druid.

ds abr de ***dans***.

DS [deɛs] **nf** [voiture] *now legendary futuristic car produced by Citroën in the 1950s.*

DST (abr de ***Direction de la surveillance du territoire***) **nf** *internal state security department,* ≃ MI5 *UK,* ≃ FBI *US.*

DT (abr de ***diphtérie, tétanos***) **nm** *vaccine against diphtheria and tetanus.*

D.T.COQ. (abr de ***diphtérie, tétanos, coqueluche***) [detekɔk] **nm** *vaccine against diphtheria, tetanus and whooping cough.*

du art partitif ➤ ***de***.

dû, due [dy] ■ **pp** ➤ ***devoir***.
■ **adj** due, owing.
◆ ***dû*** **nm** due ▸ **réclamer son dû** to demand one's due.

dualité [dɥalite] **nf** duality.

Dubayy [dybaj] **npr** Dubai.

dubitatif, ive [dybitatif, iv] **adj** doubtful.

Dublin [dyblɛ̃] **npr** Dublin.

dublinois, e [dyblinwa, waz] **adj** of/from Dublin.
◆ ***Dublinois, e*** **nm, f** Dubliner.

duc [dyk] **nm** duke.

ducal, e, aux [dykal, o] **adj** ducal.

duché [dyʃe] **nm** duchy.

duchesse [dyʃɛs] **nf** duchess.

duel [dɥɛl] **nm** duel.

duffel-coat (pl **duffel-coats**), ***duffle-coat*** (pl **duffle-coats**) [dœfœlkot] **nm** duffel coat.

dûment [dymɑ̃] **adv** duly.

dumping [dœmpiŋ] **nm** COMM dumping.

dune [dyn] **nf** dune.

duo [dɥo] **nm 1.** MUS duet ▸ **chanter en duo** to sing a duet **2.** [couple] duo.

dupe [dyp] ■ **nf** dupe.
■ **adj** gullible ▸ **être/ne pas être dupe** to be/not to be taken in.

duper [3] [dype] **vt** *sout* to dupe, to take sb in.

duplex [dyplɛks] **nm 1.** [appartement] split-level flat *UK*, maisonette *UK*, duplex *US* **2.** RADIO & TV link-up ▸ **en duplex** link-up *(avant n).*

duplicata [dyplikata] **nm inv** duplicate.

duplicité [dyplisite] **nf** duplicity.

dupliquer [3] [dyplike] **vt** [document] to duplicate.

duquel [dykɛl] ➤ ***lequel***.

dur, e [dyr] ■ **adj 1.** [matière, personne, travail] hard ▸ **dur comme du bois** rock-hard ▸ **d'une voix dure** in a harsh voice ▸ **il est parfois dur d'accepter la vérité** accepting the truth can be hard *ou* difficult ▸ **la route est dure à monter** it's a hard road to climb **2.** [carton] stiff **3.** [viande] tough **4.** [climat, punition, loi] harsh ▸ **les temps sont durs** these are hard times.
■ **nm, f** *fam* **: dur (à cuire)** tough nut.
◆ ***dur*** **adv** hard ▸ **le soleil tape dur aujourd'hui** the sun is beating down today ▸ **il travaille dur sur son nouveau projet** he's working hard *ou* he's hard at work on his new project.
◆ ***à la dure*** **loc adv : coucher à la dure** to sleep outside *ou* rough *UK* ▸ **être élevé à la dure** to be brought up the hard way.
◆ ***en dur*** **loc adj : construction/maison en dur** building/house built with non-temporary materials.

durable [dyrabl] **adj** lasting.

durablement [dyrabləmɑ̃] **adv** durably.

durant [dyrɑ̃] **prép 1.** [pendant] for **2.** [au cours de] during.

durcir [32] [dyrsir] ■ **vt** *litt* & *fig* to harden.
■ **vi** to harden, to become hard.
◆ ***se durcir*** **vp** *litt* & *fig* to harden.

durcissement [dyrsismɑ̃] **nm** hardening.

durée [dyre] **nf 1.** [période] length ▸ **'durée de conservation...'** 'best before...' **2.** [persistance] **: (de) longue durée** long-lasting **3.** [film, émission] running time.

durement [dyrmɑ̃] **adv 1.** [violemment] hard, vigorously **2.** [péniblement] severely **3.** [méchamment] harshly.

durer [3] [dyre] **vi** to last ▸ **ça ne peut plus durer!** it can't go on like this! ▸ **ce soleil ne va pas durer** this sunshine won't last long ▸ **faire durer le plaisir** to spin things out ▸ **la situation n'a que trop duré** the situation has gone on far too long.

dureté [dyrte] **nf 1.** [de matériau, de l'eau] hardness **2.** [de problème] difficulty **3.** [d'époque, de climat, de personne] harshness **4.** [de punition] severity.

durillon [dyrijɔ̃] **nm** [sur le pied] corn / [sur la main] callus.

dus, dut ➤ ***devoir***.

DUT (abr de ***diplôme universitaire de technologie***) **nm** *university diploma in technology.*

duvet [dyvɛ] **nm 1.** [plumes, poils fins] down **2.** [sac de couchage] sleeping bag.

DVD (abr de ***Digital Video ou Versatile Disc***) **nm inv** DVD.

DVD-ROM [dvdrɔm] (abr de ***Digital Video ou Versatile Disc Read Only Memory***) **nm** DVD-ROM.

dynamique [dinamik] ■ **nf 1.** PHYS dynamics *(U)* **2.** *fig* : **dynamique de groupe** group dynamics *pl.*
■ **adj** dynamic.

dynamiser [3] [dinamize] **vt** to inspire with energy.

dynamisme [dynamism] **nm** dynamism.

dynamite [dinamit] **nf** dynamite.

dynamiter [3] [dinamite] **vt** to dynamite.

dynamo [dinamo] **nf** dynamo.

dynamomètre [dinamɔmɛtr] **nm** dynamometer.

dynastie [dinasti] **nf** dynasty.

dysenterie [disɑ̃tri] **nf** dysentery.

dysfonctionnel, elle [disfɔksjɔnɛl] **adj** dysfunctional.

dysfonctionnement [disfɔ̃ksjɔnmɑ̃] **nm** malfunction, malfunctioning.

dyslexique [dislɛksik] ■ **nmf** dyslexic (person).
■ **adj** dyslexic.

dyspepsie [dispɛpsi] **nf** dyspepsia.

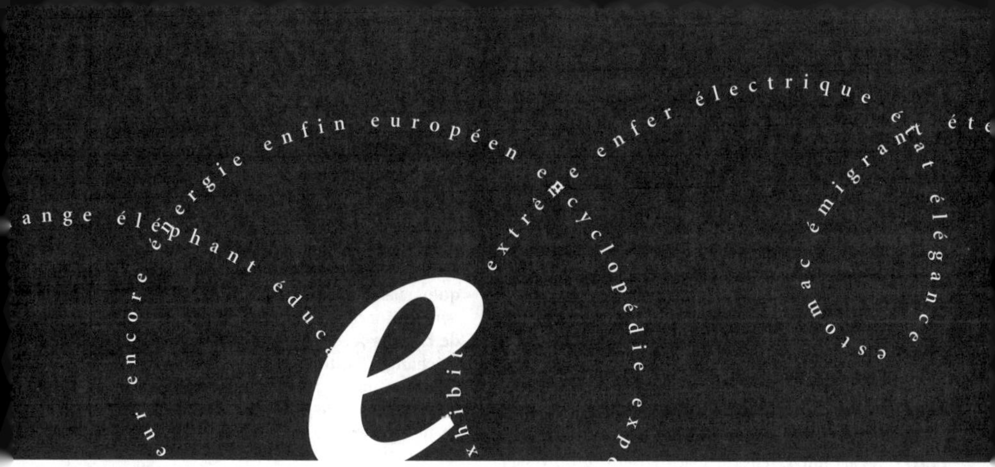

e, ***E*** [ə] **nm inv** e, E.
◆ ***E*** (abr écrite de ***est***) E.

EAO (abr de ***enseignement assisté par ordinateur***) **nm** CAL.

eau, ***x*** [o] **nf** water ▸ **laver à grande eau** [au jet] to hose down / [dans un évier, une bassine] to wash in a lot of water ▸ **prendre l'eau** to leak ▸ **eau calcaire** *ou* **dure** hard water ▸ **eau déminéralisée/distillée** demineralized/distilled water ▸ **eau douce/salée/de mer** fresh/salt/sea water ▸ **eau gazeuse/plate** fizzy/still water ▸ **eau bénite** holy water ▸ **eau de Cologne** (eau de) Cologne ▸ **eau courante** running water ▸ **eau écarlate** stain-remover ▸ **eau de Javel** bleach, Clorox® *US* ▸ **eau minérale** mineral water ▸ **eau oxygénée** hydrogen peroxide ▸ **eau de pluie** rainwater ▸ **eau du robinet** tap water ▸ **eau de Seltz** soda water ▸ **eau de source** spring water ▸ **eau de toilette** toilet water ▸ **eaux côtières** inshore waters ▸ **dans les eaux de** in the wake of ▸ **eaux dormantes** still waters ▸ **les Eaux et Forêts** ≃ the Forestry Commission *UK ou* Service *US* ▸ **eaux internationales/territoriales** international/territorial waters ▸ **les eaux usées** waste water *(U)* ▸ **à l'eau de rose** soppy, sentimental ▸ **ils étaient en eau** the sweat was pouring off them ▸ **mettre** *ou* **faire venir l'eau à la bouche** to make one's mouth water ▸ **mettre de l'eau dans son vin** to calm down, to tone it down a bit ▸ **se jeter à l'eau** *fig* to take the plunge ▸ **tomber à l'eau** *fig* to fall through ▸ **tu apportes de l'eau à mon moulin** you're adding weight to my argument.

EAU (abr de ***Émirats arabes unis***) **nmpl** UAE.

eau-de-vie [odvi] (pl **eaux-de-vie**) **nf** brandy.

eau-forte [ofɔrt] (pl **eaux-fortes**) **nf** etching.

ébahi, ***e*** [ebai] **adj** staggered, astounded.

ébahissement [ebaismɑ̃] **nm** amazement.

ébats [eba] **nmpl** *littéraire* frolics ▸ **ébats amoureux** lovemaking *(U)*.

ébattre [83] [ebatr] ◆ ***s'ébattre*** **vp** *littéraire* to frolic.

ébauche [eboʃ] **nf** [esquisse] sketch / *fig* outline ▸ **l'ébauche d'un sourire** the ghost of a smile.

ébaucher [3] [eboʃe] **vt 1.** [esquisser] to rough out **2.** *fig* [commencer] **: ébaucher des négociations** to start the process of negotiation ▸ **ébaucher un geste** to start to make a gesture.
◆ ***s'ébaucher*** **vpi** to (take) form, to start up.

ébène [ebɛn] **nf** ebony.

ébéniste [ebenist] **nm** cabinet-maker.

ébénisterie [ebenistəri] **nf 1.** [métier] cabinet-making **2.** [travail] cabinet work.

éberlué, ***e*** [ebɛrlɥe] **adj** flabbergasted.

éblouir [32] [ebluir] **vt** to dazzle.

éblouissant, ***e*** [ebluisɑ̃, ɑ̃t] **adj** dazzling.

éblouissement [ebluismɑ̃] **nm 1.** [aveuglement] glare, dazzle **2.** [vertige] dizziness **3.** [émerveillement] amazement.

ébonite [ebɔnit] **nf** vulcanite, ebonite.

éborgner [3] [ebɔrɲe] **vt : éborgner qqn** to put sb's eye out.
◆ ***s'éborgner*** **vp** *(emploi réfléchi)* to put one's eye out.

éboueur [ebwœr] **nm** dustman *UK*, garbage collector *US*.

ébouillanter [3] [ebujɑ̃te] **vt** to scald.
◆ ***s'ébouillanter*** **vp** to scald o.s.

éboulement [ebulmɑ̃] **nm** cave-in, fall.

éboulis [ebuli] **nm** mass of fallen rocks.

ébouriffer [3] [eburife] **vt 1.** [cheveux] to ruffle **2.** *fam* [étonner] to amaze.

ébranler [3] [ebrɑ̃le] **vt 1.** [bâtiment, opinion] to shake **2.** [gouvernement, nerfs] to weaken.
◆ ***s'ébranler*** **vp** [train] to move off.

ébrécher [18] [ebreʃe] **vt** [assiette, verre] to chip / *fam fig* to break into.

ébriété [ebrijete] **nf** drunkenness.

ébrouer [3] [ebrue] ◆ ***s'ébrouer*** **vp** [animal] to shake o.s.

ébruiter [3] [ebrɥite] **vt** to spread.
◆ ***s'ébruiter*** **vp** to become known.

ébullition [ebylisjɔ̃] **nf 1.** [de liquide] boiling point ▸ **porter à ébullition** CULIN to bring to the boil **2.** [effervescence] **: en ébullition** *fig* in a state of agitation.

écaille [ekaj] **nf 1.** [de poisson, reptile] scale / [de tortue] shell **2.** [de plâtre, peinture, vernis] flake **3.** [matière] tortoiseshell ▸ **en écaille** [lunettes] horn-rimmed.

écailler[1], ***ère*** [ekaje, ɛr] **nm, f** oyster seller.

écailler[2] [3] [ekaje] **vt 1.** [poisson] to scale **2.** [huîtres] to open.

◆ ***s'écailler*** **vp** to flake *ou* peel off.

écarlate [ekarlat] **adj & nf** scarlet ▸ **devenir écarlate** to turn crimson *ou* scarlet.

écarquiller [3] [ekarkije] **vt : écarquiller les yeux** to stare wide-eyed.

écart [ekar] **nm 1.** [espace] space ▸ **réduire *ou* resserrer l'écart entre** to close *ou* to narrow the gap between **2.** [temps] gap **3.** [différence] difference ▸ **écart de poids/température** difference in weight/temperature ▸ **écart type** standard deviation **4.** ÉCON gap ▸ **écart inflationniste** inflationary gap ▸ **écart de prix** price differential **5.** FIN [comptabilité] margin / [Bourse] spread / [statistiques] deviation **6.** [excès] **: écart de conduite** misdemeanour *(U) UK*, misdemeanor *(U) US*, misbehaviour *(U) UK*, misbehavior *(U) US* ▸ **écarts de langage** strong language **7.** [déviation] **: faire un écart** [personne] to step aside / [cheval] to shy ▸ **j'ai fait un petit écart aujourd'hui: j'ai mangé deux gâteaux** I broke my diet today: I ate two cakes ▸ **être à l'écart** to be in the background ▸ **mettre qqn à l'écart** to put sb on the sidelines / *fig* **: tenir qqn à l'écart de** to keep sb out of *ou* away from ▸ **il essaie de la tenir à l'écart de tous ses problèmes** he's trying not to involve her in all his problems **8.** [gymnastique] **: grand écart** splits *pl* ▸ **faire le grand écart** to do the splits / *fig* to do a balancing act.

écarteler [25] [ekartəle] **vt** *fig* to tear apart.

écartement [ekartəmɑ̃] **nm : écartement entre** space between.

écarter [3] [ekarte] **vt 1.** [bras, jambes] to open, to spread ▸ **écarter qqch de** to move sthg away from **2.** [obstacle, danger] to brush aside **3.** [foule, rideaux] to push aside / [solution] to dismiss ▸ **écarter qqn de** to exclude sb from.

◆ ***s'écarter*** **vp 1.** [se séparer] to part **2.** [se détourner] **: s'écarter de** to deviate from.

ecchymose [ekimoz] **nf** bruise.

ecclésiastique [eklezjastik] ■ **nm** clergyman.
■ **adj** ecclesiastical.

écervelé, e [esɛrvəle] ■ **adj** scatty, scatterbrained.
■ **nm, f** scatterbrain.

échafaud [eʃafo] **nm** scaffold.

échafaudage [eʃafodaʒ] **nm 1.** CONSTR scaffolding **2.** [amas] pile.

échafauder [3] [eʃafode] ■ **vt 1.** [empiler] to pile up **2.** [élaborer] to construct.
■ **vi** to put up scaffolding.

échalas [eʃala] **nm 1.** [perche] stake, pole **2.** *péj* [personne] beanpole.

échalote [eʃalɔt] **nf** shallot.

échancré, e [eʃɑ̃kre] **adj 1.** [vêtement] low-necked **2.** [côte] indented.

échancrure [eʃɑ̃kryr] **nf 1.** [de robe] low neckline **2.** [de côte] indentation.

échange [eʃɑ̃ʒ] **nm 1.** [de choses] exchange ▸ **faire un échange** to swap, to do a swap ▸ **en échange (de)** in exchange (for) ▸ **échange de balles** [avant un match] knocking up / [pendant le match] rally ▸ **échange (linguistique)** (language) exchange ▸ **échange standard** *replacement of faulty goods with the same item* ▸ **échange de bons procédés** exchange of favours *UK ou* favors *US* ▸ **échanges culturels** cultural exchanges **2.** COMM **: les échanges** trade *sg* ▸ **échanges internationaux** international trade ▸ **libre-échange** free trade **3.** INFORM **: échange de fichiers** file-sharing ▸ **site d'échange gratuit de fichiers** free file-sharing site.

échangeable [eʃɑ̃ʒabl] **adj** exchangeable.

échanger [17] [eʃɑ̃ʒe] **vt 1.** [troquer] to swap, to exchange **2.** [marchandise] **: échanger qqch (contre)** to change sthg (for) **3.** [communiquer] to exchange.

échangeur [eʃɑ̃ʒœr] **nm** interchange.

échangisme [eʃɑ̃ʒism] **nm** [de partenaires sexuels] partner-swapping.

échantillon [eʃɑ̃tijɔ̃] **nm** [de produit, de population] sample / ÉCON **: échantillon probabiliste** probability sample ▸ **échantillon promotionnel** promotional sample ▸ **échantillon type** representative sample / *fig* example.

échantillonnage [eʃɑ̃tijɔnaʒ] **nm** [série d'échantillons] range of samples / COMM **: échantillonnage aléatoire** random sampling ▸ **échantillonnage aréolaire *ou* par grappes** cluster sampling.

échappatoire [eʃapatwar] **nf** way out.

échappé, e [eʃape] **nm, f** *competitor who has broken away* ▸ **les échappés du peloton** runners who have broken away from the rest of the field.

◆ ***échappée*** **nf 1.** SPORT breakaway **2.** [espace ouvert à la vue] vista, view.

◆ ***par échappées*** **loc adv** every now and then, in fits and starts.

échappement [eʃapmɑ̃] **nm 1.** AUTO exhaust, ➤ **po**
2. [d'horloge] escapement.

échapper [3] [eʃape] **vi 1.** [éviter] **: échapper à** [personne, situation] to escape from / [danger, mort] to escape [suj: détail, parole, sens] to escape ▸ **échapper à ses obligations** to evade one's duties ▸ **ce détail m'a échappé** that detail escaped me ▸ **la victoire lui a échappé** victory eluded him ▸ **son nom m'échappe** his name escapes me *o* has slipped my mind **2.** [glisser] **: échapper de** to slip from *ou* out of ▸ **le vase lui a échappé des mains** the vase slipped out of her hands ▸ **laisser échapper** to let slip ▸▸ **l'échapper belle** to have a narrow escape.

◆ ***s'échapper*** **vp : s'échapper (de)** to escape (from) ▸ **s'échapper d'un camp** to escape from a camp ▸ **des mèches s'échappaient de son foulard** wisps of hair poked out from underneath her scarf.

écharde [eʃard] **nf** splinter.

écharpe [eʃarp] **nf** scarf ▸ **en écharpe** in a sling ▸ **l'écharpe tricolore** *mayoral sash worn by French mayors at civic functions* ▸ **prendre en écharpe** *fig* to hit on the side.

écharper [3] [eʃarpe] **vt** to rip to pieces *ou* shreds.

échasse [eʃas] **nf** [de berger, oiseau] stilt.

échassier [eʃasje] **nm** wader.

échauder [3] [eʃode] **vt 1.** [ébouillanter] to scald **2.** *fam fig* [enseigner] **: échauder qqn** to teach sb a lesson.

échauffement [eʃofmɑ̃] **nm 1.** [de moteur] overheating / [de terre] heating up **2.** SPORT warm-up **3.** [surexcitation] overheating **4.** MÉD inflammation.

échauffer [3] [eʃofe] **vt 1.** [chauffer] to overheat **2.** [exciter] to excite **3.** [énerver] to irritate.
◆ ***s'échauffer*** **vp 1.** SPORT to warm up **2.** *fig* [s'animer] to become heated.

échauffourée [eʃofure] **nf** brawl, skirmish.

échéance [eʃeɑ̃s] **nf 1.** [délai] expiry ▸ **à courte *ou* brève échéance** in the short term ▸ **à longue échéance** in the long term **2.** [date] payment date ▸ **arriver à échéance** to fall due.

échéancier [eʃeɑ̃sje] **nm** bill-book *UK*, tickler *US* ▸ **échéancier (de paiement)** payment schedule.

échéant [eʃeɑ̃] **adj : le cas échéant** if necessary, if need be.

échec [eʃɛk] **nm 1.** [insuccès] failure ▸ **un échec cuisant** a bitter defeat ▸ **essuyer un échec** to suffer a defeat ▸ **être en situation d'échec scolaire** to have learning difficulties ▸ **tenir qqn en échec** to hold sb in check ▸ **voué à l'échec** doomed to failure **2.** [jeux] **: échec et mat** checkmate.
◆ ***échecs*** **nmpl** chess *(U)*.

échelle [eʃɛl] **nf 1.** [objet] ladder ▸ **échelle de corde** rope ladder ▸ **échelle d'incendie** fireman's ladder ▸ **faire la courte échelle à qqn** *litt & fig* to give sb a leg up ▸ **monter dans l'échelle sociale** *fig* to climb the social ladder **2.** [ordre de grandeur] scale ▸ **à l'échelle de** on the scaleof ▸ **sur une grande échelle** on a large scale ▸ **à l'échelle nationale** nationwide ▸ **des événements à l'échelle mondiale** world events ▸ **une carte à l'échelle 1/10 000** a map on a scale of 1/10,000 ▸ **dessiner une carte à l'échelle** to draw a map to scale ▸ **sur l'échelle de Richter** on the Richter scale ▸ **échelle (mobile) des salaires** (sliding) salary scale.

échelon [eʃlɔ̃] **nm 1.** [barreau] rung **2.** *fig* [niveau] level ▸ **gravir les échelons (de)** to climb the rungs (of).

échelonner [3] [eʃlɔne] **vt** [espacer] to spread out.
◆ ***s'échelonner*** **vp** to be spread out.

écheveau, x [eʃvo] **nm** skein.

échevelé, e [eʃəvle] **adj 1.** [ébouriffé] dishevelled *UK*, disheveled *US* **2.** [frénétique] wild.

échine [eʃin] **nf** ANAT spine ▸ **courber l'échine** *fig* to submit.

échiner [3] [eʃine] ◆ ***s'échiner*** **vp** *fam* [s'épuiser] **: s'échiner (à faire qqch)** to exhaust o.s. (doing sthg).

échiquier [eʃikje] **nm 1.** [jeux] chessboard **2.** *fig* [scène] scene ▸ **l'échiquier politique** the political scene.

écho [eko] **nm** echo ▸ **il se fait l'écho de la direction** he repeats what the managers say ▸ **rester sans écho** to get no response.

échographie [ekɔgrafi] **nf** [examen] ultrasound (scan).

échoir [70] [eʃwar] **vi 1.** [être dévolu] **: échoir à** to fall to **2.** [expirer] to fall due.

échoppe [eʃɔp] **nf** stall.

échouer [6] [eʃwe] **vi 1.** [ne pas réussir] to fail ▸ **échouer à un examen** to fail an exam **2.** [navire] to run aground **3.** *fam fig* [aboutir] to end up.
◆ ***s'échouer*** **vp** [navire] to run aground.

échu, e [eʃy] **pp** ➤ ***échoir***.

éclabousser [3] [eklabuse] **vt 1.** [suj: liquide] to spatter **2.** *fig* [compromettre] to compromise.

éclaboussure [eklabusyr] **nf 1.** [de liquide] splash **2.** *fig* blot (on one's reputation).

éclair [eklɛr] ■ **nm 1.** [de lumière] flash of lightning **2.** *fig* [instant] **: éclair de** flash of ▸ **en un éclair** in a flash **3.** [gâteau] **: éclair au chocolat/café** chocolate/coffee éclair.
■ **adj inv : visite éclair** flying visit ▸ **guerre éclair** blitzkrieg.

éclairage [eklɛraʒ] **nm 1.** [lumière] lighting **2.** *fig* [point de vue] light.

éclairagiste [eklɛraʒist] **nmf 1.** CINÉ, THÉÂTRE & TV lighting engineer **2.** COMM dealer in lights and lamps.

éclaircie [eklɛrsi] **nf** bright interval, sunny spell.

éclaircir [32] [eklɛrsir] **vt 1.** [rendre plus clair] to lighten **2.** [rendre moins épais] to thin **3.** *fig* [clarifier] to clarify.
◆ ***s'éclaircir*** **vp 1.** [devenir plus clair] to clear **2.** [devenir moins épais] to thin **3.** [se clarifier] to become clearer.

éclaircissement [eklɛrsismɑ̃] **nm** [explication] explanation.

éclairer [4] [eklere] **vt 1.** [de lumière] to light up **2.** [expliquer] to clarify **3.** *littéraire* [renseigner] **: éclairer qqn sur qqch** to throw light on sthg for sb.
◆ ***s'éclairer*** **vp 1.** [personne] to light one's way **2.** [regard, visage] to light up **3.** [situation] to become clear **4.** [rue, ville] to light up.

éclaireur [eklɛrœr] **nm** scout ▸ **partir en éclaireur** to have a scout around.

éclat [ekla] **nm 1.** [de verre, d'os] splinter / [de pierre] chip ▸ **voler en éclats** to fly into pieces **2.** [de lumière] brilliance **3.** [de couleur] vividness **4.** [beauté] radiance **5.** [faste] splendour *UK*, splendor *US* **6.** [bruit] burst ▸ **éclat de rire** burst of laughter ▸ **éclats de voix** shouts ▸ **faire un éclat** to cause a scandal
▸▸| **rire aux éclats** to roar *ou* shriek with laughter.

éclatant, e [eklatɑ̃, ɑ̃t] **adj 1.** [brillant, resplendissant] brilliant, bright / [teint, beauté] radiant ▸ **éclatant de** bursting with **2.** [admirable] resounding **3.** [perçant] loud.

éclater [3] [eklate] **vi 1.** [exploser - pneu] to burst / [- verre] to shatter / [- obus] to explode ▸ **faire éclater** [- ballon] to burst / [- bombe] to explode / [- pétard] to let off **2.** [incendie, rires] to break out **3.** [joie] to shine ▸ **laisser éclater** to give vent to **4.** [bijou] to sparkle, to glitter **5.** *fig* [nouvelles, scandale] to break.
◆ ***s'éclater*** **vp** *fam* to have a great time.

éclectique [eklɛktik] **adj** eclectic.

éclipse [eklips] **nf 1.** ASTRON eclipse ▸ **éclipse de lune/soleil** eclipse of the moon/sun **2.** *fig* [période de défaillance] eclipse **3.** *fig* [disparition] disappearance.

éclipser [3] [eklipse] **vt** to eclipse.
◆ ***s'éclipser*** **vp 1.** ASTRON to go into eclipse **2.** *fam* [s'esquiver] to slip away.

éclopé**, **e [eklɔpe] ■ **adj** lame.
■ **nm, f** lame person.

éclore [113] [eklɔr] **vi 1.** [s'ouvrir - fleur] to open out, to blossom / [- œuf] to hatch ▸ **faire éclore** [- œuf] to hatch / *fig* [- vocation] to develop **2.** *fig* [naître] to dawn.

éclos**, e* [eklo, oz] **pp** ➤ ***éclore.

éclosion [eklozjɔ̃] **nf 1.** [de fleur] blossoming **2.** [d'œuf] hatching **3.** *fig* [naissance] blossoming, birth.

écluse [eklyz] **nf** lock.

écluser [3] [eklyze] **vt 1.** [NAUT - fleuve] to construct locks on / [- bateau] to take through a lock **2.** *fam* [boire] to knock back.

écœurant**, **e [ekœrɑ̃, ɑ̃t] **adj 1.** [gén] disgusting **2.** [démoralisant] sickening.

écœurement [ekœrmɑ̃] **nm 1.** [nausée] nausea **2.** [répugnance] disgust **3.** [découragement] discouragement.

écœurer [5] [ekœre] **vt 1.** [dégoûter] to sicken, to disgust **2.** *fig* [indigner] to sicken **3.** [décourager] to discourage.

écoguerrier [ekɔgɛrje] **nm** eco-warrior.

école [ekɔl] **nf 1.** [gén] school ▸ **aller à l'école** to go to school ▸ **école de commerce** business school ▸ **école communale** local primary *UK ou* grade *US* school ▸ **école de conduite** driving school ▸ **école maternelle** nursery school ▸ **école normale** ≃ teacher training college *UK*, ≃ teachers college *US* ▸ **École normale supérieure** *grande école for secondary and university teachers* ▸ **école primaire/secondaire** primary/secondary school *UK*, grade/high school *US* ▸ **école privée** private school ▸ **école publique** state school *UK*, public school *US* ▸ **grande école** *specialist training establishment, entered by competitive exam and highly prestigious* ▸ **faire l'école buissonnière** to play truant *UK ou* hooky *US* ▸ **être à bonne école** to be in good hands ▸ **faire école** to attract a following ▸ **il est de la vieille école** he's one of the old school *ou* guard **2.** [éducation] schooling ▸ **l'école laïque** secular education ▸ **l'école libre** education at an école libre *(Catholic school, partly state-funded)* ▸ **l'école obligatoire** compulsory schooling ▸ **l'école privée** private education.

écolier**, **ère [ekɔlje, ɛr] **nm, f 1.** [élève] pupil **2.** *fig* [novice] beginner.

écolo [ekɔlɔ] **nmf** *fam* ecologist ▸ **les écolos** the Greens.

écologie [ekɔlɔʒi] **nf** ecology.

écologique [ekɔlɔʒik] **adj** ecological.

écologiste [ekɔlɔʒist] **nmf** ecologist.

écomusée [ekɔmyze] **nm** museum of the environment.

éconduire [98] [ekɔ̃dɥir] **vt** [repousser - demande] to dismiss / [- visiteur, soupirant] to show to the door.

économat [ekɔnɔma] **nm 1.** [fonction] bursarship **2.** [magasin] staff shop.

économe [ekɔnɔm] ■ **nmf** bursar.
■ **adj** careful, thrifty ▸ **être économe de** to be sparing of.

économie [ekɔnɔmi] **nf 1.** [science] economics *(U)* **2.** POLIT economy ▸ **économie de bulle** bubble economy ▸ **économie dirigée** state-controlled economy ▸ **économie duale** dual economy ▸ **économie libérale** free-market economy ▸ **économie en ligne** e-economy ▸ **économie de marché** market economy ▸ **économie mixte** mixed economy ▸ **économie noire** hidden economy ▸ **économie à ressources sous-exploitées** sleeping economy ▸ **économie souterraine** *ou* **immergée** underground economy **3.** [parcimonie] economy, thrift **4.** *litt* & *fig* [épargne] saving ▸ **faire une économie de temps/d'argent** to save time/money.
◆ ***économies*** **fpl** [pécule] savings *pl* ▸ **économies d'énergie** energy savings ▸ **faire des économies** to save up ▸ **économies d'échelle** economies of scale.

économique [ekɔnɔmik] **adj 1.** ÉCON economic **2.** [avantageux] economical.

> PARONYME / CONFUSABLE
>
> **économique**
>
> Ce mot français peut se traduire de deux façons : *economic* signifie ce qui se rapporte à l'économie, alors que *economical* désigne ce qui n'est pas cher, ce qui permet d'économiser.

économiquement [ekɔnɔmikmɑ̃] **adv** economically.

économiser [3] [ekɔnɔmize] **vt** *litt* & *fig* to save.

économiste [ekɔnɔmist] **nmf** economist.

écoper [3] [ekɔpe] ■ **vt 1.** NAUT to bale out **2.** *fam* [sanction] **: écoper (de) qqch** to get sthg.
■ **vi** *fam* [être puni] to get the blame.

écoproduit [ekɔprɔdɥi] **nm** green product.

écorce [ekɔrs] **nf 1.** [d'arbre] bark **2.** [d'agrume] peel ▸ **écorce d'orange** orange peel **3.** GÉOL crust.

écorché [ekɔrʃe] **nm 1.** ANAT *cutaway anatomical figure* **2.** TECHNOL cutaway
▸▸ **un écorché vif** a soul in torment.

écorcher [3] [ekɔrʃe] **vt 1.** [lapin] to skin **2.** [bras, jambe] to scratch **3.** *fig* [langue, nom] to mispronounce.
◆ ***s'écorcher*** **vp** to graze o.s.

écorchure [ekɔrʃyr] **nf** graze, scratch.

écorecharge [ekɔrəʃarʒ] **nf** ecorefill.

écorner [3] [ekɔrne] **vt** [endommager - meuble] to damage / [- page] to dog-ear.

écossais**, **e [ekɔsɛ, ɛz] **adj 1.** [de l'Écosse] Scottish / [whisky] Scotch **2.** [tissu] tartan.
◆ ***écossais*** **nm 1.** [langue] Scots **2.** [tissu] tartan.
◆ ***Écossais**, **e*** **nm, f** Scot, Scotsman (f Scotswoman).

Écosse [ekɔs] **nf : l'Écosse** Scotland.

écosser [3] [ekɔse] **vt** to shell.

écosystème [ekɔsistɛm] **nm** ecosystem.

écot [eko] **nm** share ▸ **payer son écot** to pay one's share

écotaxe [ekɔtaks] **nf** green tax.

écotourisme [ekɔturism] **nm** ecotourism.

écoulement [ekulmɑ̃] **nm 1.** [gén] flow **2.** [du temps] passing **3.** [de marchandises] selling.

écouler [3] [ekule] **vt** to sell.
◆ ***s'écouler*** **vp 1.** [eau] to flow **2.** [personnes] to flow out **3.** [temps] to pass.

écourter [3] [ekurte] **vt** to shorten.

écoutant, e [ekutɑ̃, ɑ̃t] **nm, f** helpline volunteer, trained listener.

écoute [ekut] **nf 1.** [action d'écouter] listening ▸ **être à l'écoute de** to be listening to **2.** [audience] audience ▸ **heures d'écoute** RADIO listening time / TV viewing hours ▸ **heure de grande écoute** RADIO prime time, peak listening time / TV prime time, peak viewing time **3.** [surveillance] **: les écoutes téléphoniques** phone tapping *(U)* ▸ **être sur table d'écoute** *ou* **sur écoute(s)** to have one's phone tapped.

écouter [3] [ekute] **vt** to listen to.
◆ ***s'écouter*** **vp** *fig* **1.** [écouter soi-même] to listen to o.s. **2.** [s'observer] to coddle o.s.

écouteur [ekutœr] **nm** [de téléphone] earpiece.
◆ ***écouteurs*** **nmpl** [de radio] headphones.

écoutille [ekutij] **nf** hatchway.

écrabouiller [3] [ekrabuje] **vt** *fam* [écraser] to crush, to squash.

écran [ekrɑ̃] **nm 1.** CINÉ, TV & INFORM screen ▸ **le grand écran** the big screen, the cinema *UK* ▸ **le petit écran** the small screen, television ▸ **écran à cristaux liquides** liquid crystal display ▸ **écran orientable** tiltable screen ▸ **écran (à) plasma** plasma screen ▸ **écran plat** flat-faced screen ▸ **écran tactile** touch screen, tactile screen ▸ **à l'écran** *ou* **sur les écrans, cette semaine** what's on this week at the cinema *UK ou* movies *US*) ▸ **porter un roman à l'écran** to adapt a novel for the screen **2.** [de protection] shield ▸ **écran antibruit** noise-reduction screen ▸ **écran de fumée** smoke screen ▸ **écran solaire** sun screen ▸ **crème écran total** total protection sun cream *ou* block ▸ **les citations font écran à la clarté de l'article** the quotations make the article difficult to understand.

écrasant, e [ekrazɑ̃, ɑ̃t] **adj 1.** [lourd] crushing **2.** *fig* [accablant] overwhelming.

écraser [3] [ekraze] ■ **vt 1.** [comprimer - cigarette] to stub out / [- pied] to tread on / [- insecte, raisin] to crush ▸ **écraser un moustique** to swat a mosquito ▸ **écraser l'accélérateur** *ou* **le champignon** *fam* to step on it, to step on the gas *US* **2.** [accabler] **: écraser qqn (de)** to burden sb (with) ▸ **écraser un pays d'impôts** to overburden a country with taxes **3.** [vaincre] to crush ▸ **se faire écraser par l'équipe adverse** to get crushed by the opposing team **4.** [renverser] to run over ▸ **il s'est fait écraser** he was run over.
■ **vi** *fam* **: en écraser** to sleep like a log.
◆ ***s'écraser*** **vp 1.** [avion, automobile] **: s'écraser (contre)** to crash (into) ▸ **s'écraser contre un mur** to crash against a wall **2.** [foule] to be crushed ▸ **les gens s'écrasent pour entrer** there's a great crush to get in **3.** *fam* [se taire] to shut up ▸ **il vaut mieux s'écraser** better keep quiet *ou* mum.

écrémer [18] [ekreme] **vt 1.** [lait] to skim **2.** *fig* [bibliothèque, collection] to cream off the best from.

écrevisse [ekrəvis] **nf** crayfish ▸ **rouge comme une écrevisse** (as) red as a beetroot *UK ou* beet *US*.

écrier [10] [ekrije] ◆ ***s'écrier*** **vp** to cry out.

écrin [ekrɛ̃] **nm** case.

écrire [99] [ekrir] **vt 1.** [phrase, livre] to write **2.** [orthographier] to spell.
◆ ***s'écrire*** **vp** [s'épeler] to be spelled.

écrit, e [ekri, it] ■ **pp** ➤ ***écrire***.
■ **adj** written ▸ **bien/mal écrit** well/badly written.
◆ ***écrit*** **nm 1.** [ouvrage] writing **2.** [examen] written exam **3.** [document] piece of writing.
◆ ***par écrit*** **loc adv** in writing.

écriteau, x [ekrito] **nm** notice.

écriture [ekrityr] **nf 1.** [gén] writing ▸ **écriture idéographique** ideographic writing **2.** [bible] **: l'Écriture sainte** the Holy Scripture.
◆ ***écritures*** **nfpl** COMM accounts, entries ▸ **tenir les écritures** to do the bookkeeping ▸ **jeu d'écritures** dummy entry.

écrivain [ekrivɛ̃] **nm** writer, author ▸ **écrivain public** (public) letter-writer.

écrivais, écrivions ➤ ***écrire***.

écrou [ekru] **nm** TECHNOL nut.

écrouer [3] [ekrue] **vt** to imprison.

écroulement [ekrulmɑ̃] **nm** *litt* & *fig* collapse.

écrouler [3] [ekrule] ◆ ***s'écrouler*** **vp** *litt* & *fig* to collapse.

écru, e [ekry] **adj** [naturel] unbleached.

ecsta [ɛksta] (abr de ***ecstasy***) **nm** E, ecstasy.

ecstasy [ɛkstazi] **nm** [drogue] ecstasy.

ectoplasme [ɛktɔplasm] **nm** ectoplasm.

écu [eky] **nm 1.** [bouclier, armoiries] shield **2.** [monnaie ancienne] crown.

écueil [ekœj] **nm 1.** [rocher] reef **2.** *fig* [obstacle] stumbling block.

écuelle [ekɥɛl] **nf 1.** [objet] bowl **2.** [contenu] bowlful.

éculé, e [ekyle] **adj 1.** [chaussure] down-at-heel **2.** *fig* [plaisanterie] hackneyed.

écume [ekym] **nf 1.** [mousse, bave] foam **2.** *fig* [lie] dregs *pl*.

écumer [3] [ekyme] ■ **vt 1.** [confiture] to skim **2.** *fig* [mer, ville] to scour.
■ **vi 1.** [mer] to foam, to boil **2.** [animal] to foam at the mouth **3.** *fig* [être furieux] **: écumer (de)** to boil (with).

écumoire [ekymwar] **nf** skimmer.

écureuil [ekyrœj] **nm** squirrel ▸ **l'Écureuil** *nickname for the Caisse d'Épargne (whose logo is a squirrel).*

écurie [ekyri] **nf 1.** [pour chevaux & SPORT] stable **2.** *fig* [local sale] pigsty.

écusson [ekysɔ̃] **nm 1.** [d'armoiries] coat-of-arms **2.** MIL badge.

écuyer, ère [ekɥije, ɛr] **nm, f** [de cirque] rider.
◆ ***écuyer*** **nm** [de chevalier] squire.

eczéma [ɛgzema] **nm** eczema.

éd. (abr écrite de ***édition***) ed., edit.

edelweiss [edɛlvɛs] **nm** edelweiss.

éden [edɛn] **nm : un éden** a garden of Eden ▸ **l'Éden** the garden of Eden.

édenté, e [edɑ̃te] **adj** toothless.

EDF**, **Edf (abr de ***Électricité de France***) **nf** *French national electricity company*.

édifiant**, **e [edifjɑ̃, ɑ̃t] **adj** edifying.

édification [edifikasjɔ̃] **nf 1.** [de temple, empire] building **2.** *fig* [de fidèles] edification.

édifice [edifis] **nm 1.** [construction] building ▸ **édifice public** public building **2.** *fig* [institution] **: l'édifice social** the fabric of society.

édifier [9] [edifje] **vt 1.** [ville, église] to build **2.** *fig* [théorie] to construct **3.** [personne] to edify / *iron* to enlighten.

Édimbourg [edɛ̃bur] **npr** Edinburgh.

édit [edi] **nm** edict.

édit. abr de ***éditeur***.

éditer [3] [edite] **vt** to publish.

éditeur**, **trice [editœr, tris] **nm, f** publisher.

édition [edisjɔ̃] **nf 1.** [profession] publishing ▸ **travailler dans l'édition** to be in publishing *ou* in the publishing business **2.** [de journal, livre] edition ▸ **dernière édition** latest edition ▸ **édition de poche** paperback edition ▸ **édition électronique** electronic publishing ▸ **édition originale** first edition ▸ **édition revue et corrigée** revised edition ▸ **édition spéciale** [de journal] special edition / [de revue] special issue **3.** TV **: édition du journal télévisé** (television) news bulletin ▸ **édition spéciale en direct de Budapest** special report live from Budapest.

édito [edito] **nm** *fam* editorial.

éditorial**, **aux [editɔrjal, o] **nm** editorial, leader *UK*.

éditorialiste [editɔrjalist] **nmf** editorialist, leader writer *UK*.

édredon [edrədɔ̃] **nm** eiderdown *UK*, comforter *US*.

éducateur**, **trice [edykatœr, tris] ■ **adj** educational. ■ **nm, f** teacher ▸ **éducateur spécialisé** special needs teacher.

éducatif**, **ive [edykatif, iv] **adj** educational.

éducation [edykasjɔ̃] **nf 1.** [apprentissage] education ▸ **éducation civique** civics *(U)* ▸ **l'Éducation nationale** ≃ the Department for Education *UK*, ≃ the Department of Education *US* ▸ **éducation physique** physical education ▸ **éducation sexuelle** sex education **2.** [parentale] upbringing **3.** [savoir-vivre] breeding.

édulcorant [edylkɔrɑ̃] **nm : édulcorant (de synthèse)** (artificial) sweetener.

édulcorer [3] [edylkɔre] **vt 1.** *sout* [tisane] to sweeten **2.** *fig* [propos] to tone down.

éduquer [3] [edyke] **vt** [enfant] to bring up / [élève] to educate.

édutainment [edytɛnmɑ̃nt] **m** edutainment.

effacé**, **e [efase] **adj 1.** [teinte] faded **2.** [modeste - rôle] unobtrusive / [- personne] self-effacing.

effacer [16] [efase] **vt 1.** [mot] to erase, to rub out / INFORM to delete **2.** [souvenir] to erase **3.** [réussite] to eclipse.
◆ ***s'effacer*** **vp 1.** [s'estomper] to fade (away) **2.** *sout* [s'écarter] to move aside **3.** *fig* [s'incliner] to give way.

effaceur [efasœr] **nm : effaceur (d'encre)** ink eraser *ou* rubber *UK*.

effarant**, **e [efarɑ̃, ɑ̃t] **adj** frightening.

effaré**, **e [efare] **adj** frightened, scared.

effarement [efarmɑ̃] **nm** fear, alarm.

effarer [3] [efare] **vt** to frighten, to scare.

effaroucher [3] [efaruʃe] **vt 1.** [effrayer] to scare off **2.** [intimider] to overawe.

effectif**, **ive [efɛktif, iv] **adj 1.** [remède] effective **2.** [aide] positive.
◆ ***effectif*** **nm 1.** MIL strength **2.** [de groupe] total number.

effectivement [efɛktivmɑ̃] **adv 1.** [réellement] effectively **2.** [confirmation] in fact.

effectuer [7] [efɛktɥe] **vt** [réaliser - manœuvre] to carry out / [- trajet, paiement] to make.
◆ ***s'effectuer*** **vp** to be made.

efféminé**, **e [efemine] **adj** effeminate.

effervescence [efɛrvesɑ̃s] **nf 1.** PHYS effervescence **2.** [agitation] turmoil ▸ **en effervescence** in turmoil.

effervescent**, **e [efɛrvesɑ̃, ɑ̃t] **adj** [boisson] effervescent / *fig* [pays] in turmoil.

effet [efɛ] **nm 1.** [gén] effect ▸ **avoir pour effet de faire qqch** to have the effect of doing sthg ▸ **créer un effet de surprise** to create a surprise effect ▸ **à effet rétroactif** DR retrospective ▸ **effet de contraste/d'optique** contrasting/visual effect ▸ **effet de halo** [lumière] halo effect ▸ **effet de lumière** THÉÂTRE lighting effect ▸ **effets personnels** personal effects *ou* belongings ▸ **effet secondaire** MÉD side-effect ▸ **effets spéciaux** CINÉ special effects ▸ **rester sans effet** to be ineffective ▸ **sous l'effet de** under the effects of / [alcool] under the influence of ▸ **j'ai dit des choses regrettables sous l'effet de la colère** anger made me say things which I later regretted ▸ **effet de serre** greenhouse effect **2.** [impression recherchée] impression ▸ **faire son effet** to cause a stir ▸ **faire beaucoup d'effet/peu d'effet** to be impressive/unimpressive ▸ **quel effet cela t'a-t-il fait de le revoir?** how did seeing him again affect you? **3.** COMM [titre] bill ▸ **effet de commerce** bill of exchange ▸ **effet à courte échéance** short *ou* short-dated bill ▸ **effet à longue échéance** long *ou* long-dated bill ▸ **effet escomptable/négociable** discountable/negotiable bill ▸ **effet au porteur** bill payable to bearer ▸ **effet à vue** sight bill, demand bill *ou* draft.
◆ ***en effet*** **loc adv** in fact, indeed ▸ **c'est en effet la meilleure solution** it's actually *ou* in fact the best solution ▸ **il n'a pas pu venir; en effet, il était malade** he was unable to come since he was ill.
◆ ***à cet effet*** **loc adv** with this end in view.

effeuiller [5] [efœje] **vt** [arbre] to remove the leaves from / [fleur] to remove the petals from.
◆ ***s'effeuiller*** **vp** [arbre] to lose its leaves / [fleur] to lose its petals.

efficace [efikas] **adj 1.** [remède, mesure] effective **2.** [personne, machine] efficient.

efficacité [efikasite] **nf 1.** [de remède, mesure] effectiveness **2.** [de personne, machine] efficiency.

efficience [efisjɑ̃s] **nf** efficiency.

effigie [efiʒi] **nf** effigy.

effilé**, **e [efile] **adj** [doigt, silhouette] slim, slender / [lame] sharp / [voiture] streamlined.

effiler [3] [efile] **vt 1.** [tissu] to fray **2.** [lame] to sharpen **3.** [cheveux] to thin.
◆ ***s'effiler*** **vp** to fray.

effilocher [3] [efilɔʃe] **vt** to fray.
◆ ***s'effilocher*** **vp** to fray.

***efflanqué**, e* [eflɑ̃ke] **adj** emaciated.

effleurer [5] [eflœre] **vt 1.** [visage, bras] to brush (against) **2.** *fig* [problème, thème] to touch on **3.** *fig* [suj: pensée, idée] **: effleurer qqn** to cross sb's mind.

effluve [eflyv] **nm** exhalation / *fig* [d'enfance, du passé] breath.

effondrement [efɔ̃drəmɑ̃] **nm** *litt* & *fig* collapse.

effondrer [3] [efɔ̃dre] ◆ ***s'effondrer*** **vp** *litt* & *fig* to collapse.

efforcer [16] [efɔrse] ◆ ***s'efforcer*** **vp** to force o.s. ▸ **s'efforcer de faire qqch** to make an effort to do sthg.

effort [efɔr] **nm 1.** [de personne] effort ▸ **faire un effort** to make an effort ▸ **faire l'effort de faire qqch** to make the effort to do sthg ▸ **sans effort** [victoire] effortless **2.** TECHNOL stress.

effraction [efraksjɔ̃] **nf** breaking in ▸ **entrer par effraction dans** to break into.

effranger [17] [efrɑ̃ʒe] **vt** to fray into a fringe.
◆ ***s'effranger*** **vpi** to fray.

***effrayant**, e* [efrɛjɑ̃, ɑ̃t] **adj 1.** [cauchemar] terrifying **2.** *fam* [appétit, prix] tremendous, awful.

effrayer [11] [efreje] **vt** to frighten, to scare.
◆ ***s'effrayer*** **vp** to be frightened, to take fright.

***effréné**, e* [efrene] **adj 1.** [course] frantic **2.** [désir] unbridled.

effriter [3] [efrite] **vt** to cause to crumble.
◆ ***s'effriter*** **vp 1.** [mur] to crumble **2.** *fig* [majorité] to be eroded.

effroi [efrwa] **nm** fear, dread.

***effronté**, e* [efrɔ̃te] ■ **adj** insolent.
■ **nm, f** insolent person.

effrontément [efrɔ̃temɑ̃] **adv** insolently.

effronterie [efrɔ̃tri] **nf** insolence.

effroyable [efrwajabl] **adj 1.** [catastrophe, misère] appalling **2.** [laideur] hideous.

effusion [efyzjɔ̃] **nf 1.** [de liquide] effusion ▸ **sans effusion de sang** without bloodshed **2.** [de sentiments] effusiveness.

égal**, e, **aux [egal, o] ■ **adj 1.** [équivalent] equal **2.** [régulier] even **3.** *fam* [indifférent] **: ça m'est égal, c'est égal** I don't mind.
■ **nm, f** equal ▸ **d'égal à égal** as an equal ▸ **sans égal** unequalled *UK*, unequaled *US*.

également [egalmɑ̃] **adv 1.** [avec égalité] equally **2.** [aussi] as well, too.

égaler [3] [egale] **vt 1.** MATH to equal **2.** [beauté] to match, to compare with.

égalisation [egalizasjɔ̃] **nf** equalization / SPORT equalizing *UK*, tying *US*.

égaliser [3] [egalize] ■ **vt** [haie, cheveux] to trim.
■ **vi** SPORT to equalize *UK*, to tie *US*.

égalitaire [egalitɛr] **adj** egalitarian.

égalitarisme [egalitarism] **nm** egalitarianism.

égalité [egalite] **nf 1.** [gén] equality ▸ **être à égalité** to be level *ou* equal **2.** [d'humeur] evenness **3.** SPORT **: être à égalité** to be level, to be tied **4.** [au tennis] deuce.

égard [egar] **nm** consideration ▸ **à bien des égards** in many respects ▸ **à cet égard** in this respect ▸ **par égard pour** *sout* out of consideration for ▸ **eu égard à** considering ▸ **être plein d'égards** *ou* **avoir beaucoup d'égards pour qqn** to show great consideration for *ou* to be very considerate towards sb ▸ **manquer d'égards envers qqn** to show a lack of consideration for *ou* to be inconsiderate towards sb.
◆ ***à l'égard de*** **loc prép** with regard to, towards *UK*, toward *US* ▸ **être dur/tendre à l'égard de qqn** to be hard on/gentle with sb.
◆ ***à certains égards*** **loc adv** in some respects.
◆ ***sans égard pour*** **loc prép** with no respect *ou* consideration for, without regard for.

***égaré**, e* [egare] **adj 1.** [perdu - voyageur] lost / [- animal] stray *(avant n)* **2.** [regard, air] distraught.

égarement [egarmɑ̃] **nm 1.** [de jeunesse] wildness **2.** [de raisonnement] aberration.
◆ ***égarements*** **nmpl** *littéraire* **: les égarements de la passion** the follies of passion ▸ **revenir de ses égarements** to see the error of one's ways.

égarer [3] [egare] **vt 1.** [objet] to mislay, to lose **2.** [personne] to mislead **3.** *fig* & *sout* [suj: passion] to lead astray.
◆ ***s'égarer*** **vp 1.** [lettre] to get lost, to go astray / [personne] to get lost, to lose one's way **2.** [discussion] to wander from the point **3.** *fig* & *sout* [personne] to stray from the point.

égayer [11] [egeje] **vt 1.** [personne] to cheer up **2.** [pièce] to brighten up.
◆ ***s'égayer*** **vp** to enjoy o.s.

égérie [eʒeri] **nf** muse.

égide [eʒid] **nf** protection ▸ **sous l'égide de** *littéraire* under the aegis of.

églantier [eglɑ̃tje] **nm** wild rose (bush).

églantine [eglɑ̃tin] **nf** wild rose.

églefin**, **aiglefin [egləfɛ̃] **nm** haddock.

église [egliz] **nf** church ▸ **aller à l'église** to go to church.
◆ ***Église*** **nf : l'Église** the Church ▸ **l'Église catholique/protestante** the Catholic/Protestant Church.

ego [ego] **nm** ego.

égocentrique [egɔsɑ̃trik] ■ **nmf** self-centred *UK ou* self-centered *US* person.
■ **adj** self-centred *UK*, self-centered *US*, egocentric.

égocentrisme [egɔsɑ̃trism] **nm** self-centredness *UK*, self-centeredness *US*.

égoïsme [egɔism] **nm** selfishness, egoism.

égoïste [egɔist] ■ **nmf** selfish person.
■ **adj** selfish, egoistic.

égorger [17] [egɔrʒe] **vt 1.** [animal, personne] to cut the throat of **2.** *fig* [client] to bleed dry.

égosiller [3] [egɔzije] ◆ ***s'égosiller*** **vp** *fam* **1.** [crier] to bawl, to shout **2.** [chanter] to sing one's head off.

égout [egu] **nm** sewer.
égoutter [3] [egute] **vt 1.** [vaisselle] to leave to drain **2.** [légumes, fromage] to drain.
◆ ***s'égoutter*** **vp** to drip, to drain.
égouttoir [egutwar] **nm 1.** [à légumes] colander, strainer **2.** [à vaisselle] draining rack.
égratigner [3] [egratiɲe] **vt** to scratch / *fig* to have a go *ou* dig at.
◆ ***s'égratigner*** **vp : s'égratigner la main** to scratch one's hand.
égratignure [egratiɲyr] **nf** scratch, graze / *fig* dig.
égrener [19] [egrəne] **vt 1.** [détacher les grains de - épi, cosse] to shell / [- grappe] to pick grapes from **2.** [chapelet] to tell **3.** *fig* [marquer] to mark.
◆ ***s'égrener*** **vp 1.** [raisins] to drop off the bunch **2.** [personnes] to spread out.
égrillard, e [egrijar, ard] **adj** ribald, bawdy.
Égypte [eʒipt] **nf : l'Égypte** Egypt.
égyptien, enne [eʒipsjɛ̃, ɛn] **adj** Egyptian.
◆ ***égyptien*** **nm** [langue] Egyptian.
◆ ***Égyptien, enne*** **nm, f** Egyptian.
égyptologie [eʒiptɔlɔʒi] **nf** Egyptology.
eh [e] **interj** hey! ▸ **eh bien** well.
éhonté, e [eɔ̃te] ■ **adj** shameless.
■ **nm, f** shameless person.
Eiffel [efɛl] **npr : la tour Eiffel** the Eiffel Tower.
éjaculation [eʒakylasjɔ̃] **nf** ejaculation ▸ **éjaculation précoce** premature ejaculation.
éjaculer [3] [eʒakyle] **vt & vi** to ejaculate.
éjectable [eʒɛktabl] **adj : siège éjectable** ejector *UK ou* ejection *US* seat.
éjecter [4] [eʒɛkte] **vt 1.** [douille] to eject **2.** *fam* [personne] to kick out ▸ **se faire éjecter** to get kicked *ou* chucked *ou* booted out.
◆ ***s'éjecter*** **vp** *(emploi réfléchi)* AÉRON to eject.
élaboration [elabɔrasjɔ̃] **nf** [de plan, système] working out, development.
élaboré, e [elabɔre] **adj** elaborate.
élaborer [3] [elabɔre] **vt** [plan, système] to work out, to develop.
élagage [elagaʒ] **nm** *litt & fig* pruning.
élaguer [3] [elage] **vt** *litt & fig* to prune.
élan [elɑ̃] **nm 1.** ZOOL elk **2.** [athlétisme] run-up ▸ **prendre de l'élan** to gather speed *ou* momentum ▸ **prendre son élan** to take a run-up, to gather speed ▸ **saut avec/sans élan** running/standing jump **3.** *Québec* [golf] swing **4.** *fig* [de joie] outburst ▸ **élan de générosité** generous impulse ▸ **élans de tendresse** surges *ou* rushes of affection ▸ **donner de l'élan à une campagne** to give impetus to *ou* to provide impetus for a campaign.
élancé, e [elɑ̃se] **adj** slender.
élancement [elɑ̃smɑ̃] **nm** [douleur] shooting pain.
élancer [16] [elɑ̃se] **vi** MÉD to give shooting pains.
◆ ***s'élancer*** **vp 1.** [se précipiter] to rush, to dash **2.** SPORT to take a run-up **3.** *fig* [s'envoler] to soar.
élargir [32] [elarʒir] ■ **vt** to widen / [vêtement] to let out / *fig* to expand.
■ **vi** *fam* [forcir] to fill out.
◆ ***s'élargir*** **vp 1.** [s'agrandir] to widen / [vêtement] to stretch / *fig* to expand **2.** *fam* [grossir] to put on weight.
élargissement [elarʒismɑ̃] **nm** widening / [de vêtement] letting out / *fig* expansion.
élasticité [elastisite] **nf 1.** PHYS elasticity **2.** [de personne, corps] flexibility.
élastique [elastik] ■ **nm 1.** [pour attacher] rubber *ou* elastic *UK* band **2.** [matière] elastic.
■ **adj 1.** PHYS elastic **2.** [corps] flexible **3.** *fig* [conscience] accommodating.
élastomère [elastɔmɛr] **nm** elastomer.
eldorado [ɛldɔrado] **nm** El Dorado.
électeur, trice [elɛktœr, tris] **nm, f** voter, elector.
élection [elɛksjɔ̃] **nf 1.** [vote] election ▸ **élections municipales** local elections ▸ **élection partielle** by-election *UK*, off-year election *US* ▸ **élection présidentielle** presidential election ▸ **élections pour la présidence *ou* la tête (d'un parti)** POLIT leadership election **2.** *fig* [choix] choice ▸ **d'élection** chosen.
électoral, e, aux [elɛktɔral, o] **adj** electoral / [campagne, réunion] election *(avant n)*.
électoralisme [elɛktɔralism] **nm** electioneering.
électorat [elɛktɔra] **nm** electorate.
électricien, enne [elɛktrisjɛ̃, ɛn] **nm, f** electrician.
électricité [elɛktrisite] **nf** electricity ▸ **il y a de l'électricité dans l'air** *fig* the atmosphere is electric.
électrification [elɛktrifikasjɔ̃] **nf** electrification.
électrifier [9] [elɛktrifje] **vt** to electrify.
électrique [elɛktrik] **adj** *litt & fig* electric.

PARONYME / CONFUSABLE

électrique

Attention à la traduction de **électrique**, qui peut être ***electrical*** si l'on veut parler de l'énergie électrique, ou ***electric*** si l'on veut qualifier une atmosphère tendue.

électriser [3] [elɛktrize] **vt** *litt & fig* to electrify.
électroaimant [elɛktrɔɛmɑ̃] **nm** electro-magnet.
électrocardiogramme [elɛktrɔkardjɔgram] **nm** electrocardiogram.
électrochoc [elɛktrɔʃɔk] **nm** electroshock therapy.
électrocuter [3] [elɛktrɔkyte] **vt** to electrocute.
◆ ***s'électrocuter*** **vp** *(emploi réfléchi)* to electrocute o.s to be electrocuted ▸ **il a failli s'électrocuter** he nearl electrocuted himself.
électrode [elɛktrɔd] **nf** electrode.
électroencéphalogramme [elɛktrɔɑ̃sefalɔgram] **nm** electroencephalogram.
électrogène [elɛktrɔʒɛn] **adj : groupe électrogène** generating unit.
électrolyse [elɛktrɔliz] **nf** electrolysis.

électromagnétique [elɛktrɔmaɲetik] **adj** electromagnetic.

électroménager [elɛktrɔmenaʒe] ■ **adj : appareil électroménager** household electrical appliance.
■ **nm** household electrical appliances *pl*.

électron [elɛktrɔ̃] **nm** electron.

électronicien, enne [elɛktrɔnisjɛ̃, ɛn] **nm, f** electronics specialist.

électronique [elɛktrɔnik] ■ **nf** [sciences] electronics *(U)*.
■ **adj** electronic / [microscope] electron *(avant n)*.

électrophone [elɛktrɔfɔn] **nm** record player.

élégamment [elegamɑ̃] **adv** elegantly.

élégance [elegɑ̃s] **nf 1.** [de personne, style] elegance **2.** [délicatesse - de solution, procédé] elegance / [- de conduite] generosity.

élégant, e [elegɑ̃, ɑ̃t] **adj 1.** [personne, style] elegant **2.** [délicat - solution, procédé] elegant / [- conduite] generous.

élément [elemɑ̃] **nm 1.** [gén] element ▸ **éléments blindés/motorisés** armoured *UK ou* armored *US*/motorized units ▸ **éléments d'information** facts, information ▸ **il n'y a aucun élément nouveau** there are no new developments ▸ **élément radioactif** radioactive element ▸ **éléments de rangement** storage units ▸ **les bons/mauvais éléments** the good/bad elements ▸ **les quatre éléments** the four elements ▸ **être dans son élément** to be in one's element **2.** [de machine] component.

élémentaire [elemɑ̃tɛr] **adj 1.** [gén] elementary **2.** [installation, besoin] basic.

éléphant [elefɑ̃] **nm** elephant.

éléphanteau, x [elefɑ̃to] **nm** baby *ou* young elephant.

éléphantesque [elefɑ̃tɛsk] **adj** *fam* gigantic.

élevage [ɛlvaʒ] **nm** breeding, rearing / [installation] farm.

élévateur, trice [elevatœr, tris] **adj** elevator *(avant n)*.
◆ ***élévateur*** **nm** lift *UK*, elevator *US*.

élévation [elevasjɔ̃] **nf 1.** [gén] raising ▸ **élévation à** MATH raising to / *fig* elevation to **2.** [tertre] rise, mound **3.** [de sentiments] nobility.

élève [elɛv] **nmf 1.** [écolier, disciple] pupil **2.** MIL cadet.

élevé, e [ɛlve] **adj 1.** [haut] high **2.** *fig* [sentiment, âme] noble **3.** [enfant] **: bien/mal élevé** well/badly brought up.

élever [19] [ɛlve] **vt 1.** [gén] to raise ▸ **élever la voix** *ou* **le ton** to raise one's voice **2.** [fardeau] to lift, to raise **3.** [statue] to put up, to erect **4.** [à un rang supérieur] to elevate ▸ **élever qqn au grade d'officier** to promote *ou* to raise sb to (the rank of) officer **5.** [esprit] to improve **6.** [enfant] to bring up ▸ **élever qqn dans du coton** to overprotect sb, to mollycoddle sb **7.** [poulets] to rear, to breed.
◆ ***s'élever*** **vp 1.** [gén] to rise ▸ **la température s'est élevée de 10 degrés** the temperature has risen by *ou* has gone up 10 degrees ▸ **s'élever dans l'échelle sociale** to work one's way up *ou* to climb the social ladder **2.** [montant] **: s'élever à** to add up to ▸ **le bilan s'élève à 10 morts et 12 blessés** the number of casualties is 10 dead and 12 injured **3.** [protester] **: s'élever contre qqn/qqch** to protest against sb/sthg ▸ **on entend s'élever des voix** you can hear voices being raised.

éleveur, euse [ɛlvœr, øz] **nm, f** breeder.

elfe [ɛlf] **nm** elf.

élider [3] [elide] **vt** to elide.
◆ ***s'élider*** **vp** to be elided.

éligible [eliʒibl] **adj** eligible.

élimé, e [elime] **adj** threadbare.

élimination [eliminasjɔ̃] **nf** elimination ▸ **procéder par élimination** to proceed by elimination.

éliminatoire [eliminatwar] ■ **nf** *(gén pl)* SPORT qualifying heat *ou* round.
■ **adj** qualifying *(avant n)*.

éliminer [3] [elimine] **vt** to eliminate.

élire [106] [elir] **vt** to elect.

élisais, élisions ➤ ***élire***.

élision [elizjɔ̃] **nf** elision.

élite [elit] **nf** elite ▸ **d'élite** choice, select.

élitiste [elitist] **nmf & adj** elitist.

élixir [eliksir] **nm** elixir.

elle [ɛl] **pron pers 1.** [sujet - personne] she / [- animal] it, she / [- chose] it **2.** [complément - personne] her / [- animal] it, her / [- chose] it.
◆ ***elles*** **pron pers pl 1.** [sujet] they **2.** [complément] them.
◆ ***elle-même*** **pron pers** [personne] herself / [animal] itself, herself / [chose] itself.
◆ ***elles-mêmes*** **pron pers pl** themselves.

ellipse [elips] **nf 1.** GÉOM ellipse **2.** LING ellipsis.

elliptique [eliptik] **adj** elliptical.

élocution [elɔkysjɔ̃] **nf** delivery ▸ **défaut d'élocution** speech defect.

éloge [elɔʒ] **nm 1.** [discours] eulogy **2.** [louange] praise ▸ **faire l'éloge de qqn/qqch** [louer] to speak highly of sb/sthg ▸ **couvrir qqn d'éloges** to shower sb with praise.

élogieux, euse [elɔʒjø, øz] **adj** laudatory.

éloigné, e [elwaɲe] **adj** distant.

éloignement [elwaɲmɑ̃] **nm 1.** [mise à l'écart] removal **2.** [séparation] absence **3.** [dans l'espace, le temps] distance.

éloigner [3] [elwaɲe] **vt 1.** [écarter] to move away ▸ **éloigner qqch de** to move sthg away from **2.** [détourner] to turn away ▸ **ça nous éloignerait du sujet** that would take us away from the point ▸ **mon travail m'a éloigné de ma famille** my work's kept me away from my family **3.** [chasser] to dismiss ▸ **éloigner les soupçons de qqn** to avert suspicion from sb.
◆ ***s'éloigner*** **vp 1.** [partir] to move *ou* go away ▸ **ne vous éloignez pas trop, les enfants** don't go too far (away), children ▸ **éloignez-vous du bord de la falaise** move away *ou* get back from the edge of the cliff **2.** *fig* **: s'éloigner du sujet** to stray from the point **3.** [se détacher] to distance o.s. ▸ **s'éloigner de la réalité** to lose touch with reality ▸ **peu à peu ils se sont éloignés l'un de l'autre** they gradually drifted apart.

élongation [elɔ̃gasjɔ̃] **nf** MÉD **: élongation de muscle** pulled muscle.

éloquence [elɔkɑ̃s] **nf 1.** [d'orateur, d'expression] eloquence **2.** [de données] significance.

éloquent, e [elɔkɑ̃, ɑ̃t] **adj 1.** [avocat, silence] eloquent **2.** [données] significant.

élu, e [ely] ■ **pp** ➤ ***élire***.
■ **adj** POLIT elected.
■ **nm, f 1.** POLIT elected representative **2.** RELIG chosen one ▸ **l'élu de son cœur** *hum* & *sout* one's heart's desire.

élucider [3] [elyside] **vt** to clear up.

élucubration [elykybrasjɔ̃] **nf** raving.

éluder [3] [elyde] **vt** to evade.

Élysée [elize] **nm : l'Élysée** *the official residence of the French President and, by extension, the President himself.*

CULTURE
L'Élysée

Erected in 1717, the **Palais de l'Élysée** has been the French president's official residence since 1876. The building is near the Champs-Élysées, the famous thoroughfare to which it lends its name. In the media, **l'Élysée** is used as a synonym for presidential authority, much in the way that 'Number Ten' is used in the UK or 'the White House' in the US: **Une déclaration de l'Élysée est attendue dans la matinée.** Each year during the **Journées du Patrimoine**, parts of the building are opened to the public for guided tours. The president also gives a yearly reception for political journalists in the palace's gardens.

émacié, e [emasje] **adj** *littéraire* emaciated.

e-mail [imɛl] (pl **e-mails**) **nm** e-mail, E-mail.

émail, aux [emaj, emo] **nm** enamel ▸ **en émail** enamel, enamelled *UK*, enameled *US*.
◆ ***émaux*** **nmpl** enamelwork *(U)*.

émanation [emanasjɔ̃] **nf** emanation ▸ **être l'émanation de** *fig* to emanate from.

émancipation [emɑ̃sipasjɔ̃] **nf** emancipation.

émancipé, e [emɑ̃sipe] **adj** [peuple] emancipated / [femme] emancipated, liberated.

émanciper [3] [emɑ̃sipe] **vt** to emancipate.
◆ ***s'émanciper*** **vp 1.** [se libérer] to become free *ou* liberated **2.** *fam* [se dévergonder] to become emancipated.

émaner [3] [emane] **vi : émaner de** to emanate from.

émarger [17] [emarʒe] ■ **vt 1.** [signer] to sign **2.** [enlever la marge de] to trim the margins of.
■ **vi** to sign.

émasculer [3] [emaskyle] **vt** to emasculate.

emballage [ɑ̃balaʒ] **nm** packaging.

emballage-bulle **m** bubble wrap.

emballement [ɑ̃balmɑ̃] **nm 1.** [enthousiasme] sudden craze **2.** [de moteur] racing *(U)*.

emballer [3] [ɑ̃bale] **vt 1.** [objet] to pack (up), to wrap (up) **2.** [moteur] to race **3.** *fam* [plaire à] to thrill.
◆ ***s'emballer*** **vp 1.** [moteur] to race **2.** [cheval] to bolt **3.** *fam* [personne - s'enthousiasmer] to get carried away / [- s'emporter] to lose one's temper.

embarcadère [ɑ̃barkadɛr] **nm** landing stage.

embarcation [ɑ̃barkasjɔ̃] **nf** small boat.

embardée [ɑ̃barde] **nf** swerve ▸ **faire une embardée** to swerve.

embargo [ɑ̃bargo] **nm** embargo ▸ **embargo sur les armes** arms embargo.

embarquement [ɑ̃barkəmɑ̃] **nm 1.** [de marchandises] loading **2.** [de passagers] boarding ▸ **embarquement immédiat** immediate boarding.

embarquer [3] [ɑ̃barke] ■ **vt 1.** [marchandises] to load **2.** [passagers] to (take on) board **3.** *fam* [dans une voiture] to take, to give a lift to **4.** *fam* [arrêter] to pick up **5.** *fam fig* [engager] **: embarquer qqn dans** to involve sb in **6.** *fam* [emmener] to cart off.
■ **vi : embarquer (pour)** to sail (for).
◆ ***s'embarquer*** **vp 1.** [sur un bateau] to (set) sail **2.** *fam fig* [s'engager] **: s'embarquer dans** to get involved in.

embarras [ɑ̃bara] **nm 1.** [incertitude] (state of) uncertainty ▸ **avoir l'embarras du choix** to be spoilt for choice ▸ **on les a en dix teintes, vous avez l'embarras du choix** they come in ten different shades: you're spoilt for choice **2.** [situation difficile] predicament ▸ **être dans l'embarras** to be in a predicament ▸ **mettre qqn dans l'embarras** to place sb in an awkward position ▸ **ma question l'a mis dans l'embarras** my question put him on the spot ▸ **tirer qqn d'embarras** to get sb out of a tight spot **3.** [perplexité] confusion **4.** [gêne] embarrassment ▸ **à mon grand embarras, il m'a embrassé** to my great embarrassment, he kissed me **5.** [souci] difficulty, worry ▸ **avoir des embarras financiers** *ou* **d'argent** to be in financial difficulties, to have money problems.

embarrassant, e [ɑ̃barasɑ̃, ɑ̃t] **adj 1.** [encombrant] cumbersome **2.** [délicat] embarrassing.

embarrassé, e [ɑ̃barase] **adj 1.** [encombré - pièce, bureau] cluttered ▸ **avoir les mains embarrassées** to have one's hands full **2.** [gêné] embarrassed **3.** [confus] confused.

embarrasser [3] [ɑ̃barase] **vt 1.** [encombrer - pièce] to clutter up / [- personne] to hamper **2.** [gêner] to put in an awkward position.
◆ ***s'embarrasser*** **vp 1.** [se charger] **: s'embarrasser de qqch** to burden o.s. with sthg / *fig* to bother about sthg **2.** [s'empêtrer] **: s'embarrasser dans** to get tangled up in.

embauchage [ɑ̃boʃaʒ] **nm** = ***embauche***.

embauche [ɑ̃boʃ] **nf** hiring, employment.

embaucher [3] [ɑ̃boʃe] **vt 1.** [employer] to employ, to take on **2.** *fam* [occuper] **: je t'embauche!** I need you help!

embaumer [3] [ɑ̃bome] ■ **vt 1.** [cadavre] to embalm **2.** [parfumer] to scent.
■ **vi** to be fragrant.

embellie [ɑ̃beli] **nf** [éclaircie] bright *ou* clear spell / *fig* (temporary) improvement.

embellir [32] [ɑ̃belir] ■ **vt 1.** [agrémenter] to brighten up **2.** *fig* [enjoliver] to embellish.
■ **vi** [devenir plus beau] to become more attractive / *fig hum* to grow, to increase.

embellissement [ɑ̃belismɑ̃] **nm 1.** [fait d'améliorer] embellishment, embellishing **2.** [apport - à un décor] embellishment / [- à une histoire] embellishment, frill ▸ **il y a beaucoup d'embellissements dans son récit** there's a lot of poetic licence in his story.

emberlificoter [3] [ɑ̃bɛrlifikɔte] **vt** *fam fig* to sweet-talk.
◆ ***s'emberlificoter*** **vp** *fam* to get tangled up.

embêtant, e [ɑ̃bɛtɑ̃, ɑ̃t] **adj** *fam* annoying.

embêtement [ɑ̃bɛtmɑ̃] **nm** *fam* trouble.

embêter [4] [ɑ̃bɛte] **vt** *fam* [contrarier, importuner] to annoy.
◆ ***s'embêter*** **vp** *fam* [s'ennuyer] to be bored.

emblée [ɑ̃ble] ◆ ***d'emblée*** **loc adv** right away.

emblématique [ɑ̃blematik] **adj** emblematic.

emblème [ɑ̃blɛm] **nm** emblem.

embobiner [3] [ɑ̃bɔbine] **vt 1.** [fil] to wind **2.** *fam* [personne] to fool.

emboîter [3] [ɑ̃bwate] **vt : emboîter qqch dans qqch** to fit sthg into sthg ▸ **emboîter le pas à qqn** [suivre] to follow close on sb's heels / *fig* to follow sb's lead.
◆ ***s'emboîter*** **vp** to fit together.

embolie [ɑ̃bɔli] **nf** embolism.

embonpoint [ɑ̃bɔ̃pwɛ̃] **nm** stoutness ▸ **prendre de l'embonpoint** to get stout.

embouché, e [ɑ̃buʃe] **adj** *fam* **: mal embouché** foul-mouthed.

embouchure [ɑ̃buʃyr] **nf 1.** [d'instrument] mouthpiece **2.** [de fleuve] mouth ▸ **l'embouchure du Rhône** the mouth of the Rhône.

embourber [3] [ɑ̃burbe] ◆ ***s'embourber*** **vp** [s'enliser] to get stuck in the mud / *fig* to get bogged down.

embourgeoisement [ɑ̃burʒwazmɑ̃] **nm** [de personne] adoption of middle-class values / [de quartier] gentrification.

embourgeoiser [3] [ɑ̃burʒwaze] **vt** [personne] to instil *UK ou* instill *US* middle-class values in / [quartier] to gentrify.
◆ ***s'embourgeoiser*** **vp** [personne] to adopt middle-class values / [quartier] to become gentrified.

embout [ɑ̃bu] **nm** [protection] tip / [extrémité d'un tube] nozzle.

embouteillage [ɑ̃butɛjaʒ] **nm 1.** [circulation] traffic jam **2.** [mise en bouteilles] bottling.

emboutir [32] [ɑ̃butir] **vt 1.** *fam* [voiture] to crash into **2.** TECHNOL to stamp.

embranchement [ɑ̃brɑ̃ʃmɑ̃] **nm 1.** [carrefour] junction **2.** [division] branching (out) / *fig* branch.

embraser [3] [ɑ̃braze] **vt** [incendier, éclairer] to set ablaze / *fig* [d'amour] to (set on) fire, to inflame.
◆ ***s'embraser*** **vp** [prendre feu, s'éclairer] to be ablaze / *fig & littéraire* to be inflamed.

embrassade [ɑ̃brasad] **nf** embrace.

embrasse [ɑ̃bras] **nf** tieback.

embrasser [3] [ɑ̃brase] **vt 1.** [donner un baiser à] to kiss **2.** [étreindre] to embrace **3.** *fig* [du regard] to take in.
◆ ***s'embrasser*** **vp** to kiss (each other).

embrasure [ɑ̃brazyr] **nf : dans l'embrasure de la fenêtre** in the window.

embrayage [ɑ̃brɛjaʒ] **nm 1.** [action] engaging the clutch **2.** [mécanisme] clutch.

embrayer [11] [ɑ̃breje] **vi 1.** AUTO to engage the clutch **2.** *fam fig* [s'engager] **: embrayer sur** to get onto the subject of.

embrigader [3] [ɑ̃brigade] **vt** to recruit.
◆ ***s'embrigader*** **vp** to join.

embringuer [3] [ɑ̃brɛ̃ge] **vt** *fam* to involve.
◆ ***s'embringuer*** **vp** *fam* **: s'embringuer dans** to get mixed up in.

embrocher [3] [ɑ̃brɔʃe] **vt** to skewer.
◆ ***s'embrocher*** **vp** *fam* to stab o.s.

embrouillamini [ɑ̃brujamini] **nm** *fam* muddle.

embrouille [ɑ̃bruj] **nf** *fam* shenanigans *pl.*

embrouiller [3] [ɑ̃bruje] **vt 1.** [mélanger] to mix (up), to muddle (up) **2.** *fig* [compliquer] to confuse.

embruns [ɑ̃brœ̃] **nmpl** spray *(U).*

embryologie [ɑ̃brijɔlɔʒi] **nf** embryology.

embryon [ɑ̃brijɔ̃] **nm** *litt & fig* embryo.

embryonnaire [ɑ̃brijɔnɛr] **adj** *litt & fig* embryonic.

embûche [ɑ̃byʃ] **nf** pitfall.

embuer [7] [ɑ̃bɥe] **vt 1.** [de vapeur] to steam up **2.** [de larmes] to mist (over).

embuscade [ɑ̃byskad] **nf** ambush.

embusquer [3] [ɑ̃byske] **vt 1.** [poster] to position for an ambush **2.** [mettre à l'abri] to post away from the front line.
◆ ***s'embusquer*** **vp 1.** [se poster] to lie in ambush **2.** [se mettre à l'abri] to be posted away from the front line.

éméché, e [emeʃe] **adj** *fam* tipsy, merry *UK*.

émeraude [emrod] ■ **nf** emerald.
■ **adj inv** *(en apposition)* **: vert émeraude** emerald (green).

émergence [emɛrʒɑ̃s] **nf** emergence.

émergent, e [emɛrʒɑ̃, ɑ̃t] **adj : pays émergent** emerging country.

émerger [17] [emɛrʒe] **vi 1.** [gén] to emerge **2.** *fig &* NAUT to surface.

émeri [ɛmri] **nm : papier *ou* toile émeri** emery paper.

émérite [emerit] **adj** distinguished, eminent.

émerveillement [emɛrvɛjmɑ̃] **nm** wonder.

émerveiller [4] [emɛrveje] **vt** to fill with wonder.
◆ ***s'émerveiller*** **vp : s'émerveiller (de)** to marvel (at).

émets ➤ ***émettre.***

émetteur, trice [emetœr, tris] **adj** transmitting *(avant n)* ▸ **poste émetteur** transmitter.
◆ ***émetteur*** **nm** [appareil] transmitter ▸ **émetteur-récepteur** transmitter-receiver.

émettre [84] [emɛtr] **vt 1.** [produire] to emit **2.** [diffuser] to transmit, to broadcast **3.** [mettre en circulation] to issue **4.** [exprimer] to express.

émeus, émeut ➤ ***émouvoir.***

émeute [emøt] **nf** riot.

émeutier**, **ère [emøtje, ɛr] **nm, f** rioter.

émietter [4] [emjete] **vt 1.** [du pain] to crumble **2.** [morceler] to divide up.

émigrant**, **e [emigrɑ̃, ɑ̃t] **adj & nm, f** emigrant ▸ **émigrant économique** economic migrant.

émigration [emigrasjɔ̃] **nf 1.** [de personnes] emigration **2.** ZOOL migration.

émigré**, **e [emigre] ■ **adj** migrant.
■ **nm, f** emigrant.

émigrer [3] [emigre] **vi 1.** [personnes] to emigrate **2.** [animaux] to migrate.

émincé**, **e [emɛ̃se] **adj** thinly sliced.
◆ ***émincé*** **nm** *thin slices of meat served in a sauce.*

éminemment [eminamɑ̃] **adv** eminently.

éminence [eminɑ̃s] **nf** hill.
◆ ***Éminence*** **nf** Eminence ▸ **Son Éminence** His Eminence.
◆ ***éminence grise*** **nf** éminence grise.

éminent**, **e [eminɑ̃, ɑ̃t] **adj** eminent, distinguished.

émir [emir] **nm** emir.

émirat [emira] **nm** emirate.
◆ ***Émirat*** **nm : les Émirats arabes unis** the United Arab Emirates.

émis**, **e [emi, iz] **pp** ➤ ***émettre***.

émissaire [emisɛr] ■ **nm 1.** [envoyé] emissary, envoy **2.** TECHNOL outlet, drainage channel.
■ **adj 1.** ANAT emissary **2.** ➤ ***bouc***.

émission [emisjɔ̃] **nf 1.** [de gaz, de son] emission **2.** [RADIO & TV - transmission] transmission, broadcasting / [- programme] programme *UK*, program *US* ▸ **émission de télévision** broadcast ▸ **émission en direct/différé** live/recorded broadcast ▸ **émission (retransmise) par satellite** satellite broadcast **3.** [mise en circulation] issue.

emmagasiner [3] [ɑ̃magazine] **vt 1.** [stocker] to store **2.** *fig* [accumuler] to store up.

emmailloter [3] [ɑ̃majɔte] **vt** to wrap up.

emmanchure [ɑ̃mɑ̃ʃyr] **nf** armhole.

Emmaüs [emays] **npr : Emmaüs International** *charity helping the poor and homeless.*

emmêler [4] [ɑ̃mele] **vt 1.** [fils] to tangle up **2.** *fig* [idées] to muddle up, to confuse.
◆ ***s'emmêler*** **vp 1.** [fils] to get into a tangle **2.** *fig* [personne] to get mixed up.

emménagement [ɑ̃menaʒmɑ̃] **nm** moving in.

emménager [17] [ɑ̃menaʒe] **vi** to move in.

emmener [19] [ɑ̃mne] **vt** to take.

emment(h)al [emɛ̃tal] **nm** Emmenthal, Emmental.

emmerdant**, **e [ɑ̃mɛrdɑ̃, ɑ̃t] **adj** *tfam* damned *ou* bloody *UK* annoying.

emmerdement [ɑ̃mɛrdəmɑ̃] **nm** *tfam* hassle, damned *ou* bloody *UK* nuisance ▸ **avoir des emmerdements** to have problems.

emmerder [3] [ɑ̃mɛrde] **vt** *tfam* to piss off.
◆ ***s'emmerder*** **vp** *tfam* [s'embêter] to be bored stiff.

emmerdeur**, **euse [ɑ̃mɛrdœr, øz] **nm, f** *tfam* pain in the arse *UK ou* ass *US*.

emmitoufler [3] [ɑ̃mitufle] **vt** to wrap up.
◆ ***s'emmitoufler*** **vp** to wrap o.s. up.

émoi [emwa] **nm 1.** *sout* [agitation] agitation, commotion ▸ **en émoi** in turmoil **2.** [émotion] emotion.

émollient**, **e [emɔljɑ̃, ɑ̃t] **adj** emollient.
◆ ***émollient*** **nm** emollient.

émoluments [emɔlymɑ̃] **nmpl** [d'un employé] salary *sg*, wages / [d'un notaire] fees.

emoticon [emɔtikɔ] **nm** INFORM emoticon.

émotif**, **ive [emɔtif, iv] ■ **adj** emotional.
■ **nm, f** emotional person.

émotion [emosjɔ̃] **nf 1.** [sentiment] emotion **2.** [peur] fright, shock ▸ **donner des émotions à qqn** to give sb a fright *ou* shock.

émotionnel**, **elle [emosjɔnel] **adj** emotional.

émotionner [3] [emosjɔne] **vt** *fam* to move (to the brink of tears).

émotivité [emɔtivite] **nf** emotionalism.

émoulu**, **e [emuly] ➤ ***frais***.

émousser [3] [emuse] **vt** *litt* & *fig* to blunt.
◆ ***s'émousser*** **vp** [lame] to become blunt / *fig* to die down, to lessen.

émoustiller [3] [emustije] **vt 1.** [rendre gai] to liven up **2.** [exciter] to arouse, to excite.

émouvant**, **e [emuvɑ̃, ɑ̃t] **adj** moving.

émouvoir [55] [emuvwar] **vt 1.** [troubler] to disturb, to upset **2.** [susciter la sympathie de] to move, to touch.
◆ ***s'émouvoir*** **vp** to show emotion, to be upset.

empailler [3] [ɑ̃paje] **vt 1.** [animal] to stuff **2.** [chaise] to upholster (with straw).

empaler [3] [ɑ̃pale] **vt** to impale.
◆ ***s'empaler*** **vp : s'empaler sur** to be impaled on *ou* upon.

empaqueter [27] [ɑ̃pakte] **vt** to pack (up), to wrap (up).

emparer [3] [ɑ̃pare] ◆ ***s'emparer*** **vp : s'emparer de** [suj: personne] to seize / [suj: sentiment] to take hold of.

empâté**, **e [ɑ̃pate] **adj** [visage, traits] bloated / [bouche, langue] coated.

empâter [3] [ɑ̃pate] **vt 1.** [visage, traits] to fatten ou[t] **2.** [bouche, langue] to coat, to fur up.
◆ ***s'empâter*** **vp** to put on weight.

empattement [ɑ̃patmɑ̃] **nm 1.** AUTO wheelbas[e] **2.** TYPO serif.

empêchement [ɑ̃pɛʃmɑ̃] **nm** obstacle ▸ **j'ai un empêchement** something has come up.

empêcher [4] [ɑ̃peʃe] **vt** to prevent ▸ **empêcher qqn [/] qqch de faire qqch** to prevent sb/sthg from doing sth[g] ▸ **empêcher que qqn (ne) fasse qqch** to prevent sb fro[m] doing sthg ▸ **(il) n'empêche que** nevertheless, all th[e] same.
◆ ***s'empêcher*** **vp : s'empêcher de faire qqch** to sto[p] o.s. doing sthg ▸ **je ne peux pas m'empêcher de pleure[r]** I can't help crying.

empêcheur, euse [ɑ̃pɛʃœr, øz] **nm, f** *fam* **: empêcheur de tourner en rond** killjoy.

empeigne [ɑ̃pɛɲ] **nf** upper.

empereur [ɑ̃prœr] **nm** emperor.

empesé, e [ɑ̃pəze] **adj 1.** [linge] starched **2.** *fig* [style] stiff.

empester [3] [ɑ̃pɛste] ■ **vt** to stink out.
■ **vi** to stink.

empêtrer [4] [ɑ̃petre] **vt : être empêtré dans** to be tangled up in.
◆ ***s'empêtrer*** **vp : s'empêtrer (dans)** to get tangled up (in).

emphase [ɑ̃faz] **nf** *péj* pomposity.

emphatique [ɑ̃fatik] **adj** *péj* pompous.

empiècement [ɑ̃pjɛsmɑ̃] **nm** yoke.

empiéter [18] [ɑ̃pjete] **vi : empiéter sur** to encroach on.

empiffrer [3] [ɑ̃pifre] ◆ ***s'empiffrer*** **vp** *fam* to stuff o.s.

empilement [ɑ̃pilmɑ̃], ***empilage*** [ɑ̃pilaʒ] **nm** [action] piling up, stacking up / [pile] pile, stack.

empiler [3] [ɑ̃pile] **vt 1.** [entasser] to pile up, to stack up **2.** *tfam* [duper] to rip off.
◆ ***s'empiler*** **vp** to pile up.

empire [ɑ̃pir] **nm 1.** *fig* & HIST empire ▸ **l'Empire** *the Empire under Napoleon I* ▸ **le Second Empire** the Second Empire *(under Napoleon III)* ▸ **pour un empire** *fig* for the world **2.** *sout* [contrôle] influence ▸ **sous l'empire de** [la boisson] under the influence of / [la colère] gripped by.

empirer [3] [ɑ̃pire] **vi** & **vt** to worsen.

empirique [ɑ̃pirik] **adj** empirical.

empirisme [ɑ̃pirism] **nm** empiricism.

emplacement [ɑ̃plasmɑ̃] **nm** [gén] site, location / [dans un camping] place.

emplâtre [ɑ̃platr] **nm 1.** [pommade] plaster **2.** *péj* [incapable] lazy lump.

emplette [ɑ̃plɛt] **nf** *(gén pl)* purchase ▸ **faire des emplettes** to go shopping ▸ **faire l'emplette de** to purchase.

emplir [32] [ɑ̃plir] **vt** *sout* **: emplir (de)** to fill (with).
◆ ***s'emplir*** **vp : s'emplir (de)** to fill (with).

emploi [ɑ̃plwa] **nm 1.** [utilisation] use ▸ **faire double emploi** to be unnecessary *ou* redundant ▸ **emploi du temps** SCOL timetable *UK*, schedule *US* ▸ **mode d'emploi** instructions *pl* (for use) **2.** [travail] job.

employable [ɑ̃plwajabl] **adj** [personne] employable / [objet] usable.

employé, e [ɑ̃plwaje] **nm, f** employee ▸ **employé de bureau** office worker.

employer [13] [ɑ̃plwaje] **vt 1.** [utiliser] to use **2.** [salarier] to employ.
◆ ***s'employer*** **vp** to be used ▸ **s'employer à qqch** to be working on sthg, to apply o.s. to sthg ▸ **s'employer à faire qqch** to apply o.s. to doing sthg.

employeur, euse [ɑ̃plwajœr, øz] **nm, f** employer.

empocher [3] [ɑ̃pɔʃe] **vt** *fam* to pocket.

empoignade [ɑ̃pwaɲad] **nf** row.

empoigne [ɑ̃pwaɲ] ➤ ***foire***.

empoigner [3] [ɑ̃pwaɲe] **vt 1.** [saisir] to grasp **2.** *fig* [émouvoir] to grip.
◆ ***s'empoigner*** **vp** *fig* to come to blows.

empoisonnant, e [ɑ̃pwazɔnɑ̃, ɑ̃t] **adj 1.** [ennuyeux] boring **2.** [insupportable] irritating.

empoisonnement [ɑ̃pwazɔnmɑ̃] **nm 1.** [intoxication] poisoning **2.** *fam fig* [souci] trouble *(U)*.

empoisonner [3] [ɑ̃pwazɔne] **vt 1.** [gén] to poison **2.** [empuantir] to stink out **3.** *fam* [ennuyer] to annoy, to bug.

emporté, e [ɑ̃pɔrte] **adj** short-tempered.

emportement [ɑ̃pɔrtəmɑ̃] **nm** anger.

emporte-pièce [ɑ̃pɔrtəpjɛs] **nm inv** punch.
◆ ***à l'emporte-pièce*** **loc adj** incisive.

emporter [3] [ɑ̃pɔrte] **vt 1.** [emmener] to take (away) ▸ **à emporter** [plats] to take away *UK*, to take out *US*, to go *US* **2.** [entraîner] to carry along **3.** [arracher] to tear off, to blow off **4.** [faire mourir] to carry off **5.** [gagner] to win **6.** [surpasser] **: l'emporter sur** to get the better of.
◆ ***s'emporter*** **vp** to get angry, to lose one's temper.

empoté, e [ɑ̃pɔte] *fam* ■ **adj** clumsy.
■ **nm, f** clumsy person.

empourprer [3] [ɑ̃purpre] ◆ ***s'empourprer*** **vp** *littéraire* to turn crimson.

empreinte [ɑ̃prɛ̃t] **nf** [trace] print / *fig* mark, trace ▸ **empreinte génétique** genetic fingerprint ▸ **empreintes digitales** fingerprints.

empressé, e [ɑ̃prese] ■ **adj** attentive.
■ **nm, f** attentive person.

empressement [ɑ̃prɛsmɑ̃] **nm 1.** [zèle] attentiveness **2.** [enthousiasme] eagerness.

empresser [4] [ɑ̃prese] ◆ ***s'empresser*** **vp : s'empresser de faire qqch** to hurry to do sthg ▸ **s'empresser auprès de qqn** to be attentive to sb.

emprise [ɑ̃priz] **nf 1.** [ascendant] influence ▸ **sous l'emprise de** [l'alcool] under the influence of / [la colère] gripped by **2.** DR expropriation.

emprisonnement [ɑ̃prizɔnmɑ̃] **nm** imprisonment.

emprisonner [3] [ɑ̃prizɔne] **vt 1.** [voleur] to imprison **2.** [partie du corps] to fit tightly around.

emprunt [ɑ̃prœ̃] **nm 1.** FIN loan ▸ **couvrir un emprunt** to guarantee a loan ▸ **lancer un emprunt** to float a loan ▸ **emprunt d'État** government loan **2.** *fig* & LING borrowing.

emprunté, e [ɑ̃prœ̃te] **adj** awkward, self-conscious.

emprunter [3] [ɑ̃prœ̃te] **vt 1.** [gén] to borrow ▸ **emprunter qqch à** to borrow sthg from **2.** [route] to take.

empuantir [32] [ɑ̃pɥɑ̃tir] **vt** to stink out.

EMT (abr de ***éducation manuelle et technique***) **nf** practical sciences *pl*.

ému, e [emy] ■ **pp** ➤ ***émouvoir***.
■ **adj** [personne] moved, touched / [regard, sourire] emotional.

émulation [emylasjɔ̃] **nf** **1.** [concurrence] rivalry **2.** [imitation] emulation.

émule [emyl] **nmf** **1.** [imitateur] emulator **2.** [concurrent] rival.

émulsion [emylsjɔ̃] **nf** emulsion.

en [ɑ̃] ■ **prép** **1.** [temps] in ▸ **en 1994** in 1994 ▸ **en hiver/septembre** in winter/September ▸ **en deux heures c'était fini** it was over in two hours
2. [lieu] in / [direction] to ▸ **une maison en Suède** a house in Sweden ▸ **habiter en Sicile/ville** to live in Sicily/town ▸ **aller en Sicile/ville** to go to Sicily/town ▸ **aller de ville en ville** to go from town to town ▸ **se promener en forêt/en ville** to walk in the forest/around the town
3. [matière] made of ▸ **c'est en métal** it's (made of) metal ▸ **une théière en argent** a silver teapot
4. [état, forme, manière] **: les arbres sont en fleurs** the trees are in blossom ▸ **du sucre en morceaux** sugar cubes ▸ **du lait en poudre** powdered milk ▸ **je la préfère en vert** I prefer it in green ▸ **agir en traître** to behave treacherously ▸ **je l'ai eu en cadeau** I was given it as a present ▸ **dire qqch en anglais** to say sthg in English ▸ **être en colère/en rage** to be angry/in a rage ▸ **en vacances** on holiday *UK ou* vacation *US* ▸ **se déguiser en fille** to dress up as a girl
5. [moyen] by ▸ **en avion/bateau/train** by plane/boat/train ▸ **payer en liquide** to pay cash
6. [mesure] in ▸ **vous l'avez en 38?** do you have it in a 38? ▸ **compter en dollars** to calculate in dollars
7. [devant un participe présent] **: c'est en le voyant que j'ai compris** when I saw him I understood ▸ **en arrivant à Paris** on arriving in Paris, as he/she *etc* arrived in Paris ▸ **en faisant un effort** by making an effort ▸ **en mangeant** while eating ▸ **en supposant que...** supposing that... ▸ **elle répondit en souriant** she replied with a smile.
■ **pron pers** **1.** [complément de verbe, de nom, d'adjectif] **: il s'en est souvenu** he remembered it ▸ **nous en avons déjà parlé** we've already spoken about it ▸ **on en meurt, de ce genre de maladie** people die from this sort of illness ▸ **je m'en porte garant** I'll vouch for it ▸ **j'en garde un très bon souvenir** I have very happy memories of it ▸ **sa maison en est pleine** his house is full of them
2. [avec un indéfini, exprimant une quantité] **: j'en connais un/plusieurs** I know one/several of them ▸ **j'ai du chocolat, tu en veux?** I've got some chocolate; do you want some? ▸ **tu en as?** have you got any?, do you have any? ▸ **tu n'en as pas dit assez** you haven't said enough ▸ **il y en a plusieurs** there are several (of them)
3. [provenance] from there ▸ **j'en viens à l'instant** I've just come from there
4. [locutions verbales] **: il en va de même pour lui** the same goes for him ▸ **il n'en croit pas ses oreilles/yeux** he can't believe his ears/eyes.

ENA, **Ena** [ena] (abr de ***École nationale d'administration***) **nf** *prestigious grande école training future government officials.*

enamourer [3] [ɑ̃namure] ◆ ***s'enamourer de*** **v + prep** *littéraire* to become enamoured *UK ou* enamored *US* of.

énarque [enark] **nmf** *graduate of the École nationale d'administration (ENA).*

encablure [ɑ̃kablyr] **nf** cable length.

encadré [ɑ̃kadre] **nm** TYPO box.

encadrement [ɑ̃kadrəmɑ̃] **nm** **1.** [de tableau, porte] frame **2.** [dans une entreprise] managerial staff / [à l'armée] officers *pl* / [à l'école] staff **3.** [du crédit] restriction.

encadrer [3] [ɑ̃kadre] **vt** **1.** [photo, visage] to frame **2.** [employés] to supervise / [soldats] to be in command of / [élèves] to teach **3.** [détenu] to flank **4.** *fam* [arbre] to crash into.

encadreur [ɑ̃kadrœr] **nm** framer.

encaisse [ɑ̃kɛs] **nf** ready cash.

encaissé, **e** [ɑ̃kese] **adj** [vallée] deep and narrow / [rivière] steep-banked.

encaisser [4] [ɑ̃kese] **vt** **1.** [argent, coups, insultes] to take **2.** [chèque] to cash
▸▸▸ **ne pas pouvoir encaisser qqn** *fam* not to be able to stand sb.

encanailler [3] [ɑ̃kanaje] ◆ ***s'encanailler*** **vp** to slum it.

encart [ɑ̃kar] **nm** insert ▸ **encart publicitaire** advertising insert.

en-cas, **encas** [ɑ̃ka] **nm inv** snack.

encastrable [ɑ̃kastrabl] **adj** able to be fitted (in).

encastrer [3] [ɑ̃kastre] **vt** to fit.
◆ ***s'encastrer*** **vp** to fit (exactly).

encaustique [ɑ̃kostik] **nf** **1.** [cire] polish **2.** [peinture] encaustic.

encaustiquer [3] [ɑ̃kostike] **vt** to polish.

enceinte [ɑ̃sɛ̃t] ■ **adj f** pregnant ▸ **enceinte de 4 mois** 4 months pregnant.
■ **nf** **1.** [muraille] wall **2.** [espace] **: dans l'enceinte de** within (the confines of) **3.** [baffle] **: enceinte (acoustique)** speaker.

encens [ɑ̃sɑ̃] **nm** incense.

encenser [3] [ɑ̃sɑ̃se] **vt** **1.** [brûler de l'encens dans] to burn incense in **2.** *fig* [louer] to flatter.

encensoir [ɑ̃sɑ̃swar] **nm** censer.

encéphalopathie [ɑ̃sefalɔpati] **nf** encephelopathy ▸ **encéphalopathie spongiforme bovine** bovine spongiform encephalopathy.

encercler [3] [ɑ̃sɛrkle] **vt** **1.** [cerner, environner] to surround **2.** [entourer] to circle.

enchaînement [ɑ̃ʃɛnmɑ̃] **nm** **1.** [succession] series **2.** [liaison] link **3.** MUS progression.

enchaîner [4] [ɑ̃ʃene] ■ **vt** **1.** [attacher] to chain up **2.** *fig* [asservir] to enslave **3.** [coordonner] to link.
■ **vi : enchaîner (sur)** to move on (to).
◆ ***s'enchaîner*** **vp** [se suivre] to follow on from each other.

enchanté, **e** [ɑ̃ʃɑ̃te] **adj** **1.** [ravi] delighted ▸ **enchanté de faire votre connaissance** pleased to meet you **2.** [ensorcelé] enchanted.

enchantement [ɑ̃ʃɑ̃tmɑ̃] **nm** **1.** [sortilège] magic spell ▸ **comme par enchantement** as if by magic **2.** *sout* [ravissement] delight **3.** [merveille] wonder.

enchanter [3] [ɑ̃ʃɑ̃te] **vt** **1.** [ensorceler, charmer] to enchant **2.** [ravir] to delight.

enchanteur**, **eresse [ɑ̃ʃɑ̃tœr, trɛs] ■ **adj** enchanting. ■ **nm, f 1.** [magicien] enchanter **2.** [charmeur] charmer.

enchâsser [3] [ɑ̃ʃase] **vt 1.** [encastrer] to fit **2.** [sertir] to set.

enchère [ɑ̃ʃɛr] **nf** bid ▸ **faire monter les enchères** *litt* to raise the bidding / *fig* to raise the stakes ▸ **vendre qqch aux enchères** to sell sthg at *ou* by auction.

enchérir [32] [ɑ̃ʃerir] **vi : enchérir sur** to bid higher than / *fig* & *littéraire* [dépasser] to go beyond.

enchevêtrement [ɑ̃ʃəvɛtrəmɑ̃] **nm 1.** [objets emmêlés] tangle, tangled mass ▸ **un enchevêtrement de branches** tangled branches, a tangle of branches **2.** [confusion] tangle, tangled state, confusion.

enchevêtrer [4] [ɑ̃ʃəvɛtre] **vt** [emmêler] to tangle up / *fig* to muddle, to confuse ▸ **une intrigue enchevêtrée** a complicated *ou* muddled plot.
◆ ***s'enchevêtrer*** **vpi 1.** [être emmêlé - fils] to become entangled, to get into a tangle / [- branchages] to become entangled **2.** [être confus - idées, événements] to become confused *ou* muddled.

enclave [ɑ̃klav] **nf** enclave.

enclencher [3] [ɑ̃klɑ̃ʃe] **vt 1.** [mécanisme] to engage **2.** *fig* [projet] to set in motion.
◆ ***s'enclencher*** **vp 1.** TECHNOL to engage **2.** *fig* [commencer] to begin.

enclin**, **e [ɑ̃klɛ̃, in] **adj : enclin à qqch/à faire qqch** inclined to sthg/to do sthg.

enclore [113] [ɑ̃klɔr] **vt** to fence in, to enclose.

enclos**, **e [ɑ̃klo, oz] **pp** ➤ ***enclore***.
◆ ***enclos*** **nm** enclosure.

enclume [ɑ̃klym] **nf** anvil.

encoche [ɑ̃kɔʃ] **nf** notch.

encoder [3] [ɑ̃kɔde] **vt** to encode.

encodeur [ɑ̃kɔdœr] **nm** INFORM encoder.

encoignure [ɑ̃kwaɲyr, ɑ̃kɔɲyr] **nf 1.** [coin] corner **2.** [meuble] corner cupboard.

encolure [ɑ̃kɔlyr] **nf** neck.

encombrant**, **e [ɑ̃kɔ̃brɑ̃, ɑ̃t] **adj** cumbersome / *fig* [personne] undesirable.

encombre [ɑ̃kɔ̃br] ◆ ***sans encombre*** **loc adv** without a hitch.

encombré**, **e [ɑ̃kɔ̃bre] **adj** [lieu] busy, congested / *fig* saturated.

encombrement [ɑ̃kɔ̃brəmɑ̃] **nm 1.** [d'une pièce] clutter **2.** [d'un objet] overall dimensions *pl* **3.** [embouteillage] traffic jam **4.** INFORM footprint.

encombrer [3] [ɑ̃kɔ̃bre] **vt** to clutter (up).
◆ ***s'encombrer*** **vp** *fam* **: s'encombrer de qqn** to be stuck *ou* lumbered *UK* with sb ▸ **s'encombrer de qqch** to burden o.s. with sthg / *fig* to bother about sthg.

encontre [ɑ̃kɔ̃tr] ◆ ***à l'encontre de*** **loc prép : aller à l'encontre de** to go against, to oppose.

encorbellement [ɑ̃kɔrbɛlmɑ̃] **nm** corbelled structure ▸ **en encorbellement** corbelled *UK*, corbeled *US*, overhanging.

encorder [3] [ɑ̃kɔrde] ◆ ***s'encorder*** **vp** to rope up.

encore [ɑ̃kɔr] **adv 1.** [toujours] still ▸ **il dort encore** he's still asleep ▸ **je te sers encore un verre?** will you have another drink? ▸ **encore un mois** one more month ▸ **pas encore** not yet ▸ **elle ne travaille pas encore** she's not working yet
2. [de nouveau] again ▸ **il m'a encore menti** he's lied to me again ▸ **quoi encore?** what now? ▸ **l'ascenseur est en panne - encore!** the lift's out of order - not again! ▸ **encore de la glace?** some more ice cream? ▸ **encore une fois** once more, once again
3. [marque le renforcement] even ▸ **encore mieux/pire** even better/worse ▸ **il est encore plus gentil que je n'imaginais** he is even nicer than I'd imagined (he'd be)
4. [marque une restriction] **: il ne suffit pas d'être beau, encore faut-il être intelligent** it's not enough to be good-looking: you have to be intelligent too ▸ **encore heureux!** thank goodness for that!
◆ ***et encore*** **loc adv : j'ai eu le temps de prendre un sandwich, et encore!** I had time for a sandwich, but only just! ▸ **ça vaut 15 euros, et encore** it's worth 15 euros, if that.
◆ ***mais encore*** **loc adv** what else? ▸ **elle est bien élevée, charmante, mais encore?** she's well brought-up and charming, and (apart from that)?
◆ ***si encore*** **loc adv** if only ▸ **si encore il était franc, on lui pardonnerait** if only *ou* if at least he was honest, you could forgive him.
◆ ***encore que*** **loc conj** *(+ subjonctif)* although ▸ **j'aimerais y aller, encore qu'il soit tard** I'd like to go even though it's late.

encourageant**, **e [ɑ̃kuraʒɑ̃, ɑ̃t] **adj** encouraging.

encouragement [ɑ̃kuraʒmɑ̃] **nm 1.** [parole] (word of) encouragement **2.** [action] encouragement.

encourager [17] [ɑ̃kuraʒe] **vt** to encourage ▸ **encourager qqn à faire qqch** to encourage sb to do sthg.

encourir [45] [ɑ̃kurir] **vt** *sout* to incur.

encourrai**, **encourras ➤ ***encourir***.

encouru**, **e [ɑ̃kury] **pp** ➤ ***encourir***.

COMMENT EXPRIMER...

ses encouragements à quelqu'un

Go on, ask her! / Vas-y, demande-lui !
Oh, come on - you know you'll enjoy it / Allez, tu sais bien que ça va te plaire
I have a good feeling about this / Je trouve tout cela très positif
You look just fine / Tu es très bien
You can't give up now! / Tu ne vas pas laisser tomber maintenant !

encrasser [3] [ãkrase] **vt** **1.** TECHNOL to clog up **2.** *fam* [salir] to make dirty ***ou*** filthy.
◆ ***s'encrasser*** **vp** **1.** TECHNOL to clog up **2.** *fam* [se salir] to get dirty ***ou*** filthy.

encre [ãkr] **nf** ink ▸ **encre de Chine** Indian *UK* ***ou*** India *US* ink.

encrer [3] [ãkre] **vt** to ink.

encreur [ãkrœr] ➤ ***tampon***, ***rouleau***.

encrier [ãkrije] **nm** inkwell.

encroûter [3] [ãkrute] ◆ ***s'encroûter*** **vp** *fam* to get into a rut ▸ **s'encroûter dans ses habitudes** to become set in one's ways.

enculé [ãkyle] **nm** *vulg* arsehole *UK*, asshole *US*.

enculer [3] [ãkyle] **vt** *vulg* to bugger.

encyclique [ãsiklik] **nf** RELIG encyclical.

encyclopédie [ãsiklɔpedi] **nf** encyclopedia.

encyclopédique [ãsiklɔpedik] **adj** encyclopedic.

endémique [ãdemik] **adj** endemic.

endettement [ãdɛtmã] **nm** debt.

endetter [4] [ãdete] ◆ ***s'endetter*** **vp** to get into debt.

endeuiller [5] [ãdœje] **vt** to plunge into mourning.

endiablé, ***e*** [ãdjable] **adj** [frénétique] frantic, frenzied.

endiguer [3] [ãdige] **vt** **1.** [fleuve] to dam **2.** *fig* [réprimer] to stem.

endimanché, ***e*** [ãdimãʃe] **adj** in one's Sunday best.

endimancher [3] [ãdimãʃe] ◆ ***s'endimancher*** **vp** to put on one's Sunday best.

endive [ãdiv] **nf** chicory *(U)* *UK*, endive *US*.

endocrine [ãdɔkrin] **adj** endocrine.

endoctrinement [ãdɔktrinmã] **nm** indoctrination.

endoctriner [3] [ãdɔktrine] **vt** to indoctrinate.

endolori, ***e*** [ãdɔlɔri] **adj** painful, aching ▸ **le corps tout endolori** aching all over ▸ **mon pied était endolori** my foot hurt ***ou*** was aching.

endommager [17] [ãdɔmaʒe] **vt** to damage.

endormi, ***e*** [ãdɔrmi] **adj** **1.** [personne] sleeping, asleep **2.** *fig* [village] sleepy / [jambe] numb / [passion] dormant / *fam* [apathique] sluggish.

PARONYME / CONFUSABLE
endormi

Attention lorsque vous traduisez endormi : *asleep* s'emploie toujours comme attribut alors que *sleeping* peut s'utiliser comme épithète.

endormir [36] [ãdɔrmir] **vt** **1.** [assoupir, ennuyer] to send to sleep **2.** [anesthésier - patient] to anaesthetize, anesthetize *US* / [- douleur] to ease **3.** *fig* [tromper] to allay **4.** *fig* [affaiblir] to dull.
◆ ***s'endormir*** **vp** **1.** [s'assoupir] to fall asleep **2.** [s'affaiblir] to be allayed **3.** *fig* [jambe] to go to sleep.

endoscopie [ãdɔskɔpi] **nf** endoscopy.

endosser [3] [ãdose] **vt** **1.** [vêtement] to put on **2.** FIN & DR to endorse ▸ **endosser un chèque** to endorse a cheque *UK* ***ou*** check *US* **3.** *fig* [responsabilité] to take on.

endroit [ãdrwa] **nm** **1.** [lieu, point] place ▸ **à quel endroit?** where? ▸ **cela fait mal à quel endroit?** where does it hurt? ▸ **ce n'est pas au bon endroit** it's not in the right place ▸ **un endroit tranquille** a quiet place ***ou*** spot **2.** [passage] part ▸ **c'est l'endroit le plus drôle du livre** it's the funniest part ***ou*** passage in the book **3.** [côté] right side ▸ **à l'endroit** the right way around ▸ **remettre son pull à l'endroit** to put one's pullover on again the right way around ▸ **un rang à l'endroit** knit one row.
◆ ***à l'endroit de*** **prép** *littéraire* with regard to.

enduire [98] [ãdɥir] **vt** : **enduire qqch (de)** to coat sthg (with).

enduisais, ***enduisions*** ➤ ***enduire***.

enduit, ***e*** [ãdɥi, it] **pp** ➤ ***enduire***.
◆ ***enduit*** **nm** coating.

endurance [ãdyrãs] **nf** endurance.

endurant, ***e*** [ãdyrã, ãt] **adj** tough, resilient.

endurci, ***e*** [ãdyrsi] **adj** **1.** [aguerri] hardened **2.** *fig* [insensible] hard.

endurcir [32] [ãdyrsir] **vt** to harden.
◆ ***s'endurcir*** **vp** : **s'endurcir à** to become hardened to.

endurer [3] [ãdyre] **vt** to endure.

énergétique [enɛrʒetik] **adj** **1.** [ressource] energy *(avant n)* **2.** [aliment] energy-giving.

énergie [enɛrʒi] **nf** energy ▸ **énergie nucléaire/solaire** nuclear/solar energy ▸ **énergie éolienne** wind power ▸ **énergie renouvelable** renewable energy.

énergique [enɛrʒik] **adj** [gén] energetic / [remède] powerful / [mesure] drastic.

énergiquement [enɛrʒikmã] **adv** energetically.

énergisant, ***e*** [enɛrʒizã, ãt] **adj** stimulating.
◆ ***énergisant*** **nm** tonic.

énergumène [enɛrgymɛn] **nmf** rowdy character.

énervant, ***e*** [enɛrvã, ãt] **adj** annoying, irritating.

énervé, ***e*** [enɛrve] **adj** **1.** [irrité] annoyed, irritated **2.** [surexcité] overexcited.

énervement [enɛrvəmã] **nm** **1.** [irritation] irritation **2.** [surexcitation] excitement.

énerver [3] [enɛrve] **vt** to irritate, to annoy.
◆ ***s'énerver*** **vp** [être irrité] to get annoyed / [être excité] to get worked up ***ou*** excited.

enfance [ãfãs] **nf** **1.** [âge] childhood ▸ **retomber en enfance** to lapse into one's second childhood **2.** [enfants] children *pl* **3.** *fig* [débuts] infancy / [de civilisation, de l'humanité] dawn ▸ **l'enfance de l'art** *fig* child's play.

enfant [ãfã] **nmf** **1.** [gén] child ▸ **enfant de chœur** choirboy, altarboy ▸ **enfant gâté** spoilt child ▸ **enfant illégitime** ***ou*** **naturel** illegitimate child ▸ **enfant martyr** abused child ▸ **enfant prodige** child prodigy ▸ **enfant sauvage** [vivant à l'état sauvage] wolf child ▸ **attendre un enfant** to be expecting a baby ▸ **faire un enfant** to have a child ▸ **faire l'enfant** to act like a child **2.** [originaire] native ▸ **c'est un**

enfant de la balle his/her parents were in the theatre/circus *etc* ▸ **enfant du pays** [homme] son of the soil / [femme] daughter of the soil.
◆ ***bon enfant*** loc adj good-natured ▸ **d'un ton bon enfant** good-naturedly.

enfantement [ɑ̃fɑ̃tmɑ̃] **nm** *littéraire* childbirth / *fig* creation.

enfanter [3] [ɑ̃fɑ̃te] **vt** *littéraire* to give birth to.

enfantillage [ɑ̃fɑ̃tijaʒ] **nm** childishness *(U)*.

enfantin, e [ɑ̃fɑ̃tɛ̃, in] **adj 1.** [propre à l'enfance] childlike / *péj* childish / [jeu, chanson] children's *(avant n)* **2.** [facile] childishly simple.

enfariné, e [ɑ̃farine] **adj** covered with white powder ▸ **il est arrivé, la gueule enfarinée** *fig* he breezed in as if nothing was the matter.

enfer [ɑ̃fɛr] **nm 1.** *fig* & RELIG hell ▸ **d'enfer** *fig* hellish, infernal **2.** [de bibliothèque] restricted books department.
◆ ***Enfers*** **nmpl : les Enfers** the Underworld *sg*.

enfermer [3] [ɑ̃fɛrme] **vt 1.** [séquestrer, ranger] to shut away ▸ **enfermer qqn dans une cellule** to shut sb up in a cell ▸ **enfermer qqn dans un rôle** *litt* & *fig* to typecast sb ▸ **faire enfermer qqn** to have sb locked away ▸ **ne restez pas enfermés, voilà le soleil!** don't stay indoor:, the sun's come out! **2.** *littéraire* [enclore] to enclose.
◆ ***s'enfermer*** **vp** to shut o.s. away *ou* up ▸ **s'enfermer dans** *fig* to retreat into ▸ **s'enfermer dans ses contradictions** to become caught up in one's own contradictions ▸ **s'enfermer dans le silence** to retreat into silence.

enfilade [ɑ̃filad] **nf 1.** row ▸ **une enfilade de peupliers** a row of poplars **2.** MIL enfilade.
◆ ***en enfilade*** ■ **loc adj** in a row ▸ **des pièces en enfilade** a suite of adjoining rooms.
■ **loc adv : prendre en enfilade** MIL to enfilade ▸ **prendre les rues en enfilade** to follow along in a straight line from one street to the next.

enfiler [3] [ɑ̃file] **vt 1.** [aiguille, sur un fil] to thread **2.** [vêtements] to slip on.
◆ ***s'enfiler*** **vp** *fam* [ingurgiter] to put away.

enfin [ɑ̃fɛ̃] **adv 1.** [en dernier lieu] finally, at last ▸ **enfin, j'aimerais vous remercier de votre hospitalité** finally, I would like to thank you for your hospitality ▸ **un accord a été enfin conclu** an agreement has at last been reached **2.** [dans une liste] lastly **3.** [avant une récapitulation] in a word, in short **4.** [introduit une rectification] that is, well ▸ **elle est jolie, enfin, à mon avis** she's pretty, (or) at least I think she is **5.** [introduit une concession] anyway, still, however ▸ **elle est triste, mais enfin elle s'en remettra** she's sad, but still, she'll get over it **6.** [emploi expressif] **: enfin, reprends-toi!** come on, pull yourself together! ▸ **tu ne peux pas faire ça, enfin!** you can't **do** that!

enflammé, e [ɑ̃flame] **adj 1.** [en flammes] burning **2.** *fig* [déclaration, discours] passionate / [discussion] heated.

enflammer [3] [ɑ̃flame] **vt 1.** [bois] to set fire to **2.** *fig* [exalter] to inflame.
◆ ***s'enflammer*** **vp 1.** [bois] to catch fire **2.** *fig* [s'exalter] to flare up.

enflé, e [ɑ̃fle] **adj** [style] turgid.

enfler [3] [ɑ̃fle] **vi** to swell (up).

enflure [ɑ̃flyr] **nf** [de corps] swelling.

enfoiré, e [ɑ̃fware] **nm, f** *tfam* bastard.

enfoncé, e [ɑ̃fɔ̃se] **adj** deep-set.

enfoncement [ɑ̃fɔ̃smɑ̃] **nm 1.** [destruction - d'un mur] breaking down / [- d'une porte] breaking down, bashing in **2.** [cavité] depression, hollow **3.** MÉD fracture ▸ **enfoncement de la boîte crânienne** skull fracture ▸ **enfoncement du thorax** flail chest.

enfoncer [16] [ɑ̃fɔ̃se] **vt 1.** [faire pénétrer] to drive in ▸ **il a enfoncé le pieu d'un seul coup** he drove the stake home in one ▸ **enfoncer qqch dans qqch** to drive sthg into sthg **2.** [enfouir] **: enfoncer ses mains dans ses poches** to thrust one's hands into one's pockets ▸ **il enfonça son chapeau jusqu'aux oreilles** he rammed his hat onto his head **3.** [défoncer] to break down ▸ **la voiture a enfoncé la barrière** the car crashed through the fence **4.** *fam* [vaincre] to hammer, to thrash ▸ **enfoncer un adversaire** *fam* to crush an opponent.
◆ ***s'enfoncer*** **vp 1. : s'enfoncer dans** [eau, boue] to sink into / [bois, ville] to disappear into ▸ **ils s'enfoncèrent dans la neige jusqu'aux genoux** they sank knee-deep into the snow ▸ **le chemin s'enfonce dans la forêt** the path disappears into the forest **2.** [s'affaisser] to give way **3.** [aggraver son cas] to get into deep *ou* deeper waters, to make matters worse.

enfouir [32] [ɑ̃fwir] **vt 1.** [cacher] to hide **2.** [ensevelir] to bury.
◆ ***s'enfouir*** **vp** to bury o.s.

enfourcher [3] [ɑ̃furʃe] **vt** to get on, to mount.

enfourner [3] [ɑ̃furne] **vt 1.** [pain] to put in the oven **2.** *fam* [avaler] to gobble up.

enfreignais, enfreignions ➤ ***enfreindre***.

enfreindre [81] [ɑ̃frɛ̃dr] **vt** to infringe.

enfreint, e [ɑ̃frɛ̃, ɛ̃t] **pp** ➤ ***enfreindre***.

enfuir [35] [ɑ̃fɥir] ◆ ***s'enfuir*** **vp 1.** [fuir] to run away **2.** *littéraire* [passer] to slip away.

enfumé, e [ɑ̃fyme] **adj** [pièce] smoky, smoke-filled / [paroi] sooty.

enfumer [3] [ɑ̃fyme] **vt** to fill with smoke.

enfuyais, enfuyions ➤ ***enfuir***.

engagé, e [ɑ̃gaʒe] **adj** committed.

engageant, e [ɑ̃gaʒɑ̃, ɑ̃t] **adj** engaging.

engagement [ɑ̃gaʒmɑ̃] **nm 1.** [promesse] commitment ▸ **sans engagement** COMM without obligation **2.** DR contract **3.** [embauche] engagement, taking on **4.** [MIL - de soldats] enlistment / [- combat] engagement **5.** [football, rugby] kickoff **6.** [encouragement] encouragement.

engager [17] [ɑ̃gaʒe] ■ **vt 1.** [lier] to commit ▸ **cela ne t'engage à rien** it doesn't commit you to anything **2.** [embaucher] to take on, to engage **3.** [faire entrer] **: engager qqch dans** to insert sthg into ▸ **engager une péniche dans une écluse** to move a barge into a lock **4.** [commencer] to start ▸ **engager la conversation avec qqn** to engage sb in conversation, to strike up a conversation with sb **5.** [impliquer] to involve **6.** [encourager] **: engager qqn à faire qqch** to urge sb to do sthg ▸ **je vous engage à la prudence** I advise you to be prudent.

■ vi **1.** [football, rugby] to kick off **2.** [lier] : **cela n'engage à rien** there is no obligation.
◆ ***s'engager*** vp **1.** [promettre] : **s'engager à qqch/à faire qqch** to commit o.s. to sthg/to doing sthg **2.** MIL : **s'engager (dans)** to enlist (in) ▸ **s'engager avant l'appel** to volunteer before conscription **3.** [pénétrer] : **s'engager dans** to enter ▸ **la voiture s'est engagée dans une rue étroite** the car drove *ou* turned into a narrow street **4.** *fig* [débuter] to begin **5.** [militer] to be committed ▸ **s'engager contre la peine de mort** to campaign against *ou* to take a stand against the death penalty.

engeance [ɑ̃ʒɑ̃s] **nf** *littéraire* riffraff.

engelure [ɑ̃ʒlyr] **nf** chilblain.

engendrer [3] [ɑ̃ʒɑ̃dre] **vt 1.** *littéraire* to father **2.** MATH to generate **3.** *fig* [produire] to cause, to give rise to / [sentiment] to engender.

engin [ɑ̃ʒɛ̃] **nm 1.** [machine] machine **2.** MIL missile **3.** *fam péj* [objet] thing.

engineering [ɛnʒiniriŋ] **nm** engineering.

englober [3] [ɑ̃glɔbe] **vt** to include.

engloutir [32] [ɑ̃glutir] **vt 1.** [dévorer] to gobble up **2.** [faire disparaître] to engulf **3.** *fig* [dilapider] to squander.
◆ ***s'engloutir*** **vp** to be engulfed.

engluer [3] [ɑ̃glɥe] **vt 1.** [oiseau] to catch (using birdlime) **2.** [piège] to smear with birdlime.
◆ ***s'engluer*** **vp : s'engluer (de)** to get sticky (with) ▸ **s'engluer (dans)** *fig* to become bogged down (in).

engorgement [ɑ̃gɔrʒəmɑ̃] **nm 1.** MÉD engorgement **2.** *fig* [de marché] glutting, swamping.

engorger [17] [ɑ̃gɔrʒe] **vt 1.** [obstruer] to block, to obstruct **2.** MÉD to engorge.
◆ ***s'engorger*** **vp** to become blocked.

engouement [ɑ̃gumɑ̃] **nm 1.** [enthousiasme] infatuation **2.** MÉD strangulation *(of hernia)*.

engouer [6] [ɑ̃gue] ◆ ***s'engouer*** **vp : s'engouer de** to become infatuated with.

engouffrer [3] [ɑ̃gufre] **vt** *fam* **1.** [dévorer] to wolf down **2.** [dilapider] to squander.
◆ ***s'engouffrer*** **vp : s'engouffrer dans** to rush into.

engourdi, ***e*** [ɑ̃gurdi] **adj** numb / *fig* dull.

engourdir [32] [ɑ̃gurdir] **vt** to numb / *fig* to dull.
◆ ***s'engourdir*** **vp** to go numb.

engourdissement [ɑ̃gurdismɑ̃] **nm 1.** [raideur] numbness **2.** [torpeur] torpor.

engrais [ɑ̃grɛ] **nm** fertilizer ▸ **engrais chimique** chemical fertilizer.

engraisser [4] [ɑ̃grese] ■ **vt 1.** [animal] to fatten **2.** [terre] to fertilize.
■ **vi** to put on weight.
◆ ***s'engraisser*** **vp** *fam fig* to grow fat.

engranger [17] [ɑ̃grɑ̃ʒe] **vt 1.** [foin] to bring in **2.** *fig* [accumuler] to store up.

engrenage [ɑ̃grənaʒ] **nm 1.** TECHNOL gears *pl* **2.** *fig* [circonstances] : **être pris dans l'engrenage** to be caught up in the system.

engrosser [3] [ɑ̃grose] **vt** *fam* to get pregnant.

engueulade [ɑ̃gœlad] **nf** *fam* bawling out.

engueuler [5] [ɑ̃gœle] **vt** *fam* : **engueuler qqn** to bawl sb out.
◆ ***s'engueuler*** **vp** *fam* to have a row, to have a slanging match *UK*.

enguirlander [3] [ɑ̃girlɑ̃de] **vt 1.** *fam* [gronder] to tell off **2.** *littéraire* [décorer] to decorate.

enhardir [32] [ɑ̃ardir] **vt** to make bold.
◆ ***s'enhardir*** **vp** to pluck up one's courage.

ENI [eni] (abr de ***École normale d'instituteurs***) **nf** *training college for primary school teachers*.

énième [enjɛm] **adj** *fam* : **la énième fois** the nth time.

énigmatique [enigmatik] **adj** enigmatic.

énigme [enigm] **nf 1.** [mystère] enigma **2.** [jeu] riddle.

enivrant, ***e*** [ɑ̃nivrɑ̃, ɑ̃t] **adj** *litt* & *fig* intoxicating.

enivrer [3] [ɑ̃nivre] **vt** *litt* to get drunk / *fig* to intoxicate.
◆ ***s'enivrer*** **vp : s'enivrer (de)** *litt* to get drunk (on) / *fig* to become intoxicated (with).

enjambée [ɑ̃ʒɑ̃be] **nf** stride ▸ **marcher à grandes enjambées** to stride (along).

enjamber [3] [ɑ̃ʒɑ̃be] ■ **vt 1.** [obstacle] to step over **2.** [cours d'eau] to straddle.
■ **vi** [empiéter] : **enjamber sur** to encroach on.

enjeu [ɑ̃ʒø] **nm** [mise] stake ▸ **quel est l'enjeu ici?** *fig* what's at stake here?

enjoignais, ***enjoignions*** ➤ ***enjoindre***.

enjoindre [82] [ɑ̃ʒwɛ̃dr] **vt** *littéraire* : **enjoindre à qqn de faire qqch** to enjoin sb to do sthg.

enjoint [ɑ̃ʒwɛ̃] **pp inv** ➤ ***enjoindre***.

enjôler [3] [ɑ̃ʒole] **vt** to coax.

enjôleur, ***euse*** [ɑ̃ʒolœr, øz] ■ **adj** wheedling.
■ **nm, f** wheedler.

enjoliver [3] [ɑ̃ʒɔlive] **vt** to embellish.

enjoliveur [ɑ̃ʒɔlivœr] **nm** [de roue] hubcap / [de calandre] badge.

enjoué, ***e*** [ɑ̃ʒwe] **adj** cheerful.

enlacer [16] [ɑ̃lase] **vt 1.** [prendre dans ses bras] to embrace, to hug **2.** [entourer] to wind around.
◆ ***s'enlacer*** **vp 1.** [s'entrelacer] to intertwine **2.** [s'embrasser] to embrace, to hug.

enlaidir [32] [ɑ̃ledir] ■ **vt** to make ugly ▸ **enlaidir le paysage** to be a blot on the landscape *ou* an eyesore.
■ **vi** to become ugly.
◆ ***s'enlaidir*** **vpi** to make o.s. (look) ugly.

enlevé, ***e*** [ɑ̃lve] **adj : (bien) enlevé** spirited.

enlèvement [ɑ̃lɛvmɑ̃] **nm 1.** [action d'enlever] removal ▸ **l'enlèvement des ordures (ménagères)** refuse collection **2.** [rapt] abduction.

enlever [19] [ɑ̃lve] **vt 1.** [gén] to remove / [vêtement] to take off **2.** [prendre] : **enlever qqch à qqn** to take sthg away from sb **3.** [obtenir] to win **4.** [kidnapper] to abduct **5.** *littéraire* [faire mourir] to carry off.
◆ ***s'enlever*** **vp** to be removable.

enliser [3] [ɑ̃lize] ◆ ***s'enliser*** **vp 1.** [s'embourber] to sink, to get stuck **2.** *fig* [piétiner] : **s'enliser dans qqch** to get bogged down in sthg.

enluminure [ɑ̃lyminyr] **nf** illumination.

ENM (abr de ***École nationale de la magistrature***) nf *grande école training lawyers.*

enneigé, e [ɑ̃neʒe] **adj** snow-covered.

enneigement [ɑ̃nɛʒmɑ̃] **nm** snow cover ▸ **bulletin d'enneigement** snow report.

ennemi, e [ɛnmi] ■ **adj** enemy *(avant n)*.
■ **nm, f** enemy ▸ **passer à l'ennemi** to defect ▸ **ennemi juré** sworn enemy ▸ **ennemi public** public enemy.

ennui [ɑ̃nɥi] **nm** **1.** [lassitude] boredom **2.** [contrariété] annoyance ▸ **l'ennui, c'est que...** the annoying thing is that... **3.** [problème] problem ▸ **attirer des ennuis à qqn** to cause trouble for sb ▸ **s'attirer des ennuis** to cause trouble for o.s. ▸ **avoir des ennuis** to have problems.

ennuyer [14] [ɑ̃nɥije] **vt** **1.** [agacer, contrarier] to annoy ▸ **cela t'ennuierait de venir me chercher?** would you mind picking me up? **2.** [lasser] to bore **3.** [inquiéter] to bother.
◆ ***s'ennuyer*** **vp** **1.** [se morfondre] to be bored **2.** [déplorer l'absence] **: s'ennuyer de qqn/qqch** to miss sb/sthg.

ennuyeux, euse [ɑ̃nɥijø, øz] **adj** **1.** [lassant] boring **2.** [contrariant] annoying.

énoncé [enɔ̃se] **nm** **1.** [libellé] wording **2.** LING utterance.

énoncer [16] [enɔ̃se] **vt** **1.** [libeller] to word **2.** [exposer] to expound / [théorème] to set forth.

énonciation [enɔ̃sjasjɔ̃] **nf** **1.** [libellé] wording **2.** LING utterance.

enorgueillir [32] [ɑ̃nɔrgœjir] ◆ ***s'enorgueillir*** **vp : s'enorgueillir de qqch/de faire qqch** to pride o.s. on sthg/on doing sthg.

énorme [enɔrm] **adj** **1.** *litt* & *fig* [immense] enormous **2.** *fam fig* [incroyable] far-fetched.

énormément [enɔrmemɑ̃] **adv** enormously ▸ **énormément de** a great deal of.

énormité [enɔrmite] **nf** **1.** [gigantisme] enormity **2.** [absurdité] **: dire des énormités** to say the most awful things.

enquérir [39] [ɑ̃kerir] ◆ ***s'enquérir*** **vp** *sout* **: s'enquérir de qqn** to ask after sb ▸ **s'enquérir de qqch** to inquire about sthg.

enquête [ɑ̃kɛt] **nf** **1.** [de police, recherches] investigation ▸ **enquête de routine** routine inquiry **2.** [sondage] survey ▸ **enquête de marché** market survey.

enquêter [4] [ɑ̃kete] **vi** **1.** [police, chercheur] to investigate **2.** [sonder] to conduct a survey.

enquêteur, euse ou ***trice*** [ɑ̃kɛtœr, øz, tris] **nm, f** investigator.

enquiers, enquiert ➤ ***enquérir.***

enquiquinant, e [ɑ̃kikinɑ̃, ɑ̃t] **adj** *fam* annoying.

enquiquiner [3] [ɑ̃kikine] *fam* **vt** **1.** [ennuyer] to bore (stiff) **2.** [irriter] to bug **3.** [importuner] **: se faire enquiquiner** to be hassled.
◆ ***s'enquiquiner*** **vpi** **1.** [s'ennuyer] to be bored (stiff) **2.** [se donner du mal] **: s'enquiquiner à : je ne vais pas m'enquiquiner à tout recopier** I don't feel like copying it out again.

enquis, e [ɑ̃ki, iz] **pp** ➤ ***enquérir.***

enraciner [3] [ɑ̃rasine] **vt** **1.** [planter] to dig in **2.** *fig* [idée, préjugé] to implant.
◆ ***s'enraciner*** **vp** **1.** [plante, idée] to take root **2.** [personne] to put down roots.

enragé, e [ɑ̃raʒe] ■ **adj** **1.** [chien] rabid, with rabies **2.** *fig* [invétéré] keen.
■ **nm, f : c'est un enragé de football** he's mad about *ou* on football.

enrageant, e [ɑ̃raʒɑ̃, ɑ̃t] **adj** infuriating.

enrager [17] [ɑ̃raʒe] **vi** to be furious ▸ **faire enrager qqn** to infuriate sb.

enrayer [11] [ɑ̃reje] **vt** **1.** [épidémie] to check, to stop **2.** [mécanisme] to jam.
◆ ***s'enrayer*** **vp** [mécanisme] to jam.

enrégimenter [3] [ɑ̃reʒimɑ̃te] **vt** [dans l'armée] to enlist / [dans un groupe] to enrol *UK*, to enroll *US*.

enregistrement [ɑ̃rəʒistrəmɑ̃] **nm** **1.** [de son, d'images, d'informations] recording ▸ **enregistrement pirate** pirate recording **2.** [inscription] registration **3.** [à l'aéroport] check-in ▸ **enregistrement des bagages** baggage registration.

enregistrer [3] [ɑ̃rəʒistre] **vt** **1.** [son, images, informations] to record **2.** INFORM to store **3.** [inscrire] to register **4.** [à l'aéroport] to check in **5.** *fam* [mémoriser] to make a mental note of.

enregistreur, euse [ɑ̃rəʒistrœr, øz] **adj** recording *(avant n)* ▸ **caisse enregistreuse** cash register.

enrhumé, e [ɑ̃ryme] **adj : je suis enrhumé** I have a cold.

enrhumer [3] [ɑ̃ryme] ◆ ***s'enrhumer*** **vp** to catch (a) cold.

enrichi, e [ɑ̃riʃi] **adj** **1.** [personne] nouveau riche **2.** [matériau] enriched **3.** *fig* [orné] **: enrichi de** enhanced by.

enrichir [32] [ɑ̃riʃir] **vt** **1.** [financièrement] to make rich **2.** *fig* [terre] to enrich.
◆ ***s'enrichir*** **vp** **1.** [financièrement] to grow rich **2.** *fig* [sol] to become enriched.

enrichissant, e [ɑ̃riʃisɑ̃, ɑ̃t] **adj** enriching.

enrichissement [ɑ̃riʃismɑ̃] **nm** **1.** [gén] enrichment **2.** [financier] increased wealth.

enrobé, e [ɑ̃rɔbe] **adj** **1.** [recouvert] **: enrobé de** coated with **2.** *fam* [grassouillet] plump.

enrober [3] [ɑ̃rɔbe] **vt** **1.** [recouvrir] **: enrober qqch de** to coat sthg with **2.** *fig* [requête, nouvelle] to wrap up.
◆ ***s'enrober*** **vp** to put on weight.

enrôlement [ɑ̃rolmɑ̃] **nm** enrolment *UK*, enrollment *US*.

enrôler [3] [ɑ̃role] **vt** to enrol *UK*, to enroll *US* / MIL to enlist.
◆ ***s'enrôler*** **vp** to enrol *UK*, to enroll *US* / MIL to enlist.

enroué, e [ɑ̃rwe] **adj** hoarse.

enrouer [6] [ɑ̃rwe] ◆ ***s'enrouer*** **vp** to become hoarse.

enroulement [ɑ̃rulmɑ̃] **nm** rolling up.

enrouler [3] [ɑ̃rule] **vt** to roll up ▸ **enrouler qqch autour de qqch** to wind sthg around sthg.
◆ ***s'enrouler*** **vp 1.** [entourer] **: s'enrouler sur** *ou* **autour de qqch** to wind around sthg **2.** [se pelotonner] **: s'enrouler dans qqch** to wrap o.s. up in sthg.

enrouleur, euse [ɑ̃rulœr, øz] **adj** winding.

ENS (abr de ***École normale supérieure***) **nf** *grande école training secondary school and university teachers.*

ensabler [3] [ɑ̃sable] **vt** to silt up.
◆ ***s'ensabler*** **vp** to silt up.

ENSAD, Ensad [ɛnsad] (abr de ***École nationale supérieure des arts décoratifs***) **nf** *grande école for applied arts.*

ENSAM, Ensam [ɛnsam] (abr de ***École nationale supérieure des arts et métiers***) **nf** *grande école for engineering.*

enseignant, e [ɑ̃sɛɲɑ̃, ɑ̃t] ■ **adj** teaching *(avant n).*
■ **nm, f** teacher.

enseigne [ɑ̃sɛɲ] **nf 1.** [de commerce] sign ▸ **enseigne lumineuse** neon sign **2.** [drapeau, soldat] ensign
▸▸ **être logé à la même enseigne** to be in the same boat.
◆ ***à telle enseigne que*** **loc conj** so much so that.

enseignement [ɑ̃sɛɲmɑ̃] **nm 1.** [gén] teaching ▸ **enseignement assisté par ordinateur** computer-aided learning ▸ **enseignement par correspondance** correspondence courses ▸ **enseignement primaire** primary education ▸ **enseignement privé** private education ▸ **enseignement professionnel** vocational education ▸ **enseignement public** state education *ou* schools ▸ **enseignement secondaire** secondary education ▸ **enseignement technique** technical education ▸ **travailler dans l'enseignement** to work in education *ou* the teaching profession **2.** [leçon] lesson ▸ **tirer un enseignement de qqch** to learn (a lesson) from sthg.

enseigner [4] [ɑ̃seɲe] **vt** *litt* & *fig* to teach ▸ **enseigner qqch à qqn** to teach sb sthg, to teach sthg to sb.

ensemble [ɑ̃sɑ̃bl] ■ **adv** together ▸ **aller ensemble** to go together.
■ **nm 1.** [totalité] whole ▸ **l'ensemble de** all of ▸ **idée d'ensemble** general idea ▸ **dans l'ensemble** on the whole **2.** [harmonie] unity **3.** [vêtement] outfit **4.** [série] collection **5.** MATH set **6.** ARCHIT development ▸ **grand ensemble** housing estate *UK ou* project *US* **7.** MUS ensemble.

ensemblier [ɑ̃sɑ̃blije] **nm** interior decorator / CINÉ & TV set designer.

ensemencer [16] [ɑ̃səmɑ̃se] **vt 1.** [terre] to sow **2.** [rivière] to stock.

enserrer [4] [ɑ̃sere] **vt** [entourer] to encircle / *fig* to imprison.

ENSET, Enset [ɛnsɛt] (abr de ***École nationale supérieure de l'enseignement technique***) **nf** *grande école training science and technology teachers.*

ensevelir [32] [ɑ̃səvlir] **vt** *litt* & *fig* to bury.
◆ ***s'ensevelir*** **vp** to bury o.s. (away).

ensoleillé, e [ɑ̃sɔleje] **adj** sunny.

ensoleillement [ɑ̃sɔlɛjmɑ̃] **nm** sunshine.

ensommeillé, e [ɑ̃sɔmeje] **adj** sleepy.

ensorceler [24] [ɑ̃sɔrsəle] **vt** to bewitch.

ensorcellement [ɑ̃sɔrsɛlmɑ̃] **nm** bewitching.

ensuite [ɑ̃sɥit] **adv 1.** [après, plus tard] after, afterwards, later **2.** [puis] then, next, after that ▸ **et ensuite?** what then?, what next?

ensuivre [89] [ɑ̃sɥivr] ◆ ***s'ensuivre*** **vp** to follow ▸ **il s'ensuit que** it follows that ▸ **et tout ce qui s'ensuit** and all that that entails.

entaille [ɑ̃taj] **nf** cut.

entailler [3] [ɑ̃taje] **vt** to cut.
◆ ***s'entailler*** **vp : s'entailler le doigt** to cut one's finger.

entame [ɑ̃tam] **nf** first slice.

entamer [3] [ɑ̃tame] **vt 1.** [gâteau, fromage] to start (on) / [bouteille, conserve] to start, to open **2.** [capital] to dip into **3.** [cuir, réputation] to damage **4.** [courage] to shake.

entartrer [3] [ɑ̃tartre] **vt** to scale, to fur up.
◆ ***s'entartrer*** **vp** to scale, to fur up.

entassement [ɑ̃tasmɑ̃] **nm 1.** [d'objets] pile / [action] piling up **2.** [de personnes] squeezing.

entasser [3] [ɑ̃tase] **vt 1.** [accumuler, multiplier] to pile up **2.** [serrer] to squeeze.
◆ ***s'entasser*** **vp 1.** [objets] to pile up **2.** [personnes] **: s'entasser dans** to squeeze into.

entendement [ɑ̃tɑ̃dmɑ̃] **nm** understanding ▸ **dépasser l'entendement (de qqn)** to be beyond (sb's) comprehension.

entendeur [ɑ̃tɑ̃dœr] **nm : à bon entendeur salut!** so be warned!

entendre [73] [ɑ̃tɑ̃dr] **vt 1.** [percevoir, écouter] to hear ▸ **parlez plus fort, on n'entend rien** speak up: we can't hear a word (you're saying) ▸ **entendre dire que** to hear (that) ▸ **j'ai entendu dire qu'il était parti** I heard that he had left ▸ **entendre parler de qqch** to hear of *ou* about sthg ▸ **on n'entend parler que de lui/de sa pièce** he's/his play's the talk of the town ▸ **à l'entendre...** to hear him/her talk... ▸ **qu'est-ce qu'il ne faut pas entendre!** *fam* give me a break! **2.** *sout* [comprendre] to understand ▸ **laisser entendre que** to imply that ▸ **ne rien y entendre à qqch** not to know the first thing about sthg **3.** *sout* [vouloir] **: entendre faire qqch** to intend to do sthg ▸ **il entend bien partir demain** he's determined to go tomorrow **4.** [vouloir dire] to mean ▸ **sans y entendre malice** without meaning any harm (by it).
◆ ***s'entendre*** **vp 1.** [sympathiser] **: s'entendre avec qqn** to get on with sb ▸ **s'entendre comme larrons en foire** to be as thick as thieves **2.** [s'accorder] to agree **3.** [savoir] **: s'entendre en qqch/à faire qqch** to be very good at sthg at doing sthg ▸ **s'y entendre** to know all about it ▸ **il s'entend en mécanique** he's good at *ou* he knows (a lot) about mechanics **4.** [être compris] to be understood ▸ **cela s'entend** that is understood ▸ **après l'hiver, (cela) s'entend** when the winter is over, of course *ou* it goes without saying **5.** [s'écouter] **: on ne s'entend plus** we can't hear ourselves think.

entendu, e [ɑ̃tɑ̃dy] ■ **pp** ➤ ***entendre***.
■ **adj 1.** [compris] agreed, understood ▸ **entendu!** right O.K.! **2.** [complice] knowing.

entente [ɑ̃tɑ̃t] **nf 1.** [harmonie] understanding **2.** [accord] agreement **3.** [compréhension] **: à double entente** with a double meaning.

entériner [3] [ɑ̃terine] **vt** to ratify.

entérite [ɑ̃terit] **nf** enteritis *(U)*.

enterrement [ɑ̃tɛrmɑ̃] **nm** burial.

enterrer [4] [ɑ̃tere] **vt** *litt* & *fig* to bury ▸ **enterrer sa vie de garçon** to have a stag party.
◆ ***s'enterrer*** **vp** *fig* to bury o.s. (away).

entêtant, e [ɑ̃tɛtɑ̃, ɑ̃t] **adj** heady.

en-tête [ɑ̃tɛt] (pl **en-têtes**) **nm** heading.

entêté, e [ɑ̃tete] ■ **adj** stubborn.
■ **nm, f** stubborn person.

entêtement [ɑ̃tɛtmɑ̃] **nm** stubbornness.

entêter [4] [ɑ̃tete] ◆ ***s'entêter*** **vp** to persist ▸ **s'entêter à faire qqch** to persist in doing sthg ▸ **s'entêter dans qqch** to persist in sthg.

enthousiasme [ɑ̃tuzjasm] **nm** enthusiasm.

enthousiasmer [3] [ɑ̃tuzjasme] **vt** to fill with enthusiasm.
◆ ***s'enthousiasmer*** **vp : s'enthousiasmer pour** to be enthusiastic about.

enthousiaste [ɑ̃tuzjast] ■ **nmf** enthusiast.
■ **adj** enthusiastic.

enticher [3] [ɑ̃tiʃe] ◆ ***s'enticher*** **vp : s'enticher de qqn/qqch** to become obsessed with sb/sthg.

entier, ère [ɑ̃tje, ɛr] **adj** whole, entire.
◆ ***en entier*** **loc adv** in its/their entirety.

entièrement [ɑ̃tjɛrmɑ̃] **adv 1.** [complètement] fully **2.** [pleinement] wholly, entirely.

entité [ɑ̃tite] **nf** entity.

entomologie [ɑ̃tɔmɔlɔʒi] **nf** entomology.

entonner [3] [ɑ̃tɔne] **vt** [chant] to strike up.

entonnoir [ɑ̃tɔnwar] **nm 1.** [instrument] funnel **2.** [cavité] crater.

entorse [ɑ̃tɔrs] **nf** MÉD sprain ▸ **se faire une entorse à la cheville/au poignet** to sprain one's ankle/wrist ▸ **faire une entorse à** *fig* [loi, règlement] to bend.

entortiller [3] [ɑ̃tɔrtije] **vt 1.** [entrelacer] to twist **2.** [envelopper] **: entortiller qqch autour de qqch** to wrap sthg around sthg **3.** *fam fig* [personne] to sweet-talk **4.** *fam* [tromper] to hoodwink, to con ▸ **se faire entortiller** to be taken in.
◆ ***s'entortiller*** **vpi 1.** [s'enrouler - lierre] to twist, to wind **2.** [être empêtré] to get caught *ou* tangled up ▸ **s'entortiller dans ses explications** to get tangled up in one's explanations.

entourage [ɑ̃turaʒ] **nm 1.** [milieu] entourage **2.** [clôture] surround.

entouré, e [ɑ̃ture] **adj 1.** [enclos] surrounded **2.** [soutenu] popular.

entourer [3] [ɑ̃ture] **vt 1.** [enclore, encercler] **: entourer (de)** to surround (with) **2.** *fig* [soutenir] to rally round.
◆ ***s'entourer*** **vp : s'entourer de** to surround o.s. with.

entourloupette [ɑ̃turlupɛt] **nf** *fam* dirty trick.

entournure [ɑ̃turnyr] **nf : être gêné aux entournures** *fig* [financièrement] to feel the pinch / [être mal à l'aise] to feel awkward.

entracte [ɑ̃trakt] **nm** interval *UK*, intermission *US* / *fig* interlude.

entraide [ɑ̃trɛd] **nf** mutual assistance.

entraider [4] [ɑ̃trede] ◆ ***s'entraider*** **vp** to help each other.

entrailles [ɑ̃traj] **nfpl 1.** [intestins] entrails **2.** *sout* [profondeurs] depths **3.** *fig* [siège des sentiments] soul *sg*.

entrain [ɑ̃trɛ̃] **nm** drive.

entraînement [ɑ̃trɛnmɑ̃] **nm 1.** [mécanisme] drive **2.** [préparation] practice / SPORT training ▸ **manquer d'entraînement** to be out of training / *fig* to be out of practice.

entraîner [4] [ɑ̃trene] **vt 1.** TECHNOL to drive **2.** [tirer] to pull **3.** [susciter] to lead to **4.** SPORT to coach **5.** [emmener] to take along **6.** [séduire] to influence ▸ **entraîner qqn à faire qqch** to talk sb into sthg.
◆ ***s'entraîner*** **vp** to practise *UK*, to pratice *US* / SPORT to train ▸ **s'entraîner à faire qqch** to practise *UK ou* practice *US* doing sthg.

entraîneur, euse [ɑ̃trɛnœr, øz] **nm, f** trainer, coach.
◆ ***entraîneuse*** **nf** [dans un cabaret] hostess.

entrant, e [ɑ̃trɑ̃, ɑ̃t] **adj** incoming *(avant n)*.

entrapercevoir, entr'apercevoir [52] [ɑ̃trapɛrsəvwar] **vt** to glimpse.

entrave [ɑ̃trav] **nf** hobble / *fig* obstruction.

entraver [3] [ɑ̃trave] **vt** to hobble / *fig* to hinder.

entre [ɑ̃tr] **prép 1.** [gén] between ▸ **ils ont invité entre 15 et 20 personnes** they've invited 15 to 20 people ▸ **il passa la main entre les barreaux** he put his hand through the bars ▸ **tenir qqch entre ses mains** to hold sthg in one's hands ▸ **une couleur entre le jaune et le vert** a colour *UK ou* color *US* between yellow and green **2.** [parmi] among ▸ **entre nous** between you and me, between ourselves ▸ **entre nous, il n'a pas tort** [à deux] between you and me, he's right / [à plusieurs] between us, he's right ▸ **l'un d'entre nous ira** one of us will go ▸ **généralement ils restent entre eux** they tend to keep themselves to themselves ▸ **ils se battent entre eux** they're fighting among *ou* amongst themselves ▸ **parle, nous sommes entre amis** you can talk: we're among friends *ou* we're all friends here.
◆ ***entre autres*** **loc prép : entre autres (personnes)** among others ▸ **entre autres (choses)** among other things ▸ **sont exposés, entre autres, des objets rares, des œuvres de jeunesse du peintre, etc.** the exhibition includes, among other things, rare objects, examples of the artist's early work etc.

entrebâillement [ɑ̃trəbajmɑ̃] **nm** slight opening ▸ **dans l'entrebâillement de la porte** through the half-open door.

entrebâiller [3] [ɑ̃trəbaje] **vt** to open slightly.

entrechat [ɑ̃trəʃa] **nm 1.** [danse] entrechat **2.** [saut] leap ▸ **faire des entrechats** to leap around.

entrechoquer [3] [ɑ̃trəʃɔke] **vt** to bang together.
◆ ***s'entrechoquer*** **vp** to bang into each other.

entrecôte [ɑ̃trəkot] **nf** entrecôte.

entrecoupé**, **e [ɑ̃trəkupe] **adj : entrecoupé de** interspersed with.

entrecouper [3] [ɑ̃trəkupe] **vt** to intersperse.

entrecroiser [3] [ɑ̃trəkrwaze] **vt** to interlace.
◆ ***s'entrecroiser*** **vp** to intersect.

entre-déchirer [3] [ɑ̃trədeʃire] ◆ ***s'entre-déchirer*** **vp** to tear each other to pieces.

entre-deux [ɑ̃trədø] **nm inv** gap, space ▸ **dans l'entre-deux** *fig* in the interim.

entre-deux-guerres [ɑ̃trədøgɛr] **nm inv** inter-war years *pl*.

entrée [ɑ̃tre] **nf 1.** [arrivée, accès] entry, entrance ▸ **à l'entrée de la grotte** at the entrance *ou* mouth of the cave ▸ **'entrée interdite'** 'no admittance' ▸ **'entrée libre'** [dans un musée] 'admission free' / [dans une boutique] 'browsers welcome' ▸ **'entrée réservée au personnel'** 'staff only' ▸ **entrée en scène** entrance ▸ **il a fait une entrée remarquée** he made quite an entrance, he made a dramatic entrance
2. [porte] entrance ▸ **entrée des artistes** stage door ▸ **entrée de service** tradesmen's entrance ▸ **entrée principale** main entrance
3. [vestibule] (entrance) hall
4. [billet] ticket ▸ **le film a fait deux millions d'entrées** two million people have seen the film
5. [plat] starter, first course
6. [début] onset ▸ **l'entrée en guerre de la France** France's entry into the war ▸ **entrée en matière** introduction ▸ **l'entrée en vigueur d'une loi** the implementation of a law
7. [rubrique] entry
8. INFORM input, entry ▸ **entrée des données** [généralement] inputting of data, data input / [par saisie] keying in *ou* keyboarding of data
▸▸ **d'entrée de jeu** from the outset ▸ **avoir ses entrées chez qqn** to have sb's ear.

entrefaites [ɑ̃trəfɛt] **nfpl : sur ces entrefaites** just at that moment.

entrefilet [ɑ̃trəfilɛ] **nm** paragraph.

entregent [ɑ̃trəʒɑ̃] **nm : avoir de l'entregent** to know how to behave.

entrejambe**, **entre-jambes [ɑ̃trəʒɑ̃b] **nm** crotch.

entrelacer [16] [ɑ̃trəlase] **vt** to intertwine.
◆ ***s'entrelacer*** **vp** to intertwine.

entrelarder [3] [ɑ̃trəlarde] **vt 1.** CULIN to lard **2.** *fam fig* [discours] **: entrelarder de** to lace with.

entremêler [4] [ɑ̃trəmele] **vt** to mix ▸ **entremêler de** to mix with.
◆ ***s'entremêler*** **vp** to mingle.

entremets [ɑ̃trəmɛ] **nm** dessert.

entremettais**, **entremettions ➤ ***entremettre***.

entremetteur**, **euse [ɑ̃trəmɛtœr, øz] **nm, f** mediator.
◆ ***entremetteuse*** **nf** *péj* go-between.

entremettre [84] [ɑ̃trəmɛtr] ◆ ***s'entremettre*** **vp : s'entremettre (dans)** to mediate (in).

entremis**, **e [ɑ̃trəmi, iz] **pp** ➤ ***entremettre***.

entremise [ɑ̃trəmiz] **nf** intervention ▸ **par l'entremise de** through.

entrepont [ɑ̃trəpɔ̃] **nm** steerage.

entreposer [3] [ɑ̃trəpoze] **vt** to store.

entrepôt [ɑ̃trəpo] **nm** warehouse.

entreprenais**, **entreprenions ➤ ***entreprendre***.

entreprenant**, **e [ɑ̃trəprənɑ̃, ɑ̃t] **adj** enterprising / [auprès des femmes] forward.

entreprendre [79] [ɑ̃trəprɑ̃dr] **vt** to undertake / [commencer] to start ▸ **entreprendre de faire qqch** to undertake to do sthg ▸ **entreprendre qqn sur** to engage sb in conversation about.

entrepreneur**, **euse [ɑ̃trəprənœr, øz] **nm, f 1.** [de services & CONSTR] contractor **2.** [patron] businessman (f businesswoman).

entreprenne**, **entreprennes ➤ ***entreprendre***.

entrepris**, **e [ɑ̃trəpri, iz] **pp** ➤ ***entreprendre***.

entreprise [ɑ̃trəpriz] **nf 1.** [travail, initiative] enterprise ▸ **libre entreprise** ÉCON free enterprise **2.** [société] company ▸ **entreprise nationalisée** nationalized industry ▸ **petite entreprise** small business.

entrer [3] [ɑ̃tre] ■ **vi** *(v aux : être)* **1.** [pénétrer] to enter, to go/come in ▸ **entrer en gare** to pull in (to the station) ▸ **entrer au port** to come into *ou* to enter harbour *UK ou* harbor *US* ▸ **entrer dans** [gén] to enter / [pièce] to go/come into / [bain, voiture] to get into / *fig* [sujet] to go into ▸ **entrer dans un mur** to crash into a wall ▸ **entrer dans le monde du travail** to start work ▸ **cela n'entre pas dans mes attributions** this is not within my responsibilities ▸ **entrer par** to go in *ou* enter by ▸ **entrez!** come in! ▸ **entrez sans frapper** go (straight) in ▸ **faire entrer qqn** to show sb in ▸ **faire entrer qqch** to bring sthg in
2. [faire partie] **: entrer dans** to go into, to be part of
3. [être admis, devenir membre] **: entrer à** [club, parti] to join ▸ **entrer dans** [les affaires, l'enseignement] to go into / [la police, l'armée] to join ▸ **entrer en politique** to go into politics ▸ **entrer en religion** to enter the religious life ▸ **entrer à l'université** to go to university *UK ou* college *US* ▸ **elle entre à la maternelle/en troisième année** she's going to nursery school/moving up into the Year 3 ▸ **entrer à l'hôpital** to go into hospital *UK*, to enter the hospital *US*
4. [débuter] **: entrer en** to start, to begin ▸ **entrer en conversation avec qqn** to strike up a conversation with sb ▸ **entrer en guerre** to go to war.
■ **vt** *(aux : avoir)* **1.** [gén] to bring in
2. INFORM to enter, to input.

entresol [ɑ̃trəsɔl] **nm** mezzanine.

entre-temps [ɑ̃trətɑ̃] **adv** meanwhile.

entretenir [40] [ɑ̃trətnir] **vt 1.** [faire durer] to keep alive **2.** [cultiver] to maintain **3.** [soigner] to look after **4.** [personne, famille] to support **5.** [parler à] **: entretenir qqn de qqch** to speak to sb about sthg.
◆ ***s'entretenir*** **vp 1.** [se parler] **: s'entretenir (de)** to talk (about) **2.** [prendre soin de soi] to look after o.s.

entretenu**, **e [ɑ̃trətny] ■ **pp** ➤ ***entretenir***.
■ **adj 1.** [soigné] well-kept ▸ **bien/mal entretenu** well/badly kept **2.** [femme] kept *(avant n)*.

entretien [ɑ̃trətjɛ̃] **nm 1.** [de voiture, jardin] maintenance, upkeep **2.** [conversation] discussion / [colloque] debate ▸ **entretien d'embauche** job interview ▸ **entretien en profondeur** in-depth interview.

entretiendrai, entretiendras ➤ ***entretenir.***

entre-tuer [7] [ɑ̃trətɥe] ◆ ***s'entre-tuer*** **vp** to kill each other.

entreverrai, entreverras ➤ ***entrevoir.***

entrevoir [62] [ɑ̃trəvwar] **vt 1.** [distinguer] to make out **2.** [voir rapidement] to see briefly **3.** *fig* [deviner] to glimpse.
◆ ***s'entrevoir*** **vp 1.** [se voir] to see each other briefly **2.** [se profiler] to be visible.

entrevoyais, entrevoyions ➤ ***entrevoir.***

entrevu, e [ɑ̃trəvy] **pp** ➤ ***entrevoir.***

entrevue [ɑ̃trəvy] **nf** meeting.

entrouvert, e [ɑ̃truvɛr, ɛrt] ■ **pp** ➤ ***entrouvrir.***
■ **adj** half-open.

entrouvrir [34] [ɑ̃truvrir] **vt** to open partly.
◆ ***s'entrouvrir*** **vp** to open partly.

énumération [enymerasjɔ̃] **nf** enumeration.

énumérer [18] [enymere] **vt** to enumerate.

env. (abr écrite de ***environ***) approx.

envahir [32] [ɑ̃vair] **vt 1.** [gén & MIL] to invade **2.** *fig* [suj: sommeil, doute] to overcome **3.** *fig* [déranger] to intrude on.

envahissant, e [ɑ̃vaisɑ̃, ɑ̃t] **adj 1.** [herbes] invasive **2.** [personne] intrusive.

envahissement [ɑ̃vaismɑ̃] **nm** invasion.

envahisseur [ɑ̃vaisœr] **nm** invader.

enveloppe [ɑ̃vlɔp] **nf 1.** [de lettre] envelope ▸ **mettre sous enveloppe** to put in an envelope ▸ **enveloppe à fenêtre** window envelope ▸ **enveloppe timbrée** stamped addressed envelope *UK*, self-addressed stamped envelope *US* **2.** [d'emballage] covering **3.** [membrane] membrane / [de graine] husk **4.** *fig & littéraire* [apparence] exterior.
◆ ***enveloppe budgétaire*** **nf** budget.

envelopper [3] [ɑ̃vlɔpe] **vt 1.** [emballer] to wrap (up) **2.** [suj: brouillard] to envelop **3.** [déguiser] to mask.
◆ ***s'envelopper*** **vp : s'envelopper dans** to wrap o.s. up in.

envenimer [3] [ɑ̃vnime] **vt 1.** [blessure] to infect **2.** *fig* [querelle] to poison.
◆ ***s'envenimer*** **vp 1.** [s'infecter] to become infected **2.** *fig* [se détériorer] to become poisoned.

envergure [ɑ̃vɛrgyr] **nf 1.** [largeur] span / [d'oiseau, d'avion] wingspan **2.** *fig* [qualité] calibre *UK* *ou* caliber *US* **3.** *fig* [importance] scope ▸ **prendre de l'envergure** to expand.

enverrai, enverras ➤ ***envoyer.***

envers[1] [ɑ̃vɛr] **prép** towards *UK*, toward *US* ▸ **envers et contre tous** in spite of all opposition.

envers[2] [ɑ̃vɛr] **nm 1.** [de tissu] wrong side / [de feuillet] back / [de médaille] reverse **2.** [face cachée] other side ▸ **l'envers du décor** *fig* behind the scenes.
◆ ***à l'envers*** **loc adv** [vêtement] inside out / [portrait, feuille] upside down / *fig* the wrong way.

envi [ɑ̃vi] ◆ ***à l'envi*** **loc adv** *littéraire* trying to outdo each other.

enviable [ɑ̃vjabl] **adj** enviable.

envie [ɑ̃vi] **nf 1.** [désir] desire ▸ **avoir envie de qqch/de faire qqch** to feel like sthg/like doing sthg, to want sthg/to do sthg ▸ **avoir envie de rire/pleurer** to feel like laughing/crying ▸ **elle n'a pas envie que tu restes** she doesn't want you to stay ▸ **mourir d'envie de faire qqch** to be dying to do sthg ▸ **ça m'a donné envie de les revoir** it made me want to see *ou* feel like seeing them again ▸ **voilà qui lui ôtera l'envie de revenir** this'll make sure he's not tempted to come back **2.** [convoitise] envy ▸ **ce tailleur me fait envie** I'd love to buy that suit ▸ **sa réussite me fait envie** I envy her success.

envier [9] [ɑ̃vje] **vt** to envy ▸ **n'avoir rien à envier à qqn/à qqch** to have no reason to envy sb/sthg.

envieux, euse [ɑ̃vjø, øz] ■ **adj** envious.
■ **nm, f** envious person ▸ **faire des envieux** to make other people envious.

environ [ɑ̃virɔ̃] **adv** [à peu près] about.

environnant, e [ɑ̃virɔnɑ̃, ɑ̃t] **adj** surrounding.

environnement [ɑ̃virɔnmɑ̃] **nm** environment / INFORM environment, platform.

environnemental, e, aux [ɑ̃virɔnmɑ̃tal, o] **adj** environmental.

environnementaliste [ɑ̃virɔnmɑ̃talist] **nmf** environmentalist.

environner [3] [ɑ̃virɔne] **vt** to surround.

environs [ɑ̃virɔ̃] **nmpl** (surrounding) area *sg* ▸ **dans les environs de** in the vicinity of ▸ **aux environs de** [lieu] near / [époque] around, round about *UK*.

envisageable [ɑ̃vizaʒabl] **adj** conceivable ▸ **ce n'est guère envisageable** it hardly seems possible.

COMMENT EXPRIMER...

ses idées lors d'un entretien d'embauche

As you can see from my CV / Comme vous le voyez sur mon CV
I have been in publishing for almost ten years / Cela fait presque dix ans que je travaille dans l'édition
I think I'm good at dealing with people / Je crois être doué pour les relations humaines
I like working as part of a team / J'aime travailler au sein d'une équipe
What does the job involve? / En quoi consiste le travail ?
Who would I be reporting to? / Qui serait mon supérieur direct ?
Is it a permanent contract? / S'agit-il d'un contrat à durée indéterminée ?
What are the normal working hours? / Quels sont les horaires de travail ?

envisager [17] [ɑ̃vizaʒe] **vt** to consider ▸ **envisager de faire qqch** to be considering doing sthg.

envoi [ɑ̃vwa] **nm 1.** [action] sending, dispatch ▸ **faire un envoi** [colis] to send a parcel *UK ou* package *US* / [lettre] to send a letter ▸ **envoi contre remboursement** cash on delivery ▸ **envoi groupé** joint consignment ▸ **un envoi en nombre** a (mass) mailing
2. [colis] parcel *UK*, package *US* ▸ **envoi recommandé** [colis] registered parcel / [lettre] registered letter
3. SPORT **: coup d'envoi** kick-off ▸ **donner le coup d'envoi d'un match** [arbitre] to give the sign for the match to start / [joueur] to kick off ▸ **donner le coup d'envoi d'une campagne** *fig* to get a campaign off the ground
4. INFORM **: envoi multiple** crossposting ▸ **faire un envoi multiple de** to cross-post.

envoie, envoies ➤ *envoyer*.

envol [ɑ̃vɔl] **nm** takeoff.

envolée [ɑ̃vɔle] **nf 1.** [d'oiseaux] flight **2.** [augmentation] **: l'envolée du dollar** the rapid rise in the value of the dollar ▸ **envolée du marché boursier** stock market boom.

envoler [3] [ɑ̃vɔle] ◆ ***s'envoler*** **vp 1.** [oiseau] to fly away **2.** [avion] to take off **3.** [disparaître] to disappear into thin air **4.** [se disperser] to blow away.

envoûtement [ɑ̃vutmɑ̃] **nm** enchantment.

envoûter [3] [ɑ̃vute] **vt** to bewitch.

envoyé, e [ɑ̃vwaje] ■ **adj : bien envoyé** well-aimed.
■ **nm, f** envoy ▸ **envoyé spécial** special correspondent.

envoyer [30] [ɑ̃vwaje] **vt** to send ▸ **envoyer qqch à qqn** [expédier] to send sb sthg, to send sthg to sb / [jeter] to throw sb sthg, to throw sthg to sb ▸ **envoyer qqch par bateau** to ship sthg, to send sthg by ship ▸ **envoyer un (petit) mot à qqn** to drop sb a line ▸ **envoyer un enfant à l'école** to send a child (off) to school ▸ **envoyer qqn faire qqch** to send sb to do sthg ▸ **envoyer chercher qqn/qqch** to send for sb/sthg ▸ **envoyer un adversaire à terre** *ou* **au tapis** to knock an opponent down *ou* to the ground ▸ **envoyer des baisers à qqn** to blow sb kisses ▸ **envoyer des coups de pied/poing à qqn** to kick/to punch sb ▸ **envoyer promener qqn** *fam fig* to send sb packing ▸ **j'avais envie de tout envoyer promener** *fam ou* **valser** *fam* I felt like chucking the whole thing in.
◆ ***s'envoyer*** **vp** *(emploi réciproque)* to send one another ▸ **s'envoyer des lettres** to write to one another.

envoyeur, euse [ɑ̃vwajœr, øz] **nm, f** sender.

enzyme [ɑ̃zym] **nmf** enzyme.

éolien, enne [eɔljɛ̃, ɛn] **adj** wind *(avant n)*.
◆ ***éolienne*** **nf** windmill *(for generating power)*, wind turbine.

épagneul [epaɲœl] **nm** spaniel.

épais, aisse [epɛ, ɛs] **adj 1.** [large, dense] thick **2.** [trapu] thickset **3.** [grossier] crude.

épaisseur [epɛsœr] **nf 1.** [largeur, densité] thickness **2.** *fig* [consistance] depth.

épaissir [32] [epesir] **vt & vi** to thicken.
◆ ***s'épaissir*** **vp 1.** [liquide] to thicken **2.** *fig* [mystère] to deepen.

épanchement [epɑ̃ʃmɑ̃] **nm 1.** [effusion] outpouring **2.** MÉD effusion ▸ **épanchement de synovie** water on the knee.

épancher [3] [epɑ̃ʃe] **vt** to pour out.
◆ ***s'épancher*** **vp** [se confier] to pour one's heart out.

épanoui, e [epanwi] **adj 1.** [fleur] in full bloom **2.** [expression] radiant **3.** [corps] fully formed ▸ **aux formes épanouies** well-rounded.

épanouir [32] [epanwir] **vt** [personne] to make happy.
◆ ***s'épanouir*** **vp 1.** [fleur] to open **2.** [visage] to light up **3.** [corps] to fill out **4.** [personnalité] to blossom.

épanouissement [epanwismɑ̃] **nm 1.** [de fleur] blooming, opening **2.** [de visage] brightening **3.** [de corps] filling out **4.** [de personnalité] flowering.

épargnant, e [eparɲɑ̃, ɑ̃t] ■ **adj** thrifty.
■ **nm, f** saver ▸ **les petits épargnants** small savers.

épargne [eparɲ] **nf 1.** [action, vertu] saving **2.** [somme] savings *pl* ▸ **épargne logement** savings account *(to buy property)* ; voir aussi ***plan***.

CULTURE
Plan d'épargne

The **plan d'épargne logement** lets people save for at least four years to buy or build a home while the account earns interest. At the end of the fourth year, holders can apply for a loan lasting up to 15 years. The **plan d'épargne en actions** lets people deposit up to 132,000 euros earned through investment in French and European stocks, but funds are frozen for five years. The holder can amass investment revenue without paying tax on it. Finally, the **plan d'épargne entreprise** lets a company's employees build a portfolio of stocks and bonds. Employees decide how much to invest in the plan and at what intervals.

épargner [3] [eparɲe] **vt 1.** [gén] to spare ▸ **épargner qqch à qqn** to spare sb sthg **2.** [économiser] to save.
◆ ***s'épargner*** **vp** to save *ou* spare o.s.

éparpiller [3] [eparpije] **vt 1.** [choses, personnes] to scatter **2.** *fig* [forces] to dissipate.
◆ ***s'éparpiller*** **vp 1.** [se disperser] to scatter **2.** *fig* [perdre son temps] to lack focus.

épars, e [epar, ars] **adj** *sout* [objets] scattered / [végétation, cheveux] sparse.

épatant, e [epatɑ̃, ɑ̃t] **adj** *fam* great.

épate [epat] **nf** *fam* **: faire de l'épate** to show off.

épaté, e [epate] **adj 1.** [nez] flat **2.** *fam* [étonné] amazed.

épater [3] [epate] **vt** *fam* [étonner] to amaze.

épaule [epol] **nf** shoulder ▸ **hausser les épaules** to shrug (one's shoulders) ▸ **épaule d'agneau** CULIN shoulder of lamb.

épaulé-jeté [epoleʒəte] (pl **épaulés-jetés**) **nm** clean and-jerk.

épaulement [epolmɑ̃] **nm 1.** [mur] retaining wall **2.** GÉOL escarpment.

épauler [3] [epole] ■ **vi** to raise one's rifle.
■ **vt** to support, to back up.
◆ ***s'épauler*** **vp** *(emploi réciproque)* to help *ou* to support one another.

épaulette [epolɛt] **nf 1.** MIL epaulet **2.** [rembourrage] shoulder pad.

épave [epav] **nf** wreck.

épeautre [epotr] **nm** spelt *(wheat)*.

épée [epe] **nf** sword ▸ **épée de Damoclès** sword of Damocles ▸ **coup d'épée dans l'eau** *fig* wasted effort.

épeler [24] [eple] **vt** to spell.

épépiner [3] [epepine] **vt** to seed.

éperdu, ***e*** [epɛrdy] **adj** [sentiment] passionate ▸ **éperdu de** [personne] overcome with.

éperdument [epɛrdymɑ̃] **adv 1.** [travailler] frantically **2.** [aimer] passionately.

éperlan [epɛrlɑ̃] **nm** smelt.

éperon [eprɔ̃] **nm** [de cavalier, de montagne] spur / [de navire] ram ▸ **éperon rocheux** rocky outcrop.

éperonner [3] [eprɔne] **vt** to spur on.

épervier [epɛrvje] **nm** sparrowhawk.

éphèbe [efɛb] **nm** *hum* Adonis.

éphémère [efemɛr] ■ **adj** [bref] ephemeral, fleeting.
■ **nm** ZOOL mayfly.

éphéméride [efemerid] **nf** tear-off calendar.

épi [epi] **nm 1.** [de céréale] ear ▸ **épi de maïs** CULIN corn on the cob **2.** [cheveux] tuft ▸ **épi rebelle** unruly tuft of hair.

épice [epis] **nf** spice.

épicé, ***e*** [epise] **adj** spicy.

épicéa [episea] **nm** spruce.

épicentre [episɑ̃tr] **nm** epicentre *UK*, epicenter *US*.

épicer [16] [epise] **vt 1.** [plat] to spice **2.** [récit] to spice up.

épicerie [episri] **nf 1.** [magasin] grocer's (shop) *UK*, grocery (store) *US* **2.** [denrées] groceries *pl* ▸ **épicerie fine** delicatessen.

épicier, ***ère*** [episje, ɛr] **nm, f** grocer.

épicurien, ***enne*** [epikyrjɛ̃, ɛn] ■ **adj** epicurean.
■ **nm, f** epicure.

épidémie [epidemi] **nf** epidemic.

épidémique [epidemik] **adj** contagious.

épiderme [epidɛrm] **nm** epidermis.

épidermique [epidɛrmik] **adj** [de l'épiderme] skin *(avant n)* ▸ **réaction épidermique** *fig* kneejerk reaction.

épier [9] [epje] **vt 1.** [espionner] to spy on **2.** [observer] to look for.

épieu [epjø] **nm 1.** [de guerre] pike **2.** [de chasse] spear.

épigramme [epigram] **nf** epigram.

épilation [epilasjɔ̃] **nf** hair removal ▸ **épilation à la cire** waxing.

épilepsie [epilɛpsi] **nf** epilepsy.

épileptique [epilɛptik] **nmf & adj** epileptic.

épiler [3] [epile] **vt** [jambes] to remove hair from / [sourcils] to pluck.
◆ ***s'épiler*** **vp : s'épiler les jambes** to remove the hair from one's legs / [à la cire] to wax one's legs / **: s'épiler les sourcils** to pluck one's eyebrows.

épilogue [epilɔg] **nm 1.** [de roman] epilogue **2.** [d'affaire] outcome.

épiloguer [3] [epilɔge] **vi** to hold forth.

épinards [epinar] **nmpl** spinach *(U)* ▸ **épinards en branches** leaf spinach.

épine [epin] **nf 1.** [arbrisseau] thorn bush **2.** [piquant - de rosier] thorn / [- de hérisson] spine ▸ **tirer une épine du pied à qqn** *fig* to get sb out of a tight corner.
◆ ***épine dorsale*** **nf** backbone, spine.

épineux, ***euse*** [epinø, øz] **adj** thorny.

épingle [epɛ̃gl] **nf** [instrument] pin ▸ **épingle à cheveux** hairpin ▸ **épingle à nourrice** *ou* **de sûreté** safety pin ▸ **monter qqch en épingle** *fig* to blow sthg up ▸ **tirer son épingle du jeu** *fig* to extricate o.s. ▸ **tiré à quatre épingles** *fig* impeccably turned out.

épingler [3] [epɛ̃gle] **vt 1.** [fixer] to pin (up) **2.** *fam fig* [arrêter] to nab, to nick *UK*.

épinière [epinjɛr] ➤ ***moelle***.

Épiphanie [epifani] **nf** Epiphany.

épiphénomène [epifenɔmɛn] **nm** epiphenomenon.

épique [epik] **adj** epic.

épiscopal, ***e***, ***aux*** [episkɔpal, o] **adj** episcopal.

épiscopat [episkɔpa] **nm** episcopate.

épisiotomie [epizjɔtɔmi] **nf** episiotomy.

épisode [epizɔd] **nm** episode.

épisodique [epizɔdik] **adj 1.** [occasionnel] occasional **2.** [secondaire] minor.

épistémologie [epistemɔlɔʒi] **nf** epistemology.

épistolaire [epistɔlɛr] **adj 1.** [échange] of letters ▸ **être en relations épistolaires avec qqn** to be in (regular) correspondence with sb **2.** [roman] epistolary.

épitaphe [epitaf] **nf** epitaph.

épithète [epitɛt] ■ **nf 1.** GRAMM attribute **2.** [qualificatif] term.
■ **adj** attributive.

épître [epitr] **nf** epistle.

éploré, ***e*** [eplɔre] **adj** [personne] in tears / [visage, air] tearful.

épluchage [eplyʃaʒ] **nm 1.** [de légumes] peeling **2.** [de textes] dissection / [de comptes] scrutiny.

épluche-légumes [eplyʃlegym] **nm inv** potato peeler.

éplucher [3] [eplyʃe] **vt 1.** [légumes] to peel **2.** [textes] to dissect / [comptes] to scrutinize.

épluchure [eplyʃyr] **nf** peelings *pl*.

éponge [epɔ̃ʒ] **nf** sponge ▸ **jeter l'éponge** *fig* to throw in the towel ▸ **passer l'éponge** *fig* to wipe the slate clean.

éponger [17] [epɔ̃ʒe] **vt 1.** [liquide, déficit] to mop up **2.** [visage] to mop, to wipe.
◆ ***s'éponger*** **vp** [personne] to mop o.s. ▸ **s'éponger le front** to mop one's brow.

épopée [epɔpe] **nf** epic.

époque [epɔk] **nf 1.** [de l'année] time **2.** [de l'histoire] period ▸ **à l'époque** at the time ▸ **d'époque** period ▸ **la Belle Époque** ≃ the Edwardian era **3.** GÉOL period, age.

épouiller [3] [epuje] **vt** to delouse.

époumoner [3] [epumɔne] ◆ ***s'époumoner*** **vp** to shout o.s. hoarse.

épouse ➤ ***époux***.

épouser [3] [epuze] **vt 1.** [personne] to marry **2.** [forme] to hug **3.** *fig* [idée, principe] to espouse.

épousseter [27] [epuste] **vt** to dust.

époustouflant, ***e*** [epustuflɑ̃, ɑ̃t] **adj** *fam* amazing.

époustoufler [3] [epustufle] **vt** *fam* to flabbergast, to amaze.

épouvantable [epuvɑ̃tabl] **adj** dreadful.

épouvantail [epuvɑ̃taj] **nm** [à moineaux] scarecrow / *fig* bogeyman.

épouvante [epuvɑ̃t] **nf** terror, horror ▸ **film d'épouvante** horror film *UK ou* movie *US*.

épouvanter [3] [epuvɑ̃te] **vt** to terrify.

époux, ***épouse*** [epu, epuz] **nm, f** spouse ▸ **prendre pour époux** to marry.

éprendre [79] [eprɑ̃dr] ◆ ***s'éprendre*** **vp** *sout* : **s'éprendre de** to fall in love with.

épreuve [eprœv] **nf 1.** [essai, examen] test ▸ **à l'épreuve du feu** fireproof ▸ **à l'épreuve des balles** bullet-proof ▸ **mettre à l'épreuve** to put to the test ▸ **mettre les nerfs de qqn à rude épreuve** to put sb's nerves to the test ▸ **à toute épreuve** unfailing ▸ **épreuve écrite/orale** written/oral test ▸ **épreuve de force** *fig* trial of strength **2.** [malheur] ordeal ▸ **vie remplie d'épreuves** life of hardship **3.** SPORT event ▸ **épreuves d'athlétisme** track events ▸ **épreuve éliminatoire** heat **4.** TYPO proof ▸ **corriger les épreuves d'un livre** to proofread a book **5.** PHOTO print ▸ **épreuves de tournage** CINÉ rushes.

épris, ***e*** [epri, iz] ■ **pp** ➤ ***éprendre***.
■ **adj** *sout* : **épris de** in love with.

éprouvant, ***e*** [epruvɑ̃, ɑ̃t] **adj** testing, trying.

éprouvé, ***e*** [epruve] **adj 1.** [méthode] tried and tested **2.** [personne] sorely tried.

éprouver [3] [epruve] **vt 1.** [tester] to test **2.** [ressentir] to feel **3.** [faire souffrir] to distress ▸ **être éprouvé par** to be afflicted by **4.** [difficultés, problèmes] to experience.

éprouvette [epruvɛt] **nf 1.** [tube à essai] test tube **2.** [échantillon] sample.

EPS (abr de ***éducation physique et sportive***) **nf** PE.

épuisant, ***e*** [epɥizɑ̃, ɑ̃t] **adj** exhausting.

épuisé, ***e*** [epɥize] **adj 1.** [personne, corps] exhausted **2.** [marchandise] sold out, out of stock / [livre] out of print.

épuisement [epɥizmɑ̃] **nm** exhaustion ▸ **jusqu'à épuisement des stocks** while stocks last.

épuiser [3] [epɥize] **vt 1.** [gén] to exhaust **2.** [exploiter - puits] to work dry / [- gisement, veine] to exhaust, to work out / [- sol, sujet] to exhaust.
◆ ***s'épuiser*** **vpi 1.** [être très réduit - provisions, munitions] to run out, to give out / [- source] to dry up / [- filon] to be worked out **2.** [se fatiguer - athlète] to wear o.s. out, to exhaust o.s. / [- corps] to wear itself out, to run out of steam ▸ **s'épuiser à faire qqch** [s'évertuer à faire qqch] to wear o.s. out doing sthg.

épuisette [epɥizɛt] **nf** landing net.

épurateur [epyratœr] **nm** filter, purifier ▸ **épurateur d'air** air filter ▸ **épurateur d'eau** water filter.

épuration [epyrasjɔ̃] **nf 1.** [des eaux] purification **2.** POLIT purge.

épure [epyr] **nf** technical drawing.

épurer [3] [epyre] **vt 1.** [eau, huile] to purify **2.** POLIT to purge **3.** *fig* [langage] to refine.

équarrir [32] [ekarir] **vt 1.** [animal] to cut up **2.** [poutre] to square **3.** *fig* [personne] : **mal équarri** rough, crude.

équarrissage [ekarisaʒ] **nm 1.** [du bois, de la pierre] squaring (off) **2.** [d'un animal] cutting up.

équateur [ekwatœr] **nm** equator.

Équateur [ekwatœr] **nm : l'Équateur** Ecuador.

équation [ekwasjɔ̃] **nf** equation ▸ **équation du premier/second degré** simple/quadratic equation.

équatorial, ***e***, ***aux*** [ekwatɔrjal, o] **adj** equatorial.

équatorien, ***enne*** [ekwatɔrjɛ̃, ɛn] **adj** Ecuadoran, Ecuadorian.
◆ ***Équatorien***, ***enne*** **nm, f** Ecuadoran, Ecuadorian.

équerre [ekɛr] **nf** [instrument] set square *UK*, triangle *US* / [en T] T-square ▸ **en équerre** at right angles.

équestre [ekɛstr] **adj** equestrian.

équeuter [3] [ekøte] **vt** to remove the stalk *ou* stalks from.

équidistance [ekɥidistɑ̃s] **nf** equidistance ▸ **à équidistance de... et de...** equidistant between... and...

équidistant, ***e*** [ekɥidistɑ̃, ɑ̃t] **adj** equidistant.

équilatéral, ***e***, ***aux*** [ekɥilateral, o] **adj** equilateral.

équilibre [ekilibr] **nm 1.** [gén] balance ▸ **en équilibre** balanced ▸ **perdre l'équilibre** to lose one's balance **2.** [psychique] stability.

équilibré, ***e*** [ekilibre] **adj 1.** [personne] well-balanced **2.** [vie] stable **3.** ARCHIT : **aux proportions équilibrées** well-proportioned.

équilibrer [3] [ekilibre] **vt** to balance.
◆ ***s'équilibrer*** **vp** to balance each other out.

équilibriste [ekilibrist] **nmf** tightrope walker.

équinoxe [ekinɔks] **nm** equinox ▸ **équinoxe de printemps/d'automne** spring/autumn *ou* fall *US* equinox.

équipage [ekipaʒ] **nm** crew.

équipe [ekip] **nf** team ▸ **d'équipe** team *(avant n)* ▸ **équipe de création** creative team ▸ **équipe de tournage** camera crew, film crew ▸ **faire équipe avec** to team up with ▸ **travailler en équipe** to work together *ou* as a team ▸ **équipe de secours** rescue team.

équipé, ***e*** [ekipe] **adj : cuisine équipée** fitted kitchen.

équipée [ekipe] **nf 1.** [aventure] venture **2.** [promenade] outing.

équipement [ekipmɑ̃] **nm 1.** [matériel] equipment **2.** [aménagement] facilities *pl* ▸ **plan d'équipement national** national development plan ▸ **équipements sportifs/scolaires** sports/educational facilities.

équiper [3] [ekipe] **vt 1.** [navire, armée] to equip **2.** [personne, local] to equip, to fit out ▸ **équiper qqn/qqch de** to equip sb/sthg with, to fit sb/sthg out with.
◆ ***s'équiper*** **vp : s'équiper (de)** to equip o.s. (with).

équipier, ère [ekipje, ɛr] **nm, f** team member.

équitable [ekitabl] **adj** fair.

équitablement [ekitabləmɑ̃] **adv** fairly.

équitation [ekitasjɔ̃] **nf** riding, horse-riding *UK*, horseback riding *US* ▸ **faire de l'équitation** to go riding *ou* horse-riding *UK ou* horseback riding *US*, to ride.

équité [ekite] **nf** fairness.

équivalent, e [ekivalɑ̃, ɑ̃t] **adj** equivalent.
◆ ***équivalent*** **nm** equivalent.

équivaloir [60] [ekivalwar] ◆ ***équivaloir à*** **v + prep** [être égal à] to be equal *ou* equivalent to / [revenir à] to amount to ▸ **ça équivaut à s'avouer vaincu** it amounts to admitting defeat.

équivalu [ekivaly] **pp inv** ➤ ***équivaloir***.

équivaut ➤ ***équivaloir***.

équivoque [ekivɔk] ■ **adj 1.** [ambigu] ambiguous **2.** [mystérieux] dubious.
■ **nf** ambiguity ▸ **sans équivoque** unequivocal *(adj)*, unequivocally *(adv)*.

érable [erabl] **nm** maple.

érablière [erablijɛr] **nf** maple grove, sugar bush *US*.

éradication [eradikasjɔ̃] **nf 1.** [suppression] eradication **2.** [ablation] removal.

éradiquer [3] [eradike] **vt** to eradicate.

érafler [3] [erafle] **vt 1.** [peau] to scratch **2.** [mur, voiture] to scrape.
◆ ***s'érafler*** **vp** to scratch o.s.

éraflure [eraflyr] **nf 1.** [de peau] scratch **2.** [de mur, voiture] scrape.

éraillé, e [eraje] **adj** [voix] hoarse.

ère [ɛr] **nf** era ▸ **l'an 813 de notre ère** the year 813 A.D.

érection [erɛksjɔ̃] **nf** erection ▸ **en érection** erect.

éreintant, e [erɛ̃tɑ̃, ɑ̃t] **adj** exhausting.

éreinter [3] [erɛ̃te] **vt 1.** [fatiguer] to exhaust ▸ **être éreinté** to be worn out **2.** [critiquer] to pull to pieces.
◆ ***s'éreinter*** **vpi** to wear o.s. out ▸ **s'éreinter à faire qqch** to wear o.s. out doing sthg.

érémiste [eremist] **nmf** *fam* = ***RMiste***.

ergonomie [ɛrgɔnɔmi] **nf** ergonomics *(U)*.

ergonomique [ɛrgɔnɔmik] **adj** ergonomic.

ergot [ɛrgo] **nm 1.** [de coq] spur ▸ **se dresser sur ses ergots** to get one's hackles up **2.** [de mammifère] dewclaw **3.** [de blé] ergot.

ergoter [3] [ɛrgɔte] **vi** to quibble.

ergothérapie [ɛrgɔterapi] **nf** occupational therapy.

ériger [17] [eriʒe] **vt 1.** [monument] to erect **2.** [tribunal] to set up **3.** *fig* [transformer] **: ériger qqn en** to set sb up as.
◆ ***s'ériger*** **vp : s'ériger en** to set o.s. up as.

ermite [ɛrmit] **nm** hermit.

éroder [3] [erɔde] **vt** to erode.

érogène [erɔʒɛn] **adj** erogenous.

érosion [erozjɔ̃] **nf** erosion.

érotique [erɔtik] **adj** erotic.

érotisme [erɔtism] **nm** eroticism.

errance [ɛrɑ̃s] **nf** wandering.

errant, e [ɛrɑ̃, ɑ̃t] **adj** [chien, chat] stray *(avant n)*.

erratum [eratɔm] (pl **errata** [erata]) **nm** erratum.

errements [ɛrmɑ̃] **nmpl** bad habits.

errer [4] [ɛre] **vi** to wander.

erreur [ɛrœr] **nf** mistake ▸ **par erreur** by mistake ▸ **sauf erreur de ma part** unless I'm mistaken ▸ **faire erreur** to be mistaken ▸ **faire une erreur** to make a mistake ▸ **erreur judiciaire** miscarriage of justice.

erroné, e [ɛrɔne] **adj** *sout* wrong.

ersatz [ɛrzats] **nm inv** ersatz.

éructer [3] [erykte] **vi** to belch.

érudit, e [erydi, it] ■ **adj** erudite, learned.
■ **nm, f** learned person, scholar.

érudition [erydisjɔ̃] **nf** learning, erudition, scholarship.

éruption [erypsjɔ̃] **nf 1.** MÉD rash **2.** [de volcan] eruption.

érythème [eritɛm] **nm** erythema ▸ **érythème fessier** nappy *UK ou* diaper *US* rash.

es ➤ ***être***.

ès [ɛs] **prép** of *(in certain titles)* ▸ **docteur ès lettres** ≃ PhD, doctor of philosophy.

E/S (abr écrite de ***entrée/sortie***) I/O.

ESA, Esa [eza] (abr de ***European Space Agency***) **nf** ESA.

esbroufe [ɛzbruf] **nf** *fam* showing-off ▸ **faire de l'esbroufe** to show off.

escabeau, x [ɛskabo] **nm 1.** [échelle] stepladder **2.** *vieilli* [tabouret] stool.

escadre [ɛskadr] **nf 1.** [navires] fleet **2.** [avions] wing.

escadrille [ɛskadrij] **nf 1.** [navires] flotilla **2.** [avions] flight.

escadron [ɛskadrɔ̃] **nm** squadron.

escalade [ɛskalad] **nf 1.** [de montagne, grille] climbing **2.** [des prix, de violence] escalation.

escalader [3] [ɛskalade] **vt** to climb.

escale [ɛskal] **nf 1.** [lieu - pour navire] port of call / [- pour avion] stopover **2.** [arrêt - de navire] call / [- d'avion] stopover, stop ▸ **escale technique** refuelling stop ▸ **faire escale à** [- navire] to put in at, to call at / [- avion] to stop over at.

escalier [ɛskalje] nm stairs *pl* ▸ **descendre/monter l'escalier** to go downstairs/upstairs ▸ **escalier en colimaçon** spiral staircase ▸ **escalier de secours** fire escape ▸ **escalier de service** backstairs ▸ **escalier roulant** *ou* **mécanique** escalator.

escalope [ɛskalɔp] nf escalope ▸ **escalope panée** escalope in breadcrumbs.

escamotable [ɛskamɔtabl] adj **1.** [train d'atterrissage] retractable / [antenne] telescopic **2.** [table] folding.

escamoter [3] [ɛskamɔte] vt **1.** [faire disparaître] to make disappear **2.** [voler] to lift **3.** [rentrer] to retract **4.** [phrase, mot] to swallow **5.** [éluder - question] to evade / [- objection] to get around.

escampette [ɛskɑ̃pɛt] ➤ ***poudre***.

escapade [ɛskapad] nf **1.** [voyage] outing **2.** [fugue] escapade.

escarbille [ɛskarbij] nf cinder.

escargot [ɛskargo] nm snail ▸ **comme un escargot** [très lentement] at a snail's pace.

escarmouche [ɛskarmuʃ] nf skirmish.

escarpé, e [ɛskarpe] adj steep.

escarpement [ɛskarpəmɑ̃] nm **1.** [de pente] steep slope **2.** GÉOGR escarpment.

escarpin [ɛskarpɛ̃] nm court shoe *UK*, pump *US*.

escarre [ɛskar] nf bedsore, pressure sore.

Escaut [ɛsko] nm : **l'Escaut** the River Scheldt.

escient [esjɑ̃] nm : **à bon escient** advisedly ▸ **à mauvais escient** ill-advisedly.

esclaffer [3] [ɛsklafe] ◆ ***s'esclaffer*** vp to burst out laughing.

esclandre [ɛsklɑ̃dr] nm *sout* scene ▸ **faire un esclandre** to make a scene.

esclavage [ɛsklavaʒ] nm slavery.

esclavagisme [ɛsklavaʒism] nm slavery.

esclave [ɛsklav] ■ nmf slave.
■ adj : **être esclave de** to be a slave to.

escogriffe [ɛskɔgrif] nm *fam* : **un grand escogriffe** a beanpole.

escompte [ɛskɔ̃t] nm discount ▸ **escompte de caisse** cash discount.

escompter [3] [ɛskɔ̃te] vt **1.** [prévoir] to count on **2.** FIN to discount.

escorte [ɛskɔrt] nf escort.

escorter [3] [ɛskɔrte] vt to escort.

escouade [ɛskwad] nf squad.

escrime [ɛskrim] nf fencing.

escrimer [3] [ɛskrime] ◆ ***s'escrimer*** vp : **s'escrimer à faire qqch** to work (away) at doing sthg.

escroc [ɛskro] nm swindler.

escroquer [3] [ɛskrɔke] vt to swindle ▸ **escroquer qqch à qqn** to swindle sb out of sthg.

escroquerie [ɛskrɔkri] nf swindle, swindling *(U)*.

eskimo, Eskimo ➤ ***esquimau***.

ésotérique [ezɔterik] adj esoteric.

espace [ɛspas] nm space ▸ **espace publicitaire** advertising space ▸ **espace vert** green space, green area ▸ **espace vital** living space / INFORM : **espace Web** web space.

espacement [ɛspasmɑ̃] nm **1.** [spatial] spacing **2.** [temporel] spacing out.

espacer [16] [ɛspase] vt **1.** [dans l'espace] to space out **2.** [dans le temps - visites] to space out / [- paiements] to spread out.
◆ ***s'espacer*** vp to become less frequent.

espadon [ɛspadɔ̃] nm **1.** [poisson] swordfish **2.** [épée] two-handed sword.

espadrille [ɛspadrij] nf espadrille.

Espagne [ɛspaɲ] nf : **l'Espagne** Spain.

espagnol, e [ɛspaɲɔl] adj Spanish.
◆ ***espagnol*** nm [langue] Spanish.
◆ ***Espagnol, e*** nm, f Spaniard ▸ **les Espagnols** the Spanish.

espagnolette [ɛspaɲɔlɛt] nf latch *(for window or shutter)*.

espalier [ɛspalje] nm **1.** [arbre] espalier **2.** SPORT wall bars *pl*.

espèce [ɛspɛs] nf **1.** BIOL, BOT & ZOOL species ▸ **l'espèce humaine** the human race, mankind ▸ **des espèces animales/végétales** animal/plant species ▸ **espèce en voie de disparition** endangered species **2.** [sorte] kind, sort ▸ **espèce d'idiot!** you stupid fool! ▸ **c'est un menteur de la pire espèce** he's the worst kind of liar, he's a terrible liar ▸ **des escrocs de ton/son espèce** crooks like you/him ▸ **ça n'a aucune espèce d'importance!** that is of absolutely no importance! **3.** [circonstance] : **en l'espèce** *littéraire* in the case in point ▸ **nous avions de bons rapports, mais en l'espèce l'affaire a fini au tribunal** we had a good relationship, but in this instance, the matter finished up in court **4.** DR particular *ou* specific case.
◆ ***espèces*** nfpl cash ▸ **payer en espèces** to pay (in) cash ▸ **espèces sonnantes et trébuchantes** hard cash.

espérance [ɛsperɑ̃s] nf hope ▸ **espérance de vie** life expectancy.

espéranto [ɛsperɑ̃to] nm Esperanto.

espérer [18] [ɛspere] ■ vt to hope for ▸ **espérer que** to hope (that) ▸ **espérer faire qqch** to hope to do sthg.
■ vi to hope ▸ **espérer en qqn/qqch** to trust in sb/sthg.

espiègle [ɛspjɛgl] ■ nmf little rascal.
■ adj mischievous.

espièglerie [ɛspjɛgləri] nf **1.** [malice] mischievousness **2.** [tour, farce] prank.

espion, onne [ɛspjɔ̃, ɔn] nm, f spy.

espionnage [ɛspjɔnaʒ] nm spying ▸ **espionnage industriel** industrial espionage.

espionner [3] [ɛspjɔne] vt to spy on.

esplanade [ɛsplanad] nf esplanade.

espoir [ɛspwar] nm hope ▸ **avoir bon espoir que** to be confident that ▸ **nourrir l'espoir de faire qqch** to live in hope of doing sthg ▸ **sans espoir** hopeless ▸ **sans espoir de** without hope of.

esprit [ɛspri] **nm 1.** [entendement, personne, pensée] mind ▸ **avoir l'esprit mal tourné** to have a dirty *ou* filthy mind ▸ **avoir l'esprit de synthèse** to be good at drawing ideas together ▸ **esprit d'analyse** analytical mind ▸ **être large d'esprit** to be broad-minded ▸ **ouvrir l'esprit de qqn** to open sb's eyes ▸ **reprendre ses esprits** to recover ▸ **venir à l'esprit de qqn** to cross sb's mind ▸ **ça m'a traversé l'esprit** it occurred to me, it crossed my mind
2. [attitude] spirit ▸ **esprit de caste** class consciousness ▸ **esprit de compétition** competitive spirit ▸ **esprit de contradiction** argumentative nature, contrariness ▸ **esprit critique** critical acumen ▸ **esprit d'équipe** team spirit ▸ **esprit maison** company spirit ▸ **avoir l'esprit de clocher** to be parochial ▸ **avoir l'esprit de famille** to be family-minded ▸ **dans un esprit de justice** in a spirit of justice, in an effort to be fair ▸ **faire preuve de mauvais esprit** to be a troublemaker
3. [humour] wit ▸ **avoir de l'esprit** to be witty ▸ **faire de l'esprit** to try to be funny
4. [fantôme] spirit, ghost ▸ **esprit frappeur** poltergeist.

esquif [ɛskif] **nm** *littéraire* skiff.

esquimau, aude, aux [ɛskimo, od] **adj** Eskimo.
◆ ***esquimau*** **nm** [langue] Eskimo.
◆ ***Esquimau, aude, Eskimo*** **nm, f** Eskimo *(beware: the term 'Esquimau', like its English equivalent, is often considered offensive in North America. The term 'Inuit' is preferred).*

Esquimau®**, *x*** [ɛskimo] **nm inv : Esquimau (glacé)** choc-ice *(on a stick) UK*, Eskimo *US*.

esquinter [3] [ɛskɛ̃te] **vt** *fam* **1.** [abîmer] to ruin **2.** [critiquer] to pan, to slate *UK*.
◆ ***s'esquinter*** **vp : s'esquinter à faire qqch** to kill o.s. doing sthg.

esquisse [ɛskis] **nf** [croquis] sketch / *fig* [de projet] outline / *fig* [de geste, sourire] trace.

esquisser [3] [ɛskise] **vt** to sketch ▸ **esquisser un sourire** *fig* to give a half-smile.
◆ ***s'esquisser*** **vp** to take shape.

esquiver [3] [ɛskive] **vt** to dodge.
◆ ***s'esquiver*** **vp** to slip away.

essai [esɛ] **nm 1.** [vérification] test, testing *(U)* ▸ **à l'essai** on trial ▸ **engager qqn à l'essai** to appoint sb for a trial period ▸ **mettre qqn/qqch à l'essai** to put sb/sthg to the test ▸ **faire l'essai de qqch** to try sthg (out) ▸ **coup d'essai** first attempt *ou* try ▸ **période d'essai** trial period **2.** [tentative] attempt ▸ **nous avons fait plusieurs essais** we had several tries, we made several attempts **3.** [étude] **: essai (sur)** essay (on) **4.** [rugby] try **5.** ÉCON [test] [gén pl] **: essais comparatifs** comparative testing ▸ **essais de produits** product testing.

essaie, essaies ➤ ***essayer***.

essaim [esɛ̃] **nm** *litt & fig* swarm.

essaimer [4] [eseme] **vi** *litt* to swarm / *fig* to spread.

essayage [esɛjaʒ] **nm** fitting.

essayer [11] [eseje] **vt** to try ▸ **essayer de faire qqch** to try to do sthg ▸ **essaie un peu, pour voir!** go on then, why don't you try?
◆ ***s'essayer*** **vp : s'essayer à qqch/à faire qqch** to try one's hand at sthg/at doing sthg.

ESSEC, Essec [esɛk] (abr de ***École supérieure des sciences économiques et commerciales***) **nf** *grande école for management and business studies.*

essence [esɑ̃s] **nf 1.** [fondement, de plante] essence ▸ **par essence** *sout* in essence **2.** [carburant] petrol *UK*, gas *US* ▸ **prendre de l'essence** to get some petrol **3.** [d'arbre] species.

essentiel, elle [esɑ̃sjɛl] **adj 1.** [indispensable] essential **2.** [fondamental] basic.
◆ ***essentiel*** **nm 1.** [point] **: l'essentiel** [le principal] the essential *ou* main thing / [objets] the essentials *pl* ▸ **l'essentiel est que** *(+ subjonctif)* the essential *ou* main thing is that **2.** [quantité] **: l'essentiel de** the main *ou* greater part of.

essentiellement [esɑ̃sjɛlmɑ̃] **adv 1.** [avant tout] above all **2.** [par essence] essentially.

esseulé, e [esœle] **adj** *littéraire* forsaken.

essieu, x [esjø] **nm** axle.

essor [esɔr] **nm** flight, expansion, boom ▸ **en plein essor** booming ▸ **prendre son essor** to take flight / *fig* to take off.

essorage [esɔraʒ] **nm** [manuel, à rouleaux] wringing (out) / [à la machine] drying, spin-drying *UK*.

essorer [3] [esɔre] **vt** [à la main, à rouleaux] to wring out / [à la machine] to dry, to spin-dry *UK*, to tumble-dry *UK* / [salade] to spin, to dry.

essoreuse [esɔrøz] **nf** [à rouleaux] mangle / [électrique] dryer, spin-dryer *UK*, tumble-dryer *UK* / [à salade] salad spinner.

essouffler [3] [esufle] **vt** to make breathless.
◆ ***s'essouffler*** **vp** to be breathless *ou* out of breath / *fig* to run out of steam.

essuie, essuies ➤ ***essuyer***.

essuie-glace [esɥiglas] (pl **essuie-glaces**) **nm** windscreen wiper *UK*, windshield wiper *US*.

essuie-mains [esɥimɛ̃] **nm inv** hand towel.

essuie-tout [esɥitu] **nm inv** paper towels *pl*, kitchen roll *UK*.

essuyer [14] [esɥije] **vt 1.** [sécher] to dry **2.** [nettoyer] to wipe **3.** *fig* [subir] to suffer.
◆ ***s'essuyer*** **vp** to dry o.s.

est[1] [ɛst] ■ **nm** east ▸ **un vent d'est** an easterly wind ▸ **le vent d'est** the east wind ▸ **à l'est** in the east ▸ **à l'est (de)** to the east (of).
■ **adj inv** [gén] east / [province, région] eastern.

est[2] [ɛ] ➤ ***être***.

establishment [ɛstabliʃmɛnt] **nm : l'establishment** the Establishment.

estafette [ɛstafɛt] **nf** dispatch rider / MIL liaison officer.

estafilade [ɛstafilad] **nf** slash, gash.

est-allemand, e [ɛstalmɑ̃, ɑ̃d] **adj** East German.

estaminet [ɛstaminɛ] **nm** ≃ inn.

estampe [ɛstɑ̃p] **nf** print.

estamper [3] [ɛstɑ̃pe] **vt 1.** [monnaie] to mint **2.** *fam* [escroquer] to fleece.

estampille [ɛstɑ̃pij] **nf** stamp.

est-ce que [ɛskə] **adv interr : est-ce qu'il fait beau?** is the weather good? ▸ **est-ce que vous aimez l'accordéon?** do you like the accordion? ▸ **où est-ce que tu es?** where are you?

esthète [ɛstɛt] **nmf** aesthete, esthete *US*.

esthéticien, enne [ɛstetisjɛ̃, ɛn] **nm, f 1.** [spécialiste] beautician **2.** PHILO aesthetician, esthetician *US*.

esthétique [ɛstetik] ■ **nf : l'esthétique** aesthetics *(U)*, esthetics *(U) US*.
■ **adj 1.** [relatif à la beauté] aesthetic, esthetic *US* **2.** [harmonieux] attractive.

estimable [ɛstimabl] **adj 1.** [digne d'estime] honorable, respected **2.** [évaluable] **: facilement/difficilement estimable** easy/difficult to estimate.

estimatif, ive [ɛstimatif, iv] **adj** estimated.

estimation [ɛstimasjɔ̃] **nf** estimate, estimation.

estime [ɛstim] **nf** respect, esteem ▸ **avoir de l'estime pour qqn** to respect sb.

estimer [3] [ɛstime] **vt 1.** [expertiser] to value **2.** [évaluer] to estimate ▸ **j'estime la durée du voyage à 2 heures** I reckon the journey time is 2 hours **3.** [respecter] to respect **4.** [penser] **: estimer que** to feel (that).
◆ ***s'estimer*** **vp** to consider o.s.

estival, e, aux [ɛstival, o] **adj** summer *(avant n)*.

estivant, e [ɛstivɑ̃, ɑ̃t] **nm, f** (summer) holiday-maker *UK ou* vacationer *US*.

estocade [ɛstɔkad] **nf** death blow.

estomac [ɛstɔma] **nm 1.** ANAT stomach ▸ **avoir l'estomac barbouillé** to feel sick ▸ **avoir un estomac d'autruche** *fig* to have a cast-iron digestion ▸ **avoir l'estomac dans les talons** *fig* to be starving **2.** [culot, cran] nerve.

estomaquer [3] [ɛstɔmake] **vt** *fam* to stagger.

estomper [3] [ɛstɔ̃pe] **vt** to blur / *fig* [douleur] to lessen.
◆ ***s'estomper*** **vp** to become blurred / *fig* [douleur] to lessen.

Estonie [ɛstɔni] **nf : l'Estonie** Estonia.

estonien, enne [ɛstɔnjɛ̃, ɛn] **adj** Estonian.
◆ ***estonien*** **nm** [langue] Estonian.
◆ ***Estonien, enne*** **nm, f** Estonian.

estrade [ɛstrad] **nf** dais.

estragon [ɛstragɔ̃] **nm** tarragon.

estropié, e [ɛstrɔpje] ■ **adj** crippled.
■ **nm, f** cripple.

estropier [9] [ɛstrɔpje] **vt** [personne] to cripple / *fig* [nom, mot] to mispronounce.
◆ ***s'estropier*** **vp** to cripple o.s.

estuaire [ɛstɥɛr] **nm** estuary.

estudiantin, e [ɛstydjɑ̃tɛ̃, in] **adj** student *(avant n)*.

esturgeon [ɛstyrʒɔ̃] **nm** sturgeon.

et [e] **conj 1.** [gén] and ▸ **une robe courte et sans manches** a short sleeveless dress ▸ **il y a mensonge et mensonge** there are lies, and then there are lies ▸ **et moi?** what about me? ▸ **j'ai bien aimé ce film, et toi ?** I really liked the film; how *ou* what about you ? ▸ **c'est fini et bien fini!** that's the end of that! ▸ **et pourquoi pas?** (and) why not ? **2.** [dans les fractions et les nombres composés] **: vingt et un** twenty-one ▸ **il y a deux ans et demi** two and a half years ago ▸ **à deux heures et demie** at half past two.

ét. (abr écrite de ***étage***) fl.

ETA (abr de ***Euskadi ta Askatasuna***) **nf** ETA.

étable [etabl] **nf** cowshed.

établi [etabli] **nm** workbench.

établir [32] [etablir] **vt 1.** [gén] to establish / [record] to set **2.** [dresser] to draw up.
◆ ***s'établir*** **vp 1.** [s'installer] to settle **2.** [créer son entreprise] to set o.s. up **3.** [s'instaurer] to become established.

établissement [etablismɑ̃] **nm 1.** [institution] establishment ▸ **établissement hospitalier** hospital ▸ **établissement public** public body ▸ **établissement scolaire** educational establishment
2. COMM firm ▸ **les établissements Leroy** Leroy and Co ▸ **établissement financier** financial institution ▸ **établissement d'utilité publique** public utility
3. [installation] **: l'établissement des Français en Afrique** the settlement of the French in Africa
4. [preuve] establishment ▸ **rien n'est possible sans l'établissement de son identité** nothing can be done if his identity cannot be established.

étage [etaʒ] **nm 1.** [de bâtiment] floor, storey *UK*, story *US* ▸ **à l'étage** upstairs ▸ **un immeuble de quatre étages** a four-storey block of flats *UK*, a five-story block of apartments *US* ▸ **au premier étage** on the first floor *UK*, on the second floor *US* ▸ **elle est dans les étages** she's upstairs somewhere ▸ **monter les étages à pied/en courant** to walk/run up the stairs **2.** [de fusée] stage **3.** [de terrain, placard] level **4.** [condition] **: de bas étage** second-rate.

étager [17] [etaʒe] **vt** to arrange in tiers.
◆ ***s'étager*** **vp** to be terraced.

étagère [etaʒɛr] **nf 1.** [rayon] shelf **2.** [meuble] shelves *pl*, set of shelves.

étain [etɛ̃] **nm 1.** [métal] tin / [alliage] pewter **2.** [objet] piece of pewter.

étais, était ➤ *être*.

étal [etal] (pl -s *ou* **étaux** [eto]) **nm 1.** [éventaire] stal[l]
2. [de boucher] butcher's block.

étalage [etalaʒ] **nm 1.** [action, ensemble d'objets] display ▸ **faire étalage de** *fig* to flaunt **2.** [devanture] window display.

étalagiste [etalaʒist] **nmf 1.** [décorateur] window dresser **2.** [vendeur] stallholder *UK*.

étalement [etalmɑ̃] **nm 1.** [dans l'espace] spreading ou[t]
2. [dans le temps] staggering.

étaler [3] [etale] **vt 1.** [exposer] to display **2.** [étendre] to spread out **3.** [dans le temps] to stagger **4.** [mettre une couche de] to spread **5.** [exhiber] to parade.
◆ ***s'étaler*** **vp 1.** [s'étendre] to spread **2.** [dans le temps] **s'étaler (sur)** to be spread (over) **3.** *fam* [s'avachir] to sprawl **4.** *fam* [tomber] to fall flat on one's face, to come a cropper *UK*.

étalon [etalɔ̃] **nm 1.** [cheval] stallion **2.** [mesure] standar[d]
▸ **étalon-or** gold standard.

étalonner [3] [etalɔne] **vt** [graduer] to calibrate.

étamine [etamin] **nf 1.** [de fleur] stamen **2.** [tissu] muslin.

étanche [etɑ̃ʃ] **adj** watertight / [montre] waterproof.

étanchéité [etɑ̃ʃeite] **nf** watertightness.

étancher [3] [etɑ̃ʃe] **vt 1.** [sang, larmes] to stem (the flow of) **2.** [rendre étanche] to make watertight **3.** [assouvir] to quench.

étang [etɑ̃] **nm** pond.

étant **p prés** ➤ ***être***.

étant donné [etɑ̃dɔne] **loc prép** given ▸ **étant donné les circonstances** given *ou* in view of the circumstances.
◆ ***étant donné que*** **loc conj** since ▸ **étant donné qu'il pleuvait...** since *ou* as it was raining...

étape [etap] **nf 1.** [gén] stage ▸ **brûler les étapes** *fig* to race ahead **2.** [halte] stop ▸ **faire étape à** to break one's journey at.

état [eta] **nm 1.** [manière d'être] state ▸ **être en état/hors d'état de faire qqch** to be in a/in no fit state to do sthg ▸ **dans l'état actuel des choses** as things stand at the moment, in the present state of affairs ▸ **en bon/mauvais état** in good/poor condition ▸ **en état d'ivresse** under the influence of alcohol ▸ **en état de marche** in working order ▸ **laisser les choses en l'état** to leave things as they stand ▸ **remettre en état** to repair ▸ **état d'âme** mood ▸ **je me fiche de vos états d'âme!** I don't care whether you're happy about it or not! ▸ **état d'esprit** state of mind ▸ **état général** general state of health ▸ **le malade est dans un état grave** the patient's condition is serious ▸ **état de santé** (state of) health ▸ **être dans un état second** to be in a daze ▸ **état de siège** state of siege ▸ **état stationnaire** stable condition ▸ **état d'urgence** state of emergency ▸ **être en état d'arrestation** to be under arrest ▸ **être dans tous ses états** to be in a state ▸ **se mettre dans tous ses états** [en colère] to go off the deep end *UK*, to go off at the deep end *US*, to go spare *UK* ▸ **réduit à l'état de cendres/poussière** reduced to ashes/a powder ▸ **état de grâce** POLIT [pour un premier ministre, un président] honeymoon period ▸ **être en état de grâce** RELIG to be in a state of grace **2.** [métier, statut] status ▸ **de son état** by profession ▸ **il est cordonnier de son état** he's a shoemaker by trade ▸ **état civil** ADMIN ≃ marital status **3.** [inventaire - gén] inventory / [- de dépenses] statement ▸ **faire état de qqch** to give an account of sthg ▸ **état des lieux** *inventory and inspection of rented property* ▸ **états de service** MIL service record / [- professionnellement] professional record.
◆ ***État*** **nm** [nation] state ▸ **l'État** the State ▸ **État membre** member state ▸ **les États du Golfe** the Gulf States ▸ **État paternaliste** nanny state.
◆ ***en tout état de cause*** **loc adv** in any case.

étatique [etatik] **adj** state *(avant n)*.

étatiser [3] [etatize] **vt** to bring under state control.

étatisme [etatism] **nm** state control.

état-major [etamaʒɔr] (pl **états-majors**) **nm 1.** ADMIN & MIL staff / [de parti] leadership **2.** [lieu] headquarters *sg*.

États-Unis [etazyni] **nmpl : les États-Unis (d'Amérique)** the United States (of America) ▸ **aux États-Unis** in the United States.

étau, x [eto] **nm** vice *UK*, vise *US*.

étayer [11] [eteje] **vt** to prop up / *fig* to back up.

etc. (abr écrite de ***et cætera***) etc.

été [ete] ■ **pp inv** ➤ ***être***.
■ **nm** summer ▸ **en été** in (the) summer ▸ **été indien** Indian summer.

éteignais, éteignions ➤ ***éteindre***.

éteindre [81] [etɛ̃dr] **vt 1.** [incendie, bougie, cigarette] to put out / [radio, chauffage, lampe] to turn off, to switch off **2.** [soif] to quench **3.** DR [annuler] to extinguish **4.** INFORM to shut down.
◆ ***s'éteindre*** **vp 1.** [feu, lampe] to go out **2.** [bruit, souvenir] to fade (away) **3.** *fig & littéraire* [personne] to pass away **4.** [race] to die out.

éteint, e [etɛ̃, ɛ̃t] ■ **pp** ➤ ***éteindre***.
■ **adj 1.** [couleur] faded **2.** [voix] faint / [regard] dull.

étendage [etɑ̃daʒ] **nm** hanging out.

étendard [etɑ̃dar] **nm** standard.

étendre [73] [etɑ̃dr] **vt 1.** [déployer] to stretch / [journal] to spread (out) ▸ **étendre ses bras/jambes** to stretch (out) one's arms/legs ▸ **étendre du linge** [dehors] to put the washing out to dry, to hang out the washing / [à l'intérieur] to hang up the washing **2.** [coucher] to lay ▸ **étendre un blessé sur une civière** to place an injured person on a stretcher **3.** [appliquer] to spread **4.** [accroître] to extend ▸ **étendre une grève au secteur privé** to extend a strike to the private sector ▸ **étendre son vocabulaire** to increase *ou* to extend one's vocabulary **5.** *fam fig* [candidat] to fail **6.** [diluer] to dilute / [sauce] to thin.
◆ ***s'étendre*** **vp 1.** [se coucher] to lie down **2.** [s'étaler au loin] **: s'étendre (de/jusqu'à)** to stretch (from/as far as) ▸ **les banlieues s'étendaient à l'infini** the suburbs stretched out endlessly ▸ **la période qui s'étend du XVIIe au XIXe siècle** the period stretching from the 17th to the 19th century **3.** [croître] to spread **4.** [s'attarder] **: s'étendre sur** to elaborate on ▸ **je ne m'étendrai pas davantage sur ce sujet** I won't discuss this subject any further.

étendu, e [etɑ̃dy] ■ **pp** ➤ ***étendre***.
■ **adj 1.** [bras, main] outstretched **2.** [plaine, connaissances] extensive.
◆ ***étendue*** **nf 1.** [surface] area, expanse **2.** [durée] length **3.** [importance] extent **4.** MUS range.

éternel, elle [etɛrnɛl] **adj** eternal ▸ **ce ne sera pas éternel** this won't last for ever.
◆ ***Éternel*** **nm : l'Éternel** the Eternal.

éternellement [etɛrnɛlmɑ̃] **adv** eternally.

éterniser [3] [etɛrnize] **vt** [prolonger] to drag out.
◆ ***s'éterniser*** **vp 1.** [se prolonger] to drag out **2.** *fam* [rester] to stay for ever.

éternité [etɛrnite] **nf** eternity ▸ **il y a une éternité que je ne t'ai pas vu** I haven't seen you for ages.

éternuement [etɛrnymɑ̃] **nm** sneeze.

éternuer [7] [etɛrnɥe] **vi** to sneeze.

êtes ➤ ***être***.

étêter [4] [etete] **vt** to cut the head off.

éther [etɛr] **nm** ether.

éthéré, e [etere] **adj** ethereal.

Éthiopie [etjɔpi] **nf : l'Éthiopie** Ethiopia.

éthiopien, enne [etjɔpjɛ̃, ɛn] **adj** Ethiopian.
◆ ***Éthiopien, enne*** **nm, f** Ethiopian.

éthique [etik] ■ **nf** ethics *(U or pl)*.
■ **adj** ethical.

ethnie [ɛtni] **nf** ethnic group.

ethnique [ɛtnik] **adj** ethnic.

ethnographie [ɛtnɔgrafi] **nf** ethnography.

ethnologie [ɛtnɔlɔʒi] **nf** ethnology.

ethnologue [ɛtnɔlɔg] **nmf** ethnologist.

éthologie [etolɔʒi] **nf** ethology.

éthylique [etilik] ■ **nmf** alcoholic.
■ **adj** alcoholic ▸ **alcool éthylique** ethyl alcohol, ethanol.

éthylisme [etilism] **nm** alcoholism.

étiez, étions ➤ ***être***.

étincelant, e [etɛ̃slɑ̃, ɑ̃t] **adj** sparkling.

étinceler [24] [etɛ̃sle] **vi** to sparkle.

étincelle [etɛ̃sɛl] **nf** spark.

étioler [3] [etjɔle] ◆ ***s'étioler*** **vp** [plante] to wilt / [personne] to weaken / [mémoire] to go.

étique [etik] **adj** *littéraire* [plante] stunted / [personne] skinny.

étiqueter [27] [etikte] **vt** *litt* & *fig* to label.

étiquette [etikɛt] **nf** **1.** [marque] label **2.** [protocole] etiquette.

étirer [3] [etire] **vt** to stretch.
◆ ***s'étirer*** **vp** to stretch.

Etna [ɛtna] **nm : l'Etna** Mount Etna.

étoffe [etɔf] **nf** fabric, material ▸ **avoir l'étoffe de** *fig* to have the makings of.

étoffer [3] [etɔfe] **vt** to flesh out.
◆ ***s'étoffer*** **vp** to fill out.

étoile [etwal] **nf** star ▸ **ciel parsemé *ou* semé d'étoiles** starry sky, sky studded with stars ▸ **une nuit sans étoiles** a starless night ▸ **l'étoile du berger** the evening star ▸ **étoile filante** shooting star ▸ **étoile Polaire** pole star ▸ **un trois étoiles** a three-star hotel ▸ **à la belle étoile** *fig* under the stars ▸ **être né sous une bonne étoile** *fig* to be born under a lucky star ▸ **carrefour en étoile** multi-lane junction ▸ **l'étoile jaune/rouge** the yellow/red star.
◆ ***étoile de mer*** **nf** starfish.

étoilé, e [etwale] **adj** **1.** [ciel, nuit] starry ▸ **la bannière étoilée** the Star-Spangled Banner **2.** [vitre, pare-brise] shattered.

étole [etɔl] **nf** stole.

étonnamment [etɔnamɑ̃] **adv** surprisingly, astonishingly.

étonnant, e [etɔnɑ̃, ɑ̃t] **adj** astonishing.

étonné, e [etɔne] **adj** astonished, surprised.

étonnement [etɔnmɑ̃] **nm** astonishment, surprise ▸ **au grand étonnement de** to the great astonishment of.

étonner [3] [etɔne] **vt** to astonish, to surprise ▸ **ça m'étonnerait!** I'd be (very) surprised!
◆ ***s'étonner*** **vp : s'étonner (de)** to be surprised (by) ▸ **s'étonner que** *(+ subjonctif)* to be surprised (that).

étouffant, e [etufɑ̃, ɑ̃t] **adj** stifling.

étouffée [etufe] ◆ ***à l'étouffée*** **loc adv** steamed / [viande] braised ▸ **faire cuire à l'étouffée** to steam / [viande] to braise.

étouffement [etufmɑ̃] **nm** **1.** [asphyxie] suffocation **2.** [répression] suppression.

étouffer [3] [etufe] ■ **vt** **1.** [gén] to stifle ▸ **ce n'est pas la politesse qui l'étouffe** *fam hum* politeness isn't exactly his strong point **2.** [asphyxier] to suffocate ▸ **mourir étouffé** to die of suffocation, to choke to death **3.** [feu] to smother **4.** [scandale, révolte] to suppress.
■ **vi** to suffocate ▸ **j'ai failli étouffer en avalant de travers** I almost choked when I swallowed the wrong way.
◆ ***s'étouffer*** **vp** **1.** [s'étrangler] to choke ▸ **une sardine et une demi-tomate, on ne risque pas de s'étouffer!** *hum* a sardine and half a tomato! there's no fear of us choking on that! **2.** *fig* [se presser, s'écraser] to stifle.

étouffoir [etufwar] **nm** *fam* oven.

étourderie [eturdəri] **nf** **1.** [distraction] thoughtlessness **2.** [bévue] careless mistake / [acte irréfléchi] thoughtless act.

étourdi, e [eturdi] ■ **adj** scatterbrained.
■ **nm, f** scatterbrain.

étourdiment [eturdimɑ̃] **adv** without thinking.

étourdir [32] [eturdir] **vt** **1.** [assommer] to daze **2.** [fatiguer] to wear out.
◆ ***s'étourdir*** **vp** to be *ou* become dazed ▸ **s'étourdir de** to get drunk on.

étourdissant, e [eturdisɑ̃, ɑ̃t] **adj** **1.** [fatigant] wearing **2.** [sensationnel] stunning.

étourdissement [eturdismɑ̃] **nm** dizzy spell.

étourneau, x [eturno] **nm** starling.

étrange [etrɑ̃ʒ] **adj** strange.

étrangement [etrɑ̃ʒmɑ̃] **adv** strangely.

étranger, ère [etrɑ̃ʒe, ɛr] ■ **adj** **1.** [gén] foreign **2.** [différent, isolé] unknown, unfamiliar ▸ **être étranger à qqn** to

be unknown to sb ▸ **être étranger à qqch** to have no connection with sthg ▸ **se sentir étranger** to feel like an outsider.
■ **nm, f 1.** [de nationalité différente] foreigner **2.** [inconnu] stranger **3.** [exclu] outsider.
◆ ***étranger*** **nm : l'étranger** foreign countries *pl* ▸ **à l'étranger** abroad.

PARONYME / CONFUSABLE
étranger
Attention lorsque vous traduisez ce mot : *stranger* désigne un inconnu, tandis que *foreigner* désigne un habitant d'un autre pays.

étrangeté [etrɑ̃ʒte] **nf** strangeness.

étranglement [etrɑ̃gləmɑ̃] **nm 1.** [strangulation] strangulation **2.** [rétrécissement] constriction.

étrangler [3] [etrɑ̃gle] **vt 1.** [gén] to choke **2.** [stranguler] to strangle **3.** [réprimer] to stifle **4.** [serrer] to constrict ▸ **elle avait la taille étranglée par une grosse ceinture** she had a wide belt pulled in tight around the waist.
◆ ***s'étrangler*** **vp 1.** [s'étouffer] to choke ▸ **s'étrangler avec un os** to choke on a bone ▸ **s'étrangler de rire** to choke with laughter ▸ **s'étrangler d'indignation** to be speechless with indignation **2.** [sanglots] to catch.

étrave [etrav] **nf** stem.

être [2] [ɛtr] ■ **nm 1.** BIOL & PHILO being ▸ **les êtres vivants/humains** living/human beings.
2. [personne] person ▸ **un être cher** a loved one.
■ **v aux 1.** [pour les temps composés] to have/to be ▸ **il est parti hier** he left yesterday ▸ **il est déjà arrivé** he has already arrived ▸ **il est né en 1952** he was born in 1952
2. [pour le passif] to be ▸ **la maison a été vendue** the house has been *ou* was sold.
■ **v att 1.** [état] to be ▸ **il est grand/heureux** he's tall/happy ▸ **la maison est blanche** the house is white ▸ **il est médecin** he's a doctor ▸ **sois sage!** be good! ▸ **je suis comme je suis** I am what I am
2. [possession] **: être à qqn** to be sb's, to belong to sb ▸ **c'est à vous, cette voiture?** is this your car?, is this car yours? ▸ **cette maison est à lui/eux** this house is his/theirs, this is his/their house.
■ **v impers 1.** [exprimant le temps] **: quelle heure est-il?** what time is it?, what's the time? ▸ **il est dix heures dix** it's ten past ten, it's ten after ten *US*
2. [suivi d'un adjectif] **: il est...** it is... ▸ **il est inutile de** it's useless to ▸ **il serait bon de/que** it would be good to/if, it would be a good idea to/if.
■ **vi 1.** [exister] to be ▸ **n'être plus** *sout* [être décédé] to be no more ▸ **le plus petit ordinateur qui soit** the tiniest computer ever ▸ **soit une droite AB** let AB be a straight line
2. [indique une situation, un état] to be ▸ **il est à Paris** he's in Paris ▸ **nous sommes au printemps/en été** it's spring/summer ▸ **je suis à vous dans un instant** I'll be with you in a moment ▸ **vous êtes (bien) au 01.40.06.24.08** this is 01 40 06 24 08
3. [indiquant une origine] **: il est de Paris** he's from Paris ▸ **l'église est du XVIe** the church is from *ou* dates back to the 16th century ▸ **les œufs sont d'hier** the eggs were laid yesterday.
◆ ***être à*** **v + prep 1.** [indiquant une obligation] **: c'est à vérifier** it needs to be checked ▸ **cette chemise est à laver** this shirt needs washing ▸ **c'est à voir** that remains to be seen
2. [indiquant une continuité] **: il est toujours à ne rien faire** he never does a thing ▸ **il est toujours à s'inquiéter** he's always worrying
3. [avec «en»] **: en être à : le projet n'en est qu'au début** the project has only just started ▸ **où en es-tu avec Michel?** how is it going with Michel?

étreindre [81] [etrɛ̃dr] **vt 1.** [embrasser] to hug, to embrace **2.** *fig* [tenailler] to grip, to clutch.
◆ ***s'étreindre*** **vp** to embrace each other.

étreinte [etrɛ̃t] **nf 1.** [enlacement] embrace **2.** [pression] stranglehold.

étrenner [4] [etrene] **vt** to use for the first time.

étrennes [etrɛn] **nfpl** Christmas box *(sg) UK*.

étrier [etrije] **nm** stirrup.

étriller [3] [etrije] **vt 1.** [cheval] to curry **2.** [personne] to wipe the floor with / [film] to tear to pieces.

étriper [3] [etripe] **vt 1.** [animal] to disembowel **2.** *fam fig* [tuer] to murder.
◆ ***s'étriper*** **vp** *fam* to tear each other to pieces.

étriqué, e [etrike] **adj 1.** [vêtement] tight / [appartement] cramped **2.** [esprit] narrow.

étroit, e [etrwa, at] **adj 1.** [gén] narrow **2.** [intime] close **3.** [serré] tight.
◆ ***à l'étroit*** **loc adj : être à l'étroit** to be cramped.

étroitement [etrwatmɑ̃] **adv** closely.

étroitesse [etrwatɛs] **nf** narrowness ▸ **étroitesse d'esprit** *fig* narrow-mindedness.

étrusque [etrysk] **adj** Etruscan, Etrurian.
◆ ***Étrusque*** **nmf** Etruscan, Etrurian.

étude [etyd] **nf 1.** [gén & ÉCON] study ▸ **à l'étude** under consideration ▸ **étude de faisabilité** feasibility study ▸ **étude de médias** media research *(U)* ▸ **étude de marché** market research *(U)* ▸ **étude de positionnement** positioning study ▸ **études qualitatives** qualitative research *(U)* ▸ **études quantitatives** quantitative research *(U)* **2.** [de notaire - local] office / [- charge] practice **3.** MUS étude.
◆ ***études*** **nfpl** studies ▸ **faire des études** to study ▸ **études primaires/secondaires** primary/secondary education *(U)*.

étudiant, e [etydjɑ̃, ɑ̃t] ■ **adj** student *(avant n)*.
■ **nm, f** student.

étudié, e [etydje] **adj** studied.

étudier [9] [etydje] ■ **vt 1.** [apprendre - gén] to study / [- leçon] to learn / [- piano] to learn (to play), to study / [- auteur, période] to study ▸ **étudier la géographie** SCOL to study geography / UNIV to study *ou UK* to read geogra-

phy **2.** [examiner - contrat] to study, to examine / [- liste] to go through ▸ **étudier le terrain** to survey the land **3.** [observer - passant, adversaire] to watch, to observe **4.** [concevoir to devise, to design ▸ **être très étudié** to be specially designed ▸ **c'est étudié pour** *fam* that's what it's for.
■ **vi 1.** [faire ses études] to study, to be a student **2.** [travailler] to study.
◆ ***s'étudier*** **vp** *(emploi réfléchi)* [se regarder soi-même] to gaze at *ou* to study o.s..

étui [etɥi] **nm** case ▸ **étui à cigarettes/lunettes** cigarette/glasses case.

étuve [etyv] **nf 1.** [local] steam room / *fig* oven **2.** [appareil] sterilizer.

étuvée [etyve] ◆ ***à l'étuvée*** **loc adv** braised ▸ **faire cuire à l'étuvée** to braise.

étymologie [etimɔlɔʒi] **nf** etymology.

étymologique [etimɔlɔʒik] **adj** etymological.

étymologiquement [etimɔlɔʒikmɑ̃] **adv** etymologically.

eu, e [y] **pp** ➤ ***avoir***.

E-U, E-U A (**abr de *États-Unis (d'Amérique)***) **nmpl** US, USA.

eucalyptus [økaliptys] **nm** eucalyptus.

eucharistie [økaristi] **nf** Eucharist.

euh [ø] **interj** er.

eunuque [ønyk] **nm** eunuch.

euphémisme [øfemism] **nm** euphemism ▸ **par euphémisme** euphemistically.

euphorie [øfɔri] **nf** euphoria.

euphorique [øfɔrik] **adj** euphoric.

euphorisant, e [øfɔrizɑ̃, ɑ̃t] **adj** exhilarating.
◆ ***euphorisant*** **nm** antidepressant.

eurasien, enne [ørazjɛ̃, ɛn] **adj** Eurasian.
◆ ***Eurasien, enne*** **nm, f** Eurasian.

eurent ➤ ***avoir***.

euro [ørɔ] **nm** euro ▸ **zone euro** euro zone, euro area.

eurocentrisme [ørɔsɑ̃trism] **nm** Eurocentrism.

eurochèque [ørɔʃɛk] **nm** Eurocheque.

eurocrate [ørɔkrat] **nmf** Eurocrat.

eurodéputé [ørɔdepyte] **nm** Euro MP.

eurodevise [ørɔdəviz] **nf** Eurocurrency.

eurodollar [ørɔdɔlar] **nm** Eurodollar.

euromissile [ørɔmisil] **nm** Euromissile.

Europe [ørɔp] **nf : l'Europe** Europe ▸ **l'Europe centrale** Central Europe ▸ **l'Europe de l'Est** Eastern Europe ▸ **ils ont parlé de l'Europe verte** they discussed agriculture in the EU.

européen, enne [ørɔpeɛ̃, ɛn] **adj** European.
◆ ***Européen, enne*** **nm, f** European.
◆ ***européennes*** **nfpl** POLIT European elections, Euro-elections, elections for the European Parliament.

Eurostar® [ørɔstar] **npr m** Eurostar®.

Eurotunnel® [ørɔtynɛl] **npr m** Eurotunnel®.

Eurovision® [ørovizjɔ̃] **npr f** Eurovision®.

eu, e ➤ ***avoir***.

eût ➤ ***avoir***.

euthanasie [øtanazi] **nf** euthanasia.

euthanasier [9] [øtanazje] **vt** [animal] to put down, to put to sleep / [personne] to practise *UK ou* practice *US* euthanasia on, to help to die.

eux [ø] **pron pers 1.** [sujet] they ▸ **ce sont eux qui me l'ont dit** they're the ones who told me **2.** [complément] them.
◆ ***eux-mêmes*** **pron pers** themselves.

eV (**abr écrite de *électron-volt***) eV.

EV (**abr écrite de *en ville***) by hand.

évacuation [evakɥasjɔ̃] **nf 1.** [gén] evacuation **2.** [de liquide] draining.

évacuer [7] [evakɥe] **vt 1.** [gén] to evacuate **2.** [liquide] to drain.

évadé, e [evade] **nm, f** escaped prisoner.

évader [3] [evade] ◆ ***s'évader*** **vp : s'évader (de)** to escape (from).

évaluation [evalɥasjɔ̃] **nf** [action] valuation / [résultat] estimate.

évaluer [7] [evalɥe] **vt** [distance] to estimate / [tableau] to value / [risque] to assess.

évanescent, e [evanesɑ̃, ɑ̃t] **adj** *littéraire* fleeting.

évangélique [evɑ̃ʒelik] **adj** evangelical.

évangélisation [evɑ̃ʒelizasjɔ̃] **nf** evangelization, evangelizing.

évangéliser [3] [evɑ̃ʒelize] **vt** to evangelize.

évangéliste [evɑ̃ʒelist] **nm 1.** [auteur] Evangelist **2.** [prédicateur] evangelist.

évangile [evɑ̃ʒil] **nm** gospel ▸ **l'Évangile selon Saint Jean** the Gospel according to St. John.

évanouir [32] [evanwir] ◆ ***s'évanouir*** **vp 1.** [défaillir] to faint **2.** [disparaître] to fade.

évanouissement [evanwismɑ̃] **nm 1.** [syncope] fainting fit **2.** [disparition] fading.

évaporation [evapɔrasjɔ̃] **nf** evaporation.

évaporer [3] [evapɔre] ◆ ***s'évaporer*** **vp** to evaporate.

évasé, e [evaze] **adj** flared.

évaser [3] [evaze] **vt** to flare.
◆ ***s'évaser*** **vp** to flare.

évasif, ive [evazif, iv] **adj** evasive.

évasion [evazjɔ̃] **nf** escape.

évasivement [evazivmɑ̃] **adv** evasively.

évêché [eveʃe] **nm** [territoire] diocese / [résidence] bishop's palace.

éveil [evɛj] **nm** awakening ▸ **en éveil** on the alert.

éveillé, e [eveje] **adj 1.** [qui ne dort pas] wide awake **2.** [vif, alerte] alert.

éveiller [4] [eveje] **vt** to arouse / [intelligence, dormeur] to awaken.
◆ ***s'éveiller*** **vp** **1.** [dormeur] to wake, to awaken **2.** [curiosité] to be aroused **3.** [esprit, intelligence] to be awakened **4.** [s'ouvrir] **: s'éveiller à qqch** to discover sthg.

événement [evɛnmɑ̃] **nm** event.

événementiel, ***elle*** [evɛnmɑ̃sjɛl] **adj** [histoire] factual.

éventail [evɑ̃taj] **nm** **1.** [objet] fan ▸ **en éventail** fan-shaped **2.** [choix] range.

éventaire [evɑ̃tɛr] **nm** **1.** [étalage] stall, stand **2.** [corbeille] tray.

éventé, ***e*** [evɑ̃te] **adj** stale.

éventer [3] [evɑ̃te] **vt** **1.** [rafraîchir] to fan **2.** [divulguer] to give away.
◆ ***s'éventer*** **vp** **1.** [se rafraîchir] to fan o.s. **2.** [parfum, vin] to go stale.

éventrer [3] [evɑ̃tre] **vt** **1.** [étriper] to disembowel **2.** [fendre] to rip open.

éventualité [evɑ̃tɥalite] **nf** **1.** [possibilité] possibility **2.** [circonstance] eventuality ▸ **dans l'éventualité de** in the event of ▸ **parer à toute éventualité** to be ready for any eventuality.

éventuel, ***elle*** [evɑ̃tɥɛl] **adj** possible.

éventuellement [evɑ̃tɥɛlmɑ̃] **adv** possibly.

FAUX AMIS / FALSE FRIENDS

éventuellement

Eventually is not a translation of the French word *éventuellement*. Eventually is translated by *finalement*.
▸ Eventually, I decided to give up / *J'ai finalement décidé d'abandonner*

évêque [evɛk] **nm** bishop.

évertuer [7] [evɛrtɥe] ◆ ***s'évertuer*** **vp : s'évertuer à faire qqch** to strive to do sthg.

éviction [eviksjɔ̃] **nf** eviction.

évidemment [evidamɑ̃] **adv** obviously.

évidence [evidɑ̃s] **nf** [caractère] evidence / [fait] obvious fact ▸ **à l'évidence** obviously ▸ **mettre en évidence** to emphasize, to highlight ▸ **se rendre à l'évidence** to face facts.

évident, ***e*** [evidɑ̃, ɑ̃t] **adj** obvious ▸ **ce n'est pas évident** [pas facile] it's not that easy.

évider [3] [evide] **vt** to hollow out.

évier [evje] **nm** sink.

évincer [16] [evɛ̃se] **vt : évincer qqn (de)** to oust sb (from).

évitement [evitmɑ̃] **nm** RAIL shunting.
◆ ***d'évitement*** **loc adj** **1.** RAIL **: voie d'évitement** siding **2.** PSYCHO avoidance *(avant n)*.

éviter [3] [evite] **vt** **1.** [esquiver] to avoid ▸ **la catastrophe a été évitée de justesse** a catastrophe was averted by a hair's breadth **2.** [s'abstenir] **: éviter de faire qqch** to avoid doing sthg ▸ **elle évite la foule** she shies away from crowds **3.** [épargner] **: éviter qqch à qqn** to save sb sthg ▸ **évitons-lui tout souci** let's keep him from worrying (about anything) *ou* spare him any worries.
◆ ***s'éviter*** **vp** **1.** [se bouder] to avoid each other **2.** [s'épargner] to spare o.s. ▸ **s'éviter qqch** to save *ou* to spare o.s. sthg.

évocateur, ***trice*** [evɔkatœr, tris] **adj** **1.** [film, roman] **: évocateur (de)** evocative (of) **2.** [geste, regard] meaningful.

évocation [evɔkasjɔ̃] **nf** evocation.

évolué, ***e*** [evɔlɥe] **adj** **1.** [développé] developed **2.** [libéral, progressiste] broad minded.

évoluer [7] [evɔlɥe] **vi** **1.** [changer] to evolve / [personne] to change **2.** [se mouvoir] to move around.

évolutif, ***ive*** [evɔlytif, iv] **adj** **1.** [système] evolutionary **2.** MÉD progressive **3.** [travail] **: un poste évolutif** a job with prospects.

évolution [evɔlysjɔ̃] **nf** **1.** [transformation] development **2.** BIOL evolution **3.** MÉD progress.
◆ ***évolutions*** **nfpl** movements.

évoquer [3] [evɔke] **vt** **1.** [souvenir] to evoke ▸ **son nom ne m'évoque rien** his name means nothing to me **2.** [problème] to refer to **3.** [esprits, démons] to call up.

ex [ɛks] **nmf** ex.

ex- [ɛks] **préf** ex-.

ex. abr de ***exemple***.

exacerbé, ***e*** [ɛgzasɛrbe] **adj** exacerbated.

exacerber [3] [ɛgzasɛrbe] **vt** to exacerbate.

exact, ***e*** [ɛgzakt] **adj** **1.** [calcul] correct **2.** [récit, copie] exact **3.** [ponctuel] punctual.

exactement [ɛgzaktəmɑ̃] **adv** exactly.

exaction [ɛgzaksjɔ̃] **nf** extortion.

exactitude [ɛgzaktityd] **nf** **1.** [de calcul, montre] accuracy **2.** [ponctualité] punctuality.

ex æquo [ɛgzeko] ■ **adj inv & nmf** equal.
■ **adv** equal ▸ **troisième ex æquo** third equal, tied for third.

exagération [ɛgzaʒerasjɔ̃] **nf** exaggeration.

exagéré, ***e*** [ɛgzaʒere] **adj** exaggerated.

exagérément [ɛgzaʒeremɑ̃] **adv** exaggeratedly.

exagérer [18] [ɛgzaʒere] **vt & vi** to exaggerate.
◆ ***s'exagérer*** **vp** to exaggerate.

exaltant, ***e*** [ɛgzaltɑ̃, ɑ̃t] **adj** exhilarating.

exalté, ***e*** [ɛgzalte] ■ **adj** [sentiment] elated / [tempérament] over-excited / [imagination] vivid.
■ **nm, f** fanatic.

exalter [3] [ɛgzalte] **vt** to excite.
◆ ***s'exalter*** **vp** to get carried away.

examen [ɛgzamɛ̃] **nm** examination / SCOL exam, examination ▸ **examen médical** medical (examination) *UK*, physical (examination) *US* ▸ **mise en examen** DR indictment.

examinateur, trice [ɛgzaminatœr, tris] **nm, f** examiner.

examiner [3] [ɛgzamine] **vt** to examine.

exaspérant, e [ɛgzasperɑ̃, ɑ̃t] **adj** exasperating.

exaspération [ɛgzasperasjɔ̃] **nf** exasperation.

exaspérer [18] [ɛgzaspere] **vt** to exasperate.

exaucer [16] [ɛgzose] **vt** to grant ▸ **exaucer qqn** to answer sb's prayers.

ex cathedra [ɛkskatedra] **loc adv** with authority.

excédant, e [ɛksedɑ̃, ɑ̃t] **adj** exasperating.

excédent [ɛksedɑ̃] **nm** surplus ▸ **en excédent** surplus *(avant n)* ▸ **excédent de bagages** [dans l'avion] excess baggage *ou* luggage *UK* ▸ **excédent commercial** trade surplus.

excédentaire [ɛksedɑ̃tɛr] **adj** surplus *(avant n)*.

excéder [18] [ɛksede] **vt 1.** [gén] to exceed **2.** [exaspérer] to exasperate.

excellemment [ɛkselamɑ̃] **adv** excellently.

excellence [ɛkselɑ̃s] **nf** excellence ▸ **par excellence** par excellence.
◆ ***Excellence* nf : Son Excellence** His/Her Excellency.

excellent, e [ɛkselɑ̃, ɑ̃t] **adj** excellent.

exceller [4] [ɛksele] **vi : exceller en *ou* dans qqch** to excel at *ou* in sthg ▸ **exceller à faire qqch** to excel at doing sthg.

excentré, e [ɛksɑ̃tre] **adj : c'est très excentré** it's quite a long way out.

excentrique [ɛksɑ̃trik] ■ **nmf** eccentric.
■ **adj 1.** [gén] eccentric **2.** [quartier] outlying.

excepté, e [ɛksepte] **adj : tous sont venus, lui excepté** everyone came except (for) him.
◆ ***excepté*** **prép** apart from, except.

exception [ɛksɛpsjɔ̃] **nf 1.** [hors norme] exception ▸ **cette règle admet des exceptions** there are (some) exceptions to this rule ▸ **les collisions entre avions restent l'exception** plane collisions are still very rare ▸ **faire exception** to be an exception ▸ **faire une exception pour qqn/qqch** to make an exception for sb/sthg ▸ **faire une exception à** to make an exception to ▸ **d'exception** exceptional ▸ **c'est un être d'exception** [homme] he's an exceptional man / [femme] she's an exceptional woman ▸ **à l'exception de** except for ▸ **sortez tous, sans exception!** out, every (single) one of you! **2.** DR plea ▸ **exception péremptoire** peremptory plea.

exceptionnel, elle [ɛksɛpsjɔnɛl] **adj** exceptional.

exceptionnellement [ɛksɛpsjɔnɛlmɑ̃] **adv 1.** [par exception] in this (one) instance **2.** [extrêmement] exceptionally.

excès [ɛksɛ] ■ **nm** excess ▸ **excès de vitesse** speeding ▸ **excès de zèle** overzealousness ▸ **à l'excès** to excess, excessively ▸ **sans excès** moderately.
■ **nmpl** excesses.

excessif, ive [ɛksesif, iv] **adj 1.** [démesuré] excessive **2.** *fam* [extrême] extreme.

excessivement [ɛksesivmɑ̃] **adv 1.** [démesurément] excessively **2.** *fam* [extrêmement] extremely.

excipient [ɛksipjɑ̃] **nm** excipient.

excision [ɛksizjɔ̃] **nf** excision.

excitant, e [ɛksitɑ̃, ɑ̃t] **adj 1.** [stimulant, passionnant] exciting **2.** MÉD stimulating.
◆ ***excitant*** **nm** stimulant.

excitation [ɛksitasjɔ̃] **nf 1.** [énervement] excitement **2.** [stimulation] encouragement **3.** MÉD stimulation.

excité, e [ɛksite] ■ **adj** [énervé] excited.
■ **nm, f** hothead.

exciter [3] [ɛksite] **vt 1.** [gén] to excite **2.** [inciter] **: exciter qqn (à qqch/à faire qqch)** to incite sb (to sthg/to do sthg) **3.** MÉD to stimulate.
◆ ***s'exciter*** **vp : s'exciter (sur)** to lose one's temper (with).

exclamation [ɛksklamasjɔ̃] **nf** exclamation.

exclamer [3] [ɛksklame] ◆ ***s'exclamer*** **vp : s'exclamer (devant)** to exclaim (at *ou* over).

exclu, e [ɛkskly] ■ **pp** ➤ ***exclure***.
■ **adj** excluded.
■ **nm, f** outsider.

exclure [96] [ɛksklyr] **vt** to exclude / [expulser] to expel.

COMMENT EXPRIMER...

les excuses

Présenter ses excuses

Sorry! / Pardon !

I'm very sorry / Je suis vraiment désolé

Pardon me! *OR* Excuse me! *(après avoir éternué, par exemple)* / Pardon ! *OR* Excusez-moi !

I'm sorry I forgot to phone you / Je suis désolé d'avoir oublié de vous téléphoner

I'm sorry about the confusion / Je suis désolé pour le malentendu

I'm really sorry, but I can't come on Saturday / Je suis désolé, mais je ne peux pas venir samedi

I do apologize for my late arrival / Je vous prie de bien vouloir m'excuser pour ce retard

We apologize for the mistake on your invoice / Nous nous excusons de l'erreur commise sur votre facture

Please accept our apologies for the double booking / Veuillez accepter nos excuses pour la surréservation

Répondre à des excuses

That's OK / Ce n'est pas grave

Don't worry about it / Ne t'en fais pas

It doesn't matter / Ça ne fait rien

Let's say no more about it / N'en parlons plus

There's no need to apologize / Ne vous excusez pas

exclusif, ive [ɛksklyzif, iv] **adj** exclusive ▸ **exclusif de** exclusive of.

exclusion [ɛksklyzjɔ̃] **nf** expulsion ▸ **à l'exclusion de** to the exclusion of.

exclusivement [ɛksklyzivmɑ̃] **adv** **1.** [uniquement] exclusively **2.** [non inclus] exclusive.

exclusivité [ɛksklyzivite] **nf** **1.** COMM exclusive rights *pl*, exclusivity ▸ **avoir l'exclusivité (de)** to have exclusive rights (to) **2.** CINÉ sole screening rights *pl* ▸ **en exclusivité** exclusively **3.** [de sentiment] exclusiveness.

excommunier [9] [ɛkskɔmynje] **vt** to excommunicate.

excrément [ɛkskremɑ̃] **nm** *(gén pl)* excrement *(U)*.

excroissance [ɛkskrwasɑ̃s] **nf** excrescence.

excursion [ɛkskyrsjɔ̃] **nf** excursion ▸ **faire une excursion** to go on a trip.

excursionniste [ɛkskyrsjɔnist] **nmf** day-tripper.

excusable [ɛkskyzabl] **adj** excusable.

excuse [ɛkskyz] **nf** excuse ▸ **avoir une excuse** to have an excuse ▸ **se confondre en excuses** to apologize profusely ▸ **présenter ses excuses à qqn** to apologize to sb.

excuser [3] [ɛkskyze] **vt** to excuse ▸ **excusez-moi** [pour réparer] I'm sorry / [pour demander] excuse me ▸ **excuse-moi d'appeler si tard** forgive me *ou* I do apologize for phoning so late ▸ **je vous prie de** *ou* **veuillez m'excuser** I (do) beg your pardon, I do apologize ▸ **se faire excuser** to ask to be excused ▸ **excuse-moi auprès de lui** apologize to him for me.
◆ ***s'excuser*** **vp** [demander pardon] to apologize ▸ **s'excuser de qqch/de faire qqch** to apologize for sthg/for doing sthg ▸ **je m'excuse de mon retard/de vous interrompre** sorry for being late/for interrupting you.

exécrable [ɛgzekrabl] **adj** atrocious.

exécrer [18] [ɛgzekre] **vt** to loathe.

exécutable [ɛgzekytabl] **adj** possible, feasible ▸ **ce n'est pas exécutable en trois jours** it can't possibly be done in three days.

exécutant, e [ɛgzekytɑ̃, ɑ̃t] **nm, f** **1.** [personne] underling **2.** MUS performer.

exécuter [3] [ɛgzekyte] **vt** **1.** [réaliser] to carry out / [tableau] to paint **2.** MUS to play, to perform **3.** [mettre à mort] to execute.
◆ ***s'exécuter*** **vp** to comply.

exécuteur, trice [ɛgzekytœr, tris] **nmf** : **exécuteur testamentaire** executor.

exécutif, ive [ɛgzekytif, iv] **adj** executive.
◆ ***exécutif*** **nm** : **l'exécutif** the executive.

exécution [ɛgzekysjɔ̃] **nf** **1.** [réalisation] carrying out / [de tableau] painting ▸ **mettre à exécution** to carry out **2.** MUS performance **3.** [mise à mort] execution.

exécutoire [ɛgzekytwar] **adj** binding.

exégèse [ɛgzeʒɛz] **nf** exegesis.

exemplaire [ɛgzɑ̃plɛr] ■ **adj** exemplary.
■ **nm** copy / [d'un livre, d'une revue] : **exemplaire de lancement** advance copy ▸ **exemplaire de service de presse** review copy.

exemple [ɛgzɑ̃pl] **nm** example ▸ **par exemple** for example, for instance ▸ **ça, par exemple!** [exprime la surprise] well, well!, good heavens! ▸ **pour l'exemple** as an example ▸ **citer qqn en exemple** to quote sb as an example ▸ **montrer l'exemple** to set an example ▸ **prendre exemple sur qqn** to take a leaf out of sb's book ▸ **à l'exemple de** following in the footsteps of.

exempt, e [ɛgzɑ̃, ɑ̃t] **adj** **1.** : **exempt de** [dispensé de] exempt from / [dépourvu de] free of **2.** [impôts] : **exempt de taxes** tax-free, tax-exempt.

exempté, e [ɛgzɑ̃te] **adj** : **exempté (de)** exempt (from).

exempter [3] [ɛgzɑ̃te] **vt** : **exempter qqn de qqch** : **il a été exempté du service militaire** he has been exempted from doing military service ▸ **exempter qqn d'impôts** to exempt sb from tax.

exemption [ɛgzɑ̃psjɔ̃] **nf** exemption.

exercer [16] [ɛgzɛrse] **vt** **1.** [entraîner, mettre en usage] to exercise / [autorité, influence] to exert **2.** [métier] to carry on / [médecine] to practise *UK*, to practice *US*.
◆ ***s'exercer*** **vp** **1.** [s'entraîner] to practise *UK*, to practice *US* ▸ **s'exercer à qqch/à faire qqch** to practise *UK ou* to practice *US* sthg/doing sthg **2.** [se manifester] : **s'exercer (sur *ou* contre)** to be exerted (on).

exercice [ɛgzɛrsis] **nm** **1.** [gén] exercise ▸ **exercices d'assouplissement** keep-fit exercises *UK* ▸ **faire de l'exercice** to take exercise, to exercise ▸ **je manque d'exercice** I don't get enough exercise ▸ **exercice de chimie** chemistry exercise
2. [entraînement] practice ▸ **exercices de tir** shooting drill *ou* practice
3. [de métier, fonction] carrying out ▸ **dans l'exercice de ses fonctions** in the execution of one's duties ▸ **en exercice** in office ▸ **l'exercice du pouvoir/d'un droit** exercising power/a right
4. FIN fiscal year, financial year *UK* ▸ **exercice budgétaire** budgetary year ▸ **exercice (financier)** accounting period.

exergue [ɛgzɛrg] **nm** inscription ▸ **mettre qqch en exergue** to emphasize sthg.

exfoliant, e [ɛksfɔljɑ̃, ɑ̃t] **adj** exfoliating *(avant n)*.
◆ ***exfoliant*** **nm** exfoliant.

exhalaison [ɛgzalɛzɔ̃] **nf** *littéraire* odour *UK*, odor *US*.

exhaler [3] [ɛgzale] **vt** *littéraire* **1.** [odeur] to give off **2.** *fig* [colère, rage] to vent **3.** [plainte, soupir] to utter.
◆ ***s'exhaler*** **vp** **1.** [odeur] to rise **2.** [plainte, soupir] : **s'exhaler de** to rise from.

exhausser [3] [ɛgzose] **vt** to raise.

exhaustif, ive [ɛgzostif, iv] **adj** exhaustive.

exhiber [3] [ɛgzibe] **vt** [présenter] to show / [faire étalage de] to show off.
◆ ***s'exhiber*** **vp** to make an exhibition of o.s.

exhibitionniste [ɛgzibisjɔnist] **nmf** exhibitionist.

exhortation [ɛgzɔrtasjɔ̃] **nf** exhortation.

exhorter [3] [ɛgzɔrte] **vt : exhorter qqn à qqch/à faire qqch** to urge sb to sthg/to do sthg.

exhumer [3] [ɛgzyme] **vt** to exhume / *fig* to unearth, to dig up.

exigeant**, **e [ɛgziʒɑ̃, ɑ̃t] **adj** demanding.

exigence [ɛgziʒɑ̃s] **nf 1.** [caractère] demanding nature **2.** [demande] demand.

exiger [17] [ɛgziʒe] **vt 1.** [demander] to demand ▸ **exiger que** *(+ subjonctif)* to demand that ▸ **exiger qqch de qqn** to demand sthg from sb **2.** [nécessiter] to require.

exigible [ɛgziʒibl] **adj** payable.

exigu**, **ë [ɛgzigy] **adj** cramped.

exiguïté [ɛgzigɥite] **nf** lack of space.

exil [ɛgzil] **nm** exile ▸ **en exil** exiled.

exilé**, **e [ɛgzile] **nm, f** exile.

exiler [3] [ɛgzile] **vt** to exile.
◆ ***s'exiler*** **vp 1.** POLIT to go into exile **2.** *fig* [partir] to go into seclusion.

existence [ɛgzistɑ̃s] **nf** existence.

existentialisme [ɛgzistɑ̃sjalism] **nm** existentialism.

existentiel**, **elle [ɛgzistɑ̃sjɛl] **adj** existential.

exister [3] [ɛgziste] ■ **vi** to exist.
■ **v impers : il existe** [il y a] there is/are.

exode [ɛgzɔd] **nm** exodus ▸ **exode rural** rural depopulation.

exonération [ɛgzɔnerasjɔ̃] **nf** exemption ▸ **exonération de qqch** exemption from sthg ▸ **exonération d'impôts** tax exemption.

exonérer [18] [ɛgzɔnere] **vt : exonérer qqn de qqch** to exempt sb from sthg.

exorbitant**, **e [ɛgzɔrbitɑ̃, ɑ̃t] **adj** exorbitant.

exorbité**, **e [ɛgzɔrbite] ➤ ***œil***.

exorciser [3] [ɛgzɔrsize] **vt** to exorcize.

exotique [ɛgzɔtik] **adj** exotic.

exotisme [ɛgzɔtism] **nm** exoticism.

expansé**, **e [ɛkspɑ̃se] **adj** expanded.

expansif**, **ive [ɛkspɑ̃sif, iv] **adj** expansive.

expansion [ɛkspɑ̃sjɔ̃] **nf** expansion ▸ **expansion démographique** population growth.

expansionniste [ɛkspɑ̃sjɔnist] **nmf & adj** expansionist.

expatrié**, **e [ɛkspatrije] **adj & nm, f** expatriate.

expatrier [10] [ɛkspatrije] **vt** to expatriate.
◆ ***s'expatrier*** **vp** to leave one's country.

expectative [ɛkspɛktativ] **nf : être dans l'expectative** to wait and see.

expectorant**, **e [ɛkspɛktɔrɑ̃, ɑ̃t] **adj** expectorant.
◆ ***expectorant*** **nm** expectorant.

expédient [ɛkspedjɑ̃] **nm** expedient ▸ **vivre d'expédients** to live by one's wits.

expédier [9] [ɛkspedje] **vt 1.** [lettre, marchandise] to send, to dispatch **2.** [personne] to get rid of / [question] to dispose of **3.** [travail] to dash off.

expéditeur**, **trice [ɛkspeditœr, tris] ■ **adj** dispatching *(avant n)*.
■ **nm, f** sender.

expéditif**, **ive [ɛkspeditif, iv] **adj** quick, expeditious.

expédition [ɛkspedisjɔ̃] **nf 1.** [envoi] sending **2.** [voyage, campagne militaire] expedition ▸ **expédition punitive** punitive raid.

expéditionnaire [ɛkspedisjɔnɛr] ➤ ***corps***.

expérience [ɛksperjɑ̃s] **nf 1.** [pratique] experience ▸ **avoir de l'expérience** to have experience, to be experienced **2.** [essai] experiment ▸ **faire l'expérience de qqch** to experience *ou* try sthg ▸ **tenter l'expérience** to try.

PARONYME / CONFUSABLE

expérience

Ce mot se traduit de deux façons différentes selon que l'on parle d'une expérience de type scientifique : *experiment*, ou bien d'un ensemble de connaissances, de la pratique d'une activité : *experience.*

expérimental**, **e**, **aux [ɛksperimɑ̃tal, o] **adj** experimental.

expérimentation [ɛksperimɑ̃tasjɔ̃] **nf** experimentation.

expérimenté**, **e [ɛksperimɑ̃te] **adj** experienced.

expérimenter [3] [ɛksperimɑ̃te] **vt** to test.

expert**, **e [ɛkspɛr, ɛrt] **adj** expert ▸ **être expert (en la matière)** to be an expert (on the subject).
◆ ***expert*** **nm** expert.

expert-comptable [ɛkspɛrkɔ̃tabl] (**pl experts-comptables**) **nm** chartered accountant *UK*, certified public accountant *US*.

expertise [ɛkspɛrtiz] **nf 1.** [examen] expert appraisal / [estimation] (expert) valuation **2.** [compétence] expertise.

expertiser [3] [ɛkspɛrtize] **vt** to value / [dégâts] to assess.

expiation [ɛkspjasjɔ̃] **nf** atonement.

expier [9] [ɛkspje] **vt** to pay for.

expiration [ɛkspirasjɔ̃] **nf 1.** [d'air] exhalation **2.** [de contrat] expiry *UK*, expiration *US* ▸ **arriver à expiration** to expire ▸ **date d'expiration** expiry *UK ou* expiration *US* date.

expirer [3] [ɛkspire] ■ **vt** to breathe out.
■ **vi 1.** [personne] to pass away **2.** [contrat] to expire.

explicable [ɛksplikabl] **adj** explicable.

explicatif**, **ive [ɛksplikatif, iv] **adj** explanatory.

explication [ɛksplikasjɔ̃] **nf** explanation ▸ **demander des explications à qqn** to demand an explanation from sb ▸ **explication de texte** (literary) criticism.

explicite [ɛksplisit] **adj** explicit.

explicitement [ɛksplisitmɑ̃] **adv** explicitly.

expliciter [3] [ɛksplisite] **vt** to make explicit.

expliquer [3] [ɛksplike] **vt 1.** [gén] to explain **2.** [texte] to criticize.
◆ ***s'expliquer*** **vp 1.** [se justifier] to explain o.s. **2.** [comprendre] to understand **3.** [discuter] to have it out **4.** [devenir compréhensible] to be explained, to become clear.

exploit [ɛksplwa] **nm** exploit, feat / *iron* [maladresse] achievement.

exploitable [ɛksplwatabl] **adj** [gisement] exploitable / [renseignement] usable / INFORM machine-readable.

exploitant, e [ɛksplwatɑ̃, ɑ̃t] **nm, f** farmer.

exploitation [ɛksplwatasjɔ̃] **nf 1.** [mise en valeur] running / [de mine] working **2.** [entreprise] operation, concern ▸ **exploitation agricole** farm **3.** [d'une personne] exploitation.

exploiter [3] [ɛksplwate] **vt 1.** [gén] to exploit **2.** [entreprise] to operate, to run.

exploiteur, euse [ɛksplwatœr, øz] **nm, f** exploiter.

explorateur, trice [ɛksplɔratœr, tris] **nm, f** explorer.

exploration [ɛksplɔrasjɔ̃] **nf** exploration.

exploratoire [ɛksplɔratwar] **adj** exploratory.

explorer [3] [ɛksplɔre] **vt** to explore.

exploser [3] [ɛksploze] **vi** to explode.

explosif, ive [ɛksplozif, iv] **adj** explosive.
◆ ***explosif*** **nm** explosive.

explosion [ɛksplozjɔ̃] **nf** explosion / [de colère, joie] outburst.

expo [ɛkspo] **nf** *fam* exhibition.

exponentiel, elle [ɛkspɔnɑ̃sjɛl] **adj** exponential.

exportateur, trice [ɛkspɔrtatœr, tris] ■ **adj** exporting.
■ **nm, f** exporter.

exportation [ɛkspɔrtasjɔ̃] **nf** export.

exporter [3] [ɛkspɔrte] **vt** to export.

exposant, e [ɛkspozɑ̃, ɑ̃t] **nm, f** exhibitor.
◆ ***exposant*** **nm** exponent.

exposé, e [ɛkspoze] **adj 1.** [orienté] **: bien exposé** facing the sun **2.** [vulnérable] exposed.
◆ ***exposé*** **nm** account / SCOL talk.

exposer [3] [ɛkspoze] **vt 1.** [orienter, mettre en danger] to expose ▸ **exposer sa vie** to risk one's life **2.** [présenter] to display / [tableaux] to show, to exhibit **3.** [expliquer] to explain, to set out.
◆ ***s'exposer*** **vp : s'exposer à qqch** to expose o.s. to sthg.

exposition [ɛkspozisjɔ̃] **nf 1.** [présentation] exhibition **2.** [orientation] aspect **3.** [explication] exposition **4.** [vente] **: exposition sur le lieu de vente** point-of-sale display, point-of-purchase display.

exposition-vente [ɛkspozisjɔ̃vɑ̃t] (pl **expositions-ventes**) **nf** exhibition *(where purchases can be made)*.

expo-vente [ɛkspovɑ̃t] abr écrite de ***exposition-vente***.

exprès¹, esse [ɛksprɛs] **adj** [formel] formal, express.
◆ ***exprès*** **adj inv** [urgent] express ▸ **en exprès** by special *ou* express *UK* delivery.

exprès² [ɛksprɛ] **adv** on purpose ▸ **faire exprès de faire qqch** to do sthg deliberately *ou* on purpose.

express [ɛksprɛs] ■ **nm inv 1.** [train] express **2.** [café] espresso.
■ **adj inv** express.

expressément [ɛkspresemɑ̃] **adv** expressly.

expressif, ive [ɛkspresif, iv] **adj** expressive.

expression [ɛkspresjɔ̃] **nf** expression ▸ **expression idiomatique** idiom, idiomatic expression ▸ **réduire qqch à sa plus simple expression** *fig* to reduce sthg to its simplest form ▸ **selon l'expression consacrée** as the saying goes.

expressionnisme [ɛksprɛsjɔnism] **nm** expressionism.

expressivité [ɛkspresivite] **nf** expressiveness.

COMMENT EXPRIMER...

l'explication

Demander une explication

Can you explain what this means? / Peux-tu m'expliquer ce que ça veut dire ?
What do you mean exactly? / Qu'est-ce que tu veux dire au juste ?
What makes you say that? / Qu'est-ce qui te fait dire ça ?
Why do you say that? / Pourquoi est-ce que tu dis ça ?
How do you mean? / Comment ça ?
Could you be a little more specific? / Pourriez-vous être un peu plus précis ?
I would be grateful if you could explain the proposal in more detail / Auriez-vous l'obligeance de m'expliquer la proposition en détail ?

Fournir une explication

Let me explain / Je m'explique
If you'll just give me a chance to explain / Permettez-moi de vous expliquer
What I meant was / Ce que je voulais dire, c'est
The point I'm trying to make is / Ce que j'essaie de dire, c'est
Let me put it another way / Je vais présenter ça autrement

expresso [ɛkspreso] **nm** espresso.

exprimable [ɛksprimabl] **adj** able to be expressed ▸ **difficilement exprimable** difficult to express.

exprimer [3] [ɛksprime] **vt** [pensées, sentiments] to express ▸ **exprimer qqch par qqch** to express sthg with sthg ▸ **exprimer une quantité en kilos** to state a quantity in kilos ▸ **comment vous exprimer toute mon admiration?** how can I tell you how much I admire you?
◆ ***s'exprimer*** **vp** to express o.s. ▸ **chacun doit s'exprimer** all opinions must be heard ▸ **je me suis exprimée sur ce sujet** I've expressed myself *ou* made my opinions known on the subject ▸ **laisse ton cœur s'exprimer** let your heart speak ▸ **si je peux m'exprimer ainsi** if I can put it that way ▸ **s'exprimer par signes** to use sign language.

expropriation [ɛksprɔprijasjɔ̃] **nf** expropriation.

exproprier [10] [ɛksprɔprije] **vt** to expropriate.

expulser [3] [ɛkspylse] **vt : expulser (de)** to expel (from) / [locataire] to evict (from).

expulsion [ɛkspylsjɔ̃] **nf** expulsion / [de locataire] eviction.

expurger [17] [ɛkspyrʒe] **vt** to expurgate.

exquis**, **e [ɛkski, iz] **adj 1.** [délicieux] exquisite **2.** [distingué, agréable] delightful.

exsangue [ɛksɑ̃g] **adj** [blême] deathly pale.

extase [ɛkstaz] **nf** ecstasy ▸ **tomber en extase devant** to go into ecstasies over.

extasier [9] [ɛkstazje] ◆ ***s'extasier*** **vp : s'extasier devant** to go into ecstasies over.

extatique [ɛkstatik] **adj** ecstatic.

extenseur [ɛkstɑ̃sœr] ■ **nm** [gymnastique] chest expander.
■ **adj** ➤ ***muscle***.

extensible [ɛkstɑ̃sibl] **adj** stretchable.

extensif**, **ive [ɛkstɑ̃sif, iv] **adj** extensive.

extension [ɛkstɑ̃sjɔ̃] **nf 1.** [étirement] stretching **2.** [développement] spread **3.** [élargissement] extension ▸ **par extension** by extension ▸ **extension de nom de fichier** INFORM (filename) extension.

exténuant**, **e [ɛkstenɥɑ̃, ɑ̃t] **adj** exhausting.

exténuer [7] [ɛkstenɥe] **vt** to exhaust.

extérieur**, **e [ɛksterjœr] **adj 1.** [au dehors] outside / [étranger] external / [apparent] outward **2.** ÉCON & POLIT foreign.
◆ ***extérieur*** **nm 1.** [dehors] outside / [de maison] exterior ▸ **à l'extérieur de qqch** outside sthg **2.** ÉCON & POLIT **: l'extérieur** foreign countries *pl* **3.** CINÉ **: extérieur** location shot.

extérieurement [ɛksterjœrmɑ̃] **adv 1.** [à l'extérieur] on the outside, externally **2.** [en apparence] outwardly.

extérioriser [3] [ɛksterjɔrize] **vt** to show.
◆ ***s'extérioriser*** **vp** to show one's feelings.

extermination [ɛkstɛrminasjɔ̃] **nf** extermination.

exterminer [3] [ɛkstɛrmine] **vt** to exterminate.

externalisation [ɛkstɛrnalizasjɔ̃] **nf** outsourcing.

externaliser [3] [ɛkstɛrnalize] **vt** to outsource.

externat [ɛkstɛrna] **nm 1.** SCOL day school **2.** MÉD *non-resident medical studentship*.

externe [ɛkstɛrn] ■ **nmf 1.** SCOL day pupil **2.** MÉD *non-resident medical student*, ≃ extern ***US***.
■ **adj** outer, external ▸ **externe à qqch** outside sthg.

extincteur [ɛkstɛ̃ktœr] **nm** (fire) extinguisher.

extinction [ɛkstɛ̃ksjɔ̃] **nf 1.** [action d'éteindre] putting out, extinguishing ▸ **extinction des feux** lights out **2.** *fig* [disparition] extinction ▸ **extinction de voix** loss of one's voice.

extirper [3] [ɛkstirpe] **vt : extirper (de)** [épine, racine] to pull out(of) / [plante] to uproot (from) / [réponse, secret] to drag (out of) / [erreur, préjugé] to root out (of).
◆ ***s'extirper*** **vp : s'extirper de qqch** to struggle out of sthg.

extorquer [3] [ɛkstɔrke] **vt : extorquer qqch à qqn** to extort sthg from sb.

extorsion [ɛkstɔrsjɔ̃] **nf** extortion ▸ **extorsion de fonds** extortion of money.

extra [ɛkstra] ■ **nm inv 1.** [employé] extra help *(U)* **2.** [chose inhabituelle] (special) treat.
■ **adj inv 1.** [de qualité] top-quality **2.** *fam* [génial] great, fantastic.

extraction [ɛkstraksjɔ̃] **nf** extraction.

extrader [3] [ɛkstrade] **vt** to extradite.

extradition [ɛkstradisjɔ̃] **nf** extradition.

extraire [112] [ɛkstrɛr] **vt 1.** [charbon] to extract, to mine / [pétrole] to extract / [pierre] to extract, to quarry **2.** [ôter] to extract, to remove, to pull out ▸ **extraire qqch de : extraire une balle d'une jambe** to extract *ou* to remove a bullet from a leg ▸ **extraire un ticket de sa poche** to take *ou* to dig a ticket out of one's pocket **3.** CHIM & CULIN to extract / [en pressant] to squeeze out / [en écrasant] to crush out / [en tordant] to wring out **4.** MATH to extract ▸ **extraire la racine carrée/cubique d'un nombre** to extract the square/cube root of a number **5.** [citer - passage, proverbe] **: extraire de** to take *ou* to extract from.
◆ ***s'extraire*** **vp** *(emploi réfléchi)* **: s'extraire de qqch** to climb out of sthg ▸ **s'extraire d'une voiture** [rescapé d'un accident] to extricate o.s. from (the wreckage of) a car.

extrait**, **e [ɛkstrɛ, ɛt] **pp** ➤ ***extraire***.
◆ ***extrait*** **nm** extract ▸ **extrait de café** coffee extract ▸ **extrait de naissance** birth certificate.

extralucide [ɛkstralysid] ➤ ***voyant***.

extraordinaire [ɛkstraɔrdinɛr] **adj** extraordinary.

extraplat**, **e [ɛkstrapla, at] **adj** wafer-thin.

extrapoler [3] [ɛkstrapɔle] **vt & vi** to extrapolate.

extraterrestre [ɛkstraterɛstr] **nmf & adj** extraterrestrial.

extravagance [ɛkstravagɑ̃s] **nf** extravagance.

extravagant**, **e [ɛkstravagɑ̃, ɑ̃t] **adj** extravagant / [idée, propos] wild.

extraverti**, **e [ɛkstravɛrti] **nm, f** & **adj** extrovert.

extrême [ɛkstrɛm] ■ **nm** extreme ▸ **d'un extrême à l'autre** from one extreme to the other.
■ **adj** extreme / [limite] furthest ▸ **les sports extrêmes** extreme sports.

extrêmement [ɛkstrɛmmɑ̃] **adv** extremely.

extrême-onction [ɛkstrɛmɔ̃ksjɔ̃] (pl **extrêmes-onctions**) **nf** last rites *pl*, extreme unction.

Extrême-Orient [ɛkstrɛmɔrjɑ̃] **nm : l'Extrême-Orient** the Far East.

extrémiste [ɛkstremist] **nmf** & **adj** extremist.

extrémité [ɛkstremite] **nf 1.** [bout] end **2.** [situation critique] straits *pl* ▸ **à la dernière extrémité** *fig* at death's door.

exubérant**, **e [ɛgzyberɑ̃, ɑ̃t] **adj 1.** [personne] exuberant **2.** [végétation] luxuriant.

exulter [3] [ɛgzylte] **vi** to exult.

exutoire [ɛgzytwar] **nm** outlet.

ex-voto [ɛksvɔto] **nm inv** votive offering.

eye-liner [ajlajnɛr] (pl **eye-liners**) **nm** eyeliner.

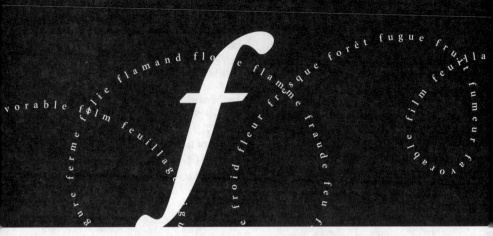

f, F [ɛf] **nm inv** f, F ▸ **F3** three-room flat *UK* *ou* apartment *US*.
◆ ***F*** **1.** abr de ***femme*** **2.** abr de ***féminin*** **3.** (abr écrite de ***Fahrenheit***) F **4.** (abr écrite de ***franc***) F, Fr.

fa [fa] **nm inv** F / [chanté] fa, fah *UK*.

FAB [fab] (abr de ***franco à bord***) FOB, fob.

fable [fabl] **nf** fable.

fabricant, e [fabrikɑ̃, ɑ̃t] **nm, f** manufacturer.

fabrication [fabrikasjɔ̃] **nf** manufacture, manufacturing ▸ **de fabrication artisanale** hand-made.

fabrique [fabrik] **nf** [usine] factory.

fabriquer [3] [fabrike] **vt** **1.** [confectionner] to manufacture, to make ▸ **fabriqué en France** made in France **2.** *fam* [faire] **: qu'est-ce que tu fabriques?** what are you up to? **3.** [inventer] to fabricate.

fabulation [fabylasjɔ̃] **nf** fabrication.

fabuleusement [fabyløzmɑ̃] **adv** fabulously.

fabuleux, euse [fabylø, øz] **adj** fabulous.

fac [fak] **nf** *fam* college, uni *UK*.

FAC (abr de ***franc d'avarie commune***) **adj** FGA, fga.

façade [fasad] **nf** *litt* & *fig* facade.

face [fas] **nf** **1.** [visage] face ▸ **perdre la face** to lose face ▸ **sauver la face** to save face ▸ **se voiler la face** *littéraire* to avert one's gaze **2.** [côté] side ▸ **disquette double face** double-sided disk ▸ **examiner un problème sous toutes ses faces** to consider every aspect of a problem ▸ **faire face à qqch** [maison] to face sthg, to be opposite sthg / *fig* [affronter] to face up to sthg ▸ **de face** from the front ▸ **photo/portrait de face** ART & PHOTO full-face photograph/portrait ▸ **vue de face** ARCHIT front view *ou* elevation ▸ **loge de face** THÉÂTRE box facing the stage ▸ **en face de qqn/qqch** opposite sb/sthg ▸ **sa maison est en face de l'église** his house is opposite *ou* faces the church ▸ **d'en face** across the street, opposite ▸ **face à** facing ▸ **face à qqch** [situation] faced with sthg ▸ **face à face** face to face ▸ **regarder qqch en face** *fig* to face up to sthg ▸ **regarder la mort en face** to face up to death ▸ **regarder les choses en face** to face facts ▸ **je lui ai dit la vérité en face** I told him the truth to his face **3.** [dans l'espace] in front of ▸ **face à l'ennemi/aux médias** faced with the enemy/media.

face-à-face [fasafas] **nm inv** debate.

facétie [fasesi] **nf** practical joke.

facétieux, euse [fasesjø, øz] ■ **adj** playful.
■ **nm, f** joker.

facette [fasɛt] **nf** *litt* & *fig* facet.

fâché, e [faʃe] **adj** **1.** [en colère] angry / [contrarié] annoyed **2.** [brouillé] on bad terms.

fâcher [3] [faʃe] **vt** [mettre en colère] to anger, to make angry / [contrarier] to annoy, to make annoyed.
◆ ***se fâcher*** **vp** **1.** [se mettre en colère] **: se fâcher (contre qqn)** to get angry (with sb) **2.** [se brouiller] **: se fâcher (avec qqn)** to fall out (with sb).

fâcherie [faʃri] **nf** disagreement.

fâcheusement [faʃøzmɑ̃] **adv** [malheureusement] unfortunately / [désagréablement] unpleasantly.

fâcheux, euse [faʃø, øz] **adj** unfortunate.

facho [faʃo] **nmf** & **adj** *fam* fascist.

facial, e, aux [fasjal, o] **adj** facial.

faciès [fasjɛs] **nm** *péj* [visage] features *pl*.

facile [fasil] **adj** **1.** [aisé] easy ▸ **facile à faire/prononcer** easy to do/pronounce **2.** [peu subtil] facile **3.** [conciliant] easy-going ▸ **facile à vivre** easy to get on with.

facilement [fasilmɑ̃] **adv** easily.

facilité [fasilite] **nf** **1.** [de tâche, problème] easiness ▸ **céder à la facilité** *péj* to take the easy way out
2. [capacité] ease ▸ **avoir beaucoup de facilité pour** to have a gift for ▸ **avec facilité** easily, with ease ▸ **avec une grande facilité** with the greatest of ease
3. [dispositions] aptitude
4. COMM **: facilités de caisse** overdraft facility ▸ **facilités de crédit** credit facilities ▸ **facilité de vente** *ou* **d'écoulement** saleability ▸ **facilités de paiement** easy (payment) terms, payment facilities.

faciliter [3] [fasilite] **vt** to make easier.

façon [fasɔ̃] **nf** **1.** [manière] way ▸ **d'une façon générale** generally speaking ▸ **de façon systématique** systematically

▸ **sa façon d'être** the way she is ▸ **façon de parler** figure of speech **2.** [travail] work / COUT making-up **3.** [imitation] **: façon cuir** imitation leather.
◆ ***façons*** **nfpl** manner *sg*, ways ▸ **en voilà des façons!** manners!, what a way to behave! ▸ **faire des façons** to make a fuss ▸ **sans plus de façons** without further ado.
◆ ***à façon*** **loc adj** [artisan] jobbing.
◆ ***à ma façon, à sa façon*** ■ **loc adj : une recette à ma/ta façon** a recipe of mine/yours ▸ **un tour à sa façon** one of his tricks.
■ **loc adv : chante-le à ta façon** sing it your way *ou* any way you like.
◆ ***de façon à*** **loc prép** so as to.
◆ ***de façon que*** *(+ subjonctif)* **loc conj** so that.
◆ ***de toute façon*** **loc adv** anyway, in any case.
◆ ***sans façon*** ■ **loc adj** unpretentious.
■ **loc adv 1.** [sincèrement] really, honestly / [accepter] without fuss **2.** [familièrement] **: elle m'a pris le bras sans façon *ou* façons** she took my arm quite naturally.

façonner [3] [fasɔne] **vt 1.** [travailler, former] to shape **2.** [fabriquer] to manufacture, to make.

fac-similé [faksimile] (pl **fac-similés**) **nm** facsimile.

facteur, trice [faktœr, tris] **nm, f** [des postes] postman (f postwoman) *UK*, mailman *US*, mail *ou* letter carrier *US*.
◆ ***facteur*** **nm 1.** MUS [fabricant] maker ▸ **facteur d'orgues** organ-builder **2.** [élément & MATH] factor ▸ **facteur rhésus** MÉD Rhesus factor ▸ **facteur vent** *Québec* windchill factor **3.** ÉCON **: facteur coût** cost factor.

factice [faktis] **adj** artificial.

faction [faksjɔ̃] **nf 1.** [groupe] faction **2.** MIL **: être en *ou* de faction** to be on guard (duty) *ou* on sentry duty.

factoring [faktɔriŋ] **m** FIN factoring.

factotum [faktɔtɔm] **nm** odd-job man *UK*, odd jobber *US*.

factuel, elle [faktɥɛl] **adj** factual.

facturation [faktyrasjɔ̃] **nf 1.** [action] invoicing **2.** [bureau] invoice office.

facture [faktyr] **nf 1.** COMM invoice / [de gaz, d'électricité] bill **2.** ART technique **3.** MUS [fabrication] making.

facturer [3] [faktyre] **vt** COMM to invoice.

facturette [faktyrɛt] **nf** (credit card sales) receipt, record of charge form.

facultatif, ive [fakyltatif, iv] **adj** optional.

facultativement [fakyltativmɑ̃] **adv** optionally.

faculté [fakylte] **nf 1.** [don & UNIV] faculty ▸ **faculté de lettres/de droit/de médecine** Faculty of Arts/Law/Medicine **2.** [possibilité] freedom **3.** [pouvoir] power.
◆ ***facultés*** **nfpl** (mental) faculties.

fada [fada] *fam* ■ **nm** nutcase.
■ **adj** nuts.

fadaises [fadɛz] **nfpl** drivel *(U)*.

fade [fad] **adj 1.** [sans saveur] bland **2.** [sans intérêt] insipid.

fagot [fago] **nm** bundle of sticks ▸ **de derrière les fagots** *fig* kept for a special occasion.

fagoté, e [fagɔte] **adj** *fam* dressed.

fagoter [3] [fagɔte] **vt** *fam* to dress up.
◆ ***se fagoter*** **vp** *fam* to dress o.s. up.

Fahrenheit [farɛnajt] **npr** Fahrenheit.

faible [fɛbl] ■ **adj 1.** [gén] weak ▸ **avoir la vue faible** to have weak *ou* poor eyesight ▸ **être de faible constitution** to have a weak constitution ▸ **être faible en maths** to be not very good at maths *UK ou* math *US* **2.** [petit - montant, proportion] small ▸ **avoir de faibles chances de succès** to have slight *ou* slender chances of succeeding / [- revenu] low **3.** [lueur, bruit] faint.
■ **nmf** weak person ▸ **faible d'esprit** feeble-minded person ▸ **c'est un faible** he's weak-willed.
■ **nm** weakness ▸ **avoir un faible pour qqch** to be partial to sthg ▸ **avoir un faible pour qqn** to have a soft spot for sb.

faiblement [fɛbləmɑ̃] **adv 1.** [mollement] weakly, feebly **2.** [imperceptiblement] faintly **3.** [peu] slightly.

faiblesse [fɛblɛs] **nf 1.** [gén] weakness ▸ **faiblesse d'esprit** feeble-mindedness **2.** [petitesse] smallness.

faiblir [32] [feblir] **vi 1.** [personne, monnaie] to weaken **2.** [forces] to diminish, to fail **3.** [tempête, vent] to die down.

faïence [fajɑ̃s] **nf** earthenware.

faignant, e = ***fainéant***.

faille [faj] ■ ➤ ***falloir***.
■ **nf 1.** GÉOL fault **2.** [défaut] flaw.

faillible [fajibl] **adj** fallible.

faillir [46] [fajir] **vi 1.** [manquer] **: faillir à** [promesse] not to keep / [devoir] not to do **2.** [être sur le point de] **: faillir faire qqch** to nearly *ou* almost do sthg.

faillite [fajit] **nf** FIN bankruptcy ▸ **faire faillite** to go bankrupt ▸ **en faillite** bankrupt.

faim [fɛ̃] **nf** hunger ▸ **avoir faim** to be hungry ▸ **avoir faim de** *fig* to hunger for ▸ **mourir de faim** to be starving ▸ **ne pas manger à sa faim** not to eat one's fill ▸ **rester sur sa faim** to be still hungry / *fig* to be unsatisfied *ou* disappointed ▸ **avoir une faim de loup** to be starving.

fainéant, e [feneɑ̃, ɑ̃t], ***feignant, e, faignant, e*** [fɛɲɑ̃, ɑ̃t] ■ **adj** lazy, idle.
■ **nm, f** lazybones.

fainéanter [3] [feneɑ̃te] **vi** to laze around.

faire [109] [fɛr] ■ **vt 1.** [fabriquer, préparer] to make ▸ **faire une maison** to build a house ▸ **faire une tarte/du café/un film** to make a tart/coffee/a film ▸ **qu'as-tu fait (à manger) pour ce soir ?** what have you made for dinner tonight? ▸ **il sait tout faire** he can turn his hand to anything ▸ **faire qqch de qqch** [transformer] to make sthg into sthg ▸ **et ta robe bleue ? – j'en ai fait une jupe** what about your blue dress ? – I made it into a skirt ▸ **faire qqch de qqn** *fig* to make sthg of sb ▸ **il veut en faire un avocat** he wants him to be a lawyer, he wants to make a lawyer of him
2. [s'occuper à, entreprendre] to do ▸ **qu'est-ce qu'il fait dans la vie?** what does he do (for a living)? ▸ **que fais-tu dimanche?** what are you doing on Sunday? ▸ **qu'est-ce que je peux faire pour vous aider?** what can I do to help you?

3. [étudier] to do ▸ **faire de l'anglais/des maths/du droit** to do English/maths/law ▸ **elle voulait faire l'ENA** she wanted to go to the ENA
4. [sport, musique] to play ▸ **faire du football/de la clarinette** to play football/the clarinet
5. [effectuer] to do ▸ **faire le ménage** to do the housework ▸ **faire la cuisine** to cook, to do the cooking ▸ **faire la lessive** to do the washing ▸ **faire la tête** *ou* **la gueule** *tfam* to sulk
6. [occasionner] **: faire de la peine à qqn** to hurt sb ▸ **faire du mal à** to harm ▸ **faire du bruit** to make a noise ▸ **ça m'a fait quelque chose** it affected me ▸ **ça ne fait rien** it doesn't matter
7. [tenir le rôle de] to be, to play ▸ **il fait le Père Noël dans les rues** he goes around the streets disguised as Father Christmas
8. [imiter] **: faire le sourd/l'innocent** to act deaf/(the) innocent
9. [calcul, mesure] **: un et un font deux** one and one are *ou* make two ▸ **ça fait combien (de kilomètres) jusqu'à la mer?** how far is it to the sea? ▸ **la table fait 2 mètres de long** the table is 2 metres *UK ou* meters *US* long ▸ **faire du 38** to take a size 38
10. [en tant que verbe substitutif] to do ▸ **je lui ai dit de prendre une échelle mais il ne l'a pas fait** I told him to use a ladder but he didn't ▸ **faites!** please do!
11. [coûter] to be, to cost ▸ **ça vous fait 10 euros en tout** that'll be 10 euros altogether
12. [dire] **: «tiens», fit-elle** "really", she said ▸ **il fit oui/non de la tête** he nodded/he shook his head
13. : ne faire que [faire sans cesse] to do nothing but ▸ **elle ne fait que bavarder** she does nothing but gossip, she's always gossiping ▸ **je ne fais que passer** I've just popped in.
■ **vi** [agir] to do, to act ▸ **fais vite!** hurry up! ▸ **que faire?** what is to be done? ▸ **tu ferais bien d'aller voir ce qui se passe** you ought to *ou* you'd better go and see what's happening ▸ **faire comme chez soi** to make o.s. at home ▸ **ça commence à bien faire!** enough is enough!
■ **v att** [avoir l'air] to look ▸ **faire démodé/joli** to look old-fashioned/pretty ▸ **ça fait jeune** it makes you look young.
■ **v impers 1.** [climat, temps] **: il fait beau/froid** it's fine/cold ▸ **il fait 20 degrés** it's 20 degrees ▸ **il fait jour/nuit** it's light/dark ▸ **il fait bon se reposer** it's *ou* it feels good to have a rest
2. [exprime la durée, la distance] **: ça fait six mois que je ne l'ai pas vu** it's six months since I last saw him ▸ **ça fait deux mois que je fais du portugais** I've been going to Portuguese classes for two months ▸ **ça fait 30 kilomètres qu'on roule sans phares** we've been driving without lights for 30 kilometres *UK ou* kilometers *US*
▸▸ **c'est bien fait pour toi** it serves you right.
■ **v aux 1.** [à l'actif] to make ▸ **faire baisser** ÉCON [prix] to deflate ▸ **faire démarrer une voiture** to start a car ▸ **faire tomber qqch** to make sthg fall ▸ **l'aspirine fait baisser la fièvre** aspirin brings down the temperature ▸ **faire travailler qqn** to make sb work ▸ **faire traverser la rue à un aveugle** to help a blind man cross the road
2. [au passif] **: faire faire qqch (par qqn)** to have sthg done (by sb) ▸ **faire réparer sa voiture/nettoyer ses vitres** to have one's car repaired/one's windows cleaned.

◆ ***se faire*** **vp 1.** [avoir lieu] to take place
2. [être à la mode] to be in ▸ **les salopettes ne se font plus** dungarees *UK ou* overalls *US* are out of fashion
3. [être convenable] **: ça ne se fait pas (de faire qqch)** it's not done (to do sthg)
4. [devenir] **: se faire** *(+ adj)* to get, to become ▸ **il se fait tard** it's getting late ▸ **se faire beau** to make o.s. beautiful
5. *(+ nom)* [causer] **: se faire mal** to hurt o.s. ▸ **se faire des amis** to make friends ▸ **se faire une idée sur qqch** to get some idea about sthg
6. *(+ infinitif)* **: se faire écraser** to get run over ▸ **se faire opérer** to have an operation ▸ **se faire aider (par qqn)** to get help (from sb) ▸ **se faire faire un costume** to have a suit made (for o.s.) ▸ **se faire tuer** to get o.s. killed
▸▸ **comment se fait-il que...?** how is it that...?, how come...? ▸ **s'en faire** to worry ▸ **ne vous en faites pas!** don't worry!
◆ ***se faire à*** **v + prep** to get used to.

faire-part [fɛrpar] **nm inv** announcement ▸ **faire-part de naissance/mariage** birth/wedding announcement.

faire-valoir [fɛrvalwar] **nm inv** [personne] foil.

fair-play [fɛrplɛ] **adj inv** sporting ▸ **se montrer fair-play** to be sporting.

fais, fait ➤ ***faire.***

faisable [fəzabl] **adj** feasible.

faisan, e [fəzɑ̃, ɑn] **nm, f** pheasant.

faisandé, e [fəzɑ̃de] **adj** CULIN high.

faisceau, x [fɛso] **nm 1.** [rayon] beam ▸ **faisceau cathodique** cathode ray ▸ **faisceau électronique** electron beam ▸ **faisceau hertzien** radio beam ▸ **faisceau lumineux** beam of light **2.** [fagot] bundle ▸ **faisceau de fils** wiring harness ▸ **faisceau de preuves** *fig* accumulation of evidence.

faiseur, euse [fəzœr, øz] **nm, f** maker ▸ **faiseur d'embarras** fusspot.

faisons ➤ ***faire.***

faisselle [fɛsɛl] **nf 1.** [récipient] cheese basket **2.**[fromage] fromage frais *(packaged in its own draining basket).*

fait, e [fɛ, fɛt] ■ **pp** ➤ ***faire.***
■ **adj 1.** [fabriqué] made ▸ **être fait pour** *litt & fig* to be made *ou* meant for ▸ **il n'est pas fait pour mener cette vie** he's not cut out for this kind of life ▸ **ils sont faits l'un pour l'autre** they are made for each other ▸ **fait sur mesure** made to measure **2.** [physique] **: bien fait** well-built ▸ **une femme fort bien faite** a very good-looking woman
3. [fromage] ripe
▸▸ **c'est bien fait pour lui** (it) serves him right ▸ **c'en est fait de nous** we're done for.
◆ ***fait*** **nm 1.** [acte] act ▸ **mettre qqn devant le fait accompli** to present sb with a fait accompli ▸ **prendre qqn sur le fait** to catch sb in the act ▸ **prendre fait et cause pour qqn** to side with sb ▸ **venons-en au fait** let's come *ou* get to the point ▸ **faits et gestes** doings, actions ▸ **hauts faits** heroic deeds **2.** [événement] event ▸ **faits divers** news in brief ▸ **fait notoire** fact of common knowledge

▸ **racontez-nous les faits** tell us what happened **3.** [réalité] fact ▸ **le fait est que...** the fact is (that)... ▸ **c'est un fait** it's a (matter of) fact.

◆ ***au fait*** **loc adv** by the way ▸ **au fait, on pourrait peut-être y aller à pied?** by the way, couldn't we walk there?

◆ ***en fait*** **loc adv** in (actual) fact ▸ **en fait, il n'est pas mon père** actually *ou* in fact he isn't my father.

◆ ***en fait de*** **loc prép** by way of ▸ **en fait de chien, c'était un loup** it wasn't a dog at all: it was a wolf.

◆ ***du fait de*** **loc prép** because of.

faîte [fɛt] **nm 1.** [de toit] ridge **2.** [d'arbre] top **3.** *fig* [sommet] pinnacle.

faites ➤ *faire*.

faîtière [fɛtjɛr] **nf** skylight.

fait-tout (pl fait-tout), ***faitout*** (pl faitouts) [fɛtu] **nm** stewpan.

fakir [fakir] **nm** fakir.

falaise [falɛz] **nf** cliff.

falbalas [falbala] **nmpl** furbelows.

fallacieux, ***euse*** [falasjø, øz] **adj 1.** [promesse] false **2.** [argument] fallacious.

falloir [69] [falwar] **v impers : il me faut du temps** I need (some) time ▸ **il lui faudra de l'énergie** he'll need (a lot of) energy ▸ **il te faut un peu de repos** you need some rest ▸ **faut-il vraiment tout ce matériel?** is all this equipment really necessary? ▸ **c'est tout ce qu'il vous fallait?** [dans une boutique] anything else? ▸ **il faut que tu partes** you must go *ou* leave, you'll have to go *ou* leave ▸ **il faut toujours qu'elle intervienne!** she always has to interfere! ▸ **il faut agir** we/you *etc* must act ▸ **il faut faire attention** we/you *etc* must be careful, we'll/you'll *etc* have to be careful ▸ **s'il le faut** if necessary ▸ **il ne fallait pas** *fam* [en recevant un cadeau] you shouldn't have ▸ **il faut le voir pour le croire!** *fam* it has to be seen to be believed! ▸ **il a fallu que le téléphone sonne juste à ce moment-là!** the phone had to ring just then!

◆ ***s'en falloir*** **v impers : il s'en faut de peu pour qu'il puisse acheter cette maison** he can almost afford to buy the house ▸ **il s'en faut de 20 cm pour que l'armoire tienne dans le coin** the cupboard is 20 cm too big to fit into the corner ▸ **il s'en faut de beaucoup pour qu'il ait l'examen** it'll take a lot for him to pass the exam ▸ **peu s'en est fallu qu'il démissionne** he very nearly resigned, he came close to resigning ▸ **tant s'en faut** far from it, on the contrary.

fallu [faly] **pp inv** ➤ *falloir*.

falot, ***e*** [falo, ɔt] **adj** dull.

◆ ***falot*** **nm** lantern.

falsificateur, ***trice*** [falsifikatœr, tris] **nm, f** falsifier, forger.

falsification [falsifikasjɔ̃] **nf 1.** [de document] forgery / [de monnaie] counterfeiting **2.** [de produit alimentaire] adulteration.

falsifier [9] [falsifje] **vt 1.** [document, signature, faits] to falsify **2.** [pensée, paroles] to misrepresent **3.** [produit alimentaire] to adulterate.

famé, ***e*** [fame] **adj : mal famé** with a (bad) reputation.

famélique [famelik] **adj** half-starved.

fameusement [famøzmɑ̃] **adv** *fam* really.

fameux, ***euse*** [famø, øz] **adj 1.** [célèbre] famous **2.** *fam* [remarquable] great ▸ **pas fameux** not up to much, nothing great.

familial, ***e***, ***aux*** [familjal, o] **adj** family *(avant n)*.

◆ ***familiale*** **nf** estate car *UK*, station wagon *US*.

familiarisation [familjarizasjɔ̃] **nf** familiarization.

familiariser [3] [familjarize] **vt : familiariser qqn avec** to familiarize sb with.

◆ ***se familiariser*** **vp : se familiariser avec** to get used to.

familiarité [familjarite] **nf** familiarity.

◆ ***familiarités*** **nfpl** liberties.

familier, ***ère*** [familje, ɛr] **adj 1.** [connu] familiar ▸ **le problème m'est familier** I am familiar with the problem ▸ **ce spectacle/bruit lui était familier** it looked/sounded familiar to him **2.** [apprivoisé] domestic, tame **3.** *péj* [cavalier] overfamiliar ▸ **je n'aime pas les gens trop familiers** I don't like people who are overfamiliar.

◆ ***familier*** **nm** regular (customer) ▸ **les familiers de ce café** this café's regulars.

famille [famij] **nf** family / [ensemble des parents] relatives, relations ▸ **de bonne famille** of good family ▸ **fonder une famille** to start a family ▸ **c'est** *ou* **cela tient de famille** it runs in the family, it's in the blood ▸ **c'est une famille de danseurs** they're all dancers in their family, they're a family of dancers ▸ **ils sont de la même famille** they're related ▸ **passer Noël en famille** to spend Christmas with one's family *ou* at home ▸ **prévenir la famille** to inform the relatives / DR to inform the next of kin ▸ **famille d'accueil** [lors d'un séjour linguistique] host family / [pour enfant en difficulté] foster home ▸ **famille monoparentale** single-parent *ou* lone-parent *ou* one-parent *UK* family ▸ **famille nombreuse** large family ▸ **famille recomposée** blended family ▸ **famille de langues** group of languages ▸ **de la même famille politique** of the same political persuasion.

famine [famin] **nf** famine ▸ **crier famine** *fig* to complain of one's poverty.

fan [fan] **nmf** *fam* fan.

fanal, ***aux*** [fanal, o] **nm 1.** [de phare] beacon **2.** [de train] headlight **3.** [lanterne] lantern.

fanatique [fanatik] ■ **nmf** fanatic.

■ **adj** fanatical.

fanatiser [3] [fanatize] **vt** to make a fanatic out of.

fanatisme [fanatism] **nm** fanaticism.

fan-club [fanklœb] (pl **fans-clubs**) **nm 1.** [d'un artiste] fan club **2.** *hum* admirers, supporters, fan club *fig*.

fane [fan] **nf 1.** [de carotte] top **2.** [d'arbre] fallen leaf.

faner [3] [fane] ■ **vt** [altérer] to fade.

■ **vi 1.** [fleur] to wither **2.** [beauté, couleur] to fade.

◆ ***se faner*** **vp 1.** [fleur] to wither **2.** [beauté, couleur] to fade.

fanfare [fɑ̃far] **nf 1.** [orchestre] brass band **2.** [musique] fanfare ▸ **en fanfare** noisy.

fanfaron, ***onne*** [fɑ̃farɔ̃, ɔn] ■ **adj** boastful.

■ **nm, f** braggart.

fanfaronnade [fɑ̃farɔnad] **nf** boasting *(U)*.

fanfreluche [fɑ̃frəlyʃ] **nf** trimming.

fange [fɑ̃ʒ] **nf** *littéraire* mire ▸ **traîner qqn dans la fange** to drag sb through the mire.

fanion [fanjɔ̃] **nm** pennant.

fantaisie [fɑ̃tezi] ■ **nf 1.** [caprice] whim ▸ **et s'il lui prend la fantaisie de partir?** what if he should take it into his head to leave? ▸ **cette (petite) fantaisie va vous coûter cher** *péj* you'll regret this little extravagance **2.** *(U)* [goût] fancy **3.** [imagination] imagination ▸ **de fantaisie** imaginary ▸ **être plein de fantaisie** to be fanciful ▸ **le récit relève de la plus haute fantaisie** the story is highly imaginative ▸ **manquer de fantaisie** [personne] to lack imagination, to be lacking in imagination / [vie] to be monotonous *ou* uneventful **4.** MUS fantasia.
■ **adj inv : chapeau fantaisie** fancy hat ▸ **bijoux fantaisie** fake/costume jewellery *UK ou* jewelry *US*.

fantaisiste [fɑ̃tezist] ■ **nmf** entertainer.
■ **adj 1.** [fumiste] dilettante **2.** [bizarre] fanciful.

fantasmagorique [fɑ̃tasmagɔrik] **adj** phantasmagorical, extraordinary.

fantasme [fɑ̃tasm] **nm** fantasy.

fantasmer [3] [fɑ̃tasme] **vi** to fantasize.

fantasque [fɑ̃task] **adj 1.** [personne] whimsical **2.** [humeur] capricious **3.** [chose] fantastic.

fantassin [fɑ̃tasɛ̃] **nm** infantryman.

fantastique [fɑ̃tastik] ■ **adj** fantastic.
■ **nm : le fantastique** the fantastic.

fantoche [fɑ̃tɔʃ] ■ **adj** puppet *(avant n)*.
■ **nm** puppet.

fantomatique [fɑ̃tɔmatik] **adj** ghostly.

fantôme [fɑ̃tom] ■ **nm** ghost.
■ **adj 1.** [spectral] ghostly **2.** [inexistant] phantom.

FAO **nf 1.** (abr de ***fabrication assistée par ordinateur***) CAM **2.** (abr de ***Food and Agriculture Organisation***) FAO.

faon [fɑ̃] **nm** fawn.

FAP (abr de ***franc d'avarie particulière***) **adj** FPA, fpa.

FAQ [fak] (abr de ***Frequently Asked Questions***) **nf** FAQ.

far [far] **nm : far breton** *sweet flan containing plums.*

faramineux, ***euse*** [faraminø, øz] **adj** *fam* **1.** [prix] astronomical **2.** [génial] fantastic.

farandole [farɑ̃dɔl] **nf** farandole.

farce [fars] **nf 1.** CULIN stuffing **2.** [blague] (practical) joke ▸ **faire une farce à qqn** to play a (practical) joke on sb ▸ **farces et attrapes** jokes and novelties **3.** LITTÉR farce.

farceur, ***euse*** [farsœr, øz] **nm, f** (practical) joker.

farci, ***e*** [farsi] **adj 1.** CULIN stuffed **2.** *fig* [plein] stuffed, crammed.

farcir [32] [farsir] **vt 1.** CULIN to stuff **2.** [remplir] **: farcir qqch de** to stuff *ou* cram sthg with.
◆ ***se farcir*** **vp** *fam* **1.** [faire] **: se farcir qqch** to get stuck with sthg **2.** [supporter] **: se farcir qqn** to put up with sb **3.** [manger] **: se farcir qqch** to scoff *UK ou* scarf *US* sthg.

fard [far] **nm** make-up ▸ **fard à joues** blusher ▸ **fard à paupières** eyeshadow ▸ **piquer un fard** *fam fig* to blush.

fardeau, ***x*** [fardo] **nm** [poids] load / *fig* burden ▸ **fardeau de la dette** debt burden.

farder [3] [farde] **vt 1.** [maquiller] to make up **2.** *fig* [masquer] to disguise.
◆ ***se farder*** **vp** to make o.s. up, to put on one's make-up.

farfadet [farfadɛ] **nm** sprite.

farfelu, ***e*** [farfəly] *fam* ■ **adj** weird.
■ **nm, f** weirdo.

farfouiller [3] [farfuje] **vi** *fam* to rummage.

farine [farin] **nf** flour ▸ **farine animale** animal flour ▸ **rouler qqn dans la farine** *fig* to take sb for a ride.

fariner [3] [farine] **vt** to flour, to sprinkle flour over ▸ **farinez le moule** dredge the tin with flour, flour the tin all over.

farineux, ***euse*** [farinø, øz] **adj 1.** [aspect, goût] floury **2.** [aliment] farinaceous.
◆ ***farineux*** **nm** starchy food.

farniente [farnjɛnte] **nm** idleness.

farouche [faruʃ] **adj 1.** [animal] wild, not tame / [personne] shy, withdrawn **2.** [sentiment] fierce.

farouchement [faruʃmɑ̃] **adv** fiercely.

fart [far(t)] **nm** (ski) wax.

farter [3] [farte] **vt** to wax.

fascicule [fasikyl] **nm** part, instalment *UK*, installment *US*.

fascinant, ***e*** [fasinɑ̃, ɑ̃t] **adj 1.** [regard] alluring, captivating **2.** [personne, histoire] fascinating.

fascination [fasinasjɔ̃] **nf** fascination.

fasciner [3] [fasine] **vt** to fascinate.

fascisant, ***e*** [faʃizɑ̃, ɑ̃t] **adj** fascistic.

fascisme [faʃism] **nm** fascism.

fasciste [faʃist] **nmf & adj** fascist.

fasse, ***fassions*** ➤ ***faire***.

faste [fast] ■ **nm** splendour *UK*, splendor *US*.
■ **adj** [favorable] lucky.

fast-food [fastfud] (pl **fast-foods**) **nm** fast food.

fastidieux, ***euse*** [fastidjø, øz] **adj** boring.

fastoche [fastɔʃ] **adj** *fam* dead easy ▸ **c'est fastoche** it's dead easy, it's a doddle *UK*.

fastueux, ***euse*** [fastyø, øz] **adj** luxurious.

fatal, ***e*** [fatal] **adj 1.** [mortel, funeste] fatal **2.** [inévitable] inevitable.

fatalement [fatalmɑ̃] **adv** inevitably.

fataliste [fatalist] ■ **nmf** fatalist.
■ **adj** fatalistic.

fatalité [fatalite] **nf 1.** [destin] fate **2.** [inéluctabilité] inevitability.

fatidique [fatidik] **adj** fateful.

fatigant[1]**, *e*** [fatigɑ̃, ɑ̃t] **adj 1.** [épuisant] tiring **2.** [ennuyeux] tiresome.

> PARONYME / CONFUSABLE
> **fatigant**
> Pour traduire **fatigant**, ne confondez pas *tiring* qui signifie épuisant, et *tiresome* qui signifie ennuyeux.

fatiguant[2] [fatigɑ̃] **p prés** ➤ ***fatiguer***.

fatigue [fatig] **nf** tiredness ▸ **tomber de fatigue, être mort de fatigue** to be dead tired.

fatigué*, *e [fatige] **adj** tired / [cœur, yeux] strained.

fatiguer [3] [fatige] ■ **vt 1.** [épuiser] to tire **2.** [cœur, yeux] to strain **3.** [ennuyer] to wear out.
■ **vi 1.** [personne] to grow tired **2.** [moteur] to strain.
◆ ***se fatiguer*** **vp** to get tired ▸ **se fatiguer de qqch** to get tired of sthg ▸ **se fatiguer à faire qqch** to wear o.s. out doing sthg.

fatras [fatra] **nm** jumble.

fatuité [fatɥite] **nf** *littéraire* complacency.

faubourg [fobur] **nm** suburb.

fauché*, *e [foʃe] **adj** *fam* broke, hard-up.

faucher [3] [foʃe] **vt 1.** [couper - herbe, blé] to cut **2.** *fam* [voler] **: faucher qqch à qqn** to steal *ou* pinch *UK* sthg from sb **3.** [piéton] to run over **4.** *fig* [suj: mort, maladie] to cut down.

faucille [fosij] **nf** sickle.

faucon [fokɔ̃] **nm** hawk.

faudra ➤ ***falloir***.

faufil [fofil] **nm** tacking *ou* basting thread.

faufiler [3] [fofile] **vt** to tack, to baste.
◆ ***se faufiler*** **vp : se faufiler dans** to slip into ▸ **se faufiler entre** to thread one's way between.

faune [fon] ■ **nf 1.** [animaux] fauna **2.** *péj* [personnes] **: la faune qui fréquente ce bar** the sort of people who hang around that bar.
■ **nm** MYTHOL faun.

faussaire [fosɛr] **nmf** forger.

fausse [fos] **f** ➤ ***faux***.

faussement [fosmɑ̃] **adv 1.** [à tort] wrongly **2.** [prétendument] falsely.

fausser [3] [fose] **vt 1.** [déformer] to bend **2.** [rendre faux] to distort.
◆ ***se fausser*** **vp** [voix] to become strained.

fausset [fosɛ] ➤ ***voix***.

fausseté [foste] **nf 1.** [hypocrisie] duplicity **2.** [de jugement, d'idée] falsity.

faut ➤ ***falloir***.

faute [fot] **nf 1.** [erreur] mistake, error ▸ **faire une faute** to make a mistake *ou* an error ▸ **faute de calcul** miscalculation ▸ **faute de frappe** [à la machine à écrire] typing error / [à l'ordinateur] keying error ▸ **faute de goût** error of taste ▸ **faute de grammaire** grammatical error *ou* mistake ▸ **faute d'inattention** careless mistake ▸ **faute d'orthographe** spelling mistake
2. [méfait, infraction] offence *UK*, offense *US* ▸ **commettre une faute** to go wrong ▸ **prendre qqn en faute** to catch sb out *UK* ▸ **faute grave** serious offence *UK ou* offense *US* ▸ **faute professionnelle** professional misdemeanour *UK ou* misdemeanor *US*
3. TENNIS fault / FOOTBALL foul
4. [responsabilité] fault ▸ **de ma/ta** *etc* **faute** my/your *etc* fault ▸ **par la faute de qqn** because of sb ▸ **imputer la faute à qqn** to lay the blame at sb's door ▸ **rejeter la faute sur qqn** to shift the blame onto sb.
◆ ***faute de*** **loc prép** for want *ou* lack of ▸ **faute de mieux** for want *ou* lack of anything better ▸ **faute de pouvoir aller au théâtre, il a regardé la télévision** since he couldn't go to the theatre he watched television (instead).
◆ ***sans faute*** ■ **loc adv** without fail.
■ **loc adj** faultless ▸ **faire un parcours sans faute** [coureur] to run a perfect race / [dans sa carrière] not to put a foot wrong.

fauteuil [fotœj] **nm 1.** [siège] armchair ▸ **fauteuil à bascule** rocking chair ▸ **fauteuil roulant** wheelchair **2.** [de théâtre] seat ▸ **fauteuil d'orchestre** seat in the stalls *UK ou* orchestra *US* **3.** [de président] chair / [d'académicien] seat.

fauteur*, *trice [fotœr, tris] **nm, f : fauteur de troubles** troublemaker.

fautif*, *ive [fotif, iv] ■ **adj 1.** [coupable] guilty **2.** [défectueux] faulty.
■ **nm, f** guilty party.

fauve [fov] ■ **nm 1.** [animal] big cat **2.** [couleur] fawn **3.** ART Fauve.
■ **adj 1.** [animal] wild **2.** [cuir, cheveux] tawny **3.** ART Fauvist.

fauvette [fovɛt] **nf** warbler.

faux*, *fausse [fo, fos] **adj 1.** [incorrect] wrong ▸ **t'as tout faux** *fam* you're completely wrong ▸ **tu te fais une fausse idée de lui** you've got the wrong idea about him **2.** [postiche, mensonger, hypocrite] false ▸ **faux témoignage** DR perjury **3.** [monnaie, papiers] forged, fake ▸ **fabriquer de la fausse monnaie** to counterfeit money / [bijou, marbre] imitation, fake ▸ **c'est un faux Renoir** it's a fake Renoir **4.** [injustifié] **: fausse alerte** false alarm ▸ **c'est un faux problème** that's not an issue (here).
◆ ***faux*** ■ **nm** [document, tableau] forgery, fake ▸ **inculper qqn pour faux et usage de faux** to prosecute sb for forgery and use of forgeries.
■ **nf** scythe.
■ **adv : chanter/jouer faux** MUS to sing/play out of tune ▸ **sonner faux** *fig* not to ring true.
◆ ***faux ami*** **nm** false friend.
◆ ***fausse couche*** **nf** miscarriage ▸ **faire une fausse couche** to have a miscarriage.
◆ ***faux départ*** **nm** *litt* & *fig* false start.
◆ ***faux jeton*** *fam* ■ **adj inv** hypocritical.
■ **nmf** hypocrite.
◆ ***faux pas*** **nm 1.** [en marchant] **: faire un faux pas** to trip, to stumble **2.** [maladresse] faux pas, gaffe.

faux-filet (**pl faux-filets**), ***faux filet*** (**pl faux filets**) [fofilɛ] **nm** sirloin.

faux-fuyant [fofɥijɑ̃] (**pl faux-fuyants**) **nm** excuse.

faux-monnayeur [fomɔnɛjœr] (pl **faux-monnayeurs**) **nm** counterfeiter.

faux-semblant [fosɑ̃blɑ̃] (pl **faux-semblants**) **nm** pretence *UK*, pretense *US*.

faux-sens [fosɑ̃s] **nm inv** mistranslation.

faveur [favœr] **nf** favour *UK*, favor *US* ▸ **faire une faveur à qqn** to do sb a favour *UK ou* favor *US* ▸ **intercéder en faveur de qqn** to intercede on sb's behalf.
◆ ***à la faveur de*** **loc prép** thanks to.
◆ ***en faveur de*** **loc prép** in favour *UK ou* favor *US* of.

favorable [favɔrabl] **adj : favorable (à)** favourable *UK ou* favorable *US* (to).

favorablement [favɔrabləmɑ̃] **adv** favourably *UK*, favorably *US*.

favori, ***ite*** [favɔri, it] **adj & nm, f** favourite *UK*, favorite *US* ▸ **c'est elle la favorite** [dans la famille] she's their darling / [en classe] she's the teacher's pet.
◆ ***favorite*** **nf** HIST **: la favorite** the King's mistress.
◆ ***favoris*** **nmpl** side whiskers.

favoriser [3] [favɔrize] **vt 1.** [avantager] to favour *UK*, to favor *US* **2.** [contribuer à] to promote **3.** [aider] to assist.

favoritisme [favɔritism] **nm** favouritism *UK*, favoritism *US*.

fax [faks] **nm** fax.

faxer [3] [fakse] **vt** to fax.

fayot [fajo] **nm** *fam* [personne] creep, crawler.

fayoter [3] [fajɔte] **vi** *fam* to lick sb's boots ▸ **il est toujours à fayoter** he's always bootlicking.

FB (abr écrite de ***franc belge***) BF.

FBI [ɛfbiaj] (abr de ***Federal Bureau of Investigation***) **nm** FBI.

FC (abr de ***Football club***) **nm** FC.

FCFA (abr écrite de ***franc CFA***) *currency still used in former French colonies in Africa.*

FCFP (abr écrite de ***franc CFP***) *currency still used in former French colonies in the Pacific.*

fébrile [febril] **adj** feverish.

fébrilement [febrilmɑ̃] **adv** feverishly.

fébrilité [febrilite] **nf** feverishness / MÉD febrility.

fécal, ***e, aux*** [fekal, o] ➤ ***matière***.

fécond, ***e*** [fekɔ̃, ɔ̃d] **adj 1.** [femelle, terre, esprit] fertile **2.** [écrivain] prolific **3.** [histoire, situation] **: fécond en qqch** rich in sthg.

fécondation [fekɔ̃dasjɔ̃] **nf** fertilization ▸ **fécondation in vitro** in vitro fertilization.

féconder [3] [fekɔ̃de] **vt 1.** [ovule] to fertilize **2.** [femme, femelle] to impregnate **3.** *littéraire* [fertiliser] to make fertile.

fécondité [fekɔ̃dite] **nf 1.** [gén] fertility **2.** [d'écrivain] productiveness.

fécule [fekyl] **nf** starch.

féculent, ***e*** [fekylɑ̃, ɑ̃t] **adj** starchy.
◆ ***féculent*** **nm** starchy food.

fedayin [fedajin] **nm** fedayee ▸ **les fedayins** the Fedayeen.

fédéral, ***e, aux*** [federal, o] **adj** federal.

fédéralisme [federalism] **nm** federalism.

fédérateur, ***trice*** [federatœr, tris] ■ **adj** federative, federating *(avant n)*.
■ **nm, f** unifier.

fédératif, ***ive*** [federatif, iv] **adj** federative.

fédération [federasjɔ̃] **nf** federation.

fée [fe] **nf** fairy ▸ **fée du logis** model housekeeper.

feed-back [fidbak] **nm inv** feedback.

feeling [filiŋ] **nm** *fam* **: on va y aller au feeling** we'll play it by ear ▸ **j'ai un bon feeling** I have a good feeling about it.

féerie [fe(e)ri] **nf 1.** THÉÂTRE spectacular / CINÉ fantasy **2.** [de lieu] enchantment / [de vision] enchanting sight.

féerique [fe(e)rik] **adj** [enchanteur] enchanting.

feignais, ***feignions*** ➤ ***feindre***.

feignant, ***e*** = ***fainéant***.

feindre [81] [fɛ̃dr] ■ **vt** to feign ▸ **feindre de faire qqch** to pretend to do sthg.
■ **vi** to pretend.

feint, ***e*** [fɛ̃, fɛ̃t] **pp** ➤ ***feindre***.

feinte [fɛ̃t] **nf 1.** [ruse] ruse **2.** [football] dummy / [boxe] feint.

fêlé, ***e*** [fele] ■ **adj 1.** [assiette] cracked **2.** *fam* [personne] nutty, loony.
■ **nm, f** *fam* nut, nutter *UK*.

fêler [4] [fele] **vt** to crack.
◆ ***se fêler*** **vp** to crack.

félicitations [felisitasjɔ̃] **nfpl** congratulations ▸ **ave[c] les félicitations du jury** highly commended.

féliciter [3] [felisite] **vt** to congratulate.
◆ ***se féliciter*** **vp : se féliciter de** to congratulate o.s. o[n]

félin, ***e*** [felɛ̃, in] **adj** feline.
◆ ***félin*** **nm** big cat.

COMMENT EXPRIMER...

les félicitations

Congratulations! / Félicitations !
Congratulations on your promotion! / Félicitations pour votre promotion !
Congratulations on passing your exams / Je te félicite d'avoir réussi ton examen
I hear congratulations are in order / Alors, il paraît qu'il faut te féliciter ?
That's great news! / C'est formidable !
I'm so happy for you! / Je suis vraiment content pour toi !
Well done! *UK*, Good job! *US* / Bravo !
Nice one! / Bien joué !

félon, onne [felɔ̃, ɔn] **adj 1.** *littéraire* [perfide] disloyal, treacherous, felonious *littéraire* **2.** HIST rebellious.
◆ ***félon*** **nm 1.** *littéraire* [traître] traitor **2.** HIST felon.

fêlure [felyr] **nf** crack.

femelle [fəmɛl] **nf & adj** female.

féminin, e [feminɛ̃, in] **adj 1.** [gén] feminine **2.** [revue, équipe] women's *(avant n).*
◆ ***féminin*** **nm** GRAMM feminine.

PARONYME / CONFUSABLE

féminin

Attention à la traduction de féminin : *female* se réfère au genre féminin, tandis que *feminine* signifie qui possède des caractéristiques traditionnellement associées aux femmes.

féminiser [3] [feminize] **vt 1.** [efféminer] to make effeminate **2.** BIOL to feminize.
◆ ***se féminiser*** **vp 1.** [institution] to attract more women **2.** [homme] to become effeminate.

féminisme [feminism] **nm** feminism.

féministe [feminist] **nmf & adj** feminist.

féminité [feminite] **nf** femininity.

femme [fam] **nf 1.** [personne de sexe féminin] woman ▸ **bonne femme** *péj* woman ▸ **contes/remèdes de bonne femme** old wives' tales/remedies ▸ **femme d'affaires** businesswoman ▸ **femme de chambre** chambermaid ▸ **femme fatale** femme fatale ▸ **femme au foyer** housewife ▸ **femme de ménage** cleaning woman ▸ **femme du monde** society woman ▸ **femme de tête** forceful woman **2.** [épouse] wife ▸ **prendre femme** *vieilli* to take a wife.

femmelette [famlɛt] **nf** *péj* weakling.

fémur [femyr] **nm** femur.

FEN [fɛn] (abr de ***Fédération de l'éducation nationale***) **nf** *teachers' trade union.*

fenaison [fənɛzɔ̃] **nf** haymaking.

fendiller [3] [fɑ̃dije] **vt** to crack.
◆ ***se fendiller*** **vp** to crack.

fendre [73] [fɑ̃dr] **vt 1.** [bois] to split ▸ **fendre une bûche en deux** to split *ou* to chop a log down the middle ▸ **c'est à vous fendre le cœur** *fig* it breaks your heart, it's heartbreaking, it's heartrending **2.** [foule, flots] to cut through ▸ **fendre les flots/l'air/le vent** *littéraire & hum* to cleave through the seas/the air/the breeze.
◆ ***se fendre*** **vp 1.** [se crevasser] to crack **2.** *fam* [d'une somme] **: se fendre de qqch** to part with sthg ▸ **se fendre de 100 euros** to fork out *ou* to shell out 100 euros.

fendu, e [fɑ̃dy] **pp** ➤ *fendre.*

fenêtre [fənɛtr] **nf 1.** [gén] window ▸ **fenêtre à guillotine** sash window **2.** INFORM **: fenêtre active** *ou* **activée** active window.

fennec [fenɛk] **nm** fennec.

fenouil [fənuj] **nm** fennel.

fente [fɑ̃t] **nf 1.** [fissure] crack **2.** [interstice, de vêtement] slit.

féodal, e, aux [feɔdal, o] **adj** feudal.
◆ ***féodal, aux*** **nm** feudal lord.

féodalité [feɔdalite] **nf** feudalism.

fer [fɛr] **nm** iron ▸ **en fer, de fer** iron *(avant n)* ▸ **fer à cheval** horseshoe ▸ **en fer à cheval** [escalier, table] horseshoe-shaped, horseshoe *(avant n)* ▸ **fer forgé** wrought iron ▸ **fer à friser** curling tongs *UK ou* iron *US* ▸ **fer de lance** spearhead ▸ **fer à repasser** iron ▸ **passer un coup de fer sur un pantalon** to give a pair of trousers *UK ou* pants *US* a quick iron ▸ **fer rouge** brand ▸ **fer à souder** soldering iron ▸ **les quatre fers en l'air** flat on one's back ▸ **croire qqch dur comme fer** to firmly believe sthg ▸ **il faut battre le fer quand il est chaud** you have to strike while the iron is hot ▸ **marquer qqn au fer rouge** to brand sb ▸ **mettre qqn aux fers** to put sb in irons.

ferai, feras ➤ *faire.*

fer-blanc [fɛrblɑ̃] (pl **fers-blancs**) **nm** tinplate, tin ▸ **en fer-blanc** tin *(avant n).*

ferblanterie [fɛrblɑ̃tri] **nf 1.** [commerce] tin industry **2.** [ustensiles] tinware.

férié, e [ferje] ➤ *jour.*

férir [ferir] **vt : sans coup férir** without meeting any resistance *ou* obstacle.

ferme¹ [fɛrm] **nf** farm.

ferme² [fɛrm] ■ **adj** firm ▸ **être ferme sur ses jambes** to be steady on one's feet.
■ **adv 1.** [beaucoup] a lot **2.** [définitivement] **: acheter/vendre ferme** to make a firm purchase/sale
▸▸ **tenir ferme** to stand firm.

fermé, e [fɛrme] **adj 1.** [passage] closed, blocked ▸ **'col fermé'** 'pass closed to traffic' **2.** [porte, récipient] closed, shut ▸ **j'ai laissé la porte à demi fermée** I left the door ajar *ou* half-open ▸ **une boîte fermée** a box which is shut, a closed box ▸ **fermé à clef** locked ▸ **fermé à double tour** double-locked **3.** [radiateur, robinet] off **4.** [bouche, œil] shut, closed (up) **5.** [magasin, bureau, restaurant] closed ▸ **fermé le lundi** closed on Mondays, closing day Monday **6.** [chasse, pêche] closed **7.** [méfiant - visage] closed, inscrutable, impenetrable / [- regard] impenetrable ▸ **une personnalité fermée** a secretive *ou* an uncommunicative personality **8.** [exclusif - milieu, cercle] exclusive, select **9.** [syllabe, voyelle] closed **10.** SPORT [jeu] tight **11.** INFORM & MATH closed.

fermement [fɛrməmɑ̃] **adv** firmly.

ferment [fɛrmɑ̃] **nm 1.** [levure] ferment **2.** *fig* [germe] seed, seeds *pl.*

fermentation [fɛrmɑ̃tasjɔ̃] **nf** CHIM fermentation / *fig* ferment.

fermenter [3] [fɛrmɑ̃te] **vi** *fig* & CHIM to ferment.

fermer [3] [fɛrme] ■ **vt 1.** [porte, tiroir, yeux] to close, to shut / [store] to pull down / [enveloppe] to seal ▸ **fermer une porte à double tour** to double-lock a door ▸ **fermer les rideaux** to close *ou* draw the curtains ▸ **fermer les yeux sur qqch** to turn a blind eye to sthg **2.** [bloquer] to close ▸ **fermer son esprit à qqch** to close one's mind to sthg ▸ **fermer son cœur à qqn** to harden one's heart

to sb **3.** [gaz, lumière] to turn off **4.** [vêtement] to do up **5.** [entreprise] to close down ▸ **la police a fait fermer l'établissement** the police had the place closed down **6.** [interdire] **: fermer qqch à qqn** to close sthg to sb ▸ **cette filière vous fermerait toutes les carrières scientifiques** this course would prevent you from following any scientific career
▸▸ **la ferme!, ferme-la!** *fam* shut up!
■ **vi 1.** [gén] to shut, to close ▸ **le portail ferme mal** the gate is difficult to close *ou* won't close properly **2.** [vêtement] to do up **3.** [entreprise] to close down.
◆ ***se fermer*** **vp 1.** [porte, partie du corps] to close, to shut ▸ **mes yeux se ferment tout seuls** I can't keep my eyes open **2.** [plaie] to close up **3.** [vêtement] to do up **4.** *fig* [s'endurcir] **: se fermer (à qqch)** to close o.s. off (from sthg) ▸ **son cœur s'est fermé à la pitié** he has become impervious to pity.

fermeté [fɛrmәte] **nf** firmness.

fermeture [fɛrmәtyr] **nf 1.** [de porte] closing ▸ **fermeture automatique des portes** doors close automatically **2.** [de vêtement, sac] fastening ▸ **fermeture Éclair®** zip *UK*, zipper *US* **3.** [d'établissement - temporaire] closing / [- définitive] closure ▸ **fermeture hebdomadaire/annuelle** weekly/annual closing.

fermier, ère [fɛrmje, ɛr] ■ **adj** farm *(avant n)*.
■ **nm, f** farmer.

fermoir [fɛrmwar] **nm** clasp.

féroce [ferɔs] **adj** [animal, appétit] ferocious / [personne, désir] fierce.

férocement [ferɔsmɑ̃] **adv** fiercely.

férocité [ferɔsite] **nf** ferocity.

Féroé [ferɔe] **npr fpl : aux Féroé** in the Faeroes ; voir aussi ***île***.

ferraille [fɛraj] **nf 1.** [vieux fer] scrap iron *(U)* ▸ **bon à mettre à la ferraille** fit for the scrap heap **2.** *fam* [monnaie] loose change.

ferré, e [fɛre] **adj 1.** [soulier] hobnailed **2.** *fam fig* [calé] **: être ferré en** to be well up on.

ferrer [4] [fɛre] **vt 1.** [cheval] to shoe **2.** [poisson] to strike **3.** [soulier] to put hobnails on.

ferreux, euse [fɛrø, øz] **adj** ferrous.

ferronnerie [fɛrɔnri] **nf 1.** [objet, métier] ironwork *(U)* **2.** [atelier] ironworks *sg*.

ferroviaire [fɛrɔvjɛr] **adj** rail *(avant n)*.

ferrugineux, euse [fɛryʒinø, øz] **adj** ferruginous.

ferrure [fɛryr] **nf 1.** [de porte] fitting **2.** [de cheval] shoeing.

ferry-boat [fɛribot] (pl **ferry-boats**) **nm** ferry.

fertile [fɛrtil] **adj** *litt* & *fig* fertile ▸ **fertile en** *fig* filled with, full of.

fertilisant, e [fɛrtilizɑ̃, ɑ̃t] **adj** fertilizing.

fertiliser [3] [fɛrtilize] **vt** to fertilize.

fertilité [fɛrtilite] **nf** fertility.

féru, e [fery] **adj** *sout* [passionné] **: être féru de qqch** to have a passion for sthg.

férule [feryl] **nf : (être) sous la férule de qqn** *sout* (to be) under sb's iron rule.

fervent, e [fɛrvɑ̃, ɑ̃t] ■ **adj** [chrétien] fervent / [amoureux, démocrate] ardent.
■ **nm, f** devotee.

ferveur [fɛrvœr] **nf 1.** [dévotion] fervour *UK*, fervor *US* **2.** [zèle] zeal.

fesse [fɛs] **nf** buttock.

fessée [fese] **nf** spanking, smack (on the bottom).

fessier, ère [fesje, ɛr] **adj** buttock *(avant n)*.
◆ ***fessier*** **nm** buttocks *pl*.

festif, ive [fɛstif, iv] **adj** *sout* festive.

festin [fɛstɛ̃] **nm** banquet, feast.

festival, als [fɛstival] **nm** festival ▸ **festival cinématographique** *ou* **du cinéma** film *UK ou* movie *US* festival.

festivités [fɛstivite] **nfpl** festivities.

feston [fɛstɔ̃] **nm 1.** ARCHIT festoon **2.** COUT scallop.

festoyer [13] [fɛstwaje] **vi** to feast.

feta [feta] **nf** feta (cheese).

fêtard, e [fɛtar, ard] **nm, f** fun-loving person.

fête [fɛt] **nf 1.** [congé] holiday ▸ **les fêtes (de fin d'année)** the Christmas holidays ▸ **fête légale** public holiday ▸ **fête nationale** national holiday ▸ **la fête du Travail** May Day ▸ **demain, c'est fête** tomorrow we have a day off
2. [réunion, réception] celebration ▸ **fête de famille** family celebration ▸ **on organise une petite fête pour son anniversaire** we're giving a party for his birthday, we're giving him a birthday party ▸ **que la fête commence!** let the festivities begin!
3. [kermesse] fair ▸ **en fête** in festive mood ▸ **fête foraine** funfair *UK*, carnival *US* ▸ **la fête de l'Humanité** *annual festival organized by the Communist daily newspaper 'l'Humanité'* ▸ **la fête de la musique** *annual music festival which takes place in the streets* ▸ **la ville/les rues en fête** the festive town/streets
4. [jour de célébration - de personne] name-day, saint's day / [- de saint] feast (day) ▸ **souhaiter sa fête à qqn** to wish sb a happy name-day *ou* saint's day ▸ **fête des mères/des pères** Mother's/Father's Day
5. [soirée] party

▶▶ **ça va être ta fête** *fam* you'll get it in the neck ▶ **faire la fête** to have a good time ▶ **faire (la) fête à qqn** to make a fuss of sb ▶ **mon chien m'a fait (la) fête quand je suis revenu** my dog was all over me when I got back.

CULTURE
Fête

French custom is to wish **bonne fête** to people who have the same name as the saint commemorated on a given day, sometimes through a telephone call and sometimes with a card (particularly for children). Television weather forecasters always mention the next day's saint along with the forecast: **Demain, vous fêterez les Patrice !**

CULTURE
La Fête de la musique

This yearly festival, begun in 1982, is celebrated every 21st of June throughout France. Free concerts by both professional and amateur musicians are organized in streets and public squares, and big-city streets become pedestrian walkways. One can hear everything from jazz to classical to rap to electronic. The festival has been so successful that it is now celebrated in several other countries.

Fête-Dieu [fɛtdjø] (pl **Fête-Dieu** *ou* **Fêtes-Dieu**) **nf** Corpus Christi.

fêter [4] [fete] **vt** [événement] to celebrate / [personne] to have a party for.

fétiche [fetiʃ] **nm 1.** [objet de culte] fetish **2.** [mascotte] mascot.

fétichisme [fetiʃism] **nm 1.** [culte, perversion] fetishism **2.** [vénération] idolatry.

fétide [fetid] **adj** fetid.

fétu [fety] **nm : fétu (de paille)** wisp (of straw).

feu[1], ***e*** [fø] **adj : feu M. X** the late Mr X ▶ **feu mon mari** my late husband.

feu[2], ***x*** [fø] **nm 1.** [flamme, incendie] fire ▶ **au feu!** fire! ▶ **en feu** *litt* & *fig* on fire ▶ **j'ai la bouche/gorge en feu** my mouth/throat is burning ▶ **avez-vous du feu?** have you got a light? ▶ **faire du** *ou* **un feu** to make a fire ▶ **faire feu** MIL to fire ▶ **cesser le feu** to cease fire ▶ **mettre le feu à qqch** to set fire to sthg, to set sthg on fire ▶ **mettre le feu aux poudres** *litt* to spark off an explosion / *fig* to spark things off ▶ **prendre feu** to catch fire ▶ **feu de bois** wood fire ▶ **feu de camp** camp fire ▶ **feu de cheminée** chimney fire ▶ **feu follet** will-o'-the-wisp ▶ **feu de joie** bonfire ▶ **être pris entre deux feux** to be caught in the crossfire ▶ **jouer avec le feu** to play with fire ▶ **mettre à feu et à sang** to ravage
2. [signal] light ▶ **feu rouge/vert** red/green light ▶ **feu (tricolore** *ou* **de signalisation)** traffic lights ▶ **feux de brouillard** fog lamps ▶ **feux de croisement** dipped *UK ou* dimmed *US* headlights ▶ **feux de détresse** warning lights ▶ **feux de position** sidelights ▶ **feux de route** headlights on full beam *UK ou* high beams *US* ▶ **feux de stationnement** parking lights ▶ **tous feux éteints** without any lights ▶ **donner son** *ou* **le feu vert (à qqn)** to give (sb) the go-ahead
3. CULIN ring *UK*, burner *US* ▶ **à feu doux/vif** on a low/high flame ▶ **à petit feu** gently ▶ **mijoter** *ou* **faire cuire à petit feu** to cook slowly ▶ **avoir qqch sur le feu** to be (in the middle of) cooking sthg
4. CINÉ & THÉÂTRE light *(U)* ▶ **les feux de la rampe** the footlights
▶▶ **dans le feu de l'action** in the heat of the moment ▶ **il n'y a vu que du feu** he never saw a thing, he was completely taken in ▶ **ne pas faire long feu** not to last long ▶ **tout feu tout flamme** burning with enthusiasm.
◆ ***feu d'artifice*** **nm** firework.

feuillage [fœjaʒ] **nm** foliage.

feuille [fœj] **nf 1.** [d'arbre] leaf ▶ **feuille morte** dead leaf ▶ **feuille de vigne** BOT vine leaf ▶ **feuilles de vigne farcies** dolmades, stuffed vine leaves ▶ **il a les oreilles en feuille de chou** *fam* his ears stick out
2. [page] sheet ▶ **feuille blanche** blank sheet ▶ **feuille de papier** sheet of paper ▶ **feuille volante** loose leaf ▶ **les feuilles d'un cahier** the sheets *ou* leaves *ou* pages of a notebook
3. [document] form ▶ **feuille d'impôts** tax form, tax return ▶ **feuille de présence** attendance sheet ▶ **feuille de soins** *claim form for reimbursement of medical expenses*
4. [journal] paper ▶ **feuille de chou** *fam péj* rag.

feuillet [fœjɛ] **nm** page.

feuilleté, e [fœjte] **adj 1.** CULIN **: pâte feuilletée** puff pastry **2.** GÉOL foliated.
◆ ***feuilleté*** **nm** pastry.

feuilleter [27] [fœjte] **vt** to flick through.

feuilleton [fœjtɔ̃] **nm** serial ▶ **feuilleton télévisé** soap opera.

feuillu, e [fœjy] **adj** leafy.
◆ ***feuillu*** **nm** broad-leaved tree.

feutre [føtr] **nm 1.** [étoffe] felt **2.** [chapeau] felt hat **3.** [crayon] felt-tip pen.

feutré, e [føtre] **adj 1.** [garni de feutre] trimmed with felt / [qui a l'aspect du feutre] felted **2.** [bruit, cri] muffled.

feutrer [3] [føtre] ■ **vt 1.** [garnir de feutre] to trim with felt **2.** [bruit, cri] to muffle.
■ **vi** to felt (up).
◆ ***se feutrer*** **vp** to felt (up).

feutrine [føtrin] **nf** lightweight felt.

fève [fɛv] **nf** broad bean.

février [fevrije] **nm** February ; voir aussi ***septembre***.

FF (abr écrite de ***francs français***) FF.

FFI (abr de ***Forces françaises de l'intérieur***) **nfpl** *French Resistance forces operating within France during World War II.*

FFL (abr de ***Forces françaises libres***) **nfpl** *Free French Army during World War II.*

FFR (abr de ***Fédération française de rugby***) **nf** *French rugby federation.*

fg abr de ***faubourg***.

FGEN (abr de ***Fédération générale de l'éducation nationale***) **nf** *teachers' trade union.*

fi [fi] **interj : faire fi de** to scorn.

fiabiliser [3] [fjabilize] **vt** [système] **: fiabiliser qqch** to safeguard sthg / [document, label] to guarantee the accuracy of sthg.

fiabilité [fjabilite] **nf** reliability.

fiable [fjabl] **adj** reliable.

FIAC [fjak] (abr de ***Foire internationale d'art contemporain***) **nf** *international contemporary art fair held annually in Paris.*

fiacre [fjakr] **nm** (horse-drawn) carriage.

fiançailles [fjɑ̃saj] **nfpl** engagement *sg.*

fiancé, ***e*** [fjɑ̃se] **nm, f** fiancé (f fiancée).

fiancer [16] [fjɑ̃se] ◆ ***se fiancer*** **vp : se fiancer (avec)** to get engaged (to).

fiasco [fjasko] **nm** fiasco ▸ **faire fiasco** to be a fiasco.

fibre [fibr] **nf 1.** ANAT, BIOL & TECHNOL fibre *UK*, fiber *US* ▸ **fibre optique** fibre *UK* ***ou*** fiber *US* optics *(U)* ▸ **fibre de verre** fibreglass *UK* ***ou*** fiberglass *US*, glass fibre *UK* ***ou*** fiber *US* **2.** *fig* [sentiment] feeling ▸ **avoir la fibre maternelle** to have the maternal instinct.

fibreux, ***euse*** [fibrø, øz] **adj** fibrous / [viande] stringy.

fibrome [fibrom] **nm** fibroma.

ficelé, ***e*** [fisle] **adj** *fam* dressed ▸ **être mal ficelé** to be scruffy.

ficeler [24] [fisle] **vt** [lier] to tie up.

ficelle [fisɛl] **nf 1.** [fil] string ▸ **tirer les ficelles** to pull the strings **2.** [pain] *very thin baguette* **3.** *(gén pl)* [truc] trick.

fiche [fiʃ] **nf 1.** [document] card ▸ **fiche de paie** pay slip *UK*, paystub *US* ▸ **fiche signalétique** identification sheet ▸ **fiche technique** technical data sheet **2.** ÉLECTR & TECHNOL pin.

ficher [3] [fiʃe] **vt 1.** *(participe passé* **fiché***)* [enfoncer] **: ficher qqch dans** to stick sthg into ▸ **un couteau fiché entre les omoplates** a knife stuck right between the shoulderblades **2.** *(participe passé* **fiché***)* [inscrire] to put on file ▸ **il est fiché** the police have got a file on him **3.** *(participe passé* **fichu***)* *fam* [faire] **: je n'ai rien fichu aujourd'hui** I haven't done a thing today ▸ **qu'est-ce qu'il fiche?** what's he doing? **4.** *(participe passé* **fichu***)* *fam* [mettre] to put ▸ **ficher qqn par terre** to send sb flying ▸ **ficher qqch par terre** *fig* to mess ***ou*** muck *UK* sthg up ▸ **ce contretemps fiche tout en l'air** this last-minute hitch really messes everything up ▸ **je lui ai fichu mon poing dans la figure** I punched him in the face ▸ **ficher qqn dehors *ou* à la porte** to throw sb out **5.** *(participe passé* **fichu***)* *fam* [donner] **: ça m'a fichu la chair de poule/la trouille** it gave me the creeps/the willies ▸ **fiche-moi la paix!** leave me alone!

◆ ***se ficher*** **vp 1.** [s'enfoncer - suj: clou, pique] **: se ficher dans** to go into ▸ **ils se sont fichus dans un fossé** [- en voiture] they drove into a ditch / [- pour passer inaperçus] they jumped into a ditch **2.** *fam* [se moquer] **: se ficher de** to make fun of ▸ **tu te fiches de moi ou quoi?** are you kidding me? **3.** *fam* [ne pas tenir compte] **: se ficher de** not to give a damn about ▸ **je me fiche de ce que disent les gens** I don't care what ***ou*** I don't give a damn about what people say

▸▸ **se ficher dedans** *fam* to get it all wrong.

fichier [fiʃje] **nm** file / INFORM **: fichier actif** active file.

fichu, ***e*** [fiʃy] **adj 1.** *fam* [cassé, fini] done for **2.** *(avant n)* [désagréable] nasty

▸▸ **être mal fichu** *fam* [personne] to feel rotten / [objet] to be badly made ▸ **il n'est même pas fichu de faire son lit** *fam* he can't even make his own bed.

◆ ***fichu*** **nm** scarf.

fictif, ***ive*** [fiktif, iv] **adj 1.** [imaginaire] imaginary **2.** [faux] false **3.** [valeur] face *(avant n).*

fiction [fiksjɔ̃] **nf 1.** LITTÉR fiction **2.** [monde imaginaire] dream world.

ficus [fikys] **nm** ficus.

fidèle [fidɛl] ■ **nmf 1.** RELIG believer **2.** [adepte] fan.
■ **adj 1.** [loyal, exact, semblable] **: fidèle (à)** faithful (to) ▸ **fidèle à la réalité** accurate **2.** [habitué] regular.

fidèlement [fidɛlmɑ̃] **adv 1.** [loyalement, exactement] faithfully **2.** [régulièrement] regularly.

fidéliser [3] [fidelize] **vt** to attract and keep.

fidélité [fidelite] **nf** faithfulness / [clientèle] **: fidélité de la clientèle** customer loyalty ▸ **fidélité à la marque** brand loyalty.

Fidji [fidzi] **npr** Fiji ▸ **à Fidji** in Fiji.

fidjien, ***enne*** [fidzjɛ̃, ɛn] **adj** Fijian.

◆ ***Fidjien***, ***enne*** **nm, f** Fijian.

fief [fjɛf] **nm** fief / *fig* stronghold.

fieffé, ***e*** [fjefe] **adj** arrant.

fiel [fjɛl] **nm** *litt* & *fig* gall.

fiente [fjɑ̃t] **nf** droppings *pl.*

fier[1], ***fière*** [fjɛr] **adj 1.** [gén] proud ▸ **fier de qqn/qqch** proud of sb/sthg ▸ **fier de faire qqch** proud to be doing sthg **2.** [noble] noble.

fier[2] [9] [fje] ◆ ***se fier*** **vp : se fier à** to trust, to rely on.

fièrement [fjɛrmɑ̃] **adv** proudly.

fierté [fjɛrte] **nf 1.** [satisfaction, dignité] pride **2.** [arrogance] arrogance.

fièvre [fjɛvr] **nf 1.** MÉD fever ▸ **avoir de la fièvre** to have a fever ▸ **avoir 40 de fièvre** to have a temperature of 104 (degrees) **2.** [vétérinaire] **: fièvre aphteuse** foot and mouth disease **3.** *fig* [excitation] excitement.

fiévreusement [fjevrøzmɑ̃] **adv** feverishly.

fiévreux, ***euse*** [fjevrø, øz] **adj** *litt* & *fig* feverish.

fig. abr de ***figure***.

figé, ***e*** [fiʒe] **adj** fixed.

figer [17] [fiʒe] **vt** to paralyse *UK*, to paralyze *US* ▸ **être figé sur place** to be rooted to the spot.
◆ ***se figer*** **vp** **1.** [s'immobiliser] to freeze **2.** [se solidifier] to congeal.

fignoler [3] [fiɲɔle] **vt** to put the finishing touches to.

figue [fig] **nf** fig.

figuier [figje] **nm** fig tree.

figurant, e [figyrɑ̃, ɑ̃t] **nm, f** extra.

figuratif, ive [figyratif, iv] **adj** figurative.

figuration [figyrasjɔ̃] **nf** CINÉ & THÉÂTRE **: faire de la figuration** to work as an extra.

figure [figyr] **nf** **1.** [gén] figure ▸ **faire figure de** to look like ▸ **figures imposées/libres** SPORT compulsory/freestyle section ▸ **figure de proue** figurehead / *fig* leading light ▸ **figure de rhétorique** LING figure of speech ▸ **figure de style** LING stylistic device **2.** [visage] face ▸ **faire bonne figure** *fig* to put on a good face.

figuré, e [figyre] **adj** [sens] figurative.
◆ ***figuré*** **nm : au figuré** in the figurative sense.

figurer [3] [figyre] ■ **vt** to represent.
■ **vi : figurer dans/parmi** to figure in/among ▸ **votre nom ne figure pas sur la liste** your name doesn't appear *ou* isn't on the list ▸ **figurer au nombre des élus** to be among the successful candidates.
◆ ***se figurer*** **vpt** **1.** [imaginer] to imagine **2.** [croire] to believe ▸ **figure-toi qu'il n'a même pas appelé!** he didn't even call; can you believe it! ▸ **eh bien figure-toi que moi non plus, je n'ai pas le temps!** surprising though it may seem, I haven't got the time either!

figurine [figyrin] **nf** figurine.

fil [fil] **nm** **1.** [brin] thread ▸ **fil à plomb** plumb line ▸ **fil conducteur** *fig* main idea ▸ **fil dentaire** dental floss ▸ **c'est cousu de fil blanc** it doesn't fool anybody ▸ **de fil en aiguille** gradually ▸ **donner du fil à retordre** *fig* to make life difficult ▸ **perdre le fil (de qqch)** *fig* to lose the thread (of sthg) ▸ **le fil des événements** the chain of events ▸ **ne tenir qu'à un fil** *fig* to hang by a thread
2. [câble] wire ▸ **fil électrique** wire ▸ **fil de fer** wire ▸ **fil de fer barbelé** barbed wire ▸ **avoir qqn au bout du fil** *fig* to have sb on the line
3. [cours] course ▸ **au fil de** in the course of ▸ **au fil du temps** as time goes by
4. [tissu] linen ▸ **draps de fil** linen sheets
5. [tranchant] edge ▸ **être sur le fil du rasoir** to be on a knife-edge.
◆ ***sans fil*** **loc adj** [télégraphie, téléphonie] wireless *(avant n)* / [rasoir, téléphone] cordless.

filaire[1] [filɛr] **adj** telegraphic.

filaire[2] [filɛr] **nf** filaria.

filament [filamɑ̃] **nm** **1.** ANAT & ÉLECTR filament **2.** [végétal] fibre *UK*, fiber *US* **3.** [de colle, bave] thread.

filandreux, euse [filɑ̃drø, øz] **adj** [viande] stringy.

filant, e [filɑ̃, ɑ̃t] ➤ ***étoile***.

filasse [filas] ■ **nf** tow.
■ **adj inv** flaxen.

filature [filatyr] **nf** **1.** [usine] mill / [fabrication] spinning **2.** [poursuite] tailing ▸ **prendre qqn en filature** to tail sb.

file [fil] **nf** line ▸ **à la file** in a line ▸ **en double file** in two lines ▸ **se garer en double file** to double-park ▸ **en file indienne** in single *ou* Indian file ▸ **se mettre en file** to line up ▸ **file d'attente** queue *UK*, line *US*.

filer [3] [file] ■ **vt** **1.** [soie, coton] to spin ▸ **filer un mauvais coton** *fig fam* [être malade] to be in bad shape / [se préparer des ennuis] to be heading for trouble
2. [personne] to tail
3. *fam* [donner] **: filer qqch à qqn** to slip sthg to sb, to slip sb sthg ▸ **il m'a filé un coup de poing** he landed *ou* beaned *US* me one ▸ **elle m'a filé la grippe** she's given me the flu.
■ **vi** **1.** [bas] to ladder *UK*, to run *US*
2. [aller vite - temps, véhicule] to fly (by) ▸ **filer à toute vitesse** [voiture] to bomb along
3. *fam* [partir] to dash off ▸ **bon, je file!** right, I'm off! ▸ **il a filé dans sa chambre** he dashed *ou* flew into his bedroom ▸ **filer à l'anglaise** to sneak off, to take French leave
▸▸ **filer doux** to behave nicely.

filet [filɛ] **nm** **1.** [à mailles] net ▸ **filet (à bagages)** (luggage) rack ▸ **filet à papillons** butterfly net ▸ **filet de pêche** fishing net ▸ **filet à provisions** string bag ▸ **attirer qqn dans ses filets** *fig* to entrap *ou* to ensnare sb ▸ **envoyer la balle dans le filet** to hit the ball into the net ▸ **monter au filet** to come to the net ▸ **travailler sans filet** *fig* to take risks ▸ **tendre un filet** *fig* to set a trap
2. CULIN fillet, filet *US* ▸ **filet de bœuf** fillet *ou* filet *US* of beef ▸ **filet de sole** fillet *ou* filet *US* of sole
3. [de liquide] drop, dash ▸ **un filet de citron/vinaigre** a dash of lemon/vinegar ▸ **un filet d'eau** a trickle of water / [de lumière] shaft ▸ **un (petit) filet de voix** a thin (reedy) voice
4. [de vis] thread.

filial, e, aux [filjal, o] **adj** filial.
◆ ***filiale*** **nf** ÉCON subsidiary.

filiation [filjasjɔ̃] **nf** **1.** [lien de parenté] line **2.** *fig* [enchaînement] logical relationship.

filière [filjɛr] **nf** **1.** [voie] **: suivre la filière** [professionnelle] to work one's way up ▸ **suivre la filière hiérarchique** to go through the right channels **2.** [réseau] network.

filiforme [filifɔrm] **adj** skinny.

filigrane [filigran] **nm** [dessin] watermark ▸ **en filigrane** *fig* between the lines.

filin [filɛ̃] **nm** rope.

fille [fij] **nf** **1.** [enfant] daughter ▸ **tu es bien la fille de ton père!** you're just like your father! **2.** [femme] girl ▸ **jeune fille** girl ▸ **fille de joie** prostitute ▸ **fille mère** *péj* single mother ▸ **une fille de la campagne** a country girl ▸ **vieille fille** *péj* spinster ▸ **courir les filles** *fig* to chase women ▸ **tu es une grande fille maintenant** you're a big girl now.

fillette [fijɛt] **nf** little girl.

filleul, e [fijœl] **nm, f** godchild.

film [film] **nm** **1.** [gén] film *UK*, movie *US* ▸ **film d'action** action film *UK ou* movie *US* ▸ **film catastrophe** disaster film *UK ou* movie *US* ▸ **film culte** cult film *UK ou* movie *US* ▸ **film d'épouvante** horror film *UK ou* movie *US* ▸ **film noir** film noir ▸ **film policier** detective film *UK ou* movie *US* **2.** *fig* [déroulement] course.

filmer [3] [filme] **vt** to film.

filmographie [filmɔgrafi] **nf** filmography, films *pl UK*, movies *pl US*.

filon [filɔ̃] **nm 1.** [de mine] vein **2.** *fam fig* [possibilité] cushy number.

filou [filu] **nm** rogue.

filouterie [filutri] **nf** fraud.

fils [fis] **nm** son ▸ **fils de famille** boy from a privileged background ▸ **fils à papa** *péj* daddy's boy ▸ **le fils prodigue** the prodigal son.

filtrage [filtraʒ] **nm** filtering / *fig* screening.

filtrant, ***e*** [filtrɑ̃, ɑ̃t] **adj** [verre] tinted.

filtre [filtr] **nm 1.** filter ▸ **filtre à café** coffee filter **2.** AUTO **: filtre à air** air filter **3.** INFORM **: filtre parental** internet filter, parental control filter **4.** COMM [dans le service des achats] gatekeeper.

filtrer [3] [filtre] ■ **vt** to filter / *fig* to screen.
■ **vi** to filter / *fig* to filter through.

fin, ***fine*** [fɛ̃, fin] ■ **adj 1.** [gén] fine ▸ **haricots verts fins** high-quality green beans ▸ **pluie fine** drizzle **2.** [partie du corps] slender / [couche, papier] thin **3.** [subtil] shrewd ▸ **ce n'était pas très fin de ta part** it wasn't very smart *ou* clever of you **4.** [ouïe, vue] keen **5.** *(avant n)* [spécialiste] expert ▸ **un fin gourmet** a gourmet ▸ **un fin tireur** a crack shot.
■ **adv** finely ▸ **c'est écrit trop fin** it's written too small ▸ **fin prêt** quite ready.
◆ ***fin*** **nf** end ▸ **fin mars** at the end of March ▸ **mettre fin à** to put a stop *ou* an end to ▸ **on n'en voit pas la fin** there doesn't seem to be any end to it ▸ **opposer une fin de non-recevoir à qqn** *fig* to turn down sb's request bluntly ▸ **prendre fin** to come to an end ▸ **tirer *ou* toucher à sa fin** to draw to a close ▸ **la fin approche** the end is near ▸ **fin de citation** (quote) unquote ▸ **fin de saison** end of season ▸ **arrondir ses fins de mois** to make ends meet ▸ **avoir des fins de mois difficiles** to find it hard to make ends meet (at the end of the month) ▸ **arriver *ou* parvenir à ses fins** to achieve one's ends *ou* aims ▸ **avoir une fin tragique/lente** to die a tragic/slow death ▸ **c'est la fin des haricots** it's the last straw ▸ **ce n'est quand même pas la fin du monde!** it's not the end of the world, is it! ▸ **mener à bonne fin** to bring to a successful conclusion ▸ **mettre fin à ses jours** to put an end to one's life ▸ **à toutes fins utiles** just in case ▸ **à des fins politiques/religieuses** for political/religious ends.
◆ ***fin de race*** **loc adj** degenerate.
◆ ***fin de série*** **nf** oddment.
◆ ***fin de siècle*** **loc adj** decadent, fin-de-siècle.
◆ ***à la fin*** **loc adv : tu vas m'écouter, à la fin?** will you listen to me? ▸ **tu es énervant, à la fin!** you're beginning to get on my nerves!
◆ ***à la fin de*** **loc prép** at the end of.
◆ ***en fin de*** **loc prép** at the end of ▸ **être en fin de liste** to be *ou* to come at the end of the list ▸ **en fin de soirée/match** towards *UK ou* toward *US* the end of the evening/match ▸ **être en fin de droit** to come to the end of one's entitlement *(to an allowance)*.
◆ ***sans fin*** **loc adj** endless.

final, ***e*** [final] (pl **finals *ou* finaux** [fino]) **adj** final.
◆ ***final(e)*** **nm** MUS finale.
◆ ***final cut*** **nm** CINÉ **: le final cut** the final cut.
◆ ***finale*** **nf 1.** SPORT final **2.** [de mot] last syllable.

finalement [finalmɑ̃] **adv** finally.

finaliser [3] [finalize] **vt** to finalize.

finaliste [finalist] **nmf & adj** finalist.

finalité [finalite] **nf** *sout* [fonction] purpose.

finance [finɑ̃s] **nf** finance ▸ **finance d'entreprise** corporate finance ▸ **la haute finance** high finance.
◆ ***finances*** **nfpl** finances.
◆ ***Finances*** **nfpl : les Finances** ≃ the Treasury, the Exchequer *UK*.

financement [finɑ̃smɑ̃] **nm** financing, funding.

financer [16] [finɑ̃se] **vt** to finance, to fund.

financier, ***ère*** [finɑ̃sje, ɛr] **adj** financial.
◆ ***financier*** **nm** financier.

financièrement [finɑ̃sjɛrmɑ̃] **adv** financially.

finasser [3] [finase] **vi** *fam* to resort to tricks.

finaud, ***e*** [fino, od] **adj** wily, crafty.

fine [fin] **nf** *type of brandy*.

finement [finmɑ̃] **adv 1.** [délicatement] finely **2.** [adroitement] cleverly **3.** [subtilement] subtly.

finesse [finɛs] **nf 1.** [gén] fineness **2.** [minceur] slenderness **3.** [perspicacité] shrewdness **4.** [subtilité] subtlety.

fini, ***e*** [fini] **adj 1.** *péj* [fieffé] **: un crétin fini** a complete idiot **2.** *fam* [usé, diminué] finished **3.** [limité] finite.
◆ ***fini*** **nm** [d'objet] finish.

finir [32] [finir] ■ **vt 1.** [gén] to finish, to end ▸ **il a fini ses jours à Cannes** he ended his days in Cannes ▸ **finir de faire qqch** to finish doing sthg
2. [vider] to empty ▸ **finis ton assiette** *fam* clear your plate
3. *fam* [user] to wear out.
■ **vi 1.** [gén] to finish, to end ▸ **la réunion a fini dans les hurlements** the meeting ended in uproar ▸ **finir par faire qqch** to do sthg eventually ▸ **tu vas finir par tomber!** you're going to fall! ▸ **mal finir** to end badly ▸ **ça va mal finir** no good will come of it, it will all end in disaster ▸ **pour finir** in the end, finally
2. [arrêter] **: finir de faire qqch** to stop doing sthg ▸ **en finir (avec)** to finish (with) ▸ **à n'en plus finir** never-ending ▸ **cette journée/son discours n'en finit pas** there's no end to this day/his speech.

finish [finiʃ] **nm** finish ▸ **au finish** to the finish.

finition [finisjɔ̃] **nf 1.** [action] finishing **2.** [d'objet] finish.

finlandais, ***e*** [fɛ̃lɑ̃dɛ, ɛz] **adj** Finnish.
◆ ***Finlandais***, ***e*** **nm, f** Finn.

Finlande [fɛ̃lɑ̃d] **nf : la Finlande** Finland.

finnois, ***e*** [finwa, az] **adj** Finnish.
◆ ***finnois*** **nm** [langue] Finnish.
◆ ***Finnois***, ***e*** **nm, f** Finn.

FINUL, ***Finul*** [finyl] (abr de ***Forces intérimaires des Nations unies au Liban***) **nfpl** UNIFIL.

fiole [fjɔl] **nf** flask.

fioriture [fjɔrityr] **nf** flourish.

fioul = ***fuel***.

FIP [fip] (abr de ***France Inter Paris***) **nf** *French national radio station broadcasting music and traffic information*.

firmament [firmamɑ̃] **nm** firmament.

firme [firm] **nf** firm.

fis, fit ➤ ***faire***.

FIS [fis] (abr de ***Front islamique du salut***) **nm : le FIS** the Islamic Salvation Front.

fisc [fisk] **nm** ≃ Inland Revenue *UK*, ≃ Internal Revenue Service *US*.

fiscal, e, aux [fiskal, o] **adj** tax *(avant n)*, fiscal.

fiscaliser [3] [fiskalize] **vt** to (make) subject to tax.

fiscalité [fiskalite] **nf** tax system.

fission [fisjɔ̃] **nf** fission ▸ **fission nucléaire** nuclear fission.

fissure [fisyr] **nf** *litt* & *fig* crack.

fissurer [3] [fisyre] **vt** *litt* [fendre] to crack / *fig* to split.
◆ ***se fissurer*** **vp** to crack.

fiston [fistɔ̃] **nm** *fam* son.

fitness [fitnɛs] **nm** keep-fit *UK*.

FIV [fiv] (abr de ***fécondation in vitro***) **nf** IVF.

FIVETE, Fivete [fivɛt] (abr de ***fécondation in vitro et transfert d'embryon***) **nf** GIFT ▸ **une FIVETE** a test-tube baby.

fixateur, trice [fiksatœr, tris] **adj 1.** PHOTO fixing *(avant n)* **2.** [lotion, crème] setting *(avant n)*.
◆ ***fixateur*** **nm** PHOTO fixer.

fixatif [fiksatif] **nm** fixative.

fixation [fiksasjɔ̃] **nf 1.** [action de fixer] fixing **2.** [attache] fastening, fastener / [de ski] binding **3.** PSYCHO fixation **4.** ÉCON : **fixation des prix compétitifs** competitive pricing ▸ **fixation des prix prédateurs** predatory pricing.

fixe [fiks] **adj** fixed / [encre] permanent ▸ **à heure fixe** at set *ou* fixed times.
◆ ***fixe*** **nm** fixed salary.

fixement [fiksəmɑ̃] **adv** fixedly ▸ **regarder fixement qqn/qqch** to stare at sb/sthg.

fixer [3] [fikse] **vt 1.** [gén] to fix / [règle] to set ▸ **fixer son choix sur** to decide on **2.** [monter] to hang **3.** [regarder] to stare at **4.** [renseigner] **: fixer qqn sur qqch** to put sb in the picture about sthg ▸ **être fixé sur qqch** to know all about sthg.
◆ ***se fixer*** **vp** to settle ▸ **se fixer sur** [suj: choix, personne] to settle on / [suj: regard] to rest on.

fixité [fiksite] **nf** steadiness.

fjord [fjɔrd] **nm** fjord.

fl. (abr écrite de ***fleuve***) R.

FL (abr écrite de ***florin***) Fl, F, G.

flacon [flakɔ̃] **nm** small bottle ▸ **flacon à parfum** perfume bottle.

flageller [4] [flaʒɛle] **vt 1.** [fouetter] to flagellate **2.** *fig* [fustiger] to denounce.

flageoler [3] [flaʒɔle] **vi** to tremble.

flageolet [flaʒɔlɛ] **nm 1.** [haricot] flageolet bean **2.** MUS flageolet.

flagornerie [flagɔrnəri] **nf** flattery.

flagrant, e [flagrɑ̃, ɑ̃t] **adj** flagrant, ➤ ***délit***.

flair [flɛr] **nm** sense of smell ▸ **avoir du flair** *fig* to be intuitive.

flairer [4] [flɛre] **vt** to sniff, to smell / *fig* to scent.

flamand, e [flamɑ̃, ɑ̃d] **adj** Flemish.
◆ ***flamand*** **nm** [langue] Flemish.
◆ ***Flamand, e*** **nm, f** Flemish person, Fleming.

flamant [flamɑ̃] **nm** flamingo ▸ **flamant rose** pink flamingo.

flambant, e [flɑ̃bɑ̃, ɑ̃t] **adj : flambant neuf** brand new.

flambé, e [flɑ̃be] **adj 1.** CULIN flambéed **2.** *fam* [personne] ruined ▸ **être flambé** to have gambled all one's money away.

flambeau, x [flɑ̃bo] **nm** torch / *fig* flame ▸ **se passer le flambeau** *fig* to hand on the torch.

flambée [flɑ̃be] **nf 1.** [feu] blaze **2.** *fig* [de colère] outburst / [de violence] outbreak ▸ **il y a eu une flambée des prix** prices have sky-rocketed.

flamber [3] [flɑ̃be] ■ **vi 1.** [brûler] to blaze **2.** *fam* [jeux] to play for high stakes.
■ **vt 1.** [crêpe] to flambé **2.** [volaille] to singe.

flamboie, flamboies ➤ ***flamboyer***.

flamboyant, e [flɑ̃bwajɑ̃, ɑ̃t] **adj 1.** [ciel, regard] blazing / [couleur] flaming **2.** ARCHIT flamboyant.

flamboyer [13] [flɑ̃bwaje] **vi** to blaze.

flamiche [flamiʃ] **nf** leek pie *ou* quiche.

flamingant, e [flamɛ̃gɑ̃, ɑ̃t] **adj 1.** [nationaliste] Flemish-nationalist **2.** [de langue] Flemish-speaking.
◆ ***Flamingant, e*** **nm, f 1.** [nationaliste] Flemish nationalist **2.** [de langue] Flemish speaker.

flamme [flam] **nf** flame / *fig* fervour *UK*, fervor *US*, fire ▸ **discours plein de flamme** impassioned speech.
◆ ***flammes*** **nfpl : périr dans les flammes** to burn to death, to be burnt alive
▸▸| **les flammes éternelles** *ou* **de l'enfer** *fig* hell fire.
◆ ***à la flamme de*** **loc prép** by the light of ▸ **lire à la flamme d'un briquet** to read by the light of a cigarette lighter.
◆ ***en flammes*** ■ **loc adj** burning, blazing.
■ **loc adv : l'avion est tombé en flammes** the plane went down in flames ▸ **descendre un auteur en flammes** *fam* to pan an author.

flan [flɑ̃] **nm** baked custard.

flanc [flɑ̃] **nm** [de personne, navire, montagne] side / [d'animal, d'armée] flank ▸ **à flanc de coteau** on the hillside ▸ **être sur le flanc** *fig* to feel washed out ▸ **tirer au flanc** *fam fig* to shirk, to skive *UK*.

flancher [3] [flɑ̃ʃe] **vi** *fam* to give up.

flanelle [flanɛl] **nf** flannel.

flâner [3] [flane] **vi 1.** [se promener] to stroll **2.** [s'attarder] to hang around, to lounge around.

flânerie [flanri] **nf** stroll.

flâneur, euse [flanœr, øz] **nm, f** stroller.

flanquer [3] [flɑ̃ke] vt **1.** *fam* [jeter] **: flanquer qqch par terre** to fling sthg to the ground ▸ **il a flanqué les bouquins par terre** [volontairement] he chucked the books on the floor / [par maladresse] he knocked the books onto the floor ▸ **j'ai tellement voulu réussir et toi tu vas tout flanquer par terre** *fig* I wanted to succeed so badly and now you're going to mess it all up (for me) ▸ **flanquer qqn dehors** to chuck *ou* fling sb out **2.** *fam* [donner] **: flanquer un coup de poing à qqn** to punch sb ▸ **flanquer une gifle à qqn** to smack *ou* slap sb ▸ **flanquer la frousse à qqn** to scare the pants off sb, to put the wind up sb *UK* **3.** [accompagner] **: être flanqué de** to be flanked by ▸ **elle est arrivée, flanquée de ses deux frères** she came in with her two brothers at her side *ou* flanked by her two brothers.
◆ ***se flanquer*** vp *fam* **: se flanquer par terre** to fall flat on one's face.

flapi, e [flapi] adj *fam* dead beat.

flaque [flak] nf pool ▸ **flaque (d'eau)** puddle.

flash [flaʃ] nm **1.** PHOTO flash **2.** RADIO & TV **: flash (d'information)** newsflash ▸ **flash de publicité** commercial.

flash-back [flaʃbak] (pl **flash-back** *ou* **flash-backs**) nm CINÉ flashback.

flasher [3] [flaʃe] vi *fam* **: flasher sur qqn/qqch** to be turned on by sb/sthg ▸ **faire flasher qqn** to turn sb on.

flasque [flask] ■ nf flask.
■ adj flabby, limp.

flatter [3] [flate] vt **1.** [louer] to flatter **2.** [caresser] to stroke.
◆ ***se flatter*** vp to flatter o.s. ▸ **je me flatte de le convaincre** I flatter myself that I can convince him ▸ **se flatter de faire qqch** to pride o.s. on doing sthg.

flatterie [flatri] nf flattery.

flatteur, euse [flatœr, øz] ■ adj flattering.
■ nm, f flatterer.

flatulence [flatylɑ̃s] nf flatulence, wind.

FLE, fle [flə] (abr de ***français langue étrangère***) nm *French as a foreign language.*

fléau, x [fleo] nm **1.** *litt* & *fig* [calamité] scourge **2.** [instrument] flail.

flèche [flɛʃ] nf **1.** [gén] arrow **2.** [d'église] spire **3.** *fig* [critique] shaft
▸▸ **monter en flèche** to shoot up ▸ **partir comme une flèche** to shoot off.

flécher [18] [fleʃe] vt to mark (with arrows).

fléchette [fleʃɛt] nf dart.
◆ ***fléchettes*** nfpl darts *sg.*

fléchir [32] [fleʃir] ■ vt to bend, to flex / *fig* to sway.
■ vi to bend / *fig* to weaken.

fléchissement [fleʃismɑ̃] nm bending, flexing / *fig* weakening.

flegmatique [flɛgmatik] adj phlegmatic.

flegme [flɛgm] nm composure.

flemmard, e [flɛmar, ard] *fam* ■ adj lazy.
■ nm, f lazybones *sg.*

flemmarder [3] [flɛmarde] vi *fam* to lounge around.

flemme [flɛm] nf *fam* laziness ▸ **j'ai la flemme (de sortir)** I can't be bothered (to go out) *UK.*

flétan [fletɑ̃] nm halibut.

flétrir [32] [fletrir] vt [fleur, visage] to wither.
◆ ***se flétrir*** vp to wither.

fleur [flœr] nf *fig* & BOT flower ▸ **en fleur, en fleurs** [arbre] in flower, in blossom ▸ **à fleurs** [motif] flowered ▸ **la fine fleur de** *fig* the flower *ou* the cream of ▸ **fleur de farine** fine wheat flour ▸ **fleur de lotus** lotus blossom ▸ **fleur de lys** fleur-de-lis ▸ **fleur d'oranger** [fleur] orange flower / [essence] orange flower water ▸ **fleurs de rhétorique** rhetorical flourishes ▸ **dans la fleur de l'âge** in the prime of life ▸ **arriver comme une fleur** to turn up out of the blue ▸ **être fleur bleue** to be a romantic, to be sentimental ▸ **faire une fleur à qqn** *fam* to do sb a good turn ▸ **avoir les nerfs à fleur de peau** to be all on edge ▸ **une sensibilité à fleur de peau** hypersensitivity.

fleurer [5] [flœre] vt **: fleurer bon la vanille** to have a pleasant smell of vanilla.

fleuret [flœrɛ] nm foil.

fleurette [flœrɛt] nf **: conter fleurette à qqn** *vieilli* & *hum* to whisper sweet nothings to sb.

fleuri, e [flœri] adj **1.** [jardin, pré] in flower / [vase] of flowers / [tissu] flowered / [table, appartement] decorated with flowers **2.** *fig* [style] flowery.

fleurir [32] [flœrir] ■ vi to blossom / *fig* to flourish.
■ vt [maison] to decorate with flowers / [tombe] to lay flowers on.

fleuriste [flœrist] nmf florist.

fleuron [flœrɔ̃] nm *fig* jewel.

fleuve [flœv] nm **1.** [cours d'eau] river **2.** *(en apposition)* [interminable] lengthy, interminable ▸ **un discours-fleuve** an interminable speech.

flexibilité [flɛksibilite] nf **1.** [d'un matériau] pliability **2.** [d'un arrangement, d'un horaire] flexibility, adaptability / [d'un dispositif] versatility.

flexible [flɛksibl] adj flexible.

flexion [flɛksjɔ̃] nf **1.** [de genou, de poutre] bending **2.** LING inflexion.

flibustier [flibystje] nm buccaneer.

flic [flik] nm *fam* cop.

flingue [flɛ̃g] nm *fam* gun.

flinguer [3] [flɛ̃ge] vt *fam* to gun down.
◆ ***se flinguer*** vp *fam* to blow one's brains out.

flipper[1] [flipœr] nm pinball machine.

flipper[2] [3] [flipe] vi *fam* **1.** [être déprimé] to feel down **2.** [planer] to freak out.

flirt [flœrt] nm **1.** [amourette] flirtation **2.** [personne] boyfriend (f girlfriend).

flirter [3] [flœrte] vi **: flirter (avec qqn)** to flirt (with sb) ▸ **flirter avec qqch** *fig* to flirt with sthg.

FLN (abr de ***Front de libération nationale***) nm *Algerian national liberation front.*

FLNC (abr de ***Front de libération nationale corse***) nm *Corsican national liberation front.*

FLNKS (abr de ***Front de libération nationale kanak et socialiste***) **nm** *political movement in New Caledonia.*

flocon [flɔkɔ̃] **nm** flake ▸ **flocon de neige** snowflake ▸ **flocons d'avoine** oat flakes.

flonflon [flɔ̃flɔ̃] **nm** *(gén pl)* blare.

flop [flɔp] **nm** [échec] flop, failure.

flopée [flɔpe] **nf** *fam* **: une flopée de** heaps of, masses of.

floraison [flɔrɛzɔ̃] **nf** *litt & fig* flowering, blossoming.

floral, e, aux [flɔral, o] **adj** floral.

floralies [flɔrali] **nfpl** flower show *sg.*

flore [flɔr] **nf** flora.

Florence [flɔrɑ̃s] **npr** Florence.

florentin, e [flɔrɑ̃tɛ̃, in] **adj** Florentine.

◆ ***Florentin, e*** **nm, f** Florentine.

◆ ***florentin*** **nm** Florentine *(biscuit containing almonds and candied fruit with a chocolate base).*

Floride [flɔrid] **nf : la Floride** Florida.

florilège [flɔrilɛʒ] **nm** anthology.

florissant, e [flɔrisɑ̃, ɑ̃t] **adj** [santé] blooming / [économie] flourishing.

flot [flo] **nm** flood, stream ▸ **être à flot** [navire] to be afloat / *fig* to be back to normal ▸ **couler à flots** *fig* to flow like water.

◆ ***flots*** **nmpl** *littéraire* waves.

flottage [flɔtaʒ] **nm** floating *(of logs).*

flottaison [flɔtɛzɔ̃] **nf** floating.

flottant, e [flɔtɑ̃, ɑ̃t] **adj 1.** [gén] floating / [esprit] irresolute **2.** [robe] loose-fitting.

flotte [flɔt] **nf 1.** AÉRON & NAUT fleet ▸ **flotte aérienne** air fleet **2.** *fam* [eau] water **3.** *fam* [pluie] rain.

flottement [flɔtmɑ̃] **nm 1.** [de drapeau] fluttering **2.** [indécision] hesitation, wavering **3.** [de monnaie] floating.

flotter [3] [flɔte] ■ **vi 1.** [sur l'eau] to float **2.** [drapeau] to flap / [brume, odeur] to drift **3.** [dans un vêtement] **: tu flottes dedans** it's baggy on you.

■ **v impers** *fam* **: il flotte** it's raining.

flotteur [flɔtœr] **nm** [de ligne de pêche, d'hydravion] float / [de chasse d'eau] ballcock.

flou, e [flu] **adj 1.** [couleur, coiffure] soft **2.** [photo] blurred, fuzzy **3.** [pensée] vague, woolly *UK ou* wooly *US.*

◆ ***flou*** **nm** [de photo] fuzziness / [de décision] vagueness ▸ **le flou artistique** CINÉ & PHOTO soft focus / *fig* vagueness.

flouer [3] [flue] **vt** *fam* to swindle, to do *UK.*

fluctuant, e [flyktɥɑ̃, ɑ̃t] **adj** fluctuating.

fluctuation [flyktɥasjɔ̃] **nf** fluctuation.

fluctuer [3] [flyktɥe] **vi** to fluctuate.

fluet, ette [flyɛ, ɛt] **adj** [personne] thin, slender / [voix] thin.

fluide [flɥid] ■ **nm 1.** [matière] fluid **2.** *fig* [pouvoir] (occult) power.

■ **adj** [matière] fluid / [circulation] flowing freely.

fluidifier [9] [flɥidifje] **vt** [trafic] to improve the flow of.

fluidité [flɥidite] **nf** [gén] fluidity / [de circulation] easy flow.

fluo [flyo] **adj** fluorescent, Day-Glo®.

fluor [flyɔr] **nm** fluorine.

fluoré, e [flyɔre] **adj** fluoridated.

fluorescent, e [flyɔresɑ̃, ɑ̃t] **adj** fluorescent.

flûte [flyt] ■ **nf 1.** MUS flute ▸ **flûte à bec** recorder ▸ **flûte traversière** flute **2.** [verre] flute (glass) ▸ **flûte à champagne** champagne flute **3.** [pain] thin loaf of French bread.

■ **interj** *fam* darn!, bother! *UK*

flûtiste [flytist] **nmf** flautist *UK*, flutist *US.*

fluvial, e, aux [flyvjal, o] **adj** [eaux, pêche] river *(avant n)* / [alluvions] fluvial.

flux [fly] **nm 1.** [écoulement] flow ▸ **un flux de** *fig* a flood of **2.** [marée] flood tide ▸ **le flux et le reflux** the ebb and flow **3.** PHYS flux **4.** [sociologie] **: flux migratoire** massive population movement.

fluxion [flyksjɔ̃] **nf** inflammation ▸ **fluxion de poitrine** pneumonia.

FM (abr de ***frequency modulation***) **nf** FM.

FMI (abr de ***Fonds monétaire international***) **nm** IMF.

FN (abr de ***Front national***) **nm** *extreme right-wing French political party.*

FNAC, Fnac [fnak] (abr de ***Fédération nationale des achats des cadres***) **nf** *chain of large stores selling books, records, audio and video equipment etc.*

FNEF, Fnef [fnɛf] (abr de ***Fédération nationale des étudiants de France***) **nf** *students' union.*

FNSEA (abr de ***Fédération nationale des syndicats d'exploitants agricoles***) **nf** *farmers' union.*

FO (abr de ***Force ouvrière***) **nf** *workers' trade union.*

foc [fɔk] **nm** jib.

focal, e, aux [fɔkal, o] **adj** focal.

focaliser [3] [fɔkalize] **vt** to focus.

◆ ***se focaliser*** **vp** *fig* **: se focaliser sur qqch** to focus on sthg.

fœtal, e, aux [fetal, o] **adj** foetal *UK*, fetal *US.*

fœtus [fetys] **nm** foetus *UK*, fetus *US.*

foi [fwa] **nf 1.** RELIG faith ▸ **avoir la foi** to have faith **2.** [confiance] trust ▸ **avoir foi en qqn/qqch** to trust sb/sthg, to have faith in sb/sthg ▸ **elle a une foi aveugle en lui** she trusts him blindly

▸▸ **ajouter foi à** *sout* to lend credence to ▸ **faire foi** to serve as proof ▸ **il n'y a qu'une pièce officielle qui fasse foi** only an official paper is valid ▸ **être de bonne/mauvaise foi** to be in good/bad faith ▸ **il a agi en toute bonne foi** he acted in good faith ▸ **en foi de quoi** DR in witness whereof ▸ **ma foi...** well... ▸ **sur la foi de** on the strength of ▸ **sur la foi de ses déclarations** on the strength of his statement ▸ **sous la foi du serment** on *ou* under oath.

foie [fwa] **nm** ANAT & CULIN liver ▸ **foie de veau/de volaille** calf's/chicken liver ▸ **foie gras** foie gras ▸ **avoir les foies** *fam fig* to be scared out of one's wits.

foin [fwɛ̃] **nm** hay ▸ **faire les foins** to make hay ▸ **faire du foin** *fam fig* to make a din.

foire [fwar] **nf 1.** [fête] funfair *UK*, carnival *US* **2.** [exposition, salon] trade fair **3.** *fam* [agitation] circus ▸ **foire d'empoigne** free-for-all ▸ **faire la foire** *fam fig* to have a wild time.

foire-exposition [fwarɛkspozisjɔ̃] (pl **foires-expositions**) **nf** trade fair.

foirer [3] [fware] **vi** *fam* [projet] to fall through.

foireux, ***euse*** [fwarø, øz] **adj** *fam* [raté] disastrous / [qui va rater] doomed.

fois [fwa] **nf** time ▸ **une fois** once ▸ **deux fois** twice ▸ **trois/quatre fois** three/four times ▸ **trois fois rien** virtually nothing, hardly anything ▸ **deux fois plus long** twice as long ▸ **neuf fois sur dix** nine times out of ten ▸ **deux fois trois** two times three ▸ **cette fois** this time ▸ **ça ira pour cette fois, mais ne recommencez pas** it's alright this once, but don't do it again ▸ **par deux fois** *littéraire* twice ▸ **il était une fois...** once upon a time there was... ▸ **payez en six fois** pay in six instalments ▸ **pour une fois (que)** for once ▸ **pour la énième fois** for the umpteenth time ▸ **une autre fois** another time ▸ **une fois nettoyé, il sera comme neuf** once *ou* after it's been cleaned, it'll be as good as new ▸ **une (bonne) fois pour toutes** once and for all ▸ **une fois n'est pas coutume** just the once won't hurt.

◆ ***à la fois*** **loc adv** at the same time, at once ▸ **pas tous à la fois!** one at a time!, not all at once! ▸ **elle est (tout) à la fois auteur et traductrice** she's both an author and a translator.

◆ ***des fois*** **loc adv** [parfois] sometimes ▸ **non, mais des fois!** *fam* look here!

◆ ***des fois que*** **loc conj** *fam* **: je préfère l'appeler, des fois qu'elle aurait oublié** I'd rather call her in case she's forgotten.

◆ ***si des fois*** **loc conj** *fam* if ever.

◆ ***une fois que*** **loc conj** once ▸ **une fois que tu auras compris, tout sera plus facile** once you've understood, you'll find everything's easier.

foison [fwazɔ̃] ◆ ***à foison*** **loc adv** in abundance.

foisonnement [fwazɔnmɑ̃] **nm** abundance.

foisonner [3] [fwazɔne] **vi** to abound ▸ **foisonner en** *ou* **de** to abound in.

fol [fɔl] **m** ➤ ***fou***.

folâtrer [3] [fɔlatre] **vi** to romp (around).

folichon, ***onne*** [fɔliʃɔ̃, ɔn] **adj : ça n'est pas folichon** *fam* it's not much fun.

folie [fɔli] **nf** *litt* & *fig* madness ▸ **à la folie** madly ▸ **c'est de la folie** it's madness *ou* lunacy ▸ **avoir la folie des grandeurs** to have delusions of grandeur ▸ **faire des folies** *fig* to be extravagant.

folio [fɔljo] **nm** folio.

folk [fɔlk] ■ **nm** folk music.
■ **adj inv** folk ▸ **la musique folk** folk music.

folklo [fɔlklo] **adj inv** *fam* weird ▸ **c'est un type plutôt folklo** he's a bit of a weirdo.

folklore [fɔlklɔr] **nm** [de pays] folklore ▸ **c'est du folklore** *fig* you can't take it seriously.

folklorique [fɔlklɔrik] **adj 1.** [danse] folk **2.** *fig* [situation, personne] bizarre, quaint.

folle ➤ ***fou***.

follement [fɔlmɑ̃] **adv** madly, wildly ▸ **follement amoureux** madly in love.

follet [fɔlɛ] ➤ ***feu***.

fomenter [3] [fɔmɑ̃te] **vt** to foment.

foncé, ***e*** [fɔ̃se] **adj** dark.

foncer [16] [fɔ̃se] ■ **vt** to darken, to make darker.
■ **vi 1.** [teinte] to darken **2.** [se ruer] **: foncer sur** to rush at **3.** *fam* [se dépêcher] to get a move on.

fonceur, ***euse*** [fɔ̃sœr, øz] ■ **adj** dynamic, go-ahead.
■ **nm, f** dynamic person.

foncier, ***ère*** [fɔ̃sje, ɛr] **adj 1.** [impôt] land *(avant n)* ▸ **propriétaire foncier** landowner **2.** [fondamental] basic, fundamental.

foncièrement [fɔ̃sjɛrmɑ̃] **adv** basically.

fonction [fɔ̃ksjɔ̃] **nf 1.** [gén] function ▸ **faire fonction de** to act as **2.** [profession] post ▸ **se démettre de ses fonctions** to resign ▸ **entrer en fonction** to take up one's post *ou* duties ▸ **la fonction publique** the civil service.

◆ ***en fonction de*** **loc prép** according to.

◆ ***de fonction*** **loc adj : appartement** *ou* **logement de fonction** tied accommodation *UK*, accommodations that go with the job *US*.

CULTURE

La fonction publique

The state is France's largest employer. With public hospitals and the territorial governments included in the figure, it employs more than 4.5 million people – about a quarter of France's total population. (This number does not include state-owned companies.) Those who work in the private sector often decry what they see as government employees' special privileges, some of which are quite significant. State employees enjoy greater job stability and often can retire earlier.

fonctionnaire [fɔ̃ksjɔnɛr] **nmf** [de l'État] state employee / [dans l'administration] civil servant ▸ **haut fonctionnaire** senior civil servant.

fonctionnariat [fɔ̃ksjɔnarja] **nm** employment by the state.

fonctionnariser [3] [fɔ̃ksjɔnarize] **vt 1.** [personne] to make a state employee **2.** [service] to take into the public sector.

fonctionnel, ***elle*** [fɔ̃ksjɔnɛl] **adj** functional.

fonctionnement [fɔ̃ksjɔnmɑ̃] **nm** working, functioning.

fonctionner [3] [fɔ̃ksjɔne] **vi** to work, to function.

fond [fɔ̃] **nm 1.** [de récipient, puits, mer] bottom / [de pièce] back ▸ **le fond d'œil** MÉD the back of the eye ▸ **un fond** [petite quantité] a drop ▸ **couler par 100 m de fond** to sink to a depth of 100 m ▸ **je vous remercie du fond du cœur** I thank you from the bottom of my heart ▸ **toucher le fond (du désespoir)** to reach the depths of despair ▸ **sans fond** bottomless ▸ **au fin fond de** in the depths of ▸ **de fond en comble** from top to bottom ▸ **revoir un texte de fond en**

comble *fig* to revise a text thoroughly **2.** [substance] heart, root ▸ **avoir un très bon fond** to be a good person at heart ▸ **le fond de ma pensée** what I really think ▸ **le fond et la forme** content and form ▸ **aller au fond des choses** to go to the heart *ou* root of things **3.** [arrière-plan] background ▸ **fond sonore** background music ▸ **le fond de l'air est frais** there's a chill *ou* nip in the air.
◆ ***fond d'artichaut*** **nm** artichoke heart.
◆ ***fond de bouteille*** **nm** lees *pl*, dregs *pl* ▸ **boire** *ou* **vider les fonds de bouteilles** to drink up the dregs.
◆ ***fond de teint*** **nm** foundation.
◆ ***à fond*** **loc adv 1.** [entièrement] thoroughly ▸ **se donner à fond** to give one's all ▸ **respirer à fond** to breathe deeply **2.** [très vite] at top speed.
◆ ***au fond, dans le fond*** **loc adv** basically ▸ **au fond, on pourrait y aller en janvier** in fact, we could go in January.
◆ ***au fond de*** **loc prép : au fond de moi-même/lui-même** *etc* at heart, deep down ▸ **au fond de la rivière** at the bottom of the river.

fondais, fondions ➤ ***fondre.***

fondamental, e, aux [fɔ̃damɑ̃tal, o] **adj** fundamental.

fondamentalement [fɔ̃damɑ̃talmɑ̃] **adv** fundamentally.

fondamentalisme [fɔ̃damɑ̃talism] **nm** (religious) fundamentalism.

fondamentaliste [fɔ̃damɑ̃talist] **nmf & adj** fundamentalist.

fondant, e [fɔ̃dɑ̃, ɑ̃t] **adj** [neige, glace] melting / [aliment] melting in the mouth.
◆ ***fondant*** **nm** [gâteau] fondant.

fondateur, trice [fɔ̃datœr, tris] **nm, f** founder.

fondation [fɔ̃dasjɔ̃] **nf** foundation.
◆ ***fondations*** **nfpl** CONSTR foundations.

fondé, e [fɔ̃de] **adj 1.** [craintes, reproches] justified, well-founded ▸ **non fondé** unfounded **2.** [raisons] **: être fondé à faire qqch** to have good reason to do sthg **3.** [marketing] based ▸ **marché fondé sur les besoins** needs-based market.
◆ ***fondé de pouvoir*** **nm** authorized representative.

fondement [fɔ̃dmɑ̃] **nm** [base, motif] foundation ▸ **sans fondement** groundless, without foundation.

fonder [3] [fɔ̃de] **vt 1.** [créer] to found **2.** [baser] **: fonder qqch sur** to base sthg on ▸ **fonder de grands espoirs sur qqn** to pin one's hopes on sb.
◆ ***se fonder*** **vp : se fonder sur** [suj: personne] to base o.s. on / [suj: argument] to be based on.

fonderie [fɔ̃dri] **nf** [usine] foundry.

fondeur, euse [fɔ̃dœr, øz] **nm, f** SKI cross-country skier.

fondre [75] [fɔ̃dr] ■ **vt 1.** [beurre, neige] to melt / [sucre, sel] to dissolve / [métal] to melt down **2.** [mouler] to cast **3.** [mêler] to blend.
■ **vi 1.** [beurre, neige] to melt / [sucre, sel] to dissolve / *fig* to melt away **2.** [maigrir] to lose weight **3.** [se ruer] **: fondre sur** to swoop down on.
◆ ***se fondre*** **vp : se fondre dans la brume/la foule** to melt away into the fog/the crowd.

fonds [fɔ̃] ■ **nm 1.** [ressources] fund ▸ **fonds d'amortissement** sinking fund ▸ **fonds de consolidation** umbrella fund ▸ **fonds commun de placement** unit trust *UK*, mutual fund *US* ▸ **fonds géré** managed fund ▸ **fonds indiciel** *ou* **à gestion indicielle** tracker fund ▸ **le Fonds monétaire international** the International Monetary Fund ▸ **fonds off-shore** offshore fund ▸ **fonds de réserve** reserve fund ▸ **fonds de roulement** working capital ▸ **le Fonds social européen** European Social Fund
2. [bien immobilier] **: fonds (de commerce)** business.
■ **nmpl 1.** [ressources] funds ▸ **collecte de fonds** financial appeal, fundraising *(U)* ▸ **être en fonds** to be in funds ▸ **rentrer dans ses fonds** to recoup one's costs
2. ÉCON & FIN **: fonds de pension** (private) pension fund ▸ **fonds de prévoyance** contingency fund ▸ **les fonds propres** shareholders' *UK ou* stockholders' *US* equity ▸ **fonds publics/secrets** public/secret funds.

fondu, e [fɔ̃dy] **pp** ➤ ***fondre.***
◆ ***fondu*** **nm 1.** [CINÉ - ouverture] fade-in / [- fermeture] fade-out ▸ **fondu enchaîné** dissolve **2.** [de couleurs] blend.
◆ ***fondue*** **nf** fondue ▸ **fondue au fromage** *ou* **savoyarde** cheese fondue ▸ **fondue bourguignonne** meat fondue.

fongicide [fɔ̃ʒisid] ■ **nm** fungicide.
■ **adj** fungicidal.

font ➤ ***faire.***

fontaine [fɔ̃tɛn] **nf** [naturelle] spring / [publique] fountain.

fontanelle [fɔ̃tanɛl] **nf** fontanelle.

fonte [fɔ̃t] **nf 1.** [de glace, beurre] melting / [de métal] melting down ▸ **la fonte des neiges** the thaw **2.** [alliage] cast iron ▸ **en fonte** cast-iron.

fonts [fɔ̃] **nmpl : fonts baptismaux** (baptismal) font *sg*.

foot [fut] *fam* = ***football.***

football [futbol] **nm** soccer, football *UK* ▸ **football américain** American football *UK*, football *US*.

footballeur, euse [futbolœr, øz] **nm, f** soccer player, footballer *UK*.

footing [futiŋ] **nm** jogging ▸ **faire du footing** to go jogging.

for [fɔr] **nm : dans son for intérieur** in his/her heart of hearts.

FOR (abr écrite de ***forint***) F, Ft.

forage [fɔraʒ] **nm** drilling.

forain, e [fɔrɛ̃, ɛn] **adj** ➤ ***fête.***
◆ ***forain*** **nm** stallholder *UK*.

forban [fɔrbɑ̃] **nm 1.** [corsaire] pirate **2.** [escroc] crook.

forçat [fɔrsa] **nm** convict.

force [fɔrs] **nf 1.** [vigueur] strength ▸ **avoir de la force** to be strong ▸ **avoir recours à la force** to resort to force ▸ **en force** [passer] by (physical) effort / [arriver] in force ▸ **être une force de la nature** to be a human dynamo ▸ **être de force à faire qqch** to be up to doing sthg ▸ **c'est ce qui fait sa force** that's where his strength lies ▸ **force de caractère** strength of character ▸ **dans la force de l'âge** *fig* in the prime of life ▸ **grimper à la force des bras** to climb by the strength of one's arms ▸ **s'élever à la force du poignet** *fig* to go up in the world by the sweat of one's brow **2.** [violence, puissance, MIL & PHYS] force ▸ **faire faire qqch**

à qqn de force to force sb to do sthg ▸ **on les a fait sortir de force** they were made to leave ▸ **par la force des choses** by force of circumstances ▸ **avoir force de loi** to have force of law ▸ **obtenir qqch par la force** to obtain sthg by force ▸ **force centrifuge** PHYS centrifugal force ▸ **force de dissuasion** deterrent power ▸ **force de frappe** strike force ▸ **force d'inertie** PHYS force of inertia ▸ **force d'intervention** task force ▸ **force de vente** COMM sales force.

◆ ***forces*** **nfpl 1.** [physique] strength *(U)* ▸ **être à bout de forces** to have no strength left ▸ **c'est au-dessus de mes forces** it's beyond me ▸ **de toutes ses forces** with all one's strength ▸ **recouvrer ses forces** to get one's strength back ▸ **reprendre des forces** to recover one's strength **2.** [organisation] **: les forces armées** the armed forces ▸ **forces d'intervention** rapid deployment force *sg* ▸ **les forces de l'ordre** the police *sg* ▸ **les forces de police** the police force *sg*.

◆ ***à force*** **loc adv** *fam* **: tu vas le casser, à force!** you'll break it if you go on like that!

◆ ***à force de*** **loc prép** by dint of ▸ **à force de parler** by dint of talking.

forcé**, **e [fɔrse] **adj** forced.

forcément [fɔrsemɑ̃] **adv** inevitably.

forcené**, **e [fɔrsəne] ■ **adj** [haine, critique] frenzied / [partisan] fanatical.
■ **nm, f** maniac.

forceps [fɔrsɛps] **nm** forceps *pl*.

forcer [16] [fɔrse] ■ **vt 1.** [gén] to force ▸ **forcer qqn à qqch/à faire qqch** to force sb into sthg/to do sthg **2.** [admiration, respect] to compel, to command **3.** [talent, voix] to strain.
■ **vi : ça ne sert à rien de forcer, ça ne passe pas** there's no point in forcing it: it won't go through ▸ **forcer sur qqch** to overdo sthg.

◆ ***se forcer*** **vp** [s'obliger] **: se forcer à faire qqch** to force o.s. to do sthg.

forcing [fɔrsiŋ] **nm** *fig* & SPORT pressure ▸ **faire du forcing** to push o.s.

forcir [32] [fɔrsir] **vi** to put on weight.

forer [3] [fɔre] **vt** to drill.

forestier**, **ère [fɔrɛstje, ɛr] **adj** forest *(avant n)*.

◆ ***forestier*** **nm** forestry worker.

foret [fɔrɛ] **nm** drill.

forêt [fɔrɛ] **nf** forest.

Forêt-Noire [fɔrɛnwar] **npr f : la Forêt-Noire** the Black Forest.

foreuse [fɔrøz] **nf** drill.

forfait [fɔrfɛ] **nm 1.** [prix fixe] fixed price ▸ **être au forfait** [pour l'imposition] to pay an estimated amount of tax **2.** [séjour] package deal **3.** SPORT **: déclarer forfait** [abandonner] to withdraw / *fig* to give up **4.** *littéraire* [crime] heinous crime.

forfaitaire [fɔrfɛtɛr] **adj** inclusive.

forfaiture [fɔrfetyr] **nf 1.** DR abuse of authority **2.** HIST forfeiture.

forfait-vacances [fɔrfɛvakɑ̃s] (pl **forfaits-vacances**) **nm** package tour *ou* holiday *UK*.

forfanterie [fɔrfɑ̃tri] **nf** bragging.

forge [fɔrʒ] **nf** forge.

forger [17] [fɔrʒe] **vt 1.** [métal] to forge **2.** *fig* [caractère] to form **3.** [plan, excuse] to concoct ▸ **une histoire forgée de toutes pièces** a fabricated story.

◆ ***se forger*** **vpt : se forger une réputation** to earn o.s. a reputation ▸ **se forger le caractère** to build up one's character.

forgeron [fɔrʒərɔ̃] **nm** blacksmith.

formaliser [3] [fɔrmalize] **vt** to formalize.

◆ ***se formaliser*** **vp : se formaliser (de)** to take offence *UK ou* offense *US* (at).

formalisme [fɔrmalism] **nm** formality.

formaliste [fɔrmalist] ■ **nmf** formalist.
■ **adj** [milieu] conventional / [personne] **: être formaliste** to be a stickler for the rules.

formalité [fɔrmalite] **nf** formality ▸ **les formalités d'usage** the usual formalities.

format [fɔrma] **nm 1.** [dimension] size ▸ **grand/petit format** large/small size **2.** INFORM format ▸ **format JPEG** JPEG format ▸ **format MJPEG** MJPEG format.

formatage [fɔrmataʒ] **nm** INFORM formatting.

formater [3] [fɔrmate] **vt** INFORM to format.

formateur**, **trice [fɔrmatœr, tris] ■ **adj** formative.
■ **nm, f** trainer.

formation [fɔrmasjɔ̃] **nf 1.** [gén] formation ▸ **formation politique** political group ▸ **architecte de formation, elle est devenue cinéaste** having trained as an architect, she turned to making films ▸ **elle a une bonne formation littéraire/scientifique** she has a good literary/scientific background **2.** [apprentissage] training ▸ **formation en alternance** sandwich course *UK* ▸ **formation continue** continuing education ▸ **formation professionnelle** vocational training.

forme [fɔrm] **nf 1.** [aspect] shape, form ▸ **en forme de** in the shape of ▸ **en forme de poisson** shaped like a fish, fish-shaped ▸ **sous forme de** in the form of ▸ **un médicament qui existe sous forme de comprimés** a drug available in tablet form ▸ **sous toutes ses formes** in all its forms ▸ **mettez vos idées en forme** give your ideas some shape ▸ **mettre un verbe à la forme interrogative** to put a verb into the interrogative (form) ▸ **prendre forme** to take shape **2.** [état] form ▸ **être en (pleine) forme** to be in (great) shape, to be on *UK ou* in *US* (top) form ▸ **être en bonne forme physique** to be fit
▸▸ **en bonne et due forme** in due form ▸ **faire qqch dans les formes** to do sthg in the correct way ▸ **pour la forme** for form's sake ▸ **sans autre forme de procès** without further ado ▸ **y mettre les formes** to be tactful.

◆ ***formes*** **nfpl** figure *sg* ▸ **avoir des formes** to have a shapely figure.

formel**, **elle [fɔrmɛl] **adj 1.** [définitif, ferme] positive, definite **2.** [poli] formal.

formellement [fɔrmɛlmɑ̃] **adv 1.** [refuser] positively / [promettre] definitely **2.** [raisonner] formally.

former [3] [fɔrme] vt **1.** [gén] to form ▸ **ils ont formé un cortège/attroupement** they formed a procession/a mob ▸ **ils forment un couple uni** they're a united couple ▸ **former des vœux pour le succès de qqn/qqch** to wish sb/sthg success **2.** [personnel, élèves] to train ▸ **former les jeunes en entreprise** to give young people industrial training ▸ **former son personnel à l'informatique** to give one's staff computer training **3.** [goût, sensibilité] to develop.
◆ ***se former*** vp **1.** [se constituer] to form **2.** [s'instruire] to train o.s. ▸ **se former sur le tas** to learn on the job *ou* as one goes along.

Formica® [fɔrmika] nm inv Formica®.

formidable [fɔrmidabl] adj **1.** [épatant] great, tremendous **2.** [incroyable] incredible.

formidablement [fɔrmidabləmɑ̃] adv tremendously ▸ **elle sait formidablement bien s'occuper des enfants** she's great *ou* marvellous *UK ou* marvelous *US* with children.

formol [fɔrmɔl] nm formalin.

formosan, e [fɔrmɔzɑ̃, an] adj Formosan.
◆ ***Formosan, e*** nm, f Formosan.

Formose [fɔrmoz] npr Formosa ▸ **à Formose** in Formosa.

formulaire [fɔrmylɛr] nm form ▸ **remplir un formulaire** to fill in a form.

formulation [fɔrmylasjɔ̃] nf wording, formulation.

formule [fɔrmyl] nf **1.** [expression] expression ▸ **formule consacrée** accepted expression ▸ **la formule magique** the magic words ▸ **formule de politesse** [orale] polite phrase / [épistolaire] letter ending
2. CHIM & MATH formula
3. [méthode] way, method ▸ **ils ont (trouvé) la formule pour ne pas avoir d'ennuis** they've found a way of not having any problems ▸ **une nouvelle formule de spectacle/restaurant** a new kind of show/restaurant ▸ **nous vous proposons plusieurs formules de crédit** we offer you several credit options ▸ **une formule économique pour vos vacances** an economical way to spend your holidays *UK ou* vacation *US* ▸ **formules de remboursement** repayment options
4. [slogan] **: formule publicitaire** advertising slogan.
◆ ***formule 1*** nf Formula One.

formuler [3] [fɔrmyle] vt to formulate, to express.

fornication [fɔrnikasjɔ̃] nf *littéraire* & *hum* fornication.

forniquer [3] [fɔrnike] vi to fornicate.

forsythia [fɔrsisja] nm forsythia.

fort, e [fɔr, fɔrt] ■ adj **1.** [gén] strong ▸ **mer forte** MÉTÉOR rough sea ▸ **fort comme un Turc** *ou* **un bœuf** as strong as an ox ▸ **elle a une forte personnalité** she's got a strong personality ▸ **et le plus fort, c'est que...** and the most amazing thing about it is... ▸ **c'est un peu fort!** *fam* that's a bit much! ▸ **tu y vas un peu fort!** you're going a bit far! ▸ **c'est plus fort que moi** I can't help it **2.** [corpulent] heavy, big ▸ **avoir la taille forte** to be big around the waist **3.** [doué] gifted ▸ **être fort en qqch** to be good at sthg **4.** [puissant - voix] loud / [- vent, lumière, accent] strong **5.** [considérable] large ▸ **il est prêt à payer le prix fort** he's willing to pay the full price ▸ **il y a de fortes chances qu'il gagne** there's a good chance he'll win.
■ adv **1.** [frapper, battre] hard / [sonner, parler] loud, loudly ▸ **sentir fort** to smell **2.** *sout* [très] very ▸ **j'en suis fort aise!** *hum* I'm very pleased to hear it! ▸ **avoir fort à faire (avec qqn)** to have a hard job (with sb).
■ nm **1.** [château] fort **2.** [personne] **: un fort en qqch** a person who is good at sthg ▸ **un fort en thème** *vieilli* a swot *UK ou* grind *US* **3.** [spécialité] **: ce n'est pas mon fort** it's not my forte *ou* strong point.
◆ ***au plus fort de*** loc prép [hiver] in the depths of ▸ **au (plus) fort de l'été** in the height of summer / [tempête, dispute] at the height of.

forte [fɔrte] adj & nm MUS forte.

fortement [fɔrtəmɑ̃] adv **1.** [avec force] hard **2.** [très - intéressé, ému] deeply **3.** [beaucoup - bégayer, loucher] badly.

forteresse [fɔrtərɛs] nf fortress.

fortiche [fɔrtiʃ] adj *fam* **: elle est fortiche en anglais!** she's dead *UK ou* real *US* good at English!

fortifiant, e [fɔrtifjɑ̃, ɑ̃t] adj fortifying.
◆ ***fortifiant*** nm tonic.

fortification [fɔrtifikasjɔ̃] nf fortification.

fortifier [9] [fɔrtifje] vt [personne, ville] to fortify ▸ **fortifier qqn dans qqch** *fig* to strengthen sb in sthg ▸ **une ville fortifiée** a walled *ou* fortified town.

fortiori [fɔrsjɔri] ➤ ***a fortiori***.

fortuit, e [fɔrtɥi, it] adj chance *(avant n)*, fortuitous.

fortune [fɔrtyn] nf **1.** [richesse] fortune ▸ **faire fortune** to make one's fortune **2.** [hasard] luck, fortune.

fortuné, e [fɔrtyne] adj **1.** [riche] wealthy **2.** [chanceux] fortunate, lucky.

forum [fɔrɔm] nm forum ▸ **forum de discussion** INFORM chat room.

fosse [fos] nf **1.** [trou] pit ▸ **fosse septique** septic tank ▸ **fosse aux lions** lions' den ▸ **fosse d'orchestre** orchestra pit ▸ **fosse de sable** *Québec* [golf] bunker, sand trap *US* **2.** [tombe] grave ▸ **fosse commune** common grave.

fossé [fose] nm ditch / *fig* gap.

fossette [fosɛt] nf dimple.

fossile [fosil] ■ adj fossil *(avant n)*, fossilized.
■ nm **1.** [de plante, d'animal] fossil **2.** *fig* & *péj* [personne] fossil, fogey.

fossiliser [3] [fosilize] vt to fossilize.
◆ ***se fossiliser*** vpi to become fossilized.

fossoyeur, euse [foswajœr, øz] nm, f gravedigger.

fou, folle [fu, fɔl] ■ adj *(fol devant voyelle ou 'h' muet)* mad, insane / [prodigieux] tremendous ▸ **c'est fou, ce qui lui est arrivé** what happened to him is incredible ▸ **être fou de qqn/qqch** to be mad about sb/sthg ▸ **être fou d'inquiétude** to be mad with worry ▸ **être fou de joie** to be deliriously happy ▸ **il y avait un monde fou** there was a huge crowd ▸ **rendre qqn fou** to drive *ou* to send sb mad ▸ **ton projet est complètement fou** your plan is completely crazy *ou* mad ▸ **fou à lier** raving mad.
■ nm, f madman (f madwoman) ▸ **fou furieux** manic ▸ **comme un fou** *litt* dementedly / [intensément] like mad *ou* crazy ▸ **c'est un fou de moto** he's mad on *ou* crazy about motorbikes *UK ou* motorcycles *US* ▸ **faire le fou** *fig* to act the fool.

foudre [fudr] **nf** lightning ▸ **rapide comme la foudre** (as) quick as lightning ▸ **encourir** *ou* **s'attirer les foudres de qqn** *fig* to bring down sb's wrath on o.s.
◆ ***foudre de guerre*** **nm 1.** [guerrier] great warrior **2.** *fig* **: ce n'est pas un foudre de guerre** *hum* he wouldn't say boo to a goose.

foudroyant, e [fudrwajɑ̃, ɑ̃t] **adj 1.** [progrès, vitesse] lightning *(avant n)* / [succès] stunning **2.** [nouvelle] devastating / [regard] withering.

foudroyer [13] [fudrwaje] **vt 1.** [suj: foudre] to strike ▸ **l'arbre a été foudroyé** the tree was struck by lightning **2.** *fig* [abattre] to strike down, to kill ▸ **foudroyer qqn du regard** to glare at sb.

fouet [fwɛ] **nm 1.** [en cuir] whip ▸ **de plein fouet** direct ▸ **il prit la pluie de plein fouet** the rain hit him full in the face **2.** CULIN whisk.

fouetter [4] [fwete] **vt 1.** [gén] to whip / [suj: pluie] to lash (against) **2.** [stimuler] to stimulate.

fougasse [fugas] **nf** *type of unleavened bread.*

fougère [fuʒɛr] **nf** fern.

fougue [fug] **nf** ardour *UK*, ardor *US*.

fougueux, euse [fugø, øz] **adj** ardent, spirited.

fouille [fuj] **nf 1.** [de personne, maison] search **2.** [du sol] dig, excavation.
◆ ***fouilles*** **nfpl** *fam* pockets.

fouiller [3] [fuje] ■ **vt 1.** [gén] to search **2.** *fig* [approfondir] to examine closely.
■ **vi : fouiller dans** to go through.

fouillis [fuji] **nm** jumble, muddle.

fouine [fwin] **nf** stone-marten.

fouiner [3] [fwine] **vi** to ferret around.

foulard [fular] **nm** scarf.

foule [ful] **nf 1.** [de gens] crowd ▸ **en foule** in great numbers ▸ **attirer les foules** *fig* to draw the crowds ▸ **il y a foule** *fam* there are crowds *ou* masses of people ▸ **il n'y a pas foule** *fam* there's hardly anyone around **2.** *péj* [peuple] **: la foule** the masses *pl* **3.** *fig* [multitude] **: une foule de** masses of ▸ **il m'a donné une foule de détails** he gave me a whole mass of details.

foulée [fule] **nf** [de coureur] stride ▸ **je suis sorti faire des courses et dans la foulée...** I went out to do some shopping and while I was at it...

fouler [3] [fule] **vt** [raisin] to press / [sol] to walk on.
◆ ***se fouler*** **vp 1.** MÉD **: se fouler le poignet/la cheville** to sprain one's wrist/ankle **2.** *fam fig* [se fatiguer] **: ne pas se fouler** not to strain o.s.

foulure [fulyr] **nf** sprain.

four [fur] **nm 1.** [de cuisson] oven ▸ **cuit au four** baked ▸ **four électrique/à micro-ondes** electric/microwave oven ▸ **four crématoire** HIST oven ▸ **je ne peux pas être (à la fois) au four et au moulin** *fig* I haven't got two pairs of hands, I can't be in two places at once ▸ **noir comme dans un four** *fig* black as pitch **2.** THÉÂTRE flop ▸ **faire un four** to flop.

fourbe [furb] ■ **adj** treacherous, deceitful.
■ **nmf** rogue.

fourbi [furbi] **nm** *fam* **1.** [attirail] gear **2.** [fouillis] mess.

fourbir [32] [furbir] **vt** *litt & fig* to polish.

fourbu, e [furby] **adj** tired out, exhausted.

fourche [furʃ] **nf 1.** [outil] pitchfork **2.** [de vélo, route] fork **3.** *Belgique* SCOL free period.

fourcher [3] [furʃe] **vi** [cheveux] to split
▸▸ **sa langue a fourché** he made a slip of the tongue.

fourchette [furʃɛt] **nf 1.** [couvert] fork **2.** [écart] range, bracket.

fourchu, e [furʃy] **adj** forked.

fourgon [furgɔ̃] **nm 1.** [camionnette] van ▸ **fourgon cellulaire** police van *UK*, patrol wagon *US* ▸ **fourgon mortuaire** hearse **2.** [ferroviaire] **: fourgon à bestiaux** cattle truck ▸ **fourgon postal** mail van *UK*, mail truck *US*.

fourgonnette [furgɔnɛt] **nf** small van.

fourguer [3] [furge] **vt** *fam* **: fourguer qqch à qqn** to palm sthg off on sb.

fourmi [furmi] **nf** [insecte] ant / *fig* hard worker ▸ **avoir des fourmis dans les bras/les jambes** to have pins and needles in one's arms/legs.

fourmilière [furmiljɛr] **nf** anthill.

fourmillement [furmijmɑ̃] **nm 1.** [d'insectes, de personnes] swarming **2.** [picotement] pins and needles *pl*.

fourmiller [3] [furmije] **vi** [pulluler] to swarm ▸ **fourmiller de** *fig* to be swarming with.

fournaise [furnɛz] **nf** furnace.

fourneau, x [furno] **nm 1.** [cuisinière, poêle] stove **2.** [de fonderie] furnace **3.** [de pipe] bowl.

fournée [furne] **nf** batch.

fourni, e [furni] **adj** [barbe, cheveux] thick.

fournil [furnil] **nm** bakery.

fournir [32] [furnir] ■ **vt 1.** [procurer] **: fournir qqch à qqn** to supply *ou* provide sb with sthg ▸ **c'est la France qui leur fournit des armes** it's France who is providing *ou* supplying them with weapons ▸ **fournir un alibi à qqn** to provide sb with an alibi **2.** [produire] **: fournir un effort** to make an effort **3.** [approvisionner] **: fournir qqn (en)** to supply sb (with) ▸ **fournir une entreprise en matières premières** to supply a firm with raw materials.
■ **vi : fournir à** to provide for ▸ **fournir aux besoins de qqn** to provide for sb's needs.
◆ ***se fournir*** **vp : se fournir chez/en** to get supplies from/of ▸ **je me fournis toujours chez le même boucher** I always shop at the same butcher's, I get all my meat from the same place.

fournisseur, euse [furnisœr, øz] **nm, f** supplier ▸ **fournisseur d'accès (Internet)** INFORM (Internet) service provider, Internet Access Provider.

fourniture [furnityr] **nf** supply, supplying *(U)*.
◆ ***fournitures*** **nfpl : fournitures de bureau** office supplies ▸ **fournitures scolaires** school supplies.

fourrage [furaʒ] **nm** fodder.

fourrager[1], ère [furaʒe, ɛr] **adj** fodder *(avant n)*.

fourrager[2] [17] [furaʒe] **vi** *fam* **: fourrager dans qqch** to rummage through sthg.

fourré [fure] **nm** thicket.

fourreau, x [furo] **nm 1.** [d'épée] sheath / [de parapluie] cover **2.** [robe] sheath dress.

fourrer [3] [fure] **vt 1.** CULIN to stuff, to fill **2.** *fam* [mettre] : **fourrer qqch (dans)** to stuff sthg (into).
◆ ***se fourrer*** **vp : se fourrer dans le pétrin** to get into a mess ▸ **se fourrer une idée dans la tête** to get an idea into one's head ▸ **je ne savais plus où me fourrer** I didn't know where to put myself.

fourre-tout [furtu] **nm inv 1.** [pièce] lumber room *UK*, junk room *US* **2.** [sac] holdall *UK*, carryall *US* **3.** *fig & péj* [d'idées] hotchpotch *UK*, hodgepodge *US*.

fourreur [furœr] **nm** furrier.

fourrière [furjɛr] **nf** pound ▸ **mettre à la fourrière** [voiture] to tow away.

fourrure [furyr] **nf** fur ▸ **un manteau en fausse fourrure** a fake fur coat.

fourvoyer [13] [furvwaje] ◆ ***se fourvoyer*** **vp** *sout* [s'égarer] to lose one's way / [se tromper] to go off on the wrong track.

foutaise [futɛz] **nf** *fam* crap *(U)*.

foutoir [futwar] **nm** *fam* pigsty.

foutre [116] [futr] **vt** *tfam* **1.** [mettre] to shove, to stick ▸ **foutre qqn dehors** *ou* **à la porte** to chuck sb out ▸ **foutre qqch par la fenêtre** to chuck sthg out of the window ▸ **foutre un rêve/un projet par terre** *fig* to wreck a dream/a project **2.** [donner] : **foutre le cafard à qqn** to get sb down ▸ **foutre la paix à qqn** to leave sb alone, to get out of sb's hair ▸ **foutre la trouille à qqn** to scare the pants off sb, to put the wind up sb *UK* ▸ **il lui a foutu une baffe** he thumped him one **3.** [faire] to do ▸ **ne rien foutre de la journée** to not do a damn thing all day ▸ **j'en ai rien à foutre** I don't give a damn *ou* toss *UK* ▸ **fous le camp de chez moi!** get the hell out of my house! *tfam* ▸ **qu'est-ce que ça peut te/lui foutre?** what the hell does it matter to you/him? *tfam* ▸ **va te faire foutre!** *vulg* piss *tfam* *ou* fuck *vulg* off!
◆ ***se foutre*** **vp** *tfam* **1.** [se mettre] : **se foutre dans** [situation] to get o.s. into ▸ **se foutre dedans** to blow it **2.** [se moquer] : **se foutre de (la gueule de) qqn** to laugh at sb, to take the mickey out of sb *UK* ▸ **tu te fous de moi ou quoi!** are you taking the piss? *UK* **3.** [ne pas s'intéresser] : **je m'en fous** I don't give a damn *ou* toss *UK* about it.

foutu, e [futy] **adj** *fam* **1.** [maudit] damned, bloody *UK* / [caractère] nasty **2.** [fait, conçu] : **bien foutu** [projet, maison] great ▸ **elle est bien foutue, celle-là** [femme] she's a real stunner **3.** [perdu] : **il est foutu** he's/it'shad it **4.** [capable] : **être foutu de faire qqch** to be liable *ou* quite likely to do sthg.

fox-terrier [fɔkstɛrje] (pl **fox-terriers**) **nm** fox terrier.

foyer [fwaje] **nm 1.** [maison] home ▸ **rentrer au foyer** to go home ▸ **être mère au foyer** to be a housewife and mother ▸ **femme au foyer** housewife **2.** [famille] family ▸ **fonder un foyer** to set up home ▸ **foyer fiscal** household **3.** [résidence] home, hostel ▸ **foyer d'étudiants** (students) hall ▸ **foyer d'immigrés** immigrant workers' hostel **4.** [point central] centre *UK*, center *US* ▸ **un foyer d'incendie** a fire **5.** [de lunettes] focus ▸ **verres à double foyer** bifocals.

FP (abr de ***franchise postale***) PP.

FPA (abr de ***formation professionnelle des adultes***) **nf** *state-run adult training scheme*.

FPLP (abr de ***Front populaire de libération de la Palestine***) **nm** PFLP.

frac [frak] **nm** tails *pl*.

fracas [fraka] **nm** roar.

fracassant, e [frakasɑ̃, ɑ̃t] **adj** [bruyant] thunderous / *fig* staggering, sensational.

fracasser [3] [frakase] **vt** to smash, to shatter.
◆ ***se fracasser*** **vp : se fracasser contre/sur** to crash against/into.

fractal, e, aux [fraktal, o] **adj** fractal.
◆ ***fractale*** **nf** fractal.

fraction [fraksjɔ̃] **nf** fraction.

fractionner [3] [fraksjɔne] **vt** to divide (up), to split up.
◆ ***se fractionner*** **vp** to split up.

fracture [fraktyr] **nf** MÉD fracture ▸ **fracture du crâne** fractured skull ▸ **fracture sociale** gap between the rich and the poor.

fracturer [3] [fraktyre] **vt 1.** MÉD to fracture **2.** [coffre, serrure] to break open.
◆ ***se fracturer*** **vp** to break, to fracture.

fragile [fraʒil] **adj** [gén] fragile / [peau, santé] delicate.

fragiliser [3] [fraʒilize] **vt** to weaken.

fragilité [fraʒilite] **nf** fragility.

fragment [fragmɑ̃] **nm 1.** [morceau] fragment **2.** [extrait - d'œuvre] extract / [- de conversation] snatch.

fragmentaire [fragmɑ̃tɛr] **adj** fragmentary.

fragmenter [3] [fragmɑ̃te] **vt** to fragment, to break up.
◆ ***se fragmenter*** **vp** to fragment, to break up.

fraîche ➤ ***frais***.

fraîchement [frɛʃmɑ̃] **adv 1.** [récemment] recently **2.** [froidement] coolly.

fraîcheur [frɛʃœr] **nf 1.** [d'air, d'accueil] coolness **2.** [de teint, d'aliment] freshness.

fraîchir [32] [frɛʃir] **vi** to freshen.

frais, fraîche [frɛ, frɛʃ] **adj 1.** [air, accueil] cool ▸ **boisson fraîche** cold drink **2.** [récent - trace] fresh / [- encre] wet ▸ **frais émoulu (de)** fresh (from) ▸ **œufs frais de ce matin** eggs newly laid this morning ▸ **j'ai reçu des nouvelles fraîches** I've got some recent news **3.** [teint] fresh, clear ▸ **frais et dispos** hale and hearty ▸ **être frais comme un gardon** to be on top form **4.** ÉCON : **argent frais** ready cash.
◆ ***frais*** ■ **nm : mettre qqch au frais** to put sthg in a cool place ▸ **prendre le frais** to take a breath of fresh air.
■ **nmpl** [dépenses] expenses, costs ▸ **faux frais** incidentals ▸ **frais d'abonnement** [sur une facture] standing charges ▸ **frais d'administration** administrative costs ▸ **frais bancaires** bank charges ▸ **frais de déplacement** travelling expenses ▸ **frais différés** deferred charges ▸ **frais directs** direct costs ▸ **frais d'entretien** upkeep ▸ **frais d'équipement** capital expenditure ▸ **frais d'envoi** *ou* **d'expédition** postage ▸ **frais de fabrication** manufacturing costs ▸ **frais facturables** FIN chargeable expenses ▸ **frais fixes** fixed costs ▸ **frais généraux** overheads *UK*, overhead *US* ▸ **frais de gestion** running costs ▸ **frais d'inscription**

registration fee, membership fee / FIN set-up fee ▸ **frais de justice** legal costs ▸ **frais de lancement** set-up costs ▸ **frais professionnels** professional expenses ▸ **frais de représentation** entertainment allowance ▸ **frais de tenue de compte** account charges ▸ **frais de sortie** exit charge(s) ▸ **frais variables** variable costs
▸▸ **à grands frais** at a high price ▸ **aux frais de la maison** at the company's expense ▸ **à peu de frais** cheaply ▸ **faire des frais** to spend a lot of money ▸ **tous frais payés** all expenses paid ▸ **faire les frais de qqch** to bear the brunt of sthg ▸ **en être pour ses frais** to waste one's time ▸ **rentrer dans ses frais** to cover one's expenses.
■ **adv : il fait frais** it's cool ▸ **'servir frais'** 'serve chilled'.

fraise [frɛz] **nf 1.** [fruit] strawberry ▸ **fraise des bois** wild strawberry **2.** [de dentiste] drill / [de menuisier] bit.

fraiser [4] [frɛze] **vt** to countersink.

fraiseuse [frɛzøz] **nf** milling machine.

fraisier [frezje] **nm 1.** [plante] strawberry plant **2.** [gâteau] strawberry sponge.

framboise [frɑ̃bwaz] **nf 1.** [fruit] raspberry **2.** [liqueur] raspberry liqueur.

framboisier [frɑ̃bwazje] **nm 1.** [plante] raspberry bush **2.** [gâteau] raspberry sponge.

franc, ***franche*** [frɑ̃, frɑ̃ʃ] **adj 1.** [sincère] frank ▸ **être franc du collier** to be straightforward ▸ **jouer franc jeu** to play fair ▸ **pour être franc avec vous** to be honest with you **2.** [net] clear, definite ▸ **l'ambiance n'était pas à la franche gaieté** the atmosphere wasn't exactly a happy one ▸ **rencontrer une franche hostilité** to encounter outright hostility **3.** COMM & FIN free ▸ **port franc** free port ▸ **zone franche** free zone.
◆ ***franc*** **nm** franc ▸ **ancien/nouveau franc** old/newfranc ▸ **franc français/belge/suisse** French/Belgian/Swiss franc.

français, ***e*** [frɑ̃sɛ, ɛz] **adj** French.
◆ ***français*** **nm** [langue] French.
◆ ***Français***, ***e*** **nm, f** Frenchman (f Frenchwoman) ▸ **les Français** the French ▸ **le Français moyen** the average Frenchman.

France [frɑ̃s] **nf : la France** France ▸ **France 2, France 3** TV *French state-owned television channels* ▸ **France-Inter** RADIO *radio station broadcasting mainly current affairs programmes, interviews and debates.*

franche ➤ ***franc***.

franchement [frɑ̃ʃmɑ̃] **adv 1.** [sincèrement] frankly **2.** [nettement] clearly **3.** [tout à fait] completely, downright.

franchir [32] [frɑ̃ʃir] **vt 1.** [obstacle] to get over **2.** [porte] to go through / [seuil] to cross **3.** [distance] to cover.

franchise [frɑ̃ʃiz] **nf 1.** [sincérité] frankness **2.** COMM franchise ▸ **agent en franchise** franchise holder **3.** [d'assurance] excess **4.** [détaxe] exemption ▸ **franchise de TVA** zero-rating.

franchouillard, ***e*** [frɑ̃ʃujar, ard] **adj** *fam péj* typically French.

francilien, ***enne*** [frɑ̃siljɛ̃, ɛn] **adj** of/from the Île-de-France.
◆ ***Francilien***, ***enne*** **nm, f** preson from the Île-de-France.

franciscain, ***e*** [frɑ̃siskɛ̃, ɛn] **adj & nm, f** Franciscan.

franciser [3] [frɑ̃size] **vt** to frenchify.

franc-jeu [frɑ̃ʒø] **nm : jouer franc-jeu** to play fair.

franc-maçon, ***onne*** [frɑ̃masɔ̃, ɔn] (mpl **francs-maçons**) (fpl **franc-maçonnes**) **adj** masonic.
◆ ***franc-maçon*** **nm** freemason.

franc-maçonnerie [frɑ̃masɔnri] (pl **franc-maçonneries**) **nf** freemasonry *(U)*.

franco [frɑ̃ko] **adv 1.** *fam* [franchement] **: y aller franco** to go straight to the point **2.** COMM **: franco à bord** free on board ▸ **franco de port** carriage paid.

francophile [frɑ̃kɔfil] **nmf & adj** francophile.

francophone [frɑ̃kɔfɔn] ■ **adj** French-speaking.
■ **nmf** French speaker.

francophonie [frɑ̃kɔfɔni] **nf : la francophonie** French-speaking nations *pl.*

CULTURE

Francophonie

This word designates both a collective movement to promote the French language and the world's French-speaking populations. The movement's ultimate cultural, and perhaps even political, goal is to create a sort of French Commonwealth. Frequent summits dedicated to the topic allow French-speaking nations' leaders to discuss the movement's objectives and how they can best promote French around the world. There is even the **prix de la francophonie**, given annually to someone who has been an outstanding advocate for the language.

franc-parler [frɑ̃parle] (pl **francs-parlers**) **nm : avoir son franc-parler** to speak one's mind.

franc-tireur [frɑ̃tirœr] (pl **francs-tireurs**) **nm 1.** MIL irregular **2.** *fig* [indépendant] freelance ▸ **agir en franc-tireur** to act independently.

frange [frɑ̃ʒ] **nf** fringe.

frangin, ***e*** [frɑ̃ʒɛ̃, frɑ̃ʒin] **nm, f** *fam* brother (f sister).

frangipane [frɑ̃ʒipan] **nf** almond paste.

franglais [frɑ̃glɛ] **nm** Franglais.

franquette [frɑ̃kɛt] ◆ ***à la bonne franquette*** **loc adv** informally, without ceremony.

frappant, ***e*** [frapɑ̃, ɑ̃t] **adj** striking.

frappe [frap] **nf 1.** [de monnaie] minting, striking **2.** [à la machine] typing / INFORM keying **3.** [de boxeur] punch **4.** *péj* [voyou] lout, yob *UK*.

frappé, ***e*** [frape] **adj 1.** [champagne] chilled **2.** *fam* [personne] crazy, nutty.

frapper [3] [frape] ■ **vt 1.** [gén] to strike ▸ **frapper un grand coup** *fig* to strike a decisive blow ▸ **ce qui me frappe chez lui, c'est sa désinvolture** what strikes me about him is his offhandedness ▸ **être frappé par la foudre** to be struck by lightning ▸ **le deuil/mal qui nous frappe** the bereavement/pain we are suffering **2.** [boisson] to chill.
■ **vi** to knock ▸ **on a frappé** someone knocked at the door ▸ **frapper à la bonne/mauvaise porte** *fig* to go to the right/wrong place.

frasques [frask] **nfpl** pranks, escapades.

fraternel, elle [fratɛrnɛl] **adj** fraternal, brotherly.

fraterniser [3] [fratɛrnize] **vi** to fraternize.

fraternité [fratɛrnite] **nf** brotherhood.

fratricide [fratrisid] ■ **nmf** fratricide.
■ **adj** fratricidal.

fratrie [fratri] **nf** siblings *pl*, brothers and sisters *pl*.

fraude [frod] **nf** fraud ▸ **passer qqch en fraude** to smuggle sthg in ▸ **fraude électorale** ballot-rigging ▸ **fraude fiscale** tax evasion ▸ **fraude informatique** computer crime.

frauder [3] [frode] **vt & vi** to cheat.

fraudeur, euse [frodœr, øz] **nm, f** cheat.

frauduleux, euse [frodylø, øz] **adj** fraudulent.

frayer [11] [frɛje] ■ **vt : frayer la voie à qqn** to clear the way for sb.
■ **vi** [fréquenter] **: frayer avec** to associate *ou* mix with.
◆ ***se frayer*** **vp : se frayer un chemin (à travers une foule)** to force one's way through (a crowd).

frayeur [frɛjœr] **nf** fright, fear.

fredaines [frədɛn] **nfpl** pranks.

fredonner [3] [frədɔne] **vt & vi** to hum.

free-lance [frilɑ̃s] (pl **free-lances**) ■ **adj** freelance.
■ **nmf** freelance, freelancer.
■ **nm** freelancing, freelance work ▸ **travailler** *ou* **être en free-lance** to work on a freelance basis *ou* as a freelancer.

freezer [frizœr] **nm** freezer compartment.

frégate [fregat] **nf 1.** [bateau] frigate **2.** [oiseau] frigatebird.

frein [frɛ̃] **nm 1.** AUTO brake ▸ **frein à main** handbrake ▸ **frein moteur** engine brake **2.** *fig* [obstacle] brake, check ▸ **mettre un frein à** to curb
▸▸ **ronger son frein** *fig* to champ at the bit.

freinage [frɛnaʒ] **nm** braking.

freiner [4] [frene] ■ **vt 1.** [mouvement, véhicule] to slow down / [inflation, dépenses] to curb **2.** [personne] to restrain.
■ **vi** to brake.

frelaté, e [frəlate] **adj** [vin] adulterated / *fig* corrupt.

frêle [frɛl] **adj 1.** [enfant, voix] frail **2.** [construction] flimsy, fragile.

frelon [frəlɔ̃] **nm** hornet.

freluquet [frəlykɛ] **nm** *péj* whippersnapper.

frémir [32] [fremir] **vi 1.** [corps, personne] to tremble **2.** [eau] to simmer.

frémissement [fremismɑ̃] **nm 1.** [de corps, personne] shiver, trembling *(U)* **2.** [d'eau] simmering.

frêne [frɛn] **nm** ash.

frénésie [frenezi] **nf** frenzy.

frénétique [frenetik] **adj** frenzied.

frénétiquement [frenetikmɑ̃] **adv** [applaudir] furiously.

fréquemment [frekamɑ̃] **adv** frequently.

fréquence [frekɑ̃s] **nf** frequency.

fréquent, e [frekɑ̃, ɑ̃t] **adj** frequent.

fréquentable [frekɑ̃tabl] **adj** respectable.

fréquentation [frekɑ̃tasjɔ̃] **nf 1.** [d'endroit] frequenting **2.** [de personne] association **3.** COMM footfall.
◆ ***fréquentations*** **nfpl** company *(U)* ▸ **avoir de mauvaises fréquentations** to keep bad company.

fréquenté, e [frekɑ̃te] **adj : très fréquenté** busy ▸ **c'est très bien/mal fréquenté** the right/wrong sort of people go there.

fréquenter [3] [frekɑ̃te] **vt 1.** [endroit] to frequent **2.** [personne] to associate with / [petit ami] to go out with, to see.

frère [frɛr] ■ **nm** brother ▸ **faux frère** false friend ▸ **frère de lait** foster brother ▸ **frère aîné/cadet** older/younger brother ▸ **frères d'armes** brothers in arms ▸ **frère jumeau** twin brother ▸ **grand frère** big brother ▸ **ce sont des frères ennemis** a friendly rivalry exists between them.
■ **adj** [parti, pays] sister *(avant n)*.

fresque [frɛsk] **nf** fresco.

fret [frɛ] **nm** freight.

frétiller [3] [fretije] **vi** [poisson, personne] to wriggle ▸ **frétiller de joie** *fig* to quiver with delight.

fretin [frətɛ̃] **nm : le menu fretin** the small fry.

freudien, enne [frødjɛ̃, ɛn] **adj** Freudian.

friable [frijabl] **adj** crumbly.

friand, e [frijɑ̃, ɑ̃d] **adj : être friand de** to be partial to.
◆ ***friand*** **nm** *meat pie in puff pastry.*

friandise [frijɑ̃diz] **nf** delicacy.

fric [frik] **nm** *fam* cash.

fricassée [frikase] **nf** fricassee.

fric-frac [frikfrak] **nm inv** *fam* break-in.

friche [friʃ] **nf** fallow land ▸ **en friche** fallow.

fricoter [3] [frikɔte] **vt** *fam litt & fig* to cook up.

friction [friksjɔ̃] **nf 1.** [massage] massage **2.** *fig* [désaccord] friction.

frictionner [3] [friksjɔne] **vt** to rub.
◆ ***se frictionner*** **vp** *(emploi réfléchi)* to rub o.s. ▸ **frictionne-toi bien** give yourself a good rub down.

Frigidaire® [friʒidɛr] **nm** fridge *UK*, refrigerator.

frigide [friʒid] **adj** frigid.

frigidité [friʒidite] **nf** frigidity.

frigo [frigo] **nm** *fam* fridge *UK*.

frigorifié, e [frigɔrifje] **adj** *fam* frozen.

frigorifique [frigɔrifik] **adj** refrigerated.

frileux, euse [frilø, øz] **adj 1.** [craignant le froid] sensitive to the cold **2.** [prudent] unadventurous.

frimas [frima] **nm** *littéraire* foggy winter weather.

frime [frim] **nf** *fam* showing off.

frimer [3] [frime] **vi** *fam* [bluffer] to pretend / [se mettre en valeur] to show off.

frimeur, euse [frimœr, øz] **nmf** show-off.

frimousse [frimus] **nf** *fam* dear little face.

fringale [frɛ̃gal] **nf** *fam* **: avoir la fringale** to be starving.

fringant, e [frɛ̃gɑ̃, ɑ̃t] **adj** high-spirited.

fringuer [3] [frɛ̃ge] *fam* **vt** to dress.
◆ ***se fringuer*** **vp** to get dressed.

fringues [frɛ̃g] **nfpl** *fam* clothes.

fripe [frip] **nf : la fripe, les fripes** secondhand clothes.

friper [3] [fripe] **vt** to crumple.
◆ ***se friper*** **vp** to crumple.

fripier, ère [fripje, ɛr] **nm, f** secondhand-clothes dealer.

fripon, onne [fripɔ̃, ɔn] ■ **nm, f** *fam vieilli* rogue, rascal.
■ **adj** mischievous, cheeky.

fripouille [fripuj] **nf** *fam* scoundrel ▸ **petite fripouille** little devil.

frire [115] [frir] ■ **vt** to fry.
■ **vi** to fry ▸ **faire frire** to fry.

Frisbee® [frizbi] **nm** Frisbee®.

frise [friz] **nf** ARCHIT frieze.

frisé, e [frize] **adj** [cheveux] curly / [personne] curly-haired.
◆ ***frisée*** **nf** [salade] frisée, curly endive.

friser [3] [frize] ■ **vt 1.** [cheveux] to curl **2.** *fig* [ressembler à] to border on.
■ **vi** to curl.

frisette [frizɛt] **nf** curl.

frisotter [3] [frizɔte] ■ **vt** to crimp, to frizz.
■ **vi** to be frizzy.

frisquet, ette [friskɛ] **adj : il fait frisquet** it's chilly.

frisson [frisɔ̃] **nm** [gén] shiver / [de dégoût] shudder.

frissonner [3] [frisɔne] **vi 1.** [trembler] to shiver / [de dégoût] to shudder **2.** [s'agiter - eau] to ripple / [- feuillage] to tremble.

frit, e [fri, frit] **pp** ➤ ***frire***.

frite [frit] **nf** chip *UK*, (French) fry *US*.

friterie [fritri] **nf** ≃ chip shop *UK*.

friteuse [fritøz] **nf** deep-fat fryer.

friture [frityr] **nf 1.** [action de frire] frying **2.** [poisson] fried fish ▸ **petite friture** fried whitebait **3.** *fam* RADIO crackle.

frivole [frivɔl] **adj** frivolous.

frivolité [frivɔlite] **nf** frivolity.

froc [frɔk] **nm 1.** RELIG habit **2.** *fam* [pantalon] trousers *pl UK*, pants *pl US*.

froid, froide [frwa, frwad] **adj** *litt* & *fig* cold ▸ **des murs froids et nus** cold bare walls ▸ **par un matin très froid** on a raw morning ▸ **rester froid** to be unmoved ▸ **ça me laisse froid** it leaves me cold.
◆ ***froid*** ■ **nm 1.** [température] cold ▸ **prendre froid** to catch (a) cold ▸ **crever de froid** *fam* to be freezing to death ▸ **conserver qqch au froid** to store sthg in a cold place ▸ **grand froid** intense cold ▸ **ça me donne froid dans le dos** it makes my blood run cold, it sends shivers down my spine **2.** [tension] coolness ▸ **cela a jeté un froid** it cast a chill over the proceedings ▸ **être en froid (avec qqn)** to be on bad terms (with sb).
■ **adv : il fait froid** it's cold ▸ **il fait un froid de canard** it's freezing cold ▸ **avoir froid** to be cold ▸ **j'ai froid aux mains** my hands are cold ▸ **n'avoir pas froid aux yeux** *fig* to be bold *ou* adventurous ▸ **manger froid** to have something cold (to eat).
◆ ***à froid*** **loc adv** [dire, faire] coolly, unemotionally ▸ **je ne peux pas répondre à froid** I can't answer off the top of my head.

froidement [frwadmɑ̃] **adv 1.** [accueillir] coldly **2.** [écouter, parler] coolly **3.** [tuer] cold-bloodedly.

froideur [frwadœr] **nf 1.** [indifférence] coldness **2.** [impassibilité] coolness.

froisser [3] [frwase] **vt 1.** [tissu, papier] to crumple, to crease **2.** *fig* [offenser] to offend.
◆ ***se froisser*** **vp 1.** [tissu] to crumple, to crease **2.** MÉD **: se froisser un muscle** to strain a muscle **3.** [se vexer] to take offence *UK ou* offense *US*.

frôler [3] [frole] **vt** to brush against / *fig* to have a brush with, to come close to.

fromage [frɔmaʒ] **nm** cheese ▸ **fromage à pâte molle/dure** soft/hardcheese ▸ **fromage de brebis** sheep's milk cheese ▸ **fromage de chèvre** goat's cheese ▸ **fromage de tête** brawn *UK*, headcheese *US*.

fromager, ère [frɔmaʒe, ɛr] ■ **adj** cheese *(avant n)*.
■ **nm, f** [fabricant] cheesemaker.

fromagerie [frɔmaʒri] **nf** cheese shop *UK ou* store *US*.

froment [frɔmɑ̃] **nm** wheat.

fronce [frɔ̃s] **nf** gather.

froncement [frɔ̃smɑ̃] **nm : froncement de sourcils** frown.

froncer [16] [frɔ̃se] **vt 1.** COUT to gather **2.** [plisser] **: froncer les sourcils** to frown.

frondaison [frɔ̃dɛzɔ̃] **nf 1.** [phénomène] foliation **2.** [feuillage] foliage.

fronde [frɔ̃d] **nf 1.** [arme] sling / [jouet] catapult *UK* slingshot *US* **2.** [révolte] rebellion.

frondeur, euse [frɔ̃dœr, øz] ■ **nm, f** rebel.
■ **adj** rebellious.

front [frɔ̃] **nm 1.** ANAT forehead ▸ **baisser le front** *litt* to lower one's head ▸ **le front haut** proudly, with one's head held high **2.** *fig* [audace] nerve, cheek *UK* ▸ **avoir le front de faire qqch** to have the nerve *ou* cheek *UK* to do sth **3.** [avant] [gén] front / [de bâtiment] front, façade ▸ **front de mer** (sea) front ▸ **de front** [attaquer] head on ▸ **aborder une difficulté de front** to tackle a problem head-on ▸ **se heurter de front** [véhicules] to collide head-on / [adversaires] to come into direct confrontation **4.** MÉTÉOR, MIL & POLIT front ▸ **front froid/chaud** cold/warm front
▸▸ **faire front à** to face up to ▸ **faire front commun contre qqn/qqch** to make common cause against sb/sth ▸ **mener plusieurs activités de front** to do several thing at the same time.

frontal, e, aux [frɔ̃tal, o] **adj 1.** ANAT frontal **2.** [collision, attaque] head-on.

frontalier, ère [frɔ̃talje, ɛr] ■ **adj** frontier *(avant n)* ▸ **travailleur frontalier** *person who lives on one side of border and works on the other.*
■ **nm, f** person from a border area.

frontière [frɔ̃tjɛr] ■ **adj** border *(avant n)*.
■ **nf** frontier, border / *fig* frontier.

frontispice [frɔ̃tispis] **nm** frontispiece.

fronton [frɔ̃tɔ̃] **nm** **1.** ARCHIT pediment **2.** SPORT *upper part of the wall in the game of pelota.*

frottement [frɔtmɑ̃] **nm** **1.** [action] rubbing **2.** [contact, difficulté] friction.

frotter [3] [frɔte] ■ **vt** to rub / [parquet] to scrub.
■ **vi** to rub, to scrape.
◆ ***se frotter*** **vp** **1.** [se blottir] **: se frotter contre** *ou* **à** to rub (up) against ▸ **il ne faut pas s'y frotter** *fig* don't cross swords with him **2.** [se laver] to rub o.s.

frottis [frɔti] **nm** smear ▸ **frottis vaginal** cervical smear *UK*, Pap smear *US*.

froufrou, ***s*** [frufru] **nm** rustle, swish.
◆ ***froufrous*** **nmpl** [de robe] frills.

froussard, ***e*** [frusar, ard] **adj** & **nm, f** *fam* chicken.

frousse [frus] **nf** *fam* fright ▸ **avoir la frousse** to be scared stiff.

fructifier [9] [fryktifje] **vi** **1.** [investissement] to give *ou* yield a profit ▸ **faire fructifier son argent** to make one's money grow **2.** [terre] to be productive **3.** [arbre, idée] to bear fruit.

fructose [fryktoz] **nm** fructose.

fructueux, ***euse*** [fryktɥø, øz] **adj** fruitful, profitable.

frugal, ***e***, ***aux*** [frygal, o] **adj** frugal.

fruit [frɥi] **nm** *litt* & *fig* fruit ▸ **fruit confit** candied fruit ▸ **le fruit défendu** the forbidden fruit ▸ **fruit sec** dried fruit *(U)* ▸ **fruits de mer** seafood *(U)*.

fruité, ***e*** [frɥite] **adj** fruity.

fruitier, ***ère*** [frɥitje, ɛr] ■ **adj** [arbre] fruit *(avant n)*.
■ **nm, f** fruit seller, fruiterer *UK*.
◆ ***fruitier*** **nm** [local] storeroom for fruit.

frusques [frysk] **nfpl** gear *(U)*, clobber *(U) UK*.

fruste [fryst] **adj** uncouth.

frustrant, ***e*** [frystrɑ̃, ɑ̃t] **adj** frustrating.

frustration [frystrasjɔ̃] **nf** frustration.

frustré, ***e*** [frystre] ■ **adj** frustrated.
■ **nm, f** frustrated person.

frustrer [3] [frystre] **vt** **1.** [priver] **: frustrer qqn de** to deprive sb of **2.** [décevoir] to frustrate.

FS (abr écrite de ***franc suisse***) SFr.

FSE (abr de ***Fonds Social Européen***) **m** ESF *(European Social Fund)*.

FTP (abr de ***francs-tireurs et partisans***) **nmpl** *Communist Resistance forces during World War II.*

fuchsia [fyʃja] **nm** fuchsia.

fuel, ***fioul*** [fjul] **nm** **1.** [de chauffage] fuel **2.** [carburant] fuel oil.

fugace [fygas] **adj** fleeting.

fugitif, ***ive*** [fyʒitif, iv] ■ **adj** fleeting.
■ **nm, f** fugitive.

fugue [fyg] **nf** **1.** [de personne] flight ▸ **faire une fugue** to run off *ou* away **2.** MUS fugue.

fuguer [3] [fyge] **vi** to run off *ou* away.

fugueur, ***euse*** [fygœr, øz] **adj** & **nm, f** runaway.

fui [fɥi] **pp inv** ➤ ***fuir***.

fuir [35] [fɥir] ■ **vi** **1.** [détaler] to flee ▸ **fuir à toutes jambes** to run for dear *ou* one's life ▸ **fuir devant le danger** to flee in the face of danger **2.** [tuyau] to leak **3.** *fig* [s'écouler] to fly by **4.** [se dérober] to run away ▸ **fuir devant ses responsabilités** to shirk *ou* to evade one's responsibilities.
■ **vt** [éviter] to avoid, to shun ▸ **fuir le danger** to keep away from *ou* to avoid danger ▸ **fuir le regard de qqn** to avoid looking sb in the eye.

fuis, ***fuit*** ➤ ***fuir***.

fuite [fɥit] **nf** **1.** [de personne] escape, flight ▸ **en fuite** on the run ▸ **prendre la fuite** to take flight ▸ **mettre qqn en fuite** to put sb to flight **2.** [écoulement, d'information] leak.

fulgurant, ***e*** [fylgyrɑ̃, ɑ̃t] **adj** **1.** [découverte] dazzling **2.** [vitesse] lightning *(avant n)* **3.** [douleur] searing **4.** *littéraire* [regard] of thunder.

fulminant, ***e*** [fylminɑ̃, ɑ̃t] **adj** [menaçant] threatening.

fulminer [3] [fylmine] **vi** **1.** [personne] **: fulminer (contre)** to fulminate (against) **2.** CHIM to detonate.

fumant, ***e*** [fymɑ̃, ɑ̃t] **adj** **1.** [cheminée] smoking **2.** [plat] steaming.

fumé, ***e*** [fyme] **adj** **1.** CULIN smoked **2.** [verres] tinted.

fumée [fyme] **nf** **1.** [de combustion] smoke ▸ **partir en fumée** *fig* to go up in smoke **2.** [vapeur] steam.
◆ ***fumées*** **nfpl** *littéraire* fumes.

fumer [3] [fyme] ■ **vi** **1.** [personne, cheminée] to smoke **2.** [bouilloire, plat] to steam **3.** *fam* [être furieux] to fume, to rage.
■ **vt** **1.** [cigarette, aliment] to smoke **2.** AGRIC to spread manure on.

fumet [fymɛ] **nm** **1.** [odeur] aroma **2.** CULIN greatly reduced stock.

fumette [fymɛt] **nf** *fam* marijuana smoking ▸ **se faire une fumette** to get stoned.

fumeur, ***euse*** [fymœr, øz] **nm, f** smoker.

fumeux, ***euse*** [fymø, øz] **adj** confused, woolly *UK ou* wooly *US*.

fumier [fymje] **nm** **1.** AGRIC dung, manure **2.** *vulg* [salaud] shit.

fumigation [fymigasjɔ̃] **nf** fumigation.

fumiste [fymist] **nmf** *péj* shirker, skiver *UK*.

fumisterie [fymistəri] **nf** *fam* shirking, skiving *UK*.

fumoir [fymwar] **nm** **1.** [pour aliments] smokehouse **2.** [pièce] smoking room.

funambule [fynɑ̃byl] **nmf** tightrope walker.

funèbre [fynɛbr] **adj** **1.** [de funérailles] funeral *(avant n)* **2.** [lugubre] funereal / [sentiments] dismal.

funérailles [fyneraj] **nfpl** funeral *sg*.

funéraire [fynerɛr] **adj** funeral *(avant n)*.

funeste [fynɛst] **adj** **1.** [accident] fatal **2.** [initiative, erreur] disastrous **3.** [présage] of doom.

funiculaire [fynikylɛr] **nm** funicular railway.

FUNU, ***Funu*** [fyny] (abr de ***Force d'urgence des Nations unies***) **nf** UNEF.

fur [fyr] ◆ ***au fur et à mesure*** loc adv as I/you *etc* go along ▸ **au fur et à mesure des besoins** as (and when) needed. ◆ ***au fur et à mesure que*** loc conj as (and when).

furax [fyraks] adj inv *fam* hopping mad.

furet [fyrɛ] nm **1.** [animal] ferret **2.** [personne] nosy parker **3.** [jeu] hunt-the-slipper.

fureter [28] [fyrte] vi **1.** [fouiller] to ferret around **2.** [chasser] to go ferreting.

fureur [fyrœr] nf **1.** [colère] fury ▸ **accès de fureur** fit of anger *ou* rage ▸ **entrer en fureur** to fly into a rage *ou* fury ▸ **se mettre dans une fureur noire** to fly into a terrible rage **2.** [passion] passion ▸ **la fureur de vivre** a lust for life ▸ **faire fureur** to be all the rage.

furibard**, **e [fyribar, ard] adj *fam* hopping mad.

furibond**, **e [fyribɔ̃, ɔ̃d] adj furious.

furie [fyri] nf **1.** [colère, agitation] fury ▸ **en furie** [personne] infuriated / [éléments] raging **2.** *fig* [femme] shrew **3.** [passion] passion.

furieusement [fyrjøzmɑ̃] adv **1.** [avec fureur] furiously **2.** [extrêmement] tremendously.

furieux**, **euse [fyrjø, øz] adj **1.** [personne] furious **2.** [violent] violent **3.** [énorme] tremendous.

furoncle [fyrɔ̃kl] nm boil.

furtif**, **ive [fyrtif, iv] adj furtive.

furtivement [fyrtivmɑ̃] adv furtively.

fus**, **fut ➤ *être*.

fusain [fyzɛ̃] nm **1.** [crayon] charcoal **2.** [dessin] charcoal drawing **3.** [arbre] spindle tree.

fuseau**, **x [fyzo] nm **1.** [outil] spindle **2.** [pantalon] ski pants *pl*.
◆ ***fuseau horaire*** nm time zone.

fusée [fyze] nf **1.** [pièce d'artifice & AÉRON] rocket ▸ **fusée de détresse** flare ▸ **fusée à étages multiples** multiple-stage rocket ▸ **partir comme une fusée** to be off like a shot, to shoot off **2.** TECHNOL spindle / AUTO stub axle.

fuselage [fyzlaʒ] nm fuselage.

fuselé**, **e [fyzle] adj [doigts] tapering / [jambes] slender.

fuser [3] [fyze] vi [cri, rire] to burst forth *ou* out.

fusible [fyzibl] nm fuse.

fusil [fyzi] nm **1.** [arme] gun ▸ **changer son fusil d'épaule** *fig* to change one's approach **2.** [personne] marksman.

fusillade [fyzijad] nf **1.** [combat] gunfire *(U)*, fusillade **2.** [exécution] shooting.

fusiller [3] [fyzije] vt **1.** [exécuter] to shoot ▸ **fusiller qqn du regard** *fig* to look daggers at sb **2.** *fam* [bousiller] to ruin, to mess *ou* muck *UK* up.

fusil-mitrailleur [fyzimitrajœr] (pl **fusils-mitrailleurs**) nm machine gun.

fusion [fyzjɔ̃] nf **1.** [gén] fusion **2.** [fonte] smelting ▸ **en fusion** molten **3.** ÉCON & POLIT merger.

fusionnel**, **elle [fyʒjɔnɛl] adj [couple] inseparable / [relation] intense.

fusionner [3] [fyzjɔne] vt & vi to merge.

fustiger [17] [fystiʒe] vt to castigate.

fut ➤ *être*.

fût [fy] nm **1.** [d'arbre] trunk **2.** [tonneau] barrel, cask **3.** [d'arme] stock **4.** [de colonne] shaft.

futaie [fytɛ] nf wood.

futé**, **e [fyte] *fam* ■ adj cunning.
■ nm, f smart cookie.

futile [fytil] adj **1.** [insignifiant] futile **2.** [frivole] frivolous.

futilité [fytilite] nf **1.** [d'action] futility **2.** [vétille] triviality.

futon [fytɔ̃] nm futon.

futur**, **e [fytyr] ■ adj future *(avant n)* ▸ **la vie future** RELIG the life to come ▸ **futurs mariés** bride- and groom-to-be.
■ nm, f [fiancé] intended.
◆ ***futur*** nm future ▸ **futur antérieur** LING future perfect.

futuriste [fytyrist] ■ nmf futurist.
■ adj futuristic.

futurologue [fytyrɔlɔg] nmf futurologist.

fuyant**, **e [fɥijɑ̃, ɑ̃t] adj **1.** [perspective, front] receding *(avant n)* **2.** [regard] evasive.

fuyard**, **e [fɥijar, ard] nm, f runaway.

fuyez**, **fuyons ➤ *fuir*.

FV (abr de ***fréquence vocale***) VF.

g[1], ***G*** [ʒe] **nm inv** g, G.

g[2] (abr écrite de ***gauche***) L, l.
◆ ***G*** (abr écrite de ***giga***) G.

G7 ÉCON & POLIT **: le G7** G7 *(the seven most industrialised countries).*

G8 ÉCON & POLIT **: le G8** G8 *(the eight most industrialised countries).*

GAB [gab] (abr de ***guichet automatique de banque***) **nm** ATM, cash dispenser *UK*.

gabardine [gabardin] **nf** gabardine.

gabarit [gabari] **nm 1.** [appareil de mesure] gauge **2.** [dimension] size **3.** [valeur] calibre *UK* ***ou*** caliber *US* ▸ **du même gabarit** of the same calibre *UK* ***ou*** caliber *US*.

gabegie [gabʒi] **nf** muddle, disorder.

Gabon [gabɔ̃] **nm : le Gabon** Gabon ▸ **au Gabon** in Gabon.

gabonais, e [gabɔnɛ, ɛz] **adj** Gabonese.
◆ ***Gabonais, e* nm, f** Gabonese.

gâche [gaʃ] **nf 1.** [de serrure] striking plate **2.** [outil] trowel.

gâcher [3] [gaʃe] **vt 1.** [gaspiller] to waste **2.** [gâter] to spoil **3.** CONSTR to mix.

gâchette [gaʃɛt] **nf** trigger ▸ **appuyer sur la gâchette** to pull the trigger.

gâchis [gaʃi] **nm 1.** [gaspillage] waste *(U)* **2.** [désordre] mess **3.** CONSTR mortar.

gadelle [gadɛl] **nf** *Québec* currant.

gadget [gadʒɛt] **nm** gadget.

gadin *tfam* [gadɛ̃] **nm** *vieilli* **: prendre *ou* ramasser un gadin** to fall flat on one's face, to come a cropper *UK*.

gadoue [gadu] **nf** *fam* [boue] mud / [engrais] sludge.

gaélique [gaelik] ■ **adj** Gaelic.
■ **nm** Gaelic ▸ **gaélique d'Écosse** Scots Gaelic ▸ **gaélique d'Irlande** Irish Gaelic.

gaffe [gaf] **nf 1.** *fam* [maladresse] boo-boo, clanger *UK* ▸ **faire une gaffe** to make a boo-boo, to drop a clanger *UK* **2.** [outil] boat hook
▸▸ **faire gaffe** *fam* to take care.

gaffer [3] [gafe] ■ **vt** to hook.
■ **vi** *fam* to put one's foot in it.

gaffeur, euse [gafœr, øz] *fam* ■ **adj** blundering.
■ **nm, f** blunderer.

gag [gag] **nm** gag.

gaga [gaga] **adj** *fam* gaga, doddering.

gage [gaʒ] **nm 1.** [dépôt] pledge ▸ **mettre qqch en gage** to pawn sthg **2.** [assurance, preuve] proof ▸ **en gage de** as a token of ▸ **en gage de ma bonne volonté** as a token of my goodwill **3.** [dans jeu] forfeit.

gager [17] [gaʒe] **vt : gager que** to bet (that).

gageure [gaʒyr] **nf** challenge.

gagnant, e [gaɲɑ̃, ɑ̃t] ■ **adj** winning *(avant n)*.
■ **nm, f** winner.

gagne-pain [gaɲpɛ̃] **nm inv** livelihood.

gagne-petit [gaɲpəti] **nm inv** person earning a pittance.

gagner [3] [gaɲe] ■ **vt 1.** [salaire, argent, repos] to earn ▸ **gagner sa vie *ou* sa croûte** *fam* to earn a living ***ou*** one's daily bread **2.** [course, prix, affection] to win ▸ **gagner une fortune à la loterie** to win a fortune in the lottery **3.** [obtenir, économiser] to gain ▸ **gagner du temps/de la place** to gain time/space ▸ **qu'est-ce que j'y gagne?** what do I get out of it? **4.** [vaincre] **: gagner qqn de vitesse** to outpace sb **5.** [atteindre - gén] to reach ▸ **il gagna la sortie** he made his way to the exit / [- suj: feu, engourdissement] to spread to / [- suj: sommeil, froid] to overcome ▸ **je sentais la panique me gagner** I could feel panic creeping over me **6.** [se concilier] to win over ▸ **gagner qqn à une cause** to win sb over to a cause.
■ **vi 1.** [être vainqueur] to win ▸ **on a gagné (par) 3 buts à 2** we won (by) 3 goals to 2, we won 3-2 **2.** [bénéficier] to gain ▸ **gagner à faire qqch** to be better off doing sthg **3.** [s'améliorer] **: gagner en** to increase in ▸ **notre production gagne en qualité** the quality of our product is improving ▸ **gagner à être connu** to improve on acquaintance ▸ **vin qui gagne à vieillir** wine for laying down ***ou*** which improves with age.

gagneur, euse [gaɲœr, øz] **nm, f** winner.

gai, ***e*** [gɛ] **adj 1.** [joyeux] cheerful, happy **2.** [vif, plaisant] bright.

gaiement [gemɑ̃] **adv** cheerfully.

gaieté [gete] **nf 1.** [joie] cheerfulness ▸ **de gaieté de cœur** enthusiastically **2.** [vivacité] brightness.

gaillard, ***e*** [gajar, ard] ■ **adj 1.** [alerte] sprightly, spry **2.** [licencieux] ribald.
■ **nm, f** strapping individual.

gain [gɛ̃] **nm 1.** [profit] gain, profit **2.** [succès] winning ▸ **avoir** *ou* **obtenir gain de cause** to win one's case **3.** [économie] saving.
◆ ***gains*** **nmpl** earnings ▸ **gains visibles** visible earnings.

gaine [gɛn] **nf 1.** [étui, enveloppe] sheath **2.** [sous-vêtement] girdle, corset.

gaine-culotte [gɛnkylɔt] (pl **gaines-culottes**) **nf** panty girdle.

gainer [4] [gene] **vt** to sheathe.

gala [gala] **nm** gala, reception ▸ **de gala** gala *(avant n)*.

galamment [galamɑ̃] **adv** politely, gallantly.

galant, ***e*** [galɑ̃, ɑ̃t] **adj 1.** [courtois] gallant **2.** [amoureux] flirtatious.
◆ ***galant*** **nm** admirer.

galanterie [galɑ̃tri] **nf 1.** [courtoisie] gallantry, politeness **2.** [flatterie] compliment.

galantine [galɑ̃tin] **nf** *boned meat or poultry pressed into a loaf shape.*

galaxie [galaksi] **nf** galaxy.

galbe [galb] **nm** curve.

galbé, ***e*** [galbe] **adj 1.** [objet] curved **2.** [jambe] shapely.

gale [gal] **nf** MÉD scabies *(U)*.

galère [galɛr] **nf** NAUT galley ▸ **quelle galère!** *fig* what a hassle!, what a drag!

galérer [18] [galere] **vi** *fam* to have a hard time.

galerie [galri] **nf 1.** [gén] gallery ▸ **galerie marchande** *ou* **commerciale** shopping arcade *UK ou* mall *US* ▸ **galerie de peinture** picture gallery **2.** THÉÂTRE circle ▸ **amuser la galerie** *fig* to play to the gallery **3.** [porte-bagages] roof *UK ou* luggage *US* rack.

galérien [galerjɛ̃] **nm** galley slave ▸ **travailler comme un galérien** to work like a Trojan.

galet [galɛ] **nm 1.** [caillou] pebble **2.** TECHNOL wheel, roller.

galette [galɛt] **nf 1.** CULIN pancake *(made from buckwheat flour)* ▸ **galette des Rois** *cake eaten on Twelfth Night* **2.** *fam* [argent] dough, cash.

galeux, ***euse*** [galø, øz] ■ **adj 1.** MÉD scabious **2.** ➤ ***brebis***.
■ **nm, f** scruffy person.

galimatias [galimatja] **nm** gibberish *(U)*.

galipette [galipɛt] **nf** *fam* somersault ▸ **faire des galipettes** to do somersaults.

Galles [gal] ➤ ***pays***.

gallicisme [galisism] **nm** [expression] French idiom / [dans une langue étrangère] gallicism.

gallinacé, ***e*** [galinase] **adj** domestic.
◆ ***gallinacé*** **nm** domestic fowl.

gallois, ***e*** [galwa, az] **adj** Welsh.
◆ ***gallois*** **nm** [langue] Welsh.
◆ ***Gallois***, ***e*** **nm, f** Welshman (f Welshwoman) ▸ **les Gallois** the Welsh.

gallo-romain, ***e*** [galɔrɔmɛ̃, ɛn] (mpl **gallo-romains**, fpl **gallo-romaines**) **adj** Gallo-Roman.
◆ ***Gallo-Romain***, ***e*** **nm, f** Gallo-Roman.

galoche [galɔʃ] **nf** clog.

galon [galɔ̃] **nm 1.** COUT braid *(U)* **2.** MIL stripe ▸ **prendre du galon** *fig* to be promoted.

galop [galo] **nm** [allure] gallop ▸ **au galop** [cheval] at a gallop / *fig* at the double *UK*, on the double *US*.

galopade [galɔpad] **nf 1.** [de cheval] gallop **2.** [de personne] (mad) rush.

galopant, ***e*** [galɔpɑ̃, ɑ̃t] **adj** *fig* galloping, runaway.

galoper [3] [galɔpe] **vi 1.** [cheval] to gallop **2.** [personne] to run around **3.** [imagination] to run riot.

galopin [galɔpɛ̃] **nm** *fam* brat.

galvaniser [3] [galvanize] **vt** *litt & fig* to galvanize.

galvauder [3] [galvode] **vt** [ternir] to tarnish.
◆ ***se galvauder*** **vp** to demean o.s.

gambade [gɑ̃bad] **nf** leap.

gambader [3] [gɑ̃bade] **vi** [sautiller] to leap around / [agneau] to gambol.

gamberger [17] [gɑ̃bɛrʒe] **vi** *fam* to think hard.

gambette [gɑ̃bɛt] **nf** *fam* leg, pin.

Gambie [gɑ̃bi] **nf : la Gambie** Gambia.

gambien, ***enne*** [gɑ̃bjɛ̃, ɛn] **adj** Gambian.
◆ ***Gambien***, ***enne*** **nm, f** Gambian.

gamelle [gamɛl] **nf 1.** [plat] mess tin *UK ou* kit *US* **2.** *fam* [chute] **: se ramasser une gamelle** to fall flat on one's face, to come a cropper *UK*.

gamète [gamɛt] **nm** gamete.

gamin, ***e*** [gamɛ̃, in] ■ **adj 1.** [espiègle] lively, mischievous **2.** [puéril] childish.
■ **nm, f 1.** *fam* [enfant] kid **2.** [des rues] street urchin.

gaminerie [gaminri] **nf 1.** [espièglerie] mischievousness **2.** [enfantillage] childishness ▸ **faire des gamineries** to be childish.

gamme [gam] **nf 1.** [série] range ▸ **gamme de produits** product range ▸ **haut/bas de gamme** at the top/bottom of the range **2.** MUS scale.

Gand [gɑ̃] **npr** Ghent.

gang [gɑ̃g] **nm** gang.

Gange [gɑ̃ʒ] **nm : le Gange** the (River) Ganges.

ganglion [gɑ̃glijɔ̃] **nm** ganglion.

gangrène [gɑ̃grɛn] **nf** gangrene / *fig* corruption, canker.

gangrener [19] [gɑ̃grəne] **vt 1.** MÉD to cause to become gangrenous, to gangrene **2.** [corrompre] to corrupt, to rot.
◆ ***se gangrener*** **vpi** to become gangrenous ▸ **la jambe risque de se gangrener** the leg may become gangrenous *ou* may get gangrene.

gangster [gɑ̃gstɛr] **nm** gangster / *fig* crook.

gangue [gɑ̃g] **nf 1.** [de minerai] gangue **2.** *fig* [carcan] straitjacket.

gant [gɑ̃] **nm** glove ▸ **gant de boxe** boxing glove ▸ **gant de caoutchouc** rubber glove ▸ **gant de crin** friction glove ▸ **gant de toilette** facecloth, flannel *UK*, washcloth *US* ▸ **aller comme un gant à qqn** to fit sb like a glove ▸ **prendre des gants** to be cautious ▸ **prendre des gants avec qqn** to handle sb with kid gloves.

garage [garaʒ] **nm** garage.

garagiste [garaʒist] **nmf** [propriétaire] garage owner / [réparateur] garage mechanic.

garant, e [garɑ̃, ɑ̃t] **nm, f** [responsable] guarantor ▸ **se porter garant de** to vouch for.
◆ ***garant*** **nm** [garantie] guarantee.

garantie [garɑ̃ti] **nf 1.** [gén] guarantee **2.** [de police d'assurance] cover *UK*, coverage *US*.
◆ ***sous garantie*** **loc adj** under guarantee ▸ **un appareil sous garantie** an appliance under guarantee.

garantir [32] [garɑ̃tir] **vt 1.** [assurer, COMM & FIN] to guarantee, to collateralize *US* ▸ **garantir à qqn que** to assure *ou* guarantee sb that **2.** [protéger] : **garantir qqch (de)** to protect sthg (from).

garce [gars] **nf** *péj* bitch.

garçon [garsɔ̃] **nm 1.** [enfant] boy ▸ **garçon d'honneur** best man ▸ **garçon manqué** tomboy ▸ **c'est un bon *ou* brave garçon** he's a good sort ▸ **c'est un mauvais garçon** he's bad news, he's a bad lot *UK* ▸ **il est plutôt joli garçon** he's quite good-looking **2.** [célibataire] : **vieux garçon** confirmed bachelor **3.** [serveur] : **garçon (de café)** waiter ▸ **garçon!** waiter! **4.** *fam* [en appellatif] : **attention, mon garçon!** watch it, sonny!

garçonne [garsɔn] **nf : coiffure à la garçonne** urchin cut.

garçonnet [garsɔnɛ] **nm** little boy.

garçonnière [garsɔnjɛr] **nf** bachelor flat *UK ou* apartment *US*.

garde [gard] ■ **nf 1.** [surveillance] protection ▸ **assurer la garde d'un immeuble** [police] to guard a building / [concierge] to look after a building, to be caretaker *UK ou* janitor *US* of a building
2. [veille] : **de garde** on duty ▸ **elle est de garde trois nuits par semaine** she's on duty three nights a week ▸ **pharmacie de garde** duty chemist *UK*, emergency drugstore *US* ▸ **garde de nuit** night duty
3. MIL guard ▸ **garde montante/descendante** relief/old guard ▸ **monter la garde** to go on guard
4. DR : **avoir la garde d'un enfant** to have custody of a child ▸ **garde alternée** divided *ou* alternated custody *(of the children)* ▸ **garde à vue** ≃ police custody
▸▸ **être/se tenir sur ses gardes** to be/stay on one's guard ▸ **mettre qqn en garde contre qqch** to put sb on their guard about sthg ▸ **je l'avais mise en garde contre les dangers du tabac** I had warned her against the dangers of smoking ▸ **mise en garde** warning ▸ **prendre garde à qqch** to watch out for sthg ▸ **prendre garde à ne pas faire qqch** to take care not to do sthg ▸ **prendre garde que** *(+ subjonctif)* to take care that ▸ **ton argent est sous bonne garde** your money is in safe hands.
■ **nmf** keeper ▸ **garde du corps** bodyguard ▸ **garde d'enfants** babysitter, childminder *UK* ▸ **garde forestier** forest ranger ▸ **garde mobile** member of the (State) security police ▸ **garde républicain** Republican guardsman *(on duty at French state occasions)* ▸ **le garde des Sceaux** the Minister of Justice, ≃ Lord Chancellor *UK*, ≃ Attorney General *US*.
◆ ***Garde*** ■ **nf : la Garde républicaine** the Republican Guard.
■ **npr** ➤ *lac*.

garde-à-vous [gardavu] **nm inv** attention ▸ **se mettre au garde-à-vous** to stand to attention.

garde-barrière [gardəbarjɛr] (pl **gardes-barrière** *ou* **gardes-barrières**) **nmf** level-crossing keeper *UK*, gateman at a grade crossing *US*.

garde-boue [gardəbu] **nm inv** mudguard.

garde-chasse [gardəʃas] (pl **gardes-chasse** *ou* **gardes-chasses**) **nm** gamekeeper.

garde-chiourme [gardəʃjurm] (pl **gardes-chiourme** *ou* **gardes-chiourmes**) **nm** prison warder *UK ou* guard *US* / *fig* slavedriver.

garde-fou [gardəfu] (pl **garde-fous**) **nm** railing, parapet.

garde-malade [gardəmalad] (pl **gardes-malades**) **nmf** nurse.

garde-manger [gardəmɑ̃ʒe] **nm inv** [pièce] pantry, larder / [armoire] meat safe *UK*, cooler *US*.

garde-meuble [gardəmœbl] (pl **garde-meuble** *ou* **garde-meubles**) **nm** warehouse.

gardénia [gardenja] **nm** gardenia.

garde-pêche [gardəpɛʃ] (pl **gardes-pêche**) ■ **nm** [personne] water bailiff *UK*, fishwarden *US*.
■ **nm inv** [bateau] fishery protection vessel.

garder [3] [garde] **vt 1.** [gén] to keep ▸ **garde-le, un jour il aura de la valeur** hold onto it *ou* keep it: one day it will be valuable **2.** [vêtement] to keep on ▸ **puis-je garder mon chapeau/manteau?** may I keep my hat/coat on? **3.** [surveiller] to mind, to look after ▸ **elle garde des enfants** she does some baby-sitting *ou* childminding *UK* **4.** [défendre] to guard **5.** [protéger] : **garder qqn de qqch** to save sb from sthg **6.** [maintenir - attitude, sentiment] to keep ▸ **garder l'anonymat** to remain anonymous ▸ **garder son calme** to keep calm *ou* cool ▸ **garder le silence** to keep silent.
◆ ***se garder*** **vp 1.** [se conserver] to keep ▸ **les framboises ne se gardent pas (longtemps)** raspberries do not keep (long) **2.** [se méfier] : **se garder de qqn/qqch** to beware of sb/sthg **3.** [s'abstenir] : **se garder de faire qqch** to take care not to do sthg ▸ **je me garderai bien de lui en parler** I'll be very careful not to talk to him about it.

garderie [gardəri] **nf** crèche *UK*, day nursery *UK*, day-care center *US*.

garde-robe [gardərɔb] (pl **garde-robes**) **nf** wardrobe.

gardien, enne [gardjɛ̃, ɛn] **nm, f 1.** [surveillant] guard, keeper ▸ **gardien de but** goalkeeper ▸ **gardien de nuit** night watchman ▸ **gardien de prison** prison warder *UK ou* guard *US* **2.** *fig* [défenseur] protector, guardian **3.** [agent] : **gardien de la paix** police officer.

gardiennage [gardjɛnaʒ] **nm** caretaking *UK*, job of janitor *US*.

gardon [gardɔ̃] **nm** roach ▸ **frais comme un gardon** *fig* fresh as a daisy.

gare[1] [gar] **nf** station ▸ **gare maritime** harbour *UK ou* harbor *US* station ▸ **gare routière** [de marchandises] road haulage depot *UK* / [pour passagers] bus station ▸ **gare de triage** marshalling yard *UK*, switchyard *US*.

gare[2] [gar] **interj 1.** [attention] watch out! ▸ **gare aux voleurs** watch out for pickpockets ▸ **sans crier gare** *fig* without warning **2.** [menace] **: gare à toi!** watch out!, watch it!

garer [3] [gare] **vt 1.** [ranger] to park **2.** [mettre à l'abri] to put in a safe place.
◆ ***se garer*** **vp 1.** [stationner] to park **2.** [se ranger] to pull over **3.** [éviter] **: se garer de qqch** to avoid sthg.

gargariser [3] [gargarize] ◆ ***se gargariser*** **vp 1.** [se rincer] to gargle **2.** *péj* [se délecter] **: se gargariser de** to delight *ou* revel in.

gargarisme [gargarism] **nm** gargle.

gargote [gargɔt] **nf** cheap restaurant, greasy spoon.

gargouille [garguj] **nf** gargoyle.

gargouillement [gargujmɑ̃] **nm** gurgling *(U)*.

gargouiller [3] [garguje] **vi 1.** [eau] to gurgle **2.** [intestins] to rumble.

garnement [garnəmɑ̃] **nm** rascal, pest.

garni [garni] **nm** *vieilli* furnished accommodation *(U) UK ou* accommodations *(pl) US*.

Garnier [garnje] **npr : le palais Garnier** *the old Paris Opera House*.

garnir [32] [garnir] **vt 1.** [équiper] to fit out, to furnish **2.** [couvrir] **: garnir qqch (de)** to cover sthg (with) **3.** [remplir] to fill **4.** [orner] **: garnir qqch de** to decorate sthg with / COUT to trim sthg with.
◆ ***se garnir*** **vp** to fill up.

garnison [garnizɔ̃] **nf** garrison.

garniture [garnityr] **nf 1.** [ornement] trimming / [de lit] bed linen **2.** AUTO **: garniture de frein** brake lining ▸ **garniture (intérieure)** upholstery **3.** [CULIN - pour accompagner] garnish, fixings *pl US* / [- pour remplir] filling ▸ **garniture de légumes** vegetables *pl*.

garrigue [garig] **nf** scrub.

garrot [garo] **nm 1.** [de cheval] withers *pl* **2.** MÉD tourniquet **3.** [de torture] garrotte.

garrotter [3] [garɔte] **vt 1.** [attacher] to tie up **2.** *fig* [museler] to muzzle.

gars [ga] **nm** *fam* **1.** [garçon, homme] lad **2.** [type] guy, bloke *UK*.

gascon, onne [gaskɔ̃, ɔn] **adj** Gascon.
◆ ***Gascon, onne*** **nm, f** Gascon.

gas-oil [gazɔjl, gazwal], ***gazole*** [gazɔl] **nm** diesel oil.

gaspacho [gaspatʃo] **nm** = ***gazpacho***.

gaspillage [gaspijaʒ] **nm** waste.

gaspiller [3] [gaspije] **vt** to waste.

gastrique [gastrik] **adj** gastric.

gastrite [gastrit] **nf** gastritis *(U)*.

gastro-entérite [gastroɑ̃terit] (pl **gastro-entérites**) **nf** gastroenteritis *(U)*.

gastronome [gastrɔnɔm] **nmf** gourmet.

gastronomie [gastrɔnɔmi] **nf** gastronomy.

gastronomique [gastrɔnɔmik] **adj** gastronomic.

gâteau, x [gato] **nm** cake ▸ **gâteau d'anniversaire** birthday cake ▸ **gâteau de miel** honeycomb ▸ **gâteau sec** biscuit *UK*, cookie *US* ▸ **c'est du gâteau** *fam* it's a piece of cake.

gâter [3] [gate] **vt 1.** [gén] to spoil / [vacances, affaires] to ruin, to spoil **2.** *iron* [combler] to be too good to ▸ **on est gâté!** just marvellous!
◆ ***se gâter*** **vp 1.** [aliments] to spoil, to go off *UK* **2.** [temps] to change for the worse **3.** [situation] to take a turn for the worse.

gâterie [gatri] **nf** treat.

gâteux, euse [gatø, øz] ■ **adj** senile ▸ **être gâteux de** *fig* to be crazy about.
■ **nm, f 1.** [sénile] doddering old man (f woman) **2.** [radoteur] old bore.

gâtisme [gatism] **nm 1.** [vieillissement] senility **2.** [stupidité] stupidity.

GATT, Gatt [gat] (abr de ***General Agreement on Tariffs and Trade***) **nm** GATT.

gauche [goʃ] ■ **nf 1.** [côté] left, left-hand side ▸ **rouler sur la gauche** to drive on the left ▸ **à gauche (de)** on the left (of) ▸ **à ma/ta** *etc* **gauche** on my/your *etc* left ▸ **de gauche** on the left **2.** POLIT **: la gauche** the left (wing) ▸ **de gauche** left-wing.
■ **nm** [boxe] left.
■ **adj 1.** [côté] left **2.** [personne] clumsy.

gauchement [goʃmɑ̃] **adv** clumsily.

gaucher, ère [goʃe, ɛr] ■ **adj** left-handed.
■ **nm, f** left-handed person.

gauchir [32] [goʃir] ■ **vi** to warp.
■ **vt** *fig* to distort.

gauchisant, e [goʃizɑ̃, ɑ̃t] **adj** leftist.

gauchisme [goʃism] **nm** leftism.

gauchiste [goʃist] ■ **nmf** leftist.
■ **adj** left-wing.

gaufre [gofr] **nf** waffle.

gaufrer [3] [gofre] **vt** to emboss.

gaufrette [gofrɛt] **nf** wafer.

gaule [gol] **nf 1.** [perche] pole **2.** [canne à pêche] fishing rod.

gauler [3] [gole] **vt** to bring *ou* shake down.

gaulliste [golist] **nmf & adj** Gaullist.

gaulois, e [golwa, az] **adj 1.** [de Gaule] Gallic **2.** [osé] ribald.
◆ ***Gaulois, e*** **nm, f** Gaul.

gauloiserie [golwazri] **nf** bawdy story.

gausser [3] [gose] ◆ ***se gausser*** **vp : se gausser d[e]** *littéraire* to make fun of.

gaver [3] [gave] **vt 1.** [animal] to force-feed **2.** [person]ne] **: gaver qqn de** to feed sb full of.
◆ ***se gaver*** **vp : se gaver de** to gorge o.s. on.

gay [gɛ] **adj inv & nm** gay.

gaz [gaz] **nm inv** gas ▸ **avoir le gaz** to have gas, to be o[n] gas *UK* ▸ **employé du gaz** gasman ▸ **à pleins gaz** *fam* AUT[O] flat out ▸ **mettre les gaz** *fam* to put one's foot down *U[K]* to step on the gas *US* ▸ **gaz carbonique** carbon dioxide ▸ **gaz d'échappement** exhaust fumes ▸ **gaz lacrymogène** tear gas ▸ **gaz naturel** natural gas ▸ **gaz propulseur** propellant.

Gaza [gaza] **npr** Gaza ▸ **la bande de Gaza** the Gaza Strip.

gaze [gaz] **nf** gauze.

gazelle [gazɛl] **nf** gazelle.

gazer [3] [gaze] ■ **vt** to gas.
■ **vi** *fam* to go at top speed ▸ **ça gaze!** everything's great! ▸ **ça gaze?** how are things?

gazette [gazɛt] **nf** newspaper, gazette.

gazeux, euse [gazø, øz] **adj 1.** CHIM gaseous **2.** [boisson] fizzy.

gazinière [gazinjɛr] **nf** gas stove, gas cooker *UK*.

gazoduc [gazɔdyk] **nm** gas pipeline.

gazole = ***gas-oil***.

gazomètre [gazɔmɛtr] **nm** gasometer.

gazon [gazɔ̃] **nm** [herbe] grass / [terrain] lawn.

gazouiller [3] [gazuje] **vi 1.** [oiseau] to chirp, to twitter **2.** [bébé] to gurgle.

gazouillis [gazuji] **nm 1.** [d'oiseau] chirping, twittering **2.** [de bébé] gurgling.

gazpacho, gaspacho [gaspatʃo] **nm** gazpacho.

GB, G-B (abr écrite de ***Grande-Bretagne***) **nf** GB.

gd abr de ***grand***.

GDF, Gdf (abr de ***Gaz de France***) *French national gas company*.

geai [ʒɛ] **nm** jay.

géant, e [ʒeɑ̃, ɑ̃t] ■ **adj** gigantic, giant.
■ **nm, f** giant.

geignement [ʒɛɲəmɑ̃] **nm** moaning.

geindre [81] [ʒɛ̃dr] **vi 1.** [gémir] to moan **2.** *fam* [pleurnicher] to whine.

gel [ʒɛl] **nm 1.** MÉTÉOR frost **2.** [d'eau] freezing **3.** [cosmétique] gel **4.** ÉCON freezing ▸ **gel des prix** price freeze ▸ **gel des salaires** wage freeze.

gélatine [ʒelatin] **nf** gelatine.

gélatineux, euse [ʒelatinø, øz] **adj** gelatinous.

gelée [ʒəle] **nf 1.** MÉTÉOR frost ▸ **gelée blanche** hoarfrost **2.** CULIN jelly ▸ **en gelée** in jelly ▸ **gelée royale** royal jelly.

geler [25] [ʒəle] **vt & vi 1.** [gén] to freeze **2.** [projet] to halt.
◆ ***se geler*** **vp** *fam* to freeze.

gélule [ʒelyl] **nf** capsule.

Gémeaux [ʒemo] **nmpl** ASTROL Gemini ▸ **être Gémeaux** to be (a) Gemini.

gémir [32] [ʒemir] **vi 1.** [gén] to moan **2.** [par déception] to groan.

gémissement [ʒemismɑ̃] **nm 1.** [gén] moan / [du vent] moaning *(U)* **2.** [de déception] groan.

gemme [ʒɛm] **nf** gem, precious stone.

gênant, e [ʒenɑ̃, ɑ̃t] **adj 1.** [encombrant] in the way **2.** [embarrassant] awkward, embarrassing **3.** [énervant] : **être gênant** to be a nuisance.

gencive [ʒɑ̃siv] **nf** gum.

gendarme [ʒɑ̃darm] **nm** policeman.

gendarmerie [ʒɑ̃darməri] **nf 1.** [corps] police force **2.** [lieu] police station.

gendre [ʒɑ̃dr] **nm** son-in-law.

gène [ʒɛn] **nm** gene.

gêne [ʒɛn] **nf 1.** [physique] difficulty **2.** [psychologique] embarrassment ▸ **être sans gêne** to be inconsiderate **3.** [financière] difficulty ▸ **être dans la gêne** to be in financial difficulties.

gêné, e [ʒene] **adj 1.** [physiquement] : **être gêné pour marcher** to have difficulty walking **2.** [psychologiquement] embarrassed **3.** [financièrement] in financial difficulties.

généalogie [ʒenealɔʒi] **nf** genealogy.

généalogique [ʒenealɔʒik] **adj** genealogical ▸ **arbre généalogique** family tree.

gêner [4] [ʒene] **vt 1.** [physiquement - gén] to be too tight for / [- suj: chaussures] to pinch ▸ **j'ai oublié mes lunettes, ça me gêne pour lire** I've left my glasses behind and I'm finding it difficult to read **2.** [moralement] to embarrass ▸ **les plaisanteries de son ami la gênaient** her friend's jokes embarrassed her *ou* made her feel uncomfortable **3.** [incommoder] to bother ▸ **ça vous gêne si j'ouvre la fenêtre?** do you mind if I open the window? ▸ **ça ne gêne pas que tu viennes, il y a de la place** it'll be no trouble *ou* bother *UK* at all if you come: there's enough room **4.** [encombrer] to hamper ▸ **ce camion gêne la circulation** that truck is holding up the traffic ▸ **ne bougez pas, vous ne me gênez pas du tout** don't move: you're not in my *ou* the way at all.
◆ ***se gêner*** **vp** to put o.s out ▸ **je vais me gêner, tiens!** just watch me! ▸ **ne pas se gêner pour faire qqch** to feel free to do sthg / *hum* to make no bones about doing sthg ▸ **ne vous gênez pas!** *hum* don't mind me!

général, e, aux [ʒeneral, o] **adj** general ▸ **à la demande générale** by popular request ▸ **à la surprise/l'indignation générale** to everybody's surprise/indignation ▸ **en général** generally, in general ▸ **répétition générale** dress rehearsal ▸ **il s'en est tenu à des remarques générales** he confined himself to generalities *ou* to some general remarks ▸ **le phénomène est général** the phenomenon is widespread, it's a general phenomenon.
◆ ***général*** **nm** MIL general ▸ **général de corps d'armée** lieutenant general ▸ **général en chef** commander in chief.
◆ ***générale*** **nf 1.** THÉÂTRE dress rehearsal **2.** MIL alarm ▸ **battre *ou* sonner la générale** to sound the alarm.

généralement [ʒeneralmɑ̃] **adv** generally.

généralisation [ʒeneralizasjɔ̃] **nf** generalization.

généraliser [3] [ʒeneralize] **vt & vi** to generalize.
◆ ***se généraliser*** **vp** to become general *ou* widespread.

généraliste [ʒeneralist] ■ **nmf** family doctor, GP.
■ **adj** general.

généralité [ʒeneralite] **nf 1.** [idée] generality **2.** [universalité] general nature.
◆ ***généralités*** **nfpl** generalities.

générateur, trice [ʒeneratœr, tris] adj generating *(avant n)* ▸ **un fanatisme générateur de violence** a fanaticism that breeds violence ▸ **une industrie génératrice d'emplois** a job-creating industry.
◆ ***générateur*** nm TECHNOL generator ▸ **générateur automatique de programmes** report program generator ▸ **générateur d'électricité** electricity generator ▸ **générateur de système expert** generic expert system tool.
◆ ***génératrice*** nf ÉLECTR generator.

génération [ʒenerasjɔ̃] nf generation ▸ **la nouvelle génération** the younger generation ▸ **génération spontanée** spontaneous generation ▸ **de troisième génération** INFORM & TÉLÉCOM third-generation.

générer [18] [ʒenere] vt to generate.

généreusement [ʒenerøzmɑ̃] adv generously.

généreux, euse [ʒenerø, øz] adj generous / [terre] fertile.

générique [ʒenerik] ■ adj generic ▸ **médicament générique** MÉD generic drug.
■ nm **1.** CINÉ & TV credits *pl* ▸ **générique déroulant** rolling credits **2.** MÉD generic drug.

générosité [ʒenerɔzite] nf generosity.

genèse [ʒənɛz] nf [création] genesis.
◆ ***Genèse*** nf [bible] Genesis.

genêt [ʒənɛ] nm broom.

génétique [ʒenetik] ■ adj genetic.
■ nf genetics *(U)*.

gêneur, euse [ʒenœr, øz] nm, f nuisance.

Genève [ʒənɛv] npr Geneva.

genevois, e [ʒənvwa, az] adj Genevan.

génial, e, aux [ʒenjal, o] adj **1.** [personne] of genius **2.** [idée, invention] inspired **3.** *fam* [formidable] **: c'est génial!** that's great!, that's terrific!

génie [ʒeni] nm **1.** [personne, aptitude] genius ▸ **avoir du génie** to be a genius ▸ **elle a le génie des affaires** she has a genius for business ▸ **à 15 ans, c'était déjà un génie de l'électronique** at 15 he was already an electronics wizard **2.** MYTHOL spirit, genie ▸ **être le bon/mauvais génie de qqn** to be a good/bad influence on sb **3.** TECHNOL engineering ▸ **le génie** MIL ≃ the Royal Engineers *UK*, ≃ the (Army) Corps of Engineers *US* ▸ **génie civil** civil engineering ▸ **génie maritime** [corps] marine architects.
◆ ***de génie*** loc adj [musicien, inventeur] of genius / [idée] brilliant.

genièvre [ʒənjɛvr] nm juniper.

génisse [ʒenis] nf heifer.

génital, e, aux [ʒenital, o] adj genital.

géniteur, trice [ʒenitœr, tris] nm, f parent / [d'animal] sire (f dam).

génitif [ʒenitif] nm genitive (case).

génocide [ʒenɔsid] nm genocide.

génoise [ʒenwa, az] nf sponge cake.

génome [ʒenom] nm genome *m*.

génothérapie [ʒenɔterapi] nf MÉD gene therapy.

génotype [ʒenɔtip] nm genotype.

genou, x [ʒənu] nm knee ▸ **on était dans la neige jusqu'aux genoux** we were knee-deep *ou* up to our knees in snow ▸ **à genoux** on one's knees, kneeling ▸ **être à genoux devant qqn** *fig* to worship sb ▸ **se mettre à genoux** to kneel (down) ▸ **je ne vais pas me mettre à genoux devant lui** [le supplier] I'm not going to go down on my knees to him ▸ **mettre un genou à terre** to go down on one knee ▸ **tenir *ou* avoir qqn sur ses genoux** to hold *ou* have sb in one's lap *ou* on one's knee ▸ **être sur les genoux** *fam fig* to be worn out, to be on one's last legs ▸ **faire du genou à qqn** to play footsie with sb.

genouillère [ʒənujɛr] nf **1.** [bandage] knee bandage **2.** SPORT kneepad.

genre [ʒɑ̃r] nm **1.** [type] type, kind ▸ **en tous genres** of all kinds ▸ **elle est unique en son genre** she's in a class of her own ▸ **le genre humain** the human race ▸ **partir sans payer, ce n'est pas son genre** it's not like him to leave without paying ▸ **un genre de** [une sorte de] a kind *ou* sort of **2.** LITTÉR genre ▸ **le genre policier** the detective genre, detective stories **3.** [style de personne] style ▸ **avoir mauvais genre** to be coarse-looking ▸ **se donner un genre** to put on airs, to give o.s. airs **4.** GRAMM gender.

gens [ʒɑ̃] nmpl people.

gentiane [ʒɑ̃sjan] nf gentian.

gentil, ille [ʒɑ̃ti, ij] adj **1.** [agréable] nice **2.** [aimable] nice, kind ▸ **être gentil avec qqn** to be nice *ou* kind to sb.

gentilhomme [ʒɑ̃tijɔm] (pl **gentilshommes**) nm gentleman.

gentillesse [ʒɑ̃tijɛs] nf kindness ▸ **avoir la gentillesse de faire qqch** to be so kind as to do sthg.

gentillet, ette [ʒɑ̃tijɛ, ɛt] adj **1.** [petit et gentil] nice little **2.** *péj* [assez agréable] nice enough.

gentiment [ʒɑ̃timɑ̃] adv **1.** [sagement] nicely **2.** [aimablement] nicely, kindly **3.** *Suisse* [tranquillement] calmly, quietly.

gentleman [dʒɛntləman] (pl **gentlemen** [dʒɛntləmɛn]) nm gentleman.

génuflexion [ʒenyflɛksjɔ̃] nf genuflexion.

géographe [ʒeɔgraf] nmf geographer.

géographie [ʒeɔgrafi] nf geography.

géographique [ʒeɔgrafik] adj geographical.

geôlier, ère [ʒolje, ɛr] nm, f jailer, gaoler *UK*.

géologie [ʒeɔlɔʒi] nf geology.

géologique [ʒeɔlɔʒik] adj geological.

géologue [ʒeɔlɔg] nmf geologist.

géomètre [ʒeɔmɛtr] nmf **1.** [spécialiste] geometer, geometrician **2.** [technicien] surveyor.

géométrie [ʒeɔmetri] nf geometry.

géométrique [ʒeɔmetrik] adj geometric.

géophysique [ʒeɔfizik] ■ nf geophysics *(U)*.
■ adj geophysical.

géopolitique [ʒeɔpɔlitik] ■ nf geopolitics *(U)*.
■ adj geopolitical.

géosphère [ʒeɔsfɛr] nf geosphere.

gérance [ʒerɑ̃s] nf management.

géranium [ʒeranjɔm] nm geranium.

gérant, e [ʒerɑ̃, ɑ̃t] **nm, f** manager.

gerbe [ʒɛrb] **nf 1.** [de blé] sheaf / [de fleurs] spray **2.** [d'étincelles, d'eau] shower.

gerber [3] [ʒɛrbe] ■ **vt 1.** [blé] to bind into sheaves **2.** [sacs, caisses] to pile (up).
■ **vi 1.** [fusée] to burst in a shower of sparks **2.** *tfam* [vomir] to puke.

gerboise [ʒɛrbwaz] **nf** jerboa.

gercé, e [ʒɛrse] **adj** chapped.

gercer [16] [ʒɛrse] **vt & vi** to crack, to chap.
◆ ***se gercer*** **vp** to crack, to chap.

gerçure [ʒɛrsyr] **nf 1.** [des mains, des lèvres] crack, chapping *(U)* ▶ **j'ai des gerçures aux mains/lèvres** I've got chapped hands/lips **2.** TECHNOL [d'un métal, d'un enduit] hairline crack / [d'un diamant, du bois] flaw / [d'un tronc] shake.

gérer [18] [ʒere] **vt** to manage.

gériatrie [ʒerjatri] **nf** geriatrics *(U)*.

gériatrique [ʒerjatrik] **adj** geriatric.

germain, e [ʒɛrmɛ̃, ɛn] ➤ ***cousin***.

germanique [ʒɛrmanik] **adj** Germanic.

germaniste [ʒɛrmanist] **nmf 1.** [spécialiste] German specialist **2.** [étudiant] German student, student of German.

germe [ʒɛrm] **nm 1.** BOT & MÉD germ / [de pomme de terre] eye ▶ **germes de soja** beansprouts **2.** *fig* [origine] seed, cause.

germer [3] [ʒɛrme] **vi** to germinate.

germination [ʒɛrminasjɔ̃] **nf** germination.

gérondif [ʒerɔ̃dif] **nm** [latin] gerundive / [français] gerund.

gérontologie [ʒerɔ̃tɔlɔʒi] **nf** gerontology.

gésier [ʒezje] **nm** gizzard.

gésir [49] [ʒezir] **vi** *littéraire* to lie.

gestation [ʒɛstasjɔ̃] **nf** gestation ▶ **en gestation** *fig* in gestation.

geste [ʒɛst] **nm 1.** [mouvement] gesture **2.** [acte] act, deed ▶ **faire un geste** *fig* to make a gesture.

gesticuler [3] [ʒɛstikyle] **vi** to gesticulate.

gestion [ʒɛstjɔ̃] **nf 1.** [activité] management **2.** DR administration **3.** ÉCON **: gestion des coûts** cost management ▶ **gestion d'entreprise** business administration ▶ **gestion de fonds** fund management ▶ **gestion de produits** product management **4.** INFORM **: gestion de fichiers** file management.

gestionnaire [ʒɛstjɔnɛr] ■ **nmf** [personne] manager.
■ **adj** management *(avant n)*.
■ **nm** INFORM **: gestionnaire de données** data manager.

gestuel, elle [ʒɛstɥɛl] **adj** [langage] gestural ▶ **langage gestuel** gestural language.
◆ ***gestuelle*** **nf 1.** [généralement] non-verbal communication **2.** [danse & THÉÂTRE] gesture.

geyser [ʒezɛr] **nm** geyser.

Ghana [gana] **nm : le Ghana** Ghana.

ghanéen, enne [ganeɛ̃, ɛn] **adj** Ghanaian.
◆ ***Ghanéen, enne*** **nm, f** Ghanaian.

ghetto [gɛto] **nm** *litt & fig* ghetto.

ghettoïsation [gɛtoizasjɔ̃] **nf** ghettoization.

gibecière [ʒibsjɛr] **nf** game bag / [d'écolier] satchel.

gibelotte [ʒiblɔt] **nf** *rabbit cooked in white wine*.

gibet [ʒibɛ] **nm** gallows *sg*, gibbet.

gibier [ʒibje] **nm** game / *fig* [personne] prey ▶ **gros gibier** big game / *fig* [personne] important catch.

giboulée [ʒibule] **nf** sudden shower.

giboyeux, euse [ʒibwajø, øz] **adj** abounding in game.

Gibraltar [ʒibraltar] **nm** Gibraltar ▶ **à Gibraltar** in Gibraltar.

GIC (abr de ***Groupe interministériel de contrôle***) **nm** *official body controlling the use of telephone tapping*.

giclée [ʒikle] **nf** squirt, spurt.

gicler [3] [ʒikle] **vi** to squirt, to spurt.

gicleur [ʒiklœr] **nm** jet.

GIE (abr de ***groupement d'intérêt économique***) **nm** intercompany management syndicate.

gifle [ʒifl] **nf** slap ▶ **donner une gifle à qqn** to slap sb.

gifler [3] [ʒifle] **vt** to slap / *fig* [suj: vent, pluie] to whip, to lash.

GIG (abr de ***grand invalide de guerre***) **nm** war invalid.

gigantesque [ʒigɑ̃tɛsk] **adj** gigantic.

giga-octet [ʒigaɔktɛ] **nm** INFORM gigabyte.

GIGN (abr de ***Groupe d'intervention de la gendarmerie nationale***) **nm** *special crack force of the French police*, ≃ SAS *UK*, ≃ SWAT *US*.

gigogne [ʒigɔɲ] ➤ ***lit***, ***table***.

gigolo [ʒigɔlo] **nm** gigolo.

gigot [ʒigo] **nm** CULIN leg.

gigoter [3] [ʒigɔte] **vi** to squirm, to wriggle.

gilet [ʒilɛ] **nm 1.** [cardigan] cardigan **2.** [sans manches] waistcoat *UK*, vest *US* ▶ **gilet pare-balles** bulletproof vest ▶ **gilet de sauvetage** life jacket.

gin [dʒin] **nm** gin.

gingembre [ʒɛ̃ʒɑ̃br] **nm** ginger.

gingivite [ʒɛ̃ʒivit] **nf** inflammation of the gums, gingivitis *(U)*.

girafe [ʒiraf] **nf** giraffe.

giratoire [ʒiratwar] **adj** gyrating ▶ **sens giratoire** roundabout *UK*, traffic circle *US*.

girofle [ʒirɔfl] ➤ ***clou***.

giroflée [ʒirɔfle] **nf** stock.

girolle [ʒirɔl] **nf** chanterelle.

giron [ʒirɔ̃] **nm** lap ▶ **le giron familial** *fig* the bosom of one's family.

girouette [ʒirwɛt] **nf** weathercock.

gisait, gisions ➤ ***gésir***.

gisant [ʒizɑ̃] ■ **p prés** ➤ ***gésir***.
■ **nm** recumbent figure *(on tomb)*.

gisement [ʒizmɑ̃] **nm** deposit.

gît ➤ ***gésir***.

gitan, ***e*** [ʒitɑ̃, an] **adj** Gipsy *(avant n)*.
◆ ***Gitan***, ***e*** **nm, f** Gipsy.

Gitane® [ʒitan] **nf** [cigarette] Gitane®.

gîte [ʒit] **nm 1.** [logement] **: gîte (rural)** gîte *self-catering accommodation in the country* **2.** *littéraire* [abri] lodging ▸ **le gîte et le couvert** board and lodging **3.** [du lièvre] form **4.** [du bœuf] shank, shin *UK*.

gîter [3] [ʒite] **vi 1.** [lièvre] to lie **2.** [bateau] to list.

givrant, ***e*** [ʒivrɑ̃, ɑ̃t] **adj** freezing.

givre [ʒivr] **nm** frost.

givré, ***e*** [ʒivre] **adj 1.** CULIN **: orange** *etc* **givrée** orange *etc* sorbet *ou* sherbet *US (served in the hollowed-out fruit)* **2.** *fam* [personne] crazy, round the twist *UK*.

glabre [glabr] **adj** hairless.

glaçage [glasaʒ] **nm 1.** [de gâteau] icing, frosting *US* **2.** [de tissu] glazing.

glaçant, ***e*** [glasɑ̃, ɑ̃t] **adj** cold.

glace [glas] **nf 1.** [eau congelée] ice ▸ **rester de glace** *fig* to be unmoved ▸ **rompre la glace** *fig* to break the ice **2.** [crème glacée] ice cream **3.** [vitre] pane / [de voiture] window **4.** [miroir] mirror ▸ **glace sans tain** two-way mirror.
◆ ***glaces*** **nfpl** ice floes.

glacé, ***e*** [glase] **adj 1.** [gelé] frozen **2.** [très froid] freezing **3.** *fig* [hostile] cold **4.** [dessert] iced / [viande] glazed / [fruit] glacé.

glacer [16] [glase] **vt 1.** [geler, paralyser] to chill **2.** [étoffe, papier] to glaze **3.** [gâteau] to ice *UK*, to frost *US*.
◆ ***se glacer*** **vp** [sang] to run cold.

glaciaire [glasjɛr] **adj** glacial.

glacial, ***e***, ***aux*** [glasjal, o] **adj** *litt* & *fig* icy.

glaciel, ***elle*** [glasjɛl] **adj** *Québec* of an ice floe.
◆ ***glaciel*** **nm** *Québec* ice floe.

glacier [glasje] **nm 1.** GÉOGR glacier **2.** [marchand] ice cream seller *ou* man.

glacière [glasjɛr] **nf** icebox.

glaçon [glasɔ̃] **nm 1.** [dans boisson] ice cube **2.** [sur toit] icicle **3.** *fam fig* [personne] iceberg.

gladiateur [gladjatœr] **nm** gladiator.

glaïeul [glajœl] **nm** gladiolus.

glaire [glɛr] **nf 1.** MÉD phlegm **2.** [d'œuf] white.

glaise [glɛz] **nf** clay.

glaive [glɛv] **nm** sword.

gland [glɑ̃] **nm 1.** [de chêne] acorn **2.** [ornement] tassel **3.** ANAT glans.

glande [glɑ̃d] **nf** gland ▸ **glande endocrine** endocrine gland.

glander [3] [glɑ̃de] **vi** *tfam* to piss around.

glaner [3] [glane] **vt** to glean.

glapir [32] [glapir] **vi** to yelp, to yap.

glapissement [glapismɑ̃] **nm** yelping, yapping.

glas [gla] **nm** knell ▸ **sonner le glas** to toll the bell ▸ **sonner le glas de** *fig* to sound the death knell for.

glaucome [glokom] **nm** glaucoma.

glauque [glok] **adj 1.** [couleur] bluey-green **2.** *fam* [lugubre] gloomy **3.** *fam* [sordide] sordid.

glissade [glisad] **nf** slip ▸ **faire des glissades** to slide.

glissant, ***e*** [glisɑ̃, ɑ̃t] **adj** slippery.

glissement [glismɑ̃] **nm 1.** [action de glisser] gliding, sliding ▸ **glissement de terrain** landslip, landslide **2.** *fig* [électoral] swing, shift.

glisser [3] [glise] ■ **vi 1.** [se déplacer] **: glisser (sur)** to glide (over), to slide (over) ▸ **il se laissa glisser à terre** he slid to the ground **2.** [déraper] **: glisser (sur)** to slip (on) ▸ **attention, ça glisse par terre** watch out, it's slippery underfoot *ou* the ground's slippery **3.** *fig* [passer rapidement] **: glisser sur** to skate over ▸ **glissons sur ce sujet!** let's say no more about it **4.** [surface] to be slippery **5.** [progresser] to slip ▸ **glisser dans** to slip into, to slide into ▸ **glisser vers** to slip towards *UK ou* toward *US*, to slide towards *UK ou* toward *US* **6.** INFORM to drag.
■ **vt** to slip ▸ **glisser un regard à qqn** *fig* to give sb a sidelong glance ▸ **glisser une lettre sous la porte** to slip a letter under the door ▸ **glisser un petit mot à qqn** to slip sb a note.
◆ ***se glisser*** **vp** to slip ▸ **se glisser dans** [lit] to slip *ou* slide into / *fig* to slip *ou* creep into ▸ **des fautes ont pu se glisser dans l'article** some mistakes may have crept into the article.

glisser-lâcher **m** INFORM drag-and-drop.

glissière [glisjɛr] **nf** runner ▸ **à glissière** sliding ▸ **glissière de sécurité** crash barrier.

glissoire [gliswar] **nf** slide.

global, ***e***, ***aux*** [glɔbal, o] **adj** global.

globalement [glɔbalmɑ̃] **adv** on the whole.

globalisation [glɔbalizasjɔ̃] **nf** [d'un marché] globalization.

globalité [glɔbalite] **nf** entirety.

globe [glɔb] **nm 1.** [sphère, terre] globe ▸ **le globe terrestre** the globe **2.** [de verre] glass cover.

globe-trotter [glɔbtrɔtœr] (**pl globe-trotters**) **nmf** globetrotter.

globule [glɔbyl] **nm** corpuscle, blood cell ▸ **globule blanc/rouge** white/red corpuscle.

globuleux [glɔbylø] ➤ ***œil***.

gloire [glwar] **nf 1.** [renommée] glory / [de vedette] fame stardom ▸ **au sommet de sa gloire** at the height *ou* pinnacle of his fame ▸ **connaître la gloire** to find fame **2.** [mérite] credit ▸ **à la gloire de** in praise of ▸ **toute la gloire vous en revient** the credit is all yours.

glorieux, ***euse*** [glɔrjø, øz] **adj** [mort, combat] glorious / [héros, soldat] renowned.

glorifier [9] [glɔrifje] **vt** to glorify, to praise.
◆ ***se glorifier*** **vp : se glorifier de** to glory in.

gloriole [glɔrjɔl] **nf** vainglory.

glose [gloz] **nf** gloss.

gloser [3] [gloze] ■ **vi : gloser sur** to gossip about.
■ **vt** to gloss.

glossaire [glɔsɛr] **nm** glossary.

glotte [glɔt] **nf** glottis.

glouglou [gluglu] **nm 1.** *fam* [de liquide] gurgling **2.** [de dindon] gobbling.

gloussement [glusmɑ̃] **nm 1.** [de poule] cluck, clucking *(U)* **2.** *fam* [de personne] chortle, chuckle.

glousser [3] [gluse] **vi 1.** [poule] to cluck **2.** *fam* [personne] to chortle, to chuckle.

glouton, onne [glutɔ̃, ɔn] ■ **adj** greedy.
■ **nm, f** glutton.

gloutonnerie [glutɔnri] **nf** gluttony, greed.

glu [gly] **nf 1.** [colle] glue **2.** *fam fig* [personne] limpet, leech.

gluant, e [glyɑ̃, ɑ̃t] **adj** sticky.

glucide [glysid] **nm** glucide.

glucose [glykoz] **nm** glucose.

gluten [glytɛn] **nm** gluten.

glycémie [glisemi] **nf** glycaemia *UK* ***ou*** glycemia *US*.

glycérine [gliserin] **nf** glycerine.

glycine [glisin] **nf** wisteria.

GMT (abr de ***Greenwich Mean Time***) GMT.

gnangnan [ɲɑ̃ɲɑ̃] **adj inv** *fam* spineless, wet *UK*.

GNL (abr de ***gaz naturel liquéfié***) **nm** LNG.

gnognot(t)e [ɲɔɲɔt] **nf** *fam* **: c'est de la gnognotte** [c'est facile] that's ***ou*** it's a cinch / [c'est sans valeur] that's ***ou*** it's rubbish *UK* ***ou*** garbage *US*.

gnôle [ɲol] **nf** brandy.

gnome [gnom] **nm** gnome.

gnon [ɲɔ̃] **nm** *fam* thump.

go [go] ◆ ***tout de go*** **loc adv** straight.

GO (abr de ***grandes ondes***) **nfpl** LW.

goal [gol] **nm** goalkeeper.

gobelet [gɔblɛ] **nm** beaker, tumbler.

gober [3] [gɔbe] **vt 1.** [avaler] to gulp down **2.** *fam* [croire] to swallow **3.** *fam* [aimer] **: je ne peux pas la gober** I can't stand her.

goberger [17] [gɔbɛrʒe] ◆ ***se goberger*** **vp** *fam* **1.** [manger] to stuff o.s. **2.** [se prélasser] to take it easy.

godasse [gɔdas] **nf** *fam* shoe.

godet [gɔdɛ] **nm 1.** [récipient] jar, pot **2.** COUT flare.

godiller [3] [gɔdije] **vi 1.** [rameur] to scull **2.** [skieur] to wedeln.

goéland [gɔelɑ̃] **nm** gull, seagull.

goélette [gɔelɛt] **nf** schooner.

goémon [gɔemɔ̃] **nm** wrack.

gogo [gogo] ◆ ***à gogo*** **loc adv** *fam* galore.

goguenard, e [gɔgnar, ard] **adj** mocking.

goguette [gɔgɛt] ◆ ***en goguette*** **loc adv** *fam* a bit tight ***ou*** tipsy.

goinfre [gwɛ̃fr] **nmf** *fam* pig.

goinfrer [3] [gwɛ̃fre] ◆ ***se goinfrer*** **vp : se goinfrer de** *fam* to stuff o.s. with, to pig out on.

goitre [gwatr] **nm** goitre.

golden [gɔldɛn] **nf** Golden Delicious.

golf [gɔlf] **nm** [sport] golf / [terrain] golf course.

golfe [gɔlf] **nm** gulf, bay ▸ **le golfe de Gascogne** the Bay of Biscay ▸ **le golfe Persique** the (Persian) Gulf.

gominer [3] [gɔmine] ◆ ***se gominer*** **vp** *(emploi réfléchi)* to put Brylcreem® ***ou*** hair cream on.

gommage [gɔmaʒ] **nm 1.** [d'écriture] erasing, rubbing out **2.** [cosmétique] face scrub.

gomme [gɔm] **nf 1.** [substance, bonbon] gum **2.** [pour effacer] eraser, rubber *UK*
⏭ **à la gomme** *fam* hopeless, useless.

gommé, e [gɔme] **adj** gummed.

gommer [3] [gɔme] **vt** to rub out, to erase / *fig* to erase.

gond [gɔ̃] **nm** hinge ▸ **sortir de ses gonds** *fam fig* to fly off the handle.

gondole [gɔ̃dɔl] **nf** gondola.

gondoler [3] [gɔ̃dɔle] **vi** [bois] to warp / [carton] to curl.
◆ ***se gondoler*** **vp 1.** [bois] to warp **2.** *fam* [rire] to split one's sides laughing.

gonflable [gɔ̃flabl] **adj** inflatable.

gonflé, e [gɔ̃fle] **adj 1.** [enflé] swollen, puffed up **2.** *fam* [locution] **: t'es gonflé!** you've got a nerve ***ou*** some cheek *UK*! ▸ **être gonflé à bloc** [en pleine forme] to be full of beans / [plein d'ardeur] to be itching ***ou*** raring to go.

gonfler [3] [gɔ̃fle] ■ **vt 1.** [ballon, pneu] to blow up, to inflate / [rivière, poitrine, yeux] to swell / [joues] to blow out **2.** *fig* [grossir] to exaggerate
⏭ **être gonflé** *fam* [être courageux] to have guts / [exagérer] to have a nerve ***ou*** cheek *UK*.
■ **vi** to swell.
◆ ***se gonfler*** **vp 1.** [se distendre] to swell **2.** [être envahi] **: se gonfler de** [orgueil] to swell with / [espoir] to be filled with.

gonflette [gɔ̃flɛt] **nf** *fam* **: faire de la gonflette** to pump iron.

gonfleur [gɔ̃flœr] **nm** pump.

gong [gɔ̃g] **nm** gong.

gonzesse [gɔ̃zɛs] **nf** *tfam* chick, bird *UK*.

goret [gɔrɛ] **nm 1.** [cochon] piglet **2.** *fam* [garçon] dirty little pig.

gorge [gɔrʒ] **nf 1.** [gosier, cou] throat ▸ **avoir la gorge serrée** to have a lump in one's throat ▸ **s'éclaircir la gorge** to clear one's throat ▸ **faire des gorges chaudes de qqch** to laugh sthg to scorn ▸ **prendre qqn à la gorge** to put sb in a difficult situation ▸ **rire à gorge déployée** to laugh heartily **2.** *littéraire* [poitrine] breast, bosom **3.** *(gén pl)* [vallée] gorge.

gorgée [gɔrʒe] **nf** mouthful ▸ **à petites gorgées** in sips.

gorger [17] [gɔrʒe] **vt : gorger qqn de qqch** [gaver] to stuff sb with sthg / [combler] to heap sthg on sb ▸ **gorger qqch de** to fill sthg with.
◆ ***se gorger*** **vp : se gorger de** to gorge o.s. on.

gorille [gɔrij] **nm 1.** [animal] gorilla **2.** *fam* [personne] bodyguard.

gosier [gozje] **nm** throat, gullet.

gosse [gɔs] **nmf** *fam* kid.

gothique [gɔtik] adj 1. ARCHIT Gothic 2. TYPO : **écriture gothique** Gothic script.
◆ ***gothique*** nm : **le gothique** the Gothic style.

gouache [gwaʃ] nf gouache.

gouaille [gwaj] nf *vieilli* cheeky humour *UK*, sassy humor *US*.

goudron [gudrɔ̃] nm tar.

goudronner [3] [gudrɔne] vt to tar.

gouffre [gufr] nm abyss ▸ **le gouffre de l'oubli/du désespoir** the depths of oblivion/despair ▸ **gouffre financier** COMM [produit, entreprise] financial disaster ▸ **au bord du gouffre** *fig* on the edge of the abyss.

goujat [guʒa] nm boor.

goujaterie [guʒatri] nf boorishness.

goujon [guʒɔ̃] nm [poisson] gudgeon ▸ **taquiner le goujon** to do a bit of fishing.

goulet [gulɛ] nm narrows *pl* ▸ **goulet d'étranglement** bottleneck.

goulot [gulo] nm neck ▸ **boire au goulot** to drink straight from the bottle.

goulu, e [guly] ■ adj greedy, gluttonous.
■ nm, f glutton.

goulûment [gulymɑ̃] adv greedily.

goupille [gupij] nf pin.

goupiller [3] [gupije] vt *fam* to fix.
◆ ***se goupiller*** vp *fam* to work out.

goupillon [gupijɔ̃] nm 1. RELIG (holy water) sprinkler 2. [à bouteille] bottle brush.

gourd, e [gur, gurd] adj numb.

gourde [gurd] ■ nf 1. [récipient] flask, water bottle 2. *fam* [personne] idiot, clot *UK*.
■ adj *fam* thick.

gourdin [gurdɛ̃] nm club.

gourer [3] [gure] ◆ ***se gourer*** vp *fam* to slip up.

gourgane [gurgan] nf *Québec* broad bean.

gourmand, e [gurmɑ̃, ɑ̃d] ■ adj greedy ▸ **gourmand de** fond of.
■ nm, f glutton.

gourmandise [gurmɑ̃diz] nf 1. [caractère] greed, greediness 2. [sucrerie] sweet thing.

gourme [gurm] nf 1. MÉD impetigo 2. [maladie du cheval] strangles *(U)*
▸▸ **jeter sa gourme** *vieilli* to sow one's wild oats.

gourmet [gurmɛ] nm : **(fin) gourmet** gourmet.

gourmette [gurmɛt] nf chain bracelet.

gourou [guru] nm guru.

gousse [gus] nf pod ▸ **gousse d'ail** clove of garlic.

gousset [gusɛ] nm [de gilet] fob pocket.

goût [gu] nm taste ▸ **au goût du jour** fashionable ▸ **remettre qqch au goût du jour** to update sthg ▸ **avoir du goût** to have taste ▸ **avoir le goût de qqch** to have a taste *ou* liking for sthg ▸ **avoir un drôle de goût** to taste funny ▸ **ça n'a aucun goût** it's tasteless, it's got no taste ▸ **avoir des goûts de luxe** to have expensive tastes ▸ **de bon goût** [élégant] tasteful, in good taste / *hum* [bienséant] advisable ▸ **de mauvais goût** tasteless, in bad taste ▸ **cette plaisanterie est d'un goût douteux** that joke is in poor *ou* doubtful taste ▸ **faire qqch par goût** to do sthg out of *ou* by inclination ▸ **il n'a goût à rien** he doesn't feel like doing anything ▸ **le décor est tout à fait à mon goût** the decor is exactly to my liking ▸ **prendre goût à qqch** to take a liking to sthg ▸ **chacun ses goûts** each to his own ▸ **c'est (une) affaire *ou* question de goût** it's a matter of taste.

goûter [3] [gute] ■ vt 1. [déguster] to taste 2. [savourer] to enjoy 3. *littéraire* [estimer] to appreciate.
■ vi to have an afternoon snack ▸ **goûter à** to taste ▸ **goûter de** *littéraire* & *fig* to have a taste of.
■ nm *afternoon snack for children, typically consisting of bread, butter, chocolate and a drink.*

goutte [gut] ■ nf 1. [de pluie, d'eau] drop ▸ **la goutte (d'eau) qui fait déborder le vase** *fig* the last straw ▸ **une goutte dans l'océan** a drop in the ocean ▸ **se ressembler comme deux gouttes d'eau** to be as like as two peas in a pod 2. *fam* [alcool] : **la goutte** the hard stuff 3. MÉD [maladie] gout.
■ adv *(de négation) littéraire* : **ne... goutte** not a thing, nothing ▸ **je n'y vois goutte** I can't see a thing.
◆ ***gouttes*** nfpl MÉD drops ▸ **gouttes pour le nez/les oreilles/les yeux** [pharmacie] nose/ear/eye drops.
◆ ***goutte à goutte*** loc adv drop by drop ▸ **tomber goutte à goutte** to drip ▸ **ils laissent filtrer les informations goutte à goutte** *fig* they are letting the news filter out bit by bit.

goutte-à-goutte [gutagut] nm inv (intravenous) drip, IV *US*.

gouttelette [gutlɛt] nf droplet.

gouttière [gutjɛr] nf 1. [CONSTR - horizontale] gutter / [- verticale] drainpipe 2. MÉD splint.

gouvernail [guvɛrnaj] nm rudder.

gouvernante [guvɛrnɑ̃t] nf 1. [d'enfants] governess 2. [de maison] housekeeper.

gouverne [guvɛrn] nf AÉRON control surface ▸ **gouverne de direction** rudder ▸ **pour ma/ta gouverne** *fig* for my yourguidance.

gouvernement [guvɛrnəmɑ̃] nm POLIT government ▸ **gouvernement de coalition** coalition government ▸ **gouvernement à la majorité absolue** majority rule.

gouvernemental, e, aux [guvɛrnəmɑ̃tal, o] adj [politique, organisation] government *(avant n)* / [journal] pro-government.

gouverner [3] [guvɛrne] vt to govern.

gouverneur [guvɛrnœr] nm governor.

GPL (abr de ***gaz de pétrole liquéfié***) nm LPG.

GPS (abr de ***global positionning system***) nm GPS.

GQG (abr de ***grand quartier général***) nm GHQ.

gr abr de ***grade***.

GR (abr de ***(sentier de) grande randonnée***) nm *long distance hiking path*.

grabataire [grabatɛr] ■ nmf invalid.
■ adj bedridden.

grabuge [grabyʒ] nm *fam* trouble.

grâce [gras] **nf 1.** [charme] grace ▸ **de bonne grâce** with good grace, willingly ▸ **de mauvaise grâce** with bad grace, reluctantly ▸ **plein de grâce** graceful **2.** [faveur] favour *UK*, favor *US* ▸ **accorder sa grâce à qqn** to pardon sb ▸ **demander grâce** to beg for mercy ▸ **être dans les bonnes grâces de qqn** to be in sb's good books ▸ **faire grâce de qqch à qqn** to spare sb sthg ▸ **je te fais grâce du récit complet** I'll spare you the full story ▸ **trouver grâce aux yeux de qqn** to find favour with sb **3.** [miséricorde] mercy ▸ **par la grâce de Dieu** by the grace of God ▸ **rendre grâce à** *littéraire* to give thanks to.
◆ ***de grâce*** **interj** for heaven's sake!
◆ ***grâce à*** **loc prép** thanks to.

gracier [9] [grasje] **vt** to pardon.

gracieusement [grasjøzmɑ̃] **adv 1.** [avec grâce] graciously **2.** [gratuitement] free (of charge).

gracieux, euse [grasjø, øz] **adj 1.** [charmant] graceful **2.** [gratuit] free.

gracile [grasil] **adj** slender.

gradation [gradasjɔ̃] **nf** gradation.

grade [grad] **nm** [échelon] rank / [universitaire] qualification ▸ **monter en grade** to be promoted ▸ **en prendre pour son grade** to get hauled over the coals.

gradé, e [grade] ■ **adj** non-commissioned.
■ **nm, f** non-commissioned officer, NCO.

gradin [gradɛ̃] **nm** [de stade, de théâtre] tier / [de terrain] terrace ▸ **en gradins** terraced.

graduation [gradɥasjɔ̃] **nf** graduation.

gradué, e [gradɥe] *Belgique* ■ **adj** [étudiant] college *(avant n)*.
■ **nm, f** college graduate.

graduel, elle [gradɥɛl] **adj** gradual / [difficultés] increasing.

graduellement [gradɥɛlmɑ̃] **adv** gradually.

graduer [7] [gradɥe] **vt 1.** [récipient, règle] to graduate **2.** *fig* [effort, travail] to increase gradually.

graff [graf] (abr de ***graffiti***) **nm** (piece of) graffiti.

graffeur, euse [grafœ, øz] **nm, f** graffiti artist, graffitist.

graffiti [grafiti] **nm inv** graffiti *(U)*.

grailler [3] [graje] **vi** *fam* to nosh *UK*, to chow down *US*.

graillon [grajɔ̃] **nm** *péj* burnt fat.

grain [grɛ̃] **nm 1.** [gén] grain / [de moutarde] seed / [de café] bean ▸ **grain de cassis/groseille** blackcurrant/redcurrant (berry) ▸ **grain de poivre** peppercorn ▸ **grain de raisin** grape ▸ **moulu ou en grains?** ground or not?, ground or whole?
2. [point] **: grain de beauté** mole, beauty spot
3. [averse] squall
4. *fig* [petite quantité] **: un grain de** a touch of ▸ **un grain de bon sens** an ounce of common sense ▸ **un grain de folie** a touch of madness
5. [aspect - de la peau] grain, texture / [- du bois, du papier] grain ▸ **à gros grain** coarse-grained ▸ **à petit grain** close-grained, fine-grained
▸▸| **avoir un grain** *fam* to be a bit touched ▸ **mettre son grain de sel** *péj* to put one's oar in ▸ **veiller au grain** to be on one's guard.

graine [grɛn] **nf** BOT seed ▸ **mauvaise graine** *fig* bad lot ▸▸| **être de la graine de voleur** to be a thief in the making ▸ **en prendre de la graine** *fam* to follow my/his *etc* example ▸ **monter en graine** [salade] to bolt, to run to seed / *fig* to shoot up.

grainetier, ère [grɛntje, ɛr] **nm, f** seed merchant.

graissage [grɛsaʒ] **nm** lubrication.

graisse [grɛs] **nf 1.** ANAT & CULIN fat **2.** [pour lubrifier] grease.

graisser [4] [grɛse] **vt 1.** [machine] to grease, to lubricate **2.** [vêtements] to get grease on.

graisseux, euse [grɛsø, øz] **adj 1.** [papier] greasy **2.** [bourrelet] of fat.

graminée [gramine] **nf** grass ▸ **les graminées** [gén] (the) grasses / BOT the gramineae *(terme spécialisé)*.

grammaire [gramɛr] **nf** grammar.

grammatical, e, aux [gramatikal, o] **adj** grammatical.

grammaticalement [gramatikalmɑ̃] **adv** grammatically.

gramme [gram] **nm** gram, gramme *UK* ▸ **il n'a pas un gramme de jugeote** he hasn't got an ounce of common sense.

grand, e [grɑ̃, grɑ̃d] ■ **adj 1.** [en hauteur] tall ▸ **une grande tour** a high *ou* tall tower / [en dimensions] big, large ▸ **de grandes jambes** long legs / [en quantité, nombre] large, great ▸ **une grande partie de** a large *ou* great proportion of ▸ **un grand nombre de** a large *ou* great number of ▸ **en grand** [dimension] full-size
2. [âgé] grown-up ▸ **les grandes personnes** grown-ups ▸ **grand frère** big *ou* older brother ▸ **grande sœur** big *ou* older sister ▸ **il est assez grand pour...** he's old enough to...
3. [puissant] big, leading *(avant n)* ▸ **les grands dignitaires du régime** the leading dignitaries of the regime
4. [important, remarquable] great ▸ **les grands problèmes de notre temps** the main *ou* major *ou* key issues of our time ▸ **les grands couturiers** the top fashion designers ▸ **un grand homme** a great man
5. [intense] **: un grand blessé/brûlé** a person with serious wounds/burns ▸ **un grand buveur/fumeur** a heavy drinker/smoker ▸ **c'était un grand moment** it was a great moment ▸ **un grand merci à ta sœur** lots of thanks to *ou* a big thank you to your sister ▸ **faire grand bien : ça m'a fait le plus grand bien** it did me a power of good *ou* the world of good.
■ **nm, f** *(gén pl)* **1.** [personnage] great man (f woman) ▸ **c'est l'un des grands de l'électroménager** he's one of the big names in electrical appliances ▸ **les grands de ce monde** the people in (positions of) power *ou* in high places

2. [enfant] older *ou* bigger boy (f girl) ▸ **allons, ma grande, ne pleure pas!** come on now, dear, don't cry!
◆ ***grand*** **adv : voir grand** to think big ▸ **tailler grand : ça devrait vous aller, ça taille grand** it should fit you: it's cut large.
◆ ***grande école*** **nf** *competitive-entrance higher education establishment.*
◆ ***grande surface*** **nf** hypermarket.

CULTURE

Grande école

These respected establishments of higher education enrol far fewer students than French universities, and students must take two years of gruelling **classes préparatoires** and pass extremely difficult exams to gain admission. Once enrolled, students often benefit from partnerships between their college and prestigious companies. The most renowned are l'**École des hautes études commerciales**, or HEC (management and business); l'**École polytechnique**, also known as **l'X** (engineering); and l'**École normale supérieure**, or **Normale Sup** (humanities). Degrees from these colleges are comparable to an Oxbridge degree in the United Kingdom or an Ivy League degree in the United States.

grand-angle [grɑ̃tɑ̃gl] (pl **grands-angles**), ***grand-angulaire*** [grɑ̃tɑ̃gylɛr] (pl **grands-angulaires**) ■ **adj** wide-angle.
■ **nm** wide-angle lens.

grand-chose [grɑ̃ʃoz] ◆ ***pas grand-chose*** ■ **pron indéf** not much.
■ **nmf** *fam* worthless person.

grand-duché [grɑ̃dyʃe] (pl **grands-duchés**) **nm** grand duchy.

Grande-Bretagne [grɑ̃dbrətaɲ] **nf : la Grande-Bretagne** Great Britain.

grandement [grɑ̃dmɑ̃] **adv 1.** [beaucoup] greatly **2.** [largement] a lot ▸ **avoir grandement de quoi vivre** to have plenty to live on.

grandeur [grɑ̃dœr] **nf 1.** [taille] size ▸ **grandeur nature** life-size, life-sized **2.** *fig* [apogée] greatness ▸ **avec grandeur** nobly ▸ **grandeur d'âme** *fig* magnanimity ▸ **la grandeur humaine** the greatness of man **3.** [sciences] **: grandeurs énergétiques** energy consumption and supply ▸ **grandeur de sortie** output.

grand-guignolesque [grɑ̃giɲɔlɛsk] **adj** bloodthirsty and melodramatic.

grandiloquent*, e* [grɑ̃dilɔkɑ̃, ɑ̃t] **adj** grandiloquent.

grandiose [grɑ̃djoz] **adj** imposing.

grandir [32] [grɑ̃dir] ■ **vt : grandir qqn** [suj: chaussures] to make sb look taller / *fig* to increase sb's standing.
■ **vi** [personne, plante] to grow / [obscurité, bruit] to increase, to grow ▸ **grandir dans l'estime de qqn** to go up in sb's estimation.
◆ ***se grandir*** **vp** to make o.s. (appear) taller / *fig* to increase one's standing.

grandissant*, e* [grɑ̃disɑ̃, ɑ̃t] **adj** growing.

grand-maman [grɑ̃mamɑ̃] (pl **grand-mamans** *ou* **grands-mamans**) **nf** granny, grandma.

grand-mère [grɑ̃mɛr] (pl **grand-mères** *ou* **grands-mères**) **nf** grandmother / *fam fig* old biddy ▸ **grand-mère maternelle/paternelle** maternal/paternalgrandmother.

grand-messe [grɑ̃mɛs] (pl **grand-messes** *ou* **grands-messes**) **nf** high mass.

grand-oncle [grɑ̃tɔ̃kl] (pl **grands-oncles**) **nm** great-uncle.

grand-papa [grɑ̃papa] (pl **grands-papas**) **nm** grandpa, grandad *UK*, granddad *US*.

grand-peine [grɑ̃pɛn] ◆ ***à grand-peine*** **loc adv** with great difficulty.

grand-père [grɑ̃pɛr] (pl **grands-pères**) **nm** grandfather / *fam fig* grandad *UK*, granddad *US*, old timer *US* ▸ **grand-père maternel/ paternel** maternal/ paternal grandfather.

grands-parents [grɑ̃parɑ̃] **nmpl** grandparents.

grand-tante [grɑ̃tɑ̃t] (pl **grand-tantes** *ou* **grands-tantes**) **nf** great-aunt.

grand-voile [grɑ̃vwal] (pl **grands-voiles**) **nf** mainsail.

grange [grɑ̃ʒ] **nf** barn.

granit(e) [granit] **nm** granite.

granité*, e* [granite] **adj** [tissu] pebble-weave.
◆ ***granité*** **nm 1.** [tissu] pebble weave **2.** [glace] granita.

granule [granyl] **nm 1.** [grain] granule **2.** MÉD pill.

granulé*, e* [granyle] **adj** [surface] granular.
◆ ***granulé*** **nm** tablet.

granuleux*, euse* [granylø, øz] **adj** granular.

grape-fruit [grɛpfrut] (pl **grape-fruits**) **nm** grapefruit.

graphe [graf] **nm** graph.

graphie [grafi] **nf** spelling.

graphique [grafik] ■ **nm** diagram / [courbe] graph / [tracé] **: graphique à** ***ou*** **en barres** bar graph *ou* chart *UK* ▸ **graphique en colonnes** bar graph *ou* chart *UK*.
■ **adj** graphic.

graphisme [grafism] **nm 1.** [écriture] handwriting **2.** ART style of drawing.

graphiste [grafist] **nmf** graphic artist.

graphologie [grafɔlɔʒi] **nf** graphology.

graphologue [grafɔlɔg] **nmf** graphologist, handwriting expert.

grappe [grap] **nf 1.** [de fruits] bunch / [de fleurs] stem ▸ **grappe de raisin** bunch of grapes **2.** *fig* [de gens] knot

grappiller [3] [grapije] ■ **vt** *litt* & *fig* to gather, to pick up.
■ **vi** [financièrement] to make money.

grappin [grapɛ̃] **nm** [ancre] grapnel ▸ **mettre le grappin sur** *fig* & *péj* to get one's claws into sb.

gras*, grasse* [gra, gras] **adj 1.** [personne, animal] fa **2.** [plat, aliment] fatty ▸ **matières grasses** fats ▸ **ne mettez pas trop de matière grasse** do not add too much fa ▸ **fromage gras** full-fat cheese **3.** [cheveux, mains] greas

4. [sol] clayey / [crayon] soft 5. *fig* [plaisanterie] crude 6. *fig* [rire] throaty / [toux] phlegmy 7. *fig* [plante] succulent

▸▸ **faire la grasse matinée** to stay in bed (very) late, to have a lie-in *UK*.

◆ ***gras*** ■ **nm** 1. [du jambon] fat 2. [de jambe] soft *ou* fleshy part 3. TYPO bold (type) 4. [substance] grease ▸ **des taches de gras** greasy stains.

■ **adv : manger gras** to eat fatty foods ▸ **parler gras** to speak coarsely *ou* gutturally ▸ **tousser gras** to have a loose cough.

gras-double [gradubl] (pl **gras-doubles**) **nm** tripe.

grassement [grasmɑ̃] **adv** 1. [rire] coarsely 2. [payer] a lot.

grassouillet, ette [grasujɛ, ɛt] **adj** *fam* plump.

gratifiant, e [gratifjɑ̃, ɑ̃t] **adj** gratifying.

gratification [gratifikasjɔ̃] **nf** 1. [en argent] bonus 2. [psychologique] gratification.

gratifier [9] [gratifje] **vt** 1. [accorder] **: gratifier qqn de qqch** to present sb with sthg, to present sthg to sb / *fig* to reward sb with sthg 2. [stimuler] to gratify.

gratin [gratɛ̃] **nm** 1. CULIN *dish sprinkled with breadcrumbs or cheese and browned* ▸ **gratin dauphinois** *sliced potatoes baked with cream and browned on top* 2. *fam fig* [haute société] upper crust.

gratiné, e [gratine] **adj** 1. CULIN *sprinkled with breadcrumbs or cheese and browned* 2. *fam fig* [ardu] stiff 3. *fam fig* [déroutant] weird.

◆ ***gratinée*** **nf** *onion soup sprinkled with cheese and browned.*

gratiner [3] [gratine] **vt** *to sprinkle with breadcrumbs or cheese and then brown.*

gratis [gratis] **adv** free.

gratitude [gratityd] **nf : gratitude (envers)** gratitude (to *ou* towards).

gratte-ciel [gratsjɛl] **nm inv** skyscraper.

grattement [gratmɑ̃] **nm** scratching.

gratte-papier [gratpapje] **nm inv** *fam* penpusher.

gratter [3] [grate] ■ **vt** 1. [gén] to scratch / [pour enlever] to scrape off 2. *fam* [gagner] to make 3. *fam* [devancer] to overtake.

■ **vi** 1. [démanger] to itch, to be itchy 2. *fam* [écrire] to scribble 3. [frapper] **: gratter à la porte** to tap at the door 4. *fam* [travailler] to slave, to slog 5. *fam* [jouer] **: gratter de** [violon] to scrape away at / [guitare] to strum on.

◆ ***se gratter*** **vp** to scratch.

grattoir [gratwar] **nm** 1. [outil] scraper 2. [de boîte d'allumettes] striking surface.

gratuit, e [gratɥi, it] **adj** 1. [entrée] free 2. [hypothèse] unwarranted 3. [violence] gratuitous.

gratuité [gratɥite] **nf** 1. [d'entrée] free nature 2. [d'hypothèse] unwarranted nature.

gratuitement [gratɥitmɑ̃] **adv** 1. [sans payer] free, for nothing 2. [sans raison] gratuitously.

gravats [grava] **nmpl** rubble *(U)*.

grave [grav] ■ **adj** 1. [attitude, faute, maladie] serious, grave ▸ **ce n'est pas grave** [ce n'est rien] don't worry about it 2. [voix] deep 3. LING **: accent grave** grave accent.

■ **nm** *(gén pl)* MUS low register.

graveleux, euse [gravlø, øz] **adj** 1. [sol] gravelly 2. [fruit] gritty 3. [propos] crude.

gravement [gravmɑ̃] **adv** gravely, seriously.

graver [3] [grave] **vt** 1. [gén] to engrave 2. [bois] to carve 3. INFORM to burn.

graveur, euse [gravœr, øz] **nm, f** engraver.

◆ ***graveur*** **nm** INFORM CD-RW drive, (CD-)burner ▸ **graveur de CD** CD writer *ou* burner.

gravier [gravje] **nm** gravel *(U)*.

gravillon [gravijɔ̃] **nm** fine gravel *(U)*.

gravir [32] [gravir] **vt** to climb.

gravité [gravite] **nf** 1. [importance] seriousness, gravity ▸ **sans gravité** not serious 2. PHYS gravity.

graviter [3] [gravite] **vi** 1. [astre] to revolve 2. *fig* [évoluer] to gravitate.

gravure [gravyr] **nf** 1. [technique] **: gravure (sur)** engraving (on) ▸ **gravure sur bois** woodcutting 2. [reproduction] print / [dans livre] plate.

gré [gre] **nm** 1. [goût] **: à mon/son gré** for my/his taste, for my/his liking 2. [volonté] **: bon gré mal gré** willy-nilly ▸ **contre mon/son gré** against my/hiswill ▸ **de gré ou de force** *fig* whether you/they *etc* like it or not ▸ **de mon/son plein gré** of my/his own free will ▸ **au gré de qqn/qqch** at the will of sb/sthg, at the pleasure of sb/sthg 3. [gratitude] **: je vous saurais gré de bien vouloir...** *littéraire* I should be grateful if you would...

grec, grecque [grɛk] **adj** Greek.

◆ ***grec*** **nm** [langue] Greek ▸ **grec ancien/moderne** ancient/modern Greek.

◆ ***grecque*** **nf** CULIN **: à la grecque** *stewed in oil (with tomatoes) and served cold.*

◆ ***Grec, Grecque*** **nm, f** Greek.

Grèce [grɛs] **nf : la Grèce** Greece.

gredin, e [grədɛ̃, in] **nm, f** rogue.

gréement [gremɑ̃] **nm** rigging.

green [grin] **nm** [golf] green.

Greenwich [grinwitʃ] **npr** Greenwich ▸ **le méridien de Greenwich** the Greenwich Meridian.

gréer [15] [gree] **vt** to rig.

greffe [grɛf] ■ **nf** 1. MÉD transplant / [de peau] graft ▸ **greffe du cœur** heart transplant 2. BOT graft.

■ **nm** DR **: greffe (du tribunal)** office of the clerk of court.

greffer [4] [grɛfe] **vt** 1. MÉD to transplant / [peau] to graft ▸ **greffer un rein/un cœur à qqn** to give sb a kidney/heart transplant 2. BOT to graft.

◆ ***se greffer*** **vp : se greffer sur qqch** to be added to sthg.

greffier [grɛfje] **nm** clerk of the court.

grégaire [gregɛr] **adj** gregarious.

grège [grɛʒ] ➤ ***soie***.

grégorien, enne [gregɔrjɛ̃, ɛn] **adj** Gregorian.

grêle [grɛl] ■ **nf** hail.
■ **adj 1.** [jambes] spindly **2.** [son] shrill.

grêlé, e [grele] **adj** pockmarked.

grêler [4] [grele] ■ **v impers** to hail ▸ **il grêle** it's hailing.
■ **vt** to devastate by hail.

grêlon [grɛlɔ̃] **nm** hailstone.

grelot [grəlo] **nm** bell.

grelotter [3] [grəlɔte] **vi : grelotter (de)** to shiver (with).

grenade [grənad] **nf 1.** [fruit] pomegranate **2.** MIL grenade ▸ **grenade lacrymogène** tear-gas grenade.

Grenade [grənad] ■ **npr f** [île] **: la Grenade** Grenada ▸ **à la Grenade** in Grenada.
■ **npr** [ville d'Espagne] Granada.

grenadier [grənadje] **nm 1.** [arbre] pomegranate tree **2.** MIL grenadier.

grenadine [grənadin] **nf** grenadine *(pomegranate syrup)*.

grenat [grəna] ■ **nm** garnet.
■ **adj inv** dark red.

grenier [grənje] **nm 1.** [de maison] attic **2.** [à foin] loft **3.** *fig* [région] breadbasket.

grenouille [grənuj] **nf** frog ▸ **grenouille de bénitier** *fig* fanatical churchgoer.

grenouiller [3] [grənuje] **vi** *fam* to plot, to scheme, to connive.

grenouillère [grənujɛr] **nf** [de bébé] all-in-one.

grenu, e [grəny] **adj 1.** [cuir] grained **2.** [roche] granular.

grès [grɛ] **nm 1.** [roche] sandstone **2.** [poterie] stoneware.

grésil [grezil] **nm** hail.

grésillement [grezijmɑ̃] **nm** [de friture] sizzling / [de feu] crackling.

grésiller [3] [grezije] **vi 1.** [friture] to sizzle / [feu] to crackle **2.** [radio] to crackle.

GRETA, Greta [greta] (abr de ***groupements d'établissements pour la formation continue***) **npr m** *state body organizing adult training programmes.*

grève [grɛv] **nf 1.** [arrêt du travail] strike ▸ **être en grève** to be on strike ▸ **faire grève** to strike, to go on strike ▸ **grève de la faim** hunger strike ▸ **grève générale** general strike ▸ **grève sauvage** wildcat strike ▸ **grève sur le tas** sit-down strike ▸ **grève tournante** rotating strike ▸ **grève du zèle** work-to-rule **2.** [rivage] shore.

grever [19] [grəve] **vt** to burden / [budget] to put a strain on.

gréviste [grevist] ■ **nmf** striker.
■ **adj** striking.

GRH (abr de ***gestion des ressources humaines***) **nf** personnel management.

gribouillage [gribujaʒ] **nm 1.** [écriture] scrawl **2.** [dessin] doodle.

gribouiller [3] [gribuje] **vt & vi 1.** [écrire] to scrawl **2.** [dessiner] to doodle.

gribouillis [gribuji] = ***gribouillage***.

grief [grijɛf] **nm** grievance ▸ **faire grief de qqch à qqn** to hold sthg against sb.

grièvement [grijɛvmɑ̃] **adv** seriously.

griffe [grif] **nf 1.** [d'animal] claw ▸ **montrer les griffes** *litt & fig* to bare *ou* show one's claws ▸ **tomber dans les griffes de qqn** *fig* to fall into sb's clutches **2.** [de créateur] hallmark / [de couturier] label **3.** *Belgique* [éraflure] scratch.

griffé, e [grife] **adj** [vêtement] designer *(modif)*.

griffer [3] [grife] **vt 1.** [suj: chat] to claw **2.** [suj: créateur] to put one's name to.

griffonner [3] [grifɔne] ■ **vt 1.** [écrire] to scrawl **2.** [dessiner] to make a rough sketch of.
■ **vi 1.** [écrire] to scrawl **2.** [dessiner] to make a rough sketch.

griffure [grifyr] **nf** scratch.

grignoter [3] [griɲɔte] ■ **vt 1.** [manger] to nibble **2.** *fam fig* [réduire - capital] to eat away (at) **3.** *fam fig* [gagner - avantage] to gain.
■ **vi 1.** [manger] to nibble **2.** *fam fig* [prendre] **: grignoter sur** to nibble away at.

grigou [grigu] **nm** *fam* skinflint.

gri-gri (pl **gris-gris**), **grigri** (pl **grigris**) [grigri] **nm** talisman, charm.

gril [gril] **nm** grill ▸ **sur le gril** on the grill ▸ **être sur le gril** *fig* to be like a cat on hot bricks *UK ou* a hot tin roof *US*.

grillade [grijad] **nf** CULIN grilled meat.

grillage [grijaʒ] **nm 1.** [de porte, de fenêtre] wire netting **2.** [clôture] wire fence.

grillager [17] [grijaʒe] **vt** to put wire netting on.

grille [grij] **nf 1.** [portail] gate **2.** [d'orifice, de guichet] grille / [de fenêtre] bars *pl* **3.** [de mots croisés, de loto] grid **4.** [tableau] table ▸ **grille des programmes** programme *UK ou* program *US* listings *pl* ▸ **grille des salaires** salary scale.

grillé, e [grije] **adj 1.** [amandes, noisettes] roasted / [viande] grilled *UK*, broiled *US* ▸ **une tartine grillée** a piece of toast **2.** *fam* [personne] **: il est grillé** his cover's blown.

grille-pain [grijpɛ̃] **nm inv** toaster.

griller [3] [grije] ■ **vt 1.** [viande] to grill *UK*, to broil *US* / [pain] to toast / [café, marrons] to roast ▸ **griller une cigarette** *fam* to have a smoke **2.** *fig* [au soleil - personne] to burn / [- végétation] to shrivel ▸ **grillé par la chaleur** scorched by the heat **3.** [moteur] to burn out **4.** *fam fig* [dépasser - concurrents] to outstrip ▸ **griller un feu rouge** to jump the lights ▸ **griller une étape** to rush ahead **5.** *fig* [compromettre] to ruin ▸ **il nous a grillés auprès du patron** he's really landed us in it with the boss.
■ **vi 1.** [viande] to grill *UK*, to broil *US* ▸ **faire griller du pain** to toast some bread **2.** [ampoule] to blow **3.** [personne] **: griller de** [envie, impatience] to be burning with ▸ **griller de faire qqch** to be longing to do sthg.
◆ ***se griller*** **vp** *fam* to be done for ▸ **se griller auprès de qqn** to blow it with sb ▸ **il s'est grillé en disant cela** he gave himself away by saying that.

grillon [grijɔ̃] **nm** [insecte] cricket.

grimace [grimas] **nf** grimace ▸ **faire des grimaces** to pull faces ▸ **faire la grimace** to pull a face.

grimacer [16] [grimase] **vi** to grimace.

grimer [3] [grime] **vt** CINÉ & THÉÂTRE to make up.
◆ ***se grimer*** **vp** CINÉ & THÉÂTRE to make (o.s.) up.

grimoire [grimwar] **nm** [de sorcier] book of spells.

grimpant, e [grɛ̃pɑ̃, ɑ̃t] **adj** climbing *(avant n)*.

grimper [3] [grɛ̃pe] ■ **vt** to climb.
■ **vi** to climb ▸ **grimper à un arbre/une échelle** to climb a tree/a ladder.

grimpeur, euse [grɛ̃pœr, øz] ■ **adj** climbing *(avant n)*.
■ **nm, f** climber.

grinçant, e [grɛ̃sɑ̃, ɑ̃t] **adj** **1.** [charnière] squeaking / [porte, plancher] creaking **2.** *fig* [ironie] jarring.

grincement [grɛ̃smɑ̃] **nm** [de charnière] squeaking / [de porte, plancher] creaking ▸ **grincements de dents** *fig* gnashing of teeth.

grincer [16] [grɛ̃se] **vi** [charnière] to squeak / [porte, plancher] to creak.

grincheux, euse [grɛ̃ʃø, øz] ■ **adj** grumpy.
■ **nm, f** moaner, grumbler.

gringalet [grɛ̃galɛ] **nm** weakling.

gringue *tfam* [grɛ̃g] **nm : faire du gringue (à qqn)** to sweet-talk (sb), to chat (sb) up *UK*.

griotte [grijɔt] **nf** morello (cherry).

grippal, e, aux [gripal, o] **adj** flu *(avant n)*, influenzal *(terme spécialisé)* ▸ **état grippal** influenza, flu.

grippe [grip] **nf** MÉD flu *(U)* ▸ **avoir la grippe** to have (the) flu ▸ **grippe intestinale** gastric flu ▸ **prendre qqn/qqch en grippe** *fig* to take a sudden dislike to sb/sthg.

grippé, e [gripe] **adj** [malade] **: être grippé** to have (the) flu.

gripper [3] [gripe] **vi** **1.** [mécanisme] to jam **2.** *fig* [processus] to stall.
◆ ***se gripper*** **vp** **1.** [mécanisme] to jam **2.** *fig* [système] to seize up.

grippe-sou [gripsu] (pl **grippe-sou** *ou* **grippe-sous**) **nm** *fam* skinflint.

gris, e [gri, griz] **adj** **1.** [couleur] grey *UK*, gray *US* **2.** *fig* [morne] dismal **3.** [saoul] tipsy.
◆ ***gris*** **nm** **1.** [couleur] grey *UK*, gray *US* **2.** [tabac] shag.

grisaille [grizaj] **nf** **1.** [de ciel] greyness *UK*, grayness *US* **2.** *fig* [de vie] dullness.

grisant, e [grizɑ̃, ɑ̃t] **adj** intoxicating.

grisâtre [grizatr] **adj** greyish *UK*, grayish *US*.

grisé [grize] **nm** grey *UK ou* gray *US* shading.

griser [3] [grize] **vt** to intoxicate.
◆ ***se griser*** **vp : se griser de** [vin] to get tipsy on / [air, succès] to get drunk on.

grisonnant, e [grizɔnɑ̃, ɑ̃t] **adj** greying *UK*, graying *US*.

grisonner [3] [grizɔne] **vi** to turn grey *UK ou* gray *US*.

grisou [grizu] **nm** firedamp.

grive [griv] **nf** thrush.

grivois, e [grivwa, az] **adj** ribald.

Groenland [grɔɛnlɑ̃d] **nm : le Groenland** Greenland ▸ **au Groenland** in Greenland.

groenlandais, e [grɔɛnlɑ̃dɛ, ɛz] **adj** of/from Greenland, Greenland *(modif)*.
◆ ***Groenlandais, e*** **nm, f** Greenlander.

grog [grɔg] **nm** (hot) toddy.

groggy [grɔgi] **adj inv** **1.** [boxeur] groggy **2.** *fig* [assommé] stunned.

grogne [grɔɲ] **nf** discontent, grumbling.

grognement [grɔɲmɑ̃] **nm** **1.** [son] grunt / [d'ours, de chien] growl **2.** [protestation] grumble.

grogner [3] [grɔɲe] **vi** **1.** [émettre un son] to grunt / [ours, chien] to growl **2.** [protester] to grumble.

grognon, onne [grɔɲɔ̃, ɔn] **adj** grumpy.

groin [grwɛ̃] **nm** snout.

grommeler [24] [grɔmle] **vt & vi** to mutter.

grondement [grɔ̃dmɑ̃] **nm** [d'animal] growl / [de tonnerre, de train] rumble / [de torrent] roar.

gronder [3] [grɔ̃de] ■ **vi** **1.** [animal] to growl / [tonnerre] to rumble **2.** *littéraire* [grommeler] to mutter.
■ **vt** to scold.

groom [grum] **nm** page, bellboy, bellhop *US*.

gros, grosse [gro, gros] ■ **adj** *(gén avant n)* **1.** [gén] large, big / *péj* big ▸ **de grosses chaussures** heavy shoes ▸ **une grosse tranche** a thick slice **2.** *(avant ou après n)* [corpulent] fat ▸ **un homme grand et gros** a tall fat man **3.** [grossier] coarse ▸ **gros drap** coarse linen **4.** [fort, sonore] loud ▸ **un gros bruit** a loud *ou* big noise **5.** [important, grave - ennuis] serious / [- dépense] major ▸ **de gros dégâts** extensive *ou* widespread damage ▸ **de grosses pertes** heavy losses **6.** [plein] **: gros de** full of ▸ **un cœur gros de tendresse** a heart full of tenderness.
■ **nm, f** **1.** [personne corpulente] fat person ▸ **un petit gros** a fat little man **2.** [personnage important] big shot.
◆ ***gros*** ■ **adv** [beaucoup] a lot ▸ **en avoir gros sur le cœur** to be upset.
■ **nm** **1.** [partie] **: le (plus) gros (de qqch)** the main part (of sthg) ▸ **le (plus) gros du travail** the bulk of the work **2.** COMM **: le gros** wholesale.
◆ ***de gros*** **loc adj** COMM wholesale.
◆ ***en gros*** **loc adv & loc adj** **1.** COMM wholesale ▸ **vente en gros** wholesaling **2.** [en grands caractères] in large letters ▸ **c'est imprimé en gros** it's printed in big letters **3.** [grosso modo] roughly ▸ **je sais en gros de quoi il s'agit** I know roughly what it's about.
◆ ***gros bonnet*** **nm** *fam* bigwig, big shot.
◆ ***grosse légume*** **nf** *fam* [personne influente] bigwig, big shot.

groseille [grozɛj] ■ **nf** currant ▸ **groseille blanche** white currant ▸ **groseille à maquereau** gooseberry ▸ **groseille rouge** redcurrant.
■ **adj inv** red.

groseillier [grozeje] **nm** currant bush.

gros-porteur [gropɔrtœr] (pl **gros-porteurs**) **nm** jumbo (jet).

grosse [gros] ■ **nf 1.** [douze douzaines] gross **2.** DR engrossment.
■ **adj** ➤ ***gros***.

grossesse [grosɛs] **nf** pregnancy ▸ **grossesse extra-utérine** ectopic pregnancy ▸ **grossesse nerveuse** phantom pregnancy.

grosseur [grosœr] **nf 1.** [dimension, taille] size **2.** [corpulence] fatness **3.** MÉD lump.

grossier, ère [grosje, ɛr] **adj 1.** [matière] coarse **2.** [sommaire] rough **3.** [insolent] rude **4.** [vulgaire] crude **5.** [erreur] crass.

grossièrement [grosjɛrmɑ̃] **adv 1.** [sommairement] roughly **2.** [vulgairement] crudely.

grossièreté [grosjɛrte] **nf 1.** [vulgarité] crudeness **2.** [parole grossière] crude remark **3.** [superficialité] superficiality.

grossir [32] [grosir] ■ **vi 1.** [prendre du poids] to put on weight ▸ **elle a beaucoup grossi** she's put on a lot of weight ▸ **faire grossir** to add pounds, to make you put on weight / [être calorique] to be fattening ▸ **ça fait grossir** it's fattening **2.** [augmenter] to grow **3.** [s'intensifier] to increase ▸ **le bruit grossit** the noise is getting louder ▸ **le malaise qui règne dans le groupe grossit** there is a growing sense of unease within the group **4.** [cours d'eau] to swell.
■ **vt 1.** [suj: microscope, verre] to magnify **2.** [suj: vêtement] : **grossir qqn** to make sb look fatter ▸ **ta robe te grossit** your dress makes you look fatter **3.** [exagérer] to exaggerate ▸ **on a grossi l'affaire** the affair was blown up out of all proportion.

grossissant, e [grosisɑ̃, ɑ̃t] **adj** [verre] magnifying.

grossissement [grosismɑ̃] **nm 1.** [de personne] increase in weight **2.** [de loupe, de microscope] magnification **3.** [exagération] exaggeration.

grossiste [grosist] **nmf** wholesaler.

grosso modo [grosomɔdo] **adv** roughly.

grotesque [grɔtɛsk] ■ **adj** grotesque, ludicrous.
■ **nm : le grotesque** the grotesque.

grotte [grɔt] **nf** cave.

grouillant, e [grujɑ̃, ɑ̃t] **adj 1.** [foule] milling **2.** [lieu] : **grouillant (de)** swarming (with).

grouiller [3] [gruje] **vi : grouiller (de)** to swarm (with).
◆ ***se grouiller*** **vp** *fam* to get a move on ▸ **se grouiller de faire qqch** to rush to do sthg.

groupage [grupaʒ] **nm** [de paquets] bulking / [de commandes, d'envois, de livraisons] groupage, consolidation.

groupe [grup] **nm** group ▸ **ils sont venus par groupes de quatre ou cinq** they came in groups of four or five *ou* in fours and fives ▸ **en groupe** as a group ▸ **groupe armé** armed group ▸ **groupe hospitalier** hospital complex ▸ **groupe parlementaire** parliamentary group ▸ **groupe de parole** support group ▸ **groupe de presse** press consortium *ou* group ▸ **groupe de pression** pressure group ▸ **groupe de rock** rock band *ou* group ▸ **groupe scolaire** school complex ▸ **groupe-témoin** focus group ▸ **groupe de travail** working group *ou* party *UK*.
◆ ***groupe électrogène*** **nm** generator.
◆ ***groupe sanguin*** **nm** blood group.

groupement [grupmɑ̃] **nm 1.** [action] grouping **2.** [groupe] group.

grouper [3] [grupe] **vt** to group.
◆ ***se grouper*** **vp** to come together.

groupie [grupi] **nmf** groupie.

groupuscule [grupyskyl] **nm** faction.

gruau [gryo] **nm** [farine] wheat flour.

grue [gry] **nf** TECHNOL & ZOOL crane ▸ **faire le pied de grue** *fig* to stand about.

gruger [17] [gryʒe] **vt** *littéraire* to dupe.

grumeau, x [grymo] **nm** lump.

grumeleux, euse [grymlø, øz] **adj 1.** [pâte] lumpy **2.** [fruit] gritty **3.** [peau] bumpy.

grunge [grʌnʒ] **adj** grunge.

gruyère [gryjɛr] **nm** Gruyère (cheese).

GSM (abr de ***global system for mobile communication***) **m** TÉLÉCOM GSM.

guacamole [gwakamol(e)] **nm** guacamole.

Guadeloupe [gwadlup] **nf : la Guadeloupe** Guadeloupe ▸ **à la Guadeloupe** in Guadeloupe.

guadeloupéen, enne [gwadlupeɛ̃, ɛn] **adj** of/from Guadeloupe.
◆ ***Guadeloupéen, enne*** **nm, f** person from Guadeloupe.

Guatemala [gwatemala] **nm : le Guatemala** Guatemala ▸ **au Guatemala** in Guatemala.

guatémaltèque [gwatemaltɛk] **adj** Guatemalan.
◆ ***Guatémaltèque*** **nmf** Guatemalan.

gué [ge] **nm** ford ▸ **traverser à gué** to ford.

guenilles [gənij] **nfpl** rags.

guenon [gənɔ̃] **nf** female monkey.

guépard [gepar] **nm** cheetah.

guêpe [gɛp] **nf** wasp.

guêpier [gepje] **nm** wasp's nest / *fig* hornet's nest ▸ **alle[r] se fourrer dans un guêpier** to stir up a hornet's nest.

guère [gɛr] **adv** [peu] hardly ▸ **ne** *(+ verbe)* **guère** [peu] hardly ▸ **il ne l'aime guère** he doesn't like him/her ver[y] much ▸ **l'appel n'a guère eu de succès** the appeal me[t] with very little success ▸ **ne** *(+ verbe)* **plus guère : il n[e] m'écrit plus guère** he hardly (ever) writes (to me) now *o[r]* any more ▸ **il n'y a guère plus de six ans** barely more tha[n] six years ago ▸ **il n'y a guère de** there are hardly any.

guéridon [geridɔ̃] **nm** pedestal table.

guérilla [gerija] **nf** guerrilla warfare.

guérir [32] [gerir] ■ **vt** to cure ▸ **guérir qqn de** *litt* & *fi[g]* to cure sb of.
■ **vi** to recover, to get better ▸ **elle est guérie de sa rou[]geole** she's cured of *ou* recovered from her measles.
◆ ***se guérir*** **vp** *(emploi réfléchi)* to cure o.s..

guérison [gerizɔ̃] **nf 1.** [de malade] recovery **2.** [de ma[]ladie] cure.

guérissable [gerisabl] **adj** curable.

guérisseur, euse [gerisœr, øz] **nm, f** healer.

guérite [gerit] **nf** MIL sentry box.

Guernesey [gɛrnəzɛ] **npr** Guernsey ▸ **à Guernesey** on Guernsey.

guerre [gɛr] **nf 1.** *fig* & MIL war ▸ **en guerre** at war ▸ **déclarer la guerre** to declare war ▸ **faire la guerre à un pays** to make *ou* wage war on a country ▸ **faire la guerre à qqch** to wage war on sthg ▸ **Première/Seconde Guerre mondiale** World War I/II, First/Second World War *UK* ▸ **guerre atomique/nucléaire** atomic/nuclear war ▸ **guerre civile** civil war ▸ **guerre économique** trade war ▸ **guerre froide** cold war ▸ **guerre des nerfs** war of nerves ▸ **guerre de religion** war of religion ▸ **guerre sainte** holy war **2.** [technique] warfare *(U)* ▸ **guerre biologique/chimique** biological/chemical warfare ▸ **guerre bactériologique** germ warfare
▸▸ **à la guerre comme à la guerre** you'll/we'll *etc* just have to make the best of things ▸ **c'est de bonne guerre** that's fair enough *ou* perfectly fair ▸ **de guerre lasse** for the sake of peace.

guerrier, ère [gɛrje, ɛr] **adj 1.** [de guerre] war *(avant n)* **2.** [peuple] warlike.
◆ ***guerrier*** **nm** warrior.

guerroyer [13] [gɛrwaje] **vi** *littéraire* to wage war.

guet [gɛ] **nm : faire le guet** to be on the look-out.

guet-apens [gɛtapɑ̃] (pl **guets-apens**) **nm** ambush / *fig* trap ▸ **tomber dans un guet-apens** to fall into an ambush *ou* a trap.

guêtre [gɛtr] **nf** gaiter ▸ **traîner ses guêtres** *fam* to lounge around.

guetter [4] [gete] **vt 1.** [épier] to lie in wait for **2.** [attendre] to be on the look-out for, to watch for **3.** [menacer] to threaten.

gueulante [gœlɑ̃t] **nf** *fam* uproar ▸ **pousser une gueulante** to yell (one's head off).

gueulard, e [gœlar, ard] *fam* ■ **adj** shouting a lot.
■ **nm, f** person who shouts a lot.
◆ ***gueulard*** **nm** TECHNOL throat.

gueule [gœl] **nf 1.** [d'animal, ouverture] mouth **2.** *tfam* [bouche de l'homme] gob *UK*, yap *US* ▸ **ta gueule!** shut it!, shut your gob! *UK* ▸ **c'est une grande gueule** he/she is all mouth **3.** *fam* [visage] face ▸ **quelle sale gueule (il a)!** [il est laid] what an ugly mug he's got! *tfam* / [il est malade] he looks terrible! ▸ **gueule cassée** WW1 veteran *(with bad facial injuries)*
▸▸ **avoir la gueule de bois** to have a hangover ▸ **casser la gueule à qqn** to smash sb's face in ▸ **se casser la gueule** *fam* [tomber] to fall flat on one's face ▸ **faire la gueule** *fam* to pull a long face, to sulk ▸ **j'en ai pris plein la gueule** I got a right mouthful ▸ **se jeter dans la gueule du loup** to enter the lion's den ▸ **leur maison a vraiment de la gueule** their house really has got style ▸ **pousser un coup de gueule** to yell out ▸ **se soûler la gueule** to get plastered *ou* pissed *tfam UK*.

ueule-de-loup [gœldəlu] (pl **gueules-de-loup**) **nf** napdragon.

ueuler [5] [gœle] *fam* ■ **vt** to yell.
■ **vi 1.** [crier] to yell **2.** [protester] to kick up a stink, to cream and shout.

gueuleton [gœltɔ̃] **nm** *fam* blowout.

gueux, gueuse [gø, gøz] **nm, f** *littéraire* beggar.

gui [gi] **nm** mistletoe.

guichet [giʃɛ] **nm** counter / [de gare, de théâtre] ticket office ▸ **jouer à guichets fermés** *fig* to be sold out.

guichetier, ère [giʃtje, ɛr] **nm, f** counter clerk.

guide [gid] ■ **nm 1.** [gén] guide ▸ **guide de montagne** mountain guide **2.** [livre] guidebook.
■ **nf** Girl Guide *UK*, Girl Scout *US*.
◆ ***guides*** **nfpl** reins.

guider [3] [gide] **vt** to guide.
◆ ***se guider*** **vpi : il s'est guidé sur le soleil** he used the sun as a guide.

guidon [gidɔ̃] **nm** handlebars *pl*.

guigne [giɲ] **nf** *fam* bad *ou* rotten luck.

guigner [3] [giɲe] **vt** *fam* **1.** [regarder] to eye **2.** [convoiter] to have one's eye on.

guignol [giɲɔl] **nm 1.** [marionnette] glove puppet **2.** [théâtre] ≃ Punch and Judy show ▸ **faire le guignol** *fig* to act *ou* play the fool.

guillemet [gijmɛ] **nm** quotation mark, inverted comma *UK* ▸ **entre guillemets** in quotation marks *ou* inverted commas *UK* ▸ **ouvrir/fermer les guillemets** to open/close quotation marks *ou* inverted commas *UK*.

guilleret, ette [gijrɛ, ɛt] **adj** perky.

guillotine [gijɔtin] **nf 1.** [instrument] guillotine **2.** [de fenêtre] sash.

guillotiner [3] [gijɔtine] **vt** to guillotine.

guimauve [gimov] **nf 1.** [confiserie, plante] marshmallow **2.** *fam* [sentimentalité] mush.

guimbarde [gɛ̃bard] **nf 1.** MUS Jew's harp **2.** *fam* [voiture] jalopy.

guindé, e [gɛ̃de] **adj** stiff.

Guinée [gine] **nf : la Guinée** Guinea ▸ **la Guinée-Bissau** Guinea-Bissau ▸ **la GuinéeÉquatoriale** Equatorial Guinea.

guinéen, enne [gineɛ̃, ɛn] **adj** Guinean.
◆ ***Guinéen, enne*** **nm, f** Guinean.

guingois [gɛ̃gwa] ◆ ***de guingois*** **adv** *sout* lopsidedly.

guinguette [gɛ̃gɛt] **nf** open-air dance floor.

guirlande [girlɑ̃d] **nf 1.** [de fleurs] garland **2.** [de papier] chain / [de Noël] tinsel *(U)*.

guise [giz] **nf : à ma guise** as I please *ou* like ▸ **en guise de** by way of.

guitare [gitar] **nf** guitar ▸ **guitare électrique** electric guitar.

guitariste [gitarist] **nmf** guitarist.

Gulf Stream [gœlfstrim] **nm : le Gulf Stream** the Gulf Stream.

gustatif, ive [gystatif, iv] **adj : sensibilité gustative** sense of taste.

guttural, e, aux [gytyral, o] **adj** guttural.

Guyana [gɥijana] **nf : la Guyana** Guyana.

Guyane [gɥijan] **nf : la Guyane** French Guiana.

gym [ʒim] **nf** gym *(U)*.

gymkhana [ʒimkana] **nm** rally.

gymnase [ʒimnaz] **nm** gymnasium.

gymnaste [ʒimnast] **nmf** gymnast.

gymnastique [ʒimnastik] **nf** *fig* & SPORT gymnastics *(U)* ▸ **faire de la gymnastique** to do exercises ▸ **gymnastique corrective** remedial gymnastics.

gynécée [ʒinese] **nm** HIST gynaeceum.

gynéco [ʒineko] **nmf** *fam* gynaecologist *UK*, gynecologist *US*.

gynécologie [ʒinekɔlɔʒi] **nf** gynaecology *UK*, gynecology *US*.

gynécologique [ʒinekɔlɔʒik] **adj** gynaecological *UK*, gynecological *US*.

gynécologue [ʒinekɔlɔg] **nmf** gynaecologist *UK*, gynecologist *US*.

gypse [ʒips] **nm** gypsum.

gyrophare [ʒirɔfar] **nm** flashing light.

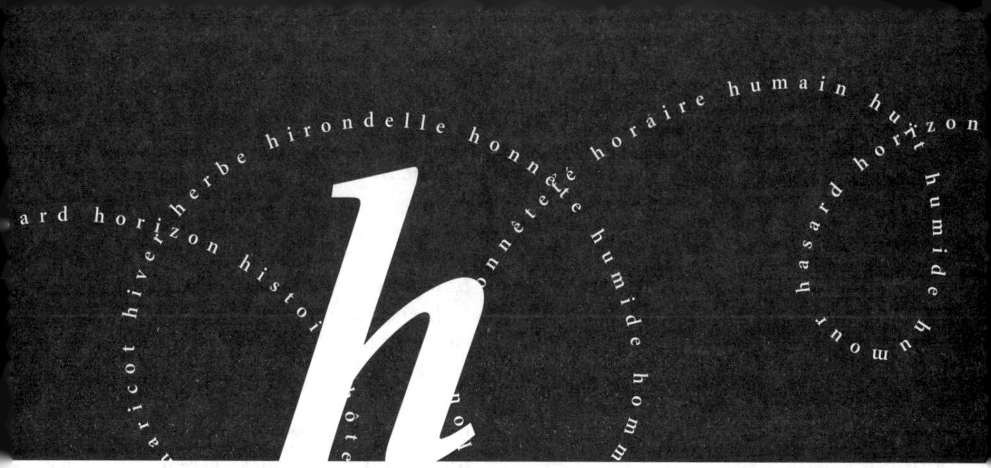

h*[1], *H [aʃ] **nm inv** h, H ▸ **h aspiré/muet** aspirate/silent h.

h*[2]** **1.** (abr écrite de ***heure) hr **2.** (abr écrite de ***hecto***) h.

H **1.** abr de ***homme*** **2.** (abr écrite de ***hydrogène***) H.

ha (abr écrite de ***hectare***) ha.

hab. abr de ***habitant***.

habile [abil] **adj** skilful *UK*, skillful *US* ⁄ [démarche] clever.

habilement [abilmɑ̃] **adv** skilfully *UK*, skillfully *US* ⁄ [manœuvrer] cleverly.

habileté [abilte] **nf** skill.

habiliter [3] [abilite] **vt** to authorize ▸ **être habilité à faire qqch** to be authorized to do sthg.

habillage [abijaʒ] **nm** **1.** [action] dressing **2.** [enveloppe, protection] covering.

habillé, e [abije] **adj** [tenue] dressy ⁄ [réception] smart.

habillement [abijmɑ̃] **nm** **1.** [action] clothing **2.** [tenue] outfit **3.** [profession] clothing trade.

habiller [3] [abije] **vt** **1.** [vêtir] **: habiller qqn (de)** to dress sb (in) ▸ **il est mal habillé** [sans goût] he's badly dressed **2.** [suj: fournisseur] to provide with clothing ⁄ [suj: fabricant] to make clothes for ▸ **j'habille toute la famille** I make clothes for all the family ▸ **elle est habillée par un grand couturier** she gets her clothes from a top designer **3.** [recouvrir] to cover ▸ **habiller un mur de toile de jute** to cover a wall with hessian.
◆ ***s'habiller*** **vp** **1.** [se vêtir] to dress, to get dressed ▸ **habille-toi chaudement** wrap up well *ou* warmly ▸ **tu t'habilles mal** you have no dress sense ▸ **s'habiller de** to dress in **2.** [se vêtir élégamment] to dress up ▸ **s'habiller pour le dîner** to dress for dinner **3.** [se fournir en vêtements] to buy one's clothes ▸ **s'habiller sur mesure** to have one's clothes made to measure *ou* tailor-made.

habilleur, euse [abijœr, øz] **nm, f** dresser.

habit [abi] **nm** **1.** [costume] suit ▸ **habit de neige** *Québec* snowsuit ▸ **habit de soirée** evening dress **2.** RELIG habit.
◆ ***habits*** **nmpl** [vêtements] clothes.

habitable [abitabl] **adj** habitable.

habitacle [abitakl] **nm** [d'avion] cockpit ⁄ [de voiture] passenger compartment.

habitant, e [abitɑ̃, ɑ̃t] **nm, f** **1.** [de pays] inhabitant ▸ **loger chez l'habitant** to stay with local people **2.** [d'immeuble] occupant **3.** *Québec* [paysan] farmer.

habitat [abita] **nm** **1.** [conditions de logement] housing conditions *pl* **2.** [mode de peuplement] settlement **3.** [d'animal] habitat.

habitation [abitasjɔ̃] **nf** **1.** [fait d'habiter] housing **2.** [résidence] house, home.

habité, e [abite] **adj** [maison] occupied ⁄ [planète] inhabited ▸ **engin spatial habité** manned spacecraft.

habiter [3] [abite] ■ **vt** **1.** [résider] to live in **2.** [suj: passion, sentiment] to dwell within.
■ **vi** to live ▸ **habiter à** to live in.

habitude [abityd] **nf** **1.** [façon de faire] habit ▸ **avoir l'habitude de faire qqch** to be in the habit of doing sthg ▸ **d'habitude** usually ▸ **comme d'habitude** as usual ▸ **par habitude** out of habit ▸ **prendre l'habitude de faire qqch** to get into the habit of doing sthg **2.** [coutume] custom.

habitué, e [abitɥe] **nm, f** regular.

habituel, elle [abitɥɛl] **adj** **1.** [coutumier] usual, customary **2.** [caractéristique] typical.

habituellement [abitɥɛlmɑ̃] **adv** usually.

habituer [7] [abitɥe] **vt : habituer qqn à qqch/à faire qqch** to get sb used to sthg/to doing sthg.
◆ ***s'habituer*** **vp : s'habituer à qqch/à faire qqch** to get used to sthg/to doing sthg.

hâbleur, euse [ˈablœr, øz] *littéraire* ■ **adj** boastful.
■ **nm, f** braggart.

hache [ˈaʃ] **nf** axe, ax *US* ▸ **enterrer la hache de guerre** *fig* to bury the hatchet.

haché, e [ˈaʃe] **adj** **1.** [coupé - gén] finely chopped ⁄ [- viande] minced *UK*, ground *US* **2.** [entrecoupé] jerky.

hacher [3] [ˈaʃe] **vt** **1.** [couper - gén] to chop finely ⁄ [- viande] to mince *UK*, to grind *US* **2.** [entrecouper] to interrupt.

hachette [ˈaʃɛt] **nf** hatchet.

hachis [ˈaʃi] **nm : un hachis de persil** finely chopped parsley ▸ **un hachis de porc** minced pork *UK*, ground pork *US* ▸ **hachis Parmentier** ≃ shepherd's pie, ≃ cottage pie.

hachisch = ***haschisch***.

hachoir ['aʃwar] **nm 1.** [couteau] chopper **2.** [appareil] mincer *UK*, grinder *US* **3.** [planche] chopping board *UK*, cutting board *US*.

hachure ['aʃyr] **nf** hatching.

hachurer [3] ['aʃyre] **vt** to hatch.

haddock ['adɔk] **nm** smoked haddock.

hagard, e ['agar, ard] **adj** haggard.

hagiographie [aʒjɔgrafi] **nf** hagiography.

haï, e ['ai] **pp** ➤ ***haïr***.

haie ['ɛ] **nf 1.** [d'arbustes] hedge **2.** [de personnes] row / [de soldats, d'agents de police] line ▸ **haie d'honneur** guard of honour *UK* ***ou*** honor *US* **3.** SPORT hurdle ▸ **400 mètres haies** 400 metres *UK* ***ou*** meters *US* hurdles.

haillons ['ajɔ̃] **nmpl** rags.

haine ['ɛn] **nf** hatred.

haineusement ['ɛnøzmɑ̃] **adv** with hatred.

haineux, euse ['ɛnø, øz] **adj** full of hatred.

haïr [33] ['air] **vt** to hate.

hais, hait ➤ ***haïr***.

haïssable ['aisabl] **adj** hateful.

haïssais, haïssions ➤ ***haïr***.

Haïti [aiti] **npr** Haiti ▸ **à Haïti** in Haiti.

haïtien, enne [aisjɛ̃, ɛn] **adj** Haitian.
◆ ***Haïtien, enne*** **nm, f** Haitian.

hâle ['al] **nm** tan.

hâlé, e ['ale] **adj** tanned *UK*, tan *US*.

haleine [alɛn] **nf** breath ▸ **avoir l'haleine forte, avoir mauvaise haleine** to have bad breath ▸ **courir à perdre haleine** to run until one is breathless ▸ **hors d'haleine** out of breath ▸ **de longue haleine** exacting and time-consuming ▸ **reprendre haleine** to catch one's breath ▸ **tenir qqn en haleine** to keep sb in suspense.

haler [3] ['ale] **vt 1.** [tirer] to haul in **2.** [remorquer] to tow.

haletant, e ['altɑ̃, ɑ̃t] **adj** panting.

halètement ['alɛtmɑ̃] **nm** panting.

haleter [28] ['alte] **vi** to pant.

hall ['ol] **nm 1.** [vestibule, entrée] foyer, lobby **2.** [salle publique] concourse ▸ **hall d'arrivée/de départ** arrival/departure hall.

hallali [alali] **nm : l'hallali** [sonnerie] the mort.

halle ['al] **nf** covered market.
◆ ***halles*** **nfpl** wholesale food market *sg*.

hallebarde ['albard] **nf** [armement] halberd, halbert ▸▸ **il pleut *ou* il tombe des hallebardes** *fam* it's raining cats and dogs.

hallucinant, e [alysinɑ̃, ɑ̃t] **adj 1.** [incroyable] extraordinary **2.** [grandiose] impressive.

hallucination [alysinasjɔ̃] **nf** hallucination.

halluciné, e [alysine] ■ **adj** crazed.
■ **nm, f** lunatic.

halluciner [3] [alysine] **vi 1.** PSYCHO to hallucinate, to suffer from ***ou*** to have hallucinations **2.** *fam fig* **: mais j'hallucine ou quoi?** I don't believe it!

hallucinogène [alysinɔʒɛn] ■ **nm** hallucinogen.
■ **adj** hallucinogenic.

halo ['alo] **nm 1.** [cercle lumineux] halo **2.** *fig* [rayonnement] aura.

halogène [alɔʒɛn] **nm & adj** halogen.

halte ['alt] ■ **nf** stop ▸ **faire halte** to stop.
■ **interj** stop!

halte-garderie ['altəgardəri] (pl **haltes-garderies**) **nf** ≃ day nursery.

haltère [altɛr] **nm** dumbbell.

haltérophile [alterɔfil] ■ **nmf** weightlifter.
■ **adj** weightlifting *(avant n)*.

haltérophilie [alterɔfili] **nf** weightlifting.

hamac ['amak] **nm** hammock.

hamburger ['ɑ̃burgœr] **nm** hamburger.

hameau, x ['amo] **nm** hamlet.

hameçon [amsɔ̃] **nm** fishhook ▸ **mordre à l'hameçon** *fig* to rise to the bait.

hammam ['amam] **nm** Turkish baths *pl*.

hampe ['ɑ̃p] **nf** [de drapeau] pole.

hamster ['amstɛr] **nm** hamster.

hanche ['ɑ̃ʃ] **nf** hip ▸ **rouler des hanches** to swing one's hips.

handball ['ɑ̃dbal] **nm** handball.

handicap ['ɑ̃dikap] **nm** handicap.

handicapé, e ['ɑ̃dikape] ■ **adj** handicapped ▸ **être handicapé par qqch** *fig* to be handicapped by sthg.
■ **nm, f** handicapped person ▸ **handicapé mental** mentally handicapped person ▸ **handicapé moteur** person with cerebral palsy.

handicaper [3] ['ɑ̃dikape] **vt** to handicap.

handisport ['ɑ̃dispɔr] **adj : activité handisport** spor for the disabled.

hangar ['ɑ̃gar] **nm** shed / AÉRON hangar.

hanneton ['antɔ̃] **nm** cockchafer.

Hanoi ['anɔj] **npr** Hanoi.

hanté, e ['ɑ̃te] **adj** [maison, forêt] haunted.

hanter [3] ['ɑ̃te] **vt** to haunt.

hantise ['ɑ̃tiz] **nf** obsession ▸ **avoir la hantise de qqch de faire qqch** to be obsessed by the fear of sthg/of doin sthg.

happer [3] ['ape] **vt 1.** [attraper] to snap up **2.** [accro cher] to strike.

hara-kiri ['arakiri] **nm : (se) faire hara-kiri** to comm hara-kiri.

harangue ['arɑ̃g] **nf** harangue.

haranguer [3] ['arɑ̃ge] **vt** to harangue.

haras ['ara] **nm** stud (farm).

harassant, e ['arasɑ̃, ɑ̃t] **adj** exhausting.

harasser [3] ['arase] **vt** to exhaust.

harcèlement ['arsɛlmɑ̃] **nm** harassment ▸ **harcèlement moral** bullying *(in the workplace)* ▸ **harcèlement sexuel** sexual harassment.

harceler [25] ['arsəle] **vt 1.** [relancer] to harass **2.** MIL to harry **3.** [importuner] **: harceler qqn (de)** to pester sb (with).

hardes ['ard] **nfpl** old clothes.

hardi, e ['ardi] **adj** bold, daring.

hardiesse ['ardjɛs] **nf** boldness, daring

hardware ['ardwɛr] **nm** INFORM hardware.

harem ['arɛm] **nm** harem.

hareng ['arɑ̃] **nm** herring ▸ **hareng saur** kipper.

harfang ['arfɑ̃] **nm** snowy owl.

hargne ['arɲ] **nf** spite *(U)*, bad temper.

hargneux, euse ['arɲø, øz] **adj** [personne] spiteful, bad-tempered / [remarque] spiteful, vicious.

haricot ['ariko] **nm** bean ▸ **haricots verts/blancs/rouges** green *ou* string/haricot/kidney beans.

harmonica [armɔnika] **nm** harmonica, mouth organ.

harmonie [armɔni] **nf 1.** [gén] harmony ▸ **vivre en harmonie (avec qqn)** to live in harmony (with sb) **2.** [de visage] symmetry **3.** [fanfare] wind band.

harmonieusement [armɔnjøzmɑ̃] **adv** harmoniously.

harmonieux, euse [armɔnjø, øz] **adj 1.** [gén] harmonious **2.** [voix] melodious **3.** [traits, silhouette] regular.

harmonique [armɔnik] **adj** harmonic.

harmonisation [armɔnizasjɔ̃] **nf 1.** [coordination] harmonization **2.** MUS harmonizing.

harmoniser [3] [armɔnize] **vt** *fig* & MUS to harmonize / [salaires] to bring into line.

harmonium [armɔnjɔm] **nm** harmonium.

harnachement ['arnaʃmɑ̃] **nm 1.** [équipement de cheval] harness **2.** [action] harnessing **3.** *fig* [attirail] gear.

harnacher [3] ['arnaʃe] **vt** [cheval] to harness ▸ **être harnaché** *fig* to be got up.

harnais ['arnɛ] **nm 1.** [de cheval, de parachutiste] harness **2.** TECHNOL train.

aro ['aro] **nm** *sout* **: crier haro sur** to rail against.

arpagon [arpagɔ̃] **nm** ≃ Scrooge.

arpe ['arp] **nf** harp.

arpie ['arpi] **nf** harpy.

arpon ['arpɔ̃] **nm** harpoon.

arponner [3] ['arpɔne] **vt 1.** [poisson] to harpoon **2.** *fam* [personne] to collar.

asard ['azar] **nm** chance ▸ **le hasard fait bien les choses** there are some lucky coincidences ▸ **les hasards de la vie** life's ups and downs, life's vicissitudes *sout* ▸ **quel heureux hasard!** what a fantastic coincidence! ▸ **jeu de hasard** game of chance ▸ **au hasard** at random ▸ **aller** *ou* **marcher au hasard** [par indifférence] to walk aimlessly / [par plaisir] to go where one's fancy takes one ▸ **ne rien laisser au hasard** to leave nothing to chance ▸ **je me suis fait des amis au hasard de mes voyages** I made friends with people I happened to meet on my travels ▸ **à tout hasard** on the off chance ▸ **par hasard** by accident, by chance ▸ **par un curieux hasard, il était né le même jour** by a strange coincidence he was born on the same day ▸ **comme par hasard** *iron* as if by chance ▸ **comme par hasard, elle n'a rien entendu** surprisingly enough, she didn't hear a thing! ▸ **si par hasard** if by chance ▸ **si par hasard vous la voyez** if by any chance you should see her, should you happen to see her.

FAUX AMIS / FALSE FRIENDS

hasard

Hazard is not a translation of the French word *hasard*. Hazard is translated by *danger*.
▸ the hazards of smoking / *les dangers du tabac*

hasarder [3] ['azarde] **vt 1.** [tenter] to venture **2.** [risquer] to hazard.
◆ ***se hasarder*** **vp : se hasarder à faire qqch** to risk doing sthg.

hasardeux, euse ['azardø, øz] **adj** risky.

haschisch, haschich, hachisch ['aʃiʃ] **nm** hashish.

hâte ['at] **nf** haste ▸ **à la hâte, en hâte** hurriedly, hastily ▸ **avoir hâte de faire qqch** to be eager to do sthg.

hâter [3] ['ate] **vt 1.** [activer] to hasten **2.** [avancer] to bring forward.
◆ ***se hâter*** **vp** to hurry ▸ **se hâter de faire qqch** to hurry to do sthg.

hâtif, ive ['atif, iv] **adj** [précipité] hurried, hasty.

hauban ['obɑ̃] **nm** NAUT shroud.

hausse ['os] **nf** [augmentation] rise, increase ▸ **à la hausse, en hausse** rising ▸ **hausse des prix** price increase.

haussement ['osmɑ̃] **nm : haussement d'épaules** shrug (of the shoulders).

hausser [3] ['ose] **vt** to raise.

haut, e [o, ot] **adj 1.** [gén] high ▸ **haut de 20 m** 20 m high ▸ **la partie haute de l'arbre** the top of the tree ▸ **les pièces sont hautes de plafond** the rooms have high ceilings **2.** [classe sociale, pays, région] upper ▸ **de haut niveau** top-level, high-level **3.** [responsable] senior ▸ **les hauts fonctionnaires** top *ou* top-ranking civil servants **4.** FIN & COMM high.
◆ ***haut*** ■ **adv 1.** [gén] high ▸ **levez haut la jambe** raise your leg (up) high *ou* high up **2.** [placé] highly ▸ **des amis haut placés** friends in high places **3.** [fort] loudly ▸ **dire bien haut ce que l'on pense tout bas** to say out loud what everyone else is thinking.
■ **nm 1.** [hauteur] height ▸ **faire 2 m de haut** to be 2 m high *ou* in height **2.** [sommet, vêtement] top

▸▸ **avoir** *ou* **connaître des hauts et des bas** to have one's ups and downs.

◆ ***de haut*** **loc adv** [avec dédain] haughtily ▸ **le prendre de haut** to react haughtily ▸ **regarder qqn de haut** to look down on sb ▸ **tomber de haut** [être surpris] to be flabbergasted / [être déçu] to come down (to earth) with a bump.

◆ ***de haut en bas*** **loc adv** from top to bottom ▸ **regarder** *ou* **considérer qqn de haut en bas** to look sb up and down.

◆ ***du haut de*** **loc prép** from the top of ▸ **il nous regarde du haut de sa grandeur** he looks down his nose at us.

◆ ***en haut*** **loc adv** at the top / [dans une maison] upstairs ▸ **nous sommes passés par en haut** [par la route du haut] we took the high road.

◆ ***en haut de*** **loc prép** at the top of ▸ **tout en haut d'une colline** high up on a hill ▸ **regarde en haut de l'armoire** look on top of the wardrobe.

◆ ***là-haut*** **loc adv** up there.

hautain**, **e ['otɛ̃, ɛn] **adj** haughty.

hautbois ['obwa] **nm** oboe.

haut-de-forme ['odfɔrm] (pl **hauts-de-forme**) **nm** top hat.

haut de gamme [odgam] ■ **adj** upmarket, high-end, top-of-the-line *US* ▸ **une chaîne haut de gamme** a state-of-the-art hi-fi system.

■ **nm** top of the range, top of the line *US*.

haute-fidélité [otfidelite] (pl **hautes-fidélités**) **nf** high fidelity, hi-fi.

hautement ['otmɑ̃] **adv** highly.

hauteur ['otœr] **nf** height ▸ **il est tombé de toute sa hauteur** he fell headlong ▸ **il y a de la neige sur les hauteurs** there's snow on the higher slopes ▸ **prendre de la hauteur** to gain altitude *ou* height ▸ **à hauteur d'épaule** at shoulder level *ou* height ▸ **ne pas être à la hauteur de qqch** not to be up to sthg ▸ **tu ne t'es pas montré à la hauteur** you weren't up to it *ou* equal to the task ▸ **une carrière à la hauteur de ses ambitions** a career commensurate with her ambitions ▸ **range ces cartons en hauteur** put these boxes up out of the way ▸ **elle habite à la hauteur de l'église** she lives up by the church.

Haute-Volta ['otvɔlta] **npr f : (la) Haute-Volta** Upper Volta.

haut-fond ['ofɔ̃] (pl **hauts-fonds**) **nm** shallows *pl*.

haut-fourneau ['ofurno] (pl **hauts-fourneaux**) **nm** blast furnace.

haut-le-cœur ['olkœr] **nm inv** retch ▸ **avoir des haut-le-cœur** to retch.

haut-le-corps ['olkɔr] **nm inv : avoir un haut-le-corps** to start, to jump.

haut-parleur ['oparlœr] (pl **haut-parleurs**) **nm** loudspeaker.

havanais**, **e ['avanɛ, ɛz] **adj** of/from Havana.

◆ ***Havanais**, **e*** **nm, f** person from Havana.

◆ ***havanaise*** **nf** habanera.

havane ['avan] ■ **nm** Havana cigar.

■ **adj inv** tobacco-coloured *UK*, tobacco-colored *US*.

Havane ['avan] **npr : La Havane** Havana.

hâve ['av] **adj** *littéraire* haggard.

havre ['avr] **nm** [refuge] haven.

Hawaii ['awaj] **npr** Hawaii ▸ **à Hawaii** in Hawaii.

hawaiien**, **enne ['awajɛ̃, ɛn] **adj** Hawaiian.

◆ ***Hawaiien**, **enne*** **nm, f** Hawaiian.

Haye ['ɛ] **npr : La Haye** the Hague.

hayon ['ajɔ̃] **nm** hatchback.

HCR (abr de ***Haut-commissariat des Nations unies pour les réfugiés***) **nm** UN-HCR.

hé ['e] **interj** hey!

hebdo [ɛbdo] **nm** *fam* weekly.

hebdomadaire [ɛbdɔmadɛr] **nm & adj** weekly.

hébergement [ebɛrʒəmɑ̃] **nm** **1.** accommodation *UK*, accommodations *(pl) US* **2.** INFORM hosting ▸ **hébergement de sites Web** web hosting.

héberger [17] [ebɛrʒe] **vt** **1.** [loger] to put up **2.** [suj: hôtel] to take in.

hébété**, **e [ebete] **adj** dazed.

hébétement [ebɛtmɑ̃] **nm** stupor.

hébétude [ebetyd] **nf** *littéraire* stupor.

hébraïque [ebraik] **adj** Hebrew.

hébreu**, **x [ebrø] **adj** Hebrew.

◆ ***hébreu*** **nm** [langue] Hebrew.

◆ ***Hébreu**, **x*** **nm** Hebrew.

Hébrides [ebrid] **npr fpl : les (îles) Hébrides** the Hebrides ▸ **aux Hébrides** in the Hebrides.

HEC (abr de ***(école des) Hautes études commerciales***) **npr** *grande école for management and business studies.*

hécatombe [ekatɔ̃b] **nf** *litt* & *fig* slaughter.

hectare [ɛktar] **nm** hectare.

hecto [ɛkto] **nm** *fam* **1.** (abr de ***hectogramme***) hectogram, hectogramme *UK* **2.** (abr de ***hectolitre***) hectolitre *UK*, hectoliter *US*.

hectolitre [ɛktɔlitr] **nm** hectolitre *UK*, hectoliter *US*.

hédonisme [edɔnism] **nm** hedonism.

hédoniste [edɔnist] ■ **nmf** hedonist.

■ **adj** hedonistic.

hégémonie [eʒemɔni] **nf** hegemony.

hégémonisme [eʒemɔnism] **nm** hegemonic tendencies *pl*.

hégire [eʒir] **nf** hegira.

hein ['ɛ̃] **interj** *fam* eh?, what? ▸ **tu m'en veux, hein** you're angry with me, aren't you?

hélas [elas] **interj** unfortunately, alas.

héler [18] ['ele] **vt** *sout* to hail.

hélice [elis] **nf** **1.** [d'avion, de bateau] propeller **2.** MATH helix.

hélico [eliko] **nm** *fam* AÉRON chopper.

hélicoïdal**, **e**, **aux [elikɔidal, o] **adj** **1.** [forme] spiral, helical **2.** MATH helical.

hélicoptère [elikɔptɛr] **nm** helicopter.

héliomarin**, **e [eljɔmarɛ̃, in] **adj** MÉD [cure] using sun and sea air.

héliport [elipɔr] **nm** heliport.

héliporté, e [elipɔrte] **adj** [troupes, fournitures] transported by helicopter / [opération] helicopter *(avant n).*

hélitreuiller [elitrœje] **vt** to wind to safety.

hélium [eljɔm] **nm** helium.

Helsinki ['ɛlsiŋki] **npr** Helsinki.

helvétique [ɛlvetik] **adj** Swiss, Helvetian.

helvétisme [ɛlvetism] **nm** Swiss expression.

CULTURE

Helvétisme

Switzerland's **Délégation à la langue française** promotes free discussion on the evolution and current state of French in the country. It works with similar bodies in other French-speaking countries and makes recommendations for the political authorities. The **Délégation** was created after France, Belgium, and Québec worked together to propose some spelling reforms in January 1991. Switzerland had no official French language authority at that time.

hem ['ɛm] **interj** [indique le doute] hmm.

hématologie [ematɔlɔʒi] **nf** haematology *UK*, hematology *US*.

hématome [ematom] **nm** MÉD haematoma *UK*, hematoma *US*.

hémicycle [emisikl] **nm** POLIT **: l'hémicycle** the Assemblée Nationale.

hémiplégique [emipleʒik] **nmf** & **adj** hemiplegic.

hémisphère [emisfɛr] **nm** hemisphere ▸ **l'hémisphère nord/sud** northern/southern hemisphere ▸ **hémisphère cérébral** ANAT cerebral hemisphere.

hémoglobine [emɔglɔbin] **nf** haemoglobin *UK*, hemoglobin *US*.

hémophile [emɔfil] ■ **nmf** haemophiliac *UK*, hemophiliac *US*.
■ **adj** haemophilic *UK*, hemophilic *US*.

iémophilie [emɔfili] **nf** haemophilia *UK*, hemophilia *US*.

iémorragie [emɔraʒi] **nf** **1.** MÉD haemorrhage *UK*, hemorrhage *US* ▸ **hémorragie cérébrale** brain haemorrhage *UK ou* hemorrhage *US* ▸ **hémorragie interne** internal bleeding *(U)* **2.** *fig* [perte, fuite] loss.

iémorroïdes [emɔrɔid] **nfpl** haemorrhoids *UK*, hemorrhoids *US*, piles.

ienné ['ene] **nm** henna.

iennir [32] ['enir] **vi** to neigh, to whinny.

iennissement ['enismɑ̃] **nm** neigh, whinny.

iep ['ɛp] **interj** hey!

iépatique [epatik] ■ **nmf** person with liver problems.
■ **adj** liver *(avant n).*

épatite [epatit] **nf** MÉD hepatitis *(U)* ▸ **hépatite B** hepatitis B ▸ **hépatite C** hepatitis C ▸ **hépatite virale** viral hepatitis.

eptagone [ɛptagɔn] **nm** heptagon.

heptathlon [ɛptatlɔ̃] **nm** heptathlon.

herbacé, e [ɛrbase] **adj** herbaceous.

herbage [ɛrbaʒ] **nm** pasture.

herbe [ɛrb] **nf** **1.** BOT grass ▸ **mauvaise herbe** weed **2.** CULIN & MÉD herb ▸ **fines herbes** herbs **3.** *fam* [marijuana] grass
▸▸ **en herbe** budding ▸ **couper l'herbe sous les pieds de qqn** to cut the ground from under sb's feet.

herbeux, euse [ɛrbø, øz] **adj** grassy.

herbicide [ɛrbisid] ■ **nm** weedkiller, herbicide.
■ **adj** herbicidal.

herbier [ɛrbje] **nm** herbarium.

herbivore [ɛrbivɔr] ■ **nm** herbivore.
■ **adj** herbivorous.

herboriste [ɛrbɔrist] **nmf** herbalist.

herboristerie [ɛrbɔristəri] **nf** herbalist's (shop).

herculéen, enne [ɛrkyleɛ̃, ɛn] **adj** Herculean.

hère ['ɛr] **nm : pauvre hère** poor wretch.

héréditaire [ereditɛr] **adj** hereditary.

hérédité [eredite] **nf** **1.** [génétique] heredity **2.** [de biens, de titre] inheritance.

hérésie [erezi] **nf** heresy.

hérétique [eretik] ■ **nmf** heretic.
■ **adj** heretical.

hérissé, e ['erise] **adj** **1.** [cheveux, poils - naturellement raides] bristly / [- dressés de peur] bristling, standing on end ▸ **un chien à l'échine hérissée** a dog with its hackles up **2.** [parsemé] **: hérissé de** full of, stuffed with ▸ **un texte hérissé de difficultés** a text bristling with *ou* full of difficult points **3.** BOT spiny.

hérisser [3] ['erise] **vt** **1.** [dresser] **: hérisser son poil** to bristle **2.** [garnir] **: être hérissé de** [de clous] to be studded with / *fig* [de difficultés] to be fraught with **3.** [irriter] **: hérisser qqn** to get sb's back up.
◆ ***se hérisser*** **vpi** **1.** [se dresser - pelage] to bristle / [- cheveux] to stand on end **2.** [s'irriter] to bristle ▸ **elle se hérisse facilement** she's easily ruffled.

hérisson ['erisɔ̃] **nm** **1.** ZOOL hedgehog **2.** [brosse] chimneysweep's brush.

héritage [eritaʒ] **nm** **1.** [de biens] inheritance ▸ **faire un héritage** to come into an inheritance ▸ **en héritage** as an inheritance **2.** [culturel] heritage.

hériter [3] [erite] ■ **vi** to inherit ▸ **hériter de qqch** to inherit sthg.
■ **vt : hériter qqch de qqn** *litt* & *fig* to inherit sthg from sb.

héritier, ère [eritje, ɛr] **nm, f** heir (f heiress).

hermaphrodite [ɛrmafrɔdit] **nmf** & **adj** hermaphrodite.

hermétique [ɛrmetik] **adj** **1.** [étanche] hermetic **2.** [incompréhensible] inaccessible, impossible to understand **3.** [impénétrable] impenetrable.

hermétiquement [ɛrmetikmɑ̃] **adv** hermetically.

hermétisme [ɛrmetism] **nm** [de texte] obscurity.

hermine [ɛrmin] **nf** **1.** [animal] stoat **2.** [fourrure] ermine.

hernie ['ɛrni] **nf** hernia ▸ **hernie discale** slipped disc *UK* *ou* disk *US*.

héroïne [erɔin] **nf 1.** [personne] heroine **2.** [drogue] heroin.

héroïnomane [erɔinɔman] **nmf** heroin addict.

héroïque [erɔik] **adj** heroic.

héroïquement [erɔikmɑ̃] **adv** heroically.

héroïsme [erɔism] **nm** heroism.

héron ['erɔ̃] **nm** heron.

héros ['ero] **nm** hero.

herpès [ɛrpɛs] **nm** herpes.

herse ['ɛrs] **nf 1.** AGRIC harrow **2.** [grille] portcullis.

hertz ['ɛrts] **nm inv** hertz.

hésitant, e [ezitɑ̃, ɑ̃t] **adj** hesitant.

hésitation [ezitasjɔ̃] **nf** hesitation ▸ **avec hésitation** hesitantly ▸ **sans hésitation** without hesitation, unhesitatingly.

hésiter [3] [ezite] **vi** to hesitate ▸ **hésiter entre/sur** to hesitate between/over ▸ **hésiter à faire qqch** to hesitate to do sthg.

hétéro [etero] **adj & nmf** hetero, straight.

hétéroclite [eterɔklit] **adj** motley.

hétérogène [eterɔʒɛn] **adj** heterogeneous.

hétérogénéité [eterɔʒeneite] **nf** heterogeneity.

hétérosexuel, elle [eterɔsɛksɥɛl] **adj & nm, f** heterosexual.

hétérozygote [eterɔzigɔt] ■ **adj** heterozygous.
■ **nmf** heterozygote.

hêtre ['ɛtr] **nm** beech.

heure [œr] **nf 1.** [unité de temps] hour ▸ **250 km à l'heure** 250 km per *ou* an hour ▸ **faire des heures supplémentaires** to work overtime ▸ **heure homme** FIN man-hour ▸ **24 heures sur 24** around-the-clock, 24 hours a day ▸ **d'heure en heure** by the hour ▸ **un travail (payé) à l'heure** a job paid by the hour
2. [moment du jour] time ▸ **il est deux heures** it's two o'clock ▸ **heure d'affluence** [dans les transports] rush hour / [au magasin] peak time ▸ **à quelle heure?** when?, (at) what time? ▸ **l'heure d'aller au lit** bedtime ▸ **heure de battement** break ▸ **heures de bureau** office hours ▸ **heure creuse** off-peak time, slack period ▸ **l'heure du déjeuner** lunchtime ▸ **heures de grande écoute** peak viewing time ▸ **heure d'ouverture/de fermeture** opening/closing time ▸ **heure de pointe** rush hour ▸ **heures de réception** office/surgery *UK* hours
3. [Indication de temps] time ▸ **donner/demander l'heure à qqn** to tell/ask sb the time ▸ **être à l'heure** to be on time ▸ **mettre à l'heure** [montre, pendule] to put right ▸ **quelle heure est-il?** what time is it? ▸ **vous avez l'heure?** do you have the time?
4. [fuseau horaire] **: l'heure d'été** British Summer Time *UK*, daylight (saving) time *US* ▸ **passer à l'heure d'été/d'hiver** to put the clocks forward/back
5. INFORM **: heures machine** computer time
6. SCOL class, period ▸ **une heure de chimie** SCOL a chemistry class *ou* period
▸▸ **à heure fixe** at a set time ▸ **à l'heure actuelle** at the present time ▸ **à l'heure qu'il est** at this moment in time ▸ **à la bonne heure!** that's wonderful! ▸ **à la première heure** at the crack of dawn ▸ **c'est sa dernière heure** his time is near ▸ **à toute heure** at any time ▸ **à tout à l'heure!** see you later! ▸ **c'est l'heure (de faire qqch)** it's time (to do sthg) ▸ **de bonne heure** early ▸ **de la première heure** right from the start ▸ **sur l'heure** at once ▸ **l'heure de vérité** the moment of truth.
◆ ***heures*** **nfpl** RELIG hours ▸ **livre d'heures** Book of Hours.

heureusement [œrøzmɑ̃] **adv 1.** [par chance] luckily, fortunately **2.** [favorablement] successfully.

heureux, euse [œrø, øz] ■ **adj 1.** [gén] happy ▸ **rendre qqn heureux** to make sb happy ▸ **l'heureux élu** the lucky man *(to be married or recently married)* ▸ **l'heureuse élue** the lucky girl *(to be married or recently married)* ▸ **heureux en ménage** happily married ▸ **être heureux de faire qqch** to be happy to do sthg ▸ **(très) heureux de faire votre connaissance** pleased *ou* nice to meet you **2.** [favorable] fortunate **3.** [réussi] successful, happy ▸ **un heureux événement** *euphém* a happy event
▸▸ **encore heureux (que)** *(+ subjonctif)***...** *fam* it's just as well (that)...
■ **nm, f : faire un heureux** to make somebody's day ▸ **faire des heureux** to make some people happy.

heurt ['œr] **nm 1.** [choc] collision, impact **2.** [désaccord] clash ▸ **sans heurts** smoothly.

heurté, e ['œrte] **adj 1.** [style] jerky, abrupt **2.** [mouvement] halting, jerky.

heurter [3] ['œrte] ■ **vt 1.** [rentrer dans - gén] to hit / [- suj: personne] to bump into **2.** [offenser - personne, sensibilité] to offend **3.** [bon sens, convenances] to go against.
■ **vi : heurter contre qqch** to bump into sthg.
◆ ***se heurter*** **vp 1.** [gén] **: se heurter (contre)** to collide (with) **2.** [rencontrer] **: se heurter à qqch** to come up against sthg.

heurtoir ['œrtwar] **nm** knocker.

hexagonal, e, aux [ɛgzagɔnal, o] **adj 1.** GÉOM hexagonal **2.** [français] French.

hexagone [ɛgzagɔn] **nm** GÉOM hexagon.
◆ ***Hexagone*** **nm : l'Hexagone** (metropolitan) France.

HF (abr écrite de ***hautes fréquences***) HF.

hiatus [jatys] **nm inv** hiatus.

hibernation [ibɛrnasjɔ̃] **nf** hibernation.

hiberner [3] [ibɛrne] **vi** to hibernate.

hibiscus [ibiskys] **nm** hibiscus.

hibou, x ['ibu] **nm** owl.

hic ['ik] **nm** *fam* snag.

hideux, euse ['idø, øz] **adj** hideous.

hier [ijɛr] **adv** yesterday ▸ **hier matin/soir** yesterday morning/evening.

hiérarchie ['jerarʃi] **nf** hierarchy.

hiérarchique ['jerarʃik] **adj** hierarchical.

hiératique [jeratik] **adj** hieratic.

hiéroglyphe [jerɔglif] **nm** hieroglyph, hieroglyphic.
◆ ***hiéroglyphes*** **nmpl** hieroglyphics.

hi-fi ['ifi] **nf inv** hi-fi.

hilarant, e [ilarɑ̃, ɑ̃t] **adj** hilarious.

hilare [ilar] **adj** beaming.

hilarité [ilarite] **nf** hilarity ▸ **provoquer l'hilarité générale** to give rise to general hilarity.

Himalaya [imalaja] **nm : l'Himalaya** the Himalayas *pl*.

himalayen, enne [imalajɛ̃, jɛn] **adj** Himalayan.

hindi ['indi] **nm** LING Hindi.

hindou, e [ɛ̃du] **adj** Hindu.
◆ ***Hindou, e*** **nm, f** Hindu.

hindouisme [ɛ̃duism] **nm** Hinduism.

hippie, hippy ['ipi] (pl **hippies**) **nmf** & **adj** hippy.

hippique [ipik] **adj** horse *(avant n)*.

hippisme [ipism] **nm** horse riding *UK*, horseback riding *US*.

hippocampe [ipɔkɑ̃p] **nm** seahorse.

hippodrome [ipɔdrom] **nm** racecourse, racetrack.

hippopotame [ipɔpɔtam] **nm** hippopotamus.

hirondelle [irɔ̃dɛl] **nf** swallow.

hirsute [irsyt] **adj** [chevelure, barbe] shaggy.

hispanique [ispanik] **adj 1.** [gén] Hispanic **2.** [aux États-Unis] Hispanic, Spanish-American.
◆ ***Hispanique*** **nmf** [aux États-Unis] Hispanic, Spanish American.

hispano-américain, e [ispanɔamerikɛ̃, ɛn] (mpl **hispano-américains**, fpl **hispano-américaines**) **adj** Hispanic, Spanish-American.
◆ ***Hispano-Américain, e*** **nm, f** Hispanic, Spanish-American, Hispanic.

hispanophone [ispanɔfɔn] ■ **nmf** Spanish-speaker.
■ **adj** Spanish-speaking.

hisser [3] ['ise] **vt 1.** [voile, drapeau] to hoist **2.** [charge] to heave, to haul.
◆ ***se hisser*** **vp 1.** [grimper] **: se hisser (sur)** to heave *ou* haul o.s. up (onto) **2.** *fig* [s'élever] **: se hisser à** to pull o.s. up to.

histoire [istwar] **nf 1.** [science] history ▸ **histoire ancienne/moderne/contemporaine** ancient/modern/contemporary history ▸ **histoire de l'art** art history ▸ **histoire économique** economic history ▸ **histoire de France** French history ▸ **histoire naturelle** natural history ▸ **histoire sainte** Biblical history ▸ **histoire sociale** social history ▸ **un lieu chargé d'histoire** a place steeped in history ▸ **on va leur téléphoner, histoire de voir s'ils sont là** let's ring them up, just to see if they're there
2. [récit, mensonge] story ▸ **c'est une autre histoire** that's another story ▸ **c'est une histoire vraie** it's a true story ▸ **allez, tu me racontes des histoires!** come on, you're pulling my leg! ▸ **histoire à dormir debout** tall story ▸ **elle en a fait (toute) une histoire** she kicked up a (huge) fuss about it
3. [aventure] funny *ou* strange thing
4. *(gén pl)* [ennui] trouble *(U)* ▸ **faire des histoires** *fam* to make a fuss ▸ **si tu ne veux pas avoir d'histoires** if you want to keep *ou* to stay out of trouble.
◆ ***sans histoires*** **loc adj** [gens] ordinary / [voyage] uneventful, trouble-free.

> PARONYME / CONFUSABLE
> **histoire**
>
> Le mot français **histoire** se traduit par ***history*** quand on se réfère à la discipline, et par ***story*** si l'on veut parler d'un récit.

historicité [istɔrisite] **nf** historicity.

historien, enne [istɔrjɛ̃, ɛn] **nm, f** historian.

historiographie [istɔrjɔgrafi] **nf** historiography.

historique [istɔrik] **adj 1.** [roman, recherches] historical **2.** [monument, événement] historic.

> PARONYME / CONFUSABLE
> **historique**
>
> Ne pas confondre les deux traductions de **historique.** On utilise ***historic*** pour désigner ce qui est important sur le plan historique, et ***historical*** pour qualifier ce qui se rapporte à l'histoire.

historiquement [istɔrikmɑ̃] **adv** historically.

hit-parade ['itparad] (pl **hit-parades**) **nm : le hit-parade** the charts *pl*.

HIV (abr de ***human immunodeficiency virus***) **nm** HIV ▸ **être atteint du virus HIV** to be HIV-positive.

hiver [ivɛr] **nm** winter ▸ **en hiver** in (the) winter.

hivernal, e, aux [ivɛrnal, o] **adj** winter *(avant n)*.

hiverner [3] [ivɛrne] **vi** to (spend the) winter.

hl (abr écrite de ***hectolitre***) hl.

HLM (abr de ***habitation à loyer modéré***) **nm** & **nf** *low-rent, state-owned housing*, ≃ council house/flat *UK*, ≃ public housing unit *US*.

hm (abr écrite de ***hectomètre***) hm.

ho ['o] **interj** oh!

hobby ['ɔbi] (pl **hobbies**) **nm** hobby.

hochement ['ɔʃmɑ̃] **nm : hochement de tête** [affirmatif] nod (of the head) / [négatif] shake of the head.

hocher [3] ['ɔʃe] **vt : hocher la tête** [affirmativement] to nod (one's head) / [négativement] to shake one's head.

hochet ['ɔʃɛ] **nm** rattle.

hockey ['ɔkɛ] **nm** hockey ▸ **hockey sur glace** ice hockey *UK*, hockey *US* ▸ **hockey sur gazon** hockey *UK*, field hockey *US*.

holà ['ɔla] ■ **interj 1.** [pour appeler] hey! **2.** [pour arrêter] hold on!
■ **nm : mettre le holà à qqch** *fam* to put a stop to sthg.

holding [ˈɔldiŋ] **nm & nf** holding company.

hold-up [ˈɔldœp] **nm inv** holdup.

hollandais, e [ˈɔlɑ̃dɛ, ɛz] **adj** Dutch.
◆ ***hollandais*** **nm** [langue] Dutch.
◆ ***Hollandais, e*** **nm, f** Dutchman (f Dutchwoman).

Hollande [ˈɔlɑ̃d] **nf : la Hollande** Holland ▸ **en Hollande** in Holland.

holocauste [ɔlɔkost] **nm** holocaust.

hologramme [ɔlɔgram] **nm** hologram.

homard [ˈɔmar] **nm** lobster ▸ **homard à l'armoricaine** *ou* **l'américaine** *lobster sautéed in oil with white wine, garlic and tomatoes.*

home [ˈom] **nm : home d'enfants** holiday centre *UK ou* vacation center *US* for children.

homélie [ɔmeli] **nf** homily.

homéopathe [ɔmeɔpat] ■ **nmf** homeopath.
■ **adj** homeopathic.

homéopathie [ɔmeɔpati] **nf** homeopathy.

homéopathique [ɔmeɔpatik] **adj** homeopathic.

homicide [ɔmisid] ■ **nm** [meurtre] murder ▸ **homicide involontaire** manslaughter ▸ **homicide volontaire** murder.
■ **adj** homicidal.

hominidé [ɔminide] **nm** hominid ▸ **les hominidés** the Hominidae.

hommage [ɔmaʒ] **nm** [témoignage d'estime] tribute ▸ **rendre hommage à qqn/qqch** to pay tribute to sb/sthg.
◆ ***hommages*** **nmpl** [salutations] respects ▸ **mes hommages** *sout* my respects.

hommasse [ɔmas] **adj** *péj* mannish, butch.

homme [ɔm] **nm** man ▸ **vêtements d'homme** menswear *(U)* ▸ **un magazine pour hommes** a men's magazine ▸ **grand homme** great man ▸ **homme d'action** man of action ▸ **homme d'affaires** businessman ▸ **l'homme des cavernes** caveman ▸ **homme d'Église** man of the Church *ou* cloth ▸ **homme d'État** statesman ▸ **homme de loi** lawyer ▸ **homme de main** hired man ▸ **homme du monde** man about town ▸ **homme de paille** stooge ▸ **homme politique** politician ▸ **l'homme de la rue** the man in the street ▸ **homme à tout faire** jack-of-all-trades ▸ **d'homme à homme** man to man ▸ **comme un seul homme** as one (man) ▸ **un homme à la mer!** man overboard!

homme-grenouille [ɔmgrənuj] (pl **hommes-grenouilles**) **nm** frogman.

homme-orchestre [ɔmɔrkɛstr] (pl **hommes-orchestres**) **nm** one-man band.

homme-sandwich [ɔmsɑ̃dwitʃ] (pl **hommes-sandwiches**) **nm** sandwich man.

homo [ɔmo] **adj & nmf** *fam* [homosexuel] gay.

homogène [ɔmɔʒɛn] **adj** homogeneous.

homogénéisé, e [ɔmɔʒeneize] **adj** homogenized.

homogénéité [ɔmɔʒeneite] **nf** homogeneity.

homologue [ɔmɔlɔg] ■ **nm** counterpart, opposite number.
■ **adj** equivalent.

homologuer [3] [ɔmɔlɔge] **vt** [ratifier] to approve / SPORT to recognize, to ratify.

homonyme [ɔmɔnim] **nm 1.** LING homonym **2.** [personne, ville] namesake.

homophobe [ɔmɔfɔb] **adj** homophobic.

homophobie [ɔmɔfɔbi] **nf** homophobia.

homosexualité [ɔmɔsɛksɥalite] **nf** homosexuality.

homosexuel, elle [ɔmɔsɛksɥɛl] **adj & nm, f** homosexual.

homozygote [ɔmɔzigɔt] ■ **adj** homozygous.
■ **nmf** homozygote.

Honduras [ˈɔ̃dyras] **nm : le Honduras** Honduras ▸ **au Honduras** in Honduras ▸ **le Honduras britannique** British Honduras.

hondurien, enne [ˈɔ̃dyrjɛ̃, ɛn] **adj** Honduran.
◆ ***Hondurien, enne*** **nm, f** Honduran.

Hongkong, Hong Kong [ˈɔ̃gkɔ̃g] **npr** Hong Kong.

hongre [ˈɔ̃gr] ■ **adj m** gelded.
■ **nm** gelding.

Hongrie [ˈɔ̃gri] **nf : la Hongrie** Hungary.

hongrois, e [ˈɔ̃grwa, az] **adj** Hungarian.
◆ ***hongrois*** **nm** [langue] Hungarian.
◆ ***Hongrois, e*** **nm, f** Hungarian.

honnête [ɔnɛt] **adj 1.** [intègre] honest **2.** [correct] honourable *UK*, honorable *US* **3.** [convenable - travail, résultat] reasonable.

honnêtement [ɔnɛtmɑ̃] **adv 1.** [de façon intègre, franchement] honestly **2.** [correctement] honourably *UK*, honorably *US*.

honnêteté [ɔnɛtte] **nf** honesty.

honneur [ɔnœr] **nm** honour *UK*, honor *US* ▸ **à vous l'honneur!** after you! ▸ **c'est tout à son honneur** it's entirely to his credit ▸ **en l'honneur de** in honour *UK ou* honor *US* of ▸ **une fête en mon/son honneur** a party for me/him ▸ **être à l'honneur** to be in favour *UK ou* favor *US* ▸ **à qui ai-je l'honneur?** *sout* to whom do I have the honour *UK ou* honor *US* of speaking? ▸ **faire honneur à qqn/à qqch** to be a credit to sb/to sthg ▸ **faites-nous l'honneur de venir nous voir** would you honour *UK ou* honor *US* us with a visit? ▸ **faire honneur à un repas** *fig* to do justice to a meal ▸ **jurer sur l'honneur** to swear on one's honour *UK ou* honor *US* ▸ **mettre qqch en honneur** to bring sthg into favour *UK ou* favor *US* ▸ **mettre un point d'honneur à faire qqch** to make a point of honour *UK ou* honor *US* of doing sthg ▸ **sauver l'honneur** to save one's honour *UK ou* honor *US*.
◆ ***honneurs*** **nmpl** honours *UK*, honors *US* ▸ **les honneurs dus à son rang** the honours due to his rank ▸ **rendre les honneurs à qqn** to pay sb one's last respects *or* honours *UK ou* honors *US*.

Honolulu [ˈonolyly] **npr** Honolulu.

honorable [ɔnɔrabl] **adj 1.** [digne] honourable *UK* honorable *US* **2.** [convenable] respectable.

honorablement [ɔnɔrabləmɑ̃] **adv** honourably *UK* honorably *US*.

honoraire [ɔnɔrɛr] **adj** honorary.
◆ ***honoraires*** **nmpl** fee *sg*, fees.

honorer [3] [ɔnɔre] **vt 1.** [vénérer, gratifier] **: honorer qqn (de)** to honour *UK ou* honor *US* sb (with) **2.** [faire honneur à] to be a credit to **3.** [payer] to honour *UK*, to honor *US*.
◆ ***s'honorer*** **vp : s'honorer de qqch** to pride o.s. on sthg.

honorifique [ɔnɔrifik] **adj** honorary *UK*, ceremonial *US*.

honte ['ɔ̃t] **nf 1.** [sentiment] shame ▸ **à ma grande honte** to my shame ▸ **avoir honte de qqn/qqch** to be ashamed of sb/sthg ▸ **avoir honte de faire qqch** to be ashamed of doing sthg ▸ **j'ai honte d'arriver les mains vides** I feel *ou* I'm ashamed at arriving empty-handed ▸ **faire honte à qqn** to make sb (feel) ashamed ▸ **il fait honte à son père** [il lui est un sujet de mécontentement] his father is ashamed of him / [il lui donne un sentiment d'infériorité] he puts his father to shame ▸ **vous pouvez parler sans honte** you may talk quite openly **2.** [action scandaleuse] **: c'est une honte!** it's a disgrace!

honteusement ['ɔ̃tøzmɑ̃] **adv** shamefully.

honteux, ***euse*** ['ɔ̃tø, øz] **adj** shameful / [personne] ashamed.

hooligan, ***houligan*** ['uligan] **nm** hooligan.

hop ['ɔp] **interj 1.** [pour faire sauter] hup! **2.** [pour stimuler] off you go!

hôpital, ***aux*** [ɔpital, o] **nm** hospital ▸ **hôpital militaire/psychiatrique** military/psychiatric hospital ▸ **hôpital de jour** outpatients unit.

hoquet ['ɔkɛ] **nm** hiccup ▸ **avoir le hoquet** to have (the) hiccups.

hoqueter [27] ['ɔkte] **vi** to hiccup.

horaire [ɔrɛr] ■ **nm 1.** [de départ, d'arrivée] timetable *UK*, schedule *US* **2.** [de travail] hours *pl* (of work) ▸ **horaire mobile *ou* flexible *ou* à la carte** flexitime, flextime *US*.
■ **adj** hourly.

horde ['ɔrd] **nf** horde.

horions ['ɔrjɔ̃] **nmpl** *littéraire* blows.

horizon [ɔrizɔ̃] **nm 1.** [ligne, perspective] horizon ▸ **à l'horizon** *litt* & *fig* on the horizon ▸ **rien à l'horizon** *litt* & *fig* nothing in sight *ou* view ▸ **horizon économique/politique** ÉCON economic/political prospects ▸ **les prévisions à l'horizon 2010** the forecast for 2010 **2.** [panorama] view ▸ **changer d'horizon** to have a change of scene *ou* scenery.

horizontal, ***e***, ***aux*** [ɔrizɔ̃tal, o] **adj** horizontal.
◆ ***horizontale*** **nf** MATH horizontal ▸ **à l'horizontale** horizontal, in a horizontal position / [couché] flat out.

horizontalement [ɔrizɔ̃talmɑ̃] **adv** horizontally.

horloge [ɔrlɔʒ] **nf** clock ▸ **horloge parlante** speaking clock *UK*, Time *US*.

horloger, ***ère*** [ɔrlɔʒe, ɛr] ■ **adj** clockmaking *(avant n)*, watchmaking *(avant n)*.
■ **nm, f** clockmaker, watchmaker.

horlogerie [ɔrlɔʒri] **nf** clockmaking, watchmaking.

hormis ['ɔrmi] **prép** save.

hormonal, ***e***, ***aux*** [ɔrmɔnal, o] **adj** hormonal.

hormone [ɔrmɔn] **nf** hormone.

hormonothérapie [ɔrmɔnɔterapi] **nf** MÉD hormone therapy / [pour femmes ménopausées] hormone replacement therapy.

horodateur [ɔrɔdatœr] **nm** [à l'usine] clock / [au parking] ticket machine.

horoscope [ɔrɔskɔp] **nm** horoscope.

horreur [ɔrœr] **nf** horror ▸ **avoir horreur de qqn/qqch** to hate sb/sthg ▸ **avoir horreur de faire qqch** to hate doing sthg ▸ **j'ai horreur qu'on me dérange** I hate *ou* I can't stand being disturbed ▸ **avoir qqn/qqch en horreur** to hate sb/sthg ▸ **faire horreur à qqn** to disgust sb ▸ **quelle horreur!** how awful!
◆ ***horreurs*** **nfpl 1.** [crimes] horrors ▸ **les horreurs de la guerre** the horrors of war **2.** [calomnies] **: on m'a raconté des horreurs sur lui** I've heard terrible things about him.

horrible [ɔribl] **adj 1.** [affreux] horrible **2.** *fig* [terrible] terrible, dreadful.

horriblement [ɔribləmɑ̃] **adv** horribly.

horrifiant, ***e*** [ɔrifjɑ̃, ɑ̃t] **adj** horrifying.

horrifier [9] [ɔrifje] **vt** to horrify.

horripilant, ***e*** [ɔripilɑ̃, ɑ̃t] **adj** exasperating.

horripiler [3] [ɔripile] **vt** to exasperate.

hors ['ɔr] **prép : hors antenne** off the air ▸ **hors cadre** ADMIN on temporary assignment, seconded *UK*, on secondment *UK* ▸ **hors catégorie** outstanding, exceptional ▸ **mettre une lampe hors circuit** to disconnect a lamp ▸ **être hors circuit** *fig* to be out of circulation ▸ **hors sujet** irrelevant, off the subject / ➤ ***pair***, ***service***.
◆ ***hors de*** **loc prép** outside ▸ **hors d'ici!** get out of here! ▸ **hors de portée (de)** [trop loin] out of reach *ou* range (of) / *fig* out of reach (of) ▸ **hors de prix** prohibitively *ou* ruinously expensive ▸ **c'est hors de question** it's out of the question ▸ **être hors de soi** to be beside o.s. ▸ **ici, vous êtes hors de danger** you're safe *ou* out of harm's reach here.

hors-bord ['ɔrbɔr] **nm inv** speedboat.

hors-d'œuvre ['ɔrdœvr] **nm inv** hors d'oeuvre, appetizer, starter *UK*.

hors-jeu ['ɔrʒø] **nm inv** & **adj inv** offside.

hors-la-loi ['ɔrlalwa] **nm inv** outlaw.

hors-piste ['ɔrpist] ■ **adj inv : le ski hors-pistes** off-piste skiing.
■ **nm inv** off-piste skiing ▸ **faire du hors-pistes** to ski off piste.

hors-série [ɔrseri] ■ **adj inv** special.
■ **nm** special issue *ou* edition.

hortensia [ɔrtɑ̃sja] **nm** hydrangea.

horticole [ɔrtikɔl] **adj** horticultural.

horticulteur, ***trice*** [ɔrtikyltœr, tris] **nm, f** horticulturalist.

horticulture [ɔrtikyltyr] **nf** horticulture.

hospice [ɔspis] **nm** home.

hospitalier, ***ère*** [ɔspitalje, ɛr] **adj 1.** [accueillant] hospitable **2.** [relatif aux hôpitaux] hospital *(avant n)*.

hospitalisation [ɔspitalizasjɔ̃] **nf** hospitalization.

hospitaliser [3] [ɔspitalize] **vt** to hospitalize.

hospitalité [ɔspitalite] **nf** hospitality.

hostie [ɔsti] **nf** host.

hostile [ɔstil] **adj : hostile (à)** hostile (to).

hostilité [ɔstilite] **nf** hostility.
◆ ***hostilités*** **nfpl** hostilities.

hôte, hôtesse [ot, otɛs] **nm, f** host (f hostess) ▸ **hôtesse d'accueil** receptionist ▸ **hôtesse de l'air** stewardess, air hostess *UK*.
◆ ***hôte*** **nm 1.** [invité] guest **2.** [client] patron, guest ▸ **un hôte de marque** an important guest ▸ **hôte payant** paying guest **3.** BIOL host.

hôtel [otɛl] **nm 1.** [d'hébergement] hotel ▸ **descendre à un hôtel** to stay at a hotel ▸ **hôtel trois étoiles** three-star hotel **2.** [établissement public] public building ▸ **hôtel de ville** town *UK ou* city *US* hall **3.** [demeure] **: hôtel (particulier)** (private) mansion, town house.

hôtelier, ère [otəlje, ɛr] ■ **adj** hotel *(avant n).*
■ **nm, f** hotelier.

hôtellerie [otɛlri] **nf 1.** [métier] hotel trade **2.** [hôtel-restaurant] inn.

hôtesse [otɛs] **f** ➤ ***hôte.***

hot line [ˈɔtlaɪn] (pl **hot lines**) **nf** hot line.

hotte [ˈɔt] **nf 1.** [panier] basket **2.** [d'aération] hood ▸ **hotte aspirante** extractor *ou* cooker *UK* hood.

houblon [ˈublɔ̃] **nm 1.** BOT hop **2.** [de la bière] hops *pl.*

houe [ˈu] **nf** hoe.

houille [ˈuj] **nf** coal ▸ **houille blanche** hydroelectric power.

houiller, ère [ˈuje, ɛr] **adj** coal *(avant n).*
◆ ***houillère*** **nf** coalmine.

houle [ˈul] **nf** swell.

houlette [ˈulɛt] **nf** *sout* **: sous la houlette de qqn** under the guidance of sb.

houleux, euse [ˈulø, øz] **adj** *litt* & *fig* turbulent.

houppe [ˈup] **nf 1.** [à poudre] powder puff **2.** [de cheveux] tuft.

houppette [ˈupɛt] **nf** powder puff.

hourra, hurrah [ˈura] ■ **nm** cheer.
■ **interj** hurrah!, hurray!

house [aws], ***house music*** [awsmjuzik] **nf** house (music).

houspiller [3] [ˈuspije] **vt** to tell off.

housse [ˈus] **nf** cover ▸ **housse de couette** duvet *UK ou* comforter *US* cover.

houx [ˈu] **nm** holly.

HS (abr de ***hors service***) **adj** out of order ▸ **la télé est complètement HS** *fam* the telly's on the blink ▸ **je suis HS** *fam* I'm completely washed out.

HT (abr de ***hors taxe***) ■ **adj** exclusive of tax ▸ **300 euros HT** ≃ 300 euros plus VAT.
■ **nf** (abr de ***haute tension***) HT.

HTML (abr de ***hypertext markup language***) **nm** INFORM HTML.

huard [ˈɥar] **nm** *Québec* (black-throated) diver *UK ou* loon *US*.

hublot [ˈyblo] **nm 1.** [de bateau] porthole **2.** [de four, cuisinière] window.

huche [ˈyʃ] **nf : huche à pain** bread bin *UK*, bread box *US*.

hue [ˈy] **interj** gee up!, giddy up!

huées [ˈɥe] **nfpl** boos.

huer [7] [ˈɥe] ■ **vt** [siffler] to boo.
■ **vi** [chouette, hibou] to hoot.

huile [ɥil] **nf 1.** [gén] oil ▸ **huile d'amandes douces** sweet almond oil ▸ **huile d'arachide** groundnut *UK ou* peanut *US* oil ▸ **huile de coude** *fam fig* elbow grease ▸ **huile de cuisson** cooking oil ▸ **huile essentielle** essential oil ▸ **huile de foie de morue** cod-liver oil ▸ **huile d'olive** olive oil ▸ **huile de paraffine** paraffin *UK*, kerosene *US* ▸ **huile solaire** suntan oil/lotion ▸ **huile végétale** vegetable oil ▸ **huile de vidange** waste (lubricating) oil ▸ **jeter de l'huile sur le feu** to add fuel to the flames ▸ **la mer était d'huile** the sea was like glass *ou* a mill pond **2.** [peinture] oil painting **3.** *fam* [personnalité] bigwig ▸ **les huiles du régiment** the regimental (top) brass *ou* big shots.

huiler [3] [ɥile] **vt** to oil.

huileux, euse [ɥilø, øz] **adj** oily.

huilier [ɥilje] **nm 1.** [accessoire] oil and vinegar set **2.** [fabricant] oil producer.

huis [ɥi] **nm** *littéraire* door ▸ **à huis clos** DR in camera.

huissier [ɥisje] **nm 1.** [appariteur] usher **2.** DR bailiff.

huit [ˈɥit] ■ **adj num inv** eight.
■ **nm** eight ▸ **lundi en huit** a week on Monday *UK*, Monday week *UK*, a week from Monday *US* ; voir aussi ***six.***

huitaine [ˈɥitɛn] **nf : sous *ou* à huitaine** in a week's time, a week today *UK*.

huitième [ˈɥitjɛm] ■ **adj num inv** & **nmf** eighth.
■ **nm** eighth ▸ **le huitième de finale** *round before the quarterfinal.*
■ **nf** SCOL ≃ Year 2 *(at junior school) UK*, ≃ fourth grade *US* ; voir aussi ***sixième.***

huître [ɥitr] **nf** oyster.

hululement = ***ululement.***

hululer = ***ululer.***

hum [ˈœm] **interj 1.** [marque le doute] hmm! **2.** [pour attirer l'attention] ahem!

humain, e [ymɛ̃, ɛn] **adj 1.** [gén] human **2.** [sensible] humane.
◆ ***humain*** **nm** [être humain] human (being).

PARONYME / CONFUSABLE
humain

Pour traduire humain, ne confondez pas ***human*** qui se rapporte à l'être humain et ***humane*** qui signifie compréhensif, bienveillant.

humainement [ymɛnmɑ̃] **adv 1.** [matériellement] humanly **2.** [avec bonté] humanely.

humaniser [3] [ymanize] **vt** to humanize.
◆ ***s'humaniser*** **vp** to become more human.

humaniste [ymanist] ■ **nmf 1.** [philosophe] humanist **2.** [lettré] classicist.
■ **adj** humanistic.

humanitaire [ymanitɛr] ■ **adj** humanitarian ▸ **couloir humanitaire** humanitarian *ou* safe corridor.
■ **nm : l' humanitaire** humanitarian *ou* relief work ▸ **travailler dans l'humanitaire** to work for a humanitarian organization.

humanité [ymanite] **nf** humanity.
◆ ***humanités*** **nfpl** *Belgique* humanities.

humanoïde [ymanɔid] **nmf & adj** humanoid.

humble [œ̃bl] **adj** humble.

humblement [œbləmɑ̃] **adv** humbly.

humecter [4] [ymɛkte] **vt** to moisten.
◆ ***s'humecter*** **vp** to moisten.

humer [3] ['yme] **vt** to smell.

humérus [ymerys] **nm** humerus.

humeur [ymœr] **nf 1.** [disposition] mood ▸ **être de bonne/mauvaise humeur** to be in a good/bad mood **2.** [caractère] nature **3.** *sout* [irritation] temper ▸ **avec humeur** angrily **4.** *vieilli* & ANAT [liquide] humour *UK*, humor *US*.

humide [ymid] **adj** [air, climat] humid / [terre, herbe, mur] wet, damp / [saison] rainy / [front, yeux] moist.

humidificateur [ymidifikatœr] **nm** humidifier.

humidifier [9] [ymidifje] **vt** to humidify.

humidité [ymidite] **nf** [de climat, d'air] humidity / [de terre, mur] dampness.

humiliant, e [ymiljɑ̃, ɑ̃t] **adj** humiliating.

humiliation [ymiljasjɔ̃] **nf** humiliation.

humilier [9] [ymilje] **vt** to humiliate.
◆ ***s'humilier*** **vp : s'humilier devant qqn** to grovel to sb.

humilité [ymilite] **nf** humility.

humoriste [ymɔrist] ■ **nmf** humorist.
■ **adj** humoristic.

humoristique [ymɔristik] **adj** humorous.

humour [ymur] **nm** humour *UK*, humor *US* ▸ **avoir de l'humour** to have a sense of humour *UK ou* humor *US* ▸ **manquer d'humour** to have no sense of humour *UK ou* humor *US* ▸ **humour noir** black humour *UK ou* humor *US*, gallows humour *UK ou* humor *US*.

humus [ymys] **nm** humus.

huppé, e ['ype] **adj 1.** *fam* [société] upper-crust **2.** [oiseau] crested.

hurlant, e ['yrlɑ̃, ɑ̃t] **adj 1.** [gén] howling **2.** *fig* [couleurs] clashing.

hurlement ['yrləmɑ̃] **nm** howl.

hurler [3] ['yrle] **vi 1.** [gén] to howl **2.** [couleurs] to clash.

hurluberlu, e [yrlybɛrly] **nm, f** *fam* crank.

hurrah = ***hourra***.

hussard ['ysar] **nm** hussar.
◆ ***hussarde*** **nf : à la hussarde** brutally.

hutte ['yt] **nf** hut.

hybride [ibrid] **nm & adj** hybrid.

hydratant, e [idratɑ̃, ɑ̃t] **adj** moisturizing.
◆ ***hydratant*** **nm** moisturizer.

hydratation [idratasjɔ̃] **nf 1.** CHIM hydration **2.** [de peau] moisturizing.

hydrate [idrat] **nm** hydrate ▸ **hydrate de carbone** carbohydrate.

hydrater [3] [idrate] **vt 1.** CHIM to hydrate **2.** [peau] to moisturize.
◆ ***s'hydrater*** **vpi 1.** [peau] to become moisturized **2.** CHIM to become hydrated, to hydrate.

hydraulique [idrolik] ■ **nf** hydraulics *(U)*.
■ **adj** hydraulic.

hydravion [idravjɔ̃] **nm** seaplane, hydroplane.

hydre [idr] **nf** hydra.

hydrocarbure [idrɔkarbyr] **nm** hydrocarbon.

hydrocéphale [idrɔsefal] ■ **adj** hydrocephalic, hydrocephalous.
■ **nmf** hydrocephalic.

hydrocution [idrɔkysjɔ̃] **nf** immersion syncope.

hydroélectrique [idrɔelɛktrik] **adj** hydroelectric.

hydrogène [idrɔʒɛn] **nm** hydrogen.

hydrogéné, e [idrɔʒene] **adj** hydrogenated.

hydroglisseur [idrɔglisœr] **nm** jetfoil, hydroplane.

hydrographie [idrɔgrafi] **nf** hydrography.

hydrologie [idrɔlɔʒi] **nf** hydrology.

hydrophile [idrɔfil] **adj 1.** [qui absorbe] absorbent **2.** ➤ ***coton***.

hyène [jɛn] **nf** hyena.

hygiène [iʒjɛn] **nf** hygiene ▸ **hygiène dentaire/intime** dental/personal hygiene.

hygiénique [iʒjenik] **adj 1.** [sanitaire] hygienic **2.** [bon pour la santé] healthy.

hymen [imɛn] **nm 1.** ANAT hymen **2.** *littéraire* [mariage] marriage.

hymne [imn] **nm** hymn ▸ **hymne national** national anthem.

hyperactif, ive [ipɛraktif, iv] **adj** hyperactive.

hyperactivité [ipɛraktivite] **nf** hyperactivity.

hyperbole [ipɛrbɔl] **nf 1.** MATH hyperbola **2.** LING hyperbole.

hyperglycémie [ipɛrglisemi] **nf** hyperglycaemia *UK*, hyperglycemia *US*.

hypermarché [ipɛrmarʃe] **nm** hypermarket.

hypermétrope [ipɛrmetrɔp] ■ **nmf** longsighted *UK ou* farsighted *US* person.
■ **adj** longsighted *UK*, farsighted *US*.

hypernerveux, euse [ipɛrnɛrvø, øz] ■ **adj** overexcitable.
■ **nm, f** overexcitable person.

hypersensible [ipɛrsɑ̃sibl] ■ **nmf** hypersensitive person.
■ **adj** hypersensitive.

hypertendu, e [ipɛrtɑ̃dy] ■ **adj** suffering from hypertension *ou* high blood pressure.
■ **nm, f** hypertensive.

hypertension [ipɛrtɑ̃sjɔ̃] **nf** high blood pressure, hypertension ▸ **faire de l'hypertension** to have high blood pressure.

hypertexte [ipɛrtɛkst] ■ **adj : lien hypertexte** hyperlink.
■ **nm** hypertext.

hypertrophié [ipɛrtrɔfje] **adj** hypertrophic / *fig* exaggerated.

hypnose [ipnoz] **nf** hypnosis.

hypnotique [ipnɔtik] **nm & adj** hypnotic.

hypnotiser [3] [ipnɔtize] **vt** to hypnotize / *fig* to mesmerize.
◆ ***s'hypnotiser*** **vp : s'hypnotiser sur qqch** to be mesmerized by sthg.

hypoallergénique [ipɔalɛrʒenik] **adj** hypoallergenic.

hypocondriaque [ipɔkɔ̃drijak] **nmf & adj** hypochondriac.

hypocrisie [ipɔkrizi] **nf** hypocrisy.

hypocrite [ipɔkrit] ■ **nmf** hypocrite.
■ **adj** hypocritical.

hypocritement [ipɔkritmɑ̃] **adv** hypocritically.

hypodermique [ipɔdɛrmik] **adj** hypodermic.

hypoglycémie [ipɔglisemi] **nf** hypoglycaemia *UK*, hypoglycemia *US*.

hypokhâgne [ipɔkaɲ] **nf** *first year of a two-year preparatory arts course taken prior to the competitive examination for entry to the École normale supérieure.*

hypophyse [ipɔfiz] **nf** pituitary gland.

hypotension [ipɔtɑ̃sjɔ̃] **nf** low blood pressure ▸ **faire de l'hypotension** to have low blood pressure.

hypoténuse [ipɔtenyz] **nf** hypotenuse.

hypothécaire [ipɔtekɛr] **adj** [prêt, contrat] mortgage *(avant n).*

hypothèque [ipɔtɛk] **nf** mortgage ▸ **grevé d'hypothèques** [maison] heavily mortgaged.

hypothéquer [18] [ipɔteke] **vt** to mortgage.

hypothèse [ipɔtɛz] **nf** hypothesis ▸ **dans l'hypothèse où** assuming.

hypothétique [ipɔtetik] **adj** hypothetical.

hystérie [isteri] **nf** hysteria ▸ **hystérie collective** mass hysteria.

hystérique [isterik] ■ **nmf** hysterical person.
■ **adj** hysterical.

Hz (abr écrite de ***hertz***) Hz.

i, I [i] nm inv i, I ▸ **mettre les points sur les i** to dot the i's and cross the t's.

IA (abr de ***intelligence artificielle***) nf AI.

IAC (abr de ***insémination artificielle entre conjoints***) nf AIH.

IAD (abr de ***insémination artificielle par donneur extérieur***) nf AID.

ibérique [iberik] adj **: la péninsule ibérique** the Iberian Peninsula.

ibid. (abr écrite de ***ibidem***) ibid.

iceberg [ajsbɛrg] nm iceberg.

ici [isi] adv **1.** [lieu] here ▸ **d'ici** from around here ▸ **les gens d'ici** the locals, the people from around here ▸ **ici même** on this very spot ▸ **par ici** [direction] this way / [alentour] around here ▸ **elle est passée par ici avant d'aller à la gare** she stopped off here on her way to the station ▸ **c'est ici que j'ai mal** this is where it hurts ▸ **vous êtes ici chez vous** make yourself at home **2.** [temps] now ▸ **d'ici (à) jeudi** between now and Thursday ▸ **d'ici (à) une semaine** in a week's time, a week from now ▸ **d'ici là** by then ▸ **d'ici là, tout peut arriver!** in the meantime *ou* until then *ou* between now and then anything can happen! ▸ **d'ici peu** soon **3.** [au téléphone] **: ici Jacques** Jacques speaking *ou* here.

ici-bas [isiba] adv here below, on earth ▸ **d'ici-bas** in this life *ou* world.

icône [ikon] nf INFORM & RELIG icon.

iconique [ikɔnik] adj iconic.

iconoclaste [ikɔnɔklast] ■ nmf iconoclast.
■ adj iconoclastic.

iconographie [ikɔnɔgrafi] nf iconography.

id. (abr écrite de ***idem***) id.

idéal, e [ideal] (pl **idéals** *ou* **idéaux** [ideo]) adj ideal.
◆ ***idéal*** nm ideal.

idéalement [idealmɑ̃] adv ideally.

idéalisation [idealizasjɔ̃] nf idealization.

idéaliser [3] [idealize] vt to idealize.

idéalisme [idealism] nm idealism.

idéaliste [idealist] ■ nmf idealist.
■ adj idealistic.

idée [ide] nf idea ▸ **à l'idée de/que** at the idea of/that ▸ **aucune idée!** no idea!, I haven't got a clue! ▸ **avoir dans l'idée que...** to have a feeling that... ▸ **avoir une idée derrière la tête** to be up to something ▸ **avoir une haute idée de qqn/qqch** to have a high opinion of sb/sthg, to think highly of sb/sthg ▸ **changer d'idée** to change one's mind ▸ **ne pas avoir la moindre idée (de)** not to have the slightest idea (about) ▸ **se faire des idées** to imagine things ▸ **se faire des idées sur qqn/qqch** to get ideas about sb/sthg ▸ **s'il croit obtenir le rôle, il se fait des idées** if he thinks he's going to get the part, he's deceiving himself ▸ **se faire une idée de** to get an idea of ▸ **cela ne m'est jamais venu à l'idée** it never occurred to me ▸ **idée fixe** obsession ▸ **c'est une idée fixe chez toi!** it's an obsession with you! ▸ **idée de génie** brainwave *UK*, brainstorm *US* ▸ **idées noires** black thoughts ▸ **idées reçues** assumptions ▸ **avoir des idées bien arrêtées sur** to have set ideas *ou* definite views about ▸ **donner des idées à qqn** to give sb ideas *ou* to put ideas in *ou* into sb's head ▸ **se rafraîchir les idées** to refresh one's memory.

idem [idɛm] adv idem.

identifiant [idɑ̃tifjɑ̃] nm INFORM user name, login name.

identification [idɑ̃tifikasjɔ̃] nf **: identification (à)** identification (with) ▸ **identification de la marque** [marketing] brand recognition ▸ **identification des besoins** ÉCON needs identification.

identifier [9] [idɑ̃tifje] vt to identify ▸ **identifier qqn à qqch** to identify sb with sthg.
◆ ***s'identifier*** vp **: s'identifier à qqn/qqch** to identify with sb/sthg.

identique [idɑ̃tik] adj **: identique (à)** identical (to).

identité [idɑ̃tite] nf identity.

idéologie [ideɔlɔʒi] nf ideology.

idéologique [ideɔlɔʒik] adj ideological.

idiomatique [idjɔmatik] adj idiomatic.

idiome [idjom] nm idiom.

idiot**, **e [idjo, ɔt] ■ **adj** idiotic / MÉD idiot *(avant n)*.
■ **nm, f** idiot.

idiotie [idjɔsi] **nf 1.** [stupidité] idiocy **2.** [action, parole] idiotic thing.

idoine [idwan] **adj** *sout* appropriate.

idolâtrer [3] [idɔlatre] **vt** to idolize.

idole [idɔl] **nf** idol.

IDS (abr de ***initiative de défense stratégique***) **nf** SDI.

idylle [idil] **nf 1.** [amour] romance **2.** [poème] idyll.

idyllique [idilik] **adj** [idéal] idyllic.

if [if] **nm** yew.

IFOP**, **Ifop [ifɔp] (abr de ***Institut français d'opinion publique***) **nm** *French market research institute.*

Ifremer [ifrəmɛr] (abr de ***Institut français de recherche pour l'exploitation de la mer***) **nm** *research establishment for marine resources.*

IGF (abr de ***impôt sur les grandes fortunes***) **nm** *former wealth tax.*

IGH (abr de ***immeuble de grande hauteur***) **nm** very high building.

igloo**, **iglou [iglu] **nm** igloo.

IGN (abr de ***Institut géographique national***) **nm** *national geographical institute*, ≃ Ordnance Survey *UK*, ≃ US Geological Survey *US*.

ignare [iɲar] ■ **nmf** ignoramus.
■ **adj** ignorant.

ignifuge [ignifyʒ] ■ **nm** fireproofing material.
■ **adj** fireproof.

ignoble [iɲɔbl] **adj 1.** [abject] base **2.** [hideux] vile.

ignominie [iɲɔmini] **nf 1.** [état] disgrace **2.** [action] disgraceful act.

ignominieux**, **euse [iɲɔminjø, øz] **adj** ignominious.

ignorance [iɲɔrɑ̃s] **nf** ignorance ▸ **dans l'ignorance de** in the dark about, in ignorance of.

ignorant**, **e [iɲɔrɑ̃, ɑ̃t] ■ **adj** ignorant ▸ **ignorant en/de qqch** ignorant of sthg.
■ **nm, f** ignoramus.

ignoré**, **e [iɲɔre] **adj** unknown.

ignorer [3] [iɲɔre] **vt 1.** [ne pas savoir] not to know, to be unaware of ▸ **ignorer que** not to know that **2.** [ne pas tenir compte de] to ignore **3.** [ne pas connaître] to have no experience of.
◆ ***s'ignorer*** **vp 1.** [se bouder] to ignore each other **2.** [méconnaître ses possibilités] to be unaware of one's talent.

IGPN (abr de ***Inspection générale de la police nationale***) **nf** *police disciplinary body.*

IGS (abr de ***Inspection générale des services***) **nf** *police disciplinary body for Paris.*

il [il] **pron pers 1.** [sujet - personne] he / [- animal] it, he / [- chose] it **2.** [sujet d'un verbe impersonnel] it ▸ **il pleut** it's raining.
◆ ***ils*** **pron pers pl** they.

île [il] **nf** island ▸ **les îles Anglo-Normandes** the Channel Islands ▸ **les îles Baléares** the Balearic Islands ▸ **les îles Britanniques** the British Isles ▸ **les îles Canaries** the Canary Islands ▸ **l'Île-de-France** the Île-de-France ▸ **les îles Malouines** the Falkland Islands ▸ **l'île de Man** the Isle of Man ▸ **l'île Maurice** Mauritius.

CULTURE

Île-de-France

This region has eight **départements** arranged in a circle with Paris (**le département de la Seine**) at its centre. The three that immediately surround Paris – Hauts-de-Seine, Seine-Saint-Denis and Val-de-Marne – are collectively called **la petite couronne.** The four others, Seine-et-Marne, Yvelines, Essonne, and Val d'Oise, make up **la grande couronne.** The region's inhabitants are known as **Franciliens. La Francilienne** is the motorway that will eventually connect four roads in the Parisian suburbs.

illégal**, **e**, **aux [ilegal, o] **adj** illegal.

illégalité [ilegalite] **nf 1.** [fait d'être illégal] illegality **2.** [action illégale] illegal act.

illégitime [ileʒitim] **adj 1.** [enfant] illegitimate / [union] unlawful **2.** [non justifié] unwarranted.

illettré**, **e [iletre] **adj & nm, f** illiterate.

illicite [ilisit] **adj** illicit.

illico [iliko] **adv** *fam* right away, pronto.

illimité**, **e [ilimite] **adj 1.** [sans limites] unlimited **2.** [indéterminé] indefinite.

illisible [ilizibl] **adj 1.** [indéchiffrable] illegible **2.** [incompréhensible & INFORM] unreadable.

illogique [ilɔʒik] **adj** illogical.

illumination [ilyminasjɔ̃] **nf 1.** [éclairage] lighting **2.** [idée soudaine] inspiration.
◆ ***illuminations*** **nfpl** illuminations.

illuminé**, **e [ilymine] ■ **adj** illuminated.
■ **nm, f** *péj* crank.

illuminer [3] [ilymine] **vt** to light up / [bâtiment, rue] to illuminate.
◆ ***s'illuminer*** **vp : s'illuminer de joie** to light up with joy.

illusion [ilyzjɔ̃] **nf** illusion ▸ **se faire des illusions** to fool o.s. ▸ **illusion d'optique** optical illusion ▸ **se bercer d'illusions** to live in cloud-cuckoo-land.

illusionner [3] [ilyzjɔne] **vt** to delude.
◆ ***s'illusionner*** **vp** to delude o.s.

illusionniste [ilyzjɔnist] **nmf** conjurer.

illusoire [ilyzwar] **adj** illusory.

illustrateur**, **trice [ilystratœr, tris] **nm, f** illustrator.

illustration [ilystrasjɔ̃] **nf** illustration.

illustre [ilystr] **adj** illustrious.

illustré**, **e [ilystre] **adj** illustrated.
◆ ***illustré*** **nm** illustrated magazine.

illustrer [3] [ilystre] **vt 1.** [gén] to illustrate **2.** [rendre célèbre] to make famous.
◆ ***s'illustrer*** **vp** to distinguish o.s.

îlot [ilo] **nm 1.** [île] small island, islet **2.** [de maisons] block **3.** [lieu isolé] island **4.** *fig* [de résistance] pocket.

ils ➤ *il.*

IMA [ima] (abr de ***Institut du monde arabe***) **nm** *Paris exhibition centre for Arab culture and art.*

image [imaʒ] **nf 1.** [vision mentale, comparaison, ressemblance] image ▸ **donner une fausse image de qqch** to misrepresent sthg, to give a false impression of sthg ▸ **ce jardin est à l'image de son propriétaire** this garden is a reflection of its owner ▸ **être l'image de qqn** to be the image of sb ▸ **image de marque** [de personne] image / [d'entreprise] corporate image ▸ **image réelle/virtuelle** real/virtual image ▸ **l'image est floue** [télévision] the picture is fuzzy **2.** [dessin] picture ▸ **image d'Épinal** sentimental picture / *fig* simplistic argument/theory ▸ **livre d'images** picture book ▸ **sage comme une image** as good as gold **3.** INFORM [imprimée] hard copy / [sur l'écran] image ▸ **image mémoire** dump.

imagé, e [imaʒe] **adj** full of imagery.

imagerie [imaʒri] **nf** MÉD **: imagerie médicale** medical imaging.

imaginable [imaʒinabl] **adj** imaginable.

imaginaire [imaʒinɛr] ■ **nm : l'imaginaire** the imaginary.
■ **adj** imaginary.

imaginatif, ive [imaʒinatif, iv] **adj** imaginative.

imagination [imaʒinasjɔ̃] **nf** imagination ▸ **avoir de l'imagination** to be imaginative.
◆ ***imaginations*** **nfpl** *littéraire* & *péj* [chimères] fancies.

imaginer [3] [imaʒine] **vt 1.** [supposer, croire] to imagine **2.** [trouver] to think of.
◆ ***s'imaginer*** **vp 1.** [se voir] to see o.s. **2.** [croire] to imagine.

imam [imam] **nm** imam.

imbattable [ɛ̃batabl] **adj** unbeatable.

imbécile [ɛ̃besil] ■ **nmf** imbecile.
■ **adj** idiotic.

imbécillité [ɛ̃besilite] **nf 1.** [manque d'intelligence] imbecility **2.** [acte, parole] stupid thing.

imberbe [ɛ̃bɛrb] **adj** beardless.

imbiber [3] [ɛ̃bibe] **vt : imbiber qqch de qqch** to soak sthg with *ou* in sthg.
◆ ***s'imbiber*** **vp : s'imbiber de** to soak up.

imbriqué, e [ɛ̃brike] **adj** overlapping.

imbriquer [3] [ɛ̃brike] ◆ ***s'imbriquer*** **vp** [se chevaucher] to overlap / *fig* to intertwine.

imbroglio [ɛ̃brɔljo] **nm** imbroglio.

imbu, e [ɛ̃by] **adj : être imbu de** to be full of ▸ **être imbu de soi-même** to be full of oneself.

imbuvable [ɛ̃byvabl] **adj 1.** [eau] undrinkable **2.** *fam* [personne] unbearable.

imitateur, trice [imitatœr, tris] **nm, f 1.** [comique] impersonator **2.** *péj* [copieur] imitator.

imitation [imitasjɔ̃] **nf** imitation ▸ **imitation cuir** imitation leather ▸ **à l'imitation de** in imitation of.
◆ ***en imitation*** **loc adj** imitation.

imiter [3] [imite] **vt 1.** [s'inspirer de, contrefaire] to imitate **2.** [reproduire l'aspect de] to look (just) like.

immaculé, e [imakyle] **adj** immaculate ▸ **L'Immaculée Conception** The Immaculate Conception.

immanent, e [imanɑ̃, ɑ̃t] **adj** immanent ▸ **immanent à** inherent in.

immangeable [ɛ̃mɑ̃ʒabl] **adj** inedible.

immanquable [ɛ̃mɑ̃kabl] **adj** impossible to miss / [sort, échec] inevitable.

immanquablement [ɛ̃mɑ̃kabləmɑ̃] **adv** inevitably.

immatériel, elle [imaterjɛl] **adj 1.** PHILO immaterial **2.** [beauté] unreal **3.** [investissement] intangible.

immatriculation [imatrikylasjɔ̃] **nf** registration.

immatriculer [3] [imatrikyle] **vt** to register.

immature [imatyr] **adj** immature.

immaturité [imatyrite] **nf** immaturity.

immédiat, e [imedja, at] ■ **adj** immediate.
■ **nm : dans l'immédiat** for the time being.

immédiatement [imedjatmɑ̃] **adv** immediately.

immémorial, e, aux [imemɔrjal, o] **adj** ancient.

immense [imɑ̃s] **adj** immense.

immensément [imɑ̃semɑ̃] **adv** immensely.

immensité [imɑ̃site] **nf** immensity, vastness.

immergé, e [imɛrʒe] **adj** [au-dessous de l'eau] submerged ▸ **la majeure partie d'un iceberg est immergée** the bulk of an iceberg is underwater ▸ **l'épave est immergée par 500 m de fond** the wreck is lying 500 m underwater
▸▸ **plante immergée** aquatic plant ▸ **terres immergées** submerged areas of land.

immerger [17] [imɛrʒe] **vt** to submerge.
◆ ***s'immerger*** **vp** to submerge o.s.

immérité, e [imerite] **adj** undeserved.

immersion [imɛrsjɔ̃] **nf** immersion.

immettable [ɛ̃metabl] **adj** unwearable.

immeuble [imœbl] ■ **nm** building.
■ **adj** DR real.

immigrant, e [imigrɑ̃, ɑ̃t] **nm, f** immigrant.

immigration [imigrasjɔ̃] **nf** immigration ▸ **immigration clandestine** illegal immigration.

immigré, e [imigre] **adj** & **nm, f** immigrant ▸ **immigré clandestin** illegal immigrant.

immigrer [3] [imigre] **vi** to immigrate.

imminence [iminɑ̃s] **nf** imminence.

imminent, e [iminɑ̃, ɑ̃t] **adj** imminent.

immiscer [16] [imise] ◆ ***s'immiscer*** **vp : s'immiscer dans** to interfere in *ou* with.

immixtion [imiksjɔ̃] **nf** interference.

immobile [imɔbil] **adj 1.** [personne, visage] motionless **2.** [mécanisme] fixed, stationary **3.** *fig* [figé] immovable.

immobilier**, **ère [imɔbilje, ɛr] **adj : biens immobiliers** property *(U)*, real estate *(U)* *US* ▸ **société immobilière** property *ou* real estate *US* company.
◆ ***immobilier*** **nm : l'immobilier** property, real estate *US*.

immobilisation [imɔbilizasjɔ̃] **nf** immobilization.
◆ ***immobilisations*** **nfpl** FIN fixed assets.

immobiliser [3] [imɔbilize] **vt** to immobilize.
◆ ***s'immobiliser*** **vp** to stop.

immobilisme [imɔbilism] **nm** *péj* opposition to progress.

immobilité [imɔbilite] **nf** immobility / [de paysage, de lac] stillness.

immodéré**, **e [imɔdere] **adj** inordinate.

immoler [3] [imɔle] **vt** to sacrifice / RELIG to immolate ▸ **immoler qqn/qqch à** to sacrifice sb/sthg to.
◆ ***s'immoler*** **vp** to immolate o.s.

immonde [imɔ̃d] **adj 1.** [sale] foul **2.** [abject] vile.

immondices [imɔ̃dis] **nfpl** waste *(U)*, refuse *(U)*.

immoral**, **e**, **aux [imɔral, o] **adj** immoral.

immoralité [imɔralite] **nf 1.** [dépravation] immorality **2.** [obscénité] obscenity.

immortaliser [3] [imɔrtalize] **vt** to immortalize.
◆ ***s'immortaliser*** **vp** to gain immortality.

immortalité [imɔrtalite] **nf** immortality.

immortel**, **elle [imɔrtɛl] **adj** immortal.
◆ ***immortelle*** **nf** BOT everlasting flower.
◆ ***Immortel**, **elle*** **nm, f** *fam member of the Académie française.*

immuable [imɥabl] **adj 1.** [éternel - loi] immutable **2.** [constant] unchanging.

immunisation [imynizasjɔ̃] **nf** immunization.

immuniser [3] [imynize] **vt 1.** [vacciner] to immunize **2.** *fig* [garantir] **: immuniser qqn contre qqch** to make sb immune to sthg.

immunitaire [imynitɛr] **adj** immune *(avant n)*.

immunité [imynite] **nf** immunity ▸ **immunité diplomatique/parlementaire** diplomatic/parliamentary immunity.

immunodéficience [imynɔdefisjɑ̃s] **nf** immunodeficiency.

immunologique [imynɔlɔʒik] **adj** immunological.

impact [ɛ̃pakt] **nm** impact ▸ **avoir de l'impact sur** to have an impact on ▸ **étude d'impact** impact study.

impair**, **e [ɛ̃pɛr] **adj** odd.
◆ ***impair*** **nm** [faux-pas] gaffe.

imparable [ɛ̃parabl] **adj 1.** [coup] unstoppable **2.** [argument] unanswerable.

impardonnable [ɛ̃pardɔnabl] **adj** unforgivable.

imparfait**, **e [ɛ̃parfɛ, ɛt] **adj 1.** [défectueux] imperfect **2.** [inachevé] incomplete.
◆ ***imparfait*** **nm** GRAMM imperfect (tense).

imparfaitement [ɛ̃parfɛtmɑ̃] **adv** imperfectly.

impartial**, **e**, **aux [ɛ̃parsjal, o] **adj** impartial.

impartialité [ɛ̃parsjalite] **nf** impartiality.

impartir [32] [ɛ̃partir] **vt : impartir qqch à qqn** *littéraire* [délai, droit] to grant sthg to sb / [don] to bestow sthg upon sb / [tâche] to assign sthg to sb.

impasse [ɛ̃pas] **nf 1.** [rue] dead end **2.** *fig* [difficulté] impasse, deadlock ▸ **être dans une impasse** *ou* **dans l'impasse** to be at an impasse, to be deadlocked **3.** SCOL & UNIV **: faire une impasse sur un sujet** *to give a subject a miss when revising for an exam* **4.** [jeux] **: faire une impasse** to finesse **5.** FIN **: impasse budgétaire** budget deficit.

impassibilité [ɛ̃pasibilite] **nf** impassivity.

impassible [ɛ̃pasibl] **adj** impassive ▸ **rester impassible** to be *ou* remain impassive.

impatiemment [ɛ̃pasjamɑ̃] **adv** impatiently.

impatience [ɛ̃pasjɑ̃s] **nf** impatience ▸ **bouillir d'impatience** to be burning with impatience.

impatient**, **e [ɛ̃pasjɑ̃, ɑ̃t] ■ **adj** impatient ▸ **être impatient de faire qqch** to be impatient *ou* longing to do sthg.
■ **nmf** impatient person.

impatienter [3] [ɛ̃pasjɑ̃te] **vt** to annoy.
◆ ***s'impatienter*** **vp : s'impatienter (de/contre)** to get impatient (at/with).

impayable [ɛ̃pɛjabl] **adj** *fam* priceless.

impayé**, **e [ɛ̃pɛje] **adj** unpaid, outstanding.
◆ ***impayé*** **nm** outstanding payment.

impec [ɛ̃pɛk] **adj** *fam* perfect.

impeccable [ɛ̃pekabl] **adj 1.** [parfait] impeccable, faultless **2.** [propre] spotless, immaculate.

impénétrable [ɛ̃penetrabl] **adj** impenetrable.

impénitent**, **e [ɛ̃penitɑ̃, ɑ̃t] **adj** unrepentant.

impensable [ɛ̃pɑ̃sabl] **adj** unthinkable.

imper [ɛ̃pɛr] **nm** *fam* raincoat, mac *UK*.

impératif**, **ive [ɛ̃peratif, iv] **adj 1.** [ton, air] imperious **2.** [besoin] imperative, essential.
◆ ***impératif*** **nm** GRAMM imperative.

impérativement [ɛ̃perativmɑ̃] **adv : il faut impérativement faire qqch** it is imperative to do sthg.

impératrice [ɛ̃peratris] **nf** empress.

imperceptible [ɛ̃pɛrsɛptibl] **adj** imperceptible.

imperceptiblement [ɛ̃pɛrsɛptibləmɑ̃] **adv** imperceptibly.

imperfection [ɛ̃pɛrfɛksjɔ̃] **nf** imperfection.

impérial**, **e**, **aux [ɛ̃perjal, o] **adj** imperial.
◆ ***impériale*** **nf** top deck.

impérialisme [ɛ̃perjalism] **nm** POLIT imperialism / *fi*[g] dominance.

impérialiste [ɛ̃perjalist] **nmf & adj** imperialist.

impérieusement [ɛ̃perjøzmɑ̃] **adv** imperiously.

impérieux**, **euse [ɛ̃perjø, øz] **adj 1.** [ton, air] imperious **2.** [nécessité] urgent.

impérissable [ɛ̃perisabl] **adj** undying.

imperméabilisation [ɛ̃pɛrmeabilizasjɔ̃] **nf** waterproofing.

imperméabiliser [3] [ɛ̃pɛrmeabilize] **vt** to waterproof.

imperméable [ɛ̃pɛrmeabl] ■ **adj** waterproof ▸ **imperméable à** [étanche] impermeable to / *fig* impervious *ou* immune to.
■ **nm** raincoat.

impersonnel, elle [ɛ̃pɛrsɔnɛl] **adj** impersonal.

impertinence [ɛ̃pɛrtinɑ̃s] **nf** impertinence *(U)*.

impertinent, e [ɛ̃pɛrtinɑ̃, ɑ̃t] ■ **adj** impertinent.
■ **nm, f** impertinent person.

imperturbable [ɛ̃pɛrtyrbabl] **adj** imperturbable.

impétigo [ɛ̃petigo] **nm** impetigo.

impétueux, euse [ɛ̃petɥø, øz] **adj 1.** [personne, caractère] impetuous **2.** *littéraire* [vent, torrent] raging.

impétuosité [ɛ̃petɥozite] **nf** impetuousness.

impie [ɛ̃pi] *littéraire* & *vieilli* ■ **nmf** ungodly person.
■ **adj** impious.

impiété [ɛ̃pjete] **nf** *littéraire* & *vieilli* impiety.

impitoyable [ɛ̃pitwajabl] **adj** merciless, pitiless.

impitoyablement [ɛ̃pitwajabləmɑ̃] **adv** mercilessly, pitilessly.

implacable [ɛ̃plakabl] **adj** implacable.

implant [ɛ̃plɑ̃] **nm** MÉD implant.

implantation [ɛ̃plɑ̃tasjɔ̃] **nf 1.** [d'usine, de système] establishment **2.** [de cheveux] implant.

implanter [3] [ɛ̃plɑ̃te] **vt 1.** [entreprise, système] to establish **2.** *fig* [préjugé] to implant.
◆ ***s'implanter*** **vp** [entreprise] to set up / [coutume] to become established.

implication [ɛ̃plikasjɔ̃] **nf 1.** [participation] **: implication (dans)** involvement (in) **2.** *(gén pl)* [conséquence] implication.

implicite [ɛ̃plisit] **adj** implicit.

implicitement [ɛ̃plisitmɑ̃] **adv** implicitly.

impliquer [3] [ɛ̃plike] **vt 1.** [compromettre] **: impliquer qqn dans** to implicate sb in **2.** [requérir, entraîner] to imply.
◆ ***s'impliquer*** **vp : s'impliquer dans** *fam* to become involved in.

implorer [3] [ɛ̃plɔre] **vt** to beseech.

imploser [3] [ɛ̃ploze] **vi** to implode.

implosion [ɛ̃plozjɔ̃] **nf** implosion.

impoli, e [ɛ̃pɔli] **adj** rude, impolite.

impoliment [ɛ̃pɔlimɑ̃] **adv** rudely, impolitely.

impolitesse [ɛ̃pɔlitɛs] **nf** rudeness, impoliteness.

impondérable [ɛ̃pɔ̃derabl] **adj** imponderable.
◆ ***impondérables*** **nmpl** imponderables.

impopulaire [ɛ̃pɔpylɛr] **adj** unpopular.

impopularité [ɛ̃pɔpylarite] **nf** unpopularity.

import [ɛ̃pɔr] **nm 1.** COMM import **2.** *Belgique* [montant] total.

importance [ɛ̃pɔrtɑ̃s] **nf 1.** [gén] importance / [de problème, montant] magnitude ▸ **attacher de l'importance à** to attach importance to ▸ **avoir de l'importance** to be important ▸ **d'importance** [non négligeable] of some importance ▸ **sans importance** [gén] unimportant / [accident] minor **2.** [de dommages] extent **3.** [de ville] size.

important, e [ɛ̃pɔrtɑ̃, ɑ̃t] ■ **adj 1.** [personnage, découverte, rôle] important / [événement, changement] important, significant **2.** [quantité, collection, somme] considerable, sizeable / [dommages] extensive.
■ **nm, f : faire l'important** *péj* to act important.
◆ ***important*** **nm : l'important** the (most) important thing, the main thing.

importateur, trice [ɛ̃pɔrtatœr, tris] **adj** importing *(avant n)*.
◆ ***importateur*** **nm** importer.

importation [ɛ̃pɔrtasjɔ̃] **nf** *fig* & COMM import.

importer [3] [ɛ̃pɔrte] ■ **vt** to import.
■ **v impers : importer (à)** to matter (to) ▸ **il importe de/que** it is important to/that ▸ **qu'importe!, peu importe!** it doesn't matter! ▸ **n'importe qui** anyone (at all) ▸ **n'importe quoi** anything (at all) ▸ **n'importe où** anywhere (at all) ▸ **n'importe quand** at any time (at all) ▸ **n'importe comment** anyhow.

import-export [ɛ̃pɔrɛkspɔr] (pl **imports-exports**) **nm** import-export.

importun, e [ɛ̃pɔrtœ̃, yn] ■ **adj 1.** [indiscret] irksome, troublesome **2.** [embarrassant] awkward.
■ **nmf** *vieilli* intruder.

importuner [3] [ɛ̃pɔrtyne] **vt** to irk.

imposable [ɛ̃pozabl] **adj** taxable ▸ **non imposable** non-taxable.

imposant, e [ɛ̃pozɑ̃, ɑ̃t] **adj** imposing.

imposé, e [ɛ̃poze] ■ **adj 1.** [contribuable] taxed ▸ **imposé à 33 %** taxed at 33% **2.** SPORT [figure] compulsory.
■ **nm, f** [contribuable] taxpayer.

imposer [3] [ɛ̃poze] **vt 1.** [gén] **: imposer qqn/qqch à qqn** to impose sb/sthg on sb ▸ **imposer sa volonté/son point de vue** to impose one's will/one's point of view **2.** [impressionner] **: en imposer à qqn** to impress sb **3.** [provoquer] **: imposer l'admiration/le respect** to command admiration/respect **4.** [taxer] to tax.
◆ ***s'imposer*** **vp 1.** [être nécessaire] to be essential *ou* imperative ▸ **cette dernière remarque ne s'imposait pas** that last remark was unnecessary *ou* uncalled for **2.** [forcer le respect] to stand out ▸ **elle s'impose par son talent** her talent makes her stand out **3.** [avoir pour règle] **: s'imposer de faire qqch** to make it a rule to do sthg ▸ **s'imposer un effort/un sacrifice** to force o.s. to make an effort/a sacrifice.

imposition [ɛ̃pozisjɔ̃] **nf 1.** FIN taxation ▸ **double imposition** double taxation **2.** RELIG laying on.

impossibilité [ɛ̃pɔsibilite] **nf** impossibility ▸ **être dans l'impossibilité de faire qqch** to find it impossible to *ou* to be unable to do sthg.

impossible [ɛ̃pɔsibl] ■ **adj** impossible.
■ **nm : tenter l'impossible** to attempt the impossible.

imposteur [ɛ̃pɔstœr] **nm** impostor.

imposture [ɛ̃pɔstyr] **nf** imposture.

impôt [ɛ̃po] **nm** tax ▸ **impôt sur les denrées** commodity tax ▸ **impôt direct/indirect** direct/indirect tax ▸ **impôt extraordinaire** emergency tax ▸ **impôts locaux** council tax *UK*, local tax *US* ▸ **impôt sur les gains exceptionnels** windfall tax ▸ **impôt sur les grandes fortunes** wealth tax ▸ **impôt sur les plus-values** capital gains tax ▸ **impôt sur le revenu** income tax ▸ **être assujetti à l'impôt** to be subject to tax.

CULTURE

Impôts

In France, two types of tax are taken directly from an employee's gross pay: the **contribution sociale généralisée**, which goes towards national social security programmes, and the **remboursement de la dette sociale**, which helps relieve company debt. There are also **impôts sur le revenu des personnes physiques** – income tax for businesses and private individuals – and different types of **impôts locaux**, including taxes paid by both tenants and homeowners, and the **taxe professionnelle** for businesses.

impotence [ɛ̃pɔtɑ̃s] **nf** infirmity.

impotent, e [ɛ̃pɔtɑ̃, ɑ̃t] ■ **adj** disabled.
■ **nm, f** disabled person.

impraticable [ɛ̃pratikabl] **adj 1.** [inapplicable] impracticable **2.** [inaccessible] impassable.

imprécation [ɛ̃prekasjɔ̃] **nf** *littéraire* imprecation.

imprécis, e [ɛ̃presi, iz] **adj** imprecise.

imprécision [ɛ̃presizjɔ̃] **nf** imprecision.

imprégner [18] [ɛ̃preɲe] **vt** [imbiber] : **imprégner qqch de qqch** to soak sthg in sthg ▸ **imprégner qqn de qqch** *fig* to fill sb with sthg.
◆ ***s'imprégner*** **vp** : **s'imprégner de qqch** [s'imbiber] to soak sthg up / *fig* to soak sthg up, to steep o.s. in sthg.

imprenable [ɛ̃prənabl] **adj 1.** [forteresse] impregnable **2.** [vue] unimpeded.

imprésario, impresario [ɛ̃presarjo] **nm** impresario.

impression [ɛ̃presjɔ̃] **nf 1.** [gén] impression ▸ **avoir l'impression que** to have the impression *ou* feeling that ▸ **j'ai l'impression qu'elle ne viendra plus** I have a feeling (that) she won't come ▸ **j'ai l'impression d'avoir déjà vécu cette scène** I've got a strong sense of déjà vu ▸ **faire (une) bonne/mauvaise impression (à)** to make a good/bad impression (on) ▸ **il donne l'impression de s'ennuyer** he seems to be bored **2.** [de livre, tissu] printing ▸ **envoyer un manuscrit à l'impression** to send a manuscript off to press *ou* the printer's **3.** PHOTO print.

impressionnable [ɛ̃presjɔnabl] **adj 1.** [émotif] impressionable **2.** PHOTO sensitive.

impressionnant, e [ɛ̃presjɔnɑ̃, ɑ̃t] **adj 1.** [imposant] impressive **2.** [effrayant] frightening.

impressionner [3] [ɛ̃presjɔne] **vt 1.** [frapper] to impress **2.** [choquer] to shock, to upset **3.** [intimider] to frighten **4.** PHOTO to expose.

impressionnisme [ɛ̃presjɔnism] **nm** impressionism.

impressionniste [ɛ̃presjɔnist] **nmf** & **adj** impressionist.

imprévisible [ɛ̃previzibl] **adj** unforeseeable.

imprévoyance [ɛ̃prevwajɑ̃s] **nf** lack of foresight, improvidence.

imprévoyant, e [ɛ̃prevwajɑ̃, ɑ̃t] **adj** improvident.

imprévu, e [ɛ̃prevy] **adj** unforeseen.
◆ ***imprévu*** **nm** unforeseen situation ▸ **sauf imprévu** barring unforeseen circumstances.

imprimante [ɛ̃primɑ̃t] **nf** printer ▸ **imprimante laser/à jet d'encre/matricielle** laser/ink-jet/dot-matrix printer.

imprimé, e [ɛ̃prime] **adj** printed.
◆ ***imprimé*** **nm 1.** [mention postale] printed matter *(U)* **2.** [formulaire] printed form **3.** [tissu] print.

imprimer [3] [ɛ̃prime] **vt 1.** [texte, tissu] to print **2.** [mouvement] to impart ▸ **imprimer un mouvement à qqch** to impart *ou* to transmit movement to sthg **3.** [marque, empreinte] to leave.
◆ ***s'imprimer*** **vpi** to be printed.

imprimerie [ɛ̃primri] **nf 1.** [technique] printing **2.** [usine] printing works *sg*.

imprimeur [ɛ̃primœr] **nm** printer.

improbable [ɛ̃prɔbabl] **adj** improbable.

improductif, ive [ɛ̃prɔdyktif, iv] **adj** unproductive.

impromptu, e [ɛ̃prɔ̃pty] **adj** impromptu.
◆ ***impromptu*** ■ **adv** impromptu.
■ **nm** impromptu.

imprononçable [ɛ̃prɔnɔ̃sabl] **adj** unpronounceable.

impropre [ɛ̃prɔpr] **adj 1.** GRAMM incorrect **2.** [inadapté] : **impropre à** unfit for.

impropriété [ɛ̃prɔprijete] **nf** [emploi erroné] incorrectness / [expression] (language) error.

improvisation [ɛ̃prɔvizasjɔ̃] **nf** improvisation.

improvisé, e [ɛ̃prɔvize] **adj** [discours] improvised, extempore *sout* / [explication] off-the-cuff, ad hoc / [mesure, réforme] makeshift, improvised / [décision] snap *(avant n)* ▸ **un repas improvisé** a makeshift meal.

improviser [3] [ɛ̃prɔvize] **vt** to improvise.
◆ ***s'improviser*** **vp 1.** [s'organiser] to be improvised **2.** [devenir] : **s'improviser metteur en scène** to act as director.

improviste [ɛ̃prɔvist] ◆ ***à l'improviste*** **loc adv** unexpectedly, without warning.

imprudemment [ɛ̃prydamɑ̃] **adv** rashly.

imprudence [ɛ̃prydɑ̃s] **nf 1.** [de personne, d'acte] rashness **2.** [acte] rash act.

imprudent, e [ɛ̃prydɑ̃, ɑ̃t] ■ **adj** rash.
■ **nm, f** rash person.

impubère [ɛ̃pybɛr] ■ **adj** [avant la puberté] pre-pubescent.
■ **nmf** DR ≃ minor.

impudence [ɛ̃pydɑ̃s] **nf 1.** [de personne, propos] impudence **2.** [propos] impudent remark.

impudent, e [ɛ̃pydɑ̃, ɑ̃t] ■ **adj** impudent.
■ **nm, f** impudent person.

impudeur [ɛ̃pydœr] **nf** shamelessness.

impudique [ɛ̃pydik] **adj** shameless.

impuissance [ɛ̃pɥisɑ̃s] **nf 1.** [incapacité] **: impuissance (à faire qqch)** powerlessness (to do sthg) **2.** [sexuelle] impotence.

impuissant, e [ɛ̃pɥisɑ̃, ɑ̃t] **adj 1.** [incapable] **: impuissant (à faire qqch)** powerless (to do sthg) **2.** [homme, fureur] impotent.
◆ ***impuissant*** **nm** impotent man.

impulsif, ive [ɛ̃pylsif, iv] ■ **adj** impulsive.
■ **nm, f** impulsive person.

impulsion [ɛ̃pylsjɔ̃] **nf 1.** [poussée, essor] impetus **2.** [instinct] impulse, instinct **3.** *fig* **: sous l'impulsion de qqn** [influence] at the prompting *ou* instigation of sb ▸ **sous l'impulsion de qqch** [effet] impelled by sthg.

impulsivement [ɛ̃pylsivmɑ̃] **adv** impulsively.

impulsivité [ɛ̃pylsivite] **nf** impulsiveness.

impunément [ɛ̃pynemɑ̃] **adv** with impunity.

impuni, e [ɛ̃pyni] **adj** unpunished.

impunité [ɛ̃pynite] **nf** impunity ▸ **en toute impunité** with impunity.

impur, e [ɛ̃pyr] **adj** impure.

impureté [ɛ̃pyrte] **nf** impurity.

imputable [ɛ̃pytabl] **adj 1.** [accident, erreur] **: imputable à** attributable to **2.** FIN **: imputable à** *ou* **sur** chargeable to.

imputation [ɛ̃pytasjɔ̃] **nf 1.** [accusation] charge **2.** FIN charging.

imputer [3] [ɛ̃pyte] **vt : imputer qqch à qqn/qqch** to attribute sthg to sb/sthg ▸ **imputer qqch à qqch** FIN to charge sthg to sthg.

imputrescible [ɛ̃pytresibl] **adj** [bois] rotproof / [déchets] non-degradable.

in [in] **adj inv** *vieilli* in, with it.

INA [ina] (abr de ***Institut national de l'audiovisuel***) **nm** *national television archive.*

inabordable [inabɔrdabl] **adj 1.** [prix] prohibitive **2.** GÉOGR inaccessible *(by boat)* **3.** [personne] unapproachable.

inacceptable [inaksɛptabl] **adj** unacceptable.

inaccessible [inaksesibl] **adj** [destination, domaine, personne] inaccessible / [objectif, poste] unattainable ▸ **inaccessible à** [sentiment] impervious to.

inaccoutumé, e [inakutyme] **adj** unaccustomed.

inachevé, e [inaʃve] **adj** unfinished, uncompleted.

inactif, ive [inaktif, iv] **adj 1.** [sans occupation, non utilisé] idle **2.** [sans effet] ineffective **3.** [sans emploi] non-working.

inaction [inaksjɔ̃] **nf** inaction.

inactivité [inaktivite] **nf 1.** [oisiveté] inactivity **2.** ADMIN **: en inactivité** out of active service.

inadapté, e [inadapte] ■ **adj 1.** [non adapté] **: inadapté (à)** unsuitable (for), unsuited (to) **2.** [asocial] maladjusted.
■ **nm, f** maladjusted person.

inadéquat, e [inadekwa, at] **adj : inadéquat (à)** inadequate (for).

inadéquation [inadekwasjɔ̃] **nf : inadéquation (à)** inadequacy (for).

inadmissible [inadmisibl] **adj** [conduite] unacceptable.

inadvertance [inadvɛrtɑ̃s] **nf** *littéraire* oversight ▸ **par inadvertance** inadvertently.

inaliénable [inaljenabl] **adj** inalienable.

inaltérable [inalterabl] **adj 1.** [matériau] stable **2.** [sentiment] unfailing.

inamical, e, aux [inamikal, o] **adj** unfriendly.

inamovible [inamɔvibl] **adj** fixed.

inanimé, e [inanime] **adj 1.** [sans vie] inanimate **2.** [inerte, évanoui] senseless.

inanité [inanite] **nf** futility.

inanition [inanisjɔ̃] **nf : tomber/mourir d'inanition** to faint with/die of hunger.

inaperçu, e [inapɛrsy] **adj** unnoticed ▸ **passer inaperçu** to go *ou* pass unnoticed.

inapplicable [inaplikabl] **adj** inapplicable.

inappliqué, e [inaplike] **adj 1.** [étourdi] lazy, lacking in application **2.** [inemployé] not applied *ou* practised *UK ou* practiced *US*.

inappréciable [inapresjabl] **adj 1.** [infime] imperceptible **2.** [précieux] invaluable.

inapprochable [inaprɔʃabl] **adj : il est vraiment inapprochable en ce moment** you can't say anything to him at the moment.

inapproprié, e [inaprɔprije] **adj : inapproprié à** not appropriate for.

inapte [inapt] **adj 1.** [incapable] **: inapte à qqch/à faire qqch** incapable of sthg/of doing sthg **2.** MIL unfit.

inaptitude [inaptityd] **nf 1.** [incapacité] **: inaptitude à qqch/à faire qqch** incapacity for sthg/for doing sthg **2.** MIL unfitness.

inarticulé, e [inartikyle] **adj** inarticulate.

inassouvi, e [inasuvi] **adj** [faim] unsatisfied / [soif] unquenched / *fig* [sentiment] unsatisfied, unfulfilled.

inattaquable [inatakabl] **adj 1.** [imprenable] impregnable **2.** [irréprochable] irreproachable, beyond reproach **3.** [irréfutable] irrefutable.

inattendu, e [inatɑ̃dy] **adj** unexpected.

inattentif, ive [inatɑ̃tif, iv] **adj : inattentif à** inattentive to.

inattention [inatɑ̃sjɔ̃] **nf** inattention ▸ **faute d'inattention** careless mistake.

inaudible [inodibl] **adj 1.** [impossible à entendre] inaudible **2.** [inécoutable] impossible to listen to.

inaugural, e, aux [inogyral, o] **adj** inaugural *(avant n)*, opening *(avant n)* / [voyage] maiden *(avant n)*.

inauguration [inogyrasjɔ̃] **nf 1.** [cérémonie] inauguration, opening (ceremony) **2.** [début] dawn.

inaugurer [3] [inogyre] **vt 1.** [monument] to unveil / [installation, route] to open / [procédé, édifice] to inaugurate **2.** [époque] to usher in.

inavouable [inavwabl] **adj** unmentionable.

inavoué, e [inavwe] **adj** unconfessed.

INC (abr de ***Institut national de la consommation***) **nm** *consumer research organization.*

inca [ɛ̃ka] **adj** Inca.
◆ ***Inca*** **nmf** Inca.

incalculable [ɛ̃kalkylabl] **adj** incalculable.

incandescence [ɛ̃kɑ̃desɑ̃s] **nf** incandescence.

incandescent, e [ɛ̃kɑ̃desɑ̃, ɑ̃t] **adj** incandescent.

incantation [ɛ̃kɑ̃tasjɔ̃] **nf** incantation.

incapable [ɛ̃kapabl] ■ **nmf 1.** [raté] incompetent **2.** DR incapable person.
■ **adj : incapable de faire qqch** [inapte à] incapable of doing sthg / [dans l'impossibilité de] unable to do sthg ▸ **elle était incapable de répondre** she was unable to answer, she couldn't answer ▸ **je serais bien incapable de le dire** I really wouldn't know, I really couldn't tell you ▸ **elle est incapable d'amour** she's incapable of loving *ou* love.

incapacité [ɛ̃kapasite] **nf 1.** [impossibilité] **: incapacité à** *ou* **de faire qqch** inability to do sthg ▸ **être dans l'incapacité de** to be unable to **2.** [invalidité] disability ▸ **incapacité de travail** industrial disability **3.** DR incapacity **4.** [incompétence] incompetence.

incarcération [ɛ̃karserasjɔ̃] **nf** incarceration.

incarcérer [18] [ɛ̃karsere] **vt** to incarcerate.

incarnation [ɛ̃karnasjɔ̃] **nf** incarnation.

incarné, e [ɛ̃karne] **adj** incarnate.

incarner [3] [ɛ̃karne] **vt 1.** [personnifier] to be the incarnation of **2.** CINÉ & THÉÂTRE to play.
◆ ***s'incarner*** **vp 1.** RELIG to be *ou* become incarnate **2.** [se réaliser] to be incarnated **3.** MÉD [ongle] to become ingrowing *UK ou* ingrown *US*.

incartade [ɛ̃kartad] **nf** misdemeanour *UK*, misdemeanor *US*.

incassable [ɛ̃kasabl] **adj** unbreakable.

incendiaire [ɛ̃sɑ̃djɛr] ■ **nmf** arsonist.
■ **adj** [bombe] incendiary / *fig* inflammatory.

incendie [ɛ̃sɑ̃di] **nm** fire / *fig* flames *pl* ▸ **incendie de forêt** forest fire.

incendier [9] [ɛ̃sɑ̃dje] **vt 1.** [mettre le feu à] to set alight, to set fire to **2.** *fig* [faire rougir] to make burn **3.** *fam* [réprimander] **: incendier qqn** to to give sb hell.

incertain, e [ɛ̃sɛrtɛ̃, ɛn] **adj 1.** [gén] uncertain / [temps] unsettled **2.** [vague - lumière] dim / [- contour] blurred.

incertitude [ɛ̃sɛrtityd] **nf** uncertainty ▸ **être dans l'incertitude** to be uncertain.

incessamment [ɛ̃sesamɑ̃] **adv** at any moment, any moment now.

incessant, e [ɛ̃sesɑ̃, ɑ̃t] **adj** incessant.

incessible [ɛ̃sesibl] **adj** inalienable.

inceste [ɛ̃sɛst] **nm** incest.

incestueux, euse [ɛ̃sɛstɥø, øz] ■ **adj 1.** [liaison, parent] incestuous **2.** [enfant] born of incest.
■ **nm, f** incestuous person.

inchangé, e [ɛ̃ʃɑ̃ʒe] **adj** unchanged.

incidemment [ɛ̃sidamɑ̃] **adv 1.** [accidentellement] accidentally **2.** [entre parenthèses] in passing.

incidence [ɛ̃sidɑ̃s] **nf 1.** [conséquence] effect, impact *(U)* **2.** FIN & PHYS incidence.

incident, e [ɛ̃sidɑ̃, ɑ̃t] **adj** [accessoire] incidental.
◆ ***incident*** **nm 1.** [gén] incident / [ennui] hitch ▸ **sans incident** without incident *ou* a hitch ▸ **incident diplomatique** diplomatic incident ▸ **incident de parcours** (minor) setback **2.** DR point of law.

incinérateur [ɛ̃sineratœr] **nm** incinerator.

incinération [ɛ̃sinerasjɔ̃] **nf 1.** [de corps] cremation **2.** [d'ordures] incineration.

incinérer [18] [ɛ̃sinere] **vt 1.** [corps] to cremate **2.** [ordures] to incinerate.

incise [ɛ̃siz] **nf** LING interpolated clause.

inciser [3] [ɛ̃size] **vt** to incise, to make an incision in.

incisif, ive [ɛ̃sizif, iv] **adj** incisive.
◆ ***incisive*** **nf** incisor.

incision [ɛ̃sizjɔ̃] **nf** incision.

incitation [ɛ̃sitasjɔ̃] **nf 1.** [provocation] **: incitation à qqch/à faire qqch** incitement to sthg/to do sthg **2.** [encouragement] **: incitation à qqch/à faire qqch** incentive to sthg/to do sthg.

inciter [3] [ɛ̃site] **vt 1.** [provoquer] **: inciter qqn à qqch/à faire qqch** to incite sb to sthg/to do sthg **2.** [encourager] **: inciter qqn à faire qqch** to encourage sb to do sthg.

COMMENT EXPRIMER...

l'incertitude

I'm not sure that's such a good idea / Je ne suis pas sûr que ce soit une très bonne idée
I'm not at all sure (that) I want to go / Je ne suis pas sûr du tout d'avoir envie d'y aller
I don't know if I'll be able to open the door / Je ne sais pas si je vais pouvoir ouvrir la porte
I doubt (that) he'll pass / Je doute qu'il réussisse
It's still not certain whether the contract will be signed / Il y a encore une incertitude sur la signature du contrat
We are unable to inform you whether there will be any job losses / Nous ne sommes pas en mesure de vous dire s'il y aura des suppressions d'emplois

incivilité [ɛ̃sivilite] **nf 1.** [manque de courtoisie] rudeness, disrespect **2.** [fraude] petty crime / [insultes, vandalismes] antisocial behaviour *UK* ***ou*** behavior *US*.

inclassable [ɛ̃klasabl] **adj** unclassifiable.

inclinable [ɛ̃klinabl] **adj** reclinable, reclining.

inclinaison [ɛ̃klinɛzɔ̃] **nf 1.** [pente] incline **2.** [de tête, chapeau] angle, tilt.

inclination [ɛ̃klinasjɔ̃] **nf 1.** [salut - de tête] nod / [- du corps entier] bow **2.** [tendance] inclination ▸ **avoir une inclination à** to have an inclination ***ou*** a tendency to ▸ **avoir une inclination pour** [aimer] to have a liking for **3.** *littéraire* [amour] (romantic) attachment.

incliné, e [ɛ̃kline] **adj** [en pente] sloping / [penché - mur] leaning / [- dossier, siège] reclining.

incliner [3] [ɛ̃kline] ■ **vt 1.** [pencher] to tilt, to lean ▸ **incliner la tête *ou* le front** to bow ***ou*** to incline one's head / [pour acquiescer ou saluer] to nod (one's head) **2.** [pousser] **: incliner qqn à qqch/à faire qqch** to incline sb to sthg/to do sthg ▸ **cette information m'incline à revoir mon point de vue** this news leads me ***ou*** makes me inclined to reconsider my position.
■ **vi : incliner à qqch/à faire qqch** to be inclined to sthg/ to do sthg ▸ **j'incline à penser qu'elle a tort** I tend ***ou*** I'm inclined to think she's wrong.
◆ ***s'incliner*** **vp 1.** [se pencher] to tilt, to lean **2.** [céder] **: s'incliner (devant)** to give in (to), to yield (to) ▸ **s'incliner devant les faits** to submit to ***ou*** to accept the facts **3.** [respecter] **: s'incliner devant** to bow down before ▸ **s'incliner devant le talent** to bow before talent.

inclure [96] [ɛ̃klyr] **vt** [mettre dedans] **: inclure qqch dans qqch** to include sthg in sthg / [joindre] to enclose sthg with sthg.

inclus, e [ɛ̃kly, yz] ■ **pp** ➤ ***inclure***.
■ **adj 1.** [compris - taxe, frais] included / [joint - lettre] enclosed / **: jusqu'à la page 10 incluse** up to and including page 10 **2.** [dent] impacted **3.** MATH **: être inclus dans** to be a subset of.

inclusion [ɛ̃klyzjɔ̃] **nf** inclusion.

inclusivement [ɛ̃klyzivmɑ̃] **adv** inclusive.

incoercible [ɛ̃kɔɛrsibl] **adj** *sout* uncontrollable.

incognito [ɛ̃kɔɲito] ■ **adv** incognito.
■ **nm : garder l'incognito** to remain incognito.

incohérence [ɛ̃kɔerɑ̃s] **nf** [de paroles] incoherence / [d'actes] inconsistency.

incohérent, e [ɛ̃kɔerɑ̃, ɑ̃t] **adj** [paroles] incoherent / [actes] inconsistent.

incollable [ɛ̃kɔlabl] **adj 1.** [riz] nonstick **2.** *fam* [imbattable] unbeatable.

incolore [ɛ̃kɔlɔr] **adj** colourless *UK*, colorless *US*.

incomber [3] [ɛ̃kɔ̃be] **vi 1.** [revenir à] **: incomber à qqn** to be sb's responsibility ▸ **cette tâche vous incombe** this task is your responsibility ▸ **à qui en incombe la responsabilité?** who is responsible for it? ▸ **les frais de déplacement incombent à l'entreprise** travelling expenses are to be paid by the company **2.** *(emploi impersonnel)* **: il incombe à qqn de faire qqch** it falls to sb ***ou*** it is incumbent on sb to do sthg ▸ **il vous incombe de la recevoir** it's your duty ***ou*** it's incumbent on you to see her **3.** DR [être rattaché à] **: cette pièce incombe au dossier Falon** this document belongs in the Falon file.

incombustible [ɛ̃kɔ̃bystibl] **adj** incombustible.

incommensurable [ɛ̃kɔmɑ̃syrabl] **adj 1.** [immense] immeasurable **2.** MATH **: incommensurable avec** incommensurable with.

incommodant, e [ɛ̃kɔmɔdɑ̃, ɑ̃t] **adj** unpleasant.

incommode [ɛ̃kɔmɔd] **adj 1.** [heure, lieu] inconvenient **2.** [position, chaise] uncomfortable.

incommoder [3] [ɛ̃kɔmɔde] **vt** *sout* to trouble.

incommodité [ɛ̃kɔmɔdite] **nf 1.** [d'installation] impracticality **2.** [malaise] indisposition **3.** [de situation] awkwardness.

incommunicable [ɛ̃kɔmynikabl] **adj 1.** [indicible] inexpressible **2.** DR non-transferable.

incomparable [ɛ̃kɔ̃parabl] **adj 1.** [différent] not comparable **2.** [sans pareil] incomparable.

incomparablement [ɛ̃kɔ̃parabləmɑ̃] **adv** incomparably.

incompatibilité [ɛ̃kɔ̃patibilite] **nf** incompatibility ▸ **incompatibilité d'humeur** (mutual) incompatibility.

incompatible [ɛ̃kɔ̃patibl] **adj** incompatible.

incompétence [ɛ̃kɔ̃petɑ̃s] **nf 1.** [incapacité] incompetence **2.** [ignorance] **: incompétence en qqch** ignorance about sthg.

incompétent, e [ɛ̃kɔ̃petɑ̃, ɑ̃t] **adj 1.** [incapable] incompetent **2.** [ignorant] **: incompétent en qqch** ignorant about sthg.

incomplet, ète [ɛ̃kɔ̃plɛ, ɛt] **adj** incomplete.

incomplètement [ɛ̃kɔ̃plɛtmɑ̃] **adv** incompletely.

incompréhensible [ɛ̃kɔ̃preɑ̃sibl] **adj** incomprehensible.

incompréhensif, ive [ɛ̃kɔ̃preɑ̃sif, iv] **adj** unsympathetic.

incompréhension [ɛ̃kɔ̃preɑ̃sjɔ̃] **nf** lack of understanding.

incompressible [ɛ̃kɔ̃presibl] **adj 1.** TECHNOL incompressible **2.** *fig* [dépenses] impossible to reduce **3.** DR ➤ ***peine***.

incompris, e [ɛ̃kɔ̃pri, iz] ■ **adj** misunderstood, not appreciated.
■ **nm, f** misunderstood person.

inconcevable [ɛ̃kɔ̃svabl] **adj** unimaginable.

inconciliable [ɛ̃kɔ̃siljabl] **adj** irreconcilable.

inconditionnel, elle [ɛ̃kɔ̃disjɔnɛl] ■ **adj 1.** [total] unconditional **2.** [fervent] ardent.
■ **nm, f** ardent supporter ***ou*** admirer.

inconditionnellement [ɛ̃kɔ̃disjɔnɛlmɑ̃] **adv** unconditionally.

inconduite [ɛ̃kɔ̃dɥit] **nf** *littéraire* scandalous behaviour *UK* ***ou*** behavior *US*.

inconfort [ɛ̃kɔ̃fɔr] **nm** discomfort.

inconfortable [ɛ̃kɔ̃fɔrtabl] **adj** uncomfortable.

incongru**, **e [ɛ̃kɔ̃gry] **adj 1.** [malséant] unseemly, inappropriate **2.** [bizarre] incongruous.

incongruité [ɛ̃kɔ̃grɥite] **nf 1.** [qualité bizarre] incongruity *(U)* **2.** [parole malséante] unseemly remark.

inconnu**, **e [ɛ̃kɔny] ■ **adj** unknown.
■ **nm, f** stranger ▸ **la personne qui a eu le prix Goncourt cette année est un illustre inconnu** *hum* no one has ever heard of the renowned winner of the prix Goncourt this year.
◆ ***inconnue*** **nf 1.** MATH unknown **2.** [variable] unknown (factor).

inconsciemment [ɛ̃kɔ̃sjamɑ̃] **adv 1.** [sans en avoir conscience] unconsciously, unwittingly **2.** [à la légère] thoughtlessly.

inconscience [ɛ̃kɔ̃sjɑ̃s] **nf 1.** [évanouissement] unconsciousness **2.** [légèreté] thoughtlessness.

inconscient**, **e [ɛ̃kɔ̃sjɑ̃, ɑ̃t] **adj 1.** [évanoui, machinal] unconscious **2.** [irresponsable] thoughtless.
◆ ***inconscient*** **nm : l'inconscient** the unconscious.

inconséquence [ɛ̃kɔ̃sekɑ̃s] **nf** inconsistency.

inconséquent**, **e [ɛ̃kɔ̃sekɑ̃, ɑ̃t] **adj** inconsistent.

inconsidéré**, **e [ɛ̃kɔ̃sidere] **adj** ill-considered, thoughtless.

inconsistant**, **e [ɛ̃kɔ̃sistɑ̃, ɑ̃t] **adj 1.** [aliment] thin, watery **2.** [caractère] frivolous.

inconsolable [ɛ̃kɔ̃sɔlabl] **adj** inconsolable.

inconstance [ɛ̃kɔ̃stɑ̃s] **nf** fickleness.

inconstant**, **e [ɛ̃kɔ̃stɑ̃, ɑ̃t] ■ **adj** fickle.
■ **nm, f** *vieilli* fickle person.

incontestable [ɛ̃kɔ̃tɛstabl] **adj** unquestionable, indisputable.

incontestablement [ɛ̃kɔ̃tɛstabləmɑ̃] **adv** unquestionably, indisputably.

incontesté**, **e [ɛ̃kɔ̃tɛste] **adj** uncontested, unchallenged.

incontinence [ɛ̃kɔ̃tinɑ̃s] **nf 1.** MÉD incontinence **2.** [excès] lack of restraint.

incontinent**, **e [ɛ̃kɔ̃tinɑ̃, ɑ̃t] **adj 1.** MÉD incontinent **2.** [sans retenue] unrestrained.
◆ ***incontinent*** **adv** *littéraire* forthwith.

incontournable [ɛ̃kɔ̃turnabl] **adj** unavoidable.

incontrôlable [ɛ̃kɔ̃trolabl] **adj 1.** [personne] out of control **2.** [non vérifiable] unverifiable, unconfirmable.

inconvenance [ɛ̃kɔ̃vnɑ̃s] **nf** impropriety.

inconvenant**, **e [ɛ̃kɔ̃vnɑ̃, ɑ̃t] **adj** improper, unseemly.

inconvénient [ɛ̃kɔ̃venjɑ̃] **nm 1.** [obstacle] problem ▸ **si vous n'y voyez pas d'inconvénient** if that is convenient (for you), if you have no objection **2.** [désavantage] disadvantage, drawback **3.** [risque] risk.

incorporation [ɛ̃kɔrpɔrasjɔ̃] **nf 1.** [intégration] incorporation / CULIN mixing, blending **2.** MIL enlistment.

incorporé**, **e [ɛ̃kɔrpɔre] **adj** [intégré] built-in.

incorporel**, **elle [ɛ̃kɔrpɔrɛl] **adj 1.** [immatériel] incorporeal **2.** DR intangible.

incorporer [3] [ɛ̃kɔrpɔre] **vt 1.** [gén] to incorporate ▸ **incorporer qqch dans** to incorporate sthg into ▸ **incorporer qqch à** CULIN to mix *ou* blend sthg into **2.** MIL to enlist.
◆ ***s'incorporer*** **vp : s'incorporer à qqch** to become part of sthg.

incorrect**, **e [ɛ̃kɔrɛkt] **adj 1.** [faux] incorrect **2.** [inconvenant] inappropriate / [impoli] rude **3.** [déloyal] unfair ▸ **être incorrect avec qqn** to treat sb unfairly.

incorrection [ɛ̃kɔrɛksjɔ̃] **nf 1.** [impolitesse] impropriety **2.** [de langage] grammatical mistake **3.** [malhonnêteté] dishonesty.

incorrigible [ɛ̃kɔriʒibl] **adj** incorrigible.

incorruptible [ɛ̃kɔryptibl] **adj** incorruptible.

incrédule [ɛ̃kredyl] ■ **nmf 1.** [sceptique] sceptic *UK*, skeptic *US* **2.** RELIG unbeliever.
■ **adj 1.** [sceptique] incredulous, sceptical *UK*, skeptical *US* **2.** RELIG unbelieving.

incrédulité [ɛ̃kredylite] **nf 1.** [scepticisme] incredulity, scepticism *UK*, skepticism *US* **2.** RELIG unbelief, lack of belief.

incrémenter [ɛ̃kremte] **vt** INFORM to increment.

incrémentiel**, **elle [ɛ̃kremɑ̃sjɛl] **adj** INFORM incremental.

increvable [ɛ̃krəvabl] **adj 1.** [ballon, pneu] puncture-proof **2.** *fam fig* [personne] tireless / [machine] able to withstand rough treatment.

incriminer [3] [ɛ̃krimine] **vt 1.** [personne] to incriminate **2.** [conduite] to condemn.

incroyable [ɛ̃krwajabl] **adj** incredible, unbelievable.

incroyablement [ɛ̃krwajabləmɑ̃] **adv** incredibly, unbelievably.

incroyant**, **e [ɛ̃krwajɑ̃, ɑ̃t] ■ **adj** unbelieving.
■ **nm, f** unbeliever.

incrustation [ɛ̃krystasjɔ̃] **nf 1.** [ornement] inlay **2.** [dépôt] deposit, scale *(U)*, fur *(U)* *UK*.

incruster [3] [ɛ̃kryste] **vt 1.** [insérer] **: incruster qqch dans qqch** to inlay sthg into sthg **2.** [décorer] **: incruster qqch de qqch** to inlay sthg with sthg **3.** [couvrir d'un dépôt] to scale, to fur up *UK*.
◆ ***s'incruster*** **vp 1.** [s'insérer] **: s'incruster dans qqch** to become embedded in sthg **2.** [chaudière] to scale, to fur up *UK* **3.** *fam fig* [personne] to take root.

incubateur**, **trice [ɛ̃kybatœr, tris] **adj** incubating.
◆ ***incubateur*** **nm** incubator.

incubation [ɛ̃kybasjɔ̃] **nf** [d'œuf, de maladie] incubation / *fig* hatching.

inculpation [ɛ̃kylpasjɔ̃] **nf** charge ▸ **sous l'inculpation de** on a charge of.

inculpé**, **e [ɛ̃kylpe] **nm, f : l'inculpé** the accused.

inculper [3] [ɛ̃kylpe] **vt** to charge ▸ **inculper qqn de** to charge sb with.

inculquer [3] [ɛ̃kylke] **vt : inculquer qqch à qqn** to instil *UK* *ou* instill *US* sthg in sb.

inculte [ɛ̃kylt] **adj 1.** [terre] uncultivated **2.** [barbe] unkempt **3.** *péj* [personne] uneducated.

inculture [ɛ̃kyltyr] **nf** **1.** [intellectuelle] lack of education **2.** [de terre] lack of cultivation.

incurable [ɛ̃kyrabl] ■ **nmf** incurably ill person.
■ **adj** incurable.

incurie [ɛ̃kyri] **nf** negligence.

incursion [ɛ̃kyrsjɔ̃] **nf** incursion, foray.

incurver [3] [ɛ̃kyrve] **vt** to curve, to bend.
◆ ***s'incurver*** **vp** to curve, to bend.

Inde [ɛ̃d] **nf : l'Inde** India.

Indes [ɛ̃d] **npr fpl** Indies ▸ **les Indes occidentales/orientales** HIST the West/East Indies ▸ **la Compagnie des Indes orientales** HIST the East India Company.

indéboulonnable [ɛ̃debylɔnabl] **adj : il est indéboulonnable** *hum* they'll never be able to sack him.

indécence [ɛ̃desɑ̃s] **nf** **1.** [impudeur, immoralité] indecency **2.** [propos] indecent remark / [action] indecent act.

indécent, e [ɛ̃desɑ̃, ɑ̃t] **adj** **1.** [impudique] indecent **2.** [immoral] scandalous.

indéchiffrable [ɛ̃deʃifrabl] **adj** **1.** [texte, écriture] indecipherable **2.** [énigme] inexplicable **3.** *fig* [regard] inscrutable, impenetrable.

indéchirable [ɛ̃deʃirabl] **adj** tear-proof.

indécis, e [ɛ̃desi, iz] ■ **adj** **1.** [personne - sur le moment] undecided / [- de nature] indecisive **2.** [sourire] vague **3.** [résultat] uncertain.
■ **nm, f** indecisive person.
◆ ***indécis*** **nmpl** [dans sondage] don't knows.

indécision [ɛ̃desizjɔ̃] **nf** indecision / [perpétuelle] indecisiveness.

indécrottable [ɛ̃dekrɔtabl] **adj** *fam* **1.** [borné] incredibly dumb **2.** [incorrigible] hopeless.

indéfectible [ɛ̃defɛktibl] **adj** indestructible.

indéfendable [ɛ̃defɑ̃dabl] **adj** indefensible.

indéfini, e [ɛ̃defini] **adj** **1.** [quantité, pronom] indefinite **2.** [sentiment] vague.
◆ ***indéfini*** **nm** GRAMM indefinite.

indéfiniment [ɛ̃definimɑ̃] **adv** indefinitely.

indéfinissable [ɛ̃definisabl] **adj** indefinable.

indéformable [ɛ̃defɔrmabl] **adj** able to retain its shape.

indélébile [ɛ̃delebil] **adj** indelible.

indélicat, e [ɛ̃delika, at] **adj** **1.** [mufle] indelicate **2.** [malhonnête] dishonest.

indémaillable [ɛ̃demajabl] ■ **nm** run-resistant material.
■ **adj** run-resistant.

indemne [ɛ̃dɛmn] **adj** unscathed, unharmed ▸ **sortir indemne de qqch** to come out of sthg unscathed *ou* unharmed.

indemnisation [ɛ̃dɛmnizasjɔ̃] **nf** compensation.

indemniser [3] [ɛ̃dɛmnize] **vt : indemniser qqn de qqch** [perte, préjudice] to compensate sb for sthg / [frais] to reimburse sb for sthg.

indemnité [ɛ̃dɛmnite] **nf** **1.** [de perte, préjudice] compensation ▸ **indemnité de licenciement** redundancy payment *UK*, severance pay *US* **2.** [de frais] allowance ▸ **indemnité journalière** daily allowance ▸ **indemnité de logement** accommodation *UK ou* housing *US* allowance **3.** [allocation] **: indemnité parlementaire** MP's *UK ou* Congressman's (f Congresswoman's) *US* salary.

indémodable [ɛ̃demɔdabl] **adj : ce style est indémodable** this style doesn't date.

indéniable [ɛ̃denjabl] **adj** undeniable.

indéniablement [ɛ̃denjabləmɑ̃] **adv** undeniably.

indépendamment [ɛ̃depɑ̃damɑ̃] **adv : indépendamment de** [abstraction faite de] regardless *ou* irrespective of / [outre] apart from / [sans rapport avec] independently of.

indépendance [ɛ̃depɑ̃dɑ̃s] **nf** independence ▸ **accéder à l'indépendance** to gain independence.

indépendant, e [ɛ̃depɑ̃dɑ̃, ɑ̃t] **adj** **1.** [gén] independent / [entrée] separate ▸ **indépendant de** independent of ▸ **indépendant de ma volonté** beyond my control **2.** [travailleur] self-employed.

indépendantiste [ɛ̃depɑ̃dɑ̃tist] ■ **nmf** advocate of political independence.
■ **adj** independence *(avant n)*.

indéracinable [ɛ̃derasinabl] **adj** [arbre] impossible to uproot / *fig* ineradicable.

indescriptible [ɛ̃dɛskriptibl] **adj** indescribable.

indésirable [ɛ̃dezirabl] **nmf & adj** undesirable.

indestructible [ɛ̃dɛstryktibl] **adj** indestructible.

indéterminé, e [ɛ̃detɛrmine] **adj** **1.** [indéfini] indeterminate, indefinite **2.** [vague] vague **3.** [personne] undecided.

indétrônable [ɛ̃detronabl] **adj** inoustable.

index [ɛ̃dɛks] **nm** **1.** [doigt] index finger **2.** [aiguille] pointer, needle **3.** [registre] index ▸ **mettre à l'index** *fig* to blacklist.

indexation [ɛ̃dɛksasjɔ̃] **nf** indexing.

indexer [4] [ɛ̃dɛkse] **vt** **1.** ÉCON **: indexer qqch sur qqch** to index sthg to sthg **2.** [livre] to index.

indic [ɛ̃dik] **nm** *fam* (police) informer.

indicateur, trice [ɛ̃dikatœr, tris] **adj : poteau indicateur** signpost ▸ **panneau indicateur** road sign.
◆ ***indicateur*** **nm** **1.** [guide] directory, guide ▸ **indicateur des chemins de fer** railway timetable *UK*, train schedule *US* **2.** TECHNOL gauge ▸ **indicateur d'altitude** altimeter ▸ **indicateur de vitesse** speedometer **3.** ÉCON indicator ▸ **indicateur de marché** market indicator **4.** [de police] informer.

indicatif, ive [ɛ̃dikatif, iv] **adj** indicative.
◆ ***indicatif*** **nm** **1.** RADIO & TV signature tune **2.** [code] **: indicatif (téléphonique)** dialling code *UK*, area code *US* **3.** GRAMM **: l'indicatif** the indicative.

indication [ɛ̃dikasjɔ̃] **nf** **1.** [mention] indication **2.** [renseignement] information *(U)* **3.** [directive] instruction / THÉÂTRE direction ▸ **sauf indication contraire** unless otherwise instructed.

indice [ɛ̃dis] **nm 1.** [signe] sign **2.** [dans une enquête] clue **3.** [taux] rating ▸ **indice de confiance** ÉCON consumer confidence index ▸ **indice du coût de la vie** ÉCON cost-of-living index ▸ **indice des prix** ÉCON price index ▸ **indice de refroidissement** *Québec* windchill factor **4.** MATH index.

indicible [ɛ̃disibl] **adj** inexpressible.

indien, enne [ɛ̃djɛ̃, ɛn] **adj 1.** [d'Inde] Indian **2.** [d'Amérique] Native American, American Indian.
◆ ***Indien, enne*** **nm, f 1.** [d'Inde] Indian **2.** [d'Amérique] Native American, American Indian.

indifféremment [ɛ̃diferamɑ̃] **adv** indifferently.

indifférence [ɛ̃diferɑ̃s] **nf** indifference.

indifférencié, e [ɛ̃diferɑ̃sje] **adj** undifferentiated.

indifférent, e [ɛ̃diferɑ̃, ɑ̃t] ■ **adj 1.** [gén] **: indifférent à** indifferent to **2.** *sout* [égal] immaterial.
■ **nm, f** unconcerned person.

indifférer [18] [ɛ̃difere] **vt** to be a matter of indifference to.

indigence [ɛ̃diʒɑ̃s] **nf** poverty.

indigène [ɛ̃diʒɛn] ■ **nmf** native.
■ **adj** [peuple] native / [faune, flore] indigenous.

indigent, e [ɛ̃diʒɑ̃, ɑ̃t] ■ **adj** [pauvre] destitute, poverty-stricken / *fig* [intellectuellement] impoverished.
■ **nm, f** poor person ▸ **les indigents** the poor, the destitute.

indigeste [ɛ̃diʒɛst] **adj** indigestible.

indigestion [ɛ̃diʒɛstjɔ̃] **nf 1.** [alimentaire] indigestion *(U)* ▸ **avoir une indigestion** to have indigestion **2.** *fig* [saturation] surfeit ▸ **avoir une indigestion de** to have had one's fill of.

indignation [ɛ̃diɲasjɔ̃] **nf** indignation.

indigne [ɛ̃diɲ] **adj : indigne (de)** unworthy (of).

indigné, e [ɛ̃diɲe] **adj** indignant.

indigner [3] [ɛ̃diɲe] **vt** to make indignant.
◆ ***s'indigner*** **vp : s'indigner de** *ou* **contre qqch** to get indignant about sthg ▸ **s'indigner que** *(+ subjonctif)* to be indignant that.

indigo [ɛ̃digo] ■ **nm** indigo.
■ **adj inv** indigo (blue).

indiqué, e [ɛ̃dike] **adj 1.** [convenable] appropriate **2.** [recommandé] advisable ▸ **ce n'est pas très indiqué** it's not very advisable **3.** [fixé] appointed.

indiquer [3] [ɛ̃dike] **vt 1.** [désigner] to indicate, to point out ▸ **indiquer qqn/qqch du doigt** to point at sb/sthg, to point sb/sthg out ▸ **indiquer qqn/qqch du regard** to glance towards *UK* *ou* toward *US* sb/sthg **2.** [afficher, montrer - suj: carte, pendule, aiguille] to show, to indicate **3.** [recommander] **: indiquer qqn/qqch à qqn** to tell sb of sb/sthg, to suggest sb/sthg to sb **4.** [dire, renseigner sur] to tell ▸ **indiquer à qqn comment faire qqch** to tell sb how to do sthg ▸ **pourriez-vous m'indiquer l'heure?** could you tell me the time? **5.** [fixer - heure, date, lieu] to name, to indicate **6.** [dénoter] to indicate, to point to.

indirect, e [ɛ̃dirɛkt] **adj** [gén] indirect / [itinéraire] roundabout.

indirectement [ɛ̃dirɛktəmɑ̃] **adv** indirectly.

indiscipline [ɛ̃disiplin] **nf** lack of discipline.

indiscipliné, e [ɛ̃disipline] **adj 1.** [écolier, esprit] undisciplined, unruly **2.** *fig* [mèches de cheveux] unmanageable.

indiscret, ète [ɛ̃diskrɛ, ɛt] ■ **adj** indiscreet / [curieux] inquisitive.
■ **nm, f** indiscreet person.

indiscrètement [ɛ̃diskrɛtmɑ̃] **adv** indiscreetly / [avec curiosité] inquisitively.

indiscrétion [ɛ̃diskresjɔ̃] **nf** indiscretion / [curiosité] curiosity ▸ **sans indiscrétion...** without wishing to be indiscreet...

indiscutable [ɛ̃diskytabl] **adj** indisputable, unquestionable.

indiscutablement [ɛ̃diskytabləmɑ̃] **adv** indisputably, unquestionably.

indiscuté, e [ɛ̃diskyte] **adj** undisputed, unquestioned.

indispensable [ɛ̃dispɑ̃sabl] ■ **adj** indispensable, essential ▸ **indispensable à** indispensable to, essential to ▸ **il est indispensable que** *(+ subjonctif)* it is essential *ou* vital that ▸ **il est indispensable de faire qqch** it is essential *ou* vital to do sthg.
■ **nm : l'indispensable** the essentials *pl.*

indisponibilité [ɛ̃dispɔnibilite] **nf** unavailability.

indisponible [ɛ̃dispɔnibl] **adj** unavailable.

indisposé, e [ɛ̃dispoze] **adj** [malade] unwell ▸ **être indisposée** [femme] to be indisposed.

indisposer [3] [ɛ̃dispoze] **vt 1.** *sout* [rendre malade] to indispose **2.** *littéraire* [fâcher] to vex.

indisposition [ɛ̃dispozisjɔ̃] **nf 1.** [malaise] indisposition **2.** [règles] period.

indissociable [ɛ̃disɔsjabl] **adj** indissociable.

indissoluble [ɛ̃disɔlybl] **adj** indissoluble.

indistinct, e [ɛ̃distɛ̃(kt), ɛ̃kt] **adj** indistinct / [souvenir] hazy.

indistinctement [ɛ̃distɛ̃ktəmɑ̃] **adv 1.** [confusément] indistinctly **2.** [indifféremment] equally well.

individu [ɛ̃dividy] **nm** individual.

individualisme [ɛ̃dividɥalism] **nm** individualism.

COMMENT EXPRIMER...

l'indifférence

I don't mind either way / Ça m'est égal
It makes absolutely no difference to me / Pour moi, ça revient au même
I don't care one way or the other / Peu importe, ça m'est égal
I don't mind: you choose / Peu importe, choisis
It all comes down to the same thing / Cela revient au même

individualiste [ɛ̃dividɥalist] ■ **nmf** individualist.
■ **adj** individualistic.

individualité [ɛ̃dividɥalite] **nf 1.** [personne] individual **2.** [unicité, originalité] individuality.

individuel**, **elle [ɛ̃dividɥɛl] **adj** individual.

individuellement [ɛ̃dividɥɛlmɑ̃] **adv** individually.

indivis**, **e [ɛ̃divi, iz] **adj 1.** [propriété] undivided **2.** [héritier] joint ▸ **par indivis** jointly.

indivisible [ɛ̃divizibl] **adj** indivisible.

Indochine [ɛ̃dɔʃin] **nf : l'Indochine** Indochina ▸ **la guerre d'Indochine** the Indochinese War.

indo-européen**, **enne [ɛ̃dɔœrɔpeɛ̃, ɛn] (mpl **indo-européens**, fpl **indo-européennes**) **adj** Indo-European.

indolence [ɛ̃dɔlɑ̃s] **nf 1.** [de personne] indolence, lethargy **2.** [d'organisation] apathy **3.** [de geste, regard] languidness.

indolent**, **e [ɛ̃dɔlɑ̃, ɑ̃t] **adj 1.** [personne] indolent, lethargic **2.** [geste, regard] languid.

indolore [ɛ̃dɔlɔr] **adj** painless.

indomptable [ɛ̃dɔ̃tabl] **adj 1.** [animal] untamable **2.** [personne] indomitable **3.** [sentiment] uncontrollable.

Indonésie [ɛ̃dɔnezi] **nf : l'Indonésie** Indonesia.

indonésien**, **enne [ɛ̃dɔnezjɛ̃, ɛn] **adj** Indonesian.
◆ ***indonésien*** **nm** [langue] Indonesian.
◆ ***Indonésien**, **enne*** **nm, f** Indonesian.

indu**, **e [ɛ̃dy] **adj 1.** [heure] ungodly, unearthly **2.** [dépenses, remarque] unwarranted.

indubitable [ɛ̃dybitabl] **adj** indubitable, undoubted ▸ **il est indubitable que** it is indisputable *ou* beyond doubt that.

indubitablement [ɛ̃dybitabləmɑ̃] **adv** undoubtedly, indubitably.

induction [ɛ̃dyksjɔ̃] **nf** induction ▸ **par induction** by induction.

induire [98] [ɛ̃dɥir] **vt** to induce ▸ **induire qqn à faire qqch** to induce sb to do sthg ▸ **induire qqn en erreur** to mislead sb ▸ **en induire que** to infer *ou* gather that.

induit**, **e [ɛ̃dɥi, ɥit] ■ **pp** ➤ ***induire***.
■ **adj 1.** [consécutif] resulting **2.** ÉLECTR induced.

indulgence [ɛ̃dylʒɑ̃s] **nf** [de juge] leniency / [de parent] indulgence ▸ **avec indulgence** [juge] leniently / [parent] indulgently.

indulgent**, **e [ɛ̃dylʒɑ̃, ɑ̃t] **adj** [juge] lenient / [parent] indulgent.

indûment [ɛ̃dymɑ̃] **adv** unduly.

industrialisation [ɛ̃dystrijalizasjɔ̃] **nf** industrialization.

industrialisé**, **e [ɛ̃dystrijalize] **adj** industrialized ▸ **pays industrialisé** industrialized country.

industrialiser [3] [ɛ̃dystrijalize] **vt** to industrialize.
◆ ***s'industrialiser*** **vp** to become industrialized.

industrie [ɛ̃dystri] **nf** industry ▸ **industrie alimentaire** food industry ▸ **industrie automobile** car industry ▸ **industrie cinématographique** *ou* **du cinéma** movie *ou* film *UK* industry ▸ **industrie chimique** chemical industry ▸ **industrie lourde** heavy industry ▸ **industrie naissante** infant industry ▸ **industrie subventionnée** subsidized industry.

industriel**, **elle [ɛ̃dystrijɛl] **adj** industrial.
◆ ***industriel*** **nm** industrialist.

industrieux**, **euse [ɛ̃dystrijø, øz] **adj** industrious.

inébranlable [inebrɑ̃labl] **adj 1.** [roc] solid, immovable **2.** *fig* [conviction] unshakeable.

INED**, **Ined [inɛd] (abr de ***Institut national d'études démographiques***) **nm** *national institute for demographic research*.

inédit**, **e [inedi, it] **adj 1.** [texte] unpublished **2.** [trouvaille] novel, original.
◆ ***inédit*** **nm** unpublished work.

ineffable [inefabl] **adj** ineffable.

ineffaçable [inefasabl] **adj** indelible.

inefficace [inefikas] **adj 1.** [personne, machine] inefficient **2.** [solution, remède, mesure] ineffective.

inefficacité [inefikasite] **nf 1.** [de personne, machine] inefficiency **2.** [de solution, remède, mesure] ineffectiveness.

inégal**, **e**, **aux [inegal, o] **adj 1.** [différent, disproportionné] unequal **2.** [irrégulier] uneven **3.** [changeant] changeable / [artiste, travail] erratic.

inégalable [inegalabl] **adj** matchless.

inégalé**, **e [inegale] **adj** unequalled *UK*, unequaled *US*.

inégalement [inegalmɑ̃] **adv** [gén] unequally / [irrégulièrement] unevenly.

inégalité [inegalite] **nf 1.** [injustice, disproportion] inequality ▸ **inégalités sociales** social inequalities **2.** [différence] difference, disparity **3.** [irrégularité] unevenness **4.** [d'humeur] changeability.

inélégant**, **e [inelegɑ̃, ɑ̃t] **adj 1.** [dans l'habillement] inelegant **2.** *fig* [indélicat] discourteous.

COMMENT EXPRIMER...

l'indignation

You can't be serious! / Tu plaisantes !
You must be joking! / Tu veux rire !
I beg your pardon! / Pardon ?!
How dare she call me a liar! / Comment ose-t-elle me traiter de menteur !
Who does he think he is! / Pour qui est-ce qu'il se prend !
What business is it of yours? / Qu'est-ce que ça peut te faire ?
The way we have been treated is quite unacceptable / La façon dont on nous a traités est inadmissible

inéligible [inelizibl] **adj** ineligible.

inéluctable [inelyktabl] **adj** inescapable.

inéluctablement [inelyktabləmɑ̃] **adv** inescapably.

inénarrable [inenarabl] **adj** very funny.

inepte [inɛpt] **adj** inept.

ineptie [inɛpsi] **nf 1.** [bêtise] ineptitude **2.** [chose idiote] nonsense *(U)* ▸ **dire des inepties** to talk nonsense.

inépuisable [inepɥizabl] **adj** inexhaustible.

inerte [inɛrt] **adj 1.** [corps, membre] lifeless **2.** [personne] passive, inert **3.** PHYS inert.

inertie [inɛrsi] **nf 1.** [manque de réaction] apathy, inertia **2.** PHYS inertia.

inespéré**, **e [inɛspere] **adj** unexpected, unhoped-for.

inesthétique [inɛstetik] **adj** unaesthetic *UK*, unesthetic *US*.

inestimable [inɛstimabl] **adj : d'une valeur inestimable** priceless / *fig* invaluable.

inévitable [inevitabl] **adj** [obstacle] unavoidable / [conséquence] inevitable.

inévitablement [inevitabləmɑ̃] **adv** inevitably.

inexact**, **e [inɛgza(kt), akt] **adj 1.** [faux, incomplet] inaccurate, inexact **2.** [en retard] unpunctual.

inexactitude [inɛgzaktityd] **nf 1.** [erreur, imprécision] inaccuracy **2.** [retard] unpunctuality.

inexcusable [inɛkskyzabl] **adj** unforgivable, inexcusable.

inexistant**, **e [inɛgzistɑ̃, ɑ̃t] **adj** nonexistent.

inexistence [inɛgzistɑ̃s] **nf** nonexistence.

inexorable [inɛgzɔrabl] **adj** inexorable.

inexorablement [inɛgzɔrabləmɑ̃] **adv** inexorably.

inexpérience [inɛksperjɑ̃s] **nf** lack of experience, inexperience.

inexpérimenté**, **e [inɛksperimɑ̃te] **adj 1.** [personne] inexperienced **2.** [gestes] inexpert **3.** [produit] untested.

inexplicable [inɛksplikabl] **adj** inexplicable, unexplainable.

inexpliqué**, **e [inɛksplike] **adj** unexplained.

inexploré**, **e [inɛksplɔre] **adj** *litt* & *fig* unexplored / [mers] uncharted.

inexpressif**, **ive [inɛkspresif, iv] **adj** inexpressive.

inexprimable [inɛksprimabl] **adj** inexpressible.

inexprimé**, **e [inɛksprime] **adj** unexpressed.

inexpugnable [inɛkspygnabl] **adj** impregnable.

inextensible [inɛkstɑ̃sibl] **adj 1.** [matériau] unstretchable **2.** [étoffe] non-stretch.

inextinguible [inɛkstɛ̃gibl] **adj** [passion] inextinguishable / [soif] unquenchable / [rire] uncontrollable.

in extremis [inɛkstremis] **adv** at the last minute.

inextricable [inɛkstrikabl] **adj 1.** [fouillis] inextricable **2.** *fig* [affaire, mystère] impossible to unravel.

inextricablement [inɛkstrikabləmɑ̃] **adv** inextricably.

infaillible [ɛ̃fajibl] **adj** [personne, méthode] infallible / [instinct] unerring.

infaisable [ɛ̃fəzabl] **adj** unfeasible.

infamant**, **e [ɛ̃famɑ̃, ɑ̃t] **adj** [marché] dishonourable *UK*, dishonorable *US* / [propos] defamatory.

infâme [ɛ̃fam] **adj 1.** [ignoble] despicable **2.** *hum* & *littéraire* [dégoûtant] vile.

infamie [ɛ̃fami] **nf** infamy.

infanterie [ɛ̃fɑ̃tri] **nf** infantry.

infanticide [ɛ̃fɑ̃tisid] ■ **nmf** infanticide, child-killer.
■ **adj** infanticidal.

infantile [ɛ̃fɑ̃til] **adj 1.** [maladie] childhood *(avant n)* **2.** [médecine] for children **3.** [comportement] infantile.

infantiliser [3] [ɛ̃fɑ̃tilize] **vt** to treat like a child.

infarctus [ɛ̃farktys] **nm** infarction, infarct ▸ **infarctus du myocarde** coronary thrombosis, myocardial infarction.

infatigable [ɛ̃fatigabl] **adj 1.** [personne] tireless **2.** [attitude] untiring.

infatué**, **e [ɛ̃fatɥe] **adj** *péj* & *sout* **: infatué de** conceited about ▸ **infatué de soi-même** self-important.

infect**, **e [ɛ̃fɛkt] **adj 1.** [dégoûtant] vile **2.** *littéraire* [marais] foul.

infecter [4] [ɛ̃fɛkte] **vt 1.** [eau] to contaminate **2.** [plaie] to infect **3.** [empoisonner] to poison.
◆ ***s'infecter*** **vp** to become infected, to turn septic.

infectieux**, **euse [ɛ̃fɛksjø, øz] **adj** infectious.

infection [ɛ̃fɛksjɔ̃] **nf 1.** MÉD infection **2.** *fig* & *péj* [puanteur] stench.

inféoder [3] [ɛ̃feɔde] ◆ ***s'inféoder*** **vp : s'inféoder à** to pledge one's allegiance to.

inférer [18] [ɛ̃fere] **vt** *littéraire* **: inférer qqch de qqch** to infer sthg from sthg.

inférieur**, **e [ɛ̃ferjœr] ■ **adj 1.** [qui est en bas] lower ▸ **c'est à l'étage inférieur** it's on the floor below *ou* on the next floor down **2.** [dans une hiérarchie] inferior ▸ **inférieur à** [qualité] inferior to / [quantité] less than ▸ **des températures inférieures à 10° C** temperatures below 10°C *ou* lower than 10°C ▸ **inférieur ou égal à 8** MATH less than or equal to 8 ▸ **nous (leur) étions inférieurs en nombre** there were fewer of us (than of them) ▸ **se sentir inférieur (par rapport à qqn)** to feel inferior (to sb) ▸ **animaux/végétaux inférieurs** BOT & ZOOL lower animals/plants.
■ **nm, f** inferior.

infériorité [ɛ̃ferjɔrite] **nf** inferiority.

infernal**, **e**, **aux [ɛ̃fɛrnal, o] **adj 1.** [personne] fiendish **2.** *fig* [bruit, chaleur, rythme] infernal / [vision] diabolical.

infester [3] [ɛ̃fɛste] **vt** to infest ▸ **être infesté de** [rats, moustiques] to be infested with / [touristes] to be overrun by.

infidèle [ɛ̃fidɛl] ■ **adj 1.** [mari, femme, ami] **: infidèle (à)** unfaithful (to) **2.** [traducteur, historien] inaccurate **3.** *vieilli* & RELIG infidel.
■ **nmf** *vieilli* & RELIG infidel.

infidélité [ɛ̃fidelite] **nf 1.** [trahison] infidelity ▸ **faire des infidélités à** to be unfaithful to **2.** [de traduction] inaccuracy **3.** [de mémoire] unreliability.

infiltration [ɛ̃filtrasjɔ̃] **nf** infiltration.

infiltrer [3] [ɛ̃filtre] **vt** to infiltrate.
◆ ***s'infiltrer*** **vp 1.** [pluie, lumière] **: s'infiltrer par/dans** to filter through/into **2.** [hommes, idées] to infiltrate.

infime [ɛ̃fim] **adj** minute, infinitesimal.

infini, e [ɛ̃fini] **adj 1.** [sans bornes] infinite, boundless **2.** MATH, PHILO & RELIG infinite **3.** *fig* [interminable] endless, interminable.
◆ ***infini*** **nm** infinity.
◆ ***à l'infini*** **loc adv 1.** MATH to infinity **2.** [discourir] ad infinitum, endlessly.

infiniment [ɛ̃finimɑ̃] **adv** extremely, immensely.

infinité [ɛ̃finite] **nf** infinity, infinite number.

infinitésimal, e, aux [ɛ̃finitezimal, o] **adj** infinitesimal.

infinitif, ive [ɛ̃finitif, iv] **adj** infinitive.
◆ ***infinitif*** **nm** infinitive.

infirme [ɛ̃firm] ■ **adj** [handicapé] disabled / [avec l'âge] infirm.
■ **nmf** disabled person ▸ **infirme de guerre** disabled ex-serviceman (f ex-servicewoman).

infirmer [3] [ɛ̃firme] **vt 1.** [démentir] to invalidate **2.** DR to annul.

infirmerie [ɛ̃firməri] **nf** infirmary.

infirmier, ère [ɛ̃firmje, ɛr] **nm, f** nurse ▸ **infirmier diplômé** ≃ registered nurse.

infirmité [ɛ̃firmite] **nf** [handicap] disability / [de vieillesse] infirmity.

inflammable [ɛ̃flamabl] **adj** inflammable, flammable.

inflammation [ɛ̃flamasjɔ̃] **nf** inflammation.

inflation [ɛ̃flasjɔ̃] **nf** ÉCON inflation ▸ **inflation galopante** galoping inflation / *fig* increase.

inflationniste [ɛ̃flasjɔnist] **adj & nmf** inflationist.

infléchir [32] [ɛ̃fleʃir] **vt** *fig* [politique] to modify.
◆ ***s'infléchir*** **vp 1.** [route] to bend **2.** *fig* [politique] to shift.

inflexible [ɛ̃flɛksibl] **adj** inflexible.

inflexion [ɛ̃flɛksjɔ̃] **nf 1.** [de tête] nod **2.** [de voix] inflection **3.** [de route] bend **4.** *fig* [de politique] shift.

infliger [17] [ɛ̃fliʒe] **vt : infliger qqch à qqn** to inflict sthg on sb / [amende] to impose sthg on sb.

influençable [ɛ̃flyɑ̃sabl] **adj** easily influenced.

influence [ɛ̃flyɑ̃s] **nf** influence / [de médicament] effect ▸ **avoir de l'influence sur qqn** to have an influence on sb ▸ **avoir une bonne/mauvaise influence sur** [suj: personne] to have a good/bad influence on, to be a good/bad influence on / [suj: chose] to have a good/bad effect on ▸ **agir sous l'influence de qqch** to act under the influence of sthg.

influencer [16] [ɛ̃flyɑ̃se] **vt** to influence.

influent, e [ɛ̃flyɑ̃, ɑ̃t] **adj** influential.

influer [3] [ɛ̃flye] **vi : influer sur qqch** to influence sthg, to have an effect on sthg.

influx [ɛ̃fly] **nm : influx nerveux** nerve impulse.

info [ɛ̃fo] **nf** *fam* info *(U)* ▸ **c'est lui qui m'a donné cette info** I got the info from him.
◆ ***infos*** **nfpl** *fam* **: les infos** the news *(U)*.

Infographie® [ɛ̃fɔgrafi] **nf** computer graphics *(U)*.

infographique [ɛ̃fɔgrafik] **adj** computer graphics *(avant n)*.

informateur, trice [ɛ̃fɔrmatœr, tris] **nm, f 1.** [qui renseigne] informant **2.** [de police] informer.

informaticien, enne [ɛ̃fɔrmatisjɛ̃, ɛn] **nm, f** computer scientist.

information [ɛ̃fɔrmasjɔ̃] **nf 1.** [renseignement] piece of information ▸ **demander des informations sur** to ask (for information) about, to inquire about **2.** [renseignements & INFORM] information *(U)* ▸ **l'information circule mal entre les services** there's poor communication between departments ▸ **la liberté d'information** freedom of information ▸ **protection de l'information** data protection ▸ **réunion d'information** briefing session ▸ **informations sur le lieu de vente** point-of-sale information, point-of-purchase information **3.** [nouvelle] piece of news ▸ **voici une information de dernière minute** here is some last minute news **4.** DR inquiry ▸ **ouvrir une information** to set up a preliminary inquiry.
◆ ***informations*** **nfpl** [média] news *sg* ▸ **c'est passé aux informations** it was on the news.

informatique [ɛ̃fɔrmatik] ■ **nf 1.** [technique] computers ▸ **informatique de gestion** business applications *pl* **2.** [science] computer science, information technology.
■ **adj** computer *(avant n)*.

informatisation [ɛ̃fɔrmatizasjɔ̃] **nf** computerization.

informatiser [3] [ɛ̃fɔrmatize] **vt** to computerize.
◆ ***s'informatiser*** **vp** to become computerized.

informe [ɛ̃fɔrm] **adj 1.** [masse, vêtement, silhouette] shapeless **2.** *fig* [projet] sketchy, rough.

informé, e [ɛ̃fɔrme] **adj** informed ▸ **bien/mal informé** well/badly informed.
◆ ***informé*** **nm : jusqu'à plus ample informé** pending further information.

informel, elle [ɛ̃fɔrmɛl] **adj** informal.

informer [3] [ɛ̃fɔrme] ■ **vt** to inform ▸ **informer qqn sur** *ou* **de qqch** to inform sb about sthg.
■ **vi** DR **: informer contre qqn/sur qqch** to investigate sb/sthg.
◆ ***s'informer*** **vp** to inform o.s. ▸ **s'informer de qqch** to ask about sthg ▸ **s'informer sur qqch** to find out about sthg.

infortune [ɛ̃fɔrtyn] **nf** misfortune.

***infortuné**, e* [ɛ̃fɔrtyne] *littéraire* & *vieilli* ■ **adj** wretched.
■ **nm, f** *(gén pl)* unfortunate.

infraction [ɛ̃fraksjɔ̃] **nf** offence *UK ou* offense *US* ▸ **infraction à** infringement *ou* breach of ▸ **être en infraction** to be in breach of the law.

infranchissable [ɛ̃frɑ̃ʃisabl] **adj** insurmountable.

infrarouge [ɛ̃fraruʒ] **nm** & **adj** infrared.

infrastructure [ɛ̃frastryktyr] **nf** infrastructure ▸ **infrastructure hôtelière** hotel facilities *pl*.

infréquentable [ɛ̃frekɑ̃tabl] **adj 1.** [personne] **: il est infréquentable** you shouldn't mix with him **2.** [lieu] **: ce café est infréquentable** it's not the kind of café you should go to.

infroissable [ɛ̃frwasabl] **adj** crease-resistant.

***infructueux**, euse* [ɛ̃fryktɥø, øz] **adj** fruitless.

infuse [ɛ̃fyz] ➤ ***science***.

infuser [3] [ɛ̃fyze] ■ **vt 1.** [tisane] to infuse / [thé] to brew ▸ **laisser infuser** to leave to infuse *ou* brew **2.** *fig* & *littéraire* **: infuser qqch à qqn/qqch** to infuse sb/sthg with sthg.
■ **vi** [tisane] to infuse / [thé] to brew.

infusion [ɛ̃fyzjɔ̃] **nf** infusion.

ingambe [ɛ̃gɑ̃b] **adj** spry.

ingénier [9] [ɛ̃ʒenje] ◆ ***s'ingénier*** **vp : s'ingénier à faire qqch** to try hard to do sthg.

ingénierie [ɛ̃ʒeniri] **nf** engineering.

ingénieur [ɛ̃ʒenjœr] **nm** engineer ▸ **ingénieur agronome/chimiste/électronicien** agricultural/chemical/electronics engineer ▸ **ingénieur des mines** mining engineer ▸ **ingénieur des ponts et chaussées** civil engineer ▸ **ingénieur du son** sound engineer ▸ **ingénieur des travaux publics** civil engineer.

***ingénieux**, euse* [ɛ̃ʒenjø, øz] **adj** ingenious.

ingéniosité [ɛ̃ʒenjozite] **nf** ingenuity.

***ingénu**, e* [ɛ̃ʒeny] ■ **adj** *littéraire* [candide] artless / *hum* & *péj* [trop candide] naïve.
■ **nm, f** *littéraire* [candide] naïve person / THÉÂTRE ingénue ▸ **jouer les ingénus** THÉÂTRE to play ingénue roles / [dans la vie] to act the sweet young thing.

ingénuité [ɛ̃ʒenɥite] **nf** naïvety.

ingénument [ɛ̃ʒenymɑ̃] **adv** naïvely.

ingérable [ɛ̃ʒerabl] **adj** unmanageable.

ingérence [ɛ̃ʒerɑ̃s] **nf : ingérence dans** interference in.

ingérer [18] [ɛ̃ʒere] **vt** to ingest.
◆ ***s'ingérer*** **vp : s'ingérer dans** to interfere in.

***ingrat**, e* [ɛ̃gra, at] ■ **adj 1.** [personne] ungrateful **2.** [métier] thankless, unrewarding **3.** [sol] barren **4.** [physique] unattractive.
■ **nm, f** ungrateful person, ingrate.

ingratitude [ɛ̃gratityd] **nf** ingratitude.

ingrédient [ɛ̃gredjɑ̃] **nm** ingredient.

inguérissable [ɛ̃gerisabl] **adj** incurable.

ingurgiter [3] [ɛ̃gyrʒite] **vt 1.** [avaler] to swallow **2.** *fig* [connaissances] to absorb.

inhabitable [inabitabl] **adj** uninhabitable.

***inhabité**, e* [inabite] **adj** uninhabited.

FAUX AMIS / FALSE FRIENDS

inhabité

Inhabited is not a translation of the French word *inhabité*. Inhabited is translated by ***habité***.
▸ The island is no longer inhabited / *L'île n'est plus habitée*

***inhabituel**, elle* [inabitɥɛl] **adj** unusual.

***inhalateur**, trice* [inalatœr, tris] **adj : appareil inhalateur** inhaler.
◆ ***inhalateur*** **nm** inhaler.

inhalation [inalasjɔ̃] **nf** inhalation.

inhaler [3] [inale] **vt** to inhale, to breathe in.

***inhérent**, e* [inerɑ̃, ɑ̃t] **adj : inhérent à** inherent in.

inhiber [3] [inibe] **vt** to inhibit.

inhibition [inibisjɔ̃] **nf** inhibition.

***inhospitalier**, ère* [inɔspitalje, ɛr] **adj** inhospitable.

***inhumain**, e* [inymɛ̃, ɛn] **adj** inhuman.

inhumation [inymasjɔ̃] **nf** burial.

inhumer [3] [inyme] **vt** to bury.

inimaginable [inimaʒinabl] **adj** incredible, unimaginable.

inimitable [inimitabl] **adj** inimitable.

inimitié [inimitje] **nf : inimitié contre** *ou* **à l'égard de** enmity towards *UK ou* toward *US*.

ininflammable [inɛ̃flamabl] **adj** non-flammable.

inintelligible [inɛ̃teliʒibl] **adj** unintelligible.

***inintéressant**, e* [inɛ̃terɛsɑ̃, ɑ̃t] **adj** uninteresting.

***ininterrompu**, e* [inɛ̃tɛrɔ̃py] **adj** [file, vacarme] uninterrupted / [ligne, suite] unbroken / [travail, effort] continuous.

inique [inik] **adj** iniquitous.

iniquité [inikite] **nf** iniquity.

***initial**, e, aux* [inisjal, o] **adj** [lettre] initial.
◆ ***initiale*** **nf** initial.

initialement [inisjalmɑ̃] **adv** initially.

initialiser [3] [inisjalize] **vt** INFORM to initialize.

***initiateur**, trice* [inisjatœr, tris] ■ **adj** innovative.
■ **nm, f 1.** [maître] initiator **2.** [précurseur] innovator.

initiation [inisjasjɔ̃] **nf : initiation (à)** [discipline] introduction (to) / [rituel] initiation (into).

initiatique [inisjatik] **adj** [rite] initiation *(avant n)*.

initiative [inisjativ] **nf** initiative ▸ **avoir de l'initiative** to have initiative ▸ **prendre l'initiative de qqch/de faire qqch** to take the initiative for sthg/in doing sthg ▸ **de sa propre initiative** on one's own initiative.

***initié**, e* [inisje] ■ **adj** initiated.
■ **nm, f** initiate.

initier [9] [inisje] **vt : initier qqn à** to initiate sb into.
◆ ***s'initier*** **vp : s'initier à** to familiarize o.s. with.

injecté, e [ɛ̃ʒɛkte] **adj : yeux injectés de sang** bloodshot eyes.

injecter [4] [ɛ̃ʒɛkte] **vt** to inject.
◆ ***s'injecter*** **vp** [yeux] **: s'injecter (de sang)** to become bloodshot.

injection [ɛ̃ʒɛksjɔ̃] **nf** injection.

injoignable [ɛ̃jwaɲabl] **adj : j'ai essayé de lui téléphoner mais il est injoignable** I tried to phone him but I couldn't get through to him *ou* reach him *ou* get hold of him.

injonction [ɛ̃ʒɔ̃ksjɔ̃] **nf** injunction.

injure [ɛ̃ʒyr] **nf** insult ▸ **abreuver qqn d'injures** to hurl insults at sb.

FAUX AMIS / FALSE FRIENDS
injure

Injury is not a translation of the French word *injure*. Injury is translated by *blessure*.
▸ He suffered a serious injury / *Il souffre d'une grave blessure*

injurier [9] [ɛ̃ʒyrje] **vt** to insult.
◆ ***s'injurier*** **vp** *(emploi réciproque)* to insult each other ▸ **les chauffeurs de taxi se sont injuriés** the taxi drivers hurled insults at each other.

injurieux, euse [ɛ̃ʒyrjø, øz] **adj** abusive, insulting.

injuste [ɛ̃ʒyst] **adj** unjust, unfair.

injustement [ɛ̃ʒystəmɑ̃] **adv** unjustly, unfairly.

injustice [ɛ̃ʒystis] **nf** injustice.

injustifiable [ɛ̃ʒystifjabl] **adj** unjustifiable.

injustifié, e [ɛ̃ʒystifje] **adj** unjustified.

inlassable [ɛ̃lasabl] **adj** tireless.

inlassablement [ɛ̃lasabləmɑ̃] **adv** tirelessly.

inné, e [ine] **adj** innate.

innocemment [inɔsamɑ̃] **adv** innocently.

innocence [inɔsɑ̃s] **nf** innocence.

innocent, e [inɔsɑ̃, ɑ̃t] ■ **adj** innocent.
■ **nm, f 1.** DR innocent person **2.** [inoffensif, candide] innocent ▸ **faire l'innocent** *fig* to play the innocent **3.** *vieilli* [idiot] simpleton.

innocenter [3] [inɔsɑ̃te] **vt 1.** DR to clear **2.** *fig* [excuser] to justify.

innocuité [inɔkɥite] **nf** harmlessness, innocuousness.

innombrable [inɔ̃brabl] **adj** innumerable / [foule] vast.

innovateur, trice [inɔvatœr, tris] ■ **adj** innovatory.
■ **nm, f** innovator.

innovation [inɔvasjɔ̃] **nf** innovation.

innover [3] [inɔve] **vi** to innovate ▸ **innover en matière de** to innovate in the field of.

inobservation [inɔpsɛrvasjɔ̃] **nf** inobservance.

inoccupé, e [inɔkype] **adj 1.** [lieu] empty, unoccupied **2.** [personne, vie] idle.

inoculation [inɔkylasjɔ̃] **nf** [volontaire] inoculation / [accidentelle] infection.

inoculer [3] [inɔkyle] **vt** MÉD **: inoculer qqch à qqn** [volontairement] to inoculate sb with sthg / [accidentellement] to infect sb with sthg.

inodore [inɔdɔr] **adj** odourless *UK*, odorless *US*.

inoffensif, ive [inɔfɑ̃sif, iv] **adj** harmless.

inondable [inɔ̃dabl] **adj** liable to flooding.

inondation [inɔ̃dasjɔ̃] **nf 1.** [action] flooding **2.** [résultat] flood.

inonder [3] [inɔ̃de] **vt** to flood ▸ **inonder de** *fig* to flood with.

inopérable [inɔperabl] **adj** inoperable.

inopérant, e [inɔperɑ̃, ɑ̃t] **adj** ineffective.

inopiné, e [inɔpine] **adj** unexpected.

inopinément [inɔpinemɑ̃] **adv** unexpectedly.

inopportun, e [inɔpɔrtœ̃, yn] **adj** inopportune.

inorganisé, e [inɔrganize] ■ **adj 1.** [sans organisation] disorganized **2.** [politiquement] independent / [syndicalement] non-union *(avant n)*.
■ **nm, f** [politiquement] independent / [syndicalement] non-union member.

inoubliable [inublijabl] **adj** unforgettable.

inouï, e [inwi] **adj** incredible, extraordinary.

Inox® [inɔks] **nm inv & adj inv** stainless steel.

inoxydable [inɔksidabl] ■ **adj** stainless / [casserole] stainless-steel.
■ **nm** stainless steel.

inqualifiable [ɛ̃kalifjabl] **adj** unspeakable.

inquiet, ète [ɛ̃kjɛ, ɛt] ■ **adj 1.** [gén] anxious **2.** [tourmenté] feverish.
■ **nm, f** worrier.

inquiétant, e [ɛ̃kjetɑ̃, ɑ̃t] **adj** disturbing, worrying.

inquiéter [18] [ɛ̃kjete] **vt 1.** [donner du souci à] to worry ▸ **il n'est pas encore arrivé? tu m'inquiètes!** hasn't he arrived yet? you've got me worried now! ▸ **son silence m'inquiète beaucoup** I find her silence quite disturbing *ou* worrying **2.** [déranger] to disturb ▸ **le magistrat ne fut jamais inquiété par la police** the police never troubled the magistrate.
◆ ***s'inquiéter*** **vp 1.** [s'alarmer] to be worried ▸ **s'inquiéter au sujet de** *ou* **pour qqn** to be worried *ou* concerned about sb **2.** [se préoccuper] **: s'inquiéter de** [s'enquérir de] to enquire about / [se soucier de] to worry about ▸ **et son cadeau? – je m'en inquiéterai plus tard** what about her present? – I'll see about that *ou* take care of that later ▸ **où tu vas? – t'inquiète!** *fam* where are you off to? – mind your own business! *ou* what's it to you?

inquiétude [ɛ̃kjetyd] **nf** anxiety, worry.

inquisiteur, trice [ɛ̃kizitœr, tris] **adj** prying.

INR (abr de ***Institut national de radiodiffusion***) **nm** *Belgian broadcasting company*.

INRA, Inra [inra] (abr de ***Institut national de la recherche agronomique***) **nm** *national institute for agronomic research*.

insaisissable [ɛ̃sezisabl] **adj 1.** [personne] elusive **2.** *fig* [nuance] imperceptible.

insalubre [ɛ̃salybr] **adj** unhealthy.

insalubrité [ɛ̃salybrite] **nf** unhealthiness.

insanité [ɛ̃sanite] **nf 1.** [déraison] insanity, madness **2.** [propos] **: dire *ou* proférer des insanités** to say insane things **3.** [acte] insane act.

insatiable [ɛ̃sasjabl] **adj** insatiable.

insatisfait, e [ɛ̃satisfɛ, ɛt] ■ **adj 1.** [personne] dissatisfied **2.** [sentiment] unsatisfied.
■ **nm, f** malcontent.

insaturé, e [ɛ̃satyre] **adj** unsaturated.

inscriptible [ɛ̃skriptibl] **adj** INFORM recordable.

inscription [ɛ̃skripsjɔ̃] **nf 1.** [action, écrit] inscription **2.** [enregistrement] enrolment *UK*, enrollment *US*, registration **3.** DR registration.

inscrire [99] [ɛ̃skrir] **vt 1.** [écrire] to write down ▸ **inscris ton nom au tableau/sur la feuille** write your name (up) on the board/(down) on the sheet **2.** [graver] to inscribe **3.** [personne] **: inscrire qqn à qqch** to enrol *UK ou* enroll *US* sb for sthg, to register sb for sthg ▸ **les étudiants inscrits en droit** the students enrolled on *UK ou* in *US* the law course ▸ **être inscrit à un club** to be a member of a club ▸ **inscrire qqn sur qqch** to put sb's name down on sthg ▸ **se faire inscrire sur les listes électorales** to register as a voter, to put one's name on the electoral register **4.** SPORT [but] to score **5.** [inclure] to list, to include ▸ **inscrire qqch au budget** to budget for sthg ▸ **inscrire une question à l'ordre du jour** to put *ou* to place a question on the agenda.
◆ ***s'inscrire*** **vp 1.** [personne] **: s'inscrire à qqch** to enrol *UK ou* enroll *US* for sthg, to register for sthg ▸ **s'inscrire au chômage** to register as unemployed ▸ **s'inscrire sur qqch** to put one's name down on sthg ▸ **s'inscrire sur une liste électorale** to register to vote **2.** [s'insérer] **: s'inscrire dans** to come within the scope of ▸ **cette mesure s'inscrit dans le cadre de notre campagne** this measure comes *ou* lies within the framework of our campaign
▸▸ **s'inscrire en faux contre qqch** to deny sthg vigorously.

inscrit, e [ɛ̃skri, it] ■ **pp** ➤ ***inscrire***.
■ **adj** [sur liste] registered ▸ **être inscrit sur une liste** to have one's name on a list.
■ **nm, f** registered person.

inscrivais, inscrivions ➤ ***inscrire***.

INSEAD [insead] (abr de ***Institut européen d'administration***) **nm** *European business school in Fontainebleau*.

insecte [ɛ̃sɛkt] **nm** insect.

insecticide [ɛ̃sɛktisid] **nm & adj** insecticide.

insectivore [ɛ̃sɛktivɔr] ■ **adj** insectivorous.
■ **nm** insectivore.

insécurité [ɛ̃sekyrite] **nf** insecurity.

INSEE, Insee [inse] (abr de ***Institut national de la statistique et des études économiques***) **nm** *national institute of statistics and information about the economy*.

insémination [ɛ̃seminasjɔ̃] **nf** insemination ▸ **insémination artificielle** artificial insemination.

insensé, e [ɛ̃sɑ̃se] **adj 1.** [déraisonnable] insane **2.** [incroyable, excentrique] extraordinary.

insensibiliser [3] [ɛ̃sɑ̃sibilize] **vt** to anaesthetize, to anesthetize *US* ▸ **insensibiliser qqn (à)** *fig* to make sb insensitive (to).

insensibilité [ɛ̃sɑ̃sibilite] **nf : insensibilité (à)** insensitivity (to).

insensible [ɛ̃sɑ̃sibl] **adj 1.** [gén] **: insensible (à)** insensitive (to) **2.** [imperceptible] imperceptible.

insensiblement [ɛ̃sɑ̃sibləmɑ̃] **adv** imperceptibly.

inséparable [ɛ̃separabl] **adj : inséparable (de)** inseparable (from).
◆ ***inséparables*** **nmpl** [perruches] lovebirds.

insérer [18] [ɛ̃sere] **vt** to insert ▸ **insérer une annonce dans un journal** to put an advertisement in a newspaper.
◆ ***s'insérer*** **vp 1.** [s'intégrer] **: s'insérer dans** to fit into **2.** [s'attacher] to be attached.

INSERM, Inserm [insɛrm] (abr de ***Institut national de la santé et de la recherche médicale***) **nm** *national institute for medical research*.

insertion [ɛ̃sɛrsjɔ̃] **nf 1.** [d'objet, de texte] insertion **2.** [de personne] integration.

insidieusement [ɛ̃sidjøzmɑ̃] **adv** insidiously.

insidieux, euse [ɛ̃sidjø, øz] **adj** insidious.

insigne [ɛ̃siɲ] ■ **nm** badge.
■ **adj 1.** *littéraire* [honneur] distinguished **2.** *hum* [maladresse] remarkable.

insignifiant, e [ɛ̃siɲifjɑ̃, ɑ̃t] **adj** insignificant.

insinuant, e [ɛ̃sinɥɑ̃, ɑ̃t] **adj** ingratiating.

insinuation [ɛ̃sinɥasjɔ̃] **nf** insinuation, innuendo.

insinuer [7] [ɛ̃sinɥe] **vt** to insinuate, to imply.
◆ ***s'insinuer*** **vp : s'insinuer dans** [eau, humidité, odeur] to seep into / *fig* [personne] to insinuate o.s. into.

insipide [ɛ̃sipid] **adj** [aliment] insipid, tasteless / *fig* insipid.

insistance [ɛ̃sistɑ̃s] **nf** insistence ▸ **avec insistance** insistently.

insistant, e [ɛ̃sistɑ̃, ɑ̃t] **adj** insistent.

insister [3] [ɛ̃siste] **vi** to insist ▸ **insister sur** to insist on ▸ **insister pour faire qqch** to insist on doing sthg.

insolation [ɛ̃sɔlasjɔ̃] **nf 1.** [malaise] sunstroke *(U)* **2.** [ensoleillement] sunshine.

insolence [ɛ̃sɔlɑ̃s] **nf** insolence *(U)*.

insolent, e [ɛ̃sɔlɑ̃, ɑ̃t] ■ **adj 1.** [personne, acte] insolent **2.** [joie, succès] unashamed, blatant.
■ **nm, f** insolent person.

insolite [ɛ̃sɔlit] **adj** unusual.

insoluble [ɛ̃sɔlybl] **adj 1.** CHIM insoluble, insolvable *US* **2.** [problème] insoluble, insolvable *US*.

insolvable [ɛ̃sɔlvabl] ■ **adj** insolvent.
■ **nmf** bankrupt.

insomniaque [ɛ̃sɔmnjak] **nmf & adj** insomniac.

insomnie [ɛ̃sɔmni] **nf** insomnia *(U)* ▸ **avoir des insomnies** to suffer from insomnia.

insondable [ɛ̃sɔ̃dabl] **adj** [gouffre, mystère] unfathomable / [bêtise] abysmal.

insonore [ɛ̃sɔnɔr] **adj** soundproof.

insonorisation [ɛ̃sɔnɔrizasjɔ̃] **nf** soundproofing.

insonoriser [3] [ɛ̃sɔnɔrize] **vt** to soundproof.

insouciance [ɛ̃susjɑ̃s] **nf 1.** [inconscience] **: insouciance (de)** lack of concern (about) **2.** [légèreté] carefree attitude.

insouciant, e [ɛ̃susjɑ̃, ɑ̃t] **adj 1.** [sans-souci] carefree **2.** [inconscient] **: insouciant (de)** unconcerned (about).

insoumis, e [ɛ̃sumi, iz] **adj 1.** [caractère] rebellious **2.** [peuple] unsubjugated **3.** [soldat] deserting *(avant n).*
◆ ***insoumis*** **nm** deserter, draft dodger *US*.

insoumission [ɛ̃sumisjɔ̃] **nf 1.** [caractère rebelle] rebelliousness **2.** MIL desertion.

insoupçonné, e [ɛ̃supsɔne] **adj** unsuspected.

insoutenable [ɛ̃sutnabl] **adj 1.** [rythme] unsustainable **2.** [scène, violence] unbearable **3.** [théorie] untenable.

inspecter [4] [ɛ̃spɛkte] **vt** to inspect.

inspecteur, trice [ɛ̃spɛktœr, tris] **nm, f** inspector ▸ **inspecteur des finances** ≃ tax inspector *UK*, ≃ Internal Revenue Service agent *US* ▸ **inspecteur de police** police inspector.

inspection [ɛ̃spɛksjɔ̃] **nf 1.** [contrôle] inspection ▸ **faire l'inspection de qqch** to inspect sthg **2.** [fonction] inspectorate ▸ **inspection générale des Finances** ≃ Inland Revenue *UK*, ≃ Internal Revenue Service *US*.

inspiration [ɛ̃spirasjɔ̃] **nf 1.** [gén] inspiration / [idée] bright idea, brainwave *UK*, brainstorm *US* ▸ **avoir de l'inspiration** to be inspired ▸ **avoir une bonne/mauvaise inspiration** to have a good/bad idea **2.** [d'air] breathing in.

inspiré, e [ɛ̃spire] **adj** inspired ▸ **être bien inspiré de faire qqch** be well-advised to do sthg.

inspirer [3] [ɛ̃spire] **vt 1.** [gén] to inspire ▸ **inspirer qqch à qqn** to inspire sb with sthg **2.** [air] to breathe in, to inhale.
◆ ***s'inspirer*** **vp** [prendre modèle sur] **: s'inspirer de qqn/qqch** to be inspired by sb/sthg.

instabilité [ɛ̃stabilite] **nf 1.** [gén] instability **2.** [du temps] unsettled nature.

instable [ɛ̃stabl] ■ **adj 1.** [gén] unstable **2.** [vie, temps] unsettled.
■ **nmf** unstable person.

installateur, trice [ɛ̃stalatœr, tris] **nm, f** fitter *UK*.

installation [ɛ̃stalasjɔ̃] **nf 1.** [de gaz, eau, électricité] installation **2.** [de personne - comme médecin, artisan] setting up / [- dans appartement] settling in **3.** [d'appartement] fitting out **4.** [de rideaux, étagères] putting up / [de meubles] putting in **5.** *(gén pl)* [équipement] installations *pl*, fittings *pl* / [usine] plant *(U)* / [de loisirs] facilities *pl* ▸ **installation électrique** wiring ▸ **installations sanitaires** plumbing *(U)*.

installer [3] [ɛ̃stale] **vt 1.** [gaz, eau, électricité] to install, to put in ▸ **nous avons dû faire installer l'eau/le gaz/l'électricité** we had to have the water laid on/the gas put in/the house wired **2.** INFORM to install **3.** [appartement] to fit out ▸ **nous avons installé la salle de jeu au grenier** we've turned the attic into a playroom **4.** [rideaux, étagères] to put up / [meubles] to put in **5.** [personne] **: installer qqn** to get sb settled, to install sb ▸ **les blessés furent installés dans la tour** the wounded were put in the tower.
◆ ***s'installer*** **vp 1.** [comme médecin, artisan] to set (o.s.) up ▸ **s'installer (à son compte)** to set up one's own business *ou* on one's own **2.** [emménager] to settle in ▸ **s'installer chez qqn** to move in with sb ▸ **s'installer dans une maison** to move into a house **3.** [dans fauteuil] to settle down **4.** *fig* [maladie, routine] to set in ▸ **le pays s'installe peu à peu dans la crise** the country is gradually learning to live with the crisis.

instamment [ɛ̃stamɑ̃] **adv** insistently.

instance [ɛ̃stɑ̃s] **nf 1.** [autorité] authority ▸ **instances (dirigeantes)** ÉCON ruling body **2.** DR proceedings *pl*.
◆ ***instances*** **nfpl** *sout* entreaties ▸ **sur les instances de** on the insistence of.
◆ ***en instance*** **loc adj** pending.
◆ ***en instance de*** **loc adv** on the point of ▸ **en instance de divorce** waiting for a divorce.

instant [ɛ̃stɑ̃] **nm** instant ▸ **à l'instant** [il y a peu de temps] a moment ago / [immédiatement] this minute ▸ **à l'instant où** (just) as ▸ **à tout instant** [en permanence] at all times / [d'un moment à l'autre] at any moment ▸ **pour l'instant** for the moment ▸ **dans un instant** in a moment *ou* minute ▸ **dès l'instant où** from the moment (when) ▸ **un instant!** one moment! ▸ **en un instant** in a flash *ou* an instant ▸ **ne pas avoir un instant de répit** not to have a moment's respite.

instantané, e [ɛ̃stɑ̃tane] **adj 1.** [immédiat] instantaneous **2.** [soluble] instant.
◆ ***instantané*** **nm** snapshot.

instantanément [ɛ̃stɑ̃tanemɑ̃] **adv** instantaneously, at once.

instar [ɛ̃star] ◆ ***à l'instar de*** **loc prép** following the example of.

instaurer [3] [ɛ̃stɔre] **vt** [instituer] to establish / *fig* [peur, confiance] to instil *UK*, to instill *US*.

instigateur, trice [ɛ̃stigatœr, tris] **nm, f** instigator.

instigation [ɛ̃stigasjɔ̃] **nf** instigation.
◆ ***à l'instigation de, sur l'instigation de*** **loc prép** at the instigation of.

instiller [3] [ɛ̃stile] **vt 1.** [substance] to drip **2.** [sentiment] to instil *UK*, to instill *US*.

instinct [ɛ̃stɛ̃] **nm** instinct ▸ **d'instinct** instinctively ▸ **instinct de conservation** instinct for self-preservation ▸ **instinct grégaire** herd instinct ▸ **instinct maternel** maternal instinct.

instinctif, ive [ɛ̃stɛ̃ktif, iv] ■ **adj** instinctive.
■ **nm, f** instinctive person.

instinctivement [ɛ̃stɛ̃ktivmɑ̃] **adv** instinctively.

instituer [7] [ɛ̃stitɥe] **vt 1.** [pratique] to institute **2.** DR [personne] to appoint.
◆ ***s'instituer*** **vp** to be set up *ou* established.

institut [ɛ̃stity] **nm 1.** [établissement] institute ▸ **l'Institut (de France)** the Institut de France ▸ **institut médico-légal** mortuary, morgue ▸ **l'institut Pasteur** *important medical research centre* ▸ **institut de recherches/scientifique** research/scientific institute ▸ **l'Institut du Monde**

Arabe *Paris exhibition centre for Arab culture and art* **2.** [de soins] **: institut de beauté** beauty salon ▸ **institut dentaire** ≃ dental hospital.

instituteur, trice [ɛ̃stitytœr, tris] **nm, f** primary school teacher *UK*, grade school teacher *US*.

institution [ɛ̃stitysjɔ̃] **nf 1.** [gén] institution **2.** [école privée] private school **3.** DR nomination.

◆ ***institutions*** **nfpl** POLIT institutions.

institutionnaliser [3] [ɛ̃stitysjɔnalize] **vt** to institutionalize.

◆ ***s'institutionnaliser*** **vp** to become institutionalized.

instructeur [ɛ̃stryktœr] ■ **nm** instructor.

■ **adj** MIL **: sergent instructeur** drill sergeant.

instructif, ive [ɛ̃stryktif, iv] **adj** instructive, educational.

instruction [ɛ̃stryksjɔ̃] **nf 1.** [enseignement, savoir] education ▸ **avoir de l'instruction** to be educated ▸ **instruction civique** civics *(U)* ▸ **instruction publique** state education ▸ **instruction religieuse** religious education **2.** [formation] training **3.** [directive] order **4.** DR (pre-trial) investigation.

◆ ***instructions*** **nfpl** instructions.

instruire [98] [ɛ̃strɥir] **vt 1.** [éduquer] to teach, to instruct **2.** *sout* [informer] to inform **3.** DR [affaire] to investigate ▸ **instruire contre qqn** to investigate sb.

◆ ***s'instruire*** **vp 1.** [se former] to learn **2.** *sout* [s'informer] **: s'instruire de qqch auprès de qqn** to find out about sthg from sb.

instruisais, instruisions ➤ ***instruire***.

instruit, e [ɛ̃strɥi, it] ■ **pp** ➤ ***instruire***.

■ **adj** educated.

instrument [ɛ̃strymɑ̃] **nm** instrument ▸ **instrument à cordes/percussion/vent** stringed/percussion/wind instrument ▸ **instrument contondant** blunt instrument ▸ **instrument de musique** musical instrument ▸ **instrument de travail** tool.

instrumental, e, aux [ɛ̃strymɑ̃tal, o] **adj** instrumental.

◆ ***instrumental*** **nm** instrumental.

instrumentaliser [3] [ɛ̃strymɑ̃talize] **vt** to use, to manipulate.

instrumentation [ɛ̃strymɑ̃tasjɔ̃] **nf** instrumentation.

instrumentiste [ɛ̃strymɑ̃tist] **nmf** instrumentalist.

insu [ɛ̃sy] ◆ ***à l'insu de*** **loc prép : à l'insu de qqn** without sb knowing ▸ **ils ont tout organisé à mon insu** they organized it all without my knowing.

insubmersible [ɛ̃sybmɛrsibl] **adj** unsinkable.

insubordination [ɛ̃sybɔrdinasjɔ̃] **nf** insubordination.

insubordonné, e [ɛ̃sybɔrdɔne] **adj** insubordinate.

insuccès [ɛ̃syksɛ] **nm** failure.

insuffisamment [ɛ̃syfizamɑ̃] **adv** insufficiently, inadequately.

insuffisance [ɛ̃syfizɑ̃s] **nf 1.** [manque] insufficiency **2.** MÉD deficiency ▸ **insuffisance cardiaque** cardiac insufficiency.

◆ ***insuffisances*** **nfpl** [faiblesses] shortcomings.

insuffisant, e [ɛ̃syfizɑ̃, ɑ̃t] **adj 1.** [en quantité] insufficient **2.** [en qualité] inadequate, unsatisfactory.

insuffler [3] [ɛ̃syfle] **vt 1.** [air] to blow **2.** *fig* [sentiment] **: insuffler qqch à qqn** to inspire sb with sthg.

insulaire [ɛ̃sylɛr] ■ **nmf** islander.

■ **adj 1.** GÉOGR island *(avant n)* **2.** *fig* [attitude] insular.

insularité [ɛ̃sylarite] **nf** insularity.

insuline [ɛ̃sylin] **nf** insulin.

insultant, e [ɛ̃syltɑ̃, ɑ̃t] **adj** insulting.

insulte [ɛ̃sylt] **nf** insult.

insulter [3] [ɛ̃sylte] **vt** to insult.

◆ ***s'insulter*** **vp** to insult each other.

insupportable [ɛ̃sypɔrtabl] **adj** unbearable.

insurgé, e [ɛ̃syrʒe] **adj & nm, f** insurgent, rebel.

insurger [17] [ɛ̃syrʒe] ◆ ***s'insurger*** **vp** to rebel, to revolt ▸ **s'insurger contre qqn** to rebel *ou* rise up against sb ▸ **s'insurger contre qqch** to protest against sthg.

insurmontable [ɛ̃syrmɔ̃tabl] **adj** [difficulté] insurmountable / [dégoût] uncontrollable.

insurrection [ɛ̃syrɛksjɔ̃] **nf** insurrection.

insurrectionnel, elle [ɛ̃syrɛksjɔnɛl] **adj** insurrectionary.

intact, e [ɛ̃takt] **adj** intact.

intangible [ɛ̃tɑ̃ʒibl] **adj 1.** *littéraire* [impalpable] intangible **2.** [sacré] inviolable.

intarissable [ɛ̃tarisabl] **adj** inexhaustible ▸ **il est intarissable** he could go on talking for ever.

intégral, e, aux [ɛ̃tegral, o] **adj 1.** [paiement] in full / [texte] unabridged, complete ▸ **bronzage intégral** all-over tan **2.** MATH **: calcul intégral** integral calculus.

◆ ***intégrale*** **nf 1.** MUS complete works *pl* **2.** MATH integral.

intégralement [ɛ̃tegralmɑ̃] **adv** fully, in full.

intégralité [ɛ̃tegralite] **nf** whole ▸ **dans son intégralité** in full.

intégrant, e [ɛ̃tegrɑ̃, ɑ̃t] ➤ ***parti***.

intégration [ɛ̃tegrasjɔ̃] **nf** integration ▸ **intégration latérale** ÉCON lateral integration.

intègre [ɛ̃tɛgr] **adj** honest.

intégré, e [ɛ̃tegre] **adj 1.** [logiciel] integrated **2.** [élément] built-in.

intégrer [18] [ɛ̃tegre] **vt** [assimiler] **: intégrer (à** *ou* **dans)** to integrate (into).

◆ ***s'intégrer*** **vp 1.** [s'incorporer] **: s'intégrer dans** *ou* **à** to fit into **2.** [s'adapter] to integrate.

intégrisme [ɛ̃tegrism] **nm** fundamentalism.

intégriste [ɛ̃tegrist] **nmf & adj** fundamentalist.

intégrité [ɛ̃tegrite] **nf 1.** [totalité] entirety **2.** [honnêteté] integrity.

intellect [ɛ̃telɛkt] **nm** intellect.

intellectualisme [ɛ̃telɛktɥalism] **nm** intellectualism.

intellectuel, elle [ɛ̃telɛktɥɛl] **adj & nm, f** intellectual.

intellectuellement [ɛ̃telɛktɥɛlmɑ̃] **adv** intellectually

intelligemment [ɛ̃teliʒamɑ̃] **adv** intelligently.

intelligence [ɛ̃teliʒɑ̃s] **nf 1.** [facultés mentales] intelligence ▸ **intelligence artificielle** artificial intelligence **2.** [personne] brain **3.** [compréhension, complicité] understanding ▸ **agir d'intelligence avec qqn** to act in complicity with sb.
◆ ***intelligences*** **nfpl** secret contacts.

intelligent, e [ɛ̃teliʒɑ̃, ɑ̃t] **adj** intelligent.

intelligentsia [ɛ̃teligɛnsja] **nf** intelligentsia.

intelligible [ɛ̃teliʒibl] **adj 1.** [voix] clear **2.** [concept, texte] intelligible.

intello [ɛ̃tɛlo] **adj inv & nmf** *péj* intellectual.

intempérance [ɛ̃tɑ̃perɑ̃s] **nf 1.** [abus] excessiveness **2.** [excès de plaisirs] overindulgence.

intempéries [ɛ̃tɑ̃peri] **nfpl** bad weather *(U)*.

intempestif, ive [ɛ̃tɑ̃pɛstif, iv] **adj** untimely.

intemporel, elle [ɛ̃tɑ̃pɔrɛl] **adj 1.** [sans durée] timeless **2.** *littéraire* [immatériel] immaterial.

intenable [ɛ̃tənabl] **adj 1.** [chaleur, personne] unbearable **2.** [position] untenable, indefensible.

intendance [ɛ̃tɑ̃dɑ̃s] **nf 1.** MIL commissariat / SCOL & UNIV bursar's office **2.** *fig* [questions matérielles] housekeeping.

intendant, e [ɛ̃tɑ̃dɑ̃, ɑ̃t] **nm, f 1.** SCOL & UNIV bursar **2.** [de manoir] steward.
◆ ***intendant*** **nm** MIL quartermaster.

intense [ɛ̃tɑ̃s] **adj 1.** [gén] intense **2.** [circulation] heavy.

intensément [ɛ̃tɑ̃semɑ̃] **adv** intensely.

intensif, ive [ɛ̃tɑ̃sif, iv] **adj** intensive.

intensification [ɛ̃tɑ̃sifikasjɔ̃] **nf** intensification.

intensifier [9] [ɛ̃tɑ̃sifje] **vt** to intensify.
◆ ***s'intensifier*** **vp** to intensify.

intensité [ɛ̃tɑ̃site] **nf** intensity.

intenter [3] [ɛ̃tɑ̃te] **vt** DR **: intenter qqch contre qqn** *ou* **à qqn** to bring sthg against sb.

intention [ɛ̃tɑ̃sjɔ̃] **nf** intention ▸ **avoir l'intention de faire qqch** to intend to do sthg ▸ **intention d'achat** COMM purchasing intention, intention to buy ▸ **intention de vote** voting intention ▸ **les intentions de vote pour le président** those leaning towards *UK ou* toward *US* the president ▸ **agir dans une bonne intention** to act with good intentions.
◆ ***à l'intention de*** **loc prép** for.

intentionné, e [ɛ̃tɑ̃sjɔne] **adj : bien intentionné** well-meaning ▸ **mal intentionné** ill-disposed.

intentionnel, elle [ɛ̃tɑ̃sjɔnɛl] **adj** intentional.

intentionnellement [ɛ̃tɑ̃sjɔnɛlmɑ̃] **adv** intentionally.

inter [ɛ̃tɛr] **nm 1.** *vieilli* = ***interurbain*** **2.** SPORT **: inter gauche/droit** inside left/right.

interactif, ive [ɛ̃tɛraktif, iv] **adj** interactive.

interaction [ɛ̃tɛraksjɔ̃] **nf** interaction.

interbancaire [ɛ̃tɛrbɑ̃kɛr] **adj** interbank *(avant n)*.

intercalaire [ɛ̃tɛrkalɛr] ■ **nm** insert.
■ **adj : feuillet intercalaire** insert ▸ **jour intercalaire** *extra day in a leap year.*

intercaler [3] [ɛ̃tɛrkale] **vt : intercaler qqch dans qqch** [feuillet, citation] to insert sthg in sthg / [dans le temps] to fit sthg into sthg.
◆ ***s'intercaler*** **vp : s'intercaler entre** to come between.

intercéder [18] [ɛ̃tɛrsede] **vi : intercéder pour** *ou* **en faveur de qqn auprès de qqn** to intercede with sb on behalf of sb.

intercepter [4] [ɛ̃tɛrsɛpte] **vt 1.** [lettre, ballon] to intercept **2.** [chaleur] to block.

intercession [ɛ̃tɛrsesjɔ̃] **nf** intercession.

interchangeable [ɛ̃tɛrʃɑ̃ʒabl] **adj** interchangeable.

interclasse [ɛ̃tɛrklas] **nm** break *UK*, recess *US*.

intercommunal, e, aux [ɛ̃tɛrkɔmynal, o] **adj** intermunicipal.

intercontinental, e, aux [ɛ̃tɛrkɔ̃tinɑ̃tal, o] **adj** intercontinental.

interculturel, elle [ɛ̃tɛrkyltyrɛl] **adj** cross-cultural.

interdépartemental, e, aux [ɛ̃tɛrdepartəmɑ̃tal, o] **adj** interdepartmental.

interdépendance [ɛ̃tɛrdepɑ̃dɑ̃s] **nf** interdependence.

interdépendant, e [ɛ̃tɛrdepɑ̃dɑ̃, ɑ̃t] **adj** interdependent.

interdiction [ɛ̃tɛrdiksjɔ̃] **nf 1.** [défense] **: 'interdiction de stationner'** 'strictly no parking' **2.** [prohibition, suspension] **: interdiction (de)** ban (on), banning (of) ▸ **enfreindre/lever une interdiction** to break/lift a ban ▸ **interdiction d'exporter** export ban ▸ **interdiction d'importation** import ban ▸ **interdiction de séjour** *order banning released prisoner from living in certain areas.*

COMMENT EXPRIMER...

l'interdiction

Smoking is not permitted in the office / Il est interdit de fumer dans les bureaux
"Smoking strictly forbidden" / "Défense absolue de fumer"
We're not supposed to leave the office before 5.30 / Nous ne sommes pas censés terminer notre journée de travail avant 17 h 30
I'm afraid I'm not allowed to give you those details / Je regrette, mais je n'ai pas le droit de vous donner ces renseignements
You must not tell anyone about this meeting / Vous ne devez pas parler à qui que ce soit de cette réunion

interdire [103] [ɛ̃tɛrdir] **vt 1.** [prohiber] **: interdire qqch à qqn** to forbid sb sthg ▸ **interdire à qqn de faire qqch** to forbid sb to do sthg **2.** [empêcher] to prevent ▸ **interdire à qqn de faire qqch** to prevent sb from doing sthg **3.** [d'exercer] to ban **4.** [bloquer] to block.
◆ ***s'interdire*** **vp : s'interdire qqch/de faire qqch** to refrain from sthg/from doing sthg.

interdisais, ***interdisions*** ➤ ***interdire***.

interdisciplinaire [ɛ̃tɛrdisiplinɛr] **adj** interdisciplinary.

interdise, ***interdises*** ➤ ***interdire***.

interdit, ***e*** [ɛ̃tɛrdi, it] ■ **pp** ➤ ***interdire***.
■ **adj 1.** [défendu] forbidden ▸ **'interdit au public'** 'no admittance' ▸ **'film interdit aux moins de 18 ans'** ≃ (18) ▸ **il est interdit de fumer** you're not allowed to smoke ▸ **la zone piétonne est interdite aux véhicules** vehicles are not allowed in the pedestrian area **2.** [ébahi] **: rester interdit** to be stunned ▸ **elle le dévisagea, interdite** she stared at him in bewilderment **3.** [privé] **: être interdit de chéquier** to have had one's chequebook *UK* *ou* checkbook *US* facilities withdrawn, to be forbidden to write cheques *UK* *ou* checks *US* ▸ **interdit de séjour** banned from entering the country.
◆ ***interdit*** **nm** BANQUE **: interdit bancaire** stopping of payment on all cheques *UK* *ou* checks *US*
▸▸ **lever un interdit** to lift a ban.

intéressant, ***e*** [ɛ̃terɛsɑ̃, ɑ̃t] ■ **adj 1.** [captivant] interesting **2.** [avantageux] advantageous, good.
■ **nm, f : faire l'intéressant** *péj* to show off.

intéressé, ***e*** [ɛ̃terese] ■ **adj** [concerné] concerned, involved / *péj* [motivé] self-interested.
■ **nm, f** person concerned ▸ **le principal intéressé** the main person concerned.

intéressement [ɛ̃terɛsmɑ̃] **nm** profit-sharing (scheme).

intéresser [4] [ɛ̃terese] **vt 1.** [captiver] to interest ▸ **intéresser qqn à qqch** to interest sb in sthg **2.** COMM [faire participer] **: intéresser les employés (aux bénéfices)** to give one's employees a share in the profits ▸ **intéresser qqn dans son commerce** to give sb a financial interest in one's business **3.** [concerner] to concern.
◆ ***s'intéresser*** **vp : s'intéresser à qqn/qqch** to take an interest in sb/sthg, to be interested in sb/sthg.

intérêt [ɛ̃terɛ] **nm 1.** [gén] interest ▸ **intérêt pour** interest in ▸ **avoir *ou* éprouver de l'intérêt pour qqch** to be interested *ou* to take an interest in sthg ▸ **agir par intérêt** to act in one's own interest ▸ **avoir intérêt à faire qqch** to be well advised to do sthg ▸ **dans l'intérêt général** in everyone's interest ▸ **je ne vois pas l'intérêt de continuer cette discussion** I see no point in carrying on this discussion **2.** [importance] significance ▸ **ses observations sont du plus haut *ou* grand intérêt** his comments are of the greatest interest *ou* importance ▸ **son essai offre peu d'intérêt** her essay is of no great interest ▸ **c'est sans intérêt pour la suite de l'enquête** it's of no importance for *ou* relevance to the rest of the inquiry **3.** [avantage] advantage ▸ **agir dans/contre son intérêt** to act in/against one's own interest **4.** FIN interest ▸ **intérêt de participation** participating interest.
◆ ***intérêts*** **nmpl 1.** FIN interest *(U)* ▸ **intérêts composés** compound interest ▸ **intérêts moratoires** interest on overdue payment ▸ **cela rapporte des intérêts** it yields *ou* bears interest **2.** COMM **: avoir des intérêts dans** to have a stake in **3.** [d'une personne, d'un pays] interests ▸ **servir les intérêts de qqn/d'une société** to serve sb's/a company's interests.

interface [ɛ̃tɛrfas] **nf** INFORM interface ▸ **interface commune de passerelle** common gateway interface ▸ **interface graphique** graphic interface ▸ **interface utilisateur graphique** graphical user interface.

interférence [ɛ̃tɛrferɑ̃s] **nf 1.** PHYS & POLIT interference **2.** *fig* [conjonction] convergence.

interférer [18] [ɛ̃tɛrfere] **vi 1.** PHYS to interfere **2.** *fig* [se rencontrer] to converge **3.** *fig* [s'immiscer] **: interférer dans qqch** to interfere in sthg.

intergalactique [ɛ̃tɛrgalaktik] **adj** intergalactic.

intérieur, ***e*** [ɛ̃terjœr] **adj 1.** [gén] inner ▸ **les peintures intérieures de la maison** the interior decoration of the house ▸ **les problèmes intérieurs d'un parti** a party's internal problems **2.** [de pays] domestic ▸ **la dette intérieure** the national debt.
◆ ***intérieur*** **nm 1.** [gén] inside ▸ **l'Intérieur** ≃ the Home Office *UK*, ≃ the Department of the Interior *US* ▸ **de l'intérieur** from the inside ▸ **à l'intérieur de soi-même** *fig & littéraire* inwardly ▸ **à l'intérieur (de qqch)** inside (sthg) ▸ **à l'intérieur des terres** inland ▸ **reste à l'intérieur de la voiture** stay in *ou* inside the car ▸ **homme d'intérieur, femme d'intérieur** homebody **2.** [de pays] interior ▸ **les villages de l'intérieur** inland villages.

intérieurement [ɛ̃terjœrmɑ̃] **adv** inwardly.

intérim [ɛ̃terim] **nm 1.** [période] interim period ▸ **assurer l'intérim (de qqn)** to deputize (for sb) ▸ **par intérim** acting *(avant n)* **2.** [travail temporaire] temporary *ou* casual work / [dans un bureau] temping ▸ **faire de l'intérim, travailler en intérim** to temp.

intérimaire [ɛ̃terimɛr] ■ **adj 1.** [ministre, directeur] acting *(avant n)* **2.** [employé, fonctions] temporary.
■ **nmf 1.** [ministre] acting minister **2.** [employé] temp.

intérioriser [3] [ɛ̃terjɔrize] **vt** to internalize.

interjection [ɛ̃tɛrʒɛksjɔ̃] **nf 1.** LING interjection **2.** DR lodging of an appeal.

interjeter [27] [ɛ̃tɛrʒəte] **vt** DR **: interjeter appel** to lodge an appeal.

interligne [ɛ̃tɛrliɲ] ■ **nm** (line) spacing ▸ **simple/double interligne** single/double spacing.
■ **nf** TYPO lead, leading.

interlocuteur, ***trice*** [ɛ̃tɛrlɔkytœr, tris] **nm, f 1.** [dans conversation] speaker ▸ **mon interlocuteur** the person to whom I am/was speaking **2.** [dans négociation] negotiator.

interlope [ɛ̃tɛrlɔp] **adj 1.** [illégal] illegal **2.** *fig* [louche] suspect, shady.

interloquer [3] [ɛ̃tɛrlɔke] **vt** to disconcert.

interlude [ɛ̃tɛrlyd] **nm** interlude.

intermède [ɛ̃tɛrmɛd] **nm** interlude.

intermédiaire [ɛ̃tɛrmedjɛr] ■ **nm** intermediary, go-between ▸ **sans intermédiaire** without an intermediary ▸ **par l'intermédiaire de qqn/qqch** through sb/sthg.
■ **adj** intermediate.

interminable [ɛ̃tɛrminabl] **adj** never-ending, interminable.

interministériel, elle [ɛ̃tɛrministerjɛl] **adj** interdepartmental.

intermittence [ɛ̃tɛrmitɑ̃s] **nf** [discontinuité] **: par intermittence** intermittently, off and on.

intermittent, e [ɛ̃tɛrmitɑ̃, ɑ̃t] **adj** intermittent ▸ **les intermittents du spectacle** *people working in the performing arts.*

internat [ɛ̃tɛrna] **nm** **1.** [SCOL - établissement] boarding school / [- système] boarding **2.** MÉD & UNIV [- concours] entrance examination / [- période de stage] period spent as a houseman *UK* ***ou*** an intern *US*.

international, e, aux [ɛ̃tɛrnasjɔnal, o] ■ **adj** international.
■ **nm, f** SPORT international.
◆ ***Internationale*** **nf** **1.** [association] International **2.** [hymne] Internationale.
◆ ***internationaux*** **nmpl** SPORT internationals ▸ **les internationaux de France de tennis** the French Open.

internationalisation [ɛ̃tɛrnasjɔnalizasjɔ̃] **nf** internationalization.

internaute [ɛ̃tɛrnɔt] **nmf** INFORM (net) surfer, cybersurfer, cybernaut, Internet user.

interne [ɛ̃tɛrn] ■ **nmf** **1.** [élève] boarder **2.** MÉD & UNIV houseman *UK*, intern *US*.
■ **adj** **1.** ANAT internal / [oreille] inner **2.** [du pays] domestic.

interné, e [ɛ̃tɛrne] **nm, f** **1.** POLIT internee **2.** MÉD inmate *(of psychiatric hospital)*.

internement [ɛ̃tɛrnəmɑ̃] **nm** **1.** POLIT internment **2.** MÉD confinement *(to psychiatric hospital)*.

interner [3] [ɛ̃tɛrne] **vt** **1.** POLIT to intern **2.** MÉD to commit *(to psychiatric hospital)*.

Internet, internet [ɛ̃tɛrnɛt] **nm : (l') Internet** the Internet.

interpellation [ɛ̃tɛrpelasjɔ̃] **nf** **1.** [apostrophe] call, shout **2.** [par la police] (arrest for) questioning ▸ **la police a procédé à plusieurs interpellations** several people were detained ***ou*** taken in by the police for questioning **3.** POLIT question / *(terme spécialisé)* interpellation.

interpeller [26] [ɛ̃tɛrpəle] **vt** **1.** [apostropher] to call ***ou*** shout out to **2.** [interroger] to take in for questioning.
◆ ***s'interpeller*** **vp** to exchange insults.

Interphone® [ɛ̃tɛrfɔn] **nm** intercom / [d'un immeuble] Entryphone®.

interplanétaire [ɛ̃tɛrplanetɛr] **adj** interplanetary.

INTERPOL, Interpol [ɛ̃tɛrpɔl] **npr** Interpol.

interpoler [3] [ɛ̃tɛrpɔle] **vt** to interpolate.

interposer [3] [ɛ̃tɛrpoze] **vt** to interpose.
◆ ***s'interposer*** **vp : s'interposer dans qqch** to intervene in sthg ▸ **s'interposer entre qqn et qqn** to intervene ***ou*** come between sb and sb.

interprétariat [ɛ̃tɛrpretarja] **nm** interpreting.

interprétation [ɛ̃tɛrpretasjɔ̃] **nf** interpretation.

interprète [ɛ̃tɛrprɛt] **nmf** **1.** [gén] interpreter **2.** [porte-parole] spokesperson **3.** CINÉ, MUS & THÉÂTRE performer.

interpréter [18] [ɛ̃tɛrprete] **vt** to interpret.

interprofessionnel, elle [ɛ̃tɛrprɔfɛsjɔnɛl] **adj** interprofessional.

interrogateur, trice [ɛ̃terɔgatœr, tris] ■ **adj** inquiring.
■ **nm, f** SCOL & UNIV oral examiner.

interrogatif, ive [ɛ̃terɔgatif, iv] **adj** **1.** GRAMM interrogative **2.** [air, ton] inquiring.
◆ ***interrogatif*** **nm** GRAMM interrogative.

interrogation [ɛ̃terɔgasjɔ̃] **nf** **1.** [de prisonnier] interrogation / [de témoin] questioning **2.** [question] question ▸ **interrogation directe/indirecte** GRAMM direct/indirect question **3.** SCOL test, quiz *US*.

interrogatoire [ɛ̃terɔgatwar] **nm** **1.** [de police, juge] questioning **2.** [procès-verbal] statement.

interrogeable [ɛ̃terɔʒabl] **adj : répondeur interrogeable à distance** answering machine ***ou*** answerphone *UK* with remote playback facility.

interroger [17] [ɛ̃terɔʒe] **vt** **1.** [questionner] to question / [accusé, base de données] to interrogate ▸ **interroger qqn (sur qqch)** to question sb (about sthg) **2.** [faits, conscience] to examine.
◆ ***s'interroger*** **vp : s'interroger sur** to wonder about.

interrompre [78] [ɛ̃terɔ̃pr] **vt** to interrupt.
◆ ***s'interrompre*** **vp** to stop.

interrompu, e [ɛ̃terɔ̃py] **pp** ➤ ***interrompre***.

interrupteur [ɛ̃teryptœr] **nm** switch ▸ **interrupteur à bascule** toggle switch.

interruption [ɛ̃terypsjɔ̃] **nf** **1.** [arrêt] break ▸ **sans interruption** without a break **2.** [action] interruption.

intersection [ɛ̃tɛrsɛksjɔ̃] **nf** intersection.

intersidéral, e, aux [ɛ̃tɛrsideral, o] **adj** interstellar.

interstice [ɛ̃tɛrstis] **nm** chink, crack.

intersyndical, e, aux [ɛ̃tɛrsɛ̃dikal, o] **adj** interunion.
◆ ***intersyndicale*** **nf** interunion committee.

intertitre [ɛ̃tɛrtitr] **nm** **1.** PRESSE subheading **2.** CINÉ subtitle.

interurbain, e [ɛ̃teryrbɛ̃, ɛn] **adj** long-distance.
◆ ***interurbain*** **nm : l'interurbain** the long-distance telephone service.

intervalle [ɛ̃tɛrval] **nm 1.** [spatial] space, gap **2.** [temporel] interval, period (of time) ▸ **à 6 jours d'intervalle** after 6 days ▸ **dans l'intervalle** in the meantime **3.** MUS interval.

intervenant, e [ɛ̃tɛrvənɑ̃, ɑ̃t] **nm, f 1.** [orateur] speaker **2.** DR intervening party.

intervenir [40] [ɛ̃tɛrvənir] **vi 1.** [personne] to intervene ▸ **intervenir auprès de qqn** to intervene with sb ▸ **intervenir dans qqch** to intervene in sthg ▸ **faire intervenir qqn** to bring *ou* call in sb **2.** [événement] to take place.

intervention [ɛ̃tɛrvɑ̃sjɔ̃] **nf 1.** [gén] intervention ▸ **intervention en faveur de qqn** intervention in sb's favour *UK ou* favor *US* ▸ **l'intervention des forces armées** military intervention ▸ **malgré l'intervention rapide des secours** despite swift rescue action **2.** MÉD operation ▸ **subir une intervention chirurgicale** to have an operation, to have surgery **3.** [discours] speech ▸ **j'ai fait deux interventions** I spoke twice.

interventionnisme [ɛ̃tɛrvɑ̃sjɔnism] **nm** interventionism.

interventionniste [ɛ̃tɛrvɑ̃sjɔnist] **nmf & adj** interventionist.

intervenu, e [ɛ̃tɛrvəny] **pp** ➤ ***intervenir***.

intervertir [32] [ɛ̃tɛrvɛrtir] **vt** to reverse, to invert.

interviendrai, interviendras ➤ ***intervenir***.

intervienne, interviennes ➤ ***intervenir***.

interviens, intervient ➤ ***intervenir***.

interview [ɛ̃tɛrvju] **nf** interview ▸ **accorder une interview à qqn** to give *ou* grant an interview to sb.

interviewer[1] [3] [ɛ̃tɛrvjuve] **vt** to interview.

interviewer[2] [ɛ̃tɛrvjuvœr] **nm** interviewer.

intestat [ɛ̃tɛsta] ■ **nmf** DR *person who dies intestate.*
■ **adj** DR intestate.

intestin, e [ɛ̃tɛstɛ̃, in] **adj** *sout* internal.

intestin [ɛ̃tɛstɛ̃] **nm** intestine ▸ **intestin grêle** small intestine ▸ **gros intestin** large intestine.

intestinal, e, aux [ɛ̃tɛstinal, o] **adj** intestinal.

intime [ɛ̃tim] ■ **nmf** close friend.
■ **adj** [gén] intimate / [vie, journal] private.

intimement [ɛ̃timmɑ̃] **adv 1.** [persuadé] firmly **2.** [lié] intimately.

intimer [3] [ɛ̃time] **vt 1.** [enjoindre] **: intimer qqch à qqn** to notify sb of sthg **2.** DR to summon.

intimidant, e [ɛ̃timidɑ̃, ɑ̃t] **adj** intimidating.

intimidation [ɛ̃timidasjɔ̃] **nf** intimidation.

intimider [3] [ɛ̃timide] **vt** to intimidate.

intimiste [ɛ̃timist] **adj** ART & LITTÉR intimist.

intimité [ɛ̃timite] **nf 1.** [secret] depths *pl* **2.** [familiarité, confort] intimacy **3.** [vie privée] privacy ▸ **dans l'intimité** amongst friends, in private ▸ **dans la plus stricte intimité** in complete privacy, in private.

intitulé [ɛ̃tityle] **nm** [titre] title / [de paragraphe] heading.

intituler [3] [ɛ̃tityle] **vt** to call, to entitle.
◆ ***s'intituler*** **vp 1.** [ouvrage] to be called *ou* entitled **2.** [personne] to call o.s.

intolérable [ɛ̃tɔlerabl] **adj** intolerable.

intolérance [ɛ̃tɔlerɑ̃s] **nf 1.** [religieuse, politique] intolerance **2.** [de l'organisme] **: intolérance à qqch** inability to tolerate sthg.

intolérant, e [ɛ̃tɔlerɑ̃, ɑ̃t] **adj** intolerant.

intonation [ɛ̃tɔnasjɔ̃] **nf** intonation.

intouchable [ɛ̃tuʃabl] **nmf & adj** untouchable.

intox [ɛ̃tɔks] **nf** *fam* propaganda, brainwashing ▸ **tout ça, c'est de l'intox** all that's just propaganda.

intoxication [ɛ̃tɔksikasjɔ̃] **nf 1.** [empoisonnement] poisoning ▸ **intoxication alimentaire** food poisoning **2.** *fig* [propagande] brainwashing.

intoxiqué, e [ɛ̃tɔksike] ■ **adj : intoxiqué (de)** addicted (to).
■ **nm, f** addict.

intoxiquer [3] [ɛ̃tɔksike] **vt : intoxiquer qqn par** [empoisonner] to poison sb with / *fig* to indoctrinate sb with.
◆ ***s'intoxiquer*** **vp** to poison o.s.

intraduisible [ɛ̃tradɥizibl] **adj 1.** [texte] untranslatable **2.** [sentiment] inexpressible.

intraitable [ɛ̃trɛtabl] **adj : intraitable (sur)** inflexible (about).

intranet [ɛ̃tranɛt] **nm** intranet.

intransigeance [ɛ̃trɑ̃ziʒɑ̃s] **nf** intransigence.

intransigeant, e [ɛ̃trɑ̃ziʒɑ̃, ɑ̃t] **adj** intransigent.

intransitif, ive [ɛ̃trɑ̃zitif, iv] **adj** intransitive.

intransportable [ɛ̃trɑ̃spɔrtabl] **adj : il est intransportable** he/it cannot be moved.

intra-utérin, e [ɛ̃trayterɛ̃, in] (mpl **intra-utérins**, fpl **intra-utérines**) **adj** intrauterine ▸ **la vie intra-utérine** life in the womb, life in utero *sout*.

intraveineux, euse [ɛ̃travenø, øz] **adj** intravenous.
◆ ***intraveineuse*** **nf** intravenous injection.

intrépide [ɛ̃trepid] **adj** bold, intrepid.

intrépidité [ɛ̃trepidite] **nf** boldness.

intrigant, e [ɛ̃trigɑ̃, ɑ̃t] ■ **adj** scheming.
■ **nm, f** schemer.

intrigue [ɛ̃trig] **nf 1.** [liaison amoureuse] affair **2.** [manœuvre] intrigue **3.** CINÉ, LITTÉR & THÉÂTRE plot.

intriguer [3] [ɛ̃trige] ■ **vt** to intrigue.
■ **vi** to scheme, to intrigue.

intrinsèque [ɛ̃trɛ̃sɛk] **adj** intrinsic.

introductif, ive [ɛ̃trɔdyktif, iv] **adj** DR introductory.

introduction [ɛ̃trɔdyksjɔ̃] **nf 1.** [gén] **: introduction (à)** introduction (to) **2.** [insertion] insertion.

introduire [98] [ɛ̃trɔdɥir] **vt 1.** [gén] to introduce **2.** [faire entrer] to show in **3.** [insérer] to insert **4.** INFORM to input, to enter.
◆ ***s'introduire*** **vp 1.** [pénétrer] to enter ▸ **s'introduire dans une maison** [cambrioleur] to get into *ou* enter a house **2.** [s'implanter] to be introduced.

introduisais, introduisions ➤ ***introduire***.

introduit, e [ɛ̃trɔdɥi, it] pp ➤ ***introduire***.

intronisation [ɛ̃trɔnizasjɔ̃] **nf** RELIG enthronement / *fig* establishment.

introniser [3] [ɛ̃trɔnize] **vt 1.** [roi, évêque] to enthrone ▸ **il s'est fait introniser à l'âge de 60 ans** [roi] he came to the throne when he was 60 / [évêque] he was made bishop at the age of 60 **2.** *fig* [établir] to establish.

introspection [ɛ̃trɔspɛksjɔ̃] **nf** introspection.

introuvable [ɛ̃truvabl] **adj** nowhere ***ou*** no-place *US* to be found.

introverti, e [ɛ̃trɔvɛrti] ■ **adj** introverted.
■ **nm, f** introvert.

intrus, e [ɛ̃try, yz] ■ **adj** intrusive.
■ **nm, f** intruder.

intrusion [ɛ̃tryzjɔ̃] **nf 1.** [gén & GÉOL] intrusion **2.** [ingérence] interference.

intuitif, ive [ɛ̃tɥitif, iv] ■ **adj** intuitive.
■ **nm, f** intuitive person.

intuition [ɛ̃tɥisjɔ̃] **nf** intuition ▸ **avoir de l'intuition** to be intuitive, to have intuition ▸ **avoir l'intuition de qqch** to have an intuition about sthg.

intuitivement [ɛ̃tɥitivmɑ̃] **adv** intuitively.

inuit [inɥit] **adj inv** Inuit.
◆ ***Inuit*** **nmf** Inuit.

inusable [inyzabl] **adj** hardwearing.

inusité, e [inyzite] **adj** unusual, uncommon.

in utero [inyterɔ] **loc adj & loc adv** in utero.

inutile [inytil] **adj** [objet, personne] useless / [effort, démarche] pointless ▸ **inutile d'insister** it's pointless insisting.

inutilement [inytilmɑ̃] **adv** needlessly, unnecessarily.

inutilisable [inytilizabl] **adj** unusable.

inutilisé, e [inytilize] **adj** unused.

inutilité [inytilite] **nf** [de personne, d'objet] uselessness / [de démarche, d'effort] pointlessness.

inv. (abr écrite de ***invariable***) inv.

invaincu, e [ɛ̃vɛ̃ky] **adj 1.** SPORT unbeaten **2.** [peuple] unconquered.

invalide [ɛ̃valid] ■ **nmf** disabled person ▸ **invalide de guerre** *officially recognized war invalid* ▸ **invalide du travail** *person disabled in an industrial accident.*
■ **adj** disabled.

invalider [3] [ɛ̃valide] **vt** to invalidate.

invalidité [ɛ̃validite] **nf 1.** DR invalidity **2.** MÉD disability.

invariable [ɛ̃varjabl] **adj 1.** [immuable] unchanging **2.** GRAMM invariable.

invariablement [ɛ̃varjabləmɑ̃] **adv** invariably.

invasion [ɛ̃vazjɔ̃] **nf** invasion.

invective [ɛ̃vɛktiv] **nf** invective, abuse.

invectiver [3] [ɛ̃vɛktive] **vt** to abuse.
◆ ***s'invectiver*** **vp** to hurl abuse at each other.

invendable [ɛ̃vɑ̃dabl] **adj** unsaleable, unsellable.

invendu, e [ɛ̃vɑ̃dy] **adj** unsold.
◆ ***invendu*** *(gén pl)* **nm** remainder.

inventaire [ɛ̃vɑ̃tɛr] **nm 1.** [gén] inventory ▸ **faire l'inventaire de qqch** to make an inventory of sthg **2.** [COMM - activité] stocktaking *UK*, inventory *US* / [- liste] list.

inventer [3] [ɛ̃vɑ̃te] **vt 1.** [créer] to invent ▸ **il n'a pas inventé la poudre** he'll never set the world on fire **2.** [imaginer] to think up ▸ **je ne sais plus quoi inventer** I've run out of ideas **3.** [forger] **: je n'invente rien!** I'm not inventing a thing! ▸ **une histoire inventée de toutes pièces** an entirely made-up story, a complete fabrication **4.** DR [trésor] to discover, to find.
◆ ***s'inventer*** **vp** *(emploi passif)* **: ça ne s'invente pas** nobody could make up a thing like that, you don't make that sort of thing up.

inventeur [ɛ̃vɑ̃tœr] **nm 1.** [de machine] inventor **2.** DR [de trésor] finder.

inventif, ive [ɛ̃vɑ̃tif, iv] **adj** inventive.

invention [ɛ̃vɑ̃sjɔ̃] **nf 1.** [découverte, mensonge] invention **2.** [imagination] inventiveness.

inventorier [9] [ɛ̃vɑ̃tɔrje] **vt** to make an inventory of.

invérifiable [ɛ̃verifjabl] **adj** unverifiable.

inverse [ɛ̃vɛrs] ■ **nm** opposite, reverse ▸ **à l'inverse de** contrary to.
■ **adj 1.** [sens] opposite / [ordre] reverse ▸ **en sens inverse (de)** in the opposite direction (to) **2.** [rapport] inverse.

inversé, e [ɛ̃vɛrse] **adj** PRESSE & TYPO **: inversé (en noir au blanc)** reversed-out.

inversement [ɛ̃vɛrsəmɑ̃] **adv 1.** MATH inversely ▸ **inversement proportionnel à** in inverse proportion to **2.** [au contraire] on the other hand **3.** [vice versa] vice versa.

inverser [3] [ɛ̃vɛrse] **vt** to reverse.

inversion [ɛ̃vɛrsjɔ̃] **nf** reversal.

invertébré, e [ɛ̃vɛrtebre] **adj** invertebrate.
◆ ***invertébré*** **nm** invertebrate.

investigation [ɛ̃vɛstigasjɔ̃] **nf** investigation.

investir [32] [ɛ̃vɛstir] **vt** to invest ▸ **investir qqn d'une fonction** to invest ***ou*** vest sb with an office.
◆ ***s'investir dans*** **v + prep : s'investir dans son métier** to be involved ***ou*** absorbed in one's job ▸ **une actrice qui s'investit entièrement dans ses rôles** an actress who throws herself heart and soul into every part she plays ▸ **je me suis énormément investie dans le projet** the project really meant a lot to me.

investissement [ɛ̃vɛstismɑ̃] **nm** investment ▸ **investissement de l'étranger** inward investment.

investisseur, euse [ɛ̃vɛstisœr, øz] **nm, f** investor ▸ **investisseur institutionnel** institutional investor.

investiture [ɛ̃vɛstityr] **nf** investiture.

invétéré, e [ɛ̃vetere] **adj** *péj* inveterate.

invincible [ɛ̃vɛ̃sibl] **adj** [gén] invincible / [difficulté] insurmountable / [charme] irresistible.

inviolabilité [ɛ̃vjɔlabilite] **nf 1.** DR inviolability **2.** [de parlementaire] immunity **3.** [de coffre] impregnability.

inviolable [ɛ̃vjɔlabl] **adj 1.** DR inviolable **2.** [parlementaire] immune **3.** [coffre] impregnable.

invisible [ɛ̃vizibl] **adj** invisible ▸ **rester invisible** [personne] to stay out of sight.

invitation [ɛ̃vitasjɔ̃] **nf : invitation (à)** invitation (to) ▸ **à** *ou* **sur l'invitation de qqn** at sb's invitation ▸ **sur invitation** by invitation ▸ **décliner une invitation** to turn down an invitation.

invite [ɛ̃vit] **nf** invitation.

invité, ***e*** [ɛ̃vite] ■ **adj** [hôte] invited / [professeur, conférencier] guest *(avant n)*.
■ **nm, f** guest.

inviter [3] [ɛ̃vite] **vt** to invite ▸ **inviter qqn à faire qqch** to invite sb to do sthg / *fig* [suj: chose] to be an invitation to sb to do sthg ▸ **le beau temps invite à la promenade** this fine weather puts one in the mood for a walk ▸ **je vous invite!** it's my treat!

in vitro [invitro] ➤ ***fécondation***.

invivable [ɛ̃vivabl] **adj** unbearable.

invocation [ɛ̃vɔkasjɔ̃] **nf** invocation ▸ **invocation à** call for.

involontaire [ɛ̃vɔlɔ̃tɛr] **adj 1.** [acte] involuntary **2.** [personne] unwilling.

involontairement [ɛ̃vɔlɔ̃tɛrmɑ̃] **adv** involuntarily, unintentionally.

invoquer [3] [ɛ̃vɔke] **vt 1.** [alléguer] to put forward **2.** [citer, appeler à l'aide] to invoke / [paix] to call for.

invraisemblable [ɛ̃vrɛsɑ̃blabl] **adj 1.** [incroyable] unlikely, improbable **2.** [extravagant] incredible.

invraisemblance [ɛ̃vrɛsɑ̃blɑ̃s] **nf** improbability.

invulnérable [ɛ̃vylnerabl] **adj** invulnerable.

iode [jɔd] **nm** iodine.

iodé, ***e*** [jɔde] **adj** containing iodine.

ion [jɔ̃] **nm** ion.

IPC (abr de ***indice des prix à la consommation***) **nm** RPI *UK*, CPI *US*.

Ipsos [ipsos] **npr** *French market research institute*.

IR (abr de ***infra-rouge***) **adj** IR.

IRA [ira] (abr de ***Irish Republican Army***) **nf** IRA.

irai, ***iras*** ➤ ***aller***.

Irak, ***Iraq*** [irak] **nm : l'Irak** Iraq.

irakien, ***enne***, ***iraquien***, ***enne*** [irakjɛ̃, ɛn] **adj** Iraqi.
◆ ***Irakien***, ***enne***, ***Iraquien***, ***enne*** **nm, f** Iraqi.

Iran [irɑ̃] **nm : l'Iran** Iran.

iranien, ***enne*** [iranjɛ̃, ɛn] **adj** Iranian.
◆ ***iranien*** **nm** [langue] Iranian.
◆ ***Iranien***, ***enne*** **nm, f** Iranian.

Iraq = ***Irak***.

iraquien = ***irakien***.

irascible [irasibl] **adj** irascible.

IRC (abr de ***Internet Relay Chat***) **m** IRC.

iris [iris] **nm** ANAT & BOT iris.

irisé, ***e*** [irize] **adj** iridescent.

irlandais, ***e*** [irlɑ̃dɛ, ɛz] **adj** Irish.
◆ ***irlandais*** **nm** [langue] Irish.
◆ ***Irlandais***, ***e*** **nm, f** Irishman (f Irishwoman).

Irlande [irlɑ̃d] **nf : l'Irlande** Ireland ▸ **l'Irlande du Nord/Sud** Northern/Southern Ireland.

IRM [iɛrɛm] (abr de ***Imagerie par résonance magnétique***) **nm** MÉD MRI.

ironie [irɔni] **nf** irony ▸ **ironie du sort** twist of fate.

ironique [irɔnik] **adj** ironic.

ironiquement [irɔnikmɑ̃] **adv** ironically.

ironiser [3] [irɔnize] **vi** to speak ironically.

IRPP (abr de ***impôt sur le revenu des personnes physiques***) **nm** income tax.

irradiation [iradjasjɔ̃] **nf** [rayons] radiation / [action] irradiation.

irradier [9] [iradje] ■ **vi** to radiate.
■ **vt** to irradiate.

irraisonné, ***e*** [irɛzɔne] **adj** irrational.

irrationnel, ***elle*** [irasjɔnɛl] **adj** irrational.

irréalisable [irealizabl] **adj** unrealizable.

irréaliste [irealist] **adj** unrealistic.

irréalité [irealite] **nf** unreality.

irrecevable [irəsəvabl] **adj** inadmissible.

COMMENT EXPRIMER...

les invitations

Inviter quelqu'un

Would you like to join us for a drink? / Voulez-vous prendre un verre avec nous ?
Do you want to go for something to eat? / Ça te dirait d'aller manger quelque chose ?
Let's go to the cinema / Allons au cinéma
Why don't you come round some time? / Passez donc me voir un de ces jours
Why don't we meet next weekend? / Et si on se voyait le week-end prochain ?
Are you free for lunch tomorrow? / Tu es libre pour déjeuner demain ?
Sarah and Tim are pleased to invite you to their housewarming party / Sarah et Tim sont heureux de vous inviter à pendre la crémaillère

Répondre à une invitation

Thanks, I'd love to / Avec plaisir, merci
That'd be lovely / Ça me plairait beaucoup
That's very kind of you / C'est très gentil à vous
I look forward to it / Ce sera un plaisir
Sure. When did you have in mind? / D'accord. Quand ça ?
Why not? / Oui, pourquoi pas ?
I'm afraid not. How about the week after? / Non, je regrette. La semaine d'après, ça irait ?
I'm afraid I'll be away that week / Malheureusement, je suis absent cette semaine-là
Can we do it another time? / On remet ça à une autre fois ?

irréconciliable [irekɔ̃siljabl] **adj** irreconcilable.

irrécupérable [irekyperabl] **adj 1.** [irrécouvrable] irretrievable **2.** [irréparable] beyond repair **3.** *fam* [personne] beyond hope.

irrécusable [irekyzabl] **adj** unimpeachable.

irréductible [iredyktibl] ■ **nmf** diehard.
■ **adj 1.** CHIM, MATH & MÉD irreducible **2.** *fig* [volonté] indomitable / [personne] implacable / [communiste] diehard *(before n)*.

irréel, elle [ireɛl] **adj** unreal.

irréfléchi, e [irefleʃi] **adj** unthinking.

irréfutable [irefytabl] **adj** irrefutable.

irrégularité [iregylarite] **nf 1.** [gén] irregularity **2.** [de terrain, performance] unevenness.

irrégulier, ère [iregylje, ɛr] **adj 1.** [gén] irregular **2.** [terrain, surface] uneven, irregular **3.** [employé, athlète] erratic.

irrégulièrement [iregyljɛrmɑ̃] **adv** irregularly.

irrémédiable [iremedjabl] **adj 1.** [irréparable] irreparable **2.** [incurable] incurable.

irrémédiablement [iremedjabləmɑ̃] **adv** irreparably.

irremplaçable [irɑ̃plasabl] **adj** irreplaceable.

irréparable [ireparabl] ■ **nm : commettre l'irréparable** to do the unforgivable.
■ **adj 1.** [objet] beyond repair **2.** *fig* [perte, erreur] irreparable.

irrépressible [irepresibl] **adj** irrepressible.

irréprochable [ireprɔʃabl] **adj** irreproachable.

irrésistible [irezistibl] **adj 1.** [tentation, femme] irresistible **2.** [amusant] entertaining.

irrésistiblement [irezistibləmɑ̃] **adv** irresistibly.

irrésolu, e [irezɔly] **adj 1.** [indécis] irresolute **2.** [sans solution] unresolved.

irrespirable [irɛspirabl] **adj 1.** [air] unbreathable **2.** *fig* [oppressant] oppressive.

irresponsable [irɛspɔ̃sabl] ■ **nmf** irresponsible person.
■ **adj** irresponsible.

irrévérencieux, euse [ireverɑ̃sjø, øz] **adj** irreverent.

irréversible [irevɛrsibl] **adj** irreversible.

irrévocable [irevɔkabl] **adj** irrevocable.

irrévocablement [irevɔkabləmɑ̃] **adv** irrevocably.

irrigation [irigasjɔ̃] **nf** irrigation.

irriguer [3] [irige] **vt** to irrigate.

irritabilité [iritabilite] **nf** irritability.

irritable [iritabl] **adj** irritable.

irritant, e [iritɑ̃, ɑ̃t] **adj 1.** [agaçant] irritating, annoying **2.** MÉD irritant.

irritation [iritasjɔ̃] **nf** irritation.

irriter [3] [irite] **vt 1.** [exaspérer] to irritate, to annoy **2.** MÉD to irritate.
◆ ***s'irriter*** **vp** to get irritated ▸ **s'irriter contre qqn/de qqch** to get irritated with sb/at sthg.

irruption [irypsjɔ̃] **nf 1.** [invasion] invasion **2.** [entrée brusque] irruption ▸ **faire irruption dans** to burst into.

ISBN (abr de ***International standard book number***) **nm** ISBN.

ISF (abr de ***impôt de solidarité sur la fortune***) **nm** wealth tax.

islam [islam] **nm** Islam.

islamique [islamik] **adj** Islamic.

islamisation [islamizasjɔ̃] **nf** Islamization.

islamiser [3] [islamize] **vt** to Islamize.

islamisme [islamism] **nm** Islamism.

islandais, e [islɑ̃dɛ, ɛz] **adj** Icelandic.
◆ ***islandais*** **nm** [langue] Icelandic.
◆ ***Islandais, e*** **nm, f** Icelander.

Islande [islɑ̃d] **nf : l'Islande** Iceland.

ISO [izo] (abr de ***International Standards Organisation***) f ISO.

isocèle [izɔsɛl] **adj** isoceles.

isolant, e [izɔlɑ̃, ɑ̃t] **adj** insulating.
◆ ***isolant*** **nm** insulator, insulating material.

isolateur, trice [izɔlatœr, tris] **adj** insulating.
◆ ***isolateur*** **nm** insulator.

isolation [izɔlasjɔ̃] **nf** insulation ▸ **isolation phonique** soundproofing ▸ **isolation thermique** thermal insulation.

isolationnisme [izɔlasjɔnism] **nm** isolationism.

isolé, e [izɔle] **adj** isolated.

isolement [izɔlmɑ̃] **nm 1.** [gén] isolation **2.** CONSTR & ÉLECTR insulation.

isolément [izɔlemɑ̃] **adv** individually.

isoler [3] [izɔle] **vt 1.** [séparer] to isolate ▸ **isoler qqch de qqch** to isolate sthg from sthg **2.** CONSTR & ÉLECTR to insulate ▸ **isoler qqch du froid** to insulate sthg (against the cold) ▸ **isoler qqch du bruit** to soundproof sthg.
◆ ***s'isoler*** **vp : s'isoler (de)** to isolate o.s. (from).

isoloir [izɔlwar] **nm** polling *UK ou* voting *US* booth.

isotherme [izɔtɛrm] ■ **nf** isotherm.
■ **adj** isothermal.

isotope [izɔtɔp] ■ **adj** isotopic.
■ **nm** isotope.

Israël [israɛl] **npr** Israel.

israélien, enne [israeljɛ̃, ɛn] **adj** Israeli.
◆ ***Israélien, enne*** **nm, f** Israeli.

israélite [israelit] **adj** Jewish.
◆ ***Israélite*** **nmf** Jew.

issu, e [isy] **adj : être issu de** [résulter de] to emerge *ou* stem from / [personne] to come from.
◆ ***issue*** **nf 1.** [sortie] exit ▸ **issue de secours** emergency exit **2.** *fig* [solution] way out, solution ▸ **sans issue** hopeless **3.** [terme] outcome ▸ **à l'issue de** at the end *ou* close of.

Istanbul [istɑ̃bul] **npr** Istanbul.

isthme [ism] **nm** isthmus.

Italie [itali] **nf : l'Italie** Italy.

italien, enne [italjɛ̃, ɛn] **adj** Italian.
◆ ***italien*** **nm** [langue] Italian.
◆ ***Italien, enne*** **nm, f** Italian.

italique [italik] ■ **nm 1.** HIST & LING Italic **2.** TYPO italics *pl* ▸ **en italique** in italics.
■ **adj 1.** HIST & LING Italic **2.** TYPO italic.

itinéraire [itinerɛr] **nm** itinerary, route ▸ **itinéraire bis** diversion.

itinérant, e [itinerɑ̃, ɑ̃t] **adj 1.** [spectacle, troupe] itinerant **2.** [ambassadeur] roving *(avant n).*

itou [itu] **adv** *fam* as well.

ITP (abr de ***ingénieur des travaux publics***) **nm** civil engineer.

IUFM (abr de ***institut universitaire de formation des maîtres***) **nm** ≃ teacher training college *UK*, ≃ teachers college *US*.

IUP (abr de ***institut universitaire professionnel***) **nm** business school.

IUT (abr de ***institut universitaire de technologie***) **nm** ≃ technical college.

IVG (abr de ***interruption volontaire de grossesse***) **nf** abortion.

ivoire [ivwar] **nm** ivory.

ivoirien, enne [ivwarjɛ̃, ɛn] **adj** of/from the Ivory Coast.
◆ ***Ivoirien, enne*** **nm, f** person from the Ivory Coast.

ivre [ivr] **adj** drunk ▸ **ivre de colère** wild with anger ▸ **ivre de joie** drunk *ou* mad with joy ▸ **ivre mort** dead drunk.

ivresse [ivrɛs] **nf** drunkenness / [extase] rapture.

ivrogne [ivrɔɲ] **nmf** drunkard.

ivrognerie [ivrɔɲri] **nf** drunkenness.

j, ***J*** [ʒi] **nm inv** j, J.
◆ ***J*** **1.** (abr écrite de ***joule***) J **2.** abr de ***jour***.

j' ➤ ***je***.

jabot [ʒabo] **nm** **1.** [d'oiseau] crop **2.** [de chemise] frill.

jacassement [ʒakasmɑ̃] **nm** *péj* chattering, jabbering.

jacasser [3] [ʒakase] **vi** *péj* to chatter, to jabber.

jachère [ʒaʃɛr] **nf : en jachère** fallow.

jacinthe [ʒasɛ̃t] **nf** hyacinth.

jackpot [dʒakpɔt] **nm** **1.** [combinaison] jackpot ▸ **toucher le jackpot** *litt* & *fig* to hit the jackpot **2.** [machine] slot machine.

jacobin, ***e*** [ʒakɔbɛ̃, in] **adj** Jacobin.
◆ ***Jacobin*** **nm** HIST Jacobin.

Jacuzzi® [ʒakuzi] **nm** Jacuzzi®.

jade [ʒad] **nm** jade.

jadis [ʒadis] **adv** formerly, in former times.

jaguar [ʒagwar] **nm** jaguar.

jaillir [32] [ʒajir] **vi** **1.** [liquide] to gush / [flammes] to leap **2.** [cri] to ring out **3.** [personne] to spring out.

jais [ʒɛ] **nm** jet ▸ **noir comme le jais, noir de jais** jet-black.

Jakarta = ***Djakarta***.

jalon [ʒalɔ̃] **nm** marker pole ▸ **poser les (premiers) jalons de** *fig* to pave the way for.

jalonner [3] [ʒalɔne] **vt** to mark (out) ▸ **jalonné de** [bordé de] lined with / *fig* punctuated with.

jalousement [ʒaluzmɑ̃] **adv** jealously.

jalouser [3] [ʒaluze] **vt** to be jealous of.

jalousie [ʒaluzi] **nf** **1.** [envie] jealousy ▸ **être malade** *ou* **crever de jalousie** *fig* to be green with envy **2.** [store] blind.

jaloux, ***ouse*** [ʒalu, uz] **adj : jaloux (de)** jealous (of).

jamaïquain, ***e***, ***jamaïcain***, ***e*** [ʒamaikɛ̃, ɛn] **adj** Jamaican.
◆ ***Jamaïquain***, ***e***, ***Jamaïcain***, ***e*** **nm, f** Jamaican.

Jamaïque [ʒamaik] **nf : la Jamaïque** Jamaica.

jamais [ʒamɛ] **adv** **1.** [sens négatif] never ▸ **ne... jamais, jamais ne** never ▸ **je ne reviendrai jamais, jamais je ne reviendrai** I'll never come back ▸ **(ne)... jamais plus, plus jamais (ne)** never again ▸ **je ne viendrai jamais plus, plus jamais je ne viendrai** I'll never come here again ▸ **plus jamais!** never again! **2.** [sens positif] **: plus que jamais** more than ever ▸ **elle l'aimait plus que jamais** she loved him more than ever ▸ **il est plus triste que jamais** he's sadder than ever ▸ **si jamais tu le vois** if you should happen to see him, should you happen to see him.
◆ ***à jamais*** **loc adv** for ever.
◆ ***pour jamais*** **loc adv** for ever.

jambage [ʒɑ̃baʒ] **nm** [de lettre] downstroke.

jambe [ʒɑ̃b] **nf** leg ▸ **courir à toutes jambes** to run flat out ▸ **il s'enfuit à toutes jambes** he ran away as fast as his legs would carry him ▸ **prendre ses jambes à son cou** to take to one's heels ▸ **tenir la jambe à qqn** *fam fig* to keep sb talking ▸ **ça me fait une belle jambe!** *fam fig* that's no good to me!

jambières [ʒɑ̃bjɛr] **nfpl** [de football] shin pads *ou* guards / [de cricket] pads.

jambon [ʒɑ̃bɔ̃] **nm** ham ▸ **jambon blanc** ham ▸ **jambon fumé** smoked ham ▸ **un jambon beurre** *fam* a ham sandwich.

jambonneau, ***x*** [ʒɑ̃bɔno] **nm** knuckle of ham.

jante [ʒɑ̃t] **nf** (wheel) rim.

janvier [ʒɑ̃vje] **nm** January ; voir aussi ***septembre***.

Japon [ʒapɔ̃] **nm : le Japon** Japan ▸ **au Japon** in Japan.

japonais, ***e*** [ʒapɔnɛ, ɛz] **adj** Japanese.
◆ ***japonais*** **nm** [langue] Japanese.
◆ ***Japonais***, ***e*** **nm, f** Japanese (person) ▸ **les Japonais** the Japanese.

jappement [ʒapmɑ̃] **nm** yap, yapping *(U)*.

japper [3] [ʒape] **vi** to yap.

jaquette [ʒakɛt] **nf** **1.** [vêtement] jacket **2.** [de livre] (dust) jacket.

jardin [ʒardɛ̃] **nm** [espace clos] garden / [attaché à une maison] yard ▸ **jardin d'enfants** nursery school, kindergarten *UK* ▸ **jardin public** park ▸ **jardin zoologique** zoo.

jardinage [ʒardinaʒ] **nm** gardening.

jardiner [3] [ʒardine] **vi** to garden.

jardinet [ʒardinɛ] **nm** small garden.

jardinier, ***ère*** [ʒardinje, ɛr] **nm, f** gardener.
◆ ***jardinière*** **nf 1.** [bac à fleurs] window box **2.** CULIN **: jardinière de légumes** mixed vegetables *pl.*

jargon [ʒargɔ̃] **nm 1.** [langage spécialisé] jargon **2.** *fam* [charabia] gibberish.

jarret [ʒarɛ] **nm 1.** ANAT back of the knee **2.** CULIN knuckle of veal.

jarretelle [ʒartɛl] **nf** suspender *UK*, garter *US*.

jarretière [ʒartjɛr] **nf** garter.

jars [ʒar] **nm** gander.

jaser [3] [ʒaze] **vi** [bavarder] to gossip.

jasmin [ʒasmɛ̃] **nm** jasmine.

JAT (abr de ***juste à temps***) **adj** JIT *(just-in-time)*.

jatte [ʒat] **nf** bowl.

jauge [ʒoʒ] **nf** [instrument] gauge ▸ **jauge de niveau d'huile** dipstick.

jauger [17] [ʒoʒe] **vt** to gauge.

jaunâtre [ʒonatr] **adj** yellowish.

jaune [ʒon] ■ **nm** [couleur] yellow.
■ **adj** yellow.
■ **adv : rire jaune** *fig* to force o.s. to laugh.
◆ ***jaune d'œuf*** **nm** (egg) yolk.

jaunir [32] [ʒonir] **vt & vi** to turn yellow.

jaunisse [ʒonis] **nf** MÉD jaundice ▸ **en faire une jaunisse** *fam fig* [de jalousie] to be green with envy / [de déception] to take it badly.

jaunissement [ʒonismɑ̃] **nm** yellowing.

java [ʒava] **nf** java *type of popular dance* ▸ **faire la java** *fam fig* to live it up.

Java [ʒava] **npr** Java ▸ **à Java** in Java.

javanais, ***e*** [ʒavanɛ, ɛz] **adj** Javanese.
◆ ***javanais*** **nm** [langue] Javanese.
◆ ***Javanais***, ***e*** **nm, f** Javanese (person) ▸ **les Javanais** the Javanese.

Javascript [ʒavaskript] **m** INFORM Java script.

Javel [ʒavɛl] **nf : eau de Javel** bleach.

javelliser [3] [ʒavelize] **vt** to chlorinate.

javelot [ʒavlo] **nm** javelin.

jazz [dʒaz] **nm** jazz.

J.-C. (abr écrite de ***Jésus-Christ***) J.C.

je [ʒə], ***j'*** *(devant voyelle ou 'h' muet)* **pron pers** I.

jean [dʒin], ***jeans*** [dʒins] **nm** jeans *pl*, pair of jeans.

Jeep® [dʒip] **nf** Jeep®.

je-m'en-foutisme [ʒmɑ̃futism] **nm** couldn't-give-a-damn attitude.

jérémiades [ʒeremjad] **nfpl** moaning *(U)*, whining *(U)*.

jerrycan, ***jerricane*** [ʒerikan] **nm** jerry can.

jersey [ʒɛrzɛ] **nm** jersey ▸ **point de jersey** stocking stitch.

Jersey [ʒɛrzɛ] **npr** Jersey ▸ **à Jersey** on Jersey.

Jérusalem [ʒeryzalɛm] **npr** Jerusalem.

jésuite [ʒezɥit] ■ **nm** Jesuit.
■ **adj** Jesuit / *péj* jesuitical.

Jésus-Christ [ʒezykri] **nm** Jesus Christ.

jet[1] [ʒɛ] **nm 1.** [action de jeter] throw ▸ **d'un seul jet** *fig* in one go **2.** [de liquide] jet ▸ **jet d'eau** fountain **3.** [esquisse] **: premier jet** rough outline *ou* draft.

jet[2] [dʒɛt] **nm** [avion] jet.

jetable [ʒətabl] **adj** disposable.

jetais, ***jetions*** ➤ ***jeter***.

jeté, ***e*** [ʒəte] **pp** ➤ ***jeter***.

jetée [ʒəte] **nf** jetty.

jeter [27] [ʒəte] **vt 1.** [gén] to throw / [se débarrasser de] to throw away ▸ **ne jetez pas de papiers par terre** don't drop litter ▸ **jeter qqch à qqn** [lancer] to throw sthg to sb, to throw sb sthg / [pour faire mal] to throw sthg at sb ▸ **jeter des injures à la tête de qqn** to hurl *ou* to fling insults at sb ▸ **jeter qqn dehors** to throw sb out ▸ **jeter qqn en prison** to throw sb in jail *ou* prison ▸ **jeter qqch par la fenêtre** to throw sthg out of the window ▸ **jeter un coup d'œil (à)** to take a look (at) **2.** [émettre - étincelle] to throw *ou* to give out / [- lumière] to cast, to shed ▸ **elle en jette, ta moto!** *fam* that's some *ou* a neat bike you've got there! **3.** *fam* [expulser] **: on a essayé d'aller en boîte mais on s'est fait jeter par un videur** we tried to get into a nightclub but got thrown out by a bouncer.
◆ ***se jeter*** **vp : se jeter sur** to pounce on ▸ **les chiens se sont jetés sur la viande** the dogs fell on the meat ▸ **se jeter dans** [suj: rivière] to flow into ▸ **là où la Marne se jette dans la Seine** where the river Marne flows *ou* runs into the Seine ▸ **se jeter dans les bras de qqn** to throw o.s. into sb's arms ▸ **se jeter à l'eau** *fig* to take the plunge.

jeton [ʒətɔ̃] **nm** [de jeu] counter / [de téléphone] token ▸▸ **avoir les jetons** *fam* to have the jitters.
◆ ***faux-jeton*** **nm** hypocrite.
◆ ***jeton de présence*** **nm** *fees paid to non-executive directors of a company*.

jet-set [dʒɛtsɛt], ***jet-society*** [dʒɛtsɔsajti] **nf** jet set ▸ **membre de la jet-set** jet-setter.

jette, ***jettes*** ➤ ***jeter***.

jetterai, ***jetteras*** ➤ ***jeter***.

jeu, ***x*** [ʒø] **nm 1.** [divertissement] play *(U)*, playing *(U)* ▸ **par jeu** for fun ▸ **jeu de mots** play on words, pun **2.** [régi par des règles] game ▸ **en jeu** in (play) ▸ **hors jeu** out (of play) ▸ **mettre un joueur hors jeu** to put a player offside ▸ **jeu électronique/vidéo** electronic/video game ▸ **jeu de l'oie** ≃ snakes and ladders ▸ **jeu de rôle** role play ▸ **jeu de société** parlour *UK ou* parlor *US* game ▸ **jeu télévisé** game show **3.** [d'argent] **: le jeu** gambling ▸ **jeu de hasard** game of chance **4.** [d'échecs, de clés] set ▸ **jeu de cartes** pack *UK ou* deck *US* of cards **5.** [manière de jouer] MUS playing / THÉÂTRE acting / SPORT game ▸ **il a un jeu défensif/offensif** he plays a defensive/an attacking game **6.** TECHNOL play ▸ **il y a du jeu** there's a bit of play, it's rather loose ▸▸ **cacher son jeu** to play one's cards close to one's chest ▸ **ce n'est pas du jeu!** that's not fair! ▸ **c'est un jeu d'enfant!** this is child's play! ▸ **être en jeu** to be at stake ▸ **les forces en jeu sur le marché** the competing forces *ou* th

forces at play *ou* the forces at work on the market ▸ **être pris à son propre jeu** to be caught at one's own game ▸ **entrer en jeu** to come into play ▸ **entrer dans le jeu de qqn** to play sb's game ▸ **mettre qqch en jeu** [risquer qqch] to put sthg at stake ▸ **mettre le ballon en jeu** FOOTBALL to throw in the ball ▸ **voir clair** *ou* **lire dans le jeu de qqn** to see through sb's little game, to see what sb is up to.
◆ ***Jeux Olympiques*** **nmpl : les Jeux Olympiques** the Olympic Games.

jeudi [ʒødi] **nm** Thursday ▸ **jeudi saint** Maundy Thursday ; voir aussi ***samedi***.

jeun [ʒœ̃] ◆ ***à jeun*** **loc adv** on an empty stomach.

jeune [ʒœn] ■ **adj** young ▸ **jeune chien** puppy, young dog ▸ **de jeunes enfants** young *ou* small children / [style, apparence] youthful ▸ **jeune homme/femme** young man/woman ▸ **jeune fille** girl ▸ **jeunes gens** [gén] young people / [garçons] young men ▸ **jeune pousse** ÉCON start up (company) ▸ **étant donné son jeune âge** given his youth *ou* how young he is ▸ **être jeune d'esprit** *ou* **de caractère** to be young at heart.
■ **adv : faire jeune** to look young ▸ **s'habiller jeune** to wear young-looking clothes.
■ **nm** young person ▸ **les jeunes** young people ▸ **une bande de jeunes** a bunch of kids.

jeûne [ʒøn] **nm** fast.

jeûner [3] [ʒøne] **vi** to fast.

jeunesse [ʒœnɛs] **nf 1.** [âge] youth ▸ **dans ma jeunesse** in my youth, when I was young, in my early years ▸ **ses amours/œuvres de jeunesse** the loves/works of his youth **2.** [de style, apparence] youthfulness ▸ **j'apprécie la jeunesse d'esprit** *ou* **de caractère** I appreciate a youthful outlook *ou* frame of mind **3.** [jeunes gens] young people *pl* ▸ **émissions pour la jeunesse** TV programmes *UK ou* programs *US* for younger viewers ▸ **les jeunesses communistes/socialistes** Young Communists/Socialists.

JF, ***jf*** abr de ***jeune fille***.

JH abr de ***jeune homme***.

jingle [dʒingəl] **nm** jingle.

JO ■ **nm** (abr de ***Journal officiel***) *bulletin giving details of laws and official announcements.*
■ **nmpl** (abr de ***Jeux Olympiques***) *Olympic Games.*

joaillerie [ʒɔajri] **nf 1.** [métier] jewel trade **2.** [magasin] jeweller's *UK ou* jeweler's *US* (shop).

joaillier, ***ère*** [ʒɔaje, ɛr] **nm, f** jeweller *UK*, jeweler *US*.

job [dʒɔb] **nm** *fam* job.

jobard, ***e*** [ʒɔbar, ard] **adj** *fam* gullible.

jockey [ʒɔkɛ] **nm** jockey.

jogging [dʒɔgiŋ] **nm 1.** [activité] jogging ▸ **faire du jogging** to go jogging, to go for a jog **2.** [vêtement] tracksuit, jogging suit.

joie [ʒwa] **nf** joy ▸ **avec joie** with pleasure ▸ **joie de vivre** joie de vivre, joy of living ▸ **être fou de joie** to be wild with joy ▸ **pousser un cri de joie** to shout *ou* to whoop for joy ▸ **il a accepté avec joie** he was delighted to accept ▸ **faire une fausse joie** to get sb excited for nothing.
◆ ***joies*** **nfpl** [plaisirs] joys ▸ **les joies de la vie/retraite** the joys of life/retirement.

joignable [ʒwaɲabl] **adj** contactable.

joignais, ***joignions*** ➤ ***joindre***.

joindre [82] [ʒwɛ̃dr] **vt 1.** [rapprocher] to join / [mains] to put together ▸ **(ne pas) arriver à joindre les deux bouts** *fam fig* (to be unable) to make ends meet ▸ **joindre la technique à l'efficacité** to combine technical know-how and efficiency **2.** [mettre avec] **: joindre qqch (à)** to attach sthg (to) / [ajouter] **joindre un fichier à un message électronique** to attach a file to an email message / [adjoindre] to enclose sthg (with) ▸ **je joins à ce pli un chèque de 300 euros** please find enclosed a cheque for 300 euros **3.** [par téléphone] to contact, to reach ▸ **où pourrai-je vous joindre?** how can I get in touch with you *ou* contact you?
◆ ***se joindre*** **vp : se joindre à qqn** to join sb ▸ **tu veux te joindre à nous?** would you like to come with us? ▸ **se joindre à qqch** to join in sthg ▸ **se joindre à une conversation/partie de rami** to join in a conversation/game of rummy.

joint, ***e*** [ʒwɛ̃, ɛ̃t] **pp** ➤ ***joindre***.
◆ ***joint*** **nm 1.** [d'étanchéité] seal **2.** *fam* [drogue] joint.
◆ ***joint de culasse*** **nm** cylinder head gasket.

jointure [ʒwɛ̃tyr] **nf** ANAT joint.

joker [ʒɔkɛr] **nm** joker.

joli, ***e*** [ʒɔli] **adj 1.** [femme, chose] pretty, attractive ▸ **très joli** [enfant, vêtement] lovely ▸ **il est joli garçon** he's nice-looking *ou* attractive **2.** [somme, situation] nice ▸ **elle s'est taillé un joli succès** she's been most *ou* very successful ▸▸ **c'est bien joli, mais...** that's all very well, but... ▸ **c'est du joli travail!** *iron* well done! ▸ **tu l'as cassé? c'est du joli!** you broke it? that's great! ▸ **faire le joli cœur** to flirt ▸ **tu nous as mis dans un joli pétrin** *fam* you got us into a fine mess.

joliment [ʒɔlimɑ̃] **adv 1.** [bien] prettily, attractively / *iron* nicely **2.** *fam* [beaucoup] really.

jonc [ʒɔ̃] **nm** rush, bulrush.

joncher [3] [ʒɔ̃ʃe] **vt** to strew ▸ **être jonché de** to be strewn with.

jonction [ʒɔ̃ksjɔ̃] **nf** [de routes] junction.

jongler [3] [ʒɔ̃gle] **vi** to juggle.

jongleur, ***euse*** [ʒɔ̃glœr, øz] **nm, f** juggler.

jonquille [ʒɔ̃kij] **nf** daffodil.

Jordanie [ʒɔrdani] **nf : la Jordanie** Jordan.

jordanien, ***enne*** [ʒɔrdanjɛ̃, ɛn] **adj** Jordanian.
◆ ***Jordanien***, ***enne*** **nm, f** Jordanian.

jouable [ʒwabl] **adj 1.** SPORT playable **2.** [situation] feasible.

joual [ʒwal] **nm** *Québec French-Canadian dialect.*

joue [ʒu] **nf** cheek ▸ **tenir** *ou* **mettre qqn en joue** *fig* to take aim at sb.

jouer [6] [ʒwe] ■ **vi 1.** [gén] to play ▸ **jouer avec qqn/qqch** to play with sb/sthg ▸ **jouer avec les sentiments de qqn** to play *ou* to trifle with sb's feelings ▸ **jouer à qqch** [jeu, sport] to play sthg ▸ **jouer à la marchande/au docteur** to play (at) shops/doctors and nurses ▸ **jouer de** MUS to play ▸ **tu joues d'un instrument?** do *ou* can you play an instrument? ▸ **à toi de jouer!** (it's) your turn! / *fig* your move! **2.** CINÉ & THÉÂTRE to act ▸ **jouer dans un film/une pièce** to be in a film/a play **3.** [parier] to gamble ▸ **jouer aux courses** to bet on horses ▸ **jouer à la roulette** to play roulette **4.** [s'appliquer] to apply ▸ **il a fait jouer ses relations pour obtenir le poste** he pulled some strings to get the job

▸▸ **jouer des coudes** to use one's elbows ▸ **jouer de malchance** to be dogged by bad luck ▸ **jouer sur les mots** to play with words.

■ **vt 1.** [carte, partie] to play ▸ **ils jouent la balle de match** they're at match point **2.** [somme d'argent] to bet, to wager / *fig* to gamble with ▸ **il joue d'énormes sommes** he gambles vast sums, he plays for high stakes *ou* big money **3.** [THÉÂTRE - pièce] to put on, to perform / [- personnage, rôle] to play ▸ **il a très bien joué Cyrano** he gave an excellent performance as Cyrano **4.** [avoir à l'affiche] to show ▸ **qu'est-ce qu'on joue en ce moment?** what's on at the moment? **5.** MUS to perform, to play ▸ **jouer du Chopin** to play (some) Chopin

▸▸ **jouer la comédie** to put on an act ▸ **jouer le jeu** to play the game ▸ **jouer un rôle** *litt* & *fig* to play a part ▸ **jouer un tour à qqn** to play a trick on sb.

◆ ***se jouer*** **vp : se jouer de qqch** to make light of sthg ▸ **se jouer de qqn** to deceive sb.

jouet [ʒwɛ] **nm** toy ▸ **être le jouet de** *fig* to be the victim of.

joueur, euse [ʒwœr, øz] **nm, f 1.** SPORT player ▸ **joueur de football** soccer *ou* football *UK* player, footballer *UK* ▸ **être beau/mauvais joueur** to be a good/bad loser **2.** [au casino] gambler.

joufflu, e [ʒufly] **adj** [personne] chubby-cheeked.

joug [ʒu] **nm** yoke.

jouir [32] [ʒwir] **vi 1.** [profiter] **: jouir de** to enjoy **2.** [sexuellement] to have an orgasm.

jouissance [ʒwisɑ̃s] **nf 1.** DR [d'un bien] use **2.** [sexuelle] orgasm.

jouisseur, euse [ʒwisœr, øz] **nm, f** sensualist.

jouissif, ive [ʒwisif, iv] **adj** *fam* **: ce film, c'était jouissif** that film *UK ou* movie *US* was a treat!

joujou, x [ʒuʒu] **nm** toy.

jour [ʒur] **nm 1.** [unité de temps] day ▸ **huit jours** a week ▸ **quinze jours** two weeks, a fortnight *UK* ▸ **tous les jours** every day ▸ **l'autre jour** the other day ▸ **de jour en jour** day by day ▸ **jour après jour** day after day ▸ **au jour le jour** from day to day ▸ **jour et nuit** night and day ▸ **du jour au lendemain** overnight ▸ **jour pour jour** to the day ▸ **le jour de l'an** New Year's Day ▸ **jour chômé** public holiday ▸ **jour de congé** day off ▸ **jour férié** public holiday ▸ **jour de fête** holiday ▸ **le jour J** D-Day ▸ **jour ouvrable** working day ▸ **un jour de repos** a day of rest ▸ **un jour de travail** a workday, a working day *UK*

2. [lumière] daylight ▸ **de jour** in the daytime, by day ▸ **il fait jour** it's light ▸ **au petit jour** at the crack of dawn ▸ **au grand jour** in broad daylight ▸ **le jour se lève** the sun is rising

3. [époque] day ▸ **comme au premier jour** as it was in the beginning ▸ **son manteau/son discours des grands jours** the coat she wears/the speech she makes on important occasions ▸ **le jour où** the day (that) ▸ **un beau jour** one fine day ▸ **les beaux jours** [printemps] springtime / [été] summertime ▸ **un de ces jours** one of these days ▸ **à un de ces jours!** see you soon!

4. [aspect] **: sous un certain jour** in a certain light ▸ **voir qqch sous son vrai** *ou* **véritable jour** to see sthg in its true light ▸ **sous un faux jour** in a false light

5. COUT opening *(made by drawing threads)* ▸ **des jours** openwork, drawn work

▸▸ **être à jour** to be up-to-date ▸ **être à jour de ses cotisations** to have paid one's subscription ▸ **mettre qqch à jour** to update sthg, to bring sthg up to date ▸ **se faire jour** to become clear ▸ **sous un jour nouveau** in a new light ▸ **donner le jour à** to give birth to ▸ **voir le jour** [bébé] to be born / [théorie, invention] to appear.

◆ ***jours*** **nmpl 1.** [vie] days, life ▸ **mettre fin à ses jours** to put an end to one's life ▸ **ses jours sont comptés** his days are numbered

2. [époque] **: passer des jours heureux** to have a good time

▸▸ **les mauvais jours** [les moments difficiles] unhappy days, hard times / [les jours où rien ne va] bad days ▸ **il a sa tête des mauvais jours** it looks like he's in a bad mood ▸ **ce manteau a connu des jours meilleurs** this coat has seen better days ▸ **ses vieux jours** his old age ▸ **de nos jours** these days, nowadays ▸ **les beaux jours** [printemps] springtime / [été] summertime.

journal, aux [ʒurnal, o] **nm 1.** [publication] newspaper, paper ▸ **journal à scandale** *ou* **à sensation** scandal sheet ▸ **journal du matin/soir/dimanche** morning/evening/Sunday paper *ou* newspaper ▸ **c'est dans** *ou* **sur le journal** it's in the paper ▸ **le Journal officiel (de la République française)** *official publication in which public notices appear* **2.** TV **: journal télévisé** television news ▸ **ils l'ont dit au journal** *fam* they said so on the news ▸ **journal vidéo** video diary **3.** [écrit] **: journal (intime)** diary, journal ▸ **tenir un journal** to keep a diary ▸ **journal de bord** NAUT ship's log / INFORM log.

CULTURE

Le Journal officiel

This daily bulletin, available online and on paper, provides information about new laws and parliamentary debates as well as any other important government business. New companies must also publish an announcement of their creation in its pages. Laws take effect no more than 48 hours after the particular day's **Journal** arrives at an **arrondissement**'s administrative headquarters.

journalier, ère [ʒurnalje, ɛr] **adj** daily.

journalisme [ʒurnalism] **nm** journalism ▸ **journalisme électronique** electronic news gathering ▸ **journalisme d'investigation** *ou* **d'enquête** investigative journalism.

journaliste [ʒurnalist] **nmf** journalist, reporter.

journalistique [ʒurnalistik] **adj** journalistic.

journée [ʒurne] **nf** day ▸ **faire la journée continue** to work through lunch.

FAUX AMIS / FALSE FRIENDS
journée
Journey is not a translation of the French word *journée.* Journey is translated by *voyage.*
▸ They set out on a journey / *Ils sont partis en voyage*

journellement [ʒurnɛlmɑ̃] **adv** daily.

joute [ʒut] **nf** joust / *fig* duel.

jouxter [3] [ʒukste] **vt** to adjoin.

jovial, e, aux [ʒɔvjal, o] **adj** jovial, jolly.

jovialité [ʒɔvjalite] **nf** joviality, jolliness.

joyau, x [ʒwajo] **nm** jewel.

joyeusement [ʒwajøzmɑ̃] **adv** joyfully.

joyeux, euse [ʒwajø, øz] **adj** joyful, happy ▸ **joyeux Noël!** Merry Christmas!

JPEG (abr de ***Joint Photographic Experts Group***) m INFORM **: JPEG** JPEG.

JT (abr de ***journal télévisé***) **nm** television news.

jubilation [ʒybilasjɔ̃] **nf** jubilation.

jubilé [ʒybile] **nm** jubilee.

jubiler [3] [ʒybile] **vi** *fam* to be jubilant.

jucher [3] [ʒyʃe] **vt : jucher qqn sur qqch** to perch sb on sthg.
◆ ***se jucher*** **vp : se jucher sur qqch** to perch on sthg.

judaïque [ʒydaik] **adj** [loi] Judaic / [tradition, religion] Jewish.

judaïsme [ʒydaism] **nm** Judaism.

judas [ʒyda] **nm** [ouverture] peephole.

Judée [ʒyde] **nf : la Judée** Judaea, Judea.

judéo-chrétien, enne [ʒydeɔkretjɛ̃, ɛn] (mpl **judéo-chrétiens**, fpl **judéo-chrétiennes**) **adj** Judaeo-Christian.

judiciaire [ʒydisjɛr] **adj** judicial.

judicieusement [ʒydisjøzmɑ̃] **adv** judiciously.

judicieux, euse [ʒydisjø, øz] **adj** judicious.

judo [ʒydo] **nm** judo.

juge [ʒyʒ] **nm** judge ▸ **juge d'instruction** examining magistrate ▸ **juge d'enfants** children's judge, juvenile magistrate *UK* ▸ **juge de ligne** TENNIS line judge ▸ **juge de paix** justice of the peace ▸ **juge de touche** [football] linesman / [rugby] touch judge.

jugé [ʒyʒe] ◆ ***au jugé*** **loc adv** by guesswork ▸ **tirer au jugé** to fire blind.

jugement [ʒyʒmɑ̃] **nm** judgment ▸ **prononcer un jugement** to pass sentence ▸ **jugement de valeur** value judgment.
◆ ***Jugement*** **nm : le Jugement dernier** the Last Judgment.

jugeote [ʒyʒɔt] **nf** *fam* common sense ▸ **manquer de jugeote** to have no common sense.

juger [17] [ʒyʒe] ■ **vt** to judge / [accusé] to try ▸ **elle a été jugée coupable/non coupable** she was found guilty/not guilty ▸ **juger un différend** to arbitrate in a dispute ▸ **juger que** to judge (that),to consider (that) ▸ **juger qqn bien/mal** to have a good/poor opinion of sb ▸ **juger qqn/qqch inutile** to consider sb/sthg useless ▸ **juger bon de faire qqch** to consider it appropriate to do sthg ▸ **son état est jugé très préoccupant** his condition is believed to be serious.
■ **vi** to judge ▸ **juger de qqch** to judge sthg ▸ **à en juger par son large sourire** if her broad smile is anything to go by ▸ **si j'en juge d'après mon expérience** judging from my experience ▸ **jugez de ma surprise!** imagine my surprise!
◆ ***se juger*** **vp** *(emploi passif)* **1.** DR **: l'affaire se jugera mardi** the case will be heard on Tuesday **2.** [se considérer] **: les commerçants se jugent lésés** shopkeepers consider *ou* think themselves hard done by.

juguler [3] [ʒygyle] **vt** [maladie] to halt / [révolte] to put down / [inflation] to curb.

juif, ive [ʒɥif, iv] **adj** Jewish.
◆ ***Juif, ive*** **nm, f** Jew.

juillet [ʒɥijɛ] **nm** July ▸ **la fête du 14 Juillet** *national holiday to mark the anniversary of the storming of the Bastille* ; voir aussi ***septembre***.

juin [ʒyɛ̃] **nm** June ; voir aussi ***septembre***.

juke-box [dʒukbɔks] **nm inv** jukebox.

julienne [ʒyljɛn] **nf : julienne de légumes** *(clear soup with) very thin strips of vegetable.*

jumeau, elle, x [ʒymo, ɛl, o] ■ **adj** twin *(avant n).*
■ **nm, f** twin ▸ **vrais/faux jumeaux** identical/fraternal twins.
◆ ***jumelles*** **nfpl** [en optique] binoculars.

jumelage [ʒymlaʒ] **nm** twinning.

jumelé, e [ʒymle] **adj** [villes] twinned / [maisons] semi-detached ▸ **roues jumelées** double wheels.

jumeler [24] [ʒymle] **vt** to twin.

jumelle ➤ ***jumeau***.

jument [ʒymɑ̃] **nf** mare.

jungle [ʒœ̃gl] **nf** jungle.

junior [ʒynjɔr] **adj** & **nmf** SPORT junior.

junte [ʒœ̃t] **nf** junta.

jupe [ʒyp] **nf** skirt.

jupe-culotte [ʒypkylɔt] (pl **jupes-culottes**) **nf** culottes *pl.*

Jupiter [ʒypitɛr] **npr 1.** ASTRON Jupiter **2.** MYTHOL Jupiter, Jove.

jupon [ʒypɔ̃] **nm** petticoat, slip.

Jura [ʒyra] **nm : le Jura** the Jura (Mountains).

jurassien, enne [ʒyrasjɛ̃, ɛn] **adj** from the Jura.

juré [ʒyre] **nm** DR juror.

juré, e [ʒyre] **adj : ennemi juré** sworn enemy.

jurer [3] [ʒyre] ■ **vt : jurer qqch à qqn** to swear *ou* pledge sthg to sb ▸ **jurer fidélité/obéissance à qqn** to

swear *ou* to pledge loyalty/obedience to sb ▸ **jurer (à qqn) que...** to swear (to sb) that... ▸ **jurer de faire qqch** to swear *ou* vow to do sthg ▸ **j'ai juré de garder le secret** I'm sworn to secrecy ▸ **je le jure** I swear ▸ **je vous jure!** *fam* honestly! ▸ **jurer sur la tête de qqn** to swear on one's mother's grave ▸ **ne plus jurer que par** to swear by ▸ **ils ne jurent que par leur nouvel entraîneur** they swear by their new coach.
■ **vi 1.** [blasphémer] to swear, to curse ▸ **jurer comme un charretier** to swear like a trooper **2.** [ne pas aller ensemble] **: jurer (avec)** to clash (with).
◆ ***jurer de*** v + prep [affirmer] **: jurer de sa bonne foi** to swear that one is sincere ▸ **il ne faut jurer de rien** you never can tell.
◆ ***se jurer*** vp **: se jurer de faire qqch** to swear *ou* vow to do sthg.

juridiction [ʒyridiksjɔ̃] **nf** jurisdiction.

juridictionnel, elle [ʒyridiksjɔnɛl] **adj** jurisdictional.

juridique [ʒyridik] **adj** legal.

juridiquement [ʒyridikmɑ̃] **adv** legally.

jurisprudence [ʒyrisprydɑ̃s] **nf** jurisprudence ▸ **faire jurisprudence** to set a precedent.

juriste [ʒyrist] **nmf** lawyer.

juron [ʒyrɔ̃] **nm** swearword, oath.

jury [ʒyri] **nm 1.** DR jury **2.** [SCOL - d'examen] examining board / [- de concours] admissions board.

jus [ʒy] **nm 1.** [de fruits, légumes] juice ▸ **jus d'orange/de pomme** orange/apple juice **2.** [de viande] gravy.

jusqu'au-boutiste [ʒyskobutist] **nmf** hard-liner.

jusque, jusqu' [ʒysk(ə)] ◆ ***jusqu'à*** loc prép **1.** [sens temporel] until, till ▸ **jusqu'à nouvel ordre** until further notice ▸ **jusqu'à présent** up until now, so far ▸ **la pièce dure jusqu'à quelle heure?** what time does the play finish? ▸ **tu vas attendre jusqu'à quand?** how long are you going to wait? **2.** [sens spatial] as far as ▸ **jusqu'à Marseille** as far as Marseilles ▸ **elle avait de l'eau jusqu'aux genoux** she was up to her knees in water ▸ **jusqu'au bout** to the end **3.** [même] even ▸ **aller jusqu'à faire qqch** *fig* to go as far as to do sthg ▸ **j'irais jusqu'à dire que c'était délibéré** I would go as far as to say it was done on purpose.
◆ ***jusqu'à ce que*** loc conj until, till ▸ **tout allait bien jusqu'à ce qu'il arrive** everything was going fine until he turned up. ◆ ***jusqu'en*** loc prép up until. ◆ ***jusqu'ici*** **loc adv** [lieu] up to here ▸ **je ne suis pas venu jusqu'ici pour rien!** I haven't come all this way *ou* as far as this for nothing! / [temps] up until now, so far. ◆ ***jusque-là*** **loc adv** [lieu] up to there ▸ **on avait de l'eau jusque-là** the water was up to here / [temps] up until then ▸ **jusque-là, tout va bien** so far so good.

justaucorps [ʒystokɔr] **nm** [maillot] leotard.

juste [ʒyst] ■ **adj 1.** [équitable] fair ▸ **être juste envers *ou* avec qqn** to be fair to sb ▸ **c'est pas juste!** *fam* it's not fair *ou* right! **2.** [exact] right, correct ▸ **ta remarque est tout à fait juste!** your comment is quite right! ▸ **as-tu l'heure juste?** have you got the right *ou* exact time? **3.** [trop petit, trop court] tight ▸ **une heure pour aller à l'aéroport, c'est trop juste** an hour to get to the airport: that's not enough ▸ **la nappe est un peu juste en longueur/largeur** the tablecloth is a bit on the short/narrow side **4.** [de justesse] **: elle a réussi, mais c'était juste** she passed, but it was a close thing.
■ **adv 1.** [bien] correctly, right ▸ **chanter juste** to sing in tune ▸ **tu as vu *ou* deviné juste!** you guessed correctly *ou* right! **2.** [exactement, seulement] just ▸ **juste à temps** just in time ▸ **il vient juste d'arriver** he's just (this minute) arrived.
◆ ***au juste*** **loc adv** exactly ▸ **combien sont-ils au juste?** how many (of them) are there exactly?
◆ ***tout juste*** **loc adv** only just ▸ **il s'est fait renvoyer? – tout juste!** so he was dismissed? – he was indeed!
◆ ***au plus juste*** **loc adv : calculer qqch au plus juste** to calculate sthg to the nearest penny.
◆ ***comme de juste*** **loc adv** of course, needless to say ▸ **comme de juste, elle avait oublié** she'd forgotten, of course.

justement [ʒystəmɑ̃] **adv 1.** [avec raison] rightly **2.** [précisément] exactly, precisely.

justesse [ʒystɛs] **nf** [de remarque] aptness / [de raisonnement] soundness.
◆ ***de justesse*** **loc adv** only just.

justice [ʒystis] **nf 1.** DR justice ▸ **se faire justice** [se suicider] to take one's life ▸ **passer en justice** to stand trial ▸ **rendre la justice** to dispense justice ▸ **rendre justice à qqn/qqch** to do justice to sb/sthg **2.** [équité] fairness.

justiciable [ʒystisjabl] **adj : être justiciable de** DR to be answerable to.

justicier, ère [ʒystisje, ɛr] **nm, f** righter of wrongs.

justifiable [ʒystifjabl] **adj** justifiable.

justificatif, ive [ʒystifikatif, iv] **adj** supporting *(avant n)*.
◆ ***justificatif*** **nm** written proof *(U)*.

justification [ʒystifikasjɔ̃] **nf** justification.

justifier [9] [ʒystifje] **vt 1.** [gén] to justify **2.** TYPO **: justifier à gauche/à droite** to left-justify/right-justify.
◆ ***se justifier*** **vp** to justify o.s.

jute [ʒyt] **nm** jute.

juter [3] [ʒyte] **vi** [fruit] to be juicy.

juteux, euse [ʒytø, øz] **adj** juicy ▸ **une affaire juteuse** *fam* a gold mine, a nice little earner *UK*.

juvénile [ʒyvenil] **adj** youthful.

juxtaposé, e [ʒykstapoze] **adj** juxtaposed.

juxtaposer [3] [ʒykstapoze] **vt** to juxtapose, to place side by side.

juxtaposition [ʒykstapozisjɔ̃] **nf** juxtaposition.

k

k, ***K*** [ka] **nm inv** k, K.

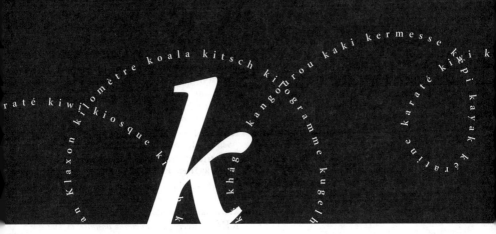

K7 [kasɛt] (abr de ***cassette***) **nf** cassette ▸ **radio-K7** radio-cassette.

Kaboul [kabul] **npr** Kabul.

kabyle [kabil] ■ **adj** Kabyle.
■ **nm** [langue] Kabyle.
◆ ***Kabyle*** **nmf** Kabyle.

Kabylie [kabili] **nf : la Kabylie** Kabylia.

kaki [kaki] ■ **nm 1.** [couleur] khaki **2.** [fruit] persimmon.
■ **adj inv** khaki.

kaléidoscope [kaleidɔskɔp] **nm** kaleidoscope.

kamikaze [kamikaz] **nm** kamikaze pilot.

Kampuchéa [kɑ̃pyʃea] **nm : le Kampuchéa** Kampuchea.

kanak = ***canaque***.

kangourou [kɑ̃guru] **nm** kangaroo.

kapok [kapɔk] **nm** kapok.

karaoké [karaɔke] **nm** karaoke.

karaté [karate] **nm** karate.

karité [karite] **nm** shea.

kart [kart] **nm** go-kart *UK*, go-cart *US*.

karting [kartiŋ] **nm** go-karting *UK*, go-carting *US*.

kas(c)her, ***cascher*** [kaʃɛr] **adj inv** kosher ▸ **manger kascher** to eat kosher food.

Katar = ***Qatar***.

kayak [kajak] **nm** kayak.

KCS (abr écrite de ***couronne tchécoslovaque***) Kcs.

kendo [kɛndo] **nm** kendo.

Kenya [kenja] **nm : le Kenya** Kenya ▸ **au Kenya** in Kenya.

kenyan, ***e*** [kenjɑ̃, an] **adj** Kenyan.
◆ ***Kenyan***, ***e*** **nm, f** Kenyan.

képi [kepi] **nm** kepi.

kératine [keratin] **nf** keratin.

kermesse [kɛrmɛs] **nf 1.** [foire] fair **2.** [fête de bienfaisance] fête.

kérosène [kerɔzɛn] **nm** kerosene.

ketchup [kɛtʃœp] **nm** ketchup.

keuf [kœf] **nm** *fam* cop.

keum [kœm] **nm** *fam* guy, bloke.

KF abr écrite de ***kilofranc***, ***café***.

kg (abr écrite de ***kilogramme***) kg.

KGB (abr de ***Komitet Gossoudarstvennoï Bezopasnosti***) **nm** KGB.

khâgne [kaɲ] **nf** *second year of a two-year preparatory arts course taken prior to the competitive examination for entry to the École normale supérieure.*

Khartoum [kartum] **npr** Khartoum.

khmer, ***ère*** [kmɛr] **adj** Khmer.
◆ ***khmer*** **nm** [langue] Khmer.
◆ ***Khmer***, ***ère*** **nm, f** Khmer.

khôl [kol], ***kohol*** [kɔɔl] **nm** kohl.

kibboutz [kibuts] **nm inv** kibbutz.

kidnapper [3] [kidnape] **vt** to kidnap.

kidnappeur, ***euse*** [kidnapœr, øz] **nm, f** kidnapper.

kidnapping [kidnapiŋ] **nm** kidnap.

kif-kif [kifkif] **adj inv** *fam* **: c'est kif-kif** it's all the same, it makes no odds *UK*.

kiki [kiki] **nm** *fam* [cou] neck / [gorge] throat ▸ **serrer le kiki à qqn** to throttle *ou* to strangle sb
▸▸ **c'est parti, mon kiki!** here we go!

kilo [kilo] **nm** kilo.

kilofranc [kilofrɑ̃] **nm** *one thousand francs.*

kilogramme [kilɔgram] **nm** kilogram, kilogramme *UK*.

kilométrage [kilɔmetraʒ] **nm 1.** [de voiture] ≃ mileage ▸ **kilométrage illimité** ≃ unlimited mileage **2.** [distance] distance.

kilomètre [kilɔmɛtr] **nm** kilometre *UK*, kilometer *US*.

kilométrique [kilɔmetrik] **adj** kilometric.

kilo-octet [kilɔɔktɛ] **nm** INFORM kilobyte.

kilowatt [kilɔwat] **nm** kilowatt.

kilowatt-heure [kilowatœr] (pl **kilowatts-heures**) **nm** kilowatt-hour.

kilt [kilt] **nm** kilt.

kimono [kimɔno] **nm** kimono.

kiné [kine] *fam* ■ **nmf** (abr de ***kinésithérapeute***) physio *UK*, physical therapist *US*.
■ **nmf** (abr de ***kinésithérapie***) physio *UK*, physical therapy *US* ▸ **5 séances de kiné** 5 sessions of physio *UK ou* physical therapy *US*.

kinésithérapeute [kineziterapøt] **nmf** physiotherapist *UK*, physical therapist *US*.

kinésithérapie [kineziterapi] **nf** physiotherapy *UK*, physical therapy *US*.

Kinshasa [kinʃasa] **npr** Kinshasa.

kiosque [kjɔsk] **nm 1.** [de vente] kiosk ▸ **kiosque à journaux** newspaper kiosk **2.** [pavillon] pavilion **3.** [de navire] pilot house, wheelhouse.

kir [kir] **nm** kir *apéritif made with white wine and blackcurrant liqueur*.

kirsch [kirʃ] **nm** cherry brandy.

kit [kit] **nm** kit ▸ **en kit** in kit form ▸ **kit mains libres** TÉLÉCOM hands-free kit.

kitchenette [kitʃənɛt] **nf** kitchenette.

kitsch [kitʃ] **adj inv** kitsch.

kiwi [kiwi] **nm 1.** [oiseau] kiwi **2.** [fruit] kiwi, kiwi fruit *(U)*.

Klaxon® [klaksɔ̃] **nm** horn.

klaxonner [3] [klaksɔne] **vi** to hoot, to honk.

kleptomane [klɛptɔman] **nmf** kleptomaniac.

kleptomanie [klɛptɔmani] **nf** kleptomania.

km (abr écrite de ***kilomètre***) km.

km/h (abr écrite de ***kilomètre par heure***) kph.

Ko (abr écrite de ***kilo-octet***) K.

K.-O. [kao] **nm : mettre qqn K.-O.** to knock sb out.

koala [kɔala] **nm** koala (bear).

kohol = ***khôl***.

kosovar, e [kɔsɔvar] **adj** Kosovan.
◆ ***Kosovar, e*** [kɔsɔvar] **nm, f** Kosovar.

Kosovo [kɔsɔvɔ] **nm : le Kosovo** Kosovo ▸ **au Kosovo** in Kosovo.

kouglof, kugelhof [kuglɔf] **nm** *cake made with dried fruit and almonds*.

Koweït [kɔwɛt] **nm** [pays, ville] Kuwait ▸ **le Koweït** Kuwait ▸ **au Koweït** in Kuwait.

koweïtien, enne [kɔwɛtjɛ̃, ɛn] **adj** Kuwaiti.
◆ ***Koweïtien, enne*** **nm, f** Kuwaiti.

krach [krak] **nm** crash ▸ **krach boursier** stock market crash.

kraft [kraft] **nm** kraft ▸ **papier kraft** brown paper.

KRD (abr écrite de ***couronne danoise***) Kr, DKr.

KRN (abr écrite de ***couronne norvégienne***) Kr, NKr.

KRS (abr écrite de ***couronne suédoise***) Kr, Skr.

Kuala Lumpur [kyalalympyr] **npr** Kuala Lumpur.

kugelhof = ***kouglof***.

kumquat [kumkwat] **nm** kumquat.

kung-fu [kuŋfu] **nm** kung fu.

kurde [kyrd] ■ **adj** Kurdish.
■ **nm** [langue] Kurdish.
◆ ***Kurde*** **nmf** Kurd.

Kurdistan [kyrdistɑ̃] **nm : le Kurdistan** Kurdistan ▸ **au Kurdistan** in Kurdistan.

K-way® [kawɛ] **nm inv** cagoule.

kWh (abr écrite de ***kilowatt-heure***) kW/hr.

Kyoto [kjɔtɔ] **npr** Kyoto.

kyrielle [kirjɛl] **nf** *fam* stream / [d'enfants] horde.

kyste [kist] **nm** cyst.

l

l, L [ɛl] ■ **nm inv** l, L.
■ (abr écrite de ***litre***) l.

l' ➤ ***le***.

la[1] [la] **art déf & pron pers** ➤ ***le***.

la[2] [la] **nm inv** MUS A / [chanté] la, lah *UK*.

là [la] ■ **adv 1.** [lieu] there ▸ **à 3 kilomètres de là** 3 kilometres from there ▸ **passe par là** go that way ▸ **c'est là que je travaille** that's where I work ▸ **je suis là** I'm here ▸ **les faits sont là** those are the facts **2.** [temps] then ▸ **à quelques jours de là** a few days later, a few days after that ▸ **attendons demain et là nous déciderons** let's wait until tomorrow and then (we'll) decide **3.** [dans cela] **: la santé, tout est là** (good) health is everything ▸ **là est le vrai problème** that's the real problem **4.** [avec une proposition relative] **: là où** [lieu] where / [temps] when **5.** [emploi expressif] **: alors là, tu exagères!** you've got a nerve! ▸ **que me chantes-tu là?** *fam* what are you on about?
▸▸ **de là à dire qu'elle est sympathique, il y a loin!** there's a big difference between saying that and saying that she's a nice person ▸ **comment en es-tu arrivé là?** how did you manage to let things go so far? ▸ **nous en sommes là** that's the stage we've reached ▸ **je n'ai pas l'intention d'en rester là** I don't intend leaving it at that ▸ **s'en tenir là** to call a halt (there) ▸ **que voulez-vous dire par là?** what do you mean by that?
■ voir aussi ***ce***, ***là-bas***, ***là-dedans*** *etc*.

là-bas [laba] **adv** (over) there.

label [labɛl] **nm 1.** [étiquette] **: label de qualité** label guaranteeing quality **2.** [commerce] label, brand name.

labeur [labœr] **nm** *sout* labour *UK*, labor *US*.

labial, e, aux [labjal, o] **adj** labial.

labo [labo] (abr de ***laboratoire***) **nm** *fam* lab.

laborantin, e [labɔrɑ̃tɛ̃, in] **nm, f** laboratory assistant.

laboratoire [labɔratwar] **nm** laboratory ▸ **laboratoire d'analyses** test laboratory ▸ **laboratoire de langues** language laboratory.

laborieusement [labɔrjøzmɑ̃] **adv** laboriously.

laborieux, euse [labɔrjø, øz] **adj 1.** [difficile] laborious **2.** [travailleur] industrious ▸ **les classes laborieuses** the working class *sg*.

labour [labur] **nm 1.** [labourage] ploughing *UK*, plowing *US* **2.** *(gén pl)* [terres] ploughed *UK* ***ou*** plowed *US* field.

labourage [laburaʒ] **nm** ploughing *UK*, plowing *US*.

labourer [3] [labure] **vt 1.** AGRIC to plough *UK*, to plow *US* **2.** *fig* [creuser] to make a gash in.

laboureur [laburœr] **nm** ploughman *UK*, plowman *US*.

labrador [labradɔr] **nm** labrador.

labyrinthe [labirɛ̃t] **nm** labyrinth.

lac [lak] **nm** lake ▸ **les Grands Lacs** the Great Lakes ▸ **le lac Léman** Lake Geneva ▸ **le lac Majeur** Lake Maggiore.

lacer [16] [lase] **vt** to tie.

lacérer [18] [lasere] **vt 1.** [déchirer] to shred **2.** [blesser, griffer] to slash.

lacet [lasɛ] **nm 1.** [cordon] lace **2.** [de route] bend **3.** [piège] snare.

lâche [laʃ] ■ **nmf** coward.
■ **adj 1.** [nœud] loose **2.** [personne, comportement] cowardly.

lâchement [laʃmɑ̃] **adv** like a coward.

lâcher [3] [laʃe] ■ **vt 1.** [libérer - bras, objet] to let go of ▸ **lâcher la pédale du frein** to take one's foot off the brake (pedal) / [- animal] to let go, to release ▸ **lâcher les chiens sur qqn** to set the dogs on sb **2.** [émettre - son, mot] to let out, to come out with ▸ **lâcher un juron** to let out an oath **3.** [desserrer] to loosen ▸ **lâcher la bride à un cheval** to give a horse its head **4.** [laisser tomber] **: lâcher qqch** to drop sthg ▸ **elle a lâché la pile d'assiettes** she dropped the pile of plates **5.** *fam* [abandonner - ami] **: lâcher qqn** to drop sb ▸ **le moteur nous a lâchés le deuxième jour** the engine broke down on us on the second day.
■ **vi** to give way.
■ **nm : un lâcher de** a release of ▸ **lâcher de ballons** balloon release.

lâcheté [laʃte] **nf 1.** [couardise] cowardice **2.** [acte] cowardly act.

lâcheur, euse [laʃœr, øz] **nm, f** *fam* unreliable person.

lacis [lasi] **nm** [labyrinthe] maze.

laconique [lakɔnik] **adj** laconic.

laconiquement [lakɔnikmɑ̃] **adv** laconically.

lacrymal**, **e**, **aux [lakrimal, o] **adj** lacrimal.

lacrymogène [lakrimɔʒɛn] **adj** tear *(avant n)*.

lactation [laktasjɔ̃] **nf** lactation.

lacté**, **e [lakte] **adj** [régime] milk *(avant n)*.

lactique [laktik] **adj** lactic.

lacunaire [lakynɛr] **adj** [insuffisant] incomplete.

lacune [lakyn] **nf** [manque] gap.

lacustre [lakystr] **adj** [faune, plante] lake *(avant n)* / [cité, village] on stilts.

lad [lad] **nm** stable lad.

là-dedans [ladədɑ̃] **adv** inside, in there ▸ **il y a quelque chose qui m'intrigue là-dedans** there's something in that which intrigues me.

là-dessous [ladsu] **adv** underneath, under there / *fig* behind that.

là-dessus [ladsy] **adv** on that ▸ **là-dessus, il partit** at that point *ou* with that, he left ▸ **je suis d'accord là-dessus** I agree about that.

ladite ➤ ***ledit***.

lagon [lagɔ̃] **nm** lagoon.

lagune [lagyn] **nf** = ***lagon***.

là-haut [lao] **adv** up there.

laïc**, **laïque [laik] ■ **adj** lay *(avant n)* / [juridiction] civil *(avant n)* / [école] state *(avant n)*.
■ **nm, f** layman (f laywoman).

laïcisation [laisizasjɔ̃] **nf** secularization.

laid**, **e [lɛ, lɛd] **adj 1.** [esthétiquement] ugly **2.** [moralement] wicked.

laideron [lɛdrɔ̃] **nm** ugly woman.

laideur [lɛdœr] **nf 1.** [physique] ugliness **2.** [morale] wickedness.

laie [lɛ] **nf** ZOOL wild sow.

lainage [lɛnaʒ] **nm** [étoffe] woollen *UK ou* woolen *US* material / [vêtement] woollen *UK ou* woolen *US* garment, woolly *UK*.

laine [lɛn] **nf** wool ▸ **laine polaire** polar fleece ▸ **laine de verre** glass wool ▸ **pure laine vierge** pure new wool.

laineux**, **euse [lɛnø, øz] **adj** woolly *UK*, wooly *US*.

lainier**, **ère [lɛnje, ɛr] ■ **adj** wool *(avant n)*.
■ **nm, f** [marchand] wool merchant / [ouvrier] wool worker.

laïque = ***laïc***.

laisse [lɛs] **nf** [corde] lead *UK*, leash *US* ▸ **tenir en laisse** [chien] to keep on a lead *UK ou* leash *US* ▸ **tenir qqn en laisse** *fig* to keep sb on a short lead *UK ou* leash *US*.

laissé-pour-compte**, **laissée-pour-compte [lesepurkɔ̃t] (mpl **laissés-pour-compte**, fpl **laissées-pour-compte**) ■ **adj 1.** [article] unsold **2.** *fig* [personne] rejected.
■ **nm, f** [personne] social reject, outcast.
◆ ***laissé-pour-compte*** **nm** [article] unsold item.

laisser [4] [lɛse] ■ **v aux** to let, to allow, to permit ▸ **laisser qqn faire qqch** to let sb do sthg ▸ **laisse-le dormir** let him sleep, leave him to sleep ▸ **laisse-le faire** leave him alone, don't interfere ▸ **laisser tomber qqch** *litt & fig* to drop sthg ▸ **laisser tomber qqn** *fam* to drop *ou* ditch sb ▸ **laisse tomber!** *fam* drop it! ▸ **laisser voir** [montrer] to show, to reveal.
■ **vt 1.** [gén] to leave ▸ **c'est à prendre ou à laisser** (it's) take it or leave it ▸ **laisser qqch à qqn** [léguer] to leave sthg to sb, to leave sb sthg ▸ **laisser qqn/qqch à qqn** [confier] to leave sb/sthg with sb ▸ **j'ai laissé mes enfants chez mon frère** I left my children at my brother's ▸ **laissez le passage à l'ambulance** let the ambulance through ▸ **laisse-lui le temps de le faire** leave *ou* give her time to do it **2.** [céder] **: laisser qqch à qqn** to let sb have sthg
▸▸ **laisser qqn tranquille** to leave sb in peace *ou* alone ▸ **laisser derrière soi** *litt & fig* to leave behind ▸ **laisser à désirer** to leave something to be desired ▸ **cela me laisse froid *ou* indifférent** it leaves me cold *ou* unmoved.
◆ ***se laisser*** **vp : se laisser faire** to let o.s. be persuaded ▸ **ne te laisse pas faire!** stand up for yourself!, don't let yourself be taken advantage of! ▸ **se laisser aller** to relax / [dans son apparence] to let o.s. go ▸ **se laisser aller dans un fauteuil** to collapse into an armchair ▸ **se laisser aller à qqch** to indulge in sthg ▸ **il se laisse boire, ton petit vin** your little wine goes down nicely *ou* is very drinkable ▸ **se laisser tenter par** to be tempted by.

laisser-aller [lɛseale] **nm inv** carelessness.

laissez-passer [lɛsepase] **nm inv** pass.

lait [lɛ] **nm 1.** [gén] milk ▸ **lait de chèvre** goat's milk ▸ **lait concentré *ou* condensé** [sucré] condensed milk / [non sucré] evaporated milk ▸ **lait écrémé** skimmed *ou* skim *US* milk ▸ **lait entier** whole milk ▸ **lait maternel** mother's milk ▸ **lait en poudre** powdered milk ▸ **lait de poule** egg flip ▸ **lait de vache** cow's milk **2.** [cosmétique] **: lait démaquillant** cleansing milk *ou* lotion.
◆ ***au lait*** **loc adj** with milk.

laitage [lɛtaʒ] **nm** dairy product.

laiterie [lɛtri] **nf** dairy.

laiteux**, **euse [lɛtø, øz] **adj** milky.

laitier**, **ère [lɛtje, ɛr] ■ **adj** dairy *(avant n)*.
■ **nm, f** milkman (f milkwoman).
◆ ***laitier*** **nm** TECHNOL slag.

laiton [lɛtɔ̃] **nm** brass.

laitue [lety] **nf** lettuce.

laïus [lajys] **nm** *fam* long speech.

lama [lama] **nm 1.** ZOOL llama **2.** RELIG lama.

lambeau**, **x [lɑ̃bo] **nm 1.** [morceau] shred ▸ **mettre qqch en lambeaux** to tear sthg to pieces *ou* shreds **2.** *fig* [fragment] fragment.

lambiner [3] [lɑ̃bine] **vi** *fam* to dawdle.

lambris [lɑ̃bri] **nm** panelling *UK*, paneling *US*.

lambswool [lɑ̃bswul] **nm** lambswool.

lame [lam] **nf 1.** [fer] blade ▸ **lame de rasoir** razor blade **2.** [lamelle] strip **3.** [vague] wave ▸ **lame de fond** groundswell.

lamé**, **e [lame] **adj** lamé ▸ **lamé or/argent** gold/silver lamé.
◆ ***lamé*** **nm** lamé ▸ **de *ou* en lamé** lamé.

lamelle [lamɛl] **nf 1.** [de champignon] gill **2.** [tranche] thin slice **3.** [de verre] slide.

lamentable [lamɑ̃tabl] **adj 1.** [résultats, sort] appalling **2.** [ton] plaintive.

lamentablement [lamɑ̃tabləmɑ̃] **adv** miserably.

lamentation [lamɑ̃tasjɔ̃] **nf 1.** [plainte] lamentation **2.** *(gén pl)* [jérémiade] moaning *(U)*.

lamenter [3] [lamɑ̃te] ◆ ***se lamenter*** **vp** to complain ▸ **se lamenter sur qqch** to bemoan sthg ▸ **se lamenter d'avoir fait qqch** to complain about having done sthg.

laminage [laminaʒ] **nm** lamination.

laminer [3] [lamine] **vt** [dans l'industrie] to laminate / *fig* [personne, revenus] to eat away at.

laminoir [laminwar] **nm** rolling mill.

lampadaire [lɑ̃padɛr] **nm** [d'intérieur] floor lamp, standard lamp *UK* / [de rue] street lamp *ou* light.

lampe [lɑ̃p] **nf** lamp, light ▸ **lampe à bronzer** sunlamp ▸ **lampe de chevet** bedside lamp ▸ **lampe halogène** halogen light ▸ **lampe à incandescence** incandescent lamp ▸ **lampe à pétrole** oil lamp ▸ **lampe de poche** torch *UK*, flashlight *US* ▸ **lampe à souder** blowtorch, blowlamp *UK* ▸ **lampe témoin** pilot light ▸ **s'en mettre plein la lampe** *fam fig* to stuff o.s.

lampée [lɑ̃pe] **nf** *fam* swig.

lampion [lɑ̃pjɔ̃] **nm** Chinese lantern.

lampiste [lɑ̃pist] **nm** [employé, subalterne] underling, dogsbody *UK*.

lance [lɑ̃s] **nf 1.** [arme] spear **2.** [de tuyau] nozzle ▸ **lance d'incendie** fire hose.

lancée [lɑ̃se] **nf : continuer sur sa lancée** to keep going.

lance-flammes [lɑ̃sflam] **nm inv** flame-thrower.

lancement [lɑ̃smɑ̃] **nm 1.** [d'entreprise, produit, navire] launching ▸ **lancement sur le marché** market entry **2.** [de javelot, projectile] throwing.

lance-pierres [lɑ̃spjɛr] **nm inv** catapult *UK*, slingshot *US*.

lancer [16] [lɑ̃se] ■ **vt 1.** [pierre, javelot] to throw ▸ **elle m'a lancé la balle** she threw me the ball, she threw the ball to me ▸ **lancer qqch sur qqn** to throw sthg at sb **2.** [fusée, produit, style] to launch ▸ **lancer un projectile téléguidé** to fire a remote-controlled missile **3.** [émettre] to give off / [cri] to let out / [injures] to hurl / [ultimatum] to issue **4.** [moteur] to start up ▸ **une fois le moteur lancé** once the engine is running **5.** [INFORM - programme] to start / [- système] to boot (up) **6.** *fig* [sur un sujet] **: lancer qqn sur qqch** to get sb started on sthg ▸ **une fois qu'il est lancé sur ce sujet, on ne peut plus l'arrêter** once he gets going on the subject, there's no stopping him **7.** [faire connaître] to launch ▸ **c'est ce roman/cette émission qui l'a lancé** this novel/programme made him famous.

■ **nm 1.** [à la pêche] casting **2.** SPORT throwing ▸ **le lancer du disque** (throwing) the discus ▸ **le lancer du javelot** (throwing) the javelin ▸ **lancer du poids** the shotput, putting the shot.

◆ ***se lancer*** **vp 1.** [débuter] to make a name for o.s **2.** [s'engager] **: se lancer dans** [dépenses, explication, lecture] to embark on ▸ **ne te lance pas dans de grosses dépenses** don't go spending a lot of money.

lanceur, euse [lɑ̃sœr, øz] **nm, f** SPORT thrower ▸ **lanceur de javelot** javelin thrower ▸ **lanceur de poids** shot putter.

◆ ***lanceur*** **nm** AÉRON launcher.

lancinant, e [lɑ̃sinɑ̃, ɑ̃t] **adj 1.** [douleur] shooting **2.** *fig* [obsédant] haunting **3.** [monotone] insistent.

lanciner [3] [lɑ̃sine] ■ **vi** to throb.

■ **vt** *fig* to haunt.

landau [lɑ̃do] **nm 1.** [d'enfant] pram *UK*, baby carriage *US* **2.** [carrosse] landau.

lande [lɑ̃d] **nf** moor.

langage [lɑ̃gaʒ] **nm 1.** [gén] language ▸ **le langage enfantin** baby talk ▸ **langage familier** colloquial language ▸ **le langage musical** the musical idiom ▸ **langage populaire** popular language ▸ **tenir un tout autre langage** to change one's tune **2.** INFORM **: langage auteur** authoring language ▸ **langage Javascript** Java script ▸ **langage machine** machine language ▸ **langage du Net** netspeak ▸ **langage de programmation** programming language.

lange [lɑ̃ʒ] **nm** nappy *UK*, diaper *US*.

langer [17] [lɑ̃ʒe] **vt** to change.

langoureusement [lɑ̃gurøzmɑ̃] **adv** languorously.

langoureux, euse [lɑ̃gurø, øz] **adj** languorous.

langouste [lɑ̃gust] **nf** crayfish.

langoustine [lɑ̃gustin] **nf** langoustine.

langue [lɑ̃g] **nf 1.** *fig* & ANAT tongue ▸ **avoir la langue blanche** *ou* **chargée** to have a coated *ou* furred tongue ▸ **tirer la langue à qqn** to stick out one's tongue at sb ▸ **langue de bœuf** CULIN ox tongue ▸ **mauvaise langue** *fig* gossip ▸ **les mauvaises langues prétendent que...** some (ill-intentioned) gossips claim that... ▸ **c'est une langue de vipère** she's got a venomous *ou* spiteful tongue ▸ **as-tu avalé** *ou* **perdu ta langue?** have you lost *ou* (has the) cat got your tongue? ▸ **avoir la langue bien pendue** to be a chatterbox ▸ **donner sa langue au chat** to give up ▸ **ne pas avoir sa langue dans sa poche** never to be at a loss for words ▸ **tenir sa langue** *fig* to hold one's tongue ▸ **tourne sept fois ta langue dans ta bouche avant de parler** *fam* think twice before you open your mouth **2.** LING language ▸ **de langue française** [livre] French / [personne] French-speaking ▸ **les politiciens qui parlent la langue de bois** politicians who talk in clichés ▸ **langues étrangères** foreign languages ▸ **langue maternelle** mother tongue ▸ **langue morte/vivante** dead/modern language ▸ **langue officielle** official language ▸ **un professeur de langues** a language teacher **3.** [forme] tongue ▸ **des langues de feu léchaient le mur** tongues of fire were licking the wall ▸ **une langue de terre** a strip of land, a narrow piece of land.

langue-de-chat [lɑ̃gdəʃa] (pl **langues-de-chat**) **nf** *light finger-biscuit*.

languette [lɑ̃gɛt] **nf** tongue.

langueur [lɑ̃gœr] **nf 1.** [dépérissement, mélancolie] languor **2.** [apathie] apathy.

languir [32] [lɑ̃gir] **vi 1.** [dépérir] **: languir (de)** to languish (with) **2.** *sout* [attendre] to wait ▸ **faire languir qqn** to keep sb waiting **3.** *littéraire* [désirer] **: languir après** to pine for.

lanière [lanjɛr] **nf** strip.

lanoline [lanɔlin] **nf** lanolin.

lanterne [lɑ̃tɛrn] **nf 1.** [éclairage] lantern **2.** [phare] light ▸▸ **éclairer la lanterne de qqn** *fig* to put sb in the know ▸ **être la lanterne rouge** *fam fig* to bring up the rear.

lanterner [3] [lɑ̃tɛrne] **vi** *fam* to dawdle ▸ **faire lanterner qqn** to keep sb hanging around.

Laos [laɔs] **nm : le Laos** Laos ▸ **au Laos** in Laos.

laotien, enne [laosjɛ̃, ɛn] **adj** Laotian.
◆ ***laotien*** **nm** [langue] Laotian.
◆ ***Laotien, enne*** **nm, f** Laotian.

lapalissade [lapalisad] **nf** statement of the obvious.

laper [3] [lape] **vt & vi** to lap.

lapereau, x [lapro] **nm** baby rabbit.

lapidaire [lapidɛr] ■ **nm** lapidary.
■ **adj** lapidary / *fig* [style] terse.

lapider [3] [lapide] **vt** [tuer] to stone.

lapin, e [lapɛ̃, in] **nm, f 1.** CULIN & ZOOL rabbit ▸ **lapin de garenne** wild rabbit **2.** *fam* [personne] **: mon lapin** my darling ▸ **chaud lapin** stud
▸▸ **poser un lapin à qqn** *fam* to stand sb up.
◆ ***lapin*** **nm** [fourrure] rabbit fur.

lapon, onne ou one [lapɔ̃, ɔn] **adj** Lapp.
◆ ***lapon*** **nm** [langue] Lapp.
◆ ***Lapon, onne ou one*** **nm, f** Lapp, Laplander.

Laponie [lapɔni] **nf : la Laponie** Lapland.

laps [laps] **nm : (dans) un laps de temps** (in) a while.

lapsus [lapsys] **nm** slip (of the tongue/pen) ▸ **faire un lapsus** to make a slip (of the tongue/pen).

laquais [lakɛ] **nm** lackey.

laque [lak] **nf 1.** [vernis, peinture] lacquer **2.** [pour cheveux] hair spray, lacquer *UK*.

laqué, e [lake] **adj** lacquered.

laquelle ➤ ***lequel.***

laquer [3] [lake] **vt** to lacquer.

larbin [larbɛ̃] **nm 1.** [domestique] servant **2.** [personne servile] yes-man.

larcin [larsɛ̃] **nm 1.** [vol] larceny, theft **2.** [butin] spoils *pl.*

lard [lar] **nm 1.** [graisse de porc] lard **2.** [viande] bacon **3.** *fam* [graisse d'homme] blubber.

larder [3] [larde] **vt 1.** CULIN to lard **2.** *fig* [piquer] **: larder qqn de coups/d'injures** to rain blows/insults on sb **3.** *fig* [truffer] **: larder qqch de** to cram sthg with.

lardon [lardɔ̃] **nm 1.** CULIN *cube or strip of bacon* **2.** *fam* [enfant] kid.

large [larʒ] ■ **adj 1.** [étendu, grand] wide ▸ **large de 5 mètres** 5 metres *UK ou* meters *US* wide ▸ **être large de hanches/d'épaules** to have broad hips/shoulders
2. [important, considérable] big ▸ **elle a une large part de responsabilité** she must bear a large *ou* major share of the blame ▸ **jouissant d'une large diffusion** widely distributed
3. [esprit, sourire] broad ▸ **leur père a l'esprit large** their father is open-minded *ou* broad-minded
4. [généreux - personne] generous.
■ **adv** amply ▸ **calculer ou prévoir large** to allow a good margin for error ▸ **voir large** to think big ▸ **ne pas en mener large** *fig* to be afraid.
■ **nm 1.** [largeur] **: 5 mètres de large** 5 metres *UK ou* meters *US* wide
2. [mer] **: le large** the open sea ▸ **le vent du large** offshore wind ▸ **au large de la côte française** off the French coast ▸ **prendre le large** [navire] to put to sea / *fig* to be off.

largement [larʒəmɑ̃] **adv 1.** [diffuser, répandre] widely ▸ **la porte était largement ouverte** the door was wide open **2.** [donner, payer] generously / [dépasser] considerably / [récompenser] amply ▸ **avoir largement le temps** to have plenty of time **3.** [au moins] easily.

largesse [larʒɛs] **nf 1.** [générosité] generosity **2.** *(gén pl)* [don] gift.

largeur [larʒœr] **nf 1.** [d'avenue, de cercle] width **2.** *fig* [d'idées, d'esprit] breadth.

largué, e [large] **adj : être largué** to be all at sea.

larguer [3] [large] **vt 1.** [voile] to unfurl **2.** [bombe, parachutiste] to drop **3.** *fam fig* [abandonner] to dump, to chuck *UK* ▸ **se faire larguer** to be dumped *ou* chucked *UK*.

larme [larm] **nf 1.** [pleur] tear ▸ **être en larmes** to be in tears ▸ **fondre en larmes** to burst into tears ▸ **pleurer à chaudes larmes** to cry bitterly ▸ **ravaler ses larmes** to hold back one's tears ▸ **rire aux larmes** to laugh until one cries ▸ **larmes de crocodile** *fig* crocodile tears **2.** *fam* [goutte] **: une larme de** a drop of.

larmoyant, e [larmwajɑ̃, ɑ̃t] **adj 1.** [yeux, personne] tearful **2.** *péj* [histoire] tearjerking.

larmoyer [13] [larmwaje] **vi 1.** [pleurer - personne] to weep / [- yeux] to water **2.** *péj* [se lamenter] to moan.

larron [larɔ̃] **nm** *vieilli* [voleur] thief.

larve [larv] **nf 1.** ZOOL larva **2.** *péj* [personne] wimp.

larvé, e [larve] **adj 1.** MÉD larvate **2.** [latent] latent.

laryngite [larɛ̃ʒit] **nf** laryngitis *(U)*.

larynx [larɛ̃ks] **nm** larynx.

las, lasse [la, las] **adj 1.** *littéraire* [fatigué] weary **2.** [dégoûté, ennuyé] tired ▸ **las de faire qqch** tired of doing sthg ▸ **las de qqn/qqch** tired of sb/sthg.
◆ ***las*** **interj** *littéraire* alas!

lascar [laskar] **nm** *fam* **1.** [homme louche] shady character / [homme rusé] rogue **2.** [enfant] rascal.

lascif, ive [lasif, iv] **adj** lascivious.

laser [lazɛr] ■ **nm** laser.
■ **adj inv** laser *(avant n)*.

lassant, e [lasɑ̃, ɑ̃t] **adj** tiresome.

lasser [3] [lase] **vt** *sout* [personne] to weary / [patience] to try.
◆ ***se lasser*** **vp** to weary ▸ **ne pas se lasser de qqch/de faire qqch** not to weary of sthg/of doing sthg.

lassitude [lasityd] **nf** lassitude.

lasso [laso] **nm** lasso.

lat. (abr écrite de ***latitude***) lat.

latent, e [latɑ̃, ɑ̃t] **adj** latent.

latéral, e, aux [lateral, o] **adj** lateral.

latex [latɛks] **nm inv** latex.

latin, e [latɛ̃, in] **adj** Latin.
◆ ***latin*** **nm** [langue] Latin ▸ **y perdre son latin** *fig* to be at a loss.

latiniste [latinist] **nmf** [spécialiste] Latinist / [étudiant] Latin student.

latino-américain, e [latinɔamerikɛ̃, ɛn] (mpl **latino-américains**, fpl **latino-américaines**) **adj** Latin-American, Hispanic.

latitude [latityd] **nf** *litt & fig* latitude.

latrines [latrin] **nfpl** latrines.

latte [lat] **nf** lath, slat.

lattis [lati] **nm** lathwork *(U)*.

laudatif, ive [lodatif, iv] **adj** laudatory.

lauréat, e [lɔrea, at] ■ **adj** prizewinning *(avant n)*, winning *(avant n)*.
■ **nm, f** prizewinner, winner.

laurier [lɔrje] **nm** BOT laurel.
◆ ***lauriers*** **nmpl** [gloire] laurels ▸ **s'endormir** *ou* **se reposer sur ses lauriers** to rest on one's laurels.

laurier-rose [lɔrjeroz] (pl **lauriers-roses**) **nm** oleander.

laurier-sauce [lɔrjesos] (pl **lauriers-sauce**) **nm** bay (tree).

Lausanne [lozan] **npr** Lausanne.

lavable [lavabl] **adj** washable.

lavabo [lavabo] **nm** **1.** [cuvette] basin *UK*, washbowl *US* **2.** *(gén pl)* [local] toilet *UK*, washroom *US*.

lavage [lavaʒ] **nm** washing ▸ **lavage à la main/en machine** hand/machine washing ▸ **lavage de cerveau** *fig* brainwashing ▸ **subir un lavage d'estomac** MÉD to have one's stomach pumped.

lavande [lavɑ̃d] ■ **nf** **1.** BOT lavender **2.** [eau] lavender water.
■ **adj inv** lavender.

lavasse [lavas] **nf** *fam* dishwater *(U)*.

lave [lav] **nf** lava.

lave-glace [lavglas] (pl **lave-glaces**) **nm** windscreen washer *UK*, windshield washer *US*.

lave-linge [lavlɛ̃ʒ] **nm inv** washing machine.

lavement [lavmɑ̃] **nm** enema.

laver [3] [lave] **vt** **1.** [nettoyer] to wash ▸ **laver à grande eau** to swill out *ou* down ▸ **laver la tête** *ou* **les cheveux à qqn** to wash sb's hair **2.** *fig* [disculper] **: laver qqn de qqch** to clear sb of sthg ▸ **laver qqn d'une accusation** to clear sb of an accusation ▸ **être lavé de tout soupçon** to be cleared of all suspicion.
◆ ***se laver*** **vp** **1.** [se nettoyer] to wash o.s., to have a wash *UK*, to wash up *US* ▸ **se laver les dents** to clean *ou* to brush one's teeth ▸ **se laver les mains/les cheveux** to wash one's hands/hair **2.** [se disculper] **: se laver (de)** to clear o.s. (of) ▸ **se laver de ses péchés** to cleanse o.s. of one's sins.

laverie [lavri] **nf** [commerce] laundry ▸ **laverie automatique** launderette, laundrette, Laundromat® *US*.

lavette [lavɛt] **nf** **1.** [brosse] washing-up brush *UK*, dish mop *US* / [en tissu] dishcloth **2.** *fam* [homme] drip.

laveur, euse [lavœr, øz] **nm, f** washer ▸ **laveur de carreaux** window cleaner *(person)*.

lave-vaisselle [lavvesɛl] **nm inv** dishwasher.

lavis [lavi] **nm** [procédé] washing / [dessin] wash (painting).

lavoir [lavwar] **nm** **1.** [lieu] laundry **2.** [bac] washtub.

laxatif, ive [laksatif, iv] **adj** laxative.
◆ ***laxatif*** **nm** laxative.

laxisme [laksism] **nm** laxity.

laxiste [laksist] ■ **nmf** over-lenient person.
■ **adj** lax.

layette [lɛjɛt] **nf** layette.

le, la [lə, la] (pl **les** [le]) (**l'** *devant une voyelle ou un 'h' muet*)
■ **art déf** **1.** [gén] the ▸ **le lac** the lake ▸ **la fenêtre** the window ▸ **l'homme** the man ▸ **les enfants** the children
2. [devant les noms abstraits] **: l'amour** love ▸ **la liberté** freedom ▸ **la vieillesse** old age
3. [devant les noms géographiques] **: la France** France ▸ **les États-Unis** America, the United States (of America) ▸ **la Seine** the Seine ▸ **les Alpes** the Alps
4. [temps] **: le 15 janvier 1953** 15th January 1953 *UK*, January 15th, 1953 *US* ▸ **je suis arrivé le 15 janvier 1953** I arrived on the 15th of January 1953 *ou* on January 15th, 1953 *US* ▸ **le lundi** [habituellement] on Mondays / [jour précis] on (the) Monday
5. [possession] **: se laver les mains** to wash one's hands ▸ **secouer la tête** to shake one's head ▸ **avoir les cheveux blonds** to have fair hair
6. [distributif] per, a ▸ **2 euros le mètre** 2 euros per metre *UK ou* meter *US*, 2 euros a metre *UK ou* meter *US* ▸ **j'y vais le soir** I go there in the evening
7. [dans les fractions] a, an ▸ **le quart/tiers de** a quarter/third of
8. [marquant l'approximation] **: il va sur la quarantaine** he's getting on for forty ▸ **vers les 4 h** about *ou* around 4 o'clock
9. [avec un nom propre] the ▸ **nous sommes invités chez les Durand** we are invited to the Durands' (house).
■ **pron pers** **1.** [personne] him (f her), them *pl* / [chose] it, them *pl* / [animal] it, him (f her), them *pl* ▸ **ce bordeaux, je l'ai déjà goûté** I've already tasted that Bordeaux ▸ **je le/la/les connais bien** I know him/her/them well ▸ **tu dois avoir la clé, donne-la moi** you must have the key: give it to me
2. [représente une proposition] **: je le sais bien** I know, I'm well aware (of it) ▸ **je te l'avais bien dit!** I told you so!

LEA (abr de ***langues étrangères appliquées***) **nfpl** *applied modern languages*.

leader [lidœr] ■ **nm** [de parti, course] leader ▸ **lutte pour la position de leader** leadership battle, leadership contest.
■ **adj** leading *(avant n)*.

leadership [lidœrʃip] **nm** leadership.

lèche [lɛʃ] **nf** *tfam* bootlicking ▸ **faire de la lèche à qqn** to lick sb's boots.

léché, e [leʃe] **adj** *fam* [fignolé] polished.

lèchefrite [lɛʃfrit] **nf** dripping pan *UK*, broiler pan *US*.

lécher [18] [leʃe] **vt 1.** [passer la langue sur, effleurer] to lick / [suj: vague] to wash against **2.** *fam* [fignoler] to polish (up).
◆ ***se lécher*** **vp : se lécher les doigts** *fam* to lick one's fingers.

lèche-vitrines [lɛʃvitrin] **nm inv** window-shopping ▸ **faire du lèche-vitrines** to go window-shopping.

leçon [ləsɔ̃] **nf 1.** [gén] lesson ▸ **leçons de conduite** driving lessons ▸ **leçons particulières** private lessons *ou* classes **2.** [conseil] advice *(U)* ▸ **faire la leçon à qqn** to lecture sb.

lecteur, trice [lɛktœr, tris] **nm, f 1.** [de livres] reader **2.** UNIV foreign language assistant.
◆ ***lecteur*** **nm 1.** [gén] head ▸ **lecteur de cassettes/CD** cassette/CD player ▸ **lecteur laser universel** audio-video CD player **2.** INFORM reader ▸ **lecteur de disques** disk drive ▸ **lecteur de CD-ROM** *ou* **de disque optique** CD-ROM drive.

lecture [lɛktyr] **nf** reading ▸ **faire la lecture à qqn** to read to sb ▸ **la photocopie ne facilite pas la lecture du plan** the plan is more difficult to read because it has been photocopied ▸ **une lecture publique de qqch** a public reading of sthg ▸ **le texte a été adopté en première lecture** the bill was passed on its first reading ▸ **lecture optique** optical reading, optical character recognition.

FAUX AMIS / FALSE FRIENDS
lecture

Lecture is not a translation of the French word *lecture*. Lecture is translated by *conférence* or *cours*.
▸ He gave a lecture / *Il a donné une conférence*
▸ Have you been to his linguistics lectures? / *Avez-vous suivi ses cours de linguistique ?*

LED (abr de ***light emitting diode***) **nf** LED.

ledit, ladite [lədi, ladit] (mpl **lesdits** [ledi]) (fpl **lesdites** [ledit]) **adj** the said, the aforementioned.

légal, e, aux [legal, o] **adj** legal.

légalement [legalmɑ̃] **adv** legally.

légalisation [legalizasjɔ̃] **nf 1.** [légitimation] legalization **2.** [authentification] authentication.

légaliser [3] [legalize] **vt 1.** [rendre légal] to legalize **2.** [certifier authentique] to authenticate.

légalisme [legalism] **nm** legalism.

légalité [legalite] **nf 1.** [de contrat, d'acte] legality, lawfulness **2.** [loi] law.

légataire [legatɛr] **nmf** legatee ▸ **légataire universel** sole legatee.

légation [legasjɔ̃] **nf** legation.

légendaire [leʒɑ̃dɛr] **adj** legendary.

légende [leʒɑ̃d] **nf 1.** [fable] legend **2.** *péj* [invention] story **3.** [de carte, de schéma] key / [de photo] caption.

léger, ère [leʒe, ɛr] **adj 1.** [objet, étoffe, repas] light **2.** [bruit, différence, odeur] slight **3.** [alcool, tabac] low-strength **4.** [femme] flighty **5.** [insouciant - ton] light-hearted / [- conduite] thoughtless.
◆ ***à la légère*** **loc adv** lightly, thoughtlessly.

légèrement [leʒɛrmɑ̃] **adv 1.** [s'habiller, poser] lightly **2.** [agir] thoughtlessly **3.** [blesser, remuer] slightly.

légèreté [leʒɛrte] **nf 1.** [d'objet, de repas, de punition] lightness **2.** [de style] gracefulness **3.** [de conduite] thoughtlessness **4.** [de personne] flightiness.

légiférer [18] [leʒifere] **vi** to legislate.

légion [leʒjɔ̃] **nf 1.** MIL legion **2.** [grand nombre] **: une légion de** a host of ▸ **être légion** *fig* to be legion.
◆ ***Légion*** **nf : la Légion étrangère** the Foreign Legion ▸ **la Légion d'honneur** the Legion of Honour *UK ou* Honor *US*.

légionnaire [leʒjɔnɛr] **nm** legionary.

légion(n)ellose [leʒjɔnɛloz] **nf** MÉD legionnaires' disease.

législateur, trice [leʒislatœr, tris] **nm, f** legislator.

législatif, ive [leʒislatif, iv] **adj** legislative.
◆ ***législatif*** **nm** legislature.
◆ ***législatives*** **nfpl : les législatives** the legislative elections, ≃ the general election *(sg) UK*, ≃ the Congressional election *(sg) US*.

législation [leʒislasjɔ̃] **nf** legislation ▸ **législation du travail** labor *UK ou* labour *US* laws.

législature [leʒislatyr] **nf 1.** [période] term of office **2.** [corps] legislature.

légiste [leʒist] **adj 1.** [juriste] jurist **2.** ➤ ***médecin***.

légitimation [leʒitimasjɔ̃] **nf 1.** [d'enfant] legitimization **2.** *littéraire* [justification] justification.

légitime [leʒitim] **adj** legitimate.

légitimement [leʒitimmɑ̃] **adv 1.** [légalement] legitimately **2.** [justement] fairly.

légitimer [3] [leʒitime] **vt 1.** [reconnaître] to recognize / [enfant] to legitimize **2.** [justifier] to justify.

légitimité [leʒitimite] **nf 1.** [de pouvoir, d'enfant] legitimacy **2.** [de récompense] fairness.

legs [lɛg] **nm** legacy.

léguer [18] [lege] **vt : léguer qqch à qqn** DR to bequeath sthg to sb / *fig* to pass sthg on to sb.

légume [legym] ■ **nm** vegetable.
■ **nf** *fam* **: une grosse légume** a bigwig.

leitmotiv [lajtmɔtif, lɛtmɔtif] **nm** leitmotif.

Léman [lemɑ̃] ➤ ***lac***.

lendemain [lɑ̃dmɛ̃] **nm 1.** [jour] day after ▸ **le lendemain matin** the next morning ▸ **au lendemain de** after, in the days following **2.** [avenir] tomorrow ▸ **sans lendemain** short-lived.

lénifiant, e [lenifjɑ̃, ɑ̃t] **adj** *litt* & *fig* soothing.

léniniste [leninist] **nmf** & **adj** Leninist.

lent, e [lɑ̃, lɑ̃t] **adj** slow ▸ **lent à faire qqch** slow to do sthg.

lente [lɑ̃t] nf nit.

lentement [lɑ̃tmɑ̃] adv slowly.

lenteur [lɑ̃tœr] nf slowness *(U)*.

lentille [lɑ̃tij] nf **1.** BOT & CULIN lentil **2.** [d'optique] lens ▸ **lentilles de contact** contact lenses.

léonin, e [leɔnɛ̃, in] adj **1.** [du lion] leonine **2.** [injuste] one-sided.

léopard [leɔpar] nm leopard.

LEP, Lep (abr de ***lycée d'enseignement professionnel***) nm *former secondary school for vocational training*.

lèpre [lɛpr] nf **1.** MÉD leprosy **2.** *fig* [mal] disease.

lépreux, euse [leprø, øz] ■ adj **1.** MÉD leprous **2.** *fig* [mur, maison] peeling.
■ nm, f leper.

lequel, laquelle [ləkɛl, lakɛl] (mpl **lesquels** [lekɛl], fpl **lesquelles** [lekɛl]) *(contraction de "à + lequel"* = **auquel** *; "de + lequel"* = **duquel** *; "à + lesquels/lesquelles"* = **auxquels/auxquelles** *"de + lesquels/lesquelles"* = **desquels/desquelles**)
■ pron rel **1.** [complément - personne] whom / [- chose] which **2.** [sujet - personne] who / [- chose] which.
■ pron interr : **lequel?** which (one)?

es ➤ *le*.

esbienne [lɛsbjɛn] nf lesbian.

esdits, lesdites ➤ *ledit*.

èse-majesté [lɛzmaʒɛste] nf inv lese-majesty.

éser [18] [leze] vt **1.** [frustrer] to wrong **2.** MÉD to injure, to damage.

ésiner [3] [lezine] vi to skimp ▸ **ne pas lésiner sur** not to skimp on.

ésion [lezjɔ̃] nf lesion.

esotho [lɛsɔtɔ] nm : **le Lesotho** Lesotho.

esquels, lesquelles ➤ *lequel*.

ssive [lɛsiv] nf **1.** [nettoyage, linge] laundry, washing *UK* **2.** [produit] washing powder *UK*, laundry detergent *US*.

ssiver [3] [lɛsive] vt **1.** [nettoyer] to wash **2.** CHIM to each **3.** *fam* [épuiser] to wipe out.

st [lɛst] nm ballast ▸ **lâcher du lest** to jettison ballast / *fig* to make concessions.

ste [lɛst] adj **1.** [agile] nimble, agile **2.** [licencieux] crude.

stement [lɛstəmɑ̃] adv **1.** [agilement] nimbly, agilely **2.** [grivoisement] crudely.

ster [3] [lɛste] vt **1.** [garnir de lest] to ballast **2.** *fam* charger] to fill, to cram.

tchi = ***litchi***.

thargie [letarʒi] nf *litt* & *fig* lethargy ▸ **tomber en léthargie** to become lethargic.

thargique [letarʒik] adj lethargic.

tton, onne [lɛtɔ̃, ɔn] adj Latvian.
◆ ***letton*** nm [langue] Latvian.
◆ ***Letton, onne*** nm, f Latvian.

ettonie [lɛtɔni] nf : **la Lettonie** Latvia.

lettre [lɛtr] nf **1.** [gén] letter ▸ **un mot de neuf lettres** a nine-letter word ▸ **en toutes lettres** in words, in full ▸ **c'est écrit en toutes lettres dans le contrat** it's written in black and white *ou* it's spelled out plainly in the contract ▸ **lettre d'amour** love letter ▸ **lettre anonyme** anonymous letter ▸ **lettre de couverture** cover note *UK* ▸ **lettre de motivation** covering *UK ou* cover *US* letter *(in support of one's application)* ▸ **lettre ouverte** open letter ▸ **lettre piégée** letter bomb ▸ **lettre de rappel** reminder ▸ **lettre de recommandation** (letter of) recommendation ▸ **lettre recommandée** [avec accusé de réception] recorded delivery letter *UK*, letter sent by certified mail *US* / [avec valeur déclarée] registered letter ▸ **lettre de remerciements** letter of thanks, thank-you letter ▸ **mettre une lettre à la poste** to post *UK ou* mail *US* a letter ▸ **passer comme une lettre à la poste** *fam* [entretien, examen] to go smoothly / [personne] to get through easily **2.** [sens des mots] : **à la lettre** to the letter ▸ **suivre des ordres au pied de la lettre** to follow orders to the letter.
◆ ***lettres*** nfpl **1.** [culture littéraire] letters ▸ **un homme/une femme de lettres** a man/a woman of letters **2.** UNIV arts, humanities ▸ **étudiant en lettres** arts *ou* humanities student ▸ **lettres classiques** classics ▸ **lettres modernes** French language and literature ▸ **lettres supérieures** preparatory class *(leading to the École Normale Supérieure and lasting two years)* **3.** [titre] : **lettres de noblesse** letters patent of nobility.
◆ ***lettre de change*** nf bill of exchange.

leucémie [løsemi] nf leukaemia *UK*, leukemia *US*.

leucocyte [løkɔsit] nm leucocyte.

leucorrhée [løkɔre] nf leucorrhoea *UK*, leukorrhea *US*, leucorrhea *US*.

leur [lœr] pron pers inv (to) them ▸ **je voudrais leur parler** I'd like to speak to them ▸ **je leur ai donné la lettre** I gave them the letter, I gave the letter to them.
◆ ***leur*** (pl **leurs**) adj poss their ▸ **c'est leur tour** it's their turn ▸ **leurs enfants** their children.
◆ ***le leur, la leur*** (pl **les leurs**) pron poss theirs ▸ **il faudra qu'ils y mettent du leur** they've got to pull their weight.

leurre [lœr] nm **1.** [appât] lure **2.** *fig* [illusion] illusion **3.** *fig* [tromperie] deception, trap.

leurrer [5] [lœre] vt to deceive.
◆ ***se leurrer*** vp to deceive o.s.

levain [ləvɛ̃] nm **1.** CULIN : **pain au levain/sans levain** leavened/unleavened bread **2.** *fig* [germe] seeds *pl*, germ.

levant [ləvɑ̃] ■ nm east.
■ adj ➤ ***soleil***.

levé, e [ləve] adj [debout] up.
◆ ***levée*** nf **1.** [de scellés, difficulté] removal / [de blocus, de siège, d'interdiction] lifting **2.** [de séance] close, closing **3.** [d'impôts, du courrier] collection **4.** [d'armée] raising **5.** [remblai] dyke **6.** [jeux de cartes] trick.
◆ ***levée de boucliers*** nf (general) outcry.

lever [19] [ləve] ■ vt **1.** [objet, blocus, interdiction] to lift **2.** [main, tête, armée] to raise ▸ **lever les yeux** [de son livre] to look up ▸ **levons nos verres à sa réussite** let's raise our glasses to *ou* let's drink to his success **3.** [scellés, difficulté]

to remove **4.** [séance] to close, to end **5.** [impôts, courrier] to collect **6.** [plan, carte] to draw (up) **7.** [enfant, malade] : **lever qqn** to get sb up.
■ **vi 1.** [plante] to come up **2.** [pâte] to rise.
■ **nm 1.** [d'astre] rising, rise ▸ **lever du jour** daybreak ▸ **lever du soleil** sunrise **2.** [de personne] : **il est toujours de mauvaise humeur au lever** he's always in a bad mood when he gets up ▸ **le lever du roi** the levee of the king **3.** THÉÂTRE : **lever de rideau** curtain, curtain-up / *fig* curtain raiser.
◆ ***se lever*** **vp 1.** [personne] to get up, to rise ▸ **je ne peux pas me lever le matin** I can't get up *ou* I can't get out of bed in the morning ▸ **se lever de sa chaise** to get up *ou* to rise from one's chair / [vent] to get up **2.** [soleil, lune] to rise / [jour] to break **3.** [temps] to clear ▸ **le temps se lève** [il fait meilleur] the sky's clearing (up).

lève-tard [lɛvtar] **nmf** late riser.

lève-tôt [lɛvto] **nmf** early riser.

levier [ləvje] **nm** *litt* & *fig* lever ▸ **levier de vitesses** gear stick *UK*, gear lever *UK*, gearshift *US*.

lévitation [levitasjɔ̃] **nf** levitation.

lèvre [lɛvr] **nf 1.** ANAT lip / [de vulve] labium ▸ **être suspendu aux lèvres de qqn** *fig* to hang on sb's every word ▸ **se mordre les lèvres** *fig* to bite one's lip **2.** [bord] edge.

lévrier, ***levrette*** [levrije, ləvrɛt] **nm, f** greyhound.

levure [ləvyr] **nf** yeast ▸ **levure chimique** baking powder.

lexical, ***e***, ***aux*** [lɛksikal, o] **adj** lexical.

lexicographie [lɛksikɔgrafi] **nf** lexicography.

lexique [lɛksik] **nm 1.** [dictionnaire] glossary **2.** [vocabulaire] vocabulary.

lézard [lezar] **nm 1.** [animal] lizard ▸ **faire le lézard** *fam fig* to bask in the sun **2.** [peau] lizard (skin).

lézarde [lezard] **nf** crack.

lézarder [3] [lezarde] ■ **vt** to crack.
■ **vi** *fam* [paresser] to bask.
◆ ***se lézarder*** **vp** to crack.

Lhassa [lasa] **npr** Lhasa.

liaison [ljɛzɔ̃] **nf 1.** [jonction, enchaînement] connection **2.** CULIN & LING liaison **3.** [contact, relation] contact ▸ **avoir une liaison** to have an affair ▸ **être/entrer en liaison avec** to be in/establish contact with ▸ **par liaison radio** by radio link ▸ **liaison par satellite** satellite link **4.** [transports] link.

liane [ljan] **nf** creeper.

liant, ***e*** [ljɑ̃, ɑ̃t] **adj** sociable.
◆ ***liant*** **nm 1.** [substance] binder **2.** [élasticité] elasticity.

liasse [ljas] **nf** bundle / [de billets de banque] wad.

Liban [libɑ̃] **nm** : **le Liban** Lebanon ▸ **au Liban** in Lebanon.

libanais, ***e*** [libanɛ, ɛz] **adj** Lebanese.
◆ ***Libanais***, ***e*** **nm, f** Lebanese (person) ▸ **les Libanais** the Lebanese.

Libé [libe] (abr de ***Libération***) **nm** *French left-of-centre newspaper.*

libelle [libɛl] **nm** lampoon.

libellé [libele] **nm** wording.

libeller [4] [libele] **vt 1.** [chèque] to make out **2.** [lettre] to word.

libellule [libelyl] **nf** dragonfly.

libéral, ***e***, ***aux*** [liberal, o] ■ **adj** [attitude, idée, parti] liberal.
■ **nm, f** POLIT liberal.

libéralement [liberalmɑ̃] **adv** liberally.

libéralisation [liberalizasjɔ̃] **nf** liberalization.

libéraliser [3] [liberalize] **vt** to liberalize.

libéralisme [liberalism] **nm** liberalism.

libéralité [liberalite] **nf 1.** [générosité] generosity **2.** *(gén pl)* [don] generous gift.

libérateur, ***trice*** [liberatœr, tris] ■ **adj** [rire] liberating ▸ **guerre libératrice** war of liberation.
■ **nm, f** liberator.

libération [liberasjɔ̃] **nf 1.** [de prisonnier] release, freeing **2.** [de pays, de la femme] liberation ▸ **la Libération** HIST the Liberation **3.** [d'énergie] release.

libéré, ***e*** [libere] **nm, f** freed prisoner.

libérer [18] [libere] **vt 1.** [prisonnier, fonds] to release, to free **2.** [pays, la femme] to liberate ▸ **libérer qqn de qqch** to free sb from sthg **3.** [passage] to clear **4.** [énergie] to release **5.** [instincts, passions] to give free rein to.
◆ ***se libérer*** **vp 1.** [se rendre disponible] to get away **2.** [se dégager] : **se libérer de** [lien] to free o.s. from / [engagement] to get out of.

Liberia [liberja] **nm** : **le Liberia** Liberia ▸ **au Liberia** in Liberia.

libérien, ***enne*** [liberjɛ̃, ɛn] **adj** Liberian.
◆ ***Libérien***, ***enne*** **nm, f** Liberian.

libertaire [libɛrtɛr] **nmf** & **adj** libertarian.

liberté [libɛrte] **nf 1.** [gén] freedom ▸ **avoir toute liberté pour décider** to be totally free *ou* to have full freedom to decide ▸ **en liberté** free ▸ **Liberté, Égalité, Fraternité** Liberty, Equality, Fraternity ▸ **parler en toute liberté** to speak freely ▸ **rendre la liberté à un oiseau** to set a bird free ▸ **rendre la liberté à un otage** to release a hostage ▸ **vivre en liberté** to live in freedom ▸ **un parc national où les animaux vivent en liberté** a national park where animals roam free ▸ **liberté d'entreprise** free enterprise ▸ **liberté d'expression** freedom of expression ▸ **liberté d'information** freedom of information ▸ **liberté d'opinion** freedom of thought ▸ **liberté des prix** freedom from price control ▸ **liberté des rédacteurs** PRESSE editorial freedom ▸ **libertés publiques** civil liberties **2.** DR release ▸ **liberté conditionnelle** parole ▸ **liberté provisoire** bail ▸ **liberté surveillée** probation **3.** [loisir] free time ▸ **je n'ai pas un instant de liberté** I haven't got a minute to myself.

libertin, ***e*** [libɛrtɛ̃, in] ■ **adj** [dissolu] dissolute / [propos, livre] lewd.
■ **nm, f** libertine.

libertinage [libɛrtinaʒ] **nm** [débauche] dissoluteness / [de propos, livre] lewdness.

libidineux, ***euse*** [libidinø, øz] **adj** lecherous.

libido [libido] **nf** libido.

libraire [librɛr] **nmf** bookseller.

librairie [librɛri] **nf 1.** [magasin] bookshop *UK*, bookstore *US* **2.** [commerce, activité] book trade.

FAUX AMIS / FALSE FRIENDS
librairie

Library is not a translation of the French word *librairie*. Library is translated by ***bibliothèque***.
▸ This is a public library / *C'est une bibliothèque municipale*

ibrairie-papeterie [librɛripapɛtri] (pl **librairies-papeteries**) **nf** bookseller's and stationer's *UK* ***ou*** stationery store *US*.

ibre [libr] **adj 1.** [gén] free ▸ **libre de qqch** free from sthg ▸ **être libre de ses mouvements** to be free to do what one likes ▸ **être libre de faire qqch** to be free to do sthg ▸ **libre à toi/à elle de refuser** you're/she's free to say no ▸ **la ligne n'est pas libre** [au téléphone] the line is engaged *UK* ***ou*** busy *US* ▸ **l'entrée de l'exposition est libre** entrance to the exhibition is free ▸ **tu as un moment de libre?** have you got a minute (to spare)? **2.** [école, secteur] private **3.** [passage] clear ▸ **la voie est libre** the way is clear.

ibre-échange [librɛʃɑ̃ʒ] (pl **libres-échanges**) **nm** free trade *(U)*.

ibrement [librəmɑ̃] **adv** freely.

ibre-penseur, euse [librəpɑ̃sœr, øz] (mpl **libres-penseurs**) (fpl **libres-penseuses**) **nm, f** freethinker.

ibre-service [librəsɛrvis] (pl **libres-services**) **nm 1.** [système] **: le libre-service** self-service **2.** [magasin] self-service shop *UK* ***ou*** store *US* / [restaurant] self-service restaurant.

ibrettiste [librɛtist] **nmf** librettist.

ibye [libi] **nf : la Libye** Libya.

byen, enne [libjɛ̃, ɛn] **adj** Libyan.
◆ ***Libyen, enne*** **nm, f** Libyan.

ce [lis] **nf : en lice** *fig* in the fray ▸ **entrer en lice** *fig* to oin the fray.

cence [lisɑ̃s] **nf 1.** [permis] permit / COMM licence *UK*, icense *US* ▸ **licence exclusive** exclusive licence *UK* ***ou*** liense *US* **2.** UNIV (first) degree ▸ **licence ès lettres/en droit** ≃ Bachelor of Arts/Law degree **3.** INFORM **: licence indiiduelle d'utilisation** single-user licence *UK* ***ou*** license *JS* **4.** *littéraire* [liberté] licence *UK*, license *US* ▸ **licence oétique** poetic licence *UK* ***ou*** license *US*.

cencié, e [lisɑ̃sje] ■ **adj 1.** UNIV graduate *(avant n)* **.** [autorisé] permit-holding *(avant n)* / COMM licensed.
■ **nm, f 1.** UNIV graduate **2.** [titulaire d'un permis] permit older / COMM licence *UK* ***ou*** license *US* holder.

cenciement [lisɑ̃simɑ̃] **nm** dismissal / [économique] yoff, redundancy *UK* ▸ **licenciement économique** ***ou*** **our raisons économiques** layoff ***ou*** redundancy *UK* for conomic reasons.

cencier [9] [lisɑ̃sje] **vt** [pour faute] to dismiss, to fire / pour raison économique] to lay off, to make redundant *UK* **se faire licencier** to be laid off, to be made redunant *UK*.

licencieux, euse [lisɑ̃sjø, øz] **adj** licentious.

lichen [likɛn] **nm** lichen.

licite [lisit] **adj** lawful, legal.

licol [likɔl], ***licou*** [liku] **nm** halter.

licorne [likɔrn] **nf** unicorn.

licou = ***licol***.

lie [li] **nf** [dépôt] dregs *pl*, sediment ▸ **la lie de la société** *fig* & *littéraire* the dregs *pl* of society.

lié, e [lje] **adj 1.** [mains] bound **2.** [amis] **: être très lié avec** to be great friends with.

lie-de-vin [lidəvɛ̃] **adj inv** burgundy, wine-coloured *UK*, wine-colored *US*.

liège [ljɛʒ] **nm** cork ▸ **en *ou* de liège** cork.

liégeois, e [ljeʒwa, az] **adj 1.** GÉOGR of/from Liège **2.** CULIN **: café/chocolat liégeois** *coffee or chocolate ice cream topped with whipped cream.*

lien [ljɛ̃] **nm 1.** [sangle] bond **2.** [relation, affinité] bond, tie ▸ **avoir des liens de parenté avec** to be related to **3.** *fig* [enchaînement] connection, link.

lier [9] [lje] **vt 1.** [attacher] to tie (up) ▸ **lier qqn/qqch à** to tie sb/sthg to **2.** [suj: contrat, promesse] to bind ▸ **lier qqn/qqch par** to bind sb/sthg by **3.** [relier par la logique] to link, to connect ▸ **lier qqch à** to link sthg to, to connect sthg with **4.** [commencer] **: lier connaissance/conversation avec** to strike up an acquaintance/a conversation with **5.** [suj: sentiment, intérêt] to unite **6.** CULIN to thicken.
◆ ***se lier*** **vp 1.** [s'attacher] **: se lier (d'amitié) avec qqn** to make friends with sb **2.** [s'astreindre] **: se lier par une promesse** to be bound by a promise.

lierre [ljɛr] **nm** ivy.

liesse [ljɛs] **nf** jubilation.

lieu, x [ljø] **nm** [endroit] place ▸ **en lieu sûr** in a safe place ▸ **lieu d'achat** point of purchase ▸ **lieu de mémoire** memorial / *fig* repository of culture ▸ **lieu de naissance** birthplace ▸ **lieu de passage** port of call ▸ **lieu de perdition** den of vice ▸ **lieu public** public place ▸ **lieu saint** holy place ▸ **lieu de vente** point of sale ▸ **haut lieu de qqch** *fig* centre *UK* ***ou*** center *US* of sthg ▸ **en haut lieu** *fig* in high places ▸ **ça se décidera en haut lieu** the decision will be made at a high level ▸ **sur votre lieu de travail** at your place of work
▸▸ **avoir lieu** to take place ▸ **avoir lieu de faire qqch** to have grounds for doing sthg ▸ **il y a tout lieu de croire** there is every reason to believe ▸ **donner lieu à** to give rise to ▸ **tenir lieu de** to take the place of.
◆ ***lieux*** **nmpl 1.** [scène] scene *sg*, spot *sg* ▸ **sur les lieux (d'un crime/d'un accident)** at the scene (of a crime/an accident) **2.** [domicile] premises ▸ **les grévistes occupent les lieux** the strikers are occupying the premises.
◆ ***lieu commun*** **nm** commonplace.
◆ ***au lieu de*** **loc prép : au lieu de qqch/de faire qqch** instead of sthg/of doing sthg ▸ **elle aurait dû me remercier, au lieu de ça, elle m'en veut** she should have thanked me, instead of which she bears a grudge against me.
◆ ***en dernier lieu*** **loc adv** lastly ▸ **n'ajoutez le sucre qu'en tout dernier lieu** do not add the sugar until the last moment.
◆ ***en premier lieu*** **loc adv** in the first place.
◆ ***en second lieu*** **loc adv** in the second place.

lieu-dit [ljødi] (pl **lieux-dits**) **nm** locality, place.

lieue [ljø] **nf** league ▸ **j'étais à cent lieues de penser cela** *fig* I never thought that for a moment.

lieutenant [ljøtnɑ̃] **nm** lieutenant.

lieutenant-colonel [ljøtnɑ̃kɔlɔnɛl] (pl **lieutenants-colonels**) **nm** lieutenant-colonel.

lièvre [ljɛvr] **nm** hare ▸ **courir deux lièvres à la fois** *fig* to do more than one thing at a time ▸ **lever un lièvre** *fig* to ask an awkward question.

lifter [3] [lifte] **vt** TENNIS to put topspin on.

lifting [liftiŋ] **nm** face-lift.

ligament [ligamɑ̃] **nm** ligament.

ligature [ligatyr] **nf** MÉD [lien] ligature / [opération] ligation, ligature ▸ **ligature des trompes** MÉD tubal ligation.

ligaturer [3] [ligatyre] **vt 1.** MÉD to ligature, to ligate **2.** AGRIC to bind.

lige [liʒ] **adj : homme lige** liege man.

ligne [liɲ] **nf 1.** [gén] line ▸ **à la ligne** new line *ou* paragraph ▸ **en ligne** [personnes] in a line / INFORM on line ▸ **descendre en ligne directe de** to be directly descended from ▸ **restez en ligne!** TÉLÉCOM hold the line! ▸ **il est en ligne, vous patientez?** he's on another call just now: will you hold the line? ▸ **en ligne droite** as the crow flies ▸ **lire entre les lignes** *fig* to read between the lines ▸ **dans sa ligne de mire** in one's line of sight ▸ **ligne de départ/d'arrivée** starting/finishing *UK ou* finish *US* line ▸ **ligne aérienne** airline ▸ **ligne d'autobus** [service] bus service / [itinéraire] bus route ▸ **ligne de métro** underground line *UK*, subway line *US* ▸ **ligne blanche/jaune** white/yellow line *(on roads)* ▸ **ligne de commande** INFORM command line ▸ **ligne de conduite** line of conduct ▸ **ligne de crédit *ou* de découvert** line of credit, credit line ▸ **ligne de démarcation** demarcation line ▸ **ligne directrice** guideline ▸ **ligne de flottaison** water line ▸ **ligne d'horizon** skyline ▸ **ligne de partage des eaux** watershed ▸ **lignes de la main** lines of the hand ▸ **les lignes ennemies** the enemy lines ▸ **être/monter en première ligne** *fig* & MIL to be in/to go to the front line ▸ **les grandes lignes** [transports] the main lines
2. [forme - de voiture, meuble] lines *pl*
3. [silhouette] **: avoir la ligne** to have a good figure ▸ **garder la ligne** to keep one's figure ▸ **surveiller sa ligne** to watch one's waistline
4. [de pêche] fishing line ▸ **pêcher à la ligne** to go angling
▸▸| **dans les grandes lignes** in outline ▸ **entrer en ligne de compte** to be taken into account ▸ **se tromper sur toute la ligne** to be completely mistaken.

lignée [liɲe] **nf** [famille] descendants *pl* ▸ **dans la lignée de** *fig* [d'écrivains, d'artistes] in the tradition of.

lignite [liɲit] **nm** lignite.

ligoter [3] [ligɔte] **vt 1.** [attacher] to tie up ▸ **ligoter qqn à qqch** to tie sb to sthg **2.** *fig* [entraver] to bind.

ligue [lig] **nf** league.

liguer [3] [lige] ◆ ***se liguer*** **vp** to form a league ▸ **se liguer contre** to conspire against.

lilas [lila] **nm & adj inv** lilac.

limace [limas] **nf 1.** ZOOL slug **2.** *fig* [personne] slowcoach *UK*, slowpoke *US*.

limaille [limaj] **nf** filings *pl*.

limande [limɑ̃d] **nf** dab.

limbes [lɛ̃b] **nmpl** RELIG limbo *sg* ▸ **être dans les limbes** *fig* to be in limbo.

lime [lim] **nf 1.** [outil] file ▸ **lime à ongles** nail file **2.** BOT lime.

limer [3] [lime] **vt** [ongles] to file / [aspérités] to file down / [barreau] to file through.

limier [limje] **nm 1.** [chien] bloodhound **2.** [détective] sleuth ▸ **fin limier** first-rate detective.

liminaire [liminɛr] **adj** introductory.

limitatif, ive [limitatif, iv] **adj** restrictive.

limitation [limitasjɔ̃] **nf** limitation / [de naissances] control ▸ **limitation de vitesse** speed limit.

limite [limit] ■ **nf 1.** [gén] limit ▸ **à la limite** [au pire] at worst ▸ **à la limite, j'accepterais de le voir** if pushed I'd agree to see him **2.** [terme, échéance] deadline ▸ **limite d'âge** age limit.
■ **adj** [extrême] maximum *(avant n)* ▸ **cas limite** borderline case ▸ **date limite** deadline ▸ **date limite de vente/consommation** sell-by/use-by date.
◆ ***limites*** **nfpl : sans limites** limitless.

limité, e [limite] **adj** [peu important] limited.

limiter [3] [limite] **vt 1.** [borner] to border, to bound **2.** [restreindre] to limit.
◆ ***se limiter*** **vp 1.** [se restreindre] **: se limiter à qqch/faire qqch** to limit o.s. to sthg/to doing sthg **2.** [se borner] **se limiter à** to be limited to.

limitrophe [limitrɔf] **adj 1.** [frontalier] border *(avant n)* ▸ **être limitrophe de** to border on **2.** [voisin] adjacent.

limogeage [limɔʒaʒ] **nm** dismissal.

limoger [17] [limɔʒe] **vt** to dismiss.

limon [limɔ̃] **nm 1.** GÉOL alluvium, silt **2.** CONSTR string board.

limonade [limɔnad] **nf** lemonade *UK*.

limpide [lɛ̃pid] **adj 1.** [eau] limpid **2.** [ciel, regard] clear **3.** [explication, style] clear, lucid.

limpidité [lɛ̃pidite] **nf 1.** [d'eau] limpidity **2.** [du ciel, de regard] clearness **3.** [d'explication, de style] clarity, lucidity.

lin [lɛ̃] **nm 1.** BOT flax **2.** [tissu] linen.

linceul [lɛ̃sœl] **nm** shroud.

linéaire [lineɛr] **adj 1.** [mesure, perspective] linear **2.** [récit] one-dimensional.

linge [lɛ̃ʒ] **nm 1.** [lessive] laundry, washing *UK* **2.** [de lit, de table] linen **3.** [sous-vêtements] underwear ▸ **linge sale** dirty laundry *ou* washing *UK* ▸ **laver son linge sale en famille** not to wash one's dirty linen *ou* laundry in public **4.** [morceau de tissu] cloth
▸▸| **blanc *ou* pâle comme un linge** as white as a sheet.

lingerie [lɛ̃ʒri] **nf 1.** [sous-vêtements] lingerie **2.** [local] linen room.

lingette [lɛ̃ʒɛt] **nf** wipe ▸ **lingette antibactérienne** antibacterial wipe ▸ **lingette démaquillante** eye makeup remover pad.

lingot [lɛ̃go] **nm** ingot ▸ **lingot d'or** gold ingot.

linguiste [lɛ̃gɥist] **nmf** linguist.

linguistique [lɛ̃gɥistik] ■ **nf** linguistics *(U)*.
■ **adj** linguistic.

linoléum [linɔleɔm] **nm** lino, linoleum.

linotte [linɔt] **nf** ZOOL linnet ▸ **tête de linotte** *fig* featherbrain.

linteau, x [lɛ̃to] **nm** lintel.

lion, lionne [ljɔ̃, ljɔn] **nm, f** lion (f lioness).
◆ ***Lion*** **nm** ASTROL Leo ▸ **être Lion** to be (a) Leo.

lionceau, x [ljɔ̃so] **nm** lion cub.

lipide [lipid] **nm** lipid.

lippu, e [lipy] **adj** thick-lipped.

liquéfier [9] [likefje] **vt** to liquefy.
◆ ***se liquéfier*** **vp 1.** [matière] to liquefy **2.** *fig* [personne] to turn to jelly.

liqueur [likœr] **nf** liqueur.

liquidation [likidasjɔ̃] **nf 1.** [de compte & FIN] settlement **2.** [de société, stock] liquidation ▸ **liquidation de fin de mois** end-of-month settlement **3.** *arg crime* [de témoin] liquidation, elimination **4.** *fam fig* [de problème] elimination.

liquide [likid] ■ **nm 1.** [substance] liquid ▸ **liquide vaisselle** washing-up liquid *UK*, dishwashing liquid *US*, dish soap *US* **2.** [argent] cash ▸ **en liquide** in cash.
■ **nf** LING liquid.
■ **adj 1.** [corps & LING] liquid **2.** [en argent] cash *(avant n)*.

liquider [3] [likide] **vt 1.** [compte & FIN] to settle **2.** [société, stock] to liquidate **3.** *fam* [importun] to get rid of **4.** *arg crime* [témoin] to liquidate, to eliminate / *fig* [problème] to eliminate, to get rid of.

liquidité [likidite] **nf** liquidity.
◆ ***liquidités*** **nfpl** liquid assets ▸ **liquidités internationales** international liquidity.

liquoreux, euse [likɔrø, øz] **adj** syrupy.

ire[1] [106] [lir] **vt** to read ▸ **lire un rapport en diagonale** to flick *ou* to skim through a report ▸ **lire entre les lignes** to read between the lines ▸ **lire sur les lèvres** to lip-read ▸ **lire dans les pensées de qqn** to read sb's thoughts *ou* mind ▸ **ça se lit facilement** it's easy to read ▸ **l'inquiétude se lisait sur son visage** anxiety showed on *ou* was written all over his face ▸ **lu et approuvé** read and approved ▸ **allemand lu et parlé** [dans un curriculum] fluent German.

re[2] [lir] **nf** lira.

s, lys [lis] **nm** lily.

sais, lisions ➤ *lire*[1].

isbonne [lizbɔn] **npr** Lisbon.

se, lises ➤ *lire*[1].

seré [lizre], ***liséré*** [lizere] **nm 1.** [ruban] binding **2.** [bande] border, edging.

seron [lizrɔ̃] **nm** bindweed.

seuse [lizøz] **nf 1.** [couvre-livre] book cover **2.** [signet] paper knife *(cum bookmark)* **3.** [vêtement] bedjacket **4.** [lampe] reading light.

sible [lizibl] **adj 1.** [écriture] legible **2.** [roman] readable.

siblement [lizibləmɑ̃] **adv** legibly.

sière [lizjɛr] **nf 1.** [limite] edge **2.** COUT selvage.

lisse [lis] ■ **nf 1.** [rambarde] handrail **2.** NAUT rib.
■ **adj 1.** [surface, peau] smooth **2.** [cheveux] straight.

lisser [3] [lise] **vt 1.** [papier, vêtements] to smooth (out) **2.** [moustache, cheveux] to smooth (down) **3.** [plumes] to preen.

listage [listaʒ] **nm** listing.

liste [list] **nf** list ▸ **liste d'attente** waiting list, waitlist *US* ▸ **liste de clients** client list ▸ **liste de diffusion** INFORM mailing list ▸ **liste électorale** electoral register *UK*, electoral roll *UK*, list of registered voters *US* ▸ **la liste des invités** the guest list ▸ **liste de mariage** wedding present list ▸ **liste noire** blacklist ▸ **elle est sur la liste noire** she has been blacklisted ▸ **être sur la liste rouge** to be ex-directory *UK*, to have an unlisted number *US* ▸ **liste de vérification** AÉRON checklist ▸ **faire *ou* dresser une liste** to make (out) *ou* to draw up a list.

lister [3] [liste] **vt** to list.

listeriose, listériose [listerjoz] **nf** MÉD listeriosis *(U)*.

listing [listiŋ] **nm** listing.

lit [li] **nm 1.** [gén] bed ▸ **faire son lit** to make one's bed ▸ **garder le lit** to stay in bed ▸ **se mettre au lit** to go to bed ▸ **lit à baldaquin** four-poster bed ▸ **lit de camp** camp bed *UK*, cot *US* ▸ **lit d'enfant** cot *UK*, crib *US* ▸ **lit gigogne** pull-out bed ▸ **lits jumeaux** twin beds ▸ **lit nuptial** marriage bed ▸ **lits superposés** bunk beds **2.** DR marriage ▸ **d'un premier lit** of a first marriage.

LIT (abr écrite de ***lire italienne***) L, Lit.

litanie [litani] **nf** litany.

litchi [litʃi], ***letchi*** [lɛtʃi] **nm** lychee.

literie [litri] **nf** bedding.

lithographie [litɔgrafi] **nf 1.** [procédé] lithography **2.** [image] lithograph.

litière [litjɛr] **nf** litter.

litige [litiʒ] **nm 1.** DR lawsuit **2.** [désaccord] dispute.

litigieux, euse [litiʒjø, øz] **adj 1.** DR litigious **2.** [douteux] disputed.

litote [litɔt] **nf** understatement, litotes.

litre [litr] **nm 1.** [mesure, quantité] litre *UK*, liter *US* **2.** [récipient] litre *UK ou* liter *US* bottle.

litron [litrɔ̃] **nm** *tfam* litre *UK ou* liter *US* of wine.

littéraire [literɛr] ■ **nmf** *person who is strong in arts subjects.*
■ **adj** literary.

littéral, e, aux [literal, o] **adj 1.** [gén] literal **2.** [écrit] written.

littéralement [literalmɑ̃] **adv** literally.

littérature [literatyr] **nf 1.** [gén] literature ▸ **littérature comparée** comparative literature **2.** [profession] writing.

littoral, e, aux [litɔral, o] **adj** coastal.
◆ ***littoral*** **nm** coast, coastline.

Lituanie [litɥani] **nf : la Lituanie** Lithuania.

lituanien, enne [litɥanjɛ̃, ɛn] **adj** Lithuanian.
◆ ***lituanien*** **nm** [langue] Lithuanian.
◆ ***Lituanien, enne*** **nm, f** Lithuanian.

liturgie [lityrʒi] **nf** liturgy.

liturgique [lityrʒik] **adj** liturgical.

livide [livid] **adj** [blême] pallid.

livrable [livrabl] **adj** able to be delivered.

livraison [livrɛzɔ̃] **nf** [de marchandise] delivery ▸ **livraison à domicile** home delivery ▸ **payer à la livraison** to pay cash on delivery ▸ **prendre livraison de qqch** to take delivery of sthg.

livre [livr] ■ **nm 1.** [gén] book ▸ **livre de bord** log, logbook ▸ **livre de classe** schoolbook, textbook ▸ **livre de comptes** (account) books ▸ **livre de cuisine** cookbook, cookery book *UK* ▸ **livre électronique** e-book ▸ **livres pour enfants** children's books ▸ **livre d'images** picture book ▸ **livre de messe** missal ▸ **livre d'or** visitors' book ▸ **livre de poche** paperback ▸ **à livre ouvert** *fig* at sight ▸ **c'est mon livre de chevet** it's a book I read and re-read ▸ **l'industrie du livre** the book industry **2.** [industrie] book trade.
■ **nf** pound ▸ **livre sterling** pound sterling ▸ **livre irlandaise** Irish pound, punt ▸ **livre verte** green pound.

livre-cassette [livrəkasɛt] (pl **livres-cassettes**) **nm** spoken-word cassette.

livrée [livre] **nf** [uniforme] livery.

livrer [3] [livre] **vt 1.** COMM to deliver ▸ **livrer qqch à qqn** [achat] to deliver sthg to sb ▸ **livrer qqch à domicile** to deliver sthg *(to the customer's home)* **2.** *fig* to reveal ▸ **dans ses romans, elle livre peu d'elle-même** she doesn't reveal much about herself in her novels ▸ **livrer qqch à qqn** [secret] to reveal *ou* give away sthg to sb **3.** [coupable, complice] **: livrer qqn à qqn** to hand sb over to sb **4.** [abandonner] **: livrer qqch à qqch** to give sthg over to sthg ▸ **le pays est livré à la corruption** the country has been given over to *ou* has sunk into corruption ▸ **livrer qqn à lui-même** to leave sb to his own devices ▸ **livrer passage à qqn** *fig* to let sb pass.
◆ ***se livrer*** **vp 1.** [se rendre] **: se livrer à** [police, ennemi] to give o.s. up to / [amant] to give o.s. to **2.** [se confier] **: se livrer à** [ami] to open up to, to confide in ▸ **elle ne se livre jamais** she never confides in anybody, she never opens up **3.** [se consacrer] **: se livrer à** [occupation] to devote o.s. to / [excès] to indulge in ▸ **se livrer à une enquête** to hold *ou* to conduct an investigation ▸ **ils se livraient au chantage** they were engaged in blackmail.

livresque [livrɛsk] **adj** bookish.

livret [livrɛ] **nm 1.** [carnet] booklet ▸ **livret de caisse d'épargne** bankbook, passbook *UK* ▸ **livret de famille** *official family record book, given by registrar to newlyweds* ▸ **livret scolaire** ≃ school report *UK*, ≃ report card *US* **2.** [catalogue] catalogue *UK*, catalog *US* **3.** MUS book, libretto.

livreur, euse [livrœr, øz] **nm, f** delivery man (f woman).

Ljubljana [ljubljana] **npr** Ljubljana.

LO (abr de ***Lutte ouvrière***) **nf** *left-wing political party.*

lobby [lɔbi] (pl **lobbies**) **nm** lobby.

lobe [lɔb] **nm 1.** ANAT & BOT lobe **2.** ARCHIT foil.

lober [3] [lɔbe] **vt** to lob.

local, e, aux [lɔkal, o] **adj** local / [douleur] localized.
◆ ***local*** **nm** room, premises *pl.*
◆ ***locaux*** **nmpl** premises, offices.

localement [lɔkalmɑ̃] **adv** locally.

localisation [lɔkalizasjɔ̃] **nf 1.** [d'un avion, d'un bruit] location **2.** [d'une épidémie, d'un conflit, d'un produit multimédia] localization.

localiser [3] [lɔkalize] **vt 1.** [avion, bruit] to locate **2.** [épidémie, conflit, produit multimédia] to localize.
◆ ***se localiser*** **vp** to be confined.

localité [lɔkalite] **nf** (small) town.

locataire [lɔkatɛr] **nmf** tenant.

locatif, ive [lɔkatif, iv] **adj** [relatif à la location] rental *(avant n).*
◆ ***locatif*** **nm** GRAMM locative.

location [lɔkasjɔ̃] **nf 1.** [de propriété - par propriétaire] renting, letting *UK* / [- par locataire] renting / [de machine] leasing ▸ **location de voitures/vélos** car/bicycle hire *UK* car/bicycle rental *US* **2.** [bail] lease **3.** [maison, appartement] rented property, rental *US* **4.** [réservation] booking
◆ ***en location*** **loc adj : être en location** [locataire] to be renting *(a house)* / [appartement] to be available for rent, to be up for rent.

FAUX AMIS / FALSE FRIENDS

location

Location is not a translation of the French word *location.* Location is translated by *emplacement.*
▸ The firm has moved to a location in the city centre / *La société a déménagé à un emplacement en centre-ville*

location-vente [lɔkasjɔ̃vɑ̃t] (pl **locations-ventes**) ≃ hire purchase *UK*, ≃ installment plan *US*.

loc. cit. (abr écrite de ***loco citato***) loc. cit.

lock-out [lɔkaut] **nm inv** lockout.

locomoteur, trice [lɔkɔmɔtœr, tris] **adj** locomotive *(avant n).*

locomotion [lɔkɔmɔsjɔ̃] **nf** locomotion.

locomotive [lɔkɔmɔtiv] **nf 1.** [machine] locomotive **2.** *fig* [leader] pacesetter.

locuteur, trice [lɔkytœr, tris] **nm, f** speaker.

locution [lɔkysjɔ̃] **nf** expression, phrase.

loden [lɔdɛn] **nm** [étoffe] loden / [vêtement] loden overcoat.

loft [lɔft] **nm** (converted) loft.

logarithme [lɔgaritm] **nm** logarithm.

loge [lɔʒ] **nf 1.** [de concierge, de francs-maçons] lodge **2.** [d'acteur] dressing room **3.** [de spectacle] box ▸ **être aux premières loges** *fig* to have a ringside seat **4.** [d'écurie] loose box **5.** ARCHIT loggia.

'ogement [lɔʒmɑ̃] **nm 1.** [hébergement] accommodation *UK*, accommodations *(pl) US* **2.** [appartement] flat *UK*, apartment *US* ▸ **logement de fonction** company flat *UK* ***ou*** apartment *US*.

oger [17] [lɔʒe] ■ **vi** [habiter] to live.
■ **vt 1.** [amis, invités] to put up **2.** [clé] to put **3.** [suj: hôtel, maison] to accommodate, to take.
◆ ***se loger*** **vp 1.** [trouver un logement] to find accommodation *UK* ***ou*** accommodations *US* **2.** [se placer - ballon, balle] **: se loger dans** to lodge in, to stick in ▸ **se loger dans** *fig* [angoisse] to take hold of.

ogeur, euse [lɔʒœr, øz] **nm, f** landlord (f landlady).

oggia [lɔdʒja] **nf** loggia.

ogiciel [lɔʒisjɛl] **nm** software *(U)* ▸ **logiciel auteur** authoring software ▸ **logiciel de filtrage** filtering ***ou*** blocking software ▸ **logiciel intégré** integrated software ▸ **logiciel de navigation** browser ▸ **logiciel de réseau** network software.

gique [lɔʒik] ■ **nf** logic ▸ **c'est dans la logique des choses** it's in the nature of things ▸ **ton raisonnement manque de logique** your argument isn't very logical ***ou*** consistent ▸ **logique programmable** INFORM field programmable logic array.
■ **adj** logical ▸ **ah oui, c'est logique, je n'y avais pas pensé!** ah, that makes sense; I hadn't thought of that! ▸ **tu la brimes, elle t'en veut, c'est logique** if you pick on her she'll hold it against you;that's only normal ***ou*** natural ***ou*** logical.

giquement [lɔʒikmɑ̃] **adv** logically.

gis [lɔʒi] **nm** abode.

gistique [lɔʒistik] ■ **nf** logistics *pl*.
■ **adj** logistic.

go [logo] **nm** logo.

gorrhée [lɔgɔre] **nf** logorrhoea *UK*, logorrhea *US*.

i [lwa] **nf 1.** [gén] law ▸ **faire la loi** to lay down the law ▸ **loi d'exception** emergency legislation ▸ **loi fondamentale** fundamental law ▸ **la loi du plus fort** might is right ▸ **la loi de la gravitation universelle *ou* de la pesanteur** the law of gravity ▸ **la loi de la jungle** the law of the jungle ▸ **loi de l'offre et de la demande** law of supply and demand ▸ **la loi du silence** the law of silence ▸ **la loi du talion** an eye for an eye ▸ **la loi de 1901** *law concerning the setting up of non-profit organizations* ▸ **selon la loi en vigueur** according to the law as it stands ▸ **tomber sous le coup de la loi** to be an offence *UK* ***ou*** offense *US* **2.** [convention] rule ▸ **les lois de l'hospitalité/du savoir-vivre** the rules of hospitality/etiquette ▸ **les lois de l'honneur** the code of honour.

CULTURE
Lois

French laws are often known by the name of the legislator who initiated the parliamentary debate on them. The **loi Veil** (1975) legalized abortion and provided for easier access to contraceptives, while the **loi Badinter**, passed in 1981, abolished the death penalty. The **loi Defferre** of 1982 decentralized the government; the **loi Evin** (1992) banned cigarettes and advertisements for alcoholic drinks in public places.

loin [lwɛ̃] **adv 1.** [dans l'espace] far ▸ **plus loin** farther, further ▸ **ils habitent loin** they live a long way away ▸ **ils ont poussé les recherches très loin** *fig* they took the research as far as possible **2.** [dans le temps - passé] a long time ago / [- futur] a long way off ▸ **c'est loin tout ça!** [- dans le passé] that was a long time ago!, that seems a long way off now! / [- dans le futur] that's a long way off!
◆ ***au loin*** **loc adv** in the distance, far off ▸ **on voyait, au loin, une rangée de peupliers** a row of poplars could be seen in the far distance ***ou*** far off in the distance.
◆ ***de loin*** **loc adv 1.** [depuis une grande distance] from a distance ▸ **de très loin** from a great distance ▸ **de plus loin** from farther ***ou*** further away ▸ **je vois mal de loin** I can't see very well from a distance **2.** [assez peu] from a distance, from afar ▸ **suivre les événements de loin** to follow events from a distance **3.** [de beaucoup] by far ▸ **je le préfère à ses collègues, et de loin** I much prefer him to his colleagues.
◆ ***de loin en loin*** **loc adv 1.** [dans l'espace] here and there **2.** [dans le temps] every now and then, from time to time.
◆ ***loin de*** **loc prép 1.** [gén] far from ▸ **loin de là!** *fig* far from it! **2.** [dans le temps] **: il n'est pas loin de 9 h** it's nearly 9 o'clock, it's not far off 9 o'clock ▸ **ça ne fait pas loin de quatre ans qu'ils sont mariés** they've been married nearly four years.

lointain, e [lwɛ̃tɛ̃, ɛn] **adj 1.** [pays, avenir, parent] distant **2.** [ressemblance] vague.
◆ ***lointain*** **nm : au *ou* dans le lointain** in the distance.

loir [lwar] **nm** dormouse ▸ **dormir comme un loir** *fig* to sleep like a log.

loisible [lwazibl] **adj** *sout* **: il m'est loisible de participer** I am at liberty to take part.

loisir [lwazir] **nm 1.** [temps libre] leisure ▸ **avoir le loisir de faire qqch** *sout* to have the time to do sthg ▸ **à loisir** [à satiété] as much as one likes / [sans hâte] at leisure **2.** *(gén pl)* [distractions] leisure activities *pl*.

lombago = ***lumbago***.

lombaire [lɔ̃bɛr] ■ **nf** lumbar vertebra.
■ **adj** lumbar.

lombes [lɔ̃b] **nfpl** loins.

Lomé [lome] **npr** Lomé.

londonien, enne [lɔ̃dɔnjɛ̃, ɛn] **adj** London *(avant n)*.
◆ **Londonien, enne nm, f** Londoner.

Londres [lɔ̃dr] **npr** London.

long, longue [lɔ̃, lɔ̃g] **adj 1.** [gén] long ▸ **j'ai trouvé le temps long** the time seemed to go (by) really slowly ▸ **une longue rangée d'arbres** a long row of trees ▸ **une robe longue** a full-length *ou* long dress ▸ **long de** [mesurant] : **tunnel long de deux kilomètres** two-kilometre *UK ou* two-kilometer *US* long tunnel **2.** [lent] slow ▸ **être long à faire qqch** to take a long time doing sthg ▸ **ne soyez pas trop long à me répondre** don't take too long answering me ▸ **il est long à venir, ce café!** that coffee's a long time coming! **3.** [qui existe depuis longtemps] long, long-standing ▸ **sa longue expérience de journaliste** his many years spent *ou* his long experience as a journalist.
◆ **long** ■ **nm 1.** [longueur] : **4 mètres de long** 4 metres *UK ou* meters *US* long *ou* in length ▸ **de long en large** up and down, to and fro ▸ **en long et en large** in great detail ▸ **en long, en large et en travers** [examiner] from every (conceivable) angle / [raconter] in the minutest detail, at some considerable length ▸ **(tout) le long de** [espace] all along ▸ **tout le long du jour** the whole day long ▸ **tout au long de** [année, carrière] throughout ▸ **tomber de tout son long** to go full length **2.** [vêtement] : **le long** long clothes *pl* ▸ **la mode est au long** long styles are in fashion.
■ **adv 1.** [beaucoup] : **en dire long : geste/regard qui en dit long** eloquent gesture/look ▸ **en savoir long sur qqch** to know a lot about sthg **2.** [s'habiller] : **elle est habillée trop long** her clothes are too long.
◆ **longue nf 1.** LING long vowel **2.** MUS long note **3.** [suite de cartes] long suit.
◆ **à la longue loc adv** in the end ▸ **à la longue, tout se sait** everything comes out in the end.

long. (abr écrite de ***longitude***) long.

long-courrier [lɔ̃kurje] **adj** [navire] ocean-going / [vol] long-haul.

longe [lɔ̃ʒ] **nf 1.** [courroie] halter **2.** [viande] loin.

longer [17] [lɔ̃ʒe] **vt 1.** [border] to go along *ou* alongside **2.** [marcher le long de] to walk along / [raser] to stay close to, to hug.

longévité [lɔ̃ʒevite] **nf** longevity.

longiligne [lɔ̃ʒiliɲ] **adj** long-limbed.

longitude [lɔ̃ʒityd] **nf** longitude.

longitudinal, e, aux [lɔ̃ʒitydinal, o] **adj** longitudinal.

longtemps [lɔ̃tɑ̃] **adv** (for) a long time ▸ **avant longtemps** before long ▸ **il ne reviendra pas avant longtemps** he won't be back for some time ▸ **depuis longtemps** (for) a long time ▸ **il y a longtemps que...** it's been a long time since... ▸ **il y a longtemps qu'il est là** he's been here a long time ▸ **mettre longtemps à faire qqch** to take a long time to do sthg ▸ **je n'en ai pas pour longtemps** I won't be long.

longue ➤ **long**.

longuement [lɔ̃gmɑ̃] **adv 1.** [longtemps] for a long time **2.** [en détail] at length.

longuet, ette [lɔ̃gɛ, ɛt] **adj** *fam* longish, a bit long.

longueur [lɔ̃gœr] **nf** length ▸ **faire 5 mètres de longueur** to be 5 metres *UK ou* meters *US* long ▸ **disposer qqch en longueur** to put sthg lengthways ▸ **le jardin est tout en longueur** the garden is long and narrow ▸ **à longueur de journée/temps** the entire day/time ▸ **à longueur d'année** all year long ▸ **longueur d'onde** wavelength ▸ **être sur la même longueur d'onde** *fig* to be on the same wavelength ▸ **saut en longueur** long jump ▸ **il l'a emporté d'une longueur** he won by a length ▸ **longueur de bloc/de mot** INFORM block/word length.
◆ **longueurs nfpl** [de film, de livre] boring parts ▸ **il y a des longueurs dans le film** the film *UK ou* movie *US* is a little tedious in parts.

longue-vue [lɔ̃gvy] (pl **longues-vues**) **nf** telescope.

look [luk] **nm** look ▸ **avoir un look** to have a style.

looping [lupiŋ] **nm** loop-the-loop.

lopin [lɔpɛ̃] **nm : lopin (de terre)** patch *ou* plot of land.

loquace [lɔkas] **adj** loquacious.

loquacité [lɔkasite] **nf** loquacity.

loque [lɔk] **nf 1.** [lambeau] rag ▸ **en loques** in rags **2.** *fig* [personne] wreck.

loquet [lɔkɛ] **nm** latch.

lorgner [3] [lɔrɲe] **vt** *fam* **1.** [observer] to eye **2.** [guigner] to have one's eye on.

lorgnette [lɔrɲɛt] **nf** opera glasses *pl*.

lorgnon [lɔrɲɔ̃] **nm** lorgnette.

lors [lɔr] **adv : depuis lors** since that time ▸ **lors de** at the time of.

lorsque [lɔrsk(ə)] **conj** when.

losange [lɔzɑ̃ʒ] **nm** lozenge.

lot [lo] **nm 1.** [part] share / [de terre] plot **2.** [stock] batch **3.** [prix] prize ▸ **le gros lot** the jackpot **4.** *fig* [destin] fate, lot.

loterie [lɔtri] **nf** lottery ▸ **la Loterie nationale** the National Lottery.

loti, e [lɔti] **adj : être bien/mal loti** to be well/badly off.

lotion [lɔsjɔ̃] **nf** lotion ▸ **lotion après-rasage** aftershave (lotion).

lotir [32] [lɔtir] **vt** to divide up ▸ **lotir qqn de qqch** to allot sthg to sb.

lotissement [lɔtismɑ̃] **nm 1.** [terrain] plot **2.** [division de terrain] parcelling out *UK*, parceling out *US*.

loto [lɔto] **nm 1.** [jeu de société] lotto **2.** [loterie] *popular* national lottery.

lotte [lɔt] **nf** monkfish.

lotus [lɔtys] **nm** lotus.

louable [lwabl] **adj 1.** [méritoire] praiseworthy **2.** [location] **: facilement/difficilement louable** easy/difficult to rent, easy/difficult to let *UK*.

louage [lwaʒ] **nm** hire *UK*, rental *US* ▸ **voiture de louage** hire *UK* ***ou*** rental *US* car.

louange [lwɑ̃ʒ] **nf** praise ▸ **chanter les louanges de qqn** *fig* to sing sb's praises.

loubar(d) [lubar] **nm** *fam* hooligan.

louche[1] [luʃ] **nf** ladle.

louche[2] [luʃ] **adj** *fam* [personne, histoire] suspicious.

loucher [3] [luʃe] **vi 1.** [être atteint de strabisme] to squint **2.** *fam fig* [lorgner] **: loucher sur** to have one's eye on.

louer [6] [lwe] **vt 1.** [glorifier] to praise ▸ **Dieu soit loué** thank God ▸ **louer qqn de qqch** to praise sb for sthg ▸ **on ne peut que vous louer d'avoir agi ainsi** you deserve nothing but praise for having acted in this way **2.** [donner en location] to rent (out), to let (out) *UK* ▸ **le propriétaire me le loue pour 1 000 euros** the landlord rents it out to me for 1,000 euros ▸ **à louer** for rent, to let *UK* **3.** [prendre en location] to rent ▸ **on a loué le hall d'exposition à une grosse compagnie** we've leased the exhibition hall from a big firm **4.** [réserver] to book ▸ **pour ce spectacle, il est conseillé de louer les places à l'avance** advance booking is advisable for this show.
◆ ***se louer*** **vp 1.** *sout* [se féliciter] **: se louer de qqch/de faire qqch** to be very pleased about sthg/about doing sthg ▸ **je peux me louer d'avoir vu juste** I can congratulate myself for having got it right **2.** [appartement] to be for rent ***ou*** to let *UK* ▸ **cette chambre se louerait aisément** you'd have no problem finding somebody to rent this room ***ou*** letting this room **3.** *péj* [se vanter] to sing one's own praises.

oufoque [lufɔk] *fam* ■ **nmf** nut.
■ **adj** nuts, crazy.

oup [lu] **nm 1.** [carnassier] wolf **2.** [poisson] bass **3.** [masque] mask **4.** *fig* [personne] **: (vieux) loup de mer** (old) sea dog.

ɔupe [lup] **nf 1.** [optique] magnifying glass ▸ **regarder qqch à la loupe** *fig* to put sthg under the microscope **2.** BOT burr.

ɔuper [3] [lupe] **vt** *fam* [travail] to make a mess of / [train] to miss.

ɔup-garou [lugaru] (pl **loups-garous**) **nm** werewolf.

ɔupiot, otte [lupjo, ɔt] **nm, f** *fam* kid.

ɔurd, e [lur, lurd] **adj 1.** [gén] heavy ▸ **des repas trop ourds** excessively rich meals ▸ **tu as là une lourde responsabilité** that is a heavy responsibility for you ▸ **lourd le** *fig* full of ▸ **cette décision est lourde de conséquences** this decision will have far-reaching consequences **2.** [tâche] difficult / [faute] serious **3.** [maladroit] clumsy, heavy-handed ▸ **des plaisanteries plutôt lourdes** rather unsubtle jokes **4.** MÉTÉOR close **5.** [esprit] slow ▸ **tu ne comprends pas? ce que tu peux être lourd!** don't you understand? how slow can you get!
◆ ***lourd*** **adv : peser lourd** to be heavy, to weigh a lot ▸ **il fait très lourd** it is very close ▸ **il n'en fait pas lourd** *fam* he doesn't do much.

lourdaud, e [lurdo, od] ■ **adj** clumsy.
■ **nm, f** oaf.

lourdement [lurdəmɑ̃] **adv 1.** [pesamment] heavily **2.** [maladroitement] heavily, clumsily / [insister] strenuously.

lourdeur [lurdœr] **nf 1.** [gén] heaviness **2.** MÉTÉOR closeness **3.** [d'esprit] slowness.

loustic [lustik] **nm** *fam* **1.** [enfant] kid **2.** [farceur] joker **3.** *péj* [type] guy.

loutre [lutr] **nf** otter.

louve [luv] **nf** she-wolf.

louveteau, x [luvto] **nm 1.** ZOOL wolf cub **2.** [scout] cub.

louvoyer [13] [luvwaje] **vi 1.** NAUT to tack **2.** *fig* [tergiverser] to beat around ***ou*** about *UK* the bush.

Louvre [luvr] **npr : le Louvre** the Louvre (museum) ▸ **l'école du Louvre** *art school in Paris.*

lover [3] [lɔve] ◆ ***se lover*** **vp** [serpent] to coil up.

loyal, e, aux [lwajal, o] **adj 1.** [fidèle] loyal **2.** [honnête] fair.

loyalement [lwajalmɑ̃] **adv 1.** [fidèlement] loyally **2.** [honnêtement] fairly.

loyauté [lwajote] **nf 1.** [fidélité] loyalty **2.** [honnêteté] fairness.

loyer [lwaje] **nm** rent.

LP (abr de ***lycée professionnel***) **nm** *secondary school for vocational training.*

LSD (abr de ***lysergic acid diethylamide***) **nm** LSD.

lu, e [ly] **pp** ➤ ***lire***[1].

lubie [lybi] **nf** *fam* whim.

lubricité [lybrisite] **nf** lechery.

lubrifiant, e [lybrifjɑ̃, ɑ̃t] **adj** lubricating.
◆ ***lubrifiant*** **nm** lubricant.

lubrification [lybrifikasjɔ̃] **nf** lubrication.

lubrifier [9] [lybrifje] **vt** to lubricate.

lubrique [lybrik] **adj** lewd.

lucarne [lykarn] **nf 1.** [fenêtre] skylight **2.** FOOTBALL top corner of the net.

lucide [lysid] **adj** lucid.

lucidement [lysidmɑ̃] **adv** lucidly.

lucidité [lysidite] **nf** lucidity.

luciole [lysjɔl] **nf** firefly.

lucratif, ive [lykratif, iv] **adj** lucrative.

lucre [lykr] **nm** *péj* lucre.

ludique [lydik] **adj** play *(avant n).*

ludo-éducatif [lydoedykatif] **nm** edutainment.

ludothèque [lydɔtɛk] **nf** toy library.

luette [lɥɛt] **nf** uvula.

lueur [lɥœr] **nf 1.** [de bougie, d'étoile] light ▸ **à la lueur de** by the light of **2.** *fig* [de colère] gleam / [de raison] spark ▸ **lueur d'espoir** glimmer of hope.

luge [lyʒ] **nf** toboggan.

lugubre [lygybr] **adj** lugubrious.

lui[1] [lɥi] **pp inv** ➤ ***luire***.

lui[2] [lɥi] **pron pers 1.** [complément d'objet indirect - homme] (to) him / [- femme] (to) her / [- animal, chose] (to) it ▸ **donne-le-lui** give it to him/her ▸ **je lui ai parlé** I've spoken to him/to her ▸ **il le lui a présenté** he introduced him to her ▸ **il lui a serré la main** he shook his/her hand
2. [sujet, en renforcement de "il"] he ▸ **qui t'accompagnera? - lui** who will go with you? - he will ▸ **il sait de quoi je parle, lui** HE knows what I'm talking about ▸ **lui aussi se pose des questions** he is wondering about it too
3. [objet, après préposition, comparatif - personne] him / [- animal, chose] it ▸ **je n'ai vu que lui** I saw no one else but him ▸ **si j'étais lui...** if I were him... ▸ **lui, tout le monde le connaît** everyone knows HIM ▸ **sans lui** without him ▸ **je vais chez lui** I'm going to his place ▸ **elle est plus jeune que lui** she's younger than him *ou* than he is ▸ **une amie à lui** a friend of his
4. [remplaçant 'soi' en fonction de pronom réfléchi - personne] himself / [- animal, chose] itself ▸ **il est content de lui** he's pleased with himself ▸ **il ne pense qu'à lui** he only thinks of himself.
◆ ***lui-même*** **pron pers** [personne] himself ▸ **lui-même paraissait surpris** he himself seemed surprised ▸ **de lui-même, il a parlé du prix** he mentioned the price without being prompted *ou* asked / [animal, chose] itself.

luire [97] [lɥir] **vi** [soleil, métal] to shine / *fig* [espoir] to glow, to glimmer.

luisais, luisions ➤ ***luire***.

luisant, e [lɥizɑ̃, ɑ̃t] **adj** gleaming.
◆ ***luisant*** **nm** sheen.

lumbago, lombago [lɔ̃bago] **nm** lumbago.

lumière [lymjɛr] **nf 1.** *fig* [éclairage] light ▸ **lumière tamisée** subdued light ▸ **allumer la lumière** to turn *ou* to switch on the light ▸ **éteindre la lumière** to turn *ou* to switch off the light ▸ **à la lumière de** by the light of ▸ **faire toute la lumière sur qqch** to make sthg clear ▸ **toute la lumière sera faite** we'll get to the bottom of this ▸ **mettre qqch en lumière** to highlight sthg ▸ **j'ai besoin de tes lumières** I need the benefit of your wisdom ▸ **le siècle des Lumières** the Enlightenment **2.** [personne] leading light ▸ **ce n'est pas une lumière** *fam* he's/she's not very bright.

luminaire [lyminɛr] **nm** light.

luminescent, e [luminɛsɑ̃, ɑ̃t] **adj** luminescent.

lumineux, euse [lyminø, øz] **adj 1.** [couleur, cadran] luminous **2.** *fig* [visage] radiant / [idée] brilliant **3.** [explication] clear.

luminosité [lyminozite] **nf 1.** [du regard, ciel] radiance **2.** [sciences] luminosity.

lump [lœ̃p] **nm : œufs de lump** lumpfish roe.

lunaire [lynɛr] **adj 1.** ASTRON lunar **2.** *fig* [visage] moon *(avant n)* / [paysage] lunar.

lunatique [lynatik] ■ **nmf** temperamental person.
■ **adj** temperamental.

lunch [lœʃ] **nm** buffet lunch.

lundi [lœ̃di] **nm** Monday ▸ **lundi de Pâques/Pentecôte** Easter/Whit Monday ; voir aussi ***samedi***.

lune [lyn] **nf 1.** ASTRON moon ▸ **nouvelle lune** new moon ▸ **pleine lune** full moon ▸ **lune de miel** honeymoon / *fig* & POLIT honeymoon period ▸ **dans la lune** *fig* in the clouds ▸ **décrocher la lune** *fig* to move heaven and earth ▸ **promettre la lune** *fig* to promise the earth **2.** *fam fig* [derrière] backside.

luné, e [lyne] **adj : être bien/mal luné** to be in a good/bad mood.

lunetier, ère [lyntje, ɛr] ■ **adj** spectacle-making *(avant n).*
■ **nm, f** optician.

lunette [lynɛt] **nf 1.** [ouverture] **: la lunette des W.-C.** [cuvette] the toilet bowl ▸ **lunette arrière** rear window **2.** ASTRON telescope ▸ **lunette astronomique** astronomical telescope ▸ **lunette de tir/pointage** sights/sighting telescope.
◆ ***lunettes*** **nfpl** glasses ▸ **porter des lunettes** to wear glasses ▸ **une paire de lunettes** a pair of glasses ▸ **lunettes noires** dark glasses ▸ **lunettes de ski** skiing goggles ▸ **lunettes de soleil** sunglasses ▸ **lunettes de vue** *ou* **correctrices** spectacles.

lunule [lynyl] **nf** [d'ongle] half-moon.

lupanar [lypanar] **nm** *sout* brothel.

lupin [lypɛ̃] **nm** lupin *UK*, lupine *US*.

lurette [lyrɛt] **nf : il y a belle lurette que...** *fam* it's been ages since...

luron, onne [lyrɔ̃, ɔn] **nm, f** *fam* **: un joyeux luron** a bit of a lad *UK*.

lustre [lystr] **nm 1.** [luminaire] chandelier **2.** [éclat] sheen, shine / *fig* reputation **3.** *littéraire* [cinq ans] period of five years ▸ **ça fait des lustres que...** *fig* it's been ages since...

ıstrer [3] [lystre] **vt 1.** [faire briller] to make shine **:.** [user] to wear.

ıth [lyt] **nm** lute.

ıthérien, enne [lyterjɛ̃, ɛn] **adj & nm, f** Lutheran.

ıthier [lytje] **nm** maker of stringed instruments.

ıtin, e [lytɛ̃, in] **adj** mischievous.
◆ ***lutin*** **nm** imp.

ıtrin [lytrɛ̃] **nm** lectern.

ıtte [lyt] **nf 1.** [combat] fight, struggle ▸ **se livrer à une utte acharnée** to fight tooth and nail ▸ **de haute lutte** vith a hard-fought struggle ▸ **lutte armée** armed struggle **la lutte contre le sida** the fight against AIDS ▸ **la lutte les classes** the class struggle ▸ **lutte d'influence** power truggle ▸ **la lutte d'un malade contre la mort** a sick erson's struggle for life *ou* battle against death ▸ **nos ca-narades en lutte** our struggling comrades **2.** SPORT wres-ing ▸ **lutte libre** all-in wrestling ▸ **lutte gréco-romaine** ireco-Roman *ou* Graeco-Roman *UK* wrestling.

ıtter [3] [lyte] **vi** to fight, to struggle ▸ **lutter contre** to ght (against).

ıtteur, euse [lytœr, øz] **nm, f** SPORT wrestler / *fig* fight-r.

ıxation [lyksasjɔ̃] **nf** dislocation.

ıxe [lyks] **nm** luxury ▸ **de luxe** luxury ▸ **ce n'est pas un** *ou* **du luxe** *fig* it is a necessity ▸ **s'offrir** *ou* **se payer le ıxe de** *fig* to afford the luxury of.

ıxembourg [lyksɑ̃bur] **nm 1.** [pays] **: le Luxem-ourg** Luxembourg ▸ **au Luxembourg** in Luxembourg **.** [ville] Luxembourg ▸ **à Luxembourg** in (the city of) Lux-mbourg **3.** [jardins] **: le Luxembourg** the Luxembourg ardens.

ıxembourgeois, e [lyksɑ̃burʒwa, az] **adj** of/from uxembourg.
◆ ***Luxembourgeois, e*** **nm, f** person from Luxembourg.

ıxer [3] [lykse] **vt** to dislocate.
◆ ***se luxer*** **vp : se luxer l'épaule** to dislocate one's houlder.

ıxueux, euse [lyksɥø, øz] **adj** luxurious.

ıxure [lyksyr] **nf** lust.

ıxuriant, e [lyksyrjɑ̃, ɑ̃t] **adj** luxuriant.

ızerne [lyzɛrn] **nf** lucerne, alfalfa.

lycée [lise] **nm** ≃ secondary school *UK*, ≃ high school *US* ▸ **lycée pilote** experimental school ▸ **lycée professionnel** *vocational secondary school* ▸ **lycée technique** ≃ technical college.

CULTURE

Lycée

The **lycée**, which students enter around the age of 15, represents the final part of their secondary education. After three years of study (**seconde**, **première** and **terminale**), students take the **baccalauréat**, a written and oral exam covering all material learned in the final year. Successful candidates can go on to university or enrol in **classes préparatoires** in the hope of gaining admission to a **grande école**. Students can attend one of three types of **lycée: général** (offering specializations in literature, social sciences and economics, or the sciences); **technologique** (offering specialized technical studies); or **professionnel** (focusing on preparing students for a specific career). The specialization determines the type of **baccalauréat** a student will take. Some students at the professional schools do not pursue the **baccalauréat** but instead take two-year diplomas based on their chosen profession.

lycéen, enne [liseɛ̃, ɛn] **nm, f** secondary school pupil *UK*, high school pupil *US*.

lymphatique [lɛ̃fatik] **adj 1.** MÉD lymphatic **2.** *fig* [apathique] sluggish.

lymphe [lɛ̃f] **nf** lymph.

lyncher [3] [lɛ̃ʃe] **vt** to lynch.

lynx [lɛ̃ks] **nm** lynx.

Lyon [ljɔ̃] **npr** Lyons.

lyonnais, e [ljɔnɛ, ɛz] **adj** of/from Lyons.
◆ ***Lyonnais, e*** **nm, f** person from Lyons.

lyre [lir] **nf** lyre.

lyrique [lirik] **adj** *fig* [poésie] lyrical / [drame, chanteur, poète] lyric.

lyrisme [lirism] **nm 1.** [poésie] lyricism **2.** [exaltation] enthusiasm.

lys = ***lis***.

m [1], ***M*** [ɛm] ■ **nm inv** m, M.
■ (abr écrite de ***mètre***) m.
◆ ***M*** **1.** (abr écrite de ***maxwell***) Mx **2.** (abr écrite de ***mile (marin)***) nm **3.** (abr écrite de ***méga***) M **4.** (abr écrite de ***Major***) M **5.** (abr écrite de ***Monsieur***) Mr *UK*, Mr. *US* **6.** (abr écrite de ***million***) M **7.** (abr écrite de ***masculin***) M.

m [2] (abr écrite de ***milli***) m.

m' ➤ ***me***.

M6 **npr** *private television channel broadcasting a high proportion of music and aimed at a younger audience.*

ma ➤ ***mon***.

MA (abr de ***maître auxiliaire***) **nm** supply *UK* ***ou*** substitute *US* teacher.

Maastricht [mastriʃt] **npr** Maastricht ▸ **le traité de Maastricht** the Maastricht treaty.

maboul, ***e*** [mabul] *fam* ■ **adj** crazy.
■ **nm, f** nut.

macabre [makabr] **adj** macabre.

macadam [makadam] **nm** [revêtement] macadam / [route] road.

Macao [makao] **npr** Macao ▸ **à Macao** in Macao.

macaque [makak] **nm 1.** ZOOL macaque **2.** *fam* [personne] ape.

macareux [makarø] **nm** puffin.

macaron [makarɔ̃] **nm 1.** [pâtisserie] macaroon **2.** [coiffure] coil **3.** [autocollant] sticker.

macaronis [makarɔni] **nmpl 1.** CULIN macaroni *(U)* **2.** *tfam* [Italiens] *offensive term used with reference to Italians* wops, Eyeties *UK*.

macchabée [makabe] **nm** *tfam* stiff.

macédoine [masedwan] **nf 1.** CULIN **: macédoine de fruits** fruit salad ▸ **macédoine de légumes** mixed vegetables **2.** *fig* [mélange] jumble.

macérer [18] [masere] ■ **vt** to steep.
■ **vi 1.** [mariner] to steep ▸ **faire macérer** to steep **2.** *fig* & *péj* [personne] to wallow.

mâche [maʃ] **nf** lamb's lettuce.

mâcher [3] [maʃe] **vt 1.** [mastiquer] to chew **2.** TECHNO to chew up.

machiavélique [makjavelik] **adj** Machiavellian.

mâchicoulis [maʃikuli] **nm** machicolation.

machin [maʃɛ̃] **nm** *fam* [chose] thing, thingamajig.

Machin, ***e*** [maʃɛ̃, in] **nm, f** *fam* what's his nam (f what's her name).

machinal, ***e***, ***aux*** [maʃinal, o] **adj** mechanical.

machinalement [maʃinalmɑ̃] **adv** mechanically.

machination [maʃinasjɔ̃] **nf** machination.

machine [maʃin] **nf 1.** TECHNOL machine ▸ **machine à coudre** sewing machine ▸ **coudre qqch à la machine** t sew sthg on the machine, to machine ***ou*** to machine-se sthg ▸ **machine à écrire** typewriter ▸ **taper qqch à la ma chine** to type sthg ▸ **machine à laver** washing machin ▸ **machine à sous** slot machine, one-armed bandit, fru machine *UK* ▸ **machine à tricoter** knitting machine ▸ **ma chines agricoles** agricultural machinery **2.** [organisatio machinery *(U)* ▸ **les lourdeurs de la machine judiciai** the cumbersome machinery of the law **3.** NAUT engir ▸ **faire machine arrière** to reverse engines / *fig* to bac pedal ▸ **salle des machines** engine room **4.** [locomotiv engine, locomotive.

machine-outil [maʃinuti] (pl **machines-outils**) machine tool.

machiner [3] [maʃine] **vt** to plot.

machiniste [maʃinist] **nm 1.** CINÉ & THÉÂTRE sce shifter **2.** [transports] driver.

machisme [matʃism] **nm** machismo.

macho [matʃo] *péj* ■ **nm** macho man.
■ **adj inv** macho.

mâchoire [maʃwar] **nf** jaw ▸ **mâchoire supérieure/i férieure** upper/lower jaw.

mâchonner [3] [maʃɔne] **vt 1.** [mâcher, mordiller] chew **2.** [marmonner] to mutter.

mâchouiller [3] [maʃuje] **vt** *fam* to chew.

maçon [masɔ̃] **nm** mason.

maçonner [3] [masɔne] **vt** [construire] to build / [re tir] to face / [boucher] to brick up.

maçonnerie [masɔnri] **nf** [travaux] building / [construction] masonry / [franc-maçonnerie] freemasonry.

maçonnique [masɔnik] **adj** masonic.

macramé [makrame] **nm** macramé.

macro [makro] **nf** INFORM macro.

macrobiotique [makrɔbjɔtik] ■ **nf** macrobiotics *(U)*. ■ **adj** macrobiotic.

macroéconomie [makrɔekɔnɔmi] **nf** macroeconomy.

macromarketing [makrɔmarkɛtiŋ] **m** macromarketing.

maculer [3] [makyle] **vt** to stain.

Madagascar [madagaskar] **npr** Madagascar ▸ **à Madagascar** in Madagascar.

madame [madam] (pl **mesdames** [medam]) **nf 1.** [titre] **: madame X** Mrs X ▸ **bonjour madame!** good morning! / [dans hôtel, restaurant] good morning, madam! ▸ **bonjour mesdames!** good morning (ladies)! ▸ **Chère madame** Dear Mrs Duval ▸ **Madame la Ministre n'est pas là** the Minister is out ▸ **adressez-vous à madame Duval** go and see Mrs Duval ▸ **madame votre mère** *sout* your (good) mother ▸ **et en plus, madame exige des excuses!** and so Her Ladyship wants an apology as well, does she? **2.** HIST Madame *(title given to the wife of the brother of the King of France)*.

nadeleine [madlɛn] **nf** madeleine *small sponge cake*. ◆ ***Madeleine*** **nf : pleurer comme une Madeleine** to cry one's eyes out.

nademoiselle [madmwazɛl] (pl **mesdemoiselles** [medmwazɛl]) **nf 1.** [titre] **: mademoiselle X** Miss X ▸ **bonjour mademoiselle!** good morning! / [à l'école, dans hôtel] good morning, miss! ▸ **bonjour mesdemoiselles!** good morning (ladies)! ▸ **Chère mademoiselle** Dear Miss Duval ▸ **c'est mademoiselle Duval qui s'en occupe** Miss Duval is dealing with it ▸ **mademoiselle, j'ai fini mon dessin!** (please) Miss (Duval), I've finished my drawing! ▸ **et en plus, mademoiselle se plaint!** *iron* so, Her Ladyship is complaining as well, is she? **2.** HIST Mademoiselle *(title given to a Princess of France)*.

nadère [madɛr] **nm** Madeira (wine).

Aadère [madɛr] **nf** Madeira ▸ **à Madère** in Madeira.

nadone [madɔn] **nf** ART & RELIG Madonna.

Aadrid [madrid] **npr** Madrid.

nadrier [madrije] **nm** beam.

nadrilène [madrilɛn] **adj** of/fromMadrid. ◆ ***Madrilène*** **nmf** person from Madrid.

naestria [maɛstrija] **nf** mastery ▸ **avec maestria** brilliantly.

naf(f)ia [mafja] **nf** Mafia.

nagasin [magazɛ̃] **nm 1.** [boutique] shop *UK*, store *US* **en magasin** in stock ▸ **grand magasin** department store **faire les magasins** *fig* to go around the shops *UK ou* tores *US* ▸ **magasin de (vente au) détail** retail outlet **magasin vitrine** flagship store **2.** [entrepôt] warehouse **.** [d'arme, d'appareil photo] magazine.

nagasinage [magazinaʒ] **nm** warehousing, storing.

magasinier [magazinje] **nm** warehouseman, storeman.

magazine [magazin] **nm** magazine.

mage [maʒ] **nm : les Rois mages** the Three Wise Men.

Maghreb [magrɛb] **nm : le Maghreb** the Maghreb.

maghrébin, e [magrebɛ̃, in] **adj** North African. ◆ ***Maghrébin, e*** **nm, f** North African.

magicien, enne [maʒisjɛ̃, ɛn] **nm, f** magician.

magie [maʒi] **nf** magic ▸ **comme par magie** as if by magic ▸ **magie noire** black magic.

magique [maʒik] **adj 1.** [occulte] magic **2.** [merveilleux] magical.

> PARONYME / CONFUSABLE
>
> **magique**
>
> Lorsque vous traduisez **magique**, ne confondez pas ***magic*** qui désigne ce qui est en rapport avec la magie, et ***magical*** qui signifie merveilleux.

magistère [maʒistɛr] **nm** authority.

magistral, e, aux [maʒistral, o] **adj 1.** [œuvre, habileté] masterly **2.** [dispute, fessée] enormous **3.** [attitude, ton] authoritative.

magistralement [maʒistralmɑ̃] **adv** authoritatively, brilliantly.

magistrat [maʒistra] **nm** magistrate.

magistrature [maʒistratyr] **nf** magistracy, magistrature.

magma [magma] **nm 1.** GÉOL magma **2.** *fig* [mélange] muddle.

magnanerie [maɲanri] **nf 1.** [bâtiment] silk farm **2.** [sériciculture] silkworm breeding, sericulture.

magnanime [maɲanim] **adj** magnanimous.

magnanimité [maɲanimite] **nf** magnanimity.

magnat [maɲa] **nm** magnate, tycoon.

magner [3] [maɲe] ◆ ***se magner*** **vp** *fam* to get a move on.

magnésium [maɲezjɔm] **nm** magnesium.

magnétique [maɲetik] **adj** magnetic.

magnétiser [3] [maɲetize] **vt 1.** PHYS to magnetize **2.** [hypnotiser, fasciner] to hypnotize.

magnétisme [maɲetism] **nm 1.** PHYS [fascination] magnetism **2.** [hypnotisme] hypnotism.

magnéto(phone) [maɲetɔ(fɔn)] **nm** tape recorder.

magnétoscope [maɲetɔskɔp] **nm** video cassette recorder, videorecorder *UK*.

magnificence [maɲifisɑ̃s] **nf** magnificence.

magnifier [9] [maɲifje] **vt** to magnify.

magnifique [maɲifik] **adj** magnificent.

magnifiquement [maɲifikmɑ̃] **adv** magnificently.

magnitude [maɲityd] **nf** magnitude.

magnolia [maɲɔlja] **nm** magnolia.

magnum [magnɔm] **nm** magnum.

magot [mago] **nm** *fam* tidy sum, packet.

magouille [maguj] **nf** *fam* plot, scheme.

magouiller [3] [maguje] **vi** *fam* to plot, to scheme.

magret [magrɛ] **nm** fillet, filet *US* ▸ **magret de canard** breast of duck.

magyar, ***e*** [magjar] **adj** Magyar.

mai [mɛ] **nm** May ▸ **le premier mai** May Day ▸ **(les événements de) mai 1968** May 1968 ; voir aussi ***septembre***.

CULTURE

Mai 68

This crisis began in Paris with a university student revolt and was aggravated by a general strike that paralysed the entire country. Recognized as a key turning point in French social history, it was marked by intense political, economic, and social debate and nearly brought down the French government. The then president Charles de Gaulle resigned a year later after a failed referendum. The events of May 1968 have left their mark on the French language itself: **soixante-huitard** today designates a person or idea marked by the driving ideology of these events. It can also describe someone who stubbornly questions every point of the status quo in a rather old-fashioned way. The expression **post-68** is also heard.

maigre [mɛgr] ■ **adj 1.** [très mince] thin **2.** [aliment] low-fat / [viande] lean **3.** [peu important] meagre *UK*, meager *US* / [végétation] sparse.
■ **adv : faire maigre** not to eat meat.
■ **nmf** thin person.
■ **nm** lean meat.

maigrelet, ***ette*** [mɛgrəlɛ, ɛt] **adj** scrawny.

maigreur [mɛgrœr] **nf** thinness.

maigrir [32] [megrir] ■ **vi** to lose weight.
■ **vt : maigrir qqn** to make sb look thinner *ou* slimmer.

mail [mel] **nm** INFORM email (message), mail.

mailing [mɛliŋ] **nm** mailing, mailshot *UK*.

maille [maj] **nf 1.** [de tricot] stitch ▸ **maille à l'endroit/l'envers** plain/purl stitch **2.** [de filet] mesh
▸▸ **avoir maille à partir avec** to have a set-to with.

maillet [majɛ] **nm** mallet.

maillon [majɔ̃] **nm** link.

maillot [majo] **nm** [de sport] shirt, jersey ▸ **maillot de bain** swimsuit ▸ **maillot (de bain) une pièce/deux pièces** one-piece/two-piece swimsuit ▸ **maillot de corps** vest *UK*, undershirt *US* ▸ **le maillot jaune** *the yellow shirt worn by the leading cyclist in the Tour de France or the cyclist himself*.

main [mɛ̃] ■ **nf** hand ▸ **à main levée** [voter] by a show of hands / [dessiner] freehand ▸ **à pleines mains** by the handful ▸ **à quatre mains** fourhanded, for four hands ▸ **de main de maître** in a masterly fashion ▸ **en sous main** secretly ▸ **attaque à main armée** armed attack ▸ **main courante** handrail, banister ▸ **main libres** [téléphone, kit] hands-free ▸ **avoir la main heureuse** to be lucky ▸ **avoir la main leste** to be quick with one's hands ▸ **avoir/prendre qqch en main** to have/to take sthg in hand ▸ **avoir qqch sous la main** to have sthg at hand ▸ **demander la main de qqn** to ask for sb's hand (in marriage) ▸ **donner la main à qqn** to take sb's hand ▸ **faire main basse sur qqch** to help o.s. to sthg ▸ **se faire la main** to practise *UK ou* practice *US* ▸ **forcer la main à qqn** to force sb's hand ▸ **se frotter les mains** to rub one's hands ▸ **haut la main** effortlessly, hands down ▸ **haut les mains!** hands up! ▸ **se laver les mains de qqch** to wash one's hands of sthg ▸ **lever la main sur qqn** *fig* to raise one's hand to sb ▸ **mettre la dernière main à** to put the finishing touches to ▸ **mettre la main à la pâte** to lend a helping hand ▸ **mettre la main sur qqch** to lay *ou* to put one's hands on sthg ▸ **ne pas y aller de main morte** not to pull one's punches ▸ **passer la main** [jeux de cartes] to pass the deal ▸ **perdre la main** *fig* to lose one's touch ▸ **remettre en main(s) propre(s)** to hand over personally ▸ **tomber dans les *ou* aux mains de** to fall into the hands *ou* clutches *of* ▸ **en venir aux mains** to come to blows.
■ **adv** [fabriqué, imprimé] by hand ▸ **fait/tricoté/trié main** hand-made/-knitted/-picked.

◆ ***à la main*** **loc adv 1.** by hand / [artisanalement] **: fait à la main** hand-made **2.** [dans les mains] **: avoir *ou* tenir qqch à la main** to hold sthg in one's hand.

◆ ***à main*** **loc adj** [levier, outil] hand *(avant n)*, manual.

◆ ***à main droite*** **loc adv** on the right-hand side.

◆ ***à main gauche*** **loc adv** on the left-hand side.

◆ ***de la main*** **loc adv** with one's hand ▸ **saluer qqn de la main** [pour dire bonjour] to wave (hello) to sb / [pour dire au revoir] to wave (goodbye) to sb, to wave sb goodbye ▸ **de la main, elle me fit signe d'approcher** she waved me over.

◆ ***de la main à la main*** **loc adv** directly, without any middleman ▸ **j'ai payé le plombier de la main à la main** I paid the plumber cash in hand.

◆ ***de la main de*** **loc prép 1.** [fait par] by ▸ **la lettre est de la main même de Proust/de ma main** the letter is in Proust's own hand/in my handwriting **2.** [donné par] from (the hand of) ▸ **elle a reçu son prix de la main du président** she received her award from the President himself.

◆ ***de main en main*** **loc adv** from hand to hand, from one person to the next.

◆ ***de première main*** ■ **loc adj** [information] first-hand / [érudition, recherche] original.
■ **loc adv : nous tenons de première main que...** we have it on the best authority that...

◆ ***de seconde main*** **loc adj** [information, voiture] secondhand.

◆ ***d'une main*** **loc adv** [ouvrir, faire] with one hand [prendre] with *ou* in one hand ▸ **donner qqch d'une main et le reprendre de l'autre** to give sthg with one hand and take it back with the other.

◆ ***en main*** ■ **loc adj : l'affaire est en main** the question is in hand *ou* is being dealt with ▸ **le livre est actuellement en main** [il est consulté] the book is out on loan *ou* is being consulted at the moment.
■ **loc adv : avoir qqch en main** to be holding sthg ▸ **avoir *ou* tenir qqch (bien) en main** *fig* to have sthg well in hand *ou* under control ▸ **quand tu auras la voiture bien en main** when you've got the feel of the car ▸ **prend**

ch en main to take control of *ou* over sthg ▸ **prendre**
n en main to take sb in hand ▸ **la société a été reprise**
main the company was taken over.
la main dans la main **loc adv** [en se tenant par la
ain] hand in hand / *fig* together / *péj* hand in glove.

ain-d'œuvre [mɛ̃dœvr] **nf** [travail] labour *UK*, labor
S / [personne] workforce ▸ **main-d'œuvre féminine/
rangère** female/foreign labour *UK* ou labor *US* ▸ **les be-
ins en main-d'œuvre** manpower requirements.

ain-forte [mɛ̃fɔrt] **nf : prêter main-forte à qqn** to
me to sb's assistance.

ainmise [mɛ̃miz] **nf** seizure.

aint, e [mɛ̃, mɛ̃t] **adj** *littéraire* many a ▸ **maints** many
maintes fois time and time again.

aintenance [mɛ̃tnɑ̃s] **nf** maintenance.

aintenant [mɛ̃tnɑ̃] **adv** now.
maintenant que **loc prép** now that.

aintenir [40] [mɛ̃tnir] **vt 1.** [soutenir] to support
maintenir qqn à distance to keep sb away **2.** [garder,
nserver] to maintain **3.** [affirmer] **: maintenir que** to
aintain (that).
se maintenir **vp 1.** [durer] to last **2.** [rester] to remain.

aintenu, e [mɛ̃tny] **pp** ➤ ***maintenir***.

aintien [mɛ̃tjɛ̃] **nm 1.** [conservation] maintenance /
e tradition] upholding ▸ **le maintien de l'ordre** the
aintenance of law and order **2.** [tenue] posture.

aintiendrai, maintiendras ➤ ***maintenir***.

aire [mɛr] **nm** mayor.

airie [meri] **nf 1.** [bâtiment] town hall *UK*, city hall *US*
[administration] town council *UK*, city hall *US*.

ais [mɛ] ■ **conj** but ▸ **mais non!** of course not! ▸ **mais
ors, tu l'as vu ou non?** so did you see him or not? ▸ **mais
saignes!** you're bleeding! ▸ **j'ai trouvé le même, mais
oins cher** I found the same thing, only *ou* but cheaper
il a pleuré, mais pleuré! he cried, and how! ▸ **nous
lons à Venise, mais aussi à Florence et à Sienne** we're
oing to Venice, and to Florence and Siena too ▸ **non mais
ne va pas!** that's just not on! ▸ **non mais tu plaisantes?**
ou can't be serious!, you must be joking! ▸ **non seule-
ent tu arrives en retard, mais (en plus) tu oublies
n livre** not only do you arrive late, but (on top of that)
ou forget your book.
adv but ▸ **vous êtes prêts? - mais bien sûr!** are you
ady? - but of course! ▸ **mais certainement** but of course
mais enfin but after all / [marquant l'impatience] really!
nm : il y a un mais there's a hitch *ou* a snag ▸ **il n'y a
as de mais** (there are) no buts.

aïs [mais] **nm** maize *UK*, corn *US*.

aison [mɛzɔ̃] **nf 1.** [habitation, lignée & ASTROL] house
maison de campagne house in the country ▸ **maison in-
ividuelle** detached house ▸ **maisons mitoyennes** semi-
etached houses ▸ **maison de poupée** doll's house ▸ **gros
omme une maison** *fam* plain for all to see
. [foyer] home / [famille] family ▸ **à la maison** [au domi-
le] at home / [dans la famille] in my/your *etc* family ▸ **les
épenses de la maison** household expenditure ▸ **toute la
aison est partie pour Noël** all the people in the house
ave *ou* the whole family has gone away for Christmas
3. COMM company ▸ **maison de couture** fashion house
▸ **maison d'édition** publishing house ▸ **maison mère**
parent company ▸ **'la maison n'accepte pas les chèques'**
'no cheques (accepted)'
4. [institut] **: maison d'arrêt** prison ▸ **maison close** *ou* **de
tolérance** *vieilli* brothel ▸ **maison de la culture** arts centre
UK ou center *US* ▸ **maison de quartier** ≃ community
centre *UK ou* center *US* ▸ **maison de repos** rest *ou* convalescent home ▸ **maison de retraite** old people's home
5. *(en apposition)* [artisanal] homemade / [dans restaurant -
vin] house *(avant n)* ▸ **spécialité maison** speciality of the
house.

> PARONYME / CONFUSABLE
> **maison**
> Le mot **maison** peut se traduire de deux façons : Utilisez ***house*** pour parler de l'habitation, l'établissement, et ***home*** lorsque vous faites référence au foyer personnel.

Maison-Blanche [mɛzɔ̃blɑ̃ʃ] **nf : la Maison-Blanche** the White House.

maisonnée [mɛzɔne] **nf** household.

maisonnette [mɛzɔnɛt] **nf** small house.

maître, esse [mɛtr, mɛtrɛs] **nm, f 1.** [professeur] teacher ▸ **maître auxiliaire** supply teacher *UK*, substitute teacher *US* ▸ **maître chanteur** blackmailer ▸ **maître de conférences** UNIV ≃ senior lecturer *UK*, ≃ assistant professor
US ▸ **maître d'école** schoolteacher ▸ **maître nageur** swimming instructor
2. *fig* [modèle, artiste] master ▸ **les grands maîtres** the Old
Masters ▸ **un tableau** *ou* **une toile de maître** an old master ▸ **maître à penser** mentor ▸ **passer maître dans l'art
de faire qqch** to be a past master in the art of doing sthg
▸ **un coup de maître** *fig* a masterstroke
3. [dirigeant] ruler / [d'animal] master (f mistress) ▸ **maître de cérémonie** master of ceremonies ▸ **maître d'hôtel**
head waiter ▸ **maître de maison** host ▸ **maîtresse de maison** hostess, lady of the house *sout* & *hum* ▸ **maître d'œuvre** CONSTR project manager / *fig* artisan, architect ▸ **être
maître de soi** to be in control of oneself, to have self-
control ▸ **être** *ou* **rester maître de faire qqch** to be free
to do sthg
4. *(en apposition)* [principal] main, principal.
◆ ***Maître*** **nm** *form of address for lawyers*.
◆ ***maîtresse*** **nf** [amie] mistress ▸ **devenir la maîtresse
de qqn** to become sb's mistress.

maître-assistant, e [mɛtrasistɑ̃, ɑ̃t] (mpl **maîtres-
assistants**) (fpl **maîtres-assistantes**) **nm, f** ≃ lecturer *UK*,
≃ assistant professor *US*.

maître-autel [mɛtrotɛl] (pl **maîtres-autels**) **nm** high
altar.

maîtresse ➤ ***maître***.

maîtrisable [metrizabl] **adj** controllable.

maîtrise [metriz] **nf 1.** [sang-froid, domination] control
▸ **maîtrise de soi** self-control **2.** [connaissance] mastery,
command / [habileté] skill **3.** UNIV ≃ master's degree.

maîtriser [3] [metrize] **vt 1.** [animal, forcené] to subdue **2.** [émotion, réaction] to control, to master **3.** [incendie] to bring under control **4.** [dépenses] to curb.
◆ ***se maîtriser*** **vp** to control o.s.

majesté [maʒɛste] **nf** majesty.
◆ ***Majesté*** **nf : Sa Majesté** His/Her Majesty.

majestueux, euse [maʒɛstɥø, øz] **adj** majestic.

majeur, e [maʒœr] **adj 1.** [gén] major **2.** [personne] of age.
◆ ***majeur*** **nm** middle finger.

Majeur [mazœr] ➤ ***lac***.

major [maʒɔr] **nm 1.** MIL ≃ adjutant **2.** SCOL **: major (de promotion)** first in *ou* top of one's year.

majoration [maʒɔrasjɔ̃] **nf** increase.

majordome [maʒɔrdɔm] **nm** majordomo.

majorer [3] [maʒɔre] **vt** to increase.

majorette [maʒɔrɛt] **nf** majorette.

majoritaire [maʒɔritɛr] ■ **nmf** member of majority group.
■ **adj** majority *(avant n)* ▸ **être majoritaire** to be in the majority.

majorité [maʒɔrite] **nf** majority ▸ **en (grande) majorité** in the majority ▸ **majorité absolue/relative** POLIT absolute/relative majority ▸ **majorité civile** voting age.

Majorque [majɔrk] **npr** Majorca ▸ **à Majorque** in Majorca.

majorquin, e [majɔrkɛ̃, in] **adj** Majorcan.
◆ ***Majorquin, e*** **nm, f** Majorcan.

majuscule [maʒyskyl] ■ **nf** capital (letter) ▸ **en majuscules** in capitals, in capital letters.
■ **adj** capital *(avant n)*.

mal, maux [mal, mo] **nm 1.** [ce qui est contraire à la morale] evil ▸ **dire du mal de qqn** to say bad things about sb ▸ **vouloir du mal à qqn** to wish sb ill *ou* harm
2. [souffrance physique] pain ▸ **avoir mal au bras** to have a sore arm ▸ **avoir mal au cœur** to feel sick ▸ **avoir mal au dos** to have backache *UK ou* a backache *US* ▸ **avoir mal à la gorge** to have a sore throat ▸ **avoir le mal de mer** to be seasick ▸ **avoir mal aux dents** to have toothache *UK ou* a toothache *US* ▸ **avoir mal à la tête** to have a headache ▸ **avoir des maux de tête** to get headaches ▸ **avoir le mal des transports** to be travelsick ▸ **avoir mal au ventre** to have (a) stomachache ▸ **faire mal à qqn** to hurt sb ▸ **ça fait mal** it hurts ▸ **se faire mal** to hurt o.s.
3. [difficulté] difficulty ▸ **avoir du mal à faire qqch** to have difficulty doing sthg ▸ **se donner du mal (pour faire qqch)** to take trouble (to do sthg) ▸ **ne vous donnez pas tant de mal pour moi** please don't go to all this trouble on my behalf
4. [douleur morale] pain, suffering *(U)* ▸ **avoir le mal du pays** to be *ou* feelhomesick ▸ **être en mal de qqch** to long for sthg ▸ **faire du mal (à qqn)** to hurt (sb) ▸ **c'est un moindre mal** it's the lesser of two evils.
◆ ***mal*** **adv 1.** [malade] ill ▸ **aller mal** not to be well ▸ **se sentir mal** to feel ill ▸ **être au plus mal** to be extremely ill
2. [respirer] with difficulty
3. [informé, se conduire] badly ▸ **être mal reçu** to get a poor welcome ▸ **mal prendre qqch** to take sthg badly ▸ **mal tourner** to go wrong ▸ **tu te tiens mal** [tu es voûté] you've got poor posture / [à table] you don't have any table manners
▸▸ **de mal en pis** from bad to worse ▸ **mal à propos** inappropriate ▸ **pas mal** not bad *(adj)*, not badly *(adv)* ▸ **pas mal de** quite a lot of ▸ **se trouver mal** [s'évanouir] to faint to pass out, to swoon *sout* ▸ **si je n'y vais pas, ça la fiche mal** it won't look good if I don't go.
◆ ***mal à l'aise*** **loc adj** uncomfortable, ill at ease ▸ **être/se sentir mal à l'aise** to be/feel uncomfortable *ou* ill at ease **je suis mal à l'aise devant elle** I feel ill at ease with her.

malabar [malabar] **nm** *fam* big guy, well-built guy.

malade [malad] ■ **nmf** invalid, sick person ▸ **malade mental** mentally ill person ▸ **c'est un malade imaginaire** he's a hypochondriac ▸ **on a travaillé comme des malades pour finir à temps** we worked like lunatics to finish on time.
■ **adj 1.** [souffrant - personne] ill, sick / [- organe] bad ▸ **gravement malade** gravely *ou* seriously ill ▸ **tomber malade** to fall ill *ou* sick ▸ **être malade du cœur/des reins** to have heart/kidney trouble ▸ **je suis malade en bateau/avion** I suffer from seasickness/airsickness ▸ **être malade d'inquiétude** *fig* to be sick with worry
2. *fam* [fou] crazy ▸ **avoir l'esprit malade** to be mentally ill
3. *fig* [en mauvais état] in bad shape, in a bad way ▸ **nous avons une économie malade** our economy is sick *or* shaky *ou* ailing.

maladie [maladi] **nf 1.** MÉD illness ▸ **maladie d'Alzheimer** Alzheimer's disease ▸ **maladie contagieuse** contagious disease ▸ **maladie de Creutzfeldt-Jakob** Creutzfeldt-Jakob disease ▸ **maladie héréditaire** hereditary disease ▸ **maladie de Parkinson** Parkinson's disease ▸ **maladie sexuellement transmissible** sexually transmissible *ou* transmitted disease ▸ **maladie de la vache folle** mad cow disease ▸ **il en fait une maladie** he's really worked up about it **2.** [passion, manie] mania.

maladif, ive [maladif, iv] **adj 1.** [enfant] sickly **2.** [pâleur] unhealthy.

maladresse [maladrɛs] **nf 1.** [inhabileté] clumsiness **2.** [bévue] blunder.

maladroit, e [maladrwa, at] ■ **adj** clumsy.
■ **nm, f** clumsy person.

maladroitement [maladrwatmɑ̃] **adv** clumsily.

mal-aimé, e [malɛme] (mpl **mal-aimés**) (fpl **mal-aimées**) **nm, f** unloved person.

malais, e [malɛ, ɛz] **adj** Malay, Malaysian ▸ **la presqu'île Malaise** the Malay Peninsula.
◆ ***malais*** **nm** [langue] Malay.
◆ ***Malais, e*** **nm, f** Malay, Malaysian.

malaise [malɛz] **nm 1.** [indisposition] discomfort ▸ **avoir un malaise** to feel faint **2.** [trouble] unease *(U)* **3.** [crise] discontent *(U)*.

malaisé, e [maleze] **adj** difficult.

Malaisie [malezi] **nf : la Malaisie** Malaya ▸ **en Malaisie** in Malaya.

malappris, e [malapri, iz] ■ **adj** uncouth, ill-mannered.
■ **nm, f** lout.

malaria [malarja] **nf** malaria.

malaudition [malodisjɔ̃] **nf** MÉD hearing loss, hardness of hearing ▸ **souffrir de malaudition** to be hearing-impaired *ou* hard of hearing.

malavisé, e [malavize] **adj** *littéraire* ill-advised, unwise.

malaxer [3] [malakse] **vt** to knead.

Malaysia [malɛzja] **nf : la Malaysia** Malaysia ▸ **la Malaysia occidentale** Malaya.

malbouffe [malbuf] **nf** junk food, bad food.

malchance [malʃɑ̃s] **nf** bad luck *(U)* ▸ **jouer de malchance** to be dogged by bad luck.

malchanceux, euse [malʃɑ̃sø, øz] ■ **adj** unlucky.
■ **nm, f** unlucky person.

malcommode [malkɔmɔd] **adj** inconvenient / [meuble] impractical.

Maldives [maldiv] **nfpl : les (îles) Maldives** the Maldives.

maldonne [maldɔn] **nf** misdeal ▸ **il y a maldonne** the cards have been misdealt / *fig* there's been a misunderstanding.

mâle [mal] ■ **adj 1.** [enfant, animal, hormone] male **2.** [voix, assurance] manly **3.** ÉLECTR male.
■ **nm** male.

malédiction [malediksjɔ̃] **nf** curse.

maléfice [malefis] **nm** *sout* evil spell.

maléfique [malefik] **adj** *sout* evil.

malencontreusement [malɑ̃kɔ̃trøzmɑ̃] **adv** inopportunely.

malencontreux, euse [malɑ̃kɔ̃trø, øz] **adj** [hasard, rencontre] unfortunate.

mal-en-point, mal en point [malɑ̃pwɛ̃] **adj inv** in a bad way *ou* sorry state.

malentendant, e [malɑ̃tɑ̃dɑ̃, ɑ̃t] ■ **adj** hard of hearing.
■ **nm, f** person who is hard of hearing.

malentendu [malɑ̃tɑ̃dy] **nm** misunderstanding.

malfaçon [malfasɔ̃] **nf** defect.

malfaisant, e [malfəzɑ̃, ɑ̃t] **adj** harmful.

malfaiteur [malfɛtœr] **nm** criminal.

malfamé, e, mal famé, e [malfame] **adj** disreputable.

malformation [malfɔrmasjɔ̃] **nf** malformation.

malfrat [malfra] **nm** *fam* crook.

malgache [malgaʃ] **adj** Madagascan, Malagasy.
◆ ***malgache*** **nm** [langue] Malagasy.
◆ ***Malgache*** **nmf** Madagascan, Malagasy.

malgré [malgre] **prép** in spite of ▸ **malgré tout** [quoi qu'il arrive] in spite of everything / [pourtant] even so, yet.
◆ ***malgré que*** **loc conj** *(+ subjonctif) fam* although, in spite of the fact that.

malhabile [malabil] **adj** clumsy.

malheur [malœr] **nm** misfortune ▸ **le malheur** misfortune, bad luck ▸ **par malheur** unfortunately ▸ **porter malheur à qqn** to bring sb bad luck ▸ **malheur à toi!** woe betide you! ▸ **faire un malheur** *fam fig* [faire un éclat] to do some damage / [avoir du succès] to be a great hit.

malheureusement [malœrøzmɑ̃] **adv** unfortunately.

malheureux, euse [malœrø, øz] ■ **adj 1.** [triste] unhappy ▸ **rendre qqn malheureux** to make sb miserable *ou* unhappy **2.** [désastreux, regrettable] unfortunate ▸ **par un malheureux hasard** by an unfortunate coincidence, as bad luck would have it ▸ **ce serait malheureux de ne pas en profiter** it would be a pity *ou* shame not to take advantage of it **3.** [malchanceux] unlucky ▸ **il est malheureux au jeu/en amour** he has no luck with gambling/women **4.** *(avant n)* [sans valeur] pathetic, miserable ▸ **ne nous battons pas pour quelques malheureux centimes** let's not fight over a few measly cents.
■ **nm, f 1.** [infortuné] poor soul ▸ **il est bien seul maintenant, le pauvre malheureux** he's very much on his own now, the poor devil **2.** [indigent] poor person ▸ **secourir les malheureux** to help the poor *ou* the needy *ou* those in need.

malhonnête [malɔnɛt] ■ **nmf** dishonest person.
■ **adj 1.** [personne, affaire] dishonest **2.** *hum* [proposition, propos] indecent.

malhonnêteté [malɔnɛtte] **nf 1.** [de personne] dishonesty **2.** [action] dishonest action.

Mali [mali] **nm : le Mali** Mali ▸ **au Mali** in Mali.

malice [malis] **nf** mischief ▸ **sans malice** without malice.

malicieux, euse [malisjø, øz] ■ **adj** mischievous.
■ **nm, f** mischievous person.

malien, enne [maljɛ̃, ɛn] **adj** Malian.
◆ ***Malien, enne*** **nm, f** Malian.

malignité [maliɲite] **nf 1.** [méchanceté] malice, spite **2.** MÉD malignancy.

malin, igne [malɛ̃, iɲ] ■ **adj 1.** [rusé] crafty, cunning ▸ **ce n'est pas malin!** *fig* that's not very clever! / [regard, sourire] knowing **2.** [méchant] malicious, spiteful **3.** MÉD malignant.
■ **nm, f** cunning *ou* crafty person ▸ **faire le malin** to show off.

malingre [malɛ̃gr] **adj** sickly.

malle [mal] **nf** [coffre] trunk / [de voiture] boot *UK*, trunk *US* ▸ **se faire la malle** *fam fig* to beat it.

malléable [maleabl] **adj** malleable.

mallette [malɛt] **nf** briefcase.

mal-logé, e [mallɔʒe] (mpl **mal-logés**) (fpl **mal-logées**) **nm, f** *person living in poor accommodation.*

malmener [19] [malməne] **vt 1.** [brutaliser] to handle roughly, to ill-treat **2.** [dominer] to have the better of.

malnutrition [malnytrisjɔ̃] **nf** malnutrition.

malodorant, e [malɔdɔrɑ̃, ɑ̃t] **adj** smelly.

malotru, e [malɔtry] **nm, f** lout.

Malouines [malwin] **nfpl : les (îles) Malouines** the Falkland Islands, the Falklands.

malpoli, e [malpɔli] ■ **adj** rude.
■ **nm, f** rude person.

malpropre [malprɔpr] **adj** [sale] dirty.

malpropreté [malprɔprəte] **nf** [saleté] dirtiness.

malsain, e [malsɛ̃, ɛn] **adj** unhealthy.

malséant, e [malseɑ̃, ɑ̃t] **adj** unbecoming.

malt [malt] **nm 1.** [céréale] malt **2.** [whisky] malt (whisky) *UK ou* (whiskey) *US*.

maltais, e [maltɛ, ɛz] **adj** Maltese.
◆ **maltais nm** [langue] Maltese.
◆ **Maltais, e nm, f** Maltese (person) ▸ **les Maltais** the Maltese.

Malte [malt] **npr** Malta ▸ **à Malte** in Malta.

maltraiter [4] [maltrete] **vt** to ill-treat / [en paroles] to attack, to run down.

malus [malys] **nm** *increase in car insurance charges resulting from loss of no-claims bonus.*

malveillance [malvɛjɑ̃s] **nf** spite.

malveillant, e [malvɛjɑ̃, ɑ̃t] **adj** spiteful.

malvenu, e [malvəny] **adj** out of place ▸ **être malvenu de faire qqch** *sout* to be wrong to do sthg.

malversation [malvɛrsasjɔ̃] **nf** embezzlement.

malvoyant, e [malvwajɑ̃, ɑ̃t] ■ **adj** partially sighted.
■ **nm, f** person who is partially sighted.

maman [mamɑ̃] **nf** mummy *UK*, mommy *US*.

mamelle [mamɛl] **nf** teat / [de vache] udder.

mamelon [mamlɔ̃] **nm 1.** [du sein] nipple **2.** [butte] hillock.

mamie, mamy [mami] **nf** granny, grandma.

mammifère [mamifɛr] **nm** mammal.

mammographie [mamɔgrafi] **nf** mammography.

mammouth [mamut] **nm** mammoth.

mamours [mamur] **nmpl** *fam* billing and cooing *(U)* ▸ **se faire des mamours** to bill and coo.

mamy = ***mamie***.

Man [man] ➤ ***île***.

management [manadʒmɛnt] **nm** management.

manager[1] [manadʒɛr] **nm** manager.

manager[2] [17] [manadʒe] **vt** to manage.

manche [mɑ̃ʃ] ■ **nf 1.** [de vêtement] sleeve ▸ **sans manches** sleeveless ▸ **manches courtes/longues** short/long sleeves ▸ **manches raglan** raglan sleeves ▸ **avoir qqn dans sa manche** *fam fig* to have sb in one's pocket ▸ **être en manches de chemise** to be in one's shirtsleeves **2.** [de jeu] round, game / TENNIS set ▸ **gagner la première manche** *fig* to win the first round
▸▸ **faire la manche** *fam* to pass the hat around.'
■ **nm 1.** [d'outil] handle ▸ **manche à balai** broomstick / [d'avion] joystick **2.** MUS neck
▸▸ **tu t'y prends comme un manche** *fam* you're making a right mess of it.

Manche [mɑ̃ʃ] **nf 1.** [Normandie] **: la Manche** the Manche (region) **2.** [mer] **: la Manche** the English Channel **3.** [en Espagne] **: la Manche** La Mancha.

manchette [mɑ̃ʃɛt] **nf 1.** [de chemise] cuff **2.** [de journal] headline, banner headline **3.** [coup] forearm blow.

manchon [mɑ̃ʃɔ̃] **nm 1.** [en fourrure] muff **2.** TECHNOL casing, sleeve.

manchot, ote [mɑ̃ʃo, ɔt] ■ **adj** one-armed.
■ **nm, f** one-armed person.
◆ **manchot nm** penguin.

mandarin [mɑ̃darɛ̃] **nm 1.** [en Chine] mandarin **2.** *péj* [personnage important] mandarin **3.** [langue] Mandarin.

mandarine [mɑ̃darin] **nf** mandarin (orange).

mandat [mɑ̃da] **nm 1.** [pouvoir, fonction] mandate **2.** DR warrant ▸ **mandat d'amener** summons ▸ **mandat d'arrêt** arrest warrant ▸ **mandat de perquisition** search warrant **3.** [titre postal] money order ▸ **mandat postal** postal order *UK*, money order *US*.

mandataire [mɑ̃datɛr] **nmf** proxy, representative.

mandat-carte [mɑ̃dakart] (pl **mandats-cartes**) **nm** postal order *UK*, money order *US*.

mandater [3] [mɑ̃date] **vt 1.** [personne] to appoint **2.** [somme] to pay by postal *UK ou* money *US* order.

mandat-lettre [mɑ̃dalɛtr] (pl **mandats-lettres**) **nm** postal order *UK*, money order *US*.

mander [3] [mɑ̃de] **vt** *littéraire* **1.** [appeler] to summon **2.** [faire savoir] **: mander qqch à qqn** to inform sb of sthg

mandibule [mɑ̃dibyl] **nf** mandible.

mandoline [mɑ̃dɔlin] **nf** mandolin.

mandrill [mɑ̃dril] **nm** mandrill.

mandrin [mɑ̃drɛ̃] **nm** [de serrage] chuck / [de perçage] punch.

manège [manɛʒ] **nm 1.** [attraction] merry-go-round, roundabout *UK*, carousel *US* **2.** [de chevaux - lieu] riding school **3.** [manœuvre] scheme, game.

manette [manɛt] **nf** lever.

manga [mɑ̃ga] **nf** manga (comic).

manganèse [mɑ̃ganɛz] **nm** manganese.

mangeable [mɑ̃ʒabl] **adj** edible.

mangeoire [mɑ̃ʒwar] **nf** manger.

manger [17] [mɑ̃ʒe] ■ **vt 1.** [nourriture] to eat ▸ **elle a tout mangé** she's eaten it all up ▸ **elle ne va pas te manger!** *fig* she's not going to eat *ou* to bite you! **2.** [étoffe, fer] to eat away ▸ **couvertures mangées par les mites** moth-eaten blankets **3.** [fortune] to get through, to squander ▸ **manger son capital** to eat up one's capital.
■ **vi** to eat ▸ **manger à sa faim** to eat one's fill ▸ **c'est un restaurant simple mais on y mange bien** it's an unpretentious restaurant, but the food is good ▸ **faire manger qqn** to feed sb ▸ **faire à manger à qqn** to make something to eat for sb.
◆ **se manger vp** *(emploi passif)* to be eaten ▸ **ça se mange avec de la mayonnaise** you eat it *ou* it is served with mayonnaise.

mange-tout [mɑ̃ʒtu] ■ **adj inv : haricots mange-tout** runner beans *UK*, string beans *US*.
■ **nm inv** [haricot] runner bean *UK*, string bean *US* / [pois] mangetout *UK*, snow pea *US*.

mangeur, euse [mɑ̃ʒœr, øz] **nm, f** eater ▸ **gros mangeur** big eater.

mangue [mɑ̃g] **nf** mango.

maniable [manjabl] **adj 1.** [instrument] manageable **2.** [personne] easily influenced.

maniaque [manjak] ■ **nmf 1.** [méticuleux] fusspot *UK*, fussbudget *US* **2.** [fou] maniac.
■ **adj 1.** [méticuleux] fussy **2.** [fou] maniacal.

maniaquerie [manjakri] **nf** fussiness.

manichéisme [manikeism] **nm** Manicheism.

manie [mani] **nf 1.** [habitude] funny habit ▸ **avoir la manie de qqch/de faire qqch** to have a mania for sthg/for doing sthg **2.** [obsession] mania.

maniement [manimɑ̃] **nm** handling.

manier [9] [manje] **vt** [manipuler, utiliser] to handle / *fig* [ironie, mots] to handle skilfully *UK ou* skillfully *US*.

manière [manjɛr] **nf 1.** [méthode] manner, way ▸ **recourir à la manière forte** to resort to strong-arm tactics ▸ **sa manière de marcher/s'habiller** his way of walking/dressing, the way he walks/dresses ▸ **de toute manière** at any rate ▸ **de toute manière, tu as tort** in any case, you're wrong ▸ **d'une manière générale** generally speaking ▸ **d'une certaine manière, je suis content que ce soit fini** in a way, I'm glad it's over ▸ **c'est une manière de parler** it's just my/his *etc* way of putting it ▸ **elle dit qu'elle l'aime à sa manière** she says she loves him in her own way ▸ **est-ce de sa faute? – en aucune manière** is it his fault? – no, not in the slightest *ou* least **2.** [style propre à un artiste] style ▸ **à la manière de** in the style of ▸ **une chanson à la manière de Cole Porter** a song in the style of Cole Porter.

◆ ***manières*** **nfpl** manners ▸ **les bonnes manières** good manners ▸ **faire des manières** *fig* to pussyfoot around ▸ **qu'est-ce que c'est que ces** *ou* **en voilà des manières!** what a way to behave!

◆ ***de manière à*** **loc conj** (in order) to ▸ **de manière à ce que** *(+ subjonctif)* so that ▸ **laisse la porte ouverte, de manière que les gens puissent entrer** leave the door open so people can come in.

◆ ***de manière que*** **loc conj** *(+ subjonctif)* in such a way that.

maniéré, e [manjere] **adj** affected.

maniérisme [manjerism] **nm** mannerism.

manif [manif] **nf** *fam* demonstration, demo *UK*.

manifestant, e [manifɛstɑ̃, ɑ̃t] **nm, f** demonstrator.

manifestation [manifɛstasjɔ̃] **nf 1.** [témoignage] expression **2.** [mouvement collectif] demonstration **3.** [apparition - de maladie] appearance.

manifeste [manifɛst] ■ **nm** [déclaration] manifesto.
■ **adj** obvious.

manifestement [manifɛstəmɑ̃] **adv** obviously.

manifester [3] [manifɛste] ■ **vt** to show, to express.
■ **vi** to demonstrate.
◆ ***se manifester*** **vp 1.** [apparaître] to show *ou* manifest itself **2.** [se montrer] to turn up, to appear.

manigance [manigɑ̃s] **nf** *fam* scheme, intrigue.

manigancer [16] [manigɑ̃se] **vt** *fam* to scheme, to plot.

Manille [manij] **npr** Manila.

manioc [manjɔk] **nm** manioc.

manipulateur, trice [manipylatœr, tris] **nm, f 1.** [opérateur] technician **2.** *fig & péj* [de personnes] manipulator.
◆ ***manipulateur*** **nm** TÉLÉCOM key.

manipulation [manipylasjɔ̃] **nf 1.** [de produits, d'explosifs] handling ▸ **manipulations génétiques** genetic engineering **2.** *fig & péj* [manœuvre] manipulation *(U)*.

manipuler [3] [manipyle] **vt 1.** [colis, appareil] to handle **2.** [statistiques, résultats] to falsify, to rig **3.** *péj* [personne] to manipulate.

manivelle [manivɛl] **nf** crank.

manne [man] **nf** RELIG manna / *fig & littéraire* godsend.

mannequin [mankɛ̃] **nm 1.** [forme humaine] model, dummy **2.** [personne] model, mannequin.

manœuvre [manœvr] ■ **nf 1.** [d'appareil, de véhicule] driving, handling ▸ **fausse manœuvre** driver error / *fig* false move **2.** MIL manoeuvre *UK*, maneuver *US*, exercise **3.** [machination] ploy, scheme.
■ **nm** labourer *UK*, laborer *US*.

manœuvrer [5] [manœvre] ■ **vi** to manoeuvre *UK*, to maneuver *US*.
■ **vt 1.** [faire fonctionner] to operate, to work / [voiture] to manoeuvre *UK*, to maneuver *US* **2.** [influencer] to manipulate.

manoir [manwar] **nm** manor, country house.

manomètre [manɔmɛtr] **nm** manometer.

manquant, e [mɑ̃kɑ̃, ɑ̃t] **adj** missing.

manque [mɑ̃k] **nm 1.** [pénurie] lack, shortage ▸ **par manque de** for want of **2.** [de toxicomane] withdrawal symptoms *pl* ▸ **être en (état de) manque** to have *ou* experience withdrawal symptoms **3.** [lacune] gap ▸ **manque à gagner** COMM loss of earnings.
◆ ***à la manque*** **loc adj** *fam* second-rate.

manqué, e [mɑ̃ke] **adj** [raté] failed / [rendez-vous] missed.

manquement [mɑ̃kmɑ̃] **nm : manquement (à)** breach (of).

manquer [3] [mɑ̃ke] ■ **vi 1.** [faire défaut] to be lacking, to be missing ▸ **l'argent/le temps me manque** I don't have enough money/time ▸ **la force/le courage lui manqua** (his) strength/courage failed him ▸ **tu me manques** I miss you
2. [être absent] **: manquer (à)** to be absent (from), to be missing (from) ▸ **manquer à l'appel** MIL to be absent (at roll call) / *fig & hum* to be missing
3. [échouer] to fail
4. [ne pas avoir assez] **: manquer de qqch** to lack sthg, to be short of sthg ▸ **manquer de personnel** to be short-staffed, to be short of staff ▸ **je manque de sommeil** I'm not getting enough sleep
5. [faillir] **: il a manqué de se noyer** he nearly *ou* almost drowned ▸ **ne manquez pas de lui dire** don't forget to tell him ▸ **je n'y manquerai pas** I certainly will, I'll definitely do it
6. [ne pas respecter] **: manquer à** [devoir] to fail in ▸ **manquer à sa parole** to break one's word.
■ **vt 1.** [gén] to miss ▸ **manquer son but** *fig* to fail to reach one's goal ▸ **manquer une occasion** to miss (out on) an opportunity ▸ **c'est une émission à ne pas manquer** this programme shouldn't be missed *ou* is a must
2. [échouer à] to bungle, to botch ▸ **coup manqué** failure, botch-up.

■ v impers : **il manque quelqu'un** somebody is missing ▸ **il me manque 3 euros** I'm 3 euros short ▸ **il ne manquait plus que ça** *fig* that's all I/you *etc* needed.
◆ ***se manquer*** vp *(emploi réciproque)* : **nous nous sommes manqués à l'aéroport** we missed each other at the airport.

mansarde [mɑ̃sard] nf attic.

mansardé**, **e [mɑ̃sarde] adj attic *(avant n)*.

mansuétude [mɑ̃sɥetyd] nf *littéraire* indulgence.

mante [mɑ̃t] nf HIST mantle.
◆ ***mante religieuse*** nf praying mantis.

manteau**, **x [mɑ̃to] nm **1.** [vêtement] coat ▸ **sous le manteau** *fig* secretly, clandestinely **2.** *fig* [de neige] mantle, blanket.

manucure [manykyr] nmf manicurist.

manuel**, **elle [manɥɛl] ■ adj manual.
■ nm, f manual worker.
◆ ***manuel*** nm manual.

manufacture [manyfaktyr] nf [fabrique] factory.

manuscrit**, **e [manyskri, it] adj handwritten.
◆ ***manuscrit*** nm manuscript.

manutention [manytɑ̃sjɔ̃] nf handling.

manutentionnaire [manytɑ̃sjɔnɛr] nmf warehouseman.

MAP (abr de ***mise au point***) nf focusing.

mappemonde [mapmɔ̃d] nf **1.** [carte] map of the world **2.** [sphère] globe.

maquereau**, **elle**, **x [makro, ɛl, o] nm, f *fam* pimp (f madam).
◆ ***maquereau*** nm mackerel.

maquette [makɛt] nf **1.** [ébauche] paste-up **2.** [modèle réduit] model.

maquettiste [makɛtist] nmf model maker.

maquignon [makiɲɔ̃] nm **1.** [marchand de chevaux] horse dealer **2.** *péj* [homme d'affaires] crook.

maquillage [makijaʒ] nm **1.** [action, produits] make-up **2.** [falsification - gén] disguising / [- de chiffres] doctoring / [- de passeport] falsification.

maquiller [3] [makije] vt **1.** [farder] to make up **2.** [fausser - gén] to disguise / [- chiffres] to doctor / [- passeport] to falsify.
◆ ***se maquiller*** vp to make up, to put on one's make-up.

maquilleur**, **euse [makijœr, øz] nm, f make-up artist.

maquis [maki] nm **1.** [végétation] scrub, brush, maquis **2.** HIST Maquis, French Resistance ▸ **prendre le maquis** HIST to take to the maquis / *fig* to go underground **3.** *fig* [méli-mélo] maze.

maquisard [makizar] nm member of the Maquis *ou* the French Resistance.

marabout [marabu] nm **1.** ZOOL marabou **2.** [guérisseur] marabout.

maraîcher**, **ère [mareʃe, ɛr] ■ adj market garden *(avant n)* *UK*, truck farming *(avant n)* *US*.
■ nm, f market gardener *UK*, truck farmer *US*.

marais [marɛ] nm [marécage] marsh, swamp ▸ **marais salant** saltpan ▸ **le Marais** *historic district in central Paris*.

marasme [marasm] nm **1.** [récession] stagnation **2.** [accablement] depression.

marathon [maratɔ̃] nm marathon.

marâtre [maratr] nf *vieilli* **1.** [mauvaise mère] bad mother **2.** [belle-mère] stepmother.

maraudage [marodaʒ] nm = ***maraude***.

maraude [marod] nf pilfering.

marbre [marbr] nm **1.** [roche, objet] marble ▸ **en *ou* de marbre** marble *(avant n)* ▸ **rester de marbre** *fig* to remain impassive **2.** [dans imprimerie] stone **3.** *Québec* [baseball] home base *ou* plate.

marbré**, **e [marbre] adj **1.** [gâteau] marble *(avant n)* **2.** [peau, teint] mottled.

marbrier [marbrije] nm monumental mason.

marbrure [marbryr] nf **1.** [imitation du marbre] marbling **2.** [sur la peau] mottling.

marc [mar] nm **1.** [eau-de-vie] marc (brandy) *(distilled from grape residue)* **2.** [de fruits] residue / [de thé] leaves ▸ **marc de café** grounds *pl*.

marcassin [markasɛ̃] nm young wild boar.

marchand**, **e [marʃɑ̃, ɑ̃d] ■ adj [valeur] market *(avant n)* / [prix] trade *(avant n)*.
■ nm, f [commerçant] merchant / [détaillant] shopkeeper *UK*, storekeeper *US* ▸ **marchand de journaux** newsagent *UK*, newsdealer *US* ▸ **marchand des quatre-saisons** fruit-and-vegetable seller.
◆ ***marchand de sable*** nm *fig* sandman.

marchandage [marʃɑ̃daʒ] nm bargaining.

marchander [3] [marʃɑ̃de] ■ vt **1.** [prix] to haggle over **2.** [appui] to begrudge.
■ vi to bargain, to haggle.

marchandise [marʃɑ̃diz] nf merchandise *(U)*, goods *p* ▸ **marchandise en gros/au détail** wholesale/retail good ▸ **gare de marchandises** [train] goods *UK* ou freight *U* station.

marche [marʃ] nf **1.** [d'escalier] step ▸ **attention à l marche** mind the step ▸ **la première/dernière march** the bottom/top step
2. [activité, sport] walking ▸ **être à deux heures de marche (de)** to be two hours' walk *ou* a two-hour walk (from ▸ **fermer la marche** to bring up the rear ▸ **ouvrir la marche** to lead the way ▸ **marche à pied** walking ▸ **marche suivre** *fig* correct procedure ▸ **en avant, marche!** MIL forward, march!
3. [promenade] walk ▸ **nous avons fait une marche de km** we did an 8 km walk
4. [défilé] : **marche silencieuse/de protestation** silen protest march
5. MUS march ▸ **marche funèbre/nuptiale** funeral/wedding march
6. [déplacement - du temps, d'astre] course ▸ **assis dans sens de la marche** [en train] sitting facing the engine ▸ **marche arrière** in reverse ▸ **faire marche arrière** to reverse / *fig* to backpedal, to backtrack ▸ **monter/descend d'un train en marche** to get on/off a moving train
7. [fonctionnement] running, working ▸ **en marche** running ▸ **se mettre en marche** to start (up) ▸ **mettre qq**

en marche to start sthg (up) ▸ **remettre qqch en marche** to restart sthg ▸ **pour assurer la bonne marche de notre coopérative** to ensure the smooth running of our co-op.

marché [marʃe] **nm 1.** [lieu de vente] market ▸ **aller au marché** to go to the market ▸ **faire son marché** to go shopping, to do one's shopping ▸ **mettre un produit sur le marché** to launch a product ▸ **marché couvert** covered market ▸ **marché aux puces** flea market **2.** FIN & ÉCON **: marché des changes** foreign exchange market ▸ **marché cible** target market ▸ **marché de concurrence** competitive marketplace ▸ **marché du crédit** credit market ▸ **marché financier** financial market ▸ **marché global** *ou* **international** global marketplace ▸ **marché des matières premières** commodity market ▸ **marché noir** black market ▸ **faire du marché noir** to deal on the black market ▸ **marché porteur** growth market ▸ **marché primaire** primary market ▸ **le marché du travail** the labour *UK ou* labor *US* market **3.** [contrat] bargain, deal ▸ **conclure** *ou* **passer un marché avec qqn** to make a deal with sb ▸ **marché conclu!** it's a deal!, that's settled! ▸ **(à) bon marché** cheap ▸ **meilleur marché** cheaper ▸ **par-dessus le marché** *fam fig* into the bargain.

◆ ***Marché commun*** **nm : le Marché commun** the Common Market.

◆ ***Marché unique européen*** **nm : le Marché unique européen** the European Single Market.

narchéage [marʃeaʒ] **m** marketing mix.

narchepied [marʃəpje] **nm** [de train] step / [escabeau] steps *pl UK*, stepladder / *fig* stepping-stone.

narcher [3] [marʃe] **vi 1.** [aller à pied] to walk ▸ **marcher à grands pas** *ou* **à grandes enjambées** to stride (along) ▸ **marcher tranquillement** to amble along **2.** [poser le pied] to step ▸ **marcher sur les pieds de qqn** to tread *ou* to stand *ou* to step on sb's feet **3.** [avancer] **: marcher sur** [ville, ennemi] to march on *ou* upon **4.** [fonctionner, tourner] to work ▸ **si ça marche, je monterai une exposition** if it works out, I'll organize an exhibition ▸ **son affaire marche bien** his business is doing well ▸ **tu sais faire marcher la machine à laver?** do you know how to work the washing machine? **5.** *fam* [accepter] to agree ▸ **je ne marche pas!** nothing doing!, count me out!

▸▸ **faire marcher qqn** *fam* to take sb for a ride.

ıarcheur, euse [marʃœr, øz] **nm, f** walker.

ıarcottage [markɔtaʒ] **nm** layering.

ıardi [mardi] **nm** Tuesday ▸ **mardi gras** Shrove Tuesday ; voir aussi ***samedi***.

ıare [mar] **nf** pool.

ıarécage [marekaʒ] **nm** marsh, bog.

ıarécageux, euse [marekaʒø, øz] **adj 1.** [terrain] marshy, boggy **2.** [plante] marsh *(avant n)*.

ıaréchal, aux [mareʃal, o] **nm** marshal.

◆ ***maréchal des logis*** **nm** sergeant.

ıaréchal-ferrant [mareʃalferɑ̃] (pl **maréchaux-errants** [mareʃoferɑ̃]) **nm** blacksmith.

ıaréchaussée [mareʃose] **nf** *vieilli* constabulary.

ıarée [mare] **nf 1.** [de la mer] tide ▸ **(à) marée haute/ basse** (at) high/low tide **2.** *fig* [de personnes] wave, surge **3.** [poissons] seafood.

◆ ***marée noire*** **nf** oil slick.

marelle [marɛl] **nf** hopscotch.

marémoteur, trice [maremɔtœr, tris] **adj** [énergie] tidal / [usine] tidal power *(avant n)*.

mareyeur, euse [marɛjœr, øz] **nm, f** wholesale fish merchant.

margarine [margarin] **nf** margarine.

marge [marʒ] **nf 1.** [espace] margin ▸ **marge de tête** head *ou* top margin ▸ **marge de pied** tail ▸ **annotations** *ou* **notes en marge** notes in the margin, marginalia *fml* ▸ **vivre en marge de la société** *fig* to live on the fringes of society **2.** [latitude] leeway ▸ **avoir de la marge** to have some leeway ▸ **marge d'erreur** margin of error ▸ **marge de manœuvre** room for manoeuvre *UK ou* maneuver *US* ▸ **marge de sécurité** safety margin **3.** COMM margin ▸ **marge brute** gross margin ▸ **marge bénéficiaire** profit margin ▸ **marge commerciale** gross margin ▸ **marge de fluctuation** fluctuation band.

margelle [marʒɛl] **nf** coping.

marginal, e, aux [marʒinal, o] ■ **adj 1.** [gén] marginal **2.** [groupe] dropout *(avant n)*.

■ **nm, f** dropout.

marginaliser [3] [marʒinalize] **vt** to marginalize.

marginalité [marʒinalite] **nf** living on the fringes of society.

margoulin [margulɛ̃] **nm** *fam* shark, conman.

marguerite [margərit] **nf 1.** BOT daisy **2.** [d'imprimante] daisy wheel.

mari [mari] **nm** husband.

mariage [marjaʒ] **nm 1.** [union, institution] marriage ▸ **donner qqn en mariage** to give sb away ▸ **mariage d'amour** love match ▸ **mariage blanc** unconsummated marriage ▸ **mariage consanguin** marriage between blood relations ▸ **mariage de raison** marriage of convenience **2.** [cérémonie] wedding ▸ **mariage civil/religieux** civil/ church wedding **3.** *fig* [de choses] blend.

Marianne [marjan] **npr** *personification of the French Republic.*

marié, e [marje] ■ **adj** married.

■ **nm, f** groom, bridegroom (f bride) ▸ **jeunes mariés** newlyweds.

marier [9] [marje] **vt 1.** [personne] to marry **2.** *fig* [couleurs] to blend.

◆ ***se marier*** **vp 1.** [personnes] to get married ▸ **se marier avec qqn** to marry sb **2.** *fig* [couleurs] to blend.

marihuana [marirwana], ***marijuana*** [mariʒɥana] **nf** marijuana.

marin, e [marɛ̃, in] **adj 1.** [de la mer] sea *(avant n)* / [faune, biologie] marine **2.** NAUT [carte, mille] nautical.

◆ ***marin*** **nm 1.** [navigateur] seafarer **2.** [matelot] sailor ▸ **marin pêcheur** deep-sea fisherman.

◆ ***marine*** ■ **nf 1.** [navigation] seamanship, navigation **2.** [navires] navy ▸ **marine marchande** merchant navy *UK ou* marine *US* ▸ **marine nationale** navy.

■ **nm 1.** MIL marine **2.** [couleur] navy (blue).

■ **adj inv** navy.

marinade [marinad] **nf** marinade.

mariner [3] [marine] ■ **vt** to marinate.
■ **vi 1.** [aliment] to marinate ▸ **faire mariner qqch** to marinate sthg **2.** *fam fig* [attendre] to hang around ▸ **faire mariner qqn** to let sb stew.

marinier [marinje] **nm** bargee *UK*, bargeman *US*.

marinière [marinjɛr] **nf** smock.

marionnette [marjɔnɛt] **nf** puppet.

marital**, **e**, **aux [marital, o] **adj : autorisation maritale** husband's permission.

maritalement [maritalmɑ̃] **adv : vivre maritalement** to cohabit.

maritime [maritim] **adj** [navigation] maritime / [ville] coastal.

marivaudage [marivodaʒ] **nm** *littéraire* banter.

marjolaine [marʒɔlɛn] **nf** marjoram.

mark [mark] **nm** [monnaie] mark.

marketing [markɛtiŋ] **nm** marketing ▸ **marketing ciblé** niche marketing ▸ **marketing concentré** concentrated marketing ▸ **marketing direct** direct marketing ▸ **marketing mix** marketing mix ▸ **marketing de relance** remarketing ▸ **marketing relationnel** relationship marketing ▸ **marketing téléphonique** telemarketing.

marmaille [marmaj] **nf** *fam* brood (of kids).

marmelade [marməlad] **nf** stewed fruit ▸ **en marmelade** cooked to a pulp / *fam fig* [nez] smashed to a pulp ▸ **marmelade d'oranges** marmalade.

marmite [marmit] **nf** [casserole] pot ▸ **faire bouillir la marmite** *fig* to be the breadwinner.

marmiton [marmitɔ̃] **nm** kitchen boy.

marmonner [3] [marmɔne] **vt & vi** to mutter, to mumble.

marmot [marmo] **nm** *fam* kid.

marmotte [marmɔt] **nf** marmot.

marmotter [3] [marmɔte] **vt** to mutter, to mumble.

marner [3] [marne] **vi** *fam* to slog.

Maroc [marɔk] **nm : le Maroc** Morocco ▸ **au Maroc** in Morocco.

marocain**, **e [marɔkɛ̃, ɛn] **adj** Moroccan.
◆ ***Marocain**, **e*** **nm, f** Moroccan.

maroquin [marɔkɛ̃] **nm** morocco (leather).

maroquinerie [marɔkinri] **nf 1.** [fabrication] fine-leather production / [commerce] fine-leather trade **2.** [magasin] leather-goods shop *UK* ***ou*** store *US*.

maroquinier [marɔkinje] **nm 1.** [artisan] leatherworker **2.** [commerçant] leather-goods dealer.

marotte [marɔt] **nf** [dada] craze.

marquant**, **e [markɑ̃, ɑ̃t] **adj** outstanding.

marque [mark] **nf 1.** [signe, trace] mark / *fig* stamp, mark ▸ **marques de coups** bruises ***ou*** marks of blows ▸ **on reconnaît la marque du génie** that's the hallmark ***ou*** stamp of genius **2.** [label, fabricant] make, brand ▸ **de marque** designer *(avant n)* / *fig* important ▸ **articles de marque** branded goods ▸ **personnage de marque** VIP ▸ **une grande marque** a well-known make ***ou*** brand ▸ **marque déposée** registered trademark ▸ **marque dominante** dominant brand ▸ **marque de fabrique** trademark ▸ **marque générique** generic brand ▸ **marque phare** core brand ▸ **marque vedette** masterbrand **3.** SPORT score ▸ **à vos marques, prêts, partez!** on your marks, get set, go!, ready, steady, go! *UK* **4.** [insigne] badge **5.** [témoignage] sign, token ▸ **marque d'affection** sign ***ou*** token of affection.

marqué**, **e [marke] **adj 1.** [net] marked, pronounced **2.** [personne, visage] marked.

marquer [3] [marke] ■ **vt 1.** [gén] to mark ▸ **ce jour est à marquer d'une pierre blanche** this will go down as a red-letter day **2.** *fam* [écrire] to write down, to note down ▸ **marqué à la craie/au crayon sur le mur** marked in chalk/pencil on the wall, chalked/pencilled on the wall **3.** [indiquer, manifester] to show ▸ **la balance marque 3 kg** the scales register ***ou*** read 3 kg ▸ **les lignes bleues marquent les frontières** the blue lines show ***ou*** indicate where the border is **4.** [SPORT - but, point] to score / [- joueur] to mark ▸ **marquer les points** to keep the score ▸ **l'argument est judicieux, vous marquez un point** *fig* the argument is valid: that's one to you ***ou*** you've scored a point **5.** [impressionner] to mark, to affect, to make an impression on ▸ **ça m'a beaucoup marqué** it made a big ***ou*** lasting impression on me.
■ **vi 1.** [événement, expérience] to leave its mark ▸ **les grands hommes qui ont marqué dans l'histoire** the great men who have left their mark on history **2.** SPORT to score.

marqueterie [markɛtri] **nf** marquetry.

marqueur [markœr] **nm 1.** [crayon] marker (pen) **2.** SPORT scorer.

marqueuse [markøz] **nf** labelling ***ou*** labeling *US* machine.

marquis**, **e [marki, iz] **nm, f** marquis (f marchioness).
◆ ***marquise*** **nf** [auvent] canopy.

Marquises [markiz] **nfpl : les Marquises** the Marquesas Islands.

marraine [marɛn] **nf 1.** [de filleul] godmother **2.** [de navire] christener.

marrant**, **e [marɑ̃, ɑ̃t] **adj** *fam* funny.

marre [mar] **adv : en avoir marre (de)** *fam* to be fed up (with).

marrer [3] [mare] ◆ ***se marrer*** **vp** *fam* to split one's sides.

marron**, **onne [marɔ̃, ɔn] **adj** *péj* [médecin] quack *(avant n)* / [avocat] crooked.
◆ ***marron*** ■ **nm 1.** [fruit] chestnut ▸ **marron glacé** marron glacé, candied chestnut ▸ **marron d'Inde** horse chestnut **2.** [couleur] brown **3.** *fam* [coup de poing] thump.
■ **adj inv** brown.

marronnier [marɔnje] **nm** chestnut tree.

mars [mars] **nm** March ; voir aussi ***septembre***.

marseillais**, **e [marsɛjɛ, ɛz] **adj** of/from Marseilles.
◆ ***Marseillais**, **e*** **nm, f** person from Marseilles.
◆ ***Marseillaise*** **nf : la Marseillaise** the Marseillaise *(French national anthem)*.

Marseille [marsɛj] **npr** Marseilles.

marsouin [marswɛ̃] **nm** porpoise.

marsupial**, **e**, **aux [marsypjal, o] **adj** marsupial.
◆ ***marsupial*** **nm** marsupial.

marte = *martre*.

marteau**, **x [marto] ■ **nm 1.** [gén] hammer ▸ **marteau piqueur** *ou* **pneumatique** pneumatic drill *UK*, jackhammer *US* **2.** [heurtoir] knocker.
■ **adj** *fam* nuts, barmy *UK*.

marteau-pilon [martopilɔ̃] (pl **marteaux-pilons**) **nm** power hammer.

martel [martɛl] **nm : se mettre martel en tête** to get worked up.

marteler [25] [martəle] **vt 1.** [pieu] to hammer / [table, porte] to hammer on, to pound **2.** [phrase] to rap out.

martial**, **e**, **aux [marsjal, o] **adj** martial.

martien**, **enne [marsjɛ̃, ɛn] **adj** & **nm, f** Martian.

martinet [martinɛ] **nm 1.** ZOOL swift **2.** [fouet] whip.

martingale [martɛ̃gal] **nf 1.** [de vêtement] half-belt **2.** [jeux] winning system.

Martini® [martini] **nm** Martini®.

martiniquais**, **e [martinikɛ, ɛz] **adj** of/from Martinique.
◆ ***Martiniquais**, **e*** **nm, f** person from Martinique.

Martinique [martinik] **nf : la Martinique** Martinique ▸ **à la Martinique** in Martinique.

martin-pêcheur [martɛ̃pɛʃœr] (pl **martins-pêcheurs**) **nm** kingfisher.

martre [martr], ***marte*** [mart] **nf** marten.

martyr**, **e [martir] ■ **adj** martyred.
■ **nm, f** martyr.
◆ ***martyre*** **nm** martyrdom ▸ **souffrir le martyre** to suffer agonies.

martyriser [3] [martirize] **vt** to torment.

marxisme [marksism] **nm** Marxism.

marxiste [marksist] **nmf** & **adj** Marxist.

mas [mas] **nm** *country house or farm in the South of France*.

mascara [maskara] **nm** mascara.

mascarade [maskarad] **nf 1.** [mise en scène] masquerade **2.** *péj* [accoutrement] getup.

mascotte [maskɔt] **nf** mascot.

masculin**, **e [maskylɛ̃, in] **adj** [apparence & GRAMM] masculine / [métier, population, sexe] male.
◆ ***masculin*** **nm** GRAMM masculine.

maso [mazo] *fam* ■ **nm** masochist.
■ **adj** masochistic.

masochisme [mazɔʃism] **nm** masochism.

masochiste [mazɔʃist] ■ **nmf** masochist.
■ **adj** masochistic.

masque [mask] **nm 1.** [gén] mask ▸ **masque funéraire** *ou* **mortuaire** death mask ▸ **masque à gaz** gas mask ▸ **masque de plongée** diving mask **2.** [crème] **: masque (de beauté)** face pack **3.** *fig* [façade] front, façade ▸ **lever le masque** *fig* to show one's true colours *UK* *ou* colors *US* ▸ **sa bonté n'est qu'un masque** his kindness is just a front *ou* is only skin-deep **4.** MÉD **: masque de grossesse** (pregnancy) chloasma **5.** INFORM **: masque de saisie** template.

masqué**, **e [maske] **adj** masked.

masquer [3] [maske] **vt 1.** [vérité, crime, problème] to conceal **2.** [maison, visage] to conceal, to hide.

massacrant**, **e [masakrɑ̃, ɑ̃t] **adj : être d'une humeur massacrante** to be in a foul temper.

massacre [masakr] **nm** *litt* & *fig* massacre.

massacrer [3] [masakre] **vt** to massacre / [voiture] to smash up.

massage [masaʒ] **nm** massage ▸ **faire un massage à qqn** to give sb a massage.

masse [mas] **nf 1.** [de pierre] block / [d'eau] volume ▸ **masse d'air** MÉTÉOR mass of air ▸ **tomber comme une masse** *fig* to drop like a stone **2.** [de gens] **: la masse** the majority ▸ **les masses** the masses ▸ **communication/culture de masse** mass communication/culture **3.** [grande quantité] **: une masse de** masses *pl* *ou* loads *pl* of ▸ **des amis, il n'en a pas des masses** he hasn't got that many friends **4.** PHYS mass ▸ **masse molaire** molar weight ▸ **masse moléculaire** molecular weight **5.** ÉLECTR earth *UK*, ground *US* ▸ **mettre à la masse** to earth *UK*, to ground *US* **6.** [maillet] sledgehammer.
◆ ***masse monétaire*** **nf** FIN money supply.
◆ ***masse salariale*** **nf** payroll.
◆ ***en masse*** **loc adv** [venir] en masse, all together / *fam* [acheter] in bulk ▸ **produire** *ou* **fabriquer en masse** to mass-produce ▸ **se déplacer en masse** to go in a body *ou* en masse.

massepain [maspɛ̃] **nm** marzipan.

masser [3] [mase] **vt 1.** [assembler] to assemble **2.** [frotter] to massage.
◆ ***se masser*** **vp 1.** [s'assembler] to assemble, to gather **2.** [se frotter] **: se masser le bras** to massage one's arm.

masseur**, **euse [masœr, øz] **nm, f** [personne] masseur (f masseuse).
◆ ***masseur*** **nm** [appareil] massager.

massicot [masiko] **nm** guillotine.

massif**, **ive [masif, iv] **adj 1.** [monument, personne, dose] massive ▸ **sa silhouette massive** his huge frame ▸ **un apport massif d'argent liquide** a massive cash injection **2.** [or, chêne] solid ▸ **argent massif** solid silver ▸ **armoire en acajou massif** solid mahogany wardrobe.
◆ ***massif*** **nm 1.** [de plantes] clump ▸ **un massif de roses** a rosebed, a bed of roses **2.** [de montagnes] massif ▸ **massif ancien** primary *ou* Caledonian massif ▸ **le Massif central** the Massif Central.

massivement [masivmɑ̃] **adv 1.** [construit] massively **2.** [répondre] en masse.

massue [masy] ■ **adj inv** crushing.
■ **nf** club.

mastic [mastik] **nm** mastic, putty.

mastiquer [3] [mastike] **vt 1.** [mâcher] to chew **2.** [coller] to putty.

mastoc [mastɔk] **adj inv** *péj* hulking.

mastodonte [mastɔdɔ̃t] **nm 1.** [mammifère] mastodon **2.** *fam* [personne] hulk.

masturbation [mastyrbasjɔ̃] **nf** masturbation.

masturber [3] [mastyrbe] ◆ ***se masturber*** **vp** to masturbate.

m'as-tu-vu [matyvy] **nmf** show-off.

masure [mazyr] **nf** hovel.

mat, e [mat] **adj 1.** [peinture, surface] matt *UK*, matte *US* **2.** [peau, personne] dusky **3.** [bruit, son] dull **4.** [aux échecs] checkmated.
◆ ***mat*** **nm** checkmate.

mât [ma] **nm 1.** NAUT mast ▸ **mât d'artimon** mizzen, mizzenmast ▸ **grand mât** main mast **2.** [poteau] pole, post ▸ **mât de cocagne** greasy pole **3.** TECHNOL : **mât de charge** cargo beam, derrick ▸ **mât de forage** [industrie du pétrole] drilling mast.

match [matʃ] (pl **matches** *ou* **matchs**) **nm** match ▸ **(faire) match nul** (to) tie, (to) draw *UK* ▸ **match aller/retour** first/second leg *UK*.

matelas [matla] **nm inv** [de lit] mattress ▸ **matelas de crin** horsehair mattress ▸ **matelas pneumatique** airbed.

matelassé, e [matlase] **adj** padded.

matelot [matlo] **nm** sailor.

mater [3] [mate] **vt 1.** [soumettre, neutraliser] to subdue **2.** *fam* [regarder] to eye up.

matérialiser [3] [materjalize] ◆ ***se matérialiser*** **vp** [aspirations] to be realized.

matérialisme [materjalism] **nm** materialism.

matérialiste [materjalist] ■ **nmf** materialist.
■ **adj** materialistic.

matériau, x [materjo] **nm** material.
◆ ***matériaux*** **nmpl 1.** CONSTR material *(U)*, materials ▸ **matériaux de construction** building material *ou* materials **2.** [documents] material *(U)*.

matériel, elle [materjɛl] **adj 1.** [être, substance] material, physical ⁄ [confort, avantage, aide] material **2.** [considération] practical.
◆ ***matériel*** **nm 1.** [gén] equipment *(U)* ▸ **matériel d'exploitation** plant *(U)* ▸ **matériel de publicité sur le lieu de vente** *ou* **matériel de PLV** point-of-sale material, point-of-purchase material ▸ **matériel de promotion** promotional material ▸ **matériel roulant** rolling stock *(U)* **2.** INFORM hardware *(U)*.

matériellement [materjɛlmɑ̃] **adv** materially.

maternel, elle [maternɛl] **adj** maternal ⁄ [langue] mother *(avant n)* ▸ **lait maternel** mother's milk.
◆ ***maternelle*** **nf** nursery school.

materner [3] [materne] **vt** to mother.

maternité [maternite] **nf 1.** [qualité] maternity, motherhood **2.** [hôpital] maternity hospital.

mathématicien, enne [matematisjɛ̃, ɛn] **nm, f** mathematician.

mathématique [matematik] **adj** mathematical.
◆ ***mathématiques*** **nfpl** mathematics *(U)*.

matheux, euse [matø, øz] **nm, f** *fam* mathematician.

maths [mat] **nfpl** *fam* maths *UK*, math *US*.

matière [matjɛr] **nf 1.** [substance] matter ▸ **matières fécales** faeces *UK*, feces *US* ▸ **matières grasses** fat ▸ **60 % de matières grasses** 60% fat content ▸ **sans matières grasses** fat-free, non-fat ▸ **matière grise** grey *UK* *ou* gray *US* matter ▸ **fais travailler ta matière grise!** use your brains *ou* head! **2.** [matériau] material ▸ **matière plastique** plastic ▸ **matières premières** raw materials **3.** [discipline, sujet] subject ▸ **les matières à l'écrit/à l'oral** the subjects for the written/oral examination ▸ **en matière de sport/littérature** as far as sport/literature is concerned ▸ **je suis incompétent en la matière** I'm ignorant on the subject ▸▸ **donner matière à** to give cause for ▸ **il y a matière à discussion** there are a lot of things to be said about that ▸ **une entrée en matière** an introduction, a lead-in.

MATIF, Matif [matif] (abr de ***Marché à terme international de France***) **nm** *body regulating activities on the French stock exchange*, ≃ LIFFE *UK*.

Matignon [matiɲɔ̃] **npr : (l'hôtel) Matignon** *building in Paris which houses the offices of the Prime Minister.*

CULTURE

Matignon

Built in the reign of Philippe II in the 18th century, this building in the rue de Varenne in Paris has been home to the French Prime Minister's offices since 1935. The media often use **Matignon** to mean the Prime Minister and his team: **Matignon envisage une réforme avant l'été.**

matin [matɛ̃] ■ **nm** morning ▸ **le matin** in the morning ▸ **ce matin** this morning ▸ **à trois heures du matin** at 3 o'clock in the morning ▸ **de bon** *ou* **de grand matin** early in the morning ▸ **du matin au soir** *fig* from dawn to dusk ▸ **je suis du matin** [actif le matin] I'm an early riser ⁄ [de service le matin] I'm on *ou* I do the morning shift, I'm on mornings ▸ **par un matin d'été/de juillet** one summer/July morning ▸ **un beau matin** one fine day, one of these (fine) days.
■ **adv : demain/hier matin** tomorrow/yesterday morning ▸ **tous les dimanches matin** every Sunday morning.

matinal, e, aux [matinal, o] **adj 1.** [gymnastique, émission] morning *(avant n)* **2.** [personne] **: être matinal** to be an early riser.

mâtiné, e [matine] **adj : mâtiné de** [chien] crossed with ⁄ *fig* [mélangé de] mixed with.

matinée [matine] **nf 1.** [matin] morning ▸ **faire la grass matinée** to sleep late, to have a lie in *UK* **2.** [spectacle matinée, afternoon performance.

matines [matin] **nfpl** matins.

matois, e [matwa, az] *littéraire* ■ **adj** wily.
■ **nm, f** wily person.

maton, onne [matɔ̃, ɔn] **nm, f** *fam arg crime* screw *UK*

matou [matu] **nm** tom, tomcat.

matraquage [matrakaʒ] **nm 1.** [bastonnade] beating clubbing **2.** *fig* [intoxication] bombardment ▸ **matraquag publicitaire** bombardment with advertisements.

matraque [matrak] **nf** truncheon *UK*, billy club *U* nightstick *US*.

matraquer [3] [matrake] **vt 1.** [frapper] to beat, to clu **2.** *fig* [intoxiquer] to bombard.

matriarcal, e, aux [matrijarkal, o] **adj** matriarchal

matriarcat [matrijarka] **nm** matriarchy.

matrice [matris] **nf 1.** [moule] mould *UK*, mold *US* **2.** MATH matrix **3.** ANAT womb.

matricule [matrikyl] ■ **nm : (numéro) matricule** number.
■ **nf** register.

matrimonial, e, aux [matrimɔnjal, o] **adj** matrimonial.

matrone [matrɔn] **nf** *péj* old bag.

maturation [matyrasjɔ̃] **nf** maturing.

mature [matyr] **adj** mature.

mâture [matyr] **nf** masts *pl*.

maturité [matyrite] **nf** maturity / [de fruit] ripeness.

maudire [104] [modir] **vt** to curse.

maudit, e [modi, it] ■ **pp** ➤ ***maudire***.
■ **adj 1.** [réprouvé] accursed **2.** *(avant n)* [exécrable] damned.
■ **nm, f** person who is damned.

maugréer [15] [mogree] ■ **vt** to mutter.
■ **vi : maugréer (contre)** to grumble (about).

maure, more [mɔr] **adj** Moorish.
◆ ***Maure, More*** **nmf** Moor.

mauresque, moresque [morɛsk] **adj** Moorish.
◆ ***Mauresque, Moresque*** **nf** Moorish woman.

Maurice [moris] ➤ ***île***.

mauricien, enne [morisjɛ̃, ɛn] **adj** Mauritian.
◆ ***Mauricien, enne*** **nm, f** Mauritian.

Mauritanie [moritani] **nf : la Mauritanie** Mauritania.

mauritanien, enne [moritanjɛ̃, ɛn] **adj** Mauritanian.
◆ ***Mauritanien, enne*** **nm, f** Mauritanian.

mausolée [mozɔle] **nm** mausoleum.

maussade [mosad] **adj 1.** [personne, air] sullen **2.** [temps] gloomy.

mauvais, e [movɛ, ɛz] ■ **adj 1.** [gén] bad ▸ **c'est (un) mauvais signe** it's a bad sign ▸ **en mauvais état** in bad *ou* poor condition ▸ **je suis mauvaise en économie** I'm bad *ou* poor at economics ▸ **mauvais goût** [de la nourriture, d'un médicament] bad *ou* nasty *ou* unpleasant taste ▸ **le mauvais temps** bad weather ▸ **un produit de mauvaise qualité** a poor-quality product **2.** [moment, numéro, réponse] wrong ▸ **faire un mauvais calcul** *fig* to miscalculate **3.** [mer] rough **4.** [personne, regard] nasty ▸ **avoir l'air mauvais** to look nasty ▸ **faire un mauvais coup à qqn** to play a dirty trick on sb.
■ **nm** [ce qui est critiquable] **: il y a du bon et du mauvais dans leur proposition** there are some good points and some bad points in their proposal.
◆ ***mauvais*** **adv : il fait mauvais** the weather is bad ▸ **sentir mauvais** to smell bad.

mauve [mov] **nm & adj** mauve.

mauviette [movjɛt] **nf** *fam* **1.** [physiquement] weakling **2.** [moralement] coward, wimp.

maux ➤ ***mal***.

max [maks] (abr de ***maximum***) **nm** *fam* **: un max de fric** loads of money ▸ **il en a rajouté un max** he went completely overboard.

max. (abr écrite de ***maximum***) max.

maxillaire [maksilɛr] **nm** jawbone.

maximal, e, aux [maksimal, o] **adj** maximum *(avant n)* / [degré] highest.

maxime [maksim] **nf** maxim.

maximum [maksimɔm] (pl **maxima** [maksima]) ■ **nm** maximum ▸ **le maximum de vitesse/capacité** maximum speed/capacity ▸ **le maximum de personnes** the greatest (possible) number of people ▸ **nous ferons le maximum le premier jour** we'll do as much as we can on the first day ▸ **il y a eu un maximum de visiteurs le premier jour** we had an enormous number of visitors the first day ▸ **pour ça il faut un maximum d'organisation** that sort of thing needs a huge amount of *ou* needs loads of organization ▸ **au maximum** at the most ▸ **en rentrant, on a mis le chauffage au maximum** when we got home, we turned the heating on full ▸ **je nettoie au maximum mais c'est quand même sale** I do as much cleaning as possible but it's still dirty ▸ **un espace utilisé au maximum** an area used to full advantage.
■ **adj** maximum *(avant n)* ▸ **vitesse maximum** maximum *ou* top speed.

maya [maja] **adj** Mayan.
◆ ***Maya*** **nmf : les Mayas** the Maya.

mayonnaise [majɔnɛz] **nf** mayonnaise.

Mazarine [mazarin] **npr : la bibliothèque Mazarine** *the oldest public library in Paris.*

mazout [mazut] **nm** fuel oil.

mazouté, e [mazute] **adj** polluted with oil.

MDM **nmpl** abr écrite de ***Médecins du monde***.

me [mə], ***m'*** *(devant voyelle ou 'h' muet)* **pron pers 1.** [complément d'objet direct] me **2.** [complément d'objet indirect] (to) me **3.** [réfléchi] myself **4.** [avec un présentatif] **: me voici** here I am.

Me (abr écrite de ***maître***) *title for barristers,* ≃ QC *UK*.

mea culpa [meakulpa] **nm inv : faire son mea culpa** *fig* to admit one's mistake.

méandre [meɑ̃dr] **nm** [de rivière] meander, bend.
◆ ***méandres*** **nmpl** [détours sinueux] meanderings *pl*.

mec [mɛk] **nm** *fam* guy, bloke *UK*.

mécanicien, enne [mekanisjɛ̃, ɛn] ■ **adj** mechanized.
■ **nm, f 1.** [de garage] mechanic **2.** [conducteur de train] train driver *UK*, engineer *US*.

mécanique [mekanik] ■ **nf 1.** TECHNOL mechanical engineering **2.** MATH & PHYS mechanics *(U)* **3.** [mécanisme] mechanism.
■ **adj** mechanical.

mécaniquement [mekanikmɑ̃] **adv** mechanically.

mécanisation [mekanizasjɔ̃] **nf** mechanization.

mécaniser [3] [mekanize] **vt** to mechanize.

mécanisme [mekanism] **nm** mechanism.

mécano [mekano] **nm** *fam* mechanic.

mécénat [mesena] **nm** patronage.

mécène [mesɛn] **nm** patron.

méchamment [meʃamɑ̃] **adv 1.** [cruellement] nastily **2.** *fam* [beaucoup] really, terribly.

méchanceté [meʃɑ̃ste] **nf 1.** [attitude] nastiness **2.** *fam* [rosserie] nasty thing.

méchant, e [meʃɑ̃, ɑ̃t] ■ **adj 1.** [malveillant, cruel] nasty, wicked / [animal] vicious **2.** [désobéissant] naughty.
■ **nm, f 1.** [moralement] wicked person **2.** [en langage enfantin] bad boy.

mèche [mɛʃ] **nf 1.** [de bougie] wick **2.** [de cheveux] lock ▸ **mèche rebelle** cowlick **3.** [de bombe] fuse **4.** [de perceuse] bit
▸▸ **être de mèche avec qqn** to be hand in glove with sb ▸ **vendre la mèche** to give the game away.

méchoui [meʃwi] **nm** *whole roast sheep.*

méconnaissable [mekɔnɛsabl] **adj** unrecognizable.

méconnaissance [mekɔnɛsɑ̃s] **nf** ignorance.

méconnu, e [mekɔny] **adj** unrecognized.

mécontent, e [mekɔ̃tɑ̃, ɑ̃t] ■ **adj** unhappy.
■ **nm, f** malcontent.

mécontentement [mekɔ̃tɑ̃tmɑ̃] **nm** displeasure, annoyance ▸ **mécontentement populaire** popular unrest.

mécontenter [3] [mekɔ̃tɑ̃te] **vt** to displease.

Mecque [mɛk] **npr : La Mecque** Mecca.

mécréant, e [mekreɑ̃, ɑ̃t] **nm, f** non-believer.

méd. abr de ***médecin***.

médaille [medaj] **nf 1.** [pièce, décoration] medal **2.** [bijou] medallion **3.** [de chien] identification tag, identification disc *UK* ***ou*** disk *US*.

médaillé, e [medaje] ■ **adj** MIL decorated / SPORT medal-winning *(avant n)*.
■ **nm, f** MIL holder of a medal / SPORT medal-winner, medallist *UK*, medalist *US*.

médaillon [medajɔ̃] **nm 1.** [bijou] locket **2.** PRESSE **: en médaillon** inset **3.** ART & CULIN medallion.

médecin [medsɛ̃] **nm** doctor ▸ **médecin conventionné** ≃ National Health doctor *UK* ▸ **médecin de famille** family doctor, GP ▸ **médecin de garde** doctor on duty, duty doctor ▸ **médecin généraliste** general practitioner, GP ▸ **médecin légiste** (forensic) pathologist *UK*, medical examiner *US* ▸ **votre médecin traitant** your (usual) doctor ▸ **Médecins du monde, Médecins sans frontières** *organizations providing medical aid to victims of war and disasters, especially in the Third World,* Doctors Without Borders *US*.

médecine [medsin] **nf** medicine ▸ **médecine générale** general medicine.

Medef [medɛf] (abr de ***Mouvement des entreprises de France***) **nm** *national council of French employers,* ≃ CBI *UK*.

média [medja] **nm : les médias** the (mass) media ▸ **médias électroniques** electronic media.

médian, e [medjɑ̃, an] **adj** median.
◆ ***médiane*** **nf** median.

médiateur, trice [medjatœr, tris] ■ **adj** mediating *(avant n)*.
■ **nm, f** mediator / [dans un conflit de travail] arbitrator.
◆ ***médiateur*** **nm** ADMIN ombudsman.
◆ ***médiatrice*** **nf** median.

médiathèque [medjatɛk] **nf** media library.

médiation [medjasjɔ̃] **nf** mediation / [dans un conflit de travail] arbitration.

médiatique [medjatik] **adj** media *(avant n)*.

médiatisation [medjatizasjɔ̃] **nf** (saturation) media coverage.

médiatiser [3] [medjatize] **vt** *péj* to turn into a media event.

médical, e, aux [medikal, o] **adj** medical.

médicalisation [medikalizasjɔ̃] **nf** [d'établissement, de service] provision of medical equipment / [de population] provision of medical care.

médicament [medikamɑ̃] **nm** medicine, drug.

médicamenteux, euse [medikamɑ̃tø, øz] **adj** medicinal.

médication [medikasjɔ̃] **nf** (course of) treatment.

médicinal, e, aux [medisinal, o] **adj** medicinal.

Médicis [medisis] **npr : le prix Médicis** *French literary prize.*

médico-légal, e, aux [medikɔlegal, o] **adj** forensic.

médico-social, e, aux [medikɔsɔsjal, o] **adj** public health *(avant n)*.

médiéval, e, aux [medjeval, o] **adj** medieval.

médiocre [medjɔkr] ■ **nmf** mediocre person.
■ **adj** mediocre.

médiocrité [medjɔkrite] **nf** mediocrity.

médire [103] [medir] **vi** to gossip ▸ **médire de qqn** to speak ill of sb.

médisance [medizɑ̃s] **nf 1.** [calomnie] slander **2.** [ragot] piece of gossip.

médisant, e [medizɑ̃, ɑ̃t] ■ **adj** slanderous.
■ **nm, f** slanderer, scandalmonger.

médit [medi] **pp inv** ➤ ***médire***.

méditatif, ive [meditatif, iv] ■ **adj** thoughtful, reflective.
■ **nm, f** thoughtful person.

méditation [meditasjɔ̃] **nf** meditation.

méditer [3] [medite] ■ **vt 1.** [projeter] to plan ▸ **méditer de faire qqch** to plan to do sthg **2.** [approfondir] to meditate on.
■ **vi : méditer (sur)** to meditate (on).

Méditerranée [mediterane] **nf : la Méditerranée** the Mediterranean (Sea).

méditerranéen, enne [mediteraneɛ̃, ɛn] **adj** Mediterranean.
◆ ***Méditerranéen, enne*** **nm, f** person from the Mediterranean.

médium [medjɔm] **nm 1.** [personne] medium **2.** MUS middle register.

médius [medjys] **nm** middle finger.

méduse [medyz] **nf** jellyfish.

méduser [3] [medyze] **vt** to dumbfound.

meeting [mitiŋ] **nm** meeting ▸ **meeting aérien** air show.

méfait [mefɛ] **nm** misdemeanour *UK*, misdemeanor *US*, misdeed.
◆ ***méfaits*** **nmpl** [du temps] ravages.

méfiance [mefjɑ̃s] **nf** suspicion, distrust.

méfiant, e [mefjɑ̃, ɑ̃t] **adj** suspicious, distrustful.

méfier [9] [mefje] ◆ ***se méfier*** **vp** to be wary *ou* careful ▸ **se méfier de qqn/qqch** to distrust sb/sthg.

méga [mega] **adj** mega.

mégalo [megalo] **nmf & adj** *fam* megalomaniac ▸ **il est complètement mégalo** he thinks he's God.

mégalomane [megalɔman] **nmf & adj** megalomaniac.

mégalomanie [megalɔmani] **nf** megalomania.

méga-octet [megaɔktɛ] **nm** megabyte.

mégaphone [megafɔn] **nm** megaphone, bullhorn *US*.

mégapole [megapɔl] **nf** megalopolis, megacity.

mégarde [megard] ◆ ***par mégarde*** **loc adv** by mistake.

mégère [meʒɛr] **nf** *péj* shrew.

mégot [mego] **nm** *fam* butt, fag-end *UK*.

mégoter [3] [megɔte] **vi** *fam* **: mégoter sur qqch** to skimp on sthg.

meilleur, e [mɛjœr] ■ **adj** *(compar)* better / *(superl)* best.
■ **nm, f** best ▸ **c'est la meilleure!** that takes the biscuit *UK ou* cake *US*!
◆ ***meilleur*** ■ **nm : le meilleur** the best.
■ **adv** better.

méjuger [17] [meʒyʒe] *littéraire* ■ **vt** to misjudge.
■ **vi : méjuger de qqn/qqch** to underestimate sb/sthg.
◆ ***se méjuger*** **vp** to underestimate o.s.

mél [mel] **nm** INFORM email.

mélancolie [melɑ̃kɔli] **nf** melancholy.

mélancolique [melɑ̃kɔlik] **adj** melancholy.

Mélanésie [melanezi] **nf : la Mélanésie** Melanesia.

mélanésien, enne [melanezjɛ̃, ɛn] **adj** Melanesian.
◆ ***Mélanésien, enne*** **nm, f** Melanesian.

mélange [melɑ̃ʒ] **nm 1.** [action] mixing ▸ **sans mélange** *fig* unadulterated **2.** [mixture] mixture.

mélanger [17] [melɑ̃ʒe] **vt 1.** [mettre ensemble] to mix **2.** [déranger] to mix up, to muddle up.
◆ ***se mélanger*** **vp 1.** [se mêler] to mix **2.** [se brouiller] to get mixed up.

mélangeur [melɑ̃ʒœr] **nm 1.** CINÉ mixer **2. : (robinet) mélangeur** mixer tap *UK*, mixing faucet *US*.

mélasse [melas] **nf 1.** [liquide] treacle *UK*, molasses *(U) US* **2.** *fam* [mélange] mess ▸ **être dans la mélasse** *fig* to be in a fix.

mêlée [mele] **nf 1.** [combat] fray **2.** [rugby] scrum ▸ **mêlée ouverte** ruck.

mêler [4] [mele] **vt 1.** [mélanger] to mix **2.** [déranger] to muddle up, to mix up **3.** [impliquer] **: mêler qqn à qqch** to involve sb in sthg **4.** [joindre] **: mêler qqch à qqch** to mix *ou* combine sthg with sthg.
◆ ***se mêler*** **vp 1.** [se joindre] **: se mêler à** [groupe] to join **2.** [s'ingérer] **: se mêler de qqch** to get mixed up in sthg ▸ **mêlez-vous de ce qui vous regarde!** mind your own business!

mélèze [melɛz] **nm** larch.

méli-mélo [melimelo] (pl **mélis-mélos**) **nm** muddle / [d'objets] jumble.

mélo [melo] **nm** *fam* melodrama.

mélodie [melɔdi] **nf** melody.

mélodieux, euse [melɔdjø, øz] **adj** melodious, tuneful.

mélodique [melɔdik] **adj** melodic.

mélodramatique [melɔdramatik] **adj** melodramatic.

mélodrame [melɔdram] **nm** melodrama.

mélomane [melɔman] ■ **nmf** music lover.
■ **adj** music-loving.

melon [məlɔ̃] **nm 1.** [fruit] melon **2.** [chapeau] bowler (hat) *UK*, derby (hat) *US*.

melting-pot [mɛltiŋpɔt] **nm** melting pot.

membrane [mɑ̃bran] **nf** membrane.

membre [mɑ̃br] ■ **nm 1.** [du corps] limb ▸ **membres supérieurs/inférieurs** upper/lower limbs ▸ **membres antérieurs/postérieurs** front/back legs ▸ **membre (viril)** (male) member **2.** [personne, pays, partie] member ▸ **membre fondateur** founder member *UK*, charter member *US*.
■ **adj** member *(avant n)*.

mémé = *mémère*.

même [mɛm] ■ **adj indéf 1.** [indique une identité ou une ressemblance] same ▸ **il a le même âge que moi** he's the same age as me **2.** [sert à souligner] **: ce sont ses paroles mêmes** those are his very words ▸ **elle est la bonté même** she's kindness itself.
■ **pron indéf : le/la même** the same one ▸ **ce sont toujours les mêmes qui gagnent** it's always the same people who win ▸ **elle est toujours la même** she's always the same.
■ **adv** even ▸ **il n'est même pas diplômé** he isn't even qualified ▸ **elle ne va même plus au cinéma** she doesn't even go to the cinema any more.
◆ ***de même*** **loc adv** similarly, likewise ▸ **il en va de même pour lui** the same goes for him.
◆ ***de même que*** **loc conj** just as.
◆ ***tout de même*** **loc adv** all the same.
◆ ***à même*** **loc prép : il boit à même la bouteille** he drinks (straight) from the bottle ▸ **s'asseoir à même le sol** to sit on the bare ground.
◆ ***à même de*** **loc prép : être à même de faire qqch** to be able to do sthg, to be in a position to do sthg.
◆ ***même si*** **loc conj** even if.

mémento [memɛ̃to] **nm 1.** [agenda] pocket diary **2.** [ouvrage] notes *(title of school textbook)*.

mémère [memɛr], ***mémé*** [meme] **nf** *fam* **1.** [grand-mère] granny **2.** *péj* [vieille femme] old biddy.

mémoire [memwar] ■ **nf** [gén & INFORM] memory ▸ **de mémoire** from memory ▸ **avoir bonne/mauvaise mémoire** to have a good/bad memory ▸ **si j'ai bonne mémoire** if I remember correctly ▸ **avoir de la mémoire** to have a good memory ▸ **je n'ai aucune mémoire!** I can never remember anything! ▸ **avoir la mémoire des chiffres/noms** to have a good memory for figures/names ▸ **avoir une mémoire d'éléphant** *fam* to have a memory like an elephant ▸ **perdre la mémoire** to lose one's memory ▸ **se rafraîchir la mémoire** to refresh one's memory

▶ **ce détail est resté à jamais** *ou* **s'est gravé dans ma mémoire** this detail has stayed with me ever since *ou* has forever remained engraved in my memory ▶ **mettre en mémoire** INFORM to store ▶ **mémoire tampon** INFORM buffer ▶ **mémoire virtuelle** INFORM virtual memory ▶ **mémoire vive** INFORM random access memory ▶ **à la mémoire de** in memory of ▶ **de mémoire d'homme** in living memory ▶ **pour mémoire** for the record.
■ **nm 1.** ADMIN memorandum, report **2.** UNIV dissertation, paper ▶ **mémoire de maîtrise** ≃ MA thesis *ou* dissertation.
◆ ***mémoires*** **nmpl** memoirs.

mémorable [memɔrabl] **adj** memorable.

mémorandum [memɔrɑ̃dɔm] **nm 1.** [note diplomatique] memorandum **2.** [carnet] notebook.

mémorial, ***aux*** [memɔrjal, o] **nm** [monument] memorial.

mémorisable [memɔrizabl] **adj** INFORM storable.

mémorisation [memɔrizasjɔ̃] **f : mémorisation du produit** product awareness.

mémoriser [3] [memɔrize] **vt 1.** [suj: personne] to memorize **2.** INFORM to store.

menaçant, ***e*** [mənasɑ̃, ɑ̃t] **adj** threatening.

menace [mənas] **nf : menace (pour)** threat (to).

menacer [16] [mənase] ■ **vt** to threaten ▶ **menacer de faire qqch** to threaten to do sthg ▶ **menacer qqn de qqch** to threaten sb with sthg.
■ **vi : la pluie menace** it looks like rain.

ménage [menaʒ] **nm 1.** [nettoyage] housework *(U)* ▶ **faire le ménage** to do the housework ▶ **faire des ménages** to work as a cleaner **2.** [couple] couple ▶ **se mettre en ménage** to set up house together ▶ **ménage à trois** ménage à trois **3.** ÉCON household
▶▶| **faire bon ménage (avec)** to get on well (with).

ménagement [menaʒmɑ̃] **nm** [égards] consideration ▶ **sans ménagement** brutally.

ménager[1], ***ère*** [menaʒe, ɛr] **adj** household *(avant n)*, domestic.
◆ ***ménagère*** **nf 1.** [femme] housewife **2.** [de couverts] canteen *UK*.

ménager[2] [17] [menaʒe] **vt 1.** [bien traiter] to treat gently **2.** [économiser - réserves] to use sparingly / [- argent, temps] to use carefully ▶ **ménager ses forces** to conserve one's strength ▶ **ménager sa santé** to take care of one's health **3.** [préparer - surprise] to prepare.
◆ ***se ménager*** **vp** to take care of o.s., to look after o.s.

ménagerie [menaʒri] **nf** menagerie.

mendiant, ***e*** [mɑ̃djɑ̃, ɑ̃t] **nm, f** beggar.

mendicité [mɑ̃disite] **nf** begging.

mendier [9] [mɑ̃dje] ■ **vt 1.** [argent] to beg for **2.** [éloges] to seek.
■ **vi** to beg.

menées [məne] **nfpl** scheming *(U)*.

mener [19] [məne] ■ **vt 1.** [emmener] to take ▶ **mener qqn en bateau** to lead sb up the garden path ▶ **mener qqn par le bout du nez** to lead sb by the nose **2.** [suj: escalier, route] to take, to lead ▶ **cette porte mène à la cave** this door leads to the cellar **3.** [diriger - débat, enquête] to conduct / [- affaires] to manage, to run ▶ **mener qqch à bonne fin** *ou* **à bien** to see sthg through, to bring sthg to a successful conclusion ▶ **il n'en menait pas large avant la publication des résultats** his heart was in his boots before the results were released **4.** [être en tête de] to lead ▶ **mener le jeu** SPORT to be in the lead / *fig* to have the upper hand, to call the tune.
■ **vi** to lead ▶ **l'équipe locale mène par 3 buts à 0** the local team is leading by 3 goals to 0 ▶ **de combien on mène?** what's our lead?

meneur, ***euse*** [mənœr, øz] **nm, f** [chef] ringleader ▶ **meneur d'hommes** born leader ▶ **meneur de jeu** host.

menhir [menir] **nm** standing stone.

méninge [menɛ̃ʒ] **nf** meninx.
◆ ***méninges*** **nfpl** *fam* brains.

méningite [menɛ̃ʒit] **nf** meningitis *(U)*.

ménisque [menisk] **nm** meniscus.

ménopause [menɔpoz] **nf** menopause.

menotte [mənɔt] **nf** [main] little hand.
◆ ***menottes*** **nfpl** handcuffs ▶ **passer les menottes à qqn** to handcuff sb.

mens ➤ ***mentir***.

mensonge [mɑ̃sɔ̃ʒ] **nm 1.** [propos] lie ▶ **un pieux mensonge** a white lie **2.** [acte] lying.

mensonger, ***ère*** [mɑ̃sɔ̃ʒe, ɛr] **adj** false.

menstruation [mɑ̃stryasjɔ̃] **nf** menstruation.

menstruel, ***elle*** [mɑ̃stryɛl] **adj** menstrual.

mensualiser [3] [mɑ̃sɥalize] **vt** to pay monthly.

mensualité [mɑ̃sɥalite] **nf 1.** [traite] monthly instalment *UK* *ou* installment *US* **2.** [salaire] (monthly) salary.

mensuel, ***elle*** [mɑ̃sɥɛl] ■ **adj** monthly.
■ **nm, f** salaried employee.
◆ ***mensuel*** **nm** monthly (magazine).

mensuellement [mɑ̃sɥɛlmɑ̃] **adv** monthly, every month.

COMMENT EXPRIMER...

les menaces

Get out or I'll call the police! / Sortez d'ici ou j'appelle la police !
I'm warning you: you'd better not say anything / Je te préviens, tu as intérêt à ne rien dire
It'll be ready tomorrow – It'd better be! / Ce sera prêt demain – Il y a intérêt !
Give it to me right now, or else! / Donne-moi ça tout de suite, sinon !
You'll be sorry for this! / Tu le regretteras !
If you ever do that again... / Si jamais tu recommences...

mensuration [mɑ̃syrasjɔ̃] **nf** measuring.
◆ ***mensurations*** **nfpl** measurements.

ment ➤ ***mentir***.

mental, ***e***, ***aux*** [mɑ̃tal, o] **adj** mental.

mentalement [mɑ̃talmɑ̃] **adv** mentally.

mentalité [mɑ̃talite] **nf** mentality.

menteur, ***euse*** [mɑ̃tœr, øz] ■ **adj** false.
■ **nm, f** liar.

menthe [mɑ̃t] **nf** mint ▸ **menthe à l'eau** peppermint cordial.

mentholé, ***e*** [mɑ̃tɔle] **adj** mentholated, menthol *(avant n)*.

menti [mɑ̃ti] **pp inv** ➤ ***mentir***.

mention [mɑ̃sjɔ̃] **nf 1.** [citation] mention ▸ **faire mention de qqch** to mention sthg **2.** [note] note ▸ **'rayer la mention inutile'** 'delete as appropriate' **3.** UNIV **: avec mention** with distinction ▸ **avec mention très bien/bien/passable** ≃ with first-/second-/third-class honours *UK*, ≃ summa cum laude/magna cum laude/cum laude *US*.

mentionner [3] [mɑ̃sjɔne] **vt** to mention.

mentir [37] [mɑ̃tir] **vi : mentir (à)** to lie (to) ▸ **sans mentir** honestly.

menton [mɑ̃tɔ̃] **nm** chin ▸ **menton en galoche** prominent chin ▸ **double menton** double chin.

menu, ***e*** [məny] **adj** [très petit] tiny ⁄ [mince] thin.
◆ ***menu*** ■ **adv : hacher menu** to chop finely.
■ **nm 1.** [liste, carte] menu ⁄ [repas à prix fixe] set menu ▸ **menu gastronomique/touristique** gourmet/tourist menu **2.** INFORM menu ▸ **menu d'aide** INFORM help menu ▸ **menu déroulant** INFORM pull-down menu ▸ **menu local** pop-up menu.

menuiserie [mənɥizri] **nf 1.** [métier] carpentry, joinery *UK* **2.** [atelier] carpenter's workshop, joinery (workshop) *UK* **3.** [ouvrages] carpentry *(U)*, joinery *(U)* *UK*.

menuisier [mənɥizje] **nm** carpenter, joiner *UK*.

méprenais, ***méprenions*** ➤ ***méprendre***.

méprendre [79] [meprɑ̃dr] ◆ ***se méprendre*** **vp** *littéraire* **: se méprendre sur** to be mistaken about ▸ **se ressembler à s'y méprendre** to be as like as two peas in a pod.

mépris, ***e*** [mepri, iz] **pp** ➤ ***méprendre***.
◆ ***mépris*** **nm 1.** [dédain] **: mépris (pour)** contempt (for), scorn (for) **2.** [indifférence] **: mépris de** disregard for.
◆ ***au mépris de*** **loc prép** regardless of.

méprisable [meprizabl] **adj** contemptible, despicable.

méprisant, ***e*** [meprizɑ̃, ɑ̃t] **adj** contemptuous, scornful.

méprise [mepriz] **nf** mistake, error.

mépriser [3] [meprize] **vt** to despise ⁄ [danger, offre] to scorn.

mer [mɛr] **nf** sea ▸ **en mer** at sea ▸ **prendre la mer** to put to sea ▸ **haute** *ou* **pleine mer** open sea ▸ **ce n'est pas la mer à boire** it's no big deal ▸ **la mer Adriatique** the Adriatic ▸ **la mer Baltique** the Baltic Sea ▸ **la mer d'Irlande** the Irish Sea ▸ **la mer Morte** the Dead Sea ▸ **la mer Noire** the Black Sea ▸ **la mer du Nord** the North Sea.

mercantile [mɛrkɑ̃til] **adj** *péj* mercenary.

mercenaire [mɛrsənɛr] **nm & adj** mercenary.

mercerie [mɛrsəri] **nf 1.** [articles] haberdashery *UK*, notions *(pl)* *US* **2.** [boutique] haberdasher's shop *UK*, notions store *US*.

merci [mɛrsi] ■ **interj** thank you!, thanks! ▸ **merci beaucoup!** thank you very much!
■ **nm : merci (de** *ou* **pour)** thank you (for) ▸ **dire merci à qqn** to thank sb, to say thank you to sb.
■ **nf** mercy ▸ **sans merci** merciless ▸ **être à la merci de** to be at the mercy of.

mercier, ***ère*** [mɛrsje, ɛr] **nm, f** haberdasher *UK*, notions dealer *US*.

mercredi [mɛrkrədi] **nm** Wednesday ▸ **mercredi des Cendres** Ash Wednesday ; voir aussi ***samedi***.

mercure [mɛrkyr] **nm** mercury.

merde [mɛrd] *tfam* ■ **nf** shit.
■ **interj** shit!

merdier [mɛrdje] **nm** *tfam* **: on est dans un merdier** we're in the shit.

mère [mɛr] **nf 1.** [génitrice] mother ▸ **mère adoptive** adoptive mother ▸ **mère biologique** MÉD & BIOL biological *ou* natural mother ▸ **mère célibataire** single *ou* unmarried mother ▸ **mère de famille** mother ▸ **mère indigne** unfit mother ▸ **mère poule** mother hen **2.** RELIG Mother ▸ **Mère supérieure** Mother Superior **3.** *(comme adj)* **: carte mère** INFORM motherboard ▸ **maison mère** COMM headquarters *sg*, head office.

merguez [mɛrgɛz] **nf** *North African spiced sausage*.

méridien, ***enne*** [meridjɛ̃, ɛn] **adj** [ligne] meridian.
◆ ***méridien*** **nm** meridian.

méridional, ***e***, ***aux*** [meridjɔnal, o] **adj** southern ⁄ [du sud de la France] Southern (French).
◆ ***Méridional***, ***e***, ***aux*** **nm, f** person from the Mediterranean ⁄ [du sud de la France] person from the South (of France).

meringue [mərɛ̃g] **nf** meringue.

mérinos [merinos] **nm** merino.

merisier [mərizje] **nm 1.** [arbre] wild cherry (tree) **2.** [bois] cherry.

méritant, ***e*** [meritɑ̃, ɑ̃t] **adj** deserving.

mérite [merit] **nm** merit ▸ **il a du mérite à y prendre part** it is to his credit that he is taking part.

mériter [3] [merite] **vt 1.** [être digne de, encourir] to deserve **2.** [valoir] to be worth, to merit.

méritoire [meritwar] **adj** commendable.

merlan [mɛrlɑ̃] **nm** whiting.

merle [mɛrl] **nm** blackbird.

merveille [mɛrvɛj] **nf** marvel, wonder ▸ **à merveille** marvellously *UK*, marvelously *US*, wonderfully ▸ **la huitième merveille du monde** *hum* the eighth wonder of the world.

merveilleusement [mɛrvɛjøzmɑ̃] **adv** marvellously *UK*, marvelously *US*, wonderfully.

merveilleux, ***euse*** [mɛrvɛjø, øz] **adj** **1.** [remarquable, prodigieux] marvellous *UK*, marvelous *US*, wonderful **2.** [magique] magic, magical.
◆ ***merveilleux*** **nm : le merveilleux** the supernatural.

mes ➤ ***mon***.

mésalliance [mezaljɑ̃s] **nf** unsuitable marriage, misalliance.

mésange [mezɑ̃ʒ] **nf** ZOOL tit ▸ **mésange bleue** bluetit ▸ **mésange charbonnière** coal tit.

mésaventure [mezavɑ̃tyr] **nf** misfortune.

mesdames ➤ ***madame***.

mesdemoiselles ➤ ***mademoiselle***.

mésentente [mezɑ̃tɑ̃t] **nf** disagreement.

mésestimer [3] [mezɛstime] **vt** *littéraire* to underestimate.

mesquin, ***e*** [mɛskɛ̃, in] **adj** mean, petty.

mesquinerie [mɛskinri] **nf** **1.** [étroitesse d'esprit] meanness, pettiness **2.** [action mesquine] petty act.

mess [mɛs] **nm** mess.

message [mɛsaʒ] **nm** message ▸ **message d'alerte** INFORM alert box ▸ **laisser un message à qqn** to leave a message for sb ▸ **message publicitaire** COMM commercial / INFORM junk e-mail.

messager, ***ère*** [mɛsaʒe, ɛr] **nm, f** messenger.

messagerie [mɛsaʒri] **nf** **1.** *(gén pl)* [transport de marchandises] freight *(U)* ▸ **les messageries aériennes** air freight company *sg* **2.** INFORM **: messagerie électronique** electronic mail ▸ **messagerie rose** *computerized dating service* ▸ **messagerie vocale électronique** INFORM voice messaging.

messe [mɛs] **nf** mass ▸ **aller à la messe** to go to mass ▸ **messe de minuit** midnight mass ▸ **faire des messes basses** *fam* to mutter.

messie [mɛsi] **nm** Messiah / *fig* saviour *UK*, savior *US*.

messieurs ➤ ***monsieur***.

mesure [məzyr] **nf** **1.** [disposition, acte] measure, step ▸ **prendre des mesures** to take measures *ou* steps ▸ **mesures d'austérité** austerity measures ▸ **mesure incitative** initiative ▸ **mesures de rétorsion** retaliatory measures ▸ **mesure de sécurité** safety measure **2.** [évaluation, dimension] measurement ▸ **prendre les mesures de qqn/qqch** to measure sb/sthg **3.** [étalon, récipient] measure ▸ **la mesure est (à son) comble** *fig* enough's enough **4.** MUS time, tempo ▸ **battre la mesure** to beat time **5.** [modération] moderation ▸ **garder une juste mesure** to keep a sense of moderation ▸ **tu passes *ou* dépasses la mesure** you're going too far
▸▸| **dans la mesure du possible** as far as possible ▸ **dans une large mesure** to a large extent, in large measure *sout* ▸ **être en mesure de** to be in a position to ▸ **c'est sans commune mesure** there's no possible comparison ▸ **prendre la (juste) mesure de qqch** to understand the full extent of sthg.
◆ ***à la mesure de*** **loc prép** worthy of ▸ **elle a un adversaire à sa mesure** she's got an opponent worthy of her *ou* who is a match for her.
◆ ***à mesure que*** **loc conj** as.
◆ ***outre mesure*** **loc adv** excessively ▸ **ils ne s'aiment pas outre mesure** they're not overkeen *ou* excessively keen on each other.
◆ ***sur mesure*** **loc adj** custom-made / [costume] made-to-measure ▸ **fabriquer des vêtements sur mesure** to make clothes to measure.

mesuré, ***e*** [məzyre] **adj** [modéré] measured.

mesurer [3] [məzyre] **vt** **1.** [gén] to measure ▸ **elle mesure 1,50 m** she's 5 feet tall ▸ **la table mesure 1,50 m** the table is 5 feet long **2.** [risques, portée, ampleur] to weigh, to weigh up *UK* ▸ **mesurer ses paroles** to weigh one's words **3.** [limiter] to limit **4.** [proportionner] **: mesurer qqch à qqch** to match sthg to sthg.
◆ ***se mesurer*** **vp : se mesurer avec *ou* à qqn** to pit o.s. against sb.

métabolisme [metabɔlism] **nm** metabolism.

métairie [metɛri] **nf** sharecropping farm.

métal, ***aux*** [metal, o] **nm** metal.

métallique [metalik] **adj** **1.** [en métal] metal *(avant n)* **2.** [éclat, son] metallic.

métallo [metalo] **nm** *fam* metalworker.

métallurgie [metalyrʒi] **nf** **1.** [industrie] metallurgica industry **2.** [technique] metallurgy.

métallurgique [metalyrʒik] **adj** metallurgical.

métallurgiste [metalyrʒist] **nm** **1.** [ouvrier] metalworker **2.** [industriel] metallurgist.

métamorphose [metamɔrfoz] **nf** metamorphosis.

métamorphoser [3] [metamɔrfoze] **vt : métamorphoser qqn/qqch (en)** to transform sb/sthg (into).
◆ ***se métamorphoser*** **vp** BIOL to metamorphose / *fig* **se métamorphoser (en)** to be transformed (into).

métaphore [metafɔr] **nf** metaphor.

métaphorique [metafɔrik] **adj** metaphorical.

métaphysique [metafizik] ■ **nf** metaphysics *(U)*.
■ **adj** metaphysical.

métayer, ***ère*** [meteje, metɛjɛr] **nm, f** tenant farmer.

météo [meteo] **nf** **1.** [bulletin] weather forecast ▸ **prévisions météo** (weather) forecast **2.** [service] ≃ Met Offic *UK*, ≃ National Weather Service *US*.

météore [meteɔr] **nm** meteor.

météorite [meteɔrit] **nm & nf** meteorite.

météorologie [meteɔrɔlɔʒi] **nf** **1.** [sciences] meteoro ogy **2.** [service] ≃ Meteorological Office *UK*, ≃ Nation Weather Service *US*.

météorologique [meteɔrɔlɔʒik] **adj** meteorologica weather *(avant n)*.

métèque [metɛk] **nm** *vulg racist term used with referenc to people from Mediterranean countries living in France.*

méthane [metan] **nm** methane.

méthode [metɔd] **nf 1.** [gén] method **2.** [ouvrage - gén] manual / [- de lecture, de langue] primer **3.** INFORM **: méthode du chemin critique** critical path method.

méthodique [metɔdik] **adj** methodical.

méthodiquement [metɔdikmɑ̃] **adv** methodically.

méthodiste [metɔdist] **nmf & adj** Methodist.

méthodologie [metɔdɔlɔʒi] **nf** methodology.

méthylène [metilɛn] **nm 1.** [alcool] methanol **2.** CHIM methylene.

méticuleusement [metikyløzmɑ̃] **adv** meticulously.

méticuleux, euse [metikylø, øz] **adj** meticulous.

métier [metje] **nm 1.** [profession - manuelle] occupation, trade / [- intellectuelle] occupation, profession ▸ **de son métier** by trade ▸ **il est du métier** he's in the same trade *ou* same line of work ▸ **avoir du métier** to have experience **2.** [machine] **: métier (à tisser)** loom.

métis, isse [metis] ■ **adj 1.** [personne] mixed-race, biracial *US* **2.** [tissu] cotton and linen.
■ **nm, f** person of mixed race.
◆ ***métis*** **nm** [tissu] cotton-linen mix.

métissage [metisaʒ] **nm** [de personnes] interbreeding.

métisser [3] [metise] **vt** to cross, to crossbreed.

métrage [metraʒ] **nm 1.** [mesure] measurement, measuring **2.** [COUT - coupon] length **3.** CINÉ footage ▸ **long métrage** feature film ▸ **court métrage** short (film) *UK ou* (movie) *US*.

mètre [mɛtr] **nm 1.** LITTÉR & MATH metre *UK*, meter *US* ▸ **mètre carré** square metre *UK ou* meter *US* ▸ **mètre cube** cubic metre *UK ou* meter *US* **2.** [instrument] rule.

métrer [18] [metre] **vt** [terrain] to survey / [tissu] to measure out.

métreur, euse [metrœr, øz] **nm, f** surveyor.

métrique [metrik] ■ **nf** LITTÉR metrics *(U)*.
■ **adj 1.** MATH metric **2.** LITTÉR metrical.

métro [metro] **nm** underground *UK*, subway *US*.

métronome [metrɔnɔm] **nm** metronome.

métropole [metrɔpɔl] **nf 1.** [ville] metropolis **2.** [pays] home country.

métropolitain, e [metrɔpɔlitɛ̃, ɛn] **adj** metropolitan ▸ **la France métropolitaine** metropolitan *ou* mainland France.

mets [mɛ] ■ **v** ➤ ***mettre***.
■ **nm** CULIN dish.

mettable [mɛtabl] **adj** wearable.

mette ➤ ***mettre***.

metteur [metœr] **nm : metteur en ondes** RADIO producer ▸ **metteur en scène** THÉÂTRE producer / CINÉ director.

mettre [84] [mɛtr] **vt 1.** [placer] to put ▸ **mettre de l'eau à bouillir** to put some water on to boil ▸ **mettre de l'argent sur son compte** to put *ou* to pay some money into one's account ▸ **mettre qqn au travail** to set sb to work, to get sb working
2. [revêtir] to put on ▸ **mets ta robe noire** put your black dress on ▸ **je ne mets plus ma robe noire** I don't wear my black dress any more ▸ **mets une barrette** put a (hair) slide *UK ou* barrette *US* in
3. [consacrer - temps] to take ▸ **combien de temps met-on pour y aller?** how long does it take to get there? / [- argent] to spend ▸ **mettre longtemps à faire qqch** to take a long time to do sthg
4. [allumer - radio, chauffage] to put on, to switch on ▸ **mets de la musique** put some music on, play some music
5. [installer] to put in ▸ **faire mettre l'électricité** to have electricity put in ▸ **faire mettre de la moquette** to have a carpet put down *ou* fitted
6. [inscrire] to put (down) ▸ **mets qu'il a refusé de signer** *fam* write *ou* put down that he refused to sign
▸▸ **mettre bas** [animal] to drop, to give birth ▸ **mettre qqn en boîte** *fam* to pull sb's leg ▸ **y mettre du sien** to do one's bit.
◆ ***se mettre*** **vp 1.** [se placer] **: où est-ce que ça se met?** where does this go? ▸ **se mettre au lit** to get into bed ▸ **se mettre à côté de qqn** to sit/stand near to sb
2. [devenir] **: se mettre en colère** to get angry
3. [commencer] **: se mettre à qqch/à faire qqch** to start sthg/doing sthg ▸ **se mettre au judo** to take up judo ▸ **se mettre à l'ouvrage** to set to work, to get down to work ▸ **s'y mettre** [au travail] to get down to it / [à une activité nouvelle] to have a try
4. [revêtir] to put on ▸ **je n'ai rien à me mettre** I haven't got a thing to wear ▸ **se mettre une belle robe/du parfum** to put on a nice dress/some perfume
5. *fam* [se donner des coups] **: qu'est-ce qu'ils se sont mis!** they really set about each other!

meuble [mœbl] ■ **nm** piece of furniture ▸ **meubles** furniture *(U)* ▸ **meubles de bureau/jardin** office/garden furniture *(U)* ▸ **sauver les meubles** *fig* not to lose everything.
■ **adj 1.** [terre, sol] easily worked **2.** DR movable.

meublé, e [mœble] **adj** furnished.
◆ ***meublé*** **nm** furnished room/flat *UK ou* apartment *US*.

meubler [5] [mœble] ■ **vt 1.** [pièce, maison] to furnish **2.** *fig* [occuper] **: meubler qqch (de)** to fill sthg (with).
■ **vi** to be decorative.
◆ ***se meubler*** **vp** to furnish one's home.

meuf [mœf] **nf** *fam* woman.

meugler [5] [møgle] **vi** to moo.

meule [møl] **nf 1.** [à moudre] millstone **2.** [à aiguiser] grindstone **3.** [de fromage] round **4.** AGRIC stack ▸ **meule de foin** haystack.

meunier, ère [mønje, ɛr] ■ **adj 1.** [industrie] milling *(avant n)* **2.** CULIN *coated in flour and fried*.
■ **nm, f** miller (f miller's wife).

meurs, meurt ➤ ***mourir***.

meurtre [mœrtr] **nm** murder.

meurtrier, ère [mœrtrije, ɛr] ■ **adj** [épidémie, arme] deadly / [fureur] murderous / [combat] bloody.
■ **nm, f** murderer.
◆ ***meurtrière*** **nf** ARCHIT loophole.

meurtrir [32] [mœrtrir] **vt 1.** [contusionner] to bruise **2.** *fig* [blesser] to wound.

meurtrissure [mœrtrisyr] **nf 1.** [marque] bruise **2.** *fig* [blessure] wound.

meute [møt] **nf** pack.

mévente [mevɑ̃t] **nf** poor sales *pl*.

mexicain**, **e [mɛksikɛ̃, ɛn] adj Mexican.
◆ ***Mexicain**, **e*** nm, f Mexican.

Mexico [mɛksiko] npr Mexico City.

Mexique [mɛksik] nm : **le Mexique** Mexico ▸ **au Mexique** in Mexico.

mezzanine [mɛdzanin] nf mezzanine.

mezzo-soprano [mɛdzosɔprano] (pl **mezzo-sopranos**) nm mezzo-soprano.

MF ■ nf (abr de ***modulation de fréquence***) FM.
■ **1.** (abr écrite de ***mark finlandais***) Mk, Fmk **2.** abr de ***million de francs***.

Mgr (abr écrite de ***Monseigneur***) Mgr.

mi [mi] nm inv E / [chanté] mi.

mi- [mi] ■ adj inv half ▸ **à la mi-juin** in mid-June.
■ adv half-.

miaou [mjau] nm miaow *UK*, meow *US*.

miasme [mjasm] nm *(gén pl)* putrid *ou* foul smell.

miaulement [mjolmɑ̃] nm miaowing *UK*, meowing *US*.

miauler [3] [mjole] vi to miaow *UK*, to meow *US*.

mi-bas [miba] nm inv knee-sock.

mica [mika] nm mica.

mi-carême [mikarɛm] nf *feast day on third Thursday in Lent.*

miche [miʃ] nf [de pain] *large round loaf.*
◆ ***miches*** nfpl *fam* **1.** [fesses] bum *(sg) UK*, butt *(sg) US* **2.** [seins] boobs.

mi-chemin [miʃmɛ̃] ◆ ***à mi-chemin*** loc adv halfway (there).

mi-clos**, **e [miklo, oz] adj half-closed.

micmac [mikmak] nm *fam* **1.** [manigance] game, scheme **2.** [embrouillamini] muddle, chaos.

mi-côte [mikot] ◆ ***à mi-côte*** loc adv halfway up/downthe hill.

micro [mikro] ■ nm **1.** [microphone] mike **2.** [micro-ordinateur] micro.
■ nf microcomputing.

microbe [mikrɔb] nm **1.** MÉD microbe, germ **2.** *péj* [avorton] (little) runt.

microbien**, **enne [mikrɔbjɛ̃, ɛn] adj bacterial.

microbiologie [mikrɔbjɔlɔʒi] nf microbiology.

microchirurgie [mikrɔʃiryrʒi] nf microsurgery.

microclimat [mikrɔklima] nm microclimate.

microcosme [mikrɔkɔsm] nm microcosm.

micro-édition [mikrɔedisjɔ̃] nf desktop publishing.

micro-électronique [mikrɔelɛktrɔnik] ■ nf microelectronics *(U)*.
■ adj microelectronic.

microfiche [mikrɔfiʃ] nf microfiche.

microfilm [mikrɔfilm] nm microfilm.

micromarketing [mikrɔmarkɛtiŋ] m micromarketing.

micron [mikrɔ̃] nm micron.

Micronésie [mikronezi] nf : **la Micronésie** Micronesia ▸ **les États fédérés de Micronésie** the Federated States of Micronesia.

micro-ondes [mikrɔɔ̃d] nfpl microwaves ▸ **four à micro-ondes** microwave (oven).

micro-ordinateur [mikrɔɔrdinatœr] (pl **micro-ordinateurs**) nm micro, microcomputer.

micro-organisme [mikrɔɔrganism] (pl **micro-organismes**) nm micro-organism.

microphone [mikrɔfɔn] nm microphone.

microprocesseur [mikrɔprɔsesœr] nm microprocessor.

microprogramme [mikrɔprɔgram] nm INFORM firmware.

microscope [mikrɔskɔp] nm microscope ▸ **microscope électronique** electron microscope.

microscopique [mikrɔskɔpik] adj microscopic.

microsillon [mikrɔsijɔ̃] nm LP, long-playing record.

MIDEM**, **Midem [midɛm] (abr de ***Marché international du disque et de l'édition musicale***) nm *music industry trade fair.*

midi [midi] nm **1.** [période du déjeuner] lunchtime **2.** [heure] midday, noon ▸ **chercher midi à quatorze heures** *fam* to look for complications (where there are none) **3.** [sud] south.
◆ ***Midi*** nm : **le Midi** the South of France.

midinette [midinɛt] nf *péj* empty-headed girl.

mie [mi] nf **1.** [de pain] soft part, inside **2.** *vieilli* [bien-aimée] : **ma mie** sweetheart.

miel [mjɛl] nm honey.

mielleux**, **euse [mjɛlø, øz] adj [personne] unctuous / [paroles, air] honeyed.

mien [mjɛ̃] ◆ ***le mien**, **la mienne*** [ləmjɛn, lamjɛn] (mpl **les miens** [lemjɛ̃], fpl **les miennes** [lemjɛn]) pron poss mine ▸ **les miens** my family ▸ **j'y mets du mien** I put in a lot of effort.

miette [mjɛt] nf **1.** [de pain] crumb, breadcrumb **2.** *(gén pl)* [débris] shreds *pl* ▸ **en miettes** in bits *ou* pieces.

mieux [mjø] ■ adv **1.** [comparatif] **: mieux (que)** better (than) ▸ **il travaille mieux** he's working better ▸ **il pourrait mieux faire** he could do better ▸ **il va mieux** he's better ▸ **faire mieux de faire qqch** to do better to do sth ▸ **vous feriez mieux de vous taire** you would do better to keep quiet, you would be well-advised to keep quiet ▸ **mieux je le comprends, plus/moins j'ai envie de le lire** the better I understand it, the more/less I want to read it ▸ **on ne peut pas mieux dire** you can't say better or fairer than that
2. [superlatif] best ▸ **il est le mieux payé du service** he's the best *ou* highest paid member of the department ▸ **le mieux qu'il peut** as best he can ▸ **voilà ce qui me convient le mieux** this is what suits me best.

■ **adj** better ▸ **c'est mieux que rien** it's better than nothing ▸ **elle est mieux avec les cheveux courts** she looks better with short hair ▸ **on est mieux dans ce fauteuil** this armchair is more comfortable.

■ **nm 1.** *(sans déterminant)* **: c'est pas mal, mais il y a mieux** it's not bad, but there's better ▸ **j'espérais mieux** I was hoping for something better ▸ **faute de mieux** for lack of anything better

2. *(avec déterminant)* best ▸ **il y a un** *ou* **du mieux** there's been an improvement ▸ **le mieux est de ne pas y aller** it's best not to go ▸ **faire de son mieux** to do one's best.

◆ ***au mieux*** **loc adv** at best ▸ **faire au mieux** to do whatever's best, to act for the best.

◆ ***des mieux*** **loc adv : un appareil des mieux conçus** one of the best-designed devices.

◆ ***pour le mieux*** **loc adv** for the best ▸ **tout va pour le mieux** everything is for the best.

◆ ***on ne peut mieux*** **loc adv : c'est on ne peut mieux** it couldn't be better.

◆ ***de mieux en mieux*** **loc adv** better and better ▸ **et maintenant, de mieux en mieux, j'ai perdu mes clefs!** *iron* and now, to cap it all, I've lost my keys!

◆ ***à qui mieux mieux*** **loc adv : on criait à qui mieux mieux** it was a case of who could shout (the) loudest.

mieux-être [mjøzɛtr] **nm inv** improvement.

mieux perçu [mjøpɛrsy] **m** best-perceived.

mièvre [mjɛvr] **adj** insipid.

mièvrerie [mjɛvrəri] **nf** insipidness.

mignon, onne [miɲɔ̃, ɔn] ■ **adj 1.** [charmant] sweet, cute **2.** [gentil] nice.

■ **nm, f** darling, sweetheart.

◆ ***mignon*** **nm** *vieilli* favourite *UK*, favorite *US*.

migraine [migrɛn] **nf** headache / MÉD migraine.

migrant, e [migrɑ̃, ɑ̃t] ■ **adj** migrant *(avant n)*.

■ **nm, f** migrant.

migrateur, trice [migratœr, tris] **adj** migratory.

◆ ***migrateur*** **nm** migratory bird.

migration [migrasjɔ̃] **nf** migration.

mijaurée [miʒore] **nf** affected woman ▸ **faire la mijaurée** to put on airs.

mijoter [3] [miʒɔte] ■ **vt 1.** CULIN to simmer **2.** *fam* [tramer] to cook up.

■ **vi** CULIN to simmer.

mi-journée [miʒurne] **nf : les informations de la mi-journée** the lunchtime news.

mil[1] [mij] **nm** millet.

mil[2] **adj =** ***mille***.

milan [milɑ̃] **nm** kite *(bird)*.

mildiou [mildju] **nm** mildew.

milice [milis] **nf** militia.

milicien, enne [milisjɛ̃, ɛn] **nm, f** militiaman (f militiawoman).

milieu, x [miljø] **nm 1.** [centre] middle ▸ **au milieu de** [au centre de] in the middle of / [parmi] among, surrounded by ▸ **au milieu de l'hiver/l'été** in midwinter/midsummer ▸ **elle est partie au milieu de mon cours** she left in the middle of *ou* halfway through my lesson ▸ **au beau** *ou* **en plein milieu de qqch** right in the middle of sthg ▸ **en milieu de trimestre** in mid-term ▸ **milieu proche** inner circle ▸ **dans les milieux proches du pouvoir** in the inner circles of power

2. [stade intermédiaire] middle course ▸ **juste milieu** happy medium

3. [sociologie] environment, milieu ▸ **milieu familial** family background ▸ **dans les milieux autorisés** in official circles ▸ **des gens de tous les milieux** people from all walks of life *ou* backgrounds

4. BIOL environment, habitat ▸ **dans un milieu acide** in an acid medium

5. [pègre] **: le milieu** the underworld

6. FOOTBALL **: milieu de terrain** midfielder, midfield player.

militaire [militɛr] ■ **nm** soldier ▸ **militaire de carrière** professional soldier.

■ **adj** military.

militant, e [militɑ̃, ɑ̃t] **adj & nm, f** militant.

militantisme [militɑ̃tism] **nm** militancy.

militarisation [militarizasjɔ̃] **nf** militarization.

militariste [militarist] ■ **nmf** militarist.

■ **adj** militaristic.

militer [3] [milite] **vi** to be active ▸ **militer pour** to militate in favour *UK ou* favor *US* of ▸ **militer contre** to militate against.

milk-shake [milkʃɛk] (pl **milk-shakes**) **nm** milk shake.

mille, mil [mil] ■ **nm inv 1.** [unité] a *ou* one thousand ▸ **il y a une chance sur mille que ça marche** there's a one-in-a-thousand chance that it'll work **2.** [de cible] bull's-eye ▸ **dans le mille** on target **3.** NAUT **: mille marin** nautical mile **4.** *Québec* [distance] mile

▸▸ **des mille et des cents** *fam* loads *ou* pots *UK* of money ▸ **je te le donne en mille!** *fam* I bet you'll never guess!

■ **adj inv** thousand ▸ **c'est mille fois trop** it's far too much ▸ **en mille morceaux** in pieces ▸ **je lui ai dit mille fois** I've told him a thousand times ▸ **mille mercis, merci mille fois** many thanks ▸ **voilà un exemple entre mille** here's just one of the countless examples I could choose ; voir aussi ***six***.

mille-feuille (pl **mille-feuilles**) [milfœj] **nm** ≃ vanilla slice *UK*, ≃ napoleon *US*.

millénaire [milenɛr] ■ **nm** millennium, thousand years *pl*.

■ **adj** thousand-year-old *(avant n)*.

mille-pattes [milpat] **nm inv** centipede, millipede.

millésime [milezim] **nm 1.** [de pièce] date **2.** [de vin] vintage, year.

millésimé, e [milezime] **adj** [vin] vintage *(avant n)*.

millet [mijɛ] **nm** millet.

milliard [miljar] **nm** thousand million *UK*, billion *US* ▸ **par milliards** *fig* in (their) millions.

milliardaire [miljardɛr] **nmf** multimillionaire *UK*, billionaire *US*.

millième [miljɛm] **adj, nm & nmf** thousandth ; voir aussi ***sixième***.

millier [milje] **nm** thousand ▸ **un millier d'euros** about a thousand euros ▸ **un millier de personnes** about a thousand people ▸ **des milliers de** thousands of ▸ **par milliers** in (their) thousands.

milligramme [miligram] **nm** milligram, milligramme *UK*.

millilitre [mililitr] **nm** millilitre *UK*, milliliter *US*.

millimètre [milimɛtr] **nm** millimetre *UK*, millimeter *US*.

millimétrique [milimetrik] **adj** : **papier millimétrique** graph paper.

million [miljɔ̃] **nm** million ▸ **un million d'euros** a million euros.

millionième [miljɔnjɛm] **adj, nm** & **nmf** millionth.

millionnaire [miljɔnɛr] **nmf** millionaire.

mime [mim] ■ **nm** mime.
■ **nmf** mime (artist).

mimer [3] [mime] **vt 1.** [exprimer sans parler] to mime **2.** [imiter] to mimic.

mimétisme [mimetism] **nm** mimicry.

mimique [mimik] **nf 1.** [grimace] face **2.** [geste] sign language *(U)*.

mimosa [mimɔza] **nm** mimosa.

min (abr écrite de ***minute***) min.

min. (abr écrite de ***minimum***) min.

MIN (abr de ***marché d'intérêt national***) **nm** *wholesale market for agricultural produce.*

minable [minabl] **adj** *fam* **1.** [misérable] seedy, shabby **2.** [médiocre] pathetic.

minaret [minarɛ] **nm** minaret.

minauder [3] [minode] **vi** to simper.

mince [mɛ̃s] ■ **adj 1.** [maigre - gén] thin / [- personne, taille] slender, slim **2.** *fig* [faible] small, meagre *UK*, meager *US*.
■ **interj** *fam* : **mince alors!** drat!

minceur [mɛ̃sœr] **nf 1.** [gén] thinness / [de personne] slenderness, slimness **2.** *fig* [insuffisance] meagreness *UK*, meagerness *US*.

mincir [32] [mɛ̃sir] **vi** to get thinner *ou* slimmer.

mine [min] **nf 1.** [expression] look ▸ **avoir bonne/mauvaise mine** to look well/ill ▸ **avoir une mine de déterré** *fam* to look like death warmed up ▸ **faire grise mine** to look annoyed ▸ **je lui trouve meilleure mine** I think she looks better *ou* in better health
2. [apparence] appearance ▸ **faire mine de faire qqch** to make as if to do sthg / [faire semblant] to pretend to do sthg ▸ **elle fit mine de raccrocher, puis se ravisa** she made as if to hang up, but then changed her mind ▸ **mine de rien, il est très costaud** *fam* he's very strong, though he doesn't look it ▸ **ne pas payer de mine** to be not much to look at
3. [gisement] mine / [exploitation] mining ▸ **mine de charbon** coalmine ▸ **une mine d'or** *litt* & *fig* a gold mine ▸ **une mine d'informations** *fig* a mine of information
4. [explosif] mine ▸ **ouvrir une roche à coups de mine** to blast a rock
5. [de crayon] lead ▸ **crayon à mine grasse/dure** soft/hard pencil.

miner [3] [mine] **vt 1.** MIL to mine **2.** [ronger] to undermine, to wear away / *fig* to wear down.
◆ ***se miner*** **vp** to worry o.s. sick.

minerai [minrɛ] **nm** ore.

minéral, e, aux [mineral, o] **adj 1.** CHIM inorganic **2.** [eau, source] mineral *(avant n)*.
◆ ***minéral*** **nm** mineral.

minéralisé, e [mineralize] **adj** mineralized.

minéralogie [mineralɔʒi] **nf** mineralogy.

minéralogique [mineralɔʒik] **adj 1.** AUTO : **numéro minéralogique** registration number *UK*, license number *US* ▸ **plaque minéralogique** numberplate *UK*, license plate *US* **2.** GÉOL mineralogical.

minet, ette [minɛ, ɛt] **nm, f** *fam* **1.** [chat] pussy cat, pussy **2.** [personne] trendy.

mineur, e [minœr] ■ **adj** minor.
■ **nm, f** DR minor.
◆ ***mineur*** **nm** [ouvrier] miner ▸ **mineur de fond** face worker.

mini abr écrite de ***minimum***.

miniature [minjatyr] ■ **nf** miniature ▸ **en miniature** in miniature.
■ **adj** miniature.

miniaturiser [3] [minjatyrize] **vt** to miniaturize.

minibar [minibar] **nm** minibar.

minibus [minibys] **nm** minibus.

minichaîne [miniʃɛn] **nf** portable hi-fi.

MiniDisc®, ***minidisque*** [minidisk] **nm** MiniDisc®.

minier, ère [minje, ɛr] **adj** mining *(avant n)*.

minijupe [miniʒyp] **nf** miniskirt.

minimal, e, aux [minimal, o] **adj** minimum *(avant n)*.

minimalisme [minimalism] **nm** minimalism.

minime [minim] ■ **nmf** SPORT ≃ junior.
■ **adj** minimal.

minimiser [3] [minimize] **vt** to minimize.

minimum [minimɔm] (pl **minimums** *ou* **minima** [mi-nima]) ■ **nm 1.** [gén & MATH] minimum ▸ **au minimum** a[t] least ▸ **le strict minimum** the bare minimum ▸ **le mini[mum] vital** a living wage **2.** DR minimum penalty.
■ **adj** minimum *(avant n)*.

mini-ordinateur [miniɔrdinatœr] (pl **mini-ordina-teurs**) **nm** minicomputer.

ministère [ministɛr] **nm 1.** [département] departmen[t], ministry *UK* **2.** [cabinet] government **3.** RELIG ministry.
◆ ***ministère public*** **nm** ≃ Crown Prosecution Servic[e] *UK*, ≃ District Attorney's office *US*.

ministériel, elle [ministerjɛl] **adj 1.** [du ministère] de-partmental, ministerial *UK* **2.** [pro-gouvernemental] pr[o-]government.

ministre [ministr] **nm** secretary, minister *UK* ▸ **ministr[e] délégué à** secretary for, minister of *UK* ▸ **ministre d**

Affaires étrangères ≃ Foreign Secretary *UK*, ≃ Secretary of State *US* ▸ **ministre des Affaires sociales** ≃ Social Services Secretary ▸ **ministre de l'Éducation nationale** ≃ Education Secretary ▸ **ministre d'État** secretary of state, cabinet minister *UK* ▸ **ministre des Finances** ≃ Chancellor of the Exchequer *UK*, ≃ Secretary of the Treasury *US* ▸ **ministre de l'Intérieur** ≃ Home Secretary *UK*, ≃ Secretary of the Interior *US* ▸ **ministre de la Santé** ≃ Health Secretary ▸ **premier ministre** prime minister.

Minitel® [minitɛl] **nm** *teletext system run by the French national telephone company to provide an information and communications network.*

minitéliste [minitelist] **nmf** Minitel® user.

minois [minwa] **nm** sweet (little) face.

minorer [3] [minɔre] **vt** to reduce.

minoritaire [minɔritɛr] ■ **nmf** member of a minority.
■ **adj** minority *(avant n)* ▸ **être minoritaire** to be in the minority.

minorité [minɔrite] **nf** minority ▸ **en minorité** in the minority ▸ **minorité ethnique** ethnic minority.

Minorque [minɔrk] **npr** Minorca ▸ **à Minorque** in Minorca.

minorquin, e [minɔrkɛ̃, in] **adj** Minorcan.
◆ ***Minorquin, e*** **nm, f** Minorcan.

minoterie [minɔtri] **nf** **1.** [moulin] flourmill **2.** [industrie] (flour) milling industry.

minuit [minɥi] **nm** midnight.

minuscule [minyskyl] ■ **nf** [lettre] small letter ▸ **en minuscules** in small letters.
■ **adj** **1.** [lettre] small **2.** [très petit] tiny, minuscule.

minutage [minytaʒ] **nm** (precise) timing.

minute [minyt] ■ **nf** minute ▸ **il n'y a pas une minute à perdre** there's not a minute to lose ▸ **dans une minute** in a minute ▸ **on n'est pas à la minute près** *ou* **à la minute!** *fam* there's no hurry! ▸ **à la minute** at once ▸ **je veux que ce soit fait à la minute** I want it done this instant ▸ **d'une minute à l'autre** in next to no time ▸ **il sera là d'une minute à l'autre** he'll be arriving any minute, he won't be a minute ▸ **une minute de silence** a minute's silence.
■ **interj** *fam* hang on (a minute)! ▸ **minute, je n'ai pas dit ça!** hang on *ou* wait a minute, I never said that!

minuter [3] [minyte] **vt** **1.** [chronométrer] to time (precisely) **2.** DR to draw up.

minuterie [minytri] **nf** [d'éclairage] time switch, timer.

minuteur [minytœr] **nm** timer.

minutie [minysi] **nf** [soin] meticulousness / [précision] attention to detail ▸ **avec minutie** [avec soin] meticulously / [dans le détail] in minute detail.

minutieusement [minysjøzmɑ̃] **adv** [avec soin] meticulously / [dans le détail] minutely, in minute detail.

minutieux, euse [minysjø, øz] **adj** [méticuleux] meticulous / [détaillé] minutely detailed ▸ **un travail minutieux** a job requiring great attention to detail.

mioche [mjɔʃ] **nmf** *fam* kiddy.

mirabelle [mirabɛl] **nf** **1.** [fruit] mirabelle (plum) **2.** [alcool] plum brandy.

miracle [mirakl] **nm** miracle ▸ **par miracle** by some *ou* a miracle, miraculously ▸ **croire aux miracles** to believe in miracles.

miraculé, e [mirakyle] ■ **adj** lucky to be alive.
■ **nm, f** *person who is lucky to be alive.*

miraculeusement [mirakyløzmɑ̃] **adv** miraculously.

miraculeux, euse [mirakylø, øz] **adj** miraculous.

mirador [miradɔr] **nm** MIL watchtower.

mirage [miraʒ] **nm** mirage.

mire [mir] **nf** **1.** TV test card *UK*, test pattern *US* **2.** [visée] **: ligne de mire** line of sight.

mirer [3] [mire] **vt** **1.** [œuf] to candle **2.** *littéraire* [refléter] to reflect.
◆ ***se mirer*** **vp** *littéraire* **1.** [se regarder] to gaze at o.s. **2.** [se refléter] to be reflected *ou* mirrored.

mirifique [mirifik] **adj** fabulous.

mirobolant, e [mirɔbɔlɑ̃, ɑ̃t] **adj** fabulous, fantastic.

miroir [mirwar] **nm** mirror ▸ **miroir aux alouettes** *fig* lure ▸ **miroir de poche** handbag mirror.

miroiter [3] [mirwate] **vi** to sparkle, to gleam ▸ **faire miroiter qqch à qqn** to hold out the prospect of sthg to sb.

miroiterie [mirwatri] **nf** **1.** [industrie] mirror manufacturing **2.** [atelier] mirror workshop.

miroton [mirɔtɔ̃] **nm** *boiled beef in an onion sauce.*

mis, e [mi, miz] **pp** ➤ ***mettre***.

misaine [mizɛn] **nf** foresail.

misanthrope [mizɑ̃trɔp] ■ **nmf** misanthropist, misanthrope.
■ **adj** misanthropic.

mise [miz] **nf** **1.** [action] putting ▸ **mise en demeure** formal notice ▸ **mise à jour** updating ▸ **mise en liberté provisoire** DR freeing on bail ▸ **mise en page** making up, composing ▸ **mise en plis** [coiffure] set ▸ **mise au point** PHOTO focusing / TECHNOL adjustment / *fig* clarification ▸ **mise en scène** production ▸ **mise en service** putting into operation **2.** [d'argent] stake ▸ **sauver la mise à qqn** *fig* to get sb out of a tight corner ▸ **mise de fonds** capital investment **3.** [tenue] clothing
▸▸ **ne pas être de mise** to be unacceptable.

miser [3] [mize] ■ **vt** to bet.
■ **vi : miser sur** to bet on / *fig* to count on.

misérabilisme [mizerabilism] **nm** miserabilism.

misérable [mizerabl] ■ **nmf** **1.** [pauvre] poor person **2.** [coquin] wretch.
■ **adj** **1.** [pauvre] poor, wretched **2.** [déplorable] pitiful **3.** [sans valeur] paltry, miserable.

misérablement [mizerabləmɑ̃] **adv** **1.** [pauvrement] in poverty, wretchedly **2.** [pitoyablement] miserably.

misère [mizɛr] **nf 1.** [indigence] poverty ▸ **misère noire** utter destitution **2.** *fig* [bagatelle] trifle.
◆ ***misères*** **nfpl** [ennuis] woes *pl*, miseries *pl* ▸ **faire des misères à qqn** *fam* to put sb through it.

FAUX AMIS / FALSE FRIENDS
misère
Misery is not a translation of the French word *misère*. Misery is translated by *malheur*.
▸ Her wealth brought her nothing but misery / *Sa fortune ne lui a apporté que des malheurs*

miséreux, euse [mizerø, øz] ■ **adj** poverty-stricken.
■ **nm, f** down-and-out.

miséricorde [mizerikɔrd] ■ **nf** [clémence] mercy.
■ **interj** mercy (me)!

miséricordieux, euse [mizerikɔrdjø, øz] **adj** merciful.

misogyne [mizɔʒin] ■ **nmf** misogynist.
■ **adj** misogynous.

misogynie [mizɔʒini] **nf** misogyny.

missel [misɛl] **nm** missal.

missile [misil] **nm** missile ▸ **missile balistique** ballistic missile.

mission [misjɔ̃] **nf** mission ▸ **en mission** on a mission.

missionnaire [misjɔnɛr] ■ **nmf** missionary.
■ **adj** missionary *(avant n)*.

missive [misiv] **nf** letter.

mistral [mistral] **nm** mistral *strong cold wind that blows down the Rhône Valley and through Southern France*.

mitaine [mitɛn] **nf** fingerless glove.

mite [mit] **nf** (clothes) moth.

mité, e [mite] **adj** moth-eaten.

mi-temps [mitɑ̃] ■ **nf inv** [SPORT - période] half / [- pause] half-time ▸ **à la mi-temps** at half-time ▸ **première/seconde mi-temps** first/second half.
■ **nm** part-time work.
◆ ***à mi-temps*** **loc adj & loc adv** part-time.

miteux, euse [mitø, øz] *fam* ■ **adj** seedy, dingy.
■ **nm, f** shabby person.

mitigé, e [mitiʒe] **adj 1.** [tempéré] lukewarm **2.** *fam* [mélangé] mixed.

mitonner [3] [mitɔne] ■ **vt 1.** [faire cuire] to simmer **2.** [préparer avec soin] to prepare lovingly **3.** *fig* [affaire] to plot, to cook up.
■ **vi** CULIN to simmer.
◆ ***se mitonner*** **vp : se mitonner qqch** to cook sthg up for o.s.

mitoyen, enne [mitwajɛ̃, ɛn] **adj** [commun] common / [attenant] adjoining ▸ **mur mitoyen** party wall.

mitrailler [3] [mitraje] **vt 1.** MIL to machinegun **2.** *fam* [photographier] to click away at **3.** *fig* [assaillir] **: mitrailler qqn (de)** to bombard sb (with).

mitraillette [mitrajɛt] **nf** submachine gun.

mitrailleur [mitrajœr] **nm** machinegunner.

mitrailleuse [mitrajøz] **nf** machinegun.

mitre [mitr] **nf 1.** [d'évêque] mitre *UK*, miter *US* **2.** [de cheminée] cowl.

mi-voix [mivwa] ◆ ***à mi-voix*** **loc adv** in a low voice.

mix **m : mix média** media mix ▸ **mix de produits** product mix.

mixage [miksaʒ] **nm** CINÉ & RADIO (sound) mixing.

mixer[1], ***mixeur*** [miksœr] **nm** (food) mixer.

mixer[2] [3] [mikse] **vt** to mix.

mixité [miksite] **nf** coeducation.

mixte [mikst] **adj** mixed ▸ **mariage mixte** mixed marriage.

mixture [mikstyr] **nf 1.** CHIM & CULIN mixture **2.** *péj* [mélange] concoction.

MJC (abr de ***maison des jeunes et de la culture***) **nf** *youth and cultural centre*.

MJPEG (abr de ***Moving Joint Photographic Expert Group***) **m** INFORM MJPEG.

ml (abr écrite de ***millilitre***) ml.

MLF (abr de ***Mouvement de libération de la femme***) **nm** *women's movement*, ≃ NOW *US*.

Mlle (abr écrite de ***Mademoiselle***) Miss.

mm (abr écrite de ***millimètre***) mm.

MM (abr écrite de ***Messieurs***) Messrs.

Mme (abr écrite de ***Madame***) Mrs.

MMX (abr de ***multimedia extensions***) **m** INFORM MMX

mn (abr écrite de ***minute***) min.

mnémotechnique [mnemɔtɛknik] **adj** mnemonic.

MNS (abr de ***maître nageur sauveteur***) **nm** lifeguard.

Mo (abr de ***méga-octet***) MB.

mobile [mɔbil] ■ **nm 1.** [objet] mobile **2.** [motivation] motive.
■ **adj 1.** [gén] movable, mobile / [partie, pièce] moving **2.** [population, main-d'œuvre] mobile **3.** [fête] movable [échelle] sliding.

mobilier, ère [mɔbilje, ɛr] **adj** DR movable.
◆ ***mobilier*** **nm** furniture.

mobilisation [mɔbilizasjɔ̃] **nf** mobilization ▸ **mobilisation générale** MIL general mobilization.

mobiliser [3] [mɔbilize] **vt 1.** [gén] to mobilize **2.** [moralement] to rally.
◆ ***se mobiliser*** **vp** to mobilize, to rally.

mobilité [mɔbilite] **nf** mobility ▸ **mobilité sociale** ÉCO upward mobility.

Mobylette® [mɔbilɛt] **nf** moped.

mocassin [mɔkasɛ̃] **nm** moccasin.

moche [mɔʃ] **adj** *fam* **1.** [laid] ugly **2.** [triste, méprisable] lousy, rotten.

modalité [mɔdalite] **nf 1.** [convention] form ▸ **modalités de paiement** methods of payment **2.** DR clause.

mode [mɔd] ■ **nf 1.** [gén] fashion ▸ **à la mode** in fashion, fashionable ▸ **ce n'est plus à la mode** it's out of fashion ▸ **lancer une mode** to start a fashion ▸ **lancer la mode**

qqch to start the fashion for sthg ▸ **passé de mode** out of fashion ▸ **suivre la mode** to follow fashion ▸ **la mode des années 80** the style of the eighties
2. [coutume] custom, style ▸ **à la mode de** in the style of ▸ **cousin à la mode de Bretagne** distant cousin, first cousin once removed.
■ **nm 1.** [manière] mode, form ▸ **mode d'action** form *ou* mode of action ▸ **mode de vie** way of life
2. [méthode] method ▸ **mode d'emploi** instructions (for use) ▸ **mode de paiement** mode *ou* method of payment
3. GRAMM mood
4. MUS mode
5. INFORM mode ▸ **mode autonome** *ou* **local** *ou* **hors ligne** off-line mode ▸ **mode connecté** *ou* **en ligne** on-line mode ▸ **mode utilisateur** user mode.

modelage [mɔdlaʒ] **nm** [action] modelling *UK*, modeling *US*.

modelé [mɔdle] **nm 1.** [de visage] contours *pl* **2.** ART & GÉOGR relief.

modèle [mɔdɛl] ■ **nm 1.** [gén] model ▸ **dessiner d'après un modèle** ART to draw from life ▸ **prendre modèle sur qqch** to use sthg as a model ▸ **sur le modèle de** on the model of ▸ **modèle déposé** patented design ▸ **modèle réduit** scale model ▸ **modèle réduit d'avion** model aircraft
2. [exemplaire] model ▸ **c'est le modèle du parfait employé** he's a model employee ▸ **c'est un modèle de discrétion** he's a model of discretion ▸ **prendre qqn pour modèle** to model o.s. on sb.
■ **adj 1.** [parfait] model *(avant n)* ▸ **il a eu un comportement modèle** he was a model of good behaviour *UK ou* behavior *US*
2. [qui sert de référence] **: ferme/prison modèle** model farm/prison.

modeler [25] [mɔdle] **vt** to shape ▸ **modeler qqch sur qqch** *fig* to model sthg on sthg.
◆ ***se modeler*** **vp** *littéraire* **: se modeler sur** *fig* to model o.s. on.

modélisme [mɔdelism] **nm** modelling *UK ou* modeling *US (of scale models)*.

modem [mɔdɛm] **nm** TÉLÉCOM modem ▸ **modem d'appel** dial-up modem ▸ **modem fax** fax modem ▸ **modem RNIS** *ou* **Numéris** ISDN line.

modérateur, trice [mɔderatœr, tris] **adj** moderating.
◆ ***modérateur*** **nm 1.** [personne] moderator **2.** [mécanisme] regulator.

modération [mɔderasjɔ̃] **nf** moderation.

modéré, e [mɔdere] **adj & nm, f** moderate.

modérément [mɔderemɑ̃] **adv** in moderation, moderately.

modérer [18] [mɔdere] **vt** to moderate.
◆ ***se modérer*** **vp** to restrain o.s., to control o.s.

moderne [mɔdɛrn] ■ **nm : le moderne** modern things *pl*, (the) modern style.
■ **adj** modern / [mathématiques] new.

modernisation [mɔdɛrnizasjɔ̃] **nf** modernization.

moderniser [3] [mɔdɛrnize] **vt** to modernize.
◆ ***se moderniser*** **vp** to become (more) modern.

modernisme [mɔdɛrnism] **nm** [style] modernism.

modernité [mɔdɛrnite] **nf** modernity.

modeste [mɔdɛst] **adj** modest / [origine] humble.

modestement [mɔdɛstəmɑ̃] **adv** modestly.

modestie [mɔdɛsti] **nf** modesty ▸ **fausse modestie** false modesty.

modicité [mɔdisite] **nf** [de prix, salaire] lowness, moderateness.

modifiable [mɔdifjabl] **adj** modifiable, alterable.

modification [mɔdifikasjɔ̃] **nf** alteration, modification.

modifier [9] [mɔdifje] **vt** to alter, to modify.
◆ ***se modifier*** **vp** to alter.

modique [mɔdik] **adj** modest.

modiste [mɔdist] **nf** milliner.

modulation [mɔdylasjɔ̃] **nf** modulation.

module [mɔdyl] **nm** module.

moduler [3] [mɔdyle] **vt 1.** [air] to warble **2.** [structure] to adjust **3.** RADIO to modulate.

modus vivendi [mɔdysviɛ̃di] **nm inv** modus vivendi.

moelle [mwal] **nf** ANAT marrow ▸ **moelle osseuse** bone marrow ▸ **jusqu'à la moelle** *fig* to the core.
◆ ***moelle épinière*** **nf** spinal cord.

moelleux, euse [mwalø, øz] **adj 1.** [canapé, tapis] soft **2.** [fromage, vin] mellow.

moellon [mwalɔ̃] **nm** rubble stone.

mœurs [mœr(s)] **nfpl 1.** [morale] morals ▸ **c'est contraire aux bonnes mœurs** it goes against accepted standards of behaviour *UK ou* behavior *US* ▸ **elle a des mœurs vraiment bizarres** she behaves in a really odd way ▸ **la police/brigade des mœurs, les Mœurs** *fam* ≃ the vice squad **2.** [coutumes] customs, habits ▸ **c'est entré dans les mœurs** it's become part of everyday life ▸ **les mœurs de notre temps** the social mores of our time **3.** ZOOL behaviour *(U) UK*, behavior *(U) US*.

mohair [mɔɛr] **nm** mohair.

moi [mwa] ■ **pron pers 1.** [objet, après préposition, comparatif] me ▸ **aide-moi** help me ▸ **il me l'a dit, à moi** he told ME ▸ **c'est pour moi** it's for me ▸ **plus âgé que moi** older than me *ou* than I (am) ▸ **à moi!** [au secours] help! / [de jouer] it's my turn! / [d'essayer] let me have a go! ▸ **je suis contente de moi** I'm pleased with myself
2. [sujet] I ▸ **moi non plus, je n'en sais rien** I don't know anything about it either ▸ **moi qui vous parle, je l'ai vu de mes propres yeux** I'm telling you, I saw him with my very own eyes ▸ **qui est là? - (c'est) moi** who's there? - (it's) me ▸ **je l'ai vu hier - moi aussi** I saw him yesterday - me too ▸ **c'est moi qui lui ai dit de venir** I was the one who told him to come ▸ **moi, je n'ai rien dit!** I didn't say anything!
3. [emploi expressif] **: regardez-moi ça!** just look at that!
■ **nm : le moi** the ego, the self.
◆ ***moi-même*** **pron pers** myself ▸ **je préfère vérifier par moi-même** I prefer to check for myself ▸ **mon épouse et moi-même** my wife and I.

moignon [mwaɲɔ̃] **nm** stump.

moindre [mwɛ̃dr] ■ **adj** *(superlatif)* **: le/la moindre** the least ▸ *(avec négation)* the least *ou* slightest ▸ **les moindres**

détails the smallest details ▸ sans la moindre difficulté without the slightest problem ▸ c'est la moindre des choses it's the least I/you *etc* could do.
■ adj compar less / [prix] lower ▸ à un moindre degré to a lesser extent.

moine [mwan] nm monk.

moineau, x [mwano] nm sparrow.

moins [mwɛ̃] ■ adv 1. [quantité] less ▸ **moins de** less (than) ▸ **moins de lait** less milk ▸ **moins de gens** fewer people ▸ **moins de dix** less than ten ▸ **il est un peu moins de 10 heures** it's nearly 10 o'clock
2. [comparatif] : **moins (que)** less (than) ▸ **il n'en est pas moins vrai que...** it is nonetheless true that... ▸ **il est moins vieux que ton frère** he's not as old as your brother, he's younger than your brother ▸ **il vient moins souvent que Pierre** he doesn't come as often as Pierre, he comes less often than Pierre ▸ **bien moins grand que** much smaller than ▸ **c'est moins bien que l'an dernier** it's not as good a last year ▸ **moins il mange, moins il travaille** the less he eats, the less he works ▸ **moins tu parles, mieux ça vaut** the less you speak, the better
3. [superlatif] : **le moins** (the) least ▸ **le moins riche des hommes** the poorest man ▸ **il est le moins fort** he's the least strong ▸ **c'est lui qui vient le moins souvent** he comes (the) least often ▸ **c'est lui qui travaille le moins** he works (the) least ▸ **le moins possible** as little as possible ▸ **pas le moins du monde** not in the least.
■ prép 1. [gén] minus ▸ **dix moins huit font deux** ten minus eight is two, ten take away eight is two ▸ **il fait moins vingt** it's twenty below, it's minus twenty
2. [servant à indiquer l'heure] : **il est 3 heures moins le quart** it's quarter to *ou* of *US* 3 ▸ **il est moins dix** it's ten to, it's ten of *US*.
■ nm [signe] minus (sign)
▸▸ **le moins qu'on puisse dire, c'est que...** it's an understatement to say... ▸ **c'est le moins qu'on puisse dire!** that's the least you can say!
◆ ***à moins de*** loc prép : **à moins de battre le record** unless I/you *etc* beat the record.
◆ ***à moins que*** loc conj *(+ subjonctif)* unless ▸ **à moins que vous ne vouliez le faire vous-même...** unless you wanted to do it yourself...
◆ ***au moins*** loc adv at least ▸ **ça fait au moins un mois qu'on ne l'a pas vu** we haven't seen him for at least a month.
◆ ***de moins en moins*** loc adv less and less ▸ **de moins en moins souvent** less and less often.
◆ ***du moins*** loc adv at least ▸ **ils devaient venir samedi, c'est du moins ce qu'ils nous avaient dit** they were supposed to come on saturday, at least that's what they told us.
◆ ***en moins*** loc adv : **il a une dent en moins** he's missing *ou* minus a tooth ▸ **c'était le paradis, les anges en moins** it was heaven, minus the angels.
◆ ***en moins de*** loc prép in less than ▸ **en moins de rien** in less than no time.
◆ ***on ne peut moins*** loc adv far from ▸ **c'est on ne peut moins compliqué!** it couldn't be less complicated!
◆ ***pour le moins*** loc adv at (the very) least ▸ **il y a pour le moins une heure d'attente** there's an hour's wait at the very least.
◆ ***tout au moins*** loc adv at (the very) least.

moins-value [mwɛ̃valy] (pl **moins-values**) nf capital loss.

moire [mwar] nf [étoffe] moiré.

moiré, e [mware] adj 1. [tissu] watered 2. *littéraire* [reflet] shimmering.

mois [mwa] nm 1. [laps de temps] month 2. [salaire] (monthly) salary ▸ **le treizième mois** extra month's salary 3. *fam* [loyer] month's rent.

moise [mɔiz] nm wicker cradle.

moisi, e [mwazi] adj mouldy *UK*, moldy *US*.
◆ ***moisi*** nm mould *UK*, mold *US*.

moisir [32] [mwazir] vi 1. [pourrir] to go mouldy *UK ou* moldy *US* 2. *fig* [personne] to rot.

moisissure [mwazisyr] nf mould *UK*, mold *US*.

moisson [mwasɔ̃] nf 1. [récolte] harvest ▸ **faire la moisson *ou* les moissons** to harvest, to bring in the harvest 2. *fig* [d'idées, de projets] wealth.

moissonner [3] [mwasɔne] vt to harvest, to gather (in) / *fig* to collect, to gather.

moissonneur, euse [mwasɔnœr, øz] nm, f [personne] harvester.
◆ ***moissonneuse*** nf [machine] harvester, reaper.

moissonneuse-batteuse [mwasɔnøzbatøz] (pl **moissonneuses-batteuses**) nf combine (harvester).

moite [mwat] adj [peau, mains] moist, sweaty / [atmosphère] muggy.

moiteur [mwatœr] nf [de peau, mains] moistness / [d'atmosphère] mugginess.

moitié [mwatje] nf 1. [gén] half ▸ **à moitié vide** half-empty ▸ **faire qqch à moitié** to half-do sthg ▸ **la moitié du temps** half the time ▸ **à la moitié de qqch** halfway through sthg ▸ **faire moitié-moitié** to go halves 2. [épouse, époux] : **ma/ta moitié** *fam hum* my/your better half.

moka [mɔka] nm 1. [café] mocha (coffee) 2. [gâteau] coffee cake.

mol ➤ ***mou.***

molaire [mɔlɛr] nf molar.

Moldavie [mɔldavi] nf : **la Moldavie** Moldavia.

mole [mɔl] nf CHIM mole.

môle [mol] nm [quai] jetty.

moléculaire [mɔlekylɛr] adj molecular.

molécule [mɔlekyl] nf molecule.

moleskine [mɔlɛskin] nf imitation leather.

molester [3] [mɔlɛste] vt to manhandle.

molette [mɔlɛt] nf 1. [de réglage] toothed wheel 2. [outil] glasscutter.

mollasse [mɔlas] adj *fam* 1. [mou] flabby 2. *fig* [personne] lethargic.

mollasson, onne [mɔlasɔ̃, ɔn] nm, f *fam* (lazy) lump.

molle ➤ ***mou.***

mollement [mɔlmɑ̃] adv 1. [faiblement] weakly, feebly 2. *littéraire* [paresseusement] sluggishly, lethargically.

mollesse [mɔlɛs] nf 1. [de chose] softness 2. [de personne] lethargy.

mollet [mɔlɛ] ■ nm calf.
■ adj ➤ *œuf.*

molletière [mɔltjɛr] adj : **bande molletière** puttee.

molleton [mɔltɔ̃] nm flannelette / [pour table] felt.

mollir [32] [mɔlir] vi **1.** [physiquement, moralement] to give way **2.** [matière] to soften, to go soft **3.** [vent] to drop, to die down.

mollo [mɔlo] adv *fam* easy ▸ **y aller mollo** to go easy, to take it easy.

mollusque [mɔlysk] nm **1.** ZOOL mollusc *UK*, mollusk *US* **2.** *fam fig* [personne] (lazy) lump.

molosse [mɔlɔs] nm **1.** [chien] watchdog **2.** *fig & péj* [personne] hulking great brute.

môme [mom] *fam* ■ nmf [enfant] kid, youngster.
■ nf [jeune fille] chick, bird *UK*.

moment [mɔmɑ̃] nm **1.** [gén] moment ▸ **attend un moment!** wait a minute! ▸ **au moment de l'accident** at the time of the accident, when the accident happened ▸ **au moment de partir** just as we/you *etc* were leaving ▸ **au moment où** just as ▸ **juste au moment où le téléphone a sonné** just when *ou* as the phone rang ▸ **dans un moment** in a moment ▸ **d'un moment à l'autre, à tout moment** (at) any moment, any moment now ▸ **il peut téléphoner d'un moment à l'autre *ou* à tout moment** he may phone any minute now ▸ **pendant un bon moment** for quite some time, for quite a while ▸ **ne pas avoir un moment à soi** not to have a moment to oneself ▸ **à aucun moment il ne s'est plaint** at no time *ou* point did he complain ▸ **à un moment donné** at a given moment ▸ **à un moment donné, il a refusé** at one point he refused ▸ **à ce moment-là, tu aurais dû me le dire!** in that case *ou* if that was the case, you should have told me! ▸ **par moments** at times, now and then ▸ **sur le moment** at the time ▸ **sur le moment, ça n'a pas fait mal** it didn't hurt at the time ▸ **en ce moment** at the moment ▸ **pour le moment** for the moment ▸ **il eut un moment d'hésitation** he hesitated for a moment **2.** [durée] (short) time ▸ **avoir de bons moments avec qqn** to have (some) good times with sb ▸ **passer un mauvais moment** to have a bad time **3.** [occasion] time ▸ **ce n'est pas le moment (de faire qqch)** this is not the time (to do sthg) ▸ **c'est le moment d'intervenir** now's the time to speak up ▸ **c'est le moment ou jamais** it's now or never.
◆ ***du moment que*** loc prép since, as ▸ **du moment que je te le dis!** *fam* you can take my word for it!

momentané, e [mɔmɑ̃tane] adj temporary.

momentanément [mɔmɑ̃tanemɑ̃] adv temporarily.

momie [mɔmi] nf mummy.

mon, ma [mɔ̃, ma] (pl **mes** [me]) adj poss my.

monacal, e, aux [mɔnakal, o] adj monastic.

Monaco [mɔnako] npr : **(la principauté de) Monaco** (the principality of) Monaco.

monarchie [mɔnarʃi] nf monarchy ▸ **monarchie absolue/constitutionnelle** absolute/constitutional monarchy.

monarchique [mɔnarʃik] adj monarchical.

monarchiste [mɔnarʃist] nmf & adj monarchist.

monarque [mɔnark] nm monarch.

monastère [mɔnastɛr] nm monastery.

monastique [mɔnastik] adj monastic.

monceau, x [mɔ̃so] nm **1.** [tas] heap **2.** *fig* [de fautes, de bêtises] mass.

mondain, e [mɔ̃dɛ̃, ɛn] ■ adj **1.** [chronique, journaliste] society *(avant n)* **2.** *péj* [futile] frivolous, superficial.
■ nm, f socialite.

FAUX AMIS / FALSE FRIENDS
mondain

Mundane is not a translation of the French word *mondain*. Mundane is translated by *banal, ordinaire.*

mondanités [mɔ̃danite] nfpl **1.** [événements] society life *(U)* **2.** [paroles] small talk *(U)* / [comportements] formalities.

monde [mɔ̃d] nm **1.** [gén] world ▸ **dans le monde entier** all over the world ▸ **le/la plus... au monde, le/la plus... du monde** the most... in the world ▸ **le plus simplement/gentiment du monde** in the simplest/kindest possible way ▸ **je vous dérange? – pas le moins du monde!** am I interrupting? – not in the least! ▸ **pour rien au monde** not for the world, not for all the tea in China ▸ **mettre un enfant au monde** to bring a child into the world ▸ **venir au monde** to come into the world ▸ **en ce bas monde** RELIG in this world ▸ **l'autre monde** RELIG the other world ▸ **le quart monde** the Fourth World ▸ **fréquenter le beau *ou* grand monde** to mix with high society *ou* in society ▸ **femme du monde** socialite ▸ **homme du monde** man-about-town ▸ **le monde des affaires** the business world **2.** [gens] people *pl* ▸ **beaucoup/peu de monde** a lot of/not many people ▸ **il n'y avait pas grand monde au spectacle** there weren't many people at the show ▸ **j'ai du monde à dîner** *fam* I've got people coming for dinner ▸ **tout le monde** everyone, everybody
▸▸ **c'est un monde!** that's really the limit! ▸ **se faire un monde de qqch** to make too much of sthg ▸ **se moquer du monde** to have a nerve ▸ **noir de monde** packed with people ▸ **tromper son monde** not to be what one seems.
◆ ***Monde*** nm : **le Nouveau Monde** the New World.

mondial, e, aux [mɔ̃djal, o] adj world *(avant n)*.

mondialement [mɔ̃djalmɑ̃] adv throughout *ou* all over the world.

mondialisation [mɔ̃djalizasjɔ̃] nf globalization.

mondialiste [mɔ̃djalist] adj pro-globalization.

monégasque [mɔnegask] adj of/from Monaco.
◆ ***Monégasque*** nmf person from Monaco.

monétaire [mɔnetɛr] adj monetary.

monétarisme [mɔnetarism] nm monetarism.

mongol, e [mɔ̃gɔl] adj Mongolian.
◆ ***mongol*** nm [langue] Mongolian.
◆ ***Mongol, e*** nm, f Mongolian.

Mongolie [mɔ̃gɔli] nf : **la Mongolie** Mongolia ▸ **la Mongolie-Extérieure** Outer Mongolia ▸ **la Mongolie-Intérieure** Inner Mongolia.

mongolien, enne [mɔ̃gɔljɛ̃, ɛn] *vieilli* ■ adj mongol *(avant n) péj & vieilli.*
■ nm, f mongol *péj & vieilli.*

mongolisme [mɔ̃gɔlism] **nm** *vieilli* mongolism *péj* & *vieilli*.

mongoloïde [mɔ̃gɔlɔid] **adj** *vieilli* mongol *(avant n) péj* & *vieilli*.

moniteur, trice [mɔnitœr, tris] **nm, f 1.** [enseignant] instructor, coach ▸ **moniteur d'auto-école** driving instructor ▸ **moniteur de ski** ski instructor **2.** [de colonie de vacances] supervisor, leader.
◆ ***moniteur*** **nm** [appareil & INFORM] monitor.

monnaie [mɔnɛ] **nf 1.** [moyen de paiement] money ▸ **monnaie commune** common currency ▸ **monnaie faible** soft currency ▸ **fausse monnaie** forged currency, counterfeit money ▸ **monnaie fiduciaire** paper *ou* fiat money ▸ **monnaie d'échange** *fig* currency ▸ **c'est monnaie courante** *fig* it's commonplace, it's common practice **2.** [de pays] currency ▸ **monnaie unique** single currency **3.** [pièces] change ▸ **avoir de la monnaie** to have change ▸ **avoir la monnaie** to have the change ▸ **avoir la monnaie de 20 euros** to have change of *ou* for 20 euros ▸ **rendre la monnaie à qqn** to give sb his/her change ▸ **faire (de) la monnaie** to get (some) change ▸ **menue monnaie** small *ou* loose change.

monnayable [mɔnɛjabl] **adj** convertible (into cash) / *fig* valuable.

monnayer [11] [mɔnɛje] **vt 1.** [biens] to convert into cash **2.** *fig* [silence] to buy.

monochrome [mɔnɔkrom] **adj** monochrome, monochromatic.

monocle [mɔnɔkl] **nm** monocle.

monocoque [mɔnɔkɔk] **nm & adj** [bateau] monohull.

monocorde [mɔnɔkɔrd] **adj 1.** MUS single-stringed **2.** [monotone] monotonous.

monoculture [mɔnɔkyltyr] **nf** monoculture.

monogame [mɔnɔgam] **adj** monogamous.

monogamie [mɔnɔgami] **nf** monogamy.

monogramme [mɔnɔgram] **nm** monogram.

monolingue [mɔnɔlɛ̃g] **adj** monolingual.

monolithique [mɔnɔlitik] **adj** monolithic.

monologue [mɔnɔlɔg] **nm 1.** THÉÂTRE soliloquy **2.** [discours individuel] monologue ▸ **monologue intérieur** stream of consciousness, interior monologue.

monologuer [3] [mɔnɔlɔge] **vi 1.** THÉÂTRE to soliloquize **2.** *fig* & *péj* [parler] to talk away.

monôme [mɔnom] **nm 1.** MATH monomial **2.** *arg scol* [procession] ≃ rag day procession *UK*.

mononucléose [mɔnɔnykleoz] **nf : mononucléose infectieuse** glandular fever *UK*, mono *US*, (infectious) mononucleosis *US*.

monoparental, e, aux [mɔnɔparɑ̃tal, o] **adj** single-parent *(avant n)*, lone-parent *(avant n)*, one-parent *(avant n) UK*.

monophasé, e [mɔnɔfaze] **adj** ÉLECTR single-phase.
◆ ***monophasé*** **nm** single-phase current.

monoplace [mɔnɔplas] ■ **nm** single-seater.
■ **adj** single-seater *(avant n)*.

monopole [mɔnɔpɔl] **nm** monopoly ▸ **avoir le monopole de qqch** *litt* & *fig* to have a monopoly of *ou* on sthg ▸ **monopole d'État** state monopoly.

monopoliser [3] [mɔnɔpɔlize] **vt** to monopolize.

monorail [mɔnɔraj] ■ **nm** monorail.
■ **adj inv** monorail *(avant n)*.

monoski [mɔnɔski] **nm 1.** [objet] monoski **2.** SPORT monoskiing.

monospace [mɔnɔspas] **nm** minivan, people carrier *UK*.

monosyllabe [mɔnɔsilab] ■ **nm** monosyllable.
■ **adj** monosyllabic.

monosyllabique [mɔnɔsilabik] **adj** monosyllabic.

monothéisme [mɔnɔteism] **nm** monotheism.

monotone [mɔnɔtɔn] **adj** monotonous.

monotonie [mɔnɔtɔni] **nf** monotony ▸ **rompre la monotonie** to break the monotony.

monseigneur [mɔ̃sɛɲœr] (pl **messeigneurs** [mesɛɲœr]) **nm 1.** [titre - d'évêque, de duc] His Grace / [- de cardinal] His Eminence / [- de prince] His (Royal) Highness **2.** [formule d'adresse - à évêque, à duc] Your Grace / [- à cardinal] Your Eminence / [- à prince] Your (Royal) Highness.

monsieur [məsjø] (pl **messieurs** [mesjø]) **nm 1.** [titre] : **monsieur X** Mr X ▸ **bonjour monsieur** good morning / [dans hôtel, restaurant] good morning, sir ▸ **bonjour messieurs** good morning (gentlemen) ▸ **messieurs dames** ladies and gentlemen ▸ **Messieurs, un peu de silence s'il vous plaît!** [à des garçonnets] boys, please be quiet! / [à des jeunes gens] gentlemen, would you please be quiet ▸ **Monsieur le Ministre n'est pas là** the Minister is ou[t] ▸ **monsieur, j'ai fini mon addition!** (please) Sir, I've done my addition! **2.** [homme quelconque] gentleman ▸ **monsieur Tout le Monde** the man in the street, Joe Public *UK* Joe Blow *US* **3.** *fam* [en appellatif] **: et en plus, monsieu[r] exige des excuses!** His Lordship wants an apology as wel[l] does he?

monstre [mɔ̃str] **nm 1.** [gén] monster ▸ **monstre mari[n]** sea monster ▸ **monstre sacré** idol **2.** *(en apposition) fa[m]* [énorme] colossal.

monstrueusement [mɔ̃stryøzmɑ̃] **adv** [gros, laid] monstrously / [intelligent] prodigiously.

monstrueux, euse [mɔ̃stryø, øz] **adj 1.** [gén] mon[-]strous **2.** *fig* [erreur] terrible.

monstruosité [mɔ̃stryozite] **nf** monstrosity.

mont [mɔ̃] **nm 1.** *littéraire* [montagne] mountain ▸ **pa[r] monts et par vaux** *fig* up hill and down dale ▸ **prome[t]tre monts et merveilles** to promise the earth **2.** GÉOG Mount ▸ **le mont Blanc** Mont Blanc ▸ **le mont Cervin** th[e] Matterhorn **3.** ANAT **: mont de Vénus** mons veneris.

montage [mɔ̃taʒ] **nm 1.** [assemblage] assembly / [de b[i]jou] setting **2.** PHOTO photomontage **3.** CINÉ editi[ng] ▸ **montage définitif** final cut **4.** ÉLECTR wiring.

montagnard, e [mɔ̃taɲar, ard] ■ **adj** mounta[in] *(avant n)*.
■ **nm, f** mountain dweller.

montagne [mɔ̃taɲ] **nf 1.** [gén] mountain ▸ **les montagnes Rocheuses** the Rocky Mountains **2.** [région] **: la montagne** the mountains *pl* ▸ **à la montagne** in the mountains ▸ **en haute montagne** at high altitudes ▸ **faire de la haute montagne** to go mountain climbing
▸▸ **se faire une montagne de qqch** to make a great song and dance about sthg.
◆ ***montagnes russes*** **nfpl** roller coaster *sg*, big dipper *sg UK*.

montagneux, euse [mɔ̃taɲø, øz] **adj** mountainous.

montant, e [mɔ̃tɑ̃, ɑ̃t] **adj 1.** [mouvement] rising **2.** [vêtement] high-necked.
◆ ***montant*** **nm 1.** [pièce verticale] upright **2.** [somme] total (amount).

mont-blanc [mɔ̃blɑ̃] (pl **monts-blancs**) **nm** *pureed chestnuts with whipped cream.*

mont-de-piété [mɔ̃dpjete] (pl **monts-de-piété**) **nm** pawnshop.

monté, e [mɔ̃te] **adj 1.** [pourvu] **: être monté en qqch** to be well off for sthg ▸ **elle est bien montée en vaisselle** she's got a lot of crockery **2.** MIL mounted ▸ **troupes montées** mounted troops **3.** CULIN **: oeufs montés en neige** whisked egg whites.

monte-charge [mɔ̃tʃarʒ] **nm inv** goods lift *UK*, service elevator *US*.

montée [mɔ̃te] **nf 1.** [de montagne] climb, ascent ▸ **la montée jusqu'au chalet** the climb up *ou* the ascent to the chalet **2.** [de prix] rise ▸ **face à la montée en flèche des prix du pétrole** in the face of rocketing *ou* soaring oil prices **3.** [relief] slope, gradient.

Monténégro [mɔ̃tenegro] **nm : le Monténégro** Montenegro.

monte-plats [mɔ̃tpla] **nm inv** dumbwaiter.

monter [3] [mɔ̃te] ■ **vi** *(v aux : être)* **1.** [personne] to come/go up / [température, niveau] to rise / [route, avion] to climb ▸ **monter sur qqch** to climb onto sthg ▸ **monte par l'ascenseur** go up in *ou* use the lift ▸ **faire monter les prix** [surenchère] to send *ou* to put prices up / [marchand] to put up *ou* to increase prices ▸ **son plâtre monte jusqu'au genou** his leg is in a plaster cast up to the knee
2. [passager] to get on ▸ **monter dans un bus** to get on a bus ▸ **monter dans une voiture** to get into a car ▸ **monter sur un *ou* à bord d'un bateau** to board a ship
3. [cavalier] to ride ▸ **monter à cheval** to ride ▸ **monter à cheval sur qqch** *fig* to straddle sthg
4. [marée] to go/come in
▸▸ **monter à l'attaque *ou* à l'assaut** MIL to go onto the attack ▸ **monter en grade** to be promoted.
■ **vt** *(v aux : être)* **1.** [escalier, côte] to climb, to come/go up ▸ **monter la rue en courant** to run up the street ▸ **la voiture a du mal à monter la côte** the car has difficulty getting up the hill
2. [chauffage, son] to turn up
3. [valise] to take/bring up ▸ **je lui ai monté son journal** I took his newspaper up to him
4. [meuble] to assemble / COUT to assemble, to put *ou* sew together / [tente] to put up
5. CINÉ to edit, to cut (together)
6. [cheval] to mount
7. [dispositif] to assemble ▸ **il a monté un moteur plus puissant sur sa voiture** he has put a more powerful engine in his car
8. THÉÂTRE to put on
9. [société, club] to set up
10. CULIN to beat, to whisk (up) ▸ **monter des blancs en neige** to whisk egg whites
▸▸ **monter qqn contre qqn** to set sb against sb.
◆ ***se monter*** **vp 1.** [s'assembler] **: se monter facilement** to be easy to assemble
2. [atteindre] **: se monter à** to amount to, to add up to.

monteur, euse [mɔ̃tœr, øz] **nm, f 1.** TECHNOL fitter **2.** CINÉ editor.

Montevideo [mɔ̃tevideo] **npr** Montevideo.

monticule [mɔ̃tikyl] **nm** mound / *Québec* [baseball] pitcher's mound.

montre [mɔ̃tr] **nf** watch ▸ **montre à quartz** quartz watch ▸ **montre en main** to the minute, exactly ▸ **contre la montre** [sport] time-trialling *UK*, time-trialing *US* / [épreuve] time trial ▸ **une course contre la montre** *fig* a race against time.

Montréal [mɔ̃real] **npr** Montreal.

montre-bracelet [mɔ̃trəbraslɛ] (pl **montres-bracelets**) **nf** wristwatch.

montrer [3] [mɔ̃tre] **vt 1.** [gén] to show ▸ **montrer qqch à qqn** to show sb sthg, to show sthg to sb ▸ **il m'a montré son usine** he showed me (around) his factory ▸ **la brochure montre comment s'en servir** the booklet explains *ou* shows how to use it **2.** [désigner] to show, to point out ▸ **montrer la sortie** [de la tête] to nod towards the exit / [du doigt] to point to the exit / [de la main] to gesture towards the exit ▸ **montrer qqch du doigt** to point at *ou* to sthg.
◆ ***se montrer*** **vp 1.** [se faire voir] to appear ▸ **le voilà, ne te montre pas!** here he is; stay out of sight! **2.** *fig* [se présenter] to show o.s. ▸ **elle adore se montrer** she loves to be seen (in public) **3.** *fig* [se révéler] to prove (to be) ▸ **ce soir-là, il s'est montré odieux/charmant** he was obnoxious/charming that evening.

montreur, euse [mɔ̃trœr, øz] **nm, f : montreur de marionnettes** puppeteer.

monture [mɔ̃tyr] **nf 1.** [animal] mount **2.** [de lunettes] frame **3.** [de bijou] setting.

monument [mɔnymɑ̃] **nm 1.** [gén] **: monument (à)** monument (to) ▸ **monument aux morts** war memorial **2.** *fig & hum* [chef-d'œuvre] masterpiece.

monumental, e, aux [mɔnymɑ̃tal, o] **adj** monumental.

moquer [3] [mɔke] ◆ ***se moquer*** **vp : se moquer de** [plaisanter sur] to make fun of, to laugh at / [ne pas se soucier de] not to give a damn about ▸ **ne vous moquez pas!** don't mock!, don't laugh!

moquerie [mɔkri] **nf** mockery *(U)*, jibe.

moquette [mɔkɛt] **nf** wall-to-wall carpet, fitted carpet *UK*.

moqueur, euse [mɔkœr, øz] ■ **adj** mocking.
■ **nm, f** mocker.

moraine [mɔrɛn] **nf** moraine.

moral**, **e**, **aux [mɔral, o] **adj 1.** [éthique - conscience, jugement] moral ▸ **il n'a aucun sens moral** he has no sense of morality ▸ **se sentir dans l'obligation morale de faire qqch** to feel morally obliged *ou* a moral obligation to do sthg ▸ **prendre l'engagement moral de faire qqch** to be morally committed to do sthg **2.** [édifiant - auteur, conte, réflexion] moral ▸ **la fin de la pièce n'est pas très morale!** the end of the play is rather immoral! **3.** [spirituel - douleur] mental / [- soutien, victoire, résistance] moral.
◆ ***moral*** **nm 1.** [mental] **: au moral comme au physique** mentally as well as physically **2.** [état d'esprit] morale, spirits *pl* ▸ **avoir/ne pas avoir le moral** to be in good/bad spirits ▸ **j'ai le moral à zéro** *fam* I feel down in the dumps *ou* really low ▸ **remonter le moral à qqn** to cheer sb up ▸ **se remonter le moral** to cheer (o.s.) up.
◆ ***morale*** **nf 1.** [science] moral philosophy, morals *pl* **2.** [règle] morality **3.** [mœurs] morals *pl* **4.** [leçon] moral ▸ **faire la morale à qqn** to preach at *ou* lecture sb.

moralement [mɔralmɑ̃] **adv** morally.

moralisateur**, **trice [mɔralizatœr, tris] ■ **adj** moralizing.
■ **nm, f** moralizer.

moralisme [mɔralism] **nm** morality.

moraliste [mɔralist] ■ **nmf** moralist.
■ **adj** moralistic.

moralité [mɔralite] **nf 1.** [gén] morality **2.** [enseignement] morals *pl*.

moratoire [mɔratwar] **nm** moratorium.

morbide [mɔrbid] **adj** morbid.

morbidité [mɔrbidite] **nf** morbidity.

morceau**, **x [mɔrso] **nm 1.** [gén] piece ▸ **morceau de sucre** lump of sugar, sugar lump ▸ **sucre en morceaux** lump sugar ▸ **manger un morceau** *fam* to have a bite to eat ▸ **mettre en morceaux** to pull *ou* tear to pieces ▸ **cracher le morceau** *fam fig* to spill the beans ▸ **emporter le morceau** *fam* to carry it off ▸ **tomber en morceaux** to fall apart, to fall to pieces **2.** [de poème, de film] passage ▸ **un morceau de bravoure** a purple passage ▸ **cette scène est un véritable morceau d'anthologie** it's a truly memorable scene ▸ **(recueil de) morceaux choisis** (collection of) selected passages *ou* extracts.

morceler [24] [mɔrsəle] **vt** to break up, to split up.
◆ ***se morceler*** **vp** to break up.

morcellement [mɔrselmɑ̃] **nm** breaking up, splitting up.

mordant**, **e [mɔrdɑ̃, ɑ̃t] **adj** biting.
◆ ***mordant*** **nm** [vivacité] keenness, bite.

mordicus [mɔrdikys] **adv** *fam* stubbornly, stoutly.

mordiller [3] [mɔrdije] **vt** to nibble.

mordoré**, **e [mɔrdɔre] **adj** bronze.

mordre [76] [mɔrdr] ■ **vt 1.** [blesser] to bite ▸ **se faire mordre** to get bitten **2.** [dépasser] to go over ▸ **mordre la ligne** [saut en longueur] to cross the (take-off) board / [sur la route] to cross the white line **3.** *fig* [entamer, ronger] to eat into *ou* away.
■ **vi 1.** [saisir avec les dents] **: mordre à** to bite ▸ **ça ne mord pas beaucoup par ici** [à la pêche] the fish aren't biting much around here **2.** [croquer] **: mordre dans qqch** to bite into sthg **3.** SPORT **: mordre sur la ligne** to step over the line.
◆ ***se mordre*** **vpt : se mordre la langue** to bite one's tongue *litt* ▸ **il va s'en mordre les doigts** he'll be sorry he did it, he'll live to regret it.

mordu**, **e [mɔrdy] ■ **pp** ➤ ***mordre***.
■ **adj** [amoureux] hooked.
■ **nm, f : mordu de foot/ski** football/ski addict.

more = ***maure***.

moresque = ***mauresque***.

morfondre [75] [mɔrfɔ̃dr] ◆ ***se morfondre*** **vp** to mope.

morgue [mɔrg] **nf 1.** [attitude] pride **2.** [lieu] morgue.

moribond**, **e [mɔribɔ̃, ɔ̃d] ■ **adj** dying.
■ **nm, f** dying person.

morigéner [18] [mɔriʒene] **vt** *littéraire* to rebuke.

morille [mɔrij] **nf** morel.

mormon**, **e [mɔrmɔ̃, ɔn] **adj & nm, f** Mormon.

morne [mɔrn] **adj** [personne, visage] gloomy / [paysage, temps, ville] dismal, dreary.

Moroni [mɔrɔni] **npr** Moroni.

morose [mɔroz] **adj** gloomy.

morosité [mɔrozite] **nf** gloominess.

morphine [mɔrfin] **nf** morphine.

morphologie [mɔrfɔlɔʒi] **nf** morphology.

morphologique [mɔrfɔlɔʒik] **adj** morphological.

morpion [mɔrpjɔ̃] **nm 1.** *fam* MÉD crab **2.** *fam* [enfant] brat **3.** [jeu] ≃ noughts and crosses *(U) UK*, ≃ tick-tack-toe *US*.

mors [mɔr] **nm** bit ▸ **prendre le mors aux dents** to get the bit between one's teeth.

morse [mɔrs] **nm 1.** ZOOL walrus **2.** [code] Morse (code).

morsure [mɔrsyr] **nf** bite.

mort**, **e [mɔr, mɔrt] ■ **pp** ➤ ***mourir***.
■ **adj** dead ▸ **raide mort** stone dead ▸ **mort ou vif** dead or alive ▸ **mort de fatigue** *fig* dead tired ▸ **mort de peur** *fig* frightened to death ▸ **laisser qqn pour mort** to leave sb for dead.
■ **nm, f 1.** [cadavre] corpse, dead body **2.** [défunt] dead person ▸ **les morts vivants** the living dead ▸ **jour *ou* fête des morts** All Souls' Day.
◆ ***mort*** ■ **nm 1.** [victime] fatality ▸ **les émeutes ont fait 300 morts** 300 people died *ou* were killed in the rioting **2.** [partie de cartes] dummy.
■ **nf** *litt & fig* death ▸ **de mort** [silence] deathly ▸ **menace/pulsion de mort** death threat/wish ▸ **être en danger de mort** to be in mortal danger ▸ **condamner qqn à mort** DR to sentence sb to death ▸ **se donner la mort** to take one's own life, to commit suicide ▸ **frôler la mort** to have a brush with death ▸ **trouver la mort** to meet one's death, to die ▸ **jusqu'à ce que mort s'ensuive** to death ▸ **en vouloir à mort à qqn** to hate sb's guts ▸ **ils sont brouillés *ou* fâchés à mort** they're mortal enemies ▸ **frapper qqn à mort** to strike sb dead ▸ **mettre qqn à mort** to put sb to death

▸ **mort naturelle/violente** natural/violent death ▸ **la mort dans l'âme** sick at heart, with a heavy heart ▸ **pâle comme la mort** deathly pale.

mortadelle [mɔrtadɛl] **nf** mortadella.

mortalité [mɔrtalite] **nf** mortality, death rate ▸ **mortalité infantile** infant mortality.

mort-aux-rats [mɔrora] **nf inv** rat poison.

Morte ➤ ***mer***.

mortel, ***elle*** [mɔrtɛl] ■ **adj 1.** [humain] mortal **2.** [accident, maladie] fatal **3.** *fig* [ennuyeux] deadly (dull).
■ **nm, f** mortal.

mortellement [mɔrtɛlmɑ̃] **adv 1.** [à mort] fatally **2.** [extrêmement] mortally, deeply ▸ **s'ennuyer mortellement** to be bored to death.

morte-saison [mɔrtsɛzɔ̃] (pl **mortes-saisons**) **nf** off-season.

mortier [mɔrtje] **nm** mortar.

mortification [mɔrtifikasjɔ̃] **nf** mortification.

mortifier [9] [mɔrtifje] **vt** to mortify.

mort-né, ***e*** [mɔrne] (mpl **mort-nés**, fpl **mort-nées**) ■ **adj** [enfant] still-born / *fig* [projet] abortive.
■ **nm, f** still-born child.

mortuaire [mɔrtɥɛr] **adj** funeral *(avant n)*.

morue [mɔry] **nf 1.** ZOOL cod **2.** *injur* [prostituée] whore.

morve [mɔrv] **nf** snot.

morveux, ***euse*** [mɔrvø, øz] ■ **adj** runny-nosed, snotty.
■ **nm, f** *fam* brat.

mosaïque [mɔzaik] **nf** *litt* & *fig* mosaic.

Moscou [mɔsku] **npr** Moscow.

moscovite [mɔskɔvit] **adj** of/from Moscow, Muscovite.
◆ ***Moscovite*** **nmf** Muscovite.

mosquée [mɔske] **nf** mosque.

mot [mo] **nm 1.** [gén] word ▸ **avoir toujours le mot pour rire** to be always able to raise a laugh ▸ **chercher ses mots** to try to find *ou* to search for the right words ▸ **les mots me manquent** words fail me ▸ **au bas mot** at the lowest estimate ▸ **à mots couverts** in veiled terms ▸ **le fin mot de l'histoire** the real story ▸ **mot clé** key word ▸ **mot composé** compound (word) ▸ **mots croisés** crossword (puzzle) *sg* ▸ **mot d'esprit** witty remark ▸ **mot d'excuse** SCOL note from one's parents ▸ **mot de la fin** concluding message, closing words ▸ **gros mot** swearword ▸ **mot d'ordre** watchword ▸ **mot d'ordre de grève** call for strike action ▸ **mot à mot, mot pour mot** word for word ▸ **faire du mot à mot** to translate word for word ▸ **c'est ce qu'elle a dit, mot pour mot** those were her very words, that's what she said, word for word ▸ **en un mot** in a word ▸ **avoir son mot à dire** to have one's say ▸ **avoir des mots avec qqn** to have words with sb ▸ **avoir le dernier mot** to have the last word ▸ **avoir deux mots à dire à qqn** *fam* to give sb a piece of one's mind ▸ **se donner** *ou* **se passer le mot** to pass the word around ▸ **ne pas mâcher ses mots** not to mince one's words ▸ **prendre qqn au mot** to take sb at his/her word ▸ **en toucher un mot à qqn** *fam* to have a word with sb **2.** [message] note, message.
◆ ***mot de passe*** **nm** password ▸ **protégé par un mot de passe** INFORM password-protected.

motard [mɔtar] **nm 1.** [motocycliste] motorcyclist **2.** [policier] motorcycle policeman.

motel [mɔtɛl] **nm** motel.

moteur, ***trice*** [mɔtœr, tris] **adj 1.** [force, énergie] driving *(avant n)* ▸ **à quatre roues motrices** AUTO with four-wheel drive **2.** [muscles, nerfs] motor *(avant n)*.
◆ ***moteur*** **nm** TECHNOL motor, engine / *fig* driving force ▸ **moteur électrique** electric motor ▸ **moteur à explosion** combustion engine ▸ **moteur à injection** fuel-injection engine ▸ **moteur à réaction** jet engine ▸ **moteur de recherche** INFORM search engine.
◆ ***motrice*** **nf** RAIL locomotive (engine).

motif [mɔtif] **nm 1.** [raison] motive, grounds *pl* **2.** [dessin, impression] motif.

motion [mɔsjɔ̃] **nf** POLIT motion ▸ **motion de censure** censure motion.

motivant, ***e*** [mɔtivɑ̃, ɑ̃t] **adj** motivating.

motivation [mɔtivasjɔ̃] **nf** motivation ▸ **motivation par le profit** profit motive.

motiver [3] [mɔtive] **vt 1.** [stimuler] to motivate **2.** [justifier] to justify.

moto [mɔto] **nf** motorcycle, motorbike *UK*.

motocross [mɔtɔkrɔs] **nm** motocross.

motoculteur [mɔtɔkyltœr] **nm** ≃ Rotavator® *UK*, ≃ rototiller® *US*.

motocyclette [mɔtɔsiklɛt] **nf** motorcycle, motorbike *UK*.

motocyclisme [mɔtɔsiklism] **nm** motorcyle racing.

motocycliste [mɔtɔsiklist] **nmf** motorcyclist.

motomarine [mɔtɔmarin] **nf** *Québec* jet ski, aquaskooter *US*.

motoneige [mɔtɔnɛʒ] **nf** *Québec* snowmobile.

motorisé, ***e*** [mɔtɔrize] **adj** motorized ▸ **être motorisé** *fam* to have a car, to have wheels.

motrice ➤ ***moteur***.

motricité [mɔtrisite] **nf** motor functions *pl*.

motte [mɔt] **nf : motte (de terre)** clod, lump of earth ▸ **motte de beurre** slab of butter.

motus [mɔtys] **interj** not a word! ▸ **motus et bouche cousue!** mum's the word!

mou, ***molle*** [mu, mɔl] **adj** (**mol** *devant voyelle ou 'h' muet*) **1.** [gén] soft **2.** [faible] weak **3.** [résistance, protestation] half-hearted **4.** *fam* [de caractère] wet, wimpy.
◆ ***mou*** **nm 1.** *fam* [personne] wimp **2.** [de corde] **: avoir du mou** to be slack **3.** [abats] lungs *pl*, lights *pl*.

mouchard, ***e*** [muʃar, ard] **nm, f** *fam* [personne] sneak.
◆ ***mouchard*** **nm** *fam* [dans camion, train] spy in the cab.

moucharder [3] [muʃarde] **vi** *fam* to sneak.

mouche [muʃ] **nf 1.** ZOOL fly ▸ **mouche tsé-tsé** tsetse fly ▸ **fine mouche** *fig* shrewd individual **2.** [accessoire féminin] beauty spot
▸▸ **faire mouche** to hit the bull's eye.

moucher [3] [muʃe] **vt 1.** [nez] to wipe ▸ **moucher un enfant** to wipe a child's nose **2.** [chandelle] to snuff out **3.** *fam fig* [personne] **: moucher qqn** to put sb in his/her place.
◆ ***se moucher*** **vp** to blow *ou* wipe one's nose.

moucheron [muʃrɔ̃] **nm** [insecte] gnat.

moucheté, ***e*** [muʃte] **adj 1.** [laine] flecked **2.** [animal] spotted, speckled.

mouchoir [muʃwar] **nm** handkerchief ▸ **mouchoir en papier** tissue, paper handkerchief *UK* ▸ **grand comme un mouchoir de poche** *fig* no bigger than a pocket handkerchief.

moudre [85] [mudr] **vt** to grind.

mouds ➤ ***moudre***.

moue [mu] **nf** pout ▸ **faire la moue** to pull a face.

mouette [mwɛt] **nf** seagull.

moufle [mufl] **nf** mitten.

mouflet, ***ette*** [muflɛ, ɛt] **nm, f** *fam* kid, brat.

mouflon [muflɔ̃] **nm** wild sheep.

mouillage [mujaʒ] **nm 1.** [coupage] watering (down) **2.** [NAUT - emplacement] anchorage, moorings *pl* / [- manœuvre] anchoring, mooring.

mouillé, ***e*** [muje] **adj** wet.

mouiller [3] [muje] ■ **vt 1.** [personne, objet] to wet ▸ **se faire mouiller** to get wet *ou* soaked **2.** [vin, lait] to water down / CULIN to add liquid to **3.** NAUT **: mouiller l'ancre** to drop anchor **4.** LING to palatalize **5.** *fam fig* [compromettre] to involve.
■ **vi** NAUT to anchor.
◆ ***se mouiller*** **vp 1.** [se tremper] to get wet **2.** *fam fig* [prendre des risques] to stick one's neck out.

mouillette [mujɛt] **nf** finger of bread, soldier *UK*.

mouise [mwiz] **nf : être dans la mouise** *fam* to be broke.

moulage [mulaʒ] **nm 1.** [action] moulding *UK*, molding *US*, casting **2.** [objet] cast.

moulant, ***e*** [mulɑ̃, ɑ̃t] **adj** close-fitting.

moule [mul] ■ **nm** mould *UK*, mold *US* ▸ **moule à gâteau** cake tin *UK ou* pan *US* ▸ **moule à gaufre** waffle-iron ▸ **moule à tarte** flan dish.
■ **nf** ZOOL mussel ▸ **moules marinières** CULIN *mussels cooked in white wine.*

mouler [3] [mule] **vt 1.** [objet] to mould *UK*, to mold *US* **2.** [forme] to make a cast of **3.** [corps] to hug.

moulin [mulɛ̃] **nm** mill ▸ **moulin à café** coffee mill ▸ **moulin à eau** watermill ▸ **moulin à paroles** *fig* chatterbox ▸ **moulin à poivre** peppermill ▸ **moulin à prières** RELIG prayer wheel ▸ **moulin à scie** *Québec* sawmill ▸ **moulin à vent** windmill ▸ **on entre chez elle comme dans un moulin** her door's always open.

mouliner [3] [muline] **vt** [aliments] to put through a food mill.

moulinet [mulinɛ] **nm 1.** [à la pêche] reel **2.** [mouvement] **: faire des moulinets** to whirl one's arms around.

Moulinette® [mulinɛt] **nf** food mill ▸ **passer qqn à la Moulinette** *fam fig* to tear sb to pieces.

moult [mult] **adv** *vieilli* many.

moulu, ***e*** [muly] **adj 1.** [en poudre] ground **2.** *fig* [brisé] **: être moulu (de fatigue)** to be worn out.

moulure [mulyr] **nf** moulding *UK*, molding *US*.

mourais, ***mourions*** ➤ ***mourir***.

mourant, ***e*** [murɑ̃, ɑ̃t] ■ **adj 1.** [moribond] dying **2.** *fig* [voix] faint.
■ **nm, f** dying person.

mourir [42] [murir] **vi 1.** [personne] to die ▸ **mourir d'envie de faire qqch** to be dying to do sthg ▸ **mourir de froid/soif** to be dying of cold/thirst ▸ **mourir de peur** to be scared to death ▸ **s'ennuyer à mourir** to be bored to death ▸ **c'est à mourir de rire** it's a scream ▸ **mourir de mort naturelle** *ou* **de sa belle mort** to die a natural death ▸ **mourir sur le coup** to die instantly ▸ **plus rapide/bête que lui, tu meurs!** *fam* you'd be hard put to be quicker/more stupid than him! ▸ **tu n'en mourras pas!** *fam* it won't kill you! **2.** [civilisation] to die out **3.** [feu] to die down.

mouroir [murwar] **nm** *péj* old people's home.

mouron [murɔ̃] **nm** BOT pimpernel ▸ **se faire du mouron** *fam fig* to worry o.s. sick.

mourrai, ***mourras*** ➤ ***mourir***.

mousquetaire [muskətɛr] **nm** musketeer.

moussant, ***e*** [musɑ̃, ɑ̃t] **adj** foaming.

mousse [mus] ■ **nf 1.** BOT moss **2.** [substance] foam ▸ **mousse carbonique** foam *(for extinguishing fires)* ▸ **mousse à raser** shaving foam **3.** CULIN mousse ▸ **mousse au chocolat** chocolate mousse **4.** [matière plastique] foam rubber.
■ **nm** NAUT cabin boy.

mousseline [muslin] ■ **nf** muslin.
■ **adj inv** *lightened with cream or milk.*

mousser [3] [muse] **vi** to foam, to lather ▸ **se faire mousser** *fam fig* to blow one's own trumpet.

mousseux, ***euse*** [musø, øz] **adj 1.** [shampooing] foaming, frothy **2.** [vin, cidre] sparkling.
◆ ***mousseux*** **nm** sparkling wine.

mousson [musɔ̃] **nf** monsoon.

moussu, ***e*** [musy] **adj** mossy, moss-covered.

moustache [mustaʃ] **nf** moustache, mustache *US*.
◆ ***moustaches*** **nfpl** [d'animal] whiskers.

moustachu, ***e*** [mustaʃy] **adj** with a moustache *ou* mustache *US*.
◆ ***moustachu*** **nm** *man with a moustache.*

moustiquaire [mustikɛr] **nf** mosquito net.

moustique [mustik] **nm** mosquito.

moutard [mutar] **nm** *fam* kid.

moutarde [mutard] ■ **nf** mustard ▸ **la moutarde m[e] monte au nez** *fig* I'm losing my temper.
■ **adj inv** mustard *(avant n).*

mouton [mutɔ̃] **nm 1.** *fig* & ZOOL sheep **2.** [viande] mu[t]ton **3.** *fam* [poussière] piece of fluff, fluff *(U)*
▸▸ **revenons à nos moutons** let's get back to the subje[ct] in hand.
◆ ***moutons*** **nmpl** [vagues] white horses *UK*, whit[e]caps *US*.

mouture [mutyr] **nf** **1.** [de céréales, de café] grinding **2.** [de thème, d'œuvre] rehash.

mouvance [muvɑ̃s] **nf** [domaine] sphere of influence.

mouvant, e [muvɑ̃, ɑ̃t] **adj** **1.** [terrain] unstable **2.** [situation] uncertain.

mouvement [muvmɑ̃] **nm** **1.** [gén] movement ▸ **avoir un mouvement de recul** to start (back) ▸ **en mouvement** on the move ▸ **le balancier se mit en mouvement** the pendulum started moving ▸ **le cortège se mit en mouvement** the procession started *ou* set off ▸ **faux mouvement** clumsy *ou* awkward movement ▸ **faire un faux mouvement** to pull something ▸ **mouvement alternatif** TECHNOL reciprocating movement ▸ **mouvements de capitaux** *ou* **de fonds** movement of capital ▸ **mouvement de contestation** protest movement ▸ **mouvement d'horlogerie** movement, mechanism *(of a clock or watch)* ▸ **mouvement social** industrial action ▸ **mouvement de terrain** undulation ▸ **mouvements de troupes** troop movements **2.** [de colère, d'indignation] burst, fit ▸ **mouvement d'humeur** fit of bad temper.

mouvementé, e [muvmɑ̃te] **adj** **1.** [terrain] rough **2.** [réunion, soirée] eventful.

mouvoir [54] [muvwar] **vt** to move.
◆ ***se mouvoir*** **vp** to move.

moyen, enne [mwajɛ̃, ɛn] **adj** **1.** [intermédiaire] medium **2.** [médiocre, courant] average.
◆ ***moyen*** **nm** means *sg*, way ▸ **par tous les moyens** by any means possible ▸ **y a-t-il moyen de...?** is there any way of...? ▸ **moyen de communication** means of communication ▸ **moyen d'expression** means of expression ▸ **moyen de locomotion** *ou* **transport** means of transport ▸ **employer les grands moyens** to resort to extreme measures.
◆ ***moyenne*** **nf** average ▸ **en moyenne** on average ▸ **la moyenne** SCOL the passmark ▸ **la moyenne d'âge** the average age.
◆ ***moyens*** **nmpl** **1.** [ressources] means ▸ **avoir les moyens** to be comfortably off ▸ **avoir les moyens de faire qqch** to have the means to do sthg ▸ **avec les moyens du bord** with the means at one's disposal **2.** [capacités] powers, ability ▸ **faire qqch par ses propres moyens** to do sthg on one's own ▸ **perdre tous ses moyens** to panic.
◆ ***au moyen de*** **loc prép** by means of.

Moyen Âge [mwajɛnaʒ] **nm : le Moyen Âge** the Middle Ages *pl*.

moyenâgeux, euse [mwajɛnaʒø, øz] **adj** medieval.

moyen-courrier [mwajɛ̃kurje] (pl **moyens-courriers**) ■ **nm** medium-haul aircraft.
■ **adj** medium-haul *(avant n)*.

moyennant [mwajɛnɑ̃] **prép** for, in return for.

moyennement [mwajɛnmɑ̃] **adv** moderately, fairly.

Moyen-Orient [mwajɛnɔrjɑ̃] **nm : le Moyen-Orient** the Middle East ▸ **au Moyen-Orient** in the Middle East.

moyen-oriental, e [mwayɛnɔrjɑ̃tal] **adj** Middle Eastern.

moyeu, x [mwajø] **nm** hub.

mozambicain, e [mɔzɑ̃bikɛ̃, ɛn] **adj** Mozambican.
◆ ***Mozambicain, e*** **nm, f** Mozambican.

Mozambique [mɔzɑ̃bik] **nm : le Mozambique** Mozambique ▸ **au Mozambique** in Mozambique.

MRAP [mrap] (abr de ***Mouvement contre le racisme, l'antisémitisme et pour la paix***) **nm** *pacifist anti-racist organization.*

MRG (abr de ***Mouvement des radicaux de gauche***) **nm** *centre-left political party.*

ms (abr écrite de ***manuscrit***) ms.

MSF (abr de ***Médecins sans frontières***) **nmpl** *organization providing medical aid to victims of war and disasters, especially in the Third World* Doctors Without Borders *US*.

MST **nf** **1.** (abr de ***maladie sexuellement transmissible***) STD **2.** (abr de ***maîtrise de sciences et techniques***) *masters degree in science and technology.*

MT (abr écrite de ***moyenne tension***) MT.

mû, mue [my] **pp** ➤ ***mouvoir***.

mucosité [mykozite] **nf** mucus *(U)*.

mucus [mykys] **nm** mucus *(U)*.

mue [my] **nf** **1.** [de pelage] moulting *UK*, molting *US* **2.** [de serpent] skin, slough **3.** [de voix] breaking.

muer [7] [mɥe] **vi** **1.** [mammifère] to moult *UK*, to molt *US* **2.** [serpent] to slough its skin **3.** [voix] to break / [jeune homme] **: il mue** his voice is breaking.
◆ ***se muer*** **vp** *littéraire* **: se muer en** to turn into.

muesli [mysli] **nm** muesli.

muet, muette [mɥɛ, ɛt] ■ **adj** **1.** MÉD dumb **2.** [silencieux] silent ▸ **muet d'admiration/d'étonnement** speechless with admiration/surprise **3.** LING silent, mute.
■ **nm, f** dumb person, mute.
◆ ***muet*** **nm : le muet** CINÉ silent films *pl UK ou* movies *US*.

muezzin [mɥɛdzin] **nm** muezzin.

mufle [myfl] **nm** **1.** [d'animal] muzzle, snout **2.** *fig* [goujat] lout.

muflerie [myfləri] **nf** loutishness.

mufti, muphti [myfti] **nm** mufti.

mugir [32] [myʒir] **vi** **1.** [vache] to moo **2.** [vent, sirène] to howl.

mugissement [myʒismɑ̃] **nm** **1.** [de vache] mooing **2.** [de vent, sirène] howling.

muguet [mygɛ] **nm** **1.** [fleur] lily of the valley **2.** MÉD thrush.

mulâtre, mulâtresse [mylatr, trɛs] **nm, f** mulatto *injur*.
◆ ***mulâtre*** **adj** mulatto *injur*.

mule [myl] **nf** mule.

mulet [mylɛ] **nm** **1.** [âne] mule **2.** [poisson] mullet.

muletier, ère [myltje, ɛr] **adj** mule *(avant n)*.
◆ ***muletier*** **nm** muleteer.

mulot [mylo] **nm** field mouse.

multicolore [myltikɔlɔr] **adj** multicoloured *UK*, multicolored *US*.

multicoque [myltikɔk] ■ **adj : (bateau) multicoque** multihull *ou* multihulled boat.
■ **nm** multihull.

multiculturel**, **elle [myltikyltyrɛl] **adj** multicultural.

multifonction [myltifɔ̃ksjɔ̃] **adj inv** multifunction.

multiforme [myltifɔrm] **adj** multiform.

multilatéral**, **e**, **aux [myltilateral, o] **adj** multilateral.

multimedia [myltimedja] **adj** INFORM multimedia.

multimillionnaire [myltimiljɔnɛr] **nmf & adj** multimillionaire.

multinational**, **e**, **aux [myltinasjɔnal, o] **adj** multinational.
◆ ***multinationale*** **nf** multinational (company).

multiplateforme [myltiplatfɔrm] **nf** cross-platform.

multiple [myltipl] ■ **nm** multiple.
■ **adj 1.** [nombreux] multiple, numerous **2.** [divers] many, various.

multiplication [myltiplikasjɔ̃] **nf** multiplication.

multiplicité [myltiplisite] **nf** multiplicity.

multiplier [10] [myltiplije] **vt 1.** [accroître] to increase **2.** MATH to multiply ▸ **X multiplié par Y égale Z** X multiplied by *ou* times Y equals Z.
◆ ***se multiplier*** **vp** to multiply.

multipropriété [myltiprɔprijete] **nf** timeshare.

multiracial**, **e**, **aux [myltirasjal, o] **adj** multiracial.

multirisque [myltirisk] **adj** comprehensive.

multitude [myltityd] **nf : multitude (de)** multitude (of).

municipal**, **e**, **aux [mynisipal, o] **adj** municipal.
◆ ***municipales*** **nfpl : les municipales** the local government elections.

municipalité [mynisipalite] **nf 1.** [commune] municipality **2.** [conseil] town council *UK*, city council *US*.

munir [32] [mynir] **vt : munir qqn/qqch de** to equip sb/sthg with.
◆ ***se munir*** **vp : se munir de** to equip o.s. with.

munitions [mynisjɔ̃] **nfpl** ammunition *(U)*, munitions.

munster [mœ̃stɛr] **nm** Munster *strong semi-hard cheese.*

muphti = ***mufti***.

muqueuse [mykøz] **nf** mucous membrane.

mur [myr] **nm 1.** [gén] wall ▸ **mur antibruit** soundproof wall ▸ **mur mitoyen** party wall ▸ **raser les murs** to hug the walls / *fig* to tread warily **2.** *fig* [obstacle] barrier, brick wall ▸ **mur du son** AÉRON sound barrier.

mûr**, **mûre [myr] **adj** ripe / [personne] mature ▸ **après mûre réflexion** *fig* after careful consideration.
◆ ***mûre*** **nf 1.** [de mûrier] mulberry **2.** [de ronce] blackberry, bramble.

muraille [myraj] **nf** wall.

mural**, **e**, **aux [myral, o] **adj** wall *(avant n).*

mûrement [myrmɑ̃] **adv : après avoir mûrement réfléchi** after careful consideration.

murène [myrɛn] **nf** moray eel.

murer [3] [myre] **vt 1.** [boucher] to wall up, to block up **2.** [enfermer] to wall in.
◆ ***se murer*** **vp** to shut o.s. up *ou* away ▸ **se murer dans** *fig* to retreat into.

muret [myrɛ] **nm** low wall.

mûrier [myrje] **nm 1.** [arbre] mulberry tree **2.** [ronce] blackberry bush, bramble bush.

mûrir [32] [myrir] **vi 1.** [fruits, légumes] to ripen **2.** *fig* [idée, projet] to develop **3.** [personne] to mature.

murmure [myrmyr] **nm** murmur.

murmurer [3] [myrmyre] **vt & vi** to murmur.

musaraigne [myzarɛɲ] **nf** shrew.

musarder [3] [myzarde] **vi** *fam* to dawdle.

musc [mysk] **nm** musk.

muscade [myskad] **nf** nutmeg.

muscadet [myskadɛ] **nm** Muscadet *dry white wine.*

muscat [myska] **nm 1.** [raisin] muscat grape **2.** [vin] Muscat, Muscatel *sweet wine.*

muscle [myskl] **nm** muscle ▸ **muscle extenseur** extensor muscle.

musclé**, **e [myskle] **adj 1.** [personne] muscular **2.** *fig* [mesure, décision] forceful.

muscler [3] [myskle] **vt : muscler son corps** to build up one's muscles.
◆ ***se muscler*** **vp** to build up one's muscles.

musculaire [myskylɛr] **adj** muscular.

musculation [myskylasjɔ̃] **nf : faire de la musculation** to do muscle-building exercises.

musculature [myskylatyr] **nf** musculature.

muse [myz] **nf** muse.

museau [myzo] **nm 1.** [d'animal] muzzle, snout **2.** *fam* [de personne] face.

musée [myze] **nm** museum / [d'art] art gallery.

museler [24] [myzle] **vt** *litt & fig* to muzzle.

muselière [myzəljɛr] **nf** muzzle.

musette [myzɛt] ■ **nf** knapsack / [d'écolier] satchel.
■ **nm : le musette** *dance music played on the accordion.*

muséum [myzeɔm] **nm** museum.

musical**, **e**, **aux [myzikal, o] **adj 1.** [son] musical **2.** [émission, critique] music *(avant n).*

music-hall [myzikol] (pl **music-halls**) **nm** music hall *UK*, vaudeville *US*.

musicien**, **enne [myzisjɛ̃, ɛn] ■ **adj** musical.
■ **nm, f** musician.

musicographie [myzikɔgrafi] **nf** musicography.

musicologue [myzikɔlɔg] **nmf** musicologist.

musique [myzik] **nf** music ▸ **musique de chambre** chamber music ▸ **musique de film** film *UK ou* movie *US* score ▸ **connaître la musique** *fam fig* to know the score.

musqué**, **e [myske] **adj 1.** [parfum] musky **2.** [animal] **rat musqué** muskrat.

must [mœst] **nm** *fam* must.

musulman**, **e [myzylmɑ̃, an] **adj & nm, f** Muslim.

mutant**, **e [mytɑ̃, ɑ̃t] **adj** & **nm, f** mutant.

mutation [mytasjɔ̃] **nf 1.** BIOL mutation **2.** *fig* [changement] transformation ▸ **en pleine mutation** undergoing a (complete) transformation **3.** [de fonctionnaire] transfer.

muter [3] [myte] **vt** to transfer.

mutilation [mytilasjɔ̃] **nf** mutilation.

mutilé**, **e [mytile] **nm, f** disabled person.

mutiler [3] [mytile] **vt** to mutilate ▸ **il a été mutilé du bras droit** he lost his right arm.

mutin**, **e [mytɛ̃, in] **adj** *littéraire* impish.
◆ ***mutin*** **nm** rebel / MIL & NAUT mutineer.

mutiner [3] [mytine] ◆ ***se mutiner*** **vp** to rebel / MIL & NAUT to mutiny.

mutinerie [mytinri] **nf** rebellion / MIL & NAUT mutiny.

mutisme [mytism] **nm** silence.

mutualiste [mytɥalist] ■ **nmf** mutualist.
■ **adj : société mutualiste** mutual insurance company.

mutualité [mytɥalite] **nf** [assurance] mutual insurance.

mutuel**, **elle [mytɥɛl] **adj** mutual.
◆ ***mutuelle*** **nf** mutual insurance company.

CULTURE

Mutuelle

Every employed French citizen benefits from national health insurance, which covers some of the cost of doctor visits and prescriptions. Most people also buy insurance from an **organisme de mutuelle** to make up some or all of their remaining health care costs. As is the case in national health insurance, spouses and children can be beneficiaries of **mutuelle** plans.

mutuellement [mytɥɛlmɑ̃] **adv** mutually.

mycose [mikoz] **nf** mycosis, fungal infection.

myocarde [mjɔkard] **nm** myocardium.

myopathie [mjɔpati] **nf** myopathy.

myope [mjɔp] ■ **nmf** shortsighted *UK* ***ou*** nearsighted ***US*** person.
■ **adj** shortsighted *UK*, nearsighted *US*, myopic.

myopie [mjɔpi] **nf** shortsightedness *UK*, nearsightedness *US*, myopia.

myosotis [mjozɔtis] **nm** forget-me-not.

myriade [mirjad] **nf : une myriade de** a myriad of.

myrtille [mirtij] **nf** blueberry, bilberry.

mystère [mistɛr] **nm 1.** [gén] mystery **2.** CULIN *ice cream covered in meringue and flaked almonds.*

mystérieusement [misterjøzmɑ̃] **adv** mysteriously.

mystérieux**, **euse [misterjø, øz] **adj** mysterious.

mysticisme [mistisism] **nm** mysticism.

mystification [mistifikasjɔ̃] **nf** [tromperie] hoax, practical joke.

mystifier [9] [mistifje] **vt** [duper] to take in.

mystique [mistik] ■ **nmf** mystic.
■ **adj** mystic, mystical.

mythe [mit] **nm** myth.

mythifier [9] [mitifje] **vt** to mythicize.

mythique [mitik] **adj** mythical.

mytho [mito] **adj** *fam* **: il est complètement mytho** you can't believe anything he says.

mythologie [mitɔlɔʒi] **nf** mythology.

mythologique [mitɔlɔʒik] **adj** mythological.

mythomane [mitɔman] **nmf** pathological liar.

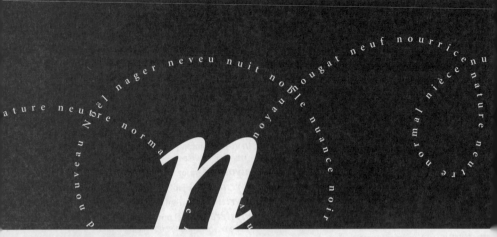

n, ***N*** [ɛn] **nm inv** [lettre] n, N.

◆ ***N*** **1.** (abr écrite de ***newton***) N **2.** (abr écrite de ***nord***) N.

n' ➤ ***ne***.

n^o^ (abr écrite de ***numéro***) no.

nabot, ***e*** [nabo, ɔt] **nm, f** *péj* midget.

nac [nak] (abr de ***nouvel animal de compagnie***) **nm** *wild animal kept as a pet.*

nacelle [nasɛl] **nf** [de montgolfière] basket.

nacre [nakr] **nf** mother-of-pearl.

nacré, ***e*** [nakre] **adj** pearly.

nage [naʒ] **nf** [natation] swimming ▸ **nage indienne** side stroke ▸ **nage papillon** butterfly (stroke) ▸ **à la nage** CULIN *poached in wine and herbs* ▸ **traverser à la nage** to swim across

▸▸ **en nage** bathed in sweat.

nageoire [naʒwar] **nf** fin.

nager [17] [naʒe] ■ **vi 1.** [se baigner] to swim **2.** [flotter] to float **3.** *fig* [dans vêtement] **: nager dans** to be lost in ▸ **nager dans la joie** to be incredibly happy.

■ **vt** to swim.

nageur, ***euse*** [naʒœr, øz] **nm, f** swimmer.

naguère [nagɛr] **adv** *littéraire* a short time ago.

naïade [najad] **nf** water nymph, naiad.

naïf, ***naïve*** [naif, iv] ■ **adj 1.** [ingénu, art] naive **2.** *péj* [crédule] gullible.

■ **nm, f 1.** *péj* [niais] fool **2.** [peintre] naive painter.

nain, ***e*** [nɛ̃, nɛn] ■ **adj** dwarf *(avant n).*

■ **nm, f** dwarf ▸ **nain de jardin** garden gnome.

Nairobi [nɛrɔbi] **npr** Nairobi.

naissais, ***naissions*** ➤ ***naître***.

naissance [nɛsɑ̃s] **nf 1.** [de personne] birth ▸ **donner naissance à** to give birth to ▸ **de naissance** [aveugle] from birth ▸ **le contrôle des naissances** birth control **2.** [endroit] source / [du cou] nape **3.** *fig* [de science, nation] birth ▸ **donner naissance à** to give rise to ▸ **prendre naissance dans** to originate in.

naissant, ***e*** [nɛsɑ̃, ɑ̃t] **adj 1.** [brise] rising / [jour] dawning **2.** [barbe] incipient.

naître [92] [nɛtr] **vi 1.** [enfant] to be born ▸ **elle est née en 1965** she was born in 1965 ▸ **il est né de parents inconnus** he is of unknown parentage ▸ **je ne suis pas né d'hier** *ou* **de la dernière pluie** I wasn't born yesterday **2.** [espoir] to spring up ▸ **naître de** to arise from ▸ **de là sont nées toutes nos difficultés** that's the cause of all our difficulties ▸ **faire naître qqch** to give rise to sthg ▸ **faire naître des soupçons/la sympathie** to arouse suspicion/ sympathy ▸ **son intervention a fait naître une polémique au sein du gouvernement** his intervention gave rise to *ou* caused much controversy in the government.

naïvement [naivmɑ̃] **adv** naively.

naïveté [naivte] **nf 1.** [candeur] innocence **2.** *péj* [crédulité] gullibility.

naja [naʒa] **nm** cobra.

Namibie [namibi] **nf : la Namibie** Namibia.

namibien, ***enne*** [namibjɛ̃, ɛn] **adj** Namibian.

◆ ***Namibien***, ***enne*** **nm, f** Namibian.

nana [nana] **nf** *fam* [jeune fille] girl.

nanti, ***e*** [nɑ̃ti] ■ **adj** wealthy.

■ **nm, f** wealthy person ▸ **les nantis** the rich.

nantir [32] [nɑ̃tir] *littéraire* **vt : nantir qqn de** to provide sb with.

◆ ***se nantir*** **vp : se nantir de** to provide o.s. with.

NAP [nap] (abr écrite de ***Neuilly Auteuil Passy***) ■ **ad** ≃ Sloaney *UK*, ≃ preppie *US*.

■ **nf** ≃ Sloane *UK*, ≃ preppie *US*.

naphtaline [naftalin] **nf** mothballs *pl*.

nappage [napaʒ] **nm** CULIN coating.

nappe [nap] **nf 1.** [de table] tablecloth, cloth **2.** *fig* [étendue - gén] sheet / [- de brouillard] blanket **3.** [couche] laye ▸ **nappe de mazout** *ou* **pétrole** oil slick.

napper [3] [nape] **vt** CULIN to coat.

napperon [naprɔ̃] **nm** tablemat.

naquis, ***naquit*** ➤ ***naître***.

narcisse [narsis] **nm** BOT narcissus.

narcissique [narsisik] ■ **nmf** narcissist.

■ **adj** narcissistic.

narcissisme [narsisism] **nm** narcissism.

narcodollars [narkodɔlar] **nmpl** drug money *(U)*, narcodollars.

narcotique [narkɔtik] **nm** & **adj** narcotic.

narguer [3] [narge] **vt** [danger] to flout / [personne] to scorn, to scoff at.

narine [narin] **nf** nostril.

narquois, e [narkwa, az] **adj** sardonic.

narrateur, trice [naratœr, tris] **nm, f** narrator.

narratif, ive [naratif, iv] **adj** narrative.

narration [narasjɔ̃] **nf 1.** [récit] narration **2.** SCOL essay.

narrer [3] [nare] **vt** *littéraire* to narrate.

NASA, Nasa [naza] (abr de ***National Aeronautics and Space Administration***) **nf** NASA.

nasal, e, aux [nazal, o] **adj** nasal.

nasaliser [3] [nazalize] **vt** to nasalize.

naseau, x [nazo] **nm** nostril.

nasillard, e [nazijar, ard] **adj** nasal.

nasiller [3] [nazije] **vi 1.** [personne] to speak through one's nose **2.** [machine] to whine.

nasse [nas] **nf** keep net.

natal, e, als [natal] **adj** [d'origine] native.

natalité [natalite] **nf** birth rate.

natation [natasjɔ̃] **nf** swimming ▸ **faire de la natation** to swim.

natif, ive [natif, iv] ■ **adj 1.** [originaire] native ▸ **natif de** native of **2.** [inné] innate.
■ **nm, f** native.

nation [nasjɔ̃] **nf** nation.
◆ ***Nations unies*** **nfpl : les Nations unies** the United Nations.

national, e, aux [nasjɔnal, o] **adj** national.
◆ ***nationale*** **nf : (route) nationale** ≃ A road *UK*, ≃ state highway *US*.

nationalisation [nasjɔnalizasjɔ̃] **nf** nationalization.

nationaliser [3] [nasjɔnalize] **vt** to nationalize.

nationalisme [nasjɔnalism] **nm** nationalism.

nationaliste [nasjɔnalist] **nmf** & **adj** nationalist.

nationalité [nasjɔnalite] **nf** nationality ▸ **de nationalité française** of French nationality ▸ **double nationalité** dual nationality.

nativité [nativite] **nf** nativity.

natte [nat] **nf 1.** [tresse] plait *UK*, braid *US* **2.** [tapis] mat.

natter [3] [nate] **vt** to plait *UK*, to braid *US*.

naturalisation [natyralizasjɔ̃] **nf 1.** [de personne, de plante] naturalization **2.** [taxidermie] stuffing.

naturalisé, e [natyralize] ■ **adj 1.** [personne, plante] naturalized **2.** [empaillé] stuffed.
■ **nm, f** naturalized person.

naturaliser [3] [natyralize] **vt 1.** [personne, plante] to naturalize ▸ **se faire naturaliser** to become naturalized **2.** [empailler] to stuff.

naturaliste [natyralist] ■ **nmf 1.** LITTÉR & ZOOL naturalist **2.** [empailleur] taxidermist.
■ **adj** naturalistic.

nature [natyr] ■ **nf** nature ▸ **c'est contre nature** it's not natural, it goes against nature ▸ **c'est une petite nature** he's the feeble type *ou* a weakling ▸ **disparaître** *ou* **s'évanouir dans la nature** to vanish into thin air ▸ **elle est anxieuse de nature** she's the worrying kind *ou* anxious type ▸ **il est généreux de nature** he's generous by nature, it's (in) his nature to be generous ▸ **je ne suis pas de nature à me laisser faire** I'm not the kind *ou* type of person you can push around ▸ **les raisonnements de cette nature** this kind of argument, arguments of this kind ▸ **par nature** by nature ▸ **payer en nature** to pay in kind.
■ **adj inv 1.** [simple] plain **2.** *fam* [spontané] natural.
◆ ***nature morte*** **nf** still life.

naturel, elle [natyrɛl] **adj** natural ▸ **ce n'est pas ma couleur naturelle** it's not my natural *ou* real hair colour *UK ou* color *US* ▸ **c'est bien** *ou* **tout naturel que je t'aide** it's only natural that I should help you ▸ **trouver naturel de faire qqch** to think nothing of doing sthg ▸ **'soie naturelle'** 'pure *ou* 100% silk'.
◆ ***naturel*** **nm 1.** [tempérament] nature ▸ **être d'un naturel affable/sensible** to be affable/sensitive by nature **2.** [aisance, spontanéité] naturalness ▸ **avec beaucoup de naturel** with perfect ease, completely naturally ▸ **ce que j'aime chez elle c'est son naturel** what I like about her is she's so natural **3.** CULIN **: thon au naturel** tuna in brine.

naturellement [natyrɛlmɑ̃] **adv 1.** [gén] naturally **2.** [logiquement] rationally.

naturisme [natyrism] **nm** naturism.

naturiste [natyrist] ■ **nmf** naturist.
■ **adj** naturist *(avant n)*.

naturopathie [natyrɔpati] **nf** naturopathy.

naufrage [nofraʒ] **nm 1.** [navire] shipwreck ▸ **faire naufrage** to be wrecked **2.** *fig* [effondrement] collapse.

naufragé, e [nofraʒe] ■ **adj** shipwrecked.
■ **nm, f** shipwrecked person.

nauséabond, e [nozeabɔ̃, ɔ̃d] **adj** nauseating.

nausée [noze] **nf 1.** MÉD nausea ▸ **avoir la nausée** to feel nauseous *ou* sick *UK* ▸ **donner la nausée à qqn** *litt* & *fig* to make sb (feel) sick **2.** [dégoût] disgust.

nautique [notik] **adj** nautical / [ski, sport] water *(avant n)*.

nautisme [notism] **nm** water sports *pl*.

naval, e, als [naval] **adj** naval.

navarin [navarɛ̃] **nm** *lamb stew*.

navet [navɛ] **nm 1.** BOT turnip **2.** *fam péj* [œuvre] trash *(U)*.

navette [navɛt] **nf** shuttle ▸ **navette spatiale** AÉRON space shuttle ▸ **faire la navette** to shuttle.

navigable [navigabl] **adj** navigable.

navigant, e [navigɑ̃, ɑ̃t] ■ **adj** navigation *(avant n)*.
■ **nm, f** member of the flight crew.

navigateur, trice [navigatœr, tris] **nm, f** navigator.
◆ ***navigateur*** **nm** INFORM browser.

navigation [navigasjɔ̃] **nf** navigation / COMM shipping ▸ **navigation aérienne/spatiale** air/space travel / INFORM browsing.

naviguer [3] [navige] **vi 1.** [voguer] to sail **2.** *fam* [voyager] to travel **3.** [piloter] to navigate **4.** INFORM to browse.

navire [navir] **nm** ship ▸ **navire de guerre** warship ▸ **navire marchand** merchant ship.

navrant, e [navrɑ̃, ɑ̃t] **adj 1.** [triste] upsetting, distressing **2.** [regrettable, mauvais] unfortunate.

navrer [3] [navre] **vt** to upset ▸ **être navré de qqch/de faire qqch** to be sorry about sthg/to do sthg.

nazi, e [nazi] ■ **adj** Nazi *(avant n)*.
■ **nm, f** Nazi.

nazisme [nazism] **nm** Nazism.

NB (abr de ***Nota Bene***) NB.

NBC (abr de ***nucléaire, bactériologique, chimique***) **adj** NBC.

nbreuses (abr écrite de ***nombreuses***), ➤ ***nombreux***.

nbrx abr de ***nombreux***.

n.c. **1.** (abr écrite de ***non communiqué***) n.a. **2.** (abr écrite de ***non connu***) n.a.

n.d. **1.** (abr écrite de ***non daté***) n.d **2.** (abr écrite de ***non disponible***) n.a.

N-D (abr écrite de ***Notre-Dame***) OL.

NDA (abr écrite de ***note de l'auteur***) author's note.

NDLR (abr écrite de ***note de la rédaction***) editor's note.

NDT (abr écrite de ***note du traducteur***) translator's note.

ne [nə], ***n'*** *(devant voyelle ou 'h' muet)* **adv 1.** [négation] **: je n'ai pas d'autre solution que celle-là** I have no other solution but that / ➤ ***pas***[2], ***plus, rien*** *etc* **2.** [négation implicite] **: il ne cesse de m'appeler** he won't stop calling me ▸ **il se porte mieux que je ne (le) croyais** he's in better health than I thought (he would be) ▸ **prenez garde qu'on ne vous voie** be careful (that) nobody sees you ▸ **que ne ferais-je pour vous?** what wouldn't I do for you? **3.** [avec verbes ou expressions marquant le doute, la crainte etc] **: je crains qu'il n'oublie** I'm afraid he'll forget ▸ **j'ai peur qu'il n'en parle** I'm frightened he'll talk about it.

né, e [ne] **adj** born ▸ **né en 1965** born in 1965 ▸ **né le 17 juin** born on the 17th June *UK*, born on June 17th *US* ▸ **né de** born to *ou* of ▸ **Mme X, née Y** Mrs X née Y ▸ **je ne suis pas né d'hier** I wasn't born yesterday.

néanmoins [neɑ̃mwɛ̃] **adv** nevertheless.

néant [neɑ̃] **nm 1.** [absence de valeur] worthlessness **2.** [absence d'existence] nothingness ▸ **réduire à néant** to reduce to nothing.

nébuleux, euse [nebylø, øz] **adj 1.** [ciel] cloudy **2.** [idée, projet] nebulous.
◆ ***nébuleuse*** **nf 1.** ASTRON nebula **2.** *fig* [groupe] nebulous group.

nécessaire [nesesɛr] ■ **adj** necessary ▸ **nécessaire à** necessary for ▸ **cette introduction est nécessaire à la compréhension du texte** it is necessary to read this introduction to understand the text ▸ **l'eau est nécessaire aux plantes** plants need water ▸ **il est nécessaire de faire qqch** it is necessary to do sthg ▸ **il est nécessaire que** *(+ subjonctif)* **: il est nécessaire qu'elle vienne** she must come ▸ **si (c'est) nécessaire** if necessary, if need be.
■ **nm 1.** [biens] necessities *pl* ▸ **le strict nécessaire** the bare essentials *pl*
2. [mesures] **: faire le nécessaire** to do the necessary ▸ **je ferai le nécessaire pour vos réservations** I'll see to your reservations
3. [trousse] bag ▸ **nécessaire de couture** sewing kit ▸ **nécessaire de toilette** toilet bag ▸ **nécessaire de voyage** overnight bag.

nécessairement [nesesɛrmɑ̃] **adv 1.** [fatalement] necessarily, of necessity **2.** [absolument] absolutely, positively.

nécessité [nesesite] **nf 1.** [obligation, situation] necessity ▸ **être dans la nécessité de faire qqch** to have no choice *ou* alternative but to do sthg **2.** [besoin] need.
◆ ***nécessités*** **nfpl** necessities.

nécessiter [3] [nesesite] **vt** to necessitate.

nec plus ultra [nɛkplyzyltra] **nm inv : le nec plus ultra de** the last word in.

nécrologie [nekrɔlɔʒi] **nf** [notice] obituary / [rubrique] deaths *pl*.

nécrologique [nekrɔlɔʒik] **adj** obituary *(avant n)*.

nécromancien, enne [nekrɔmɑ̃sjɛ̃, ɛn] **nm, f** necromancer.

nécrose [nekroz] **nf** necrosis.

nectar [nɛktar] **nm** nectar ▸ **nectar d'abricot/de pêche** apricot/peach nectar.

nectarine [nɛktarin] **nf** nectarine.

néerlandais, e [neɛrlɑ̃dɛ, ɛz] **adj** Dutch.
◆ ***néerlandais*** **nm** [langue] Dutch.
◆ ***Néerlandais, e*** **nm, f** Dutchman (f Dutchwoman) ▸ **le Néerlandais** the Dutch.

nef [nɛf] **nf 1.** [d'église] nave **2.** *littéraire* [bateau] vessel.

néfaste [nefast] **adj 1.** [jour, événement] fateful **2.** [influence] harmful.

nèfle [nɛfl] **nf** medlar.

néflier [nɛflije] **nm** medlar tree.

négatif, ive [negatif, iv] **adj** negative.
◆ ***négatif*** **nm** PHOTO negative.
◆ ***négative*** **nf : répondre par la négative** to reply in the negative.

négation [negasjɔ̃] **nf 1.** [rejet] denial **2.** GRAMM negative.

négativement [negativmɑ̃] **adv** negatively.

négligé, e [negliʒe] **adj 1.** [travail, tenue] untidy **2.** [ami, jardin] neglected.
◆ ***négligé*** **nm 1.** [laisser-aller] untidiness **2.** [déshabillé] negligée.

négligeable [negliʒabl] **adj** negligible.

négligemment [negliʒamɑ̃] **adv 1.** [sans soin] carelessly **2.** [avec indifférence] casually.

négligence [neglizɑ̃s] **nf 1.** [laisser-aller] carelessness **2.** [omission] negligence ▸ **par négligence** out of negligence.

négligent, e [negliʒɑ̃, ɑ̃t] ■ **adj 1.** [sans soin] careless **2.** [indifférent] casual.
■ **nm, f** casual person.

négliger [17] [negliʒe] **vt 1.** [ami, jardin] to neglect ▸ **négliger de faire qqch** to fail to do sthg **2.** [avertissement] to ignore.
◆ ***se négliger*** **vp** to neglect o.s.

négoce [negɔs] **nm** business.

négociable [negɔsjabl] **adj** negotiable.

négociant, e [negɔsjɑ̃, ɑ̃t] **nm, f** dealer.

négociateur, trice [negɔsjatœr, tris] **nm, f** negotiator.

négociation [negɔsjasjɔ̃] **nf** negotiation ▸ **négociations de paix** peace negotiations ▸ **négociations au sommet** summit meeting *sg*.

négocier [9] [negɔsje] **vt** to negotiate.

nègre, négresse [nɛgr, negrɛs] **nm, f** Negro (f negress) *(beware: the terms 'nègre' and 'négresse' are considered racist)*.
◆ ***nègre*** ■ **nm** *fam* ghost writer.
■ **adj** negro *(avant n) (beware: the term 'nègre' is considered racist)*.

négrier [negrije] **nm 1.** [esclavagiste] slave trader **2.** *fig* [exploiteur] slave driver.

négro [negro] **nm** *racist term used with reference to a black person*.

neige [nɛʒ] **nf** [flocons] snow ▸ **aller à la neige** ≃ to go skiing ▸ **blanc comme neige** as white as snow / *fig* pure as the driven snow ▸ **neige fabriquée** *Québec* artificial snow ▸▸ **battre en neige** CULIN to beat *ou* whip until stiff.
◆ ***neige carbonique*** **nf** dry ice.

neiger [23] [neʒe] **v impers : il neige** it is snowing.

neigeux, euse [nɛʒø, øz] **adj** snowy.

nénuphar [nenyfar] **nm** water lily.

néo-calédonien, enne [neɔkaledɔnjɛ̃, ɛn] (mpl **néo-calédoniens**) (fpl **néo-calédoniennes**) **adj** New Caledonian.
◆ ***Néo-Calédonien, enne*** **nm, f** New Caledonian.

néo-colonialiste [neɔkɔlɔnjalist] (pl **néo-colonialistes**) **nmf & adj** neo-colonialist.

néologisme [neɔlɔʒism] **nm** neologism.

néon [neɔ̃] **nm 1.** [gaz] neon **2.** [enseigne] neon light.

néonatal, e, als [neɔnatal] **adj** neonatal.

néophyte [neɔfit] ■ **nmf** novice.
■ **adj** novice *(avant n)*.

néo-zélandais, e [neɔzelɑ̃dɛ, ɛz] (mpl **néo-zélandais**) (fpl **néo-zélandaises**) **adj** New Zealand *(avant n)*, of/from New Zealand.
◆ ***Néo-Zélandais, e*** **nm, f** New Zealander.

Népal [nepal] **nm : le Népal** Nepal ▸ **au Népal** in Nepal.

népalais, e [nepalɛ, ɛz] **adj** Nepalese.
◆ ***népalais*** **nm** [langue] Nepali, Nepalese.
◆ ***Népalais, e*** **nm, f** Nepalese (person) ▸ **les Népalais** the Nepalese.

néphrite [nefrit] **nf** nephritis.

népotisme [nepɔtism] **nm** nepotism.

nerf [nɛr] **nm 1.** ANAT nerve ▸ **nerf optique/rachidien** optic/spinal nerve **2.** *fig* [vigueur] spirit ▸ **son style manque de nerf** his style is a bit weak ▸ **allez, du nerf!** come on, put some effort into it!
◆ ***nerfs*** **nmpl** nerves ▸ **avoir les nerfs à fleur de peau** *ou* **à vif** to be a bundle of nerves ▸ **avoir les nerfs solides/d'acier** to have strong nerves/nerves of steel ▸ **être à bout de nerfs** to be at the end of one's tether ▸ **ses nerfs ont fini par lâcher** she eventually cracked ▸ **être sur les nerfs** to be tense ▸ **ne passe pas tes nerfs sur moi** *fam* don't take it out on me ▸ **taper sur les nerfs de qqn** *fam* to get on sb's nerves.

nerveusement [nɛrvøzmɑ̃] **adv** nervously.

nerveux, euse [nɛrvø, øz] ■ **adj 1.** [gén] nervous **2.** [viande] stringy **3.** [style] vigorous / [voiture] responsive.
■ **nm, f** nervous person.

nervosité [nɛrvozite] **nf** nervousness.

nervure [nɛrvyr] **nf 1.** [de feuille, d'aile] vein **2.** [de voûte] rib.

n'est-ce pas [nɛspa] **adv : vous me croyez, n'est-ce pas?** you believe me, don't you? ▸ **c'est délicieux, n'est-ce pas?** it's delicious, isn't it? ▸ **n'est-ce pas que vous vous êtes bien amusés?** you enjoyed yourselves, didn't you?

net, nette [nɛt] **adj 1.** [écriture, image, idée] clear ▸ **sa position est nette** her position is clear ▸ **un refus net** a flat refusal **2.** [propre, rangé] clean, neat ▸ **une chemise pas très nette** a grubby shirt **3.** COMM & FIN net ▸ **net d'impôt** tax-free, tax-exempt ▸ **bénéfice net** net profit ▸ **revenu net** net income **4.** [visible, manifeste] definite, distinct ▸ **la cassure est nette** the break is clean ▸ **il y a une nette amélioration** there's a marked improvement.
◆ ***net*** **adv 1.** [sur le coup] on the spot ▸ **s'arrêter net** to stop dead ▸ **se casser net** to break clean off **2.** [franchement - parler] plainly ▸ **je vous le dis tout net** I'm telling you straight **3.** COMM & FIN net ▸ **je gagne 200 euros net par semaine** *ou* **200 euros par semaine net** I take home *ou* my take-home pay is 200 euros a week.

Net [nɛt] **nm** *fam* **: le Net** the Net, the net ▸ **surfer sur le Net** to surf the Net.

netéconomie [nɛtekɔnomi] **nf** (Inter)net economy.

nettement [nɛtmɑ̃] **adv 1.** [clairement] clearly **2.** [incontestablement] definitely ▸ **nettement mieux** definitely better ▸ **nettement plus/moins** much more/less.

netteté [nɛtte] **nf** clearness.

nettoie, nettoies ➤ ***nettoyer***.

nettoyage [netwajaʒ] **nm** [de vêtement] cleaning ▸ **nettoyage à sec** dry cleaning.

nettoyant [netwajɑ̃] **nm** cleaning fluid.

nettoyer [13] [netwaje] **vt 1.** [gén] to clean ▸ **nettoyer une maison à fond** to give a house a thorough clean, to spring-clean a house *UK* ▸ **donner un vêtement à nettoyer** to have a garment cleaned, to take a garment to the cleaner's **2.** [vider] to clear out ▸ **en un instant, elle avait nettoyé son assiette** she cleared her plate in a flash **3.** [suj: police, soldats] to clean up.

neuf[1], ***neuve*** [nœf, nœv] **adj** new ▸ **flambant neuf** brand new ▸ **mon appareil photo n'est plus tout neuf** my camera is a bit old now ▸ **porter un regard neuf sur qqn/qqch** to take a fresh look at sb/sthg.
◆ ***neuf*** **nm : ici, on vend du neuf et de l'occasion** here we sell both new and second-hand items ▸ **vêtu de neuf** wearing new clothes ▸ **quoi de neuf?** what's new? ▸ **rien de neuf** nothing new ▸ **il y a eu du neuf dans l'affaire Peters** there have been new developments in the Peters case ▸ **donner un coup de neuf à qqch** to spruce sthg up ▸ **refaire** *ou* **remettre à neuf** to make as good as new, to refurbish.

neuf[2] [nœf] **adj num inv & nm** nine ; voir aussi ***six***.

neurasthénie [nørasteni] **nf** depression.

neurasthénique [nørastenik] **nmf & adj** depressive.

neurochirurgie [nørɔʃiryrʒi] **nf** neurosurgery.

neurodégénératif, ***ive*** [nørɔdeʒeneratif, iv] **adj** MÉD neurodegenerative.

neuroleptique [nørɔlɛptik] ■ **nm** neuroleptic drug.
■ **adj** neuroleptic.

neurologie [nørɔlɔʒi] **nf** neurology.

neurologique [nørɔlɔʒik] **adj** neurological.

neurologue [nørɔlɔg] **nmf** neurologist.

neuropsychiatre [nøropsikjatr] **nmf** neuropsychiatrist.

neurovégétatif, ***ive*** [nørovεʒetatif, iv] **adj : système neurovégétatif** nervous system.

neutralisation [nøtralizasjɔ̃] **nf** neutralization.

neutraliser [3] [nøtralize] **vt** to neutralize.

neutralité [nøtralite] **nf** neutrality.

neutre [nøtr] ■ **nm** LING neuter.
■ **adj 1.** [gén] neutral **2.** LING neuter.

neutron [nøtrɔ̃] **nm** neutron.

neuve ➤ ***neuf***[1].

neuvième [nœvjɛm] ■ **adj num inv, nm & nmf** ninth.
■ **nf** SCOL ≃ Year 3 *(at junior school) UK*, ≃ third grade *US* ; voir aussi ***sixième***.

névé [neve] **nm** snowbank.

neveu, ***x*** [nəvø] **nm** nephew.

névralgie [nevralʒi] **nf 1.** MÉD neuralgia **2.** [mal de tête] headache.

névralgique [nevralʒik] **adj 1.** [douloureux] neuralgic **2.** *fig* [sensible] sensitive.

névrite [nevrit] **nf** neuritis.

névrose [nevroz] **nf** neurosis.

névrosé, ***e*** [nevroze] **adj & nm, f** neurotic.

névrotique [nevrɔtik] **adj** neurotic.

New Delhi [njudeli] **npr** New Delhi.

New York [njujɔrk] **npr 1.** [ville] New York (City) ▸ **à New York** in New York (City) **2.** [état] New York State ▸ **dans l'État de New York** in New York State.

new-yorkais, ***e*** [njujɔrkɛ, ɛz] (**mpl new-yorkais, fpl new-yorkaises**) **adj** of/from New York.
◆ ***New-Yorkais***, ***e*** **nm, f** New Yorker.

nez [ne] **nm** nose ▸ **avoir le nez bouché** to have a stuffed up *ou* blocked nose ▸ **avoir le nez qui coule** to have a runny nose ▸ **parler du nez** to talk *ou* to speak through one's nose ▸ **saigner du nez** to have a nosebleed ▸ **nez aquilin** aquiline nose ▸ **nez busqué** hooked nose ▸ **nez camus** pug nose ▸ **nez retroussé** snub nose ▸ **avoir du nez** to have good judgment ▸ **avoir le nez fin** to have a good sense of smell / *fig* to have foresight ▸ **nez à nez** face to face ▸ **se trouver nez à nez avec qqn** to find o.s. face to face with sb ▸ **ça lui pend au nez** *fam* he's got it coming to him ▸ **ça se voit comme le nez au milieu de la figure** it's as plain as the nose on your face ▸ **faire qqch au nez et à la barbe de qqn** to do sthg (right) under sb's nose ▸ **le dernier billet m'est passé sous le nez** I just missed the last ticket ▸ **mettre le nez dehors** to put one's nose outside ▸ **mettre le nez à la fenêtre** to show one's face at the window ▸ **mettre** *ou* **fourrer son nez dans les affaires de qqn** *fam* to poke *ou* to stick one's nose into sb's business ▸ **raccrocher au nez de qqn** to hang up on sb ▸ **rire au nez de qqn** to laugh in sb's face.

NF (abr de ***Norme française***) *French industrial standard*, ≃ BS *UK*, ≃ US standard *US*.

ni [ni] **conj : sans pull ni écharpe** without a sweater or a scarf ▸ **je ne peux ni ne veux venir** I neither can nor want to come.
◆ ***ni... ni*** **loc correlative** neither... nor ▸ **ni lui ni moi** neither of us ▸ **ni l'un ni l'autre n'a parlé** neither of them spoke ▸ **je ne les aime ni l'un ni l'autre** I don't like either of them.

niable [njabl] **adj** deniable.

Niagara [njagara] **nm : les chutes du Niagara** Niagara Falls.

niais, ***e*** [njɛ, njɛz] ■ **adj** silly, foolish.
■ **nm, f** fool.

niaisement [njɛzmɑ̃] **adv** foolishly.

niaiserie [njɛzri] **nf** foolishness *(U)* ▸ **dire des niaiseries** to talk nonsense.

Nicaragua [nikaragwa] **nm : le Nicaragua** Nicaragua ▸ **au Nicaragua** in Nicaragua.

nicaraguayen, ***enne*** [nikaragwajɛ̃, ɛn] **adj** Nicaraguan.
◆ ***Nicaraguayen***, ***enne*** **nm, f** Nicaraguan.

niche [niʃ] **nf 1.** [de chien] kennel *UK*, doghouse *US* **2.** [de statue] niche **3.** *fam* [farce] trick **4.** ÉCON (market) niche.

nicher [3] [niʃe] **vi 1.** [oiseaux] to nest **2.** *fam* [personne] to live.
◆ ***se nicher*** **vp** to hide.

nickel [nikɛl] ■ **nm** nickel.
■ **adj inv** *fam* spotless, spick and span.

niçois, e [niswa, az] **adj** of/from Nice ◗ **salade niçoise** *salad made out of lettuce, green peppers, tuna fish, tomatoes, anchovy and hard-boiled egg.*
◆ ***Niçois, e*** **nm, f** person fromNice.

nicotine [nikɔtin] **nf** nicotine.

nid [ni] **nm** nest ◗ **nid-d'abeilles** [tissu] waffle cloth ◗ **nid à poussière** *fig* dust trap.
◆ ***nid de poule*** **nm** pothole.

nièce [njɛs] **nf** niece.

nier [9] [nje] **vt** to deny.

nigaud, e [nigo, od] ■ **adj** silly.
■ **nm, f** halfwit.

Niger [niʒɛr] **nm** **1.** [fleuve] **: le Niger** the River Niger **2.** [État] **: le Niger** Niger ◗ **au Niger** in Niger.

Nigeria [niʒerja] **nm : le Nigeria** Nigeria ◗ **au Nigeria** in Nigeria.

nigérian, e [niʒerjɑ̃, ɑn] **adj** Nigerian.
◆ ***Nigérian, e*** **nm, f** Nigerian.

nigérien, enne [niʒerjɛ̃, ɛn] **adj** Nigerien.
◆ ***Nigérien, enne*** **nm, f** Nigerien.

night-club [najtklœb] (pl **night-clubs**) **nm** nightclub.

Nil [nil] **nm : le Nil** the Nile ◗ **le Nil Blanc** the White Nile ◗ **le Nil Bleu** the Blue Nile.

n'importe ➤ ***importer***.

nippes [nip] **nfpl** *fam* gear *(U)*.

nippon, one [nipɔ̃, ɔn] **adj** Japanese.
◆ ***Nippon, one*** **nm, f** Japanese (person) ◗ **les Nippons** the Japanese.

nirvana [nirvana] **nm** nirvana.

nitrate [nitrat] **nm** nitrate.

nitrique [nitrik] **adj** nitric.

nitroglycérine [nitrɔgliserin] **nf** nitroglycerine.

niveau, x [nivo] **nm** **1.** [gén] level ◗ **un parking à trois niveaux** a car park *UK ou* parking lot *US*on three levels ◗ **de même niveau** *fig* of the same standard ◗ **les deux terrains ne sont pas de niveau** the two plots of land are not level (with each other) ◗ **niveau à bulle** spirit level ◗ **au-dessus du niveau de la mer** above sea level ◗ **niveau scolaire** standard of education ◗ **j'ai un bon niveau/un niveau moyen en russe** I'm good/average at Russian ◗ **niveau de vie** standard of living ◗ **dans deux mois, vous serez au niveau** in two months' time you'll have caught up ◗ **au niveau de** at the level of / *fig* [en ce qui concerne] as regards ◗ **je ressens une douleur au niveau de la hanche** I've got a pain in my hip ◗ **ce problème sera traité au niveau du syndicat** this problem will be dealt with at union level **2.** LING **: niveau de langue** register.

niveler [24] [nivle] **vt** to level / *fig* to level out.

nivellement [nivɛlmɑ̃] **nm** levelling *UK*, leveling *US* / *fig* levelling *UK ou* leveling *US* out ◗ **nivellement par le bas** levelling *UK ou* leveling *US* down.

NN (abr écrite de ***nouvelle norme***) *revised standard of hotel classification.*

noble [nɔbl] ■ **nmf** nobleman (f noblewoman).
■ **adj** noble.

noblement [nɔbləmɑ̃] **adv** nobly.

noblesse [nɔblɛs] **nf** nobility.

noce [nɔs] **nf** **1.** [mariage] wedding **2.** [invités] wedding party
▶▶ **faire la noce** *fam* to live it up.
◆ ***noces*** **nfpl** wedding *sg* ◗ **convoler en justes noces** to be married ◗ **elle l'a épousé en secondes noces** he is her second husband ◗ **noces d'or/d'argent** golden/silver wedding (anniversary).

nocif, ive [nɔsif, iv] **adj** **1.** [produit, gaz] noxious **2.** *fig* [théorie, doctrine] harmful.

nocivité [nɔsivite] **nf** **1.** [de produit, gaz] noxiousness **2.** *fig* [de théorie, doctrine] harmfulness.

noctambule [nɔktɑ̃byl] **nmf** night bird.

nocturne [nɔktyrn] ■ **nm** **1.** MUS nocturne **2.** ZOOL night hunter.
■ **nm & nf** **1.** [d'un magasin] late opening ◗ **ouvert en nocturne** open late **2.** SPORT **: match en nocturne** evening game.
■ **adj** **1.** [émission, attaque] night *(avant n)* **2.** [animal] nocturnal.

nodule [nɔdyl] **nm** nodule.

Noël [nɔɛl] **nm** Christmas ◗ **joyeux Noël!** Happy *ou* Merry Christmas!

nœud [nø] **nm** **1.** [de fil, de bois] knot ◗ **nœud coulant** slipknot ◗ **double nœud** double knot **2.** NAUT knot ◗ **filer à 10 nœuds** NAUT to do 10 knots **3.** *fig & littéraire* [attachement] bond **4.** [de l'action, du problème] crux **5.** [ornement] bow ◗ **nœud de cravate** knot *(in one's tie)* ◗ **nœud papillon** bow tie **6.** ANAT, ASTRON, ÉLECTR & RAIL node.

noie, noies ➤ ***noyer***.

noierai, noieras ➤ ***noyer***.

noir, e [nwar] **adj** **1.** [gén] black ◗ **noir de** [poussière] black with ◗ **noir de suie** black with soot ◗ **noir de monde** *fig* teeming with people **2.** [pièce, couloir] dark ◗ **dans les rues noires** in the pitch-black *ou* pitch-dark streets **3.** *fig* [maléfique] sombre *UK*, somber *US* ◗ **il m'a regardé d'un œil noir** he gave me a black look **4.** *fig* [ivre] drunk.
◆ ***Noir, e*** **nm, f** black ◗ **Noir américain** African American.
◆ ***noir*** **nm** **1.** [couleur] black ◗ **une photo/un film en noir et blanc** a black and white photo/film *UK ou* movie *US* ◗ **noir sur blanc** *fig* in black and white **2.** [obscurité] dark ◗ **dans le noir** in the dark, in darkness
▶▶ **acheter qqch au noir** to buy sthg on the black market ◗ **je l'ai eu au noir** I got it on the black market ◗ **broyer du noir** to be down in the dumps ◗ **travail au noir** moonlighting ◗ **travailler au noir** to moonlight ◗ **voir tout en noir** to see the dark side of everything.
◆ ***noire*** **nf** crotchet *UK*, quarter note *US*.

noirâtre [nwaratr] **adj** blackish.

noiraud, e [nwaro, od] ■ **adj** swarthy.
■ **nm, f** swarthy person.

noirceur [nwarsœr] **nf** **1.** *littéraire* [couleur] blackness **2.** *fig* [méchanceté] wickedness.

noircir [32] [nwarsir] ■ **vi** to darken.
■ **vt** *litt* & *fig* to blacken.
◆ ***se noircir*** **vp** [devenir noir] to darken.

Noire ➤ ***mer***.

noise [nwaz] **nf** *littéraire* **: chercher noise à qqn** to pick a quarrel with sb.

noisetier [nwaztje] **nm** hazel tree.

noisette [nwazɛt] ■ **nf 1.** [fruit] hazelnut **2.** [petite quantité] **: une noisette de beurre** a knob of butter.
■ **adj inv** hazel.

noix [nwa] **nf 1.** [fruit] walnut ▸ **noix de cajou** cashew (nut) ▸ **noix de coco** coconut ▸ **noix de muscade** nutmeg **2.** [de viande] **: noix de veau** cushion of veal
▸▸| **à la noix** *fam* dreadful.

nom [nɔ̃] **nm 1.** [gén] name ▸ **au nom de** in the name of ▸ **nom de Dieu!** *tfam* God damn it!, bloody hell! *UK* ▸ **nom d'un chien** *ou* **d'une pipe!** *fam* drat! ▸ **faux nom** false name ▸ **nom de domaine** domain name ▸ **nom déposé** trade name ▸ **nom d'emprunt** assumed name ▸ **nom de famille** surname ▸ **nom de fichier** INFORM filename ▸ **nom de jeune fille** maiden name ▸ **nom de marque sous licence** licensed brand name ▸ **nom de l'utilisateur** *ou* **d'utilisateur** user name ▸ **nom de login** login name ▸ **traiter qqn de tous les noms** to call sb all the names under the sun **2.** [prénom] (first) name **3.** GRAMM noun ▸ **nom composé** compound noun ▸ **nom propre/commun** proper/common noun.

nomade [nɔmad] ■ **nmf** nomad.
■ **adj** nomadic.

nombre [nɔ̃br] **nm** number ▸ **au nombre de** among ▸ **les invités sont au nombre de cent** there are a hundred guests ▸ **bon nombre de** a large number of, a good many ▸ **je te l'ai déjà dit (un) bon nombre de fois** I've already told you several times ▸ **un bon nombre d'entre nous/eux** many of us/them ▸ **un certain nombre de** a (certain) number of ▸ **un grand nombre de** a lot of, a great number of, a great many ▸ **venir en nombre** to come in large numbers ▸ **nous ne sommes pas en nombre suffisant** there aren't enough of us ▸ **nombre pair/impair** even/odd number ▸ **un nombre de trois chiffres** a three-digit *ou* three-figure number.

nombreux, ***euse*** [nɔ̃brø, øz] **adj 1.** [famille, foule] large **2.** [erreurs, occasions] numerous ▸ **peu nombreux** few.

nombril [nɔ̃bril] **nm** navel ▸ **il se prend pour le nombril du monde** he thinks the world revolves around him.

nombrilisme [nɔ̃brilism] **nm** *fam péj* navel-gazing.

nomenclature [nɔmɑ̃klatyr] **nf 1.** [terminologie] nomenclature **2.** [liste] word list.

nominal, ***e***, ***aux*** [nɔminal, o] **adj 1.** [liste] of names **2.** [valeur, autorité] nominal **3.** GRAMM noun *(avant n)*.

nominalement [nɔminalmɑ̃] **adv 1.** [désigner] by name **2.** GRAMM nominally.

nominatif, ***ive*** [nɔminatif, iv] **adj** [liste] of names.
◆ ***nominatif*** **nm** GRAMM nominative.

nomination [nɔminasjɔ̃] **nf** nomination, appointment.

nommé, ***e*** [nɔme] ■ **adj 1.** [désigné] named **2.** [choisi] appointed.
■ **nm, f** aforementioned.

nommément [nɔmemɑ̃] **adv** [citer] by name.

nommer [3] [nɔme] **vt 1.** [appeler] to name, to call **2.** [qualifier] to call **3.** [promouvoir] to appoint, to nominate **4.** [dénoncer, mentionner] to name.
◆ ***se nommer*** **vp 1.** [s'appeler] to be called **2.** [se désigner] to give one's name.

non [nɔ̃] ■ **adv 1.** [réponse négative] no ▸ **ah ça non!** definitely not! **2.** [se rapportant à une phrase précédente] not ▸ **moi non** not me ▸ **moi non plus** (and) neither am/do *etc* I ▸ **elle ne travaille pas aujourd'hui, moi non plus** she's not working today and neither am I **3.** [sert à demander une confirmation] **: c'est une bonne idée, non?** it's a good idea, isn't it? ▸ **il devait prendre une semaine de vacances, non?** he was supposed to take a week's holiday *UK* *ou* vacation *US*, wasn't he? **4.** [modifie un adjectif ou un adverbe] not ▸ **non loin d'ici** not far from here ▸ **une difficulté non négligeable** a not inconsiderable problem **5.** [emploi expressif] **: non! pas possible!** no *ou* never! I don't believe it! ▸ **non mais (des fois)!** honestly!, I ask you!
■ **nm inv** no.
◆ ***non moins*** **loc adv** no less.
◆ ***non (pas)... mais*** **loc correlative** not... but ▸ **non pas maigre, mais mince** not skinny but slim.
◆ ***non plus... mais*** **loc correlative** no longer... but.
◆ ***non (pas) que... mais*** **loc correlative** not that... but ▸ **non (pas) que je m'en méfie, mais...** it's not that I don't trust him, but...

nonagénaire [nɔnaʒenɛr] **nmf** & **adj** nonagenarian.

non-agression [nɔnagrɛsjɔ̃] **nf** non-aggression.

non-aligné, ***e*** [nɔnaliɲe] **adj** non-aligned ▸ **les pays non-alignés** the non-aligned countries.

nonante [nɔnɑ̃t] **adj num inv** *Belgique* & *Suisse* ninety.

non-assistance [nɔnasistɑ̃s] **nf** non-assistance ▸ **non-assistance à personne en danger** failure to give assistance to a person in danger.

nonchalance [nɔ̃ʃalɑ̃s] **nf** nonchalance, casualness.

nonchalant, ***e*** [nɔ̃ʃalɑ̃, ɑ̃t] **adj** nonchalant, casual.

non-combattant, ***e*** [nɔ̃kɔ̃batɑ̃, ɑ̃t] ■ **adj** noncombatant.
■ **nm, f** noncombatant.

non-conformiste [nɔ̃kɔ̃fɔrmist] ■ **nmf** nonconformist.
■ **adj** unconventional.

non-conformité [nɔ̃kɔ̃fɔrmite] **nf** nonconformity.

non-dit [nɔ̃di] **nm** unvoiced feeling.

non-fumeur, ***euse*** [nɔ̃fymœr, øz] ■ **nm, f** non-smoker.
■ **adj** non-smoking *(avant n)*.

non-ingérence [nɔnɛ̃ʒerɑ̃s] **nf** noninterference.

non-inscrit, ***e*** [nɔnɛ̃skri, it] **adj** & **nm, f** POLIT independent.

non-intervention [nɔnɛ̃tɛrvɑ̃sjɔ̃] **nf** nonintervention.

non-lieu [nɔ̃ljø] (pl **non-lieux**) **nm** DR dismissal through lack of evidence ▸ **rendre un non-lieu** to dismiss a case for lack of evidence.

nonne [nɔn] **nf** nun.

nonobstant [nɔnɔpstɑ̃] *sout* ■ **prép** notwithstanding.
■ **adv** nevertheless.

non-paiement [nɔ̃pɛmɑ̃] **nm** nonpayment.

non-recevoir [nɔ̃rəsəvwar] ◆ ***fin de non-recevoir*** **nf** DR objection.

non-résident, e [nɔ̃rezidɑ̃] **nm, f** nonresident.

non-retour [nɔ̃rətur] ◆ ***point de non-retour*** **nm** point of no return.

non-sens [nɔ̃sɑ̃s] **nm inv 1.** [absurdité] nonsense **2.** [contresens] meaningless word.

non-stop [nɔnstɔp] **adj inv** non-stop.

non-violence [nɔ̃vjɔlɑ̃s] **nf** non-violence.

non-voyant, e [nɔ̃vwajɑ̃, ɑ̃t] **adj** visually handicapped *UK*, visually impaired *US*.

nord [nɔr] ■ **nm** north ▸ **un vent du nord** a northerly wind ▸ **le vent du nord** the north wind ▸ **au nord** in the north ▸ **au nord (de)** to the north (of) ▸ **le grand Nord** the frozen North ▸ **perdre le nord** *fam fig* to lose one's head.
■ **adj inv** north / [province, région] northern.

nord-africain, e [nɔrafrikɛ̃, ɛn] (mpl **nord-africains**) (fpl **nord-africaines**) **adj** North African.
◆ ***Nord-Africain, e*** **nm, f** North African.

nord-américain, e [nɔramerikɛ̃, ɛn] (mpl **nord-américains**) (fpl **nord-américaines**) **adj** North American.
◆ ***Nord-Américain, e*** **nm, f** North American.

nord-coréen, enne [nɔrkɔreɛ̃, ɛn] (mpl **nord-coréens**) (fpl **nord-coréennes**) **adj** North Korean.
◆ ***Nord-Coréen, enne*** **nm, f** North Korean.

nord-est [nɔrɛst] **nm & adj inv** northeast.

nordicité [nɔrdisite] **nf** *Québec* northerliness.

nordique [nɔrdik] **adj** Nordic, Scandinavian.
◆ ***Nordique*** **nmf 1.** [Scandinave] Scandinavian **2.** *Québec* North Canadian.

nord-ouest [nɔrwɛst] **nm & adj inv** north-west.

normal, e, aux [nɔrmal, o] **adj** normal ▸ **en temps normal** in normal circumstances, normally ▸ **il n'est pas rentré, ce n'est pas normal** he's not back yet, something must have happened (to him) ▸ **la situation est redevenue normale** the situation is back to normal ▸ **mais c'est bien normal, voyons** it's only natural, don't worry about it.
◆ ***normale*** **nf 1.** [moyenne] **: la normale** the norm ▸ **intelligence supérieure à la normale** above average intelligence ▸ **température au-dessous de la normale (saisonnière)** temperature below the (seasonal) average **2.** *Québec* [golf] par.

normalement [nɔrmalmɑ̃] **adv** normally, usually ▸ **normalement il devrait déjà être arrivé** he should have arrived by now.

normalien, enne [nɔrmaljɛ̃, ɛn] **nm, f 1.** [élève d'une école normale] student at teacher training college *UK ou* teachers college *US* **2.** [ancien élève de l'École normale supérieure] graduate of the École normale supérieure.

normalisation [nɔrmalizasjɔ̃] **nf 1.** [stabilisation] normalization **2.** [standardisation] standardization.

normaliser [3] [nɔrmalize] **vt 1.** [situation] to normalize **2.** [produit] to standardize.
◆ ***se normaliser*** **vp** to return to normal.

normalité [nɔrmalite] **nf** normality, normalcy *US*.

normand, e [nɔrmɑ̃, ɑ̃d] **adj** Norman.
◆ ***Normand, e*** **nm, f** Norman.

Normandie [nɔrmɑ̃di] **nf : la Normandie** Normandy.

normatif, ive [nɔrmatif, iv] **adj** prescriptive.

norme [nɔrm] **nf 1.** [gén] standard, norm ▸ **être dans la norme** to be within the norm ▸ **être hors normes** to be non-standard **2.** [critère] criterion.

Norvège [nɔrvɛʒ] **nf : la Norvège** Norway.

norvégien, enne [nɔrveʒjɛ̃, ɛn] **adj** Norwegian.
◆ ***norvégien*** **nm** [langue] Norwegian.
◆ ***Norvégien, enne*** **nm, f** Norwegian.

nos ➤ ***notre***.

nosocomial, e, aux [nɔzɔkɔmjal, o] **adj** nosocomial, contracted in hospital.

nostalgie [nɔstalʒi] **nf** nostalgia ▸ **avoir la nostalgie de** to feel nostalgia for.

nostalgique [nɔstalʒik] **adj** nostalgic.

nota bene [nɔtabene] **nm inv** nota bene, NB.

notable [nɔtabl] ■ **adj** noteworthy, notable.
■ **nm** notable.

notablement [nɔtabləmɑ̃] **adv** notably.

notaire [nɔtɛr] **nm** ≃ solicitor *UK*, ≃ lawyer.

notamment [nɔtamɑ̃] **adv** in particular.

notarial, e, aux [nɔtarjal, o] **adj** notarial.

notarié, e [nɔtarje] **adj** ≃ drawn up by a solicitor *UK ou* lawyer.

notation [nɔtasjɔ̃] **nf 1.** [système] notation **2.** [remarque] note **3.** SCOL marking, grading *US*.

note [nɔt] **nf 1.** [gén & MUS] note ▸ **apporter une note personnelle à qqch** to give sthg a personal touch ▸ **prendre des notes** to take notes ▸ **prendre qqch en note** to make a note of sthg ▸ **prendre bonne note de qqch** to take good note of sthg ▸ **fausse note** MUS false note / *fig* sour note ▸ **la cérémonie s'est déroulée sans une fausse note** the ceremony went (off) without a hitch ▸ **note de bas de page** footnote ▸ **note de service** memo **2.** SCOL & UNIV mark, grade *US* ▸ **avoir une bonne/mauvaise note** to have a good/bad mark **3.** [facture] bill ▸ **note de frais** [à remplir] expense *ou* expenses claim (form) ▸ **présenter sa note de frais** to put in for expenses ▸ **note d'honoraires** invoice *(for work done by a self-employed person)* ▸ **une note salée** *fam* a hefty *ou* steep bill.

noter [3] [nɔte] **vt 1.** [écrire] to note down **2.** [constater] to note, to notice **3.** SCOL & UNIV to mark, to grade *US* **4.** [marquer] to mark.

notice [nɔtis] **nf** instructions *pl* ▸ **notice explicative** directions for use.

notification [nɔtifikasjɔ̃] **nf** notification.

notifier [9] [nɔtifje] **vt : notifier qqch à qqn** to notify sb of sthg.

notion [nɔsjɔ̃] **nf 1.** [conscience, concept] notion, concept **2.** *(gén pl)* [rudiment] smattering *(U)*.

notoire [nɔtwar] **adj** [fait] well-known / [criminel] notorious.

notoirement [nɔtwarmɑ̃] **adv** notoriously.

notoriété [nɔtɔrjete] **nf 1.** [de fait] notoriety ▸ **être de notoriété publique** to be common *ou* public knowledge **2.** [célébrité] fame **3.** ÉCON **: notoriété du produit** product awareness.

notre [nɔtr] (pl **nos** [no]) **adj poss** our.

nôtre [notr] ◆ ***le nôtre***, ***la nôtre*** (pl **les nôtres**) **pron poss** ours ▸ **les nôtres** our family *sg* ▸ **serez-vous des nôtres demain?** will you be joining us tomorrow? ▸ **il faut y mettre du nôtre** we'll all have to pull our weight.

nouba [nuba] **nf : faire la nouba** *fam* to paint the town red.

nouer [6] [nwe] **vt 1.** [corde, lacet] to tie / [bouquet] to tie up **2.** *fig* [gorge, estomac] to knot **3.** *sout* [alliance, amitié] to make, to form.
◆ ***se nouer*** **vp 1.** [gorge] to tighten up **2.** [alliance, amitié] to be formed **3.** [intrigue] to start.

noueux, ***euse*** [nwø, øz] **adj** [bois] knotty / [mains] gnarled.

nougat [nuga] **nm** nougat.

nouille [nuj] **nf** *fam péj* idiot.
◆ ***nouilles*** **nfpl** [pâtes] pasta *(U)*, noodles *pl*.

Nouméa [numea] **npr** Nouméa.

nounou [nunu] **nf** nanny.

nourrice [nuris] **nf 1.** [garde d'enfants] nanny *UK*, childminder *UK*, nursemaid *US* / [qui allaite] wet nurse **2.** [réservoir] jerrycan *UK*, can *US*.

nourrir [32] [nurir] **vt 1.** [gén] to feed ▸ **j'ai trois enfants à nourrir** I've got three children to feed *ou* to provide for ▸ **nourri-logé-blanchi** board, lodging and laundry ▸ **être bien nourri** to be well-fed ▸ **être mal nourri** [sous-alimenté] to be undernourished **2.** [sentiment, projet] to nurture ▸ **elle nourrissait déjà des projets ambitieux** she was already turning over some ambitious projects in her mind **3.** [style, esprit] to improve.
◆ ***se nourrir*** **vp** to eat ▸ **il se nourrit mal** he doesn't feed himself *ou* eat properly ▸ **se nourrir de qqch** *litt* & *fig* to live on sthg ▸ **se nourrir d'illusions** to revel in illusions.

nourrissant, ***e*** [nurisɑ̃, ɑ̃t] **adj** nutritious, nourishing.

nourrisson [nurisɔ̃] **nm** infant.

nourriture [nurityr] **nf** food.

nous [nu] **pron pers 1.** [sujet] we **2.** [objet] us.
◆ ***nous-mêmes*** **pron pers** ourselves.

nouveau, ***elle***, ***x*** [nuvo, ɛl, o] **(nouvel** *devant une voyelle ou un 'h' muet)* ■ **adj** new ▸ **nouveaux mariés** newlyweds ▸ **ce nouvel attentat a fait 52 morts** 52 people died in this latest bomb attack ▸ **ce dossier est nouveau pour moi** this case is new to me, I'm new to this case ▸ **il est encore (un peu) nouveau en politique** he's still (a bit of) a newcomer to politics ▸ **porter un regard nouveau sur qqn/qqch** to take a fresh look at sb/sthg ▸ **pommes de terre nouvelles** new potatoes.
■ **nm, f** new boy (f new girl).
◆ ***nouveau*** **nm : il y a du nouveau** there's something new ▸ **rien de nouveau depuis la dernière fois** nothing new *ou* special since last time.
◆ ***nouvelle*** **nf 1.** [information] (piece of) news *(U)* ▸ **j'ai une bonne/mauvaise nouvelle pour toi** I have (some) good/bad news for you ▸ **première nouvelle!** that's news to me! **2.** [court récit] short story.
◆ ***nouvelles*** **nfpl** news ▸ **les nouvelles** [média] the news *sg* ▸ **il a donné de ses nouvelles** I/we *etc* have heard from him ▸ **être sans nouvelles de qqn/qqch** to have no news of sb/sthg ▸ **aux dernières nouvelles...** the latest is...
◆ ***à nouveau*** **loc adv 1.** [encore] again ▸ **je tiens à vous remercier à nouveau** I'd like to thank you once again **2.** [de manière différente] afresh, anew.
◆ ***de nouveau*** **loc adv** again ▸ **tu as fait de nouveau la même bêtise** you've made the same mistake again.

nouveau-né, ***e*** [nuvone] (mpl **nouveau-nés**, fpl **nouveau-nées**) ■ **adj** newborn.
■ **nm, f** newborn baby.

nouveauté [nuvote] **nf 1.** [actualité] novelty **2.** [innovation] something new **3.** [ouvrage] new book/film *etc*.

nouvel, ***nouvelle*** ➤ ***nouveau***.

Nouvelle-Calédonie [nuvɛlkaledɔni] **nf : la Nouvelle-Calédonie** New Caledonia.

Nouvelle-Écosse [nuvɛlekɔs] **nf : la Nouvelle-Écosse** Nova Scotia.

Nouvelle-Guinée [nuvɛlgine] **nf : la Nouvelle-Guinée** New Guinea.

nouvellement [nuvɛlmɑ̃] **adv** recently.

Nouvelle-Orléans [nuvɛlɔrleɑ̃] **npr : La Nouvelle-Orléans** New Orleans.

Nouvelle-Zélande [nuvɛlzelɑ̃d] **nf : la Nouvelle-Zélande** New Zealand.

novateur, ***trice*** [nɔvatœr, tris] ■ **adj** innovative.
■ **nm, f** innovator.

novembre [nɔvɑ̃br] **nm** November ; voir aussi ***septembre***.

novice [nɔvis] ■ **nmf** novice ▸ **(internaute) novice** INFORM newbie *fam*.
■ **adj** inexperienced.

noyade [nwajad] **nf** drowning.

noyau, ***x*** [nwajo] **nm 1.** [de fruit] stone *UK*, pit **2.** ASTRON, BIOL & PHYS nucleus **3.** *fig* [d'amis] group, circle [d'opposants, de résistants] cell ▸ **noyau dur** hard core **4.** *fig* [centre] core.

noyauter [3] [nwajote] **vt** to infiltrate.

noyé, e [nwaje] ■ **adj 1.** [personne] drowned **2.** [inondé] flooded ▸ **yeux noyés de larmes** eyes swimming with tears.
■ **nm, f** drowned person.

noyer [13] [nwaje] **vt 1.** [animal, personne] to drown ▸ **noyer son chagrin** to drown one's sorrows **2.** [terre, moteur] to flood **3.** [estomper, diluer] to swamp / [contours] to blur.
◆ ***se noyer*** **vp 1.** [personne] to drown **2.** *fig* [se perdre] : **se noyer dans** to become bogged down in **3.** [s'estomper] to be swamped.

NPI (abr de ***nouveaux pays industrialisés***) **nmpl** NICs.

N/Réf (abr écrite de ***Notre référence***) O/Ref.

NRF (abr de ***Nouvelle Revue Française***) **nf 1.** [revue] *literary review* **2.** [mouvement] *literary movement*.

nu, e [ny] **adj 1.** [personne] naked ▸ **être à demi nu** *ou* **à moitié nu** to be half-naked ▸ **être pieds nus** to be barefoot *ou* barefooted ▸ **il travaillait torse nu** he was working without a shirt on ▸ **poser nu pour un photographe** to pose in the nude for a photographer ▸ **ça ne se voit pas/ça se voit à l'œil nu** you can't/you can see it with the naked eye **2.** [paysage, fil électrique] bare **3.** [style, vérité] plain.
◆ ***nu*** **nm** nude ▸ **une photo de nu** a nude photo ▸ **à nu** stripped, bare ▸ **le fil est à nu** [accidentellement] the wire is bare / [exprès] the wire has been stripped ▸ **mettre à nu** to strip bare ▸ **mettre un fil électrique à nu** to strip a wire ▸ **mettre son cœur à nu** to bare one's soul.

nuage [nɥaʒ] **nm 1.** [gén] cloud ▸ **ciel chargé de nuages** cloudy *ou* overcast sky ▸ **sous un ciel sans nuages** under cloudless blue skies ▸ **être dans les nuages** *fig* to have one's head in the clouds ▸ **il y avait de gros nuages à l'horizon économique de 2004** the economic outlook for 2004 was very gloomy *ou* bleak **2.** [petite quantité] : **un nuage de lait** a drop of milk **3.** [masse légère] : **un nuage de tulle** a mass *ou* swathe of tulle **4.** *Québec* [foulard] scarf.

nuageux, euse [nɥaʒø, øz] **adj 1.** [temps, ciel] cloudy **2.** *fig* [esprit] hazy.

nuance [nɥɑ̃s] **nf 1.** [de couleur] shade / [de son, de sens] nuance ▸ **tout en nuances** extremely subtle **2.** [touche] : **nuance de** touch of, trace of.

nuancer [16] [nɥɑ̃se] **vt 1.** [couleurs] to shade **2.** [pensée] to qualify.

nubile [nybil] **adj** nubile.

nucléaire [nykleɛr] ■ **nm** nuclear energy.
■ **adj** nuclear.

nudisme [nydism] **nm** nudism, naturism.

nudiste [nydist] **nmf & adj** nudist.

nudité [nydite] **nf 1.** [de personne] nudity, nakedness **2.** [de lieu, style] bareness.

nuée [nɥe] **nf 1.** [multitude] : **une nuée de** a horde of **2.** *littéraire* [nuage] cloud.

nues [ny] **nfpl : tomber des nues** to be completely taken aback.

nui [nɥi] **pp inv** ➤ ***nuire***.

nuire [97] [nɥir] **vi : nuire à** to harm, to injure.
◆ ***se nuire*** **vp** to harm o.s.

nuisais, nuisions ➤ ***nuire***.

nuisance [nɥizɑ̃s] **nf** nuisance *(U)*, harm *(U)* ▸ **nuisances sonores** noise pollution.

nuise, nuises ➤ ***nuire***.

nuisette [nɥizɛt] **nf** short nightgown, babydoll nightgown.

nuisible [nɥizibl] **adj** harmful.

nuit [nɥi] **nf 1.** [laps de temps] night ▸ **cette nuit** [la nuit dernière] last night / [la nuit prochaine] tonight ▸ **en pleine nuit** in the middle of the night ▸ **toute la nuit** all night (long), through the night ▸ **toutes les nuits** nightly, every night ▸ **de nuit** at night ▸ **animaux/oiseaux de nuit** nocturnal animals/birds ▸ **bateau/vol de nuit** night ferry/flight ▸ **travailler de nuit** to work nights *ou* the night shift *ou* at night ▸ **passer la nuit à l'hôtel** to spend the night in a hotel ▸ **nuit blanche** sleepless night ▸ **la nuit de noces** the wedding night ▸ **une nuit étoilée** a starry night **2.** [obscurité] darkness, night ▸ **il fait nuit** it's dark ▸ **la nuit tombe** it's getting dark, night is falling *sout* ▸ **perdu dans la nuit des temps** lost in the mists of time.

nuitamment [nɥitamɑ̃] **adv** *littéraire* by night.

nuitée [nɥite] **nf** overnight stay.

nul, nulle [nyl] ■ **adj indéf** *(avant n) littéraire* no.
■ **adj** *(après n)* **1.** [égal à zéro] nil **2.** [sans valeur] useless, hopeless ▸ **c'est nul!** *fam* it's rubbish! ▸ **être nul en maths** to be hopeless *ou* useless at maths **3.** [sans résultat] : **match nul** draw *UK*, tie *US* **4.** [caduc] : **nul et non avenu** DR null and void.
■ **nm, f** *péj* nonentity.
■ **pron indéf** *sout* no one, nobody.
◆ ***nulle part*** **loc adv** nowhere, no place *US*.

nullement [nylmɑ̃] **adv** by no means.

nullité [nylite] **nf 1.** [médiocrité] incompetence **2.** *péj* [personne] nonentity **3.** DR invalidity, nullity.

numéraire [nymerɛr] ■ **nm** cash.
■ **adj** [espèces] legal.

numéral, e, aux [nymeral, o] **adj** numeral.
◆ ***numéral, aux*** **nm** numeral.

numérateur [nymeratœr] **nm** numerator.

numération [nymerasjɔ̃] **nf 1.** MATH numeration **2.** MÉD : **numération globulaire** blood count.

numérique [nymerik] **adj 1.** [gén] numerical **2.** INFORM digital.

numériquement [nymerikmɑ̃] **adv** numerically.

numéro [nymero] **nm 1.** [gén] number ▸ **composer** *ou* **faire un numéro** to dial a number ▸ **faire un faux numéro** to dial a wrong number ▸ **j'ai changé de numéro** my number has changed ▸ **'il n'y a pas d'abonné au numéro que vous avez demandé'** there's no subscriber at the number you've dialled ▸ **numéro de commande** order number ▸ **numéro minéralogique** *ou* **d'immatriculation** registration *UK* *ou* license *US* number ▸ **numéro**

d'accès [à un fournisseur d'accès Internet] access number ▸ **numéro de compte** account number ▸ **numéro azur** *telephone number for which calls are charged at the local rate irrespective of the actual distance covered* ▸ **numéro de poste** extension number ▸ **numéro de téléphone** telephone number ▸ **numéro vert** ≃ freefone number *UK*, ≃ 800 *ou* tollfree number *US* ▸ **il y a un article intéressant dans le numéro de ce mois-ci** there's an interesting article in this month's issue ▸ **tirer le mauvais numéro** *fig* to get a raw deal ▸ **lui, il a tiré le bon numéro!** *fig* he's really picked a winner! **2.** [de spectacle] act, turn ▸ **il fait le numéro le plus important du spectacle** he's top of the bill ▸ **faire son numéro** *fig* to do one's little act **3.** *fam* [personne] **: quel numéro!** what a character!

numéroter [3] [nymerɔte] **vt** to number.

numerus clausus [nymerysklɔzys] **nm** *restricted intake of students.*

numismatique [nymismatik] ■ **nf** numismatics *(U)*. ■ **adj** numismatic.

nu-pieds [nypje] **nm inv** [sandale] sandal.

nuptial, e, aux [nypsjal, o] **adj** nuptial.

nuque [nyk] **nf** nape.

nurse [nœrs] **nf** children's nurse, nanny *UK*.

nursery [nœrsəri] (pl **nurseries**) **nf 1.** [dans un hôpital] nursery **2.** [dans un lieu public] parent-and-baby clinic.

nutritif, ive [nytritif, iv] **adj** nutritious.

nutritionniste [nytrisjɔnist] **nmf** nutritionist, dietician.

Nylon® [nilɔ̃] **nm** nylon.

nymphe [nɛ̃f] **nf** nymph.

nymphomane [nɛ̃fɔman] **nf & adj** nymphomaniac.

o, ***O*** [o] **nm inv** [lettre] o, O.
◆ ***O*** (abr écrite de ***Ouest***) W.

ô [o] **interj** oh!, O!

OACI (abr de ***Organisation de l'aviation civile internationale***) **nf** ICAO.

OAS (abr de ***Organisation de l'armée secrète***) **nf** *organization opposed to independence in Algeria in the 1960s.*

oasis [ɔazis] **nf 1.** [dans désert] oasis **2.** *fig* [de calme] haven, oasis.

obédience [ɔbedjɑ̃s] **nf 1.** [appartenance] allegiance, persuasion ▸ **être d'obédience marxiste/catholique** to be a Marxist/Catholic **2.** [obéissance] obedience.

obéir [32] [ɔbeir] **vi 1.** [personne] **: obéir à qqn/qqch** to obey sb/sthg **2.** [freins] to respond.

obéissance [ɔbeisɑ̃s] **nf** obedience ▸ **devoir obéissance à qqn** to owe sb allegiance.

obéissant, ***e*** [ɔbeisɑ̃, ɑ̃t] **adj** obedient.

obélisque [ɔbelisk] **nm** obelisk.

obèse [ɔbɛz] ■ **nmf** obese person.
■ **adj** obese.

obésité [ɔbezite] **nf** obesity.

objecter [4] [ɔbʒɛkte] **vt 1.** [répliquer] to raise as an objection ▸ **objecter que** to object that **2.** [prétexter] **: objecter qqch (à qqn)** to put forward sthg as an excuse (to sb).

objecteur [ɔbʒɛktœr] **nm** objector ▸ **objecteur de conscience** conscientious objector.

objectif, ***ive*** [ɔbʒɛktif, iv] **adj** objective.
◆ ***objectif*** **nm 1.** PHOTO lens **2.** [but, cible] objective, target.

objection [ɔbʒɛksjɔ̃] **nf** objection ▸ **faire objection à** to object to.

objectivement [ɔbʒɛktivmɑ̃] **adv** objectively.

objectivité [ɔbʒɛktivite] **nf** objectivity.

objet [ɔbʒɛ] **nm 1.** [chose] object ▸ **objet d'art** objet d'art ▸ **objet de luxe** luxury item ▸ **objets personnels** personal belongings *ou* effects ▸ **objet de valeur** valuable ▸ **objets trouvés** lost property office *UK*, lost-and-found (office) *US*
2. [sujet] subject ▸ **l'objet de leurs discussions était toujours la politique** politics was always the subject of their discussions ▸ **être *ou* faire l'objet de** to be the subject of ▸ **faire l'objet d'attaques répétées** to be the victim of repeated attacks ▸ **faire l'objet de controverses** to be a controversial subject
3. [but] aim, object ▸ **cette réunion a pour objet de...** the aim of this meeting is to... ▸ **exposer l'objet de sa visite** to explain the purpose of *ou* reason for one's visit ▸ **sans objet** pointless ▸ **ces arguments sont maintenant sans objet** these arguments no longer apply *ou* are no longer applicable
4. DR matter ▸ **l'objet du litige** the matter at issue.

objurgations [ɔbʒyrgasjɔ̃] **nfpl 1.** [remontrances] objurgations **2.** [prières] pleas.

obligation [ɔbligasjɔ̃] **nf 1.** [gén] obligation ▸ **être dans l'obligation de faire qqch** to be obliged to do sthg ▸ **je suis dans l'obligation de vous expulser** I'm obliged *ou* forced to evict you ▸ **sans obligation d'achat** COMM (with) no obligation to buy ▸ **avoir une obligation envers qqn** to be under an obligation to sb ▸ **obligation alimentaire** alimony, maintenance (order) *UK* ▸ **obligation de réserve** duty of confidentiality **2.** FIN bond, debenture ▸ **obligation échue/négociable** matured/marketable bond ▸ **obligation d'entreprise** bond, debenture (stock) *UK* ▸ **obligation d'État** (government) bond ▸ **obligation hypothécaire** mortgage bond.
◆ ***obligations*** **nfpl** obligations, duties ▸ **avoir des obligations** to have obligations, to have a duty ▸ **mes obligations de président de la société** my duties as the chair-

man of the company ▸ **obligations militaires** military duties.

obligatoire [ɔbligatwar] **adj 1.** [imposé] compulsory, obligatory **2.** *fam* [inéluctable] inevitable.

obligeance [ɔbliʒɑ̃s] **nf** *sout* obligingness ▸ **avoir l'obligeance de faire qqch** to be good *ou* kind enough to do sthg.

obligeant, e [ɔbliʒɑ̃, ɑ̃t] **adj** helpful, obliging.

obliger [17] [ɔbliʒe] **vt 1.** [forcer] **: obliger qqn à qqch** to impose sthg on sb ▸ **obliger qqn à faire qqch** to force sb to do sthg ▸ **être obligé de faire qqch** to be obliged to do sthg **2.** DR to bind **3.** [rendre service à] to oblige.
◆ ***s'obliger*** **vp : s'obliger à qqch** to impose sthg on o.s. ▸ **s'obliger à faire qqch** to force o.s. to do sthg.

oblique [ɔblik] ■ **adj** oblique ▸ **en oblique** diagonally.
■ **nf** oblique line.

obliquer [3] [ɔblike] **vi** to turn off.

oblitérer [18] [ɔblitere] **vt 1.** [tamponner] to cancel **2.** MÉD to obstruct **3.** [effacer] to obliterate.

oblong, oblongue [ɔblɔ̃, ɔ̃g] **adj** oblong.

obnubiler [3] [ɔbnybile] **vt** to obsess ▸ **être obnubilé par** to be obsessed with *ou* by.

obole [ɔbɔl] **nf** small contribution.

obscène [ɔpsɛn] **adj** obscene.

obscénité [ɔpsenite] **nf** obscenity.

obscur, e [ɔpskyr] **adj 1.** [sombre] dark **2.** [confus] vague **3.** [inconnu, douteux] obscure.

obscurantisme [ɔpskyrɑ̃tism] **nm** obscurantism.

obscurcir [32] [ɔpskyrsir] **vt 1.** [assombrir] to darken **2.** [embrouiller] to confuse.
◆ ***s'obscurcir*** **vp 1.** [s'assombrir] to grow dark **2.** [s'embrouiller] to become confused.

obscurément [ɔpskyremɑ̃] **adv** obscurely.

obscurité [ɔpskyrite] **nf 1.** [nuit] darkness **2.** [anonymat] obscurity **3.** [hermétisme] abstruseness.

obsédant, e [ɔpsedɑ̃, ɑ̃t] **adj** haunting.

obsédé, e [ɔpsede] ■ **adj** obsessed.
■ **nm, f** obsessive ▸ **obsédé sexuel** sex maniac.

obséder [18] [ɔpsede] **vt** to obsess, to haunt.

obsèques [ɔpsɛk] **nfpl** funeral *sg*.

obséquieux, euse [ɔpsekjø, øz] **adj** obsequious.

obséquiosité [ɔpsekjozite] **nf** obsequiousness.

observance [ɔpsɛrvɑ̃s] **nf** observance.

observateur, trice [ɔpsɛrvatœr, tris] ■ **adj** observant.
■ **nm, f** observer.

observation [ɔpsɛrvasjɔ̃] **nf 1.** [gén] observation ▸ **être en observation** MÉD to be under observation **2.** [critique] remark **3.** [conformité] observance.

observatoire [ɔpsɛrvatwar] **nm 1.** ASTRON observatory **2.** [lieu de surveillance] observation post.

observer [3] [ɔpsɛrve] **vt 1.** [regarder, remarquer, respecter] to observe **2.** [épier] to watch **3.** [constater] **: observer que** to note that ▸ **faire observer qqch à qqn** to point sthg out to sb **4.** *sout* [attitude] to keep, to maintain.
◆ ***s'observer*** **vp 1.** [se surveiller] to be careful of one's behaviour *UK ou* behavior *US* **2.** [s'épier] to watch each other.

obsession [ɔpsesjɔ̃] **nf** obsession.

obsessionnel, elle [ɔpsesjɔnɛl] **adj** obsessional.

obsolète [ɔpsɔlɛt] **adj** obsolete.

obstacle [ɔpstakl] **nm 1.** [entrave] obstacle **2.** *fig* [difficulté] hindrance ▸ **faire obstacle à qqch/qqn** to hinder sthg/sb ▸ **rencontrer un obstacle** to meet an obstacle.

obstétricien, enne [ɔpstetrisjɛ̃, ɛn] **nm, f** obstetrician.

obstétrique [ɔpstetrik] **nf** obstetrics *(U)*.

obstination [ɔpstinasjɔ̃] **nf** stubbornness, obstinacy.

obstiné, e [ɔpstine] ■ **adj 1.** [entêté] stubborn, obstinate **2.** [acharné] dogged.
■ **nm, f** stubborn *ou* obstinate person.

obstinément [ɔpstinemɑ̃] **adv 1.** [refuser] obstinately **2.** [travailler] doggedly.

obstiner [3] [ɔpstine] ◆ ***s'obstiner*** **vp** to insist ▸ **s'obstiner à faire qqch** to persist stubbornly in doing sthg ▸ **s'obstiner dans qqch** to cling stubbornly to sthg.

obstruction [ɔpstryksjɔ̃] **nf 1.** MÉD obstruction, blockage **2.** POLIT & SPORT obstruction.

COMMENT EXPRIMER...

l'obligation

You have to be there at 8 o'clock / Il faut que tu y sois à 8 heures
You must talk to your boss about this / Tu dois en parler à ton chef
We will have to get approval from the board / Il nous faudra obtenir l'autorisation de la direction
It's essential that you call us as soon as you arrive / Il faut absolument que vous nous appeliez dès votre arrivée
You're under no obligation to buy / Vous n'avez pas l'obligation d'acheter
You don't have to stay / Tu n'es pas obligé de rester
There's no need to ask / Ce n'est pas la peine de demander
Do I really have to go? / Est-ce qu'il faut vraiment que j'y aille ?
Do you have to make an appointment? / Est-ce qu'il faut prendre rendez-vous ?
Do you require a deposit? / Vous exigez un acompte ?

obstructionnisme [ɔpstryksjɔnism] **m** POLIT obstructionism.

obstructionniste [ɔpstryksjɔnist] **nmf & adj** POLIT obstructionist.

obstruer [3] [ɔpstrye] **vt** to block, to obstruct.
◆ ***s'obstruer*** **vp** to become blocked.

obtempérer [18] [ɔptɑ̃pere] **vi : obtempérer à** to comply with.

obtenir [40] [ɔptənir] **vt** to get, to obtain ▸ **obtenir qqch de qqn** to get sthg from sb ▸ **obtenir de faire qqch** to get permission to do sthg ▸ **obtenir qqch à *ou* pour qqn** to obtain sthg for sb.

obtention [ɔptɑ̃sjɔ̃] **nf** obtaining.

obtenu, e [ɔptəny] **pp** ➤ ***obtenir***.

obtiendrai, obtiendras ➤ ***obtenir***.

obtienne, obtiennes ➤ ***obtenir***.

obturateur, trice [ɔptyratœr, tris] **adj** closing *(avant n)*.
◆ ***obturateur*** **nm 1.** [valve] stop valve **2.** PHOTO shutter.

obturation [ɔptyrasjɔ̃] **nf** closing, sealing.

obturer [3] [ɔptyre] **vt** to close, to seal / [dent] to fill.

obtus, e [ɔpty, yz] **adj** obtuse.

obus [ɔby] **nm** shell.

OC (abr écrite de ***ondes courtes***) SW.

occasion [ɔkazjɔ̃] **nf 1.** [possibilité, chance] opportunity, chance ▸ **saisir l'occasion (de faire qqch)** to seize *ou* grab the chance (to do sthg) ▸ **rater une occasion (de faire qqch)** to miss a chance (to do sthg) ▸ **être l'occasion de** to give rise to ▸ **à l'occasion** some time / [de temps en temps] sometimes, on occasion ▸ **à l'occasion, passez nous voir** drop by some time *ou* if you get the chance ▸ **à la première occasion** at the first opportunity ▸ **je le lui dirai à la première occasion** I'll tell him as soon as I get a chance ▸ **si l'occasion se présente** if the opportunity arises **2.** [circonstance] occasion ▸ **à l'occasion de** on the occasion of ▸ **dans les grandes occasions** on important occasions ▸ **ces retrouvailles furent l'occasion de grandes réjouissances** there were great festivities to celebrate this reunion **3.** [bonne affaire] bargain ▸ **pour ce prix-là, c'est une occasion!** it's a (real) bargain at that price!
◆ ***d'occasion*** **loc adv & loc adj** second-hand ▸ **voiture d'occasion** secondhand *ou* used car ▸ **j'ai fini par le trouver d'occasion** in the end I found a secondhand one.

occasionnel, elle [ɔkazjɔnɛl] **adj** [irrégulier - visite, problème] occasional / [- travail] casual.

occasionner [3] [ɔkazjɔne] **vt** to cause.

occident [ɔksidɑ̃] **nm** west.
◆ ***Occident*** **nm : l'Occident** the West.

occidental, e, aux [ɔksidɑ̃tal, o] **adj** western.
◆ ***Occidental, e*** (pl **-aux**) **nm, f** Westerner.

occiput [ɔksipyt] **nm** back of the head.

occitan, e [ɔksitɑ̃, an] **adj** Provençal French.
◆ ***occitan*** **nm** [langue] Provençal French.
◆ ***Occitan, e*** **nm, f** speaker of Provençal French.

occlusion [ɔklyzjɔ̃] **nf 1.** MÉD blockage, obstruction **2.** LING & CHIM occlusion.

occulte [ɔkylt] **adj** occult.

occulter [3] [ɔkylte] **vt** [sentiments] to conceal.

occupant, e [ɔkypɑ̃, ɑ̃t] ■ **adj** occupying.
■ **nm, f** occupant, occupier.
◆ ***occupant*** **nm : l'occupant** the occupying power *ou* forces *pl*.

occupation [ɔkypasjɔ̃] **nf 1.** [activité] occupation, job ▸ **vaquer à ses occupations** to go about one's business **2.** MIL occupation **3.** DR occupancy.
◆ ***Occupation*** **nf : l'Occupation** the Occupation (of France).

occupé, e [ɔkype] **adj 1.** [personne] busy ▸ **être occupé à qqch** to be busy with sthg **2.** [appartement, zone] occupied **3.** [place] taken / [toilettes] engaged *UK* ▸ **c'est occupé** [téléphone] it's engaged *UK ou* busy *US*.

occuper [3] [ɔkype] **vt 1.** [gén] to occupy ▸ **les grévistes occupent les bureaux** the strikers have occupied the offices **2.** [espace] to take up ▸ **le bar occupe le fond de la pièce/trop de place** the bar stands at the back of the room/takes up too much space **3.** [place, poste] to hold ▸ **Liverpool occupe la seconde place du championnat** Liverpool are (lying) second in the league table **4.** [main-d'œuvre] to employ.
◆ ***s'occuper*** **vp 1.** [s'activer] to keep o.s. busy ▸ **s'occuper à qqch/à faire qqch** to be busy with sthg/doing sthg ▸ **à quoi s'occupent les citadins au mois d'août?** how do city dwellers spend their time in August? **2. : s'occuper de qqch** [se charger de] to take care of sthg, to deal with sthg / [s'intéresser à] to take an interest in, to be interested in ▸ **je m'en occuperai plus tard** I'll see to *ou* attend to it later ▸ **qui s'occupe de votre dossier?** who's dealing with *ou* handling your file? ▸ **occupez-vous de vos affaires!** mind your own business! **3.** [prendre soin] **: s'occuper de qqn** to take care of sb, to look after sb ▸ **s'occuper d'un malade** to care for a patient.

occurrence [ɔkyrɑ̃s] **nf 1.** [circonstance] **: en l'occurrence** in this case **2.** LING occurrence.

OCDE (abr de ***Organisation de coopération et de développement économique***) **nf** OECD.

océan [ɔseɑ̃] **nm** ocean ▸ **l'océan Antarctique** the Antarctic Ocean ▸ **l'océan Arctique** the Arctic Ocean ▸ **l'océan Atlantique** the Atlantic Ocean ▸ **l'océan Indien** the Indian Ocean ▸ **l'océan Pacifique** the Pacific Ocean.

Océanie [ɔseani] **nf : l'Océanie** Oceania.

océanien, enne [ɔseanjɛ̃, ɛn] **adj** Oceanian.
◆ ***Océanien, enne*** **nm, f** Oceanian.

océanique [ɔseanik] **adj** ocean *(avant n)*.

océanographie [ɔseanɔgrafi] **nf** oceanography.

ocelot [ɔslo] **nm** ocelot.

ocre [ɔkr] **adj inv & nf** ochre *UK*, ocher *US*.

octane [ɔktan] **nm : indice d'octane** octane rating.

octante [ɔktɑ̃t] **adj num inv** *Belgique & Suisse* eighty.

octave [ɔktav] **nf** octave.

octet [ɔktɛ] **nm** INFORM byte.

octobre [ɔktɔbr] **nm** October ; voir aussi ***septembre***.

octogénaire [ɔktɔʒenɛr] **nmf & adj** octogenarian.

octogone [ɔktɔgɔn] **nm** octagon.

octroie, octroies ➤ ***octroyer***.

octroyer [13] [ɔktrwaje] **vt : octroyer qqch à qqn** to grant sb sthg, to grant sthg to sb.
◆ ***s'octroyer*** **vp** to grant o.s., to treat o.s. to.

oculaire [ɔkylɛr] ■ **nm** eyepiece.
■ **adj** ocular, eye *(avant n)* ▸ **témoin oculaire** eyewitness.

oculiste [ɔkylist] **nmf** ophthalmologist.

ode [ɔd] **nf** ode.

odeur [ɔdœr] **nf** smell ▸ **ne pas être en odeur de sainteté (auprès de)** *fig* to be out of favour *UK* *ou* favor *US* (with).

odieusement [ɔdjøzmɑ̃] **adv** abominably.

odieux, euse [ɔdjø, øz] **adj 1.** [crime] odious, abominable **2.** [personne, attitude] unbearable, obnoxious.

odorant, e [ɔdɔrɑ̃, ɑ̃t] **adj** sweet-smelling, fragrant.

odorat [ɔdɔra] **nm** (sense of) smell.

odoriférant, e [ɔdɔriferɑ̃, ɑ̃t] **adj** sweet-smelling, fragrant.

odyssée [ɔdise] **nf** odyssey.

OEA (abr de ***Organisation des États américains***) **nf** OAS.

œdème [edɛm] **nm** oedema *UK*, edema *US*.

œil [œj] (pl **yeux** [jø]) **nm 1.** [gén] eye ▸ **yeux bridés/exorbités/globuleux** slanting/bulging/protruding eyes ▸ **avoir de bons yeux** to have good eyesight ▸ **avoir de mauvais yeux** to have bad *ou* poor eyesight ▸ **avoir les yeux cernés** to have bags under one's eyes ▸ **baisser/lever les yeux** to look down/up, to lower/raise one's eyes ▸ **du coin de l'œil** out of the corner of one's eye ▸ **chercher qqn des yeux** to look around for sb ▸ **écarquiller les yeux** to stare wide-eyed ▸ **à l'œil nu** to the naked eye ▸ **sous mes/tes** *etc* **yeux** before my/your *etc* very eyes ▸ **à vue d'œil** visibly ▸ **rien n'échappait à l'œil du professeur** nothing escaped the teacher's notice **2.** [bulle de graisse] blob of grease *ou* fat
▸▸ **attention les yeux!** *fam* get an eyeful of that! ▸ **avoir qqch/qqn à l'œil** to have one's eye on sthg/sb ▸ **j'ai eu deux tickets à l'œil** I got two tickets gratis *ou* (for) free *ou* on the house ▸ **avoir un œil au beurre noir** to have a black eye ▸ **n'avoir pas froid aux yeux** not to be afraid of anything, to have plenty of nerve ▸ **avoir des yeux de lynx** to have eyes like a hawk ▸ **ne pas avoir les yeux dans sa poche** to be very observant ▸ **couver qqch/qqn des yeux** to look fondly at sthg/sb, to look lovingly at sthg/sb ▸ **ça crève les yeux** *fam* it's staring you in the face, it's as plain as the nose on your face ▸ **ne pas en croire ses yeux** not to believe one's eyes ▸ **dévorer qqn/qqch des yeux** [avec insistance] to eye sb/sthg intently / [avec convoitise] to eye sb/sthg greedily ▸ **faire de l'œil à qqn** *fam* to give sb the eye, to eye sb up ▸ **faire les gros yeux à qqn** to glare at sb ▸ **faire qqch pour les beaux yeux de qqn** to do sthg for the love of sb ▸ **fermer les yeux sur qqch** to close one's eyes to sthg ▸ **jeter le mauvais œil à qqn** to give sb the evil eye ▸ **mon œil!** *fam* like hell! ▸ **généreux, mon œil!** generous, my foot! ▸ **ouvrir l'œil** to keep one's eyes open ▸ **se rincer l'œil** *fam* to get an eyeful ▸ **cela saute aux yeux** it's obvious ▸ **tourner de l'œil** *fam* to pass out ▸ **voir qqch d'un bon/mauvais œil** to look favourably/unfavourably upon sthg.

œil-de-bœuf [œjdəbœf] (pl **œils-de-bœuf**) **nm** bull's-eye window.

œillade [œjad] **nf** wink ▸ **lancer une œillade à qqn** to wink at sb.

œillère [œjɛr] **nf** eyebath.
◆ ***œillères*** **nfpl** blinkers *UK*, blinders *US* ▸ **avoir des œillères** *fam fig* to be blinkered.

œillet [œjɛ] **nm 1.** [fleur] carnation **2.** [de chaussure] eyelet.

œnologie [enɔlɔʒi] **nf** wine appreciation.

œnologue [enɔlɔg] **nmf** wine expert.

œsophage [ezɔfaʒ] **nm** oesophagus *UK*, esophagus *US*.

œstrogène [ɛstrɔʒɛn] **nm** oestrogen *UK*, estrogen *US*.

œuf [œf] **nm** egg ▸ **œuf à la coque/au plat/poché** boiled/fried/poached egg ▸ **œuf mollet/dur** soft-boiled/hard-boiled egg ▸ **œuf de Pâques** Easter egg ▸ **œufs brouillés** scrambled eggs ▸ **œufs en** *ou* **à la neige** whipped egg whites ▸ **dans l'œuf** *fig* in the bud.

œuvre [œvr] ■ **nf 1.** [travail] work ▸ **être à l'œuvre** to be working *ou* at work ▸ **se mettre à l'œuvre** to get down to work ▸ **mettre qqch en œuvre** to make use of sthg / [loi, accord, projet] to implement sthg **2.** [artistique] work / [ensemble de la production d'un artiste] works *pl* ▸ **œuvre d'art** work of art ▸ **œuvre de bienfaisance** charity, charitable organization / [organisation] charity.
■ **nm 1.** [d'artiste] works *pl*, work **2.** [de bâtiment] **: le gros œuvre** the shell.

œuvrer [5] [œvre] **vi** *littéraire* **: œuvrer (pour)** to work (for).

OFCE (abr de ***Observatoire français des conjonctures économiques***) **nm** *economic research institute.*

off [ɔf] **adj inv 1.** CINÉ [voix, son] off **2.** [festival] fringe *(avant n).*

offensant, e [ɔfɑ̃sɑ̃, ɑ̃t] **adj** offensive.

offense [ɔfɑ̃s] **nf 1.** [insulte] insult **2.** RELIG trespass.

offenser [3] [ɔfɑ̃se] **vt 1.** [personne] to offend **2.** [bon goût] to offend against.
◆ ***s'offenser*** **vp : s'offenser de** to take offence *UK* *ou* offense *US* at, to be offended by.

offenseur [ɔfɑ̃sœr] **nm** offender, offending party.

offensif, ive [ɔfɑ̃sif, iv] **adj** offensive.
◆ ***offensive*** **nf 1.** MIL offensive ▸ **passer à l'offensive** to go on the offensive ▸ **prendre l'offensive** to take the offensive **2.** *fig* [du froid] (sudden) onset.

offert, e [ɔfɛr, ɛrt] **pp** ➤ ***offrir.***

offertoire [ɔfɛrtwar] **nm** offertory.

office [ɔfis] **nm 1.** [bureau] office, agency ▸ **office de tourisme** tourist office **2.** [fonction] **: faire office de** to act as ▸ **remplir son office** to do its job, to fulfil its function **3.** RELIG service
▸▸ **recourir aux offices de qqn** to turn to sb for help.
◆ ***d'office*** **loc adv** automatically, as a matter of course ▸ **commis d'office** officially appointed.

officialiser [3] [ɔfisjalize] **vt** to make official.

officiel, elle [ɔfisjɛl] **adj & nm, f** official.

officiellement [ɔfisjɛlmɑ̃] **adv** officially.

officier[1] [9] [ɔfisje] **vi** to officiate.

officier[2] [ɔfisje] **nm** officer ▸ **officier d'ordonnance** aide-de-camp.

officieusement [ɔfisjøzmɑ̃] **adv** unofficially.

officieux, euse [ɔfisjø, øz] **adj** unofficial.

officine [ɔfisin] **nf 1.** [pharmacie] pharmacy **2.** *péj* [repaire] agency.

offrande [ɔfrɑ̃d] **nf 1.** [don] offering **2.** RELIG offertory.

offrant [ɔfrɑ̃] **nm : au plus offrant** to the highest bidder.

offre [ɔfr] **nf 1.** [proposition] offer / [aux enchères] bid / [pour contrat] tender ▸ **'offres d'emploi'** 'situations vacant *UK*', 'help wanted *US*', 'vacancies' ▸ **offre d'essai** trial offer ▸ **offre de lancement** introductory offer ▸ **offre promotionnelle** promotional offer ▸ **offre de remboursement** money-back offer ▸ **offre publique d'achat** takeover bid ▸ **offre de prix** price bid **2.** ÉCON supply ▸ **la loi de l'offre et de la demande** the law of supply and demand.

offrir [34] [ɔfrir] **vt 1.** [faire cadeau] **: offrir qqch à qqn** to give sb sthg, to give sthg to sb ▸ **offrir qqch en cadeau à qqn** to give sb sthg as a present **2.** [proposer] **: offrir qqch à qqn** to offer sb sthg *ou* sthg to sb ▸ **elle nous a offert sa maison pour l'été** she offered us her house for the summer ▸ **offrir (à qqn) de faire qqch** to offer to do sthg (for sb) **3.** [présenter] to offer, to present ▸ **cette solution offre l'avantage d'être équitable** this solution has *ou* presents the advantage of being fair ▸ **son visage n'offrait rien d'accueillant** his/her face showed no sign of welcome.
◆ ***s'offrir*** **vp 1.** [croisière, livre] to treat o.s. to **2.** [se présenter] to present itself ▸ **un seul moyen s'offrait à moi** there was only one course of action open to me **3.** [s'exposer] **: s'offrir à qqch** to expose o.s. to sthg **4.** [se proposer] to offer one's services, to offer o.s. ▸ **s'offrir à faire qqch** to offer to do sthg ▸ **s'offrir à payer les dégâts** to offer to pay for the damage.

offset [ɔfsɛt] ■ **adj inv** offset.
■ **nm inv** offset (lithography).
■ **nf inv** offset press.

offshore [ɔfʃɔr] ■ **adj inv 1.** [exploitation] offshore **2.** SPORT speedboat *(avant n)* ▸ **bateau offshore** speedboat.
■ **nm** SPORT speedboat racing.

offusquer [3] [ɔfyske] **vt** to offend.
◆ ***s'offusquer*** **vp : s'offusquer (de)** to take offence *UK* *ou* offense *US* (at).

ogive [ɔʒiv] **nf 1.** ARCHIT ogive ▸ **en ogive** ribbed **2.** MIL [d'obus] head / [de fusée] nosecone ▸ **ogive nucléaire** nuclear warhead.

OGM (abr de ***organisme génétiquement modifié***) **nm** GMO.

ogre, ogresse [ɔgr, ɔgrɛs] **nm, f** ogre (f ogress).

oh [o] ■ **interj** oh! ▸ **oh là là!** dear oh dear!
■ **nm inv : pousser des oh et des ah** to ooh and ah.

ohé [ɔe] **interj** hey!

OHQ (abr de ***ouvrier hautement qualifié***) **nm** highly skilled worker.

oie [wa] **nf** goose ▸ **oie blanche** *fig* innocent young girl.

oignon [ɔɲɔ̃] **nm 1.** [plante] onion ▸ **mêle-toi de tes oignons** *fam fig* mind your own business ▸ **soigner qqn aux petits oignons** *fam fig* to take care of sb's every need **2.** [bulbe] bulb **3.** MÉD bunion.

oindre [82] [wɛ̃dr] **vt** *littéraire* **1.** [corps] to (rub with) oil **2.** RELIG to anoint.

oiseau, x [wazo] **nm 1.** ZOOL bird ▸ **oiseau de proie** bird of prey **2.** *fam péj* [individu] character.

oiseau-mouche [wazomuʃ] (pl **oiseaux-mouches**) **nm** hummingbird.

oiseleur [waslœr] **nm** bird catcher.

oiseux, euse [wazø, øz] **adj** pointless.

oisif, ive [wazif, iv] ■ **adj** idle.
■ **nm, f** man of leisure (f woman of leisure).

oisillon [wazijɔ̃] **nm** fledgling.

oisiveté [wazivte] **nf** idleness.

oison [wazɔ̃] **nm** gosling.

OIT (abr de ***Organisation internationale du travail***) **nf** ILO.

O.K. [ɔke] **interj** *fam* okay.

OL (abr écrite de ***ondes longues***) LW.

ola [ɔla] **nf** Mexican wave *UK*, wave *US*.

oléagineux, euse [ɔleaʒinø, øz] **adj** oleaginous.
◆ ***oléagineux*** **nm** oleaginous plant.

oléoduc [ɔleɔdyk] **nm** (oil) pipeline.

olfactif, ive [ɔlfaktif, iv] **adj** olfactory.

oligo-élément [ɔligɔelemɑ̃] (pl **oligo-éléments**) **nm** trace element.

olivâtre [ɔlivatr] **adj** [verdâtre] olive-coloured *UK*, olive-colored *US* / [teint] sallow.

olive [ɔliv] ■ **nf** olive.
■ **adj inv** olive, olive-green.

oliveraie [ɔlivrɛ] **nf** olive grove.

olivier [ɔlivje] **nm** [arbre] olive tree / [bois] olive wood.

OLP (abr de ***Organisation de libération de la Palestine***) **nf** PLO.

Olympe [ɔlɛ̃p] **nm : l'Olympe** Olympus.

olympiade [ɔlɛ̃pjad] *(gén pl)* **nf** olympiad *sg*.

olympien, enne [ɔlɛ̃pjɛ̃, ɛn] **adj** Olympian.

olympique [ɔlɛ̃pik] **adj** Olympic *(avant n)*.

OM ■ **nm** (abr de ***Olympique de Marseille***) *Marseilles football team*.
■ **nfpl** (abr écrite de ***ondes moyennes***) MW.

Oman [ɔman] **npr** Oman ▸ **le sultanat d'Oman** the Sultanate of Oman.

ombilic [ɔ̃bilik] **nm 1.** [de personne] navel **2.** BOT navelwort.

ombilical, e, aux [ɔ̃bilikal, o] **adj** umbilical.

omble [ɔ̃bl] **nm : omble chevalier** *fish found especially in Lake Geneva, with a light texture and flavour*.

ombrage [ɔ̃braʒ] **nm** shade ▸ **porter ombrage à qqn** *fig* to offend sb ▸ **prendre ombrage de qqch** *fig* to take offence *UK* *ou* offense *US* at sthg, to take umbrage at sthg.

ombragé, e [ɔ̃braʒe] **adj** shady.

ombrageux**, **euse [ɔ̃braʒø, øz] **adj 1.** [personne] touchy, prickly **2.** [cheval] nervous, skittish.

ombre [ɔ̃br] **nf 1.** [zone sombre] shade ▸ **il fait 30°C à l'ombre** it's 30°C in the shade ▸ **faire de l'ombre à qqn** to get in sb's light ▸ **à l'ombre de** [arbre] in the shade of / [personne] in the shadow of ▸ **dans l'ombre des sous-bois** in the shadowy undergrowth ▸ **rester dans l'ombre de qqn** *fig* to live in sb's shadow ▸ **laisser qqch dans l'ombre** *fig* to deliberately ignore sthg ▸ **vivre dans l'ombre** *fig* to live in obscurity ▸ **ceux qui œuvrent dans l'ombre pour la paix** those who work behind the scenes to bring about peace
2. [forme, fantôme] shadow ▸ **ombres chinoises** [spectacle] shadow play *ou* pantomime *sg* / [jeu] Chinese shadows ▸ **il n'est plus que l'ombre de lui-même** he's but a shadow of his former self ▸ **il y a une ombre au tableau** *fig* there's a fly in the ointment
3. [trace] hint ▸ **ça ne fait pas l'ombre d'un doute** there's not the shadow of a doubt
4. [cosmétique] **: ombre à paupières** eye shadow.

PARONYME / CONFUSABLE
ombre
Il existe deux traductions du mot ombre. *Shadow* désigne l'ombre portée au sol, tandis que *shade* désigne l'endroit à l'abri du soleil.

ombrelle [ɔ̃brɛl] **nf** parasol.

ombrer [3] [ɔ̃bre] **vt 1.** [paupières] to put eye shadow on **2.** [dessin] to shade (in).

OMC (abr de ***Organisation mondiale du commerce***) **nf** WTO.

omelette [ɔmlɛt] **nf** omelette ▸ **omelette norvégienne** baked Alaska.

omets ➤ ***omettre***.

omettre [84] [ɔmɛtr] **vt** to omit ▸ **omettre de faire qqch** to omit to do sthg.

OMI (abr de ***Organisation maritime internationale***) **nf** IMO.

omis**, **e [ɔmi, iz] **pp** ➤ ***omettre***.

omission [ɔmisjɔ̃] **nf** omission ▸ **par omission** by omission.

OMM (abr de ***Organisation météorologique mondiale***) **nf** WMO.

omnibus [ɔmnibys] ■ **nm** stopping *UK ou* local *US* train. ■ **adj inv : ce train est omnibus pour...** this train stops at all stations to...

omnipotent**, **e [ɔmnipɔtɑ̃, ɑ̃t] **adj** omnipotent.

omniprésence [ɔmniprezɑ̃s] **nf** omnipresence.

omniprésent**, **e [ɔmniprezɑ̃, ɑ̃t] **adj** omnipresent.

omniscient**, **e [ɔmnisjɑ̃, ɑ̃t] **adj** omniscient.

omnisports [ɔmnispɔr] **adj inv** sports *(avant n)*.

omnivore [ɔmnivɔr] ■ **nm** omnivore.
■ **adj** omnivorous.

omoplate [ɔmɔplat] **nf** [os] shoulder blade / [épaule] shoulder.

OMS (abr de ***Organisation mondiale de la santé***) **nf** WHO.

on [ɔ̃] **pron indéf 1.** [indéterminé] you, one ▸ **on dirait qu'il va pleuvoir** it looks like rain ▸ **on n'a pas le droit de fumer ici** you're not allowed *ou* one isn't allowed to smoke here, smoking isn't allowed here **2.** [les gens, l'espèce humaine] they, people ▸ **on dit que la vie là-bas n'est pas chère** they say that the cost of living over there is cheap ▸ **on vit de plus en plus vieux en Europe** people in Europe are living longer and longer **3.** [quelqu'un] someone ▸ **est-ce qu'on vous sert, Monsieur?** are you being served, Sir? ▸ **on vous a appelé au téléphone ce matin** there was a telephone call for you this morning **4.** *fam* [nous] we ▸ **on s'en va** we're off, we're going **5.** [se substituant à d'autres pronoms personnels] **: alors, on ne répond pas au téléphone?** *fam* aren't you going to answer the phone? ▸ **ça va, on a compris!** *fam* all right, I've got the message!

onanisme [ɔnanism] **nm** onanism.

once [ɔ̃s] **nf : une once (de)** an ounce (of).

oncle [ɔ̃kl] **nm** uncle.

onction [ɔ̃ksjɔ̃] **nf** unction.

onctueux**, **euse [ɔ̃ktɥø, øz] **adj** smooth.

onctuosité [ɔ̃ktɥozite] **nf** smoothness.

onde [ɔ̃d] **nf 1.** PHYS wave **2.** *littéraire* [eau] **: l'onde** the waters *pl.*
◆ ***ondes*** **nfpl** [radio] air *sg.*

ondée [ɔ̃de] **nf** shower (of rain).

on-dit [ɔ̃di] **nm inv** rumour *UK*, rumor *US*, hearsay *(U)*.

ondoyant**, **e [ɔ̃dwajɑ̃, ɑ̃t] **adj** [ondulant] rippling / [démarche] swaying.

ondoyer [13] [ɔ̃dwaje] **vi** to ripple.

ondulant**, **e [ɔ̃dylɑ̃, ɑ̃t] **adj** [ondoyant] undulating, wavy / [démarche] swaying.

ondulation [ɔ̃dylasjɔ̃] **nf 1.** [mouvement] rippling / [de sol, terrain] undulation **2.** [de coiffure] wave.

ondulé**, **e [ɔ̃dyle] **adj** [surface] undulating / [chevelure] wavy / [tôle, carton] corrugated.

onduler [3] [ɔ̃dyle] **vi** [drapeau] to ripple, to wave / [cheveux] to be wavy / [route] to undulate.

one-man-show [wanmanʃo] **nm inv** one-man show

onéreux**, **euse [ɔnerø, øz] **adj** costly.

ONF (abr de ***Office national des forêts***) **nm** *French national forestry agency*, ≃ Forestry Commission *UK*, ≃ National Forestry Service *US*.

ONG (abr de ***organisation non gouvernementale***) **nf** NGO.

ongle [ɔ̃gl] **nm 1.** [de personne] fingernail, nail ▸ **se faire les ongles** to do one's nails ▸ **se ronger les ongles** to bite one's nails **2.** [d'animal] claw.

onglée [ɔ̃gle] **nf : j'ai l'onglée** my fingers are numb with cold.

onglet [ɔ̃glɛ] **nm 1.** [de reliure] tab **2.** [de lame] thumbnail groove **3.** CULIN top skirt.

onguent [ɔ̃gɑ̃] **nm** ointment.

onirique [ɔnirik] **adj** [relatif au rêve] dream *(avant n)* / [semblable au rêve] dreamlike.

onomastique [ɔnɔmastik] ■ **nf** onomastics *(U)*.
■ **adj** onomastic.

onomatopée [ɔnɔmatɔpe] **nf** onomatopoeia.

ont ➤ ***avoir***.

ONU, Onu [ɔny] (abr de ***Organisation des Nations unies***) **nf** UN, UNO.

ONUDI, Onudi [ɔnydi] (abr de ***Organisation des Nations unies pour le développement industriel***) **nf** UNIDO.

onyx [ɔniks] **nm** onyx.

onze [ɔ̃z] ■ **adj num inv** eleven.
■ **nm** [chiffre & SPORT] eleven ; voir aussi ***six***.

onzième [ɔ̃zjɛm] ■ **adj num inv, nm & nmf** eleventh.
■ **nf** [classe] ≃ second year ***ou*** form *(at primary school)* ***UK***, ≃ first grade ***US*** / voir aussi ***sixième, sixième***.

OP (abr de ***ouvrier professionnel***) **nm** skilled worker.

OPA (abr de ***offre publique d'achat***) **nf** takeover bid ▸ **OPA amicale** friendly takeover bid ▸ **OPA hostile** hostile takeover bid.

opacité [ɔpasite] **nf** opacity.

opale [ɔpal] **nf & adj inv** opal.

opaline [ɔpalin] **nf** opaline.

opaque [ɔpak] **adj : opaque (à)** opaque (to).

op. cit. (abr écrite de ***opere citato***) op. cit.

OPE (abr de ***offre publique d'échange***) **nf** *takeover bid where bidder offers to exchange shares.*

OPEP, Opep [ɔpɛp] (abr de ***Organisation des pays exportateurs de pétrole***) **nf** OPEC.

opéra [ɔpera] **nm 1.** MUS opera **2.** [théâtre] opera house ▸ **l'Opéra Bastille** *opera house built on the site of the Bastille* ▸ **l'Opéra de Paris** the Paris Opera (House).

opérable [ɔperabl] **adj** operable.

opéra-bouffe [ɔperabuf] (pl **opéras-bouffes**) **nm** comic opera.

opéra-comique [ɔperakɔmik] (pl **opéras-comiques**) **nm** light opera.

opérateur, trice [ɔperatœr, tris] **nm, f** operator ▸ **opérateur de saisie** keyboarder.

opération [ɔperasjɔ̃] **nf 1.** [gén] operation ▸ **pratiquer une opération** to carry out surgery ***ou*** an operation ▸ **subir une grave/petite opération** to undergo major/minor surgery, to have a major/minor operation ▸ **la police a effectué une opération coup de poing dans le quartier** the police swooped on the area ▸ **crois-tu que tu y arriveras par l'opération du Saint-Esprit?** *hum* do you think you'll succeed just waiting for things to happen? **2.** COMM deal, transaction ▸ **opération bancaire** bank transaction ▸ **opération boursière** stock exchange transaction ***ou*** dealing ▸ **opérations de Bourse** share dealing.

opérationnel, elle [ɔperasjɔnɛl] **adj** operational.

opératoire [ɔperatwar] **adj** MÉD operating *(avant n)* ▸ **choc opératoire** post-operative shock.

opérer [18] [ɔpere] ■ **vt 1.** MÉD to operate on **2.** [exécuter] to carry out, to implement / [choix, tri] to make.
■ **vi** [agir] to take effect / [personne] to operate, to proceed.
◆ ***s'opérer*** **vp** to come about, to take place.

opérette [ɔperɛt] **nf** operetta.

ophtalmique [ɔftalmik] **adj** ophthalmic.

ophtalmologiste [ɔftalmɔlɔʒist] **nmf** ophthalmologist.

Opinel® [ɔpinɛl] **nm** *folding knife used especially for outdoor activities, scouting etc.*

opiner [3] [ɔpine] **vi** *sout* **: opiner à qqch** to give one's consent to sthg.

COMMENT EXPRIMER...

l'opinion

Pour exprimer son opinion

In my opinion, ... / À mon avis, ...
As I see it, ... / Selon moi, ...
As far as I'm concerned, ... / En ce qui me concerne, ...
Personally, I feel that... / Personnellement, j'ai le sentiment que...
It seems to me that... / Il me semble que...
If you ask me, ... / Si vous voulez mon avis, ...
Quite frankly, I'm not impressed / Franchement, je ne trouve pas ça terrible
On balance, I think it's a good idea / Tout bien considéré, je pense que c'est une bonne idée
If you don't mind my saying so, it seems rather complicated / Excusez-moi, mais ça semble plutôt compliqué
I don't know about you, but I quite like it / Je ne sais pas ce que vous en pensez, mais moi, j'aime bien

Pour solliciter une opinion

What do you think of their proposal? / Que pensez-vous de leur proposition ?
What's your opinion on the fashion industry? / Quel est votre avis sur l'industrie de la mode ?
I'd like to hear your views / J'aimerais connaître votre point de vue
Anne, what do you think? / Qu'est-ce que tu en penses, Anne ?
What's your take on the situation? / Qu'est-ce que t'en dis ?

Pour éviter de prendre position

That depends / Ça dépend
I don't know really / Je ne sais pas vraiment
It's difficult to say / C'est difficile à dire
I wouldn't like to say / Je préférerais ne rien dire
I haven't really thought about it / Je n'y ai pas vraiment réfléchi

opiniâtre [ɔpinjatr] **adj 1.** [caractère, personne] stubborn, obstinate **2.** [effort] dogged / [travail] unrelenting / [fièvre, toux] persistent.

opiniâtreté [ɔpinjatrəte] **nf** [de caractère, personne] stubbornness, obstinacy.

opinion [ɔpinjɔ̃] **nf** opinion ▸ **conforter *ou* renforcer qqn dans son opinion** to confirm sb's opinion ▸ **avoir (une) bonne/mauvaise opinion de** to have a good/bad opinion of ▸ **l'opinion publique** public opinion.

opium [ɔpjɔm] **nm** opium.

opportun**, **e [ɔpɔrtœ̃, yn] **adj** opportune, timely.

opportunément [ɔpɔrtynemɑ̃] **adv** opportunely.

opportunisme [ɔpɔrtynism] **nm** opportunism.

opportuniste [ɔpɔrtynist] ■ **nmf** opportunist.
■ **adj** opportunistic.

opportunité [ɔpɔrtynite] **nf 1.** [à-propos] opportuneness, timeliness **2.** [occasion] opportunity.

opposant**, **e [ɔpozɑ̃, ɑ̃t] ■ **adj** opposing.
■ **nm, f : opposant (à)** opponent (of).

opposé**, **e [ɔpoze] **adj 1.** [direction, côté, angle] opposite **2.** [intérêts, opinions] conflicting / [forces] opposing **3.** [hostile] **: opposé à** opposed to.
◆ ***opposé*** **nm : l'opposé** the opposite ▸ **à l'opposé de** in the opposite direction from / *fig* unlike, contrary to.

opposer [3] [ɔpoze] **vt 1.** [mettre en opposition - choses, notions] **: opposer qqch (à)** to contrast sthg (with) **2.** [mettre en présence - personnes, armées] to oppose ▸ **opposer deux équipes** to bring two teams together ▸ **opposer qqn à qqn** to pit *ou* set sb against sb ▸ **qui peut-on opposer au président sortant?** who can we put up against the outgoing president? **3.** [refus, protestation, objection] to put forward ▸ **opposer une objection à qqn** to raise an objection with sb, to put forward an objection to sb **4.** [diviser] to divide ▸ **deux guerres ont opposé nos pays** two wars have brought our countries into conflict.
◆ ***s'opposer*** **vp 1.** [contraster] to contrast **2.** [entrer en conflit] to clash **3. : s'opposer à** [se dresser contre] to oppose, to be opposed to ▸ **il s'opposera ce soir au président dans un débat télévisé** he'll face the president tonight in a televised debate ▸ **s'opposer à ce que qqn fasse qqch** to be opposed to sb's doing sthg ▸ **je m'oppose à ce que tu reviennes** I'm against *ou* opposed to your coming back.

opposition [ɔpozisjɔ̃] **nf 1.** [gén] opposition ▸ **nous avons rencontré une forte opposition** we encountered strong opposition ▸ **faire opposition à** [décision, mariage] to oppose / [chèque] to stop *UK* ▸ **entrer en opposition avec** to come into conflict with ▸ **je me suis trouvée en opposition avec elle sur plusieurs points** I found myself at odds *ou* at variance with her on several points **2.** DR **: opposition (à)** objection (to) ▸ **faire opposition à un acte** to lodge an objection to a deed **3.** [contraste] contrast ▸ **opposition de *ou* entre deux styles** clash of *ou* between two styles ▸ **par opposition à** in contrast with, as opposed to **4.** POLIT **: les dirigeants/partis de l'opposition** the leaders/parties of the Opposition.

oppressant**, **e [ɔpresɑ̃, ɑ̃t] **adj** oppressive.

oppresser [4] [ɔprese] **vt 1.** [étouffer] to suffocate, to stifle **2.** *fig* [tourmenter] to oppress.

oppresseur [ɔpresœr] ■ **nm** oppressor.
■ **adj** oppressive.

oppressif**, **ive [ɔpresif, iv] **adj** oppressive.

oppression [ɔpresjɔ̃] **nf 1.** [asservissement] oppression **2.** [malaise] tightness of the chest.

opprimé**, **e [ɔprime] ■ **adj** oppressed.
■ **nm, f** oppressed person.

opprimer [3] [ɔprime] **vt 1.** [asservir] to oppress **2.** [étouffer] to stifle.

opprobre [ɔprɔbr] **nm : jeter l'opprobre sur qqn** to cast opprobrium on sb.

opter [3] [ɔpte] **vi : opter pour** to opt for.

opticien**, **enne [ɔptisjɛ̃, ɛn] **nm, f** optician.

optimal**, **e**, **aux [ɔptimal, o] **adj** optimal.

optimiser [ɔptimize], ***optimaliser*** [3] [ɔptimalize] **vt** to optimize.

optimisme [ɔptimism] **nm** optimism.

optimiste [ɔptimist] ■ **nmf** optimist.
■ **adj** optimistic.

optimum [ɔptimɔm] (pl **optimums *ou* optima** [-ma]) **nm & adj** optimum.

option [ɔpsjɔ̃] **nf 1.** [gén] option ▸ **prendre une option sur** FIN to take (out) an option on **2.** [accessoire] optional extra.

optionnel**, **elle [ɔpsjɔnɛl] **adj** optional.

optique [ɔptik] ■ **nf 1.** [science, technique] optics (U) **2.** [perspective] viewpoint ▸ **dans l'optique de faire qqch** with a mind *ou* view to doing sthg.
■ **adj** [nerf] optic / [verre] optical.

opulence [ɔpylɑ̃s] **nf 1.** [richesse] opulence ▸ **vivre ou nager dans l'opulence** to live a life of luxury **2.** [ampleur] fullness, ampleness.

opulent**, **e [ɔpylɑ̃, ɑ̃t] **adj 1.** [riche] rich **2.** [gros] ample

OQ (abr de ***ouvrier qualifié***) **nm** skilled worker.

or[1] [ɔr] **nm 1.** [métal, couleur] gold ▸ **en or** [objet] gold (avant n) ▸ **une bague en or** a gold ring ▸ **une occasion en or** a golden opportunity ▸ **une affaire en or** [achat] an excellent bargain / [commerce] a lucrative line of business ▸ **j'ai une femme en or** I've a wonderful wife ▸ **or blanc** white gold ▸ **or massif** solid gold ▸ **or noir** *fig* oil ▸ **le cours de l'or** the price of gold ▸ **l'étalon-or** the gold standard ▸ **pour tout l'or du monde** *fig* for all the tea in China ▸ **rouler sur l'or** *fig* to be rolling in it ▸ **un cœur d'or** heart of gold **2.** [dorure] gilding.

or[2] [ɔr] **conj** [au début d'une phrase] now ▸ **il faut tenir les délais; or, ce n'est pas toujours possible** deadlines must be met; now this is not always possible / [pour introduire un contraste] well, but ▸ **je devais y aller, or au dernier moment j'ai eu un empêchement** I was supposed to go but then at the last moment something came up.

oracle [ɔrakl] **nm** oracle.

orage [ɔraʒ] **nm 1.** [tempête] storm ▸ **il y a de l'orage dans l'air** *fig* there's a storm brewing **2.** *fig* [tumulte, revers] turmoil.

orageux**, **euse [ɔraʒø, øz] **adj** stormy.

oraison [ɔrɛzɔ̃] **nf** prayer ▸ **oraison funèbre** funeral oration.

oral**, **e**, **aux [ɔral, o] **adj** oral.
◆ ***oral*** **nm** oral (examination) ▸ **oral de rattrapage** *oral examination taken after failing written exams.*

oralement [ɔralmɑ̃] **adv** orally.

orange [ɔrɑ̃ʒ] ■ **nf** orange ▸ **orange pressée** freshly squeezed orange juice.
■ **nm & adj inv** [couleur] orange.

orangé**, **e [ɔrɑ̃ʒe] **adj** orangey.
◆ ***orangé*** **nm** orangey colour *UK* *ou* color *US*.

orangeade [ɔrɑ̃ʒad] **nf** orange squash *UK*, orangeade *US*.

oranger [ɔrɑ̃ʒe] **nm** orange tree.

orangeraie [ɔrɑ̃ʒrɛ] **nf** orange grove.

Orangina® [ɔrɑ̃ʒina] **nm** Orangina®.

orang-outan (pl **orangs-outans**), ***orang-outang*** (pl **orangs-outangs**) [ɔrɑ̃utɑ̃] **nm** orang-utang.

orateur**, **trice [ɔratœr, tris] **nm, f** **1.** [conférencier] speaker **2.** [personne éloquente] orator.

orbital**, **e**, **aux [ɔrbital, o] **adj** [mouvement] orbital / [station] orbiting.

orbite [ɔrbit] **nf** **1.** ANAT (eye) socket **2.** *fig* & ASTRON orbit ▸ **mettre sur orbite** AÉRON to put into orbit / *fig* to launch.

Orcades [ɔrkad] **nfpl : les Orcades** the Orkney Islands, the Orkneys.

orchestral**, **e**, **aux [ɔrkɛstral, o] **adj** orchestral.

orchestration [ɔrkɛstrasjɔ̃] **nf** orchestration.

orchestre [ɔrkɛstr] **nm** **1.** MUS orchestra **2.** CINÉ & THÉÂTRE stalls *pl* *UK*, orchestra *US* ▸ **fauteuil d'orchestre** seat in the stalls *UK*, orchestra seat *US*.

orchestrer [3] [ɔrkɛstre] **vt** *litt* & *fig* to orchestrate.

orchidée [ɔrkide] **nf** orchid.

ordinaire [ɔrdinɛr] ■ **adj** **1.** [usuel, standard] ordinary, normal ▸ **en temps ordinaire** usually, normally ▸ **peu** *ou* **pas ordinaire** [attitude, méthode, journée] unusual / [volonté] unusual, extraordinary **2.** *péj* [commun] ordinary, common.
■ **nm** **1.** [moyenne] **: l'ordinaire** the ordinary ▸ **comme à l'ordinaire, il arriva en retard** as usual, he turned up late ▸ **sortir de l'ordinaire** to be out of the ordinary, to be unusual **2.** [alimentation] usual diet.
◆ ***d'ordinaire*** **loc adv** normally, usually ▸ **plus tôt que d'ordinaire** earlier than usual.

ordinal**, **e**, **aux [ɔrdinal, o] **adj** ordinal.
◆ ***ordinal**, **aux*** **nm** ordinal (number).

ordinateur [ɔrdinatœr] **nm** computer ▸ **ordinateur individuel** personal computer, PC ▸ **ordinateur de bureau** desktop (computer) ▸ **ordinateur portable** laptop (computer) ▸ **ordinateur de poche** palmtop.

ordonnance [ɔrdɔnɑ̃s] ■ **nf** **1.** MÉD prescription **2.** [de gouvernement, juge] order.
■ **nmf** MIL orderly.

ordonnateur**, **trice [ɔrdɔnatœr, tris] **nm, f** organizer.

ordonné**, **e [ɔrdɔne] **adj** [maison, élève] tidy.

ordonner [3] [ɔrdɔne] **vt** **1.** [ranger] to organize, to put in order **2.** [enjoindre] to order, to tell ▸ **ordonner à qqn de faire qqch** to order sb to do sthg **3.** MÉD **: ordonner qqch à qqn** to prescribe sb sthg **4.** RELIG to ordain **5.** MATH to arrange in order.
◆ ***s'ordonner*** **vp** to be arranged *ou* put in order.

ordre [ɔrdr] **nm** **1.** [gén, MIL & RELIG] order ▸ **par ordre alphabétique/chronologique/décroissant** in alphabetical/chronological/descending order ▸ **par ordre d'apparition à l'écran** in order of appearance ▸ **par ordre d'entrée en scène** in order of appearance ▸ **procéder par ordre** to take one thing at a time ▸ **rentrer dans l'ordre : puis tout est rentré dans l'ordre** then order was restored, then everything went back to normal ▸ **rétablir l'ordre** to restore order ▸ **rappeler qqn à l'ordre** to call sb to order ▸ **donner un ordre à qqn** to give sb an order ▸ **être aux ordres de qqn** to be at sb's disposal ▸ **intimer à qqn l'ordre de faire qqch** to order sb to do sthg ▸ **jusqu'à nouvel ordre** until further notice ▸ **entrer dans les ordres** RELIG to take holy orders ▸ **l'ordre établi** the established order ▸ **ordre de mission** MIL orders *pl (for a particular mission)* ▸ **ordre de passage** running order ▸ **l'ordre public** law and order ▸ **troubler l'ordre public** to disturb the peace
2. [bonne organisation] tidiness, orderliness ▸ **en ordre** orderly, tidy ▸ **avoir de l'ordre** to be orderly *ou* tidy ▸ **mettre en ordre** to put in order, to tidy (up) ▸ **mettre de l'ordre dans ses idées** to order one's ideas ▸ **mettre bon ordre à** to sort out
3. [catégorie] **: de premier ordre** first-rate ▸ **de second ordre** second-rate ▸ **d'ordre privé/pratique** of a private/practical nature ▸ **dans le même ordre d'idées** similarly ▸ **dans un tout autre ordre d'idées** in a quite different connection ▸ **pouvez-vous me donner un ordre de grandeur?** can you give me some idea of the size/amount *etc* ?
4. [corporation] professional association ▸ **l'Ordre des médecins** ≃ the British Medical Association *UK*, ≃ the American Medical Association *US*

COMMENT EXPRIMER...

les ordres

Move back a little, please / Reculez un peu, s'il vous plaît
Quiet, please / Un peu de silence, s'il vous plaît
Please leave a message after the tone / Merci de laisser un message après le bip sonore
Give me a call back when you get this message / Rappelle-moi quand tu auras ce message
Go and get my glasses, will you? / Va me chercher mes lunettes, veux-tu ?
Don't walk on the grass / Ne marche pas sur l'herbe
Put that down now! / Pose ça tout de suite !

5. FIN **: à l'ordre de** payable to ▸ **c'est à quel ordre?** who shall I make it payable to?

◆ ***ordre du jour*** **nm 1.** [de réunion] agenda ▸ **à l'ordre du jour** [de réunion] on the agenda / *fig* topical ▸ **mettre qqch à l'ordre du jour** to put *ou* to place sthg on the agenda

2. MIL order of the day ▸ **cité à l'ordre du jour** mentioned in dispatches.

ordure [ɔrdyr] **nf 1.** *fig* [grossièreté] filth *(U)* **2.** *péj* [personne] scum *(U)*, bastard.

◆ ***ordures*** **nfpl** [déchets] rubbish *(U) UK*, garbage *(U) US*.

ordurier, ***ère*** [ɔrdyrje, ɛr] **adj** filthy, obscene.

orée [ɔre] **nf** edge.

oreille [ɔrɛj] **nf 1.** ANAT ear **2.** [ouïe] hearing ▸ **avoir de l'oreille** to have a good ear (for music) ▸ **être dur d'oreille** to be hard of hearing **3.** [de fauteuil, écrou] wing / [de marmite, tasse] handle

▸▸ **se boucher les oreilles** to close one's ears ▸ **dormir sur ses deux oreilles** to rest easy ▸ **dresser *ou* tendre l'oreille** to prick up one's ears ▸ **écorcher les oreilles** to grate on the ear ▸ **écouter d'une oreille distraite, n'écouter que d'une oreille** to only half-listen ▸ **il ne l'entend pas de cette oreille** he's dead (set) against it ▸ **faire la sourde oreille** to turn a deaf ear ▸ **se faire tirer l'oreille** to need talking round ▸ **prêter l'oreille (à qqch)** to lend an ear (to sthg) ▸ **rebattre les oreilles à qqn** *fam* to go on at sb.

oreiller [ɔreje] **nm** pillow.

oreillette [ɔrɛjɛt] **nf 1.** [du cœur] auricle **2.** [de casquette] earflap.

oreillons [ɔrɛjɔ̃] **nmpl** mumps *sg*.

ores [ɔr] ◆ ***d'ores et déjà*** **loc adv** from now on.

orfèvre [ɔrfɛvr] **nm** goldsmith / [d'argent] silversmith ▸ **être orfèvre en la matière** *fig* to be (an) expert on the subject.

orfèvrerie [ɔrfɛvrəri] **nf 1.** [art] goldsmith's art / [d'argent] silversmith's art **2.** [commerce] goldsmith's trade / [d'argent] silversmith's trade.

orfraie [ɔrfrɛ] **nf** sea eagle.

organdi [ɔrgɑ̃di] **nm** organdie.

organe [ɔrgan] **nm 1.** ANAT organ ▸ **organes génitaux** genitals, genitalia ▸ **organes des sens** sense organs **2.** [institution] organ, body ▸ **les organes de l'État** the apparatus of the state ▸ **organe de presse** newspaper, publication **3.** [mécanisme] mechanism, system ▸ **organes de commande** controls ▸ **organes de transmission** transmission system **4.** *littéraire* [voix] voice **5.** *fig* [porte-parole] representative.

organigramme [ɔrganigram] **nm 1.** [hiérarchique] organization chart **2.** INFORM flow chart.

organique [ɔrganik] **adj** organic.

organisateur, ***trice*** [ɔrganizatœr, tris] ■ **adj** organizing *(avant n)*.

■ **nm, f** organizer / [campagne électorale] **: organisateur de la publicité** campaign organizer *UK*, advance man *US*.

organisation [ɔrganizasjɔ̃] **nf** organization ▸ **avoir le sens de l'organisation** to be well-organized ▸ **Organisation internationale de normalisation** International Standards Organization ▸ **Organisation mondiale du commerce** World Trade Organization.

organisé, ***e*** [ɔrganize] **adj** organized ▸ **organisé en qqch** organized in sthg.

organiser [3] [ɔrganize] **vt** to organize.

◆ ***s'organiser*** **vp 1.** [personne] to be *ou* get organized **2.** [prendre forme] to take shape.

organiseur [ɔrganisœr] **nm** [agenda, ordinateur] (personal) organizer.

organisme [ɔrganism] **nm 1.** BIOL & ZOOL organism ▸ **organisme génétiquement modifié** genetically modified organism **2.** [institution] body, organization.

organiste [ɔrganist] **nmf** organist.

orgasme [ɔrgasm] **nm** orgasm.

orge [ɔrʒ] **nf** barley.

orgeat [ɔrʒa] **nm : sirop d'orgeat** barley water.

orgelet [ɔrʒəlɛ] **nm** stye.

orgie [ɔrʒi] **nf** orgy.

orgue [ɔrg] **nm** organ.

◆ ***orgues*** **nfpl 1.** MUS organ *sg* **2.** GÉOL columns.

orgueil [ɔrgœj] **nm** pride.

orgueilleux, ***euse*** [ɔrgœjø, øz] ■ **adj** proud.

■ **nm, f** proud person.

orient [ɔrjɑ̃] **nm** east.

◆ ***Orient*** **nm : l'Orient** the Orient, the East.

orientable [ɔrjɑ̃tabl] **adj** adjustable.

oriental, ***e***, ***aux*** [ɔrjɑ̃tal, o] **adj** [région, frontière] eastern / [d'Extrême-Orient] oriental.

◆ ***Oriental***, ***e***, ***aux*** **nm, f** Oriental.

orientation [ɔrjɑ̃tasjɔ̃] **nf 1.** [direction] orientation ▸ **avoir le sens de l'orientation** to have a good sense of direction **2.** SCOL career ▸ **orientation professionnelle** careers advice *UK*, vocational guidance **3.** [de maison] aspec[t] **4.** *fig* [de politique, recherche] direction, trend.

orienté, ***e*** [ɔrjɑ̃te] **adj** [tendancieux] biased.

orienter [3] [ɔrjɑ̃te] **vt 1.** [disposer] to position **2.** [voyageur, élève, recherches] to guide, to direct **3.** [navire] to steer / [voile] to trim.

◆ ***s'orienter*** **vp 1.** [se repérer] to find *ou* get one's bearings **2.** *fig* [se diriger] **: s'orienter vers** to move towards *UK ou* toward *US*.

orifice [ɔrifis] **nm** orifice.

oriflamme [ɔriflam] **nf** banner.

origan [ɔrigɑ̃] **nm** oregano.

originaire [ɔriʒinɛr] **adj 1.** [natif] **: être originaire d[e]** to originate from / [personne] to be a native of **2.** [premier] original.

original, ***e***, ***aux*** [ɔriʒinal, o] ■ **adj 1.** [premier, inédit] original **2.** [singulier] eccentric.

■ **nm, f** [personne] (outlandish) character.

◆ ***original***, ***aux*** **nm** [œuvre, document] original.

originalité [ɔriʒinalite] **nf 1.** [nouveauté] originality [/] [caractéristique] original feature **2.** [excentricité] eccentricity.

origine [ɔriʒin] **nf 1.** [gén] origin ▸ **d'origine** [originel] original / [de départ] of origin ▸ **ma voiture a encore son moteur d'origine** my car has still got its original engine ▸ **pays d'origine** country of origin ▸ **d'origine anglaise** of English origin ▸ **à l'origine** originally ▸ **être à l'origine d'une querelle** [personne] to be behind *ou* to be the cause of an argument / [malentendu] to be at the origin *ou* root of an argument ▸ **avoir son origine dans, tirer son origine de** to have one's origins in, to originate in ▸ **il ne sait rien de ses origines** he doesn't know anything about his origins *ou* where he comes from **2.** [souche] origins *pl* ▸ **les origines de la civilisation** the origins of civilization **3.** [provenance] source ▸ **quelle est l'origine de ces pêches?** where are these peaches from?

originel, elle [ɔriʒinɛl] **adj** original.

orignal, aux [ɔriɲal, o] **nm** moose.

oripeaux [ɔripo] **nmpl** rags.

ORL ■ **nmf** (abr de ***oto-rhino-laryngologiste***) ENT specialist.
■ **nf** (abr de ***oto-rhino-laryngologie***) ENT.

orme [ɔrm] **nm** elm.

ormeau, x [ɔrmo] **nm** young elm.

ornement [ɔrnəmɑ̃] **nm 1.** [gén & MUS] ornament ▸ **d'ornement** [plante, arbre] ornamental **2.** ARCHIT embellishment.

ornemental, e, aux [ɔrnəmɑ̃tal, o] **adj** ornamental.

ornementation [ɔrnəmɑ̃tasjɔ̃] **nf** ornamentation.

ornementer [3] [ɔrnəmɑ̃te] **vt** to ornament.

orner [3] [ɔrne] **vt 1.** [décorer] **: orner (de)** to decorate (with) **2.** [agrémenter] to adorn.

ornière [ɔrnjɛr] **nf** rut.

ornithologie [ɔrnitɔlɔʒi] **nf** ornithology.

orphelin, e [ɔrfəlɛ̃, in] ■ **adj** orphan *(avant n)*, orphaned ▸ **orphelin de père** fatherless ▸ **orphelin de mère** motherless.
■ **nm, f** orphan.

orphelinat [ɔrfəlina] **nm** orphanage.

Orsay [ɔrsɛ] **npr : le musée d'Orsay** *art museum in Paris specialized in the second half of the 19th century and the early 20th century.*

ORSEC, Orsec [ɔrsɛk] (abr de ***Organisation des secours***) **adj : le plan Orsec** *disaster contingency plan.*

ORSECRAD, Orsecrad [ɔrsɛkrad] (abr de ***Orsec en cas d'accident nucléaire***) **adj : plan Orsecrad** *disaster contingency plan in case of nuclear accident.*

orteil [ɔrtɛj] **nm** toe ▸ **gros orteil** big toe.

orthodontiste [ɔrtɔdɔ̃tist] **nmf** orthodontist.

orthodoxe [ɔrtɔdɔks] ■ **adj 1.** RELIG Orthodox **2.** [conformiste] orthodox.
■ **nmf 1.** RELIG Orthodox Christian **2.** POLIT conformist.

orthodoxie [ɔrtɔdɔksi] **nf** orthodoxy.

orthogonal, e, aux [ɔrtɔgɔnal, o] **adj** orthogonal.

orthographe [ɔrtɔgraf] **nf** spelling.

orthographier [9] [ɔrtɔgrafje] **vt** to spell ▸ **mal orthographier** to misspell.

orthographique [ɔrtɔgrafik] **adj** orthographic.

orthopédique [ɔrtɔpedik] **adj** orthopa(e)dic.

orthopédiste [ɔrtɔpedist] **nmf** orthopa(e)dist.

orthophoniste [ɔrtɔfɔnist] **nmf** speech therapist.

ortie [ɔrti] **nf** nettle.

ortolan [ɔrtɔlɑ̃] **nm** ortolan.

orvet [ɔrvɛ] **nm** slowworm.

os [ɔs] (pl **os** [o]) **nm 1.** [gén] bone ▸ **os à moelle** marrowbone ▸ **os de seiche** cuttlebone **2.** *fam fig* [difficulté] snag, hitch.

OS (abr de ***ouvrier spécialisé***) **nm** semiskilled worker.

oscar [ɔskar] **nm** CINÉ Oscar.

oscariser [3] [ɔskarize] **vt** to award an Oscar to.

oscillation [ɔsilasjɔ̃] **nf** oscillation / [de navire] rocking.

oscillatoire [ɔsilatwar] **adj** swinging, oscillatory.

osciller [3] [ɔsile] **vi 1.** [se balancer] to swing / [navire] to rock **2.** [vaciller, hésiter] to waver.

osé, e [oze] **adj** daring, audacious.

oseille [ozɛj] **nf 1.** BOT sorrel **2.** *fam* [argent] bread.

oser [3] [oze] **vt** to dare ▸ **oser faire qqch** to dare (to) do sthg ▸ **si j'ose dire** if I may say so.

osier [ozje] **nm 1.** BOT osier **2.** [fibre] wicker.

Oslo [ɔslo] **npr** Oslo.

osmose [ɔsmoz] **nf** osmosis ▸ **en osmose** by osmosis.

ossature [ɔsatyr] **nf 1.** ANAT skeleton **2.** *fig* [structure] framework.

osselet [ɔslɛ] **nm 1.** ANAT ossicle **2.** [élément de jeu] jack ▸ **jouer aux osselets** to play jacks.

ossements [ɔsmɑ̃] **nmpl** bones.

osseux, euse [ɔsø, øz] **adj 1.** ANAT & MÉD bone *(avant n)* **2.** [maigre] bony.

ossification [ɔsifikasjɔ̃] **nf** ossification.

ossuaire [ɔsɥɛr] **nm** ossuary.

ostensible [ɔstɑ̃sibl] **adj** conspicuous.

ostensiblement [ɔstɑ̃sibləmɑ̃] **adv** conspicuously.

ostensoir [ɔstɑ̃swar] **nm** monstrance.

ostentation [ɔstɑ̃tasjɔ̃] **nf** ostentation.

ostentatoire [ɔstɑ̃tatwar] **adj** ostentatious.

ostéopathe [ɔsteɔpat] **nmf** osteopath.

ostéoporose [ɔsteɔpɔroz] **nf** MÉD osteoporosis.

ostracisme [ɔstrasism] **nm** ostracism.

otage [ɔtaʒ] **nm** hostage ▸ **prendre qqn en otage** to take sb hostage.

OTAN, Otan [ɔtɑ̃] (abr de ***Organisation du traité de l'Atlantique Nord***) **nf** NATO.

otarie [ɔtari] **nf** sea lion.

OTASE [ɔtaz] (abr de ***Organisation du traité de l'Asie du sud-est***) **nf** SEATO.

ôter [3] [ote] **vt 1.** [enlever] to take off **2.** [soustraire] to take away **3.** [retirer, prendre] **: ôter qqch à qqn** to take sthg away from sb.
◆ ***s'ôter*** **vp** *fam* **: ôte-toi de là!** get out of the way!

otite [ɔtit] **nf** ear infection.

oto-rhino-laryngologie [ɔtɔrinɔlarɛ̃gɔlɔʒi] **nf** ear, nose and throat medicine, ENT.

oto-rhino-laryngologiste, **s** [ɔtɔrinɔlarɛ̃gɔlɔʒist] **nmf** ear, nose and throat specialist.

Ottawa [ɔtawa] **npr** Ottawa.

ou [u] **conj 1.** [indique une alternative, une approximation] or **2.** [sinon] **: ou (bien)** or (else).
◆ ***ou (bien)... ou (bien)*** **loc correlative** either... or ▸ **ou c'est elle, ou c'est moi!** it's either her or me!

où [u] ■ **pron rel 1.** [spatial] where ▸ **le village où j'habite** the village where I live, the village I live in ▸ **pose-le là où tu l'as trouvé** put it back where you found it ▸ **partout où vous irez** wherever you go
2. [temporel] that ▸ **à l'époque où...** in the days when... ▸ **le jour où je suis venu** the day (that) I came.
■ **adv** where ▸ **je vais où je veux** I go where I please ▸ **où que vous alliez** wherever you go.
■ **adv interr** where? ▸ **où vas-tu?** where are you going? ▸ **où est la voiture?** where's the car? ▸ **par où commencer?** where to begin?, where should I begin? ▸ **dites-moi où il est allé** tell me where he's gone.
◆ ***d'où*** **loc adv** [conséquence] hence ▸ **d'où on conclut que...** from which it may be concluded that... ▸ **je ne savais pas qu'il était déjà arrivé, d'où ma surprise** I didn't know that he'd already arrived, which is why I was so surprised.

OUA (abr de ***Organisation de l'unité africaine***) **nf** OAU.

ouailles [waj] **nfpl** flock *sg*.

ouais [wɛ] **interj** *fam* yeah!

ouananiche [wananiʃ] **nf** *Québec type of freshwater salmon*.

ouaouaron [wawarɔ̃] **nm** *Québec* bullfrog.

ouate [wat] **nf 1.** [pansement] cotton wool *UK*, (absorbent) cotton *US* **2.** [rembourrage] (cotton) wadding.

ouaté, **e** [wate] **adj 1.** [garni d'ouate] cotton wool *UK (avant n)*, cotton *US (avant n)* / [vêtement] quilted **2.** *fig* [feutré] muffled.

oubli [ubli] **nm 1.** [acte d'oublier] forgetting **2.** [négligence] omission / [étourderie] oversight **3.** [abnégation] **: oubli de soi** self-effacement **4.** [général] oblivion ▸ **tomber dans l'oubli** to sink into oblivion.

oublier [10] [ublije] **vt** to forget / [laisser quelque part] to leave behind ▸ **oublier de faire qqch** to forget to do sthg ▸ **j'ai oublié la lettre à la maison** I left the letter at home ▸ **n'oublie pas le rendez-vous** don't forget (that) you have an appointment ▸ **oublions ce malentendu** let's forget (all) about this misunderstanding.
◆ ***s'oublier*** **vp 1.** [emploi passif] to be forgotten ▸ **une fois acquise, la technique ne s'oublie jamais** once you've learnt the technique, it stays with you forever *ou* you'll never forget it **2.** [emploi réfléchi] to forget o.s. ▸ **tu ne t'es pas oublié, à ce que je vois!** *hum* I see you've not forgotten yourself! **3.** *euphém* [chat, enfant] to have an accident.

oubliettes [ublijɛt] **nfpl** dungeon *sg* ▸ **jeter qqch aux oubliettes** *fam fig* to shelve sthg.

oublieux, **euse** [ublijø, øz] **adj** forgetful.

ouest [wɛst] ■ **nm** west ▸ **un vent d'ouest** a westerly wind ▸ **le vent d'ouest** the west wind ▸ **à l'ouest** in the west ▸ **à l'ouest (de)** to the west (of).
■ **adj inv** [gén] west / [province, région] western.

ouest-allemand, **e** [wɛstalmɑ̃, ɑ̃d] **adj** West German.

ouf [uf] **interj** phew!

Ouganda [ugɑ̃da] **nm : l'Ouganda** Uganda.

ougandais, **e** [ugɑ̃dɛ, ɛz] **adj** Ugandan.
◆ ***Ougandais***, **e** **nm, f** Ugandan.

oui [wi] ■ **adv** yes ▸ **tu viens? - oui** are you coming? - yes (I am) ▸ **tu viens, oui ou non?** are you coming or not?, are you coming or aren't you? ▸ **je crois que oui** I think so ▸ **faire signe que oui** to nod ▸ **mais oui, bien sûr que oui** yes, of course.
■ **nm inv** yes ▸ **pour un oui pour un non** for no apparent reason.

ouï-dire [widir] **nm inv : par ouï-dire** by *ou* from hearsay.

ouïe [wi] **nf** hearing ▸ **avoir l'ouïe fine** to have excellent hearing.
◆ ***ouïes*** **nfpl** [de poisson] gills.

ouistiti [wistiti] **nm 1.** ZOOL marmoset **2.** *fam* [type] bloke *UK*, guy.

ouragan [uragɑ̃] **nm 1.** MÉTÉOR hurricane **2.** *fig* [tempête] storm.

ourdir [32] [urdir] **vt** *fig & littéraire* [complot] to hatch.

ourler [3] [urle] **vt 1.** COUT to hem **2.** *littéraire* [border] to edge.

ourlet [urlɛ] **nm 1.** COUT hem ▸ **faire un ourlet à** to hem **2.** [de l'oreille] helix.

ours [urs] **nm** bear ▸ **ours (en peluche)** teddy (bear) ▸ **ours polaire** polar bear.

ourse [urs] **nf** she-bear.
◆ ***Ourse*** **nf : la Grande/Petite Ourse** the Great/Little Bear.

oursin [ursɛ̃] **nm** sea urchin.

ourson [ursɔ̃] **nm** bear cub.

oust, ***ouste*** [ust] **interj** *fam* [dehors!] clear off! / [vite!] get a move on!

outarde [utard] **nf** bustard.

outil [uti] **nm** tool ▸ **boîte *ou* caisse à outils** toolbox ▸ **outil auteur** INFORM authoring tool ▸ **outil de marketing** marketing tool.

outillage [utijaʒ] **nm** [équipement] tools *pl*, equipment.

outrage [utraʒ] **nm 1.** *sout* [insulte] insult ▸ **faire subir les derniers outrages à qqn** *fig & littéraire* to ravish s[omeone] **2.** DR **: outrage aux bonnes mœurs** affront to public decency ▸ **outrage à magistrat** contempt of court ▸ **outrage à la pudeur** indecent behaviour *(U) UK ou* behavior *(U) U[S]*.

outrageant, **e** [utraʒɑ̃, ɑ̃t] **adj** insulting, offensive.

outrager [17] [utraʒe] **vt 1.** [offenser] to insu[lt] **2.** [contrevenir] to offend.

outrageusement [utraʒøzmɑ̃] **adv** outrageously.

outrance [utrɑ̃s] **nf** excess ▸ **à outrance** excessively.

outrancier, **ère** [utrɑ̃sje, ɛr] **adj** extravagant.

outre[1] [utr] **nf** wineskin.

outre[2] [utr] ■ **prép** besides, as well as.
■ **adv : passer outre** to go on, to proceed further ▸ **passer outre à qqch** to disregard sthg.
◆ ***en outre*** **loc adv** moreover, besides.
◆ ***outre que*** **loc conj** apart from the fact that.

outré, e [utre] **adj** indignant.

outre-Atlantique [utratlɑ̃tik] **loc adv** across the Atlantic.

outrecuidance [utrəkɥidɑ̃s] **nf** *littéraire* presumptuousness.

outrecuidant, e [utrəkɥidɑ̃, ɑ̃t] **adj** *littéraire* presumptuous.

outre-Manche [utrəmɑ̃ʃ] **loc adv** across the Channel.

outremer [utrəmɛr] ■ **nm** [pierre] lapis lazuli / [couleur] ultramarine.
■ **adj inv** ultramarine.

outre-mer [utrəmɛr] **loc adv** overseas ▸ **d'outre-mer** overseas.

outrepasser [3] [utrəpase] **vt** to exceed.

outrer [3] [utre] **vt** [personne] to outrage.

outre-Rhin [utrərɛ̃] **loc adv** across the Rhine.

outsider [awtsajdœr] **nm** outsider.

ouvert, e [uvɛr, ɛrt] ■ **pp** ➤ ***ouvrir***.
■ **adj 1.** [gén] open ▸ **grand ouvert** wide open **2.** [robinet] on, running.

ouvertement [uvɛrtəmɑ̃] **adv** openly.

ouverture [uvɛrtyr] **nf 1.** [gén] opening / [d'hostilités] outbreak ▸ **l'ouverture de la chasse** the start of the hunting season ▸ **une ouverture dans le mur** an opening *ou* a hole in the wall ▸ **'ouverture des portes à 20 h'** 'doors open at eight' ▸ **heures d'ouverture** opening hours ▸ **pour faciliter l'ouverture d'un compte courant** to make it easier to open a current account ▸ **ouverture d'esprit** open-mindedness **2.** MUS overture **3.** PHOTO aperture ▸ **ouverture du diaphragme** f-stop.
◆ ***ouvertures*** **nfpl** [propositions] overtures ▸ **faire des ouvertures de paix** to make peace overtures.

ouvrable [uvrabl] **adj** working ▸ **heures ouvrables** hours of business.

ouvrage [uvraʒ] **nm 1.** [travail] work *(U)*, task ▸ **se mettre à l'ouvrage** to start work **2.** [objet produit] (piece of) work / COUT work *(U)* **3.** [livre, écrit] work ▸ **ouvrage de référence** reference work.

ouvragé, e [uvraʒe] **adj** elaborate.

ouvrant, e [uvrɑ̃, ɑ̃t] **adj : toit ouvrant** sunroof.

ouvré, e [uvre] **adj : jour ouvré** working day.

ouvre-boîtes [uvrəbwat] **nm inv** tin opener *UK*, can opener.

ouvre-bouteilles [uvrəbutɛj] **nm inv** bottle opener.

ouvreur, euse [uvrœr, øz] **nm, f** usher (f usherette).

ouvrier, ère [uvrije, ɛr] ■ **adj** [quartier, enfance] working-class / [conflit] industrial / [questions, statut] labour *(avant n) UK*, labor *(avant n) US* ▸ **classe ouvrière** working class.
■ **nm, f** worker ▸ **ouvrier agricole** farm worker ▸ **ouvrier qualifié** skilled worker ▸ **ouvrier spécialisé** semi-skilled worker.
◆ ***ouvrière*** **nf** ZOOL worker.

ouvrir [34] [uvrir] ■ **vt 1.** [gén] to open ▸ **ouvrir une porte par effraction** to force a door ▸ **ouvrir qqch à qqn** to open sthg to sb ▸ **va ouvrir** go and answer the door **2.** [chemin, voie] to open up ▸ **le diplôme vous ouvre de nombreuses possibilités** the diploma opens up a whole range of possibilities for you
3. [gaz] to turn on.
■ **vi** to open ▸ **la chasse au faisan/la conférence ouvrira en septembre** the pheasant season/the conference will open in September ▸ **ouvrir par qqch** to open with sthg ▸ **ouvrir sur qqch** to open onto sthg ▸ **le vasistas ouvre sur le parking** the fanlight opens onto *ou* looks out over the car park.
◆ ***s'ouvrir*** **vp 1.** [porte, fleur] to open
2. [route, perspectives] to open up
3. [personne] **: s'ouvrir (à qqn)** to confide (in sb), to open up (to sb)
4. [se blesser] **: s'ouvrir le genou** to cut one's knee open ▸ **s'ouvrir les veines** to slash *ou* cut one's wrists
5. [se sensibiliser] **: s'ouvrir à qqch** to start to take an interest in sthg ▸ **s'ouvrir à la poésie** to become sensitive to poetry.

ovaire [ɔvɛr] **nm** ovary.

ovale [ɔval] **adj & nm** oval.

ovation [ɔvasjɔ̃] **nf** ovation ▸ **faire une ovation à qqn** to give sb an ovation.

ovationner [3] [ɔvasjɔne] **vt** to give an ovation to.

overbooking [ɔvœrbukiŋ] **nm** overbooking.

overdose [ɔvœrdoz] **nf** overdose.

ovin, e [ɔvɛ̃, in] **adj** ovine.
◆ ***ovin*** **nm** sheep.

OVNI, Ovni [ɔvni] (abr de ***objet volant non identifié***) **nm** UFO.

ovoïde [ɔvɔid] **adj** egg-shaped.

ovuler [3] [ɔvyle] **vi** to ovulate.

oxydable [ɔksidabl] **adj** liable to rust.

oxydation [ɔksidasjɔ̃] **nf** oxidation, oxidization.

oxyde [ɔksid] **nm** oxide ▸ **oxyde de carbone** carbon monoxide.

oxyder [3] [ɔkside] **vt** to oxidize.
◆ ***s'oxyder*** **vp** to become oxidized.

oxygène [ɔksiʒɛn] **nm** oxygen ▸ **ballon d'oxygène** oxygen cylinder.

oxygéné, e [ɔksiʒene] **adj 1.** CHIM oxygenated, ➤ ***eau*** **2.** [cheveux] peroxide-blond, bleached.

oxygéner [18] [ɔksiʒene] **vt 1.** CHIM to oxygenate **2.** [cheveux] to bleach, to peroxide.
◆ ***s'oxygéner*** **vp** *fam* to get some fresh air.

ozone [ɔzon] **nm** ozone.

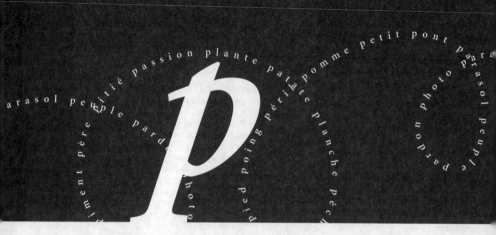

p[1], ***P*** [pe] **nm inv** p, P.

p[2] **1.** (abr écrite de ***pico***) p **2.** (abr écrite de ***page***) p **3.** (abr écrite de ***passable***) *fair grade (as assessment of schoolwork)*, ≃ C **4.** abr de ***pièce***.

Pa (abr écrite de ***pascal***) Pa.

PA (abr écrite de ***petites annonces***) **nfpl** small ads *UK*, want ads *US*.

PAC, ***Pac*** [pak] (abr de ***politique agricole commune***) **nf** CAP.

pacage [pakaʒ] **nm** pasture.

pacemaker [pɛsmekœr] **nm** pacemaker.

pacha [paʃa] **nm** pasha ▸ **mener une vie de pacha** *fam fig* to live a life of ease.

pachyderme [paʃidɛrm] **nm** elephant ▸ **les pachydermes** (the) pachyderms.

pacificateur, ***trice*** [pasifikatœr, tris] ■ **adj** pacifying.
■ **nm, f** peacemaker.

pacification [pasifikasjɔ̃] **nf** pacification.

pacifier [9] [pasifje] **vt** to pacify.

pacifique [pasifik] **adj** peaceful.

Pacifique [pasifik] **nm : le Pacifique** the Pacific (Ocean).

pacifiquement [pasifikmɑ̃] **adv** peacefully.

pacifiste [pasifist] **nmf & adj** pacifist.

pack [pak] **nm** pack.

package [pakadʒ] **nm** INFORM package.

packaging [pakadʒiŋ] **nm** packaging.

pacotille [pakɔtij] **nf** shoddy goods *pl*, rubbish ▸ **de pacotille** cheap.

PACS [paks] (abr de ***Pacte civil de solidarité***) **nm** Civil Solidarity Pact *civil contract conferring marital rights on the contracting parties*.

pacsé, ***e*** [pakse] **nm, f** *fam person who has signed a PACS agreement*, ≃ (life) partner.

pacser [3] [pakse] ◆ ***se pacser*** [pakse] **vpi** to sign a PACS agreement *to have one's relationship legally recognized*.

pacte [pakt] **nm** pact.

pactiser [3] [paktize] **vi : pactiser avec** [faire un pacte avec] to make a pact with / [transiger avec] to come to terms with.

pactole [paktɔl] **nm** gold mine *fig*.

paddock [padɔk] **nm 1.** [d'un hippodrome] paddock **2.** *tfam* [lit] **: se mettre au paddock** to hit the sack.

paddy [padi] **nm** paddy (rice).

paella [paela] **nf** paella.

paf [paf] ■ **interj** wham!
■ **adj inv** *fam* [ivre] plastered.

PAF [paf] ■ **nf** (abr de ***Police de l'air et des frontières***) *police authority responsible for civil aviation etc.*
■ **nm** (abr de ***paysage audiovisuel français***) *French radio and television*.

pagaie [pagɛ] **nf** paddle.

pagaille, ***pagaye***, ***pagaïe*** [pagaj] **nf** *fam* mess ▸ **en pagaille** [en désordre] in a mess ▸ **des fruits en pagaille** loads of fruit.

paganisme [paganism] **nm** paganism.

pagaye = ***pagaille***.

pagayer [11] [pagɛje] **vi** to paddle.

pagayeur, ***euse*** [pagɛjœr, øz] **nm, f** paddler.

page [paʒ] ■ **nf 1.** [feuillet] page ▸ **page blanche** blank page ▸ **double page** PRESSE & TYPO double-page spread ▸ **mettre en pages** TYPO to make up (into pages) ▸ **page de garde** flyleaf
2. INFORM page ▸ **page d'accueil** home page ▸ **page précédente** page up ▸ **page suivante** page down
3. *fig* [passage] passage / [événement] episode, page
▸▸ **être à la page** to be up-to-date ▸ **tourner la page** to turn the page.
■ **nm** page (boy).

pagination [paʒinasjɔ̃] **nf** pagination.

pagne [paɲ] **nm** loincloth.

pagode [pagɔd] **nf** pagoda.

paie[1], ***paies*** *etc* ➤ ***payer***.

paie[2], ***paye*** [pɛ] **nf** pay *(U)*, wages *pl*.

paiement, payement [pɛmɑ̃] **nm** payment ▸ **paiement anticipé** advance payment ▸ **paiement différé** deferred payment ▸ **paiement minimum** minimum payment ▸ **paiement partiel** part payment.

païen, ïenne [pajɛ̃, ɛn] **adj & nm, f** pagan, heathen.

paierai, paieras ➤ ***payer***.

paillard, e [pajar, ard] ■ **adj** bawdy.
■ **nm, f** rake (f slut).

paillasse [pajas] ■ **nf** **1.** [matelas] straw mattress **2.** [d'évier] draining board *UK*, drainboard *US*.
■ **nm** clown.

paillasson [pajasɔ̃] **nm** **1.** [tapis] doormat **2.** AGRIC (roll of) matting.

paille [paj] **nf** **1.** BOT straw ▸ **être sur la paille** *fam fig* to be down and out **2.** [pour boire] straw.
◆ ***paille de fer*** **nf** steel wool.

pailleté, e [pajte] **adj** sequined.

paillette [pajɛt] **nf** *(gén pl)* **1.** [sur vêtements] sequin, spangle **2.** [d'or] grain of gold dust **3.** [de lessive, savon] flake ▸ **savon en paillettes** soap flakes *pl*.

pain [pɛ̃] **nm** **1.** [aliment] bread ▸ **un pain** a loaf ▸ **petit pain** (bread) roll ▸ **pain azyme** unleavened bread ▸ **pain bénit** consecrated bread ▸ **pain brioché** brioche-like bread ▸ **pain de campagne** ≃ farmhouse loaf ▸ **pain aux céréales** granary bread ▸ **pain au chocolat** *sweet roll with chocolate filling* ▸ **pain complet** wholemeal *UK* *ou* whole wheat *US* bread ▸ **pain d'épice** ≃ gingerbread ▸ **pain grillé** toast ▸ **pain au lait** sweet roll, bun ▸ **pain de mie** sandwich loaf ▸ **pain perdu** ≃ French toast ▸ **pain de seigle** rye bread ▸ **pain au son** wholemeal bread ▸ **avoir du pain sur la planche** *fam fig* to have a lot on one's plate ▸ **ôter le pain de la bouche de qqn** *fig* to take the bread out of sb's mouth **2.** [de savon, cire] bar ▸ **pain de glace** block of ice ▸ **pain de sucre** CULIN sugarloaf **3.** *tfam* [coup] punch ▸ **je lui ai filé un de ces pains!** I socked him one!

pair, e [pɛr] **adj** even.
◆ ***pair*** **nm** peer.
◆ ***paire*** **nf** pair ▸ **une paire de** [lunettes, ciseaux, chaussures] a pair of ▸ **c'est une autre paire de manches** *fig* that's another story.
◆ ***au pair*** **loc adv** for board and lodging, for one's keep ▸ **jeune fille au pair** au pair (girl).
◆ ***de pair*** **loc adv** : **aller de pair avec** to go hand in hand with.
◆ ***hors pair*** **loc adj** unrivalled *UK*, unrivaled *US*.

paisible [pɛzibl] **adj** peaceful.

paisiblement [pɛzibləmɑ̃] **adv** peacefully.

paître [91] [pɛtr] ■ **vi** to graze.
■ **vt** to feed on.

paix [pɛ] **nf** peace ▸ **en paix** [en harmonie] at peace / [tranquillement] in peace ▸ **vivre en paix** to live in peace ▸ **en temps de paix** in peacetime ▸ **avoir la paix** to have peace and quiet ▸ **j'ai enfin la paix depuis qu'il est parti** I've at last got some peace and quiet now that he's left ▸ **avoir la conscience en paix** to have a clear conscience ▸ **faire la paix avec qqn** to make peace with sb ▸ **ficher la paix à qqn** *fam* to stop hassling sb ▸ **laisser qqn en paix** to leave sb alone *ou* in peace ▸ **pourparlers/offres de paix** peace talks/proposals.

Pakistan [pakistɑ̃] **nm** : **le Pakistan** Pakistan ▸ **au Pakistan** in Pakistan.

pakistanais, e [pakistanɛ, ɛz] **adj** Pakistani.
◆ ***Pakistanais, e*** **nm, f** Pakistani.

PAL, Pal [pal] (abr de ***Phase Alternation Line***) **adj** PAL.

palabrer [3] [palabre] **vi** to have interminable discussions.

palabres [palabr] **nmpl & nfpl** interminable discussions.

palace [palas] **nm** luxury hotel.

palais [palɛ] **nm** **1.** [château] palace **2.** [grand édifice] centre *UK*, center *US* ▸ **palais des expositions** exhibition centre *UK* *ou* center *US* ▸ **le palais Garnier** *the (old) Paris opera house* ▸ **palais de justice** DR law courts *pl* ▸ **le palais du Luxembourg** *palace in Paris where the French Senate is situated* ▸ **palais omnisports** (multi-purpose) sports centre *UK* *ou* center *US* ▸ **le palais des Papes** *the Papal Palace in Avignon* ▸ **le Grand Palais** the Grand Palais ▸ **le Petit Palais** the Petit Palais **3.** ANAT palate.

palan [palɑ̃] **nm** block and tackle, hoist.

pale [pal] **nf** [de rame, d'hélice] blade.

pâle [pal] **adj** pale.

palefrenier [palfrənje] **nm** groom.

paléographie [paleɔgrafi] **nf** paleography.

paléolithique [paleɔlitik] ■ **nm** : **le paléolithique** the Paleolithic (age).
■ **adj** paleolithic.

paléontologie [paleɔ̃tɔlɔʒi] **nf** paleontology.

Palerme [palɛrm] **npr** Palermo.

Palestine [palɛstin] **nf** : **la Palestine** Palestine.

palestinien, enne [palɛstinjɛ̃, ɛn] **adj** Palestinian.
◆ ***Palestinien, enne*** **nm, f** Palestinian.

palet [palɛ] **nm** [hockey] puck.

paletot [palto] **nm** (short) overcoat.

palette [palɛt] **nf** **1.** [de peintre] palette **2.** CULIN shoulder **3.** [de chariot élévateur] pallet.

palétuvier [paletyvje] **nm** mangrove.

pâleur [palœr] **nf** [de visage] pallor.

pâlichon, onne [paliʃɔ̃, ɔn] **adj** *fam* pale, sickly-looking.

palier [palje] **nm** **1.** [d'escalier] landing **2.** [étape] level **3.** TECHNOL bearing.

pâlir [32] [palir] ■ **vt** to turn pale.
■ **vi** [couleur, lumière] to fade / [personne] to turn *ou* go pale ▸ **pâlir de** [angoisse] to turn *ou* go pale with / [jalousie] to turn *ou* go green with.

palissade [palisad] **nf** [clôture] fence / [de verdure] hedge.

palissandre [palisɑ̃dr] **nm** rosewood.

palliatif, ive [paljatif, iv] **adj** palliative.
◆ ***palliatif*** **nm** **1.** MÉD palliative **2.** *fig* stopgap measure.

pallier [9] [palje] **vt** to make up for.

Palma [palma] **npr** : **Palma (de Majorque)** Palma (de Majorca).

palmarès [palmarɛs] **nm 1.** [de lauréats] list of (medal) winners / SCOL list of prizewinners **2.** [de succès] record (of achievements).

palme [palm] **nf 1.** [de palmier] palm leaf **2.** [de nageur] flipper **3.** [décoration, distinction] **: avec palme** MIL ≃ with bar ▸ **la palme d'or** *award given to best film at the Cannes Film Festival* ▸ **palmes académiques** *decoration awarded for services to education.*

palmé**, **e [palme] **adj 1.** BOT palmate **2.** ZOOL web-footed / [patte] webbed.

palmeraie [palmərɛ] **nf** palm grove.

palmier [palmje] **nm 1.** BOT palm tree **2.** CULIN *sweet pastry shaped like a palm leaf.*

palmipède [palmipɛd] ■ **nm** web-footed bird.
■ **adj** web-footed.

palombe [palɔ̃b] **nf** woodpigeon.

pâlot**, **otte [palo, ɔt] **adj** pale, sickly-looking.

palourde [palurd] **nf** clam.

palpable [palpabl] **adj** palpable, tangible.

palper [3] [palpe] **vt 1.** [toucher] to feel, to finger / MÉD to palpate **2.** *fam* [de l'argent] to get.

palpitant**, **e [palpitɑ̃, ɑ̃t] **adj** exciting, thrilling.

palpitation [palpitasjɔ̃] **nf** palpitation.

palpiter [3] [palpite] **vi 1.** [paupières] to flutter / [cœur] to pound **2.** [personne] **: palpiter de** to tremble *ou* quiver with **3.** *littéraire* [flamme] to tremble, to quiver.

palu [paly] **nm** *fam* malaria.

paludisme [palydism] **nm** malaria.

pâmer [3] [pame] ◆ ***se pâmer*** **vp 1.** *littéraire* [s'évanouir] to swoon (away) **2.** *fig* **: se pâmer de** to be overcome with.

pâmoison [pamwazɔ̃] **nf** *littéraire* swoon.

pampa [pɑ̃pa] **nf** pampas *pl.*

pamphlet [pɑ̃flɛ] **nm** satirical tract.

pamplemousse [pɑ̃pləmus] **nm** grapefruit.

pan [pɑ̃] ■ **nm 1.** [de vêtement] tail **2.** [d'affiche] piece, bit ▸ **pan de mur** section of wall **3.** [d'écrou] side.
■ **interj** bang!

panacée [panase] **nf** panacea.

panachage [panaʃaʒ] **nm 1.** [mélange] mix **2.** POLIT *splitting one's vote.*

panache [panaʃ] **nm 1.** [de plumes, fumée] plume **2.** [éclat] panache.

panaché**, **e [panaʃe] **adj 1.** [de plusieurs couleurs] multicoloured *UK*, multicolored *US* **2.** [mélangé] mixed.
◆ ***panaché*** **nm** shandy *UK*.

panacher [3] [panaʃe] **vt 1.** [mélanger] to mix **2.** POLIT **: panacher une liste électorale** to split one's vote among several candidates.

panafricanisme [panafrikanism] **nm** Pan-Africanism.

panama [panama] **nm** panama (hat).

Panama [panama] **nm 1.** [pays] **: le Panama** Panama ▸ **au Panama** in Panama **2.** [ville] Panama City.

panaméen**, **enne [panameɛ̃, ɛn], ***pana-mien**, **enne*** [panamjɛ̃, ɛn] **adj** Panamanian.
◆ ***Panaméen**, **enne**, **Panamien**, **enne*** **nm, f** Panamanian.

panard [panar] **nm** *fam* foot.

panaris [panari] **nm** whitlow.

pan-bagnat [pɑ̃baɲa] (pl **pans-bagnats**) **nm** *roll fillec with lettuce, tomatoes, anchovies and olives.*

pancarte [pɑ̃kart] **nf 1.** [de manifestant] placard **2.** [de signalisation] sign.

pancréas [pɑ̃kreas] **nm** pancreas.

panda [pɑ̃da] **nm** panda.

pané**, **e [pane] **adj** breaded, in breadcrumbs.

panégyrique [paneʒirik] **nm** panegyric.

panel [panel] **nm** [groupe] sample (group) / [jury] panel

paner [3] [pane] **vt** to coat with breadcrumbs.

panier [panje] **nm** basket ▸ **panier à provisions** shopping basket ▸ **c'est un panier de crabes** *fig* they're alway at each other's throats ▸ **panier à salade** CULIN salad shaker / *fig* police van ▸ **mettre au panier** *fig* to throw out.

panier-repas [panjerəpa] (pl **paniers-repas**) **nm** packed lunch.

panini [panini] (pl **paninis**) **nm** panini.

panique [panik] ■ **nf** panic.
■ **adj** panicky ▸ **être pris d'une peur panique** to be panic stricken.

paniquer [3] [panike] **vt & vi** to panic.
◆ ***se paniquer*** **vp** *fam* to panic.

panne [pan] **nf** [arrêt] breakdown ▸ **tomber en panne** t break down ▸ **panne de courant** *ou* **d'électricité** powe failure ▸ **tomber en panne d'essence** *ou* **en panne sèch** to run out of petrol *UK* *ou* gas *US* ▸ **panne de secteu** ÉLECTR mains failure ▸ **panne (du système)** INFORM syster failure.

panneau**, **x [pano] **nm 1.** [pancarte] sign ▸ **pannea d'affichage** noticeboard *UK*, bulletin board *US* / [pour pu blicité] (advertising) hoarding *UK*, billboard *US* ▸ **pannea indicateur** signpost ▸ **panneau publicitaire** (advertisin hoarding *UK*, billboard *US* ▸ **panneau de signalisatio** road sign ▸ **tomber dans le panneau** *fig* to fall into th trap **2.** [élément] panel ▸ **panneau de commande** INFOR control panel ▸ **panneau de particules** chipboard ▸ **pa neau solaire** solar panel.

panonceau**, **x [panɔ̃so] **nm 1.** [plaque] plaque **2.** [e seigne] sign.

panoplie [panɔpli] **nf 1.** [jouet] outfit **2.** [d'armes] di play **3.** *fig* [de mesures] package.

panorama [panɔrama] **nm** [vue] view, panorama / f overview.

panoramique [panɔramik] ■ **adj** panoramic.
■ **nm** CINÉ pan, panning shot.

panse [pɑ̃s] **nf 1.** [d'estomac] first stomach, rumen **2.** fa [gros ventre] belly, paunch ▸ **se remplir** *ou* **s'en mett plein la panse** to stuff o.s. **3.** [partie arrondie] bulge.

pansement [pɑ̃smɑ̃] **nm** dressing, bandage ▸ **pans ment (adhésif)** (sticking) plaster *UK*, Band-Aid®.

panser [3] [pɑ̃se] **vt 1.** [plaie] to dress, to bandage / [jambe] to put a dressing on, to bandage / [avec pansement adhésif] to put a plaster *UK* *ou* Band-Aid® on **2.** [cheval] to groom.

pantacourt [pɑ̃takur] **nm** capri pants, capris, clamdiggers.

pantagruélique [pɑ̃tagryelik] **adj** gargantuan.

pantalon [pɑ̃talɔ̃] **nm** trousers *pl UK*, pants *pl US*, pair of trousers *UK ou* pants *US*.

pantelant, e [pɑ̃tlɑ̃, ɑ̃t] **adj** panting, gasping.

panthéisme [pɑ̃teism] **nm** pantheism.

panthéiste [pɑ̃teist] ■ **nmf** pantheist.
■ **adj** pantheistic.

panthéon [pɑ̃teɔ̃] **nm : le Panthéon** the Pantheon *(where famous Frenchmen and Frenchwomen are buried)*.

panthère [pɑ̃tɛr] **nf** panther ▸ **panthère noire** black panther.

pantin [pɑ̃tɛ̃] **nm 1.** [jouet] jumping jack **2.** *péj* [personne] puppet.

pantois, e [pɑ̃twa, az] **adj** astounded, dumbstruck ▸ **rester pantois** to be astounded *ou* dumbstruck.

pantomime [pɑ̃tɔmim] **nf 1.** [art, pièce] mime **2.** *fig & péj* [manège ridicule] **: qu'est-ce que c'est que cette pantomime?** what are you playing at?

pantouflard, e [pɑ̃tuflar, ard] *fam* **adj & nm, f** stay-at-home.

pantoufle [pɑ̃tufl] **nf** slipper.

panure [panyr] **nf** breadcrumbs *pl*, coating of breadcrumbs.

PAO (abr de ***publication assistée par ordinateur***) **nf** DTP.

paon [pɑ̃] **nm** peacock ▸ **fier comme un paon** (as) proud as a peacock.

papa [papa] **nm** dad, daddy ▸ **papa gâteau** indulgent father.

papal, e, aux [papal, o] **adj** papal.

paparazzi [paparadzi] (pl **paparazzi** *ou* **paparazzis**) **nm** *péj* paparazzi ▸ **les paparazzis** the paparazzi.

papauté [papote] **nf** papacy.

papaye [papaj] **nf** papaya, pawpaw.

pape [pap] **nm 1.** RELIG pope ▸ **sérieux comme un pape** deadly serious **2.** *fig* [de mouvement] leading light.

papelard [paplar] **nm** *fam* [papier] bit of paper.

paperasse [papras] **nf** *péj* **1.** [papier sans importance] bumf *(U) UK*, papers *pl* **2.** [papiers administratifs] paperwork *(U)*.

paperasserie [paprasri] **nf** *péj* paperwork.

papet [papɛ] **nm : papet vaudois** *stew of leeks and potatoes plus sausage made from cabbage and pigs' liver, a speciality of the canton of Vaud in Switzerland.*

papeterie [papɛtri] **nf** [magasin] stationer's / [fabrique] paper mill.

papetier, ère [papətje, ɛr] **nm, f** [commerçant] stationer / [fabricant] paper manufacturer.

papi, papy [papi] **nm** grandpa, grandad.

papier [papje] **nm 1.** [matière, écrit] paper ▸ **jeter qqch sur le papier** to jot sthg down ▸ **noircir du papier** to scribble ▸ **papier alu** *ou* **aluminium** aluminium *UK ou* aluminum *US* foil, tinfoil ▸ **papier brouillon** rough paper ▸ **papier buvard** blotting paper ▸ **papier cadeau** wrapping paper ▸ **papier carbone** carbon paper ▸ **papier continu** continuous stationery ▸ **papier crépon** crêpe paper ▸ **papier d'emballage** wrapping paper ▸ **papier à en-tête** headed notepaper ▸ **papier glacé** glazed paper ▸ **papier hygiénique** *ou* **toilette** toilet paper ▸ **papier journal** newsprint / [vieux journaux] newspaper ▸ **papier kraft** brown paper ▸ **papier à lettres** writing paper, notepaper ▸ **papier mâché** papier-mâché ▸ **papier machine** typing paper ▸ **papier millimétré** graph paper ▸ **papier peint** wallpaper ▸ **papier de soie** tissue paper ▸ **papier thermique** thermal paper ▸ **papier tue-mouches** fly paper ▸ **papier de verre** glasspaper *UK*, sandpaper **2.** [article de journal] article ▸ **faire un papier sur** to do a piece *ou* an article on.
◆ ***papiers*** **nmpl : papiers (d'identité)** (identity) papers ▸ **les papiers du véhicule, s'il vous plaît** may I see your logbook *UK ou* (vehicle) registration papers, please?

papier-calque [papjekalk] (pl **papiers-calque**) **nm** tracing paper.

papier-filtre [papjefiltr] (pl **papiers-filtres**) **nm** filter paper.

papier-monnaie [papjemɔnɛ] (pl **papiers-monnaies**) **nm** paper money.

papille [papij] **nf : papilles gustatives** taste buds.

papillon [papijɔ̃] **nm 1.** ZOOL butterfly ▸ **papillon de nuit** moth **2.** [contravention] (parking) ticket **3.** [écrou] wing nut **4.** [nage] butterfly (stroke).

papillonner [3] [papijɔne] **vi** to flit about *ou* around.

papillote [papijɔt] **nf 1.** [de bonbon] sweet paper *ou* wrapper *UK*, candy paper *US* **2.** [de cheveux] curl paper **3.** CULIN **: en papillotes** *baked in tinfoil or greaseproof paper.*

papilloter [3] [papijɔte] **vi** [lumière] to twinkle / [yeux] to blink.

papoter [3] [papɔte] **vi** *fam* to chatter.

papou, e [papu] **adj** Papuan.
◆ ***papou*** **nm** [langue] Papuan.
◆ ***Papou, e*** **nm, f** Papuan.

Papouasie-Nouvelle-Guinée [papwazinyvɛlgine] **nf : la Papouasie-Nouvelle-Guinée** Papua New Guinea.

paprika [paprika] **nm** paprika.

papy = ***papi***.

papyrus [papirys] **nm** papyrus.

Pâque [pak] **nf : la Pâque** Passover ; voir aussi ***Pâques***.

paquebot [pakbo] **nm** liner.

pâquerette [pakrɛt] **nf** daisy.

Pâques [pak] **nfpl** Easter *sg* ▸ **joyeuses Pâques** Happy Easter ▸ **île de Pâques** Easter Island.

paquet [pakɛ] **nm 1.** [colis] parcel *UK*, package *US* ▸ **faire un paquet de vieux journaux** to make up a bundle of old newspapers **2.** [emballage] packet *UK*, package *US* ▸ **un paquet de sucre/de farine** a bag of sugar/flour ▸ **un**

paquet de cigarettes a packet *UK ou* a pack *US* (of cigarettes) ▸ **paquet-cadeau** gift-wrapped parcel *UK ou* package *US* ▸ **paquet de présentation** presentation pack ▸▸ **mettre le paquet** *fam* to pull out all the stops, to give it all one's got ▸ **sa mère est un paquet de nerfs** her mother's a bundle *ou* bag of nerves.

paquetage [paktaʒ] **nm** MIL kit.

par [par] **prép 1.** [spatial] through, by (way of) ▸ **passer par la Suède et le Danemark** to go via Sweden and Denmark ▸ **regarder par la fenêtre** to look out of the window ▸ **par endroits** in places ▸ **par ici/là** this/that way ▸ **mon cousin habite par ici** my cousin lives round here ▸ **de par le monde** all over *ou* throughout the world
2. [temporel] on ▸ **par un beau jour d'été** on a lovely summer's day ▸ **par deux fois** twice ▸ **par moments** at times, from time to time ▸ **par le passé** in the past
3. [moyen, manière, cause] by ▸ **par bateau/train/avion** by boat/train/plane ▸ **par pitié** out of *ou* from pity ▸ **par accident** by accident, by chance ▸ **je l'ai rencontré par hasard** I met him by chance ▸ **répondre par oui ou par non** to answer yes or no
4. [introduit le complément d'agent] by ▸ **faire faire qqch par qqn** to have sthg done by sb ▸ **le logiciel est protégé par un code** the software is protected by *ou* with a code
5. [sens distributif] per, a ▸ **une heure par jour** one hour a *ou* per day ▸ **deux par deux** two at a time ▸ **marcher deux par deux** to walk in twos
6. [avec les verbes commencer et finir] **: commence par travailler** start (off) by working ▸ **il a fini par avouer** he eventually owned up.
◆ ***par-ci par-là*** **loc adv** here and there ▸ **des livres traînaient par-ci par-là** books were lying around here and there.

para [para] (abr de ***parachutiste***) **nm** *fam* para *UK*.

parabole [parabɔl] **nf 1.** [récit] parable **2.** MATH parabola.

parabolique [parabɔlik] **adj** parabolic.

paracétamol [parasetamɔl] **nm** paracetamol.

parachever [19] [paraʃve] **vt** to put the finishing touches to.

parachutage [paraʃytaʒ] **nm** parachuting, dropping by parachute.

parachute [paraʃyt] **nm** parachute ▸ **parachute ascensionnel** parachute *(for parascending)* ▸ **faire du parachute ascensionnel** to go parascending.

parachuter [3] [paraʃyte] **vt** to parachute, to drop by parachute ▸ **ils l'ont parachuté directeur** *fig* he was unexpectedly given the job of manager.

parachutisme [paraʃytism] **nm** parachuting.

parachutiste [paraʃytist] **nmf** parachutist / MIL paratrooper.

parade [parad] **nf 1.** [spectacle] parade **2.** [défense] parry / *fig* riposte **3.** [étalage] show.

parader [3] [parade] **vi** to show off.

paradis [paradi] **nm** paradise ▸ **paradis fiscal** tax haven ▸ **le Paradis terrestre** [bible] the Garden of Eden / *fig* heaven on earth.

paradisiaque [paradizjak] **adj** heavenly.

paradoxal, e, aux [paradɔksal, o] **adj** paradoxical.

paradoxalement [paradɔksalmɑ̃] **adv** paradoxically.

paradoxe [paradɔks] **nm** paradox.

parafe, paraphe [paraf] **nm** initials *pl*.

parafer, parapher [3] [parafe] **vt** to initial.

paraffine [parafin] **nf** paraffin *UK*, kerosene *US* / [solide] paraffin wax.

parages [paraʒ] **nmpl : être *ou* se trouver dans les parages** *fig* to be in the area *ou* vicinity.

paragraphe [paragraf] **nm** paragraph.

Paraguay [paragwɛ] **nm : le Paraguay** Paraguay ▸ **au Paraguay** in Paraguay.

paraguayen, enne [paragwejɛ̃, ɛn] **adj** Paraguayan.
◆ ***Paraguayen, enne*** **nm, f** Paraguayan.

paraissais, paraissions ➤ *paraître*.

paraître [91] [parɛtr] ■ **v attr** to look, to seem, to appear.
■ **vi 1.** [se montrer] to appear **2.** [être publié] to come out, to be published **3.** [se manifester] to show (through) ▸ **laisser paraître** to show ▸ **ne rien laisser paraître** to let nothing show **4.** [briller] to be noticed.
■ **v impers : il paraît/paraîtrait que** it appears/would appear that ▸ **paraît-il** apparently, it seems.

parallèle [paralɛl] ■ **nm** parallel ▸ **mettre en parallèle** *fig* to compare ▸ **établir un parallèle entre** *fig* to draw a parallel between.
■ **nf** parallel (line).
■ **adj 1.** [action, en maths] parallel **2.** [marché] unofficial / [médecine, énergie] alternative.

parallèlement [paralɛlmɑ̃] **adv** in parallel / *fig* at the same time.

parallélépipède [paralelepipɛd] **nm** parallelepiped.

parallélisme [paralelism] **nm** parallelism / [de roues] alignment.

parallélogramme [paralelɔgram] **nm** parallelogram.

paralysant, e [paralizɑ̃, ɑ̃t] **adj** paralysing *UK*, paralyzing *US*.

paralyser [3] [paralize] **vt** to paralyse *UK*, to paralyze *US*.

paralysie [paralizi] **nf** paralysis.

paralytique [paralitik] **adj & nmf** paralytic.

paramédical, e, aux [paramedikal, o] **adj** paramedical.

paramètre [paramɛtr] **nm** parameter.

paramilitaire [paramilitɛr] **adj** paramilitary.

parangon [parɑ̃gɔ̃] **nm** *littéraire* paragon.

parano [parano] **adj** *fam* paranoid.

paranoïa [paranɔja] **nf** paranoia.

paranoïaque [paranɔjak] ■ **adj** paranoid.
■ **nmf** paranoiac.

paranormal, e, aux [paranɔrmal, o] **adj** paranormal.

parapente [parapɑ̃t] **nm** paragliding ▸ **faire du parapente** to go paragliding.

parapet [parapɛ] **nm** parapet.

paraphe = *parafe*.

parapher = *parafer*.

paraphrase [parafraz] **nf** paraphrase.

paraphraser [3] [parafraze] **vt** to paraphrase.

paraplégique [paraplezik] **nmf & adj** paraplegic.

parapluie [paraplɥi] **nm** umbrella ▸ **parapluie atomique** *ou* **nucléaire** nuclear umbrella.

parapsychologie [parapsikɔlɔʒi] **nf** parapsychology.

parascolaire [paraskɔlɛr] **adj** extracurricular.

parasite [parazit] ■ **nm** parasite.
■ **adj** parasitic ▸ **bruits parasites** RADIO & TV interference *(U)*.
◆ ***parasites*** **nmpl** RADIO & TV interference *(U)*.

parasiter [3] [parazite] **vt 1.** [suj: ver, insecte] to live parasitically on, to parasitize **2.** [suj: personne] to leech *ou* live off **3.** RADIO & TV to cause interference on.

parasol [parasɔl] **nm** parasol, sunshade.

paratonnerre [paratɔnɛr] **nm** lightning conductor *UK* *ou* rod *US*.

paravent [paravɑ̃] **nm** screen.

parbleu [parblø] **interj** (but) of course!

parc [park] **nm 1.** [jardin] park / [de château] grounds *pl* ▸ **parc d'attractions** amusement park ▸ **parc de loisirs** ≃ leisure park ▸ **parc national** national park ▸ **parc à thème** ≃ theme park **2.** [pour l'élevage] pen ▸ **parc à huîtres** oyster bed **3.** [de bébé] playpen **4.** [de voitures] fleet ▸ **le parc automobile** the number of cars on the roads.
◆ ***parc des Princes*** **npr m** *Paris sports stadium, home to football team Paris Saint-Germain.*

parcelle [parsɛl] **nf 1.** [petite partie] fragment, particle **2.** [terrain] parcel of land.

parce que [parsk(ə)] **loc conj** because.

parchemin [parʃəmɛ̃] **nm** parchment.

parcheminé, ***e*** [parʃəmine] **adj** wrinkled.

parcimonie [parsimɔni] **nf** parsimoniousness ▸ **avec parcimonie** sparingly, parsimoniously.

parcimonieusement [parsimɔnjøzmɑ̃] **adv** parsimoniously.

parcimonieux, ***euse*** [parsimɔnjø, øz] **adj** parsimonious.

parcmètre [parkmɛtr] **nm** parking meter.

parcourir [45] [parkurir] **vt 1.** [région, route] to cover **2.** [journal, dossier] to skim *ou* glance through, to scan.

parcourrai, ***parcourras*** ➤ ***parcourir***.

parcours[1], ***parcourt*** etc ➤ ***parcourir***.

parcours[2] [parkur] **nm 1.** [trajet, voyage] journey / [itinéraire] route ▸ **parcours du combattant** assault course ▸ **parcours santé** *trail in the countryside where signs encourage people to do exercises for their health* **2.** [golf] [terrain] course / [trajet] round.

parcouru, ***e*** [parkury] **pp** ➤ ***parcourir***.

par-delà [pardəla] **prép** beyond.

par-derrière [pardɛrjɛr] **adv 1.** [par le côté arrière] round *UK* *ou* around *US* the back **2.** [en cachette] behind one's back.

par-dessous [pardəsu] **prép & adv** under, underneath.

pardessus [pardəsy] **nm inv** overcoat.

par-dessus [pardəsy] ■ **prép** over, over the top of ▸ **par-dessus tout** above all.
■ **adv** over, over the top.

par-devant [pardəvɑ̃] ■ **prép** in front of.
■ **adv** in front.

pardi [pardi] **interj** *fam* of course!

pardon [pardɔ̃] ■ **nm** forgiveness ▸ **demander pardon** to say (one is) sorry.
■ **interj** [excuses] (I'm) sorry! / [pour attirer l'attention] excuse me! ▸ **pardon?** (I beg your) pardon? *UK*, pardon me? *US*

pardonnable [pardɔnabl] **adj** forgiveable.

pardonner [3] [pardɔne] ■ **vt** to forgive ▸ **pardonner qqch à qqn** to forgive sb for sthg ▸ **pardonner à qqn d'avoir fait qqch** to forgive sb for doing sthg.
■ **vi : ce genre d'erreur ne pardonne pas** this kind of mistake is fatal.

paré, ***e*** [pare] **adj** [prêt] ready.

pare-balles [parbal] ■ **nm inv** [gilet] bullet-proof vest / [plaque] bullet-proof shield.
■ **adj inv** bullet-proof.

pare-brise [parbriz] **nm inv** windscreen *UK*, windshield *US*.

pare-chocs [parʃɔk] **nm inv** bumper.

pare-feu [parfø] **nm inv** [dispositif] fireguard / [en forêt] firebreak.

pareil, ***eille*** [parɛj] ■ **adj 1.** [semblable] **: pareil (à)** similar (to) **2.** [tel] such ▸ **un pareil film** such a film, a film like this ▸ **de pareils films** such films, films like these.
■ **nm, f : mes pareils** my equals ▸ **sans pareil** matchless ▸ **c'est du pareil au même** it comes to much the same thing ▸ **rendre la pareille à qqn** to pay sb back in his/her own coin, to give sb a taste of his/her own medicine.
◆ ***pareil*** **adv** *fam* the same (way).

pareillement [parɛjmɑ̃] **adv** [de même] in the same way / [également, aussi] likewise, also.

parement [parmɑ̃] **nm** facing.

parent, ***e*** [parɑ̃, ɑ̃t] ■ **adj : parent (de)** related (to).
■ **nm, f** relative, relation ▸ **parent éloigné** distant relation *ou* relative.
◆ ***parents*** **nmpl 1.** [père et mère] parents, mother and father **2.** *littéraire* [ancêtres] forefathers.

parental, ***e***, ***aux*** [parɑ̃tal, o] **adj** parental.

parenté [parɑ̃te] **nf 1.** [lien, affinité] relationship **2.** [famille] relatives *pl*, relations *pl*.

parenthèse [parɑ̃tɛz] **nf 1.** [digression] digression, parenthesis **2.** TYPO bracket *UK*, parenthesis ▸ **entre parenthèses** in brackets *UK* / *fig* incidentally, by the way ▸ **mettre entre parenthèses** to put in brackets *UK* *ou* parentheses *US*, to bracket *UK* / *fig* to put to one side ▸ **ouvrir/fermer la parenthèse** to open/close brackets *UK* *ou* parentheses *US*.

paréo [pareo] **nm** pareo.

parer [3] [pare] ■ **vt 1.** *sout* [orner] to adorn **2.** [vêtir] **: parer qqn de qqch** to dress sb up in sthg, to deck sb out in sthg / *fig* to attribute sthg to sb **3.** [contrer] to ward off, to parry.
■ **vi : parer à** [faire face à] to deal with / [pourvoir à] to prepare for ▸ **parer au plus pressé** to see to what is most urgent.
◆ ***se parer*** **vp** to dress up, to put on all one's finery ▸ **se parer de** to adorn o.s. with / *fig* [titre] to assume.

pare-soleil [parsɔlɛj] **nm inv** sun visor.

paresse [parɛs] **nf 1.** [fainéantise] laziness, idleness **2.** MÉD sluggishness.

paresser [4] [parɛse] **vi** to laze about *ou* around.

paresseusement [parɛsøzmɑ̃] **adv** lazily, idly.

paresseux, euse [parɛsø, øz] ■ **adj 1.** [fainéant] lazy **2.** MÉD sluggish.
■ **nm, f** [personne] lazy *ou* idle person.
◆ ***paresseux*** **nm** [animal] sloth.

parfaire [109] [parfɛr] **vt** to complete, to perfect.

parfait, e [parfɛ, ɛt] **adj** perfect ▸ **c'est le parfait homme du monde** he's a perfect gentleman ▸ **c'est un parfait goujat/idiot** he's an utter boor/fool ▸ **dans la plus parfaite indifférence** in utter *ou* complete *ou* total indifference ▸ **le rôle est parfait pour lui** the part is ideal *ou* made for him ▸ **son russe est parfait** her Russian is perfect *ou* flawless, she speaks perfect Russian.
◆ ***parfait*** **nm 1.** CULIN parfait **2.** GRAMM perfect (tense).

parfaitement [parfɛtmɑ̃] **adv 1.** [admirablement, très] perfectly **2.** [marque l'assentiment] absolutely.

parfois [parfwa] **adv** sometimes.

parfum [parfœ̃] **nm 1.** [de fleur] scent, fragrance **2.** [à base d'essences] perfume, scent **3.** [de glace] flavour *UK*, flavor *US*
▸▸ **être/mettre qqn au parfum** to be/put sb in the know.

parfumé, e [parfyme] **adj 1.** [fleur] fragrant **2.** [mouchoir] perfumed **3.** [femme] **: elle est trop parfumée** she's wearing too much perfume.

parfumer [3] [parfyme] **vt 1.** [suj: fleurs] to perfume **2.** [mouchoir] to perfume, to scent **3.** CULIN to flavour.
◆ ***se parfumer*** **vp** to put perfume on.

parfumerie [parfymri] **nf** perfumery.

parfumeur, euse [parfymœr, øz] **nm, f** perfumer.

pari [pari] **nm 1.** [entre personnes] bet ▸ **faire un pari** to make *ou* lay a bet ▸ **gagner/perdre son pari** to win/lose one's bet **2.** [jeu] betting *(U)*.

paria [parja] **nm** pariah.

parier [9] [parje] **vt : parier (sur)** to bet (on) ▸ **je l'aurais parié!** *fig* I thought as much!

parieur [parjœr] **nm** punter.

parigot, ote [parigo, ɔt] **adj** *fam* Parisian.
◆ ***Parigot, ote*** **nm, f** *fam* Parisian.

Paris [pari] **npr** Paris.

paris-brest [paribrɛst] **nm inv** *choux pastry ring with cream and almonds.*

parisianisme [parizjanism] **nm** [expression] Parisian idiom / [habitude] Parisian custom.

parisien, enne [parizjɛ̃, ɛn] **adj** [vie, société] Parisian / [métro, banlieue, région] Paris *(avant n).*
◆ ***Parisien, enne*** **nm, f** Parisian.

paritaire [paritɛr] **adj : commission paritaire** joint commission *(with both sides equally represented).*

parité [parite] **nf** parity.

parjure [parʒyr] ■ **nmf** [personne] perjurer.
■ **nm** [faux serment] perjury.

parjurer [3] [parʒyre] ◆ ***se parjurer*** **vp** to perjure o.s.

parka [parka] **nm & nf** parka.

parking [parkiŋ] **nm** [parc] car park *UK*, parking lot *US*.

parlant, e [parlɑ̃, ɑ̃t] **adj 1.** [qui parle] **: le cinéma parlant** talking pictures ▸ **l'horloge parlante** TÉLÉCOM the speaking clock **2.** *fig* [chiffres, données] eloquent / [portrait] vivid.

parlé, e [parle] **adj** [anglais, langue] spoken.
◆ ***parlé*** **nm** [à l'opéra] spoken part, dialogue.

parlement [parləmɑ̃] **nm** parliament ▸ **le Parlement européen** the European Parliament.

parlementaire [parləmɑ̃tɛr] ■ **nmf** [député] membe of parliament ▸ **parlementaire rebelle** rebel MP / [négo ciateur] negotiator.
■ **adj** parliamentary.

parlementarisme [parləmɑ̃tarism] **nm** (system of parliamentary government.

parlementer [3] [parləmɑ̃te] **vi 1.** [négocier] to nego tiate, to parley **2.** [parler longtemps] to talk at length.

parler [3] [parle] ■ **vi 1.** [gén] to talk, to speak ▸ **le faits parlent d'eux-mêmes** the facts speak for themselve ▸ **tout le monde en parle** everybody's talking about ▸ **parler à/avec qqn** to speak to/with sb, to talk to/with s ▸ **puis-je parler à Virginie?** [au téléphone] may I speak t Virginie? ▸ **parler de qqch à qqn** to speak *ou* talk to s about sthg ▸ **elle nous a parlé de ses projets** she talke to us about her plans ▸ **parler de qqn/qqch** to talk abou sb/sthg ▸ **parler de faire qqch** to talk about doing sth ▸ **parler en français** to speak in French ▸ **parler tout seu** to talk to o.s. ▸ **sans parler de** apart from, not to mentio ▸ **sans parler du fait que...** to say nothing of..., withou mentioning the fact that... ▸ **à proprement parler** strict speaking ▸ **parler pour ne rien dire** to talk for the sak of talking ▸ **parle pour toi!** speak for yourself! ▸ **tu parle** *fam* you can say that again! ▸ **ça t'a plu? – tu parles!** [bie sûr] did you like it? – you bet! / [pas du tout] did you lik it? – you must be joking! ▸ **sa timidité? parlons-en!** h shyness? that's a good one *ou* you must be joking! ▸ **n'e parlons plus** we'll say no more about it
2. [avouer] to talk ▸ **faire parler qqn** to make sb talk, get sb to talk.
■ **vt** [langue] to speak ▸ **parler (le) français** to spea French ▸ **parler politique/affaires** to talk politics/busine ▸ **nous ne parlons pas la même langue** *ou* **le mêm langage** *fig* we don't speak the same language.
■ **nm 1.** [manière de parler] speech ▸ **dans le parler d tous les jours** in common parlance
2. [patois] dialect.
◆ ***se parler*** **vp : il faudrait qu'on se parle tous l deux** I think we two should have a talk ▸ **ils ne se parler pas** they're not on speaking terms.

parleur [parlœr] **nm : beau parleur** *péj* fine talker.

parloir [parlwar] **nm** parlour *UK*, parlor *US*.

parlo(t)te [parlɔt] **nf** chat.

parme [parm] **nm & adj inv** violet.

parmesan [parməzɑ̃] **nm** Parmesan (cheese).

parmi [parmi] **prép** among.

parnassien, enne [parnasjɛ̃, ɛn] **adj** Parnassian.
◆ ***Parnassien, enne*** **nm, f** Parnassian *(member of the Parnassian school of French poets).*

parodie [parɔdi] **nf** parody.

parodier [9] [parɔdje] **vt** to parody.

paroi [parwa] **nf 1.** [mur] wall / [cloison] partition ▸ **paroi rocheuse** rock face **2.** [de récipient] inner side.

paroisse [parwas] **nf** parish.

paroissial, e, aux [parwasjal, o] **adj** parish *(avant n).*

paroissien, enne [parwasjɛ̃, ɛn] **nm, f** parishioner.

parole [parɔl] **nf 1.** [faculté de parler] **: la parole** speech ▸ **perdre l'usage de la parole** to lose one's power of speech **2.** [propos, discours] **: adresser la parole à qqn** to speak to sb ▸ **couper la parole à qqn** to cut sb off ▸ **demander la parole** to ask for the right to speak / DR to request leave to speak ▸ **prendre la parole** to speak ▸ **donner** *ou* **passer la parole à qqn** to hand over to sb ▸ **temps de parole** speaking time ▸ **c'est parole d'Évangile** it's the gospel truth ▸ **ce ne sont que des paroles en l'air** all that's just idle talk ▸ **en paroles et en actes** in word and deed **3.** [promesse, mot] word ▸ **tenir parole** to keep one's word ▸ **donner sa parole d'honneur** to give one's word of honour *UK ou* honor *US* ▸ **croire qqn sur parole** to take sb's word for it ▸ **libérer qqn sur parole** to free sb on parole.
◆ ***paroles*** **nfpl** MUS words, lyrics.

parolier, ère [parɔlje, ɛr] **nm, f** [de chanson] lyricist / [d'opéra] librettist.

paroxysme [parɔksism] **nm** height.

parpaing [parpɛ̃] **nm** breezeblock *UK*, cinderblock *US*.

parquer [3] [parke] **vt 1.** [animaux] to pen in *ou* up **2.** [prisonniers] to shut up *ou* in **3.** [voiture] to park.

parquet [parkɛ] **nm 1.** [plancher] parquet floor **2.** DR ≃ Crown Prosecution Service *UK*, ≃ District Attorney's office *US*.

parqueter [27] [parkəte] **vt** to lay a parquet floor in.

parrain [parɛ̃] **nm 1.** [d'enfant] godfather **2.** [de festival, sportif] sponsor.

parrainage [parɛnaʒ] **nm** sponsorship ▸ **parrainage d'entreprises** corporate sponsorship.

parrainer [4] [parɛne] **vt** to sponsor, to back.

parricide [parisid] ■ **nm** [crime] parricide.
■ **adj** parricidal.

pars, part ➤ ***partir.***

parsemer [19] [parsəme] **vt : parsemer (de)** to strew (with).

part [par] **nf 1.** [de gâteau] portion / [de bonheur, d'héritage] share / [partie] part ▸ **réclamer sa part** to claim one's share ▸ **part de marché** ÉCON market share ▸ **faire la part belle à qqn** to give sb a good deal ▸ **se tailler la part du lion** *fig* to take the lion's share **2.** [participation] **: prendre part à qqch** to take part in sthg ▸ **prendre part à la joie/peine de qqn** to share (in) sb's joy/sorrow
▸▸ **de la part de** from / [appeler, remercier] on behalf of *UK*, in behalf of *US* ▸ **c'est de la part de qui?** [au téléphone] who's speaking *ou* calling? ▸ **dites-lui de ma part que...** tell him from me that... ▸ **ce serait bien aimable de votre part** it would be very kind of you ▸ **pour ma part** as far as I'm concerned ▸ **faire part à qqn de qqch** to inform sb of sthg ▸ **faire la part des choses** to make allowances.
◆ ***à part*** ■ **loc adv** aside, separately ▸ **mets les dossiers bleus à part** put the blue files to one side ▸ **prendre qqn à part** to take sb aside *ou* to one side.
■ **loc adj** exceptional ▸ **ce sont des gens à part** these people are rather special.
■ **loc prép** apart from ▸ **à part cela** apart from that, that aside.
◆ ***à part entière*** **loc adj : citoyen à part entière** person with full citizenship (status) ▸ **elle est devenue une actrice à part entière** she's now a proper *ou* a fully-fledged actress.
◆ ***autre part*** **loc adv** somewhere *ou* someplace *US* else.
◆ ***d'autre part*** **loc adv** besides, moreover.
◆ ***de part en part*** **loc adv** right through ▸ **la poutre est fendue de part en part** the beam is split from end to end.
◆ ***de part et d'autre*** **loc adv** on both sides.
◆ ***d'une part..., d'autre part*** **loc correlative** on the one hand..., on the other hand.
◆ ***quelque part*** **loc adv** somewhere, someplace *US*.

part. abr de ***particulier.***

partage [partaʒ] **nm 1.** [action] sharing (out) **2.** DR distribution.

partagé, e [partaʒe] **adj 1.** [opposé] split, divided ▸ **j'ai lu des critiques partagées** I've read mixed reviews ▸ **il était partagé entre la joie et la crainte** he was torn between joy and fear **2.** [mutuel - haine] mutual, reciprocal / [- amour] mutual **3.** INFORM **: en temps partagé** on a time-sharing basis.

partager [17] [partaʒe] **vt 1.** [morceler] to divide (up) ▸ **partager qqch en deux** to divide sthg in two ▸ **être partagé** *fig* to be divided **2.** [mettre en commun] **: partager qqch avec qqn** to share sthg with sb **3.** [prendre part à] to share (in) ▸ **partager la joie/peine de qqn** to share (in) sb's joy/sorrow ▸ **voici une opinion partagée par beaucoup de gens** this is an opinion shared *ou* held by many (people).
◆ ***se partager*** **vp 1.** [se diviser] to be divided ▸ **se partager en** to be split *ou* divided into **2.** [partager son temps] to divide one's time ▸ **elles se partagent entre leur carrière et leurs enfants** their time is divided between their professional lives and their families **3.** [se répartir] **: se partager qqch** to share sthg between themselves/ourselves etc ▸ **se partager la tâche** to share (out) the work.

partagiciel [partaʒisjɛl] **nm** shareware.

partance [partɑ̃s] **nf : en partance** outward bound ▸ **en partance pour** bound for.

partant, e [partɑ̃, ɑ̃t] **adj : être partant pour** to be ready for.
◆ ***partant*** **nm** starter.

partenaire [partənɛr] **nmf** partner ▸ **partenaire économique** business partner ▸ **partenaires sociaux** labour *UK ou* labor *US* and management.

partenariat [partənarja] **nm** partnership.

parterre [partɛr] **nm** **1.** [de fleurs] (flower) bed **2.** THÉÂTRE stalls *pl UK*, orchestra *US*.

parti, e [parti] ■ **pp** ➤ ***partir***.
■ **adj** *fam* [ivre] tipsy.
◆ ***parti*** **nm** **1.** POLIT party ▸ **les partis de droite/gauche** the parties of the right/left, the right-wing/left-wing parties ▸ **parti d'opposition** opposition party **2.** [choix, décision] course of action ▸ **prendre parti** to make up one's mind ▸ **prendre parti pour/contre qqch** to come out for/against sthg ▸ **prendre le parti de faire qqch** to make up one's mind to do sthg ▸ **en prendre son parti** to be resigned ▸ **être de parti pris** to be prejudiced *ou* biased ▸ **être sans parti pris** to be unbiased *ou* objective ▸ **tirer parti de** to make (good) use of ▸ **elle ne sait pas tirer parti de ses qualifications** she doesn't know how to get the most out of her qualifications **3.** [personne à marier] match ▸ **un beau parti** a good match.
◆ ***partie*** **nf** **1.** [élément, portion] part ▸ **en grande partie** largely ▸ **en majeure partie** for the most part ▸ **faire partie (intégrante) de qqch** to be (an integral) part of sthg ▸ **une grande/petite partie de l'électorat** a large/small part of the electorate, a large/small section of the electorate ▸ **parties communes/privatives** communal/private areas *(in a building or an estate)* **2.** [domaine d'activité] field, subject ▸ **elle est de la partie** it's her line **3.** SPORT [jeux] game ▸ **faire une partie de cartes** to have a game of cards ▸ **partie de golf** round of golf **4.** DR party ▸ **la partie adverse** the opposing party ▸ **se constituer** *ou* **se porter partie civile** to act jointly with the public prosecutor
⏭ **prendre qqn à partie** to attack sb ▸ **ça n'est pas une partie de plaisir!** *fam* it's no picnic *ou* fun! ▸ **ce n'est que partie remise** there'll be other opportunities, I'll reschedule it, I'll take a rain check *US* ▸ **être partie prenante dans qqch** *fig* to be directly involved *ou* concerned in sthg.
◆ ***parties*** **nfpl** *fam* private parts, privates.
◆ ***en partie*** **loc adv** partly, in part ▸ **c'est en partie vrai** it's partly true ▸ **je ne l'ai cru qu'en partie** I only half believed him.

partial, e, aux [parsjal, o] **adj** biased.

partialement [parsjalmɑ̃] **adv** in a biased way, with bias.

partialité [parsjalite] **nf** partiality, bias.

participant, e [partisipɑ̃, ɑ̃t] ■ **adj** participating.
■ **nm, f** **1.** [à réunion] participant **2.** SPORT competitor **3.** [à concours] entrant.

participatif, ive [partisipatif, iv] **adj** : **prêt participatif** participating capital loan.

participation [partisipasjɔ̃] **nf** **1.** [collaboration] participation ▸ **sa participation aux jeux Olympiques semble compromise** there's a serious question mark hanging over his participation in the Olympic Games ▸ **apporter sa participation à qqch** to contribute to sthg ▸ **'avec la participation des frères Jarry'** 'featuring the Jarry Brothers' **2.** ÉCON interest ▸ **participation aux frais** (financial) contribution ▸ **participation aux bénéfices** profit sharing ▸ **participation majoritaire/minoritaire** majority/minority interest ▸ **il détient une participation de 6% dans l'entreprise** he holds a 6% share in the company ▸ **prendre des participations dans une entreprise** to buy into a company **3.** POLIT : **participation (électorale)** (voter) turnout.

participe [partisip] **nm** participle ▸ **participe passé/présent** past/present participle.

participer [3] [partisipe] **vi** **1.** : **participer à** [réunion, concours] to take part in ⁄ [frais] [payer pour] to contribute to ⁄ [bénéfices] to share in **2.** : **participer de** *littéraire* to have some of the characteristics of.

particularisme [partikylarism] **nm** (sense of) identity.

particularité [partikylarite] **nf** distinctive feature.

particule [partikyl] **nf** **1.** [gén & LING] particle **2.** [nobiliaire] nobiliary particle.

particulier, ère [partikylje, ɛr] **adj** **1.** [personnel, privé] private **2.** [spécial] particular, special ⁄ [propre] peculiar, characteristic ▸ **particulier à** peculiar to, characteristic of **3.** [remarquable] unusual, exceptional ▸ **cas particulier** special case **4.** [assez bizarre] peculiar.
◆ ***particulier*** **nm** [personne] private individual.
◆ ***en particulier*** **loc adv** **1.** [seul à seul] in private **2.** [surtout] in particular, particularly **3.** [à part] separately.

PARONYME / CONFUSABLE
particulier
Attention à ne pas confondre les deux traductions de particulier : *particular* signifie spécifique, propre à une entité, alors que *peculiar* signifie bizarre.

particulièrement [partikyljɛrmɑ̃] **adv** particularly ▸ **tout particulièrement** especially.

partie ➤ ***parti***.

partiel, elle [parsjɛl] **adj** partial.
◆ ***partiel*** **nm** UNIV ≃ end-of-term exam *UK*.

partiellement [parsjɛlmɑ̃] **adv** partially, partly.

partir [43] [partir] **vi** **1.** [personne] to go, to leave ▸ **partir à** to go to ▸ **partir à la campagne/montagne/mer** to go (off) to the countryside/mountains/seaside ▸ **partir à la recherche de** to set off in search of, to go looking for ▸ **partir pour** to leave for ▸ **partir de** [bureau] to leave ⁄ [aéroport, gare] to leave from ⁄ [date] to run from ⁄ [hypothèse, route] to start from ▸ **la rue part de la mairie** the street starts at the town hall ▸ **partir dans une explication** to embark on an explanation **2.** [voiture] to start ▸ **c'est bien/mal parti** *fig* it got off on the right/wrong foot ▸ **elle a l'air bien partie pour remporter l'élection** she seems well set to win the election **3.** [coup de feu] to go off ⁄ [bouchon] to pop **4.** [tache] to come out, to go ▸ **faire partir** [salissure] to get rid of, to remove ⁄ [odeur] to get rid of, to clear ⁄ [douleur] to ease.
◆ ***à partir de*** **loc prép** from ▸ **à partir de mardi** starting from Tuesday, from Tuesday onwards ▸ **c'est fait à partir d'huiles végétales** it's made from *ou* with vegetable oil ▸ **j'ai fait un résumé à partir de ses notes** I've made a summary based on his notes.

partisan, e [partizɑ̃, an] **adj** [partial] partisan ▸ **être partisan de** to be in favour *UK ou* favor *US* of.
◆ ***partisan*** **nm 1.** [adepte] supporter, advocate **2.** MIL partisan.

partitif, ive [partitif, iv] **adj** partitive.
◆ ***partitif*** **nm** partitive.

partition [partisjɔ̃] **nf 1.** [séparation] partition **2.** MUS score.

partout [partu] **adv** everywhere ▸ **partout ailleurs** everywhere else ▸ **un peu partout** all over, everywhere.

paru, e [pary] **pp** ➤ ***paraître***.

parure [paryr] **nf** (matching) set.

parution [parysjɔ̃] **nf** publication.

parvenir [40] [parvənir] **vi : parvenir à** [atteindre] to reach / [obtenir] to achieve ▸ **parvenir à faire qqch** to manage to do sthg ▸ **faire parvenir qqch à qqn** to send sthg to sb.

parvenu, e [parvəny] ■ **pp** ➤ ***parvenir***.
■ **nm, f** *péj* parvenu, upstart.

parviendrai, parviendras ➤ ***parvenir***.

parvis [parvi] **nm** square *(in front of church)*.

pas[1] [pa] **nm 1.** [gén] step ▸ **allonger le pas** to quicken one's pace ▸ **faire ses premiers pas** *litt* to learn to walk ▸ **marcher d'un bon pas** to walk at a good *ou* brisk pace ▸ **marcher à grands pas** to stride along ▸ **marquer le pas** to mark time ▸ **ralentir le pas** to slow one's pace, to slow down ▸ **revenir sur ses pas** to retrace one's steps ▸ **pas à pas** step by step ▸ **au pas cadencé** in quick time ▸ **à pas de loup** *fig* stealthily ▸ **à pas feutrés** *fig* with muffled footsteps ▸ **au pas de charge** MIL at the charge / *fig* charging along **2.** TECHNOL thread
▸▸ **c'est à deux pas (d'ici)** it's very near (here) ▸ **emboîter le pas à qqn** to fall into step with sb ▸ **faire les cent pas** to pace up and down ▸ **faire un faux pas** to slip / *fig* to make a faux pas ▸ **faire le premier pas** to make the first move ▸ **franchir** *ou* **sauter le pas** to take the plunge ▸ **je vais de ce pas lui dire ma façon de penser** I'm going to waste no time in telling him what I think ▸ **mettre qqn/qqch au pas** to bring sb/sthg to heel ▸ **prendre le pas (sur qqn/qqch)** to take precedence (over sb/sthg),to dominate (sb/sthg) ▸ **(rouler) au pas** (to move) at a snail's pace ▸ **sur le pas de la porte** on the doorstep ▸ **tirer qqn d'un mauvais pas** to get sb out of a tight spot.

pas[2] [pa] **adv 1.** [avec ne] not ▸ **elle ne vient pas** she's not *ou* she isn't coming ▸ **elle n'a pas mangé** she hasn't eaten ▸ **je ne le connais pas** I don't know him ▸ **il n'y a pas de vin** there's no wine, there isn't any wine ▸ **je ne m'en suis pas mal tiré** I handled it quite well ▸ **je préférerais ne pas le rencontrer** I would prefer not to meet him, I would rather not meet him
2. *fam* [avec omission du 'ne'] **: c'est vraiment pas drôle!** [pas comique] it's not in the least *ou* slightest bit funny / [ennuyeux] it's no fun at all ▸ **elle sait pas** she doesn't know
3. [sans ne] not ▸ **l'as-tu vu ou pas?** have you seen him or not? ▸ **il est très satisfait, moi pas** he's very pleased, but I'm not ▸ **pourquoi pas?** why not? ▸ **sincère ou pas** (whether) sincere or not ▸ **une histoire pas drôle** a story which isn't funny ▸ **pas encore** not yet ▸ **pas du tout** not at all ▸ **pas un geste!** not one move!
4. [avec pron indéf] **: pas un** [aucun] none, not one ▸ **il sait faire les crêpes comme pas un** he makes pancakes like nobody else (on earth) ▸ **pas un d'eux n'est venu** none of them *ou* not one of them came.

Pas-de-Calais [padkalɛ] **nm** *"département" in the north of France, containing the port of Calais.*

pascal, e [paskal] (pl **pascals** *ou* **pascaux** [pasko]) **adj** Easter *(avant n)*.
◆ ***pascal*** **nm 1.** INFORM Pascal **2.** PHYS pascal.

pas-de-porte [padpɔrt] **nm inv** key money.

pashmina [paʃmina] **nm** pashmina.

passable [pasabl] **adj** passable, fair.

passablement [pasabləmɑ̃] **adv 1.** [assez bien] fairly well **2.** [beaucoup] quite a bit.

passage [pasaʒ] **nm 1.** [action - de passer] going past / [- de traverser] crossing ▸ **être de passage** to be passing through ▸ **je suis de passage à Paris** I'm in Paris for a few days ▸ **au passage** [- en passant] as he/she *etc* goes by / *fig* in passing ▸ **lors de son dernier passage à la télévision** [- personne] last time he was on TV / [- film] last time it was shown on TV ▸ **prochain passage du car dans deux heures** the coach will be back *ou* will pass through again in two hours' time
2. [endroit] passage, way ▸ **se frayer un passage à travers** *ou* **dans** to force a way through ▸ **'passage interdit'** 'no entry' ▸ **passage clouté** *ou* **pour piétons** pedestrian crossing *UK*, crosswalk *US* ▸ **passage couvert** passageway ▸ **passage à niveau** level crossing *UK*, grade crossing *US* ▸ **passage protégé** *priority given to traffic on the main road* ▸ **passage secret** secret passage ▸ **passage souterrain** underpass, subway *UK*
3. [changement d'état] **: passage de qqch à qqch** change *ou* transition from sthg to sthg ▸ **le passage de l'autocratie à la démocratie** the changeover *ou* transition from autocracy to democracy ▸ **le passage dans la classe supérieure** SCOL going *ou* moving up to the next class *UK ou* grade *US* ▸ **passage à tabac** beating up ▸ **passage à vide** dizzy spell / *fig* bad patch ▸ **avoir un passage à vide** [syncope] to feel faint, to faint / [moralement] to go through a bad patch / [intellectuellement] to have a lapse in concentration
4. [extrait] passage ▸ **tu te souviens du passage où ils se rencontrent?** do you remember the bit where they meet?

passager, ère [pasaʒe, ɛr] ■ **adj 1.** [bonheur] fleeting, short-lived **2.** [hôte] short-stay *(avant n)* ▸ **oiseau passager** bird of passage.
■ **nm, f** passenger ▸ **passager clandestin** stowaway.

passant, e [pasɑ̃, ɑ̃t] ■ **adj** busy.
■ **nm, f** passerby.
◆ ***passant*** **nm** [de ceinture] (belt) loop.

passation [pasasjɔ̃] **nf 1.** [conclusion] signing **2.** [transmission] handover ▸ **passation des pouvoirs** transfer of power.

passe [pas] ■ **nm** passkey.
■ **nf 1.** [au sport] pass **2.** NAUT channel **3.** *fam* [prostitution] **: maison de passe** ≃ brothel
▸▸ **être en passe de faire qqch** to be on the way to doing sthg ▸ **être dans une mauvaise passe** to be in a fix.

passé*, *e [pase] **adj 1.** [qui n'est plus] past / [précédent] : **la semaine passée** last week ▸ **au cours de la semaine passée** in the last week ▸ **il est trois heures passées** it's gone three *UK*, it's after three ▸ **elle songeait au temps passé** she was thinking of times *ou* days gone by **2.** [fané] faded.

◆ ***passé*** ■ **nm** past ▸ **il a un lourd passé** he's a man with a past ▸ **oublions le passé** let bygones be bygones, let's forget the past ▸ **soyons amis, comme par le passé** let's be friends, like before ▸ **passé composé** perfect tense ▸ **passé simple** past historic ▸ **verbe au passé** verb in the past tense.

■ **prép** after.

passe-droit [pasdrwa] (pl **passe-droits**) **nm** privilege.

passementerie [pasmɑ̃tri] **nf** haberdashery *UK*, notions *pl US*.

passe-montagne [pasmɔ̃taɲ] (pl **passe-montagnes**) **nm** balaclava (helmet).

passe-partout [paspartu] **nm inv 1.** [clé] passkey **2.** *(en apposition)* [tenue] all-purpose / [phrase] stock *(avant n)*.

passe-passe [paspas] **nm inv : tour de passe-passe** [prestidigitation] conjuring trick / *fig* [tromperie] trick.

passe-plat [paspla] (pl **passe-plats**) **nm** serving hatch.

passeport [paspɔr] **nm** passport.

passer [3] [pase] ■ **vi** *(v aux : être)* **1.** [se frayer un chemin] to pass, to get past **2.** [défiler] to go by *ou* past ▸ **regarder passer les coureurs** to watch the runners go past **3.** [aller] to go ▸ **passer à *ou* au travers *ou* par** to come *ou* pass through ▸ **le voleur est passé par la fenêtre** the burglar got in through the window ▸ **passer chez qqn** to call on sb, to drop in on sb ▸ **passer de qqch à qqch** [changer d'état] to go from sthg to sthg / [changer d'activité] to change from sthg to sthg ▸ **passer devant** [bâtiment] to pass / [juge] to come before ▸ **en passant** in passing ▸ **ne faire que passer** to stay only a short while ▸ **où est-il passé?** where's he gone (to)? ▸ **l'affaire passera en justice le mois prochain** the case will be heard next month **4.** [venir - facteur] to come, to call ▸ **le facteur passe deux fois par jour** the postman delivers *ou* comes twice a day **5.** SCOL to pass, to be admitted ▸ **passer dans la classe supérieure** to move up *UK*, to be moved up (a class) *UK* **6.** [être accepté] to be accepted ▸ **qu'il soit toujours en retard, passe encore, mais...** it's one thing *ou* it's all very well to be late all the time but... **7.** [fermer les yeux] **: passer sur qqch** to pass over sthg **8.** [temps] to pass, to go by ▸ **comme le temps passe!** how time flies! **9.** [disparaître - souvenir, couleur] to fade / [- douleur] to pass, to go away ▸ **le papier peint a passé au soleil** the sun has faded the wallpaper **10.** CINÉ, TV & THÉÂTRE to be on ▸ **passer à la radio/télévision** to be on the radio/television ▸ **sa dernière pièce passe au Galatée** her latest play is on at the Galatée **11.** [aux cartes] to pass **12.** [devenir] **: passer président/directeur** to become president/director, to be appointed president/director

▸▸ **passer inaperçu** to pass *ou* go unnoticed ▸ **passons...** let's move on... ▸ **passer pour** to be regarded as ▸ **se faire passer pour qqn** to pass o.s. off as sb ▸ **il y est passé** *fam* [mort] he kicked the bucket ▸ **tout son argent y passe** *fam* all his money goes on that.

■ **vt** *(v aux : être)* **1.** [franchir - frontière, rivière] to cross / [- douane] to go through ▸ **passer un ruisseau à gué** to ford a stream **2.** [soirée, vacances] to spend **3.** [sauter - ligne, tour] to miss ▸ **je passe toutes les descriptions dans ses romans** I miss out *ou* I skip all the descriptions in her novels **4.** [défauts] **: passer qqch à qqn** to overlook sthg in sb ▸ **elle lui passe tout** she lets him get away with anything **5.** [faire aller - bras] to pass, to put ▸ **passer son bras autour de la taille de qqn** to put *ou* to slip one's arm round sb's waist **6.** [peinture] to lay on, to spread **7.** [filtrer - huile] to strain / [- café] to filter **8.** [film, disque] to put on **9.** [vêtement] to slip on ▸ **je passe une robe moins chaude et j'arrive** I'll put on a cooler dress and I'll be with you **10.** [vitesses] to change ▸ **passer la *ou* en troisième** to change into third (gear) **11.** [donner] **: passer qqch à qqn** to pass sb sthg ; **passe-moi le sel** pass me the salt **12.** MÉD **: passer qqch à qqn** to give sb sthg **13.** [accord] **: passer un contrat avec qqn** to have an agreement with sb **14.** SCOL & UNIV [examen] to sit *UK*, to take **15.** [au téléphone] **: je vous passe Mme Ledoux** [transmettre] I'll put you through to Mme Ledoux / [donner l'écouteur à] I'll hand you Mme Ledoux.

◆ ***se passer*** **vp 1.** [événement] to happen, to take place ▸ **comment ça s'est passé?** how did it go? ▸ **ça ne se passera pas comme ça!** I'm not putting up with that! ▸ **l'opération s'est bien/mal passée** the operation went (off) smoothly/badly **2.** [s'enduire - crème] to put on **3.** [s'abstenir] **: se passer de qqch/de faire qqch** to do without sthg/doing sthg ▸ **il ne peut pas se passer de télévision** he can't live without the television.

passereau [pasro] **nm** sparrow.

passerelle [pasrɛl] **nf 1.** [pont] footbridge **2.** [passage mobile] gangway.

passe-temps [pastɑ̃] **nm inv** pastime.

passe-thé [paste] **nm inv** tea strainer.

passible [pasibl] **adj : passible de** DR liable to.

passif*, *ive [pasif, iv] **adj** passive.

◆ ***passif*** **nm 1.** GRAMM passive **2.** FIN liabilities *pl*.

passing-shot [pasiŋʃɔt] (pl **passing-shots**) **nm** passing shot.

passion [pasjɔ̃] **nf** passion ▸ **avoir la passion de qqch** to have a passion for sthg.

◆ ***Passion*** **nf** MUS & RELIG Passion.

passionnant*, *e [pasjɔnɑ̃, ɑ̃t] **adj** exciting, fascinating.

passionné*, *e [pasjɔne] ■ **adj 1.** [personne] passionate **2.** [récit, débat] impassioned.

■ **nm, f** passionate person ▸ **passionné de ski/d'échecs** *etc* skiing/chess *etc* fanatic.

passionnel*, *elle [pasjɔnɛl] **adj** [crime] of passion.

passionnément [pasjɔnemɑ̃] **adv** passionately.

passionner [3] [pasjɔne] **vt** [personne] to grip, to fascinate.

◆ ***se passionner*** **vp : se passionner pour** to have a passion for.

passivement [pasivmɑ̃] **adv** passively.

passivité [pasivite] **nf** passivity.

passoire [paswar] **nf** [à liquide] sieve / [à légumes] colander.

pastel [pastɛl] ■ **nm** pastel.
■ **adj inv** [couleur] pastel *(avant n)*.

pastèque [pastɛk] **nf** watermelon.

pasteur [pastœr] **nm** **1.** *littéraire* [berger] shepherd **2.** RELIG pastor, minister.
◆ ***Pasteur*** [pastœr] **npr m : l'Institut Pasteur** *important medical research centre.*

pasteurisation [pastœrizasjɔ̃] **nf** pasteurization.

pasteurisé, e [pastœrize] **adj** pasteurized.

pasteuriser [3] [pastœrize] **vt** to pasteurize.

pastiche [pastiʃ] **nm** pastiche.

pastille [pastij] **nf** [bonbon] pastille, lozenge.

pastis [pastis] **nm** *aniseed-flavoured aperitif.*

pastoral, e, aux [pastɔral, o] **adj** *littéraire* pastoral.
◆ ***pastorale*** **nf** ART & LITTÉR pastoral / MUS pastorale.

patagon, one [patagɔ̃, ɔn] **adj** Patagonian.
◆ ***Patagon, one*** **nm, f** Patagonian.

Patagonie [patagɔni] **nf : la Patagonie** Patagonia.

patapouf [patapuf] **nm** *fam* fatty.

patate [patat] **nf** **1.** *fam* [pomme de terre] spud **2.** *fam* [imbécile] fathead.
◆ ***patate douce*** **nf** sweet potato.

patati [patati] **interj : et patati et patata** *fam* and so on and so forth.

patatras [patatra] **interj** crash!

pataud, e [pato, od] ■ **adj** clumsy.
■ **nm, f** clumsy person.

pataugeoire [patoʒwar] **nf** paddling pool *UK*, wading pool *US*.

patauger [17] [patoʒe] **vi** **1.** [barboter] to splash about **2.** *fam fig* [s'embrouiller] to flounder.

patch [patʃ] **nm** MÉD patch.

patchouli [patʃuli] **nm** patchouli.

patchwork [patʃwœrk] **nm** patchwork.

pâte [pat] **nf** **1.** [à tarte] pastry / [à pain] dough ▸ **pâte brisée** shortcrust pastry ▸ **pâte feuilletée** puff pastry ▸ **pâte à frire** batter ▸ **pâte à pain** bread dough ▸ **pâte sablée** sweet biscuit *ou* sweet flan pastry *UK*, sweet *ou* sugar dough *US* ▸ **pâte à tarte** pastry **2.** [mélange] paste ▸ **pâte d'amandes** almond paste ▸ **pâte de fruits** *jelly made from fruit paste* ▸ **une pâte de fruits** a fruit jelly *(sweet)* ▸ **pâte à modeler** modelling *UK ou* modeling *US* clay ▸ **pâte à papier** paper pulp ▸ **pâte de verre** [pour l'industrie] molten glass / [en joaillerie] paste ▸ **des bijoux en pâte de verre** paste (jewellery)
▸▸ **être bonne pâte** to be easy-going.
◆ ***pâtes*** **nfpl** pasta *sg* ▸ **les pâtes sont trop cuites** the pasta's overcooked.

pâté [pate] **nm** **1.** CULIN pâté ▸ **pâté de campagne** farmhouse pâté ▸ **pâté en croûte** *pâté baked in a pastry case* ▸ **pâté de foie** liver pâté ▸ **pâté impérial** spring roll **2.** [tache] ink blot **3.** [bloc] **: pâté de maisons** block (of houses).

pâtée [pate] **nf** mash, feed.

patelin [patlɛ̃] **nm** *fam* village, place.

patène [patɛn] **nf** paten.

patente [patɑ̃t] **nf** licence *UK ou* license *US* fee *(for traders and professionals).*

patenté, e [patɑ̃te] **adj** **1.** [commerçant] licensed **2.** *fam* [voleur, menteur] habitual.

patère [patɛr] **nf** [portemanteau] coat hook.

paternalisme [patɛrnalism] **nm** paternalism.

paternaliste [patɛrnalist] ■ **nmf** paternalist.
■ **adj** paternalistic.

paternel, elle [patɛrnɛl] **adj** [devoir, autorité] paternal / [amour, ton] fatherly.
◆ ***paternel*** **nm** *fam* old man.

paternité [patɛrnite] **nf** paternity, fatherhood / *fig* authorship, paternity.

pâteux, euse [patø, øz] **adj** **1.** [aliment] doughy / [encre] thick **2.** [style] leaden.

pathétique [patetik] ■ **nm** *littéraire* pathos.
■ **adj** moving, pathetic.

pathogène [patɔʒɛn] **adj** pathogenic.

pathologie [patɔlɔʒi] **nf** pathology.

pathologique [patɔlɔʒik] **adj** pathological.

pathos [patos] **nm** *littéraire* & *péj* pathos.

patibulaire [patibylɛr] **adj** *péj* sinister.

patiemment [pasjamɑ̃] **adv** patiently.

patience [pasjɑ̃s] **nf** **1.** [gén] patience ▸ **s'armer de patience** to be patient, to have patience ▸ **perdre patience** to lose patience ▸ **prendre son mal en patience** to put up with it **2.** [jeu de cartes] patience *UK*, solitaire *US*.

patient, e [pasjɑ̃, ɑ̃t] ■ **adj** patient.
■ **nm, f** **1.** [qui a de la patience] patient person **2.** MÉD patient.

patienter [3] [pasjɑ̃te] **vi** to wait ▸ **'veuillez patienter'** 'please wait'.

patin [patɛ̃] **nm** **1.** SPORT skate ▸ **patin à glace/à roulettes** ice/roller skate ▸ **faire du patin à glace/à roulettes** to go ice-/roller-skating **2.** [de feutre] *cloth pad used under shoes to protect wooden floor.*

patinage [patinaʒ] **nm** SPORT skating ▸ **patinage artistique/de vitesse** figure/speed skating.

patine [patin] **nf** patina.

patiner [3] [patine] ■ **vi** **1.** SPORT to skate **2.** [véhicule] to skid.
■ **vt** [objet] to give a patina to / [avec vernis] to varnish.
◆ ***se patiner*** **vp** to take on a patina.

patineur, euse [patinœr, øz] **nm, f** skater.

patinoire [patinwar] **nf** ice *ou* skating rink.

patio [patjo, pasjo] **nm** patio.

pâtir [32] [patir] **vi : pâtir de** to suffer the consequences of.

pâtisserie [patisri] **nf** **1.** [gâteau] pastry **2.** [art, métier] pastry-making **3.** [commerce] ≃ cake shop *UK*, bakery *US*, ≃ bakery *US*.

pâtissier, ère [patisje, ɛr] ■ **adj : crème pâtissière** confectioner's custard.
■ **nm, f** pastrycook.

patois [patwa] **nm** patois.

patraque [patrak] **adj** *fam* [personne] out of sorts.

patriarcal, e, aux [patrijarkal, o] **adj** patriarchal.

patriarcat [patrijarka] **nm 1.** RELIG patriarchate **2.** [sociologie] patriarchy.

patriarche [patrijarʃ] **nm** patriarch.

patrie [patri] **nf** country, homeland ▸ **patrie d'adoption** country of adoption.

patrimoine [patrimwan] **nm** [familial] inheritance / [collectif] heritage.

patriote [patrijɔt] ■ **nmf** patriot.
■ **adj** patriotic.

patriotique [patrijɔtik] **adj** patriotic.

patriotisme [patrijɔtism] **nm** patriotism.

patron, onne [patrɔ̃, ɔn] **nm, f 1.** [d'entreprise] head **2.** [chef] boss **3.** RELIG patron saint.
◆ ***patron*** **nm** [modèle] pattern.

patronage [patrɔnaʒ] **nm 1.** [protection] patronage / [de saint] protection **2.** [organisation] youth club.

patronal, e, aux [patrɔnal, o] **adj** [organisation, intérêts] employers' *(avant n).*

patronat [patrɔna] **nm** employers.

patronnesse [patrɔnɛs] **nf : (dame) patronnesse** *iron* patroness.

patronyme [patrɔnim] **nm** patronymic.

patronymique [patrɔnimik] **adj** patronymic.

patrouille [patruj] **nf** patrol.

patrouiller [3] [patruje] **vi** to patrol.

patte [pat] **nf 1.** [d'animal] paw / [d'oiseau] foot ▸ **montrer patte blanche** *fig* to give the password ▸ **à quatre pattes** four-legged / *fig* on all fours, on one's hands and knees ▸ **retomber sur ses pattes** *fig* to land on one's feet **2.** *fam* [jambe] leg / [pied] foot / [main] hand, paw ▸ **graisser la patte à qqn** to grease sb's palm **3.** [favori] sideburn **4.** [de poche, de portefeuille] fastening.

patte-d'oie [patdwa] (pl **pattes-d'oie**) **nf** crow's foot.

pattemouille [patmuj] **nf** damping cloth.

pâturage [patyraʒ] **nm** [lieu] pasture land.

pâture [patyr] **nf** [nourriture] food, fodder / *fig* intellectual nourishment ▸ **donner qqn/qqch en pâture à, offrir qqn/qqch en pâture à** to feed sb/sthg to.

paume [pom] **nf 1.** [de main] palm **2.** SPORT real tennis.

paumé, e [pome] *fam* ■ **adj** lost.
■ **nm, f** down and out.

paumer [3] [pome] *fam* **vt** to lose.
◆ ***se paumer*** **vp** to get lost.

paupérisation [poperizasjɔ̃] **nf** pauperization.

paupière [popjɛr] **nf** eyelid.

paupiette [popjɛt] **nf** *thin slice of meat or fish stuffed and rolled* ▸ **paupiettes de veau** ≃ veal olives *UK*.

pause [poz] **nf 1.** [arrêt] break ▸ **pause-café** coffee-break **2.** MUS pause.

pauvre [povr] ■ **nmf** poor person ▸ **le/la pauvre!** the poor thing! ▸ **tu es vraiment trop bête, ma pauvre/mon pauvre!** [avec mépris] you're really too stupid for words, my dear girl/boy! ▸ **les pauvres** the poor.
■ **adj** poor ▸ **laisse donc ce pauvre chien tranquille!** do leave that poor *ou* wretched dog alone! ▸ **pauvre de moi!** woe is me! *(archaïque) hum* ▸ **pauvre crétin, va!** you idiot! ▸ **une végétation pauvre** sparse vegetation ▸ **pauvre en** low in ▸ **alimentation pauvre en sels minéraux** food lacking (in) minerals ▸ **régime pauvre en calories** low-calorie diet ▸ **pauvre d'esprit** feeble-minded.

pauvrement [povrəmɑ̃] **adv** poorly.

pauvreté [povrəte] **nf** poverty.

pavage [pavaʒ] **nm** paving.

pavaner [3] [pavane] ◆ ***se pavaner*** **vp** to strut.

pavé, e [pave] **adj** cobbled.
◆ ***pavé*** **nm 1.** [chaussée] **: être sur le pavé** *fig* to be out on the streets ▸ **battre le pavé** *fig* to walk the streets ▸ **tenir le haut du pavé** *fig* to be on top **2.** [de pierre] cobblestone, paving stone ▸ **un pavé dans la mare** a bombshell *fig* **3.** *fam* [livre] tome **4.** [de viande] slab ▸ **pavé de romsteck** thick rump steak **5.** INFORM **: pavé numérique** numeric keypad.

paver [3] [pave] **vt** to pave.

pavillon [pavijɔ̃] **nm 1.** [bâtiment] detached house *UK* ▸ **pavillon de banlieue** ≃ bungalow ▸ **pavillon de chasse** hunting lodge **2.** [de trompette] bell **3.** [d'oreille] pinna, auricle **4.** [drapeau] flag.

pavoiser [3] [pavwaze] ■ **vt** to decorate with flags.
■ **vi** *fam* to crow.

pavot [pavo] **nm** poppy.

payable [pɛjabl] **adj** payable.

payant, e [pɛjɑ̃, ɑ̃t] **adj 1.** [hôte] paying *(avant n)* **2.** [spectacle] with an admission charge **3.** *fam* [affaire] profitable.

paye = ***paie***[2].

payement = ***paiement***.

payer [11] [peje] ■ **vt 1.** [gén] to pay / [achat] to pay for ▸ **payer qqch à qqn** to buy sthg for sb, to buy sb sthg, to treat sb to sthg ▸ **payer sa dette à la société** to pay one's debt to society ▸ **payer à boire à qqn** to buy sb a drink ▸ **payer qqn de qqch** *fig* [efforts, peine] to reward sb for sthg ▸ **ses félicitations me paient de mes efforts** his congratulations repay me my efforts **2.** [expier - crime, faute] to pay for ▸ **il me le paiera!** he'll pay for this! ▸ **payer les pots cassés** to foot the bill *fig*.
■ **vi : c'est un travail qui paie mal** it's badly paid work, it's not a well paid job ▸ **payer (pour)** to pay (for) ▸ **payer de sa poche** to pay out of one's own pocket ▸ **payer de sa personne** [s'exposer au danger] to put o.s. on the line / [se donner du mal] to put in a lot of effort ▸ **payer d'audace** to risk one's all ▸ **la maison ne paie pas de mine, mais elle est confortable** the house isn't much to look at *ou* the house doesn't look much but it's very comfortable.
◆ ***se payer*** **vp** [s'offrir] **: se payer qqch** to buy o.s. sthg to treat o.s. to sthg ▸ **j'ai envie de me payer une robe** I feel like treating myself to a dress *ou* like buying myself a dress ▸ **se payer la tête de qqn** *fig* to make fun of sb.

payeur, euse [pɛjœr, øz] **adj** payments *(avant n).*
◆ ***payeur*** **nm** payer ▸ **mauvais payeur** bad debtor.

ays [pei] **nm 1.** [gén] country ▸ **le pays d'accueil** the host country ▸ **pays d'adoption** country of adoption ▸ **pays de cocagne** *fig* land of plenty ▸ **les pays de l'Est** the Eastern bloc (countries) ▸ **pays moins développé** less-developed country ▸ **pays parmi les moins avancés** least-developed country ▸ **pays natal** native land, native country ▸ **comme en pays conquis** like the lord of the manor ▸ **voir du pays** to travel a lot **2.** [région, province] region ▸ **avoir le mal du pays** to be homesick ▸ **être du pays** to be a local ▸ **c'est un enfant du pays** he's from these parts ▸ **saucisson de pays** traditional *ou* country-style sausage **3.** [village] village ▸ **un petit pays de 2 000 âmes** a small town of 2,000 souls.

◆ ***pays de Galles*** **nm : le pays de Galles** Wales ▸ **au pays de Galles** in Wales.

aysage [peizaʒ] **nm 1.** [site, vue] landscape, scenery **2.** [tableau] landscape **3.** *fig* [contexte] scene.

aysager, ère [peizaʒe, ɛr] **adj** landscaped.

aysagiste [peizaʒist] ■ **nmf 1.** [peintre] landscape artist **2.** [concepteur de parcs] landscape gardener.

■ **adj** landscape *(avant n).*

aysan, anne [peizɑ̃, an] ■ **adj** [vie, coutume] country *(avant n)*, rural / [organisation, revendication] farmers' *(avant n)* / *péj* peasant *(avant n).*

■ **nm, f 1.** [agriculteur] (small) farmer **2.** *péj* [rustre] peasant.

aysannat [peizana] **nm** peasantry.

aysannerie [peizanri] **nf** peasantry, peasant class.

ays-Bas [peiba] **nmpl : les Pays-Bas** the Netherlands ▸ **aux Pays-Bas** in the Netherlands.

C **nm 1.** (abr de ***Parti communiste***) Communist Party **2.** (abr de ***personal computer***) PC **3.** (abr de ***prêt conventionné***) *special loan for house purchase* **4.** (abr de ***permis de construire***) planning permission *UK* **5.** (abr de ***poste de commandement***) HQ **6.** (abr de ***Petite Ceinture***) *bus following the inner ring road in Paris.*

cc (abr écrite de ***pour copie conforme***) certified accurate.

CF (abr de ***Parti communiste français***) **nm** *French Communist Party.*

CV (abr de ***à percevoir***) **nm** reverse-charge call *UK*, collect call *US*.

-DG (abr de ***président-directeur général***) **nm** Chairman and Managing Director *UK*, President and Chief Executive Officer *US*.

DV (abr de ***point de vente***) **m** POS *(point of sale).*

.-ê. abr de ***peut-être***.

EA (abr de ***plan d'épargne en actions***) **nm** *savings scheme* / ≃ ISA *(individual savings account) UK*.

éage [peaʒ] **nm** toll.

eau [po] **nf 1.** [gén] skin ▸ **peau de banane** banana skin ▸ **peau d'orange** orange peel / MÉD ≃ cellulite ▸ **n'avoir que la peau sur les os** to be just skin and bones ▸ **être bien/mal dans sa peau** [en général] to feel great/terrible / [en situation] to feel at ease/ill at ease ▸ **risquer sa peau** to risk one's neck ▸ **sauver sa peau** to save one's skin **2.** [cuir] hide, leather *(U)* ▸ **peau de vache** *fam fig* [homme] bastard / [femme] bitch.

peaufiner [3] [pofine] **vt** *fig* [travail] to polish up.

pécan [pekɑ̃] **nm : (noix de) pécan** pecan.

pécari [pekari] **nm 1.** ZOOL peccary **2.** [cuir] peccary (skin).

peccadille [pekadij] **nf** peccadillo.

péché [peʃe] **nm** sin ▸ **les sept péchés capitaux** the seven deadly sins ▸ **le péché originel** original sin ▸ **un péché mignon** a weakness.

pêche [pɛʃ] **nf 1.** [fruit] peach ▸ **pêche Melba** peach Melba **2.** [activité] fishing / [poissons] catch ▸ **aller à la pêche** to go fishing ▸ **pêche à la dandinette** jigging ▸ **pêche sous la glace** ice fishing ▸ **pêche à la ligne** angling ▸ **pêche sous-marine** underwater fishing

▸▸ **avoir la pêche** *fam* to feel great.

pécher [18] [peʃe] **vi** to sin ▸ **pécher contre la bienséance** *fig* to break the rules of correct behaviour ▸ **pécher par omission** *fig* to commit the sin of omission ▸ **cet exposé pèche par manque d'exemples** *fig* this report falls down because it lacks examples.

pêcher [1] [4] [peʃe] **vt 1.** [poisson] to catch **2.** *fam* [trouver] to dig up.

pêcher [2] [peʃe] **nm** peach tree.

pécheresse [peʃrɛs] **f** ➤ ***pécheur***.

pêcherie [pɛʃri] **nf** fishery, fishing ground.

pécheur, eresse [peʃœr, peʃrɛs] ■ **adj** sinful.

■ **nm, f** sinner.

pêcheur, euse [pɛʃœr, øz] **nm, f** fisherman (f fisherwoman).

pecnot = ***péquenot***.

pectine [pɛktin] **nf** pectin.

pectoral, e, aux [pɛktɔral, o] **adj 1.** [muscle] pectoral **2.** [sirop] cough *(avant n).*

◆ ***pectoraux*** **nmpl** pectorals.

pécule [pekyl] **nm** [économies] savings *pl.*

pécuniaire [pekynjɛr] **adj** financial.

pédagogie [pedagɔʒi] **nf 1.** [science] education, pedagogy **2.** [qualité] teaching ability.

pédagogique [pedagɔʒik] **adj** educational / [méthode] teaching *(avant n).*

pédagogue [pedagɔg] ■ **nmf** teacher.

■ **adj : être pédagogue** to be a good teacher.

pédale [pedal] **nf 1.** [gén] pedal ▸ **perdre les pédales** *fam fig* to lose one's head **2.** *fam injur* [homosexuel] queer.

pédaler [3] [pedale] **vi** [à bicyclette] to pedal ▸ **pédaler dans la choucroute** *fam fig* to be all at sea.

pédalier [pedalje] **nm 1.** [de vélo] (bicycle) drive **2.** [d'orgue] pedals *pl.*

Pédalo® [pedalo] **nm** pedal boat.

pédant, e [pedɑ̃, ɑ̃t] ■ **adj** pedantic.

■ **nm, f** pedant.

pédé [pede] **nm** *tfam péj* queer.

pédéraste [pederast] **nm** homosexual, pederast.

pédérastie [pederasti] **nf** homosexuality.

pédestre [pedɛstr] **adj : randonnée pédestre** hike, ramble ▸ **chemin pédestre** footpath.

pédiatre [pedjatr] **nmf** pediatrician.

pédiatrie [pedjatri] **nf** pediatrics *(U)*.

pédicule [pedikyl] **nm** BOT peduncle.

pédicure [pedikyr] **nmf** chiropodist, podiatrist *US*.

pedigree [pedigre] **nm** pedigree.

pédophile [pedɔfil] ■ **nm** pedophile.
■ **adj** pedophiliac.

pédopsychiatre [pedɔpsikjatr] **nmf** child psychiatrist.

peeling [piliŋ] **nm** face scrub.

PEGC (abr de ***professeur d'enseignement général de collège***) **nmf** *teacher qualified to teach one or two subjects to 11-to-15-year-olds in French secondary schools*.

pègre [pɛgr] **nf** underworld.

peignais, ***peignions*** ➤ ***peindre***.

peigne [pɛɲ] **nm 1.** [démêloir, barrette] comb ▸ **se donner un coup de peigne** to run a comb through one's hair ▸ **passer qqch au peigne fin** *fig* to go through sthg with a fine-tooth comb ▸ **sale comme un peigne** *fig* filthy dirty **2.** [de tissage] card.

peigner [4] [peɲe] **vt 1.** [cheveux] to comb **2.** [fibres] to card.
◆ ***se peigner*** **vp** to comb one's hair.

peignoir [pɛɲwar] **nm** dressing gown *UK*, robe *US*, bathrobe *US* ▸ **peignoir de bain** bathrobe.

peinard, ***e***, ***pénard***, ***e*** [pɛnar, ard] **adj** *fam* [emploi] cushy / [personne] comfortable.

peindre [81] [pɛ̃dr] **vt** to paint / *fig* [décrire] to depict.
◆ ***se peindre*** **vp** *fig* [émotion] **: se peindre sur** to be written on.

peine [pɛn] **nf 1.** [châtiment] punishment, penalty / DR sentence ▸ **sous peine de qqch** on pain of sthg ▸ **'défense de fumer sous peine d'amende'** 'smokers will be prosecuted' ▸ **peine capitale** *ou* **de mort** capital punishment, death sentence ▸ **peine incompressible** sentence without remission ▸ **peine de prison** prison sentence ▸ **infliger une lourde peine à qqn** to pass a harsh sentence on sb
2. [chagrin] sorrow, sadness *(U)* ▸ **avoir de la peine** to be sad ▸ **faire de la peine à qqn** to upset sb, to distress sb ▸ **il me fait vraiment de la peine** I feel really sorry for him
3. [effort] trouble ▸ **se donner de la peine** to go to a lot of trouble ▸ **il ne s'est même pas donné la peine de répondre** he didn't even bother replying ▸ **c'est peine perdue** it's a waste of effort ▸ **prendre la peine de faire qqch** to go to the trouble of doing sthg ▸ **ça ne vaut pas** *ou* **ce n'est pas la peine** it's not worth it ▸ **ce n'est pas la peine de tout récrire/que tu y ailles** there's no point writing it all out again/your going ▸ **l'exposition vaut la peine d'être vue** the exhibition is worth seeing
4. [difficulté] difficulty ▸ **avoir de la peine à faire qqch** to have difficulty *ou* trouble doing sthg ▸ **il monte l'escalier avec peine** he has trouble climbing stairs ▸ **à grand-peine** with great difficulty ▸ **sans peine** without difficulty, easily ▸ **je suis arrivé à le faire en deux heures sans peine** I had no trouble doing it in two hours.
◆ ***à peine*** **loc adv** scarcely, hardly ▸ **à peine... que** hardly... than ▸ **à peine était-elle couchée que le téléphone se mit à sonner** no sooner had she gone to bed than o she'd only just gone to bed when the phone rang ▸ **c'est peine si on se parle** we hardly speak (to each other).

peiner [4] [pene] ■ **vt** [affliger] to distress, to sadden.
■ **vi 1.** [travailler] to work hard **2.** [se fatiguer] to struggl to labour *UK*, to labor *US*.

peint, ***e*** [pɛ̃, pɛ̃t] **pp** ➤ ***peindre***.

peintre [pɛ̃tr] **nm** painter ▸ **peintre en bâtiment** hous painter.

peinture [pɛ̃tyr] **nf 1.** [gén] painting ▸ **la peinture fla mande** Flemish painting ▸ **peinture sur soie** silk paintin ▸ **une peinture de la société médiévale** a picture of me diaeval society **2.** [produit] paint ▸ **donner un petit cou de peinture à qqch** to freshen sthg up, to give sthg a lic of paint ▸ **refaire la peinture d'une porte** to repaint door ▸ **'peinture fraîche'** 'wet paint' ▸ **peinture à l'ea** CONSTR water *ou* water-based paint ▸ **peinture à l'huil** ART oil paint.

peinturlurer [3] [pɛ̃tyrlyre] **vt** *péj* to daub.
◆ ***se peinturlurer*** **vp** *péj* to plaster one's face wit make-up.

péjoratif, ***ive*** [peʒɔratif, iv] **adj** pejorative.

Pékin [pekɛ̃] **npr** Peking, Beijing.

pékinois, ***e*** [pekinwa, az] **adj** of/from Peking.
◆ ***pékinois*** **nm 1.** [langue] Mandarin **2.** [chien] pekinese
◆ ***Pékinois***, ***e*** **nm, f** native *ou* inhabitant of Peking ▸ **le Pékinois** the people of Peking.

PEL, ***Pel*** [pɛl] (abr de ***plan d'épargne logement***) **nn** *savings scheme offering low-interest mortgages*.

pelage [pəlaʒ] **nm** coat, fur.

pelé, ***e*** [pəle] **adj 1.** [crâne] bald **2.** *fig* [colline, paysage bare.

pêle-mêle [pɛlmɛl] **adv** pell-mell.

peler [25] [pəle] **vt** & **vi** to peel.

pèlerin [pɛlrɛ̃] **nm** pilgrim.

pèlerinage [pɛlrinaʒ] **nm 1.** [voyage] pilgrimage ▸ **er pèlerinage** on a pilgrimage **2.** [lieu] place of pilgrimage.

pèlerine [pɛlrin] **nf** cape.

pélican [pelikɑ̃] **nm** pelican.

pelisse [pəlis] **nf** pelisse.

pelle [pɛl] **nf 1.** [instrument] shovel ▸ **pelle à tarte** pie server ▸ **à la pelle** *fam fig* by the bucketful ▸ **ils ramassen des fraises à la pelle dans leur jardin** they get loads o strawberries from their garden **2.** [machine] digger.

pelletée [pɛlte] **nf** shovelful.

pelleter [27] [pɛlte] **vt** to shovel.

pelleteuse [pɛltøz] **nf** mechanical digger.

pellicule [pelikyl] **nf** film.
◆ ***pellicules*** **nfpl** dandruff *(U)*.

pelote [pəlɔt] **nf 1.** [de laine, ficelle] ball **2.** COUT pir cushion.
◆ ***pelote basque*** **nf** pelota.

peloter [3] [plɔte] **vt** *fam* to paw.

peloton [plɔtɔ̃] **nm 1.** [de ficelle] small ball **2.** [de soldats] squad ▸ **peloton d'exécution** firing squad **3.** [de concurrents] pack ▸ **le peloton de tête** SPORT the leading group / *fig* the top few.

pelotonner [3] [pəlɔtɔne] ◆ ***se pelotonner*** **vp** to curl up ▸ **se pelotonner contre** to snuggle up to.

pelouse [pəluz] **nf 1.** [de jardin] lawn **2.** [de champ de courses] public enclosure **3.** FOOTBALL [rugby] field.

peluche [pəlyʃ] **nf 1.** [jouet] soft toy, stuffed animal **2.** [tissu] plush **3.** [d'étoffe] piece of fluff.

pelucheux, euse [pəlyʃø, øz] **adj** fluffy.

pelure [pəlyr] **nf 1.** [fruit] peel **2.** *fam péj* [habit] coat.

pénal, e, aux [penal, o] **adj** penal.

pénalisation [penalizasjɔ̃] **nf** penalty.

pénaliser [3] [penalize] **vt** to penalize.

pénalité [penalite] **nf** penalty.

penalty [penalti] (pl **penaltys** *ou* **penalties**) **nm** penalty.

pénard = ***peinard***.

pénates [penat] **nmpl : regagner ses pénates** *fam* to go home.

penaud, e [pəno, od] **adj** sheepish.

penchant [pɑ̃ʃɑ̃] **nm 1.** [inclination] tendency **2.** [sympathie] **: penchant pour** liking *ou* fondness for.

penché, e [pɑ̃ʃe] **adj 1.** [tableau] crooked, askew / [mur, écriture] sloping, slanting / [objet] tilting **2.** [personne] **: il est toujours penché sur ses livres** he's always got his head in a book.

pencher [3] [pɑ̃ʃe] ■ **vi** to lean ▸ **pencher vers** *fig* to incline towards *ou* toward *US* ▸ **pencher pour** to incline in favour *UK ou* favor *US* of.
■ **vt** to bend.
◆ ***se pencher*** **vp** [s'incliner] to lean over / [se baisser] to bend down ▸ **se pencher sur qqn/qqch** to lean over sb/sthg ▸ **se pencher sur qqch** *fig* [problème, cas] to look into sthg.

pendable [pɑ̃dabl] **adj : tour pendable** dirty trick ▸ **ce n'est pas un cas pendable** it's not a hanging matter.

pendaison [pɑ̃dɛzɔ̃] **nf** hanging ▸ **pendaison de crémaillère** housewarming.

pendant[1], e [pɑ̃dɑ̃, ɑ̃t] **adj 1.** [bras] hanging, dangling **2.** [question] pending.
◆ ***pendant*** **nm 1.** [bijou] **: pendant d'oreilles** (drop) earring **2.** [de paire] counterpart ▸ **se faire pendant** *fig* to make a pair.

pendant[2] [pɑ̃dɑ̃] **prép** during.
◆ ***pendant que*** **loc conj** while, whilst *UK* ▸ **pendant que j'y suis,...** while I'm at it,...

pendeloque [pɑ̃dlɔk] **nf 1.** [bijou] pendant **2.** [de lustre] crystal.

pendentif [pɑ̃dɑ̃tif] **nm** pendant.

penderie [pɑ̃dri] **nf** wardrobe *UK*, walk-in closet *US*.

pendouiller [3] [pɑ̃duje] **vi** *fam* to dangle, to hang down.

pendre [73] [pɑ̃dr] ■ **vi 1.** [être fixé en haut] **: pendre (à)** to hang (from) ▸ **du linge pendait aux fenêtres** washing was hanging out of the windows **2.** [descendre trop bas] to hang down ▸ **sa natte pendait dans son dos** her plait was hanging down her back.
■ **vt 1.** [rideaux, tableau] to hang (up), to put up ▸ **pendre un tableau à un clou** to hang a picture from a nail ▸ **pendre la crémaillère** to have a housewarming (party) **2.** [personne] to hang ▸ **il sera pendu à l'aube** he'll hang *ou* be hanged at dawn.
◆ ***se pendre*** **vp 1.** [s'accrocher] **: se pendre à** to hang from ▸ **les chauves-souris se pendent aux branches** the bats hang from the branches ▸ **se pendre au cou de qqn** to fling one's arms around sb's neck **2.** [se suicider] to hang o.s.

pendu, e [pɑ̃dy] ■ **pp** ➤ ***pendre***.
■ **adj 1.** [objet] hung up, hanging up / *fig* **: il est toujours pendu au téléphone** he's never off the phone **2.** [personne] hanged.
■ **nm, f** hanged person.

pendule [pɑ̃dyl] ■ **nm** pendulum.
■ **nf** clock.

pendulette [pɑ̃dylɛt] **nf** small clock.

pêne [pɛn] **nm** bolt.

pénétrant, e [penetrɑ̃, ɑ̃t] **adj** penetrating / [odeur] pervasive.

pénétration [penetrasjɔ̃] **nf 1.** [de projectile, d'idée] penetration ▸ **pénétration du marché** ÉCON market penetration **2.** [sagacité] shrewdness.

pénétré, e [penetre] **adj** earnest ▸ **elle est pénétrée de son importance** she's full of her own importance.

pénétrer [18] [penetre] ■ **vi** to enter ▸ **pénétrer dans la maison de qqn** [avec sa permission] to enter sb's house / [par effraction] to break into sb's house ▸ **faire pénétrer la crème en massant doucement** gently rub *ou* massage the cream in.
■ **vt 1.** [mur, vêtement] to penetrate ▸ **un froid glacial me pénétra** I was chilled to the bone *ou* to the marrow **2.** *fig* [mystère, secret] to fathom out ▸ **pénétrer les intentions de qqn** to guess sb's intentions.
◆ ***se pénétrer*** **vp** [s'imprégner] **: se pénétrer d'une idée** to let an idea sink in ▸ **se pénétrer d'une vérité** to become convinced of a truth.

pénible [penibl] **adj 1.** [travail] laborious **2.** [nouvelle, maladie] painful **3.** *fam* [personne] tiresome.

péniblement [peniblәmɑ̃] **adv 1.** [avec difficulté] with difficulty, laboriously **2.** [cruellement] painfully **3.** [à peine] just about.

péniche [peniʃ] **nf** barge.

pénicilline [penisilin] **nf** penicillin.

péninsule [penɛ̃syl] **nf** peninsula ▸ **la péninsule d'Arabie** the Arabian Peninsula ▸ **la péninsule Ibérique** the Iberian peninsula.

pénis [penis] **nm** penis.

pénitence [penitɑ̃s] **nf 1.** [repentir] penitence **2.** [peine, punition] penance.

pénitencier [penitɑ̃sje] **nm** prison, penitentiary *US*.

pénitent**, **e [penitɑ̃, ɑ̃t] ■ **adj** penitent. ■ **nm, f** penitent.

pénitentiaire [penitɑ̃sjɛr] **adj** prison *(avant n)*.

penne [pɛn] **nf** ZOOL quill.

pénombre [penɔ̃br] **nf** half-light.

pensable [pɑ̃sabl] **adj : ce n'est pas pensable** it's unthinkable.

pensant**, **e [pɑ̃sɑ̃, ɑ̃t] **adj** thinking.

pense-bête [pɑ̃sbɛt] (pl **pense-bêtes**) **nm** reminder.

pensée [pɑ̃se] **nf 1.** [idée, faculté] thought ▸ **avoir une pensée claire** to be clear-thinking ▸ **être tout à** *ou* **perdu dans ses pensées** to be lost in thought **2.** [esprit] mind, thoughts *pl* ▸ **par la** *ou* **en pensée** in one's mind *ou* thoughts ▸ **avec nos affectueuses** *ou* **meilleures pensées** with (all) our love *ou* fondest regards **3.** [opinion] thoughts *pl*, feelings *pl* ▸ **j'avais deviné ta pensée** I'd guessed what you'd been thinking ▸ **allez donc jusqu'au bout de votre pensée** come on, say what you really think *ou* what's really on your mind **4.** [doctrine] thought, thinking ▸ **pensée conceptuelle/logique/mathématique** conceptual/logical/mathematical thought **5.** BOT pansy.

penser [3] [pɑ̃se] ■ **vi** to think ▸ **penser à qqn/qqch** [avoir à l'esprit] to think of sb/sthg, to think about sb/sthg / [se rappeler] to remember sb/sthg ▸ **essaye de penser un peu aux autres** try to think of others ▸ **penser à faire qqch** [avoir à l'esprit] to think of doing sthg / [se rappeler] to remember to do sthg ▸ **qu'est-ce que tu en penses?** what do you think (of it)? ▸ **c'est simple mais il fallait y penser** it's a simple enough idea but somebody had to think of it (in the first place) ▸ **faire penser à qqn/qqch** to make one think of sb/sthg ▸ **faire penser à qqn à faire qqch** to remind sb to do sthg ▸ **sans penser à mal** without meaning any harm ▸ **n'y pensons plus!** let's forget it! ▸ **laisser** *ou* **donner à penser (que)** to make one think (that) ▸ **même s'il ne dit rien, il n'en pense pas moins** even if he doesn't say anything, he's thinking it nonetheless.
■ **vt** to think ▸ **je ne sais jamais ce que tu penses** I can never tell what you're thinking *ou* what's on your mind ▸ **penser que...** to think (that)... ▸ **je pense que oui** I think so ▸ **je pense que non** I don't think so ▸ **je pensais la chose faisable, mais on me dit que non** I thought it was possible (to do), but I'm told it's not ▸ **penser faire qqch** to be planning to do sthg ▸ **je pense avoir réussi** [examen] I think I passed ▸ **pensez-vous!** don't be silly! ▸ **je n'aurais/on n'aurait jamais pensé que...** I'd never/nobody'd ever have thought that... ▸ **tu penses bien que je lui ai tout raconté!** *fam* I told him everything, as you can well imagine.

penseur [pɑ̃sœr] **nm** thinker.

pensif**, **ive [pɑ̃sif, iv] **adj** pensive, thoughtful.

pension [pɑ̃sjɔ̃] **nf 1.** [allocation] pension ▸ **pension alimentaire** [dans un divorce] alimony **2.** [hébergement] board and lodgings ▸ **pension complète** full board ▸ **demi-pension** half board **3.** [hôtel] guesthouse ▸ **pension de famille** guesthouse, boarding house ▸ **pension de l'État** state pension **4.** [prix de l'hébergement] ≃ rent, keep **5.** [internat] boarding school ▸ **être en pension** to be a boarder *ou* at boarding school.

pensionnaire [pɑ̃sjɔnɛr] **nmf 1.** [élève] boarder **2.** [hôte payant] lodger.

pensionnat [pɑ̃sjɔna] **nm 1.** [internat] boarding school **2.** [élèves] boarders *pl*.

pensivement [pɑ̃sivmɑ̃] **adv** pensively, thoughtfully.

pensum [pɛ̃sɔm] **nm 1.** [travail ennuyeux] chore **2.** *vieilli* [punition] imposition.

pentagone [pɛ̃tagɔn] **nm** pentagon.
◆ ***Pentagone*** **nm : le Pentagone** the Pentagon.

pentathlon [pɛ̃tatlɔ̃] **nm** pentathlon.

pente [pɑ̃t] **nf** slope ▸ **en pente** sloping, inclined ▸ **être sur une mauvaise pente** *fig* to be on a downward path ▸ **remonter la pente** *fig* to claw one's way back again.

pentecôte [pɑ̃tkot] **nf** [juive] Pentecost / [chrétienne] Whitsun.

pénurie [penyri] **nf** shortage ▸ **pénurie de main-d'œuvre** labour shortage.

people [pipɔl] **adj : la presse people** celebrity (gossip) magazines.

PEP**, **Pep [pɛp] (abr de ***plan d'épargne populaire***) **nm** personal pension plan.

pépé [pepe] **nm** *fam* **1.** [grand-père] grandad, grandpa **2.** [homme âgé] old man.

pépère [pepɛr] *fam* ■ **nm** [grand-père] grandad, grandpa. ■ **adj** cushy.

pépier [9] [pepje] **vi** to chirp.

pépin [pepɛ̃] **nm 1.** [graine] pip **2.** *fam* [ennui] hitch **3.** *fam* [parapluie] umbrella, brolly *UK*.

pépinière [pepinjɛr] **nf** tree nursery / *fig* [école, établissement] nursery.

pépiniériste [pepinjerist] **nmf** nursery man (f woman).

pépite [pepit] **nf** nugget.

péquenaud**, **e [pekno, od] **nm, f** = ***péquenot***.

péquenot**, **pecnot [pekno] **nm** *fam péj* country bumpkin.

PER**, **Per [pɛr] (abr de ***plan d'épargne retraite***) **nm** former personal pension plan.

percale [pɛrkal] **nf** percale.

perçant**, **e [pɛrsɑ̃, ɑ̃t] **adj 1.** [regard, son] piercing **2.** [froid] bitter, biting.

percée [pɛrse] **nf 1.** [trouée] opening **2.** *fig* & MIL & SPORT breakthrough.

percement [pɛrsəmɑ̃] **nm** opening (up) / [d'oreilles] piercing.

perce-neige [pɛrsənɛʒ] **nm inv** & **nf inv** snowdrop.

perce-oreille [pɛrsɔrɛj] (pl **perce-oreilles**) **nm** earwig.

percepteur [pɛrsɛptœr] **nm** tax collector.

perceptible [pɛrsɛptibl] **adj** perceptible.

perception [pɛrsɛpsjɔ̃] **nf 1.** [d'impôts] collection **2.** [bureau] tax office **3.** [sensation] perception.

percer [16] [pɛrse] ■ **vt 1.** [mur, roche] to make a hole in / [coffre-fort] to crack **2.** [trou] to make / [avec perceuse] to drill ▸ **percer une porte dans un mur** to put a door in *ou* into a wall ▸ **percer un tunnel dans la montagne** to drive *ou* to build a tunnel through the mountain **3.** [silence, oreille] to pierce ▸ **un bruit à vous percer les tympans** an ear-splitting noise ▸ **se faire percer les oreilles** to have

one's ears pierced **4.** [foule] to make one's way through **5.** *fig* [mystère] to penetrate ▸ **percer qqn/qqch à jour** to see right through sb/sthg.
■ **vi 1.** [soleil] to break through **2.** [abcès] to burst ▸ **avoir une dent qui perce** to be cutting a tooth **3.** [réussir] to make a name for o.s., to break through ▸ **un jeune chanteur en train de percer** an up-and-coming young singer.

perceuse [pɛrsøz] **nf** drill.

percevoir [52] [pɛrsəvwar] **vt 1.** [intention, nuance] to perceive **2.** [retraite, indemnité] to receive **3.** [impôts] to collect.

perchaude [pɛrʃod] **nf** *Québec* yellow *ou* lake perch.

perche [pɛrʃ] **nf 1.** [poisson] perch **2.** [de bois, métal] pole ▸ **tendre la perche à qqn** *fig* to throw sb a line.

percher [3] [pɛrʃe] ■ **vi 1.** [oiseau] to perch **2.** *fam* [personne] to live.
■ **vt** to perch.
◆ ***se percher*** **vp** to perch.

percheron [pɛrʃərɔ̃] **nm** ZOOL Percheron.

perchiste [pɛrʃist] **nmf 1.** SPORT pole vaulter **2.** CINÉ & TV boom operator.

perchoir [pɛrʃwar] **nm** perch.

perclus, e [pɛrkly, yz] **adj : perclus de** [rhumatismes] crippled with / *fig* [crainte] paralysed *UK ou* paralyzed *US* with.

perçois, perçoit ➤ ***percevoir.***

percolateur [pɛrkɔlatœr] **nm** percolator.

perçu, e [pɛrsy] **pp** ➤ ***percevoir.***

percussion [pɛrkysjɔ̃] **nf** percussion.

percussionniste [pɛrkysjɔnist] **nmf** percussionist.

percussions [pɛrkysjɔ̃] **nfpl** percussion *sg.*

percutant, e [pɛrkytɑ̃, ɑ̃t] **adj 1.** [obus] explosive **2.** *fig* [argument] forceful.

percuter [3] [pɛrkyte] ■ **vt** to strike, to smash into.
■ **vi** to explode.

perdant, e [pɛrdɑ̃, ɑ̃t] ■ **adj** losing.
■ **nm, f** loser.

perdition [pɛrdisjɔ̃] **nf 1.** [ruine morale] perdition **2.** [détresse] **: en perdition** in distress.

perdre [77] [pɛrdr] ■ **vt 1.** [gén] to lose ▸ **perdre le contrôle de** to lose control of ▸ **perdre son emploi** to lose one's job ▸ **perdre patience** to run out of *ou* to lose patience ▸ **perdre pied** *litt* & *fig* to get out of one's depth ▸ **les actions ont perdu de leur valeur** the shares have partially depreciated ▸ **tu perds des papiers/un gant!** you've dropped some documents/a glove!
2. [temps] to waste / [occasion] to miss, to waste
3. [suj: bonté, propos] to be the ruin of ▸ **c'est le jeu qui le perdra** gambling will be the ruin of him *ou* his downfall
▸▸ **vous ne perdez rien pour attendre!** just wait until I get my hands on you!
■ **vi** to lose ▸ **perdre à la loterie/aux élections** to lose at the lottery/polls ▸ **je n'ai pas perdu au change** *litt* & *fig* I've come out of it quite well ▸ **on perd toujours à agir sans réfléchir** you're bound to be worse off if you act without thinking.
◆ ***se perdre*** ■ **vpi 1.** [coutume] to die out, to become lost **2.** [personne] to get lost, to lose one's way ▸ **se perdre dans les détails** *fig* to get bogged down in details.
■ **vp** *(emploi réciproque)* **: se perdre de vue** to lose sight of each other.

perdreau, x [pɛrdro] **nm** young partridge.

perdrix [pɛrdri] **nf** partridge.

perdu, e [pɛrdy] ■ **pp** ➤ ***perdre.***
■ **adj 1.** [égaré] lost **2.** [endroit] out-of-the-way **3.** [balle] stray **4.** [emballage] non-returnable **5.** [temps, occasion] wasted **6.** [malade] dying **7.** [récolte, robe] spoilt, ruined.

perdurer [3] [pɛrdyre] **vi** *littéraire* to endure.

père [pɛr] **nm 1.** [gén] father ▸ **mon père** RELIG Father ▸ **le Père éternel** the Heavenly Father ▸ **père de famille** father ▸ **être bon père de famille** to be a (good) father *ou* family man ▸ **père nourricier** foster father ▸ **de père en fils** from father to son ▸ **ils sont menuisiers de père en fils** they've been carpenters for generations ▸ **je suis né de père inconnu** it's not known who my father was **2.** [d'animal] sire **3.** *fam* [homme mûr] **: le père Martin** old Martin.
◆ ***pères*** **nmpl** [ancêtres] forefathers, ancestors.
◆ ***père Noël*** **nm : le père Noël** Father Christmas *UK*, Santa Claus.

pérégrination [peregrinasjɔ̃] **nf** *(gén pl)* wanderings *pl.*

Père-Lachaise [pɛrlaʃɛz] **npr : le (cimetière du) Père-Lachaise** *the chief cemetery of Paris, where many famous people are buried.*

péremption [perɑ̃psjɔ̃] **nf** time limit ▸ **date de péremption** best-before date.

péremptoire [perɑ̃ptwar] **adj** peremptory.

pérenniser [3] [perenize] **vt** *sout* to perpetuate.

pérennité [perenite] **nf** durability.

péréquation [perekwasjɔ̃] **nf** equalization.

perfectible [pɛrfɛktibl] **adj** perfectible.

perfection [pɛrfɛksjɔ̃] **nf 1.** [qualité] perfection ▸ **à la perfection** to perfection **2.** [chose parfaite] jewel, gem.

perfectionné, e [pɛrfɛksjɔne] **adj** sophisticated.

perfectionnement [pɛrfɛksjɔnmɑ̃] **nm** improvement.

perfectionner [3] [pɛrfɛksjɔne] **vt** to perfect.
◆ ***se perfectionner*** **vp** to improve.

perfectionnisme [pɛrfɛksjɔnism] **nm** perfectionism.

perfectionniste [pɛrfɛksjɔnist] **nmf** & **adj** perfectionist.

perfide [pɛrfid] **adj** perfidious.

perfidement [pɛrfidmɑ̃] **adv** perfidiously.

perfidie [pɛrfidi] **nf** perfidy.

perforateur, trice [pɛrfɔratœr, tris] **adj** perforating.
◆ ***perforateur*** **nm** punch card operator.
◆ ***perforatrice*** **nf** [perceuse] drill / [de bureau] hole punch.

perforation [pɛrfɔrasjɔ̃] **nf** perforation.

perforer [3] [pɛrfɔre] **vt** to perforate.

performance [pɛrfɔrmɑ̃s] **nf** performance ▸ **les performances d'une voiture** a car's performance.

performant*, *e [pɛrfɔrmɑ̃, ɑ̃t] **adj 1.** [personne] efficient **2.** [machine] high-performance *(avant n)*.

perfusion [pɛrfyzjɔ̃] **nf** perfusion.

pergola [pɛrgɔla] **nf** pergola.

péricliter [3] [periklite] **vi** to collapse.

péridurale [peridyral] **nf** epidural.

péril [peril] **nm** peril ▸ **au péril de ma vie** at the risk of my life.

périlleux*, *euse [perijø, øz] **adj** perilous, dangerous.

périmé*, *e [perime] **adj** out-of-date / *fig* [idées] outdated.

périmètre [perimɛtr] **nm 1.** [contour] perimeter **2.** [contenu] area.

périnatal*, *e*, *aux [perinatal, o] **adj** perinatal.

périnée [perine] **nm** perineum.

période [perjɔd] **nf** period ▸ **période comptable** accounting period.

périodique [perjɔdik] ■ **nm** periodical.
■ **adj** periodic.

périodiquement [perjɔdikmɑ̃] **adv** periodically.

péripatéticienne [peripatetisjɛn] **nf** streetwalker.

péripétie [peripesi] **nf** event.

périph [perif] **nm** *fam* abr écrite de ***périphérique***.

périphérie [periferi] **nf 1.** [de ville] outskirts *pl* **2.** [bord] periphery / [de cercle] circumference.

périphérique [periferik] ■ **nm 1.** [route] ring road *UK*, beltway *US* **2.** INFORM peripheral device.
■ **adj** peripheral ▸ **boulevard périphérique** ring road *UK*, beltway *US*.

périphrase [perifraz] **nf** periphrasis.

périple [peripl] **nm 1.** NAUT voyage **2.** [voyage] trip.

périr [32] [perir] **vi** to perish.

périscolaire [periskɔlɛr] **adj** extracurricular.

périscope [periskɔp] **nm** periscope.

périssable [perisabl] **adj 1.** [denrée] perishable **2.** *littéraire* [sentiment] transient.

péristyle [peristil] **nm** peristyle.

péritonite [peritɔnit] **nf** peritonitis.

perle [pɛrl] **nf 1.** [de nacre] pearl **2.** [de bois, verre] bead **3.** [de sang, d'eau] drop **4.** [personne] gem **5.** *fam* [erreur] howler.

perlé*, *e [pɛrle] **adj** beaded ▸ **grève perlée** go-slow *UK*, slowdown *US*.

perler [3] [pɛrle] **vi** to form beads.

perlimpinpin [pɛrlɛ̃pɛ̃pɛ̃] **nm : poudre de perlimpinpin** miracle cure.

permanence [pɛrmanɑ̃s] **nf 1.** [continuité] permanence ▸ **en permanence** constantly **2.** [service] **: être de permanence** to be on duty **3.** SCOL **: (salle de) permanence** study room *UK*, study hall *US*.

permanent*, *e [pɛrmanɑ̃, ɑ̃t] ■ **adj** permanent / [cinéma] with continuous showings / [comité] standing *(avant n)*.
■ **nm, f** official.
◆ ***permanente*** **nf** perm.

perméable [pɛrmeabl] **adj : perméable (à)** permeable (to) / *fig* open (to),receptive (to).

permets ➤ ***permettre***.

permettais*, *permettions ➤ ***permettre***.

permettre [84] [pɛrmɛtr] **vt** to permit, to allow ▸ **si le temps/sa santé le permet** weather/(his) health permitting ▸ **vous permettez?** may I? ▸ **si vous me permettez l'expression** if I may be allowed to say so, if you don't mind my saying ▸ **permettre qqch à qqn** to allow sb sthg ▸ **permettre à qqn de faire qqch** to permit *ou* allow sb to do sthg ▸ **il ne permettra pas qu'on insulte son frère** he won't allow his brother to be insulted ▸ **il n'est pas/il est permis de boire de l'alcool** drinking is not/is allowed *ou* permitted.
◆ ***se permettre*** **vp : se permettre qqch** to allow o.s sthg / [avoir les moyens de] to be able to afford sthg ▸ **il se permet de petites entorses au règlement** he's not averse to bending the rules now and then ▸ **se permettre de faire qqch** to take the liberty of doing sthg ▸ **puis-je me permettre de vous rappeler nos accords signés?** may I remind you of our binding agreements?

permis*, *e [pɛrmi, iz] **pp** ➤ ***permettre***.
◆ ***permis*** **nm** licence *UK*, license *US*, permit ▸ **permis de conduire** driving licence *UK*, driver's license *US* ▸ **permis de construire** planning permission *UK*, building per-

COMMENT EXPRIMER...

la permission

Demander la permission

Can I use the computer? / Est-ce que je peux me servir de l'ordinateur ?

Do you mind if I phone home? / Je peux téléphoner chez moi ?

Is it OK if I borrow your car? / J'emprunte ta voiture, d'accord ?

Donner la permission

Yes, of course / Oui, bien sûr

Go ahead / Allez-y

Yes, feel free / Mais certainement

Please do / Je vous en prie

Help yourself / Servez-vous

No, I don't mind / Non, ça ne me dérange pas

Refuser la permission

I'm afraid that's not possible / Je regrette, mais ce n'est pas possible

I'd rather you didn't / J'aimerais mieux pas

Actually, I'd prefer you to stay / En fait, je préférerais que vous restiez

mit *US* ▸ **permis à points** *driving licence with a penalty points system, introduced in France in 1992* ▸ **permis de séjour** residence permit ▸ **permis de travail** work permit.

permissif, ive [pɛrmisif, iv] **adj** permissive.

permission [pɛrmisjɔ̃] **nf 1.** [autorisation] permission **2.** MIL leave.

permutable [pɛrmytabl] **adj** which can be changed round.

permutation [pɛrmytasjɔ̃] **nf** [de mots, figures] transposition / MATH permutation.

permuter [3] [pɛrmyte] ■ **vt** to change round / [mots, figures] to transpose.
■ **vi** to change, to switch.

pernicieux, euse [pɛrnisjø, øz] **adj 1.** MÉD pernicious **2.** [conseil, habitude] harmful.

péroné [perɔne] **nm** fibula.

péroraison [perɔrɛzɔ̃] **nf** peroration.

pérorer [3] [perɔre] **vi** *péj* to hold forth.

Pérou [peru] **nm : le Pérou** Peru ▸ **au Pérou** in Peru.

perpendiculaire [pɛrpɑ̃dikylɛr] ■ **nf** perpendicular.
■ **adj : perpendiculaire (à)** perpendicular (to).

perpendiculairement [pɛrpɑ̃dikylɛrmɑ̃] **adv** perpendicularly ▸ **perpendiculairement à** perpendicular to.

perpète, perpette [pɛrpɛt] ◆ ***à perpète*** **loc adv** *fam* [loin] miles away / [longtemps] for ever.

perpétrer [18] [pɛrpetre] **vt** to perpetrate.

perpette = ***perpète***.

perpétuel, elle [pɛrpetɥɛl] **adj 1.** [fréquent, continu] perpetual **2.** [rente] life *(avant n)* / [secrétaire] permanent.

perpétuellement [pɛrpetɥɛlmɑ̃] **adv** perpetually.

perpétuer [7] [pɛrpetɥe] **vt** to perpetuate.
◆ ***se perpétuer*** **vp** to continue / [espèce] to perpetuate itself.

perpétuité [pɛrpetɥite] **nf** perpetuity ▸ **à perpétuité** for life ▸ **être condamné à perpétuité** to be sentenced to life imprisonment.

perplexe [pɛrplɛks] **adj** perplexed.

perplexité [pɛrplɛksite] **nf** perplexity.

perquisition [pɛrkizisjɔ̃] **nf** search.

perquisitionner [3] [pɛrkizisjɔne] ■ **vi** to make a search.
■ **vt** to search, to make a search of.

perron [pɛrɔ̃] **nm** steps *pl (at entrance to building)*.

perroquet [pɛrɔkɛ] **nm** [animal] parrot.

perruche [peryʃ] **nf** budgerigar *UK*, parakeet *US*.

perruque [peryk] **nf** wig.

pers [pɛr(s)] **adj** *littéraire* blue-green.

persan, e [pɛrsɑ̃, an] **adj** Persian.
◆ ***persan*** **nm 1.** [langue] Persian **2.** [chat] Persian (cat).
◆ ***Persan, e*** **nm, f** Persian.

persécuter [3] [pɛrsekyte] **vt 1.** [martyriser] to persecute **2.** [harceler] to harass.

persécuteur, trice [pɛrsekytœr, tris] ■ **adj** persecuting.
■ **nm, f** persecutor.

persécution [pɛrsekysjɔ̃] **nf** persecution.

persévérance [pɛrseverɑ̃s] **nf** perseverance.

persévérant, e [pɛrseverɑ̃, ɑ̃t] **adj** persevering.

persévérer [18] [pɛrsevere] **vi : persévérer (dans)** to persevere (in).

persienne [pɛrsjɛn] **nf** shutter.

persiflage [pɛrsiflaʒ] **nm** mockery.

persifler [3] [pɛrsifle] **vt** *littéraire* to mock.

persifleur, euse [pɛrsiflœr, øz] ■ **adj** mocking.
■ **nm, f** mocker.

persil [pɛrsi] **nm** parsley.

persillé, e [pɛrsije] **adj 1.** [plat] with parsley **2.** [viande] marbled / [fromage] veined, blue-veined.

Persique [pɛrsik] ➤ ***golfe***.

persistance [pɛrsistɑ̃s] **nf** persistence.

persistant, e [pɛrsistɑ̃, ɑ̃t] **adj** persistent ▸ **arbre à feuillage persistant** evergreen (tree).

persister [3] [pɛrsiste] **vi** to persist ▸ **persister à faire qqch** to persist in doing sthg ▸ **persister dans qqch** to persist in sthg.

perso [pɛrso] (abr de ***personnel***) **adj** *fam* personal, private.

personnage [pɛrsɔnaʒ] **nm 1.** [dignitaire] figure **2.** THÉÂTRE character ▸ **personnage principal** main *OU* leading character / ART figure **3.** [personnalité] image **4.** *péj* [individu] character, individual.

personnaliser [3] [pɛrsɔnalize] **vt** to personalize.

personnalité [pɛrsɔnalite] **nf 1.** [gén] personality **2.** DR status.

personne [pɛrsɔn] ■ **nf** person ▸ **personnes** people ▸ **en personne** in person, personally ▸ **j'y veillerai en personne** I'll see to it personally ▸ **en la personne de** in the person of ▸ **personne âgée** elderly person ▸ **personne à charge** dependant ▸ **la personne humaine** the individual ▸ **personne morale** legal entity ▸ **personne physique** natural person ▸ **les grandes personnes** grown-ups ▸ **ma personne** myself.
■ **pron indéf 1.** [quelqu'un] anybody, anyone ▸ **il est parti sans que personne le remarque** he left without anybody *OU* anyone noticing him ▸ **je me demande si personne arrivera un jour à le convaincre** I wonder if anyone will ever convince him ▸ **tu le sais mieux que personne** you know it better than anybody *OU* anyone (else) ▸ **personne de blessé?** nobody *OU* anybody injured? **2.** [aucune personne] nobody, no one ▸ **personne ne viendra** nobody will come ▸ **il n'y a jamais personne** there's never anybody there, nobody is ever there ▸ **je ne connais personne d'aussi gentil qu'elle** I don't know anyone *OU* anybody as nice as her ▸ **personne d'autre** nobody *OU* no one else.

personnel, elle [pɛrsɔnɛl] **adj 1.** [gén] personal **2.** [égoïste] self-centred *UK*, self-centered *US*.
◆ ***personnel*** **nm** staff, personnel ▸ **personnel navigant** flight crew.

personnellement [pɛrsɔnɛlmɑ̃] **adv** personally.

personnification [pɛrsɔnifikasjɔ̃] **nf** personification.

personnifier [9] [pɛrsɔnifje] **vt** to personify.

perspective [pɛrspɛktiv] **nf 1.** ART [point de vue] perspective **2.** [panorama] view **3.** [éventualité] prospect.

perspicace [pɛrspikas] **adj** perspicacious.

perspicacité [pɛrspikasite] **nf** perspicacity.

persuader [3] [pɛrsɥade] **vt : persuader qqn de qqch/de faire qqch** to persuade sb of sthg/to do sthg, to convince sb of sthg/to do sthg.
◆ ***se persuader*** **vp : se persuader que** to persuade *ou* convince o.s. (that) ▸ **se persuader de** to persuade *ou* convince o.s. of.

persuasif, ive [pɛrsɥazif, iv] **adj** persuasive.

persuasion [pɛrsɥazjɔ̃] **nf** persuasion.

perte [pɛrt] **nf 1.** [gén] loss ▸ **perte de connaissance** fainting, blackout ▸ **perte de mémoire** (memory) blank ▸ **perte de poids** weight loss ▸ **à perte** COMM at a loss ▸ **perte sèche** dead loss ▸ **en perte de vitesse** AUTO losing speed / *fig* losing momentum ▸ **déclarer une perte** to declare the loss (of a thing) ▸ **l'entreprise a enregistré une perte de deux millions** the company has chalked up losses of two million **2.** [gaspillage - de temps] waste ▸ **en pure perte** for absolutely nothing **3.** [ruine, déchéance] ruin ▸ **courir/aller à sa perte** to be on the road to ruin ▸ **jurer la perte de qqn** to vow to ruin sb.
◆ ***pertes*** **nfpl** [morts] losses ▸ **passer qqch aux *ou* par pertes et profits** *litt* & *fig* to write sthg off (as a total loss).
◆ ***à perte de vue*** **loc adv** as far as the eye can see.

pertinemment [pɛrtinamɑ̃] **adv** pertinently.

pertinence [pɛrtinɑ̃s] **nf** pertinence, relevance.

pertinent, e [pɛrtinɑ̃, ɑ̃t] **adj** pertinent, relevant.

perturbant, e [pɛrtyrbɑ̃, ɑ̃t] **adj** disturbing.

perturbateur, trice [pɛrtyrbatœr, tris] ■ **adj** disruptive.
■ **nm, f** troublemaker.

perturbation [pɛrtyrbasjɔ̃] **nf** disruption / ASTRON & MÉTÉOR disturbance.

perturber [3] [pɛrtyrbe] **vt 1.** [gén] to disrupt ▸ **perturber l'ordre public** to disturb the peace **2.** PSYCHO to disturb.

péruvien, enne [peryvjɛ̃, ɛn] **adj** Peruvian.
◆ ***Péruvien, enne*** **nm, f** Peruvian.

pervenche [pɛrvɑ̃ʃ] ■ **nf 1.** BOT periwinkle **2.** *fam* [contractuelle] traffic warden *UK*, meter maid *US*.
■ **adj inv** (periwinkle) blue.

pervers, e [pɛrvɛr, ɛrs] ■ **adj 1.** [vicieux] perverted **2.** [effet] unwanted.
■ **nm, f** pervert.

perversion [pɛrvɛrsjɔ̃] **nf** perversion.

perversité [pɛrvɛrsite] **nf** perversity.

pervertir [32] [pɛrvɛrtir] **vt** to pervert.
◆ ***se pervertir*** **vp** to become perverted.

pesage [pəzaʒ] **nm 1.** [pesée] weighing **2.** [de jockey] weigh-in.

pesamment [pəzamɑ̃] **adv** heavily.

pesant, e [pəsɑ̃, ɑ̃t] **adj 1.** [lourd] heavy **2.** [style, architecture] ponderous.
◆ ***pesant*** **nm : valoir son pesant d'or** *fig* to be worth its/one's weight in gold.

pesanteur [pəzɑ̃tœr] **nf 1.** PHYS gravity **2.** [lourdeur] heaviness.

pèse-bébé [pɛzbebe] (pl **pèse-bébé** *ou* **pèse-bébés**) **nm** (pair of) baby scales *pl*.

pesée [pəze] **nf 1.** [opération] weighing **2.** [quantité] weight **3.** [pression] pressure, force.

pèse-lettre [pɛzlɛtr] (pl **pèse-lettre** *ou* **pèse-lettres**) **nm** letter scales *pl*.

pèse-personne [pɛzpɛrsɔn] (pl **pèse-personne** *ou* **pèse-personnes**) **nm** scales *pl*.

peser [19] [pəze] ■ **vt** to weigh ▸ **tout bien pesé** *fig* all things considered ▸ **peser ses mots** to weigh *ou* to choose one's words ▸ **peser le pour et le contre** to weigh (up) the pros and cons.
■ **vi 1.** [avoir un certain poids] to weigh ▸ **combien pèses-tu/pèse le paquet?** how much do you/does the parcel weigh?
2. [être lourd] to be heavy ▸ **il ne pèse pas lourd face à lui** he's no match for him ▸ **peser à qqn** *fig* to weigh on sb ▸ **ton absence me pèse** I find your absence difficult to bear ▸ **peser sur** *fig* [accabler] to weigh heavy on / *fig* [influer sur] to influence ▸ **ça me pèse sur l'estomac/la conscience** it's lying on my stomach/weighing on my conscience ▸ **les responsabilités qui pèsent sur moi** the responsibilities I have to bear
3. [appuyer] **: peser sur qqch** to press (down) on sthg.
◆ ***se peser*** **vp** to weigh o.s. ▸ **les mangues ne se pèsent pas** [au magasin] mangoes are not sold by weight.

peseta [pezeta] **nf** peseta.

pessimisme [pesimism] **nm** pessimism.

pessimiste [pesimist] ■ **nmf** pessimist.
■ **adj** pessimistic.

peste [pɛst] **nf 1.** MÉD plague ▸ **craindre qqn/qqch comme la peste** *fig* to be terrified of sb/sthg ▸ **fuir qqn/qqch comme la peste** *fig* to avoid sb/sthg like the plague **2.** [personne] pest.

pester [3] [pɛste] **vi : pester (contre qqn/qqch)** to curse (sb/sthg).

COMMENT EXPRIMER...
la persuasion

Are you sure you won't come? / Tu es sûr que tu ne veux pas venir ?
Do you really think you should go? / Tu penses vraiment devoir y aller ?
Could you possibly stay a bit longer? / Restez donc encore un peu
I really think you should tell her / Je crois vraiment que tu devrais le lui dire
I really wish you'd have supper with us / Ça me ferait vraiment plaisir que vous dîniez avec nous
I wish I could persuade you to stay / J'aimerais pouvoir vous convaincre de rester

pesticide [pɛstisid] ■ **nm** pesticide.
■ **adj** pesticidal.

pestiféré, e [pɛstifere] ■ **adj** plague-stricken.
■ **nm, f** plague victim.

pestilentiel, elle [pɛstilɑ̃sjɛl] **adj** pestilential.

pet [pɛ] **nm** *fam* fart.

pétale [petal] **nm** petal.

pétanque [petɑ̃k] **nf** ≃ bowls *(U)*.

pétant, e [petɑ̃, ɑ̃t] **adj** *fam* on the dot.

pétarader [3] [petarade] **vi** to backfire.

pétard [petar] **nm 1.** [petit explosif] banger *UK*, firecracker **2.** *fam* [revolver] gun **3.** *fam* [postérieur] bum *UK*, butt *US* **4.** *fam* [haschich] joint.

pet-de-nonne [pɛdnɔn] (pl **pets-de-nonne**) **nm** *very light fritter.*

péter [18] [pete] ■ **vi 1.** *tfam* [personne] to fart **2.** *fam* [câble, élastique] to snap **3.** *tfam* **: péter plus haut que son cul** *tfam* to be full of oneself.
■ **vt** *fam* to bust.

pète-sec [pɛtsɛk] **adj inv** *fam* bossy.

pétillant, e [petijɑ̃, ɑ̃t] **adj** *littéraire & fig* sparkling.

pétiller [3] [petije] **vi 1.** [vin, eau] to sparkle, to bubble **2.** [feu] to crackle **3.** *fig* [yeux] to sparkle ▸ **pétiller de** [personne] to bubble with / [yeux] to sparkle with.

petiot, e [pətjo, ɔt] ■ **adj** teeny.
■ **nm, f** little one.

petit, e [pəti, it] ■ **adj 1.** [de taille, jeune] small, little ▸ **petit frère** little *ou* younger brother ▸ **petite sœur** little *ou* younger sister ▸ **une personne de petite taille** a small *ou* short person
2. [voyage, visite] short, little ▸ **un petit séjour** a short *ou* brief stay
3. [faible, infime - somme d'argent] small / [- bruit] faint, slight ▸ **c'est une petite nature** he/she is slightly built ▸ **expédition/émission à petit budget** low-budget expedition/programme ▸ **on y sera dans une petite heure** we'll be there in a bit less than *ou* in under an hour ▸ **un petit bout de papier** a scrap of paper
4. [de peu d'importance, de peu de valeur] minor
5. [médiocre, mesquin] petty
6. [de rang modeste - commerçant, propriétaire, pays] small / [- fonctionnaire] minor ▸ **les petites gens** people of modest means ▸ **les petits salaires** [- sommes] low salaries, small wages / [- employés] low-paid workers
7. [avec une valeur affective] **: alors, mon petit Paul, comment ça va?** [dit par une femme] how's life, Paul, dear? / [dit par un homme plus âgé] how's life, young Paul? / [pour encourager] **: tu mangeras bien une petite glace!** come on, have an ice cream!
■ **nm, f 1.** [personne de petite taille] small man (f woman) **2.** [enfant] little one, child ▸ **bonjour, mon petit/ma petite** good morning, my dear ▸ **mon petit, je suis fier de toi** [à un garçon] young man, I'm proud of you / [à une fille] young lady, I'm proud of you ▸ **pauvre petit!** poor little thing! ▸ **la classe des petits** SCOL the infant class ▸ **c'est le petit de Monique** it's Monique's son.
■ **nm 1.** [jeune animal] young *(U)* ▸ **faire des petits** to have puppies/kittens *etc*
2. *(gén pl)* [personne modeste] little man ▸ **c'est toujours les petits qui doivent payer** it's always the little man who's got to pay.
◆ ***petit à petit*** **loc adv** little by little, gradually.

petit-beurre [p(ə)tibœr] (pl **petits-beurre**) **nm** *small biscuit.*

petit-bourgeois, petite-bourgeoise [p(ə)tiburʒwa, p(ə)titburʒwaz] (mpl **petits-bourgeois**, fpl **petites-bourgeoises**) *péj* ■ **adj** lower middle-class.
■ **nm, f** lower middle-class person.

petit déjeuner [p(ə)tidezøne] (pl **petits déjeuners**) **nm** breakfast.

petit-déjeuner [5] [p(ə)tideʒøne] **vi** to have breakfast, to breakfast.

petite-fille [p(ə)titfij] (pl **petites-filles**) **nf** granddaughter.

petitement [p(ə)titmɑ̃] **adv 1.** [être logé] in cramped conditions **2.** [chichement - vivre] poorly **3.** [mesquinement] pettily.

petitesse [p(ə)titɛs] **nf 1.** [de personne, de revenu] smallness **2.** [d'esprit] pettiness.

petit-fils [p(ə)tifis] (pl **petits-fils**) **nm** grandson.

petit-four [p(ə)tifur] (pl **petits-fours**) **nm** petit four.

pétition [petisjɔ̃] **nf** petition.

pétitionner [3] [petisjɔne] **vi** to petition.

petit-lait [p(ə)tilɛ] (pl **petits-laits**) **nm** whey.

petit-nègre [p(ə)tinɛgr] **nm inv** *fam* pidgin French.

petits-enfants [p(ə)tizɑ̃fɑ̃] **nmpl** grandchildren.

petit-suisse [p(ə)tisɥis] (pl **petits-suisses**) **nm** *fresh soft cheese, eaten with sugar.*

peton [pətɔ̃] **nm** *fam* foot.

pétrifier [9] [petrifje] **vt** *littéraire & fig* to petrify.
◆ ***se pétrifier*** **vp** to become petrified.

pétrin [petrɛ̃] **nm 1.** [de boulanger] kneading machine **2.** *fam* [embarras] pickle ▸ **se fourrer/être dans le pétrin** to get into/to be in a pickle.

pétrir [32] [petrir] **vt 1.** [pâte, muscle] to knead **2.** *fig & littéraire* [personne] to mould ▸ **pétri d'orgueil** filled with pride.

pétrochimie [petrɔʃimi] **nf** petrochemistry.

pétrochimique [petrɔʃimik] **adj** petrochemical.

pétrodollar [petrɔdɔlar] **nm** petrodollar.

pétrole [petrɔl] **nm** oil, petroleum ▸ **pétrole lampant** paraffin (oil) *UK*, kerosene *US*.

pétrolier, ère [petrɔlje, ɛr] **adj** oil *(avant n)*, petroleum *(avant n)*.
◆ ***pétrolier*** **nm 1.** [navire] oil tanker **2.** [personne] oil magnate.

pétrolifère [petrɔlifɛr] **adj** oil-bearing.

pétulant, e [petylɑ̃, ɑ̃t] **adj** exuberant.

pétunia [petynja] **nm** petunia.

peu [pø] ■ **adv 1.** *(avec verbe, adjectif, adverbe)* **: il a peu dormi** he didn't sleep much, he slept little ▸ **c'est un livre peu intéressant** it's not a very interesting book ▸ **peu**

avant shortly *ou* not long before ▸ **peu après** soon after, shortly *ou* not long after ▸ **peu souvent** not very often, rarely ▸ **très peu** very little
2. : peu de *(+ n sg)* little, not much ▸ **peu de** *(+ n pl)* few, not many ▸ **il a peu de travail** he hasn't got much work, he has little work ▸ **c'est (bien) peu de chose** it's not much ▸ **il reste peu de jours** there aren't many days left ▸ **peu d'élèves l'ont compris** few *ou* not many students understood him ▸ **peu de gens le connaissent** few *ou* not many know him ▸ **peu de temps : je ne reste que peu de temps** I'm only staying for a short while, I'm not staying long.
■ **nm 1.** [petite quantité] **: le peu de** *(+ n sg)* the little / *(+ n pl)* the few ▸ **avec mon peu de moyens** with the little I possess ▸ **le peu que tu gagnes** the little you earn
2. *(précédé de un)* a little, a bit ▸ **je le connais un peu** I know him slightly *ou* a little ▸ **un (tout) petit peu** a little bit ▸ **fais voir un peu...** let me have a look... ▸ **elle est un peu sotte** she's a bit stupid ▸ **tu parles un peu fort** you're talking a little too loudly ▸ **un peu de** a little ▸ **un peu de vin/patience** a little wine/patience ▸ **un peu plus de** [suivi d'un nom comptable] a few more / [suivi d'un nom non comptable] a little (bit) more ▸ **un peu moins de** [suivi d'un nom comptable] slightly fewer, not so many / [suivi d'un nom non comptable] a little (bit) less ▸ **un peu plus et je me faisais écraser!** I was within an inch of being run over!
◆ ***avant peu*** **loc adv** soon, before long.
◆ ***depuis peu*** **loc adv** recently.
◆ ***peu à peu*** **loc adv** gradually, little by little ▸ **on s'habitue, peu à peu** you get used to things, bit by bit *ou* gradually.
◆ ***pour peu que*** *(+ subjonctif)* **loc conj** if ever, if only ▸ **pour peu qu'il le veuille, il réussira** if he wants to, he'll succeed.
◆ ***pour un peu*** **loc adv** nearly, almost ▸ **pour un peu, j'oubliais mes clés** I nearly forgot my keys.
◆ ***si peu que*** *(+ subjonctif)* **loc conj** however little ▸ **si peu que j'y aille, j'apprécie toujours beaucoup l'opéra** although I don't go very often, I always like the opera very much.
◆ ***sous peu*** **loc adv** soon, shortly ▸ **vous recevrez sous peu les résultats de vos analyses** you will receive the results of your tests in a short while.

peul, e [pøl] **adj** Fulani.
◆ ***peul*** **nm** [langue] Fulani.
◆ ***Peul, e*** **nm, f** Fulani.

peuplade [pœplad] **nf** tribe.

peuple [pœpl] **nm 1.** [gén] people ▸ **le peuple** the (common) people **2.** *fam* [multitude] **: quel peuple!** what a crowd!

peuplé, e [pœple] **adj** populated.

peuplement [pœpləmɑ̃] **nm 1.** [action] populating **2.** [population] population.

peupler [5] [pœple] **vt 1.** [pourvoir d'habitants - région] to populate / [- bois, étang] to stock **2.** [habiter, occuper] to inhabit **3.** *fig* [remplir] to fill.
◆ ***se peupler*** **vp 1.** [région] to become populated **2.** [rue, salle] to be filled.

peuplier [pøplije] **nm** poplar.

peur [pœr] **nf** fear ▸ **avoir peur de qqn/qqch** to be afraid of sb/sthg ▸ **avoir peur de faire qqch** to be afraid of doing sthg ▸ **avoir peur que** *(+ subjonctif)* to be afraid that ▸ **j'ai peur qu'il ne vienne pas** I'm afraid he won't come ▸ **faire peur à qqn** to frighten sb ▸ **par *ou* de peur de qqch** for fear of sthg ▸ **par *ou* de peur de faire qqch** for fear of doing sthg ▸ **il n'a pas peur du ridicule** he doesn't mind making a fool of himself ▸ **avoir une peur bleue de** to be scared stiff of ▸ **avoir plus de peur que de mal** to be more frightened than hurt ▸ **laid à faire peur** horribly ugly ▸ **mourir de peur** to die of fright ▸ **prendre peur** to take fright.

peureux, euse [pœrø, øz] ■ **adj** fearful, timid.
■ **nm, f** fearful *ou* timid person.

peut ➤ ***pouvoir***.

peut-être [pøtɛtr] **adv** perhaps, maybe ▸ **peut-être qu'ils ne viendront pas, ils ne viendront peut-être pas** perhaps *ou* maybe they won't come ▸ **peut-être pas** perhaps *ou* maybe not.

peux ➤ ***pouvoir***.

p. ex. (abr écrite de ***par exemple***) e.g.

pH (abr de ***potential of hydrogen***) **nm** pH.

phalange [falɑ̃ʒ] **nf 1.** ANAT phalanx **2.** POLIT falange.

phallique [falik] **adj** phallic.

phallocrate [falɔkrat] ■ **nm** male chauvinist.
■ **adj** male chauvinist *(avant n)* / [milieu] male-dominated.

phallus [falys] **nm** phallus.

phantasme [fɑ̃tasm] = ***fantasme***.

pharamineux, euse [faraminø, øz] *fam* = ***faramineux***.

pharaon [faraɔ̃] **nm** pharaoh.

phare [far] ■ **nm 1.** [tour] lighthouse **2.** AUTO headlight ▸ **phare antibrouillard** fog lamp *UK*, fog light *US*.
■ **adj** landmark *(avant n)* ▸ **une industrie phare** a flagship *ou* pioneering industry.

pharmaceutique [farmasøtik] **adj** pharmaceutical.

pharmacie [farmasi] **nf 1.** [science] pharmacology **2.** [magasin] chemist's *UK*, drugstore *US* **3.** [meuble] **: (armoire à) pharmacie** medicine cupboard *UK* *ou* chest *US*.

pharmacien, enne [farmasjɛ̃, ɛn] **nm, f** chemist *UK*, druggist *US*.

pharmacologie [farmakɔlɔʒi] **nf** pharmacology.

pharyngite [farɛ̃ʒit] **nf** pharyngitis *(U)*.

pharynx [farɛ̃ks] **nm** pharynx.

phase [faz] **nf** phase ▸ **être en phase avec qqn** to be on the same wavelength as sb ▸ **phase terminale** final phase.

phénix [feniks] **nm 1.** MYTHOL phoenix **2.** [personne] paragon.

phénoménal, e, aux [fenɔmenal, o] **adj** phenomenal.

phénomène [fenɔmɛn] **nm 1.** [fait] phenomenon **2.** [être anormal] freak **3.** *fam* [excentrique] character.

philanthropie [filɑ̃trɔpi] **nf** philanthropy.

philanthropique [filɑ̃trɔpik] **adj** philanthropic.

philatélie [filateli] **nf** philately, stamp collecting.

philatéliste [filatelist] **nmf** philatelist, stamp collector.

philharmonique [filarmɔnik] **adj** philharmonic.

philippin, e [filipɛ̃, in] **adj** Filipino.
◆ ***Philippin, e*** **nm, f** Filipino.

Philippines [filipin] **nfpl : les Philippines** the Philippines ▸ **aux Philippines** in the Philippines.

philistin [filistɛ̃] **nm** philistine.

philo [filo] **nf** *fam* philosophy.

philodendron [filɔdɛ̃drɔ̃] **nm** philodendron.

philologie [filɔlɔʒi] **nf** philology.

philosophe [filɔzɔf] ■ **nmf** philosopher.
■ **adj** philosophical.

philosopher [3] [filɔzɔfe] **vi** to philosophize.

philosophie [filɔzɔfi] **nf** philosophy.

philosophique [filɔzɔfik] **adj** philosophical.

philosophiquement [filɔzɔfikmɑ̃] **adv** philosophically.

philtre [filtr] **nm** love potion.

phlébite [flebit] **nf** phlebitis.

Phnom Penh [pnɔmpɛn] **npr** Phnom Penh.

phobie [fɔbi] **nf** phobia.

phobique [fɔbik] **nmf & adj** phobic.

phonème [fɔnɛm] **nm** phoneme.

phonétique [fɔnetik] ■ **nf** phonetics *(U)*.
■ **adj** phonetic.

phonétiquement [fɔnetikmɑ̃] **adv** phonetically.

phono [fɔno] **nm** *fam vieilli* gramophone *UK*, phonograph *US*.

phonographe [fɔnɔgraf] **nm** *vieilli* gramophone *UK*, phonograph *US*.

phoque [fɔk] **nm** seal.

phosphate [fɔsfat] **nm** phosphate.

phosphaté, e [fɔsfate] **adj : engrais phosphaté** phosphate fertilizer.

phosphore [fɔsfɔr] **nm** phosphorus.

phosphorescent, e [fɔsfɔresɑ̃, ɑ̃t] **adj** phosphorescent.

photo [fɔto] ■ **nf 1.** [technique] photography **2.** [image] photo, picture ▸ **prendre qqn en photo** to take a photo of sb ▸ **photo d'identité** passport photo ▸ **photo noir et blanc** black and white photo ▸ **photo couleur** colour *UK* *ou* color *US* photo ▸ **y'a pas photo** *fam* there's no comparison.
■ **adj inv : appareil photo** camera.

photocomposition [fɔtɔkɔ̃pozisjɔ̃] **nf** filmsetting *UK*, photocomposition *US*.

photocopie [fɔtɔkɔpi] **nf 1.** [procédé] photocopying **2.** [document] photocopy.

photocopier [9] [fɔtɔkɔpje] **vt** to photocopy.

photocopieur [fɔtɔkɔpjœr] **nm** photocopier.

photocopieuse [fɔtɔkɔpjøz] **nf** = ***photocopieur***.

photoélectrique [fɔtɔelɛktrik] **adj** photoelectric.

photogénique [fɔtɔʒenik] **adj** photogenic.

photographe [fɔtɔgraf] **nmf 1.** [artiste, technicien] photographer **2.** [commerçant] camera dealer.

FAUX AMIS / FALSE FRIENDS

photographe

Photograph is not a translation of the French word *photographe*. Photograph is translated by *photographie* or *photo*.
▸ a black-and-white photograph / *une photographie en noir et blanc*
▸ To take a photograph / *Prendre une photo*

photographie [fɔtɔgrafi] **nf 1.** [technique] photography **2.** [cliché] photograph.

photographier [9] [fɔtɔgrafje] **vt** to photograph.

photographique [fɔtɔgrafik] **adj** photographic.

Photomaton® [fɔtɔmatɔ̃] **nm** photo booth.

photomontage [fɔtɔmɔ̃taʒ] **nm** photomontage.

photoreportage [fɔtɔrəpɔrtaʒ] **nm** PRESSE report *(consisting mainly of photographs)*.

photosensible [fɔtɔsɑ̃sibl] **adj** photosensitive.

photothèque [fɔtɔtɛk] **nf** photograph library.

phrase [fraz] **nf 1.** LING sentence ▸ **phrase toute faite** stock phrase **2.** MUS phrase.

phraséologie [frazeɔlɔʒi] **nf** phraseology / *péj* verbiage.

phraseur, euse [frazœr, øz] **nm, f** *péj* verbose person.

phréatique [freatik] **adj : nappe phréatique** water table.

phrygien, enne [friʒjɛ̃, ɛn] **adj** Phrygian.
◆ ***Phrygien, enne*** **nm, f** Phrygian.

phtisie [ftizi] **nf** *vieilli* consumption.

phylloxéra, phylloxera [filɔksera] **nm** phylloxera.

physicien, enne [fizisjɛ̃, ɛn] **nm, f** physicist.

physiologie [fizjɔlɔʒi] **nf** physiology.

physiologique [fizjɔlɔʒik] **adj** physiological.

physiologiquement [fizjɔlɔʒikmɑ̃] **adv** physiologically.

physionomie [fizjɔnɔmi] **nf 1.** [faciès] face **2.** [apparence] physiognomy.

physionomiste [fizjɔnɔmist] ■ **nmf** person with a good memory for faces.
■ **adj : être physionomiste** to have a good memory for faces.

physiothérapie [fizjɔterapi] **nf** *natural medicine based on treatment using water, air, light etc.*

physique [fizik] ■ **adj** physical.
■ **nf** [sciences] physics *(U)*.
■ **nm 1.** [constitution] physical well-being **2.** [apparence] physique.

physiquement [fizikmɑ̃] **adv** physically.

phytoplancton [fitɔplɑ̃ktɔ̃] **nm** phytoplankton.

phytothérapie [fitɔterapi] **nf** herbal medicine.

p.i. abr de ***par intérim***.

piaf [pjaf] **nm** *fam* sparrow.

piaffer [3] [pjafe] **vi 1.** [cheval] to paw the ground **2.** [personne] to fidget.

piaillement [pjajmɑ̃] **nm 1.** [d'oiseau] cheeping **2.** [d'enfant] squawking.

piailler [3] [pjaje] **vi 1.** [oiseaux] to cheep **2.** [enfant] to squawk.

pianiste [pjanist] **nmf** pianist.

piano [pjano] ■ **nm** piano ▸ **piano demi-queue** baby grand (piano) ▸ **piano droit** upright (piano) ▸ **piano mécanique** player piano ▸ **piano à queue** grand (piano).
■ **adv 1.** MUS piano **2.** [doucement] gently.

pianoter [3] [pjanɔte] **vi 1.** [jouer du piano] to plunk away (on the piano) **2.** [sur table] to drum one's fingers.

piaule [pjol] **nf** *fam* [hébergement] place ⁄ [chambre] room.

piauler [3] [pjole] **vi 1.** [oiseau] to cheep **2.** [enfant] to whimper.

PIB (abr de ***produit intérieur brut***) **nm** GDP.

pic [pik] **nm 1.** [outil] pick, pickaxe *UK*, pickax *US* **2.** [montagne] peak **3.** [oiseau] woodpecker **4.** *fig* [maximum] **: pic d'audience** top (audience) ratings ▸ **on a observé des pics de pollution** pollution levels reached a peak, pollution levels peaked.
◆ ***à pic*** **loc adv 1.** [verticalement] vertically ▸ **couler à pic** to sink like a stone **2.** *fam fig* [à point nommé] just at the right moment.

picard, e [pikar, ard] **adj** from Picardy.
◆ ***picard*** **nm** LING Picard *ou* Picardy dialect.

pichenette [piʃnɛt] **nf** flick (of the finger).

pichet [piʃɛ] **nm** jug *UK*, pitcher *US*.

pickpocket [pikpɔkɛt] **nm** pickpocket.

pick-up [pikœp] **nm inv 1.** *vieilli* [tourne-disque] record player **2.** [camionnette] pick-up (truck).

picoler [3] [pikɔle] **vi** *fam* to booze.

picorer [3] [pikɔre] **vi & vt** to peck.

picotement [pikɔtmɑ̃] **nm** prickling *(U)*, prickle.

picoter [3] [pikɔte] **vt 1.** [yeux] to make sting **2.** [pain] to peck (at).

pictogramme [piktɔgram] **nm** pictogram.

pictural, e, aux [piktyral, o] **adj** pictorial.

pic-vert = ***pivert***.

pie [pi] ■ **nf 1.** [oiseau] magpie **2.** *fig & péj* [bavard] chatterbox.
■ **adj inv** [cheval] piebald.

pièce [pjɛs] **nf 1.** [élément] piece ⁄ [de moteur] part ▸ **mettre en pièces** [vêtement] to tear to pieces ⁄ [assiette, tasse] to smash to pieces ▸ **pièce de collection** collector's item ▸ **pièce détachée** spare part ▸ **en pièces détachées** *fig* in little bits *ou* pieces ▸ **pièce de musée** museum piece ▸ **une pièce de viande** [flanc] a side of meat ⁄ [morceau découpé] a piece *ou* cut of meat ▸ **créer/inventer qqch de toutes pièces** to create/invent sthg from start to finish ▸ **la pièce maîtresse d'une argumentation** the main part *ou* the linchpin of an argument ▸ **pièce de résistance** *litt* main dish ⁄ *fig* pièce de résistance
2. [unité] **: deux euros pièce** deux euros each *ou* apiece ▸ **acheter/vendre qqch à la pièce** to buy/sell sthg singly, to buy/sell sthg separately ▸ **travailler à la pièce** to do piecework ▸ **on n'est pas aux pièces!** *fam* what's the big hurry?, where's the fire?
3. [document] document, paper ▸ **pièce à conviction** object produced as evidence, exhibit ▸ **pièce d'identité** identification papers *pl* ▸ **pièce jointe** [e-mail] attachment ▸ **pièce jointes** [document] enclosures ▸ **pièce justificative** written proof *(U)*, supporting document
4. [œuvre littéraire ou musicale] piece ▸ **pièce (de théâtre)** play ▸ **monter une pièce** to put on *ou* to stage a play
5. [argent] **: pièce (de monnaie)** coin ▸ **une pièce de 2 euros** a 2-euro coin *ou* piece
6. [de maison] room ▸ **un deux-pièces** a one-bedroom flat *UK ou* apartment *US*
7. COUT patch ▸ **pièce rapportée** *litt* patch ⁄ *fig* [personne] odd person out.
◆ ***pièce d'eau*** **nf** large pond, ornamental lake.
◆ ***pièce montée*** **nf** tiered cake.

piécette [pjesɛt] **nf** small coin.

pied [pje] **nm 1.** [gén] foot ▸ **à pied** on foot ▸ **on ira au stade à pied** we'll walk to the stadium ▸ **avoir pied** to be able to touch the bottom ▸ **avoir les pieds plats** to have flat feet *litt*, to be flat-footed *litt* ▸ **perdre pied** *litt & fig* to be out of one's depth ▸ **à pieds joints** with one's feet together ▸ **être/marcher pieds nus** *ou* **nu-pieds** to be/to go barefoot ▸ **pied bot** [handicap] clubfoot **2.** CULIN **: pied de porc** pig's trotter **3.** [base - de montagne, table] foot ⁄ [- de verre] stem ⁄ [- de lampe] base **4.** [plant - de tomate] stalk ⁄ [- de vigne] stock
▸▸ **attendre qqch/qqn de pied ferme** to be ready for sb/sthg ▸ **avoir le pied marin** to be a good sailor ▸ **c'est le pied** *fam* it's great ▸ **casser les pieds à qqn** *fam* to get on sb's nerves ▸ **comme un pied** *fam* [chanter, conduire] terribly ▸ **être à pied d'œuvre** to be ready to get down to the job ▸ **être au pied du mur** to have one's back to the wall ▸ **être sur pied** to be (back) on one's feet, to be up and about ▸ **être sur un pied d'égalité (avec)** to be on an equal footing (with) ▸ **faire du pied à** to play footsie with ▸ **faire le pied de grue** to wait about ▸ **faire des pieds et des mains** to move heaven and earth, to do one's utmost ▸ **faire un pied de nez à qqn** to thumb one's nose at sb ▸ **ça te fera les pieds!** *fam* it'll serve you right! ▸ **fouler qqch aux pieds** to ride roughshod over sthg ▸ **il a fallu lui mettre le pied à l'étrier** he had to be given a leg up *fig* ▸ **je suis pieds et poings liés** my hands are tied ▸ **se lever du bon pied/du pied gauche** to get out of bed on the right/wrong side ▸ **mettre qqch sur pied** to get sthg on its feet, to get sthg off the ground ▸ **mettre qqn au pied du mur** to drive sb to the wall ▸ **mettre les pieds dans le plat** *fam* to put one's foot in it ▸ **je n'ai jamais mis les pieds chez lui** I've never set foot in his house ▸ **au pied de la lettre** literally, to the letter ▸ **il faut que tu sois prêt**

à le faire au pied levé you must be ready to drop everything and do it ▸ **de pied en cap** from head to toe ▸ **en vert de pied en cap** dressed in green from top *ou* head to toe ▸ **ne pas savoir sur quel pied danser** not to know which way to turn ▸ **ne pas se laisser marcher sur les pieds** not to let anyone tread on one's toes ▸ **prendre son pied** *fam* [sexuellement] to come / *fig* to be in seventh heaven ▸ **retomber sur ses pieds** to land on one's feet.
◆ ***en pied*** **loc adj** [portrait] full-length.

pied-à-terre [pjetatɛr] **nm inv** pied-à-terre.

pied-bot [pjebo] (pl **pieds-bots**) **nm** club-footed person ▸ **c'est un pied-bot** he's got a *ou* he's a club-foot.

pied-de-biche [pjedbiʃ] (pl **pieds-de-biche**) **nm** **1.** [outil] nail claw **2.** COUT presser foot.

pied-de-poule [pjedpul] (pl **pieds-de-poule**) ■ **nm** houndstooth (material).
■ **adj inv** houndstooth *(avant n)*.

piédestal, aux [pjedɛstal, o] **nm** pedestal.

piedmont = ***piémont***.

pied-noir (pl **pieds-noirs**) [pjenwar] **nmf** *French settler in Algeria*.

piège [pjɛʒ] **nm** *litt & fig* trap ▸ **être pris au piège** to be trapped ▸ **piège de la dette** debt trap ▸ **tendre un piège** to set a trap.

piéger [22] [pjeʒe] **vt** **1.** [animal, personne] to trap **2.** [colis, véhicule] to boobytrap.

piémont, piedmont [pjemɔ̃] **nm** piedmont glacier/plain.

piercing [pi:rsiŋ] **nm** body piercing.

pierraille [pjɛraj] **nf** loose stones *pl*.

pierre [pjɛr] **nf** stone ▸ **investir dans la pierre** to invest in property *ou* in bricks and mortar ▸ **il a construit sa fortune pierre par pierre** he built up his fortune from nothing ▸ **sculpter la pierre** to carve in stone ▸ **pierre d'achoppement** *fig* stumbling block ▸ **pierre à feu** *ou* **fusil** gun flint ▸ **pierre fine** *ou* **semi-précieuse** semi-precious stone ▸ **pierre funéraire** *ou* **tombale** tombstone, gravestone ▸ **pierre philosophale** philosopher's stone ▸ **pierre ponce** pumice stone ▸ **pierre précieuse** precious stone ▸ **pierre de taille** *ou* **d'appareil** freestone ▸ **poser la première pierre** CONSTR to lay the foundation stone / *fig* to lay the foundations ▸ **c'est une pierre dans ton jardin** that remark was (meant) for you ▸ **faire d'une pierre deux coups** *fig* to kill two birds with one stone ▸ **jeter la pierre à qqn** to cast a stone at sb.

pierreries [pjɛrri] **nfpl** precious stones, jewels.

piété [pjete] **nf** piety.

piétiner [3] [pjetine] ■ **vi** **1.** [trépigner] to stamp (one's feet) **2.** *fig* [ne pas avancer] to make no progress, to be at a standstill.
■ **vt** **1.** [personne, parterre] to trample **2.** *fig* [principes] to ride roughshod over.

piéton, onne [pjetɔ̃, ɔn] ■ **nm, f** pedestrian.
■ **adj** pedestrian *(avant n)*.

piétonnier, ère [pjetɔnje, ɛr] **adj** pedestrian *(avant n)*.

piètre [pjɛtr] **adj** poor.

pieu, x [pjø] **nm** **1.** [poteau] post, stake **2.** *fam* [lit] pit *UK*, sack *US*.

pieusement [pjøzmɑ̃] **adv** **1.** RELIG piously **2.** *fig* [conserver] religiously.

pieuter [3] [pjøte] ◆ ***se pieuter*** **vp** *fam* to hit the hay.

pieuvre [pjœvr] **nf** octopus / *fig & péj* leech.

pieux, pieuse [pjø, pjøz] **adj** **1.** [personne, livre] pious **2.** [soins] devoted **3.** [silence] reverent.

pif [pif] **nm** *fam* conk *UK*, hooter *UK*, schnoz(zle) *US* ▸ **au pif** *fig* by guesswork.

pige [piʒ] **nf** **1.** PRESSE **: travailler à la pige** to work freelance **2.** *fam* [an] **: avoir 30 piges** to be 30 (years old).

pigeon [piʒɔ̃] **nm** **1.** [oiseau] pigeon ▸ **pigeon voyageur** carrier pigeon, homing pigeon **2.** *fam péj* [personne] sucker.

pigeonnant, e [piʒɔnɑ̃, ɑ̃t] **adj** [soutien-gorge] uplift *(avant n)* / [poitrine] prominent.

pigeonner [3] [piʒɔne] **vt** *fam* to cheat.

pigeonnier [piʒɔnje] **nm** **1.** [pour pigeons] pigeon loft, dovecote **2.** *fig & vieilli* [logement] garret.

piger [17] [piʒe] *fam* ■ **vt** to understand.
■ **vi** to catch on, to get it.

pigiste [piʒist] **nmf** freelance.

pigment [pigmɑ̃] **nm** pigment.

pigmentation [pigmɑ̃tasjɔ̃] **nf** pigmentation.

pignon [piɲɔ̃] **nm** **1.** [de mur] gable ▸ **avoir pignon sur rue** *fig* to be a person of substance **2.** [d'engrenage] gearwheel **3.** [de pomme de pin] pine kernel.

pilaf [pilaf] ➤ ***riz***.

pile [pil] ■ **nf** **1.** [de livres, journaux] pile
2. ÉLECTR battery ▸ **une radio à piles** a radio run on batteries, a battery radio ▸ **pile atomique** pile reactor ▸ **pile solaire** solar cell
3. [de pièce] **: pile ou face** heads or tails ▸ **tirer à pile ou face** to toss a coin.
■ **adv** *fam* on the dot ▸ **s'arrêter pile** to stop dead ▸ **ça commence à 8 h pile** it begins at 8 o'clock sharp *ou* on the dot ▸ **tomber/arriver pile** to come/to arrive at just the right time ▸ **vous tombez pile, j'allais vous appeler** you're right on cue, I was about to call you.

piler [3] [pile] ■ **vt** **1.** [amandes] to crush, to grind **2.** *fam fig* [adversaire] to thrash.
■ **vi** *fam* AUTO to jam on the brakes.

pileux, euse [pilø, øz] **adj** hairy *(avant n)* ▸ **système pileux** hair.

pilier [pilje] **nm** **1.** [de construction] pillar **2.** *fig* [soutien] mainstay, pillar **3.** *fig & péj* [habitué] **: c'est un pilier de bar** he's always propping up the bar **4.** [rugby] prop (forward).

pillage [pijaʒ] **nm** looting.

pillard, e [pijar, ard] ■ **nm, f** looter.
■ **adj** looting *(avant n)*.

piller [3] [pije] **vt** **1.** [ville, biens] to loot **2.** *fig* [ouvrage, auteur] to plagiarize.

pilon [pilɔ̃] **nm** **1.** [instrument] pestle ▸ **mettre au pilon** to pulp **2.** [de poulet] drumstick **3.** [jambe de bois] wooden leg.

pilonner [3] [pilɔne] **vt** to pound.

pilori [pilɔri] **nm** pillory ▸ **mettre *ou* clouer qqn au pilori** *fig* to pillory sb.

pilotage [pilɔtaʒ] **nm** piloting ▸ **pilotage automatique** automatic piloting.

pilote [pilɔt] ■ **nm 1.** [d'avion] pilot / [de voiture] driver ▸ **pilote automatique** autopilot ▸ **pilote de chasse** fighter pilot ▸ **pilote de course** racing *UK ou* race *US* driver ▸ **pilote d'essai** test pilot ▸ **pilote de ligne** airline pilot **2.** [poisson] pilot fish.
■ **adj** pilot *(avant n)*, experimental.

piloter [3] [pilɔte] **vt 1.** [avion] to pilot / [voiture] to drive **2.** [personne] to show around.

pilotis [pilɔti] **nm** pile.

pilule [pilyl] **nf** pill ▸ **prendre la pilule** to be on the pill ▸ **dorer la pilule à qqn** *fig* to sugar the pill for sb.

pimbêche [pɛ̃bɛʃ] *péj* ■ **nf** stuck-up woman, stuck-up girl.
■ **adj** stuck-up.

piment [pimɑ̃] **nm 1.** [plante] pepper, capsicum ▸ **piment rouge** chilli pepper, hot red pepper **2.** *fig* [piquant] spice, pizzazz *US* ▸ **donner du piment à qqch** to spice sthg up, to add pizzazz to sthg *US*.

pimenté, e [pimɑ̃te] **adj** [sauce] hot, spicy.

pimenter [3] [pimɑ̃te] **vt 1.** [plat] to put chillis in **2.** *fig* [récit] to spice up.

pimpant, e [pɛ̃pɑ̃, ɑ̃t] **adj** smart.

pin [pɛ̃] **nm** pine ▸ **pin parasol** umbrella pine ▸ **pin sylvestre** Scots pine.

PIN [pin] (abr de ***produit intérieur net***) **m** ÉCON NDP *(net domestic product)*.

pin's [pinz] **nm inv** badge.

pinacle [pinakl] **nm** ARCHIT pinnacle ▸ **porter qqn au pinacle** *fig* to praise sb to the skies.

pinailler [3] [pinaje] **vi** *fam* to split hairs ▸ **pinailler sur** to quibble about.

pinard [pinar] **nm** *fam* wine, *péj* plonk *UK*, jug wine *US*.

pince [pɛ̃s] **nf 1.** [grande] pliers *pl* **2.** [petite] **: pince (à épiler)** tweezers *pl* ▸ **pince à linge** clothes peg *UK*, clothespin *US* **3.** [de crabe] pincer **4.** *fam* [main] mitt **5.** *fam* [jambe] **: à pinces** on foot **6.** COUT dart.

pincé, e [pɛ̃se] **adj 1.** [air, sourire] prim **2.** [nez] pinched.

pinceau, x [pɛ̃so] **nm 1.** [pour peindre] brush **2.** *fam* [pied] foot.

pincée [pɛ̃se] **nf** pinch.

pincement [pɛ̃smɑ̃] **nm** pinching ▸ **pincement au cœur** *fig* pang of sorrow.

pince-monseigneur [pɛ̃smɔ̃seɲœr] (pl **pinces-monseigneur**) **nf** jemmy *UK*, jimmy *US*.

pince-nez [pɛ̃sne] **nm inv** pince-nez.

pincer [16] [pɛ̃se] ■ **vt 1.** [serrer] to pinch / MUS to pluck / [lèvres] to purse **2.** *fam fig* [arrêter] to nick *UK*, to catch ▸ **se faire pincer** to get nicked *UK*, to get caught **3.** [suj: froid] to nip.
■ **vi** *fam* **1.** [faire froid] **: ça pince!** it's a bit nippy! **2.** *fig* [avoir le béguin] **: en pincer pour qqn** to be crazy about sb.
◆ ***se pincer*** **vp : se pincer le doigt** to jam *ou* catch one's finger ▸ **se pincer le nez** to hold one's nose.

pince-sans-rire [pɛ̃ssɑ̃rir] **nmf** person with a deadpan face.

pincettes [pɛ̃sɛt] **nfpl** [ustensile] tongs ▸ **il n'est pas à prendre avec des pincettes** *fig* he's like a bear with a sore head.

pinçon [pɛ̃sɔ̃] **nm** pinch mark.

pinède [pinɛd], ***pineraie*** [pinrɛ], ***pinière*** [pinjɛr] **nf** pinewood.

pingouin [pɛ̃gwɛ̃] **nm** penguin.

ping-pong [piŋpɔ̃g] (pl **ping-pongs**) **nm** ping pong, table tennis.

pingre [pɛ̃gr] *péj* ■ **nmf** skinflint.
■ **adj** stingy.

pingrerie [pɛ̃grəri] **nf** *péj* stinginess.

pinière = ***pinède***.

pinson [pɛ̃sɔ̃] **nm** chaffinch ▸ **gai comme un pinson** *fig* happy as a lark.

pintade [pɛ̃tad] **nf** guinea fowl.

pintadeau, x [pɛ̃tado] **nm** young guinea fowl.

pinte [pɛ̃t] **nf 1.** [mesure anglo-saxonne] pint **2.** *vieilli* [mesure française] quart **3.** *Suisse* [débit de boissons] drinking establishment.

pin-up [pinœp] **nf inv** pinup (girl).

pioche [pjɔʃ] **nf 1.** [outil] pick **2.** [jeux] pile.

piocher [3] [pjɔʃe] ■ **vt 1.** [terre] to dig **2.** [jeux] to take **3.** *fig* [choisir] to pick at random.
■ **vi 1.** [creuser] to dig **2.** [jeux] to pick up ▸ **piocher dan[s]** [tas] to delve into / [économies] to dip into.

piolet [pjɔlɛ] **nm** ice axe *UK ou* ax *US*.

pion, pionne [pjɔ̃, pjɔn] **nm, f** *fam* SCOL *supervisor (often a student who does this as a part-time job)*.
◆ ***pion*** **nm** [aux échecs] pawn / [aux dames] piece ▸ **dame[r] le pion à qqn** *fig* to get the better of sb ▸ **n'être qu'u[n] pion** *fig* to be just a pawn in the game.

pionnier, ère [pjɔnje, ɛr] **nm, f** pioneer.

pipe [pip] **nf** pipe.

pipeau [pipo] **nm** MUS (reed) pipe ▸ **c'est du pipeau** *fa[m]* that's nonsense.

pipeline, pipe-line [pajplajn, piplin] (pl **pipe-line[s]**) **nm** pipeline.

piper [3] [pipe] **vt** [cartes] to mark / [dés] to load
▸▸ **ne pas piper mot** not to breathe a word.

piperade [piperad] **nf** *eggs cooked with tomatoes, pe[p]pers and onions*.

pipette [pipɛt] **nf** pipette.

pipi [pipi] **nm** *fam* wee *UK*, weewee ▸ **faire pipi** to ha[ve] a wee.

piquant, e [pikɑ̃, ɑ̃t] **adj** **1.** [barbe, feuille] prickly **2.** [sauce] spicy, hot **3.** [froid] biting **4.** *fig* [détail] spicy, juicy.
◆ ***piquant*** **nm** **1.** [d'animal] spine / [de végétal] thorn, prickle **2.** *fig* [d'histoire] spice.

pique [pik] ■ **nf** **1.** [arme] pike **2.** *fig* [mot blessant] barbed comment.
■ **nm** [aux cartes] spade.

piqué, e [pike] **adj** **1.** [vin] sour, vinegary **2.** [meuble] worm-eaten **3.** [tissu] spotted, flecked **4.** *fam* [personne] loony.
◆ ***piqué*** **nm** **1.** [tissu] piqué **2.** AÉRON dive.

pique-assiette [pikasjɛt] (pl **pique-assiette** *ou* **pique-assiettes**) **nmf** *péj* sponger.

pique-nique [piknik] (pl **pique-niques**) **nm** picnic.

pique-niquer [3] [piknike] **vi** to picnic.

piquer [3] [pike] ■ **vt** **1.** [suj: guêpe, méduse] to sting ▸ **être piqué** *ou* **se faire piquer par une abeille** to get stung by a bee / [suj: serpent, moustique] to bite ▸ **se faire piquer par un moustique** to get bitten by a mosquito **2.** [avec pointe] to prick ▸ **piquer qqch de** CULIN to stick sthg with ▸ **piquer un rôti d'ail** to stick garlic into a roast **3.** MÉD to give an injection to ▸ **se faire piquer contre** *fam* to have o.s. inoculated *ou* vaccinated against **4.** [animal] to put down ▸ **faire piquer un chien** to have a dog put down **5.** [fleur] **: piquer qqch dans** to stick sthg into ▸ **piquer une broche sur un chemisier** to pin a brooch on *ou* onto a blouse **6.** [suj: tissu, barbe] to prickle ▸ **un tissu rêche qui pique la peau** a rough material which chafes the skin **7.** [suj: fumée, froid] to sting **8.** COUT to sew, to machine **9.** *fam* [voler] to pinch *UK* **10.** *fig* [curiosité] to excite, to arouse **11.** *fam* [voleur, escroc] to nick *UK*, to catch ▸ **se faire piquer** to get nicked *UK*, to get caught.
■ **vi** **1.** [ronce] to prick / [ortie] to sting **2.** [guêpe, méduse] to sting / [serpent, moustique] to bite **3.** [épice] to burn ▸ **radis/moutarde qui pique** hot radish/mustard **4.** COUT to machine **5.** *fam* [voler] **: piquer (dans)** to pinch (from) **6.** [avion] to dive.
◆ ***se piquer*** **vp** **1.** [avec une épingle, des ronces] to prick o.s. **2.** [avec des orties] to sting o.s. **3.** *fam* [se droguer] to shoot up ▸ **il se pique à l'héroïne** he shoots *ou* does heroin **4.** *littéraire* [se vexer] to become irritated **5.** *littéraire* & *péj* [avoir la prétention] **: se piquer de qqch/de faire qqch** to pride o.s. on one's knowledge of sthg/on one's ability to do sthg ▸ **il se pique de connaissances médicales** he prides himself on his knowledge of medicine
▸▸ **elle s'est piquée au jeu** it grew on her.

piquet [pikɛ] **nm** **1.** [pieu] peg, stake **2.** [jeux] piquet.
◆ ***piquet de grève*** **nm** picket.

piqueter [27] [pikte] **vt** to dot, to spot.

piquette [pikɛt] **nf** **1.** [vin] cheap wine *ou* plonk *UK* **2.** *fam* [défaite] **: prendre une** *ou* **la piquette** *fig* to get a hammering *ou* a thrashing.

piqûre [pikyr] **nf** **1.** [de guêpe, de méduse] sting / [de serpent, de moustique] bite **2.** [d'ortie] sting **3.** [injection] jab *UK*, shot **4.** COUT stitching *(U)*.

piranha [piraɲa], ***piraya*** [piraja] **nm** piranha.

piratage [pirataʒ] **nm** piracy ▸ **piratage musical** music piracy / INFORM hacking / *fam* TÉLÉCOM **: piratage du téléphone** phreaking.

pirate [pirat] ■ **nm** **1.** [corsaire] pirate ▸ **pirate de l'air** hijacker, skyjacker **2.** *fig* [escroc] swindler / *fam* TÉLÉCOM **: pirate du téléphone** phreaker.
■ **adj** pirate *(avant n)*.

pirater [3] [pirate] **vt** to pirate.

piraterie [piratri] **nf** **1.** [flibuste] piracy *(U)* **2.** [acte] act of piracy **3.** *fig* [escroquerie] swindling.

piraya = ***piranha***.

pire [pir] ■ **adj** **1.** [comparatif relatif] worse **2.** [superlatif] **: le/la pire** the worst.
■ **nm : le pire (de)** the worst (of) ▸ **s'attendre au pire** to expect the worst.

Pirée [pire] **nm : Le Pirée** Piraeus.

pirogue [pirɔg] **nf** dugout canoe.

pirouette [pirwɛt] **nf** **1.** [saut] pirouette **2.** *fig* [faux-fuyant] prevarication, evasive answer ▸ **répondre par une pirouette** to answer evasively ▸ **s'en tirer par une pirouette** to evade the issue.

pis [pi] ■ **adj** *littéraire* [pire] worse.
■ **adv** worse ▸ **de mal en pis** from bad to worse ▸ **de pis en pis** worse and worse.
■ **nm** udder.

pis-aller [pizale] **nm inv** last resort.

pisciculture [pisikyltyr] **nf** fish farming.

piscine [pisin] **nf** swimming pool ▸ **piscine couverte/découverte** indoor/open-air swimming pool.

Pise [piz] **npr** Pisa ▸ **la tour de Pise** the Leaning Tower of Pisa.

pisse [pis] **nf** *tfam* pee, piss.

pisse-froid [pisfrwa] **nm inv** *fam péj* wet blanket.

pissenlit [pisɑ̃li] **nm** dandelion ▸ **manger les pissenlits par la racine** *fig* to be pushing up daisies.

pisser [3] [pise] *fam* ■ **vt** **1.** [suj: personne] **: pisser du sang** to pass blood **2.** [suj: plaie] **: son genou pissait le sang** blood was gushing from his knee ▸ **le moteur commençait à pisser de l'huile** oil started to gush from the engine.
■ **vi** to pee, to piss ▸ **pisser au lit** to wet the bed ▸ **il ne se sent plus pisser** he's too big for his boots.

pissotière [pisɔtjɛr] **nf** *fam* public urinal.

pistache [pistaʃ] ■ **nf** [fruit] pistachio (nut).
■ **adj inv** [couleur] pistachio (green).

piste [pist] **nf** **1.** [trace] trail ▸ **être sur la piste de qqn** to be on sb's track *ou* trail ▸ **suivre/perdre une piste** to follow/to lose a trail ▸ **brouiller les pistes** *fig* to cover one's tracks ▸ **la police cherche une piste** the police are looking for leads
2. [zone aménagée] **: piste d'atterrissage** runway ▸ **en bout de piste** at the end of the runway ▸ **piste de cirque** circus ring ▸ **piste cyclable** (bi)cycle path ▸ **piste de danse** dance floor ▸ **piste de ski** ski run ▸ **entrer en piste** to come into play, to join in
3. [chemin] path, track
4. [d'enregistrement] track ▸ **piste sonore** soundtrack
5. [divertissement] **: jeu de piste** treasure hunt.

pister [3] [piste] **vt** [gibier] to track / [suspect] to tail.

pisteur [pistœr] **nm** ski patrol member.

pistil [pistil] nm pistil.

pistolet [pistɔlɛ] nm 1. [arme] pistol, gun 2. [à peinture] spray gun.

pistolet-mitrailleur [pistɔlɛmitrajœr] (pl **pistolets-mitrailleurs**) nm submachine gun.

piston [pistɔ̃] nm 1. [de moteur] piston 2. MUS [d'instrument] valve 3. *fig* [appui] string-pulling ▸ **avoir du piston** to have friends in the right places.

pistonner [3] [pistɔne] vt to pull strings for ▸ **se faire pistonner** to have strings pulled for one.

pistou [pistu] nm *dish of vegetables served with sauce made from basil.*

pita [pita] nf pitta (bread).

pitance [pitɑ̃s] nf *péj* & *vieilli* sustenance.

pitbull, ***pit-bull*** [pitbul] (pl **pit-bulls**) nm pitbull (terrier).

piteux, ***euse*** [pitø, øz] adj piteous.

pithiviers [pitivje] nm *puff pastry cake filled with almond cream.*

pitié [pitje] nf pity ▸ **avoir pitié de qqn** to have pity on sb, to pity sb ▸ **sans pitié** pitiless, ruthless ▸ **par pitié** for pity's sake.

piton [pitɔ̃] nm 1. [clou] piton 2. [pic] peak.

pitoyable [pitwajabl] adj pitiful.

pitre [pitr] nm clown ▸ **faire le pitre** to fool about.

pitrerie [pitrəri] nf tomfoolery.

pittoresque [pitɔrɛsk] ■ nm : **le pittoresque** [de description] the vividness / [d'histoire] the amusing part.
■ adj 1. [région] picturesque 2. [détail] colourful *UK*, colorful *US*, vivid.

pivert, ***pic-vert*** (pl **pic-verts**) [pivɛr] nm green woodpecker.

pivoine [pivwan] nf peony.

pivot [pivo] nm 1. [de machine, au basket] pivot 2. [de dent] post 3. *fig* [centre] mainspring.

pivotant, ***e*** [pivɔtɑ̃, ɑ̃t] adj [fauteuil] swivel *(avant n).*

pivoter [3] [pivɔte] vi to pivot / [porte] to revolve ▸ **faire pivoter qqch** to swivel sthg around, to pivot sthg.

pixel [piksɛl] nm pixel.

pizza [pidza] nf pizza.

pizzeria [pidzerja] nf pizzeria.

PJ ■ nf (abr de ***police judiciaire***) ≃ CID *UK*, ≃ FBI *US*.
■ (abr écrite de ***pièce jointe***) Encl.

Pl., ***pl.*** abr de ***place***.

PL (abr écrite de ***poids lourd***) HGV.

placage [plakaʒ] nm [de bois] veneer.

placard [plakar] nm 1. [armoire] cupboard ▸ **mettre qqn au placard** *fam fig* to elbow sb out ▸ **mettre qqch au placard** *fam fig* to shelve sthg 2. [affiche] poster, notice ▸ **placard publicitaire** display advertisement 3. TYPO galley (proof).

placarder [3] [plakarde] vt [affiche] to put up, to stick up / [mur] to placard, to stick a notice on.

place [plas] nf 1. [espace] space, room ▸ **prendre de la place** to take up (a lot of) space ▸ **faire place à** [amour, haine] to give way to ▸ **faire place nette** *litt* to tidy up / *fig* to clear up, to make a clean sweep ▸ **la musique tient une grande place dans ma vie** music is very important in *ou* is an important part of my life
2. [emplacement, position] position ▸ **changer qqch de place** to put sthg in a different place, to move sthg ▸ **prendre la place de qqn** to take sb's place ▸ **ne pas tenir *ou* rester en place** to be unable to stay still ▸ **il ne tient pas en place** [il est turbulent] he can't keep still / [il est anxieux] he's nervous / [il voyage beaucoup] he's always on the move ▸ **reprendre sa place** [sa position] to go back to one's place / [son rôle] to go back to where one belongs ▸ **se faire une place au soleil** to make a success of things, to find one's place in the sun ▸ **à la place de qqn** instead of sb, in sb's place ▸ **à ta place** if I were you, in your place
3. [siège] seat ▸ **céder sa place à qqn** to give up one's seat to sb ▸ **prendre place** to take a seat ▸ **place assise** seat ▸ **j'ai trois places de concert** I have three tickets for the concert
4. [rang] place ▸ **avoir la première place** to come first *ou* top
5. [de ville] square
6. [emploi] position, job ▸ **perdre sa place** to lose one' job
7. COMM market ▸ **place financière internationale** money market
8. MIL [de garnison] garrison (town) ▸ **place forte** fortifie town
▸▸ **j'ai rapporté la jupe et j'ai pris un pantalon à place** I returned the skirt and exchanged it for a pair c trousers ▸ **se mettre à la place de qqn** to put o.s. in sb' place *ou* shoes ▸ **la méthode sera mise en place progressivement** the method will be phased in (gradually) ▸ **remettre qqn à sa place** to put sb in his/her place.
◆ ***sur place*** loc adv there, on the spot ▸ **je serai déjà su place** I'll already be there.

placebo [plasebo] nm placebo.

placement [plasmɑ̃] nm 1. [d'argent] investment ▸ **placement offshore** offshore investment 2. [d'employé] placing 3. CINÉ & TV placement ▸ **placement de produits** product placement.

placenta [plasɛ̃ta] nm ANAT placenta.

placer [16] [plase] vt 1. [gén] to put, to place / [invite spectateurs] to seat ▸ **placer sa voix** MUS to pitch one voice ▸ **placer qqn à l'hospice** to put sb in an old people home ▸ **l'ouvreuse va vous placer** the usherette will sho you to your seats ▸ **être bien/mal placé** to have a good/b seat ▸ **être bien/mal placé pour faire qqch** *fig* to be in position/in no position to do sthg ▸ **être haut placé** *fig* be highly placed ▸ **orchestre placé sous la direction de** orchestra conducted by... 2. [mot, anecdote] to put in,

get in ▸ **il essaie toujours de placer quelques boutades** he always tries to slip in a few jokes ▸ **je n'ai pas pu placer un mot** I couldn't get a word in edgeways **3.** [argent] to invest.
◆ ***se placer*** vp **1.** [prendre place - debout] to stand ▸ **placez-vous en cercle** get into a circle / [- assis] to sit (down) ▸ **venez vous placer autour de la table** come and sit at the table **2.** *fig* [dans une situation] to put o.s. ▸ **si l'on se place de son point de vue** if you look at things from his point of view **3.** [se classer] to come, to be ▸ **se placer premier/troisième** to finish first/third.

placide [plasid] adj placid.

placidité [plasidite] nf placidity.

plafond [plafɔ̃] nm **1.** *litt* & *fig* ceiling **2.** [bâtiment] : **faux plafond** false ceiling **3.** ÉCON : **plafond de découvert** overdraft limit ▸ **plafond de prix** price ceiling.

plafonner [3] [plafɔne] ■ vt to put a ceiling in.
■ vi [prix, élève] to peak / [avion] to reach its ceiling.

plafonnier [plafɔnje] nm ceiling light.

plage [plaʒ] nf **1.** [de sable] beach **2.** [ville balnéaire] resort **3.** [d'ombre, de prix] band / *fig* [de temps] slot **4.** [de disque] track **5.** [dans une voiture] : **plage arrière** back shelf.

plagiaire [plaʒjɛr] nmf plagiarist.

plagiat [plaʒja] nm plagiarism.

plagier [9] [plaʒje] vt to plagiarize.

plagiste [plaʒist] nm beach attendant.

plaid [plɛd] nm car rug.

plaider [4] [plede] ■ vt DR to plead.
■ vi DR to plead ▸ **plaider contre qqn** to plead against sb ▸ **plaider pour qqn** DR to plead for sb / [justifier] to plead sb's cause.

plaideur, euse [plɛdœr, øz] nm, f litigant.

plaidoirie [plɛdwari] nf DR speech for the defence *UK* *ou* defense *US* / *fig* plea.

plaidoyer [plɛdwaje] nm = ***plaidoirie***.

plaie [plɛ] nf **1.** *litt* & *fig* wound **2.** *fam* [personne] pest.

plaignais, plaignions ➤ ***plaindre***.

plaignant, e [plɛɲɑ̃, ɑ̃t] ■ adj DR litigant *(avant n)*.
■ nm, f DR plaintiff.

plaindre [80] [plɛ̃dr] vt to pity ▸ **ne pas être à plaindre** to be not to be pitied.
◆ ***se plaindre*** vp to complain ▸ **se plaindre de** [souffrir de] to complain of / [être mécontent de] to complain about.

plaine [plɛn] nf plain.

plain-pied [plɛ̃pje] ◆ ***de plain-pied*** loc adv **1.** [pièce] on one floor ▸ **de plain-pied avec** *litt* & *fig* on a level with **2.** *fig* [directement] straight.

plaint, e [plɛ̃, plɛ̃t] pp ➤ ***plaindre***.

plainte [plɛ̃t] nf **1.** [gémissement] moan, groan / *fig* & *litt* [du vent] moan **2.** [doléance & DR] complaint ▸ **porter plainte** to lodge a complaint ▸ **retirer sa plainte** DR to withdraw one's action *ou* suit ▸ **plainte contre X** ≃ complaint against person or persons unknown.

plaintif, ive [plɛ̃tif, iv] adj plaintive.

plaire [110] [plɛr] vi to be liked ▸ **il me plaît** I like him ▸ **ça te plairait d'aller au cinéma?** would you like to go to the cinema? ▸ **cette idée ne me plaît pas du tout** I'm not at all keen on this idea ▸ **elle ne lit que ce qui lui plaît** she only reads what she feels like (reading) ▸ **il cherche à plaire aux femmes** he tries hard to make himself attractive to women ▸ **s'il vous/te plaît** please ▸ **plaît-il?** I beg your pardon?
◆ ***se plaire*** vp **1.** [s'aimer] to get on well together ▸ **ces deux jeunes gens se plaisent, c'est évident** it's obvious that those two like each other **2.** [prendre plaisir] : **se plaire à faire qqch** to take pleasure in doing sthg ▸ **il se plaît à la contredire** he loves contradicting her ▸ **se plaire avec qqn** to enjoy being with sb ▸ **se plaire à Paris** to enjoy being in Paris.

plaisance [plɛzɑ̃s] ◆ ***de plaisance*** loc adj pleasure *(avant n)* ▸ **navigation de plaisance** sailing ▸ **port de plaisance** marina.

plaisancier, ère [plɛzɑ̃sje, ɛr] nm, f (amateur) sailor.

plaisant, e [plɛzɑ̃, ɑ̃t] adj pleasant.
◆ ***mauvais plaisant*** nm *péj* hoaxer.

plaisanter [3] [plɛzɑ̃te] ■ vi to joke ▸ **plaisanter avec qqch** to joke about sthg ▸ **ne pas plaisanter avec** *ou* **sur qqch** to take sthg seriously ▸ **tu plaisantes?** you must be joking!
■ vt *sout* [personne] to tease.

COMMENT EXPRIMER...

les plaintes

I have a complaint about the telephone you sold me / J'ai une réclamation au sujet du téléphone que vous m'avez vendu
There's a problem with the heating / Il y a un problème avec le chauffage
There must be some mistake / Je crois qu'il y a un malentendu
It seems very expensive for what we've eaten / Ça me paraît très cher pour ce qu'on a mangé
I'm not very happy with the service / Je ne suis pas très content du service
I want my money back / Je veux être remboursé
I'd like to see the manager / Je voudrais voir le directeur
This is just not good enough / Ça ne va pas du tout
I expect something to be done about this / Je compte sur vous pour régler le problème

plaisanterie [plɛzɑ̃tri] nf joke ▸ **c'est une plaisanterie?** *iron* you must be joking! ▸ **c'était une plaisanterie** *fig* it was child's play.

plaisantin [plɛzɑ̃tɛ̃] nm joker.

plaise ➤ ***plaire.***

plaisir [plezir] nm pleasure ▸ **les plaisirs de la chair** pleasures of the flesh ▸ **les plaisirs de la vie** life's pleasures ▸ **avoir du/prendre plaisir à faire qqch** to have/to take pleasure in doing sthg ▸ **faire plaisir à qqn** to please sb ▸ **cela fait plaisir de vous voir en bonne santé** it's a pleasure to see you in good health ▸ **avec plaisir** with pleasure ▸ **j'ai le plaisir de vous annoncer que...** I have the (great) pleasure of announcing that... ▸ **pour le** *ou* **son plaisir** for pleasure ▸ **il joue aux cartes par plaisir, non pas pour l'argent** he doesn't play cards for money, just for the fun of it ▸ **prendre un malin plaisir à faire qqch** to take a malicious pleasure in doing sthg ▸ **se faire un plaisir de faire qqch** to be only too pleased to do sthg ▸ **je me ferai un plaisir de vous renseigner** I'll be delighted *ou* happy to give you all the information ▸ **tout le plaisir est pour moi** the pleasure is all mine, (it's) my pleasure.

plan*[1]*, e [plɑ̃, plan] adj level, flat.

***plan*[2]** [plɑ̃] nm **1.** [dessin - de ville] map / [- de maison] plan ▸ **plan de métro** underground *UK ou* subway *US* map ▸ **plan de vol** flight plan
2. [projet] plan ▸ **faire des plans** to make plans ▸ **avoir son plan** to have something in mind ▸ **un plan d'action** a plan of action ▸ **un plan de carrière** a career strategy
3. [domaine] **: sur tous les plans** in all respects ▸ **sur le plan affectif** emotionally ▸ **sur le plan familial** as far as the family is concerned
4. [surface] **: plan d'eau** lake ▸ **plan de travail** work surface, worktop *UK*
5. GÉOM plane ▸ **plan horizontal/incliné/médian/tangent** level/inclined/median/tangent plane
6. CINÉ take ▸ **gros plan** close-up ▸ **plan général/moyen/rapproché** long/medium/close shot
7. BANQUE **: plan d'épargne** savings plan ▸ **plan d'épargne logement** *savings scheme offering low-interest mortgages* ▸ **plan d'épargne retraite** *former personal pension plan*
8. [sécurité] **: plan vigipirate** security measures to protect against terrorist attacks
9. ÉCON **: plan marketing** marketing plan ▸ **plan d'occupation des sols** *document laying out local land development plans* ▸ **Plan quinquennal** Five-Year Plan ▸ **plan de restructuration** restructuring plan ▸ **plan social** redundancy scheme *ou* plan *UK*.
◆ ***à l'arrière-plan*** loc adv in the background.
◆ ***au premier plan*** loc adv **1.** [dans l'espace] in the foreground
2. [dans un ordre] **: c'est au premier plan de nos préoccupations** it's our chief concern, it's uppermost in our minds.
◆ ***de tout premier plan*** loc adj exceptional ▸ **jouer un rôle de tout premier plan dans** to play a leading *ou* major part in.
◆ ***en plan*** loc adv **: laisser qqn en plan** to leave sb stranded, to abandon sb ▸ **il a tout laissé en plan** he dropped everything ▸ **tous mes projets sont restés en plan** none of my plans came to anything.
◆ ***sur le même plan*** loc adj on the same level.

CULTURE
Plan

The French authorities can use four types of plans to respond to emergencies. The **plan Vigipirate**, decreed when there is risk of a terrorist attack, has several levels. It calls for the deployment of armed forces in public places. The **plan blanc**, used to respond to public health crises, took effect during the heat wave of summer 2003. Hospital beds were requisitioned to deal with the staggering number of illnesses and deaths caused by record temperatures. The **plan rouge** calls for establishment of an evacuation centre in the wake of an emergency with multiple victims (such as an accident). The **plan Orsec**, or **organisation des secours**, is administered by the chief of police and comes into effect during disasters or other widespread emergencies.

planche [plɑ̃ʃ] nf **1.** [en bois] plank ▸ **planche à dessin** drawing board ▸ **planche à neige** snowboard ▸ **planche à repasser** ironing board ▸ **planche de salut** *fig* mainstay ▸ **planche à voile** [planche] sailboard / [sport] windsurfing ▸ **faire la planche** *fig* to float **2.** [d'illustration] plate.
◆ ***planches*** nfpl **1.** *fig* & THÉÂTRE boards ▸ **monter sur les planches** to go on the stage **2.** *fam* [skis] skis.

***plancher*[1]** [plɑ̃ʃe] nm **1.** [de maison, de voiture] floor ▸ **débarrasser le plancher** *fam fig* to clear off **2.** *fig* [limite] floor, lower limit.

***plancher*[2]** [3] [plɑ̃ʃe] vi **1.** *arg scol* to be given a test **2.** *fam fig* [travailler] **: plancher (sur)** to work hard (at).

planchiste [plɑ̃ʃist] nmf windsurfer.

plancton [plɑ̃ktɔ̃] nm plankton.

planer [3] [plane] vi **1.** [avion, oiseau] to glide **2.** [nuage, fumée, brouillard] to float **3.** *fig* [danger] **: planer sur qqn** to hang over sb **4.** *fam fig* [personne] to be out of touch with reality, to have one's head in the clouds ▸ **planer au dessus de qqch** to be above sthg.

planétaire [planetɛr] adj **1.** ASTRON planetary **2.** [mondial] world *(avant n)*.

planétarium [planetarjɔm] nm planetarium.

planète [planɛt] nf planet.

planeur [planœr] nm glider.

planificateur, trice [planifikatœr, tris] ■ adj planning *(avant n)*.
■ nm, f planner.

planification [planifikasjɔ̃] nf ÉCON planning.

planifier [9] [planifje] vt ÉCON to plan.

planisphère [planisfɛr] nm map of the world, planisphere.

planning [planiŋ] nm **1.** [de fabrication] workflow schedule **2.** [agenda personnel] schedule ▸ **planning familial** [contrôle] family planning / [organisme] family planning clinic.

planque [plɑ̃k] **nf** *fam* **1.** [cachette] hideout **2.** *fig* [situation, travail] cushy number.

planquer [3] [plɑ̃ke] **vt** *fam* to hide.
◆ ***se planquer*** **vp** *fam* to hide.

plant [plɑ̃] **nm** **1.** [plante] seedling **2.** [culture] bed, patch.

plantain [plɑ̃tɛ̃] **nm** plantain.

plantaire [plɑ̃tɛr] **adj** plantar.

plantation [plɑ̃tasjɔ̃] **nf** **1.** [exploitation - d'arbres, de coton, de café] plantation / [- de légumes] patch **2.** [action] planting.

plante [plɑ̃t] **nf** **1.** BOT plant ▸ **plantes médicinales** medicinal herbs ▸ **plante verte *ou* d'appartement *ou* d'intérieur** house *ou* pot *UK* plant **2.** ANAT sole.

planté, e [plɑ̃te] **adj** *fam* **1.** [personne] **: rester planté** to be rooted to the spot **2.** [machine] broken-down.

planter [3] [plɑ̃te] ■ **vt** **1.** [arbre, terrain] to plant ▸ **planter qqch de qqch** to plant sthg with sthg **2.** [clou] to hammer in, to drive in / [pieu] to drive in / [couteau, griffes] to stick in **3.** [tente] to pitch **4.** *fam fig* [laisser tomber] to dump ▸ **tout planter là** to drop everything **5.** *fig* [chapeau] to stick / [baiser] to plant ▸ **planter son regard dans celui de qqn** to look sb right in the eyes.
■ **vi** *fam* INFORM to crash.
◆ ***se planter*** **vp** **1.** [se camper] to plant o.s. **2.** *fam* [tomber] to go flying / [en voiture] to have a prang *UK* **3.** *fam* [se tromper] to be wrong.

planteur [plɑ̃tœr, øz] **nm** planter.

planton [plɑ̃tɔ̃] **nm** orderly.

plantureux, euse [plɑ̃tyrø, øz] **adj** **1.** [repas] lavish **2.** [femme] buxom **3.** [terre] fertile.

plaque [plak] **nf** **1.** [de métal, de verre, de verglas] sheet / [de marbre] slab ▸ **plaque chauffante *ou* de cuisson** hotplate ▸ **plaque de cheminée** fire back ▸ **plaque de chocolat** bar of chocolate ▸ **plaque de verglas** icy patch **2.** [gravée] plaque ▸ **plaque d'immatriculation *ou* minéralogique** numberplate *UK*, license plate *US* **3.** [insigne] badge **4.** [sur la peau] patch ▸ **plaques d'eczéma** eczema patches ▸ **des plaques rouges dues au froid** red blotches due to the cold **5.** [dentaire] plaque
▸▸ **être à côté de la plaque** to be wide of the mark.
◆ ***plaque tournante*** **nf** RAIL turntable / *fig* hub ▸ **la plaque tournante du trafic de drogue** the nerve centre of the drug-running industry.

plaqué, e [plake] **adj** **1.** [métal] plated ▸ **plaqué or/argent** gold-/silver-plated **2.** [bois] veneered.
◆ ***plaqué*** **nm** **1.** [métal] **: du plaqué or/argent** gold/silver plate **2.** [bois] veneered wood.

plaquer [3] [plake] **vt** **1.** [métal] to plate **2.** [bois] to veneer **3.** [aplatir] to flatten ▸ **plaquer qqn contre qqch** to pin sb against sthg ▸ **plaquer qqch contre qqch** to stick sthg onto sthg **4.** [rugby] to tackle **5.** MUS [accord] to play **6.** *fam* [travail, personne] to chuck.
◆ ***se plaquer*** **vp : se plaquer contre qqch** to flatten o.s. against sthg ▸ **se plaquer au sol** to lie flat on the ground ▸ **se plaquer les cheveux** to flatten (down) one's hair.

plaquette [plakɛt] **nf** **1.** [de métal] plaque / [de marbre] tablet **2.** [de chocolat] bar / [de beurre] pat **3.** [de comprimés] packet, strip **4.** *(gén pl)* BIOL platelet **5.** [petit livre] slim volume **6.** AUTO **: plaquette de frein** brake pad.

plasma [plasma] **nm** plasma.

plastic [plastik] **nm** plastic explosive.

plasticage [plastikaʒ] **nm** [de coffre] blowing ▸ **un plasticage de la banque** a bomb attack on the bank.

plastifié, e [plastifje] **adj** plastic-coated.

plastifier [9] [plastifje] **vt** to coat with plastic, to plastic-coat.

plastique [plastik] ■ **adj & nm** plastic.
■ **nf** **1.** [en sculpture] art of modelling **2.** [beauté] form **3.** [arts] plastic arts *pl*.

plastiquer [3] [plastike] **vt** to blow up *(with plastic explosives)*.

plastron [plastrɔ̃] **nm** [de chemise] shirt front.

plastronner [3] [plastrɔne] **vi** [parader] to swagger.

plat, e [pla, plat] **adj** **1.** [gén] flat **2.** [eau] still.
◆ ***plat*** **nm** **1.** [partie plate] flat **2.** [récipient] dish ▸ **mettre les petits plats dans les grands** *fig* to go to town **3.** [mets] course ▸ **plat cuisiné** ready-cooked meal *ou* dish ▸ **plat du jour** today's special ▸ **plat préparé** ready meal ▸ **plat de résistance** main course ▸ **en faire tout un plat** *fig* to make a song and dance about it **4.** [plongeon] belly-flop.
◆ ***à plat*** **loc adv** **1.** [horizontalement, dégonflé] flat **2.** *fam* [épuisé] exhausted.

platane [platan] **nm** plane tree.

plateau, x [plato] **nm** **1.** [de cuisine] tray ▸ **plateau de/à fromages** cheeseboard ▸ **plateau de fruits de mer** seafood platter ▸ **il attend que tout lui soit apporté sur un plateau (d'argent)** *fig* he expects everything to be handed to him on a (silver) plate **2.** [de balance] pan **3.** *fig* & GÉOGR plateau ▸ **hauts plateaux** high plateau **4.** THÉÂTRE stage / CINÉ & TV set ▸ **nous avons un beau plateau ce soir** TV we have a wonderful line-up for you in the studio tonight **5.** [de vélo] chain wheel **6.** [mécanique] **: plateau d'embrayage** pressure plate ▸ **plateau de frein** brake backing plate.

plateau-repas [platorəpa] (pl **plateaux-repas**) **nm** tray (of food).

plate-bande [platbɑ̃d] (pl **plates-bandes**) **nf** flowerbed.

platée [plate] **nf** dishful, plateful.

plate-forme [platfɔrm] (pl **plates-formes**) **nf** **1.** [gén] platform ▸ **plate-forme de forage** drilling platform **2.** GÉOGR shelf.

platement [platmɑ̃] **adv** **1.** [sans imagination] dully **2.** [servilement] humbly.

platine [platin] ■ **adj inv** platinum.
■ **nm** [métal] platinum.
■ **nf** [de tourne-disque] deck ▸ **platine laser** compact disc player.

platiné, e [platine] **adj** platinum *(avant n)*.

platitude [platityd] **nf** **1.** [médiocrité] banality **2.** [propos sans intérêt] platitude ▸ **débiter des platitudes** to spout platitudes.

platonique [platɔnik] **adj** **1.** [amour, amitié] platonic **2.** *littéraire* [protestation] ineffective.

plâtras [platra] **nm** [gravats] rubble.

plâtre [platr] **nm** **1.** CONSTR & MÉD plaster ▸ **essuyer les plâtres** *fig* to be the first to suffer **2.** [sculpture] plaster cast **3.** *péj* [fromage] **: c'est du vrai plâtre** it's like sawdust.

plâtrer [3] [platre] **vt** **1.** [mur] to plaster **2.** MÉD to put in plaster.

plâtrier [platrije] ■ **nm** plasterer.
■ **adj m : ouvrier plâtrier** plasterer.

plausible [plozibl] **adj** plausible.

play-back [plɛbak] **nm inv** miming ▸ **chanter en play-back** to mime.

play-boy [plɛbɔj] (pl **play-boys**) **nm** playboy.

plèbe [plɛb] **nf** **1.** *péj* [populace] **: la plèbe** the plebs *pl* **2.** HIST **: la plèbe** the plebeians *pl*.

plébéien**, **enne [plebejɛ̃, ɛn] **adj** plebeian.

plébiscite [plebisit] **nm** plebiscite.

plébisciter [3] [plebisite] **vt** **1.** POLIT to elect by plebiscite **2.** [approuver] to endorse overwhelmingly.

pléiade [plejad] **nf** pleiad.

plein**, **e [plɛ̃, plɛn] **adj** **1.** [rempli, complet] full ▸ **c'est la pleine forme** I am/they are *etc* in top form ▸ **être en pleine forme** to be on top form ▸ **en plein jour** in broad daylight ▸ **en pleine nuit** in the middle of the night ▸ **en plein air** outdoor, open-air ▸ **en plein cœur de la ville** right in the heart of the city ▸ **plein à craquer** *fig* full to bursting ▸ **être plein d'enthousiasme/de bonne volonté** to show great enthusiasm/willingness ▸ **foncer/rouler (à) plein tube** to go/to drive flat out ▸ **une pièce pleine de livres** a room full of books **2.** [non creux] solid ▸ **en bois plein** solid-wood **3.** [femelle] pregnant **4.** *fam* [saoul] plastered ▸ **être plein (comme) une barrique** *ou* **une outre** *fam* to be (well) tanked up.
◆ ***plein*** ■ **adv** *fam* **: avoir de l'argent plein les poches** *fig* to have loads of money ▸ **il a de l'encre plein les doigts** he has ink all over his fingers ▸ **j'en ai plein le dos** *fam* I've had it up to here ▸ **plein de** lots of ▸ **il y avait plein de gens dans la rue** there were crowds *ou* masses of people in the street ▸ **en plein dans/sur qqch** right in/on sthg ▸ **tomber en plein dans un piège** to fall right into a trap.
■ **nm** [de réservoir] full tank ▸ **le plein, s'il vous plaît** fill her up, please ▸ **faire le plein** to fill up
▸▸ **battre son plein** to be at its height.

plein-air [plɛnɛr] **nm inv** SCOL games.
◆ ***de plein-air**, **en plein-air*** **loc adj** open-air *(modif)*, outdoor *(modif)*.

pleinement [plɛnmɑ̃] **adv** fully, totally.

plein-temps [plɛ̃tɑ̃] (pl **pleins-temps**) **nm** full-time job.

plénier**, **ère [plenje, ɛr] **adj** plenary.

plénipotentiaire [plenipɔtɑ̃sjɛr] **nm & adj** plenipotentiary.

plénitude [plenityd] **nf** fullness.

pléonasme [pleɔnasm] **nm** pleonasm.

pléthorique [pletɔrik] **adj** *sout* [classe] overfull.

pleurer [5] [plœre] ■ **vi** **1.** [larmoyer] to cry ▸ **pleurer de joie** to weep for joy, to cry with joy **2.** *péj* [se plaindre] to whinge *UK* **3.** [réclamer] **: pleurer après** to cry for **4.** [se lamenter] **: pleurer sur** to lament.
■ **vt** to mourn.

pleurésie [plœrezi] **nf** pleurisy.

pleureur**, **euse [plœrœr, øz] ■ **adj** whining.
■ **nm, f** whinger *UK*.
◆ ***pleureuse*** **nf** professional mourner.

pleurnicher [3] [plœrniʃe] **vi** to whine, to whinge *UK*.

pleurnicheur**, **euse [plœrniʃœr, øz] ■ **adj** whining, whingeing *UK*.
■ **nm, f** whinger *UK*.

pleurs [plœr] **nmpl : être en pleurs** to be in tears.

pleut ➤ ***pleuvoir***.

pleutre [pløtr] *littéraire* ■ **nm** coward.
■ **adj** cowardly.

pleuvoir [68] [pløvwar] **v impers** *litt* & *fig* to rain ▸ **il pleut** it is raining.

Plexiglas® [plɛksiglas] **nm** Plexiglass®.

plexus [plɛksys] **nm** plexus ▸ **plexus solaire** solar plexus.

pli [pli] **nm** **1.** [de tissu] pleat / [de pantalon] crease ▸ **faux pli** crease **2.** [forme] shape ▸ **prendre le pli (de faire qqch)** *fig* to get into the habit (of doing sthg) **3.** [du front] line / [du cou] fold **4.** [lettre] letter / [enveloppe] envelope ▸ **sous pli séparé** under separate cover **5.** [aux cartes] trick **6.** GÉOL fold.

pliable [plijabl] **adj** pliable.

pliant**, **e [plijɑ̃, ɑ̃t] **adj** folding *(avant n)*.
◆ ***pliant*** **nm** folding chair.

plier [10] [plije] ■ **vt** **1.** [papier, tissu] to fold **2.** [vêtement, vélo] to fold (up) **3.** [branche, bras] to bend **4.** *fig* [personne] **: plier qqn à sa volonté** to bend sb to one's will ▸ **plier qqn à la discipline** to impose discipline on sb.
■ **vi** **1.** [se courber] to bend **2.** *fig* [céder] to bow.
◆ ***se plier*** **vp** **1.** [être pliable] to fold (up) **2.** *fig* [se soumettre] **: se plier à qqch** to bow to sthg.

plinthe [plɛ̃t] **nf** plinth.

plissé**, **e [plise] **adj** **1.** [jupe] pleated **2.** [peau] wrinkled.
◆ ***plissé*** **nm** pleats *pl*, pleating.

plissement [plismɑ̃] **nm** **1.** [de front] creasing / [d'yeux] screwing up **2.** GÉOL fold.

plisser [3] [plise] ■ **vt** **1.** COUT to pleat **2.** [front] to crease / [lèvres] to pucker / [yeux] to screw up.
■ **vi** [étoffe] to crease.
◆ ***se plisser*** **vp** **1.** [étoffe] to crease **2.** [front] to crease.

pliure [plijyr] **nf** **1.** [de tissu, de papier] fold **2.** [d'articulation] crook.

plomb [plɔ̃] **nm 1.** [métal, de vitrail] lead **2.** [de chasse] shot ▸ **avoir du plomb dans l'aile** *fig* to be in a bad way **3.** ÉLECTR fuse ▸ **les plombs ont sauté** a fuse has blown *ou* gone **4.** [de pêche] sinker.

plombage [plɔ̃baʒ] **nm 1.** [de dent] filling **2.** [de ligne] weighting (with lead).

plombé, e [plɔ̃be] **adj 1.** [dent] filled **2.** [ligne] weighted (with lead) **3.** [teinte] leaden.

plomber [3] [plɔ̃be] **vt 1.** [ligne] to weight (with lead) **2.** [dent] to fill.
◆ ***se plomber*** **vp** [ciel] to become leaden.

plomberie [plɔ̃bri] **nf** plumbing.

plombier [plɔ̃bje] **nm** plumber.

plombières [plɔ̃bjɛr] **nf** tutti-frutti ice cream.

plonge [plɔ̃ʒ] **nf** *fam* dishwashing ▸ **faire la plonge** to wash dishes.

plongeant, e [plɔ̃ʒɑ̃, ɑ̃t] **adj 1.** [vue] from above **2.** [décolleté] plunging.

plongée [plɔ̃ʒe] **nf 1.** [immersion] diving ▸ **plongée sous-marine** scuba diving **2.** CINÉ & PHOTO high-angle shot.

plongeoir [plɔ̃ʒwar] **nm** diving board.

plongeon [plɔ̃ʒɔ̃] **nm** [dans l'eau, au football] dive ▸ **faire un plongeon** to plunge ▸ **faire le plongeon** *fig* to hit rock bottom.

plonger [17] [plɔ̃ʒe] ■ **vt 1.** [immerger, enfoncer] to plunge ▸ **plonger la tête sous l'eau** to put one's head under the water **2.** *fig* [précipiter] **: plonger qqn dans qqch** to throw sb into sthg ▸ **plonger une pièce dans l'obscurité** to plunge a room into darkness ▸ **il est plongé dans ses dossiers** he's engrossed in his files ▸ **plongé dans un sommeil profond, il ne nous a pas entendus** as he was sound asleep, he didn't hear us.
■ **vi 1.** [dans l'eau, gardien de but] to dive ▸ **il plongea du haut du rocher** he dived off the rock **2.** [avion, oiseau] **: plonger sur** to dive (down) onto **3.** *fig* [se lancer] to dive *ou* jump in ▸ **elle plongea dans la dépression** she plunged into depression **4.** *fam* [échouer] to decline, to fall off ▸ **c'est ce qui l'a fait plonger** that's what caused his demise.
◆ ***se plonger*** **vp 1.** [s'immerger] to submerge **2.** *fig* [s'absorber] **: se plonger dans qqch** to immerse o.s. in sthg.

plongeur, euse [plɔ̃ʒœr, øz] **nm, f 1.** [dans l'eau] diver **2.** [dans restaurant] dishwasher.

plot [plo] **nm** ÉLECTR contact.

plouc [pluk] **nmf** *fam péj* country bumpkin.

plouf [pluf] **interj** splash!

ployer [13] [plwaje] **vt** & **vi** *litt* & *fig* to bend.

plu [ply] ■ **pp inv** ➤ ***plaire***.
■ **pp inv** ➤ ***pleuvoir***.

plug-and-play [plœgɛ̃dple] **m** INFORM plug-and-play.

pluie [plɥi] **nf 1.** [averse] rain *(U)* ▸ **sous la pluie** in the rain ▸ **une pluie battante** driving rain ▸ **une pluie fine** drizzle ▸ **des pluies diluviennes** torrential rain ▸ **il fait la pluie et le beau temps** *fig* what he says goes ▸ **ne pas être né de la dernière pluie** *fig* not to be born yesterday **2.** *fig* [grande quantité] **: une pluie de** a shower of.

plumage [plymaʒ] **nm** plumage.

plumard [plymar] **nm** *fam* bed, sack *US*.

plume [plym] ■ **nf 1.** [d'oiseau] feather ▸ **y laisser/perdre des plumes** *fig* to come off badly **2.** [pour écrire - d'oiseau] quill pen / [- de stylo] nib ▸ **un homme de plume** *fig* a man of letters.
■ **nm** *fam* [plumard] bed, sack *US*.

plumeau, x [plymo] **nm** feather duster.

plumer [3] [plyme] **vt 1.** [volaille] to pluck **2.** *fam fig* & *péj* [personne] to fleece.

plumier [plymje] **nm** pencil box.

plupart [plypar] **nf : la plupart de** most of, the majority of ▸ **la plupart du temps** most of the time, mostly ▸ **pour la plupart** mostly, for the most part.

pluralisme [plyralism] **nm** pluralism.

pluralité [plyralite] **nf** plurality.

pluridimensionnel, elle [plyridimɑ̃sjɔnɛl] **adj** multidimensional.

pluridisciplinaire [plyridisipliner] **adj** multidisciplinary.

pluriel, elle [plyrjɛl] **adj 1.** GRAMM plural **2.** [société] pluralist.
◆ ***pluriel*** **nm** plural ▸ **au pluriel** in the plural.

plus [ply(s)] ■ **adv 1.** [quantité] more ▸ **je ne peux vous en dire plus** I can't tell you anything more ▸ **il a plus de travail cette année** he has more work this year ▸ **il en veut plus** he wants more (of it/them) ▸ **beaucoup plus de** *(suivi d'un nom au singulier)* a lot more, much more / *(suivi d'un nom au pluriel)* a lot more, many more ▸ **un peu plus de** *(suivi d'un nom au singulier)* a little more / *(suivi d'un nom au pluriel)* a few more ▸ **il y a (un peu) plus de 15 ans** (a little) more than 15 years ago ▸ **plus j'y pense, plus je me dis que...** the more I think about it, the more I'm sure...
2. [comparaison] more ▸ **c'est plus court par là** it's shorter that way ▸ **viens plus souvent** come more often ▸ **c'est un peu plus loin** it's a (little) bit further ▸ **plus jeune (que)** younger (than) ▸ **c'est plus simple qu'on ne le croit** it's simpler than you think ▸ **plus tôt** earlier ▸ **plus tard** later
3. [superlatif] **: le plus** the most ▸ **c'est lui qui travaille le plus** he's the hardest worker, he's the one who works (the) hardest ▸ **un de ses tableaux les plus connus** one of his best-known paintings ▸ **le plus souvent** the most often ▸ **le plus loin** the furthest ▸ **le plus souvent possible** as often as possible ▸ **le plus vite possible** as quickly as possible
4. [négation] no more ▸ **plus un mot!** not another word! ▸ **ne... plus** no longer, no more ▸ **il n'a plus d'amis** he no longer has any friends, he has no friends any more ▸ **il ne vient plus me voir** he doesn't come to see me any more, he no longer comes to see me ▸ **je n'y vais plus du tout** I don't go there any more.
■ **nm 1.** [signe] plus (sign)
2. *fig* [atout] plus ▸ **la connaissance de l'anglais est toujours un plus** knowledge of English is always a plus.
■ **prép** plus ▸ **trois plus trois font six** three plus three is six, three and three are six ▸ **le transport, plus le**

logement, plus la nourriture, ça revient cher travel, plus *ou* and accommodation, plus *ou* then food, (all) work out quite expensive.
◆ ***au plus*** loc adv at the most ▸ **ça coûtera au plus 30 euros** it'll cost a maximum of 30 euros *ou* 30 euros at most ▸ **tout au plus** at the very most ▸ **c'est une mauvaise grippe, tout au plus** it's a bad case of flu, at the most.
◆ ***de plus*** loc adv **1.** [en supplément, en trop] more ▸ **elle a cinq ans de plus que moi** she's five years older than me **2.** [en outre] furthermore, what's more ▸ **de plus, il m'a menti** what's more, he lied to me.
◆ ***de plus en plus*** loc adv more and more ▸ **de plus en plus souvent** more and more often ▸ **les prix augmentent de plus en plus** prices are increasing all the time.
◆ ***de plus en plus de*** loc prép more and more ▸ **il y a de plus en plus de demande pour ce produit** demand for this product is increasing, there is more and more demand for this product.
◆ ***en plus*** loc adv **1.** [en supplément] extra ▸ **les boissons sont en plus** drinks are extra, you pay extra for the drinks **2.** [d'ailleurs] moreover, what's more ▸ **elle a une excellente technique et en plus, elle a de la force** her technique's first-class and she's got strength too.
◆ ***en plus de*** loc prép in addition to ▸ **en plus du squash, elle fait du tennis** besides (playing) squash, she plays tennis.
◆ ***ni plus ni moins*** loc adv no more no less ▸ **je te donne une livre, ni plus ni moins** I'll give you one pound, no more no less.
◆ ***on ne peut plus*** loc adv **: il est on ne peut plus bête** he's as stupid as can be.
◆ ***plus ou moins*** loc adv more or less ▸ **c'est plus ou moins cher, selon les endroits** prices vary according to where you are.
◆ ***sans plus*** loc adv **: elle est gentille, sans plus** she's nice, but no more than that.

plusieurs [plyzjœr] **adj indéf pl** & **pron indéf pl** several.

plus-que-parfait [plyskəparfɛ] **nm** GRAMM pluperfect.

plus-value [plyvaly] (pl **plus-values**) **nf 1.** [d'investissement] appreciation **2.** [excédent] surplus **3.** [bénéfice] profit / [à la revente] capital gain.

plutonium [plytɔnjɔm] **nm** plutonium.

plutôt [plyto] **adv** rather ▸ **plutôt que de faire qqch** instead of doing sthg, rather than doing *ou* do sthg.

pluvial, e, aux [plyvjal, o] **adj : eau pluviale** rainwater.

pluvieux, euse [plyvjø, øz] **adj** rainy.

pluviométrie [plyvjɔmetri] **nf** rainfall measurement.

pluviosité [plyvjozite] **nf** rainfall.

PLV (abr de ***publicité sur le lieu de vente***) f point-of-sale promotion, point-of-purchase promotion.

p.m. (abr écrite de ***pour mémoire***) p.m.

PM ■ **nf 1.** (abr de ***préparation militaire***) *training before military service* **2.** (abr de ***police militaire***) MP.
■ **nm** abr écrite de ***petit modèle***.

PMA ■ **nf** (abr de ***procréation médicalement assistée***) assisted reproduction.
■ **nmpl** (abr de ***pays les moins avancés***) LDCs *(less-developed countries)*.

PmaC (abr de ***propension moyenne à consommer***) ÉCON APC *(average propensity to consume)*.

PmaE (abr de ***propension moyenne à économiser***) ÉCON & ÉCON APS *(average propensity to save)*.

PMD (abr de ***Pays les Moins Développés***) m LLDC *(least-developed country)*.

PME (abr de ***petite et moyenne entreprise***) **nf** SME / [société] small business.

PMI **nf 1.** (abr de ***petite et moyenne industrie***) small industrial firm **2.** (abr de ***protection maternelle et infantile***) *social service concerned with child welfare*.

PMU (abr de ***Pari mutuel urbain***) **nm** *system for betting on horses*.

PNB (abr de ***produit national brut***) **nm** GNP.

pneu, x [pnø] **nm 1.** [de véhicule] tyre *UK*, tire *US* ▸ **pneu avant** front tyre *UK ou* tire *US* ▸ **pneu arrière** rear tyre *UK ou* tire *US* ▸ **pneu clouté** studded tyre *UK ou* tire *US* ▸ **pneu-neige** winter tyre *UK ou* tire *US* **2.** *vieilli* [message] *letter sent by network of pneumatic tubes*.

pneumatique [pnømatik] ■ **nf** PHYS pneumatics *(U)*.
■ **nm** *vieilli* **1.** [de véhicule] tyre *UK*, tire *US* **2.** [message] *letter sent by network of pneumatic tubes*.
■ **adj 1.** [fonctionnant à l'air] pneumatic **2.** [gonflé à l'air] inflatable.

pneumonie [pnømɔni] **nf** pneumonia.

PNUD, Pnud [pnyd] (abr de ***Programme des Nations unies pour le développement***) **nm** UNDP.

PNUE, Pnue [pny] (abr de ***Programme des Nations unies pour l'environnement***) **nm** UNEP.

p.o. abr de ***par ordre***.

PO (abr écrite de ***petites ondes***) MW.

poche [pɔʃ] **nf 1.** [de vêtement, de sac, d'air] pocket ▸ **de poche** pocket *(avant n)* ▸ **poche intérieure** inside (breast) pocket ▸ **poche revolver** back *ou* hip pocket ▸ **poche d'eau/de gaz** pocket of water/gas ▸ **c'est dans la poche** *fig* it's in the bag ▸ **faire les poches de qqn** *fig* to go through sb's pockets ▸ **il a mis tout le monde dans sa poche** he twisted everyone round his little finger, he took everyone in ▸ **s'en mettre plein *ou* se remplir les poches** *fig* to make a packet **2.** [sac, sous les yeux] bag ▸ **avoir des poches sous les yeux** to have bags under one's eyes ▸ **faire des poches** [vêtement] to bag **3.** MÉD sac ▸ **poche des eaux** (sac of) waters **4.** MIL **: poche de résistance** pocket of resistance.

poché, e [pɔʃe] **adj 1.** [œuf] poached **2.** [meurtri] **: avoir un œil poché** to have a black eye.

pocher [3] [pɔʃe] **vt 1.** CULIN to poach **2.** [blesser] **: pocher l'œil à qqn** to give sb a black eye.

pochette [pɔʃɛt] **nf 1.** [enveloppe] envelope / [d'allumettes] book / [de photos] packet **2.** [de disque] sleeve, jacket *US* **3.** [mouchoir] (pocket) handkerchief.

pochette-surprise [pɔʃɛtsyrpriz] (pl **pochettes-surprises**) **nf** lucky bag.

pochoir [pɔʃwar] **nm** stencil.

podium [pɔdjɔm] **nm** podium.

podologie [pɔdɔlɔʒi] **nf** chiropody, podiatry *US*.

podologue [pɔdɔlɔg] **nmf** chiropodist, podiatrist *US*.

poêle [pwal] ■ **nf** pan ▸ **poêle à frire** frying pan.
■ **nm** stove.

poêlée [pwale] **nf** panful.

poêlon [pwalɔ̃] **nm** casserole.

poème [pɔɛm] **nm** poem.

poésie [pɔezi] **nf 1.** [genre, émotion] poetry **2.** [pièce écrite] poem.

poète [pɔɛt] ■ **adj** poetic.
■ **nm 1.** [écrivain] poet **2.** *fig & hum* [rêveur] dreamer.

poétique [pɔetik] **adj** poetic.

poétiquement [pɔetikmɑ̃] **adv** poetically.

ognon [pɔɲɔ̃] **nm** *tfam* dosh *UK*, dough.

ogrom(e) [pɔgrɔm] **nm** pogrom.

oids [pwa] **nm 1.** [gén] weight ▸ **poids à vide** unladen weight, tare ▸ **quel poids fait-il?** how heavy is it/he? ▸ **perdre/prendre du poids** to lose/gain weight ▸ **vendre au poids** to sell by weight ▸ **avoir du poids** *fig* to carry a lot of weight ▸ **son avis a du poids auprès du reste du groupe** her opinion carries weight with the rest of the group ▸ **donner du poids à** *fig* to lend weight to ▸ **écrasé sous le poids des responsabilités** weighed down by responsibilities ▸ **poids léger** lightweight ▸ **poids lourd** [boxe] heavyweight / [camion] heavy goods vehicle *UK* ▸ **poids mort** [produit, entreprise & COMM] dead weight ▸ **poids plume** [boxe] featherweight ▸ **de poids** [argument] weighty ▸ **un homme de poids** an influential man ▸ **il ne fait pas le poids** *fig* he's not up to it ▸ **j'ai peur de ne pas faire le poids** I'm afraid of being out of my depth
2. SPORT [lancer] shot ▸ **poids et haltères** weightlifting.

oignant, e [pwaɲɑ̃, ɑ̃t] **adj** poignant.

oignard [pwaɲar] **nm** dagger.

oignarder [3] [pwaɲarde] **vt** to stab.

oigne [pwaɲ] **nf** grip / *fig* authority ▸ **avoir de la poigne** to have a strong grip / *fig* to have authority.

oignée [pwaɲe] **nf 1.** [quantité, petit nombre] handful **2.** [manche] handle.
◆ ***poignée de main*** **nf** handshake.

oignet [pwaɲɛ] **nm 1.** ANAT wrist **2.** [de vêtement] cuff.

oil [pwal] **nm 1.** [du corps] hair ▸ **il n'a plus un poil sur e caillou** *fam* he's bald as a coot *UK ou* an egg ▸ **à poil** *fam* [tout nu] starkers *UK* ▸ **se mettre à poil** to strip (off)
. [d'animal] hair, coat ▸ **chien à poil ras/long** smooth-aired/long-haired dog ▸ **en poils de sanglier** made of ristle ▸ **de tout poil** *fig* of all kinds ▸ **voleurs et escrocs le tout poil** all manner of thieves and crooks
. [de pinceau] bristle / [de tapis] strand
. *fam* [peu] **: il s'en est fallu d'un poil que je réussisse** came within a hair's breadth of succeeding
▸▸ **avoir un poil dans la main** *fam* to be bone-idle ▸ **être de bon/mauvais poil** *fam fig* to be in a good/bad mood ▸ **reprendre du poil de la bête** *fig* to regain strength ▸ **tu peux venir samedi, au poil!** you can come on Saturday, great!

poil-de-carotte [pwaldəkarɔt] **adj inv** *fam* [personne] red-headed / [cheveux] carroty.

poiler [3] [pwale] ◆ ***se poiler*** **vp** *fam* to kill o.s. (laughing).

poilu, e [pwaly] **adj** hairy.
◆ ***poilu*** **nm** *fam* French First World War soldier.

poinçon [pwɛ̃sɔ̃] **nm 1.** [outil] awl **2.** [marque] hallmark.

poinçonner [3] [pwɛ̃sɔne] **vt 1.** [bijou] to hallmark **2.** [billet, tôle] to punch.

poinçonneuse [pwɛ̃sɔnøz] **nf** punch.

poindre [82] [pwɛ̃dr] **vi** *littéraire* **1.** [jour] to break **2.** [plante] to come up **3.** *fig* [sentiment] to break through.

poing [pwɛ̃] **nm** fist ▸ **dormir à poings fermés** *fig* to sleep like a log.

point [pwɛ̃] ■ **nm 1.** COUT [tricot] stitch ▸ **faire un point à** to put a stitch *ou* a few stitches in ▸ **points de suture** MÉD stitches
2. [de ponctuation] **: point (final)** full stop *UK*, period *US* ▸ **point d'interrogation/d'exclamation** question/exclamation mark ▸ **points de suspension** suspension points ▸ **mettre les points sur les i** *fig* to get things straight ▸ **il a fait une bêtise, point à la ligne!** *fig* he did something stupid, let's leave it at that!
3. [petite tache] dot ▸ **point noir** [sur la peau] blackhead / *fig* [problème] problem
4. [endroit] spot, point / *fig* point ▸ **point d'appui** [support] something to lean on ▸ **point chaud** POLIT key issue / [zone dangereuse] trouble spot, hot spot ▸ **j'ai un point de chute à Milan** I have somewhere to stay in Milan ▸ **point culminant** [en montagne] summit / *fig* climax ▸ **les investissements sont à leur point culminant** investment has reached a peak ▸ **point d'eau** water supply point ▸ **point de mire** *fig* focal point ▸ **point névralgique** *fig* sensitive spot ▸ **point de ralliement** rallying point ▸ **point de rencontre** meeting point ▸ **point de repère** [temporel] reference point / [spatial] landmark ▸ **point de vente** point of sale, sale outlet ▸ **point de vue** [panorama] viewpoint / *fig* [opinion, aspect] point of view ▸ **avoir un point commun avec qqn** to have something in common with sb
5. [degré] point ▸ **au point que, à tel point que** to such an extent that ▸ **les choses en étaient arrivées à un tel point que...** things had reached such a pitch that... ▸ **je ne pensais pas que cela le vexerait à ce point** I didn't think it would make him so cross ▸ **être... au point de faire qqch** to be so... as to do sthg ▸ **il n'est pas stupide au point de le leur répéter** he's not so stupid as to tell them ▸ **je le respecte au plus haut point** I have the utmost respect for him
6. *fig* [position] position ▸ **faire le point** to take stock (of the situation) ▸ **et maintenant, le point sur la circulation** and now, the latest traffic news
7. [réglage] **: mettre au point** [machine] to adjust / [idée, projet] to finalize ▸ **ton revers n'est pas encore au point** your backhand isn't good enough *ou* up to scratch yet ▸ **à point** [cuisson] just right ▸ **à point (nommé)** just in time

8. [question, détail] point, detail ▸ **point faible** weak point
9. [score] point ▸ **il me manquait 12 points pour avoir l'examen** I was 12 marks short of passing the exam ▸ **marquer un point** *fig* & SPORT to score a point
10. [douleur] pain ▸ **point de côté** stitch
11. [début] **: être sur le point de faire qqch** to be on the point of doing sthg, to be about to do sthg ▸ **j'étais sur le point de partir** I was about to *ou* going to leave ▸ **au point du jour** *sout* at daybreak
12. ÉCON **: point de (vente au) détail** retail outlet
13. AUTO **: au point mort** in neutral
14. GÉOGR **: points cardinaux** points of the compass.
■ **adv** *vieilli* **: ne point** not (at all) ▸ **ne vous en faites point** don't worry.

pointage [pwɛ̃taʒ] **nm 1.** [au travail - d'entrée] clocking in / [- de sortie] clocking out **2.** [d'arme] aiming.

pointe [pwɛ̃t] **nf 1.** [extrémité] point / [de nez] tip ▸ **se hausser sur la pointe des pieds** to stand on tiptoe ▸ **en pointe** pointed ▸ **tailler en pointe** to taper ▸ **se terminer en pointe** to taper ▸ **pointe d'asperge** asparagus tip **2.** [clou] tack **3.** [sommet] peak, summit ▸ **à la pointe de** *fig* at the peak of ▸ **à la pointe de la technique** at the forefront *ou* cutting edge of technology **4.** [accélération] **: faire** *ou* **pousser une pointe (jusqu'à)** to put on a spurt (and reach) **5.** *fig* [trait d'esprit] witticism **6.** *fig* [petite quantité] **: une pointe de** a touch of.
◆ ***pointes*** **nfpl** [danse] points ▸ **faire des** *ou* **les pointes** to dance on one's points.
◆ ***de pointe*** **loc adj 1.** [vitesse] maximum, top **2.** [industrie, secteur] leading / [technique] latest.

pointer [3] [pwɛ̃te] ■ **vt 1.** [cocher] to tick (off) **2.** [employés - à l'entrée] to check in / [- à la sortie] to check out **3.** [diriger] **: pointer qqch vers** to point sthg towards *ou* toward *US* ▸ **pointer qqch sur** to point sthg at.
■ **vi 1.** [à l'usine - à l'entrée] to clock in / [- à la sortie] to clock out **2.** [à la pétanque] to get as close to the jack as possible **3.** [être en pointe] to stick up **4.** [jour] to break **5.** *fig* [sentiment] to show through.
◆ ***se pointer*** **vp** *fam* to turn up.

pointillé [pwɛ̃tije] **nm 1.** [ligne] dotted line ▸ **en pointillé** [ligne] dotted / *fig* [par sous-entendus] obliquely **2.** [perforations] perforations *pl*.

pointilleux, euse [pwɛ̃tijø, øz] **adj : pointilleux (sur)** particular (about).

pointu, e [pwɛ̃ty] **adj 1.** [objet] pointed **2.** [voix, ton] sharp **3.** [étude, formation] specialized.

pointure [pwɛ̃tyr] **nf** (shoe) size.

point-virgule [pwɛ̃virgyl] (pl **points-virgules**) **nm** semi-colon.

poire [pwar] ■ **nf 1.** [fruit] pear ▸ **poire Belle-Hélène** pear *ou* poire Belle-Hélène ▸ **couper la poire en deux** *fig* to compromise **2.** MÉD **: poire à injections** syringe **3.** *fam* [visage] face **4.** *fam* [naïf] dope.
■ **adj** *fam* **: être poire** to be a sucker *ou* a mug *UK*.

poireau, x [pwaro] **nm** leek ▸ **poireaux vinaigrette** leeks with vinaigrette dressing.

poireauter, poiroter [3] [pwarote] **vi** *fam* to hang around.

poirier [pwarje] **nm** pear tree ▸ **faire le poirier** *fig* to do a headstand.

poiroter = ***poireauter***.

pois [pwa] **nm 1.** BOT pea ▸ **pois chiche** chickpea ▸ **petits pois** garden peas, petits pois ▸ **pois de senteur** sweet pea **2.** *fig* [motif] dot, spot ▸ **à pois** spotted, polka-dot.

poison [pwazɔ̃] ■ **nm** [substance] poison.
■ **nmf** *fam fig* [personne] drag, pain / [enfant] brat.

poisse [pwas] **nf** *fam* bad luck ▸ **porter la poisse** to be bad luck.

poisseux, euse [pwasø, øz] **adj** sticky.

poisson [pwasɔ̃] **nm** fish ▸ **poisson d'avril** [farce] April fool / [en papier] *paper fish pinned to someone's back as a prank on April Fools' Day* ▸ **poisson-chat** catfish ▸ **poisson rouge** goldfish ▸ **noyer le poisson** *fig* to confuse the issue.
◆ ***Poissons*** **nmpl** ASTROL Pisces *sg* ▸ **être Poissons** to be (a) Pisces.

poissonnerie [pwasɔnri] **nf 1.** [boutique] fish shop, fishmonger's (shop) *UK* **2.** [métier] fish trade.

poissonneux, euse [pwasɔnø, øz] **adj** full of fish.

poissonnier, ère [pwasɔnje, ɛr] **nm, f** fishmonger *UK*.

poitevin, e [pwatvɛ̃, in] **adj** [de Poitiers] of/from Poitiers / [du Poitou] of/from Poitou.
◆ ***Poitevin, e*** **nm, f** [de Poitiers] person from Poitiers / [du Poitou] person from Poitou.

poitrail [pwatraj] **nm** breast, chest.

poitrinaire [pwatrinɛr] **nmf & adj** consumptive.

poitrine [pwatrin] **nf 1.** [thorax] chest / [de femme] chest, bust **2.** [viande] breast.

poivre [pwavr] **nm** pepper ▸ **poivre blanc** white pepper ▸ **poivre gris, poivre noir** black pepper ▸ **poivre et sel** *fig* pepper-and-salt.

poivré, e [pwavre] **adj 1.** CULIN peppery **2.** [parfum] peppery, spicy **3.** [chanson, histoire] spicy, racy.

poivrer [3] [pwavre] **vt** to put pepper on.
◆ ***se poivrer*** **vp** *fam* to get plastered.

poivrier [pwavrije] **nm** pepper pot *UK*, pepperbox *US*.

poivrière [pwavrijɛr] **nf** = ***poivrier***.

poivron [pwavrɔ̃] **nm** pepper, capsicum ▸ **poivron rouge/vert** red/green pepper.

poivrot, e [pwavro, ɔt] **nm, f** *fam* boozer.

poix [pwa] **nf** pitch.

poker [pɔkɛr] **nm** poker.

polaire [pɔlɛr] ■ **adj** polar.
■ **nf** [textile] (polar) fleece.

polar [pɔlar] **nm** *fam* thriller, whodunnit.

polariser [3] [pɔlarize] **vt 1.** TECHNOL to polarize **2.** *fig* [attention] to focus.
◆ ***se polariser*** **vp : se polariser sur** to be centred *UK* *ou* centered *US ou* focussed on.

Polaroïd® [pɔlarɔid] **nm** Polaroid®.

older [pɔldɛr] **nm** polder.

ôle [pol] **nm** pole ▸ **pôle Nord/Sud** North/South Pole.

olémique [pɔlemik] ■ **nf** controversy.
■ **adj** [style, ton] polemical.

olémiquer [3] [pɔlemike] **vi** to engage in controversy.

olenta [pɔlɛnta] **nf** polenta.

ole position [polpozisjɔ̃] (pl **pole positions**) **nf** SPORT pole position.

oli, e [pɔli] **adj 1.** [personne] polite **2.** [surface] polished.
◆ ***poli*** **nm** polish.

olice [pɔlis] **nf 1.** [force de l'ordre] police ▸ **être de** *ou* **dans la police** to be in the police ▸ **police judiciaire** *plain-clothes police force responsible for criminal investigation and arrests,* ≃ CID *UK,* ≃ FBI *US* ▸ **police secours** *emergency service provided by the police* ▸ **police secrète** secret police **2.** [contrat] policy ▸ **police d'assurance** insurance policy **3.** TYPO **: police (de caractères)** font.

olicé, e [pɔlise] **adj** *littéraire* civilized.

olichinelle [pɔliʃinɛl] **nm 1.** [personnage] Punch ▸ **secret de polichinelle** *fig* open secret **2.** *fam fig* [guignol] buffoon.

olicier, ère [pɔlisje, ɛr] **adj 1.** [de la police] police *(avant n)* **2.** [film, roman] detective *(avant n).*
◆ ***policier*** **nm** police officer.

oliclinique [pɔliklinik] **nf** [partie d'hôpital] ≃ outpatients department.

oliment [pɔlimɑ̃] **adv** politely.

olio [pɔljo] **nf** polio.

oliomyélite [pɔljɔmjelit] **nf** poliomyelitis.

olir [32] [pɔlir] **vt** to polish.

olissage [pɔlisaʒ] **nm** polishing.

olisson, onne [pɔlisɔ̃, ɔn] ■ **adj 1.** [chanson, propos] lewd, suggestive **2.** [enfant] naughty.
■ **nm, f** [enfant] naughty child.

olitesse [pɔlitɛs] **nf 1.** [courtoisie] politeness **2.** [action] polite action ▸ **se faire des politesses** *iron* to exchange favours *UK ou* favors *US.*

oliticard, e [pɔlitikar, ard] *péj* ■ **adj** politicking.
■ **nm, f** (political) schemer, politico.

oliticien, enne [pɔlitisjɛ̃, ɛn] ■ **adj** *péj* politicking, politically unscrupulous.
■ **nm, f** politician, politico ▸ **politicien véreux** shyster *fam.*

olitique [pɔlitik] ■ **nf 1.** [de gouvernement, de personne] policy ▸ **politique étrangère/intérieure** foreign/domestic policy ▸ **politique monétaire** monetary policy ▸ **politique du stop-and-go** ÉCON stop-and-go-policy *UK* ▸ **pratiquer la politique de l'autruche** *fig* to bury one's head in the sand
2. [affaires publiques] politics *(U)* ▸ **faire de la politique** to be involved in politics ▸ **la politique politicienne** *péj* party politics
3. PRESSE **: politique éditoriale** editorial policy.
■ **nm** politician.
■ **adj 1.** [pouvoir, théorie] political ▸ **homme/femme politique** politician, political figure ▸ **dans les milieux politiques** in political circles ▸ **quelles sont ses opinions politiques?** what are his politics?
2. *littéraire* [choix, réponse] politic ▸ **ce n'était pas très politique de le licencier** it wasn't a very wise move to fire him.

PARONYME / CONFUSABLE
politique

Le mot **politique** correspond à deux termes distincts. Ne confondez pas ***politics*** qui signifie la politique en tant que discipline, et ***policy*** qui désigne un ensemble de mesures.

politiquement [pɔlitikmɑ̃] **adv** politically ▸ **politiquement correct** politically correct, PC.

politisation [pɔlitizasjɔ̃] **nf** politicization.

politiser [3] [pɔlitize] **vt** to politicize.

politologue [pɔlitɔlɔg] **nmf** political expert *ou* analyst.

polka [pɔlka] **nf** polka.

pollen [pɔlɛn] **nm** pollen.

polluant [pɔlɥɑ̃] **nm** pollutant.

pollué, e [pɔlɥe] **adj** polluted.

polluer [7] [pɔlɥe] **vt** to pollute.

pollution [pɔlysjɔ̃] **nf** pollution.

polo [pɔlo] **nm 1.** [sport] polo **2.** [chemise] polo shirt.

polochon [pɔlɔʃɔ̃] **nm** *fam* bolster.

Pologne [pɔlɔɲ] **nf : la Pologne** Poland.

polonais, e [pɔlɔnɛ, ɛz] **adj** Polish.
◆ ***polonais*** **nm** [langue] Polish.
◆ ***polonaise*** **nf 1.** [danse] polonaise **2.** [gâteau] *brioche with an almond filling covered in meringue.*
◆ ***Polonais, e*** **nm, f** Pole.

poltron, onne [pɔltrɔ̃, ɔn] ■ **nm, f** coward.
■ **adj** cowardly.

polyamide [pɔliamid] **nm** polyamide.

polychrome [pɔlikrom] **adj** polychrome, polychromatic.

polyclinique [pɔliklinik] **nf** general hospital.

polycopie [pɔlikɔpi] **nf** duplicating.

polycopié, e [pɔlikɔpje] **adj** duplicate *(avant n).*
◆ ***polycopié*** **nm** duplicated lecture notes *pl.*

polycopier [9] [pɔlikɔpje] **vt** to duplicate.

polyculture [pɔlikyltyr] **nf** mixed farming.

polyester [pɔliɛstɛr] **nm** polyester.

polygame [pɔligam] ■ **nm** polygamist.
■ **adj** polygamous.

polygamie [pɔligami] **nf** polygamy.

polyglotte [pɔliglɔt] **nmf & adj** polyglot.

polygone [pɔligɔn] **nm 1.** MATH polygon **2.** MIL : **polygone de tir** rifle range.

polymère [pɔlimɛr] ■ **nm** polymer.
■ **adj** polymeric.

polymorphe [pɔlimɔrf] **adj** polymorphous.

Polynésie [pɔlinezi] **nf : la Polynésie** Polynesia ▸ **la Polynésie française** French Polynesia.

polynésien, enne [pɔlinezjɛ̃, ɛn] **adj** Polynesian.
◆ ***polynésien*** **nm** [langue] Polynesian.
◆ ***Polynésien, enne*** **nm, f** Polynesian.

polype [pɔlip] **nm** polyp.

polyphonie [pɔlifɔni] **nf** polyphony.

polysémique [pɔlisemik] **adj** polysemous, polysemic.

polystyrène [pɔlistirɛn] **nm** polystyrene.

polytechnicien, enne [pɔlitɛknisjɛ̃, ɛn] **nm, f** *student or ex-student of the École Polytechnique.*

Polytechnique [pɔlitɛknik] **npr : l'École Polytechnique** *prestigious engineering college.*

polythéisme [pɔliteism] **nm** polytheism.

polythéiste [pɔliteist] ■ **nmf** polytheist.
■ **adj** polytheistic.

polyvalent, e [pɔlivalɑ̃, ɑ̃t] **adj 1.** [salle] multi-purpose **2.** [professeur] non-specialized **3.** CHIM & MÉD polyvalent **4.** [personne] versatile.
◆ ***polyvalent*** **nm** *tax inspector specializing in company taxation.*

pomelo [pɔmelo] **nm** grapefruit.

pommade [pɔmad] **nf** [médicament] ointment.

pommader [3] [pɔmade] **vt** to pomade.

pomme [pɔm] **nf 1.** [fruit] apple ▸ **pomme d'amour** toffee apple ▸ **pomme de pin** pine *ou* fir cone ▸ **pomme de reinette** pippin **2.** [pomme de terre] : **pommes allumettes** *very thin chips* ▸ **pommes dauphine/duchesse** dauphine/duchesse potatoes ▸ **pommes frites** chips *UK*, (French) fries *US* ▸ **pommes noisettes** deep-fried potato balls ▸ **pommes vapeur** steamed potatoes **3.** [objet rond] : **pomme d'arrosoir** rose *(of a watering can)* ▸ **pomme de douche** shower head
▸▸| **pomme de discorde** bone of contention ▸ **tomber dans les pommes** *fam* to pass out, to faint.
◆ ***pomme d'Adam*** **nf** Adam's apple.

pommeau, x [pɔmo] **nm 1.** [de parapluie, de canne] knob **2.** [de sabre] pommel.

pomme de terre [pɔmdətɛr] **nf** potato ▸ **pomme de terres à l'eau** boiled potatoes ▸ **pomme de terres au four** baked potatoes ▸ **pomme de terres frites** chips *UK*, (French) fries *US* ▸ **pomme de terres en robe des champs** jacket potatoes ▸ **pomme de terres sautées** sauté potatoes.

pommelé, e [pɔmle] **adj** dappled ▸ **gris pommelé** dapple grey *UK ou* gray *US*.

pommette [pɔmɛt] **nf** cheekbone.

pommier [pɔmje] **nm** apple tree.

pompe [pɔ̃p] **nf 1.** [appareil] pump ▸ **pompe à essence** petrol pump *UK*, gas pump *US* ▸ **pompe à incendie** fire engine, fire truck *US* **2.** [magnificence] pomp, ceremony ▸ **en grande pompe** with great ceremony **3.** *fam* [chaussure] shoe ▸ **être à côté de ses pompes** *fam fig* to be completely out of it.
◆ ***pompes funèbres*** **nfpl** undertaker's *sg*, funeral director's *(sg) UK*, mortician's *(sg) US*.

Pompéi [pɔ̃pei] **npr** Pompeii.

pomper [3] [pɔ̃pe] **vt 1.** [eau, air] to pump **2.** [avec éponge] to soak up **3.** *arg scol* [copier] : **pomper qqch (sur qqn)** to crib sthg (from sb).

pompette [pɔ̃pɛt] **adj** *fam* merry, tipsy.

pompeusement [pɔ̃pøzmɑ̃] **adv** pompously.

pompeux, euse [pɔ̃pø, øz] **adj** pompous.

pompier, ère [pɔ̃pje, ɛr] **adj** pretentious.

pompier [pɔ̃pje] **nm** fireman, firefighter.

pompiste [pɔ̃pist] **nmf** petrol *UK ou* gas *US* pump attendant.

pompon [pɔ̃pɔ̃] **nm** pompom ▸ **décrocher le pompon** *fam fig* to take the biscuit *UK ou* cake.

pomponner [3] [pɔ̃pɔne] ◆ ***se pomponner*** **vp** to get dressed up.

ponce [pɔ̃s] **adj : pierre ponce** pumice (stone).

poncer [16] [pɔ̃se] **vt** [bois] to sand (down).

ponceuse [pɔ̃søz] **nf** sander, sanding machine.

poncif [pɔ̃sif] **nm** [banalité] commonplace, cliché.

ponction [pɔ̃ksjɔ̃] **nf 1.** [MÉD - lombaire] puncture / [- pulmonaire] tapping **2.** *fig* [prélèvement] withdrawal.

ponctionner [3] [pɔ̃ksjɔne] **vt 1.** [MÉD - région lombaire] to puncture / [- poumon] to tap **2.** *fig* [contribuable] to take money from / [argent] to withdraw.

ponctualité [pɔ̃ktɥalite] **nf** punctuality.

ponctuation [pɔ̃ktɥasjɔ̃] **nf** punctuation.

ponctuel, elle [pɔ̃ktɥɛl] **adj 1.** [action] specific, selective **2.** [personne] punctual.

ponctuellement [pɔ̃ktɥɛlmɑ̃] **adv** punctually.

ponctuer [7] [pɔ̃ktɥe] **vt** to punctuate ▸ **ponctuer qqch de qqch** *fig* to punctuate sthg with sthg.

pondéral, e, aux [pɔ̃deral, o] **adj** weight *(avant n).*

pondération [pɔ̃derasjɔ̃] **nf 1.** [de personne] levelheadedness **2.** ÉCON weighting.

pondéré, e [pɔ̃dere] **adj 1.** [personne] level-headed **2.** ÉCON weighted.

pondérer [18] [pɔ̃dere] **vt 1.** [pouvoirs] to balance (out), to counterbalance **2.** économie; [bourse] to weight.

Pondichéry [pɔ̃diʃeri] **npr** Pondicherry.

pondre [75] [pɔ̃dr] **vt 1.** [œufs] to lay **2.** *fam fig* [projet, texte] to produce.

pondu, e [pɔ̃dy] **pp** ➤ ***pondre***.

poney [pɔnɛ] **nm** pony.

pongiste [pɔ̃ʒist] **nmf** table-tennis player.

pont [pɔ̃] **nm 1.** CONSTR bridge ▸ **ponts et chaussées** ADMIN ≃ highways department ▸ **pont autoroutier** motorway *UK ou* freeway *US* flyover ▸ **pont ferroviaire** railway bridge ▸ **pont mobile/suspendu** movable/suspension bridge ▸ **faire/promettre un pont d'or à qqn** *fig* to offe to promise sb a fortune *(so that they'll take on a job)* **2.** [lien] link, connection ▸ **pont aérien** airlift ▸ **couper les ponts avec qqn** *fig* to break with sb **3.** [congé] *day off granted by an employer to fill the gap between a national holiday and a weekend* ▸ **faire le pont** to have a long weekend **4.** [de navire] deck ▸ **pont inférieur/principal** lower/main deck **5.** [structure de manutention] **: pont élévateur** *ou* **de graissage** garage ramp, car lift, elevator platform ▸ **pont de chargement** loading platform.

ponte [pɔ̃t] ■ **nf** [action] laying / [œufs] clutch.
■ **nm 1.** [jeux] punter **2.** *fam* [autorité] big shot.

pontife [pɔ̃tif] **nm** pontiff.

pontifical, e, aux [pɔ̃tifikal, o] **adj** papal.

pontificat [pɔ̃tifika] **nm** pontificate.

pontifier [9] [pɔ̃tifje] **vi** *fam* to pontificate.

pont-levis [pɔ̃ləvi] (pl **ponts-levis**) **nm** drawbridge.

ponton [pɔ̃tɔ̃] **nm 1.** [plate-forme] pontoon **2.** [chaland] lighter, barge.

pool [pul] **nm** pool.

pop [pɔp] ■ **nm** pop.
■ **adj** pop *(avant n)*.

pop-corn [pɔpkɔrn] **nm inv** popcorn *(U)*.

pope [pɔp] **nm** priest *(in the Orthodox church)*.

popeline [pɔplin] **nf** poplin.

popote [pɔpɔt] *fam* ■ **adj inv** homeloving.
■ **nf : faire la popote** to do the cooking ▸ **préparer la popote** to prepare the meal.

populace [pɔpylas] **nf** *péj* mob.

populaire [pɔpylɛr] **adj 1.** [du peuple - volonté] popular, of the people / [- quartier] working-class / [- art, chanson] folk **2.** [personne] popular.

populariser [3] [pɔpylarize] **vt** to popularize.

popularité [pɔpylarite] **nf** popularity.

population [pɔpylasjɔ̃] **nf** population ▸ **population active** working population.

populiste [pɔpylist] **nmf & adj** populist.

populo [pɔpylo] **nm** *fam* **1.** [peuple] hoi polloi **2.** [foule] crowd.

porc [pɔr] **nm 1.** [animal] pig, hog *US* **2.** *fig & péj* [personne] pig, swine **3.** [viande] pork **4.** [peau] pigskin.

porcelaine [pɔrsəlɛn] **nf 1.** [matière] china, porcelain **2.** [objet] piece of china *ou* porcelain **3.** [mollusque] cowrie shell.

porcelet [pɔrsəlɛ] **nm** piglet.

porc-épic [pɔrkepik] (pl **porcs-épics**) **nm** porcupine.

porche [pɔrʃ] **nm** porch.

porcherie [pɔrʃəri] **nf** *litt & fig* pigsty.

porcin, e [pɔrsɛ̃, in] **adj 1.** [élevage] pig *(avant n)* **2.** *fig & péj* [yeux] piggy.
◆ ***porcin*** **nm** pig.

pore [pɔr] **nm** pore.

poreux, euse [pɔrø, øz] **adj** porous.

porno [pɔrno] *fam* ■ **adj** [film, magazine, scène] porn, porno ▸ **des photos pornos** dirty pictures.
■ **nm 1.** [activité] **: le porno** [genre] porn / [industrie] the porn industry **2.** [film] porno film *UK*, blue movie.

pornographie [pɔrnɔgrafi] **nf** pornography.

pornographique [pɔrnɔgrafik] **adj** pornographic.

porridge [pɔridʒ] **nm** porridge.

port [pɔr] **nm 1.** [lieu] port ▸ **arriver à bon port** [personne] to arrive safe and sound / [chose] to arrive in good condition ▸ **port d'attache** home port ▸ **port de commerce/pêche** commercial/fishing port **2.** [fait de porter sur soi - d'objet] carrying / [- de vêtement, décoration] wearing ▸ **port d'armes** carrying of weapons **3.** [transport] carriage ▸ **franco de port** carriage paid **4.** [allure] bearing.

portable [pɔrtabl] ■ **nm** TV portable / INFORM laptop, portable / [téléphone] mobile *UK*, cell(phone) *US*.
■ **adj 1.** [vêtement] wearable **2.** [ordinateur, machine à écrire] portable, laptop.

portage [pɔrtaʒ] **nm** *Québec* NAUT portage / FIN piggybacking.

portail [pɔrtaj] **nm** [gén & INFORM] portal.

portant, e [pɔrtɑ̃, ɑ̃t] **adj : être bien/mal portant** to be in good/poor health.
◆ ***portant*** **nm** upright.

portatif, ive [pɔrtatif, iv] **adj** portable.

Port-au-Prince [pɔroprɛ̃s] **npr** Port-au-Prince.

porte [pɔrt] **nf 1.** [de maison, voiture] door ▸ **claquer la porte** to slam the door ▸ **claquer/fermer la porte au nez de qqn** to slam/shut the door in sb's face ▸ **écouter aux portes** to listen at keyholes ▸ **être à la porte** to be locked out ▸ **ficher** *ou* **foutre qqn à la porte** *fam* to throw *ou* chuck sb out ▸ **mettre qqn à la porte** to throw sb out ▸ **ouvrir sa porte à qqn** to welcome sb ▸ **prendre la porte** to leave ▸ **je mets 40 minutes de porte à porte** it takes me 40 minutes door-to-door ▸ **porte cochère** carriage entrance ▸ **porte de communication** communicating door ▸ **porte coulissante** sliding door ▸ **porte coupe-feu** firedoor ▸ **porte à deux battants** double door ▸ **porte d'entrée** front door ▸ **porte de secours** emergency exit ▸ **porte de service** trademen's entrance ▸ **porte vitrée** glass door **2.** gate / AÉRON **: embarquement porte 6** boarding gate 6 / SKI **: elle a chuté à la troisième porte** she fell at the third gate / [de ville] **: la porte de Versailles** *site of a large exhibition complex in Paris where major trade fairs take place* ▸ **les portes de Paris** *the old city gates around Paris* **3.** *fig* [de région] gateway.

porte-à-faux [pɔrtafo] **nm inv** [roche] overhang / CONSTR cantilever ▸ **en porte-à-faux** overhanging / CONSTR cantilevered / *fig* in a delicate situation.

porte-à-porte [pɔrtapɔrt] **nm inv : faire du porte-à-porte** to sell from door to door.

porte-avions [pɔrtavjɔ̃] **nm inv** aircraft carrier.

porte-bagages [pɔrtbagaʒ] **nm inv** luggage rack *UK* / [de voiture] roof rack *UK*.

porte-bébé [pɔrtbebe] (pl **porte-bébés**) **nm** baby sling, papoose.

porte-bonheur [pɔrtbɔnœr] **nm inv** lucky charm.

porte-bouteilles [pɔrbutɛj] **nm inv** [casier] wine rack.

porte-cartes, porte-carte [pɔrtəkart] **nm inv** card holder.

porte-cigarettes [pɔrtsigarɛt] **nm inv** cigarette case.

porte-clefs, porte-clés [pɔrtəkle] **nm inv** keyring.

porte-couteau [pɔrkuto] (pl **porte-couteaux**) **nm** knife rest.

porte-documents [pɔrtdɔkymɑ̃] **nm inv** attaché *ou* document case.

porte-drapeau [pɔrtdrapo] (pl **porte-drapeaux**) **nm** standard-bearer.

portée [pɔrte] **nf 1.** [de missile] range ▸ **à portée de** within range of ▸ **à portée de main** within reach ▸ **à portée de voix** within earshot ▸ **à portée de vue** in sight ▸ **à la portée de qqn** *fig* within sb's reach ▸ **hors de la portée de** out of reach of **2.** [d'événement] impact, significance **3.** MUS stave, staff **4.** [de femelle] litter.

porte-fenêtre [pɔrtfənɛtr] (pl **portes-fenêtres**) **nf** French window *ou* door *US*.

portefeuille [pɔrtəfœj] **nm 1.** [pour billets] wallet **2.** FIN & POLIT portfolio.

porte-jarretelles [pɔrtʒartɛl] **nm inv** suspender belt *UK*, garter belt *US*.

porte-malheur [pɔrtmalœr] **nm inv** jinx.

portemanteau, x [pɔrtmɑ̃to] **nm** [au mur] coat-rack / [sur pied] coat stand.

portemine [pɔrtəmin] **nm** propelling pencil *UK*, mechanical pencil *US*.

porte-monnaie [pɔrtmɔnɛ] **nm inv** purse.

porte-parapluies [pɔrtparaplɥi] **nm inv** umbrella stand.

porte-parole [pɔrtparɔl] **nm inv** spokesman (f spokeswoman) ▸ **porte-parole officiel du gouvernement** official government spokesman.

porte-plume [pɔrtəplym] **nm inv** penholder.

porter [3] [pɔrte] ■ **vt 1.** [gén] to carry ▸ **porter qqn sur son dos/dans ses bras** to carry sb on one's back/in one's arms **2.** [vêtement, lunettes, montre] to wear ▸ **elle porte toujours du noir** she always dresses in *ou* wears black / [barbe] to have **3.** [nom, date, inscription] to bear ▸ **l'étui portait ses initiales gravées** the case was engraved with his initials ▸ **elle porte le nom de son mari** she has taken her husband's name **4.** [apporter] to take ▸ **porter des fleurs sur la tombe de qqn** to take flowers to sb's grave **5.** [inciter] **: porter qqn à faire qqch** to lead sb to do sthg ▸ **l'alcool peut porter les gens à des excès/à la violence** alcohol can drive people to excesses/induce people to be violent **6.** [inscrire] to put down, to write down ▸ **porté disparu** reported missing.

■ **vi 1.** [s'appuyer - balcon] **: porter sur** to be supported by **2.** [traiter] **: porter sur qqn/qqch** to be about sb/sthg ▸ **le détournement porte sur plusieurs millions d'euros** the embezzlement concerns several million euros **3.** [remarque] to strike home **4.** [voix, tir] to carry ▸ **sa voix ne porte pas assez** his voice doesn't carry well ▸ **aussi loin que porte la vue** as far as the eye can see.

◆ ***se porter*** ■ **vp 1.** [se sentir] **: se porter bien/mal** to be well/unwell ▸ **à bientôt, portez-vous bien!** see you soon, look after yourself! **2.** [se diriger] **: se porter sur** [choix, regard] to fall on / [conversation] to turn to ▸ **tous les regards se portèrent sur elle** all eyes turned towards her **3.** [se livrer] **: se porter à** [violences] to carry out ▸ **se porter à des extrémités** to go to extremes.

■ **v attr : se porter garant de qqch** to guarantee sthg, to vouch for sthg ▸ **se porter candidat à** to stand for election to *UK*, to run for *US* ▸ **se porter volontaire pour faire** to volunteer to do.

porte-savon [pɔrtsavɔ̃] (pl **porte-savon** *ou* **porte-savons**) **nm** soap dish.

porte-serviettes [pɔrtsɛrvjɛt] **nm inv** towel rail.

porteur, euse [pɔrtœr, øz] ■ **adj : marché porteur** COMM growth market ▸ **mère porteuse** surrogate mother ▸ **mur porteur** load-bearing wall.

■ **nm, f 1.** [de message, nouvelle] bringer, bearer **2.** [de bagages] porter **3.** [détenteur - de papiers, d'actions] holder / [- de chèque] bearer **4.** [de maladie] carrier.

porte-voix [pɔrtəvwa] **nm inv** megaphone, loudhailer *UK*, bullhorn *US*.

portier [pɔrtje] **nm** doorman, commissionaire *UK*.

portière [pɔrtjɛr] **nf** [de voiture, train] door.

portillon [pɔrtijɔ̃] **nm** barrier, gate.

portion [pɔrsjɔ̃] **nf 1.** [de gâteau] portion, helping **2.** [d'héritage] portion, part ▸ **être réduit à la portion congrue** *fig* to get the smallest share.

portique [pɔrtik] **nm 1.** ARCHIT portico **2.** SPORT crossbeam *(for hanging apparatus)*.

Port-Louis [pɔrlwi] **npr** Port Louis.

porto [pɔrto] **nm** port.

portoricain, e [pɔrtɔrikɛ̃, ɛn] **adj** Puerto Rican.

◆ ***Portoricain, e*** **nm, f** Puerto Rican.

Porto Rico [pɔrtoriko], ***Puerto Rico*** [pwɛrtoriko] **npr** Puerto Rico.

portrait [pɔrtrɛ] **nm** portrait / PHOTO photograph ▸ **être tout le portrait de qqn** *fig* to be the spitting *ou* very image of sb ▸ **faire le portrait de qqn** *fig* to describe sb.

portraitiste [pɔrtretist] **nmf** portrait painter.

portrait-robot [pɔrtrɛrɔbo] (pl **portraits-robots**) **nm** Photofit® picture, Identikit® picture.

portuaire [pɔrtɥɛr] **adj** port *(avant n)*, harbour *(avant n) UK*, harbor *(avant n) US*.

portugais, e [pɔrtygɛ, ɛz] **adj** Portuguese.

◆ ***portugais*** **nm** [langue] Portuguese.

◆ ***Portugais, e*** **nm, f** Portuguese (person) ▸ **les Portugais** the Portuguese.

Portugal [pɔrtygal] **nm : le Portugal** Portugal ▸ **au Portugal** in Portugal.

POS, Pos [pɔs] (abr de ***plan d'occupation des sols***) **nm** *land use scheme.*

pose [poz] **nf 1.** [de pierre, moquette] laying / [de papier peint, rideaux] hanging **2.** [position] pose ▸ **prendre la pose** to pose **3.** PHOTO exposure.

posé, e [poze] **adj** sober, steady.

posément [pozemɑ̃] **adv** calmly.

poser [3] [poze] ■ **vt 1.** [mettre] to put down ▸ **poser qqch sur qqch** to put sthg on sthg ▸ **poser ses coudes sur la table** to rest *ou* to put one's elbows on the table ▸ **poser un sac par terre** to put a bag (down) on the floor
2. [installer - rideaux, papier peint] to hang / [- étagère] to put up / [- moquette, carrelage] to lay ▸ **faire poser un double vitrage** to have double-glazing put in *ou* fitted
3. [établir] to lay down, to set out ▸ **poser qqch comme condition/principe** to lay sthg down as a condition/principle
4. [donner à résoudre - problème, difficulté] to pose ▸ **elle me pose de gros problèmes** she's a great problem *ou* source of anxiety to me ▸ **poser une question** to ask a question ▸ **poser sa candidature** to apply / POLIT to stand *UK ou* run *US* for election.
■ **vi** to pose ▸ **poser pour une photo/un magazine** to pose for a photo/magazine.
◆ ***se poser*** **vp 1.** [oiseau, avion] to land ▸ **se poser en douceur** to make a smooth landing / *fig* [choix, regard] : **se poser sur** to fall on ▸ **il sentit leurs yeux se poser sur lui** he could feel their eyes on him
2. [question, problème] to arise, to come up ▸ **la question qui se pose maintenant est la suivante** the question which must now be asked is the following
3. [personne] **: se poser en** to pose as ▸ **je ne me suis jamais posé en expert** I never set myself up to be *ou* I never pretended I was an expert.

poseur, euse [pozœr, øz] **nm, f** *vieilli* show-off, poser.

positif, ive [pozitif, iv] **adj** positive.

position [pozisjɔ̃] **nf** position ▸ **position de repli** *fig* & MIL fall-back position ▸ **position de place** FIN market position ▸ **arriver en première/dernière position** [coureur] to come first/last / [candidat] to come top/be last ▸ **déterminer la position de qqch** to locate sthg ▸ **être en position de faire qqch** to be in a position to do sthg ▸ **mettez le siège en position inclinée** tilt the seat back ▸ **prendre position** *fig* to take up a position, to take a stand ▸ **rester sur ses positions** *litt* & *fig* to stand one's ground, to stick to one's guns.

positionnement [pɔzisjɔnmɑ̃] **nm** positioning ▸ **positionnement sur le marché** market positioning.

positionner [3] [pozisjɔne] **vt** to position.
◆ ***se positionner*** **vp** to position o.s.

positivement [pozitivmɑ̃] **adv** positively.

posologie [pozɔlɔʒi] **nf** dosage.

possédant, e [pɔsedɑ̃, ɑ̃t] ■ **adj** property-owning *(avant n).*
■ **nm, f** *person from the property-owning classes.*

possédé, e [pɔsede] ■ **adj** possessed.
■ **nm, f** person possessed.

posséder [18] [pɔsede] **vt 1.** [détenir - voiture, maison] to possess, to own / [- diplôme] to have / [- capacités, connaissances] to possess, to have **2.** [langue, art] to have mastered **3.** *fam* [personne] to have.

possesseur [pɔsesœr] **nm 1.** [de bien] possessor, owner **2.** [de secret, diplôme] holder.

possessif, ive [pɔsesif, iv] **adj** possessive.
◆ ***possessif*** **nm** GRAMM possessive.

possession [pɔsesjɔ̃] **nf 1.** [gén] possession ▸ **être en ma/ta** *etc* **possession** to be in my/your *etc* possession ▸ **prendre possession de** to take possession of ▸ **être en possession de** to be in possession of ▸ **possession de soi** self-possession, composure **2.** [de langue] knowledge, command.

possibilité [pɔsibilite] **nf 1.** [gén] possibility **2.** [moyen] chance, opportunity **3.** [pour des objets, un produit] **: possibilité de commercialisation** marketability.
◆ ***possibilités*** **nfpl** [capacités] potential *sg.*

possible [pɔsibl] ■ **adj** possible ▸ **c'est/ce n'est pas possible** that's possible/impossible ▸ **dès que** *ou* **aussitôt que possible** as soon as possible ▸ **il est toujours possible d'annuler la réunion** the meeting can always be cancelled ▸ **je l'ai cherché dans tous les endroits possibles** I looked for it everywhere imaginable *ou* in every possible place ▸ **je veux un rapport aussi détaillé que possible** I want as detailed a report as possible ▸ **serait-il possible qu'il m'ait menti?** could he (possibly) have lied to me?
■ **nm : faire tout son possible** to do one's utmost, to do everything possible ▸ **dans la mesure du possible** as far as possible ▸ **ennuyeux au possible** extremely boring.

postal, e, aux [pɔstal, o] **adj** postal.

postdater [3] [pɔstdate] **vt** to postdate.

poste [pɔst] ■ **nf 1.** [service] post *UK*, mail *US* ▸ **envoyer/recevoir qqch par la poste** to send/receive sthg by post ▸ **mettre une lettre à la poste** to post *UK ou* to mail *US* a letter ▸ **travailler à la poste** ≃ to work for the Post Office ▸ **poste aérienne** airmail
2. [bureau] post office ▸ **poste centrale** central post office ▸ **poste restante** poste restante *UK*, general delivery *US*.
■ **nm 1.** [emplacement] post ▸ **poste de combat** action *ou* battle station ▸ **poste de contrôle** checkpoint ▸ **poste de garde** guardroom ▸ **poste d'incendie** fire point ▸ **poste de police** police station ▸ **poste de secours** first-aid post ▸ **être fidèle au poste** *fig* to stay at one's post
2. [emploi] position, post ▸ **un poste à pourvoir** a post to be filled, a vacancy
3. [appareil] **: poste émetteur** transmitter ▸ **poste de radio** radio ▸ **poste de télévision** television (set)
4. TÉLÉCOM extension ▸ **passez-moi le poste 1421** give me extension 1421.

poster [1] [pɔstɛr] **nm** poster.

poster[2] [3] [pɔste] **vt 1.** [lettre] to post *UK*, to mail *US* **2.** [sentinelle] to post.
◆ ***se poster*** **vp** to position o.s., to station o.s.

postérieur, ***e*** [pɔsterjœr] **adj 1.** [date] later, subsequent **2.** [membre] hind *(avant n)*, back *(avant n)*.
◆ ***postérieur*** **nm** *hum* posterior.

postérieurement [pɔsterjœrmɑ̃] **adv** subsequently.

posteriori [pɔsterjɔri] ◆ ***a posteriori*** **loc adv** a posteriori.

postériorité [pɔsterjɔrite] **nf** *sout* posteriority.

postérité [pɔsterite] **nf 1.** [générations à venir] posterity **2.** *littéraire* [descendance] descendants *pl*.

postface [pɔstfas] **nf** postscript.

posthume [pɔstym] **adj** posthumous.

postiche [pɔstiʃ] ■ **nm** hairpiece.
■ **adj** false.

postier, ***ère*** [pɔstje, ɛr] **nm, f** post-office worker.

postillon [pɔstijɔ̃] **nm** [salive] droplet of saliva.

postillonner [3] [pɔstijɔne] **vi** to splutter.

postindustriel, ***elle*** [pɔstɛ̃dystrijɛl] **adj** post-industrial.

Post-it® [pɔstit] **nm inv** Post-it®, Post-it® note.

postmoderne [pɔstmɔdɛrn] **adj** postmodern.

postnatal, ***e*** [pɔstnatal] (pl **postnatals** *ou* **postnataux** [pɔstnato]) **adj** postnatal.

postopératoire [pɔstɔperatwar] **adj** postoperative.

post-scriptum [pɔstskriptɔm] **nm inv** postscript.

postsynchronisation [pɔstsɛ̃krɔnizasjɔ̃] **nf** dubbing.

postulant, ***e*** [pɔstylɑ̃, ɑ̃t] **nm, f 1.** [pour emploi] applicant **2.** RELIG postulant.

postuler [3] [pɔstyle] **vt 1.** [emploi] to apply for **2.** PHILO to postulate.

posture [pɔstyr] **nf** posture ▸ **être** *ou* **se trouver en mauvaise posture** *fig* to be in a difficult position.

pot [po] **nm 1.** [récipient] pot, jar ⁄ [à eau, à lait] jug *UK*, pitcher *US* ▸ **pot de chambre** chamber pot ▸ **pot à confiture** jam jar ▸ **pot de confiture/miel** jar of jam/honey ▸ **pot de fleurs** flowerpot ▸ **pot de peinture** pot *ou* can of paint ▸ **pot de yaourt** yoghurt pot ▸ **petit pot (pour bébé)** (jar of) baby food ▸ **découvrir le pot aux roses** to get to the bottom of something ▸ **tourner autour du pot** *fam* to beat about the bush **2.** AUTO **: pot catalytique** catalytic convertor *ou* converter ▸ **pot d'échappement** exhaust (pipe) ⁄ [silencieux] silencer *UK*, muffler *US* **3.** *fam* [boisson] drink ▸ **boire** *ou* **prendre un pot** to have a drink ▸ **faire un pot** to have a drinks party *UK* ▸ **ils font un pot pour son départ à la retraite** they're having a little get-together for his retirement
▸▸ **avoir du/manquer de pot** *fam* to be lucky/unlucky ▸ **coup de pot** stroke of luck ▸ **payer plein pot** *fam* to pay full fare *ou* full whack *UK* ▸ **elle est pot de colle** she sticks to you like glue, you just can't get rid of her.

CULTURE

Pot

In France, workers often gather to toast a colleague who is retiring or leaving the firm because of an expired contract or completed work experience period. Pots, get-togethers with drinks and often light snacks, are also organized to celebrate someone's return from maternity leave and the new addition to her family. Sometimes colleagues give a gift to the person in whose honour the celebration is being held.

potable [pɔtabl] **adj 1.** [liquide] drinkable ▸ **eau potable** drinking water **2.** *fam* [travail] acceptable.

potache [pɔtaʃ] **nm** *fam* schoolkid.

potage [pɔtaʒ] **nm** soup ▸ **potage aux légumes** vegetable soup.

potager, ***ère*** [pɔtaʒe, ɛr] **adj : jardin potager** vegetable garden ▸ **plante potagère** vegetable.
◆ ***potager*** **nm** kitchen *ou* vegetable garden.

potasse [pɔtas] **nf** potash.

potasser [3] [pɔtase] **vt** *fam* [cours] to swot up *UK*, to bone up on ⁄ [examen] to swot up for *UK*, to bone up for.

potassium [pɔtasjɔm] **nm** potassium.

pot-au-feu [pɔtofø] **nm inv** ≃ beef-and-vegetable stew.

pot-de-vin [podvɛ̃] (pl **pots-de-vin**) **nm** bribe.

pote [pɔt] **nm** *fam* mate *UK*, buddy *US*.

poteau, ***x*** [pɔto] **nm** post ▸ **poteau de but** goalpost ▸ **poteau indicateur** signpost ▸ **poteau télégraphique** telegraph pole *UK*, telephone pole *US* ▸ **coiffer qqn au poteau** to pip sb at the post *UK*.

potée [pɔte] **nf** *pot-au-feu made with salt pork*.

potelé, ***e*** [pɔtle] **adj** plump, chubby.

potence [pɔtɑ̃s] **nf 1.** CONSTR bracket **2.** [de pendaison] gallows *sg*.

potentat [pɔtɑ̃ta] **nm** potentate.

potentiel, ***elle*** [pɔtɑ̃sjɛl] **adj** potential.
◆ ***potentiel*** **nm** potential ▸ **potentiel de croissance** growth potentiel ▸ **potentiel industriel** industrial potential ▸ **potentiel nucléaire** nuclear capability.

potentiellement [pɔtɑ̃sjɛlmɑ̃] **adv** potentially.

poterie [pɔtri] **nf 1.** [art] pottery **2.** [objet] piece of pottery.

potiche [pɔtiʃ] **nf 1.** [vase] vase **2.** *fam* [personne] figurehead.

potier, ère [pɔtje, ɛr] **nm, f** potter.

potin [pɔtɛ̃] **nm** *fam* [bruit] din.
◆ ***potins*** **nmpl** *fam* [ragots] gossip *(U)*.

potion [posjɔ̃] **nf** potion.

potiron [pɔtirɔ̃] **nm** pumpkin.

pot-pourri [popuri] (pl **pots-pourris**) **nm** potpourri.

pou, x [pu] **nm** louse.

pouah [pwa] **interj** ugh!

poubelle [pubɛl] **nf** dustbin *UK*, trashcan *US* / INFORM recycle bin.

pouce [pus] **nm 1.** [de main] thumb / [de pied] big toe ▸ **sucer son pouce** to suck one's thumb ▸ **manger sur le pouce** to grab something to eat **2.** [mesure] inch ▸ **ne pas bouger/céder d'un pouce** not to move/give an inch.

pouding [pudiŋ] **nm** *sweet cake made from bread and candied fruit* ▸ **pouding de cochon** *French-Canadian dish of meatloaf made from chopped pork and pigs' livers.*

poudre [pudr] **nf** powder ▸ **réduire qqch en poudre** to reduce sthg to powder, to pulverize ***ou*** to powder sthg ▸ **se mettre de la poudre** to powder one's face ***ou*** nose ▸ **poudre à canon** gunpowder ▸ **poudre à éternuer** sneezing powder ▸ **poudre à laver** washing *UK* ***ou*** soap powder ▸ **poudre à récurer** scouring powder ▸ **poudre de riz** face powder ▸ **poudre vermifuge** worming powder ▸ **chocolat en poudre** drinking chocolate ▸ **prendre la poudre d'escampette** to make off ▸ **jeter de la poudre aux yeux à qqn** to try to dazzle ***ou*** to impress sb.

poudrerie [pudrəri] **nf** *Québec* snowdrift.

poudreux, euse [pudrø, øz] **adj** powdery.
◆ ***poudreuse*** **nf** powder (snow).

poudrier [pudrije] **nm 1.** [boîte] powder compact **2.** [fabricant] explosives manufacturer.

poudrière [pudrijɛr] **nf** powder magazine / *fig* powder keg.

poudroyer [13] [pudrwaje] **vi** *littéraire* to rise (up) in clouds.

pouf [puf] ■ **nm** pouffe.
■ **interj** thud!

pouffer [3] [pufe] **vi : pouffer (de rire)** to snigger.

pouilleux, euse [pujø, øz] ■ **adj 1.** [personne, animal] flea-ridden **2.** [endroit] squalid.
■ **nm, f 1.** [couvert de poux] person with fleas **2.** [misérable] down-and-out.

poulailler [pulaje] **nm 1.** [de ferme] henhouse **2.** *fam* THÉÂTRE gods *sg*.

poulain [pulɛ̃] **nm** foal / *fig* protégé.

poulamon [pulamɔ̃] **nm** *Québec* tomcod.

poularde [pulard] **nf** fattened chicken.

poule [pul] **nf 1.** ZOOL hen ▸ **la poule aux œufs d'or** the goose that lays the golden egg ▸ **poule mouillée** wimp, wet *UK* **2.** *fam péj* [femme] bird *UK*, broad *US* **3.** SPORT [compétition] round robin / [rugby] [groupe] pool.

poulet [pulɛ] **nm 1.** ZOOL chicken ▸ **poulet rôti** roast chicken ▸ **poulet fermier** free-range chicken ▸ **poulet de grain** corn-fed chicken **2.** *fam* [policier] cop.

poulette [pulɛt] **nf 1.** ZOOL pullet **2.** *fam péj* [fille] bird *UK*, broad *US*.

pouliche [puliʃ] **nf** filly.

poulie [puli] **nf** pulley.

poulpe [pulp] **nm** octopus.

pouls [pu] **nm** pulse.

poumon [pumɔ̃] **nm** lung ▸ **à pleins poumons** deeply.

poupe [pup] **nf** stern.

poupée [pupe] **nf 1.** [jouet] doll **2.** [pansement] finger bandage.

poupin, e [pupɛ̃, in] **adj** chubby.

poupon [pupɔ̃] **nm 1.** [bébé] little baby **2.** [jouet] baby doll.

pouponner [3] [pupɔne] **vi** to play mother.

pouponnière [pupɔnjɛr] **nf** nursery.

pour [pur] ■ **prép 1.** [gén] for ▸ **condamné pour vol** found guilty of theft ▸ **il y en a bien pour 80 euros de réparation** the repairs will cost at least 80 euros ▸ **j'en ai bien pour cinq heures** it'll take me at least five hours ▸ **mot pour mot** word for word ▸ **partir pour l'Italie** to leave for Italy ▸ **pour la plus grande joie des enfants** to the children's great delight ▸ **prendre qqn pour époux/épouse** to take sb to be one's husband/wife ▸ **c'est fait pour** that's what it's (there) for
2. *(+ infinitif)* **: pour faire** in order to do, (so as) to do ▸ **je suis venu pour vous voir** I've come to see you ▸ **pour m'avoir aidé** for having helped me, for helping me
3. [indique un rapport] for ▸ **avancé pour son âge** advanced for his/her age ▸ **pour moi** for my part, as far as I'm concerned ▸ **pour ce qui est de** as regards, with regard to.
■ **adv : je suis pour** I'm (all) for it.
■ **nm : le pour et le contre** the pros and cons *pl* ▸ **peser le pour et le contre** to weigh up the pros and cons.
◆ ***pour que*** **loc conj** *(+ subjonctif)* so that, in order that ▸ **j'ai pris des places non-fumeurs pour que vous ne soyez pas incommodés par la fumée** I've got non-smoking seats so that you won't be bothered by the smoke ▸ **mon appartement est trop petit pour qu'on puisse tous y dormir** my flat is too small for us all to be able to sleep there.

pourboire [purbwar] **nm** tip.

pourceau, x [purso] **nm** *littéraire* swine.

pourcentage [pursɑ̃taʒ] **nm** percentage.

pourchasser [3] [purʃase] **vt 1.** [criminel] to chase, to pursue ▸ **pourchassé par ses créanciers** pursued ***ou***

hounded by his creditors **2.** *sout* [erreur, abus] to track down *(sep)* ▸ **nous pourchasserons les injustices** we'll root out injustice wherever we find it.

pourfendeur**, **euse [purfɑ̃dœr, øz] **nm, f** *littéraire* : **pourfendeur d'abus** righter of wrongs.

pourlécher [18] [purleʃe] ◆ ***se pourlécher*** ■ **vpi** to lick one's lips.
■ **vpt : je m'en pourlèche les babines à l'avance** *hum* my mouth is watering already.

pourparlers [purparle] **nmpl** talks ▸ **pourparlers de paix** peace talks.

pourpre [purpr] ■ **nf 1.** [colorant] purple (dye) **2.** [couleur] purple.
■ **nm & adj** crimson.

pourquoi [purkwa] ■ **adv** why ▸ **pourquoi pas?** why not? ▸ **c'est pourquoi...** that's why...
■ **nm inv : le pourquoi (de)** the reason (for) ▸ **les pourquoi** the questions ▸ **le pourquoi et le comment** the whys and wherefores.

pourrai**, **pourras ➤ ***pouvoir***.

pourri**, **e [puri] **adj 1.** [fruit] rotten **2.** [personne, milieu] corrupt **3.** [enfant] spoiled rotten, ruined.
◆ ***pourri*** **nm 1.** [de fruit] rotten part **2.** *fam* [personne] creep.

pourrir [32] [purir] ■ **vt 1.** [matière, aliment] to rot, to spoil **2.** [enfant] to ruin, to spoil rotten.
■ **vi** [matière] to rot / [fruit, aliment] to go rotten *ou* bad.

pourrissement [purismɑ̃] **nm 1.** [de fruits, du bois, de la viande] rotting / [de chairs] putrefaction / [d'une dent, de la végétation] decay, rotting, decaying **2.** [d'une situation] deterioration.

pourriture [purityr] **nf 1.** [d'aliment] rot **2.** *fig* [de personne, de milieu] corruption **3.** *injur* [personne] bastard.

poursuis**, **poursuit ➤ ***poursuivre***.

poursuite [pursɥit] **nf 1.** [de personne] chase ▸ **se lancer à la poursuite de** to set off after **2.** [d'argent, de vérité] pursuit **3.** [de négociations] continuation.
◆ ***poursuites*** **nfpl** DR (legal) proceedings ▸ **engager des poursuites judiciaires** to take legal action.

poursuivant**, **e [pursɥivɑ̃, ɑ̃t] **nm, f** pursuer.

poursuivi**, **e [pursɥivi] **pp** ➤ ***poursuivre***.

poursuivre [89] [pursɥivr] ■ **vt 1.** [voleur] to pursue, to chase / [gibier] to hunt **2.** [rêve, vengeance] to pursue **3.** [enquête, travail] to carry on with, to continue **4.** DR [criminel] to prosecute / [voisin] to sue.
■ **vi** to go on, to carry on.
◆ ***se poursuivre*** **vp** to continue.

pourtant [purtɑ̃] **adv** nevertheless, even so.

pourtour [purtur] **nm** perimeter.

pourvoi [purvwa] **nm** DR appeal ▸ **présenter un pourvoi en cassation** to take one's case to the Appeal Court.

pourvoir [64] [purvwar] ■ **vt : pourvoir qqn de** to provide sb with ▸ **pourvoir qqch de** to equip *ou* fit sthg with.
■ **vi : pourvoir à** to provide for.
◆ ***se pourvoir*** **vp 1.** [se munir] **: se pourvoir de** to provide o.s. with **2.** DR to appeal.

pourvoirie [purvwari] **nf** *Québec* outfitter *(for hunting and fishing)*.

pourvoyeur**, **euse [purvwajœr, øz] **nm, f** supplier.

pourvu**, **e [purvy] **pp** ➤ ***pourvoir***.
◆ ***pourvu que*** *(+ subjonctif)* **loc conj 1.** [condition] providing, provided (that) **2.** [souhait] let's hope (that).

pousse [pus] **nf 1.** [croissance] growth **2.** [bourgeon] shoot ▸ **pousses de bambou** bamboo shoots **3.** ÉCON : **jeune pousse** start-up.

poussé**, **e [puse] **adj 1.** [travail] meticulous **2.** [moteur] souped-up.

pousse-café [puskafe] **nm inv** *fam* liqueur.

poussée [puse] **nf 1.** [pression] pressure **2.** [coup] push **3.** [de fièvre, inflation] rise ▸ **poussée démographique** population increase.

pousse-pousse [puspus] **nm inv 1.** [voiture] rickshaw **2.** *Suisse* [poussette] pushchair.

pousser [3] [puse] ■ **vt 1.** [personne, objet] to push ▸ **ils essayaient de pousser les manifestants vers la place** they were trying to drive *ou* to push the demonstrators towards the square ▸ **pousser une porte** [doucement, pour l'ouvrir] to push a door open / [doucement, pour la fermer] to push a door to *ou* shut ▸ **pousser qqn du coude** [pour l'alerter, accidentellement] to nudge sb with one's elbow ▸ **pousser qqn à bout** *fig* to push sb to breaking point **2.** [moteur, voiture] to drive hard **3.** [recherches, études] to carry on, to continue **4.** [cri, soupir] to give **5.** [inciter] : **pousser qqn à faire qqch** to urge sb to do sthg **6.** [au crime, au suicide] **: pousser qqn à** to drive sb to ▸ **pousser qqn au désespoir** to drive sb to despair.
■ **vi 1.** [exercer une pression] to push **2.** [croître] to grow ▸ **elle a laissé pousser ses cheveux** she's let her hai[r] grow ▸ **les plants de tomates poussent bien** the tomato plants are doing well **3.** [poursuivre son chemin] to push on ▸ **poussons un peu plus loin** let's go *ou* push on a bi[t] further **4.** *fam* [exagérer] to overdo it ▸ **faut pas pousser** enough's enough!
◆ ***se pousser*** **vp** to move up ▸ **pousse-toi de là, tu voi[s] bien que tu gênes!** *fam* move over *ou* shove over, can'[t] you see you're in the way?

poussette [pusɛt] **nf** pushchair *UK*, stroller *US*.

poussière [pusjɛr] **nf 1.** [gén] dust ▸ **mordre la poussière** to bite the dust ▸ **réduire en poussière** to reduc[e] to dust ▸ **et des poussières** *fam* and a bit **2.** *littéraire* [d[e] mort] ashes *pl*.

poussiéreux**, **euse [pusjerø, øz] **adj 1.** [meuble] dust[y] **2.** [teint] dull **3.** *fig* [organisation] old-fashioned.

poussif**, **ive [pusif, iv] **adj** *fam* wheezy.

poussin [pusɛ̃] **nm 1.** ZOOL chick **2.** SPORT under-11.

poussoir [puswar] **nm** push button.

poutine [putin] **nf** *Can fried potato topped with grate[d] cheese and brown sauce.*

poutre [putr] **nf** beam.

poutrelle [putrɛl] **nf** girder.

pouvoir [58] [puvwar] ■ **nm 1.** [gén] power ▸ **pouvo[ir] d'achat** purchasing power ▸ **les pouvoirs publics** the au[thorities] ▸ **arriver au pouvoir** to come to power ▸ **exerce[r] le pouvoir** to exercise power, to govern, to rule ▸ **prendr[e]**

le pouvoir [élus] to take office / [dictateur] to seize power ▸ **je ferai tout ce qui est en mon pouvoir pour t'aider** I'll do everything *ou* all in my power to help you
2. DR proxy, power of attorney ▸ **avoir pouvoir de décision** to have the authority to decide.
■ **vt 1.** [avoir la possibilité de, parvenir à] **: pouvoir faire qqch** to be able to do sthg ▸ **je ne peux pas venir ce soir** I can't come tonight ▸ **pouvez-vous...?** can you...?, could you...? ▸ **je peux vous aider?** [généralement, dans un magasin] can I help you? ▸ **je n'en peux plus** [exaspéré] I'm at the end of my tether / [fatigué] I'm exhausted ▸ **je/tu n'y peux rien** there's nothing I/you can do about it ▸ **tu aurais pu me le dire!** you might have *ou* could have told me! ▸ **il est on ne peut plus bête/gentil** nobody could be stupider/kinder
2. [avoir la permission de] **: je peux prendre la voiture?** can I borrow the car? ▸ **aucun élève ne peut partir** no pupil may leave
3. [indiquant l'éventualité] **: il peut pleuvoir** it may rain ▸ **vous pourriez rater votre train** you could *ou* might miss your train
4. [exprime une suggestion, une hypothèse] **: tu peux toujours essayer de lui téléphoner** you could always try phoning him
5. [en intensif] **: où ai-je bien pu laisser mes lunettes?** what on earth can I have done with my glasses?
◆ ***se pouvoir*** **v impers : il se peut que je me trompe** I may be mistaken ▸ **il se pourrait bien qu'il n'y ait plus de places** it might *ou* could well be fully booked ▸ **cela se peut/pourrait bien** that's quite possible.

pp (abr écrite de ***pages***) pp.

p.p. (abr écrite de ***par procuration***) pp.

PQ ■ **nm** *fam* (abr de ***papier-cul***) bog paper *UK*.
■ **1.** (abr écrite de ***province de Québec***) PQ **2.** (abr écrite de ***premier quartier (de lune)***) first quarter.

Pr (abr écrite de ***professeur***) Prof.

PR ■ **nm** (abr de ***Parti républicain***) *French political party*.
■ **nf** (abr écrite de ***poste restante***) PR.

pragmatique [pragmatik] **adj** pragmatic.

pragois**, **e**, **praguois**, **e [pragwa, az] **adj** of/from Prague.
◆ ***Pragois**, **e**, **Praguois**, **e*** **nm, f** native *ou* inhabitant of Prague.

Prague [prag] **npr** Prague.

praguois**, **e = ***pragois***.

praire [prɛr] **nf** clam.

prairie [preri] **nf** meadow / [aux États-Unis] prairie.

praline [pralin] **nf 1.** [amande] sugared almond **2.** *Belgique* [chocolat] chocolate.

praliné [praline] **nm** *almond-flavoured sponge covered with praline*.

praticable [pratikabl] ■ **adj 1.** [route] passable **2.** [plan] feasible, practicable.
■ **nm** CINÉ & THÉÂTRE [- plate-forme] (tray) dolly / [- élément de décor] prop.

praticien**, **enne [pratisjɛ̃, ɛn] **nm, f** practitioner / MÉD medical practitioner.

pratiquant**, **e [pratikɑ̃, ɑ̃t] ■ **adj** practising *UK*, practicing *US*.
■ **nm, f** practising *UK ou* practicing *US* Christian/Jew/Muslim *etc*.

pratique [pratik] ■ **nf 1.** [expérience] practical experience **2.** [usage] practice ▸ **mettre qqch en pratique** to put sthg into practice.
■ **adj** practical / [gadget, outil] handy.

pratiquement [pratikmɑ̃] **adv 1.** [en fait] in practice **2.** [quasiment] practically.

pratiquer [3] [pratike] ■ **vt 1.** [métier] to practise *UK*, to practice *US* / [sport] to do / [jeu de ballon] to play / [méthode] to apply ▸ **pratiquer la pêche/le football** to be a keen fisherman/football player **2.** [ouverture] to make.
■ **vi** RELIG to be a practising *UK ou* practicing *US* Christian/Jew/Muslim *etc*.
◆ ***se pratiquer*** **vp 1.** SPORT to be played **2.** [politique, tradition] to be the practice / [prix] to apply.

pré [pre] **nm** meadow.

préado [preado] **nmf** *fam* preadolescent.

préalable [prealabl] ■ **adj** prior, previous ▸ **préalable à** prior to, preceding ▸ **sans avis préalable** without prior warning *ou* notice.
■ **nm** precondition.
◆ ***au préalable*** **loc adv** first, beforehand.

préalablement [prealabləmɑ̃] **adv** first, beforehand ▸ **préalablement à** prior to.

préambule [preɑ̃byl] **nm 1.** [introduction, propos] preamble ▸ **sans préambule** immediately **2.** [prélude] **: préambule de** prelude to.

préau**, **x [preo] **nm 1.** [d'école] (covered) play area **2.** [de prison] (covered) exercise yard.

préavis [preavi] **nm inv** advance notice *ou* warning.

CULTURE

Préavis de licenciement

It is neither easy nor common to fire employees in France. In rare cases where it happens, employers give an employee notice of his or her dismissal. The **préavis de licenciement** ("notice period") varies from one to two months (according to length of service) and gives employees who have been fired time to look for other work while they are still earning their current salary. If a company wants to get rid of an employee more quickly, it can dispense with all or part of the **préavis** period, but it must pay the employee what he or she would have earned during that time.

précaire [prekɛr] **adj** [incertain] precarious.

précancéreux**, **euse [prekɑ̃serø, øz] **adj** precancerous.

précarisation [prekarizasjɔ̃] **nf** loss of security *ou* stability ▸ **la précarisation du travail** reduced job security.

précariser [prekarize] **vt** to make (sthg) less secure *ou* stable ▸ **précariser l'emploi** to threaten job security ▸ **la crise a précarisé leur situation** the recession has made them more vulnerable.

précarité [prekarite] **nf** [instabilité] precariousness.

précaution [prekosjɔ̃] **nf 1.** [prévoyance] precaution ▸ **par précaution** as a precaution ▸ **prendre des précautions** to take precautions **2.** [prudence] caution.

précautionneux, ***euse*** [prekosjɔnø, øz] **adj** cautious.

précédemment [presedamɑ̃] **adv** previously, before.

précédent, ***e*** [presedɑ̃, ɑ̃t] **adj** previous.
◆ ***précédent*** **nm** precedent ▸ **sans précédent** unprecedented.

précéder [18] [presede] **vt 1.** [dans le temps - gén] to precede / [- suj: personne] to arrive before **2.** [marcher devant] to go in front of **3.** *fig* [devancer] to get ahead of.

précepte [presɛpt] **nm** precept.

précepteur, ***trice*** [presɛptœr, tris] **nm, f** (private) tutor.

préchauffer [3] [preʃofe] **vt** to preheat.

prêche [prɛʃ] **nm** sermon / *fig* lecture.

prêcher [4] [preʃe] **vt & vi** to preach.

prêcheur, ***euse*** [prɛʃœr, øz] ■ **adj** preaching, moralizing.
■ **nm, f 1.** RELIG preacher **2.** *fig* [moralisateur] moralizer.

prêchi-prêcha [preʃipreʃa] **nm inv** preachifying.

précieusement [presjøzmɑ̃] **adv** preciously.

précieux, ***euse*** [presjø, øz] **adj 1.** [pierre, métal] precious / [objet] valuable / [collaborateur] invaluable, valued **2.** *péj* [style] precious, affected.

préciosité [presjozite] **nf** *péj* [affectation] preciosity, affectation.

précipice [presipis] **nm** precipice.

précipitamment [presipitamɑ̃] **adv** hastily.

précipitation [presipitasjɔ̃] **nf 1.** [hâte] haste **2.** CHIM precipitation.
◆ ***précipitations*** **nfpl** MÉTÉOR precipitation *(U)*.

précipité, ***e*** [presipite] **adj 1.** [pressé - pas] hurried / [- fuite] headlong **2.** [rapide - respiration] rapid ▸ **tout cela a été si précipité** it all happened so fast **3.** [hâtif - retour] hurried, hasty / [- décision] hasty, rash.
◆ ***précipité*** **nm** precipitate.

précipiter [3] [presipite] **vt 1.** [objet, personne] to throw, to hurl ▸ **précipiter qqn/qqch du haut de** to throw sb/sthg off, to hurl sb/sthg off **2.** [départ] to hasten.
◆ ***se précipiter*** **vp 1.** [se jeter] to throw o.s., to hurl o.s. **2.** [s'élancer] **: se précipiter (vers qqn)** to rush *ou* hurry (towards sb) **3.** [s'accélérer - gén] to speed up / [- choses, événements] to move faster.

précis, ***e*** [presi, iz] **adj 1.** [exact] precise, accurate ▸ **à cet instant précis** at that precise *ou* very moment ▸ **à 20 h précises** at precisely 8 p.m., at 8 p.m. sharp ▸ **la balance n'est pas très précise** the scales aren't very accurate **2.** [fixé] definite, precise ▸ **sans raison précise** for no particular reason ▸ **tu penses à quelqu'un de précis?** do you have a specific person in mind? **3.** [clair, net] **: je voudrais une réponse précise** I'd like a clear answer.
◆ ***précis*** **nm** handbook.

précisément [presizemɑ̃] **adv** precisely, exactly.

préciser [3] [presize] **vt 1.** [heure, lieu] to specify **2.** [pensée] to clarify.
◆ ***se préciser*** **vp** to become clear.

précision [presizjɔ̃] **nf 1.** [de style, d'explication] precision **2.** [détail] detail ▸ **apporter** *ou* **donner des précisions** to give further information.

précité, ***e*** [presite] **adj** above-mentioned.

précoce [prekɔs] **adj 1.** [plante, fruit] early **2.** [enfant] precocious.

précocité [prekɔsite] **nf 1.** [de plante, de saison] earlines **2.** [d'enfant] precociousness.

précolombien, ***enne*** [prekɔlɔ̃bjɛ̃, ɛn] **adj** pre Columbian.

préconçu, ***e*** [prekɔ̃sy] **adj** preconceived.

préconiser [3] [prekɔnize] **vt** to recommend ▸ **préco niser de faire qqch** to recommend doing sthg ▸ **préco niser que** *(+ subjonctif)* to recommend that.

précuit, ***e*** [prekɥi, it] **adj** precooked.

précurseur [prekyrsœr] ■ **nm** precursor, forerunner.
■ **adj** precursory.

prédateur, ***trice*** [predatœr, tris] **adj** predatory.
◆ ***prédateur*** **nm** predator.

prédécesseur [predesesœr] **nm** predecessor.

prédécoupé, ***e*** [predekupe] **adj** pre-cut.

prédestination [predɛstinasjɔ̃] **nf** predestination.

prédestiner [3] [predɛstine] **vt** to predestine ▸ **êtr prédestiné à qqch/à faire qqch** to be predestined f sthg/to do sthg.

prédéterminer [3] [predetɛrmine] **vt** to predete mine.

prédicat [predika] **nm** predicate.

prédicateur, ***trice*** [predikatœr, tris] **nm, f** preache

prédication [predikasjɔ̃] **nf** preaching / [discour sermon.

prédiction [prediksjɔ̃] **nf** prediction.

prédilection [predilɛksjɔ̃] **nf** partiality ▸ **avoir u prédilection pour** to have a partiality *ou* liking for ▸ **prédilection** favourite *(avant n)* *UK*, favorite *(avant n)* *U*

prédire [103] [predir] **vt** to predict.

prédisposer [3] [predispoze] **vt : prédisposer qqn qqch** to predispose sb to sthg.

prédisposition [predispozisjɔ̃] **nf : prédisposition** predisposition to *ou* towards.

prédit, ***e*** [predi, it] **pp** ➤ ***prédire***.

prédominant**, **e [predɔminɑ̃, ɑ̃t] **adj** predominant.

prédominer [3] [predɔmine] **vt** to predominate.

préélectoral**, **e**, **aux [preelɛktɔral, o] **adj** pre-election *(avant n)*.

préemballé**, **e [preɑ̃bale] **adj** prepacked, pre-packaged.

prééminence [preeminɑ̃s] **nf** preeminence.

préemption [preɑ̃psjɔ̃] **nf** preemption.

préétabli**, **e [preetabli] **adj** pre-established.

préexistant**, **e [preɛgzistɑ̃, ɑ̃t] **adj** preexisting.

préfabriqué**, **e [prefabrike] **adj** **1.** [maison] prefabricated **2.** [accusation, sourire] false.
◆ ***préfabriqué*** **nm** prefabricated material.

préface [prefas] **nf** preface.

préfacer [16] [prefase] **vt** [livre, texte] to preface ▸ **préfacer un ouvrage** to write a preface to *ou* to preface a book.

préfectoral**, **e**, **aux [prefɛktɔral, o] **adj** prefectorial.

préfecture [prefɛktyr] **nf** prefecture.

préférable [preferabl] **adj** preferable.

préféré**, **e [prefere] **adj** & **nm, f** favourite *UK*, favorite *US*.

préférence [preferɑ̃s] **nf** preference ▸ **de préférence** preferably ▸ **préférence du consommateur** consumer preference.

préférentiel**, **elle [preferɑ̃sjɛl] **adj** preferential.

préférer [18] [prefere] **vt : préférer qqn/qqch (à)** to prefer sb/sthg (to) ▸ **préférer faire qqch** to prefer to do sthg ▸ **je préfère rentrer** I would rather go home, I would prefer to go home ▸ **je préfère ça!** I like that better!, I prefer that!

préfet [prefɛ] **nm** prefect.

préfigurer [3] [prefigyre] **vt** to prefigure.

préfixe [prefiks] **nm** prefix.

préhistoire [preistwar] **nf** prehistory.

préhistorique [preistɔrik] **adj** prehistoric.

préinscription [preɛ̃skripsjɔ̃] **nf** preregistration.

préinstallé [logiciel] preinstalled.

préjudice [preʒydis] **nm** harm *(U)*, detriment *(U)* ▸ **porter préjudice à qqn** to harm sb.

préjudiciable [preʒydisjabl] **adj : préjudiciable (à)** harmful (to), detrimental (to).

préjugé [preʒyʒe] **nm : préjugé (contre)** prejudice (against).

préjuger [17] [preʒyʒe] **vt** *littéraire* to prejudge ▸ **autant qu'on puisse préjuger** as far as one can judge beforehand.
◆ ***préjuger de*** **v + prep** *littéraire* **: préjuger de qqch** to judge sthg in advance, to prejudge sthg ▸ **son attitude ne laisse rien préjuger de sa décision** his attitude gives us no indication of what he is going to decide ▸ **je crains d'avoir préjugé de mes forces** I'm afraid I've overestimated my strength.

prélasser [3] [prelase] ◆ ***se prélasser*** **vp** to lounge.

prélat [prela] **nm** prelate.

prélavage [prelavaʒ] **nm** pre-wash.

prélèvement [prelɛvmɑ̃] **nm** **1.** MÉD removal / [de sang] sample **2.** FIN deduction ▸ **prélèvement (de l'impôt) à la source** taxation at source, pay-as-you-earn *UK* ▸ **prélèvement automatique** direct debit *UK* ▸ **prélèvement mensuel** monthly standing order *UK* ▸ **prélèvements obligatoires** tax and social security contributions.

prélever [19] [prelve] **vt** **1.** FIN **: prélever de l'argent (sur)** to deduct money (from) **2.** MÉD to remove ▸ **prélever du sang** to take a blood sample.

préliminaire [preliminɛr] **adj** preliminary.
◆ ***préliminaires*** **nmpl** **1.** [de paix] preliminary talks **2.** [de discours] preliminaries.

prélude [prelyd] **nm : prélude (à)** prelude (to).

préluder [3] [prelyde] **vi** **1.** [marquer le début] **: préluder à** to be a prelude to **2.** MUS to warm up.

prématuré**, **e [prematyre] ■ **adj** premature.
■ **nm, f** premature baby.

prématurément [prematyremɑ̃] **adv** prematurely.

préméditation [premeditasjɔ̃] **nf** premeditation ▸ **avec préméditation** [meurtre] premeditated / [agir] with premeditation.

prémédité**, **e [premedite] **adj** **1.** DR [crime] premeditated, wilful **2.** [insulte, réponse] deliberate.

COMMENT EXPRIMER...
la préférence

I like going to the cinema / J'aime aller au cinéma
I'm fond of (listening to) music / J'aime beaucoup la musique
I enjoy Peter's company / J'aime bien être avec Peter
I think she's really nice / Je la trouve très sympa
I prefer red wine to white wine / J'aime mieux le vin rouge que le vin blanc
I much prefer baseball to cricket / Je préfère de loin le base-ball au cricket
I'd rather fly than go by train / J'aimerais mieux y aller en avion plutôt qu'en train
Saturday would suit me better / Samedi me conviendrait davantage
I'd rather you went instead of me / Je préférerais que tu y ailles à ma place
Would you rather meet somewhere else? / Préférez-vous qu'on se retrouve ailleurs ?

préméditer [3] [premedite] vt to premeditate ▸ **préméditer de faire qqch** to plan to do sthg.

prémices [premis] nfpl *sout* beginnings.

premier, ère [prəmje, ɛr] ■ adj **1.** [gén] first ▸ **au premier abord** at first ▸ **au premier rang** CINÉ & THÉÂTRE in the first *ou* front row / SCOL in the first row ▸ **on s'est arrêtés dans le premier hôtel venu** we stopped at the first hotel we came to *ou* happened to come to ▸ **ses premières œuvres** her early works / [étage] first *UK*, second *US*
2. [qualité] top ▸ **elle a eu le premier prix d'interprétation** she's won the award for best actress ▸ **le premier pays producteur de vin au monde** the world's leading wine-producing country ▸ **le premier personnage de l'État** the country's Head of State
3. [état] original ▸ **l'idée première était de...** the original idea was to...
■ **nm, f** first ▸ **être/sortir premier** to be/come first, to be/come top ▸ **elle est la première de sa classe/au hit-parade** she's top of her class/the charts ▸ **jeune premier** CINÉ leading man.
◆ ***premier*** nm [étage] first floor *UK*, second floor *US* ▸ **la dame du premier** the lady on the first floor.
◆ ***première*** nf **1.** CINÉ première / THÉÂTRE première, first night
2. [exploit] first ▸ **c'est une (grande) première chirurgicale** it's a first for surgery
3. [première classe] first class ▸ **voyager en première** to travel first class
4. SCOL ≃ lower sixth year *ou* form *UK*, ≃ eleventh grade *US*
5. AUTO first (gear) ▸ **être/passer en première** to be in/to go into first.
◆ ***premier de l'an*** nm : **le premier de l'an** New Year's Day.
◆ ***en premier*** loc adv first, firstly ▸ **je dois m'occuper en premier de mon visa** the first thing I must do is to see about my visa.

premièrement [prəmjɛrmɑ̃] adv first, firstly.

premier-né, première-née [prəmjene, prəmjɛrne] (mpl **premiers-nés**) (fpl **premières-nées**) nm, f first-born (child).

prémisse [premis] nf premise.

prémolaire [premɔlɛr] nf premolar.

prémonition [premɔnisjɔ̃] nf premonition.

prémonitoire [premɔnitwar] adj premonitory.

prémunir [32] [premynir] vt : **prémunir qqn (contre)** to protect sb (against).
◆ ***se prémunir*** vp to protect o.s. ▸ **se prémunir contre qqch** to guard against sthg.

prenais, prenions ➤ ***prendre***.

prenant, e [prənɑ̃, ɑ̃t] ■ p prés ➤ ***prendre***.
■ adj **1.** [film, histoire] absorbing **2.** DR : **partie prenante** payee.

prénatal, e [prenatal] (pl **prénatals** *ou* **prénataux** [prenato]) adj antenatal, prenatal *US* / [allocation] maternity *(avant n)*.

prendre [79] [prɑ̃dr] ■ vt **1.** [gén] to take ▸ **prends la casserole par le manche** pick the pan up by the handle ▸ **prendre qqch/qqn (en photo)** to take a picture *ou* photo *ou* photograph of sthg/sb ▸ **prendre un jour de congé** to take *ou* to have the day off
2. [enlever] to take (away) ▸ **prendre qqch à qqn** to take sthg from sb
3. [aller chercher - objet] to get, to fetch / [- personne] to pick up ▸ **inutile de prendre un parapluie** there's no need to take *ou* no need for an umbrella ▸ **(passer) prendre qqn : je suis passé la prendre chez elle à midi** I picked her up at *ou* collected her from her home at midday
4. [repas, boisson] to have ▸ **vous prendrez quelque chose?** would you like something to eat/drink?
5. [voleur] to catch ▸ **se faire prendre** to get caught
6. [responsabilité] to take (on) ▸ **prendre sur soi de faire qqch** to take it upon o.s. to do sthg
7. [aborder - personne] to handle / [- problème] to tackle ▸ **prendre qqn en pitié** to take pity on sb ▸ **prendre qqn par qqch** to win sb over by sthg ▸ **prendre qqn par surprise** to take sb by surprise ▸ **à tout prendre** on the whole, all things considered ▸ **prendre de bonnes résolutions pour l'avenir** to resolve to do better in the future ▸ **on me prend souvent pour ma sœur** I'm often mistaken for my sister
8. [réserver] to book / [louer] to rent, to take / [acheter] to buy ▸ **j'ai pris des artichauts pour ce soir** I've got *ou* bought some artichokes for tonight
9. [poids] to gain, to put on
10. [embaucher] to take on.
■ **vi 1.** [ciment, sauce] to set
2. [plante, greffe] to take / [mode] to catch on
3. [feu] to catch ▸ **je n'arrive pas à faire prendre le feu les brindilles** I can't get the fire going/the twigs to catch
4. [se diriger] : **prendre à droite** to turn right.
◆ ***se prendre*** vp **1.** [vêtement] to get caught ▸ **le foulard s'est pris dans la portière** the scarf got caught *ou* shut in the door ▸ **se prendre à** to catch on
2. [se considérer] : **pour qui se prend-il?** who does he think he is?
▸▸ **s'en prendre à qqn** [physiquement] to set about sb *UK* / [verbalement] to take it out on sb ▸ **pourquoi faut-il toujours que tu t'en prennes à moi?** why do you always take it out on me? ▸ **je sais comment m'y prendre** I know how to do it *ou* go about it.

preneur, euse [prənœr, øz] nm, f [locataire] lessee [acheteur] purchaser.

prenne, prennes ➤ ***prendre***.

prénom [prenɔ̃] nm first name.

prénommer [3] [prenɔme] vt to name, to call.
◆ ***se prénommer*** vp to be called.

prénuptial, e, aux [prenypsjal, o] adj premarital.

préoccupant, e [preɔkypɑ̃, ɑ̃t] adj preoccupying.

préoccupation [preɔkypasjɔ̃] nf preoccupation.

préoccupé, e [preɔkype] adj preoccupied.

préoccuper [3] [preɔkype] vt to preoccupy.
◆ ***se préoccuper*** vp : **se préoccuper de qqch** to be worried about sthg, to think about.

préparateur, trice [preparatœr, tris] **nm, f** lab *ou* laboratory assistant ▸ **préparateur en pharmacie** chemist's assistant *UK*, druggist's assistant *US*.

préparatifs [preparatif] **nmpl** preparations.

préparation [preparasjɔ̃] **nf** preparation.

préparatoire [preparatwar] **adj** preparatory.

préparer [3] [prepare] **vt 1.** [gén] to prepare / [plat, repas] to cook, to prepare ▸ **préparer qqn à qqch** to prepare sb for sthg **2.** [réserver] **: préparer qqch à qqn** to have sthg in store for sb **3.** [congrès] to organize.
◆ ***se préparer*** **vp 1.** [personne] **: se préparer à qqch/à faire qqch** to prepare for sthg/to do sthg **2.** [tempête] to be brewing.

prépondérance [prepɔ̃derɑ̃s] **nf : prépondérance (sur)** dominance (over), supremacy (over).

prépondérant, e [prepɔ̃derɑ̃, ɑ̃t] **adj** dominating.

préposé, e [prepoze] **nm, f** (minor) official / [de vestiaire] attendant / [facteur] postman (f postwoman) *UK*, mailman *US*, mail *ou* letter carrier *US* ▸ **préposé à qqch** person in charge of sthg.

préposer [3] [prepoze] **vt** to put in charge ▸ **être préposé à qqch/à faire qqch** to be (put) in charge of sthg/of doing sthg.

préposition [prepozisjɔ̃] **nf** preposition.

prépuce [prepys] **nm** foreskin.

préréglé, e [preregle] **adj** preset, preprogrammed.

préretraite [prerətrɛt] **nf** early retirement / [allocation] early retirement pension.

prérogative [prerɔgativ] **nf** prerogative.

près [prɛ] **adv** near, close ▸ **le bureau est tout près** the office is very near *ou* just around the corner ▸ **jeudi c'est trop près, disons plutôt samedi** Thursday is too soon, let's say Saturday.
◆ ***de près*** **loc adv** closely ▸ **regarder qqch de près** to watch sthg closely ▸ **de plus/très près** more/very closely ▸ **il est rasé de près** he's clean-shaven.
◆ ***près de*** **loc prép 1.** [dans l'espace] near, close to ▸ **assieds-toi près de lui** sit near him *ou* next to him **2.** [dans le temps] close to ▸ **il est près de partir** he's about to leave ▸ **il doit être près de la retraite** he must be about to retire **3.** [presque] nearly, almost ▸ **on était près de cinquante** there were almost *ou* nearly fifty of us.
◆ ***à peu près*** **loc adv** more or less, just about ▸ **il est à peu près cinq heures** it's about five o'clock ▸ **il sait à peu près comment y aller** he knows more or less *ou* roughly how to get there.
◆ ***à peu de chose(s) près*** **loc adv** more or less, approximately ▸ **à peu de choses près, il y en a cinquante** there are fifty of them, more or less *ou* give or take a few.
◆ ***à ceci près que, à cela près que*** **loc conj** except that, apart from the fact that.
◆ ***à... près*** **loc adv : à dix centimètres près** to within ten centimetres ▸ **il n'en est pas à un ou deux jours près** a day or two more or less won't make any difference.

présage [prezaʒ] **nm** omen.

présager [17] [prezaʒe] **vt 1.** [annoncer] to portend **2.** [prévoir] to predict ▸ **laisser présager de qqch** to hint at sthg.

pré-salé [presale] (pl **prés-salés**) **nm** *lamb reared on salt marshes.*

presbyte [prɛsbit] ■ **nmf** longsighted person *UK*, farsighted person *US*.
■ **adj** longsighted *UK*, farsighted *US*.

presbytère [prɛsbitɛr] **nm** presbytery.

presbytérien, enne [prɛsbiterjɛ̃, ɛn] **nm, f & adj** Presbyterian.

presbytie [prɛsbisi] **nf** longsightedness *UK*, farsightedness *US*.

prescience [presjɑ̃s] **nf** *littéraire* foresight.

préscolaire [preskɔlɛr] **adj** preschool *(avant n)*.

prescription [prɛskripsjɔ̃] **nf 1.** MÉD prescription **2.** DR limitation.

prescrire [99] [prɛskrir] **vt 1.** [mesures, conditions] to lay down, to stipulate **2.** MÉD to prescribe.
◆ ***se prescrire*** **vp** MÉD to be prescribed.

prescrit, e [prɛskri, it] **pp** ➤ ***prescrire***.

prescrivais, prescrivions ➤ ***prescrire***.

préséance [preseɑ̃s] **nf** precedence.

présélection [preselɛksjɔ̃] **nf** preselection / [pour concours] making a list of finalists, short-listing *UK*.

présélectionner [3] [preselɛksjɔne] **vt** to preselect / [candidats] to put on a list of finalists, to short-list *UK*.

présence [prezɑ̃s] **nf 1.** [gén] presence ▸ **en présence** face to face ▸ **honorer qqn de sa présence** to honour sb with one's presence ▸ **en présence de** in the presence of ▸ **en sa *etc* présence** in his/her *etc* presence **2.** [compagnie] company *(U)* **3.** [assiduité] attendance ▸ **feuille de présence** attendance sheet.
◆ ***présence d'esprit*** **nf** presence of mind.

présent, e [prezɑ̃, ɑ̃t] **adj 1.** [gén] present ▸ **le présent ouvrage** this work ▸ **la présente loi** this law ▸ **avoir qqch présent à l'esprit** to remember sthg ▸ **être présent à une conférence** to be present at *ou* to attend a conference ▸ **dans le cas présent** in the present case **2.** [actif] attentive, involved ▸ **les Français ne sont pas du tout présents dans le jeu** the French team is making no impact on the game at all.
◆ ***présent*** **nm 1.** [gén] present ▸ **faire présent à qqn de qqch** *sout* to make sb a present of sthg ▸ **à présent** at present ▸ **je travaille à présent dans une laiterie** I'm working in a dairy at present ▸ **à présent que** now that ▸ **jusqu'à présent** up to now, so far ▸ **dès à présent** right away ▸ **vivre dans le présent** to live in the present **2.** GRAMM **: le présent** the present tense ▸ **au présent** in the present.
◆ ***présente*** **nf : je vous informe par la présente que...** I hereby inform you that...

présentable [prezɑ̃tabl] **adj 1.** [d'aspect] presentable **2.** [d'attitude] **: tu n'es pas présentable** I can't take you anywhere.

présentateur, trice [prezɑ̃tatœr, tris] **nm, f** presenter *UK*, anchorman (f anchorwoman).

présentation [prezɑ̃tasjɔ̃] **nf 1.** [de personne] **: faire les présentations** to make the introductions **2.** [aspect extérieur] appearance ▸ **avoir une bonne/mauvaise présentation** to be of a pleasing/disagreeable appearance **3.** [de papiers, de produit, de film] presentation ▸ **sur présentation de** on presentation of ▸ **présentation de la marque** brand presentation **4.** [de magazine] layout.

présentement [prezɑ̃tmɑ̃] **adv** at the moment, at present.

présenter [3] [prezɑ̃te] ■ **vt 1.** [gén] to present ▸ **présenter sa candidature à un poste** to apply for a position ▸ **présenter l'avantage de** to have the advantage of / [projet] to present, to submit **2.** [invité] to introduce ▸ **je te présente ma sœur Blanche** this is *ou* let me introduce my sister Blanche **3.** [condoléances, félicitations, avantages] to offer ▸ **présenter ses excuses** to offer (one's) apologies / [hommages] to pay ▸ **présenter ses hommages à qqn** to pay one's respects to sb ▸ **présenter qqch à qqn** to offer sb sthg.
■ **vi** *fam* **: présenter bien/mal** to make a good/bad impression.
◆ ***se présenter*** **vp 1.** [se faire connaître] **: se présenter (à)** to introduce o.s. (to) **2.** [être candidat] **: se présenter à** to stand in *UK*, to run in *US* ; **se présenter aux présidentielles** to run for president **3.** [examen] to sit *UK*, to take ▸ **se présenter pour un poste** to apply for a job **4.** [paraître] to appear **5.** [occasion, situation] to arise, to present itself ▸ **si une difficulté se présente** if any difficulty should arise **6.** [affaire, contrat] **: se présenter bien/mal** to look good/bad ▸ **l'affaire se présente sous un jour nouveau** the matter can be seen *ou* appears in a new light.

présentoir [prezɑ̃twar] **nm** display stand.

préservatif [prezɛrvatif] **nm** condom.

préservation [prezɛrvasjɔ̃] **nf** preservation.

préserver [3] [prezɛrve] **vt** to preserve.
◆ ***se préserver*** **vp : se préserver de** to protect o.s. from.

présidence [prezidɑ̃s] **nf 1.** [de groupe] chairmanship **2.** [d'État] presidency **3.** [lieu] presidential residence *ou* palace.

président, e [prezidɑ̃, ɑ̃t] **nm, f 1.** [d'assemblée] chairman (f chairwoman) ▸ **président du conseil d'administration** chairman of the board **2.** [d'État] president ▸ **Monsieur/Madame le Président** Mr/Madam President ▸ **président de la République** President (of the Republic) of France **3.** DR [de tribunal] presiding judge / [de jury] foreman (f forewoman).
◆ ***présidente*** **nf** *vieilli* president's wife.
◆ ***président-directeur général*** **nm** (chairman and) managing director *UK*, president and chief executive officer *US*.

présidentiable [prezidɑ̃sjabl] **nmf** would-be presidential candidate.

présidentiel, elle [prezidɑ̃sjɛl] **adj** presidential ▸ **régime présidentiel** presidential system.

présider [3] [prezide] ■ **vt 1.** [réunion] to chair **2.** [banquet, dîner] to preside over.
■ **vi : présider à** to be in charge of / *fig* to govern, to preside at.

présomptif, ive [prezɔ̃ptif, iv] **adj : héritier présomptif** heir apparent.

présomption [prezɔ̃psjɔ̃] **nf 1.** [hypothèse] presumption **2.** DR presumption ▸ **présomption d'innocence** presumption of innocence **3.** *littéraire* [prétention] presumptuousness.

présomptueux, euse [prezɔ̃ptɥø, øz] ■ **adj** presumptuous.
■ **nm, f** *littéraire* presumptuous person.

presque [prɛsk] **adv** almost, nearly ▸ **presque rien** next to nothing, scarcely anything ▸ **presque jamais** hardly ever.

presqu'île [prɛskil] **nf** peninsula.

pressant, e [prɛsɑ̃, ɑ̃t] **adj** pressing.

COMMENT EXPRIMER...
les présentations

Se présenter
Hello, my name's Robert / Bonjour, je m'appelle Robert
I'm Charlotte Martin from the Maonia Bank / Je suis Charlotte Martin de la banque Maonia
I'd like to introduce myself, I'm Tanya / Je me présente, je m'appelle Tanya
Hi, I'm Tom / Salut ! Moi, c'est Tom
I don't think we've met / Je ne crois pas que nous nous connaissions

Présenter quelqu'un
I'd like you to meet Miss Fouquet / J'aimerais vous présenter Mlle Fouquet
Can I introduce you to our Head of Sales? / Laissez-moi vous présenter à notre directeur/directrice des ventes
This is Emma / Je te présente Emma
Paul, do you know Katie? / Paul, tu connais Katie ?
Have you two met? / Est-ce que vous avez été présentés ?
Do you know everybody? / Tu connais tout le monde ?
Shall I do the introductions? / Je vais faire les présentations :

Une fois que les présentations sont faites
How do you do? / Enchanté
Pleased to meet you / Très heureux de vous rencontrer
I'm sorry, I didn't catch your name / Excusez-moi, je n'ai pas saisi votre nom

press-book [presbuk] (pl **press-books**) **nm** portfolio.

presse [pres] **nf 1.** [journaux] press ▸ **avoir bonne/mauvaise presse** to have a good/bad press ▸ **presse féminine/financière/nationale/sportive** women's/financial/national/sports magazines ▸ **presse à sensation** *OU* **à scandale** popular press, gutter press, ≃ tabloids **2.** [d'imprimerie] press ▸ **être mis sous presse** to go to press ▸ **sortir de presse** to come out.

CULTURE

Presse régionale/nationale

French daily newspapers are divided into two categories: the **presse nationale** and the **presse (quotidienne) régionale.** Among the national dailies, the centre-left **Le Monde** is often considered the best. The others are the right-wing **Le Figaro; Libération,** a left-leaning paper often called **Libé; France-Soir,** known for its features content; and **Les Échos,** which covers the economy. **L'Humanité** is published by the Communist Party; **L'Équipe** is a popular sports daily. Dailies focusing on local issues are published in each of France's regions. Weekly publications include news magazines like **L'Express, Le Point, Le Nouvel Observateur (Nouvel Obs), Paris Match, VSD,** and **Le Figaro Magazine** (sold with the paper). **Le Canard Enchaîné** is a satirical investigative weekly paper.

pressé, e [prese] **adj 1.** [travail] urgent ▸ **aller au plus pressé** to do first things first **2.** [personne] **: être pressé** to be in a hurry **3.** [citron, orange] freshly squeezed.

presse-citron [pressitrɔ̃] **nm inv** lemon squeezer.

pressentiment [presɑ̃timɑ̃] **nm** premonition.

pressentir [37] [presɑ̃tir] **vt 1.** [événement] to have a premonition of **2.** *sout* [personne] to sound out.

presse-papiers [prespapje] **nm inv** paperweight.

presse-purée [prespyre] **nm inv** potato masher.

presser [4] [prese] ■ **vt 1.** [écraser - olives] to press / [- citron, orange] to squeeze ▸ **presser qqn comme un citron** *fam fig* to exploit sb to the full, to squeeze sb dry **2.** [disque] to press **3.** [dans ses bras] to squeeze ▸ **il pressait sur son cœur la photo de sa fille** he was clasping a picture of his daughter to his heart **4.** [bouton] to press, to push **5.** *sout* [harceler] **: presser qqn de faire qqch** to press sb to do sthg ▸ **presser qqn de questions** to bombard sb with questions **6.** [faire se hâter] to speed up, to rush ▸ **j'ai horreur qu'on me presse** I hate being rushed ▸ **presser le pas** to speed up, to walk faster.
■ **vi : le temps presse** time is short ▸ **rien ne presse, ça ne presse pas** there's no (need to) rush *OU* hurry.
◆ ***se presser*** **vp 1.** [se dépêcher] to hurry (up) ▸ **sans se presser** without hurrying *OU* rushing ▸ **se presser de faire qqch** to be in a hurry to do sthg **2.** [s'agglutiner] **: se presser (autour de)** to crowd (around) ▸ **les gens se pressaient au guichet** there was a crush at the box office **3.** [se serrer] to huddle ▸ **il se pressait contre moi tant il avait peur** he was pressing up against me from fright.

pressing [presiŋ] **nm** steam pressing / [établissement] dry cleaner's.

pression [presjɔ̃] **nf 1.** [gén] pressure ▸ **exercer une pression sur qqch** to exert pressure on sthg ▸ **une simple pression de la main suffit** you just have to press lightly ▸ **exercer une pression sur qqn, faire pression sur qqn** to put pressure on sb ▸ **sous pression** *fig* [liquide] under pressure / [cabine] pressurized ▸ **mettre sous pression** to pressurize ▸ **pression artérielle** blood pressure ▸ **pression atmosphérique** atmospheric pressure ▸ **pression fiscale** tax burden **2.** [sur vêtement] press stud *UK*, popper *UK*, snap fastener *US* **3.** [bière] draught *UK ou* draft *US* beer.

pressoir [preswar] **nm 1.** [machine] press **2.** [lieu] press house.

pressurer [3] [presyre] **vt 1.** [objet] to press, to squeeze **2.** *fig* [contribuable] to squeeze.

pressurisation [presyrizasjɔ̃] **nf** pressurization.

pressuriser [3] [presyrize] **vt** to pressurize.

prestance [prestɑ̃s] **nf** bearing ▸ **avoir de la prestance** to have presence.

prestataire [prestater] **nmf 1.** [bénéficiaire] person in receipt of benefit, claimant **2.** [fournisseur] provider ▸ **prestataire de service** service provider.

prestation [prestasjɔ̃] **nf 1.** [allocation] benefit *UK* ▸ **prestation en nature** payment in kind ▸ **prestations familiales** ≃ family allowance *UK* **2.** [de comédien] performance **3.** [de serment] taking.

preste [prest] **adj** *littéraire* nimble.

prestement [prestəmɑ̃] **adv** nimbly.

prestidigitateur, trice [prestidiʒitatœr, tris] **nm, f** conjurer.

prestidigitation [prestidiʒitasjɔ̃] **nf** conjuring.

prestige [prestiʒ] **nm** prestige.

prestigieux, euse [prestiʒjø, øz] **adj 1.** [magnifique] splendid **2.** [réputé] prestigious.

présumé, e [prezyme] **adj** presumed.

présumer [3] [prezyme] ■ **vt** to presume, to assume ▸ **présumer que** to presume (that), to assume (that) ▸ **être présumé coupable/innocent** to be presumed guilty/innocent.
■ **vi : présumer de qqch** to overestimate sthg.

présupposé [presypoze] **nm** presupposition.

présupposer [3] [presypoze] **vt** to presuppose.

présure [prezyr] **nf** rennet.

prêt, e [prɛ, prɛt] **adj** ready ▸ **prêt à qqch/à faire qqch** ready for sthg/to do sthg ▸ **prêt à tout** ready for anything ▸ **prêts? partez!** SPORT get set, go!, ready, steady, go! *UK*
◆ ***prêt*** **nm** [action] lending *(U)* / [objet, matériel] **: prêt à l'usage** off-the-shelf / [somme] loan ▸ **prêt bancaire** bank loan ▸ **prêt non-garanti** unsecured loan ▸ **prêt-logement** repayment mortgage ▸ **prêt sans intérêt** interest-free loan ▸ **prêt personnel** *OU* **personnalisé** personal loan.

prêt-à-porter [prɛtapɔrte] (pl **prêts-à-porter**) **nm** ready-to-wear clothing *(U)*.

prétendant [pretɑ̃dɑ̃] **nm** **1.** [au trône] pretender **2.** [amoureux] suitor.

prétendre [73] [pretɑ̃dr] ■ **vt** **1.** [affecter] **: prétendre faire qqch** to claim to do sthg **2.** [affirmer] **: prétendre que** to claim (that), to maintain (that) **3.** *littéraire* [exiger] **: prétendre faire qqch** to intend to do sthg.
■ **vi** [aspirer] **: prétendre à qqch** to aspire to sthg.
◆ ***se prétendre*** **vp : se prétendre acteur/écrivain** to claim to be an actor/an author.

FAUX AMIS / FALSE FRIENDS
prétendre
Pretend is not a translation of the French word *prétendre.* Pretend is translated by *faire semblant.*
▸ He pretended not to be interested / *Il a fait semblant de ne pas être intéressé*

prétendu, e [pretɑ̃dy] ■ **pp** ➤ ***prétendre***.
■ **adj** *(avant n)* so-called.

prétendument [pretɑ̃dymɑ̃] **adv** supposedly.

prête-nom [prɛtnɔ̃] (pl **prête-noms**) **nm** front man.

prétentieux, euse [pretɑ̃sjø, øz] ■ **adj** pretentious.
■ **nm, f** pretentious person.

prétention [pretɑ̃sjɔ̃] **nf** **1.** [suffisance] pretentiousness **2.** [ambition] pretension, ambition ▸ **avoir la prétention de faire qqch** to claim *ou* pretend to do sthg.

prêter [4] [prete] ■ **vt** **1.** [fournir] **: prêter qqch (à qqn)** [objet, argent] to lend (sb) sthg / *fig* [concours, appui] to lend (sb) sthg, to give (sb) sthg ▸ **peux-tu me prêter ta voiture?** can you lend me *ou* can I borrow your car? ▸ **prêter attention à** to pay attention to **2.** [attribuer] **: prêter qqch à qqn** to attribute sthg to sb ▸ **prêter de l'importance à qqch** to attach importance to sthg ▸ **on lui a parfois prêté des pouvoirs magiques** he was sometimes alleged *ou* claimed to have magical powers.
■ **vi : prêter à** to lead to, to generate ▸ **le texte prête à confusion** the text is open to misinterpretation.
◆ ***se prêter*** **vp : se prêter à** [participer à] to go along with / [convenir à] to fit, to suit ▸ **se prêter au jeu** to enter into the spirit of the game ▸ **si le temps s'y prête** weather permitting.

prétérit [preterit] **nm** preterite.

prêteur, euse [prɛtœr, øz] ■ **adj** generous.
■ **nm, f : prêteur sur gages** pawnbroker ▸ **prêteur hypothécaire** mortgage lender.

prétexte [pretɛkst] **nm** pretext, excuse ▸ **sous prétexte de faire qqch/que** on the pretext of doing sthg/that, under the pretext of doing sthg/that ▸ **sous aucun prétexte** on no account.

prétexter [4] [pretɛkste] **vt** to give as an excuse.

prétimbré, e [pretɛ̃bre] **adj** prepaid.

Pretoria [pretɔrja] **npr** Pretoria.

prêtre [prɛtr] **nm** priest.

prêtresse [prɛtrɛs] **nf** priestess.

preuve [prœv] **nf** **1.** [gén] proof **2.** DR evidence **3.** [témoignage] sign, token ▸ **faire preuve de qqch** to show sthg ▸ **faire ses preuves** to prove o.s./itself.

preux [prø] *littéraire* ■ **nm** knight valiant.
■ **adj m** valiant.

prévaloir [61] [prevalwar] **vi** [dominer] **: prévaloir (sur)** to prevail (over).
◆ ***se prévaloir*** **vp : se prévaloir de** to boast about.

prévalu [prevaly] **pp inv** ➤ ***prévaloir***.

prévarication [prevarikasjɔ̃] **nf** *sout* breach of trust.

prévaudrai, prévaux **v** ➤ ***prévaloir***.

prévaut ➤ ***prévaloir***.

prévenance [prevnɑ̃s] **nf** **1.** [attitude] thoughtfulness, consideration **2.** [action] considerate *ou* thoughtful act.

prévenant, e [prevnɑ̃, ɑ̃t] **adj** considerate, attentive.

prévenir [40] [prevnir] **vt** **1.** [employé, élève] **: prévenir qqn (de)** to warn sb (about) **2.** [police] to inform **3.** [désirs] to anticipate **4.** [maladie] to prevent **5.** *littéraire* [prédisposer] **: prévenir qqn contre qqn** to prejudice sb against sb.

préventif, ive [prevɑ̃tif, iv] **adj** **1.** [mesure, médecine] preventive **2.** DR **: être en détention préventive** to be on remand.

prévention [prevɑ̃sjɔ̃] **nf** **1.** [protection] **: prévention (contre)** prevention (of) ▸ **prévention routière** road safety (measures) **2.** DR remand.

prévenu, e [prevny] ■ **pp** ➤ ***prévenir***.
■ **nm, f** accused, defendant.

préviendrai, préviendras ➤ ***prévenir***.

prévisible [previzibl] **adj** foreseeable.

prévision [previzjɔ̃] **nf** forecast, prediction ▸ **les prévisions météorologiques** the weather forecast / [de coûts] estimate / ÉCON forecast ▸ **prévisions budgétaires** budget forecast ▸ **prévision des ventes** sales forecast.
◆ ***en prévision de*** **loc prép** in anticipation of.

prévisionnel, elle [previzjɔnɛl] **adj** anticipatory ▸ **budget prévisionnel** budget estimate.

prévoir [63] [prevwar] **vt** **1.** [s'attendre à] to expect **2.** [prédire] to predict **3.** [anticiper] to foresee, to anticipate **4.** [programmer] to plan ▸ **n'être pas prévu** to be unforeseen ▸ **comme prévu** as planned, according to plan.

prévoyais, prévoyions ➤ ***prévoir***.

prévoyance [prevwajɑ̃s] **nf** [de personne] foresight voir aussi ***caisse***.

prévoyant, e [prevwajɑ̃, ɑ̃t] **adj** provident.

prévu, e [prevy] **pp** ➤ ***prévoir***.

prie-Dieu [pridjø] **nm inv** prie-dieu.

prier [10] [prije] ■ **vt** **1.** RELIG to pray to ▸ **je prie Dieu et tous ses saints que...** I pray (to) God and all his saints that... **2.** [implorer] to beg ▸ **(ne pas) se faire prier (pour faire qqch)** (not) to need to be persuaded (to do sthg) ▸ **je vous en prie** [de grâce] please, I beg you / [de rien] don't mention it, not at all **3.** *sout* [demander] **: prier qqn de faire qqch** to request sb to do sthg ▸ **prier instamment qqn de faire qqch** to insist that sb does sthg ▸ **je vous pri**

de croire à mes sentiments distingués yours sincerely ▸ **vous êtes priés de** you are requested to **4.** *littéraire* [convier] to invite ▸ **prier qqn à** to ask *ou* to invite sb for, to request sb to *littéraire*.
■ **vi** RELIG to pray ▸ **prions pour la paix** let us pray for peace.

prière [prijɛr] **nf 1.** [RELIG - recueillement] prayer *(U)*, praying *(U)* / [- formule] prayer / [- office] prayers *pl* **2.** *littéraire* [demande] entreaty ▸ **prière de frapper avant d'entrer** please knock before entering.

prieuré [prijœre] **nm** priory.

primaire [primɛr] **adj 1.** [premier] **: couleur primaire** primary colour *UK ou* color *US* ▸ **élection primaire** primary (election) ▸ **ère primaire** Palaeozoic era ▸ **études primaires** primary education *(U)* **2.** *péj* [primitif] limited.

primate [primat] **nm 1.** ZOOL primate **2.** *fam* [brute] gorilla.

primauté [primote] **nf** primacy.

prime [prim] ■ **nf 1.** [d'employé] bonus ▸ **prime d'ancienneté** seniority bonus ▸ **prime d'intéressement** profit-related bonus ▸ **prime de licenciement** redundancy payment, severance pay ▸ **prime d'objectif** incentive bonus ▸ **prime de précarité** *bonus paid to compensate for lack of job security*
2. [allocation - de déménagement, de transport] allowance *UK* ▸ **prime au retour** repatriation allowance / [- à l'exportation] incentive
3. [d'assurance] premium ▸ **ils ne toucheront pas la prime** [bonus] they will not qualify for the no-claims bonus
4. [cadeau] free gift ▸ **en prime** as a free gift / *fig* in addition ▸ **en prime, vous gagnez trois tasses à café** as a bonus, you get a free gift of three coffee cups ▸ **non seulement il ne fait rien mais en prime il se plaint!** not only does he do nothing, but he complains as well!
■ **adj 1.** [premier] **: de prime abord** at first glance ▸ **de prime jeunesse** in the first flush of youth
2. MATH prime.

primer [3] [prime] ■ **vi** to take precedence, to come first.
■ **vt 1.** [être supérieur à] to take precedence over **2.** [récompenser] to award a prize to ▸ **le film a été primé au festival** the film won an award at the festival.

primerose [primroz] **nf** hollyhock.

primesautier, ère [primsotje, ɛr] **adj** impulsive.

primeur [primœr] **nf** immediacy ▸ **avoir la primeur de qqch** to be the first to hear sthg.
◆ ***primeurs*** **nfpl** early produce *(U)*.

primevère [primvɛr] **nf** primrose.

primitif, ive [primitif, iv] ■ **adj 1.** [gén] primitive **2.** [aspect] original.
■ **nm, f** primitive.

primo [primo] **adv** firstly.

primordial, e, aux [primɔrdjal, o] **adj** essential.

prince [prɛ̃s] **nm** prince ▸ **prince consort** prince consort.

prince-de-Galles [prɛ̃sdəgal] **nm inv & adj inv** Prince of Wales check.

princesse [prɛ̃sɛs] **nf** princess.

princier, ère [prɛ̃sje, ɛr] **adj** princely.

principal, e, aux [prɛ̃sipal, o] ■ **adj 1.** [gén] main, principal **2.** GRAMM main.
■ **nm, f 1.** [important] **: le principal** the main thing **2.** SCOL headmaster (f headmistress) *UK*, principal *US*.

principalement [prɛ̃sipalmɑ̃] **adv** mainly, principally.

principauté [prɛ̃sipote] **nf** principality.

principe [prɛ̃sip] **nm** principle ▸ **j'ai des principes** I've got principles ▸ **je pars du principe que...** I start from the principle *ou* I assume that... ▸ **le principe de la vente par correspondance, c'est...** the (basic) principle of mail-order selling is... ▸ **le principe de la vie** the origin of life ▸ **par principe** on principle ▸ **il refuse de l'écouter par principe** he refuses to listen to her on principle ▸ **tu refuses de signer pour le principe ou pour des raisons personnelles?** are you refusing to sign for reasons of principle or for personal reasons?
◆ ***en principe*** **loc adv** theoretically, in principle ▸ **en principe, nous descendons à l'hôtel** we usually stop at a hotel.

printanier, ère [prɛ̃tanje, ɛr] **adj 1.** [temps] spring-like **2.** *fig* [humeur] bright and cheerful.

printemps [prɛ̃tɑ̃] **nm 1.** [saison] spring **2.** *fig* [de la vie] springtime **3.** *fam* [année] **: avoir 20 printemps** to be 20.

prion [prijɔ̃] **nm** BIOL & MÉD prion.

priori [prijɔri] ◆ ***a priori*** ■ **loc adv** in principle.
■ **nm inv** initial reaction.
■ **adj inv** a priori.

prioritaire [prijɔritɛr] **adj 1.** [industrie, mesure] priority *(avant n)* **2.** AUTO with right of way.

priorité [prijɔrite] **nf 1.** [importance primordiale] priority ▸ **en priorité** first **2.** AUTO right of way ▸ **priorité à droite** give way to the right.

pris, e [pri, priz] ■ **pp** ➤ ***prendre***.
■ **adj 1.** [place] taken / [personne] busy / [mains] full ▸ **aide-moi, tu vois bien que j'ai les mains prises** help me, can't you see my hands are full? **2.** [nez] blocked / [gorge] sore **3.** [envahi] **: pris de** seized with ▸ **pris de panique** panic-stricken ▸ **pris d'une violente douleur** seized with a terrible pain.
◆ ***prise*** **nf 1.** [sur barre, sur branche] grip, hold ▸ **lâcher prise** to let go / *fig* to give up ▸ **avoir prise sur qqch** to have hold of sthg ▸ **avoir prise sur qqn** *fig* to have a hold over sb ▸ **être aux prises avec** *fig* to grapple with **2.** [action de prendre - de ville] seizure, capture ▸ **prise de conscience** realization ▸ **prise de contact** meeting ▸ **prise en charge** [par Sécurité sociale] (guaranteed) reimbursement ▸ **prise d'otages** hostage taking ▸ **prise de participation** ÉCON acquisition of holdings ▸ **prise de pouvoir** [- légale] (political) takeover / [- illégale] seizure of power ▸ **prise de sang** blood test ▸ **la prise de son est de Raoul Fleck** sound (engineer), Raoul Fleck ▸ **prise de tête** *tfam* hassle ▸ **prise de vue** shot ▸ **prise de vue *ou* vues** [action] filming, shooting **3.** [à la pêche] haul **4.** ÉLECTR **: prise (de courant)** [mâle] plug / [femelle] socket ▸ **prise multiple** adaptor ▸ **prise de terre** earth *UK*, ground *US* **5.** [de judo] hold ▸ **faire une prise à qqn** SPORT to get sb in a hold **6.** INFORM outlet.

prisé**, **e [prize] **adj** valued ▸ **des qualités très prisées** highly valued qualities.

priser [3] [prize] **vt 1.** *sout* [apprécier] to appreciate, to value **2.** [aspirer] **: priser du tabac** to take snuff.

prisme [prism] **nm** prism.

prison [prizɔ̃] **nf 1.** [établissement] prison **2.** [réclusion] imprisonment.

prisonnier**, **ère [prizɔnje, ɛr] ■ **nm, f** prisoner ▸ **faire qqn prisonnier** to take sb prisoner, to capture sb.
■ **adj** imprisoned / *fig* trapped ▸ **être prisonnier de** to be the prisoner of / *fig* to be a prisoner of *ou* a slave to.

privatif**, **ive [privatif, iv] **adj 1.** DR private **2.** GRAMM privative.

privation [privasjɔ̃] **nf** deprivation.
◆ ***privations*** **nfpl** privations, hardships.

privatisation [privatizasjɔ̃] **nf** privatization.

privatiser [3] [privatize] **vt** to privatize.

privé**, **e [prive] **adj** private.
◆ ***privé*** **nm 1.** ÉCON private sector **2.** [détective] private eye **3.** [intimité] **: en privé** in private ▸ **dans le privé** in private life.

priver [3] [prive] **vt : priver qqn (de)** to deprive sb (of).
◆ ***se priver*** **vp 1.** [s'abstenir] **: se priver de** to go *ou* do without, to deprive o.s. of ▸ **ne pas se priver de faire qqch** not to hesitate to do sthg ▸ **ne pas se priver de qqch** to indulge in sthg **2.** *(emploi absolu)* [économiser] to do *ou* go without.

privilège [privilɛʒ] **nm** privilege.
◆ ***privilèges*** **nmpl : les privilèges** *the privileges of the aristocracy, cities, corporations, guilds etc abolished in 1789.*

privilégié**, **e [privileʒje] ■ **adj 1.** [personne] privileged **2.** [climat, site] favoured *UK*, favored *US*.
■ **nm, f** privileged person.

privilégier [9] [privileʒje] **vt** to favour *UK*, to favor *US*.

prix [pri] **nm 1.** [coût] price ▸ **à aucun prix** on no account ▸ **je ne quitterais le pays à aucun prix!** nothing would induce me to leave the country! ▸ **il veut se faire un nom à n'importe quel prix** he'll stop at nothing to make a name for himself ▸ **au prix fort** at a very high price ▸ **ma mère m'a élevé au prix de grands sacrifices** my mother made great sacrifices to bring me up ▸ **hors de prix** too expensive ▸ **à moitié prix** at half price ▸ **à tout prix** at all costs ▸ **tu dois à tout prix être rentré à minuit** you must be back by midnight at all costs ▸ **prix d'ami** reduced price ▸ **prix comptant** cash price ▸ **acheter** *ou* **payer qqch à prix d'or** to pay through the nose for sthg ▸ **mettre la tête de qqn à prix** to put a price on sb's head ▸ **y mettre le prix** to pay a lot / ÉCON **: à** *ou* **au prix coûtant** at cost (price) ▸ **prix d'achat** purchase price ▸ **à prix fixe** set-price *(avant n)* ▸ **prix exceptionnel** bargain price ▸ **prix hors taxes** price before tax *ou* duties ▸ **prix de lancement** introductory price ▸ **prix net** net (price) ▸ **prix coûtant** *ou* **de revient** cost price ▸ **prix optimum** optimal price ▸ **prix de prestige** premium price ▸ **prix promotionnel** promotional price ▸ **prix de revient** cost price ▸ **prix (sortie) usine** factory price **2.** [importance] value ▸ **le prix de la vie/liberté** the price of life/freedom ▸ **donner du prix à qqch** to make sthg worthwhile **3.** [récompense] prize ▸ **elle a eu le prix de la meilleure interprétation** she got the award for best actress ▸ **prix Goncourt** *the most prestigious French annual literary prize* ▸ **prix Nobel** Nobel prize / [lauréat] Nobel prizewinner.
◆ ***Grand Prix*** **nm** Grand Prix.

PARONYME / CONFUSABLE
prix
Attention à la traduction de prix : on utilise *price* pour parler du coût, de l'équivalent financier, tandis que *prize* désigne une récompense.

pro [pro] **nmf & adj** *fam* pro.

probabilité [prɔbabilite] **nf 1.** [chance] probability **2.** [vraisemblance] probability, likelihood ▸ **selon toute probabilité** in all probability.

probable [prɔbabl] **adj** probable, likely ▸ **il est probable que** it is likely *ou* probable that.

probablement [prɔbabləmɑ̃] **adv** probably.

probant**, **e [prɔbɑ̃, ɑ̃t] **adj** convincing, conclusive.

probatoire [prɔbatwar] **adj** [période] trial *(avant n)* / [examen] qualifying.

probité [prɔbite] **nf** integrity.

problématique [prɔblematik] ■ **nf** problems *pl*.
■ **adj** problematic.

problème [prɔblɛm] **nm** problem ▸ **poser un problème** to cause *ou* pose a problem ▸ **sans problème!, (il n'y a) pas de problème!** *fam* no problem! ▸ **faux problème** imaginary problem ▸ **ça ne lui pose aucun problème** *hum* that doesn't worry him/her.

procédé [prɔsede] **nm 1.** [méthode] process **2.** [conduite] behaviour *(U) UK*, behavior *(U) US*.

procéder [18] [prɔsede] **vi 1.** [agir] to proceed **2.** [exécuter] **: procéder à qqch** to set about sthg ▸ **il sera procédé au démantèlement de l'entreprise** the company will be dismantled **3.** *sout* [provenir] **: procéder de** to come from, to originate in.

procédure [prɔsedyr] **nf** procedure / [démarche] proceedings *pl*.

procédurier**, **ère [prɔsedyrje, ɛr] ■ **adj** quibbling.
■ **nm, f** quibbler.

procès [prɔsɛ] **nm** DR trial ▸ **intenter un procès à qqn** to sue sb ▸ **faire le procès de** *fig* to make a case against ▸ **procès en diffamation** libel suit.

processeur [prɔsesœr] **nm** processor.

procession [prɔsesjɔ̃] **nf** procession ▸ **en procession** in procession.

processus [prɔsesys] **nm** process.

procès-verbal [prɔsɛvɛrbal] (pl **procès-verbaux** [prɔsɛvɛrbo]) **nm 1.** [contravention - gén] ticket / [- pour stationnement interdit] parking ticket **2.** [compte-rendu] minutes.

prochain**, **e [prɔʃɛ̃, ɛn] **adj 1.** [suivant] next ▸ **à la prochaine!** *fam* see you! **2.** [imminent] impending.
◆ ***prochain*** **nm** *littéraire* [semblable] fellow man.

prochainement [prɔʃɛnmɑ̃] **adv** soon, shortly.

proche [prɔʃ] **adj 1.** [dans l'espace] near ▸ **le bureau est tout proche** the office is close at hand *ou* very near ▸ **proche de** near, close to / [semblable à] very similar to, closely related to ▸ **plus proche de chez lui** closer to his home ▸ **je me sens très proche de ce qu'il dit** my feelings are very close *ou* similar to his ▸ **portrait proche de la réalité** accurate *ou* lifelike portrait **2.** [dans le temps] imminent, near ▸ **dans un proche avenir** in the immediate future ▸ **le dénouement est proche** the end is in sight **3.** [ami, parent] close.

◆ ***proches*** **nmpl : les proches** close friends and relatives *sg*.

◆ ***de proche en proche*** **loc adv** *sout* gradually ▸ **de proche en proche, j'ai fini par reconstituer les événements** step by step, I finally reconstructed the events.

Proche-Orient [prɔʃɔrjɑ̃] **nm : le Proche-Orient** the Near East.

proclamation [prɔklamasjɔ̃] **nf** proclamation.

proclamer [3] [prɔklame] **vt** to proclaim, to declare.

procréation [prɔkreasjɔ̃] **nf** procreation ▸ **procréation artificielle** artificial reproduction ▸ **procréation médicalement assistée** medically assisted conception *ou* procreation *ou* reproduction.

procréer [15] [prɔkree] **vt** *littéraire* to procreate.

procuration [prɔkyrasjɔ̃] **nf** proxy ▸ **par procuration** by proxy.

procurer [3] [prɔkyre] **vt : procurer qqch à qqn** [suj: personne] to obtain sthg for sb / [suj: chose] to give *ou* bring sb sthg.

◆ ***se procurer*** **vp : se procurer qqch** to obtain sthg.

procureur [prɔkyrœr] **nm : Procureur de la République** *public prosecutor at a 'tribunal de grande instance'*, ≃ Attorney General ▸ **procureur général** *public prosecutor at the 'Parquet'*, ≃ Director of Public Prosecutions *UK*, ≃ district attorney *US*.

prodigalité [prɔdigalite] **nf** extravagance *(U)*.

prodige [prɔdiʒ] **nm 1.** [miracle] miracle **2.** [tour de force] marvel, wonder ▸ **c'est un prodige d'ingéniosité** it's incredibly ingenious **3.** [génie] prodigy.

prodigieusement [prɔdiʒjøzmɑ̃] **adv** fantastically, incredibly.

prodigieux, euse [prɔdiʒjø, øz] **adj** fantastic, incredible.

prodigue [prɔdig] **adj** [dépensier] extravagant ▸ **prodigue de** *fig* lavish with.

prodiguer [3] [prɔdige] **vt** *littéraire* [soins, amitié] **: prodiguer qqch (à)** to lavish sthg (on).

producteur, trice [prɔdyktœr, tris] ■ **nm, f 1.** [gén] producer **2.** AGRIC producer, grower.

■ **adj : producteur de pétrole** oil-producing *(avant n)* ▸ **producteur d'emplois** which creates jobs.

productif, ive [prɔdyktif, iv] **adj** productive.

production [prɔdyksjɔ̃] **nf 1.** [gén] production ▸ **coût de production** production cost ▸ **production JAT/juste à temps** JIT/just-in-time production ▸ **la production littéraire d'un pays** the literature of a country **2.** [producteurs] producers *pl*.

productique [prɔdyktik] **nf** computer-aided *ou* computer-integrated manufacturing.

productivité [prɔdyktivite] **nf** productivity.

produire [98] [prɔdɥir] **vt 1.** [gén] to produce **2.** [provoquer] to cause.

◆ ***se produire*** **vp 1.** [arriver] to occur, to take place **2.** [acteur, chanteur] to appear.

produisais, produisions ➤ ***produire***.

produit, e [prɔdɥi, it] **pp** ➤ ***produire***.

◆ ***produit*** **nm 1.** [gén] product ▸ **produits alimentaires** foodstuffs, foods ▸ **produit de beauté** cosmetic, beauty product ▸ **produits chimiques** chemicals ▸ **produits de consommation** consumable goods, consumables ▸ **produit dérivé** by-product ▸ **produits d'entretien** cleaning products ▸ **produit générique** generic product ▸ **produit financier** financial product ▸ **produit de grande consommation** mass consumption product ▸ **produits manufacturés** manufactured goods ▸ **produit de substitution** substitute **2.** [d'investissement] profit, income ▸ **produit de l'impôt** tax revenue ▸ **le produit de la vente** the profit made on the sale **3.** ÉCON **: produit brut** gross income ▸ **produit ciblé** niche product ▸ **produit intérieur brut** gross (domestic) product ▸ **produit intérieur net** net domestic product ▸ **produit national brut** gross national product ▸ **produit de prestige** premium product ▸ **produit sous licence** licensed product.

proéminent, e [prɔeminɑ̃, ɑ̃t] **adj** prominent.

prof [prɔf] **nmf** *fam* teacher.

profanation [prɔfanasjɔ̃] **nf** desecration.

profane [prɔfan] ■ **nmf 1.** [non religieux] non-believer **2.** [novice] layman.

■ **adj 1.** [laïc] secular **2.** [ignorant] ignorant.

profaner [3] [prɔfane] **vt 1.** [église] to desecrate **2.** *fig* [mémoire] to defile.

proférer [18] [prɔfere] **vt** to utter.

professer [4] [prɔfese] **vt** to profess.

professeur [prɔfɛsœr] **nm** [gén] teacher / [dans l'enseignement supérieur] lecturer / [titulaire] professor.

profession [prɔfɛsjɔ̃] **nf 1.** [métier] occupation ▸ **de profession** by trade/profession ▸ **sans profession** unemployed **2.** [corps de métier - libéral] profession ▸ **profession libérale** (liberal) profession ▸ **être en profession libérale** to work in a liberal profession / [- manuel] trade.

◆ ***profession de foi*** **nf 1.** RELIG profession of faith **2.** [manifeste] manifesto.

professionnel, elle [prɔfɛsjɔnɛl] ■ **adj 1.** [gén] professional **2.** [école] technical / [enseignement] vocational.

■ **nm, f** professional.

professionnellement [prɔfɛsjɔnɛlmɑ̃] **adv** professionally.

professoral, e, aux [prɔfɛsɔral, o] **adj** [ton, attitude] professorial / [corps] teaching *(avant n)*.

professorat [prɔfɛsɔra] **nm** teaching.

profil [prɔfil] **nm 1.** [de personne, d'emploi] profile ▸ **profil psychologique** psychological profile / [de bâtiment] outline ▸ **de profil** [visage, corps] in profile / [objet] from the side **2.** [coupe] section **3.** ÉCON **: profil de la clientèle** customer profile ▸ **profil du consommateur** consumer profile ▸ **profil démographique** demographic profile ▸ **profil du marché** market profile **4.** INFORM **: profil (utilisateur)** (user) profil.

profilage [prɔfilaʒ] **nm** streamlining.

profiler [3] [prɔfile] **vt** to shape.
◆ ***se profiler*** **vp 1.** [bâtiment, arbre] to stand out **2.** [solution] to emerge.

profileur**, **euse [prɔfilœr, øz] **nm, f** profiler.

profit [prɔfi] **nm 1.** [avantage] benefit ▸ **au profit de** in aid of ▸ **tirer profit de** to profit from, to benefit from **2.** [gain] profit ▸ **profits inattendus** *ou* **exceptionnels** windfall profits.

profitable [prɔfitabl] **adj** profitable ▸ **être profitable à qqn** to benefit sb, to be beneficial to sb.

profiter [3] [prɔfite] **vi 1.** [tirer avantage] **: profiter de** [vacances] to benefit from / [personne] to take advantage of ▸ **profiter de qqch pour faire qqch** to take advantage of sthg to do sthg ▸ **en profiter** to make the most of it ▸ **en profiter pour faire qqch** to take the opportunity to do sthg **2.** [servir] **: profiter à qqn** to be beneficial to sb.

profiteroles [prɔfitrɔl] **nfpl : profiteroles au chocolat** chocolate profiteroles.

profiteur**, **euse [prɔfitœr, øz] **nm, f** *péj* profiteer.

profond**, **e [prɔfɔ̃, ɔ̃d] **adj 1.** [gén] deep **2.** [pensée] deep, profound **3.** PSYCHO **: un débile profond** a profoundly subnormal person.
◆ ***profond*** ■ **nm : au plus profond de** in the depths of. ■ **adv** deep.

profondément [prɔfɔ̃demɑ̃] **adv 1.** [enfoui] deep **2.** [intensément - aimer, intéresser] deeply / [- dormir] soundly ▸ **être profondément endormi** to be fast asleep **3.** [extrêmement - convaincu, ému] deeply, profoundly / [- différent] profoundly.

profondeur [prɔfɔ̃dœr] **nf** depth ▸ **en profondeur** in depth ▸ **profondeur de champ** CINÉ & PHOTO depth of field.
◆ ***profondeurs*** **nfpl** depths.

profusion [prɔfyzjɔ̃] **nf : une profusion de** a profusion of ▸ **à profusion** in abundance, in profusion.

progéniture [prɔʒenityr] **nf** offspring.

progiciel [prɔʒisjɛl] **nm** software package.

programmable [prɔgramabl] **adj** programmable.

programmateur**, **trice [prɔgramatœr, tris] **nm, f** programme *UK* *ou* program *US* planner.
◆ ***programmateur*** **nm** automatic control unit.

programmation [prɔgramasjɔ̃] **nf 1.** INFORM programming ▸ **faire de la programmation** to program ▸ **programmation linéaire** linear programming **2.** RADIO & TV programme *UK* *ou* program *US* planning.

programme [prɔgram] **nm 1.** [gén] programme *UK*, program *US* ▸ **programmes d'été** TV summer schedule *ou* programmes ▸ **il y a un bon programme ce soir à la télé** it's a good night on TV tonight ▸ **le programme des réjouissances** *hum* the treats in store ▸ **c'est tout un programme** it's quite an undertaking ▸ **le programme nucléaire/spatial français** the French nuclear/space programme
2. INFORM program ▸ **programme antivirus** antivirus program ▸ **programme d'application** applications program ▸ **programme de chargement** loader ▸ **programme de diagnostic** malfunction routine
3. [planning] schedule ▸ **qu'avons-nous au programme aujourd'hui?** what's on (our schedule) today?
4. SCOL syllabus ▸ **Shakespeare figure au programme cette année** Shakespeare is on this year's syllabus.

programmé**, **e [prɔgrame] **adj** programmed.

programmer [3] [prɔgrame] **vt 1.** [organiser] to plan **2.** RADIO & TV to schedule **3.** INFORM to program.

programmeur**, **euse [prɔgramœr, øz] **nm, f** INFORM (computer) programmer.

progrès [prɔgrɛ] **nm** progress *(U)* ▸ **être en progrès** to be making (good) progress ▸ **faire des progrès** to make progress.

progresser [4] [prɔgrese] **vi 1.** [avancer] to progress, to advance **2.** [maladie] to spread **3.** [élève] to make progress.

progressif**, **ive [prɔgresif, iv] **adj** progressive / [difficulté] increasing.

progression [prɔgresjɔ̃] **nf 1.** [avancée] advance **2.** [de maladie, du nationalisme] spread.

progressiste [prɔgresist] **nmf & adj** progressive.

progressivement [prɔgresivmɑ̃] **adv** progressively.

prohiber [3] [prɔibe] **vt** to ban, to prohibit.

prohibitif**, **ive [prɔibitif, iv] **adj 1.** [dissuasif] prohibitive **2.** DR prohibitory.

prohibition [prɔibisjɔ̃] **nf** ban, prohibition.
◆ ***Prohibition*** **nf : la Prohibition** HIST Prohibition.

proie [prwa] **nf** prey ▸ **être la proie de qqn** *fig* to be the prey *ou* victim of sb ▸ **être la proie de qqch** *fig* to be the victim of sthg ▸ **être en proie à** [sentiment] to be prey to

projecteur [prɔʒɛktœr] **nm 1.** [de lumière] floodlight THÉÂTRE spotlight **2.** [d'images] projector.

projectile [prɔʒɛktil] **nm** missile.

projection [prɔʒɛksjɔ̃] **nf 1.** [gén] projection **2.** [jet] throwing **3.** CINÉ **: projection privée** private screening *o*[r] showing.

projectionniste [prɔʒɛksjɔnist] **nmf** projectionist.

projet [prɔʒɛ] **nm 1.** [perspective] plan **2.** [étude, ébauche] draft ▸ **projet de loi** bill.

projeter [27] [prɔʃte] **vt 1.** [envisager] to plan ▸ **projeter de faire qqch** to plan to do sthg **2.** [missile, pierre] to throw **3.** [film, diapositives] to show **4.** GÉOM & PSYCHO to project.
◆ ***se projeter*** **vp** [ombre] to be cast.

prolétaire [prɔletɛr] **nmf & adj** proletarian.

prolétariat [prɔletarja] **nm** proletariat.

prolétarien, enne [prɔletarjɛ̃, ɛn] **adj** proletarian.

prolifération [prɔliferasjɔ̃] **nf** proliferation.

proliférer [18] [prɔlifere] **vi** to proliferate.

prolifique [prɔlifik] **adj** prolific.

prolixe [prɔliks] **adj** *sout* wordy, verbose.

prolo [prɔlo] **nmf** *fam* prole, pleb.

prologue [prɔlɔg] **nm** prologue.

prolongation [prɔlɔ̃gasjɔ̃] **nf** [extension] extension, prolongation.
◆ ***prolongations*** **nfpl** SPORT extra time *(U) UK*, overtime *US* ▸ **jouer les prolongations** to go into extra time *UK ou* overtime *US*.

prolongement [prɔlɔ̃ʒmɑ̃] **nm** [de mur, quai] extension ▸ **être dans le prolongement de** to be a continuation of.
◆ ***prolongements*** **nmpl** [conséquences] repercussions.

prolonger [17] [prɔlɔ̃ʒe] **vt 1.** [dans le temps] **: prolonger qqch (de)** to prolong sthg (by) **2.** [dans l'espace] **: prolonger qqch (de)** to extend sthg (by).
◆ ***se prolonger*** **vp 1.** [événement] to go on, to last **2.** [route] to go on, to continue.

promenade [prɔmnad] **nf 1.** [balade] walk, stroll / *fig* trip, excursion ▸ **promenade en voiture** drive ▸ **promenade à vélo** (bike) ride ▸ **faire une promenade** to go for a walk **2.** [lieu] promenade.

promener [19] [prɔmne] **vt 1.** [personne] to take out (for a walk) / [en voiture] to take for a drive **2.** *littéraire* [chagrin] to carry (about) **3.** *fig* [regard, doigts] **: promener qqch sur** to run sthg over.
◆ ***se promener*** **vp** to go for a walk.

promeneur, euse [prɔmnœr, øz] **nm, f** walker, stroller.

promesse [prɔmɛs] **nf 1.** [serment] promise ▸ **manquer à sa promesse** to break one's promise ▸ **tenir sa promesse** to keep one's promise ▸ **promesses en l'air** empty promises **2.** [engagement] undertaking ▸ **promesse d'achat/de vente** DR agreement to purchase/to sell ▸ **promesse électorale** election promise **3.** *fig* [espérance] **: être plein de promesses** to be very promising.

promets ➤ ***promettre***.

prometteur, euse [prɔmetœr, øz] **adj** promising.

promettre [84] [prɔmɛtr] ■ **vt** to promise ▸ **promettre qqch à qqn** to promise sb sthg ▸ **je ne peux rien vous promettre** I can't promise anything ▸ **promettre de faire qqch** to promise to do sthg ▸ **promettre à qqn que** to promise sb that ▸ **je te promets que je ne dirai rien** I promise (you) I won't say anything ▸ **ses récents succès le promettent à une brillante carrière** considering his recent successes, he has a brilliant career ahead of him ▸ **tout cela ne promet rien de bon** it doesn't look *ou* sound too good.
■ **vi** to be promising ▸ **ça promet!** *iron* that bodes well!
◆ ***se promettre*** **vp : se promettre de faire qqch** to resolve to do sthg ▸ **ils se sont promis de se revoir** they promised (each other) that they would meet again ▸ **je me suis bien promis de ne jamais recommencer** I swore never to do it again, I promised myself I would never do it again.

promis, e [prɔmi, iz] ■ **pp** ➤ ***promettre***.
■ **adj** promised ▸ **promis à qqch** destined for sthg.
■ **nm, f** *hum* intended.

promiscuité [prɔmiskɥite] **nf** overcrowding ▸ **promiscuité sexuelle** (sexual) promiscuity.

promontoire [prɔmɔ̃twar] **nm** promontory.

promoteur, trice [prɔmɔtœr, tris] **nm, f 1.** [novateur] instigator **2.** [constructeur] property developer.

promotion [prɔmɔsjɔ̃] **nf 1.** [gén] promotion ▸ **promotion des ventes** sales promotion ▸ **promotion sur le lieu de vente** point-of-sale promotion, point-of-purchase promotion ▸ **en promotion** [produit] on special offer **2.** MIL & SCOL year.

promotionnel, elle [prɔmɔsjɔnɛl] **adj** promotional.

promouvoir [56] [prɔmuvwar] **vt** to promote.

prompt, e [prɔ̃, prɔ̃t] **adj** *sout* **: prompt (à faire qqch)** swift (to do sthg).

promptitude [prɔ̃tityd] **nf** *sout* swiftness.

promu, e [prɔmy] **pp** ➤ ***promouvoir***.

promulgation [prɔmylgasjɔ̃] **nf** promulgation.

promulguer [3] [prɔmylge] **vt** to promulgate.

prôner [3] [prone] **vt** *sout* to advocate.

pronom [prɔnɔ̃] **nm** pronoun ▸ **pronom personnel/possessif/relatif** personal/possessive/relative pronoun.

pronominal, e, aux [prɔnɔminal, o] **adj** pronominal.

prononcé, e [prɔnɔ̃se] **adj** marked.
◆ ***prononcé*** **nm** [d'arrêt] delivery / [de sentence] passing.

prononcer [16] [prɔnɔ̃se] **vt 1.** DR & LING to pronounce **2.** [dire] to utter.
◆ ***se prononcer*** **vp 1.** [se dire] to be pronounced ▸ **comme ça se prononce** as it is pronounced **2.** [trancher - assemblée] to decide, to reach a decision / [- magistrat] to deliver a verdict ▸ **se prononcer sur** to give one's opinion of.

prononciation [prɔnɔ̃sjasjɔ̃] **nf 1.** LING pronunciation **2.** DR pronouncement.

pronostic [prɔnɔstik] **nm 1.** *(gén pl)* [prévision] forecast **2.** MÉD prognosis.

pronostiquer [3] [prɔnɔstike] **vt 1.** [annoncer] to forecast **2.** MÉD to make a prognosis of.

pronostiqueur, euse [prɔnɔstikœr, øz] **nm, f** forecaster.

propagande [prɔpagɑ̃d] **nf 1.** [endoctrinement] propaganda **2.** *fig* & *hum* [publicité] **: faire de la propagande pour qqch** to plug sthg.

propagation [prɔpagasjɔ̃] **nf 1.** *fig* [de flammes, de maladie] spread, spreading **2.** BIOL & PHYS propagation.

propager [17] [prɔpaʒe] **vt** to spread.
◆ ***se propager*** **vp** to spread / BIOL to be propagated / PHYS to propagate.

propane [prɔpan] **nm** propane.

propension [prɔpɑ̃sjɔ̃] **nf : propension à qqch/à faire qqch** propensity for sthg/to do sthg / ÉCON **: propension moyenne à consommer** average propensity to consume ▸ **propension moyenne à épargner** average propensity to save.

prophète, prophétesse [prɔfɛt, prɔfetɛs] **nm, f** prophet (f prophetess).
◆ ***Prophète*** **nm : le Prophète** the Prophet.

prophétie [prɔfesi] **nf** prophecy.

prophétique [prɔfetik] **adj** prophetic.

prophétiser [3] [prɔfetize] **vt** to prophesy.

prophylactique [prɔfilaktik] **adj** prophylactic.

prophylaxie [prɔfilaksi] **nf** prophylaxis.

propice [prɔpis] **adj** favourable *UK*, favorable *US* ▸ **propice à** [changement] conducive to / [culture, élevage] good for.

proportion [prɔpɔrsjɔ̃] **nf** proportion ▸ **en proportion de** in proportion to ▸ **toutes proportions gardées** relatively speaking.

proportionné, e [prɔpɔrsjɔne] **adj : bien/mal proportionné** well-/badly-proportioned ▸ **proportionné à** proportionate to.

proportionnel, elle [prɔpɔrsjɔnɛl] **adj : proportionnel (à)** proportional (to).
◆ ***proportionnelle*** **nf : la proportionnelle** proportional representation.

proportionnellement [prɔpɔrsjɔnɛlmɑ̃] **adv** proportionally.

propos [prɔpo] ■ **nm 1.** [discours] talk **2.** [but] intention ▸ **c'est à quel propos?** what is it about? ▸ **de propos délibéré** deliberately, on purpose ▸ **hors de propos** at the wrong time.
■ **nmpl** [paroles] talk *(U)*, words ▸ **tenir des propos d'une extrême banalité** to say extremely banal things.
◆ ***à propos*** ■ **loc adv 1.** [opportunément] at (just) the right time **2.** [au fait] by the way.
■ **loc adj** [opportun] opportune.
◆ ***à propos de*** **loc prép** about.

proposer [3] [prɔpoze] **vt 1.** [offrir] to offer, to propose ▸ **proposer qqch à qqn** to offer sb sthg, to offer sthg to sb ▸ **il a proposé sa place à la vieille dame** he offered the old lady his seat ▸ **proposer à qqn de faire qqch** to offer to do sthg for sb **2.** [suggérer] to suggest, to propose ▸ **proposer de faire qqch** to suggest *ou* propose doing sthg ▸ **je propose qu'on aille au cinéma** I suggest going to the cinema **3.** [loi, candidat] to propose ▸ **proposer un ordre du jour** to move an agenda.
◆ ***se proposer*** **vp 1.** [offrir ses services] to offer one's services ▸ **je me propose pour coller les enveloppes** I'm volunteering to stick the envelopes **2.** [décider] **: se proposer de faire qqch** to intend *ou* mean to do sthg ▸ **ils se proposaient de passer ensemble une semaine tranquille** they intended to spend a quiet week together.

proposition [prɔpozisjɔ̃] **nf 1.** [offre] offer, proposal ▸ **proposition malhonnête** improper suggestion ▸ **faire des propositions à qqn** to proposition sb ▸ **refuser une proposition** to turn down an offer **2.** [suggestion] suggestion, proposal ▸ **quelqu'un a-t-il une autre proposition à faire?** has anyone any other suggestion *ou* anything else to suggest? **3.** GRAMM clause ▸ **proposition consécutive** *ou* **de conséquence** consecutive *ou* result clause **4.** POLIT **: propositions et contre-propositions** proposals and counterproposals ▸ **la proposition est votée** the motion is passed **5.** ÉCON **: proposition unique de vente** unique selling proposition, USP.
◆ ***proposition de loi*** **nf** bill.

propre [prɔpr] ■ **adj 1.** [nettoyé] clean ▸ **gardez votre ville propre** don't drop litter! *UK*, don't litter! *US* **2.** [soigné] neat, tidy ▸ **chez eux c'est bien propre** their house is neat and tidy **3.** [éduqué - enfant] toilet-trained / [- animal] house-trained *UK*, housebroken *US* **4.** [personnel] own ▸ **de mes propres yeux** with my own eyes **5.** [particulier] **: propre à** peculiar to ▸ **sa méthode de travail lui est propre** he has his own particular way of working **6.** [appro-

COMMENT EXPRIMER...

les propositions

Faire une proposition

Can I make a suggestion? / Je peux faire une suggestion ?
Can I help you? / Je peux vous aider ?
Is there anything I can do to help? / Est-ce que je peux faire quelque chose ?
Would you like me to call him for you? / Tu veux que je l'appelle ?
Why don't I come and pick you up? / Et si je passais te prendre ?
Perhaps we could buy him a watch / On pourrait peut-être lui acheter une montre
Shall I open another bottle of wine? / Est-ce que j'ouvre une autre bouteille de vin ?
How about a game of cards? / Une partie de cartes, ça te dit ?

Répondre à une proposition

What a good idea! / Quelle bonne idée !
All right then / Alors c'est d'accord
Thank you, that's very kind of you / Oui, merci, c'est très gentil
If you don't mind / Je veux bien, si ça ne vous dérange pas
No thanks, I'm fine / Non merci, ça va aller
No thank you, it's not necessary / Non merci, ce n'est pas la peine
Thanks, but I'd rather do it myself / Merci, mais je préfère le faire moi-même

prié] : **propre (à)** suitable (for), appropriate (for) **7.** [de nature] : **propre à faire qqch** capable of doing sthg ▸ **mesures propres à stimuler la production** appropriate measures for boosting production **8.** *fig* [honnête] respectable ▸ **une affaire pas très propre** a shady business / *hum* : **nous voilà propres!** we're in a fine mess! **9.** FIN : **capitaux** *ou* **fonds propres** capital stock.
■ **nm 1.** [propreté] cleanness, cleanliness ▸ **recopier qqch au propre** to make a fair copy of sthg, to copy sthg up **2.** [particularité] : **le propre de** the characteristic feature of ▸ **la raison est le propre de l'homme** reason is unique to man ▸ **avoir qqch en propre** DR to be the sole owner of sthg ▸ **la fortune qu'il a en propre** his own fortune, the fortune that's his by rights.
◆ ***au propre*** **loc adv** LING literally ▸ **le mot peut s'employer au propre et au figuré** the word can be used both literally and figuratively.

FAUX AMIS / FALSE FRIENDS
propre
Proper is not a translation of the French word *propre*. Proper is translated by *vrai* or *correct*.
▸ He's not a proper doctor / *Ce n'est pas un vrai docteur*
▸ That's not a proper solution / *Ce n'est pas la bonne solution*

propre-à-rien [prɔprarjɛ̃] (pl **propres-à-rien**) **nmf** good-for-nothing.

proprement [prɔprəmɑ̃] **adv 1.** [convenablement - habillé] neatly, tidily / [- se tenir] correctly **2.** [véritablement] completely ▸ **à proprement parler** strictly *ou* properly speaking ▸ **l'événement proprement dit** the event itself, the actual event **3.** [exclusivement] peculiarly.

propret, ette [prɔprɛ, ɛt] **adj** neat and tidy.

propreté [prɔprəte] **nf** cleanness, cleanliness.

propriétaire [prɔprijetɛr] **nmf 1.** [possesseur] owner ▸ **propriétaire foncier** property owner ▸ **propriétaire terrien** landowner **2.** [dans l'immobilier] landlord.

propriété [prɔprijete] **nf 1.** [gén] property ▸ **propriété industrielle** DR patent rights *pl* ▸ **propriété privée** private property **2.** [droit] ownership ▸ **propriété commerciale** leasehold ownership *(covenant to extend lease)* ▸ **propriété littéraire et artistique** copyright **3.** [terres] property *(U)* ▸ **une grande/une petite propriété** a large/a small property **4.** [convenance] suitability **5.** [qualité] property, characteristic, feature ▸ **la codéine a des propriétés antitussives** codeine suppresses coughing.

propulser [3] [prɔpylse] **vt** *litt* & *fig* to propel.
◆ ***se propulser*** **vp** to move forward, to propel o.s. forward *ou* along / *fig* to shoot.

propulsion [prɔpylsjɔ̃] **nf** propulsion.

prorata [prɔrata] ◆ ***au prorata de*** **loc prép** in proportion to.

prorogation [prɔrɔgasjɔ̃] **nf 1.** DR extension **2.** POLIT adjournment.

proroger [17] [prɔrɔʒe] **vt 1.** DR to extend **2.** POLIT to adjourn.

prosaïque [prozaik] **adj** prosaic, mundane.

proscription [prɔskripsjɔ̃] **nf** [interdiction] banning, prohibition.

proscrire [99] [prɔskrir] **vt 1.** [interdire] to ban, to prohibit **2.** *littéraire* [chasser] : **proscrire qqn (de)** to exile sb (from), to banish sb (from).

proscrit, e [prɔskri, it] ■ **pp** ➤ ***proscrire***.
■ **adj 1.** [interdit] banned, prohibited **2.** *littéraire* [chassé] exiled.
■ **nm, f** *littéraire* exile.

proscrivais, proscrivions ➤ ***proscrire***.

prose [proz] **nf** prose ▸ **en prose** in prose.

prosélyte [prɔzelit] **nmf** convert.

prosélytisme [prɔzelitism] **nm** proselytizing.

prospecter [4] [prɔspɛkte] **vt 1.** [pays, région] to prospect **2.** COMM to canvass.

prospecteur, trice [prɔspɛktœr, tris] **nm, f 1.** [de ressources] prospector **2.** COMM canvasser.

prospectif, ive [prɔspɛktif, iv] **adj : analyse prospective** COMM forecast.
◆ ***prospective*** **nf** futurology.

prospection [prɔspɛksjɔ̃] **nf 1.** [de ressources] prospecting **2.** COMM canvassing.

prospectus [prɔspɛktys] **nm** (advertising) leaflet.

prospère [prɔspɛr] **adj 1.** [commerce] prosperous **2.** [santé] blooming.

prospérer [18] [prɔspere] **vi** to prosper, to thrive / [plante, insecte] to thrive.

prospérité [prɔsperite] **nf 1.** [richesse] prosperity **2.** [bien-être] well-being.

prostate [prɔstat] **nf** prostate (gland).

prosterner [3] [prɔstɛrne] ◆ ***se prosterner*** **vp** to bow down ▸ **se prosterner devant** to bow down before / *fig* to kowtow to.

prostitué [prɔstitɥe] **nm** male prostitute.

prostituée [prɔstitɥe] **nf** prostitute.

prostituer [7] [prɔstitɥe] ◆ ***se prostituer*** **vp** to prostitute o.s.

prostitution [prɔstitysjɔ̃] **nf** prostitution.

prostration [prɔstrasjɔ̃] **nf** prostration.

prostré, e [prɔstre] **adj** prostrate.

protagoniste [prɔtagɔnist] **nmf** protagonist, hero (f heroine).

protecteur, trice [prɔtɛktœr, tris] ■ **adj** protective.
■ **nm, f 1.** [défenseur] protector **2.** [des arts] patron **3.** [souteneur] pimp **4.** *Québec* POLIT : **le Protecteur du citoyen** the ombudsman.

protection [prɔtɛksjɔ̃] **nf 1.** [défense] protection ▸ **protection contre** protection from *ou* against ▸ **se mettre sous la protection de qqn** to put o.s. under sb's protection ▸ **prendre qqn sous sa protection** to take sb under one's wing ▸ **protection sociale** social welfare **2.** [des arts] patronage.

protectionnisme [prɔtɛksjɔnism] **nm** protectionism.

protectionniste [prɔtɛksjɔnist] **nmf & adj** protectionist.

protectorat [prɔtɛktɔra] **nm** protectorate.

protégé, e [prɔteʒe] ■ **adj** protected.
■ **nm, f** protégé.

protège-cahier [prɔtɛʒkaje] (pl **protège-cahiers**) **nm** exercise book cover *US*, notebook cover *US*.

protège-matelas [prɔtɛʒmatla] **nm inv** mattress cover.

protège-poignets [prɔtɛʒpwanjɛ] **nm inv** wrist guard, wrist protector.

protéger [22] [prɔteʒe] **vt 1.** [gén] to protect ▸ **protéger qqn de *ou* contre qqch** to protect sb from *ou* against sthg **2.** [arts] to be a patron of.
◆ ***se protéger*** **vp** [se préserver] to protect o.s. ▸ **protégez-vous contre la grippe** protect yourself against the flu ▸ **se protéger contre le *ou* du soleil** to shield o.s. from the sun / [mettre un préservatif] to use a condom ▸ **les jeunes sont encouragés à se protéger lors de leurs relations sexuelles** young people are encouraged to protect themselves (by using a condom).

protège-slip [prɔtɛʒslip] (pl **protège-slips**) **nm** panty liner.

protège-tibia [prɔtɛʒtibja] (pl **protège-tibias**) **nm** shin pad.

protéine [prɔtein] **nf** protein.

protestant, e [prɔtɛstɑ̃, ɑ̃t] **adj & nm, f** Protestant.

protestantisme [prɔtɛstɑ̃tism] **nm** Protestantism.

protestataire [prɔtɛstatɛr] ■ **nmf** protestor.
■ **adj** *sout* [vote, écrits] protest *(avant n)* / [cri] of protest.

protestation [prɔtɛstasjɔ̃] **nf 1.** [contestation] protest **2.** *littéraire* [déclaration] protestation.

protester [3] [prɔtɛste] **vi** to protest ▸ **protester contre qqch** to protest against sthg, to protest sthg *US* ▸ **protester de qqch** *littéraire* to protest sthg.

prothèse [prɔtɛz] **nf** prosthesis ▸ **prothèse dentaire** dentures *(pl)*, false teeth *pl*.

prothésiste [prɔtezist] **nmf** prosthetist ▸ **prothésiste dentaire** prosthodontist, dental prosthetist.

protide [prɔtid] **nm** protein.

protocolaire [prɔtɔkɔlɛr] **adj** [poli] conforming to etiquette.

protocole [prɔtɔkɔl] **nm** protocol / INFORM **: protocole Internet** Internet protocol ▸ **protocole SET®** secure electronic transaction, SET®.

proton [prɔtɔ̃] **nm** proton.

prototype [prɔtɔtip] **nm** prototype.

protubérance [prɔtyberɑ̃s] **nf** bulge, protuberance.

protubérant, e [prɔtyberɑ̃, ɑ̃t] **adj** bulging, protruding.

proue [pru] **nf** bows *pl*, prow.

prouesse [pruɛs] **nf** feat.

prouver [3] [pruve] **vt 1.** [établir] to prove **2.** [montrer] to demonstrate, to show.
◆ ***se prouver*** **vp** to prove to o.s.

provenance [prɔvnɑ̃s] **nf** origin ▸ **en provenance de** from.

provençal, e, aux [prɔvɑ̃sal, o] **adj 1.** [de Provence] of/from Provence **2.** CULIN *with tomatoes, garlic and onions*.
◆ ***provençal*** **nm** [langue] Provençal.
◆ ***Provençal, e, aux*** **nm, f** native *ou* inhabitant of Provence.
◆ ***à la provençale*** **loc adv** CULIN *with tomatoes, garlic and onions*.

Provence [prɔvɑ̃s] **nf : la Provence** Provence ▸ **herbes de Provence** ≃ mixed herbs.

provenir [40] [prɔvnir] **vi : provenir de** to come from / *fig* to be due to, to be caused by.

provenu, e [prɔvny] **pp** ➤ ***provenir***.

proverbe [prɔvɛrb] **nm** proverb.

proverbial, e, aux [prɔvɛrbjal, o] **adj** proverbial.

providence [prɔvidɑ̃s] **nf** providence / *fig* guardian angel.
◆ ***Providence*** **nf** Providence.

providentiel, elle [prɔvidɑ̃sjɛl] **adj** providential.

proviendrai, proviendras ➤ ***provenir***.

proviens, provient ➤ ***provenir***.

province [prɔvɛ̃s] **nf 1.** [gén] province **2.** [campagne] provinces *pl*.

provincial, e, aux [prɔvɛ̃sjal, o] **adj & nm, f** provincial.

proviseur [prɔvizœr] **nm** ≃ head *UK*, ≃ headteacher *UK*, ≃ headmaster (, headmistress *f*) *UK*, ≃ principal *US*.

provision [prɔvizjɔ̃] **nf 1.** [réserve] stock, supply ▸ **faire provision de qqch** to stock up on *ou* with sthg **2.** FIN retainer / **: provision pour créances douteuses** bad debt provision.
◆ ***provisions*** **nfpl** provisions.

provisionnel, elle [prɔvizjɔnɛl] **adj** provisional.

provisoire [prɔvizwar] ■ **adj** temporary / DR provisional.
■ **nm : ce n'est que du provisoire** it's only a temporary arrangement.

provisoirement [prɔvizwarmɑ̃] **adv** temporarily.

provocant, e [prɔvɔkɑ̃, ɑ̃t] **adj** provocative.

provocateur, trice [prɔvɔkatœr, tris] ■ **adj** provocative.
■ **nm, f** agitator, troublemaker.

provocation [prɔvɔkasjɔ̃] **nf** provocation.

provoquer [3] [prɔvɔke] **vt 1.** [entraîner] to cause **2.** [personne] to provoke.
◆ ***se provoquer*** **vp** to provoke each other.

proxénète [prɔksenɛt] **nm** pimp.

proxénétisme [prɔksenetism] **nm** pimping, procuring.

proximité [prɔksimite] **nf 1.** [de lieu] proximity, nearness ▸ **à proximité de** near **2.** [d'événement] closeness.
◆ ***de proximité*** **loc adj 1.** TECHNOL proximity *(modif)* **2.** [de quartier] **: commerces de proximité** local shops ▸ **police de proximité** community policing ▸ **élu de**

proximité [de la communauté] local councillor, local representative / [faisant valoir ses liens avec la communauté] local man *ou* woman ▸ **médias de proximité** locals *ou* community media.

prude [pryd] ■ **nf** prude.
■ **adj** prudish.

prudemment [prydamɑ̃] **adv** cautiously.

prudence [prydɑ̃s] **nf** care, caution.

prudent, e [prydɑ̃, ɑ̃t] **adj** careful, cautious ▸ **sois prudent!** be careful!

prud'homme [prydɔm] **nm** ≃ member of an industrial tribunal ▸ **Conseil de prud'hommes** ≃ industrial tribunal.

prune [pryn] ■ **nf** plum ▸ **compter pour des prunes** *fam* to count for nothing.
■ **adj inv** plum-coloured *UK*, plum-colored *US*.

pruneau, x [pryno] **nm** **1.** [fruit] prune **2.** *fam* [balle] slug.

prunelle [prynɛl] **nf** ANAT pupil ▸ **j'y tiens comme à la prunelle de mes yeux** it's the apple of my eye.

prunier [prynje] **nm** plum tree ▸ **secouer qqn comme un prunier** *fam* to shake sb until his/her teeth rattle.

prurit [pryrit] **nm** pruritus.

Prusse [prys] **nf : la Prusse** Prussia.

prussien, enne [prysjɛ̃, ɛn] **adj** Prussian.
◆ ***Prussien, enne*** **nm, f** Prussian.

PS [1] (abr de ***Parti socialiste***) **nm** *French socialist party.*

PS [2], ***P-S*** (abr de ***post-scriptum***) **nm** PS.

psalmodie [psalmɔdi] **nf** chanting.

psalmodier [9] [psalmɔdje] ■ **vt** to chant / *fig & péj* to drone.
■ **vi** to drone.

psaume [psom] **nm** psalm.

pseudonyme [psødɔnim] **nm** pseudonym.

PS-G (abr de ***Paris St-Germain***) **nm** *Paris football team.*

PSIG (abr de ***Peloton de surveillance et d'intervention de la gendarmerie***) **nm** *gendarmerie commando squad.*

PSU (abr de ***Parti socialiste unifié***) **nm** *socialist party.*

psy [psi] *fam* ■ **nmf** (abr de ***psychiatre***) shrink.
■ **adj : elle est très psy** she's really into psychology.

psychanalyse [psikanaliz] **nf** psychoanalysis ▸ **faire la psychanalyse de qqn** to psychoanalyse *UK ou* psychoanalyze *US* sb.

psychanalyser [3] [psikanalize] **vt** to psychoanalyse *UK*, to psychoanalyze *US*.

psychanalyste [psikanalist] **nmf** psychoanalyst, analyst.

psychanalytique [psikanalitik] **adj** psychoanalytic, psychoanalytical.

psyché [psiʃe] **nf** cheval glass.

psychédélique [psikedelik] **adj** psychedelic.

psychiatre [psikjatr] **nmf** psychiatrist.

psychiatrie [psikjatri] **nf** psychiatry.

psychiatrique [psikjatrik] **adj** psychiatric.

psychique [psiʃik] **adj** psychic / [maladie] psychosomatic.

psychisme [psiʃism] **nm** psyche, mind.

psychodrame [psikɔdram] **nm** psychodrama / *fig* melodrama.

psychologie [psikɔlɔʒi] **nf** psychology.

psychologique [psikɔlɔʒik] **adj** psychological.

psychologiquement [psikɔlɔʒikmɑ̃] **adv** psychologically.

psychologue [psikɔlɔg] ■ **nmf** psychologist.
■ **adj** psychological.

psychomoteur, trice [psikɔmɔtœr, tris] **adj** psychomotor.

psychopathe [psikɔpat] **nmf** psychopath.

psychose [psikoz] **nf** **1.** MÉD psychosis **2.** [crainte] obsessive fear.

psychosomatique [psikɔsɔmatik] **adj** psychosomatic.

psychothérapeute [psikɔterapøt] **nmf** psychotherapist.

psychothérapie [psikɔterapi] **nf** psychotherapy.

PTA (abr écrite de ***peseta***) Pta, P.

Pte abr de ***porte, pointe***.

PTT (abr de ***Postes, télécommunications et télédiffusion***) **nfpl** *former French post office and telecommunications network.*

pu [py] **pp** ➤ ***pouvoir***.

puant, e [pɥɑ̃, ɑ̃t] **adj** **1.** [fétide] smelly, stinking **2.** *fam fig* [personne] bumptious, full of oneself.

puanteur [pɥɑ̃tœr] **nf** stink, stench.

pub [1] [pyb] **nf** *fam* ad, advert *UK* / [métier] advertising.

pub [2] [pœb] **nm** pub.

pubère [pybɛr] **adj** pubescent.

puberté [pybɛrte] **nf** puberty.

pubis [pybis] **nm** [zone] pubis.

publiable [pyblijabl] **adj** publishable ▸ **ce n'est guère publiable** it's hardly fit for publication *ou* to be printed.

public, ique [pyblik] **adj** public.
◆ ***public*** **nm** **1.** [auditoire] audience ▸ **en public** in public **2.** [population] public ▸ **grand public** general public.

publication [pyblikasjɔ̃] **nf** publication ▸ **publication à compte d'auteur** vanity publishing.

publiciste [pyblisist] **nmf** **1.** DR specialist in public law **2.** [publicitaire] advertiser, advertising man *(nm)*.

publicitaire [pyblisitɛr] ■ **nmf** person in advertising.
■ **adj** [campagne] advertising *(avant n)* / [vente, film] promotional.

publicité [pyblisite] **nf** **1.** [domaine] advertising ▸ **publicité comparative** comparative advertising ▸ **publicité institutionnelle** corporate advertising ▸ **publicité mensongère** misleading advertising, deceptive advertising ▸ **publicité sur le lieu de vente** point-of-sale advertising, POS advertising
2. [réclame] advertisement, advert *UK* ▸ **publicité d'amorçage** advance publicity ▸ **publicité comparative**

dénigrante knocking copy ▸ **publicité directe** direct advertising ▸ **publicité sur le lieu de vente** point-of-sale promotion, point-of-purchase promotion ▸ **publicité au/en prime time** prime time advertising ▸ **publicité rédactionnelle** advertorial
3. [autour d'une affaire] publicity *(U)*
4. [caractère public] public nature.

publier [10] [pyblije] **vt 1.** [livre] to publish / [communiqué] to issue, to release **2.** [nouvelle] to make public.

publipostage [pyblipɔstaʒ] **nm** mailing ▸ **publipostage d'essai** test *ou* cold mailing ▸ **publipostage massif** blanket mailing.

publiquement [pyblikmɑ̃] **adv** publicly.

publireportage [pyblirəpɔrtaʒ] **nm** advertorial, free write-up *UK*, special advertising section *US*.

puce [pys] **nf 1.** [insecte] flea **2.** INFORM (silicon) chip **3.** *fig* [terme affectueux] pet, love
▸▸ **mettre la puce à l'oreille de qqn** to make sb suspicious ▸ **secouer les puces à qqn** *fam* to tear sb off a strip *UK*.
◆ ***puces*** **nfpl : les puces** flea market *sg*.

puceau, elle, x [pyso, ɛl, o] **nm, f & adj** *fam* virgin.

puceron [pysrɔ̃] **nm** aphid.

pudding [pudiŋ] **nm** plum *ou* Christmas pudding.

pudeur [pydœr] **nf 1.** [physique] modesty, decency **2.** [morale] restraint.

pudibond, e [pydibɔ̃, ɔ̃d] **adj** prudish, prim and proper.

pudibonderie [pydibɔ̃dri] **nf** *littéraire* prudishness, primness.

pudique [pydik] **adj 1.** [physiquement] modest, decent **2.** [moralement] restrained.

pudiquement [pydikmɑ̃] **adv** modestly.

puer [7] [pɥe] ■ **vi** to stink ▸ **ça pue ici!** it stinks in here!
■ **vt** to reek of, to stink of.

puériculteur, trice [pɥerikyltœr, tris] **nm, f** nursery nurse.

puéricultrice [pɥerikyltris] **nf** nursery nurse.

puériculture [pɥerikyltyr] **nf** childcare.

puéril, e [pɥeril] **adj** childish.

puérilité [pɥerilite] **nf** childishness.

Puerto Rico = ***Porto Rico***.

PUF, Puf [pyf] (abr de ***Presses Universitaires de France***) **nfpl** *French publishing house*.

pugilat [pyʒila] **nm** fight.

pugnace [pygnas] **adj** *littéraire* pugnacious.

pugnacité [pygnasite] **nf** *littéraire* pugnacity.

puis [pɥi] **adv** then ▸ **et puis** [d'ailleurs] and moreover *ou* besides ▸ **et puis quoi** *ou* **après?** *fam* so what?

puisard [pɥizar] **nm** cesspool.

puiser [3] [pɥize] **vt** [liquide] to draw ▸ **puiser qqch dans qqch** *fig* to draw *ou* take sthg from sthg.

puisque [pɥiskə] **conj 1.** [gén] since **2.** [renforce une affirmation] **: mais puisqu'il m'attend!** but he's waiting for me!

puissamment [pɥisamɑ̃] **adv** powerfully.

puissance [pɥisɑ̃s] **nf** power ▸ **un État au sommet de sa puissance** a state at the height of its power ▸ **une grande puissance de travail** a great capacity for work ▸ **puissance économique** economic power ▸ **puissance nucléaire** nuclear capability ▸ **les grandes puissances** the great powers ▸ **les puissances des ténèbres** the powers of darkness ▸ **un client en puissance** a prospective customer ▸ **puissance de vente** selling power ▸ **puissance d'entrée/de sortie** ÉLECTR input/output (power) ▸ **six puissance cinq** six to the power (of) five.
◆ ***en puissance*** **loc adj** potential.

puissant, e [pɥisɑ̃, ɑ̃t] **adj** powerful.
◆ ***puissant*** **nm : les puissants** the powerful.

puisse, puisses ➤ ***pouvoir***.

puits [pɥi] **nm 1.** [d'eau] well ▸ **puits artésien** artesian well **2.** [de gisement] shaft ▸ **puits d'extraction** extraction shaft ▸ **puits de mine** mine shaft ▸ **puits de pétrole** oil well ▸ **puits de sciences** *fig* fount of all knowledge.

pull [pyl], ***pull-over*** [pylɔvɛr] (pl **pull-overs**) **nm** jumper *UK*, sweater.

pulluler [3] [pylyle] **vi** to swarm.

pulmonaire [pylmɔnɛr] **adj** lung *(avant n)*, pulmonary.

pulpe [pylp] **nf** pulp.

pulpeux, euse [pylpø, øz] **adj 1.** [fruit] pulpy / [jus] containing pulp **2.** *fig* [femme] curvaceous.

pulsation [pylsasjɔ̃] **nf** beat, beating *(U)*.

pulsion [pylsjɔ̃] **nf** impulse.

pulvérisateur [pylverizatœr] **nm** spray.

pulvérisation [pylverizasjɔ̃] **nf 1.** [d'insecticide] spraying **2.** MÉD spray / [traitement] spraying.

pulvériser [3] [pylverize] **vt 1.** [projeter] to spray **2.** [détruire] to pulverize / *fig* to smash.

puma [pyma] **nm** puma.

punaise [pynɛz] ■ **nf 1.** [insecte] bug **2.** *fig* [femme] shrew **3.** [clou] drawing pin *UK*, thumbtack *US*.
■ **interj** good grief!

punch [pɔ̃ʃ] **nm** punch.

punching-ball [pœnʃiŋbol] (pl **punching-balls**) **nm** punchball *UK*, punching bag *US*.

puni, e [pyni] **adj** punished.

punir [32] [pynir] **vt : punir qqn (de)** to punish sb (with).

punitif, ive [pynitif, iv] **adj** punitive.

punition [pynisjɔ̃] **nf** punishment.

punk [pœnk] **nmf & adj inv** punk.

pupille [pypij] ■ **nf** ANAT pupil.
■ **nmf** [orphelin] ward ▸ **pupille de l'État** ≃ child in care *UK* ▸ **pupille de la Nation** war orphan *(in care)*.

pupitre [pypitr] **nm 1.** [d'orateur] lectern / MUS stand **2.** TECHNOL console **3.** [d'écolier] desk.

pur, e [pyr] **adj 1.** [gén] pure ▸ **à l'état pur** pure, unalloyed, unadulterated ▸ **biscuits pur beurre** (100 %) butter biscuits ▸ **le cognac se boit pur** cognac should be taken straight *ou* neat **2.** *fig* [absolu] pure, sheer ▸ **par pure méchanceté** out of sheer malice ▸ **pur et simple** pure and simple **3.** *fig* & *littéraire* [intention] honourable *UK*, honorable *US* ▸ **le regard pur d'un enfant** a child's innocent gaze **4.** [lignes] pure, clean.

purée [pyre] **nf** purée ▸ **purée de pois** *fig* peasouper *UK* ▸ **purée de pommes de terre** mashed potatoes *pl*.

purement [pyrmɑ̃] **adv** purely ▸ **purement et simplement** purely and simply.

pureté [pyrte] **nf 1.** [gén] purity **2.** [de sculpture, de diamant] perfection **3.** [d'intention] honourableness *UK*, honorableness *US*.

purgatif, ive [pyrgatif, iv] **adj** purgative.
◆ ***purgatif*** **nm** purgative.

purgatoire [pyrgatwar] **nm** purgatory.

purge [pyrʒ] **nf 1.** MÉD & POLIT purge **2.** [de radiateur] bleeding.

purger [17] [pyrʒe] **vt 1.** MÉD & POLIT to purge **2.** [radiateur] to bleed **3.** [peine] to serve.
◆ ***se purger*** **vp** to take a purgative.

purificateur, trice [pyrifikatœr, tris] **adj** purifying, cleansing.
◆ ***purificateur*** **nm** purifier.

purification [pyrifikasjɔ̃] **nf** purification ▸ **purification ethnique** ethnic cleansing.

purifier [9] [pyrifje] **vt** to purify.
◆ ***se purifier*** **vp** to become pure *ou* clean / *fig* to purify *ou* cleanse o.s.

purin [pyrɛ̃] **nm** slurry.

puriste [pyrist] **nmf & adj** purist.

puritain, e [pyritɛ̃, ɛn] ■ **adj 1.** [pudibond] puritanical **2.** RELIG Puritan *(avant n)*.
■ **nm, f 1.** [prude] puritan **2.** RELIG Puritan.

puritanisme [pyritanism] **nm** puritanism / RELIG Puritanism.

pur-sang [pyrsɑ̃] **nm inv** thoroughbred.

purulent, e [pyrylɑ̃, ɑ̃t] **adj** purulent.

pus [py] **nm** pus.

pusillanime [pyzilanim] **adj** pusillanimous.

pusillanimité [pyzilanimite] **nf** pusillanimity.

pustule [pystyl] **nf** pustule.

putain [pytɛ̃] ■ **nf** *vulg* **1.** *péj* [prostituée] whore **2.** *péj* [femme facile] tart, slag *UK* **3.** *fig* [pour exprimer le mécontentement] **: (ce) putain de...** this/that sodding... *UK*, this/that goddam... *US*
■ **interj** sod it! *UK*, bugger! *UK*, goddam! *US* / [exprime l'étonnement] (well) bugger me! *UK*, goddam it! *US*

pute [pyt] **nf** *vulg péj* [prostituée] whore.

putois [pytwa] **nm** polecat.

putréfaction [pytrefaksjɔ̃] **nf** putrefaction ▸ **en putréfaction** rotting, putrefying.

putréfier [9] [pytrefje] ◆ ***se putréfier*** **vp** to putrefy, to rot.

putrescent, e [pytrɛsɑ̃, ɑ̃t] **adj** putrescent, rotting.

putride [pytrid] **adj 1.** [corps] putrid **2.** [odeur, miasme] fetid, foul.

putsch [putʃ] **nm** uprising, coup.

putschiste [putʃist] ■ **nmf** rebel.
■ **adj** rebel *(avant n)*.

puzzle [pœzl] **nm** jigsaw (puzzle).

P-V **nm** abr écrite de ***procès-verbal***.

PVC (abr de ***polyvinyl chloride***) **nm** PVC.

PVD (abr de ***pays en voie de développement***) **nm** developing country.

px (abr écrite de ***prix***) **: px à déb.** offers.

pygmée [pigme] **adj** pygmy.
◆ ***Pygmée*** **nmf** Pygmy.

pyjama [piʒama] **nm** pyjamas *pl UK*, pajamas *pl US*.

pylône [pilon] **nm** pylon.

Pyongyang [pjɔngjɑ̃g] **npr** Pyongyang.

pyramide [piramid] **nf** pyramid ▸ **la Pyramide du Louvre** *glass pyramid in the courtyard of the Louvre which serves as its main entrance.*

pyrénéen, enne [pireneɛ̃, ɛn] **adj** Pyrenean.
◆ ***Pyrénéen, enne*** **nm, f** Pyrenean.

Pyrénées [pirene] **nfpl : les Pyrénées** the Pyrenees.

Pyrex® [pirɛks] **nm** Pyrex®.

pyrogravure [pirɔgravyr] **nf** pokerwork, pyrography *(terme spécialisé)*.

pyromane [pirɔman] **nmf** arsonist / MÉD pyromaniac.

pyrotechnique [pirɔtɛknik] **adj** firework *(avant n)*, pyrotechnic.

python [pitɔ̃] **nm** python.

q*[1], *Q [ky] **nm inv** [lettre] q, Q.

q*[2]** abr de ***quintal.

Qatar*, *Katar [katar] **nm : le Qatar** Qatar.

QCM (abr de ***questionnaire à choix multiple***) **nm** multiple choice questionnaire.

QG (abr de ***quartier général***) **nm** HQ.

QHS (abr de ***quartier de haute sécurité***) **nm** high-security wing.

QI (abr de ***quotient intellectuel***) **nm** IQ.

qqch (abr écrite de ***quelque chose***) sthg.

qqe abr de ***quelque***.

qqes (abr écrite de ***quelques***), ➤ ***quelque***.

qqf abr de ***quelquefois***.

qqn (abr écrite de ***quelqu'un***) s.o., sb.

qu' ➤ ***que***.

quad [kwad] **nm** [moto] four-wheel motorbike, quad bike / [rollers] roller skate.

quadra [k(w)adra] **nm** POLIT fortysomething, babyboomer.

quadragénaire [kwadraʒenɛr] ■ **nmf** forty year old.
■ **adj : être quadragénaire** to be in one's forties.

quadrangulaire [kwadrɑ̃gylɛr] **adj** quadrangular.

quadrature [kwadratyr] **nf** quadrature ▸ **c'est la quadrature du cercle** it's like trying to square the circle.

quadrichromie [kwadrikrɔmi] **nf** four-colour *UK ou* four-color *US* printing.

quadrilatère [kwadrilatɛr] **nm** quadrilateral.

quadrillage [kadrijaʒ] **nm 1.** [de papier, de tissu] crisscross pattern **2.** [policier] combing.

quadrille [kadrij] **nm** quadrille.

quadrillé*, *e [kadrije] **adj** squared, cross-ruled.

quadriller [3] [kadrije] **vt 1.** [papier] to mark with squares **2.** [ville - suj: rues] to criss-cross / [- suj: police] to comb.

quadrimoteur [kwadrimɔtœr] ■ **nm** four-engined plane.
■ **adj** four-engined.

quadriphonie [kwadrifɔni] **nf** quadraphony.

quadrupède [k(w)adrypɛd] **nm & adj** quadruped.

quadruple [k(w)adrypl] **nm & adj** quadruple.

quadrupler [3] [k(w)adryple] **vt & vi** to quadruple, to increase fourfold.

quadruplés*, *ées [k(w)adryple] **nmf pl** quadruplets, quads.

quai [kɛ] **nm 1.** [de gare] platform **2.** [de port] quay, wharf **3.** [de rivière] embankment.

CULTURE

Quai

In the French press, **quai d'Orsay** and **quai des Orfèvres** are often used to designate the government bodies located at these Parisian addresses: the Ministry of Foreign Affairs and the city's police headquarters, respectively. **Quai de Conti** refers to the **Académie française**, whose offices are located at the **palais de l'Institut** there.

qualifiable [kalifjabl] **adj** [conduite, attitude] **: peu qualifiable** indescribable.

qualificatif*, *ive [kalifikatif, iv] **adj** qualifying.
◆ ***qualificatif*** **nm** term.

qualification [kalifikasjɔ̃] **nf 1.** [gén] qualification **2.** [désignation] designation.

qualifié*, *e [kalifje] **adj 1.** [compétent] skilled, qualified ▸ **non qualifié pour** ineligible for **2.** SPORT [choisi] qualifying **3.** DR aggravated.

qualifier [9] [kalifje] **vt 1.** [gén] to qualify ▸ **être qualifié pour qqch/pour faire qqch** to be qualified for sthg/to do sthg **2.** [caractériser] **: qualifier qqn/qqch de qqch** to describe sb/sthg as sthg, to call sb/sthg sthg.
◆ ***se qualifier*** **vp** to qualify.

qualitatif*, *ive [kalitatif, iv] **adj** qualitative.

qualitativement [kalitativmɑ̃] **adv** qualitatively.

qualité [kalite] **nf 1.** [gén] quality ▸ **de bonne/mauvaise qualité** of good/poor quality ▸ **qualité de vie** quality of life **2.** [impression] **: qualité brouillon** *ou* **listing** [pour une impression] draft quality ▸ **qualité liste rapide** [pour une impression] draft quality ▸ **qualité perçue** perceived quality **3.** [condition] position, capacity ▸ **en qualité de** in my/his *etc* capacity as.

quand [kɑ̃] ■ **conj 1.** [lorsque, alors que] when ▸ **quand tu le verras, demande-lui de me téléphoner** when you see him, ask him to phone me ▸ **pourquoi rester ici quand on pourrait partir en week-end?** why stay here when we could go away for the weekend? **2.** *sout* [introduit une hypothèse] even if.
■ **adv interr** when ▸ **quand arriveras-tu?** when will you arrive? ▸ **je ne sais pas encore quand je pars** I don't know yet when I'm leaving ▸ **jusqu'à quand restez-vous?** how long are you staying for?
◆ ***quand même*** ■ **loc conj** *sout* even though, even if.
■ **loc adv** all the same ▸ **je pense qu'il ne viendra pas, mais je l'inviterai quand même** I don't think he'll come but I'll invite him all the same ▸ **tu pourrais faire attention quand même!** you might at least be careful!
■ **interj : quand même, à son âge!** really, at his/her age!
◆ ***quand bien même*** **loc conj** *sout* even though, even if ▸ **j'irai, quand bien même je devrais y aller à pied!** I'll go, even if I have to walk!
◆ ***n'importe quand*** **loc adv** any time.

quant [kɑ̃] ◆ ***quant à*** **loc prép** as for.

quant-à-soi [kɑ̃taswa] **nm inv** reserve ▸ **rester sur son quant-à-soi** to remain aloof.

quantième [kɑ̃tjɛm] **nm** date.

quantifiable [kɑ̃tifjabl] **adj** quantifiable.

quantifier [9] [kɑ̃tifje] **vt** to quantify.

quantitatif, ive [kɑ̃titatif, iv] **adj** quantitative.

quantitativement [kɑ̃titativmɑ̃] **adv** quantitatively.

quantité [kɑ̃tite] **nf 1.** [mesure] quantity, amount **2.** [abondance] **: (une) quantité de** a great many, a lot of ▸ **en quantité** in large numbers ▸ **des exemplaires en quantité** a large number of copies **3.** LING [sciences] quantity.

quarantaine [karɑ̃tɛn] **nf 1.** [nombre] **: une quarantaine de** about forty **2.** [âge] **: avoir la quarantaine** to be in one's forties **3.** [isolement] quarantine ▸ **mettre qqn en quarantaine** *fig* to send sb to Coventry.

quarante [karɑ̃t] **adj num inv & nm** forty ; voir aussi ***six***.

quarantième [karɑ̃tjɛm] **adj num inv, nm & nmf** fortieth ; voir aussi ***sixième***.

quart [kar] **nm 1.** [fraction] quarter ▸ **deux heures moins le quart** (a) quarter to two, (a) quarter of two *US* ▸ **deux heures et quart** (a) quarter past two, (a) quarter after two *US* ▸ **il est moins le quart** it's (a) quarter to, it's a quarter of *US* ▸ **un quart de** a quarter of ▸ **un quart de cercle** [gén] a quarter (of a) circle / GÉOM a quadrant ▸ **démarrer au quart de tour** to start first time / *fig* to fly off the handle ▸ **un quart d'heure** a quarter of an hour ▸ **passer un mauvais quart d'heure** to have a bad time of it ▸ **quart de ton** quarter tone **2.** NAUT watch ▸ **être de quart** to be on watch *ou* duty **3.** SPORT **: quart de finale** quarter-final.

quart-arrière [kararjɛr] **nmf** *Québec* SPORT quarterback.

quarté [karte] **nm** *system of betting involving the first four horses in a race.*

quarteron, onne [kartərɔ̃, ɔn] **nm, f** [métis] quadroon.
◆ ***quarteron*** **nm** *péj* [petit nombre] bunch, gang ▸ **un quarteron de politiciens véreux** a bunch of shady politicians.

quartette [kwartɛt] **nm** jazz quartet.

quartier [kartje] **nm 1.** [de ville] area, district ▸ **les beaux quartiers** the smart areas ▸ **le quartier latin** the Latin quarter ▸ **quartier résidentiel** residential area ▸ **restaurant de quartier** local restaurant
2. [de fruit] piece ▸ **un quartier d'orange** an orange segment / [de viande] quarter
3. [héraldique, de lune] quarter
4. *(gén pl)* MIL quarters *pl* ▸ **quartier général** headquarters *pl* ▸ **avoir/donner quartier libre** to have/give permission to leave barracks / *fig* to have/give permission to go out ▸ **prendre ses quartiers d'hiver à** to winter at
5. [partie d'une prison] wing ▸ **quartier de haute sécurité** high-security wing
6. [degré de descendance noble] **: quartiers de noblesse** degree of noble descent.

quartier-maître [kartjemɛtr] (pl **quartiers-maîtres**) **nm** leading seaman.

quart-monde [karmɔ̃d] (pl **quarts-mondes**) **nm : le quart-monde** the Fourth World.

quartz [kwarts] **nm** quartz ▸ **montre à quartz** quartz watch.

quasi [kazi] **adv** almost, nearly.

quasi- [kazi] **préf** near ▸ **quasi-collision** near collision.

quasiment [kazimɑ̃] **adv** *fam* almost, nearly.

quaternaire [kwatɛrnɛr] ■ **adj 1.** GÉOL Quaternary ▸ **ère quaternaire** Quaternary era **2.** CHIM & MATH quaternary.
■ **nm** GÉOL Quaternary (period).

quatorze [katɔrz] **adj num inv & nm** fourteen ; voir aussi ***six***.

CULTURE

Quatorze juillet

The 14th of July, Bastille Day, celebrates the taking of the Bastille prison on that day in 1789 – the symbolic beginning of the French Revolution. A grand military parade featuring students from the country's military schools assembles on the Champs-Elysées and large fireworks displays are part of the annual celebrations.

quatorzième [katɔrzjɛm] **adj num inv, nm & nmf** fourteenth ; voir aussi ***sixième***.

quatrain [katrɛ̃] **nm** quatrain.

quatre [katr] ■ **adj num inv** four ▸ **monter l'escalier quatre à quatre** to take the stairs four at a time ▸ **se mettre en quatre pour qqn** to bend over backwards for sb.
■ **nm** four ; voir aussi ***six***.

quatre-quarts [katkar] **nm inv** pound cake.

quatre-quatre [katkatr] ■ **adj inv** four-wheel drive. ■ **nm inv & nf inv** four-wheel drive (vehicle).

quatre-vingt = ***quatre-vingts***.

quatre-vingt-dix [katrəvɛ̃dis] **adj num inv & nm** ninety ; voir aussi ***six***.

quatre-vingt-dixième [katrəvɛ̃dizjɛm] **adj num inv, nm & nmf** ninetieth ; voir aussi ***sixième***.

quatre-vingtième [katrəvɛ̃tjɛm] **adj num inv, nm & nmf** eightieth ; voir aussi ***sixième***.

quatre-vingts, ***quatre-vingt*** [katrəvɛ̃] **adj num inv & nm** eighty ; voir aussi ***six***.

quatrième [katrijɛm] ■ **adj num inv, nm & nmf** fourth. ■ **nf 1.** SCOL ≃ third year ***ou*** form *UK*, ≃ eighth grade *US* **2.** [en danse] fourth position ; voir aussi ***sixième***.

quatuor [kwatɥɔr] **nm** quartet / *Québec* [golf] foursome.

que [k(ə)] ■ **conj 1.** [introduit une subordonnée] that ▸ **je sais que tu mens** I know (that) you're lying ▸ **il a dit qu'il viendrait** he said (that) he'd come ▸ **il veut que tu viennes** he wants you to come
2. [introduit une hypothèse] whether ▸ **que vous le vouliez ou non** whether you like it or not
3. [reprend une autre conjonction] **: s'il fait beau et que nous avons le temps...** if the weather is good and we have time... ▸ **quand je serai grande et que j'aurai un métier** when I'm grown up and (I) have a job
4. [indique un ordre, un souhait] **: qu'il entre!** let him come in! ▸ **que tout le monde sorte!** everybody out! ▸ **que Dieu nous pardonne** may God forgive us
5. [après un présentatif] **: voilà/voici que ça recommence!** here we go again! ▸ **je croyais l'affaire faite et voilà qu'elle n'est pas d'accord** I thought the deal was clinched and now I find she disagrees
6. [comparatif - après moins, plus] than / [- après autant, aussi, même] as ▸ **plus jeune que moi** younger than I (am) ***ou*** than me ▸ **elle a la même robe que moi** she has the same dress as I do ***ou*** as me
7. [seulement] **: ne... que** only ▸ **je n'ai qu'une sœur** I've only got one sister.
■ **pron rel** [chose, animal] which, that ▸ **le contrat que j'ai signé** the contract (which) ***ou*** that I signed ▸ **le livre qu'il m'a prêté** the book (which ***ou*** that) he lent me / [personne] whom, that ▸ **la femme que j'aime** the woman (whom ***ou*** that) I love.
■ **pron interr** what ▸ **que savez-vous au juste?** what exactly do you know? ▸ **que faire?** what can I/we/one do? ▸ **je me demande que faire** I wonder what I should do.
■ **adv excl : qu'elle est belle!** how beautiful she is! ▸ **que de monde!** what a lot of people! ▸ **que tu es naïf!** you're so naive!, aren't you naive!
◆ ***c'est que*** **loc conj** it's because ▸ **si je vais me coucher, c'est que j'ai sommeil** if I'm going to bed, it's because I'm tired.
◆ ***qu'est-ce que*** **pron interr** what ▸ **qu'est-ce que tu veux encore?** what else do you want?
◆ ***qu'est-ce qui*** **pron interr** what ▸ **qu'est-ce qui se passe?** what's going on?

Québec [kebɛk] **nm 1.** [province] **: le Québec** Quebec ▸ **la province de *ou* du Québec** Quebec State ▸ **au Québec** in Quebec **2.** [ville] Quebec ▸ **à Québec** in (the city of) Quebec.

CULTURE

Le Québec

This Canadian province and the city of the same name were founded by Samuel de Champlain in 1608. Although Canada came under British control in 1763, the province has remained 90% French-speaking. Even several American attempts at annexation have not erased Quebec's Francophone heritage: French has been the province's only official language for 30 years. **L'Office québecois de la langue française**, founded in 1977, aims to preserve and promote the French language and its use in the workplace, government, commerce, and communication. It reports on the state of the language in Quebec every five years.

québécois, ***e*** [kebekwa, az] **adj** Quebec *(avant n)*.
◆ ***québécois*** **nm** [langue] Quebec French.
◆ ***Québécois***, ***e*** **nm, f** Quebecker, Québecois.

quel, ***quelle*** (mpl **quels**, fpl **quelles**) [kɛl] ■ **adj interr** [personne] which / [chose] what, which ▸ **quel homme?** which man? ▸ **quel est cet homme?** who is this man? ▸ **quel livre voulez-vous?** what ***ou*** which book do you want? ▸ **de quel côté es-tu?** what ***ou*** which side are you on? ▸ **je ne sais quels sont ses projets** I don't know what his plans are ▸ **quelle heure est-il?** what time is it?, what's the time?
■ **adj excl : quel idiot!** what an idiot! ▸ **quelle honte!** the shame of it! ▸ **quel beau temps!** what lovely weather!
■ **adj indéf : quel que** *(+ subjonctif)* [chose, animal] whatever / [personne] whoever ▸ **il se baigne, quel que soit le temps** he goes swimming whatever the weather ▸ **il refuse de voir les nouveaux arrivants, quels qu'ils soient** he refuses to see new arrivals, whoever they may be.
■ **pron interr** which (one) ▸ **de vous trois, quel est le plus jeune?** which (one) of you three is the youngest?

quelconque [kɛlkɔ̃k] **adj 1.** [n'importe lequel] any ▸ **donner un prétexte quelconque** to give any old excuse ▸ **si pour une raisonquelconque...** if for any reason... ▸ **une quelconque observation** some remark or other **2.** *(après n) péj* [banal] ordinary, mediocre.

quelque [kɛlk(ə)] ■ **adj indéf** some ▸ **à quelque distance de là** some way away (from there) ▸ **j'ai quelques lettres à écrire** I have some ***ou*** a few letters to write ▸ **vous n'avez pas quelques livres à me montrer?** don't you have any books to show me? ▸ **les quelques fois où j'étais absent** the few times I wasn't there ▸ **les quelques millions de téléspectateurs qui nous regardent** the few million viewers watching us ▸ **les quelques 30 euros qu'il m'a prêté** the 30 euros or so (that) he lent me ▸ **quelque route que je prenne** whatever route I take ▸ **dans quelque pays que tu sois** whichever ***ou*** whatever country you may be in ▸ **quelque peu** somewhat, rather ▸ **dans quelque temps** in a while ▸ **c'est en quelque sorte un cheval avec un buste d'homme** it is, as it were ***ou*** so to speak, a horse with the head and shoulders of a man ▸ **elle est bizarre depuis quelque temps** she's been acting strangely for a *ou* some time now.

■ **adv** [environ] about ▸ **30 euros et quelque** some *ou* about 30 euros ▸ **il est midi et quelque** *fam* it's just after midday ▸ **quelque volontaire qu'il se montrât** however willing he was.

◆ ***quelques*** **adj 1.** [plusieurs] some, a few ▸ **j'ai quelques lettres à écrire** I have some letters to write ▸ **aurais-tu quelques pièces pour le téléphone?** have you got any change for the phone? **2.** [dans des expressions] **: 50 euros et quelques** just over 50 euros ▸ **il est midi et quelques** it's just gone midday.

quelque chose [kɛlkəʃoz] **pron indéf** something ▸ **quelque chose de différent** something different ▸ **quelque chose d'autre** something else ▸ **tu veux boire quelque chose?** do you want something *ou* anything to drink? ▸ **apporter un petit quelque chose à qqn** to give sb a little something ▸ **c'est quelque chose!** [ton admiratif] it's really something! ▸ **cela m'a fait quelque chose** I really felt it.

quelquefois [kɛlkəfwa] **adv** sometimes, occasionally.

quelque part [kɛlkəpar] **adv** somewhere, someplace *US* ▸ **l'as-tu vu quelque part?** did you see him anywhere *ou* anyplace *US*?, have you seen him anywhere *ou* anyplace *US*?

quelques-uns, ***quelques-unes*** [kɛlkəzœ̃, yn] **pron indéf** some, a few.

quelqu'un [kɛlkœ̃] **pron indéf m** someone, somebody ▸ **c'est quelqu'un d'ouvert/d'intelligent** he's/she's a frank/an intelligent person.

quémander [3] [kemɑ̃de] **vt** to beg for ▸ **quémander qqch à qqn** to beg sb for sthg.

qu'en-dira-t-on [kɑ̃diratɔ̃] **nm inv** *fam* tittle-tattle.

quenelle [kənɛl] **nf** *very finely chopped mixture of fish or chicken cooked in stock.*

quenotte [kənɔt] **nf** *fam* tooth.

querelle [kərɛl] **nf** quarrel ▸ **chercher querelle à qqn** to pick a quarrel with sb.

quereller [4] [kərele] ◆ ***se quereller*** **vp : se quereller (avec)** to quarrel (with).

querelleur, ***euse*** [kərɛlœr, øz] ■ **adj** quarrelsome.

■ **nm, f** quarrelsome person.

quérir [kerir] **vt** *littéraire* **: faire quérir qqn** to summon sb ▸ **aller quérir qqn** to go and fetch sb.

qu'est-ce que [kɛskə] ➤ ***que***.

qu'est-ce qui [kɛski] ➤ ***que***.

questeur [kɛstœr] **nm 1.** HIST quaestor **2.** POLIT parliamentary administrator.

question [kɛstjɔ̃] **nf** question ▸ **y a-t-il des questions?** (are there) any questions? ▸ **poser une question à qqn** to ask sb a question ▸ **il est question de faire qqch** it's a question *ou* matter of doing sthg ▸ **de quoi est-il question dans ce paragraphe?** what is this paragraph about? ▸ **il n'en est pas question** there is no question of it ▸ **poser la question de confiance** POLIT to ask for a vote of confidence ▸ **remettre qqn/qqch en question** to question sb/sthg, to challenge sb/sthg ▸ **mettez-vous mon honnêteté en question?** are you questioning my honesty? ▸ **question piège** [dans un jeu] trick question / [dans un interrogatoire] loaded *ou* leading question ▸ **question subsidiaire** tie-breaker ▸ **c'est une question de vie ou de mort** it's a matter of life and death ▸ **là n'est pas la question** that's not the point (at issue) *ou* the issue.

questionnaire [kɛstjɔnɛr] **nm** questionnaire.

questionner [3] [kɛstjɔne] **vt** to question.

quête [kɛt] **nf 1.** *sout* [d'objet, de personne] quest ▸ **se mettre en quête de** to go in search of **2.** [d'aumône] **: faire la quête** to take a collection.

quêter [4] [kete] ■ **vi** to collect.

■ **vt** *fig* to seek, to look for.

quetsche [kwɛtʃ] **nf 1.** [fruit] variety of plum **2.** [eau-de-vie] *type of plum brandy.*

queue [kø] **nf 1.** [d'animal] tail ▸ **faire une queue de poisson à qqn** AUTO to cut in front of sb ▸ **histoire sans queue ni tête** *fig* cock-and-bull story **2.** [de fruit] stalk **3.** [de poêle] handle **4.** [de liste, de classe] bottom / [de file, peloton] rear **5.** [file] queue *UK*, line *US* ▸ **faire la queue** to queue *UK*, to stand in line *US* ▸ **à la queue leu leu** in single file **6.** *vulg* [sexe masculin] dick.

queue-de-cheval [kødʃəval] (pl **queues-de-cheval**) **nf** ponytail.

queue-de-pie [kødpi] (pl **queues-de-pie**) **nf** *fam* tails *pl.*

qui [ki] ■ **pron rel 1.** *(sujet)* [personne] who / [chose] which, that ▸ **l'homme qui parle** the man who's talking ▸ **je l'ai vu qui passait** I saw him pass ▸ **le chien qui aboie** the barking dog, the dog which *ou* that is barking ▸ **donne-moi le magazine qui est sur la table** give me the magazine (that) *ou* which is on the table ▸ **qui plus est** (and) what's more ▸ **qui mieux est** even better, better still

2. *(complément d'objet direct)* who ▸ **tu vois qui je veux dire** you see who I mean ▸ **invite qui tu veux** invite whoever *ou* anyone you like

3. *(après une prép)* who, whom ▸ **la personne à qui je parle** the person I'm talking to, the person to whom I'm talking ▸ **les personnes au nom de qui ils ont agi** the people in whose name they acted

4. *(indéfini)* **: qui que tu sois** whoever you are ▸ **qui que ce soit** whoever it may be.

■ **pron interr 1.** *(sujet)* who ▸ **qui es-tu?** who are you? ▸ **je voudrais savoir qui est là** I would like to know who's there

2. *(complément d'objet, après une prép)* who, whom ▸ **qui demandez-vous?** who do you want to see? ▸ **dites-moi qui vous demandez** tell me who you want to see ▸ **à qui vas-tu le donner?** who are you going to give it to?, to whom are you going to give it? ▸ **de qui parles-tu?** who *ou* whom *sout* are you talking about?

◆ ***qui est-ce qui*** **pron interr** who ▸ **qui est-ce qui en veut?** who wants some?

◆ ***qui est-ce que*** **pron interr** who, whom ▸ **qui est-ce que tu connais ici?** who do you know around here?

quiche [kiʃ] **nf** quiche.

quiconque [kikɔ̃k] ■ **pron indéf** anyone, anybody.

■ **pron indéf** *sout* anyone who, whoever.

quid [kwid] **pron interr** *sout* & *hum* **: quid de...?** what about...?

Quid [kwid] **npr : le Quid** *annually updated one-volume encyclopedia of facts and figures.*

quidam [kidam] **nm** *fam* chap *UK*, guy *US*.

quiétude [kjetyd] **nf** tranquillity *UK*, tranquility *US*.

quignon [kiɲɔ̃] **nm** *fam* hunk.

quille [kij] **nf 1.** [de bateau] keel **2.** *arg mil* **: la quille** discharge, demob *UK*.

◆ ***quilles*** **nfpl 1.** [jeu] **: (jeu de) quilles** skittles *(U)* **2.** *fam* [jambes] pins.

quincaillerie [kɛ̃kajri] **nf 1.** [ustensiles] ironmongery *UK*, hardware **2.** [magasin] ironmonger's (shop) *UK*, hardware shop **3.** *fam fig* [bijoux] jewellery *UK*, jewelry *US*.

quincaillier, ère [kɛ̃kaje, ɛr] **nm, f** ironmonger *UK*, hardware dealer.

quinconce [kɛ̃kɔ̃s] **nm : en quinconce** in a staggered arrangement.

quinine [kinin] **nf** quinine.

quinqua [kɛ̃ka] **nmf** fiftysomething.

quinquagénaire [kɛ̃kaʒenɛr] ■ **nmf** fifty year old.
■ **adj : être quinquagénaire** to be in one's fifties.

quinquennal, e, aux [kɛ̃kenal, o] **adj** [plan] five-year *(avant n)* / [élection] five-yearly.

quinquennat [kɛ̃kena] **nm** five-year period of office, quinquennium, lustrum.

quinquina [kɛ̃kina] **nm 1.** [pharmacie & BOT] cinchona **2.** [boisson] quinine tonic wine.

quintal, aux [kɛ̃tal, o] **nm** quintal.

quinte [kɛ̃t] **nf** MUS fifth.

◆ ***quinte de toux*** **nf** coughing fit.

quintessence [kɛ̃tesɑ̃s] **nf** quintessence.

quintette [kɛ̃tɛt] **nm** quintet.

quintuple [kɛ̃typl] **nm & adj** quintuple.

quintupler [3] [kɛ̃typle] **vt & vi** to quintuple, to increase fivefold.

quinzaine [kɛ̃zɛn] **nf 1.** [nombre] fifteen (or so) ▸ **une quinzaine de** about fifteen **2.** [deux semaines] fortnight *UK*, two weeks *pl* ▸ **quinzaine publicitaire/commerciale** two-week advertising campaign/sale.

quinze [kɛ̃z] ■ **adj num inv** fifteen ▸ **dans quinze jours** in a fortnight *UK*, in two weeks.
■ **nm 1.** [chiffre] fifteen **2.** [rugby] **: le Quinze de France** the French fifteen ; voir aussi ***six***.

quinzième [kɛ̃zjɛm] **adj num inv, nm & nmf** fifteenth ; voir aussi ***sixième***.

quiproquo [kiprɔko] **nm** misunderstanding.

Quito [kito] **npr** Quito.

quittance [kitɑ̃s] **nf** receipt.

quitte [kit] **adj** quits ▸ **être quitte de qqch** to be clear of sthg ▸ **en être quitte pour qqch/pour faire qqch** to get off with sthg/doing sthg ▸ **quitte à faire qqch** even if it means doing sthg ▸ **quitte ou double** double or quits *UK*, double or nothing *US*.

quitter [3] [kite] **vt 1.** [gén] to leave ▸ **ne quittez pas!** [au téléphone] hold the line, please! **2.** [fonctions] to give up **3.** [vêtement] to take off **4.** INFORM to exit.

◆ ***se quitter*** **vp** to part.

quitus [kitys] **nm** discharge.

qui-vive [kiviv] ■ **interj** who goes there?
■ **nm inv : être sur le qui-vive** to be on the alert.

quoi [kwa] ■ **pron rel** *(après prép)* **: ce à quoi je me suis intéressé** what I was interested in ▸ **c'est en quoi vous avez tort** that's where you're wrong ▸ **après quoi** after which ▸ **avoir de quoi vivre** to have enough to live on ▸ **avez-vous de quoi écrire?** have you got something to write with? ▸ **merci – il n'y a pas de quoi** thank you – don't mention it.
■ **pron interr** what ▸ **à quoi penses-tu?** what are you thinking about? ▸ **je ne sais pas quoi dire** I don't know what to say ▸ **à quoi bon?** what's the point *ou* use? ▸ **quoi de neuf?** what's new? ▸ **quoi de plus?** what else? ▸ **décide-toi, quoi!** *fam* make your mind up, will you? ▸ **tu viens ou quoi?** *fam* are you coming or what?

◆ ***quoi que*** **loc conj** *(+ subjonctif)* whatever ▸ **quoi qu'il arrive** whatever happens ▸ **quoi qu'il dise** whatever he says ▸ **quoi qu'il en soit** be that as it may.

quoique [kwakə] **conj** although, though.

quolibet [kɔlibɛ] **nm** *sout* jeer, taunt.

quorum [k(w)ɔrɔm] **nm** quorum.

quota [k(w)ɔta] **nm** quota.

quote-part [kɔtpar] **(pl quotes-parts) nf** share.

quotidien, enne [kɔtidjɛ̃, ɛn] **adj** daily.

◆ ***quotidien*** **nm 1.** [routine] daily life ▸ **au quotidien** on a day-to-day basis **2.** [journal] daily (newspaper).

quotidiennement [kɔtidjɛnmɑ̃] **adv** daily, every day.

quotient [kɔsjɑ̃] **nm** quotient ▸ **quotient intellectuel** intelligence quotient.

QWERTY [kwɛrti] **adj inv : clavier QWERTY** QWERTY keyboard.

r[1], ***R*** [ɛr] **nm inv** [lettre] r, R.
◆ ***R*** (abr écrite de ***rand***) R.

r[2] abr de ***rue***.

rab [rab] **nm** *fam* [portion] seconds *pl* / [travail] overtime.

rabâchage [rabaʃaʒ] **nm** *fam* constant harping on *(U)*.

rabâcher [3] [rabaʃe] ■ **vi** *fam* to harp on.
■ **vt** to go over (and over).

rabais [rabɛ] **nm** reduction, discount ▸ **au rabais** *péj* [artiste] third-rate / [travailler] for a pittance.

rabaisser [4] [rabese] **vt 1.** [réduire] to reduce / [orgueil] to humble **2.** [personne] to belittle.
◆ ***se rabaisser*** **vp 1.** [se déprécier] to belittle o.s. **2.** [s'humilier] **: se rabaisser à faire qqch** to demean o.s. by doing sthg.

rabat [raba] **nm 1.** [partie rabattue] flap **2.** [de robe d'avocat] bands *pl*.

Rabat [raba] **npr** Rabat.

rabat-joie [rabaʒwa] ■ **nm inv** killjoy.
■ **adj inv : être rabat-joie** to be a killjoy.

rabattable [rabatabl] **adj** [siège] folding.

rabatteur, ***euse*** [rabatœr, øz] **nm, f 1.** [de gibier] beater **2.** *fig & péj* [de clientèle] tout.

rabattre [83] [rabatr] **vt 1.** [col] to turn down **2.** [siège] to tilt back / [couvercle] to shut ▸ **rabats le capot de la voiture** close the bonnet of the car **3.** [somme] to deduct ▸ **il a rabattu 5 % sur le prix affiché** he took *ou* knocked 5% off the marked price **4.** [gibier] to drive **5.** *fam* [clients] to tout for
▸▸| **en rabattre** to climb down.
◆ ***se rabattre*** **vp 1.** [siège] to tilt back / [couvercle] to shut **2.** [voiture, coureur] to cut in ▸ **le car s'est rabattu juste devant moi** the bus cut in just in front of me **3.** [se contenter] **: se rabattre sur** to fall back on ▸ **il a dû se rabattre sur un emploi de veilleur de nuit** he had to make do with a night watchman's job.

rabattu, ***e*** [rabaty] **pp** ➤ ***rabattre***.

rabbin [rabɛ̃] **nm** rabbi.

rabibocher [3] [rabibɔʃe] **vt 1.** *fam* [époux] to reconcile, to get back together **2.** *vieilli* [voiture] to patch up.
◆ ***se rabibocher*** **vp** *fam* to make (it) up.

rabiot [rabjo] **nm** *fam* [portion] seconds *pl*, more / [travail] overtime.

râble [rabl] **nm** [de lapin] back / CULIN saddle.

râblé, ***e*** [rable] **adj** stocky.

rabot [rabo] **nm** plane.

raboter [3] [rabɔte] **vt** to plane.

raboteux, ***euse*** [rabɔtø, øz] **adj** uneven, rugged.
◆ ***raboteuse*** **nf** planing machine.

rabougri, ***e*** [rabugri] **adj 1.** [plante] stunted **2.** [personne] shrivelled, wizened.

rabrouer [3] [rabrue] **vt** to snub.

racaille [rakaj] **nf** *péj* riffraff.

raccommodage [rakɔmɔdaʒ] **nm** mending.

raccommoder [3] [rakɔmɔde] **vt 1.** [vêtement] to mend **2.** *fam fig* [personnes] to reconcile, to get back together.
◆ ***se raccommoder*** **vp** *fam* to make (it) up.

raccompagner [3] [rakɔ̃paɲe] **vt** to see home, to take home.

raccord [rakɔr] **nm 1.** [liaison] join **2.** [pièce] connector, coupling **3.** CINÉ link.

raccordement [rakɔrdəmɑ̃] **nm** connection, linking.

raccorder [3] [rakɔrde] **vt : raccorder qqch (à)** to connect sthg (to), to join sthg (to).
◆ ***se raccorder*** **vp : se raccorder par** to be connected *ou* joined by ▸ **se raccorder à** to be connected to / *fig* [faits] to tie in with.

raccourci [rakursi] **nm** shortcut ▸ **en raccourci** in miniature ▸ **raccourci clavier** keyboard shortcut.

raccourcir [32] [rakursir] ■ **vt** to shorten.
■ **vi** to grow shorter.

raccroc [rakro] ◆ ***par raccroc*** **loc adv** by a fluke.

raccrocher [3] [rakrɔʃe] ■ **vt** to hang back up.
■ **vi 1.** [au téléphone] **: raccrocher (au nez de qqn)** to hang up (on sb), to put the phone down (on sb) **2.** *fam* [coureur] to give up.
◆ ***se raccrocher*** **vp : se raccrocher à** to cling to, to hang on to.

race [ras] **nf** [humaine] race / [animale] breed ▸ **de race** pedigree / [cheval] thoroughbred.

racé, e [rase] **adj 1.** [animal] purebred **2.** [voiture] of distinction.

rachat [raʃa] **nm 1.** [transaction] repurchase ▸ **rachat d'actions** FIN buy-back ▸ **rachat d'entreprise financé par l'endettement** leveraged buyout ▸ **rachat d'entreprise par les salariés** staff *ou* employee buyout **2.** *fig* [de péchés] atonement.

racheter [28] [raʃte] **vt 1.** [acheter en plus - gén] to buy another / [- pain, lait] to buy some more **2.** [acheter d'occasion] to buy **3.** [acheter après avoir vendu] to buy back **4.** *fig* [péché, faute] to atone for / [défaut, lapsus] to make up for **5.** [prisonnier] to ransom **6.** [honneur] to redeem **7.** COMM [société] to buy out.
◆ ***se racheter*** **vp** *fig* to redeem o.s.

rachidien, enne [raʃidjɛ̃, ɛn] **adj** rachidian, rachidial.

rachitique [raʃitik] **adj** suffering from rickets.

rachitisme [raʃitism] **nm** rickets *(U)*.

racial, e, aux [rasjal, o] **adj** racial.

racine [rasin] **nf** root / [de nez] base ▸ **racine carrée/cubique** MATH square/cube root.

racisme [rasism] **nm** racism.

raciste [rasist] **nmf** & **adj** racist.

racket [rakɛt] **nm** racket.

racketter [4] [rakɛte] **vt : racketter qqn** to subject sb to a protection racket.

racketteur [rakɛtœr] **nm** racketeer.

raclée [rakle] **nf** *fam* hiding, thrashing.

raclement [rakləmɑ̃] **nm** scraping (noise) ▸ **on entendit quelques raclements de gorge** some people could be heard clearing their throats.

racler [3] [rakle] **vt** to scrape ▸ **ce vin racle le gosier** this wine is a bit rough (on the throat).
◆ ***se racler*** **vp : se racler la gorge** to clear one's throat.

raclette [raklɛt] **nf 1.** CULIN *melted Swiss cheese served with jacket potatoes* **2.** [outil] scraper.

racloir [raklwar] **nm** scraper.

racolage [rakɔlaʒ] **nm** *fam péj* [par commerçant] touting / [par prostituée] soliciting.

racoler [3] [rakɔle] **vt** *fam péj* [suj: commerçant] to tout for / [suj: prostituée] to solicit.

racoleur, euse [rakɔlœr, øz] **adj** *fam péj* [air, sourire] come-hither / [publicité] strident.
◆ ***racoleur*** **nm** *fam péj* tout.
◆ ***racoleuse*** **nf** *fam péj* streetwalker.

racontar [rakɔ̃tar] **nm** *fam péj* piece of gossip.
◆ ***racontars*** **nmpl** *fam péj* tittle-tattle *(U)*.

raconter [3] [rakɔ̃te] **vt 1.** [histoire] to tell, to relate / [événement] to relate, to tell about ▸ **raconter qqch à qqn** to tell sb sthg, to relate sthg to sb **2.** [ragot, mensonge] to tell ▸ **qu'est-ce que tu racontes?** what are you on about?

racorni, e [rakɔrni] **adj 1.** [vieillard] wizened, shrivelled / [mains] gnarled / [plante] shrivelled / [parchemin] dried-up **2.** *sout* [esprit] hardened.

racornir [32] [rakɔrnir] **vt** to harden.
◆ ***se racornir*** **vp** to become hard.

radar [radar] **nm** radar ▸ **marcher au radar** *fam* to be on automatic pilot.

rade [rad] **nf** (natural) harbour *UK ou* harbor *US* ▸ **rester en rade** *fam fig* to be left stranded.

radeau, x [rado] **nm 1.** [embarcation] raft **2.** [train de bois] timber raft.

radial, e, aux [radjal, o] **adj** radial.

radiateur [radjatœr] **nm** radiator.

radiation [radjasjɔ̃] **nf 1.** PHYS radiation **2.** [de liste, du barreau] striking off.

radical, e, aux [radikal, o] **adj** radical.
◆ ***radical*** **nm 1.** [gén] radical **2.** LING stem.

radicalement [radikalmɑ̃] **adv** radically.

radicaliser [3] [radikalize] **vt** to radicalize, to make more radical.
◆ ***se radicaliser*** **vpi : le mouvement étudiant s'est radicalisé** the student movement has become more radical.

radier [9] [radje] **vt** to strike off.

radiesthésiste [radjɛstezist] **nmf** diviner *(by radiation)*.

radieux, euse [radjø, øz] **adj** radiant / [soleil] dazzling.

radin, e [radɛ̃, in] *fam péj* ■ **adj** stingy.
■ **nm, f** skinflint.

radiner [3] [radine] ◆ ***se radiner*** **vp** *fam* to get one's skates on, to get a move on.

radio [radjo] ■ **nf 1.** [station, poste] radio ▸ **à la radio** on the radio ▸ **allumer** *ou* **mettre la radio** to switch on the radio ▸ **éteindre la radio** to switch off the radio ▸ **passer à la radio** [personne] to be on the radio / [chanson] to be played on the radio ▸ **radio locale** *ou* **privée** *ou* **libre** independent local radio station ▸ **radio numérique** digital radio ▸ **radio pirate** pirate radio **2.** MÉD **: passer une radio** to have an X-ray, to be X-rayed.
■ **nm** radio operator.

radioactif, ive [radjɔaktif, iv] **adj** radioactive.

radioactivité [radjɔaktivite] **nf** radioactivity.

radioamateur [radjɔamatœr] **nm** (radio) ham.

radiocassette [radjɔkasɛt] **nf** radio cassette player.

radiodiffuser [3] [radjɔdifyze] **vt** to broadcast.

radiodiffusion [radjɔdifyzjɔ̃] **nf** broadcasting.

radioélectrique [radjɔelɛktrik] **adj** radio *(avant n)*.

radiographie [radjɔgrafi] **nf 1.** [technique] radiography **2.** [image] X-ray.

radiographier [9] [radjɔgrafje] **vt** to X-ray.

radiographique [radjɔgrafik] **adj** [technique] radiographic / [examen] X-ray *(modif)*.

radiologie [radjɔlɔʒi] **nf** radiology.

radiologue [radjɔlɔg], ***radiologiste*** [radjɔlɔʒist] **nmf** radiologist.

radiophonique [radjɔfɔnik] **adj** radio *(avant n)*.

radioréveil (pl radioréveils), ***radio-réveil*** (pl radios-réveils) [radjɔrevɛj] **nm** radio alarm, clock radio.

radioscopie [radjɔskɔpi] **nf** radioscopy.

radioscopique [radjɔskɔpik] **adj** X-ray *(modif)*.

radio-taxi [radjɔtaksi] (pl **radio-taxis**) **nm** radio taxi, radio-cab.

radiotéléphone [radjɔtelefɔn] **nm** cordless telephone, portable telephone.

radiotélévisé, e [radjɔtelevize] **adj** broadcast on both radio and television.

radiothérapie [radjɔterapi] **nf** radiotherapy.

radis [radi] **nm** radish ▸ **n'avoir plus un radis** *fig* not to have a penny *UK ou* cent *US* (to one's name).

radium [radjɔm] **nm** radium.

radius [radjys] **nm** radius.

radotage [radɔtaʒ] **nm** rambling.

radoter [3] [radɔte] **vi** to ramble.

radouber [3] [radube] **vt** to repair.

radoucir [32] [radusir] **vt** to soften.
◆ ***se radoucir*** **vp** [temps] to become milder / [personne] to calm down.

radoucissement [radusismɑ̃] **nm 1.** [d'attitude] softening **2.** [de température] rise ▸ **un radoucissement du temps** a spell of milder weather.

rafale [rafal] **nf 1.** [de vent] gust ▸ **en rafales** in gusts *ou* bursts **2.** [de coups de feu, d'applaudissements] burst.

raffermir [32] [rafɛrmir] **vt 1.** [muscle] to firm up **2.** *fig* [pouvoir] to strengthen.
◆ ***se raffermir*** **vp 1.** [muscle] to firm up **2.** *fig* [prix, autorité] to strengthen.

raffinage [rafinaʒ] **nm** refining.

raffiné, e [rafine] **adj** refined.

raffinement [rafinmɑ̃] **nm** refinement.

raffiner [3] [rafine] ■ **vt** to refine.
■ **vi : raffiner sur** to be meticulous about.

raffinerie [rafinri] **nf** refinery.

raffoler [3] [rafɔle] **vi : raffoler de qqn/qqch** to adore sb/sthg, to be mad about sb/sthg.

raffut [rafy] **nm** *fam* row, racket.

rafiot, rafiau [rafjo] **nm** *fam péj* tub *(boat)*.

rafistoler [3] [rafistɔle] **vt** *fam* to patch up.

rafle [rafl] **nf** raid.

rafler [3] [rafle] **vt** to swipe.

rafraîchir [32] [rafreʃir] ■ **vt 1.** [nourriture, vin] to chill, to cool / [air] to cool **2.** [vêtement, appartement] to smarten up / *fig* [mémoire, idées] to refresh / [connaissances] to brush up **3.** INFORM to refresh / [navigateur] to reload.
■ **vi** to cool (down).
◆ ***se rafraîchir*** **vp 1.** [se refroidir] to cool (down) **2.** [en buvant] to have a drink.

rafraîchissant, e [rafrɛʃisɑ̃, ɑ̃t] **adj** refreshing.

rafraîchissement [rafrɛʃismɑ̃] **nm 1.** [de climat] cooling **2.** [boisson] cold drink ▸ **prendre un rafraîchissement** to have a drink **3.** [de vêtement, d'appartement] smartening up.

raft(ing) [raft(iŋ)] **nm** whitewater rafting.

ragaillardir [32] [ragajardir] **vt** *fam* to buck up, to perk up.

rage [raʒ] **nf 1.** [fureur] rage ▸ **être ivre *ou* fou de rage** to be mad with rage ▸ **la rage au ventre *ou* cœur** seething with rage ▸ **faire rage** [tempête] to rage **2.** [manie] **: rage de faire qqch** mania for doing sthg **3.** [maladie] rabies *(U)*.
◆ ***rage de dents*** **nf** (raging) toothache.

rageant, e [raʒɑ̃, ɑ̃t] **adj** *fam* infuriating.

rager [17] [raʒe] **vi** *fam* to fume.

rageur, euse [raʒœr, øz] **adj** bad-tempered.

rageusement [raʒøzmɑ̃] **adv** furiously.

raglan [raglɑ̃] ■ **nm inv** raglan coat.
■ **adj inv** raglan *(avant n)*.

ragot [rago] **nm** *(gén pl) fam* gossip *sg*, (malicious) rumour *UK ou* rumor *US*, tittle-tattle *(U)*.

ragoût [ragu] **nm** stew.

ragoûtant, e [ragutɑ̃, ɑ̃t] **adj : peu *ou* pas très ragoûtant** *péj* [plat] not very appetizing / *fig* [idée] not very inviting.

rai [rɛ] **nm** *littéraire* [de soleil] ray.

raid [rɛd] **nm 1.** AÉRON, FIN & MIL raid ▸ **raid aérien** air raid **2.** SPORT long-distance rally.

raide [rɛd] ■ **adj 1.** [cheveux] straight **2.** [tendu - corde] taut / [- membre, cou] stiff **3.** [pente] steep **4.** [personne - attitude physique] stiff, starchy / [- caractère] inflexible **5.** *fam* [histoire] hard to swallow, farfetched **6.** *fam* [chanson] rude, blue **7.** *fam* [sans le sou] broke.
■ **adv** [abruptement] steeply
▸▸ **tomber raide mort** to fall down dead.

raideur [rɛdœr] **nf 1.** [de membre] stiffness **2.** [de personne - attitude physique] stiffness, starchiness / [- caractère] inflexibility.

raidillon [rɛdijɔ̃] **nm** steep (section of) road.

raidir [32] [rɛdir] **vt** [muscle] to tense / [corde] to tighten, to tauten.
◆ ***se raidir*** **vp 1.** [se contracter] to grow stiff, to stiffen **2.** *fig* [résister] **: se raidir contre** to steel o.s. against.

raie [rɛ] **nf 1.** [rayure] stripe **2.** [dans les cheveux] parting *UK*, part *US* **3.** [des fesses] crack **4.** [poisson] skate.

raifort [rɛfɔr] **nm** horseradish.

rail [raj] **nm** rail ▸ **remettre qqn/qqch sur les rails** to put sb/sthg back on the rails, to get sb/sthg back on the rails.

railler [3] [raje] **vt** *sout* to mock (at).
◆ ***se railler*** **vp : se railler de** *sout* to mock (at).

raillerie [rajri] **nf** *sout* mockery *(U)*.

railleur, euse [rajœr, øz] *sout* ■ **adj** mocking.
■ **nm, f** scoffer.

rails [raj] **nmpl** tracks.

rainette [renɛt] **nf** tree frog.

rainure [renyr] **nf** [longue] groove, channel / [courte] slot.

raisin [rɛzɛ̃] **nm** [fruit] grapes *pl* ▸ **raisin blanc/noir** white/black grapes ▸ **raisins de Corinthe** currants ▸ **raisins secs** raisins.

raison [rɛzɔ̃] **nf 1.** [gén] reason ▸ **perdre la raison** not to be in one's right mind ▸ **pour la (bonne et) simple raison que** for the simple reason that ▸ **pour quelle raison?** why? ▸ **recouvrer la raison** to come to one's senses ▸ **à plus forte raison** all the more (so) ▸ **faire entendre raison à qqn, ramener qqn à la raison** to make sb see reason ▸ **se faire une raison** to resign o.s. ▸ **fais-toi une raison, c'est trop tard** you'll just have to put up with *ou* to accept the fact that it's too late ▸ **raison de plus pour faire qqch** all the more reason to do sthg ▸ **sans raison** for no reason (at all) ▸ **le gouvernement a invoqué la raison d'État pour justifier cette mesure** the government said that it had done this for reasons of State ▸ **le vol est annulé en raison du mauvais temps** the flight has been cancelled because of bad weather **2.** [justesse, équité] **: avoir raison** to be right ▸ **avoir raison de faire qqch** to be right to do sthg ▸ **avoir raison de qqn/qqch** to get the better of sb/sthg ▸ **donner raison à qqn** to prove sb right.
◆ ***à raison de*** **loc prép** at (the rate of).
◆ ***en raison de*** **loc prép** owing to, because of.

raisonnable [rɛzɔnabl] **adj** reasonable.

raisonnablement [rɛzɔnabləmɑ̃] **adv 1.** [agir, parler] reasonably **2.** [manger, boire] in moderation.

raisonné, e [rɛzɔne] **adj 1.** [analyse, projet, décision] reasoned **2.** [grammaire, méthode] structured.

raisonnement [rɛzɔnmɑ̃] **nm 1.** [faculté] reason, power of reasoning **2.** [argumentation] reasoning, argument.

raisonner [3] [rɛzɔne] ■ **vt** [personne] to reason with.
■ **vi 1.** [penser] to reason **2.** [discuter] **: raisonner avec** to reason with.
◆ ***se raisonner*** **vp** [personne] to be reasonable.

raisonneur, euse [rɛzɔnœr, øz] ■ **adj** reasoning / *péj* argumentative.
■ **nm, f** argumentative person.

rajeunir [32] [raʒœnir] ■ **vt 1.** [suj: couleur, vêtement] **: rajeunir qqn** to make sb look younger **2.** [suj: personne] **: rajeunir qqn de trois ans** to take three years off sb's age **3.** [vêtement, canapé] to renovate, to do up / [meubles] to modernize **4.** *fig* [parti] to rejuvenate.
■ **vi 1.** [personne] to look younger / [se sentir plus jeune] to feel younger *ou* rejuvenated **2.** [faubourg] to be modernized.
◆ ***se rajeunir*** **vp** to lie about one's age.

rajeunissement [raʒœnismɑ̃] **nm** [de population] drop in age.

rajout [raʒu] **nm** addition.

rajouter [3] [raʒute] **vt** to add ▸ **en rajouter** *fam* to exaggerate.

rajuster [raʒyste], ***réajuster*** [3] [reaʒyste] **vt** to adjust / [cravate] to straighten.
◆ ***se rajuster*** **vp** to straighten one's clothes.

râle [ral] **nm** moan / [de mort] death rattle.

ralenti, e [ralɑ̃ti] **adj** slow.
◆ ***ralenti*** **nm 1.** AUTO idling speed ▸ **tourner au ralenti** AUTO to idle / *fig* to tick over *UK* ▸ **vivre au ralenti** *fig* to take things easy **2.** CINÉ slow motion.

ralentir [32] [ralɑ̃tir] ■ **vt 1.** [allure, expansion] to slow (down) **2.** [rythme] to slacken.
■ **vi** to slow down *ou* up.
◆ ***se ralentir*** **vp** to slow down *ou* up.

ralentissement [ralɑ̃tismɑ̃] **nm 1.** [d'allure, d'expansion] slowing (down) **2.** [de rythme] slackening **3.** [embouteillage] holdup **4.** PHYS deceleration.

râler [3] [rale] **vi 1.** [malade] to breathe with difficulty **2.** *fam* [grogner] to moan.

râleur, euse [ralœr, øz] *fam* ■ **adj** moaning *(avant n).*
■ **nm, f** grumbler, moaner.

ralliement [ralimɑ̃] **nm** rallying.

rallier [9] [ralje] **vt 1.** [poste, parti] to join **2.** [suffrages] to win **3.** [troupes] to rally.
◆ ***se rallier*** **vp** to rally ▸ **se rallier à** [parti] to join / [cause] to rally to / [avis] to come round *UK ou* around *US* to.

rallonge [ralɔ̃ʒ] **nf 1.** [de table] leaf, extension **2.** [électrique] extension (lead) **3.** *fam* [de crédit] extension (of credit).

rallonger [17] [ralɔ̃ʒe] ■ **vt** to lengthen.
■ **vi** to lengthen, to get longer.

rallumer [3] [ralyme] **vt 1.** [feu, cigarette] to relight / *fig* [querelle] to revive **2.** [appareil, lumière électrique] to switch (back) on again.
◆ ***se rallumer*** **vp 1.** [feu, guerre, colère] to flare up again **2.** [lumière électrique] to come on again.

rallye [rali] **nm** rally.

RAM, Ram [ram] (abr de ***Random access memory***) **nf** RAM.

ramadan [ramadɑ̃] **nm** Ramadan.

ramage [ramaʒ] **nm** *littéraire* [d'oiseau] song.
◆ ***ramages*** **nmpl** leafy design, foliage *(U).*

ramassage [ramasaʒ] **nm** collection ▸ **ramassage scolaire** [action] pick-up (of school children), busing *US* / [service] school bus.

ramasse-miettes [ramasmjɛt] **nm inv** crumb-brush and tray (set).

COMMENT EXPRIMER...

qu'on donne raison à quelqu'un

I see what you mean / Je vois ce que vous voulez dire	You're probably right / Vous avez probablement raison
I take your point / Je comprends votre point de vue	I guess so / C'est possible
You've got a point there / C'est juste	I'll have to take your word for it / Je suis bien obligé de vous croire
That's a fair comment / C'est une remarque pertinente	

ramasser [3] [ramase] **vt 1.** [récolter, réunir] to gather, to collect ▸ **ramasser du bois** to gather wood / *fig* [forces] to gather **2.** [prendre] to pick up ▸ **il était à ramasser à la petite cuillère** *fam* [épuisé] he was all washed out / [blessé] you could have scraped him off the ground **3.** *fig* [pensée] to sum up ▸ **ramassez vos idées en quelques lignes** condense your ideas into just a few lines **4.** *fam* [claque, rhume] to get ▸ **qu'est-ce que tu vas ramasser!** you're in for it!
◆ ***se ramasser*** **vp 1.** [se replier] to crouch **2.** *fam* [tomber, échouer] to come a cropper.

ramasseur, euse [ramasœr, øz] **nm, f** gatherer ▸ **ramasseur/ramasseuse de balles** [au tennis] ball boy/girl.
◆ ***ramasseur*** **nm** [machine & AGRIC] pick-up.

ramassis [ramasi] **nm** *péj* **: un ramassis de** a collection of.

rambarde [rɑ̃bard] **nf** (guard) rail.

rame [ram] **nf 1.** [aviron] oar **2.** RAIL train ▸ **rame de métro** underground *UK ou* subway *US* train **3.** [de papier] ream **4.** [tuteur] stake, pole.

rameau, x [ramo] **nm** branch.
◆ ***Rameaux*** **nmpl : les Rameaux** Palm Sunday.

ramener [19] [ramne] **vt 1.** [remmener] to take back ▸ **son chauffeur le ramène tous les soirs** his chauffeur drives him back every evening **2.** [rapporter, restaurer] to bring back ▸ **ramène-moi un journal** bring me back a newspaper **3.** [remettre] to put back ▸ **elle ramena le châle sur ses épaules** she pulled the shawl around her shoulders **4.** [réduire] **: ramener qqch à qqch** to reduce sthg to sthg, to bring sthg down to sthg ▸ **cela ramène le problème à sa dimension financière** it reduces the problem to its purely financial aspects
▸▸ **il ramène tout à lui** he sees things only in terms of how they affect him ▸ **la ramener** *fam* to stick one's oar in.
◆ ***se ramener*** **vp 1.** [problème] **: se ramener à** to come down to ▸ **toute l'affaire se ramenait finalement à une querelle de famille** in the end the whole business boiled down to *ou* was nothing more than a family quarrel **2.** *fam* [arriver] to turn up ▸ **ramène-toi en vitesse!** come on, hurry up!

ramequin [ramkɛ̃] **nm** ramekin.

ramer [3] [rame] **vi 1.** [rameur] to row **2.** *fam fig* [peiner] to slog.

rameur, euse [ramœr, øz] **nm, f** rower.

rameuter [3] [ramøte] **vt** to round up.

ramier [ramje] **nm** wood pigeon.

ramification [ramifikasjɔ̃] **nf 1.** [division] branch **2.** *(gén pl) fig* [de complot] ramification.

ramifier [9] [ramifje] ◆ ***se ramifier*** **vp** to branch out.

ramolli, e [ramɔli] ■ **adj** soft / *fig* soft (in the head).
■ **nm, f** *fam fig* thicko *UK*, half-wit.

ramollir [32] [ramɔlir] **vt 1.** [beurre] to soften **2.** *fam fig* [ardeurs] to cool.
◆ ***se ramollir*** **vp 1.** [beurre] to go soft, to soften **2.** *fam fig* [courage] to weaken.

ramonage [ramɔnaʒ] **nm** chimney sweeping.

ramoner [3] [ramɔne] **vt** to sweep.

ramoneur [ramɔnœr] **nm** (chimney) sweep.

rampant, e [rɑ̃pɑ̃, ɑ̃t] **adj 1.** [animal] crawling **2.** [plante] creeping **3.** *fig* [attitude] grovelling.
◆ ***rampants*** **nmpl** *fam* AÉRON ground staff *(U)*.

rampe [rɑ̃p] **nf 1.** [d'escalier] banister, handrail ▸ **lâcher la rampe** *fam fig* to kick the bucket **2.** [d'accès] ramp ▸ **rampe de lancement** launch pad **3.** THÉÂTRE **: la rampe** the footlights *pl.*

ramper [3] [rɑ̃pe] **vi 1.** [animal, soldat, enfant] to crawl **2.** [plante] to creep **3.** *fig* [personne] **: ramper devant** to grovel to **4.** *fig* [inquiétude] to creep.

rampon [rɑ̃pɔ̃] **nm** *Suisse* lamb's lettuce.

rancard, rencard [rɑ̃kar] **nm** *fam* [rendez-vous] date, meeting.

rancarder [3] [rɑ̃karde] **vt 1.** *arg crime* [renseigner] to fill in *(sep)*, to clue up *(sep)* ▸ **qui t'a rancardé?** who tipped you off? **2.** *tfam* [donner un rendez-vous à] **: rancarder qqn** to arrange to meet sb.
◆ ***se rancarder*** *tfam* **vp** *(emploi réfléchi) arg crime* to get information.

rancart, rencart [rɑ̃kar] **nm : mettre au rancart** to chuck out.

rance [rɑ̃s] ■ **nm : sentir le rance** to smell rancid.
■ **adj 1.** [beurre] rancid **2.** *fig* [idéologie] stale.

ranch [rɑ̃tʃ] **nm** ranch.

rancir [32] [rɑ̃sir] **vi** to go rancid.

rancœur [rɑ̃kœr] **nf** rancour *UK*, rancor *US*, resentment.

rançon [rɑ̃sɔ̃] **nf** ransom / *fig* price.

rancune [rɑ̃kyn] **nf** rancour *UK*, rancor *US*, spite ▸ **garder *ou* tenir rancune à qqn de qqch** to hold a grudge against sb for sthg ▸ **sans rancune!** no hard feelings!

rancunier, ère [rɑ̃kynje, ɛr] ■ **adj** vindictive, spiteful.
■ **nm, f** vindictive *ou* spiteful person.

randonnée [rɑ̃dɔne] **nf 1.** [promenade - à pied] walk / [- à cheval, à bicyclette] ride / [- en voiture] drive **2.** [activité] **: la randonnée** [à pied] walking / [à cheval] riding ▸ **faire de la randonnée** to go trekking.

randonneur, euse [rɑ̃dɔnœr, øz] **nm, f** walker, rambler.

rang [rɑ̃] **nm 1.** [d'objets, de personnes] row ▸ **on était au premier rang** we were in the front row ▸ **ce problème devrait être au premier rang de nos préoccupations** this problem should be at the top of our list of priorities ▸ **se mettre en rang par deux** to line up in twos ▸ **en rang d'oignons** *fig* in a row *ou* line ▸ **entrez/sortez en rang** go in/out in single file ▸ **élever qqn au rang de ministre** to raise *ou* to promote sb to the rank of minister
2. MIL rank ▸ **de haut rang** high-ranking ▸ **se mettre sur les rangs** to be in the running ▸ **grossir les rangs de** to swell the ranks of ▸ **sortir du rang** *litt* to come up through the ranks / *fig* to stand out
3. [position sociale] station ▸ **tenir son rang** to maintain one's position in society
4. *Québec* [peuplement rural] rural district
5. *Québec* [chemin] country road.

rangé, e [rɑ̃ʒe] **adj** [sérieux] well-ordered, well-behaved.

rangée [rɑ̃ʒe] **nf** row.

rangement [rɑ̃ʒmɑ̃] **nm** tidying up.

ranger [17] [rɑ̃ʒe] **vt** **1.** [élèves, soldats] to line up **2.** [chambre] to tidy **3.** [objets] to arrange **4.** [voiture] to park **5.** *fig* [livre, auteur] **: ranger parmi** to rank among.
◆ ***se ranger*** **vp** **1.** [élèves, soldats] to line up **2.** [voiture] to pull in **3.** [piéton] to step aside **4.** [s'assagir] to settle down **5.** *fig* [se rallier] **: se ranger à** to go along with ▸ **se ranger à côté de** to side with.

ranimer [3] [ranime] **vt** **1.** [personne] to revive, to bring round **2.** [feu] to rekindle **3.** *fig* [sentiment] to rekindle, to reawaken.
◆ ***se ranimer*** **vp** **1.** [personne] to come round *UK ou* around *US*, to come to **2.** *fig* [haine, ressentiment] to reawaken, to be renewed / [volcan] to become active again.

rap [rap] **nm** rap (music).

rapace [rapas] ■ **nm** bird of prey.
■ **adj** [cupide] rapacious, grasping.

rapacité [rapasite] **nf** rapaciousness.

rapatrié, e [rapatrije] ■ **nm, f** repatriated settler.
■ **adj** repatriated.

rapatriement [rapatrimɑ̃] **nm** repatriation.

rapatrier [10] [rapatrije] **vt** to repatriate.

râpe [rap] **nf** **1.** [de cuisine] grater ▸ **râpe à fromage** cheese grater **2.** [de menuisier] rasp **3.** *Suisse fam* [avare] miser, skinflint.

râpé, e [rape] **adj** **1.** CULIN grated **2.** [manteau] threadbare **3.** *fam* [raté] **: c'est râpé!** we've had it!
◆ ***râpé*** **nm** grated Gruyère cheese.

râper [3] [rape] **vt** **1.** CULIN to grate **2.** [bois, métal] to rasp.

rapetasser [3] [raptase] **vt** *fam péj* to patch up.

rapetisser [3] [raptise] ■ **vt** **1.** [rendre plus petit] to make smaller **2.** [faire paraître plus petit] **: rapetisser qqn/qqch** to make sb/sthg seem smaller **3.** [dévaloriser] to belittle.
■ **vi** to get smaller ▸ **la piste rapetissait à vue d'œil** the runway looked smaller and smaller by the minute.
◆ ***se rapetisser*** **vp** *(emploi réfléchi)* [se dévaloriser] **: se rapetisser aux yeux de qqn** to belittle o.s. in front of sb.

râpeux, euse [rapø, øz] **adj** **1.** [tissu] rough **2.** [vin] harsh.

raphia [rafja] **nm** raffia.

rapiat, e [rapja, at] **nm, f** *très familier* skinflint, meany *UK*.
◆ ***rapiat*** *tfam* **adj** [avare] tightfisted, stingy.

rapide [rapid] ■ **adj** **1.** [gén] rapid ▸ **une réponse rapide** a quick *ou* speedy reply ▸ **rapide comme l'éclair** quick as lightning **2.** [train, coureur] fast **3.** [pente] steep **4.** [musique, intelligence] lively, quick ▸ **être rapide à la détente** to be quick off the mark ▸ **jeter un coup d'œil rapide sur qqch** to have a quick glance at sthg.
■ **nm** **1.** [train] express (train) **2.** [de fleuve] rapid.

rapidement [rapidmɑ̃] **adv** rapidly.

rapidité [rapidite] **nf** rapidity.

rapiécer [20] [rapjese] **vt** to patch.

rapière [rapjɛr] **nf** rapier.

rappel [rapɛl] **nm** **1.** [de réservistes, d'ambassadeur] recall ▸ **rappel sous les drapeaux** (reservists) call-up *ou* recall **2.** [souvenir] reminder ▸ **rappel d'échéance** reminder of due date ▸ **rappel à l'ordre** call to order ▸ **rappel des titres de l'actualité** a summary of today's news **3.** TÉLÉCOM **: rappel automatique** recall **4.** [de paiement] back pay ▸ **rappel de cotisation** payment of contribution arrears **5.** [de vaccination] booster ▸ **ne pas oublier le rappel l'an prochain** don't forget to renew the vaccination next year **6.** [au spectacle] curtain call, encore **7.** SPORT abseiling *UK*, rapelling *US* ▸ **descendre en rappel** to abseil *UK ou* rappel *US* (down) ▸ **faire un rappel** to abseil **8.** TECHNOL **: ressort de rappel** return spring.

rappeler [24] [raple] **vt** **1.** [gén] to call back ▸ **rappelez-moi votre nom** what was your name again, please? ▸ **rappeler qqn à l'ordre** to call sb to order ▸ **rappeler qqn à qqch** *fig* to bring sb back to sthg ▸ **la mort de sa mère l'a rappelé à Aix** the death of his mother took him back to Aix **2.** [faire penser à] **: rappeler qqch à qqn** to remind sb of sthg ▸ **ça me rappelle les vacances** it reminds me of my holidays ▸ **son collier de turquoise rappelle la couleur de ses yeux** her turquoise necklace echoes the colour of her eyes.
◆ ***se rappeler*** **vp** to remember ▸ **elle se rappelle avoir reçu une lettre** she remembers receiving a letter ▸ **rappelle-toi que je t'attends!** remember *ou* don't forget (that) I'm waiting for you!

> PARONYME / CONFUSABLE
> **se rappeler**
> Quand vous traduisez rappeler, ne confondez pas *to remember* qui signifie se souvenir de quelque chose, et *to remind* qui signifie faire penser, rappeler quelque chose à quelqu'un.

rappelle, rappelles ➤ *rappeler*.

rappliquer [3] [raplike] **vi** *fam* to turn up, to show up.

rapport [rapɔr] **nm** **1.** [corrélation] link, connection ▸ **rapport de causalité** causal link ▸ **je ne vois pas le rapport** I don't see the connection ▸ **n'avoir aucun rapport avec qqch** to have no connection with *ou* to bear no relation to sthg
2. [contact] **: mettre qqn en rapport avec qqn** to put sb in touch with sb ▸ **se mettre en rapport avec qqn** to get in touch with sb
3. [compte-rendu] report ▸ **faire un rapport sur les conditions de travail** to report on working conditions ▸ **rapport annuel** annual report ▸ **rapport de police** police report
4. [profit] return, yield ▸ **il vit du rapport de son capital** he lives on the income from his investments
5. MATH ratio ▸ **un excellent rapport qualité-prix** excellent value for money.
◆ ***rapports*** **nmpl** **1.** [relations] relations ▸ **entretenir de bons rapports avec qqn** to be on good terms with sb **2.** [sexuels] **: rapports (sexuels)** intercourse *sg* ▸ **avoir des rapports (sexuels) avec qqn** to have sex with sb.
◆ ***par rapport à*** **loc prép** in comparison to, compared with ▸ **on constate un retrait de l'euro par rapport aux autres monnaies européennes** the euro has dropped sharply against other European currencies.

rapporter [3] [rapɔrte] **vt** to bring back ▸ **as-tu rapporté le journal?** did you get *ou* buy the paper? ▸ **le chien rapporte la balle** the dog brings back the ball ▸ **quelqu'un a rapporté le sac que tu avais oublié** somebody has brought back *ou* returned the bag you left behind ▸ **rapporter des intérêts** to yield interest ▸ **sa boutique lui rapporte beaucoup d'argent** her shop brings in a lot of money ▸ **rapporter un projet de loi** to throw out a bill.
◆ ***se rapporter*** **vp : se rapporter à** to refer *ou* relate to.

rapporteur, euse [rapɔrtœr, øz] ■ **adj** sneaky, telltale *(avant n)*.
■ **nm, f** sneak, telltale.
◆ ***rapporteur*** **nm 1.** [de commission] rapporteur **2.** GÉOM protractor.

rapproché, e [raprɔʃe] **adj** close.

rapprochement [raprɔʃmɑ̃] **nm 1.** [d'objets, de personnes] bringing together **2.** *fig* [entre événements] link, connection **3.** *fig* [de pays, de parti] rapprochement, coming together.

rapprocher [3] [raprɔʃe] **vt 1.** [mettre plus près] **: rapprocher qqn/qqch de qqch** to bring sb/sthg nearer to sthg, to bring sb/sthg closer to sthg **2.** *fig* [personnes] to bring together **3.** *fig* [idée, texte] **: rapprocher qqch (de)** to compare sthg (with).
◆ ***se rapprocher*** **vp 1.** [approcher] **: se rapprocher (de qqn/qqch)** to approach (sb/sthg) **2.** [se ressembler] **: se rapprocher de qqch** to be similar to sthg **3.** [se réconcilier] **: se rapprocher de qqn** to become closer to sb.

rapsodie = ***rhapsodie***.

rapt [rapt] **nm** abduction.

raquette [rakɛt] **nf 1.** [de tennis, de squash] racket / [de ping-pong] bat *UK*, paddle **2.** [à neige] snowshoe.

rare [rar] **adj 1.** [peu commun, peu fréquent] rare ▸ **plantes/timbres rares** rare plants/stamps ▸ **les visiteurs se font rares** there are fewer and fewer visitors ▸ **ses rares amis** his few friends **2.** [peu dense] sparse ▸ **il a le cheveu rare** his hair is thinning **3.** [surprenant] unusual, surprising ▸ **il n'est pas rare de le voir ici** it's not uncommon *ou* unusual to see him here.

raréfaction [rarefaksjɔ̃] **nf** scarcity / [d'air] rarefaction.

raréfier [9] [rarefje] **vt** to rarefy.
◆ ***se raréfier*** **vp** to become rarefied.

rarement [rarmɑ̃] **adv** rarely.

rareté [rarte] **nf 1.** [de denrées, de nouvelles] scarcity **2.** [de visites, de lettres] infrequency **3.** [objet précieux] rarity.

rarissime [rarisim] **adj** extremely rare.

ras, e [ra, raz] **adj 1.** [herbe, poil] short **2.** [mesure] full.
◆ ***ras*** **adv** short ▸ **à ras** short ▸ **à ras de** level with ▸ **en avoir ras le bol** *fam* to be fed up.
◆ ***ras du cou, ras le cou*** **loc adj** crew-neck, round-neck.

RAS (abr de ***rien à signaler***) nothing to report.

rasade [razad] **nf** glassful.

rasage [razaʒ] **nm** shaving.

rasant, e [razɑ̃, ɑ̃t] **adj 1.** [lumière] low-angled **2.** *fam* [film, discours] boring.

rascasse [raskas] **nf** scorpion fish.

rase-mottes [razmɔt] **nm inv** hedge-hopping.

raser [3] [raze] **vt 1.** [barbe, cheveux] to shave off ▸ **raser qqn** to give sb a shave, to shave sb ▸ **être rasé de près** to be close-shaven **2.** [mur, sol] to hug ▸ **l'hirondelle rase le sol** the swallow is skimming the ground **3.** [village] to raze ▸ **la vieille église a été rasée** the old church was razed to the ground **4.** *fam* [personne] to bore.
◆ ***se raser*** **vp 1.** [avec rasoir] to shave ▸ **se raser la barbe** to shave off one's beard ▸ **se raser les jambes** to shave one's legs **2.** *fam* [s'ennuyer] to be bored ▸ **on se rase ici, allons-nous-en** it's deadly boring here, let's go.

raseur, euse [razœr, øz] ■ **adj** boring.
■ **nm, f** bore.

ras-le-bol [ralbɔl] **nm inv** *fam* discontent ▸ **ras-le-bol!** *fam* that's enough!

rasoir [razwar] ■ **nm** razor ▸ **rasoir électrique** electric shaver ▸ **rasoir mécanique** safety razor.
■ **adj inv** *fam* boring.

rassasié, e [rasazje] **adj** full (up).

rassasier [9] [rasazje] **vt** to satisfy.
◆ ***se rassasier*** **vp : se rassasier de** to tire of, to have one's fill of.

rassemblement [rasɑ̃bləmɑ̃] **nm 1.** [d'objets] collecting, gathering **2.** [foule] crowd, gathering **3.** [union, parti] union **4.** MIL parade ▸ **rassemblement!** fall in!

rassembler [3] [rasɑ̃ble] **vt 1.** [personnes, documents] to collect, to gather **2.** [courage] to summon up / [idées] to collect.
◆ ***se rassembler*** **vp 1.** [manifestants] to assemble **2.** [famille] to get together.

rasseoir [65] [raswar] ◆ ***se rasseoir*** **vp** to sit down again.

rasséréner [18] [raserene] **vt** *sout* to calm down.
◆ ***se rasséréner*** **vp** *sout* to recover one's serenity.

rassir [32] [rasir] **vi** [gâteau, pain] to go stale / [viande] **: laisser rassir un morceau de bœuf** to let a piece of beef hang.
◆ ***se rassir*** **vpi** to go stale.

rassis, e [rasi, iz] **adj 1.** [pain] stale **2.** *sout* [esprit] calm, sober.

rassurant, e [rasyrɑ̃, ɑ̃t] **adj** reassuring.

rassuré, e [rasyre] **adj** confident, at ease.

rassurer [3] [rasyre] **vt** to reassure.
◆ ***se rassurer*** **vp** to feel at ease *ou* reassured ▸ **rassurez-vous** don't worry.

rat [ra] ■ **nm** rat ▸ **rat des champs** field mouse ▸ **petit rat** *fig* young ballet pupil ▸ **être fait comme un rat** to be cornered ▸ **rat de bibliothèque** *fig* bookworm.
■ **adj** *fam* [avare] mean, stingy.

ratage [rataʒ] **nm** bungling, messing up.

ratatiné, e [ratatine] **adj 1.** [fruit, personne] shrivelled *UK ou* shriveled *US* **2.** *fam fig* [vélo, bagnole] wrecked.

ratatiner [3] [ratatine] **vt 1.** [fruit, personne] to shrivel **2.** *fam* [démolir] to wreck.
◆ ***se ratatiner*** **vp** to shrivel up, to become wrinkled.

ratatouille [ratatuj] **nf** ratatouille.

rate [rat] **nf 1.** [animal] female rat **2.** [organe] spleen.

raté, e [rate] **nm, f** [personne] failure.
◆ ***raté*** **nm 1.** *(gén pl)* AUTO misfiring *(U)* ▸ **faire des ratés** to misfire **2.** *fig* [difficulté] problem.

râteau, x [rato] **nm** rake.

râtelier [ratəlje] **nm 1.** [à fourrage, à outils] rack ▸ **manger à tous les râteliers** *fig* to have a finger in every pie **2.** *fam* [dentier] false teeth *pl*.

rater [3] [rate] ■ **vt 1.** [train, occasion] to miss ▸ **elle a raté la marche** she missed the step ▸ **c'est une émission à ne pas rater** this programme is a must **2.** [plat, affaire] to make a mess of ▸ **il rate toujours les mayonnaises** his mayonnaise always goes wrong ▸ **tais-toi, tu vas tout faire rater!** shut up or you'll ruin everything! / [examen] to fail.
■ **vi** to go wrong.
◆ ***se rater*** **vp** *(emploi réfléchi) fam* **: il s'est coupé les cheveux lui-même, il s'est complètement raté!** he cut his hair himself and made a complete mess of it! ▸ **elle s'est ratée pour la troisième fois** that's her third (unsuccessful) suicide attempt.

ratiboiser [3] [ratibwaze] **vt** *fam* **1.** [voler] to pinch, to nick *esp UK* **2.** [ruiner] to clean out *(sep)* **3.** [tuer] to bump off *(sep)*, to do in *(sep)* **4.** [cheveux] **: je suis ressorti ratiboisé de chez le coiffeur** I got scalped at the hairdresser's.

ratification [ratifikasjɔ̃] **nf** ratification.

ratifier [9] [ratifje] **vt** to ratify.

ration [rasjɔ̃] **nf** [quantité] portion / *fig* share ▸ **ration alimentaire** food intake.

rationalisation [rasjɔnalizasjɔ̃] **nf** rationalization.

rationaliser [3] [rasjɔnalize] **vt** to rationalize.

rationnel, elle [rasjɔnɛl] **adj** rational.

rationnellement [rasjɔnɛlmɑ̃] **adv** rationally.

rationnement [rasjɔnmɑ̃] **nm** rationing ▸ **carte de rationnement** ration card.

rationner [3] [rasjɔne] **vt** to ration.
◆ ***se rationner*** **vp** to ration o.s.

ratissage [ratisaʒ] **nm 1.** [de jardin] raking **2.** [de quartier] search.

ratisser [3] [ratise] **vt 1.** [jardin] to rake **2.** [quartier] to search, to comb ▸ **ratisser large** to cast one's net wide **3.** *fam fig* [au jeu] to clean out **4.** [rugby] to heel.

raton [ratɔ̃] **nm 1.** ZOOL young rat **2.** *tfam* [Arabe] *racist term used with reference to North African Arabs.*
◆ ***raton laveur*** **nm** racoon.

raton(n)ade [ratɔnad] **nf** *tfam racist term used to describe an attack on North African Arab immigrants.*

RATP (abr de ***Régie autonome des transports parisiens***) **nf** *Paris transport authority.*

rattachement [rataʃmɑ̃] **nm** uniting, joining.

rattacher [3] [rataʃe] **vt 1.** [attacher de nouveau] to do up, to fasten again **2.** [relier] **: rattacher qqch à** to join sthg to / *fig* to link sthg with **3.** [unir] **: rattacher qqn à** to bind sb to.
◆ ***se rattacher*** **vp : se rattacher à** to be linked to.

ratte [rat] **nf** BOT & CULIN fingerling potato, (La) Ratte potato.

rattrapage [ratrapaʒ] **nm 1.** SCOL **: cours de rattrapage** remedial class **2.** [de salaires, prix] adjustment.

rattraper [3] [ratrape] **vt 1.** [animal, prisonnier] to recapture **2.** [temps] **: rattraper le temps perdu** to make up for lost time **3.** [rejoindre] to catch up with **4.** [bus] to catch **5.** [erreur] to correct **6.** [personne qui tombe] to catch.
◆ ***se rattraper*** **vp 1.** [se retenir] **: se rattraper à qqn/qqch** to catch hold of sb/sthg **2.** [compenser] to catch up **3.** [se faire pardonner] to make amends.

rature [ratyr] **nf** alteration.

raturer [3] [ratyre] **vt** to alter.

rauque [rok] **adj** hoarse, husky.

ravage [ravaʒ] **nm** [destruction] devastation ▸ **les ravages de la maladie/du temps** the ravages of disease/of time ▸ **faire des ravages** *litt* to wreak havoc ▸ **l'alcoolisme faisait des ravages** *fig* alcoholism was rife ▸ **notre cousin fait des ravages (dans les cœurs)!** our cousin is a heartbreaker!

ravagé, e [ravaʒe] **adj** *fam* [fou] **: être ravagé** to be off one's head.

ravager [17] [ravaʒe] **vt** [gén] to devastate, to ravage.

ravalement [ravalmɑ̃] **nm** cleaning, restoration.

ravaler [3] [ravale] **vt 1.** [façade] to clean, to restore **2.** [personne] **: ravaler qqn au rang de** to lower sb to the level of **3.** [salive] to swallow **4.** *fig* [larmes, colère] to stifle, to hold back.
◆ ***se ravaler*** **vp** to debase o.s., to demean o.s.

ravaudage [ravodaʒ] **nm** mending, repairing.

ravauder [3] [ravode] **vt** to mend, to repair.

rave[1] [rav] **nf 1.** BOT rape **2.** [fête] rave (party).

rave[2] [rɛv], ***rave-party*** [rɛvparti] **nf** rave (party).

ravi, e [ravi] **adj : ravi (de)** delighted (with) ▸ **je suis ravi de l'avoir trouvé** I'm delighted that I found it, I'm delighted to have found it ▸ **je suis ravi qu'il soit venu** I'm delighted (that) he has come ▸ **ravi de vous connaître** pleased to meet you.

ravier [ravje] **nm** small dish.

ravigotant, e [ravigɔtɑ̃, ɑ̃t] **adj** *fam* refreshing, stimulating.

ravigote [ravigɔt] **nf** *sauce of mustard, gherkins and capers.*

ravigoter [3] [ravigɔte] **vt** *fam* to perk up, to buck up.

ravin [ravɛ̃] **nm** ravine, gully.

raviné, e [ravine] **adj** [visage] furrowed.

raviner [3] [ravine] **vt** to gully.

ravioli [ravjɔli] (pl **ravioli** *ou* **raviolis**) **nm** ravioli *(U)*.

ravir [32] [ravir] **vt 1.** [charmer] to delight ▸ **à ravir** beautifully **2.** *littéraire* [arracher] **: ravir qqch à qqn** to rob sb of sthg.

raviser [3] [ravize] ◆ ***se raviser*** **vp** to change one's mind.

ravissant, e [ravisɑ̃, ɑ̃t] **adj** delightful, beautiful.

ravissement [ravismɑ̃] **nm 1.** [enchantement] delight **2.** *littéraire* [rapt] rape, ravishing.

ravisseur, euse [ravisœr, øz] **nm, f** abductor.

ravitaillement [ravitajmɑ̃] **nm** [en denrées] resupplying / [en carburant] refuelling *UK*, refueling *US*.

ravitailler [3] [ravitaje] **vt** [en denrées] to resupply / [en carburant] to refuel.
◆ ***se ravitailler*** **vp** [en denrées] to get fresh supplies / [en carburant] to refuel.

raviver [3] [ravive] **vt** **1.** [feu] to rekindle **2.** [couleurs] to brighten up **3.** *fig* [douleur] to revive **4.** [plaie] to reopen.

ravoir [ravwar] **vt** **1.** [jouet, livre] to get back **2.** *fam* [linge] to get clean.

rayé, e [rɛje] **adj** **1.** [tissu] striped **2.** [disque, vitre] scratched **3.** [canon] rifled.

rayer [11] [rɛje] **vt** **1.** [disque, vitre] to scratch **2.** [nom, mot] to cross out ▸ **rayer qqn d'une liste** to cross sb's name off a list **3.** [canon] to rifle.

rayon [rɛjɔ̃] **nm** **1.** [de lumière] beam, ray / *fig* [d'espoir] ray ▸ **un rayon de soleil** a ray of sunshine, a sunbeam / MÉTÉOR a brief sunny spell / *fig* a ray of sunshine ▸ **rayon vert** green flash
2. *(gén pl)* [radiation] radiation *(U)* ▸ **rayon cathodique** cathode ray ▸ **rayons infrarouges/ultraviolets** infrared/ultraviolet light ▸ **rayon laser** laser beam ▸ **rayons X** X-rays ▸ **passer qqch aux rayons X** to X-ray sthg
3. [de roue] spoke
4. GÉOM radius ▸ **dans un rayon de** *fig* within a radius of ▸ **dans un rayon de vingt kilomètres** within (a radius of) twenty kilometres ▸ **rayon d'action** range ▸ **étendre son rayon d'action** *fig* to increase *ou* to widen the scope of one's activities
5. [étagère] shelf
6. [dans un magasin] department ▸ **nous n'en avons plus en rayon** we're out of stock
7. *fam* [domaine] : **demande à ton père, c'est son rayon** ask your father, that's his department ▸ **il en connaît un rayon en électricité** he really knows a thing or two about electricity.

rayonnage [rɛjɔnaʒ] **nm** shelving.

rayonnant, e [rɛjɔnɑ̃, ɑ̃t] **adj** *litt* & *fig* radiant.

rayonne [rɛjɔn] **nf** rayon.

rayonnement [rɛjɔnmɑ̃] **nm** **1.** [gén] radiance / [des arts] influence **2.** PHYS radiation.

rayonner [3] [rɛjɔne] **vi** **1.** [soleil] to shine ▸ **rayonner de joie** *fig* to radiate happiness **2.** [culture] to be influential **3.** [avenues, lignes, chaleur] to radiate **4.** [touriste] to tour around *(from a base)*.

rayure [rɛjyr] **nf** **1.** [sur étoffe] stripe **2.** [sur disque, sur meuble] scratch **3.** [de fusil] groove.

raz [ra] ◆ ***raz de marée*** **nm** tidal wave / *fig* & POLIT landslide.

razzia [razja] **nf** *fam* raid ▸ **faire une razzia sur** to raid, to plunder.

razzier [9] [razje] **vt** to raid, to plunder.

RBE (abr de ***revenu brut d'exploitation***) **nm** gross profit.

RBL (abr écrite de ***rouble***) R, Rub.

R-C abr de ***rez-de-chaussée***.

r.d. (abr écrite de ***rive droite***) *right (north) bank of the Seine*.

R-D (abr de ***recherche-développement***) **nf** R & D.

RDA (abr de ***République démocratique allemande***) **nf** GDR.

RDB (abr de ***revenu disponible brut***) **nm** gross disposable income.

RdC abr de ***rez-de-chaussée***.

ré [re] **nm inv** MUS D / [chanté] re.

ré(-) [re] **préf** re(-).

réa [rea] **nm** pulley (wheel).

réabonnement [reabɔnmɑ̃] **nm** subscription renewal.

réabonner [3] [reabɔne] **vt : réabonner qqn à** to renew sb's subscription to.
◆ ***se réabonner*** **vp : se réabonner à** to renew one's subscription to.

réac [reak] **nmf** & **adj** *péj* reactionary.

réaccoutumer [3] [reakutyme] **vt** to reaccustom.
◆ ***se réaccoutumer*** **vp : se réaccoutumer à** to reaccustom o.s. to.

réacheminer [3] [reaʃmine] **vt** to forward.

réacteur [reaktœr] **nm** [d'avion] jet engine ▸ **réacteur nucléaire** nuclear reactor.

réactif, ive [reaktif, iv] **adj** reactive.
◆ ***réactif*** **nm** reagent.

réaction [reaksjɔ̃] **nf : réaction (à/contre)** reaction (to/against) ▸ **réaction en chaîne** chain reaction.

réactionnaire [reaksjɔnɛr] **nmf** & **adj** *péj* reactionary.

réactiver [3] [reaktive] **vt** to reactivate.

réactualisation [reaktɥalizasjɔ̃] **nf** [modernisation] updating, bringing up to date.

réactualiser [3] [reaktɥalize] **vt** [moderniser] to update, to bring up to date.

réadaptation [readaptasjɔ̃] **nf** rehabilitation.

réadapter [3] [readapte] **vt** to readapt / [accidenté] to rehabilitate.
◆ ***se réadapter*** **vp : se réadapter à** to readapt to.

réaffirmer [3] [reafirme] **vt** to reaffirm.

réagir [32] [reaʒir] **vi : réagir (à/contre)** to react (to/against) ▸ **réagir sur** to affect.

réajustement [reaʒystəmɑ̃] **nm** adjustment.

réajuster = ***rajuster***.

réalisable [realizabl] **adj** **1.** [projet] feasible **2.** FIN realizable.

réalisateur, trice [realizatœr, tris] **nm, f** CINÉ & TV director.

réalisation [realizasjɔ̃] **nf** **1.** [de projet] carrying out **2.** CINÉ & TV production.

réaliser [3] [realize] **vt** **1.** [projet] to carry out / [ambitions, rêves] to achieve, to realize **2.** CINÉ & TV to produce **3.** [s'apercevoir de] to realize.
◆ ***se réaliser*** **vp** **1.** [ambition] to be realized / [rêve] to come true **2.** [personne] to fulfil *UK ou* fulfill *US* o.s.

réalisme [realism] **nm** realism.

réaliste [realist] ▪ **nmf** realist.
▪ **adj** **1.** [personne, objectif] realistic **2.** ART & LITTÉR realist.

réalité [realite] **nf** reality ▸ **en réalité** in reality ▸ **réalité virtuelle** INFORM virtual reality, VR.

reality-show, ***reality show*** [realitiʃo] (pl **reality(-)shows**) **nm** *talk show focussing on real-life drama.*

réaménagement [reamenaʒmɑ̃] **nm 1.** [de projet] restructuring **2.** [de taux d'intérêt] readjustment.

réamorcer [16] [reamɔrse] **vt** to start up again.

réanimation [reanimasjɔ̃] **nf** resuscitation ▸ **en réanimation** in intensive care.

réanimer [3] [reanime] **vt** to resuscitate.

réapparaître [91] [reaparɛtr] **vi** to reappear.

réapparition [reaparisjɔ̃] **nf** reappearance.

réapprendre [79] [reaprɑ̃dr] **vt** to relearn.

réarmement [rearməmɑ̃] **nm** rearmament.

réassort [reasɔr] **nm 1.** [action] restocking **2.** [result] fresh stock.

réassortiment [reasɔrtimɑ̃] **nm 1.** COMM [d'un magasin] restocking / [d'un stock] renewing / [de marchandises] new stock, fresh supplies **2.** [de pièces d'un service] matching (up) / [d'une soucoupe] replacing.

réassurance [reasyrɑ̃s] **nf** reinsurance.

rébarbatif, ***ive*** [rebarbatif, iv] **adj 1.** [personne, visage] forbidding **2.** [travail] daunting.

rebâtir [32] [rəbatir] **vt** to rebuild.

rebattre [83] [rəbatr] **vt** [cartes] to reshuffle.

rebattu, ***e*** [rəbaty] ■ **pp** ➤ ***rebattre***.
■ **adj** overworked, hackneyed.

rebelle [rəbɛl] **adj 1.** [personne] rebellious / [troupes] rebel *(avant n)* ▸ **rebelle à** [discipline] unamenable to **2.** [mèche, boucle] unruly.

rebeller [4] [rəbɛle] ◆ ***se rebeller*** **vp : se rebeller (contre)** to rebel (against).

rébellion [rebɛljɔ̃] **nf** rebellion.

rebelote [rəbəlɔt] **nf** [jeu de cartes] rebelote *(said when playing the second card of a pair of king and queen of trumps while playing belote)*
▸▸ **rebelote!** *fam* here we go again!

rebiffer [3] [rəbife] ◆ ***se rebiffer*** **vp** *fam* **: se rebiffer (contre)** to rebel (against).

reblochon [rəblɔʃɔ̃] **nm** *cow's-milk cheese from Haute-Savoie.*

reboiser [3] [rəbwaze] **vt** to reafforest *UK*, to reforest *US*.

rebond [rəbɔ̃] **nm** bounce.

rebondi, ***e*** [rəbɔ̃di] **adj** rounded.

rebondir [32] [rəbɔ̃dir] **vi 1.** [objet] to bounce / [contre mur] to rebound **2.** *fig* [affaire] to come to life (again).

rebondissement [rəbɔ̃dismɑ̃] **nm** [d'affaire] new development.

rebord [rəbɔr] **nm** [de table] edge / [de fenêtre] sill, ledge.

reboucher [3] [rəbuʃe] **vt** [bouteille] to put the cork back in, to recork / [trou] to fill in.

rebours [rəbur] ◆ ***à rebours*** **loc adv** the wrong way / *fig* the wrong way round *UK* ***ou*** around *US*, back to front.

rebouteux, ***euse*** [rəbutø, øz], ***rebouteur***, ***euse*** [rəbutœr, øz] **nm, f** *fam* bonesetter.

reboutonner [3] [rəbutɔne] **vt** to rebutton.

rebrousse-poil [rəbruspwal] ◆ ***à rebrousse-poil*** **loc adv** the wrong way ▸ **prendre qqn à rebrousse-poil** *fig* to rub sb up the wrong way.

rebrousser [3] [rəbruse] **vt** to brush back ▸ **rebrousser chemin** *fig* to retrace one's steps.

rebuffade [rəbyfad] **nf** rebuff ▸ **essuyer une rebuffade** to be rebuffed.

rébus [rebys] **nm** rebus.

rebut [rəby] **nm** scrap ▸ **mettre qqch au rebut** to get rid of sthg, to scrap sthg.

rebutant, ***e*** [rəbytɑ̃, ɑ̃t] **adj 1.** [travail] disheartening **2.** [manières] disgusting.

rebuter [3] [rəbyte] **vt 1.** [suj: travail] to dishearten **2.** [suj: manières] to disgust.

récalcitrant, ***e*** [rekalsitrɑ̃, ɑ̃t] ■ **adj** recalcitrant, stubborn.
■ **nm, f** recalcitrant.

recaler [3] [rəkale] **vt** *fam* to fail.

récapitulatif, ***ive*** [rekapitylatif, iv] **adj** summary *(avant n)*.
◆ ***récapitulatif*** **nm** summary.

récapitulation [rekapitylasjɔ̃] **nf** recapitulation, recap.

récapituler [3] [rekapityle] **vt** to recapitulate, to recap.

recaser [3] [rəkaze] **vt** *fam* [personne] to find a new job for.
◆ ***se recaser*** **vp** *(emploi réfléchi) fam* [retrouver un emploi] to get fixed up with a new job / [se remarier] to get hitched again.

recel [rəsɛl] **nm** [action] receiving ***ou*** handling stolen goods / [délit] possession of stolen goods.

receler [25] [rəsəle] **vt 1.** [objet volé] to receive, to handle **2.** *fig* [secret, trésor] to contain.

receleur, ***euse*** [rəsəlœr, øz] **nm, f** receiver *(of stolen goods)*.

récemment [resamɑ̃] **adv** recently.

recensement [rəsɑ̃smɑ̃] **nm 1.** [de population] census **2.** [d'objets] inventory.

recenser [3] [rəsɑ̃se] **vt 1.** [population] to take a census of **2.** [objets] to take an inventory of.

récent, ***e*** [resɑ̃, ɑ̃t] **adj** recent.

recentrer [3] [rəsɑ̃tre] **vt** to refocus.

récépissé [resepise] **nm** receipt.

réceptacle [resɛptakl] **nm** [lieu] gathering place.

récepteur, ***trice*** [resɛptœr, tris] **adj** receiving.
◆ ***récepteur*** **nm** receiver.

réceptif, ***ive*** [resɛptif, iv] **adj** receptive.

réception [resɛpsjɔ̃] **nf 1.** [gén] reception ▸ **donner une réception** to hold a reception **2.** [de marchandises] receipt **3.** [bureau] reception (desk), front desk *US* **4.** SPORT [de sauteur, skieur] landing / [du ballon, avec la main] catch ▸ **bonne réception de X** [avec le pied] X traps the ball.

réceptionnaire [resɛpsjɔnɛr] **nmf 1.** [de marchandises] receiving clerk **2.** [à l'hôtel] head of reception.

réceptionner [3] [resɛpsjɔne] **vt 1.** [marchandises] to take delivery of **2.** [SPORT - avec la main] to catch / [- avec le pied] to control.

réceptionniste [resɛpsjɔnist] **nmf** receptionist, desk clerk *US*.

récessif, ive [resesif, iv] **adj** recessive.

récession [resesjɔ̃] **nf** recession.

recette [rəsɛt] **nf 1.** COMM takings *pl* ▸ **faire recette** *fig* to be a success **2.** [entreprise] incomings, earnings *(pl)* ▸ **recette(s) annuelle(s)** annual earnings ▸ **recettes nettes** net receipts **3.** CULIN recipe / *fig* [méthode] recipe, formula.

recevable [rəsəvabl] **adj 1.** [excuse, offre] acceptable **2.** DR admissible.

receveur, euse [rəsəvœr, øz] **nm, f 1.** ADMIN **: receveur des impôts** tax collector ▸ **receveur des postes** postmaster (f postmistress) **2.** [de bus] conductor (f conductress) **3.** [de greffe] recipient.

recevoir [52] [rəsəvwar] ■ **vt 1.** [gén] to receive ▸ **voilà longtemps que je n'ai pas reçu de ses nouvelles** it's a long time since I last heard from him **2.** [coup] to get, to receive ▸ **recevoir un coup sur la tête** to receive a blow to *ou* to get hit on the head **3.** [invités] to entertain / [client] to see ▸ **recevoir qqn à dîner** to have sb to dinner ▸ **j'ai été très bien reçu** I was made (to feel) most welcome **4.** SCOL & UNIV **: être reçu à un examen** to pass an exam ▸ **elle a été reçue à l'épreuve de français** she passed her French exam.

■ **vi 1.** [donner une réception] to entertain ▸ **elle sait merveilleusement recevoir** she's marvellous at entertaining, she's a marvellous hostess **2.** [avocat, médecin] to be available (to see clients) ▸ **le médecin reçoit/ne reçoit pas aujourd'hui** the doctor is/isn't seeing patients today.

◆ ***se recevoir*** **vp** SPORT to land.

rechange [rəʃɑ̃ʒ] ◆ ***de rechange*** **loc adj** spare / *fig* alternative.

réchapper [3] [reʃape] **vi : réchapper de** to survive.

recharge [rəʃarʒ] **nf 1.** [cartouche] refill **2.** [action - de batterie] recharging.

rechargeable [rəʃarʒabl] **adj** [batterie] rechargeable / [briquet] refillable.

recharger [17] [rəʃarʒe] **vt 1.** [batterie] to recharge **2.** [stylo, briquet] to refill **3.** [arme, camion, appareil-photo] to reload.

réchaud [reʃo] **nm** (portable) stove.

réchauffé, e [reʃofe] **adj** [plat] reheated / *fig* rehashed.

réchauffement [reʃofmɑ̃] **nm** warming (up).

réchauffer [3] [reʃofe] **vt 1.** [nourriture] to reheat **2.** [personne] to warm up.

◆ ***se réchauffer*** **vp** to warm up.

rêche [rɛʃ] **adj** rough.

recherche [rəʃɛrʃ] **nf 1.** [quête & INFORM] search ▸ **être à la recherche de** to be in search of ▸ **se mettre** *ou* **partir à la recherche de** to go in search of ▸ **faire** *ou* **effectuer des recherches** to make inquiries **2.** [sciences] research ▸ **faire de la recherche** to do research **3.** [raffinement] elegance.

recherché, e [rəʃɛrʃe] **adj 1.** [ouvrage] sought-after **2.** [raffiné - vocabulaire] refined / [- mets] exquisite.

rechercher [3] [rəʃɛrʃe] **vt 1.** [objet, personne] to search for, to hunt for **2.** [compagnie] to seek out.

rechigner [3] [rəʃiɲe] **vi : rechigner à** to balk at.

rechute [rəʃyt] **nf** relapse.

rechuter [3] [rəʃyte] **vi** to relapse.

récidive [residiv] **nf 1.** DR repeat offence *UK ou* offense *US* **2.** MÉD recurrence.

récidiver [3] [residive] **vi 1.** DR to commit another offence *UK ou* offense *US* **2.** MÉD to recur.

récidiviste [residivist] **nmf** repeat *ou* persistent offender.

récif [resif] **nm** reef ▸ **récif de corail** coral reef.

récipiendaire [resipjɑ̃dɛr] **nmf** *sout* **1.** [dans assemblée] newly elected member **2.** [de diplôme] recipient.

récipient [resipjɑ̃] **nm** container.

réciproque [resiprɔk] ■ **adj** reciprocal.

■ **nf : la réciproque** the reverse.

réciproquement [resiprɔkmɑ̃] **adv** mutually ▸ **et réciproquement** and vice versa.

récit [resi] **nm** story.

récital, als [resital] **nm** recital.

récitatif [resitatif] **nm** recitative.

récitation [resitasjɔ̃] **nf** recitation.

réciter [3] [resite] **vt** to recite.

réclamation [reklamasjɔ̃] **nf** complaint ▸ **faire/déposer une réclamation** to make/lodge a complaint.

réclame [reklam] **nf 1.** [annonce] advert *UK*, advertisement **2.** [publicité] **: la réclame** advertising **3.** [promotion] **: en réclame** on special offer.

réclamer [3] [reklame] **vt 1.** [demander] to ask for, to request / [avec insistance] to demand **2.** [nécessiter] to require, to demand.

◆ ***se réclamer*** **vp : se réclamer de** [mouvement] to identify with.

reclasser [3] [rəklase] **vt 1.** [dossiers] to refile **2.** [chômeur] to find a new job for **3.** ADMIN to regrade.

reclus, e [rəkly, yz] ■ **adj** *sout* reclusive.

■ **nm, f** recluse.

réclusion [reklyzjɔ̃] **nf** imprisonment ▸ **réclusion à perpétuité** life imprisonment.

recoiffer [3] [rəkwafe] **vt : recoiffer qqn** to do sb's hair again.

◆ ***se recoiffer*** **vp** to do one's hair again.

recoin [rəkwɛ̃] **nm** nook.

reçois, reçoit ➤ *recevoir*.

recoller [3] [rəkɔle] **vt** [objet brisé] to stick back together.

récolte [rekɔlt] **nf 1.** [AGRIC - action] harvesting *(U)*, gathering *(U)* / [- produit] harvest, crop **2.** *fig* collection.

récolter [3] [rekɔlte] **vt** to harvest / *fig* to collect.

recommandable [rəkɔmɑ̃dabl] **adj** commendable ▸ **peu recommandable** undesirable.

recommandation [rəkɔmɑ̃dasjɔ̃] **nf** recommendation.

recommandé, e [rəkɔmɑ̃de] **adj 1.** [envoi] registered ▸ **envoyer qqch en recommandé** to send sthg by registered post *UK ou* mail *US* **2.** [conseillé] advisable ▸ **ce n'est pas très recommandé** it's not really a good idea, it's not very advisable.

recommander [3] [rəkɔmɑ̃de] **vt** to recommend ▸ **recommander à qqn de faire qqch** to advise sb to do sthg ▸ **recommander qqn à qqn** to recommend sb to sb.
◆ ***se recommander*** **vp 1.** [se réclamer] **: se recommander de qqn** to use sb as a referee **2.** [invoquer la protection de] **: se recommander à qqn** to commend o.s. to sb **3.** *Suisse* [insister] to be persistent.

recommencement [rəkɔmɑ̃smɑ̃] **nm** new beginning.

recommencer [16] [rəkɔmɑ̃se] ■ **vt** [travail] to start *ou* begin again / [erreur] to make again ▸ **recommencer à faire qqch** to start *ou* begin doing sthg again.
■ **vi** to start *ou* begin again ▸ **ne recommence pas!** don't do that again!

recommercialiser [rəkɔmɛrsjalize] **adj** to remarket.

récompense [rekɔ̃pɑ̃s] **nf** reward ▸ **en récompense de** as a reward for.

récompenser [3] [rekɔ̃pɑ̃se] **vt** to reward.

recompter [3] [rəkɔ̃te] **vt** to recount.

réconciliation [rekɔ̃siljasjɔ̃] **nf** reconciliation.

réconcilier [9] [rekɔ̃silje] **vt** to reconcile.
◆ ***se réconcilier*** **vp : se réconcilier avec** to make it up with.

reconductible [rəkɔ̃dyktibl] **adj** renewable.

reconduction [rəkɔ̃dyksjɔ̃] **nf** renewal.

reconduire [98] [rəkɔ̃dɥir] **vt 1.** [personne] to accompany, to take **2.** [politique, bail] to renew.

reconduit, e [rəkɔ̃dɥi, it] **pp** ➤ ***reconduire***.

reconfigurer INFORM to reconfigure.

réconfort [rekɔ̃fɔr] **nm** comfort ▸ **chercher réconfort dans** to seek comfort *ou* solace in.

réconfortant, e [rekɔ̃fɔrtɑ̃, ɑ̃t] **adj** comforting.

réconforter [3] [rekɔ̃fɔrte] **vt** to comfort.

reconnaissable [rəkɔnɛsabl] **adj** recognizable.

reconnaissance [rəkɔnɛsɑ̃s] **nf 1.** [gén] recognition ▸ **reconnaissance de la parole/vocale** INFORM speech/voice recognition ▸ **reconnaissance optique de caractères** optical character recognition, OCR **2.** [aveu] acknowledgment, admission ▸ **la reconnaissance de ses torts lui a valu l'indulgence du jury** his admission of his wrongs won him the leniency of the jury ▸ **reconnaissance de dette** acknowledgment of a debt, IOU **3.** MIL reconnaissance ▸ **aller/partir en reconnaissance** to go out on reconnaissance ▸ **envoyer des hommes en reconnaissance** to send men out on reconnaissance **4.** [gratitude] gratitude ▸ **avoir/éprouver de la reconnaissance envers qqn** to be/to feel grateful to *ou* towards sb ▸ **exprimer sa reconnaissance à qqn** to show *ou* express one's gratitude to sb.

reconnaissant, e [rəkɔnɛsɑ̃, ɑ̃t] **adj** grateful ▸ **je vous en suis très reconnaissant** I am very grateful to you (for it) ▸ **je vous serais reconnaissant de m'aider** I would be grateful if you would help me.

reconnaître [91] [rəkɔnɛtr] **vt 1.** [gén] to recognize ▸ **je t'ai reconnu à ta démarche** I recognized you *ou* I could tell it was you by your walk **2.** [erreur] to admit, to acknowledge ▸ **l'accusé reconnaît-il les faits?** does the accused acknowledge the facts? ▸ **je reconnais que j'ai eu tort** I admit I was wrong **3.** MIL to reconnoitre ▸ **il envoya dix hommes reconnaître le terrain** he ordered ten men to go and reconnoitre the ground.
◆ ***se reconnaître*** **vp 1.** [s'identifier] to recognize o.s. ▸ **se reconnaître dans** *ou* **en qqn** to see o.s. in sb ▸ **je me reconnais dans la réaction de ma sœur** I can see myself reacting in the same way as my sister **2.** [s'orienter] to know where one is, to get one's bearings ▸ **mets des étiquettes sur tes dossiers, sinon comment veux-tu qu'on s'y reconnaisse?** label your files, otherwise we'll get completely confused **3.** [s'avouer] **: se reconnaître coupable** to admit one's guilt.

reconnecter [rəkɔnɛkte] **vt** to reconnect.
◆ ***se reconnecter*** **vpi** INFORM to reconnect o.s., to get back on line.

reconnu, e [rəkɔny] ■ **pp** ➤ ***reconnaître***.
■ **adj** well-known.

reconquérir [39] [rəkɔ̃kerir] **vt** to reconquer.

reconquête [rəkɔ̃kɛt] **nf** reconquest.

reconquiers, reconquiert ➤ ***reconquérir***.

reconquis, e [rəkɔ̃ki, iz] **pp** ➤ ***reconquérir***.

reconsidérer [18] [rəkɔ̃sidere] **vt** to reconsider.

reconstituant, e [rəkɔ̃stitɥɑ̃, ɑ̃t] **adj** invigorating.
◆ ***reconstituant*** **nm** tonic.

reconstituer [7] [rəkɔ̃stitɥe] **vt 1.** [puzzle] to put together **2.** [crime, délit] to reconstruct.

reconstitution [rəkɔ̃stitysjɔ̃] **nf 1.** [de puzzle] putting together **2.** [de crime, délit] reconstruction ▸ **reconstitution historique** CINÉ & TV dramatic reconstruction.

reconstruction [rəkɔ̃stryksjɔ̃] **nf** reconstruction, rebuilding.

reconstruire [98] [rəkɔ̃strɥir] **vt** to reconstruct, to rebuild.

reconstruit, e [rəkɔ̃strɥi, it] **pp** ➤ ***reconstruire***.

reconversion [rəkɔ̃vɛrsjɔ̃] **nf 1.** [d'employé] redeployment **2.** [d'usine, de société] conversion ▸ **opérer une reconversion** to restructure ▸ **reconversion économique/technique** economic/technical restructuring.

reconvertir [32] [rəkɔ̃vɛrtir] **vt 1.** [employé] to redeploy **2.** [économie] to restructure.
◆ ***se reconvertir*** **vp : se reconvertir dans** to move into / [profession] to go into.

recopier [9] [rəkɔpje] **vt** to copy out.

record [rəkɔr] ■ **nm** record ▸ **détenir/améliorer/battre un record** to hold/improve/beat a record.
■ **adj inv** record *(avant n)*.

recordman [rəkɔrdman] (pl **recordmen** [-mɛn]) **nm** record holder.

recoucher [3] [rəkuʃe] **vt** to put back to bed.
◆ ***se recoucher*** **vp** to go back to bed.

recoudre [86] [rəkudr] **vt** to sew (up) again.

recoupement [rəkupmɑ̃] **nm** cross-check ▸ **par recoupement** by cross-checking.

recouper [3] [rəkupe] **vt** **1.** [pain] to cut again **2.** COUT to recut **3.** *fig* [témoignages] to compare, to cross-check.
◆ ***se recouper*** **vp** **1.** [lignes] to intersect **2.** [témoignages] to match up.

recourbé, e [rəkurbe] **adj** [cils] curved / [nez] hooked.

recourber [3] [rəkurbe] **vt** to bend (over).

recourir [45] [rəkurir] **vi** : **recourir à** [médecin, agence] to turn to / [force, mensonge] to resort to.

recourrai, recourras ➤ ***recourir***.

recours[1], ***recourt*** *etc* ➤ ***recourir***.

recours[2] [rəkur] **nm** **1.** [emploi] : **recours à** use of ▸ **avoir recours à** [médecin, agence] to turn to / [force, mensonge] to resort to, to have recourse to **2.** [solution] solution, way out ▸ **en dernier recours** as a last resort **3.** DR action ▸ **recours en cassation** appeal ▸ **recours en justice** legal action ▸ **sans recours** without appeal / *fig* final.

recouru [rəkury] **pp inv** ➤ ***recourir***.

recouvert, e [rəkuvɛr, ɛrt] **pp** ➤ ***recouvrir***.

recouvrable [rəkuvrabl] **adj** recoverable.

recouvrement [rəkuvrəmɑ̃] **nm** **1.** [de surface] covering **2.** [de dettes, d'impôts] collection.

recouvrer [3] [rəkuvre] **vt** **1.** [vue, liberté] to regain **2.** [dettes, impôts] to collect.

recouvrir [34] [rəkuvrir] **vt** **1.** [gén] to cover / [fauteuil] to re-cover **2.** [personne] to cover (up).
◆ ***se recouvrir*** **vp** **1.** [tuiles] to overlap **2.** [surface] : **se recouvrir (de)** to be covered (with).

recracher [3] [rəkraʃe] **vt** to spit out.

récréatif, ive [rekreatif, iv] **adj** entertaining.

récréation [rekreasjɔ̃] **nf** **1.** [détente] relaxation, recreation **2.** SCOL break *UK*, recess *US*.

recréer [15] [rəkree] **vt** to recreate.

récrier [10] [rekrije] ◆ ***se récrier*** **vp** *sout* : **se récrier (à)** to exclaim (at).

récrimination [rekriminasjɔ̃] **nf** complaint.

récriminer [3] [rekrimine] **vi** to complain.

récrire [rekrir], ***réécrire*** [99] [reekrir] **vt** to rewrite.

recroqueviller [3] [rəkrɔkvije] ◆ ***se recroqueviller*** **vp** to curl up.

recru, e [rəkry] **adj** : **recru de fatigue** *littéraire* exhausted.
◆ ***recrue*** **nf** recruit.

recrudescence [rəkrydɛsɑ̃s] **nf** renewed outbreak.

recrutement [rəkrytmɑ̃] **nm** recruitment.

recruter [3] [rəkryte] **vt** to recruit.

rectal, e, aux [rɛktal, o] **adj** rectal.

rectangle [rɛktɑ̃gl] **nm** rectangle.

rectangulaire [rɛktɑ̃gylɛr] **adj** rectangular.

recteur [rɛktœr] **nm** SCOL *chief administrative officer of an education authority*, ≃ (Chief) Education Officer *UK*.

rectificatif, ive [rɛktifikatif, iv] **adj** correcting.
◆ ***rectificatif*** **nm** correction.

rectification [rɛktifikasjɔ̃] **nf** **1.** [correction] correction **2.** [de tir] adjustment.

rectifier [9] [rɛktifje] **vt** **1.** [tir] to adjust **2.** [erreur] to rectify, to correct / [calcul] to correct.

rectiligne [rɛktiliɲ] **adj** rectilinear.

recto [rɛkto] **nm** right side ▸ **recto verso** on both sides.

rectorat [rɛktɔra] **nm** SCOL *offices of the education authority*, ≃ Education Offices *UK*.

rectum [rɛktɔm] **nm** rectum.

reçu, e [rəsy] **pp** ➤ ***recevoir***.
◆ ***reçu*** **nm** receipt.

recueil [rəkœj] **nm** collection.

recueillement [rəkœjmɑ̃] **nm** meditation.

recueilli, e [rəkœji] **adj** contemplative, meditative ▸ **un public très recueilli** a very attentive audience ▸ **un visage recueilli** a composed expression.

recueillir [41] [rəkœjir] **vt** **1.** [fonds] to collect **2.** [suffrages] to win **3.** [enfant] to take in.
◆ ***se recueillir*** **vp** to meditate.

recuire [98] [rəkɥir] **vt & vi** to recook.

recul [rəkyl] **nm** **1.** [mouvement arrière] step backwards / MIL retreat **2.** [d'arme à feu] recoil **3.** [de civilisation] decline / [d'inflation, de chômage] : **recul (de)** downturn (in) **4.** *fig* [retrait] : **prendre du recul** to stand back ▸ **avec du recul** with hindsight.

reculade [rəkylad] **nf** retreat.

reculé, e [rəkyle] **adj** distant.

reculer [3] [rəkyle] ■ **vt** **1.** [voiture] to back up **2.** [date] to put back, to postpone.
■ **vi** **1.** [aller en arrière] to move backwards / [voiture] to reverse ▸ **il a heurté le mur en reculant** he backed *ou* reversed into the wall ▸ **mets le frein à main, la voiture recule!** put the handbrake on, the car is rolling backwards! ▸ **ne reculer devant rien** *fig* to stop at nothing ▸ **reculer devant l'ennemi** to retreat in the face of the enemy ▸ **le prix m'a fait reculer** I backed down when I saw the price **2.** [maladie, pauvreté] to be brought under control **3.** [faiblir - cours, valeur] to fall, to weaken ▸ **le yen recule par rapport au dollar** the yen is losing ground *ou* falling against the dollar.

reculons [rəkylɔ̃] ◆ ***à reculons*** **adv** backwards.

récupérateur, trice [rekyperatœr, tris] ■ **adj** **1.** [qui recycle] : **industrie récupératrice** *industry based on reclaimed or recycled materials* **2.** [qui repose] : **sommeil récupérateur** refreshing *ou* restorative *sout* sleep.
■ **nm, f** *industrialist or builder working with reclaimed materials*.
◆ ***récupérateur*** **nm** [armement & TECHNOL] recuperator.

récupération [rekyperasjɔ̃] **nf** [de déchets] salvage.

récupérer [18] [rekypere] ■ **vt** **1.** [objet] to get back **2.** [déchets] to salvage **3.** [idée] to pick up **4.** [journée] to make up.
■ **vi** to recover, to recuperate.

récurer [3] [rekyre] **vt** to scour.

récurrent, e [rekyrɑ̃, ɑ̃t] **adj** recurrent.

récuser [3] [rekyze] **vt 1.** DR to challenge **2.** *sout* [refuser] to reject.
◆ ***se récuser*** **vp** *sout* to decline to give an opinion.

recyclage [rəsiklaʒ] **nm 1.** [d'employé] retraining **2.** [de déchets] recycling.

recycler [3] [rəsikle] **vt 1.** [employé] to retrain **2.** [déchets] to recycle.
◆ ***se recycler*** **vp** [employé] to retrain.

rédacteur, trice [redaktœr, tris] **nm, f** [de journal] subeditor ⁄ [d'ouvrage de référence] editor ▸ **rédacteur en chef** editor-in-chief.

rédaction [redaksjɔ̃] **nf 1.** [de texte] editing **2.** SCOL essay **3.** [personnel] editorial staff.

rédactionnel, elle [redaksjɔnɛl] **adj** editorial.

reddition [redisjɔ̃] **nf** surrender.

redécouvrir [34] [rədekuvrir] **vt** to rediscover.

redéfinir [32] [rədefinir] **vt** to redefine.

redéfinition [rədefinisjɔ̃] **nf** redefinition.

redemander [3] [rədəmɑ̃de] **vt** to ask again for.

redémarrer [3] [rədemare] **vi** to start again ⁄ *fig* to get going again ⁄ INFORM to reboot, to restart.

rédempteur, trice [redɑ̃ptœr, tris] ■ **adj** redeeming.
■ **nm, f** redeemer.

rédemption [redɑ̃psjɔ̃] **nf** redemption.

redéploiement [rədeplwamɑ̃] **nm** redeployment.

redescendre [73] [rədesɑ̃dr] ■ **vt** *(v aux : être)* **1.** [escalier] to go/come down again **2.** [objet - d'une étagère] to take down again.
■ **vi** *(v aux : être)* to go/come down again.

redevable [rədəvabl] **adj : être redevable de 20 euros à qqn** to owe sb 20 euros ▸ **être redevable à qqn de qqch** [service] to be indebted to sb for sthg.

redevance [rədəvɑ̃s] **nf** [de radio, télévision] licence *UK* *ou* license *US* fee ⁄ [téléphonique] rental (fee).

redevenir [40] [rədəvnir] **vi** to become again.

rédhibitoire [redibitwar] **adj** [défaut] crippling ⁄ [prix] prohibitive.

rediffuser [3] [rədifyze] **vt** to broadcast again, to repeat.

rediffusion [rədifyzjɔ̃] **nf** repeat.

rédiger [17] [rediʒe] **vt** to write.

redimensionner [3] [radimɑ̃sjɔne] **vt** INFORM to resize.

redingote [rədɛ̃gɔt] **nf** [de femme] coat ⁄ HIST frock coat.

redire [102] [rədir] **vt** to repeat ▸ **avoir *ou* trouver à redire à qqch** *fig* to find fault with sthg.

redistribuer [7] [rədistribɥe] **vt** to redistribute.

redistribution [rədistribysjɔ̃] **nf** redistribution.

redit, e [rədi, it] **pp** ➤ ***redire***.

redite [rədit] **nf** repetition.

redondance [rədɔ̃dɑ̃s] **nf** redundancy.

redonner [3] [rədɔne] **vt** to give back ⁄ [confiance, forces] to restore.

redoublant, e [rədublɑ̃, ɑ̃t] **nm, f** pupil who is repeating a year.

redoublé, e [rəduble] **adj : à coups redoublés** twice as hard.

redoubler [3] [rəduble] ■ **vt 1.** [syllabe] to reduplicate **2.** [efforts] to intensify **3.** SCOL to repeat.
■ **vi** to intensify ▸ **redoubler d'efforts** to redouble one's efforts ▸ **le vent redoubla de fureur** the wind blew twice as hard.

redoutable [rədutabl] **adj** formidable.

Redoute [rədut] **npr f : la Redoute** *French mail order firm*.

redouter [3] [rədute] **vt** to fear.

redoux [rədu] **nm** thaw.

redressement [rədrɛsmɑ̃] **nm 1.** [de pays, d'économie] recovery **2.** DR **: redressement fiscal** payment of back taxes.

redresser [4] [rədrɛse] ■ **vt 1.** [poteau, arbre] to put *ou* set upright ▸ **redresser la tête** to raise one's head ⁄ *fig* to hold up one's head **2.** [situation] to set right.
■ **vi** AUTO to straighten up.
◆ ***se redresser*** **vp 1.** [personne] to stand *ou* sit straight **2.** [pays] to recover.

redresseur [rədrɛsœr] **nm : redresseur de torts** righter of wrongs.

réducteur, trice [redyktœr, tris] **adj 1.** [de quantité] reducing **2.** [limitatif] simplistic.
◆ ***réducteur*** **nm** CHIM reducing agent.

réduction [redyksjɔ̃] **nf 1.** [gén] reduction ▸ **bénéficier d'une réduction** to get a reduction **2.** MÉD setting.

réduire [98] [redɥir] ■ **vt 1.** [gén] to reduce ▸ **réduire qqch de moitié** to cut sthg by half, to halve sthg ▸ **réduire en** to reduce to ▸ **réduire qqch en cendres** to reduce sthg to ashes ▸ **il a réussi à réduire à néant le travail de dix années** he managed to reduce ten years' work to nothing ▸ **réduire qqn à qqch/à faire qqch** to reduce sb to sthg/to doing sthg ▸ **réduire la presse/l'opposition au silence** to silence the press/the opposition ▸ **être réduit à faire qqch** to be reduced to doing sthg **2.** INFORM to minimize **3.** MÉD to set **4.** *Suisse* [ranger] to put away.
■ **vi** CULIN to reduce ▸ **faire réduire** to reduce.
◆ ***se réduire*** **vp 1.** [se restreindre] to cut down **2.** [se ramener] **: se réduire à** to come *ou* boil down to **3.** [se transformer] **: se réduire en** to be reduced to.

réduisais, réduisions ➤ ***réduire***.

réduit, e [redɥi, it] ■ **pp** ➤ ***réduire***.
■ **adj** reduced.
◆ ***réduit*** **nm 1.** [local] small room **2.** [renfoncement] recess.

rééchelonnement [reeʃlɔnemɑ̃] **nm** rescheduling ▸ **rééchelonnement des dettes** debt rescheduling.

rééchelonner [3] [reeʃlɔne] **vt** to reschedule.

réécrire = ***récrire***.

rééditer [3] [reedite] **vt 1.** [œuvre, auteur] to republish **2.** *fam* [méfaits] to give a repeat performance of.

réédition [reedisjɔ̃] **nf** new edition.

rééducation [reedykasjɔ̃] **nf 1.** [de membre] re-education **2.** [de délinquant, malade] rehabilitation, rehab *US*.

rééduquer [3] [reedyke] **vt 1.** [membre] to re-educate **2.** [délinquant, malade] to rehabilitate, to rehab *US*.

réel, elle [reɛl] **adj** real.
◆ ***réel*** **nm : le réel** reality.

réélection [reelɛksjɔ̃] **nf** reelection.

réélire [106] [reelir] **vt** to reelect.

réellement [reɛlmɑ̃] **adv** really.

réembaucher [3] [reɑ̃boʃe] **vt** to take on again.

réemploi = ***remploi***.

réemployer = ***remployer***.

réengager = ***rengager***.

rééquilibrer [3] [reekilibre] **vt** to balance (again).

réescompte [reɛskɔ̃t] **nm** rediscount.

réessayer [reeseje], ***ressayer*** [11] [rɛseje] **vt** to try again.

réévaluer [7] [reevalɥe] **vt** to revalue.

réexaminer [3] [reɛgzamine] **vt** to re-examine.

réexpédier [9] [reɛkspedje] **vt** to send back.

réexporter [3] [reɛkspɔrte] **vt** to reexport.

réf. (abr écrite de ***référence***) ref.

refaire [109] [rəfɛr] **vt 1.** [faire de nouveau - travail, devoir] to do again / [- voyage] to make again **2.** [mur, toit] to repair **3.** *fam* [personne] to take in.
◆ ***se refaire*** **vp 1.** [se rétablir] **: se refaire une santé** to recover (one's health) **2.** [se réhabituer] **: se refaire à qqch** to get used to sthg again **3.** *fam* [au jeu] to make up ***ou*** win back one's losses.

refaisais, refaisions ➤ ***refaire***.

refait, e [rəfɛ, ɛt] **pp** ➤ ***refaire***.

refasse, refasses ➤ ***refaire***.

réfection [refɛksjɔ̃] **nf** repair.

réfectoire [refɛktwar] **nm** refectory.

référé [refere] **nm** [procédure] special hearing / [arrêt] temporary ruling / [ordonnance] temporary injunction.

référence [referɑ̃s] **nf** reference ▸ **faire référence à** to refer to.
◆ ***références*** **nfpl** references.

référencement [referɑ̃smɑ̃] **nm 1.** COMM listing **2.** INFORM (website) referencing.

référendum [referɛ̃dɔm] **nm** referendum.

référer [18] [refere] **vi : en référer à qqn** to refer the matter to sb.
◆ ***se référer*** **vp : se référer à** to refer to.

refermer [3] [rəfɛrme] **vt** to close ***ou*** shut again.

refiler [3] [rəfile] **vt** *fam* **: refiler qqch à qqn** [objet] to palm sthg off on sb / [maladie] to give sthg to sb.

refinancement [rəfinɑ̃səmɑ̃] **nm** refinancing.

refinancer [sərəfinɑ̃se] ◆ ***se refinancer*** [rəfinɑ̃se] **vi** [pour une entreprise] to refinance.

réfléchi, e [refleʃi] **adj 1.** [action] considered ▸ **c'est tout réfléchi** I've made up my mind, I've decided **2.** [personne] thoughtful **3.** GRAMM reflexive.

réfléchir [32] [refleʃir] ■ **vt 1.** [refléter] to reflect **2.** [penser] **: réfléchir que** to think ***ou*** reflect that.
■ **vi** to think, to reflect ▸ **réfléchir à *ou* sur qqch** to think about sthg.
◆ ***se réfléchir*** **vp** to be reflected.

réfléchissant, e [refleʃisɑ̃, ɑ̃t] **adj** reflective.

réflecteur [reflɛktœr] **nm** reflector.

reflet [rəflɛ] **nm 1.** [image] reflection **2.** [de lumière] glint.

refléter [18] [rəflete] **vt** to reflect.
◆ ***se refléter*** **vp 1.** [se réfléchir] to be reflected **2.** [transparaître] to be mirrored.

refleurir [32] [rəflœrir] **vi 1.** [fleurir à nouveau] to flower again **2.** *fig* [art] to flourish again.

reflex [reflɛks] ■ **nm** reflex camera.
■ **adj** reflex *(avant n)*.

réflexe [reflɛks] ■ **nm** reflex.
■ **adj** reflex *(avant n)*.

réflexion [reflɛksjɔ̃] **nf 1.** [de lumière, d'ondes] reflection **2.** [pensée] reflection, thought ▸ **à la réflexion** on second thoughts ▸ **réflexion faite** on reflection **3.** [remarque] remark.

refluer [3] [rəflye] **vi 1.** [liquide] to flow back **2.** [foule] to flow back / [avec violence] to surge back.

reflux [rəfly] **nm 1.** [d'eau] ebb **2.** [de personnes] backward surge.

refondre [75] [rəfɔ̃dr] **vt 1.** [métal] to remelt **2.** [ouvrage] to recast.

refonte [rəfɔ̃t] **nf 1.** [de métal] remelting **2.** [d'ouvrage] recasting **3.** [d'institution, de système] overhaul, reshaping.

reforestation [rəfɔrɛstasjɔ̃] **nf** reforestation.

réformateur, trice [refɔrmatœr, tris] ■ **adj** reforming.
■ **nm, f 1.** [personne] reformer **2.** RELIG Reformer.

réforme [refɔrm] **nf** reform ▸ **réforme monétaire** monetary reform.

réformé, e [refɔrme] **adj & nm, f** Protestant.
◆ ***réformé*** **nm** MIL *soldier who has been invalided out.*

reformer [3] [rəfɔrme] **vt** to re-form.
◆ ***se reformer*** **vp** to reform.

réformer [3] [refɔrme] **vt 1.** [améliorer] to reform, to improve **2.** MIL to invalid out *UK* **3.** [matériel] to scrap.

réformisme [refɔrmism] **nm** reformism.

réformiste [refɔrmist] **adj & nmf** reformist.

reformulation [rəfɔrmylasjɔ̃] **nf** rewording.

refoulé, e [rəfule] ■ **adj** repressed, frustrated.
■ **nm, f** repressed person.

refoulement [rəfulmɑ̃] **nm 1.** [de personnes] repelling **2.** PSYCHO repression.

refouler [3] [rəfule] **vt 1.** [personnes] to repel, to repulse **2.** PSYCHO to repress.

réfractaire [refraktɛr] ■ **adj** **1.** [rebelle] insubordinate ▸ **réfractaire à** resistant to ▸ **être réfractaire à la loi** to flout the law **2.** HIST [prêtre] non-juring **3.** [matière] refractory.
■ **nmf** insubordinate.

réfraction [refraksjɔ̃] **nf** refraction ▸ **indice de réfraction** refractive index.

refrain [rəfrɛ̃] **nm** MUS refrain, chorus ▸ **c'est toujours le même refrain** *fam fig* it's always the same old story.

refréner [18] [rəfrene] **vt** to check, to hold back.
◆ ***se refréner*** **vp** to control o.s.

réfrigérant, e [refriʒerɑ̃, ɑ̃t] **adj** **1.** [liquide] refrigerating, refrigerant **2.** *fam* [accueil] icy.

réfrigérateur [refriʒeratœr] **nm** refrigerator.

réfrigération [refriʒerasjɔ̃] **nf** refrigeration.

réfringent, e [refrɛ̃ʒɑ̃, ɑ̃t] **adj** refractive.

refroidir [32] [rəfrwadir] ■ **vt** **1.** [plat] to cool **2.** [décourager] to discourage **3.** *fam* [tuer] to rub out, to do in.
■ **vi** to cool.
◆ ***se refroidir*** **vp** **1.** [temps] to get *ou* turn colder **2.** [ardeur] to cool.

refroidissement [rəfrwadismɑ̃] **nm** **1.** [de température] drop, cooling **2.** [grippe] chill **3.** *fig* [de sentiment] cooling off.

refuge [rəfyʒ] **nm** **1.** [abri] refuge ▸ **chercher refuge auprès de qqn** to seek refuge with sb **2.** [de montagne] hut **3.** [sur chaussée] traffic island.

réfugié, e [refyʒje] ■ **adj** refugee *(avant n).*
■ **nm, f** refugee.

réfugier [9] [refyʒje] ◆ ***se réfugier*** **vp** to take refuge.

refus [rəfy] **nm inv** refusal ▸ **ce n'est pas de refus** *fam* I wouldn't say no ▸ **essuyer un refus** to meet with a refusal.

refuser [3] [rəfyze] **vt** **1.** [repousser] to refuse ▸ **refuser de faire qqch** to refuse to do sthg **2.** [contester] **: refuser qqch à qqn** to deny sb sthg **3.** [clients, spectateurs] to turn away **4.** [candidat] **: être refusé** to fail.
◆ ***se refuser*** **vp : se refuser à faire qqch** to refuse to do sthg ▸ **se refuser à tout commentaire** to refuse to make any comment ▸ **ne rien se refuser** not to stint o.s.

réfutation [refytasjɔ̃] **nf** refutation.

réfuter [3] [refyte] **vt** to refute.

regagner [3] [rəgaɲe] **vt** **1.** [reprendre] to regain, to win back **2.** [revenir à] to get back to.

regain [rəgɛ̃] **nm** **1.** [herbe] second crop **2.** [retour] **: un regain de** a revival of, a renewal of ▸ **un regain de vie** a new lease of life.

régal, als [regal] **nm** treat, delight.

régalade [regalad] **nf : boire à la régalade** *to drink without letting the bottle touch one's lips.*

régaler [3] [regale] **vt** to treat ▸ **c'est moi qui régale!** it's my treat!
◆ ***se régaler*** **vp : je me régale** [nourriture] I'm thoroughly enjoying it / [activité] I'm having the time of my life.

regard [rəgar] **nm** look ▸ **un regard méfiant** a suspicious look ▸ **attirer les regards** to be the centre of attention ▸ **chercher du regard** to look (around) for ▸ **couver qqch/qqn du regard** to stare at sthg/sb with greedy eyes ▸ **il a détourné le regard** he averted his gaze, he looked away ▸ **fusiller *ou* foudroyer qqn du regard** *fig* to glare at sb, to look daggers at sb ▸ **lancer un regard à qqn** to look at sb, to glance at sb ▸ **porter un regard nouveau sur qqn/qqch** *fig* to look at sb/sthg in a new light ▸ **soutenir le regard de qqn** *fig* to be able to look sb straight in the eye.
◆ ***au regard de*** **loc prép** in relation to, with regard to ▸ **mes papiers sont en règle au regard de la loi** my papers are in order from a legal point of view.
◆ ***en regard de*** **loc prép** **1.** [face à] **: en regard de la colonne des chiffres** facing *ou* opposite the column of figures **2.** [en comparaison avec] compared with.

regardant, e [rəgardɑ̃, ɑ̃t] **adj** **1.** *fam* [économe] mean **2.** [minutieux] **: être très/peu regardant sur qqch** to be very/not very particular about sthg.

regarder [3] [rəgarde] ■ **vt** **1.** [observer, examiner, consulter] to look at / [télévision, spectacle] to watch ▸ **regarde s'il arrive** see if he's coming ▸ **regarde-moi ça!** *fam* just look at that! ▸ **as-tu eu le temps de regarder le dossier?** did you have time to look at *ou* to examine the file? ▸ **regarder qqn faire qqch** to watch sb doing sthg ▸ **regarder les trains passer** to watch the trains go by **2.** [considérer] to consider, to regard ▸ **il regarde avec envie la réussite de son frère** he casts an envious eye upon his brother's success, he looks upon his brother's success with envy ▸ **regarder qqn/qqch comme** to regard sb/sthg as, to consider sb/sthg as

COMMENT EXPRIMER...

le refus

No, I'm sorry, I can't / Non, je suis désolé, je ne peux pas
I'm afraid I can't possibly do that / Je regrette, mais je ne peux vraiment pas
I'm sorry, but it's not up to me / Désolé, ça ne dépend pas de moi
There's really nothing I can do / Je ne peux vraiment rien faire
I am afraid I cannot accept your suggestion / Je regrette, mais je ne peux pas accepter votre suggestion
I refuse to do her job for her / Je refuse de faire son travail à sa place
It's out of the question / Il n'en est pas question
Certainly not! / Certainement pas !
No way! / Pas question !
Forget it! / Alors là, tu peux toujours courir !

3. [concerner] to concern ▸ **cela ne te regarde pas** it's none of your business.

■ **vi 1.** [observer, examiner] to look ▸ **nous avons regardé partout** we looked *ou* searched everywhere
2. [faire attention] **: sans regarder à la dépense** regardless of the expense ▸ **y regarder à deux fois** to think twice about it ▸ **à y bien regarder, à y regarder de plus près** when you think it over, on thinking it over.

◆ ***se regarder*** **vp 1.** [emploi réfléchi] to look at o.s. ▸ **tu ne t'es pas regardé!** *fam* you should take a (good) look at yourself!
2. [emploi réciproque] to look at one another.

FAUX AMIS / FALSE FRIENDS
regarder

Regard is not a translation of the French word *regarder*. Regard is translated by *considérer*.
▸ I regard him as a brother / *Je le considère comme un frère*

regarnir [32] [rəgarnir] **vt** to refill, to restock.

régate [regat] **nf** *(gén pl)* regatta.

régence [reʒɑ̃s] **nf** regency.
◆ ***Régence*** **nf** HIST **: la Régence** the Regency.

régénérer [18] [reʒenere] **vt** to regenerate.
◆ ***se régénérer*** **vp** to regenerate.

régent, e [reʒɑ̃, ɑ̃t] **nm, f** regent.

régenter [3] [reʒɑ̃te] **vt : vouloir tout régenter** *péj* to want to be the boss.

reggae [rege] **nm & adj inv** reggae.

régie [reʒi] **nf 1.** [entreprise] state-controlled company **2.** RADIO & TV [pièce] control room / CINÉ, THÉÂTRE & TV [équipe] production team.

regimber [3] [rəʒɛ̃be] **vi** to balk.

régime [reʒim] **nm 1.** [politique] regime ▸ **régime militaire/totalitaire** military/totalitarian regime ▸ **l'Ancien Régime** the Ancien Regime
2. [administratif] system ▸ **régime carcéral** prison regime ▸ **régime de Sécurité sociale** *subdivision of the French social security system applying to certain professional groups* ▸ **être marié sous le régime de la communauté** to opt for a marriage based on joint ownership of property
3. [alimentaire] diet ▸ **se mettre au/suivre un régime** to go on/to be on a diet ▸ **régime amincissant** slimming diet ▸ **régime sans sel** salt-free diet
4. [de moteur] speed
5. ÉCON **: fonctionner à plein régime** [usine] to work to full capacity ▸ **régime de croisière** economic *ou* cruising speed
6. [de fleuve, des pluies] cycle ▸ **le régime des vents** the prevailing winds *ou* wind system
7. [de bananes, dattes] bunch.

régiment [reʒimɑ̃] **nm 1.** MIL regiment **2.** *fam* [grande quantité] **: un régiment de** masses of, loads of.

région [reʒjɔ̃] **nf** region ▸ **région parisienne** Paris area *ou* region.

CULTURE
Région

France's European territory (including the island of Corsica off the Riviera coast) is divided into 21 regions. Collectively, they are known as the **métropole.** The region is France's largest administrative division; each is run by a prefect and a regional council with the power to oversee education, cultural programmes, and regional development and planning. The word **région** encapsulates the distinction between Parisian and provincial life that is firmly anchored in the French psyche, although decentralization initiatives may have helped blur this difference. Regional council elections are known for their low voter turnout. Belgium has three regions, each of which plays a distinct role in the national economy: Brussels, the capital; Flemish-speaking Flanders; and Wallonia, in the south.

régional, e, aux [reʒjɔnal, o] **adj** regional.

régionalisation [reʒjɔnalizasjɔ̃] **nf** regionalization.

régionalisme [reʒjɔnalism] **nm** regionalism.

régionaliste [reʒjɔnalist] **nmf & adj** regionalist.

régir [32] [reʒir] **vt** to govern.

régisseur [reʒisœr] **nm 1.** [intendant] steward **2.** [de théâtre] stage manager.

registre [rəʒistr] **nm** [gén] register ▸ **registre du commerce** trade register ▸ **registre de comptabilité** ledger ▸ **registres publics d'état civil** register *(sg)* of births, marriages and deaths.

réglable [reglabl] **adj 1.** [adaptable] adjustable **2.** [payable] payable.

réglage [reglaʒ] **nm** adjustment, setting.

règle [rɛgl] **nf 1.** [instrument] ruler ▸ **règle graduée** graduated ruler **2.** [principe, loi] rule ▸ **je suis en règle** my papers are in order ▸ **mets-toi en règle** get your papers in order ▸ **être de règle** to be the rule.
◆ ***en règle générale*** **loc adv** as a general rule.
◆ ***règles*** **nfpl** [menstruation] period *sg*.

réglé, e [regle] **adj 1.** [organisé] regular, well-ordered **2.** [papier] lined, ruled.

réglée [regle] **adj f : être réglée** to have periods, to menstruate.

règlement [rɛgləmɑ̃] **nm 1.** [résolution] settling ▸ **règlement de comptes** *fig* settling of scores ▸ **règlement**

judiciaire liquidation **2.** [règle] regulation ▸ **observer le règlement** to follow the rules *ou* regulations **3.** [paiement] settlement.

réglementaire [rɛgləmɑ̃tɛr] **adj 1.** [régulier] statutory **2.** [imposé] regulation *(avant n)*.

réglementation [rɛgləmɑ̃tasjɔ̃] **nf 1.** [action] regulation **2.** [ensemble de règles] regulations *pl*, rules *pl* ▸ **réglementation du travail/commerce** work/commercial regulations.

réglementer [3] [rɛgləmɑ̃te] **vt** to control, to regulate.

régler [18] [regle] **vt 1.** [affaire, conflit] to settle, to sort out ▸ **c'est une affaire réglée** it is (all) settled now ▸ **quelques détails à régler** a few details to be settled **2.** [appareil] to adjust ▸ **j'ai réglé mon réveil sur 7 h/le four à 200°** I've set my alarm for seven o'clock/the oven at 200 degrees **3.** [payer - note] to settle, to pay / [- commerçant] to pay ▸ **régler l'addition** to pay *ou* settle the bill ▸ **régler qqch par chèque/par carte de crédit** to pay for sthg by cheque/by credit card.
◆ ***se régler*** **vp 1.** [suivre] **: se régler sur qqn** to model o.s. on sb ▸ **elle a tendance à se régler sur (l'exemple de) sa mère** she has a tendency to model herself on her mother **2.** [affaire, conflit] to be sorted out, to be settled.

réglisse [reglis] **nf** liquorice *UK*, licorice *US*.

réglo [reglo] **adj inv** *fam* straight.

régnant, e [reɲɑ̃, ɑ̃t] **adj** [monarque] reigning.

règne [rɛɲ] **nm 1.** [de souverain] reign ▸ **sous le règne de** in the reign of **2.** [pouvoir] rule **3.** BIOL kingdom.

régner [18] [reɲe] **vi 1.** [souverain] to rule, to reign **2.** [silence] to reign.

regonfler [3] [rəgɔ̃fle] **vt 1.** [pneu, ballon] to blow up again, to reinflate **2.** *fam* [personne] to cheer up.

regorger [17] [rəgɔrʒe] **vi : regorger de** to be abundant in.

régresser [4] [regrese] **vi 1.** [sentiment, douleur] to diminish **2.** [personne] to regress.

régressif, ive [regresif, iv] **adj** regressive, backward.

régression [regresjɔ̃] **nf 1.** [recul] decline ▸ **régression sociale** ÉCON downward mobility **2.** PSYCHO regression.

regret [rəgrɛ] **nm : regret (de)** regret (for) ▸ **tous mes regrets** I'm very sorry ▸ **à regret** with regret ▸ **sans regret** with no regrets ▸ **avoir le** *ou* **être au regret d'informer qqn de** to be sorry *ou* to regret to inform sb of.

regrettable [rəgrɛtabl] **adj** regrettable.

regretter [4] [rəgrɛte] ■ **vt 1.** [époque] to miss, to regret / [personne] to miss **2.** [faute] to regret ▸ **regretter d'avoir fait qqch** to regret having done sthg **3.** [déplorer] **: regretter que** *(+ subjonctif)* to be sorry *ou* to regret that.
■ **vi** to be sorry.

regroupement [rəgrupmɑ̃] **nm 1.** [action] gathering together **2.** [groupe] group, assembly.

regrouper [3] [rəgrupe] **vt 1.** [grouper à nouveau] to regroup, to reassemble **2.** [réunir] to group together.
◆ ***se regrouper*** **vp** to gather, to assemble.

régulariser [3] [regylarize] **vt 1.** [documents] to sort out, to put in order / [situation] to straighten out **2.** [circulation, fonctionnement] to regulate.

régularité [regylarite] **nf 1.** [gén] regularity **2.** [de travail, résultats] consistency.

régulateur, trice [regylatœr, tris] **adj** regulating.
◆ ***régulateur*** **nm** regulator.

régulation [regylasjɔ̃] **nf** [contrôle] control, regulation ▸ **régulation des naissances** birth control.

réguler [3] [regyle] **vt** to regulate.

régulier, ère [regylje, ɛr] **adj 1.** [gén] regular **2.** [uniforme, constant] steady, regular **3.** [travail, résultats] consistent **4.** [légal] legal ▸ **être en situation régulière** to have all the legally required documents **5.** *fam* [correct] straight, above board.

régulièrement [regyljɛrmɑ̃] **adv 1.** [gén] regularly **2.** [uniformément] steadily, regularly / [étalé, façonné] evenly.

réhabilitation [reabilitasjɔ̃] **nf** rehabilitation.

réhabiliter [3] [reabilite] **vt 1.** [accusé] to rehabilitate, to clear / *fig* [racheter] to restore to favour *UK* *ou* favor *US* **2.** [rénover] to restore.
◆ ***se réhabiliter*** **vp** to redeem o.s.

réhabituer [7] [reabitɥe] **vt** to reaccustom.
◆ ***se réhabituer*** **vp : se réhabituer à qqch** to get used to sthg again.

rehausser [3] [rəose] **vt 1.** [surélever] to heighten **2.** *fig* [mettre en valeur] to enhance.

rehausseur [rəosœr] **nm** booster seat.

réimporter [3] [reɛ̃pɔrte] **vt** to reimport.

COMMENT EXPRIMER...

des regrets

I shouldn't have eaten so much / Je n'aurais pas dû manger autant
I only wish I'd told him earlier / Je regrette de ne pas le lui avoir dit plus tôt
I'd like to have visited the museum / J'aurais bien aimé visiter le musée
I'm sorry I ever mentioned it now! / J'aurais mieux fait de ne pas en parler !
If only I could drive! / Si seulement je savais conduire !
What a pity she isn't here! / Quel dommage qu'elle ne soit pas là !
Unfortunately, we didn't get there on time / Malheureusement, nous ne sommes pas arrivés à temps

réimposer [3] [reɛ̃poze] **vt** to retax.

réimpression [reɛ̃prɛsjɔ̃] **nf** reprinting, reprint.

réimprimer [3] [reɛ̃prime] **vt** to reprint.

rein [rɛ̃] **nm** kidney ▸ **rein artificiel** dialysis *ou* kidney machine.
◆ ***reins*** **nmpl** small of the back *sg* ▸ **avoir mal aux reins** to have backache *UK ou* a backache *US* ▸ **avoir les reins solides** *fam* [être résistant] to have a strong back / [être riche] not to be short of money.

réincarnation [reɛ̃karnasjɔ̃] **nf** reincarnation.

réincarner [3] [reɛ̃karne] ◆ ***se réincarner*** **vpi** to be reincarnated ▸ **il voulait se réincarner en oiseau** he wanted to be reincarnated as a bird.

reine [rɛn] **nf** queen ▸ **la reine mère** the Queen Mother ▸ **la reine de Suède/des Pays-Bas** the Queen of Sweden/of the Netherlands ▸ **la reine de cœur/pique** the queen of hearts/spades ▸ **la reine de la soirée** the belle of the ball, the star of the party ▸ **la reine des abeilles/termites** the queen bee/termite.

reine-claude [rɛnklod] (pl **reines-claudes**) **nf** greengage.

reinette [renɛt] **nf** *variety of apple similar to pippin.*

réinfecter [4] [reɛ̃fɛkte] **vt** to reinfect.
◆ ***se réinfecter*** **vpi** to become reinfected.

réinscriptible [reɛ̃skriptibl] **adj** INFORM (re-)recordable / [cédérom] rewritable.

réinscrire [99] [reɛ̃skrir] **vt : réinscrire qqn à** to re-enrol *UK ou* re-enroll *US* sb for.
◆ ***se réinscrire*** **vp : se réinscrire à** to re-enrol *UK ou* re-enroll *US* for.

réinsérer [18] [reɛ̃sere] **vt** to reinsert.
◆ ***se réinsérer*** **vp** to become reintegrated.

réinsertion [reɛ̃sɛrsjɔ̃] **nf** [de délinquant] rehabilitation / [dans la vie professionnelle] reintegration.

réintégrer [18] [reɛ̃tegre] **vt 1.** [rejoindre] to return to **2.** DR to reinstate.

réintroduire [98] [reɛ̃trɔdɥir] **vt** to reintroduce.

réitérer [18] [reitere] **vt** [promesse, demande] to repeat, to reiterate / [attaque] to repeat.

rejaillir [32] [rəʒajir] **vi** to splash up ▸ **rejaillir sur qqn** *fig* to rebound on sb.

rejet [rəʒɛ] **nm 1.** [gén] rejection **2.** [pousse] shoot.

rejeter [27] [rəʒte] **vt 1.** [relancer] to throw back **2.** [expulser] to bring up, to vomit **3.** [offre, personne] to reject **4.** [partie du corps] **: rejeter la tête/les bras en arrière** to throw back one's head/one's arms **5.** [imputer] **: rejeter la responsabilité de qqch sur qqn** to lay the responsibility for sthg at sb's door.
◆ ***se rejeter*** **vp : se rejeter la faute l'un sur l'autre** to blame one another for sthg ▸ **se rejeter la responsabilité (de qqch) l'un sur l'autre** to hold one another responsible (for sthg).

rejeton [rəʒtɔ̃] **nm** offspring *(U).*

rejette, rejettes ➤ ***rejeter.***

rejoindre [82] [rəʒwɛ̃dr] **vt 1.** [retrouver] to join **2.** [regagner] to return to **3.** [concorder avec] to agree with **4.** [rattraper] to catch up with.
◆ ***se rejoindre*** **vp 1.** [personnes, routes] to meet **2.** [opinions] to agree.

rejoignais, rejoignions ➤ ***rejoindre.***

rejoint, e [rəʒwɛ̃, ɛ̃t] **pp** ➤ ***rejoindre.***

réjoui, e [reʒwi] **adj** joyful.

réjouir [32] [reʒwir] **vt** to delight.
◆ ***se réjouir*** **vp** to be delighted ▸ **se réjouir de qqch** to be delighted at *ou* about sthg.

réjouissance [reʒwisɑ̃s] **nf** rejoicing.
◆ ***réjouissances*** **nfpl** festivities.

réjouissant, e [reʒwisɑ̃, ɑ̃t] **adj** joyful, cheerful.

relâche [rəlaʃ] **nf 1.** [pause] **: sans relâche** without respite *ou* a break **2.** THÉÂTRE **: demain c'est le jour de relâche** we're closed tomorrow ▸ **faire relâche** to be closed.

relâché, e [rəlaʃe] **adj** lax, loose.

relâchement [rəlaʃmɑ̃] **nm** relaxation.

relâcher [3] [rəlaʃe] **vt 1.** [étreinte, cordes] to loosen **2.** [discipline, effort] to relax, to slacken **3.** [prisonnier] to release.
◆ ***se relâcher*** **vp 1.** [se desserrer] to loosen **2.** [faiblir - discipline] to become lax / [- attention] to flag **3.** [se laisser aller] to slacken off.

relaie, relaies ➤ ***relayer.***

relais [rəlɛ] **nm 1.** [auberge] post house ▸ **relais routier** transport cafe *UK*, truck stop *US* **2.** SPORT & TV **: prendre/passer le relais** to take/hand over ▸ **(course de) relais** relay **3.** COMM [dans le service des achats] gatekeeper.

relance [rəlɑ̃s] **nf 1.** [économique] revival, boost / [de projet] relaunch **2.** [au jeu] stake.

relancer [16] [rəlɑ̃se] **vt 1.** [renvoyer] to throw back **2.** [faire reprendre - économie] to boost / [- projet] to relaunch / [- moteur, machine] to restart / INFORM to restart.

relater [3] [rəlate] **vt** *littéraire* to relate.

relatif, ive [rəlatif, iv] **adj** relative ▸ **relatif à** relating to ▸ **tout est relatif** it's all relative.
◆ ***relative*** **nf** GRAMM relative clause.

relation [rəlasjɔ̃] **nf** relationship ▸ **relation de cause à effet** relation *ou* relationship of cause and effect ▸ **entrer en relation avec qqn** [le contacter] to get in touch *ou* to make contact with sb ▸ **mettre qqn en relation avec qqn** to put sb in touch with sb.
◆ ***relations*** **nfpl 1.** [rapport] relationship *sg* ▸ **en excellentes/mauvaises relations avec ses collègues** on excellent/bad terms with one's colleagues ▸ **relations sexuelles** sexual relations, intercourse *(U)* **2.** [connaissance] acquaintance ▸ **avoir des relations** to have connections ▸ **j'ai trouvé à me loger par relations** I found a place to live through knowing the right people *ou* through the grapevine **3.** [communication] **: relations humaines** [gén]

dealings between people / [en sociologie] human relations ▸ **relations internationales** international relations ▸ **relations publiques** public relations.

PARONYME / CONFUSABLE

relations

Attention lorsque vous traduisez le mot **relation** : *relation* signifie un parent, un proche, tandis que *relationship* désigne les rapports affectifs, éventuellement sexuels, entre des personnes.

relationnel**, **elle [rəlasjɔnɛl] **adj** [problèmes] relationship *(avant n)*.

relative ➤ ***relatif***.

relativement [rəlativmɑ̃] **adv** **1.** [passablement] relatively, comparatively, reasonably **2.** *sout* [de façon relative] relatively, contingently *sout*.

◆ ***relativement à*** **loc prép** **1.** [par rapport à] compared to, in relation to **2.** [concernant] concerning ▸ **entendre un témoin relativement à une affaire** to hear a witness in relation to a case.

relativiser [3] [rəlativize] **vt** to relativize.

relativité [rəlativite] **nf** relativity.

relax**, **relaxe [rəlaks] **adj** *fam* relaxed.

relaxant**, **e [rəlaksɑ̃, ɑ̃t] **adj** relaxing, soothing.

relaxation [rəlaksasjɔ̃] **nf** relaxation.

relaxe = ***relax***.

relaxer [3] [rəlakse] **vt** **1.** [reposer] to relax **2.** DR to discharge.

◆ ***se relaxer*** **vp** to relax.

relayer [11] [rəleje] **vt** to relieve.

◆ ***se relayer*** **vp** to take over from one another.

relecture [rəlɛktyr] **nf** second reading, rereading.

relégation [rəlegasjɔ̃] **nf** **1.** SPORT relegation **2.** HIST & DR banishment, relegation.

reléguer [18] [rəlege] **vt** to relegate.

relent [rəlɑ̃] **nm** **1.** [odeur] stink, stench **2.** *fig* [trace] whiff.

relevé**, **e [rəlve] **adj** **1.** [style] elevated **2.** CULIN spicy.

◆ ***relevé*** **nm** reading ▸ **faire le relevé de qqch** to read sthg ▸ **relevé de compte** bank statement ▸ **relevé de fin de mois** end-of-month statement ▸ **relevé d'identité bancaire** bank account number, bank details.

relève [rəlɛv] **nf** relief ▸ **prendre la relève** to take over.

relèvement [rəlɛvmɑ̃] **nm** **1.** [redressement] rebuilding **2.** [hausse] raising **3.** [majoration] increase.

relever [19] [rəlve] ■ **vt** **1.** [redresser - personne] to help up ▸ **ils m'ont relevé** [- debout] they helped me (back) to my feet / [- assis] they sat me up *ou* helped me to sit up / [- pays, économie] to rebuild / [- moral, niveau] to raise ▸ **relever le moral des troupes** to boost the troops' morale **2.** [ramasser] to collect ▸ **relever les copies** SCOL to collect the papers **3.** [tête, col, store] to raise / [manches] to push up **4.** [CULIN - mettre en valeur] to bring out / [- pimenter] to season ▸ **relevez l'assaisonnement** make the seasoning more spicy **5.** *fig* [récit] to liven up, to spice up **6.** [noter] to note down / [compteur] to read ▸ **températures relevées à 16 h** MÉTÉOR temperatures recorded at 4 p.m. **7.** [relayer] to take over from, to relieve ▸ **relever qqn de ses fonctions** to relieve sb of his/her duties **8.** [erreur] to note.

■ **vi** **1.** [se rétablir] **: relever de** to recover from ▸ **elle relève d'une grippe** she is recovering from flu **2.** [être du domaine] **: relever de** to come under ▸ **cela relève des tribunaux/de la psychiatrie** it's a matter for the courts/the psychiatrists.

◆ ***se relever*** **vp** **1.** [se mettre debout] to stand up ▸ **il l'aida à se relever** he helped her to her feet again / [sortir du lit] to get up **2.** [se rétablir] **: se relever de qqch** to recover from sthg, to get over sthg ▸ **le parti se relève de ses cendres** *ou* **ruines** the party is rising from the ashes **3.** [se rehausser] to lift ▸ **les commissures de ses lèvres se relevèrent** the corners of his mouth curled up.

relief [rəljɛf] **nm** relief ▸ **sans aucun relief** completely flat ▸ **en relief** in relief, raised ▸ **une carte en relief** relief map ▸ **mettre en relief** *fig* to enhance, to bring out.

◆ ***reliefs*** **nmpl** *vieilli* remains.

relier [9] [rəlje] **vt** **1.** [livre] to bind **2.** [attacher] **: relier qqch à qqch** to link sthg to sthg **3.** [joindre] to connect **4.** *fig* [associer] to link up.

relieur**, **euse [rəljœr, øz] **nm, f** binder.

religieuse ➤ ***religieux***.

religieusement [rəliʒjøzmɑ̃] **adv** **1.** [gén] religiously / [solennellement] reverently **2.** [se marier] in church.

religieux**, **euse [rəliʒjø, øz] **adj** **1.** [vie, chant] religious / [mariage] religious, church *(avant n)* **2.** [respectueux] reverent.

◆ ***religieux*** **nm** monk.

◆ ***religieuse*** **nf** **1.** RELIG nun **2.** CULIN **: religieuse au café, religieuse au chocolat** *choux pastry filled with coffee or chocolate confectioner's custard*.

religion [rəliʒjɔ̃] **nf** **1.** [culte] religion **2.** [foi] faith **3.** [croyance] religion, faith ▸ **entrer en religion** to take one's vows.

reliquaire [rəlikɛr] **nm** reliquary.

reliquat [rəlika] **nm** balance, remainder.

relique [rəlik] **nf** relic.

relire [106] [rəlir] **vt** **1.** [lire] to reread **2.** [vérifier] to read over.

◆ ***se relire*** **vp** to read what one has written.

reliure [rəljyr] **nf** binding.

relocalisation [rəlokalizasjɔ̃] **nf** relocation.

relocaliser [rəlokalize] **vt** to relocate.

relogement [rəlɔʒmɑ̃] **nm** rehousing.

reloger [17] [rəlɔʒe] **vt** to rehouse.

relu**, **e [rəly] **pp** ➤ ***relire***.

reluire [97] [rəlɥir] **vi** to shine, to gleam ▸ **faire reluire qqch** to shine *ou* polish sthg.

reluisant**, **e [rəlɥizɑ̃, ɑ̃t] **adj** shining, gleaming ▸ **peu** *ou* **pas très reluisant** *fig* [avenir, situation] not all that brilliant / [personne] shady.

?luquer [3] [rəlyke] **vt** *fam* [personne] to ogle, to eye ıp / [objet] to have one's eye on, to covet ▸ **se faire reluquer** to be *ou* get stared at.

?mâcher [3] [rəmaʃe] **vt** *fig* to brood over.

?mailler [3] [rəmaje] **vt** [filet] to mend / [tricot] to ɟarn.

?make [rimɛjk] **nm** CINÉ remake.

?manent, e [remanɑ̃, ɑ̃t] **adj** residual.

?maniement [rəmanimɑ̃] **nm** restructuring ▸ **remaıiement ministériel** cabinet reshuffle.

?manier [9] [rəmanje] **vt** to restructure / [ministère] to eshuffle.

?maquiller [3] [rəmakije] **vt** to make up *(sep)* again.
◆ ***se remaquiller*** **vp** *(emploi réfléchi)* [entièrement] to eapply one's make-up / [partiellement] to touch up one's nake-up.

?marier [9] [rəmarje] ◆ ***se remarier*** **vp** to remarry.

?marquable [rəmarkabl] **adj** remarkable.

?marquablement [rəmarkabləmɑ̃] **adv** remarkably.

?marque [rəmark] **nf** **1.** [observation] remark / [critiıue] critical remark **2.** [annotation] note.

?marquer [3] [rəmarke] ■ **vt** **1.** [apercevoir] to notice
· **faire remarquer qqch (à qqn)** to point sthg out (to sb)
· **se faire remarquer** *péj* to draw attention to o.s. **2.** [noer] to remark, to comment.
■ **vi : ce n'est pas l'idéal, remarque!** it's not ideal, nind you!
◆ ***se remarquer*** **vp** to be noticeable.

?mballer [3] [rɑ̃bale] **vt** [marchandise] to pack up.

?mbarquer [3] [rɑ̃barke] **vt** to reembark.
◆ ***se rembarquer*** **vp** to reembark.

?mbarrer [3] [rɑ̃bare] **vt** *fam* to snub.

?mblai [rɑ̃blɛ] **nm** embankment.

?mblayer [11] [rɑ̃bleje] **vt** [hausser] to bank up / combler] to fill in.

?mbobiner [3] [rɑ̃bɔbine] **vt** to rewind.

?mbourrage [rɑ̃buraʒ] **nm** stuffing, padding.

?mbourré, e [rɑ̃bure] **adj** [fauteuil, veste] padded.

?mbourrer [3] [rɑ̃bure] **vt** to stuff, to pad.

?mboursable [rɑ̃bursabl] **adj** refundable.

remboursement [rɑ̃bursəmɑ̃] **nm** refund, repayment.

rembourser [3] [rɑ̃burse] **vt** **1.** [dette] to pay back, to repay **2.** [personne] to pay back ▸ **rembourser qqn de qqch** to reimburse sb for sthg ▸ **tu t'es fait rembourser pour ton trajet en taxi?** did they reimburse you for your taxi journey? **3.** [dépense, achat] **: se faire rembourser** to get a refund.

rembrunir [32] [rɑ̃brynir] ◆ ***se rembrunir*** **vp** to cloud over, to become gloomy.

remède [rəmɛd] **nm** *litt* & *fig* remedy, cure.

remédier [9] [rəmedje] **vi** **1. : remédier à qqch** to put sthg right, to remedy sthg **2.** [problème] to solve **3.** [situation] to put right.

remembrement [rəmɑ̃brəmɑ̃] **nm** land regrouping.

remémorer [3] [rəmemɔre] ◆ ***se remémorer*** **vp** to recollect.

remerciement [rəmɛrsimɑ̃] **nm** thanks *pl* ▸ **une lettre de remerciement** a thank-you letter ▸ **avec tous mes remerciements** with all my thanks, with many thanks.

remercier [9] [rəmɛrsje] **vt** **1.** [dire merci à] to thank ▸ **remercier qqn de *ou* pour qqch** to thank sb for sthg ▸ **non, je vous remercie** no, thank you **2.** [congédier] to dismiss.

remets ➤ ***remettre***.

remettre [84] [rəmɛtr] **vt** **1.** [replacer] to put back ▸ **remets le livre où tu l'as trouvé** put the book back where you found it ▸ **remettre en question** to call into question ▸ **remettre qqn à sa place** to put sb in his place
2. [enfiler de nouveau] to put back on
3. [rétablir - lumière, son] to put back on ▸ **remettre qqch en marche** to restart sthg ▸ **remettre qqch à neuf** to restore sthg ▸ **remettre de l'ordre dans qqch** to tidy sthg up ▸ **remettre une montre à l'heure** to put a watch right ▸ **remettre qqch en état de marche** to put sthg back in working order
4. [donner] **: remettre qqch à qqn** to hand sthg over to sb / [médaille, prix] to present sthg to sb ▸ **on lui a remis le prix Nobel** he was presented with *ou* awarded the Nobel prize
5. [ajourner] **: remettre qqch (à)** to put sthg off (until) ▸ **la réunion a été remise à lundi** the meeting has been put off *ou* postponed until Monday
6. *fig* [reconnaître] to place

OMMENT EXPRIMER...

es remerciements

Remercier quelqu'un
Thank you (very much)! / Merci (beaucoup) !
Thanks, it's lovely! / Merci, c'est très joli !
Thank you for your help / Merci pour votre aide
Thank you for being so patient with me / Merci d'avoir autant de patience avec moi
t's very kind of you to take me back to the hotel / C'est très gentil à vous de me raccompagner à 'hôtel
 really appreciate this / Je vous suis vraiment reconnaissant
I don't know how to thank you / Je ne sais comment vous remercier

Réponses
Not at all / De rien
Don't mention it / Je vous en prie
It was nothing / Ce n'est rien
My pleasure / Je vous en prie
Any time! / N'hésite pas !

7. MÉD **: remettre qqn** to put sb back on his feet ▸ **sa cheville n'est pas vraiment encore remise** her ankle isn't reset yet.

◆ ***se remettre*** **vp 1.** [recommencer] **: se remettre à qqch** to take up sthg again ▸ **je me suis remis à l'espagnol** I've taken up Spanish again ▸ **se remettre à fumer** to start smoking again
2. [se rétablir] to get better ▸ **se remettre de qqch** to get over sthg ▸ **se remettre d'un accident** to recover from *ou* to get over an accident
3. [redevenir] **: se remettre debout** to stand up again ▸ **le temps s'est remis au beau** the weather has cleared up ▸▸ **je m'en remets à toi** it's up to you, I'll leave it up to you.

rémige [remiʒ] **nf** remex ▸ **les rémiges** remiges.

réminiscence [reminisɑ̃s] **nf** reminiscence.

remis, ***e*** [rəmi, iz] **pp** ➤ *remettre*.

remise [rəmiz] **nf 1.** [action] **: remise en jeu** throw-in ▸ **remise en marche** restarting ▸ **remise à neuf** restoration ▸ **remise en place** putting back in place ▸ **remise en question** *ou* **cause** calling into question ▸ **faire une remise de chèque** to pay in a cheque
2. [de message, colis] handing over ▸ **remise d'une lettre/d'un paquet en mains propres** personal delivery of a letter/package / [de médaille, prix] presentation ▸ **remise des prix** SCOL prize-giving
3. [réduction] discount ▸ **faire une remise à qqn** to give sb a discount *ou* a reduction ▸ **remise sur paiement (au) comptant** cash discount ▸ **remise de peine** DR remission
4. [hangar] shed.

remiser [3] [rəmize] **vt** to put away.

rémission [remisjɔ̃] **nf** remission ▸ **sans rémission** [punir, juger] without mercy / [pleuvoir] unremittingly.

remix [rəmiks] **nm** MUS [enregistrement, disque] remix / [technique] remixing.

remixé, ***e*** [rəmikse] **adj** remastered ▸ **remixé en numérique** digitally remastered.

remmener [19] [rɑ̃mne] **vt** to take *ou* bring back.

remodeler [25] [rəmɔdle] **vt 1.** [forme] to remodel **2.** [remanier] to restructure.

rémois, ***e*** [remwa, az] **adj** of/from Rheims.

◆ ***Rémois***, ***e*** **nm, f** native *ou* inhabitant of Rheims.

remontant, ***e*** [rəmɔ̃tɑ̃, ɑ̃t] **adj** [tonique] invigorating.

◆ ***remontant*** **nm** tonic.

remontée [rəmɔ̃te] **nf 1.** [des eaux] rising **2.** [de pente, rivière] ascent **3.** SPORT recovery **4.** SKI **: remontées mécaniques** ski lifts **5.** [des mineurs] bringing to the surface.

remonte-pente [rəmɔ̃tpɑ̃t] (**pl remonte-pentes**) **nm** ski tow.

remonter [3] [rəmɔ̃te] ■ **vt** *(v aux : être)* **1.** [escalier, pente] to go/come back up ▸ **remonter la rue** to go *ou* to walk back up the street ▸ **en remontant le cours du temps** going back several centuries **2.** [assembler] to put together again **3.** [manches] to turn up **4.** [horloge, montre] to wind up **5.** [ragaillardir] to put new life into, to cheer up ▸ **remonter le moral à qqn** to cheer sb up.

■ **vi** *(v aux : être)* **1.** [monter à nouveau - personne] to go/come back up ▸ **remonte dans ta chambre** go back up to your room ▸ **tu remontes dans mon estime** you've gone up in my esteem / [- baromètre] to rise again / [- prix, température] to go up again, to rise / [- sur vélo] to get back on ▸ **remonter à cheval** [- se remettre en selle] to remount / [- refaire de l'équitation] to take up riding again ▸ **remonter dans une voiture** to get back into a car **2.** [dater] **: remonter à** to date *ou* go back to ▸ **on fait généralement remonter la crise à 1910** the crisis is generally believed to have started in 1910.

remontoir [rəmɔ̃twar] **nm** winder.

remontrance [rəmɔ̃trɑ̃s] **nf** *(gén pl)* remonstrance, reprimand.

remontrer [3] [rəmɔ̃tre] **vt** to show again ▸ **vouloir en remontrer à qqn** to try to show sb up.

remords [rəmɔr] **nm** remorse ▸ **être bourrelé de remords** *fam* to be conscience-stricken.

remorque [rəmɔrk] **nf** trailer ▸ **être en remorque** to be on tow ▸ **être à la remorque** *fig* to drag behind.

remorquer [3] [rəmɔrke] **vt 1.** [voiture, bateau] to tow **2.** *fam* [personne] to drag along.

remorqueur [rəmɔrkœr] **nm** tug, tugboat.

rémoulade [remulad] **nf** remoulade (sauce).

rémouleur [remulœr] **nm** knife grinder.

remous [rəmu] ■ **nm** [de bateau] wash, backwash / [de rivière] eddy.

■ **nmpl** *fig* stir, upheaval.

rempailler [3] [rɑ̃paje] **vt** to re-cane.

rempart [rɑ̃par] **nm** *(gén pl)* rampart.

rempiler [3] [rɑ̃pile] ■ **vt** to pile up again.

■ **vi** *fam* MIL to sign on again.

remplaçable [rɑ̃plasabl] **adj** replaceable.

remplaçant, ***e*** [rɑ̃plasɑ̃, ɑ̃t] **nm, f** [suppléant] stand-in / SPORT substitute.

remplacement [rɑ̃plasmɑ̃] **nm 1.** [changement] replacing, replacement **2.** [intérim] substitution ▸ **faire des remplacements** to stand in / [docteur] to act as a locum *UK*.

remplacer [16] [rɑ̃plase] **vt 1.** [gén] to replace **2.** [prendre la place de] to stand in for / SPORT to substitute.

rempli, ***e*** [rɑ̃pli] **adj : j'ai eu une journée bien rempli**e I've had a very full *ou* busy day ▸ **un emploi du temps trè**s *ou* **bien rempli** a very busy schedule ▸ **j'ai le ventre bie**n **rempli, ça va mieux!** *fam* I feel a lot better for that meal

remplir [32] [rɑ̃plir] **vt 1.** [gén] to fill ▸ **remplir de** to fi[ll] with ▸ **remplir qqn de joie/d'orgueil** to fill sb with happ[i]ness/pride **2.** [questionnaire] to fill in *ou* out **3.** [missio[n], fonction] to complete, to fulfil.

◆ ***se remplir*** **vp** to fill up.

◆ ***se remplir (de)*** **v + prep** to fill (with).

remplissage [rɑ̃plisaʒ] **nm 1.** [de récipient] filling u[p] **2.** *fig & péj* [de texte] padding out.

remploi [rɑ̃plwa], ***réemploi*** [reɑ̃plwa] **nm** reuse.

remployer [rɑ̃plwaje], ***réemployer*** [13] [reɑ̃plw[a]je] **vt** to reuse.

remplumer [3] [rɑ̃plyme] ◆ ***se remplumer*** **vp** *fa[m]* **1.** [financièrement] to get o.s. back in funds **2.** [se rétabli[r]] to fill out again.

rempocher [3] [rɑ̃pɔʃe] **vt** to pocket again, to put back in one's pocket.

remporter [3] [rɑ̃pɔrte] **vt 1.** [repartir avec] to take away again **2.** [gagner] to win.

rempoter [3] [rɑ̃pɔte] **vt** to repot.

remuant, e [rəmɥɑ̃, ɑ̃t] **adj** restless, overactive.

remue-ménage [rəmymenaʒ] **nm inv** commotion, confusion.

remuer [7] [rəmɥe] ■ **vt 1.** [bouger, émouvoir] to move **2.** [café, thé] to stir / [salade] to toss.
■ **vi** to move, to stir ▸ **arrête de remuer comme ça** stop being so restless.
◆ ***se remuer*** **vp 1.** [se mouvoir] to move **2.** *fig* [réagir] to make an effort.

rémunérateur, trice [remyneratœr, tris] **adj** profitable, lucrative.

rémunération [remynerasjɔ̃] **nf** remuneration ▸ **rémunération de départ** starting salary.

rémunérer [18] [remynere] **vt 1.** [personne] to remunerate, to pay **2.** [activité] to pay for.

renâcler [3] [rənakle] **vi** *fam* to make a fuss ▸ **renâcler devant** *ou* **à qqch** to balk at sthg.

renaissance [rənɛsɑ̃s] **nf** rebirth.
◆ ***Renaissance*** **nf : la Renaissance** the Renaissance.

renaître [92] [rənɛtr] **vi 1.** [ressusciter] to come back to life, to come to life again ▸ **se sentir renaître** to feel like a new person ▸ **faire renaître** [passé, tradition] to revive ▸ **renaître à la vie** to take on a new lease of life **2.** [revenir - sentiment, printemps] to return / [- économie] to revive, to recover.

rénal, e, aux [renal, o] **adj** renal, kidney *(avant n)*.

renard [rənar] **nm** fox.

renardeau, x [rənardo] **nm** fox cub.

Renaudot [rənodo] **npr : le prix Renaudot** *annual literary prize for a work of fiction.*

rencard = ***rancard***.

rencart = ***rancart***.

renchérir [32] [rɑ̃ʃerir] **vi 1.** [augmenter] to become more expensive / [prix] to go up **2.** [surenchérir] **: renchérir sur** to add to.

renchérissement [rɑ̃ʃerismɑ̃] **nm** increase in price ▸ **renchérissement des prix** price increase.

rencontre [rɑ̃kɔ̃tr] **nf 1.** [gén] meeting ▸ **faire une bonne rencontre** to meet somebody interesting ▸ **faire une mauvaise rencontre** to meet an unpleasant person ▸ **aller/venir à la rencontre de qqn** to go/come to meet sb **2.** [choc, collision] collision.

rencontrer [3] [rɑ̃kɔ̃tre] **vt 1.** [gén] to meet **2.** [heurter] to strike.
◆ ***se rencontrer*** **vp 1.** [gén] to meet **2.** [opinions] to agree.

rendement [rɑ̃dmɑ̃] **nm** [de machine, travailleur] output / [de terre, placement] yield / ÉCON **: rendement croissant** increasing returns.

rendez-vous [rɑ̃devu] **nm inv 1.** [rencontre] appointment / [amoureux] date ▸ **on a tous rendez-vous au café** we're all meeting at the café ▸ **lors de notre dernier rendez-vous** at our last meeting ▸ **prendre rendez-vous avec qqn** to make an appointment with sb ▸ **donner rendez-vous à qqn** to arrange to meet sb ▸ **se donner rendez-vous** to arrange to meet **2.** [lieu] meeting place.

rendormir [36] [rɑ̃dɔrmir] ◆ ***se rendormir*** **vp** to go back to sleep.

rendre [73] [rɑ̃dr] ■ **vt 1.** [restituer] **: rendre qqch à qqn** to give sthg back to sb, to return sthg to sb ▸ **donne-moi trente euros, je te les rendrai demain** give me thirty euros, I'll pay you back *ou* I'll give it back to you tomorrow **2.** [invitation, coup] to return **3.** DR to pronounce ▸ **rendre une sentence** to pass *ou* to pronounce sentence **4.** [produire un effet] to produce ▸ **les photos n'ont pas rendu grand-chose** the pictures didn't come out very well ▸ **mes recherches n'ont encore rien rendu** my research hasn't come up with anything yet *ou* hasn't produced any results yet **5.** [vomir] to vomit, to cough up **6.** MIL [céder] to surrender ▸ **rendre les armes** to lay down one's arms **7.** *(+ adj)* [faire devenir] to make ▸ **rendre qqch public** to make sthg public ▸ **rendre qqn fou** to drive sb mad **8.** [exprimer] to render.
■ **vi 1.** [produire - champ] to yield ▸ **cette terre ne rend pas** this land is unproductive *ou* yields no return **2.** [vomir] to vomit, to be sick *UK*.
◆ ***se rendre*** **vp 1.** [céder, capituler] to give in ▸ **se rendre à la police** to give o.s. up to the police ▸ **j'ai dû me rendre à l'évidence** I had to face facts ▸ **se rendre à la raison** to give in to reason **2.** [aller] **: se rendre à** to go to ▸ **il s'y**

COMMENT EXPRIMER...

la prise de rendez-vous

Can I see you tonight? / Est-ce qu'on peut se voir ce soir ?
Could we arrange to meet soon? / Pouvons-nous convenir d'un rendez-vous bientôt ?
Could I make an appointment to see you? / Puis-je prendre rendez-vous avec vous ?
Are you free any time next week? / Êtes-vous libre la semaine prochaine ?
When's a good time for you? / Quand est-ce que ça t'arrange ?
How about Friday? / Vendredi, ça te va ?
Would Wednesday morning be convenient? / Mercredi matin, est-ce que ça vous convient ?
Where shall we meet? / Où est-ce qu'on se retrouve ?
Shall I come to your office? / Voulez-vous que je vienne à votre bureau ?
Could we meet some other time? / Pourrions-nous nous voir un autre jour ?
Right, that's settled then / Bon, alors c'est réglé
See you on Friday! / À vendredi !

rend en train he goes *ou* gets *ou* travels there by train **3.** *(+ adj)* [se faire tel] **: se rendre utile/malade** to make o.s. useful/ill.

rêne [rɛn] **nf** rein.

renégat**, **e [rənega, at] **nm, f** *sout* renegade.

renégocier [9] [rənegɔsje] **vt** to renegotiate.

reneiger [23] [rəneʒe] **vi** to snow again.

renfermé**, **e [rɑ̃fɛrme] **adj** introverted, withdrawn.
◆ ***renfermé*** **nm : ça sent le renfermé** it smells stuffy in here.

renfermer [3] [rɑ̃fɛrme] **vt** [contenir] to contain.
◆ ***se renfermer*** **vp** to withdraw.

renfiler [3] [rɑ̃file] **vt 1.** [perles] to restring **2.** [aiguille] to rethread **3.** [vêtement] to slip on again.

renflé**, **e [rɑ̃fle] **adj** bulging.

renflement [rɑ̃fləmɑ̃] **nm** bulge.

renflouer [3] [rɑ̃flue] **vt 1.** [bateau] to refloat **2.** *fig* [entreprise, personne] to bail out.
◆ ***se renflouer*** **vp** *fam fig* to get back on one's feet (financially).

renfoncement [rɑ̃fɔ̃smɑ̃] **nm** recess.

renfoncer [16] [rɑ̃fɔ̃se] **vt** to push (further) down.

renforcer [16] [rɑ̃fɔrse] **vt** to reinforce, to strengthen ▸ **cela me renforce dans mon opinion** that confirms my opinion.

renfort [rɑ̃fɔr] **nm** reinforcement ▸ **envoyer des renforts** to send reinforcements ▸ **venir en renfort** to come as reinforcements ▸ **à grand renfort de** *fig* with the help of a lot of.

renfrogné**, **e [rɑ̃frɔɲe] **adj** scowling.

renfrogner [3] [rɑ̃frɔɲe] ◆ ***se renfrogner*** **vp** to scowl, to pull a face.

rengager [rɑ̃gaʒe], ***réengager*** [17] [reɑ̃gaʒe] ■ **vt** [personnel] to take on again.
■ **vi** MIL to re-enlist, to join up again.
◆ ***se rengager*** **vp** MIL to re-enlist, to join up again.

rengaine [rɑ̃gɛn] **nf 1.** [formule répétée] (old) story **2.** [chanson] (old) song.

rengainer [4] [rɑ̃gɛne] **vt 1.** [épée] to sheathe / [pistolet] to put back in its holster **2.** *fam fig* [compliment] to withold.

rengorger [17] [rɑ̃gɔrʒe] ◆ ***se rengorger*** **vp** *fig* to puff o.s. up.

reniement [rənimɑ̃] **nm** renunciation.

renier [9] [rənje] **vt 1.** [famille, ami] to disown **2.** [foi, opinion] to renounce, to repudiate **3.** [signature] to refuse to acknowledge.

renifler [3] [rənifle] ■ **vi** to sniff.
■ **vt** to sniff ▸ **renifler quelque chose de louche** to smell a rat.

renne [rɛn] **nm** reindeer *(inv)*.

renom [rənɔ̃] **nm** renown, fame ▸ **de grand renom** of great renown, famous.

renommé**, **e [rənɔme] **adj** renowned, famous.
◆ ***renommée*** **nf** renown, fame ▸ **de renommée internationale** world-famous, internationally renowned.

renoncement [rənɔ̃smɑ̃] **nm : renoncement (à)** renunciation (of).

renoncer [16] [rənɔ̃se] **vi** *littéraire* to give up.
◆ ***renoncer à*** **v + prep** to give up ▸ **renoncer à** to give up ▸ **renoncer à comprendre qqch** to give up trying to understand sthg ▸ **renoncer à voir qqn** to give up *ou* abandon the idea of seeing sb ▸ **renoncer à faire qqch** to give up doing sthg.

renoncule [rənɔ̃kyl] **nf** buttercup.

renouer [6] [rənwe] ■ **vt 1.** [lacet, corde] to re-tie, to tie up again **2.** [contact, conversation] to resume.
■ **vi : renouer avec qqn** to take up with sb again ▸ **renouer avec sa famille** to make it up with one's family again.

renouveau**, **x [rənuvo] **nm 1.** [transformation] revival **2.** [regain] **: un renouveau de succès** renewed success.

renouvelable [rənuvlabl] **adj** renewable / [expérience] repeatable.

renouveler [24] [rənuvle] **vt 1.** [gén] to renew ▸ **renouveler un abonnement/un permis de séjour** to renew a subscription/a residence permit ▸ **renouveler un exploit/une tentative** to repeat a feat/an attempt ▸ **j'ai préféré ne pas renouveler l'expérience** I chose not to repeat the experience ▸ **renouveler sa garde-robe** to get *ou* to buy some new clothes **2.** [rajeunir] to revive ▸ **elle a renouvelé le genre policier** she gave the detective story new life.
◆ ***se renouveler*** **vp 1.** [être remplacé] to be renewed **2.** [changer, innover] to have new ideas ▸ **c'est un bon acteur mais il ne se renouvelle pas assez** he's a good actor but he doesn't vary his roles enough **3.** [se répéter] to be repeated, to recur ▸ **je te promets que cela ne se renouvellera pas** I promise you it won't happen again.

renouvelle**, **renouvelles ➤ ***renouveler***.

renouvellement [rənuvɛlmɑ̃] **nm** renewal.

rénovateur**, **trice [renɔvatœr, tris] ■ **adj** reformist, reforming.
■ **nm, f** reformer ▸ **les grands rénovateurs de la science** the people who revolutionized *ou* radically transformed science.
◆ ***rénovateur*** **nm** [pour nettoyer] restorer.

rénovation [renɔvasjɔ̃] **nf** renovation, restoration.

rénover [3] [renɔve] **vt 1.** [immeuble] to renovate, to restore **2.** [système, méthodes] to reform.

renseignement [rɑ̃sɛɲəmɑ̃] **nm** information *(U)* ▸ **un renseignement** a piece of information ▸ **prendre des renseignements (sur)** to make enquiries (about).
◆ ***renseignements*** **nmpl 1.** [service d'information] enquiries *UK*, information ▸ **appeler les renseignements** TÉLÉCOM to call directory enquiries *UK* *ou* information *US* **2.** [sécurité] intelligence *(U)* ▸ **les renseignements généraux** *police department responsible for political security.*

renseigner [4] [rɑ̃seɲe] **vt : renseigner qqn (sur)** to give sb information (about), to inform sb (about).
◆ ***se renseigner*** **vp 1.** [s'enquérir] to make enquiries, to ask for information **2.** [s'informer] to find out.

rentabiliser [3] [rɑ̃tabilize] **vt** to make profitable.

rentabilité [rɑ̃tabilite] **nf** profitability ▸ **seuil de rentabilité** breakeven point.

rentable [rɑ̃tabl] **adj 1.** COMM profitable **2.** *fam* [qui en vaut la peine] worthwhile.

rente [rɑ̃t] **nf 1.** [d'un capital] revenue, income ▸ **vivre de ses rentes** to have a private income **2.** [pension] pension, annuity ▸ **rente viagère** life annuity **3.** [emprunt d'État] government bond.

rentier, ère [rɑ̃tje, ɛr] **nm, f** person of independent means ▸ **mener une vie de rentier** *fig* to lead a life of leisure.

rentrée [rɑ̃tre] **nf 1.** [fait de rentrer] return
2. [reprise des activités] **: la rentrée parlementaire** the reopening of parliament ▸ **faire sa rentrée politique** [après les vacances] to start the new political season *(after the summer)* / [après une absence] to make one's (political) comeback ▸ **la rentrée des classes** the start of the new school year ▸ **la rentrée est fixée au 6 septembre** school starts again *ou* schools reopen on September 6th
3. CINÉ & THÉÂTRE comeback ▸ **la rentrée musicale/théâtrale** the new musical/theatrical season *(after the summer break)* ▸ **faire sa rentrée** to make one's comeback
4. [recette] income ▸ **avoir une rentrée d'argent** to come into some money ▸ **rentrées de caisse** cash receipts ▸ **rentrées fiscales** tax receipts *ou* revenue.

CULTURE

La rentrée

The beginning of the French school year in September marks more than just the start of school: it means a return to normal life for the rest of the country and is considered the start of the new year. People head back to work after the long summer holidays, and commercial activity, usually very sluggish in August, picks up again. Politics is on people's minds once again after Parliament reconvenes in early October. Autumn also marks the **rentrée littéraire**, when publishers release a large number of works from both new and established authors. University students return to their studies in October.

rentrer [3] [rɑ̃tre] ■ **vi** *(v aux : être)* **1.** [entrer de nouveau] to go/come back in ▸ **tout a fini par rentrer dans l'ordre** everything returned to normal **2.** [entrer] to go/come in ▸ **la clé ne rentre pas dans la serrure** the key won't go in **3.** [revenir chez soi] to go/come back, to go/come home ▸ **je vous laisse, il faut que je rentre** I'll leave you now, I must go home *ou* get (back) home **4.** [recouvrer, récupérer] **: rentrer dans** to recover, to get back ▸ **rentrer dans ses fonds** to recoup (one's) costs ▸ **rentrer dans ses frais** to cover one's costs, to break even **5.** [se jeter avec violence] **: rentrer dans** to crash into **6.** [s'emboîter] to go in, to fit ▸ **rentrer les uns dans les autres** to fit together **7.** [être compris] **: rentrer dans** to be included in ▸ **cela ne rentre pas dans mes attributions** that is not part of my duties **8.** [être perçu - fonds] to come in ▸ **faire rentrer l'argent/les devises** to bring in money/foreign currency.
■ **vt** *(v aux : être)* **1.** [mettre ou remettre à l'intérieur] to bring in ▸ **rentrer une clé dans une serrure** to put a key in a lock / [chemise] to tuck in **2.** [ventre] to pull in / [griffes] to retract, to draw in **3.** *fig* [rage, larmes] to hold back ▸ **rentrer son humiliation** to swallow one's humiliation.

renversant, e [rɑ̃vɛrsɑ̃, ɑ̃t] **adj** staggering, astounding.

renverse [rɑ̃vɛrs] **nf : tomber à la renverse** to fall over backwards.

renversé, e [rɑ̃vɛrse] **adj 1.** [à l'envers] upside down **2.** [qu'on a fait tomber] overturned **3.** [incliné en arrière] tilted back **4.** [stupéfait] staggered.

renversement [rɑ̃vɛrsəmɑ̃] **nm 1.** [inversion] turning upside down **2.** [de situation] reversal **3.** [de régime] overthrow **4.** [de tête, buste] tilting back.

renverser [3] [rɑ̃vɛrse] **vt 1.** [mettre à l'envers] to turn upside down **2.** [faire tomber - objet] to knock over / [- piéton] to run over / [- liquide] to spill **3.** *fig* [obstacle] to overcome / [régime] to overthrow / [ministre] to throw out of office **4.** [tête, buste] to tilt back **5.** [étonner] to bowl over **6.** [accident] **: se faire renverser par une voiture** to get *ou* be knocked over by a car.
◆ ***se renverser*** **vp 1.** [incliner le corps en arrière] to lean back **2.** [tomber] to overturn.

renvoi [rɑ̃vwa] **nm 1.** [licenciement] dismissal ▸ **notifier à qqn son renvoi** to give sb his/her notice **2.** [de colis, lettre] return, sending back **3.** [ajournement] postponement **4.** [référence] cross-reference **5.** DR referral **6.** [éructation] belch.

renvoie, renvoies ➤ *renvoyer*.

renvoyer [30] [rɑ̃vwaje] **vt 1.** [faire retourner] to send back **2.** [congédier] to dismiss **3.** [colis, lettre] to send back, to return **4.** [balle] to throw back **5.** [réfléchir - lumière] to reflect / [- son] to echo **6.** [référer] **: renvoyer qqn à** to refer sb to **7.** [différer] to postpone, to put off.

réorganisation [reɔrganizasjɔ̃] **nf** reorganization.

réorganiser [3] [reɔrganize] **vt** to reorganize.

réorienter [3] [reɔrjɑ̃te] **vt** to reorient, to reorientate.

réouverture [reuvɛrtyr] **nf** reopening.

repaire [rəpɛr] **nm** den.

repaître [91] [rəpɛtr] **vt : repaître ses yeux (de)** to feast one's eyes (on).
◆ ***se repaître*** **vp : se repaître de** [se rassasier] to eat one's fill of / *fig* to revel in.

répandre [74] [repɑ̃dr] **vt 1.** [verser, renverser] to spill / [larmes] to shed **2.** [diffuser, dégager] to give off **3.** *fig* [bienfaits] to pour out / [effroi, terreur, nouvelle] to spread.
◆ ***se répandre*** **vp 1.** [gén] to spread **2.** [liquide] to spill **3.** [personne] **: se répandre en injures** to let out a stream of insults ▸ **se répandre en remerciements** to give one's heartfelt thanks.

répandu, e [repɑ̃dy] ■ **pp** ➤ *répandre*.
■ **adj** [opinion, maladie] widespread.

réparable [reparabl] **adj 1.** [objet] repairable **2.** [erreur] that can be put right.

reparaître [91] [rəparɛtr] **vi** to reappear.

réparateur, trice [reparatœr, tris] ■ **adj** [sommeil] refreshing.
■ **nm, f** repairer.

réparation [reparasjɔ̃] **nf 1.** [d'objet - action] repairing / [- résultat] repair ▸ **en réparation** under repair **2.** [de faute] **: réparation (de)** atonement (for) **3.** [indemnité] reparation, compensation.

réparer [3] [repare] **vt 1.** [objet] to repair **2.** [faute, oubli] to make up for ▸ **réparer ses torts** to make amends.

reparler [3] [rəparle] **vi : reparler de qqn/qqch** to talk about sb/sthg again ▸ **reparler à qqn** to speak to sb again.
◆ ***se reparler*** **vp** to speak to each other again.

repartie [rəparti] **nf** retort ▸ **avoir de la repartie** to be good at repartee.

repartir [43] [rəpartir] ■ **vt** *littéraire* to reply.
■ **vi 1.** [retourner] to go back, to return **2.** [partir de nouveau] to set off again **3.** [recommencer] to start again.

répartir [32] [repartir] **vt 1.** [partager] to share out, to divide up **2.** [dans l'espace] to spread out, to distribute **3.** [échelonner] to spread out **4.** [classer] to divide *ou* split up.
◆ ***se répartir*** **vp** to divide up.

répartition [repartisjɔ̃] **nf 1.** [partage] sharing out / [de tâches] allocation **2.** [dans l'espace] distribution.

reparu [rəpary] **pp** ➤ ***reparaître***.

repas [rəpa] **nm** meal ▸ **prendre son repas** to eat ▸ **repas d'affaires** business meal, working lunch/dinner.

repassage [rəpasaʒ] **nm** ironing.

repasser [3] [rəpase] ■ **vi** *(v aux : être)* [passer à nouveau] to go/come back ▸ **repasser par le même chemin** to go back the way one came / [film] to be on again.
■ **vt** *(v aux : être)* **1.** [frontière, montagne] to cross again, to recross **2.** [examen] to resit *UK* ▸ **je dois repasser l'allemand/le permis demain** I have to retake German/my driving test tomorrow **3.** [film] to show again **4.** *fam* [transmettre] to pass on **5.** [linge] to iron **6.** [leçon] to go over ▸ **repasser le programme de physique** SCOL to go over the physics course **7.** [remettre] **: repasser une couche de vernis** to put on another coat of varnish **8.** [au téléphone] **: repassez-moi le standard** put me through to the switchboard again.

repasseuse [rəpasøz] **nf 1.** [ouvrière] ironer **2.** [machine] ironing machine.

repayer [11] [rəpeje] **vt** to pay again.

repêchage [rəpeʃaʒ] **nm** [de noyé, voiture] recovery.

repêcher [4] [rəpeʃe] **vt 1.** [noyé, voiture] to fish out **2.** *fam* [candidat] to let through.

repeindre [81] [rəpɛ̃dr] **vt** to repaint.

repeint**, **e [rəpɛ̃, ɛ̃t] **pp** ➤ ***repeindre***.

repenser [3] [rəpɑ̃se] **vt** to rethink.

repentir [37] [rəpɑ̃tir] **nm** repentance.
◆ ***se repentir*** **vp** to repent ▸ **se repentir de qqch/d'avoir fait qqch** to be sorry for sthg/for having done sthg.

repérable [rəperabl] **adj : difficilement repérable** difficult to spot.

repérage [rəperaʒ] **nm** location.

répercussion [reperkysjɔ̃] **nf** repercussion.

répercuter [3] [reperkyte] **vt 1.** [lumière] to reflect / [son] to throw back **2.** [ordre, augmentation] to pass on.
◆ ***se répercuter*** **vp 1.** [lumière] to be reflected / [son] to echo **2.** [influer] **: se répercuter sur** to have repercussions on.

repère [rəpɛr] **nm** [marque] mark / [objet concret] landmark ▸ **point de repère** point of reference.

repérer [18] [rəpere] **vt 1.** [situer] to locate, to pinpoint **2.** *fam* [remarquer] to spot ▸ **se faire repérer** to be spotted.
◆ ***se repérer*** **vp** *fam* to find one's way around.

répertoire [repertwar] **nm 1.** [agenda] thumb-indexed notebook **2.** [inventaire] catalogue, catalog *US*, list **3.** [de théâtre, d'artiste] repertoire **4.** INFORM directory.

répertorier [9] [repertɔrje] **vt** to make a list of.

répéter [18] [repete] ■ **vt 1.** [gén] to repeat ▸ **je n'arrête pas de vous le répéter** that's what I've been trying to tell you ▸ **ne pas se le faire répéter deux fois** not to have to be told twice ▸ **ne va pas le répéter (à tout le monde)** don't go telling everybody **2.** [leçon] to go over, to learn / [rôle] to rehearse.
■ **vi** to rehearse ▸ **on ne répète pas demain** there's no rehearsal tomorrow.
◆ ***se répéter*** **vp 1.** [radoter] to repeat o.s. ▸ **au risque de me répéter** at the risk of repeating myself **2.** [se reproduire] to be repeated ▸ **que cela ne se répète pas!** don't let it happen again! ▸ **l'histoire se répète** history repeats itself.

répétitif**, **ive [repetitif, iv] **adj** repetitive.

répétition [repetisjɔ̃] **nf 1.** [réitération] repetition **2.** MUS & THÉÂTRE rehearsal.

repeupler [5] [rəpœple] **vt 1.** [région, ville] to repopulate **2.** [forêt] to replant / [étang] to restock.

repiquage [rəpikaʒ] **nm 1.** [plantation] planting ou[t] **2.** [enregistrement] re-recording.

repiquer [3] [rəpike] ■ **vt 1.** [replanter] to plant ou[t] **2.** [disque, cassette] to tape.
■ **vi** *fam* **: repiquer à qqch** to take sthg up again ▸ **repiquer au plat** to have a second helping.

répit [repi] **nm** respite ▸ **sans répit** without respite.

replacer [16] [rəplase] **vt 1.** [remettre] to replace, to pu[t] back **2.** [situer] to place, to put.
◆ ***se replacer*** **vp** to find new employment.

replanter [3] [rəplɑ̃te] **vt** to replant.

replat [rəpla] **nm** ledge.

replâtrer [3] [rəplatre] **vt 1.** [mur, fissure] to replaste[r] **2.** *fam fig* to patch up.

replet**, **ète [rəplɛ, ɛt] **adj** chubby.

repli [rəpli] **nm 1.** [de tissu] fold / [de rivière] bend **2.** [d]e troupes] withdrawal.

replier [10] [rəplije] **vt 1.** [plier de nouveau] to fold u[p] again **2.** [ramener en pliant] to fold back **3.** [armée] to with[draw].
◆ ***se replier*** **vp 1.** [armée] to withdraw **2.** [personne] **: s[e] replier sur soi-même** to withdraw into o.s. **3.** [journa[l], carte] to fold.

réplique [replik] **nf 1.** [riposte] reply ▸ **sans répliq[ue]** [argument] irrefutable **2.** [d'acteur] line ▸ **donner la répl[i]que à qqn** to play opposite sb **3.** [copie] replica / [sos[ie]] double.

répliquer [3] [replike] ■ **vt : répliquer à qqn que** reply to sb that.
■ **vi 1.** [répondre] to reply / [avec impertinence] to answ[er] back **2.** *fig* [riposter] to retaliate.

replonger [17] [rəplɔ̃ʒe] ■ **vt** to plunge back.
■ **vi** to dive back.
◆ ***se replonger*** **vp : se replonger dans qqch** to immerse o.s. in sthg again.

répondant, e [repɔ̃dɑ̃, ɑ̃t] **nm, f** guarantor.
◆ ***répondant*** **nm** *fam* **: avoir du répondant** to have money behind one.

répondeur [repɔ̃dœr] **nm : répondeur (téléphonique** *OU* **automatique** *OU* **-enregistreur)** answering machine.

répondre [75] [repɔ̃dr] ■ **vi : répondez par oui ou par non** answer *OU* say yes or no ▸ **répondre à qqn** [faire connaître sa pensée] to answer sb, to reply to sb / [riposter] to answer sb back ▸ **répondre à ses parents/professeurs** to answer one's parents/teachers back ▸ **répondre à qqch** [faire une réponse] to reply to sthg, to answer sthg / [en se défendant] to respond to sthg ▸ **répondez au questionnaire suivant** answer the following questions, fill in the following questionnaire ▸ **répondre au téléphone** to answer the telephone ▸ **ça ne répond pas** nobody's answering, there's no answer.
■ **vt** to answer, to reply ▸ **ils m'ont répondu des bêtises** they answered me with a lot of nonsense ▸ **répondre que** to reply that, to answer that ▸ **elle m'a répondu de le faire moi-même** she told me to do it myself.
◆ ***répondre à*** **vt 1.** [correspondre à - besoin] to answer / [- conditions] to meet ▸ **les dédommagements ne répondent pas à l'attente des sinistrés** the amount offered in compensation falls short of the victims' expectations **2.** [ressembler à - description] to match ▸ **au bleu du ciel répond le bleu de la mer** the blue of the sky matches the blue of the sea.
◆ ***répondre de*** **vt** to answer for ▸ **répondre de l'exactitude de qqch/de l'intégrité de qqn** to vouch for the accuracy of sthg/sb's integrity ▸ **les ministres répondent de leurs actes devant le Parlement** ministers are accountable for their actions before Parliament.

épondu, e [repɔ̃dy] **pp** ➤ ***répondre***.

éponse [repɔ̃s] **nf 1.** [action de répondre] answer, reply ▸ **elle a toujours réponse à tout** [elle sait tout] she has an answer for everything / [elle a de la repartie] she's never at a loss for *OU* she's always ready with an answer ▸ **en réponse à votre lettre...** in reply *OU* in answer *OU* in response to your letter... ▸ **réponse par retour du courrier** reply by return of post ▸ **bulletin-réponse** reply slip ▸ **coupon-réponse** reply coupon **2.** [solution] answer ▸ **la réponse à la question nº 5 est fausse** the answer to number 5 is wrong **3.** [réaction] response ▸ **la réponse du gouvernement fut d'imposer le couvre-feu** the government's response was to impose a curfew **4.** TECHNOL response ▸ **temps de réponse d'un appareil** response time of a device.

eport [rəpɔr] **nm 1.** [de réunion, rendez-vous] postponement **2.** COMM [d'écritures] carrying forward **3.** POLIT [de voix] transfer.

portage [rəpɔrtaʒ] **nm 1.** [article, enquête] report **2.** [métier] reporting.

porter[1] [rəpɔrtɛr] **nm** reporter ▸ **grand reporter** international reporter ▸ **reporter d'investigation** *OU* **d'enquête** investigative reporter.

reporter[2] [3] [rəpɔrte] **vt 1.** [rapporter] to take back **2.** [différer] **: reporter qqch à** to postpone sthg till, to put sthg off till **3.** [somme] **: reporter (sur)** to carry forward (to) **4.** [transférer] **: reporter sur** to transfer to.
◆ ***se reporter*** **vp : se reporter à** [se référer à] to refer to / [se transporter en pensée à] to cast one's mind back to.

repos [rəpo] **nm 1.** [gén] rest ▸ **prendre un jour de repos** to take a day off **2.** [tranquillité] peace and quiet ▸ **ce n'est pas de tout repos** it's not exactly restful **3.** MIL **: repos!** at ease!

reposant, e [rəpozɑ̃, ɑ̃t] **adj** restful.

reposé, e [rəpoze] **adj** rested ▸ **à tête reposée** with a clear head.

reposer [3] [rəpoze] ■ **vt 1.** [poser à nouveau] to put down again, to put back down **2.** [remettre] to put back **3.** [poser de nouveau - question] to ask again **4.** [appuyer] to rest **5.** [délasser] to rest, to relax.
■ **vi 1.** [pâte] to sit, to stand / [vin] to stand **2.** [mort] **: ici repose...** here lies... **3.** [théorie] **: reposer sur** to rest on.
◆ ***se reposer*** **vp 1.** [se délasser] to rest **2.** [faire confiance] **: se reposer sur qqn** to rely on sb.

repositionnable [rəpɔzisjɔnabl] **adj** repositionable, removable.

repositionnement [rəpɔzisjɔnmɑ̃] **m** [d'une marque, d'un produit] repositioning.

repositionner [3] [rəpozisjɔne] **vt** to reposition.
◆ ***se repositionner*** **vp** to reposition o.s.

repoussant, e [rəpusɑ̃, ɑ̃t] **adj** repulsive.

repoussé [rəpuse] ■ **adj m** repoussé *(modif)*.
■ **nm** [technique - généralement] repoussé (work) / [- au marteau] chasing / [relief] repoussé.

repousser [3] [rəpuse] ■ **vi** to grow again, to grow back.
■ **vt 1.** [écarter] to push away, to push back / [l'ennemi] to repel, to drive back **2.** [éconduire] to reject **3.** [proposition] to reject, to turn down **4.** [différer] to put back, to postpone.
◆ ***se repousser*** **vp** [aimants] to repel one another.

repoussoir [rəpuswar] **nm : servir de repoussoir à qqn** to be a foil to sb.

répréhensible [repreɑ̃sibl] **adj** reprehensible.

reprenais, reprenions ➤ ***reprendre***.

reprendre [79] [rəprɑ̃dr] ■ **vt 1.** [prendre de nouveau] to take again ▸ **je passe te reprendre dans une heure** I'll come by and pick you up again in an hour ▸ **reprendre la route** to take to the road again ▸ **reprendre haleine** to get one's breath back **2.** [récupérer - objet prêté] to take back ▸ **tu peux reprendre ton parapluie, je n'en ai plus besoin** I don't need your umbrella anymore, you can take it back / [- prisonnier, ville] to recapture **3.** COMM [entreprise, affaire] to take over ▸ **ni repris ni échangé** goods may not be returned or exchanged ▸ **ils m'ont repris ma voiture pour 1000 euros** I traded my car in for 1,000 euros **4.** [se resservir] **: reprendre un gâteau/de la viande** to take another cake/some more meat ▸ **reprends un biscuit** have another biscuit **5.** [recommencer] to resume ▸ **"et ainsi" reprit-il...** "and so", he continued... **6.** [retoucher] to repair / [jupe] to alter ▸ **reprendre une maille** to pick up a

stitch **7.** [corriger] to correct ▸ **c'était parfait, je n'ai rien eu à reprendre** it was perfect, I didn't have to make a single correction *ou* alteration.
■ **vi 1.** [affaires, plante] to pick up **2.** [recommencer] to start again ▸ **la tempête reprit de plus belle** the storm started again with renewed ferocity.
◆ ***se reprendre*** **vp 1.** [rectifier ce qu'on a dit] to correct o.s. ▸ **se reprendre à temps** [avant une bévue] to stop o.s. in time **2.** [recommencer] **: se reprendre à espérer** to find new hope ▸ **s'y reprendre à plusieurs fois** to make several attempts **3.** [se ressaisir] to pull o.s. together.

repreneur [rəprənœr] **nm** *person who takes over a company with the aim of revitalizing it.*

représailles [rəprezaj] **nfpl** reprisals ▸ **par représailles** as a reprisal, in reprisal.

représentant**, **e [rəprezɑ̃tɑ̃, ɑ̃t] **nm, f** representative.

représentatif**, **ive [rəprezɑ̃tatif, iv] **adj** representative.

représentation [rəprezɑ̃tasjɔ̃] **nf 1.** [gén] representation **2.** [spectacle] performance **3.** [métier] commercial travelling *UK ou* traveling *US*.

représentativité [rəprezɑ̃tativite] **nf** representativeness.

représenter [3] [rəprezɑ̃te] **vt** to represent.
◆ ***se représenter*** **vp 1.** [s'imaginer] **: se représenter qqch** to visualize sthg **2.** [se présenter à nouveau] **: se représenter à** [aux élections] to stand *UK ou* run *US* again at / [à un examen] to resit *UK*, to represent.

répressif**, **ive [represif, iv] **adj** repressive.

répression [represjɔ̃] **nf 1.** [de révolte] repression **2.** [de criminalité, d'injustices] suppression.

réprimande [reprimɑ̃d] **nf** reprimand.

réprimander [3] [reprimɑ̃de] **vt** to reprimand.

réprimer [3] [reprime] **vt 1.** [émotion, rire] to repress, to check **2.** [révolte, crimes] to put down, to suppress.

repris**, **e [rəpri, iz] **pp** ➤ ***reprendre***.
◆ ***repris*** **nm : repris de justice** habitual criminal.

reprisage [rəprizaʒ] **nm** mending.

reprise [rəpriz] **nf 1.** [recommencement - des hostilités] resumption, renewal / [- des affaires] revival, recovery / [- de pièce] revival ▸ **à plusieurs reprises** on several occasions, several times **2.** [boxe] round **3.** [accélération] acceleration **4.** [raccommodage] mending **5.** COMM trade-in, part exchange *UK* / [somme payée à un locataire] *sum paid for fixtures and fittings left by outgoing tenant*.

repriser [3] [rəprize] **vt** to mend.

réprobateur**, **trice [reprɔbatœr, tris] **adj** reproachful.

réprobation [reprɔbasjɔ̃] **nf** disapproval.

reproche [rəprɔʃ] **nm** reproach ▸ **faire des reproches à qqn** to reproach sb ▸ **avec reproche** reproachfully ▸ **sans reproche** blameless.

reprocher [3] [rəprɔʃe] **vt : reprocher qqch à qqn** to reproach sb for sthg ▸ **je ne vous reproche rien** I don't reproach *ou* blame you for anything.
◆ ***se reprocher*** **vp : se reprocher (qqch)** to blame o.s. (for sthg) ▸ **ne rien avoir à se reprocher** to have nothing to reproach o.s. for.

reproducteur**, **trice [rəprɔdyktœr, tris] **adj** reproductive.

reproduction [rəprɔdyksjɔ̃] **nf** reproduction ▸ **reproduction interdite** all rights (of reproduction) reserved.

reproduire [98] [rəprɔdɥir] **vt** to reproduce.
◆ ***se reproduire*** **vp 1.** BIOL to reproduce, to breed **2.** [se répéter] to recur.

reproduisais**, **reproduisions ➤ ***reproduire***.

reproduit**, **e [rəprɔdɥi, it] **pp** ➤ ***reproduire***.

reprogrammer [3] [rəprɔgrame] **vt** to reprogram.

reprographie [rəprɔgrafi] **nf** reproduction.

réprouvé**, **e [repruve] ■ **adj** rejected.
■ **nm, f** outcast.

réprouver [3] [repruve] **vt** [blâmer] to reprove.

reptation [rɛptasjɔ̃] **nf** creeping.

reptile [rɛptil] **nm** reptile.

repu**, **e [rəpy] ■ **pp** ➤ ***repaître***.
■ **adj** full, sated.

républicain**, **e [repyblikɛ̃, ɛn] **adj & nm, f** republican

république [repyblik] **nf** republic ▸ **la République centrafricaine** Central African Republic ▸ **la République française** the French Republic ▸ **la République populaire de Chine** the People's Republic of China ▸ **la République tchèque** the Czech Republic.

répudiation [repydjasjɔ̃] **nf** repudiation.

répudier [9] [repydje] **vt 1.** [femme] to repudiat **2.** [principes, engagements] to renounce.

répugnance [repyɲɑ̃s] **nf 1.** [horreur] repugnanc **2.** [réticence] reluctance ▸ **avoir *ou* éprouver de la répugnance à faire qqch** to be reluctant to do sthg ▸ **avec répugnance** reluctantly.

répugnant**, **e [repyɲɑ̃, ɑ̃t] **adj** repugnant.

répugner [3] [repyɲe] **vi : répugner à qqn** to disgu sb, to fill sb with repugnance ▸ **répugner à faire qqch** be reluctant to do sthg, to be loath to do sthg.

répulsion [repylsjɔ̃] **nf** repulsion.

réputation [repytasjɔ̃] **nf** reputation ▸ **avoir une réputation de** to have a reputation for ▸ **avoir la réputatic d'être généreux** to have a reputation for being genero ▸ **connaître qqn/qqch de réputation** to know sb/sthg reputation ▸ **avoir bonne/mauvaise réputation** to ha a good/bad reputation.

réputé**, **e [repyte] **adj** famous, well-known ▸ **être répu pour** to be famous *ou* well-known for.

requérir [39] [rəkerir] **vt 1.** [nécessiter] to require, to c for **2.** [solliciter] to solicit **3.** DR [réclamer au nom de la l to demand.

requête [rəkɛt] **nf 1.** [prière] petition ▸ **à *ou* sur la requête de** at the request of **2.** DR appeal **3.** INFORM query.

requiem [rekɥijɛm] **nm inv** requiem.

requiers, requiert ➤ ***requérir***.

requin [rəkɛ̃] **nm** shark.

requinquer [3] [rəkɛ̃ke] **vt** *fam* to perk up, to buck up.
◆ ***se requinquer*** **vp** *fam* to perk up, to buck up.

requis, e [rəki, iz] ■ **pp** ➤ ***requérir***.
■ **adj** required, requisite.

réquisition [rekizisj̃ɔ] **nf 1.** MIL requisition **2.** DR closing speech for the prosecution.

réquisitionner [3] [rekizisjɔne] **vt** to requisition.

réquisitoire [rekizitwar] **nm** DR closing speech for the prosecution ▸ **réquisitoire (contre)** *fig* indictment (of).

RER (abr de ***réseau express régional***) **nm** *train service linking central Paris with its suburbs and airports.*

rescapé, e [rɛskape] ■ **adj** rescued.
■ **nm, f** survivor.

rescousse [rɛskus] ◆ ***à la rescousse*** **loc adv : venir à la rescousse de qqn** to come to sb's rescue ▸ **appeler qqn à la rescousse** to call on sb for help.

réseau, x [rezo] **nm** network ▸ **réseau de distribution** distribution network ▸ **réseau d'espionnage** spy ring, network of spies ▸ **réseau ferroviaire/routier** rail/road network ▸ **réseau fluvial** river system ▸ **réseau local** INFORM LAN *(local area network)* ▸ **réseau urbain** city bus network ▸ **en réseau** INFORM networked.

réséda [rezeda] **nm** mignonette.

réservation [rezɛrvasjɔ̃] **nf** reservation.

réserve [rezɛrv] **nf 1.** [gén] reserve ▸ **réserves monétaires/de devises** monetary/currency reserves ▸ **en réserve** in reserve ▸ **avoir de la nourriture en réserve** to have food put by, to have food in reserve ▸ **officier de réserve** MIL reserve officer ▸ **faire des réserves de** to lay in supplies *ou* provisions of
2. [restriction] reservation ▸ **faire des réserves (sur)** to have reservations (about) ▸ **sous toute réserve *ou* toutes réserves** subject to confirmation ▸ **la nouvelle a été publiée sous toute réserve** the news was published with no guarantee as to its accuracy ▸ **sous réserve de** subject to ▸ **sans réserve** unreservedly ▸ **éloges sans réserve** unreserved praise
3. [d'animaux, de plantes] reserve ▸ **réserve ornithologique *ou* d'oiseaux** bird sanctuary / [d'Indiens] reservation ▸ **réserve faunique** *Québec* wildlife reserve ▸ **réserve naturelle** nature reserve
4. [local] storeroom.
◆ ***Réserve fédérale*** **nf** Federal Reserve.

réservé, e [rezɛrve] **adj** reserved.

réserver [3] [rezɛrve] **vt 1.** [destiner] **: Mesdames, bonsoir, avez-vous réservé?** good evening, ladies, have you booked *UK ou* do you have a reservation? ▸ **réserver qqch (à qqn)** [chambre, place] to reserve *ou* book sthg (for sb) / *fig* [surprise, désagrément] to have sthg in store (for sb) ▸ **réserver un accueil glacial/chaleureux à qqn** to reserve an icy/a warm welcome for sb **2.** [mettre de côté, garder] **: réserver qqch (pour)** to put sthg on one side (for), to keep sthg (for) ▸ **j'avais réservé des fonds pour l'achat d'une maison** I had put *ou* set some money aside to buy a house ▸ **réserver le meilleur pour la fin** to keep *ou* to save the best till last.
◆ ***se réserver*** **vp 1.** [s'accorder] **: se réserver qqch** to keep sthg for o.s. ▸ **se réserver de faire qqch** to wait to do sthg ▸ **se réserver le droit de faire qqch** to reserve the right to do sthg **2.** [se ménager] to save o.s.

réserviste [rezɛrvist] **nm** reservist.

réservoir [rezɛrvwar] **nm 1.** [cuve] tank **2.** [bassin] reservoir **3.** *fig* [de main-d'œuvre] reserve, pool / [d'idées] source.

résidant, e [rezidɑ̃, ɑ̃t] **adj** resident.

résidence [rezidɑ̃s] **nf 1.** [habitation] residence ▸ **résidence principale** main residence *ou* home ▸ **résidence secondaire** second home ▸ **résidence universitaire** hall of residence *UK*, dormitory *US* **2.** [immeuble] block of luxury flats *UK*, luxury apartment block *US*.
◆ ***résidence surveillée*** **nf : en résidence surveillée** under house arrest.

résident, e [rezidɑ̃, ɑ̃t] **nm, f 1.** [de pays] **: les résidents français en Écosse** French nationals resident in Scotland **2.** [habitant d'une résidence] resident.

résidentiel, elle [rezidɑ̃sjɛl] **adj** residential.

résider [3] [rezide] **vi 1.** [habiter] **: résider à/dans/en** to reside in **2.** [consister] **: résider dans** to lie in.

résidu [rezidy] **nm** [reste] residue / [déchet] waste.

résiduel, elle [rezidɥɛl] **adj** residual.

résignation [reziɲasjɔ̃] **nf** resignation.

résigné, e [reziɲe] ■ **adj** resigned.
■ **nm, f** resigned person.

résigner [3] [reziɲe] ◆ ***se résigner*** **vp : se résigner (à)** to resign o.s. (to) ▸ **se résigner à faire qqch** to resign o.s. to doing sthg.

résiliation [reziljasjɔ̃] **nf** cancellation, termination.

résilience [reziljɑ̃s] **nf** PSYCHO resilience.

résilier [9] [rezilje] **vt** to cancel, to terminate.

résille [rezij] **nf 1.** [pour cheveux] hairnet **2.** [pour les jambes] **: bas résille** fishnet stockings.

résine [rezin] **nf** resin.

résiné, e [rezine] **adj** flavoured *UK ou* flavored *US* with resin.
◆ ***résiné*** **nm** retsina.

résineux, euse [rezinø, øz] **adj** resinous.
◆ ***résineux*** **nm** conifer.

résistance [rezistɑ̃s] **nf 1.** [gén, ÉLECTR & PHYS] resistance ▸ **manquer de résistance** to lack stamina ▸ **opposer une résistance** to put up resistance ▸ **résistance passive** passive resistance **2.** [de radiateur, chaudière] element.
◆ ***Résistance*** **nf : la Résistance** HIST the Resistance.

résistant**, **e [rezistɑ̃, ɑ̃t] ■ **adj** [personne] tough / [tissu] hard-wearing, tough ▸ **être résistant au froid/aux infections** to be resistant to the cold/to infection.
■ **nm, f** [gén] resistance fighter / [de la Résistance] member of the Resistance.

résister [3] [reziste] **vi** to resist ▸ **résister à** [attaque, désir] to resist / [tempête, fatigue] to withstand / [personne] to stand up to, to oppose.

résolu**, **e [rezɔly] ■ **pp** ➤ ***résoudre***.
■ **adj** resolute ▸ **être bien résolu à faire qqch** to be determined to do sthg.

résolument [rezɔlymɑ̃] **adv** resolutely.

résolution [rezɔlysjɔ̃] **nf** **1.** [décision] resolution ▸ **prendre la résolution de faire qqch** to make a resolution to do sthg **2.** [détermination] resolve, determination **3.** [solution] solving.

résolvais**, **résolvions ➤ ***résoudre***.

résonance [rezɔnɑ̃s] **nf** **1.** ÉLECTR & PHYS resonance **2.** *fig* [écho] echo.

résonner [3] [rezɔne] **vi** [retentir] to resound / [renvoyer le son] to echo ▸ **résonner de** to resound with.

résorber [3] [rezɔrbe] **vt** **1.** [déficit] to absorb **2.** MÉD to resorb.
◆ ***se résorber*** **vp** **1.** [déficit] to be absorbed **2.** MÉD to be resorbed.

résoudre [88] [rezudr] **vt** **1.** [problème] to solve, to resolve **2.** [décider] **: résoudre qqn à faire qqch** to get sb to make up his/her mind to do sthg **3.** [décomposer] **: résoudre en** to break up *ou* resolve into.
◆ ***se résoudre*** **vp : se résoudre à faire qqch** to make up one's mind to do sthg, to decide *ou* resolve to do sthg.

respect [rɛspɛ] **nm** respect ▸ **manquer de respect à qqn** to be disrespectful to sb, to show disrespect for sb ▸ **sauf votre respect** with all (due) respect ▸ **avec tout le respect que je vous dois** with all (due) respect, with the greatest of respect ▸ **tenir qqn en respect** *fig* to keep sb at bay.
◆ ***respects*** **nmpl** respects, regards.

respectabilité [rɛspɛktabilite] **nf** respectability.

respectable [rɛspɛktabl] **adj** respectable.

respecter [4] [rɛspɛkte] **vt** to respect ▸ **faire respecter la loi** to enforce the law.
◆ ***se respecter*** **vp : un professeur qui se respecte ne ferait pas cela** no self-respecting teacher would do that.

respectif**, **ive [rɛspɛktif, iv] **adj** respective.

respectivement [rɛspɛktivmɑ̃] **adv** respectively.

respectueusement [rɛspɛktɥøzmɑ̃] **adv** respectfully.

respectueux**, **euse [rɛspɛktɥø, øz] **adj** respectful ▸ **être respectueux de** to have respect for.

respirable [rɛspirabl] **adj : l'air n'est plus respirable** the air is no longer breathable.

respiration [rɛspirasjɔ̃] **nf** breathing *(U)* ▸ **retenir sa respiration** to hold one's breath ▸ **respiration artificielle** artificial respiration.

respiratoire [rɛspiratwar] **adj** respiratory.

respirer [3] [rɛspire] ■ **vi** **1.** [inspirer-expirer] to breathe **2.** *fig* [se reposer] to get one's breath / [être soulagé] to be able to breathe again.
■ **vt** **1.** [aspirer] to breathe in **2.** *fig* [exprimer] to exude.

resplendir [32] [rɛsplɑ̃dir] **vi** **1.** [lune] to shine **2.** *fig* [personne] **: resplendir de joie/santé** to be radiant with joy/health.

resplendissant**, **e [rɛsplɑ̃disɑ̃, ɑ̃t] **adj** radiant.

responsabilisation [rɛspɔ̃sabilizasjɔ̃] **nf** making sb aware of his/her responsibilities.

responsabiliser [3] [rɛspɔ̃sabilize] **vt : responsabiliser qqn** to make sb aware of his/her responsibilities.

responsabilité [rɛspɔ̃sabilite] **nf** **1.** [morale] responsibility ▸ **décliner toute responsabilité** to disclaim all responsibility ▸ **avoir la responsabilité de** to be responsible for, to have the responsibility of **2.** DR liability ▸ **responsabilité civile** civil liability ▸ **responsabilité collective/pénale** collective/criminal responsibility.

responsable [rɛspɔ̃sabl] ■ **adj** **1.** [gén] **: responsable (de)** responsible (for) / [légalement] liable (for) / [chargé de] in charge (of), responsible (for) ▸ **il n'est pas responsable de ses actes** DR he cannot be held responsible for his (own) actions ▸ **il est responsable du service après-vente** he's in charge of the after-sales department ▸ **l'abus des graisses animales est largement responsable des affections cardiaques** the main contributing factor to heart disease is over-consumption of animal fats **2.** [sérieux] responsible ▸ **elle s'est toujours comportée en personne responsable** she has always acted responsibly.
■ **nmf** **1.** [auteur, coupable] person responsible ▸ **qui est le responsable de l'accident?** who's responsible for the accident? **2.** [dirigeant] official ▸ **réunion avec les responsables syndicaux** meeting with the union representatives **3.** [personne compétente] person in charge.

resquillage [rɛskijaʒ] **nm** = ***resquille***.

resquille [rɛskij] **nf** **1.** [au théâtre etc] sneaking in without paying **2.** [dans autobus etc] fare-dodging.

resquiller [3] [rɛskije] **vi** **1.** [au théâtre etc] to sneak in without paying **2.** [dans autobus etc] to dodge paying the fare.

resquilleur**, **euse [rɛskijœr, øz] **nm, f** **1.** [au théâtre etc] person who sneaks in without paying **2.** [dans autobus etc] fare-dodger.

ressac [rəsak] **nm** undertow.

ressaisir [32] [rəsezir] ◆ ***se ressaisir*** **vp** to pull o.s together.

ressasser [3] [rəsase] **vt** **1.** [répéter] to keep churning out **2.** *fig* [mécontentement] to dwell on.

ressayer = ***réessayer***.

ressemblance [rəsɑ̃blɑ̃s] **nf** [gén] resemblance, likeness / [trait] resemblance.

ressemblant**, **e [rəsɑ̃blɑ̃, ɑ̃t] **adj** lifelike.

ressembler [3] [rəsɑ̃ble] **vi : ressembler à** [physiquement] to resemble, to look like / [moralement] to be like, to resemble ▸ **cela ne lui ressemble pas** that's not like him.
◆ ***se ressembler*** **vp** to look alike, to resemble each other ▸ **qui se ressemble s'assemble** birds of a feather flock together.

ressemeler [24] [rəsəmle] **vt** to resole.

ressentiment [rəsɑ̃timɑ̃] **nm** resentment.

ressentir [37] [rəsɑ̃tir] **vt** to feel.
◆ ***se ressentir*** **vp : se ressentir de** [suj: travail] to show the effects of / [suj: personne, pays] to feel the effects of.

resserre [rəsɛr] **nf** storeroom.

resserrer [4] [rəsere] **vt 1.** [ceinture, boulon] to tighten **2.** *fig* [lien] to strengthen.
◆ ***se resserrer*** **vp 1.** [route] to (become) narrow **2.** [nœud, étreinte] to tighten **3.** *fig* [relations] to grow stronger, to strengthen.

resservir [38] [rəsɛrvir] ■ **vt 1.** [plat] to serve again / *fig* [histoire] to trot out **2.** [personne] to give another helping to.
■ **vi** to be used again.
◆ ***se resservir*** **vp : se resservir de qqch** [ustensile] to use sthg again / [plat] to take another helping of sthg.

ressort [rəsɔr] **nm 1.** [mécanisme] spring **2.** *fig* [énergie] spirit **3.** *fig* [force] force **4.** *fig* [compétence] **: être du ressort de qqn** to be sb's area of responsibility, to come under sb's jurisdiction.
◆ ***en dernier ressort*** **loc adv** in the last resort, as a last resort.

ressortir[1] [43] [rəsɔrtir] ■ **vi** *(v aux : être)* **1.** [personne] to go out again **2.** *fig* [couleur] **: ressortir (sur)** to stand out (against) ▸ **faire ressortir** to highlight **3.** *fig* [résulter de] **: ressortir de** to emerge from.
■ **vt** *(v aux : être)* to take *ou* get *ou* bring out again.

ressortir[2] [32] [rəsɔrtir] **vi** [relever] **: ressortir à** DR to be in the province of / *sout* [domaine] to pertain to.

ressortissant, e [rəsɔrtisɑ̃, ɑ̃t] **nm, f** national.

ressouder [3] [rəsude] **vt** to resolder / *fig* to cement.

ressource [rəsurs] **nf** resort ▸ **elle n'a eu d'autre ressource que de le lui demander** there was no other course (of action) open *ou* left to her but to ask him ▸ **votre seule ressource est de...** the only course open to you is to... ▸ **avoir de la ressource** to be resourceful ▸ **ressource renouvelable** [écologie] renewable resource.
◆ ***ressources*** **nfpl 1.** [financières] means ▸ **être sans ressources** to be without means ▸ **ressources personnelles** private means **2.** [énergétiques, de langue] resources ▸ **ressources naturelles** natural resources ▸ **ressources humaines** human resources, personnel **3.** [de personne] resourcefulness *(U)* ▸ **nous mobilisons toutes nos ressources pour retrouver les marins disparus** we're mobilizing all our resources *ou* all the means at our disposal to find the missing sailors.

ressourcer [16] [rəsurse] ◆ ***se ressourcer*** **vp** to recharge one's batteries.

ressouvenir [40] [rəsuvnir] ◆ ***se ressouvenir*** **vp** *littéraire* **: se ressouvenir de qqn/qqch** to remember sb/sthg.

ressurgir [32] [rəsyrʒir] **vi** to reappear.

ressusciter [3] [resysite] ■ **vi** to rise (from the dead) / *fig* to revive.
■ **vt** to bring back to life, to raise / *fig* to revive.

restant, e [rɛstɑ̃, ɑ̃t] **adj** remaining, left.
◆ ***restant*** **nm** rest, remainder.

restaurant [rɛstɔrɑ̃] **nm** restaurant ▸ **manger au restaurant** to eat out ▸ **restaurant d'entreprise** staff canteen *UK ou* cafeteria *US* ▸ **restaurant universitaire** ≃ university cafeteria *ou* refectory.

restaurateur, trice [rɛstɔratœr, tris] **nm, f 1.** CULIN restaurant owner **2.** ART restorer.

restauration [rɛstɔrasjɔ̃] **nf 1.** CULIN restaurant business ▸ **restauration rapide** fast food **2.** ART & POLIT restoration.
◆ ***Restauration*** **nf : la Restauration** the Restoration.

restaurer [3] [rɛstɔre] **vt** to restore.
◆ ***se restaurer*** **vp** to have something to eat.

reste [rɛst] **nm 1.** [de lait, temps] **: le reste (de)** the rest (of) **2.** MATH remainder ▸ **ne pas être en reste (avec)** not to be outdone (by).
◆ ***restes*** **nmpl 1.** [de repas] leftovers **2.** [de mort] remains.
◆ ***au reste, du reste*** **loc adv** besides.
◆ ***pour le reste*** **loc adv** as for the rest.

rester [3] [rɛste] ■ **vi 1.** [dans lieu, état] to stay, to remain ▸ **restez calme!** stay *ou* keep calm! ▸ **rester sur** to retain **2.** [se perpétuer] to endure **3.** [subsister] to remain, to be left ▸ **le seul bien qui me reste** the only thing I have left **4.** [s'arrêter] **: en rester à qqch** to stop at sthg ▸ **en rester là** to finish there
▸▸ **y rester** *fam* [mourir] to pop one's clogs *UK*.
■ **v impers : il en reste un peu** there's still a little left ▸ **il te reste de l'argent?** do you still have some money left? ▸ **il reste beaucoup à faire** there is still a lot to be done ▸ **il reste que..., il n'en reste pas moins que...** the fact remains that... ▸ **reste à savoir si...** it remains to be seen whether...

restituer [7] [rɛstitɥe] **vt 1.** [objet volé] to return, to restore / [argent] to refund, to return **2.** [archives, texte] to reconstruct **3.** [énergie] to release **4.** [son] to reproduce.

restitution [rɛstitysjɔ̃] **nf 1.** [d'argent, objet volé] return **2.** [d'archives, de texte] reconstruction **3.** [d'énergie] release **4.** [de son] reproduction.

resto [rɛsto] **nm** *fam* restaurant ▸ **les restos du cœur** *charity food distribution centres* ▸ **resto-U** UNIV university refectory, cafeteria.

Restoroute® [rɛstorut] **nm** motorway cafe *UK*, highway restaurant *US*.

restreignais, restreignions ➤ ***restreindre***.

restreindre [81] [rɛstrɛ̃dr] **vt** to restrict.
◆ ***se restreindre*** **vp 1.** [domaine, champ] to narrow **2.** [personne] to cut back ▸ **se restreindre dans qqch** to restrict sthg.

restreint, e [rɛstrɛ̃, ɛ̃t] **pp** ➤ ***restreindre***.

restrictif, ive [rɛstriktif, iv] **adj** restrictive, limited.

restriction [rɛstriksjɔ̃] **nf** **1.** [condition] condition ▸ **sans restriction** unconditionally **2.** [limitation] restriction.
◆ ***restrictions*** **nfpl** [alimentaires] rationing *(U)*.

restructuration [rəstryktyrasjɔ̃] **nf** **1.** [d'un quartier, d'une ville] redevelopment **2.** [d'une société, d'un service] restructuring, reorganization.

restructurer [3] [rəstryktyre] **vt** to restructure.

résultant, e [rezyltɑ̃, ɑ̃t] **adj** resulting.
◆ ***résultante*** **nf** **1.** [sciences] resultant **2.** [conséquence] consequence, outcome.

résultat [rezylta] **nm** result / [d'action] outcome.
◆ ***résultats*** **nmpl** results.

résulter [3] [rezylte] ■ **vi : résulter de** to be the result of, to result from.
■ **v impers : il en résulte que...** as a result,...

résumé [rezyme] **nm** summary, résumé ▸ **en résumé** [pour conclure] to sum up / [en bref] in brief, summarized.

résumer [3] [rezyme] **vt** to summarize.
◆ ***se résumer*** **vp** **1.** [suj: personne] to sum up **2.** [se réduire] **: se résumer à qqch/à faire qqch** to come down to sthg/to doing sthg.

FAUX AMIS / FALSE FRIENDS

résumer

Resume is not a translation of the French word *résumer*. Resume is translated by *reprendre*.
▸ Normal service will be resumed by the end of the week / *Le service reprendra normalement à la fin de la semaine*

résurgence [rezyrʒɑ̃s] **nf** resurgence.

resurgir [rəsyrʒir] = ***ressurgir***.

résurrection [rezyrɛksjɔ̃] **nf** resurrection.

rétablir [32] [retablir] **vt** **1.** [gén] to restore / [malade] to restore (to health) **2.** [communications, contact] to re-establish **3.** [dans emploi] **: rétablir qqn (dans)** to reinstate sb (in).
◆ ***se rétablir*** **vp** **1.** [silence] to return, to be restored **2.** [malade] to recover **3.** [gymnastique] to pull o.s. up.

rétablissement [retablismɑ̃] **nm** **1.** [d'ordre] restoration **2.** [de communications] re-establishment **3.** [de malade] recovery **4.** [dans emploi] reinstatement **5.** [gymnastique] pull-up.

retaper [3] [rətape] **vt** **1.** [maison, canapé] to do up **2.** [lettre] to retype **3.** *fam* [personne] to set up.
◆ ***se retaper*** **vp** *fam* [personne] to get back on one's feet.

retard [rətar] **nm** **1.** [délai] delay ▸ **être en retard** [sur heure] to be late / [sur échéance] to be behind ▸ **retard de paiement** late payment ▸ **il est en retard dans ses paiements** he's behind *ou* in arrears with (his) payments ▸ **être en retard sur son temps** to be behind the times ▸ **nous avons rendu nos épreuves en retard** we were late handing in our tests ▸ **avoir du retard** to be late *ou* delayed ▸ **ma montre a plusieurs minutes de retard** my watch is several minutes slow ▸ **le peloton est arrivé avec cinq minutes de retard sur le vainqueur** the pack arrived five minutes after *ou* behind the winner ▸ **se mettre en retard** to make o.s. late ▸ **rattraper son retard** to make up lost time ▸ **après bien des retards** after much delay **2.** [de pays, peuple, personne] backwardness ▸ **retard scolaire** learning difficulties ▸ **il doit combler son retard en physique** he's got to catch up in physics ▸ **nous avons comblé notre retard industriel en quelques années** we caught up on *ou* we closed the gap in our industrial development in a few years.

retardataire [rətardatɛr] ■ **nmf** **1.** [en retard] latecomer **2.** [enfant] backward *ou* retarded person.
■ **adj** **1.** [sur heure] late **2.** [idée, enfant] backward.

retardement [rətardəmɑ̃] **nm : à retardement** belatedly ; voir aussi ***bombe***.

retarder [3] [rətarde] ■ **vt** **1.** [personne, train] to delay / [sur échéance] to put back ▸ **retarder qqn dans qqch** to delay sb in sthg **2.** [ajourner - rendez-vous] to put back *ou* off / [- départ] to put back *ou* off, to delay **3.** [montre] to put back.
■ **vi** **1.** [horloge] to be slow **2.** *fam* [ne pas être au courant] to be behind the times **3.** [être en décalage] **: retarder sur** to be out of step *ou* tune with.

retendre [73] [rətɑ̃dr] **vt** to retighten.

retenir [40] [rətnir] **vt** **1.** [physiquement - objet, personne, cri] to hold back / [- souffle] to hold ▸ **retenir qqn de faire qqch** to stop *ou* restrain sb from doing sthg ▸ **retiens le chien, il va sauter!** hold the dog back, it's going to jump! **2.** [retarder] to keep, to detain ▸ **retenir qqn à dîner** to have sb stay for dinner **3.** [montant, impôt] to keep back to withhold ▸ **sommes retenues à la base *ou* source** sums deducted at source **4.** [chambre] to reserve **5.** [leçon, cours] to remember ▸ **et surtout, retiens bien ce qu'on t'a dit** and above all, remember *ou* don't forget what you've been told **6.** [projet] to accept, to adopt **7.** [eau, chaleur] to retain **8.** MATH to carry ▸ **je pose 5 et je retiens 4** I put down

COMMENT EXPRIMER...

un résumé de ses idées

All in all, it was a great success / Dans l'ensemble, ça a été une vraie réussite
It wasn't that bad in the end / Finalement, ce n'était pas si mal
All things considered, we didn't do too badly / En fin de compte, on ne s'en est pas trop mal tiré
To cut a long story short, she's decided to come next week instead / Bref, elle a décidé de venir plutôt la semaine prochaine
What it all boils down to is we need more money / Tout ça pour dire qu'on a besoin de plus d'argent
To sum up, the majority of the feedback was positive / En résumé, la plupart des commentaires ont été positifs

5 and carry 4 **9.** [intérêt, attention] to hold ▸ **votre CV a retenu toute mon attention** I studied your CV with great interest.

◆ ***se retenir*** **vp 1.** [s'accrocher] **: se retenir à** to hold onto **2.** [se contenir] to hold on ▸ **se retenir de faire qqch** to refrain from doing sthg.

rétention [retɑ̃sjɔ̃] **nf** MÉD retention.

retentir [32] [rətɑ̃tir] **vi 1.** [son] to ring (out) **2.** [pièce, rue] **: retentir de** to resound with **3.** *fig* [fatigue, blessure] **: retentir sur** to have an effect on.

retentissant**, **e [rətɑ̃tisɑ̃, ɑ̃t] **adj** resounding.

retentissement [rətɑ̃tismɑ̃] **nm 1.** [de mesure] repercussions *pl* **2.** [de spectacle] effect.

retenu**, **e [rətny] **pp** ➤ ***retenir***.

retenue [rətny] **nf 1.** [prélèvement] deduction ▸ **retenue à la source** deduction at source **2.** MATH amount carried **3.** SCOL detention **4.** *fig* [de personne - dans relations] reticence ⁄ [- dans comportement] restraint ▸ **sans retenue** without restraint.

réticence [retisɑ̃s] **nf** [hésitation] hesitation, reluctance ▸ **avec réticence** hesitantly ▸ **sans réticence** without hesitation.

réticent**, **e [retisɑ̃, ɑ̃t] **adj** hesitant, reluctant.

retiendrai**, **retiendras ➤ ***retenir***.

retienne**, **retiennes ➤ ***retenir***.

rétif**, **ive [retif, iv] **adj** restive.

rétine [retin] **nf** retina.

retiré**, **e [rətire] **adj 1.** [lieu] remote, isolated ⁄ [vie] quiet **2.** [personne] retired.

retirer [3] [rətire] **vt 1.** [vêtement, emballage] to take off, to remove ▸ **il aida l'enfant à retirer son manteau** he helped the child off with his coat ⁄ [permis, jouet] to take away ▸ **retirer qqch à qqn** to take sthg away from sb ▸ **on lui a retiré son permis de conduire** he's been banned from driving **2.** [plainte] to withdraw, to take back **3.** [sortir - personne] to remove, to extricate ⁄ [- casserole] to remove **4.** [métal] to extract **5.** [avantages, bénéfices] **: retirer qqch de qqch** to get *ou* derive sthg from sthg ▸ **retirer un bénéfice important d'une affaire** to make a large profit out of a deal **6.** [bagages, billet] to collect ⁄ [argent] to withdraw ▸ **j'ai retiré un peu d'argent de mon compte** I drew *ou* withdrew some money from my bank account.

◆ ***se retirer*** **vp 1.** [s'isoler] to withdraw, to retreat ▸ **il est tard, je vais me retirer** *sout* it's late, I'm going to retire *ou* to withdraw **2.** [des affaires] **: se retirer (de)** to retire (from) **3.** [refluer] to recede.

retombée [rətɔ̃be] **nf 1.** *littéraire* [déclin] **: la retombée de l'enthousiasme populaire** the decline in popular enthusiasm **2.** ARCHIT & CONSTR springing.

◆ ***retombées*** **nfpl** [physique nucléaire] fallout ▸ **retombées radioactives** radioactive fallout ⁄ *fig* [répercussions] repercussions, effects ▸ **les retombées d'une campagne publicitaire** the results of an advertising campaign.

retomber [3] [rətɔ̃be] **vi 1.** [gymnaste, chat] to land ▸ **se laisser retomber sur son lit** to flop *ou* to fall back onto one's bed **2.** [redevenir] **: retomber malade** to relapse **3.** [pluie] to fall again **4.** *fig* [colère] to die away **5.** [cheveux] to hang down **6.** *fig* [responsabilité] **: retomber sur** to fall on ▸ **tous les torts sont retombés sur elle** she had to bear the brunt of all the blame **7.** [dans un état] to fall back, to lapse *sout* ▸ **retomber dans les mêmes erreurs** to make the same mistakes again ▸ **retomber en enfance** to go into one's second childhood **8.** *fam* [rencontrer à nouveau] **: retomber sur qqn** to bump into *ou* to come across sb again ▸ **retomber sur qqch** to come across sthg again.

retordre [76] [rətɔrdr] **vt** [linge] to wring (out) again.

rétorquer [3] [retɔrke] **vt** to retort ▸ **rétorquer à qqn que...** to retort to sb that...

retors**, **e [rətɔr, ɔrs] **adj** wily.

rétorsion [retɔrsjɔ̃] **nf** retaliation ▸ **mesures de rétorsion** reprisals.

retouche [rətuʃ] **nf 1.** [de texte, vêtement] alteration **2.** ART & PHOTO touching up.

retoucher [3] [rətuʃe] **vt 1.** [texte, vêtement] to alter **2.** ART & PHOTO to touch up.

retour [rətur] **nm 1.** [gén] return ▸ **à mon/ton retour** when I/you get back, on my/your return ▸ **au retour de** [étant arrivé] on my/his *etc* return from ⁄ [en cours de route] on the way back ▸ **être de retour (de)** to be back (from) ▸ **de retour de Rio, je tentai de la voir** on my return from Rio, I tried to see her ▸ **sur le chemin** *ou* **la route du retour** on the way back ▸ **'retour à l'expéditeur** *ou* **l'envoyeur'** 'return to sender' ▸ **retour en arrière** flashback ▸ **retour de bâton** kickback ▸ **retour à la case départ** [dans un jeu] back to the start ⁄ *fig* back to square one *ou* to the drawing board ▸ **retour de chariot** carriage return ▸ **retour de flamme** backfire ▸ **retour de manivelle** *ou* **de bâton** *fam fig* kickback ▸ **en retour** in return ▸ **sans retour** for ever ▸ **(être) sur le retour** *fig* (to be) over the hill ▸ **une beauté sur le retour** a waning beauty **2.** [trajet] journey back, return journey ▸ **combien coûte le retour** how much is the return fare? **3.** INFORM **: retour (d'information)** (information) feedback **4.** FIN **: retour sur investissements** return on investments.

retournement [rəturnəmɑ̃] **nm** turnaround, turnabout ▸ **retournement de situation** reversal.

retourner [3] [rəturne] ■ **vt** *(v aux : être)* **1.** [carte, matelas] to turn over ⁄ [terre] to turn (over) **2.** [pull, poche] to turn inside out **3.** [compliment, objet prêté] **: retourner qqch (à qqn)** to return sthg (to sb) ▸ **je lui ai retourné son** *ou* **le compliment** I returned the compliment **4.** [lettre, colis] to send back, to return **5.** *fam fig* [personne] to shake up ▸ **en être tout retourné** to be shaken up.

■ **vi** *(v aux : être)* to come/go back ▸ **je n'y étais pas retourné depuis des années** I had not been back there for years ▸ **retourner à** [personne] to go back *ou* return to ⁄ [objet] to be returned to ▸ **retourner à un stade antérieur** to revert to an earlier stage ▸ **retourner en arrière** *ou* **sur ses pas** to retrace one's steps.

◆ ***se retourner*** **vp 1.** [basculer] to turn over **2.** [pivoter] to turn round *UK ou* around *US* ▸ **partir sans se retourner** to leave without looking back **3.** *fam fig* [s'adapter] to sort o.s. out *UK* ▸ **ils ne me laissent pas le temps de me retourner** [de décider] they won't give me time to make a decision ⁄ [de me reprendre] they won't give me time to sort things out **4.** [rentrer] **: s'en retourner** to go back (home) **5.** *fig* [s'opposer] **: se retourner contre** to turn against ▸ **tout cela finira par se retourner contre toi** all this will eventually backfire on you.

retracer [16] [rətrase] **vt** **1.** [ligne] to redraw **2.** [événement] to relate.

rétracter [3] [retrakte] **vt** to retract.
◆ ***se rétracter*** **vp** **1.** [se contracter] to retract **2.** [se dédire] to back down.

retraduire [98] [rətradɥir] **vt** to translate again.

retrait [rətrɛ] **nm** **1.** [gén] withdrawal ▸ **retrait du permis** disqualification from driving **2.** BANQUE **: faire un retrait** to withdraw money **3.** [de bagages] collection **4.** [des eaux] ebbing.
◆ ***en retrait*** **loc adj & loc adv** **1.** [maison] set back from the road ▸ **rester en retrait** *fig* to hang back **2.** [texte] indented.

retraite [rətrɛt] **nf** **1.** [gén] retreat ▸ **battre en retraite** to beat a retreat **2.** [cessation d'activité] retirement ▸ **être à la retraite** to be retired ▸ **prendre sa retraite** to retire ▸ **retraite anticipée** early retirement ▸ **retraite complémentaire** supplementary pension, private pension **3.** [revenu] (retirement) pension.

CULTURE
Retraite

In France, workers in the private sector who have reached the retirement age of 60 and have 40 years' worth of social security contributions are entitled to the **régime de base**, which pays them half their final basic salary. This amount is reduced for those workers who are under 65 or who have not made sufficient social security contributions. There is also a **régime complémentaire** for workers in industry, mining and agriculture. As is the case in both the UK and the US, France's pension scheme is in trouble. The length of time that workers must pay contributions into the system increases every year, and it is likely that in a few years they will be forced to make even higher payments while seeing their pensions getting smaller and smaller.

retraité, e [rətrete] ■ **adj** **1.** [personne] retired **2.** TECHNOL reprocessed.
■ **nm, f** retired person, pensioner *UK*.

retraitement [rətrɛtmɑ̃] **nm** reprocessing ▸ **centre *ou* usine de retraitement (des déchets nucléaires)** (nuclear) reprocessing plant.

retranchement [rətrɑ̃ʃmɑ̃] **nm** entrenchment ▸ **poursuivre *ou* forcer qqn dans ses derniers retranchements** *fig* to drive sb into a corner.

retrancher [3] [rətrɑ̃ʃe] **vt** **1.** [passage] **: retrancher qqch (de)** to cut sthg out (from), to remove sthg (from) **2.** [montant] **: retrancher qqch (de)** to take sthg away (from), to deduct sthg (from).
◆ ***se retrancher*** **vp** to entrench o.s. ▸ **se retrancher derrière/dans** *fig* to take refuge behind/in.

retransmettre [84] [rətrɑ̃smɛtr] **vt** to broadcast.

retransmis, e [rətrɑ̃smi, iz] **pp** ➤ ***retransmettre***.

retransmission [rətrɑ̃smisjɔ̃] **nf** broadcast.

retravailler [3] [rətravaje] ■ **vt : retravailler qqch** to work on sthg again.
■ **vi** to start work again.

rétrécir [32] [retresir] ■ **vt** [tissu] to take in.
■ **vi** [tissu] to shrink.
◆ ***se rétrécir*** **vp** [tissu] to shrink.

rétrécissement [retresismɑ̃] **nm** **1.** [de vêtement] shrinkage **2.** MÉD stricture.

retremper [3] [rətrɑ̃pe] **vt** **1.** [linge] to resoak **2.** [acier] to requench.
◆ ***se retremper*** **vp** to go back into the water / *fig* to reimmerse o.s.

rétribuer [7] [retribɥe] **vt** **1.** [employé] to pay **2.** [travail] to pay for.

rétribution [retribysjɔ̃] **nf** remuneration.

rétro [retro] ■ **nm** **1.** [style] old style *ou* fashion **2.** *fam* [rétroviseur] rearview mirror.
■ **adj inv** old-style.

rétroactif, ive [retrɔaktif, iv] **adj** retrospective.

rétroactivement [retrɔaktivmɑ̃] **adv** retrospectively.

rétrocéder [18] [retrɔsede] **vt** to retrocede.

rétrocession [retrɔsɛsjɔ̃] **nf** retrocession.

rétrograde [retrɔgrad] **adj** *péj* reactionary.

rétrograder [3] [retrɔgrade] ■ **vt** to demote.
■ **vi** **1.** AUTO to change down *UK*, to downshift *US* **2.** [dans une hiérarchie] to move down.

rétroprojecteur [retrɔprɔʒɛktœr] **nm** overhead projector.

rétrospectif, ive [retrɔspɛktif, iv] **adj** retrospective.
◆ ***rétrospective*** **nf** retrospective.

rétrospectivement [retrɔspɛktivmɑ̃] **adv** retrospectively.

retroussé, e [rətruse] **adj** **1.** [manches, pantalon] rolled up **2.** [nez] turned up.

retrousser [3] [rətruse] **vt** **1.** [manches, pantalon] to roll up **2.** [lèvres] to curl.

retrouvailles [rətruvaj] **nfpl** reunion *sg*.

retrouver [3] [rətruve] **vt** **1.** [gén] to find ▸ **a-t-elle retrouvé sa clef?** [elle-même] did she find her key? / [grâce à autrui] did she get her key back? ▸ **ça y est, j'ai retrouvé le mot!** that's it, the word's come back to me now! [appétit] to recover, to regain **2.** [reconnaître] to recognize ▸ **on retrouve les mêmes propriétés dans les polymères** the same properties are to be found in polymers **3.** [ami] to meet, to see ▸ **retrouve-moi en bas** meet me downstairs.
◆ ***se retrouver*** **vp** **1.** [entre amis] to meet (up) again ▸ **on se retrouve au café?** shall we meet up *ou* see each other at the cafe? **2.** [être de nouveau] to find o.s. again ▸ **se retrouver dans la même situation (qu'avant)** to find o.s. back in the same situation (as before) **3.** [par hasard] to end up ▸ **tu vas te retrouver à l'hôpital** you'll end up

hospital **4.** [s'orienter] to find one's way ▸ **ne pas s'y retrouver** [dans ses papiers] to be completely lost **5.** [erreur, style] to be found, to crop up **6.** [financièrement] **: s'y retrouver** *fam* to break even.

rétroviseur [retrɔvizœr] **nm** rearview mirror.

réunification [reynifikasjɔ̃] **nf** reunification.

réunifier [9] [reynifje] **vt** to reunify.

réunion [reynjɔ̃] **nf 1.** [séance] meeting ▸ **dites que je suis en réunion** say that I'm at *ou* in a meeting ▸ **réunion du Parlement** Parliamentary session *UK* **2.** [jonction] union, merging **3.** [d'amis, de famille] reunion ▸ **réunion d'anciens élèves** reunion of former pupils **4.** [collection] collection **5.** SPORT meeting ▸ **réunion d'athlétisme** athletics meeting ▸ **réunion hippique** horse show.

Réunion [reunjɔ̃] **nf : (l'île de) la Réunion** Réunion ▸ **à la Réunion** in Réunion.

réunionnais, e [reynjɔnɛ, ɛz] **adj** of/from Réunion Island.
◆ ***Réunionnais, e*** **nm, f** native *ou* inhabitant of Réunion.

réunir [32] [reynir] **vt 1.** [fonds] to collect **2.** [extrémités] to put together, to bring together **3.** [qualités] to combine **4.** [personnes] to bring together / [après séparation] to reunite.
◆ ***se réunir*** **vp 1.** [personnes] to meet **2.** [entreprises] to combine / [états] to unite **3.** [fleuves, rues] to converge.

réussi, e [reysi] **adj** successful ▸ **c'est réussi!** *fig & iron* congratulations!, well done!

réussir [32] [reysir] ■ **vi 1.** [personne, affaire] to succeed, to be a success ▸ **il a réussi dans la vie** he's done well in life, he's a successful man ▸ **réussir à faire qqch** to succeed in doing sthg ▸ **j'ai réussi à le réparer** I managed to mend it **2.** [convenir] **: réussir à** to agree with ▸ **le café lui réussit/ne lui réussit pas** coffee agrees/doesn't agree with him.
■ **vt 1.** [portrait, plat] to make a success of ▸ **réussir un coup fumant** to pull off a master stroke ▸ **réussir sa vie** to make a success of one's life **2.** [examen] to pass.

réussite [reysit] **nf 1.** [succès] success **2.** [jeu de cartes] patience *UK*, solitaire *US*.

réutilisable [reytilizabl] **adj** reusable ▸ **non réutilisable** disposable, throwaway.

réutiliser [3] [reytilize] **vt** to reuse.

revaloir [60] [rəvalwar] **vt : revaloir qqch à qqn** [avec reconnaissance] to repay sb for sthg / [avec hostilité] to get even with sb for sthg.

revalorisation [rəvalɔrizasjɔ̃] **nf** [de monnaie] revaluation / [de salaires] raising / *fig* [d'idée] rehabilitation.

revaloriser [3] [rəvalɔrize] **vt** [monnaie] to revalue / [salaires] to raise / *fig* [idée, doctrine] to rehabilitate.

revanchard, e [rəvɑ̃ʃar, ard] *péj* ■ **adj** of revenge.
■ **nm, f** advocate of revenge.

revanche [rəvɑ̃ʃ] **nf 1.** [vengeance] revenge ▸ **prendre sa revanche** to take one's revenge **2.** SPORT return (match).
◆ ***en revanche*** **loc adv 1.** [par contre] on the other hand **2.** [en contrepartie] in return.

rêvasser [3] [rɛvase] **vi** to daydream.

revaudrai, revaudras ➤ ***revaloir***.

rêve [rɛv] **nm** dream ▸ **de rêve** *fig* dream *(avant n)*.

rêvé, e [rɛve] **adj** ideal.

revêche [rəvɛʃ] **adj** surly.

réveil [revɛj] **nm 1.** [de personne] waking (up) / *fig* awakening ▸ **j'attendrai ton réveil pour partir** I'll wait until you have woken up *ou* until you are awake before I leave ▸ **au réveil** on waking (up) ▸ **à mon réveil il était là** when I woke up he was there **2.** [pendule] alarm clock ▸ **réveil téléphonique** wake-up service ▸ **j'ai mis le réveil (à 7 h)** I've set the alarm (for 7 o'clock) **3.** [de volcan] reawakening.

réveiller [4] [reveje] **vt 1.** [personne] to wake up **2.** [courage] to revive.
◆ ***se réveiller*** **vp 1.** [personne] to wake (up) **2.** [ambitions] to reawaken.

réveillon [revɛjɔ̃] **nm 1.** [jour - de Noël] Christmas Eve / [- de nouvel an] New Year's Eve **2.** [repas - de Noël] Christmas Eve meal / [- de nouvel an] New Year's Eve meal.

réveillonner [3] [revɛjɔne] **vi** to have a Christmas Eve/New Year's Eve meal.

COMMENT EXPRIMER...

qu'on dirige une réunion

Good morning, everyone. Thank you for coming / Bonjour à tous. Merci d'être venus
Is there anyone still to come? / Y a-t-il des retardataires ?
Could we make a start now, please? / Pouvons-nous commencer maintenant, s'il vous plaît ?
The first item on the agenda is our new product launch / La première chose à l'ordre du jour est le lancement de notre nouveau produit
Can we move on to the second point? / Pouvons-nous passer au deuxième point ?
Let's break for coffee / Arrêtons-nous pour prendre un café
Does anyone else have any comments? / Y a-t-il d'autres commentaires ?
Any other business? / D'autres questions à l'ordre du jour ?
If no one has anything to add, I'll bring this meeting to a close / Si personne n'a rien à ajouter, nous pouvons ajourner cette réunion

révélateur, ***trice*** [revelatœr, tris] **adj** revealing.
◆ ***révélateur*** **nm** PHOTO developer / *fig* [ce qui révèle] indication.

révélation [revelasjɔ̃] **nf 1.** [gén] revelation **2.** [artiste] discovery.

révéler [18] [revele] **vt 1.** [gén] to reveal **2.** [artiste] to discover.
◆ ***se révéler*** **vp 1.** [apparaître] to be revealed **2.** [s'avérer] to prove to be.

revenant [rəvnɑ̃] **nm 1.** [fantôme] spirit, ghost **2.** *fam* [personne] stranger.

revendeur, ***euse*** [rəvɑ̃dœr, øz] **nm, f** retailer.

revendication [rəvɑ̃dikasjɔ̃] **nf** claim, demand.

revendiquer [3] [rəvɑ̃dike] **vt** [dû, responsabilité] to claim / [avec force] to demand.

revendre [73] [rəvɑ̃dr] **vt 1.** [après utilisation] to resell **2.** [vendre plus de] to sell more of.

revendu, ***e*** [rəvɑ̃dy] **pp** ➤ ***revendre***.

revenir [40] [rəvnir] **vi 1.** [gén] to come back, to return ▸ **je reviens (tout de suite)** I'll be (right) back ▸ **la lettre m'est revenue** the letter was returned to me ▸ **revenir de** to come back from, to return from ▸ **revenir à** to come back to, to return to ▸ **revenir au point de départ** to go back to the starting point / *fig* to be back to square one ▸ **revenir à une plus juste vision des choses** to come round to a more balanced view of things ▸ **revenir sur** [sujet] to go over again / [décision] to go back on ▸ **ma décision est prise, je ne reviendrai pas dessus** my mind is made up and I'm not going to change it ▸ **revenir à soi** to come to
2. [mot, sujet] to crop up
3. [à l'esprit] **: revenir à** to come back to ▸ **son nom ne me revient pas (à la mémoire)** his name escapes me *ou* has slipped my mind
4. [impliquer] **: cela revient au même/à dire que...** it amounts to the same thing/to saying (that)...
5. [coûter] **: revenir à** to come to, to amount to ▸ **revenir cher** to be expensive
6. [honneur, tâche] **: revenir à** to fall to ▸ **avec les honneurs qui lui reviennent** with the honours (which are) due to her ▸ **c'est à lui qu'il revient de...** it is up to him to... ▸ **tout le mérite t'en revient** the credit is all yours, you get all the credit for it
7. CULIN **: faire revenir** to brown
▸▸ **sa tête ne me revient pas** I don't like the look of him/her ▸ **il n'en revenait pas** he couldn't get over it ▸ **je n'en reviens pas qu'il ait dit ça!** it's amazing he should say that!, I can't get over him saying that! ▸ **revenir de loin** to have been at death's door.

revente [rəvɑ̃t] **nf** resale.

revenu, ***e*** [rəvny] **pp** ➤ ***revenir***.
◆ ***revenu*** **nm** [de pays] revenue / [de personne] earnings, income / **: revenu annuel** annual earnings *ou* income ▸ **revenu disponible** disposable income ▸ **revenu imposable** taxable income.
◆ ***revenus*** **nmpl** incomings.

rêver [4] [rɛve] ■ **vi** to dream / [rêvasser] to daydream ▸ **toi ici? (dites-moi que) je rêve!** you here? I must be dreaming! ▸ **ça fait rêver!** that's the stuff that dreams are made of! ▸ **faut pas rêver!** let's not get carried away! ▸ **rêver de/à** to dream of/about ▸ **je n'avais jamais osé rêver d'un bonheur pareil!** I'd never have dared dream of such happiness! ▸ **elle en rêve la nuit** *litt* she has dreams about it at night / *fig* she's obsessed by it ▸ **on ne saurait rêver (une) occasion plus propice** you couldn't wish for a more appropriate occasion.
■ **vt** to dream ▸ **rêver que** to dream (that).

réverbération [reverberasjɔ̃] **nf** reverberation.

réverbère [reverbɛr] **nm** street lamp *ou* light.

réverbérer [18] [reverbere] **vt** to reverberate.

reverdir [32] [rəverdir] **vi** to become green again.

révérence [reverɑ̃s] **nf 1.** [salut] bow **2.** *littéraire* [déférence] reverence.

révérencieux, ***euse*** [reverɑ̃sjø, øz] **adj** reverent.

révérend, ***e*** [reverɑ̃, ɑ̃d] **adj** reverend.
◆ ***révérend*** **nm** reverend.

révérer [18] [revere] **vt** to revere.

rêverie [rɛvri] **nf** reverie.

revers [rəvɛr] **nm 1.** [de main] back / [de pièce] reverse ▸ **prendre à revers** to capture from the rear *ou* from behind ▸ **le revers de la médaille** *fig* the other side of the coin **2.** [de veste] lapel / [de pantalon] turn-up *UK*, cuff *US* **3.** TENNIS backhand **4.** *fig* [de fortune] reversal.

reverser [3] [rəvɛrse] **vt 1.** [liquide] to pour out more of **2.** FIN **: reverser qqch sur** to pay sthg into ▸ **reverser qqch dans** to invest sthg in.

réversible [reversibl] **adj** reversible.

revêtement [rəvɛtmɑ̃] **nm** surface.

revêtir [44] [rəvetir] **vt 1.** [mur, surface] **: revêtir (de)** to cover (with) **2.** [aspect] to take on, to assume **3.** [vêtement] to put on / [personne] to dress **4.** *sout* [de dignité, de pouvoir] **: revêtir qqn de** to invest sb with.

revêts ➤ ***revêtir***.

revêtu, ***e*** [rəvety] **pp** ➤ ***revêtir***.

rêveur, ***euse*** [rɛvœr, øz] ■ **adj** dreamy.
■ **nm, f** dreamer.

reviendrai, ***reviendras*** ➤ ***revenir***.

revient [rəvjɛ̃] ➤ ***prix***.

revigorer [3] [rəvigɔre] **vt** to invigorate.

revirement [rəvirmɑ̃] **nm** [gén] change / POLIT about-turn.

révisable [revizabl] **adj** subject to review.

réviser [3] [revize] **vt 1.** [réexaminer, modifier] to revise, to review **2.** SCOL to revise *UK*, to review *US* **3.** [machine] to check.

révision [revizjɔ̃] **nf 1.** [réexamen, modification] revision, review **2.** [de machine] checkup / [d'une voiture] service.
◆ ***révisions*** **nfpl** SCOL revision *sg UK*, review *sg US*.

révisionnisme [revizjɔnism] **nm** revisionism.

révisionniste [revizjɔnist] **nmf & adj** revisionist.

revisser [3] [rəvise] **vt** to screw back again.

revitaliser [3] [rəvitalize] **vt** to revitalize.

revivre [90] [rəvivr] ■ **vi** [personne] to come back to life, to revive / *fig* [espoir] to be revived, to revive ▸ **faire revivre** to revive.

■ **vt** to relive ▸ **faire revivre qqch à qqn** to bring sthg back to sb.

révocation [revɔkasjɔ̃] **nf 1.** [de loi] revocation **2.** [de fonctionnaire] dismissal.

revoici [rəvwasi] **prép : me revoici!** it's me again!, I'm back!

revoilà [rəvwala] **prép : revoilà le printemps!** it looks like spring's here again! ▸ **enfin, te revoilà!** you're back at last! ▸ **les revoilà!** there they are again!
▸▸ **nous y revoilà, je m'y attendais!** here we go again! I just knew it.

revoir [62] [rəvwar] **vt 1.** [renouer avec] to see again **2.** [corriger, étudier] to revise *UK*, to review *US*.
◆ ***se revoir*** **vp** [amis] to see each other again / [professionnellement] to meet again.
◆ ***au revoir*** **interj** & **nm** goodbye.

révoltant, e [revɔltɑ̃, ɑ̃t] **adj** revolting.

révolte [revɔlt] **nf** revolt ▸ **inciter** *ou* **pousser qqn à la révolte** to incite sb to revolt ▸ **être en révolte contre** to be in revolt against.

révolter [3] [revɔlte] **vt** to disgust.
◆ ***se révolter*** **vp : se révolter (contre)** to revolt (against).

révolu, e [revɔly] **adj** past ▸ **avoir 15 ans révolus** ADMIN to be over 15.

révolution [revɔlysjɔ̃] **nf 1.** [gén] revolution ▸ **la Révolution française** the French Revolution **2.** *fam* [effervescence] uproar ▸ **en révolution** in an uproar.

CULTURE

La Révolution française

This popular revolt against France's Old Regime and the monarchy left a deep mark on the country's history. Revolutionaries abolished the special privileges of the monarchy and clergy, creating the middle class. The storming of the Bastille prison on the 14th of July 1789 is seen as the start of the Revolution. Among its other notable events are the Declaration of the Rights of Man (1789), the beheading of Louis XVI (1793), and the bloody Reign of Terror (1793–1794). Napoleon Bonaparte's seizure of power in 1799 effectively brought the Revolution to an end. While French radicals were inspired by the new American democracy, their own movement helped spark social change in other countries such as Poland.

révolutionnaire [revɔlysjɔnɛr] **nmf** & **adj** revolutionary.

révolutionner [3] [revɔlysjɔne] **vt 1.** [transformer] to revolutionize **2.** [mettre en émoi] to stir up.

revolver [revɔlvɛr] **nm** revolver.

révoquer [3] [revɔke] **vt 1.** [fonctionnaire] to dismiss **2.** [loi] to revoke.

revue [rəvy] **nf 1.** [gén] review ▸ **revue de presse** press review ▸ **passer en revue** *fig* to review **2.** [défilé] march-past **3.** [magazine] magazine **4.** [spectacle] revue.

révulsé, e [revylse] **adj** [traits, visage] contorted ▸ **révulsé de douleur** [visage] contorted with pain ▸ **les yeux révulsés** with his eyes rolled upwards.

révulser [3] [revylse] **vt** to disgust.
◆ ***se révulser*** **vp** to contort.

rewriting [rərajtiŋ] **nm** rewriting.

Reykjavik [rɛkjavik] **npr** Reykjavik.

rez-de-chaussée [redʃose] **nm inv** ground floor *UK*, first floor *US*.

rez-de-jardin [redʒardɛ̃] **nm inv** garden level.

RF abr de ***République française***.

RFA (abr de ***République fédérale d'Allemagne***) **nf** FRG.

RFI (abr de ***Radio France Internationale***) **nf** *French world service radio station*.

RFO (abr de ***Radio-télévision française d'outre-mer***) **nf** *French overseas broadcasting service*.

r.g. (abr écrite de ***rive gauche***) *left (south) bank of the Seine*.

RG (abr de ***Renseignements généraux***) **nmpl** *police department responsible for political security*, ≃ Special Branch *UK*.

Rh (abr écrite de ***Rhésus***) Rh.

rhabiller [3] [rabije] **vt** to dress again.
◆ ***se rhabiller*** **vp** to get dressed again ▸ **aller se rhabiller** *fam fig* to throw in the towel.

rhapsodie, rapsodie [rapsɔdi] **nf** rhapsody.

rhénan, e [renɑ̃, an] **adj** of/from the Rhine, Rhine *(avant n)*.

rhéostat [reɔsta] **nm** rheostat.

rhésus [rezys] **nm** rhesus (factor) ▸ **rhésus positif/négatif** rhesus positive/negative.

rhétorique [retɔrik] **nf** rhetoric.

Rhin [rɛ̃] **nm : le Rhin** the Rhine.

rhinite [rinit] **nf** rhinitis *(U)*.

COMMENT EXPRIMER...

au revoir

Goodbye Mrs Jones! It was nice meeting you / Au revoir, madame ! Enchanté d'avoir fait votre connaissance
See you soon / À bientôt
See you tomorrow / À demain
See you around / À la prochaine
See you! / À plus !
Bye! / Salut !
Right, I'm off / Bon, allez, j'y vais
I have to go / Je te laisse
Take care / Fais attention à toi
All the best / Bonne continuation !
Give my love to Anne / Mes amitiés à Anne
Speak to you soon *(au téléphone)* / À bientôt

rhinocéros [rinɔserɔs] **nm** rhinoceros.

rhino-pharyngite [rinɔfarɛ̃ʒit] (pl **rhino-pharyngites**) **nf** throat infection.

rhodanien, enne [rɔdanjɛ̃, ɛn] **adj** [du Rhône] from the Rhone ▸ **le couloir rhodanien** the Rhone corridor.

Rhodes [rɔd] **npr** Rhodes ▸ **le colosse de Rhodes** the Colossus of Rhodes.

rhododendron [rɔdɔdɛ̃drɔ̃] **nm** rhododendron.

Rhône [ron] **nm : le Rhône** the (River) Rhone.

rhubarbe [rybarb] **nf** rhubarb.

rhum [rɔm] **nm** rum.

rhumatisant, e [rymatizɑ̃, ɑ̃t] **adj & nm, f** rheumatic.

rhumatismal, e, aux [rymatismal, o] **adj** rheumatic.

rhumatisme [rymatism] **nm** rheumatism.

rhumatismes [rymatism] **nmpl** rheumatism *sg* ▸ **avoir des rhumatismes** to have rheumatism.

rhumatologue [rymatɔlɔg] **nmf** rheumatologist.

rhume [rym] **nm** cold ▸ **attraper un rhume** to catch a cold ▸ **rhume des foins** hay fever.

ri [ri] **pp inv** ➤ ***rire***.

RI ■ **nm** (abr de ***régiment d'infanterie***) infantry regiment.
■ **nmpl** (abr de ***Républicains indépendants***) *right-wing French political party.*

Riad = ***Riyad***.

riant, e [rijɑ̃, ɑ̃t] **adj** smiling / *fig* cheerful.

RIB, Rib [rib] (abr de ***relevé d'identité bancaire***) **nm** bank details *(bank account identification slip).*

ribambelle [ribɑ̃bɛl] **nf : ribambelle de** string of.

ricanement [rikanmɑ̃] **nm** snigger.

ricaner [3] [rikane] **vi** to snigger.

Ricard® [rikar] **nm** *brand of pastis.*

RICE, Rice [ris] (abr de ***relevé d'identité de caisse d'épargne***) **nm** *savings bank account identification slip.*

richard, e [riʃar, ard] **nm, f** *fam péj* moneybags *sg.*

riche [riʃ] ■ **adj 1.** [gén] rich / [personne, pays] rich, wealthy ▸ **être riche comme Crésus *ou* à millions** to be as rich as Croesus *ou* Midas ▸ **on n'est pas bien riche chez nous** we're not very well-off ▸ **elle a un vocabulaire/une langue riche** she has a rich vocabulary/a tremendous command of the language ▸ **riche en *ou* de** rich in ▸ **régime riche en calcium** calcium-rich diet ▸ **la journée fut riche en émotions** the day was packed full of excitement ▸ **son premier roman est riche de promesses** his first novel is full of promise *ou* shows great promise
2. *(avant le n)* [demeure, étoffe] lavish, magnificent
3. [idée] great.
■ **nmf** rich person ▸ **les riches** the rich ▸ **nouveau riche** nouveau riche ▸ **voiture de riche** rich man's car.

richement [riʃmɑ̃] **adv** richly.

richesse [riʃɛs] **nf 1.** [de personne, pays] wealth *(U)* **2.** [d'appartement] sumptuousness *(U)* **3.** [de faune, flore] abundance ▸ **richesse en vitamines** high vitamin content.
◆ ***richesses*** **nfpl 1.** [gén] wealth *(U)* **2.** [de musée] riches.

richissime [riʃisim] **adj** super-rich.

Richter [riʃtɛr] **npr : échelle de Richter** Richter scale.

ricin [risɛ̃] **nm** castor-oil plant ▸ **huile de ricin** castor oil.

ricocher [3] [rikɔʃe] **vi** *litt & fig* to rebound / [balle d'arme] to ricochet.

ricochet [rikɔʃɛ] **nm** *litt & fig* rebound / [de balle d'arme] ricochet ▸ **par ricochet** in an indirect way.

rictus [riktys] **nm** rictus.

ride [rid] **nf** wrinkle / [de surface d'eau] ripple.

ridé, e [ride] **adj** wrinkled.

rideau, x [rido] **nm** curtain, drape *US* ▸ **rideau de douche** shower curtain ▸ **rideau de fumée** smokescreer ▸ **doubles rideaux** thick curtains ▸ **tirer *ou* ouvrir les rideaux** to draw *ou* to open the curtains ▸ **tirer *ou* fermer les rideaux** to draw *ou* to close the curtains ▸ **ça suffit, rideau!** *fam* (that's) enough!, lay off! ▸ **rideau de fer** [frontière] Iron Curtain.

rider [3] [ride] **vt 1.** [peau] to wrinkle **2.** [surface] to ruffle
◆ ***se rider*** **vp** to become wrinkled.

ridicule [ridikyl] ■ **adj** ridiculous.
■ **nm : le ridicule** ridicule ▸ **se couvrir de ridicule** t make o.s. look ridiculous ▸ **tourner qqn/qqch en ridicul** to ridicule sb/sthg.

ridiculement [ridikylmɑ̃] **adv** ridiculously.

ridiculiser [3] [ridikylize] **vt** to ridicule.
◆ ***se ridiculiser*** **vp** to make o.s. look ridiculous.

ridule [ridyl] **nf** little wrinkle.

rien [rjɛ̃] ■ **pron indéf 1.** [en contexte négatif] **: ne... rie** nothing, not... anything ▸ **ça n'a rien à voir avec toi** it got nothing to do with you, it doesn't concern you ▸ **je n'a rien fait** I've done nothing, I haven't done anything ▸ **j n'en sais rien** I don't know (anything about it), I kno nothing about it ▸ **rien ne m'intéresse** nothing interes me ▸ **il n'y a plus rien dans le réfrigérateur** there's not ing left in the fridge
2. [aucune chose] nothing ▸ **que fais-tu? rien** what a you doing? nothing ▸ **rien à déclarer** nothing to decla ▸ **rien de nouveau** nothing new ▸ **rien d'autre** nothin else ▸ **rien du tout** nothing at all ▸ **un/une rien du tout** nobody ▸ **rien à faire** it's no good ▸ **j'en ai rien à fai** *fam* ***ou* à cirer** *tfam* I don't give a damn *ou* a toss *tfam* ▸ **d rien!** don't mention it!, not at all! ▸ **pour rien** for nothin ▸ **ne le dérange pas pour rien** don't disturb him for n reason ▸ **j'ai acheté ça pour rien chez un brocanteu** I bought it for next to nothing in a second-hand shop
3. [quelque chose] anything ▸ **sans rien dire** without sayir anything ▸ **y a-t-il rien que je puisse faire?** is there not ing I can do?
■ **nm : pour un rien** [se fâcher, pleurer] for nothing, at t slightest thing ▸ **il se fâche pour un rien** he loses his te per over the slightest little thing ▸ **perdre son temps des riens** to waste one's time with trivia ▸ **en un rien temps** in no time at all.
◆ ***rien que*** **loc adv** only, just ▸ **la vérité, rien que vérité** the truth and nothing but the truth ▸ **rien que l'id des vacances la comblait** just thinking about the holid filled her with joy.
◆ ***un rien*** **loc adv** a bit, a shade ▸ **sa robe est un ri trop étroite** her dress is a bit too tight.

rieur**, **rieuse [rijœr, rijøz] **adj** cheerful.

Riga [riga] **npr** Riga.

rigide [riʒid] **adj** rigid / [muscle] tense.

rigidité [riʒidite] **nf** rigidity / [de muscle] tenseness / [de principes, mœurs] strictness.

rigolade [rigɔlad] **nf** *fam* fun *(U)* ▸ **c'est de la rigolade** *fig* it's a walkover.

rigolard**, **e [rigɔlar, ard] **adj** *fam* jokey, joking.

rigole [rigɔl] **nf** channel.

rigoler [3] [rigɔle] **vi** *fam* **1.** [rire] to laugh **2.** [plaisanter] **: rigoler (de)** to joke (about).

rigolo**, **ote [rigɔlo, ɔt] *fam* ■ **adj** funny.
■ **nm, f** *péj* phoney *UK*, phony *US*.

rigoriste [rigɔrist] ■ **nmf** puritan.
■ **adj** austere, puritanical.

rigoureusement [rigurøzmɑ̃] **adv 1.** [punir] harshly **2.** [vrai, ponctuel] absolutely ▸ **c'est rigoureusement exact** it's the honest truth.

rigoureux**, **euse [rigurø, øz] **adj 1.** [discipline, hiver] harsh **2.** [analyse] rigorous.

rigueur [rigœr] **nf 1.** [de punition] severity, harshness **2.** [de climat] harshness **3.** [d'analyse] rigour *UK*, rigor *US*, exactness
▸▸ **être de rigueur** to be obligatory ▸ **tenir rigueur de qqch à qqn** to hold sthg against sb.
◆ ***à la rigueur*** **loc adv** if necessary, if need be.

rillettes [rijɛt] **nfpl** *potted pork, duck or goose.*

rime [rim] **nf** rhyme ▸ **sans rime ni raison** *fig* without rhyme or reason.

rimer [3] [rime] **vi : rimer (avec)** to rhyme (with) ▸ **ça ne rime à rien** *fig* that doesn't make sense.

Rimmel® [rimɛl] **nm** mascara.

rinçage [rɛ̃saʒ] **nm** rinsing.

rince-doigts [rɛ̃sdwa] **nm inv** finger bowl.

rincer [16] [rɛ̃se] **vt** [bouteille] to rinse out / [cheveux, linge] to rinse ▸ **se faire rincer** *fam fig* to get a soaking.
◆ ***se rincer*** **vp** to rinse o.s. ▸ **se rincer la bouche** to rinse one's mouth.

ring [riŋ] **nm 1.** [boxe] ring **2.** *Belgique* [route] bypass.

ringard**, **e [rɛ̃gar, ard] *fam* ■ **adj 1.** [chanson] corny **2.** [décor] naff *UK* **3.** [acteur] second-rate **4.** [personne] nerdy.
■ **nm, f** nerd.

ringuette [rɛ̃gɛt] **nf** ringette *(women's sport similar to ice hockey).*

Rio de Janeiro [rjodedʒanɛro] **npr** Rio de Janeiro.

ripaille [ripaj] **nf : faire ripaille** *fam vieilli* to have a feast.

riposte [ripɔst] **nf 1.** [réponse] retort, riposte **2.** [contre-attaque] counterattack.

riposter [3] [ripɔste] ■ **vt : riposter que** to retort *ou* riposte that.
■ **vi 1.** [répondre] to riposte ▸ **riposter à** [personne] to answer back / [insulte] to reply to **2.** [contre-attaquer] to counter, to retaliate.

rire [95] [rir] ■ **nm** laugh ▸ **un petit rire sot** a silly giggle ▸ **rires préenregistrés** *ou* **en boîte** *fam* RADIO & TV prerecorded *ou* canned laughter ▸ **avoir un fou rire** to giggle ▸ **éclater de rire** to burst out laughing.
■ **vi 1.** [gén] to laugh ▸ **ta lettre nous a beaucoup fait rire** your letter made us all laugh a lot ▸ **rire de** to laugh at ▸ **rire aux éclats** *ou* **à gorge déployée** to howl with laughter ▸ **c'est à mourir de rire** it's a hoot *ou* a scream ▸ **se tordre de rire** to split one's sides (with laughter), to be in stitches ▸ **rire jaune** to give a hollow laugh **2.** [plaisanter] **: tu veux/vous voulez rire?** you must be joking! ▸ **pour rire** *fam* as a joke, for a laugh ▸ **j'ai dit ça pour rire** I (only) said it in jest, I was only joking.
◆ ***se rire*** **vp** *sout* **: se rire de** to laugh at.

ris [ri] **nm 1.** *(gén pl)* CULIN **: ris de veau** sweetbread **2.** NAUT reef.

risée [rize] **nf** ridicule ▸ **être la risée de** to be the laughing-stock of.

risette [rizɛt] **nf : faire (une) risette à qqn** [enfant] to give sb a nice *ou* sweet smile / [sourire de commande] to smile politely at sb.

risible [rizibl] **adj** [ridicule] ridiculous.

risotto [rizɔto] **nm** risotto.

risque [risk] **nm** risk ▸ **courir un risque** to run a risk ▸ **évaluation des risques** ÉCON risk assessment ▸ **prendre des risques** to take risks ▸ **à tes/vos risques et périls** at your own risk.

risqué**, **e [riske] **adj 1.** [entreprise] risky, dangerous **2.** [plaisanterie] risqué, daring.

risquer [3] [riske] **vt 1.** [vie, prison] to risk ▸ **risquer de faire qqch** to be likely to do sthg ▸ **je risque de perdre tout ce que j'ai** I'm running the risk of losing everything I have ▸ **risquer que** *(+ subjonctif)* to take a risk that ▸ **cela ne risque rien** it will be all right ▸ **risquer gros** to take a big risk ▸ **risquer le tout pour le tout** *fig* to put everything on the line **2.** [tenter] to venture.
◆ ***se risquer*** **vp** to venture ▸ **se risquer à faire qqch** to dare to do sthg.

risque-tout [riskətu] **nmf** daredevil.

rissolé**, **e [risɔle] **adj** browned.

rissoler [3] [risɔle] ■ **vt** to brown.
■ **vi** to brown ▸ **faire rissoler** to brown.

ristourne [risturn] **nf** discount ▸ **faire une ristourne à qqn** to give sb a discount.

rite [rit] **nm 1.** RELIG rite **2.** *fig* [cérémonial] ritual.

ritournelle [riturnɛl] **nf 1.** *fam fig* [rabâchage] old story, old song **2.** MUS ritornello.

rituel**, **elle [ritɥɛl] **adj** ritual.
◆ ***rituel*** **nm** ritual.

rituellement [ritɥɛlmɑ̃] **adv 1.** [selon un rite] ritually, religiously **2.** *fig* [immuablement] unfailingly.

rivage [rivaʒ] **nm** shore.

rival**, **e**, **aux [rival, o] ■ **adj** rival *(avant n).*
■ **nm, f** rival.

rivaliser [3] [rivalize] **vi : rivaliser avec** to compete with ▸ **rivaliser de** to vie in.

rivalité [rivalite] **nf** rivalry.

rive [riv] **nf** [de rivière] bank ▸ **la rive droite** [à Paris] the north bank of the Seine *(generally considered more affluent than the south bank)* ▸ **la rive gauche** [à Paris] the south bank of the Seine *(generally associated with students and artists)*.

CULTURE
Rive droite, Rive gauche

The left and right banks of Paris, split by the Seine, each have defining social, economic, and political characteristics. The **rive droite** contains the smart neighbourhoods of the 8th, 16th, and 17th **arrondissements**, while the **rive gauche** is associated with the students, intellectuals, and artists traditionally concentrated in the 5th and 6th **arrondissements**. The right bank has many office buildings and luxury boutiques and is seen as more conservative. A Parisian who is nonconformist and lives a rather bohemian lifestyle, on the other hand, may be known for his or her **esprit rive gauche**.

river [3] [rive] **vt 1.** [fixer] **: river qqch à qqch** to rivet sthg to sthg **2.** [clou] to clinch ▸ **être rivé à** *fig* to be riveted *ou* glued to.

riverain, e [rivrɛ̃, ɛn] ■ **adj** riverside *(avant n)* / [de rue] roadside *(avant n)*.
■ **nm, f** resident.

rivet [rivɛ] **nm** rivet.

rivière [rivjɛr] **nf** river.
◆ ***rivière de diamants*** **nf** diamond necklace *(with largest stone in the middle)*.

rixe [riks] **nf** fight, brawl.

Riyad, Riad [rijad] **npr** Riyadh.

riz [ri] **nm** rice ▸ **riz au lait** rice pudding ▸ **riz pilaf** pilau rice.

riziculture [rizikyltyr] **nf** rice-growing.

rizière [rizjɛr] **nf** paddy (field).

RMC (abr de ***Radio Monte-Carlo***) **nf** *independent radio station*.

RMI (abr de ***revenu minimum d'insertion***) **nm** *minimum guaranteed income (for people with no other source of income)*.

CULTURE
RMI

The **revenu minimum d'insertion** is a benefit paid to French people over 25 who are earning no income and are ineligible for unemployment benefits because they have not worked long enough. The basic rate is equal to roughly one-third of the French minimum wage, or SMIC (**salaire minimum interprofessionel de croissance**), but payments are larger for those who pay rent or have dependents.

RMiste [ɛrɛmist] **nmf** *person receiving the "RMI"*.

RN (abr de ***route nationale***) **nf** ≃ A road *UK*, ≃ state highway *US*.

RNIS (abr de ***réseau numérique à intégration de services***) **nm** ISDN *(integrated services digital network)* ▸ **envoyer qqch par RNIS** to ISDN sthg ▸ **ligne RNIS** ISDN line.

ro abr de ***recto***.

robe [rɔb] **nf 1.** [de femme] dress ▸ **robe chasuble** pinafore dress ▸ **robe de grossesse** maternity dress ▸ **robe de mariée** wedding dress **2.** [peignoir] **: robe de chambre** dressing gown *UK*, (bath)robe *US* **3.** [de magistrat] robe **4.** [de cheval] coat **5.** [de vin] colour *UK*, color *US*.

robinet [rɔbinɛ] **nm** tap *UK*, faucet *US*.

robinetterie [rɔbinɛtri] **nf** [installations] taps *(pl) UK*, faucets *(pl) US*.

roboratif, ive [rɔbɔratif, iv] **adj** *sout* bracing, invigorating.

robot [rɔbo] **nm 1.** [gén] robot **2.** [ménager] food processor.

robotique [rɔbɔtik] **nf** robotics *(U)*.

robotisation [rɔbɔtizasjɔ̃] **nf** automation, robotization *US*.

robotiser [3] [rɔbɔtize] **vt** to automate, to robotize *US*

robuste [rɔbyst] **adj 1.** [personne, santé] robust **2.** [plante] hardy **3.** [voiture] sturdy.

robustesse [rɔbystɛs] **nf 1.** [de personne] robustness **2.** [de plante] hardiness **3.** [de voiture] sturdiness.

roc [rɔk] **nm** rock.

rocade [rɔkad] **nf** bypass.

rocaille [rɔkaj] ■ **nf 1.** [cailloux] loose stones *pl* **2.** [dans un jardin] rock garden, rockery.
■ **adj inv** rocaille.

rocailleux, euse [rɔkajø, øz] **adj 1.** [terrain] rocky **2.** *fig* [voix] harsh.

rocambolesque [rɔkɑ̃bɔlɛsk] **adj** fantastic.

roche [rɔʃ] **nf** rock.

rocher [rɔʃe] **nm** rock ▸ **le Rocher** *the town of Monaco* ▸ **le rocher de Gibraltar** the Rock of Gibraltar.
◆ ***rocher au chocolat*** **nm** nut chocolate.

rocheux, euse [rɔʃø, øz] **adj** rocky.
◆ ***Rocheuses*** **nfpl : les Rocheuses** the Rockies.

rock [rɔk] ■ **nm** rock ('n' roll).
■ **adj inv** rock.

rocker [rɔkœr] **nmf** = ***rockeur***.

rockeur, euse [rɔkœr, øz] **nm, f 1.** [chanteur] rock singer **2.** [fan] rock fan.

rocking-chair [rɔkiŋtʃɛr] (pl **rocking-chairs**) **nm** rocking chair.

rodage [rɔdaʒ] **nm 1.** [de véhicule] running in *UK*, breaking in *US* ▸ **en rodage** running in *UK* **2.** *fig* [de méthode] running-in *UK ou* breaking-in *US ou* debugging period.

rodéo [rɔdeo] **nm** rodeo / *fig & iron* free-for-all.

roder [3] [rɔde] **vt 1.** [véhicule] to run in *UK*, to break in *US* **2.** *fam* [méthode] to run in *UK*, to break in *US*, to debug / [personne] to break in.

rôder [3] [rode] **vi** to prowl, to wander about.

rôdeur, euse [rodœr, øz] **nm, f** prowler.

rodomontade [rɔdɔmɔ̃tad] **nf** *littéraire* boasting *(U)*.

rœsti [røʃti] **nmpl** *Suisse grated potato fried to form a sort of cake.*

rogations [rɔgasjɔ̃] **nfpl** Rogations.

rogatoire [rɔgatwar] **adj** rogatory.

rogne [rɔɲ] **nf** *fam* bad temper ▸ **être/se mettre en rogne** to be in/to get into a bad mood, to be in/to get into a temper.

rogner [3] [rɔɲe] ■ **vt 1.** [ongles] to trim **2.** [revenus] to eat into.
■ **vi : rogner sur qqch** to cut down on sthg.

rognon [rɔɲɔ̃] **nm** kidney.

rognures [rɔɲyr] **nfpl** clippings, trimmings.

rogue [rɔg] **adj** *littéraire* arrogant.

roi [rwa] **nm** king ▸ **être plus royaliste que le roi** *fig* to be more Catholic than the Pope ▸ **tirer les rois** to celebrate Epiphany.
◆ ***Rois mages*** **nmpl : les Rois mages** RELIG the Three Wise Men.

CULTURE

Tirer les rois

At Epiphany, which is celebrated on the 6th of January, the French traditionally enjoy a round, almond-flavoured cake called the **galette des rois** – in honour of the Three Wise Men who visited Jesus at his birth. The cake contains a **fève**, or small porcelain figure, hidden in it by the baker (so called because dried beans were once used instead). The person who finds the figurine is proclaimed king or queen and given a paper crown to wear. He or she must also choose a king or queen from among the other guests. This way of celebrating the feast of Epiphany is found not only in families, but also among friends, at schools, and in the workplace.

Roissy [rwasi] **npr** [aéroport] *commonly-used name for Charles-de-Gaulle airport.*

roitelet [rwatle] **nm 1.** [oiseau] wren **2.** *péj & vieilli* [petit roi] kinglet.

Roland-Garros [rɔlɑ̃garos] **npr** *tennis stadium in Paris where the French Open is held.*

CULTURE

Roland-Garros

The Roland-Garros stadium in western Paris is home to the French Open, held each May. It is one of tennis's four Grand Slam events and the only one played on clay courts. The tournament, which consists of men's and women's singles and doubles and mixed doubles, is popular in France and elsewhere and attracts large television audiences.

rôle [rol] **nm** role, part ▸ **apprendre son rôle** to learn one's part *ou* lines ▸ **distribuer les rôles** to do the casting, to cast ▸ **jouer un rôle** to play a role *ou* part ▸ **rôle de composition** character part *ou* role ▸ **petit rôle** walk-on part ▸ **premier rôle** [acteur] leading actor (f actress) / [personnage] lead ▸ **second rôle** secondary *ou* supporting role ▸ **jeu de rôle** role play ▸ **avoir le beau rôle** *fig* to come off best ▸ **ce n'est pas mon rôle de m'occuper de ça** it's not my job *ou* it's not up to me to do it.

rôle-titre [roltitr] **nm** title role.

roller [rɔllœr, rɔlœr] **nm** [sport] rollerblading ▸ **les rollers** [patins] Rollerblades® ▸ **faire du roller** to go rollerblading, to rollerblade.

rollmops [rɔlmɔps] **nm** rollmop.

ROM, Rom [rɔm] (abr de ***read only memory***) **nf** ROM.

romain, e [rɔmɛ̃, ɛn] **adj** Roman.
◆ ***romain*** **nm** TYPO roman.
◆ ***romaine*** **nf** [salade] cos (lettuce) *UK*, romaine (lettuce) *US*.
◆ ***Romain, e*** **nm, f** Roman.

roman, e [rɔmɑ̃, an] **adj 1.** [langue] Romance **2.** ARCHIT Romanesque.
◆ ***roman*** **nm 1.** LITTÉR novel ▸ **roman d'action** adventure novel ▸ **roman d'anticipation** *ou* **de science fiction** science fiction novel ▸ **roman noir** thriller **2.** *fig & iron* [exagération] story / [aventure] saga **3.** ARCHIT **: le roman** the Romanesque.

romance [rɔmɑ̃s] **nf** [chanson] love song.

romancer [16] [rɔmɑ̃se] **vt** to romanticize.

romanche [rɔmɑ̃ʃ] **nm & adj** Romansh.

romancier, ère [rɔmɑ̃sje, ɛr] **nm, f** novelist.

romand, e [rɔmɑ̃, ɑ̃d] **adj** of/from French-speaking Switzerland.
◆ ***Romand, e*** **nm, f** French-speaking Swiss.

romanesque [rɔmanɛsk] **adj 1.** LITTÉR novelistic **2.** [aventure] fabulous, storybook *(avant n)*.

roman-feuilleton [rɔmɑ̃fœjtɔ̃] (pl **romans-feuilletons**) **nm** serial / *fig* soap opera.

roman-fleuve [rɔmɑ̃flœv] (pl **romans-fleuves**) **nm** saga.

romanichel, elle [rɔmaniʃɛl] **nm, f** gipsy.

romaniste [rɔmanist] **nmf** Romanist.

roman-photo [rɔmɑ̃fɔto] (pl **romans-photos**) **nm** story told in photographs.

romantique [rɔmɑ̃tik] **nmf & adj** romantic.

romantisme [rɔmɑ̃tism] **nm 1.** ART Romantic movement **2.** [sensibilité] romanticism.

romarin [rɔmarɛ̃] **nm** rosemary.

rombière [rɔ̃bjɛr] **nf** *fam péj* old biddy.

Rome [rɔm] **npr** Rome.

rompre [78] [rɔ̃pr] ■ **vt 1.** *sout* [objet] to break **2.** [charme, marché] to break / [fiançailles, relations] to break off **3.** *sout* [exercer] **: rompre qqn à** to break sb into.
■ **vi** to break ▸ **rompre avec qqn** *fig* to break up with sb ▸ **rompre avec qqch** *fig* to break with sthg.
◆ ***se rompre*** **vp** to break ▸ **se rompre le cou/les reins** to break one's neck/back.

rompu**, **e [rɔ̃py] ■ **pp** ➤ ***rompre***.
■ **adj 1.** [exténué] exhausted ▸ **rompu de** exhausted by ▸ **rompu de fatigue** exhausted **2.** [expérimenté] **: rompu à** experienced in.

romsteck = ***rumsteck***.

ronce [rɔ̃s] **nf** [arbuste] bramble.

ronchon**, **onne [rɔ̃ʃɔ̃, ɔn] *fam* ■ **adj** grumpy.
■ **nm, f** grumbler.

ronchonner [3] [rɔ̃ʃɔne] **vi** *fam* **: ronchonner (après)** to grumble (at).

rond**, **e [rɔ̃, rɔ̃d] **adj 1.** [forme, chiffre] round **2.** [joue, ventre] chubby, plump **3.** *fam* [ivre] tight.
◆ ***rond*** ■ **nm 1.** [cercle] circle ▸ **en rond** in a circle *ou* ring ▸ **tourner en rond** *fig* to go round in circles **2.** [anneau] ring ▸ **rond de serviette** napkin ring **3.** *fam* [argent] **: je n'ai pas un rond** I haven't got a penny *ou* bean.
■ **adv : ça ne tourne pas rond** *fig* there's something up *ou* fishy.

rond-de-cuir [rɔ̃dkɥir] (pl **ronds-de-cuir**) **nm** *péj* & *vieilli* pen pusher.

ronde [rɔ̃d] **nf 1.** [de surveillance] rounds *pl* / [de policier] beat **2.** [danse] round **3.** MUS semibreve *UK*, whole note *US*.
◆ ***à la ronde*** **loc adv : à des kilomètres à la ronde** for miles around.

rondelet**, **ette [rɔ̃dlɛ, ɛt] **adj 1.** [grassouillet] plump **2.** *fig* [somme] goodish, tidy.

rondelle [rɔ̃dɛl] **nf 1.** [de saucisson] slice **2.** [de métal] washer **3.** *Québec* [hockey] puck.

rondement [rɔ̃dmɑ̃] **adv** [efficacement] efficiently, briskly.

rondeur [rɔ̃dœr] **nf 1.** [forme] roundness **2.** [partie charnue] curve **3.** [de caractère] openness.

rondin [rɔ̃dɛ̃] **nm** log.

rondouillard**, **e [rɔ̃dujar, ard] **adj** *fam* tubby.

rond-point [rɔ̃pwɛ̃] (pl **ronds-points**) **nm** roundabout *UK*, traffic circle *US*.

ronflant**, **e [rɔ̃flɑ̃, ɑ̃t] **adj** *péj* grandiose.

ronflement [rɔ̃fləmɑ̃] **nm 1.** [de dormeur] snore **2.** [de poêle, moteur] hum, purr.

ronfler [3] [rɔ̃fle] **vi 1.** [dormeur] to snore **2.** [poêle, moteur] to hum, to purr **3.** *fam* [dormir] to be in a deep sleep.

ronger [17] [rɔ̃ʒe] **vt** [bois, os] to gnaw / [métal, falaise] to eat away at / *fig* to gnaw at, to eat away at.
◆ ***se ronger*** **vp 1.** [grignoter] **: se ronger les ongles** to bite one's nails **2.** *fig* [se tourmenter] to worry, to torture o.s.

rongeur**, **euse [rɔ̃ʒœr, øz] **adj** gnawing, rodent *(avant n)*.
◆ ***rongeur*** **nm** rodent.

ronron [rɔ̃rɔ̃] **nm 1.** [de chat] purr / [de moteur] purr, hum **2.** *fig* & *péj* [routine] humdrum existence.

ronronnement [rɔ̃rɔnmɑ̃] **nm** [de chat] purring / [de moteur] purring, humming.

ronronner [3] [rɔ̃rɔne] **vi** [chat] to purr / [moteur] to purr, to hum.

röntgen [rœntgɛn] **nm** roentgen, rontgen, röntgen.

roquefort [rɔkfɔr] **nm** Roquefort *(French blue-veined cheese)*.

roquer [3] [rɔke] **vi** [échecs] to castle.

roquet [rɔkɛ] **nm** *péj* **1.** [chien] nasty little dog **2.** *fig* [personne] nasty little squirt.

roquette [rɔkɛt] **nf** rocket.

ROR [ɛroɛr *ou* rɔr] (abr de ***rougeole oreillons rubéole***) **nm** MMR (vaccine).

rosace [rozas] **nf 1.** [ornement] rose **2.** [vitrail] rose window **3.** [figure géométrique] rosette.

rosaire [rozɛr] **nm** rosary.

rosâtre [rozatr] **adj** pinkish.

rosbif [rɔsbif] **nm 1.** [viande] roast beef **2.** [Anglais] *pejorative term for a British person*.

rose [roz] ■ **nf** rose ▸ **rose blanche/rouge** white/red rose ▸ **rose pompon** fairy rose ▸ **rose trémière** hollyhock ▸ **frais comme une rose** fresh as a daisy ▸ **envoyer qqn sur les roses** *fam fig* to send sb packing.
■ **nm** pink ▸ **rose nacré** oyster pink ▸ **voir la vie en rose** to see things through rose-tinted spectacles *UK ou* glasses *US*.
■ **adj** pink ▸ **rose bonbon** bright pink ▸ **rose fluo** *fam* fluorescent *ou* dayglo pink ▸ **rose thé** tea rose ▸ **vieux rose** old rose ▸ **ce n'est pas (tout) rose** it isn't exactly a bed of roses.
◆ ***rose des sables**, **rose du désert*** **nf** gypsum flower.
◆ ***rose des vents*** **nf** compass card.

rosé**, **e [roze] **adj 1.** [vin] rosé **2.** [teinte] rosy.
◆ ***rosé*** **nm** rosé.
◆ ***rosée*** **nf** dew.

roseau**, **x [rozo] **nm** reed.

roseraie [rozrɛ] **nf** rose garden.

rosette [rozɛt] **nf 1.** [nœud] bow **2.** [insigne] rosette.
◆ ***rosette de Lyon*** **nf** *dry pork sausage*.

rosier [rozje] **nm** rose bush.

rosir [32] [rozir] **vt** & **vi** to turn pink.

rosse [rɔs] *péj* ■ **nf 1.** *vieilli* [cheval] nag **2.** *fig* [femme] bitch, cow *UK* / [homme] bastard.
■ **adj** nasty.

rosser [3] [rɔse] **vt** to thrash.

rosserie [rɔsri] **nf** *fam* nasty remark.

rossignol [rɔsiɲɔl] **nm 1.** [oiseau] nightingale **2.** *fam fig* [article invendable] piece of rubbish **3.** [passe-partout] pick lock.

rot [ro] **nm** burp.

rotatif**, **ive [rɔtatif, iv] **adj** rotary.
◆ ***rotative*** **nf** rotary press.

rotation [rɔtasjɔ̃] **nf** rotation.

roter [3] [rɔte] **vi** *fam* to burp.

rôti**, **e [roti] **adj** roast.
◆ ***rôti*** **nm** roast, joint *UK* ▸ **rôti de veau/porc** roast veal/pork.

rôtie [roti] **nf** *Québec* piece of toast.

rotin [rɔtɛ̃] **nm** rattan.

rôtir [32] [rotir] ■ **vt** to roast.
■ **vi 1.** CULIN to roast ▸ **faire rôtir** to roast **2.** *fam fig* [avoir chaud] to be roasting.
◆ ***se rôtir*** **vp : se rôtir au soleil** *fig* to bask in the sunshine.

rôtisserie [rotisri] **nf 1.** [restaurant] ≃ steakhouse **2.** [magasin] *shop selling roast meat.*

rôtissoire [rotiswar] **nf** spit.

rotonde [rɔtɔ̃d] **nf 1.** [bâtiment] rotunda **2.** [d'autobus] back seat.

rotor [rɔtɔr] **nm** rotor.

rotule [rɔtyl] **nf** kneecap.

roturier, ère [rɔtyrje, ɛr] ■ **adj 1.** [non noble] common **2.** *péj* [commun] plebeian.
■ **nm, f** *vieilli* commoner.

rouage [rwaʒ] **nm** cog, gearwheel ▸ **les rouages de l'État** *fig* the wheels of State.

roublard, e [rublar, ard] *fam* ■ **adj** cunning, crafty.
■ **nm, f** cunning *ou* crafty devil.

roublardise [rublardiz] **nf 1.** [caractère] cunning, craftiness **2.** *vieilli* [acte] cunning *ou* crafty trick.

rouble [rubl] **nm** rouble.

roucoulement [rukulmɑ̃] **nm** cooing / *fig* billing and cooing.

roucouler [3] [rukule] ■ **vt** to warble / *fig* to coo.
■ **vi** to coo / *fig* to bill and coo.

roue [ru] **nf 1.** [gén] wheel ▸ **descendre en roue libre** to freewheel downhill ▸ **roue arrière/avant** back/front wheel ▸ **roue d'angle** bevel gear wheel ▸ **roue dentée** cogwheel ▸ **roue motrice** drive *ou* driving wheel ▸ **la grande roue** the big wheel *UK*, the Ferris wheel *US* ▸ **la roue de la Fortune** the wheel of Fortune ▸ **roue de secours** spare wheel ▸ **un deux roues** a two-wheeled vehicle **2.** [de paon] **: faire la roue** to display **3.** [gymnastique] cartwheel **4.** NAUT **: roue du gouvernail** helm.

rouer [6] [rwe] **vt : rouer qqn de coups** to thrash sb, to beat sb.

rouerie [ruri] **nf** *littéraire* **1.** [caractère] cunning **2.** *vieilli* [action] cunning trick.

rouet [ruɛ] **nm** [à filer] spinning wheel.

rouge [ruʒ] ■ **nm 1.** [couleur] red **2.** *fam* [vin] red (wine) ▸ **gros rouge** *fam* cheap red wine, plonk *UK* **3.** [fard] rouge, blusher ▸ **rouge à lèvres** lipstick **4.** AUTO **: passer au rouge** to turn red / [conducteur] to go through a red light.
■ **nmf** *péj* & POLIT Red.
■ **adj 1.** [gén] red ▸ **rouge de** red with **2.** [fer, tison] red-hot **3.** *péj* & POLIT Red.
■ **adv : voir rouge** *fig* to see red.

rougeâtre [ruʒatr] **adj** reddish.

rougeaud, e [ruʒo, od] ■ **adj** red-faced.
■ **nm, f** red-faced person.

rouge-gorge [ruʒgɔrʒ] (pl **rouges-gorges**) **nm** robin.

rougeoiement [ruʒwamɑ̃] **nm** reddening.

rougeole [ruʒɔl] **nf** measles *sg.*

rougeoyer [13] [ruʒwaje] **vi** to turn red.

rouget [ruʒɛ] **nm** mullet.

rougeur [ruʒœr] **nf 1.** [teinte] redness **2.** [de visage, de chaleur, d'effort] flush / [de gêne] blush **3.** [sur peau] red spot *ou* blotch.

rougir [32] [ruʒir] ■ **vt 1.** [colorer] to turn red ▸ **des yeux rougis par les larmes** eyes red with weeping **2.** [chauffer] to make red-hot.
■ **vi 1.** [devenir rouge] to turn red **2.** [d'émotion] **: rougir (de)** [de plaisir, colère] to flush (with) / [de gêne] to blush (with) ▸ **je me sentais rougir** I could feel myself going red (in the face) ▸ **rougir jusqu'aux oreilles** to blush to the roots of one's hair **3.** *fig* [avoir honte] **: rougir de qqch** to be ashamed of sthg ▸ **tu n'as pas/il n'y a pas à en rougir** there's nothing for you/nothing to be ashamed of.

rougissant, e [ruʒisɑ̃, ɑ̃t] **adj** [ciel] reddening / [jeune fille] blushing.

rouille [ruj] ■ **nf 1.** [oxyde] rust **2.** CULIN *spicy garlic sauce for fish soup.*
■ **adj inv** rust.

rouillé, e [ruje] **adj 1.** [grille, clef] rusty, rusted ▸ **la serrure est complètement rouillée** the lock is rusted up **2.** *fig* [muscles] stiff ▸ **être rouillé** [physiquement] to feel stiff / [intellectuellement] to feel a bit rusty ▸ **mes réflexes au volant sont un peu rouillés** my driving reflexes are a bit rusty **3.** BOT [blé] affected by rust, rusted / [feuille] mouldy.

rouiller [3] [ruje] ■ **vt** to rust, to make rusty.
■ **vi** to rust.
◆ ***se rouiller*** **vp** to rust / *fig* to get rusty.

roulade [rulad] **nf 1.** [galipette] roll **2.** CULIN rolled meat.

roulant, e [rulɑ̃, ɑ̃t] **adj 1.** [meuble] on wheels, on castors **2.** RAIL **: personnel roulant** train crew.

roulé, e [rule] **adj** rolled ▸ **bien roulée** *fam fig* curvy, shapely.
◆ ***roulé*** **nm** CULIN ≃ swiss roll.

rouleau, x [rulo] **nm 1.** [gén & TECHNOL] roller ▸ **rouleau compresseur** steamroller ▸ **rouleau encreur** ink roller **2.** [de papier] roll **3.** [à pâtisserie] rolling pin **4.** CULIN **: rouleau de printemps** spring roll, egg roll *US*.

roulé-boulé [rulebule] (pl **roulés-boulés**) **nm** roll.

roulement [rulmɑ̃] **nm 1.** [gén] rolling **2.** [de hanches] swaying **3.** [de personnel] rotation ▸ **travailler par roulement** to work to a rota *UK* **4.** [de tambour, tonnerre] roll **5.** TECHNOL rolling bearing ▸ **roulement à billes** ball bearing **6.** FIN circulation.

rouler [3] [rule] ■ **vt 1.** [déplacer] to wheel **2.** [enrouler - tapis] to roll up / [- cigarette] to roll **3.** *fam* [balancer] to sway ▸ **rouler des mécaniques** *fam* to sway one's shoulders / *fig* to come *ou* to play the hard guy **4.** LING to roll ▸ **rouler les r** to roll one's r's **5.** [faire tourner sur soi] to roll **6.** *fam fig* [duper] to swindle, to do *UK* ▸ **elle m'a roulé de 30 euros** she diddled *ou* did me out of 30 euros ▸ **se faire rouler** to be conned *ou* had.
■ **vi 1.** [ballon, bateau] to roll **2.** [véhicule] to go, to run ▸ **une voiture qui a peu/beaucoup roulé** a car with a low/high mileage / [suj: personne] to drive ▸ **'roulez au pas'** 'dead slow' ▸ **roule moins vite** slow down, drive more

slowly **3.** [tonnerre] to rumble **4.** [suj: conversation] **: rouler sur** to turn on **5.** *fam* [aller bien] **: ça roule** everything's OK *ou* going well

▸▸ **rouler pour qqn** *fam* to be for sb, to back sb ▸ **rouler sur l'or** *fam* to be rolling in money *ou* in it.

◆ ***se rouler*** **vp** to roll about ▸ **se rouler par terre** to roll on the ground ▸ **c'était à se rouler par terre** [de rire] it was hysterically funny / [de douleur] it was so painful ▸ **se rouler en boule** to roll o.s. into a ball.

roulette [rulɛt] **nf 1.** [petite roue] castor ▸ **comme sur des roulettes** *fam fig* like clockwork **2.** [de dentiste] drill **3.** [jeux] roulette ▸ **roulette russe** Russian roulette.

roulis [ruli] **nm** roll.

roulotte [rulɔt] **nf** [de gitan] caravan / [de tourisme] caravan *UK*, trailer *US* / *fig* **: vol à la roulotte** theft of goods in car.

roulure [rulyr] **nf** *fam péj* tart, whore.

roumain, e [rumɛ̃, ɛn] **adj** Romanian.

◆ ***roumain*** **nm** [langue] Romanian.

◆ ***Roumain, e*** **nm, f** Romanian.

Roumanie [rumani] **nf : la Roumanie** Romania.

round [rawnd] **nm** round.

roupiller [3] [rupije] **vi** *fam* to snooze.

roupillon [rupijɔ̃] **nm** *fam* snooze.

rouquin, e [rukɛ̃, in] *fam* ■ **adj** redheaded.

■ **nm, f** redhead.

rouspéter [18] [ruspete] **vi** *fam* to grumble, to moan.

rousse ➤ ***roux***.

rousseur [rusœr] **nf** redness.

◆ ***taches de rousseur*** **nfpl** freckles.

roussi [rusi] **nm** burning ▸ **ça sent le roussi** *fam fig* trouble's on its way.

roussir [32] [rusir] ■ **vt 1.** [rendre roux] to turn brown / CULIN to brown **2.** [brûler légèrement] to singe.

■ **vi** to turn brown / CULIN to brown.

routage [rutaʒ] **nm** sorting and mailing.

routard, e [rutar, ard] **nm, f** *fam* backpacker.

route [rut] **nf 1.** [gén] road ▸ **route à grande circulation** busy road ▸ **faire de la route** to do a lot of mileage ▸ **en route** on the way ▸ **en route!** let's go! ▸ **les accidents de la route** road accidents ▸ **mettre en route** [démarrer] to start up / *fig* to get under way ▸ **prendre la** *ou* **se mettre en route** to set off, to get going ▸ **route départementale** secondary road ▸ **route nationale** ≃ A road *UK*, ≃ highway *US* ▸ **route de montagne** mountain road ▸ **tenir la route** AUTO to hold the road / *fig* to hold water ▸ **cette politique ne tient pas la route** *fig* there's no mileage in that policy **2.** [itinéraire] route ▸ **montrer la route à qqn** to show sb the way ▸ **faire fausse route** to go the wrong way / *fig* to be on the wrong track ▸ **prendre la route des vacances/du soleil** to set off on holiday/to the south ▸ **la route des Indes** the road to India **3.** *fig* [voie] path ▸ **la route du succès** the road to success ▸ **la route est toute tracée pour lui** the path is all laid out for him.

routier, ère [rutje, ɛr] **adj** road *(avant n)*.

◆ ***routier*** **nm 1.** [chauffeur] long-distance lorry driver *UK* *ou* trucker *US* **2.** [restaurant] ≃ transport cafe *UK*, ≃ truck stop *US*.

routine [rutin] **nf** routine.

routinier, ère [rutinje, ɛr] **adj** routine.

rouvert, e [ruvɛr, ɛrt] **pp** ➤ ***rouvrir***.

rouvrir [34] [ruvrir] **vt** to reopen, to open again.

◆ ***se rouvrir*** **vp** to reopen, to open again.

roux, rousse [ru, rus] ■ **adj 1.** [cheveux] red **2.** [feuilles] russet, red-brown **3.** [sucre] brown.

■ **nm, f** [personne] redhead.

◆ ***roux*** **nm 1.** [couleur] red, russet **2.** CULIN roux.

royal, e, aux [rwajal, o] **adj 1.** [de roi] royal **2.** [magnifique] princely.

royalement [rwajalmɑ̃] **adv 1.** [recevoir] royally / [vivre] like royalty **2.** *fig* [complètement] **: elle s'en moque royalement** she couldn't care less.

royaliste [rwajalist] **nmf & adj** royalist.

royalties [rwajalti(z)] **nfpl** royalties.

royaume [rwajom] **nm** kingdom.

Royaume-Uni [rwajomyni] **nm : le Royaume-Uni** the United Kingdom.

royauté [rwajɔte] **nf 1.** [fonction] kingship **2.** [régime] monarchy.

RP ■ **nfpl** (abr de ***relations publiques***) PR *sg*.

■ **nf 1.** (abr de ***recette principale***) main post office **2.** abr écrite de ***région parisienne***.

R.P. (abr écrite de ***révérend père***) Holy Father.

RPR (abr de ***Rassemblement pour la République***) **nm** *French political party to the right of the political spectrum*.

RSVP (abr de ***répondez s'il vous plaît***) RSVP.

RTB (abr de ***Radio-télévision belge***) **nf** *Belgian broadcasting company*.

rte abr de ***route***.

RTL (abr de ***Radio-télévision Luxembourg***) **nf** *Luxembourg broadcasting company*.

RTT [ɛrtete] (abr de ***réduction du temps de travail***) ■ **nf** (statutory) reduction in working hours.

■ **nm** (extra) day off *(as a result of shorter working hours)* ▸ **poser/prendre un RTT** to book *ou* claim a day's holiday to take a day off *US*.

CULTURE

RTT

Meant to combat relatively high unemployment, the law mandating a 35-hour working week – commonly called **les trente-cinq heures** – has not exactly met its goal, but it does give salaried workers more leisure time. Most now have **journées de RTT** (short for **réduction du temps de travail**) once or twice a month. Some companies have kept the 39-hour working week, however, and the Medef, France's main employers' organization, is trying to get the law absolished.

RU (abr de ***restaurant universitaire***) [ʀy] **nm** universit[y] refectory, cafeteria.

ruade [ryad] **nf** kick.

Ruanda, Rwanda [ryɑ̃nda] **nm : le Ruanda** Rwanda ▸ **au Ruanda** in Rwanda.

ruandais, e [ryɑ̃dɛ, ɛz] **adj** Rwandan.
◆ ***ruandais*** **nm** [langue] Rwandan.
◆ ***Ruandais, e*** **nm, f** Rwandan.

ruban [rybɑ̃] **nm** ribbon ▸ **ruban adhésif** adhesive tape.

rubéole [rybeɔl] **nf** German measles *sg*, rubella.

rubicond, e [rybikɔ̃, ɔ̃d] **adj** rubicund.

rubis [rybi] ■ **nm 1.** [pierre précieuse] ruby **2.** [de montre] jewel
▸▸ **payer rubis sur l'ongle** to pay cash on the nail.
■ **adj inv** [couleur] ruby.

rubrique [rybrik] **nf 1.** [chronique] column **2.** [dans classement] heading.

ruche [ryʃ] **nf 1.** [abeilles] hive **2.** [abri] hive, beehive / *fig* hive of activity.

rucher [ryʃe] **nm** apiary.

ude [ryd] **adj 1.** [surface] rough **2.** [voix] harsh **3.** [personne, manières] rough, uncouth **4.** [hiver, épreuve] harsh, severe / [tâche, adversaire] tough **5.** [appétit] hearty.

udement [rydmɑ̃] **adv 1.** [brutalement - tomber] hard / [- répondre] harshly **2.** *fam* [très] damn.

udesse [rydɛs] **nf** harshness, severity.

udimentaire [rydimɑ̃tɛr] **adj** rudimentary.

udiments [rydimɑ̃] **nmpl** rudiments.

udoie, rudoies ➤ ***rudoyer***.

udoyer [13] [rydwaje] **vt** to treat harshly.

ue [ry] **nf** street ▸ **rue piétonne** *ou* **piétonnière** pedestrian area *ou* street ▸ **descendre dans la rue** to take to the streets ▸ **jeter/mettre/être à la rue** *fig* to throw/to put/to be out on the streets ▸ **ne pas courir les rues** *fig* not to grow on trees, to be thin on the ground.

uée [rɥe] **nf** rush.

uelle [rɥɛl] **nf** [rue] alley, lane.

uer [7] [rɥe] **vi** to kick.
◆ ***se ruer*** **vp : se ruer sur** to pounce on.

ugby [rygbi] **nm** rugby ▸ **rugby à treize/quinze** Rugby League/Union.

ugir [32] [ryʒir] ■ **vt** to roar, to bellow.
■ **vi** to roar / [vent] to howl / [personne] **: rugir de** to roar with.

ugissement [ryʒismɑ̃] **nm** roar, roaring *(U)* / [de vent] howling.

ugosité [rygozite] **nf 1.** [de surface] roughness **2.** [aspérité] rough patch.

ugueux, euse [rygø, øz] **adj** rough.

uine [rɥin] **nf 1.** [gén] [financière] ruin **2.** [château] **: en ruine** ruined ▸ **tomber en ruine** to crumble **3.** [effondrement] ruin, downfall **4.** [humaine] wreck **5.** [acquisition] **: c'est une vraie ruine** it costs me/you *etc* an arm and a leg.
◆ ***ruines*** **nfpl** ruins ▸ **tomber en ruines** to fall into ruins.

uiné, e [rɥine] **adj** ruined.

uiner [3] [rɥine] **vt** to ruin.
◆ ***se ruiner*** **vp** to ruin o.s., to bankrupt o.s.

uineux, euse [rɥinø, øz] **adj** ruinous.

ruisseau, x [rɥiso] **nm 1.** [cours d'eau] stream ▸ **des ruisseaux de larmes** floods of tears **2.** *fig & péj* [caniveau] gutter.

ruisseler [24] [rɥisle] **vi : ruisseler (de)** to stream (with).

ruissellement [rɥisɛlmɑ̃] **nm** streaming.

rumba [rumba] **nf** rumba.

rumeur [rymœr] **nf 1.** [bruit] murmur **2.** [nouvelle] rumour *UK*, rumor *US*.

ruminant [ryminɑ̃] **nm** ruminant.

ruminer [3] [rymine] **vt** to ruminate / *fig* to mull over.

rumsteck, romsteck [rɔmstɛk] **nm** rump steak.

rupestre [rypɛstr] **adj 1.** ART cave *(avant n)*, rock *(avant n)* **2.** BOT rock *(avant n)*.

rupin, e [rypɛ̃, in] *fam* ■ **adj** plush.
■ **nm, f** moneybags *sg*.

rupture [ryptyr] **nf 1.** [cassure] breaking **2.** *fig* [changement] abrupt change ▸ **en rupture de ban avec** *fig* at odds with **3.** [manque] **: être en rupture de stock** to be out of stock **4.** [de négociations, fiançailles] breaking off / [de contrat] breach **5.** [amoureuse] breakup, split.

rural, e, aux [ryral, o] ■ **adj** country *(avant n)*, rural.
■ **nm, f** country dweller.

ruse [ryz] **nf 1.** [habileté] cunning, craftiness **2.** [subterfuge] ruse.

rusé, e [ryze] ■ **adj** cunning, crafty.
■ **nm, f** cunning *ou* crafty person.

ruser [3] [ryze] **vi** to use trickery.

rush [rœʃ] (pl **rushs** *ou* **rushes**) **nm** rush.

russe [rys] ■ **adj** Russian.
■ **nm** [langue] Russian.
◆ ***Russe*** **nmf** Russian.

Russie [rysi] **nf : la Russie** Russia.

rustine [rystin] **nf** *small rubber patch for repairing bicycle tyres.*

rustique [rystik] ■ **nm** [style] rustic style.
■ **adj** rustic.

rustre [rystr] *péj* ■ **nmf** lout.
■ **adj** loutish.

rut [ryt] **nm : être en rut** [mâle] to be rutting / [femelle] to be on *UK ou* in *US* heat.

rutabaga [rytabaga] **nm** swede *UK*, rutabaga *US*.

rutilant, e [rytilɑ̃, ɑ̃t] **adj** [brillant] gleaming.

rutiler [3] [rytile] **vi** to gleam.

R-V abr de ***rendez-vous***.

Rwanda = ***Ruanda***.

rythme [ritm] **nm 1.** MUS rhythm ▸ **en rythme** in rhythm ▸ **avoir le sens du rythme** [personne] to have rhythm ▸ **suivre le rythme** to keep up **2.** [de travail, production] pace, rate ▸ **travailler à un rythme soutenu** to work at a sustained pace ▸ **à ce rythme-là** at that rate ▸ **au rythme de** at the rate of ▸ **rythme cardiaque** heart rate ▸ **rythme respiratoire** breathing rate.

rythmer [3] [ritme] **vt** to give rhythm to.

rythmique [ritmik] ■ **nf** rhythmics *(U)*.
■ **adj** rhythmical.

S

s*[1], *S [ɛs] **nm inv 1.** [lettre] s, S **2.** [forme] zigzag.
◆ ***S*** (abr écrite de ***Sud***) S.

s*[2]** (abr écrite de ***seconde) s.

s' ➤ ***se***, ***si***.

s/ abr de ***sur***.

sa ➤ ***son***[2].

SA (abr de ***société anonyme***) **nf** ≃ Ltd *UK*, ≃ Inc. *US*

S.A. (abr écrite de ***Son Altesse***) H.H.

sabayon [sabajɔ̃] **nm** zabaglione.

sabbat [saba] **nm 1.** RELIG Sabbath **2.** [de sorciers] sabbath.

sabbatique [sabatik] **adj 1.** RELIG Sabbath *(avant n)* **2.** [congé] sabbatical.

sable [sabl] ■ **nm** sand ▸ **de sable** [plage] sandy / [tempête] sand *(avant n)* ▸ **sables mouvants** quicksand *(sg)*, quicksands.
■ **adj inv** [couleur] sandy.

sablé, ***e*** [sable] **adj 1.** [route] sandy **2.** CULIN **: gâteau sablé** ≃ shortbread *(U)*.
◆ ***sablé*** **nm** ≃ shortbread *(U)*.

sabler [3] [sable] **vt 1.** [route] to sand **2.** [façade] to sandblast **3.** [boire] **: sabler le champagne** to crack a bottle of champagne.

sableux, ***euse*** [sablø, øz] **adj** sandy.
◆ ***sableuse*** **nf** sandblaster.

sablier [sablije] **nm** hourglass.

sablière [sablijɛr] **nf 1.** [carrière] sand quarry **2.** [poutre] stringer.

sablonneux, ***euse*** [sablɔnø, øz] **adj** sandy.

saborder [3] [sabɔrde] **vt** [navire] to scuttle / *fig* [entreprise] to wind up / *fig* [projet] to scupper *UK*.
◆ ***se saborder*** **vp 1.** [navire] to be scuttled **2.** *fig* [entreprise] to wind up.

sabot [sabo] **nm 1.** [chaussure] clog **2.** [de cheval] hoof **3.** AUTO **: sabot de Denver** wheel clamp, Denver boot ▸ **sabot de frein** brake shoe.

sabotage [sabɔtaʒ] **nm 1.** [volontaire] sabotage **2.** [bâclage] bungling.

saboter [3] [sabɔte] **vt 1.** [volontairement] to sabotage **2.** [bâcler] to bungle.

saboteur, ***euse*** [sabɔtœr, øz] **nm, f** MIL & POLIT saboteur.

sabre [sabr] **nm** sabre *UK*, saber *US*.

sabrer [3] [sabre] **vt 1.** *vieilli* [avec sabre] to cut down **2.** *fam* [biffer] to slash **3.** *fam* [critiquer] to slam **4.** *fam* [candidat] to fail.

sac [sak] **nm 1.** [gén] bag / [pour grains] sack / [contenu] bag, bagful, sack, sackful ▸ **sac de couchage** sleeping bag ▸ **sac à dos** rucksack ▸ **sac à main** handbag ▸ **sac en papier** paper bag ▸ **sac de plage** beach bag ▸ **sac (en) plastique** [petit] plastic bag / [solide et grand] plastic carrier (bag) *UK*, large plastic bag *US* ▸ **sac poubelle** bin liner *UK*, garbage can liner *US* / [noir] black bag ▸ **sac à provisions** shopping bag ▸ **sac de voyage** overnight ou travelling *UK* or traveling *US* bag ▸ **vider son sac** *fig* to get it off one's chest **2.** *fam* [10 francs] 10 francs **3.** *littéraire* [pillage] sack ▸ **mettre à sac** [ville] to sack / [maison] to ransack
▸▸ **méfie-toi, c'est un sac de nœuds, leur affaire** *fam* be careful, that business of theirs is a real hornets' nest ▸ **sac à puces** *fam* [chien] fleabag ▸ **ça y est, l'affaire est ou c'est dans le sac!** *fam* it's as good as done!, it's in the bag ▸ **ils sont tous à mettre dans le même sac** *fam* they're as bad as each other.

saccade [sakad] **nf** jerk.

saccadé, ***e*** [sakade] **adj** jerky.

saccage [sakaʒ] **nm** havoc.

saccager [17] [sakaʒe] **vt 1.** [piller] to sack **2.** [dévaster] to destroy.

saccharine [sakarin] **nf** saccharin.

SACEM, ***Sacem*** [sasɛm] (abr de ***Société des auteurs, compositeurs et éditeurs de musique***) **nf** *society that safeguards the rights of French writers and musicians*

sacerdoce [sasɛrdɔs] **nm** priesthood / *fig* vocation.

sacerdotal, ***e***, ***aux*** [sasɛrdɔtal, o] **adj** priestly.

sachant **p prés** ➤ ***savoir***.

sache, ***saches*** ➤ ***savoir***.

sachet [saʃɛ] **nm** [de bonbons] bag / [de shampooing] sachet ▸ **sachet de thé** teabag ▸ **soupe en sachet** packet soup *UK*, package soup *US*.

sacoche [sakɔʃ] **nf 1.** [de médecin, d'écolier] bag **2.** [de cycliste] pannier.

sac-poubelle [sakpubɛl] (pl **sacs-poubelle**) **nm** [petit] dustbin *UK ou* garbage can *US* liner / [grand] rubbish bag *UK*, garbage bag *US*.

sacquer, ***saquer*** [3] [sake] **vt** *fam* **1.** [renvoyer] to sack *UK*, to fire **2.** [élève] to fail
▸▸ **je ne peux pas le sacquer** I can't stand *ou* stomach him.

sacraliser [3] [sakralize] **vt** to hold as sacred.

sacre [sakr] **nm** [de roi] coronation / [d'évêque] consecration.

sacré, ***e*** [sakre] **adj 1.** [gén] sacred **2.** RELIG [ordres, écritures] holy **3.** *(avant n) fam* [maudit] bloody *UK (avant n)*, goddam *US (avant n)* **4.** *(avant n)* [considérable] **: un sacré...** a hell of a...

Sacré-Cœur [sakrekœr] **npr m 1.** [édifice] **: le Sacré-Cœur, la basilique du Sacré-Cœur** Sacré-Cœur *(one of the landmarks of Paris, the church situated on the butte Montmartre)* **2.** [fête] **: le Sacré-Cœur, la fête du Sacré-Cœur** the (Feast of the) Sacred Heart.

sacrement [sakrəmɑ̃] **nm** sacrament ▸ **les derniers sacrements** the last rites.

sacrément [sakremɑ̃] **adv** *fam vieilli* dashed.

sacrer [3] [sakre] **vt 1.** [roi] to crown / [évêque] to consecrate **2.** *fig* [déclarer] to hail.

acrifice [sakrifis] **nm** sacrifice ▸ **faire un sacrifice/des sacrifices** *fig* to make a sacrifice/sacrifices.

acrifié, ***e*** [sakrifje] **adj 1.** [personne] sacrificed **2.** [prix] giveaway *(avant n)*.

acrifier [9] [sakrifje] ■ **vt** [gén] to sacrifice ▸ **sacrifier qqch pour qqn/qqch** to sacrifice sthg for sb/sthg ▸ **sacrifier qqch pour faire qqch** to sacrifice sthg to do sthg ▸ **sacrifier qqn/qqch à** to sacrifice sb/sthg to.
■ **vi** *littéraire* [se conformer] **: sacrifier à** to conform to.
◆ ***se sacrifier*** **vp : se sacrifier à/pour** to sacrifice o.s. to/for.

acrilège [sakrilɛʒ] ■ **nm** sacrilege.
■ **nmf** sacrilegious person.
■ **adj** sacrilegious.

acristain [sakristɛ̃] **nm** sacristan.

acristie [sakristi] **nf** sacristy.

acro-saint, ***e*** [sakrɔsɛ̃, ɛ̃t] **adj** *hum* sacrosanct.

dique [sadik] ■ **nmf** sadist.
■ **adj** sadistic.

disme [sadism] **nm** sadism.

domaso [sadɔmazo] *fam* ■ **adj** sadomasochistic.
■ **nmf** sadomasochist.

domasochiste [sadɔmazɔʃist] ■ **nmf** sadomasochist.
■ **adj** sadomasochistic.

fari [safari] **nm** safari ▸ **safari-photo** photographic safari.

SAFER, ***Safer*** [safɛr] (abr de ***Société d'aménagement foncier et d'établissement régional***) **nf** *agency entitled to buy land and earmark it for agricultural use.*

safran [safrɑ̃] ■ **nm 1.** [épice] saffron **2.** NAUT rudder blade.
■ **adj inv** [couleur] saffron.

saga [saga] **nf** saga.

sagace [sagas] **adj** sagacious.

sagacité [sagasite] **nf** sagacity.

sagaie [sagɛ] **nf** assegai.

sage [saʒ] ■ **adj 1.** [personne, conseil] wise, sensible **2.** [enfant, chien] good **3.** [goûts] modest / [propos, vêtement] sober.
■ **nm** wise man, sage.

sage-femme [saʒfam] (pl **sages-femmes**) **nf** midwife.

sagement [saʒmɑ̃] **adv 1.** [avec bon sens] wisely, sensibly **2.** [docilement] like a good girl/boy.

sagesse [saʒɛs] **nf 1.** [bon sens] wisdom, good sense **2.** [docilité] good behaviour *UK ou* behavior *US*.

Sagittaire [saʒitɛr] **nm** ASTROL Sagittarius ▸ **être Sagittaire** to be (a) Sagittarius.

sagouin, ***e*** [sagwɛ̃, in] **nm, f** *fam* slob.
◆ ***sagouin*** **nm** ZOOL squirrel monkey.

Sahara [saara] **nm : le Sahara** the Sahara ▸ **au Sahara** in the Sahara ▸ **le Sahara occidental** the Western Sahara.

saharien, ***enne*** [saarjɛ̃, ɛn] **adj** Saharan.
◆ ***saharienne*** **nf** safari jacket.
◆ ***Saharien***, ***enne*** **nm, f** Saharan.

saignant, ***e*** [sɛɲɑ̃, ɑ̃t] **adj 1.** [blessure] bleeding **2.** [viande] rare, underdone **3.** *fam fig* [critique] hurtful.

saignée [seɲe] **nf 1.** *vieilli* & MÉD bloodletting, bleeding **2.** [pli du bras] crook of the arm **3.** [sillon - dans un sol] ditch / [- dans un mur] groove.

saignement [sɛɲmɑ̃] **nm** bleeding.

saigner [4] [seɲe] ■ **vt 1.** [malade, animal] to bleed **2.** [financièrement] **: saigner qqn (à blanc)** to bleed sb (white).
■ **vi** to bleed ▸ **je saigne du nez** my nose is bleeding, I've got a nosebleed.
◆ ***se saigner*** **vp : se saigner pour qqn** *fig* to bleed o.s. white for sb.

saillant, ***e*** [sajɑ̃, ɑ̃t] **adj 1.** [proéminent] projecting, protruding / [muscles] bulging / [pommettes] prominent **2.** *fig* [événement] salient, outstanding.

sailli, ***e*** [saji] **pp** ➤ ***saillir***[1], ***saillir***[2].

saillie [saji] **nf 1.** [avancée] projection ▸ **en saillie** projecting **2.** ZOOL covering.

saillir[1] [50] [sajir] **vi** [balcon] to project, to protrude / [muscles] to bulge.

saillir[2] [32] [sajir] **vt** ZOOL to cover.

sain, ***e*** [sɛ̃, sɛn] **adj 1.** [gén] healthy ▸ **sain et sauf** safe and sound **2.** [lecture] wholesome **3.** [fruit] fit to eat / [mur, gestion] sound.

saindoux [sɛ̃du] **nm** lard.

sainement [sɛnmɑ̃] **adv 1.** [vivre] healthily **2.** [raisonner] soundly.

saint, e [sɛ̃, sɛ̃t] ■ **adj 1.** [sacré] holy ▸ **le Saint-Esprit** the Holy Spirit ▸ **la Saint-Sylvestre** New Year's Eve ▸ **la Sainte Vierge** the Blessed Virgin ▸ **leur saint patron** their patron saint ▸ **le saint suaire (de Turin)** the Turin Shroud **2.** [pieux] saintly ▸ **sa mère était une sainte femme** his mother was a real saint **3.** [extrême] **: avoir une sainte horreur de qqch** to detest sthg.
■ **nm, f** saint ▸ **le saint des saints** *fig* the holy of holies ▸ **je ne sais (plus) à quel saint me vouer** I don't know which way to turn (any more).

saint-bernard [sɛ̃bɛrnar] **nm inv 1.** [chien] St Bernard **2.** *fig* [personne] good Samaritan.

Sainte-Catherine [sɛ̃tkatrin] **npr : coiffer Sainte-Catherine** *to be 25 and still unmarried on Saint Catherine's Day (25th November).*

Sainte-Chapelle [sɛ̃tʃapɛl] **npr f : la Sainte-Chapelle** *thirteenth-century church within the Palais de Justice on the île de la Cité.*

saintement [sɛ̃tmɑ̃] **adv : vivre saintement** to lead a saintly life.

saint-émilion [sɛ̃temiljɔ̃] **nm inv** *red wine from the Bordeaux region.*

sainte-nitouche [sɛ̃tnituʃ] (pl **saintes-nitouches**) **nf** *péj* **: c'est une sainte-nitouche** butter wouldn't melt in her mouth.

sainteté [sɛ̃tte] **nf** holiness.
◆ ***Sainteté*** **nf : Sa Sainteté** His Holiness.

saint-glinglin [sɛ̃glɛ̃glɛ̃] ◆ ***à la saint-glinglin*** **loc adv** *fam* till Doomsday.

Saint-Guy [sɛ̃gi] **npr : danse de Saint-Guy** Saint Vitus's dance.

saint-honoré [sɛ̃tɔnɔre] **nm inv** *choux pastry ring filled with confectioner's custard.*

Saint-Marin [sɛ̃marɛ̃] **npr** San Marino ▸ **à Saint-Marin** in San Marino.

saint-marinais, e [sɛ̃marinɛ, ɛz] **adj** of/from San Marino.
◆ ***Saint-Marinais, e*** **nm, f** native *ou* inhabitant of San Marino.

Saint-Père [sɛ̃pɛr] **nm** Holy Father.

Saint-Pétersbourg [sɛ̃petɛrsbur] **npr** Saint Petersburg.

saint-pierre [sɛ̃pjɛr] **nm inv** [poisson] John Dory.

Saint-Pierre [sɛ̃pjɛr] **npr : la basilique Saint-Pierre** Saint Peter's Basilica.

Saint-Siège [sɛ̃sjɛʒ] **nm : le Saint-Siège** the Holy See.

Saint-Sylvestre [sɛ̃silvɛstr] **npr f : la Saint-Sylvestre** *New Year's Eve* ▸ **le réveillon de la Saint-Sylvestre** *traditional French New Year's Eve celebration.*

sais, sait ➤ ***savoir.***

saisie [sezi] **nf 1.** [fiscalité & DR] distraint, seizure **2.** INFORM input ▸ **erreur de saisie** input error ▸ **saisie de données** data capture.

saisir [32] [sezir] **vt 1.** [empoigner] to take hold of / [avec force] to seize ▸ **saisir qqn à la gorge** to seize *ou* grab sb by the throat **2.** FIN & DR to seize, to distrain **3.** INFORM to capture **4.** [comprendre] to grasp **5.** [suj: sensation, émotion] to grip, to seize **6.** [surprendre] **: être saisi par** to be struck by **7.** CULIN to seal.
◆ ***se saisir*** **vp : se saisir de qqn/qqch** to seize sb/sthg, to grab sb/sthg.

saisissant, e [sezisɑ̃, ɑ̃t] **adj 1.** [spectacle] gripping / [ressemblance] striking **2.** [froid] biting.

saisissement [sezismɑ̃] **nm** [émotion] emotion.

saison [sɛzɔ̃] **nf** season ▸ **la belle saison** the summer months *pl* ▸ **c'est la bonne/mauvaise saison pour** it's the right/wrong time of year for ▸ **ce n'est pas un temps de saison** this weather's unusual for the time of the year ▸ **la saison des amours** the mating season ▸ **la saison des pluies** the rainy season, the rains ▸ **la saison touristique** the tourist season ▸ **en/hors saison** in/out of season ▸ **en pleine saison** at the height of the season ▸ **la haute/basse/morte saison** the high/low/off season ▸ **en cette saison** at this time of (the) year ▸ **en toutes saisons** all year round.

saisonnalité [sɛzɔnalite] **nf** seasonal nature.

saisonnier, ère [sɛzɔnje, ɛr] ■ **adj** seasonal.
■ **nm, f** seasonal worker.

saké [sake] **nm** sake.

salace [salas] **adj** salacious.

salade [salad] **nf 1.** [plante] lettuce **2.** [plat] (green) salad ▸ **salade composée** mixed salad ▸ **salade de fruits** fruit salad ▸ **salade niçoise** *salad containing anchovies and tuna* **3.** *fam fig* [méli-mélo] mess **4.** *fam fig* [baratin] story ▸ **raconter des salades** to tell stories ▸ **vendre sa salade** to lay it on thick.

saladier [saladje] **nm** salad bowl.

salaire [salɛr] **nm 1.** [rémunération] salary, wage ▸ **salaire brut/net/de base** gross/net/basic salary, gross/net/basic wage ▸ **salaire de départ** starting salary ▸ **salaire lié aux bénéfices** profit-related pay **2.** *fig* [récompense] reward.

salaison [salɛzɔ̃] **nf 1.** [procédé] salting **2.** [aliment] salted food.

salamalecs [salamalɛk] **nmpl** *fam péj* bowing and scraping *(U).*

salamandre [salamɑ̃dr] **nf** [animal] salamander.

salami [salami] **nm** salami.

salant [salɑ̃] ➤ ***marais.***

salarial, e, aux [salarjal, o] **adj** wage *(avant n).*

salariat [salarja] **nm 1.** [système] paid employment **2.** [salariés] wage-earners *pl.*

salarié, e [salarje] ■ **adj 1.** [personne] wage-earning **2.** [travail] paid.
■ **nm, f** salaried employee.

salaud [salo] *vulg* ■ **nm** bastard.
■ **adj m** shitty.

sale [sal] **adj 1.** [linge, mains] dirty / [couleur] dirty, dingy **2.** *(avant n)* [type, gueule, coup] nasty / [tour, histoire] dirty / [bête, temps] filthy.

salé, e [sale] **adj 1.** [eau, saveur] salty / [beurre] salted / [viande, poisson] salt *(avant n)*, salted **2.** *fig* [histoire] spicy **3.** *fam fig* [addition, facture] steep.
◆ ***salé*** **nm 1.** [aliment salé] savoury *UK ou* savory *US* food **2.** [porc] salt pork.

salement [salmɑ̃] adv **1.** [malproprement] dirtily, disgustingly **2.** *fam* [très] bloody *UK*, damn.

saler [3] [sale] vt **1.** [gén] to salt **2.** *fam fig* [note] to bump up.

saleté [salte] nf **1.** [malpropreté] dirtiness, filthiness ▸ **les rues sont d'une saleté incroyable** the streets are incredibly dirty *ou* filthy **2.** [crasse] dirt *(U)*, filth *(U)* ▸ **faire des saletés** to make a mess ▸ **tu as une saleté sur ta veste** you've got some dirt on your jacket **3.** *fam* [pacotille] junk *(U)*, rubbish *(U)* ▸ **c'est de la saleté** it's rubbish **4.** *fam* [maladie] bug ▸ **j'ai attrapé cette saleté à la piscine** I caught this blasted thing at the swimming pool **5.** [obscénité] dirty thing, obscenity ▸ **il m'a dit des saletés** he used obscenities to me **6.** [action] disgusting thing ▸ **faire une saleté à qqn** to play a dirty trick on sb **7.** [calomnie] (piece of) dirt ▸ **tu as encore raconté des saletés sur mon compte** you've been spreading filthy rumours about me again **8.** *fam péj* [personne] nasty piece of work *UK*.

salière [saljɛr] nf saltcellar, saltshaker *US* ▸ **salière-poivrière** cruet.

salin, e [salɛ̃, in] adj saline ⁄ [eau] salt *(avant n)*.

salir [32] [salir] vt **1.** [linge, mains] to (make) dirty, to soil **2.** *fig* [réputation, personne] to sully.
◆ ***se salir*** vp to get dirty.

salissant, e [salisɑ̃, ɑ̃t] adj **1.** [tissu] easily soiled **2.** [travail] dirty, messy.

salissure [salisyr] nf stain.

salivaire [salivɛr] adj salivary.

salive [saliv] nf saliva ▸ **dépenser beaucoup de salive** *fig* to talk nineteen to the dozen *UK* ▸ **perdre sa salive** *fig* to waste one's breath.

saliver [3] [salive] vi to salivate.

salle [sal] nf **1.** [pièce] room ▸ **en salle** [dans un café] inside ▸ **salle d'attente** waiting room ▸ **salle de bains** bathroom ▸ **salle de cinéma** cinema *UK*, movie theater *US* ▸ **salle de classe** classroom ▸ **salle d'eau, salle de douches** shower room ▸ **salle d'embarquement** departure lounge ▸ **salle des machines** engine room ▸ **salle à manger** dining room ▸ **salle non-fumeur** ≃ no smoking area ▸ **salle d'opération** operating theatre *UK ou* room *US* ▸ **salle de séjour** living room ▸ **salle de spectacle** theatre *UK*, theater *US* ▸ **salle des ventes** saleroom *UK*, salesroom *US* **2.** [de spectacle] auditorium **3.** [public] audience, house ▸ **jouer à salle pleine** to play to a full house ▸ **faire salle comble** to have a full house.

salmigondis [salmigɔ̃di] nm hotchpotch *UK*, hodgepodge *US*.

salmis [salmi] nm *half-roasted game or poultry finished in wine sauce.*

salmonellose [salmɔneloz] nf salmonella poisoning.

salon [salɔ̃] nm **1.** [de maison] lounge *UK*, living room ▸ **salon en cuir** leather suite ▸ **salon de jardin** garden set **2.** [commerce] **: salon de coiffure** hairdressing salon, hairdresser's ▸ **salon d'essayage** fitting room, changing room ▸ **salon de thé** tearoom **3.** [foire-exposition] show ▸ **Salon de l'automobile** Motor *UK ou* Car *ou* Automobile *US* Show ▸ **Salon du livre** *annual book fair in Paris.*

salopard [salɔpar] nm *tfam* bastard.

salope [salɔp] nf *vulg* bitch.

saloper [3] [salɔpe] vt *fam* to mess up, to make a mess of.

saloperie [salɔpri] nf *fam* **1.** [pacotille] rubbish *(U)* **2.** [maladie] bug **3.** [saleté] junk *(U)*, rubbish *(U)* ▸ **faire des saloperies** to make a mess **4.** [action] dirty trick ▸ **faire des saloperies à qqn** to play dirty tricks on sb **5.** [propos] dirty comment.

salopette [salɔpɛt] nf [d'ouvrier] overalls *pl* ⁄ [à bretelles] dungarees *(pl) UK*, overalls *US*.

salpêtre [salpɛtr] nm saltpetre *UK*, saltpeter *US*.

salsa [salsa] nf salsa.

salsifis [salsifi] nm salsify.

SALT [salt] (abr de ***Strategic Arms Limitation Talks***) SALT.

saltimbanque [saltɛ̃bɑ̃k] nmf acrobat.

salubre [salybr] adj healthy.

salubrité [salybrite] nf healthiness ▸ **la salubrité publique** public health.

saluer [7] [salɥe] vt **1.** [accueillir] to greet **2.** [dire au revoir à] to take one's leave of **3.** *fig* & MIL to salute.
◆ ***se saluer*** vp to say hello/goodbye (to one another).

salut [saly] ■ nm **1.** [de la main] wave ⁄ [de la tête] nod ⁄ [propos] greeting **2.** MIL salute **3.** [d'acteur] bow **4.** [sauvegarde] safety **5.** RELIG salvation.
■ interj *fam* [bonjour] hi! ⁄ [au revoir] bye!, see you!

salutaire [salytɛr] adj **1.** [conseil, expérience] salutary **2.** [remède, repos] beneficial.

salutation [salytasjɔ̃] nf *littéraire* salutation, greeting.
◆ ***salutations*** nfpl **: veuillez agréer, Monsieur, mes salutations distinguées** *ou* **mes sincères salutations** *sout* yours faithfully *UK*, yours sincerely.

salutiste [salytist] nmf & adj Salvationist.

Salvador [salvadɔr] nm **: le Salvador** El Salvador ▸ **au Salvador** in El Salvador.

salvadorien, enne [salvadɔrjɛ̃, ɛn] adj Salvadorian.
◆ ***Salvadorien, enne*** nm, f Salvadorian.

salve [salv] nf salvo.

Salzbourg [salzbur] npr Salzburg.

samaritain, e [samaritɛ̃, ɛn] adj Samaritan.
◆ ***samaritain*** nm *Suisse* first-aid worker.

samba [sɑ̃ba] nf samba.

samedi [samdi] nm Saturday ▸ **nous sommes partis samedi** we left on Saturday ▸ **samedi 13 septembre** Saturday 13th September *UK*, Saturday September 13th *US* ▸ **samedi dernier/prochain** last/next Saturday ▸ **samedi matin/midi/après-midi/soir** Saturday morning/lunchtime/afternoon/evening ▸ **de/du samedi** Saturday *(avant n)* ▸ **le samedi d'avant** the Saturday before ▸ **le samedi** on Saturdays ▸ **samedi en huit** a week on Saturday *UK*, Saturday week *UK*, a week from Saturday *US* ▸ **samedi en quinze** two weeks on *UK ou* from *US* Saturday ▸ **un samedi sur deux** every other Saturday ▸ **nous sommes *ou* c'est samedi** it's Saturday (today) ▸ **tous les samedis** every Saturday.

Samoa [samɔa] npr fpl Samoa.

samouraï, **samuraï** [samuraj] **nm** samurai.

samovar [samɔvar] **nm** samovar.

SAMU, **Samu** [samy] (abr de ***Service d'aide médicale d'urgence***) **nm 1.** MÉD *French ambulance and emergency service*, ≃ Ambulance Brigade *UK*, ≃ Paramedics *US* **2.** [aide sociale] **: le SAMU social** *a municipal service that deals with the homeless and assists persons in need.*

samuraï = ***samouraï***.

sanatorium [sanatɔrjɔm] **nm** sanatorium.

sanctifier [9] [sɑ̃ktifje] **vt 1.** [rendre saint] to sanctify **2.** [révérer] to hallow.

sanction [sɑ̃ksjɔ̃] **nf** sanction / *fig* [conséquence] penalty, price ▸ **prendre des sanctions contre** to impose sanctions on.

sanctionner [3] [sɑ̃ksjɔne] **vt** to sanction.

sanctuaire [sɑ̃ktɥɛr] **nm 1.** [d'église] sanctuary **2.** [lieu saint] shrine.

sandale [sɑ̃dal] **nf** sandal.

sandalette [sɑ̃dalɛt] **nf** sandal.

Sandow® [sɑ̃do] **nm 1.** [attache] elastic cable *(for securing luggage etc)* **2.** AÉRON catapult.

sandwich [sɑ̃dwitʃ] (pl **sandwiches** *ou* **sandwichs**) **nm** sandwich ▸ **être pris en sandwich entre** *fam* to be sandwiched between.

sandwicherie [sɑ̃dwitʃri] **nf** sandwich shop / [avec possibilité de manger sur place] sandwich bar.

sang [sɑ̃] **nm** blood ▸ **en sang** bleeding ▸ **pur-sang** thoroughbred ▸ **dans le sang** *fig* in the blood ▸ **se faire du mauvais sang** *ou* **un sang d'encre** *fig* to get really worried *ou* upset ▸ **suer sang et eau** *fig* to sweat blood.

sang-froid [sɑ̃frwa] **nm inv** calm ▸ **de sang-froid** in cold blood ▸ **perdre/garder son sang-froid** to lose/to keep one's head.

sanglant, **e** [sɑ̃glɑ̃, ɑ̃t] **adj** bloody / *fig* cruel.

sangle [sɑ̃gl] **nf** strap / [de selle] girth.
◆ ***sangles*** **nfpl** webbing *(U)*.

sangler [3] [sɑ̃gle] **vt** [attacher] to strap / [cheval] to girth.

sanglier [sɑ̃glije] **nm** boar.

sanglot [sɑ̃glo] **nm** sob ▸ **éclater en sanglots** to burst into sobs.

sangloter [3] [sɑ̃glɔte] **vi** to sob.

sangria [sɑ̃grija] **nf** sangria.

sangsue [sɑ̃sy] **nf** leech / *fig* [personne] bloodsucker.

sanguin, **e** [sɑ̃gɛ̃, in] **adj 1.** ANAT blood *(avant n)* **2.** [rouge - visage] ruddy / [- orange] blood *(avant n)* **3.** [emporté] quick-tempered.
◆ ***sanguine*** **nf 1.** [dessin] red chalk drawing **2.** [fruit] blood orange.

sanguinaire [sɑ̃ginɛr] **adj 1.** [tyran] bloodthirsty **2.** [lutte] bloody.

sanguinolent, **e** [sɑ̃ginɔlɑ̃, ɑ̃t] **adj** stained with blood.

Sanibroyeur® [sanibrwajœr] **nm** Saniflo® *(toilet with macerator unit)*.

Sanisette® [sanizɛt] **nf** ≃ superloo *UK*; *(automatic public toilet)*.

sanitaire [sanitɛr] ■ **nm** bathroom fittings and plumbing.
■ **adj 1.** [service, mesure] health *(avant n)* **2.** [installation, appareil] bathroom *(avant n)*.
◆ ***sanitaires*** **nmpl** toilets and showers.

sans [sɑ̃] ■ **prép** without ▸ **sans argent** without any money ▸ **sans faire un effort** without making an effort.
■ **adv : passe-moi mon manteau, je ne veux pas sortir sans** pass me my coat, I don't want to go out without it.
◆ ***sans que*** **loc conj** *(+ subjonctif)* **: sans que vous le sachiez** without your knowing.

sans-abri [sɑ̃zabri] **nmf** homeless person.

San Salvador [sɑ̃salvadɔr] **npr** San Salvador.

sanscrit [sɑ̃skri] **nm** Sanskrit.

sans-emploi [sɑ̃zɑ̃plwa] **nmf** unemployed person.

sans-gêne [sɑ̃ʒɛn] ■ **nm inv** [qualité] rudeness, lack of consideration.
■ **nmf** [personne] rude *ou* inconsiderate person.
■ **adj inv** rude, inconsiderate.

sans-le-sou [sɑ̃lsu] **nmf** *fam* person who is broke *ou* hard up.

sans-logis [sɑ̃lɔʒi] **nmf** homeless person.

sansonnet [sɑ̃sɔnɛ] **nm** starling.

sans-papiers [sɑ̃papje] **nmf** *immigrant without proper identity or working papers.*

sans-plomb [sɑ̃plɔ̃] **nm inv** unleaded, unleaded petrol *UK ou* gas *US*, lead-free petrol *UK ou* gas *US*.

santal [sɑ̃tal] **nm** sandalwood.

santé [sɑ̃te] **nf** health ▸ **recouvrer la santé** to get one's health back ▸ **santé de fer** strong *ou* iron constitution ▸ **à ta/votre santé!** cheers!, good health! ▸ **boire à la santé de qqn** to drink sb's health, to toast sb.

santiag [sɑ̃tjag] **nf** cowboy boot.

Santiago [sɑ̃tjago] **npr** Santiago.

santon [sɑ̃tɔ̃] **nm** *figure placed in Christmas crib.*

São Paulo [saopolo] **npr 1.** [ville] São Paulo **2.** [État] **: l'État de São Paulo** São Paulo (State).

saoudien, **enne** [saudjɛ̃, ɛn] **adj** Saudi (Arabian).
◆ ***Saoudien***, ***enne*** **nm, f** Saudi (Arabian).

saoul = ***soûl***.

saouler = ***soûler***.

sape [sap] **nf 1.** [travaux publics & MIL] sapping / [tranchée] sap **2.** *fig* **: travail de sape** (insidious) undermining ▸ **par un patient travail de sape, ils ont fini par avoir raison de lui** they chipped away at him until he gave in **3.** *(gén pl) fam* [vêtement] rig-out *UK*, gear.

saper [3] [sape] **vt** to undermine.
◆ ***se saper*** **vp** *fam* to dress o.s. up.

sapeur [sapœr] **nm** sapper.

sapeur-pompier [sapœrpɔ̃pje] (pl **sapeurs-pompiers**) **nm** fireman, firefighter.

saphir [safir] **nm** sapphire.

sapidité [sapidite] **nf** sapidity.

sapin [sapɛ̃] **nm** **1.** [arbre] fir, firtree ▸ **sapin de Noël** Christmas tree **2.** [bois] fir, deal *UK*.

sapinière [sapinjɛr] **nf** fir forest.

sapristi [sapristi] **interj** *fam* goodness me!, my goodness!

saquer = ***sacquer***.

S.A.R. (abr écrite de ***son altesse royale***) H.R.H.

sarabande [sarabɑ̃d] **nf** **1.** [danse] saraband **2.** *fam* [vacarme] din, racket.

Sarajevo [sarajɛvo] **npr** Sarajevo.

sarbacane [sarbakan] **nf** [arme] blowpipe, blowgun / [jouet] peashooter.

sarcasme [sarkasm] **nm** sarcasm.

sarcastique [sarkastik] **adj** sarcastic.

sarcler [3] [sarkle] **vt** to weed.

sarcloir [sarklwar] **nm** hoe.

sarcophage [sarkɔfaʒ] **nm** sarcophagus.

Sardaigne [sardɛɲ] **nf : la Sardaigne** Sardinia.

sarde [sard] **adj** Sardinian.
◆ ***Sarde*** **nmf** Sardinian.

sardine [sardin] **nf** sardine ▸ **sardines à l'huile** sardines in oil ▸ **être serrés comme des sardines** *fam fig* to be packed like sardines.

sardinerie [sardinri] **nf** sardine cannery.

sardonique [sardɔnik] **adj** sardonic.

sari [sari] **nm** sari, saree.

SARL, ***Sarl*** (abr de ***société à responsabilité limitée***) **nf** limited liability company *UK* ▸ **Leduc, SARL** ≃ Leduc Ltd *UK*, ≃ Leduc Inc *US*.

sarment [sarmɑ̃] **nm** **1.** [de vigne] shoot **2.** [tige] stem.

sarrasin, ***e*** [sarazɛ̃, in] **adj** Saracen.
◆ ***sarrasin*** **nm** buckwheat.
◆ ***Sarrasin***, ***e*** **nm, f** Saracen.

sarrau [saro] **nm** smock.

sarriette [sarjɛt] **nf** savory.

sas [sas] **nm** **1.** AÉRON & NAUT airlock **2.** [d'écluse] lock **3.** [tamis] sieve.

S.A.S. (abr écrite de ***son altesse sérénissime***) H.S.H.

satané, ***e*** [satane] **adj** *(avant n)* *fam* damned.

satanique [satanik] **adj** satanic.

satellisation [satelizasjɔ̃] **nf** **1.** [de fusée] putting into orbit **2.** [de pays] becoming a satellite.

satelliser [3] [satelize] **vt** **1.** [fusée] to put into orbit **2.** [pays] to make a satellite.

satellite [satelit] ■ **nm** satellite ▸ **satellite artificiel/météorologique/de télécommunications** artificial/meteorological/communications satellite ▸ **par satellite** by satellite ▸ **satellite-relais** telecommunications satellite.
■ **adj** satellite *(avant n)*.

satiété [sasjete] **nf : à satiété** [boire, manger] one's fill / [répéter] ad nauseam.

satin [satɛ̃] **nm** satin.

satiné, ***e*** [satine] **adj** satin *(avant n)* / [peau] satiny-smooth.
◆ ***satiné*** **nm** satin-like quality.

satinette [satinɛt] **nf** **1.** [coton et soie] satinet **2.** [coton seul] sateen.

satire [satir] **nf** satire.

satirique [satirik] **adj** satirical.

satisfaction [satisfaksjɔ̃] **nf** satisfaction ▸ **donner (entière) satisfaction à qqn** [personne] to give sb (complete) satisfaction / [travail] to fulfil *UK ou* to fulfill *US* sb completely, to give sb a lot of (job) satisfaction ▸ **éprouver de la satisfaction/une grande satisfaction à faire qqch** to feel satisfaction/great satisfaction in doing sthg ▸ **le problème fut résolu à la satisfaction générale** the problem was solved to everybody's satisfaction ▸ **mon fils m'apporte de nombreuses satisfactions** my son is a great satisfaction to me.

satisfaire [109] [satisfɛr] **vt** to satisfy ▸ **satisfaire à** [condition, revendication] to meet, to satisfy / [engagement] to fulfil *UK*, to fulfill *US*.
◆ ***se satisfaire*** **vp : se satisfaire de** to be satisfied with.

satisfaisait, ***satisfaisions*** ➤ ***satisfaire***.

satisfaisant, ***e*** [satisfəzɑ̃, ɑ̃t] **adj** **1.** [travail] satisfactory **2.** [expérience] satisfying.

PARONYME / CONFUSABLE

satisfaisant

Attention en traduisant le mot satisfaisant : *satisfactory* signifie convenable, qui donne satisfaction, tandis que *satisfying* désigne ce qui contente.

satisfait, ***e*** [satisfɛ, ɛt] ■ **pp** ➤ ***satisfaire***.
■ **adj** satisfied ▸ **être satisfait de** to be satisfied with ▸ **'satisfait ou remboursé'** 'satisfaction guaranteed or your money back'.

satisfasse, ***satisfasses*** ➤ ***satisfaire***.

saturation [satyrasjɔ̃] **nf** saturation.

saturé, ***e*** [satyre] **adj : saturé (de)** saturated (with).

saturer [3] [satyre] **vt : saturer qqch (de)** to saturate sthg (with).

saturne [satyrn] **nm** *vieilli* lead.
◆ ***Saturne*** **nf** ASTRON Saturn.

saturnisme [satyrnism] **nm** (chronic) lead poisoning, saturnism *(terme spécialisé)*.

satyre [satir] **nm** satyr / *fig* sex maniac.

sauce [sos] **nf** **1.** CULIN sauce ▸ **en sauce** in a sauce ▸ **sauce hollandaise** hollandaise sauce ▸ **sauce tartare** tartare sauce ▸ **sauce tomate/blanche/piquante** tomato/white/spicy sauce **2.** *fig* [accompagnement] presentation ▸ **mettre qqn à toutes les sauces** to use sb as a dogsbody *UK*.

saucer [16] [sose] **vt** **1.** [assiette] to wipe **2.** *fam* [personne] **: se faire saucer** to get soaked.

saucière [sosjɛr] **nf** sauceboat.

saucisse [sosis] **nf** **1.** CULIN sausage ▸ **saucisse de Francfort** frankfurter ▸ **saucisse sèche** dried sausage **2.** *fam vieilli* & AÉRON barrage balloon.

saucisson [sosisɔ̃] **nm** slicing sausage.

saucissonner [3] [sosisɔne] ■ **vi** *fam* to have a picnic. ■ **vt 1.** [colis] to truss up **2.** [baguette] to slice up.

sauf[1], ***sauve*** [sof, sov] **adj** [personne] safe, unharmed / *fig* [honneur] saved, intact.

sauf[2] [sof] **prép 1.** [à l'exclusion de] except, apart from **2.** [sous réserve de] barring ▸ **sauf que** except (that).

sauf-conduit [sofkɔ̃dɥi] (pl **sauf-conduits**) **nm** safe-conduct.

sauge [soʒ] **nf 1.** CULIN sage **2.** [plante ornementale] salvia.

saugrenu, ***e*** [sogrəny] **adj** ridiculous, nonsensical.

saule [sol] **nm** willow ▸ **saule pleureur** weeping willow.

saumâtre [somatr] **adj 1.** [eau] brackish **2.** *fig* [plaisanterie] distasteful.

saumon [somɔ̃] ■ **nm** salmon ▸ **saumon fumé** CULIN smoked salmon *UK*, lox *US*.
■ **adj inv** salmon pink.

saumoné, ***e*** [somɔne] **adj** salmon *(avant n)*.

saumure [somyr] **nf** brine.

sauna [sona] **nm** sauna.

saupoudrer [3] [sopudre] **vt : saupoudrer qqch de** to sprinkle sthg with.

saupoudreuse [sopudrøz] **nf** dredger.

saur [sɔr] ➤ ***hareng***.

saurai, ***sauras*** ➤ ***savoir***.

saurien [sorjɛ̃] **nm** saurian.

saut [so] **nm 1.** [bond] leap, jump ▸ **au saut du lit** [en se levant] on *ou* upon getting up / [tôt] first thing in the morning **2.** SPORT **: saut de l'ange** swallow *UK ou* swan *US* dive ▸ **saut à la corde** skipping ▸ **saut de haies** hurdling ▸ **saut en hauteur** high jump ▸ **saut en longueur** long jump, broad jump *US* ▸ **saut à l'élastique** bungee-jumping ▸ **faire du saut à l'élastique** to go bungee-jumping ▸ **saut en parachute** [discipline] parachuting, skydiving / [épreuve] parachute jump ▸ **saut à la perche** [discipline] pole vaulting / [épreuve] pole vault ▸ **saut périlleux** somersault **3.** [visite] **: faire un saut chez qqn** *fig* to pop in and see sb ▸ **elle a fait un saut chez nous hier** she dropped by (our house) yesterday **4.** INFORM **: (insérer un) saut de page** (insert) page break ▸ **saut de colonne** (insert) column break.

saute [sot] **nf** sudden change ▸ **avoir des sautes d'humeur** to have mood swings, to be temperamental.

sauté, ***e*** [sote] **adj** sautéed.
◆ ***sauté*** **nm : sauté de veau** sautéed veal.

saute-mouton [sotmutɔ̃] **nm inv : jouer à saute-mouton** to play leapfrog.

sauter [3] [sote] ■ **vi 1.** [bondir] to jump, to leap ▸ **sauter à la corde** to skip *UK*, to skip *ou* jump rope *US* ▸ **sauter en hauteur/longueur** to do the high/long jump ▸ **sauter en parachute** to (parachute) jump, to parachute ▸ **sauter à la perche** to pole-vault ▸ **sauter dans un taxi** to jump *ou* to leap into a taxi ▸ **sauter par la fenêtre** to jump out of the window ▸ **sauter d'un sujet à l'autre** *fig* to jump from one subject to another ▸ **sauter de joie** *fig* to jump for joy ▸ **sauter au cou de qqn** *fig* to throw one's arms around sb **2.** [exploser] to blow up ▸ **faire sauter un pont** to blow up a bridge / [fusible] to blow **3.** [être projeté - bouchon] to fly out / [- serrure] to burst off / [- bouton] to fly off / [- chaîne de vélo] to come off **4.** *fam* [personne] to get the sack *UK* ▸ **faire sauter un directeur** to kick out *ou* to fire a manager **5.** [être annulé] to be cancelled **6.** CULIN **: faire sauter qqch** to sauté sthg ▸ **faire sauter des crêpes** to toss pancakes
▸▸ **et que ça saute!** *fam* and get a move on!
■ **vt 1.** [fossé, obstacle] to jump *ou* leap over ▸ **sauter le pas** *fig* to take the plunge **2.** *fig* [page, repas] to skip **3.** *vulg* [personne] **: sauter qqn** to have it off with sb.

sauterelle [sotrɛl] **nf 1.** ZOOL grasshopper **2.** *fam fig* [personne] beanpole.

sauterie [sotri] **nf** *vieilli* do *UK*, party.

sauternes [sotɛrn] **nm** *sweet dessert wine*.

sauteur, ***euse*** [sotœr, øz] ■ **adj** [insecte] jumping *(avant n)*.
■ **nm, f** [athlète] jumper.
◆ ***sauteur*** **nm** [cheval] jumper.
◆ ***sauteuse*** **nf** CULIN frying pan.

sautiller [3] [sotije] **vi** to hop.

sautoir [sotwar] **nm 1.** [bijou] chain ▸ **sautoir de perles** string of pearls ▸ **porter qqch en sautoir** to wear sthg on a chain round one's neck **2.** SPORT jumping area.

sauvage [sovaʒ] ■ **adj 1.** [plante, animal] wild **2.** [farouche - animal familier] shy, timid / [- personne] unsociable **3.** [conduite, haine] savage.
■ **nmf 1.** [solitaire] recluse **2.** *péj* [brute, indigène] savage.

sauvagement [sovaʒmɑ̃] **adv** savagely.

sauvageon, ***onne*** [sovaʒɔ̃, ɔn] **nm, f** little savage.

sauvagerie [sovaʒri] **nf 1.** [férocité] brutality, savagery **2.** [insociabilité] unsociableness.

sauvagine [sovaʒin] **nf** *littéraire* wildfowl.

sauve ➤ ***sauf***.

sauvegarde [sovgard] **nf 1.** [protection] safeguard **2.** INFORM saving / [copie] backup.

sauvegarder [3] [sovgarde] **vt 1.** [protéger] to safeguard **2.** INFORM to save / [copier] to back up.

sauve-qui-peut [sovkipø] ■ **nm inv** [débandade] stampede.
■ **interj** every man for himself!

sauver [3] [sove] **vt 1.** [gén] to save ▸ **sauver qqn/qqch de** to save sb/sthg from, to rescue sb/sthg from ▸ **sauver qqch de l'oubli** to rescue sthg from oblivion ▸ **sauver qqn de** MÉD to cure sb of ▸ **sauver la vie à qqn** to save sb's life ▸ **sauver sa peau** *fam* to save one's skin *ou* hide ▸ **être sauvé** [sain et sauf] to be safe / [par quelqu'un] to have been saved *ou* rescued **2.** [navire, biens] to salvage.
◆ ***se sauver*** **vp : se sauver (de)** to run away (from) [prisonnier] to escape (from) ▸ **se sauver à toutes jambe**[s] to take to one's heels (and run).

sauvetage [sovtaʒ] **nm 1.** [de personne] rescue **2.** [d]e navire, biens] salvage.

sauveteur [sovtœr] **nm** rescuer.

sauvette [sovɛt] ◆ ***à la sauvette*** **loc adv** hurriedly, a[t] great speed.

sauveur [sovœr] **nm** saviour *UK*, savior *US*.

SAV [sav] (abr de ***service après-vente***) **nm** after-sales service.

savamment [savamɑ̃] **adv 1.** [avec érudition] learnedly **2.** [avec habileté] skilfully *UK*, skillfully *US*, cleverly.

savane [savan] **nf** savanna.

savant, e [savɑ̃, ɑ̃t] **adj 1.** [érudit] scholarly **2.** [habile] skilful, clever **3.** [animal] performing *(avant n)*.
◆ ***savant*** **nm** scientist.

savarin [savarɛ̃] **nm** *ring-shaped cake containing rum.*

savate [savat] **nf 1.** [pantoufle] worn-out slipper / [soulier] worn-out shoe **2.** SPORT kick boxing **3.** *fam fig* [personne] clumsy oaf.

saveur [savœr] **nf** flavour *UK*, flavor *US* / *fig* savour *UK*, savor *US*.

savoir [59] [savwar] ■ **vt 1.** [gén] to know ▸ **faire savoir qqch à qqn** to tell sb sthg, to inform sb of sthg ▸ **si j'avais su...** had I but known..., if I had only known... ▸ **je l'ai su par son frère** I heard it from her brother ▸ **je ne savais plus où me mettre** *ou* **me fourrer** *fam* [de honte] I didn't know where to put myself ▸ **je ne sais où, on ne sait où** God knows where ▸ **sans le savoir** unconsciously, without being aware of it ▸ **en savoir long sur qqn/qqch** to know a lot about sb/sthg ▸ **tu (ne) peux pas savoir** *fam* you have no idea ▸ **pas que je sache** not as far as I know ▸ **(ne pas) savoir de quoi il retourne** (not) to know what it's all about ▸ **que savez-vous de lui?** what do you know about *ou* of him? **2.** [être capable de] to know how to ▸ **sais-tu conduire?** can you drive? ▸ **je n'ai pas su la réconforter** I wasn't able to comfort her ▸ **elle ne sait ni lire ni écrire** she can't read or write ▸ **savoir s'y prendre avec les enfants** to know how to handle children, to be good with children.
■ **nm** learning.
◆ ***se savoir*** **vp** *(emploi passif)* to become known ▸ **tout se sait dans le village** news travels fast in the village ▸ **ça se saurait s'il était si doué que ça** *fam* if he was that good, you'd know about it.
◆ ***à savoir*** **loc conj** namely, that is.

savoir-faire [savwarfɛr] **nm inv** know-how, expertise.

savoir-vivre [savwarvivr] **nm inv** good manners *pl.*

savon [savɔ̃] **nm 1.** [matière] soap / [pain] cake *ou* bar of soap ▸ **savon de Marseille** ≃ household soap **2.** *fam* [réprimande] telling-off ▸ **passer un savon à qqn** to give sb a telling-off.

savonner [3] [savɔne] **vt 1.** [linge] to soap **2.** *fam* [enfant] to tell off.
◆ ***se savonner*** **vp** to soap o.s.

savonnette [savɔnɛt] **nf** guest soap.

savonneux, euse [savɔnø, øz] **adj** soapy.

savourer [3] [savure] **vt** to savour *UK*, to savor *US*.

savoureux, euse [savurø, øz] **adj 1.** [mets] tasty **2.** *fig* [anecdote] juicy.

savoyard, e [savwajar, ard] **adj** of/from Savoy.
◆ ***Savoyard, e*** **nm, f** native *ou* inhabitant of Savoy.

saxo [sakso] **nm** *fam* **1.** [instrument] sax **2.** [musicien] sax (player).

saxophone [saksɔfɔn] **nm** saxophone.

saxophoniste [saksɔfɔnist] **nmf** saxophonist, saxophone player.

saynète [sɛnɛt] **nf** playlet.

SBB (abr de ***Schweizerische Bundesbahn***) *Swiss federal railways.*

sbire [sbir] **nm** *péj* henchman.

sbrinz [ʃbrints] **nm** *hard crumbly Swiss cheese made from cow's milk.*

sc. (abr écrite de ***scène***) sc.

s/c (abr écrite de ***sous couvert de***) c/o.

scabreux, euse [skabrø, øz] **adj 1.** [propos] shocking, indecent **2.** [entreprise] risky.

scalp [skalp] **nm 1.** [action] scalping **2.** [trophée] scalp.

scalpel [skalpɛl] **nm** scalpel.

scalper [3] [skalpe] **vt** to scalp.

scampi [skɑ̃pi] **nmpl** scampi *(U).*

scandale [skɑ̃dal] **nm 1.** [fait choquant] scandal **2.** [indignation] uproar **3.** [tapage] scene ▸ **faire du** *ou* **un scandale** to make a scene.

scandaleusement [skɑ̃daløzmɑ̃] **adj** scandalously, outrageously.

scandaleux, euse [skɑ̃dalø, øz] **adj** scandalous, outrageous.

scandaliser [3] [skɑ̃dalize] **vt** to shock, to scandalize.
◆ ***se scandaliser*** **vp** to be shocked, to be scandalized.

scander [3] [skɑ̃de] **vt 1.** [vers] to scan **2.** [slogan] to chant.

scandinave [skɑ̃dinav] **adj** Scandinavian.
◆ ***Scandinave*** **nmf** Scandinavian.

Scandinavie [skɑ̃dinavi] **nf : la Scandinavie** Scandinavia.

scanner[1] [4] [skane] **vt** to scan.

scanner[2] [skanɛr] **nm** scanner.

scaphandre [skafɑ̃dr] **nm 1.** [de plongeur] diving suit ▸ **scaphandre autonome** aqualung **2.** [d'astronaute] spacesuit.

scaphandrier [skafɑ̃drije] **nm** deep-sea diver.

scarabée [skarabe] **nm** beetle, scarab.

scarlatine [skarlatin] **nf** scarlet fever.

scarole [skarɔl] **nf** endive.

scatologique [skatɔlɔʒik] **adj** scatological.

sceau, x [so] **nm** seal / *fig* stamp, hallmark ▸ **sous le sceau du secret** *fig* under the seal of secrecy.

scélérat, e [selera, at] *littéraire* ■ **adj** wicked.
■ **nm, f** villain / *péj* rogue, rascal.

sceller [4] [sele] **vt 1.** [gén] to seal **2.** CONSTR [fixer] to embed.

scellés [sele] **nmpl** seals ▸ **sous scellés** sealed.

scénario [senarjo] **nm 1.** CINÉ, LITTÉR & THÉÂTRE [canevas] scenario **2.** CINÉ & TV [découpage, synopsis] screenplay, script **3.** *fig* [rituel] pattern.

scénariste [senarist] **nmf** scriptwriter.

scène [sɛn] **nf 1.** [gén] scene ▸ **la scène finale** the last *ou* closing scene ▸ **la scène se passe à Montréal** the action takes place in *ou* the scene is set in Montreal ▸ **la scène internationale/politique** the international/political scene ▸ **scène de ménage** domestic row *ou* scene ▸ **faire une scène (à qqn)** to make a scene **2.** [estrade] stage ▸ **adapter un livre pour la scène** to adapt a book for the stage *ou* theatre ▸ **entrée en scène** THÉÂTRE entrance / *fig* appearance ▸ **entrer en scène** THÉÂTRE to come on stage / *fig* to come *ou* to step in ▸ **mettre en scène** THÉÂTRE to stage / CINÉ to direct ▸ **monter sur scène** to go on the stage.

scénique [senik] **adj** theatrical.

scepticisme [sɛptisism] **nm** scepticism *UK*, skepticism *US*.

sceptique [sɛptik] ■ **nmf** sceptic *UK*, skeptic *US*.
■ **adj 1.** [incrédule] sceptical *UK*, skeptical *US* **2.** PHILO sceptic *UK*, skeptic *US*.

sceptre [sɛptr] **nm** sceptre *UK*, scepter *US*.

SCH (abr écrite de ***schilling***) S, Sch.

schah, ***shah*** [ʃa] **nm** shah.

schéma [ʃema] **nm 1.** [diagramme] diagram **2.** [résumé] outline.

schématique [ʃematik] **adj 1.** [dessin] diagrammatic **2.** [interprétation, exposé] simplified.

schématiquement [ʃematikmɑ̃] **adv 1.** [par dessin] diagrammatically **2.** [en résumé] briefly.

schématisation [ʃematizasjɔ̃] **nf 1.** [présentation graphique] diagrammatic representation **2.** *péj* [généralisation] oversimplification.

schématiser [3] [ʃematize] **vt 1.** [présenter en schéma] to represent diagrammatically **2.** *péj* [généraliser] to oversimplify.

schisme [ʃism] **nm 1.** RELIG schism **2.** [d'opinion] split.

schiste [ʃist] **nm** shale.

schizo [skizo] **adj** *fam* schizophrenic.

schizoïde [skizɔid] **adj** schizoid.

schizophrène [skizɔfrɛn] **nmf & adj** schizophrenic.

schizophrénie [skizɔfreni] **nf** schizophrenia.

schizophrénique [skizɔfrenik] **adj** schizophrenic.

schlinguer, ***chlinguer*** [3] [ʃlɛ̃ge] **vi** *tfam* to stink.

schnock, ***chnoque*** [ʃnɔk] **nm** *fam* **: du schnock!** dummy!, dimwit!

schublig [ʃublig] **nm** *Suisse type of sausage.*

schuss [ʃus] ■ **nm** schuss.
■ **adv : descendre (tout) schuss** to schuss down.

sciatique [sjatik] ■ **nf** sciatica.
■ **adj** sciatic.

scie [si] **nf 1.** [outil] saw ▸ **scie à métaux** hacksaw ▸ **scie sauteuse** jigsaw **2.** [rengaine] catchphrase **3.** *fam* [personne] bore.

sciemment [sjamɑ̃] **adv** knowingly.

science [sjɑ̃s] **nf 1.** [connaissances scientifiques] science ▸ **les sciences économiques** economics ▸ **sciences humaines *ou* sociales** UNIV social sciences ▸ **sciences naturelles** SCOL biology *sg* ▸ **sciences occultes** the occult (sciences) ▸ **les sciences politiques** politics, political sciences **2.** [érudition] knowledge ▸ **avoir la science infuse** *fig* to know a lot ▸ **il faut toujours qu'il étale sa science** he's always trying to impress everybody with what he knows **3.** [art] art.

science-fiction [sjɑ̃sfiksjɔ̃] **nf** science fiction.

sciences-po [sjɑ̃spo] **nfpl** UNIV political science *sg*.
◆ ***Sciences-Po*** **npr** *grande école for political science.*

scientifique [sjɑ̃tifik] ■ **nmf** scientist.
■ **adj** scientific.

scientifiquement [sjɑ̃tifikmɑ̃] **adv** scientifically.

scientisme [sjɑ̃tism] **nm** Christian Science.

scientologie [sjɑ̃tɔlɔʒi] **nf** Scientology®.

scier [9] [sje] **vt 1.** [branche] to saw **2.** *fam* [personne] to stagger.

scierie [siri] **nf** sawmill.

scinder [3] [sɛ̃de] **vt : scinder (en)** to split (into), to divide (into).
◆ ***se scinder*** **vp : se scinder (en)** to split (into), to divide (into).

scintillant, ***e*** [sɛ̃tijɑ̃, ɑ̃t] **adj** sparkling.

scintillement [sɛ̃tijmɑ̃] **nm** sparkle.

scintiller [3] [sɛ̃tije] **vi** to sparkle.

scission [sisjɔ̃] **nf** split.

sciure [sjyr] **nf** sawdust.

sclérose [skleroz] **nf** sclerosis / *fig* ossification ▸ **sclérose en plaques** multiple sclerosis.

sclérosé, ***e*** [skleroze] ■ **adj** sclerotic / *fig* ossified.
■ **nm, f** person suffering from sclerosis / *fig* person set in his/her ways.

scléroser [3] [skleroze] ◆ ***se scléroser*** **vp** to become sclerotic / *fig* to become ossified.

scolaire [skɔlɛr] **adj** school *(avant n)* / *péj* bookish.

scolarisable [skɔlarizabl] **adj** of school age.

scolarisation [skɔlarizasjɔ̃] **nf** schooling.

scolariser [3] [skɔlarize] **vt** to provide with schooling.

scolarité [skɔlarite] **nf** schooling ▸ **prolonger la scolarité** to raise the school-leaving age *UK* ▸ **frais de scolarité** SCOL school fees / UNIV tuition fees.

scolastique [skɔlastik] ■ **nf** scholasticism.
■ **adj** scholastic.

scoliose [skɔljoz] **nf** curvature of the spine.

scoop [skup] **nm** scoop.

scooter [skutœr] **nm** scooter ▸ **scooter des mers** jet sk ▸ **scooter des neiges** snowmobile.

scorbut [skɔrbyt] **nm** scurvy.

score [skɔr] **nm 1.** SPORT score **2.** POLIT result.

scorie [skɔri] **nf 1.** *(gén pl)* GÉOL scoria **2.** [dans l'industrie slag *(U)* / *fig* dregs *pl*.

scorpion [skɔrpjɔ̃] **nm** scorpion.
◆ ***Scorpion*** **nm** ASTROL Scorpio ▸ **être Scorpion** to be (a Scorpio.

scotch [skɔtʃ] **nm** [alcool] whisky, Scotch.

Scotch® [skɔtʃ] **nm** [adhésif] ≃ Sellotape® *UK*, ≃ Scotc tape® *US*.

scotché, e [skɔtʃe] **adj : être scotché devant la télévision** to be glued to the television.

scotcher [3] [skɔtʃe] **vt** to sellotape *UK*, to scotch-tape *US*.

scout, e [skut] **adj** scout *(avant n)*.
◆ ***scout*** **nm** scout.

scoutisme [skutism] **nm** scouting.

Scrabble® [skrabl] **nm** Scrabble®.

scratcher [skratʃe] ◆ ***scratcher (se)*** **vp** *fam* to crash ▸ **se scratcher contre un arbre** to crash into a tree.

scribe [skrib] **nm** HIST scribe.

scribouillard, e [skribujar, ard] **nm, f** *péj* pen pusher.

script [skript] **nm 1.** TYPO printing, print **2.** CINÉ & TV script.

scripte [skript] **nmf** CINÉ & TV continuity person.

scriptural, e, aux [skriptyral, o] **adj : monnaie scripturale** substitute money.

scrotum [skrɔtɔm] **nm** scrotum.

scrupule [skrypyl] **nm** scruple ▸ **avec scrupule** scrupulously ▸ **sans scrupules** [être] unscrupulous / [agir] unscrupulously.

scrupuleusement [skrypyløzmɑ̃] **adv** scrupulously.

scrupuleux, euse [skrypylø, øz] **adj** scrupulous.

scrutateur, trice [skrytatœr, tris] **adj** searching.
◆ ***scrutateur*** **nm** POLIT ≃ scrutineer *UK*, ≃ teller *US*.

scruter [3] [skryte] **vt** to scrutinize.

scrutin [skrytɛ̃] **nm 1.** [vote] ballot ▸ **dépouiller un scrutin** to count the votes **2.** [système] voting system ▸ **scrutin majoritaire** first-past-the-post system *UK* ▸ **scrutin proportionnel** proportional representation system.

sculpter [3] [skylte] **vt** to sculpt.

sculpteur [skyltœr] **nm** sculptor.

sculptural, e, aux [skyltyral, o] **adj** sculptural / *fig* statuesque.

sculpture [skyltyr] **nf** sculpture.

sdb abr de ***salle de bains***.

SDF (abr de ***sans domicile fixe***) **nmf : les SDF** the homeless.

SDN (abr de ***Société des Nations***) **nf** League of Nations.

se [sə], ***s'*** *(devant voyelle ou 'h' muet)* **pron pers 1.** *(réfléchi)* [personne] oneself, himself (f herselfpl themselves) / [chose, animal] itself (, themselves *pl*) ▸ **elle se regarde dans le miroir** she looks at herself in the mirror ▸ **se salir** to get dirty **2.** *(réciproque)* each other, one another ▸ **elles se sont parlé** they spoke to each other *ou* to one another ▸ **ils se sont rencontrés hier** they met yesterday **3.** *(passif)* **: ce produit se vend bien/partout** this product is selling well/is sold everywhere ▸ **ça se mange?** can you eat it? **4.** [remplace l'adjectif possessif] **: se laver les mains** to wash one's hands ▸ **se couper le doigt** to cut one's finger **5.** [dans des tournures impersonnelles] **: il se fait tard** it's getting late ▸ **il se peut qu'ils arrivent plus tôt** it's possible that they'll arrive earlier, they might arrive earlier.

S.E. (abr écrite de ***son excellence***) H.E.

S-E (abr écrite de ***Sud-Est***) SE.

séance [seɑ̃s] **nf 1.** [réunion] meeting, sitting, session ▸ **lever la séance** *fig* to adjourn the meeting *ou* session ▸ **la séance est levée!** [au tribunal] the court will adjourn! ▸ **la séance est ouverte!** [au tribunal] this court is now in session! ▸ **séance extraordinaire** special session, extraordinary meeting ▸ **en séance publique** [au tribunal] in open court
2. [période] session ▸ **séance d'information** briefing session ▸ **séance de rééducation** (session of) physiotherapy / [de pose] sitting
3. CINÉ & THÉÂTRE performance ▸ **séance à 19 h 10, film à 19 h 30** program 7.10, film starts 7.30 ▸ **à la séance** TV pay-per-view ▸ **la dernière séance** the last showing ▸ **séance privée** private screening *ou* showing
4. *fam* [scène] performance
5. [à la Bourse] **: ce fut une bonne/mauvaise séance aujourd'hui à la Bourse** it was a good/bad day today on the Stock Exchange
▸▸▸ **séance tenante** right away, forthwith.

séant, e [seɑ̃, ɑ̃t] **adj** fitting, seemly.
◆ ***séant*** **nm : se dresser** *ou* **se mettre sur son séant** *littéraire* to sit up.

seau, x [so] **nm 1.** [récipient] bucket ▸ **seau à glace** ice bucket **2.** [contenu] bucketful.

sébile [sebil] **nf** (begging) bowl.

sébum [sebɔm] **nm** sebum.

sec, sèche [sɛk, sɛʃ] **adj 1.** [gén] dry **2.** [fruits] dried **3.** [alcool] neat **4.** [personne - maigre] lean / [- austère] austere **5.** *fig* [cœur] hard / [voix, ton] sharp **6.** [sans autre prestation] **: vol sec** flight only **7.** *fam* **: être sec sur un sujet** to have nothing to say on a subject.
◆ ***sec*** ■ **adv 1.** [beaucoup] **: boire sec** to drink heavily **2.** [frapper] hard **3.** [démarrer] sharply
▸▸▸ **aussi sec** *fam* right away ▸ **être à sec** [puits] to be dry *ou* dried up / *fam* [personne] to be broke.
■ **nm : tenir au sec** to keep in a dry place.

sécable [sekabl] **adj** divisible.

SECAM, Secam [sekam] (abr de ***procédé séquentiel à mémoire***) **nm & adj** *French TV broadcasting system.*

sécateur [sekatœr] **nm** secateurs *pl*.

sécession [sesesjɔ̃] **nf** secession ▸ **faire sécession (de)** to secede (from).

sécessionniste [sesesjɔnist] **adj & nmf** secessionist.

séchage [seʃaʒ] **nm** drying.

sèche [sɛʃ] **nf** *fam* cigarette, fag *UK*.

sèche-cheveux [sɛʃʃəvø] **nm inv** hairdryer.

sèche-linge [sɛʃlɛ̃ʒ] **nm inv** tumble-dryer.

sèche-mains [sɛʃmɛ̃] **nm inv** hand-dryer.

sèchement [sɛʃmɑ̃] **adv 1.** [durement] dryly, curtly, tersely ▸ **ne comptez pas sur moi, répondit-elle sèchement** don't count on me, she snapped back **2.** [brusquement] sharply ▸ **prendre un virage un peu sèchement** to take a bend rather sharply **3.** [sans fioritures] dryly ▸ **il expose toujours ses arguments un peu sèchement** he always sets out his arguments rather unimaginatively.

sécher [18] [seʃe] ■ **vt 1.** [linge] to dry **2.** *arg scol* [cours] to skip, to skive off *UK*.
■ **vi 1.** [linge] to dry **2.** [peau] to dry out / [rivière] to dry up **3.** *arg scol* [ne pas savoir répondre] to dry up.

sécheresse [seʃrɛs] **nf 1.** [de terre, climat, style] dryness **2.** [absence de pluie] drought **3.** [de réponse] curtness.

séchoir [seʃwar] **nm 1.** [local] drying shed **2.** [tringle] airer, clotheshorse **3.** [électrique] dryer ▸ **séchoir à cheveux** hairdryer.

second**, **e [səgɔ̃, ɔ̃d] ■ **adj num inv** second ▸ **dans un état second** dazed ▸ **en second lieu** secondly, in the second place ▸ **le second marché** FIN the unlisted securities market ▸ **être doué de seconde vue** to be clairvoyant.
■ **nm, f** second ; voir aussi ***sixième***.
◆ ***second*** **nm** [assistant] assistant.
◆ ***seconde*** **nf 1.** [unité de temps & MUS] second ▸ **une seconde!** just a second! **2.** SCOL ≃ fifth year *ou* form *UK*, ≃ tenth grade *US* **3.** [transports] second class ▸ **voyager en seconde** to travel second class **4.** AUTO second gear ▸ **passe en seconde** change into *ou* to second gear.

secondaire [səgɔ̃dɛr] ■ **nm : le secondaire** GÉOL the Mesozoic / SCOL secondary education / ÉCON the secondary sector.
■ **adj 1.** [gén & SCOL] secondary ▸ **effets secondaires** MÉD side effects **2.** GÉOL Mesozoic.

seconder [3] [səgɔ̃de] **vt** to assist.

secouer [6] [səkwe] **vt 1.** [gén] to shake **2.** *fam* [réprimander] to shake up.
◆ ***se secouer*** **vp** *fam* to snap out of it.

secourable [səkurabl] **adj** helpful ▸ **main secourable** helping hand.

secourir [45] [səkurir] **vt** [blessé, miséreux] to help / [personne en danger] to rescue.

secourisme [səkurism] **nm** first aid.

secouriste [səkurist] **nmf** first-aid worker.

secourrai, ***secourras*** ➤ ***secourir***.

secours [1], ***secourt*** etc ➤ ***secourir***.

secours [2] [səkur] **nm 1.** [aide] help ▸ **appeler au secours** to call for help ▸ **les secours** emergency services ▸ **au secours!** help! ▸ **porter secours à qqn** to help sb ▸ **voler au secours de qqn** *fig* to rush to sb's aid **2.** [dons] aid, relief **3.** [renfort] relief, reinforcements *pl* **4.** [soins] aid ▸ **les premiers secours** first aid *(U)*.
◆ ***de secours*** **loc adj 1.** [trousse, poste] first-aid *(avant n)* **2.** [éclairage, issue] emergency *(avant n)* **3.** [roue] spare.

secouru**, **e [səkury] **pp** ➤ ***secourir***.

secousse [səkus] **nf 1.** [mouvement] jerk, jolt **2.** *fig* [bouleversement] upheaval / [psychologique] shock **3.** [tremblement de terre] tremor.

secret**, **ète [səkrɛ, ɛt] **adj 1.** [gén] secret ▸ **garder *ou* tenir qqch secret** to keep sthg secret ▸ **une vie secrète** a secret life **2.** [personne] reticent.
◆ ***secret*** **nm 1.** [gén] secret ▸ **confier un secret à qqn** to let sb into a secret ▸ **c'est un secret de Polichinelle** it's an open secret *ou* not much of a secret ▸ **être/mettre qqn dans le secret de** to be/let sb in on the secret of ▸ **être dans le secret des dieux** to have privileged information ▸ **...dont il a le secret** ...which he alone knows ▸ **secret d'alcôve** pillow talk *(U)* ▸ **secret d'État** official secret, state secret ▸ **secret de fabrication** COMM trade secret ▸ **secret professionnel** confidentiality ▸ **trahir le secret professionnel** to commit a breach of (professional) confidence **2.** [discrétion] secrecy ▸ **dans le plus grand secret** in the utmost secrecy ▸ **je vous demande le secret sur cette affaire** I want you to keep silent about this matter.
◆ ***au secret*** **loc adv** DR in solitary confinement ▸ **mettre qqn au secret** to detain sb in solitary confinement.
◆ ***en secret*** **loc adv 1.** [écrire, économiser] in secret, secretly **2.** [croire, espérer] secretly, privately.

secrétaire [səkretɛr] ■ **nmf** [personne] secretary ▸ **secrétaire de direction** executive secretary ▸ **secrétaire d'État** minister of state ▸ **secrétaire général** COMM company secretary ▸ **secrétaire de rédaction** subeditor.
■ **nm** [meuble] writing desk, secretaire.

secrétariat [səkretarja] **nm 1.** [bureau] secretary's office / [d'organisation internationale] secretariat **2.** [personnel] secretarial staff ▸ **assurer le secrétariat de qqn** to act as sb's secretary **3.** [métier] secretarial work.

secrètement [səkrɛtmɑ̃] **adv** secretly.

sécréter [18] [sekrete] **vt** to secrete / *fig* to exude.

sécrétion [sekresjɔ̃] **nf** secretion.

sectaire [sɛktɛr] **nmf & adj** sectarian.

sectarisme [sɛktarism] **nm** sectarianism.

secte [sɛkt] **nf** sect.

secteur [sɛktœr] **nm 1.** [zone] area ▸ **se trouver dans le secteur** *fam* to be somewhere *ou* someplace *US* around **2.** ADMIN district **3.** ÉCON, GÉOM & MIL sector ▸ **secteur d'affaires** business sector ▸ **secteur en expansion** growth area ▸ **secteur primaire/secondaire/tertiaire** primary/secondary/tertiary sector ▸ **secteur privé/public** private/public sector ▸ **secteur tertiaire** business sector **4.** ÉLECTR mains ▸ **sur secteur** off *ou* from the mains.

section [sɛksjɔ̃] **nf 1.** [gén] section / [de parti] branch **2.** [action] cutting **3.** MIL platoon.

sectionnement [sɛskjɔnmɑ̃] **nm 1.** *fig* [division] division into sections **2.** [coupure] severing.

sectionner [3] [sɛksjɔne] **vt 1.** *fig* [diviser] to divide into sections **2.** [trancher] to sever.
◆ ***se sectionner*** **vp** to split, to be severed.

sectoriel**, **elle [sɛktɔrjɛl] **adj** sector *(avant n)*, sector-based.

sectorisation [sɛktɔrizasjɔ̃] **nf** division into sectors.

sectoriser [3] [sɛktɔrize] **vt** to divide into sectors.

Sécu [seky] (abr de ***Sécurité sociale***) **nf** *fam* **: la Sécu** *French social security system.*

séculaire [sekylɛr] **adj** [ancien] age-old.

séculariser [3] [sekylarize] **vt** to secularize.

séculier**, **ère [sekylje, ɛr] **adj** secular.

secundo [səgɔ̃do] **adv** in the second place, secondly.

sécurisant**, **e [sekyrizɑ̃, ɑ̃t] **adj** [milieu] secure / [attitude] reassuring.

sécuriser [3] [sekyrize] **vt : sécuriser qqn** to make sb feel secure.

sécuritaire [sekyritɛr] adj **: programme sécuritaire** security-conscious programme ▸ **mesures sécuritaires** drastic security measures ▸ **idéologie sécuritaire** law-and-order ideology.

sécurité [sekyrite] nf **1.** [d'esprit] security **2.** [absence de danger] safety ▸ **la sécurité routière** road safety ▸ **en toute sécurité** safe and sound **3.** [dispositif] safety catch **4.** [organisme] **: la Sécurité sociale** ≃ the DSS *UK*, ≃ Social Security *US*.

PARONYME / CONFUSABLE
sécurité

Pour la traduction de **sécurité**, ne confondez pas ***security*** qui désigne le sentiment de stabilité, d'ordre, et ***safety*** qui signifie l'absence de danger.

CULTURE
Sécurité sociale

The French social security system, popularly called **la Sécu**, was created in October 1945. It provides health, disability, and life insurance; worker's compensation; retirement pensions; and benefits for dependents. **La Sécu** is divided into several benefit schemes: the **régime général** for most private-sector workers; the **régime agricole** for the farming community; **régimes spéciaux** for certain segments of the population (sailors, miners, government workers, students and others); and **régimes particuliers** for independent workers. **Régimes complémentaires** provide benefits not offered in the basic schemes. Social security is paid for by both employers and their employees, who make compulsory monthly contributions.

sédatif, ive [sedatif, iv] **adj** sedative.
◆ ***sédatif*** **nm** sedative.

sédentaire [sedɑ̃tɛr] ■ **nmf** sedentary person / [casanier] stay-at-home.
■ **adj** [personne, métier] sedentary / [casanier] stay-at-home.

sédentarisation [sedɑ̃tarizasjɔ̃] **nf** settlement (process).

sédentariser [3] [sedɑ̃tarize] ◆ ***se sédentariser*** **vp** [tribu] to settle, to become settled.

sédentarité [sedɑ̃tarite] **nf** settled state.

sédiment [sedimɑ̃] **nm** sediment.

sédimentaire [sedimɑ̃tɛr] **adj** sedimentary.

sédimentation [sedimɑ̃tasjɔ̃] **nf** sedimentation.

séditieux, euse [sedisjø, øz] *littéraire* ■ **adj** seditious.
■ **nm, f** rebel.

sédition [sedisjɔ̃] **nf** sedition.

séducteur, trice [sedyktœr, tris] ■ **adj** seductive.
■ **nm, f** seducer (f seductress).

séduction [sedyksjɔ̃] **nf 1.** [action] seduction **2.** [attrait] seductive power.

séduire [98] [sedɥir] **vt 1.** [plaire à] to attract, to appeal to **2.** [abuser de] to seduce.

séduisais, séduisions ➤ ***séduire***.

séduisant, e [sedɥizɑ̃, ɑ̃t] **adj** attractive.

séduit, e [sedɥi, it] **pp** ➤ ***séduire***.

séfarade [sefarad] ■ **nmf** Sephardi.
■ **adj** Sephardic.

segment [sɛgmɑ̃] **nm 1.** GÉOM segment **2.** TECHNOL **: segment de frein** brake shoe ▸ **segment de piston** piston ring **3.** COMM **: segment de marché** market segment.

segmentation [sɛgmɑ̃tasjɔ̃] **nf** segmentation ▸ **segmentation démographique** demographic segmentation.

segmenter [3] [sɛgmɑ̃te] **vt** to segment.

ségrégation [segregasjɔ̃] **nf** segregation.

ségrégationniste [segregasjɔnist] **nmf & adj** segregationist.

seiche [sɛʃ] **nf** cuttlefish.

seigle [sɛgl] **nm** rye.

seigneur [sɛɲœr] **nm** lord ▸ **faire le grand seigneur** *fig* to throw money about ▸ **vivre en grand seigneur** *fig* to live like a lord.
◆ ***Seigneur*** **nm : le Seigneur** the Lord.

seigneurial, e, aux [sɛɲœrjal, o] **adj** lordly / HIST seigneurial.

sein [sɛ̃] **nm** breast / *fig* bosom ▸ **donner le sein (à un bébé)** to breast-feed (a baby).
◆ ***au sein de*** **loc prép** within.

Seine [sɛn] **nf : la Seine** the (River) Seine.

seing [sɛ̃] **nm** [signature] signature.
◆ ***sous seing privé*** **loc adj : acte sous seing privé** private agreement, simple contract.

séisme [seism] **nm** earthquake.

SEITA, Seita [sejta] (abr de ***Société nationale d'exploitation industrielle des tabacs et allumettes***) **nf** *French tobacco and match manufacturer.*

seize [sɛz] **adj num inv & nm** sixteen ; voir aussi ***six***.

seizième [sɛzjɛm] **adj num inv, nm & nmf** sixteenth ▸ **le seizième** *wealthy district of Paris* ; voir aussi ***sixième***.

CULTURE
Le seizième

This term often designates something more than the chic western Paris neighbourhood of the 16th **arrondissement**: wealth, a good education, a taste for fine clothes, and perhaps a stuffy manner. People who fit this stereotyped image of the upper middle class in the city's **beaux quartiers** are also labelled **BCBG**, or **bon chic bon genre**.

séjour [seʒur] **nm 1.** [durée] stay ▸ **interdit de séjour** ≃ banned ▸ **séjour linguistique** stay abroad *(to develop language skills)* **2.** [pièce] living room.

séjourner [3] [seʒurne] **vi** to stay.

sel [sɛl] **nm** salt / *fig* piquancy ▸ **gros sel** coarse salt.
◆ ***sels*** **nmpl** smelling salts ▸ **sels de bain** bath salts.

sélect**, **e [selɛkt] adj *fam* select.

sélecteur [selɛktœr] nm **1.** [dispositif] selector ▸ **sélecteur de température** thermostat **2.** [de moto] gear lever *UK*, gearshift *US*.

sélectif**, **ive [selɛktif, iv] adj selective.

sélection [selɛksjɔ̃] nf selection.

sélectionné**, **e [selɛksjɔne] adj selected.

sélectionner [3] [selɛksjɔne] vt to select, to pick / INFORM to select.

sélectionneur**, **euse [selɛksjɔnœr, øz] nm, f selector.

sélectivement [selɛktivmɑ̃] adv selectively.

self [sɛlf] nm *fam* self-service (cafeteria).

self-control [sɛlfkɔ̃trol] nm inv self-control.

self-made-man [sɛlfmɛdman] (pl **self-made-men** [sɛlfmɛdmɛn]) nm self-made man.

self-service [sɛlfsɛrvis] (pl **self-services**) nm self-service cafeteria.

selle [sɛl] nf **1.** [gén] saddle ▸ **se mettre en selle** to mount **2.** [toilettes] **: aller à la selle** to open one's bowels.

seller [4] [sele] vt to saddle.

sellerie [sɛlri] nf **1.** [commerce] saddlery **2.** [lieu] tack room.

sellette [sɛlɛt] nf hot seat ▸ **mettre qqn/être sur la sellette** *fig* to put sb/be in the hot seat.

sellier [selje] nm saddler.

selon [səlɔ̃] prép **1.** [conformément à] in accordance with **2.** [d'après] according to ▸ **c'est selon** *fam fig* that (all) depends.

◆ ***selon que*** loc conj depending on whether.

S.Em (abr écrite de ***son éminence***) H.E.

semailles [səmaj] nfpl **1.** [action] sowing *(U)* **2.** [période] sowing season *sg*.

semaine [səmɛn] nf **1.** [période] week ▸ **à la semaine** [être payé] by the week ▸ **dans une semaine** in a week's time ▸ **deux visites par semaine** two visits a week *ou* per week ▸ **en semaine** during the week ▸ **toutes les semaines** [nettoyer, recevoir] every *ou* each week / [publier, payer] weekly, on a weekly basis ▸ **la semaine sainte** Holy Week ▸ **semaine commerciale** week-long promotion *ou* sale ▸ **faire qqch à la petite semaine** *fig* to do sthg on a short-term basis ▸ **vivre à la petite semaine** to live from day to day *ou* from hand to mouth **2.** [salaire] weekly wage.

semainier**, **ère [səmenje, ɛr] nm, f person on duty for the week.

◆ ***semainier*** nm **1.** [bijou] seven-band bracelet **2.** [meuble] *small chest of drawers* **3.** [calendrier] desk diary.

sémantique [semɑ̃tik] ■ nf semantics *(U)*.

■ adj semantic.

sémaphore [semafɔr] nm **1.** NAUT semaphore **2.** RAIL semaphore, semaphore signals *pl*.

semblable [sɑ̃blabl] ■ nm [prochain] fellow man ▸ **il n'a pas son semblable** there's nobody like him.

■ adj **1.** [analogue] similar ▸ **semblable à** like, similar to **2.** *(avant n)* [tel] such.

semblant [sɑ̃blɑ̃] nm **: un semblant de** a semblance of ▸ **faire semblant (de faire qqch)** to pretend (to do sthg).

sembler [3] [sɑ̃ble] ■ vi to seem.

■ v impers **: il (me/te) semble que** it seems (to me/you) that.

semelle [səmɛl] nf **1.** [de chaussure - dessous] sole / [- à l'intérieur] insole ▸ **bottes à semelles fines/épaisses** thin-soled/thick-soled boots ▸ **semelles compensées** platform soles ▸ **semelle intérieure** insole, inner sole **2.** [de ski] underside **3.** CONSTR foundation / [de poutre] flange **4.** *fam* [viande dure] **: c'est de la semelle, ce steak!** this steak is like (shoe) leather *ou* old boots *UK*

▸▸ **battre la semelle** to stamp one's feet to keep warm ▸ **ne pas quitter qqn d'une semelle** to stick to sb like glue.

semence [səmɑ̃s] nf **1.** [graine] seed **2.** [sperme] semen *(U)*.

semer [19] [səme] vt **1.** *fig* [planter] to sow ▸ **semer un champ** to sow a field **2.** [répandre] to scatter ▸ **semer qqch de** to scatter sthg with, to strew sthg with ▸ **parcours semé d'embûches** course littered with obstacles ▸ **il sème ses affaires partout** he leaves his things everywhere **3.** *fam* [se débarrasser de] to shake off ▸ **semer le peloton** to leave the pack behind **4.** *fam* [perdre] to lose **5.** [propager] to bring ▸ **semer la pagaille** to wreak havoc ▸ **semer le doute dans l'esprit de qqn** to sow *ou* to plant a seed of doubt in sb's mind.

semestre [səmɛstr] nm half year, six-month period / SCOL semester.

semestriel**, **elle [səmɛstrijɛl] adj **1.** [qui a lieu tous les six mois] half-yearly, six-monthly **2.** [qui dure six mois] six months', six-month.

semeur**, **euse [səmœr, øz] nm, f sower / *fig* disseminator.

semi-automatique [səmiotɔmatik] adj semiautomatic.

semi-conducteur**, **trice [səmikɔ̃dyktœr, tris] adj semiconducting.

◆ ***semi-conducteur*** nm semiconductor.

semi-fini**, **e [səmifini] adj semi-finished.

semi-liberté [səmilibɛrte] (pl **semi-libertés**) nf temporary release from prison.

sémillant**, **e [semijɑ̃, ɑ̃t] adj vivacious.

séminaire [seminɛr] nm **1.** RELIG seminary **2.** UNIV [colloque] seminar.

séminal**, **e**, **aux [seminal, o] adj seminal.

séminariste [seminarist] nm seminarist.

sémiologie [semjɔlɔʒi] nf semiology.

semi-précieux**, **euse [səmipresjø, øz] adj semi-precious.

semi-public**, **ique [səmipyblik] adj semi-public.

semi-remorque [səmirəmɔrk] (pl **semi-remorques**) nm articulated lorry *UK*, semitrailer *US*, rig *US*.

semis [səmi] **nm** **1.** [méthode] sowing broadcast **2.** [terrain] seedbed **3.** [plant] seedling.

sémite [semit] **adj** Semitic.
◆ ***Sémite*** **nmf** Semite.

sémitique [semitik] **adj** Semitic.

semoir [səmwar] **nm** **1.** [machine] drill **2.** [sac] seedbag.

semonce [səmɔ̃s] **nf** **1.** [réprimande] reprimand **2.** MIL : **coup de semonce** warning shot.

semoule [səmul] **nf** semolina.

sempiternel**, **elle [sɑ̃pitɛrnɛl] **adj** eternal.

sénat [sena] **nm** senate ▸ **le Sénat** *upper house of the French parliament.*

CULTURE

Le Sénat

The Senate, whose headquarters is in the **Palais du Luxembourg** in Paris, is the upper chamber of the French parliament. Senators are chosen for six-year terms by a group including members of the National Assembly and members of France's departmental and regional councils. Half of the senators come up for re-election every three years. Until 2003, they served nine-year terms. All laws must be approved by both the Senate and the National Assembly, but the annual budget goes through the Assembly first.

sénateur**, **trice [senatœr, tris] **nm** senator.

Sénégal [senegal] **nm : le Sénégal** Senegal ▸ **au Sénégal** in Senegal.

sénégalais**, **e [senegalɛ, ɛz] **adj** Senegalese.
◆ ***Sénégalais**, **e*** **nm, f** Senegalese person.

sénile [senil] **adj** senile.

sénilité [senilite] **nf** senility.

senior [senjɔr] **adj & nmf** **1.** SPORT senior **2.** [tourisme] for the over-50s, for the young at heart / [menu] over 50s' ▸ **notre clientèle senior** our over-50s customers **3.** [personnes de plus de 50 ans] over-50 *(gén pl).*

sens[1], ***sent*** etc ➤ ***sentir.***

sens[2] [sɑ̃s] ■ **nm** **1.** [fonction, instinct, raison] sense ▸ **le sens du toucher** the sense of touch ▸ **avoir un sixième sens** to have sixth sense ▸ **avoir le sens de la nuance** to be subtle ▸ **avoir le sens de l'humour** to have a sense of humour *UK ou* humor *US* ▸ **avoir le sens de l'orientation** to have a (good) sense of direction ▸ **ne pas avoir le sens des réalités** to have no grasp of reality ▸ **bon sens** good sense ▸ **tomber sous le sens** *fig* to be perfectly obvious
2. [opinion, avis] : **abonder dans le sens de qqn** to agree completely with sb ▸ **à mon sens** to my way of thinking, to my mind
3. [direction] direction ▸ **dans le sens de la longueur** lengthways ▸ **dans le sens de la marche** in the direction of travel ▸ **dans le sens contraire de la marche** facing the rear *(of a vehicle)* ▸ **dans le sens des aiguilles d'une montre** clockwise ▸ **dans le sens contraire des aiguilles d'une montre** anticlockwise *UK*, counterclockwise *US* ▸ **dans tous les sens** *litt* in all directions, all over the place ▸ **en sens inverse** in the opposite direction ▸ **sens dessus dessous** upside down ▸ **la maison était sens dessus dessous** [en désordre] the house was all topsy-turvy ▸ **sens giratoire** roundabout *UK*, traffic circle *US* ▸ **sens interdit** *ou* **unique** one-way street
4. [signification] meaning ▸ **cela n'a pas de sens!** it's nonsensical! ▸ **ce que tu dis n'a pas de sens** [c'est inintelligible, déraisonnable] what you're saying doesn't make sense ▸ **dans** *ou* **en un sens** in one sense ▸ **à double sens** with a double meaning ▸ **au sens strict (du terme)** strictly speaking ▸ **porteur de sens** meaningful ▸ **lourd** *ou* **chargé de sens** meaningful ▸ **vide de sens** meaningless ▸ **en ce sens que** in the sense that ▸ **au sens propre/figuré** in the literal/ figurative sense
5. *fig* [orientation] line ▸ **des mesures allant dans le sens d'une plus grande justice** measures directed at greater justice.
■ **nmpl** senses ▸ **pour le plaisir des sens** for the gratification of the senses ▸ **reprendre ses sens** *litt* to come to / *fig* to come to one's senses.

sensass [sɑ̃sas] **adj inv** *fam* [sensationnel] terrific, sensational.

sensation [sɑ̃sasjɔ̃] **nf** **1.** [perception] sensation, feeling ▸ **à sensation** sensational ▸ **faire sensation** to cause a sensation **2.** [impression] feeling.

sensationnel**, **elle [sɑ̃sasjɔnɛl] **adj** sensational.

sensé**, **e [sɑ̃se] **adj** sensible.

sensément [sɑ̃semɑ̃] **adv** sensibly.

sensibilisation [sɑ̃sibilizasjɔ̃] **nf** **1.** MÉD & PHOTO sensitization **2.** *fig* [du public] consciousness raising.

sensibiliser [3] [sɑ̃sibilize] **vt** **1.** MÉD & PHOTO to sensitize **2.** *fig* [public] : **sensibiliser (à)** to make aware (of).

sensibilité [sɑ̃sibilite] **nf : sensibilité (à)** sensitivity (to).

sensible [sɑ̃sibl] **adj** **1.** [gén] : **sensible (à)** sensitive (to) ▸ **sensible à la vue** visible ▸ **sensible à l'ouïe** audible **2.** [notable] considerable, appreciable.

FAUX AMIS / FALSE FRIENDS

sensible

Sensible is not a translation of the French word *sensible.* Sensible is translated by *judicieux* or *pratique.*
▸ We need a sensible solution / *Il nous faut une solution judicieuse*
▸ You need sensible walking shoes / *Il te faut des chaussures de marche pratiques*

sensiblement [sɑ̃sibləmɑ̃] **adv** **1.** [à peu près] more or less **2.** [notablement] appreciably, considerably.

sensiblerie [sɑ̃sibləri] **nf** *péj* [morale] sentimentality / [physique] squeamishness.

sensoriel**, **elle [sɑ̃sɔrjɛl] **adj** sensory.

sensualité [sɑ̃sɥalite] **nf** [lascivité] sensuousness / [charnelle] sensuality.

sensuel, elle [sɑ̃sɥɛl] **adj 1.** [charnel] sensual **2.** [lascif] sensuous.

PARONYME / CONFUSABLE

sensuel

Quand vous traduisez le mot sensuel, employez *sensual* pour parler de ce qui se rapporte aux sens, et *sensuous* pour désigner ce qui est voluptueux.

sentence [sɑ̃tɑ̃s] **nf 1.** [jugement] sentence **2.** [maxime] adage.

sentencieux, euse [sɑ̃tɑ̃sjø, øz] **adj** *péj* sententious.

senteur [sɑ̃tœr] **nf** *littéraire* perfume.

senti, e [sɑ̃ti] ■ **pp** ➤ ***sentir***.
■ **adj : bien senti** [mots] well-chosen.

sentier [sɑ̃tje] **nm** path ▸ **sortir des sentiers battus** *fig* to go off the beaten track.

sentiment [sɑ̃timɑ̃] **nm** feeling ▸ **j'ai le sentiment de l'avoir déjà vu** I have the feeling that I've seen him before ▸ **faire appel aux bons sentiments de qqn** to appeal to sb's better *ou* finer feelings ▸ **plein de bons sentiments** full of good intentions ▸ **prendre qqn par les sentiments** to appeal to sb's feelings ▸ **ramener qqn à de meilleurs sentiments** to bring sb round to a more generous point of view ▸ **si vous voulez savoir mon sentiment** if you want to know what I think *ou* feel ▸ **veuillez agréer, Monsieur, l'expression de mes sentiments distingués/cordiaux/les meilleurs** yours faithfully *UK*/sincerely/truly.

sentimental, e, aux [sɑ̃timɑ̃tal, o] ■ **adj 1.** [amoureux] love *(avant n)* **2.** [sensible, romanesque] sentimental.
■ **nm, f** sentimentalist.

sentimentalisme [sɑ̃timɑ̃talism] **nm** sentimentalism.

sentinelle [sɑ̃tinɛl] **nf** sentry.

sentir [37] [sɑ̃tir] ■ **vt 1.** [percevoir - par l'odorat] to smell ▸ **je sens une odeur de gaz** I can smell gas / [- par le goût] to taste / [- par le toucher] to feel ▸ **je n'ai rien senti!** I didn't feel a thing! **2.** [exhaler - odeur] to smell of ▸ **ça sent bon le lilas, ici** there's a nice smell of lilac in here **3.** [colère, tendresse] to feel **4.** [affectation, plagiat] to smack of ▸ **son interprétation/style sent un peu trop le travail** her performance/style is rather too constrained **5.** [danger] to sense, to be aware of ▸ **sentir que** to feel (that) ▸ **j'ai senti qu'on me suivait** I felt *ou* sensed (that) I was being followed **6.** [beauté] to feel, to appreciate
▸▸ **je ne peux pas le sentir** *fam* I can't stand him ▸ **le/la sentir passer** *fam* to really feel it ▸ **vous allez la sentir passer, l'amende!** you'll certainly know about it when you get the fine!
■ **vi : sentir bon/mauvais** to smell good/bad ▸ **le fromage sent fort** the cheese smells strong.
◆ ***se sentir*** ■ **v att : se sentir bien/fatigué** to feel well/tired ▸ **se sentir en sécurité/danger** to feel safe/threatened ▸ **se sentir la force de faire qqch** to feel strong enough to do sthg ▸ **elle ne se sent plus depuis qu'elle a eu le rôle** *fam* she's been really full of it since she landed the part.
■ **vp** [être perceptible] **: ça se sent!** you can really tell!

seoir [67] [swar] ■ **vi** *sout* [aller bien] **: seoir à qqn** to become sb.
■ **v impers : comme il sied** as is fitting.

Séoul [seul] **npr** Seoul.

séparable [separabl] **adj** separable.

séparation [separasjɔ̃] **nf** separation.

séparatisme [separatism] **nm** separatism.

séparatiste [separatist] **nmf** separatist.

séparé, e [separe] **adj 1.** [intérêts] separate **2.** [couple] separated.

séparément [separemɑ̃] **adv** separately.

séparer [3] [separe] **vt 1.** [gén] **: séparer (de)** to separate (from) **2.** [suj: divergence] to divide **3.** [maison] **: séparer (en)** to divide (into).
◆ ***se séparer*** **vp 1.** [se défaire] **: se séparer de** to part with **2.** [conjoints] to separate, to split up ▸ **se séparer de** to separate from, to split up with **3.** [participants] to disperse **4.** [route] **: se séparer (en)** to split (into), to divide (into).

sépia [sepja] ■ **nf 1.** [matière] sepia **2.** [dessin] sepia (drawing).
■ **adj inv** sepia.

sept [sɛt] **adj num inv & nm** seven ; voir aussi ***six***.

septante [sɛptɑ̃t] **adj num inv** *Belgique* & *Suisse* seventy.

septembre [sɛptɑ̃br] **nm** September ▸ **de septembre** September *(avant n)* ▸ **en septembre, au mois de septembre** in September ▸ **début septembre, au début du mois de septembre** at the beginning of September ▸ **fin septembre, à la fin du mois de septembre** at the end of September ▸ **d'ici septembre** by September ▸ **(à la) mi-septembre** (in) mid-September ▸ **le premier/deux/dix septembre** the first/second/tenth of September.

septennat [sɛptena] **nm** seven-year term (of office).

septentrional, e, aux [sɛptɑ̃trijɔnal, o] **adj** northern.

septicémie [sɛptisemi] **nf** septicaemia *UK*, septicemia *US*, blood poisoning.

septième [sɛtjɛm] ■ **adj num inv, nm & nmf** seventh.
■ **nf** SCOL ≃ third year *ou* form *(at junior school) UK*, ≃ fifth grade *US* ; voir aussi ***sixième***.

septièmement [sɛtjɛmmɑ̃] **adv** seventhly, in (the) seventh place.

septique [sɛptik] **adj** [infecté] septic.

septuagénaire [sɛptɥaʒenɛr] ■ **nmf** 70-year-old.
■ **adj : être septuagénaire** to be in one's seventies.

sépulcral, e, aux [sepylkral, o] **adj** sepulchral.

sépulcre [sepylkr] **nm** sepulchre *UK*, sepulcher *US*.

sépulture [sepyltyr] **nf 1.** [lieu] burial place **2.** [inhumation] burial.

séquelle [sekɛl] **nf** *(gén pl)* aftermath / MÉD aftereffect.

séquence [sekɑ̃s] **nf** sequence / [cartes à jouer] run, sequence.

séquentiel, elle [sekɑ̃sjɛl] **adj** sequential.

séquestration [sekɛstrasjɔ̃] **nf 1.** [de personne] confinement **2.** [de biens] impoundment.

séquestre [sekɛstr] **nm** DR pound ▸ **mettre** *ou* **placer sous séquestre** to impound.

séquestrer [3] [sekɛstre] **vt 1.** [personne] to confine **2.** [biens] to impound.

serai, seras ➤ *être*.

sérail [seraj] **nm** seraglio.

serbe [sɛrb] **adj** Serbian.
◆ ***Serbe*** **nmf** Serb.

Serbie [sɛrbi] **nf : la Serbie** Serbia.

serbo-croate [sɛrbɔkrɔat] (pl **serbo-croates**) ■ **nm** [langue] Serbo-Croat.
■ **adj** Serbo-Croat, Serbo-Croatian.
◆ ***Serbo-Croate*** **nmf** Serbo-Croat speaker.

séré [sere] **nm** *Suisse* fromage frais.

serein, e [sərɛ̃, ɛn] **adj 1.** [calme] serene **2.** [impartial] calm, dispassionate.

sereinement [sərɛnmɑ̃] **adv** serenely, calmly.

sérénade [serenad] **nf 1.** MUS serenade **2.** *fam* [tapage] hullabaloo.

sérénité [serenite] **nf** serenity.

serf, serve [sɛrf, sɛrv] **nm, f** serf.

serge [sɛrʒ] **nf** serge.

sergent [sɛrʒɑ̃] **nm** sergeant.

sergent-chef [sɛrʒɑ̃ʃɛf] (pl **sergents-chefs**) **nm** staff sergeant.

sériciculture [serisikyltyr] **nf** silkworm farming.

série [seri] **nf 1.** [gén] series *sg* ▸ **série B** CINÉ & TV B movie **2.** SPORT rank / [au tennis] seeding **3.** COMM [dans l'industrie] **: produire qqch en série** to mass-produce sthg ▸ **de série** standard ▸ **hors série** custom-made / *fig* outstanding, extraordinary.
◆ ***série noire*** **nf 1.** [roman] **: un roman de série noire** a detective novel ▸ **c'est un vrai personnage de série noire** he's like something out of a detective novel **2.** [catastrophes] chapter of accidents.

sérier [9] [serje] **vt** to classify.

sérieusement [serjøzmɑ̃] **adv** seriously.

sérieux, euse [serjø, øz] **adj 1.** [grave] serious ▸ **être sérieux comme un pape** to look as solemn as a judge **2.** [digne de confiance] reliable / [client, offre] genuine **3.** [consciencieux] responsible ▸ **ce n'est pas sérieux** it's irresponsible ▸ **être sérieux dans son travail** to be a conscientious worker, to take one's work seriously **4.** [considérable] considerable ▸ **il a de sérieuses chances de gagner** he stands a good chance of winning ▸ **on a de sérieuses raisons de le penser** we have good reasons to think so.
◆ ***sérieux*** **nm 1.** [application] sense of responsibility ▸ **elle fait son travail avec sérieux** she's serious about her work **2.** [gravité] seriousness ▸ **garder son sérieux** to keep a straight face ▸ **prendre qqn/qqch au sérieux** to take sb/sthg seriously ▸ **se prendre au sérieux** to take o.s. (too) seriously.

sérigraphie [serigrafi] **nf** silk-screen printing.

serin, e [sərɛ̃, in] **nm, f 1.** [oiseau] canary **2.** *fam* [niais] idiot, twit *UK*.

seriner [3] [sərine] **vt** *fam* [rabâcher] **: seriner qqch à qqn** to drum sthg into sb.

seringue [sərɛ̃g] **nf** syringe.

serment [sɛrmɑ̃] **nm 1.** [affirmation solennelle] oath ▸ **prêter serment** to take an oath ▸ **sous serment** on *ou* under oath ▸ **serment d'Hippocrate** Hippocratic oath **2.** [promesse] vow, pledge.

sermon [sɛrmɔ̃] **nm** *litt* & *fig* sermon.

sermonner [3] [sɛrmɔne] **vt** to lecture.

SERNAM, Sernam [sɛrnam] (abr de ***Service national de messageries***) **nm** *rail delivery service*, ≃ Red Star® *UK*.

séronégatif, ive [serɔnegatif, iv] **adj** HIV-negative.

séropositif, ive [serɔpozitif, iv] **adj** HIV-positive.

séropositivité [serɔpozitivite] **nf** HIV infection.

serpe [sɛrp] **nf** billhook.

serpent [sɛrpɑ̃] **nm** ZOOL snake ▸ **serpent à sonnette** *ou* **sonnettes** rattlesnake.
◆ ***serpent monétaire*** **nm** (currency) snake.

serpenter [3] [sɛrpɑ̃te] **vi** to wind.

serpentin [sɛrpɑ̃tɛ̃] **nm 1.** [de papier] streamer **2.** [tuyau] coil.

serpillière [sɛrpijɛr] **nf** floor cloth *UK*, mop *US*.

serpolet [sɛrpɔlɛ] **nm** wild thyme.

serre [sɛr] **nf** [bâtiment] greenhouse, glasshouse *UK*.
◆ ***serres*** **nfpl** ZOOL talons, claws.

serré, e [sere] **adj 1.** [écriture] cramped / [tissu] closely-woven / [rangs] serried **2.** [style] dense, concise **3.** [vêtement, chaussure] tight **4.** [discussion] closely argued / [match] close-fought **5.** [poing, dents] clenched ▸ **la gorge serrée** with a lump in one's throat ▸ **j'en avais le cœur serré** *fig* it was heartbreaking **6.** [café] strong.
◆ ***serré*** **adv : jouer serré** to be cautious.

serre-livres [sɛrlivr] **nm inv** bookend ▸ **deux serre-livres** a pair of bookends.

serrement [sɛrmɑ̃] **nm 1.** [de main] handshake **2.** [de cœur] anguish **3.** [de gorge] tightening.

serrer [4] [sere] ■ **vt 1.** [saisir] to grip, to hold tight ▸ **serrer la main à qqn** to shake sb's hand ▸ **serrer qqch contre son cœur** to clasp sthg to one's breast ▸ **serrer qqn dans ses bras** to hug sb **2.** *fig* [rapprocher] to bring together ▸ **serrer les rangs** to close ranks ▸ **être serrés comme des sardines** to be squashed up like sardines **3.** [poing, dents] to clench / [lèvres] to purse / *fig* [cœur] to wring **4.** [suj: vêtement, chaussure] to be too tight for ▸ **la chaussure droite/le col me serre un peu** the right shoe/the collar is a bit tight **5.** [vis, ceinture] to tighten **6.** [trottoir, bordure] to hug.
■ **vi** AUTO **: serrer à droite/gauche** to keep right/left.
◆ ***se serrer*** **vp 1.** [se blottir] **: se serrer contre** to huddle up to *ou* against ▸ **se serrer les uns contre les autres** to

huddle together ▸ **se serrer autour de** to crowd *ou* press around **2.** [se rapprocher] to squeeze up **3.** [se contracter] to tighten ▸ **mon cœur se serra en les voyant** my heart sank when I saw them ▸ **je sentais ma gorge se serrer** I could feel a lump in my throat.

serre-tête [sɛrtɛt] **nm inv** headband.

serrure [seryr] **nf** lock.

serrurerie [seryrri] **nf 1.** [métier] locksmith's trade **2.** [ouvrage] metalwork.

serrurier [seryrje] **nm** locksmith.

sers, sert ➤ *servir*.

sertir [32] [sɛrtir] **vt 1.** [pierre précieuse] to set **2.** TECHNOL [assujettir] to crimp.

sérum [serɔm] **nm** serum ▸ **sérum physiologique** saline.

servage [sɛrvaʒ] **nm** serfdom / *fig* bondage.

servante [sɛrvɑ̃t] **nf 1.** [domestique] maidservant **2.** TECHNOL tool rest.

serve ➤ *serf*.

serveur, euse [sɛrvœr, øz] **nm, f 1.** [de restaurant] waiter (f waitress) / [de bar] barman (f barmaid) *UK*, bartender *US* **2.** [joueur de cartes] dealer **3.** TENNIS server.

◆ ***serveur*** **nm** INFORM server ▸ **serveur sécurisé** secure server.

servi, e [sɛrvi] **pp** ➤ *servir*.

serviable [sɛrvjabl] **adj** helpful, obliging.

service [sɛrvis] **nm 1.** [gén] service ▸ **être en service** to be in use, to be set up ▸ **cet hélicoptère/cette presse entrera en service en mai** this helicopter will be put into service/this press will come on stream in May ▸ **mettre en service** to set up ▸ **hors service** out of order

2. [travail] duty ▸ **pendant le service** while on duty ▸ **être de service** to be on duty ▸ **prendre son service** to go on *ou* to report for duty ▸ **finir son service** to come off duty

3. [département] department ▸ **service des achats** purchasing department ▸ **service après-vente** after-sales service ▸ **service du personnel** personnel department *ou* division ▸ **service de presse** [département] press office / [personnes] press officers, press office staff ▸ **service de réanimation** intensive care (unit) ▸ **service de renseignements** intelligence service ▸ **service d'ordre** police and stewards *UK (at a demonstration)* ▸ **assurer le service d'ordre dans un périmètre** to police a perimeter

4. MIL **: service (militaire)** military *ou* national service ▸ **service civil** non-military national service

5. [aide, assistance] favour *UK*, favor *US* ▸ **rendre un service à qqn** to do sb a favour *UK ou* favor *US* ▸ **rendre service** to be helpful ▸ **ça peut encore/toujours rendre service** it can still/it'll always come in handy ▸ **service après-vente** after-sales service ▸ **offrir ses services à qqn** to offer one's services to sb, to offer to help sb out ▸ **service de bavardage Internet** *ou* **de chat** Internet Relay Chat, IRC

6. [à table] **: premier/deuxième service** first/second sitting

7. [pourboire] service (charge) ▸ **service compris/non compris** service included/not included

8. [assortiment - de porcelaine] service, set / [- de linge] set ▸ **acheter un service de 6 couverts en argent** to buy a 6-place canteen of silver cutlery

9. SPORT service, serve ▸ **prendre le service de qqn** to break sb's serve *ou* service.

serviette [sɛrvjɛt] **nf 1.** [de table] serviette, napkin **2.** [de toilette] towel ▸ **serviette de bain** bath towel **3.** [porte-documents] briefcase.

◆ ***serviette hygiénique*** **nf** sanitary towel *UK ou* napkin *US*.

serviette-éponge [sɛrvjɛtepɔ̃ʒ] (pl **serviettes-éponges**) **nf** terry towel.

servile [sɛrvil] **adj 1.** [gén] servile **2.** [traduction, imitation] slavish.

servir [38] [sɛrvir] ■ **vt 1.** [gén] to serve ▸ **servir qqch à qqn** to serve sb sthg, to help sb to sthg ▸ **qu'est-ce que je vous sers?** what can I get you? ▸ **c'est difficile de se faire servir ici** it's difficult to get served here ▸ **le dîner est servi!** dinner's ready *ou* served! ▸ **sers-moi à boire** give *ou* pour me a drink

2. [avantager] to serve (well), to help ▸ **servir les ambitions de qqn** to serve *ou* to aid *ou* to further sb's ambitions ▸ **sa mémoire la sert beaucoup** her memory's a great help to her.

■ **vi 1.** [avoir un usage] to be useful *ou* of use ▸ **ça peut toujours/encore servir** it may/may still come in useful ▸ **ça n'a jamais servi** it's never been used

2. [être utile] **: servir à qqch/à faire qqch** to be used for sthg/for doing sthg ▸ **sa connaissance du russe lui a servi dans son métier** her knowledge of Russian helped her *ou* was of use to her in her job ▸ **tu vois bien que ça a servi à quelque chose de faire une pétition!** as you see, getting up a petition did serve some purpose! ▸ **ça ne sert à rien** it's pointless

3. [tenir lieu] **: servir de** [personne] to act as / [chose] to serve as ▸ **je lui ai servi d'interprète** I acted as his interpreter ▸ **le coffre me sert aussi de table** I also use the trunk as a table

4. [domestique] to be in service ▸ **elle sert au château depuis 40 ans** she's worked as a servant *ou* been in service at the castle for 40 years

5. MIL & SPORT to serve ▸ **à toi de servir!** your serve *ou* service!

6. [jeu de cartes] to deal.

◆ ***se servir*** **vp 1.** [prendre] **: se servir (de)** to help o.s. (to) ▸ **je me suis servi un verre de lait** I poured myself a glass of milk ▸ **servez-vous!** help yourself!

2. [utiliser] **: se servir de qqn/qqch** to use sb/sthg ▸ **c'est une arme dont on ne se sert plus** it's a weapon which is no longer used *ou* in use.

serviteur [sɛrvitœr] **nm** servant.

servitude [sɛrvityd] **nf 1.** [esclavage] servitude **2.** *(gén pl)* [contrainte] constraint **3.** DR easement.

ses ➤ *son*[2].

sésame [sezam] **nm 1.** BOT sesame **2.** *fig* [formule magique] **: sésame ouvre-toi** open sesame.

session [sesjɔ̃] **nf 1.** [d'assemblée] session, sitting **2.** UNIV exam session **3.** INFORM **: ouvrir une session** to log in *ou* on ▸ **fermer** *ou* **clore une session** to log out *ou* off.

set [sɛt] **nm 1.** TENNIS set **2.** [napperon] **: set (de table)** set of table *ou* place mats.

SET® (abr de ***secure electronic transaction***) INFORM SET®.

setter [setɛr] **nm** setter.

seuil [sœj] **nm** *litt* & *fig* threshold ▸ **seuil de rentabilité** COMM breakeven point.

seul, e [sœl] ■ **adj 1.** [isolé] alone ▸ **seul à seul** alone (together),privately ▸ **je voudrais te parler seul à seul** I'd like to talk to you in private
2. [sans compagnie] alone, by o.s. ▸ **parler tout seul** to talk to o.s.
3. [sans aide] on one's own, by o.s. ▸ **il a bâti sa maison tout seul** he built his house all by himself
4. [unique] **: le seul...** the only... ▸ **un seul...** a single... ▸ **pas un seul...** not one..., not a single... ▸ **je l'ai vue une seule et unique fois** I saw her only once ▸ **il n'a qu'un seul défaut** he's only got one fault
5. [esseulé] lonely
6. [sans partenaire, non marié] alone, on one's own ▸ **elle est seule avec trois enfants** she's bringing up three children on her own.
■ **nm, f : le seul** the only one ▸ **tu voudrais t'arrêter de travailler? t'es pas le seul!** *fam* you'd like to stop work? you're not the only one! ▸ **un seul** a single one, only one ▸ **pas un seul (de ses camarades) n'était prêt à l'épauler** not a single one (of her friends) was prepared to help her.

PARONYME / CONFUSABLE
seul
Attention lorsque vous traduisez le mot seul. *Alone* signifie unique, tranquille, alors que *lonely* signifie solitaire et évoque toujours un sentiment de solitude.

seulement [sœlmɑ̃] **adv 1.** [gén] only / [exclusivement] only, solely **2.** [même] even.
◆ ***non seulement... mais (encore)*** **loc correlative** not only... but (also).

sève [sɛv] **nf 1.** BOT sap **2.** *fig* [vigueur] vigour *UK*, vigor *US*.

sévère [sevɛr] **adj** severe.

sévèrement [sevɛrmɑ̃] **adv** severely.

sévérité [severite] **nf** severity.

sévices [sevis] **nmpl** *sout* ill treatment *(U)*.

Séville [sevij] **npr** Seville.

sévir [32] [sevir] **vi 1.** [gouvernement] to act ruthlessly *ou* severely **2.** [épidémie, guerre] to rage **3.** [punir] to give out a punishment.

sevrage [səvraʒ] **nm 1.** [d'enfant] weaning **2.** [de toxicomane] withdrawal.

sevrer [19] [səvre] **vt** to wean ▸ **sevrer qqn de** *fig* to deprive sb of.

sexagénaire [sɛksaʒenɛr] ■ **nmf** sixty-year-old.
■ **adj : être sexagénaire** to be in one's sixties.

sex-appeal [sɛksapil] **nm** sex appeal.

S.Exc (abr écrite de ***son excellence***) H.E.

sexe [sɛks] **nm 1.** [gén] sex ▸ **le sexe fort/faible** *fam fig* the stronger/weaker sex **2.** [organe] genitals *pl*.

sexisme [sɛksism] **nm** sexism.

sexiste [sɛksist] **nmf** & **adj** sexist.

sexologie [sɛksɔlɔʒi] **nf** sexology.

sexologue [sɛksɔlɔg] **nmf** sexologist.

sex-shop [sɛksʃɔp] (pl **sex-shops**) **nm** sex shop.

sextant [sɛkstɑ̃] **nm** sextant.

sextuple [sɛkstypl] ■ **nm : le sextuple de 3** 6 times 3.
■ **adj** sixfold.

sexualité [sɛksɥalite] **nf** sexuality.

sexué, e [sɛksɥe] **adj** [animal] sexed / [reproduction] sexual.

sexuel, elle [sɛksɥɛl] **adj** sexual.

sexuellement [sɛksɥɛlmɑ̃] **adv** sexually.

sexy [sɛksi] **adj inv** *fam* sexy.

seyais, seyait ➤ ***seoir***.

seyant, e [sɛjɑ̃, ɑ̃t] **adj** becoming.

Seychelles [seʃɛl] **nfpl : les Seychelles** the Seychelles ▸ **aux Seychelles** in the Seychelles.

SFIO (abr de ***Section française de l'internationale ouvrière***) **nf** *former name of the French socialist party*.

SG abr écrite de ***secrétaire général***.

SGA abr écrite de ***secrétaire général adjoint***.

SGEN (abr de ***Syndicat général de l'éducation nationale***) **nm** *teachers' trade union*.

SGML (abr de ***Standard Generalized Markup Language***) **m** INFORM SGML.

shah = ***schah***.

shaker [ʃɛkœr] **nm** cocktail shaker.

shampoing = ***shampooing***.

shampooiner = ***shampouiner***.

shampooineur = ***shampouineur***.

shampooing [ʃɑ̃pwɛ̃] **nm** shampoo.

shampouiner, shampooiner [3] [ʃɑ̃pwine] **vt** to shampoo.

shampouineur, euse, shampooineur, euse [ʃɑ̃pwinœr, øz] **nm, f** shampooer.

Shanghai [ʃɑ̃gaj] **npr** Shanghai.

shérif [ʃerif] **nm** sheriff.

sherry [ʃeri] **nm** sherry.

shetland [ʃɛtlɑ̃d] **nm 1.** [laine] Shetland wool **2.** [cheval] Shetland pony.

Shetland [ʃɛtlɑ̃d] **nfpl : les Shetland** the Shetlands.

shit [ʃit] *fam* **nm** hash.

shooter [3] [ʃute] **vi** to shoot ▸ **shooter dans qqch** *fam* to kick sthg.
◆ ***se shooter*** **vp** *fam arg crime* to shoot up.

shopping [ʃɔpiŋ] **nm** shopping ▸ **faire du shopping** to go (out) shopping.

short [ʃɔrt] **nm** shorts *pl*, pair of shorts.

show [ʃo] **nm** show.

show-business [ʃobiznɛs] **nm inv** show business.

si [1] [si] **nm inv** MUS B / [chanté] ti.

si[2] [si] ■ adv **1.** [tellement] so ▸ **elle est si belle** she is so beautiful ▸ **elle a de si beaux cheveux!** she has such beautiful hair! ▸ **il roulait si vite qu'il a eu un accident** he was driving so fast (that) he had an accident ▸ **ce n'est pas si facile que ça** it's not as easy as that ▸ **si vieux qu'il soit** however old he may be, old as he is ▸ **il est si mignon!** he's (ever) so sweet! ▸ **je la vois si peu** I see so little of her, I see her so rarely ▸ **il n'est pas si bête qu'il en a l'air** he's not as stupid as he seems
2. [oui] yes ▸ **tu n'aimes pas le café? si** don't you like coffee? yes, I do ▸ **je n'y arriverai jamais – mais si!** I'll never manage – of course you will! ▸ **ce n'est pas fermé? – si** isn't it closed? – yes (it is) ▸ **ça n'a pas d'importance – si, ça en a!** it doesn't matter – it **does** *ou* yes it does! ▸ **tu n'aimes pas ça? – si, si!** don't you like that? – oh yes I do!
■ **conj 1.** [gén] if ▸ **si tu veux, on y va** we'll go if you want ▸ **si tu faisais cela, je te détesterais** I would hate you if you did that ▸ **si seulement** if only
2. [exprimant une hypothèse] if ▸ **si tu venais de bonne heure, on pourrait finir avant midi** if you came early we would be able to finish before midday ▸ **s'il m'arrivait quelque chose, prévenez John** should anything happen to me *ou* if anything should happen to me, call John ▸ **ah toi, si je ne me retenais pas...!** just count yourself lucky I'm restraining myself! ▸ **si j'avais su, je me serais méfié** if I had known *ou* had I known, I would have been more cautious
3. [dans une question indirecte] if, whether ▸ **dites-moi si vous venez** tell me if *ou* whether you're coming
4. [emploi exclamatif] **: si je m'attendais à te voir ici!** well, I (certainly) didn't expect to meet you here *ou* fancy meeting you here!
■ **nm inv : il y a toujours des si et des mais** there are always ifs and buts ▸ **avec des si, on mettrait Paris en bouteille** *proverbe* if ifs and buts were pots and pans, there'd be no trade for tinkers *proverbe*.
◆ ***si bien que*** loc conj so that, with the result that ▸ **il ne sait pas lire une carte, si bien qu'on s'est perdus** he can't read a map, and so we got lost.
◆ ***si ce n'est que*** loc conj apart from the fact that, except (for the fact) that ▸ **il n'a pas de régime, si ce n'est qu'il ne doit pas fumer** he has no special diet, except that he mustn't smoke.
◆ ***si tant est que*** loc conj *(+ subjonctif)* providing, provided (that) ▸ **on se retrouvera à 18 h, si tant est que l'avion arrive à l'heure** we'll meet at 6 p.m. provided (that) *ou* if the plane arrives on time.

SI nm **1.** (abr de ***syndicat d'initiative***) tourist office **2.** (abr de ***système international***) SI.

siamois**, **e [sjamwa, az] adj Siamese ▸ **frères siamois, sœurs siamoises** MÉD Siamese twins / *fig* inseparable companions.
◆ ***Siamois**, **e*** nm, f *vieilli* Siamese person.

Sibérie [siberi] nf **: la Sibérie** Siberia.

sibérien**, **enne [siberjɛ̃, ɛn] adj Siberian.
◆ ***Sibérien**, **enne*** nm, f Siberian.

sibyllin**, **e [sibilɛ̃, in] adj enigmatic.

sic [sik] adv sic.

SICAV**, **Sicav [sikav] (abr de ***société d'investissement à capital variable***) nf **1.** [société] unit trust *UK*, mutual fund *US* **2.** [action] share in a unit trust *UK ou* mutual fund *US*.

Sicile [sisil] nf **: la Sicile** Sicily.

sicilien**, **enne [sisiljɛ̃, ɛn] adj Sicilian.
◆ ***Sicilien**, **enne*** nm, f Sicilian.

SICOB**, **Sicob [sikɔb] (abr de ***Salon des industries, du commerce et de l'organisation du bureau***) nm **: le Sicob** *annual information technology fair in Paris.*

SIDA**, **Sida [sida] (abr de ***syndrome immunodéficitaire acquis***) nm AIDS.

side-car [sidkar] (pl **side-cars**) nm sidecar.

sidéen**, **enne [sideɛ̃, ɛn] nm, f person with AIDS.

sidéral**, **e**, **aux [sideral, o] adj sidereal.

sidérant**, **e [siderɑ̃, ɑ̃t] adj *fam* staggering.

sidérer [18] [sidere] vt *fam* to stagger.

sidérurgie [sideryrʒi] nf **1.** [industrie] iron and steel industry **2.** [technique] iron and steel metallurgy.

sidérurgique [sideryrʒik] adj steel *(avant n)*.

sidérurgiste [sideryrʒist] nmf steelworker.

sidologue [sidɔlɔg] nmf AIDS specialist.

siècle [sjɛkl] nm **1.** [cent ans] century ▸ **l'affaire du siècle** the bargain of the century **2.** [époque, âge] age ▸ **le siècle des lumières** the (Age of) Enlightenment ▸ **le siècle de l'atome** the atomic age **3.** *(gén pl) fam* [longue durée] ages *pl* ▸ **ça fait des siècles que...** it's ages since...

sied**, **siéra ➤ ***seoir***.

siège [sjɛʒ] nm **1.** [meuble & POLIT] seat ▸ **siège avant/arrière** front/back seat ▸ **siège éjectable** ejector *UK ou* ejection *US* seat ▸ **siège de voiture pour bébé** baby car seat **2.** MIL siege ▸ **faire le siège d'une ville** to lay siege to *ou* to besiege a town ▸ **lever le siège** to lift the siege **3.** [d'organisme] headquarters, head office ▸ **siège social** registered office ▸ **le siège du gouvernement** the seat of government **4.** MÉD **: se présenter par le siège** to be in the breech position **5.** DR bench.

siéger [22] [sjeʒe] vi **1.** [juge, assemblée] to sit **2.** *littéraire* [mal] to have its seat / [maladie] to be located.

sien [sjɛ̃] ◆ ***le sien**, **la sienne*** [ləsjɛn, lasjɛn] (mpl **les siens** [lesjɛ̃], fpl **les siennes** [lesjɛn]) **pron poss** [d'homme] his / [de femme] hers / [de chose, d'animal] its ▸ **les siens** his/her family ▸ **faire des siennes** to be up to one's usual tricks.

sierra [sjera] nf sierra.

sieste [sjɛst] nf siesta.

sifflant**, **e [siflɑ̃, ɑ̃t] adj [son] whistling / [voix] hissing / LING sibilant.

sifflement [sifləmɑ̃] nm [son] whistling / [de serpent] hissing.

siffler [3] [sifle] ■ vi to whistle / [serpent] to hiss.
■ vt **1.** [air de musique] to whistle **2.** [femme] to whistle at **3.** [chien] to whistle (for) **4.** [acteur] to boo, to hiss **5.** *fam* [verre] to knock back.

sifflet [siflɛ] nm whistle.
◆ ***sifflets*** nmpl hissing *(U)*, boos.

sifflotement [siflɔtmɑ̃] **nm** whistling.

siffloter [3] [siflɔte] **vi** & **vt** to whistle.

sigle [sigl] **nm** acronym, (set of) initials.

signal, aux [siɲal, o] **nm 1.** [geste, son] signal ▸ **signal d'alarme** alarm (signal) ▸ **signal de détresse** distress signal ▸ **donner le signal (de)** to give the signal (for) ▸ **signal du marché** market indicator **2.** [panneau] sign.

signalement [siɲalmɑ̃] **nm** description.

signaler [3] [siɲale] ■ **vt 1.** [fait] to point out ▸ **rien à signaler** nothing to report **2.** [à la police] to denounce.
■ **vi** [à train, navire] **: signaler à** to signal to.
◆ ***se signaler*** **vp : se signaler par** to become known for, to distinguish o.s. by.

signalétique [siɲaletik] **adj** identifying.

signalisation [siɲalizasjɔ̃] **nf 1.** [action] signposting **2.** [panneaux] signs *pl* / [au sol] (road) markings *pl* / NAUT signals *pl*.

signataire [siɲatɛr] **nmf** signatory.

signature [siɲatyr] **nf 1.** [nom, marque] signature ▸ **signature électronique** digital signature **2.** [acte] signing **3.** ÉCON strapline.

signe [siɲ] **nm 1.** [gén] sign ▸ **en signe de** as a sign of ▸ **mettre un brassard en signe de deuil** to wear an armband as a sign of mourning ▸ **être né sous le signe de** ASTROL to be born under the sign of ▸ **être placé sous le signe de** *fig* [conférence, transaction] to be marked by ▸ **faire signe à qqn** to signal to sb ▸ **faire un signe de la main à qqn** [pour saluer, attirer l'attention] to wave to sb, to wave one's hand at sb ▸ **quand vous serez à Paris, faites-moi signe** *fig* when you're in Paris, let me know ▸ **signe avant-coureur** advance indication ▸ **signe de la croix** RELIG sign of the cross ▸ **signe dollar** dollar sign ▸ **signe de ponctuation** punctuation mark ▸ **signe de ralliement** rallying symbol ▸ **signe de reconnaissance** means of recognition ▸ **signes extérieurs de richesse** outward signs of wealth ▸ **c'est bon/mauvais signe** it's a good/bad sign ▸ **donner signe de vie** to get in touch
2. [trait] mark ▸ **signe distinctif** characteristic ▸ **signe particulier** distinguishing mark ▸ **'signes particuliers: néant'** 'distinguishing marks: none'
3. [indication] sign ▸ **c'est un signe** [mauvais] that's ominous / [bon] that's a good sign ▸ **c'est signe de : c'est signe de pluie/de beau temps** it's a sign of rain/of good weather ▸ **c'est signe que...** it's a sign that... ▸ **c'est bon signe** it's a good sign, it augurs well *sout* ▸ **c'est mauvais signe** it's a bad sign, it's ominous ▸ **(un) signe de : il n'y a aucun signe d'amélioration** there's no sign of (any) improvement ▸ **c'est un signe des temps** it's a sign of the times ▸ **il n'a pas donné signe de vie depuis janvier** there's been no sign of him since January ▸ **donner des signes d'impatience** to give *ou* to show signs of impatience ▸ **la voiture donne des signes de fatigue** the car is beginning to show its age ▸ **signe annonciateur** *ou* **avant-coureur** forerunner ▸ **signes extérieurs de richesse** DR outward signs of wealth
4. LING, MATH, MÉD & MUS sign ▸ **le signe moins/plus** the minus/plus sign
5. [imprimerie] **: signe de correction** proofreading mark *ou* symbol ▸ **signe de ponctuation** punctuation mark.

signer [3] [siɲe] **vt** to sign.
◆ ***se signer*** **vp** to cross o.s.

signet [siɲɛ] **nm** bookmark *(attached to spine of book)*.

significatif, ive [siɲifikatif, iv] **adj** significant.

signification [siɲifikasjɔ̃] **nf 1.** [sens] meaning **2.** DR service (of documents).

signifier [9] [siɲifje] **vt 1.** [vouloir dire] to mean ▸ **de telles menaces ne signifient rien de sa part** such threats mean nothing coming from him ▸ **que signifie ceci?** what's the meaning of this? **2.** [faire connaître] to make known ▸ **signifier son congé à qqn** to give sb notice of dismissal *sout*,to give sb his/her notice ▸ **signifier ses intentions à qqn** to make one's intentions known *ou* to state one's intentions to sb **3.** DR to serve notice of.

silence [silɑ̃s] **nm 1.** [gén] silence ▸ **demander** *ou* **réclamer le silence** to call for silence ▸ **garder le silence (sur)** to remain silent (about) ▸ **imposer le silence à qqn** to shut sb up ▸ **dans le silence de la nuit** in the still *ou* silence of the night ▸ **silence de glace** stony silence ▸ **silence de mort** deathly hush ▸ **il régnait un silence de mort** it was as quiet *ou* silent as the grave ▸ **silence radio** radio silence ▸ **il devait me rappeler après son voyage mais depuis un mois silence radio** he was supposed to call me back after his trip but I haven't heard a peep *ou* a dicky bird *vieilli* out of him for a month ▸ **passer qqch sous silence** *fig* to avoid mentioning sthg **2.** MUS rest **3.** CINÉ **: silence on tourne!** quiet on the set! **4.** [lacune] **: le silence de la loi en la matière** the absence of legislation regarding this matter.

silencieusement [silɑ̃sjøzmɑ̃] **adv** in silence, silently.

silencieux, euse [silɑ̃sjø, øz] **adj 1.** [lieu, appareil] quiet **2.** [personne - taciturne] quiet / [- muet] silent.
◆ ***silencieux*** **nm** AUTO silencer *UK*, muffler *US*.

silex [silɛks] **nm** flint.

silhouette [silwɛt] **nf 1.** [de personne] silhouette / [de femme] figure / [d'objet] outline **2.** ART silhouette.

silice [silis] **nf** silica.

siliceux, euse [silisø, øz] **adj** silicious, siliceous.

silicium [silisjɔm] **nm** silicon.

silicone [silikon] **nf** silicone.

sillage [sijaʒ] **nm** wake.

sillon [sijɔ̃] **nm 1.** [tranchée, ride] furrow **2.** [de disque] groove.

sillonner [3] [sijɔne] **vt 1.** [champ] to furrow **2.** [ciel] to crisscross.

silo [silo] **nm** silo.

simagrées [simagre] **nfpl** *péj* **: faire des simagrées** to make a fuss.

simiesque [simjɛsk] **adj** simian.

similaire [similɛr] **adj** similar.

similarité [similarite] **nf** similarity.

simili [simili] ■ **nm 1.** *fam* [imitation] imitation ▸ **en simili** imitation *(avant n)* **2.** [de photogravure] halftone plate *ou* block.
■ **nf** *fam* halftone illustration.

similicuir [similikɥir] **nm** imitation leather.

similitude [similityd] **nf** similarity.

simple [sɛ̃pl] ■ **adj 1.** [gén] simple ▸ **simple d'esprit** simple-minded **2.** [ordinaire] ordinary **3.** [billet] **: un aller simple** a single ticket.
■ **nm** TENNIS singles *sg*.
◆ ***simples*** **nmpl** medicinal plants *ou* herbs.

simplement [sɛ̃pləmɑ̃] **adv** simply ▸ **tout simplement** quite simply, just.

simplet, ette [sɛ̃plɛ, ɛt] **adj 1.** [personne] simple **2.** *péj* [raisonnement] simplistic.

simplicité [sɛ̃plisite] **nf** simplicity ▸ **d'une simplicité enfantine** childishly simple.

simplificateur, trice [sɛ̃plifikatœr, tris] **adj** simplifying.

simplification [sɛ̃plifikasjɔ̃] **nf** simplification.

simplifier [9] [sɛ̃plifje] **vt 1.** [procédé] to simplify **2.** [explication] to simplify, to make simpler ▸ **en simplifiant à outrance** by oversimplifying ▸ **cela simplifierait les choses** it would make things easier **3.** MATH [fraction] to reduce, to simplify / [équation] to simplify.
◆ ***se simplifier*** ■ **vpi** to become simplified *ou* simpler.
■ **vpt** to simplify ▸ **elle se simplifie l'existence** she makes her life simpler.

simplisme [sɛ̃plism] **nm** *péj* oversimplification.

simpliste [sɛ̃plist] **adj** *péj* simplistic.

simulacre [simylakr] **nm 1.** [semblant] **: un simulacre de** a pretence of, a sham **2.** [action simulée] enactment.

simulateur, trice [simylatœr, tris] **nm, f** pretender / [de maladie] malingerer.
◆ ***simulateur*** **nm** TECHNOL simulator.

simulation [simylasjɔ̃] **nf 1.** [gén] simulation **2.** [comédie] shamming, feigning / [de maladie] malingering.

simuler [3] [simyle] **vt 1.** [gén] to simulate **2.** [feindre] to feign, to sham.

simultané, e [simyltane] **adj** simultaneous.

simultanéité [simyltaneite] **nf** simultaneousness.

simultanément [simyltanemɑ̃] **adv** simultaneously.

Sinaï [sinaj] **npr : le Sinaï** Sinai ▸ **le mont Sinaï** Mount Sinai.

sincère [sɛ̃sɛr] **adj** sincere.

sincèrement [sɛ̃sɛrmɑ̃] **adv 1.** [franchement] honestly, sincerely ▸ **sincèrement vôtre** yours sincerely **2.** [vraiment] really, truly.

sincérité [sɛ̃serite] **nf** sincerity ▸ **en toute sincérité** in all sincerity.

sinécure [sinekyr] **nf** sinecure ▸ **ce n'est pas une sinécure** *fam fig* it's not exactly a cushy job.

sine qua non [sinekwanɔn] **adj : condition sine qua non** prerequisite.

Singapour [sɛ̃gapur] **npr** Singapore ▸ **à Singapour** in Singapore.

singe [sɛ̃ʒ] **nm** ZOOL monkey / [de grande taille] ape.

singer [17] [sɛ̃ʒe] **vt 1.** [personne] to mimic, to ape **2.** [sentiment] to feign.

singerie [sɛ̃ʒri] **nf 1.** [grimace] face **2.** [manières] fuss *(U)*.

singulariser [3] [sɛ̃gylarize] **vt** to draw *ou* call attention to.
◆ ***se singulariser*** **vp** to draw *ou* call attention to o.s.

singularité [sɛ̃gylarite] **nf 1.** *littéraire* [bizarrerie] strangeness **2.** [particularité] peculiarity.

singulier, ère [sɛ̃gylje, ɛr] **adj 1.** *sout* [bizarre] strange / [spécial] uncommon **2.** GRAMM singular **3.** [d'homme à homme] **: combat singulier** single combat.
◆ ***singulier*** **nm** GRAMM singular.

singulièrement [sɛ̃gyljɛrmɑ̃] **adv 1.** *littéraire* [bizarrement] strangely **2.** [beaucoup, très] particularly.

sinistre [sinistr] ■ **nm 1.** [catastrophe] disaster **2.** DR damage *(U)*.
■ **adj 1.** [personne, regard] sinister / [maison, ambiance] gloomy **2.** *(avant n) péj* [crétin, imbécile] dreadful, terrible.

sinistré, e [sinistre] ■ **adj** [région] disaster *(avant n)*, disaster-stricken / [famille] disaster-stricken.
■ **nm, f** disaster victim.

sinistrose [sinistroz] **nf** pessimism.

sinologue [sinɔlɔg] **nmf** Sinologist, China-watcher.

sinon [sinɔ̃] **conj 1.** [autrement] or else, otherwise ▸ **je ne peux pas, sinon je l'aurais fait** I can't, otherwise I would have done it ▸ **j'essaierai d'être à l'heure, sinon partez sans moi** I'll try to be on time, but if I'm not go without me ▸ **tais-toi, sinon...!** be quiet or else...! **2.** [sauf] except, apart from ▸ **elle l'a, sinon aimé, du moins apprécié** although *ou* if she didn't like it she did at least appreciate it ▸ **que faire, sinon attendre?** what can we do other than wait? **3.** [si ce n'est] if not.
◆ ***sinon que*** **loc conj** except that.

sinueux, euse [sinɥø, øz] **adj** winding / *fig* tortuous.

sinuosité [sinɥozite] **nf** bend, twist.
◆ ***sinuosités*** **nfpl** *fig* tortuousness, convolutions.

sinus [sinys] **nm 1.** ANAT sinus **2.** MATH sine.

sinusite [sinyzit] **nf** sinusitis *(U)*.

sionisme [sjɔnism] **nm** Zionism.

sioniste [sjɔnist] **nmf & adj** Zionist.

sioux [sju] **adj** [anthropologie] Siouan.
◆ ***Sioux*** **nmf** Sioux ▸ **les Sioux** the Sioux (Indians).
◆ ***sioux*** **nm** LING Sioux.

siphon [sifɔ̃] **nm 1.** [tube] siphon **2.** [bouteille] soda siphon.

siphonné, e [sifɔne] **adj** *fam* [fou] batty, crackers *UK*.

siphonner [3] [sifɔne] **vt** to siphon.

sire [sir] **nm** HIST lord
▸▸ **un triste sire** a sad character.
◆ ***Sire*** **nm** Sire.

sirène [sirɛn] **nf** siren.

sirocco [sirɔko] **nm** sirocco.

sirop [siro] **nm** syrup ▸ **sirop d'érable** maple syrup ▸ **sirop de grenadine** (syrup of) grenadine ▸ **sirop de menthe** mint cordial ▸ **sirop d'orgeat** barley water ▸ **sirop contre la toux** cough mixture *ou* syrup.

siroter [3] [sirɔte] **vt** *fam* to sip.

SIRPA, ***Sirpa*** [sirpa] (abr de ***Service d'information et de renseignement du public de l'armée***) **nm** *French army public information service.*

sirupeux, ***euse*** [sirypø, øz] **adj** syrupy.

sis, ***e*** [si, siz] **adj** DR located.

sismique [sismik] **adj** seismic.

sismographe [sismɔgraf] **nm** seismograph.

sismologie [sismɔlɔʒi] **nf** seismology.

sitcom [sitkɔm] **nm** & **nf** sitcom.

site [sit] **nm 1.** [emplacement] site ▸ **site archéologique/historique** archaeological/historic site ▸ **site naturel** unspoiled site **2.** [paysage] beauty spot **3.** INFORM **: site FTP** FTP site ▸ **site Web** web site, Web site.

sitôt [sito] **adv : sitôt après** immediately after ▸ **pas de sitôt** not for some time, not for a while ▸ **sitôt arrivé,...** as soon as I/he *etc* arrived,... ▸ **sitôt dit, sitôt fait** no sooner said than done.
◆ ***sitôt que*** **loc conj** as soon as.

situation [sitɥasjɔ̃] **nf 1.** [position, emplacement] position, location **2.** [contexte, circonstance] situation ▸ **situation de famille** marital status ▸ **être en situation de faire qqch** to be in a position to do sthg ▸ **ma situation financière n'est pas brillante!** my financial situation is *ou* my finances are none too healthy! ▸ **je n'aimerais pas être dans ta situation** I wouldn't like to be in your position ▸ **tu vois un peu la situation!** do you get the picture? **3.** [emploi] job, position ▸ **avoir une bonne situation** [être bien payé] to have a well-paid job / [être puissant] to have a high-powered job **4.** FIN financial statement, account ▸ **situation de compte** account balance ▸ **situation de trésorerie** cash budget.
◆ ***en situation*** **loc adv** in real life ▸ **voyons comment elle va aborder les choses en situation** let's see how she gets on in real life *ou* when faced with the real thing.
◆ ***en situation de*** **loc prép : être en situation de faire qqch** to be in a position to do sthg.

situé, ***e*** [sitɥe] **adj** situated ▸ **bien/mal situé** well/badly situated.

situer [7] [sitɥe] **vt 1.** [maison] to site, to situate **2.** [sur carte] to locate **3.** *fam* [personne] to size up.
◆ ***se situer*** **vp** [scène] to be set / [dans classement] to be.

SIVOM, ***Sivom*** [sivɔm] (abr de ***Syndicat intercommunal à vocation multiple***) **nm** *group of local authorities pooling public services.*

six *(en fin de phrase* [sis], *devant consonne ou 'h' aspiré* [si], *devant voyelle ou 'h' muet* [siz]*)* ■ **adj num inv** six ▸ **il a six ans** he is six (years old) ▸ **il est six heures** it's six (o'clock) ▸ **le six janvier** (on) the sixth of January *UK*, (on) January sixth *US* ▸ **daté du six septembre** dated the sixth of September *UK ou* September sixth *US* ▸ **Charles Six** Charles the Sixth ▸ **page six** page six.
■ **nm inv 1.** [gén] six ▸ **six de pique** six of spades
2. [adresse] (number) six
3. SPORT **: le six** number six.
■ **pron** six ▸ **ils étaient six** there were six of them ▸ **ils sont venus à six** six (of them) came ▸ **couper/partager en six** to cut/divide into six ▸ **six par six** six at a time ▸ **six d'entre eux/nous/vous** six of them/us/you ▸ **cinq sur six** five out of six.

sixième [sizjɛm] ■ **adj num inv** sixth.
■ **nmf** sixth ▸ **arriver/se classer sixième** to come (in)/to be placed sixth.
■ **nf** SCOL ≃ first year *ou* form *UK*, ≃ sixth grade *US* ▸ **être en sixième** to be in the first year *ou* form *UK*, to be in sixth grade *US* ▸ **entrer en sixième** to go to secondary school.
■ **nm 1.** [part] **: le/un sixième de** one/a sixth of ▸ **cinq sixièmes** five sixths **2.** [arrondissement] sixth arrondissement **3.** [étage] sixth floor *UK*, seventh floor *US*.

sixièmement [sizjɛmmɑ̃] **adv** sixthly, in (the) sixth place.

six-quatre-deux [siskatdø] ◆ ***à la six-quatre-deux*** **loc adv** *fam* in a slapdash way.

Skaï® [skaj] **nm inv** leatherette.

skateboard [skɛtbɔrd] **nm** skateboard.

sketch [skɛtʃ] (pl **sketches**) **nm** sketch *(in a revue etc).*

ski [ski] **nm 1.** [objet] ski **2.** [sport] skiing ▸ **faire du ski** to ski ▸ **ski acrobatique/alpin/de fond** freestyle/alpine/cross-country skiing ▸ **ski nautique** water skiing ▸ **ski de randonnée** ski-touring ▸ **ski sauvage** *ou* **hors piste** off-piste skiing / AÉRON landing skid.
◆ ***de ski*** **loc adj** [chaussures, lunettes] ski *(modif)* / [vacances, séjour] skiing *(modif).*

skier [10] [skje] **vi** to ski.

skieur, ***euse*** [skjœr, øz] **nm, f** skier.

skinhead [skinɛd] **nm** skinhead.

skipper [skipœr] **nm 1.** [capitaine] skipper **2.** [barreur] helmsman.

slalom [slalɔm] **nm 1.** SKI slalom ▸ **slalom géant/spécial** giant/special slalom **2.** [zigzags] **: faire du slalom** to zigzag.

slalomer [3] [slalɔme] **vi 1.** SKI to slalom **2.** [zigzaguer] to zigzag.

slalomeur, ***euse*** [slalɔmœr, øz] **nm, f** slalom skier.

slave [slav] **adj** Slavonic.
◆ ***Slave*** **nmf** Slav.

slip [slip] **nm** briefs *pl*, underpants *pl* ▸ **slip de bain** [d'homme] swimming trunks *pl* / [de femme] bikini bottoms *pl*.

s.l.n.d. (abr de ***sans lieu ni date***) date and origin unknown.

sloche [slɔʃ] **nf** *Québec* slush.

slogan [slɔgɑ̃] **nm** slogan.

slovaque [slɔvak] ■ **adj** Slovak.
■ **nm** [langue] Slovak.
◆ ***Slovaque*** **nmf** Slovak.

Slovaquie [slɔvaki] **nf : la Slovaquie** Slovakia.

slovène [slɔvɛn] ■ **adj** Slovenian.
■ **nm** [langue] Slovenian.
◆ ***Slovène*** **nmf** Slovenian.

Slovénie [slɔveni] **nf : la Slovénie** Slovenia.

slow [slo] **nm** slow dance.

SM, ***S-M*** (abr de ***sado-masochisme***) **nm** S & M.

SM (abr écrite de ***sa majesté***) HM.

SMAG, ***Smag*** [smag] (abr de ***salaire minimum agricole garanti***) **nm** *guaranteed minimum wage for agricultural workers.*

smala(h) [smala] **nf 1.** [de chef arabe] retinue **2.** *fam* [famille] brood.

smasher [3] [sma(t)ʃe] **vi** TENNIS to smash (the ball).

SME (abr de ***Système monétaire européen***) **nm** EMS.

SMI (abr de ***Système Monétaire International***) **m** ÉCON IMS *(International Monetary System).*

SMIC, ***Smic*** [smik] (abr de ***salaire minimum interprofessionnel de croissance***) **nm** *index-linked guaranteed minimum wage.*

smicard, ***e*** [smikar, ard] ■ **adj** *minimum-wage-earning.*
■ **nm, f** *minimum-wage earner.*

smiley [smaılı] **nm** smiley.

smocks [smɔk] **nmpl** smocking *(U).*

smoking [smɔkiŋ] **nm** dinner jacket, tuxedo *US.*

SMUR, ***Smur*** [smyr] (abr de ***Service médical d'urgence et de réanimation***) **nm** *French ambulance and emergency unit.*

snack [snak] **nm 1.** = ***snack-bar*** **2.** [collation] snack.

snack-bar [snakbar] (pl **snack-bars**) **nm** snack bar, self-service restaurant, cafeteria.

SNC (abr de ***service non compris***) service not included.

SNCB (abr de ***Société nationale des chemins de fer belges***) **nf** *Belgian railways board.*

SNCF (abr de ***Société nationale des chemins de fer français***) **nf** *French railways board.*

SNES, ***Snes*** [snɛs] (abr de ***Syndicat national de l'enseignement secondaire***) **nm** *secondary school teachers' union.*

Sne-sup [snɛsyp] (abr de ***Syndicat national de l'enseignement supérieur***) **nm** *university teachers' union.*

SNI (abr de ***Syndicat national des instituteurs***) **nm** *primary school teachers' union.*

SNJ (abr de ***Syndicat national des journalistes***) **nm** *national union of journalists.*

snob [snɔb] ■ **nmf** snob.
■ **adj** snobbish.

snober [3] [snɔbe] **vt** to snub, to cold-shoulder.

snobinard, ***e*** [snɔbinar, ard] *fam péj* ■ **adj** rather snobbish.
■ **nm, f** a bit of a snob.

snobisme [snɔbism] **nm** snobbery, snobbishness.

SNSM (abr de ***Société nationale de sauvetage en mer***) **nf** *national sea-rescue association.*

soap opera [sopɔpera] (pl **soap operas**), ***soap*** [sop] (pl **soaps**) **nm** soap (opera).

sobre [sɔbr] **adj 1.** [personne] temperate **2.** [style] sober / [décor, repas] simple.

sobrement [sɔbrəmɑ̃] **adv 1.** [boire] in moderation **2.** [se vêtir] soberly.

sobriété [sɔbrijete] **nf** sobriety.

sobriquet [sɔbrikɛ] **nm** nickname.

soc [sɔk] **nm** ploughshare *UK*, plowshare *US.*

sociabilité [sɔsjabilite] **nf** sociability.

sociable [sɔsjabl] **adj** sociable.

social, ***e***, ***aux*** [sɔsjal, o] **adj 1.** [rapports, classe, service] social **2.** COMM : **capital social** share capital ▸ **raison sociale** company name.
◆ ***social*** **nm : le social** social affairs *pl.*

social-démocrate, ***sociale-démocrate*** [sɔsjaldemɔkrat] (mpl **sociaux-démocrates** [sɔsjodemɔkrat]) (fpl **sociales-démocrates**) ■ **nmf** social democrat.
■ **adj** social democratic.

socialement [sɔsjalmɑ̃] **adv** socially.

socialisation [sɔsjalizasjɔ̃] **nf 1.** [développement social] socialization **2.** POLIT nationalization.

socialiser [3] [sɔsjalize] **vt 1.** [enfant] to socialize **2.** POLIT to nationalize.

socialisme [sɔsjalism] **nm** socialism.

socialiste [sɔsjalist] **nmf & adj** socialist.

sociétaire [sɔsjetɛr] **nmf** member.

société [sɔsjete] **nf 1.** [communauté, classe sociale, groupe] society ▸ **la société de consommation** the consumer society ▸ **en société** in society ▸ **cela ne se fait pas dans la bonne société** it's not done in good company *ou* in the best society ▸ **la haute société** high society ▸ **société littéraire/savante** literary/learned society ▸ **la Société protectrice des animaux** = ***SPA*** ▸ **société secrète** secret society ▸ **jeux de société** games *(for playing indoors, often with boards or cards)*
2. SPORT club
3. [présence] company, society
4. COMM company, firm ▸ **société d'affacturage** factoring company ▸ **société de bourse** securities house, brokerage firm ▸ **société de capitaux (à responsabilité limitée)** limited liability company ▸ **société (de capitaux) par actions (à responsabilité limitée)** (limited liability) joint-stock company ▸ **société de commerce en ligne** online retailer ▸ **société d'économie mixte** government-controlled corporation ▸ **société financière/de crédit** finance/credit company ▸ **société mère** parent company ▸ **société en participation** joint-venture company ▸ **société de personnes** partnership, joint-stock company *UK* ▸ **société de services** service company ▸ **société sœur** sister company.

socioculturel, ***elle*** [sɔsjɔkyltyrɛl] **adj** social and cultural.

socio-économique [sɔsjɔekɔnɔmik] **adj** socioeconomic.

sociologie [sɔsjɔlɔʒi] **nf** sociology.

sociologique [sɔsjɔlɔʒik] **adj** sociological.

sociologue [sɔsjɔlɔg] **nmf** sociologist.

socioprofessionnel, ***elle*** [sɔsjɔprɔfɛsjɔnɛl] **adj** socioprofessional.

socle [sɔkl] **nm 1.** [de statue] plinth, pedestal **2.** [de lampe] base **3.** GÉOGR : **socle continental** continental shelf.

socquette [sɔkɛt] **nf** ankle *ou* short sock.

soda [sɔda] **nm** fizzy drink.

sodium [sɔdjɔm] **nm** sodium.

sodomie [sɔdɔmi] **nf** buggery, sodomy.

sodomiser [3] [sɔdɔmize] **vt** to sodomize.

sœur [sœr] **nf 1.** [gén] sister ▸ **grande/petite sœur** big/little sister ▸ **sœur de lait** foster sister **2.** RELIG nun, sister.

sofa [sɔfa] **nm** sofa.

Sofia [sɔfja] **npr** Sofia.

SOFRES**, **Sofres [sɔfrɛs] (abr de ***Société française d'enquête par sondages***) **nf** *French opinion poll company*.

software [sɔftwɛr] **nm** software.

soi [swa] **pron pers** oneself ▸ **chacun pour soi** every man for himself ▸ **en soi** in itself, per se ▸ **cela va de soi** that goes without saying ▸ **il va de soi que** it goes without saying that.

◆ ***chez soi*** **loc adv** at home ▸ **se sentir chez soi** to feel at home.

◆ ***soi-même*** **pron pers** oneself.

soi-disant [swadizɑ̃] ■ **adj inv** *(avant n)* so-called.

■ **adv** *fam* supposedly.

soie [swa] **nf 1.** [textile] silk ▸ **en soie** silk ▸ **soie grège** raw silk ▸ **soie sauvage** wild silk **2.** [poil] bristle.

soierie [swari] **nf 1.** *(gén pl)* [textile] silk **2.** [industrie] silk trade.

soif [swaf] **nf** thirst ▸ **soif (de)** *fig* thirst (for), craving (for) ▸ **avoir soif** to be thirsty ▸ **étancher sa soif** to quench one's thirst ▸ **jusqu'à plus soif** to excess / *fig* until one has had one's fill.

soigné**, **e [swaɲe] **adj 1.** [travail] meticulous **2.** [personne] well-groomed / [jardin, mains] well-cared-for **3.** *fam fig* [cuite, raclée] awful, massive.

soigner [3] [swaɲe] **vt 1.** [suj: médecin] to treat / [suj: infirmière, parent] to nurse **2.** [invités, jardin, mains] to look after **3.** [travail, présentation] to take care over.

◆ ***se soigner*** **vp** to take care of o.s., to look after o.s.

soigneur [swaɲœr] **nm** SPORT trainer / [boxe] second.

soigneusement [swaɲøzmɑ̃] **adv** carefully.

soigneux**, **euse [swaɲø, øz] **adj 1.** [personne] tidy, neat **2.** [travail] careful ▸ **soigneux de** careful with.

soin [swɛ̃] **nm 1.** [attention] care ▸ **avoir *ou* prendre soin de** to take care of, to look after ▸ **avoir *ou* prendre soin de faire qqch** to be sure to do sthg ▸ **confier à qqn le soin de faire qqch** to entrust sb with the task of doing sthg ▸ **aux bons soins de** in the care of, in the hands of ▸ **aux bons soins de** [dans le courrier] care of ▸ **avec soin** carefully ▸ **sa maison est toujours rangée avec soin** his house is always very neat *ou* tidy ▸ **sans soin** [procéder] carelessly / [travail] careless ▸ **être aux petits soins pour qqn** *fig* to wait on sb hand and foot **2.** [souci] concern.

◆ ***soins*** **nmpl** care *(U)* ▸ **prodiguer des soins à un nouveau-né** to care for a newborn baby ▸ **les premiers soins** first aid *sg* ▸ **soins dentaires** dental treatment *ou* care ▸ **soins (médicaux)** medical care *ou* treatment ▸ **soins du visage** skin care *(for the face)*.

soir [swar] **nm** evening ▸ **demain soir** tomorrow evening *ou* night ▸ **le soir** in the evening ▸ **à ce soir!** see you tonight!

soirée [sware] **nf 1.** [soir] evening ▸ **en soirée** CINÉ & THÉÂTRE evening *(avant n)* **2.** [réception] party ▸ **de soirée** evening *(avant n)* ▸ **charmante soirée!** *iron* wonderful evening!

sois ➤ ***être***.

soit[1] [swat] **adv** so be it.

soit[2] [swa] ■ **v** ➤ ***être***.

■ **conj 1.** [c'est-à-dire] in other words, that is to say **2.** MATH [étant donné] **: soit une droite AB** given a straight line AB.

◆ ***soit... soit*** **loc correlative** either... or.

◆ ***soit que... soit que*** **loc correlative** *(+ subjonctif)* whether... or (whether).

soixantaine [swasɑ̃tɛn] **nf 1.** [nombre] **: une soixantaine (de)** about sixty, sixty-odd **2.** [âge] **: avoir la soixantaine** to be in one's sixties.

soixante [swasɑ̃t] ■ **adj num inv** sixty ▸ **les années soixante** the Sixties.

■ **nm** sixty ; voir aussi ***six***.

soixante-dix [swasɑ̃tdis] ■ **adj num inv** seventy ▸ **les années soixante-dix** the Seventies.

■ **nm** seventy ; voir aussi ***six***.

soixante-dixième [swasɑ̃tdizjɛm] **adj num inv, nm & nmf** seventieth ; voir aussi ***sixième***.

soixante-huitard**, **e [swasɑ̃tɥitar, ard] ■ **adj** of May 1968.

■ **nm, f** *person who participated in the events of May 1968*.

soixantième [swasɑ̃tjɛm] **adj num inv, nm & nmf** sixtieth ; voir aussi ***sixième***.

soja [sɔʒa] **nm** soya.

sol [sɔl] **nm 1.** [terre] ground **2.** [de maison] floor **3.** [territoire] soil **4.** MUS G / [chanté] so.

solaire [sɔlɛr] **adj 1.** [énergie, four] solar **2.** [crème] sun *(avant n)*.

solarium [sɔlarjɔm] **nm** solarium.

soldat [sɔlda] **nm 1.** MIL soldier / [grade] private ▸ **le soldat inconnu** the Unknown Soldier **2.** [jouet] (toy) soldier ▸ **soldat de plomb** tin soldier, toy soldier.

solde [sɔld] ■ **nm 1.** [de compte, facture] balance ▸ **solde créditeur/débiteur** credit/debit balance ▸ **solde à découvert** outstanding balance ▸ **solde d'ouverture** opening balance ▸ **solde de fin de mois** end-of-month balance **2.** [rabais] **: en solde** [acheter] in a sale.

■ **nf** MIL pay ▸ **à la solde de qqn** *fig* in the pay of sb.

◆ ***soldes*** **nmpl** sales.

soldé**, **e [sɔlde] **adj** [article] reduced.

solder [3] [sɔlde] **vt 1.** [compte] to close **2.** [marchandises] to sell off.

◆ ***se solder*** **vp : se solder par** FIN to show / *fig* [aboutir] to end in.

soldeur**, **euse [sɔldœr, øz] **nm, f** *buyer and seller of discount goods*.

sole [sɔl] **nf** sole ▸ **sole meunière** *sole coated with flour and fried in butter*.

solécisme [sɔlesism] **nm** solecism.

soleil [sɔlɛj] **nm 1.** [astre, motif] sun ▸ **soleil couchant/levant** setting/rising sun ▸ **le soleil de minuit** the midnight sun ▸ **sous un soleil de plomb** *fig* in the blazing sun **2.** [lumière, chaleur] sun, sunlight ▸ **au soleil** in the sun ▸ **en plein soleil** right in the sun ▸ **il fait (du) soleil** it's sunny ▸ **il y aura beaucoup de soleil sur le sud de la France** it'll be very sunny in *ou* over southern France ▸ **prendre le soleil** to sunbathe ▸ **une journée sans soleil** a day with no sunshine **3.** [tournesol] sunflower.

solennel, elle [sɔlanɛl] **adj 1.** [cérémonieux] ceremonial **2.** [grave] solemn **3.** *péj* [pompeux] pompous.

solennellement [sɔlanɛlmɑ̃] **adv 1.** [avec importance] ceremonially **2.** [avec sérieux] solemnly.

solennité [sɔlanite] **nf 1.** [gravité] solemnity **2.** [raideur] stiffness, formality **3.** [fête] special occasion.

Solex® [sɔlɛks] **nm** ≃ moped.

solfège [sɔlfɛʒ] **nm : apprendre le solfège** to learn the rudiments of music.

solfier [9] [sɔlfje] **vt** to sol-fa.

solidaire [sɔlidɛr] **adj 1.** [lié] **: être solidaire de qqn** to be behind sb, to show solidarity with sb **2.** [relié] interdependent, integral.

solidariser [3] [sɔlidarize] ◆ ***se solidariser*** **vp : se solidariser (avec)** to show solidarity (with).

solidarité [sɔlidarite] **nf** [entraide] solidarity ▸ **par solidarité** [se mettre en grève] in sympathy.

solide [sɔlid] ■ **adj 1.** [état, corps] solid **2.** [construction] solid, sturdy ▸ **peu solide** [chaise, pont] rickety **3.** [personne] sturdy, robust ▸ **solide sur ses jambes** steady on one's feet ▸ **avoir une solide constitution** to have an iron constitution **4.** [argument] solid, sound ▸ **attitude empreinte d'un solide bon sens** no-nonsense attitude, attitude based on sound common sense **5.** [relation] stable, strong.
■ **nm** solid ▸ **il nous faut du solide** *fig* we need something solid *ou* concrete ▸ **les voitures suédoises, c'est du solide** Swedish cars are built to last ▸ **son dernier argument, c'est du solide!** *fam* her last argument is rock solid!

solidement [sɔlidmɑ̃] **adv 1.** [gén] firmly **2.** [attaché] firmly, securely.

solidifier [9] [sɔlidifje] **vt 1.** [ciment, eau] to solidify **2.** [structure] to reinforce.
◆ ***se solidifier*** **vp** to solidify.

solidité [sɔlidite] **nf 1.** [de matière, construction] solidity **2.** [de mariage] stability, strength **3.** [de raisonnement, d'argument] soundness.

soliloque [sɔlilɔk] **nm** *sout* soliloquy.

soliste [sɔlist] **nmf** soloist.

solitaire [sɔlitɛr] ■ **adj 1.** [de caractère] solitary **2.** [esseulé, retiré] lonely.
■ **nmf** [personne] loner, recluse.
■ **nm** [jeu, diamant] solitaire.
◆ ***en solitaire*** ■ **loc adj** [course, vol] solo *(modif)* / [navigation] single-handed.
■ **loc adv** [vivre, travailler] on one's own / [naviguer] single-handed ▸ **il vit en solitaire dans sa vieille maison** he lives on his own in his old house.

solitude [sɔlityd] **nf 1.** [isolement] loneliness **2.** [retraite] solitude.

solive [sɔliv] **nf** joist.

sollicitation [sɔlisitasjɔ̃] **nf** *(gén pl)* entreaty.

solliciter [3] [sɔlisite] **vt 1.** [demander - entretien, audience] to request / [- attention, intérêt] to seek ▸ **solliciter qqch de qqn** to ask sb for sthg, to seek sthg from sb **2.** [s'intéresser à] **: être sollicité** to be in demand **3.** [faire appel à] **: solliciter qqn pour faire qqch** to appeal to sb to do sthg.

sollicitude [sɔlisityd] **nf** solicitude, concern.

solo [sɔlo] ■ **nm** solo ▸ **en solo** solo.
■ **adj** solo *(avant n)*.

solstice [sɔlstis] **nm : solstice d'été/d'hiver** summer/winter solstice.

solubilité [sɔlybilite] **nf** solubility.

soluble [sɔlybl] **adj 1.** [matière] soluble / [café] instant **2.** *fig* [problème] solvable.

soluté [sɔlyte] **nm** solution.

solution [sɔlysjɔ̃] **nf 1.** [résolution] solution, answer ▸ **chercher/trouver la solution** to seek/to find the solution, to seek/to find the answer ▸ **solution de facilité** easy answer, easy way out **2.** [liquide] solution.
◆ ***solution de continuité*** **nf** break ▸ **sans solution de continuité** without a break.

solutionner [3] [sɔlysjɔne] **vt** to solve.

solvabilité [sɔlvabilite] **nf** solvency.

solvable [sɔlvabl] **adj** solvent, creditworthy.

solvant [sɔlvɑ̃] **nm** solvent.

somali = ***somalien.***

Somalie [sɔmali] **nf : la Somalie** Somalia.

somalien, enne [sɔmaljɛ̃, ɛn], ***somali, e*** [sɔmali] **adj** Somali.
◆ ***Somalien, enne, Somali, e*** **nm, f** Somali.

sombre [sɔ̃br] **adj 1.** [couleur, costume, pièce] dark **2.** *fig* [pensées, avenir] dark, gloomy **3.** *fig* [complot] murky **4.** *(avant n) fam* [profond] **: c'est un sombre crétin** he's a prize idiot.

sombrer [3] [sɔ̃bre] **vi** to sink ▸ **sombrer dans** *fig* to sink into.

sommaire [sɔmɛr] ■ **adj 1.** [explication] brief **2.** [exécution] summary **3.** [installation] basic.
■ **nm** summary.

sommairement [sɔmɛrmɑ̃] **adv 1.** [expliquer] briefly **2.** [délibérer] summarily **3.** [peu - vêtu] scantily / [- meublé] basically.

sommation [sɔmasjɔ̃] **nf 1.** [assignation] summons *sg* **2.** [ordre - de payer] demand / [- de se rendre] warning.

somme [sɔm] ■ **nf 1.** [addition] total, sum ▸ **faire la somme de plusieurs choses** to add up several things ▸ **somme de travail/d'énergie** amount of work/energy **2.** [d'argent] sum, amount ▸ **c'est une somme!** that's a lot of money! ▸ **j'ai dépensé des sommes folles** I spent huge amounts of money ▸ **la somme totale** the grand total **3.** [ouvrage] overview.
■ **nm** nap ▸ **faire un (petit) somme** to have a nap.
◆ ***en somme*** **loc adv** in short ▸ **en somme, tu refuses** in short, your answer is no.
◆ ***somme toute*** **loc adv** when all's said and done ▸ **somme toute, tu as eu de la chance** all things considered, you've been lucky.

sommeil [sɔmɛj] **nm** sleep ▸ **avoir sommeil** to be sleepy ▸ **tomber de sommeil** to be asleep on one's feet ▸ **dormir d'un sommeil de plomb** *fig* to be in a deep sleep ▸ **je manque de sommeil** I haven't been getting enough sleep ▸ **j'ai le sommeil léger/profond** I'm a light/heavy sleeper

⏭ **sommeil lent/paradoxal** NREM/REM sleep ▸ **le premier sommeil** the first hours of sleep.
◆ ***en sommeil*** ■ **loc adj** [volcan, économie] inactive, dormant.
■ **loc adv : rester en sommeil** to remain dormant *ou* inactive ▸ **mettre un secteur économique en sommeil** to put an economic sector in abeyance.

sommeiller [4] [sɔmeje] **vi 1.** [personne] to doze **2.** *fig* [qualité] to be dormant.

sommelier, ***ère*** [sɔməlje, ɛr] **nm, f** wine waiter (f wine waitress).

sommer [3] [sɔme] **vt : sommer qqn de faire qqch** *sout* to order sb to do sthg.

sommes ➤ *être*.

sommet [sɔmɛ] **nm 1.** [de montagne] summit, top **2.** *fig* [de hiérarchie] top / [de perfection] height ▸ **conférence au sommet** summit (meeting *ou* conference) **3.** GÉOM apex.

sommier [sɔmje] **nm** base, bed base.

sommité [sɔmite] **nf 1.** [personne] leading light **2.** BOT head.

somnambule [sɔmnɑ̃byl] ■ **nmf** sleepwalker.
■ **adj : être somnambule** to be a sleepwalker.

somnifère [sɔmnifɛr] **nm** sleeping pill.

somnolence [sɔmnɔlɑ̃s] **nf** sleepiness, drowsiness.

somnolent, ***e*** [sɔmnɔlɑ̃, ɑ̃t] **adj** [personne] sleepy, drowsy / *fig* [vie] dull / *fig* [économie] sluggish.

somnoler [3] [sɔmnɔle] **vi** to doze.

somptueusement [sɔ̃ptɥøzmɑ̃] **adv** sumptuously, lavishly.

somptueux, ***euse*** [sɔ̃ptɥø, øz] **adj** sumptuous, lavish.

somptuosité [sɔ̃ptɥozite] **nf** lavishness *(U)*.

son[1] [sɔ̃] **nm 1.** [bruit] sound ▸ **au son de** to the sound of ▸ **son et lumière** son et lumière **2.** [céréale] bran.

son[2], ***sa***, ***ses*** [sɔ̃, sa, se] **adj poss 1.** [possesseur défini - homme] his / [- femme] her / [- chose, animal] its ▸ **à sa vue, elle s'évanouit** on seeing him/her, she fainted ▸ **il aime son père** he loves his father ▸ **elle aime ses parents** she loves her parents ▸ **la ville a perdu son charme** the town has lost its charm **2.** [possesseur indéfini] one's / [après «chacun», «tout le monde» etc] his/her, their ▸ **il faut faire ses preuves** one has to show one's mettle *sout*, you have to show your mettle ▸ **tout le monde a ses problèmes** everybody has (his *ou* their) problems **3.** [emploi expressif] **: ça a son charme** it's got its own charm *ou* a certain charm ▸ **il a réussi à avoir son samedi** *fam* he managed to get Saturday off.

sonar [sɔnar] **nm** sonar.

sonate [sɔnat] **nf** sonata.

sondage [sɔ̃daʒ] **nm 1.** [enquête] poll, survey ▸ **sondage d'opinion** opinion poll **2.** TECHNOL drilling **3.** MÉD probing.

sonde [sɔ̃d] **nf 1.** MÉTÉOR sonde / [spatiale] probe **2.** MÉD probe **3.** NAUT sounding line **4.** TECHNOL drill.

sondé, ***e*** [sɔ̃de] **nm, f** poll respondent.

sonder [3] [sɔ̃de] **vt 1.** MÉD & NAUT to sound **2.** [terrain] to drill **3.** *fig* [opinion, personne] to sound out.

sondeur, ***euse*** [sɔ̃dœr, øz] **nm, f** pollster.
◆ ***sondeur*** **nm** TECHNOL sounder.

songe [sɔ̃ʒ] **nm** *littéraire* dream ▸ **en songe** in a dream.

songer [17] [sɔ̃ʒe] ■ **vt : songer que** to consider that.
■ **vi : songer à** to think about.

songeur, ***euse*** [sɔ̃ʒœr, øz] **adj** pensive, thoughtful.

sonnant, ***e*** [sɔnɑ̃, ɑ̃t] **adj : à six heures sonnantes** at six o'clock sharp.

sonné, ***e*** [sɔne] **adj 1.** [passé] **: il est trois heures sonnées** it's gone three o'clock ▸ **il a quarante ans bien sonnés** *fam fig* he's the wrong side of forty **2.** *fig* [étourdi] groggy **3.** *fam fig* [fou] cracked.

sonner [3] [sɔne] ■ **vt 1.** [cloche] to ring ▸ **sonner les cloches à qqn** *fam* to give sb a telling-off *ou* roasting **2.** [retraite, alarme] to sound **3.** [domestique] to ring for **4.** *fam fig* [siffler] **: je ne t'ai pas sonné!** who asked you! **5.** *fam* [assommer] to knock out *(sep)*, to stun / [abasourdir] to stun, to stagger, to knock (out) ▸ **ça l'a sonné!** he was reeling under the shock!
■ **vi 1.** [gén] to ring ▸ **j'ai mis le réveil à sonner pour** *ou* **à 8 h** I've set the alarm for 8 o'clock ▸ **sonner chez qqn** to ring sb's bell ▸ **on a sonné** there's someone at the door ▸ **sonner creux** to sound hollow, to give a hollow sound / *fig* to have a hollow ring ▸ **sonner faux** to be out of tune / *fig* to ring false ▸ **l'heure de la vengeance a sonné** *fig* the time for revenge has come **2.** [jouer] **: sonner de** to sound ▸ **sonner du cor** to sound the horn.

sonnerie [sɔnri] **nf 1.** [bruit] ringing **2.** [mécanisme] striking mechanism **3.** [signal] call.

sonnet [sɔnɛ] **nm** sonnet.

sonnette [sɔnɛt] **nf** bell.

sono [sɔno] **nf** *fam* [de salle] P.A. (system) / [de discothèque] sound system.

sonore [sɔnɔr] **adj 1.** CINÉ & PHYS sound *(avant n)* **2.** [voix, rire] ringing, resonant **3.** [salle] resonant.

sonorisation [sɔnɔrizasjɔ̃] **nf 1.** [action - de film] addition of the soundtrack / [- de salle] wiring for sound **2.** [matériel - de salle] public address system, P.A. (system) / [- de discothèque] sound system.

sonoriser [3] [sɔnɔrize] **vt 1.** [film] to add the soundtrack to **2.** [salle] to wire for sound.

sonorité [sɔnɔrite] **nf 1.** [de piano, voix] tone **2.** [de salle] acoustics *pl*.

sont ➤ *être*.

Sopalin® [sɔpalɛ̃] **nm** kitchen roll *UK*, paper towels *US*.

sophisme [sɔfism] **nm** sophism.

sophistication [sɔfistikasjɔ̃] **nf** sophistication.

sophistiqué, ***e*** [sɔfistike] **adj** sophisticated.

soporifique [sɔpɔrifik] ■ **adj** soporific.
■ **nm** sleeping drug, soporific.

soprano [soprano] (pl **sopranos** *ou* **soprani** [sɔprani]) **nm & nmf** soprano.

sorbet [sɔrbɛ] **nm** sorbet *UK*, sherbet *US*.

sorbetière [sɔrbətjɛr] **nf** ice-cream maker.

sorbier [sɔrbje] **nm** sorb, service tree.

Sorbonne [sɔrbɔn] **nf : la Sorbonne** the Sorbonne *(highly respected Paris university)*.

sorcellerie [sɔrsɛlri] **nf** witchcraft, sorcery.

sorcier, **ère** [sɔrsje, ɛr] ■ **nm, f** sorcerer (f witch). ■ **adj : ce n'est pas sorcier** *fig* there's no magic involved.

sordide [sɔrdid] **adj** squalid / *fig* sordid.

Sorlingues [sɔrlɛ̃g] **nfpl : les (îles) Sorlingues** the Scilly Isles.

sornettes [sɔrnɛt] **nfpl** nonsense *(U)*.

sors ➤ *sortir*.

sort [sɔr] **nm 1.** [maléfice] spell ▸ **jeter un sort (à qqn)** to cast a spell (on sb) **2.** [destinée] fate ▸ **faire un sort à qqch** *fam fig* to polish sthg off **3.** [condition] lot **4.** [hasard] **: le sort** fate ▸ **tirer au sort** to draw lots.

sortable [sɔrtabl] **adj** presentable ▸ **tu n'es pas sortable!** I can't take you anywhere!

sortant, **e** [sɔrtɑ̃, ɑ̃t] **adj 1.** [numéro] winning **2.** [président, directeur] outgoing *(avant n)*.

sorte [sɔrt] ■ **nf** sort, kind ▸ **une sorte de** a sort of, a kind of ▸ **une sorte de grand dadais** *péj* a big clumsy oaf ▸ **toutes sortes de** all kinds of, all sorts of ▸ **de la sorte** in that way, in that manner ▸ **comment osez-vous me traiter de la sorte?** how dare you treat me in that way *ou* like that! ▸ **de telle sorte que** so that, in such a way that ▸ **en quelque sorte** in a way, as it were ▸ **faire en sorte que** to see to it that ▸ **fais en sorte d'arriver à l'heure** try to be there on time.
■ **v** ➤ *sortir*.

sortie [sɔrti] **nf 1.** [issue] exit, way out / [d'eau, d'air] outlet ▸ **'attention, sortie de garage/véhicules'** 'caution, garage entrance/vehicle exit' ▸ **sortie d'autoroute** motorway junction *ou* exit *UK*, freeway exit *US* ▸ **sortie de secours** emergency exit ▸ **attends-moi à la sortie** wait for me outside ▸ **par ici la sortie!** this way out, please!
2. [départ] **: c'est la sortie de l'école** it's home time *UK* ▸ **à ma sortie de prison/d'hôpital** when I come (*ou* came) out of prison/hospital, on my release from prison/discharge from hospital ▸ **à la sortie du travail** when work finishes, after work
3. [de produit] launch, launching / [de disque] release / [film] **: sortie directement sur cassette vidéo** straight-to-video / [de livre] publication
4. *(gén pl)* [dépense] outgoings *pl UK*, expenditure *(U)*
5. [excursion] outing ▸ **sortie scolaire** school outing ▸ **on a organisé une petite sortie en famille/à vélo** we've organized a little family outing/cycle ride / [au cinéma, au restaurant] evening *ou* night out ▸ **faire une sortie** to go out ▸ **c'est son jour de sortie** [d'un domestique] it's his/her day off
6. MIL sortie
7. [écoulement - de liquide, gaz] escape
8. INFORM **: sortie imprimante** printout ▸ **sortie papier** hard copy.

sortie-de-bain [sɔrtidbɛ̃] (pl **sorties-de-bain**) **nf** bathrobe.

sortilège [sɔrtilɛʒ] **nm** spell.

sortir [43] [sɔrtir] ■ **vi** *(v aux : être)* **1.** [de la maison, du bureau etc] to leave, to go/come out ▸ **sors !** get out (of here)! ▸ **elle est sortie déjeuner/se promener** she's gone (out) for lunch/for a walk ▸ **sortir de** to go/come out of, to leave ▸ **sortir d'une pièce** to leave a room ▸ **sortir de prison** to come out of *ou* to be released from prison ▸ **sortir de l'école/du bureau** [finir sa journée] to finish school/work ▸ **sortir d'une voiture** to get out of a car ▸ **sortir du lit** to get out of bed ▸ **sortir par la fenêtre** to get out *ou* to leave by the window
2. [pour se distraire] to go out ▸ **je sors très peu** I hardly ever go out ▸ **sortir avec qqn** to go out with sb
3. *fig* [quitter] **: sortir de** [réserve, préjugés] to shed ▸ **elle est sortie de son silence pour écrire son second roman** she broke her silence to write her second novel
4. *fig* **: sortir de** [coma] to come out of / [de maladie] to get over, to recover from ▸ **je sors d'une grippe** I'm just recovering from a bout of flu
5. [film, livre, produit] to come out / [disque] to be released ▸ **ça vient de sortir!** it's just (come) out!, it's (brand) new!
6. [au jeu - carte, numéro] to come up
7. [s'écarter de] **: sortir de** [sujet] to get away from / [légalité, compétence] to be outside
8. [s'échapper] to get out ▸ **faire sortir qqn/des marchandises d'un pays** to smuggle sb/goods out of a country
9. INFORM **: sortir (d'un système)** to exit (from a system) ▸ **sortir d'un fichier** to close a file
10. NAUT & AÉRON **: sortir du port** to leave harbour ▸ **sortir en mer** to put out to sea ▸ **aujourd'hui, les avions/bateaux ne sont pas sortis** the planes were grounded/the boats stayed in port today
▸▸ **sortir de l'ordinaire** to be out of the ordinary ▸ **ça m'est complètement sorti de la tête** it went clean out of my mind ▸ **d'où il sort, celui-là?** where did HE spring from?
■ **vt** *(v aux : être)* **1.** [gén] **: sortir qqch (de)** to take sthg out (of)
2. [de situation difficile] to get out, to extract ▸ **je vais te sortir d'affaire** I'll get you out of it
3. [produit] to launch / [disque] to bring out, to release / [livre] to bring out, to publish
4. *fam* [bêtise] to come out with ▸ **il m'a sorti que j'étais trop vieille!** he told me I was too old, just like that!
5. [mettre dehors - vu de l'intérieur] to put out *ou* outside / [- vu de l'extérieur] to bring out *ou* outside *(sep)* ▸ **sortir la poubelle** to take out the rubbish bin *UK ou* the trash *US*
6. *fam* [expulser] to get *ou* to throw out *(sep)* ▸ **elle a sorti la Suédoise en trois sets** she disposed of *ou* beat the Swedish player in three sets
7. [s'écarter de] **: attention à ne pas sortir du sujet!** be careful not to get off *ou* to stray from the subject!

◆ ***au sortir de*** **loc prép** [dans le temps] **: au sortir de l'hiver** as winter draws to a close ▸ **au sortir de la guerre** towards the end of the war.

◆ ***se sortir*** **vp 1.** *fig* [de pétrin] to get out ▸ **se sortir d'une situation embarrassante** to get (o.s.) out of *ou sout* to extricate o.s. from an embarrassing situation ▸ **s'en sortir** [en réchapper] to come out of it
2. : il s'en est finalement sorti [il a survécu] he pulled through in the end / [il a réussi] he won through in the end
3. [y arriver] to get through it, to pull through ▸ **malgré les allocations, on ne s'en sort pas** in spite of the benefit, we're not making ends meet ▸ **tu t'en es très bien sorti** you did very well
4. : s'en sortir pour *fam* [avoir à payer] to be stung for.

SOS **nm** SOS ▸ **SOS médecins/dépannage** emergency medical/repair service ▸ **SOS-Racisme** *voluntary organization set up to combat racism in French society* ▸ **lancer un SOS** to send out an SOS.

sosie [sozi] **nm** double.

sot, sotte [so, sɔt] ■ **adj** silly, foolish.
■ **nm, f** fool.

sottement [sɔtmɑ̃] **adv** stupidly, foolishly.

sottise [sɔtiz] **nf** stupidity *(U)*, foolishness *(U)* ▸ **dire/faire une sottise** to say/do something stupid.

sottisier [sɔtizje] **nm** *collection of howlers*.

sou [su] **nm : être sans le sou** to be penniless ▸ **je n'ai pas le premier sou pour acheter une voiture** I really can't afford a car.
◆ ***sous*** **nmpl** *fam* money *(U)* ▸ **être près de ses sous** to be tightfisted ▸ **parler gros sous** to talk big money.

souahéli = ***swahili***.

soubassement [subasmɑ̃] **nm** base.

soubresaut [subrəso] **nm 1.** [de voiture] jolt **2.** [de personne] start.

soubrette [subrɛt] **nf** maid.

souche [suʃ] **nf 1.** [d'arbre] stump ▸ **dormir comme une souche** *fig* to sleep like a log **2.** [de carnet] counterfoil, stub **3.** [de famille] founder ▸ **de vieille souche** of old stock **4.** LING root.

souci [susi] **nm 1.** [tracas] worry ▸ **donner du souci à qqn** to worry sb ▸ **se faire du souci** to worry **2.** [préoccupation] concern ▸ **avoir des soucis** to have worries ▸ **c'est le dernier *ou* le cadet de mes soucis** that's the least of my worries **3.** [fleur] marigold.
◆ ***sans souci*** ■ **loc adj** [vie, personne - insouciant] carefree ▸ **être sans souci** [sans tracas] to be free of worries.
■ **loc adv : vivre sans souci** [de façon insouciante] to live a carefree life / [sans tracas] to live a life free of worries.

soucier [9] [susje] ◆ ***se soucier*** **vp : se soucier de** to care about.

soucieux, euse [susjø, øz] **adj 1.** [préoccupé] worried, concerned **2.** [concerné] **: être soucieux de qqch/de faire qqch** to be concerned about sthg/about doing sthg.

soucoupe [sukup] **nf 1.** [assiette] saucer **2.** [vaisseau] **: soucoupe volante** flying saucer.

soudain, e [sudɛ̃, ɛn] **adj** sudden.
◆ ***soudain*** **adv** suddenly, all of a sudden.

soudainement [sudɛnmɑ̃] **adv** suddenly.

Soudan [sudɑ̃] **nm : le Soudan** the Sudan ▸ **au Soudan** in the Sudan.

soudanais, e [sudanɛ, ɛz] **adj** Sudanese.
◆ ***Soudanais, e*** **nm, f** Sudanese person.

soude [sud] **nf** soda ▸ **soude caustique** caustic soda.

souder [3] [sude] **vt 1.** TECHNOL to weld, to solder **2.** MÉD to knit **3.** *fig* [unir] to bind together.

soudeur, euse [sudœr, øz] **nm, f** [personne] welder, solderer.
◆ ***soudeuse*** **nf** [machine] welding machine.

soudoyer [13] [sudwaje] **vt** to bribe.

soudure [sudyr] **nf 1.** TECHNOL welding / [résultat] weld ▸ **faire la soudure** *fig* to bridge the gap **2.** MÉD knitting.

souffert, e [sufɛr, ɛrt] **pp** ➤ ***souffrir***.

souffle [sufl] **nm 1.** [respiration] breathing ▸ **jusqu'à mon dernier souffle** as long as I live and breathe, to my dying day / [expiration] puff, breath ▸ **un souffle d'air** *fig* a breath of air, a puff of wind **2.** *fig* [inspiration] inspiration **3.** [d'explosion] blast **4.** MÉD **: souffle au cœur** heart murmur
▸▸ **avoir le souffle coupé** to have one's breath taken away ▸ **couper le souffle à qqn** to take sb's breath away ▸ **être à bout de souffle** [haletant] to be out of breath ▸ **reprendre son souffle** to get one's breath *ou* wind back ▸ **retenir son souffle** to hold one's breath.

soufflé, e [sufle] **adj 1.** CULIN soufflé *(avant n)* **2.** *fam fig* [étonné] flabbergasted.
◆ ***soufflé*** **nm** soufflé ▸ **soufflé au fromage** cheese soufflé.

souffler [3] [sufle] ■ **vt 1.** [bougie] to blow out **2.** [verre] to blow **3.** [vitre] to blow out, to shatter **4.** [chuchoter] **: souffler qqch à qqn** to whisper sthg to sb ▸ **on ne souffle pas!** no whispering!, don't whisper (the answer)! **5.** *fam* [prendre] **: souffler qqch à qqn** to pinch sthg from sb *UK* ▸ **je me suis fait souffler ma place** someone's pinched my seat **6.** *fam* [époustoufler - suj: événement, personne] to take aback, to stagger, to knock out *(sep)* ▸ **son insolence m'a vraiment soufflé!** I was quite staggered at her rudeness!
■ **vi 1.** [gén] to blow ▸ **ils m'ont fait souffler dans le ballon** they gave me a breath test ▸ **quand le vent souffle de l'ouest** when the wind blows *ou* comes from the west **2.** [respirer] to puff, to pant ▸ **souffler comme un bœuf** *fam* to wheeze like a pair of old bagpipes **3.** [se reposer] to have a break ▸ **au bureau, on n'a pas le temps de souffler!** it's all go at the office!

soufflerie [sufləri] **nf 1.** [d'orgue] bellows *sg* **2.** AÉRON wind tunnel.

soufflet [suflɛ] **nm 1.** [instrument] bellows *sg* **2.** [de train] connecting corridor, concertina vestibule **3.** COUT gusset **4.** *littéraire* [claque] slap.

souffleur, euse [suflœr, øz] **nm, f** THÉÂTRE prompt.
◆ ***souffleur*** **nm** [de verre] blower.
◆ ***souffleuse*** **nf : souffleuse (à neige)** snowblower.

souffrance [sufrɑ̃s] **nf** suffering.
◆ ***en souffrance*** **loc adv : être *ou* rester en souffrance** to be held up ▸ **dossiers en souffrance** files pending.

souffrant, e [sufrɑ̃, ɑ̃t] **adj** poorly.

souffre-douleur [sufrədulœr] **nm inv** whipping boy.

souffreteux, euse [sufrətø, øz] **adj** sickly.

souffrir [34] [sufrir] ■ **vi** to suffer ▸ **souffrir de** to suffer from ▸ **souffrir de la chaleur** [être très sensible à] to suffer in the heat / [être atteint par] to suffer from the heat ▸ **souffrir du dos/cœur** to have back/heart problems ▸ **c'est le sud du pays qui a le plus souffert** the southern part of the country was the worst hit ▸ **c'est une intervention bénigne, vous ne souffrirez pas** it's a very minor operation, you won't feel any pain ▸ **faire souffrir** [faire mal] to cause pain to, to hurt ▸ **les récoltes n'ont pas trop souffert** the crops didn't suffer too much *ou* weren't too badly damaged ▸ **c'est le sud du pays qui a le plus souffert** the southern part of the country was the worst hit.

■ **vt 1.** [ressentir] to suffer ▸ **souffrir le martyre** to go through *ou* to suffer agonies **2.** *littéraire* [supporter] to stand, to bear ▸ **elle ne souffre pas d'être critiquée** she can't stand *ou* take criticism ▸ **son dossier ne peut souffrir aucun délai** his case simply cannot be postponed.

◆ ***se souffrir*** **vp** *(emploi réciproque) littéraire* **: ils ne peuvent pas se souffrir** they can't stand *ou* bear each other.

soufi [sufi] **adj inv** Sufic.

◆ ***Soufi*** **nm** Sufi.

soufisme [sufism] **nm** Sufism.

soufre [sufr] **nm** sulphur *UK*, sulfur *US* ▸ **sentir le soufre** *fig* to smack of heresy.

souhait [swɛ] **nm** wish ▸ **tous nos souhaits de** our best wishes for ▸ **à souhait** to perfection ▸ **à tes/vos souhaits!** bless you!

souhaitable [swɛtabl] **adj** desirable ▸ **il est souhaitable que** *(+ subjonctif)* it is desirable that...

souhaiter [4] [swete] **vt : souhaiter qqch** to wish for sthg ▸ **souhaiter faire qqch** to hope to do sthg ▸ **souhaiter qqch à qqn** to wish sb sthg ▸ **souhaiter à qqn de faire qqch** to hope that sb does sthg ▸ **souhaiter que...** *(+ subjonctif)* to hope that...

souiller [3] [suje] **vt** *littéraire* [salir] to soil / *fig* & *sout* to sully.

souillon [sujɔ̃] **nf** *péj* slut.

souillure [sujyr] **nf** *littéraire* **1.** *(gén pl)* [déchet] waste *(U)* **2.** *fig* [morale] stain.

souk [suk] **nm** souk / *fam fig* chaos.

soul [sul] **nf & adj inv** MUS soul.

soûl, e, saoul, e [su, sul] **adj** drunk ▸ **être soûl de** *fig* to be drunk on.

◆ ***soûl*** **nm : tout mon/son soûl** *fig* to my/his/her heart's content.

soulagement [sulaʒmɑ̃] **nm** relief.

soulager [17] [sulaʒe] **vt 1.** [gén] to relieve **2.** [véhicule] to lighten.

◆ ***se soulager*** **vp 1.** [se libérer] to find relief **2.** [satisfaire un besoin naturel] to relieve o.s.

soûler, saouler [3] [sule] **vt 1.** *fam* [enivrer] **: soûler qqn** to get sb drunk / *fig* to intoxicate sb **2.** *fig* & *péj* [de plaintes] **: soûler qqn** to bore sb silly.

◆ ***se soûler*** **vp** *fam* to get drunk.

soûlerie [sulri] **nf** drinking spree.

soulèvement [sulɛvmɑ̃] **nm** uprising.

soulever [19] [sulve] **vt 1.** [fardeau, poids] to lift / [rideau] to raise **2.** *fig* [question] to raise, to bring up **3.** *fig* [enthousiasme] to generate, to arouse / [tollé] to stir up ▸ **soulever qqn contre** to stir sb up against **4.** [foule] to stir.

◆ ***se soulever*** **vp 1.** [s'élever] to raise o.s., to lift o.s. **2.** [se révolter] to rise up.

soulier [sulje] **nm** shoe ▸ **être dans ses petits souliers** *fig* to feel awkward.

souligner [3] [suliɲe] **vt 1.** [par un trait] to underline **2.** *fig* [insister sur] to underline, to emphasize **3.** [mettre en valeur] to emphasize.

soumets ➤ *soumettre*.

soumettre [84] [sumɛtr] **vt 1.** [astreindre] **: soumettre qqn à** to subject sb to **2.** [ennemi, peuple] to subjugate **3.** [projet, problème] **: soumettre qqch (à)** to submit sthg (to).

◆ ***se soumettre*** **vp : se soumettre (à)** to submit (to) / [loi, obligation] to abide by.

soumis, e [sumi, iz] ■ **pp** ➤ ***soumettre***.

■ **adj 1.** [gén] submissive **2.** [impôt] liable, subject to ▸ **soumis à l'impôt** liable to tax.

soumission [sumisjɔ̃] **nf** submission.

soupape [supap] **nf** valve ▸ **soupape de sûreté** safety valve.

soupçon [supsɔ̃] **nm 1.** [suspicion, intuition] suspicion ▸ **être au-dessus/à l'abri de tout soupçon** to be above/free from all suspicion **2.** *fig* [quantité] **: un soupçon de** a hint of.

soupçonner [3] [supsɔne] **vt** [suspecter] to suspect ▸ **soupçonner qqn de qqch/de faire qqch** to suspect sb of sthg/of doing sthg ▸ **soupçonner que** *(+ subjonctif)* to suspect that.

soupçonneux, euse [supsɔnø, øz] **adj** suspicious.

soupe [sup] **nf 1.** CULIN soup ▸ **soupe à l'oignon** onion soup ▸ **soupe populaire** soup kitchen ▸ **être soupe au lait** *fig* to have a quick temper ▸ **cracher dans la soupe** *fig* to bite the hand that feeds **2.** *fam fig* [neige] slush.

soupente [supɑ̃t] **nf** cupboard under the stairs.

souper [3] [supe] ■ **nm** supper.

■ **vi** to have supper ▸ **en avoir soupé de qqch/de faire qqch** *fam fig* to be sick and tired of sthg/of doing sthg.

soupeser [19] [supəze] **vt 1.** [poids] to feel the weight of **2.** *fig* [évaluer] to weigh up.

soupière [supjɛr] **nf** tureen.

soupir [supir] **nm 1.** [souffle] sigh ▸ **pousser un soupir** to let out *ou* give a sigh ▸ **pousser des soupirs** to sigh ▸ **rendre le dernier soupir** to breathe one's last **2.** MUS crotchet rest *UK*, quarter-note rest *US*.

COMMENT EXPRIMER...

les souhaits

I wish it would stop raining / Si seulement il pouvait s'arrêter de pleuvoir !

I wish you could have seen her face! / J'aurais voulu que tu voies sa tête !

I'd love you to meet them / J'aimerais tellement que vous fassiez leur connaissance

I hope we meet again / J'espère que nous nous reverrons

I just hope she says yes! / Pourvu qu'elle dise oui !

It would be great if we could all go / Ça serait vraiment bien si on pouvait tous y aller

I'd give anything to be there! / Je donnerais n'importe quoi pour être là-bas !

soupirail, aux [supiraj, o] **nm** barred basement window *(for ventilation purposes)*.

soupirant [supirɑ̃] **nm** suitor.

soupirer [3] [supire] ■ **vt** to sigh.
■ **vi 1.** [souffler] to sigh **2.** *fig & littéraire* [rechercher] **: soupirer après qqch** to sigh for sthg, to yearn after sthg.

souple [supl] **adj 1.** [gymnaste] supple **2.** [pas] lithe **3.** [paquet, col] soft **4.** [tissu, cheveux] flowing **5.** [tuyau, horaire, caractère] flexible.

souplesse [suplɛs] **nf 1.** [de gymnaste] suppleness **2.** [flexibilité - de tuyau] pliability, flexibility / [- de matière] suppleness **3.** [de personne] flexibility.

sourate = *surate*.

source [surs] **nf 1.** [gén] source ▸ **tenir de bonne source** *ou* **de source sûre** to have sthg on good authority *ou* from a reliable source ▸ **puiser à la source** *fig* to go to the source ▸ **imposer à la source** to tax at the source ▸ **retenir les impôts à la source** to deduct tax at source, to operate a pay-as-you-earn system *UK* ▸ **ça coule de source** *fig* it's obvious
2. [d'eau] spring ▸ **source chaude** hot spring ▸ **prendre sa source à** to rise in ▸ **remonter jusqu'à la source** [d'un fleuve] to go upriver until one finds the source / [d'une habitude, d'un problème] to go back to the root
3. [cause] source ▸ **cette formulation peut être source de malentendus** the way it's worded could give rise to misinterpretations ▸ **une source de revenus** a source of income
4. ÉLECTR **: source de courant** power supply.

sourcier, ère [sursje, ɛr] **nm, f** water diviner.

sourcil [sursi] **nm** eyebrow ▸ **froncer les sourcils** to frown.

sourcilière [sursiljɛr] ➤ *arcade*.

sourciller [3] [sursije] **vi : sans sourciller** without batting an eyelid.

sourcilleux, euse [sursijø, øz] **adj** fussy, finicky.

sourd[1], e [sur, surd] ■ **adj 1.** [personne] deaf ▸ **être/rester sourd à qqch** *fig* to be/to remain deaf to sthg **2.** [bruit, voix] muffled **3.** [douleur] dull **4.** [lutte, hostilité] silent.
■ **nm, f** deaf person.

sourd[2], sourdait *etc* ➤ *sourdre*.

sourdement [surdəmɑ̃] **adv 1.** [avec un bruit sourd] dully **2.** *fig* [secrètement] silently.

sourdine [surdin] **nf** mute ▸ **en sourdine** [sans bruit] softly / [secrètement] in secret ▸ **mettre une sourdine à qqch** to tone sthg down.

sourd-muet, sourde-muette [surmɥɛ, surdmɥɛt] (mpl **sourds-muets**, fpl **sourdes-muettes**) ■ **adj** deaf-mute, deaf-and-dumb.
■ **nm, f** deaf-mute, deaf-and-dumb person.

sourdre [73] [surdr] **vi** to well up.

souriant, e [surjɑ̃, ɑ̃t] **adj** smiling, cheerful.

souriceau [suriso] **nm** baby mouse.

souricière [surisjɛr] **nf** mousetrap / *fig* trap.

sourire [95] [surir] ■ **vi** to smile ▸ **sourire à qqn** to smile at sb / *fig* [campagne] to appeal to sb / [destin, chance] to smile on sb ▸ **sourire de qqn/qqch** [être amusé par] to smile at sb/sthg.
■ **nm** smile ▸ **garder le sourire** to keep smiling.

souris [suri] **nf 1.** INFORM & ZOOL mouse ▸ **souris infrarouge** infrared mouse **2.** [viande] knuckle **3.** *fam fig* [fille] bird *UK*, chick *US*.

sournois, e [surnwa, az] ■ **adj 1.** [personne] underhand **2.** *fig* [maladie, phénomène] unpredictable.
■ **nm, f** underhanded person.

sournoisement [surnwazmɑ̃] **adv** in an underhand way.

sous [su] **prép 1.** [gén] under ▸ **ça s'est passé sous nos yeux** it took place before our very eyes ▸ **être sous la douche** to be in the *ou* having a shower ▸ **emballé sous vide** vacuum-packed ▸ **nager sous l'eau** to swim underwater ▸ **parfait sous tous rapports** perfect in every respect ▸ **sous son air calme...** beneath his calm appearance... ▸ **sous le coup de l'émotion** in the grip of the emotion ▸ **sous ses ordres** under his command ▸ **sous la pluie** in the rain ▸ **sous cet aspect** *ou* **angle** from that point of view **2.** [dans un délai de] within ▸ **sous huit jours** within a week.

sous-alimentation [suzalimɑ̃tasjɔ̃] **nf** malnutrition, undernourishment.

sous-alimenté, e [suzalimɑ̃te] **adj** malnourished, underfed.

sous-bois [subwa] **nm inv** undergrowth.

sous-chef [suʃɛf] (pl **sous-chefs**) **nm** second-in-command.

souscripteur, trice [suskriptœr, tris] **nm, f** subscriber.

souscription [suskripsjɔ̃] **nf** subscription ▸ **lancer** *ou* **ouvrir une souscription** to start a fund ▸ **uniquement en souscription** available to subscribers only.

souscrire [99] [suskrir] ■ **vt** [gén] to sign.
■ **vi** FIN to apply for ▸ **souscrire à** to subscribe to.

sous-cutané, e [sukytane] **adj** MÉD subcutaneous.

sous-développé, e [sudevlɔpe] **adj** ÉCON underdeveloped / *fig & péj* backward.

sous-directeur, trice [sudirɛktœr, tris] (mpl **sous-directeurs**, fpl **sous-directrices**) **nm, f** assistant manager (f assistant manageress).

sous-employé, e [suzɑ̃plwaje] **adj** underemployed.

sous-ensemble [suzɑ̃sɑ̃bl] (pl **sous-ensembles**) **nm** subset.

sous-entendre [73] [suzɑ̃tɑ̃dr] **vt** to imply.

sous-entendu [suzɑ̃tɑ̃dy] (pl **sous-entendus**) **nm** insinuation.

sous-équipé, e [suzekipe] **adj** underequipped.

sous-estimer [3] [suzɛstime] **vt** to underestimate, to underrate.
◆ ***se sous-estimer*** **vp** to underrate o.s.

sous-évaluer [7] [suzevalɥe] **vt** to underestimate.

sous-exploiter [3] [suzɛksplwate] **vt** to underexploit.

sous-exposer [3] [suzɛkspoze] **vt** to underexpose.

sous-fifre [sufifr] (pl **sous-fifres**) **nm** *fam* underling.

sous-jacent**, **e [suʒasɑ̃, ɑ̃t] **adj** underlying.

Sous-le-Vent [suləvɑ̃] **npr : les îles Sous-le-Vent** [en Polynésie] the Leeward Islands, the Western Society Islands / [aux Antilles] the Netherlands (and Venezuelan) Antilles ; voir aussi ***île***.

sous-lieutenant [suljøtnɑ̃] (pl **sous-lieutenants**) **nm** MIL sub-lieutenant.

sous-location [sulɔkasjɔ̃] (pl **sous-locations**) **nf** subletting.

sous-louer [6] [sulwe] **vt** to sublet.

sous-main [sumɛ̃] **nm inv** desk blotter.

sous-marin**, **e [sumarɛ̃, in] **adj** underwater *(avant n)*.
◆ ***sous-marin*** (pl **sous-marins**) **nm** submarine.

sous-marque [sumark] **nf** sub-brand.

sous marque double [sumaʀkdubl] **adj : sous marque double** dual-branded.

sous-œuvre [suzœvr] ◆ ***en sous-œuvre*** **loc adv : reprise en sous-œuvre** underpinning.

sous-officier [suzɔfisje] (pl **sous-officiers**) **nm** non-commissioned officer.

sous-ordre [suzɔrdr] (pl **sous-ordres**) **nm 1.** [personne] subordinate **2.** [espèce] suborder.

sous-payer [11] [supeje] **vt** to underpay.

sous-peuplé**, **e [supœple] **adj** underpopulated.

sous-préfecture [suprefɛktyr] (pl **sous-préfectures**) **nf** sub-prefecture.

sous-préfet [suprefɛ] (pl **sous-préfets**) **nm** sub-prefect.

sous-produit [suprɔdɥi] (pl **sous-produits**) **nm 1.** [objet] by-product **2.** *fig* [imitation] pale imitation.

sous-pull**, **s [supyl] **nm** *lightweight polo-neck sweater*.

sous-répertoire [surepɛrtwar] (pl **sous-répertoires**) **nm** INFORM sub-directory.

sous-secrétaire [susəkretɛr] (pl **sous-secrétaires**) **nm : sous-secrétaire d'État** Under-Secretary of State.

soussigné**, **e [susiɲe] ■ **adj : je soussigné** I the undersigned ▸ **nous soussignés** we the undersigned.
■ **nm, f** undersigned.

sous-sol [susɔl] (pl **sous-sols**) **nm 1.** [de bâtiment] basement **2.** [naturel] subsoil.

sous-tasse [sutas] (pl **sous-tasses**) **nf** saucer.

sous-tendre [73] [sutɑ̃dr] **vt** to underpin.

sous-titre [sutitr] (pl **sous-titres**) **nm** subtitle.

sous-titré**, **e**, **s [sutitre] **adj** subtitled, with subtitles.

sous-titrer [3] [sutitre] **vt** to subtitle.

soustraction [sustraksjɔ̃] **nf** MATH subtraction.

soustraire [112] [sustrɛr] **vt 1.** [retrancher] **: soustraire qqch de** to subtract sthg from **2.** *sout* [voler] **: soustraire qqch de qqch** to remove sthg from sthg ▸ **soustraire qqch à qqn** to take sthg away from sb **3.** [faire échapper] **: soustraire qqn à qqch** to shield sb from sthg.
◆ ***se soustraire*** **vp : se soustraire à** to escape from.

sous-traitance [sutrɛtɑ̃s] (pl **sous-traitances**) **nf** subcontracting ▸ **donner qqch en sous-traitance** to subcontract sthg.

sous-traitant**, **e [sutrɛtɑ̃, ɑ̃t] **adj** subcontracting.
◆ ***sous-traitant*** (pl **sous-traitants**) **nm** subcontractor.

sous-traiter [4] [sutrete] **vt** to subcontract.

soustrayais**, **soustrayions ➤ ***soustraire***.

sous-verre [suvɛr] **nm inv** *picture or document framed between a sheet of glass and a rigid backing*.

sous-vêtement [suvɛtmɑ̃] (pl **sous-vêtements**) **nm** undergarment ▸ **sous-vêtements** underwear *(U)*, underclothes.

soutane [sutan] **nf** cassock.

soute [sut] **nf** hold.

soutenable [sutnabl] **adj 1.** [défendable] tenable **2.** [supportable] bearable.

soutenance [sutnɑ̃s] **nf** viva *UK*.

soutènement [sutɛnmɑ̃] **nm 1.** CONSTR support **2.** [de mines] timbering.
◆ ***de soutènement*** **loc adj** support *(modif)*, supporting.

souteneur [sutnœr] **nm** procurer.

soutenir [40] [sutnir] **vt 1.** [immeuble, personne] to support, to hold up **2.** [effort, intérêt] to sustain **3.** [encourager] to support / POLIT to back, to support **4.** [affirmer] **: soutenir que** to maintain (that) **5.** [résister à] to withstand / [regard, comparaison] to bear.
◆ ***se soutenir*** **vp 1.** [se maintenir] to hold o.s. up, to support o.s. **2.** [s'aider] to support each other, to back each other (up).

soutenu**, **e [sutny] **adj 1.** [style, langage] elevated **2.** [attention, rythme] sustained **3.** [couleur] vivid.

souterrain**, **e [sutɛrɛ̃, ɛn] **adj** underground.
◆ ***souterrain*** **nm** underground passage.

soutien [sutjɛ̃] **nm** support ▸ **apporter son soutien à** to give one's support to ▸ **soutien de famille** breadwinner.

soutien-gorge [sutjɛ̃gɔrʒ] (pl **soutiens-gorge**) **nm** bra.

soutirer [3] [sutire] **vt 1.** [liquide] to decant **2.** *fig* [tirer] **: soutirer qqch à qqn** to extract sthg from sb.

souvenance [suvnɑ̃s] **nf** *littéraire* recollection.

souvenir [40] [suvnir] **nm 1.** [réminiscence, mémoire] memory ▸ **en souvenir de** in memory of ▸ **rappeler qqn au bon souvenir de qqn** to remember sb to sb ▸ **avec mes meilleurs souvenirs** with kind regards **2.** [objet] souvenir.
◆ ***se souvenir*** **vp** [ne pas oublier] **: se souvenir de qqch/de qqn** to remember sthg/sb ▸ **se souvenir que** to remember (that).

souvent [suvɑ̃] **adv** often ▸ **le plus souvent** more often than not.

souvenu**, **e [suvny] **pp** ➤ ***souvenir***.

souverain**, **e [suvrɛ̃, ɛn] ■ **adj 1.** [remède, état] sovereign **2.** [indifférence] supreme.
■ **nm, f** [monarque] sovereign, monarch.

souverainement [suvrɛnmɑ̃] **adv 1.** [extrêmement] intensely **2.** [avec autorité] regally **3.** [absolument - bon] supremely / [- parfait] absolutely.

souveraineté [suvrɛnte] **nf** sovereignty.

souviendrai**, **souviendras ➤ ***souvenir***.

souvienne**, **souviennes ➤ ***souvenir***.

souviens, souvient ➤ ***souvenir.***

soviet [sɔvjɛt] **nm** soviet ▸ **Soviet suprême** Supreme Soviet.

soviétique [sɔvjetik] **adj** Soviet.
◆ ***Soviétique*** **nmf** Soviet (citizen).

soviétologue [sɔvjetɔlɔg] **nmf** Kremlinologist.

soyeux, euse [swajø, øz] **adj** silky.

soyez ➤ ***être.***

SPA (abr de ***Société protectrice des animaux***) **nf** *French society for the protection of animals,* ≃ RSPCA *UK,* ≃ SPCA *US.*

spacieux, euse [spasjø, øz] **adj** spacious.

spaghettis [spagɛti] **nmpl** spaghetti *(U).*

sparadrap [sparadra] **nm** sticking plaster *UK*, Band-Aid®.

spartiate [sparsjat] **adj** [austère] Spartan ▸ **à la spartiate** *fig* in a Spartan fashion.
◆ ***spartiates*** **nfpl** [sandales] Roman sandals.
◆ ***Spartiate*** **nmf** Spartan.

spasme [spasm] **nm** spasm.

spasmodique [spasmɔdik] **adj** spasmodic.

spasmophilie [spasmɔfili] **nf** spasmophilia.

spatial, e, aux [spasjal, o] **adj** space *(avant n).*

spatio-temporel, elle [spasjɔtɑ̃pɔrɛl] **adj** spatio-temporal.

spatule [spatyl] **nf** **1.** [ustensile] spatula **2.** [de ski] tip.

spätzli [ʃpetsli] **nmpl** *Suisse* small dumplings.

speaker, speakerine [spikœr, spikrin] **nm, f** announcer.

spécial, e, aux [spesjal, o] **adj** **1.** [particulier] special ▸ **spécial à** special to **2.** *fam* [bizarre] peculiar.

spécialement [spesjalmɑ̃] **adv** **1.** [exprès] specially **2.** [particulièrement] particularly, especially ▸ **pas spécialement** *fam* not particularly, not specially.

spécialisation [spesjalizasjɔ̃] **nf** specialization.

spécialisé, e [spesjalize] **adj** [généralement] specialized / INFORM dedicated, special-purpose ▸ **des chercheurs spécialisés dans l'intelligence artificielle** researchers specializing in artificial intelligence.

spécialiser [3] [spesjalize] **vt** to specialize.
◆ ***se spécialiser*** **vp : se spécialiser (dans)** to specialize (in).

spécialiste [spesjalist] **nmf** specialist ▸ **spécialiste de la prise de risques** ÉCON venture capitalist.

spécialité [spesjalite] **nf** speciality *UK*, specialty *US*.

spécieux, euse [spesjø, øz] **adj** *littéraire* specious.

spécification [spesifikasjɔ̃] **nf** specification.

spécificité [spesifisite] **nf** specificity.

spécifier [9] [spesifje] **vt** to specify.

spécifique [spesifik] **adj** specific.

spécifiquement [spesifikmɑ̃] **adv** specifically.

spécimen [spesimɛn] **nm** **1.** [représentant] specimen **2.** [exemplaire] sample.

spectacle [spɛktakl] **nm** **1.** [représentation] show **2.** [domaine] show business, entertainment **3.** [tableau] spectacle, sight ▸ **se donner en spectacle** *fig* to make a spectacle *ou* an exhibition of o.s.

spectaculaire [spɛktakylɛr] **adj** spectacular.

spectateur, trice [spɛktatœr, tris] **nm, f** **1.** [témoin] witness **2.** [de spectacle] spectator.

spectre [spɛktr] **nm** **1.** [fantôme] spectre *UK*, specter *US* ▸ **le spectre de** *fig* the spectre *UK ou* specter *US* of **2.** PHYS spectrum.

spéculateur, trice [spekylatœr, tris] **nm, f** speculator ▸ **spéculateur à la baisse** bear ▸ **spéculateur à la hausse** bull ▸ **spéculateur sur devises** currency speculator.

spéculatif, ive [spekylatif, iv] **adj** speculative.

spéculation [spekylasjɔ̃] **nf** speculation ▸ **spéculation à la baisse/hausse** bear/bull trading ▸ **spéculation à la journée** day trading.

spéculer [3] [spekyle] **vi : spéculer sur** FIN to speculate in / *fig* [miser] to count on ▸ **spéculer en Bourse** to speculate on the stock exchange ▸ **spéculer sur l'or** to speculate in gold.

speculo(o)s [spekylos] **nm** *Belgique crunchy sweet biscuit flavoured with cinnamon.*

speech [spitʃ] (pl **speeches**) **nm** speech.

speed [spid] **adj** *fam* hyper ▸ **il est très speed** he's really hyper.

speedé, e [spide] **adj** *fam* hyper.

speeder [spide] **vi** *fam* to hurry.

spéléologie [speleɔlɔʒi] **nf** [exploration] potholing *UK*, spelunking *US* / [science] speleology.

spéléologue [speleɔlɔg] **nmf** [explorateur] potholer *UK*, spelunker *US* / [scientifique] speleologist.

spencer [spɛnsɛr] **nm** *short fitted jacket or coat.*

spermatozoïde [spɛrmatɔzɔid] **nm** sperm, spermatozoon.

sperme [spɛrm] **nm** sperm, semen.

spermicide [spɛrmisid] ■ **adj** spermicidal.
■ **nm** spermicide, spermatocide.

sphère [sfɛr] **nf** sphere ▸ **les hautes sphères de** the higher reaches of ▸ **sphère d'influence** sphere of influence.

sphérique [sferik] **adj** spherical.

sphincter [sfɛ̃ktɛr] **nm** sphincter.

sphinx [sfɛ̃ks] **nm inv** **1.** *fig* & MYTHOL sphinx **2.** ZOOL hawk moth.

spirale [spiral] **nf** spiral ▸ **en spirale** spiral.

spiritisme [spiritism] **nm** spiritualism.

spiritualité [spiritɥalite] **nf** spirituality.

spirituel, elle [spiritɥɛl] **adj** **1.** [de l'âme, moral] spiritual **2.** [vivant, drôle] witty.

spirituellement [spiritɥɛlmɑ̃] **adv** **1.** [moralement] spiritually **2.** [avec humour] wittily.

spiritueux [spiritɥø] **nm** spirit.

spleen [splin] **nm** *littéraire* spleen.

splendeur [splɑ̃dœr] **nf 1.** [beauté, prospérité] splendour *UK*, splendor *US* **2.** [merveille] **: c'est une splendeur!** it's magnificent!

splendide [splɑ̃did] **adj** magnificent, splendid.

spolier [9] [spɔlje] **vt** to despoil.

spongieux, euse [spɔ̃ʒjø, øz] **adj** spongy.

sponsor [spɔ̃sɔr] **nm** sponsor.

sponsoring [spɔ̃sɔriŋ] **nm** sponsoring, corporate sponsorship.

sponsorisation [spɔ̃sɔrizasjɔ̃] **nf** sponsoring, sponsorship.

sponsoriser [3] [spɔ̃sɔrize] **vt** to sponsor.

spontané, e [spɔ̃tane] **adj** spontaneous.

spontanéité [spɔ̃taneite] **nf** spontaneity.

spontanément [spɔ̃tanemɑ̃] **adv** spontaneously.

sporadique [spɔradik] **adj** sporadic.

sporadiquement [spɔradikmɑ̃] **adv** sporadically.

sport [spɔr] ■ **nm** sport ▸ **de sport** sports *(avant n)* ▸ **sport d'équipe/de combat** team/combat sport ▸ **sports d'hiver** winter sports ▸ **aller aux sports d'hiver** to go on a skiing holiday.
■ **adj inv 1.** [vêtement] sports *(avant n)* **2.** [fair play] sporting.

sportif, ive [spɔrtif, iv] ■ **adj 1.** [association, résultats] sports *(avant n)* **2.** [personne, physique] sporty, athletic **3.** [fair play] sportsmanlike, sporting.
■ **nm, f** sportsman (f sportswoman).

spot [spɔt] **nm 1.** [lampe] spot, spotlight **2.** [publicité] **: spot (publicitaire)** commercial, advert *UK*, spot advertisement.

SPOT, Spot [spɔt] (abr de ***satellite pour l'observation de la terre***) **nm** earth observation satellite.

sprint [sprint] **nm** [SPORT - accélération] spurt / [- course] sprint ▸ **piquer un sprint** *fam* to put on a spurt.

sprinter[1] [3] [sprinte] **vi** to sprint.

sprinter[2] [sprintœr] **nm** sprinter.

squale [skwal] **nm** dogfish.

square [skwar] **nm** small public garden.

squash [skwaʃ] **nm** squash.

squat [skwat] **nm** squat.

squatter[1] [skwatœr] **nm** squatter.

squatter[2] [3] [skwate] ■ **vt** to squat in.
■ **vi** to squat.

squelette [skəlɛt] **nm** skeleton.

squelettique [skəletik] **adj 1.** [corps] emaciated **2.** [exposé] sketchy, skeletal.

Sri Lanka [ʃrilɑ̃nka] **nm : le Sri Lanka** Sri Lanka ▸ **au Sri Lanka** in Sri Lanka.

sri lankais, e [ʃrilɑ̃kɛ, ɛz] **adj** Sri Lankan.
◆ ***Sri Lankais, e*** **nm, f** Sri Lankan.

SS ■ **nf 1.** (abr de ***Sécurité sociale***) ≃ DSS *UK*, ≃ SSA *US* **2.** (abr de ***SchutzStaffel***) SS ▸ **un SS** a member of the SS.
■ (abr de ***steamship***) SS.

S.S. (abr écrite de ***Sa Sainteté***) H.H.

S/S (abr écrite de ***steamship***) S/S.

SSR (abr de ***Société suisse romande***) **nf** *French-language Swiss broadcasting company.*

St (abr écrite de ***saint***) St.

stabilisateur, trice [stabilizatœr, tris] **adj** stabilizing.

stabilisation [stabilizasjɔ̃] **nf** stabilization.

stabiliser [3] [stabilize] **vt 1.** [gén] to stabilize / [meuble] to steady **2.** [terrain] to make firm.
◆ ***se stabiliser*** **vp 1.** [véhicule, prix, situation] to stabilize **2.** [personne] to settle down.

stabilité [stabilite] **nf** stability.

stable [stabl] **adj 1.** [gén] stable **2.** [meuble] steady, stable.

stade [stad] **nm 1.** [terrain] stadium **2.** [étape & MÉD] stage ▸ **en être au stade de/où** to reach the stage of/at which.

Stade de France [staddəfrɑ̃s] **nm** Stade de France *(stadium built for the 1998 World Cup in the north of Paris).*

staff [staf] **nm** staff.

stage [staʒ] **nm** SCOL work placement *UK*, internship *US* / [sur le temps de travail] in-service training ▸ **faire un stage** [cours] to go on a training course / [expérience professionnelle] to go on a work placement *UK*, to undergo an internship *US*.

FAUX AMIS / FALSE FRIENDS
stage

Stage is not a translation of the French word *stage*. Stage is translated by *phase*.
▸ The project is at an early stage / *Le projet en est aux premières phases*

stagiaire [staʒjɛr] ■ **nmf** trainee, intern *US*.
■ **adj** trainee *(avant n)*.

stagnant, e [stagnɑ̃, ɑ̃t] **adj** stagnant.

stagnation [stagnasjɔ̃] **nf** stagnation.

stagner [3] [stagne] **vi** to stagnate.

stakhanoviste [stakanɔvist] **nmf & adj** Stakhanovite, hard worker.

stalactite [stalaktit] **nf** stalactite.

stalagmite [stalagmit] **nf** stalagmite.

stalle [stal] **nf** stall.

stand [stɑ̃d] **nm 1.** [d'exposition] stand **2.** [de fête] stall ▸ **stand de tir** shooting range, firing range.

standard [stɑ̃dar] ■ **adj inv** standard.
■ **nm 1.** [norme] standard **2.** [téléphonique] switchboard.

standardisation [stɑ̃dardizasjɔ̃] **nf** standardization.

standardiser [3] [stɑ̃dardize] **vt** to standardize.

standardiste [stɑ̃dardist] **nmf** switchboard operator.

standing [stɑ̃diŋ] **nm** standing ▸ **immeuble de grand standing** prestigious block of flats *UK*, luxury apartment building *US* ▸ **quartier de grand standing** select district.

staphylocoque [stafilɔkɔk] **nm** staphylococcus.

star [star] **nf** CINÉ star.

starlette [starlɛt] **nf** starlet.

starter [startɛr] **nm** AUTO choke ▸ **mettre le starter** to pull the choke out.

starting-block [startiŋblɔk] (pl **starting-blocks**) **nm** starting block.

start up [startɔp] **nf** start-up.

station [stasjɔ̃] **nf 1.** [arrêt - de bus] stop / [- de métro] station ▸ **à quelle station dois-je descendre?** which stop do I get off at? ▸ **station de taxis** taxi stand
2. [installations] station ▸ **station d'épuration** sewage treatment plant ▸ **station météorologique** weather station ▸ **station orbitale** orbital station ▸ **station spatiale** space station
3. [ville] resort ▸ **station balnéaire** seaside resort ▸ **station de ski/de sports d'hiver** ski/winter sports resort ▸ **station thermale** spa (town)
4. [position] position ▸ **station debout** standing position ▸ **station verticale** upright position
5. INFORM **: station de travail** work station.

stationnaire [stasjɔnɛr] **adj** stationary.

stationnement [stasjɔnmɑ̃] **nm** parking ▸ **'stationnement interdit'** 'no parking' ▸ **stationnement bilatéral** parking on both sides of the road ▸ **stationnement en double file** double-parking ▸ **stationnement en épi** angle *ou* angled parking ▸ **stationnement unilatéral** parking on one side (only) ▸ **stationnement payant** parking fee payable.

stationner [3] [stasjɔne] **vi** to park.

station-service [stasjɔ̃sɛrvis] (pl **stations-service**) **nf** service station, petrol station *UK*, gas station *US*.

statique [statik] **adj** static.

statisticien, enne [statistisjɛ̃, ɛn] **nm, f** statistician.

statistique [statistik] ■ **adj** statistical.
■ **nf 1.** [science] statistics *(U)* **2.** [donnée] statistic ▸ **statistiques démographiques** demographics.

statistiquement [statistikmɑ̃] **adv** statistically.

statuaire [statɥɛr] **nf & adj** statuary.

statue [staty] **nf** statue.

statuer [7] [statɥe] **vi : statuer sur** to give a decision on.

statuette [statɥɛt] **nf** statuette.

statu quo [statykwo] **nm inv** status quo.

stature [statyr] **nf** stature.

statut [staty] **nm** status.
◆ ***statuts*** **nmpl** statutes, by laws *US*.

statutaire [statytɛr] **adj** statutory.

Ste (abr écrite de ***sainte***) St.

Sté (abr écrite de ***société***) Co.

steak [stɛk] **nm** steak ▸ **steak frites** steak and chips *UK* *ou* fries *US* ▸ **steak haché** mince *UK*, ground beef *US* ▸ **steak tartare** steak tartare.

stèle [stɛl] **nf** stele.

stellaire [stelɛr] **adj** stellar.

stencil [stɛnsil] **nm** stencil.

sténo [steno] ■ **nmf** stenographer.
■ **nf** shorthand.

sténodactylo [stenɔdaktilo] **nmf** shorthand typist *UK*, stenographer *US*.

sténodactylographie [stenɔdaktilɔgrafi] **nf** shorthand typing.

sténographe [stenɔgraf] **nmf** stenographer.

sténographie [stenɔgrafi] **nf** shorthand ▸ **en sténographie** in shorthand.

sténographier [9] [stenɔgrafje] **vt** to take down in shorthand.

sténographique [stenɔgrafik] **adj** shorthand *(avant n)*.

sténotypiste [stenɔtipist] **nmf** stenotypist.

stentor [stɑ̃tɔr] ➤ ***voix***.

steppe [stɛp] **nf** steppe.

stéréo [stereo] ■ **adj inv** stereo.
■ **nf** stereo ▸ **en stéréo** in stereo.

stéréotype [stereɔtip] **nm** stereotype.

stéréotypé, e [stereɔtipe] **adj** stereotyped.

stérile [steril] **adj 1.** [personne] sterile, infertile / [terre] barren **2.** *fig* [inutile - discussion] sterile / [- efforts] futile **3.** MÉD sterile.

stérilet [sterilɛ] **nm** IUD, intrauterine device.

stérilisateur [sterilizatœr] **nm** sterilizer.

stérilisation [sterilizasjɔ̃] **nf** sterilization.

stériliser [3] [sterilize] **vt** to sterilize.

stérilité [sterilite] **nf** *litt & fig* sterility / [d'efforts] futility.

sterling [stɛrliŋ] **adj inv & nm inv** sterling.

sternum [stɛrnɔm] **nm** breastbone, sternum.

stéthoscope [stetɔskɔp] **nm** stethoscope.

steward [stiwart] **nm** steward.

stick [stik] **nm** [tube] stick ▸ **de la colle en stick** a stick of glue ▸ **un déodorant en stick** a stick deodorant.

stigmate [stigmat] **nm** *(gén pl)* mark, scar.
◆ ***stigmates*** **nmpl** RELIG stigmata.

stigmatiser [3] [stigmatize] **vt** *littéraire* [dénoncer] to denounce.

stimulant, e [stimylɑ̃, ɑ̃t] **adj** stimulating.
◆ ***stimulant*** **nm 1.** [remontant] stimulant **2.** [motivation] incentive, stimulus.

stimulateur [stimylatœr] **nm : stimulateur cardiaque** pacemaker.

stimulation [stimylasjɔ̃] **nf** stimulation.

stimuler [3] [stimyle] **vt** to stimulate.

stipuler [3] [stipyle] **vt : stipuler que** to stipulate (that).

STO (abr de ***service du travail obligatoire***) **nm** HIST forced labour *(by French workers requisitioned during the Second World War)*.

stock [stɔk] **nm** stock ▸ **en stock** in stock ▸ **stock existant en magasin** in stock ▸ **tout un stock de** *fig & iron* a whole stock of, plenty of.

stockage [stɔkaʒ] **nm 1.** [de marchandises] stocking **2.** INFORM storage.

stocker [3] [stɔke] **vt 1.** [marchandises] to stock **2.** INFORM to store.

Stockholm [stɔkɔlm] **npr** Stockholm.

stock-option [stɔkɔpsjɔ̃] **nf** stock option.

stoïcisme [stɔisism] **nm 1.** PHILO Stoicism **2.** *fig* [courage] stoicism.

stoïque [stɔik] ■ **nmf** Stoic.
■ **adj** stoical.

stoïquement [stɔikmɑ̃] **adv** stoically.

stomacal**, **e**, **aux [stɔmakal, o] **adj** stomach *(avant n).*

stomatologie [stɔmatɔlɔʒi] **nf** stomatology.

stomatologiste [stɔmatɔlɔʒist], ***stomatologue*** [stɔmatɔlɔg] **nmf** stomatologist.

stop [stɔp] ■ **interj** stop! ▸ **dis-moi stop!** say when!
■ **nm 1.** [feu] brake light **2.** [panneau] stop sign **3.** [autostop] hitchhiking, hitching ▸ **faire du stop** to hitch, to hitchhike ▸ **on y est allé en stop** we hitchhiked *ou* hitched there.

stopper [3] [stɔpe] ■ **vt 1.** [arrêter] to stop, to halt **2.** COUT to repair by invisible mending.
■ **vi** to stop.

store [stɔr] **nm 1.** [de fenêtre] blind **2.** [de magasin] awning.

STP abr écrite de ***s'il te plaît***.

strabisme [strabism] **nm** squint ▸ **être atteint de strabisme** to (have a) squint.

strangulation [strɑ̃gylasjɔ̃] **nf** strangulation.

strapontin [strapɔ̃tɛ̃] **nm 1.** [siège] pull-down seat **2.** *fig* [position] minor role.

stras [stras] = ***strass***.

strass [stras] **nm** paste.

stratagème [strataʒɛm] **nm** stratagem.

strate [strat] **nf** stratum.

stratège [stratɛʒ] **nm** strategist.

stratégie [strateʒi] **nf** strategy ▸ **stratégie globale** global strategy ▸ **stratégie marketing** marketing strategy ▸ **stratégie de positionnement** positioning strategy.

stratégique [strateʒik] **adj** strategic ▸ **matières premières stratégiques** strategic raw materials.

stratifié**, **e [stratifje] **adj 1.** GÉOL stratified **2.** TECHNOL laminated.

stratosphère [stratɔsfɛr] **nf** stratosphere.

stress [strɛs] **nm** stress.

stressant**, **e [strɛsɑ̃, ɑ̃t] **adj** stressful.

stressé**, **e [strɛse] **adj** stressed.

stresser [4] [strɛse] ■ **vt : stresser qqn** to cause sb stress, to put sb under stress.
■ **vi** to be stressed.

Stretch® [strɛtʃ] **nm inv** *stretch material.*

stretching [strɛtʃiŋ] **nm** SPORT stretching, stretching exercises *pl.*

strict**, **e [strikt] **adj 1.** [personne, règlement] strict **2.** [sobre] plain **3.** [absolu - minimum] bare, absolute / [- vérité] absolute ▸ **dans la plus stricte intimité** strictly in private ▸ **au sens strict du terme** in the strict sense of the word.

strictement [striktəmɑ̃] **adv 1.** [rigoureusement] strictly **2.** [sobrement] plainly, soberly.

strident**, **e [stridɑ̃, ɑ̃t] **adj** strident, shrill.

stridulation [stridylasjɔ̃] **nf** chirping.

strie [stri] *(gén pl)* **nf 1.** [sillon] groove / [en relief] ridge **2.** [rayure] streak.

strié**, **e [strije] **adj 1.** [rayé] striped **2.** GÉOL striated.

strier [10] [strije] **vt** to streak.

string [striŋ] **nm** G-string.

strip-tease [striptiz] (pl **strip-teases**) **nm** striptease.

strip-teaseuse [striptizøz] (pl **strip-teaseuses**) **nf** stripper.

striure [strijyr] **nf 1.** [sillons] grooves *pl* / [en relief] ridges *pl* **2.** [rayures] streaks *pl.*

strophe [strɔf] **nf** verse.

structural**, **e**, **aux [stryktyral, o] **adj** structural.

structuralisme [stryktyralism] **nm** structuralism.

structure [stryktyr] **nf** structure ▸ **structure *ou* structures d'accueil** reception facilities ▸ **structures administratives/politiques** administrative/political facilities.

structurel**, **elle [stryktyrɛl] **adj** structural.

structurer [3] [stryktyre] **vt** to structure.
◆ ***se structurer*** **vp** to be/become structured.

strychnine [striknin] **nf** strychnine.

stuc [styk] **nm** stucco.

studieusement [stydjøzmɑ̃] **adv** studiously.

studieux**, **euse [stydjø, øz] **adj 1.** [personne] studious **2.** [vacances] study *(avant n).*

studio [stydjo] **nm 1.** CINÉ, PHOTO & TV studio ▸ **studio d'enregistrement** recording studio **2.** [appartement] studio flat *UK*, studio apartment *US*.
◆ ***en studio*** **loc adv : tourné en studio** shot in studio ▸ **scène tournée en studio** studio scene.

stupéfaction [stypefaksjɔ̃] **nf** astonishment, stupefaction.

stupéfait**, **e [stypefɛ, ɛt] **adj** astounded, stupefied.

stupéfiant**, **e [stypefjɑ̃, ɑ̃t] **adj** astounding, stunning.
◆ ***stupéfiant*** **nm** narcotic, drug.

stupéfier [9] [stypefje] **vt** to astonish, to stupefy.

stupeur [stypœr] **nf 1.** [stupéfaction] astonishment **2.** MÉD stupor.

stupide [stypid] **adj 1.** *péj* [abruti] stupid **2.** [insensé - mort] senseless / [- accident] stupid **3.** *littéraire* [interdit] stunned.

stupidement [stypidmɑ̃] **adv** stupidly.

stupidité [stypidite] **nf** stupidity ▸ **faire/dire des stupidités** to do/say something stupid.

stups [styp] *tfam* **nmpl** *arg crime* **: les stups** the narcotics *ou* drugs squad.

style [stil] **nm** **1.** [gén] style ▸ **de style** period *(avant n)* ▸ **style Empire/Louis XIII** Empire/Louis XIII Style ▸ **style de vie** lifestyle **2.** GRAMM **: style direct/indirect** direct/indirect speech.

styliser [3] [stilize] **vt** to stylize.

stylisme [stilism] **nm** COUT design, designing.

styliste [stilist] **nmf** COUT designer.

stylistique [stilistik] ■ **adj** stylistic.
■ **nf** stylistics *(U)*.

stylo [stilo] **nm** pen ▸ **stylo bille** ballpoint (pen) ▸ **stylo plume** fountain pen.

stylo-feutre [stiloføtr] (pl **stylos-feutres**) **nm** felt-tip pen.

su, e [sy] **pp** ➤ ***savoir***.
◆ ***au vu et au su de*** **loc prép** under the eyes of.

suave [sɥav] **adj** [voix] smooth / [parfum] sweet.

suavité [sɥavite] **nf** pleasantness.

subalpin, e [sybalpɛ̃, in] **adj** subalpine.

subalterne [sybaltɛrn] ■ **nmf** subordinate, junior.
■ **adj** [rôle] subordinate / [employé] junior.

subaquatique [sybakwatik] **adj** underwater.

subconscient, e [sybkɔ̃sjɑ̃, ɑ̃t] **adj** subconscious.
◆ ***subconscient*** **nm** subconscious.

subdiviser [3] [sybdivize] **vt** to subdivide.
◆ ***se subdiviser*** **vp** to be subdivided.

subdivision [sybdivizjɔ̃] **nf** subdivision.

subir [32] [sybir] **vt** **1.** [conséquences, colère] to suffer / [personne] to put up with **2.** [opération, épreuve, examen] to undergo **3.** [dommages, pertes] to sustain, to suffer ▸ **subir une hausse** to be increased.

subit, e [sybi, it] **adj** sudden.

subitement [sybitmɑ̃] **adv** suddenly.

subjectif, ive [sybʒɛktif, iv] **adj** **1.** [personnel, partial] subjective **2.** MÉD **: troubles subjectifs** symptoms.

subjectivité [sybʒɛktivite] **nf** subjectivity.

subjonctif [sybʒɔ̃ktif] **nm** subjunctive.

subjuguer [3] [sybʒyge] **vt** to captivate.

sublimation [syblimasjɔ̃] **nf** sublimation.

sublime [syblim] **adj** sublime.

sublimer [3] [syblime] **vt** to sublimate.

submergé, e [sybmɛrʒe] **adj** **1.** [rochers] submerged / [champs] submerged, flooded **2.** [surchargé, accablé] inundated ▸ **submergé de travail** snowed under with work ▸ **submergé de réclamations** inundated with complaints **3.** [incapable de faire face] swamped, up to one's eyes ▸ **depuis que ma secrétaire est partie, je suis submergé** since my secretary left, I've been up to my eyes in work.

submerger [17] [sybmɛrʒe] **vt** **1.** [inonder] to flood **2.** [envahir] to overcome, to overwhelm **3.** [déborder] to overwhelm ▸ **être submergé de travail** to be swamped with work.

submersible [sybmɛrsibl] **nm & adj** submersible.

subodorer [3] [sybɔdɔre] **vt** *fam* to smell, to scent.

subordination [sybɔrdinasjɔ̃] **nf** subordination.

subordonné, e [sybɔrdɔne] ■ **adj** GRAMM subordinate, dependent.
■ **nm, f** subordinate.
◆ ***subordonnée*** **nf** GRAMM subordinate clause.

subordonner [3] [sybɔrdɔne] **vt** **1.** [chose] **: subordonner qqch à qqch** to make sthg dependent on sthg **2.** [personne] **: subordonner qqn à qqn** to subordinate sb to sb.

subornation [sybɔrnasjɔ̃] **nf** bribing, subornation.

suborner [3] [sybɔrne] **vt** **1.** *littéraire* [séduire] to lead astray **2.** DR to bribe, to suborn.

subreptice [sybrɛptis] **adj** surreptitious.

subrepticement [sybrɛptismɑ̃] **adv** surreptitiously.

subroger [17] [sybrɔʒe] **vt** DR to substitute.

subséquent, e [sypsekɑ̃, ɑ̃t] **adj** *sout* subsequent.

subside [sypsid] **nm** *(gén pl)* grant, subsidy.

subsidiaire [sybzidjɛr] **adj** subsidiary.

subsidiarité [sybzidjarite] **nf** subsidiarity.

subsistance [sybzistɑ̃s] **nf** subsistence ▸ **pourvoir à la subsistance de sa famille** to support one's family.

subsister [3] [sybziste] **vi** **1.** [chose] to remain **2.** [personne] to live, to subsist.

subsonique [sypsɔnik] **adj** subsonic.

substance [sypstɑ̃s] **nf** **1.** [matière] substance **2.** [essence] gist ▸ **en substance** in substance.

substantiel, elle [sypstɑ̃sjɛl] **adj** substantial.

substantif [sypstɑ̃tif] **nm** noun.

substituer [7] [sypstitɥe] **vt : substituer qqch à qqch** to substitute sthg for sthg.
◆ ***se substituer*** **vp : se substituer à** [personne] to stand in for, to substitute for / [chose] to take the place of.

substitut [sypstity] **nm** **1.** [remplacement] substitute **2.** DR deputy public prosecutor.

substitution [sypstitysjɔ̃] **nf** substitution.

substrat [sypstra] **nm** **1.** [de récit, réflexion] basis **2.** GÉOL & LING substratum **3.** CHIM substrate.

subterfuge [syptɛrfyʒ] **nm** subterfuge.

subtil, e [syptil] **adj** subtle.

subtilement [syptilmɑ̃] **adv** subtly.

subtiliser [3] [syptilize] **vt** to steal.

subtilité [syptilite] **nf** subtlety.

subtropical, e, aux [syptrɔpikal, o] **adj** subtropical.

suburbain, e [sybyrbɛ̃, ɛn] **adj** suburban.

subvenir [40] [sybvənir] **vi : subvenir à** to meet, to cover ▸ **subvenir aux besoins de qqn** to meet sb's needs.
◆ ***subvenir à*** **v + prep** [besoins] to provide for / [dépenses] to meet.

subvention [sybvɑ̃sjɔ̃] **nf** grant, subsidy ▸ **subvention de l'État** government grant ▸ **subvention d'État** government subsidy ▸ **subventions gouvernementales** government handouts.

subventionné [sybvɑ̃sjɔne] **adj** subsidized ▸ **un projet subventionné par l'État** government-funded project ▸ **une école subventionnée (par l'État)** a grant-maintained school.

subventionner [3] [sybvɑ̃sjɔne] **vt** to give a grant to, to subsidize / ÉCON [industrie, entreprise] **: subventionner excessivement** to featherbed.

subvenu, e [sybvəny] **pp** ➤ ***subvenir***.

subversif, ive [sybvɛrsif, iv] **adj** subversive.

subversion [sybvɛrsjɔ̃] **nf** subversion.

subviendrai, subviendras ➤ ***subvenir***.

subviens, subvient ➤ ***subvenir***.

suc [syk] **nm 1.** [d'arbre] sap / [de fruit, viande] juice ▸ **suc gastrique** gastric juices *pl* **2.** *littéraire* [quintessence] essence.

succédané [syksedane] **nm** substitute.

succéder [18] [syksede] **vt : succéder à** [suivre] to follow / [remplacer] to succeed, to take over from ▸ **tous ceux qui lui ont succédé** all his successors, all those who came after him ▸ **un épais brouillard a succédé au soleil** the sun gave way to thick fog.

◆ ***se succéder*** **vpi** [se suivre] to follow each other ▸ **les crises se succèdent** it's just one crisis after another.

succès [syksɛ] **nm 1.** [gén] success ▸ **avoir du succès** to be very successful ▸ **avoir un succès fou (auprès de)** to be very successful (with) ▸ **à succès** hit *(avant n)* ▸ **sans succès** [essai] unsuccessful / [essayer] unsuccessfully ▸ **avec succès** [essai] successful / [essayer] successfully ▸ **se tailler un franc succès** *fig* to be a great *ou* huge success **2.** [chanson, pièce] hit **3.** [conquête] conquest.

successeur [syksesœr] **nm 1.** [gén] successor **2.** DR successor, heir.

successif, ive [syksesif, iv] **adj** successive.

succession [syksesjɔ̃] **nf 1.** [gén] succession ▸ **une succession de** a succession of ▸ **prendre la succession de qqn** to take over from sb, to succeed sb **2.** DR succession, inheritance ▸ **droits de succession** death duties *UK*, inheritance tax *US*.

successivement [syksesivmɑ̃] **adv** successively.

succinct, e [syksɛ̃, ɛ̃t] **adj 1.** [résumé] succinct **2.** [repas] frugal.

succinctement [syksɛ̃tmɑ̃] **adv 1.** [résumer] succinctly **2.** [manger] frugally.

succion [syksjɔ̃, sysjɔ̃] **nf** suction, sucking.

succomber [3] [sykɔ̃be] **vi : succomber (à)** to succumb (to).

succulent, e [sykylɑ̃, ɑ̃t] **adj** delicious.

succursale [sykyrsal] **nf** branch.

sucer [16] [syse] **vt** to suck ▸ **pastilles à sucer** lozenges to be sucked ▸ **sucer son pouce** to suck one's thumb.

◆ ***se sucer*** **vpt : se sucer les doigts** to suck one's fingers.

sucette [sysɛt] **nf** [friandise] lolly *UK*, lollipop ▸ **sucette au caramel** caramel lollipop.

suçon [sysɔ̃] **nm** lovebite, hickey *US*.

sucre [sykr] **nm** sugar ▸ **sucre de betterave/canne** beet/cane sugar ▸ **sucre candi** candy sugar ▸ **sucre cristallisé** granulated sugar ▸ **sucre glace** icing sugar *UK*, confectioner's sugar *US* ▸ **sucre en morceaux** lump sugar ▸ **sucre d'orge** barley sugar ▸ **sucre en poudre, sucre semoule** caster sugar *UK*, finely granulated sugar *US* ▸ **sucre roux ou brun** brown sugar ▸ **casser du sucre sur le dos de qqn** *fam fig* to talk about sb behind his/her back.

◆ ***au sucre*** **loc adj** [fruits, crêpes] (sprinkled) with sugar.

sucré, e [sykre] **adj** [goût] sweet.

sucrer [3] [sykre] **vt 1.** [café, thé] to sweeten, to sugar **2.** *fam* [permission] to withdraw / [passage, réplique] to cut ▸ **sucrer qqch à qqn** to take sthg away from sb.

◆ ***se sucrer*** **vp** *fam* **1.** [se servir en sucre] to take some sugar **2.** [s'octroyer une part] to line one's pockets.

sucrerie [sykrəri] **nf 1.** [usine] sugar refinery **2.** [friandise] sweet *UK*, candy *US*.

Sucrette® [sykrɛt] **nf** (artificial) sweetener.

sucrier [sykrije] **nm** sugar bowl.

sucrier, ère [sykrije, ɛr] **adj** sugar *(avant n)*.

sud [syd] ■ **nm** south ▸ **un vent du sud** a southerly wind ▸ **le vent du sud** the south wind ▸ **au sud** in the south ▸ **au sud (de)** to the south (of).

■ **adj inv** [gén] south / [province, région] southern.

sud-africain, e [sydafrikɛ̃, ɛn] (mpl **sud-africains**, fpl **sud-africaines**) **adj** South African.

◆ ***Sud-Africain, e*** **nm, f** South African.

sud-américain, e [sydamerikɛ̃, ɛn] (mpl **sud-américains**, fpl **sud-américaines**) **adj** South American.

◆ ***Sud-Américain, e*** **nm, f** South American.

sudation [sydasjɔ̃] **nf** sweating.

sud-coréen, enne [sydkɔreɛ̃, ɛn] (mpl **sud-coréens**, fpl **sud-coréennes**) **adj** South Korean.

◆ ***Sud-Coréen, enne*** **nm, f** South Korean.

sud-est [sydɛst] **nm & adj inv** southeast.

sud-ouest [sydwɛst] **nm & adj inv** southwest.

Suède [sɥɛd] **nf : la Suède** Sweden.

suédine [sɥedin] **nf** suedette.

suédois, e [sɥedwa, az] **adj** Swedish.

◆ ***suédois*** **nm** [langue] Swedish.

◆ ***Suédois, e*** **nm, f** Swede.

suée [sɥe] **nf** *fam* sweat.

suer [7] [sɥe] ■ **vi** [personne] to sweat ▸ **faire suer qqn** *fam fig* to give sb a hard time ▸ **se faire suer** *fam fig* to be bored to tears.

■ **vt** to exude.

sueur [sɥœr] **nf** sweat ▸ **être en sueur** to be sweating ▸ **avoir des sueurs froides** *fig* to be in a cold sweat.

Suez [sɥɛz] **npr : le canal de Suez** the Suez Canal.

suffi [syfi] **pp inv** ➤ ***suffire***.

suffire [100] [syfir] ■ **vi 1.** [être assez] **: suffire pour qqch/pour faire qqch** to be enough for sthg/to do sthg, to be sufficient for sthg/to do sthg ▸ **ça suffit!** that's enough! **2.** [satisfaire] **: suffire à** to be enough for.

■ **v impers : il suffit de...** all that is necessary is..., all that you have to do is... ▸ **il suffit d'un moment d'inattention pour que...** it only takes a moment of carelessness for... ▸ **il lui suffit de donner sa démission** all he has to do is resign ▸ **il suffit que** *(+ subjonctif)* **: il suffit que vous lui écriviez** all (that) you need do is write to him.

◆ ***se suffire*** **vp : se suffire à soi-même** to be self-sufficient.

suffisais ➤ ***suffire***.

suffisamment [syfizamɑ̃] **adv** sufficiently.

suffisance [syfizɑ̃s] **nf** [vanité] self-importance ▸ **c'est un homme plein de suffisance** he's a very self-satisfied man.

suffisant, e [syfizɑ̃, ɑ̃t] **adj 1.** [satisfaisant] sufficient **2.** [vaniteux] self-important.

suffise ➤ ***suffire***.

suffixe [syfiks] **nm** suffix.

suffocant, e [syfɔkɑ̃, ɑ̃t] **adj 1.** [chaleur, fumée] suffocating **2.** *fig* [nouvelle, révélation] astonishing, incredible.

suffocation [syfɔkasjɔ̃] **nf** suffocation.

suffoquer [3] [syfɔke] ■ **vt 1.** [suj: chaleur, fumée] to suffocate **2.** *fig* [suj: colère] to choke / [suj: nouvelle, révélation] to astonish, to stun.
■ **vi** to choke ▸ **suffoquer de** *fig* to choke with.

suffrage [syfraʒ] **nm** vote ▸ **rallier tous les suffrages** to win all the votes ▸ **recueillir des suffrages** to win votes ▸ **suffrage indirect/restreint/universel** indirect/restricted/universal suffrage.

suffragette [syfraʒɛt] **nf** POLIT suffragette.

suggérer [18] [sygʒere] **vt 1.** [proposer] to suggest ▸ **suggérer qqch à qqn** to suggest sthg to sb ▸ **suggérer à qqn de faire qqch** to suggest that sb (should) do sthg **2.** [faire penser à] to evoke.

suggestif, ive [sygʒɛstif, iv] **adj 1.** [musique] evocative **2.** [pose, photo] suggestive.

suggestion [sygʒɛstjɔ̃] **nf** suggestion.

suicidaire [sɥisidɛr] **adj** suicidal.

suicide [sɥisid] ■ **nm** suicide.
■ **adj** suicide *(avant n)*.

suicider [3] [sɥiside] ◆ ***se suicider*** **vp** to commit suicide, to kill o.s.

suie [sɥi] **nf** soot.

suif [sɥif] **nm** tallow.

suintant, e [sɥɛ̃tɑ̃, ɑ̃t] **adj** [mur] sweating / [plaie] weeping.

suintement [sɥɛ̃tmɑ̃] **nm 1.** [de mur] sweating / [de plaie] weeping **2.** [d'eau] seeping, oozing.

suinter [3] [sɥɛ̃te] **vi 1.** [eau, sang] to ooze, to seep **2.** [surface, mur] to sweat / [plaie] to weep.

suis[1] ➤ ***être***.

suis[2], ***suit*** *etc* ➤ ***suivre***.

suisse [sɥis] ■ **adj** Swiss.
■ **nm** RELIG verger.
◆ ***Suisse*** ■ **nf** [pays] **: la Suisse** Switzerland ▸ **la Suisse allemande/italienne/romande** German-/Italian-/French-speaking Switzerland.
■ **nmf** [personne] Swiss (person) ▸ **les Suisses** the Swiss.
◆ ***en suisse*** **loc adv** *fam* alone, on one's own.

Suissesse [sɥisɛs] **nf** Swiss woman.

suite [sɥit] **nf 1.** [de liste, feuilleton] continuation ▸ **suite page 17** continued on page 17 ▸ **la suite au prochain numéro** to be continued (in our next issue) ▸ **suite et fin** final instalment
2. [série - de maisons, de succès] series / [- d'événements] sequence ▸ **attendons la suite des événements** let's wait to see what happens next ▸ **une suite de malheurs** a run *ou* series of misfortunes ▸ **écoute la suite** [- du discours] listen to what comes next / [- de mon histoire] listen to what happened next
3. [succession] **: prendre la suite de** [personne] to succeed, to take over from / [affaire] to take over ▸ **à la suite** one after the other ▸ **un nom avec plusieurs chiffres inscrits à la suite** a name followed by a string of numbers ▸ **à la suite de** *fig* following ▸ **à la suite de son discours télévisé, sa cote a remonté** following her speech on TV, her popularity rating went up ▸ **avoir de la suite dans les idées** to be coherent *ou* consistent ▸ **tu as de la suite dans les idées!** *hum* you certainly know what you want!
4. [escorte] retinue
5. MUS suite
6. [appartement] suite.
◆ ***suites*** **nfpl** consequences ▸ **avoir des suites** to have repercussions ▸ **elle est morte des suites de ses blessures** she died of her wounds.
◆ ***de suite*** **loc adv 1.** [l'un après l'autre] in succession ▸ **elle est restée de garde 48 heures de suite** she was on duty for 48 hours on end
2. [immédiatement] immediately ▸ **il revient de suite** he'll be right back.
◆ ***par la suite*** **loc adv** afterwards ▸ **ils se sont mariés par la suite** they eventually got married.
◆ ***par suite de*** **loc prép** owing to, because of ▸ **par suite d'un arrêt de travail des techniciens** due to industrial action by technical staff.
◆ ***sans suite*** **loc adj 1.** [incohérent] disconnected ▸ **il tenait des propos sans suite** his talk was incoherent
2. COMM discontinued.
◆ ***suite à*** **loc prép** ADMIN **: suite à votre lettre** further to *ou* in response to *ou* with reference to your letter ▸ **suite à votre appel téléphonique** further to your phone call.

suivais, suivions ➤ ***suivre***.

suivant, e [sɥivɑ̃, ɑ̃t] ■ **adj** next, following.
■ **nm, f** next *ou* following one ▸ **au suivant!** next!
◆ ***suivant*** **prép** according to ▸ **suivant que** according to whether.

suiveur [sɥivœr] **nm** follower.

suivi, e [sɥivi] ■ **pp** ➤ ***suivre***.
■ **adj 1.** [visites] regular / [travail] sustained / [qualité] consistent **2.** [raisonnement] coherent.
◆ ***suivi*** **nm** follow-up.

suivre [89] [sɥivr] ■ **vt 1.** [gén] to follow ▸ **la police les a suivis sur plusieurs kilomètres** the police chased them for several kilometres ▸ **suivez le guide** this way (for the guided tour), please ▸ **suivre qqn des yeux *ou* du regard** to follow sb with one's eyes ▸ **'faire suivre'** 'please forward' ▸ **faire suivre son courrier** to have one's mail forwarded ▸ **à suivre** to be continued ▸ **c'est une affaire à suivre** it's something we should keep an eye on ▸ **suivre un régime** to be on a diet ▸ **suivre le mouvement** *fam* to (just) go *ou* tag along with the crowd / [comprendre] to follow ▸ **je ne te suis plus** I'm not with you any more
2. [suj: médecin] to treat ▸ **je suis suivie par un très bon médecin** I'm with *ou* under a very good doctor
3. [se dérouler après] to follow (on from), to come after ▸ **la réunion sera suivie d'une collation** refreshments will be

served after the meeting / *(en usage absolu)* **: le jour qui suivit** (the) next day, the following day / *(tournure impersonnelle)* **: il suit de votre déclaration que le témoin ment** it follows from your statement that the witness is lying.

■ **vi 1.** SCOL to keep up ▸ **il a du mal à suivre en physique** he's having difficulty keeping up in physics
2. [venir après] to follow ▸ **procéder comme suit** proceed as follows.

◆ ***se suivre*** **vp** to follow one another ▸ **les trois coureurs se suivent de très près** the three runners are very close behind one another *ou* are tightly bunched.

◆ ***à suivre*** ■ **loc adj : c'est une affaire à suivre** it's something we should keep an eye on.
■ **loc adv : 'à suivre'** 'to be continued'.

sujet**, **ette [syʒɛ, ɛt] ■ **adj : être sujet à qqch** to be subject *ou* prone to sthg ▸ **sujet à des attaques cardiaques** subject to heart attacks ▸ **nous sommes tous sujets à l'erreur** we're all prone to making mistakes ▸ **être sujet à faire qqch** to be apt *ou* liable to do sthg ▸ **être sujet à caution** *fig* to be unconfirmed ▸ **leurs informations sont sujettes à caution** their information should be taken warily.
■ **nm, f** [de souverain] subject.

◆ ***sujet*** **nm 1.** [gén] subject ▸ **c'est à quel sujet?** what is it about? ▸ **quel est le sujet du livre?** what's the book about? ▸ **sujet de conversation** topic of conversation ▸ **au sujet de** about, concerning **2.** [motif] **: sujet de** cause for, reason for ▸ **sujet de plainte** grievance ▸ **leur salaire est leur principal sujet de mécontentement** the main cause of their dissatisfaction is their salary.

◆ ***au sujet de*** **loc prép** about, concerning ▸ **c'est au sujet de Martha?** is it about Martha? ▸ **j'aimerais vous faire remarquer, à ce sujet, que...** concerning this matter, I'd like to point out to you that... ▸ **je voudrais parler au directeur – c'est à quel sujet?** I'd like to talk to the manager – what about?

sulfate [sylfat] **nm** sulphate *UK*, sulfate *US*.

sulfure [sylfyr] **nm** sulphide *UK*, sulfide *US*.

sulfureux**, **euse [sylfyrø, øz] **adj** sulphurous *UK*, sulfurous *US*.

sulfurique [sylfyrik] **adj** sulphuric *UK*, sulfuric *US*.

sulfurisé**, **e [sylfyrize] **adj : papier sulfurisé** greaseproof paper *UK*, wax paper *US*.

sultan**, **e [syltɑ̃, an] **nm, f** sultan (f sultana).

sultanat [syltana] **nm** sultanate.

Sumatra [symatra] **npr** Sumatra ▸ **à Sumatra** in Sumatra.

summum [sɔmɔm] **nm** summit, height.

sumo [sumo] **nm** sumo.

Sup de Co [sypdəko] *fam* abr écrite de ***École Supérieure de Commerce***.

super [sypɛr] *fam* ■ **adj inv** super, great.
■ **nm** four star (petrol) *UK*, premium *US*.

superbe [sypɛrb] ■ **adj** superb / [enfant, femme] beautiful.
■ **nf** *littéraire* pride, arrogance.

superbement [sypɛrbəmɑ̃] **adv** superbly.

supercarburant [sypɛrkarbyrɑ̃] **nm** high-octane petrol *UK ou* gasoline *US*.

supercherie [sypɛrʃəri] **nf** deception, trickery.

supérette [syperɛt] **nf** mini-market, superette *US*.

superfétatoire [sypɛrfetatwar] **adj** *littéraire* superfluous.

superficie [sypɛrfisi] **nf 1.** [surface] area **2.** *fig* [aspect superficiel] surface.

superficiel**, **elle [sypɛrfisjɛl] **adj** superficial.

superficiellement [sypɛrfisjɛlmɑ̃] **adv** superficially.

superflu**, **e [sypɛrfly] **adj** superfluous.
◆ ***superflu*** **nm** superfluity.

superforme [sypɛrfɔrm] **nf** *fam* top form, top shape.

super-huit [sypɛrɥit] **nm inv** super-eight.

supérieur**, **e [syperjœr] ■ **adj 1.** [étage] upper ▸ **les jouets sont à l'étage supérieur** toys are on the next floor *ou* the floor above **2.** [intelligence, qualité] superior ▸ **intelligence supérieure à la moyenne** above-average intelligence ▸ **supérieur à** [température] higher than, above / [notation] superior to ▸ **une note supérieure à 10** a mark above 10 **3.** [dominant - équipe] superior ▸ **les autorités supérieures** the powers above / [- cadre] senior **4.** [SCOL - classe] upper, senior ▸ **passer dans la classe supérieure** SCOL to move up one class / [- enseignement] higher **5.** *péj* [air] superior ▸ **ne prends pas cet air supérieur!** don't look so superior!
■ **nm, f** superior.

supériorité [syperjɔrite] **nf** superiority.

superlatif [sypɛrlatif] **nm** superlative.

supermarché [sypɛrmarʃe] **nm** supermarket.

COMMENT EXPRIMER...

un changement de sujet

By the way, who was that you were talking to before? / Au fait, à qui est-ce que tu parlais tout à l'heure ?
Before I forget, where did you say she lives? / J'allais oublier : tu m'as dit qu'elle habitait où ?
While I remember, have I told you about next week's meeting? / Pendant que j'y pense, est-ce que je t'ai parlé de la réunion de la semaine prochaine ?
Talking of holidays, are you going skiing this year? / À propos de vacances, tu vas faire du ski cette année ?
That reminds me. What time do we have to leave? / À propos, à quelle heure est-ce qu'il faut partir ?
On a completely different point, new regulations will come into effect next month / Sur un tout autre sujet, de nouvelles réglementations entrent en vigueur le mois prochain
Let's change the subject! / Changeons de sujet !

superposable [sypɛrpozabl] **adj** stacking *(avant n)*.

superposer [3] [sypɛrpoze] **vt** to stack.
◆ ***se superposer*** **vp** to be stacked / GÉOL to be superposed.

superposition [sypɛrpozisjɔ̃] **nf** **1.** [action - d'objets] stacking **2.** [état] superposition **3.** *fig* [d'influences] combination.

superproduction [sypɛrprɔdyksjɔ̃] **nf** spectacular.

superpuissance [sypɛrpɥisɑ̃s] **nf** superpower.

supersonique [sypɛrsɔnik] **adj** supersonic.

superstar [sypɛrstar] **nf** *fam* superstar.

superstitieux, ***euse*** [sypɛrstisjø, øz] ■ **adj** superstitious.
■ **nm, f** superstitious person.

superstition [sypɛrstisjɔ̃] **nf** **1.** [croyance] superstition **2.** [obsession] obsessive attachment.

superviser [3] [sypɛrvize] **vt** to supervise.

supervision [sypɛrvizjɔ̃] **nf** supervision.

supplanter [3] [syplɑ̃te] **vt** to supplant.

suppléance [sypleɑ̃s] **nf** supply post *UK*, substitute post *US*.

suppléant, ***e*** [sypleɑ̃, ɑ̃t] ■ **adj** acting *(avant n)*, temporary.
■ **nm, f** substitute, deputy.

suppléer [15] [syplee] ■ **vt** **1.** *littéraire* [carence] to compensate for **2.** [personne] to stand in for.
■ **vi : suppléer à** to compensate for, to make up for.

supplément [syplemɑ̃] **nm** **1.** [surplus] **: un supplément de détails** additional details, extra details **2.** PRESSE supplement **3.** [de billet] extra charge ▸ **en supplément** extra.

supplémentaire [syplemɑ̃tɛr] **adj** extra, additional.

suppliant, ***e*** [syplijɑ̃, ɑ̃t] ■ **adj** begging, imploring, beseeching *littéraire* ▸ **d'un ton suppliant** imploringly, pleadingly.
■ **nm, f** supplicant.

supplication [syplikasjɔ̃] **nf** plea.

supplice [syplis] **nm** torture / *fig* [souffrance] torture, agony ▸ **être un supplice** to be agony ▸ **être au supplice** to be in agony *ou* torment ▸ **mettre qqn au supplice** to torture sb ▸ **supplice de Tantale** torture.

supplicié, ***e*** [syplisje] **nm, f** victim of torture.

supplier [10] [syplije] **vt : supplier qqn de faire qqch** to beg *ou* implore sb to do sthg ▸ **je t'en** *ou* **vous en supplie** I beg *ou* implore you.

supplique [syplik] **nf** petition.

support [sypɔr] **nm** **1.** [socle] support, base **2.** *fig* [de communication] medium ▸ **supports audiovisuels** audiovisual aids ▸ **support pédagogique** teaching aid ▸ **support publicitaire** advertising medium.

supportable [sypɔrtabl] **adj** **1.** [douleur] bearable **2.** [conduite] tolerable, acceptable.

supporter[1] [3] [sypɔrte] **vt** **1.** [soutenir, encourager] to support **2.** [endurer] to bear, to stand ▸ **des plantes qui supportent/ne supportent pas le froid** plants that do well/badly in the cold ▸ **je ne supporte pas l'alcool/la pilule** drink/the pill doesn't agree with me ▸ **supporter que** *(+ subjonctif)* **: il ne supporte pas qu'on le contredise** he cannot bear being contradicted ▸ **il faudra le supporter encore deux jours** we'll have to put up with him for two more days **3.** [résister à] to withstand ▸ **leur nouvelle voiture supporte la comparaison avec la concurrence** their new car will bear *ou* stand comparison with anything produced by their competitors ▸ **sa théorie ne supporte pas une critique sérieuse** his theory won't stand up to serious criticism.
◆ ***se supporter*** **vp** [se tolérer] to bear *ou* stand each other.

supporter[2] [sypɔrtɛr] **nm** supporter.

supposé, ***e*** [sypoze] **adj** [montant] estimated / [criminel] alleged / [admis] **: la vitesse est supposée constante** the speed is assumed to be constant.

supposer [3] [sypoze] **vt** **1.** [imaginer] to suppose, to assure ▸ **en supposant que** *(+ subjonctif)* supposing (that) ▸ **à supposer que** *(+ subjonctif)* supposing (that) **2.** [impliquer] to imply, to presuppose.

supposition [sypozisjɔ̃] **nf** supposition, assumption.

suppositoire [sypozitwar] **nm** suppository.

suppôt [sypo] **nm** *littéraire* henchman ▸ **suppôt du diable** *ou* **de satan** fiend.

suppression [sypresjɔ̃] **nf** **1.** [de permis de conduire] withdrawal / [de document] suppression **2.** [de mot, passage] deletion **3.** [de loi, poste] abolition.

supprimer [3] [syprime] **vt** **1.** [document] to suppress / [obstacle, difficulté] to remove **2.** [mot, passage] to delete **3.** [loi, poste] to abolish **4.** [témoin] to do away with, to eliminate ▸ **supprimer les étapes/intermédiaires** to do away with the intermediate stages/the middlemen **5.** [permis de conduire, revenus] **: supprimer qqch à qqn** to take sthg away from sb **6.** [douleur] to take away, to suppress **7.** [retirer] **: supprimer des emplois** to lay people off, to make people redundant *UK* ▸ **j'ai partiellement**

COMMENT EXPRIMER...

la supposition

Supposing he's right and she does resign / Supposons qu'il ait raison et qu'elle démissionne
Suppose he can't come? / Et à supposer qu'il ne puisse pas venir ?
What if he decided not to sell? / Et s'il décidait de ne plus vendre ?
I assume these figures have been checked? / Je suppose que ces chiffres ont été vérifiés ?
For the sake of argument, let's say the initial cost is one million euros / Admettons que le coût initial soit d'un million d'euros

supprimé le sel I cut down on salt ▸ **ils vont supprimer des trains dans les zones rurales** train services will be cut in rural areas **8.** INFORM to delete.
◆ ***se supprimer*** **vp** *(emploi réfléchi)* to take one's own life.

suppurer [3] [sypyre] **vi** to suppurate.

supputation [sypytasjɔ̃] **nf** calculation, computation.

supputer [3] [sypyte] **vt** *littéraire* to calculate, to compute.

supranational, ***e***, ***aux*** [sypranasjɔnal, o] **adj** supranational.

suprématie [sypremasi] **nf** supremacy.

suprême [syprɛm] ■ **adj 1.** [gén] supreme **2.** *sout* [dernier - moment, pensée] last.
■ **nm** *fillets in a cream sauce.*

suprêmement [syprɛmmɑ̃] **adv** supremely.

sur [syr] **prép 1.** [position - dessus] on / [- au-dessus de] above, over ▸ **sur la table** on the table ▸ **il a jeté ses affaires sur le lit** he threw his things onto the bed ▸ **une chambre avec vue sur la mer** a room with a view of *ou* over the sea
2. [direction] towards, toward *US* ▸ **sur la droite/gauche** on the right/left, to the right/left ▸ **le malheur s'est abattu sur cette famille** unhappiness has fallen upon this family
3. [distance] **: travaux sur 10 kilomètres** roadworks for 10 kilometres *UK ou* kilometers *US* ▸ **la foire s'étend sur 3 000 m²** the fair covers 3,000 m²
4. [d'après] by ▸ **juger qqn sur sa mine** to judge sb by his/her appearance
5. [grâce à] on ▸ **ça s'ouvre sur simple pression** you open it by just pressing it ▸ **il vit sur les revenus de ses parents** he lives on *ou* off his parents' income
6. [au sujet de] on, about ▸ **faire des recherches sur qqch** to do some research into sthg ▸ **je sais peu de choses sur elle** I don't know much about her
7. [proportion] out of / [mesure] by ▸ **9 sur 10** 9 out of 10 ▸ **un mètre sur deux** one metre *UK ou* meter *US* by two ▸ **un jour sur deux** every other day ▸ **une fois sur deux** every other time
8. [indiquant une relation de supériorité] over ▸ **l'emporter sur qqn** to defeat sb ▸ **régner sur un pays** to rule over a country.
◆ ***sur ce*** **loc adv** whereupon.

sûr, ***e*** [syr] **adj 1.** [sans danger] safe **2.** [digne de confiance - personne] reliable, trustworthy / [- goût] reliable, sound / [- investissement] sound **3.** [certain] sure, certain ▸ **sûr de** sure of ▸ **sûr et certain** absolutely certain ▸ **sûr de soi** self-confident.

surabondance [syrabɔ̃dɑ̃s] **nf** overabundance.

surabondant, ***e*** [syrabɔ̃dɑ̃, ɑ̃t] **adj** overabundant.

surabonder [3] [syrabɔ̃de] **vi** *littéraire* to overabound.

suractivité [syraktivite] **nf** hyperactivity.

suraigu, ***ë*** [syregy] **adj** high-pitched, shrill.

surajouter [3] [syraʒute] **vt** to add (on top).
◆ ***se surajouter*** **vp** to be added (on top).

suralimenter [3] [syralimɑ̃te] **vt 1.** [personne] to overfeed **2.** [moteur] to supercharge.

suranné, ***e*** [syrane] **adj** *littéraire* old-fashioned, outdated.

surate [syrat], ***sourate*** [surat] **nf** sura.

surbooking [syrbukiŋ] **nm** overbooking.

surcharge [syrʃarʒ] **nf 1.** [de poids] excess load / [de bagages] excess weight **2.** *fig* [surcroît] **: une surcharge de travail** extra work **3.** [surabondance] surfeit **4.** [de document] alteration **5.** [de timbre] surcharge.

surcharger [17] [syrʃarʒe] **vt 1.** [véhicule, personne] **: surcharger (de)** to overload (with) **2.** [texte] to alter extensively **3.** [timbre] to surcharge.

surchauffe [syrʃof] **nf** overheating.

surchauffé, ***e*** [syrʃofe] **adj 1.** [trop chauffé] overheated ▸ **l'air était toujours surchauffé dans l'atelier** the air in the workshop was always too hot **2.** [surexcité] overexcited ▸ **des esprits surchauffés** reckless individuals.

surchauffer [3] [syrʃofe] **vt** to overheat.

surchemise [syrʃəmiz] **nf** overshirt.

surclasser [3] [syrklase] **vt** to outclass.

surconsommation [syrkɔ̃sɔmasjɔ̃] **nf** overconsumption.

surcroît [syrkrwa] **nm : un surcroît de travail/d'inquiétude** additional work/anxiety ▸ **de** *ou* **par surcroît** moreover, what is more.

surdimensionné, ***e*** [syrdimɑ̃sjɔne] **adj** oversize(d).

surdi-mutité [syrdimytite] **nf** deaf-muteness.

surdiplômé, ***e*** [syrdiplome] **adj** overqualified.

surdité [syrdite] **nf** deafness.

surdose [syrdoz] **nf** overdose.

surdoué, ***e*** [syrdwe] **adj** exceptionally *ou* highly gifted.

sureau, ***x*** [syro] **nm** elder.

sureffectif [syrefɛktif] **nm** overmanning, overstaffing.

surélever [19] [syrɛlve] **vt** to raise, to heighten.

sûrement [syrmɑ̃] **adv 1.** [certainement] certainly ▸ **sûrement pas!** *fam* no way!, definitely not! **2.** [sans doute] certainly, surely **3.** [sans risque] surely, safely.

surenchère [syrɑ̃ʃɛr] **nf** higher bid / *fig* overstatement, exaggeration ▸ **faire de la surenchère** *fig* to try to go one better.

surenchérir [32] [syrɑ̃ʃerir] **vi** to bid higher / *fig* to try to go one better.

surendetté, ***e*** [syrɑ̃dete] **adj** overindebted.

surendettement [syrɑ̃dɛtmɑ̃] **nm 1.** [gén] overindebtedness, debt burden **2.** [d'une entreprise] overborrowing.

surestimer [3] [syrɛstime] **vt 1.** [exagérer] to overestimate **2.** [surévaluer] to overvalue.
◆ ***se surestimer*** **vp** to overestimate o.s.

sûreté [syrte] **nf 1.** [sécurité] safety ▸ **en sûreté** safe ▸ **de sûreté** safety *(avant n)* **2.** [fiabilité] reliability **3.** DR surety.
◆ ***Sûreté*** **nf : la Sûreté (nationale)** ≃ C.I.D. *UK* ≃ F.B.I. *US*

surexcitation [syrɛksitasjɔ̃] **nf** overexcitement.

surexcité, e [syreksite] **adj** overexcited.

surexciter [3] [syrɛksite] **vt** to overexcite.

surexposer [3] [syrɛkspoze] **vt** to overexpose.

surf [sœrf] **nm** surfing ▸ **surf des neiges** snowboarding.

surface [syrfas] **nf 1.** [extérieur, apparence] surface ▸ **faire surface** *litt & fig* to surface ▸ **en surface** superficially **2.** [superficie] surface area.
◆ ***grande surface*** **nf** hypermarket *UK*, supermarket *US*.
◆ ***moyenne surface*** **nf** high-street store *UK*, superette *US*.

surfait, e [syrfɛ, ɛt] **adj** overrated.

surfer [3] [sœrfe] **vi 1.** SPORT to go surfing **2.** INFORM to surf.

surfeur, euse [sœrfœr, øz] **nm, f** surfer.

surfiler [3] [syrfile] **vt** to oversew.

surfin, e [syrfɛ̃, in] **adj** superfine, extra fine.

surgelé, e [syrʒəle] **adj** frozen.
◆ ***surgelé*** **nm** frozen food.

surgeler [25] [syrʒəle] **vt** to freeze.

surgir [32] [syrʒir] **vi** to appear suddenly / *fig* [difficulté] to arise, to come up.

surhomme [syrɔm] **nm** superman.

surhumain, e [syrymɛ̃, ɛn] **adj** superhuman.

surimi [syrimi] **nm** surimi.

surimposer [3] [syrɛ̃poze] **vt** to overtax *(financially)*.

surimpression [syrɛ̃presjɔ̃] **nf** double exposure.

Surinam(e) [syrinam] **nm : le Suriname** Surinam ▸ **au Suriname** in Surinam.

surinfection [syrɛ̃fɛksjɔ̃] **nf** secondary infection.

surjet [syrʒɛ] **nm** overcasting stitch.

sur-le-champ [syrləʃɑ̃] **loc adv** immediately, straightaway.

surlendemain [syrlɑ̃dmɛ̃] **nm : le surlendemain** two days later ▸ **le surlendemain de mon départ** two days after I left.

surligner [3] [syrliɲe] **vt** to highlight.

surligneur [syrliɲœr] **nm** highlighter (pen).

surmenage [syrmənaʒ] **nm** overwork.

surmené, e [syrməne] **nm, f** [nerveusement] person suffering from nervous exhaustion / [par le travail] overworked person.

surmener [19] [syrməne] **vt** to overwork.
◆ ***se surmener*** **vp** to overwork.

surmontable [syrmɔ̃tabl] **adj** surmountable.

surmonter [3] [syrmɔ̃te] **vt 1.** [obstacle, peur] to overcome, to surmount **2.** [suj: statue, croix] to surmount, to top.

surnager [17] [syrnaʒe] **vi 1.** [flotter] to float (on the surface) **2.** *fig* [subsister] to remain, to survive.

surnaturel, elle [syrnatyrɛl] **adj** supernatural.
◆ ***surnaturel*** **nm : le surnaturel** the supernatural.

surnom [syrnɔ̃] **nm** nickname.

FAUX AMIS / FALSE FRIENDS
surnom

Surname is not a translation of the French word *surnom*. Surname is translated by *nom de famille*.
▸ Her surname is Jones / *Son nom de famille est Jones*

surnombre [syrnɔ̃br] ◆ ***en surnombre*** **loc adv** too many.

surnommer [3] [syrnɔme] **vt** to nickname.

surpasser [3] [syrpase] **vt** to surpass, to outdo.
◆ ***se surpasser*** **vp** to surpass *ou* excel o.s.

surpayer [11] [syrpeje] **vt** [personne] to overpay / [article] to pay too much for.

surpeuplé, e [syrpœple] **adj** overpopulated.

surpeuplement [syrpœpləmɑ̃] **nm** overpopulation.

surplace [syrplas] **nm : faire du surplace** [voiture] to be stuck (in traffic).

surplis [syrpli] **nm** surplice.

surplomb [syrplɔ̃] ◆ ***en surplomb*** **loc adj** overhanging.

surplomber [3] [syrplɔ̃be] ■ **vt** to overhang.
■ **vi** to be out of plumb.

surplus [syrply] **nm 1.** [excédent] surplus **2.** [magasin] army surplus store **3.** [supplément de prix] surcharge **4.** FIN disposable income.
◆ ***au surplus*** **loc adv** besides, what is more.

surpopulation [syrpɔpylasjɔ̃] **nf** overpopulation.

surprenant, e [syrprənɑ̃, ɑ̃t] **adj** surprising, amazing.

surprendrai, surprendras ➤ ***surprendre***.

surprendre [79] [syrprɑ̃dr] **vt 1.** [voleur] to catch (in the act) **2.** [secret] to overhear **3.** [prendre à l'improviste] to surprise, to catch unawares **4.** [étonner] to surprise, to amaze.
◆ ***se surprendre*** **vp : se surprendre à faire qqch** to catch o.s. doing sthg.

surpris, e [syrpri, iz] ■ **pp** ➤ ***surprendre***.
■ **adj 1.** [pris au dépourvu] surprised ▸ **l'ennemi, surpris, n'opposa aucune résistance** caught off their guard, the enemy put up no resistance **2.** [déconcerté] surprised ▸ **je suis surpris de son absence** I'm surprised (that) she's not here **3.** [vu, entendu par hasard] **: quelques mots surpris entre deux portes** a snatch of overheard conversation.

surprise [syrpriz] ■ **nf** surprise ▸ **à la surprise générale** to everybody's surprise ▸ **avoir une surprise** to be surprised ▸ **par surprise** by surprise ▸ **faire une surprise à qqn** to give sb a surprise ▸ **on a souvent de mauvaises surprises avec lui** you often have unpleasant surprises with him ▸ **quelle (bonne) surprise!** what a (nice *ou* pleasant) surprise!

■ **adj** [inattendu] surprise *(avant n)* ▸ **attaque surprise** surprise attack ▸ **grève surprise** lightning strike ▸ **visite surprise** surprise *ou* unexpected visit.

surproduction [syrprɔdyksjɔ̃] **nf** overproduction.

surqualifié, e [syrkalifje] **adj** overqualified.

surréalisme [syrrealism] **nm** surrealism.

surréel, elle [syrreɛl] **adj** *littéraire* surreal.

surréservation [syrlresɛrvasjɔ̃] **nm** = ***overbooking***.

sursaut [syrso] **nm 1.** [de personne] jump, start ▸ **en sursaut** with a start **2.** [d'énergie] burst, surge.

sursauter [3] [syrsote] **vi** to start, to give a start.

surseoir [66] [syrswar] ◆ ***surseoir à*** **v + prep 1.** *littéraire* [différer - publication, décision] to postpone, to defer **2.** DR : **surseoir à statuer** to defer a judgment ▸ **surseoir à une exécution** to stay an execution.

sursis [syrsi] **nm** *fig* & DR reprieve ▸ **six mois avec sursis** six months' suspended sentence ▸ **en sursis** in remission.

sursitaire [syrsitɛr] **nmf** MIL *person whose call-up has been deferred*.

surtaxe [syrtaks] **nf** surcharge.

surtension [syrtɑ̃sjɔ̃] **nf** INFORM power surge.

surtout [syrtu] **adv 1.** [avant tout] above all **2.** [spécialement] especially, particularly ▸ **surtout pas** certainly not.
◆ ***surtout que*** **loc conj** *fam* especially as.

survécu [syrveky] **pp** ➤ ***survivre***.

surveillance [syrvɛjɑ̃s] **nf** supervision ∕ [de la police, de militaire] surveillance ▸ **être sous surveillance** to be under surveillance ▸ **Direction de la surveillance du territoire** counterespionage section ∕ ADMIN & DR surveillance ▸ **surveillance légale** sequestration (by the courts).
◆ ***sans surveillance*** **loc adj** & **loc adv** unattended, unsupervised.
◆ ***sous surveillance*** **loc adv 1.** [par la police] under surveillance ▸ **mettre** *ou* **placer qqch sous surveillance** to put sthg under surveillance **2.** MÉD under observation.

surveillant, e [syrvɛjɑ̃, ɑ̃t] **nm, f** supervisor ∕ [de prison] guard, warder *UK*.

surveiller [4] [syrveje] **vt 1.** [enfant] to watch, to keep an eye on ∕ [suspect] to keep a watch on **2.** [travaux] to supervise ∕ [examen] to invigilate *UK* **3.** [ligne, langage] to watch.
◆ ***se surveiller*** **vp** to watch o.s.

survenir [40] [syrvənir] **vi 1.** [personne] to arrive unexpectedly **2.** [incident] to occur.

survenu, e [syrvəny] **pp** ➤ ***survenir***.

survêtement [syrvɛtmɑ̃] **nm** tracksuit.

survie [syrvi] **nf** [de personne] survival.

surviendrai, surviendras ➤ ***survenir***.

survient ➤ ***survenir***.

survitrage [syrvitraʒ] **nm** double glazing ▸ **poser un survitrage** to fit double glazing.

survivant, e [syrvivɑ̃, ɑ̃t] ■ **nm, f** survivor.
■ **adj** surviving.

survivre [90] [syrvivr] **vi** to survive ▸ **survivre à** [personne] to outlive, to survive ∕ [accident, malheur] to survive.

survol [syrvɔl] **nm 1.** [de territoire] flying over **2.** [de texte] skimming through.

survoler [3] [syrvɔle] **vt 1.** [territoire] to fly over **2.** [texte] to skim (through).

sus [sy(s)] **interj : sus à l'ennemi!** at the enemy!
◆ ***en sus*** **loc adv** moreover, in addition ▸ **en sus de** over and above, in addition to.

susceptibilité [sysɛptibilite] **nf** touchiness, sensitivity.

susceptible [sysɛptibl] **adj 1.** [ombrageux] touchy, sensitive **2.** [en mesure de] : **susceptible de faire qqch** liable *ou* likely to do sthg ▸ **susceptible d'amélioration, susceptible d'être amélioré** open to improvement.

susciter [3] [sysite] **vt 1.** [admiration, curiosité] to arouse **2.** [ennuis, problèmes] to create ▸ **susciter qqch à qqn** *sout* to make *ou* cause sthg for sb.

susdit, e [sysdi, it] ■ **adj** above-mentioned.
■ **nm, f** above-mentioned (person).

sushi [suʃi] **nm** sushi.

susnommé, e [sysnɔme] ■ **adj** above-named.
■ **nm, f** above-named (person).

suspect, e [syspɛ, ɛkt] ■ **adj 1.** [personne] suspicious ▸ **suspect de qqch** suspected of sthg **2.** [douteux] suspect.
■ **nm, f** suspect.

suspecter [4] [syspɛkte] **vt** to suspect, to have one's suspicions about ▸ **suspecter qqn de qqch/de faire qqch** to suspect sb of sthg/of doing sthg.

suspendre [73] [syspɑ̃dr] **vt 1.** [lustre, tableau] to hang (up) ▸ **suspendre au plafond/au mur** to hang from the ceiling/on the wall **2.** [pourparlers] to suspend ∕ [séance] to adjourn ∕ [journal] to suspend publication of **3.** [fonctionnaire, constitution] to suspend **4.** [jugement] to postpone, to defer.
◆ ***se suspendre*** **vp : se suspendre à** to hang from.

suspendu, e [syspɑ̃dy] ■ **pp** ➤ ***suspendre***.

COMMENT EXPRIMER...

la surprise

I don't believe it! ∕ Pas possible !
That's amazing! ∕ C'est incroyable !
It can't be true! ∕ C'est pas vrai !
Never! ∕ Non !
Well I never! ∕ Ça alors !
Oh my God! ∕ Oh, mon Dieu !
I can't get over it! ∕ Je n'en reviens pas !
I couldn't believe my eyes ∕ Je n'en croyais pas mes yeux
What a nice surprise! ∕ Quelle bonne surprise !
I'm speechless! ∕ Je suis sans voix !
You shouldn't have! ∕ Vous n'auriez pas dû !

■ **adj 1.** [fonctionnaire] suspended **2.** [séance] adjourned **3.** [lustre, tableau] **: suspendu au plafond/au mur** hanging from the ceiling/on the wall **4.** [véhicule] **: bien/mal suspendu** with good/bad suspension.

suspens [syspɑ̃] ◆ ***en suspens*** **loc adv** in abeyance.

suspense [syspɑ̃s, syspɛns] **nm** suspense ▸ **film à suspense** thriller ▸ **roman à suspense** thriller, suspense story.

suspension [syspɑ̃sjɔ̃] **nf 1.** [gén] suspension ▸ **en suspension** in suspension, suspended **2.** [de combat] halt / [d'audience] adjournment **3.** [lustre] light fitting.

suspicieux, euse [syspisjø, øz] **adj** suspicious.

suspicion [syspisjɔ̃] **nf** suspicion.

sustentation [systɑ̃tasjɔ̃] **nf** AÉRON lift.

sustenter [3] [systɑ̃te] ◆ ***se sustenter*** **vp** *hum & sout* to take sustenance.

susurrer [3] [sysyre] **vt & vi** to murmur.

suture [sytyr] **nf** suture.

suzeraineté [syzrɛnte] **nf** suzerainty.

svastika, swastika [zvastika] **nm** swastika.

svelte [zvɛlt] **adj** slender.

sveltesse [zvɛltɛs] **nf** slenderness.

SVP (abr écrite de ***s'il vous plaît***) ➤ ***plaire***.

swahili, e [swaili], ***souahéli, e*** [swaeli] **adj** Swahili.
◆ ***swahili, souahéli*** **nm** [langue] Swahili.

swastika = ***svastika***.

Swaziland [swazilɑ̃d] **nm : le Swaziland** Swaziland.

sweat-shirt [switʃœrt] (pl **sweat-shirts**) **nm** sweatshirt.

Sydney [sidnɛ] **npr** Sydney.

syllabe [silab] **nf** syllable.

sylphide [silfid] **nf** sylph.

sylvestre [silvɛstr] **adj** *littéraire* forest *(avant n)* ➤ ***pin***.

sylviculture [silvikyltyr] **nf** forestry.

symbiose [sɛ̃bjoz] **nf** *fig* & BIOL symbiosis.
◆ ***en symbiose*** **loc adv** in symbiosis, symbiotically ▸ **ils vivent en symbiose** *fig* they're inseparable.

symbole [sɛ̃bɔl] **nm** symbol.

symbolique [sɛ̃bɔlik] ■ **adj 1.** [figure] symbolic **2.** [geste, contribution] token *(avant n)* **3.** [rémunération] nominal.
■ **nf 1.** [système] system of symbols **2.** [interprétation] interpretation.

symboliquement [sɛ̃bɔlikmɑ̃] **adv** symbolically.

symboliser [3] [sɛ̃bɔlize] **vt** to symbolize.

symbolisme [sɛ̃bɔlism] **nm** symbolism.

symétrie [simetri] **nf** symmetry.

symétrique [simetrik] **adj** symmetrical.

symétriquement [simetrikmɑ̃] **adv** symmetrically.

sympa [sɛ̃pa] **adj** *fam* [personne] likeable, nice / [soirée, maison] pleasant, nice / [ambiance] friendly.

sympathie [sɛ̃pati] **nf 1.** [pour personne, projet] liking ▸ **avoir de la sympathie pour qqn** to have a liking for sb, to be fond of sb ▸ **accueillir un projet avec sympathie** to look sympathetically *ou* favourably on a project **2.** [condoléances] sympathy.

sympathique [sɛ̃patik] **adj 1.** [personne] likeable, nice / [soirée, maison] pleasant, nice / [ambiance] friendly **2.** ANAT & MÉD sympathetic.

FAUX AMIS / FALSE FRIENDS

sympathique

Sympathetic is not the common translation of the French word *sympathique*. Sympathetic is translated by *compatissant*.
▸ She was very sympathetic about his problems / *Elle a eu beaucoup de compassion pour ses problèmes*

sympathisant, e [sɛ̃patizɑ̃, ɑ̃t] ■ **adj** sympathizing.
■ **nm, f** sympathizer.

sympathiser [3] [sɛ̃patize] **vi** to get on well ▸ **sympathiser avec qqn** to get on well with sb.

symphonie [sɛ̃fɔni] **nf** symphony.

symphonique [sɛ̃fɔnik] **adj** [musique] symphonic / [concert, orchestre] symphony *(avant n)*.

symposium [sɛ̃pozjɔm] **nm** symposium.

symptomatique [sɛ̃ptɔmatik] **adj** symptomatic.

symptôme [sɛ̃ptom] **nm** symptom.

synagogue [sinagɔg] **nf** synagogue.

synapse [sinaps] **nf 1.** ANAT synapse **2.** BIOL synapsis.

synchrone [sɛ̃krɔn] **adj** synchronous.

synchronique [sɛ̃krɔnik] **adj** synchronic.

synchronisation [sɛ̃krɔnizasjɔ̃] **nf** synchronization.

synchronisé, e [sɛ̃krɔnize] **adj** synchronized.

synchroniser [3] [sɛ̃krɔnize] **vt** to synchronize.

syncope [sɛ̃kɔp] **nf 1.** [évanouissement] blackout ▸ **tomber en syncope** to faint **2.** MUS syncopation.

syncopé, e [sɛ̃kɔpe] **adj** syncopated.

syndic [sɛ̃dik] **nm** [de copropriété] managing agent.

syndical, e, aux [sɛ̃dikal, o] **adj 1.** [délégué, revendication] (trade) union *(avant n) UK*, labor union *(avant n) US* **2.** [patronal] **: chambre syndicale** employers' association.

syndicalisme [sɛ̃dikalism] **nm 1.** [mouvement] trade unionism **2.** [activité] (trade) union *UK ou* labor union *US* activity.

syndicaliste [sɛ̃dikalist] ■ **nmf** trade unionist *UK*, union activist *US*.
■ **adj** (trade) union *(avant n) UK*, labor union *(avant n) US*.

syndicat [sɛ̃dika] **nm** [d'employés, d'agriculteurs] (trade) union *UK*, labor union *US* / [d'employeurs, de propriétaires] association.
◆ ***syndicat d'initiative*** **nm** tourist office.

syndication [sɛ̃dikasjɔ̃] **f** PRESSE [d'un article] syndication.

syndiqué, e [sɛ̃dike] ■ **adj** unionized.
■ **nm, f** (trade) union member, trade unionist *UK*.

syndiquer [3] [sɛ̃dike] **vt** to unionize.
◆ ***se syndiquer*** **vp 1.** [personne] to join a (trade *UK ou* labor *US*) union **2.** [groupe] to form a (trade *UK ou* labor *US*) union.

syndrome [sɛ̃drom] **nm** syndrome ▸ **syndrome immunodéficitaire acquis** acquired immunodeficiency syndrome.

synergie [sinɛrʒi] **nf** synergy, synergism.

synode [sinɔd] **nm** synod ▸ **le saint-synode** the holy synod.

synonyme [sinɔnim] ■ **nm** synonym.
■ **adj** synonymous.

synoptique [sinɔptik] **adj** synoptic.

synovie [sinɔvi] ➤ ***épanchement***.

syntagme [sɛ̃tagm] **nm** phrase.

syntaxe [sɛ̃taks] **nf** syntax.

synthé [sɛ̃te] **nm** *fam* synth.

synthèse [sɛ̃tɛz] **nf** **1.** [opération & CHIM] synthesis **2.** [exposé] overview.

synthétique [sɛ̃tetik] **adj** **1.** [vue] overall **2.** [produit] synthetic **3.** [personne] **: avoir l'esprit synthétique** to have a gift for summing things up.

synthétiser [3] [sɛ̃tetize] **vt** to synthesize.

synthétiseur [sɛ̃tetizœr] **nm** synthesizer.

syphilis [sifilis] **nf** syphilis.

Syrie [siri] **nf : la Syrie** Syria.

syrien, enne [sirjɛ̃, ɛn] **adj** Syrian.
◆ ***Syrien, enne*** **nm, f** Syrian.

systématique [sistematik] **adj** systematic.

systématiquement [sistematikmɑ̃] **adv** systematically.

systématiser [3] [sistematize] **vt** to systematize.
◆ ***se systématiser*** **vp** to be/become systematic.

système [sistɛm] **nm** **1.** [structure] system ▸ **système métrique** metric system ▸ **système de valeurs** values system ▸ **le système D** resourcefulness ▸ **système nerveux** nervous system ▸ **système solaire** solar system ▸ **le système d'éducation français** the French educational system
2. POLIT & ÉCON **: analyse de système** systems analysis ▸ **système monétaire européen** European Monetary System ▸ **système majoritaire** majority rule ▸ **système de production** system of production ▸ **système de retraite** pension scheme
3. INFORM **: système bureautique** office automation system ▸ **système expert** expert system ▸ **système d'exploitation** operating system ▸ **système intégré de gestion** management information system ▸ **système de nom de domaine** Domain Name System, DNS
4. AUTO **: système anti-démarrage** immobilizer.

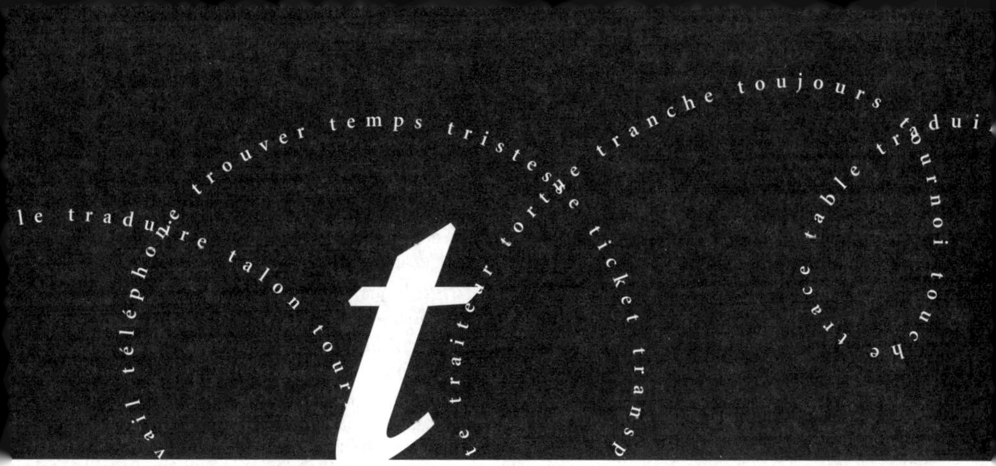

t, ***T*** [te] **nm inv** t, T.

t. (abr écrite de ***tome***) vol.

t' ➤ ***te***.

ta ➤ ***ton***[2].

TAA (abr de ***train autos accompagnées***) **nm** car-sleeper train, ≃ Motorail® *UK*.

tabac [taba] **nm 1.** [plante, produit] tobacco ▸ **tabac blond** mild *ou* Virginia tobacco ▸ **tabac brun** dark tobacco ▸ **tabac gris** shag ▸ **tabac à priser** snuff ▸ **campagne contre le tabac** anti-smoking campaign **2.** [magasin] tobacconist's *UK* ▸ **un bar tabac, un bar-tabac** *a bar with a tobacco counter*
▸▸ **et autres ennuis du même tabac** and troubles of that ilk ▸ **faire un tabac** to be a huge hit ▸ **passer à tabac** *fam* to beat up, to work over.

tabagie [tabaʒi] **nf 1.** [pièce] smoke-filled room **2.** *Québec* [bureau de tabac] tobacconist's *UK*.

tabagisme [tabaʒism] **nm 1.** [intoxication] nicotine addiction **2.** [habitude] smoking.

tabasser [3] [tabase] **vt** *fam* to beat up, to work over.

tabatière [tabatjɛr] **nf** snuffbox.

tabernacle [tabɛrnakl] **nm** tabernacle.

table [tabl] **nf 1.** [meuble] table ▸ **à table!** lunch/dinner *etc* is ready! ▸ **être à table** to be at table, to be having a meal ▸ **se mettre à table** to sit down to eat / *fig* to come clean ▸ **dresser** *ou* **mettre la table** to lay the table ▸ **sortir** *ou* **se lever de table** to leave the table, to get up from the table ▸ **quitter la table** to leave the table ▸ **table de chevet** *ou* **de nuit** bedside table ▸ **table basse** coffee table ▸ **table de cuisson** hob ▸ **table gigogne** nest of tables ▸ **table de jeu** *ou* **à jouer** gaming table ▸ **table à langer** baby changing table ▸ **table de montage** [en imprimerie & PHOTO] light table / CINÉ cutting table ▸ **table d'opération** operating table ▸ **table roulante** trolley ▸ **table de travail** desk **2.** [nourriture] **: les plaisirs de la table** good food ▸ **une des meilleures tables de Paris** one of the best restaurants in Paris.
◆ ***table d'écoute*** **nf** wiretapping set *ou* equipment ▸ **elle est sur table d'écoute** her phone is tapped ▸ **mettre qqn sur table d'écoute** to tap sb's phone.
◆ ***table des matières*** **nf** contents *pl*, table of contents.
◆ ***table de multiplication*** **nf** (multiplication) table.
◆ ***table ronde*** **nf** [conférence] round table.

tableau, ***x*** [tablo] **nm 1.** [peinture] painting, picture / *fig* [description] picture ▸ **un tableau de Goya** a painting by Goya ▸ **tableau de maître** old master ▸ **noircir le tableau** *fig* to paint a gloomy picture ▸ **vous nous faites un tableau très alarmant de la situation** you've painted an alarming picture of the situation ▸ **vous voyez d'ici le tableau!** *fam* you can imagine *ou* picture the scene!
2. THÉÂTRE scene
3. [panneau] board ▸ **tableau d'affichage** notice board *UK*, bulletin board *US* ▸ **tableau des arrivées/départs** arrivals/departures board ▸ **tableau de bord** AÉRON instrument panel / AUTO dashboard ▸ **tableau des fusibles** fuseboard ▸ **tableau noir** blackboard ▸ **aller au tableau** to go to the front of the classroom *(and answer questions or recite a lesson)*
4. [liste] register ▸ **tableau d'avancement** promotions roster *ou* list ▸ **tableau de chasse** [chasse] bag / AÉRON list of kills ▸ **tableau de chasse** bag ▸ **tableau (périodique) des éléments** CHIM periodic table ▸ **tableau d'honneur** honours board *UK*, honor roll *US* ▸ **elle a eu le tableau d'honneur ce mois-ci** she was on the roll of honour this month
5. [de données] table.

tablée [table] **nf** table.

tabler [3] [table] **vi : tabler sur** to count *ou* bank on.

tablette [tablɛt] **nf 1.** [planchette] shelf **2.** [de chewing-gum] stick / [de chocolat] bar ▸ **je vais l'inscrire** *ou* **le noter dans mes tablettes** *fig* I'll make a note of it.

tableur [tablœr] **nm** INFORM spreadsheet.

tablier [tablije] **nm 1.** [de cuisinière] apron / [d'écolier] smock **2.** [de magasin] shutter / [de cheminée] flue-shutter **3.** [de pont] roadway, deck.

tabloïd(e) [tablɔid] **nm** tabloid.

tabou, ***e*** [tabu] **adj** taboo.
◆ ***tabou*** **nm** taboo.

taboulé [tabule] **nm** *Lebanese dish of bulgur wheat, onions, tomatoes and herbs.*

tabouret [taburɛ] **nm** stool ▸ **tabouret de bar/de cuisine/de piano** bar/kitchen/piano stool.

tabulateur [tabylatœr] **nm** tabulator, tab.

tac [tak] **nm : du tac au tac** tit for tat.

TAC (abr de ***train auto-couchettes***) **nm** car-sleeper train, ≃ Motorail® *UK*.

tache [taʃ] **nf 1.** [de pelage] marking / [de peau] mark ▸ **tache de rousseur** *ou* **de son** freckle **2.** [de couleur, lumière] spot, patch **3.** [sur nappe, vêtement] stain ▸ **faire tache d'huile** *fig* to gain ground **4.** *littéraire* [morale] blemish.

tâche [taʃ] **nf** task ▸ **travailler à la tâche** to do piecework ▸ **faciliter la tâche de qqn** to make sb's task easier ▸ **se tuer à la tâche** *fig* to work o.s. to death.

tacher [3] [taʃe] **vt 1.** [nappe, vêtement] to stain, to mark **2.** *fig* [réputation] to tarnish.
◆ ***se tacher*** **vp 1.** [enfant] to get one's clothes dirty **2.** [nappe] to stain, to mark.

tâcher [3] [taʃe] ■ **vt : tâche que ça soit parfait** try to make sure it's perfect.
■ **vi : tâcher de faire qqch** to try to do sthg.

tâcheron [3] [taʃrɔ̃] **nm** *péj* drudge.

tacheté, ***e*** [taʃte] **adj** spotted.

tacheter [27] [taʃte] **vt** to spot, to speckle.

tachycardie [takikardi] **nf** tachycardia.

tacite [tasit] **adj** tacit.

tacitement [tasitmɑ̃] **adv** tacitly.

taciturne [tasityrn] **adj** taciturn.

tacot [tako] **nm** *fam* jalopy, heap.

tact [takt] **nm** [délicatesse] tact ▸ **avoir du tact** to be tactful ▸ **manquer de tact** to be tactless.

tacticien, ***enne*** [taktisjɛ̃, ɛn] **nm, f** tactician.

tactile [taktil] **adj** tactile ▸ **écran tactile** touch-sensitive.

tactique [taktik] ■ **adj** tactical.
■ **nf** tactics *pl*.

tænia = ***ténia***.

taf [taf] **nm** *fam* work.

taffe [taf] **nf** *fam* drag, puff.

taffetas [tafta] **nm 1.** [tissu] taffeta **2.** [sparadrap] plaster *UK*.

tag [tag] **nm** *identifying name written with a spray can on walls, the sides of trains etc.*

tagine = ***tajine***.

tagliatelles [taljatɛl] **nfpl** tagliatelle *(U)*.

taguer [3] [tage] **vt** to tag *(with graffiti)*.

tagueur, ***euse*** [tagœr, øz] **nm, f** *person who sprays their 'tag' on walls, the sides of trains etc.*

Tahiti [taiti] **npr** Tahiti ▸ **à Tahiti** in Tahiti.

tahitien, ***enne*** [taisjɛ̃, ɛn] **adj** Tahitian.
◆ ***tahitien*** **nm** [langue] Tahitian.
◆ ***Tahitien***, ***enne*** **nm, f** Tahitian.

taïaut, ***tayaut*** [tajo] **interj** tally-ho.

Taibei [tajbɛ], ***T'ai-pei*** [tajpɛ] **npr** Taipei.

taie [tɛ] **nf 1.** [enveloppe] **: taie (d'oreiller)** pillowcase, pillowslip **2.** [sur œil] leucoma, opaque spot.

taïga [tajga] **nf** taiga.

taillader [3] [tajade] **vt** to gash.
◆ ***se taillader*** **vpt : se taillader les poignets** to slash one's wrists.

taille [taj] **nf 1.** [action - de pierre, diamant] cutting / [- d'arbre, de haie] pruning
2. [stature] height ▸ **un homme de petite taille** a short man ▸ **être de taille** to measure up ▸ **être de taille à faire qqch** *fig* to be capable of doing sthg
3. [mesure, dimensions] size ▸ **une pièce de taille moyenne** an average-sized room ▸ **vous faites quelle taille?** what size are you?, what size do you take? ▸ **ce n'est pas à ma taille** it doesn't fit me ▸ **de taille** sizeable, considerable ▸ **une surprise de taille** a big surprise
4. [milieu du corps] waist ▸ **avoir la taille fine** to be slim-waisted *ou* slender-waisted ▸ **avoir une taille de guêpe** *fig* to be wasp-waisted
5. [partie d'un vêtement] waist ▸ **un jean (à) taille basse** low-waisted *ou* hipster *UK* *ou* hip-hugger *US* jeans.

taille-crayon [tajkrɛjɔ̃] (pl **taille-crayons**) **nm** pencil sharpener.

tailler [3] [taje] **vt 1.** [couper - chair, pierre, diamant] to cut / [- arbre, haie] to prune / [- crayon] to sharpen / [- bois] to carve **2.** [vêtement] to cut out.
◆ ***se tailler*** **vp 1.** [obtenir] to achieve **2.** *fam* [se sauver] to beat it, to clear off.

tailleur [tajœr] **nm 1.** [couturier] tailor **2.** [vêtement] (lady's) suit **3.** [de diamants, pierre] cutter
▸▸ **s'asseoir en tailleur** to sit cross-legged.

tailleur-pantalon [tajœrpɑ̃talɔ̃] (pl **tailleurs-pantalons**) **nm** trouser suit *UK*, pantsuit *US*.

taillis [taji] **nm** coppice, copse.

tain [tɛ̃] **nm** silvering ▸ **miroir sans tain** two-way mirror.

taire [111] [tɛr] **vt** to conceal.
◆ ***se taire*** **vp 1.** [rester silencieux] to be silent *ou* quiet **2.** [cesser de s'exprimer] to fall silent ▸ **faire se taire qqn** to make sb be quiet ▸ **tais-toi!** shut up! **3.** [orchestre] to fall silent / [cris] to cease.

taisais, ***taisions*** ➤ ***taire***.

taise, ***taises*** ➤ ***taire***.

Taiwan [tajwan] **npr** Taiwan ▸ **à Taiwan** in Taiwan.

taiwanais, ***e*** [tajwanɛ, ɛz] **adj** Taiwanese.
◆ ***Taiwanais***, ***e*** **nm, f** Taiwanese.

tajine, ***tagine*** [taʒin] **nm** *North African stew of mutton steamed with a variety of vegetables.*

talc [talk] **nm** talcum powder.

talent [talɑ̃] **nm** talent ▸ **avoir du talent** to be talented to have talent ▸ **les jeunes talents** young talent *(U)*.

talentueux, ***euse*** [talɑ̃tɥø, øz] **adj** talented.

talion [taljɔ̃] **nm : la loi du talion** an eye for an eye (and a tooth for a tooth).

talisman [talismɑ̃] **nm** talisman.

talkie-walkie [tɔkiwɔki] (pl **talkies-walkies**) **nm** walkie-talkie.

talk-show [tɔkʃo] **nm** tak show, chat show *UK*.

taloche [talɔʃ] **nf** *fam* [gifle] slap.

talon [talɔ̃] **nm 1.** [gén] heel ▸ **talons aiguilles/hauts** stiletto/high heels ▸ **chaussures à talons hauts** high-heeled shoes ▸ **talons plats** low *ou* flat heels ▸ **talon d'Achille** Achilles' heel ▸ **être/marcher sur les talons de qqn** *fig* to be/to follow hard on sb's heels ▸ **tourner les talons** *fig* to turn on one's heel **2.** [de chèque] counterfoil *UK*, stub **3.** [jeux de cartes] stock.

talonner [3] [talɔne] **vt 1.** [suj: poursuivant] to be hard on the heels of **2.** [suj: créancier] to harry, to hound.

talonnette [talɔnɛt] **nf 1.** [de chaussure] heel cushion, heel-pad **2.** [de pantalon] binding *(to reinforce trouser bottoms).*

talquer [3] [talke] **vt** to put talcum powder on.

talus [taly] **nm** embankment.

tamarin [tamarɛ̃] **nm** [fruit] tamarind.

tamarinier [tamarinje] **nm** tamarind tree.

tamaris [tamaris], ***tamarix*** [tamariks] **nm** tamarisk.

tambouille [tɑ̃buj] **nf** *fam* **1.** [plat] grub **2.** [cuisine] cooking.

tambour [tɑ̃bur] **nm 1.** [instrument, cylindre] drum ▸ **sans tambour ni trompette** *fig* without any fuss ▸ **tambour battant** *fig* briskly **2.** [musicien] drummer **3.** [porte à tourniquet] revolving door **4.** [à broder] embroidery hoop.

tambourin [tɑ̃burɛ̃] **nm 1.** [à grelots] tambourine **2.** [tambour] tambourin.

tambouriner [3] [tɑ̃burine] ■ **vt** to drum.
■ **vi : tambouriner sur** *ou* **à** to drum on ▸ **tambouriner contre** to drum against.

tamis [tami] **nm 1.** [crible] sieve **2.** [de raquette] strings *pl.*

Tamise [tamiz] **nf : la Tamise** the Thames.

tamisé, e [tamize] **adj** [éclairage] subdued.

tamiser [3] [tamize] **vt 1.** [farine] to sieve **2.** [lumière] to filter.

tampon [tɑ̃pɔ̃] **nm 1.** [bouchon] stopper, plug **2.** [éponge] pad ▸ **tampon à récurer** scourer **3.** [de coton, d'ouate] pad ▸ **tampon hygiénique** *ou* **périodique** tampon **4.** [cachet] stamp ▸ **tampon encreur** inking pad **5.** *litt & fig* [amortisseur] buffer.

tamponner [3] [tɑ̃pɔne] **vt 1.** [document] to stamp **2.** [plaie] to dab.
◆ ***se tamponner*** **vp** to crash into each other.

tamponneur, euse [tɑ̃pɔnœr, øz] **adj** colliding.

tamponneuse [tɑ̃pɔnøz] ➤ ***auto.***

tam-tam [tamtam] (pl **tam-tams**) **nm** tom-tom.

Tananarive [tananariv] **npr** Antananarivo.

tancer [16] [tɑ̃se] **vt** *littéraire* to rebuke.

tanche [tɑ̃ʃ] **nf** tench.

tandem [tɑ̃dɛm] **nm 1.** [vélo] tandem **2.** [duo] pair ▸ **en tandem** together, in tandem.

tandis [tɑ̃di] ◆ ***tandis que*** **loc conj 1.** [pendant que] while **2.** [alors que] while, whereas.

tangage [tɑ̃gaʒ] **nm** pitching, pitch.

tangent, e [tɑ̃ʒɑ̃, ɑ̃t] **adj : tangent à** MATH tangent to, tangential to ▸ **c'était tangent** *fig* it was close, it was touch and go.
◆ ***tangente*** **nf** tangent.

tangible [tɑ̃ʒibl] **adj** tangible.

tango [tɑ̃go] **nm** tango.

tanguer [3] [tɑ̃ge] **vi** to pitch.

tanière [tanjɛr] **nf** den, lair.

tanin, tannin [tanɛ̃] **nm** tannin.

tank [tɑ̃k] **nm** tank.

tannage [tanaʒ] **nm** tanning.

tannant, e [tanɑ̃, ɑ̃t] **adj** *fam* [assommant] irritating, maddening.

tanner [3] [tane] **vt 1.** [peau] to tan **2.** *fam* [personne] to pester, to annoy.

tannerie [tanri] **nf 1.** [usine] tannery **2.** [opération] tanning.

tanneur [tanœr] **nm 1.** [ouvrier] tanner **2.** [commerçant] leather merchant.

tannin = ***tanin.***

tant [tɑ̃] ■ **adv 1.** [quantité] **: tant de** so much ▸ **tant de travail** so much work ▸ **vous m'avez reçu avec tant de générosité que je ne sais quoi dire** you've made me so welcome that I'm lost for words
2. [nombre] **: tant de** so many ▸ **tant d'années ont passé que j'ai oublié** so many years have gone by that I've forgotten ▸ **tant de livres/d'élèves** so many books/pupils
3. [tellement] such a lot, so much ▸ **il l'aime tant** he loves her so much ▸ **le jour tant attendu arriva enfin** the long-awaited day arrived at last ▸ **tant de gens** so many people
4. [quantité indéfinie] so much ▸ **ça coûte tant** it costs so much ▸ **à tant pour cent** at so many per cent
5. [un jour indéfini] **: votre lettre du tant** your letter of such-and-such a date
6. [comparatif] **: tant que** as much as ▸ **elle ne travaille pas tant que les autres** she doesn't work as much *ou* as hard as the others
7. [valeur temporelle] **: tant que** [aussi longtemps que] as long as / [pendant que] while ▸ **tu peux rester tant que tu veux** you can stay as long as you like ▸ **tant qu'il y a de la vie, il y a de l'espoir** while there's life there's hope ▸ **tant qu'on y est** while we're at it.
■ **nm : suite à votre lettre du tant** with reference to your letter of such and such a date ▸ **vous serez payé le tant** you'll be paid on such and such a date.
◆ ***en tant que*** **loc conj** as ▸ **en tant que tel** as such.
◆ ***tant bien que mal*** **loc adv** after a fashion, somehow or other ▸ **le moteur est reparti, tant bien que mal** somehow, the engine started up again.
◆ ***tant mieux*** **loc adv** so much the better ▸ **tant mieux**

pour lui good for him ▸ **vous n'avez rien à payer – tant mieux!** you don't have anything to pay – good *ou* fine!
◆ ***tant pis*** **loc adv** too bad ▸ **tant pis pour lui** too bad for him ▸ **je reste, tant pis s'il n'est pas content** I'm staying, too bad if he doesn't like it.
◆ ***(un) tant soit peu*** **loc adv** the slightest bit ▸ **si elle avait un tant soit peu de bon sens** if she had the slightest bit of common sense.

Tantale [tɑ̃tal] ➤ ***supplice***.

tante [tɑ̃t] **nf 1.** [parente] aunt **2.** *tfam péj* [homosexuel] poof *UK*, fairy.

tantinet [tɑ̃tinɛ] **nm** tiny bit.
◆ ***un tantinet*** **loc adv** a tiny (little) bit ▸ **un tantinet exagéré/trop long** a bit exaggerated/too long ▸ **un tantinet stupide** a tiny bit stupid.

tantôt [tɑ̃to] **adv 1.** [parfois] sometimes **2.** *vieilli* [après-midi] this afternoon.

Tanzanie [tɑ̃zani] **nf : la Tanzanie** Tanzania.

tanzanien, enne [tɑ̃zanjɛ̃, ɛn] **adj** Tanzanian.
◆ ***Tanzanien, enne*** **nm, f** Tanzanian.

TAO (abr de ***traduction assistée par ordinateur***) **nf** CAT.

taoïsme [taɔism] **nm** Taoism.

taon [tɑ̃] **nm** horsefly.

tapage [tapaʒ] **nm 1.** [bruit] row ▸ **tapage nocturne** ≃ disturbance of the peace **2.** *fig* [battage] fuss *(U)*.

tapageur, euse [tapaʒœr, øz] **adj 1.** [hôte, enfant] rowdy **2.** [style] flashy **3.** [liaison, publicité] blatant.

tapant, e [tapɑ̃, ɑ̃t] **adj : à six heures tapant** *ou* **tapantes** at six sharp *ou* on the dot.

tape [tap] **nf** slap.

tape-à-l'œil [tapalœj] ■ **adj inv** flashy.
■ **nm inv** show.

tapenade [tapənad] **nf** *pounded anchovies with capers, olives and tuna fish.*

taper [3] [tape] ■ **vt 1.** [personne, cuisse] to slap ▸ **taper (un coup) à la porte** to knock at the door **2.** [à la machine] to type ▸ **taper un document à la machine** to type (out) a document **3.** *fam* [demander de l'argent à] **: taper qqn de** to touch sb for ▸ **il m'a tapé de 300 euros** he touched me for 300 euros, he cadged *UK ou* bummed *US* 300 euros off me.
■ **vi 1.** [frapper] to hit ▸ **taper du poing sur** to bang one's fist on ▸ **taper dans ses mains** to clap **2.** [à la machine] to type ▸ **il tape bien/mal** he types well/badly, he's a good/bad typist **3.** *fam* [soleil] to beat down **4.** *fig* [critiquer] **: taper sur qqn** to knock sb ▸ **elle s'est fait taper dessus dans la presse** the newspapers really panned her **5.** *fam* [puiser] **: taper dans** to dip into.
◆ ***se taper*** ■ **vpt** *fam* **1.** [chocolat, vin] to put away **2.** [corvée] to be landed with ▸ **je me suis tapé les cinq étages à pied** I had to walk up the five floors.
■ **vp** *(emploi réciproque)* to hit each other ▸ **ils ont fini par se taper dessus** eventually, they came to blows.

tapette [tapɛt] **nf 1.** [à tapis] carpet beater **2.** [à mouches] flyswatter **3.** *tfam péj* [homosexuel] poof *UK*, fairy.

tapinois [tapinwa] ◆ ***en tapinois*** **loc adv** furtively.

tapioca [tapjɔka] **nm** tapioca.

tapir[1] [tapir] **nm** ZOOL tapir.

tapir[2] [32] [tapir] ◆ ***se tapir*** **vp 1.** [se blottir] to crouch / *fig* [sentiment] to be hidden ▸ **une maison tapie au creux de la vallée** *fig* a house hidden away in the valley **2.** [se cacher] to retreat.

tapis [tapi] **nm 1.** [gén] carpet / [de gymnase] mat ▸ **tapis roulant** [pour bagages] conveyor belt / [pour personnes] travelator ▸ **tapis de sol** groundsheet ▸ **dérouler le tapis rouge** *fig* to roll out the red carpet ▸ **mettre un sujet sur le tapis** *fig* to bring up a subject **2.** INFORM **: tapis de souris** mouse mat *UK*, mouse pad *US*.

tapis-brosse [tapibrɔs] (pl **tapis-brosses**) **nm** doormat.

tapisser [3] [tapise] **vt : tapisser (de)** to cover (with).

tapisserie [tapisri] **nf** [de laine] tapestry / [papier peint] wallpaper ▸ **faire tapisserie** *fig* to be a wallflower.

tapissier, ère [tapisje, ɛr] **nm, f 1.** [artisan] tapestry maker **2.** [décorateur] (interior) decorator **3.** [commerçant] upholsterer.

tapotement [tapɔtmɑ̃] **nm** tapping.

tapoter [3] [tapɔte] ■ **vt** to tap / [joue] to pat.
■ **vi : tapoter sur** to tap on.

tapuscrit [tapyskri] **nm** typescript.

taquet [takɛ] **nm 1.** [butée] stop, catch **2.** [loquet] latch.

taquin, e [takɛ̃, in] ■ **adj** teasing.
■ **nm, f** tease.

taquiner [3] [takine] **vt** [faire enrager] to tease ▸ **cesse de la taquiner** stop teasing her
▸▸ **taquiner le piano/violon** *fam* to play the piano/violin a bit ▸ **taquiner le goujon** to do a bit of fishing.
◆ ***se taquiner*** **vp** *(emploi réciproque)* to tease each other.

taquinerie [takinri] **nf** teasing.

tarabiscoté, e [tarabiskɔte] **adj** elaborate.

tarabuster [3] [tarabyste] **vt 1.** [suj: personne] to badger **2.** [suj: idée] to niggle at *UK*.

tarama [tarama] **nm** taramasalata.

tarauder [3] [tarode] **vt** to tap / *fig* to torment.

tard [tar] **adv** late ▸ **plus tard** later ▸ **au plus tard** at the latest ▸ **sur le tard** [en fin de journée] late in the day / [dans la vie] late in life.

tarder [3] [tarde] ■ **vi : tarder à faire qqch** [attendre pour] to delay *ou* put off doing sthg / [être lent à] to take a long time to do sthg ▸ **ne pas tarder à faire qqch** not to take long to do sthg ▸ **le feu ne va pas tarder à s'éteindre** it won't be long before the fire goes out ▸ **elle ne devrait plus tarder maintenant** she should be here any time now.
■ **v impers : il me tarde de te revoir/qu'il vienne** I am longing to see you again/for him to come.

tardif, ive [tardif, iv] **adj 1.** [heure] late **2.** [excuse] belated.

tardivement [tardivmɑ̃] **adv** [arriver] late / [s'excuser] belatedly.

tare [tar] **nf 1.** [défaut] defect **2.** [de balance] tare **3.** *fam péj* [personne] cretin.

taré, e [tare] ■ **adj 1.** [héréditairement] tainted / *fig* flawed **2.** *fam péj* [idiot] cracked.
■ **nm, f 1.** [héréditaire] degenerate **2.** *fam péj* [idiot] cretin.

tarentule [tarɑ̃tyl] **nf** tarantula.

targette [tarʒɛt] **nf** bolt.

targuer [3] [targe] ◆ ***se targuer*** **vp** *sout* **: se targuer de qqch/de faire qqch** to boast about sthg/about doing sthg.

tarif [tarif] **nm 1.** [prix - de restaurant, café] price / [- de service] rate, price / [douanier] tariff ▸ **tarif douanier** customs rate ▸ **tarifs postaux** postage rates ▸ **demi-tarif** half rate ***ou*** price ▸ **plein tarif** full rate ***ou*** price ▸ **tarif dégressif** decreasing rate ▸ **tarif minimum** minimum charge ▸ **tarif préférentiel** preferential rate ▸ **tarif réduit** reduced price / [au cinéma, théâtre] concession ***UK*** ▸ **à tarif réduit** [loisirs] reduced-price / [transport] reduced-fare **2.** [tableau] price list.

tarifaire [tarifɛr] **adj** tariff *(avant n)*.

tarifer [3] [tarife] **vt** to fix the price ***ou*** rate for.

tarification [tarifikasjɔ̃] **nf** fixing of the price ***ou*** rate.

tarir [32] [tarir] ■ **vt** to dry up.
■ **vi** to dry up ▸ **elle ne tarit pas d'éloges sur son professeur** she never stops praising her teacher.
◆ ***se tarir*** **vp** to dry up.

tarot [taro] **nm** tarot.
◆ ***tarots*** **nmpl** tarot cards.

tartare [tartar] **adj** Tartar ▸ **sauce tartare** tartare sauce ▸ **steak tartare** steak tartare.
◆ ***Tartare*** **nmf** Tartar.

tarte [tart] ■ **nf 1.** [gâteau] tart, pie ***US*** ▸ **tarte aux pommes** apple tart ***UK***, apple pie ***US*** ▸ **tarte tatin** ≃ upside-down apple cake **2.** *fam fig* [gifle] slap **3.** [sujet, propos] hackneyed
▸▸ **c'est pas de la tarte !** *fam* it's no joke ***ou*** picnic! ▸ **tarte à la crème** CINÉ custard pie.
■ **adj** *(avec ou sans accord) fam* [idiot] stupid.

tartelette [tartəlɛt] **nf** tartlet.

tartiflette [tartiflɛt] **nf** *cheese and potato gratin from the Savoy region.*

tartine [tartin] **nf 1.** [de pain] piece of bread and butter ▸ **tartine de confiture** piece of bread and jam ▸ **tartine grillée** piece of toast **2.** *fam fig* [laïus] **: en mettre une tartine *ou* des tartines** to write reams.

tartiner [3] [tartine] **vt 1.** [pain] to spread ▸ **chocolat/fromage à tartiner** chocolate/cheese spread **2.** *fam fig* [pages] to cover.

tartre [tartr] **nm 1.** [de dents, vin] tartar **2.** [de chaudière] fur, scale.

tartuf(f)e [tartyf] **nm** hypocrite.

tas [ta] **nm** heap ▸ **un tas de** a lot of ▸ **apprendre sur le tas** *fig* to learn on the job ▸ **mettre en tas** [feuilles, objets] to pile ***ou*** to heap up ▸ **tas d'ordures** rubbish ***UK ou*** garbage ***US*** heap.
◆ ***sur le tas*** *fam* ■ **loc adj 1.** [formation] on-the-job **2.** CONSTR on-site.
■ **loc adv 1.** [se former] on the job ▸ **il a appris son métier sur le tas** he learned his trade as he went along **2.** CONSTR [tailler] on site.

tasse [tas] **nf** cup ▸ **tasse à café/à thé** coffee/tea cup ▸ **tasse de café/de thé** cup of coffee/tea ▸ **boire la tasse** *fig* to get a mouthful of water.

tasseau, x [taso] **nm** bracket.

tassement [tasmɑ̃] **nm 1.** [de neige] compression / [de fondations] settling **2.** *fig* [diminution] decline.

tasser [3] [tase] **vt 1.** [neige] to compress, to pack down **2.** [vêtements, personnes] **: tasser qqn/qqch dans** to stuff sb/sthg into.
◆ ***se tasser*** **vp 1.** [fondations] to settle **2.** *fig* [vieillard] to shrink **3.** [personnes] to squeeze up **4.** *fam fig* [situation] to settle down.

taste-vin [tastəvɛ̃], ***tâte-vin*** [tatvɛ̃] **nm inv** tasting cup.

tata [tata] **nf** auntie.

tâter [3] [tate] ■ **vt** to feel / *fig* to sound out.
■ **vi : tâter de** to have a taste of.
◆ ***se tâter*** **vp** *fam fig* [hésiter] to be in ***UK ou*** of ***US*** two minds.

tâte-vin = ***taste-vin***.

tatie [tati] **nf** *fam* auntie.

tatillon, onne [tatijɔ̃, ɔn] ■ **adj** finicky.
■ **nm, f** finicky person.

tâtonnement [tatɔnmɑ̃] **nm 1.** [action] groping **2.** *(gén pl)* [tentative] trial and error *(U)*.

tâtonner [3] [tatɔne] **vi** to grope around.

tâtons [tatɔ̃] ◆ ***à tâtons*** **loc adv : marcher/procéder à tâtons** to feel one's way.

tatou [tatu] **nm** armadillo.

tatouage [tatwaʒ] **nm 1.** [action] tattooing **2.** [dessin] tattoo.

tatouer [6] [tatwe] **vt** to tattoo.

taudis [todi] **nm** slum.

taulard = ***tôlard***.

taule = ***tôle***.

taulier = ***tôlier***.

taupe [top] **nf** *litt & fig* mole ▸ **être myope comme une taupe** *fig* to be as blind as a bat.

taupinière [topinjɛr] **nf** molehill.

taureau, x [tɔro] **nm** [animal] bull ▸ **prendre le taureau par les cornes** to take the bull by the horns.
◆ ***Taureau*** **nm** ASTROL Taurus ▸ **être Taureau** to be (a) Taurus.

tauromachie [tɔrɔmaʃi] **nf** bullfighting.

taux [to] **nm 1.** [proportion] rate / [de cholestérol, d'alcool] level ▸ **taux d'échec/de réussite** failure/success rate ▸ **taux de fécondité** reproduction rate ▸ **taux de mémorisation** recall rate ▸ **taux de natalité/mortalité** birth/death rate ▸ **son taux d'invalidité est de 50 %** he's 50% disabled ▸ **taux zéro** zero-rating **2.** ÉCON **: taux de base** FIN minimum lending rate ▸ **taux de change** exchange rate ▸ **taux de couverture** margin ratio ▸ **taux de crédit** lending rate ▸ **taux de croissance** growth rate ▸ **à quel taux prêtent-ils?** what is their lending rate? ▸ **taux d'escompte** rate of discount, discounted rate ▸ **taux fixe** fixed rate ▸ **taux flottant** floating rate ▸ **taux horaire** hourly rate ▸ **taux d'intérêt** interest rate ▸ **taux officiel d'escompte** minimum lending rate ▸ **taux de rendement** rate of return.

taverne [tavɛrn] **nf** tavern.

taxable [taksabl] **adj** taxable, liable to duty.

taxation [taksasjɔ̃] **nf** taxation.

taxe [taks] **nf** tax, controlled price ▸ **hors taxe** COMM exclusive of tax, before tax / [boutique, achat] duty-free ▸ **taxe sur la valeur ajoutée** value-added tax ▸ **taxe d'habitation** *tax paid on residence,* ≃ council tax *UK*, local tax *US* ▸ **toutes taxes comprises** inclusive of tax ▸ **vendre qqch à la taxe** to sell sthg at the controlled price.

CULTURE

Taxe foncière/Taxe d'habitation

In France, tax on domestic properties and commercial buildings (the **taxe foncière**) is due on the 1st of January of each year and payable by owners. Land is taxed only if it isn't cultivated or used as forest. The **taxe d'habitation** is levied on both renters and owners of furnished dwellings and is also due on the 1st of January. It is based on valuation and tax schedules that vary from town to town. Nîmes has France's highest **taxe d'habitation** rates, at around 30% of the value of a property. Reductions are available for the elderly, the handicapped, and those with modest incomes.

taxer [3] [takse] **vt 1.** [imposer] to tax **2.** [fixer] **: taxer le prix de qqch à** to fix the price of sthg at **3.** *fam* [traiter] **: taxer qqn de qqch** to call sb sthg **4.** [accuser] **: taxer qqn de qqch** to accuse sb of sthg **5.** *fam* [prendre] **: taxer qqch à qqn** to cadge sthg off *ou* from sb.

taxi [taksi] **nm 1.** [voiture] taxi, cab *US* **2.** [chauffeur] taxi driver.

taxidermiste [taksidɛrmist] **nmf** taxidermist.

taximètre [taksimɛtr] **nm** meter.

taxinomie [taksinɔmi] **nf** taxonomy.

Taxiphone® [taksifɔn] **nm** pay phone.

tayaut [tajo] = ***taïaut***.

TB, ***tb*** (abr écrite de ***très bien***) VG.

TBE, ***tbe*** (abr écrite de ***très bon état***) vgc.

TCA (abr de ***taxe sur le chiffre d'affaires***) **nf** tax on turnover.

TCF (abr de ***Touring Club de France***) **nm** *French motorists' club,* ≃ AA *UK*, ≃ AAA *US*.

Tchad [tʃad] **nm : le Tchad** Chad ▸ **au Tchad** in Chad.

tchadien, ***enne*** [tʃadjɛ̃, ɛn] **adj** of/from Chad.
◆ ***tchadien*** **nm** [langue] Chadic.
◆ ***Tchadien***, ***enne*** **nm, f** person from Chad.

tchador [tʃadɔr] **nm** chador.

tchatche [tʃatʃ] **nf** *fam* **: avoir la tchatche** to have the gift of the gab.

tchatcher [tʃatʃe] **vi** *fam* to chat (away).

tchécoslovaque [tʃekɔslɔvak] **adj** Czechoslovakian.
◆ ***Tchécoslovaque*** **nmf** Czechoslovak.

Tchécoslovaquie [tʃekɔslɔvaki] **nf : la Tchécoslovaquie** Czechoslovakia.

tchèque [tʃɛk] ■ **adj** Czech.
■ **nm** [langue] Czech.
◆ ***Tchèque*** **nmf** Czech.

tchétchène [tʃetʃɛn] **adj** Chechen.
◆ ***Tchétchène*** **nmf** Chechen.

Tchétchénie [tʃetʃeni] **nf : la Tchétchénie** Chechnya.

TCS (abr de ***Touring Club de Suisse***) **nm** *Swiss motorists' club,* ≃ AA *UK*, ≃ AAA *US*.

TD (abr de ***travaux dirigés***) **nmpl** supervised practical work.

TdF (abr de ***Télévision de France***) **nf** *French broadcasting authority.*

te [tə], ***t'*** **pron pers 1.** [complément d'objet direct] you **2.** [complément d'objet indirect] (to) you **3.** [réfléchi] yourself **4.** [avec un présentatif] **: te voici!** here you are!

té [te] ■ **nm 1.** [équerre] T-square **2.** [menuiserie] tee.
■ **interj** [dialecte] **: té! voilà Martin!** hey, here comes Martin!
◆ ***en té*** **loc adj** T-shaped.

technicien, ***enne*** [tɛknisjɛ̃, ɛn] **nm, f 1.** [professionnel] technician **2.** [spécialiste] **: technicien (de)** expert (in).

technicité [tɛknisite] **nf 1.** [de produit] technical nature **2.** [avance technologique] technological sophistication **3.** [savoir-faire] skill.

technico-commercial, ***e*** [tɛknikokɔmɛrsjal] (mpl **technico-commerciaux**, fpl **technico-commerciales**) ■ **adj** sales engineer *(avant n).*
■ **nm, f** sales engineer.

Technicolor® [tɛknikɔlɔr] **nm** Technicolor®.

technique [tɛknik] ■ **adj** technical.
■ **nf** technique.

techniquement [tɛknikmɑ̃] **adv** technically.

techno [tɛkno] **adj & nf** techno.

technocrate [tɛknɔkrat] **nmf** technocrat.

technologie [tɛknɔlɔʒi] **nf** technology ▸ **de haute technologie** high-tech.

technologique [tɛknɔlɔʒik] **adj** technological.

technologue [tɛknɔlɔg], ***technologiste*** [tɛknɔlɔʒist] **nmf** technologist.

technopole [tɛknɔpɔl] **nf** *large urban centre with teaching and research facilities to support development of hi-tech industries.*

teck, ***tek*** [tɛk] **nm** teak.

teckel [tekɛl] **nm** dachshund.

tectonique [tɛktɔnik] ■ **adj** tectonic.
■ **nf** tectonics *(U)* ▸ **la tectonique des plaques** plate tectonics.

TEE (abr de ***Trans-Europ-Express***) **nm** TEE.

teen-ager [tinedʒœr] (pl **teen-agers**) **nmf** teenager.

tee-shirt (pl **tee-shirts**), ***T-shirt*** (pl **T-shirts**) [tiʃœrt] **nm** T-shirt.

Téflon® [teflɔ̃] **nm** Teflon®.

TEG (abr de ***taux effectif garanti***) **nm** APR.

Téhéran [teerɑ̃] **npr** Tehran.

teignais, ***teignions*** ➤ ***teindre***.

teigne [tɛɲ] **nf 1.** [mite] moth **2.** MÉD ringworm **3.** *fam fig & péj* [femme] cow *UK* / [homme] bastard.

teigneux, euse [tɛɲø, øz] *fam fig & péj* ■ **adj : être teigneuse** [femme] to be a cow *UK* ▸ **être teigneux** [homme] to be a bastard.
■ **nm, f** [femme] cow *UK* / [homme] bastard.

teindre [81] [tɛ̃dr] **vt** to dye.
◆ ***se teindre*** **vp : se teindre les cheveux** to dye one's hair.

teint, e [tɛ̃, tɛ̃t] ■ **pp** ➤ ***teindre***.
■ **adj** dyed.
◆ ***teint*** **nm 1.** [carnation] complexion **2.** [couleur] **: tissu bon** *ou* **grand teint** colourfast *UK ou* colorfast *US* material ▸ **bon teint** *fig* staunch, dyed-in-the-wool.
◆ ***teinte*** **nf** colour *UK*, color *US* ▸ **une teinte de** *fig* a hint of.

teinté, e [tɛ̃te] **adj** tinted ▸ **teinté de** *fig* tinged with.

teinter [3] [tɛ̃te] **vt** to stain.
◆ ***se teinter*** **vp : se teinter de** to become tinged with.

teinture [tɛ̃tyr] **nf 1.** [action] dyeing **2.** [produit] dye.
◆ ***teinture d'iode*** **nf** tincture of iodine.

teinturerie [tɛ̃tyrri] **nf 1.** [pressing] dry cleaner's **2.** [métier] dyeing.

teinturier, ère [tɛ̃tyrje, ɛr] **nm, f 1.** [de pressing] dry cleaner **2.** [technicien] dyer.

tek = ***teck***.

tel, telle (mpl tels, fpl telles) [tɛl] ■ **adj 1.** [valeur indéterminée] such-and-such a ▸ **tel et tel** such-and-such a ▸ **il m'a demandé de lui acheter tel et tel livres** he asked me to buy him such and such books
2. [semblable] such ▸ **un tel homme** such a man ▸ **une telle générosité** such generosity ▸ **de telles gens** such people ▸ **je n'ai rien dit de tel** I never said anything of the sort
3. [valeur emphatique ou intensive] such ▸ **un tel génie** such a genius ▸ **un tel bonheur** such happiness ▸ **la douleur fut telle que je faillis m'évanouir** the pain was so bad that I nearly fainted
4. [introduit un exemple ou une énumération] **: elle a filé tel l'éclair** she shot off like a bolt of lightning ▸ **tel (que)** such as, like ▸ **des métaux tels le cuivre et le fer** metals such as copper and iron
5. [introduit une comparaison] like ▸ **il est tel que je l'avais toujours rêvé** he's just like I always dreamt he would be ▸ **tel quel** as it is/was *etc* ▸ **tout est resté tel quel depuis son départ** everything is just as he left it.
■ **pron indéf : tel veut marcher, tandis que tel autre veut courir** one will want to walk, while another will want to run ▸ **une telle m'a dit qu'il était parti** someone or other told me he'd left.
◆ ***à tel point que*** **loc conj** to such an extent that.
◆ ***de telle manière que*** **loc conj** in such a way that.
◆ ***de telle sorte que*** **loc conj** with the result that, so that.

tél. (abr écrite de ***téléphone***) tel.

télé [tele] **nf** *fam* TV, telly *UK*.
◆ ***de télé*** **loc adj** *fam* [chaîne, émission] TV *(modif)*.

téléachat [teleaʃa] **nm** TV teleshopping ▸ **chaîne de télé-achat** shopping channel.

téléacteur, trice [teleaktɛr, tris] **nm, f** telesalesperson.

télébenne [telebɛn], ***télécabine*** [telekabin] **nf** cable car.

Télécarte® [telekart] **nf** phonecard.

téléchargeable [teleʃarʒabl] **adj** downloadable.

téléchargement [teleʃarʒmɑ̃] **m** INFORM [vers un serveur] to upload.

télécharger [17] [teleʃarge] **vt** to download.

télécommande [telekɔmɑ̃d] **nf** remote control.

télécommander [3] [telekɔmɑ̃de] **vt** to operate by remote control / *fig* to mastermind.

télécommunication [telekɔmynikasjɔ̃] **nf** telecommunications *pl*.

téléconférence [telekɔ̃ferɑ̃s] **nf** teleconference.

télécopie [telekɔpi] **nf** fax.

télécopieur [telekɔpjœr] **nm** fax (machine).

télédétection [teledetɛksjɔ̃] **nf** remote sensing ▸ **satellite de télédétection** spy satellite.

télédiffuser [3] [teledifyze] **vt** to televise.

télédiffusion [teledifyzjɔ̃] **nf** televising.

télédistribution [teledistribysjɔ̃] **nf** cable television.

télé-enseignement [teleɑ̃sɛɲmɑ̃] (pl **télé-enseignements**) **nm** distance learning.

téléfilm [telefilm] **nm** film made for television.

télégramme [telegram] **nm** telegram, wire *US*, cable *US*.

télégraphe [telegraf] **nm** telegraph.

télégraphie [telegrafi] **nf** telegraphy.

télégraphier [9] [telegrafje] **vt** to telegraph, to wire *US*, to cable *US*.

télégraphique [telegrafik] **adj** [fil, poteau] telegraph *(avant n)* ▸ **en style télégraphique** in telegraphic style, in telegraphese.

télégraphiste [telegrafist] **nmf 1.** [technicien] telegraphist **2.** [employé] telegraph boy (f telegraph girl).

téléguidage [telegidaʒ] **nm** remote control.

téléguidé, e [telegide] **adj 1.** [missile] guided **2.** [piloté à distance - avion, jouet] radiocontrolled **3.** *fig* [manipulé] manipulated.

téléguider [3] [telegide] **vt** to operate by remote control / *fig* to mastermind.

téléinformatique [teleɛ̃fɔrmatik] **nf** INFORM data communication.

télématique [telematik] ■ **nf** telematics *(U)*.
■ **adj** telematic.

téléobjectif [teleɔbʒɛktif] **nm** telephoto lens *sg*.

télépaiement [telepemɑ̃] **nm** electronic payment.

télépathie [telepati] **nf** telepathy.

télépathique [telepatik] **adj** telepathic.

téléphérique [teleferik] **nm** cableway.

téléphone [telefɔn] **nm** telephone ▸ **téléphone à carte** cardphone ▸ **téléphone cellulaire** cellular telephone ▸ **téléphone sans fil** cordless telephone ▸ **téléphone portable** mobile phone *UK*, cell(phone) *US* ▸ **téléphone rouge** hotline ▸ **téléphone de voiture** carphone.

téléphoner [3] [telefɔne] ■ **vt** to telephone, to phone.
■ **vi** to telephone, to phone ▸ **téléphoner à qqn** to telephone sb, to phone sb (up) *UK*.
◆ ***se téléphoner*** **vp** *(emploi réciproque)* to call each other ▸ **on se téléphone, d'accord?** we'll talk on the phone later, OK?

téléphonique [telefɔnik] **adj** telephone *(avant n)*, phone *(avant n)*.

téléphoniste [telefɔnist] **nmf** (telephone) operator, telephonist *UK*.

téléprospection [teleprɔspɛksjɔ̃] **nf** telemarketing.

téléréalité [telerealite] **nf** TV reality TV, fly-on-the-wall television ▸ **une émission de téléréalité** fly-on-the-wall documentary / [de style feuilleton] docusoap.

télescopage [teleskɔpaʒ] **nm 1.** [de véhicules] concertinaing **2.** *fig* [d'idées] cross-fertilization.

télescope [teleskɔp] **nm** telescope.

télescoper [3] [teleskɔpe] **vt** [véhicule] to crash into.
◆ ***se télescoper*** **vp 1.** [véhicules] to concertina *UK* **2.** *fig* [idées] to influence each other.

télescopique [teleskɔpik] **adj 1.** [antenne] telescopic **2.** [planète] visible only by telescope.

téléscripteur [teleskriptœr] **nm** teleprinter *UK*, teletypewriter *US*.

télésiège [telesjɛʒ] **nm** chairlift.

téléski [teleski] **nm** ski tow.

téléspectateur, trice [telespɛktatœr, tris] **nm, f** (television) viewer.

télésurveillance [telesyrvejɑ̃s] **nf** remote surveillance.

Télétex® [teletɛks] **nm** teletex.

télétraitement [teletrɛtmɑ̃] **nm** teleprocessing.

télétransmission [teletrɑ̃smisjɔ̃] **nf** remote transmission.

télétravail, aux [teletravaj, o] **nm** teleworking.

télétravailleur, euse [teletravajœr,øz] **nm, f** teleworker.

Télétype® [teletip] **nm** Teletype®.

télévente [televɑ̃t] **nf** [à la télévision] television selling / [via Internet] online selling ***ou*** commerce, e-commerce.

télévisé, e [televize] **adj** [discours, match] televised.

téléviser [3] [televize] **vt** to televise.

téléviseur [televizœr] **nm** television (set).

télévision [televizjɔ̃] **nf** television ▸ **à la télévision** on television ▸ **télévision câblée** cable television ▸ **télévision à la carte** *ou* **à la séance** pay-per-view television ▸ **télévision interactive** interactive television ▸ **télévision numérique** digital television ▸ **télévision à plasma** plasma TV ▸ **télévision par satellite** satellite television.

télévisuel, elle [televizɥɛl] **adj** television *(avant n)*.

télex [telɛks] **nm inv** telex.

télexer [4] [telekse] **vt** to telex.

tellement [tɛlmɑ̃] **adv 1.** [si, à ce point] so / *(+ comparatif)* so much ▸ **tellement plus jeune que** so much younger than ▸ **pas tellement** not especially, not particularly ▸ **ce n'est plus tellement frais/populaire** it's no longer all that fresh/popular **2.** [autant] **: tellement de** [personnes, objets] so many / [gentillesse, travail] so much **3.** [tant] so much ▸ **elle a tellement changé** she's changed so much ▸ **je ne comprends rien tellement il parle vite** he talks so quickly that I can't understand a word.

téloche [telɔʃ] **nf** *fam* telly *UK*.

téméraire [temerɛr] ■ **adj 1.** [audacieux] bold **2.** [imprudent] rash.
■ **nmf** hothead.

témérité [temerite] **nf 1.** [audace] boldness **2.** [imprudence] rashness.

témoignage [temwaɲaʒ] **nm 1.** DR testimony, evidence *(U)* ▸ **faux témoignage** perjury **2.** [gage] token, expression ▸ **en témoignage de** as a token of **3.** [récit] account.

témoigner [3] [temwaɲe] ■ **vt 1.** [manifester] to show, to display **2.** DR **: témoigner que** to testify that.
■ **vi 1.** DR to testify ▸ **témoigner contre** to testify against ▸ **témoigner en faveur de qqn** to testify in sb's favour *UK* *ou* favor *US* **2. : témoigner de** [être le signe de] to show / [certifier] to testify (as) to.

témoin [temwɛ̃] ■ **nm 1.** [spectateur] witness ▸ **être témoin de qqch** to be a witness to sthg, to witness sthg ▸ **prendre qqn à témoin (de)** to call on sb as a witness (of) **2.** DR **: témoin à charge** DR witness for the prosecution ▸ **témoin oculaire** eyewitness ▸ **faux témoin** perjurer ▸ **c'est le témoin du marié** he's the best man **3.** INFORM indicator ▸ **témoin de connexion** cookie **4.** *littéraire* [marque] **: témoin de** evidence *(U)* of ▸ **l'architecture, témoin d'une époque** architecture that bears witness to an era **5.** [preuve] **: elle a bien mené sa carrière, témoin sa réussite** she has managed her career well, her success is a testimony to that **6.** SPORT baton ▸ **passer le témoin** to hand over *ou* to pass the baton.
■ **adj** [appartement] show *(avant n)*.

tempe [tɑ̃p] **nf** temple.

tempérament [tɑ̃peramɑ̃] **nm** temperament ▸ **avoir du tempérament** to be hot-blooded ▸ **ce n'est pas dans mon tempérament** it's not like me, it's not in my nature ▸ **il est d'un tempérament plutôt anxieux** he's the worrying kind.
◆ ***à tempérament*** ■ **loc adj** [achat] on deferred payment.
■ **loc adv** [acheter] on hire purchase *UK*, on an installment plan *US*.

tempérance [tɑ̃perɑ̃s] **nf** temperance, moderation.

tempérant, e [tɑ̃perɑ̃, ɑ̃t] **adj** temperate.

température [tɑ̃peratyr] **nf** temperature ▸ **avoir de la température** to have a temperature ▸ **prendre sa température** to take one's temperature.

tempéré, e [tɑ̃pere] **adj 1.** [climat] temperate **2.** [personne] even-tempered.

tempérer [18] [tɑ̃pere] vt 1. [adoucir] to temper / *fig* [enthousiasme, ardeur] to moderate 2. *fig & littéraire* [douleur, peine] to attenuate, to soothe.
◆ **se tempérer** vp *(emploi réfléchi)* to restrain o.s..

tempête [tɑ̃pɛt] nf storm ▸ **une tempête de** *fig* a storm of ▸ **tempête de sable** sandstorm.

tempêter [4] [tɑ̃pete] vi to rage.

tempétueux, euse [tɑ̃petyø, øz] adj *littéraire* stormy / *fig* tempestuous.

temple [tɑ̃pl] nm 1. HIST temple 2. [protestant] church.

tempo [tɛmpo] nm tempo.

temporaire [tɑ̃pɔrɛr] adj temporary.

temporairement [tɑ̃pɔrɛrmɑ̃] adv temporarily.

temporel, elle [tɑ̃pɔrɛl] adj 1. [défini dans le temps] time *(avant n)* 2. [terrestre] temporal.

temporisateur, trice [tɑ̃pɔrizatœr, tris] ■ adj 1. [stratégie] delaying *(avant n)* 2. [personne] who stalls *ou* delays.
■ nm, f person who stalls *ou* delays.

temporiser [3] [tɑ̃pɔrize] vi to play for time, to stall.

temps [tɑ̃] nm 1. [gén] time ▸ **à plein temps** full-time ▸ **à mi-temps** half-time ▸ **à temps partiel** part-time ▸ **un temps partiel** a part-time job ▸ **en un temps record** in record time ▸ **traitement en temps réel** real-time processing ▸ **au** *ou* **du temps où** (in the days) when ▸ **de mon temps** in my day ▸ **ça prend un certain temps** it takes some time ▸ **ces temps-ci, ces derniers temps** these days ▸ **pendant ce temps** meanwhile ▸ **les premiers temps** at the beginning ▸ **en temps normal** *ou* **ordinaire** usually, in normal circumstances ▸ **en temps utile** in due course ▸ **en temps de guerre/paix** in wartime/peacetime ▸ **il est grand temps de partir** it is high time that we left ▸ **il était temps!** *iron* and about time too! ▸ **avoir le temps de faire qqch** to have time to do sthg ▸ **avoir du temps devant soi** to have time to spare *ou* on one's hands ▸ **être dans les temps** [pour un travail] to be on schedule *ou* time / [pour une course] to be within the time (limit) ▸ **gagner du temps** to save time ▸ **passer le temps** to pass the time ▸ **je passe mon temps à lire** I spend (all) my time reading ▸ **prendre son temps** to take one's time ▸ **temps libre** free time ▸ **temps mort** SPORT stoppage time, injury time / *fig* break, pause ▸ **à temps** in time ▸ **je n'arriverai/je ne finirai jamais à temps!** I'll never make it/I'll never finish in time! ▸ **de temps à autre** now and then *ou* again ▸ **de temps en temps** from time to time ▸ **en même temps** at the same time ▸ **tout le temps** all the time, the whole time ▸ **ne me harcèle pas tout le temps!** don't keep on pestering me! ▸ **tuer le temps** to kill time ▸ **avoir tout son temps** to have all the time in the world ▸ **la cafetière/mon manteau a fait son temps** *fam* the coffee machine's/my coat's seen better days ▸ **ne pas laisser à qqn le temps de se retourner** not to give sb the time to catch his/her breath ▸ **rattraper le temps perdu** to catch up on *ou* make up for lost time ▸ **par les temps qui courent** in this day and age
2. MUS beat ▸ **valse à trois temps** waltz in three-four time
3. GRAMM tense
4. MÉTÉOR weather ▸ **gros temps** rough weather *ou* conditions ▸ **un temps de chien** foul weather ▸ **quel temps fait-il à Nîmes?** what's the weather like in Nîmes?

tenable [tənabl] adj bearable.

tenace [tənas] adj 1. [gén] stubborn 2. *fig* [odeur, rhume] lingering 3. [colle] strong.

ténacité [tenasite] nf 1. [d'odeur] lingering nature 2. [de préjugé, personne] stubbornness.

tenailler [3] [tənaje] vt to torment.

tenailles [tənaj] nfpl pincers.

tenancier, ère [tənɑ̃sje, ɛr] nm, f manager (f manageress).

tenant, e [tənɑ̃,ɑ̃t] nm, f : **tenant du titre** title holder.
◆ **tenant** nm *(gén pl)* [d'une opinion] supporter
▸▸ **d'un seul tenant** in one piece, intact ▸ **les tenants et les aboutissants** [d'une affaire] the ins and outs, the full details.

tendance [tɑ̃dɑ̃s] ■ nf 1. [disposition] tendency ▸ **avoir tendance à qqch/à faire qqch** to have a tendency to sthg/to do sthg, to be inclined to sthg/to do sthg ▸ **tu as un peu trop tendance à croire que tout t'est dû** you're too inclined to think that the world owes you a living 2. [économique, de mode] trend ▸ **les nouvelles tendances de l'art/la mode** the new trends in art/fashion 3. [position, opinion] : **un parti de tendance libérale** a party with liberal tendencies 4. ÉCON trend ▸ **tendance à la baisse** *ou* **baissière** downward trend ▸ **tendances de la consommation** consumer trends ▸ **tendance à la hausse** *ou* **haussière** upward trend ▸ **tendance inflationniste** inflationary trend.
■ adj : **une coupe très tendance** a very fashionable cut.

tendancieusement [tɑ̃dɑ̃sjøzmɑ̃] adv tendentiously.

tendancieux, euse [tɑ̃dɑ̃sjø, øz] adj tendentious.

tendeur [tɑ̃dœr] nm 1. [sangle] elastic strap *(for fastening luggage etc)* 2. [appareil] wire-strainer 3. [de bicyclette] chain adjuster 4. [de tente] runner.

tendinite [tɑ̃dinit] nf tendinitis.

tendon [tɑ̃dɔ̃] nm tendon ▸ **tendon d'Achille** Achilles' tendon.

tendre[1] [tɑ̃dr] ■ adj 1. [gén] tender 2. [matériau] soft 3. [couleur] delicate.
■ nmf tender-hearted person.

tendre[2] [73] [tɑ̃dr] ■ vt 1. [corde] to tighten 2. [muscle] to tense 3. [objet, main] : **tendre qqch à qqn** to hold out sthg to sb 4. [bâche] to hang 5. [piège] to set (up).
■ vi : **tendre à/vers** [évoluer vers] to tend to/towards / [viser à] to aim at.
◆ **se tendre** vp to tighten / *fig* [relations] to become strained.

tendrement [tɑ̃drəmɑ̃] adv tenderly.

tendresse [tɑ̃drɛs] nf 1. [affection] tenderness 2. [indulgence] sympathy.
◆ **tendresses** nfpl : **se faire des tendresses** to be loving with each other.

tendron [tɑ̃drɔ̃] nm *part of veal rib.*

tendu, e [tɑ̃dy] ■ pp ➤ *tendre*[2].
■ adj 1. [fil, corde] taut 2. [pièce] : **tendu de** [velours] hung with / [papier peint] covered with 3. [personne] tense 4. [atmosphère, rapports] strained 5. [main] outstretched.

ténèbres [tenɛbr] nfpl darkness *sg*, shadows / *fig* depths.

ténébreux**, **euse [tenebrø, øz] adj **1.** *littéraire* [forêt] dark, shadowy **2.** *fig* [dessein, affaire] mysterious **3.** [personne] serious, solemn.

teneur [tənœr] nf content / [de traité] terms *pl* ▸ **teneur en alcool/cuivre** alcohol/copper content.

ténia**, **tænia [tenja] nm tapeworm.

tenir [40] [tənir] ■ vt **1.** [objet, personne, solution] to hold ▸ **tenir la main de qqn** to hold sb's hand **2.** [garder, conserver, respecter] to keep ▸ **elle tient ses chiens attachés** she keeps her dogs tied up ▸ **tenir chaud** to keep warm / [avoir reçu] **: les propriétés que je tenais de ma mère** [par héritage] the properties I'd inherited from my mother **3.** [gérer - boutique] to keep, to run ▸ **tenir la caisse** to be at the cash desk, to be the cashier **4.** [apprendre] **: tenir qqch de qqn** to have sthg from sb ▸ **nous tenons de source sûre/soviétique que...** we have it on good authority/we hear from Soviet sources that... **5.** [considérer] **: tenir qqn pour** to regard sb as.

■ vi **1.** [être solide] to stay up, to hold together ▸ **tout ça tient avec de la colle** all this is held together with glue **2.** [durer] to last ▸ **aucun parfum ne tient sur moi** perfumes don't stay on me **3.** [pouvoir être contenu] to fit ▸ **on tient facilement à cinq dans la barque** the boat sits five in comfort ▸ **son histoire tient en peu de mots** his story can be summed up in a few words **4.** [être attaché] **: tenir à** [personne] to care about / [privilèges] to value ▸ **si tu tiens à la vie...** if you value your life... **5.** [vouloir absolument] **: tenir à faire qqch** to insist on doing sthg ▸ **je tiens à ce qu'ils aient une bonne éducation** I'm most concerned that they should have a good education **6.** [ressembler] **: tenir de** to take after **7.** [relever de] **: tenir de** to have something of ▸ **sa guérison tient du miracle** his recovery is something of a miracle **8.** [dépendre de] **: il ne tient qu'à toi de...** it's entirely up to you to...

⏭ **tenir bon** to stand firm ▸ **il me refusait une augmentation, mais j'ai tenu bon** he wouldn't give me a rise but I held out *ou* stood my ground ▸ **qu'à cela ne tienne** it *ou* that doesn't matter ▸ **tiens!** [en donnant] here! / [surprise] well, well! / [pour attirer attention] look!

◆ ***se tenir*** vp **1.** [réunion] to be held **2.** [personnes] to hold one another ▸ **se tenir par la main** to hold hands **3.** [être présent] to be ▸ **se tenir aux aguets** to be on the lookout, to watch out **4.** [être cohérent] to make sense ▸ **je voudrais trouver un alibi qui se tienne** I'm looking for a plausible excuse **5.** [se conduire] to behave (o.s.) ▸ **bien se tenir** to behave o.s. **6.** [se retenir] **: se tenir (à)** to hold on (to) **7.** [se borner] **: s'en tenir à** to stick to ▸ **tenez-vous-en aux ordres** confine yourself to carrying out orders.

tennis [tenis] ■ nm **1.** [sport] tennis **2.** [terrain] tennis court.

■ nmpl tennis shoes, sneakers *US*.

tennisman [tenisman] (pl **tennismen** [tenismen]) nm tennis player.

ténor [tenɔr] ■ adj [instrument de musique] tenor *(avant n)*.

■ nm **1.** [chanteur] tenor **2.** *fig* [vedette] **: un ténor de la politique** a political star performer.

tensioactif**, **ive [tɑ̃sjɔaktif, iv] adj surface-active.

tension [tɑ̃sjɔ̃] nf **1.** [contraction, désaccord] tension **2.** MÉD pressure ▸ **avoir de la tension** to have high blood pressure ▸ **tension artérielle** blood pressure ▸ **tension (nerveuse)** [État] tension, strain, nervous stress **3.** ÉLECTR voltage ▸ **haute/basse tension** high/low voltage.

◆ ***sous tension*** ■ loc adj **1.** ÉLECTR [fil] live **2.** [état physique] tense, under stress.

■ loc adv **: mettre un appareil sous tension** to switch on an appliance.

tentaculaire [tɑ̃takylɛr] adj *fig* sprawling.

tentacule [tɑ̃takyl] nm tentacle.

tentant**, **e [tɑ̃tɑ̃, ɑ̃t] adj tempting.

tentateur**, **trice [tɑ̃tatœr, tris] ■ adj tempting.

■ nm, f tempter (f temptress).

tentation [tɑ̃tasjɔ̃] nf temptation.

tentative [tɑ̃tativ] nf attempt ▸ **tentative d'homicide** attempted murder ▸ **tentative de suicide** suicide attempt.

tente [tɑ̃t] nf tent.

◆ ***tente à oxygène*** nf oxygen tent.

tenter [3] [tɑ̃te] vt **1.** [entreprendre] **: tenter qqch/de faire qqch** to attempt sthg/to do sthg **2.** [plaire] to tempt ▸ **être tenté par qqch/de faire qqch** to be tempted by sthg/to do sthg.

tenture [tɑ̃tyr] nf hanging.

tenu**, **e [təny] ■ pp ➤ ***tenir***.

■ adj **1.** [obligé] **: être tenu à qqch** to be bound by sthg ▸ **être tenu de faire qqch** to be required *ou* obliged to do sthg **2.** [en ordre] **: bien/mal tenu** [maison] well/badly kept.

ténu**, **e [teny] adj **1.** [fil] fine / *fig* [distinction] tenuous **2.** [voix] thin.

tenue [təny] nf **1.** [entretien] running ▸ **l'école est réputée pour sa tenue** the school is renowned for being well-run ▸ **tenue de la comptabilité** bookkeeping **2.** [manières] good manners *pl* ▸ **voyons, un peu de tenue!** come now, behave yourself! **3.** [maintien du corps] posture **4.** [costume] dress ▸ **'tenue correcte exigée'** 'dress code' ▸ **tenue réglementaire** regulation uniform ▸ **tenue de soirée** evening dress ▸ **une tenue de sport** sports gear *ou* kit ▸ **être en petite tenue** to be scantily dressed ▸ **officiers en grande tenue** officers in dress uniform.

◆ ***tenue de route*** nf roadholding ▸ **avoir une bonne tenue de route** to hold the road well ▸ **avoir une mauvaise tenue de route** to have poor road holding.

tequila [tekila] nf tequila.

ter [tɛr] ■ adv MUS three times.

■ adj **: 12 ter** 12B.

TER (abr de ***Train Express Régional***) nm *fast intercity train*.

térébenthine [terebɑ̃tin] nf turpentine.

Tergal® [tɛrgal] nm ≃ Terylene®.

tergiversation [tɛrʒivɛrsasjɔ̃] nf shilly-shallying *(U)*.

tergiverser [3] [tɛrʒivɛrse] vi to shilly-shally.

termaillage [tɛrmajaʒ] m ÉCON leads and lags.

terme [tɛrm] **nm 1.** [fin] end ▸ **sa convalescence touche à son terme** his convalescence will soon be over ▸ **ils arrivèrent enfin au terme de leur voyage** they finally reached the end of their journey ▸ **mettre un terme à** to put an end *ou* a stop to
2. [de grossesse] term ▸ **mener une grossesse à terme** to go full term ▸ **bébé né à terme** baby born at full term ▸ **avant terme** prematurely
3. [échéance] time limit / [de loyer] rent day ▸ **avoir plusieurs termes de retard** to be several months behind (with one's rent) ▸ **à court/moyen/long terme** [calculer] in the short/medium/long term / [projet] short-/medium-/long-term
4. [mot, élément] term ▸ **terme technique** technical term
5. FIN **: à terme** forward *(avant n)* ▸ **assurance à terme** term insurance ▸ **opérations à terme** forward transactions ▸ **passé ce terme, vous devrez payer des intérêts** after that date, interest becomes due.
◆ ***termes*** **nmpl 1.** [expressions] words ▸ **ce furent ses propres termes** those were her very words ▸ **en d'autres termes** in other words
2. [de contrat] terms ▸ **aux termes de la loi/du traité** under the terms of the law/of the treaty
3. [relations] **: être en bons/mauvais termes avec qqn** to be on good/bad terms with sb.

terminaison [tɛrminɛzɔ̃] **nf** GRAMM ending.
◆ ***terminaison nerveuse*** **nf** nerve ending.

terminal, e, aux [tɛrminal, o] **adj 1.** [au bout] final **2.** MÉD [phase] terminal.
◆ ***terminal, aux*** **nm** terminal.
◆ ***terminale*** **nf** SCOL ≃ upper sixth year *ou* form *UK*, ≃ twelfth grade *US*.

terminer [3] [tɛrmine] **vt** to end, to finish / [travail, repas] to finish ▸ **terminer qqch par** to finish sthg with ▸ **je suis bien soulagé d'en avoir terminé avec cette affaire** I'm really glad to have seen the end of this business ▸ **pour terminer, je remercie tous les participants** finally, let me thank all those who took part ▸ **un clip termine l'émission** the programme ends with a pop video.
◆ ***se terminer*** **vp** to end, to finish ▸ **se terminer par** to end *ou* finish with ▸ **l'histoire se termine par la mort du héros** the story ends with the death of the hero ▸ **se terminer en** to end in ▸ **ça s'est terminé en drame** it ended in a tragedy.

terminologie [tɛrminɔlɔʒi] **nf** terminology.

terminus [tɛrminys] **nm** terminus.

termite [tɛrmit] **nm** termite.

termitière [tɛrmitjɛr] **nf** termite nest.

ternaire [tɛrnɛr] **adj** CHIM & MATH ternary / LITTÉR & MUS triple.

terne [tɛrn] **adj** dull.

ternir [32] [tɛrnir] **vt** to dirty / [métal, réputation] to tarnish.
◆ ***se ternir*** **vp** to get dirty / [métal, réputation] to tarnish.

terrain [tɛrɛ̃] **nm 1.** [sol] soil ▸ **terrain sédimentaire/volcanique** sedimentary/volcanic formations ▸ **tout terrain** all-terrain ▸ **vélo tout terrain** mountain bike
2. [surface] piece of land ▸ **terrain accidenté** uneven terrain ▸ **terrain à bâtir** development land *(U)*,building plot ▸ **terrain cultivé/en friche** cultivated/uncultivated land ▸ **terrain vague** waste ground *(U)* *ou* land *(U)* *UK*, vacant lot *US*
3. [emplacement - de football, rugby] pitch *UK* / [- de golf] course ▸ **terrain d'aviation** airfield ▸ **terrain de camping** campsite ▸ **terrain de jeux** playground
4. MIL terrain ▸ **l'armée occupe le terrain conquis** the army is occupying the captured territory
5. *fig* [domaine] ground ▸ **en terrain glissant** *fig* on shaky ground ▸ **être sur son terrain** to be on familiar ground *fig* ▸▸ **céder du terrain à qqn** to give ground to sb ▸ **déblayer le terrain** *fig* to clear the ground ▸ **gagner du terrain** to gain ground ▸ **gagner du terrain sur qqn** to gain on sb ▸ **un homme de terrain** a man with practical experience ▸ **sur le terrain** in the field ▸ **sonde le terrain avant d'agir** see how the land lies before making a move ▸ **trouver un terrain d'entente** to find common ground.

terrasse [tɛras] **nf** terrace.

terrassement [tɛrasmɑ̃] **nm** [action] excavation.

terrasser [3] [tɛrase] **vt** [suj: personne] to bring down / [suj: émotion] to overwhelm / [suj: maladie] to conquer.

terrassier [tɛrasje] **nm** labourer *UK*, laborer *US*.

terre [tɛr] **nf 1.** [monde] world ▸ **si je suis encore sur cette terre** if I am still alive
2. [sol] ground ▸ **par terre** on the ground ▸ **tomber par terre** to fall down ▸ **sous terre** underground ▸ **j'aurais voulu rentrer sous terre** I wished the earth would swallow me up ▸ **terre à terre** *fig* down-to-earth ▸ **terre arable** farmland ▸ **terre battue** [dans une habitation] earth *ou* hard-earth *ou* mud floor / [dans une cour] bare ground / [sur un court de tennis] clay (surface)
3. [matière] earth, soil ▸ **terre cuite** terracotta ▸ **en terre cuite** earthenware *(modif)* ▸ **terre glaise** clay
4. [propriété] land *(U)* ▸ **acheter une terre** to buy a piece of land ▸ **vivre sur/de ses terres** to live on/off one's estates
5. [territoire, continent] land ▸ **sur la terre ferme** on dry land ▸ **les terres arctiques** the Arctic regions ▸ **terre d'exil** place of exile ▸ **terre natale** native land
6. ÉLECTR earth *UK*, ground *US* ▸ **mettre *ou* relier qqch à la terre** to earth *UK* *ou* to ground *US* sthg.
◆ ***Terre*** **nf : la Terre** Earth ▸ **sciences de la Terre** earth sciences ▸ **la Terre promise** the Promised Land ▸ **la Terre Sainte** the Holy Land.

terreau [tɛro] **nm** compost.

terre-neuve [tɛrnœv] **nm inv** Newfoundland (dog).

Terre-Neuve [tɛrnœv] **nf** Newfoundland ▸ **à Terre-Neuve** in Newfoundland.

terre-plein [tɛrplɛ̃] (pl **terre-pleins**) **nm** platform.

terrer [4] [tɛre] ◆ ***se terrer*** **vp** to go to earth.

terrestre [tɛrɛstr] **adj 1.** [croûte, atmosphère] of the earth **2.** [animal, transport] land *(avant n)* **3.** [plaisir, paradis] earthly **4.** [considérations] worldly.

terreur [tɛrœr] **nf** terror.

terreux, euse [tɛrø, øz] **adj 1.** [substance, goût] earthy **2.** [mains, teint] muddy.

terri = ***terril***.

terrible [tɛribl] adj **1.** [gén] terrible **2.** [appétit, soif] terrific, enormous ▸ **avoir un travail terrible** to have a terrific *ou* an enormous amount of work **3.** *fam* [excellent] brilliant.

terriblement [tɛribləmɑ̃] adv terribly.

terrien, ***enne*** [tɛrjɛ̃, ɛn] ■ adj **1.** [foncier] **: propriétaire terrien** landowner **2.** [vertu] rural.
■ nm, f [habitant de la Terre] earthling.

terrier [tɛrje] nm **1.** [tanière] burrow **2.** [chien] terrier.

terrifier [9] [tɛrifje] vt to terrify.

terril [tɛril], ***terri*** [tɛri] nm slag heap.

terrine [tɛrin] nf terrine.

territoire [tɛritwar] nm **1.** [pays, zone] territory **2.** ADMIN area.
◆ ***territoire d'outre-mer*** nm (French) overseas territory.

territorial, ***e***, ***aux*** [tɛritɔrjal, o] adj territorial.

terroir [tɛrwar] nm **1.** [sol] soil **2.** [région rurale] country ▸ **du terroir** rural.

terroriser [3] [tɛrɔrize] vt to terrorize.

terrorisme [tɛrɔrism] nm terrorism.

terroriste [tɛrɔrist] ■ nmf terrorist.
■ adj terrorist *(avant n).*

tertiaire [tɛrsjɛr] ■ nm tertiary sector.
■ adj tertiary.

tertio [tɛrsjo] adv third, thirdly.

tes ➤ ***ton***[2].

tesson [tesɔ̃] nm piece of broken glass.

test [tɛst] nm test ▸ **test d'aptitude** aptitude test ▸ **test aveugle** [marketing] blind test ▸ **tests de concept** concept testing ▸ **tests auprès des consommateurs** consumer testing ▸ **test de dépistage** screening test ▸ **test de dépistage du SIDA** AIDS test ▸ **test de grossesse** pregnancy test ▸ **faire passer un test à qqn** to give sb a test.

testament [tɛstamɑ̃] nm will / *fig* legacy.
◆ ***Testament*** nm **: Ancien/Nouveau Testament** Old/New Testament.

testamentaire [tɛstamɑ̃tɛr] adj of a will.

tester [3] [tɛste] ■ vt to test.
■ vi to make a will.

testicule [tɛstikyl] nm testicle.

tétaniser [3] [tetanize] vt to cause to go into spasm / *fig* to paralyse *UK*, to paralyze *US*.

tétanos [tetanos] nm tetanus.

têtard [tɛtar] nm tadpole.

tête [tɛt] nf **1.** [gén] head ▸ **de la tête aux pieds** from head to foot *ou* toe ▸ **la tête en bas** head down ▸ **la tête la première** head first ▸ **elle s'est trouvée à la tête d'une grosse fortune** she found herself in possession of a great fortune ▸ **calculer qqch de tête** to calculate sthg in one's head ▸ **10 euros par tête** 10 euros a head *ou* each ▸ **tête chercheuse** homing head ▸ **tête d'écriture** INFORM write head ▸ **tête de lecture** INFORM read head ▸ **tête de liste** POLIT main candidate ▸ **tête de mort** death's head ▸ **avoir mal à la tête** to have a headache ▸ **piquer une tête** *fam* to have *ou* go for a dip ▸ **se casser la tête pour faire qqch** *fam fig* to kill o.s. doing sthg ▸ **se laver la tête** to wash one's hair ▸ **se payer la tête de qqn** *fam* to make fun of sb, to take the mickey out of sb *UK* ▸ **avoir la grosse tête** *fam* to be big-headed ▸ **avoir qqch en tête** to have sthg in mind ▸ **en avoir par-dessus la tête** *fam* to be sick (and tired) of it ▸ **être tête en l'air** to have one's head in the clouds ▸ **être tombé sur la tête** *fam* to have a screw loose ▸ **excuse-moi, j'avais la tête ailleurs** sorry, I was thinking about something else *ou* I was miles away ▸ **avoir la tête sur les épaules** to have a good head on one's shoulders ▸ **faire la tête** to sulk ▸ **n'en faire qu'à sa tête** to do exactly as one pleases ▸ **garder la tête froide** to keep a cool head ▸ **perdre la tête** to lose one's head ▸ **tenir tête à qqn** to stand up to sb ▸ **tourner la tête à qqn** to turn sb's head **2.** [visage] face ▸ **avoir une bonne tête** to look like a nice person ▸ **ne fais pas cette tête!** don't pull *UK ou* make such a long face! **3.** [devant - de cortège, peloton] head, front ▸ **prendre la tête du défilé** to head *ou* to lead the procession ▸ **de tête** [- voiture] front *(avant n)* / *fig* [- personne] high-powered ▸ **en tête** SPORT in the lead ▸ **en tête des sondages** leading the polls ▸ **tête de série** SPORT seeded player.

tête-à-queue [tɛtakø] nm inv spin.

tête-à-tête [tɛtatɛt] nm inv tête-à-tête ▸ **en tête-à-tête** alone.

tête-bêche [tɛtbɛʃ] loc adv head to tail.

tête-de-nègre [tɛtdənɛgr] adj inv dark brown.

tétée [tete] nf feed.

téter [tete] vi to suckle.

tétine [tetin] nf **1.** [de biberon, mamelle] nipple, teat **2.** [sucette] dummy *UK*, pacifier *US*.

téton [tetɔ̃] nm **1.** *fam* [sein] breast **2.** TECHNOL nipple.

Tétrabrick® [tetrabrik] nm carton.

tétralogie [tetralɔʒi] nf tetralogy.

tétraplégique [tetrapleʒik] adj quadriplegic.

têtu, ***e*** [tety] adj stubborn.

teuf [tœf] nf *fam* party, rave.

teuf-teuf [tœftœf] nm inv old banger.

teuton, ***onne*** [tøtɔ̃, ɔn] *péj* ■ adj Teutonic.
■ nm, f Teuton.

tex mex [tɛksmɛks] ■ adj Tex Mex.
■ nm Tex Mex food.

texte [tɛkst] nm **1.** [écrit] wording ▸ **dans le texte** in the original ▸ **texte intégral** unabridged text ▸ **texte de loi** legal text **2.** [imprimé] text **3.** [extrait] passage.

textile [tɛkstil] ■ adj textile *(avant n).*
■ nm **1.** [matière] textile **2.** [industrie] **: le textile** textiles *pl*, the textile industry.

texto [tɛksto] ■ adv *fam* word for word, verbatim.
■ nm TÉLÉCOM text (message).

textuel, ***elle*** [tɛkstɥɛl] adj **1.** [analyse] textual / [citation] exact ▸ **il a dit ça, textuel** those were his very *ou* exact words **2.** [traduction] literal.

textuellement [tɛkstɥɛlmɑ̃] adv verbatim.

texture [tɛkstyr] nf texture.

TF1 (abr de ***Télévision Française 1***) nf *French independent television company.*

TG (abr de ***Trésorerie générale***) **nf** *local finance office*.

TGI abr écrite de ***tribunal de grande instance***.

TGV (abr de ***train à grande vitesse***) **nm** *French high-speed train*.

thaï [taj] **nm & adj inv** Thai.
◆ ***Thaï*** **nm, f** Thai.

thaïlandais, e [tajlɑ̃dɛ, ɛz] **adj** Thai.
◆ ***Thaïlandais, e*** **nm, f** Thai.

Thaïlande [tajlɑ̃d] **nf : la Thaïlande** Thailand.

thalasso [talasɔ] **nf** *fam* abr de ***thalassothérapie***.

thalassothérapie [talasɔterapi] **nf** seawater therapy.

thaumaturge [tomatyrʒ] **nm** *littéraire* miracle worker.

thé [te] **nm** tea ▸ **thé au citron/lait** tea with lemon/milk ▸ **thé nature** tea without milk, black tea *UK*.

théâtral, e, aux [teatral, o] **adj 1.** [saison] theatre *(avant n) UK*, theater *(avant n) US* **2.** [ton] theatrical.

théâtralement [teatralmɑ̃] **adv** theatrically.

théâtre [teatr] **nm 1.** [bâtiment, représentation] theatre *UK*, theater *US* ▸ **aller au théâtre** to go to the theatre **2.** [troupe] theatre *UK ou* theater *US* company ▸ **théâtre municipal** local theatre ▸ **théâtres subventionnés** state-subsidized theatres **3.** [art] **: faire du théâtre** to be on the stage ▸ **adapté pour le théâtre** adapted for the stage ▸ **le théâtre de boulevard** mainstream popular theatre *(as first played in theatres on the Paris boulevards)* ▸ **le théâtre de rue** street theatre ▸ **théâtre filmé** film of a play ▸ **metteur en scène de théâtre** (stage) director **4.** [œuvre] plays *pl* **5.** [lieu] scene ▸ **notre région a été le théâtre de nombreuses mutations** our part of the country has seen a lot of changes ▸ **théâtre d'opérations** MIL theatre *UK ou* theater *US* of operations.

théière [tejɛr] **nf** teapot.

théine [tein] **nf** caffeine.

thématique [tematik] ■ **adj** thematic.
■ **nf** themes *pl*.

thème [tɛm] **nm 1.** [sujet & MUS] theme **2.** SCOL prose.
◆ ***thème astral*** **nm** birth chart.

théocratie [teɔkrasi] **nf** theocracy.

théologie [teɔlɔʒi] **nf** theology.

théologien, enne [teɔlɔʒjɛ̃, ɛn] **nm, f** theologian.

théologique [teɔlɔʒik] **adj** theological.

théorème [teɔrɛm] **nm** theorem.

théoricien, enne [teɔrisjɛ̃, ɛn] **nm, f** theoretician.

théorie [teɔri] **nf** theory ▸ **en théorie** in theory.

théorique [teɔrik] **adj** theoretical.

théoriquement [teɔrikmɑ̃] **adv** theoretically.

théoriser [3] [teɔrize] ■ **vt** to theorize about.
■ **vi : théoriser (sur)** to theorize (about).

thérapeute [terapøt] **nmf** therapist.

thérapeutique [terapøtik] ■ **adj** therapeutic.
■ **nf** therapy.

thérapie [terapi] **nf** therapy ▸ **thérapie génique** gene therapy.

thermal, e, aux [tɛrmal, o] **adj** thermal.

thermalisme [tɛrmalism] **nm** ≃ hydrotherapy.

thermes [tɛrm] **nmpl** thermal baths.

thermique [tɛrmik] **adj** thermal.

thermodynamique [tɛrmɔdinamik] ■ **adj** thermodynamic.
■ **nf** thermodynamics *(U)*.

Thermolactyl® [tɛrmɔlaktil] **nm** *thermal clothing fabric*.

thermomètre [tɛrmɔmɛtr] **nm** [instrument] thermometer.

thermonucléaire [tɛrmɔnykleɛr] **adj** thermonuclear.

Thermos® [tɛrmos] **nm & nf** Thermos®(flask).

thermostat [tɛrmɔsta] **nm** thermostat.

thésard, e [tezar, ard] **nm, f** *fam* PhD student.

thésauriser [3] [tezɔrize] ■ **vt** to hoard.
■ **vi** to hoard money.

thésaurus, thesaurus [tezɔrys] **nm inv** thesaurus.

thèse [tɛz] **nf 1.** [opinion] argument ▸ **pièce/roman à thèse** drama/novel of ideas **2.** PHILO & UNIV thesis ▸ **thèse de doctorat** doctorate **3.** [théorie] theory.

thon [tɔ̃] **nm** tuna.

thoracique [tɔrasik] **adj** thoracic.

thorax [tɔraks] **nm** thorax.

thriller [srilœr, trilœr] **nm** thriller.

thrombose [trɔ̃boz] **nf** thrombosis.

thune, tune [tyn] **nf** *fam* cash *(U)*, dough *(U)*.

thuya [tyja] **nm** thuja ▸ **thuya occidental** white cedar.

thym [tɛ̃] **nm** thyme.

thyroïde [tirɔid] **nf** thyroid (gland).

TI abr écrite de ***tribunal d'instance***.

Tibet [tibɛ] **nm : le Tibet** Tibet ▸ **au Tibet** in Tibet.

tibétain, e [tibetɛ̃, ɛn] **adj** Tibetan.
◆ ***Tibétain, e*** **nm, f** Tibetan.

tibia [tibja] **nm** tibia.

tic [tik] **nm** tic.

ticket [tikɛ] **nm** ticket ▸ **ticket de caisse** (till) receipt *UK*, sales slip *US* ▸ **ticket modérateur** *proportion of medical expenses payable by the patient* ▸ **ticket de rationnement** ration coupon ▸ **ticket-repas** ≃ luncheon voucher *UK*, ≃ meal ticket *US* ▸ **avoir un ticket avec qqn** *fam fig* to have made a hit with sb.

tic-tac [tiktak] ■ **interj** tick-tock!
■ **nm inv** tick-tock.

tiédasse [tjedas] **adj** *péj* tepid.

tiède [tjɛd] ■ **adj 1.** [boisson, eau] tepid, lukewarm **2.** [vent] mild **3.** *fig* [accueil] lukewarm.
■ **adv : à boire tiède** serve lukewarm.

tièdement [tjɛdmɑ̃] **adv** half-heartedly.

tiédeur [tjedœr] **nf 1.** [chaleur modérée] tepidness **2.** *fig* [de climat] mildness **3.** *fig* [indifférence] half-heartedness.

tiédir [32] [tjedir] ■ **vt** to warm.
■ **vi** to become warm ▸ **faire tiédir qqch** to warm sthg.

tien [tjɛ̃] ◆ ***le tien, la tienne*** [lətjɛ̃, latjɛn] (mpl les tiens [letjɛ̃], fpl les tiennes [letjɛn]) **pron poss** yours ▸ **les tiens** your family ▸ **mets-y du tien!** make an effort! ▸ **à la tienne!** cheers! ▸ **tu as encore fais des tiennes!** you've been up to your tricks again!

tiendrai, tiendras ➤ ***tenir***.

tienne ■ v ➤ ***tenir***.
■ **pron poss** ➤ ***tien***.

tiens, tient ➤ ***tenir***.

tierce [tjɛrs] ■ **nf 1.** MUS third **2.** [cartes à jouer] [escrime] tierce **3.** TYPO final proof **4.** INFORM [pour des transactions sur Internet] **: tierce partie de confiance** trusted third party.
■ **adj** ➤ ***tiers***.

tiercé [tjɛrse] **nm** *system of betting involving the first three horses in a race.*

tiers, tierce [tjɛr, tjɛrs] **adj : une tierce personne** a third party.
◆ ***tiers*** **nm 1.** [étranger] outsider, stranger **2.** [tierce personne] third party ▸ **assurance au tiers** third-party insurance **3.** [de fraction] **: le tiers de** one-third of ▸ **tiers provisionnel** *thrice-yearly income tax payment based on estimated tax due for the previous year.*

tiers-monde [tjɛrmɔ̃d] **nm : le tiers-monde** the Third World.

tiers-mondisation [tjɛrmɔ̃dizasjɔ̃] **nf : la tiers-mondisation de ce pays** this country's economic degeneration to Third World levels.

tiers-mondiste [tjɛrmɔ̃dist] ■ **adj** favouring *UK ou* favoring *US* the Third World.
■ **nmf** champion of the Third World.

tiers-payant [tjɛrpɛjɑ̃] **nm** *system by which a proportion of the fee for medical treatment is paid directly to the hospital, doctor or pharmacist by the patient's insurer.*

tifs [tif] **nmpl** *fam* hair *(U).*

TIG (abr de ***travail d'intérêt général***) **nm** community service.

tige [tiʒ] **nf 1.** [de plante] stem, stalk **2.** [de bois, métal] rod.

tignasse [tiɲas] **nf** *fam* mop (of hair).

tigre [tigr] **nm** tiger ▸ **jaloux comme un tigre** *fig* fiercely jealous.
◆ ***tigres*** **nmpl** [Philippines, Thaïlande] **: les tigres (asiatiques)** the (Asian) tiger economies.

tigré, e [tigre] **adj 1.** [rayé] striped ⁄ [chat] tabby *(avant n)* **2.** [tacheté] spotted ⁄ [cheval] piebald.

tigresse [tigrɛs] **nf** tigress.

tilleul [tijœl] **nm** lime (tree).

tilsit [tilsit] **nm** *strong firm Swiss cheese with holes in it.*

tilt [tilt] **nm : faire tilt** *fam fig* to ring a bell.

timbale [tɛ̃bal] **nf 1.** [gobelet] (metal) cup ▸ **décrocher la timbale** *fig* to hit the jackpot **2.** CULIN timbale **3.** MUS kettledrum.

timbrage [tɛ̃braʒ] **nm** postmarking.

timbre [tɛ̃br] **nm 1.** [gén] stamp ▸ **timbre dateur** date stamp ▸ **timbre fiscal** revenue stamp ▸ **timbre tuberculinique** tuberculosis patch **2.** [de voix] timbre ▸ **un beau timbre de voix** beautiful mellow tones, a beautiful rich voice **3.** [de bicyclette] bell.

timbré, e [tɛ̃bre] ■ **adj 1.** [papier, enveloppe] stamped **2.** [voix] resonant **3.** *fam* [fou] barmy *UK*, doolally *UK*.
■ **nm, f** *fam* loony.

timbre(-poste) [tɛ̃br(əpɔst)] (pl timbres(-poste)) **nm** (postage) stamp.

timbrer [3] [tɛ̃bre] **vt** to stamp.

timide [timid] ■ **adj 1.** [personne] shy **2.** [protestation, essai] timid **3.** [soleil] uncertain.
■ **nmf** shy person.

timidement [timidmɑ̃] **adv** shyly ⁄ [protester] timidly.

timidité [timidite] **nf 1.** [de personne] shyness **2.** [de protestation] timidness.

timing [tajmiŋ] **nm 1.** [emploi du temps] schedule **2.** [organisation] timing.

timonier [timɔnje] **nm** helmsman.

timoré, e [timɔre] **adj** fearful, timorous.

tintamarre [tɛ̃tamar] **nm** *fam* racket.

tintement [tɛ̃tmɑ̃] **nm** [de cloche, d'horloge] chiming ⁄ [de pièces] jingling.

tinter [3] [tɛ̃te] **vi 1.** [cloche, horloge] to chime **2.** [pièces] to jingle.

tintin [tɛ̃tɛ̃] **interj** *fam* no way!, not a chance!

tintouin [tɛ̃twɛ̃] **nm** *fam* **1.** [vacarme] racket **2.** [souci] worry.

TIP [tip] (abr de ***titre interbancaire de paiement***) **nm** *payment slip for bills,* ≃ bank giro payment slip *UK*.

tique [tik] **nf** tick.

tiquer [3] [tike] **vi** *fam* **: tiquer (sur)** to wince (at).

tir [tir] **nm 1.** [SPORT - activité] shooting ⁄ [- lieu] **: (centre de) tir** shooting range ▸ **tir à l'arc** archery ▸ **tir au but** penalty shoot-out ▸ **tir à la carabine/au pistolet** rifle-/pistol-shooting ▸ **tir au pigeon** clay pigeon shooting
2. [trajectoire] shot
3. [salve] fire *(U)* ▸ **un tir intense/nourri/sporadique** heavy/sustained/sporadic fire ▸ **tir par rafales** firing in bursts ▸ **tir de roquette** rocket attack ▸ **rectifier le tir** *fig* to change one's angle of attache, to change one's approach to a problem
4. [manière, action de tirer] firing.

TIR (abr de ***transports internationaux routiers***) *international road transport agreement allowing lorries to avoid customs until they reach their destination.*

tirade [tirad] **nf 1.** THÉÂTRE soliloquy **2.** [laïus] tirade.

tirage [tiraʒ] **nm 1.** [de journal] circulation ⁄ [de livre] print run ▸ **à grand tirage** mass circulation ▸ **tirage limité** limited edition ▸ **un tirage de 50 000 exemplaires** a print run of 50,000 ▸ **écrivain qui fait de gros tirages** bestselling author **2.** [du loto] draw ▸ **tirage au sort** drawing lots ▸ **nous t'avons désigné par tirage au sort** we drew lots and your name came up **3.** [de cheminée] draught

UK, draft *US* ▸ **le tirage est bon/mauvais** it draws well/ doesn't draw well **4.** [d'un prêt] drawdown **5.** [de vin] drawing off

▸▸ **il y a du tirage** *fam fig* there is some friction.

tiraillement [tirajmɑ̃] **nm** *(gén pl)* **1.** [crampe] cramp **2.** *fig* [conflit] conflict.

tirailler [3] [tiraje] ■ **vt 1.** [tirer sur] to tug (at) **2.** *fig* [écarteler] **: être tiraillé par/entre qqch** to be torn by/between sthg.

■ **vi** to fire wildly.

tirailleur [tirajœr] **nm** skirmisher.

tirant [tirɑ̃] **nm 1.** NAUT **: tirant d'eau** draught ▸ **avoir cinq pieds de tirant d'eau** to draw five feet (of water) **2.** CONSTR [entrait] tie beam / [fer plat] rod **3.** [de mines] strap, tie beam.

tire [tir] **nf** *fam* [voiture] wheels *pl*

▸▸ **vol à la tire** *fam* pickpocketing ▸ **voleur à la tire** *fam* pickpocket.

tiré, e [tire] **adj** [fatigué] **: avoir les traits tirés** *ou* **le visage tiré** to look drawn / ÉCON **: tiré par la demande** demand-led.

tire-au-flanc [tiroflɑ̃] **nm inv** *fam* shirker, skiver *UK*.

tire-botte [tirbɔt] (pl **tire-bottes**) **nm** boot-jack.

tire-bouchon [tirbuʃɔ̃] (pl **tire-bouchons**) **nm** corkscrew.

◆ ***en tire-bouchon*** **loc adv** corkscrew *(avant n)*.

tire-bouchonner [3] [tirbuʃɔne] ■ **vt** to twiddle.

■ **vi** to get *ou* become twisted.

tire-d'aile [tirdɛl] ◆ ***à tire-d'aile*** **loc adv** as quickly as possible.

tire-fesses [tirfɛs] **nm inv** *fam* ski tow.

tire-lait [tirlɛ] **nm inv** breast pump.

tire-larigot [tirlarigo] ◆ ***à tire-larigot*** **loc adv** *fam* to one's heart's content.

tirelire [tirlir] **nf** piggy bank, moneybox *UK*.

tirer [3] [tire] ■ **vt 1.** [gén] to pull ▸ **elle me tira doucement par la manche** she tugged *ou* pulled at my sleeve ▸ **tirer les cheveux à qqn** to pull sb's hair ▸ **tirer la chasse d'eau** to flush the toilet / [rideaux] to draw / [tiroir] to pull open

2. [tracer - trait] to draw / [- plan] to draw up

3. [revue, livre] to print ▸ **'bon à tirer'** 'passed for press' ▸ **un bon à tirer** [épreuve] a press proof ▸ **je voudrais que cette photo soit tirée sur du papier mat** I'd like a matt print of this picture

4. [avec arme] to fire

5. [faire sortir - vin] to draw off ▸ **tirer qqn de** *litt & fig* to help *ou* get sb out of ▸ **tirer qqn de son silence** to draw sb out (of his/her silence) ▸ **tirer un revolver/un mouchoir de sa poche** to pull a gun/a handkerchief out of one's pocket ▸ **tirer la langue** to stick out one's tongue

6. [aux cartes, au loto] to draw ▸ **le gagnant sera tiré au sort** there will be a draw to decide the winner

7. [plaisir, profit] to derive

8. [déduire - conclusion] to draw / [- leçon] to learn

9. [fabriquer] **: tirer qqch de** to derive *ou* to get *ou* to make sthg from ▸ **des produits tirés du pétrole** oil-based products ▸ **tirer des sons d'un instrument** to get *ou* to draw sounds from an instrument ▸ **tirer un film d'une pièce de théâtre** to adapt a play for the screen ▸ **photos tirées d'un film** movie stills

10. [chèque, argent liquide] to draw ▸ **tirer de l'argent d'un compte** to draw money out of *ou* to withdraw money from an account

11. [obtenir, soutirer] **: tirer qqch de : tirer de l'argent de qqn** to extract money from sb, to get money out of sb ▸ **la police n'a rien pu tirer de lui** the police couldn't get anything out of him ▸ **je n'ai pas pu en tirer davantage** I couldn't get any more out of her

12. SPORT [à la pétanque, boule en main] to throw / [boule placée] to knock out *(sep)* / FOOTBALL to take ▸ **tirer un corner** to take a corner / TENNIS [passing-shot, volée] to hit / [en haltérophilie] to lift / [escrime] **: tirer des armes** to fence

▸▸ **tirer qqch au clair** to shed light on sthg.

■ **vi 1.** [tendre] **: tirer sur** to pull on *ou* at ▸ **ne tire pas sur ton gilet** don't pull your cardigan out of shape

2. [aspirer] **: tirer sur** [pipe] to draw *ou* pull on

3. [couleur] **: bleu tirant sur le vert** greenish blue

4. [cheminée] to draw ▸ **la cheminée tire mal** the fireplace doesn't draw properly

5. [avec arme] to fire, to shoot ▸ **on m'a tiré dessus** I was fired *ou* shot at ▸ **tirer à balles/à blanc** to fire bullets/ blanks ▸ **tirer sur qqn** to take a shot *ou* to shoot *ou* to fire at sb

6. SPORT to shoot.

◆ ***se tirer*** **vp 1.** *fam* [s'en aller] to push off ▸ **tire-toi!** [ton menaçant] beat it!, clear *ou* push off!

2. [se sortir] **: se tirer de** to get o.s. out of ▸ **il s'est bien/ mal tiré de l'entrevue** he did well/badly at the interview ▸ **s'en tirer** *fam* to escape ▸ **il ne s'en tirera pas comme ça** he won't get off so lightly, he won't get away with it ▸ **je m'en suis tiré avec une suspension de permis** I got away with my licence being suspended ▸ **il s'est tiré de chez lui** [s'enfuir] he's left home.

tiret [tirɛ] **nm** dash.

tirette [tirɛt] **nf 1.** [planchette] leaf **2.** *Belgique* [fermeture] zip *UK*, zipper *US* **3.** [commande] lever.

tireur, euse [tirœr, øz] **nm, f** [avec arme] gunman ▸ **tireur d'élite** marksman (f markswoman).

◆ ***tireur*** **nm** [de chèque] drawer.

◆ ***tireuse*** **nf : tireuse de cartes** fortune teller.

tiroir [tirwar] **nm** drawer.

tiroir-caisse [tirwarkɛs] (pl **tiroirs-caisses**) **nm** till.

tisane [tizan] **nf** herb(al) tea.

tison [tizɔ̃] **nm** ember.

tisonnier [tizɔnje] **nm** poker.

tissage [tisaʒ] **nm** weaving.

tisser [3] [tise] **vt** *litt & fig* to weave / [suj: araignée] to spin.

tisserand, e [tisrɑ̃, ɑ̃d] **nm, f** weaver.

tissu [tisy] **nm 1.** [étoffe] cloth, material **2.** BIOL tissue ▸ **tissu adipeux** adipose tissue ▸ **tissu conjonctif** connective tissue.

tissu-éponge [tisyepɔ̃ʒ] (pl **tissus-éponges**) **nm** towelling *(U) UK*, toweling *(U) US*.

titan [titɑ̃] **nm** Titan ▸ **de titan** *fig* titanic.

titi [titi] **nm** *fam* : **titi parisien** Parisian urchin.

titiller [3] [titije] **vt** to titillate.

titrage [titraʒ] **nm** **1.** [d'œuvre, de film] titling **2.** [de liquide] titration.

titre [titr] **nm** **1.** [gén] title ▸ **titre courant** running title **2.** [de presse] headline ▸ **faire les gros titres des quotidiens** to hit *ou* to make the front page of the daily newspapers ▸ **gros titre** headline *ou* banner headline **3.** [universitaire] diploma, qualification ▸ **recruter sur titres** to recruit on the basis of (paper) qualifications **4.** DR title ▸ **titre de propriété** title deed **5.** FIN security ▸ **avance sur titres** advance on *ou* against securities ▸ **titre nominatif** registered bond ▸ **titre au porteur** [action] bearer share / [obligation] floater *ou* bearer security ▸ **titre universel de paiement** payment slip formerly used to settle bills **6.** [de monnaie] fineness ▸ **le titre des monnaies d'or et d'argent est fixé par la loi** the precious metal content of gold and silver coins is determined by law **7.** [billet] : **titre de transport** ticket
▸▸ **à titre d'essai** on a trial basis ▸ **à titre exceptionnel** exceptionally ▸ **à titre gracieux** *ou* **gratuit** free of charge ▸ **à titre indicatif** for information ▸ **à titre privé/professionnel** in a private/professional capacity ▸ **à titre indicatif** for information only ▸ **à aucun titre** on any account, in any way ▸ **à juste titre** with just cause, justifiably so ▸ **elle s'est emportée, (et) à juste titre** she lost her temper and understandably *ou* rightly so ▸ **à quel titre?** [en vertu de quel droit] in what capacity? / [pour quelle raison] on what grounds?
◆ ***titre de transport*** **nm** ticket.
◆ ***à titre de*** **loc prép** : **à titre d'exemple** by way of example ▸ **à titre d'information** for information.
◆ ***au même titre que*** **loc prép** in the same way that ▸ **je proteste au même titre que mon voisin** I protest for the same reasons as my neighbour.
◆ ***en titre*** **loc adj** **1.** [titulaire] titular **2.** [attitré] official ▸ **le fournisseur en titre de la cour de Hollande** the official *ou* appointed supplier to the Dutch Court.

titrer [3] [titre] **vt** **1.** [œuvre] to title **2.** [liquide] to titrate.

titrisation [titrizas] **nf** securitization.

tituber [3] [titybe] **vi** to totter.

titulaire [titylɛr] ■ **adj** [employé] permanent / UNIV with tenure.
■ **nmf** [de passeport, permis] holder / [de poste, chaire] occupant / FIN account holder.

titulariser [3] [titylarize] **vt** to give tenure to.

TNP (abr de ***traité de non-prolifération***) **nm** NPT.

TNT (abr de ***trinitrotoluène***) **nm** TNT.

toast [tost] **nm** **1.** [pain grillé] toast *(U)* **2.** [discours] toast ▸ **porter un toast à** to drink a toast to.

toasteur [tɔstœr] **nm** toaster.

toboggan [tɔbɔgɑ̃] **nm** **1.** [traîneau] toboggan **2.** [de terrain de jeu] slide / [de piscine] chute **3.** AUTO flyover *UK*, overpass *US*.

toc [tɔk] ■ **interj** : **et toc!** so there!
■ **nm** *fam* : **c'est du toc** it's fake ▸ **en toc** fake *(avant n)*.
■ **adj inv** rubbishy.

TOC [tɔk] (abr de ***troubles obsessionnels compulsifs***) **nmpl** MÉD OCD.

tocard, e [tɔkar, ard] **adj** *fam* [tableau, décor] naff *UK*, tacky.
◆ ***tocard*** **nm** *fam* **1.** [cheval] old nag **2.** [personne] dead loss, (born) loser.

tocsin [tɔksɛ̃] **nm** alarm bell.

Togo [tɔgo] **nm** : **le Togo** Togo ▸ **au Togo** in Togo.

togolais, e [tɔgɔlɛ, ɛz] **adj** Togolese.
◆ ***Togolais, e*** **nm, f** Togolese person ▸ **les Togolais** the Togolese.

tohu-bohu [tɔybɔy] **nm inv** commotion.

toi [twa] **pron pers** you ▸ **à toi de jouer!** your turn! ▸ **alors, tu es content de toi?** I hope you're pleased with yourself, then! ▸ **c'est toi qui le dis!** that's what you say! ▸ **habille-toi!** get dressed! ▸ **qu'est-ce que tu en sais, toi?** what do you know about it? ▸ **un ami à toi** *fam* a friend of yours.
◆ ***toi-même*** **pron pers** yourself.

toile [twal] **nf** **1.** [étoffe] cloth / [de lin] linen ▸ **toile cirée** oilcloth **2.** [tableau] canvas, picture **3.** NAUT [voilure] sails *pl*.
◆ ***toile d'araignée*** **nf** spider's web.
◆ ***toile de fond*** **nf** backdrop.
◆ ***Toile*** **nf** : **la Toile** INFORM the Web, the web.

toilettage [twalɛtaʒ] **nm** grooming.

toilette [twalɛt] **nf** **1.** [de personne, d'animal] washing ▸ **faire sa toilette** to (have a) wash *UK*, to wash up *US* **2.** [parure, vêtements] outfit, clothes *pl* **3.** [de monument, voiture] cleaning **4.** [de texte] tidying up.
◆ ***toilettes*** **nfpl** toilet(s) *UK*, bath room *US*, rest room *US*.

toiletter [4] [twalɛte] **vt** **1.** [chien, chat] to groom ▸ **je fais toiletter le chien au moins une fois par mois** I take the dog to be groomed at least once a month **2.** *fam* [modifier légèrement - texte] to amend, to doctor.

toise [twaz] **nf** height gauge.

toiser [3] [twaze] **vt** to eye (up and down).
◆ ***se toiser*** **vp** to eye each other up and down.

toison [twazɔ̃] **nf** **1.** [pelage] fleece **2.** [chevelure] mop (of hair).

toit [twa] **nm** roof ▸ **toit ouvrant** sunroof.

toiture [twatyr] **nf** roof, roofing.

Tokyo [tɔkjo] **npr** Tokyo.

tôlard, e, taulard, e [tolar, ard] **nm, f** *tfam* jailbird, con.

tôle [tol] **nf** **1.** [de métal] sheet metal ▸ **tôle ondulée** corrugated iron **2.** *tfam* [prison] nick *UK*, clink.

tolérable [tɔlerabl] **adj** **1.** [comportement] excusable **2.** [douleur] bearable, tolerable.

tolérance [tɔlerɑ̃s] **nf** **1.** [gén] tolerance **2.** [liberté] concession.

tolérant, e [tɔlerɑ̃, ɑ̃t] **adj 1.** [large d'esprit] tolerant **2.** [indulgent] liberal.

tolérer [18] [tɔlere] **vt** to tolerate.
◆ ***se tolérer*** **vp** to put up with *ou* tolerate each other.

tôlier, ère, taulier, ère [tolje, ɛr] **nm, f** *tfam* [propriétaire] hotel owner.

tollé [tɔle] **nm** protest ▸ **soulever un tollé général** *fig* to cause a general outcry.

tomate [tɔmat] **nf** tomato ▸ **tomates à la provençale** *baked or fried tomatoes with herbs, breadcrumbs and garlic.*

tombal, e, aux [tɔ̃bal, o] **adj : pierre tombale** gravestone.

tombant, e [tɔ̃bɑ̃, ɑ̃t] **adj** [moustaches] drooping / [épaules] sloping.

tombe [tɔ̃b] **nf 1.** [fosse] grave, tomb **2.** [pierre] gravestone, tombstone.

tombeau, x [tɔ̃bo] **nm** tomb ▸ **rouler à tombeau ouvert** *fig* to drive at breakneck speed.

tombée [tɔ̃be] **nf** fall ▸ **à la tombée du jour** *ou* **de la nuit** at nightfall.

tomber [3] [tɔ̃be] ■ **vi** *(v aux : être)* **1.** [gén] to fall ▸ **faire tomber qqn** to knock sb over *ou* down ▸ **tomber de sommeil** to be asleep on one's feet ▸ **tomber raide mort** to drop down dead ▸ **je suis tombé de haut** *fig* you could have knocked me down with a feather ▸ **j'ai fait tomber mes lunettes** I've dropped my glasses ▸ **tomber bien** [robe] to hang well / *fig* [visite, personne] to come at a good time ▸ **ah, vous tombez bien, je voulais justement vous parler** ah, you've come just at the right moment, I wanted to speak to you
2. [cheveux] to fall out ▸ **ses longs cheveux lui tombaient dans le dos** her long hair hung down her back
3. [nouvelle] to break ▸ **à 20 h, la nouvelle est tombée** the news came through at 8 p.m.
4. [diminuer - prix] to drop, to fall / [- fièvre, vent] to drop / [- jour] to come to an end / [- colère] to die down ▸ **la température est tombée de 10 degrés** the temperature has dropped *ou* fallen (by) 10 degrees
5. [devenir brusquement] **: tomber malade** to fall ill ▸ **tomber amoureux** to fall in love ▸ **tomber enceinte** to become pregnant ▸ **être bien/mal tombé** to be lucky/unlucky ▸ **tomber en ruine** to go to rack and ruin
6. [trouver] **: tomber sur** to come across ▸ **je suis tombé sur ton article dans le journal** I came across your article in the newspaper
7. [attaquer] **: tomber sur** to set about ▸ **il tombe sur les nouveaux pour la moindre erreur** he comes down on the newcomers like a ton of bricks if they make the slightest mistake
8. [se placer] **: tomber sous** [loi, juridiction] to come *ou* fall under ▸ **tomber sous la main** to come to hand
9. [date, événement] to fall on ▸ **mon anniversaire tombe un dimanche** my birthday is *ou* falls on a Sunday.
■ **vt** *(v aux : être) fam* [séduire] to lay ▸ **il les tombe toutes** he's got them falling at his feet.

tombeur [tɔ̃bœr] **nm** *fam fig* womanizer, Casanova.

tombola [tɔ̃bɔla] **nf** raffle.

tome [tɔm] **nm** volume.

tomme [tɔm] **nf : tomme (de Savoie)** *semi-hard cow's milk cheese from Savoy.*

tommette [tɔmɛt] **nf** terracotta floor tile.

ton[1] [tɔ̃] **nm 1.** [de voix] tone ▸ **hausser/baisser le ton** to raise/lower one's voice ▸ **ne me parle pas sur ce ton!** don't speak to me like that *ou* in that tone of voice! ▸ **ne le prends pas sur ce ton!** don't take it like that! ▸ **on nous répète sur tous les tons que...** we're being told over and over again that..., it's being drummed into us that... ▸ **sur le ton de la plaisanterie** jokingly, in jest, in a joking tone ▸ **ton monocorde** drone ▸ **sur un ton monocorde** monotonously ▸ **ton nasillard** twang ▸ **d'un ton sec** curtly **2.** MUS key ▸ **donner le ton** to give the chord / *fig* to set the tone ▸ **le ton majeur/mineur** major/minor key ▸ **il est de bon ton de mépriser l'argent** *fig* it's quite the thing *ou* good form to despise money ▸ **tu crois que je serai dans le ton?** *fig* do you think I'll fit in? ▸ **elle a très vite donné le ton de la conversation** she quickly set the tone of the conversation **3.** [couleur] tone, shade ▸ **être dans le même ton que** to tone in with ▸ **les verts sont en tons dégradés** the greens are shaded (from dark to light).

ton[2]***, ta, tes*** [tɔ̃, ta, te] **adj poss** your ▸ **ta meilleure amie** your best friend ▸ **un de tes amis** one of your friends, a friend of yours.

tonalité [tɔnalite] **nf 1.** MUS tonality **2.** *fig* [impression] tone **3.** [au téléphone] dialling tone *UK*, dial tone *US*.

tondeuse [tɔ̃døz] **nf** [à cheveux] clippers *pl* ▸ **tondeuse (à gazon)** mower, lawnmower.

tondre [75] [tɔ̃dr] **vt** [gazon] to mow / [mouton] to shear / [caniche, cheveux] to clip ▸ **se laisser** *ou* **se faire tondre par qqn** *fig* to be fleeced by sb.

tondu, e [tɔ̃dy] **adj** [caniche, cheveux] clipped / [pelouse] mown.

tongs [tɔ̃g] **nfpl** flip-flops *UK*, thongs *US*.

tonicité [tɔnisite] **nf** [des muscles] tone.

tonifiant, e [tɔnifjɑ̃, ɑ̃t] **adj** [climat] invigorating, bracing / [lecture] stimulating.

tonifier [9] [tɔnifje] **vt** [peau] to tone / [esprit] to stimulate.

tonique [tɔnik] ■ **adj 1.** [boisson] tonic *(avant n)* / [froid] bracing / [lotion] toning **2.** LING & MUS tonic.
■ **nm** MÉD tonic.
■ **nf** MUS tonic, keynote.

tonitruant, e [tɔnitryɑ̃, ɑ̃t] **adj** booming.

tonnage [tɔnaʒ] **nm** tonnage.

tonnant, e [tɔnɑ̃, ɑ̃t] **adj** thundering, thunderous.

tonne [tɔn] **nf 1.** [1000 kg] tonne **2.** [grande quantité] **: des tonnes de** tons *ou* loads of **3.** [tonneau] tun.

tonneau, x [tɔno] **nm 1.** [baril] barrel, cask **2.** [de voiture] roll **3.** NAUT ton.

tonnelet [tɔnlɛ] **nm** keg, small cask.

tonnelle [tɔnɛl] **nf** bower, arbour.

tonner [3] [tɔne] **vi** to thunder.

tonnerre [tɔnɛr] **nm** thunder ▸ **coup de tonnerre** thunderclap / *fig* bombshell ▸ **du tonnerre** *fam fig* terrific, great.

tonsure [tɔ̃syr] **nf** tonsure.

tonte [tɔ̃t] **nf** [de mouton] shearing / [de gazon] mowing / [de caniche, cheveux] clipping.

tonton [tɔ̃tɔ̃] **nm** uncle.

tonus [tɔnys] **nm 1.** [dynamisme] energy **2.** [de muscle] tone.

top [tɔp] ■ **nm** [signal] beep.
■ **adj** *fam* : **être au top niveau** to be at the top (level).
◆ ***top secret*** **adj inv** top secret.

topaze [tɔpaz] **nf** topaz.

toper [3] [tɔpe] **vi : tope-là!** right, you're on!

topinambour [tɔpinɑ̃bur] **nm** Jerusalem artichoke.

topique [tɔpik] ■ **adj** pertinent.
■ **nm** topical *ou* local remedy.

topo [tɔpo] **nm** *fam* spiel ▸ **c'est toujours le même topo** *fig* it's always the same old story.

topographie [tɔpɔgrafi] **nf** topography.

topographique [tɔpɔgrafik] **adj** topographical.

toponymie [tɔpɔnimi] **nf** toponymy.

toquade [tɔkad] **nf : toquade (pour)** [personne] crush (on) / [style, mode] craze (for).

toque [tɔk] **nf** [de juge, de jockey] cap / [de cuisinier] hat.

toqué, e [tɔke] *fam* ■ **adj : toqué (de)** crazy (about), nuts (about).
■ **nm, f** nutter *UK*, nutcase.

torche [tɔrʃ] **nf** torch ▸ **torche électrique** (electric) torch *UK*, flashlight *US*.

torcher [3] [tɔrʃe] **vt** *fam* **1.** [assiette, fesses] to wipe **2.** [travail] to dash off **3.** [bouteille] to polish off.
◆ ***se torcher*** **vp** *tfam* to wipe one's bottom.

torchis [tɔrʃi] **nm** daub *(building material)*.

torchon [tɔrʃɔ̃] **nm 1.** [serviette] cloth **2.** *fam* [travail] mess **3.** *fam* [journal] rag.

tordant, e [tɔrdɑ̃, ɑ̃t] **adj** *fam* hilarious.

tord-boyaux [tɔrbwajo] **nm inv** *fam* gutrot.

tordre [76] [tɔrdr] **vt 1.** [gén] to twist **2.** [linge] to wring (out).
◆ ***se tordre*** **vp : se tordre la cheville** to twist one's ankle ▸ **se tordre de douleur** *fig* to be racked with pain ▸ **se tordre de rire** *fam fig* to double up with laughter.

tordu, e [tɔrdy] ■ **pp** ➤ ***tordre***.
■ **adj** *fam* [bizarre, fou] crazy / [esprit] warped.
■ **nm, f** *fam* nutcase.

toréador [tɔreadɔr], ***torero*** [tɔrero] **nm** bullfighter.

tornade [tɔrnad] **nf** tornado.

torpeur [tɔrpœr] **nf** torpor.

torpille [tɔrpij] **nf 1.** MIL torpedo **2.** [poisson] torpedo, electric ray.

torpiller [3] [tɔrpije] **vt** to torpedo.

torpilleur [tɔrpijœr] **nm** torpedo boat.

torréfaction [tɔrefaksjɔ̃] **nf** roasting.

torréfier [9] [tɔrefje] **vt** to roast.

torrent [tɔrɑ̃] **nm** torrent ▸ **pleuvoir à torrents** *fig* to pour down ▸ **un torrent de** *fig* [injures] a stream of / [lumière, larmes] a flood of.

torrentiel, elle [tɔrɑ̃sjɛl] **adj** torrential.

torride [tɔrid] **adj** torrid.

tors, e [tɔr, tɔrs] **adj** twisted.

torsade [tɔrsad] **nf 1.** [de cheveux] twist, coil **2.** [de pull] cable **3.** ARCHIT cabling, cable moulding.
◆ ***à torsades*** **loc adj** ARCHIT cabled.

torsader [3] [tɔrsade] **vt** to twist.

torse [tɔrs] **nm** chest ▸ **bomber le torse** to puff *ou* throw out one's chest / *fig* to puff up (with pride).

torsion [tɔrsjɔ̃] **nf** twisting / PHYS torsion.

tort [tɔr] **nm 1.** [erreur] fault ▸ **avoir tort** to be wrong ▸ **avoir tort de faire qqch** to be wrong to do sthg ▸ **tu as tort de ne pas la prendre au sérieux** you're making a mistake in not taking her seriously, you're wrong not to take her seriously ▸ **parler à tort et à travers** to talk nonsense ▸ **elle dépense son argent à tort et à travers** money burns a hole in her pocket, she spends money like water ▸ **donner tort à qqn** [désapprouver] to disagree with sb ▸ **être dans son *ou* en tort** to be in the wrong ▸ **dans cet accident, c'est lui qui est en tort** he is to blame for the accident ▸ **reconnaître ses torts** to acknowledge one's

COMMENT EXPRIMER...

qu'on donne tort à quelqu'un

With respect, I think you're mistaken / Sauf votre respect, je crois que vous vous trompez
I'm sorry, but you're wrong / Je regrette, mais vous avez tort
You've got it all wrong / Vous n'avez rien compris
You've got the wrong end of the stick! / Vous avez tout compris de travers !
That can't be right, surely / Ça ne peut pas être ça, si ?
Actually, that's not strictly true / En fait, ce n'est pas tout à fait exact
I'm sorry, I don't accept your assessment of my report / Je suis désolé. Je ne suis pas d'accord avec votre évaluation de mon rapport
I beg to differ / Permettez-moi de ne pas partager votre avis
Rubbish! / N'importe quoi !

faults ▸ **à tort** wrongly ▸ **condamner qqn à tort** to blame sb wrongly ▸ **à tort ou à raison** rightly or wrongly ▸ **les torts sont partagés** both parties are equally to blame **2.** [préjudice] wrong ▸ **causer** *ou* **faire du tort à qqn** to wrong sb ▸ **réparer le tort qu'on a causé** to right the wrong one has caused, to make good the wrong one has done ▸ **réparer un tort** to make amends ▸ **avoir tous les torts** [gén] to be entirely to blame / [dans un accident] to be fully responsible / [dans un divorce] to be the guilty party.

torticolis [tɔrtikɔli] **nm** stiff neck.

tortillement [tɔrtijmɑ̃] **nm** wriggling, writhing.

tortiller [3] [tɔrtije] ■ **vt** [enrouler] to twist / [moustache] to twirl.
■ **vi : tortiller des hanches** to swing one's hips ▸ **il n'y a pas à tortiller** *fig* there's no getting out of it.
◆ ***se tortiller*** **vp** to writhe, to wriggle.

tortionnaire [tɔrsjɔnɛr] ■ **nmf** torturer.
■ **adj** given to torture.

tortue [tɔrty] **nf** tortoise / *fig* slowcoach *UK*, slowpoke *US*.

tortueux, ***euse*** [tɔrtɥø, øz] **adj** winding, twisting / *fig* tortuous.

torture [tɔrtyr] **nf** torture ▸ **sous la torture** under torture.

torturer [3] [tɔrtyre] **vt** to torture.
◆ ***se torturer*** **vp** to torment o.s. ▸ **se torturer pour** to agonize over.

torve [tɔrv] **adj : œil** *ou* **regard torve** threatening look.

tôt [to] **adv 1.** [de bonne heure] early ▸ **se lever tôt** [ponctuellement] to get up early / [habituellement] to be an early riser **2.** [avant le moment prévu] soon ▸ **il est trop tôt pour le dire** it's too early *ou* soon to say that ▸ **il fallait y penser plus tôt** you should have thought about it earlier *ou* before **3.** [vite] soon, early ▸ **ce n'est pas trop tôt!** *fam* and about time too! ▸ **tôt ou tard** sooner or later ▸ **tôt ou tard, quelqu'un se plaindra** sooner or later *ou* one of these days, someone's bound to complain ▸ **le plus tôt possible** as early *ou* as soon as possible.
◆ ***au plus tôt*** **loc adv** at the earliest ▸ **samedi au plus tôt** on Saturday at the earliest.

total, ***e***, ***aux*** [tɔtal, o] **adj** total ▸ **somme totale** total (amount).
◆ ***total*** **nm** total ▸ **au total** in total / *fig* on the whole, all in all ▸ **faire le total** to work out the total.

totalement [tɔtalmɑ̃] **adv** totally.

totaliser [3] [tɔtalize] **vt 1.** [additionner] to add up, to total **2.** [réunir] to have a total of.

totalitaire [tɔtalitɛr] **adj** totalitarian.

totalitarisme [tɔtalitarism] **nm** totalitarianism.

totalité [tɔtalite] **nf 1.** [intégralité] whole ▸ **la totalité de** [inscrits] all (of) / [classe] the whole of, the entire ▸ **la totalité de la somme** the whole (of the) sum **2.** [ensemble] **: la totalité des marchandises** all the goods ▸ **la presque totalité des tableaux** almost all the paintings **3.** PHILO totality, wholeness.
◆ ***en totalité*** **loc adv : somme remboursée en totalité** sum paid back in full ▸ **le navire a été détruit en totalité** the ship was completely destroyed, the whole ship was destroyed.

totem [tɔtɛm] **nm** totem.

touareg, ***ègue*** [twarɛg] **adj** Tuareg.
◆ ***touareg*** **nm** [langue] Tuareg.
◆ ***Touareg***, ***ègue*** **nm, f** Tuareg.

toubib [tubib] **nmf** *fam* doc.

toucan [tukɑ̃] **nm** toucan.

touchant, ***e*** [tuʃɑ̃, ɑ̃t] **adj** touching.

touche [tuʃ] **nf 1.** [de clavier] key ▸ **touche alphanumérique** alphanumeric key ▸ **touche entrée/contrôle** enter/controlkey ▸ **touche fléchée** *ou* **de direction** arrow key ▸ **touche de fonction** function key
2. [de peinture] stroke ▸ **du vert en touches légères** light strokes of green ▸ **mettre la touche finale à qqch** *fig* to put the finishing touches to sthg
3. *fig* [note] **: une touche de** a touch of ▸ **une touche de cynisme** a touch *ou* tinge *ou* hint of cynicism
4. *fam* [allure] appearance, look ▸ **on avait une de ces touches avec nos cheveux mouillés!** we did look funny with our hair all wet!
5. [à la pêche] bite ▸ **faire une touche** *fig* to make a hit ▸ **avoir une touche avec qqn** *fam fig* to have something going with sb
6. [FOOTBALL - ligne] touch line / [- remise en jeu] throw-in / [rugby - ligne] touch (line) / [- remise en jeu] line-out ▸ **envoyer le ballon en touche** to kick the ball into touch ▸ **être mis/rester sur la touche** *fig* to be left/to stay on the sidelines ▸ **quand il a eu 50 ans, ils l'ont mis sur la touche** when he was fifty, they put him out to grass *ou* they threw him on the scrap heap
7. [escrime] hit.

touche-à-tout [tuʃatu] **nmf** [adulte] dabbler / [enfant] **: c'est un petit touche-à-tout** he's into everything.

toucher [3] [tuʃe] ■ **nm : le toucher** the (sense of) touch ▸ **au toucher** to the touch ▸ **doux/rude au toucher** soft/rough to the touch ▸ **il a un bon toucher de balle** he's got a nice touch.
■ **vt 1.** [palper, émouvoir] to touch ▸ **ne me touche pas!** get your hands off me!, don't touch me! ▸ **elle a été très touchée par sa disparition** she was badly shaken by his death ▸ **vos compliments me touchent beaucoup** I'm very touched by your kind words
2. [correspondant] to contact, to reach ▸ **si notre message l'avait touché...** if our message had got (through) to him *ou* reached him... ▸ **où peut-on vous toucher?** where can you be contacted *ou* reached? / [cible] to hit
3. [rivage] to reach / [cible] to hit
4. [salaire] to get, to be paid / [chèque] to cash / [gros lot] to win ▸ **toucher le tiercé** to win the tiercé
5. [concerner] to affect, to concern ▸ **une affaire qui touche la Défense nationale** a matter related to defence, a defence-related matter.
■ **vi : toucher à** to touch / [problème] to touch on / [inconscience, folie] to border *ou* verge on / [maison] to adjoin ▸ **ne touchez pas aux parcs nationaux!** hands off the

national parks! ▸ **je n'ai jamais touché à la drogue** I've never been on *ou* touched drugs ▸ **toucher à la perfection** to be close to perfection ▸ **toucher à tout** *litt* to fiddle with *ou* to touch everything / *fig* to dabble (in everything) ▸ **toucher à sa fin** to draw to a close ▸ **le projet touche à son terme** the project is nearing its end.
◆ ***se toucher*** vp [maisons] to be adjacent (to each other), to adjoin (each other).

touffe [tuf] **nf** tuft.

touffu, ***e*** [tufy] **adj** [forêt] dense / [barbe] bushy.

touiller [3] [tuje] **vt** *fam* [mélanger] to stir / [salade] to toss.

toujours [tuʒur] **adv 1.** [continuité, répétition] always ▸ **ils s'aimeront toujours** they will always love one another, they will love one another forever ▸ **elle est toujours en retard** she is always late ▸ **toujours plus** more and more ▸ **toujours moins** less and less **2.** [encore] still ▸ **toujours pas** still not ▸ **elle n'a toujours pas téléphoné** she hasn't phoned yet, she still hasn't phoned **3.** [de toute façon] anyway, anyhow.
◆ ***de toujours*** **loc adj : ce sont des amis de toujours** they are lifelong friends.
◆ ***pour toujours*** **loc adv** forever, for good.
◆ ***toujours est-il que*** **loc conj** the fact remains that.

toundra [tundra] **nf** tundra.

toupet [tupɛ] **nm 1.** [de cheveux] quiff *UK*, tuft of hair **2.** *fam fig* [aplomb] cheek ▸ **avoir du toupet, ne pas manquer de toupet** *fam* to have a cheek.

toupie [tupi] **nf** (spinning) top.

tour [tur] ■ **nm 1.** [périmètre] circumference ▸ **faire le tour de** to go round ▸ **faire le tour d'une question** *fig* to consider a problem from all angles ▸ **faire un tour** to go for a walk/drive *etc* ▸ **nous irons faire un tour dans les Pyrénées** we'll go for a trip in the Pyrenees ▸ **faire le tour du propriétaire** to go on a tour of inspection ▸ **tour d'horizon** survey ▸ **faire un tour d'horizon** to deal with all aspects of a problem ▸ **tour de piste** SPORT lap ▸ **tour de taille** waist measurement ▸ **quel est votre tour de taille/hanches?** what size waist/hips are you?
2. [rotation] turn ▸ **fermer à double tour** to double-lock ▸ **à tour de bras** *fig* nonstop ▸ **en un tour de main** *fig* in the twinkling of an eye ▸ **tour de manège** ride on a roundabout *UK ou* a merry-go-round
3. [plaisanterie] trick ▸ **avoir plus d'un tour dans son sac** to have more than one trick up one's sleeve ▸ **jouer un bon/mauvais tour à qqn** to play a joke/dirty trick on sb ▸ **tour de force** amazing feat ▸ **il a réussi le tour de force de la convaincre** he managed to convince her, and it was quite a tour de force *ou* quite an achievement
4. [succession] turn ▸ **attendre son tour** to wait one's turn ▸ **c'est à mon tour** it's my turn ▸ **j'ai fait la cuisine/la vaisselle** *etc* **plus souvent qu'à mon tour** I've done more than my fair share of cooking/washing-up *etc* ▸ **tour de garde** [d'un médecin] spell *ou* turn of duty ▸ **tour de scrutin** ballot, round of voting ▸ **à tour de rôle** in turn ▸ **tour à tour** alternately, in turn
5. [d'événements] turn ▸ **cette affaire prend un très mauvais tour** this business is going very wrong
6. [de potier] wheel.
■ **nf 1.** [monument, de château] tower / [immeuble] tower-block *UK*, high rise *US* ▸ **tour de bureaux** office (tower) block ▸ **tour d'habitation** tower *ou* high-rise block ▸ **tour d'ivoire** *fig* ivory tower
2. [échecs] rook, castle
3. [industrie du pétrole] **: tour de forage** drilling rig.
◆ ***tour de contrôle*** **nf** control tower.
◆ ***Tour de France*** **npr m : le Tour de France** the Tour de France.

CULTURE
Le Tour de France

This world-renowned cycling race, first held in 1903, is held in the first three weeks of July each year. It is divided into stages of varying length and difficulty around the country, but always ends in Paris on the Champs-Elysées. During the race, the cyclist with the best cumulative time wears a yellow jersey, because the newspaper **L'Auto** – organizer of the tour until 1939 – was printed on yellow paper. The winner of the mountain section wears a white jersey with red dots, while the best sprinter wears a green jersey. At the end of the race, the victor is awarded the yellow jersey. Despite many drugs scandals in recent years, the race remains very popular, and competitors are greeted all along the route by cheering fans. A **Tour de France** for women began in 1985.

tourbe [turb] **nf** peat.

tourbière [turbjɛr] **nf** peat bog.

tourbillon [turbijɔ̃] **nm 1.** [de vent] whirlwind ▸ **un tourbillon de** a whirl of **2.** [de poussière, fumée] swirl **3.** [d'eau] whirlpool **4.** *fig* [agitation] hurly-burly.

tourbillonnant, ***e*** [turbijɔnɑ̃, ɑ̃t] **adj** swirling, whirling.

tourbillonner [3] [turbijɔne] **vi** to whirl, to swirl / *fig* to whirl (round).

tourelle [turɛl] **nf** turret.

tourisme [turism] **nm** tourism ▸ **faire du tourisme** [dans un pays] to go touring / [dans une ville] to go sightseeing ▸ **notre région vit du tourisme** we are a tourist area

tourista [turista] **nf** traveller's *UK ou* traveler's *US* tummy, t(o)urista *US*.

touriste [turist] ■ **nmf** tourist ▸ **en touriste** as a tourist ■ **adj** tourist *(avant n)*.

touristique [turistik] **adj** tourist *(avant n)*.

tourment [turmɑ̃] **nm** *sout* torment.

tourmente [turmɑ̃t] **nf 1.** *littéraire* [tempête] storm, tempest **2.** *fig* turmoil.

tourmenté, ***e*** [turmɑ̃te] **adj 1.** [angoissé - personne] tormented, troubled, anguished / [- conscience] tormented, troubled **2.** [visage] tormented ▸ **un regard tourmenté** a haunted *ou* tormented look **3.** [agité - époque] troubled **4.** MÉTÉOR & NAUT **: mer tourmentée** rough *ou* heavy sea.

tourmenter [3] [turmɑ̃te] **vt** to torment.
◆ ***se tourmenter*** **vp** to worry o.s., to fret.

tournage [turnaʒ] **nm** CINÉ shooting.

tournailler [3] [turnaje] **vi** *fam* to prowl about ▸ **tournailler autour de qqn/qqch** to hover around sb/sthg.

tournant, ***e*** [turnɑ̃, ɑ̃t] **adj** [porte] revolving / [fauteuil] swivel *(avant n)* / [pont] swing *(avant n)*.
◆ ***tournant*** **nm** bend / *fig* turning point ▸ **je l'attends au tournant** *fam fig* I'll get even with him/her.

tournante [turnɑ̃t] **nf** gang rape, gangbang.

tourné, ***e*** [turne] **adj** [lait] sour, off
▸▸ **bien tourné** [lettre] well-worded / [personne] shapely ▸ **mal tourné** [lettre] badly-worded / [personne] unattractive / [esprit] warped.

tournebroche [turnəbrɔʃ] **nm** spit.

tourne-disque [turnədisk] (pl **tourne-disques**) **nm** record player.

tournedos [turnədo] **nm** *steak taken from the thickest part of the fillet.*

tournée [turne] **nf 1.** [voyage] tour ▸ **être en tournée** [facteur, représentant] to be off on one's rounds / [chanteur] to be on tour ▸ **faire sa tournée** [facteur, livreur] to do *ou* to make one's round / [représentant] to be on the road ▸ **faire une tournée en Europe** to go on a European tour ▸ **tournée de conférences** lecture tour **2.** *fam* [consommations] round ▸ **c'est ma tournée** it's my round ▸ **tournée générale!** drinks all round! **3.** *fam* [correction] thrashing, hiding.

tourner [3] [turne] ■ **vt 1.** [gén] to turn ▸ **tourne le bouton jusqu'au 7** turn the knob to 7 **2.** [pas, pensées] to turn, to direct ▸ **tourner son attention vers** to focus one's attention on, to turn one's attention to **3.** [obstacle, loi] to get round *UK ou* around *US* ▸ **tourner la difficulté/le règlement/la loi** *fig* to get round the problem/regulations/law **4.** CINÉ to shoot ▸ **tourner un film** to shoot *ou* to make a film *UK ou* movie *US* / [acteur] to make a film *UK ou* movie *US* **5.** *fig* [formuler] **: bien tourner qqch** to put sthg well ▸ **il tourne bien ses phrases** he's got a neat turn of phrase.
■ **vi 1.** [gén] to turn / [moteur] to turn over / [planète] to revolve ▸ **tourner autour de qqn** *fig* to hang around sb ▸ **tourner autour du pot** *ou* **du sujet** *fig* to beat about the bush ▸ **tourner au ridicule** *fig* to become ridiculous ▸ **'tournez s'il vous plaît'** 'please turn over' ▸ **tourner au coin de la rue** to turn at the corner (of the street) ▸ **tourner sur soi-même** to turn round / [vite] to spin (round and round) ▸ **la Terre tourne sur elle-même** the Earth spins on its axis ▸ **tourner de l'œil** *fam* to pass out, to faint ▸ **bien tourner** [situation, personne] to turn out well *ou* satisfactorily ▸ **mal tourner** [initiative, plaisanterie] to turn out badly, to go wrong **2.** *fam* [entreprise] to tick over *UK*, to go ok ▸ **faire tourner une entreprise** [directeur] to run a business **3.** [lait] to go off *UK*, to go bad *US*.
◆ ***se tourner*** **vp** to turn (right) round *UK ou* around *US* ▸ **je ne sais plus de quel côté me tourner** I don't know which way to turn any more ▸ **se tourner vers** to turn towards *ou* toward *UK* ▸ **tous les regards se tournèrent vers elle** all eyes turned to look at her.

ournesol [turnəsɔl] **nm 1.** [plante] sunflower **2.** [colorant] litmus.

ourneur, ***euse*** [turnœr, øz] **nm, f** turner, lathe operator.

tournevis [turnəvis] **nm** screwdriver.

tournicoter [3] [turnikɔte] **vi** *fam* to wander up and down.

tourniquet [turnikɛ] **nm 1.** [entrée] turnstile **2.** MÉD tourniquet.

tournis [turni] **nm** *fam* **: avoir le tournis** to feel dizzy *ou* giddy ▸ **donner le tournis à qqn** to make sb dizzy *ou* giddy.

tournoi [turnwa] **nm** tournament.

tournoiement [turnwamɑ̃] **nm** wheeling, whirling.

tournoyer [13] [turnwaje] **vi** to wheel, to whirl.

tournure [turnyr] **nf 1.** [apparence] turn ▸ **prendre tournure** to take shape **2.** [formulation] form ▸ **tournure de phrase** turn of phrase.

tour-opérateur [turɔperatœr] (pl **tour-opérateurs**) **nm** tour operator.

tourte [turt] **nf** pie.

tourteau, ***x*** [turto] **nm 1.** [crabe] crab **2.** [pour bétail] oil cake.

tourtereau [turtəro] **nm** young turtledove.
◆ ***tourtereaux*** **nmpl** *fam fig* [amoureux] lovebirds.

tourterelle [turtərɛl] **nf** turtledove.

tourtière [turtjɛr] **nf** pie dish.

tous ➤ *tout*.

Toussaint [tusɛ̃] **nf : la Toussaint** All Saints' Day.

tousser [3] [tuse] **vi** to cough.

toussotement [tusɔtmɑ̃] **nm** coughing.

toussoter [3] [tusɔte] **vi** to cough.

tout, ***toute*** [tu, tut] (mpl **tous** [tus], fpl **toutes** [tut]) ■ **adj 1.** *(avec substantif singulier déterminé)* all ▸ **tout le vin** all the wine ▸ **tout un gâteau** a whole cake ▸ **toute la journée/la nuit** all day/night, the whole day/night ▸ **toute sa famille** all his family, his whole family ▸ **j'ai tout mon temps** I've plenty of time *ou* all the time in the world
2. *(avec pronom démonstratif)* **: tout ceci/cela** all this/that ▸ **tout ce que je sais** all I know.
■ **adj indéf 1.** [exprime la totalité] all ▸ **tous les gâteaux** all the cakes ▸ **toutes les femmes** all the women ▸ **tous les deux** both of us/them *etc* ▸ **tous les trois** all three of us/them *etc* ▸ **il roulait tous feux éteints** he was driving with his lights off
2. [chaque] every ▸ **tous les jours** every day ▸ **tous les deux ans** every two years ▸ **tous les combien?** how often? ▸ **toutes les fois qu'on s'est rencontrés** every time we've met
3. [n'importe quel] any ▸ **à toute heure** at any time.
■ **pron indéf** everything, all ▸ **je t'ai tout dit** I've told you everything ▸ **ils voulaient tous la voir** they all wanted to see her ▸ **ce sera tout?** will that be all ▸ **c'est tout** that's all ▸ **il est tout sauf un génie** call him anything but not a genius ▸ **j'adore les prunes – prends-les toutes** I love plums – take them all *ou* all of them ▸ **on aura tout vu!** now I've *ou* we've seen everything! ▸ **tous ensemble** all together.
◆ ***tout*** ■ **adv 1.** [entièrement, tout à fait] very, quite ▸ **tout jeune/près** very young/near ▸ **tout neuf** brand new ▸ **tout**

nu stark naked ▸ **ils étaient tout seuls** they were all alone ▸ **tout en haut** right at the top ▸ **tout à côté de moi** right next to me ▸ **tout simplement** quite simply
2. [avec un gérondif] **: tout en marchant** while walking.
■ **nm : un tout** a whole ▸ **le tout est de...** the main thing is to... ▸ **le tout c'est de ne pas bafouiller** the most important thing is not to stutter ▸ **risquer le tout pour le tout** to risk everything.
◆ ***du tout au tout*** **loc adv** completely, entirely ▸ **changer du tout au tout** to change completely.
◆ ***pas du tout*** **loc adv** not at all.
◆ ***tout à fait*** **loc adv 1.** [complètement] quite, entirely ▸ **ce n'est pas tout à fait exact** it's not quite correct **2.** [exactement] exactly ▸ **c'est tout à fait ce que je cherche/le même** it's exactly what I've been looking for/the same.
◆ ***tout à l'heure*** **loc adv 1.** [futur] in a little while, shortly ▸ **à tout à l'heure!** see you later!
2. [passé] a little while ago.
◆ ***tout de suite*** **loc adv** immediately, at once ▸ **tournez à gauche tout de suite après le pont** turn left immediately after the bridge.

tout-à-l'égout [tutalegu] **nm inv** mains drainage.

toutefois [tutfwa] **adv** however.

toutou [tutu] **nm** *fam* doggie.

tout-petit [tup(ə)ti] (**pl tout-petits**) **nm** toddler, tot.

tout-puissant, ***toute-puissante*** [tupɥisɑ̃, tutpɥisɑ̃t] (**mpl tout-puissants**) (**fpl toutes-puissantes**) **adj** omnipotent, all-powerful.
◆ ***Tout-Puissant*** **nm : le Tout-Puissant** the Almighty.

tout(-)terrain, ***s*** [tutɛrɛ̃] **adj** off-road.

tout-venant [tuvnɑ̃] **nm inv : le tout-venant** ordinary people *pl*.

toux [tu] **nf** cough.

toxicité [tɔksisite] **nf** toxicity.

toxicologie [tɔksikɔlɔʒi] **nf** toxicology.

toxicomane [tɔksikɔman] **nmf** drug addict.

toxicomanie [tɔksikɔmani] **nf** drug addiction.

toxine [tɔksin] **nf** toxin.

toxique [tɔksik] **adj** toxic.

TP ■ **nmpl** (**abr de *travaux publics***) civil engineering.
■ **nm** (**abr de *Trésor public***) *public revenue office*.

TPC (**abr de *tierce partie de confiance***) **f** INFORM [pour des transactions sur Internet] TTP.

TPE [tepeø] ■ **nmpl** (**abr de *travaux personnels encadrés***) GIS.
■ **nf** (**abr de *très petite entreprise***) VSB.

TPG (**abr de *trésorier payeur général***) **nm** paymaster.

tps **abr de *temps***.

trac [trak] **nm** nerves *pl* / THÉÂTRE stage fright ▸ **avoir le trac** to get nervous / THÉÂTRE to get stage fright.

traçabilité [trasabilite] **nf** traceability.

tracas [traka] **nm** worry.

tracasser [3] [trakase] **vt** to worry, to bother.
◆ ***se tracasser*** **vp** to worry.

tracasserie [trakasri] **nf** annoyance.

tracassier, ***ère*** [trakasje, ɛr] **adj** irksome.

trace [tras] **nf 1.** [d'animal, de fugitif] track ▸ **des traces de pas** footprints, footmarks ▸ **des traces de pneus** tyre tracks *ou* wheel marks ▸ **ils sont sur la trace du bandit/d'un manuscrit** they are on the bandit's trail/tracking down a manuscript ▸ **suivre à la trace** [fuyard, gibier] to track (down) **2.** [de brûlure, fatigue] mark ▸ **il portait des traces de coups** his body showed signs of having been beaten ▸ **sans laisser de traces** without (a) trace **3.** *(gén pl)* [vestige] trace ▸ **on y a retrouvé les traces d'une civilisation très ancienne** traces of a very ancient civilization have been discovered there **4.** [très petite quantité] **: une trace de** a trace of ▸ **elle parle sans la moindre trace d'accent** she speaks without the slightest trace *ou* hint of an accent **5.** SKI trail ▸ **trace directe** direct descent ▸ **faire la trace** to break a trail **6.** [à la recherche de] on the trail of *ou* track of ▸ **ils sont sur la trace d'un dossier** they are tracking down a file.

tracé [trase] **nm** [lignes] plan, drawing / [de parcours] line.

tracer [16] [trase] ■ **vt 1.** [dessiner, dépeindre] to draw **2.** [route, piste] to mark out ▸ **tracer la voie/le chemin à qqn** *fig* to show sb the way.
■ **vi** *fam* to belt along *UK*.

traceur [trasœr] **nm** INFORM plotter.

trachée-artère [traʃeartɛr] (**pl trachées-artères**) **nf** windpipe, trachea.

trachéite [trakeit] **nf** throat infection.

tract [trakt] **nm** leaflet.

tractations [traktasjɔ̃] **nfpl** negotiations, dealings.

tracter [3] [trakte] **vt** to tow.

tracteur [traktœr] **nm** tractor.

traction [traksjɔ̃] **nf 1.** [action de tirer] towing, pulling ▸ **traction avant/arrière** front-/rear-wheel drive **2.** TECHNOL tensile stress **3.** [SPORT - au sol] press-up *UK*, push-up *US* / [- à la barre] pull-up.

tradition [tradisjɔ̃] **nf** tradition ▸ **renouer avec la tradition** to revive a tradition.

traditionaliste [tradisjɔnalist] **nmf & adj** traditionalist.

traditionnel, ***elle*** [tradisjɔnɛl] **adj 1.** [de tradition] traditional **2.** [habituel] usual.

traditionnellement [tradisjɔnɛlmɑ̃] **adv** traditionally.

traducteur, ***trice*** [tradyktœr, tris] **nm, f** translator.
◆ ***traducteur*** **nm** INFORM translator.

traduction [tradyksjɔ̃] **nf 1.** [gén] translation ▸ **traduction assistée par ordinateur** computer-aided translation **2.** *littéraire* [expression] rendering.

traduire [98] [tradɥir] **vt 1.** [texte] to translate ▸ **traduire qqch en français/anglais** to translate sthg into French/English **2.** [révéler - crise] to reveal, to betray / [- sentiments, pensée] to render, to express **3.** DR **: traduire qqn en justice** to bring sb before the courts.
◆ ***se traduire*** **vp** *(emploi passif)* **: la phrase peut se traduire de différentes façons** the sentence can be translated in different ways.
◆ ***se traduire par*** **v + prep** [avoir pour résultat] **: cela se traduit par des changements climatiques** it results i

ou entails changes in the climate ▸ **la sécheresse s'est traduite par une baisse de la production agricole** agricultural production fell as a result of the drought.

traduisible [tradɥizibl] **adj** translatable.

trafic [trafik] **nm 1.** [de marchandises] traffic, trafficking **2.** [circulation] traffic.
◆ ***trafic d'influence*** **nm** corruption, taking bribes.

trafiquant, e [trafikɑ̃, ɑ̃t] **nm, f** trafficker, dealer.

trafiquer [3] [trafike] ■ **vt 1.** [falsifier] to tamper with **2.** *fam* [manigancer] **: qu'est-ce que tu trafiques?** what are you up to?
■ **vi** to be involved in trafficking ▸ **trafiquer de qqch** to traffic in sthg.

tragédie [traʒedi] **nf** tragedy.

tragédien, enne [traʒedjɛ̃, ɛn] **nm, f** tragedian (f tragedienne), tragic actor (f actress).

tragi-comédie [traʒikɔmedi] (pl **tragi-comédies**) **nf** tragicomedy.

tragi-comique [traʒikɔmik] **adj** tragicomic, tragicomical.

tragique [traʒik] ■ **adj** tragic.
■ **nm 1.** [auteur] tragedian **2.** [caractère] **: le tragique** tragedy ▸ **prendre qqch au tragique** to act as if sthg were a tragedy ▸ **tourner au tragique** to take a tragic turn.

tragiquement [traʒikmɑ̃] **adv** tragically.

trahir [32] [trair] **vt 1.** [gén] to betray ▸ **trahir qqn** to deceive sb, to be unfaithful to sb ▸ **trahir sa promesse/ses engagements** to break one's promise/one's commitments ▸ **trahir les intérêts de qqn** to betray sb's interests ▸ **son visage ne trahit aucun émoi** he remained stony-faced **2.** [suj: moteur] to let down / [suj: forces] to fail ▸ **si ma mémoire ne me trahit pas** if my memory serves me right **3.** [pensée] to misrepresent ▸ **mes paroles ont trahi ma pensée** my words failed to express my true thoughts **4.** [révéler, démasquer] to betray, to give away *(sep)* ▸ **trahir un secret** to give away a secret ▸ **son silence l'a trahie** her silence gave her away.
◆ ***se trahir*** **vp** to give o.s. away ▸ **il s'est trahi en faisant du bruit** he gave himself away by making a noise.

trahison [traizɔ̃] **nf 1.** [gén] betrayal **2.** DR treason.

train [trɛ̃] **nm 1.** [transports] train ▸ **train de banlieue** suburban *ou* commuter train ▸ **train corail** express ▸ **train direct** non-stop *ou* through train ▸ **train (à) grande vitesse** high-speed train ▸ **train de marchandises** goods *UK* *ou* freight train ▸ **train de voyageurs** passenger train ▸ **être dans le train** to be on the train ▸ **elle voyage beaucoup en train** she travels by train a great deal ▸ **monter dans *ou* prendre le train en marche** to climb onto *ou* to jump on the bandwagon
2. AÉRON **: train d'atterrissage** landing gear
3. [allure] pace ▸ **aller à fond de train *ou* à un train d'enfer** to speed *ou* to race along ▸ **au train où vont les choses** the way things are going, at this rate ▸ **les négociations ont été menées bon train** the negotiations made good progress
4. [série] **: un train de** a series of ▸ **train de camions** convoy *ou* line of lorries *UK* *ou* trucks *US* ▸ **train de péniches** train *ou* string of barges ▸ **train de réformes** set of reforms
5. *fam* [postérieur] backside, butt *US* ▸ **courir *ou* filer au train de qqn** [le suivre partout] to stick to sb like glue / [le prendre en filature] to tail *ou* to shadow sb
▸▸ **être en train** *fig* to be on form ▸ **se mettre en train** to warm up ▸ **être en train de faire qqch** to be (busy) doing sthg.
◆ ***train de vie*** **nm** lifestyle.
◆ ***en train de*** **loc prép : être en train de lire/travailler** to be reading/working ▸ **l'opinion publique est en train d'évoluer** public opinion is changing.

traînailler [trɛnaje], ***traînasser*** [3] [trɛnase] **vi** *fam* **1.** [vagabonder] to loaf about **2.** [être lent] to dawdle.

traînant, e [trɛnɑ̃, ɑ̃t] **adj 1.** [robe] trailing **2.** [voix] drawling / [démarche] dragging.

traînard, e [trɛnar, ard] **nm, f** *fam* straggler / *fig* slowcoach *UK*, slowpoke *US*.

traînasser = ***traînailler***.

traîne [trɛn] **nf 1.** [de robe] train **2.** [à la pêche] dragnet ▸ **pêche à la traîne** trolling **3.** *Québec* **: traîne sauvage** toboggan
▸▸ **être à la traîne** to lag behind.

traîneau, x [trɛno] **nm** sleigh, sledge.

traînée [trene] **nf 1.** [trace] trail ▸ **se répandre comme une traînée de poudre** *fig* to spread like wildfire **2.** *tfam péj* [prostituée] tart, whore.

traîner [4] [trene] ■ **vt 1.** [tirer, emmener] to drag ▸ **traîner les pieds** to shuffle along, to drag one's feet ▸ **traîner qqn dans la boue** *fig* to drag sb's name through the mud **2.** [trimbaler] to lug around, to cart around **3.** [maladie] to be unable to shake off ▸ **ça fait des semaines que je traîne cette angine** this sore throat has been with *ou* plaguing me for weeks.
■ **vi 1.** [personne, animal] to dawdle ▸ **ne traîne pas, Mamie nous attend** stop dawdling *ou* do hurry up, Grandma's expecting us ▸ **des chiens traînent dans le village** dogs roam around the village **2.** [maladie, affaire] to drag on ▸ **traîner en longueur** to drag ▸ **faire traîner des pourparlers/un procès** to drag out negotiations/a trial **3.** [robe] to trail **4.** [vêtements, livres] to lie around *ou* about ▸ **laisser traîner qqch** to leave sthg lying around.
◆ ***se traîner*** **vp 1.** [personne] to drag o.s. along ▸ **je me suis traînée jusque chez le docteur** *fig* I dragged myself to the doctor's **2.** [jour, semaine] to drag.

training [trɛniŋ] **nm 1.** [entraînement] training **2.** [survêtement] tracksuit top.

train-train [trɛ̃trɛ̃] **nm** *fam* routine, daily grind.

traire [112] [trɛr] **vt 1.** [vache] to milk **2.** [lait] to draw.

trait [trɛ] **nm 1.** [ligne] line, stroke ▸ **trait d'union** hyphen ▸ **prendre un trait d'union** to be hyphenated *ou* take a hyphen ▸ **servir de trait d'union entre** *fig* to bridge the gap between, to link ▸ **tirer un trait sur qqch** *fig* to put sthg behind one ▸ **tirer un trait sur le passé** *fig* to turn over a new leaf, to make a complete break with the past ▸ **d'un trait de plume** with a stroke of the pen ▸ **voici l'intrigue, résumée à grands traits** here's a broad *ou* rough outline of the plot **2.** *(gén pl)* [de visage] feature ▸ **avoir les traits tirés** to look drawn ▸ **ressembler à qqn trait pour trait** to be the spitting image of sb, to be exactly

like sb **3.** [caractéristique] trait, feature ▸ **trait de caractère** character trait **4.** [acte] act ▸ **trait d'esprit** witticism, flash of wit ▸ **trait de génie** brainwave
▸▸ **avoir trait à** to be to do with, to concern.
◆ ***d'un trait*** **loc adv** [boire, lire] in one go.

traitant, e [trɛtɑ̃, ɑ̃t] **adj** [shampooing, crème] medicated, ➤ ***médecin***.

traite [trɛt] **nf 1.** [de vache] milking **2.** COMM bill, draft ▸ **escompter une traite** to discount a bill *ou* draft ▸ **tirer une traite sur** to draw a bill *ou* draft on **3.** [d'esclaves] **: la traite des noirs** the slave trade ▸ **la traite des blanches** the white slave trade.
◆ ***d'une seule traite*** **loc adv** without stopping, in one go.

traité [trete] **nm 1.** [ouvrage] treatise **2.** POLIT treaty ▸ **traité de non-prolifération** non-proliferation treaty.

traitement [trɛtmɑ̃] **nm 1.** [gén & MÉD] treatment ▸ **donner un traitement à qqn** to prescribe (a treatment) for sb ▸ **être sous traitement** to be being treated *ou* having treatment *ou* under treatment ▸ **mauvais traitement** ill-treatment ▸ **faire subir de mauvais traitements à qqn** to ill-treat sb ▸ **traitement de faveur** special treatment
2. [rémunération] wage
3. INFORM processing ▸ **traitement différé** off-line processing ▸ **traitement de données** data processing ▸ **traitement de texte** word processing ▸ **traitement de la parole** speech processing ▸ **traitement par lots** batch processing
4. [procédé] processing, treatment ▸ **traitement antirouille** rustproofing ▸ **le traitement des récoltes** the treating of crops / [par avion] the spraying of crops
5. [de problème] handling.

traiter [4] [trete] ■ **vt 1.** [gén & MÉD] to treat ▸ **se faire traiter** MÉD to be treated ▸ **on me traite à l'homéopathie** I'm having homeopathy ▸ **bien/mal traiter qqn** to treat sb well/badly ▸ **traiter qqn d'égal à égal** to treat sb as an equal **2.** [qualifier] **: traiter qqn d'imbécile/de lâche** *etc* to call sb an imbecile/a coward *etc* ▸ **traiter qqn de tous les noms** to call sb all the names under the sun **3.** [question, thème] to deal with ▸ **vous ne traitez pas le sujet** you're not addressing the question **4.** [dans l'industrie & INFORM] to process ▸ **traiter qqch par lots** to batch process sthg.
■ **vi 1.** [négocier] to negotiate ▸ **nous ne traiterons pas avec des terroristes** we won't bargain *ou* negotiate with terrorists **2.** [livre] **: traiter de** to deal with.
◆ ***se traiter*** ■ **vp** *(emploi passif)* [maladie] **: ça se traite aux antibiotiques** it can be treated with antibiotics.
■ **vp** *(emploi réciproque)* [personne] **: ils se traitaient de menteurs** they were calling each other liars.

traiteur [trɛtœr] **nm** caterer.

traître, esse [trɛtr, ɛs] ■ **adj** treacherous.
■ **nm, f** traitor ▸ **prendre qqn en traître** to play an underhand trick on sb.

traîtreusement [trɛtrøzmɑ̃] **adv** treacherously.

traîtrise [trɛtriz] **nf 1.** [déloyauté] treachery **2.** [acte] act of treachery.

trajectoire [traʒɛktwar] **nf** trajectory, path / *fig* path.

trajet [traʒɛ] **nm 1.** [distance] distance **2.** [itinéraire] route **3.** [voyage] journey.

trame [tram] **nf** weft / *fig* framework.

tramer [3] [trame] **vt** *sout* to plot.
◆ ***se tramer*** ■ **vp** to be plotted.
■ **v impers : il se trame quelque chose** there's something afoot.

tramontane [tramɔ̃tan] **nf** *strong cold wind that blows through Languedoc-Roussillon in southwest France.*

trampoline [trɑ̃pɔlin] **nm** trampoline.

tram(way) [tram(wɛ)] **nm** tram *UK*, streetcar *US*.

tranchant, e [trɑ̃ʃɑ̃, ɑ̃t] **adj 1.** [instrument] sharp **2.** [personne] assertive **3.** [ton] curt.
◆ ***tranchant*** **nm** edge ▸ **à double tranchant** *fig* two-edged.

tranche [trɑ̃ʃ] **nf 1.** [de gâteau, jambon] slice ▸ **tranche de bacon** [à frire] rasher (of bacon) ▸ **tranche napolitaine** CULIN Neapolitan slice *ou* ice-cream ▸ **débiter *ou* couper qqch en tranches** to slice sthg (up),to cut sthg into slices ▸ **tranche d'âge** *fig* age bracket ▸ **tranche de vie** *fig* slice of life **2.** [de livre, pièce] edge ▸ **doré sur tranche** gilt-edged **3.** [période] part, section ▸ **tranche horaire** time slot / RADIO & TV [tard dans la soirée] **: tranche nocturne** graveyard slot **4.** ÉCON & FIN [de revenus] portion / [de paiement] instalment *UK*, installment *US* / [fiscale] bracket / [d'un prêt, d'un crédit] tranche ▸ **tranche de salaire *ou* de revenu** income bracket, income group ▸ **tranche d'imposition** tax band.

tranchée [trɑ̃ʃe] **nf** MIL [Travaux Publics] trench ▸ **creuser une tranchée** to (dig a) trench.

trancher [3] [trɑ̃ʃe] ■ **vt** [couper] to cut / [pain, jambon] to slice ▸ **trancher la question** *fig* to settle the question.
■ **vi 1.** *fig* [décider] to decide **2.** [contraster] **: trancher avec *ou* sur** to contrast with.

tranchoir [trɑ̃ʃwar] **nm 1.** [couteau] chopper **2.** [planche] chopping board.

tranquille [trɑ̃kil] **adj 1.** [endroit, vie] quiet ▸ **marcher d'un pas tranquille** to stroll unhurriedly ▸ **laisser qqn/qqch tranquille** to leave sb/sthg alone ▸ **se tenir/rester tranquille** to keep/remain quiet ▸ **allons dans mon bureau, nous y serons plus tranquilles pour discuter** let's go into my office, we can talk there without being disturbed **2.** [rassuré] at ease, easy ▸ **soyez tranquille** don't worry ▸ **je serais plus tranquille s'il n'était pas seul** I'd feel easier in my mind knowing that he wasn't on his own.

tranquillement [trɑ̃kilmɑ̃] **adv 1.** [sans s'agiter] quietly **2.** [sans s'inquiéter] calmly.

tranquillisant, e [trɑ̃kilizɑ̃, ɑ̃t] **adj 1.** [nouvelle] reassuring **2.** [médicament] tranquillizing.
◆ ***tranquillisant*** **nm** tranquillizer *UK*, tranquilizer *US*.

tranquilliser [3] [trɑ̃kilize] **vt** to reassure.
◆ ***se tranquilliser*** **vp** to set one's mind at rest.

tranquillité [trɑ̃kilite] **nf 1.** [calme] peacefulness quietness **2.** [sérénité] peace, tranquillity *UK*, tranquility *US* ▸ **tranquillité d'esprit** peace of mind.

transaction [trɑ̃zaksjɔ̃] **nf** transaction ▸ **transaction boursières électroniques** FIN electronic trading.

transactionnel, elle [trɑ̃zaksjɔnɛl] **adj 1.** PSYCHO transactional **2.** DR compromise *(avant n)*.

transalpin, e [trɑ̃zalpɛ̃, in] **adj** transalpine.

transat [trɑ̃zat] ■ **nm** deckchair.
■ **nf** transatlantic race.

transatlantique [trɑ̃zatlɑ̃tik] ■ **adj** transatlantic.
■ **nm** transatlantic liner.
■ **nf** transatlantic race.

transbahuter [3] [trɑ̃sbayte] **vt** *fam* to hump *UK ou* lug along, to schlepp *US*.

transbordement [trɑ̃sbɔrdəmɑ̃] **nm** transfer.

transcendant, e [trɑ̃sɑ̃dɑ̃, ɑ̃t] **adj** *fam* [extraordinaire] special, great.

transcender [3] [trɑ̃sɑ̃de] **vt** to transcend.
◆ ***se transcender*** **vp** to surpass o.s.

transcoder [3] [trɑ̃skɔde] **vt** to transcribe.

transcription [trɑ̃skripsjɔ̃] **nf** [de document & MUS] transcription / [dans un autre alphabet] transliteration ◗ **transcription phonétique** phonetic transcription.

transcrire [99] [trɑ̃skrir] **vt** [document & MUS] to transcribe / [dans un autre alphabet] to transliterate.

transcrit, e [trɑ̃skri, it] **pp** ➤ ***transcrire***.

transe [trɑ̃s] **nf** : **être en transe** *fig* to be beside o.s.
◆ ***transes*** **nfpl** *sout* agony *(U)*.

transférer [18] [trɑ̃sfere] **vt** to transfer.

transfert [trɑ̃sfɛr] **nm** transfer ◗ **transfert de fonds électronique** INFORM electronic funds transfer.

transfigurer [3] [trɑ̃sfigyre] **vt** to transfigure.

transformable [trɑ̃sfɔrmabl] **adj** convertible.

transformateur, trice [trɑ̃sfɔrmatœr, tris] **adj** **1.** [dans l'industrie] processing *(avant n)* **2.** *fig* [pouvoir, action] for change.
◆ ***transformateur*** **nm** transformer.

transformation [trɑ̃sfɔrmasjɔ̃] **nf** **1.** [de pays, personne] transformation **2.** [dans l'industrie] processing **3.** [rugby] conversion.

transformer [3] [trɑ̃sfɔrme] **vt** **1.** [gén] to transform / [magasin] to convert ◗ **transformer qqch en** to turn sthg into **2.** [dans l'industrie] [rugby] to convert.
◆ ***se transformer*** **vp** : **se transformer en monstre/papillon** to turn into a monster/butterfly.

transfuge [trɑ̃sfyʒ] **nmf** renegade.

transfuser [3] [trɑ̃sfyze] **vt** [sang] to transfuse.

transfusion [trɑ̃sfyzjɔ̃] **nf** : **transfusion (sanguine)** (blood) transfusion.

transgénique [trɑ̃sʒenik] **adj** transgenic.

transgresser [4] [trɑ̃sgrese] **vt** [loi] to infringe / [ordre] to disobey.

transgression [trɑ̃zgrɛsjɔ̃] **nf** infringement, transgression.

transhumance [trɑ̃zymɑ̃s] **nf** transhumance.

transi, e [trɑ̃zi] **adj** : **être transi de** to be paralysed *UK ou* paralyzed *US* with, to be transfixed with ◗ **être transi de froid** to be chilled to the bone.

transiger [17] [trɑ̃ziʒe] **vi** : **transiger (sur)** to compromise (on).

transistor [3] [trɑ̃zistɔr] **nm** transistor.

transit [trɑ̃zit] **nm** transit ◗ **en transit** in transit.

transitaire [trɑ̃zitɛr] **nm** forwarding agent.

transiter [3] [trɑ̃zite] ■ **vt** to forward.
■ **vi** to pass in transit ◗ **transiter par** to pass through.

transitif, ive [trɑ̃sitif, iv] **adj** transitive.

transition [trɑ̃zisjɔ̃] **nf** transition ◗ **sans transition** with no transition, abruptly.

transitivité [trɑ̃zitivite] **nf** transitivity.

transitoire [trɑ̃zitwar] **adj** [passager] transitory.

translucide [trɑ̃slysid] **adj** translucent.

transmettre [84] [trɑ̃smɛtr] **vt** **1.** [message, salutations] : **transmettre qqch (à)** to pass sthg on (to) **2.** [tradition, propriété] : **transmettre qqch (à)** to hand sthg down (to) **3.** [fonction, pouvoir] : **transmettre qqch (à)** to hand sthg over (to) **4.** [maladie] : **transmettre qqch (à)** to transmit sthg (to), to pass sthg on (to) **5.** [concert, émission] to broadcast.
◆ ***se transmettre*** **vp** **1.** [maladie] to be passed on, to be transmitted **2.** [nouvelle] to be passed on **3.** [courant, onde] to be transmitted **4.** [tradition] to be handed down.

transmis, e [trɑ̃smi, iz] **pp** ➤ ***transmettre***.

transmissible [trɑ̃smisibl] **adj** **1.** [patrimoine] transferable **2.** [maladie] transmissible.

transmission [trɑ̃smisjɔ̃] **nf** **1.** [de biens] transfer **2.** [de maladie] transmission **3.** [de message] passing on **4.** [de tradition] handing down.

transocéanique [trɑ̃zɔseanik] **adj** transoceanic.

transpalette [trɑ̃spalɛt] **nf** pallet truck, stacker.

transparaître [91] [trɑ̃sparɛtr] **vi** to show.

transparence [trɑ̃sparɑ̃s] **nf** transparency ◗ **par transparence** against the light.

transparent, e [trɑ̃sparɑ̃, ɑ̃t] **adj** transparent.
◆ ***transparent*** **nm** transparency.

transpercer [16] [trɑ̃spɛrse] **vt** to pierce / *fig* [suj: froid, pluie] to go right through.

transpiration [trɑ̃spirasjɔ̃] **nf** [sueur] perspiration.

transpirer [3] [trɑ̃spire] **vi** **1.** [suer] to perspire **2.** *fig* [se divulguer] to leak out.

transplant [trɑ̃splɑ̃] **nm** MÉD transplant.

transplantation [trɑ̃splɑ̃tasjɔ̃] **nf** **1.** [d'arbre, de population] transplanting **2.** MÉD transplant.

transplanter [3] [trɑ̃splɑ̃te] **vt** to transplant.

transport [trɑ̃spɔr] **nm** transport *(U)*, transportation *(U) US* ◗ **transport aérien** air transport ◗ **transport ferroviaire** rail transport ◗ **transport maritime** sea transport ◗ **transports en commun** public transport *sg*.

transportable [trɑ̃spɔrtabl] **adj** [marchandise] transportable / [blessé] fit to be moved.

transporter [3] [trɑ̃spɔrte] **vt** **1.** [marchandises, personnes] to transport **2.** *fig* [enthousiasmer] to delight ◗ **être transporté de joie/bonheur** to be beside o.s. with joy/happiness.

transporteur [trɑ̃spɔrtœr] **nm** **1.** [personne] carrier ◗ **transporteur routier** road haulier *UK ou* hauler *US* **2.** [machine] conveyor.

transposer [3] [trɑ̃spoze] **vt** **1.** [déplacer] to transpose **2.** [adapter] : **transposer qqch (à)** to adapt sthg (for).

transposition [trɑ̃spozisjɔ̃] **nf 1.** [déplacement] transposition **2.** [adaptation] **: transposition (à)** adaptation (for).

transsexuel, elle [trɑ̃ssɛksɥɛl] **adj & nm, f** transsexual.

transvaser [3] [trɑ̃svaze] **vt** to decant.

transversal, e, aux [trɑ̃svɛrsal, o] **adj 1.** [coupe] cross *(avant n)* **2.** [chemin] running at right angles, cross *(avant n) US* **3.** [vallée] transverse.

transversalité [trɑ̃svɛrsalite] **nf** transversality.

trapèze [trapɛz] **nm 1.** GÉOM trapezium **2.** [gymnastique] trapeze **3.** ANAT trapezius.

trapéziste [trapezist] **nmf** trapeze artist.

trappage [trapaʒ] **nm** *Québec* trapping.

trappe [trap] **nf 1.** [ouverture] trapdoor **2.** [piège] trap.

trappeur [trapœr] **nm** trapper.

trapu, e [trapy] **adj 1.** [personne] stocky, solidly built **2.** [édifice] squat.

traquenard [traknar] **nm** trap / *fig* trap, pitfall.

traquer [3] [trake] **vt** [animal] to track / [personne, faute] to track *ou* hunt down.

traumatisant, e [tromatizɑ̃, ɑ̃t] **adj** traumatizing.

traumatiser [3] [tromatize] **vt** to traumatize.

traumatisme [tromatism] **nm** traumatism.

traumatologie [tromatɔlɔʒi] **nf** ≃ casualty department *UK*, ≃ emergency room *US*.

travail [travaj] **nm 1.** [gén] work *(U)* ▸ **se mettre au travail** to get down to work ▸ **demander du travail** [projet] to require some work ▸ **abattre du travail** *fig* to get through a lot of work ▸ **mâcher le travail à qqn** *fig* to spoon-feed sb
2. [tâche, emploi] job ▸ **chercher du** *ou* **un travail** to be job-hunting, to be looking for a job ▸ **travail de bureau** office work ▸ **travail d'intérêt général** DR community service ▸ **travail intérimaire** temporary work ▸ **le travail manuel** manual work, manual labour *UK ou* labor *US* ▸ **travail au noir** moonlighting ▸ **travail précaire** casual labour *UK ou* labor *US* ▸ **le travail saisonnier** seasonal work ▸ **le travail salarié** paid work ▸ **le travail temporaire** [gén] temporary work / [dans un bureau] temping ▸ **c'est un travail de fourmi** it's a painstaking task ▸ **contrat de travail** employment contract ▸ **mes instruments de travail** the tools of my trade
3. [du métal, du bois] working ▸ **elle est attirée par le travail du bois/de la soie** she's interested in working with wood/with silk
4. [de la mémoire] workings *pl*
5. [phénomène - du bois] warping / [- du temps, fermentation] action
6. MÉD **: être en travail** to be in labour *UK ou* labor *US* ▸ **entrer en travail** to go into labour *UK ou* labor *US*.
◆ ***travaux*** **nmpl 1.** [d'aménagement] work *(U)* / [routiers] roadworks *UK*, roadwork *US* ▸ **travaux publics** civil engineering *sg* ▸ **'attention, travaux'** 'caution: work in progress'
2. SCOL **: travaux dirigés** class work ▸ **travaux manuels** arts and crafts ▸ **travaux pratiques** practical work *(U)*.
◆ ***travaux d'approche*** **nmpl** preliminary work *(U)*.

travaillé, e [travaje] **adj 1.** [matériau] wrought, worked **2.** [style] laboured *UK*, labored *US* **3.** [tourmenté] **: être travaillé par** to be tormented by.

travailler [3] [travaje] ■ **vi 1.** [gén] to work ▸ **travailler chez/dans** to work at/in ▸ **travailler à qqch** to work on sthg ▸ **travailler à temps partiel** to work part-time ▸ **travailler dur** to work hard ▸ **travailler en free-lance** to do freelance work, to be a freelancer ▸ **elle travaille dans l'informatique** she works with computers ▸ **travailler sur ordinateur** to work on a computer **2.** [métal, bois] to warp.
■ **vt 1.** [étudier] to work at *ou* on / [piano] to practise *UK*, to practice *US* **2.** [essayer de convaincre] to work on **3.** [suj: idée, remords] to torment ▸ **être travaillé par le remords/l'angoisse** to be tormented by remorse/anxiety **4.** [matière] to work, to fashion ▸ **travailler la terre** to work *ou* to till *sout* the land.

travailleur, euse [travajœr, øz] ■ **adj** hard-working.
■ **nm, f** worker ▸ **travailleur à domicile** homeworker ▸ **travailleur émigré** migrant worker ▸ **travailleur indépendant** self-employed person ▸ **travailleur saisonnier** migrant worker.

travailliste [travajist] ■ **nmf** member of the Labour Party.
■ **adj** Labour *(avant n)*.

travée [trave] **nf 1.** [de bâtiment] bay **2.** [de sièges] row.

traveller [travlœr] **nm inv** traveller's cheque *UK*, traveler's check *US*.

traveller's cheque, traveler's check = *traveller*.

travelling [travliŋ] **nm** [mouvement] travelling *UK ou* traveling *US* shot.

travelo [travlo] **nm** *tfam* drag queen.

travers [travɛr] **nm** failing, fault ▸ **elle tombait dans les mêmes travers que ses prédécesseurs** she displayed the same shortcomings as her predecessors.
◆ ***à travers*** **loc adv & loc prép** through ▸ **à travers les âges** throughout the centuries ▸ **prendre** *ou* **passer à travers champs** to go through the fields *ou* across country.
◆ ***au travers*** **loc adv** through ▸ **passer au travers** *fig* to escape.
◆ ***au travers de*** **loc prép** through ▸ **passer au travers des dangers** to escape danger.
◆ ***de travers*** **loc adv 1.** [irrégulièrement - écrire] unevenly ▸ **marcher de travers** to stagger **2.** [nez, escalier] crooked **3.** [obliquement] sideways ▸ **regarder qqn de travers** *fig* to look askance at sb **4.** [mal] wrong ▸ **aller de travers** to go wrong ▸ **comprendre qqch de travers** to misunderstand sthg ▸ **prendre qqch de travers** to take sthg the wrong way.
◆ ***en travers*** **loc adv** crosswise ▸ **la remorque du camion s'est mise en travers** the truck jack-knifed.
◆ ***en travers de*** **loc prép** across ▸ **s'il se met en travers de mon chemin** *fig* if he stands in my way.

traverse [travɛrs] **nf 1.** [de chemin de fer] sleeper *UK*, tie *US* **2.** [chemin] short cut.

traversée [travɛrse] **nf** crossing.

traverser [3] [travɛrse] **vt 1.** [rue, mer, montagne] to cross / [ville] to go through **2.** [peau, mur] to go through to pierce **3.** [crise, période] to go through.

traversin [travɛrsɛ̃] **nm** bolster.

travesti, e [travɛsti] **adj 1.** [pour s'amuser] dressed up (in fancy dress) **2.** THÉÂTRE [comédien] playing a female part.

◆ ***travesti*** **nm** [homosexuel] transvestite.

travestir [32] [travɛstir] **vt 1.** [déguiser] to dress up **2.** *fig* [vérité, idée] to distort.

◆ ***se travestir*** **vp 1.** [pour bal] to wear fancy dress **2.** [en femme] to put on drag.

travestissement [travɛstismɑ̃] **nm 1.** [pour bal] wearing fancy dress **2.** [en femme] putting on drag **3.** *fig* [de vérité] distortion.

trayeuse [trɛjøz] **nf** milking machine.

trébucher [3] [trebyʃe] **vi : trébucher (sur/contre)** to stumble (over/against).

trèfle [trɛfl] **nm 1.** [plante] clover ▸ **trèfle à quatre feuilles** four-leaved *UK ou* four-leaf *US* clover **2.** [carte] club / [famille] clubs *pl*.

tréfonds [trefɔ̃] **nm** *littéraire* depths *pl*.

treillage [trɛjaʒ] **nm** [clôture] trellis (fencing).

treille [trɛj] **nf 1.** [vigne] climbing vine **2.** [tonnelle] trellised vines *pl*, vine arbour.

treillis [trɛji] **nm 1.** [clôture] trellis (fencing) **2.** [toile] canvas **3.** MIL combat uniform.

treize [trɛz] **adj num inv & nm** thirteen ; voir aussi ***six***.

treizième [trɛzjɛm] **adj num inv, nm & nmf** thirteenth ▸ **treizième mois** *bonus corresponding to an extra month's salary which is paid annually* ; voir aussi ***sixième***.

trekking [trɛkiŋ] **nm** trek.

tréma [trema] **nm** diaeresis *UK*, dieresis *US*.

tremblant, e [trɑ̃blɑ̃, ɑ̃t] **adj 1.** [personne - de froid] shivering / [- d'émotion] trembling, shaking ▸ **être tout tremblant** to be trembling *ou* shaking **2.** [voix] quavering **3.** [lumière] flickering.

tremble [trɑ̃bl] **nm** aspen.

tremblement [trɑ̃bləmɑ̃] **nm 1.** [de corps] trembling **2.** [de voix] quavering **3.** [de feuilles] fluttering.

◆ ***tremblement de terre*** **nm** earthquake.

trembler [3] [trɑ̃ble] **vi 1.** [personne - de froid] to shiver / [- d'émotion] to tremble, to shake **2.** *fig & sout* [avoir peur] to fear ▸ **trembler que** *(+ subjonctif)* to fear (that) ▸ **trembler de faire qqch** to be scared to do sthg **3.** [voix] to quaver **4.** [lumière] to flicker **5.** [terre] to shake.

tremblotant, e [trɑ̃blɔtɑ̃, ɑ̃t] **adj 1.** [personne] trembling **2.** [voix] quavering **3.** [lumière] flickering.

trembloter [3] [trɑ̃blɔte] **vi 1.** [personne] to tremble **2.** [voix] to quaver **3.** [lumière] to flicker.

trémière [tremjɛr] ➤ ***rose***.

trémolo [tremɔlo] **nm** tremolo ▸ **avoir des trémolos dans la voix** *hum* to have a quaver in one's voice.

trémousser [3] [tremuse] ◆ ***se trémousser*** **vp** to jig up and down.

trempe [trɑ̃p] **nf 1.** [envergure] calibre ▸ **de sa trempe** of his/her calibre **2.** *fam* [coups] thrashing.

trempé, e [trɑ̃pe] **adj 1.** [personne, vêtements] soaked, drenched / [chaussures, jardin] waterlogged ▸ **trempé de sueur** soaked with sweat ▸ **trempé de larmes** [mouchoir] tear-stained **2.** [énergique] **: avoir le caractère bien trempé** to be resilient **3.** [métallurgie] quenched **4.** [verre] toughened.

tremper [3] [trɑ̃pe] ■ **vt 1.** [mouiller] to soak ▸ **faire tremper** to soak **2.** [plonger] **: tremper qqch dans** to dip sthg into **3.** [métal] to harden, to quench.

■ **vi 1.** [linge] to soak **2.** [se compromettre] **: tremper dans** to be involved in.

◆ ***se tremper*** **vp 1.** [se mouiller] to get soaking wet **2.** [se plonger] to have a quick dip.

trempette [trɑ̃pɛt] **nf : faire trempette** [se baigner] to go for a dip / [avec biscuit] to dunk.

tremplin [trɑ̃plɛ̃] **nm** *fig* springboard / SKI ski jump.

trench-coat [trɛnʃkot] (pl **trench-coats**) **nm** trench coat.

trentaine [trɑ̃tɛn] **nf 1.** [nombre] **: une trentaine de** about thirty **2.** [âge] **: avoir la trentaine** to be in one's thirties.

trente [trɑ̃t] ■ **adj num inv** thirty ▸ **trente-trois tours** LP, long-playing record.

■ **nm** thirty ▸ **être/se mettre sur son trente et un** *fig* to be in/to put on one's Sunday best ; voir aussi ***six***.

trente-six [trɑ̃tsiz] *(en fin de phrase* [trɑ̃tsi], *devant consonne ou h aspiré* [trɑ̃tsi], *devant voyelle ou h muet* [trɑ̃tsiz]*)* ■ **dét** *fam* [pour exprimer la multitude] umpteen, dozens of ▸ **il n'y a pas trente-six solutions!** there aren't all that many solutions! ▸ **j'ai trente-six mille choses à faire** I've a hundred and one things to do

▸▸ **voir trente-six chandelles** to see stars.

■ **nm inv** *fam* **: tous les trente-six du mois** once in a blue moon ; voir aussi ***cinquante***.

trentième [trɑ̃tjɛm] **adj num inv, nm & nmf** thirtieth ; voir aussi ***sixième***.

trépaner [3] [trepane] **vt** MÉD to trepan.

trépas [trepa] **nm** *littéraire* demise.

trépasser [3] [trepase] **vi** *littéraire* to pass away.

trépidant, e [trepidɑ̃, ɑ̃t] **adj** [vie] hectic.

trépidation [trepidasjɔ̃] **nf** [vibration] vibration.

trépied [trepje] **nm 1.** [support] tripod **2.** [meuble] three-legged stool/table.

trépignement [trepiɲmɑ̃] **nm** stamping.

trépigner [3] [trepiɲe] **vi** to stamp one's feet.

très [trɛ] **adv** very ▸ **très malade** very ill ▸ **très bien** very well ▸ **être très aimé** to be much *ou* greatly liked ▸ **avoir très peur/faim** to be very frightened/hungry ▸ **j'ai très envie de...** I'd very much like to...

trésor [trezɔr] **nm** treasure ▸ **mon trésor** *fig* my precious.

◆ ***Trésor*** **nm : le Trésor public** the public revenue department.

◆ ***trésors*** **nmpl** riches, treasures ▸ **des trésors de** *fig* a wealth *(sg)* of.

trésorerie [trezɔrri] **nf 1.** [service] accounts department **2.** [gestion] accounts *pl* **3.** [fonds] finances *pl*, funds *pl*.

trésorier, ère [trezɔrje, ɛr] **nm, f** treasurer.

tressaillement [tresajmɑ̃] **nm** [de joie] thrill / [de douleur] wince.

tressaillir [47] [tresajir] **vi 1.** [de joie] to thrill / [de douleur] to wince **2.** [sursauter] to start, to jump.

tressauter [3] [tresote] **vi** [sursauter] to jump, to start / [dans véhicule] to be tossed about ▸ **faire tressauter** to toss *ou* jolt about.

tresse [trɛs] **nf 1.** [de cheveux] plait **2.** [de rubans] braid.

tresser [4] [trese] **vt 1.** [cheveux] to plait **2.** [osier] to braid **3.** [panier, guirlande] to weave.

tréteau, x [treto] **nm** trestle.

treuil [trœj] **nm** winch, windlass.

trêve [trɛv] **nf 1.** [cessez-le-feu] truce **2.** *fig* [répit] rest, respite ▸ **trêve de plaisanteries/de sottises** that's enough joking/nonsense.
◆ ***sans trêve*** **loc adv** relentlessly, unceasingly.

tri [tri] **nm** [de lettres] sorting / [de candidats] selection ▸ **faire le tri dans qqch** *fig* to sort sthg out / [déchets] **: tri sélectif (des ordures)** *sorting of rubbish into different types for recycling.*

triage [trijaʒ] **nm** [de lettres] sorting / [de candidats] selection.

triangle [trijɑ̃gl] **nm** triangle ▸ **triangle isocèle** isosceles triangle ▸ **triangle rectangle** right-angled triangle.

triangulaire [trijɑ̃gylɛr] **adj** triangular.

triathlon [trijatlɔ̃] **nm** triathlon.

tribal, e, aux [tribal, o] **adj** tribal.

tribord [tribɔr] **nm** starboard ▸ **à tribord** on the starboard side, to starboard.

tribu [triby] **nf** tribe.

tribulations [tribylasjɔ̃] **nfpl** tribulations, trials.

tribun [tribœ̃] **nm 1.** HIST tribune **2.** [orateur] popular orator.

tribunal, aux [tribynal, o] **nm 1.** DR court ▸ **tribunal correctionnel** ≃ magistrates' court *UK*, ≃ county court *US* ▸ **tribunal pour enfants** juvenile court ▸ **tribunal d'exception** special court ▸ **tribunal de grande instance** ≃ crown court *UK*, ≃ circuit court *US* ▸ **tribunal d'instance** ≃ magistrates' court *UK*, ≃ county court *US* ▸ **tribunal de police** police court **2.** *fig* [jugement] judgment.

tribune [tribyn] **nf 1.** [d'orateur] platform **2.** *(gén pl)* [de stade] stand **3.** *fig* [lieu d'expression] forum ▸ **tribune libre** PRESSE opinion column.

tribut [triby] **nm** *littéraire* tribute.

tributaire [tribytɛr] **adj : être tributaire de** to depend *ou* be dependent on.

tricentenaire [trisɑ̃tnɛr] ■ **adj** three-hundred-year-old.
■ **nm** tricentennial.

triceps [trisɛps] **nm** triceps.

triche [triʃ] **nf** *fam* cheating.

tricher [3] [triʃe] **vi 1.** [au jeu, à un examen] to cheat **2.** [mentir] **: tricher sur** to lie about.

tricherie [triʃri] **nf** cheating.

tricheur, euse [triʃœr, øz] **nm, f** cheat.

tricolore [trikɔlɔr] **adj 1.** [à trois couleurs] three-coloured *UK*, three-colored *US* **2.** [français] French.

tricot [triko] **nm 1.** [vêtement] jumper *UK*, sweater ▸ **tricot de corps** vest *UK*, undershirt *US* **2.** [ouvrage] knitting ▸ **faire du tricot** to knit **3.** [étoffe] knitted fabric, jersey.

tricoter [3] [trikɔte] **vi & vt** to knit.

tricycle [trisikl] **nm** tricycle.

trident [tridɑ̃] **nm 1.** MYTHOL trident **2.** [fourche] pitchfork.

tridimensionnel, elle [tridimɑ̃sjɔnɛl] **adj** three-dimensional.

triennal, e, aux [trienal, o] **adj 1.** [mandat] three-year **2.** [élection] three-yearly.

trier [10] [trije] **vt 1.** [classer] to sort out **2.** [sélectionner] to select ▸ **trier sur le volet** to handpick.

trifouiller [3] [trifuje] **vi** *fam* to rummage around.

trigonométrie [trigɔnɔmetri] **nf** trigonometry.

trilingue [trilɛ̃g] ■ **nmf** person who is trilingual.
■ **adj** trilingual.

trille [trij] **nm** trill.

trilogie [trilɔʒi] **nf** trilogy.

trim. **1.** (abr écrite de ***trimestre***) quarter **2.** (abr écrite de ***trimestriel***) quarterly.

trimaran [trimarɑ̃] **nm** trimaran.

trimbaler [3] [trɛ̃bale] **vt** *fam* [personne] to trail around / [chose] to cart around, to schlepp around *US*.
◆ ***se trimbaler*** **vp** *fam* to trail around.

trimer [3] [trime] **vi** *fam* to slave away.

trimestre [trimɛstr] **nm 1.** SCOL term *UK*, trimester *US*, quarter *US* **2.** [loyer] quarter's rent / [rente] quarter's income
▸▸ **par trimestre** termly.

trimestriel, elle [trimɛstrijɛl] **adj** [loyer, magazine] quarterly / SCOL end-of-term *(avant n) UK*.

trimoteur [trimɔtœr] ■ **nm** three-engined plane.
■ **adj** three-engined.

tringle [trɛ̃gl] **nf** rod ▸ **tringle à rideaux** curtain rod.

trinité [trinite] **nf** *littéraire* trinity.
◆ ***Trinité*** **nf : la Trinité** the Trinity.

trinquer [3] [trɛ̃ke] **vi 1.** [boire] to toast, to clink glasses ▸ **trinquer à** to drink to **2.** *fam* [personne] to get the worst of it / [voiture] to be damaged.

trio [trijo] **nm** trio.

triomphal, e, aux [trijɔ̃fal, o] **adj** [succès] triumphal / [accueil] triumphant.

triomphalement [trijɔ̃falmɑ̃] **adv 1.** [en triomphe] in triumph **2.** [fièrement] triumphantly.

triomphalisme [trijɔ̃falism] **nm** triumphalism.

triomphant, e [trijɔ̃fɑ̃, ɑ̃t] **adj** [équipe] winning / [air] triumphant.

triomphateur, trice [trijɔ̃fatœr, tris] ■ **adj** triumphant.
■ **nm, f** victor.

triomphe [trijɔ̃f] **nm** triumph.

triompher [3] [trijɔ̃fe] **vi 1.** [gén] to triumph ▸ **triompher de** to triumph over ▸ **faire triompher qqch** to ensure the success of sthg **2.** [crier victoire] to rejoice.

trip [trip] nm *arg crime* trip.

triparti, ***e*** [triparti], ***tripartite*** [tripartit] adj tripartite.

tripatouiller [3] [tripatuje] vt *fam* **1.** [fruits] to paw **2.** [texte, compte] to fiddle with.

triperie [tripri] nf **1.** [commerce] tripe trade **2.** [boutique] tripe shop **3.** [aliments] tripe.

tripes [trip] nfpl **1.** [d'animal, de personne] guts ▸ **prendre qqn aux tripes** *fam fig* to get sb in the guts **2.** CULIN tripe *sg*.

tripier, ***ère*** [tripje, ɛr] nm, f tripe butcher.

triple [tripl] ■ adj triple.
■ nm : **le triple (de)** three times as much (as).

triplé, ***ées*** [triple] nm **1.** [au turf] *bet on three horses winning in three different races* **2.** SPORT [trois victoires] hat-trick of victories.
◆ ***triplés***, ***ées*** nmf pl triplets.

triplement [tripləmɑ̃] ■ adv trebly.
■ nm threefold increase, tripling.

tripler [3] [triple] vt & vi to triple.

triporteur [tripɔrtœr] nm tricycle *(used for deliveries)*.

tripot [tripo] nm *péj* gambling den.

tripotage [tripɔtaʒ] nm *(gén pl) fam* [manigances] fiddling *(U)*.

tripoter [3] [tripɔte] ■ vt **1.** *fam* [stylo, montre] to play with **2.** *vulg* [femme] to feel up.
■ vi *fam* : **tripoter dans** [fouiller dans] to rummage about in / [trafiquer] to dabble in.

tripous, ***tripoux*** [tripu] nmpl *stuffed tripe*.

triptyque [triptik] nm triptych.

trique [trik] nf cudgel.

trisomie [trizɔmi] nf trisomy ▸ **trisomie 21** trisomy 21.

trisomique [trizɔmik] ■ adj : **enfant trisomique** Down's syndrome child.
■ nmf Down's syndrome child.

triste [trist] adj **1.** [personne, nouvelle] sad ▸ **être triste de qqch/de faire qqch** to be sad about sthg/about doing sthg ▸ **d'un air triste** bleakly ▸ **faire triste figure** ***ou*** **mine** *littéraire* to look pitiful **2.** [paysage, temps] gloomy ▸ **une ville triste à pleurer** a dreadfully bleak town / [couleur] dull **3.** *(avant n)* [lamentable] sorry ▸ **elle était dans un triste état** she was in a sorry state ▸ **son triste sort** his sad ***ou*** unhappy fate.

tristement [tristəmɑ̃] adv **1.** [d'un air triste] sadly **2.** [lugubrement] gloomily **3.** [de façon regrettable] sadly, regrettably ▸ **tristement célèbre** notorious.

tristesse [tristɛs] nf **1.** [de personne, nouvelle] sadness **2.** [de paysage, temps] gloominess.

tristounet, ***ette*** [tristunɛ, ɛt] adj *fam* **1.** [personne] sad **2.** *péj* [humeur] gloomy.

trithérapie [triterapi] nf combination therapy.

triton [tritɔ̃] nm triton.

triturer [3] [trityre] vt **1.** [sel] to grind **2.** *fam* [mouchoir] to knead.
◆ ***se triturer*** vp *fam* : **se triturer l'esprit** ***ou*** **les méninges** to rack one's brains.

trivial, ***e***, ***aux*** [trivjal, o] adj **1.** [banal] trivial **2.** *péj* [vulgaire] crude, coarse.

trivialité [trivjalite] nf **1.** [banalité] triviality **2.** *péj* [vulgarité] vulgar ***ou*** coarse expression.

tr/mn, ***tr/min*** (abr écrite de ***tour par minute***) r/min, rpm.

troc [trɔk] nm **1.** [échange] exchange **2.** [système économique] barter.

troène [trɔɛn] nm privet.

troglodyte [trɔglɔdit] nm cave dweller, troglodyte.

trogne [trɔɲ] nf *fam* [visage] mug.

trognon [trɔɲɔ̃] ■ nm [de fruit] core.
■ adj inv *fam* [mignon] sweet, cute.

troïka [trɔika] nf troika.

trois [trwa] ■ nm three.
■ adj num inv three ▸ **les trois-huit** shift work ▸ **trois fois rien** *fig* nothing at all ▸ **les trois jours** MIL *induction course preceding military service (now lasting one day)* / voir aussi ***six***.

trois étoiles [trwazetwal] ■ adj three-star *(avant n)*.
■ nm three-star hotel/restaurant.

troisième [trwazjɛm] ■ adj num inv & nmf third.
■ nm third / [étage] third floor ***UK***, fourth floor ***US***.
■ nf **1.** SCOL ≃ fourth year ***ou*** form ***UK***, ≃ ninth grade ***US*** **2.** [vitesse] third (gear) ; voir aussi ***sixième***.

troisièmement [trwazjɛmmɑ̃] adv thirdly.

trois-mâts [trwama] nm inv three-master.

trois-quarts [trwakar] nm inv [rugby] three-quarter.

trolley [trɔlɛ] nm **1.** *fam* [transports] = ***trolleybus*** **2.** [chariot] truck *(on cableway)* **3.** ÉLECTR trolley.

trolley(bus) [trɔlɛ(bys)] nm trolleybus.

trombe [trɔ̃b] nf water spout ▸ **passer en trombe** *fig* to zoom past, to speed past ▸ **des trombes d'eau** torrential rain *(U)*.

trombone [trɔ̃bɔn] nm **1.** [agrafe] paper clip **2.** [instrument] trombone ▸ **trombone à coulisse** slide trombone **3.** [joueur] trombone player, trombonist.

trompe [trɔ̃p] nf **1.** [instrument] trumpet **2.** [d'éléphant] trunk **3.** [d'insecte] proboscis **4.** ANAT tube.

trompe-l'œil [trɔ̃plœj] nm inv **1.** [peinture] trompe-l'oeil ▸ **en trompe-l'œil** done in trompe-l'oeil **2.** [apparence] deception.

tromper [3] [trɔ̃pe] vt **1.** [personne] to deceive ▸ **tromper qqn sur ses intentions** to mislead sb as to one's intentions ▸ **on m'a trompé sur la qualité** I was misinformed as to the quality / [époux] to be unfaithful to, to deceive ▸ **elle le trompe avec Thomas** she's having an affair with Thomas behind his back **2.** [vigilance] to elude **3.** *littéraire* [espoirs] to fall short of ▸ **tromper l'espoir de qqn** to disappoint sb **4.** [faim] to stave off.
◆ ***se tromper*** vp to make a mistake, to be mistaken ▸ **se tromper d'adresse** to go to the wrong address ▸ **se tromper de jour/maison** to get the wrong day/house ▸ **se tromper dans une addition/dictée** to get a sum/dictation wrong ▸ **si je ne me trompe** if I'm not mistaken.

tromperie [trɔ̃pri] nf deception.

trompette [trɔ̃pɛt] nf trumpet.

trompettiste [trɔ̃petist] **nmf** trumpeter.

trompeur, euse [trɔ̃pœr, øz] ■ **adj 1.** [personne] deceitful **2.** [calme, apparence] deceptive.
■ **nm, f** deceitful person.

trompeusement [trɔ̃pøzmɑ̃] **adv 1.** [hypocritement] deceitfully **2.** [apparemment] deceptively.

tronc [trɔ̃] **nm 1.** [d'arbre, de personne] trunk **2.** [d'église] collection box **3.** [de veine, nerf] stem.
◆ ***tronc commun*** **nm** [de programmes] common element *ou* feature / SCOL core syllabus.

tronche [trɔ̃ʃ] **nf** *fam péj* [visage] mug.

tronçon [trɔ̃sɔ̃] **nm 1.** [morceau] piece, length **2.** [de route, de chemin de fer] section.

tronçonner [3] [trɔ̃sɔne] **vt** to cut into pieces.

tronçonneuse [trɔ̃sɔnøz] **nf** chain saw.

trône [tron] **nm** throne.

trôner [3] [trone] **vi 1.** [personne] to sit enthroned / [objet] to have pride of place **2.** *hum* [faire l'important] to lord it.

tronquer [3] [trɔ̃ke] **vt** to truncate.

trop [tro] **adv 1.** *(devant adj, adv)* too ▸ **trop vieux/loin** too old/far ▸ **nous étions trop nombreux** there were too many of us ▸ **avoir trop chaud/froid/peur** to be too hot/cold/frightened **2.** *(avec verbe)* too much ▸ **cela n'a que trop duré** it's been going on far too long ▸ **trop c'est trop!** enough is enough! ▸ **il mange trop** he eats too much ▸ **nous étions trop** there were too many of us ▸ **on a trop chargé la voiture** we've overloaded the car ▸ **je n'aime pas trop le chocolat** I don't like chocolate very much ▸ **on ne se voit plus trop** we don't really see each other any more ▸ **sans trop savoir pourquoi** without really knowing why ▸ **en faire trop** [travailler] to overdo things / [pour plaire] to overdo it **3.** *(avec complément)* **: trop de** [quantité] too much / [nombre] too many ▸ **il y a beaucoup trop de monde** there are far too many people ▸ **j'ai trop de soucis pour me charger des vôtres** I've too many worries of my own to deal with yours.
◆ ***en trop, de trop*** **loc adv** too much/many ▸ **2 euros de** *ou* **en trop** 2 euros too much ▸ **il y a un verre en trop** there's a *ou* one glass too many ▸ **un rafraîchissement ne serait pas de trop!** a drink wouldn't go amiss! ▸ **une personne de** *ou* **en trop** one person too many ▸ **être de trop** [personne] to be in the way, to be unwelcome ▸ **se sentir en trop** to feel in the way.

trophée [trɔfe] **nm** trophy.

tropical, e, aux [trɔpikal, o] **adj** tropical.

tropique [trɔpik] **nm** tropic ▸ **tropique du Cancer/du Capricorne** Tropic of Cancer/Capricorn.
◆ ***tropiques*** **nmpl** tropics.

trop-perçu [trɔpersy] (pl **trop-perçus**) **nm** excess payment, overpayment.

trop-plein [trɔplɛ̃] (pl **trop-pleins**) **nm 1.** [excès] excess / *fig* excess, surplus **2.** [déversoir] overflow.

troquer [3] [trɔke] **vt : troquer qqch (contre)** to barter sthg (for) / *fig* to swap sthg (for).

troquet [trɔkɛ] **nm** *fam* (small) café.

trot [tro] **nm** trot ▸ **au trot** at a trot ▸ **au trot!** *fam fig* at the double!

trotter [3] [trɔte] **vi 1.** [cheval] to trot **2.** [personne] to run around.

trotteur, euse [trɔtœr, øz] **nm, f** trotter.
◆ ***trotteuse*** **nf** second hand.

trottiner [3] [trɔtine] **vi** to trot.

trottinette [trɔtinɛt] **nf** child's scooter.

trottoir [trɔtwar] **nm** pavement *UK*, sidewalk *US* ▸ **faire le trottoir** *fam fig* to walk the streets.

trou [tru] **nm 1.** [gén] hole ▸ **trou d'aération** air vent ▸ **trou d'air** air pocket ▸ **des trous d'air** turbulence ▸ **trou normand** *glass of Calvados taken between courses* ▸ **trou de serrure** keyhole ▸ **faire un trou à son collant** to make a hole in *ou* to rip one's tights ▸ **elle a fait son trou dans l'édition** she has made a nice little niche for herself in publishing **2.** [manque, espace vide] gap ▸ **trou de mémoire** memory lapse **3.** *fam* [prison] nick *UK*, clink ▸ **être au trou** to be inside **4.** *fam* [endroit reculé] (little) place, hole *péj*, one-horse-town *hum* ▸ **pas même un café, quel trou!** not even a café, what a dump!

troublant, e [trublɑ̃, ɑ̃t] **adj** disturbing.

trouble [trubl] ■ **adj 1.** [eau] cloudy **2.** [image, vue] blurred **3.** [affaire] shady.
■ **nm 1.** [désordre] trouble, discord **2.** [gêne] confusion / [émoi] agitation **3.** *(gén pl)* [dérèglement] disorder ▸ **troubles moteurs** motor disorders ▸ **troubles respiratoires** respiratory disorders.
◆ ***troubles*** **nmpl** [sociaux] unrest *(U)*.

trouble-fête [trubləfɛt] **nmf** spoilsport.

troubler [3] [truble] **vt 1.** [eau] to cloud, to make cloudy **2.** [image, vue] to blur **3.** [sommeil, événement] to disrupt, to disturb **4.** [esprit, raison] to cloud **5.** [inquiéter, émouvoir] to disturb **6.** [rendre perplexe] to trouble.
◆ ***se troubler*** **vp 1.** [eau] to become cloudy **2.** [personne] to become flustered.

trouée [true] **nf** gap / MIL breach.

trouer [3] [true] **vt 1.** [chaussette] to make a hole in **2.** *fig* [silence] to disturb.

troufion [trufjɔ̃] **nm** *fam* soldier.

trouillard, e [trujar, ard] *fam* ■ **adj** yellow, chicken.
■ **nm, f** chicken.

trouille [truj] **nf** *fam* fear, terror.

troupe [trup] **nf 1.** MIL troop **2.** [d'amis] group, band / [d singes] troop **3.** THÉÂTRE theatre *UK ou* theater *US* group

troupeau, x [trupo] **nm** [de vaches, d'éléphants] herd [de moutons, d'oies] flock / *péj* [de personnes] herd.

trousse [trus] **nf** case, bag ▸ **trousse de secours** first-ai kit ▸ **trousse de toilette** toilet bag.
◆ ***trousses*** **nfpl : avoir qqn à ses trousses** *fig* to hav sb hot on one's heels ▸ **être aux trousses de qqn** *fig* to b hot on the heels of sb.

trousseau, x [truso] **nm 1.** [de mariée] trousseau **2.** [d clefs] bunch.

trousser [3] [truse] **vt 1.** [manches] to roll up / [jupe] t hitch up **2.** CULIN to truss.

trouvaille [truvaj] **nf 1.** [découverte] find, discover **2.** [invention] new idea.

trouvé, e [truve] **adj** [découvert] **: enfant trouvé** foundling ▸ **bien trouvé** [original] well-chosen, apposite ▸ **voilà une réponse bien trouvée!** that's a (pretty) good answer! ▸ **tout trouvé** ready-made.

trouver [3] [truve] ■ **vt** to find ▸ **trouver qqch par hasard** to chance *ou* to stumble upon sthg ▸ **j'ai trouvé ce livre en faisant du rangement** I found *ou* came across this book while I was tidying up ▸ **trouver que** to feel (that) ▸ **trouver qqch à qqn : je lui trouve du charme** I think he's got charm ▸ **trouver bon/mauvais que...** to think (that) it is right/wrong that... ▸ **trouver qqch à faire/à dire** *etc* to find sthg to do/say *etc* ▸ **trouver à s'occuper** to find something to do.
■ **v impers : il se trouve que...** the fact is that... ▸ **il se trouve que quelqu'un vous a vu dans mon bureau** as it happens, somebody saw you in my office.
◆ ***se trouver*** **vp 1.** [dans un endroit] to be ▸ **où se trouve la gare?** where's the station? ▸ **si ça se trouve** *fam* maybe **2.** [dans un état] to find o.s. ▸ **se trouver dans l'impossibilité de faire qqch** to find o.s. *ou* to be unable to do sthg **3.** [se sentir] to feel ▸ **je me suis trouvé bête d'avoir crié** I felt stupid for having screamed ▸ **se trouver mal** [s'évanouir] to faint.

truand [tryɑ̃] **nm** crook.

truander [3] [tryɑ̃de] **vt** *fam* to rip off.

trublion [tryblijɔ̃] **nm** troublemaker.

truc [tryk] **nm 1.** [combine] trick ▸ **j'ai un truc pour rentrer sans payer** I know a way of getting in without paying **2.** *fam* [chose] thing, thingamajig ▸ **ce n'est pas son truc** it's not his thing ▸ **j'ai plein de trucs à faire** I've got lots to do ▸ **je pense à un truc** I've just thought of something ▸ **mange pas de ce truc-là!** don't eat any of that (stuff)!

trucage = ***truquage***.

truchement [tryʃmɑ̃] **nm : par le truchement de qqn** through sb.

trucider [3] [tryside] **vt** *fam hum* to bump off.

truculence [trykylɑ̃s] **nf** vividness, colourfulness *UK*, colorfulness *US*.

truculent, e [trykylɑ̃, ɑ̃t] **adj** colourful *UK*, colorful *US*.

truelle [tryɛl] **nf** trowel.

truffe [tryf] **nf 1.** [champignon] truffle ▸ **truffe en chocolat** chocolate truffle **2.** [museau] muzzle.

truffer [3] [tryfe] **vt 1.** [volaille] to garnish with truffles **2.** *fig* [discours] **: truffer de** to stuff with.

truie [trɥi] **nf** sow.

truite [trɥit] **nf** trout.

truquage, trucage [trykaʒ] **nm 1.** [d'élections] rigging **2.** CINÉ (special) effect.

truquer [3] [tryke] **vt 1.** [élections] to rig **2.** CINÉ to use special effects in.

trust [trœst] **nm 1.** [groupement] trust **2.** [entreprise] corporation.

ts abr de ***tous***.

tsar [tsar], ***tzar*** [dzar] **nm** tsar.

tsé-tsé [tsetse] ➤ ***mouche***.

tsigane [tsigan] **adj** Gypsyish.
◆ ***Tsigane*** **nmf** (Hungarian) Gypsy.

TSVP (abr de ***tournez s'il vous plaît***) PTO.

tt abr de ***tout***.

TT(A) (abr de ***transit temporaire (autorisé)***) *registration for vehicles bought in France for tax-free export by non-residents*.

TTC (abr de ***toutes taxes comprises***) **loc adj** inclusive of all tax, including tax.

tt conf. abr de ***tout confort***.

ttes (abr écrite de ***toutes***), ➤ ***tout***.

TTX (abr écrite de ***traitement de texte***) WP.

tu[1], ***e*** [ty] **pp** ➤ ***taire***.

tu[2] [ty] **pron pers** you ▸ **dire tu à qqn** to use the "tu" form to sb.

TU (abr de ***temps universel***) **nm** UT, GMT.

tuant, e [tɥɑ̃, ɑ̃t] **adj 1.** [épuisant] exhausting **2.** [énervant] tiresome.

tuba [tyba] **nm 1.** MUS tuba **2.** [de plongée] snorkel.

tube [tyb] **nm 1.** [gén] tube ▸ **tube cathodique** cathode ray tube ▸ **à pleins tubes** *fig* [chanter, crier] at the top of one's voice / [mettre la musique] at full blast **2.** *fam* [chanson] hit.
◆ ***tube digestif*** **nm** digestive tract.

tubercule [tybɛrkyl] **nm 1.** BOT tuber **2.** ANAT tubercle.

tuberculeux, euse [tybɛrkylø, øz] ■ **adj** tubercular.
■ **nm, f** tuberculosis sufferer.

tuberculose [tybɛrkyloz] **nf** tuberculosis.

tubulaire [tybylɛr] **adj** tubular.

TUC, Tuc [tyk] (abr de ***travail d'utilité collective***) **nm** *community work scheme for unemployed young people*.

tue-mouches [tymuʃ] ➤ ***papier***.

tuer [7] [tɥe] **vt** to kill ▸ **je t'assure, il est à tuer!** [exaspérant] honestly, I could (cheerfully) kill him! ▸ **se faire tuer** to be killed ▸ **tuer le temps** to kill time ▸ **tuer qqch dans l'œuf** to nip sthg in the bud.
◆ ***se tuer*** **vp 1.** [se suicider] to kill o.s. **2.** [par accident] to die **3.** *fig* [s'épuiser] **: se tuer à faire qqch** to wear o.s. out doing sthg ▸ **elle se tue à la tâche** she's working herself to death.

tuerie [tyri] **nf** slaughter.

tue-tête [tytɛt] ◆ ***à tue-tête*** **loc adv** at the top of one's voice.

tueur, euse [tɥœr, øz] **nm, f 1.** [meurtrier] killer ▸ **tueur à gages** hit man ▸ **tueur en série** serial killer **2.** [dans abattoir] slaughterer.

tuile [tɥil] **nf 1.** [de toit] tile **2.** *fam* [désagrément] blow.

tulipe [tylip] **nf** tulip.

tulle [tyl] **nm** tulle.

tuméfié, e [tymefje] **adj** swollen.

tumeur [tymœr] **nf** tumour *UK*, tumor *US*.

tumoral, e, aux [tymɔral, o] **adj** tumorous.

tumulte [tymylt] **nm 1.** [désordre] hubbub **2.** *littéraire* [trouble] tumult.

tumultueux, euse [tymyltɥø, øz] **adj** stormy.
tune = ***thune***.
tuner [tynɛr] **nm** tuner.
tungstène [tœ̃kstɛn] **nm** tungsten.
tunique [tynik] **nf** tunic.
Tunis [tynis] **npr** Tunis.
Tunisie [tynizi] **nf : la Tunisie** Tunisia.
tunisien, enne [tynizjɛ̃, ɛn] **adj** Tunisian.
◆ ***Tunisien, enne*** **nm, f** Tunisian.
tunnel [tynɛl] **nm** tunnel.
TUP [typ] (abr de ***titre universel de paiement***) **nm** *payment slip formerly used to settle bills.*
tuque [tyk] **nf** *Québec* wool hat, tuque *Québec*.
turban [tyrbɑ̃] **nm** turban.
turbin [turbɛ̃] **nm** *fam* **: aller au turbin** to go to work.
turbine [tyrbin] **nf** turbine.
turbo [tyrbo] **nm & nf** turbo.
turboréacteur [tyrbɔreaktœr] **nm** turbojet.
turbot [tyrbo] **nm** turbot.
turbotrain [tyrbɔtrɛ̃] **nm** turbotrain.
turbulence [tyrbylɑ̃s] **nf 1.** [de personne] boisterousness **2.** MÉTÉOR turbulence.
turbulent, e [tyrbylɑ̃, ɑ̃t] **adj** boisterous.
turc, turque [tyrk] **adj** Turkish.
◆ ***turc*** **nm** [langue] Turkish.
◆ ***Turc, Turque*** **nm, f** Turk.
turf [tœrf] **nm** [activité] **: le turf** racing.
turfiste [tœrfist] **nmf** racegoer.
turkmène [tyrkmɛn] ■ **adj** Turkmen.
■ **nm** [langue] Turkmen.
◆ ***Turkmène*** **nmf** Turkoman.
turlupiner [3] [tyrlypine] **vt** *fam* to nag.
turnover [tœrnɔvœr] **nm** turnover.
turpitude [tyrpityd] **nf** [littéraire] turpitude.
turque ➤ ***turc***.
Turquie [tyrki] **nf : la Turquie** Turkey.
turquoise [tyrkwaz] **nf & adj inv** turquoise.
tutelle [tytɛl] **nf 1.** DR guardianship **2.** [dépendance] supervision ▸ **sous la tutelle des Nations unies** under United Nations supervision **3.** [protection] protection.
tuteur, trice [tytœr, tris] **nm, f** guardian.
◆ ***tuteur*** **nm** [pour plante] stake.
tutoiement [tytwamɑ̃] **nm** use of "tu".
tutoyer [13] [tytwaje] **vt : tutoyer qqn** to use the familiar "tu" form to sb ▸ **elle tutoie son professeur** ≃ she's on first-name terms with her teacher.
◆ ***se tutoyer*** **vp** to use the familiar "tu" form with each other.
tutu [tyty] **nm** tutu.
tuyau, x [tɥijo] **nm 1.** [conduit] pipe ▸ **tuyau d'arrosage** hosepipe **2.** *fam* [renseignement] tip.
tuyauter [3] [tɥijote] **vt** *fam* to give a tip to.
tuyauterie [tɥijotri] **nf** piping *(U)*, pipes *pl*.
TV (abr de ***télévision***) **nf** TV.
TVA (abr de ***taxe à la valeur ajoutée***) **nf** ≃ VAT.

CULTURE

TVA

The **taxe sur la valeur ajoutée** is an indirect tax included in the price of most goods and services – it is even levied on taxes themselves. Created in 1954, it applies in all European Union member nations. In France, the normal rate is 19.6%. A reduced rate of 5.5% applies to books, food and entertainment, passenger transport, and some utility costs for private homes. An even lower rate applies to television licence fees and most medicine.

TVHD (abr de ***télévision haute définition***) **nf** HDTV.
tweed [twid] **nm** tweed.
twin-set [twinsɛt] (pl **twin-sets**) **nm** twin set *UK*, sweater set *US*.
tympan [tɛ̃pɑ̃] **nm 1.** ANAT eardrum **2.** ARCHIT tympanum.
type [tip] ■ **nm 1.** [exemple caractéristique] perfect example ▸ **il est le type parfait du professeur** he's the classic example of a teacher ▸ **c'est le type même du romantique** he's the typical romantic **2.** [genre] type ▸ **avoir le type nordique/méditerranéen** to have Nordic/Mediterranean features **3.** *fam* [individu] guy, bloke *UK* ▸ **c'est un drôle de type!** [bizarre] he's a pretty weird bloke! / [louche] he's a shady character! ▸ **quel sale type!** what a nasty piece of work! *UK*, what an SOB! *US*
■ **adj inv** [caractéristique] typical ▸ **contrat type** model contract ▸ **erreur type** typical *ou* classic mistake.
typé, e [tipe] **adj : il est bien** *ou* **très typé** he has all the characteristic features.
typhoïde [tifɔid] ■ **nf** typhoid.
■ **adj : fièvre typhoïde** typhoid fever.
typhon [tifɔ̃] **nm** typhoon.
typhus [tifys] **nm** typhus.
typique [tipik] **adj** typical.
typiquement [tipikmɑ̃] **adv** typically.
typographe [tipɔgraf] **nmf** typographer.
typographie [tipɔgrafi] **nf** typography.
typographique [tipɔgrafik] **adj** typographical.
typologie [tipɔlɔʒi] **nf** typology.
tyran [tirɑ̃] **nm** tyrant.
tyrannie [tirani] **nf** tyranny.
tyrannique [tiranik] **adj** tyrannical.
tyranniser [3] [tiranize] **vt** to tyrannize.
tyrolien, enne [tirɔljɛ̃, ɛn] **adj** Tyrolean.
◆ ***tyrolienne*** **nf** [air] Tyrolienne.
◆ ***Tyrolien, enne*** **nm, f** Tyrolean.
tzar = ***tsar***.
tzigane [dzigan], ***tsigane*** [tsigan] ■ **nmf** gipsy.
■ **adj** gipsy *(avant n)*.

u, ***U*** [y] **nm inv** u, U.

ubiquité [ybikɥite] **nf** ubiquity ▸ **je n'ai pas le don d'ubiquité** I can't be everywhere (at once).

UDF (abr de ***Union pour la démocratie française***) **nf** *French political party to the right of the political spectrum.*

UE (abr de ***Union européenne***) **nf** EU.

UEFA (abr de ***Union of European Football Associations***) **nf** UEFA.

UEO (abr de ***Union de l'Europe occidentale***) **nf** WEU.

UER **nf 1.** (abr de ***unité d'enseignement et de recherche***) *former name for a university department* **2.** (abr de ***Union européenne de radiodiffusion***) EBU.

UFC (abr de ***Union fédérale des consommateurs***) **nf** *French consumers' association.*

UFR (abr de ***unité de formation et de recherche***) **nf** university department.

UHF (abr de ***ultra-haute fréquence***) **nf** UHF.

UHT (abr de ***ultra-haute température***) **nf** UHT.

Ukraine [ykrɛn] **nf : l'Ukraine** the Ukraine.

ukrainien, ***enne*** [ykrɛnjɛ̃, ɛn] **adj** Ukrainian.
◆ ***ukrainien*** **nm** [langue] Ukrainian.
◆ ***Ukrainien***, ***enne*** **nm, f** Ukrainian.

ulcère [ylsɛr] **nm** ulcer.

ulcérer [18] [ylsere] **vt 1.** MÉD to ulcerate **2.** *sout* [mettre en colère] to enrage.
◆ ***s'ulcérer*** **vp** to ulcerate, to fester.

ulcéreux, ***euse*** [ylserø, øz] **adj** [plaie] ulcerous / [organe] ulcerated.

ULM (abr de ***ultra léger motorisé***) **nm** microlight.

Ulster [ylstɛr] **nm : l'Ulster** Ulster.

ultérieur, ***e*** [ylterjœr] **adj** later, subsequent.

ultérieurement [ylterjœrmɑ̃] **adv** later, subsequently.

ultimatum [yltimatɔm] **nm** ultimatum.

ultime [yltim] **adj** ultimate, final.

ultra- [yltra] **préf** ultra-.

ultraconservateur, ***trice*** [yltrakɔ̃sɛrvatœr, tris] **adj** ultraconservative.

ultramoderne [yltramɔdɛrn] **adj** ultramodern.

ultrasensible [yltrasɑ̃sibl] **adj** [personne] ultra-sensitive / [pellicule] high-speed.

ultrason [yltrasɔ̃] **nm** ultrasound *(U)*.

ultraviolet, ***ette*** [yltravjɔlɛ, ɛt] **adj** ultraviolet.
◆ ***ultraviolet*** **nm** ultraviolet.

ululement, ***hululement*** [ylylmɑ̃] **nm** hoot, hooting *(U)*.

ululer, ***hululer*** [3] [ylyle] **vi** to hoot.

UMP [yɛmpe] (abr de ***Union pour un mouvement populaire***) **nf** POLIT *French right-wing political party.*

un, ***une*** [yn, œ̃] ■ **art indéf** a, an *(devant voyelle)* ▸ **un homme** a man ▸ **un livre** a book ▸ **une femme** a woman ▸ **une pomme** an apple.
■ **pron indéf** one ▸ **l'un de mes amis** one of my friends ▸ **l'un l'autre** each other ▸ **les uns les autres** one another ▸ **l'un..., l'autre** one..., the other ▸ **les uns..., les autres** some..., others ▸ **l'un et l'autre** both (of them) ▸ **l'un ou l'autre** either (of them) ▸ **ni l'un ni l'autre** neither one nor the other, neither (of them) ▸ **un des seuls** one of the few ▸ **appelle-le un de ces jours** give him a call one of these days.
■ **adj num inv** one ▸ **une personne à la fois** one person at a time ▸ **avale les cachets un par un** swallow the tablets one by one *ou* one at a time ▸ **les enfants de un à sept ans** children (aged) from one to seven.
■ **nm** one ; voir aussi ***six***.
◆ ***une*** **nf : faire la/être à la une** PRESSE to make the/to be on the front page ▸ **ce sujet sera à la un de notre dernier journal télévisé ce soir** this will be one of the main items in our late news bulletin ▸ **ne faire ni une ni deux** not to think twice ▸ **j'en ai un (bonne) à t'apprendre** wait till you hear this.

unanime [ynanim] **adj** unanimous.

unanimement [ynanimmɑ̃] **adv** unanimously.

unanimité [ynanimite] **nf** unanimity ▸ **faire l'unanimité** to be unanimously approved ▸ **à l'unanimité** unanimously.

underground [œndœrgraɔnd] ■ **nm inv** underground.
■ **adj inv** underground *(avant n)*.

une [yn] ➤ ***un***.

UNEF, Unef [ynɛf] (abr de ***Union nationale des étudiants de France***) **nf** *students' union*, ≃ NUS *UK*.

UNESCO, Unesco [ynɛsko] (abr de ***United Nations Educational, Scientific and Cultural Organization***) **nf** UNESCO.

uni, e [yni] **adj 1.** [joint, réuni] united **2.** [famille, couple] close **3.** [surface, mer] smooth / [route] even **4.** [étoffe, robe] plain, self-coloured *UK*, self-colored *US*.

UNICEF, Unicef [ynisɛf] (abr de ***United Nations International Children's Emergency Fund***) **nm** UNICEF.

unicité [ynisite] **nf** *littéraire* uniqueness.

unième [ynjɛm] **adj num inv : cinquante et unième** fifty-first.

unificateur, trice [ynifikatœr, tris] **adj** unifying.

unification [ynifikasjɔ̃] **nf** unification.

unifier [9] [ynifje] **vt 1.** [régions, parti] to unify **2.** [programmes] to standardize.
◆ ***s'unifier*** **vp** to unite, to unify.

uniforme [ynifɔrm] ■ **adj** uniform / [régulier] regular ▸ **un paysage uniforme** an unchanging *ou* a monotonous landscape.
■ **nm** uniform.

uniformément [ynifɔrmemɑ̃] **adv** uniformly.

uniformisation [ynifɔrmizasjɔ̃] **nf** standardization.

uniformiser [3] [ynifɔrmize] **vt 1.** [couleur] to make uniform **2.** [programmes, lois] to standardize.

uniformité [ynifɔrmite] **nf 1.** [gén] uniformity / [de mouvement] regularity **2.** [monotonie] monotony.

unijambiste [ynizɑ̃bist] ■ **adj** one-legged.
■ **nmf** one-legged person.

unilatéral, e, aux [ynilateral, o] **adj** unilateral ▸ **stationnement unilatéral** parking on only one side of the street.

unilatéralement [ynilateralmɑ̃] **adv** unilaterally.

uninominal, e, aux [yninɔminal, o] **adj : scrutin uninominal** voting for a single candidat.

union [ynjɔ̃] **nf 1.** [de couleurs] blending **2.** [mariage] union ▸ **union conjugale** marriage ▸ **union libre** cohabitation ▸ **vivre en union libre** to cohabit **3.** [de pays] union ▸ **union nationale** national coalition / [de syndicats] confederation ▸ **union de consommateurs** consumer association ▸ **union douanière** customs union **4.** [entente] unity.
◆ ***Union africaine*** **nf** African Union.
◆ ***Union européenne*** **nf** European Union.
◆ ***Union soviétique*** **nf : l'(ex-)Union soviétique** the (former) Soviet Union.

unique [ynik] **adj 1.** [seul - enfant, veston] only / [- préoccupation] sole **2.** [principe, prix] single **3.** [exceptionnel] unique ▸ **tu es vraiment unique!** *iron* you're priceless!

uniquement [ynikmɑ̃] **adv 1.** [exclusivement] only, solely **2.** [seulement] only, just.

unir [32] [ynir] **vt 1.** [assembler - mots, qualités] to put together, to combine / [- pays] to unite ▸ **unir qqch à** [- pays] to unite sthg with / [- mot, qualité] to combine sthg with **2.** [réunir - partis, familles] to unite **3.** [marier] to unite, to join in marriage.
◆ ***s'unir*** **vp 1.** [s'associer] to unite, to join together **2.** [se joindre - rivières] to merge / [- couleurs] to go together **3.** [se marier] to be joined in marriage.

unisexe [ynisɛks] **adj** unisex.

unisson [ynisɔ̃] **nm** unison ▸ **à l'unisson** in unison.

unitaire [ynitɛr] **adj 1.** [à l'unité] **: prix unitaire** unit price **2.** [manifestation, politique] joint *(avant n)*.

unité [ynite] **nf 1.** [cohésion] unity ▸ **arriver à une certaine unité de pensée** *ou* **vues** to reach a certain consensus ▸ **les trois unités, l'unité d'action, l'unité de temps et l'unité de lieu** HIST & THÉÂTRE the three unities, unity of action, unity of time, and unity of place **2.** COMM, MATH & MIL unit ▸ **unité de production** ÉCON [usine] production unit ▸ **à l'unité** COMM unit *(avant n)* ▸ **prix à l'unité** unit price.
◆ ***unité centrale*** **nf** INFORM central processing unit.
◆ ***unité de valeur*** **nf** *university course unit*, ≃ credit.

univers [ynivɛr] **nm** universe / *fig* world.

universaliser [3] [ynivɛrsalize] **vt** to universalize, to make universal.
◆ ***s'universaliser*** **vp** to become universal.

universalité [ynivɛrsalite] **nf** universality.

universel, elle [ynivɛrsɛl] **adj** universal.

universellement [ynivɛrsɛlmɑ̃] **adv** universally.

universitaire [ynivɛrsitɛr] ■ **adj** university *(avant n)*.
■ **nmf** academic.

université [ynivɛrsite] **nf** university.

univoque [ynivɔk] **adj 1.** [mot, tournure] unambiguous **2.** [relation] one-to-one *UK*, one-on-one *US*.

Untel, Unetelle [œ̃tɛl, yntɛl] **nm, f** Mr so-and-so (Mrs so-and-so *f*).

uppercut [ypɛrkyt] **nm** uppercut.

uranium [yranjɔm] **nm** uranium.

urbain, e [yrbɛ̃, ɛn] **adj 1.** [de la ville] urban **2.** *littéraire* [affable] urbane.

urbanisation [yrbanizasjɔ̃] **nf** urbanization.

urbaniser [3] [yrbanize] **vt** to urbanize.
◆ ***s'urbaniser*** **vp** to become urbanized *ou* built up.

urbanisme [yrbanism] **nm** town planning *UK*, city planning *US*.

urbanité [yrbanite] **nf** urbanity.

urée [yre] **nf** urea.

urémie [yremi] **nf** uraemia.

urgence [yrʒɑ̃s] **nf 1.** [de mission] urgency **2.** MÉD emergency ▸ **les urgences** the casualty department *(sg) UK* emergency room *US*.
◆ ***d'urgence*** ■ **loc adj 1.** [mesures, soins] emergency *(modif)* ▸ **c'est un cas d'urgence** it's an emergency **2.** POLIT **: état d'urgence** state of emergency ▸ **procédure d'urgence** emergency *ou* special powers.
■ **loc adv** immediately.

urgent, e [yrʒɑ̃, ɑ̃t] **adj** urgent.

urgentiste [yrʒɑ̃tist] **nmf** MÉD A & E doctor.

urinaire [yrinɛr] **adj** urinary.

urine [yrin] **nf** urine.

uriner [3] [yrine] **vi** to urinate.

urinoir [yrinwar] **nm** urinal.

urne [yrn] **nf 1.** [vase] urn **2.** [de vote] ballot box ▸ **aller aux urnes** to go to the polls.

urologie [yrɔlɔʒi] **nf** urology.

URSS (abr de ***Union des républiques socialistes soviétiques***) **nf : l'(ex-)URSS** the (former) USSR.

URSSAF, Urssaf [yrsaf] (abr de ***Union pour le recouvrement des Cotisations de la sécurité sociale et des allocations familiales***) **nf** *administrative body responsible for collecting social security funds.*

urticaire [yrtikɛr] **nf** urticaria, hives *pl*.

Uruguay [yrygwɛ] **nm : l'Uruguay** Uruguay.

uruguayen, enne [yrygwejɛ̃, ɛn] **adj** Uruguayan.
◆ ***Uruguayen, enne*** **nm, f** Uruguayan.

us [ys] **nmpl : les us et coutumes** the ways and customs.

USA (abr de ***United States of America***) **nmpl** USA.

usage [yzaʒ] **nm 1.** [gén] use ▸ **faire usage de qqch** to use sthg ▸ **faire un usage abusif du pouvoir** to abuse power ▸ **en usage** in use ▸ **cette technique n'est plus en usage** this technique is now obsolete *ou* is no longer in use ▸ **à l'usage** [à l'emploi] with use / [vêtement] with wear ▸ **c'est à l'usage qu'on s'aperçoit des défauts d'une cuisine** you only realize what the shortcomings of a kitchen are after you've used it for a while ▸ **à l'usage de qqn** for (the use of) sb ▸ **un livre de cuisine à l'usage des enfants** a cookery book aimed at *ou* intended for children ▸ **à usage externe/interne** for external/internal use ▸ **hors d'usage** out of action ▸ **appareil d'usage courant** household appliance ▸ **à usage unique** [seringue, produit] use-once-then-throw-away ▸ **perdre l'usage de la parole** to lose one's power of speech **2.** [coutume] custom ▸ **c'est l'usage** it's the done thing ▸ **c'est conforme à l'usage** *ou* **aux usages** it's in accordance with the rules of etiquette ▸ **d'usage** customary ▸ **échanger les banalités d'usage** to exchange the customary platitudes **3.** LING usage ▸ **le mot est entré dans l'usage** the word is now in common use ▸ **le mot est sorti de l'usage** the word has become obsolete *ou* is no longer used.

usagé, e [yzaʒe] **adj** worn, old.

usager [yzaʒe] **nm** user ▸ **les usagers de la route** road-users.

usé, e [yze] **adj 1.** [détérioré] worn ▸ **eaux usées** waste water *sg* **2.** [personne] worn-out **3.** [plaisanterie] hackneyed, well-worn.

user [3] [yze] ■ **vt 1.** [consommer] to use **2.** [vêtement] to wear out **3.** [forces] to use up / [santé] to ruin / [personne] to wear out.
■ **vi 1.** [se servir] **: user de** [charme] to use / [droit, privilège] to exercise **2.** [traiter] **: en user bien avec qqn** *littéraire* to treat sb well.
◆ ***s'user*** **vp 1.** [chaussure] to wear out **2.** [personne] to wear o.s. out **3.** [amour] to burn itself out.

usinage [yzinaʒ] **nm 1.** [façonnage] machining **2.** [fabrication] manufacturing.

usine [yzin] **nf** factory.

usiner [3] [yzine] **vt 1.** [façonner] to machine **2.** [fabriquer] to manufacture.

usité, e [yzite] **adj** in common use ▸ **très/peu usité** commonly/rarely used.

USP [yɛspe] (abr de ***unité de soins palliatifs***) **nf** MÉD palliative care unit.

ustensile [ystɑ̃sil] **nm** implement, tool ▸ **ustensiles de cuisine** kitchen utensils.

usuel, elle [yzɥɛl] **adj** common, usual.

usuellement [yzɥɛlmɑ̃] **adv** usually, ordinarily.

usufruit [yzyfrɥi] **nm** usufruct.

usuraire [yzyrɛr] **adj** usurious.

usure [yzyr] **nf 1.** [de vêtement, meuble] wear / [de forces] wearing down ▸ **avoir qqn à l'usure** *fam* to wear sb down ▸ **obtenir qqch à l'usure** to get sthg through sheer persistence **2.** [intérêt] usury.

usurier, ère [yzyrje, ɛr] **nm, f** usurer.

usurpateur, trice [yzyrpatœr, tris] ■ **adj** usurping *(avant n)*.
■ **nm, f** usurper.

usurpation [3] [yzyrpasjɔ̃] **nf** usurpation.

usurper [3] [yzyrpe] **vt** to usurp.

ut [yt] **nm inv** C.

UTA (abr de ***Union des transporteurs aériens***) **nf** *French airline company.*

utérin, ine [yterɛ̃, in] **adj** uterine.

utérus [yterys] **nm** uterus, womb.

utile [ytil] **adj** useful ▸ **être utile à qqn** to be useful *ou* of help to sb, to help sb.

utilement [ytilmɑ̃] **adv** usefully, profitably.

utilisable [ytilizabl] **adj** usable.

utilisateur, trice [ytilizatœr, tris] **nm, f** user / INFORM **: utilisateur disposant d'une licence** registered user ▸ **utilisateur étranger** unauthorized user ▸ **utilisateur final** end user ▸ **utilisateur pilote** lead user ▸ **utilisateur tardif** late adopter.

utilisation [ytilizasjɔ̃] **nf** use.

utiliser [3] [ytilize] **vt** to use.

utilitaire [ytilitɛr] ■ **adj 1.** [pratique] utilitarian / [véhicule] commercial **2.** *péj* [préoccupations] material / [caractère] materialistic.
■ **nm** INFORM utility (program).

utilité [ytilite] **nf 1.** [usage] usefulness **2.** DR **: entreprise d'utilité publique** public utility ▸ **organisme d'utilité publique** registered charity
▸▸ **jouer les utilités** THÉÂTRE to play bit parts / *fig* to play second fiddle.

utopie [ytɔpi] **nf 1.** [idéal] utopia **2.** [projet irréalisable] unrealistic idea.

utopique [ytɔpik] **adj** utopian.

utopiste [ytɔpist] **nmf** utopian.

UV ■ **nf** (abr de ***unité de valeur***) *university course unit*, ≃ credit.
■ (abr de ***ultraviolet***) UV.

V

v*, *V [ve] **nm inv** v, V ▸ **pull en v** V-neck sweater.

v.[1] **1.** LITTÉR (abr écrite de ***vers***) v. **2.** (abr écrite de ***verset***) v. **3.** [environ] (abr écrite de ***vers***) approx.

v.[2], ***V.*** abr de ***voir***.

va [va] ■ ➤ ***aller***.
■ **interj : courage, va!** come on, cheer up! ▸ **va donc!** come on! ▸ **va pour 10 euros/demain** OK, let's say 10 euros/tomorrow.

VA (abr écrite de ***voltampère***) VA.

vacance [vakɑ̃s] **nf** vacancy ▸ **vacance du pouvoir** power vacuum ▸ **pendant la vacance du siège** while the seat is empty ▸ **vacance de succession** DR abeyance of succession.
◆ ***vacances*** **nfpl** holiday *(sg) UK*, vacation *(sg) US* ▸ **bonnes vacances!** have a good holiday! ▸ **être/partir en vacances** to be/go on holiday ▸ **prendre des vacances** to take a holiday, to go on holiday ▸ **rentrer de vacances** to come back from holiday *ou* vacation ▸ **les grandes vacances** the summer holidays ▸ **vacances de neige** skiing holidays *ou* vacation ▸ **vacances scolaires** school holidays *UK* *ou* break *US*.

vacancier*, *ère [vakɑ̃sje, ɛr] ■ **adj** holiday *(avant n)*.
■ **nm, f** holiday-maker *UK*, vacationer *US*.

vacant*, *e [vakɑ̃, ɑ̃t] **adj** [poste] vacant / [logement] vacant, unoccupied.

vacarme [vakarm] **nm** racket, din.

vacataire [vakatɛr] ■ **adj** [employé] temporary.
■ **nmf** temporary worker, temp.

vacation [vakasjɔ̃] **nf** [d'expert] session.

vaccin [vaksɛ̃] **nm** vaccine.

vaccination [vaksinasjɔ̃] **nf** vaccination.

vacciner [3] [vaksine] **vt : vacciner qqn (contre)** MÉD to vaccinate sb (against) / *fam fig* to make sb immune (to).

vache [vaʃ] ■ **nf 1.** ZOOL cow ▸ **vache laitière *ou* à lait** milker, dairy cow **2.** [cuir] cowhide **3.** *fam péj* [femme] cow *UK* / [homme] pig ▸ **ah les vaches, ils ne m'ont pas invité!** the swines didn't invite me! **4.** COMM [produit] **: vache à lait** cash cow, milch cow
▸▸ **la vache!** hell!
■ **adj** *fam* rotten ▸ **allez, ne sois pas vache** come on, don't be rotten, come on, be a sport *UK* ▸ **faire un coup vache à qqn** to play a dirty trick on sb.

vachement [vaʃmɑ̃] **adv** *fam* bloody *UK*, dead *UK*, real *US*.

vacherie [vaʃri] **nf** *fam* nastiness ▸ **faire/dire une vacherie** to do/say something nasty.

vacherin [vaʃrɛ̃] **nm** [dessert] *meringue filled with ice cream and fruit*.

vachette [vaʃɛt] **nf 1.** [jeune vache] calf **2.** [cuir] calfskin.

vacillant*, *e [vasijɑ̃, ɑ̃t] **adj 1.** [jambes, fondations] unsteady / [lumière] flickering **2.** [mémoire, santé] failing / [caractère] wavering, indecisive.

vaciller [3] [vasije] **vi 1.** [jambes, fondations] to shake / [lumière] to flicker ▸ **vaciller sur ses jambes** to be unsteady on one's legs **2.** [mémoire, santé] to fail.

vacuité [vakɥite] **nf** *sout* [de propos] emptiness, vacuousness.

vade-mecum [vademekɔm] **nm inv** vade mecum.

vadrouille [vadruj] **nf** *fam* **: être/partir en vadrouille** to be/to go off gallivanting.

va-et-vient [vaevjɛ̃] **nm inv 1.** [de personnes] comings and goings *pl*, toing and froing **2.** [de balancier] to-and-fro movement **3. : (porte) va-et-vient** swing door **4.** ÉLECTR two-way switch.

vagabond*, *e [vagabɔ̃, ɔ̃d] ■ **adj 1.** [chien] stray / [vie] vagabond *(avant n)* **2.** [humeur] restless.
■ **nm, f** [rôdeur] vagrant, tramp / *littéraire* [voyageur] wanderer.

vagabondage [vagabɔ̃daʒ] **nm** [délit] vagrancy / [errance] wandering, roaming.

vagabonder [3] [vagabɔ̃de] **vi 1.** [personne] to wander, to roam **2.** [esprit, imagination] to wander.

vagin [vaʒɛ̃] **nm** vagina.

vaginal*, *e*, *aux [vaʒinal, o] **adj** vaginal.

vaginite [vaʒinit] **nf** vaginitis.

vagir [32] [vaʒir] **vi** to cry, to wail.

vagissement [vaʒismɑ̃] **nm** cry, wail.

vague [vag] ■ **adj 1.** [idée, promesse] vague **2.** [vêtement] loose-fitting **3.** *(avant n)* [quelconque] **: il a un vague travail dans un bureau** he has some job or other in an office **4.** *(avant n)* [cousin] distant.
■ **nf** wave ▸ **une vague de** [touristes, immigrants] a wave of / [d'enthousiasme] a surge of ▸ **une vague de fond** *litt & fig* a groundswell ▸ **une vague de froid** a cold spell ▸ **la nouvelle vague** the new wave ▸ **vague de chaleur** heat wave ▸ **une vague de protestations/grèves** a wave of protest/strikes.
■ **nm : rester dans le vague** *fig* to remain vague ▸ **avoir du vague à l'âme** *fig* to be wistful.

vaguelette [vaglɛt] **nf** ripple, wave.

vaguement [vagmɑ̃] **adv** vaguely.

vahiné [vaine] **nf** Tahitian woman.

vaillamment [vajamɑ̃] **adv** bravely, valiantly.

vaillance [vajɑ̃s] **nf** *littéraire* bravery, courage / MIL valour *UK*, valor *US*.

vaillant, e [vajɑ̃, ɑ̃t] **adj 1.** [enfant, vieillard] hale and hearty **2.** *littéraire* [héros] valiant.

vain, e [vɛ̃, vɛn] **adj 1.** [inutile] vain, useless ▸ **en vain** in vain, to no avail **2.** *littéraire* [vaniteux] vain.

vaincre [114] [vɛ̃kr] **vt 1.** [ennemi] to defeat **2.** [obstacle, peur] to overcome.

vaincu, e [vɛ̃ky] ■ **pp** ➤ ***vaincre***.
■ **adj** defeated ▸ **s'avouer vaincu** to admit defeat.
■ **nm, f** defeated person.

vainement [vɛnmɑ̃] **adv** vainly.

vainqueur [vɛ̃kœr] ■ **nm 1.** [de combat] conqueror, victor **2.** SPORT winner.
■ **adj m** victorious, conquering.

vairon [vɛrɔ̃] ■ **adj m 1.** [yeux] of different colours **2.** [cheval] wall-eyed.
■ **nm** minnow.

vais ➤ ***aller***.

vaisseau, x [vɛso] **nm 1.** NAUT vessel, ship ▸ **vaisseau spatial** AÉRON spaceship **2.** ANAT vessel **3.** ARCHIT nave.

vaisselier [vɛsəlje] **nm** dresser.

vaisselle [vɛsɛl] **nf** crockery ▸ **faire** *ou* **laver la vaisselle** to do the dishes, to wash up *UK*.

val [val] (pl **vals** *ou* **vaux** [vo]) **nm** valley.

valable [valabl] **adj 1.** [passeport] valid **2.** [raison, excuse] valid, legitimate **3.** [œuvre] good, worthwhile.

valériane [valerjan] **nf** valerian.

valet [valɛ] **nm 1.** [serviteur] servant ▸ **valet de chambre** manservant, valet ▸ **valet de pied** footman **2.** *fig & péj* [homme servile] lackey **3.** [cartes à jouer] jack, knave.

valeur [valœr] **nf 1.** [gén & MUS] value ▸ **avoir de la valeur** to be valuable ▸ **bijoux sans valeur** worthless jewels ▸ **manuscrit d'une valeur inestimable** invaluable manuscript ▸ **prendre de la valeur** to increase in value ▸ **perdre de sa valeur** to lose its value ▸ **mettre en valeur** [talents] to bring out / [terre] to exploit ▸ **valeur absolue** absolute value ▸ **de (grande) valeur** [chose] (very) valuable / [personne] of (great) worth *ou* merit ▸ **des objets de valeur** valuables, items of value, valuable items ▸ **un collaborateur de valeur** a prized colleague ▸ **valeur nominale** face value ▸ **valeur nutritive** nutritional value, goodness
2. *(gén pl)* FIN stocks and shares *pl*, securities *pl* ▸ **valeurs (mobilières)** stocks and shares, securities ▸ **valeurs à revenu fixe/variable** fixed/variable income securities ▸ **valeur refuge** [gén] sound investment / [Bourse] currency-safe investment
3. ÉCON value ▸ **valeur ajoutée** added value ▸ **valeur au comptant** *ou* **de rachat** cash value ▸ **valeur comptable** book value ▸ **valeur marchande/vénale** market/monetary value ▸ **valeur perçue** perceived value ▸ **valeur à la revente** resale value
4. [mérite] worth, merit ▸ **avoir conscience de sa valeur** to know one's own worth
5. *fig* [importance] value, importance ▸ **attacher** *ou* **accorder une grande valeur à qqch** to prize sthg, to set great value by sthg ▸ **la valeur sentimentale d'un collier** the sentimental value of a necklace
6. [équivalent] **: la valeur de** the equivalent of ▸ **donnez-lui la valeur d'une cuillère à soupe de sirop** give him the equivalent of a tablespoonful of syrup.
◆ ***valeurs*** **nfpl** [critères de référence] values ▸ **valeurs morales/sociales/familiales** moral/social/family values / ÉCON **: valeurs matérielles** tangible assets.

valeureusement [valœrøzmɑ̃] **adv** *litt* valiantly, bravely.

valeureux, euse [valœrø, øz] **adj** *litt* valiant, brave.

validation [validasjɔ̃] **nf** validation, authentication.

valide [valid] **adj 1.** [personne] spry **2.** [contrat] valid.

valider [3] [valide] **vt** to validate, to authenticate.

validité [validite] **nf** validity.

valise [valiz] **nf** case *UK*, suitcase ▸ **faire sa valise/ses valises** *litt* to pack one's case/cases / *fam fig* [partir] to pack one's bags ▸ **valise diplomatique** diplomatic bag.

vallée [vale] **nf** valley.

vallon [valɔ̃] **nm** small valley.

vallonné, e [valɔne] **adj** undulating.

valoir [60] [valwar] ■ **vi 1.** [gén] to be worth ▸ **ça vaut combien?** how much is it? ▸ **que vaut ce film?** is this film any good? ▸ **l'émission d'hier ne valait pas grand-chose** yesterday's programme wasn't up to much ▸ **ne rien valoir** not to be any good, to be worthless ▸ **ça vaut mieux** *fam* that's best ▸ **ça ne vaut pas la peine** it's not worth it ▸ **faire valoir** [vues] to assert / [talent] to show ▸ **faire valoir ses droits à la retraite** to provide evidence for one's entitlement to a pension
2. [règle] **: valoir pour** to apply to, to hold good for ▸ **le règlement vaut pour tout le monde** the rules hold for everyone
3. COMM & ÉCON **: à ce prix-là, ça vaut le coup** at that price, you can't go wrong ▸ **à valoir sur : il y a deux euros à valoir sur votre prochain achat** you'll get two euros off your next purchase ▸ **faire valoir un capital** to turn a sum of money to (good) account, to make a sum of money yield a good profit ▸ **faire valoir une propriété** to derive profit from a property ▸ **ne pas valoir cher** to be cheap *ou* inexpensive ▸ **valoir très cher** to cost a lot, to be very expensive ▸ **verser un acompte à valoir sur une somme** to pay a deposit to be set off against a sum.

■ vt [médaille, gloire] to bring, to earn ▸ **ses efforts lui ont valu une médaille aux jeux Olympiques** his efforts earned him a medal at the Olympic Games ▸ **qu'est-ce qui me vaut l'honneur/le plaisir de ta visite?** to what do I owe the honour/pleasure of your visit?

■ **v impers : il vaudrait mieux que nous partions** it would be better if we left, we'd better leave.

◆ ***se valoir*** vp to be equally good/bad ▸ **nous nous valons au sprint** we're both equally good (as) sprinters ▸ **tu vas voter Dupond ou Dufort? – tout ça se vaut!** are you going to vote Dupond or Dufort? – it's six of one and half a dozen of the other *ou* it's all the same thing!

valorisant, ***e*** [valɔrizɑ̃, ɑ̃t] **adj** good for one's image.

valorisation [valɔrizasjɔ̃] **nf** [d'immeuble, de région] development ▸ **valorisation de soi** good self-image.

valoriser [3] [valɔrize] **vt** [immeuble, région] to develop / [individu, société] to improve the image of.

valse [vals] **nf** waltz / *fam fig* [de personnel] reshuffle.

valser [3] [valse] **vi** to waltz ▸ **envoyer valser qqch** *fam fig* to send sthg flying ▸ **envoyer valser qqn** *fam fig* [employé] to give sb the elbow.

valseur, ***euse*** [valsœr, øz] [danseur] **nm, f** waltzer.

valu [valy] **pp inv** ➤ ***valoir***.

valve [valv] **nf** valve.

vamp [vɑ̃p] **nf** vamp.

vamper [3] [vɑ̃pe] **vt** *fam* to vamp.

vampire [vɑ̃pir] **nm 1.** [fantôme] vampire **2.** *fig* [personne avide] vulture **3.** ZOOL vampire bat.

vampiriser [3] [vɑ̃pirize] **vt** *fig* to control.

van [vɑ̃] **nm** [fourgon] horsebox *UK*, horsecar *US*.

vandale [vɑ̃dal] **nmf** vandal.

vandalisme [vɑ̃dalism] **nm** vandalism.

vanille [vanij] **nf** vanilla.

vanillé, ***e*** [vanije] **adj** vanilla *(avant n)*.

vanité [vanite] **nf** vanity.

vaniteux, ***euse*** [vanitø, øz] ■ **adj** vain, conceited.

■ **nm, f** vain *ou* conceited person.

vanity-case [vanitikez] (pl **vanity-cases**) **nm** vanity case.

vanne [van] **nf 1.** [d'écluse] lockgate **2.** *fam* [remarque] gibe.

vanné, ***e*** [vane] **adj** *fam* [personne] dead beat.

vanner [3] [vane] **vt 1.** [grain] to winnow **2.** *fam* [fatiguer] to wear out **3.** *fam* [se moquer de] to make gibes at, to have a go at.

vannerie [vanri] **nf** basketwork, wickerwork.

vannier [vanje] **nm** basket maker.

vantail, ***aux*** [vɑ̃taj, o] **nm** [de porte] leaf / [d'armoire] door.

vantard, ***e*** [vɑ̃tar, ard] ■ **adj** bragging, boastful.

■ **nm, f** boaster.

vantardise [vɑ̃tardiz] **nf** boasting *(U)*, bragging *(U)*.

vanter [3] [vɑ̃te] **vt** to vaunt.

◆ ***se vanter*** **vp** to boast, to brag ▸ **se vanter de qqch** to boast *ou* brag about sthg ▸ **se vanter de faire qqch** to boast *ou* brag about doing sthg.

va-nu-pieds [vanypje] **nmf** *fam* beggar.

vapes [vap] **nfpl** *fam* : **être dans les vapes** to have one's head in the clouds ▸ **tomber dans les vapes** to pass out.

vapeur [vapœr] ■ **nf 1.** [d'eau] steam ▸ **à la vapeur** steamed ▸ **bateau à vapeur** steamboat, steamer ▸ **locomotive à vapeur** steam engine ▸ **renverser la vapeur** NAUT to reverse engines / *fig* to backpedal **2.** [émanation] vapour *UK*, vapor *US*.

■ **nm** steamer.

◆ ***vapeurs*** **nfpl** [émanations] fumes

▸▸ **avoir ses vapeurs** *vieilli* to have the vapours *UK ou* vapors *US*.

vapocuiseur [vapɔkɥizœr] **nm** pressure cooker.

vaporeux, ***euse*** [vapɔrø, øz] **adj 1.** *littéraire* [ciel, lumière] hazy **2.** [tissu] filmy.

vaporisateur [vapɔrizatœr] **nm 1.** [atomiseur] spray, atomizer **2.** [dans l'industrie] vaporizer.

vaporisation [vapɔrizasjɔ̃] **nf 1.** [de parfum, déodorant] spraying **2.** PHYS vaporization.

vaporiser [3] [vapɔrize] **vt 1.** [parfum, déodorant] to spray **2.** PHYS to vaporize.

◆ ***se vaporiser*** **vp** to vaporize.

vaquer [3] [vake] **vi : vaquer à** to see to, to attend to.

varappe [varap] **nf** rock climbing.

varappeur, ***euse*** [varapœr, øz] **nm, f** (rock) climber.

varech [varɛk] **nm** kelp.

vareuse [varøz] **nf 1.** [veste] loose-fitting jacket **2.** [de marin] pea jacket **3.** [d'uniforme] tunic.

variable [varjabl] ■ **adj 1.** [temps] changeable **2.** [distance, résultats] varied, varying **3.** [température] variable.

■ **nf** variable.

variante [varjɑ̃t] **nf** variant.

variateur [varjatœr] **nm** ÉLECTR dimmer switch.

variation [varjasjɔ̃] **nf** variation.

varice [varis] **nf** varicose vein.

varicelle [varisɛl] **nf** chickenpox.

varié, ***e*** [varje] **adj 1.** [divers] various **2.** [non monotone] varied, varying.

varier [9] [varje] **vt & vi** to vary.

variété [varjete] **nf** variety.

◆ ***variétés*** **nfpl** variety show *sg*.

variole [varjɔl] **nf** smallpox.

variqueux, ***euse*** [varikø, øz] **adj** varicose.

Varsovie [varsɔvi] **npr** Warsaw ▸ **le pacte de Varsovie** the Warsaw Pact.

vas ➤ ***aller***.

vasculaire [vaskylɛr] **adj** vascular.

vase [vaz] ■ **nm** vase ▸ **en vase clos** *fig* in a vacuum.

■ **nf** mud, silt.

vasectomie [vazɛktɔmi] **nf** vasectomy.

vaseline [vazlin] **nf** Vaseline®, petroleum jelly *UK*.

vaseux, euse [vazø, øz] **adj** **1.** [fond] muddy, silty **2.** *fam* [personne] under the weather **3.** *fam* [raisonnement, article] woolly.

vasistas [vazistas] **nm** fanlight.

vasque [vask] **nf** **1.** [de fontaine] basin **2.** [coupe] bowl.

vassal, e, aux [vasal, o] **nm, f** vassal.

vaste [vast] **adj** vast, immense.

Vatican [vatikɑ̃] **nm : le Vatican** the Vatican ▸ **l'État de la cité du Vatican** Vatican City ▸ **au Vatican** in Vatican City.

va-tout [vatu] **nm inv : jouer son va-tout** *fig* to stake one's all.

vaudeville [vodvil] **nm** vaudeville.

vaudevillesque [vodvilɛsk] **adj** ludicrous.

vaudou [vodu] **nm** voodoo.

vaudrait ➤ ***valoir***.

vau-l'eau [volo] ◆ ***à vau-l'eau*** **loc adv** *littéraire* with the flow ▸ **aller à vau-l'eau** *fig* to go down the drain.

vaurien, enne [vorjɛ̃, ɛn] **nm, f** good-for-nothing.

vaut ➤ ***valoir***.

vautour [votur] **nm** vulture.

vautrer [3] [votre] ◆ ***se vautrer*** **vp** [dans la boue, dans la débauche] to wallow / [sur l'herbe, dans un fauteuil] to sprawl.

va-vite [vavit] ◆ ***à la va-vite*** **loc adv** *fam* in a rush.

vd (abr écrite de ***vend***), ➤ ***vendre***.

VDQS (abr de ***vin délimité de qualité supérieure***) **nm** *label indicating quality of wine.*

vds abr de ***vends***.

veau, x [vo] **nm** **1.** [animal] calf ▸ **le Veau d'or** the golden calf **2.** [viande] veal **3.** [peau] calfskin **4.** *péj* [personne] lump.

vecteur [vɛktœr] **nm** **1.** GÉOM vector **2.** [intermédiaire] vehicle / MÉD carrier.

vécu, e [veky] ■ **pp** ➤ ***vivre***.
■ **adj** real.

vedettariat [vədɛtarja] **nm** stardom.

vedette [vədɛt] **nf** **1.** NAUT patrol boat ▸ **vedette de la douane** customs patrol boat **2.** [star] star ▸ **vedette du petit écran/du cinéma** TV/film star ▸ **une vedette de la politique/du rugby** a big name in politics/rugby ▸ **mettre en vedette** *fig* to turn the spotlight on ▸ **partager la vedette avec qqn** THÉÂTRE to share star billing with sb / *fig* to share the limelight with sb.

végétal, e, aux [veʒetal, o] **adj** [huile] vegetable *(avant n)* / [cellule, fibre] plant *(avant n)*.

végétalien, enne [veʒetaljɛ̃, ɛn] **adj & nm, f** vegan.

végétarien, enne [veʒetarjɛ̃, ɛn] **adj & nm, f** vegetarian.

végétarisme [veʒetarism] **nm** vegetarianism.

végétatif, tive [veʒetatif, iv] **adj** vegetative / *fig & péj* vegetable-like.

végétation [veʒetasjɔ̃] **nf** vegetation.
◆ ***végétations*** **nfpl** adenoids.

végéter [18] [veʒete] **vi** to vegetate.

véhémence [veemɑ̃s] **nf** vehemence.

véhément, e [veemɑ̃, ɑ̃t] **adj** vehement.

véhicule [veikyl] **nm** vehicle ▸ **véhicule banalisé** unmarked vehicle.

véhiculer [3] [veikyle] **vt** to transport / *fig* to convey.

veille [vɛj] **nf** **1.** [jour précédent] day before, eve ▸ **la veille au soir** the previous evening, the evening before ▸ **la veille de mon anniversaire** the day before my birthday ▸ **la veille de Noël** Christmas Eve ▸ **à la veille de** *fig* on the eve of **2.** [éveil] wakefulness / [privation de sommeil] sleeplessness **3.** [garde] **: être de veille** to be on night duty.

veillée [veje] **nf** **1.** [soirée] evening **2.** [de mort] wake, vigil.

veiller [4] [veje] ■ **vi** **1.** [rester éveillé] to stay up **2.** [rester vigilant] **: veiller à qqch** to look after sthg ▸ **veiller à faire qqch** to see that sthg is done ▸ **veiller sur** to watch over.
■ **vt** to sit up with.

veilleur [vejœr] **nm : veilleur de nuit** night watchman.

veilleuse [vejøz] **nf** **1.** [lampe] nightlight **2.** AUTO sidelight **3.** [de chauffe-eau] pilot light.

veinard, e [vɛnar, ard] *fam* ■ **adj** lucky.
■ **nm, f** lucky devil.

veine [vɛn] **nf** **1.** [gén] vein ▸ **en veine de** in the mood for ▸ **s'ouvrir les veines** to slash one's wrists ▸ **se saigner aux quatre veines** *fig* to bleed o.s. dry **2.** [de marbre] vein / [de bois] grain **3.** [filon] seam, vein **4.** *fam* [chance] luck ▸ **avoir de la veine** to be lucky ▸ **avoir une veine de cocu** *fig* to have the luck of the devil.

veiné, e [vene] **adj** [marbre] veined / [bois] grained.

veineux, euse [venø, øz] **adj** **1.** ANAT venous **2.** [marbre] veined / [bois] grainy.

veinule [venyl] **nf** venule.

Velcro® [vɛlkro] **nm** Velcro®.

vêler [4] [vele] **vi** to calve.

vélin [velɛ̃] **nm** vellum.

véliplanchiste [veliplɑ̃ʃist] **nmf** windsurfer.

velléitaire [veleitɛr] ■ **nmf** indecisive person.
■ **adj** indecisive.

velléité [veleite] **nf** whim.

vélo [velo] **nm** *fam* bike ▸ **faire du vélo** to go cycling.

véloce [velɔs] **adj** swift.

vélocité [velɔsite] **nf** swiftness, speed.

vélodrome [velɔdrom] **nm** velodrome.

vélomoteur [velɔmɔtœr] **nm** light motorcycle, moped.

velours [vəlur] **nm** velvet.

velouté, e [vəlute] **adj** velvety.
◆ ***velouté*** **nm** **1.** [de peau] velvetiness **2.** [potage] cream soup ▸ **velouté d'asperges** cream of asparagus soup.

velu, e [vəly] **adj** hairy.

venaison [vənɛzɔ̃] **nf** venison.

vénal, e, aux [venal, o] **adj** venal.

vénalité [venalite] **nf** venality.

venant [vənɑ̃] ◆ ***à tout venant*** **loc adv** to all comers.

vendange [vɑ̃dɑ̃ʒ] **nf 1.** [récolte] grape harvest, wine harvest **2.** [raisins] grape crop **3.** [période] **: les vendanges** (grape) harvest time *sg.*

vendanger [17] [vɑ̃dɑ̃ʒe] ■ **vt** to harvest grapes from. ■ **vi** to harvest the grapes.

vendangeur, euse [vɑ̃dɑ̃ʒœr, øz] **nm, f** grape-picker.

vendetta [vɑ̃deta] **nf** vendetta.

vendeur, euse [vɑ̃dœr, øz] **nm, f** salesman (f saleswoman).

vendre [73] [vɑ̃dr] **vt** to sell ▸ **'à vendre'** 'for sale' ▸ **vendre (qqch) au détail** to retail (sthg) ▸ **vendre qqch aux enchères** [généralement] to auction sthg / [pour s'en débarrasser] to auction sthg off ▸ **vendre (qqch) en gros** to sell (sthg) wholesale ▸ **vendre qqch à perte** to sell sthg at a loss
▸▸ **la publicité fait vendre** advertising sells.
◆ ***se vendre*** **vp 1.** [maison, produit] to be sold ▸ **ça se vend bien/mal actuellement** it is/isn't selling well at the moment ▸ **se vendre comme des petits pains** to sell *ou* to go like hot cakes **2.** *péj* [se laisser corrompre] to sell o.s. ▸ **se vendre à l'adversaire** to sell o.s. to *ou* to sell out to the opposite side **3.** [se trahir] to give o.s. away.

vendredi [vɑ̃drədi] **nm** Friday ▸ **Vendredi Saint** Good Friday ; voir aussi ***samedi***.

vends ➤ ***vendre***.

vendu, e [vɑ̃dy] ■ **pp** ➤ ***vendre***.
■ **adj 1.** [cédé] sold **2.** [corrompu] corrupt.
■ **nm, f** traitor.

venelle [vənɛl] **nf** alley.

vénéneux, euse [venenø, øz] **adj** poisonous.

vénérable [venerabl] **adj** venerable.

vénération [venerasjɔ̃] **nf** veneration, reverence.

vénérer [18] [venere] **vt** to venerate, to revere.

vénerie [venri] **nf** hunting.

vénérien, enne [venerjɛ̃, ɛn] **adj** venereal.

Venezuela [venezɥela] **nm : le Venezuela** Venezuela ▸ **au Venezuela** in Venezuela.

vénézuélien, enne [venezɥeljɛ̃, ɛn] **adj** Venezuelan.
◆ ***Vénézuélien, enne*** **nm, f** Venezuelan.

vengeance [vɑ̃ʒɑ̃s] **nf** vengeance.

venger [17] [vɑ̃ʒe] **vt** to avenge.
◆ ***se venger*** **vp** to get one's revenge ▸ **se venger de qqn** to take revenge on sb ▸ **se venger de qqch** to take revenge for sthg ▸ **se venger sur** to take it out on.

vengeur, vengeresse [vɑ̃ʒœr, vɑ̃ʒrɛs] ■ **adj** vengeful.
■ **nm, f** avenger.

véniel, elle [venjɛl] **adj** venial.

venimeux, euse [vənimø, øz] **adj** venomous.

venin [vənɛ̃] **nm** venom.

venir [40] [vənir] **vi 1.** [gén] to come ▸ **alors, tu viens?** are you coming? ▸ **faire venir une personne chez soi** to have somebody come round ▸ **il me vient une idée** I've got an idea ▸ **le moment est venu de** the time has come to ▸ **Roger viendra me chercher** Roger will come and collect me ▸ **venir de** [personne, mot] to come from / [échec] to be due to ▸ **le mot vient du latin** the word comes *ou* derives from Latin ▸ **c'est de là que vient le mal/problème** this is the root of the evil/problem ▸ **venir à** [maturité] to reach / [question, sujet] to come to ▸ **il lui vient à l'épaule** he comes up to his/her shoulder ▸ **venir de faire qqch** to have just done sthg ▸ **je viens de l'avoir au téléphone** I was on the phone to her just a few minutes *ou* a short while ago ▸ **je viens de la voir** I've just seen her ▸ **s'il venait à mourir...** if he was to die... ▸ **où veux-tu en venir?** what are you getting at? ▸ **en venir aux mains** *ou* **coups** to come to blows ▸ **les générations à venir** future *ou* coming generations **2.** [plante, arbre] to come on.
◆ ***s'en venir*** **vp** *littéraire* to come (along).

Venise [vəniz] **npr** Venice.

vénitien, enne [venisjɛ̃, ɛn] **adj** Venetian.
◆ ***Vénitien, enne*** **nm, f** Venetian.

vent [vɑ̃] **nm** wind ▸ **il fait** *ou* **il y a du vent** headwind ▸ **le vent souffle/tourne** the wind is blowing/changing ▸ **le vent tombe/se lève** the wind is dropping/rising ▸ **sentir d'où vient le vent** to see which way the wind blows *ou* how the land lies ▸ **vent arrière** AÉRON tail wind / NAUT rear wind ▸ **vent contraire** headwind ▸ **vent debout** head wind ▸ **vent de terre/mer** land/sea breeze ▸ **dans le vent** trendy ▸ **avoir vent de** *fig* to get wind of ▸ **bon vent!** *fig* good riddance! ▸ **contre vents et marées** *fig* come hell or high water.

vente [vɑ̃t] **nf 1.** [cession, transaction] sale ▸ **en vente** on sale *UK*, for sale *US* ▸ **mettre une maison en vente** to put a house up for sale ▸ **en vente libre** available over the counter ▸ **en vente sur/sans ordonnance** obtainable on prescription/without a prescription ▸ **vente au comptant** cash sale ▸ **promesse de ventes** sales agreement ▸ **vente à perte** dumping ▸ **vente répétée** repeat sale
2. [domaine] **: vente de charité** (charity) bazaar ▸ **vente par correspondance** mail order ▸ **vente à la criée** sale by auction ▸ **vente en demi-gros** cash-and-carry ▸ **vente au détail** retail sales ▸ **vente directe** direct selling ▸ **vente aux enchères** auction ▸ **vente forcée** forced sale ▸ **vente en gros** wholesale sales ▸ **vente en ligne** e-commerce ▸ **ventes sur le marché intérieur** home *ou* domestic sales ▸ **vente par téléphone** telesales, telemarketing
3. [service] sales (department) ▸ **le responsable des ventes** the sales manager
4. [technique] selling ▸ **vente à domicile** door-to-door selling ▸ **vente à tempérament** hire-purchase *UK ou* installment plan *US* selling.

venteux, euse [vɑ̃tø, øz] **adj** windy.

ventilateur [vɑ̃tilatœr] **nm** fan.

ventilation [vɑ̃tilasjɔ̃] **nf 1.** [de pièce] ventilation **2.** FIN breakdown.

ventiler [3] [vɑ̃tile] **vt 1.** [pièce] to ventilate **2.** FIN to break down.

ventouse [vɑ̃tuz] **nf 1.** [de caoutchouc] suction pad / [d'animal] sucker **2.** MÉD ventouse **3.** TECHNOL air vent.

ventral, e, aux [vɑ̃tral, o] **adj** ventral.

ventre [vɑ̃tr] **nm** [de personne] stomach ▸ **avoir/prendre du ventre** to have/be getting (a bit of) a paunch ▸ **avoir le ventre ballonné** to have a bloated stomach ▸ **à plat ventre** flat on one's stomach ▸ **ventre à terre** *fig* flat out ▸ **avoir quelque chose dans le ventre** *fig* to have guts.

ventricule [vɑ̃trikyl] **nm** ventricle.

ventriloque [vɑ̃trilɔk] **nmf** ventriloquist.

ventripotent, e [vɑ̃tripɔtɑ̃, ɑ̃t] **adj** *fam* pot-bellied.

ventru, e [vɑ̃try] **adj 1.** *fam* [personne] pot-bellied **2.** [cruche] round / [commode] bow-fronted.

venu, e [vəny] ■ **pp** ➤ ***venir***.
■ **adj : bien venu** welcome ▸ **mal venu** unwelcome ▸ **il serait mal venu de faire cela** it would be improper to do that.
■ **nm, f : nouveau venu** newcomer.
◆ ***venue*** **nf** coming, arrival.

Vénus [venys] **npr** Venus.

vépéciste [vepesist] **nm** mail-order company.

vêpres [vɛpr] **nfpl** vespers.

ver [vɛr] **nm** worm ▸ **ver luisant** glow-worm ▸ **ver à soie** silkworm ▸ **ver solitaire** tapeworm ▸ **ver de terre** earthworm ▸ **nu comme un ver** *fig* stark naked ▸ **tirer les vers du nez à qqn** *fig* to worm information out of sb.

véracité [verasite] **nf** truthfulness.

véranda [verɑ̃da] **nf** veranda.

verbal, e, aux [vɛrbal, o] **adj 1.** [promesse, violence] verbal **2.** GRAMM verb *(avant n)*.

verbalement [vɛrbalmɑ̃] **adv** verbally.

verbaliser [3] [vɛrbalize] ■ **vt** to verbalize.
■ **vi** to make out a report.

verbe [vɛrb] **nm 1.** GRAMM verb ▸ **verbe impersonnel** impersonal verb **2.** *littéraire* [langage] words *pl*, language.

verbeux, euse [vɛrbø, øz] **adj** wordy, verbose.

verbiage [vɛrbjaʒ] **nm** verbiage.

verdâtre [vɛrdatr] **adj** greenish.

verdeur [vɛrdœr] **nf 1.** [de personne] vigour *UK*, vigor *US*, vitality **2.** [de langage] crudeness **3.** [de fruit] tartness / [de vin] acidity **4.** [de bois] greenness.

verdict [vɛrdikt] **nm** verdict.

verdir [32] [vɛrdir] **vt & vi** to turn green.

verdoyant, e [vɛrdwajɑ̃, ɑ̃t] **adj** green.

verdoyer [13] [vɛrdwaje] **vi** to turn green.

verdure [vɛrdyr] **nf 1.** [végétation] greenery **2.** [couleur] greenness **3.** [légumes verts] green vegetables *pl*, greens *pl*.

véreux, euse [verø, øz] **adj** worm-eaten, maggoty / *fig* shady.

verge [vɛrʒ] **nf 1.** ANAT penis **2.** *littéraire* [baguette] rod, stick.

verger [vɛrʒe] **nm** orchard.

vergeture [vɛrgətyr] **nf** stretchmark.

verglacé, e [vɛrglase] **adj** icy.

verglas [vɛrgla] **nm** (black) ice.

vergogne [vɛrgɔɲ] ◆ ***sans vergogne*** **loc adv** shamelessly.

vergue [vɛrg] **nf** yard.

véridique [veridik] **adj** truthful.

vérifiable [verifjabl] **adj** verifiable.

vérificateur, trice [verifikatœr, tris] ■ **adj : comptable vérificateur** auditor.
■ **nm, f** inspector.

vérification [verifikasjɔ̃] **nf 1.** [contrôle] check, checking ▸ **vérification antivirale** INFORM antivirus check **2.** [confirmation] proof, confirmation **3.** FIN checking ▸ **vérification des comptes** audit.

vérifier [9] [verifje] **vt 1.** [contrôler] to check **2.** [confirmer] to prove, to confirm.
◆ ***se vérifier*** **vp** to prove accurate.

vérin [verɛ̃] **nm** jack.

véritable [veritabl] **adj** real / [ami] true ▸ **du cuir/de l'or véritable** real leather/gold.

véritablement [veritabləmɑ̃] **adv** really.

vérité [verite] **nf 1.** [chose vraie, réalité, principe] truth *(U)* ▸ **dire ses quatre vérités à qqn** *fam* to tell sb a few home truths **2.** [sincérité] sincerity **3.** [ressemblance - de reproduction] accuracy / [- de personnage, portrait] trueness to life.
◆ ***en vérité*** **loc adv** actually, really.

verlan [vɛrlɑ̃] **nm** back slang.

CULTURE

Verlan

Verlan, a form of slang in which syllables are reversed, is popular among young French people. Its name comes from (à) **l'envers**. Most of verlan is reversed two-syllable words: **laisse béton** for **laisse tomber**, **chanmé** for **méchant**, **ripou** for **pourri**. The latter describes corrupt policemen. Some words are altered slightly: **meuf (femme)**; **keuf (flic)**; **feuj (juif)**. **Beur** and **Beurette**, which describe French men and women of North African parentage, are among the few **verlan** words now used in everyday conversation.

vermeil, eille [vɛrmɛj] **adj** scarlet.
◆ ***vermeil*** **nm** silver-gilt.

vermicelle [vɛrmisɛl] **nm** vermicelli *(U)*.

vermifuge [vɛrmifyʒ] **nm** [pour chat, chien] worm tablet.

vermillon [vɛrmijɔ̃] **nm & adj inv** vermilion.

vermine [vɛrmin] **nf 1.** [parasites] vermin **2.** *fig* [canaille] rat.

vermisseau, x [vɛrmiso] **nm 1.** [ver] small worm **2.** *fig* [être chétif] runt.

vermoulu, e [vɛrmuly] **adj** riddled with woodworm / *fig* moth-eaten.

vermouth [vɛrmut] **nm** vermouth.

vernaculaire [vɛrnakylɛr] **adj** vernacular.

verni, e [vɛrni] **adj 1.** [bois] varnished **2.** [souliers] **: chaussures vernies** patent-leather shoes **3.** *fam* [chanceux] lucky.

vernir [32] [vɛrnir] **vt** to varnish.

vernis [vɛrni] **nm** varnish / *fig* veneer ▸ **vernis à ongles** nail polish *ou* varnish.

vernissage [vɛrnisaʒ] **nm 1.** [de meuble] varnishing **2.** [d'exposition] private viewing.

vérole [verɔl] **nf** MÉD **: petite vérole** smallpox.

verrat **[vera] nm** boar.

verre **[vɛr] nm 1.** [matière, récipient] glass / [quantité] glassful, glass ▸ **verre dépoli** frosted glass ▸ **verre incassable** shatterproof glass ▸ **verre ballon** brandy glass ▸ **verre à dents** tooth mug *ou* glass ▸ **verre doseur** measuring glass ▸ **verre à moutarde** mustard jar ▸ **verre à pied** long-stemmed glass ▸ **verre à vin** wineglass ▸ **mettre qqch sous verre** to put sthg in a clip frame ▸ **objets de verre** glassware *(U)* **2.** [optique] lens ▸ **porter des verres** to wear glasses ▸ **verres antireflet** anti-glare coated lenses ▸ **verres de contact** contact lenses ▸ **verres correcteurs** correcting lenses ▸ **verre grossissant** magnifying glass ▸ **verre optique** optical glass ▸ **verres polarisés** polaroid lenses ▸ **verres progressifs** progressive lenses, progressives *UK* **3.** [boisson] drink ▸ **boire un verre** to have a drink ▸ **je bois *ou* prends juste un petit verre** I'll just have a quick one.

verrerie **[vɛrri] nf 1.** [fabrication] glass-making **2.** [usine] glassworks *sg* **3.** [objets] glassware.

verrier **[vɛrje] nm** glassmaker.

verrière **[vɛrjɛr] nf 1.** [pièce] conservatory **2.** [toit] glass roof.

verroterie **[vɛrɔtri] nf** coloured *UK ou* colored *US* glass beads *pl*.

verrou **[vɛru] nm** bolt ▸ **mettre qqn/être sous les verrous** to put sb/to be behind bars.

verrouillage **[vɛrujaʒ] nm** AUTO **: verrouillage central** central locking.

verrouiller [3] **[vɛruje] vt 1.** [porte] to bolt **2.** [personne] to lock up.

◆ ***se verrouiller*** **vp** to lock o.s. in.

verrue **[vɛry] nf** wart ▸ **verrue plantaire** verruca.

vers[1] **[vɛr]** ■ **nm** line.

■ **nmpl : en vers** in verse ▸ **faire des vers** to write poetry.

vers[2] **[vɛr] prép 1.** [dans la direction de] towards, toward *US* **2.** [aux environs de - temporel] around, about / [- spatial] near ▸ **vers la fin du mois** towards *ou* toward *US* the end of the month.

Versailles **[vɛrsaj] npr** Versailles ▸ **le château de Versailles** (the Palace of) Versailles.

versant **[vɛrsɑ̃] nm** side.

versatile **[vɛrsatil] adj** changeable, fickle.

verse **[vɛrs]** ◆ ***à verse*** **loc adv : pleuvoir à verse** to pour down.

versé, e **[vɛrse] adj : être versé dans** to be versed *ou* well-versed in.

Verseau **[vɛrso] nm** ASTROL Aquarius ▸ **être Verseau** to be (an) Aquarius.

versement **[vɛrsəmɑ̃] nm** payment.

verser [3] **[vɛrse]** ■ **vt 1.** [eau] to pour / [larmes, sang] to shed **2.** [argent] to pay.

■ **vi** to overturn, to tip over ▸ **verser dans** *fig* to lapse into.

verset **[vɛrsɛ] nm** verse.

verseur, euse **[vɛrsœr, øz] adj** pouring *(avant n)*.

◆ ***verseur*** **nm** pourer.

◆ ***verseuse*** **nf** pot, jug *UK (for coffee maker)*.

versification **[vɛrsifikasjɔ̃] nf** versification.

version **[vɛrsjɔ̃] nf 1.** [gén] version ▸ **version française/originale** French/original version **2.** [traduction] translation *(into mother tongue)* **3.** INFORM [d'un logiciel] **: version alpha** alpha version ▸ **version bêta** beta version ▸ **version de démonstration *ou* d'évaluation** demo version.

verso **[vɛrso] nm** back.

versus **[vɛrsys] prép** versus.

vert, e **[vɛr, vɛrt] adj 1.** [couleur, fruit, légume, bois] green ▸ **être vert de peur** to be white with fear **2.** *fig* [vieillard] spry, sprightly **3.** [réprimande] sharp **4.** [à la campagne] **: le tourisme vert** country holidays *pl* ▸ **station verte** rural tourist centre **5.** *fam* [histoire] smutty ▸ **(en entendre) des vertes et des pas mûres** (to hear) all sorts of awful things ▸ **il lui en a fait voir des vertes et des pas mûres!** he's really put her through it!

◆ ***vert*** **nm 1.** [couleur] green ▸ **vert bouteille/d'eau/pomme/tendre** bottle/sea/apple/soft green ▸ **peint *ou* teint en vert** painted *ou* tinted green ▸ **le feu est passé au vert** the lights have turned (to) green **2.** [verdure] **: se mettre au vert** to take a break in the country.

◆ ***Verts*** **nmpl : les Verts** POLIT the Greens.

vert-de-gris **[vɛrdəgri]** ■ **nm** verdigris.

■ **adj** grey-green *UK*, gray-green *US*.

vertébral, e, aux **[vɛrtebral, o] adj** vertebral.

vertèbre **[vɛrtɛbr] nf** vertebra.

vertébré, e **[vɛrtebre] adj** vertebrate.

◆ ***vertébré*** **nm** vertebrate.

vertement **[vɛrtəmɑ̃] adv** sharply.

vertical, e, aux **[vɛrtikal, o] adj** vertical.

◆ ***verticale*** **nf** vertical ▸ **à la verticale** [descente] vertical / [descendre] vertically.

verticalement **[vɛrtikalmɑ̃] adv** vertically.

vertige **[vɛrtiʒ] nm 1.** [peur du vide] vertigo ▸ **donner le vertige à qqn** to make sb dizzy **2.** [étourdissement] dizziness / *fig* intoxication ▸ **avoir des vertiges** to suffer from *ou* have dizzy spells.

vertigineux, euse **[vɛrtiʒinø, øz] adj 1.** *fig* [vue, vitesse] breathtaking **2.** [hauteur] dizzy.

vertu **[vɛrty] nf 1.** [morale, chasteté] virtue ▸ **de petite vertu** of easy virtue **2.** [pouvoir] properties *pl*, power.

◆ ***en vertu de*** **loc prép** in accordance with.

vertueusement **[vɛrtɥøzmɑ̃] adv** virtuously.

vertueux, euse **[vɛrtɥø, øz] adj** virtuous.

verve **[vɛrv] nf** eloquence ▸ **être en verve** to be particularly eloquent.

verveine **[vɛrvɛn] nf 1.** [plante] verbena **2.** [infusion] verbena tea.

vésicule **[vezikyl] nf** vesicle ▸ **vésicule biliaire** gall bladder.

Vespa® **[vɛspa] nf** scooter, Vespa®.

vespasienne **[vɛspazjɛn] nf** public urinal.

vespéral, e, aux **[vɛsperal, o] adj** *littéraire* evening *(avant n)*.

vessie **[vesi] nf** bladder.

veste [vɛst] **nf 1.** [vêtement] jacket ▸ **veste croisée/droite** double-/single-breasted jacket ▸ **retourner sa veste** *fam fig* to change one's colours *UK* *ou* colors *US* **2.** *fam* [échec] **: ramasser** *ou* **prendre une veste** to come a cropper.

vestiaire [vɛstjɛr] **nm 1.** [au théâtre] cloakroom **2.** *(gén pl)* SPORT changing room *UK*, locker room *US*.

vestibule [vɛstibyl] **nm** [pièce] hall, vestibule.

vestige [vɛstiʒ] **nm** *(gén pl)* [de ville] remains *pl* / *fig* [de civilisation, grandeur] vestiges *pl*, relic.

vestimentaire [vɛstimɑ̃tɛr] **adj** [industrie] clothing *(avant n)* / [dépense] on clothes ▸ **détail vestimentaire** accessory.

veston [vɛstɔ̃] **nm** jacket.

vétéciste [vetesist] **nmf** hybrid bike rider.

vêtement [vɛtmɑ̃] **nm** garment, article of clothing ▸ **vêtements** clothing *(U)*, clothes.

vétéran [veterɑ̃] **nm** veteran.

vétérinaire [veterinɛr] ■ **adj** veterinary *(avant n)*.
■ **nmf** vet *UK*, veterinary surgeon *UK*, veterinarian *US*.

vététiste [vetetist] **nmf** mountain biker.

vétille [vetij] **nf** triviality.

vêtir [44] [vetir] **vt** to dress.
◆ ***se vêtir*** **vp** to dress, to get dressed.

vétiver [vetivɛr] **nm** vetiver.

veto [veto] **nm inv** veto ▸ **mettre son veto à qqch** to veto sthg.

véto [veto] **nmf** *fam* vet.

vêtu**, **e [vɛty] ■ **pp** ➤ ***vêtir***.
■ **adj : vêtu (de)** dressed (in) ▸ **à demi-vêtu** half-dressed.

vétuste [vetyst] **adj** dilapidated.

vétusté [vetyste] **nf** dilapidation.

veuf**, **veuve [vœf, vœv] ■ **adj** widowed.
■ **nm, f** widower (f widow).

veuille ➤ ***vouloir***.

veule [vøl] **adj** spineless.

veulerie [vølri] **nf** spinelessness.

veut ➤ ***vouloir***.

veuvage [vœvaʒ] **nm** [de femme] widowhood / [d'homme] widowerhood.

veuve ➤ ***veuf***.

veux ➤ ***vouloir***.

vexant**, **e [vɛksɑ̃, ɑ̃t] **adj 1.** [contrariant] annoying, vexing **2.** [blessant] hurtful.

vexation [vɛksasjɔ̃] **nf** [humiliation] insult.

vexatoire [vɛksatwar] **adj** offensive.

vexer [4] [vɛkse] **vt** to offend.
◆ ***se vexer*** **vp** to take offence *UK* *ou* offense *US*.

VF (abr de ***version française***) **nf** *indicates that a film has been dubbed into French*.

VHF (abr de ***very high frequency***) **nf** VHF.

via [vja] **prép** via.

viabiliser [3] [vjabilize] **vt** to service.

viabilité [vjabilite] **nf 1.** [de route] passable state **2.** [d'entreprise, organisme] viability.

viable [vjabl] **adj** viable.

viaduc [vjadyk] **nm** viaduct.

viager**, **ère [vjaʒe, ɛr] **adj** life *(avant n)*.
◆ ***viager*** **nm** life annuity ▸ **mettre qqch en viager** to sell sthg in return for a life annuity.

viande [vjɑ̃d] **nf** meat ▸ **viande blanche** white meat ▸ **viande froide** cold meat ▸ **viande rouge** red meat.

viatique [vjatik] **nm 1.** RELIG **: recevoir le viatique** to receive the last rites *pl* **2.** *littéraire* [soutien] lifeline.

vibrant**, **e [vibrɑ̃, ɑ̃t] **adj 1.** [corde] vibrating **2.** *fig* [discours] stirring.

vibraphone [vibrafɔn] **nm** vibraphone.

vibration [vibrasjɔ̃] **nf** vibration.

vibratoire [vibratwar] **adj** vibratory.

vibrer [3] [vibre] **vi 1.** [trembler] to vibrate **2.** *fig* [être ému] **: vibrer (de)** to be stirred (with).

vibreur [vibrœr] **nm** TÉLÉCOM VibraCall® (alert *ou* feature).

vibromasseur [vibromasœr] **nm** vibrator.

vicaire [vikɛr] **nm** curate.

vice [vis] **nm 1.** [de personne] vice **2.** [d'objet] fault, defect ▸ **vice caché** hidden flaw ▸ **vice de forme** DR flaw.

vice-consul [viskɔ̃syl] (pl **vice-consuls**) **nm** vice-consul.

vice-présidence [visprezidɑ̃s] (pl **vice-présidences**) **nf** POLIT vice-presidency / [de société] vice-chairmanship.

vice-président**, **e [visprezidɑ̃, ɑ̃t] (mpl **vice-présidents**, fpl **vice-présidentes**) **nm, f** POLIT vice-president / [de société] vice-chairman (f vice-chairwoman).

vice versa [vis(e)vɛrsa] **loc adv** vice versa.

vichy [viʃi] **nm 1.** [étoffe] gingham **2.** [eau] vichy (water).

vicié**, **e [visje] **adj** [air] polluted, tainted.

vicier [9] [visje] **vt 1.** [air] to pollute, to taint **2.** DR to invalidate.

vicieux**, **euse [visjø, øz] **adj 1.** [personne, conduite] perverted, depraved **2.** [animal] restive **3.** [attaque] underhand **4.** *sout* [prononciation, locution] incorrect.

vicinal**, **e, aux [visinal, o] ➤ ***chemin***.

vicissitudes [visisityd] **nfpl** vicissitudes.

vicomte**, **vicomtesse [vikɔ̃t, vikɔ̃tɛs] **nm, f** viscount (f viscountess).

victime [viktim] **nf** victim / [blessé] casualty.

victoire [viktwar] **nf** MIL victory / POLIT & SPORT win, victory ▸ **chanter** *ou* **crier victoire** to boast of one's success.

victorieux**, **euse [viktɔrjø, øz] **adj 1.** MIL victorious / POLIT & SPORT winning *(avant n)*, victorious **2.** [air] triumphant.

victuailles [viktɥaj] **nfpl** provisions.

vidange [vidɑ̃ʒ] **nf 1.** [action] emptying, draining **2.** AUTO oil change **3.** [mécanisme] waste outlet.
◆ ***vidanges*** **nfpl** sewage *(U)*.

vidanger [17] [vidɑ̃ʒe] **vt** to empty, to drain.

vide [vid] ■ nm **1.** [espace] void ▸ **le moteur tourne à vide** the engine's ticking over *ou* idling / *fig* [néant, manque] emptiness **2.** [absence d'air] vacuum ▸ **conditionné sous vide** vacuum-packed **3.** [ouverture] gap, space **4.** DR **: vide juridique** legal vacuum ▸ **il y a un vide juridique en la matière** the law is not specific on this matter
▸▸ **faire le vide** [se détendre] to have some time on one's own ▸ **faire le vide autour de soi** to drive all one's friends away ▸ **faire des promesses dans le vide** to make empty promises ▸ **parler dans le vide** [sans objet] to talk aimlessly / [sans auditeur] to talk to a brick wall *ou* to o.s. ▸ **regarder dans le vide** to stare into space.
■ adj empty ▸ **avoir le ventre vide** to have an empty stomach ▸ **un regard vide** a vacant stare ▸ **vide de** *fig* devoid of ▸ **des remarques vides de sens** meaningless remarks, remarks devoid of meaning.
◆ ***à vide*** loc adj & loc adv empty.

vidéo [video] ■ adj inv video *(avant n)*.
■ nf video ▸ **vidéo à la demande** video-on-demand.

vidéocassette [videɔkasɛt] nf video cassette.

vidéoconférence [videokɔ̃ferɑ̃s] = ***visioconférence***.

vidéodisque [videɔdisk] nm videodisc *UK*, videodisk *US*.

vidéoprojecteur [videɔprɔʒektœr] nm video projector.

vide-ordures [vidɔrdyr] nm inv rubbish chute *UK*, garbage chute *US*.

vidéosurveillance [videɔsyrvɛjɑ̃s] nf video surveillance.

vidéothèque [videɔtɛk] nf video library.

vidéotransmission [videɔtrɑ̃smisjɔ̃] nf video transmission.

vide-poches [vidpɔʃ] nm inv **1.** [chez soi] tidy **2.** [de voiture] glove compartment.

vide-pomme [vidpɔm] (pl **vide-pomme** *ou* **vide-pommes**) nm apple corer.

vider [3] [vide] vt **1.** [rendre vide] to empty ▸ **vider les ordures** to put out the rubbish *UK ou* garbage *US* ▸ **vider son verre** to drain one's glass ▸ **nous avons vidé une bouteille à deux** we downed a bottle between the two of us ▸ **vider son sac** *fig* to get things off one's chest, to unburden o.s. **2.** [évacuer] **: vider les lieux** to vacate the premises **3.** [poulet] to clean **4.** *fam* [personne - épuiser] to drain ▸ **être vidé** to be exhausted / [- expulser] to chuck out.
◆ ***se vider*** vp **1.** [eaux] **: se vider dans** to empty into, to drain into **2.** [baignoire, salle] to empty.

videur [vidœr] nm bouncer.

vie [vi] nf **1.** [gén] life ▸ **attenter à la vie de qqn** to make an attempt on sb's life ▸ **avoir la vie dure** to have a hard life ▸ **coûter la vie à qqn** to cost sb his/her life ▸ **entrer dans la vie active** to start working ▸ **sauver la vie à qqn** to save sb's life ▸ **être en vie** to be alive ▸ **être entre la vie et la mort** to be at death's door ▸ **sa vie durant** for one's entire life ▸ **à vie** for life ▸ **une vie de chien** *fam* a dog's life ▸ **mener la vie dure à qqn** to make sb's life hell ▸ **l'œuvre de toute une vie** a lifetime's work ▸ **prendre la vie du bon côté** to look on the bright side of life ▸ **rater sa vie** to make a mess of one's life ▸ **refaire sa vie** to start afresh *ou* all over again ▸ **risquer sa vie** to risk one's life ▸ **voir la vie en rose** to see life through rose-coloured *UK ou* rose-colored *US* spectacles ▸ **enterrer sa vie de garçon** to have a stag party *ou* night ▸ **membre à vie** life member **2.** [subsistance] cost of living ▸ **dans ce pays, la vie n'est pas chère** prices are very low in this country ▸ **gagner sa vie** to earn one's living **3.** TECHNOL life ▸ **à courte vie** short-lived ▸ **à longue vie** long-lived.

vieil ➤ ***vieux***.

vieillard [vjɛjar] nm old man.

vieille ➤ ***vieux***.

vieillerie [vjɛjri] nf [objet] old thing.

vieillesse [vjɛjɛs] nf **1.** [fin de la vie] old age **2.** [vieillards] **: la vieillesse** old people *pl*.

vieilli, e [vjeji] adj [mode, attitude] dated.

vieillir [32] [vjejir] ■ vi **1.** [personne] to grow old, to age ▸ **vieillir bien/mal** to age well/badly ▸ **tu ne vieillis pas** you never seem to look any older **2.** CULIN to mature, to age **3.** [tradition, idée] to become dated *ou* outdated ▸ **son roman a beaucoup vieilli** her novel seems really dated now.
■ vt **: vieillir qqn** to make sb look older ▸ **c'est fou ce que les cheveux longs la vieillissent!** [coiffure, vêtement] long hair makes her look a lot older! ▸ **ils m'ont vieilli de cinq ans** [personne] they said I was five years older than I actually am.
◆ ***se vieillir*** vp [d'apparence] to make o.s. look older / [dans les propos] to say one is older than one really is.

vieillissement [vjejismɑ̃] nm **1.** [de personne] ageing **2.** [de mot, d'idée] obsolescence **3.** [de vin, fromage] maturing, ageing.

vieillot, otte [vjejo, ɔt] adj old-fashioned.

vielle [vjɛl] nf hurdy-gurdy.

Vienne [vjɛn] npr **1.** [en France] Vienne **2.** [en Autriche] Vienna.

viennois, e [vjenwa, az] adj Viennese ▸ **pain viennois** Vienna loaf.
◆ ***Viennois, e*** nm, f Viennese.

viennoiserie [vjenwazri] nf *pastry made with sweetened dough like croissant, brioche etc.*

vierge [vjɛrʒ] ■ nf virgin ▸ **la (Sainte) Vierge** the (Blessed) Virgin.
■ adj **1.** [personne] virgin **2.** [terre] virgin / [page] blank / [casier judiciaire] clean ▸ **vierge de** unsullied by.
◆ ***Vierge*** nf ASTROL Virgo ▸ **être Vierge** to be (a) Virgo.

Viêt Nam [vjɛtnam] nm **: le Viêt Nam** Vietnam ▸ **au Viêt Nam** in Vietnam ▸ **le Nord Viêt Nam** HIST North Vietnam ▸ **le Sud Viêt Nam** HIST South Vietnam.

vietnamien, enne [vjɛtnamjɛ̃, ɛn] adj Vietnamese.
◆ ***vietnamien*** nm [langue] Vietnamese.
◆ ***Vietnamien, enne*** nm, f Vietnamese person.

vieux, vieille [vjø, vjɛj] ■ adj *(vieil devant voyelle ou 'h muet)* old ▸ **les vieilles gens** old people, elderly people, the elderly ▸ **un vieil homme** an old *ou* elderly man ▸ **sa vieille mère** her old *ou* aged mother ▸ **se faire vieux** to get old ▸ **faire vieux** to look old ▸ **vieux jeu** old-fashioned ▸ **ce que tu peux être vieux jeu!** you're so behind the times! ▸ **un vieux numéro** [de magazine] a back issue ▸ **recycler les vieux papiers** to recycle waste paper ▸ **une amitié vieille**

de 20 ans a friendship that goes back 20 years ▸ **c'est une manie de vieille fille** it's an old-maidish thing to do *péj* ▸ **des manies de vieux garçon** bachelor ways.
■ **nm, f 1.** [personne âgée] old man (f woman) ▸ **les vieux** the old ▸ **elle a pris un sacré coup de vieux** she's looking a lot older ▸ **un petit vieux** a little old man ▸ **une petite vieille** a little old lady
2. *fam* [ami] **: mon vieux** old chap *ou* boy *UK*, old buddy *US* ▸ **ma vieille** old girl
3. *tfam* [parent] old man (f woman) ▸ **ses vieux** his folks.
■ **nm** [meubles] antique furniture.

vif, vive [vif, viv] **adj 1.** [preste - enfant] lively / [- imagination] vivid ▸ **rouler à vive allure** to drive at great speed **2.** [couleur, œil] bright ▸ **avoir le regard vif** to have a lively look in one's eye ▸ **rouge/jaune vif** bright red/yellow **3.** [reproche] sharp / [discussion] bitter ▸ **je le lui dirai de vive voix** I'll tell him personally **4.** *sout* [vivant] alive **5.** [douleur, déception] acute / [intérêt] keen / [amour, haine] intense, deep ▸ **c'est avec un vif plaisir que...** it's with great pleasure that... ▸ **avec un vif soulagement** with a profound sense of relief.
◆ ***vif*** **nm 1.** DR living person **2.** [à la pêche] live bait ▸▸ **entrer dans le vif du sujet** to get to the heart of the matter ▸ **piquer au vif** to touch a raw nerve ▸ **prendre qqn sur le vif** to catch sb red-handed ▸ **une photo prise sur le vif** an action photograph.
◆ ***à vif*** **loc adj** [plaie] open ▸ **la chair était à vif** the flesh was exposed ▸ **j'ai les nerfs à vif** *fig* my nerves are frayed.

vif-argent [vifarʒɑ̃] **nm inv** quicksilver / *fig* [personne] live wire.

vigie [viʒi] **nf 1.** [NAUT - personne] lookout / [- poste] crow's nest **2.** RAIL observation box.

vigilance [viʒilɑ̃s] **nf** vigilance.

vigilant, e [viʒilɑ̃, ɑ̃t] **adj** vigilant, watchful.

vigile [viʒil] **nm** watchman.

vigne [viɲ] **nf 1.** [plante] vine, grapevine **2.** [plantation] vineyard.
◆ ***vigne vierge*** **nf** Virginia creeper.

vigneron, onne [viɲərɔ̃, ɔn] **nm, f** wine grower.

vignette [viɲɛt] **nf 1.** [timbre] label / [de médicament] price sticker *(for reimbursement by the social security services)* / AUTO tax disc *UK* **2.** [motif] vignette.

vignoble [viɲɔbl] **nm 1.** [plantation] vineyard **2.** [vignes] vineyards *pl*.

vigoureusement [vigurøzmɑ̃] **adv** vigorously.

vigoureux, euse [vigurø, øz] **adj** [corps, personne] vigorous / [bras, sentiment] strong.

vigueur [vigœr] **nf** vigour *UK*, vigor *US*.
◆ ***en vigueur*** **loc adj** in force.

VIH, V.I.H. (abr de ***virus d'immunodéficience humaine***) **nm** HIV.

vil, e [vil] **adj** vile, base.

vilain, e [vilɛ̃, ɛn] **adj 1.** [gén] nasty **2.** [laid] ugly.
◆ ***vilain*** **nm 1.** HIST villein **2.** *fam* [grabuge] **: il y aura du vilain** there's going to be trouble.

vilebrequin [vilbrəkɛ̃] **nm 1.** [outil] brace and bit **2.** AUTO crankshaft.

vilenie [vileni] **nf 1.** [caractère] vileness, baseness **2.** [action] vile deed / [parole] vile comment.

vilipender [3] [vilipɑ̃de] **vt** *littéraire* to vilify.

villa [vila] **nf** villa.

village [vilaʒ] **nm** village ▸ **village de vacances** holiday village *UK*, vacation village *US*.

villageois, e [vilaʒwa, az] ■ **adj** rustic.
■ **nm, f** villager.

ville [vil] **nf** [petite, moyenne] town / [importante] city ▸ **à la ville comme à la scène** in real life as (well as) on stage ▸ **les gens de la ville** city-dwellers, townspeople ▸ **aller en ville** to go into town ▸ **et si nous dînions en ville?** let's eat out tonight ▸ **habiter en ville** to live in town ▸ **ville champignon** town which has mushroomed ▸ **ville dortoir** dormitory town *UK*, bedroom community *US* ▸ **ville nouvelle** new town ▸ **ville d'eau** spa (town) ▸ **ville industrielle/universitaire** industrial/university town ▸ **ville nouvelle** new town ▸ **chaussures/tenue de ville** shoes/outfit for wearing in town.

villégiature [vileʒjatyr] **nf** holiday *UK*, vacation *US*.

Villette [vilɛt] **npr : la Villette** *cultural complex in north Paris (including a science museum, theatre and park).*

vin [vɛ̃] **nm** wine ▸ **vin blanc/rosé/rouge** white/rosé/red wine ▸ **vin champagnisé** champagne-style wine ▸ **vin résiné** retsina ▸ **vin de table** table wine.
◆ ***vin d'honneur*** **nm** reception.

vinaigre [vinɛgr] **nm** vinegar ▸ **vinaigre de framboise/de vin** raspberry/wine vinegar ▸ **vinaigre balsamique** balsamic vinegar ▸ **tourner au vinaigre** *fig* to turn sour.

vinaigrer [4] [vinegre] **vt** to put vinegar on.

vinaigrette [vinɛgrɛt] **nf** oil and vinegar dressing.

vinasse [vinas] **nf** *péj* plonk *UK*.

vindicatif, ive [vɛ̃dikatif, iv] **adj** vindictive.

vindicte [vɛ̃dikt] **nf : vindicte publique** DR justice.

vingt [vɛ̃] **adj num inv & nm** twenty ; voir aussi ***six***.

vingtaine [vɛ̃tɛn] **nf : une vingtaine de** about twenty.

vingtième [vɛ̃tjɛm] **adj num inv, nm & nmf** twentieth ; voir aussi ***sixième***.

vinicole [vinikɔl] **adj** wine-growing, wine-producing.

vinification [vinifikasjɔ̃] **nf** winemaking.

viol [vjɔl] **nm 1.** [de femme] rape ▸ **au viol!** rape! **2.** [de sépulture] desecration / [de sanctuaire] violation.

violacé, e [vjɔlase] **adj** purplish.

violation [vjɔlasjɔ̃] **nf** violation, breach ▸ **violation de domicile** unauthorized entry.

viole [vjɔl] **nf** viol.

violemment [vjɔlamɑ̃] **adv 1.** [frapper] violently **2.** [rétorquer] sharply.

violence [vjɔlɑ̃s] **nf** violence ▸ **se faire violence** to force o.s.

violent, e [vjɔlɑ̃, ɑ̃t] **adj 1.** [personne, tempête] violent **2.** *fig* [douleur, angoisse, chagrin] acute / [haine, passion] violent **3.** *fam* [excessif] annoying.

violenter [3] [vjɔlɑ̃te] **vt** to assault sexually.

violer [3] [vjɔle] **vt 1.** [femme] to rape **2.** [loi, traité] to break **3.** [sépulture] to desecrate / [sanctuaire] to violate.

violet**, **ette [vjɔlɛ, ɛt] **adj** purple / [pâle] violet.
◆ ***violet*** **nm** purple / [pâle] violet.

violette [vjɔlɛt] **nf** violet.

violeur [vjɔlœr] **nm** rapist.

violon [vjɔlɔ̃] **nm 1.** [instrument] violin ▸ **accorder ses violons** *fig* to come to an agreement **2.** [musicien] violin (player) **3.** *fam* [prison] nick *UK*, clink.
◆ ***violon d'Ingres*** **nm** hobby.

violoncelle [vjɔlɔ̃sɛl] **nm 1.** [instrument] cello **2.** [musicien] cello (player).

violoncelliste [vjɔlɔ̃selist] **nmf** cellist.

violoneux [vjɔlɔnø] **nm** fiddler.

violoniste [vjɔlɔnist] **nmf** violinist.

VIP (abr de ***very important person***) **nm** VIP.

vipère [vipɛr] **nf** viper.

virage [viraʒ] **nm 1.** [sur route] bend ▸ **négocier un virage** to negotiate a bend ▸ **prendre un virage** to take a bend ▸ **virage sans visibilité** blind corner ▸ **virage en épingle à cheveux** hairpin bend **2.** [changement] turn **3.** CHIM colour *UK* *ou* color *US* change **4.** MÉD positive reaction.

viral**, **e**, **aux [viral, o] **adj** viral.

virée [vire] **nf** *fam* **: faire une virée** [en voiture] to go for a spin / [dans bars] ≃ to go on a pub crawl.

virement [virmɑ̃] **nm 1.** FIN transfer ▸ **virement automatique** automatic transfer, standing order ▸ **virement bancaire/postal** bank/giro *UK* transfer ▸ **virement de crédit** credit transfer ▸ **virement interbancaire** interbank transfer ▸ **faire un virement** to transfer **2.** NAUT **: virement (de bord)** tacking.

virer [3] [vire] ■ **vi 1.** [tourner] **: virer à droite/à gauche** to turn right/left **2.** [étoffe] to change colour *UK* *ou* color *US* ▸ **virer au blanc/jaune** to go white/yellow **3.** PHOTO to tone **4.** MÉD to react positively.
■ **vt 1.** FIN to transfer **2.** *fam* [renvoyer] to kick out.

virevolte [virvɔlt] **nf 1.** [mouvement] twirl **2.** *fig* [volte-face] about-turn *UK*, about-face *US*, U-turn.

virevolter [3] [virvɔlte] **vi 1.** [tourner] to twirl *ou* spin round *UK* *ou* around *US* **2.** *fig* [changer de sujet] to flit from one subject to another.

virginal**, **e**, **aux [virʒinal, o] **adj** virginal.

virginité [virʒinite] **nf 1.** [de personne] virginity **2.** [de sentiment] purity.

virgule [virgyl] **nf** [entre mots] comma / [entre chiffres] (decimal) point.

viril**, **e [viril] **adj** virile.

virilité [virilite] **nf** virility.

virologie [virɔlɔʒi] **nf** virology.

virtualité [virtɥalite] **nf** potentiality, possibility.

virtuel**, **elle [virtɥɛl] **adj** potential ▸ **animal virtuel** cyberpet.

virtuellement [virtɥɛlmɑ̃] **adv 1.** [potentiellement] potentially **2.** [pratiquement] virtually.

virtuose [virtɥoz] **nmf** virtuoso.

virtuosité [virtɥozite] **nf** virtuosity.

virulence [virylɑ̃s] **nf** virulence.

virulent**, **e [virylɑ̃, ɑ̃t] **adj** virulent.

virus [virys] **nm** INFORM & MÉD virus / *fig* bug ▸ **dépourvu de virus** bug free ▸ **virus informatique** computer virus.

vis [vis] **nf** screw ▸ **serrer la vis à qqn** *fig* to put the screws on sb.

visa [viza] **nm** visa ▸ **visa de censure** censor's certificate ▸ **visa d'entrée** entry visa.

Visa® [viza] **nf : la (carte) Visa** Visa® (card).

visage [vizaʒ] **nm** face ▸ **à visage découvert** *fig* openly.

visagiste [vizaʒist] **nmf** beautician.

vis-à-vis [vizavi] **nm 1.** [personne] person sitting opposite **2.** [tête-à-tête] encounter **3.** [immeuble] **: avoir un vis-à-vis** to have a building opposite.
◆ ***vis-à-vis de*** **loc prép 1.** [en face de] opposite **2.** [en comparaison de] beside, compared with **3.** [à l'égard de] towards, toward *US*.

viscéral**, **e**, **aux [viseral, o] **adj 1.** ANAT visceral **2.** *fam* [réaction] gut *(avant n)* / [haine, peur] deep-seated.

viscère [visɛr] **nm** *(gén pl)* innards *pl*.

viscose [viskoz] **nf** viscose.

viscosité [viskozite] **nf 1.** [de liquide] viscosity **2.** [de surface] stickiness.

visé**, **e [vize] **adj 1.** [concerné] concerned **2.** [vérifié] stamped.

visée [vize] **nf 1.** [avec arme] aiming **2.** *(gén pl) fig* [intention, dessein] aim.

viser [3] [vize] ■ **vt 1.** [cible] to aim at **2.** *fig* [poste] to aspire to, to aim for / [personne] to be directed *ou* aimed at **3.** *fam* [fille, voiture] to get a load of **4.** [document] to check, to stamp.
■ **vi** to aim, to take aim ▸ **viser à** to aim at ▸ **viser à faire qqch** to aim to do sthg, to be intended to do sthg ▸ **viser haut** *fig* to aim high ▸ **ne pas viser juste** not to aim accurately, to aim wide.

viseur [vizœr] **nm 1.** [d'arme] sights *pl* **2.** PHOTO viewfinder.

visibilité [vizibilite] **nf** visibility.

visible [vizibl] **adj 1.** [gén] visible **2.** [personne] **: il n'est pas visible** he's not seeing visitors.

visiblement [viziblәmɑ̃] **adv** visibly.

visière [vizjɛr] **nf 1.** [de casque] visor **2.** [de casquette] peak **3.** [de protection] eyeshade.

visioconférence [vizjokɔ̃ferɑ̃s], ***vidéoconférence*** [videokɔ̃ferɑ̃s] **nf** videoconference.

vision [vizjɔ̃] **nf 1.** [faculté] eyesight, vision **2.** [représentation] view, vision **3.** [mirage] vision.

visionnaire [vizjɔnɛr] **nmf & adj** visionary.

visionner [3] [vizjɔne] **vt** to view.

visionneuse [vizjɔnøz] **nf** viewer.

visite [vizit] **nf 1.** [chez un ami, officielle] visit ▸ **avoir de la visite** *ou* **une visite** to have visitors ▸ **rendre visite à qqn** to pay sb a visit ▸ **je m'attendais à sa visite** I was expecting him to call **2.** [MÉD - à l'extérieur] call, visit / [- à l'hôpital] rounds *pl* ▸ **heures de visite** visiting hours ▸ **passer une visite médicale** to have a medical *UK ou* a physical *US* **3.** [de monument] tour ▸ **visite guidée** guided tour **4.** [d'expert] inspection ▸ **visite d'inspection** visitation, visit.

visiter [3] [vizite] **vt** **1.** [en touriste] to tour **2.** [malade, prisonnier] to visit.

visiteur, euse [vizitœr, øz] **nm, f** visitor.

vison [vizɔ̃] **nm** mink.

visqueux, euse [viskø, øz] **adj** **1.** [liquide] viscous **2.** [surface] sticky **3.** *péj* [personne, manières] slimy, smarmy.

visser [3] [vise] **vt** **1.** [planches] to screw together **2.** [couvercle] to screw down **3.** [bouchon] to screw in / [écrou] to screw on **4.** *fam fig* [enfant] to keep a tight rein on.
◆ ***se visser*** **vp** *(emploi passif)* to screw on *ou* in ▸ **ampoule qui se visse** screw-in bulb.

visualisation [vizɥalizasjɔ̃] **nf** INFORM display mode.

visualiser [3] [vizɥalize] **vt** **1.** [gén] to visualize **2.** INFORM to display / TECHNOL to make visible.

visuel, elle [vizɥɛl] **adj** visual.
◆ ***visuel*** **nm** INFORM visual display unit ▸ **visuel graphique** graphical display unit.

visuellement [vizɥɛlmɑ̃] **adv** visually.

vital, e, aux [vital, o] **adj** vital.

vitalité [vitalite] **nf** vitality.

vitamine [vitamin] **nf** vitamin.

vitaminé, e [vitamine] **adj** with added vitamins, vitamin-enriched.

vite [vit] **adv** **1.** [rapidement] quickly, fast ▸ **fais vite!** hurry up! ▸ **avoir vite fait de faire qqch** to have been quick to do sthg ▸ **ça a été vite réglé** it was settled in no time at all, it was soon settled ▸ **méfie-toi, il a vite fait de s'énerver** be careful, he loses his temper easily ▸ **on lui a repeint sa grille vite fait, bien fait** we gave her gate a nice new coat of paint in no time ▸ **va plus vite** speed up, go faster **2.** [tôt] soon ▸ **envoyez vite votre bulletin-réponse!** send your entry form now! ▸ **j'ai vite compris de quoi il s'agissait** I soon realized what it was all about, it didn't take me long to realize what it was all about.

vitesse [vitɛs] **nf** **1.** [gén] speed ▸ **prendre de la vitesse** to pick up *ou* gather speed ▸ **prendre qqn de vitesse** *fig* to outstrip sb ▸ **à toute vitesse** at top speed ▸ **vitesse de croisière** cruising speed **2.** AUTO gear ▸ **changer de vitesse** to change *UK ou* to shift gear ▸ **en quatrième vitesse** *fam fig* at the double.

viticole [vitikɔl] **adj** wine-growing.

viticulteur, trice [vitikyltœr, tris] **nm, f** wine-grower.

viticulture [vitikyltyr] **nf** wine-growing.

vitrage [vitraʒ] **nm** **1.** [vitres] windows *pl* **2.** [toit] glass roof.

vitrail, aux [vitraj, o] **nm** stained-glass window.

vitre [vitr] **nf** **1.** [de fenêtre] pane of glass, windowpane **2.** [de voiture, train] window.

vitré, e [vitre] **adj** glass *(avant n)*.

vitrer [3] [vitre] **vt** to glaze.

vitreux, euse [vitrø, øz] **adj** **1.** [roche] vitreous **2.** [œil, regard] glassy, glazed.

vitrier [vitrije] **nm** glazier.

vitrification [vitrifikasjɔ̃] **nf** **1.** [de parquet] sealing and varnishing **2.** [d'émail] vitrification.

vitrifier [9] [vitrifje] **vt** **1.** [parquet] to seal and varnish **2.** [émail] to vitrify.

vitrine [vitrin] **nf** **1.** [de boutique] (shop) window / *fig* showcase ▸ **lécher les vitrines** to go window-shopping **2.** [meuble] display cabinet.

vitriol [vitrijɔl] **nm** vitriol.

vitrocéramique [vitroseramik] **adj : plaque vitrocéramique** ceramic hob.

vitupération [vityperasjɔ̃] **nf** vituperation, vilification.

vitupérer [18] [vitypere] **vt** to rail against.

vivable [vivabl] **adj** [appartement] livable-in / [situation] bearable, tolerable / [personne] **: il n'est pas vivable** he's impossible to live with.

vivace [vivas] **adj** **1.** [plante] perennial / [arbre] hardy **2.** *fig* [haine, ressentiment] deep-rooted, entrenched / [souvenir] enduring.

vivacité [vivasite] **nf** **1.** [promptitude - de personne] liveliness, vivacity ▸ **vivacité d'esprit** quick-wittedness **2.** [de coloris, teint] intensity, brightness **3.** [de propos] sharpness.

vivant, e [vivɑ̃, ɑ̃t] **adj** **1.** [en vie] alive, living ▸ **enterré vivant** buried alive **2.** [enfant, quartier] lively **3.** [souvenir] still fresh **4.** *fig* [preuve] living.
◆ ***vivant*** **nm** **1.** [vie] **: du vivant de qqn** in sb's lifetime **2.** [personne] **: les vivants** the living ▸ **un bon vivant** *fig* a person who enjoys (the good things in) life.

PARONYME / CONFUSABLE

vivant

Ne pas confondre les deux traductions de vivant : *living* signifie existant, doué de vie, et s'utilise comme épithète, tandis que *alive* signifie en vie et ne s'utilise qu'en attribut.

vivarium [vivarjɔm] **nm** vivarium.

vivats [viva] **nmpl** cheers, cheering *sg*.

vive[1] [viv] **nf** [poisson] weever.

vive[2] [viv] **interj** three cheers for ▸ **vive le roi!** long live the King!

vivement [vivmɑ̃] ■ **adv** **1.** [agir] quickly **2.** [répondre] sharply **3.** [affecter] deeply.
■ **interj : vivement les vacances!** roll on the holidays! ▸ **vivement que l'été arrive** I'll be glad when summer comes, summer can't come quick enough.

vivier [vivje] **nm 1.** [de poissons] fish pond / [dans un restaurant] fish tank **2.** *fig* [concentration] breeding-ground.

vivifiant, e [vivifjɑ̃, ɑ̃t] **adj** invigorating, bracing.

vivifier [9] [vivifje] **vt** to invigorate.

vivipare [vivipar] **adj** viviparous.

vivisection [vivisɛksjɔ̃] **nf** vivisection.

vivoter [3] [vivɔte] **vi 1.** [personne] to live from hand to mouth **2.** [affaire, commerce] to struggle to survive.

vivre [90] [vivr] ■ **vi** to live / [être en vie] to be alive ▸ **vivre avec qqn** [maritalement] to live with sb / [en amis] to share *ou* to live with sb ▸ **vivre de** to live on ▸ **vivre de sa plume** to live by one's pen ▸ **vivre d'amour et d'eau fraîche** to live on love alone ▸ **faire vivre sa famille** to support one's family ▸ **être difficile/facile à vivre** to be hard/easy to get on with ▸ **avoir vécu** to have seen life ▸ **elle a vécu jusqu'à 95 ans** she lived to be 95 ▸ **il fait bon vivre ici** life is good *ou* it's a good life here ▸ **ils ont tout juste de quoi vivre** they've just enough to live on.
■ **vt 1.** [passer] to spend ▸ **vivre des temps difficiles** to live through *ou* to experience difficult times ▸ **vivre sa vie** to live one's own life **2.** [éprouver] to experience ▸ **elle a mal/bien vécu mon départ** she couldn't cope/she coped well after I left.
■ **nm : le vivre et le couvert** board and lodging.
◆ ***vivres*** **nmpl** provisions ▸ **couper les vivres à qqn** *fig* to cut off sb's livelihood.

vivrier, ère [vivrije, ɛr] **adj : culture vivrière** food crops *pl*.

vizir [vizir] **nm** vizier.

VL (abr de ***véhicule lourd***) **nm** HGV.

vlan [vlɑ̃] **interj** wham!, bang!

vo abr de ***verso***.

VO (abr de ***version originale***) **nf** *indicates that a film has not been dubbed* ▸ **en VO sous-titrée** in the original version with subtitles.

vocable [vɔkabl] **nm** term.

vocabulaire [vɔkabylɛr] **nm 1.** [gén] vocabulary **2.** [livre] lexicon, glossary.

vocal, e, aux [vɔkal, o] **adj : ensemble vocal** choir ➤ ***corde***.

vocalise [vɔkaliz] **nf : faire des vocalises** to do singing exercises.

vocaliser [3] [vɔkalize] **vi** to do singing exercises.

vocatif [vɔkatif] **nm** vocative (case).

vocation [vɔkasjɔ̃] **nf 1.** [gén] vocation **2.** [d'organisation] mission.

vocifération [vɔsiferasjɔ̃] **nf** shout, scream.

vociférer [18] [vɔsifere] **vt** to shout, to scream.

vodka [vɔdka] **nf** vodka.

vœu, x [vø] **nm 1.** RELIG [résolution] vow ▸ **faire le vœu de faire qqch** to vow to do sthg ▸ **faire vœu de silence** to take a vow of silence **2.** [souhait, requête] wish.
◆ ***vœux*** **nmpl** greetings ▸ **meilleurs vœux** best wishes ▸ **tous nos vœux de bonheur** our best wishes for your future happiness.

vogue [vɔg] **nf** vogue, fashion ▸ **en vogue** fashionable, in vogue.

voguer [3] [vɔge] **vi** *littéraire* to sail.

voici [vwasi] **prép 1.** [pour désigner, introduire] here is/are ▸ **le voici** here he/it is ▸ **les voici** here they are ▸ **vous cherchiez des allumettes? en voici** were you looking for matches? there are some here ▸ **l'homme que voici** this man (here) ▸ **voici ce qui s'est passé** this is what happened **2.** [il y a] **: voici trois mois** three months ago ▸ **voici quelques années que je ne l'ai pas vu** I haven't seen him for some years (now),it's been some years since I last saw him **3.** [caractérisant un état] **: me voici prêt** I'm ready now ▸ **nous voici enfin arrivés!** here we are at last! **4.** [désignant une action proche dans le temps] **: voici qu'ils recommencent avec leur musique!** their music's started (up) again! ▸ **voici venir le printemps** spring is coming.

voie [vwa] **nf 1.** [route] road ▸ **route à deux voies** two-lane road ▸ **voie de dégagement** slip road ▸ **voie express** *ou* **rapide** express way ▸ **voie navigable** waterway ▸ **la voie publique** the public highway ▸ **voie sans issue** no through road ▸ **voie privée** private road ▸ **les voies sur berges** [à Paris] *expressway running along the Seine in Paris* **2.** [rails] track, line / [quai] platform ▸ **voie ferrée** railway line *UK*, railroad line *US* ▸ **voie de garage** siding / *fig* dead-end job
3. [mode de transport] route ▸ **par la voie maritime/aérienne** by sea/air ▸ **par voie de terre** overland, by land
4. ANAT passage, tract ▸ **par voie buccale** *ou* **orale** orally, by mouth ▸ **par les voies naturelles** naturally ▸ **par voie rectale** by rectum ▸ **voie respiratoire** respiratory tract
5. *fig* [chemin] way ▸ **être en bonne voie** to be going well ▸ **votre dossier est en bonne voie** your file is being processed ▸ **être sur la bonne/mauvaise voie** to be on the right/wrong track ▸ **mettre qqn sur la voie** to put sb on

COMMENT EXPRIMER...

les vœux

Happy Birthday! / Bon anniversaire !
Many happy returns! / Heureux anniversaire !
Happy Anniversary! / Joyeux anniversaire de mariage !
Merry Christmas! / Joyeux Noël !
Happy New Year! / Bonne année !
Happy Easter! / Joyeuses Pâques !
Congratulations! / Toutes mes félicitations !
Cheers! / À la tienne !
Please raise your glasses to the bride and groom / Buvons à la santé des mariés
Here's wishing you all the best in your new job / Je te souhaite bonne chance dans ton nouveau poste

the right track ▸ **ouvrir la voie** to pave the way ▸ **la voie royale** *fig* the high road (to success) ▸ **la voie est libre** *fig* the road is clear ▸ **trouver sa voie** to find one's feet
6. [filière, moyen] means *pl* ▸ **par des voies détournées** by devious means, by a circuitous route ▸ **suivre la voie hiérarchique** to go through the official channels *pl*.
◆ ***voie de fait*** **nf** assault ▸ **se livrer à des voies de fait sur qqn** to assault sb.
◆ ***Voie lactée*** **nf : la Voie lactée** the Milky Way.
◆ ***en voie de*** **loc prép** on the way *ou* road to ▸ **en voie de développement** developing ▸ **espèces en voie de disparition** endangered species ▸ **en voie de guérison** getting better, on the road to recovery.

voilà [vwala] **prép 1.** [pour désigner] there is/are ▸ **le voilà** there he/it is ▸ **les voilà** there they are ▸ **me voilà** that's me, there I am ▸ **le voilà qui arrive** (look) he's here ▸ **vous cherchiez de l'encre? en voilà** you were looking for ink? there is some (over) there ▸ **la maison que voilà** that house (there) ▸ **nous voilà arrivés** we've arrived ▸ **en voilà un qui n'a pas peur!** *fam* He's certainly got guts! ▸ **en voilà une surprise/des manières!** what a surprise/way to behave!
2. [reprend ce dont on a parlé] that is / [introduit ce dont on va parler] this is ▸ **voilà ce que j'en pense** this is/that is what I think ▸ **voilà ce que c'est que de mentir!** that's where lying gets you! ▸ **voilà tout** that's all ▸ **et voilà!** there we are!
3. [il y a] **: voilà dix jours** ten days ago ▸ **voilà dix ans que je le connais** I've known him for ten years (now)
4. [désignant une action proche dans le temps] **: voilà que la nuit tombe** (now) it's getting dark ▸ **voilà qu'ils remettent ça avec leur musique!** *fam* they're at it again with their music!

voilage [vwalaʒ] **nm 1.** [rideau] net curtain **2.** [garniture] veil.

voile [vwal] ■ **nf 1.** [de bateau] sail ▸ **mettre les voiles** *fam fig* to shoot off, to scarper *UK* **2.** [activité] sailing.
■ **nm 1.** [textile] voile **2.** [coiffure] veil ▸ **voile de mariée** marriage veil ▸ **lever le voile sur** *fig* to lift the veil on **3.** [de brume] mist **4.** PHOTO fogging *(U)* **5.** MÉD **: voile au poumon** shadow on the lung ▸ **j'ai un voile devant** *ou* **sur les yeux** my vision *ou* sight is blurred.

voilé, e [vwale] **adj 1.** [visage, allusion] veiled **2.** [ciel, regard] dull **3.** [roue] buckled **4.** PHOTO fogged **5.** [son, voix] muffled.

voiler [3] [vwale] **vt 1.** [visage] to veil **2.** [vérité, sentiment] to hide **3.** [suj: brouillard, nuages] to cover **4.** [roue] to buckle.
◆ ***se voiler*** **vp 1.** [femme] to wear a veil **2.** [ciel] to cloud over / [yeux] to mist over **3.** [roue] to buckle.

voilette [vwalɛt] **nf** veil.

voilier [vwalje] **nm** [bateau] sailing boat *UK*, sailboat *US*.

voilure [vwalyr] **nf 1.** [de bateau] sails *pl* **2.** [d'avion] wings *pl* **3.** [de parachute] canopy.

voir [62] [vwar] ■ **vt 1.** [gén] to see ▸ **je l'ai vu tomber** I saw him fall ▸ **faire voir qqch à qqn** to show sb sthg ▸ **fais voir!** let me see!, show me! ▸ **en faire voir (de toutes les couleurs) à qqn** *fam* to give sb a hard time, to lead sb a merry dance ▸ **avoir assez vu qqn** *fam* to be fed up with sb ▸ **ne rien avoir à voir avec** *fig* to have nothing to do with ▸ **l'instruction n'a rien à voir avec l'intelligence** education has nothing to do with intelligence ▸ **je te vois bien papa!** I can just see you as a father! ▸ **je ne vois pas comment je pourrais t'aider** I can't see how I could help you ▸ **tu vois ce que je veux dire?** do you see *ou* understand what I mean? ▸ **essaie un peu, pour voir!** go on, just try it! ▸ **voyons,...** [en réfléchissant] let's see,... ▸ **un peu de courage, voyons!** come on, be brave! ▸ **ni vu ni connu** *fam* without anyone being any the wiser ▸ **j'en ai vu d'autres!** I've seen worse!, I've been through worse! ▸ **je dois aller voir le médecin** I've got to go to the doctor's ▸ **voir le jour** [bébé] to be born / [journal] to come out / [théorie, invention] to appear **2.** [dossier, affaire] to look at *ou* into, to go over.
■ **vi** to see ▸ **voir bien** to see clearly, to have good eyesight ▸ **voir mal** to have poor eyesight.
◆ ***se voir*** **vp 1.** [se regarder] to see o.s., to watch o.s. **2.** [s'imaginer] to see *ou* to imagine *ou* to picture o.s. ▸ **elle se voyait déjà championne!** she thought the championship was hers already! **3.** [se rencontrer] to see one another *ou* each other **4.** [se remarquer] to be obvious, to show ▸ **ça se voit!** you can tell! ▸ **il porte une perruque, ça se voit bien** you can tell he wears a wig.

voire [vwar] **adv** even.

voirie [vwari] **nf 1.** ADMIN ≃ Department of Transport **2.** [décharge] rubbish dump *UK*, garbage dump *US*.

voisin, e [vwazɛ̃, in] ■ **adj 1.** [pays, ville] neighbouring *UK*, neighboring *US* ▸ **les pays voisins de l'équateur/de notre territoire** the countries near the equator/bordering on our territory / [maison] next-door ▸ **il habite la maison voisine** he lives next door **2.** [idée] similar ▸ **des pratiques voisines du charlatanisme** practices akin to *ou* bordering on quackery.
■ **nm, f** neighbour *UK*, neighbor *US* ▸ **voisin d'à côté** next-door neighbour ▸ **mes voisins du dessus/dessous** the people upstairs/downstairs from me ▸ **voisin de palier** next-door neighbour *(in a flat)* ▸ **mon voisin de table** the person next to me *ou* my neighbour at table.

voisinage [vwazinaʒ] **nm 1.** [quartier] neighbourhood *UK*, neighborhood *US* **2.** [environs] vicinity **3.** [relations] **: rapports de bon voisinage** (good) neighbourliness *UK ou* neighborliness *US*.

voisiner [3] [vwazine] **vi : voisiner avec** to be next to.

voiture [vwatyr] **nf 1.** [automobile] car ▸ **voiture de fonction** company car ▸ **voiture de location** hire *UK ou* rental *US* car ▸ **voiture d'occasion/de sport** second-hand/sports car **2.** [de train] carriage *UK*, car *US*.
◆ ***voiture d'enfant*** **nf** pram *UK*, baby carriage *US*.

voiture-balai [vwatyrbalɛ] (pl **voitures-balais**) **nf** SPORT *car which follows a cycle race to pick up competitors who drop out* ▸ **faire la voiture-balai** *fig* to go round picking up the stragglers.

voix [vwa] **nf 1.** [gén] voice ▸ **voix caverneuse** hollow voice ▸ **voix de fausset** falsetto voice ▸ **voix de poitrine/tête** chest/head voice ▸ **voix de stentor** stentorian voice ▸ **voix de ténor** tenor voice ▸ **voix off** voice-over ▸ **à mi-voix** in an undertone ▸ **à voix basse** in a low voice, quietly ▸ **à voix haute** [parler] in a loud voice / [lire] aloud ▸ **de vive voix** in person ▸ **avoir de la voix** to have a strong voice ▸ **donner de la voix** [chien] to bay / [personne] to shout, to bawl ▸ **être *ou* rester sans voix** [d'épouvante] to be speechless, to be struck dumb / [d'émotion, de chagrin] to be speechless ▸ **poser sa voix** to train one's voice ▸ **avoir voix au chapitre** *fig* to have a say in the matter **2.** [suffrage] vote ▸ **donner sa voix à** to give one's vote to, to vote for ▸ **obtenir 1 500 voix** to win *ou* to get 1,500 votes ▸ **recueillir des voix** to win *ou* get votes.

vol [vɔl] **nm 1.** [d'oiseau, avion] flight ▸ **attraper qqch au vol** to catch sthg in mid-air ▸ **saisir une occasion au vol** *fig* to jump at *ou* to seize an opportunity ▸ **vol (en) charter** charter flight ▸ **vol d'essai** test flight ▸ **pratiquer le *ou* faire du vol libre** to go hang-gliding ▸ **vol à vue** sight flight ▸ **vol à voile** gliding ▸ **pratiquer le *ou* faire du vol à voile** to glide, to do gliding ▸ **prendre son vol** to fly away, to take wing *littéraire* ▸ **à vol d'oiseau** as the crow flies ▸ **en plein vol** in flight **2.** [groupe d'oiseaux] flight, flock ▸ **vol de perdreaux** flock *ou* covey of partridges **3.** [délit] theft ▸ **commettre un vol** to commit a theft, to steal ▸ **vol à l'arraché** bag snatching ▸ **vol avec effraction** breaking and entering ▸ **vol à l'étalage** shoplifting ▸ **vol à main armée** armed robbery ▸ **vol à la tire** pickpocketing.
◆ ***de haut vol*** **loc adj** [artiste, spécialiste] top *(avant n)* / [projet] ambitious, far-reaching.

vol. (abr écrite de ***volume***) vol.

volage [vɔlaʒ] **adj** *littéraire* fickle.

volaille [vɔlaj] **nf : la volaille** poultry, (domestic) fowl.

volant, e [vɔlɑ̃, ɑ̃t] **adj 1.** [qui vole] flying ▸ **personnel volant** aircrew **2.** [mobile] **: feuille volante** loose sheet.
◆ ***volant*** **nm 1.** [de voiture] steering wheel **2.** [de robe] flounce **3.** [de badminton] shuttlecock.

volatil, e [vɔlatil] **adj** volatile.
◆ ***volatile*** **nm** (domestic) fowl.

volatiliser [3] [vɔlatilize] ◆ ***se volatiliser*** **vp** to volatilize / *fig* to vanish into thin air.

vol-au-vent [vɔlovɑ̃] **nm inv** vol-au-vent.

volcan [vɔlkɑ̃] **nm** volcano / *fig* spitfire ▸ **être assis sur un volcan** *fig* to be sitting on the edge of a volcano.

volcanique [vɔlkanik] **adj** volcanic / *fig* [tempérament] fiery.

volcanologue = ***vulcanologue***.

volée [vɔle] **nf 1.** [d'oiseau] flight **2.** [de flèches] volley ▸ **une volée de coups** a hail of blows ▸ **volée d'insultes** *fig* shower of insults **3.** FOOTBALL & TENNIS volley ▸ **il n'est pas/il est très bon à la volée** he's a bad/he's a good volleyer ▸ **monter à la volée** to come to the net **4.** *fam* [gifle] thrashing, hiding ▸ **tu vas recevoir la volée!** you're really going to get it! **5.** CONSTR **: volée d'escaliers** flight of stairs.
◆ ***à la volée*** **loc adv : attraper *ou* saisir à la volée** [clés, balle] to catch in mid-air ▸ **saisir un nom à la volée** to (just) catch a name.
◆ ***de haute volée*** **loc adj** [spécialiste] top *(avant n)* / [projet] ambitious, far-reaching.

voler [3] [vɔle] ■ **vi** to fly ▸ **voler de ses propres ailes** to stand on one's own two feet, to fend for o.s. ▸ **voler en éclats** to be smashed to bits *ou* to pieces ▸ **voler au secours de qqn** to fly to sb's assistance.
■ **vt** [personne] to rob ▸ **il s'est fait voler son portefeuille** his wallet was stolen / [chose] to steal ▸ **voler qqch à qqn** to steal sthg from sb ▸ **il volait de l'argent dans la caisse** he used to steal money from the till ▸ **on m'a volé ma montre!** my watch has been stolen!

volet [vɔlɛ] **nm 1.** [de maison] shutter **2.** [de dépliant] leaf / [d'émission] part **3.** INFORM drive door.

voleter [27] [vɔlte] **vi 1.** [papillon] to flit *ou* flutter about **2.** [robe] to flutter.

voleur, euse [vɔlœr, øz] ■ **adj** thieving.
■ **nm, f** thief ▸ **au voleur!** stop thief!

volière [vɔljɛr] **nf** aviary.

volley-ball [vɔlɛbol] (pl **volley-balls**) **nm** volleyball.

volleyeur, euse [vɔlɛjœr, øz] **nm, f** volleyball player.

volontaire [vɔlɔ̃tɛr] ■ **nmf** volunteer.
■ **adj 1.** [omission] deliberate / [activité] voluntary **2.** [enfant] strong-willed.

volontairement [vɔlɔ̃tɛrmɑ̃] **adv** deliberately / [offrir] voluntarily.

volontariat [vɔlɔ̃tarja] **nm** voluntary service *(in armed forces)*.

volontariste [vɔlɔ̃tarist] **nmf & adj** voluntarist.

volonté [vɔlɔ̃te] **nf 1.** [vouloir] will ▸ **à volonté** unlimited, as much as you like ▸ **les dernières volontés** last wishes ▸ **faire les quatre volontés de qqn** *fam fig* to obey sb's every whim **2.** [disposition] **: bonne volonté** willingness, good will ▸ **mauvaise volonté** unwillingness **3.** [détermination] willpower.

volontiers [vɔlɔ̃tje] **adv 1.** [avec plaisir] with pleasure, gladly, willingly **2.** [affable, bavard] naturally.

volt [vɔlt] **nm** volt.

voltage [vɔltaʒ] **nm** voltage.

volte [vɔlt] **nf 1.** [de cheval] volt, volte **2.** *littéraire* [pirouette] pirouette.

volte-face [vɔltəfas] **nf inv** about-turn *UK*, about-face *US* / *fig* U-turn, about-turn *UK*, about-face *US*.

voltige [vɔltiʒ] **nf 1.** [au trapèze] trapeze work ▸ **haute voltige** flying trapeze act / *fam fig* mental gymnastics *(U)* **2.** [à cheval] circus riding **3.** [en avion] aerobatics *(U)*.

voltiger [17] [vɔltiʒe] **vi 1.** [acrobate] to perform on a flying trapeze **2.** [insecte, oiseau] to flit *ou* flutter about **3.** [feuilles] to flutter about.

voltigeur [vɔltiʒœr] **nm 1.** [acrobate] trapeze artist **2.** MIL light infantryman **3.** *Québec* [baseball] **: voltigeur gauche/droit** left/right fielder ▸ **voltigeur du centre** centre fielder.

volubile [vɔlybil] **adj** voluble.

volubilis [vɔlybilis] **nm** morning glory.

volubilité [vɔlybilite] **nf** volubility.

volume [vɔlym] **nm 1.** [tome] volume **2.** [en acoustique] volume ▸ **augmente *ou* monte le volume** turn the sound up ▸ **baisse *ou* descend le volume** turn the sound down **3.** [quantité globale] volume, amount ▸ **le volume des exportations** the volume of exports ▸ **volume de ventes** volume of sales **4.** [poids, épaisseur] volume ▸ **un**

permanente donnerait du volume à vos cheveux a perm would give your hair more body **5.** INFORM [unité] volume ▸ **volume mémoire** storage capacity.

volumineux, euse [vɔlyminø, øz] **adj** voluminous, bulky.

volupté [vɔlypte] **nf** [sensuelle] sensual *ou* voluptuous pleasure / [morale, esthétique] delight.

voluptueusement [vɔlyptɥøzmɑ̃] **adv** voluptuously.

voluptueux, euse [vɔlyptɥø, øz] **adj** voluptuous.

volute [vɔlyt] **nf 1.** [de fumée] wreath **2.** ARCHIT volute, helix.

vomi [vɔmi] **nm** *fam* vomit.

vomir [32] [vɔmir] **vt 1.** [aliments] to bring up **2.** [fumées] to belch, to spew (out) / [injures] to spit out.

vomissement [vɔmismɑ̃] **nm 1.** [action] vomiting **2.** [vomissure] vomit.

vomitif, ive [vɔmitif, iv] **adj** emetic / *fam fig* revolting, sickening.
◆ ***vomitif*** **nm** emetic.

vont ➤ ***aller***.

vorace [vɔras] **adj** voracious.

voracement [vɔrasmɑ̃] **adv** voraciously.

voracité [vɔrasite] **nf** voracity.

vos ➤ ***votre***.

votant, e [vɔtɑ̃, ɑ̃t] **nm, f** voter.

vote [vɔt] **nm** vote ▸ **vote à main levée** (ballot by) show of hands ▸ **vote secret, vote à bulletins secrets** secret ballot.

voter [3] [vɔte] ■ **vi** to vote.
■ **vt** POLIT to vote for / [crédits] to vote / [loi] to pass.

votre [vɔtr] (pl **vos** [vo]) **adj poss** your.

vôtre [votr] ◆ ***le vôtre, la vôtre*** (pl **les vôtres**) **pron poss** yours ▸ **les vôtres** your family ▸ **vous et les vôtres** people like you ▸ **je suis des vôtres** I'm on your side ▸ **vous devriez y mettre du vôtre** you ought to pull your weight ▸ **à la vôtre!** your good health!

vouer [6] [vwe] **vt 1.** [promettre, jurer] **: vouer qqch à qqn** to swear *ou* vow sthg to sb **2.** [consacrer] to devote **3.** [condamner] **: être voué à** to be doomed to.
◆ ***se vouer*** **vp : se vouer à** to dedicate *ou* devote o.s. to.

vouloir [57] [vulwar] ■ **vt 1.** [gén] to want ▸ **voulez-vous boire quelque chose?** would you like something to drink? ▸ **veux-tu te taire!** will you be quiet! ▸ **je voudrais savoir** I would like to know ▸ **voudriez-vous vous joindre à nous?** would you care *ou* like to join us? ▸ **vouloir que** *(+ subjonctif)* **: je veux qu'il parte** I want him to leave ▸ **vouloir qqch de qqn/qqch** to want sthg from sb/sthg ▸ **combien voulez-vous de votre maison?** how much do you want for your house? ▸ **ne pas vouloir de qqn/qqch** not to want sb/sthg ▸ **je ne veux pas entendre parler de ça!** I won't hear of it *ou* such a thing! ▸ **je veux bien** I don't mind ▸ **je veux bien être patient, mais il y a des limites!** I can be patient, but there are limits! ▸ **si tu veux** if you like, if you want ▸ **comme tu veux!** as you like! ▸ **un peu de respect, tu veux (bien)** a bit less cheek, if you don't mind! ▸ **veuillez vous asseoir** please take a seat ▸ **veuillez m'excuser un instant** (will you) please excuse me for a moment ▸ **sans le vouloir** without meaning *ou* wishing to, unintentionally ▸ **je l'ai vexé sans le vouloir** I offended him unintentionally *ou* without meaning to
2. [suj: coutume] to demand ▸ **la dignité de notre profession veut que...** the dignity of our profession demands that... ▸ **comme le veulent les usages** as convention dictates
3. [s'attendre à] to expect ▸ **que voulez-vous que j'y fasse?** what do you want me to do about it? ▸ **pourquoi voudrais-tu qu'on se fasse cambrioler?** why do you assume we might be burgled?
4. [essayer de] **: vouloir faire** to want *ou* to try to do ▸ **en voulant la sauver, il s'est noyé** he drowned in his attempt *ou* trying to rescue her ▸ **tu veux me faire peur?** are you trying to frighten me?
5. [formules de politesse] **: veuillez m'excuser un instant** (will you) please excuse me for a moment ▸ **veuillez avoir l'obligeance de...** would you kindly *ou* please... ▸ **veuillez recevoir, Monsieur, mes salutations distinguées** yours sincerely *UK ou* truly *US*
▸▸| **vouloir dire** to mean ▸ **ça veut tout dire!** that says it all! ▸ **si on veut** more or less, if you like ▸ **en vouloir** to be a real go-getter ▸ **en vouloir à qqn** to have a grudge against sb ▸ **tu ne m'en veux pas?** no hard feelings? ▸ **tu l'auras voulu!** on your own head (be it)!
■ **nm : le bon/mauvais vouloir de qqn** sb's goodwill/ill will.
◆ ***se vouloir*** **vp : elle se veut différente** she thinks she's different ▸ **le livre se veut une satire de l'aristocratie allemande** the book claims *ou* is supposed to be a satire on the German aristocracy ▸ **s'en vouloir de faire qqch** to be cross with o.s. for doing sthg ▸ **je m'en veux de l'avoir laissé partir** I feel bad at having let him go.

voulu, e [vuly] ■ **pp** ➤ ***vouloir***.
■ **adj 1.** [requis] requisite **2.** [délibéré] intentional.

vous [vu] **pron pers 1.** [sujet, objet direct] you ▸ **dire vous à qqn** to use the "vous" form to sb ▸ **eux m'ont compris, pas vous** they understood me, you didn't ▸ **je vous connais, vous!** I know **you**! ▸ **elle vous a accusés tous les trois** she accused all three of you
2. [objet indirect] (to) you ▸ **pensez un peu à vous** think of yourself a bit
3. [après préposition, comparatif] you ▸ **de vous à moi** between (the two of) us *ou* you and me ▸ **à vous trois, vous finirez bien la tarte?** surely the three of you can finish the tart?
4. [réfléchi] yourself (, yourselves *pl*) ▸ **taisez-vous!** be quiet! ▸ **regardez-vous** look at yourself ▸ **taisez-vous tous!** be quiet, all of you!
◆ ***vous-même*** **pron pers** yourself ▸ **vous pouvez vérifier par vous** you can check for yourself.
◆ ***vous-mêmes*** **pron pers** yourselves.

voûte [vut] **nf 1.** ARCHIT vault / *fig* arch ▸ **la voûte céleste** the sky **2.** ANAT **: voûte du palais** roof of the mouth ▸ **voûte plantaire** arch (of the foot).

voûté, e [vute] **adj 1.** [homme] stooping, round-shouldered / [dos] bent ▸ **avoir le dos voûté** to stoop, to have a stoop ▸ **ne te tiens pas voûté** stand up straight **2.** [galerie] vaulted, arched.

voûter [3] [vute] **vt** to arch over, to vault.
◆ ***se voûter*** **vp** to be *ou* become stooped.

vouvoiement [vuvwamɑ̃] **nm** use of the "vous" form.

vouvoyer [13] [vuvwaje] **vt : vouvoyer qqn** to use the "vous" form to sb.

◆ ***se vouvoyer*** **vp** to use the formal "vous" form with each other.

CULTURE

Vouvoyer

The **vous** form of 'you' is used among people who have just been introduced or do not know each other well, but also at work, particularly among colleagues at different levels in a hierarchy. Students from primary school to university level are expected to use **vous** with their teachers, even though professors often address students as **tu**. **Vous** is also common among relatives by marriage, even if they have known each other for many years. In some upper-class families, parents and children (and even spouses) use **vous** with each other. **Tu** is reserved for friends, animals, inanimate objects and often colleagues whom one regards as equals.

voyage [vwajaʒ] **nm** journey, trip ▸ **les voyages** travel *(sg)*, travelling *(U) UK*, traveling *(U) US* ▸ **bon voyage!** bon voyage!, have a good *ou* safe journey! ▸ **partir en voyage** to go away, to go on a trip ▸ **voyage d'affaires** business trip ▸ **voyage organisé** package tour ▸ **voyage de noces** honeymoon.

voyager [17] [vwajaʒe] **vi** to travel.

voyageur, euse [vwajaʒœr, øz] **nm, f** traveller *UK*, traveler *US* ▸ **voyageur de commerce** commercial traveller *UK*, traveling salesman *US*.

voyagiste [vwajaʒist] **nm** tour operator.

voyance [vwajɑ̃s] **nf** clairvoyance.

voyant, e [vwajɑ̃, ɑ̃t] ■ **adj** loud, gaudy.

■ **nm, f** [devin] seer ▸ **voyante extralucide** clairvoyant.

◆ ***voyant*** **nm** [lampe] light / AUTO indicator (light) ▸ **voyant d'essence/d'huile** petrol/oil warning light.

voyelle [vwajɛl] **nf** vowel.

voyeur, euse [vwajœr, øz] **nm, f** voyeur, Peeping Tom.

voyeurisme [vwajœrism] **nm** voyeurism.

voyou [vwaju] **nm 1.** [garnement] urchin **2.** [loubard] lout.

VPC (abr de ***vente par correspondance***) **nf** mail order sales.

vrac [vrak] ◆ ***en vrac*** **loc adv 1.** [sans emballage] loose **2.** [en désordre] higgledy-piggledy **3.** [au poids] in bulk.

vrai, e [vrɛ] **adj 1.** [histoire] true ▸ **c'est** *ou* **il est vrai que...** it's true that... ▸ **c'est pas vrai!** *fam* never!, I don't believe it! ▸ **il l'a bien mérité, pas vrai?** he deserved it, didn't he? **2.** [or, perle, nom] real ▸ **c'est une copie, ce n'est pas un vrai Modigliani** it's a copy, it's not a real Modigliani **3.** [personne] natural ▸ **des dialogues vrais** dialogue that rings true **4.** [ami, raison] real, true ▸ **c'est une histoire vraie** it's a true story.

◆ ***vrai*** **nm : le vrai** truth ▸ **être dans le vrai** to be right ▸ **il y a du vrai dans ses critiques** there's some truth in her criticism ▸ **à vrai dire, à dire vrai** to tell the truth ▸ **cette fois-ci, je pars pour de vrai** this time I'm really leaving.

vraiment [vrɛmɑ̃] **adv** really.

vraisemblable [vrɛsɑ̃blabl] **adj** likely, probable / [excuse] plausible.

vraisemblablement [vrɛsɑ̃blabləmɑ̃] **adv** probably, in all probability.

vraisemblance [vrɛsɑ̃blɑ̃s] **nf** likelihood, probability / [d'excuse] plausibility ▸ **contre toute vraisemblance** implausibly ▸ **selon toute vraisemblance** in all probability.

V/Réf (abr écrite de ***Votre référence***) your ref.

vrille [vrij] **nf 1.** BOT tendril **2.** [outil] gimlet **3.** [spirale] spiral **4.** AÉRON spin ▸ **descendre en vrille** to spin downwards.

vriller [3] [vrije] ■ **vi 1.** [avion] to spin **2.** [parachute] to twist.

■ **vt** to bore into.

vrombir [32] [vrɔ̃bir] **vi** to hum.

vrombissement [vrɔ̃bismɑ̃] **nm** humming *(U)*.

VRP (abr de ***voyageur, représentant, placier***) **nm** rep.

VTC [vetese] (abr de ***vélo tout chemin***) **nf** SPORT hybrid bike.

VTT (abr de ***vélo tout terrain***) **nm** mountain bike.

vu, e [vy] ■ **pp** ➤ ***voir***.

■ **adj 1.** [perçu] **: être bien/mal vu** to be acceptable/unacceptable **2.** [compris] clear.

◆ ***vu*** **prép** given, in view of.

◆ ***vue*** **nf 1.** [sens, vision] sight, eyesight ▸ **avoir une bonne vue** to have good eyesight ▸ **avoir une mauvaise vue** to have bad *ou* poor eyesight ▸ **perdre la vue** to lose one's sight, to go blind ▸ **recouvrer la vue** to get one's sight *ou* eyesight back **2.** [regard] gaze ▸ **à première vue** at first sight ▸ **à vue** on sight ▸ **de vue** by sight ▸ **je le connais de vue** I know his face, I know him by sight ▸ **en vue** [vedette] in the public eye ▸ **à vue de nez** at a rough guess ▸ **à vue d'œil** visibly ▸ **mes économies disparaissent à vue d'œil** my savings just disappear before my very eyes ▸ **il s'évanouit à la vue du sang** he faints at the sight of blood ▸ **en mettre plein la vue à qqn** *fam fig* to dazzle sb ▸ **perdre qqn de vue** to lose touch with sb **3.** [panorama, idée] view ▸ **vue d'ensemble** *fig* overview ▸ **avoir qqn/qqch en vue** to have sb/sthg in mind ▸ **vue panoramique** panoramic view ▸ **vue sur la mer** sea view.

◆ ***à vue*** ■ **loc adj** BANQUE **: dépôt à vue** call deposit ▸ **retrait à vue** withdrawal on demand.

■ **loc adv** [atterrir] visually / [tirer] on sight / [payable] at sight.

◆ ***vues*** **nfpl** plans ▸ **avoir des vues sur qqn** to have designs on sb, to have one's eye on sb ▸ **avoir des vus sur qqch** to covet sthg.

◆ ***en vue de*** **loc prép** with a view to ▸ **j'y vais en vue de préparer le terrain** I'm going in order to prepare the ground.

◆ ***vu que*** **loc conj** given that, seeing that.

vulcaniser [3] [vylkanize] **vt** to vulcanize.

vulcanologue [vylkanɔlɔg], ***volcanologue*** [vɔlkanɔlɔg] **nmf** vulcanologist, volcanologist.

vulgaire [vylgɛr] **adj 1.** [grossier] vulgar, coarse **2.** *(avant n) péj* [quelconque] common **3.** [courant] common, popular.

vulgairement [vylgɛrmɑ̃] **adv 1.** [grossièrement] vulgarly, coarsely **2.** [couramment] commonly, popularly.

vulgarisation [vylgarizasjɔ̃] **nf** popularization.

vulgariser [3] [vylgarize] **vt** to popularize.

vulgarité [vylgarite] **nf** vulgarity, coarseness.

vulnérabilité [vylnerabilite] **nf** vulnerability.

vulnérable [vylnerabl] **adj** vulnerable.

vulve [vylv] **nf** vulva.

Vve abr écrite de ***veuve***.

VVF (abr de ***village vacances famille***) **nm** *state-subsidized holiday village*.

vx abr de ***vieux***.

w, ***W*** [dubləve] **nm inv** w, W.

wagon [vagɔ̃] **nm** carriage *UK*, car *US* ▸ **wagon fumeurs** smoking carriage *UK* ***ou*** car *US* ▸ **wagon de marchandises** goods wagon ***ou*** truck *UK*, freight car *US* ▸ **wagon non-fumeurs** non-smoking carriage *UK* ***ou*** car *US* ▸ **wagon de première/seconde classe** first-class/second-class carriage *UK* ***ou*** car *US*.

wagon-citerne [vagɔ̃sitɛrn] (pl **wagons-citernes**) **nm** tank wagon *UK* ***ou*** car *US*.

wagon-lit [vagɔ̃li] (pl **wagons-lits**) **nm** sleeping car, sleeper.

wagonnet [vagɔnɛ] **nm** small truck.

wagon-restaurant [vagɔ̃rɛstɔrɑ̃] (pl **wagons-restaurants**) **nm** restaurant *UK* ***ou*** dining *US* car.

Walkman® [wɔkman] **nm** personal stereo, Walkman®.

wallon, ***onne*** [walɔ̃, ɔn] **adj** Walloon.
- ◆ ***wallon*** **nm** [langue] Walloon.
- ◆ ***Wallon***, ***onne*** **nm, f** Walloon.

Wallonie [walɔni] **nf : la Wallonie** Southern Belgium *(where French and Walloon are spoken)*.

wapiti [wapiti] **nm** wapiti.

Washington [waʃiŋtɔn] **npr 1.** [ville] Washington DC **2.** [État] Washington State.

wassingue [vasɛ̃g] **nf** floorcloth.

water-polo [watɛrpɔlo] **nm** water polo.

waterproof [watɛrpru:f] **adj inv** waterproof.

waters [watɛr] **nmpl** toilet *sg*.

waterz(o)oi [watɛrzɔj] **nm** *Belgique chicken or fish with vegetables, cooked in a cream sauce, a Flemish speciality*.

watt [wat] **nm** watt.

Wb (abr écrite de ***weber***) Wb.

W.-C. [vese] (abr de ***water closet***) **nmpl** WC *sg*, toilets.

Web [wɛb] **nm : le Web** the Web, the web.

webcam [wɛbkam] **nf** webcam.

webcast [wɛbkast] **m** INFORM webcast.

webcasting [wɛbkastiŋ] **m** INFORM webcasting.

webmestre [wɛbmɛstr], ***webmaster*** [wɛbmastœr] **nm** webmaster.

webzine [wɛbzi:n] [wɛbzin] **m** INFORM webzine.

week-end [wikɛnd] (pl **week-ends**) **nm** weekend ▸ **bon week-end!** have a good ***ou*** nice weekend! ▸ **partir en week-end** to go away for the weekend.

western [wɛstɛrn] **nm** western.

Wh (abr écrite de ***wattheure***) Wh.

whisky [wiski] (pl **whiskies**) **nm** [écossais] whisky, scotch / [irlandais ou américain] whiskey ▸ **whisky sec** straight ***ou*** neat whisky.

whist [wist] **nm** whist.

white-spirit [wajtspirit] (pl **white-spirits**) **nm** white spirit *UK*.

wok [wɔk] **nm** wok.

WORM (abr de ***write once read many times***) INFORM WORM.

WWW (abr de ***World Wide Web***) **nf** WWW.

WYSIWYG [wiziwig] (abr de ***what you see is what you get***) WYSIWYG.

x, ***X*** [iks] **nm inv** x, X ▸ **l'X** *prestigious engineering college in Paris*.

xénon [gzenɔ̃] ■ **nm** xenon.

xénophobe [gzenɔfɔb] ■ **nmf** xenophobe. ■ **adj** xenophobic.

xénophobie [gzenɔfɔbi] **nf** xenophobia.

xérès [gzerɛs, xerɛs] **nm** sherry.

xylographie [ksilɔgrafi] **nf** xylography.

xylophage [ksilɔfaʒ] ■ **adj** xylophagous. ■ **nmf** xylophage

xylophone [ksilɔfɔn] **nm** xylophone.

Y

y¹, ***Y*** [igrɛk] **nm inv** y, Y.

y² [i] ■ **adv** [lieu] there ▸ **j'y vais demain** I'm going there tomorrow ▸ **mets-y du sel** put some salt in it ▸ **va voir sur la table si les clefs y sont** go and see if the keys are on the table ▸ **on ne peut pas couper cet arbre, des oiseaux y ont fait leur nid** you can't cut down that tree, some birds have built their nest there *ou* in it ▸ **ils ont ramené des vases anciens et y ont fait pousser des fleurs exotiques** they brought back some antique vases and grew exotic flowers in them.
■ **pron pers** *(la traduction varie selon la préposition utilisée avec le verbe)* : **pensez-y** think about it ▸ **n'y comptez pas** don't count on it ▸ **j'y suis!** I've got it! ⁄ voir aussi ***aller***, ***avoir*** *etc.*

yacht [jot] **nm** yacht.

yacht-club [jotklœb] (pl **yacht-clubs**) **nm** yacht club.

yaourt [jaurt], ***yogourt***, ***yoghourt*** [jɔgurt] **nm** yoghurt ▸ **yaourt aux fruits/nature** fruit/plain yoghurt.

yaourtière [jaurtjɛr] **nf** yoghurt maker.

Yémen [jemɛn] **nm : le Yémen** Yemen ▸ **au Yémen** in Yemen ▸ **le Yémen du Nord** North Yemen ▸ **le Yémen du Sud** South Yemen.

yéménite [jemenit] **adj** Yemeni.
◆ ***Yéménite*** **nmf** Yemeni.

yen [jɛn] **nm** yen.

yeux ➤ ***œil***.

yé-yé [jeje] *vieilli* ■ **nmf** pop fan.
■ **adj inv** pop *(avant n)*.

yiddish [jidiʃ] **nm inv & adj inv** Yiddish.

yoga [jɔga] **nm** yoga.

yoghourt = ***yaourt***.

yogi [jɔgi] **nm** yogi.

yogourt = ***yaourt***.

yougoslave [jugɔslav] **adj** Yugoslav, Yugoslavian.
◆ ***Yougoslave*** **nmf** Yugoslav, Yugoslavian.

Yougoslavie [jugɔslavi] **nf : la Yougoslavie** Yugoslavia ▸ **l'ex-Yougoslavie** the former Yugoslavia.

youpala [jupala] **nm** baby bouncer.

youpi [jupi] **interj** yippee!

youyou [juju] **nm** dinghy.

yoyo [jojo] **nm** MÉD grommet.

Yo-yo® [jɔjɔ] **nm inv** yo-yo.

yucca [juka] **nm** yucca.

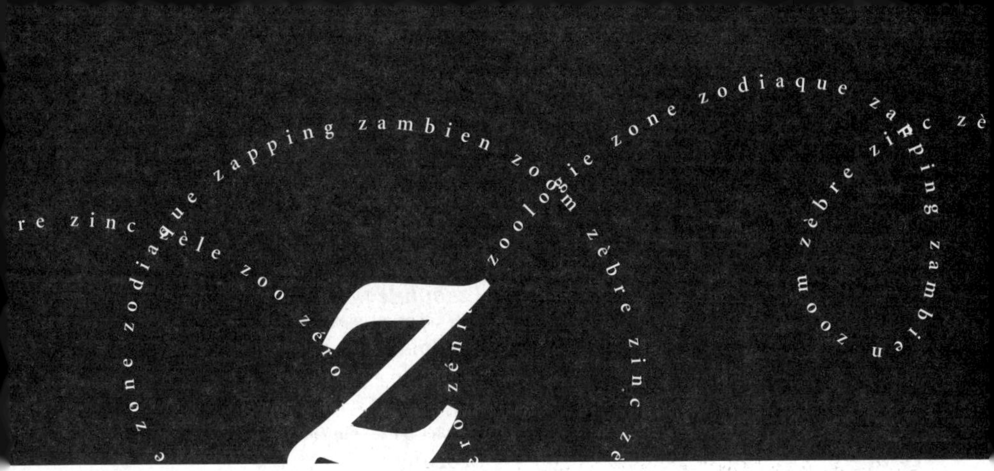

z, Z [zɛd] **nm inv** z, Z.

ZAC, Zac [zak] (abr de ***zone d'aménagement concerté***) **nf** *area earmarked for local government planning project.*

ZAD, Zad [zad] (abr de ***zone d'aménagement différé***) **nf** *area earmarked for future development.*

Zagreb [zagrɛb] **npr** Zagreb.

Zaïre [zair] **nm : le Zaïre** Zaïre ▸ **au Zaïre** in Zaïre.

zaïrois, e [zairwa, az] **adj** Zairian.
◆ ***Zaïrois, e*** **nm, f** Zairian.

zakouski [zakuski] **nmpl** zakuski, zakouski.

Zambie [zɑ̃bi] **nf : la Zambie** Zambia.

zambien, enne [zɑ̃bjɛ̃, ɛn] **adj** Zambian.
◆ ***Zambien, enne*** **nm, f** Zambian.

zapper [3] [zape] **vi** to zap, to channel-hop, to channel-flick.

zappeur, euse [zapœr, øz] **nm, f** channel hopper, zapper.

zapping [zapiŋ] **nm** zapping, channel-hopping.

zèbre [zɛbr] **nm** zebra ▸ **un drôle de zèbre** *fam fig* an oddball.

zébrer [18] [zebre] **vt** to streak, to stripe.

zébrure [zebryr] **nf 1.** [de pelage] stripe **2.** [marque] weal.

zébu [zeby] **nm** zebu.

ZEC [zɛk] (abr de ***zone d'exploitation contrôlée***) **nf** *Québec* controlled harvesting zone.

zélateur, trice [zelatœr, tris] **nm, f** zealot.

zèle [zɛl] **nm** zeal ▸ **faire du zèle** *péj* to be over-zealous.

zélé, e [zele] **adj** zealous.

zen [zɛn] ■ **nm** Zen.
■ **adj inv** Zen ▸ **rester zen** to keep cool.

zénith [zenit] **nm** zenith ▸ **être au zénith de** *fig* to be at the height *ou* peak of.

ZEP, Zep [zɛp] (abr de ***zone d'éducation prioritaire***) **nf** *designated area with special educational needs.*

zéro [zero] ■ **nm 1.** [chiffre] zero, nought *UK* / [énoncé dans un numéro de téléphone] O *UK*, zero
2. [nombre] nought *UK*, nothing ▸ **deux buts à zéro** two goals to nil *UK ou* zero ▸ **zéro partout** no score ▸ **j'ai eu zéro** I got (a) nought ▸ **zéro de conduite** black mark
3. [de graduation] freezing point, zero ▸ **à zéro** at zero ▸ **zéro absolu** absolute zero ▸ **au-dessus/au-dessous de zéro** above/below (zero) ▸ **avoir le moral à zéro** *fig* to be *ou* feel down ▸ **repartir à *ou* de zéro** to start again from scratch
4. *fam* [personne] dead loss.
■ **adj : zéro faute** no mistakes ▸ **ça te coûtera zéro centime** it'll cost you nothing at all.

zeste [zɛst] **nm** peel, zest ▸ **zeste de citron** lemon peel *ou* zest.

zézaiement [zezɛmɑ̃] **nm** lisp.

zézayer [11] [zezeje] **vi** to lisp.

ZI abr écrite de ***zone industrielle***.

zibeline [ziblin] **nf** sable.

zieuter, zyeuter [3] [zjøte] **vt** *fam* to get an eyeful of.

ZIF, Zif [zif] (abr de ***zone d'intervention foncière***) **nf** *area earmarked for local government planning project.*

zigoto [zigɔto] **nm** *fam* **: un drôle de zigoto** an oddball.

zigouiller [3] [ziguje] **vt** *fam* to bump off.

zigzag [zigzag] **nm** zigzag ▸ **en zigzag** winding.

zigzaguer [3] [zigzage] **vi** to zigzag (along).

Zimbabwe [zimbabwe] **nm : le Zimbabwe** Zimbabwe ▸ **au Zimbabwe** in Zimbabwe.

zimbabwéen, enne [zimbabweɛ̃, ɛn] **adj** Zimbabwean.
◆ ***Zimbabwéen, enne*** **nm, f** Zimbabwean.

zinc [zɛ̃g] **nm 1.** [matière] zinc **2.** *fam* [comptoir] bar **3.** *fam* [avion] crate.

zinzin [zɛ̃zɛ̃] **adj** *fam* cracked.

Zip® [zip] **nm** zip *UK*, zipper *US*.

zipper [3] [zipe] **vt** to zip up / INFORM to zip.

zizanie [zizani] **nf : semer la zizanie** *fig* to sow discord.

zizi [zizi] **nm** *fam* willy *UK*, peter *US*.

zodiacal, e, aux [zɔdjakal, o] **adj** [signe] of the zodiac / [position] in the zodiac.

zodiaque [zɔdjak] **nm** zodiac.

zombi [zɔ̃bi] **nm** *fam* zombie.

zona [zona] **nm** shingles *(U)*.

zone [zon] **nf 1.** [région] zone, area
2. [administration] **: zone bleue** restricted parking zone ▸ **zone piétonne** *ou* **piétonnière** pedestrian precinct *UK* *ou* zone *US* ▸ **zone de stationnement interdit** no parking area
3. GÉOGR **: zone de dépression, zone dépressionnaire** trough of low pressure ▸ **zone désertique** desert belt ▸ **zone forestière** forest belt ▸ **la zone d'influence de l'Asie** Asia's sphere of influence
4. FIN **: zone d'action** area of operations ▸ **la zone d'activité du directeur commercial** the commercial manager's area ▸ **zone commerciale** retail park ▸ **zone dollar** dollar area ▸ **zone franche** free zone ▸ **zone industrielle** industrial estate *UK* *ou* park *US* ▸ **zone monétaire** monetary zone ▸ **zone sterling** sterling area
5. *fam* [faubourg] **: la zone** the slum belt ▸ **cette famille, c'est vraiment la zone** they're real dropouts in that family
6. INFORM **: zone de données** data field ▸ **zone de mémoire** storage area
7. ANAT **: zone érogène** erogenous zone
8. [Astronautique] **: zone de couverture (d'un satellite)** area of coverage (of a satellite).

zoner [3] [zone] **vi** *fam* to hang about, to hang around.

zoo [zo(o)] **nm** zoo.

zoologie [zɔɔlɔʒi] **nf** zoology.

zoologique [zɔɔlɔʒik] **adj** zoological.

zoologiste [zɔɔlɔʒist] **nmf** zoologist.

zoom [zum] **nm 1.** [objectif] zoom (lens) **2.** [gros plan] zoom.

zoophile [zɔɔfil] ■ **nmf** person who practises bestiality. ■ **adj** of *ou* relating to bestiality.

zooplancton [zɔɔplɑ̃ktɔ̃] **nm** zooplankton.

zoulou, e [zulu] **adj** Zulu.
◆ ***Zoulou, e*** **nm, f : les Zoulous** the Zulus.

zozo [zozo] **nm** *fam* mug *UK*, nitwit.

zozoter [3] [zɔzɔte] **vi** to lisp.

ZUP, Zup [zyp] (abr de ***zone à urbaniser en priorité***) **nf** *area earmarked for urgent urban development*.

Zurich [zyrik] **npr** Zörich.

zut [zyt] **interj** *fam* damn!

zyeuter = ***zieuter***.

zygomatique [zigɔmatik] **adj** zygomatic.

zygote [zigɔt] **nm** zygote.

Guide de communication

Communication guide

Sommaire

Guide de communication

Communication guide

Guide de communication

Les lettres

Présentation d'une lettre

La présence de la virgule n'est pas obligatoire après la formule d'appel. Notez cependant que si la formule d'appel est suivie d'une virgule, la formule finale le sera également.

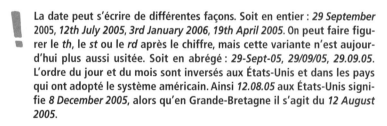

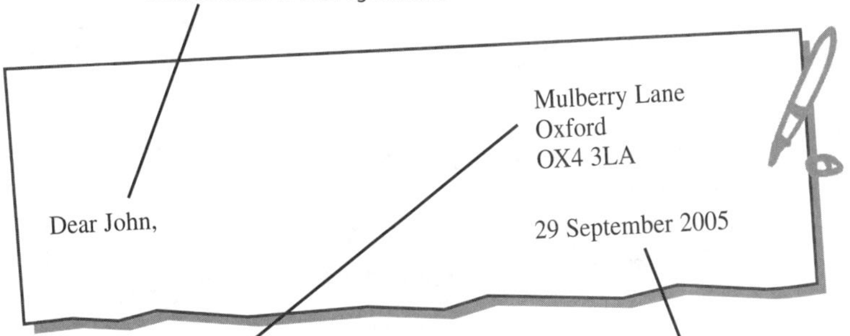

Dans votre correspondance privée, indiquez votre adresse (sans votre nom) en haut à droite. Aux États-Unis, dans les lettres à des proches, les noms et adresse de l'expéditeur n'apparaissent pas.

Le nom de la ville d'où écrit l'expéditeur n'est pas indiqué avant la date.

! **La date peut s'écrire de différentes façons. Soit en entier : *29 September* 2005, *12th July 2005, 3rd January 2006, 19th April 2005.* On peut faire figurer le *th*, le *st* ou le *rd* après le chiffre, mais cette variante n'est aujourd'hui plus aussi usitée. Soit en abrégé : *29-Sept-05, 29/09/05, 29.09.05.* L'ordre du jour et du mois sont inversés aux États-Unis et dans les pays qui ont adopté le système américain. Ainsi *12.08.05* aux États-Unis signifie *8 December 2005*, alors qu'en Grande-Bretagne il s'agit du *12 August 2005.***

Dans des lettres à caractère plus formel ou du courrier d'affaires, le nom et l'adresse de l'expéditeur figurent en haut à droite (sauf s'il s'agit de papier à en-tête, auquel cas elles sont en haut au centre de la page).

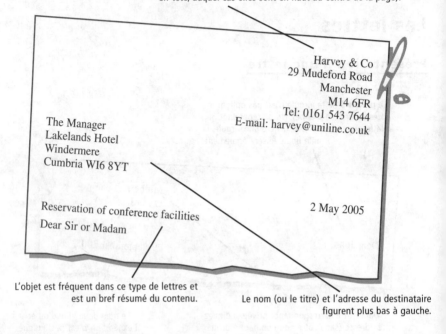

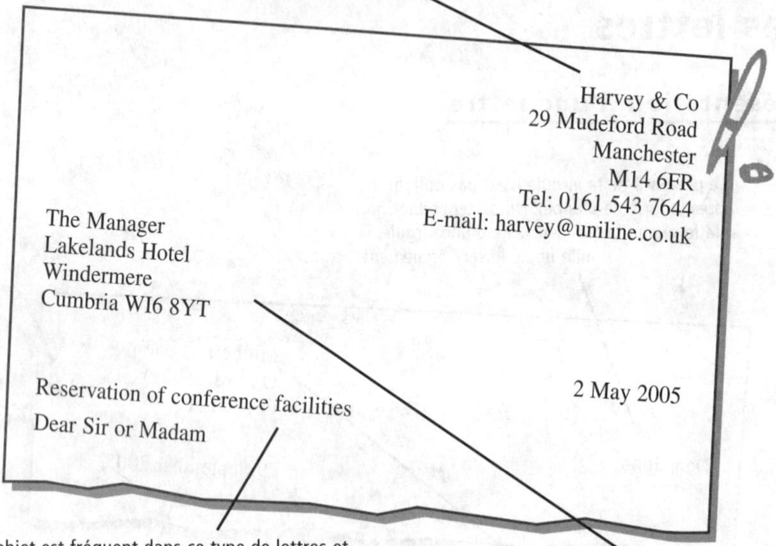

L'objet est fréquent dans ce type de lettres et est un bref résumé du contenu.

Le nom (ou le titre) et l'adresse du destinataire figurent plus bas à gauche.

Formules d'appel et formules finales

Formules d'appel

Lorsqu'on ne s'adresse pas à des amis ou à des proches, il est d'usage de faire débuter une lettre par *Dear*. Si le destinataire est inconnu ou si la lettre est adressée à une entreprise, la lettre débutera par *Dear Sir* (*Monsieur*) ou *Dear Sir/Dear Madam* (*Monsieur/Madame*). Si le nom de votre destinataire vous est connu, vous pourrez employer *Dear* suivi du titre (*Dr, Mr, Miss, Mrs, Ms* suivi du nom de la personne, par exemple : *Dear Mrs Clarke*). Pour la correspondance privée, la rédaction est plus libre :

Dear David
Cher David

My dear Lily
Ma chère Lily

Darling John
John chéri

Dans de nombreuses situations, on préfère aujourd'hui l'abréviation *Ms*, qui s'applique aussi bien à une femme mariée qu'à une femme célibataire. Utilisez *Ms* si vous ignorez le statut marital de votre correspondante ou quand celle-ci préfère qu'on l'appelle ainsi, qu'elle soit mariée ou non. Dans le doute, choisissez toujours *Ms*.

Formules finales

Dans un courrier formel, il est important d'avoir une formule finale qui corresponde à la formule d'appel. À *Dear Sir* ou *Dear Sir/Dear Madam* devront correspondre *Yours faithfully*. Pour des lettres où le destinataire a été nommément cité, la formule finale est *Yours sincerely*. Si on connaît bien la personne à qui on écrit, on peut utiliser des tournures moins formelles comme *Best wishes* ou *Kind regards*.

Présentation d'une enveloppe

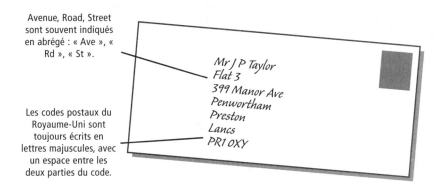

Avenue, Road, Street sont souvent indiqués en abrégé : « Ave », « Rd », « St ».

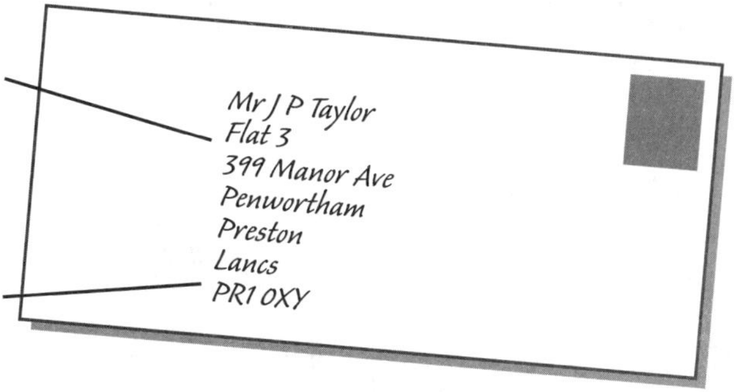

Les codes postaux du Royaume-Uni sont toujours écrits en lettres majuscules, avec un espace entre les deux parties du code.

L'adresse se place au milieu de l'enveloppe ; l'expéditeur peut éventuellement écrire son adresse au dos de l'enveloppe, en haut. Aux États-Unis, par contre, l'adresse de l'expéditeur apparaît en haut à gauche des noms et adresse des destinataires. On donne aujourd'hui couramment les abréviations des titres, les initiales et les adresses sans ponctuation :

Abréviations utilisées sur les enveloppes

Dr (=Doctor)
Docteur

Prof (=Professor)
Professeur

Mr (=Mister)
M. (=Monsieur)

Messrs (=Misters)
MM (=Messieurs)

Mrs (=Madam)
Mme (=Madame)

St (=Street)
Rue

Ave (=Avenue)
Avenue

Blvd (=Boulevard)
Boulevard

Rd (=Road)
Rue

Codes postaux

Au Royaume-Uni

Les codes postaux britanniques se présentent généralement sous la forme de deux groupes de lettres. Les premières lettres désignent le centre de distribution le plus proche (par exemple, *BN* pour *Brighton* ou *EH* pour *Edinburgh*. Seul Londres ne suit pas ce système, les deux lettres correspondant aux points cardinaux : *W* (*West*), *SW* (*South West*), etc.

Aux États-Unis

Les codes postaux américains sont composés d'une abréviation de l'État, suivie d'un numéro à cinq chiffres. Ci-dessous la liste des abréviations des États américains :

AL
Alabama
AK
Alaska
AS
American Samoa
AZ
Arizona
AR
Arkansas
CA
California
CO
Colorado
CT
Connecticut
DE
Delaware
DC
District of Columbia
FM
Federated States of Micronesia
FL
Florida
GA
Georgia
GU
Guam
HI
Hawaii

ID
Idaho
IL
Illinois
IN
Indiana
IA
Iowa
KS
Kansas
KY
Kentucky
LA
Louisiana
ME
Maine
MH
Marshall Islands
MD
Maryland
MA
Massachussetts
MI
Michigan
MN
Minnesota
MS
Mississippi
MO
Missouri
MT
Montana

NE
Nebraska
NV
Nevada
NH
New Hampshire
NJ
New Jersey
NM
New Mexico
NY
New York
NC
North Carolina
ND
North Dakota
MP
Northern Mariana Islands
OH
Ohio
OK
Oklahoma
OR
Oregon
PA
Pennsylvania
PR
Puerto Rico

RI
Rhode Island
SC
South Carolina
SD
South Dakota
TN
Tennessee
TX
Texas
UT
Utah
VT
Vermont
VI
Virgin Islands
VA
Virginia
WA
Washington
WV
West Virginia
WI
Wisconsin
WY
Wyoming

Rendez-vous

Rencontre amicale

Les rendez-vous entre amis se fixent le plus souvent par téléphone mais aussi par e-mail ou en envoyant un SMS sur le portable du destinataire. En plus du jour, de l'heure et du lieu de rendez-vous, vous pouvez suggérer une activité particulière.

What about ten o'clock?
10 heures, c'est possible ?

How about going to the cinema?
Que dis-tu d'aller au cinéma ?

Why don't we eat out tonight?
Et si on allait au resto ce soir ?

Let's have a coffee before we go home.
Que dirais-tu d'un café avant de rentrer ?

I suggest we meet up after the show.
Et si on se retrouvait après le spectacle ?

Shall we just stay in and watch TV?
D'accord pour rester à la maison ce soir et se faire une soirée télé ?

Hi Jackie!
Long time no see! Shall we meet up for a coffee after college tomorrow? How about 5pm in the City Café? Hope you can make it.
Love,
Shona

Salut Jackie !
Ça fait un bail ! Qu'est-ce que tu dis d'un café demain après les cours ? 5 heures au City Café, ça te va ? J'espère que tu pourras.
Bises,
Shona

Voici un exemple de message SMS pour un rendez-vous entre amis :

RUOK for tonite?
CU L8er! Luv Chris

Are you OK for tonight? See you later!
Love Chris

OK pour ce soir ? À plus, bises, Chris

Rendez-vous d'affaires

Il est également courant d'organiser ses réunions d'affaires par e-mail. Dans ce cas, le ton du message sera bien sûr plus formel :

```
Dear Andrew,
I've been looking at this month's
sales figures, and I was wondering
if we could meet some time this
week to discuss them. I'm free on
Wednesday afternoon, from 2pm
onwards. Does this suit you? I
suggest we meet in the meeting
room on the third floor.
Let me know if this is convenient.
George
```

```
Bonjour Andrew,
J'ai consulté le chiffre d'affaires
de ce mois et je me demandais si
nous pourrions nous rencontrer
cette semaine pour en discuter. Je
suis libre mercredi après-midi à
partir de 14 heures.
Cela vous convient-il ? Je propose la
salle de réunion au troisième étage.
Dites-moi si cela vous convient.
George
```

S'il s'agit d'une réunion importante ou plus formelle, envoyer une lettre devient impératif.

Application for post of textile designer
Dear Ms Denholm,
Thank you for your application for the above post. We would be delighted if you could attend an interview on 4 October 2005 at 3pm. Directions to our offices are enclosed. Please let us know by return of post if you are able to attend.
We look forward to meeting you on the 4th.
Yours sincerely,
Harry Fielding
Design Director

Obj. : Candidature au poste de designer textile

Chère Mme Denholm,

Nous vous remercions pour votre candidature au poste mentionné ci-dessus. Nous serions ravis de vous rencontrer pour un entretien le 4 octobre 2005 à 15 heures.

Vous trouverez ci-joint des indications pour vous rendre à nos bureaux. Nous vous prions de bien vouloir nous faire savoir par retour de courrier si vous êtes disponible ce jour-là.

Dans l'attente de vous rencontrer le 4, nous vous prions d'accepter nos cordiales salutations,

Harry Fielding
Directeur
Bureau des Études

Recherche de stage ou d'emploi

Généralités

Pour une demande de stage, une réponse à une offre d'emploi ou un acte de candidature spontanée, votre lettre doit être tapée à la machine sur format A4 et imprimée sur une imprimante de haute qualité. Seule votre signature doit être manuscrite. Recueillez le plus d'informations possibles sur l'entreprise qui vous intéresse et, si vous ne connaissez pas le nom de la personne à laquelle vous adressez votre lettre, essayez d'abord d'obtenir ce renseignement par téléphone. Tâchez d'éviter les lettres type et rédigez plutôt une lettre adaptée à chaque poste. Le ton de votre lettre n'en sera que plus convaincant. Avant de commencer à rédiger, prenez le temps de réfléchir aux compétences et qualifications exigées et décidez de l'ordre dans lequel vous allez aborder ces différents points. À la fin de votre lettre, précisez que vous êtes disponible pour un entretien.

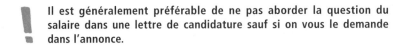

! Il est généralement préférable de ne pas aborder la question du salaire dans une lettre de candidature sauf si on vous le demande dans l'annonce.

Votre CV

Modèle de curriculum vitae

Voici un exemple de CV présenté sous sa forme la plus répandue, c'est-à-dire par ordre chronologique et en commençant par l'expérience et le diplôme les plus récents. En ce qui concerne la présentation générale, vous pouvez mentionner en premier lieu, selon ce qui vous semble le plus pertinent, vos études ou votre expérience professionnelle :

Martin Everett
Term Address:
138 Trinity Crescent
Langholm
Nottinghamshire N13 6JN
Telephone: 01378 456978
Home Address:
76 Sycamore Drive
Smallfield
Sussex RH9 4CD
Telephone: 01452 587234
Email address: meverett@whincop.com
Date of Birth: 11.6.80
Nationality: British

EDUCATION AND QUALIFICATIONS

2002:	BSc in Computer Studies. Final year project: development of a program for tracking accessibility of websites
1996-1998:	A-levels: English, Maths, Computer Studies, French
1994-1996:	GCSEs: English, Maths, Geography, History, Sciences, Computer Studies, Art and Design Work

EXPERIENCE

2001-2002:	worked part-time as an Internet cafe assistant
2000:	participated in the organisation of a conference on the future of office technology
1999:	completed a period of work experience at Compunet, Nottingham

OTHER SKILLS
In-depth knowledge of various operating systems: Windows 2000, Windows NT, Linux, Mac OS
Languages: French (fluent), German (spoken), Spanish (basic knowledge)

OTHER INFORMATION
Full clean driving licence
References available on request

Nom : Martin Everett
Adresse d'étudiant : 138 Trinity Crescent
Langholm
Nottinghamshire N13 6JN
Téléphone : 01378 456978
Adresse permanente : 76 Sycamore Drive
Smallfield
Sussex RH9 4CD
Téléphone : 01452 587234
Adresse e-mail : meverett@whincop.com
Date de naissance : 11.06.80
Nationalité : britannique

FORMATION ET QUALIFICATIONS

2002 : BSc en Informatique. Rapport de fin d'année : création d'un programme d'évaluation de l'accessibilité des sites Web
1996-1998 : A-levels : anglais, maths, informatique, français
1994-1996 : GCSEs : anglais, maths, géographie, histoire, sciences, informatique, arts graphiques

EXPÉRIENCE PROFESSIONNELLE

2001-2002 :	assistant de cybercafé à temps partiel
2000 :	participation à l'organisation d'une conférence sur l'avenir de la bureautique
1999 :	stage chez Compunet, Nottingham

AUTRES COMPÉTENCES

Connaissance approfondie de logiciels : Windows 2000, Windows NT, Linux, Mac OS
Langues : français (courant), allemand (parlé), espagnol (bases)

DIVERS

Permis de conduire
Personnes pouvant fournir leurs recommandations : adresses disponibles sur demande

Lettre de référence

Demander une lettre de recommandation

Il est de tradition dans une lettre de candidature, de donner les coordonnées de deux personnes pouvant témoigner de vos qualités et compétences pour l'emploi auquel vous vous présentez. La personne qui vous recommande est souvent un ancien professeur ou un précédent employeur. La courtoisie veut qu'on demande d'abord à cette personne si elle accepte de vous recommander. Vous pouvez ensuite, le cas échéant, inscrire son nom, sa profession et son adresse professionnelle à la fin de votre CV sous le titre : *Referees* (*Personnes pouvant fournir des références*). Ces personnes ne sont pas contactées systématiquement. Quand elles le sont, cela se passe généralement à la réception de votre lettre de candidature, ou après l'entretien si votre employeur a le sentiment que vous êtes le bon candidat. Voici un exemple de lettre envoyée à un ancien professeur :

Dear Dr Marchant

When I finished my degree in June last year, you very kindly suggested that I might use your name when applying for a job.

I am about to apply for the position of technical translator with Astral Oil, and would like to give your name as one of two referees. The company may write to you, and I hope that you will be happy to write a favourable reference for me.

It is an extremely interesting job with good prospects.

I would like to take this opportunity to thank you for all the help and guidance you offered me during my final year at Leicester.

Yours sincerely

Philip Linneman

Cher M. Marchant,
Lorsque j'ai terminé mon diplôme en juin l'année dernière, vous m'aviez gentiment suggéré de donner votre nom si je me présentais à un emploi.
J'ai l'intention de me présenter à un poste de traducteur technique chez Astra Oil et aimerais vous mentionner parmi les deux personnes pouvant me recommander.
La société vous contactera peut-être et j'espère que vous accepterez de donner une appréciation positive à mon sujet.
Il s'agit d'un travail extrêmement intéressant avec des possibilités d'évolution de carrière.
Je voudrais saisir l'occasion pour vous remercier de l'aide et des conseils judicieux dont vous m'avez fait profiter au cours de ma dernière année à Leicester.
Sentiments respectueux,
Philip Linneman

Rédiger une lettre de recommandation

Une lettre de recommandation dépourvue de conviction ferait plus de tort que de bien. Commencez par préciser quel est le lien qui vous lie à la personne que vous recommandez. Mentionnez une série de qualités en insistant sur son honnêteté dans le travail, ses réussites, ses compétences et ses contributions les plus marquantes. Évitez les termes vagues tels que : *nice* et *good*. Utilisez plutôt des mots tels que : *excellent*, *creative*, *efficient*, *dependable* et *confident*. Terminez par une recommandation pour l'emploi concerné et offrez de fournir plus d'informations si nécessaire. Donnez vos coordonnées si elles ne figurent pas déjà en en-tête.

To whom it may concern:
I have been Jonathan Kay's manager at Gateshead Social Work Department for almost four years.
I was delighted to promote him to Senior Aftercare Supervisor last year, because he has shown great skill during his time with us.
Jonathan is an enthusiastic, dedicated and reliable employee.
He is consistently successful in improving his skills, and is always willing to get involved in the work of the team.
He is efficient in planning projects, and conscientiously works towards raising standards within his department.
I highly recommend Jonathan as an excellent addition to your staff.
If you need further information, please call the phone number above.

À qui de droit

J'ai été le directeur de Jonathan Kay dans le département d'assistance sociale de Gateshead pendant presque quatre ans.

C'est avec satisfaction que je lui ai confié la responsabilité du suivi des affaires sociales l'année dernière en raison des grandes compétences dont il a fait preuve dans nos services.

Jonathan est enthousiaste, motivé et c'est aussi un employé de confiance.

Il a su accroître ses compétences et a fait la preuve de sa capacité à travailler en équipe.

Il sait organiser des projets de manière efficace et travaille avec une grande conscience professionnelle à l'amélioration de la qualité des services offerts par son département.

C'est pourquoi je recommande Jonathan sans aucune réserve et avec l'assurance qu'il apportera un complément positif à votre équipe.

Si vous désirez de plus amples informations, vous pouvez me contacter au numéro ci-dessus.

Remarque

Beaucoup d'entreprises envoient maintenant des formulaires de candidature à leurs futurs employés. Si l'on vous demande de remplir un tel formulaire, vous n'aurez besoin ni de lettre ni de CV. Cependant, une part importante du document est réservée à la description de vos compétences pour l'emploi en question. Vous pouvez utiliser les expressions suggérées ci-dessus pour parler de vos réussites et de vos qualités personnelles et pour expliquer pourquoi ce poste vous intéresse.

Structurer votre lettre

Pour toute demande d'emploi, certains éléments doivent être nécessairement mentionnés. Vous trouverez ci-dessous des expressions qui vous guideront à chaque étape. En premier lieu, précisez le poste auquel vous postulez :

I am writing to inquire as to whether you would be interested in offering me a short period of work experience in your company.

J'aimerais savoir s'il vous serait possible de m'offrir un stage pratique dans votre entreprise.

I would like to inquire as to whether there are any openings for junior sales administrators in your company.
Je voudrais savoir si votre entreprise recherche actuellement un jeune responsable des ventes.

I am writing to apply for the post of senior web developer.
Je souhaite présenter ma candidature au poste de cadre promoteur Internet.

I would like to apply for the position of computer programmer, as advertised on your website.
Je souhaite poser ma candidature au poste de programmeur en informatique, indiqué sur votre site Internet.

I am writing to apply for the above post, as advertised in the 'Independent' of 4 April 2005.
Suite à l'annonce parue dans l'« Independent » du 4 avril 2005, je souhaite poser ma candidature au poste mentionné ci-dessus.

! Utilisez la phrase ci-dessus quand vous avez déjà mentionné le titre et éventuellement le numéro de code du poste visé à la ligne « Objet ». Notez aussi qu'en anglais britannique on peut écrire *enquire* ou *inquire*.

Ensuite, donnez quelques exemples de réussite personnelle prouvant que vous convenez au poste à pourvoir :

I achieved a distinction in A Level Maths.
J'ai obtenu une mention aux épreuves de mathématiques de A level.

I contributed to the development of our accounting software.
J'ai contribué à la création d'un logiciel de comptabilité.

I coordinated the change-over from one operating system to another.
J'ai coordonné la mise en place d'un nouveau système d'exploitation.

I developed designs for a new range of table linen.
J'ai créé le design d'une nouvelle ligne de linge de table.

I gained experience in several major aspects of marketing.
J'ai acquis de l'expérience dans plusieurs secteurs-clé du marketing.

I implemented a new system to monitor production.
J'ai assuré la mise en place d'un nouveau système de contrôle de la production.

I presented our new products at the annual sales fair.
J'ai présenté nos nouveaux produits à la foire-exposition annuelle.

I have supervised a team of freelancers on several projects.
J'ai dirigé une équipe de collaborateurs freelance sur différents projets.

Vous pouvez alors énumérer vos qualités personnelles :

I see myself as systematic and methodical in my approach to work.
Je suis organisé et méthodique dans mon travail.

I am an impartial and tolerant person, with an ability to get on well with people from all walks of life.
Je suis impartial et tolérant et suis capable de bien m'entendre avec des personnes de milieux très différents.

I am hardworking and commercially-minded, and able to stay calm under pressure.

Sur le plan commercial, je suis capable de me donner à fond dans mon travail et j'ai une bonne capacité de résistance à la pression.

My last job required me to be sensitive and tactful, and I feel that my personality proved to be suited to this type of work.

Mon dernier emploi exigeait du tact et le sens de la nuance et je pense que ma personnalité correspond tout à fait à ce genre de travail.

Expliquer également pourquoi vous souhaitez obtenir ce poste :

I am keen to find a post with more responsibility where I can use my programming skills.

Je désire occuper un poste à responsabilités dans lequel je pourrai utiliser mes compétences en programmation.

I have been doing temporary work, and now wish to find a more permanent full-time position.

J'ai occupé des postes intérimaires et désire désormais un emploi permanent à temps complet.

I would now like to further my career in the field of TV journalism.

Je désirerais maintenant avancer dans ma carrière professionnelle en devenant journaliste pour la télévision.

After extensive research, I feel that your company's activities most closely match my own values and interests.

Après avoir effectué des recherches approfondies, je suis parvenue à la conclusion que les activités de votre entreprise correspondent bien à mes centres d'intérêt et à mes critères personnels.

Montrez-vous motivé et disponible pour un entretien.

I would be pleased to come for an interview at your convenience.

Je suis disponible pour un entretien selon votre convenance.

I would be delighted to meet you to discuss this further. I am available on Monday and Wednesday afternoons.

Je serais ravi de vous rencontrer pour vous donner davantage de précisions. Je suis disponible les lundis et mercredis après-midi.

Please do not hesitate to contact me if you would like to discuss this further.

N'hésitez pas à me contacter si vous le désirez pour un entretien plus approfondi.

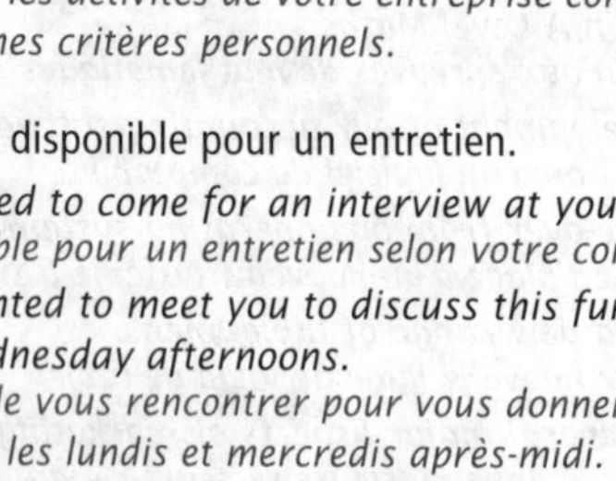

Effectuer une demande de stage

S'il s'agit d'une demande de stage, vous n'êtes sans doute qu'au début de votre carrière et n'avez peut-être pas de réussite professionnelle à mentionner. Vous pouvez toutefois réfléchir aux qualités requises pour ce genre de travail et faire remarquer que vous pensez avoir le profil qui convient.

Dear Ms Osborne
I am a student, currently in my final year of a Business Studies degree.
I am writing to inquire as to whether you have any openings for three months' work experience in your overseas department during the period July to September this year.
Throughout my course of study, I have concentrated particularly on overseas markets, imports and exports, and business English, and so I hope that while learning from your business activities, I may also be able to help out with some of the simpler tasks in the office.
I am reliable and punctual, and am looking forward to getting an insight into the world of work.
Please do not hesitate to contact me if you require any more information. I am available for interview on Wednesday and Friday afternoons. In the meantime, I look forward to hearing from you.
Yours sincerely
Jane Parkinson

Madame Osborne,
Je suis actuellement étudiante en dernière année d'études commerciales.
J'aimerais savoir si vous recherchez, dans votre service international, des stagiaires pour une durée de trois mois, durant la période de juillet à septembre.
Au cours de mes études, je me suis particulièrement intéressée aux marchés étrangers, à l'import/export ainsi qu'à l'anglais des affaires.
C'est pourquoi je pense pouvoir vous être utile pour la réalisation de tâches simples, ce qui me permettrait par la même occasion de mieux connaître les activités de votre entreprise.
Je suis fiable et ponctuel, et j'attends beaucoup d'une première expérience dans le monde du travail.
N'hésitez pas à me contacter si vous désirez de plus amples informations. Je suis disponible pour un entretien les mercredis et vendredis après-midi.
Dans l'attente d'une réponse de votre part, je vous prie d'accepter, Madame, l'expression de mes meilleurs sentiments,
Jane Parkinson

Recherche d'emploi

Candidature spontanée

Si vous recherchez un emploi précis, essayez d'obtenir de l'entreprise concernée la dénomination exacte du poste qui vous intéresse. Si vous avez déjà eu un contact avec l'entreprise concernée, vous pouvez y faire référence dans votre lettre et joindre votre CV.

Management traineeship

Dear Mr Thomson,

Thank you very much for taking the time last Wednesday to speak to me about the possibility of a training position with your company. Your advice has strongly encouraged me to pursue a career in this field, and your company's core activities closely match my own interests. I would therefore like to apply for a Trainee Manager placement. Please find attached a CV which highlights my prior professional experience and qualities which I feel make me suited to this position. In particular, I would like to bring to your attention the following, achieved during my BA in Business Studies at the University of Manchester.

I have a strong interest in and knowledge of staff management, and have gained extensive experience in handling heavy workloads and meeting deadlines.

I pride myself on being well-organised and a self-starter, and have excellent communication skills.

I am extremely motivated to develop my career with Frasers' department stores, and so would very much appreciate the opportunity to discuss further my suitability for a traineeship. Please feel free to contact me, either by email: fobrien@quickserve.com, or by leaving a message on 01625 456123. I look forward to speaking to you soon.

Yours sincerely,

Ms Fiona O'Brien

Objet : demande de stage de direction

Madame Thomson,

Je vous remercie d'avoir accepté de me recevoir en entretien mercredi dernier au sujet d'un éventuel stage de formation dans votre entreprise.

Notre conversation m'a persuadée de poursuivre ma démarche d'autant que les activités principales de votre entreprise correspondent tout à fait à mes centres d'intérêt.

Je souhaite donc soumettre ma candidature pour ce poste de stagiaire rattachée à la direction. Le CV ci-joint rend compte de mon expérience professionnelle et souligne les qualités qui paraissent faire de moi une candidate idéale.

Je voudrais particulièrement attirer votre attention sur un aspect de mes études de commerce à l'université de Manchester.

J'ai une bonne connaissance des questions d'encadrement d'entreprise auxquelles j'attache un intérêt particulier. J'ai l'habitude du travail intensif dans le respect des délais impartis.

Je suis organisée et indépendante et je possède de bonnes qualités de communication.

Je souhaite vivement poursuivre ma carrière professionnelle dans les magasins Frasers et je serais heureuse de pouvoir m'entretenir avec vous sur la possibilité d'un stage de formation dans votre service.

Vous pouvez me contacter par e-mail à l'adresse suivante : fobrien@quickserve.com, ou me laisser un message au 01625 456123.

Dans l'espoir de vous rencontrer bientôt, recevez, Madame, l'assurance de mes meilleurs sentiments,

Fiona O' Brien

Répondre à une offre d'emploi

Si vous répondez à une annonce précise, indiquez où vous en avez eu connaissance ainsi que le poste concerné.

I am responding to your advertisement for a graphic designer, which appeared in the Guardian on 22 May, 2005.

Suite à l'annonce parue dans le Guardian du 22 mai 2005, je soumets ma candidature au poste de concepteur graphique.

Modèle de réponse à une offre d'emploi

Application for post of desktop publishing manager

Dear Mrs Williams,

I am writing in response to your advertisement in the January edition of Publishing News, and am enclosing my CV for your review.

As you will see, I have gained valuable experience in book design using various types of publishing software, and have written technical specifications and supervised page design and layout for both dictionary text and illustrated books.

In my current position at Isis Press, I have initiated monitoring systems that enable pre-press controllers to work more easily with authors and other editors.

I am currently attending an evening class on the use of QuarkXpress for the advanced user, and am now looking for a post which gives me an opportunity to use my new skills.

I look forward to having the opportunity to discuss this further with you. I shall be in London for a week at the end of January, and would be available for interview any time between the 24th and the 31st.

Yours sincerely

Katie Mitchell

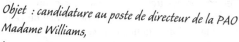

Objet : candidature au poste de directeur de la PAO

Madame Williams,

Je vous écris en réponse à l'annonce parue dans le numéro de janvier de Publishing News et je joins mon curriculum vitae.

Comme vous pourrez vous en rendre compte, je possède une solide expérience de la conception éditoriale et j'ai travaillé avec une grande variété de logiciels.

J'ai rédigé des manuels techniques et contrôlé la conception et la mise en page de dictionnaires et de livres illustrés.

À Isis Press, où je travaille actuellement, j'ai effectué la mise en place d'un système de monitoring facilitant aux contrôleurs pré-presse leurs échanges professionnels avec les auteurs et les rédacteurs.

Je suis actuellement une formation de niveau avancé sur QuarkXPress et aimerais trouver un emploi qui me permette d'utiliser mes nouvelles compétences.

J'espère que j'aurai bientôt l'occasion d'en parler avec vous. Je me trouverai à Londres une semaine à la fin janvier et par conséquent serai disponible pour un entretien entre le 24 et le 31 selon votre convenance.

Sincères salutations,

Katie Mitchell

Écrire une annonce

Le style d'une annonce est généralement très synthétique : omissions d'articles, des prépositions et recours à une seule forme verbale. Les offres de service doivent être rédigées à la troisième personne du singulier. Une annonce doit contenir le numéro de téléphone auquel vous pouvez être contacté.

Cleaner required light housework two days a week. Good rates offered.
Recherche une femme de ménage pour de menus travaux deux jours par semaine. Rémunération intéressante.

Maths undergraduate offers help with revision. Friendly approach. £12/hour.
Étudiant en mathématiques propose cours de soutien. Approche sympathique. 12 livres de l'heure.

Si vous voulez publier une annonce pour une location, indiquez précisément dans quel quartier se trouve le logement concerné, tous les détails susceptibles de le mettre en valeur et le numéro de téléphone où on peut vous joindre. Vous pouvez aussi préciser quel type de locataire vous souhaitez ou ne souhaitez pas : étudiants, fumeurs, etc.

To Let
Room in friendly shared house in Marchmont.
Central heating, access to shared kitchen and living area.
Rent £220 per calendar month.
Call 992 6755.
Non-smokers only.

À louer
Chambre dans maison collective à Marchmont, environnement sympathique.
Chauffage central, cuisine et séjour collectifs.
220 livres par mois.
Tél : 992 6755.
Non fumeurs.

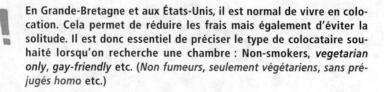

En Grande-Bretagne et aux États-Unis, il est normal de vivre en colocation. Cela permet de réduire les frais mais également d'éviter la solitude. Il est donc essentiel de préciser le type de colocataire souhaité lorsqu'on recherche une chambre : Non-smokers, *vegetarian only, gay-friendly* etc. (*Non fumeurs, seulement végétariens, sans préjugés homo* etc.)

Téléphoner

Appeler et répondre au téléphone

Si vous téléphonez à un ami à titre privé, vous pouvez utiliser :

Hello./Hi. Can I speak to Paul, please?
Allo./Salut. Je pourrais parler à Paul, s'il vous/te plaît.

Hi. Is Bernard there, please?
Bonjour. Bernard est là, s'il vous plaît ?

Hi. This is Sylvie. Is Anne around?
Salut, c'est Sylvie. Anne est dans le coin ?

Hi. Is that Marie?
Salut. C'est Marie ?

Hello. Would it be possible to speak to Sophie, please?
Allo. Est-ce que je pourrais parler à Sophie, s'il vous plaît ?

Répondre au téléphone

Hello. 432219.
Allo.

Répondre quand on vous demande

Speaking.
C'est moi./Oui.

This is he/she (US).
Oui./C'est moi.

Philip *Hi. Can I speak to Jill please?*
Jill *Speaking.*
Philip *Hi, Jill. It's Philip.*
Jill *Hi, Philip. How are you?*
Philip *Fine, thanks.*

Philip *Allo. Je pourrais parler à Jill, s'il-vous-plaît.*
Jill *C'est moi.*
Philip *Salut Jill. C'est Philip.*
Jill *Salut, Philip. Comment ça va ?*
Philip *Bien, merci.*

Passer une communication

I'll just get him/her for you.
Je vous le/la passe.

Can I ask/say who's calling?
Pardon, c'est de la part de qui ?

Who's calling, please?
Excusez-moi, c'est de la part de... ?

Just one moment. I'll put you through.
Un moment. Je vous le/la passe.

Hang/Hold on. I'll try to connect you.
Restez en ligne, je vous passe votre correspondant.

Si vous ne pouvez pas passer la communication

I'm sorry. She's not here today. Can I take a message?/Would you like to leave a message?
Désolé, elle n'est pas là aujourd'hui. Je peux prendre un message ?/Vous voulez lui laisser un message ?
I'm afraid he's not at his desk at the moment. Can I get him to call you back?
Il s'est absenté du bureau. Je lui demande de vous rappeler ?
I'm afraid she's on another call. Would you like to hold?
Désolé, mais elle est déjà en ligne. Je vous mets en attente ?

Laisser un message

Can I leave a message?
Je peux laisser un message ?
Could you give him a message?
Vous pouvez lui transmettre un message ?
Would you ask her to call me? She has my number.
Vous pouvez lui demander de me rappeler ? Elle a mon numéro.
Could you tell her I called?
Vous pouvez lui dire que j'ai appelé ?
Would you ask her to call me on 557846?
Vous pouvez lui demander de me rappeler au 557846 ?

Problèmes rencontrés pendant un appel téléphonique

Si vous comprenez mal votre interlocuteur, parce que la communication est mauvaise ou que son accent ne vous est pas familier :

I'm sorry. I didn't catch that. This is a really bad line.
Pardon, je ne vous ai pas compris. La ligne est mauvaise.
Could you say that again?
Vous pourriez répéter ?
Could you spell that for me?
Vous pourriez me l'épeler ?
Was that 'M' for 'Mark' or 'N' for 'Nigel'?
Vous avez dit "M" comme "Mark" ou "N" comme "Nigel" ?
I'm sorry. Could you repeat the first part of the number again, please?
Excusez-moi. Pourriez-vous répéter le début du numéro, s'il vous plaît ?

Si le numéro est erroné

S'excuser

I'm sorry. Wrong number.
Désolé. Vous avez fait un faux numéro.
Sorry. I've got the wrong number.
Je suis désolé. On m'a donné un faux numéro.
I'm terribly sorry. I must have dialled the wrong number.
Je suis vraiment désolé. J'ai dû faire un faux numéro.

Répondre

I'm sorry. I think you must have the wrong number.
Désolé. Je pense que vous avez fait un faux numéro.

Are you sure you've got the right number? There's no one here by that name.
Vous êtes sûr que c'est le bon numéro ? Il n'y a personne de ce nom ici.

Mettre fin à la communication

Pour mettre fin à la communication, vous pouvez utiliser ces phrases :

Thanks for calling.
Merci d'avoir appelé.

Speak to you soon.
Je vous rappelle.

I have to go. Someone's trying to get through on the other line.
Il faut que je te laisse. Il y a quelqu'un sur l'autre ligne.

Can I call you back? Someone's at the door.
Je peux te rappeler ? Il y a quelqu'un à la porte.

Le portable

Il n'y a normalement aucune différence d'utilisation par rapport à un fixe. Ci-dessous quelques situations particulières :

I'm on my mobile.
Je suis sur mon portable.

I'm sorry. You're breaking up.
Désolé. Mais ça passe de moins en moins bien.

I'm sorry. The reception's really bad.
Désolé. La réception est mauvaise.

If we get cut off, I'll call you back.
Si ça coupe, je te rappelle.

Can you text me the number?
Tu peux m'envoyer ton numéro par SMS ?

I called her three times but I keep getting her voicemail.
Je l'ai déjà appelée trois fois, mais je tombe toujours sur sa boîte vocale.

La messagerie téléphonique

Enregistrer un message

Hello. This is 483397. I'm afraid there's no one here to take your call right now but please leave your name and number and we'll get back to you as soon as possible. Thanks for calling.
Bonour vous êtes au 48 33 97. Il n'y a personne pour le moment, mais vous pouvez laisser votre nom et votre numéro et je vous rappelerai dès que possible. Merci de votre appel.

Hi. You're through to John and Luce. Please leave a message after the tone. If you want to send a fax, please press 5 now.
Salut. Vous êtes sur le répondeur de John et Luce. Merci de laisser un message après le bip. Pour envoyer un fax, appuyez sur le 5.

Laisser un message

Hi, John. This is Marc. /It's Marc here. Just wondering if you and Jean are free for dinner next Friday. Give me a call back when you get this message. Bye.

Salut John. C'est Marc. Je me demandais si Jean et toi seriez libres pour dîner vendredi prochain. Rappelle-moi quand tu auras eu mon message. Salut.

Hello. This is a message for Patrick Blanc. Could you call Annie Foyle on 476998? Thank you.

Bonjour, ce message s'adresse à Patrick Blanc. Pourriez-vous rappeler Annie Foyle au 476998 ? Merci.

Remarque

Les numéros de téléphone se lisent en énumérant les chiffres un à un et en marquant une pause après l'indicatif de ville : 01237 456789 se lit *oh, one, two, three, seven. Four, five, six, seven, eight, nine*. Si un chiffre est présent en double ou en triple vous l'indiquez en disant *double* ou *triple*. Par exemple, *01237 4667888* se lira *oh, one, two, three, seven. Four, double six, seven, triple eight.*

Les e-mails

L'en-tête

L'en-tête d'un nouveau message est composé d'une série de rubriques. La première, *To* (*À*) sert à indiquer l'adresse du destinataire, la rubrique *Cc* (*courtesy copy*) et celle appelée *Bcc* (*blind courtesy copy*) servent à envoyer des copies de l'e-mail. Cette dernière est réservée aux copies pour lesquelles vous ne voulez pas que le nom du destinataire en copie apparaisse. La rubrique *Subject* est bien sûr prévue pour l'objet du message.

Formules d'appels et de salutations

La formule d'appel n'est pas indispensable dans un e-mail. Les formules suivantes sont les plus courantes pour les messages familiers :

Hi Jenny
  Salut Jenny
Hi there!
  Salut !

! Dans un style plus formel, *Dear* (suivi du nom) est recommandé.

Un e-mail rédigé dans un style familier peut être terminé par :

See you soon
  À bientôt
Take care
  À bientôt
Love
  Bises
Lots of love
  Bises

! Si *Take care* et *see you soon* ont des sens très proches, *take care* est plus affectueux.

Dans un e-mail plus formel ou la correspondance d'affaires, on peut utiliser les exemples suivants (classés ici du plus formel au moins formel) :

Kind regards
  Meilleures salutations
Best wishes
  Salutations
All the best
  Cordialement

Abréviations

Les abréviations et les contractions sont très courantes dans les e-mails. Voici quelques exemples que vous risquez de rencontrer ou de vouloir utiliser :

AFAIK (as far as I know)
Autant que je sache

ASAP (as soon as possible)
Aussitôt que possible

B4 (before)
Avant

BTW (by the way)
Au fait

cld (could)
Pouvoir (conditionnel)

FYI (for your information)
Pour votre information

GR8 (great)
Super

HTH (hope this helps)
En espérant que cela te sera utile

IMHO (in my humble opinion)
À mon humble avis

msg (message)
Message

prhps (perhaps)
Peut-être

TNX (thanks)
Merci

WRT (with regard to)
Rapport à

Un lien *FAQ* vous dirige vers une page Web contenant les questions les plus fréquentes qui ont été posées concernant le site que vous visitez. L'expression *IMHO* n'est pas une tournure recherchée mais une abréviation ironique signifiant *je pense que*.

Les messages SMS

Envoyer un SMS

Bien que la plupart des abréviations utilisées dans les e-mails puissent être retrouvées dans les SMS, d'autres abréviations ont été inventées spécialement pour ce type de communication :

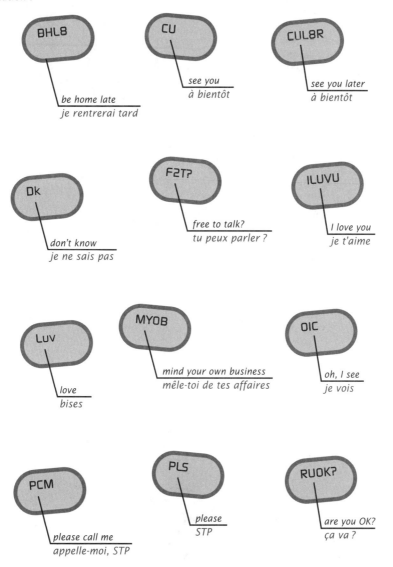

BHL8
be home late
je rentrerai tard

CU
see you
à bientôt

CUL8R
see you later
à bientôt

Dk
don't know
je ne sais pas

F2T?
free to talk?
tu peux parler ?

ILUVU
I love you
je t'aime

Luv
love
bises

MYOB
mind your own business
mêle-toi de tes affaires

OIC
oh, I see
je vois

PCM
please call me
appelle-moi, STP

PLS
please
STP

RUOK?
are you OK?
ça va ?

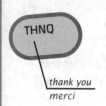

THNQ
thank you
merci

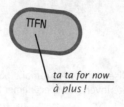

TTFN
ta ta for now
à plus !

WAN2TLK?
want to talk?
veux-tu (en) parler ?

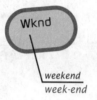

Wknd
weekend
week-end

XX
kisses
bises

Communication guide

Communication guide

Letters

Layout of a letter

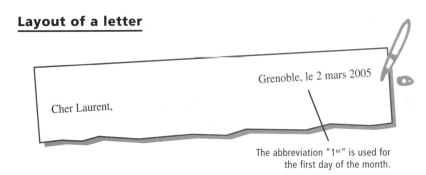

Grenoble, le 2 mars 2005

Cher Laurent,

The abbreviation "1er" is used for the first day of the month.

In an informal letter you do not need to give your own address, but in a more formal letter you write it in the top left-hand corner.

The name and address of the person the letter is going to are written in the top right-hand corner, lower down on the page than the name and address of the sender, and above the dates.

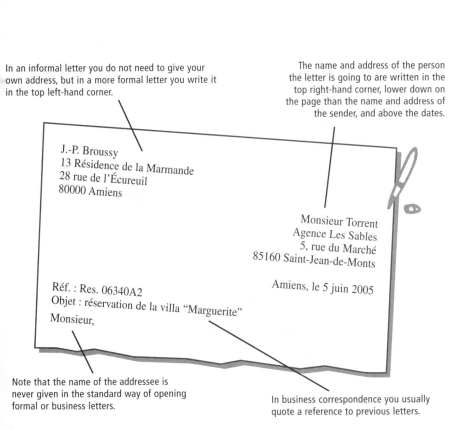

J.-P. Broussy
13 Résidence de la Marmande
28 rue de l'Écureuil
80000 Amiens

Monsieur Torrent
Agence Les Sables
5, rue du Marché
85160 Saint-Jean-de-Monts

Amiens, le 5 juin 2005

Réf. : Res. 06340A2
Objet : réservation de la villa "Marguerite"

Monsieur,

Note that the name of the addressee is never given in the standard way of opening formal or business letters.

In business correspondence you usually quote a reference to previous letters.

Standard ways of starting and ending letters

Private correspondence

The following are the commonest ways of starting a letter:

Cher Arthur,
Dear Arthur,

Chers amis,
Dear Friends,

Chère Anne, cher Éric,
Dear Anne and Éric,

! The use of *mon, ma, mes (my)* at the start of the greeting indicates a closer relationship with the person you are writing to.

Mon cher Sylvain,
My dear/Dearest Sylvain,

Mon chéri/Ma chérie,
Dearest,

Ways of ending a letter are:

(Bien) affectueusement
Best wishes

Je t'embrasse
Love

Bisous/(Grosses) Bises
Lots of love

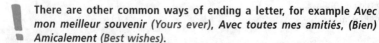

! There are other common ways of ending a letter, for example *Avec mon meilleur souvenir (Yours ever), Avec toutes mes amitiés, (Bien) Amicalement (Best wishes).*

Here is an example of a letter to a friend:

Chère Laure, Cher Vincent,

Ce petit mot pour vous donner notre nouvelle adresse.

Désolée de mon long silence, nous avons été très occupés par notre déménagement. Nous nous installons petit à petit : il ne reste plus que quelques cartons à déballer !

Nous avons maintenant le téléphone : 020 7463 8291, et mon numéro de portable est toujours le même.

J'espère que vous pourrez venir à notre pendaison de crémaillère prévue pour la fin juin.

En espérant avoir/recevoir bientôt de vos nouvelles.

Je vous embrasse.

Kate

Dear Laure and Vincent,

Just a short note to give you our new address.

I'm sorry for not having been in touch before, but we've been very busy with the move. We're slowly getting settled in: only a few more boxes to unpack!

We've got a new home phone number: 020 7463 8291, and my mobile number is still the same.

I hope you'll be able to come to our housewarming, which we've got planned for the end of June.

Hoping to hear from you soon.

Love

Kate

Formal letters

If you do not know the name of the person you are writing to, start the letter with *Madame* or *Monsieur*. If you do know it, you write *Chère Madame* or *Cher Monsieur*.

! **Except when you are talking about marital status, the form of address *mademoiselle (miss)* is less commonly used than *madame (madam)*. Note that, in French, you never use the person's surname when starting a formal letter.**

The standard ways of ending a formal letter are *Veuillez agréer, Madame/Monsieur, l'expression de mes meilleurs sentiments, Je vous prie d'accepter, Madame/Monsieur, mes salutations distinguées, Je vous prie d'agréer, Madame/Monsieur, l'expression de ma meilleure considération*, which correspond to the English *Yours faithfully*.

! **If the person sending the letter is a woman, the ending containing the word *sentiments* is avoided if the addressee is a man (and vice versa). If you know the person you are writing to, you can use less traditional endings: *Avec mes meilleurs sentiments, Avec mes meilleures salutations (With kind regards), Cordialement, Bien à vous (With best wishes).***

Example of a formal letter:

> *Madame, Monsieur,*
>
> *Objet : Confirmation de réservation de salles*
>
> *Suite à notre conversation téléphonique de ce matin, je vous confirme la location de votre salle de conférence et de deux salles de réunion plus petites, pour les ateliers du 10 au 12 avril.*
>
> *En ce qui concerne le matériel, il nous faut une sonorisation de la salle de conférence avec micro et magnétophone, un rétroprojecteur et un écran.*
>
> *Merci de prévoir également un paper board pour chacune des deux salles de réunion.*
>
> *Vous remerciant par avance, je vous prie de recevoir, Madame, Monsieur, mes salutations distinguées.*
>
> *Frances Devlin*
>
> *Direction marketing*

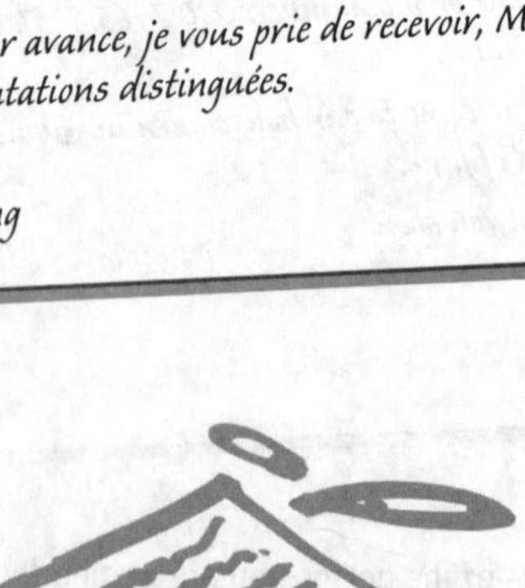

Dear Sir or Madam,

Confirmation of room reservations

Following our telephone conversation of this morning, I hereby confirm the hire of your conference room and two smaller meeting rooms for our workshops, which will be held from the 10th to the 12th of April.

With regard to equipment in the conference room, we shall need a public address system with a microphone and tape recorder, an overhead projector and a screen.

Please also provide a flipchart for each of the two meeting rooms.

Thanking you in advance.

Yours faithfully,

Frances Devlin

Marketing Director

When you do not know the name of the person you are writing to, you should start the letter with *Madame, Monsieur*. If you do know it, you still remain formal, starting the letter with *Chère madame, Cher monsieur*. At the end of the letter you address the person in the same way.

Addressing an envelope

"avenue" can be abbreviated to "av."; similarly "boulevard" becomes "bd." and "place" "pl."; "rue", however, is always written in full.

Mademoiselle Irène Hubert
Appt. 128, Bât. D
Résidence des Feuillantines
128, avenue des Feuillantines
59000 LILLE

It is conventional to avoid abbreviating the words *Monsieur* and *Madame* on the envelope of a business letter. The postal service recommends writing the name and address of the sender on the envelope, generally on the back. Before the name of the sender you write *exp.*, the abbreviation of *expéditeur (sender)*.

Only lawyers, doctors and sometimes university professors have their names preceded on the envelope by an abbreviated form of their title. For a lawyer: *Me* = *Maître*. For a doctor: *Dr* = *Docteur*. For a professor: *Pr* = *Professeur*. These are used for both men and women. Also, when you write to a university professor, prefect, member of parliament, minister etc., you use the form *Monsieur*, or *Madame*, + title + surname; for example, you write *Monsieur le Professeur Dupont* or *Madame la Ministre Delacroix*.

! If the person you are writing to is living in the care of someone else, you write *aux bon soins de Madame/Monsieur...* after the person's name on the envelope. As an alternative to this you can use the English abbreviation *c/o* (care of).

Postcodes

The first two numbers of a French postcode refer to the *départe-ment*, for example *13 = Bouches du Rhône, 38 = Isère*. For Paris, the last two numbers specify the *arrondissement*. Thus, 75006 is the postcode of the capital's sixth arrondissement. The third number, if it is a 0, indicates a prefecture. Businesses or organizations that receive a large volume of mail have a special postcode, called *CEDEX* (*Courrier d'Entreprise à Distribution EXceptionnelle*), which provides them with a special delivery service. Many businesses also have a PO Box, which is indicated on the envelope by the letters *B.P.* (*Boîte Postale*) followed by the corresponding number: for example *B.P. 1158*.

Arranging a meeting

Between friends

Meetings between friends are usually arranged by telephone, but also by e-mail or text message. Some useful expressions are given below. Note that despite the informality of the situation the *vous* form may still be used:

Venez donc prendre un verre à la maison.
Come to my place for a drink.

Vous êtes libre ce soir ?
Are you free this evening?

À quelle heure voulez-vous que je vienne vous chercher ?
What time do you want me to call for you?

If you use the *tu* form to each other:

Tu es libre ce soir ?
Are you free this evening?

Tu veux passer à la maison après le bureau ?
Do you want to come to my place after work?

Rendez-vous chez toi ou chez moi ?
Shall we meet at your place or mine?

On se retrouve à six heures au café de la poste ?
Shall we meet at six o'clock at the café by the post office?

On se voit ce soir chez Emma.
See you tonight at Emma's.

Si on déjeunait ensemble demain ?
How about having dinner together tomorrow?

A meeting is often suggested in the form of a conditional clause introduced by *si (if)* followed by the imperfect indicative, as in the last example above.

Salut,
ça fait un bail qu'on s'est pas vues ! Et si on se faisait un petit ciné ce soir ? Il y a une rétro de Jarman super intéressante.
Ça te dit ?
Bises
Anne

Hi,
It's ages since we've seen each other! How about going to a film tonight? There's a great Jarman retrospective on. Do you fancy it?
Love
Anne

Here is an example of a text message for arranging to meet a friend:

KeSKonfé ce soir ?
I 6né ?

qu'est-ce qu'on fait ce soir ? un ciné ?
wot we doin 2nite? movie?

slt, rdv o Kfé kom dab DAK ?

salut, rendez-vous au café comme d'habitude, d'accord ?
hi, CU at cafe as usl ok?

Work meetings

Work meetings too are often arranged by e-mail. In this case, the tone of the message will obviously be more formal.

```
Bonjour Florence,
Je serai à Marseille au début
de la semaine prochaine et
j'aimerais faire la connaissance
de vos nouveaux collaborateurs.
Est-ce que vous pourriez
organiser cela et me prévenir
rapidement du jour et de l'heure
qui conviendraient à tout le
monde ?
Merci
Simon
```

```
Hello Florence,
I'm going to be in Marseilles
at the beginning of next week
and I'd like to meet your new
contributors. Could you arrange
that and let me know as soon as
possible what day and time would
suit everyone best?
Thanks
Simon
```

Cher Marc,
J'ai reçu une proposition intéressante de la société Thomas et Co. et j'aimerais en discuter avec vous. Seriez-vous libre lundi après-midi vers 14 heures ? À toutes fins utiles, je retiens la salle de réunion du troisième étage car je viendrai avec l'équipe commerciale.
Dites-moi si cela vous convient.
Nicola

Dear Marc,
I've just received an interesting proposal from the firm Thomas & Co. and I'd like to discuss it with you. Would you be free Monday afternoon about 2 o'clock? Just in case, I've booked the meeting room on the third floor since I'm coming with the sales team.
Let me know if that's OK for you.
Nicola

Looking for a job or work experience

Reading a job advertisement

The style and presentation of job advertisements published in the newspapers vary according to the size of the company and the level of the position being advertised. In all cases, these advertisements contain helpful details that you should keep in mind when replying to them. Here are some of the abbreviations that are used:

H/F = homme/femme
man/woman

JH/JF = jeune homme/jeune femme
young man/young woman

CDI = contrat à durée indéterminée
permanent contract

CDD = contrat à durée déterminée
fixed-term contract

rémun. = rémunération
salary

exp. = expérience
experience

Bac + 2 = Baccalauréat + 2 ans de formation supérieure
A levels + 2 years' higher education

Fixe + % sur CA = salaire fixe + % sur chiffre d'affaires
fixed salary+ share of profits

Tps plein ou partiel = temps plein ou partiel
full-time or part-time

In an advertisement the proposed salary is given either as *mensuel brut (gross monthly)* or as *annuel brut (gross annual)* salary. From this figure, National Insurance contributions and income tax will be deducted.

Here are some examples of job advertisements:

Studio Ardéco
recrute collaborateurs H/F :
- architectes d'intérieur,
- chefs de projets et concepteurs,
- dessinateurs.
écrire au 33, rue Auguste Comte
59000 Lille

Studio Ardéco
seeks male/female
- interior designers
- project and design managers
- draughtsmen/women
Applications in writing to 33, rue Auguste Comte
59000 Lille

Groupe de sociétés spécialisées dans la vente par correspondance d'articles de sports recherche pour embauche immédiate en CDI :
Un(e) comptable confirmé(e)
Profil recherché :
Formation comptable Bac + 2, expérience minimum 3/4 ans
Autonomie, sens de l'organisation, rigueur, fiabilité, esprit d'équipe, dynamisme
Envoyez lettre de motivation + CV et prétentions salariales à :
Sports et Nature
43, avenue de la République
50000 Cherbourg

Group specializing in mail-order sales of sports equipment seeks, for immediate start, on fixed-term contract:
An experienced accountant
The ideal candidate will be:
An accountancy professional with two years' higher education and a minimum of 3–4 years' experience
He/She will have the ability to work independently, good organizational skills, attention to detail, reliability, team spirit and dynamism
Send CV with covering letter, stating expected salary to:
Sports et Nature
43, avenue de la République
50000 Cherbourg

Grand groupe de communication
Vous avez 30/35 ans (H/F), une formation commerciale de haut niveau, vous parlez plusieurs langues européennes, vous avez le sens du travail en équipe, vous aimez voyager. Rejoignez un grand groupe de presse international pour animer une équipe commerciale tonique et efficace.
Envoyez votre candidature et votre CV au cabinet Duhamel,
48, rue de Monceau
26000 Valence

Large communications group
You are 30–35 (M/F), have a high level of commercial training, speak several European languages, are a team player and like to travel.
Come and join a large international press consortium and head up a dynamic and effective sales team.
Send your letter of application and CV to: Cabinet Duhamel,
48, rue de Monceau
26000 Valence

The curriculum vitae

A CV should be clear, concise, and honest and must be capable of being adapted to all the different businesses that you will decide to contact. In France it is not uncommon to enclose a photo and limit the length of the CV to one page. Giving your age and marital status is not obligatory. If you are looking for a first job, you should give more space to the section on education and training and mention any work experience in companies, holiday jobs and voluntary work.

Lucy Kyle
44, rue de Fleurus
75006 Paris France
Téléphone : 01 58 92 77 55
E-mail : lukyle@tiscali.fr

Célibataire
24 ans
Nationalité britannique

You can also give your date of birth; in this case you write "Né(e) le 12/08/1980".

The available alternatives are: "marié(e)", "divorcé(e)", "séparé(e)", "veuf/veuve".

FORMATION

Févr. – juin 2003 : OUEBNET, Lyon. Cours de formation pour consultants en commerce électronique.
1999 – 2002 : Université de Sheffield. BSc en informatique (licence), mention très bien.
1997 – 1999 : St Mark's School, Derby. A levels (baccalauréat). Options : langue anglaise, mathématiques, physique, informatique, français.
1995 – 1997 : Pinewood School, Coventry. GCSEs : langue anglaise, littérature anglaise, mathématiques, physique, chimie, dessin industriel, géographie, français.

EXPÉRIENCE PROFESSIONNELLE

2001 – 2002 : animation d'un cybercafé à Mansfield.
Étés 1998 et 1999 : Grand Hotel de Brighton, Accueil et standard.

DIVERS

- Connaissance approfondie de nombreux logiciels.
- Anglais (langue maternelle), français (lu, écrit, parlé), notions d'allemand et d'espagnol.
- Goût pour les voyages, le cinéma et la guitare.

"lu, écrit, parlé" = "bonne connaissance du français", "français courant".

Lucy Kyle
44, rue de Fleurus
75006 Paris France
Telephone: 01 58 92 77 55
E-mail: lukyle@tiscali.fr
Single
24 years old
Nationality: British

EDUCATION AND TRAINING

Feb. – Jun. 2003: OUEBNET, Lyons. Training course for e-business consultants.
1999 – 2002: University of Sheffield. BSc in Information Technology (1st class Hons).
1997 – 1999: St Mark's School, Derby. A levels: English Language, Maths, Physics, Information Technology, French.
1995 – 1997: Pinewood School, Coventry. GCSEs: English Language, English Literature, Maths, Physics, Chemistry, Industrial Design, Geography, French.

WORK EXPERIENCE

2001 – 2002: running an Internet café in Mansfield.
Summer 1998 and 1999: Receptionist and switchboard operator at the Grand Hotel in Brighton.

INTERESTS AND OTHER QUALIFICATIONS

- Good working knowledge of numerous software packages.
- Languages: English (mother tongue), French (fluent), German and Spanish (basic knowledge).
- Enjoys travel, cinema, playing the guitar.

How to structure a letter of application

As a general rule, a letter of application should consist of three paragraphs:
- the first picks up the terms used in the job advertisement, *Vous cherchez* (*You are looking for*);
- the second describes your suitability as a candidate for the job, *Je suis celui/celle que vous cherchez* (*I am the person you are looking for*);
- the third unites the elements of the first two paragraphs, *Nous sommes faits pour nous entendre* (*We are ideally suited*).

The content of these letters varies according to the age and experience of the candidates.

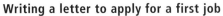

Writing a letter to apply for a first job

In this type of letter you need to make as much as possible of any experience acquired on work experience in companies or in other kinds of activities, for example in associations or clubs.

Je souhaite poser ma candidature au poste de programmeur en informatique annoncé dans « Le Monde » du 3 mars.
I would like to apply for the post of computer programmer advertised in "Le Monde" of 3rd March.

J'ai effectué plusieurs remplacements à ce type de poste pendant les vacances universitaires.
I have provided holiday cover for this type of post several times during university vacations.

J'ai créé le site Internet de mon groupe de jazz.
I set up the website for my jazz band.

En tant que président de l'association des anciens élèves de mon lycée, j'ai eu souvent l'occasion de prendre la parole en public.
As president of the Former Pupils' Association of my secondary school, I have often had the opportunity of speaking in public.

Don't be afraid of talking about your personal qualities:

Je suis organisé(e) et méthodique.
I am well-organized and methodical.

J'aime le travail en équipe.
I like working as part of a team.

Prendre des responsabilités ne me fait pas peur.
I am not afraid of responsibility.

J'ai le sens et le goût du contact.
I am a people person.

Explain the reasons why you are applying for the post in question:

Le poste que vous proposez me semble correspondre à ma formation et à mon expérience.
The post you are offering seems to match my training and experience.

Les possibilités d'évolution de carrière que vous évoquez correspondent parfaitement à mes propres aspirations.
The career development possibilities that you mention are exactly those I am looking for.

Try to appear motivated and available for interview:

Je suis à votre disposition pour vous rencontrer et vous fournir les renseignements complémentaires qui pourraient vous être utiles.
I would be happy to meet you at any time and provide you with any further information that might be useful to you.

J'aimerais avoir la possibilité de vous parler de vive voix de mes motivations professionnelles.
I would appreciate the opportunity of discussing with you in person my reasons for applying for this post.

Applying for work experience

If you are applying for work experience, it's likely that you don't have much professional experience on which to base your request for work. You can, nevertheless, concentrate on the qualities that you think you have that make you suitable for the type of work in question.

Madame la Directrice des ressources humaines,
Monsieur le Directeur des ressources humaines,
La formation que je suis actuellement à l'École de commerce d'Orléans porte principalement sur les techniques de marketing et sur les aspects logistiques de la distribution de biens de consommation. Je suis en deuxième année et je dois effectuer un stage de trois mois en entreprise.
Votre société m'a été vivement conseillée pour son dynamisme et sa créativité dans ces deux domaines et je souhaiterais être intégré à l'une de vos équipes de représentants pendant la durée de mon stage.
Comme vous le savez, ce stage doit être suivi d'un rapport qui pourrait intéresser vos services, dans la mesure où il proposerait un regard neuf, bien qu'inexpérimenté, sur une partie de vos activités.
En espérant que vous voudrez bien prendre ma demande en considération, je vous prie de recevoir, Madame la Directrice/Monsieur le Directeur, l'expression de mes respectueuses salutations.
Alexander Soames
P.J. CV

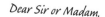

Dear Sir or Madam,

The course I am currently taking at the Orleans Business School deals principally with marketing techniques and the logistical aspects of consumer goods distribution. I am in my second year and am required to do three months' work experience within a relevant company.

Your company has been highly recommended to me for its dynamic and creative approach in these two fields and I would like to join one of your teams of sales representatives during the period of my work experience.

As you know, this work experience must be followed by a report, which might be of interest to your departments in that it would offer a fresh, although inexperienced, look at a part of your activities.

I hope that you will give my request serious consideration.

Yours faithfully,

Alexander Soames

Enc. CV

Job application

Speculative application

A speculative application is one possible way of applying for a job, but such letters are difficult to write, since your request for work does not correspond to any official advertisement. For this reason it is important to write a letter that gets you noticed, to emphasize your personal qualities and to show a certain amount of knowledge of the company you are applying to.

Ma formation et mon expérience professionnelle me situent exactement dans votre secteur d'activités.

My training and experience are ideally suited to your field of activities.

Le dynamisme bien connu de votre société et le développement actuel de vos activités me font penser que vous envisagez certainement d'augmenter vos effectifs.

Your company's well-known dynamism and the current expansion of your activities lead me to think that you must be considering recruiting new staff.

Replying to a job advertisement

If you use e-mail, you will have to use shorter sentences and more direct forms of expression. For example:

> En réponse à votre annonce sur le site emploi.fr, je vous prie de trouver ici ma candidature au poste de webmaster. En pièce jointe, mon CV ainsi qu'une liste de liens vers les sites pour lesquels j'ai déjà travaillé.

> I would like to apply for the post of webmaster as advertised on the "emploi.fr" website. I am attaching a copy of my CV and a list of links to the websites I have worked on.

> J'ai vu sur votre site que vous cherchiez des assistants pendant les mois d'été. Cette possibilité m'intéresse, je vous envoie donc mon CV. Vous pouvez me joindre par courrier électronique. Je suis disponible pour un entretien si vous le souhaitez.

> I have seen on your website that you are looking for assistants for the summer months. This job opportunity interests me, so I am sending you my CV. You can contact me by e-mail. I am available for interview if you are interested in meeting me.

Writing an advertisement

There are two kinds of advertisement: those that are asking for goods or services and those that are offering them. These advertisements are found in some newspapers or in shops. There are also free newspapers that specialize in advertisements. These are often available at newsstands, in the underground in big cities, at the entrance to supermarkets, etc.
The advertisements are written in a telegraphic style, often with abbreviations, and must give the advertiser's details clearly.

Examples of offers of goods or services:

> *Étudiant en médecine garde enfants le soir à partir de 20 heures*
> *Medical student available for baby-sitting, evenings from 8 p.m.*
>
> *Jeune fille, maîtrise de Maths, donne cours particuliers de la 6e à la Terminale. Tél : 06 08 40 00 00 (le soir)*
> *Young female Maths graduate offers private tutition. Secondary school to A level. Tel: 06 08 40 00 00 (eves.)*
>
> *Vends réfrigérateur bon état, avec compartiment congélation. 150 euros, à débattre. Tél : 02 18 53 64 75 (le matin)*
> *For sale: fridge, in good condition, with freezer compartment. 150 euros o.n.o. Tel: 02 18 53 64 75 (mornings)*

Examples of requests for goods or services:

> *Mère de famille cherche aide ménagère 6 heures/semaine*
> *Mother seeks home help: 6 hrs per wk*
>
> *Jeune femme à mobilité réduite cherche formation informatique à domicile. Pas sérieux s'abstenir. Tél : 02 15 36 57 78 (le matin)*
> *Young woman with restricted mobility seeks computer training at home. No time-wasters. Tel: 02 15 36 57 78 (mornings)*
>
> *Étudiant français échangerait heures de conversation en anglais contre heures de conversation en français, dans perspective bourse Erasmus à Manchester. Tél : 05 45 36 77 88*
> *French student seeks conversation exchange with English speaker with view to ERASMUS scholarship in Manchester. Tel: 05 45 36 77 88*

On the telephone

Making and answering telephone calls

If you call a friend at home, you can use the following phrases:

Allô Marc ? C'est Vicky.
Hello, Marc? It's Vicky.

Allô c'est toi David ? Stephen à l'appareil.
Hello, is that you, David? It's Stephen here.

Salut, c'est Joe. Est-ce qu'Anne est là ?
Hi, it's Joe. Is Anne there?

Bonjour, c'est Martin. Je voudrais parler à Lise, s'il vous plaît.
Good morning, it's Martin. I'd like to speak to Lise, please.

Bonjour, puis-je parler à Philip, s'il vous plaît. C'est de la part de Nicolas.
Good morning, can I speak to Philip, please. It's Nicolas calling.

! Note that when you're telephoning someone in France, you should always introduce yourself. Saying your first name and surname is enough. So, if John Carter is telephoning a friend, he'll say: *Allô, John Carter. Charles ?* Remember that it is considered bad manners not to give your name. If you don't do it without prompting, before anything else you'll probably be asked *Who's speaking?* with expressions like *Qui est à l'appareil ?* or *C'est de la part de qui ?*

Answering

Allô ?
Hello?

Answering someone who is asking for you

Jean Lambert ?
C'est moi./C'est lui-même./Lui-même.

Jean Lambert?
Speaking./This is he (US).

Here is an example of a telephone conversation:

Linda *Allô, est-ce que je pourrais parler à Jean, s'il vous plaît ?*
Jean *C'est moi.*
Linda *Bonjour Jean. C'est Linda.*
Jean *Linda, quelle bonne surprise ! Comment vas-tu ?*
Linda *Très bien. Écoute, je te téléphone pour savoir...*

Linda *Hello, could I speak to Jean, please?*
Jean *Speaking.*
Linda *Hello, Jean. It's Linda.*
Jean *Linda, what a nice surprise! How are you?*
Linda *Very well, thanks. Listen, I'm calling to find out...*

Transferring a call

If the person who answers isn't the person you want, they'll say:

Ne quittez pas, je vous passe madame/monsieur Verdier.
Hold on. I'll put you through to Ms/Mr Verdier.

Un moment, s'il vous plaît. Je vais vous le/la passer.
One moment, please. I'll put you through to him/her.

C'est de la part de qui, s'il vous plaît ?
Who's calling, please?

Ne quittez pas, je vous passe son poste.
Hold on. I'll put you through to his/her extension.

If you want to ask the person who answers to give a message to the person you wanted to speak to, you can say:

Pourriez-vous lui transmettre/laisser un message ?
Could you give/leave her a message?

Pourriez-vous lui demander de me rappeler ? Elle a mon numéro mais je vais vous le redonner.
Could you ask her to call me back? She has my number, but I'll give it to you again.

Pourriez-vous lui dire de m'appeler au 07 32 25 48 69 ?
Could you tell her to call me on 07 32 25 48 69?

Pourriez-vous lui dire que j'ai appelé ?
Could you tell her that I called?

Problems during a telephone call

You may get a bad connection, especially with a mobile call. Here are some expressions for asking the person you're talking to to repeat or explain something you haven't understood.

Excusez-moi, je ne vous entends pas bien. La communication est mauvaise.
Sorry, I can't hear you very well. It's a bad line.

Je n'entends rien, est-ce que tu peux me rappeler sur mon fixe ?
I can't hear anything. Can you call me back on my land line?

Pourriez-vous répéter, s'il vous plaît ?
Could you repeat that, please?

Pourriez-vous épeler votre nom, s'il vous plaît ?
Could you spell your name, please?

Pardon, pourriez-vous me répéter votre adresse, mais plus lentement s'il vous plaît ?
Sorry, could you repeat your address, more slowly this time, please?

C'est B comme Bruno ou P comme Pascal ?
Is it B for Bob or P for Peter?

If it's the wrong number

If you're calling

Excusez-moi, j'ai fait un mauvais numéro.
Sorry, I've dialled the wrong number.
Excusez-moi, je me suis trompé de numéro.
Sorry, I've got the wrong number.
Excusez-moi, c'est une erreur.
Sorry, wrong number.

If you're answering

Désolé, vous avez dû faire un mauvais numéro.
Sorry, you must have dialled the wrong number.
Je regrette, il n'y a personne de ce nom ici. Êtes-vous sûr d'avoir composé le bon numéro ?
I'm sorry, there's no one here of that name. Are you sure you dialled the right number?

Finishing a telephone conversation

To finish the conversation and say goodbye you can use one of the following ways:

Merci de votre appel/coup de téléphone. À bientôt.
Thanks for calling. Speak to you soon.
Puis-je vous rappeler plus tard ? On sonne à ma porte.
Can I call you back later? There's someone at the door.
Excusez-moi, il faut que je vous laisse. On m'appelle sur une autre ligne.
Sorry, I've got to go. There's someone on the other line.
Il faut que je te laisse sinon je vais être en retard chez le dentiste.
I've got to go or I'm going to be late for the dentist.

Mobile phones

Allô, où es-tu ? J'entends très mal.
Hello, where are you? I can hardly hear you.
Allô, je vous/t'appelle de mon portable.
Hello, I'm calling you on my mobile.
Je ne capte plus, je te rappelle.
You're breaking up. I'll call you back.
La communication est trop mauvaise, je te rappelle de la maison.
The signal's too weak. I'll call you back from home.
Si ça coupe, je te rappelle.
If we get cut off, I'll call you back.
Si tu allumais ton portable de temps en temps. J'en ai assez de tomber sur ta messagerie.
I wish you'd switch on your mobile once in a while. I'm fed up getting your voicemail.
Allô, je n'ai plus de batterie. Rappelle-moi sur mon fixe.
Hello, my battery's going. Call me back on my land line.

Answering machines

Understanding the message on an answering machine

Bonjour, vous êtes bien au 02 86 32 47 59. Nous ne sommes pas là mais si vous laissez votre nom et votre numéro de téléphone, nous vous rappellerons dès que possible.

Hello, this is 02 86 32 47 59. We're not in at the moment, but if you leave your name and number, we'll get back to you as soon as possible.

Vous n'avez pas de chance, je ne suis pas chez moi. Laissez-moi vos coordonnées. Je vous rappellerai dès que possible.

You're out of luck. I'm not in. Leave your details and I'll get back to you as soon as I can.

Leaving a message

When you leave a message, it's important to speak clearly and repeat your telephone number at least once.

Bonjour, monsieur Lautrec. C'est Jane Peterson de la société Logicom. Pourriez-vous me rappeler au 06 03 12 16 27, je répète 06 03 12 16 27, pour que nous puissions convenir d'un rendez-vous ? Merci.

Good morning, Mr Lautrec. It's Jane Peterson from Logicom. Could you call me on 06 03 12 16 27, that's 06 03 12 16 27, so that we can arrange a meeting? Thank you.

Bonjour Nicolas. C'est Mark. Est-ce qu'Anne et toi voudriez venir dîner chez nous ce vendredi vers 20 h ? Rappelle-moi à la maison pour me dire si ça vous va. Salut.

Hello Nicolas. It's Mark. Would you and Anne like to come to dinner at our place this Friday at about 8 o'clock? Call me at home to let me know if that suits you. Bye.

E-mail

Writing an e-mail

The header of a message consists of a series of sections: *De (From)* refers to the address of the sender, while *à (To)* refers to the address of the person the e-mail is sent to, *Cc* (*Cc*) refers to the addresses of other people that the e-mail is sent to. *Bcc* (*Cci*) refers to the addresses of other people that the e-mail is sent to without the other addressees knowing. *Objet* (*Subject*), which is optional and says what the message is about. *Pièces jointes* (*Attachments*) refers to a file or files sent as an attachment to the e-mail.

Standard ways of starting and ending e-mails

It isn't always necessary to start an e-mail with a standard greeting. The following are commonly used in messages between friends:

Bonjour Éric,
Hello Éric,

Salut (les amis)
Hi

Cher Denis/Chère Marion
Dear Denis/Dear Marion

To end an e-mail you can use:

(Meilleures) Salutations
(Best) Regards

Cordialement
Best wishes

À bientôt
See you soon

Salut
Bye

Bises/Bisous
Love

Here is an e-mail thanking someone for their hospitality:

À: Marie et Patrick
Date: mardi 25 juillet 15:36
Objet : un week-end de rêve
Merci pour ce bon moment de détente, de soleil, de rigolade et de bonne cuisine ; la prochaine fois ce sera chez nous.
Paul et Christine

To: Marie and Patrick
Date: Tuesday 25 July 15:36
Subject: a wonderful weekend
Thanks for last weekend. We had a great time relaxing in the sun and the food was excellent. Next time, you come to us.
Paul and Christine

Text messages

Sending a text message

Here are some examples of text messages written in an abbreviated form:

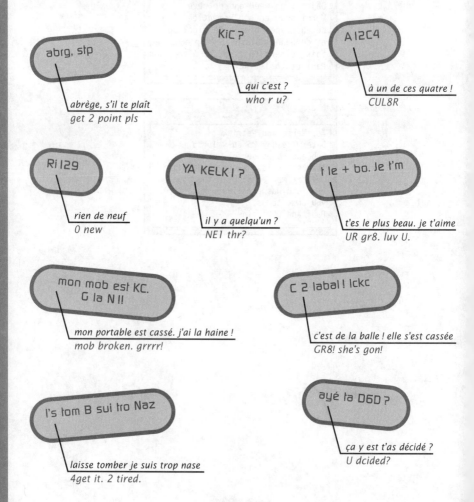

abrg, stp
abrège, s'il te plaît
get 2 point pls

KiC ?
qui c'est ?
who r u?

A12C4
à un de ces quatre !
CUL8R

Ri129
rien de neuf
0 new

YA KELKI ?
il y a quelqu'un ?
NE1 thr?

t le + bo. Je t'm
t'es le plus beau. je t'aime
UR gr8. luv U.

mon mob est KC. G la N!!
mon portable est cassé. j'ai la haine !
mob broken. grrrr!

C 2 labal ! lckc
c'est de la balle ! elle s'est cassée
GR8! she's gon!

l's tom B sui tro Naz
laisse tomber je suis trop nase
4get it. 2 tired.

ayé ta D6D ?
ça y est t'as décidé ?
U dcided?

t ou ?

t'es où ?
whr RU?

ght le p1 rentr asap

j'ai acheté le pain, je rentre dès que possible
got brd. b hom asap

kestufé ?

qu'est-ce que tu fais ?
what are you doing?

g talan tjs au resto

je t'attends toujours au restaurant
I'm still waiting for you at the restaurant

koi 2 9

quoi de neuf ?
what's new?

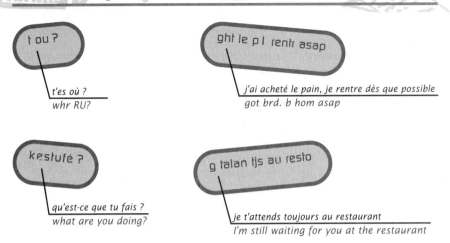

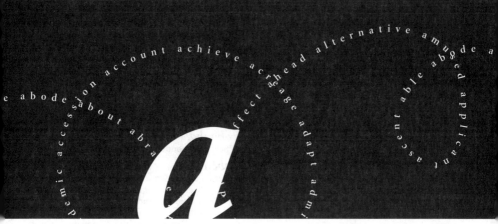

a [1] (pl a's), ***A*** (pl A's *OR* As) [eɪ] n [letter] a *m inv*, A *m inv* ▸ **to get from A to B** aller d'un point à un autre ▸ **from A to Z** de A à Z, depuis A jusqu'à Z.
◆ ***A*** n **1.** MUS la *m inv* **2.** SCH [mark] A *m inv*.

a [2] *(weak form* [ə]*, strong form* [eɪ]*, before vowel or silent 'h'* **an** *weak form* [ən]*, strong form* [æn]*)* **indef art 1.** [gen] un (une) ▸ **a boy** un garçon ▸ **a table** une table ▸ **an orange** une orange ▸ **I can't see a thing** je ne vois rien
2. [referring to occupation] **: to be a doctor/lawyer/plumber** être médecin/avocat/plombier ▸ **have you seen a doctor?** as-tu vu un médecin?
3. [before numbers, quantities] un (une) ▸ **a hundred/thousand pounds** cent/mille livres ▸ **a dozen eggs** une douzaine d'œufs ▸ **an hour and a half** une heure et demie ▸ **a few weeks/months** quelques semaines/mois ▸ **a lot of money** beaucoup d'argent
4. [to express prices, ratios] **: 20p a kilo** 20p le kilo ▸ **£10 a person** 10 livres par personne ▸ **twice a week/month** deux fois par semaine/mois ▸ **50 km an hour** 50 km à l'heure
5. [preceding person's name] un certain (une certaine) ▸ **a Mr Jones** un certain M. Jones
6. [after half, rather, such, what] **: half a glass of wine** un demi-verre de vin ▸ **what a lovely dress!** quelle jolie robe!

a. abbr of ***acre***.

A-1 adj *inf* excellent(e).

A4 n *UK* format *m* A4.

AA ▪ adj abbr of ***antiaircraft***.
▪ n **1.** (abbr of ***Automobile Association***) *automobile club britannique*, ≃ ACF *m*, ≃ TCF *m* **2.** (abbr of ***Associate in Arts***) *diplôme universitaire américain de lettres* **3.** (abbr of ***Alcoholics Anonymous***) Alcooliques Anonymes *mpl*.

AAA n **1.** (abbr of ***Amateur Athletics Association***) *fédération britannique d'athlétisme* **2.** (abbr of ***American Automobile Association***) *automobile club américain*, ≃ ACF *m*, ≃ TCF *m*.

aardvark ['ɑːdvɑːk] n oryctérope *m*.

aargh [æː] excl aargh!

AAUP (abbr of ***American Association of University Professors***) n *syndicat universitaire américain des professeurs d'université*.

AB [1] n *US* abbr of ***Bachelor of Arts***.

AB [2] abbr of ***Alberta***.

aback [ə'bæk] **adv : to be taken aback** être décontenancé(e).

abacus ['æbəkəs] (pl **-cuses** [-kəsiːz] *OR* **-ci** [-saɪ]) n boulier *m*, abaque *m*.

abandon [ə'bændən] ▪ vt abandonner ▸ **to abandon ship** abandonner *OR* quitter le navire ▸ **the match was abandoned because of bad weather** on a interrompu le match en raison du mauvais temps.
▪ **n : with abandon** avec abandon.

abandoned [ə'bændənd] **adj** abandonné(e).

abandonment [ə'bændənmənt] **n 1.** [of place, person, project] abandon *m* **2.** [of right] cession *f*.

abashed [ə'bæʃt] **adj** confus(e).

abate [ə'beɪt] **vi** [storm, fear] se calmer / [noise] faiblir.

abatement [ə'beɪtmənt] **n 1.** [of tax, rent] réduction *f*, abattement *m* **2.** [of noise, strength] diminution *f*, réduction *f*.

abattoir ['æbətwɑːʳ] **n** abattoir *m*.

abbess ['æbes] **n** abbesse *f*.

abbey ['æbɪ] **n** abbaye *f*.

abbot ['æbət] **n** abbé *m*.

abbreviate [ə'briːvɪeɪt] **vt** abréger.

abbreviated [ə'briːvɪeɪtɪd] **adj** abrégé(e).

abbreviation [əˌbriːvɪ'eɪʃn] **n** abréviation *f*.

ABC **n 1.** [alphabet] alphabet *m* **2.** *fig* [basics] B.A.-Ba *m*, abc *m* **3.** (abbr of ***American Broadcasting Company***) *chaîne de télévision américaine*.

abdicate ['æbdɪkeɪt] **vt & vi** abdiquer.

abdication [ˌæbdɪ'keɪʃn] **n** abdication *f*.

abdomen ['æbdəmən] **n** abdomen *m*.

abdominal [æb'dɒmɪnl] **adj** abdominal(e).

abduct [əb'dʌkt] **vt** enlever.

abduction [æb'dʌkʃn] **n** enlèvement *m*.

abductor [əb'dʌktəʳ] **n 1.** [of person] ravisseur *m*, -euse *f* **2.** [muscle] (muscle *m*) abducteur *m*.

aberration [ˌæbə'reɪʃn] **n** aberration *f*.

abet [ə'bet] (pt & pp **-ted**, cont **-ting**) **vt** ➤ ***aid***.

abeyance [ə'beɪəns] **n** : **in abeyance** en attente.

abhor [əb'hɔːʳ] (pt & pp **-red**, cont **-ring**) **vt** exécrer, abhorrer.

abhorrence [əb'hɒrəns] **n** *fml* aversion *f*, horreur *f* ▸ **to have an abhorrence of sthg** avoir horreur de qqch *OR* une aversion pour qqch, avoir qqch en horreur.

abhorrent [əb'hɒrənt] **adj** répugnant(e).

abide [ə'baɪd] **vt** supporter, souffrir.
◆ ***abide by*** **vt insep** respecter, se soumettre à.

abiding [ə'baɪdɪŋ] **adj** [lasting - feeling, interest] constant(e) / [- memory] éternel(elle), impérissable.

ability [ə'bɪlətɪ] (pl **-ies**) **n 1.** [capacity, capability] aptitude *f* ▸ **children at different levels of ability/of different abilities** des enfants de niveaux intellectuels différents/aux compétences diverses ▸ **to do sthg to the best of one's ability** faire qqch de son mieux **2.** [skill] talent *m*.

abject ['æbdʒekt] **adj 1.** [poverty] noir(e) **2.** [person] pitoyable / [apology] servile.

ablaze [ə'bleɪz] **adj 1.** [on fire] en feu **2.** *fig* [bright] : **to be ablaze with** être resplendissant(e) de.

able ['eɪbl] **adj 1.** [capable] : **to be able to do sthg** pouvoir faire qqch ▸ **I wasn't able to see** je ne voyais pas **2.** [accomplished] compétent(e).

able-bodied [-ˌbɒdɪd] **adj** en bonne santé, valide.

ablutions [ə'bluːʃnz] **npl** *fml* ablutions *fpl*.

ably ['eɪblɪ] **adv** avec compétence, habilement.

ABM (abbr of ***anti-ballistic missile***) **n** ABM *m*.

abnormal [æb'nɔːml] **adj** anormal(e).

abnormality [ˌæbnɔː'mælətɪ] (pl **-ies**) **n 1.** [gen] anomalie *f* **2.** [abnormal state, condition] anormalité *f* **3.** MED malformation *f*.

abnormally [æb'nɔːməlɪ] **adv** anormalement.

aboard [ə'bɔːd] ■ **adv** à bord.
■ **prep** [ship, plane] à bord de / [bus, train] dans.

abode [ə'bəʊd] **n** *fml* : **of no fixed abode** sans domicile fixe.

abolish [ə'bɒlɪʃ] **vt** abolir.

abolition [ˌæbə'lɪʃn] **n** abolition *f*.

A-bomb (abbr of ***atom bomb***) **n** bombe *f* atomique.

abominable [ə'bɒmɪnəbl] **adj** abominable.

abominable snowman **n** : **the abominable snowman** l'abominable homme *m* des neiges.

abominably [ə'bɒmɪnəblɪ] **adv** abominablement.

abomination [əˌbɒmɪ'neɪʃn] **n 1.** *fml* [loathing] abomination *f* ▸ **we hold such behaviour in abomination** ce genre de comportement nous fait horreur *OR* nous horrifie **2.** *fml* [detestable act] abomination *f*, acte *m* abominable **3.** [awful thing] abomination *f*, chose *f* abominable.

aboriginal [ˌæbə'rɪdʒənl] **adj 1.** [culture, legend] aborigène, des aborigènes **2.** BOT & ZOOL aborigène.
◆ ***Aboriginal*** **adj** aborigène, des aborigènes.

aborigine [ˌæbə'rɪdʒənɪ] **n** aborigène *mf* d'Australie.

abort [ə'bɔːt] ■ **vt 1.** [pregnancy] interrompre **2.** *fig* [plan, project] abandonner, faire avorter **3.** COMPUT abandonner.
■ **vi** COMPUT abandonner.

abortion [ə'bɔːʃn] **n** avortement *m*, interruption *f* (volontaire) de grossesse ▸ **to have an abortion** se faire avorter.

abortive [ə'bɔːtɪv] **adj** manqué(e).

abound [ə'baʊnd] **vi 1.** [be plentiful] abonder **2.** [be full] : **to abound with** *OR* **in** abonder en.

about [ə'baʊt] ■ **adv 1.** [approximately] environ, à peu près ▸ **about fifty/a hundred/a thousand** environ cinquante/cent/mille ▸ **at about five o'clock** vers cinq heures ▸ **I'm just about ready** je suis presque prêt ▸ **it's about time you started** il serait grand temps que vous vous y mettiez ▸ **I've had just about enough!** j'en ai vraiment assez!
2. [referring to place] : **to run about** courir çà et là ▸ **to leave things lying about** laisser traîner des affaires ▸ **to walk about** aller et venir, se promener ▸ **is there anyone about?** il y a quelqu'un? ▸ **there's a lot of flu about** il y a beaucoup de grippe en ce moment ▸ **stop fooling about!** *inf* arrête de faire l'imbécile!
3. [on the point of] : **to be about to do sthg** être sur le point de faire qqch ▸ **I was just about to leave** j'allais partir, j'étais sur le point de partir.
■ **prep 1.** [relating to, concerning] au sujet de ▸ **a film about Paris** un film sur Paris ▸ **what is it about?** de quoi s'agit-il? ▸ **I'm worried about her** je suis inquiet à son sujet ▸ **there's no doubt about it** cela ne fait aucun doute il n'y a aucun doute là-dessus ▸ **to talk about sthg** parler de qqch ▸ **she asked me about my mother** elle m'a demandé des nouvelles de ma mère ▸ **what do you want to see me about?** vous voulez me voir à quel sujet? ▸ **I can't do anything about it** je n'y peux rien ▸ **what do you think about modern art?** que pensez-vous de l'art moderne? ▸ **I was thinking about my father** je pensais à mon père ▸ **what I like about her is her generosity** ce que j'aime en *OR* chez elle, c'est sa générosité
2. [referring to place] : **his belongings were scattered about the room** ses affaires étaient éparpillées dans toute la pièce ▸ **to wander about the streets** errer de par les rues
3. [busy with] : **while I'm about it** pendant que j'y suis ▸ **be quick about it!** faites vite!, dépêchez-vous!

about-turn UK, ***about-face*** US **n 1.** MIL demi-tour *m* / *fig* volte-face *f inv* **2.** POL revirement *m*.

above [ə'bʌv] ■ **adv 1.** [on top, higher up] au-dessus ▸ **the people in the flat above** les voisins du dessus ▸ **to fall from above** tomber d'en haut **2.** [in text] ci-dessus, plus haut ▸ **two lines above** deux lignes plus haut **3.** [more, over] plus ▸ **children aged 5 and above** les enfants âgés de 5 ans et plus *OR* de plus de 5 ans **4.** [a higher rank or authority] en haut ▸ **we've had orders from above** nous avons reçu des ordres d'en haut.
■ **prep 1.** [on top of, higher up than] au-dessus de ▸ **they live above the shop** ils habitent au-dessus du magasin ▸ **above ground** en surface **2.** [more than] plus de ▸ **it's above my price limit** c'est au-dessus du prix *OR* ça dépasse le prix que je me suis fixé ▸ **he values friendship above success** il accorde plus d'importance à l'amitié qu'à la réussite **3.** [too good for] : **to be above doing sthg** ne p

s'abaisser à faire qqch ▸ **above suspicion/reproach** au-dessus de tout soupçon/reproche **4.** [higher in rank, quality than] au-dessus de ▸ **she's ranked above the other athletes** elle se classe devant les autres athlètes.
◆ ***above all*** **adv** avant tout.

aboveboard [əˌbʌv'bɔːd] **adj** honnête.

above-mentioned [-'menʃnd] *fml* ■ **adj** cité(e) plus haut, susmentionné(e).
■ **n** (pl **above-mentioned**) **: the above-mentioned** [person] le susmentionné, la susmentionnée.

above-named *fml* ■ **adj** susnommé(e).
■ **n** (pl **above-named**) **: the above-named** le susnommé, la susnommée.

above-the-line **adj** FIN [expenses] au-dessus de la ligne.

above-the-line accounts **n** comptes *mpl* de résultats courants.

above-the-line costs, ***above-the-line expenditure*** **n** dépenses *fpl* de création, dépenses *fpl* au-dessus de la ligne.

abracadabra [ˌæbrəkə'dæbrə] **excl** abracadabra!

abrasion [ə'breɪʒn] **n** *fml* [on skin] écorchure *f*, égratignure *f*.

abrasive [ə'breɪsɪv] ■ **adj** [substance] abrasif(ive) / *fig* caustique, acerbe.
■ **n** abrasif *m*.

abreast [ə'brest] **adv** de front, côte à côte.
◆ ***abreast of*** **prep : to keep abreast of** se tenir au courant de.

abridge [ə'brɪdʒ] **vt** [book] abréger / [article, play, speech] écourter, abréger.

abridged [ə'brɪdʒd] **adj** abrégé(e).

abroad [ə'brɔːd] **adv** à l'étranger.

abrupt [ə'brʌpt] **adj 1.** [sudden] soudain(e), brusque **2.** [brusque] abrupt(e).

abruptly [ə'brʌptlɪ] **adv 1.** [suddenly] brusquement **2.** [brusquely] abruptement.

ABS (abbr of ***Anti-lock braking system***) **n** ABS *m*.

abscess ['æbses] **n** abcès *m*.

abscond [əb'skɒnd] **vi** s'enfuir.

abseil ['æbseɪl] **vi** *UK* descendre en rappel.

absence ['æbsəns] **n** absence *f* ▸ **in the absence of** [thing] faute de.

absent ['æbsənt] **adj : absent (from)** absent(e) (de) ▸ **to be absent without leave** MIL être en absence irrégulière.

absentee [ˌæbsən'tiː] **n** absent *m*, -e *f*.

absenteeism [ˌæbsən'tiːɪzm] **n** absentéisme *m*.

absent-minded [-'maɪndɪd] **adj** distrait(e).

absent-mindedly [-'maɪndɪdlɪ] **adv** distraitement.

absent-mindedness [-'maɪndɪdnɪs] **n** distraction *f*, absence *f*.

absinth(e) ['æbsɪnθ] **n** absinthe *f*.

absolute ['æbsəluːt] **adj 1.** [complete - fool, disgrace] complet(ète) ▸ **what absolute nonsense!** quelles bêtises, vraiment! **2.** [totalitarian - ruler, power] absolu(e).

absolutely ['æbsə'luːtlɪ] **adv** absolument.

absolute majority **n** majorité *f* absolue.

absolution [ˌæbsə'luːʃn] **n** absolution *f*.

absolve [əb'zɒlv] **vt : to absolve sb (from)** absoudre qqn (de).

absorb [əb'zɔːb] **vt** [gen] absorber / [information] retenir, assimiler ▸ **to be absorbed in sthg** être absorbé(e) dans qqch.

absorbency [əb'sɔːbənsɪ] **n** [gen] pouvoir *m* absorbant / CHEM & PHYS absorptivité *f*.

absorbent [əb'zɔːbənt] **adj** absorbant(e).

absorbing [əb'zɔːbɪŋ] **adj** captivant(e).

absorption [əb'zɔːpʃn] **n** absorption *f*.

abstain [əb'steɪn] **vi : to abstain (from)** s'abstenir (de).

abstainer [əb'steɪnəʳ] **n 1.** [teetotaller] abstinent *m*, -e *f* **2.** [person not voting] abstentionniste *mf*.

abstemious [æb'stiːmjəs] **adj** *fml* frugal(e), sobre.

abstention [əb'stenʃn] **n** abstention *f*.

abstinence ['æbstɪnəns] **n** abstinence *f*.

abstract ■ **adj** ['æbstrækt] abstrait(e).
■ **n** ['æbstrækt] [summary] résumé *m*, abrégé *m*.
■ **vt** [æb'strækt] [summarize] résumer.

abstraction [æb'strækʃn] **n 1.** [distractedness] distraction *f* **2.** [abstract idea] abstraction *f*.

abstruse [æb'struːs] **adj** abstrus(e).

absurd [əb'sɜːd] **adj** absurde.

absurdity [əb'sɜːdətɪ] (pl **-ies**) **n** absurdité *f*.

absurdly [əb'sɜːdlɪ] **adv** absurdement.

ABTA ['æbtə] (abbr of ***Association of British Travel Agents***) **n** *association des agences de voyage britanniques*.

Abu Dhabi [ˌæbuː'dɑːbɪ] **n** Abou Dhabi.

abundance [ə'bʌndəns] **n** abondance *f* ▸ **in abundance** en abondance.

abundant [ə'bʌndənt] **adj** abondant(e).

abundantly [ə'bʌndəntlɪ] **adv 1.** [clear, obvious] parfaitement, tout à fait **2.** [exist, grow] en abondance.

abuse ■ **n** [ə'bjuːs] *(U)* **1.** [offensive remarks] insultes *fpl*, injures *fpl* **2.** [maltreatment] mauvais traitement *m* ▸ **child abuse** mauvais traitements infligés aux enfants ▸ **physical abuse** sévices *mpl* corporels ▸ **sexual abuse** abus *mpl* sexuels **3.** [of power, drugs] abus *m*.
■ **vt** [ə'bjuːz] **1.** [insult] insulter, injurier **2.** [maltreat] maltraiter **3.** [power, drugs] abuser de.

abuse of privilege **n** POL abus *m* de droit.

abuser [ə'bjuːzəʳ] **n 1.** [gen] **: abusers of the system** ceux qui profitent du système **2.** [of child] *personne qui a maltraité un enfant physiquement ou psychologiquement* **3.** [of drugs] **: (drug) abuser** drogué *m*, -e *f*.

abusive [ə'bjuːsɪv] **adj** grossier(ère), injurieux(euse).

abusively [ə'bjuːsɪvlɪ] **adv 1.** [speak, write] de façon offensante, grossièrement **2.** [behave, treat] brutalement **3.** [use] abusivement.

abut [ə'bʌt] (pt & pp **-ted**, cont **-ting**) **vi** [adjoin] **: to abut on to** être contigu(ë) à.

abysmal [ə'bɪzml] **adj** épouvantable, abominable.

abysmally [ə'bɪzməlɪ] adv abominablement.

abyss [ə'bɪs] n abîme *m*, gouffre *m*.

Abyssinia [ˌæbɪ'sɪnjə] n Abyssinie *f* ▸ **in Abyssinia** en Abyssinie.

Abyssinian [ˌæbɪ'sɪnɪən] ■ adj abyssinien(enne).
■ n Abyssinien *m*, -enne *f*.

a/c (abbr of ***account (current)***) cc.

AC n 1. *UK* (abbr of ***athletics club***) *club d'athlétisme* 2. (abbr of ***alternating current***) courant *m* alternatif.

acacia [ə'keɪʃə] n acacia *m*.

academic [ˌækə'demɪk] ■ adj 1. [of college, university] universitaire 2. [person] intellectuel(elle) 3. [question, discussion] théorique ▸ **out of academic interest** par simple curiosité.
■ n universitaire *mf*.

academic year n année *f* scolaire OR universitaire.

academy [ə'kædəmɪ] (pl -ies) n 1. [school, college] école *f* ▸ **academy of music** conservatoire *m* 2. [institution, society] académie *f*.

ACAS ['eɪkæs] (abbr of ***Advisory Conciliation and Arbitration Service***) n *organisme britannique de conciliation des conflits du travail*.

accede [æk'si:d] vi 1. [agree] : **to accede to** agréer, donner suite à 2. [monarch] : **to accede to the throne** monter sur le trône.

accelerate [ək'seləreɪt] vi 1. [car, driver] accélérer 2. [inflation, growth] s'accélérer.

accelerated depreciation [əkˌselə'reɪtɪd-] n FIN amortissement *m* dégressif OR accéléré.

acceleration [əkˌselə'reɪʃn] n accélération *f*.

accelerator [ək'seləreɪtəʳ] n accélérateur *m*.

accelerator board, ***accelerator card*** n COMPUT carte *f* accélérateur OR accélératrice.

accent ['æksent] n accent *m*.

accentuate [æk'sentjʊeɪt] vt accentuer.

accept [ək'sept] vt 1. [gen] accepter / [for job, as member of club] recevoir, admettre ▸ **he proposed and she accepted (him)** il la demanda en mariage et elle accepta ▸ **the machine only accepts coins** la machine n'accepte que les pièces ▸ **she's been accepted at** OR *US* **to Harvard** elle a été admise à Harvard 2. [agree] : **to accept that...** admettre que...

acceptable [ək'septəbl] adj acceptable.

Acceptable Use Policy n COMPUT *code de conduite défini par un fournisseur d'accès à l'Internet*.

acceptably [ək'septəblɪ] adv convenablement.

acceptance [ək'septəns] n 1. [gen] acceptation *f* ▸ **the idea is gaining acceptance** l'idée fait son chemin 2. [for job, as member of club] admission *f*.

accepted [ək'septɪd] adj [ideas, fact] reconnu(e).

access ['ækses] ■ n 1. [entry, way in] accès *m* ▸ **to gain access to** avoir accès à 2. [opportunity to use, see] : **to have access to sthg** avoir qqch à sa disposition, disposer de qqch.
■ vt COMPUT avoir accès à.

access code n COMPUT code *m* d'accès.

accessibility [əkˌsesə'bɪlətɪ] n 1. [of place] accessibilité *f* 2. [availability] accès *m*.

accessible [ək'sesəbl] adj 1. [reachable - place] accessible 2. [available] disponible.

accession [æk'seʃn] n [of monarch] accession *f*.

access number n COMPUT [to ISP] numéro *m* d'accès.

accessorize, ***-ise*** *UK* [ək'sesəraɪz] vt accessoiriser.

accessory [ək'sesərɪ] (pl -ies) n 1. [for car, vacuum cleaner] accessoire *m* 2. LAW complice *mf* 3. COMPUT accessoire *m*.
◆ ***accessories*** npl accessoires *mpl*.

access road n [to motorway] bretelle *f* de raccordement OR d'accès.

access time n COMPUT temps *m* d'accès.

accident ['æksɪdənt] n accident *m* ▸ **accident and emergency department** *UK* (service *m* des) urgences *fpl* ▸ **by accident** par hasard, par accident.

accidental [ˌæksɪ'dentl] adj accidentel(elle).

accidentally [ˌæksɪ'dentəlɪ] adv 1. [drop, break] par mégarde 2. [meet] par hasard.

accident-prone adj prédisposé(e) aux accidents.

acclaim [ə'kleɪm] ■ n *(U)* éloges *mpl*.
■ vt louer.

acclamation [ˌæklə'meɪʃn] *(U)* n acclamation *f*.

acclimatization *UK*, ***-isation*** *UK* [əˌklaɪmətaɪ'zeɪʃn], *US* ***acclimation*** [ˌæklə'meɪʃn] n [to climate] acclimatation *f* / [to conditions, customs] accoutumance *f*, acclimatement *m*.

acclimatize *UK*, *UK* ***-ise*** [ə'klaɪmətaɪz], *US* ***acclimate*** ['ækləmeɪt] vi : **to acclimatize (to)** s'acclimater (à).

accolade ['ækəleɪd] n accolade *f* ▸ **the ultimate accolade** la consécration suprême.

accommodate [ə'kɒmədeɪt] vt 1. [provide room for] loger ▸ **the cottage accommodates up to six people** dans la villa, on peut loger jusqu'à six (personnes) 2. [oblige - person, wishes] satisfaire.

accommodating [ə'kɒmədeɪtɪŋ] adj obligeant(e).

accommodation [əˌkɒmə'deɪʃn] n *UK* logement *m* ▸ **office accommodation** bureaux *mpl*.

accommodations [əˌkɒmə'deɪʃnz] npl *US* = ***accommodation***.

accompaniment [ə'kʌmpənɪmənt] n MUS accompagnement *m*.

accompanist [ə'kʌmpənɪst] n MUS accompagnateur *m*, -trice *f*.

accompany [ə'kʌmpənɪ] (pt & pp -ied) vt 1. [gen] accompagner 2. MUS : **to accompany sb (on)** accompagner qqn (à).

accompanying [ə'kʌmpənɪɪŋ] adj : **the accompanying documents** les documents ci-joints ▸ **children will not be allowed in without an accompanying adult** l'entrée est interdite aux enfants non accompagnés.

accomplice [ə'kʌmplɪs] n complice *mf*.

accomplish [ə'kʌmplɪʃ] vt accomplir.

accomplished [ə'kʌmplɪʃt] **adj** accompli(e).

accomplishment [ə'kʌmplɪʃmənt] **n 1.** [action] accomplissement *m* **2.** [achievement] réussite *f*.
◆ ***accomplishments*** **npl** talents *mpl*.

accord [ə'kɔ:d] **n : to do sthg of one's own accord** faire qqch de son propre chef OR de soi-même ▸ **to be in accord with** être d'accord avec ▸ **with one accord** d'un commun accord.

accordance [ə'kɔ:dəns] **n : in accordance with** conformément à.

according [ə'kɔ:dɪŋ] ◆ ***according to*** **prep 1.** [as stated or shown by] d'après ▸ **to go according to plan** se passer comme prévu **2.** [with regard to] suivant, en fonction de.

accordingly [ə'kɔ:dɪŋlɪ] **adv 1.** [appropriately] en conséquence **2.** [consequently] par conséquent.

accordion [ə'kɔ:djən] **n** accordéon *m*.

accordionist [ə'kɔ:djənɪst] **n** accordéoniste *mf*.

accost [ə'kɒst] **vt** accoster.

account [ə'kaʊnt] **n 1.** [with bank, shop, company] compte *m* ▸ **put it on OR charge it to my account** mettez cela sur mon compte ▸ **I'd like to settle my account** je voudrais régler ma note ▸ **accounts payable** comptes *mpl* fournisseurs ▸ **accounts receivable** comptes *mpl* clients **2.** [report] compte-rendu *m* ▸ **he gave his account of the accident** il a donné sa version de l'accident **3.** [business, patronage] appui *m* / [in advertising] budget *m*
▸▸ **to call sb to account** demander des comptes à qqn ▸ **to give a good account of o.s.** faire bonne impression ▸ **to put something to good account** tirer parti de qqch ▸ **to take account of sthg, to take sthg into account** prendre qqch en compte ▸ **to be of no account** n'avoir aucune importance ▸ **on no account** sous aucun prétexte, en aucun cas.
◆ ***accounts*** **npl** [of business] comptabilité *f*, comptes *mpl* ▸ **to do the accounts** faire les comptes.
◆ ***by all accounts*** **adv** d'après ce que l'on dit, au dire de tous.
◆ ***on account*** **adv** à crédit ▸ **I paid £100 on account** j'ai versé un acompte de 100 livres.
◆ ***on account of*** **prep** à cause de.
◆ ***on no account*** **adv** en aucun cas, sous aucun prétexte.
◆ ***account for*** **vt insep 1.** [explain] justifier, expliquer ▸ **he has to account for every penny he spends** il doit rendre compte de chaque euro qu'il dépense ▸ **there's no accounting for his behaviour** il n'y a aucune explication à son comportement ▸ **has everyone been accounted for?** personne n'a été oublié? **2.** [represent] représenter ▸ **wine accounts for 5% of exports** le vin représente 5 % des exportations.

accountability [ə,kaʊntə'bɪlətɪ] *(U)* **n** responsabilité *f*.

accountable [ə'kaʊntəbl] **adj 1.** [responsible] **: accountable (for)** responsable (de) **2.** [answerable] **: to be accountable to** rendre compte à, rendre des comptes à.

accountancy [ə'kaʊntənsɪ] **n** comptabilité *f*.

accountant [ə'kaʊntənt] **n** comptable *mf*.

account balance **n** [status] situation *f* de compte.

account charges **n** frais *mpl* de tenue de compte.

account holder **n** titulaire *mf*.

accounting [ə'kaʊntɪŋ] **n** comptabilité *f*.

accounting period **n** exercice *m* (financier), période *f* comptable.

account number **n** numéro *m* de compte.

accoutrements [ə'ku:trəmənts], *US* ***accouterments*** [ə'ku:tərmənts] **npl** *fml* attirail *m*.

accredit [ə'kredɪt] **vt 1.** [credit] créditer ▸ **they accredited the discovery to him** on lui a attribué cette découverte ▸ **she is accredited with having discovered radium** on lui attribue la découverte du radium **2.** [provide with credentials] accréditer ▸ **ambassador accredited to Morocco** ambassadeur accrédité au Maroc **3.** [recognize as bona fide] agréer.

accreditation [ə,kredɪ'teɪʃn] **n : to seek accreditation** chercher à se faire accréditer OR reconnaître.

accredited [ə'kredɪtɪd] **adj** attitré(e).

accrual [ə'kru:əl] **n** *fml* accumulation *f*.
◆ ***accruals*** **npl** FIN compte *m* de régularisation (du passif).

accrue [ə'kru:] **vi** [money] fructifier / [interest] courir.

accumulate [ə'kju:mjʊleɪt] ■ **vt** accumuler, amasser.
■ **vi** s'accumuler.

accumulation [ə,kju:mjʊ'leɪʃn] **n 1.** *(U)* [act of accumulating] accumulation *f* **2.** [things accumulated] amas *m*.

accuracy ['ækjʊrəsɪ] **n 1.** [of description, report] exactitude *f* **2.** [of weapon, typist, figures] précision *f*.

accurate ['ækjʊrət] **adj 1.** [description, report] exact(e) ▸ **the report was accurate in every detail** le compte rendu était fidèle jusque dans les moindres détails **2.** [weapon, typist, figures] précis(e).

accurately ['ækjʊrətlɪ] **adv 1.** [truthfully - describe, report] fidèlement **2.** [precisely - aim] avec précision / [- type] sans faute.

accusation [,ækju:'zeɪʃn] **n** accusation *f*.

accuse [ə'kju:z] **vt : to accuse sb of sthg/of doing sthg** accuser qqn de qqch/de faire qqch.

accused [ə'kju:zd] (pl **accused**) **n** LAW **: the accused** l'accusé *m*, -e *f*.

accuser [ə'kju:zə'] **n** accusateur *m*, -trice *f*.

accusing [ə'kju:zɪŋ] **adj** accusateur(trice).

accusingly [ə'kju:zɪŋlɪ] **adv** d'une manière accusatrice.

accustom [ə'kʌstəm] **vt** habituer, accoutumer ▸ **to accustom sb to sthg** habituer qqn à qqch.

accustomed [ə'kʌstəmd] **adj : to be accustomed to sthg/to doing sthg** avoir l'habitude de qqch/de faire qqch.

AC/DC ■ **n abbr of *alternating current/direct current*.**
■ **adj** *inf* [bisexual] **: to be AC/DC** marcher à voile et à vapeur.

ace [eɪs] ■ **n** as *m* ▸ **to be within an ace of** *fig* être à deux doigts de.
■ **adj** *inf* [top-class] de haut niveau.

acerbic [ə'sɜ:bɪk] **adj** acerbe.

acetate ['æsɪteɪt] **n** acétate *m*.

acetic acid [ə'si:tɪk-] **n** acide *m* acétique.

acetone ['æsɪtəʊn] **n** acétone *f*.

acetylene [ə'setɪli:n] **n** acétylène *m*.

ACGB (abbr of ***Arts Council of Great Britain***) **n** *organisme public britannique d'aide à la création artistique*.

ache [eɪk] ■ **n** douleur *f*.
■ **vi 1.** [back, limb] faire mal ▸ **my head aches** j'ai mal à la tête **2.** *fig* [want] **: to be aching for sthg/to do sthg** mourir d'envie de qqch/de faire qqch.

achieve [ə'tʃi:v] **vt** [success, victory] obtenir, remporter / [goal] atteindre / [ambition] réaliser / [fame] parvenir à.

achievement [ə'tʃi:vmənt] **n 1.** [success] réussite *f* **2.** [of goal, objective] réalisation *f*.

FALSE FRIENDS / FAUX AMIS
achievement
Achèvement n'est pas la traduction du mot anglais *achievement*. Achèvement se traduit par ***completion***.
▸ après l'achèvement des travaux / *following completion of the work* OU *after the work was completed*

achiever [ə'tʃi:vər] **n** fonceur *m*, -euse *f*.

Achilles' heel [ə'kɪli:z-] **n** talon *m* d'Achille.

Achilles' tendon **n** tendon *m* d'Achille.

aching ['eɪkɪŋ] **adj** douloureux(euse), endolori(e).

achy ['eɪkɪ] **adj** *inf* douloureux(euse), endolori(e).

acid ['æsɪd] ■ **adj** *lit* & *fig* acide.
■ **n** acide *m*.

acid house **n** MUS house *f* (music).

acidic [ə'sɪdɪk] **adj** acide.

acidity [ə'sɪdətɪ] **n** acidité *f*.

acid jazz **n** MUS acid jazz *m*.

acid rain *(U)* **n** pluies *fpl* acides.

acid test **n** *fig* épreuve *f* décisive.

acknowledge [ək'nɒlɪdʒ] **vt 1.** [fact, situation, person] reconnaître ▸ **we acknowledge (the fact) that we were wrong** nous admettons notre erreur ▸ **they acknowledged him as their leader** ils l'ont reconnu comme leur chef **2.** [letter] **: to acknowledge (receipt of)** accuser réception de **3.** [greet] saluer.

acknowledged [ək'nɒlɪdʒd] **adj** [expert, authority] reconnu(e).

acknowledg(e)ment [ək'nɒlɪdʒmənt] **n 1.** [admission] reconnaissance *f* / [of mistake] reconnaissance *f*, aveu *m* ▸ **in acknowledgement of your letter** en réponse à votre lettre ▸ **acknowledgement of receipt** accusé *m* de réception ▸ **he received a watch in acknowledgement of his work** il a reçu une montre en reconnaissance OR remerciement de son travail **2.** [letter, receipt] accusé *m* de réception / [for payment] quittance *f*, reçu *m*.
◆ ***acknowledg(e)ments*** **npl** [in article, book] remerciements *mpl*.

ACLU (abbr of ***American Civil Liberties Union***) **n** *ligue américaine des droits du citoyen*.

acme ['ækmɪ] **n** apogée *m*.

acne ['æknɪ] **n** acné *f*.

acorn ['eɪkɔ:n] **n** gland *m*.

acoustic [ə'ku:stɪk] **adj** acoustique.
◆ ***acoustics*** **npl** [of room] acoustique *f*.

acoustic guitar **n** guitare *f* sèche.

ACPO (abbr of ***Association of Chief Police Officers***) **n** *syndicat d'officiers supérieurs de la police britannique*.

acquaint [ə'kweɪnt] **vt : to acquaint sb with sthg** mettre qqn au courant de qqch ▸ **to be acquainted with sb** connaître qqn.

acquaintance [ə'kweɪntəns] **n 1.** [person] connaissance *f* **2.** [with person] **: to make sb's acquaintance** faire la connaissance de qqn.

acquiesce [,ækwɪ'es] **vi : to acquiesce (to** OR **in sthg)** donner son accord (à qqch).

acquiescence [,ækwɪ'esns] **n** consentement *m*.

acquire [ə'kwaɪər] **vt** acquérir.

acquired [ə'kwaɪəd] **adj** acquis(e) ▸ **an acquired taste** un goût acquis.

acquisition [,ækwɪ'zɪʃn] **n** acquisition *f*.

acquisitive [ə'kwɪzɪtɪv] **adj** avide de possessions.

acquit [ə'kwɪt] (pt & pp **-ted**, cont **-ting**) **vt 1.** LAW acquitter **2.** [perform] **: to acquit o.s. well/badly** bien/mal se comporter.

acquittal [ə'kwɪtl] **n** acquittement *m*.

acre ['eɪkər] **n** ≃ demi-hectare *m* (= 4046,9 m²).

acreage ['eɪkərɪdʒ] **n** superficie *f*, aire *f*.

acrid ['ækrɪd] **adj** [taste, smell] âcre / *fig* acerbe.

acrimonious [,ækrɪ'məʊnjəs] **adj** acrimonieux(euse).

acrimoniously [,ækrɪ'məʊnjəslɪ] **adv** [say] avec amertume ▸ **the meeting ended acrimoniously** la réunion s'est terminée dans l'amertume.

acrobat ['ækrəbæt] **n** acrobate *mf*.

acrobatic [,ækrə'bætɪk] **adj** acrobatique.
◆ ***acrobatics*** **npl** acrobatie *f*.

acronym ['ækrənɪm] **n** acronyme *m*.

across [ə'krɒs] ■ **adv 1.** [from one side to the other] en travers ▸ **to run across** traverser en courant ▸ **I helped him across** je l'ai aidé à traverser ▸ **she walked across to Mary** elle s'est dirigée vers Mary ▸ **I looked across at my mother** j'ai regardé ma mère
2. [in measurements] **: the river is 2 km across** la rivière mesure 2 km de large
3. [in crossword] **: 21 across** 21 horizontalement
▸▸ **to get sthg across (to sb)** faire comprendre qqch (à qqn).
■ **prep 1.** [from one side to the other] d'un côté à l'autre de, en travers de ▸ **to walk across the road** traverser la route ▸ **to run across the road** traverser la route en courant ▸ **there's a bridge across the river** il y a un pont sur la rivière ▸ **he leaned across my desk** il s'est penché par dessus mon bureau ▸ **a smile spread across her face** un sourire a éclairé son visage
2. [on the other side of] de l'autre côté de ▸ **the house across the road** la maison d'en face ▸ **he sat across the table from me** il s'assit en face de moi ▸ **she glanced across the room at us** elle nous lança un regard de l'autre bout de la pièce

3. [throughout] en travers de, à travers ▸ **the study of literature across cultures** l'étude de la littérature à travers différentes cultures ▸ **he gave speeches all across Europe** il a fait des discours dans toute l'Europe.
◆ ***across from*** **prep** en face de.

across-the-board **adj** général(e).

acrylic [ə'krılık] ■ **adj** acrylique.
■ **n** acrylique *m*.

act [ækt] ■ **n 1.** [action, deed] acte *m* ▸ **to catch sb in the act** prendre qqn sur le fait ▸ **to catch sb in the act of doing sthg** surprendre qqn en train de faire qqch **2.** LAW loi *f* **3.** [of play, opera] acte *m* / [in cabaret] numéro *m* / *fig* [pretence] **: to put on an act** jouer la comédie
▸▸ **to get in on the act** s'y mettre ▸ **to get one's act together** se reprendre en main.
■ **vi 1.** [gen] agir **2.** [behave] se comporter ▸ **to act as if** se conduire comme si, se comporter comme si ▸ **to act like** se conduire comme, se comporter comme **3.** [in play, film] jouer / *fig* [pretend] jouer la comédie **4.** [function] **: to act as** [person] être / [object] servir de ▸ **to act for sb, to act on behalf of sb** représenter qqn.
■ **vt** [part] jouer ▸ **to act the fool** faire l'imbécile ▸ **act your age!** ce n'est plus de ton âge!
◆ ***act on*** **vt insep 1.** [advice, suggestion] suivre / [order] exécuter ▸ **acting on your instructions, we have cancelled your account** selon vos instructions, nous avons fermé votre compte **2.** [chemical, drug] agir sur.
◆ ***act out*** **vt sep 1.** [feelings, thoughts] exprimer **2.** [event] mimer.
◆ ***act up*** **vi** faire des siennes.

ACT (abbr of ***American College Test***) **n** *examen américain de fin d'études secondaires.*

acting ['æktıŋ] ■ **adj** par intérim, provisoire.
■ **n** [in play, film] interprétation *f*.

action ['ækʃn] **n 1.** [gen] action *f* ▸ **to take action** agir, prendre des mesures ▸ **to put sthg into action** mettre qqch à exécution ▸ **to go into action** entrer en action ▸ **in action** [person] en action / [machine] en marche ▸ **out of action** [person] hors de combat / [machine] hors service, hors d'usage ▸ **it's time for action** il est temps d'agir, passons aux actes ▸ **to be killed in action** mourir au combat **2.** [deed] acte *m*, geste *m*, action *f* ▸ **he's not responsible for his actions** il n'est pas responsable de ses actes ▸ **actions speak louder than words** les actes en disent plus long que les mots **3.** LAW procès *m*, action *f* ▸ **to bring an action against sb** intenter un procès à *OR* contre qqn, intenter une action contre qqn **4.** [of book, film, play] intrigue *f*, action *f* ▸ **action!** CIN silence, on tourne!

actionable ['ækʃnəbl] **adj** [allegations, deed, person] passible de poursuites / [claim] recevable.

action group **n** groupe *m* de pression.

action movie **n** film *m* d'action.

action-packed **adj** [film] bourré(e) d'action / [holiday] rempli(e) d'activités, bien rempli(e).

action replay **n** *UK* répétition *f* immédiate (au ralenti).

action stations ■ **npl** MIL postes *mpl* de combat.
■ **excl : action stations!** à vos postes!

activate ['æktıveıt] **vt** mettre en marche.

active ['æktıv] **adj 1.** [gen] actif(ive) / [encouragement] vif (vive) ▸ **to be active in sthg, to take an active part in sthg** prendre une part active à qqch ▸ **to be politically active** être engagé(e) **2.** [volcano] en activité.

active duty *US* = ***active service***.

active file **n** COMPUT fichier *m* actif.

actively ['æktıvlı] **adv** activement.

active service **n : to be killed on active service** mourir au champ d'honneur.

active window **n** COMPUT fenêtre *f* active *OR* activée.

activist ['æktıvıst] **n** activiste *mf*.

activity [æk'tıvətı] (pl **-ies**) **n** activité *f*.

activity holiday **n** *UK* vacances *fpl* actives.

act of Congress **n** POL acte *m* du Congrès.

act of God **n** catastrophe *f* naturelle.

act of Parliament **n** POL acte *m* du Parlement.

actor ['æktəʳ] **n** acteur *m*, -trice *f*.

actress ['æktrıs] **n** actrice *f*.

actual ['æktʃʊəl] **adj** réel(elle) ▸ **what were her actual words?** quels étaient ses mots exacts? ▸ **the actual cost was £1,000** le coût exact était de 1 000 livres ▸ **the actual ceremony starts at ten a.m.** la cérémonie proprement dite commence à dix heures.

FALSE FRIENDS / FAUX AMIS
actual

Actuel n'est pas la traduction du mot anglais *actual*. Actuel se traduit par *present* ou *current*.
▸ sous le gouvernement actuel / *under the present government*
▸ dans les circonstances actuelles / *under the current circumstances*

actuality [,æktʃʊ'ælətı] **n : in actuality** en fait.

actually ['æktʃʊəlı] **adv 1.** [really, in truth] vraiment ▸ **what did he actually say?** qu'est-ce qu'il a dit vraiment? ▸ **she's actually older than she looks** en fait, elle est plus âgée qu'elle n'en a l'air **2.** [by the way] au fait.

FALSE FRIENDS / FAUX AMIS
actually

Actuellement n'est pas la traduction du mot anglais *actually*. Actuellement se traduit par *at the moment* ou *currently, nowadays*.
▸ Je ne suis pas libre actuellement / *I'm not free at the moment*
▸ Actuellement, nous assistons à une forte poussée des prix immobiliers / *We're currently witnessing a big rise in house prices*

actuary ['æktjʊərı] (pl **-ies**) **n** actuaire *mf*.

actuate ['æktjʊeıt] **vt** mettre en marche.

acuity [ə'kju:ətı] **n** acuité *f*.

acumen ['ækjʊmen] **n** flair *m* ▸ **business acumen** le sens des affaires.

acupuncture ['ækjʊpʌŋktʃəʳ] **n** acupuncture *f*, acuponcture *f*.

acupuncturist ['ækjʊpʌŋktʃərɪst] **n** acupuncteur *m*, -trice *f*.

acute [ə'kju:t] **adj 1.** [severe - pain, illness] aigu(ë) / [- danger] sérieux(euse), grave **2.** [perceptive - person, mind] perspicace **3.** [keen - eyesight] perçant(e) / [- hearing] fin(e) / [- sense of smell] développé(e) **4.** MATHS **: acute angle** angle *m* aigu **5.** LING **: e acute** e accent aigu.

acute accent **n** accent *m* aigu.

acutely [ə'kju:tlɪ] **adv** [extremely] extrêmement.

ad [æd] (abbr of ***advertisement***) **n** *inf* [in newspaper] annonce *f* / [on TV] pub *f*.

AD (abbr of ***Anno Domini***) ap. J.-C.

adage ['ædɪdʒ] **n** adage *m*.

adamant ['ædəmənt] **adj** résolu(e), inflexible.

adamantly ['ædəməntlɪ] **adv** résolument.

Adam's apple ['ædəmz-] **n** pomme *f* d'Adam.

adapt [ə'dæpt] ■ **vt** adapter.
■ **vi : to adapt (to)** s'adapter (à).

adaptability [ə,dæptə'bɪlətɪ] **n** souplesse *f*.

adaptable [ə'dæptəbl] **adj** [person] souple.

adaptation [,ædæp'teɪʃn] **n** [of book, play] adaptation *f*.

adapter, adaptor [ə'dæptəʳ] **n** *UK* [ELEC - for several devices] prise *f* multiple / [- for foreign plug] adaptateur *m*.

ADC **n 1.** abbr of ***aide-de-camp*** **2.** (abbr of ***Aid to Dependent Children***) *aux États-Unis, aide pour enfants assistés* **3.** (abbr of ***analogue-digital converter***) CAN *m*.

add [æd] **vt 1.** [gen] **: to add sthg (to)** ajouter qqch (à) **2.** [numbers] additionner.
◆ ***add in*** **vt sep** ajouter.
◆ ***add on*** **vt sep : to add sthg on (to)** ajouter qqch (à) / [charge, tax] rajouter qqch (à).
◆ ***add to*** **vt insep** ajouter à, augmenter.
◆ ***add up*** ■ **vt sep** additionner.
■ **vi** *inf* [make sense] **: it doesn't add up** c'est pas logique.
◆ ***add up to*** **vt insep** se monter à, s'élever à.

added ['ædɪd] **adj** supplémentaire.

addendum [ə'dendəm] (**pl -da** [-də]) **n** addenda *m inv*.

adder ['ædəʳ] **n** vipère *f*.

addict ['ædɪkt] **n 1.** drogué *m*, -e *f* ▸ **drug addict** drogué **2.** *fig* fanatique *mf*, fana *mf* ▸ **she's a film addict** c'est une fana de cinéma.

addicted [ə'dɪktɪd] **adj : addicted (to)** drogué(e) (à) / *fig* passionné(e) (de).

addiction [ə'dɪkʃn] **n : addiction (to)** dépendance *f* (à) / *fig* penchant *m* (pour).

addictive [ə'dɪktɪv] **adj** qui rend dépendant(e).

Addis Ababa ['ædɪs'æbəbə] **n** Addis-Ababa, Addis-Abeba.

addition [ə'dɪʃn] **n** addition *f* ▸ **in addition (to)** en plus (de).

additional [ə'dɪʃənl] **adj** supplémentaire.

additionally [ə'dɪʃənəlɪ] **adv 1.** [further, more] davantage, plus **2.** [moreover] en outre, de plus.

additive ['ædɪtɪv] **n** additif *m*.

addled ['ædld] **adj 1.** [egg] pourri(e) **2.** [brain] embrouillé(e).

add-on ■ **adj** COMPUT supplémentaire.
■ **n** COMPUT dispositif *m* supplémentaire.

address [ə'dres] ■ **n 1.** [place] adresse *f* ▸ **we've changed our address** nous avons changé d'adresse **2.** [speech] discours *m*.
■ **vt 1.** [gen] adresser ▸ **the letter is addressed to you** cette lettre vous est adressée ▸ **address all complaints to the manager** adressez vos doléances au directeu[r] **2.** [meeting, conference] prendre la parole à **3.** [problem, issue] aborder, examiner ▸ **to address o.s. to** s'attaquer à.

address book **n** carnet *m* d'adresses.

addressee [,ædre'si:] **n** destinataire *mf*.

Aden ['eɪdn] **n** Aden.

adenoids ['ædɪnɔɪdz] **npl** végétations *fpl*.

adept ['ædept] **adj : adept (at)** doué(e) (pour).

adequacy ['ædɪkwəsɪ] **n 1.** [of amount] quantité *f* né[]cessaire **2.** [of person] compétence *f*.

adequate ['ædɪkwət] **adj** adéquat(e).

adequately ['ædɪkwətlɪ] **adv 1.** [sufficiently] suffisam[]ment **2.** [well enough] de façon satisfaisante OR adéquate[]

adhere [əd'hɪəʳ] **vi 1.** [stick] **: to adhere (to)** adhérer (à) **2.** [observe] **: to adhere to** obéir à **3.** [keep] **: to adhere t[o]** adhérer à.

adherence [əd'hɪərəns] **n : adherence to** adhésion *f* à

adherent [əd'hɪərənt] ■ **adj** adhérent(e).
■ **n** [to party] adhérent *m*, -e *f*, partisan *m*, -e *f* / [to agree[]ment] adhérent *m*, -e *f* / [to belief, religion] adepte *mf*.

adhesive [əd'hi:sɪv] ■ **adj** adhésif(ive).
■ **n** adhésif *m*.

adhesive tape **n** ruban *m* adhésif.

ad hoc [,æd'hɒk] **adj** ad hoc *(inv)*.

ad infinitum [,ædɪnfɪ'naɪtəm] **adv** à l'infini.

adjacent [ə'dʒeɪsənt] **adj : adjacent (to)** adjacent(e) (à), contigu(ë) (à).

adjective ['ædʒɪktɪv] **n** adjectif *m*.

adjoin [ə'dʒɔɪn] **vt** être contigu(ë) à, toucher.

adjoining [ə'dʒɔɪnɪŋ] ■ **adj** voisin(e).
■ **prep** attenant à.

adjourn [ə'dʒɜ:n] ■ **vt** ajourner.
■ **vi** suspendre la séance.

adjournment [ə'dʒɜ:nmənt] **n** ajournement *m*.

Adjt (abbr of ***adjutant***) adjt.

adjudge [ə'dʒʌdʒ] **vt** déclarer.

adjudicate [ə'dʒu:dɪkeɪt] ■ **vt** juger, décider.
■ **vi : to adjudicate (on** OR **upon)** se prononcer (sur).

adjudication [ə,dʒu:dɪ'keɪʃn] **n** jugement *m*.

adjudicator [ə'dʒu:dɪkeɪtəʳ] **n** [of competition] juge[,] arbitre *m* / [of dispute] arbitre *m*.

adjunct ['ædʒʌŋkt] **n** complément *m*.

adjust [ə'dʒʌst] ■ vt ajuster, régler ▸ **figures adjusted for inflation** chiffres en monnaie constante.
■ **vi : to adjust (to)** s'adapter (à).

adjustable [ə'dʒʌstəbl] **adj** réglable.

adjustable spanner **n** *UK* clé *f* universelle.

adjusted [ə'dʒʌstɪd] **adj : to be well adjusted** être (bien) équilibré(e).

adjustment [ə'dʒʌstmənt] **n 1.** [modification] ajustement *m* / TECH réglage *m* ▸ **to make an adjustment to** apporter une modification à **2.** [change in attitude] **: adjustment (to)** adaptation *f* (à).

adjutant ['ædʒʊtənt] **n** adjudant *m*.

ad lib [ˌæd'lɪb] ■ **adj** improvisé(e).
■ **adv** à volonté.
■ **n** improvisation *f*.
◆ ***ad-lib*** (pt & pp **ad-libbed**, cont **ad-libbing**) **vi** improviser.

adman ['ædmæn] (pl **-men** [-men]) **n** publicitaire *m*.

admin ['ædmɪn] (abbr of ***administration***) **n** *UK inf* administration *f*.

administer [əd'mɪnɪstəʳ] **vt 1.** [company, business] administrer, gérer **2.** [justice, punishment] dispenser **3.** [drug, medication] administrer.

administrate [əd'mɪnɪstreɪt] **vt** = ***administer*** *(sense 1)* .

administration [ədˌmɪnɪ'streɪʃn] **n** administration *f*.
◆ ***Administration*** **n** *US* **: the Administration** le gouvernement.

administrative [əd'mɪnɪstrətɪv] **adj** administratif(ive).

administrative costs **npl** frais *mpl* d'administration OR de gestion.

administrator [əd'mɪnɪstreɪtəʳ] **n** administrateur *m*, -trice *f*.

admirable ['ædmərəbl] **adj** admirable.

admirably ['ædmərəblɪ] **adv** admirablement.

admiral ['ædmərəl] **n** amiral *m*.

Admiralty ['ædmərəltɪ] **n** *UK* **: the Admiralty** le ministère de la Marine.

admiration [ˌædmə'reɪʃn] **n** admiration *f*.

admire [əd'maɪəʳ] **vt** admirer.

admirer [əd'maɪərəʳ] **n** admirateur *m*, -trice *f*.

admiring [əd'maɪərɪŋ] **adj** admiratif(ive).

admiringly [əd'maɪərɪŋlɪ] **adv** avec admiration.

admissibility [ədˌmɪsə'bɪlətɪ] **n** [of behaviour, plan] admissibilité *f* / LAW recevabilité *f*.

admissible [əd'mɪsəbl] **adj** LAW recevable.

admission [əd'mɪʃn] **n 1.** [permission to enter] admission *f* **2.** [to museum] entrée *f* **3.** [confession] confession *f*, aveu *m* ▸ **by his/her own admission** de son propre aveu.

admit [əd'mɪt] (pt & pp **-ted**, cont **-ting**) ■ **vt 1.** [confess] reconnaître ▸ **to admit (that)...** reconnaître que... ▸ **to admit doing sthg** reconnaître avoir fait qqch ▸ **to admit defeat** *fig* s'avouer vaincu(e) **2.** [allow to enter, join] admettre ▸ **'admits two'** [on ticket] 'valable pour deux personnes' ▸ **to be admitted to hospital** *UK* OR **to the hospital** *US* être admis(e) à l'hôpital.
■ **vi : to admit to** admettre, reconnaître.

admittance [əd'mɪtəns] **n** admission *f* ▸ **to gain admittance to** parvenir à, entrer dans ▸ **'no admittance'** 'entrée interdite'.

admittedly [əd'mɪtɪdlɪ] **adv** de l'aveu général.

admixture [æd'mɪkstʃəʳ] **n** mélange *m*.

admonish [əd'mɒnɪʃ] **vt** réprimander.

admonition [ˌædmə'nɪʃn] **n 1.** [rebuke] réprimande *f*, remontrance *f*, admonestation *f* **2.** [warning] avertissement *m* / LAW admonition *f*.

ad nauseam [ˌæd'nɔːzɪæm] **adv** [talk] à n'en plus finir.

ado [ə'duː] **n : without further** OR **more ado** sans plus de cérémonie.

adolescence [ˌædə'lesns] **n** adolescence *f*.

adolescent [ˌædə'lesnt] ■ **adj** adolescent(e) / *pej* puéril(e).
■ **n** adolescent *m*, -e *f*.

adopt [ə'dɒpt] **vt** adopter.

adopted [ə'dɒptɪd] **adj** [child] adoptif(ive) / [country] d'adoption, adoptif(ive).

adoption [ə'dɒpʃn] **n** adoption *f*.

adoptive [ə'dɒptɪv] **adj** adoptif(ive).

adorable [ə'dɔːrəbl] **adj** adorable.

adoration [ˌædə'reɪʃn] **n** adoration *f*.

adore [ə'dɔːʳ] **vt** adorer.

adoring [ə'dɔːrɪŋ] **adj** [person] adorateur(trice) / [look] d'adoration.

adoringly [ə'dɔːrɪŋlɪ] **adv** avec adoration.

adorn [ə'dɔːn] **vt** orner.

adornment [ə'dɔːnmənt] **n** décoration *f*.

ADP (abbr of ***automatic data processing***) **n** *traitement automatique de données*.

adrenalin [ə'drenəlɪn] **n** adrénaline *f*.

Adriatic [ˌeɪdrɪ'ætɪk] **n : the Adriatic (Sea)** l'Adriatique *f*, la mer Adriatique.

adrift [ə'drɪft] ■ **adj** à la dérive.
■ **adv : to go adrift** *fig* aller à la dérive.

adroit [ə'drɔɪt] **adj** adroit(e).

ADSL (abbr of ***Asymmetric Digital Subscriber Line***) **n** ADSL *m*, RNA *m offic*.

ADT (abbr of ***Atlantic Daylight Time***) **n** *heure d'été de la côte est des États-Unis*.

adulation [ˌædjʊ'leɪʃn] **n** adulation *f*.

adult ['ædʌlt] ■ **adj 1.** [gen] adulte **2.** [film, literature] pour adultes.
■ **n** adulte *mf*.

adult education **n** enseignement *m* pour adultes.

adulterate [ə'dʌltəreɪt] **vt** frelater.

adulteration [əˌdʌltə'reɪʃn] **n** frelatage *m*.

adulterer [ə'dʌltərəʳ] **n** personne *f* adultère.

adulteress [ə'dʌltərɪs] **n** adultère *f*.

adulterous [ə'dʌltərəs] **adj** adultère.

adultery [ə'dʌltərɪ] **n** adultère *m*.

adulthood ['ædʌlthʊd] **n** âge *m* adulte.

adult student **n** *US* = ***mature student***.

advance [əd'vɑːns] ■ **n 1.** [gen] avance *f* ▸ **an advance on his salary** une avance sur son salaire **2.** [progress] progrès *m*.
■ **comp** à l'avance.
■ **vt 1.** [gen] avancer ▸ **the date of the meeting was advanced by one week** la réunion a été avancée d'une semaine ▸ **we advanced her £100 on her salary** nous lui avons avancé 100 livres sur son salaire **2.** [improve] faire progresser *OR* avancer.
■ **vi 1.** [gen] avancer **2.** [improve] progresser.
◆ ***advances*** **npl : to make advances to sb** [sexual] faire des avances à qqn / [business] faire des propositions à qqn.
◆ ***in advance*** **adv** à l'avance.
◆ ***in advance of*** **prep 1.** [in front of] en avance sur **2.** [prior to] en avance de, avant.

advance copy **n** [of book, magazine] exemplaire *m* de lancement.

advanced [əd'vɑːnst] **adj** avancé(e) ▸ **advanced in years** *euph* d'un âge avancé.

advance man **n** *US* POL organisateur *m* de la publicité *(pour une campagne politique)*.

advancement [əd'vɑːnsmənt] **n 1.** [promotion] avancement *m* **2.** [progress] progrès *m*.

advance publicity **n** publicité *f* d'amorçage.

advancing [əd'vɑːnsɪŋ] **adj** qui approche, qui avance ▸ **the advancing army** l'armée en marche *OR* qui avance ▸ **the advancing tide** la marée qui monte.

advantage [əd'vɑːntɪdʒ] **n : advantage (over)** avantage *m* (sur) ▸ **they have an advantage over us *OR* the advantage of us** ils ont un avantage sur nous ▸ **to be to one's advantage** être à son avantage ▸ **to take advantage of sthg** profiter de qqch ▸ **to take advantage of sb** exploiter qqn.

advantageous [ˌædvən'teɪdʒəs] **adj** avantageux (euse).

advent ['ædvənt] **n** avènement *m*.
◆ ***Advent*** **n** RELIG Avent *m*.

Advent calendar **n** calendrier *m* de l'Avent.

adventure [əd'ventʃər] **n** aventure *f*.

adventure game **n** COMPUT jeu *m* d'aventures.

adventure holiday **n** *UK* circuit *m* aventure.

adventure playground **n** *UK* terrain *m* d'aventures.

adventurer [əd'ventʃərər] **n** aventurier *m*, -ère *f*.

adventurous [əd'ventʃərəs] **adj** aventureux(euse).

adverb ['ædvɜːb] **n** adverbe *m*.

adverbial [əd'vɜːbɪəl] **adj** adverbial(e).

adversarial [ˌædvə'seərɪəl] **adj** antagoniste, hostile.

adversary ['ædvəsərɪ] (pl **-ies**) **n** adversaire *mf*.

adverse ['ædvɜːs] **adj** défavorable.

adversely ['ædvɜːslɪ] **adv** de façon défavorable.

adversity [əd'vɜːsətɪ] **n** adversité *f*.

advert ['ædvɜːt] *UK* = ***advertisement***.

advertise ['ædvətaɪz] ■ **vt** COMM faire de la publicité pour / [event] annoncer ▸ **we advertised our house in the local paper** nous avons mis *OR* passé une annonce pour vendre notre maison dans le journal local.
■ **vi** faire de la publicité ▸ **to advertise in the press/on radio/on TV** faire de la publicité dans la presse/à la radio/à la télévision ▸ **to advertise for sb/sthg** chercher qqn/qqch par voie d'annonce.

advertisement [əd'vɜːtɪsmənt] **n** [in newspaper] annonce *f* / *fig* & COMM publicité *f* ▸ **to put an advertisement in the paper** passer une annonce dans le journal.

FALSE FRIENDS / FAUX AMIS

advertisement

Avertissement n'est pas la traduction du mot anglais *advertisement*. Avertissement se traduit par *warning*.

▸ Elle a déjà eu deux avertissements / *She's already had two warnings*

advertiser ['ædvətaɪzər] **n** annonceur *m*, -euse *f*.

advertising ['ædvətaɪzɪŋ] **n** *(U)* publicité *f*.

advertising agency **n** agence *f* de publicité.

advertising campaign **n** campagne *f* de publicité.

advertorial [ædvə'tɔːrɪəl] **n** publireportage *m*, publicité *f* rédactionnelle.

HOW TO ...

reply to an advertisement

J'appelle au sujet de l'annonce parue dans le journal d'hier / I'm calling about the ad published in yesterday's paper

J'ai vu votre annonce dans le journal d'aujourd'hui / I saw your ad in today's paper

Est-ce que l'appartement est encore libre ? / Is the flat still available?

Pouvez-vous me renseigner sur les services de nettoyage de bureaux ? / I'm phoning to enquire about office cleaning services

Votre annonce concernant un poste de traducteur m'a vivement intéressé / I was very interested to see your advertisement for the post of translator

J'ai décidé de poser ma candidature pour le poste de la petite annonce parce que je veux travailler à l'étranger / I decided to apply for the advertised post because I want to work abroad

advice [əd'vaɪs] **n** *(U)* conseils *mpl* ▸ **a piece of advice** un conseil ▸ **to give sb advice** donner des conseils à qqn ▸ **to take sb's advice** suivre les conseils de qqn ▸ **letter of advice** avis *m*.

advice note **n** avis *m*.

advisability [əd,vaɪzə'bɪlətɪ] **n** bien-fondé *m*.

advisable [əd'vaɪzəbl] **adj** conseillé(e), recommandé(e).

advise [əd'vaɪz] ■ **vt 1.** [give advice to] **: to advise sb to do sthg** conseiller à qqn de faire qqch ▸ **to advise sb against sthg** déconseiller qqch à qqn ▸ **to advise sb against doing sthg** déconseiller à qqn de faire qqch **2.** [professionally] **: to advise sb on sthg** conseiller qqn sur qqch **3.** [inform] **: to advise sb (of sthg)** aviser qqn (de qqch).
■ **vi 1.** [give advice] **: to advise against sthg/against doing sthg** déconseiller qqch/de faire qqch **2.** [professionally] **: to advise on sthg** conseiller sur qqch.

advisedly [əd'vaɪzɪdlɪ] **adv** en connaissance de cause, délibérément.

adviser, *US* ***advisor*** [əd'vaɪzəʳ] **n** conseiller *m*, -ère *f*.

advisory [əd'vaɪzərɪ] **adj** consultatif(ive) ▸ **in an advisory capacity** *OR* **role** à titre consultatif.

advocacy ['ædvəkəsɪ] **n** plaidoyer *m*.

advocate ■ **n** ['ædvəkət] **1.** LAW avocat *m*, -e *f* **2.** [supporter] partisan *m*.
■ **vt** ['ædvəkeɪt] préconiser, recommander.

advt. abbr of ***advertisement***.

AEA (abbr of ***Atomic Energy Authority***) **n** *commission britannique à l'énergie nucléaire,* ≃ CEA *f*.

AEC (abbr of ***Atomic Energy Commission***) **n** *commission américaine à l'énergie nucléaire,* ≃ CEA *f*.

AEEU (abbr of ***Amalgamated Engineering and Electrical Union***) **n** *syndicat britannique d'ingénieurs et d'électriciens.*

Aegean [iː'dʒiːən] **n : the Aegean (Sea)** la mer Égée.

aegis, *US* ***egis*** ['iːdʒɪs] **n : under the aegis of** sous l'égide de.

Aeolian Islands **npl : the Aeolian Islands** les îles *fpl* Éoliennes.

aeon *UK*, ***eon*** *US* ['iːən] **n** *fig* éternité *f*.

aerate ['eəreɪt] **vt 1.** [liquid] gazéifier / [blood] oxygéner **2.** [soil] retourner.

aerial ['eərɪəl] ■ **adj** aérien(enne).
■ **n** *UK* antenne *f*.

aerobatics [,eərəʊ'bætɪks] **n** *(U)* acrobatie *f* aérienne.

aerobic [eə'rəʊbɪk] **adj** aérobie.

aerobics [eə'rəʊbɪks] **n** *(U)* aérobic *m*.

aerodrome ['eərədrəʊm] **n** *UK* aérodrome *m*.

aerodynamic [,eərəʊdaɪ'næmɪk] **adj** aérodynamique.
◆ ***aerodynamics*** ■ **n** *(U)* aérodynamique *f*.
■ **npl** [aerodynamic qualities] aérodynamisme *m*.

aerogramme ['eərəgræm] **n** aérogramme *m*.

aeronautics [,eərə'nɔːtɪks] **n** *(U)* aéronautique *f*.

aeroplane ['eərəpleɪn] **n** *UK* avion *m*.

aerosol ['eərəsɒl] **n** aérosol *m*.

aerospace ['eərəʊspeɪs] **n : the aerospace industry** l'industrie *f* aérospatiale.

aesthete, *US* ***esthete*** ['iːsθiːt] **n** esthète *mf*.

aesthetic, *US* ***esthetic*** [iːs'θetɪk] **adj** esthétique.

aesthetically, *US* ***esthetically*** [iːs'θetɪklɪ] **adv** esthétiquement.

aestheticism, *US* ***estheticism*** [iːs'θetɪsɪzm] **n** esthétisme *m*.

aesthetics, *US* ***esthetics*** [iːs'θetɪks] **n** *(U)* esthétique *f*.

afar [ə'fɑːʳ] **adv : from afar** de loin.

AFB (abbr of ***Air Force Base***) **n** *aux États-Unis, base de l'armée de l'air.*

AFDC (abbr of ***Aid to Families with Dependent Children***) **n** *aux États-Unis, aide pour les familles d'enfants assistés.*

affable ['æfəbl] **adj** affable.

affably ['æfəblɪ] **adv** affablement, avec affabilité.

affair [ə'feəʳ] **n 1.** [gen] affaire *f* **2.** [extra-marital relationship] liaison *f*.
◆ ***affairs*** **npl** affaires *fpl*.

HOW TO ...

ask for and give advice

Asking for advice

Que feriez-vous à ma place ? / What would you do, if you were me?

Qu'est-ce que tu en penses ? / What do you think?

J'aurais besoin d'un conseil / I could do with some advice

Tu crois que je devrais lui en parler ? / Do you think I should talk to him about it?

Giving advice

Tu veux mon avis ? / Do you want to know what I think?

Si tu veux mon avis, je pense que tu devrais y aller / If you want my advice, I think you should go

Tu sais, je crois que tu devrais accepter / You know, I think you should accept

À ta place je le lui dirais / If I were you, I'd tell her

Je vous conseille de le lui dire / I advise you to tell her

Tu devrais le lui dire / You really should tell her

Tu ferais peut-être mieux de le lui dire / Perhaps you should tell her

Pourquoi tu ne le lui dis pas carrément ? / Why don't you tell her straight out?

Et si tu lui en parlais ? / What about talking to her about it?

affect [ə'fekt] vt 1. [influence] avoir un effet OR des conséquences sur 2. [emotionally] affecter, émouvoir 3. [put on] affecter.

affectation [ˌæfek'teɪʃn] n affectation *f*.

affected [ə'fektɪd] adj affecté(e).

-affected suffix affecté(e) par ▸ **famine/drought-affected** affecté par la famine/sécheresse.

affectedly [ə'fektɪdlɪ] adv avec affectation, d'une manière affectée.

affection [ə'fekʃn] n affection *f*.

affectionate [ə'fekʃnət] adj affectueux(euse).

affectionately [ə'fekʃnətlɪ] adv affectueusement.

affidavit [ˌæfɪ'deɪvɪt] n *déclaration écrite sous serment*.

affiliate ■ n [ə'fɪlɪeɪt] affilié *m*, -e *f*.
■ vt [ə'fɪlɪət] affilier ▸ **to affiliate o.s. to** OR **with** s'affilier à.

affiliated [ə'fɪlɪeɪtɪd] adj [member, organization] affilié(e) ▸ **to be affiliated to** OR **with** être affilié à ▸ **an affiliated company** une filiale.

affiliation [əˌfɪlɪ'eɪʃn] n affiliation *f*.

affinity [ə'fɪnətɪ] (pl -ies) n affinité *f* ▸ **to have an affinity with sb** avoir des affinités avec qqn.

affinity card [ə'fɪnɪtɪˌkɑːd] n carte *f* affinitaire.

affirm [ə'fɜːm] vt 1. [declare] affirmer 2. [confirm] confirmer.

affirmation [ˌæfə'meɪʃn] n 1. [declaration] affirmation *f* 2. [confirmation] confirmation *f*.

affirmative [ə'fɜːmətɪv] ■ adj affirmatif(ive).
■ n : **in the affirmative** par l'affirmative.

affirmative action n *(U) US* mesures *fpl* d'embauche antidiscriminatoires *(en faveur des minorités)*.

affix [ə'fɪks] vt [stamp] coller.

afflict [ə'flɪkt] vt affliger ▸ **to be afflicted with** souffrir de.

affliction [ə'flɪkʃn] n affliction *f*.

affluence ['æflʊəns] n prospérité *f*.

affluent ['æflʊənt] adj riche.

affluent society n société *f* d'abondance.

afford [ə'fɔːd] vt 1. [buy, pay for] : **to be able to afford sthg** avoir les moyens d'acheter qqch ▸ **how much can you afford?** combien pouvez-vous mettre?, jusqu'à combien pouvez-vous aller? ▸ **I can't afford £50!** je ne peux pas mettre 50 livres! 2. [spare] : **to be able to afford the time (to do sthg)** avoir le temps (de faire qqch) 3. [harmful, embarrassing thing] : **to be able to afford sthg** pouvoir se permettre qqch 4. [provide, give] procurer.

affordable [ə'fɔːdəbl] adj que l'on peut se permettre.

afforestation [æˌfɒrɪ'steɪʃn] n boisement *m*.

affray [ə'freɪ] n *UK* bagarre *f*.

affront [ə'frʌnt] ■ n affront *m*, insulte *f*.
■ vt insulter, faire un affront à.

Afghan ['æfgæn], **Afghani** [æf'gænɪ] ■ adj afghan(e).
■ n Afghan *m*, -e *f*.

Afghan hound n lévrier *m* afghan.

Afghani = **Afghan**.

Afghanistan [æf'gænɪstæn] n Afghanistan *m* ▸ **in Afghanistan** en Afghanistan.

aficionado [əˌfɪsjə'nɑːdəʊ] (pl -s) n aficionado *m*, amoureux *m*, -euse *f* ▸ **theatre aficionados, aficionados of the theatre** les aficionados du théâtre.

afield [ə'fɪəld] adv : **far afield** loin.

AFL-CIO (abbr of **American Federation of Labor and Congress of Industrial Organizations**) n *confédération syndicale américaine*.

afloat [ə'fləʊt] adj *lit & fig* à flot.

afoot [ə'fʊt] adj en préparation.

aforementioned [ə'fɔːˌmenʃənd], **aforesaid** [ə'fɔːsed] adj susmentionné(e).

aforenamed [ə'fɔːneɪmd] adj *fml* susnommé(e), précité(e).

afraid [ə'freɪd] adj 1. [frightened] : **to be afraid (of)** avoir peur (de) ▸ **to be afraid of doing** OR **to do sthg** avoir peur de faire qqch ▸ **there's nothing to be afraid of** il n'y a rien à craindre 2. [reluctant, apprehensive] : **to be afraid of** craindre 3. [in apologies] : **to be afraid (that)...** regretter que... ▸ **I'm afraid so/not** j'ai bien peur que oui/non.

afresh [ə'freʃ] adv de nouveau.

Africa ['æfrɪkə] n Afrique *f* ▸ **in Africa** en Afrique.

African ['æfrɪkən] ■ adj africain(e).
■ n Africain *m*, -e *f*.

African-American ■ n Noir américain *m*, Noire américaine *f*.
■ adj noir américain (noire américaine).

African, Caribbean and Pacific Group of States n POL Groupe *m* des États d'Afrique, des Caraïbes et du Pacifique.

African National Congress n POL Congrès *m* national africain, ANC *m*.

African Union n POL Union *f* africaine.

African violet n saintpaulia *m*.

Afrikaans [ˌæfrɪ'kɑːns] n afrikaans *m*.

Afrikaner [ˌæfrɪ'kɑːnər] n Afrikaner *mf*.

Afro ['æfrəʊ] (pl -s) ■ adj [hairstyle] afro.
■ n coiffure *f* afro.

Afro-American ■ n Afro-Américain *m*, -e *f*.
■ adj afro-américain(e).

Afro-Asian ■ n Afro-Asiatique *mf*.
■ adj afro-asiatique.

Afro-Caribbean ■ n Afro-antillais *m*, -e *f*.
■ adj afro-antillais(e).

aft [ɑ:ft] adv sur *OR* à l'arrière.

AFT (abbr of ***American Federation of Teachers***) n *syndicat américain d'enseignants.*

after ['ɑ:ftəʳ] ■ prep **1.** [gen] après ▸ **Smith comes after Smedley** Smith vient après Smedley ▸ **to shout after sb** crier après *OR* contre qqn ▸ **they ran after him** ils lui ont couru après ▸ **close the door after you** fermez la porte derrière vous ▸ **to be after sb/sthg** *inf* [in search of] chercher qqn/qqch ▸ **after you!** après vous! ▸ **to name sb after sb** donner à qqn le nom de qqn
2. [in time] après ▸ **after dark** après la tombée de la nuit ▸ **day after day** jour après jour ▸ **the day after tomorrow** après-demain *m* ▸ **(for) mile after mile** sur des kilomètres et des kilomètres ▸ **it is after six o'clock already** il est déjà six heures passées *OR* plus de six heures ▸ **it's twenty after three** *US* il est trois heures vingt.
■ adv après ▸ **the day after** le lendemain, le jour suivant ▸ **two days after** deux jours après *OR* plus tard ▸ **the week after** la semaine d'après *OR* suivante.
■ conj après que ▸ **I came after he had left** je suis arrivé après qu'il est parti ▸ **after saying goodnight to the children** après avoir dit bonsoir aux enfants.
◆ ***afters*** npl *UK inf* dessert *m.*
◆ ***after all*** adv après tout ▸ **so she was right after all** alors elle avait raison en fait.
◆ ***one after another***, ***one after the other*** adv l'un après l'autre.

afterbirth ['ɑ:ftəbɜ:θ] n placenta *m.*

aftercare ['ɑ:ftəkeəʳ] n postcure *f.*

after-dinner adj [speaker, speech] de fin de dîner *OR* banquet ▸ **an after-dinner drink** ≃ un digestif.

aftereffect ['ɑ:ftərɪˌfekt] n *(usu pl)* [gen] suite *f* / MED séquelle *f.*

afterglow ['ɑ:ftəgləʊ] n [of sunset] dernières lueurs *fpl*, derniers reflets *mpl* / *fig* [of pleasure] sensation *f* de bien-être *(après coup).*

after-hours adj [after closing time] qui suit la fermeture / [after work] qui suit le travail ▸ **an after-hours bar** *US* un bar de nuit.
◆ ***after hours*** adv [after closing time] après la fermeture / [after work] après le travail.

afterlife ['ɑ:ftəlaɪf] (pl -lives [-laɪvz]) n vie *f* future.

aftermath ['ɑ:ftəmæθ] n conséquences *fpl*, suites *fpl.*

afternoon [ˌɑ:ftə'nu:n] n après-midi *m inv* ▸ **this afternoon** cet après-midi ▸ **tomorrow/yesterday afternoon** demain/hier après-midi ▸ **all afternoon** tout l'après-midi ▸ **in the afternoon** l'après-midi ▸ **at 2 o'clock in the afternoon** à 2 h de l'après-midi ▸ **good afternoon** bonjour.
◆ ***afternoons*** adv l'après-midi.

afternoon tea n *thé pris avec une légère collation dans le cours de l'après-midi.*

afterpains ['ɑ:ftəpeɪnz] npl tranchées *fpl* utérines.

after-sales adj après-vente *(inv).*

after-sales service n service *m* après-vente.

after-school adj [activities] extrascolaire.

aftershave ['ɑ:ftəʃeɪv] n après-rasage *m.*

aftershock ['ɑ:ftəʃɒk] n réplique *f.*

aftersun ['ɑ:ftəsʌn] adj : **aftersun cream** crème *f* après-soleil.

aftertaste ['ɑ:ftəteɪst] n *lit & fig* arrière-goût *m.*

after-tax adj [profits] après impôts, net d'impôt / [salary] net d'impôt.

afterthought ['ɑ:ftəθɔ:t] n pensée *f OR* réflexion *f* après coup.

afterwards ['ɑ:ftəwədz] *UK*, ***afterward*** ['ɑ:ftəwəd] *US* adv après.

again [ə'gen] adv encore une fois, de nouveau ▸ **to do again** refaire ▸ **to say again** répéter ▸ **to start again** recommencer ▸ **it's me again!** c'est encore moi!, me revoici! ▸ **again and again** à plusieurs reprises ▸ **all over again** une fois de plus ▸ **time and again** maintes et maintes fois ▸ **I didn't see them again** je ne les ai plus revus ▸ **half as much again** à moitié autant ▸ **(twice) as much again** deux fois autant ▸ **come again?** *inf* comment?, pardon? ▸ **then *OR* there again** d'autre part.

against [ə'genst] prep & adv contre ▸ **I banged my knee against the chair** je me suis cogné le genou contre la chaise ▸ **the fight against inflation/crime** la lutte contre l'inflation/la criminalité ▸ **to decide against sthg** décider de ne pas faire qqch ▸ **it's against the law to steal** le vol est interdit par la loi ▸ **the dollar fell against the yen** FIN le dollar a baissé par rapport au yen ▸ **(as) against** contre.

age [eɪdʒ] (cont **ageing** *UK*, **aging** *US*) ■ n **1.** [gen] âge *m* ▸ **she's 20 years of age** elle a 20 ans ▸ **at the age of 25** à l'âge de 25 ans ▸ **what age are you?** quel âge avez-vous? ▸ **when I was your age** quand j'avais votre âge ▸ **I have a son your age** j'ai un fils de votre âge ▸ **to be of age** *US* avoir l'âge légal pour consommer de l'alcool dans un lieu public ▸ **to be under age** être mineur(e) ▸ **to come of age** atteindre sa majorité **2.** [old age] vieillesse *f* **3.** [in history] époque *f* ▸ **through the ages** à travers les âges.
■ vt & vi vieillir ▸ **to age well** [person] vieillir bien / [wine, cheese] s'améliorer en vieillissant.
◆ ***ages*** npl : **ages ago** il y a une éternité ▸ **I haven't seen him for ages** je ne l'ai pas vu depuis une éternité ▸ **it took him ages to do the work** il a mis très longtemps à faire le travail.

age bracket n = ***age group***.

aged ■ adj **1.** [eɪdʒd] [of stated age] **: aged 15** âgé(e) de 15 ans **2.** ['eɪdʒɪd] [very old] âgé(e), vieux (vieille).
■ npl ['eɪdʒɪd] **: the aged** les personnes *fpl* âgées.

age group n tranche *f* d'âge.

ageing *UK*, ***aging*** *US* ['eɪdʒɪŋ] ■ adj vieillissant(e).
■ n vieillissement *m.*

ageism ['eɪdʒɪzm] n âgisme *m.*

ageist ['eɪdʒɪst] ■ adj [action, policy] qui relève de l'âgisme.
■ n *personne qui fait preuve d'âgisme.*

ageless ['eɪdʒlɪs] adj sans âge.

age limit n limite *f* d'âge.

agency ['eɪdʒənsɪ] (pl **-ies**) **n 1.** [business] agence *f* ▸ **employment agency** agence OR bureau *m* de placement ▸ **travel agency** agence de voyages **2.** [organization] organisme *m*.

agenda [ə'dʒendə] (pl **-s**) **n** ordre *m* du jour.

FALSE FRIENDS / FAUX AMIS

agenda

Agenda n'est pas la traduction du mot anglais *agenda*. Agenda se traduit par *diary*.

▸ J'ai noté le rendez-vous dans mon agenda / *I've put the meeting in my diary*

agenda setting n *fait d'influencer la direction d'un débat.*

agent ['eɪdʒənt] **n** agent *m*, -e *f*.

age-old **adj** antique.

aggravate ['ægrəveɪt] **vt 1.** [make worse] aggraver **2.** [annoy] agacer.

aggravating ['ægrəveɪtɪŋ] **adj** [annoying] agaçant(e).

aggravation [ˌægrə'veɪʃn] **n 1.** *(U)* [trouble] agacements *mpl* **2.** [annoying thing] agacement *m*.

aggregate ['ægrɪgət] ■ **adj** total(e).
■ **n 1.** [total] total *m* **2.** [material] agrégat *m*.

aggression [ə'greʃn] **n** agression *f*.

aggressive [ə'gresɪv] **adj** agressif(ive).

aggressively [ə'gresɪvlɪ] **adv** d'une manière agressive.

aggressiveness [ə'gresɪvnɪs] **n 1.** [gen] agressivité *f* **2.** COMM [of businessman] combativité *f* / [of campaign] dynamisme *m*, fougue *f*.

aggressor [ə'gresəʳ] **n** agresseur *m*.

aggrieved [ə'gri:vd] **adj** blessé(e), froissé(e).

aggro ['ægrəʊ] **n** *UK inf* enquiquinement *m*.

aghast [ə'gɑ:st] **adj : aghast (at sthg)** atterré(e) (par qqch).

agile [*UK* 'ædʒaɪl, *US* 'ædʒəl] **adj** agile.

agility [ə'dʒɪlətɪ] **n** agilité *f*.

aging *US* = *ageing*.

agitate ['ædʒɪteɪt] ■ **vt 1.** [disturb] inquiéter **2.** [shake] agiter.
■ **vi : to agitate for/against** faire campagne pour/contre.

agitated ['ædʒɪteɪtɪd] **adj** agité(e).

agitation [ˌædʒɪ'teɪʃn] **n 1.** [anxiety] agitation *f* **2.** POL campagne *f* mouvementée.

agitator ['ædʒɪteɪtəʳ] **n** agitateur *m*, -trice *f*.

agitprop ['ædʒɪtprɒp] **n** POL agit-prop *f*.

aglow [ə'gləʊ] **adj** [fire] rougeoyant(e) / [sky] embrasé(e) ▸ **to be aglow with colour** briller de couleurs vives ▸ **his face was aglow with excitement/health** son visage rayonnait d'émotion/de santé.

AGM (abbr of ***annual general meeting***) **n** *UK* AGA *f*.

agnostic [æg'nɒstɪk] ■ **adj** agnostique.
■ **n** agnostique *mf*.

agnosticism [æg'nɒstɪsɪzm] **n** agnosticisme *m*.

ago [ə'gəʊ] **adv : a long time ago** il y a longtemps ▸ **three days ago** il y a trois jours.

agog [ə'gɒg] **adj : to be agog (with)** être en ébullition (à propos de).

agonize, *UK* ***-ise*** ['ægənaɪz] **vi : to agonize over** OR **about sthg** se tourmenter au sujet de qqch.

agonized, *UK* ***-ised*** ['ægənaɪzd] **adj** [behaviour, reaction] angoissé(e), d'angoisse / [cry] déchirant(e).

agonizing, *UK* ***-ising*** ['ægənaɪzɪŋ] **adj** [situation] angoissant(e) / [decision] déchirant(e), angoissant(e) / [pain] atroce.

agonizingly, *UK* ***-isingly*** ['ægənaɪzɪŋlɪ] **adv** [difficult] extrêmement.

agony ['ægənɪ] (pl **-ies**) **n 1.** [physical pain] douleur *f* atroce ▸ **to be in agony** souffrir le martyre **2.** [mental pain] angoisse *f* ▸ **to be in agony** être angoissé(e), être torturé(e) par l'angoisse.

agony aunt n *UK inf personne qui tient la rubrique du courrier du cœur.*

agony column n *UK inf* courrier *m* du cœur.

agoraphobia [ˌægərə'fəʊbjə] **n** agoraphobie *f*.

agoraphobic [ˌægərə'fəʊbɪk] ■ **adj** agoraphobe.
■ **n** agoraphobe *mf*.

agrarian [ə'greərɪən] ■ **adj** agraire.
■ **n** agrarien *m*, -enne *f*.

agree [ə'gri:] ■ **vi 1.** [concur] **: to agree (with/about)** être d'accord (avec/au sujet de) ▸ **I quite agree** je suis tout à fait d'accord (avec vous) ▸ **to agree on** [price, terms] convenir de
2. [consent] **: to agree (to sthg)** donner son consentement (à qqch) ▸ **they agreed to share the cost** ils se sont mis d'accord pour partager les frais ▸ **to agree on a date** convenir d'une date
3. [be in favour] être d'accord ▸ **I don't agree with censorship** je suis contre OR je n'admets pas la censure
4. [be consistent] concorder
5. [suit sb] **: to agree with** réussir à ▸ **rich food doesn't agree with me** la nourriture riche ne me réussit pas
6. GRAM **: to agree (with)** s'accorder (avec).
■ **vt 1.** [concur, concede] **: to agree (that)...** admettre que... ▸ **we all agree that he's innocent** nous sommes tous d'accord pour dire qu'il est innocent, nous sommes tous d'avis qu'il est innocent ▸ **they agreed that they had made a mistake** ils ont reconnu OR convenu qu'ils avaient fait une faute
2. [arrange] **: to agree to do sthg** se mettre d'accord pour faire qqch
3. [price, conditions] accepter, convenir de ▸ **the budget has been agreed** le budget a été adopté.

agreeable [ə'grɪəbl] **adj 1.** [pleasant] agréable **2.** [willing] **: to be agreeable to** consentir à.

agreeably [ə'grɪəblɪ] **adv** agréablement.

agreed [ə'gri:d] **adj : to be agreed (on sthg)** être d'accord (à propos de qqch).

agreement [əˈgri:mənt] **n 1.** [gen] accord *m* ▸ **to be in agreement (with)** être d'accord (avec) ▸ **to reach an agreement** parvenir à un accord **2.** [consistency] concordance *f.*

agricultural [ˌægrɪˈkʌltʃərəl] **adj** agricole.

agriculture [ˈægrɪkʌltʃəʳ] **n** agriculture *f.*

aground [əˈgraʊnd] **adv : to run aground** s'échouer.

ah [ɑ:] **excl** ah!

aha [ɑ:ˈhɑ:] **excl** ah, ah!

ahead [əˈhed] **adv 1.** [in front] devant, en avant ▸ **to go/be sent on ahead** partir/être envoyé (ee) en avant ▸ **right** OR **straight ahead** droit devant ▸ **the road ahead** la route devant nous/eux *etc* **2.** [in better position] en avance ▸ **Scotland are ahead by two goals to one** l'Écosse mène par deux à un ▸ **to get ahead** [be successful] réussir **3.** [in time] à l'avance ▸ **the months ahead** les mois à venir ▸ **to plan ahead** faire des projets.
◆ ***ahead of*** **prep 1.** [in front of] devant **2.** [in time] avant ▸ **ahead of schedule** [work] en avance sur le planning ▸ **ahead of time** en avance.

ahem [əˈhem] **excl** hum!

ahoy [əˈhɔɪ] **excl** NAUT ohé! ▸ **ship ahoy!** ohé, du bateau!

AI **n 1.** (abbr of ***Amnesty International***) AI *m* **2.** (abbr of ***artificial intelligence***) IA *f* **3.** abbr of ***artificial insemination***.

AIB (abbr of ***Accident Investigation Bureau***) **n** *commission d'enquête sur les accidents aériens en Grande-Bretagne.*

aid [eɪd] ■ **n** aide *f* ▸ **with the aid of** [person] avec l'aide de / [thing] à l'aide de ▸ **to go to the aid of sb** OR **to sb's aid** aller à l'aide de qqn ▸ **in aid of** au profit de.
■ **vt 1.** [help] aider **2.** LAW **: to aid and abet sb** être complice de qqn.

AID **n 1.** (abbr of ***artificial insemination by donor***) IAD *f* **2.** (abbr of ***Agency for International Development***) AID *f.*

aide [eɪd] **n** POL aide *mf.*

aide-de-camp [eɪddəˈkɑ̃:] (pl **aides-de-camp** [ˌeɪdz-]) **n** aide *m* de camp.

aide-mémoire [ˌeɪdmemˈwɑ:] (pl **aides-mémoire** [ˈeɪdz-]) **n** aide-mémoire *m inv.*

AIDS, ***Aids*** (abbr of ***acquired immune deficiency syndrome***) [eɪdz] ■ **n** SIDA *m*, sida *m.*
■ **comp : AIDS specialist** sidologue *mf* ▸ **AIDS patient** sidéen *m*, -enne *f.*

aids-related **adj** lié(e) au sida ▸ **aids-related complex** ARC *m.*

aid worker **n** [voluntary] volontaire *mf* / [paid] employé *m*, -e *f* d'une organisation humanitaire.

AIH (abbr of ***artificial insemination by husband***) **n** IAC *f.*

ail [eɪl] **vi** souffrir.

ailing [ˈeɪlɪŋ] **adj 1.** [ill] souffrant(e) **2.** *fig* [economy, industry] dans une mauvaise passe.

ailment [ˈeɪlmənt] **n** maladie *f.*

aim [eɪm] ■ **n 1.** [objective] but *m*, objectif *m* **2.** [in firing gun, arrow] **: to take aim at** viser.
■ **vt 1.** [gun, camera] **: to aim sthg at** braquer qqch sur **2.** *fig* **: to be aimed at** [plan, campaign] être destiné(e) à, viser / [criticism] être dirigé(e) contre.
■ **vi : to aim (at)** viser ▸ **to aim at** OR **for** *fig* viser ▸ **to aim to do sthg** viser à faire qqch.

aimless [ˈeɪmlɪs] **adj** [person] désœuvré(e) / [life] sans but.

aimlessly [ˈeɪmlɪslɪ] **adv** sans but.

ain't [eɪnt] *inf* = ***am not, are not, is not, has not, have not.***

air [eəʳ] ■ **n 1.** [gen] air *m* ▸ **to throw sthg into the air** jeter qqch en l'air ▸ **the smoke rose into the air** la fumée s'éleva vers le ciel ▸ **I need some (fresh) air** j'ai besoin de prendre l'air ▸ **by air** [travel] par avion ▸ **to disappear** OR **vanish into thin air** se volatiliser, disparaître sans laisser de traces ▸ **to be (up) in the air** *fig* [plans] être vague ▸ **to clear the air** *fig* dissiper les malentendus
2. RADIO & TV **: on the air** à l'antenne ▸ **to go on the air** passer à l'antenne ▸ **to go off the air** [person] rendre l'antenne / [programme] se terminer / [station] cesser d'émettre
3. [manner, atmosphere] air *m* ▸ **an air of mystery** un air mystérieux.
■ **comp** [transport] aérien(enne).
■ **vt 1.** [room, linen] aérer
2. [make publicly known] faire connaître OR communiquer
3. [broadcast] diffuser.
■ **vi** sécher.
◆ ***airs*** **npl : airs and graces** manières *fpl* ▸ **to give o.s. airs, to put on airs** prendre de grands airs.

airbag [ˈeabæg] **n** AUT Airbag® *m.*

airbase [ˈeəbeɪs] **n** base *f* aérienne.

airbed [ˈeəbed] **n** matelas *m* pneumatique.

HOW TO ...

express agreement

Absolument ! / Absolutely!
Vous avez (absolument) raison / You're (absolutely) right
Je suis entièrement de votre avis / I couldn't agree with you more
Je suis tout à fait d'accord / I quite agree
C'est exactement ce que je pensais / That's just what I was thinking
Je suis assez d'accord (avec toi) / I'm inclined to agree (with you)
C'est aussi mon avis / I think so too
Tu as fait le bon choix / You've made the right choice
Pas de problème / That's fine by me

airborne **['eəbɔ:n] adj 1.** [troops] aéroporté(e) / [seeds] emporté(e) par le vent **2.** [plane] qui a décollé.

airbrake **['eəbreɪk] n** frein *m* à air comprimé.

airbrush **['eəbrʌʃ] ■ n** pistolet *m (pour peindre)*.
■ **vt** peindre au pistolet.

airbus **['eəbʌs] n** airbus *m*.

air-conditioned **[-kən'dɪʃnd] adj** climatisé(e), à air conditionné.

air-conditioning **[-kən'dɪʃnɪŋ] n** climatisation *f*.

aircraft **['eəkrɑ:ft] (pl aircraft) n** avion *m*.

aircraft carrier **n** porte-avions *m inv*.

aircrew **['eəkru:] n** équipage *m (d'avion)*.

air cushion **n** coussin *m* pneumatique ***OR*** gonflable.

airfare **['eəfeəʳ] n** prix *m* du billet (d'avion), tarif *m* aérien.

airfield **['eəfi:ld] n** terrain *m* d'aviation.

airforce **['eəfɔ:s] ■ n** armée *f* de l'air.
■ **comp** [base] aérien(enne).

air freight **n** fret *m* aérien.

air freshener **[-'freʃənəʳ] n** désodorisant *m (pour la maison)*.

airgun **['eəgʌn] n** carabine *f* ***OR*** fusil *m* à air comprimé.

airhead **['eəhed] n** *inf* taré *m*, -e *f*.

air hostess **['eə,həustɪs] n** *UK dated* hôtesse *f* de l'air.

airily **['eərəlɪ] adv** à la légère.

airing **['eərɪŋ] n : to give sthg an airing** aérer qqch / *fig* [opinions] exposer qqch.

airing cupboard **n** *UK* placard *m* séchoir.

air-kiss **['eəkɪs] vi** s'embrasser (avec affectation).

airlane **['eəleɪn] n** couloir *m* aérien.

airless **['eəlɪs] adj** [room] qui sent le renfermé.

air letter **['eəletəʳ] n** aérogramme *m*.

airlift **['eəlɪft] ■ n** pont *m* aérien.
■ **vt** transporter par pont aérien.

airline **['eəlaɪn] n** compagnie *f* aérienne.

airliner **['eəlaɪnəʳ] n** [short-distance] (avion *m*) moyen-courrier *m* / [long-distance] (avion *m*) long-courrier *m*.

airlock **['eəlɒk] n 1.** [in tube, pipe] poche *f* d'air **2.** [airtight chamber] sas *m*.

airmail **['eəmeɪl] n** poste *f* aérienne ▸ **by airmail** par avion.

airman **['eəmən] (pl -men [-mən]) n** [aviator] aviateur *m*.

air marshal **n** général *m* de corps aérien.

air mattress **n** matelas *m* pneumatique.

airplane **['eəpleɪn] n** *US* avion *m*.

airplay **['eəpleɪ] n** RADIO **: to get a lot of airplay** passer beaucoup à la radio.

air pocket **n** trou *m* d'air.

air pollution **n** pollution *f* atmosphérique.

airport **['eəpɔ:t] ■ n** aéroport *m*.
■ **comp** de l'aéroport.

air pressure **n** pression *f* atmosphérique.

air raid **n** raid *m* aérien, attaque *f* aérienne.

air-raid shelter **n** abri *m* antiaérien.

air rifle **n** carabine *f* à air comprimé.

air-sea rescue **n** sauvetage *m* en mer *(par hélicoptère)*.

airship **['eəʃɪp] n** (ballon *m*) dirigeable *m*.

airsick **['eəsɪk] adj : to be airsick** avoir le mal de l'air.

airspace **['eəspeɪs] n** espace *m* aérien.

airspeed **['eəspi:d] n** vitesse *f* vraie *(d'un avion)*.

air steward **n** steward *m*.

air stewardess **n** *dated* hôtesse *f* de l'air.

airstrip **['eəstrɪp] n** piste *f* (d'atterrissage).

air terminal **n** aérogare *f*.

airtight **['eətaɪt] adj** hermétique.

airtime **['eətaɪm] n** RADIO temps *m* d'antenne.

air-to-air **adj** [missile, rocket] air-air *(inv)*.

air-to-surface **adj** MIL air-sol *(inv)*.

air-traffic control **n** contrôle *m* du trafic (aérien).

air-traffic controller **n** aiguilleur *m* (du ciel).

air travel **n** déplacement *m* ***OR*** voyage *m* par avion.

airwaves **['eəweɪvz] npl** ondes *fpl* (hertziennes).

airway **['eəweɪ] n 1.** AERON [route] voie *f* aérienne [company] ligne *f* aérienne **2.** MED voies *fpl* respiratoire **3.** [shaft] conduit *m* d'air.

airworthy **['eə,wɜ:ðɪ] adj** en état de navigation.

airy **['eərɪ] (comp -ier, superl -iest) adj 1.** [room] aéré(e) **2.** [notions, promises] chimérique, vain(e) **3.** [nonchalant] nonchalant(e).

airy-fairy **adj** *UK inf* [person, notion] farfelu(e).

aisle **[aɪl] n** [in cinema, supermarket, plane] allée *f* / [o train] couloir *m* (central).

ajar **[ə'dʒɑ:ʳ] adj** entrouvert(e).

AK abbr of ***Alaska***.

aka (abbr of ***also known as***) alias.

akimbo **[ə'kɪmbəu] adv : with arms akimbo** les mair ***OR*** poings sur les hanches.

akin **[ə'kɪn] adj : to be akin to** être semblable à.

AL abbr of ***Alabama***.

Alabama **[,ælə'bæmə] n** Alabama *m* ▸ **in Alabama** dar l'Alabama.

alabaster **[,ælə'bɑ:stəʳ] n** albâtre *m*.

alacrity **[ə'lækrətɪ] n** empressement *m*.

alarm **[ə'lɑ:m] ■ n 1.** [fear] alarme *f*, inquiétude *f* **2.** [d vice] alarme *f* ▸ **fire alarm** sirène *f* d'incendie ▸ **to raise sound the alarm** donner ***OR*** sonner l'alarme.
■ **vt** alarmer, alerter.

alarm clock **n** réveil *m*, réveille-matin *m inv*.

alarmed **[ə'lɑ:md] adj 1.** [anxious] inquiet(ète) ▸ **don be alarmed** ne vous alarmez ***OR*** effrayez pas ▸ **to becon alarmed** [person] s'alarmer / [animal] s'effaroucher, pre dre peur **2.** [vehicle, building] équipé(e) d'une alarme.

alarming **[ə'lɑ:mɪŋ] adj** alarmant(e), inquiétant(e).

alarmingly [ə'lɑːmɪŋlɪ] **adv** d'une manière alarmante OR inquiétante.

alarmist [ə'lɑːmɪst] **adj** alarmiste.

alas [ə'læs] **excl** hélas!

Alaska [ə'læskə] **n** Alaska *m* ▸ **in Alaska** en Alaska.

Albania [æl'beɪnjə] **n** Albanie *f* ▸ **in Albania** en Albanie.

Albanian [æl'beɪnjən] ■ **adj** albanais(e).
■ **n 1.** [person] Albanais *m*, -e *f* **2.** [language] albanais *m*.

albatross ['ælbətrɒs] (pl **albatross** OR **-es** [-iːz]) **n** albatros *m*.

albeit [ɔːl'biːɪt] **conj** *fml* bien que *(+ subjunctive)*.

Alberta [æl'bɜːtə] **n** Alberta *f*.

Albert Hall ['ælbət-] **n : the Albert Hall** *salle de concert à Londres*.

albino [æl'biːnəʊ] ■ **n** (pl **-s**) albinos *mf*.
■ **comp** albinos *(inv)*.

album ['ælbəm] **n** album *m*.

albumen ['ælbjʊmɪn] **n** [of egg] albumen *m*.

alchemist ['ælkəmɪst] **n** alchimiste *m*.

alchemy ['ælkəmɪ] **n** alchimie *f*.

alcohol ['ælkəhɒl] **n** alcool *m*.

alcoholic [ˌælkə'hɒlɪk] ■ **adj** [person] alcoolique / [drink] alcoolisé(e).
■ **n** alcoolique *mf*.

alcoholism ['ælkəhɒlɪzm] **n** alcoolisme *m*.

alcopop ['ælkəʊpɒp] **n** *UK boisson gazeuse faiblement alcoolisée*.

alcove ['ælkəʊv] **n** alcôve *f*.

alderman ['ɔːldəmən] (pl **-men** [-mən]) **n** conseiller *m* municipal.

ale [eɪl] **n** bière *f*.

alert [ə'lɜːt] ■ **adj 1.** [vigilant] vigilant(e) **2.** [perceptive] vif (vive), éveillé(e) **3.** [aware] **: to be alert to** être conscient(e) de.
■ **n** [warning] alerte *f* ▸ **on the alert** [watchful] sur le qui-vive / MIL en état d'alerte.
■ **vt** alerter ▸ **to alert sb to sthg** avertir qqn de qqch.

alert box **n** COMPUT message *m* d'alerte.

alertness [ə'lɜːtnɪs] **n 1.** [vigilance] vigilance *f* **2.** [liveliness] vivacité *f*, esprit *m* éveillé.

Aleutian Islands [ə'luːʃjən-] **npl : the Aleutian Islands** les îles *fpl* Aléoutiennes.

A level (abbr of ***Advanced level***) **n** ≃ baccalauréat *m*.

Alexandria [ˌælɪg'zɑːndrɪə] **n** Alexandrie.

alfalfa [æl'fælfə] **n** luzerne *f*.

alfresco [æl'freskəʊ] **adj & adv** en plein air.

algae ['ældʒiː] **npl** algues *fpl*.

Algarve [æl'gɑːv] **n : the Algarve** l'Algarve *f*.

algebra ['ældʒɪbrə] **n** algèbre *f*.

Algeria [æl'dʒɪərɪə] **n** Algérie *f* ▸ **in Algeria** en Algérie.

Algerian [æl'dʒɪərɪən] ■ **adj** algérien(enne).
■ **n** Algérien *m*, -enne *f*.

Algiers [æl'dʒɪəz] **n** Alger.

algorithm ['ælgərɪðm] **n** algorithme *m*.

alias ['eɪlɪəs] ■ **adv** alias.
■ **n** (pl **-es** [-iːz]) **1.** faux nom *m*, nom *m* d'emprunt **2.** COMPUT [in e-mail, on desktop] alias *m*.

aliasing ['eɪlɪəsɪŋ] **n** COMPUT aliassage *m*, crénelage *m*.

alibi ['ælɪbaɪ] **n** alibi *m*.

Alice band **n** bandeau *m (pour les cheveux)*.

alien ['eɪljən] ■ **adj 1.** [gen] étranger(ère) **2.** [from outer space] extraterrestre.
■ **n 1.** [from outer space] extraterrestre *mf* **2.** LAW [foreigner] étranger *m*, -ère *f*.

alienate ['eɪljəneɪt] **vt** aliéner.

alienated ['eɪljəneɪtɪd] **adj : many young people feel alienated and alone** beaucoup de jeunes se sentent seuls et rejetés.

alienation [ˌeɪljə'neɪʃn] **n** PSYCHOL aliénation *f*.

alight [ə'laɪt] ■ **adj** allumé(e), en feu.
■ **vi 1.** [bird] se poser **2.** [from bus, train] **: to alight from** descendre de.

align [ə'laɪn] **vt 1.** [line up] aligner **2.** [ally] **: to align o.s. with sb** s'aligner sur qqn.

alignment [ə'laɪnmənt] **n** alignement *m*.

alike [ə'laɪk] ■ **adj** semblable ▸ **to look alike** se ressembler.
■ **adv** de la même façon.

alimentary canal [ˌælɪmentərɪ-] **n** tube *m* digestif.

alimony ['ælɪmənɪ] **n** pension *f* alimentaire.

A-line **adj** trapèze *(inv)*.

A-list **n** *liste des célébrités les plus cotées*.

alive [ə'laɪv] **adj 1.** [living] vivant(e), en vie **2.** [practice, tradition] vivace ▸ **to keep alive** préserver **3.** [lively] plein(e) de vitalité ▸ **to come alive** [story, description] prendre vie / [person, place] s'animer **4.** [aware] **: to be alive to sthg** être conscient(e) de qqch **5.** [full of] **: to be alive with sthg** grouiller de qqch, pulluler de qqch.

alkali ['ælkəlaɪ] (pl **-s** OR **-es**) **n** alcali *m*.

alkaline ['ælkəlaɪn] **adj** alcalin(e).

all [ɔːl] ■ **adj 1.** *(with sg noun)* tout (toute) ▸ **all day/night/evening** toute la journée/la nuit/la soirée ▸ **all the drink** toute la boisson ▸ **all the time** tout le temps
2. *(with pl noun)* tous (toutes) ▸ **all the boxes** toutes les boîtes ▸ **all men** tous les hommes ▸ **all three died** ils sont morts tous les trois, tous les trois sont morts.
■ **pron 1.** *(sg)* [the whole amount] tout *m* ▸ **all of the butter/the cakes** tout le beurre, tous les gâteaux ▸ **she drank it all, she drank all of it** elle a tout bu
2. *(pl)* [everybody, everything] tous (toutes) ▸ **all of them came, they all came** ils sont tous venus ▸ **all I want is to rest** tout ce que je veux c'est du repos ▸ **will that be all?** ce sera tout? ▸ **it's all his fault** c'est sa faute à lui
3. *(with superl)* **:... of all**... de tous (toutes) ▸ **I like this one best of all** je préfère celui-ci entre tous ▸ **hers was the best/worst essay of all** sa dissertation était la meilleure/la pire de toutes
4. : above all ➤ ***above*** ▸ **after all** ➤ ***after*** ▸ **at all** ➤ ***at***.

■ adv **1.** [entirely] complètement ▸ **I'd forgotten all about that** j'avais complètement oublié cela ▸ **all alone** tout seul (toute seule) ▸ **that's all very well, but...** tout cela est bien beau, mais...
2. [in sport, competitions] **: the score is five all** le score est cinq partout
3. *(with compar)* **: to run all the faster** courir d'autant plus vite ▸ **all the better** d'autant mieux.
◆ ***all but*** adv presque, pratiquement.
◆ ***all in all*** adv dans l'ensemble.
◆ ***all that*** adv si... que ça ▸ **it's not all that interesting** ce n'est pas si intéressant que ça.
◆ ***in all*** adv en tout.

Allah ['ælə] n Allah *m*.

all along adv depuis le début.

all-American adj cent pour cent américain(e) ▸ **the all-American boy** le jeune américain type.

all-around *US* = ***all-round***.

allay [ə'leɪ] vt [fears, anger] apaiser, calmer / [doubts] dissiper.

all clear n [signal, announcement] signal *m* de fin d'alerte / *fig* feu *m* vert.

all-day adj qui dure toute la journée ▸ **all-day breakfast** petit-déjeuner *m* servi toute la journée.

allegation [,ælɪ'geɪʃn] n allégation *f* ▸ **to make allegations (about)** faire des allégations (sur).

allege [ə'ledʒ] vt prétendre, alléguer ▸ **to allege (that)...** prétendre que..., alléguer que... ▸ **she is alleged to have done it** on prétend qu'elle l'a fait.

alleged [ə'ledʒd] adj prétendu(e).

allegedly [ə'ledʒɪdlɪ] adv prétendument.

allegiance [ə'li:dʒəns] n allégeance *f*.

allegorical [,ælɪ'gɒrɪkl] adj allégorique.

allegory ['ælɪgərɪ] (pl **-ies**) n allégorie *f*.

alleluia [,ælɪ'lu:jə] excl alléluia!

all-embracing [-ɪm'breɪsɪŋ] adj exhaustif(ive), complet(ète).

allergen ['ælədʒen] n allergène *m*.

allergic [ə'lɜ:dʒɪk] adj **: allergic (to)** allergique (à) ▸ **to be allergic to hard work** *hum* être allergique au travail.

allergy ['ælədʒɪ] (pl -ies) n allergie *f* ▸ **to have an allergy to sthg** être allergique à qqch.

alleviate [ə'li:vɪeɪt] vt apaiser, soulager.

alley cat n chat *m* de gouttière.

alley(way) ['ælɪ(weɪ)] n [street] ruelle *f* / [in garden] allée *f*.

all fours ◆ ***on all fours*** adv à quatre pattes.

Allhallows [,ɔ:l'hæləʊz] n Toussaint *f*.

alliance [ə'laɪəns] n alliance *f*.

allied ['ælaɪd] adj **1.** MIL allié(e) **2.** [related] connexe.

alligator ['ælɪgeɪtəʳ] (pl **alligator** *OR* -s) n alligator *m*.

all-important adj capital(e), crucial(e).

all-in adj *UK* [price] global(e).
◆ ***all in*** adv [inclusive] tout compris.

all-inclusive adj [price, tariff] net(nette), tout compris(e), forfaitaire / [insurance policy] tous risques.

all-in-one adj tout-en-un *(inv)*.

all-in wrestling n *UK* lutte *f* libre.

alliteration [ə,lɪtə'reɪʃn] n allitération *f*.

all-night adj [party] qui dure toute la nuit / [bar] ouvert(e) toute la nuit.

all-nighter [-'naɪtə] n **: the party will be an all-nighter** la fête va durer toute la nuit ▸ **we pulled an all-nighter for the physics exam** *US* on a passé la nuit à réviser l'examen de physique.

allocate ['æləkeɪt] vt [money, resources] **: to allocate sthg (to sb)** attribuer qqch (à qqn).

allocation [,ælə'keɪʃn] n **1.** [gen] attribution *f* **2.** [share of money] somme *f* allouée.

allot [ə'lɒt] (pt & pp **-ted**, cont **-ting**) vt [job] assigner / [money, resources] attribuer / [time] allouer.

allotment [ə'lɒtmənt] n **1.** *UK* [garden] jardin *m* ouvrier *(loué par la commune)* **2.** [sharing out] attribution **3.** [share] part *f*.

all out adv **: to go all out to do sthg** se donner à fond pour faire qqch.
◆ ***all-out*** adj [strike, war] total(e) / [effort] maximum *(inv)*.

allow [ə'laʊ] vt **1.** [permit - activity, behaviour] autoriser, permettre ▸ **to allow sb to do sthg** permettre à qqn de faire qqch, autoriser qqn à faire qqch ▸ **we weren't allowed in** on ne nous a pas permis d'entrer ▸ **I won't allow such behaviour!** je ne tolérerai pas une telle conduite ▸ **allow me** permettez-moi **2.** [set aside - money, time] prévoir ▸ **allow a week for delivery** il faut prévoir *OR* compter une semaine pour la livraison **3.** [grant - money, time] accorder, allouer / [- opportunity] donner / [- claim] admettre **4.** [concede] **: to allow that...** admettre que...
◆ ***allow for*** vt insep tenir compte de ▸ **we hadn't allowed for these extra costs** nous n'avions pas prévu ces frais supplémentaires ▸ **allowing for the bad weather** compte tenu du mauvais temps.

allowable [ə'laʊəbl] adj admissible.

allowance [ə'laʊəns] n **1.** *UK* [money received] indemnité *f* ▸ **maternity allowance** allocation *f* de maternité ▸ **cost-of-living allowance** indemnité de vie chère **2.** *US* [pocket money] argent *m* de poche **3.** *UK* FIN **: tax allowance** ≃ abattement *m* fiscal **4.** [excuse] **: to make allowances for sb** faire preuve d'indulgence envers qqn ▸ **to make allowances for sthg** prendre qqch en considération.

alloy ['ælɔɪ] n alliage *m*.

all-party talks n POL *discussions entre tous les partis*

all-powerful adj tout-puissant (toute-puissante).

all-purpose adj [gen] qui répond à tous les besoins, passe-partout *(inv)* / [tool, vehicle] polyvalent(e) ▸ **all-purpose cleaning fluid** détachant *m* tous usages.

all right ■ adv bien ▸ **they're doing all right** [progressing well] ça va (pour eux) / [successful] ils se débrouillent bien.
■ interj [in answer - yes] d'accord ▸ **all right, let's go!** bon, on y va?

■ **adj 1.** [healthy] en bonne santé / [unharmed] sain et sauf (saine et sauve) ▸ **are you all right?** ça va? **2.** *inf* [acceptable, satisfactory] **: it was all right** c'était pas mal ▸ **that's all right** [never mind] ce n'est pas grave ▸ **is everything all right, Madam?** tout va bien, Madame? **3.** [allowable] **: is it all right if...?** ça ne vous dérange pas si...? ▸ **it's all right** [no problem] ça va **4.** [pleasant] bien, agréable / [nice-looking] chouette ▸ **she's all right** *inf* elle est pas mal.

all-round *UK*, ***all-around*** *US* **adj 1.** [multiskilled] doué(e) dans tous les domaines **2.** [comprehensive] complet(ète).

all-rounder [-'raʊndəʳ] **n** *UK* **1.** [versatile person] **: to be an all-rounder** être bon (bonne) en tout **2.** SPORT sportif complet *m*, sportive complète *f*.

All Saints' Day **n** (le jour de) la Toussaint.

all-singing all-dancing **adj** dernier cri.

All Souls' Day **n** le jour *OR* la Fête des Morts.

all-star **adj** [show, performance] avec beaucoup de vedettes, à vedettes ▸ **with an all-star cast** avec un plateau de vedettes.

all-terrain vehicle [ɔ:ltəˌreɪn'vi:ɪkl] **n** véhicule *m* tout terrain, 4x4 *m*.

all-time **adj** [record] sans précédent ▸ **sales have reached an all-time high/low** les ventes ont connu le niveau le plus élevé jamais atteint/sont tombées au niveau le plus bas jamais atteint.

all told **adv** en tout.

allude [ə'lu:d] **vi : to allude to** faire allusion à.

allure [ə'ljʊəʳ] **n** charme *m*.

alluring [ə'ljʊərɪŋ] **adj** séduisant(e).

allusion [ə'lu:ʒn] **n** allusion *f*.

allusive [ə'lu:sɪv] **adj** allusif(ive), qui contient une allusion *OR* des allusions.

all-weather **adj** [surface] de toute saison, tous temps ▸ **all-weather court** TENNIS (terrain *m* en) quick *m*.

ally ■ **n** ['ælaɪ] (pl **-ies**) allié *m*, -e *f*.
■ **vt** (pt & pp **-ied** [ə'laɪ]) **: to ally o.s. with** s'allier à.

almanac ['ɔ:lmənæk] **n** almanach *m*.

almighty [ɔ:l'maɪtɪ] **adj** *inf* [noise] terrible.
◆ ***Almighty*** **n : the Almighty** le Tout-Puissant.

almond ['ɑ:mənd] **n** [nut] amande *f* ▸ **almond (tree)** amandier *m*.

almond paste **n** pâte *f* d'amande.

almost ['ɔ:lməʊst] **adv** presque ▸ **I almost missed the bus** j'ai failli rater le bus.

alms [ɑ:mz] **npl** *dated* aumône *f*.

aloft [ə'lɒft] **adv 1.** [in the air] en l'air **2.** NAUT dans la mâture.

alone [ə'ləʊn] ■ **adj** seul(e) ▸ **all alone** tout seul (toute seule) ▸ **she alone knows the truth** elle seule connaît la vérité.
■ **adv** seul ▸ **to leave sthg alone** ne pas toucher à qqch ▸ **leave me alone!** laisse-moi tranquille! ▸ **to go it alone** faire cavalier seul.

along [ə'lɒŋ] ■ **adv : to walk along** se promener ▸ **to move along** avancer ▸ **can I come along (with you)?** est-ce que je peux venir (avec vous)?
■ **prep** le long de ▸ **to run/walk along the street** courir/marcher le long de la rue.
◆ ***along with*** **prep** ainsi que.

alongside [əˌlɒŋ'saɪd] ■ **prep** [along] le long de, à côté de / [beside] à côté de.
■ **adv** bord à bord.

aloof [ə'lu:f] ■ **adj** distant(e).
■ **adv : to remain aloof (from)** garder ses distances (vis-à-vis de).

aloofness [ə'lu:fnɪs] **n** attitude *f* distante, réserve *f*.

aloud [ə'laʊd] **adv** à voix haute, tout haut.

alpaca [æl'pækə] **n** alpaga *m*.

alpha ['ælfə] **n 1.** [Greek letter] alpha *m* **2.** *UK* SCH ≃ mention *f* bien ▸ **alpha plus** ≃ mention *f* très bien.

alphabet ['ælfəbet] **n** alphabet *m*.

alphabetical [ˌælfə'betɪkl] **adj** alphabétique ▸ **in alphabetical order** par ordre alphabétique.

alphabetically [ˌælfə'betɪklɪ] **adv** par ordre alphabétique.

alphabetize, *UK* ***-ise*** ['ælfəbətaɪz] **vt** classer par ordre alphabétique.

alphanumeric [ˌælfənju:'merɪk] **adj** alphanumérique.

alphanumeric key **n** COMPUT touche *f* alphanumérique.

alpha version **n** COMPUT [of program] version *f* alpha.

alpine ['ælpaɪn] **adj** alpin(e).

Alps [ælps] **npl : the Alps** les Alpes *fpl*.

al-Qaeda, ***al-Qaida*** [ˌælkæ'i:də] **n** Al-Qaida *m*.

already [ɔ:l'redɪ] **adv** déjà.

alright [ˌɔ:l'raɪt] = ***all right***.

Alsace [æl'sæs] **n** Alsace *f* ▸ **in Alsace** en Alsace.

Alsatian [æl'seɪʃn] ■ **adj** alsacien(enne).
■ **n 1.** [person] Alsacien *m*, -enne *f* **2.** *UK* [dog] berger *m* allemand.

also ['ɔ:lsəʊ] **adv** aussi.

also-ran **n** [person] perdant *m*, -e *f*.

Alta. abbr of ***Alberta***.

altar ['ɔ:ltəʳ] **n** autel *m*.

alter ['ɔ:ltəʳ] ■ **vt** changer, modifier ▸ **to have a dress/suit altered** faire retoucher une robe/un costume.
■ **vi** changer.

alteration [ˌɔ:ltə'reɪʃn] **n** modification *f*, changement *m* ▸ **to make an alteration** *OR* **alterations to sthg** changer *OR* modifier qqch.

altercation [ˌɔ:ltə'keɪʃn] **n** altercation *f*.

alter ego ['ɔ:ltəʳ-] (pl **-s**) **n** alter ego *m*.

alternate ■ **adj** [*UK* ɔ:l'tɜ:nət, *US* 'ɔ:ltərnət] alterné(e), alternatif(ive) ▸ **on alternate days** tous les deux jours, un jour sur deux.
■ **vt** ['ɔ:ltərneɪt] faire alterner.

■ vi ['ɔ:ltərneɪt] : **to alternate (with)** alterner (avec) ▸ **to alternate between sthg and sthg** passer de qqch à qqch.

alternately [ɔ:l'tɜ:nətlɪ] **adv** alternativement.

alternating ['ɔ:ltəneɪtɪŋ] **adj** [gen] alternant(e), en alternance ⁄ ELEC & TECH alternatif(ive) ⁄ MATHS alterné(e).

alternating current ['ɔ:ltəneɪtɪŋ-] **n** courant *m* alternatif.

alternation [,ɔ:ltə'neɪʃn] **n** alternance *f*.

alternative [ɔ:l'tɜ:nətɪv] ■ **adj 1.** [different] autre **2.** [non-traditional - society] parallèle ⁄ [- art, energy] alternatif(ive).

■ **n 1.** [between two solutions] alternative *f* **2.** [other possibility] : **alternative (to)** solution *f* de remplacement (à) ▸ **to have no alternative** ne pas avoir le choix ▸ **to have no alternative but to do sthg** ne pas avoir d'autre choix que de faire qqch.

alternatively [ɔ:l'tɜ:nətɪvlɪ] **adv** ou bien.

alternative medicine **n** médecine *f* parallèle OR douce.

alternator ['ɔ:ltəneɪtər] **n** ELEC alternateur *m*.

although [ɔ:l'ðəʊ] **conj** bien que *(+ subjunctive)*.

altitude ['æltɪtju:d] **n** altitude *f*.

alt key [ælt-] **n** touche *f* alt.

alto ['æltəʊ] **(pl -s)** ■ **n 1.** [male voice] haute-contre *f* **2.** [female voice] contralto *m*.

■ **comp** alto.

altogether [,ɔ:ltə'geðər] **adv 1.** [completely] entièrement, tout à fait **2.** [considering all things] tout compte fait **3.** [in all] en tout.

altruism ['æltruɪzm] **n** altruisme *m*.

altruist ['æltruɪst] **n** altruiste *mf*.

altruistic [,æltru'ɪstɪk] **adj** altruiste.

aluminium *UK* [,ælju'mɪnɪəm], ***aluminum*** *US* [ə'lu:mɪnəm] ■ **n** aluminium *m*.

■ **comp** en aluminium ▸ **aluminium foil** papier *m* aluminium.

alumna [ə'lʌmna:] **(pl -nae [-ni:])** **n** ancienne étudiante *f (d'une université)*.

alumnus [ə'lʌmnəs] **(pl -ni [-naɪ])** **n** ancien étudiant *m (d'une université)*.

always ['ɔ:lweɪz] **adv** toujours.

always-on [,ɔ:lweɪz'ɑn] **adj** permanent(e).

Alzheimer's (disease) ['ælts,haɪməz -] **n** maladie *f* d'Alzheimer.

am [æm] ➤ ***be***.

a.m. (abbr of ***ante meridiem***) : **at 3 a.m.** à 3h (du matin).

AM (abbr of ***amplitude modulation***) **n** AM *f*.

AMA (abbr of ***American Medical Association***) **n** *ordre américain des médecins*.

amalgam [ə'mælgəm] **n** amalgame *m*.

amalgamate [ə'mælgəmeɪt] **vt & vi** [companies] fusionner.

amalgamation [ə,mælgə'meɪʃn] **n** [of companies] fusion *f*.

amass [ə'mæs] **vt** amasser.

amateur ['æmətər] ■ **adj** amateur *(inv)* ⁄ *pej* d'amateur *Québec*.

■ **n** amateur *m*.

amateurish [,æmətə:rɪʃ] **adj** d'amateur.

amateurism ['æmətərɪzəm] **n 1.** SPORT amateurisme *m* **2.** *pej* [lack of professionalism] amateurisme *m*, dilettantisme *m*.

amaze [ə'meɪz] **vt** étonner, stupéfier.

amazed [ə'meɪzd] **adj** stupéfait(e).

amazement [ə'meɪzmənt] **n** stupéfaction *f*.

amazing [ə'meɪzɪŋ] **adj 1.** [surprising] étonnant(e), ahurissant(e) **2.** [wonderful] excellent(e).

amazingly [ə'meɪzɪŋlɪ] **adv** étonnamment.

Amazon ['æməzn] **n 1.** [river] : **the Amazon** l'Amazone *f* **2.** [region] : **the Amazon (Basin)** l'Amazonie *f* ▸ **in the Amazon** en Amazonie ▸ **the Amazon rain forest** la forêt amazonienne.

Amazonian [,æmə'zəunjən] **adj** amazonien(enne).

ambassador [æm'bæsədər] **n** ambassadeur *m*, -drice *f*.

amber ['æmbər] ■ **adj 1.** [amber-coloured] ambré(e) **2.** *UK* [traffic light] orange *(inv)*.

■ **n 1.** [substance] ambre *m* **2.** *UK* [colour - of traffic light] orange *m*.

■ **comp** [made of amber] d'ambre.

ambiance ['æmbɪəns] = ***ambience***.

ambidextrous [,æmbɪ'dekstrəs] **adj** ambidextre.

ambience ['æmbɪəns] **n** ambiance *f*.

ambient ['æmbɪənt] **adj** ambiant(e).

ambiguity [,æmbɪ'gju:ətɪ] **(pl -ies)** **n** ambiguïté *f*.

ambiguous [æm'bɪgjuəs] **adj** ambigu(ë).

ambiguously [æm'bɪgjuəslɪ] **adv** de façon ambiguë.

ambition [æm'bɪʃn] **n** ambition *f*.

ambitious [æm'bɪʃəs] **adj** ambitieux(euse).

ambivalence [æm'bɪvələns] **n** ambivalence *f*.

ambivalent [æm'bɪvələnt] **adj** ambivalent(e).

amble ['æmbl] **vi** déambuler.

ambulance ['æmbjuləns] ■ **n** ambulance *f*.

■ **comp : ambulance man** ambulancier *m* ▸ **ambulance woman** ambulancière *f*.

ambush ['æmbuʃ] ■ **n** embuscade *f*.

■ **vt** tendre une embuscade à.

ameba [ə'mi:bə] *US* **n** = ***amoeba***.

amebic dysentery *US* **n** = ***amoebic dysentery***.

ameliorate [ə'mi:ljəreɪt] *fml* ■ **vt** améliorer.

■ **vi** s'améliorer.

amen [,ɑ:'men] **excl** amen!

amenable [ə'mi:nəbl] **adj : amenable (to)** ouvert(e) (à)

amend [ə'mend] **vt** [generally] modifier ⁄ [law] amender

◆ ***amends*** **npl : to make amends (for)** se racheter (pour).

amendment [ə'mendmənt] **n** [generally] modification *f* ⁄ [to law] amendement *m*.

amenities [ə'mi:nətɪz] **npl** **1.** [features] agréments *mpl* / [facilities] équipements *mpl* ▸ **urban amenities** équipements *mpl* collectifs **2.** [social courtesy] civilités *fpl*, politesses *fpl*.

America [ə'merɪkə] **n** Amérique *f* ▸ **in America** en Amérique.
◆ ***Americas*** **npl : the Americas** les Amériques *fpl*.

American [ə'merɪkn] ■ **adj** américain(e).
■ **n** Américain *m*, -e *f*.

American football **n** *UK* football *m* américain.

American Indian **n** Indien *m*, -enne *f* d'Amérique, Amérindien *m*, -enne *f*.

Americanism [ə'merɪkənɪzm] **n** américanisme *m*.

americanize, *UK* ***-ise*** [ə'merɪkənaɪz] **vt** américaniser.

American Samoa **n** Samoa américaines *fpl*.

amethyst ['æmɪθɪst] **n** améthyste *f*.

Amex ['æmeks] **n** (abbr of ***American Stock Exchange***) *deuxième place boursière des États-Unis*.

amiable ['eɪmjəbl] **adj** aimable.

amiably ['eɪmjəblɪ] **adv** aimablement.

amicable ['æmɪkəbl] **adj** amical(e).

amicably ['æmɪkəblɪ] **adv** amicalement.

amid(st) [ə'mɪd(st)] **prep** au milieu de, parmi.

amino acid [ə'mi:nəʊ-] **n** acide *m* aminé.

amiss [ə'mɪs] ■ **adj : is there anything amiss?** y a-t-il quelque chose qui ne va pas?
■ **adv : to take sthg amiss** prendre qqch de travers.

Amman [ə'mɑ:n] **n** Amman.

ammo ['æməʊ] **n** *(U)* *inf* munitions *fpl*.

ammonia [ə'məʊnjə] **n** [liquid] ammoniaque *f*.

ammunition [,æmjʊ'nɪʃn] *(U)* **n** **1.** MIL munitions *fpl* **2.** *fig* [argument] argument *m*.

ammunition dump **n** dépôt *m* de munitions.

amnesia [æm'ni:zjə] **n** amnésie *f*.

amnesty ['æmnəstɪ] (pl **-ies**) **n** amnistie *f*.

Amnesty International **n** Amnesty International *f*.

amniocentesis [,æmnɪəʊsen'ti:sɪs] **n** amniocentèse *f*.

amoeba, *US* ***ameba*** [ə'mi:bə] amibe *f*.

amoebic dysentery, *US* ***amebic dysentery*** [ə'mi:bɪk-] **n** dysenterie *f* amibienne.

amok [ə'mɒk] **adv : to run amok** être pris(e) d'une crise de folie furieuse.

among [ə'mʌŋ], *US* ***amongst*** [ə'mʌŋst] **prep** parmi, entre ▸ **among other things** entre autres (choses).

amoral [,eɪ'mɒrəl] **adj** amoral(e).

amorous ['æmərəs] **adj** amoureux(euse).

amorphous [ə'mɔ:fəs] **adj** informe.

amortization, *UK* ***-isation*** [ə,mɔ:tɪ'zeɪʃn] **n** amortissement *m*.

amortize, *UK* ***-ise*** [ə'mɔ:taɪz] **vt** FIN amortir.

amount [ə'maʊnt] **n** **1.** [quantity] quantité *f* ▸ **a great amount of** beaucoup de ▸ **in small/large amounts** en petites/grandes quantités **2.** [sum of money] somme *f*, montant *m* ▸ **do you have the exact amount?** avez-vous le compte (exact)? ▸ **you're in credit to the amount of £100** vous avez un crédit de 100 livres.
◆ ***amount to*** **vt insep** **1.** [total] s'élever à **2.** [be equivalent to] revenir à, équivaloir à.

amp [æmp] **n** **1.** abbr of ***ampere*** **2.** *inf* (abbr of ***amplifier***) ampli *m*.

amperage ['æmpərɪdʒ] **n** intensité *f* de courant.

ampere ['æmpeə^r] **n** ampère *m*.

ampersand ['æmpəsænd] **n** esperluette *f*.

amphetamine [æm'fetəmi:n] **n** amphétamine *f*.

amphibian [æm'fɪbɪən] **n** batracien *m*.

amphibious [æm'fɪbɪəs] **adj** amphibie.

amphitheatre *UK*, ***amphitheater*** *US* ['æmfɪ,θɪətə^r] **n** amphithéâtre *m*.

ample ['æmpl] **adj** **1.** [enough] suffisamment de, assez de **2.** [large] ample.

amplification [,æmplɪfɪ'keɪʃn] **n** **1.** [of sound] amplification *f* **2.** [of idea, statement] développement *m*.

amplifier ['æmplɪfaɪə^r] **n** amplificateur *m*.

amplify ['æmplɪfaɪ] (pt & pp **-ied**) ■ **vt** **1.** [sound] amplifier **2.** [idea, statement] développer.
■ **vi : to amplify on sthg** développer qqch.

amplitude ['æmplɪtju:d] **n** [breadth, scope] ampleur *f*, envergure *f* / ASTRON & PHYS amplitude *f*.

amply ['æmplɪ] **adv** **1.** [sufficiently] amplement **2.** [considerably] largement.

ampoule, *US* ***ampule*** ['æmpu:l] **n** ampoule *f*.

amputate ['æmpjʊteɪt] **vt & vi** amputer.

amputation [,æmpjʊ'teɪʃn] **n** amputation *f*.

amputee [,æmpjʊ'ti:] **n** amputé *m*, -e *f*.

Amsterdam [,æmstə'dæm] **n** Amsterdam.

amt abbr of ***amount***.

Amtrak® ['æmtræk] **n** *société nationale de chemins de fer aux États-Unis*.

amuck [ə'mʌk] = ***amok***.

amulet ['æmjʊlɪt] **n** amulette *f*.

amuse [ə'mju:z] **vt** **1.** [make laugh] amuser, faire rire **2.** [entertain] divertir, distraire ▸ **to amuse o.s. (by doing sthg)** s'occuper (à faire qqch).

amused [ə'mju:zd] **adj** **1.** [laughing] amusé(e) ▸ **to be amused at** *OR* **by sthg** trouver qqch amusant **2.** [entertained] **: to keep o.s. amused** s'occuper.

amusement [ə'mju:zmənt] **n** **1.** [laughter] amusement *m* **2.** [diversion, game] distraction *f*.

amusement arcade **n** *UK* galerie *f* de jeux.

amusement park **n** parc *m* d'attractions.

amusing [ə'mju:zɪŋ] **adj** amusant(e).

an *(stressed* [æn], *unstressed* [ən]*)* ➤ ***a***.

ANA **n** **1.** (abbr of ***American Newspaper Association***) *syndicat américain de la presse écrite* **2.** (abbr of ***American Nurses Association***) *syndicat américain d'infirmiers*.

anabolic steroid [,ænə'bɒlɪk-] **n** (stéroïde *m*) anabolisant *m*.

anachronism [ə'nækrənɪzm] **n** anachronisme *m*.

anachronistic [ə,nækrə'nɪstɪk] **adj** anachronique.

anaemia, ***anemia*** *US* [ə'ni:mjə] **n** anémie *f*.

anaemic, ***anemic*** *US* [ə'ni:mɪk] **adj** MED anémique / *fig* & *pej* fade, plat(e).

anaesthesia, ***anesthesia*** *US* [,ænɪs'θi:zjə] **n** anesthésie *f*.

anaesthetic, ***anesthetic*** *US* [,ænɪs'θetɪk] **n** anesthésique *m* ▸ **under anaesthetic** sous anesthésie ▸ **local/general anaesthetic** anesthésie *f* locale/générale.

anaesthetist [æ'ni:sθətɪst], ***anesthetist*** *US* [æ'ni:sθətɪst], ***anesthesiologist*** [æ,ni:sθəzɪ'ɒlədʒɪst] **n** anesthésiste *mf*.

anaesthetize, *UK* ***-ise***, *US* ***anesthetize*** [æ'ni:sθətaɪz] **vt** anesthésier.

anagram ['ænəgræm] **n** anagramme *f*.

anal ['eɪnl] **adj** anal(e).

analgesic [,ænæl'dʒi:sɪk] ■ **adj** analgésique.
■ **n** analgésique *m*.

analog = ***analogue***.

analogous [ə'næləgəs] **adj : analogous (to)** analogue (à).

analogue *UK*, ***analog*** *US* ['ænəlɒg] ■ **adj** [watch, clock] analogique.
■ **n** analogue *m*.

analogy [ə'nælədʒɪ] (pl **-ies**) **n** analogie *f* ▸ **to draw an analogy with/between** faire une comparaison avec/entre ▸ **by analogy** par analogie.

analyse *UK*, ***-yze*** *US* ['ænəlaɪz] **vt** analyser.

analysis [ə'næləsɪs] (pl **-ses** [-si:z]) **n** analyse *f* ▸ **in the final** *OR* **last analysis** en dernière analyse.

analyst ['ænəlɪst] **n** analyste *mf*.

analytic(al) [,ænə'lɪtɪk(l)] **adj** analytique.

analyze *US* = ***analyse***.

anarchic [æ'nɑ:kɪk] **adj** anarchique.

anarchist ['ænəkɪst] **n** anarchiste *mf*.

anarchistic [,ænə'kɪstɪk] **adj** anarchiste.

anarchy ['ænəkɪ] **n** anarchie *f*.

anathema [ə'næθəmə] **n** anathème *m*.

anatomical [,ænə'tɒmɪkl] **adj** anatomique.

anatomically [,ænə'tɒmɪklɪ] **adv** anatomiquement ▸ **anatomically correct** [doll, model] réaliste du point de vue anatomique.

anatomy [ə'nætəmɪ] (pl **-ies**) **n** anatomie *f*.

ANC (abbr of ***African National Congress***) **n** ANC *m*.

ancestor ['ænsestər] **n** *lit* & *fig* ancêtre *m*.

ancestral [æn'sestrəl-] **adj** ancestral(e) ▸ **ancestral home** demeure *f* ancestrale.

ancestry ['ænsestrɪ] (pl **-ies**) **n** **1.** [past] ascendance *f* **2.** *(U)* [ancestors] ancêtres *mpl*.

anchor ['æŋkər] ■ **n** **1.** NAUT ancre *f* ▸ **to drop/weigh anchor** jeter/lever l'ancre **2.** *US* TV présentateur *m*, -trice *f*.
■ **vt** **1.** [secure] ancrer **2.** *US* TV présenter.
■ **vi** NAUT jeter l'ancre.

anchorage ['æŋkərɪdʒ] **n** **1.** NAUT mouillage *m* **2.** [means of securing] ancrage *m*.

anchorman ['æŋkəmæn] (pl **-men** [-men]) **n** *US* TV présentateur *m*.

anchorwoman ['æŋkə,wʊmən] (pl **-women** [-,wɪmɪn]) **n** *US* TV présentatrice *f*.

anchovy ['æntʃəvɪ] (pl **anchovy** *OR* **-ies**) **n** anchois *m*.

ancient ['eɪnʃənt] **adj** **1.** [monument] historique / [custom] ancien(enne) **2.** *hum* [car] antique / [person] vieux (vieille).

ancillary [æn'sɪlərɪ] **adj** auxiliaire.

and *(stressed* [ænd], *unstressed* [ənd] *OR* [ən]*)* **conj** **1.** [as well as, plus] et ▸ **get your hat and coat** va chercher ton manteau et ton chapeau ▸ **he opened the door and went out** il a ouvert la porte et est sorti
2. [in numbers] **: one hundred and eighty** cent quatre-vingts ▸ **six and a half** six et demi
3. [to] **: come and look!** venez voir! ▸ **try and come** essayez de venir ▸ **wait and see** vous verrez bien
4. [indicating continuity, repetition] **: he cried and cried** il n'arrêtait pas de pleurer ▸ **for hours and hours** pendant des heures (et des heures) ▸ **louder and louder** de plus en plus fort.
◆ ***and so on***, ***and so forth*** **adv** et ainsi de suite.

Andes ['ændi:z] **npl : the Andes** les Andes *fpl*.

Andorra [æn'dɔ:rə] **n** Andorre *f* ▸ **in Andorra** en Andorre.

androgynous [æn'drɒdʒɪnəs] **adj** androgyne.

android ['ændrɔɪd] **n** androïde *m*.

anecdotal [,ænek'dəʊtl] **adj** anecdotique ▸ **anecdotal evidence** preuve *f* *OR* témoignage *m* anecdotique.

anecdote ['ænɪkdəʊt] **n** anecdote *f*.

anemia *US* = ***anaemia***.

anemic *US* = ***anaemic***.

anemone [ə'nemənɪ] **n** anémone *f*.

anesthesia *US* = ***anaesthesia*** .

anesthesiologist *US* = ***anaesthetist*** .

anesthetic *US* = ***anaesthetic*** .

anesthetist *US* = ***anaesthetist*** .

anesthetize *US* = ***anaesthetize***.

anew [ə'nju:] **adv : to start anew** recommencer (à zéro)

angel ['eɪndʒəl] **n** ange *m*.

angel cake **n** ≃ gâteau *m* de Savoie.

Angeleno [,ændʒə'li:nəʊ] **n** *habitant de Los Angeles*.

angelfish ['eɪndʒəlfɪʃ] (pl **angelfish** *OR* **-es**) **n** [fish] scalaire *m* / [shark] ange *m*.

angelic [æn'dʒelɪk] **adj** angélique.

angelus ['ændʒələs] **n** [bell, prayer] angélus *m*.

anger ['æŋgər] ■ **n** colère *f*.
■ **vt** fâcher, irriter.

angina [æn'dʒaɪnə] **n** angine *f* de poitrine.

angle ['æŋgl] ■ **n** **1.** [gen] angle *m* ▸ **at an angle** de travers, en biais ▸ **the roads intersect at an angle of 90º** le

routes se croisent à angle droit **2.** [point of view] point *m* de vue, angle *m* ▸ **from an economic angle** d'un point de vue économique.
■ **vi** pêcher (à la ligne) ▸ **to angle for** *fig* [invitation, compliments] chercher à obtenir, quêter.

angle bracket **n** crochet *m*.

Anglepoise® ['æŋglpɔɪz] **n** lampe *f* architecte.

angler ['æŋglə^r] **n** pêcheur *m* (à la ligne).

Anglican ['æŋglɪkən] ■ **adj** anglican(e).
■ **n** anglican *m*, -e *f*.

Anglicanism ['æŋglɪkənɪzm] **n** anglicanisme *m*.

anglicism ['æŋglɪsɪzm] **n** anglicisme *m*.

anglicize, -ise *UK* ['æŋglɪsaɪz] **vt** angliciser.

angling ['æŋglɪŋ] **n** pêche *f* à la ligne.

Anglo- ['æŋgləʊ] **prefix** anglo-.

Anglo-American ■ **adj** anglo-américain(e).
■ **n** Anglo-Américain *m*, -e *f*.

Anglo-French **adj** anglo-français(e), franco-anglais(e), franco-britannique.

Anglo-Irish ■ **adj** anglo-irlandais(e).
■ **n** LING anglais *m* parlé en Irlande.
■ **npl : the Anglo-Irish** les Anglo-Irlandais *mpl*.

anglophile ['æŋgləʊfaɪl] **adj** anglophile.
◆ ***Anglophile*** **n** anglophile *mf*.

anglophobe ['æŋgləʊfəʊb] **adj** anglophobe.
◆ ***Anglophobe*** **n** anglophobe *mf*.

Anglo-Saxon ■ **adj** anglo-saxon(onne).
■ **n 1.** [person] Anglo-saxon *m*, -onne *f* **2.** [language] anglo-saxon *m*.

Angola [æŋ'gəʊlə] **n** Angola *m* ▸ **in Angola** en Angola.

Angolan [æŋ'gəʊlən] ■ **adj** angolais(e).
■ **n** Angolais *m*, -e *f*.

angora [æŋ'gɔːrə] **n** angora *m*.

angrily ['æŋgrəlɪ] **adv** avec colère.

angry ['æŋgrɪ] (comp **-ier**, superl **-iest**) **adj** [person] en colère, fâché(e) / [words, quarrel] violent(e) ▸ **to be angry with** ***or*** **at sb** être en colère ***or*** fâché contre qqn ▸ **to get angry** se mettre en colère, se fâcher.

angst [æŋst] **n** anxiété *f*.

anguish ['æŋgwɪʃ] **n** angoisse *f*.

anguished ['æŋgwɪʃt] **adj** angoissé(e).

angular ['æŋgjʊlə^r] **adj** anguleux(euse).

animal ['ænɪml] ■ **n** ZOOL animal *m* / *pej* brute *f*.
■ **adj** animal(e).

animate ['ænɪmət] **adj** animé(e), vivant(e).

animated ['ænɪmeɪtɪd] **adj** animé(e).

animated cartoon **n** dessin *m* animé.

animation [ˌænɪ'meɪʃn] **n** animation *f*.

animator ['ænɪmeɪtə^r] **n** animateur *m*, -trice *f*.

animatronics [ˌænɪmə'trɒnɪks] **n** *(U)* CIN animatronique *f*.

animosity [ˌænɪ'mɒsətɪ] (pl **-ies**) **n** animosité *f*.

aniseed ['ænɪsiːd] **n** anis *m*.

ankle ['æŋkl] ■ **n** cheville *f*.
■ **comp : ankle socks** socquettes *fpl* ▸ **ankle boots** bottines *fpl*.

anklebone ['æŋkəlbəʊn] **n** astragale *m*.

ankle-deep **adj : she was ankle-deep in mud** elle était dans la boue jusqu'aux chevilles ▸ **the water is only ankle-deep** l'eau monte ***or*** vient seulement jusqu'à la cheville.

ankle-length **adj** qui descend jusqu'à la cheville.

annals ['ænlz] **npl** annales *fpl*.

annex, *UK* ***annexe*** ['æneks] **n** [building] annexe *f*.

annexation [ˌænek'seɪʃn] **n** annexion *f*.

annihilate [ə'naɪəleɪt] **vt** anéantir, annihiler.

annihilation [əˌnaɪə'leɪʃn] **n** anéantissement *m*.

anniversary [ˌænɪ'vɜːsərɪ] (pl **-ies**) **n** anniversaire *m*.

annotate ['ænəteɪt] **vt** annoter.

annotation [ˌænə'teɪʃn] **n** [action] annotation *f* / [note] annotation *f*, note *f*.

announce [ə'naʊns] **vt** annoncer.

announcement [ə'naʊnsmənt] **n 1.** [statement] déclaration *f* / [in newspaper] avis *m* **2.** *(U)* [act of stating] annonce *f*.

announcer [ə'naʊnsə^r] **n** RADIO & TV speaker *m*, speakerine *f*.

annoy [ə'nɔɪ] **vt** agacer, contrarier.

annoyance [ə'nɔɪəns] **n** contrariété *f*.

annoyed [ə'nɔɪd] **adj** mécontent(e), agacé(e) ▸ **to get annoyed** se fâcher ▸ **to be annoyed at sthg** être contrarié(e) par qqch ▸ **to be annoyed with sb** être fâché(e) contre qqn.

annoying [ə'nɔɪɪŋ] **adj** agaçant(e), énervant(e).

annoyingly [ə'nɔɪɪŋlɪ] **adv** de manière gênante ***or*** agaçante ▸ **she was annoyingly vague** elle était si vague que c'en était agaçant.

annual ['ænjʊəl] ■ **adj** annuel(elle).
■ **n 1.** [plant] plante *f* annuelle **2.** [book - gen] publication *f* annuelle / [- for children] album *m*.

annual earnings **npl 1.** [of company] recette(s) *fpl* annuelle(s) **2.** [of person] revenu *m* annuel.

annual general meeting **n** *UK* assemblée *f* générale annuelle.

annual income **n** revenu *m* annuel.

annually ['ænjʊəlɪ] **adv** annuellement.

annual turnover **n** chiffre *m* d'affaires annuel.

annuity [ə'njuːɪtɪ] (pl **-ies**) **n** rente *f*.

annul [ə'nʌl] (pt & pp **-led**, cont **-ling**) **vt** [generally] annuler / [law] abroger.

annulment [ə'nʌlmənt] **n** [generally] annulation *f* / [of law] abrogation *f*.

annum ['ænəm] **n : per annum** par an.

Annunciation [əˌnʌnsɪ'eɪʃn] **n : the Annunciation** l'Annonciation *f*.

anode ['ænəʊd] **n** anode *f*.

anoint [ə'nɔɪnt] **vt** oindre.

anomalous [ə'nɒmələs] **adj** anormal(e).

anomaly [ə'nɒməlɪ] (pl **-ies**) **n** anomalie *f*.

anon [ə'nɒn] **adv** *dated & liter* [soon] bientôt, sous peu ▸ **see you anon** *hum* à bientôt.

anon. [ə'nɒn] (abbr of ***anonymous***) anon.

anonymity [ˌænə'nɪmətɪ] **n** anonymat *m*.

anonymous [ə'nɒnɪməs] **adj** anonyme.

anonymously [ə'nɒnɪməslɪ] **adv** anonymement.

anorak ['ænəræk] **n** anorak *m*.

anorexia (nervosa) [ˌænə'reksɪə (nɜː'vəʊsə)] **n** anorexie *f* mentale.

anorexic [ˌænə'reksɪk] ■ **adj** anorexique.
■ **n** anorexique *mf*.

another [ə'nʌðəʳ] ■ **adj 1.** [additional] **: another apple** encore une pomme, une pomme de plus, une autre pomme ▸ **in another few minutes** dans quelques minutes ▸ **(would you like) another drink?** (voulez-vous) encore un verre? **2.** [different] **: another job** un autre travail.
■ **pron 1.** [additional one] un autre (une autre), encore un (encore une) ▸ **one after another** l'un après l'autre (l'une après l'autre) **2.** [different one] un autre (une autre) ▸ **one another** l'un l'autre (l'une l'autre).

A. N. Other [ˌeɪen'ʌðəʳ] **n** *UK* monsieur X, madame X.

Ansaphone® ['ɑːnsəfəʊn] **n** répondeur *m* (téléphonique).

ANSI (abbr of ***American National Standards Institute***) **n** *association américaine de normalisation*.

answer ['ɑːnsəʳ] ■ **n 1.** [gen] réponse *f* ▸ **in answer to** en réponse à ▸ **I rang the bell but there was no answer** j'ai sonné mais personne n'a répondu *OR* n'a ouvert ▸ **he has an answer for everything** il a réponse à tout **2.** [to problem] solution *f* ▸ **the (right) answer** la bonne réponse ▸ **there's no easy answer** *lit & fig* il n'y a pas de solution facile.
■ **vt** répondre à ▸ **to answer the door** aller ouvrir la porte ▸ **to answer the phone** répondre au téléphone.
■ **vi** [reply] répondre.
◆ ***answer back*** ■ **vt sep** répondre à.
■ **vi** répondre.
◆ ***answer for*** **vt insep** être responsable de, répondre de ▸ **this government has a lot to answer for** ce gouvernement a bien des comptes à rendre.

answerable ['ɑːnsərəbl] **adj : answerable to sb/for sthg** responsable devant qqn/de qqch.

answering machine ['ɑːnsərɪŋ-] **n** répondeur *m*.

answerphone ['ænsəfəʊn] **n** répondeur *m* (téléphonique).

ant [ænt] **n** fourmi *f*.

antacid [ˌænt'æsɪd] **n** (médicament *m*) alcalin *m*.

antagonism [æn'tægənɪzm] **n** antagonisme *m*, hostilité *f*.

antagonist [æn'tægənɪst] **n** antagoniste *mf*, adversaire *mf*.

antagonistic [ænˌtægə'nɪstɪk] **adj** [hostile] hostile.

antagonize, *UK* ***-ise*** [æn'tægənaɪz] **vt** éveiller l'hostilité de.

Antarctic [æn'tɑːktɪk] ■ **n : the Antarctic** l'Antarctique *m* ▸ **in the Antarctic** dans l'Antarctique.
■ **adj** antarctique.

Antarctica [æn'tɑːktɪkə] **n** Antarctique *m*, le continent *m* antarctique.

Antarctic Circle **n : the Antarctic Circle** le cercle polaire antarctique.

Antarctic Ocean **n : the Antarctic Ocean** l'océan *m* Antarctique, l'océan Austral.

ante ['æntɪ] **n** *inf fig* **: to up** *OR* **raise the ante** faire monter les enchères.

anteater ['æntˌiːtəʳ] **n** tamanoir *m*, fourmilier *m*.

antecedent [ˌæntɪ'siːdənt] **n** antécédent *m*.

antediluvian [ˌæntɪdɪ'luːvjən] **adj** antédiluvien(enne).

antelope ['æntɪləʊp] (pl **antelope** *OR* **-s**) **n** antilope *f*.

antenatal [ˌæntɪ'neɪtl] **adj** prénatal(e).

antenatal clinic **n** service *m* de consultation prénatale.

antenna [æn'tenə] **n 1.** (pl **-nae** [-niː]) [of insect] antenne *f* **2.** (pl **-s**) *US* [for TV, radio] antenne *f*.

anteroom ['æntɪrʊm] **n** antichambre *f*.

anthem ['ænθəm] **n** hymne *m*.

anthill ['ænthɪl] **n** fourmilière *f*.

anthology [æn'θɒlədʒɪ] (pl **-ies**) **n** anthologie *f*.

anthrax ['ænθræks] **n** charbon *m*.

anthropological [ˌænθrəpə'lɒdʒɪkl] **adj** anthropologique.

anthropologist [ˌænθrə'pɒlədʒɪst] **n** anthropologue *mf*.

anthropology [ˌænθrə'pɒlədʒɪ] **n** anthropologie *f*.

anti- ['æntɪ] **prefix** anti-.

antiabortion [ˌæntɪə'bɔːʃn] **adj : the antiabortion movement** le mouvement contre l'avortement.

antiaircraft [ˌæntɪ'eəkrɑːft] **adj** antiaérien(enne).

anti-aliasing **n** COMPUT anti-aliassage *m*, anti-crénelage *m*.

anti-Americanism **n** antiaméricanisme *m*.

antiapartheid [ˌæntɪə'pɑːtheɪt] **adj** anti-apartheid (*inv*).

antibacterial [ˌæntɪbæk'tiːrɪəl] **adj** antibactérien(ienne).

antiballistic missile [ˌæntɪbə'lɪstɪk-] **n** missile *m* antibalistique.

antibiotic [ˌæntɪbaɪ'ɒtɪk] **n** antibiotique *m*.

antibody ['æntɪˌbɒdɪ] (pl **-ies**) **n** anticorps *m*.

anticipate [æn'tɪsɪpeɪt] **vt 1.** [expect] s'attendre à, prévoir ▸ **I didn't anticipate leaving so early** je ne m'attendais pas à ce qu'on parte si tôt ▸ **as anticipated** comme prévu **2.** [request, movement] anticiper / [competitor] prendre de l'avance sur **3.** [look forward to] savourer à l'avance.

anticipation [ænˌtɪsɪ'peɪʃn] **n** [expectation] attente *f* [eagerness] impatience *f* ▸ **in anticipation** avec impatience ▸ **in anticipation of** en prévision de ▸ **thanking you in anticipation** en vous remerciant d'avance.

anticlimax [æntɪ'klaɪmæks] **n** déception *f*.

anticlockwise [ˌæntɪ'klɒkwaɪz] **adj & adv** *UK* dans le sens inverse des aiguilles d'une montre.

anticompetitive [ˌæntɪkəm'petətɪv] **adj** ECON anti-concurrentiel(elle).

anticonstitutional [ˌæntɪkɒnstɪ'tju:ʃənl] **adj** POL anticonstitutionnel(elle).

antics ['æntɪks] **npl 1.** [of children, animals] gambades *fpl* **2.** *pej* [of politicians] bouffonneries *fpl*.

anticyclone [ˌæntɪ'saɪkləʊn] **n** anticyclone *m*.

antidemocratic [ˌæntɪdemə'krætɪk] **adj** POL antidémocratique.

antidepressant [ˌæntɪdɪ'presnt] **n** antidépresseur *m*.

antidote ['æntɪdəʊt] **n** *lit & fig* **: antidote (to)** antidote *m* (contre).

antidumping [ˌæntɪ'dʌmpɪŋ] **adj** [law, legislation] antidumping.

anti-Establishment **adj** POL anticonformiste.

antifascism [ˌæntɪ'fæʃɪsm] **n** POL antifascisme *m*.

antifascist [ˌæntɪ'fæʃɪst] ■ **n** POL antifasciste *mf*.
■ **adj** POL antifasciste.

antifreeze ['æntɪfri:z] **n** antigel *m*.

antiglare ['æntɪgleəʳ] **adj : antiglare headlights** phares *mpl* antiéblouissants.

antiglobalization, -isation *UK* [ˌæntɪˌgləʊbəlaɪ'zeɪʃn] ■ **n** POL antimondialisation *f*.
■ **adj** POL antimondialisation *(inv)*.

Antigua [æn'ti:gə] **n** Antigua.

antihero ['æntɪˌhɪərəʊ] (pl **-es**) **n** antihéros *m*.

antihistamine [ˌæntɪ'hɪstəmɪn] **n** antihistaminique *m*.

anti-inflammatory **adj** anti-inflammatoire.

antimonopoly [ˌæntɪmə'nɒpəlɪ] **adj** *UK* ECON [law, legislation] antitrust *(inv)*.

antinuclear [ˌæntɪ'nju:klɪəʳ] **adj** antinucléaire.

antipathy [æn'tɪpəθɪ] **n : antipathy (to** *OR* **towards)** antipathie *f* (pour).

antipersonnel ['æntɪˌpɜ:sə'nel] **adj** MIL antipersonnel *(inv)*.

antiperspirant [ˌæntɪ'pɜ:spərənt] **n** antiperspirant *m*.

antipodean [ænˌtɪpə'dɪən] **adj** des antipodes.

antipodes [æn'tɪpədi:z] **npl** antipodes *mpl*.
◆ ***Antipodes*** **npl : the Antipodes** l'Australie *f* et la Nouvelle-Zélande.

antiquarian [ˌæntɪ'kweərɪən] ■ **adj : antiquarian bookshop** librairie *f* spécialisée dans les éditions anciennes.
■ **n** amateur *m* d'antiquités.

antiquated ['æntɪkweɪtɪd] **adj** dépassé(e).

antique [æn'ti:k] ■ **adj** ancien(enne).
■ **n** [object] objet *m* ancien / [piece of furniture] meuble *m* ancien.

antique dealer **n** antiquaire *mf*.

antique shop **n** magasin *m* d'antiquités.

antiquity [æn'tɪkwətɪ] (pl **-ies**) **n** antiquité *f*.

anti-Semitic [-sɪ'mɪtɪk] **adj** antisémite.

anti-Semitism [-semɪtɪzəm] **n** antisémitisme *m*.

antiseptic [ˌæntɪ'septɪk] ■ **adj** antiseptique.
■ **n** antiseptique *m*.

antisocial [ˌæntɪ'səʊʃl] **adj 1.** [against society] antisocial(e) **2.** [unsociable] peu sociable, sauvage.

antistatic [ˌæntɪ'stætɪk] **adj** antistatique.

antitank [ˌæntɪ'tæŋk] **adj** antichar *(inv)*.

antiterrorist [ˌæntɪ'terərɪst] **adj** antiterroriste.

antithesis [æn'tɪθɪsɪs] (pl **-ses** [-si:z]) **n** opposé *m*, antithèse *f*.

antivirus check [ˌæntɪ'vaɪrəs-] **n** COMPUT vérification *f* antivirale.

antivirus program [ˌæntɪ'vaɪrəs-] **n** COMPUT programme *m* antivirus.

antler ['æntləʳ] **n** corne *f*.
◆ ***antlers*** **npl** bois *mpl (de cervidés)*, ramure *f*.

antonym ['æntənɪm] **n** antonyme *m*.

Antwerp ['æntwɜ:p] **n** Anvers.

anus ['eɪnəs] **n** anus *m*.

anvil ['ænvɪl] **n** enclume *f*.

anxiety [æŋ'zaɪətɪ] (pl **-ies**) **n 1.** [worry] anxiété *f* **2.** [cause of worry] souci *m* **3.** [keenness] désir *m* farouche.

anxious ['æŋkʃəs] **adj 1.** [worried] anxieux(euse), très inquiet(ète) ▸ **to be anxious about** se faire du souci au sujet de **2.** [keen] **: to be anxious to do sthg** tenir à faire qqch ▸ **to be anxious that** tenir à ce que *(+ subjunctive)*.

anxiously ['æŋkʃəslɪ] **adv** avec anxiété.

anxiousness ['æŋkʃəsnɪs] **n =** ***anxiety***.

any ['enɪ] ■ **adj 1.** *(with negative)* de, d' ▸ **I haven't got any money/tickets** je n'ai pas d'argent/de billets ▸ **he never does any work** il ne travaille jamais ▸ **he can't stand any noise** il ne supporte pas le moindre bruit, il ne supporte aucun bruit ▸ **hardly** *OR* **barely** *OR* **scarcely any** très peu de
2. [some - with sg noun] du, de l', de la / [- with pl noun] des ▸ **have you got any money/milk/cousins?** est-ce que vous avez de l'argent/du lait/des cousins? ▸ **were you in any danger?** étiez-vous en danger?
3. [no matter which] n'importe quel (n'importe quelle) ▸ **at any time of day** à n'importe quel moment *OR* à tout moment de la journée ▸ **any box will do** n'importe quelle boîte fera l'affaire.
■ **pron 1.** *(with negative)* en ▸ **I didn't buy any (of them)** je n'en ai pas acheté ▸ **I didn't know any of the guests** je ne connaissais aucun des invités ▸ **there was hardly any of it left** il n'en restait que très peu
2. [some] en ▸ **do you have any?** est-ce que vous en avez? ▸ **can any of you change a tyre?** est-ce que l'un d'entre vous sait changer un pneu? ▸ **if any** si tant est qu'il y en ait ▸ **few, if any, are likely to be successful** il y en a très peu, si tant est qu'il y en ait, qui ont une chance de réussir
3. [no matter which one or ones] n'importe lequel (n'importe laquelle) ▸ **take any you like** prenez n'importe lequel/

laquelle, prenez celui/celle que vous voulez ▸ **any of the suspects would fit that description** cette description s'applique à tous les suspects.
■ adv **1.** *(with negative)* : **I can't see it any more** je ne le vois plus ▸ **I can't stand it any longer** je ne peux plus le supporter ▸ **we can't go any further** nous ne pouvons aller plus loin
2. [some, a little] un peu ▸ **do you want any more potatoes?** voulez-vous encore des pommes de terre? ▸ **are you finding the course any easier now?** est-ce que tu trouves le cours un peu plus facile maintenant? ▸ **is that any better/different?** est-ce que c'est mieux/différent comme ça? ⁄ see also ***case***, ***day***, ***moment***, ***rate***.

anybody ['enɪ,bɒdɪ] = ***anyone***.

anyhow ['enɪhaʊ] adv **1.** [in spite of that] quand même, néanmoins **2.** [carelessly] n'importe comment **3.** [in any case] de toute façon.

any more, US ***anymore*** ['enɪmɔːʳ] adv : **they don't live here any more** ils n'habitent plus ici.

anyone ['enɪwʌn] pron **1.** *(in negative sentences)* : **I didn't see anyone** je n'ai vu personne ▸ **there was hardly anyone there** il n'y avait presque personne **2.** *(in questions)* quelqu'un ▸ **(is) anyone home?** il y a quelqu'un? **3.** [any person] n'importe qui ▸ **invite anyone you want** invitez qui vous voulez ▸ **it could happen to anyone** ça pourrait arriver à tout le monde ***or*** n'importe qui ▸ **I don't care what anyone thinks** je me fiche de ce que pensent les gens.

anyplace ['enɪpleɪs] US = ***anywhere***.

anything ['enɪθɪŋ] pron **1.** *(in negative sentences)* : **I didn't see anything** je n'ai rien vu ▸ **don't do anything stupid!** ne fais pas de bêtise! ▸ **I don't know anything about computers** je ne m'y connais pas du tout ***or*** je n'y connais rien en informatique ▸ **he isn't anything like his father** il ne ressemble en rien à son père **2.** *(in questions)* quelque chose ▸ **did you hear anything?** avez-vous entendu quelque chose? ▸ **did you notice anything unusual?** avez-vous remarqué quelque chose de bizarre? ▸ **can't we do anything?** est-ce qu'il n'y a rien à faire? ▸ **anything else?** [in shop] et avec ceci? **3.** [any object, event] n'importe quoi ▸ **just tell him anything** racontez-lui n'importe quoi ▸ **anything you like** tout ce que vous voudrez ▸ **if anything happens...** s'il arrive quoi que ce soit... ▸ **it's as easy as anything** c'est facile comme tout.
◆ ***anything but*** adv pas du tout.

anyway ['enɪweɪ] adv [in any case] de toute façon.

anywhere ['enɪweəʳ], US ***anyplace*** ['enɪpleɪs] adv **1.** *(in negative sentences)* : **I haven't seen him anywhere** je ne l'ai vu nulle part ▸ **this isn't getting us anywhere** tout ça ne nous mène à rien ▸ **he isn't anywhere near as quick as you are** il est loin d'être aussi rapide que toi
2. *(in questions)* quelque part ▸ **have you seen my keys anywhere?** avez-vous vu mes clés (quelque part)? ▸ **are you going anywhere at Easter?** vous partez à Pâques? ▸ **do they need anywhere to stay?** ont-ils besoin d'un endroit où loger?
3. [any place] n'importe où ▸ **just put it down anywhere** posez-le n'importe où ▸ **sit anywhere you like** asseyez-vous où vous voulez
4. [any amount, number] : **anywhere between 5,000 and 10,000** quelque chose entre 5000 et 10000.

Anzac ['ænzæk] (abbr of ***Australia-New Zealand Army Corps***) n *soldat australien ou néo-zélandais.*

AOB, ***a.o.b.*** (abbr of ***any other business***) divers.

aorta [eɪ'ɔːtə] (pl -s ***or*** -tae [-tiː]) n aorte *f.*

Apache [ə'pætʃɪ] n Apache *mf.*

apart [ə'pɑːt] adv **1.** [separated] : **the houses were about 10 kilometres apart** les maisons étaient à environ 10 kilomètres l'une de l'autre ▸ **cities as far apart as Johannesburg and Hong Kong** des villes aussi éloignées l'une de l'autre que Johannesburg et Hong Kong ▸ **to keep apart** séparer ▸ **we're living apart** nous sommes séparés **2.** [to one side] à l'écart **3.** [in several parts] : **to take sthg apart** démonter qqch ▸ **to fall apart** tomber en morceaux **4.** [aside] : **joking apart** sans plaisanter, plaisanterie à part.
◆ ***apart from*** prep **1.** [except for] à part, sauf **2.** [as well as] en plus de, outre.

apartheid [ə'pɑːtheɪt] n apartheid *m.*

apartment [ə'pɑːtmənt] n appartement *m.*

apartment building n US immeuble *m (d'habitation).*

apathetic [,æpə'θetɪk] adj apathique.

apathy ['æpəθɪ] n apathie *f.*

APB (abbr of ***all points bulletin***) n US *message radiodiffusé par la police concernant une personne recherchée.*

APC (abbr of ***average propensity to consume***) n ECO PmaC *(propension moyenne à consommer).*

ape [eɪp] ■ n singe *m.*
■ vt singer.

Apennines ['æpɪnaɪnz] npl : **the Apennines** l'Apennin *m*, les Apennins *mpl.*

aperitif [əperə'tiːf] n apéritif *m.*

aperture ['æpə,tjʊəʳ] n **1.** [hole, opening] orifice *m*, ouverture *f* **2.** PHOT ouverture *f.*

apex ['eɪpeks] (pl -es [-iːz] ***or*** apices ['eɪpɪsiːz]) n sommet *m.*

APEX ['eɪpeks] (abbr of ***advance purchase excursion***) n : **APEX ticket** billet *m* APEX.

aphasia [ə'feɪzjə] n aphasie *f.*

aphid ['eɪfɪd] n puceron *m.*

aphorism ['æfərɪzm] n aphorisme *m.*

aphrodisiac [,æfrə'dɪzɪæk] n aphrodisiaque *m.*

apices ['eɪpɪsiːz] npl ➤ ***apex***.

apiece [ə'piːs] adv [for each person] chacun(e), par personne ⁄ [for each thing] chacun(e), pièce *(inv).*

aplomb [ə'plɒm] n aplomb *m*, assurance *f.*

APO (abbr of ***Army Post Office***) n US *service postal de l'armée.*

apocalypse [ə'pɒkəlɪps] n apocalypse *f.*

apocalyptic [ə,pɒkə'lɪptɪk] adj apocalyptique.

apogee ['æpədʒi:] **n** apogée *m*.

apolitical [ˌeɪpə'lɪtɪkəl] **adj** apolitique.

apologetic [əˌpɒlə'dʒetɪk] **adj** [letter] d'excuse ▸ **to be apologetic about sthg** s'excuser de qqch.

apologetically [əˌpɒlə'dʒetɪklɪ] **adv** en s'excusant, pour s'excuser.

apologist [ə'pɒlədʒɪst] **n** apologiste *mf*.

apologize, *UK* ***-ise*** [ə'pɒlədʒaɪz] **vi** s'excuser ▸ **to apologize to sb (for sthg)** faire des excuses à qqn (pour qqch).

apology [ə'pɒlədʒɪ] (pl **-ies**) **n** excuses *fpl*.

apoplectic [ˌæpə'plektɪk] **adj** **1.** MED apoplectique **2.** *inf* [very angry] hors de soi.

apoplexy ['æpəpleksɪ] **n** apoplexie *f*.

apostle [ə'pɒsl] **n** RELIG apôtre *m*.

apostrophe [ə'pɒstrəfɪ] **n** apostrophe *f*.

appal *UK* (pt & pp **-led**, cont **-ling**), ***appall*** *US* [ə'pɔ:l] **vt** horrifier.

Appalachian [ˌæpə'leɪtʃjən] **n : the Appalachians, the Appalachian Mountains** les (monts *mpl*) Appalaches *mpl*.

appall *US* = ***appal***.

appalled [ə'pɔ:ld] **adj** horrifié(e).

appalling [ə'pɔ:lɪŋ] **adj** épouvantable.

appallingly [ə'pɔ:lɪŋlɪ] **adv** épouvantablement.

apparatus [ˌæpə'reɪtəs] (pl **apparatus** *OR* **-es** [-i:z]) **n** **1.** [device] appareil *m*, dispositif *m* **2.** *(U)* [in gym] agrès *mpl* **3.** [system, organization] appareil *m*.

apparel [ə'pærəl] **n** *US* habillement *m*.

apparent [ə'pærənt] **adj** **1.** [evident] évident(e) ▸ **for no apparent reason** sans raison particulière **2.** [seeming] apparent(e).

apparently [ə'pærəntlɪ] **adv** **1.** [it seems] à ce qu'il paraît **2.** [seemingly] apparemment, en apparence.

apparition [ˌæpə'rɪʃn] **n** apparition *f*.

appeal [ə'pi:l] ■ **vi** **1.** [request] **: to appeal (to sb for sthg)** lancer un appel (à qqn pour obtenir qqch) **2.** [make a plea] **: to appeal to** faire appel à **3.** LAW **: to appeal (against)** faire appel (de) **4.** [attract, interest] **: to appeal to sb** plaire à qqn ▸ **it appeals to me** ça me plaît.
■ **n** **1.** [request] appel *m* ▸ **an appeal for help** un appel au secours **2.** LAW appel *m* ▸ **right of appeal** droit *m* d'appel ▸ **on appeal** en seconde instance **3.** [charm, interest] intérêt *m*, attrait *m*.

FALSE FRIENDS / FAUX AMIS
appeal

Appeler n'est pas la traduction du mot anglais *to appeal*. Appeler se traduit par *to call*.
▸ Appelle-moi demain / *Call me tomorrow*

appeal court **n** cour *f* d'appel.

appealing [ə'pi:lɪŋ] **adj** **1.** [attractive] attirant(e), sympathique **2.** [pleading] suppliant(e).

appear [ə'pɪəʳ] **vi** **1.** [gen] apparaître / [book] sortir, paraître **2.** [seem] sembler, paraître ▸ **to appear to do something** sembler faire qqch ▸ **she appeared nervous** elle avait l'air nerveuse ▸ **it would appear (that)...** il semblerait que... **3.** [in play, film] jouer **4.** LAW comparaître ▸ **to appear before the court** *OR* **the judge** comparaître devant le tribunal ▸ **they appeared as witnesses for the defence** ils ont témoigné pour la défense.

appearance [ə'pɪərəns] **n** **1.** [gen] apparition *f* ▸ **to make an appearance** se montrer ▸ **to put in an appearance** faire acte de présence ▸ **she's made a number of television appearances** elle est passée plusieurs fois à la télévision **2.** [look] apparence *f*, aspect *m* ▸ **don't judge by appearances** ne vous fiez pas aux apparences, il ne faut pas se fier aux apparences ▸ **by** *OR* **to all appearances** selon toute apparence ▸ **to keep up appearances** sauver les apparences.

appease [ə'pi:z] **vt** apaiser.

appeasement [ə'pi:zmənt] **n** apaisement *m*.

append [ə'pend] **vt** *fml* [document, note] joindre / [signature] apposer.

appendage [ə'pendɪdʒ] **n** appendice *m*.

appendices [ə'pendɪsi:z] **npl** ➤ ***appendix***.

appendicitis [əˌpendɪ'saɪtɪs] **n** *(U)* appendicite *f*.

appendix [ə'pendɪks] (pl **-dixes** [-dɪksi:z] *OR* **-dices** [-dɪsi:z]) **n** appendice *m* ▸ **to have one's appendix out** *OR* **removed** *OR* **taken out** *US* se faire opérer de l'appendicite.

appertain [ˌæpə'teɪn] **vi** *fml* **: to appertain to** se rapporter à.

HOW TO ...
apologize

Pardon / Sorry
Pardon ! / Excusez-moi ! *(eg: after sneezing)* / Excuse me!
Pardon ! *(eg: when trying to get past somebody)* / Excuse me!
Excusez-moi, je dois vous laisser / Excuse me, I have to go now
Désolé de vous interrompre, mais... / Sorry to interrupt, but...
Je suis désolé pour le malentendu de ce matin / I'm sorry about the misunderstanding this morning
Je suis (vraiment) désolé / I'm (terribly) sorry
J'ai bien peur que nous ne soyons obligés d'annuler / I'm afraid we're going to have to cancel

appetite ['æpɪtaɪt] **n 1.** [for food] **: appetite (for)** appétit *m* (pour) **2.** *fig* [enthusiasm] **: appetite (for)** goût *m* (de *OR* pour).

appetizer, *UK* ***-iser*** ['æpɪtaɪzəʳ] **n** [food] amuse-gueule *m inv* / [drink] apéritif *m*.

appetizing, *US* ***-ising*** ['æpɪtaɪzɪŋ] **adj** [food] appétissant(e).

applaud [ə'plɔ:d] ■ **vt 1.** [clap] applaudir **2.** [approve] approuver, applaudir à.
■ **vi** applaudir.

applause [ə'plɔ:z] **n** *(U)* applaudissements *mpl*.

apple ['æpl] **n** pomme *f* ▸ **she's the apple of her father's eye** *inf* son père tient à elle comme à la prunelle de ses yeux.

apple pie **n** tarte *f* aux pommes.

applet ['æplət] **n** COMPUT appelette *f*, appliquette *f*.

apple tree **n** pommier *m*.

appliance [ə'plaɪəns] **n** [device] appareil *m* ▸ **domestic appliance** appareil ménager.

applicable [ə'plɪkəbl] **adj : applicable (to)** applicable (à).

applicant ['æplɪkənt] **n : applicant (for)** [job] candidat *m*, -e *f* (à) / [state benefit] demandeur *m*, -euse *f* (de) / UNIV **: college** ***US OR*** **university applicant** candidat à l'inscription à l'université.

application [,æplɪ'keɪʃn] **n 1.** [gen] application *f* **2.** [for job] **: application (for)** demande *f* (de).

application form **n** [for post] dossier *m* de candidature / UNIV dossier *m* d'inscription.

applications program [,æplɪ'keɪʃns-] **n** COMPUT programme *m* d'application.

applicator ['æplɪkeɪtəʳ] **n** [for lotion, glue] applicateur *m*.

applied [ə'plaɪd] **adj** [science] appliqué(e).

appliqué [ə'pli:keɪ] **n** application *f*.

apply [ə'plaɪ] (pt & pp -ied) ■ **vt** appliquer ▸ **we apply the same rule to all students** nous appliquons la même règle à *OR* pour tous les étudiants ▸ **to apply o.s. (to sthg)** s'appliquer (à qqch) ▸ **to apply one's mind (to sthg)** s'appliquer (à qqch) ▸ **to apply pressure to sthg** exercer une pression *OR* appuyer sur qqch ▸ **to apply the brakes** freiner.
■ **vi 1.** [for work, grant] **: to apply (for)** faire une demande (de) ▸ **to apply to sb (for sthg)** s'adresser à qqn (pour obtenir qqch) ▸ **to apply for a job** faire une demande d'emploi ▸ **she has decided to apply for the job** elle a décidé de poser sa candidature pour cet emploi ▸ **'apply within'** 's'adresser à l'intérieur *OR* ici' **2.** [be relevant] **: to apply to** s'appliquer à, concerner ▸ **this law applies to all citizens** cette loi s'applique à tous les citoyens ▸ **this doesn't apply to us** nous ne sommes pas concernés.

appoint [ə'pɔɪnt] **vt 1.** [to job, position] **: to appoint sb (as sthg)** nommer qqn (qqch) ▸ **to appoint sb to sthg** nommer qqn à qqch ▸ **she was appointed to the post of director** elle a été nommée directrice ▸ **his appointed agent** son agent attitré **2.** [time, place] fixer.

appointment [ə'pɔɪntmənt] **n 1.** [to job, position] nomination *f*, désignation *f* ▸ **'by appointment to Her Majesty the Queen'** 'fournisseur de sa Majesté la Reine' **2.** [job, position] poste *m*, emploi *m* ▸ **'appointments'** 'offres *fpl* d'emploi' **3.** [arrangement to meet] rendez-vous *m* ▸ **to make an appointment** prendre un rendez-vous ▸ **do you have an appointment?** avez-vous (pris) rendez-vous? ▸ **by appointment** sur rendez-vous.

apportion [ə'pɔ:ʃn] **vt** répartir.

apposite ['æpəzɪt] **adj** pertinent(e), approprié(e).

appraisal [ə'preɪzl] **n** évaluation *f*.

appraise [ə'preɪz] **vt** évaluer.

appreciable [ə'pri:ʃəbl] **adj** [difference] sensible / [amount] appréciable.

appreciably [ə'pri:ʃəblɪ] **adv** sensiblement.

appreciate [ə'pri:ʃɪeɪt] ■ **vt 1.** [value, like] apprécier, aimer **2.** [recognize, understand] comprendre, se rendre compte de **3.** [be grateful for] être reconnaissant(e) de ▸ **I would appreciate a prompt reply to this letter** je vous serais obligé de bien vouloir me répondre dans les plus brefs délais.
■ **vi** FIN prendre de la valeur.

appreciation [ə,pri:ʃɪ'eɪʃn] **n 1.** [liking] contentement *m* **2.** [understanding] compréhension *f* **3.** [gratitude] reconnaissance *f* **4.** FIN augmentation *f* de valeur **5.** [of novel, play] critique *f*.

appreciative [ə'pri:ʃjətɪv] **adj** [person] reconnaissant(e) / [remark] élogieux(euse).

apprehend [,æprɪ'hend] **vt** *fml* [arrest] appréhender, arrêter.

apprehension [,æprɪ'henʃn] **n** [anxiety] appréhension *f*, crainte *f*.

apprehensive [,æprɪ'hensɪv] **adj** inquiet(ète) ▸ **to be apprehensive about sthg** appréhender *OR* craindre qqch.

apprehensively [,æprɪ'hensɪvlɪ] **adv** avec appréhension.

apprentice [ə'prentɪs] ■ **n** apprenti *m*, -e *f*.
■ **vt : to be apprenticed to sb** être apprenti(e) chez qqn.

apprenticeship [ə'prentɪsʃɪp] **n** apprentissage *m*.

appro. ['æprəʊ] (abbr of ***approval***) **n** *inf UK* **: on appro.** à condition, à l'essai.

approach [ə'prəʊtʃ] ■ **n 1.** [gen] approche *f* ▸ **she heard his approach** elle l'a entendu venir ▸ **the approach of spring** la venue du printemps
2. [method] démarche *f*, approche *f* ▸ **another approach to the problem** une autre façon d'aborder le problème ▸ **his approach is all wrong** il s'y prend mal
3. [to person] **: to make an approach to sb** faire une proposition à qqn.
■ **vt 1.** [come near to - place, person, thing] s'approcher de ▸ **as we approached Boston** comme nous approchions de Boston / *fig* approcher de ▸ **we are approaching a time when...** le jour approche où... ▸ **speeds approaching the speed of light** des vitesses proches de celle de la lumière **2.** [speak to] parler à ▸ **a salesman approached me** un vendeur m'a abordé ▸ **I approached him about the job**

je lui ai parlé du poste ▸ **they approached him about doing a deal** ils sont entrés en contact avec lui pour conclure un marché
3. [tackle - problem] aborder ▸ **that's not the way to approach it** ce n'est pas comme cela qu'il faut s'y prendre.
■ **vi** s'approcher.

approachable [ə'prəʊtʃəbl] **adj** accessible.

approaching [ə'prəʊtʃɪŋ] **adj** qui approche.

approach shot **n** [in golf] approche *f*.

approbation [ˌæprə'beɪʃn] **n** approbation *f*.

appropriate ■ **adj** [ə'prəʊprɪət] [clothing] convenable / [action] approprié(e) / [moment] opportun(e).
■ **vt** [ə'prəʊprɪeɪt] **1.** LAW s'approprier **2.** [allocate] affecter.

appropriately [ə'prəʊprɪətlɪ] **adv** [dress] convenablement / [behave] de manière appropriée.

appropriation [əˌprəʊprɪ'eɪʃn] **n** **1.** [taking] appropriation *f* **2.** [allocation] affectation *f*.

approval [ə'pru:vl] **n** approbation *f* ▸ **to meet with sb's approval** obtenir ***OR*** recevoir l'approbation de qqn ▸ **submit the proposal for his approval** soumettez la proposition à son approbation ▸ **on approval** COMM à condition, à l'essai.

approval rating **n** [of politician] cote *f* de popularité.

approve [ə'pru:v] ■ **vi : to approve (of sthg)** approuver (qqch) ▸ **I don't approve of him** il me déplaît.
■ **vt** [ratify] approuver, ratifier.

approved [ə'pru:vd] **adj** approuvé(e), agréé(e).

approving [ə'pru:vɪŋ] **adj** approbateur(trice).

approx. [ə'prɒks] (abbr of ***approximately***) approx., env.

approximate ■ **adj** [ə'prɒksɪmət] approximatif(ive).
■ **vi** [ə'prɒksɪmeɪt] **: to approximate to** se rapprocher de.

approximately [ə'prɒksɪmətlɪ] **adv** à peu près, environ.

approximation [əˌprɒksɪ'meɪʃn] **n : approximation (to)** approximation *f* (de).

APR **n** **1.** (abbr of ***annualized percentage rate***) TEG *m* **2.** (abbr of ***annual purchase rate***) taux *m* annuel.

Apr. (abbr of ***April***) avr.

après-ski [ˌæpreɪ'ski:] **n** *(U)* activités *fpl* après-ski.

apricot ['eɪprɪkɒt] ■ **n** abricot *m*.
■ **comp** à l'abricot.

April ['eɪprəl] **n** avril *m* ; see also ***September***.

April Fools' Day **n** le 1er avril.

apron ['eɪprən] **n** **1.** [clothing] tablier *m* ▸ **to be tied to sb's apron strings** *inf* être toujours dans les jupes de qqn **2.** AERON aire *f* de stationnement.

apropos ['æprəpəʊ] ■ **adj** pertinent(e), à propos.
■ **prep : apropos (of)** à propos (de).

APS (abbr of ***average propensity to save***) **n** ECON PmaE *(propension moyenne à épargner)*.

apt [æpt] **adj** **1.** [pertinent] pertinent(e), approprié(e) **2.** [likely] **: to be apt to do sthg** avoir tendance à faire qqch.

apt. (abbr of ***apartment***) appt.

APT (abbr of ***advanced passenger train***) **n** ≃ TGV *m*.

Apt. (abbr of ***apartment***) appt.

aptitude ['æptɪtju:d] **n** aptitude *f*, disposition *f* ▸ **to have an aptitude for** avoir des dispositions pour.

aptitude test **n** test *m* d'aptitude.

aptly ['æptlɪ] **adv** avec justesse, à propos.

aqualung ['ækwəlʌŋ] **n** scaphandre *m* autonome.

aquamarine [ˌækwəmə'ri:n] **n** [colour] bleu vert *m inv*.

aquaplane ['ækwəpleɪn] **vi** *UK* AUT faire de l'aquaplaning.

aquarium [ə'kweərɪəm] (pl **-riums *OR* -ria** [-rɪə]) **n** aquarium *m*.

Aquarius [ə'kweərɪəs] **n** Verseau *m* ▸ **to be (an) Aquarius** être Verseau.

aquarobics [ˌækwə'rəʊbɪks] **n** aquagym *f*.

aquatic [ə'kwætɪk] **adj** **1.** [animal, plant] aquatique **2.** [sport] nautique.

aqueduct ['ækwɪdʌkt] **n** aqueduc *m*.

AR abbr of ***Arkansas***.

ARA (abbr of ***Associate of the Royal Academy***) **n** *membre associé de la RA*.

Arab ['ærəb] ■ **adj** arabe.
■ **n** **1.** [person] Arabe *mf* **2.** [horse] pur-sang *m* arabe.

Arabia [ə'reɪbjə] **n** Arabie *f*.

Arabian [ə'reɪbjən] **adj** d'Arabie, arabe.

Arabian desert **n : the Arabian desert** le désert d'Arabie.

Arabian Peninsula **n : the Arabian Peninsula** la péninsule d'Arabie.

Arabian Sea **n : the Arabian Sea** la mer d'Arabie, la mer d'Oman.

Arabic ['ærəbɪk] ■ **adj** arabe.
■ **n** arabe *m*.

Arabic numeral **n** chiffre *m* arabe.

arable ['ærəbl] **adj** arable.

ARAM (abbr of ***Associate of the Royal Academy of Music***) **n** *membre associé de l'académie britannique de musique*.

arbiter ['ɑ:bɪtəʳ] **n** *fml* arbitre *m*.

arbitrary ['ɑ:bɪtrərɪ] **adj** arbitraire.

arbitrate ['ɑ:bɪtreɪt] **vi** arbitrer.

arbitration [ˌɑ:bɪ'treɪʃn] **n** arbitrage *m* ▸ **to go to arbitration** recourir à l'arbitrage.

arbitrator ['ɑ:bɪtreɪtəʳ] **n** arbitre *m*, médiateur *m*, -trice *f* ▸ **the dispute has been referred to the arbitrator** le litige a été soumis à l'arbitrage.

arc [ɑ:k] **n** arc *m*.

ARC (abbr of ***AIDS-related complex***) n ARC *m*.
arcade [ɑ:'keɪd] n **1.** [for shopping] galerie *f* marchande **2.** [covered passage] arcades *fpl* **3.** *US* galerie *f* de jeux.
arch [ɑ:tʃ] ■ adj malicieux(euse), espiègle.
■ n **1.** ARCHIT arc *m*, voûte *f* **2.** [of foot] voûte *f* plantaire, cambrure *f*.
■ vt cambrer, arquer.
■ vi former une voûte.
arch- [ɑ:tʃ] prefix grand(e), principal(e).
archaeological [ˌɑ:kɪə'lɒdʒɪkl] adj archéologique.
archaeologist [ˌɑ:kɪ'ɒlədʒɪst] n archéologue *mf*.
archaeology [ˌɑ:kɪ'ɒlədʒɪ] n archéologie *f*.
archaic [ɑ:'keɪɪk] adj archaïque.
archangel ['ɑ:kˌeɪndʒəl] n archange *m*.
archbishop [ˌɑ:tʃ'bɪʃəp] n archevêque *m*.
archduchess [ˌɑ:tʃ'dʌtʃɪs] n archiduchesse *f*.
archduke [ˌɑ:tʃ'dju:k] n archiduc *m*.
arched [ɑ:tʃt] adj **1.** ARCHIT cintré(e), courbé(e) **2.** [curved] arqué(e), cambré(e).
archenemy [ˌɑ:tʃ'enɪmɪ] (pl -ies) n ennemi *m* numéro un.
archeological = ***archaelogical***.
archeologist = ***archaeologist***.
archeology = ***archaeology*** .
archer ['ɑ:tʃəʳ] n archer *m*.
archery ['ɑ:tʃərɪ] n tir *m* à l'arc.
archetypal [ˌɑ:kɪ'taɪpl] adj typique.
archetype ['ɑ:kɪtaɪp] n archétype *m*.
archipelago [ˌɑ:kɪ'pelɪgəʊ] (pl -es ***or*** -s) n archipel *m*.
architect ['ɑ:kɪtekt] n *lit* & *fig* architecte *mf*.
architectural [ˌɑ:kɪ'tektʃərəl] adj architectural(e).
architecturally [ˌɑ:kɪ'tektʃərəlɪ] adv au ***or*** du point de vue architectural.
architecture ['ɑ:kɪtektʃəʳ] n [gen & COMPUT] architecture *f*.
archive ['ɑ:kaɪv] ■ n [repository] archives *fpl*, dépôt *m* ▸ **the archives** les archives *fpl*.
■ comp [photo] d'archives.
■ vt archiver.
archive file ['ɑ:kaɪv-] n COMPUT fichier *m* archives.
archive site n COMPUT site *m* FTP.
archivist ['ɑ:kɪvɪst] n archiviste *mf*.
archway ['ɑ:tʃweɪ] n passage *m* voûté.
ARCM (abbr of ***Associate of the Royal College of Music***) n *membre associé du conservatoire de musique britannique*.
arctic ['ɑ:ktɪk] ■ adj **1.** arctique **2.** *fig* [cold] glacial(e).
■ n *US* [overshoe] couvre-chaussure *m*.
◆ ***Arctic*** ■ n : **the Arctic (Ocean)** l'(océan *m*) Arctique *m* ▸ **in the Arctic** dans l'Arctique.
■ adj arctique.
Arctic Circle n : **the Arctic Circle** le cercle arctique.
ardent ['ɑ:dənt] adj fervent(e), passionné(e).
ardently ['ɑ:dəntlɪ] adv ardemment, passionnément.
ardour *UK*, ***ardor*** *US* ['ɑ:dəʳ] n ardeur *f*, ferveur *f*.
arduous ['ɑ:djʊəs] adj ardu(e).
are (*weak form* [əʳ], *strong form* [ɑ:ʳ]) ➤ ***be***.
area ['eərɪə] n **1.** [region] région *f* ▸ **landing area** aire d'atterrissage ▸ **parking area** aire *f* de stationnement ▸ **in the area** dans la région ▸ **in the area of** [approximately] environ, à peu près **2.** [surface size] aire *f*, superficie *f* **3.** [of knowledge, interest] domaine *m*.
area code n *US* indicatif *m* de zone.
arena [ə'ri:nə] n *lit* & *fig* arène *f*.
aren't [ɑ:nt] = ***are not***.
Argentina [ˌɑ:dʒən'ti:nə] n Argentine *f* ▸ **in Argentina** en Argentine.
Argentine ['ɑ:dʒəntaɪn], ***Argentinian*** [ˌɑ:dʒən'tɪnɪən] ■ adj argentin(e).
■ n Argentin *m*, -e *f*.
arguable ['ɑ:gjʊəbl] adj discutable, contestable.
arguably ['ɑ:gjʊəblɪ] adv : **she's arguably the best** on peut soutenir qu'elle est la meilleure.
argue ['ɑ:gju:] ■ vi **1.** [quarrel] : **to argue (with sb about sthg)** se disputer (avec qqn à propos de qqch) **2.** [reason] **to argue (for/against)** argumenter (pour/contre).
■ vt débattre de, discuter de ▸ **to argue that** soutenir ***or*** maintenir que.
argument ['ɑ:gjʊmənt] n **1.** [quarrel] dispute *f* ▸ **to have an argument (about sthg)** se disputer (à propos de qqch) **2.** [reason] argument *m* ▸ **there is a strong argument in favour of the proposal** il y a de bonnes raisons pour soutenir ***or*** appuyer cette proposition **3.** *(U)* [reasoning] discussion *f*, débat *m* ▸ **for the sake of argument** à titre d'exemple.
argumentative [ˌɑ:gjʊ'mentətɪv] adj querelleur(euse), batailleur(euse).
argy-bargy [ˌɑ:dʒɪ'bɑ:dʒɪ] n *(U) UK inf* chamailleries *fpl*.
aria ['ɑ:rɪə] n aria *f*.
arid ['ærɪd] adj *lit* & *fig* aride.
Aries ['eəri:z] n Bélier *m* ▸ **to be (an) Aries** être Bélier.
arise [ə'raɪz] (pt **arose**, pp **arisen** [ə'rɪzn]) vi [appear] surgir, survenir ▸ **to arise from** résulter de, provenir de ▸ **if the need arises** si le besoin se fait sentir.
aristocracy [ˌærɪ'stɒkrəsɪ] (pl -ies) n aristocratie *f*.
aristocrat [*UK* 'ærɪstəkræt, *US* ə'rɪstəkræt] n aristocrate *mf*.
aristocratic [*UK* ˌærɪstə'krætɪk, *US* əˌrɪstə'krætɪk] adj aristocratique.
arithmetic [ə'rɪθmətɪk] n arithmétique *f*.
Arizona [ˌærɪ'zəʊnə] n Arizona *m* ▸ **in Arizona** dans l'Arizona.
ark [ɑ:k] n arche *f*.
Arkansas ['ɑ:kənsɔ:] n Arkansas *m* ▸ **in Arkansas** dans l'Arkansas.
arm [ɑ:m] ■ n **1.** [of person, chair] bras *m* ▸ **arm in arm** bras dessus bras dessous ▸ **to chance one's arm** *fig* tente

le coup ▸ **to keep sb at arm's length** *UK fig* tenir qqn à distance ▸ **to twist sb's arm** *fig* forcer la main à qqn **2.** [of garment] manche *f* **3.** [of organization] section *f*, aile *f*.
■ **vt** armer.
◆ ***arms*** **npl** armes *fpl* ▸ **to take up arms** prendre les armes ▸ **to be up in arms about sthg** s'élever contre qqch.

armada [ɑ:'mɑ:də] **n** armada *f*.

armadillo [,ɑ:mə'dɪləʊ] (**pl -s**) **n** tatou *m*.

Armageddon [,ɑ:mə'gedn] **n** Armageddon *m*.

armaments ['ɑ:məmənts] **npl** [weapons] matériel *m* de guerre, armements *mpl*.

armband ['ɑ:mbænd] **n** brassard *m* / [mourning] brassard *m* de deuil, crêpe *m*.

arm candy ['ɑ:mkændɪ] **n** *inf pej* jeune et jolie compagne *f*.

armchair ['ɑ:mtʃeəʳ] **n** fauteuil *m*.

armed [ɑ:md] **adj** *lit & fig* : **armed (with)** armé(e) (de).

armed forces **npl** forces *fpl* armées.

Armenia [ɑ:'mi:njə] **n** Arménie *f* ▸ **in Armenia** en Arménie.

Armenian [ɑ:'mi:njən] ■ **adj** arménien(enne).
■ **n 1.** [person] Arménien *m*, -enne *f* **2.** [language] arménien *m*.

armful ['ɑ:mfʊl] **n** brassée *f* ▸ **in armfuls, by the armful** par pleines brassées, par brassées entières.

armhole ['ɑ:mhəʊl] **n** emmanchure *f*.

armistice ['ɑ:mɪstɪs] **n** armistice *m*.

armour *UK*, ***armor*** *US* ['ɑ:məʳ] **n 1.** [for person] armure *f* **2.** [for military vehicle] blindage *m*.

armoured *UK*, ***armored*** *US* ['ɑ:məd] **adj** MIL blindé(e).

armoured car *UK*, ***armored car*** *US* [,ɑ:məd-] **n** voiture *f* blindée.

armour-plated *UK*, ***armor-plated*** *US* [-pleɪtɪd] **adj** blindé(e).

armoury *UK* (**pl -ies**), ***armory*** *US* (**pl -ies**) ['ɑ:mərɪ] **n** arsenal *m*.

armpit ['ɑ:mpɪt] **n** aisselle *f*.

armrest ['ɑ:mrest] **n** accoudoir *m*.

arms control ['ɑ:mz-] **n** contrôle *m* des armements.

arms embargo ['ɑ:mz-] **n** embargo *m* sur les armes.

arms race ['ɑ:mz-] **n** course *f* aux armements.

arm-twisting [-'twɪstɪŋ] **n** *(U) inf* pressions *fpl*.

arm-wrestle **vi** : **to arm-wrestle with sb** faire une partie de bras de fer avec qqn.

arm wrestling **n** bras *m* de fer.

army ['ɑ:mɪ] (**pl -ies**) **n** *lit & fig* armée *f*.

A-road **n** *UK* ≃ route *f* nationale.

aroma [ə'rəʊmə] **n** arôme *m*.

aromatherapy [ə,rəʊmə'θerəpɪ] **n** aromathérapie *f*.

aromatic [,ærə'mætɪk] **adj** aromatique.

arose [ə'rəʊz] **pt** ➤ ***arise***.

around [ə'raʊnd] ■ **adv 1.** [about, round] : **to walk around** se promener ▸ **to lie around** [clothes] traîner ▸ **to travel around** voyager
2. [on all sides] (tout) autour ▸ **the fields all around** les champs tout autour
3. [near] dans les parages ▸ **to stay** *OR* **to stick around** rester dans les parages ▸ **he's around somewhere** il n'est pas loin, il est dans le coin
4. [in circular movement] : **to turn around** se retourner
5. [in existence] : **that firm has been around for years** cette société existe depuis des années ▸ **there wasn't much money around in those days** les gens n'avaient pas beaucoup d'argent à l'époque
▸▸ **I don't know my way around yet** je suis encore un peu perdu ▸ **he has been around** *inf* il n'est pas né d'hier, il a de l'expérience.
■ **prep 1.** [gen] autour de ▸ **to walk around a garden/town** faire le tour d'un jardin/d'une ville ▸ **all around the country** dans tout le pays ▸ **they travelled around Europe** ils ont voyagé à travers l'Europe / *fig* : **to find a way (to get) around a problem** trouver un moyen de contourner un problème
2. [near] : **around here** par ici ▸ **my keys are somewhere around here** mes clés sont quelque part par ici
3. [approximately] environ, à peu près ▸ **around five o'clock** vers cinq heures ▸ **he's around your age** il a environ *OR* à peu près votre âge.

around-the-clock **adj** : **around-the-clock protection/surveillance** protection *f*/surveillance *f* 24 heures sur 24.

arousal [ə'raʊzl] **n** éveil *m*.

arouse [ə'raʊz] **vt 1.** [excite - feeling] éveiller, susciter / [- person] exciter **2.** [wake] réveiller.

arrange [ə'reɪndʒ] ■ **vt 1.** [flowers, books, furniture] arranger, disposer **2.** [event, meeting] organiser, fixer ▸ **to arrange to do sthg** convenir de faire qqch ▸ **she arranged for him to come to Edinburgh** elle a fait le nécessaire pour qu'il vienne à Édimbourg ▸ **I can arrange a loan** je peux m'arranger pour obtenir un prêt ▸ **here is the first instalment, as arranged** voici le premier versement, comme convenu **3.** MUS arranger.
■ **vi** prendre des dispositions, s'arranger ▸ **I've arranged with the boss to leave early tomorrow** je me suis arrangé avec le patron pour partir de bonne heure demain.

arranged marriage [ə'reɪndʒd-] **n** mariage *m* arrangé.

arrangement [ə'reɪndʒmənt] **n 1.** [agreement] accord *m*, arrangement *m* ▸ **to come to an arrangement** s'entendre, s'arranger ▸ **price by arrangement** prix à débattre **2.** [of furniture, books] arrangement *m* ▸ **flower arrangement** composition *f* florale **3.** MUS arrangement *m*.
◆ ***arrangements*** **npl** dispositions *fpl*, préparatifs *mpl* ▸ **to make arrangements** prendre des mesures *OR* dispositions ▸ **could you make arrangements to change the meeting?** pouvez-vous faire le nécessaire pour changer la date de la réunion? ▸ **what are the travel arrangements?** comment le voyage est-il organisé?

array [ə'reɪ] ■ **n 1.** [of objects] étalage *m* **2.** COMPUT tableau *m*.
■ **vt** [ornaments] disposer.

arrears [ə'rɪəz] **npl** [money owed] arriéré *m* ▸ **to be in arrears** [late] être en retard / [owing money] avoir des arriérés.

arrest [ə'rest] ■ **n** [by police] arrestation *f* ▸ **under arrest** en état d'arrestation ▸ **he was put under arrest** il a été arrêté ▸ **they made several arrests** ils ont procédé à plusieurs arrestations.
■ **vt 1.** [gen] arrêter **2.** *fml* [sb's attention] attirer, retenir.

arresting [ə'restɪŋ] **adj** [striking] frappant(e), saisissant(e).

arrival [ə'raɪvl] **n 1.** [gen] arrivée *f* ▸ **late arrival** [of train] retard *m* **2.** [person - at airport, hotel] arrivant *m*, -e *f* ▸ **new arrival** [- person] nouveau venu *m*, nouvelle venue *f* / [- baby] nouveau-né *m*, nouveau-née *f*.

arrive [ə'raɪv] **vi** [generally] arriver / [baby] être né(e) ▸ **to arrive at** [conclusion, decision] arriver à.

arrogance ['ærəgəns] **n** arrogance *f*.

arrogant ['ærəgənt] **adj** arrogant(e).

arrogantly ['ærəgəntlɪ] **adv** avec arrogance.

arrow ['ærəʊ] **n** flèche *f*.

arrow key **n** COMPUT touche *f* fléchée ***OR*** de direction.

arrowroot ['ærəʊru:t] **n** arrow-root *m*.

arse *UK* [ɑ:s], ***ass*** *US* [æs] **n** *vulg* cul *m*.

arsehole *UK* ['ɑ:shəʊl], ***asshole*** *US* ['æshəʊl] **n** *vulg* trou *m* du cul ▸ **don't be such an arsehole** ne sois pas si con.

arsenal ['ɑ:sənl] **n** arsenal *m*.

arsenic ['ɑ:snɪk] **n** arsenic *m*.

arson ['ɑ:sn] **n** incendie *m* criminel ***OR*** volontaire.

arsonist ['ɑ:sənɪst] **n** incendiaire *mf*.

art [ɑ:t] ■ **n** art *m*.
■ **comp** [exhibition] d'art / [college] des beaux-arts ▸ **art student** étudiant *m*, -e *f* d'une école des beaux-arts.
◆ ***arts*** ■ **npl 1.** *UK* SCH & UNIV lettres *fpl* **2.** [fine arts] **: the arts** les arts *mpl*.
■ **comp** *UK* SCH & UNIV de lettres ▸ **arts student** étudiant *m*, -e *f* en lettres.

art deco [-'dekəʊ] **n** art *m* déco.

artefact ['ɑ:tɪfækt] = ***artifact***.

arterial [ɑ:'tɪərɪəl] **adj 1.** [blood] artériel(elle) **2.** *UK* [road] à grande circulation.

arteriosclerosis [ɑ:ˌtɪərɪəʊsklɪə'rəʊsɪs] **n** artériosclérose *f*.

artery ['ɑ:tərɪ] (pl **-ies**) **n** artère *f*.

art form **n** moyen *m* d'expression artistique.

artful ['ɑ:tfʊl] **adj** rusé(e), malin(igne).

art gallery **n** [public] musée *m* d'art / [for selling paintings] galerie *f* d'art.

art house **n** cinéma *m* d'art et d'essai.

art-house **adj** [cinema, film] d'art et d'essai.

arthritic [ɑ:'θrɪtɪk] **adj** arthritique.

arthritis [ɑ:'θraɪtɪs] **n** arthrite *f*.

artic [ɑ:'tɪk] (abbr of ***articulated lorry***) **n** *UK inf* semi-remorque *m*.

artichoke ['ɑ:tɪtʃəʊk] **n** artichaut *m*.

article ['ɑ:tɪkl] **n** article *m* ▸ **article of clothing** vêtement *m*.

articled clerk ['ɑ:tɪkld-] **n** *UK* avocat *m* stagiaire.

articles of association ['ɑ:tɪklz-] **npl** statuts *mpl* d'une société.

articulate ■ **adj** [ɑ:'tɪkjʊlət] [person] qui sait s'exprimer / [speech] net (nette), distinct(e).
■ **vt** [ɑ:'tɪkjʊleɪt] [thought, wish] formuler.

articulated lorry [ɑ:'tɪkjʊleɪtɪd-] **n** *UK* semi-remorque *m*.

articulately [ɑ:'tɪkjʊlətlɪ] **adv** [speak] distinctement / [explain] clairement.

articulation [ɑ:ˌtɪkjʊ'leɪʃn] **n** articulation *f*.

artifact ['ɑ:tɪfækt] **n** objet *m* fabriqué.

artifice ['ɑ:tɪfɪs] **n 1.** [trick] artifice *m*, ruse *f* **2.** [trickery] ingéniosité *f*, habileté *f*.

artificial [ˌɑ:tɪ'fɪʃl] **adj 1.** [not natural] artificiel(elle) **2.** [insincere] affecté(e).

artificial insemination **n** insémination *f* artificielle.

artificial intelligence **n** intelligence *f* artificielle.

artificially [ˌɑ:tɪ'fɪʃəlɪ] **adv** artificiellement.

artificial respiration **n** respiration *f* artificielle.

artillery [ɑ:'tɪlərɪ] **n** artillerie *f*.

artisan [ˌɑ:tɪ'zæn] **n** artisan *m*, -e *f*.

artist ['ɑ:tɪst] **n** artiste *mf*.

artiste [ɑ:'ti:st] **n** artiste *mf*.

artistic [ɑ:'tɪstɪk] **adj** [person] artiste / [style] artistique

artistically [ɑ:'tɪstɪklɪ] **adv** avec art, de façon artistique.

artistry ['ɑ:tɪstrɪ] **n** art *m*, talent *m* artistique.

artless ['ɑ:tlɪs] **adj** naturel(elle), ingénu(e).

art nouveau [ˌɑ:nu:'vəʊ] **n** art *m* nouveau.

artsy ['ɑ:tzɪ] (comp **-ier**, superl **-iest**) **adj** *inf* = ***arty***.

artwork ['ɑ:twɜ:k] **n** iconographie *f*, illustration *f*.

arty ['ɑ:tɪ] (comp **-ier**, superl **-iest**) **adj** *inf pej* [person] qui se veut artiste ***OR*** bohème / [clothing] de style bohème [object, film, style] prétentieux(euse).

ARV (abbr of ***American Revised Version***) **n** *traductio[n] américaine de la Bible*.

as *(stressed* [æz], *unstressed* [əz]*)* ■ **conj 1.** [referring to time] comme, alors que ▸ **she rang (just) as I was leaving** ell[e] m'a téléphoné au moment même où ***OR*** juste comme j[e] partais ▸ **I listened as she explained the plan to them** j'ai écoutée leur expliquer le projet ▸ **as time goes by** mesure que le temps passe, avec le temps
2. [like] comme ▸ **A as in Able** a comme Anatole ▸ **as told you** comme je vous l'ai dit ▸ **as you know,...** comm[e] tu le sais,... ▸ **do as I say** fais ce que je (te) dis ▸ **leave it as it is** laissez-le tel qu'il est ***OR*** tel quel ▸ **she's working to[o] hard as it is** elle travaille déjà assez dur comme ça ▸ **as i[t] turns out** finalement, en fin de compte ▸ **as things stan[d]** les choses étant ce qu'elles sont

3. [because, since] comme, puisque ▸ **let her drive, as it's her car** laissez-la conduire, puisque c'est sa voiture.
■ **prep 1.** [referring to function, characteristic] en, comme, en tant que ▸ **I'm speaking as your friend** je te parle en ami ▸ **he made a name as an actor** il s'est fait un nom comme acteur ▸ **she works as a nurse** elle est infirmière ▸ **he was dressed as a clown** il était habillé en clown
2. [referring to attitude, reaction] **: it came as a shock** cela nous a fait un choc ▸ **she treats it as a game** elle prend ça à la rigolade.
■ **adv** *(in comparisons)* **: as... as...** aussi... que... ▸ **he's as tall as I am** il est aussi grand que moi ▸ **as red as a tomato** rouge comme une tomate ▸ **twice as big as** deux fois plus gros que ▸ **as much/many as** autant que ▸ **as much wine/many chocolates as** autant de vin/de chocolats que ▸ **as often as possible** aussi souvent que possible.
◆ ***as it were*** **adv** pour ainsi dire.
◆ ***as for*** **prep** quant à.
◆ ***as from, as of*** **prep** dès, à partir de.
◆ ***as if, as though*** **conj** comme si ▸ **it looks as if** *OR* **as though it will rain** on dirait qu'il va pleuvoir.
◆ ***as to*** **prep 1.** [concerning] en ce qui concerne, au sujet de
2. = ***as for***.

AS[1] **n** (abbr of ***Associate in/of Science***) *diplômé en sciences.*

AS[2] abbr of ***American Samoa***.

ASA (abbr of ***American Standards Association***) **n** *association américaine de normalisation,* ≃ AFNOR *f.*

asafoetida, asafetida *US* [ˌæsəˈfetɪdə] **n** ase *f* fétide.

asap (abbr of ***as soon as possible***) **adv** aussitôt *OR* dès que possible.

asbestos [æsˈbestəs] **n** asbeste *m*, amiante *m*.

asbestosis [ˌæsbesˈtəʊsɪs] **n** asbestose *f*.

ascend [əˈsend] **vt & vi** monter ▸ **to ascend the throne** monter sur le trône.

ascendancy [əˈsendənsɪ] **n** ascendant *m*.

ascendant [əˈsendənt] **n : to be in the ascendant** avoir le dessus.

ascendency [əˈsendənsɪ] = ***ascendancy***.

ascendent [əˈsendənt] = ***ascendant***.

ascending [əˈsendɪŋ] **adj** croissant(e) ▸ **in ascending order** en ordre croissant.

ascension [əˈsenʃn] **n** ascension *f*.
◆ ***Ascension*** **n** RELIG **: the Ascension** l'Ascension *f*.

Ascension Island **n** île *f* de l'Ascension.

ascent [əˈsent] **n** *lit & fig* ascension *f*.

ascertain [ˌæsəˈteɪn] **vt** établir.

ascetic [əˈsetɪk] ■ **adj** ascétique.
■ **n** ascète *mf*.

ASCII [ˈæskɪ] (abbr of ***American Standard Code for Information***) **n** ASCII *m*.

ascorbic acid [əˈskɔːbɪk-] **n** acide *m* ascorbique.

ascribe [əˈskraɪb] **vt : to ascribe sthg to** attribuer qqch à / [blame] imputer qqch à.

ASCU (abbr of ***Association of State Colleges and Universities***) **n** *association des établissements universitaires d'État aux États-Unis.*

ASE (abbr of ***American Stock Exchange***) **n** *deuxième place boursière des États-Unis.*

aseptic [ˌeɪˈseptɪk] **adj** aseptique.

asexual [ˌeɪˈsekʃʊəl] **adj** asexué(e).

ash [æʃ] **n 1.** [from cigarette, fire] cendre *f* **2.** [tree] frêne *m*.
◆ ***ashes*** **npl** cendres *fpl*.

ASH [æʃ] (abbr of ***Action on Smoking and Health***) **n** *ligue antitabac britannique.*

ashamed [əˈʃeɪmd] **adj** honteux(euse), confus(e) ▸ **to be ashamed of** avoir honte de ▸ **to be ashamed to do sthg** avoir honte de faire qqch.

ashcan [ˈæʃkæn] **n** *US* poubelle *f*.

ashen [ˈæʃn] **adj 1.** [ash-coloured] cendré(e), couleur de cendre / [face] blême, livide **2.** [of ashwood] en (bois de) frêne.

ashen-faced [ˈæʃnˌfeɪst] **adj** blême.

ashore [əˈʃɔːʳ] **adv** à terre.

ashtray [ˈæʃtreɪ] **n** cendrier *m*.

Ash Wednesday **n** le mercredi des Cendres.

Asia [*UK* ˈeɪʃə, *US* ˈeɪʒə] **n** Asie *f* ▸ **in Asia** en Asie.

Asia Minor **n** Asie *f* Mineure.

Asian [*UK* ˈeɪʃn, *US* ˈeɪʒn] ■ **adj** asiatique.
■ **n** [person] Asiatique *mf*.

Asiatic [ˌeɪʒɪˈætɪk] **adj** asiatique.

aside [əˈsaɪd] ■ **adv 1.** [to one side] de côté ▸ **to move aside** s'écarter ▸ **to take sb aside** prendre qqn à part ▸ **to brush** *OR* **sweep sthg aside** balayer *OR* repousser qqch **2.** [apart] à part ▸ **aside from** à l'exception de.
■ **n 1.** [in play] aparté *m* **2.** [remark] réflexion *f*, commentaire *m*.

ask [ɑːsk] ■ **vt 1.** [gen] demander ▸ **to ask sb sthg** demander qqch à qqn ▸ **he asked me my name** il m'a demandé mon nom ▸ **she asked him about his job** elle lui a posé des questions sur son travail ▸ **to ask sb for sthg** demander qqch à qqn ▸ **to ask sb to do sthg** demander à qqn de faire qqch ▸ **he asked them a favour** il leur a demandé un service ▸ **if you ask me...** si tu veux mon avis... **2.** [put - question] poser **3.** COMM **: to ask a price** demander un prix ▸ **what are you asking for it?** combien en voulez-vous *OR* demandez-vous? **4.** [invite] inviter.
■ **vi** demander.
◆ ***ask after*** **vt insep** demander des nouvelles de.
◆ ***ask for*** **vt insep 1.** [person] demander à voir **2.** [thing] demander.

askance [əˈskæns] **adv : to look askance at sb** regarder qqn d'un air désapprobateur.

askew [əˈskjuː] **adj** [not straight] de travers.

asking price [ˈɑːskɪŋ-] **n** prix *m* demandé.

asleep [əˈsliːp] **adj** endormi(e) ▸ **to fall asleep** s'endormir ▸ **to be fast** *OR* **sound asleep** dormir profondément *OR* à poings fermés.

ASLEF [ˈæzlef] (abbr of ***Associated Society of Locomotive Engineers and Firemen***) **n** *syndicat des cheminots en Grande-Bretagne.*

AS-level [eɪ'eslevl] (abbr of ***Advanced Supplementary Level***) n SCH *examen facultatif complétant les A-levels.*

ASM (abbr of ***air-to-surface missile***) n ASM *m.*

asparagus [ə'spærəgəs] n *(U)* asperges *fpl.*

aspartame ['æspərteɪm] n aspartame *m.*

ASPCA (abbr of ***American Society for the Prevention of Cruelty to Animals***) n *société américaine protectrice des animaux.*

aspect ['æspekt] n **1.** [gen] aspect *m* **2.** [of building] orientation *f.*

aspen ['æspən] n tremble *m.*

aspersions [ə'spɜːʃnz] npl **: to cast aspersions on** jeter le discrédit sur.

asphalt ['æsfælt] n asphalte *m.*

asphyxia [əs'fɪksɪə] n asphyxie *f.*

asphyxiate [əs'fɪksɪeɪt] vt asphyxier.

asphyxiating [əs'fɪksɪeɪtɪŋ] adj asphyxiant(e).

asphyxiation [əsˌfɪksɪ'eɪʃn] n asphyxie *f.*

aspic ['æspɪk] n aspic *m.*

aspirate ['æspərət] adj LING aspiré(e).

aspiration [ˌæspə'reɪʃn] n aspiration *f.*

aspire [ə'spaɪəʳ] vi **: to aspire to sthg/to do sthg** aspirer à qqch/à faire qqch.

aspirin ['æsprɪn] n aspirine *f.*

aspiring [ə'spaɪərɪŋ] adj **: she was an aspiring writer** elle avait pour ambition de devenir écrivain.

ass [æs] n **1.** [donkey] âne *m* **2.** *inf* [idiot] imbécile *mf*, idiot *m*, -e *f* **3.** *US vulg* = ***arse***.

assail [ə'seɪl] vt assaillir.

assailant [ə'seɪlənt] n assaillant *m*, -e *f.*

assassin [ə'sæsɪn] n assassin *m.*

assassinate [ə'sæsɪneɪt] vt assassiner.

assassination [əˌsæsɪ'neɪʃn] n assassinat *m.*

assault [ə'sɔːlt] ■ n **1.** MIL **: assault (on)** assaut *m* (de), attaque *f* (de) **2.** [physical attack] **: assault (on sb)** agression *f* (contre qqn) ▸ **assault and battery** LAW coups *mpl* et blessures.

■ vt [attack - physically] agresser / [- sexually] violenter.

assault course n parcours *m* du combattant.

assemble [ə'sembl] ■ vt **1.** [gather] réunir **2.** [fit together] assembler, monter.

■ vi se réunir, s'assembler.

assembly [ə'semblɪ] (pl -ies) n **1.** [gen] assemblée *f* **2.** [fitting together] assemblage *m.*

assembly language n COMPUT langage *m* d'assemblage.

assembly line n chaîne *f* de montage.

assemblyman [ə'semblɪmən] (pl **-men** [-men]) n *US* POL *homme qui siège à une assemblée législative.*

assembly point n point *m* de rassemblement.

assemblywoman [ə'semblɪwʊmən] (pl **-women** [-ˌwɪmɪn]) n *US* POL *femme qui siège à une assemblée législative.*

assent [ə'sent] ■ n consentement *m*, assentiment *m.*

■ vi **: to assent (to)** donner son consentement *OR* assentiment (à).

assert [ə'sɜːt] vt **1.** [fact, belief] affirmer, soutenir **2.** [authority] imposer ▸ **to assert o.s.** s'imposer.

assertion [ə'sɜːʃn] n [claim] assertion *f*, affirmation *f.*

assertive [ə'sɜːtɪv] adj [generally] assuré(e) / *pej* péremptoire.

assertively [ə'sɜːtɪvlɪ] adv [generally] fermement / *pej* de façon péremptoire.

assertiveness [ə'sɜːtɪvnɪs] n manière *f* assurée / *pej* arrogance *f.*

assertiveness training n stage *m* d'affirmation de soi.

assess [ə'ses] vt évaluer, estimer.

assessment [ə'sesmənt] n **1.** [opinion] opinion *f* **2.** [calculation] évaluation *f*, estimation *f.*

assessor [ə'sesəʳ] n [of tax] contrôleur *m*, -euse *f* (des impôts).

asset ['æset] n avantage *m*, atout *m* ▸ **she will be an asset to the company** sa compétence sera un atout pour la société.

◆ ***assets*** npl COMM actif *m.*

asset-stripper n dépeceur *m* d'entreprise.

asset-stripping [-ˌstrɪpɪŋ] n *rachat d'une société pour en récupérer l'actif.*

asshole ['æshəʊl] n *vulg US* = ***arsehole***.

assiduous [ə'sɪdjʊəs] adj assidu(e).

assiduously [ə'sɪdjʊəslɪ] adv assidûment.

assign [ə'saɪn] vt **1.** [allot] **: to assign sthg (to)** assigner qqch (à) **2.** [give task to] **: to assign sb (to sthg/to do sthg)** nommer qqn (à qqch/pour faire qqch).

assignation [ˌæsɪg'neɪʃn] n rendez-vous *m* (amoureux).

assignee [ˌæsaɪ'niː] n cessionnaire *mf.*

assignment [ə'saɪnmənt] n **1.** [task] mission *f* / SCH devoir *m* **2.** [act of assigning] attribution *f.*

assimilate [ə'sɪmɪleɪt] vt assimiler.

assimilation [əˌsɪmɪ'leɪʃn] n assimilation *f.*

assist [ə'sɪst] vt **: to assist sb (with sthg/in doing sthg)** aider qqn (dans qqch/à faire qqch) / [professionally] assister qqn (dans qqch/pour faire qqch).

assistance [ə'sɪstəns] n aide *f* ▸ **to be of assistance (to)** être utile (à).

assistant [ə'sɪstənt] ■ n assistant *m*, -e *f* ▸ **(shop) assistant** *UK* vendeur *m*, -euse *f.*

■ comp [director, editor, librarian, secretary] adjoint(e) ▸ **assistant manager** sous-directeur *m*, -trice *f* ▸ **assistant referee** SPORT assistant-arbitre *m.*

associate ■ adj [ə'səʊʃɪət] associé(e).

■ n [ə'səʊʃɪət] associé *m*, -e *f.*

■ vt [ə'səʊʃɪeɪt] **: to associate sb/sthg (with)** associer qqn/qqch (à) ▸ **to be associated with** être associé(e) à.

■ vi [ə'səʊʃɪeɪt] **: to associate with sb** fréquenter qqn.

association [əˌsəʊsɪ'eɪʃn] n association *f* ▸ **in association with** avec la collaboration de.

assonance ['æsənəns] **n** assonance *f.*

assorted [ə'sɔːtɪd] **adj** varié(e).

assortment [ə'sɔːtmənt] **n** mélange *m.*

Asst. abbr of ***assistant***.

assuage [ə'sweɪdʒ] **vt** [thirst, hunger] assouvir / [grief] soulager.

assume [ə'sjuːm] **vt** **1.** [suppose] supposer, présumer **2.** [power, responsibility] assumer **3.** [appearance, attitude] adopter.

assumed [ə'sjuːmd] **adj** feint(e), faux (fausse).

assumed name [ə'sjuːmd-] **n** nom *m* d'emprunt.

assuming [ə'sjuːmɪŋ] **conj** en supposant que.

assumption [ə'sʌmpʃn] **n** **1.** [supposition] supposition *f* **2.** [of power] prise *f.*
◆ ***Assumption*** **n** RELIG **: the Assumption** l'Assomption *f.*

assurance [ə'ʃʊərəns] **n** **1.** [gen] assurance *f* **2.** [promise] garantie *f*, promesse *f.*

assure [ə'ʃʊəʳ] **vt : to assure sb (of)** assurer qqn (de).

assured [ə'ʃʊəd] **adj** assuré(e).

AST (abbr of ***Atlantic Standard Time***) **n** *heure d'hiver de la côte est des États-Unis.*

asterisk ['æstərɪsk] **n** astérisque *m.*

astern [ə'stɜːn] **adv** NAUT en poupe.

asteroid ['æstərɔɪd] **n** astéroïde *m.*

asthma ['æsmə] **n** asthme *m.*

asthmatic [æs'mætɪk] ■ **adj** asthmatique.
■ **n** asthmatique *mf.*

astigmatism [æ'stɪgmətɪzm] **n** astigmatisme *m.*

astonish [ə'stɒnɪʃ] **vt** étonner.

astonished [ə'stɒnɪʃt] **adj** surpris(e).

astonishing [ə'stɒnɪʃɪŋ] **adj** étonnant(e).

astonishingly [ə'stɒnɪʃɪŋlɪ] **adv** incroyablement ▸ **astonishingly, they both decided to leave** aussi étonnant que cela paraisse, ils ont tous les deux décidé de partir.

astonishment [ə'stɒnɪʃmənt] **n** étonnement *m.*

astound [ə'staʊnd] **vt** stupéfier.

astounded [ə'staʊndɪd] **adj** stupéfait(e).

astounding [ə'staʊndɪŋ] **adj** stupéfiant(e).

astoundingly [ə'staʊndɪŋlɪ] **adv** incroyablement ▸ **astoundingly beautiful** d'une beauté incroyable ▸ **astoundingly enough, they'd already met** chose extraordinaire, ils s'étaient déjà rencontrés.

astrakhan [ˌæstrə'kæn] **n** astrakan *m.*

astray [ə'streɪ] **adv : to go astray** [become lost] s'égarer ▸ **to lead sb astray** détourner qqn du droit chemin.

astride [ə'straɪd] ■ **adv** à cheval, à califourchon.
■ **prep** à cheval OR califourchon sur.

astringent [ə'strɪndʒənt] ■ **adj** astringent(e).
■ **n** astringent *m.*

astrologer [ə'strɒlədʒəʳ] **n** astrologue *mf.*

astrological [ˌæstrə'lɒdʒɪkl] **adj** astrologique.

astrologist [ə'strɒlədʒɪst] = ***astrologer***.

astrology [ə'strɒlədʒɪ] **n** astrologie *f.*

astronaut ['æstrənɔːt] **n** astronaute *mf.*

astronomer [ə'strɒnəməʳ] **n** astronome *mf.*

astronomical [ˌæstrə'nɒmɪkl] **adj** astronomique.

astronomically [ˌæstrə'nɒmɪklɪ] **adv** [generally] astronomiquement / *fig* **: prices have risen astronomically** les prix ont atteint des sommets astronomiques.

astronomy [ə'strɒnəmɪ] **n** astronomie *f.*

astrophysics [ˌæstrəʊ'fɪzɪks] **n** *(U)* astrophysique *f.*

Astroturf® ['æstrəʊˌtɜːf] **n** gazon *m* artificiel.

astute [ə'stjuːt] **adj** malin(igne).

astutely [ə'stjuːtlɪ] **adv** astucieusement, avec finesse OR perspicacité.

astuteness [ə'stjuːtnɪs] **n** finesse *f*, perspicacité *f.*

asunder [ə'sʌndəʳ] **adv** *liter* **: to tear asunder** déchirer en deux.

ASV (abbr of ***American Standard Version***) **n** *traduction américaine de la Bible.*

asylum [ə'saɪləm] **n** asile *m.*

asylum-seeker **n** demandeur *m*, -euse *f* d'asile.

asymmetrical [ˌeɪsɪ'metrɪkl] **adj** asymétrique.

at *(stressed* [æt], *unstressed* [ət]*)* **prep** **1.** [indicating place, position] à ▸ **they arrived at the airport** ils sont arrivés à l'aéroport ▸ **at my father's** chez mon père ▸ **at home** à la maison, chez soi ▸ **at my house/the dentist's** chez moi/le dentiste ▸ **at school** à l'école ▸ **at work** au travail
2. [indicating direction] vers ▸ **to look at sb** regarder qqn ▸ **to smile at sb** sourire à qqn ▸ **to shoot at sb** tirer sur qqn ▸ **don't shout at me!** ne me crie pas dessus!
3. [indicating a particular time] à ▸ **at midnight/noon/eleven o'clock** à minuit/midi/onze heures ▸ **at night** la nuit ▸ **I work at night** je travaille de nuit ▸ **at Christmas/Easter** à Noël/Pâques ▸ **I'm busy at the moment** je suis occupé en ce moment
4. [indicating age, speed, rate] à ▸ **at 52 (years of age)** à 52 ans ▸ **he started working at 15** il a commencé à travailler à (l'âge de) 15 ans ▸ **at 100 mph** à 160 km/h ▸ **he drove at 50 mph** il faisait du 80 (à l'heure) ▸ **the temperature stands at 30°** la température est de 30°
5. [indicating price] **: at £50 a pair** 50 livres la paire ▸ **it's a bargain at £5** à 5 livres, c'est une bonne affaire
6. [indicating particular state, condition] en ▸ **at peace/war** en paix/guerre ▸ **to be at lunch/dinner** être en train de déjeuner/dîner
7. [indicating tentativeness, noncompletion] **: to snatch at sthg** essayer de saisir qqch ▸ **to nibble at sthg** grignoter qqch
8. *(after adjectives)* **: amused/appalled/puzzled at sthg** diverti(e)/effaré(e)/intrigué(e) par qqch ▸ **delighted at sthg** ravi(e) de qqch ▸ **to be bad/good at sthg** être mauvais(e)/bon (bonne) en qqch
9. [in electronic address] ar(r)obas *f.*
◆ ***at all*** **adv** **1.** *(with negative)* **: not at all** [when thanked] je vous en prie / [when answering a question] pas du tout ▸ **she's not at all happy** elle n'est pas du tout contente ▸ **nothing at all** rien du tout

2. [in the slightest] **: anything at all will do** n'importe quoi fera l'affaire ▸ **do you know her at all?** est-ce que vous la connaissez? ▸ **if you had any feelings at all** si vous aviez le moindre sentiment.

ATC (abbr of ***Air Training Corps***) n *unité de formation de l'armée de l'air britannique.*

ate [*UK* et, *US* eɪt] pt ➤ ***eat***.

atheism ['eɪθɪɪzm] n athéisme *m*.

atheist ['eɪθɪɪst] n athée *mf*.

Athenian [ə'θi:njən] ■ adj athénien(enne).
■ n Athénien *m*, -enne *f*.

Athens ['æθɪnz] n Athènes.

athlete ['æθli:t] n athlète *mf*.

athlete's foot n *(U)* mycose *f*.

athletic [æθ'letɪk] adj athlétique.
◆ ***athletics*** npl *UK* athlétisme *m* / *US* sports *mpl*.

atishoo [ə'tɪʃu:] excl atchoum!

Atlantic [ət'læntɪk] ■ adj atlantique.
■ n **: the Atlantic (Ocean)** l'océan *m* Atlantique, l'Atlantique *m*.

Atlantis [ət'læntɪs] n Atlantide *f*.

atlas ['ætləs] n atlas *m*.

Atlas ['ætləs] n **: the Atlas Mountains** l'Atlas *m*.

atm. (abbr of ***atmosphere***) atm.

ATM (abbr of ***automatic* OR *automated teller machine***) n *esp US* DAB *m*.

atmosphere ['ætmə,sfɪər] n atmosphère *f*.

atmospheric [,ætməs'ferɪk] adj **1.** [pressure, pollution] atmosphérique **2.** [film, music] d'ambiance.

atoll ['ætɒl] n atoll *m*.

atom ['ætəm] n **1.** TECH atome *m* **2.** *fig* [tiny amount] grain *m*, parcelle *f*.

atom bomb n bombe *f* atomique.

atomic [ə'tɒmɪk] adj atomique.

atomic bomb = ***atom bomb***.

atomic energy n énergie *f* atomique.

atomic number n nombre *m* OR numéro *m* atomique.

atomizer, *UK* ***-iser*** ['ætəmaɪzər] n atomiseur *m*, vaporisateur *m*.

atone [ə'təʊn] vi **: to atone for** racheter.

atonement [ə'təʊnmənt] n **: atonement (for)** réparation *f* (de).

A to Z n plan *m* de ville.

ATP (abbr of ***Association of Tennis Professionals***) n ATP *f*.

atrocious [ə'trəʊʃəs] adj [cruel, evil] atroce, horrible / [very bad] affreux(euse), atroce.

atrociously [ə'trəʊʃəslɪ] adv **1.** [cruelly] atrocement, horriblement **2.** [badly] affreusement, atrocement.

atrocity [ə'trɒsətɪ] (pl -ies) n [terrible act] atrocité *f*.

attach [ə'tætʃ] vt **1.** [gen] **: to attach sthg (to)** attacher qqch (à) **2.** [letter] joindre.

attaché [ə'tæʃeɪ] n attaché *m*, -e *f*.

attaché case n attaché-case *m*.

attached [ə'tætʃt] adj **1.** [fastened on] attaché(e) **2.** [letter] joint(e) **3.** [for work, job] **: attached to** rattaché(e) à **4.** [fond] **: attached to** attaché(e) à.

attachment [ə'tætʃmənt] n **1.** [device] accessoire *m* **2.** [fondness] **: attachment (to)** attachement *m* (à) **3.** COMPUT pièce *f* jointe.

attack [ə'tæk] ■ n **1.** [physical, verbal] **: attack (on)** attaque *f* (contre) ▸ **to go on the attack** passer à l'attaque ▸ **to come under attack** être en butte aux attaques **2.** [of illness] crise *f*.
■ vt **1.** [gen] attaquer **2.** [job, problem] s'attaquer à.
■ vi attaquer.

attacker [ə'tækər] n **1.** [assailant] agresseur *m* **2.** SPORT attaquant *m*, -e *f*.

attain [ə'teɪn] vt atteindre, parvenir à.

attainable [ə'teɪnəbl] adj [level, objective, profits] réalisable / [position] accessible ▸ **a growth rate attainable by industrialized countries** un taux de croissance à la portée des OR accessible aux pays industrialisés.

attainment [ə'teɪnmənt] n **1.** [of success, aims] réalisation *f* **2.** [skill] talent *m*.

attempt [ə'tempt] ■ n **: attempt (at)** tentative *f* (de) ▸ **to make an attempt at doing sthg** OR **to do sthg** essayer de faire qqch ▸ **attempt on sb's life** tentative d'assassinat.
■ vt tenter, essayer ▸ **to attempt to do sthg** essayer OR tenter de faire qqch.

attend [ə'tend] ■ vt **1.** [meeting, party] assister à ▸ **she attends the same course as me** elle suit les mêmes cours que moi ▸ **the concert was well attended** il y avait beaucoup de monde au concert **2.** [school, church] aller à.
■ vi **1.** [be present] être présent(e) ▸ **let us know if you are unable to attend** prévenez-nous si vous ne pouvez pas venir **2.** [pay attention] **: to attend (to)** prêter attention (à).
◆ ***attend to*** vt insep **1.** [deal with] s'occuper de, régler **2.** [look after - customer] s'occuper de / [- patient] soigner.

attendance [ə'tendəns] n **1.** [number present] assistance *f*, public *m* **2.** [presence] présence *f*.

attendant [ə'tendənt] ■ adj [problems] qui en découle.
■ n [at museum, car park] gardien *m*, -enne *f* / [at petrol station] pompiste *mf* ▸ **swimming-pool attendant** maître *m* nageur.

attention [ə'tenʃn] ■ n *(U)* **1.** [gen] attention *f* ▸ **to bring sthg to sb's attention, to draw sb's attention to sthg** attirer l'attention de qqn sur qqch ▸ **to attract** OR **catch sb's attention** attirer l'attention de qqn ▸ **to pay attention to** prêter attention à ▸ **may I have your attention for a moment?** pourriez-vous m'accorder votre attention un instant? ▸ **the news came to his attention** il a appris la nouvelle ▸ **for the attention of** COMM à l'attention de **2.** [care

soins *mpl*, attentions *fpl* ▸ **they need medical attention** ils ont besoin de soins médicaux **3.** MIL **: to stand to attention** se mettre au garde-à-vous.
■ **excl** MIL garde-à-vous!

attentive [ə'tentɪv] **adj** [paying attention] attentif(ive) / [considerate] attentionné(e), prévenant(e).

CONFUSABLE / PARONYME
attentive
When translating **attentive**, note that *attentif* and *attentionné* are not interchangeable. *Attentif* refers to someone who pays attention and *attentionné* to someone who is considerate.

attentively [ə'tentɪvlɪ] **adv** attentivement.

attenuate [ə'tenjʊeɪt] ■ **vt** atténuer.
■ **vi** s'atténuer.

attest [ə'test] ■ **vt** attester, certifier.
■ **vi : to attest to** témoigner de.

attic ['ætɪk] **n** grenier *m*.

attire [ə'taɪər] **n** *(U) fml* tenue *f*.

attitude ['ætɪtju:d] **n 1.** [gen] **: attitude (to** *OR* **towards)** attitude *f* (envers) **2.** [posture] pose *f* **3.** *inf* **: to have attitude** [to be stylish] avoir du cran / [to be arrogant] être frimeur (euse).

attn. (abbr of ***for the attention of***) à l'attention de.

attorney [ə'tɜ:nɪ] **n** *US* avocat *m*, -e *f*.

attorney general (pl **attorneys general**) **n** [in England, Wales and Northern Ireland] *principal avocat de la couronne* / [in US] ministre *m* de la Justice.

attract [ə'trækt] **vt** attirer ▸ **to attract criticism** s'attirer des critiques ▸ **to be attracted to** être attiré(e) par.

attraction [ə'trækʃn] **n 1.** [gen] attraction *f* ▸ **attraction to sb** attirance *f* envers qqn **2.** [of thing] attrait *m*.

attractive [ə'træktɪv] **adj** [person] attirant(e), séduisant(e) / [thing, idea] attrayant(e), séduisant(e) / [investment] intéressant(e).

attractively [ə'træktɪvlɪ] **adv** [decorate, arrange] de manière attrayante / [smile, dress] de manière séduisante.

attributable [ə'trɪbjʊtəbl] **adj : attributable to** dû (due) à, attribuable à.

attribute ■ **vt** [ə'trɪbju:t] **: to attribute sthg to** attribuer qqch à.
■ **n** ['ætrɪbju:t] attribut *m*.

attribution [,ætrɪ'bju:ʃn] **n : attribution (to)** attribution *f* (à).

attrition [ə'trɪʃn] **n** usure *f* ▸ **war of attrition** guerre *f* d'usure.

attuned [ə'tju:nd] **adj : attuned to** [generally] accoutumé(e) à / [ears] habitué(e) à.

Atty. Gen. abbr of ***Attorney General***.

ATV **n 1.** (abbr of ***Associated Television***) *société britannique de télévision* **2.** (abbr of ***all terrain vehicle***) véhicule *m* tout-terrain, 4 X 4 *m*.

atypical [,eɪ'tɪpɪkl] **adj** atypique.

atypically [,eɪ'tɪpɪklɪ] **adv** pas typiquement.

aubergine ['əʊbəʒi:n] **n** *UK* aubergine *f*.

auburn ['ɔ:bən] **adj** auburn *(inv)*.

auction ['ɔ:kʃn] ■ **n** vente *f* aux enchères ▸ **at** *OR* **by auction** aux enchères ▸ **to put sthg up for auction** mettre qqch (dans une vente) aux enchères.
■ **vt** vendre aux enchères.
◆ ***auction off*** **vt sep** vendre aux enchères.

auctioneer [,ɔ:kʃə'nɪər] **n** commissaire-priseur *m*.

auction room **n** salle *f* des ventes.

audacious [ɔ:'deɪʃəs] **adj** audacieux(euse).

audacity [ɔ:'dæsətɪ] **n** audace *f*.

audible ['ɔ:dəbl] **adj** audible.

audibly ['ɔ:dəblɪ] **adv** distinctement.

audience ['ɔ:djəns] **n 1.** [of play, film] public *m*, spectateurs *mpl* / [of TV programme] téléspectateurs *mpl* **2.** [formal meeting] audience *f*.

audio ['ɔ:dɪəʊ] **adj** audio *(inv)*.

audio frequency **n** audiofréquence *f*.

audiotyping ['ɔ:dɪəʊ,taɪpɪŋ] **n** audiotypie *f*.

audiotypist ['ɔ:dɪəʊ,taɪpɪst] **n** audiotypiste *mf*.

audiovisual [,ɔ:dɪəʊvɪzjʊəl] **adj** audiovisuel(elle).

audit ['ɔ:dɪt] ■ **n** audit *m*, vérification *f* des comptes.
■ **vt 1.** vérifier, apurer **2.** *US* UNIV **: he audits several courses** il assiste à plusieurs cours en tant qu'auditeur libre.

audition [ɔ:'dɪʃn] ■ **n** THEAT audition *f* / CIN & TV (séance *f* d')essai *m*.
■ **vi : to audition (for)** THEAT passer une audition (pour) / CIN & TV faire un essai (pour).

auditor ['ɔ:dɪtər] **n** auditeur *m*, -trice *f*.

auditorium [,ɔ:dɪ'tɔ:rɪəm] (pl **-riums** *OR* **-ria** [-rɪə]) **n** salle *f*.

au fait [,əʊ'feɪ] **adj : to be au fait with sthg** être au fait de qqch, connaître qqch.

Aug. abbr of ***August***.

augment [ɔ:g'ment] **vt** augmenter, accroître.

augur ['ɔ:gər] **vi : to augur well/badly** être de bon/mauvais augure.

august [ɔ:'gʌst] **adj** auguste, noble.

August ['ɔ:gəst] **n** août *m* ; see also ***September***.

Auld Alliance [ˌɔːld-] **n : the Auld Alliance** *l'ancienne alliance unissant l'Ecosse et la France contre l'Angleterre.*

CULTURE
Auld Alliance

Le traité entre l'Écosse et la France, plus connu sous le nom de **Auld Alliance**, fut conclu en 1295 afin de déjouer l'expansion des Anglais. C'était à l'origine un accord militaire et diplomatique qui garantissait aux deux pays une aide mutuelle en cas d'offensive anglaise, mais qui accordait également aux commerçants écossais le privilège de choisir les meilleurs vins de Bordeaux. Les Anglais furent ainsi désavantagés durant de longues années en ne recevant que des produits médiocres. Ce traité a eu également une influence importante sur l'architecture et la langue écossaises, puisqu'il a suscité notamment l'emprunt de mots comme « cravate » (**gravat**) ou « assiette » (**ashet**).

Auld Lang Syne [ˌɔːldlæŋ'saɪn] **n** *chant traditionnel britannique correspondant à "Ce n'est qu'un au revoir, mes frères".*

aunt [ɑːnt] **n** tante *f.*

auntie, aunty (pl **-ies**) ['ɑːntɪ] **n** *inf* tata *f*, tantine *f.*

AUP (abbr of ***Acceptable Use Policy***) **n** COMPUT *code de conduit défini par un fournisseur d'accès à l'Internet.*

au pair [ˌəʊ'peəʳ] **n** jeune fille *f* au pair.

aura ['ɔːrə] **n** atmosphère *f.*

aural ['ɔːrəl] **adj** auditif(ive).

aurally ['ɔːrəlɪ] **adv : aurally handicapped** mal entendant(e).

aurora australis [ɔːˌrɔːrə ɒ'streɪlɪs] **n** aurore *f* australe.

aurora borealis [ɔːˌrɔːrə ˌbɔːrɪ'eɪlɪs] **n** aurore *f* boréale.

auspices ['ɔːspɪsɪz] **npl : under the auspices of** sous les auspices de.

auspicious [ɔː'spɪʃəs] **adj** prometteur(euse).

auspiciously [ɔː'spɪʃəslɪ] **adv** favorablement, sous d'heureux auspices.

Aussie ['ɒzɪ] *inf* ■ **adj** australien(enne).
■ **n** Australien *m*, -enne *f.*

austere [ɒ'stɪəʳ] **adj** austère.

austerity [ɒ'sterətɪ] **n** austérité *f.*

austerity measures **npl** restrictions *fpl.*

Australasia [ˌɒstrə'leɪʒə] **n** Australasie *f* ▸ **in Australasia** en Australasie.

Australia [ɒ'streɪljə] **n** Australie *f* ▸ **in Australia** en Australie.

Australian [ɒ'streɪljən] ■ **adj** australien(enne).
■ **n** Australien *m*, -enne *f.*

Austria ['ɒstrɪə] **n** Autriche *f* ▸ **in Austria** en Autriche.

Austrian ['ɒstrɪən] ■ **adj** autrichien(enne).
■ **n** Autrichien *m*, -enne *f.*

AUT (abbr of ***Association of University Teachers***) **n** *syndicat britannique d'enseignants universitaires.*

authentic [ɔː'θentɪk] **adj** authentique.

authenticate [ɔː'θentɪkeɪt] **vt** établir l'authenticité de.

authentication [ɔːˌθentɪ'keɪʃn] **n** authentification *f.*

authenticity [ˌɔːθen'tɪsətɪ] **n** authenticité *f.*

author ['ɔːθəʳ] **n** auteur *m.*

authoring language ['ɔːθərɪŋ-] **n** COMPUT langage *m* auteur.

authoring software ['ɔːθərɪŋ-] **n** COMPUT logiciel *m* auteur.

authoring tool ['ɔːθərɪŋ-] **n** COMPUT outil *m* auteur.

authoritarian [ɔːˌθɒrɪ'teərɪən] **adj** autoritaire.

authoritative [ɔː'θɒrɪtətɪv] **adj 1.** [person, voice] autoritaire **2.** [study] qui fait autorité.

authoritatively [ɔː'θɒrɪtətɪvlɪ] **adv** avec autorité.

authority [ɔː'θɒrətɪ] (pl **-ies**) **n 1.** [organization, power] autorité *f* ▸ **to be in authority** être le/la responsable **2.** [permission] autorisation *f* ▸ **without authority** sans autorisation ▸ **they had no authority to answer** ils n'étaient pas habilités à répondre **3.** [expert] **: authority (on sthg)** expert *m*, -e *f* (en qqch)
▸▸ **to have it on good authority** le tenir de bonne source **OR** de source sûre.
◆ ***authorities*** **npl : the authorities** les autorités *fpl.*

authorization, UK -isation [ˌɔːθəraɪ'zeɪʃn] **n** [act, permission] autorisation *f* / [official sanction] pouvoir *m*, mandat *m* ▸ **he has authorization to leave the country** il est autorisé à quitter le pays.

authorize, UK -ise ['ɔːθəraɪz] **vt : to authorize sb (to do sthg)** autoriser qqn (à faire qqch).

authorized, UK -ised ['ɔːθəraɪzd] **adj** autorisé(e) ▸ **authorized dealer** COMM distributeur *m* agréé ▸ **authorized capital** FIN capital *m* social **OR** nominal.

Authorized Version **n : the Authorized Version** la Bible de 1611.

authorship ['ɔːθəʃɪp] **n** paternité *f.*

autism ['ɔːtɪzm] **n** autisme *m.*

autistic [ɔː'tɪstɪk] **adj** [child] autiste / [behaviour] autistique.

auto ['ɔːtəʊ] (pl **-s**) **n** *US* auto *f*, voiture *f.*

autobiographic(al) ['ɔːtəˌbaɪə'græfɪk(l)] **adj** autobiographique.

autobiography [ˌɔːtəbaɪ'ɒgrəfɪ] (pl **-ies**) **n** autobiographie *f.*

autocracy [ɔː'tɒkrəsɪ] (pl **-ies**) **n** autocratie *f.*

autocrat ['ɔːtəkræt] **n** autocrate *m.*

autocratic [ˌɔːtə'krætɪk] **adj** autocratique.

autocross ['ɔːtəʊkrɒs] **n** *UK* auto-cross *m.*

Autocue® ['ɔːtəʊkjuː] **n** *UK* téléprompteur *m.*

auto-dial ['ɔːtəʊˌdaɪəl] **n : a phone with auto-dial** un poste à numérotation automatique.

autofocus ['ɔːtəʊˌfəʊkəs] **n** autofocus *m inv.*

autograph ['ɔːtəgrɑːf] ■ n autographe *m*.
■ vt signer.

Automat® ['ɔːtəmæt] n *US restaurant où les plats sont vendus dans des distributeurs automatiques.*

automata [ɔː'tɒmətə] npl ➤ ***automaton***.

automate ['ɔːtəmeɪt] vt automatiser.

automated ['ɔːtəmeɪtɪd] adj automatisé(e) ▸ **automated telling machine** *esp US*, **automated teller** *US* distributeur *m* automatique (de billets).

automatic [ˌɔːtə'mætɪk] ■ adj **1.** [gen] automatique ▸ **automatic telling machine** *esp US* distributeur *m* automatique (de billets) **2.** [gesture] machinal(e).
■ n **1.** [car] voiture *f* à transmission automatique **2.** [gun] automatique *m* **3.** [washing machine] lave-linge *m* automatique.

automatically [ˌɔːtə'mætɪklɪ] adv **1.** [gen] automatiquement **2.** [move, reply] machinalement.

automatic pilot n *lit & fig* pilote *m* automatique.

automation [ˌɔːtə'meɪʃn] n automatisation *f*, automation *f*.

automaton [ɔː'tɒmətən] (pl **-tons** *OR* **-ta** [-tə]) n *lit & fig* automate *mf*.

automobile ['ɔːtəməbiːl] n *US* automobile *f*.

automotive [ˌɔːtə'məʊtɪv] adj automobile.

autonomous [ɔː'tɒnəməs] adj autonome.

autonomy [ɔː'tɒnəmɪ] n autonomie *f*.

autopilot [ˌɔːtəʊ'paɪlət] = ***automatic pilot***.

autopsy ['ɔːtɒpsɪ] (pl **-ies**) n autopsie *f*.

autosave ['ɔːtəʊˌseɪv] n COMPUT sauvegarde *f* automatique.

autumn ['ɔːtəm] ■ n *esp UK* automne *m* ▸ **in autumn** en automne.
■ comp d'automne.

autumnal [ɔː'tʌmnəl] adj automnal(e).

auxiliary [ɔːg'zɪljərɪ] ■ adj auxiliaire.
■ n (pl **-ies**) auxiliaire *mf*.

auxiliary verb n (verbe *m*) auxiliaire *m*.

av. (abbr of ***average***) adj moyen(ne).

Av. (abbr of ***avenue***) av.

AV ■ n abbr of ***Authorized Version***.
■ abbr of ***audiovisual***.

avail [ə'veɪl] ■ n : **to no avail** en vain, sans résultat.
■ vt : **to avail o.s. of** profiter de.

availability [əˌveɪlə'bɪlətɪ] n disponibilité *f*.

available [ə'veɪləbl] adj disponible ▸ **they made the data available to us** ils ont mis les données à notre disposition.

available market n ECON marché *m* effectif.

avalanche ['ævəlɑːnʃ] n *lit & fig* avalanche *f*.

avant-garde [ˌævɒŋ'gɑːd] adj d'avant-garde.

avarice ['ævərɪs] n avarice *f*.

avaricious [ˌævə'rɪʃəs] adj avare.

avatar ['ɑːvɪtəʳ] n COMPUT avatar *m*.

avdp. (abbr of ***avoirdupois***) *système avoirdupois*.

Ave. (abbr of ***avenue***) av.

avenge [ə'vendʒ] vt venger.

avenger [ə'vendʒəʳ] n vengeur *m*, -eresse *f*.

avenue ['ævənjuː] n avenue *f*.

average ['ævərɪdʒ] ■ adj moyen(enne).
■ n moyenne *f* ▸ **above/below average** au-dessus/au-dessous de la moyenne ▸ **on average** en moyenne ▸ **we travelled an average of 100 miles a day** nous avons fait une moyenne de 100 miles par jour *OR* 100 miles par jour en moyenne.
■ vt : **the factory averages 10 machines a day** l'usine produit en moyenne 10 machines par jour ▸ **the cars were averaging 90 mph** les voitures roulaient en moyenne à 150 km/h.
◆ ***average out*** ■ vt sep établir la moyenne de.
■ vi : **to average out at** donner la moyenne de.

average propensity to consume n ECON propension *f* moyenne à consommer.

average propensity to save n ECON propension *f* moyenne à épargner.

averse [ə'vɜːs] adj : **I'm not averse to the occasional drink** *hum* je ne dis pas non à un verre de temps en temps.

aversion [ə'vɜːʃn] n : **aversion (to)** aversion *f* (pour).

aversion therapy n thérapie *f* d'aversion.

avert [ə'vɜːt] vt **1.** [avoid] écarter / [accident] empêcher **2.** [eyes, glance] détourner.

aviary ['eɪvjərɪ] (pl **-ies**) n volière *f*.

aviation [ˌeɪvɪ'eɪʃn] n aviation *f*.

aviator ['eɪvɪeɪtəʳ] n *dated* aviateur *m*, -trice *f*.

avid ['ævɪd] adj : **avid (for)** avide (de).

avidly ['ævɪdlɪ] adv avidement, avec avidité.

avocado [ˌævə'kɑːdəʊ] (pl **-s** *OR* **-es**) n : **avocado (pear)** avocat *m*.

avoid [ə'vɔɪd] vt éviter ▸ **to avoid doing sthg** éviter de faire qqch ▸ **don't avoid the issue** n'essaie pas d'éviter *OR* d'éluder la question.

avoidable [ə'vɔɪdəbl] adj qui peut être évité(e).

avoidable costs npl coûts *mpl* évitables.

avoidance [ə'vɔɪdəns] n ➤ ***tax avoidance***.

avowed [ə'vaʊd] adj **1.** [supporter, opponent] déclaré(e) **2.** [aim, belief] avoué(e).

AVP (abbr of ***assistant vice-president***) n *US vice-président adjoint*.

AWACS ['eɪwæks] (abbr of ***airborne warning and control system***) n AWACS *m*.

await [ə'weɪt] vt attendre ▸ **she's awaiting trial** elle est dans l'attente de son procès ▸ **a long-awaited holiday** des vacances qui se sont fait attendre.

awake [ə'weɪk] ■ adj **1.** [not sleeping] réveillé(e) ▸ **are you awake?** tu dors? ▸ **to be wide awake** être complètement réveillé(e) **2.** *fig* [aware] : **awake to** conscient(e) de.
■ vt (pt **awoke** *OR* **awaked**, pp **awoken**) **1.** [wake up] réveiller **2.** *fig* [feeling] éveiller.
■ vi (pt **awoke** *OR* **awaked**, pp **awoken**) **1.** [wake up] se réveiller **2.** *fig* [feeling] s'éveiller.

awaken [ə'weɪkn] ■ **vt** éveiller.
■ **vi** s'éveiller.

awakening [ə'weɪknɪŋ] **n 1.** [from sleep] réveil *m* **2.** *fig* [of feeling] éveil *m* ▸ **a rude awakening** un réveil brutal.

award [ə'wɔ:d] ■ **n 1.** [prize] prix *m* **2.** [compensation] dommages-intérêts *mpl*.
■ **vt : to award sb sthg, to award sthg to sb** [prize] décerner qqch à qqn / [compensation, free kick] accorder qqch à qqn.

award-winner **n** [person] lauréat *m*, -e *f* / [film] film *m* primé / [book] livre *m* primé.

award-winning **adj** qui a reçu un prix ▸ **he gave an award-winning performance in...** il a reçu un prix pour son rôle dans...

aware [ə'weəʳ] **adj : to be aware of sthg** se rendre compte de qqch, être conscient(e) de qqch ▸ **to be aware that** se rendre compte que, être conscient que ▸ **politically aware** politisé(e).

awareness [ə'weənɪs] **n** *(U)* conscience *f*.

awash [ə'wɒʃ] **adj** *lit* & *fig* **: awash (with)** inondé(e) (de).

away [ə'weɪ] ■ **adv 1.** [in opposite direction] **: to move** OR **walk away (from)** s'éloigner (de) ▸ **to look away** détourner le regard ▸ **to turn away** se détourner
2. [in distance] **: we live 4 miles away (from here)** nous habitons à 6 kilomètres (d'ici) ▸ **to keep sb away** empêcher qqn de s'approcher
3. [in time] **: the elections are a month away** les élections se dérouleront dans un mois
4. [absent] absent(e) ▸ **she's away on holiday** elle est partie en vacances
5. [in safe place] **: to put sthg away** ranger qqch
6. [so as to be gone or used up] **: to fade away** disparaître ▸ **to give sthg away** donner qqch, faire don de qqch ▸ **to take sthg away** emporter qqch
7. [continuously] **: to be working away** travailler sans arrêt.
■ **adj** SPORT [fans] de l'équipe des visiteurs ▸ **away game** match *m* à l'extérieur ▸ **away team** équipe *f* des visiteurs.

awe [ɔ:] **n** respect *m* mêlé de crainte ▸ **to be in awe of sb** être impressionné(e) par qqn.

awe-inspiring **adj** [impressive] impressionnant(e), imposant(e) / [amazing] stupéfiant(e) / [frightening] terrifiant(e).

awesome ['ɔ:səm] **adj** impressionnant(e).

awe-struck **adj** [intimidated] intimidé(e), impressionné(e) / [amazed] stupéfait(e) / [frightened] frappé(e) de terreur.

awful ['ɔ:fʊl] **adj 1.** [terrible] affreux(euse) **2.** *inf* [very great] **: an awful lot (of)** énormément (de).

awfully ['ɔ:flɪ] **adv** *inf* [bad, difficult] affreusement / [nice, good] extrêmement.

awhile [ə'waɪl] **adv** *liter* un moment.

awkward ['ɔ:kwəd] **adj 1.** [clumsy] gauche, maladroit(e) **2.** [embarrassed] mal à l'aise, gêné(e) ▸ **she felt awkward about going** cela la gênait d'y aller **3.** [difficult - person, problem, task] difficile **4.** [inconvenient] incommode ▸ **you've come at an awkward time** vous êtes arrivé au mauvais moment **5.** [embarrassing] embarrassant(e), gênant(e).

awkwardly ['ɔ:kwədlɪ] **adv 1.** [move] gauchement, maladroitement **2.** [with embarrassment] avec gêne OR embarras.

awkwardness ['ɔ:kwədnɪs] **n 1.** [of person, movement] gaucherie *f*, maladresse *f* **2.** [embarrassment] gêne *f*, embarras *m*.

awl [ɔ:l] **n** poinçon *m*, alêne *f*.

awning ['ɔ:nɪŋ] **n 1.** [of tent] auvent *m* **2.** [of shop] banne *f*.

awoke [ə'wəʊk] **pt** ➤ ***awake***.

awoken [ə'wəʊkn] **pp** ➤ ***awake***.

AWOL ['eɪwɒl] (abbr of ***absent without leave***) **: to be/go AWOL** MIL être/partir en absence irrégulière.

awry [ə'raɪ] ■ **adj** de travers.
■ **adv : to go awry** aller de travers, mal tourner.

axe, *US* ***ax*** [æks] ■ **n** hache *f* ▸ **to have an axe to grind** prêcher pour sa paroisse.
■ **vt** [project] abandonner / [jobs] supprimer.

axeman ['æksmæn] (pl **-men** [-mən]) **n** *lit* tueur *m* à la hache / *fig* [in company] *cadre chargé des licenciements*.

axes ['æksi:z] **npl** ➤ ***axis***.

axiom ['æksɪəm] **n** axiome *m*.

axis ['æksɪs] (pl **axes** ['æksi:z]) **n** axe *m*.

axle ['æksl] **n** essieu *m*.

ayatollah [ˌaɪə'tɒlə] **n** ayatollah *m*.

aye [aɪ] ■ **adv** [generally] oui.
■ **n** oui *m* / [in voting] voix *f* pour.

AYH (abbr of ***American Youth Hostels***) **n** *association américaine des auberges de jeunesse*.

AZ abbr of ***Arizona***.

azalea [ə'zeɪljə] **n** azalée *f*.

Azerbaijan [ˌæzəbaɪ'dʒɑ:n] **n** Azerbaïdjan *m*.

Azerbaijani [ˌæzəbaɪ'dʒɑ:nɪ] ■ **adj** azerbaïdjanais(e).
■ **n** Azerbaïdjanais *m*, -e *f*.

Azeri [ə'zerɪ] ■ **adj** azeri.
■ **n** Azeri *mf*.

AZERTY keyboard [ə'zɜ:tɪ] **n** clavier *m* AZERTY.

Azores [ə'zɔ:z] **npl : the Azores** les Açores *fpl* ▸ **in the Azores** aux Açores.

AZT (abbr of ***azidothymidine***) **n** AZT *f*.

Aztec ['æztek] ■ **adj** aztèque.
■ **n** Aztèque *mf*.

azure ['æʒəʳ] **adj** azuré(e), bleu(e) d'azur.

b (pl b's ***OR*** bs), ***B*** (pl B's ***OR*** Bs) [biː] **n** [letter] b *m inv*, B *m inv*.
◆ ***B*** **n 1.** MUS si *m* **2.** SCH [mark] B *m inv*.

b. abbr of ***born***.

B & B n abbr of ***bed and breakfast***.

B2B [ˌbiːtə'biː] (abbr of ***business to business***) **n** COMM B to B.

B2C [ˌbiːtə'siː] (abbr of ***business to customer***) **n** COMM B to C.

BA n **1.** abbr of ***Bachelor of Arts*** **2.** (abbr of ***British Academy***) *organisme public d'aide à la recherche dans le domaine des lettres* **3.** (abbr of ***British Airways***) *compagnie aérienne britannique*.

BAA (abbr of ***British Airports' Authority***) **n** *organisme autonome responsable des aéroports en Grande-Bretagne*.

babble ['bæbl] ■ **n** [of voices] murmure *m*, rumeur *f*.
■ **vi** [person] babiller / [stream] gazouiller.

babbling ['bæblɪŋ] ■ **n 1.** [of voices] rumeur *f* / [of baby] babillage *m*, babil *m* / [of stream] gazouillement *m*, babil *m* **2.** [chatter] bavardage *m*.
■ **adj** babillard(e).

babe [beɪb] **n 1.** *liter* [baby] bébé *m* **2.** *US inf* [term of affection] chéri *m*, -e *f*.

baboon [bə'buːn] **n** babouin *m*.

baby ['beɪbɪ] (pl **-ies**) **n 1.** [child] bébé *m* **2.** *inf* [darling] chéri *m*, -e *f*.

baby boom **n** baby boom *m*.

baby boomer [-ˌbuːmər] **n** *US personne née pendant le baby-boom d'après-guerre*.

baby buggy **n 1.** *UK* [foldable pushchair] **: Baby buggy®** poussette *f* **2.** *US* = ***baby carriage***.

baby carriage **n** *US* landau *m*.

baby doll **n** poupée *f*.
◆ ***baby-doll*** **adj : baby-doll pyjamas, baby-doll nightdress** baby-doll *m*.

baby face **n** visage *m* de bébé.
◆ ***baby-face*** **adj** au visage de bébé.

baby grand **n** (piano *m*) demi-queue *m*.

Baby-gro® ['beɪbɪgrəʊ] **n** grenouillère *f*.

babyish ['beɪbɪɪʃ] **adj** puéril(e), enfantin(e).

baby-minder **n** *UK* nourrice *f*.

baby-sit **vi** faire du baby-sitting.

baby-sitter **n** baby-sitter *mf*.

baby-sitting **n** garde *f* d'enfants, baby-sitting *m*.

baby sling **n** porte-bébé *m*, Kangourou® *m*.

baby-snatcher **n** ravisseur *m*, -euse *f* de bébés.

baby talk **n** langage *m* enfantin ***OR*** de bébé.

baby tooth **n** = ***milk tooth***.

baby-walker **n** trotteur *m*.

babywipe ['beɪbɪwaɪp] **n** lingette *f*.

baccalaureate [ˌbækə'lɔːrɪət] **n** UNIV ≃ licence *f*.

bachelor ['bætʃələr] **n** célibataire *m*.

bachelorette party *US* = ***hen party***.

bachelor flat **n** garçonnière *f*.

Bachelor of Arts **n** [degree] ≃ licence *f* en ***OR*** ès lettres / [person] ≃ licencié *m*, -e *f* en ***OR*** ès lettres.

Bachelor of Science **n** [degree] ≃ licence *f* en ***OR*** ès sciences / [person] ≃ licencié *m*, -e *f* en ***OR*** ès sciences.

bachelor's degree **n** [in the United Kingdom] ≃ licence *f*.

back [bæk] ■ **adv 1.** [backwards] en arrière ▸ **to step/move back** reculer ▸ **to push back** repousser ▸ **to tie one's hair back** attacher ses cheveux en arrière ▸ **he glanced back** il a regardé derrière lui

2. [to former position or state] **: I'll be back at five** je rentrerai *OR* serai de retour à dix-sept heures ▸ **I'd like my money back** [in shop] je voudrais me faire rembourser ▸ **to go back** retourner ▸ **to come back** revenir, rentrer ▸ **to drive back** rentrer en voiture ▸ **to go back and forth** [person] faire des allées et venues ▸ **to go back to sleep** se rendormir ▸ **she wants her children back** elle veut qu'on lui rende ses enfants ▸ **business soon got back to normal** les affaires ont vite repris leur cours normal ▸ **to be back (in fashion)** revenir à la mode
3. [earlier] **: six pages back** six pages plus haut ▸ **ten years back** *inf* il y a dix ans ▸ **to think back (to)** se souvenir (de) ▸ **as far back as I can remember** d'aussi loin que je m'en souvienne ▸ **back in November** déjà au mois de novembre
4. [in return] **: to phone** *OR* **call back** rappeler ▸ **to write back** répondre ▸ **to pay sb back** rembourser qqn ▸ **I hit him back** je lui ai rendu son coup.
■ **n 1.** [of person, animal] dos *m* ▸ **I fell flat on my back** je suis tombé à la renverse *OR* sur le dos ▸ **we lay on our backs** nous étions allongés sur le dos ▸ **I only saw them from the back** je ne les ai vus que de dos ▸ **to break the back of a job** faire le plus gros d'un travail ▸ **behind sb's back** *fig* derrière le dos de qqn ▸ **to stab sb in the back** *fig* poignarder qqn dans le dos ▸ **to put sb's back up** casser les pieds de qqn ▸ **to turn one's back on sb/sthg** *fig* ignorer qqn/qqch
2. [of door, book, hand] dos *m* / [of head] derrière *m* / [of envelope, cheque] revers *m* / [of page] verso *m* / [of chair] dossier *m* ▸ **to know somewhere like the back of one's hand** connaître un endroit comme sa poche
3. [of room, fridge] fond *m* / [of car] arrière *m* ▸ **the garden is out** *OR* **round the back** le jardin se trouve derrière la maison ▸ **it's the back of beyond** *UK* c'est un trou perdu
4. SPORT arrière *m*.
■ **adj** *(in compounds)* **1.** [at the back] de derrière / [wheel] arrière *(inv)* / [page] dernier(ère) ▸ **the back legs of a horse** les pattes arrière d'un cheval ▸ **the back room** la pièce qui donne sur l'arrière
2. [overdue] **: back rent** arriéré *m* de loyer.
■ **vt 1.** [reverse] reculer ▸ **I backed the car into the garage** j'ai mis la voiture dans le garage en marche arrière
2. [support] appuyer, soutenir
3. [bet on] parier sur, miser sur.
■ **vi** reculer.

◆ ***back away*** **vi** reculer.

◆ ***back down*** **vi** céder.

◆ ***back off*** **vi** reculer.

◆ ***back onto*** **vt : the house backs onto the park** l'arrière de la maison donne sur le parc.

◆ ***back out*** **vi** [of promise] se dédire.

◆ ***back up*** ■ **vt sep 1.** [support - claim] appuyer, soutenir / [- person] épauler, soutenir
2. [reverse] reculer
3. COMPUT sauvegarder, faire une copie de sauvegarde de.
■ **vi** [reverse] reculer.

backache ['bækeɪk] **n : to have backache** *UK*, **to have a backache** *US* avoir mal aux reins *OR* au dos.

backbench ['bækbentʃ] ■ **n** *banc des membres du Parlement britannique qui n'ont pas de portefeuille.*
■ **comp** [opinion, support] des "backbenchers".

backbencher [ˌbæk'bentʃəʳ] **n** *UK* POL *député qui n'a aucune position officielle au gouvernement ni dans aucun parti.*

CULTURE
Backbencher

Un backbencher est un député dit « d'arrière-banc », qui n'exerce aucune fonction au sein du Conseil des ministres ou du Conseil de l'opposition de la Chambre des communes britannique. Cette appellation est due au fait qu'ils occupent les « bancs » situés derrière les places attribuées aux ministres et aux dirigeants de l'opposition dans les assemblées parlementaires. Ces députés n'ont pas la charge d'un cabinet ministériel, mais ils possèdent à titre personnel un certain pouvoir politique : ils proposent des lois, représentent des intérêts privés et ont une plus grande liberté d'expression.

backbiting ['bækbaɪtɪŋ] **n** médisance *f*.

backbone ['bækbəʊn] **n** ANAT épine *f* dorsale, colonne *f* vertébrale / *fig* [main support] pivot *m*.

backbreaking ['bækˌbreɪkɪŋ] **adj** éreintant(e).

back burner **n : to put sthg on the back burner** *inf* mettre qqch en veilleuse.

backchat *UK* ['bæktʃæt], ***backtalk*** *US* ['bæktɔːk] **n** *inf* insolence *f*.

backcloth ['bækklɒθ] *UK* = ***backdrop***.

backcomb ['bækkəʊm] **vt** *UK* crêper.

back copy **n** vieux numéro *m* (d'un journal).

backdate [ˌbæk'deɪt] **vt** antidater.

back door **n** porte *f* de derrière ▸ **to get a job through** *OR* **by the back door** *fig* obtenir un emploi par relations.

backdrop ['bækdrɒp] **n** *lit* & *fig* toile *f* de fond.

-backed [bækt] **suffix 1.** [chair] à dos, à dossier ▸ **a broad-backed man** un homme qui a le dos large **2.** [supported by] **: US-backed rebels** des rebelles soutenus par les États-Unis.

back end **n 1.** [of car, bus] arrière *m* / [of train] queue *f* **2.** *UK inf* [autumn] **: the back end of the year** l'arrière-saison.

backer ['bækəʳ] **n** commanditaire *m*, bailleur *m* de fonds.

backfill ['bækfɪl] ■ **vt** remplir.
■ **n** matériau de construction.

backfire [ˌbæk'faɪəʳ] **vi 1.** AUT pétarader **2.** [plan] **: to backfire (on sb)** se retourner (contre qqn).

backflip ['bækflɪp] **n** [in gymnastics] culbute *f* à l'envers.

backgammon ['bækˌgæmən] **n** backgammon *m*, ≃ jacquet *m*.

background ['bækgraʊnd] ■ **n 1.** [in picture, view] arrière-plan *m* ▸ **in the background** *lit* dans le fond, à l'arrière-plan / *fig* au second plan **2.** [of event, situation] contexte *m* ▸ **the economic background to the crisis** les raisons économiques de la crise **3.** [upbringing] milieu *m* ▸ **people from a working-class background** gens *mpl* de milieu ouvrier.

■ **comp** [music, noise] de fond ▸ **background reading/information** lectures/informations générales *(pour un certain sujet)*.

backhand ['bækhænd] **n** revers *m*.

backhanded ['bækhændɪd] **adj** [compliment, remark] ambigu(ë), équivoque.

backhander ['bækhændəʳ] **n** *UK inf* pot-de-vin *m*.

backing ['bækɪŋ] **n 1.** [support] soutien *m* **2.** [lining] doublage *m* **3.** *UK* MUS accompagnement *m*.

backing group **n** *UK musiciens qui accompagnent un chanteur.*

back issue = ***back number***.

backlash ['bæklæʃ] **n** contrecoup *m*, choc *m* en retour.

backless ['bæklɪs] **adj** [dress] décolleté(e) dans le dos.

backlit ['bæklɪt] **adj** [screen] rétro-éclairé(e).

backlog ['bæklɒg] **n : backlog (of work)** arriéré *m* de travail, travail *m* en retard.

back number **n** vieux numéro *m*.

backpack ['bækpæk] **n** sac *m* à dos.

backpacker ['bækpækəʳ] **n** randonneur *m*, -euse *f (avec sac à dos)*.

backpacking ['bækpækɪŋ] **n : to go backpacking** faire de la randonnée *(avec sac à dos)*.

back passage **n** *UK euph* rectum *m*.

back pay **n** rappel *m* de salaire.

backpedal [ˌbæk'pedl] (*UK* **-led**, cont **-ling**, *US* **-ed**, cont **-ing**) **vi** *fig* **: to backpedal (on)** faire marche OR machine arrière (sur).

backrest ['bækrest] **n** dossier *m*.

back seat **n** [in car] siège *m* OR banquette *f* arrière ▸ **to take a back seat** *fig* jouer un rôle secondaire.

back-seat driver **n** *personne qui n'arrête pas de donner des conseils au conducteur.*

backside [ˌbæk'saɪd] **n** *inf* postérieur *m*, derrière *m*.

backslash ['bækslæʃ] **n** COMPUT barre *f* oblique inversée.

backslide [ˌbæk'slaɪd] (pt & pp **-slid**) **vi** rechuter, récidiver.

backspace ['bækspeɪs] ■ **n** [key] touche *f* de retour en arrière.
■ **vi** [in typing] reculer d'un espace.

backstage [ˌbæk'steɪdʒ] **adv** dans les coulisses.

backstairs [ˌbæk'steəz] ■ **npl** [secondary] escalier *m* de service / [secret] escalier *m* secret OR dérobé.
■ **adj** [secret] secret(ète), furtif(ive) / [unfair] déloyal(e) ▸ **backstairs gossip** bruits *mpl* de couloirs.

back street **n** petite rue *f*.

backstreet ['bækstri:t] **adj** [secret] secret(ète), furtif(ive) / [underhanded] louche ▸ **backstreet abortion** avortement *m* clandestin ▸ **backstreet abortionist** faiseuse *f* d'anges.

backstroke ['bækstrəʊk] **n** dos *m* crawlé.

backtalk *US* = ***backchat***.

back-to-back ■ **adj** *lit* & *fig* dos à dos.
■ **n : back-to-backs** [houses] *rangée de maisons construites dos à dos et séparées par un passage étroit, typique des régions industrielles du nord de l'Angleterre.*
◆ ***back to back*** **adv 1.** [stand] dos à dos **2.** [happen] l'un après l'autre.

back to front **adv** à l'envers.

backtrack ['bæktræk] = ***backpedal***.

backup ['bækʌp] ■ **adj 1.** [plan, team] de secours, de remplacement **2.** COMPUT de sauvegarde.
■ **n 1.** [gen] aide *f*, soutien *m* **2.** COMPUT (copie *f* de) sauvegarde *f*.

backup copy **n** COMPUT copie *f* de sauvegarde.

backward ['bækwəd] ■ **adj 1.** [movement, look] en arrière **2.** [country] arriéré(e) / [person] arriéré(e), attardé(e).
■ **adv** *US* = ***backwards***.

backward-looking [-ˌlʊkɪŋ] **adj** *pej* rétrograde.

backwardness ['bækwədnɪs] **n 1.** [of development - country] sous-développement *m* / [- person] retard *m* mental / [- of economy] retard *m* **2.** [reluctance] hésitation *f*, lenteur *f*.

backwards ['bækwədz], *US* ***backward*** ['bækwərd] **adv** [move, go] en arrière, à reculons / [read list] à rebours, à l'envers ▸ **backwards and forwards** [movement] de va-et-vient, d'avant en arrière et d'arrière en avant ▸ **to walk backwards and forwards** aller et venir.

backwash ['bækwɒʃ] **n** remous *m*.

backwater ['bækˌwɔ:təʳ] **n** [place] désert *m*.

backwoods ['bækwʊdz] **npl : to live in the backwoods of France** habiter la France profonde.

backyard [ˌbæk'jɑ:d] **n 1.** *UK* [yard] arrière-cour *f* **2.** *US* [garden] jardin *m* de derrière.

bacon ['beɪkən] **n** bacon *m*.

bacteria [bæk'tɪərɪə] **npl** bactéries *fpl*.

bacterial [bæk'tɪərɪəl] **adj** bactérien (enne).

bacteriology [bækˌtɪərɪ'ɒlədʒɪ] **n** bactériologie *f*.

bad [bæd] ■ **adj** (comp **worse**, superl **worst**) **1.** [not good] mauvais(e) ▸ **to be bad at sthg** être mauvais en qqch ▸ **he's in a bad mood** OR **bad temper** il est de mauvaise humeur ▸ **things look bad** la situation n'est pas brillante ▸ **to go from bad to worse** aller de mal en pis, empirer ▸ **too bad!** dommage! ▸ **not bad** pas mal
2. [unhealthy] malade ▸ **smoking is bad for you** fumer est mauvais pour la santé ▸ **I'm feeling bad** je ne suis pas dans mon assiette ▸ **he's in a bad way** il va mal, il est en piteux état ▸ **to have a bad heart** être cardiaque
3. [serious] **: a bad cold** un gros rhume
4. [rotten] pourri(e), gâté(e) ▸ **to go bad** se gâter, s'avarier
5. [guilty] **: to feel bad about sthg** se sentir coupable de qqch
6. [naughty] méchant(e).
■ **adv** *US* = ***badly***.

bad blood **n** ressentiment *m*, rancune *f*.

bad cheque *UK*, ***bad check*** *US* **n** chèque *m* sans provision.

bad debt **n** créance *f* irrécouvrable OR douteuse.

bad debt provision **n** provision *f* pour créances douteuses.

baddie, ***baddy*** ['bædɪ] (pl -ies) n *UK inf* méchant *m*.

bade [bæd] pt ➤ ***bid***.

bad feeling n *(U)* rancœur *f*.

badge [bædʒ] n **1.** [metal, plastic] badge *m* **2.** [sewn-on] écusson *m*.

badger ['bædʒəʳ] ■ n blaireau *m*.
■ vt : **to badger sb (to do sthg)** harceler qqn (pour qu'il fasse qqch).

badly ['bædlɪ] (comp **worse**, superl **worst**) adv **1.** [not well] mal ▶ **badly made/organized** mal fait(e)/organisé(e) ▶ **to think badly of sb** penser du mal de qqn **2.** [seriously - wounded] grièvement / [- affected] gravement, sérieusement ▶ **to be badly in need of sthg** avoir vraiment *OR* absolument besoin de qqch.

badly-off adj **1.** [poor] pauvre, dans le besoin **2.** [lacking] : **to be badly-off for sthg** manquer de qqch.

bad-mannered [-'mænəd] adj [child] mal élevé(e) / [shop assistant] impoli(e).

badminton ['bædmɪntən] n badminton *m*.

badmouth ['bædmaʊθ] vt médire de, dénigrer.

badness ['bædnɪs] n [of behaviour] méchanceté *f*.

bad-tempered [-'tempəd] adj **1.** [by nature] qui a mauvais caractère **2.** [in a bad mood] de mauvaise humeur.

baffle ['bæfl] vt déconcerter, confondre.

baffling ['bæflɪŋ] adj déconcertant(e).

bag [bæg] ■ n **1.** [gen] sac *m* ▶ **she's a bag of bones** elle n'a que la peau sur les os ▶ **it's in the bag** *inf* c'est dans la poche, l'affaire est dans le sac ▶ **to pack one's bags** *fig* plier bagage **2.** [handbag] sac *m* à main.
■ vt (pt & pp -ged, cont -ging) **1.** [put into bags] mettre en sac, ensacher **2.** *UK inf* [reserve] garder.
◆ ***bags*** npl **1.** [under eyes] poches *fpl* **2.** *UK inf* [lots] : **bags of** plein *OR* beaucoup de.

bagel ['beɪgəl] n *petit pain en couronne*.

baggage ['bægɪdʒ] n *(U)* bagages *mpl*.

baggage car n *US* fourgon *m (d'un train)*.

baggage reclaim *UK*, ***baggage claim*** *US* n retrait *m* des bagages.

baggage room n *US* consigne *f*.

baggy ['bægɪ] (comp -ier, superl -iest) adj ample.

Baghdad [bæg'dæd] n Bagdad.

bag lady n *inf* clocharde *f*.

bagpipes ['bægpaɪps] npl cornemuse *f*.

bag-snatcher [-snætʃəʳ] n voleur *m*, -euse *f* à la tire.

bah [bɑ:] excl bah!

Bahamas [bə'hɑ:məz] npl : **the Bahamas** les Bahamas *fpl* ▶ **in the Bahamas** aux Bahamas.

Bahrain, ***Bahrein*** [bɑ:'reɪn] n Bahreïn *m*, Bahrayn *m* ▶ **in Bahrain** au Bahreïn.

Bahraini, ***Bahreini*** [bɑ:'reɪnɪ] ■ adj bahreïni(e).
■ n Bahreïni *m*, -e *f*.

Bahrein [bɑ:'reɪn] = ***Bahrain***.

bail [beɪl] ■ n *(U)* caution *f* ▶ **on bail** sous caution ▶ **the judge granted/refused bail** le juge a accordé/refusé la mise en liberté provisoire sous caution.
■ vt **1.** LAW [subj: guarantor] payer la caution pour, se porter garant(e) de / [subj: judge] mettre en liberté provisoire sous caution **2.** [water] vider.
◆ ***bail out*** ■ vt sep **1.** [pay bail for] se porter garant(e) de **2.** *fig* [rescue] tirer d'affaire.
■ vi *US* [from plane] sauter (en parachute).

bailiff ['beɪlɪf] n huissier *m*.

bait [beɪt] ■ n appât *m* ▶ **to rise to *OR* take the bait** *fig* mordre à l'hameçon.
■ vt **1.** [put bait on] appâter **2.** [tease] tourmenter, tarabuster.

baize [beɪz] n feutrine *f*.

bake [beɪk] ■ vt **1.** CULIN faire cuire au four **2.** [clay, bricks] cuire.
■ vi [food] cuire au four.

baked beans [beɪkt-] npl haricots *mpl* blancs à la tomate.

baked potato [beɪkt-] n pomme *f* de terre en robe des champs *OR* de chambre.

Bakelite® ['beɪkəlaɪt] n Bakélite® *f*.

baker ['beɪkəʳ] n boulanger *m*, -ère *f* ▶ **baker's (shop)** *UK* boulangerie *f*.

bakery ['beɪkərɪ] (pl -ies) n boulangerie *f*.

baking ['beɪkɪŋ] ■ adj *inf* : **it's a baking hot day!** on cuit aujourd'hui!
■ n cuisson *f*.

baking powder n levure *f* (chimique).

baking tin n [for cakes] moule *m* à gâteau / [for meat] plat *m* à rôtir.

balaclava (helmet) [,bælə'klɑ:və-] n passe-montagne *m*.

balance ['bæləns] ■ n **1.** [equilibrium] équilibre *m* ▶ **to keep/lose one's balance** garder/perdre l'équilibre ▶ **off balance** déséquilibré(e) ▶ **to strike a balance between the practical and the idealistic** trouver un juste milieu entre la réalité et l'idéal **2.** *fig* [counterweight] contrepoids *m* / [of evidence] poids *m*, force *f* **3.** [scales] balance *f* ▶ **to be *OR* hang in the balance** *fig* être en balance ▶ **his remark tipped the balance in his favour** sa remarque a fait pencher la balance en sa faveur **4.** FIN solde *m* ▶ **balance due** solde débiteur.
■ vt **1.** [keep in balance] maintenir en équilibre **2.** [compare] : **to balance sthg against sthg** mettre qqch et qqch en balance **3.** [in accounting] : **to balance a budget** équilibrer un budget ▶ **to balance the books** clôturer les comptes, dresser le bilan.
■ vi **1.** [maintain equilibrium] se tenir en équilibre ▶ **the weights balance** les poids s'équilibrent **2.** [budget, accounts] s'équilibrer.
◆ ***on balance*** adv tout bien considéré.
◆ ***balance out*** vi insep : **the advantages and disadvantages balance out** les avantages contrebalancent *OR* compensent les inconvénients.

balanced ['bælənst] adj [fair] juste, impartial(e).

balanced diet [,bælənst-] n alimentation *f* équilibrée

balance of payments n balance *f* des paiements.

balance of power n équilibre *m* *OR* balance *f* des forces.

balance of trade **n** balance *f* commerciale.

balance sheet **n** bilan *m*.

balancing ['bælənsɪŋ] **n 1.** [physical effort] stabilisation *f* ▸ **a balancing act** un numéro d'équilibriste ▸ **it was a real balancing act keeping everyone happy** *fig* il fallait jongler pour pouvoir satisfaire tout le monde **2.** FIN [account, books - equalizing] balance *f* / [- settlement] règlement *m*, solde *m*.

balcony ['bælkənɪ] (pl **-ies**) **n** balcon *m*.

bald [bɔ:ld] **adj 1.** [head, man] chauve **2.** [tyre] lisse **3.** *fig* [blunt] direct(e).

bald eagle **n** *aigle à tête blanche (cet oiseau est le symbole des États-Unis et figure sur le sceau officiel)*.

bald-headed **adj** chauve.

balding ['bɔ:ldɪŋ] **adj** qui devient chauve.

baldness ['bɔ:ldnɪs] **n** calvitie *f*.

bale [beɪl] **n** balle *f*.

◆ ***bale out*** *UK* ■ **vt sep** [boat] écoper, vider.

■ **vi** [from plane] sauter en parachute.

Balearic Islands [,bælɪ'ærɪk-], ***Balearics*** [,bælɪ'ærɪks] **npl : the Balearic Islands** les Baléares *fpl* ▸ **in the Balearic Islands** aux Baléares.

baleful ['beɪlfʊl] **adj** *liter* sinistre.

Bali ['bɑ:lɪ] **n** Bali *m* ▸ **in Bali** à Bali.

balk [bɔ:k] **vi : to balk (at)** hésiter OR reculer (devant).

Balkan ['bɔ:lkən] **adj** balkanique.

Balkans ['bɔ:lkənz], ***Balkan States*** ['bɔ:lkən-] **npl : the Balkans** les Balkans *mpl*, les États *mpl* balkaniques ▸ **in the Balkans** dans les Balkans.

ball [bɔ:l] **n 1.** [round shape] boule *f* / [in game] balle *f* / [football] ballon *m* ▸ **to be on the ball** *fig* connaître son affaire, s'y connaître ▸ **to play ball with sb** *fig* coopérer avec qqn ▸ **to start the ball rolling** *fig* lancer la discussion **2.** [of foot] plante *f* **3.** [dance] bal *m* ▸ **to have a ball** *fig* bien s'amuser.

◆ ***balls*** *vulg* ■ **npl** [testicles] couilles *fpl*.

■ **n** *(U)* [nonsense] conneries *fpl*.

CONFUSABLE / PARONYME

ball

When translating **ball**, note that ***balle*** and ***ballon*** are not interchangeable. ***Ballon*** is a large ball used for example in football, while ***balle*** is used for games such as tennis and cricket.

ballad ['bæləd] **n** ballade *f*.

ball-and-socket joint **n** TECH rotule *f*.

ballast ['bæləst] **n** lest *m*.

ball bearing **n** bille *f* de roulement ▸ **ball bearings** roulement *m* à billes.

ball boy **n** ramasseur *m* de balles.

ballcock ['bɔ:lkɒk] **n** (robinet *m* à) flotteur *m*.

ballerina [,bælə'ri:nə] **n** ballerine *f*.

ballet ['bæleɪ] **n 1.** *(U)* [art of dance] danse *f* **2.** [work] ballet *m*.

ballet dancer **n** danseur *m*, -euse *f* de ballet.

ball game **n 1.** *US* [baseball match] match *m* de base-ball **2.** *inf* [situation] **: it's a whole new ball game** c'est une autre paire de manches.

ball girl **n** ramasseuse *f* de balles.

ballistic [bə'lɪstɪk] **adj** balistique ▸ **to go ballistic** *inf* péter les plombs.

ballistic missile **n** missile *m* balistique.

ballistics [bə'lɪstɪks] **n** *(U)* balistique *f*.

ballocks *UK* ['bɒləks] = ***bollocks***.

balloon [bə'lu:n] ■ **n 1.** [gen] ballon *m* **2.** [in cartoon] bulle *f*.

■ **vi** [swell] gonfler.

ballooning [bə'lu:nɪŋ] **n : to go ballooning** faire une ascension en ballon.

ballot ['bælət] ■ **n 1.** [voting paper] bulletin *m* de vote **2.** [voting process] scrutin *m*.

■ **vt** appeler à voter.

■ **vi : to ballot for sthg** voter pour qqch.

ballot box **n 1.** [container] urne *f* **2.** [voting process] scrutin *m*.

ballot paper **n** bulletin *m* de vote.

ballpark ['bɔ:lpɑ:k] **n 1.** *US* [stadium] stade *m* de baseball **2.** *inf* [approximate range] ordre *m* de grandeur ▸ **his guess was in the right ballpark** il avait plutôt bien deviné.

ballpark figure **n** *inf* chiffre *m* approximatif.

ballpoint ['bɔ:lpɔɪnt] ■ **adj** à bille ▸ **ballpoint pen** stylo *m* (à) bille, Bic® *m*.

■ **n** stylo *m* (à) bille, Bic® *m*.

ballroom ['bɔ:lrʊm] **n** salle *f* de bal.

ballroom dancing **n** *(U)* danse *f* de salon.

balls-up *UK*, ***ball-up*** *US* **n** *v inf* **: to make a balls-up of sthg** saloper qqch.

balm [bɑ:m] **n** baume *m*.

balmy ['bɑ:mɪ] (comp **-ier**, superl **-iest**) **adj** doux (douce).

baloney [bə'ləʊnɪ] **n** *(U) inf* foutaises *fpl*, bêtises *fpl*.

BALPA ['bælpə] (abbr of ***British Airline Pilots' Association***) **n** *syndicat britannique des pilotes de ligne*.

balsa(wood) ['bɒlsə(wʊd)] **n** balsa *m*.

balsam ['bɔ:lsəm] **n** baume *m*.

balsamic vinegar [bɔ:l'sæmɪk] **n** vinaigre *m* balsamique.

balti ['bɔ:ltɪ] **n** [pan] *récipient métallique utilisé dans la cuisine indienne* / [food] *plat épicé préparé dans un 'balti'*.

Baltic ['bɔ:ltɪk] ■ **adj** [port, coast] de la Baltique.

■ **n : the Baltic (Sea)** la Baltique.

Baltic Republic **n : the Baltic Republics** les républiques *fpl* baltes.

Baltic State **n : the Baltic States** les pays *mpl* baltes.

balustrade [,bæləs'treɪd] **n** balustrade *f*.

bamboo [bæm'bu:] **n** bambou *m*.

bamboozle [bæm'bu:zl] **vt** *inf* embobiner.

ban [bæn] ■ **n** interdiction *f* ▸ **there is a ban on smoking** il est interdit de fumer.
■ **vt** (pt & pp **-ned**, cont **-ning**) interdire ▸ **to ban sb from doing sthg** interdire à qqn de faire qqch.

banal [bəˈnɑːl] **adj** *pej* banal(e), ordinaire.

banality [bəˈnælətɪ] **n** banalité *f*.

banana [bəˈnɑːnə] **n** banane *f*.

banana republic **n** république *f* bananière.

banana skin **n** *lit* peau *f* de banane, *fig* gaffe ▸ **he slipped on a banana skin** *fig* il a fait une gaffe.

banana split **n** banana split *m*.

band [bænd] **n** **1.** [MUS - rock] groupe *m* / [- military] fanfare *f* / [- jazz] orchestre *m* **2.** [group, strip] bande *f* **3.** [stripe] rayure *f* **4.** [range] tranche *f*.
◆ ***band together*** **vi** se grouper, s'unir.

bandage [ˈbændɪdʒ] ■ **n** bandage *m*, bande *f*.
■ **vt** mettre un pansement ***OR*** un bandage sur.

Band-Aid® **n** pansement *m* adhésif.

bandan(n)a [bænˈdænə] **n** bandana *m*.

b and b, ***B and B*** **n abbr of** ***bed and breakfast***.

bandeau [ˈbændəʊ] (pl **-x** [-z]) **n** bandeau *m*.

bandit [ˈbændɪt] **n** bandit *m*.

bandleader [ˈbænd,liːdəʳ] **n** [generally] chef *m* d'orchestre / MIL chef *m* de fanfare.

bandmaster [ˈbænd,mɑːstəʳ] **n** chef *m* d'orchestre.

band saw **n** scie *f* à ruban.

bandsman [ˈbændzmən] (pl **-men** [-mən]) **n** musicien *m* (d'orchestre).

bandstand [ˈbændstænd] **n** kiosque *m* à musique.

bandwagon [ˈbændwægən] **n : to jump on the bandwagon** suivre le mouvement.

bandwidth [ˈbændwɪdθ] **n** **1.** RADIO largeur *f* de bande **2.** [in acoustics] bande *f* passante.

bandy [ˈbændɪ] (comp **-ier**, superl **-iest**) **adj** qui a les jambes arquées ▸ **to have bandy legs** avoir les jambes arquées.
◆ ***bandy about***, ***bandy around*** (pt & pp **-ied**) **vt sep** répandre, faire circuler.

bandy-legged [-,legd] **adj** = ***bandy***.

bane [beɪn] **n : he's the bane of my life** c'est le fléau de ma vie.

bang [bæŋ] ■ **adv** **1.** [exactly] **: bang in the middle** en plein milieu ▸ **to be bang on time** être pile à l'heure **2.** *inf* [away] **: bang goes my holiday!** mes vacances sont tombées à l'eau! ***OR*** dans le lac.
■ **n** **1.** [blow] coup *m* violent **2.** [of gun] détonation *f* / [of door] claquement *m* ▸ **to go with a bang** *inf fig* être du tonnerre.
■ **vt** [generally] frapper violemment / [door] claquer ▸ **to bang one's head/knee** se cogner la tête/le genou.
■ **vi** **1.** [knock] **: to bang on** frapper à **2.** [make a loud noise - gun] détoner / [- door] claquer **3.** [crash] **: to bang into** se cogner contre.
■ **excl** boum!
◆ ***bangs*** **npl** *US* frange *f*.
◆ ***bang down*** **vt sep** poser violemment.

banger [ˈbæŋəʳ] **n** *UK* **1.** *inf* [sausage] saucisse *f* **2.** *inf* [old car] vieille guimbarde *f*, vieux tacot *m* **3.** [firework] pétard *m*.

Bangkok [,bæŋˈkɒk] **n** Bangkok.

Bangladesh [,bæŋgləˈdeʃ] **n** Bangladesh *m* ▸ **in Bangladesh** au Bangladesh.

Bangladeshi [,bæŋgləˈdeʃɪ] ■ **adj** bangladais(e), bangladeshi.
■ **n** Bangladais *m*, -e *f*, Bangladeshi *mf*.

bangle [ˈbæŋgl] **n** bracelet *m*.

bang-on *inf* ■ **adv** **1.** [exactly] pile ▸ **to hit sthg bang-on** frapper qqch en plein dans le mille **2.** [punctually] à l'heure.
■ **adj : his answers were bang-on** ses réponses étaient percutantes.

banish [ˈbænɪʃ] **vt** bannir.

banister [ˈbænɪstəʳ] **n** rampe *f*.

banjo [ˈbændʒəʊ] (pl **-s** ***OR*** **-es**) **n** banjo *m*.

bank [bæŋk] ■ **n** **1.** [generally] banque *f* ▸ **she has £10,000 in the bank** elle a 10 000 livres à la banque **2.** [of river, lake] rive *f*, bord *m* **3.** [of earth] talus *m* **4.** [of clouds] masse *f* / [of fog] nappe *f*.
■ **vt** FIN mettre ***OR*** déposer à la banque.
■ **vi** **1.** FIN **: to bank with** avoir un compte à **2.** [plane] tourner.
◆ ***bank on*** **vt insep** compter sur.

CULTURE

Bank of England

Fondée en 1694 et surnommée la « Vieille Dame » de la rue Threadneedle, la Banque d'Angleterre est l'équivalent britannique de la Banque de France. Indépendante depuis 1997, elle gère les intérêts monétaires du gouvernement britannique en assurant le contrôle des taux de change, des provisions d'or, du stock de monnaie nationale en circulation et, par le biais de son comité de politique monétaire (le MPC), des taux d'intérêt officiels de la nation. De par sa position éminente dans le monde des affaires, elle participe à de nombreux forums consacrés à l'économie mondiale et aux systèmes financiers internationaux.

bankable [ˈbæŋkəbl] **adj** bancable, escomptable ▸ **to be bankable** *fig* être une valeur sûre.

bank account **n** compte *m* en banque.

bank balance **n** *UK* solde *m* bancaire.

bankbook [ˈbæŋkbʊk] **n** livret *m* de banque.

bank card = ***banker's card***.

bank charges **npl** frais *mpl* bancaires.

bank clerk **n** employé *m*, -e *f* de banque.

bank details **n** relevé *m* d'identité bancaire, RIB *m*.

bank draft **n** traite *f* bancaire.

banker [ˈbæŋkəʳ] **n** banquier *m*.

banker's card **n** *UK* carte *f* d'identité bancaire.

banker's draft **n** traite *f* bancaire.

banker's order n *UK* prélèvement *m* automatique.

bank holiday n *UK* jour *m* férié.

CULTURE

Bank Holiday

Cette fête nationale britannique coïncide avec les jours de fermeture des banques. Jusqu'en 1834, la Banque d'Angleterre célébrait plus de trente dates (jours saints et fêtes religieuses), mais, en 1871, quatre jours fériés seulement sont officialisés : le lundi de Pâques, le premier lundi du mois d'août, le 26 décembre et le **Whit Monday** (« Pentecôte »). Une moyenne de huit jours fériés est institutionnalisée en 1971, ce qui est peu par rapport aux autres pays européens : la majorité des Britanniques prennent leurs congés à ces dates, sauf ceux qui travaillent pour le service public (pompiers, ambulances, police, personnel de santé). À l'exception du jour de Noël, du **Boxing Day** (26 décembre), du Nouvel An et du Vendredi saint, les jours fériés sont déplacés au lundi suivant.

banking ['bæŋkɪŋ] n : **to go into banking** travailler dans la banque.

banking hours npl heures *fpl* d'ouverture des banques.

banking house n banque *f*, établissement *m* bancaire.

bank loan n emprunt *m* (bancaire).

bank manager n directeur *m*, -trice *f* de banque.

bank note n billet *m* de banque.

bank rate n taux *m* d'escompte.

bank robber n cambrioleur *m*, -euse *f* de banque.

bankroll ['bæŋkrəul] *US inf* ■ n fonds *mpl*, finances *fpl*.
■ vt financer.

bankrupt ['bæŋkrʌpt] ■ adj failli(e) ▸ **to go bankrupt** faire faillite.
■ n failli *m*, -e *f*.
■ vt mettre en faillite.

bankruptcy ['bæŋkrəptsɪ] (pl -ies) n **1.** [gen] faillite *f* **2.** *fig* [lack] : **moral bankruptcy** manque *m* de crédibilité.

bank statement n relevé *m* de compte.

banner ['bænəʳ] n **1.** [flag] banderole *f* **2.** COMPUT bandeau *m*.

banner campaign n *campagne publicitaire sur Internet utilisant des bandeaux publicitaires.*

banner headline n PRESS gros titre *m*, manchette *f*.

bannister ['bænɪstəʳ] n = ***banister***.

banns [bænz] npl : **to publish the banns** publier les bans.

banoffee [bə'nɑfi:] n *(U)* banoffee *m*, caramel *m* banane.

banquet ['bæŋkwɪt] n banquet *m*.

bantam ['bæntəm] n poule *f* naine.

bantamweight ['bæntəmweɪt] n poids *m* coq.

banter ['bæntəʳ] ■ n *(U)* plaisanterie *f*, badinage *m*.
■ vi plaisanter, badiner.

BAOR (abbr of ***British Army of the Rhine***) n *forces britanniques en Allemagne.*

bap [bæp] n *UK* petit pain *(rond) m*.

baptism ['bæptɪzm] n baptême *m* ▸ **baptism of fire** baptême du feu.

Baptist ['bæptɪst] n baptiste *mf*.

baptize, *UK* ***-ise*** [*UK* bæp'taɪz, *US* 'bæptaɪz] vt baptiser.

bar [bɑʳ] ■ n **1.** [piece - of gold] lingot *m* / [- of chocolate] tablette *f* ▸ **a bar of soap** une savonnette **2.** [length of wood, metal] barre *f* ▸ **an iron bar** une barre de fer ▸ **to be behind bars** être derrière les barreaux *OR* sous les verrous **3.** *fig* [obstacle] obstacle *m* **4.** [pub] bar *m* **5.** [counter of pub] comptoir *m*, zinc *m* **6.** MUS mesure *f*.
■ vt (pt & pp -red, cont -ring) **1.** [door, road] barrer / [window] mettre des barreaux à ▸ **to bar sb's way** barrer la route *OR* le passage à qqn **2.** [ban] interdire, défendre ▸ **to bar sb (from)** interdire à qqn (de).
■ prep sauf, excepté ▸ **bar none** sans exception.
◆ ***Bar*** n LAW : **the Bar** *UK* le barreau / *US* les avocats *mpl*.

Barbadian [bɑ:'beɪdɪən] ■ adj barbadien(ne).
■ n Barbadien *m*, -ne *f*.

Barbados [bɑ:'beɪdɒs] n Barbade *f* ▸ **in Barbados** à la Barbade.

barbarian [bɑ:'beərɪən] n barbare *mf*.

barbaric [bɑ:'bærɪk] adj barbare.

barbarous ['bɑ:bərəs] adj barbare.

barbecue ['bɑ:bɪkju:] ■ n barbecue *m*.
■ vt griller sur un barbecue.

barbed ['bɑ:bd] adj [arrow, hook] barbelé(e) / *fig* [comment] acerbe, acide.

barbed wire [bɑ:bd-], *US* ***barbwire*** ['bɑ:ʳbwaɪəʳ] n *(U)* fil *m* de fer barbelé.

barber ['bɑ:bəʳ] n coiffeur *m* (pour hommes) ▸ **barber's (shop)** *UK* salon *m* de coiffure (pour hommes) ▸ **to go to the barber's** *UK* aller chez le coiffeur.

barbiturate [bɑ:'bɪtjʊrət] n barbiturique *m*.

Barbour jacket® ['bɑ:bəʳ-] n *veste en toile cirée à col de velours souvent associée à un style de vie BCBG en Grande-Bretagne.*

Barcelona [,bɑ:sɪ'ləʊnə] n Barcelone.

bar chart, *US* ***bar graph*** n diagramme *m* à bâtons, graphique *m* à *OR* en barres, graphique *m* en colonnes.

bar code n code *m* à barres, code-barres *m*.

bard margin n *Ir* = ***hard shoulder***.

bare [beəʳ] ■ adj **1.** [feet, arms] nu(e) / [trees, hills] dénudé(e) ▸ **he killed a tiger with his bare hands** il a tué un tigre à mains nues ▸ **his head was bare** il était nu-tête ▸ **we had to sleep on bare floorboards** nous avons dû coucher à même le plancher
2. [absolute, minimum] : **the bare facts** les simples faits ▸ **the bare minimum** le strict minimum ▸ **the bare essentials** le strict nécessaire
3. [empty] vide

4. [mere] **: it cost us a bare £10** cela nous a coûté simplement 10 livres.

■ **vt** découvrir ▸ **to bare one's head** se découvrir la tête ▸ **to bare one's teeth** montrer les dents ▸ **to bare one's soul** mettre son âme à nu.

bareback ['beəbæk] ■ **adj** qui monte à cru *OR* à nu.
■ **adv** à cru, à nu.

barefaced ['beəfeɪst] **adj** éhonté(e).

barefoot(ed) [,beə'fʊt(ɪd)] ■ **adj** aux pieds nus.
■ **adv** nu-pieds, pieds nus.

bareheaded [,beə'hedɪd] ■ **adj** nu-tête *(inv)*.
■ **adv** nu-tête.

barelegged [,beə'legd] ■ **adj** aux jambes nues.
■ **adv** les jambes nues.

barely ['beəlɪ] **adv** [scarcely] à peine, tout juste.

Barents Sea **n : the Barents Sea** la mer de Barents.

bargain ['bɑ:gɪn] ■ **n 1.** [agreement] marché *m* ▸ **to strike** *OR* **to make a bargain with sb** conclure un marché avec qqn ▸ **into the bargain** en plus, par-dessus le marché **2.** [good buy] affaire *f*, occasion *f*.
■ **vi** négocier ▸ **to bargain with sb for sthg** négocier qqch avec qqn.
◆ ***bargain for, bargain on*** **vt insep** compter sur, prévoir ▸ **they got more than they bargained for** ils ne s'attendaient pas à un coup pareil.

bargain basement **n** [in shop] *dans certains grands magasins, sous-sol où sont regroupés les articles en solde et autres bonnes affaires.*

bargain-hunter **n** dénicheur *m*, -euse *f* de bonnes affaires.

bargaining ['bɑ:gɪnɪŋ] **n** *(U)* [haggling] marchandage *m* / [negociating] négociations *fpl*.

bargaining power **n** influence *f* sur les négociations.

bargain price **n** prix *m* exceptionnel.

barge [bɑ:dʒ] ■ **n** péniche *f*.
■ **vi** *inf* **: to barge past sb** bousculer qqn ▸ **to barge into sb** rentrer dans qqn.
◆ ***barge in*** **vi** *inf* **: to barge in (on)** interrompre.

barge pole **n** *UK* **: I wouldn't touch it with a barge pole** *inf* je ne m'y frotterais pas.

bar graph = ***bar chart***.

barista [bə'ri:stə] **n** barman *m*, barmaid *f*.

baritone ['bærɪtəʊn] **n** baryton *m*.

barium meal ['beəriəm-] **n** *UK* baryte *f*.

bark [bɑ:k] ■ **n 1.** [of dog] aboiement *m* ▸ **his bark is worse than his bite** *inf* il n'est pas si terrible qu'il en a l'air **2.** [on tree] écorce *f*.
■ **vt** [subj: person] aboyer.
■ **vi** [dog] **: to bark (at)** aboyer (après).

barking ['bɑ:kɪŋ] **n** *(U)* aboiement *m*.

barley ['bɑ:lɪ] **n** orge *f*.

barley sugar **n** *UK* sucre *m* d'orge.

barley water **n** *UK* orgeat *m*.

barmaid ['bɑ:meɪd] **n** *UK* barmaid *f*, serveuse *f* de bar.

barman ['bɑ:mən] **(pl -men [-mən]) n** *UK* barman *m*, serveur *m* de bar.

barmy ['bɑ:mɪ] (comp -ier, superl -iest) **adj** *UK inf* toqué(e), timbré(e).

barn [bɑ:n] **n** grange *f*.

barnacle ['bɑ:nəkl] **n** anatife *m*, bernache *f*.

barn dance **n 1.** [occasion] soirée *f* de danse campagnarde **2.** *UK* [type of dance] danse *f* campagnarde.

barn owl **n** chouette *f*.

barometer [bə'rɒmɪtər] **n** *lit & fig* baromètre *m*.

baron ['bærən] **n** baron *m* ▸ **press/oil baron** baron *m* de la presse/du pétrole, magnat *m* de la presse/du pétrole.

baroness ['bærənɪs] **n** baronne *f*.

baronet ['bærənɪt] **n** baronnet *m*.

baroque [bə'rɒk] **adj** baroque.

barrack ['bærək] **vt** *UK* huer, conspuer.
◆ ***barracks*** **npl** caserne *f*.

barracking ['bærəkɪŋ] **n** *UK* chahut *m*, huée *f*.

barracuda [,bærə'ku:də] **n** barracuda *m*.

barrage ['bærɑ:ʒ] **n 1.** [of firing] barrage *m* **2.** [of questions] avalanche *f*, déluge *m* **3.** *UK* [dam] barrage *m*.

barred [bɑ:d] **adj** [window] à barreaux.

barrel ['bærəl] **n 1.** [for beer, wine] tonneau *m*, fût *m* **2.** [for oil] baril *m* **3.** [of gun] canon *m*.

barrel organ **n** orgue *m* de Barbarie.

barren ['bærən] **adj** stérile.

barrette [bə'ret] **n** *US* barrette *f*.

barricade [,bærɪ'keɪd] ■ **n** barricade *f*.
■ **vt** barricader ▸ **to barricade o.s. in** se barricader.

barrier ['bærɪər] **n** *lit & fig* barrière *f*.

barrier cream **n** *UK* crème *f* protectrice.

barring ['bɑ:rɪŋ] **prep** sauf.

barrister ['bærɪstər] **n** *UK* avocat *m*, -e *f*.

bar room ['bɑ:rʊm] **n** *US* bar *m*.

barrow ['bærəʊ] **n** brouette *f*.

bar snack **n** *repas léger pris dans un pub.*

bar stool **n** tabouret *m* de bar.

Bart. abbr of ***baronet***.

bartender ['bɑ:tendər] **n** *US* barman *m*.

barter ['bɑ:tər] ■ **n** troc *m*.
■ **vt : to barter sthg (for)** troquer *OR* échanger qqch (contre).
■ **vi** faire du troc.

base [beɪs] ■ **n** base *f*.
■ **vt** baser ▸ **to base sthg on** *OR* **upon** baser *OR* fonder qqch sur ▸ **where are you based?** où êtes-vous installé? ▸ **the job is based in Tokyo** le poste est basé à Tokyo.
■ **adj** *liter* indigne, ignoble.

baseball ['beɪsbɔ:l] **n** base-ball *m*.

baseball cap **n** casquette *f* de base-ball.

base camp **n** camp *m* de base.

Basel ['bɑ:zl] **n** Bâle.

baseless ['beɪslɪs] **adj** sans fondement.

baseline ['beɪslaɪn] **n** ligne *f* de fond.

basement ['beɪsmənt] **n** sous-sol *m*.

base metal **n** *dated* métal *m* vil.

base rate **n** *UK* taux *m* de base.

bases ['beɪsi:z] **npl** ➤ ***basis***.

bash [bæʃ] *inf* ■ **n 1.** [painful blow] coup *m* **2.** *UK* [attempt] **: to have a bash** tenter le coup **3.** [party] fête *f*, boum *f*.
■ **vt 1.** [hit - gen] frapper, cogner / [- car] percuter **2.** [criticize] critiquer, attaquer.

bashful ['bæʃfʊl] **adj** timide.

-bashing ['bæʃɪŋ] **suffix** *inf* **: media-bashing** dénigration *f* systématique des médias.

basic ['beɪsɪk] **adj** [problem, theme] fondamental(e) / [vocabulary, salary] de base.
◆ ***basics*** **npl 1.** [rudiments] éléments *mpl*, bases *fpl* **2.** [essential foodstuffs] aliments *mpl* de première nécessité.

BASIC ['beɪsɪk] (abbr of ***Beginner's All-purpose Symbolic Instruction Code***) **n** basic *m*.

basically ['beɪsɪklɪ] **adv 1.** [essentially] au fond, fondamentalement **2.** [really] en fait.

basic commodity **n** denrée *f* de base.

basic rate **n** *UK* taux *m* de base.

basic wage **n** salaire *m* de base.

basil ['bæzl] **n** basilic *m*.

basin ['beɪsn] **n 1.** *UK* [bowl - for cooking] terrine *f* / [- for washing] cuvette *f* **2.** *UK* [in bathroom] lavabo *m* **3.** GEOG bassin *m*.

basis ['beɪsɪs] (pl **-ses** [-si:z]) **n** base *f* ▸ **on the basis of** sur la base de ▸ **on a regular basis** de façon régulière ▸ **to be paid on a weekly/monthly basis** toucher un salaire hebdomadaire/mensuel ▸ **the basis for assessing income tax** l'assiette de l'impôt sur le revenu.

bask [bɑ:sk] **vi : to bask in the sun** se chauffer au soleil ▸ **to bask in sb's approval** *fig* jouir de la faveur de qqn.

basket ['bɑ:skɪt] **n** [generally] corbeille *f* / [with handle] panier *m*.

basketball ['bɑ:skɪtbɔ:l] ■ **n** basket-ball *m*, basket *m*.
■ **comp** de basket.

basket case **n** *v inf* **: to be a basket case** [nervous wreck] être un paquet de nerfs / [mad person] être bon (bonne) à enfermer.

basket of currencies **n** ECON & FIN panier *m* de devises **OR** de monnaies.

basketwork ['bɑ:skɪtwɜ:k] **n** vannerie *f*.

basking shark ['bɑ:skɪŋ-] **n** requin *m* pèlerin.

Basle [bɑ:l] = ***Basel***.

basmati (rice) [,bæz'mætɪ] **n** (riz *m*) basmati *m*.

Basque [bɑ:sk] ■ **adj** basque.
■ **n 1.** [person] Basque *mf* **2.** [language] basque *m*.

bass¹ [beɪs] ■ **adj** bas (basse).
■ **n 1.** [singer] basse *f* **2.** [double bass] contrebasse *f* **3.** = ***bass guitar***.

bass² [bæs] (pl **bass OR -es** [-i:z]) **n** [fish] perche *f*.

bass clef [beɪs-] **n** clef *f* de fa.

bass drum [beɪs-] **n** grosse caisse *f*.

basset (hound) ['bæsɪt-] **n** basset *m*.

bass guitar [beɪs-] **n** basse *f*.

bassoon [bə'su:n] **n** basson *m*.

bastard ['bɑ:stəd] **n 1.** [illegitimate child] bâtard *m*, -e *f*, enfant naturel *m*, enfant naturelle *f* **2.** *v inf* [unpleasant person] salaud *m*, saligaud *m*.

baste [beɪst] **vt** arroser.

bastion ['bæstɪən] **n** bastion *m*.

BASW (abbr of ***British Association of Social Workers***) **n** *syndicat britannique des travailleurs sociaux*.

bat [bæt] ■ **n 1.** [animal] chauve-souris *f* **2.** [for cricket, baseball] batte *f* / *UK* [for table-tennis] raquette *f*
▸▸ **to do sthg off one's own bat** *UK* faire qqch de son propre chef.
■ **vt** (pt & pp **-ted**, cont **-ting**) [ball] frapper (avec la batte).
■ **vi** (pt & pp **-ted**, cont **-ting**) manier la batte.

batch [bætʃ] **n 1.** [of papers] tas *m*, liasse *f* / [of letters, applicants] série *f* **2.** [of products] lot *m*.

batch file **n** COMPUT fichier *m* de commandes.

batch processing **n** COMPUT traitement *m* par lots.

bated ['beɪtɪd] **adj : with bated breath** en retenant son souffle.

bath [bɑ:θ] ■ **n 1.** *UK* [bathtub] baignoire *f* **2.** [act of washing] bain *m* ▸ **to have** *UK* **OR take a bath** prendre un bain.
■ **vt** *UK* baigner, donner un bain à.
◆ ***baths*** **npl** *UK* piscine *f*.

bath chair **n** fauteuil *m* roulant.

bath cube **n** sels *mpl* de bain (en forme de cube).

bathe [beɪð] ■ **vt 1.** [wound] laver **2.** [subj: light, sunshine] **: to be bathed in OR with** être baigné(e) de.
■ **vi 1.** [swim] se baigner **2.** [take a bath] prendre un bain.

bather ['beɪðəʳ] **n** baigneur *m*, -euse *f*.

bathing ['beɪðɪŋ] **n** *(U)* baignade *f*.

bathing cap **n** bonnet *m* de bain.

bathing costume UK, ***bathing suit*** **n** maillot *m* de bain.

bathing trunks **npl** slip *m* **OR** caleçon *m* de bain.

bath mat **n** tapis *m* de bain.

bath oil **n** huile *f* de bain.

bathrobe ['bɑ:θrəʊb] **n** [made of towelling] sortie *f* de bain / [dressing gown] peignoir *m*.

bathroom ['bɑ:θrʊm] **n 1.** [room with bath] salle *f* de bains **2.** *US* [toilet] toilettes *fpl*.

bath salts **npl** sels *mpl* de bain.

bath towel **n** serviette *f* de bain.

bathtub ['bɑ:θtʌb] **n** baignoire *f*.

batik [bə'ti:k] **n** batik *m*.

baton ['bætən] **n 1.** [of conductor] baguette *f* **2.** [in relay race] témoin *m* **3.** *UK* [of policeman] bâton *m*, matraque *f*.

baton charge **n** *UK* [by police] charge *f* à la matraque.

batsman ['bætsmən] (pl **-men** [-mən]) **n** batteur *m*.

battalion [bə'tæljən] **n** bataillon *m*.

batten ['bætn] n planche *f*, latte *f*.
◆ ***batten down*** vt insep : **to batten down the hatches** fermer les écoutilles.

batter ['bætər] ■ n *(U)* pâte *f*.
■ vt battre.
◆ ***batter down*** vt sep [door] abattre.

battered ['bætəd] adj **1.** [child, woman] battu(e) **2.** [car, hat] cabossé(e).

battering ['bætərɪŋ] n : **to take a battering** *fig* être ébranlé(e).

battering ram n bélier *m*.

battery ['bætərɪ] (pl -ies) n [generally] batterie *f* / [of calculator, toy] pile *f*.

battery charger n chargeur *m*.

battery farming n élevage *m* intensif *OR* en batterie.

battery hen n poulet *m* de batterie.

battle ['bætl] ■ n **1.** [in war] bataille *f* **2.** [struggle] : **battle (for/against/with)** lutte *f* (pour/contre/avec), combat *m* (pour/contre/avec) ▸ **battle of wits** joute *f* d'esprit ▸ **that's half the battle** le plus dur est fait ▸ **to be fighting a losing battle** mener un combat perdu d'avance.
■ vi : **to battle (for/against/with)** se battre (pour/contre/avec), lutter (pour/contre/avec).

battleaxe *UK*, ***battleax*** *US* ['bætəlæks] n **1.** [weapon] hache *f* d'armes **2.** *pej* & *hum* [woman] virago *f*.

battledress ['bætldres] n tenue *f* de combat.

battlefield ['bætlfi:ld], ***battleground*** ['bætlgraʊnd] n **1.** MIL champ *m* de bataille **2.** *fig* [controversial subject] polémique *f*.

battlements ['bætlmənts] npl remparts *mpl*.

battle-scarred adj [army, landscape] marqué(e) par les combats / [person] marqué(e) par la vie / *hum* [car, table] abîmé(e).

battleship ['bætlʃɪp] n cuirassé *m*.

batty ['bætɪ] (comp -ier, superl -iest) adj *inf* [crazy] cinglé(e), dingue / [eccentric] bizarre.

bauble ['bɔ:bl] n babiole *f*, colifichet *m*.

baud [bɔ:d] n COMPUT baud *m*.

baud rate n COMPUT vitesse *f* de transmission.

baulk [bɔ:k] = ***balk***.

Bavaria [bə'veərɪə] n Bavière *f* ▸ **in Bavaria** en Bavière.

Bavarian [bə'veərɪən] ■ adj bavarois(e).
■ n Bavarois *m*, -e *f*.

bawdy ['bɔ:dɪ] (comp -ier, superl -iest) adj grivois(e), salé(e).

bawl [bɔ:l] vt & vi brailler.

bay [beɪ] ■ n **1.** GEOG baie *f* **2.** [for loading] aire *f* (de chargement) **3.** [for parking] place *f* (de stationnement) **4.** [horse] cheval *m* bai
▸▸ **to keep sb/sthg at bay** tenir qqn/qqch à distance, tenir qqn/qqch en échec.
■ vi hurler.

bay leaf n feuille *f* de laurier.

bayonet ['beɪənɪt] n baïonnette *f*.

bay tree n laurier *m*.

bay window n fenêtre *f* en saillie.

bazaar [bə'zɑ:r] n **1.** [market] bazar *m* **2.** [charity sale] vente *f* de charité.

bazooka [bə'zu:kə] n bazooka *m*.

BB (abbr of ***Boys' Brigade***) n *mouvement chrétien de la jeunesse en Grande-Bretagne*.

BBB (abbr of ***Better Business Bureau***) *US* & *Can* n *organisme de défense de la déontologie professionnelle dans le secteur tertiaire*.

BBC (abbr of ***British Broadcasting Corporation***) n *office national britannique de radiodiffusion* ▸ **the BBC** la BBC.

BBQ n abbr of ***barbecue***.

BC **1.** (abbr of ***before Christ***) av. J.-C. **2.** abbr of ***British Columbia***.

Bcc (abbr of ***blind carbon copy***) n Cci *m*.

BCE adv (abbr of ***before the Common Era***) av. J.-C.

BCG (abbr of ***Bacillus Calmette-Guérin***) n BCG *m*.

BD (abbr of ***Bachelor of Divinity***) n *UK* [degree] ≃ licence *f* de théologie / [person] ≃ licencié, -e *f* en théologie.

BDS (abbr of ***Bachelor of Dental Surgery***) n *UK* [degree] ≃ licence *f* de chirurgie dentaire / [person] ≃ licencié *m*, -e *f* en chirurgie dentaire.

be [bi:] (pt was *OR* were, pp been) ■ aux vb **1.** *(in combination with present participle to form continuous tense)* : **what is he doing?** qu'est-ce qu'il fait? ▸ **he is having breakfast** il prend *OR* il est en train de prendre son petit déjeuner ▸ **it's snowing** il neige ▸ **what are you going to do about it?** qu'est-ce que vous allez *OR* comptez faire? ▸ **they've been promising reform for years** ça fait des années qu'ils nous promettent des réformes
2. *(in combination with past participle to form passive)* être ▸ **to be loved** être aimé(e) ▸ **plans are being made** on fait des projets ▸ **what is left to do?** qu'est-ce qui reste à faire? ▸ **socks are sold by the pair** les chaussettes se vendent par deux ▸ **it is said/thought that...** on dit/pense que...
3. *(in tag questions and answers)* : **he's always causing trouble, isn't he? – yes, he is** il est toujours en train de créer des problèmes, n'est-ce pas? – oui, toujours ▸ **the meal was delicious, wasn't it?** le repas était délicieux, non? *OR* vous n'avez pas trouvé? ▸ **you're back, are you?** vous êtes revenu alors? ▸ **is she satisfied? – she is** est-elle satisfaite? – oui(, elle l'est)
4. *(followed by 'to' + infin)* : **the firm is to be sold** on va vendre la société ▸ **I'm to be promoted** je vais avoir de l'avancement ▸ **you're not to tell anyone** ne le dis à personne ▸ **I'm to be home by 10 o'clock** il faut que je rentre avant 10 h ▸ **there was no one to be seen** il n'y avait personne ▸ **what am I to say to them?** qu'est-ce que je vais leur dire?
■ cop vb **1.** *(with adj, n)* être ▸ **to be a doctor/lawyer/plumber** être médecin/avocat/plombier ▸ **he is American** il est américain, c'est un Américain ▸ **she's intelligent/attractive** elle est intelligente/jolie ▸ **he was angry/tired** il était fâché/fatigué ▸ **I'm hot/cold** j'ai chaud/froid ▸ **I am hungry/thirsty/afraid** j'ai faim/soif/peur ▸ **my feet/hands are frozen** j'ai les pieds gelés/mains gelées ▸ **be quiet!** tais-toi! ▸ **1 and 1 are 2** 1 et 1 font 2 ▸ **just be yourself** soyez vous-même, soyez naturel

2. [referring to health] aller, se porter ▸ **to be seriously ill** être gravement malade ▸ **she's better now** elle va mieux maintenant ▸ **how are you?** comment allez-vous? ▸ **I am fine** ça va
3. [referring to age] **: how old are you?** quel âge avez-vous? ▸ **I'm 20 (years old)** j'ai 20 ans
4. [cost] coûter, faire ▸ **how much was it?** combien cela a-t-il coûté?, combien ça faisait? ▸ **that will be £10, please** cela fait 10 livres, s'il vous plaît
5. [measure] **: the table is one metre long** la table fait un mètre de long ▸ **how tall is he?** combien mesure-t-il?
■ **vi 1.** [exist] être, exister ▸ **the greatest scientist that ever was** le plus grand savant qui ait jamais existé **OR** de tous les temps ▸ **be that as it may** quoi qu'il en soit
2. [referring to place] être ▸ **Toulouse is in France** Toulouse se trouve **OR** est en France ▸ **the school is two kilometres from here** l'école est à deux kilomètres d'ici ▸ **he will be here tomorrow** il sera là demain
3. [happen, occur] être, avoir lieu ▸ **the concert is on Saturday** le concert est **OR** a lieu samedi ▸ **when is your birthday?** quand est **OR** c'est quand ton anniversaire? ▸ **the spring holidays are in March this year** les vacances de printemps tombent en mars cette année
4. [referring to movement] aller, être ▸ **I've been to the cinema** j'ai été **OR** je suis allé au cinéma ▸ **has the plumber been?** le plombier est-il (déjà) passé?
■ **impers vb 1.** [referring to time, dates, distance] être ▸ **it's two o'clock** il est deux heures ▸ **yesterday was Monday** hier on était **OR** c'était lundi ▸ **it's 3 km to the next town** la ville voisine est à 3 km
2. [referring to the weather] faire ▸ **it's hot/cold** il fait chaud/froid ▸ **it's windy** il y a du vent
3. [with 'there'] **: there is, there are** il y a ▸ **there are six of them** ils sont **OR** il y en a six ▸ **there will be swimming** on nagera
4. [for emphasis] **: it's me/Paul/the milkman** c'est moi/Paul/le laitier ▸ **it was your mother who decided** c'est ta mère qui a décidé ▸ **this is my friend John** voici mon ami John ▸ **there are the others** voilà les autres.

B/E **abbr of** ***bill of exchange***.

beach [bi:tʃ] ■ **n** plage *f*.
■ **vt** échouer.

beach ball **n** ballon *m* de plage.

beach buggy **n** buggy *m*.

beachcomber ['bi:tʃˌkəumər] **n** *ramasseur d'objets trouvés sur la plage*.

beachhead ['bi:tʃhed] **n** MIL tête *f* de pont.

beachwear ['bi:tʃweər] **n** *(U)* tenue *f* de plage.

beacon ['bi:kən] **n 1.** [warning fire] feu *m*, fanal *m* **2.** [lighthouse] phare *m* **3.** [radio beacon] radiophare *m*.

bead [bi:d] **n 1.** [of wood, glass] perle *f* **2.** [of sweat] goutte *f*.

beaded ['bi:dɪd] **adj** orné(e) de perles.

beading ['bi:dɪŋ] **n** *(U)* baguette *f* de recouvrement.

beady ['bi:dɪ] (**comp -ier, superl -iest**) **adj : beady eyes** petits yeux perçants.

beady-eyed **adj** aux yeux perçants.

beagle ['bi:gl] **n** beagle *m*.

beak [bi:k] **n** bec *m*.

beaker ['bi:kər] **n** gobelet *m*.

be-all **n : the be-all and end-all** la seule chose qui compte.

beam [bi:m] ■ **n 1.** [of wood, concrete] poutre *f* **2.** [of light] rayon *m*.
■ **vt** [signal, news] transmettre.
■ **vi 1.** [smile] faire un sourire radieux **2.** [shine] rayonner.

beaming ['bi:mɪŋ] **adj 1.** [smiling] radieux(euse) **2.** [shining] rayonnant(e).

bean [bi:n] **n** [gen] haricot *m* / [of coffee] grain *m* ▸ **to be full of beans** *inf dated* péter le feu ▸ **to spill the beans** *inf* manger le morceau.

beanbag ['bi:nbæg] **n** [chair] sacco *m*.

beanshoot ['bi:nʃu:t], ***beansprout*** ['bi:nspraut] **n** germe *m* **OR** pousse *f* de soja.

bear [beər] ■ **n 1.** [animal] ours *m*
2. FIN baissier *m*.
■ **vt** (**pt bore, pp borne**) **1.** [carry, have] porter ▸ **I still bear the scars** j'en porte encore les cicatrices ▸ **he bears no resemblance to his father** il ne ressemble pas du tout à son père ▸ **to bear sthg in mind** ne pas oublier qqch
2. [endure, tolerate] supporter ▸ **the news was more than she could bear** elle n'a pas pu supporter la nouvelle ▸ **I can't bear to see you go** je ne supporte pas que tu t'en ailles ▸ **I can't bear Christmas** je n'aime pas Noël
3. [accept - responsibility, blame] assumer / [- costs] supporter
4. [child] donner naissance à
5. [feeling] **: to bear sb a grudge** garder rancune à qqn
6. FIN [interest] rapporter ▸ **his investment bore 8% interest** ses investissements lui ont rapporté 8 % d'intérêt.
■ **vi** (**pt bore, pp borne**) **: to bear left/right** se diriger vers la gauche/la droite ▸ **to bring pressure/influence to bear on sb** exercer une pression/une influence sur qqn.
◆ ***bear down*** **vi : to bear down on sb/sthg** s'approcher de qqn/qqch de façon menaçante.
◆ ***bear out*** **vt sep** confirmer, corroborer.
◆ ***bear up*** **vi** tenir le coup.
◆ ***bear with*** **vt insep** être patient(e) avec.

bearable ['beərəbl] **adj** [tolerable] supportable.

bearbaiting ['beəˌbeɪtɪŋ] **n** combat *m* d'ours et de chiens.

beard [bɪəd] **n** barbe *f*.

bearded ['bɪədɪd] **adj** barbu(e).

bearer ['beərər] **n 1.** [gen] porteur *m*, -euse *f* **2.** [of passport] titulaire *mf*.

bear hug **n** *inf* **: to give sb a bear hug** serrer qqn très fort.

bearing ['beərɪŋ] **n 1.** [connection] **: bearing (on)** rapport *m* (avec) **2.** [deportment] allure *f*, maintien *m* **3.** TECH [for shaft] palier *m* ▸ **rolling bearing** roulement *m* **4.** [on compass] orientation *f* ▸ **to get one's bearings** s'orienter, se repérer.

-bearing **suffix : rain-bearing clouds** des nuages chargés de pluie ▸ **fruit-bearing trees** des arbres fructifères.

bear market **n** FIN marché *m* à la baisse.

bearskin ['beəskɪn] **n 1.** [fur] peau *f* d'ours **2.** [hat] bonnet *m* à poil.

beast [bi:st] **n 1.** [animal] bête *f* **2.** *inf pej* [person] brute *f*.

beastly ['bi:stlɪ] (comp -ier, superl -iest) adj *UK dated* [person] malveillant(e), cruel(elle) / [headache, weather] épouvantable.

beat [bi:t] ■ **n 1.** [of heart, drum, wings] battement *m* **2.** MUS [rhythm] mesure *f*, temps *m* **3.** [of policeman] ronde *f*.
■ adj *inf* crevé(e).
■ vt (pt beat, pp beaten) **1.** [gen] battre ▸ **to beat sb with a stick** donner des coups de bâton à qqn ▸ **to beat a drum** battre du tambour **2.** [defeat] battre ▸ **she beat him at poker** elle l'a battu au poker ▸ **Liverpool were beaten** Liverpool a perdu ▸ **they beat us to it** ils nous ont devancés, ils sont arrivés avant nous ▸ **it beats me** *inf* ça me dépasse **3.** [be better than] être bien mieux que, valoir mieux que ▸ **nothing beats a cup of tea** rien ne vaut une tasse de thé
▸▸ **beat it!** *inf* décampe!, fiche le camp!
■ vi (pt beat, pp beaten) battre ▸ **to beat on** *OR* **at the door** cogner à la porte.
◆ ***beat down*** ■ vi **1.** [sun] taper, cogner **2.** [rain] s'abattre.
■ vt sep [seller] faire baisser son prix à.
◆ ***beat off*** vt sep [resist] repousser.
◆ ***beat up*** vt sep *inf* **1.** [attack] tabasser, passer à tabac **2.** PSYCHOL culpabiliser ▸ **to beat o.s. up (about sth)** culpabiliser (à propos de qch).

beaten ['bi:tn] adj battu(e).

beaten-up adj cabossé(e).

beater ['bi:tər] **n 1.** [for eggs] batteur *m*, fouet *m* **2.** [for carpet] tapette *f* **3.** [of wife, child] bourreau *m*.

beating ['bi:tɪŋ] **n 1.** [blows] raclée *f*, rossée *f* **2.** [defeat] défaite *f* ▸ **that will take some beating!** *inf* on ne pourra sans doute jamais faire mieux.

beating up (pl beatings up) n *inf* passage *m* à tabac.

beatnik ['bi:tnɪk] n beatnik *mf*.

beat-up adj *inf* déglingué(e).

beautician [bju:'tɪʃn] n esthéticien *m*, -enne *f*.

beautiful ['bju:tɪfʊl] adj **1.** [gen] beau (belle) **2.** *inf* [very good] joli(e).

beautifully ['bju:təflɪ] adv **1.** [attractively - dressed] élégamment / [- decorated] avec goût **2.** *inf* [very well] parfaitement, à la perfection.

beautify ['bju:tɪfaɪ] (pt & pp -ied) vt embellir, orner ▸ **to beautify o.s.** se faire une beauté.

beauty ['bju:tɪ] ■ n (pl -ies) **1.** [gen] beauté *f* ▸ **beauty is in the eye of the beholder** *prov* il n'y a pas de laides amours *prov* ▸ **beauty is only skin-deep** *prov* la beauté n'est pas tout *prov* **2.** *inf* [very good thing] merveille *f* ▸ **that's the beauty of it** c'est ça qui est formidable.
■ comp [products] de beauté.

beauty contest n concours *m* de beauté.

beauty mask n masque *m* de beauté.

beauty parade n défilé *m* d'un concours de beauté.

beauty parlour *UK*, **beauty parlor** *US* n institut *m* de beauté.

beauty queen n reine *f* de beauté.

beauty salon = ***beauty parlour***.

beauty sleep **n : I need my beauty sleep** *hum* j'ai besoin de mon compte de sommeil pour être frais le matin.

beauty spot **n 1.** [picturesque place] site *m* pittoresque **2.** [on skin] grain *m* de beauté.

beaver ['bi:vər] n castor *m*.
◆ ***beaver away*** vi travailler d'arrache-pied.

bebop ['bi:bɒp] n [music, dance] be-bop *m*.

becalmed [bɪ'kɑ:md] adj [ship] encalminé(e).

became [bɪ'keɪm] pt ➤ ***become***.

because [bɪ'kɒz] conj parce que.
◆ ***because of*** prep à cause de.

béchamel sauce [,beɪʃə'mel-] n sauce *f* béchamel, béchamel *f*.

beck [bek] **n : to be at sb's beck and call** être aux ordres *OR* à la disposition de qqn.

beckon ['bekən] ■ vt **1.** [signal to] faire signe à **2.** *fig* [draw, attract] séduire.
■ vi [signal] **: to beckon to sb** faire signe à qqn.

become [bɪ'kʌm] (pt became, pp become) vi devenir ▸ **to become quieter** se calmer ▸ **to become irritated** s'énerver ▸ **what has become of them?** que sont-ils devenus?

becoming [bɪ'kʌmɪŋ] adj **1.** [attractive] seyant(e), qui va bien **2.** [appropriate] convenable.

BECTU ['bektu:] (abbr of ***Broadcasting, Entertainment, Cinematograph and Theatre Union***) n *syndicat britannique des techniciens des médias audiovisuels*.

bed [bed] **n 1.** [to sleep on] lit *m* ▸ **to go to bed** se coucher ▸ **to go to bed with sb** *euph* coucher avec qqn ▸ **to make the bed** faire le lit **2.** [flowerbed] parterre *m* ▸ **it's not a bed of roses** *fig* ce n'est pas tout rose **3.** [of sea, river] lit *m*, fond *m*.
◆ ***bed down*** (pt & pp -ded, cont -ding) vi coucher, se coucher.

BEd [,bi:'ed] (abbr of ***Bachelor of Education***) n *UK* [degree] ≃ licence *f* de sciences de l'éducation / [person] ≃ licencié *m*, -e *f* en sciences de l'éducation.

bed and breakfast n ≃ chambre *f* d'hôte.

bedazzle [bɪ'dæzl] vt [dazzle] éblouir, aveugler / [fascinate] éblouir.

bed-bath n *UK* toilette *f* d'un malade.

bedbug ['bedbʌg] n punaise *f*.

bedclothes ['bedkləʊðz] npl draps *mpl* et couvertures *fpl*.

bedcover ['bed,kʌvər] n couvre-lit *m*, dessus-de-lit *m inv*.

bedding ['bedɪŋ] n *(U)* = ***bedclothes***.

bedding plant n plant *m* à repiquer.

bedeck [bɪ'dek] vt **: to bedeck sthg with** parer *OR* orner qqch de.

bedevil [bɪ'devl] (*UK* -led, cont -ling, *US* -ed, cont -ing) vt **: to be bedevilled with** être surchargé(e) de.

bedfellow ['bed,feləʊ] n *fig* partenaire *mf*.

bedlam ['bedləm] n pagaille *f*.

bed linen n *(U)* draps *mpl* et taies *fpl*.

Bedouin*, *Beduin ['bedʊɪn] ■ **adj** bédouin(e).
■ **n** Bédouin *m*, -e *f*.

bedpan ['bedpæn] **n** bassin *m*.

bedraggled [bɪ'drægld] **adj** [person] débraillé(e) / [hair] embroussaillé(e).

bedridden ['bed,rɪdn] **adj** grabataire.

bedrock ['bedrɒk] **n** *(U)* **1.** GEOL soubassement *m* **2.** *fig* [basis] base *f*, fondement *m*.

bedroom ['bedrʊm] **n** chambre *f* (à coucher).

-bedroomed [,bedrʊmd] **suffix : two-bedroomed flat** trois-pièces *m*.

Beds [bedz] (abbr of ***Bedfordshire***) *comté anglais*.

bedsettee [,bedse'tiː] **n** *UK* canapé-lit *m*.

bedside ['bedsaɪd] **n** chevet *m*.

bedside manner **n** [of doctor] comportement *m* envers les malades.

bedsit ['bed,sɪt], ***bedsitter*** ['bedsɪtəʳ], ***bedsitting room*** ['bed'sɪtɪŋ-] **n** *UK* chambre *f* meublée.

bedsore ['bedsɔːʳ] **n** escarre *f*.

bedspread ['bedspred] **n** couvre-lit *m*, dessus-de-lit *m inv*.

bedtime ['bedtaɪm] **n** heure *f* du coucher.

Beduin ['bedʊɪn] = ***Bedouin***.

bed-wetting [,wetɪŋ] **n** énurésie *f*, incontinence *f* nocturne.

bee [biː] **n** abeille *f* ▸ **to have a bee in one's bonnet (about)** avoir une idée fixe (à propos de).

Beeb [biːb] **n** *UK inf* **: the Beeb** la BBC.

beef [biːf] ■ **n 1.** [meat] bœuf *m* ▸ **joint of beef** rôti *m* (de bœuf), rosbif *m* **2.** *UK* (pl **beeves** [biːvz]) [animal] bœuf *m* **3.** *inf* [complaint] grief *m* ▸ **what's your beef?** tu as un problème? ▸ **to have a beef with sb/sthg** avoir des ennuis avec qqn/qqch.
■ **comp** [sausage, stew] de bœuf ▸ **beef cattle** bœufs *mpl* de boucherie.
■ **vi** *inf* râler ▸ **to beef about sthg** râler contre qqch.
◆ ***beef up*** **vt sep** *inf* [army, campaign] renforcer / [report, story] étoffer.

beefburger ['biːf,bɜːgəʳ] **n** *UK* hamburger *m*.

beehive ['biːhaɪv] **n 1.** [for bees] ruche *f* ▸ **the Beehive State** l'Utah *m* **2.** [hairstyle] *coiffure très haute maintenue avec de la laque*.

beeline ['biːlaɪn] **n : to make a beeline for** *inf* aller tout droit OR directement vers.

been [biːn] **pp** ➤ ***be***.

beep [biːp] *inf* ■ **n** bip *m* / [on anwering machine] bip sonore.
■ **vi** faire bip.

beeper **n** = ***bleeper***.

beer [bɪəʳ] **n** bière *f*.

beer garden **n** esp *UK jardin attenant à un pub*, ≃ terrasse *f*.

beeswax ['biːzwæks] **n** cire *f* d'abeille.

beet [biːt] **n** *US* betterave *f*.

beetle ['biːtl] **n** scarabée *m*.

beetroot ['biːtruːt] **n** *UK* betterave *f*.

befall [bɪ'fɔːl] (pt **befell** [-'fel], pp **befallen** [-'fɔːlən]) *liter*
■ **vt** advenir à.
■ **vi** arriver, survenir.

befit [bɪ'fɪt] (pt & pp **-ted**, cont **-ting**) **vt** seoir à.

befitting [bɪ'fɪtɪŋ] **adj** *fml* convenable, seyant(e) ▸ **in a manner befitting a statesman** d'une façon qui sied à un homme d'État.

before [bɪ'fɔːʳ] ■ **adv** auparavant, avant ▸ **I've never been there before** je n'y suis jamais allé(e) ▸ **I've seen it before** je l'ai déjà vu ▸ **haven't we met before?** est-ce que nous ne nous sommes pas OR ne nous sommes-nous pas déjà rencontrés? ▸ **the year before** l'année d'avant OR précédente ▸ **the day before** la veille ▸ **the night before** la veille au soir.
■ **prep 1.** [in time] avant ▸ **the day before the meeting** la veille de la réunion ▸ **it should have been done before now** ça devrait déjà être fait
2. [in space] devant ▸ **to appear before the court/judge** comparaître devant le tribunal/juge ▸ **we have a difficult task before us** *fig* nous avons une tâche difficile devant nous.
■ **conj** avant de *(+ infin)*, avant que *(+ subjunctive)* ▸ **before leaving** avant de partir ▸ **before you leave** avant que vous ne partiez ▸ **it was almost an hour before the ambulance arrived** il a fallu presque une heure avant que l'ambulance n'arrive.

CONFUSABLE / PARONYME
before

When translating **before**, note that *avant* and *devant* are not interchangeable. *Avant* relates to time, while *devant* is used to express position or location.

beforehand [bɪ'fɔːhænd] **adv** à l'avance.

befriend [bɪ'frend] **vt** prendre en amitié.

befuddle [bɪ'fʌdl] **vt 1.** [confuse - person] brouiller l'esprit OR les idées de, embrouiller / [- mind] embrouiller **2.** [muddle with alcohol] griser, enivrer.

befuddled [bɪ'fʌdld] **adj** [confused] embrouillé(e).

beg [beg] (pt & pp **-ged**, cont **-ging**) ■ **vt 1.** [money, food] mendier **2.** [favour] solliciter, quémander / [forgiveness] demander ▸ **to beg sb to do sthg** prier OR supplier qqn de faire qqch ▸ **to beg sb for sthg** implorer qqch de qqn ▸ **I beg your pardon** [excuse me] je vous demande pardon / [I didn't hear you] pardon? / [indignantly] pardon!
■ **vi 1.** [for money, food] **: to beg (for sthg)** mendier (qqch) **2.** [plead] supplier ▸ **to beg for** [forgiveness] demander.

began [bɪ'gæn] **pt** ➤ ***begin***.

beggar ['begəʳ] **n** mendiant *m*, -e *f*.

begging bowl ['begɪŋ-] **n** sébile *f (de mendiant)*.

begin [bɪ'gɪn] (pt **began**, pp **begun**, cont **-ning**) ■ **vt 1.** [start] commencer ▸ **to begin doing** OR **to do sthg** commencer OR se mettre à faire qqch ▸ **she began life as a waitress** elle a débuté comme serveuse ▸ **I can't begin to explain** c'est trop difficile à expliquer **2.** [found - institution, club] fonder, inaugurer / [argument, fight, war] déclencher, faire naître / [conversation] engager, amorcer.

■ vi commencer ▸ **the day began badly/well** la journée s'annonçait mal/bien ▸ **to begin again** *OR* **afresh** recommencer (à zéro) ▸ **let me begin by thanking our host** permettez-moi tout d'abord de remercier notre hôte ▸ **the play begins with a murder** la pièce débute par un meurtre ▸ **to begin with** pour commencer, premièrement ▸ **everything went well to begin with** tout s'est bien passé au début *OR* au départ.

beginner [bɪ'gɪnəʳ] n débutant *m*, -e *f*.

beginning [bɪ'gɪnɪŋ] n début *m*, commencement *m* ▸ **in** *OR* **at the beginning** au début, au commencement ▸ **from beginning to end** du début à la fin, d'un bout à l'autre.

begonia [bɪ'gəʊnjə] n bégonia *m*.

begrudge [bɪ'grʌdʒ] vt **1.** [envy] **: to begrudge sb sthg** envier qqch à qqn **2.** [do unwillingly] **: to begrudge doing sthg** rechigner à faire qqch.

beguile [bɪ'gaɪl] vt [charm] séduire.

beguiling [bɪ'gaɪlɪŋ] adj [charming] séduisant(e).

begun [bɪ'gʌn] pp ➤ ***begin***.

behalf [bɪ'hɑ:f] n **: on behalf of** *UK*, **in behalf of** *US* de la part de, au nom de.

behave [bɪ'heɪv] ■ vt **: to behave o.s.** bien se conduire *OR* se comporter.

■ vi **1.** [in a particular way] se conduire, se comporter ▸ **to well/badly** bien/mal se comporter **2.** [acceptably] bien se tenir **3.** [to function] fonctionner, marcher.

behaviour *UK*, ***behavior*** *US* [bɪ'heɪvjəʳ] n conduite *f*, comportement *m*.

behaviourism *UK*, ***behaviorism*** *US* [bɪ'heɪvjərɪzm] n béhaviorisme *m*.

behead [bɪ'hed] vt décapiter.

beheld [bɪ'held] pt & pp ➤ ***behold***.

behind [bɪ'haɪnd] ■ prep **1.** [gen] derrière **2.** [in time] en retard sur ▸ **they arrived two hours behind us** ils sont arrivés deux heures après nous.

■ adv **1.** [gen] derrière **2.** [in time] en retard ▸ **to leave sthg behind** oublier qqch ▸ **to stay behind** rester ▸ **to be behind with sthg** être en retard dans qqch.

■ n *inf* derrière *m*, postérieur *m*.

behind-the-scenes adj secret (ète) ▸ **a behind-the-scenes look at politics** un regard en coulisse sur la politique.

behold [bɪ'həʊld] (pt & pp **beheld**) vt *liter* voir, regarder.

beige [beɪʒ] ■ adj beige.

■ n beige *m* ▸ **in beige** en beige.

Beijing [ˌbeɪ'dʒɪŋ] n Beijing.

being ['bi:ɪŋ] n **1.** [creature] être *m* **2.** [existence] **: in being** existant(e) ▸ **to come into being** voir le jour, prendre naissance.

Beirut [ˌbeɪ'ru:t] n Beyrouth ▸ **East Beirut** Beyrouth-Est ▸ **West Beirut** Beyrouth-Ouest.

belated [bɪ'leɪtɪd] adj tardif(ive).

belatedly [bɪ'leɪtɪdlɪ] adv tardivement.

belch [beltʃ] ■ n renvoi *m*, rot *m*.

■ vt [smoke, fire] vomir, cracher.

■ vi **1.** [person] éructer, roter **2.** [smoke, fire] cracher, vomir.

beleaguered [bɪ'li:gəd] adj *lit* assiégé(e) / *fig* harcelé(e), tracassé(e).

belfry ['belfrɪ] (pl -ies) n beffroi *m*, clocher *m*.

Belgian ['beldʒən] ■ adj belge.

■ n Belge *mf*.

Belgium ['beldʒəm] n Belgique *f* ▸ **in Belgium** en Belgique.

Belgrade [ˌbel'greɪd] n Belgrade.

belie [bɪ'laɪ] (cont **belying**) vt **1.** [disprove] démentir **2.** [give false idea of] donner une fausse idée de.

belief [bɪ'li:f] n **1.** [faith, certainty] **: belief (in)** croyance *f* (en) ▸ **beyond belief** incroyable **2.** [principle, opinion] opinion *f*, conviction *f* ▸ **in the belief that** persuadé(e) *OR* convaincu(e) que.

believable [bɪ'li:vəbl] adj croyable.

believe [bɪ'li:v] ■ vt croire ▸ **he's getting married! – I don't believe it!** il va se marier! – c'est pas vrai! ▸ **he couldn't believe his ears/his eyes** il n'en croyait pas ses oreilles/ses yeux ▸ **believe it or not** tu ne me croiras peut-être pas.

■ vi croire ▸ **to believe in sb** croire en qqn ▸ **to believe in sthg** croire à qqch ▸ **he believes in giving the public greater access to information** il est d'avis qu'il faut donner au public un plus grand accès à l'information.

believer [bɪ'li:vəʳ] n **1.** RELIG croyant *m*, -e *f* **2.** [in idea, action] **: believer in** partisan *m*, -e *f* de.

Belisha beacon [bɪ'li:ʃə-] n *UK globe lumineux indiquant un passage clouté.*

belittle [bɪ'lɪtl] vt dénigrer, rabaisser.

Belize [be'li:z] n Belize *m* ▸ **in Belize** au Belize.

bell [bel] n [of church] cloche *f* / [handbell] clochette *f* / [on door] sonnette *f* / [on bike] timbre *m* ▸ **the name rings a bell** ce nom me dit quelque chose.

bell-bottoms npl pantalon *m* à pattes d'éléphant.

bellhop ['belhɒp] n *US* groom *m*, chasseur *m*.

belligerence [bɪ'lɪdʒərəns] n belligérance *f*.

belligerent [bɪ'lɪdʒərənt] adj **1.** [at war] belligérant(e) **2.** [aggressive] belliqueux(euse).

bellow ['beləʊ] ■ vt [order] hurler, brailler.

■ vi **1.** [person] brailler, beugler **2.** [bull] beugler.

bellows ['beləʊz] npl soufflet *m*.

bell push n *UK* bouton *m* de sonnette.

bell-ringer n carillonneur *m*, -euse *f*.

belly ['belɪ] (pl -ies) n [of person] ventre *m* / [of animal] panse *f*.

bellyache ['belɪeɪk] ■ n mal *m* de ventre.

■ vi *inf* râler, rouspéter.

bellyaching ['belɪˌeɪkɪŋ] n *(U) inf* ronchonnements *mpl*, rouspétances *fpl*.

belly button n *inf* nombril *m*.

belly dancer n danseuse *f* orientale.

belly flop n **: to do a belly flop** faire un plat.

bellyful ['belɪfʊl] n *inf* [of food] ventre *m* plein / *UK fig* **: I've had a bellyful of your complaints** j'en ai ras le bol de tes rouspétances.

belly laugh **n** *inf* gros rire *m*.

belly-up **n** *inf* **: to go belly-up** [of company] faire faillite.

belong [bɪ'lɒŋ] **vi 1.** [be property] **: to belong to sb** appartenir *OR* être à qqn **2.** [be member] **: to belong to sthg** être membre de qqch **3.** [be in right place] être à sa place ▸ **that chair belongs here** ce fauteuil va là.

belongings [bɪ'lɒŋɪŋz] **npl** affaires *fpl*.

Belorussia [ˌbeləʊ'rʌʃə] **n** Biélorussie *f* ▸ **in Belorussia** en Biélorussie.

beloved [bɪ'lʌvd] ■ **adj** bien-aimé(e).
■ **n** bien-aimé *m*, -e *f*.

below [bɪ'ləʊ] ■ **adv 1.** [lower] en dessous, en bas ▸ **the flat below** l'appartement d'en dessous *OR* du dessous ▸ **children of five and below** les enfants de cinq ans et moins **2.** [in text] ci-dessous **3.** NAUT en bas.
■ **prep** sous, au-dessous de ▸ **below the poverty line** en dessous du seuil de pauvreté ▸ **children below the age of five** les enfants de moins de cinq ans ▸ **to be below sb in rank** occuper un rang inférieur à qqn.

below-the-line **adj** FIN [expenses] au-dessous de la ligne / [accounts] de résultats exceptionnels.

belt [belt] ■ **n 1.** [for clothing] ceinture *f* ▸ **that was below the belt** *inf* c'était un coup bas ▸ **to tighten one's belt** *fig* se serrer la ceinture ▸ **under one's belt** *fig* à son actif **2.** TECH courroie *f* **3.** [of land, sea] région *f*.
■ **vt** *inf* flanquer une raclée à.
■ **vi** *UK inf* [car] rouler à toute blinde *OR* à pleins gaz / [person] foncer.
◆ ***belt out*** **vt sep** *inf* [song] beugler.
◆ ***belt up*** **vi** *UK inf* la fermer, la boucler.

beltway ['beltˌweɪ] **n** *US* route *f* périphérique.

bemused [bɪ'mju:zd] **adj** perplexe.

bench [bentʃ] **n 1.** [gen & POL] banc *m* **2.** [caned, padded] banquette *f* **3.** [in lab, workshop] établi *m*.

CONFUSABLE / PARONYME
bench
When translating **bench**, note that *banc* and *banquette* are not interchangeable. *Banc* is a bench found outdoors in a park or garden, whereas *banquette* is of the upholstered variety.

benchmark ['bentʃˌmɑ:k] ■ **n** *lit* repère *m* / [in surveying] repère *m* de nivellement / *fig* repère *m*, point *m* de référence.
■ **comp : benchmark test** COMPUT test *m* d'évaluation (de programme).

bend [bend] ■ **n 1.** [in road] courbe *f*, virage *m* **2.** [in pipe, river] coude *m*
▸▸ **round** *UK OR* **around** *US* **the bend** *inf* dingue, fou (folle).
■ **vt** (pt & pp **bent**) **1.** [arm, leg] plier ▸ **they bent their heads over their books** ils se penchèrent sur leurs livres **2.** [wire, fork] tordre, courber ▸ **he bent the rod out of shape** il a tordu la barre
▸▸ **to bend the rules** faire une entorse au règlement.
■ **vi** (pt & pp **bent**) [person] se baisser, se courber / [tree, rod] plier ▸ **she bent over the counter** elle s'est penchée par-dessus le comptoir ▸ **the road bends to the left** la route tourne à gauche ▸ **to bend over backwards for sb** se mettre en quatre pour qqn.
◆ ***bends*** **npl : the bends** la maladie des caissons.

bendy ['bendɪ] (comp **-ier**, superl **-iest**) **adj** *inf* flexible.

beneath [bɪ'ni:θ] ■ **adv** dessous, en bas.
■ **prep 1.** [under] sous **2.** [unworthy of] **: she thinks the work is beneath her** elle estime que le travail est indigne d'elle.

benediction [ˌbenɪ'dɪkʃn] **n** bénédiction *f*.

benefactor ['benɪfæktəʳ] **n** bienfaiteur *m*.

benefactress ['benɪfæktrɪs] **n** bienfaitrice *f*.

beneficial [ˌbenɪ'fɪʃl] **adj : beneficial (to sb)** salutaire (à qqn) ▸ **beneficial (to sthg)** utile (à qqch).

beneficiary [ˌbenɪ'fɪʃərɪ] (pl **-ies**) **n** bénéficiaire *mf*.

benefit ['benɪfɪt] ■ **n 1.** [advantage] avantage *m* ▸ **for the benefit of** dans l'intérêt de ▸ **to be to sb's benefit, to be of benefit to sb** être dans l'intérêt de qqn ▸ **to give sb the benefit of the doubt** laisser *OR* accorder à qqn le bénéfice du doute **2.** ADMIN [allowance of money] allocation *f*, prestation *f* ▸ **social security benefits** *UK* prestations sociales ▸ **tax benefit** *US* dégrèvement *m*, allègement *m* fiscal.
■ **comp : benefit performance** représentation *f* de bienfaisance.
■ **vt** profiter à, être avantageux pour.
■ **vi : to benefit from** tirer avantage de, profiter de.

Benelux ['benɪlʌks] **n** Bénélux *m* ▸ **the Benelux countries** les pays du Bénélux.

benevolent [bɪ'nevələnt] **adj** bienveillant(e).

BEng [ˌbi:'endʒ] (abbr of ***Bachelor of Engineering***) **n** *UK* [degree] ≃ licence *f* de mécanique / [person] ≃ licencié, -e *f* en mécanique.

Bengal [ˌbeŋ'gɔ:l] **n** Bengale *m* ▸ **in Bengal** au Bengale ▸ **the Bay of Bengal** le golfe du Bengale.

benign [bɪ'naɪn] **adj 1.** [person] gentil(ille), bienveillant(e) **2.** MED bénin(igne).

Benin [be'ni:n] **n** Bénin *m* ▸ **in Benin** au Bénin.

bent [bent] ■ **pt & pp** ➤ ***bend***.
■ **adj 1.** [wire, bar] tordu(e) **2.** [person, body] courbé(e), voûté(e) **3.** *UK inf* [dishonest] véreux(euse) **4.** [determined] **: to be bent on doing sthg** vouloir absolument faire qqch, être décidé(e) à faire qqch.
■ **n : bent (for)** penchant *m* (pour).

bento ['bentəʊ] **n** *(U)* bento *m*.

bento box **n** boîte *f* à bento.

bequeath [bɪ'kwi:ð] **vt** *lit & fig* léguer.

bequest [bɪ'kwest] **n** legs *m*.

berate [bɪ'reɪt] **vt** réprimander.

Berber ['bɜ:bəʳ] ■ **adj** berbère.
■ **n 1.** [person] Berbère *mf* **2.** [language] berbère *m*.

bereaved [bɪ'ri:vd] ■ **adj** endeuillé(e), affligé(e).
■ **n** (pl **bereaved**) **: the bereaved** la famille du défunt.

bereavement [bɪ'ri:vmənt] **n** deuil *m*.

bereft [bɪ'reft] **adj** *liter* **: bereft of** privé(e) de.

beret ['bereɪ] **n** béret *m*.

Bering Sea ['berɪŋ-] **n : the Bering Sea** la mer de Béring.

Bering Strait ['berɪŋ-] **n : the Bering Strait** le détroit de Béring.

berk [bɜ:k] **n** *UK inf* idiot *m*, -e *f*, andouille *f*.

Berks [bɑ:ks] (abbr of ***Berkshire***) *comté anglais*.

Berlin [bɜ:'lɪn] **n** Berlin ▸ **East Berlin** Berlin-Est ▸ **West Berlin** Berlin-Ouest ▸ **the Berlin Wall** le mur de Berlin.

Berliner [bɜ:'lɪnə] **n** Berlinois *m*, -e *f*.

berm [bɜ:m] **n** *US* bas-côté *m*.

Bermuda [bə'mju:də] **n** Bermudes *fpl* ▸ **in Bermuda** aux Bermudes.

Bermuda shorts **npl** bermuda *m*.

Bern [bɜ:n] **n** Berne.

berry ['berɪ] (pl **-ies**) **n** baie *f*.

berserk [bə'zɜ:k] **adj : to go berserk** devenir fou furieux (folle furieuse).

berth [bɜ:θ] ■ **n 1.** [in harbour] poste *m* d'amarrage, mouillage *m* **2.** [in ship, train] couchette *f*
⏭ **to give sb a wide berth** éviter qqn.
■ **vt** [ship] amener à quai.
■ **vi** [ship] accoster, se ranger à quai.

beseech [bɪ'si:tʃ] (pt & pp **besought** *OR* **beseeched**) **vt** *liter* **: to beseech sb (to do sthg)** implorer *OR* supplier qqn (de faire qqch).

beset [bɪ'set] ■ **adj : beset with** *OR* **by** [doubts] assailli(e) de ▸ **the plan is beset with risks** le plan comporte une multitude de risques.
■ **vt** (pt & pp **beset**, cont **-ting**) assaillir.

beside [bɪ'saɪd] **prep 1.** [next to] à côté de, auprès de **2.** [compared with] comparé(e) à, à côté de
⏭ **to be beside o.s. with anger** être hors de soi ▸ **to be beside o.s. with joy** être fou (folle) de joie.

besides [bɪ'saɪdz] ■ **adv** en outre, en plus.
■ **prep** en plus de.

besiege [bɪ'si:dʒ] **vt 1.** [town, fortress] assiéger **2.** *fig* [trouble, annoy] assaillir, harceler ▸ **to be besieged with** être assailli(e) *OR* harcelé(e) de.

besotted [bɪ'sɒtɪd] **adj : besotted (with sb)** entiché(e) (de qqn).

besought [bɪ'sɔ:t] **pt & pp** ➤ ***beseech***.

bespectacled [bɪ'spektəkld] **adj** qui porte des lunettes, à lunettes.

bespoke [bɪ'spəʊk] **adj** *UK* [clothes] fait(e) sur mesure / [tailor] à façon.

best [best] ■ **adj** le meilleur (la meilleure) ▸ **may the best man win** que le meilleur gagne ▸ **she was dressed in her best clothes** elle portait ses plus beaux vêtements ▸ **I'm doing what is best for the family** je fais ce qu'il y a de mieux pour la famille ▸ **the best thing (to do) is to keep quiet** le mieux, c'est de ne rien dire.
■ **adv** le mieux ▸ **he does it best** c'est lui qui le fait le mieux ▸ **which film did you like best?** quel est le film que vous avez préféré?
■ **n** le mieux ▸ **to do one's best** faire de son mieux ▸ **it/she is the best there is** c'est le meilleur/la meilleure qui soit ▸ **the best you can say is that...** le mieux qu'on puisse dire c'est que... ▸ **it was the best we could do** nous ne pouvions pas faire mieux ▸ **they're the best of friends** ce sont les meilleurs amis du monde ▸ **it's journalism at its best** c'est du journalisme de haut niveau ▸ **I'm not at my best in the morning** je ne suis pas en forme le matin ▸ **all the best!** meilleurs souhaits! ▸ **to be for the best** être pour le mieux ▸ **to make the best of sthg** s'accommoder de qqch, prendre son parti de qqch ▸ **he wants the best of both worlds** il veut le beurre et l'argent du beurre.
◆ ***at best*** **adv** au mieux.

best-case **adj : this is the best-case scenario** c'est le scénario le plus optimiste.

bestial ['bestjəl] **adj** bestial(e).

best man **n** garçon *m* d'honneur.

bestow [bɪ'stəʊ] **vt** *fml* **: to bestow sthg on sb** conférer qqch à qqn.

best-perceived **adj** mieux perçu(e).

best-seller **n** [book] best-seller *m*.

best-selling **adj** à succès.

bet [bet] ■ **n** pari *m* ▸ **it's a safe bet that...** *fig* il est certain que... ▸ **to hedge one's bets** se couvrir.
■ **vt** (pt & pp **bet** *OR* **-ted**, cont **-ting**) parier.
■ **vi** (pt & pp **bet** *OR* **-ted**, cont **-ting**) parier ▸ **I wouldn't bet on it** *fig* je n'en suis pas si sûr ▸ **you bet!** *inf* un peu!, et comment!

beta ['bi:tə] **n** bêta *m inv*.

beta-blocker ['bi:təˌblɒkəʳ] **n** bêtabloquant *m*.

beta version **n** COMPUT [of program] version *f* bêta.

Bethlehem ['beθlɪhem] **n** Bethléem.

betray [bɪ'treɪ] **vt** trahir.

betrayal [bɪ'treɪəl] **n 1.** [of person] trahison *f* **2. : betrayal of trust** abus *m* de confiance **3.** [of secret] révélation *f*.

betrayer [bɪ'treɪəʳ] **n** traître *m*, -esse *f*.

betrothed [bɪ'trəʊðd] **adj** *dated* **: betrothed (to)** fiancé(e) (à).

better ['betəʳ] ■ **adj** *(compar of good)* meilleur(e) ▸ **I'm better at languages than he is** je suis meilleur *OR* plus fort en langues que lui ▸ **he's a better cook than you are** il cuisine mieux que toi ▸ **that's better!** voilà qui est mieux! ▸ **to get better** [generally] s'améliorer / [after illness] se remettre, se rétablir ▸ **it's better if I don't see them** il vaut mieux *OR* il est préférable que je ne les voie pas ▸ **she's a better person for it** ça lui a fait beaucoup de bien.
■ **adv** *(compar of well)* mieux ▸ **he swims better than I do** il nage mieux que moi ▸ **I liked his last book better** j'ai préféré son dernier livre ▸ **better looking** plus beau(belle) ▸ **better paid/prepared** mieux payé(e)/préparé(e) ▸ **the less he knows the better** moins il en saura, mieux ça vaudra ▸ **I'd better leave** il faut que je parte, je dois partir ▸ **you'd better let your mother know** tu ferais mieux de le dire à ta mère ▸ **you'd better be on time!** tu as intérêt à être à l'heure!
■ **n** le meilleur (la meilleure) ▸ **the situation has taken a turn for the better** la situation a pris une meilleure tournure ▸ **for better or worse** pour le meilleur ou pour le pire ▸ **to get the better of sb** avoir raison de qqn.
■ **vt** améliorer ▸ **to better o.s.** s'élever.

better half **n** *inf* moitié *f*.

betterment ['betəmənt] **n** [generally] amélioration *f* / LAW [of property] plus-value *f*.

better off **adj 1.** [financially] plus à son aise **2.** [in better situation] mieux.
◆ ***better-off*** **npl : the better-off** les gens riches ***OR*** aisés.

betting ['betɪŋ] **n** *(U)* paris *mpl*.

betting shop **n** *UK* ≃ bureau *m* de P.M.U.

between [bɪ'twi:n] ■ **prep** entre ▸ **he sat (in) between Paul and Anne** il s'est assis entre Paul et Anne ▸ **between now and this evening** d'ici ce soir ▸ **children between the ages of 5 and 10** les enfants de 5 à 10 ans ▸ **a bus runs between the airport and the hotel** un bus fait la navette entre l'aéroport et l'hôtel ▸ **to choose between sth and sth** choisir entre qch et qch ▸ **they shared the cake between them** ils se sont partagé le gâteau ▸ **between us we saved enough money for the trip** à nous tous nous avons économisé assez d'argent pour le voyage
▸▸ **between you and me, between ourselves** entre nous.
■ **adv : (in) between** [in space] au milieu / [in time] dans l'intervalle.

bevelled *UK*, ***beveled*** *US* ['bevld] **adj** biseauté(e).

beverage ['bevərɪdʒ] **n** *fml* boisson *f*.

bevvy ['bevɪ] **n** *UK inf* breuvage, boisson alcoolisée.

bevy ['bevɪ] **(pl -ies) n** bande *f*, troupe *f*.

beware [bɪ'weəʳ] **vi : to beware (of)** prendre garde (à), se méfier (de) ▸ **beware of...** attention à...

bewilder [bɪ'wɪldəʳ] **vt** rendre perplexe, dérouter.

bewildered [bɪ'wɪldəd] **adj** déconcerté(e), perplexe.

bewildering [bɪ'wɪldərɪŋ] **adj** déconcertant(e), déroutant(e).

bewilderment [bɪ'wɪldəmənt] **n** confusion *f*, perplexité *f* ▸ **to my complete bewilderment he refused** à mon grand étonnement, il a refusé.

bewitched [bɪ'wɪtʃt] **adj** ensorcelé(e), enchanté(e).

bewitching [bɪ'wɪtʃɪŋ] **adj** charmeur(euse), ensorcelant(e).

beyond [bɪ'jɒnd] ■ **prep 1.** [in space] au-delà de **2.** [in time] après, plus tard que **3.** [exceeding] au-dessus de ▸ **it's beyond my control** je n'y peux rien ▸ **it's beyond my responsibility** cela n'entre pas dans le cadre de mes responsabilités ▸ **beyond belief** incroyable.
■ **adv** au-delà ▸ **major changes are foreseen for 2005 and beyond** des changements importants sont prévus pour 2005 et au-delà.

b/f abbr of ***brought forward***.

bhangra ['bæŋgrə] **n** MUS *combinaison de musique traditionnelle du Pendjab et de musique pop occidentale*.

bhp abbr of ***brake horsepower***.

bi- [baɪ] **prefix** bi-.

biannual [baɪ'ænjʊəl] **adj** semestriel(elle).

bias ['baɪəs] **n 1.** [prejudice] préjugé *m*, parti *m* pris **2.** [tendency] tendance *f*.

biased ['baɪəst] **adj** partial(e) ▸ **to be biased towards sb/sthg** favoriser qqn/qqch ▸ **to be biased against sb/sthg** défavoriser qqn/qqch.

biathlon [baɪ'æθlɒn] **n** biathlon *m*.

bib [bɪb] **n** [for baby] bavoir *m*, bavette *f*.

Bible ['baɪbl] **n : the Bible** la Bible.
◆ ***bible*** **n** bible *f*.

bible-basher, ***bible-thumper*** **n** *inf pej* évangéliste *mf* de carrefour.

biblical ['bɪblɪkl] **adj** biblique.

bibliography [ˌbɪblɪ'ɒgrəfɪ] **(pl -ies) n** bibliographie *f*.

bicarbonate of soda [baɪ'kɑ:bənət-] **n** bicarbonate *m* de soude.

bicentenary *UK* [ˌbaɪsen'ti:nərɪ] **(pl -ies)**, ***bicentennial*** *US* [ˌbaɪsen'tenjəl] **n** bicentenaire *m*.

biceps ['baɪseps] **(pl biceps) n** biceps *m*.

bicker ['bɪkəʳ] **vi** se chamailler.

bickering ['bɪkərɪŋ] **n** *(U)* chamailleries *fpl*.

bickie ['bɪkɪ] **n** *UK inf* biscuit *m*, petit gâteau *m*.

bicultural [ˌbaɪ'kʌltʃərəl] **adj** biculturel(elle).

bicycle ['baɪsɪkl] ■ **n** bicyclette *f*, vélo *m*.
■ **vi** aller à bicyclette ***OR*** vélo.

bicycle clip **n** pince *f* à vélo.

bicycle path **n** piste *f* cyclable.

bicycle pump **n** pompe *f* à vélo.

bicycle rack **n** [for parking] ratelier *m* à bicyclettes ***OR*** à vélos / [on car roof] porte-vélos *m inv*.

bicycle track **n** piste *f* cyclable.

bid [bɪd] ■ **n 1.** [attempt] tentative *f* ▸ **the prisoners made a bid for freedom** les prisonniers ont fait une tentative d'évasion ▸ **a rescue bid** une tentative de sauvetage **2.** [at auction] enchère *f* ▸ **a bid of £100** [gen] une offre de 100 livres / [at auction] une enchère de 100 livres **3.** COMM offre *f* ▸ **the firm made *OR* put in a bid for the contract** l'entreprise a fait une soumission ***OR*** a soumissionné pour le contrat.
■ **vt (pt & pp bid, cont bidding) 1.** [at auction] faire une enchère de ▸ **what am I bid for this table?** combien m'offre-t-on pour cette table? **2. (pt bid *OR* bade, pp bid *OR* bidden, cont bidding)** *liter* [request] **: to bid sb do sthg** prier qqn de faire qqch ▸ **he bade them enter** il les pria d'entrer **3. (pt bid *OR* bade, pp bid *OR* bidden, cont bidding)** *fml* [say] **: to bid sb good morning** souhaiter le bonjour à qqn ▸ **they bade him farewell** ils lui firent leurs adieux.
■ **vi (pt & pp bid, cont bidding) 1.** [at auction] **: to bid (for)** faire une enchère (pour) ▸ **they bid against us** ils ont surenchéri sur notre offre **2.** [attempt] **: to bid for sthg** briguer qqch ▸ **he's bidding for the presidency** il vise la présidence **3.** COMM faire une soumission, répondre à un appel d'offres.

bidder ['bɪdəʳ] **n** enchérisseur *m*, -euse *f*.

bidding ['bɪdɪŋ] **n** *(U)* enchères *fpl*.

bidding price *US* = ***bid price***.

bide [baɪd] **vt : to bide one's time** attendre son heure ***OR*** le bon moment.

bidet ['bi:deɪ] **n** bidet *m*.

bid price **n** cours *m* acheteur.

biennial [baɪ'enɪəl] ■ **adj** biennal(e).
■ **n** plante *f* bisannuelle.

bier [bɪəʳ] **n** bière *f*.

bifidus ['bɪfɪdəs] **n** bifidus *m*.

bifocals [ˌbaɪ'fəʊklz] **npl** lunettes *fpl* bifocales.

BIFU ['bɪfu:] (abbr of ***Banking, Insurance and Finance Union***) **n** *syndicat britannique des employés du secteur financier*.

big [bɪg] (comp -**ger**, superl -**gest**) **adj 1.** [gen] grand(e) ▸ **to get** ***or*** **to grow bigger** grandir ▸ **my big sister** ma grande sœur **2.** [in amount, bulk - box, crowd, book] gros (grosse) ▸ **the crowd got bigger** la foule a grossi **3.** [important, significant - decision, problem] grand (e), important (e) / [- drop, increase] fort (e), important (e) ▸ **the big day** le grand jour ▸ **he's big in publishing, he's a big man in publishing** c'est quelqu'un d'important dans l'édition
▸▸ **to do things in a big way** faire les choses en grand ▸ **to be big on sthg** *inf* adorer ***or*** être fana de qqch.

bigamist ['bɪgəmɪst] **n** bigame *mf*.

bigamy ['bɪgəmɪ] **n** bigamie *f*.

Big Apple **n : the Big Apple** *surnom de New York*.

big bang theory **n** la théorie du big-bang ***or*** big bang.

Big Ben [-'ben] **n** Big Ben *m*.

big-boned **adj** fortement charpenté(e).

big business **n** *(U)* les grandes entreprises *fpl*.

big cat **n** fauve *m*.

big deal *inf* ■ **n : it's no big deal** ce n'est pas dramatique ▸ **what's the big deal?** où est le problème?
■ **excl** tu parles!, et alors?

big dipper [-'dɪpəʳ] **n 1.** *UK* [rollercoaster] montagnes *fpl* russes **2.** *US* ASTRON **: the Big Dipper** la Grande Ourse.

big end **n** tête *f* de bielle.

big fish **n** *inf* huile *f*, gros bonnet *m*.

big game **n** gros gibier *m*.

biggie ['bɪgɪ] **n** *inf* [success - song] tube *m* / [- film, record] succès *m*.

big gun **n** *inf* gros bonnet *m*.

big hand **n 1.** [on clock] grande aiguille *f* **2.** *inf* [applause] **: let's give him a big hand** applaudissons-le bien fort.

bighead ['bɪghed] **n** *inf* crâneur *m*, -euse *f*.

bigheaded [ˌbɪg'hedɪd] **adj** *inf* crâneur(euse).

bighearted [ˌbɪg'hɑ:tɪd] **adj** au grand cœur ▸ **to be big-hearted** avoir le cœur sur la main, avoir bon ***or*** du cœur.

big money **n** *inf* **: to make big money** se faire du pognon.

bigmouth ['bɪgmaʊθ] (pl [-maʊðz]) **n** *inf* grande gueule *f* ▸ **she's such a bigmouth** elle ne sait pas la fermer.

big name **n** *inf* personne *f* connue, célébrité *f*.

big noise **n** *inf* gros bonnet *m*.

bigot ['bɪgət] **n** sectaire *mf*.

bigoted ['bɪgətɪd] **adj** sectaire.

bigotry ['bɪgətrɪ] **n** sectarisme *m*.

big screen **n : the big screen** le grand écran, le cinéma.

big shot **n** *inf* huile *f*, grosse légume *f*.

big smoke **n** *UK inf* **: the big smoke** [gen] la grande ville / [London] Londres.

big time **n** *inf* **: to make** ***or*** **to hit the big time** réussir, arriver en haut de l'échelle.

big toe **n** gros orteil *m*.

big top **n** chapiteau *m*.

big wheel **n 1.** *UK* [at fairground] grande roue *f* **2.** *inf* [big shot] huile *f*, grosse légume *f*.

bigwig ['bɪgwɪg] **n** *inf* huile *f*, gros bonnet *m*.

bike [baɪk] **n** *inf* **1.** [bicycle] vélo *m*, bécane *f* **2.** [motorcycle] bécane *f*, moto *f*.

biker ['baɪkəʳ] **n** *inf* motard *m*, motocycliste *mf*.

bikeway ['baɪkweɪ] **n** *US* piste *f* cyclable.

bikini [bɪ'ki:nɪ] **n** Bikini® *m*.

bikini line **n : to have one's bikini line done** se faire faire une épilation maillot.

bilateral [ˌbaɪ'lætərəl] **adj** bilatéral(e).

bilateral agreement **n** accord *m* bilatéral.

bilateral trade **n** commerce *m* bilatéral.

bilberry ['bɪlbərɪ] (pl -**ies**) **n** myrtille *f*.

bile [baɪl] **n 1.** [fluid] bile *f* **2.** [anger] mauvaise humeur *f*.

bilingual [baɪ'lɪŋgwəl] **adj** bilingue.

bilingualism [baɪ'lɪŋgwəlɪzm] **n** bilinguisme *m*.

bilious ['bɪljəs] **adj 1.** [sickening] écœurant(e) **2.** [nauseous] qui a envie de vomir.

bill [bɪl] ■ **n 1.** [statement of cost] **: bill (for)** note *f* ***or*** facture *f* (de) / [in restaurant] addition *f* (de) ▸ **may I have the bill please?** l'addition, s'il vous plaît ▸ **put it on my bill** mettez-le sur ma note **2.** [in parliament] projet *m* de loi ▸ **to vote on a bill** mettre un projet de loi au vote **3.** [of show, concert] programme *m* ▸ **to head** ***or*** **to top the bill** être en tête d'affiche ***or*** en vedette **4.** *US* [banknote] billet *m* de banque **5.** [poster] **: 'post** ***or*** **stick** ***UK*** **no bills'** 'défense d'afficher' **6.** [beak] bec *m*
▸▸ **to be given a clean bill of health** être déclaré(e) en parfait état de santé.
■ **vt 1.** [invoice] **: to bill sb (for)** envoyer une facture à qqn (pour) **2.** [advertise] annoncer ▸ **they're billed as the best band in the world** on les présente comme le meilleur groupe du monde.

billboard ['bɪlbɔ:d] **n** panneau *m* d'affichage.

billet ['bɪlɪt] ■ **n** logement *m* (chez l'habitant).
■ **vt** loger, cantonner.

billfold ['bɪlfəʊld] **n** *US* portefeuille *m*.

billiards ['bɪljədz] **n** billard *m*.

billion ['bɪljən] **num 1.** *US* [thousand million] milliard *m* **2.** *UK dated* [million million] billion *m*.

billionaire [ˌbɪljə'neəʳ] **n** milliardaire *mf*.

bill of exchange **n** effet *m* ***or*** lettre *f* de change.

bill of lading **n** connaissement *m*.

Bill of Rights **n : the Bill of Rights** *les dix premiers amendements à la Constitution américaine*.

bill of sale **n** acte *m* de vente.

billow ['bɪləʊ] ■ **n** nuage *m*, volute *f*.
■ **vi** [smoke, steam] tournoyer / [skirt, sail] se gonfler.

billycan ['bɪlɪkæn] **n** gamelle *f*.

billy club **n** *US* matraque *f*.

billy goat ['bɪlɪ-] **n** bouc *m*.

bimbo ['bɪmbəʊ] (pl **-s** *OR* **-es**) **n** *inf pej* **: she's a bit of a bimbo** c'est le genre 'pin-up'.

bimonthly [,baɪ'mʌnθlɪ] ■ **adj 1.** [every two months] bimestriel(elle) **2.** [twice a month] bimensuel(elle).
■ **adv 1.** [every two months] tous les deux mois **2.** [twice a month] deux fois par mois.

bin [bɪn] ■ **n 1.** *UK* [for rubbish] poubelle *f* **2.** [for grain, coal] coffre *m* **3.** [for bread] huche *f*, boîte *f*.
■ **vt** *UK inf* balancer.

binary ['baɪnərɪ] **adj** binaire.

binbag ['bɪnbæg] **n** *UK* sac-poubelle *m*.

bind [baɪnd] ■ **vt** (pt & pp **bound**) **1.** [tie up] attacher, lier **2.** [unite - people] lier **3.** [bandage] panser **4.** [book] relier **5.** [constrain] contraindre, forcer.
■ **n** *inf* **1.** *UK* [nuisance] corvée *f* **2.** [difficult situation] **: to be in a bit of a bind** être dans le pétrin.
◆ ***bind over*** **vt sep : to be bound over** être sommé(e) d'observer une bonne conduite.

binder ['baɪndəʳ] **n 1.** [machine] lieuse *f* **2.** [person] relieur *m*, -euse *f* **3.** [cover] classeur *m*.

binding ['baɪndɪŋ] ■ **adj** [contract, promise] qui lie *OR* engage / [agreement] irrévocable.
■ **n 1.** [on book] reliure *f* **2.** [on dress, tablecloth] liséré *m*.

bin-end **n** fin *f* de série *(de vin)*.

binge [bɪndʒ] *inf* ■ **n : to go on a binge** prendre une cuite.
■ **vi : to binge on sthg** se gaver *OR* se bourrer de qqch.

bingo ['bɪŋgəʊ] **n** bingo *m*, ≃ loto *m*.

bin liner **n** *UK* sac-poubelle *m*.

binman ['bɪnmæn] (pl **-men** [-men]) **n** *UK* éboueur *m*.

binoculars [bɪ'nɒkjʊləz] **npl** jumelles *fpl*.

biochemical [,baɪəʊ'kemɪkl] ■ **adj** biochimique.
■ **n** produit *m* biochimique.

biochemistry [,baɪəʊ'kemɪstrɪ] **n** biochimie *f*.

biodegradable [,baɪəʊdɪ'greɪdəbl] **adj** biodégradable.

biodiversity [,baɪəʊdaɪ'vɜːsətɪ] **n** biodiversité *f*.

bioethics [,baɪəʊ'eθɪks] **n** *(U)* bioéthique *f*.

biographer [baɪ'ɒgrəfəʳ] **n** biographe *mf*.

biographic(al) [,baɪə'græfɪk(l)] **adj** biographique.

biography [baɪ'ɒgrəfɪ] (pl **-ies**) **n** biographie *f*.

biological [,baɪə'lɒdʒɪkl] **adj** [generally] biologique / [washing powder] aux enzymes.

biological clock **n** horloge *f* interne biologique.

biological mother **n** mère *f* biologique.

biological weapon **n** arme *f* biologique.

biologist [baɪ'ɒlədʒɪst] **n** biologiste *mf*.

biology [baɪ'ɒlədʒɪ] **n** biologie *f*.

biome ['baɪəʊm] **n** biome *m*.

bionic [baɪ'ɒnɪk] **adj** bionique.

bionics [baɪ'ɒnɪks] **n** *(U)* bionique *f*.

biopic ['baɪəʊpɪk] **n** *inf* film *m* biographique.

biopsy ['baɪɒpsɪ] (pl **-ies**) **n** biopsie *f*.

biotechnology [,baɪəʊtek'nɒlədʒɪ] **n** biotechnologie *f*.

bioterrorism [,baɪəʊ'terərɪzm] **n** bioterrorisme *m*.

biowarfare [,baɪəʊ'wɔːfeə] **n** guerre *f* biologique.

bipartite [,baɪ'pɑːtaɪt] **adj** bipartite.

biplane ['baɪpleɪn] **n** biplan *m*.

bipolar disorder [baɪ'pəʊləʳ-] **n** MED trouble *m* bipolaire.

birch [bɜːtʃ] **n 1.** [tree] bouleau *m* **2.** [stick] **: the birch** la verge, le fouet.

bird [bɜːd] **n 1.** [creature] oiseau *m* ▸ **to kill two birds with one stone** faire d'une pierre deux coups **2.** *UK inf* [woman] gonzesse *f*.

bird-brained [-breɪnd] **adj** *inf* [person] écervelé(e), qui a une cervelle d'oiseau / [idea] insensé(e).

birdcage ['bɜːdkeɪdʒ] **n** cage *f* à oiseaux.

birdie ['bɜːdɪ] **n 1.** [childrens' vocabulary] petit oiseau *m* **2.** GOLF birdie *m*.

bird of paradise **n** oiseau *m* de paradis, paradisier *m*.

bird of prey **n** oiseau *m* de proie.

birdseed ['bɜːdsiːd] **n** graine *f* pour oiseaux.

bird's-eye view **n** *lit* vue *f* aérienne / *fig* vue *f* d'ensemble.

bird-watcher [-,wɒtʃəʳ] **n** observateur *m*, -trice *f* d'oiseaux.

bird-watching **n** ornithologie *f* ▸ **to go bird-watching** aller observer les oiseaux.

Biro® ['baɪərəʊ] **n** *UK* stylo *m* à bille.

birth [bɜːθ] **n** *lit & fig* naissance *f* ▸ **to give birth (to)** donner naissance (à).

birth certificate **n** acte *m* *OR* extrait *m* de naissance.

birth control **n** *(U)* régulation *f* *OR* contrôle *m* des naissances.

birthday ['bɜːθdeɪ] ■ **n** anniversaire *m*.
■ **comp** [party, present] d'anniversaire.

birthday suit **n** *inf hum* [of man] costume *m* d'Adam / [of woman] costume *m* d'Ève.

birthmark ['bɜːθmɑːk] **n** tache *f* de vin.

birth mother **n** mère *f* gestationnelle.

birthplace ['bɜːθpleɪs] **n** lieu *m* de naissance.

birthrate ['bɜːθreɪt] **n** (taux *m* de) natalité *f*.

birthright ['bɜːθraɪt] **n** droit *m* de naissance *OR* du sang.

birthstone ['bɜːθstəʊn] **n** pierre *f* porte-bonheur *(selon la date de naissance)*.

Biscay ['bɪskeɪ] **n : the Bay of Biscay** le golfe de Gascogne.

biscuit ['bɪskɪt] **n** *UK* biscuit *m*, petit gâteau *m* / *US* scone *m*.

bisect [baɪ'sekt] **vt** couper *OR* diviser en deux.

bisexual [ˌbaɪ'sekʃʊəl] ■ **adj** bisexuel(elle).
■ **n** bisexuel *m*, -elle *f*.

bisexuality [baɪˌseksjʊ'ælɪtɪ] **n** bisexualité *f*.

bishop ['bɪʃəp] **n 1.** RELIG évêque *mf* **2.** [in chess] fou *m*.

bison ['baɪsn] (pl **bison** OR **-s**) **n** bison *m*.

bisque [bɪsk] **n 1.** [colour] beige-rosé *m* **2.** [ceramics] biscuit *m* **3.** [soup] bisque *f*.

bistro ['bi:strəʊ] (pl **-s**) **n** bistro *m*.

bit [bɪt] ■ **pt** ➤ ***bite***.
■ **n 1.** [small piece - of paper, cheese] morceau *m*, bout *m* / [- of book, film] passage *m* ▸ **I just want a bit** je n'en veux qu'un petit peu ▸ **bits and pieces** *UK* petites affaires *fpl* OR choses *fpl* ▸ **to fall to bits** tomber en morceaux ▸ **to take sthg to bits** démonter qqch ▸ **you missed out the best bit** [of story, joke] tu as oublié le meilleur
2. [amount] **: a bit of money/time** un peu d'argent/de temps ▸ **a bit of shopping** quelques courses ▸ **it's a bit of a nuisance** c'est un peu embêtant ▸ **a bit of trouble** un petit problème ▸ **quite a bit of** pas mal de, beaucoup de ▸ **he's away quite a bit** il est souvent absent ▸ **they haven't changed a bit** ils n'ont pas du tout changé
3. [short time] **: for a bit** pendant quelque temps
4. [of drill] mèche *f*
5. [of bridle] mors *m* ▸ **to take the bit between one's teeth** *fig* prendre le mors aux dents
6. COMPUT bit *m*
▸▸ **to do one's bit** *UK* faire sa part ▸ **every bit as... as** tout aussi... que ▸ **it's all a bit much** [overwhelming] c'en est trop ▸ **it's a bit much** c'est un peu fort ▸ **not a bit** [not at all] pas du tout.
◆ ***a bit*** **adv** un peu ▸ **I'm a bit tired** je suis un peu fatigué(e).
◆ ***bit by bit*** **adv** petit à petit, peu à peu.

bitch [bɪtʃ] ■ **n 1.** [female dog] chienne *f* **2.** *inf pej* [woman] salope *f*, garce *f*.
■ **vi** *inf* rouspéter, râler ▸ **to bitch about sb** casser du sucre sur le dos de qqn.

bitchy ['bɪtʃɪ] (comp **-ier**, superl **-iest**) **adj** *inf* vache, rosse.

bite [baɪt] ■ **n 1.** [act of biting] morsure *f*, coup *m* de dent **2.** *inf* [food] **: to have a bite (to eat)** manger un morceau **3.** [wound] piqûre *f* **4.** *UK* [sharp flavour] piquant *m*.
■ **vt** (pt **bit**, pp **bitten**) **1.** [subj: person, animal] mordre **2.** [subj: insect, snake] piquer, mordre.
■ **vi** (pt **bit**, pp **bitten**) **1.** [animal, person] **: to bite (into)** mordre (dans) ▸ **to bite off sthg** arracher qqch d'un coup de dents ▸ **to bite off more than one can chew** *fig* avoir les yeux plus gros que le ventre **2.** [insect, snake] mordre, piquer **3.** [grip] adhérer, mordre **4.** *fig* [take effect] se faire sentir.

bite-sized [-ˌsaɪzd] **adj : cut the meat into bite-sized pieces** coupez la viande en petits dés.

biting ['baɪtɪŋ] **adj 1.** [very cold] cinglant(e), piquant(e) **2.** [humour, comment] mordant(e), caustique.

bit map ['bɪtmæp] **n** mode *m* points ▸ **bit map screen** écran *m* pixel.

bit part **n** petit rôle *m*.

bitten ['bɪtn] **pp** ➤ ***bite***.

bitter ['bɪtəʳ] ■ **adj 1.** [gen] amer(ère) ▸ **to the bitter end** jusqu'au bout **2.** [icy] glacial(e) **3.** [argument] violent(e).
■ **n** *UK bière relativement amère, à forte teneur en houblon*.

bitter lemon **n** Schweppes® *m* au citron.

bitterly ['bɪtəlɪ] **adv 1.** [of weather] **: it's bitterly cold** il fait un froid de canard **2.** [disappointed] cruellement / [cry, complain] amèrement / [criticize] âprement, violemment.

bitterness ['bɪtənɪs] **n 1.** [gen] amertume *f* **2.** [of wind, weather] âpreté *f*.

bittersweet ['bɪtəswi:t] **adj** [taste] aigre-doux(-douce) / [memory] doux-amer(douce-amère).

bitty ['bɪtɪ] (comp **-ier**, superl **-iest**) **adj** *UK inf* décousu(e).

bitumen ['bɪtjʊmɪn] **n** bitume *m*.

bivouac ['bɪvʊæk] ■ **n** bivouac *m*.
■ **vi** (pt & pp **-ked**, cont **-king**) bivouaquer.

biweekly [ˌbaɪ'wi:klɪ] ■ **adj 1.** [every two weeks] bimensuel(elle) **2.** [twice a week] bihebdomadaire.
■ **adv 1.** [every two weeks] tous les quinze jours **2.** [twice a week] deux fois par semaine.

biyearly [ˌbaɪ'jɪəlɪ] ■ **adj** [every two years] biennal(e) / [twice yearly] semestriel(elle).
■ **adv** [every two years] tous les deux ans / [twice yearly] deux fois par an.
■ **n** (pl **-ies**) biennale *f*.

biz [bɪz] **n** *inf* commerce *m*.

bizarre [bɪ'zɑ:ʳ] **adj** bizarre.

bk abbr of ***bank***, ***book***.

bl abbr of ***bill of lading***.

BL **n** *UK* **1.** (abbr of ***Bachelor of Law(s)***) [degree] ≃ licence *f* de droit / [person] ≃ licencié *m*, -e *f* en OR ès droit **2.** (abbr of ***Bachelor of Letters***) [degree] ≃ licence *f* de lettres / [person] ≃ licencié *m*, -e *f* en OR ès lettres **3.** (abbr of ***Bachelor of Literature***) [degree] ≃ licence *f* de littérature / [person] ≃ licencié *m*, -e *f* en OR ès littérature.

blab [blæb] (pt & pp **-bed**, cont **-bing**) **vi** *inf* lâcher le morceau.

blabber ['blæbəʳ] *inf* ■ **vi** jaser, babiller ▸ **to blabber on about sthg** parler de qqch à n'en plus finir.
■ **n 1.** [person] moulin *m* à paroles **2.** [prattle] bavardage *m*, papotage *m*.

blabbermouth ['blæbəˌmaʊθ] (pl **-ˌmaʊðz**]) **n** *inf* pipelette *f*.

black [blæk] ■ **adj 1.** noir(e) ▸ **as black as ink** noir comme du jais OR de l'encre **2.** [race] noir(e) ▸ **he won the black vote** il a gagné les voix de l'électorat noir ▸ **black man** Noir *m* ▸ **black woman** Noire *f* ▸ **black American** Afro-Américain *m*, -e *f* **3.** [coffee] noir(e) / [tea] nature *(inv)*.
■ **n 1.** [colour] noir *m* ▸ **to be dressed in black** [gen] être habillé de OR en noir / [in mourning] porter le deuil **2.** [person] noir *m*, -e *f*
▸▸ **in the black** [financially solvent] solvable, sans dettes.
■ **vt 1.** [make black] noircir / [shoes] cirer *(avec du cirage noir)* ▸ **he blacked his attacker's eye** il a poché l'œil de son agresseur **2.** *UK* [boycott] boycotter.
◆ ***black out*** ■ **vt sep 1.** [city] faire le black-out dans, occulter **2.** [TV programme] faire le black-out sur, occulter.
■ **vi** [faint] s'évanouir.

black and blue **adj** couvert(e) de bleus ▸ **they beat him black and blue** ils l'ont roué de coups.

black and white ■ **adj 1.** [photograph, television] noir(e) et blanc(che) ▸ **a black-and-white film** un film en noir et blanc **2.** *fig* [clear-cut] précis(e), net(nette) ▸ **there's no black-and-white solution** le problème n'est pas simple.
■ **n 1.** [drawing, print] dessin *m* en noir et blanc / [photograph] photographie *f* en noir et blanc **2.** [written down] **: to put sthg down in black and white** écrire qqch noir sur blanc.

blackball ['blækbɔːl] **vt** blackbouler.

black belt **n** ceinture *f* noire.

blackberry ['blækbərɪ] (**pl -ies**) **n** mûre *f*.

blackbird ['blækbɜːd] **n** merle *m*.

blackboard ['blækbɔːd] **n** tableau *m* (noir).

black box **n** [flight recorder] boîte *f* noire.

black cab **n** taxi *m* londonien.

black comedy **n** comédie *f* d'humour noir.

blackcurrant [ˌblæk'kʌrənt] **n** cassis *m*.

black economy **n** économie *f* parallèle.

blacken ['blækn] ■ **vt 1.** [make dark] noircir **2.** *fig* [reputation] ternir.
■ **vi** s'assombrir.

black eye **n** œil *m* poché **OR** au beurre noir.

blackhead ['blækhed] **n** [on skin] point *m* noir.

black hole **n** trou *m* noir.

black ice **n** verglas *m*.

blackjack ['blækdʒæk] ■ **n 1.** [card game] vingt-et-un *m* **2.** *US* [weapon] matraque *f*.
■ **vt** *US* matraquer.

blackleg ['blækleg] **n** *UK pej* jaune *m*.

blacklist ['blæklɪst] ■ **n** liste *f* noire.
■ **vt** mettre sur la liste noire.

black magic **n** magie *f* noire.

blackmail ['blækmeɪl] ■ **n** *lit & fig* chantage *m*.
■ **vt 1.** [for money] faire chanter **2.** *fig* [emotionally] faire du chantage à.

blackmailer ['blækmeɪlə^r] **n** maître-chanteur *m*.

black mark **n** *fig* mauvais point *m*.

black market **n** marché *m* noir.

black marketeer **n** *personne qui fait du marché noir.*

Black Monday **n** lundi *m* noir.

blackout ['blækaʊt] **n 1.** MIL & PRESS black-out *m* **2.** [power cut] panne *f* d'électricité **3.** [fainting fit] évanouissement *m*.

black pepper **n** poivre *m* gris.

Black Power **n** *mouvement séparatiste noir né dans les années 60 aux États-Unis.*

black pudding **n** *UK* boudin *m*.

Black Sea **n : the Black Sea** la mer Noire.

black sheep **n** brebis *f* galeuse.

blacksmith ['blæksmɪθ] **n** [for horses] maréchal-ferrant *m* / [for tools] forgeron *m*.

black spot **n** *UK* AUT point *m* noir.

black tie **n** *nœud papillon noir porté avec une tenue de soirée* ▸ **'black tie'** [on invitation card] 'tenue de soirée exigée'.
◆ ***black-tie*** **adj : it's black-tie** il faut être en smoking.

bladder ['blædə^r] **n** vessie *f*.

blade [bleɪd] **n 1.** [of knife, saw] lame *f* **2.** [of propeller] pale *f* **3.** [of grass] brin *m*.

blah [blɑː] *inf* ■ **n 1.** [talk] baratin *m*, bla-bla-bla *m inv* **2.** *US* [blues] **: to have the blahs** avoir le cafard.
■ **adj** *US* **1.** [uninteresting] insipide, ennuyeux(euse) **2.** [blue] **: to feel blah** avoir le cafard.

Blairism ['bleərɪzm] **n** *politique du Premier ministre britannique socialiste Tony Blair.*

Blairite ['bleəraɪt] ■ **n** partisan *m* de la politique de Tony Blair.
■ **adj** [views, policies] du gouvernement de Tony Blair.

blame [bleɪm] ■ **n** responsabilité *f*, faute *f* ▸ **to take the blame for sthg** endosser la responsabilité de qqch ▸ **they laid OR put the blame for the incident on the secretary** ils ont rejeté la responsabilité de l'incident sur la secrétaire.
■ **vt** blâmer, condamner ▸ **to blame sthg on** rejeter la responsabilité de qqch sur, imputer qqch à ▸ **to blame sb/sthg for sthg** reprocher qqch à qqn/qqch ▸ **to be to blame for sthg** être responsable de qqch ▸ **he is not to blame** ce n'est pas de sa faute.

blameless ['bleɪmlɪs] **adj** [person] innocent(e) / [life] irréprochable.

blameworthy ['bleɪmˌwɜːðɪ] **adj** *fml* [person] fautif(ive), coupable / [action] répréhensible.

blanch [blɑːntʃ] ■ **vt** blanchir.
■ **vi** blêmir, pâlir.

blancmange [blə'mɒndʒ] **n** blanc-manger *m*.

bland [blænd] **adj 1.** [person - dull] insipide, ennuyeux(euse) / [- ingratiating] mielleux(euse), doucereux(euse) **2.** [food] fade, insipide **3.** [music, style] insipide.

blandly ['blændlɪ] **adv** [say - dully] affablement, avec affabilité / [- ingratiatingly] d'un ton mielleux.

blank [blæŋk] ■ **adj 1.** [sheet of paper] blanc (blanche) / [wall] nu(e) ▸ **fill in the blank spaces** remplissez les blancs **OR** les (espaces) vides ▸ **leave this line blank** n'écrivez rien sur cette ligne **2.** *fig* [look] vide, sans expression ▸ **my mind went blank** j'ai eu un trou.
■ **n 1.** [empty space] blanc *m* **2.** [cartridge] cartouche *f* à blanc
▸▸ **to draw a blank** faire chou blanc.

blank cheque *UK*, ***blank check*** *US* **n** FIN chèque *m* en blanc / *fig* carte *f* blanche.

blanket ['blæŋkɪt] ■ **adj** global(e), général(e).
■ **n 1.** [for bed] couverture *f* **2.** [of snow] couche *f*, manteau *m* / [of fog] nappe *f*.
■ **vt** recouvrir.

blanket bath **n** *UK* toilette *f (d'un malade alité).*

blankly ['blæŋklɪ] **adv** [stare] avec les yeux vides.

blank verse **n** *(U)* vers *mpl* blancs **OR** non rimés.

blare [bleə^r] **vi** [person, voice] hurler / [radio] beugler.
◆ ***blare out*** **vi** [person, voice] hurler / [radio] beugler.

blarney ['blɑːnɪ] *inf* ■ **n** [smooth talk] baratin *m* / [flattery] flatterie *f*.
■ **vt** [smooth-talk] baratiner / [wheedle] embobiner / [flatter] flatter.

blasé [*UK* 'blɑːzeɪ, *US* ˌblɑː'zeɪ] **adj** blasé(e).

blaspheme [blæs'fiːm] ■ **vi** blasphémer.
■ **vt** blasphémer.

blasphemous ['blæsfəməs] **adj** [words] blasphématoire / [person] blasphémateur(trice).

blasphemy ['blæsfəmɪ] (*pl* **-ies**) **n** blasphème *m*.

blast [blɑːst] ■ **n 1.** [explosion] explosion *f* **2.** [of air, from bomb] souffle *m*.
■ **vt** [hole, tunnel] creuser à la dynamite.
■ **excl** *UK inf* zut!, mince!
◆ ***(at) full blast*** **adv** [play music] à pleins gaz *OR* tubes / [work] d'arrache-pied.
◆ ***blast off*** **vi** [of space shuttle] être mis à feu, décoller.

blasted ['blɑːstɪd] **adj** *inf* fichu(e), maudit(e).

blast furnace **n** haut fourneau *m*.

blast-off **n** [of space shuttle] mise *f* à feu, lancement *m*.

blatant ['bleɪtənt] **adj** criant(e), flagrant(e).

blatantly ['bleɪtəntlɪ] **adv** d'une manière flagrante.

blaze [bleɪz] ■ **n 1.** [fire] incendie *m* **2.** *fig* [of colour, light] éclat *m*, flamboiement *m* ▸ **a blaze of gunfire** des coups de feu, une fusillade ▸ **in a blaze of publicity** à grand renfort de publicité ▸ **in a sudden blaze of anger** sous le coup de la colère.
■ **vi 1.** [fire] flamber **2.** *fig* [with colour] flamboyer ▸ **he suddenly blazed with anger** il s'est enflammé de colère.

blazer ['bleɪzər] **n** blazer *m*.

blazing ['bleɪzɪŋ] **adj 1.** [sun, heat] ardent(e) ▸ **blazing hot** torride, brûlant(e) **2.** [row] violent(e).

bleach [bliːtʃ] ■ **n** eau *f* de Javel.
■ **vt** [hair] décolorer / [clothes] blanchir.

bleached [bliːtʃt] **adj** [hair] décoloré(e).

bleachers ['bliːtʃəz] **npl** *US* SPORT gradins *mpl*.

bleak [bliːk] **adj 1.** [future] sombre **2.** [place, weather, face] lugubre, triste.

bleary ['blɪərɪ] (*comp* **-ier**, *superl* **-iest**) **adj** [eyes] trouble, voilé(e).

bleary-eyed [ˌblɪərɪ'aɪd] **adj** aux yeux troubles.

bleat [bliːt] ■ **n** [of sheep] bêlement *m*.
■ **vi** [sheep] bêler / *fig* [person] se plaindre, geindre.

bleed [bliːd] (*pt & pp* **bled** [bled]) ■ **vi** saigner.
■ **vt** [radiator] purger.

bleeding ['bliːdɪŋ] ■ **n 1.** [loss of blood] saignement *m* / [haemorrhage] hémorragie *f* / [taking of blood] saignée *f* **2.** [of plant] écoulement *m* de sève.
■ **adj 1.** [wound] saignant(e), qui saigne / [person] qui saigne **2.** *UK v inf* [as intensifier] fichu(e), sacré(e).
■ **adv** *UK v inf* vachement.

bleep [bliːp] *UK* ■ **n** bip *m*, bip-bip *m*.
■ **vt** appeler avec un bip, biper.
■ **vi** faire bip-bip.

bleeper ['bliːpər] *UK* **n** bip *m*, biper *m*.

blemish ['blemɪʃ] ■ **n** *lit & fig* défaut *m*.
■ **vt** [reputation] souiller, tacher.

blend [blend] ■ **n** mélange *m*.
■ **vt : to blend sthg (with)** mélanger qqch (avec *OR* à).
■ **vi : to blend (with)** se mêler (à *OR* avec).
◆ ***blend in*** **vi** se fondre.
◆ ***blend into*** **vt insep** se fondre dans.

blender ['blendər] **n** mixer *m*.

bless [bles] (*pt & pp* **-ed** *OR* **blest**) **vt** bénir ▸ **to be blessed with** [talent] être doué(e) de / [children] avoir la chance *OR* le bonheur d'avoir ▸ **bless you!** [after sneezing] à vos souhaits! / [thank you] merci mille fois!

blessed ['blesɪd] **adj 1.** RELIG saint(e), béni(e) **2.** [relief, silence] merveilleux(euse) **3.** *inf* [blasted] fichu(e), maudit(e).

blessing ['blesɪŋ] **n** *lit & fig* bénédiction *f* ▸ **a blessing in disguise** une bonne chose en fin de compte ▸ **to count one's blessings** s'estimer heureux(euse) de ce que l'on a ▸ **a mixed blessing** quelque chose qui a du bon et du mauvais.

blest [blest] **pt & pp** ➤ ***bless***.

blew [bluː] **pt** ➤ ***blow***.

blight [blaɪt] ■ **n 1.** [plant disease] rouille *f*, charbon *m* **2.** *fig* [scourge] fléau *m*, calamité *f*.
■ **vt** gâcher, briser.

Blighty ['blaɪtɪ] **n** *UK inf dated* l'Angleterre *f*.

blimey ['blaɪmɪ] **excl** *UK inf* zut alors!, mince alors!

blind [blaɪnd] ■ **adj 1.** *lit & fig* aveugle ▸ **to go blind** devenir aveugle ▸ **he's blind in one eye** il est aveugle d'un œil, il est borgne ▸ **as blind as a bat** myope comme une taupe ▸ **to be blind to sthg** ne pas voir qqch ▸ **to turn a blind eye to sthg** fermer les yeux sur qqch
2. *UK inf* [for emphasis] **: blind drunk** complètement rond(e), bourré(e) ▸ **it doesn't make a blind bit of difference to me** cela m'est complètement égal ▸ **he didn't take a blind bit of notice** il n'a pas fait la moindre attention.
■ **adv 1.** [drive, fly - without visibility] sans visibilité / [- using only instruments] aux instruments
2. [as intensifier] **: I would swear blind he was there** j'aurais donné ma tête à couper *OR* j'aurais juré qu'il était là.
■ **n 1.** [for window] store *m*
2. *US* [for watching birds, animals] cachette *f*.
■ **npl : the blind** les aveugles *mpl* ▸ **it's a case of the blind leading the blind** c'est l'aveugle qui conduit l'aveugle.
■ **vt** aveugler ▸ **to blind sb to sthg** *fig* cacher qqch à qqn ▸ **to blind sb with science** *hum* éblouir qqn par sa science.

blind alley **n** *lit & fig* impasse *f*.

blind corner **n** *UK* AUT virage *m* sans visibilité.

blind date **n** *rendez-vous avec quelqu'un qu'on ne connaît pas.*

blinders ['blaɪndəz] **npl** *US* œillères *fpl*.

blindfold ['blaɪndfəʊld] ■ **adv** les yeux bandés.
■ **n** bandeau *m*.
■ **vt** bander les yeux à.

blinding ['blaɪndɪŋ] **adj 1.** [light] aveuglant(e) **2.** [obvious] évident(e), manifeste.

blindly ['blaɪndlɪ] **adv** [unseeingly] à l'aveuglette / [without thinking] aveuglément.

blindness ['blaɪndnɪs] **n** cécité *f* ▸ **blindness (to sthg)** *fig* aveuglement *m* (devant qqch).

blind spot **n 1.** AUT angle *m* mort **2.** *fig* [inability to understand] blocage *m*.

blind test **n** test *m* aveugle.

blind testing **n** *(U)* tests *mpl* aveugles.

blini ['blɪni:] **npl** blinis *mpl*.

blink [blɪŋk] ■ **n 1.** [of eyes] clignement *m* **2.** [of light] clignotement *m*
▸▸| **on the blink** *inf* [machine] détraqué(e).
■ **vt 1.** [eyes] cligner **2.** *US* AUT **: to blink one's lights** faire un appel de phares.
■ **vi 1.** [person] cligner des yeux **2.** [light] clignoter.

blinkered ['blɪŋkəd] **adj : to be blinkered** *lit & fig* avoir des œillères.

blinkers ['blɪŋkəz] **npl** *UK* œillères *fpl*.

blinking ['blɪŋkɪŋ] **adj** *UK inf dated* sacré(e), fichu(e).

blip [blɪp] **n 1.** [sound] bip *m* **2.** [on radar] spot *m* **3.** *fig* [temporary problem] problème *m* passager.

bliss [blɪs] **n** bonheur *m* suprême, félicité *f*.

blissful ['blɪsfʊl] **adj** [day, silence] merveilleux(euse), divin(e) / [ignorance] total(e).

blissfully ['blɪsfʊlɪ] **adv** [smile] d'un air heureux / [happy, unaware] parfaitement.

blister ['blɪstəʳ] ■ **n** [on skin] ampoule *f*, cloque *f*.
■ **vi 1.** [skin] se couvrir d'ampoules **2.** [paint] cloquer, se boursoufler.

blistering ['blɪstərɪŋ] **adj** [sun] brûlant(e), ardent(e) / [attack] caustique, cinglant(e).

blister pack **n** blister *m*.

blithe [blaɪð] **adj 1.** [unworried] insouciant(e) **2.** *dated* [cheerful] joyeux(euse), gai(e).

blithely ['blaɪðlɪ] **adv** gaiement, joyeusement.

blithering ['blɪðərɪŋ] **adj** *inf dated* sacré(e) ▸ **a blithering idiot** un crétin fini.

BLitt [ˌbi:'lɪt] (abbr of ***Bachelor of Letters***) *UK* **n** [degree] ≃ licence *f* de lettres / [person] ≃ licencié *m*, -e *f* en *OR* ès lettres.

blitz [blɪts] **n 1.** MIL bombardement *m* aérien **2.** *UK fig* **: to have a blitz on sthg** s'attaquer à qqch.

blizzard ['blɪzəd] **n** tempête *f* de neige.

BLM (abbr of ***Bureau of Land Management***) **n** *service de l'aménagement du territoire aux États-Unis*.

bloated ['bləʊtɪd] **adj 1.** [face] bouffi(e), boursouflé(e) **2.** [with food] ballonné(e).

blob [blɒb] **n 1.** [drop] goutte *f* **2.** [indistinct shape] forme *f* ▸ **a blob of colour** une tache de couleur.

bloc [blɒk] **n** bloc *m*.

block [blɒk] ■ **n 1.** [building] **: office block** *UK* immeuble *m* de bureaux ▸ **block of flats** *UK* immeuble *m* **2.** *US* [of buildings] pâté *m* de maisons ▸ **it's five blocks from here** c'est cinq rues plus loin **3.** [of stone, ice] bloc *m* **4.** [obstruction] blocage *m* ▸ **to have a (mental) block about sthg** faire un blocage sur qqch.
■ **vt 1.** [road, pipe, view] boucher ▸ **to block sb's way** barrer le chemin à qqn **2.** [prevent] bloquer, empêcher.
◆ ***block off*** **vt sep** [road] barrer / [pipe, entrance] boucher.
◆ ***block out*** **vt sep 1.** [from mind] chasser **2.** [light] empêcher d'entrer.
◆ ***block up*** ■ **vt sep** boucher.
■ **vi** se boucher.

blockade [blɒ'keɪd] ■ **n** blocus *m*.
■ **vt** faire le blocus de.

blockage ['blɒkɪdʒ] **n** obstruction *f*.

block and tackle ['blɒkɪdʒ] **n** palan *m*, moufle *f*.

block booking **n** *UK* location *f* en bloc.

blockbuster ['blɒkbʌstəʳ] **n** *inf* [book] best-seller *m* / [film] film *m* à succès, superproduction *f*.

block capitals **npl** majuscules *fpl* d'imprimerie ▸ **in block capitals** en majuscules.

blockhead ['blɒkhed] **n** *inf* crétin *m*, -e *f*, imbécile *mf*.

blocking software ['blɒkɪŋ-] **n** COMPUT logiciel *m* de filtrage.

block letters **npl** majuscules *fpl* d'imprimerie.

block release **n** *UK stage de formation de plusieurs semaines*.

block vote **n** *UK* vote *m* groupé.

blog [blɒg] (abbr of ***weblog***) **n** COMPUT blog *m*.

bloke [bləʊk] **n** *UK inf* type *m*.

blokeish ['bləʊkɪʃ], ***blokey*** ['bləʊkɪ] **adj** *UK inf* [behaviour, humour] de mec / [joke] macho.

blond [blɒnd] **adj** blond(e).

blonde [blɒnd] ■ **adj** blond(e).
■ **n** [woman] blonde *f*.

blood [blʌd] **n** sang *m* ▸ **to donate** *OR* **to give blood** donner son sang ▸ **in cold blood** de sang-froid ▸ **it made my blood boil** cela m'a mis dans une colère noire ▸ **it made my blood run cold** cela m'a glacé le sang ▸ **it's in his blood** *fig* il a cela dans le sang ▸ **new** *OR* **fresh blood** *fig* sang frais.

blood bank **n** banque *f* de sang.

bloodbath ['blʌdbɑ:θ] (pl [-bɑ:ðz]) **n** bain *m* de sang, massacre *m*.

blood brother **n** frère *m* de sang.

blood cell **n** globule *m*.

blood count **n** numération *f* globulaire.

bloodcurdling ['blʌdˌkɜ:dlɪŋ] **adj** à vous glacer le sang.

blood donor **n** donneur *m*, -euse *f* de sang.

blood group **n** *UK* groupe *m* sanguin.

bloodhound ['blʌdhaʊnd] **n** limier *m*.

bloodless ['blʌdlɪs] **adj 1.** [face, lips] exsangue, pâle **2.** [coup, victory] sans effusion de sang.

bloodletting ['blʌd,letɪŋ] **n** [killing] tuerie *f*.

blood money **n** prix *m* du sang.

blood orange **n** orange *f* sanguine.

blood poisoning **n** septicémie *f*.

blood pressure **n** tension *f* artérielle ▸ **to have high blood pressure** faire de l'hypertension.

blood relation, ***blood relative*** **n** parent *m*, -e *f* par le sang.

bloodshed ['blʌdʃed] **n** carnage *m*.

bloodshot ['blʌdʃɒt] **adj** [eyes] injecté(e) de sang.

blood sports **npl** chasse *f*.

bloodstained ['blʌdsteɪnd] **adj** taché(e) de sang, ensanglanté(e).

bloodstream ['blʌdstri:m] **n** sang *m*.

blood sugar **n** glycémie *f* ▸ **blood-sugar level** taux *m* de glycémie.

blood test **n** prise *f* de sang, examen *m* du sang.

bloodthirsty ['blʌd,θɜ:stɪ] **adj** sanguinaire.

blood transfusion **n** transfusion *f* sanguine.

blood type **n** groupe *m* sanguin.

blood vessel **n** vaisseau *m* sanguin.

bloody ['blʌdɪ] ■ **adj** (**comp -ier**, **superl -iest**) **1.** [gen] sanglant(e) **2.** *UK v inf* foutu(e) ▸ **you bloody idiot!** espèce de con!
■ **adv** *UK v inf* vachement.

bloody-minded [-'maɪndɪd] **adj** *UK inf* contrariant(e).

bloody-mindedness [-'maɪndɪdnɪs] **n** *UK inf* caractère *m* difficile ▸ **it's sheer bloody-mindedness on your part** tu le fais uniquement pour emmerder le monde.

bloom [blu:m] ■ **n** fleur *f*.
■ **vi** fleurir.

blooming ['blu:mɪŋ] ■ **adj 1.** *UK inf* [to show annoyance] sacré(e), fichu(e) **2.** [person] éclatant(e), resplendissant(e).
■ **adv** *UK inf* sacrément.

blossom ['blɒsəm] ■ **n** [of tree] fleurs *fpl* ▸ **in blossom** en fleur(s).
■ **vi 1.** [tree] fleurir **2.** *fig* [person] s'épanouir.

blot [blɒt] ■ **n** *lit* & *fig* tache *f*.
■ **vt** (**pt** & **pp -ted**, **cont -ting**) **1.** [paper] faire des pâtés sur **2.** [ink] sécher.
◆ ***blot out*** **vt sep** [light, sun] cacher, masquer / [memory, thought] effacer.

blotchy ['blɒtʃɪ] (**comp -ier**, **superl -iest**) **adj** couvert(e) de marbrures *OR* taches.

blotting paper ['blɒtɪŋ-] **n** *(U)* (papier *m*) buvard *m*.

blouse [blaʊz] **n** chemisier *m*.

blouson ['blu:zɒn] **n** *UK* blouson *m*.

blow [bləʊ] ■ **vi** (**pt blew**, **pp blown**) **1.** [gen] souffler ▸ **she blew on her hands/on her coffee** elle a soufflé dans ses mains/sur son café ▸ **he blows hot and cold** il souffle le chaud et le froid
2. [in wind] **: the trees were blowing in the wind** le vent soufflait dans les arbres ▸ **the door blew open** la porte s'ouvrit à la volée ▸ **the door blew shut** la porte a claqué ▸ **to blow off** s'envoler
3. [fuse] sauter.
■ **vt** (**pt blew**, **pp blown**) **1.** [subj: wind] faire voler, chasser
2. [with mouth, nose] **: to blow one's nose** se moucher ▸ **to blow sb a kiss** envoyer un baiser à qqn ▸ **he blew the dust off the book** il a soufflé sur le livre pour enlever la poussière
3. [trumpet] jouer de, souffler dans ▸ **to blow a whistle** donner un coup de sifflet, siffler ▸ **the referee blew his whistle for time** l'arbitre a sifflé la fin du match ▸ **to blow one's own trumpet** se vanter ▸ **to blow the whistle on sthg** dévoiler qqch
4. [bubbles] faire
5. [tyre] faire éclater / [fuse, safe] faire sauter ▸ **the house was blown to pieces** la maison a été entièrement détruite par l'explosion ▸ **the blast almost blew his hand off** l'explosion lui a presque emporté la main ▸ **he blew a gasket** *UK OR* **a fuse when he found out** quand il l'a appris, il a piqué une crise
6. *inf* [money] claquer
7. *inf* [spoil - chance] gâcher ▸ **I blew it!** j'ai tout gâché!
■ **n 1.** [hit] coup *m* ▸ **to come to blows** en venir aux mains ▸ **to soften the blow** *fig* adoucir le coup ▸ **to strike a blow for** *fig* servir la cause de ▸ **it was a big blow to her pride** son orgueil en a pris un coup
2. *UK drug sl* [marijuana] herbe *f* / *US drug sl* [cocaine] cocaïne *f*.
◆ ***blow out*** ■ **vt sep** [candle] souffler.
■ **vi 1.** [candle] s'éteindre
2. [tyre] éclater.
◆ ***blow over*** **vi** se calmer.
◆ ***blow up*** ■ **vt sep 1.** [inflate] gonfler
2. [with bomb] faire sauter
3. [photograph] agrandir.
■ **vi** exploser.

blow-by-blow **adj** *fig* détaillé(e).

blow-dry ■ **n** Brushing® *m*.
■ **vt** faire un Brushing® à.

blowfly ['bləʊflaɪ] (**pl -flies**) **n** mouche *f* bleue, mouche de la viande.

blowgun ['bləʊgʌn] = ***blowpipe***.

blowlamp *UK* ['bləʊlæmp], ***blowtorch*** ['bləʊtɔ:tʃ] **n** chalumeau *m*, lampe *f* à souder.

blown [bləʊn] **pp** ➤ ***blow***.

blowout ['bləʊaʊt] **n 1.** *esp US* [of tyre] éclatement *m* **2.** *UK inf* [big meal] grande bouffe *f*, gueuleton *m* **3.** [of gas] éruption *f*.

blowpipe ['bləʊpaɪp], ***blowgun*** ['bləʊgʌn] **n** sarbacane *f*.

blowtorch = ***blowlamp***.

blowzy ['blaʊzɪ] **adj** *UK* négligé(e).

BLS (**abbr of *Bureau of Labor Statistics***) **n** *institut de statistiques du travail aux États-Unis*.

blubber ['blʌbəʳ] ■ **n** graisse *f* de baleine.
■ **vi** *inf pej* chialer, pleurer comme un veau.

bludgeon ['blʌdʒən] **vt** matraquer.

blue [blu:] ■ **adj 1.** [colour] bleu(e) **2.** *inf* [sad] triste, cafardeux(euse) **3.** *inf dated* [pornographic] porno *(inv)*.
■ **n** bleu *m* ▸ **in blue** en bleu ▸ **out of the blue** [happen] subitement / [arrive] à l'improviste.
◆ ***blues*** **npl : the blues** MUS le blues / *inf* [sad feeling] le blues, le cafard.

blue baby **n** enfant *m* bleu.

bluebell ['blu:bel] **n** jacinthe *f* des bois.

blueberry ['blu:bərɪ] **n** myrtille *f*.

bluebird ['blu:bɜ:d] **n** oiseau *m* bleu.

blue-black **adj** bleu noir *(inv)*.

blue-blooded [-'blʌdɪd] **adj** de sang noble, qui a du sang bleu.

bluebottle ['blu:ˌbɒtl] **n** mouche *f* bleue, mouche de la viande.

blue cheese **n** (fromage *m*) bleu *m*.

blue chip **n** FIN valeur *f* sûre, titre *m* de premier ordre.
◆ ***blue-chip*** **comp** de premier ordre.

blue-collar **adj** manuel(elle).

blue-eyed boy [-aɪd-] **n** *UK inf* chouchou *m*.

blue jeans **npl** *esp US* blue-jean *m*, jean *m*.

blue moon **n : once in a blue moon** tous les trente-six du mois.

blueprint ['blu:prɪnt] **n** [photographic] photocalque *m* / *fig* plan *m*, projet *m*.

blue-sky **comp : blue-sky research** recherches *fpl* sans applications immédiates.

bluestocking ['blu:ˌstɒkɪŋ] **n** *pej* bas-bleu *m*.

blue tit **n** *UK* mésange *f* bleue.

Bluetooth ['blu:tu:θ] **n** TELEC technologie *f* Bluetooth.

bluff [blʌf] ■ **adj** franc (franche).
■ **n 1.** [deception] bluff *m* ▸ **to call sb's bluff** prendre qqn au mot **2.** [cliff] falaise *f* à pic.
■ **vt** bluffer, donner le change à.
■ **vi** faire du bluff, bluffer.

blunder ['blʌndəʳ] ■ **n** gaffe *f*, bévue *f*.
■ **vi 1.** [make mistake] faire une gaffe, commettre une bévue **2.** [move clumsily] avancer d'un pas maladroit.

blundering ['blʌndərɪŋ] **adj** maladroit(e).

blunt [blʌnt] ■ **adj 1.** [knife] émoussé(e) / [pencil] épointé(e) / [object, instrument] contondant(e) **2.** [person, manner] direct(e), carré(e).
■ **vt** *lit* & *fig* émousser.

bluntly ['blʌntlɪ] **adv** carrément, brutalement.

bluntness ['blʌntnɪs] **n** brusquerie *f*.

blur [blɜ:ʳ] ■ **n** forme *f* confuse, tache *f* floue.
■ **vt** (pt & pp **-red**, cont **-ring**) **1.** [vision] troubler, brouiller **2.** [distinction] rendre moins net (nette).

blurb [blɜ:b] **n** texte *m* publicitaire.

blurred [blɜ:d] **adj 1.** [photograph] flou(e) **2.** [vision] trouble **3.** [distinction] peu net (nette), vague.

blurt [blɜ:t] ◆ ***blurt out*** **vt sep** laisser échapper.

blush [blʌʃ] ■ **n** rougeur *f*.
■ **vi** rougir.

blusher ['blʌʃəʳ] **n** *UK* fard *m* à joues, blush *m*.

bluster ['blʌstəʳ] ■ **n** *(U)* propos *mpl* coléreux.
■ **vi** tempêter.

blustery ['blʌstərɪ] **adj** venteux(euse).

Blvd (abbr of ***Boulevard***) bd, boul.

BM **n 1.** (abbr of ***Bachelor of Medicine***) [degree] ≃ licence *f* de médecine / [person] ≃ licencié *m*, -e *f* en médecine **2.** (abbr of ***British Museum***) *grand musée et bibliothèque célèbres, situés à Londres*.

BMA (abbr of ***British Medical Association***) **n** *ordre britannique des médecins*.

BMJ (abbr of ***British Medical Journal***) **n** *organe de la BMA*.

B-movie **n** film *m* de série B.

BMus ['bi:'mʌz] (abbr of ***Bachelor of Music***) **n** [degree] ≃ licence *f* de musique / [person] ≃ licencié *m*, -e *f* en musique.

BMX (abbr of ***bicycle motorcross***) **n** bicross *m*.

BO abbr of ***body odour***.

boa constrictor ['bəʊəkən'strɪktəʳ] **n** boa *m* constricteur.

boar [bɔ:ʳ] **n 1.** [male pig] verrat *m* **2.** [wild pig] sanglier *m*.

board [bɔ:d] ■ **n 1.** [plank] planche *f* **2.** [for notices] panneau *m* d'affichage **3.** [for games - gen] tableau *m* / [- for chess] échiquier *m* **4.** [blackboard] tableau *m* (noir) **5.** [of company] **: board (of directors)** conseil *m* d'administration ▸ **who's on the board?** qui siège au conseil d'administration? **6.** [committee] comité *m*, conseil *m* ▸ **board of examiners** jury *m* d'examen **7.** *UK* [at hotel, guesthouse] pension *f* ▸ **board and lodging** pension ▸ **full board** pension complète ▸ **half board** demi-pension *f* **8. : on board** [on ship, plane, bus, train] à bord
▸▸ **to take sthg on board** [knowledge] assimiler qqch / [advice] accepter qqch ▸ **above board** régulier(ère), dans les règles ▸ **across the board** [agreement] général(e) / [apply] de façon générale ▸ **to go by the board** aller à vau-l'eau, être abandonné(e) ▸ **to sweep the board** tout rafler ***OR*** gagner.
■ **vt** [ship, aeroplane] monter à bord de / [train, bus] monter dans.
■ **vi : the flight is now boarding at gate 3** embarquement immédiat du vol porte 3.

boarder ['bɔ:dəʳ] **n 1.** [lodger] pensionnaire *mf* **2.** [at school] interne *mf*, pensionnaire *mf*.

board game **n** jeu *m* de société.

boarding card ['bɔ:dɪŋ-] **n** carte *f* d'embarquement.

boarding house ['bɔ:dɪŋhaʊs] (pl [-haʊzɪz]) **n** *dated* pension *f* de famille.

boarding pass ['bɔ:dɪŋ-] **n** carte *f* d'embarquement.

boarding school ['bɔ:dɪŋ-] **n** pensionnat *m*, internat *m*.

board meeting **n** réunion *f* du conseil d'administration.

Board of Trade **n** *UK* **: the Board of Trade** ≃ le ministère *m* du Commerce.

boardroom ['bɔ:drʊm] **n** salle *f* du conseil (d'administration).

boardwalk ['bɔ:dwɔ:k] **n** *US* trottoir *m* en planches.

boast [bəʊst] ■ **n** vantardise *f*, fanfaronnade *f*.
■ **vt** [special feature] s'enorgueillir de.
■ **vi : to boast (about)** se vanter (de).

boastful ['bəʊstfʊl] **adj** vantard(e), fanfaron(onne).

boat [bəʊt] **n** [large] bateau *m* / [small] canot *m*, embarcation *f* ▸ **by boat** en bateau ▸ **to rock the boat** semer le trouble ▸ **to be in the same boat** être logé(e) à la même enseigne.

boater ['bəʊtə^r] **n** [hat] canotier *m*.

boating ['bəʊtɪŋ] **n** canotage *m*.

boatswain ['bəʊsn] **n** maître *m* d'équipage.

boat train **n** *train qui assure la correspondance avec le bateau.*

bob [bɒb] ■ **n 1.** [hairstyle] coupe *f* au carré **2.** *UK inf dated* [shilling] shilling *m* **3.** = ***bobsleigh***.
■ **vi** (pt & pp **-bed**, cont **-bing**) [boat, ship] tanguer.

bobbin ['bɒbɪn] **n** bobine *f*.

bobble [bɒbl] **n** pompon *m*.

bobby ['bɒbɪ] (pl **-ies**) **n** *UK inf dated* agent *m* de police.

bobby pin **n** *US* pince *f* à cheveux.

bobby socks, ***bobby sox*** **npl** *US* socquettes *fpl (de fille)*.

bobsleigh ['bɒbsleɪ] *UK*, ***bobsled*** ['bɒbsled] *US* **n** bobsleigh *m*.

bode [bəʊd] **vi** *liter* **: to bode ill/well (for)** être de mauvais/bon augure (pour).

bodge [bɒdʒ] **vt** *UK inf* **1.** [spoil] saboter, bousiller **2.** [mend clumsily] rafistoler.

bodice ['bɒdɪs] **n** corsage *m*.

bodily ['bɒdɪlɪ] ■ **adj** [needs] matériel(elle) / [pain] physique.
■ **adv** [lift, move] à bras-le-corps.

body ['bɒdɪ] (pl **-ies**) **n 1.** [of person] corps *m* ▸ **to keep body and soul together** subsister **2.** [corpse] corps *m*, cadavre *m* ▸ **over my dead body!** il faudra d'abord me passer sur le corps! **3.** [organization] organisme *m*, organisation *f* **4.** [of car] carrosserie *f* / [of plane] fuselage *m* **5.** [mass] masse *f* ▸ **a body of water** un plan d'eau ▸ **a growing body of evidence** une accumulation de preuves ▸ **the body of public opinion** la majorité de l'opinion publique ▸ **the main body of voters** le gros des électeurs **6.** *(U)* [of wine] corps *m* **7.** *(U)* [of hair] volume *m* **8.** *UK* [garment] body *m*.

bodybuilder ['bɒdɪbɪldə^r] **n** [person] culturiste *mf* / [machine] extenseur *m* / [food] aliment *m* énergétique.

body building **n** culturisme *m*.

body clock **n** horloge *f* biologique.

bodyguard ['bɒdɪgɑːd] **n** garde *m* du corps.

body language **n** langage *m* du corps.

body lotion **n** lait *m* corporel.

body odour *UK*, ***body odor*** *US* **n** odeur *f* corporelle.

body piercing **n** piercing *m*.

body search **n** fouille *f* corporelle.

body shop **n 1.** [garage] atelier *m* **2.** *US inf* [gym] club *m* de gym.

body stocking **n** justaucorps *m*.

body warmer [-,wɔːmə^r] **n** gilet *m* matelassé.

bodywork ['bɒdɪwɜːk] **n** carrosserie *f*.

boffin ['bɒfɪn] **n** *UK inf* savant *m*.

bog [bɒg] **n 1.** [marsh] marécage *m* **2.** *UK v inf* [toilet] chiottes *fpl*.

bogey ['bəʊgɪ] **n** GOLF bogey *m*.

bogged down [,bɒgd-] **adj 1.** *fig* [in work] **: bogged down (in)** submergé(e) (de) **2.** [car] **: bogged down (in)** enlisé(e) (dans).

boggle ['bɒgl] **vi : the mind boggles!** ce n'est pas croyable!, on croit rêver!

boggy ['bɒgɪ] **adj** marécageux(euse).

bogie ['bəʊgɪ] **n** RAIL bogie *m*.

Bogotá [,bəʊgə'tɑː] **n** Bogotá.

bog-standard **adj** *UK inf* [restaurant, food] ordinaire, médiocre / [film, book] sans intérêt, médiocre / [hotel] standard *(inv)*, médiocre.

bogus ['bəʊgəs] **adj** faux (fausse), bidon *(inv)*.

Bohemia [bəʊ'hiːmjə] **n** Bohême *f* ▸ **in Bohemia** en Bohême.

bohemian [bəʊ'hiːmjən] ■ **adj** [person] bohème / [lifestyle] de bohème.
■ **n** bohème *mf*.
◆ ***Bohemian*** ■ **adj** bohémien(enne).
■ **n** Bohémien *m*, -enne *f*.

boil [bɔɪl] ■ **n 1.** MED furoncle *m* **2.** [boiling point] **: to bring sthg to the boil** porter qqch à ébullition ▸ **to come to the boil** venir à ébullition.
■ **vt 1.** [water, food] faire bouillir **2.** [kettle] mettre sur le feu.
■ **vi** [water] bouillir.
◆ ***boil away*** **vi** [evaporate] s'évaporer.
◆ ***boil down to*** **vt insep** *fig* revenir à, se résumer à.
◆ ***boil over*** **vi 1.** [liquid] déborder **2.** *fig* [feelings] exploser.

boiled ['bɔɪld] **adj** bouilli(e) ▸ **boiled egg** œuf *m* à la coque ▸ **boiled sweet** *UK* bonbon *m* (à sucer).

boiler ['bɔɪlə^r] **n** chaudière *f*.

boiler room **n** chaufferie *f*.

boiler suit **n** *UK* bleu *m* de travail.

boiling ['bɔɪlɪŋ] **adj 1.** [liquid] bouillant(e) **2.** *inf* [weather] très chaud(e), torride / [person] **: I'm boiling (hot)!** je crève de chaleur! **3.** [angry] **: boiling with rage** en rage, écumant(e) de rage.

boiling point **n** point *m* d'ébullition.

boisterous ['bɔɪstərəs] **adj** turbulent(e), remuant(e).

bold [bəʊld] **adj 1.** [confident] hardi(e), audacieux(euse) **2.** [lines, design] hardi(e) / [colour] vif (vive), éclatant(e) **3.** TYPO **: bold type** *OR* **print** caractères *mpl* gras.

boldly ['bəʊldlɪ] **adv** hardiment, avec audace.

boldness ['bəʊldnɪs] **n 1.** [courage] intrépidité *f*, audace **2.** [impudence] impudence *f*, effronterie *f* **3.** [force] vigueur *f*, hardiesse *f*.

Bolivia [bəˈlɪvɪə] n Bolivie *f* ▸ **in Bolivia** en Bolivie.

Bolivian [bəˈlɪvɪən] ■ adj bolivien(enne).
■ n Bolivien *m*, -enne *f*.

bollard [ˈbɒlɑːd] n *UK* [on road] borne *f*.

bollocking [ˈbɒləkɪŋ] n *UK v inf* engueulade *f* ▸ **he got/ she gave him a right bollocking** il a reçu/elle lui a passé un sacré savon.

bollocks [ˈbɒləks] *UK v inf* ■ npl couilles *fpl*.
■ excl quelles conneries!

Bolshevik [ˈbɒlʃɪvɪk] ■ adj bolchevique.
■ n bolchevique *mf*.

bolshie, bolshy *UK inf* ■ n [ˈbɒlʃɪ] rouge *mf*.
■ adj **1.** [intractable] ronchon(onne) **2.** POL rouge.

bolster [ˈbəʊlstəʳ] ■ n [pillow] traversin *m*.
■ vt renforcer, affirmer.
◆ ***bolster up*** vt sep soutenir, appuyer.

bolt [bəʊlt] ■ n **1.** [on door, window] verrou *m* **2.** [type of screw] boulon *m*.
■ adv : **bolt upright** droit(e) comme un piquet.
■ vt **1.** [fasten together] boulonner **2.** [close - door, window] verrouiller, fermer au verrou **3.** [food] engouffrer, engloutir.
■ vi [run] détaler.

bolt hole n *UK* abri *m*, refuge *m*.

bomb [bɒm] ■ n bombe *f*.
■ vt bombarder.

bombard [bɒmˈbɑːd] vt *fig* & MIL : **to bombard (with)** bombarder (de).

bombardment [bɒmˈbɑːdmənt] n bombardement *m*.

bombastic [bɒmˈbæstɪk] adj pompeux(euse).

bomb disposal squad n équipe *f* de déminage.

bomber [ˈbɒməʳ] n **1.** [plane] bombardier *m* **2.** [person] plastiqueur *m*.

bomber jacket n blouson *m* d'aviateur.

bombing [ˈbɒmɪŋ] n bombardement *m*.

bombproof [ˈbɒmpruːf] adj à l'épreuve des bombes.

bombshell [ˈbɒmʃel] n *fig* bombe *f*.

bombsight [ˈbɒmsaɪt] n viseur *m* de bombardement.

bombsite [ˈbɒmsaɪt] n lieu *m* bombardé.

bona fide [ˌbəʊnəˈfaɪdɪ] adj [genuine] véritable, authentique ⁄ [offer] sérieux(euse).

bonanza [bəˈnænzə] n aubaine *f*, filon *m*.

bonce [bɒns] n *UK inf* caboche *f*.

bond [bɒnd] ■ n **1.** [between people] lien *m* **2.** [promise] engagement *m* **3.** FIN bon *m*, titre *m*.
■ vt **1.** [glue] : **to bond sthg to sthg** coller qqch sur qqch **2.** *fig* [people] unir.
■ vi **1.** [stick together] : **to bond (together)** être collé(e) (ensemble) **2.** *fig* [people] établir des liens.

bondage [ˈbɒndɪdʒ] n servitude *f*, esclavage *m*.

bonded warehouse [ˈbɒndɪd-] n entrepôt *m* de douane.

bone [bəʊn] ■ n [generally] os *m* ⁄ [of fish] arête *f* ▸ **bone of contention** pomme *f* de discorde ▸ **to feel** OR **know sthg in one's bones** avoir le pressentiment de qqch ▸ **I have a bone to pick with you** j'ai un compte à régler avec toi ▸ **to make no bones about sthg** ne pas cacher qqch.
■ vt [meat] désosser ⁄ [fish] enlever les arêtes de.

bone china n porcelaine *f* tendre.

bone-dry adj tout à fait sec (sèche).

bonehead [ˈbəʊnhed] n *inf* crétin *m*, -e *f*, imbécile *mf*.

bone-idle adj *UK inf* paresseux(euse) comme une couleuvre OR un lézard.

boneless [ˈbəʊnlɪs] adj [meat] sans os ⁄ [fish] sans arêtes.

bone marrow n moelle *f* osseuse.

bonfire [ˈbɒnˌfaɪəʳ] n [for fun] feu *m* de joie ⁄ [to burn rubbish] feu.

Bonfire Night n *UK* le 5 novembre *(commémoration de la tentative de Guy Fawkes de faire sauter le Parlement en 1605)*.

bongo [ˈbɒŋgəʊ] (pl -s OR -es) n : **bongo (drum)** bongo *m*.

bonhomie [ˈbɒnəmiː] n *fml* bonhomie *f*.

bonk [bɒŋk] *v inf hum* ■ vi s'envoyer en l'air.
■ vt s'envoyer en l'air avec.
■ n partie *f* de jambes en l'air.

bonkers [ˈbɒŋkəz] adj *UK inf* fou *(before vowel or silent 'h'* **fol***)* (folle), cinglé(e).

Bonn [bɒn] n Bonn.

bonnet [ˈbɒnɪt] n **1.** *UK* [of car] capot *m* **2.** [hat] bonnet *m*.

bonny [ˈbɒnɪ] (comp -ier, superl -iest) adj *Scot* beau (belle), joli(e).

bonus [ˈbəʊnəs] (pl -es [-iːz]) n **1.** [extra money] prime *f*, gratification *f* **2.** *fig* [added advantage] plus *m*.

bonus issue n *UK* FIN émission *f* d'actions gratuites.

bony [ˈbəʊnɪ] (comp -ier, superl -iest) adj **1.** [person, hand, face] maigre, osseux(euse) **2.** [meat] plein(e) d'os ⁄ [fish] plein(e) d'arêtes.

boo [buː] ■ excl hou!
■ n (pl -s) huée *f*.
■ vt & vi huer.

boob [buːb] *UK*, ***boo-boo*** [buːbuː] n *inf* [mistake] gaffe *f*, bourde *f*.
◆ ***boobs*** npl *v inf* nichons *mpl*.

boob tube n **1.** *UK* [garment] bustier *m* **2.** *US inf* télé *f*.

booby prize [ˈbuːbɪ-] n prix *m* de consolation.

booby trap [ˈbuːbɪ-] n **1.** [bomb] objet *m* piégé **2.** [practical joke] farce *f*.
◆ ***booby-trap*** vt piéger.

boogie [ˈbuːgɪ] *inf* ■ n : **to have a boogie** danser.
■ vi danser.

boohoo [ˌbuːˈhuː] *inf* ■ vi pleurer à chaudes larmes, chialer.
■ excl *hum* sniff.

book [bʊk] ■ n **1.** [for reading] livre *m* ▸ **book lover** bibliophile *mf* ▸ **mathematics is a closed book to me** je ne comprends rien aux mathématiques ▸ **to do sthg by the book** faire qqch selon les règles ▸ **he can read her like a**

book pour lui elle est transparente ▸ **to throw the book at sb** donner le maximum à qqn **2.** [of stamps, tickets, cheques] carnet *m* / [of matches] pochette *f*.
■ **vt 1.** [reserve - gen] réserver / [- performer] engager ▸ **to be fully booked** être complet(ète) ▸ **have you already booked your trip?** avez-vous déjà fait les réservations pour votre voyage? **2.** [engage] embaucher, engager ▸ **he's booked solid until next week** il est complètement pris jusqu'à la semaine prochaine **3.** *inf* [subj: police] coller un PV à ▸ **he was booked for speeding** il a attrapé une contravention pour excès de vitesse **4.** *UK* FOOTBALL prendre le nom de.
■ **vi** réserver.
◆ ***books*** **npl** COMM livres *mpl* de comptes ▸ **to do the books** tenir les livres ▸ **to be in sb's bad books** être mal vu(e) de qqn ▸ **to be in sb's good books** être dans les petits papiers de qqn.
◆ ***book in*** *UK* ■ **vt sep** réserver une chambre à.
■ **vi** [at hotel] prendre une chambre.
◆ ***book up*** **vt sep** réserver, retenir.

bookable ['bʊkəbl] **adj** *UK* **1.** [seats, tickets] qu'on peut réserver *OR* louer **2.** FOOTBALL [offence] pour laquelle l'arbitre donne un carton jaune.

bookbinding ['bʊk,baɪndɪŋ] **n** reliure *f*.

bookcase ['bʊkkeɪs] **n** bibliothèque *f*.

book club **n** club *m* de livres.

bookend ['bʊkend] **n** serre-livres *m inv*, presse-livres *m inv*.

Booker Prize ['bʊkə-] **n : the Booker Prize** *prix littéraire britannique*.

bookie ['bʊkɪ] **n** *inf* bookmaker *m*, book *m*.

booking ['bʊkɪŋ] **n 1.** [reservation] réservation *f* **2.** *UK* FOOTBALL **: to get a booking** recevoir un carton jaune.

booking clerk **n** *UK* préposé *m*, -e *f* à la location *OR* la vente des billets.

booking office **n** *UK* bureau *m* de réservation *OR* location.

bookish ['bʊkɪʃ] **adj** [person] studieux(euse), qui aime la lecture.

bookkeeper ['bʊk,kiːpər] **n** comptable *mf*.

bookkeeping ['bʊk,kiːpɪŋ] **n** comptabilité *f*.

booklet ['bʊklɪt] **n** brochure *f*.

bookmaker ['bʊk,meɪkər] **n** bookmaker *m*.

bookmark ['bʊkmɑːk] **n** signet *m*.

bookseller ['bʊk,selər] **n** libraire *mf*.

bookshelf ['bʊkʃelf] (**pl -shelves** [-ʃelvz]) **n** rayon *m* *OR* étagère *f* à livres.

bookshop *UK* ['bʊkʃɒp], ***bookstore*** *esp US* ['bʊkstɔːr] **n** librairie *f*.

bookstall ['bʊkstɔːl] **n** *UK* kiosque *m* (à journaux).

bookstand ['bʊkstænd] **n** *US* [furniture] bibliothèque *f* / [small shop] étalage *m* de bouquiniste / [in station] kiosque *m* à journaux.

bookstore ['bʊkstɔːr] *esp US* = ***bookshop***.

book token **n** *UK* chèque-livre *m*.

bookworm ['bʊkwɜːm] **n** rat *m* de bibliothèque.

boom [buːm] ■ **n 1.** [loud noise] grondement *m* **2.** [in business, trade] boom *m* **3.** NAUT bôme *f* **4.** [for TV camera, microphone] girafe *f*, perche *f*.
■ **vi 1.** [make noise] gronder **2.** [business, trade] être en plein essor *OR* en hausse.

boom and bust (cycle) **n** ECON cycle *m* expansion-récession.

boom box **n** *esp US inf* grand radiocassette *m* portatif.

boomerang ['buːməræŋ] **n** boomerang *m*.

booming ['buːmɪŋ] ■ **adj 1.** [sound] retentissant(e) **2.** [business] prospère, en plein essor.
■ **n** [gen] retentissement *m* / [of guns, thunder] grondement *m* / [of waves] grondement *m*, mugissement *m* / [of organ] ronflement *m* / [of voice] rugissement *m*, grondement *m*.

boom town **n** ville *f* en plein essor, ville-champignon *f*.

boon [buːn] **n** avantage *m*, bénédiction *f*.

boor [bʊər] **n** butor *m*, rustre *m*.

boorish ['bʊərɪʃ] **adj** rustre, grossier(ère).

boost [buːst] ■ **n** [to production, sales] augmentation *f* / [to economy] croissance *f* ▸ **to give a boost to** stimuler.
■ **vt 1.** [production, sales] accroître, stimuler **2.** [popularity] accroître, renforcer ▸ **to boost sb's spirits** *OR* **morale** remonter le moral à qqn.

booster ['buːstər] **n** MED rappel *m* ▸ **booster shot** piqûre *f* de rappel.

booster seat **n** AUT (siège *m*) rehausseur *m*.

boot [buːt] ■ **n 1.** [for walking, sport] chaussure *f* **2.** [fashion item] botte *f* **3.** *UK* [of car] coffre *m*.
■ **vt** *inf* flanquer des coups de pied à.
◆ ***to boot*** **adv** par-dessus le marché, en plus.
◆ ***boot out*** **vt sep** *inf* flanquer à la porte.

boot camp **n** *US inf* MIL camp *m* d'entraînement pour nouvelles recrues.

booth [buːð] **n 1.** [at fair] baraque *f* foraine **2.** [telephone booth] cabine *f* **3.** [voting booth] isoloir *m*.

bootleg ['buːtleg] **adj** *inf* [recording] pirate / [whisky] de contrebande.

bootlegger ['buːt,legər] **n** *inf* contrebandier *m* d'alcool.

bootlicker ['buːt,lɪkər] **n** *inf* lèche-bottes *mf inv*.

booty ['buːtɪ] **n** butin *m*.

booze [buːz] *inf* ■ **n** *(U)* alcool *m*, boisson *f* alcoolisée.
■ **vi** picoler, lever le coude.

boozer ['buːzər] **n** *inf* **1.** [person] picoleur *m*, -euse *f* **2.** *UK* [pub] pub *m*.

boozy ['buːzɪ] (**comp -ier, superl -iest**) **adj** *inf* [person] soûlard(e) / [party, evening] de soûlographie.

bop [bɒp] *inf* ■ **n 1.** [hit] coup *m* **2.** [disco, dance] boum *f*.
■ **vt** (**pt & pp -ped, cont -ping**) [hit] taper, donner un coup à.
■ **vi** (**pt & pp -ped, cont -ping**) [dance] danser.

border ['bɔːdər] ■ **n 1.** [between countries] frontière **2.** [edge] bord *m* **3.** [in garden] bordure *f*.
■ **vt 1.** [country] toucher à, être limitrophe de **2.** [edge] border.
◆ ***border on*** **vt insep** friser, être voisin(e) de.

borderline ['bɔːdəlaɪn] ■ **adj : borderline case** cas *m* limite.
■ **n** *fig* limite *f*, ligne *f* de démarcation.

bore [bɔːʳ] ■ **pt** ➤ ***bear***.
■ **n 1.** [person] raseur *m*, -euse *f* / [situation, event] corvée *f* **2.** [of gun] calibre *m*.
■ **vt 1.** [not interest] ennuyer, raser ▸ **to bore sb stiff** *OR* **to tears** *OR* **to death** ennuyer qqn à mourir **2.** [drill] forer, percer.

bored [bɔːd] **adj** [person] qui s'ennuie / [look] d'ennui ▸ **to be bored with** en avoir assez de ▸ **I'm bored with this book** ce livre m'ennuie.

boredom ['bɔːdəm] **n** *(U)* ennui *m*.

boring ['bɔːrɪŋ] **adj** ennuyeux(euse), assommant(e).

born [bɔːn] **adj** né(e) ▸ **to be born** naître ▸ **I was born in 1965** je suis né(e) en 1965 ▸ **when were you born?** quelle est ta date de naissance? ▸ **born and bred** né(e) et élevé(e).

-born **suffix** originaire de.

born-again Christian **n** évangéliste *mf*.

borne [bɔːn] **pp** ➤ ***bear***.

Borneo ['bɔːnɪəʊ] **n** Bornéo *m* ▸ **in Borneo** à Bornéo.

borough ['bʌrə] **n** municipalité *f*.

borrow ['bɒrəʊ] **vt** emprunter ▸ **to borrow sthg (from sb)** emprunter qqch (à qqn).

borrower ['bɒrəʊəʳ] **n** emprunteur *m*, -euse *f*.

borrowing ['bɒrəʊɪŋ] **n** emprunt *m*.

Bosnia ['bɒznɪə] **n** Bosnie *f* ▸ **in Bosnia** en Bosnie.

Bosnia-Herzegovina [-ˌhɜːtsəgə'viːnə] **n** Bosnie-Herzégovine *f*.

Bosnian ['bɒznɪən] ■ **adj** bosniaque.
■ **n** Bosniaque *mf*.

bosom ['bʊzəm] **n** ANAT poitrine *f*, seins *mpl* / *fig* sein *m* ▸ **bosom friend** ami *m*, -e *f* intime.

Bosporus ['bɒspərəs], ***Bosphorus*** ['bɒsfərəs] **n : the Bosporus** le Bosphore.

boss [bɒs] ■ **n** patron *m*, -onne *f*, chef *m* ▸ **I'll show you who's boss!** je vais te montrer qui est le chef! ▸ **to be one's own boss** travailler à son compte.
■ **vt** *pej* donner des ordres à, régenter.
◆ ***boss about***, ***boss around*** **vt sep** *pej* donner des ordres à, régenter.

boss-eyed **adj** *UK inf* qui louche.

bossy ['bɒsɪ] (**comp -ier**, **superl -iest**) **adj** *pej* autoritaire.

bosun ['bəʊsn] = ***boatswain***.

botanic(al) [bə'tænɪk(l)] **adj** botanique.

botanical garden **n** jardin *m* botanique.

botanist ['bɒtənɪst] **n** botaniste *mf*.

botany ['bɒtənɪ] **n** botanique *f*.

botch [bɒtʃ] ◆ ***botch up*** **vt sep** *inf* bousiller, saboter.

both [bəʊθ] ■ **adj** les deux.
■ **pron : both (of them)** (tous) les deux ((toutes) les deux) ▸ **both of us are coming** on vient tous les deux.
■ **adv : she is both intelligent and amusing** elle est à la fois intelligente et drôle.

bother ['bɒðəʳ] ■ **vt 1.** [worry] ennuyer, inquiéter ▸ **to bother o.s. (about)** se tracasser (au sujet de) ▸ **I can't be bothered to do it** *esp UK* je n'ai vraiment pas envie de le faire **2.** [pester, annoy] embêter ▸ **I'm sorry to bother you** excusez-moi de vous déranger.
■ **vi : to bother about sthg** s'inquiéter de qqch ▸ **don't bother (to do it)** ce n'est pas la peine (de le faire) ▸ **don't bother getting up** ne vous donnez pas la peine de vous lever.
■ **n** *(U) esp UK* embêtement *m* ▸ **I hope I'm not putting you to any bother** j'espère que je ne vous cause pas trop de dérangement ▸ **it's no bother at all** cela ne me dérange *OR* m'ennuie pas du tout.

bothered ['bɒðəd] **adj** inquiet(ète) ▸ **I am really bothered that so many people are unemployed** cela m'inquiète que tant de personnes soient au chômage ▸ **I am bothered about it** *OR* **I am bothered by it** *UK* cela me dérange.

Botox® ['bəʊtɒks] **n** *(U)* MED Botox *m*.

Botswana [bɒ'tswɑːnə] **n** Botswana *m* ▸ **in Botswana** au Botswana.

bottle ['bɒtl] ■ **n 1.** [gen] bouteille *f* / [for medicine, perfume] flacon *m* / [for baby] biberon *m* **2.** *(U) UK inf* [courage] cran *m*, culot *m*.
■ **vt** [wine] mettre en bouteilles / [fruit] mettre en bocal.
◆ ***bottle out*** **vi** *UK inf* se dégonfler.
◆ ***bottle up*** **vt sep** [feelings] refouler, contenir.

bottle bank **n** *UK* container *m* pour verre usagé.

bottled ['bɒtld] **adj** en bouteille.

bottle-fed **adj** élevé(e) *OR* allaité(e) au biberon.

bottle-feed **vt** allaiter *OR* nourrir au biberon.

bottleneck ['bɒtlnek] **n 1.** [in traffic] bouchon *m*, embouteillage *m* **2.** [in production] goulet *m* d'étranglement.

bottle-opener **n** ouvre-bouteilles *m inv*, décapsuleur *m*.

bottle party **n** soirée *f (où chacun apporte quelque chose à boire)*.

bottom ['bɒtəm] ■ **adj 1.** [lowest] du bas ▸ **the bottom half of the chart** la partie inférieure du tableau ▸ **the bottom floor** le rez-de-chaussée ▸ **the bottom end of the table** le bas de la table
2. [in class] dernier(ère) ▸ **the bottom half of the class/list** la deuxième moitié de la classe/liste.
■ **n 1.** [of bottle, lake, garden] fond *m* / [of page, ladder, street] bas *m* / [of hill] pied *m* ▸ **at the bottom of page one** au bas de la *OR* en bas de page un ▸ **at the bottom of the street/garden** au bout de la rue/du jardin ▸ **I believe, at the bottom of my heart, that...** je crois, au fond de moi-même, que...
2. [of scale] bas *m* / [of class] dernier *m*, -ère *f* ▸ **he's (at the) bottom of his class** il est le dernier de sa classe ▸ **you're at the bottom of the list** vous êtes en queue de liste ▸ **you have to start at the bottom and work your way up** vous devez commencer au plus bas et monter dans la hiérarchie à la force du poignet
3. [buttocks] derrière *m*
4. [cause] **: what's at the bottom of it?** qu'est-ce qui en est la cause? ▸ **to get to the bottom of sthg** aller au fond de qqch, découvrir la cause de qqch ▸ **I'm sure she's at the bottom of all this** je suis sûr que c'est elle qui est à l'origine de cette histoire

5. [of two-piece garment] bas *m* ▸ **pyjama bottoms** bas de pyjama.
◆ ***bottom out*** vi atteindre son niveau le plus bas.

bottomless ['bɒtəmlɪs] adj **1.** [very deep] sans fond **2.** [endless] inépuisable.

bottom line n *fig* : **the bottom line** l'essentiel *m*.

bottommost ['bɒtəmməʊst] adj le plus bas (la plus basse).

bottom-of-the-range adj bas (basse) de gamme.

botulism ['bɒtjʊlɪzm] n botulisme *m*.

bough [baʊ] n branche *f*.

bought [bɔːt] pt & pp ➤ ***buy***.

boulder ['bəʊldər] n rocher *m*.

boulevard ['buːləvɑːd] n boulevard *m*.

bounce [baʊns] ■ vi **1.** [ball] rebondir / [person] sauter ▸ **the ball bounced down the steps** la balle a rebondi de marche en marche **2.** [light] être réfléchi(e) / [sound] être renvoyé(e) **3.** *inf* [cheque] être sans provision.
■ vt **1.** [ball] faire rebondir ▸ **he bounced the baby on his knee** il a fait sauter l'enfant sur son genou **2.** *inf* [cheque] : **the bank bounced my cheque** la banque a refusé mon chèque.
■ n rebond *m*.
◆ ***bounce back*** vi *fig* se remettre vite.

bouncer ['baʊnsər] n *inf* videur *m*.

bouncy ['baʊnsɪ] (comp -ier, superl -iest) adj **1.** [lively] dynamique **2.** [ball] qui rebondit / [bed] élastique, souple.

bound [baʊnd] ■ pt & pp ➤ ***bind***.
■ adj **1.** [certain] : **he's bound to win** il va sûrement gagner ▸ **she's bound to see it** elle ne peut pas manquer de le voir ▸ **it was bound to happen** c'était à prévoir ▸ **but he's bound to say that** mais il est certain que c'est cela qu'il va dire
2. [obliged] : **to be bound to do sthg** être obligé(e) *OR* tenu(e) de faire qqch ▸ **I'm bound to say/admit that...** je dois dire/reconnaître que... ▸ **they are bound by the treaty to take action** l'accord les oblige à prendre des mesures ▸ **the teacher felt bound to report them** l'enseignant s'est cru obligé de les dénoncer
3. [for place] : **to be bound for** [subj: person] être en route pour / [subj: plane, train] être à destination de.
■ n [leap] bond *m*, saut *m*.
■ vt : **to be bounded by** [subj: field] être limité(e) *OR* délimité(e) par / [subj: country] être limitrophe de ▸ **a country bounded on two sides by the sea** un pays limité par la mer de deux côtés.
■ vi [leap] bondir, sauter ▸ **the children bounded into/out of the classroom** les enfants sont entrés dans/sortis de la salle de classe en faisant des bonds.
◆ ***bounds*** npl limites *fpl* ▸ **the situation has gone beyond the bounds of all reason** la situation est devenue complètement aberrante *OR* insensée ▸ **her rage knew no bounds** sa colère était sans bornes ▸ **within the bounds of possibility** dans la limite du possible ▸ **out of bounds** interdit, défendu.

-bound suffix **1.** [restricted] confiné (e) ▸ **house-bound** confiné à la maison ▸ **snow-bound road** route *f* complètement enneigée **2.** [heading towards] : **a south-bound train** un train en partance pour le Sud ▸ **city-bound traffic** circulation *f* en direction du centre-ville.

boundary ['baʊndərɪ] (pl -ies) n [gen] frontière *f* / [of property] limite *f*, borne *f*.

boundless ['baʊndlɪs] adj illimité(e), sans bornes.

bountiful ['baʊntɪfʊl] adj *liter* [ample] abondant(e).

bounty ['baʊntɪ] n *liter* [generosity] générosité *f*, libéralité *f*.

bouquet [bʊ'keɪ] n bouquet *m*.

bourbon ['bɜːbən] n bourbon *m*.

bourgeois ['bɔːʒwɑː] adj *pej* bourgeois(e).

bout [baʊt] n **1.** [of illness] accès *m* ▸ **a bout of flu** une grippe **2.** [session] période *f* ▸ **a bout of drinking** une beuverie **3.** [boxing match] combat *m*.

boutique [buː'tiːk] n boutique *f*.

bovine ['bəʊvaɪn] ■ adj *lit* & *fig* bovin(e).
■ n bovin *m*.

bovver boots npl *UK inf dated* brodequins *mpl*, rangers *mpl*.

bovver boy n *UK inf dated* loubard *m*.

bow[1] [baʊ] ■ n **1.** [in greeting] révérence *f* ▸ **to take a bow** saluer **2.** [of ship] proue *f*, avant *m*.
■ vt [head] baisser, incliner.
■ vi **1.** [make a bow] saluer **2.** [defer] : **to bow to** s'incliner devant.
◆ ***bow down*** vi s'incliner.
◆ ***bow out*** vi tirer sa révérence.

bow[2] [bəʊ] n **1.** [weapon] arc *m* **2.** MUS archet *m* **3.** [knot] nœud *m* ▸ **tie it in a bow** faites un nœud.

bowel ['baʊəl] n [human] intestin *m* / [animal] boyau *m*, intestin *m* ▸ **a bowel disorder** troubles *mpl* intestinaux.
◆ ***bowels*** npl ANAT intestins *mpl* / *fig* entrailles *fpl* ▸ **the bowels of the earth** les entrailles de la terre.

bowl [bəʊl] ■ n **1.** [container - gen] jatte *f*, saladier *m* / [- small] bol *m* / [- for washing up] cuvette *f* ▸ **sugar bowl** sucrier *m* **2.** [of toilet, sink] cuvette *f* / [of pipe] fourneau *m*.
■ vt CRICKET lancer.
■ vi CRICKET lancer la balle.
◆ ***bowls*** n *(U)* boules *fpl (sur herbe)*.
◆ ***bowl over*** vt sep *lit* & *fig* renverser.

bow-legged [ˌbəʊ'legɪd] adj aux jambes arquées.

bowler ['bəʊlər] n **1.** CRICKET lanceur *m* **2.** *UK* : **bowler (hat)** chapeau *m* melon.

bowlful ['bəʊlfʊl] n bol *m*.

bowling ['bəʊlɪŋ] n *(U)* bowling *m*.

bowling alley n [building] bowling *m* / [alley] piste *f* de bowling.

bowling green n terrain *m* de boules *(sur herbe)*.

bow tie [bəʊ-] n nœud *m* papillon.

bow window [bəʊ-] n fenêtre *f* en saillie.

box [bɒks] ■ n **1.** [gen] boîte *f* **2.** THEAT loge *f* **3.** *UK inf* [television] : **the box** la télé.
■ vi boxer, faire de la boxe.
◆ ***box in*** vt sep **1.** [trap] coincer **2.** [enclose - pipes] encastrer.

boxed [bɒkst] **adj** en boîte, en coffret.

boxer ['bɒksəʳ] **n** **1.** [fighter] boxeur *m*, -euse *f* **2.** [dog] boxer *m*.

boxer shorts **npl** boxer-short *m*.

boxing ['bɒksɪŋ] **n** boxe *f*.

Boxing Day **n** *le 26 décembre*.

boxing glove **n** gant *m* de boxe.

boxing ring **n** ring *m*.

box junction **n** *UK* carrefour *m* à l'accès réglementé.

box number **n** numéro *m* d'annonce, référence *f*.

box office **n** bureau *m* de location.

boxroom ['bɒksrʊm] **n** *UK* débarras *m*.

boy [bɔɪ] ■ **n** **1.** [male child] garçon *m* **2.** *inf* [male friend] **: I'm going out with the boys tonight** je sors avec mes potes ce soir.
■ **excl** *inf* **: (oh) boy!** ben, mon vieux!, ben, dis-donc!

boycott ['bɔɪkɒt] ■ **n** boycott *m*, boycottage *m*.
■ **vt** boycotter.

boyfriend ['bɔɪfrend] **n** copain *m*, petit ami *m*.

boyhood ['bɔɪhʊd] **n** enfance *f*.

boyish ['bɔɪɪʃ] **adj** **1.** [appearance - of man] gamin(e) / [- of woman] de garçon **2.** [behaviour] garçonnier(ère).

boy scout **n** scout *m*, éclaireur *m*.

bozo ['bəʊzəʊ] **n** *inf pej* type *m*.

Bp (abbr of ***Bishop***) Mgr.

Br (abbr of ***brother***) RELIG F.

BR (abbr of ***British Rail***) **n** ≃ SNCF *f*.

bra [brɑː] **n** soutien-gorge *m*.

brace [breɪs] ■ **n** **1.** [on teeth] appareil *m* (dentaire) **2.** [on leg] appareil *m* orthopédique **3.** [pair] paire *f*, couple *m*.
■ **vt** **1.** [steady] soutenir, consolider ▸ **to brace o.s.** s'accrocher, se cramponner **2.** *fig* [prepare] **: to brace o.s. (for sthg)** se préparer (à qqch).
◆ ***braces*** **npl** **1.** *UK* [for trousers] bretelles *fpl* **2.** [for teeth] appareil *m* dentaire *OR* orthodontique.

bracelet ['breɪslɪt] **n** bracelet *m*.

bracing ['breɪsɪŋ] **adj** vivifiant(e).

bracken ['brækn] **n** fougère *f*.

bracket ['brækɪt] ■ **n** **1.** [support] support *m* **2.** [parenthesis - round] parenthèse *f* / [- square] crochet *m* ▸ **in brackets** entre parenthèses/crochets **3.** [group] **: age/income bracket** tranche *f* d'âge/de revenus.
■ **vt** **1.** [enclose in brackets] mettre entre parenthèses/crochets **2.** [group] **: to bracket sb/sthg (together) with** mettre qqn/qqch dans le même groupe que.

brackish ['brækɪʃ] **adj** saumâtre.

brag [bræg] (pt & pp **-ged**, cont **-ging**) **vi** se vanter.

braid [breɪd] ■ **n** **1.** [on uniform] galon *m* **2.** *esp US* [of hair] tresse *f*, natte *f*.
■ **vt** *esp US* [hair] tresser, natter.

braille [breɪl] **n** braille *m*.

brain [breɪn] **n** cerveau *m* ▸ **he's got money on the brain** il ne pense qu'à l'argent.
◆ ***brains*** **npl** [intelligence] intelligence *f* ▸ **to pick sb's brains** faire appel aux lumières de qqn ▸ **to rack** *OR* **cudgel one's brains** se creuser la tête *OR* la cervelle.

CONFUSABLE / PARONYME

brain

When translating **brain**, note that *cerveau* and *cervelle* are not interchangeable. *Cerveau* refers to the organ, whereas generally *cervelle* refers to brain matter or brain power.

brainbox ['breɪnbɒks] **n** *UK inf dated* [person] cerveau *m*.

brainchild ['breɪntʃaɪld] **n** *inf* idée *f* personnelle, invention *f* personnelle.

brain dead **adj** dans un coma dépassé ▸ **he's brain dead** *inf pej* il n'a rien dans le cerveau.

brain death **n** mort *f* cérébrale, coma *m* dépassé.

brain drain **n** fuite *f* *OR* exode *m* des cerveaux.

brainless ['breɪnlɪs] **adj** stupide.

brainpower ['breɪn,paʊəʳ] **n** intelligence *f*.

brainstorm ['breɪnstɔːm] **n** **1.** *UK* [mental aberration] moment *m* d'aberration **2.** *US* [brilliant idea] idée *f* géniale *OR* de génie.

brainstorming ['breɪn,stɔːmɪŋ] **n** brainstorming *m*, remue-méninges *m inv*.

brainteaser ['breɪn,tiːzəʳ] **n** colle *f*.

brainwash ['breɪnwɒʃ] **vt** faire un lavage de cerveau à.

brainwashing ['breɪnwɒʃɪŋ] **n** lavage *m* de cerveau.

brainwave ['breɪnweɪv] **n** *UK* idée *f* géniale *OR* de génie.

brainy ['breɪnɪ] (comp **-ier**, superl **-iest**) **adj** *inf* intelligent(e).

braise [breɪz] **vt** braiser.

brake [breɪk] ■ **n** *lit* & *fig* frein *m*.
■ **vi** freiner.

brake horsepower **n** puissance *f* de freinage.

brake light **n** stop *m*, feu *m* arrière.

brake lining **n** garniture *f* de frein.

brake pedal **n** (pédale *f* de) frein *m*.

brake shoe **n** sabot *m* *OR* patin *m* de frein.

bramble ['bræmbl] **n** [bush] ronce *f* / *UK* [fruit] mûre *f*.

bran [bræn] **n** son *m*.

branch [brɑːntʃ] ■ **n** **1.** [of tree, subject] branche *f* **2.** [of railway] bifurcation *f*, embranchement *m* **3.** [of company] filiale *f*, succursale *f* / [of bank] agence *f*.
■ **vi** bifurquer.
◆ ***branch off*** **vi** bifurquer.
◆ ***branch out*** **vi** [person, company] étendre ses activités, se diversifier.

branch line **n** RAIL ligne *f* secondaire.

brand [brænd] ■ **n 1.** COMM marque *f* **2.** *fig* [type, style] type *m*, genre *m*.
■ **vt 1.** [cattle] marquer au fer rouge **2.** *fig* [classify] **: to brand sb (as) sthg** étiqueter qqn comme qqch, coller à qqn l'étiquette de qqch.

brand building **n** création *f* de marque.

brand familiarity **n** connaissance *f* de la marque.

brand image **n** image *f* de marque.

brandish ['brændɪʃ] **vt** brandir.

brand leader **n** marque *f* dominante.

brand loyalty **n** fidélité *f* à la marque.

brand name **n** marque *f*.

brand-new **adj** flambant neuf (flambant neuve), tout neuf (toute neuve).

brand recognition **n** identification *f* de la marque.

brandy ['brændɪ] (**pl -ies**) **n** cognac *m*.

brash [bræʃ] **adj** effronté(e).

Brasilia [brə'zɪljə] **n** Brasilia.

brass [brɑːs] **n 1.** [metal] laiton *m*, cuivre *m* jaune **2.** MUS **: the brass** les cuivres *mpl*.

brass band **n** fanfare *f*.

brasserie ['bræsərɪ] **n** brasserie *f*.

brassiere [*UK* 'bræsɪəʳ, *US* brə'zɪr] **n** soutien-gorge *m*.

brass knuckles **npl** *US* coup-de-poing *m* américain.

brass tacks **npl** *inf* **: to get down to brass tacks** en venir aux choses sérieuses.

brat [bræt] **n** *inf pej* sale gosse *m*.

brat pack **n** [gen] jeunes loups *mpl* / CIN *terme désignant les jeunes acteurs populaires des années 80*.

bravado [brə'vɑːdəʊ] **n** bravade *f*.

brave [breɪv] ■ **adj** courageux(euse), brave.
■ **n** guerrier *m* indien, brave *m*.
■ **vt** braver, affronter.

bravely ['breɪvlɪ] **adv** courageusement, vaillamment.

bravery ['breɪvərɪ] **n** courage *m*, bravoure *f*.

bravo [ˌbrɑː'vəʊ] **excl** bravo!

bravura [brə'vʊərə] **n** [gen & MUS] bravoure *f*.

brawl [brɔːl] **n** bagarre *f*, rixe *f*.

brawn [brɔːn] **n** *(U)* **1.** [muscle] muscle *m* **2.** *UK* [meat] fromage *m* de tête.

brawny ['brɔːnɪ] (**comp -ier, superl -iest**) **adj** musclé(e).

bray [breɪ] **vi** [donkey] braire.

brazen ['breɪzn] **adj** [person] effronté(e), impudent(e) / [lie] éhonté(e).
◆ ***brazen out*** **vt sep : to brazen it out** crâner.

brazier ['breɪzjəʳ] **n** brasero *m*.

Brazil [brə'zɪl] **n** Brésil *m* ▸ **in Brazil** au Brésil.

Brazilian [brə'zɪljən] ■ **adj** brésilien(enne).
■ **n** Brésilien *m*, -enne *f*.

brazil nut **n** noix *f* du Brésil.

breach [briːtʃ] ■ **n 1.** [of law, agreement] infraction *f*, violation *f* / [of promise] rupture *f* ▸ **to be in breach of sthg** enfreindre *OR* violer qqch ▸ **breach of confidence** abus *m* de confiance ▸ **breach of contract** rupture *f* de contrat **2.** [opening, gap] trou *m*, brèche *f* ▸ **she stepped into the breach when I fell ill** elle m'a remplacé au pied levé quand je suis tombé malade **3.** [in friendship, marriage] brouille *f*.
■ **vt 1.** [agreement, contract] rompre **2.** [make hole in] faire une brèche dans.

breach of the peace **n** atteinte *f* à l'ordre public.

bread [bred] **n** pain *m* ▸ **bread and butter** [food] tartine *f* beurrée, pain *m* beurré / *fig* gagne-pain *m*.

bread bin *UK*, ***bread box*** *US* **n** boîte *f* à pain.

breadboard ['bredbɔːd] **n** planche *f* à pain.

bread box *US* = ***bread bin***.

breadcrumbs ['bredkrʌmz] **npl** chapelure *f*.

breaded ['bredɪd] **adj** pané(e).

breadline ['bredlaɪn] **n : to be on the breadline** être sans ressources *OR* sans le sou.

breadstick ['bredstɪk] **n** gressin *m*.

breadth [bretθ] **n 1.** [width] largeur *f* **2.** *fig* [scope] ampleur *f*, étendue *f*.

breadwinner ['bredˌwɪnəʳ] **n** soutien *m* de famille.

break [breɪk] ■ **n 1.** [gap] **: break (in)** trouée *f* (dans) ▸ **a break in the clouds** une éclaircie
2. [fracture] fracture *f* ▸ **a clean break** [in object] une cassure nette / [in bone] une fracture simple
3. [change] **: a break with tradition** une rupture d'avec la tradition ▸ **to make a clean break with the past** rompre avec le passé
4. [pause - gen] pause *f* / *UK* [- at school] récréation *f* ▸ **to take a break** [- short] faire une pause / [- longer] prendre des jours de congé ▸ **without a break** sans interruption ▸ **to have a break from doing sthg** arrêter de faire qqch ▸ **you need a break** [- short rest] tu as besoin de faire une pause / [- holiday] tu as besoin de vacances ▸ **a break for commercials, a (commercial) break** RADIO un intermède de publicité / TV un écran publicitaire, une page de publicité ▸ **lunch break** pause *f* de midi
5. *inf* [luck] **: (lucky) break** chance *f*, veine *f* ▸ **to have a bad break** manquer de veine
6. *liter* [of day] **: at (the) break of day** au point du jour, l'aube
7. COMPUT [key] break *m*.
■ **vt** (**pt broke, pp broken**) **1.** [gen] casser, briser ▸ **to break one's arm/leg** se casser le bras/la jambe ▸ **the fall broke his back** la chute lui a brisé les reins ▸ **is the bone broken?** y a-t-il une fracture? ▸ **the river broke its banks** la rivière est sortie de son lit ▸ **to break cover** [animal] être débusqué / [person] sortir à découvert ▸ **to break a habit** se défaire d'une (mauvaise) habitude ▸ **to break sb's heart** briser le cœur à qqn ▸ **to break sb's hold** se dégager de l'étreinte de qqn ▸ **to break new ground** innover, faire œuvre de pionnier ▸ **to break a record** battre un record ▸ **to break a strike** briser une grève ▸ **break a leg!** *inf* merde! *(pour souhaiter bonne chance à un acteur)*
2. [journey] interrompre ▸ **we broke our journey at Brussels** nous avons fait une étape à Bruxelles

3. [contact, silence] rompre ▸ **a cry broke the silence** un cri a déchiré *OR* percé le silence
4. [not keep - law, rule] enfreindre, violer / [- promise] manquer à ▸ **he broke his word to her** il a manqué à la parole qu'il lui avait donnée
5. [tell] **: to break the news (of sthg to sb)** annoncer la nouvelle (de qqch à qqn) ▸ **break it to her gently** annonce-le lui avec ménagement
6. TENNIS **: to break sb's serve** prendre le service de qqn.
■ **vi** (pt **broke**, pp **broken**) **1.** [gen] se casser, se briser ▸ **to break loose** *OR* **free** se dégager, s'échapper ▸ **the ship broke loose from its moorings** le bateau a rompu ses amarres
2. [pause] s'arrêter, faire une pause ▸ **let's break for coffee** arrêtons-nous pour prendre un café
3. [day] poindre, se lever
4. [weather] se gâter
5. [wave] se briser
6. [voice - with emotion] se briser / [- at puberty] muer
7. [news] se répandre, éclater
8. SPORT [boxers] se dégager / [ball] dévier / [in billiards, pool] donner l'acquit
⏭ **to break even** rentrer dans ses frais.
◆ ***break away*** **vi 1.** [escape] s'échapper
2. [end relationship] **: to break away from sb** abandonner qqn, quitter qqn.
◆ ***break down*** ■ **vt sep 1.** [destroy - barrier] démolir / [- door] enfoncer
2. [analyse] analyser
3. [substance] décomposer.
■ **vi 1.** [car, machine] tomber en panne / [resistance] céder / [negotiations] échouer
2. [emotionally] fondre en larmes, éclater en sanglots
3. [decompose] se décomposer.
◆ ***break in*** ■ **vi 1.** [burglar] entrer par effraction
2. [interrupt] **: to break in (on sb/sthg)** interrompre (qqn/qqch).
■ **vt sep 1.** [horse] dresser / [person] rompre, accoutumer
2. [shoes] faire.
◆ ***break into*** **vt insep 1.** [subj: burglar] entrer par effraction dans
2. [begin] **: to break into song/applause** se mettre à chanter/applaudir
3. [become involved in] **: to break into a market** pénétrer un marché ▸ **to break into the music business** percer dans la chanson.
◆ ***break off*** ■ **vt sep 1.** [detach] détacher
2. [talks, relationship] rompre / [holiday] interrompre.
■ **vi 1.** [become detached] se casser, se détacher
2. [stop talking] s'interrompre, se taire
3. [stop working] faire une pause, s'arrêter de travailler.
◆ ***break out*** **vi 1.** [begin - fire] se déclarer / [- fighting] éclater
2. [skin, person] **: to break out in spots** se couvrir de boutons
3. [escape] **: to break out (of)** s'échapper (de), s'évader (de).
◆ ***break through*** ■ **vt insep** [subj: sun] percer ▸ **she broke through the crowd** elle se fraya un chemin à travers la foule.
■ **vi** [sun] percer.
◆ ***break up*** ■ **vt sep 1.** [into smaller pieces] mettre en morceaux
2. [end - marriage, relationship] détruire / [- fight, party] mettre fin à.
■ **vi 1.** [into smaller pieces - gen] se casser en morceaux / [- ship] se briser
2. [end - marriage, relationship] se briser / [- talks, party] prendre fin / [- school] finir, fermer ▸ **to break up (with sb)** rompre (avec qqn)
3. [crowd] se disperser.
◆ ***break with*** **vt insep : to break with tradition** rompre avec la tradition.

breakable ['breɪkəbl] **adj** cassable, fragile.
breakage ['breɪkɪdʒ] **n** bris *m*.
breakaway ['breɪkəweɪ] **adj** [faction] dissident(e).
breakdance ['breɪkdɑ:ns] **n** smurf *m*.
◆ ***break-dance*** **vi** danser le smurf.
break dancing **n** smurf *m*.
breakdown ['breɪkdaʊn] **n 1.** [of vehicle, machine] panne *f* / [of negotiations] échec *m* / [in communications] rupture *f* ▸ **nervous breakdown** dépression *f* nerveuse
2. [analysis] détail *m*.
breakdown lorry, breakdown truck **n** *UK* dépanneuse *f*.
breaker ['breɪkəʳ] **n** [wave] brisant *m*.
break-even **adj : break-even point** seuil *m* de rentabilité, point *m* mort ▸ **break-even price** prix *m* d'équilibre.
breakfast ['brekfəst] ■ **n** petit déjeuner *m*.
■ **vi : to breakfast (on)** déjeuner (de).
breakfast cereal **n** céréales *fpl*.
breakfast room **n** salle *f* du petit déjeuner.
breakfast television **n** *UK* télévision *f* du matin.
break-in **n** cambriolage *m*.
breaking ['breɪkɪŋ] **n : breaking and entering** LAW entrée *f* par effraction.
breaking point **n** limite *f*.
breakneck ['breɪknek] **adj : at breakneck speed** à fond de train.
breakthrough ['breɪkθru:] **n** percée *f*.
breakup ['breɪkʌp] **n** [of marriage, relationship] rupture *f*.
breakup value **n** COMM valeur *f* liquidative.
bream [bri:m] (pl **bream** *OR* **-s**) **n** brème *f*.
breast [brest] **n 1.** [of woman] sein *m* / [of man] poitrine *f*
2. [meat of bird] blanc *m*
⏭ **to make a clean breast of it** tout avouer.
breast-fed **adj** nourri(e) au sein.
breast-feed **vt & vi** allaiter.
breast-feeding **n** allaitement *m* au sein.
breast milk **n** *(U)* lait *m* maternel.
breast pocket **n** poche *f* de poitrine.
breaststroke ['breststrəʊk] **n** brasse *f*.
breath [breθ] **n** souffle *m*, haleine *f* ▸ **to take a deep breath** inspirer profondément ▸ **to go out for a breath of (fresh) air** sortir prendre l'air ▸ **she/it was a breath of fresh air** elle représentait/c'était une véritable bouffée d'oxygène ▸ **out of breath** hors d'haleine, à bout de

souffle ▸ **to get one's breath back** reprendre haleine *OR* son souffle ▸ **to hold one's breath** *lit* & *fig* retenir son souffle ▸ **it took my breath away** cela m'a coupé le souffle.

breathable ['bri:ðəbl] **adj** respirable.

breathalyse *UK*, ***-yze*** *US* ['breθəlaɪz] **vt** ≃ faire subir l'Alcootest® à.

Breathalyser® *UK*, ***-yzer***® *US* **n** Alcootest® *m*.

breathe [bri:ð] ■ **vi** respirer ▸ **to breathe heavily** *OR* **deeply** [after exertion] souffler *OR* respirer bruyamment / [during illness] respirer péniblement ▸ **I can breathe more easily now** *fig* je respire maintenant.

■ **vt 1.** [inhale] respirer ▸ **she breathed a sigh of relief** elle poussa un soupir de soulagement **2.** [give out - smell] souffler des relents de.

◆ ***breathe in*** **vi** & **vt sep** inspirer.

◆ ***breathe out*** **vi** & **vt sep** expirer.

breather ['bri:ðəʳ] **n** *inf* moment *m* de repos *OR* répit.

breathing ['bri:ðɪŋ] **n** respiration *f*, souffle *m*.

breathing space **n** *fig* répit *m*.

breathless ['breθlɪs] **adj 1.** [out of breath] hors d'haleine, essoufflé(e) **2.** [with excitement] fébrile, fiévreux(euse).

breathtaking ['breθ,teɪkɪŋ] **adj** à vous couper le souffle.

breath test **n** Alcootest® *m*.

breathy ['breθɪ] (**comp -ier**, **superl -iest**) **adj** [generally] qui respire bruyamment / MUS qui manque d'attaque.

breed [bri:d] (**pt** & **pp bred** [bred]) ■ **n** *lit* & *fig* race *f*, espèce *f*.

■ **vt 1.** [animals, plants] élever **2.** *fig* [suspicion, contempt] faire naître, engendrer.

■ **vi** se reproduire.

breeder ['bri:dəʳ] **n** éleveur *m*, -euse *f*.

breeder reactor **n** surgénérateur *m*.

breeding ['bri:dɪŋ] **n** *(U)* **1.** [of animals, plants] élevage *m* **2.** [manners] bonnes manières *fpl*, savoir-vivre *m*.

breeding-ground **n** *fig* terrain *m* propice.

breeze [bri:z] ■ **n** brise *f*.

■ **vi : to breeze in/out** [quickly] entrer/sortir en coup de vent / [casually] entrer/sortir d'un air désinvolte.

breezeblock ['bri:zblɒk] **n** *UK* parpaing *m*.

breezy ['bri:zɪ] (**comp -ier**, **superl -iest**) **adj 1.** [windy] venteux(euse) **2.** [cheerful] jovial(e), enjoué(e).

Breton ['bretn] ■ **adj** breton(onne).

■ **n 1.** [person] Breton *m*, -onne *f* **2.** [language] breton *m*.

brevity ['brevɪtɪ] **n** brièveté *f*.

brew [bru:] ■ **vt** [beer] brasser / [tea] faire infuser / [coffee] préparer, faire.

■ **vi 1.** [tea] infuser / [coffee] se faire **2.** *fig* [trouble, storm] se préparer, couver.

brewer ['bru:əʳ] **n** brasseur *m*.

brewery ['brʊərɪ] (**pl -ies**) **n** brasserie *f*.

briar [braɪəʳ] **n** églantier *m*.

bribe [braɪb] ■ **n** pot-de-vin *m*.

■ **vt : to bribe sb (to do sthg)** soudoyer qqn (pour qu'il fasse qqch).

bribery ['braɪbərɪ] **n** corruption *f*.

bric-à-brac ['brɪkəbræk] ■ **n** bric-à-brac *m*.

■ **comp : a bric-à-brac shop/stall** une boutique/un éventaire de brocanteur.

brick [brɪk] **n** brique *f*.

◆ ***brick up*** **vt sep** murer.

bricklayer ['brɪk,leɪəʳ] **n** maçon *m*.

brick-red **adj** rouge brique *(inv)*.

brickwork ['brɪkwɜ:k] **n** briquetage *m*.

bridal ['braɪdl] **adj** [dress] de mariée / [suite] nuptial(e).

bride [braɪd] **n** mariée *f*.

bridegroom ['braɪdgrʊm] **n** marié *m*.

bridesmaid ['braɪdzmeɪd] **n** demoiselle *f* d'honneur.

bride-to-be **n** future mariée *f*.

bridge [brɪdʒ] ■ **n 1.** [gen] pont *m* ▸ **I'll cross that bridge when I come to it** chaque chose en son temps **2.** [on ship] passerelle *f* **3.** [of nose] arête *f* **4.** [card game, for teeth] bridge *m*.

■ **vt** *fig* [gap] réduire.

bridging loan ['brɪdʒɪŋ-] **n** *UK* crédit-relais *m*.

bridle ['braɪdl] ■ **n** bride *f*.

■ **vt** mettre la bride à, brider.

■ **vi : to bridle (at sthg)** se rebiffer (contre qqch).

bridle path **n** piste *f* cavalière.

brief [bri:f] ■ **adj 1.** [short] bref (brève), court(e) **2.** [revealing] très court(e).

■ **n 1.** LAW affaire *f*, dossier *m* ▸ **he took our brief** il a accepté de plaider notre cause **2.** *UK* [instructions] instructions *fpl* ▸ **my brief was to develop sales** la tâche *OR* la mission qui m'a été confiée était de développer les ventes.

■ **vt : to brief sb (on)** [bring up to date] mettre qqn au courant (de) / [instruct] briefer qqn (sur).

◆ ***briefs*** **npl** slip *m*.

◆ ***in brief*** **adv** en bref, en deux mots.

briefcase ['bri:fkeɪs] **n** serviette *f*.

briefing ['bri:fɪŋ] **n** instructions *fpl*, briefing *m*.

briefly ['bri:flɪ] **adv 1.** [for a short time] un instant **2.** [concisely] brièvement.

Brig. abbr of ***brigadier***.

brigade [brɪ'geɪd] **n** brigade *f* ▸ **fire brigade** *UK* pompiers *mpl*.

brigadier [,brɪgə'dɪəʳ] **n** général *m* de brigade.

bright [braɪt] **adj 1.** [room] clair(e) / [light, colour] vif (vive) / [sunlight] éclatant(e) ▸ **the weather will get brighter later** le temps s'améliorera en cours de journée ▸ **cloudy with bright intervals** nuageux avec des éclaircies **2.** [eyes, future] brillant(e) ▸ **to be bright and breezy** avoir l'air en pleine forme ▸ **to look on the bright side** prendre les choses du bon côté, être optimiste **3.** [intelligent] intelligent(e) ▸ **a bright idea** une idée géniale *OR* lumineuse.

◆ ***brights*** **npl** *US inf* feux *mpl* de route, phares *mpl*.

◆ ***bright and early*** **adv** de bon matin.

brighten ['braɪtn] **vi 1.** [become lighter] s'éclaircir **2.** [face, mood] s'éclairer.

◆ ***brighten up*** ■ **vt sep** égayer.

■ **vi 1.** [person] s'égayer, s'animer **2.** [weather] se dégager, s'éclaircir.

brightly ['braɪtlɪ] **adv** **1.** [shine] avec éclat **2.** [coloured] vivement **3.** [cheerfully] gaiement.

brightness ['braɪtnɪs] **n** [of light, colour] éclat *m* / [of TV] intensité *f*.

bright spark **n** *UK inf* [clever person] lumière *f*.

brilliance ['brɪljəns] **n** **1.** [cleverness] intelligence *f* **2.** [of colour, light] éclat *m*.

brilliant ['brɪljənt] **adj** **1.** [gen] brillant(e) **2.** [colour] éclatant(e) **3.** *inf* [wonderful] super *(inv)*, génial(e).

brilliantly ['brɪljəntlɪ] **adv** **1.** [cleverly] brillamment **2.** [coloured] vivement **3.** [shine] avec éclat.

Brillo pad® ['brɪləʊ-] **n** ≃ tampon *m* Jex®.

brim [brɪm] ■ **n** bord *m*.
■ **vi** (pt & pp **-med**, cont **-ming**) **: to brim with** *lit* & *fig* être plein(e) de.
◆ ***brim over*** **vi : to brim over (with)** *lit* & *fig* déborder (de).

brine [braɪn] **n** saumure *f*.

bring [brɪŋ] (pt & pp **brought**) **vt** **1.** [person] amener ▸ **her father's bringing her home today** son père la ramène à la maison aujourd'hui / **: that brings us to the next question** cela nous amène à la question suivante **2.** [object] apporter ▸ **I'll bring the books (across) tomorrow** j'apporterai les livres demain ▸ **did you bring anything with you?** as-tu apporté quelque chose? ▸ **he brought his dog with him** il a emmené son chien ▸ **black musicians brought jazz to Europe** les musiciens noirs ont introduit le jazz en Europe ▸ **that brings the total to £350** cela fait 350 livres en tout **3.** [cause - happiness, shame] entraîner, causer ▸ **it brings bad/good luck** ça porte malheur/bonheur ▸ **money does not always bring happiness** l'argent ne fait pas toujours le bonheur ▸ **to bring sthg to an end** mettre fin à qqch ▸ **to bring sthg into question** mettre *OR* remettre qqch en question ▸ **to bring sthg to sb's attention** *OR* **knowledge** *OR* **notice** attirer l'attention de qqn sur qqch ▸ **to bring sb to his/her senses** ramener qqn à la raison ▸ **the story brought tears to my eyes** l'histoire m'a fait venir les larmes aux yeux ▸ **who knows what the future will bring?** qui sait ce que l'avenir nous réserve? **4.** LAW **: to bring charges against sb** porter plainte contre qqn ▸ **to bring an action** *OR* **a suit against sb** intenter un procès à *OR* contre qqn ▸ **to be brought to trial** comparaître en justice ▸ **the case was brought before the court** l'affaire a été déférée au tribunal
▸▸ **I couldn't bring myself to do it** je ne pouvais me résoudre à le faire.
◆ ***bring about*** **vt sep** causer, provoquer.
◆ ***bring along*** **vt sep** [person] amener / [object] apporter.
◆ ***bring around*** **vt sep** [make conscious] ranimer.
◆ ***bring back*** **vt sep** **1.** [object] rapporter / [person] ramener **2.** [memories] rappeler **3.** [reinstate] rétablir.
◆ ***bring down*** **vt sep** **1.** [plane] abattre / [government] renverser **2.** [prices] faire baisser.
◆ ***bring forward*** **vt sep** **1.** [gen] avancer **2.** [in bookkeeping] reporter.
◆ ***bring in*** **vt sep** **1.** [law] introduire **2.** [money - subj: person] gagner / [- subj: deal] rapporter **3.** LAW [verdict] rendre.
◆ ***bring off*** **vt sep** [plan] réaliser, réussir / [deal] conclure, mener à bien.
◆ ***bring on*** **vt sep** [cause] provoquer, causer ▸ **you've brought it on yourself** tu l'as cherché.
◆ ***bring out*** **vt sep** **1.** [product] lancer / [book] publier, faire paraître **2.** [cause to appear] faire ressortir.
◆ ***bring round*** *UK*, ***bring to*** **vt sep** = ***bring around***.
◆ ***bring up*** **vt sep** **1.** [raise - children] élever **2.** [mention] mentionner **3.** [vomit] rendre, vomir.

CONFUSABLE / PARONYME
bring
When translating **to bring**, note that *amener* and *apporter* are not interchangeable. *Amener* is used with animate objects and *apporter* with inanimate objects.

bring-and-buy **n** *UK* **: bring-and-buy (sale)** *brocante de particuliers en Grande-Bretagne*.

brink [brɪŋk] **n : on the brink of** au bord de, à la veille de.

brisk [brɪsk] **adj** **1.** [quick] vif (vive), rapide **2.** [busy] **: business is brisk** les affaires marchent bien **3.** [manner, tone] déterminé(e) **4.** [wind] frais (fraîche).

brisket ['brɪskɪt] **n** poitrine *f* de bœuf.

briskly ['brɪsklɪ] **adv** **1.** [quickly] d'un bon pas **2.** [efficiently, confidently] avec détermination.

bristle ['brɪsl] ■ **n** poil *m*.
■ **vi** *lit* & *fig* se hérisser.
◆ ***bristle with*** **vt insep** grouiller de.

bristly ['brɪslɪ] (comp **-ier**, superl **-iest**) **adj** aux poils raides.

Brit [brɪt] (abbr of ***Briton***) **n** *inf* Britannique *mf*.

Britain ['brɪtn] **n** Grande-Bretagne *f* ▸ **in Britain** en Grande-Bretagne.

British ['brɪtɪʃ] ■ **adj** britannique.
■ **npl : the British** les Britanniques *mpl*.

British Broadcasting Corporation **n : the British Broadcasting Corporation** la BBC.

British Columbia [kə'lʌmbɪə] **n** Colombie-Britannique *f* ▸ **in British Columbia** en Colombie-Britannique.

British Council **n : the British Council** *organisme public chargé de promouvoir la langue et la culture anglaises*.

Britisher ['brɪtɪʃər] **n** *US inf* Anglais *m*, -e *f*, Britannique *mf*.

British Isles **npl : the British Isles** les îles *fpl* Britanniques.

British Library **n** *la bibliothèque nationale britannique*.

British Rail **n** *société des chemins de fer britanniques*, ≃ SNCF *f*.

British Summer Time **n** heure *f* d'été *(en Grande-Bretagne)*.

British Telecom [-'telɪkɒm] **n** *société britannique de télécommunications*.

Briton ['brɪtn] **n** Britannique *mf*.

Britpop ['brɪtpɒp] n *tendance musicale des années 1990 en Grande-Bretagne.*

Brittany ['brɪtənɪ] n Bretagne *f* ▸ **in Brittany** en Bretagne.

brittle ['brɪtl] adj fragile.

Bro [brəʊ] = ***Br.***

broach [brəʊtʃ] vt [subject] aborder.

broad [brɔːd] adj **1.** [wide - gen] large / [- range, interests] divers(e), varié(e) ▸ **we offer a broad range of products** nous offrons une large *OR* grande gamme de produits **2.** [description] général(e) ▸ **here is a broad outline** voilà les grandes lignes ▸ **his books still have a very broad appeal** ses livres plaisent toujours à *OR* intéressent toujours un vaste public **3.** [hint] transparent(e) / [accent] prononcé(e).
◆ ***in broad daylight*** adv en plein jour.

B-road n *UK* ≃ route *f* départementale *OR* secondaire.

broadband ['brɔːdbænd] n COMPUT diffusion *f* en larges bandes de fréquence.
◆ ***broadband*** adj à larges bandes.

broad bean n fève *f*, gourgane *f* ***Québec***.

broad-brush adj : **a broad-brush approach** une approche grossière.

broadcast ['brɔːdkɑːst] (pt & pp **broadcast**) ■ n RADIO & TV émission *f*.
■ vt RADIO radiodiffuser, diffuser / TV téléviser.

broadcaster ['brɔːdkɑːstər] n personnalité *f* de la télévision/de la radio.

broadcasting ['brɔːdkɑːstɪŋ] n *(U)* RADIO radiodiffusion *f* / TV télévision *f*.

broaden ['brɔːdn] ■ vt élargir.
■ vi s'élargir.
◆ ***broaden out*** ■ vt sep élargir.
■ vi s'élargir, s'étendre.

broad jump *US* n = ***long jump.***

broadly ['brɔːdlɪ] adv **1.** [generally] généralement ▸ **broadly speaking** généralement parlant **2.** [smile] jusqu'aux oreilles.

broadly-based [-'beɪst] adj varié(e), divers(e).

broad-minded [-'maɪndɪd] adj large d'esprit ▸ **to be broad-minded** avoir les idées larges ▸ **he has very broad-minded parents** ses parents sont très tolérants *OR* larges d'esprit.

broad-mindedness [-'maɪndɪdnɪs] n largeur *f* d'esprit.

broadsheet ['brɔːdʃiːt] n journal *m* de qualité.

brocade [brə'keɪd] n brocart *m*.

broccoli ['brɒkəlɪ] n *(U)* brocoli *m*.

brochure ['brəʊʃər] n brochure *f*, prospectus *m*.

brogues [brəʊgz] npl *chaussures lourdes souvent ornées de petits trous.*

broil [brɔɪl] vt *US* griller, faire cuire au gril.

broiler ['brɔɪlər] n **1.** [young chicken] poulet *m* (à rôtir) **2.** *US* [pan] gril *m*.

broke [brəʊk] ■ pt ➤ ***break.***
■ adj *inf* fauché(e) ▸ **to go broke** [company] faire faillite ▸ **to go for broke** risquer le tout pour le tout.

broken ['brəʊkn] ■ pp ➤ ***break.***
■ adj **1.** [gen] cassé(e) ▸ **to have a broken leg** avoir la jambe cassée ▸ **broken heart** cœur brisé ▸ **to die of a broken heart** mourir de chagrin **2.** [interrupted - journey, sleep] interrompu(e) / [- line] brisé(e) **3.** [promise] non respecté(e) **4.** [marriage] brisé(e), détruit(e) / [home] désuni(e) **5.** [hesitant] : **to speak in broken English** parler un anglais hésitant.

broken-down adj **1.** [not working] en panne **2.** [dilapidated] délabré(e).

broker ['brəʊkər] n courtier *m*, -ière *f* ▸ **(insurance) broker** assureur *m*, courtier, -ière *f* d'assurances.

brokerage ['brəʊkərɪdʒ] n courtage *m*.

brolly ['brɒlɪ] (pl **-ies**) n *UK inf* pépin *m*.

bronchitis [brɒŋ'kaɪtɪs] n *(U)* bronchite *f*.

bronze [brɒnz] ■ adj [colour] (couleur) bronze *(inv)*.
■ n **1.** [gen] bronze *m* **2.** = ***bronze medal.***
■ comp en bronze.

bronzed [brɒnzd] adj bronzé(e).

bronze medal n médaille *f* de bronze.

bronze medallist n : **he's the bronze medallist** il a remporté la médaille de bronze.

brooch [brəʊtʃ] n broche *f*.

brood [bruːd] ■ n **1.** [of animals] couvée *f* **2.** [of children] nichée *f*, marmaille *f*.
■ vi : **to brood (over** *OR* **about sthg)** ressasser (qqch), remâcher (qqch).

broody ['bruːdɪ] (comp **-ier**, superl **-iest**) adj **1.** [sad] triste, cafardeux(euse) **2.** [hen] couveuse ▸ **to feel broody** *UK inf fig* être en mal d'enfant.

brook [brʊk] ■ n ruisseau *m*.
■ vt *fml* tolérer, souffrir.

broom [bruːm] n balai *m*.

broomstick ['bruːmstɪk] n manche *m* à balai.

Bros, **bros** (abbr of **brothers**) Frères.

broth [brɒθ] n bouillon *m*.

brothel ['brɒθl] n bordel *m*.

brother ['brʌðər] ■ n frère *m*.
■ excl *inf* ben, dis-donc!

brotherhood ['brʌðəhʊd] n **1.** [companionship] fraternité *f* **2.** [organization] confrérie *f*, société *f*.

brother-in-law (pl **brothers-in-law**) n beau-frère *m*.

brotherly ['brʌðəlɪ] adj fraternel(elle).

brought [brɔːt] pt & pp ➤ ***bring.***

brow [braʊ] n **1.** [forehead] front *m* **2.** [eyebrow] sourcil *m* ▸ **to knit one's brows** froncer les sourcils **3.** [of hill] sommet *m*.

browbeat ['braʊbiːt] (pt **browbeat**, pp **-en**) vt rudoyer, brutaliser.

browbeaten ['braʊbiːtn] adj opprimé(e), tyrannisé(e).

brown [braʊn] ■ **adj 1.** [colour] brun(e), marron *(inv)* **2.** [tanned] bronzé(e), hâlé(e).
■ **n** [colour] marron *m*, brun *m* ▸ **in brown** en marron.
■ **vt** [food] faire dorer.

brown bread **n** *(U)* pain *m* complet **OR** bis.

brown goods **npl** COMM *biens de consommation de taille moyenne tels que téléviseur, radio ou magnétoscope.*

brownie ['braʊnɪ] **n 1.** [elf] lutin *m*, farfadet *m* **2.** [cake] brownie *m*.
◆ ***Brownie (Guide)*** **n** ≃ jeannette *f*.

Brownie point ['braʊnɪ-] **n** *inf* bon point *m*.

brownout ['braʊnaʊt] **n** *US* [electric failure] baisse *f* de tension.

brown paper **n** papier *m* d'emballage, papier kraft.

brown rice **n** riz *m* complet.

brown sugar **n** sucre *m* roux.

browse [braʊz] ■ **vi 1.** [look] **: I'm just browsing** [in shop] je ne fais que regarder ▸ **to browse through** [magazine] feuilleter **2.** [animal] brouter **3.** COMPUT naviguer.
■ **vt** [file, document] parcourir ▸ **to browse a site** COMPUT naviguer sur un site.

browser ['braʊzəʳ] **n** COMPUT navigateur *m*, browser *m*.

bruise [bru:z] ■ **n** bleu *m*.
■ **vt 1.** [skin, arm] se faire un bleu à / [fruit] taler **2.** *fig* [pride] meurtrir, blesser.
■ **vi** [person] se faire un bleu / [fruit] se taler.

bruised [bru:zd] **adj 1.** [skin, arm] qui a des bleus / [fruit] talé(e) **2.** *fig* [pride] meurtri(e), blessé(e).

bruiser ['bru:zəʳ] **n** *inf* [big man] malabar *m* / [fighter] cogneur *m*.

Brum [brʌm] **n** *UK inf surnom donné à la ville de Birmingham.*

Brummie, Brummy ['brʌmɪ] **n** *UK inf habitant de Birmingham.*

brunch [brʌntʃ] **n** brunch *m*.

Brunei ['bru:naɪ] **n** Brunei *m* ▸ **in Brunei** au Brunei.

brunette [bru:'net] **n** brunette *f*.

brunt [brʌnt] **n : to bear OR take the brunt of** subir le plus gros de.

bruschetta [brʊs'ketə] **n** CULIN bruschette *f*.

brush [brʌʃ] ■ **n 1.** [gen] brosse *f* / [of painter] pinceau *m* **2.** [encounter] **: to have a brush with the police** avoir des ennuis avec la police.
■ **vt 1.** [clean with brush] brosser **2.** [move with hand] **: he brushed away some crumbs** il a enlevé quelques miettes (avec sa main) **3.** [touch lightly] effleurer.
◆ ***brush aside*** **vt sep** *fig* écarter, repousser.
◆ ***brush off*** **vt sep** [dismiss] envoyer promener.
◆ ***brush up*** ■ **vt sep** [revise] réviser.
■ **vi : to brush up on sthg** réviser qqch.

brushed [brʌʃt] **adj** [metal] poli(e) / [cotton, nylon] peigné(e).

brush-off **n** *inf* **: to give sb the brush-off** envoyer promener qqn.

brush-up **n** *UK inf* **: to have a wash and brush-up** se donner un coup de peigne.

brushwood ['brʌʃwʊd] **n** *(U)* brindilles *fpl*.

brushwork ['brʌʃwɜ:k] **n** *(U)* [of painter] touche *f*.

brusque, *US* ***brusk*** [bru:sk] **adj** brusque.

brusquely, *US* ***bruskly*** ['bru:sklɪ] **adv** [abruptly] avec brusquerie / [curtly] avec brusquerie **OR** rudesse, brutalement.

Brussels ['brʌslz] **n** Bruxelles.

brussels sprout **n** chou *m* de Bruxelles.

brutal ['bru:tl] **adj** brutal(e).

brutality [bru:'tælətɪ] (pl **-ies**) **n** brutalité *f*.

brutalize, *UK* ***-ise*** ['bru:təlaɪz] **vt** brutaliser.

brutally ['bru:təlɪ] **adv** [attack, kill, treat] brutalement, sauvagement / [say] brutalement, franchement / [cold] extrêmement ▸ **she gave a brutally honest account of events** elle a raconté les événements avec une franchise brutale **OR** un réalisme brutal.

brute [bru:t] ■ **adj** [force] brutal(e).
■ **n** brute *f*.

brutish ['bru:tɪʃ] **adj 1.** [animal-like] animal(e), bestial(e) **2.** [cruel] brutal(e), violent(e) / [coarse] grossier(ère).

bs abbr of ***bill of sale***.

BS (abbr of ***Bachelor of Science***) **n** *US* = ***BSc***.

BSA (abbr of ***Boy Scouts of America***) **n** *association américaine de scouts.*

BSc (abbr of ***Bachelor of Science***) **n** *UK* [degree] ≃ licence *f* en **OR** ès sciences / [person] ≃ licencié *m*, -e *f* en **OR** ès sciences.

BSE (abbr of ***bovine spongiform encephalopathy***) **n** EBS *f*.

BSI (abbr of ***British Standards Institution***) **n** *association britannique de normalisation*, ≃ AFNOR *f*.

B-side **n** face *f* B.

BST **1.** (abbr of ***British Summer Time***) *heure d'été britannique* **2.** (abbr of ***British Standard Time***) *heure officielle britannique.*

BT (abbr of ***British Telecom***) **n** *société britannique de télécommunications.*

Bt. abbr of ***baronet***.

btu (abbr of ***British thermal unit***) **n** *unité de chaleur (1055 joules).*

BTW (abbr of ***by the way***) **adv** *inf* à propos.

bubble ['bʌbl] ■ **n** bulle *f*.
■ **vi 1.** [liquid] faire des bulles, bouillonner **2.** *fig* [person] **: to bubble with** déborder de.

bubble bath **n** bain *m* moussant.

bubble economy **n** économie *f* de bulle.

bubble gum **n** bubble-gum *m*.

bubblejet printer ['bʌbldʒet-] **n** imprimante *f* à jet d'encre.

bubble pack **n** [for toy, batteries] emballage *m* pelliculé / [for pills] plaquette *f*.

bubble wrap **n** emballage-bulle *m*.

bubbly ['bʌblɪ] ■ **adj** (comp **-ier**, superl **-iest**) **1.** [water] pétillant(e) **2.** *fig* [lively] plein(e) de vie.
■ **n** *inf* champagne *m*.

Bucharest [ˌbju:kə'rest] **n** Bucarest.

buck [bʌk] ■ **n 1.** [male animal] mâle *m* **2.** *US inf* [dollar] dollar *m* ▸ **to make a fast buck** gagner facilement du fric **3.** *inf* [responsibility] **: the buck stops here** maintenant, j'en prends la responsabilité ▸ **to pass the buck** refiler la responsabilité.
■ **vt 1.** [subj: horse] désarçonner d'une ruade **2.** *inf* [trend] **: to buck the trend** aller à contre-courant.
■ **vi** [horse] ruer.
◆ ***buck up*** *inf* ■ **vt sep 1.** *UK* [improve] **: buck your ideas up!** reprenez-vous! **2.** [cheer up] **: to buck sb up** remonter le moral à qqn.
■ **vi 1.** *UK dated* [hurry up] se remuer, se dépêcher **2.** [cheer up] ne pas se laisser abattre.

bucket ['bʌkɪt] **n 1.** [gen] seau *m* **2.** *inf* [lots] **: buckets of rain** des trombes d'eau ▸ **he has buckets of charm** il a énormément de charme ▸ **she has buckets of money** elle est pleine aux as.

bucket shop **n 1.** FIN bureau *m* OR maison *f* de contrepartie, bureau *m* de courtiers marrons **2.** *UK* [travel agency] *organisme de vente de billets d'avion à prix réduit*.

Buckingham Palace ['bʌkɪŋəm-] **n** le palais de Buckingham *(résidence officielle du souverain britannique)*.

buckle ['bʌkl] ■ **n** boucle *f*.
■ **vt 1.** [fasten] boucler **2.** [bend] voiler.
■ **vi** [wheel] se voiler / [knees, legs] se plier.
◆ ***buckle down*** **vi : to buckle down (to)** s'atteler (à).

Bucks [bʌks] (abbr of ***Buckinghamshire***) *comté anglais*.

buck's fizz **n** *UK cocktail composé de champagne et de jus d'orange*.

buckshot ['bʌkʃɒt] **n** chevrotine *f*.

buckskin ['bʌkskɪn] **n** *(U)* peau *f* de daim.

buckteeth [ˌbʌk'ti:θ] **npl** dents *fpl* en avant.

buckwheat ['bʌkwi:t] **n** blé *m* noir.

bud [bʌd] ■ **n** bourgeon *m* ▸ **to nip sthg in the bud** *fig* écraser OR étouffer qqch dans l'œuf.
■ **vi** (pt & pp **-ded**, cont **-ding**) bourgeonner.

Budapest [ˌbju:də'pest] **n** Budapest.

Buddha ['bʊdə] **n** Bouddha *m*.

Buddhism ['bʊdɪzm] **n** bouddhisme *m*.

Buddhist ['bʊdɪst] ■ **adj** bouddhiste.
■ **n** bouddhiste *mf*.

budding ['bʌdɪŋ] **adj** [writer, artist] en herbe.

buddy ['bʌdɪ] (pl **-ies**) **n** *inf* pote *m*.

budge [bʌdʒ] ■ **vt** faire bouger.
■ **vi** bouger.

budgerigar ['bʌdʒərɪgɑ:r] **n** perruche *f*.

budget ['bʌdʒɪt] ■ **adj** [holiday, price] pour petits budgets.
■ **n** budget *m* ▸ **the Budget** *UK* le budget.
■ **vt** budgétiser.
■ **vi** préparer un budget.
◆ ***budget for*** **vt insep** prévoir.

budget account **n** *UK* compte-crédit *m*.

budgetary ['bʌdʒɪtrɪ] **adj** budgétaire.

budget constraint **n** contrainte *f* budgétaire.

budget cuts **n** coupes *fpl* budgétaires.

budget deficit **n** déficit *m* budgétaire.

budget forecast **n** prévisions *fpl* budgétaires.

budgie ['bʌdʒɪ] **n** *inf* perruche *f*.

Buenos Aires [ˌbwenəs'aɪrɪz] **n** Buenos Aires.

buff [bʌf] ■ **adj** [brown] chamois *(inv)*.
■ **n** *inf* [expert] mordu *m*, -e *f*.

buffalo ['bʌfələʊ] (pl **buffalo, -es** OR **-s**) **n** buffle *m* / *US* bison *m*.

buffer ['bʌfər] **n 1.** [gen] tampon *m* **2.** COMPUT mémoire *f* tampon.

buffer state **n** État *m* tampon.

buffer zone **n** région *f* tampon.

buffet[1] [*UK* 'bʊfeɪ, *US* bə'feɪ] **n** [food, cafeteria] buffet *m*.

buffet[2] ['bʌfɪt] **vt** [physically] frapper.

buffet car ['bʊfeɪ-] **n** *UK* wagon-restaurant *m*.

buffoon [bə'fu:n] **n** bouffon *m*.

bug [bʌg] ■ **n 1.** [insect] punaise *f* **2.** *inf* [germ] microbe *m* **3.** *inf* [listening device] micro *m* **4.** COMPUT bogue *m*, bug *m* **5.** [enthusiasm] **: the travel bug** le virus des voyages.
■ **vt** (pt & pp **-ged**, cont **-ging**) **1.** *inf* [telephone] mettre sur table d'écoute / [room] cacher des micros dans **2.** *inf* [annoy] embêter.

bugbear ['bʌgbeər] **n** cauchemar *m*.

bug-free **adj** COMPUT [program] exempt (e) d'erreurs OR de bogues.

bugger ['bʌgər] *UK v inf* ■ **n 1.** [person] con *m*, conne *f* **2.** [job] **: this job's a real bugger!** ce travail est vraiment chiant!
■ **excl** merde!
■ **vt : bugger it!** merde alors!
◆ ***bugger off*** **vi** *UK v inf* **: bugger off!** fous le camp!

bugger all **n** *UK v inf* que dalle.

buggered ['bʌgəd] **adj** *UK v inf* **1.** [broken] foutu(e) **2.** [in surprise] **: well, I'll be buggered!** merde alors! **3.** [in annoyance] **: buggered if I know** j'en sais foutre rien.

buggy ['bʌgɪ] (pl **-ies**) **n 1.** [carriage] boghei *m* **2.** [pushchair] poussette *f* / *US* [pram] landau *m*.

bugle ['bju:gl] **n** clairon *m*.

build [bɪld] ■ **vt** (pt & pp **built**) *lit & fig* construire, bâtir ▸ **houses are being built** des maisons sont en construction.
■ **n** carrure *f* ▸ **of medium build** de taille OR corpulence moyenne.
◆ ***build into*** **vt sep 1.** CONSTR encastrer dans **2.** [include in] inclure dans.
◆ ***build on, build upon*** ■ **vt insep** [success] tirer avantage de.
■ **vt sep** [base on] baser sur.
◆ ***build up*** ■ **vt sep** [business] développer / [reputation] bâtir ▸ **to build up one's strength** reprendre des forces.
■ **vi** [clouds] s'amonceler / [traffic] augmenter.

builder ['bɪldər] **n** entrepreneur *m*, -euse *f*.

building ['bɪldɪŋ] **n** bâtiment *m*.

building and loan association **n** *US société d'épargne et de financement immobilier.*

building block **n 1.** [toy] cube *m* **2.** *fig* [element] élément *m*, composante *f*.

building contractor **n** entrepreneur *m*.

building site **n** chantier *m*.

building society **n** *UK* ≃ société *f* d'épargne et de financement immobilier.

buildup ['bɪldʌp] **n** [increase] accroissement *m*.

built [bɪlt] ■ **pt & pp** ➤ ***build***.
■ **adj** bâti(e).

built-in **adj 1.** CONSTR encastré(e) **2.** [inherent] inné(e).

built-up **adj : built-up area** agglomération *f*.

bulb [bʌlb] **n 1.** ELEC ampoule *f* **2.** BOT oignon *m* **3.** [of thermometer] cuvette *f*.

bulbous ['bʌlbəs] **adj** bulbeux(euse).

Bulgaria [bʌl'geərɪə] **n** Bulgarie *f* ▸ **in Bulgaria** en Bulgarie.

Bulgarian [bʌl'geərɪən] ■ **adj** bulgare.
■ **n 1.** [person] Bulgare *mf* **2.** [language] bulgare *m*.

bulge [bʌldʒ] ■ **n 1.** [lump] bosse *f* **2.** [in sales] croissance *f* soudaine.
■ **vi : to bulge (with)** être gonflé (e) (de).

bulging ['bʌldʒɪŋ] **adj** [pocket, bag] bourré(e), plein(e) à craquer / [muscles] gonflé(e).

bulimia (nervosa) [bjʊ'lɪmɪə (nɜː'vəʊsə)] **n** boulimie *f*.

bulk [bʌlk] ■ **n 1.** [mass] volume *m* **2.** [of person] corpulence *f* **3.** COMM **: in bulk** en gros **4.** [majority] **: the bulk of** le plus gros de.
■ **adj** en gros.

bulk buying **n** *(U)* achat *m* en gros.

bulkhead ['bʌlkhed] **n** cloison *f*.

bulk mail **n** *(U)* envois *mpl* en nombre.

bulky ['bʌlkɪ] (**comp -ier**, **superl -iest**) **adj** volumineux(euse).

bull [bʊl] **n 1.** [male cow] taureau *m* / [male elephant, seal] mâle *m* **2.** FIN haussier *m* **3.** *(U) esp US v inf* [nonsense] conneries *fpl*.

bulldog ['bʊldɒg] **n** bouledogue *m*.

bulldog clip® **n** *UK* pince *f* à dessin.

bulldoze ['bʊldəʊz] **vt 1.** CONSTR passer au bulldozer **2.** *fig* [force] **: to bulldoze one's way** forcer son chemin ▸ **to bulldoze sb into doing sthg** contraindre *OR* forcer qqn à faire qqch.

bulldozer ['bʊldəʊzəʳ] **n** bulldozer *m*.

bullet ['bʊlɪt] **n** [for gun] balle *f*.

bulletin ['bʊlətɪn] **n** bulletin *m*.

bulletin board **n 1.** *esp US* [generally] tableau *m* d'affichage **2.** COMPUT **: bulletin board (system)** babillards *mpl*.

bulletproof ['bʊlɪtpruːf] ■ **adj** [glass, vest] pare-balles *(inv)* / [vehicle] blindé(e).
■ **vt** [door, vehicle] blinder.

bullfight ['bʊlfaɪt] **n** corrida *f*.

bullfighter ['bʊlˌfaɪtəʳ] **n** toréador *mf*.

bullfighting ['bʊlˌfaɪtɪŋ] **n** *(U)* [activity] courses *fpl* de taureaux / [art] tauromachie *f*.

bullfinch ['bʊlfɪntʃ] **n** bouvreuil *m*.

bullhorn ['bʊlhɔːn] *US* = ***loudhailer***.

bullion ['bʊljən] **n** *(U)* **: gold bullion** or *m* en barres.

bullish ['bʊlɪʃ] **adj** FIN à la hausse.

bull market **n** FIN marché *m* à la hausse.

bullock ['bʊlək] **n** bœuf *m*.

bullring ['bʊlrɪŋ] **n** arène *f*.

bullrush ['bʊlrʌʃ] = ***bulrush***.

bull's-eye **n** centre *m*.

bullshit ['bʊlʃɪt] *vulg* ■ **n** *(U)* conneries *fpl*.
■ **vi** (**pt & pp -ted**, **cont -ting**) dire des conneries.

bull terrier **n** bull-terrier *m*.

bully ['bʊlɪ] ■ **n** (**pl -ies**) tyran *m*.
■ **vt** (**pt & pp -ied**) tyranniser, brutaliser ▸ **to bully sb into doing sthg** forcer *OR* obliger qqn à faire qqch.

bullyboy ['bʊlɪbɔɪ] **n** *UK inf* brute *f*, voyou *m*.

bullying ['bʊlɪɪŋ] **n** *(U)* brimades *fpl*.

bulrush ['bʊlrʌʃ] **n** jonc *m*.

bum [bʌm] (**pt & pp -med**, **cont -ming**) **n 1.** *UK inf* [bottom] derrière *m* **2.** *inf pej* [tramp] clochard *m* **3.** *inf* [idler] bon à rien *m*.
◆ ***bum around*** **vi** *inf* **1.** [waste time] perdre son temps **2.** [travel aimlessly] se balader.

bumblebee ['bʌmblbiː] **n** bourdon *m*.

bumbling ['bʌmblɪŋ] **adj** *inf* empoté(e).

bumf [bʌmf] *(U)* **n** *UK inf* paperasses *fpl*.

bummer ['bʌməʳ] **n** *v inf* [bad experience] poisse *f* ▸ **the film's a real bummer** ce film est vraiment nul *OR* un vrai navet ▸ **what a bummer!** les boules!

bump [bʌmp] ■ **n 1.** [lump] bosse *f* **2.** [knock, blow] choc *m* **3.** [noise] bruit *m* sourd.
■ **vt** [head] cogner / [car] heurter.
■ **vi** [car] **: to bump along** cahoter.
◆ ***bump into*** **vt insep** [meet by chance] rencontrer par hasard.
◆ ***bump off*** **vt sep** *inf* liquider.
◆ ***bump up*** **vt sep** *inf* faire grimper.

bumper ['bʌmpəʳ] ■ **adj** [harvest, edition] exceptionnel(elle).
■ **n 1.** AUT pare-chocs *m inv* **2.** *US* RAIL tampon *m*.

bumper cars **npl** auto *fpl* tamponneuses.

bumper sticker **n** autocollant *m (pour voiture)*.

bumper-to-bumper **adj** pare-chocs contre pare-chocs.

bumph [bʌmf] *UK inf* = ***bumf***.

bump start **n** *démarrage d'un véhicule en le poussant*.
◆ ***bump-start*** **vt** démarrer en poussant.

bumptious ['bʌmpʃəs] **adj** suffisant(e).

bumpy ['bʌmpɪ] (**comp -ier**, **superl -iest**) **adj 1.** [surface] défoncé(e) **2.** [ride] cahoteux(euse) / [sea crossing] agité(e).

bun [bʌn] **n 1.** *UK* [cake] petit pain *m* aux raisins / [bread roll] petit pain au lait **2.** [hairstyle] chignon *m*.

bunch [bʌntʃ] ■ **n** [of people] groupe *m* / [of flowers] bouquet *m* / [of grapes] grappe *f* / [of bananas] régime *m* / [of keys] trousseau *m*.
■ **vt** grouper.
■ **vi** se grouper.
◆ ***bunches*** **npl** *UK* [hairstyle] couettes *fpl*.

bundle ['bʌndl] ■ **n** [of clothes] paquet *m* / [of notes, newspapers] liasse *f* / [of wood] fagot *m* ▸ **he's a bundle of nerves** c'est un paquet de nerfs.
■ **vt** [put roughly - person] entasser / [- clothes] fourrer, entasser ▸ **he was bundled into the car** on l'a poussé dans la voiture brusquement *OR* sans ménagement.
◆ ***bundle off*** **vt sep** [person] envoyer en hâte.
◆ ***bundle up*** **vt sep** [clothes] mettre en tas / [newspapers] mettre en liasse / [wood] mettre en fagot.

bundled software ['bʌndld-] **n** *(U)* COMPUT logiciel *m* inclus à l'achat d'un ordinateur.

bundling ['bʌndlɪŋ] **n** [of products] groupage *m*.

bung [bʌŋ] ■ **n** bonde *f*.
■ **vt** *UK inf* envoyer.

bungalow ['bʌŋgələʊ] **n** bungalow *m*.

bunged up [bʌŋd-] **adj** *UK inf* bouché(e).

bungee-jumping ['bʌndʒɪ-] **n** saut *m* à l'élastique.

bungle ['bʌŋgl] **vt** gâcher, bâcler.

bunion ['bʌnjən] **n** oignon *m*.

bunk [bʌŋk] **n 1.** [bed] couchette *f* **2.** *(U) inf* [nonsense] foutaises *fpl*
▸▸ **to do a bunk** *UK inf* mettre les voiles.

bunk bed **n** lit *m* superposé.

bunker ['bʌŋkər] **n 1.** GOLF & MIL bunker *m* **2.** [for coal] coffre *m*.

bunkhouse ['bʌŋkhaʊs] (pl [-haʊzɪz]) **n** dortoir *m*.

bunny ['bʌnɪ] (pl **-ies**) **n : bunny (rabbit)** lapin *m*.

bunny hill **n** *US* [in skiing] piste *f* pour débutants.

Bunsen burner ['bʌnsn-] **n** bec *m* Bunsen.

bunting ['bʌntɪŋ] **n** *(U)* guirlandes *fpl* (de drapeaux).

buoy [*UK* bɔɪ, *US* 'bu:ɪ] **n** bouée *f*.
◆ ***buoy up*** **vt sep** [encourage] soutenir.

buoyancy ['bɔɪənsɪ] **n 1.** [ability to float] flottabilité *f* **2.** *fig* [optimism] entrain *m*.

buoyant ['bɔɪənt] **adj 1.** [able to float] qui flotte **2.** *fig* [person] enjoué(e) / [economy] florissant(e) / [market] ferme.

burden ['bɜ:dn] ■ **n** *lit* & *fig* **: burden (on)** charge *f* (pour), fardeau *m* (pour) ▸ **to be a burden to sb** être un fardeau pour qqn ▸ **the tax burden** le fardeau *OR* le poids des impôts.
■ **vt : to burden sb with** [responsibilities, worries] accabler qqn de.

bureau ['bjʊərəʊ] (pl **-x** [-z]) **n 1.** *UK* [desk] bureau *m* / *US* [chest of drawers] commode *f* **2.** [office] bureau *m* **3.** *US* POL service *m* (gouvernemental).

bureaucracy [bjʊə'rɒkrəsɪ] (pl **-ies**) **n** bureaucratie *f*.

bureaucrat ['bjʊərəkræt] **n** bureaucrate *mf*.

bureaucratic [,bjʊərə'krætɪk] **adj** bureaucratique.

bureaux ['bjʊərəʊz] **npl** ➤ ***bureau***.

burger ['bɜ:gər] **n** hamburger *m*.

burglar ['bɜ:glər] **n** cambrioleur *m*, -euse *f*.

burglar alarm **n** système *m* d'alarme.

burglarize *US* = ***burgle***.

burglary ['bɜ:glərɪ] (pl **-ies**) **n** cambriolage *m*.

burgle ['bɜ:gl], *US* **burglarize** ['bɜ:gləraɪz] **vt** cambrioler.

Burgundy ['bɜ:gəndɪ] **n** Bourgogne *f* ▸ **in Burgundy** en Bourgogne.

burial ['berɪəl] **n** enterrement *m*.

burial ground **n** cimetière *m*.

burk [bɜ:k] **n** *UK inf* idiot *m*, -e *f*, andouille *f*.

Burkina Faso [bɜ:,ki:nə'fæsəʊ] **n** Burkina *m* ▸ **in Burkina Faso** au Burkina.

burlap ['bɜ:læp] **n** jute *f*.

burly ['bɜ:lɪ] (comp **-ier**, superl **-iest**) **adj** bien charpenté(e).

Burma ['bɜ:mə] **n** Birmanie *f* ▸ **in Burma** en Birmanie.

Burmese [,bɜ:'mi:z] ■ **adj** birman(e).
■ **n 1.** [person] Birman *m*, -e *f* **2.** [language] birman *m*.

burn [bɜ:n] ■ **vt** (pt & pp **burnt** *OR* **-ed**) **1.** [heat] brûler ▸ **to burn o.s.** se brûler ▸ **I've burned my hand** je me suis brûlé la main ▸ **three people were burnt to death** trois personnes sont mortes carbonisées *OR* ont été brûlées vives ▸ **to be burnt alive** être brûlé vif ▸ **his cigarette burnt a hole in the carpet** sa cigarette a fait un trou dans la moquette ▸ **I've burnt the potatoes** j'ai laissé brûler les pommes de terre ▸ **the house was burnt to the ground** la maison fut réduite en cendres *OR* brûla entièrement ▸ **to burn one's boats** *OR* **bridges** *fig* brûler ses vaisseaux *OR* les ponts ▸ **to burn one's fingers, to get one's fingers burnt** *fig* se brûler les doigts ▸ **to have money to burn** *fig* avoir de l'argent à ne pas savoir qu'en faire
2. COMPUT graver ▸ **to burn a CD** graver un CD.
■ **vi** (pt & pp **burnt** *OR* **-ed**) brûler ▸ **this material won't burn** ce tissu est ininflammable ▸ **my skin burns easily** j'attrape facilement des coups de soleil ▸ **the church burned to the ground** l'église a été réduite en cendres ▸ **to burn with** *fig* brûler de ▸ **my face was burning** [with embarrassment] j'avais le visage en feu, j'étais tout rouge.
■ **n** brûlure *f*.
◆ ***burn down*** ■ **vt sep** [building, town] incendier.
■ **vi 1.** [building] brûler complètement
2. [fire] baisser d'intensité.
◆ ***burn out*** ■ **vt sep** [exhaust] **: to burn o.s. out** s'user
■ **vi** [fire] s'éteindre.
◆ ***burn up*** ■ **vt sep** [destroy by fire] brûler ▸ **this car burns up a lot of petrol** cette voiture consomme beaucoup d'essence ▸ **to burn up a lot of calories/energy** dépenser *OR* brûler beaucoup de calories/d'énergie.
■ **vi** [satellite] se désintégrer (sous l'effet de la chaleur).

burned-out ['bɜ:nd-] **adj** = ***burnt-out***.

burner ['bɜ:nər] **n** brûleur *m*.

burning ['bɜːnɪŋ] **adj** **1.** [on fire] en flammes **2.** [very hot] brûlant(e) / [cheeks, face] en feu **3.** [passion, desire] ardent(e) / [interest] passionné(e) ▸ **burning question** question *f* brûlante.

burnish ['bɜːnɪʃ] **vt** astiquer, polir.

burnout ['bɜːnaʊt] **n** **1.** AERON *arrêt par suite d'épuisement du combustible* **2.** ELEC **: what caused the burnout?** qu'est-ce qui a fait griller les circuits? **3.** [exhaustion] épuisement *m* total.

Burns' Night [bɜːnz-] **n** *fête célébrée en l'honneur du poète écossais Robert Burns, le 25 janvier.*

burnt [bɜːnt] **pt & pp** ➤ ***burn***.

burnt-out **adj** **1.** [building, car] détruit(e) (par le feu) **2.** *fig* [person] usé(e).

burp [bɜːp] *inf* ■ **n** rot *m*.
■ **vi** roter.

burqa [bɜːkə] **n** burqa *f*.

burrow ['bʌrəʊ] ■ **n** terrier *m*.
■ **vi** **1.** [dig] creuser un terrier **2.** *fig* [search] fouiller.

bursar ['bɜːsəʳ] **n** **1.** [treasurer] intendant *m*, -e *f* **2.** *Scot* [student] boursier *m*, -ère *f*.

bursary ['bɜːsərɪ] (pl **-ies**) **n** *UK* [scholarship, grant] bourse *f*.

burst [bɜːst] ■ **vi** (pt & pp **burst**) **1.** [break, explode] éclater ▸ **his heart felt as if it would burst with joy/grief** il crut que son cœur allait éclater de joie/se briser de chagrin **2.** [move suddenly] **: the door burst open** la porte s'est ouverte brusquement ▸ **two policemen burst into the house** deux policiers ont fait irruption dans la maison ▸ **the sun burst through the clouds** le soleil perça OR apparut à travers les nuages.
■ **vt** (pt & pp **burst**) faire éclater ▸ **the river is about to burst its banks** le fleuve est sur le point de déborder ▸ **to burst a blood vessel** se faire éclater une veine, se rompre un vaisseau sanguin.
■ **n** [of gunfire] rafale *f* / [of enthusiasm] élan *m* ▸ **a burst of applause** un tonnerre d'applaudissements ▸ **he had a sudden burst of energy** il a eu un sursaut d'énergie.
◆ ***burst into*** **vt insep** **1.** [room] faire irruption dans **2.** [begin suddenly] **: to burst into tears** fondre en larmes ▸ **to burst into song** se mettre tout d'un coup à chanter ▸ **to burst into flames** prendre feu.
◆ ***burst out*** **vt insep** [say suddenly] s'exclamer ▸ **to burst out laughing** éclater de rire ▸ **to burst out crying** fondre en larmes.

bursting ['bɜːstɪŋ] **adj** **1.** [full] plein(e), bourré(e) **2.** [with emotion] **: bursting with** débordé(e) de **3.** [eager] **: to be bursting to do sthg** mourir d'envie de faire qqch.

Burundi [bʊ'rʊndɪ] **n** Burundi *m* ▸ **in Burundi** au Burundi.

bury ['berɪ] (pt & pp **-ied**) **vt** **1.** [in ground] enterrer ▸ **to be buried at sea** être immergé(e) en haute mer ▸ **to bury o.s. in sthg** *fig* se plonger dans qqch **2.** [hide] cacher, enfouir ▸ **to bury one's face in one's hands** enfouir son visage dans ses mains.

bus [bʌs] **n** [generally] autobus *m*, bus *m* / [long-distance] car *m* ▸ **by bus** en autobus OR car.

bus conductor **n** receveur *m*, -euse *f* d'autobus.

bus driver **n** conducteur *m*, -trice *f* d'autobus.

bush [bʊʃ] **n** **1.** [plant] buisson *m* **2.** [open country] **: the bush** la brousse
▸▸ **she doesn't beat about the bush** elle n'y va pas par quatre chemins.

bushel ['bʊʃl] **n** boisseau *m*.

bushfire ['bʊʃ,faɪəʳ] **n** feu *m* de brousse.

bushy ['bʊʃɪ] (comp **-ier**, superl **-iest**) **adj** touffu(e).

busily ['bɪzɪlɪ] **adv** activement ▸ **to be busily engaged in sthg/in doing sthg** être très occupé à qqch/à faire qqch ▸ **he was busily scribbling in his notebook** il griffonnait sur son calepin d'un air affairé.

business ['bɪznɪs] ■ **n** **1.** *(U)* [commerce] affaires *fpl* ▸ **business is good/bad** les affaires vont bien/mal ▸ **we have lost business to foreign competitors** nous avons perdu une partie de notre clientèle au profit de concurrents étrangers ▸ **the travel business** les métiers OR le secteur du tourisme ▸ **she's in the publishing business** elle est dans l'édition ▸ **he's in business** il est dans les affaires ▸ **this firm has been in business for 25 years** cette entreprise tourne depuis 25 ans ▸ **on business** pour affaires ▸ **to do business with** travailler OR traiter avec ▸ **from now on I'll take my business elsewhere** désormais j'irai voir OR je m'adresserai ailleurs ▸ **to go out of business** fermer, faire faillite
2. [company] entreprise *f* ▸ **would you like to have OR to run your own business?** aimeriez-vous travailler à votre compte?
3. [concern] affaire *f* ▸ **he had no business to tell you that** ce n'était pas à lui de vous le dire ▸ **to mean business** *inf* ne pas plaisanter ▸ **it's my (own) business if I decide not to go** c'est mon affaire OR cela ne regarde que moi si je décide de ne pas y aller ▸ **it's none of your business** cela ne vous regarde pas ▸ **mind your own business!** *inf* occupe-toi de tes oignons!
4. [affair, matter] histoire *f*, affaire *f* ▸ **any other business** [on agenda] points *mpl* divers ▸ **she had important business to discuss** elle avait à parler d'affaires importantes ▸ **I'm tired of the whole business** je suis las de toute cette histoire.
■ **comp** [meeting] d'affaires.

business account **n** compte *m* professionnel OR commercial.

business address **n** adresse *f* de travail.

business associate **n** associé *m*, -e *f*.

business card **n** carte *f* de visite.

business centre *UK*, ***business center*** *US* **n** centre *m* des affaires.

business class **n** classe *f* affaires.

business college **n** *UK* [generally] école *f* de commerce / [for management training] école *f* (supérieure) de gestion.

business cycle **n** cycle *m* des affaires, cycle *m* conjoncturel.

business expenses **npl** [for individual] frais *mpl* professionnels / [for firm] frais *mpl* généraux.

business hours **npl** heures *fpl* ouvrables.

businesslike ['bɪznɪslaɪk] **adj** systématique, méthodique.

businessman ['bɪznɪsmæn] (pl **-men** [-men]) **n** homme *m* d'affaires.

business manager **n** COMM & INDUST directeur *m* commercial / SPORT manager *m* / THEAT directeur *m*.

business park **n** zone *f* d'activités.

business partner **n** partenaire *mf*.

business plan **n** projet *m* d'entreprise.

business school **n** école *f* de commerce.

business sector **n** secteur *m* tertiaire, secteur *m* d'affaires.

business trip **n** voyage *m* d'affaires.

businesswoman ['bɪznɪs,wʊmən] (pl **-women** [-,wɪmɪn]) **n** femme *f* d'affaires.

busing ['bʌsɪŋ] *US* **n** *système de ramassage scolaire aux États-Unis, qui organise la répartition des enfants noirs et des enfants blancs dans les écoles afin de lutter contre la ségrégation raciale.*

busk [bʌsk] **vi** *UK* jouer de la musique *(dans la rue ou le métro).*

busker ['bʌskəʳ] **n** *UK* chanteur *m*, -euse *f* des rues.

bus lane **n** *UK* voie *f* des bus.

busload ['bʌsləʊd] **n : a busload of workers** un autobus plein d'ouvriers ▸ **the tourists arrived by the busload** *OR* **in busloads** les touristes sont arrivés par cars entiers.

bus shelter **n** Abribus® *m*.

bus station **n** gare *f* routière.

bus stop **n** arrêt *m* de bus.

bust [bʌst] ■ **adj** *inf* **1.** [broken] foutu(e) **2.** [bankrupt] **: to go bust** faire faillite.

■ **n 1.** [bosom] poitrine *f* **2.** [statue] buste *m* **3.** *police sl* [raid] descente *f*.

■ **vt** (pt & pp **bust** *OR* **-ed**) **1.** *inf* [break] péter **2.** *police sl* [arrest] arrêter / [raid] faire une descente à.

buster ['bʌstəʳ] **n** *esp US inf* [pal] **: thanks, buster** merci, mon (petit) gars.

bustle ['bʌsl] ■ **n** *(U)* [activity] remue-ménage *m inv*.

■ **vi** s'affairer.

bustling ['bʌslɪŋ] **adj** [place] qui bourdonne d'activité.

bust-up **n** *inf* **1.** [quarrel] engueulade *f* **2.** [of marriage, relationship] rupture *f*.

busty ['bʌstɪ] (comp **-ier**, superl **-iest**) **adj** qui a une forte poitrine.

busy ['bɪzɪ] ■ **adj** (comp **-ier**, superl **-iest**) **1.** [gen] occupé(e) ▸ **to be busy doing sthg** être occupé à faire qqch ▸ **he likes to keep (himself) busy** il aime bien s'occuper ▸ **I'm afraid I'm busy tomorrow** malheureusement je suis pris demain **2.** [life, week] chargé(e) / [town, office] animé(e) ▸ **this is our busiest period** [business, shop] c'est la période où nous sommes en pleine activité **3.** *esp US* TELEC [engaged] occupé(e).

■ **vt : to busy o.s. (doing sthg)** s'occuper (à faire qqch).

busybody ['bɪzɪ,bɒdɪ] (pl **-ies**) **n** *inf pej* mouche *f* du coche.

busy signal **n** *US* TELEC tonalité *f* "occupé".

but [bʌt] ■ **conj** mais ▸ **I'm sorry, but I don't agree** je suis désolé, mais je ne suis pas d'accord ▸ **but now let's talk about you** mais parlons plutôt de toi.

■ **prep** sauf, excepté ▸ **everyone was at the party but Jane** tout le monde était à la soirée sauf Jane ▸ **he has no one but himself to blame** il ne peut s'en prendre qu'à lui-même.

■ **adv** *fml* seulement, ne... que ▸ **she has but recently joined the firm** elle n'est entrée dans la société que depuis peu ▸ **had I but known!** si j'avais su! ▸ **we can but try** on peut toujours essayer.

◆ ***but for*** **prep** sans ▸ **but for her** sans elle.

◆ ***but then*** **adv** mais ▸**... but then I've known him for years...** mais il faut dire *OR* il est vrai que je le connais depuis des années.

butane ['bju:teɪn] **n** butane *m*.

butch [bʊtʃ] **adj** *inf pej* [woman] hommasse.

butcher ['bʊtʃəʳ] ■ **n** boucher *m*, -ère *f* ▸ **butcher's (shop)** *UK* boucherie *f*.

■ **vt 1.** [animal] abattre **2.** *fig* [massacre] massacrer.

butchery ['bʊtʃərɪ] **n** *lit* & *fig* boucherie *f*.

butler ['bʌtləʳ] **n** maître *m* d'hôtel *(chez un particulier)*.

butt [bʌt] ■ **n 1.** [of cigarette, cigar] mégot *m* **2.** [of rifle] crosse *f* **3.** [for water] tonneau *m* **4.** [of joke, criticism] cible *f*.

■ **vt** donner un coup de tête à.

◆ ***butt in*** **vi** [interrupt] **: to butt in on sb** interrompre qqn ▸ **to butt in on sthg** s'immiscer *OR* s'imposer dans qqch.

butter ['bʌtəʳ] ■ **n** beurre *m* ▸ **butter wouldn't melt in her mouth** *inf* on lui donnerait le bon Dieu sans confession.

■ **vt** beurrer.

◆ ***butter up*** **vt sep** *inf* passer de la pommade à.

butter bean **n** haricot *m* beurre.

buttercup ['bʌtəkʌp] **n** *UK* bouton *m* d'or.

butter dish **n** beurrier *m*.

buttered ['bʌtəd] **adj** [bread] beurré(e).

butterfingers ['bʌtə,fɪŋgəz] (pl **butterfingers**) **n** *inf* maladroit *m*, -e *f*.

butterfly ['bʌtəflaɪ] (pl **-ies**) **n** [insect, swimming stroke] papillon *m* ▸ **to have butterflies in one's stomach** avoir le trac.

buttermilk ['bʌtəmɪlk] **n** babeurre *m*.

butterscotch ['bʌtəskɒtʃ] **n** caramel *m* dur.

butt naked **adj** *US inf* à poil.

buttocks ['bʌtəks] **npl** fesses *fpl*.

button ['bʌtn] ■ **n 1.** [gen] bouton *m* **2.** *US* [badge] badge *m*.

■ **vt** = ***button up***.

◆ ***button up*** **vt sep** boutonner.

buttonhole ['bʌtnhəʊl] ■ **n 1.** [hole] boutonnière **2.** *UK* [flower] fleur *f* à la boutonnière.

■ **vt** *inf* coincer.

button mushroom **n** champignon *m* de Paris.

buttress ['bʌtrɪs] ■ **n** contrefort *m*.

■ **vt** [wall] soutenir, étayer.

buxom ['bʌksəm] **adj** bien en chair.

buy [baɪ] ■ **vt** (pt & pp **bought**) acheter ▸ **to buy sthg for sb, to buy sb sthg** acheter qqch à *OR* pour qqn ▸ **can I buy you a coffee?** puis-je t'offrir un café? ▸ **to buy sthg from sb** acheter qqch à qqn ▸ **they bought if for £100** ils l'ont payé 100 livres ▸ **she bought herself a pair of skis** elle s'est acheté une paire de skis.
■ **n : a good buy** une bonne affaire.
◆ ***buy in*** **vt sep** *UK* stocker.
◆ ***buy into*** **vt insep** acquérir des parts dans.
◆ ***buy off*** **vt sep : to buy sb off** acheter le silence de qqn.
◆ ***buy out*** **vt sep 1.** COMM racheter la part de **2.** [from army] **: to buy o.s. out** se racheter.
◆ ***buy up*** **vt sep** acheter en masse.

buy-back **n** FIN rachat *m* d'actions.

buyer ['baɪəʳ] **n** acheteur *m*, -euse *f*.

buyer's market **n** marché *m* d'acheteurs.

buyout ['baɪaʊt] **n** rachat *m*.

buzz [bʌz] ■ **n 1.** [of insect] bourdonnement *m* **2.** *inf* [telephone call] **: to give sb a buzz** passer un coup de fil à qqn.
■ **vi : to buzz (with)** bourdonner (de).
■ **vt** [on intercom] appeler.
◆ ***buzz off*** **vi** *UK inf* **: buzz off!** file!, fous le camp!

buzzard ['bʌzəd] **n 1.** *UK* [hawk] buse *f* **2.** *US* [vulture] urubu *m*.

buzzer ['bʌzəʳ] **n** sonnerie *f*.

buzzing ['bʌzɪŋ] **n** [of insect] bourdonnement *m* / [of machine] ronronnement *m*.

buzzword ['bʌzwɜ:d] **n** *inf* mot *m* à la mode.

b/w (abbr of ***black and white***) **adj** NB.

by [baɪ] ■ **adv 1.** [past] **: she drove by without stopping** elle est passée (en voiture) sans s'arrêter ▸ **two hours have gone by** deux heures ont passé ▸ **as time went by he became less bitter** avec le temps il est devenu moins amer
2. [near] **: is there a bank close by?** y a-t-il une banque près d'ici?
3. [to, at someone's home] **: I'll stop** *OR* **drop by this evening** je passerai ce soir.
■ **prep 1.** [indicating cause, agent] par ▸ **caused/written/killed by** causé(e)/écrit(e)/tué(e) par ▸ **I was shocked by his reaction** sa réaction m'a choqué ▸ **a book by Toni Morrison** un livre de Toni Morrison
2. [indicating means, method, manner] **: to pay by cheque** payer par chèque ▸ **by letter/phone** par courrier/téléphone ▸ **to travel by bus/train/plane/ship** voyager en bus/par le train/en avion/en bateau ▸ **I know her by name/sight** je la connais de nom/vue ▸ **to dine by candlelight** dîner aux chandelles ▸ **he's a lawyer by profession** il est avocat de son métier ▸ **by doing sthg** en faisant qqch ▸ **he learned to cook by watching his mother** il a appris à faire la cuisine en regardant sa mère ▸ **she took her by the hand** elle l'a prise par la main ▸ **by nature** de nature, de tempérament
3. [to explain a word or expression] par ▸ **what do you mean by "all right"?** qu'est-ce que tu veux dire par "très bien"?
4. [beside, close to] près de ▸ **by the sea** au bord de la mer ▸ **I sat by her bed** j'étais assis à son chevet ▸ **don't stand by the door** ne restez pas debout près de la porte
5. [past] **: to pass by sb/sthg** passer devant qqn/qqch ▸ **to drive by sb/sthg** passer en voiture devant qqn/qqch ▸ **she walked right by me** elle passa juste devant moi
6. [via, through] par ▸ **come in by the back door** entrez par la porte de derrière
7. [at or before a particular time] avant, pas plus tard que ▸ **I'll be there by eight** j'y serai avant huit heures ▸ **I'll have finished by Friday** j'aurai fini pour vendredi ▸ **by 1914 it was all over** en 1914 c'était fini ▸ **by the time you read this letter I'll be in California** lorsque tu liras cette lettre, je serai en Californie ▸ **he should be in India by now** il devrait être en Inde maintenant ▸ **she had already married by then** à ce moment-là elle était déjà mariée
8. [during] **: by day** le *OR* de jour ▸ **by night** la *OR* de nuit
9. [according to] selon, suivant ▸ **they're rich, even by American standards** ils sont riches même par rapport aux normes américaines ▸ **it's 6:15 by my watch** il est 6 h 15 à *OR* d'après ma montre ▸ **by law** conformément à la loi ▸ **to play by the rules** faire les choses dans les règles ▸ **it's all right by me** *inf* moi, je suis d'accord *OR* je n'ai rien contre
10. [in quantities, amounts] à ▸ **she won by five points** elle a gagné de cinq points ▸ **by the yard** au mètre ▸ **by the thousands** par milliers ▸ **paid by the day/week/month** payé(e) à la journée/à la semaine/au mois ▸ **to cut prices by 50%** réduire les prix de 50% ▸ **his second book is better by far** son deuxième livre est nettement meilleur
11. [in arithmetic] par ▸ **divide/multiply 20 by 2** divisez/multipliez 20 par 2
12. [in measurements] **: 2 metres by 4** 2 mètres sur 4
13. [indicating gradual change] **: week by week** de semaine en semaine ▸ **day by day** jour après jour, de jour en jour ▸ **little by little** peu à peu ▸ **one by one** un à un, un par un
▸▸| **(all) by oneself** (tout) seul ((toute) seule) ▸ **I'm all by myself today** je suis tout seul aujourd'hui.
◆ ***by and by*** **adv** *liter* bientôt.
◆ ***by the by*** **adj : that's by the by** ça n'a pas d'importance.

bye(-bye) [baɪ(baɪ)] **excl** *inf* au revoir!, salut!

bye-election *UK* = ***by-election***.

byelaw ['baɪlɔ:] = ***bylaw***.

by-election *UK* **n** élection *f* partielle.

Byelorussia [bɪˌeləʊ'rʌʃə] = ***Belorussia***.

bygone ['baɪgɒn] **adj** d'autrefois.
◆ ***bygones*** **npl : to let bygones be bygones** oublier le passé.

bylaw ['baɪlɔ:] **n** arrêté *m*.

by-line, *US* ***byline*** ['baɪlaɪn] **n** PRESS signature *f*.

bypass ['baɪpɑ:s] ■ **n 1.** [road] route *f* de contournement **2.** MED **: bypass (operation)** pontage *m*.
■ **vt** [town, difficulty] contourner / [subject] éviter.

by-product, *US* ***byproduct*** ['baɪprɒdʌkt] **n 1.** [product] dérivé *m* **2.** *fig* [consequence] conséquence *f*.

bystander ['baɪˌstændəʳ] **n** spectateur *m*, -trice *f*.

byte [baɪt] **n** COMPUT octet *m*.

byway ['baɪweɪ] **n 1.** [road] chemin *m* détourné *OR* écarté **2.** *fig* [of subject] à-côté *m*.

byword ['baɪwɜ:d] **n** [symbol] **: to be a byword for** être synonyme de.

C

***c*[1]** [siː] (pl c's *OR* cs), **C** (pl C's *OR* Cs) **n** [letter] c *m inv*, C *m inv*.

◆ **C n 1.** MUS do *m* **2.** SCH [mark] C *m inv* **3.** (abbr of ***Celsius, centigrade***) C.

c*[2]** [siː] **1.** (abbr of ***century) s. **2.** (abbr of ***cent(s)***) ct.

c., ca. abbr of ***circa***.

C & G (abbr of ***City and Guilds***) **n** *diplôme britannique d'enseignement technique*.

C & W abbr of ***country and western***.

c/a abbr of ***credit account, current account***.

CA*[1]** **n 1.** abbr of ***chartered accountant **2.** (abbr of ***Consumers' Association***) *association britannique des consommateurs*.

CA*[2]** **1.** abbr of ***Central America **2.** abbr of ***California***.

CAA **n 1.** (abbr of ***Civil Aviation Authority***) *direction britannique de l'aviation civile* **2.** (abbr of ***Civil Aeronautics Authority***) *direction américaine de l'aviation civile*.

cab [kæb] **n 1.** [taxi] taxi *m* **2.** [of lorry] cabine *f*.

CAB (abbr of ***Citizens' Advice Bureau***) **n** *service britannique d'information et d'aide au consommateur*.

cabaret ['kæbəreɪ] **n** cabaret *m*.

cabbage ['kæbɪdʒ] **n** [vegetable] chou *m*.

cabbie, cabby ['kæbɪ] **n** *inf* chauffeur *m* de taxi.

caber ['keɪbəʳ] **n** *Scot* **: tossing the caber** *lancement d'un tronc d'arbre (épreuve des* **Highland Games***)*.

cabin ['kæbɪn] **n 1.** [on ship, plane] cabine *f* **2.** [house] cabane *f*.

cabin class **n** seconde classe *f*.

cabin crew **n** équipage *m*.

cabin cruiser **n** bateau *m* de croisière.

cabinet ['kæbɪnɪt] **n 1.** [cupboard] meuble *m* **2.** POL cabinet *m*.

cabinet-maker **n** ébéniste *mf*.

cabinet minister **n** *UK* ministre *mf*.

cable ['keɪbl] ■ **n** câble *m*.

■ **vt** [news] câbler / [person] câbler à.

cable car **n** téléphérique *m*.

cablegram ['keɪblgræm] **n** câblogramme *m*.

cable railway **n** funiculaire *m*.

cable television, cable TV **n** câble *m*, télévision *f* par câble.

cabling ['keɪblɪŋ] **n** câblage *m*.

caboodle [kə'buːdl] **n** *inf* **: the whole caboodle** et tout le tremblement.

cache [kæʃ] ■ **n 1.** [store] cache *f* **2.** COMPUT mémoire-cache *f*, antémémoire *f*.

■ **vt** COMPUT stocker dans la mémoire-cache.

cache memory **n** COMPUT antémémoire *f*, mémoire *f* cache.

cachet ['kæʃeɪ] **n** cachet *m*.

cack-handed [kæk-] **adj** *UK inf* maladroit(e), gauche.

cackle ['kækl] ■ **n 1.** [of hen] caquet *m* **2.** [of person] jacassement *m*.

■ **vi 1.** [hen] caqueter **2.** [person] jacasser.

cacophony [kæ'kɒfənɪ] **n** cacophonie *f*.

cactus ['kæktəs] (pl **-tuses** [-təsiːz] *OR* **-ti** [-taɪ]) **n** cactus *m*.

cad [kæd] **n** *dated* goujat *m*.

CAD (abbr of ***computer-aided design***) **n** CAO *f*.

CADCAM (abbr of ***computer-aided design and manufacture***) **n** CFAO *f*.

caddie ['kædɪ] ■ **n** GOLF caddie *m*.

■ **vi : to caddie for sb** servir de caddie à qqn.

caddy ['kædɪ] (pl **-ies**) **n** *UK* [for tea] boîte *f* à thé.

cadence ['keɪdəns] **n** [of voice] intonation *f*.

cadet [kə'det] **n** élève *m* officier.

cadge [kædʒ] *UK inf dated* ■ **vt : to cadge sthg off** *OR* **from sb** taper qqn de qqch.

■ **vi : to cadge off** *OR* **from sb** taper qqn.

Cadiz [kə'dɪz] **n** Cadix.

Caesar ['siːzəʳ] **n** César *m*.

caesarean (section) *UK, US* ***cesarean (section)*** [sɪ'zeərɪən-] **n** césarienne *f*.

CAF (abbr of ***cost and freight***) C et F.

cafe, café ['kæfeɪ] **n** café *m*.

cafeteria [ˌkæfɪ'tɪərɪə] **n** cafétéria *f*, cantine *f*.

cafetière [kæfə'tjɛəʳ] **n** *UK* cafetière *f* à piston.

caff [kæf] **n** *UK inf* snack *m*.

caffeine ['kæfi:n] **n** caféine *f*.

caffeine-free **adj** sans caféine.

caftan, ***kaftan*** ['kæftæn] **n** cafetan *m*.

cage [keɪdʒ] **n** [for animal] cage *f*.

caged [keɪdʒd] **adj** en cage.

cagey ['keɪdʒɪ] (comp **-ier**, superl **-iest**) **adj** *inf* discret(ète).

cagoule [kə'gu:l] **n** *UK* K-way® *m inv*.

cahoots [kə'hu:ts] **n** *inf* **: to be in cahoots (with)** être de mèche (avec).

CAI (abbr of ***computer-aided instruction***) **n** EAO *m*.

cairn [keən] **n** [pile of rocks] cairn *m*.

Cairo ['kaɪərəʊ] **n** Le Caire.

cajole [kə'dʒəʊl] **vt : to cajole sb (into doing sthg)** enjôler qqn (pour qu'il fasse qqch).

cake [keɪk] **n 1.** [sweet] gâteau *m* / [of fish, potato] croquette *f* ▸ **it's a piece of cake** *inf fig* c'est du gâteau ▸ **to sell like hot cakes** se vendre comme des petits pains ▸ **you can't have your cake and eat it** on ne peut pas avoir le beurre et l'argent du beurre **2.** [of soap] pain *m*.

caked [keɪkt] **adj : caked with mud** recouvert(e) de boue séchée.

cake tin *UK*, ***cake pan*** *US* **n** moule *m* à gâteau.

cal [kæl] (abbr of ***calorie***) **n** cal.

CAL (abbr of ***computer assisted (OR aided) learning***) **n** enseignement *m* assisté par ordinateur.

calamine lotion [ˌkæləmaɪn-] **n** *(U)* lotion *f* à la calamine.

calamitous [kə'læmɪtəs] **adj** catastrophique.

calamity [kə'læmətɪ] (pl **-ies**) **n** calamité *f*.

calcium ['kælsɪəm] **n** calcium *m*.

calculate ['kælkjʊleɪt] **vt 1.** [result, number] calculer / [consequences] évaluer **2.** [plan] **: to be calculated to do sthg** être calculé(e) pour faire qqch.

◆ ***calculate on*** **vi : to calculate on sthg** compter sur qqch ▸ **to calculate on doing sthg** compter faire qqch.

calculated ['kælkjʊleɪtɪd] **adj** calculé(e).

calculating ['kælkjʊleɪtɪŋ] **adj** *pej* calculateur(trice).

calculation [ˌkælkjʊ'leɪʃn] **n** calcul *m*.

calculator ['kælkjʊleɪtəʳ] **n** calculatrice *f*.

calculus ['kælkjʊləs] **n** calcul *m*.

calendar ['kælɪndəʳ] **n** calendrier *m*.

calendar month **n** mois *m* (de calendrier).

calendar year **n** année *f* civile.

calf [kɑ:f] (pl **calves** [kɑ:vz]) **n 1.** [of cow, leather] veau *m* / [of elephant] éléphanteau *m* / [of seal] bébé *m* phoque **2.** ANAT mollet *m*.

caliber ['kælɪbəʳ] *US* = ***calibre***.

calibrate ['kælɪbreɪt] **vt** [scale] étalonner / [gun] calibrer.

calibration [ˌkælɪ'breɪʃn] **n** étalonnage *m*, calibrage *m*.

calibre *UK*, *US* ***caliber*** ['kælɪbəʳ] **n** calibre *m*.

calico ['kælɪkəʊ] **n** calicot *m*.

California [ˌkælɪ'fɔ:njə] **n** Californie *f* ▸ **in California** en Californie.

Californian [ˌkælɪ'fɔ:njən] ■ **adj** californien(enne).
■ **n** Californien *m*, -enne *f*.

calipers *US* = ***callipers***.

call [kɔ:l] ■ **n 1.** [cry] appel *m*, cri *m* ▸ **a call for help** un appel à l'aide OR au secours
2. TELEC appel *m* (téléphonique) ▸ **to make a call** passer un coup de téléphone ▸ **I'll give you a call** je t'appellerai ▸ **there's a call for you** on vous demande au téléphone ▸ **to take a call** prendre un appel
3. [summons, invitation] appel *m* ▸ **to be on call** [doctor] être de garde
4. [visit] visite *f* ▸ **to pay a call on sb** rendre visite à qqn
5. [demand] **: call (for)** demande *f* (de) ▸ **there have been calls for a return to capital punishment** il y a des gens qui demandent le rétablissement de la peine de mort.
■ **vt 1.** [name, describe] appeler ▸ **what's this thing called?** comment ça s'appelle ce truc? ▸ **she's called Joan** elle s'appelle Joan ▸ **he has a cat called Felix** il a un chat qui s'appelle Félix ▸ **let's call it £10** disons 10 livres ▸ **he called me a liar** il m'a traité de menteur ▸ **Denver is where I call home** c'est à Denver que je me sens chez moi ▸ **I don't call that clean** ce n'est pas ce que j'appelle propre ▸ **let's call it a day** si on s'arrêtait là pour aujourd'hui?
2. [telephone] appeler ▸ **don't call me at work** ne m'appelle pas au bureau ▸ **we called his house** nous avons appelé chez lui ▸ **to call the police/fire brigade** appeler la police/les pompiers
3. [shout, summon] appeler ▸ **can you call the children to the table?** pouvez-vous appeler les enfants pour qu'ils viennent à table? ▸ **he called me over** il m'a appelé ▸ **he was called to the phone** on l'a demandé au téléphone ▸ **she was suddenly called home** elle a été rappelée soudainement chez elle ▸ **she was called as a witness** elle a été citée comme témoin
4. [announce - meeting] convoquer / [- strike] lancer / [- flight] appeler / [- election] annoncer
▸▸ **to call sthg to mind** rappeler qqch ▸ **to call sthg into play** faire jouer qqch ▸ **to call sthg into question** remettre qqch en question.
■ **vi 1.** [shout - person] crier / [- animal, bird] pousser un cri/des cris ▸ **to call for help** appeler à l'aide OR au secours
2. TELEC appeler ▸ **who's calling?** qui est à l'appareil? ▸ **where are you calling from?** d'où appelles-tu?
3. [visit] passer ▸ **I was out when they called** je n'étais pas là quand ils sont passés.

◆ ***call away*** **vt sep : she's often called away on business** elle doit souvent partir en déplacement OR s'absenter pour affaires.

◆ ***call back*** ■ **vt sep** rappeler.
■ **vi 1.** TELEC rappeler
2. [visit again] repasser.

◆ ***call by*** **vi** *inf* passer.

◆ ***call for*** **vt insep 1.** [collect - person] passer prendre / [- package, goods] passer chercher ▸ **he called for her at her parents' house** il est allé la chercher chez ses parents

2. [demand] demander ▸ **the situation called for quick thinking** la situation demandait *OR* exigeait qu'on réfléchisse vite.

◆ ***call in*** ▪ vt sep **1.** [expert, police] faire venir ▸ **the army was called in to assist with the evacuation** on a fait appel à l'armée pour aider à l'évacuation
2. COMM [goods] rappeler / FIN [loan] exiger le remboursement de.
▪ vi passer.

◆ ***call off*** vt sep **1.** [cancel] annuler ▸ **to call off a strike** rapporter un ordre de grève
2. [dog] rappeler.

◆ ***call on*** vt insep **1.** [visit] passer voir
2. [ask] **: to call on sb to do sthg** demander à qqn de faire qqch.

◆ ***call out*** ▪ vt sep **1.** [police, doctor] appeler
2. [order to strike] **: they called the workers out** ils ont donné la consigne de grève aux ouvriers
3. [cry out] crier ▸ **"over here" he called out** "par ici" appela-t-il.
▪ vi [cry out] crier.

◆ ***call round*** vi *UK* passer ▸ **can I call round this evening?** puis-je passer ce soir?

◆ ***call up*** vt sep **1.** MIL & TELEC appeler
2. COMPUT rappeler.

CALL (abbr of ***computer assisted (OR aided) language learning***) n enseignement *m* des langues assisté par ordinateur.

call box n *UK* cabine *f* (téléphonique).

caller ['kɔːlər] n **1.** [visitor] visiteur *m*, -euse *f* **2.** TELEC demandeur *m*.

caller ID display, ***caller display*** n TELEC présentation *f* du numéro.

call girl n call-girl *f*.

calligraphy [kə'lɪgrəfɪ] n calligraphie *f*.

call-in n *US* RADIO & TV programme *m* à ligne ouverte.

calling ['kɔːlɪŋ] n **1.** [profession] métier *m* **2.** [vocation] vocation *f*.

calling card n *US* carte *f* de visite.

callipers *UK*, ***calipers*** *US* ['kælɪpəz] npl **1.** MATHS compas *m* **2.** MED appareil *m* orthopédique.

callous ['kæləs] adj dur(e).

callously ['kæləslɪ] adv durement.

callousness ['kæləsnɪs] n dureté *f*.

call-up n ordre *m* de mobilisation.

callus ['kæləs] (pl -es [-iːz]) n cal *m*, durillon *m*.

call waiting n signal *m* d'appel.

calm [kɑːm] ▪ adj calme ▸ **keep calm!** du calme!, restons calmes!
▪ n calme *m* ▸ **the calm before the storm** le calme avant la tempête.
▪ vt calmer.

◆ ***calm down*** ▪ vt sep calmer.
▪ vi se calmer ▸ **calm down!** calmez-vous!, ne vous énervez pas!

calming ['kɑːmɪŋ] adj calmant(e).

calmly ['kɑːmlɪ] adv calmement.

calmness ['kɑːmnɪs] n calme *m*.

Calor gas® ['kælər-] n *UK* butane *m*.

calorie ['kælərɪ] n calorie *f*.

calorific [ˌkælə'rɪfɪk] adj calorifique.

calve [kɑːv] vi vêler.

calves [kɑːvz] npl ➤ ***calf***.

cam [kæm] n came *f*.

CAM (abbr of ***computer-aided manufacturing***) n FAO *f*.

camaraderie [ˌkæmə'rɑːdərɪ] n camaraderie *f*.

camber ['kæmbər] n [of road] bombement *m*.

Cambodia [kæm'bəʊdjə] n Cambodge *m* ▸ **in Cambodia** au Cambodge.

Cambodian [kæm'bəʊdjən] ▪ adj cambodgien(enne).
▪ n Cambodgien *m*, -enne *f*.

Cambs (abbr of ***Cambridgeshire***) *comté anglais*.

camcorder ['kæmˌkɔːdər] n Caméscope® *m*.

came [keɪm] pt ➤ ***come***.

camel ['kæml] ▪ adj ocre *(inv)*.
▪ n chameau *m*.

camellia [kə'miːljə] n camélia *m*.

cameo ['kæmɪəʊ] (pl -s) n **1.** [jewellery] camée *m* **2.** CIN & THEAT courte apparition *f (d'une grande vedette)*.

camera ['kæmərə] n PHOT appareil photo *m* / CIN & TV caméra *f* ▸ **video camera** caméra vidéo.

◆ ***in camera*** adv à huis clos.

cameraman ['kæmərəmæn] (pl -men [-men]) n cameraman *m*, cadreur *m*.

camera-shy adj qui n'aime pas être photographié.

camerawoman ['kæmərəˌwʊmən] (pl -women [-ˌwɪmɪn]) n cadreuse *f*.

camerawork ['kæmərəwɜːk] n *(U)* prise *f* de vue.

Cameroon [ˌkæmə'ruːn] n Cameroun *m* ▸ **in Cameroon** au Cameroun.

Cameroonian [ˌkæmə'ruːnɪən] ▪ adj camerounais(e)
▪ n Camerounais *m*, -e *f*.

camisole ['kæmɪsəʊl] n camisole *f*.

camomile ['kæməmaɪl] ▪ n camomille *f*.
▪ comp **: camomile tea** infusion *f* de camomille.

camouflage ['kæməflɑːʒ] ▪ n camouflage *m*.
▪ vt camoufler.

camp [kæmp] ▪ n camp *m*.
▪ vi camper.

◆ ***camp out*** vi camper.

campaign [kæm'peɪn] ▪ n campagne *f*.
▪ vi **: to campaign (for/against)** mener une campagne (pour/contre).

campaigner [kæm'peɪnər] n militant *m*, -e *f*.

camp bed n *UK* lit *m* de camp.

camper ['kæmpər] n **1.** [person] campeur *m*, -euse **2.** [vehicle] camping-car *m*.

camper van n *UK* camping-car *m*.

campfire ['kæmpˌfaɪər] n feu *m* de camp.

campground ['kæmpgraʊnd] **n** *US* (terrain *m* de) camping *m*.

camphor ['kæmfəʳ] **n** camphre *m*.

camping ['kæmpɪŋ] **n** camping *m* ▸ **to go camping** faire du camping.

camping site, ***campsite*** ['kæmpsaɪt] **n** (terrain *m* de) camping *m*.

campus ['kæmpəs] (pl **-es** [-i:z]) **n** campus *m*.

camshaft ['kæmʃɑ:ft] **n** arbre *m* à cames.

can[1] [kæn] ■ **n** [of drink, food] boîte *f* / [of oil] bidon *m* / [of paint] pot *m*.
■ **vt** (pt & pp **-ned**, cont **-ning**) mettre en boîte.

can[2] *(weak form* [kən], *strong form* [kæn], *conditional and preterite form* **could**; *negative form* **cannot** *and* **can't**) **modal vb 1.** [be able to] pouvoir ▸ **can you come to lunch?** tu peux venir déjeuner? ▸ **she couldn't come** elle n'a pas pu venir ▸ **I'll come if I can** je viendrai si je (le) peux ▸ **I'll come as soon as I can** je viendrai aussitôt que possible *OR* aussitôt que je pourrai ▸ **we'll do everything we can to help** nous ferons tout ce que nous pourrons *OR* tout notre possible pour aider ▸ **I can't** *OR* **cannot afford it** je ne peux pas me le payer ▸ **can you see/hear/smell something?** tu vois/entends/sens quelque chose? ▸ **can you feel it?** tu le sens? ▸ **I can't understand you** je ne te comprends pas *OR* je ne comprends pas ce que tu dis
2. [know how to] savoir ▸ **I can play the piano** je sais jouer du piano ▸ **can you drive/cook?** tu sais conduire/cuisiner? ▸ **she can speak three languages** elle parle trois langues
3. [indicating permission, in polite requests] pouvoir ▸ **you can use my car if you like** tu peux prendre ma voiture si tu veux ▸ **we can't wear jeans to work** on ne peut pas aller au travail en jeans ▸ **can I speak to John, please?** est-ce que je pourrais parler à John, s'il vous plaît? ▸ **can I borrow your sweater? – yes, you can** puis-je emprunter ton pull? – (mais oui,) bien sûr ▸ **can I just say something here?** est-ce que je peux dire quelque chose? ▸ **can I be of any assistance?** puis-je vous aider?
4. [indicating disbelief, puzzlement] pouvoir ▸ **what can she have done with it?** qu'est-ce qu'elle a bien pu en faire? ▸ **we can't just leave him here** on ne peut tout de même pas le laisser ici ▸ **you can't be serious!** tu ne parles pas sérieusement! ▸ **he can't possibly have finished already!** ce n'est pas possible qu'il ait déjà fini! ▸ **can't we at least talk about it?** est-ce que nous pouvons au moins en discuter? ▸ **how can you say that?** comment pouvez-vous *OR* osez-vous dire ça?
5. [indicating possibility] **: the contract can still be cancelled** il est toujours possible d'annuler *OR* on peut encore annuler le contrat ▸ **the job can't be finished in one day** il est impossible de finir le travail *OR* le travail ne peut pas se faire en un jour ▸ **I could see you tomorrow** je pourrais vous voir demain ▸ **the train could have been cancelled** peut-être que le train a été annulé
6. [indicating usual state or behaviour] **: she can be a bit difficult sometimes** elle peut parfois être (un peu) difficile ▸ **Edinburgh can be very chilly** il peut faire très froid à Édimbourg.

Canada ['kænədə] **n** Canada *m* ▸ **in Canada** au Canada.

Canadian [kə'neɪdjən] ■ **adj** canadien(enne).
■ **n** Canadien *m*, -enne *f*.

canal [kə'næl] **n** canal *m*.

canapé ['kænəpeɪ] **n** canapé *m (petit four)*.

Canaries [kə'neərɪz] **npl : the Canaries** les Canaries *fpl*.

canary [kə'neərɪ] (pl **-ies**) **n** canari *m*.

Canary Islands **npl : the Canary Islands** les îles *fpl* Canaries ▸ **in the Canary Islands** aux Canaries.

cancan ['kænkæn] **n** cancan *m*.

cancel ['kænsl] (*UK* **-led**, cont **-ling**, *US* **-ed**, cont **-ing**) **vt 1.** [gen] annuler / [appointment, delivery] décommander **2.** [stamp] oblitérer / [cheque] faire opposition à.
◆ ***cancel out*** **vt sep** annuler ▸ **to cancel each other out** s'annuler.

cancellation [ˌkænsə'leɪʃn] **n** annulation *f*.

cancer ['kænsəʳ] ■ **n** cancer *m*.
■ **comp : cancer patient** cancéreux *m*, -euse *f* ▸ **cancer research** lutte *f* contre le cancer ▸ **cancer ward** service *m* de cancérologie.
◆ ***Cancer*** **n** Cancer *m* ▸ **to be (a) Cancer** être Cancer.

cancerous ['kænsərəs] **adj** cancéreux(euse).

candelabra [ˌkændɪ'lɑ:brə] **n** candélabre *m*.

C and F, ***C & F*** (abbr of ***cost and freight***) C et F.

candid ['kændɪd] **adj** franc (franche).

candidacy ['kændɪdəsɪ] **n** candidature *f*.

candidate ['kændɪdət] **n : candidate (for)** candidat *m*, -e *f* (pour).

candidature ['kændɪdətʃəʳ] **n** *UK* candidature *f*.

candidly ['kændɪdlɪ] **adv** franchement.

candidness ['kændɪdnɪs] = ***candour***.

candied ['kændɪd] **adj** confit(e).

candle ['kændl] **n** bougie *f*, chandelle *f* ▸ **to burn the candle at both ends** brûler la chandelle par les deux bouts.

candlelight ['kændllaɪt] **n** lueur *f* d'une bougie *OR* d'une chandelle.

candlelit ['kændllɪt] **adj** aux chandelles.

candlestick ['kændlstɪk] **n** bougeoir *m*.

candour *UK*, ***candor*** *US* ['kændəʳ] **n** franchise *f*.

candy ['kændɪ] (pl **-ies**) **n** *US* **1.** *(U)* [confectionery] confiserie *f* **2.** [sweet] bonbon *m*.

candyfloss ['kændɪflɒs] **n** *UK* barbe *f* à papa.

cane [keɪn] ■ **n 1.** *(U)* [for furniture] rotin *m* **2.** [walking stick] canne *f* **3.** [for punishment] **: the cane** la verge **4.** [for supporting plant] tuteur *m*.
■ **comp** en rotin.
■ **vt** fouetter.

cane sugar **n** sucre *m* de canne.

canine ['keɪnaɪn] ■ **adj** canin(e).
■ **n : canine (tooth)** canine *f*.

canister ['kænɪstəʳ] **n** [for film, tea] boîte *f* / [for gas, smoke] bombe *f*.

cannabis ['kænəbɪs] **n** cannabis *m*.

canned [kænd] **adj 1.** [food, drink] en boîte **2.** *inf fig* [music] enregistré(e) / [laughter] préenregistré(e).

cannelloni [ˌkænɪ'ləʊnɪ] **n** cannelloni *m*.

cannery ['kænərɪ] (pl **-ies**) **n** conserverie *f*.

cannibal ['kænɪbl] **n** cannibale *mf*.

cannibalism ['kænɪbəlɪzm] **n** cannibalisme *m*, anthropophagie *f*.

cannibalization, *UK* ***-isation*** [ˌkænɪbəlaɪ'zeɪʃn] **n** cannibalisme *m*.

cannibalize, *UK* ***-ise*** ['kænɪbəlaɪz] **vt** cannibaliser.

cannon ['kænən] (pl **cannon** OR **-s**) **n** canon *m*.
◆ ***cannon into*** **vt insep** *UK* percuter.

cannonball ['kænənbɔːl] **n** boulet *m* de canon.

cannot ['kænɒt] *fml* = ***can²***.

canny ['kænɪ] (comp **-ier**, superl **-iest**) **adj** [shrewd] adroit(e).

canoe [kə'nuː] ■ **n** canoë *m*, kayak *m*.
■ **vi** (pt & pp **-d**, cont **canoeing**) faire du canoë.

canoeing [kə'nuːɪŋ] **n** *(U)* canoë-kayak *m*.

canoeist [kə'nuːɪst] **n** canoéiste *mf*.

canon ['kænən] **n** canon *m*.

canonize, *UK* ***-ise*** ['kænənaɪz] **vt** canoniser.

canoodle [kə'nuːdl] **vi** *inf dated* se faire des mamours.

can opener **n** ouvre-boîtes *m inv*.

canopy ['kænəpɪ] (pl **-ies**) **n 1.** [over bed] ciel *m* de lit, baldaquin *m* / [over seat] dais *m* **2.** [of trees, branches] voûte *f*.

cant [kænt] **n** *(U)* paroles *fpl* hypocrites.

can't [kɑːnt] = ***cannot***.

Cantab. (abbr of ***cantabrigiensis***) *de l'université de Cambridge*.

Cantabrian Mountains [kæn'teɪbrɪən-] **npl : the Cantabrian Mountains** les monts *mpl* Cantabriques.

cantaloup, ***cantaloupe*** ['kæntəluːp] **n** cantaloup *m*.

cantankerous [kæn'tæŋkərəs] **adj** hargneux(euse).

canteen [kæn'tiːn] *UK* **n 1.** [restaurant] cantine *f* **2.** [box of cutlery] ménagère *f*.

canter ['kæntəʳ] ■ **n** petit galop *m*.
■ **vi** aller au petit galop.

Canterbury ['kæntəbrɪ] **n** Cantorbéry.

cantilever ['kæntɪliːvəʳ] **n** cantilever *m*.

Canton [kæn'tɒn] **n** Canton.

Cantonese [ˌkæntə'niːz] ■ **adj** cantonais(e).
■ **n** [language] cantonais *m*.

canvas ['kænvəs] **n** toile *f* ▸ **under canvas** [in a tent] sous la tente.

canvass ['kænvəs] ■ **vt 1.** POL [person] solliciter la voix de **2.** [opinion] sonder.
■ **vi** POL solliciter des voix.

canvasser ['kænvəsəʳ] **n 1.** POL agent *m* électoral **2.** [for opinion poll] sondeur *m*, -euse *f*.

canvassing ['kænvəsɪŋ] **n 1.** POL démarchage *m* électoral **2.** [for opinion poll] sondage *m*.

canyon ['kænjən] **n** canyon *m*.

canyoning ['kænjənɪŋ] **n** canyoning *m*.

cap [kæp] ■ **n 1.** [hat - gen] casquette *f* ▸ **swimming cap** bonnet *m* de bain ▸ **to go cap in hand to sb** se présenter humblement devant qqn **2.** [of pen] capuchon *m* / [of bottle] capsule *f* / [of lipstick] bouchon *m* **3.** *UK* [contraceptive device] diaphragme *m*.
■ **vt** (pt & pp **-ped**, cont **-ping**) **1.** [top] **: to be capped with** être coiffé(e) de **2.** [outdo] **: to cap it all** pour couronner le tout.

CAP (abbr of ***Common Agricultural Policy***) **n** PAC *f*.

capability [ˌkeɪpə'bɪlətɪ] (pl **-ies**) **n** capacité *f*.

capable ['keɪpəbl] **adj : capable (of)** capable (de).

capably ['keɪpəblɪ] **adv** avec compétence.

capacious [kə'peɪʃəs] **adj** *fml* vaste.

capacitor [kə'pæsɪtəʳ] **n** condensateur *m*.

capacity [kə'pæsɪtɪ] ■ **n** (pl **-ies**) **1.** *(U)* [limit] capacité *f*, contenance *f* ▸ **full to capacity** plein(e), comble ▸ **to work at full capacity** [factory] travailler à plein rendement ▸ **seating capacity** nombre *m* de places (assises) **2.** [ability] **: capacity (for)** aptitude *f* (à) **3.** [role] qualité *f* ▸ **in my capacity as...** en ma qualité de... ▸ **in an advisory capacity** en tant que conseiller.
■ **comp : capacity audience** salle *f* comble.

cape [keɪp] **n 1.** GEOG cap *m* **2.** [cloak] cape *f*.

Cape Canaveral [-kə'nævərəl] **n** le cap Canaveral.

Cape Cod **n** le cap Cod.

Cape Horn **n** le cap Horn.

Cape of Good Hope **n : the Cape of Good Hope** le cap de Bonne-Espérance.

caper ['keɪpəʳ] ■ **n 1.** CULIN câpre *f* **2.** *inf* [dishonest activity] coup *m*, combine *f*.
■ **vi** gambader.

Cape Town **n** Le Cap.

Cape Verde [-vɜːd] **n : the Cape Verde Islands** les îles *fpl* du Cap-Vert ▸ **in Cape Verde** au Cap-Vert.

capful ['kæpfʊl] **n** [of liquid] capsule *f* (pleine).

capillary [kə'pɪlərɪ] (pl **-ies**) **n** capillaire *m*.

capita ➤ ***per capita***.

capital ['kæpɪtl] ■ **adj 1.** [letter] majuscule **2.** [offence] capital(e).
■ **n 1.** [of country] **: capital (city)** capitale *f* **2.** TYPO **: capital (letter)** majuscule *f* ▸ **in capitals** en lettres majuscules **3.** *(U)* [money] capital *m* ▸ **to make capital (out) of** *fig* tirer profit de.

capital allowance **n** amortissement *m* fiscal pour investissement.

capital assets **npl** actif *m* immobilisé, immobilisations *fpl*.

capital expenditure **n** *(U)* dépenses *fpl* d'investissement.

capital gains tax **n** impôt *m* sur les plus-values.

capital goods **npl** biens *mpl* d'équipement.

capital-intensive **adj** à fort coefficient de capitaux.

capitalism ['kæpɪtəlɪzm] **n** capitalisme *m*.

capitalist ['kæpɪtəlɪst] ■ **adj** capitaliste.
■ **n** capitaliste *mf*.

capitalization, *UK* ***-isation*** [ˌkæpɪtəlaɪ'zeɪʃn] **n** capitalisation *f*.

capitalize, *UK* ***-ise*** ['kæpɪtəlaɪz] **vi : to capitalize on** tirer parti de.

capital punishment **n** peine *f* capitale *OR* de mort.

capital stock **n** capital *m* social.

capital transfer tax **n** droits *mpl* de mutation.

Capitol ['kæpɪtl] **n : the Capitol** le Capitole.

Capitol Hill **n** *siège du Congrès à Washington*.

capitulate [kə'pɪtjʊleɪt] **vi** capituler.

capitulation [kəˌpɪtjʊ'leɪʃn] **n** capitulation *f*.

cappuccino [ˌkæpʊ'tʃi:nəʊ] (**pl -s**) **n** cappuccino *m*.

capricious [kə'prɪʃəs] **adj** capricieux(euse).

Capricorn ['kæprɪkɔ:n] **n** Capricorne *m* ▸ **to be (a) Capricorn** être Capricorne.

caps [kæps] (**abbr of *capital letters***) **npl** cap.

capsicum ['kæpsɪkəm] **n** poivron *m*.

capsize [kæp'saɪz] ■ **vt** faire chavirer.
■ **vi** chavirer.

capsule ['kæpsju:l] **n 1.** [gen] capsule *f* **2.** MED gélule *f*.

Capt. (**abbr of *captain***) cap.

captain ['kæptɪn] ■ **n** capitaine *mf*.
■ **vt 1.** [ship] commander **2.** [sports team] être le capitaine de.

caption ['kæpʃn] **n** légende *f*.

captivate ['kæptɪveɪt] **vt** captiver.

captivating ['kæptɪveɪtɪŋ] **adj** captivant(e).

captive ['kæptɪv] ■ **adj** captif(ive).
■ **n** captif *m*, -ive *f*.

captive audience **n** audience *f* captive.

captive market **n** clientèle *f* captive, marché *m* captif.

captivity [kæp'tɪvətɪ] **n** *(U)* captivité *f* ▸ **in captivity** en captivité.

captor ['kæptər] **n** ravisseur *m*, -euse *f*.

capture ['kæptʃər] ■ **vt 1.** [person, animal] capturer / [city] prendre / [market] conquérir **2.** [attention, imagination] captiver **3.** [subj: painting, photo] rendre **4.** COMPUT saisir.
■ **n** [of person, animal] capture *f* / [of city] prise *f*.

car [kɑ:r] ■ **n 1.** AUT voiture *f* **2.** RAIL wagon *m*, voiture *f*.
■ **comp** [door, accident] de voiture / [industry] automobile.

Caracas [kə'rækəs] **n** Caracas.

carafe [kə'ræf] **n** carafe *f*.

car alarm **n** AUT alarme *f* de voiture.

carambola [ˌkærəm'bəʊlə] **n** carambole *f*.

caramel ['kærəmel] **n** caramel *m*.

caramelize, *UK* ***-ise*** ['kærəməlaɪz] **vi** se caraméliser.

carat ['kærət] **n** *UK* carat *m* ▸ **24-carat gold** or à 24 carats.

caravan ['kærəvæn] ■ **n** [people travelling] caravane *f* / *UK* [vehicle] caravane *f* / [towed by horse] roulotte *f*.
■ **comp** *UK* [holiday] en caravane.

caravanning ['kærəvænɪŋ] **n** *UK* caravaning *m*.

caravan site **n** *UK* camping *m* pour caravanes.

caraway seed ['kærəweɪ-] **n** graine *f* de carvi.

carbohydrate [ˌkɑ:bəʊ'haɪdreɪt] **n** CHEM hydrate *m* de carbone.
◆ ***carbohydrates*** **npl** [in food] glucides *mpl*.

car bomb **n** voiture *f* piégée.

carbon ['kɑ:bən] **n 1.** [element] carbone *m* **2.** = ***carbon copy*** **3.** = ***carbon paper***.

carbonated ['kɑ:bəneɪtɪd] **adj** [mineral water] gazeux(euse).

carbon copy **n 1.** [document] carbone *m* **2.** *fig* [exact copy] réplique *f*.

carbon dating [-'deɪtɪŋ] **n** datation *f* au carbone 14.

carbon dioxide [-daɪ'ɒksaɪd] **n** gaz *m* carbonique.

carbon fibre *UK*, ***carbon fiber*** *US* **n** fibre *f* de carbone.

carbon monoxide **n** oxyde *m* de carbone.

carbon paper **n** *(U)* (papier *m*) carbone *m*.

car-boot sale **n** *UK brocante en plein air où les coffres des voitures servent d'étal*.

carburettor *UK*, ***carburetor*** *US* [ˌkɑ:bə'retər] **n** carburateur *m*.

carcass ['kɑ:kəs] **n** [of animal] carcasse *f*.

carcinogen [kɑ:'sɪnədʒən] **n** (agent *m*) carcinogène *m* *OR* cancérogène *m*.

carcinogenic [ˌkɑ:sɪnə'dʒenɪk] **adj** carcinogène, cancérogène.

carcinoma [ˌkɑ:sɪ'nəʊmə] (**pl -s** *OR* **-mata** [-mətə]) **n** carcinome *m*.

card [kɑ:d] **n 1.** [gen] carte *f* ▸ **to play one's cards right** *fig* bien jouer son jeu ▸ **to put** *OR* **lay one's cards on the table** *fig* jouer cartes sur table **2.** *(U)* [cardboard] carton *m* **3.** COMPUT carte *f*.
◆ ***cards*** **npl : to play cards** jouer aux cartes.
◆ ***on the cards*** *UK*, ***in the cards*** *US* **adv** *inf* **: it's on the cards that...** il y a de grandes chances pour que...

cardamom ['kɑ:dəməm] **n** cardamome *f*.

cardboard ['kɑ:dbɔ:d] ■ **n** *(U)* carton *m*.
■ **comp** en carton.

cardboard box **n** boîte *f* en carton.

card-carrying **adj : card-carrying member** membre *m*.

card catalogue *UK*, ***card catalog*** *US* **n** fichier *m*.

cardiac ['kɑ:dɪæk] **adj** cardiaque.

cardiac arrest **n** arrêt *m* du cœur.

cardigan ['kɑːdɪgən] **n** cardigan *m*.

cardinal ['kɑːdɪnl] ■ **adj** cardinal(e).
■ **n** RELIG cardinal *m*.

cardinal number, cardinal numeral **n** nombre *m* cardinal.

card index **n** *UK* fichier *m*.

cardiogram ['kɑːdɪəgræm] **n** cardiogramme *m*.

cardiograph ['kɑːdɪəgrɑːf] **n** cardiographe *m*.

cardiology [ˌkɑːdɪ'ɒlədʒɪ] **n** cardiologie *f*.

cardiovascular [ˌkɑːdɪəʊ'væskjʊlər] **adj** cardiovasculaire.

cardphone ['kɑːdfəʊn] **n** *UK* téléphone *m* à carte.

cardsharp(er) ['kɑːdˌʃɑːp(ər)] **n** tricheur professionnel *m*, tricheuse professionnelle *f*.

card table **n** table *f* de jeu.

card trick **n** tour *m* de cartes.

card vote **n** *UK* vote *m* par carte *(chaque carte comptant pour le nombre de voix d'adhérents représentés)*.

care [keər] ■ **n 1.** *(U)* [protection, supervision] soin *m*, attention *f* ▸ **to take care of** [look after] s'occuper de ▸ **who will take care of your cat?** qui va s'occuper *OR* prendre soin de ton chat? ▸ **I'll take care of the reservations** je me charge des réservations *OR* de faire les réservations, je vais m'occuper des réservations ▸ **I have important business to take care of** j'ai une affaire importante à expédier ▸ **I can take care of myself** je peux *OR* je sais me débrouiller (tout seul) ▸ **the problem will take care of itself** le problème va s'arranger tout seul ▸ **I'm leaving the matter in your care** je vous confie l'affaire, je confie l'affaire à vos soins ▸ **the children are in the care of a nanny** on a laissé *OR* confié les enfants à une nurse *OR* à la garde d'une nurse ▸ **take care!** faites bien attention à vous!
2. *(U)* [attention, caution] attention *f*, soin *m* ▸ **'handle with care'** [on package] 'fragile' ▸ **take care not to offend her** faites attention à *OR* prenez soin de ne pas la vexer ▸ **you should take care of that cough** vous devriez (faire) soigner cette toux ▸ **drive with care** conduisez prudemment
3. [cause of worry] souci *m* ▸ **you look as though you haven't a care in the world** on dirait que tu n'as pas le moindre souci
4. *UK* ADMIN **: the baby was put in care *OR* taken into care** on a retiré aux parents la garde de leur bébé.
■ **vi 1.** [be concerned] se sentir concerné(e) ▸ **to care about** se soucier de ▸ **they really do care about the project** le projet est vraiment important pour eux ▸ **she cares a lot about her family** elle est très attachée *OR* elle tient beaucoup à sa famille ▸ **a book for all those who care about the environment** un livre pour tous ceux qui s'intéressent à l'environnement *OR* qui se sentent concernés par les problèmes d'environnement ▸ **I don't care what people think** je me moque de ce que pensent les gens ▸ **we could be dead for all he cares** pour lui, nous pourrions aussi bien être morts
2. [mind] **: I don't care** ça m'est égal ▸ **who cares?** qu'est-ce que ça peut faire? ▸ **I couldn't care less** *inf* je m'en moque pas mal.
◆ ***care of*** **prep** chez.
◆ ***care for*** **vt insep** *dated* [like] aimer.

CARE [keər] (abbr of ***Cooperative for American Relief Everywhere***) **n** *organisation humanitaire américaine.*

career [kə'rɪər] ■ **n** carrière *f*.
■ **comp** de carrière.
■ **vi** aller à toute vitesse.

careerist [kə'rɪərɪst] **n** *pej* carriériste *mf*.

careers [kə'rɪəz] **comp** *UK* [office, teacher] d'orientation.

careers adviser **n** *UK* conseiller *m*, -ère *f* d'orientation.

career woman **n** femme *f* qui privilégie sa carrière.

carefree ['keəfriː] **adj** insouciant(e).

careful ['keəfʊl] **adj 1.** [cautious] prudent(e) ▸ **to be careful to do sthg** prendre soin de faire qqch, faire attention à faire qqch ▸ **be careful!** fais attention! ▸ **be careful of the wet floor!** attention au sol mouillé! ▸ **to be careful with one's money** regarder à la dépense **2.** [work] soigné(e) / [worker] consciencieux(euse).

carefully ['keəflɪ] **adv 1.** [cautiously] prudemment **2.** [thoroughly] soigneusement.

careless ['keəlɪs] **adj 1.** [work] peu soigné(e) / [driver] négligent(e) **2.** [unconcerned] insouciant(e).

carelessly ['keəlɪslɪ] **adv 1.** [inattentively] sans faire attention **2.** [unconcernedly] avec insouciance.

carelessness ['keəlɪsnɪs] **n 1.** [inattention] manque *m* d'attention **2.** [lack of concern] insouciance *f*.

carer ['keərər] **n** *personne qui s'occupe d'un parent malade ou handicapé.*

caress [kə'res] ■ **n** caresse *f*.
■ **vt** caresser.

caret ['kærət] **n** TYPO signe *m* d'insertion.

caretaker ['keəˌteɪkər] **n** *UK* concierge *mf*.

caretaker government **n** gouvernement *m* intérimaire.

careworn ['keəwɔːn] **adj** accablé(e) de soucis, rongé(e) par les soucis.

car ferry **n** ferry *m*.

cargo ['kɑːgəʊ] ■ **n** (pl **-es** *OR* **-s**) cargaison *f*.
■ **comp : cargo ship** cargo *m*.

car hire **n** *UK* location *f* de voitures.

Carib ['kærɪb] **n** Caraïbe *mf*.

Caribbean [*UK* kærɪ'biːən, *US* kə'rɪbɪən] ■ **adj** caraïbe
■ **n : the Caribbean (Sea)** la mer des Caraïbes *OR* des Antilles ▸ **in the Caribbean** dans les Caraïbes.

caribou ['kærɪbuː] (pl **caribou** *OR* **-s**) **n** caribou *m*.

caricature ['kærɪkəˌtjʊər] ■ **n 1.** [cartoon] caricature **2.** [travesty] parodie *f*.
■ **vt** caricaturer.

caries ['keəriːz] **n** *(U)* carie *f*.

caring ['keərɪŋ] **adj** bienveillant(e).

caring professions **npl : the caring professions** les métiers *mpl* du social.

carjack ['kɑːˌdʒæk] **vt : to be carjacked** se faire voler sa voiture sous la menace d'une arme.

carjacking ['kɑːˌdʒækɪŋ] **n** vol *m* de voiture sous la menace d'une arme.

carload ['kɑːˌləʊd] **n : a carload of boxes/people** une voiture pleine de cartons/de gens.

carnage ['kɑːnɪdʒ] **n** carnage *m*.

carnal ['kɑːnl] **adj** *liter* charnel(elle).

carnation [kɑː'neɪʃn] **n** œillet *m*.

carnival ['kɑːnɪvl] **n 1.** [festival] carnaval *m* **2.** *US* [fun fair] fête *f* foraine.

carnivore ['kɑːnɪvɔːʳ] **n** carnivore *mf*.

carnivorous [kɑː'nɪvərəs] **adj** carnivore.

carol ['kærəl] **n : (Christmas) carol** chant *m* de Noel.

carouse [kə'raʊz] **vi** faire la fête.

carousel [ˌkærə'sel] **n 1.** [at fair] manège *m* **2.** [at airport] carrousel *m*.

carp [kɑːp] ■ **n** (pl **carp** *OR* **-s**) carpe *f*.
■ **vi : to carp (about sthg)** critiquer (qqch).

car park **n** *UK* parking *m*.

Carpathians [kɑː'peɪθɪənz] **npl : the Carpathians** les Carpates *fpl* ▸ **in the Carpathians** dans les Carpates.

carpenter ['kɑːpəntəʳ] **n** [on building site, in shipyard] charpentier *m* / [furniture-maker] menuisier *m*.

carpentry ['kɑːpəntrɪ] **n** [on building site, in shipyard] charpenterie *f* / [furniture-making] menuiserie *f*.

carpet ['kɑːpɪt] ■ **n** *lit & fig* tapis *m* ▸ **(fitted) carpet** moquette *f* ▸ **to sweep sthg under the carpet** *fig* tirer le rideau sur qqch.
■ **vt** [floor] recouvrir d'un tapis / [with fitted carpet] recouvrir de moquette, moquetter ▸ **carpeted with snow** *fig* recouvert d'un tapis de neige.

carpet slipper **n** pantoufle *f*.

carpet sweeper [-ˌswiːpəʳ] **n** balai *m* mécanique.

carphone ['kɑːˌfəʊn] **n** téléphone *m* de voiture.

car pool [kɑː'puːl] **n 1.** *UK* [fleet of cars] parc *m* de voitures **2.** [group of persons] *groupe de personnes qui s'organise pour utiliser la même voiture afin de se rendre à une destination commune*.

carport ['kɑːˌpɔːt] **n** appentis *m* (pour voitures).

car rental **n** *US* location *f* de voitures.

carriage ['kærɪdʒ] **n 1.** [of train, horsedrawn] voiture *f* **2.** *(U)* *UK* [transport of goods] transport *m* ▸ **carriage paid** *OR* **free** franco de port ▸ **carriage forward** en port dû **3.** [on typewriter] chariot *m* **4.** *liter* [bearing] port *m*.

carriage clock **n** pendule *f* de voyage *(décorative)*.

carriage return **n** retour *m* chariot.

carriageway ['kærɪdʒweɪ] **n** *UK* chaussée *f*.

carrier ['kærɪəʳ] **n 1.** COMM transporteur *m* **2.** [of disease] porteur *m*, -euse *f* **3.** MIL **: (aircraft) carrier** porte-avions *m inv* **4.** [on bicycle] porte-bagages *m inv* **5.** = ***carrier bag***.

carrier bag **n** sac *m* (en plastique).

carrier pigeon **n** pigeon *m* voyageur.

carrion ['kærɪən] **n** *(U)* charogne *f*.

carrot ['kærət] **n** carotte *f*.

carry ['kærɪ] (pt & pp -ied) ■ **vt 1.** [subj: person, wind, water] porter ▸ **she carried her baby on her back/in her arms** elle portait son enfant sur son dos/dans ses bras ▸ **the porter carried the suitcases downstairs/upstairs** le porteur a descendu/monté les bagages / [subj: vehicle] transporter **2.** [disease] transmettre **3.** [responsibility] impliquer / [consequences] entraîner ▸ **this offence carries a fine of £50** ce délit entraînera une amende de 50 livres ▸ **our products carry a 6-month warranty** nos produits sont accompagnés d'une garantie de 6 mois **4.** [motion, proposal] voter **5.** [baby] attendre **6.** MATHS retenir.
■ **vi** [sound] porter.
◆ ***carry away*** **vt insep : he was carried away by his enthusiasm/imagination** il s'est laissé emporter par son enthousiasme/imagination ▸ **I got a bit carried away and spent all my money** je me suis emballé et j'ai dépensé tout mon argent.
◆ ***carry forward*** **vt sep** FIN reporter.
◆ ***carry off*** **vt sep 1.** [plan] mener à bien ▸ **she carried it off beautifully** elle s'en est très bien tirée **2.** [prize] remporter.
◆ ***carry on*** ■ **vt insep** continuer ▸ **to carry on doing sthg** continuer à *OR* de faire qqch.
■ **vi 1.** [continue] continuer ▸ **to carry on with sthg** continuer qqch **2.** *inf* [make a fuss] faire des histoires **3.** *inf* [have a love affair] **: to carry on with sb** avoir une liaison avec qqn.
◆ ***carry out*** **vt insep** [task] remplir / [plan, order] exécuter / [experiment] effectuer / [investigation] mener ▸ **he failed to carry out his promise** il a manqué à sa parole, il n'a pas tenu *OR* respecté sa promesse ▸ **to carry out one's (professional) duties** s'acquitter de ses fonctions.
◆ ***carry over*** **vt sep 1.** [defer, postpone] reporter ▸ **to carry over a loss to the following year** reporter une perte sur l'année suivante **2.** COMM **: to carry over goods from one season to another** stocker des marchandises d'une saison sur l'autre.
◆ ***carry through*** **vt sep** [accomplish] réaliser.

carryall ['kærɪɔːl] **n** *US* fourre-tout *m inv*.

carrycot ['kærɪkɒt] **n** *UK* couffin *m*.

carry-on ■ **n** *UK inf* **: what a carry-on!** quelle histoire!
■ **adj : carry-on items, carry-on luggage** *OR* **bags** bagages à main.

carry-out, *US* ***carryout*** **n** plat *m* à emporter.

carsick ['kɑːˌsɪk] **adj : to be carsick** être malade en voiture.

car sickness **n** mal *m* de la route ▸ **to suffer from car sickness** être malade en voiture.

cart [kɑːt] ■ **n** charrette *f*.
■ **vt** *inf* traîner.

carte blanche **n** carte *f* blanche.

cartel [kɑː'tel] **n** cartel *m*.

cartilage ['kɑːtɪlɪdʒ] **n** cartilage *m*.

carton ['kɑːtn] **n 1.** [box] boîte *f* en carton **2.** [of cream, yoghurt] pot *m* / [of milk] carton *m*.

cartoon [kɑːˈtuːn] **n 1.** [satirical drawing] dessin *m* humoristique **2.** [comic strip] bande *f* dessinée **3.** [film] dessin *m* animé.

cartoonist [kɑːˈtuːnɪst] **n 1.** [of satirical drawings] dessinateur *m*, -trice *f* humoristique **2.** [of comic strips] dessinateur *m*, -trice *f* de bandes dessinées.

cartridge [ˈkɑːtrɪdʒ] **n 1.** [for gun, pen] cartouche *f* **2.** [for camera] chargeur *m* **3.** [for record player] tête *f* de lecture.

cartridge paper **n** papier-cartouche *m*.

cartwheel [ˈkɑːtwiːl] **n** [movement] roue *f*.

carve [kɑːv] ■ **vt 1.** [wood, stone] sculpter / [design, name] graver **2.** [slice - meat] découper.
■ **vi** découper.
◆ ***carve out*** **vt sep** *fig* se tailler.
◆ ***carve up*** **vt sep** *fig* diviser.

carving [ˈkɑːvɪŋ] **n** [of wood] sculpture *f* / [of stone] ciselure *f*.

carving knife **n** couteau *m* à découper.

car wash **n** [process] lavage *m* de voitures / [place] station *f* de lavage de voitures.

Casablanca [ˌkæsəˈblæŋkə] **n** Casablanca.

cascade [kæˈskeɪd] ■ **n** [waterfall] cascade *f*.
■ **vi** [water] tomber en cascade.

case [keɪs] **n 1.** [gen] cas *m* ◗ **to be the case** être le cas ◗ **in case of** en cas de ◗ **in that case** dans ce cas ◗ **in this particular case** en l'occurrence ◗ **in your case** en ce qui vous concerne, dans votre cas ◗ **in which case** auquel cas ◗ **in some cases** dans certains cas ◗ **as** *OR* **whatever the case may be** selon le cas ◗ **it's a clear case of mismanagement** c'est un exemple manifeste de mauvaise gestion ◗ **it was a case of having to decide on the spur of the moment** il fallait décider sur-le-champ ◗ **a case in point** un bon exemple
2. [argument] : **case (for/against)** arguments *mpl* (pour/contre) ◗ **there is a good case against/for establishing quotas** il y a beaucoup à dire contre/en faveur de l'établissement de quotas ◗ **to make (out) a case for sthg** présenter des arguments pour *OR* en faveur de qqch
3. LAW affaire *f*, procès *m* ◗ **her case comes up next week** son procès a lieu la semaine prochaine ◗ **to try a case** juger une affaire ◗ **the case is closed** c'est une affaire classée ◗ **he's on the case** [working on it] il s'en occupe
4. [container - gen] caisse *f* / [- for glasses] étui *m*
5. *UK* [suitcase] valise *f*.
◆ ***in any case*** **adv** quoi qu'il en soit, de toute façon ◗ **in any case I shan't be coming** je ne viendrai pas en tout cas *OR* de toute façon.
◆ ***in case*** ■ **conj** au cas où ◗ **I kept a place for you, in case you were late** je t'ai gardé une place, au cas où tu serais en retard.
■ **adv : (just) in case** à tout hasard ◗ **I'll take my umbrella (just) in case** je vais prendre mon parapluie au cas où.

case-hardened [-ˈhɑːdnd] **adj** [person] endurci(e).

case history **n** MED antécédents *mpl*.

case study **n** étude *f* de cas.

casework [ˈkeɪswɜːk] **n** *travail social personnalisé*.

caseworker [ˈkeɪsˌwɜːkəʳ] **n** *travailleur social s'occupant de cas individuels et familiaux*.

cash [kæʃ] ■ **n** *(U)* **1.** [notes and coins] liquide *m* ◗ **to pay (in) cash** payer comptant *OR* en espèces ◗ **discount for cash** escompte *m* de caisse **2.** *inf* [money] sous *mpl*, fric *m* ◗ **to be short of cash** être à court (d'argent) ◗ **cash prize** prix *m* en espèces **3.** [payment] : **cash in advance** paiement *m* à l'avance ◗ **cash on delivery** paiement à la livraison.
■ **vt** encaisser.
◆ ***cash in*** **vi** *inf* : **to cash in on** tirer profit de.

cash and carry **n** *UK* libre-service *m* de gros, cash-and-carry *m*.

cashback [ˈkæʃbæk] **n** *esp UK* **1.** [in supermarket] *espèces retirées à la caisse d'un supermarché lors d'un paiement par carte* **2.** [in mortgage lending] *prime versée par une société de crédit immobilier au souscripteur d'un emprunt*.

cashbook [ˈkæʃbʊk] **n** livre *m* de caisse.

cash box **n** caisse *f*.

cash card **n** carte *f* de retrait.

cash cow **n** COMM [product] vache *f* à lait.

cash crop **n** culture *f* de rapport.

cash desk **n** *UK* caisse *f*.

cash discount **n** escompte *m* de caisse, remise *f* sur paiement (au) comptant.

cash dispenser [-dɪˌspensəʳ] **n** distributeur *m* automatique de billets.

cashew (nut) [ˈkæʃuː-] **n** noix *f* de cajou.

cash flow **n** marge *f* d'auto-financement, cash-flow *m*.

cashier [kæˈʃɪəʳ] **n** caissier *m*, -ère *f*.

cashless [ˈkæʃlɪs] **adj** sans argent ◗ **cashless pay system** système *m* de paiement électronique ◗ **cashless society** société *f* de l'argent virtuel.

cash machine **n** distributeur *m* de billets.

cashmere [kæʃˈmɪəʳ] ■ **n** cachemire *m*.
■ **comp** en *OR* de cachemire.

cash payment **n** paiement *m* comptant, versement *m* en espèces.

cash point, ***cashpoint*** **n** *UK* **1.** [cash dispenser] distributeur *m* (automatique de billets), DAB *m* **2.** [shop counter] caisse *f*.

cash price **n** prix *m* comptant.

cash purchase **n** achat *m* au comptant *OR* contre espèces.

cash register **n** caisse *f* enregistreuse.

cash sale **n** vente *f* au comptant.

cash value **n** valeur *f* au comptant *OR* de rachat.

casing [ˈkeɪsɪŋ] **n** revêtement *m* / TECH boîtier *m*.

casino [kəˈsiːnəʊ] (pl -s) **n** casino *m*.

cask [kɑːsk] **n** tonneau *m*.

casket ['kɑ:skɪt] **n** **1.** [for jewels] coffret *m* **2.** *US* [coffin] cercueil *m*.

Caspian Sea ['kæspɪən-] **n : the Caspian Sea** la (mer) Caspienne.

casserole ['kæsərəʊl] **n** **1.** [stew] ragoût *m* **2.** [pot] cocotte *f*.

cassette [kæ'set] **n** [of magnetic tape] cassette *f* / PHOT recharge *f*.

cassette deck **n** platine *f* à cassettes.

cassette player **n** lecteur *m* de cassettes.

cassette recorder **n** magnétophone *m* à cassettes.

cassock ['kæsək] **n** soutane *f*.

cast [kɑ:st] ■ **n** **1.** CIN & THEAT [actors] acteurs *mpl* / [list of actors] distribution *f* **2.** ART & TECH [act of moulding - metal] coulage *m*, coulée *f* / [- plaster] moulage *m* / [mould] moule *m* **3.** MED [for broken limb] plâtre *m* ▸ **her arm was in a cast** elle avait un bras dans le plâtre.
■ **vt** (pt & pp cast) **1.** [throw] jeter ▸ **to cast doubt on sthg** jeter le doute sur qqch ▸ **to cast a spell (on)** jeter un sort (à) ▸ **we'll have to cast our net wide to find the right candidate** il va falloir ratisser large pour trouver le bon candidat ▸ **the accident cast a shadow over their lives** l'accident a jeté une ombre sur leur existence ▸ **could you cast an eye over this report?** voulez-vous jeter un œil sur ce rapport? ▸ **the evidence cast suspicion on him** les preuves ont jeté la suspicion sur lui ▸ **to cast lots** *UK* tirer au sort **2.** CIN & THEAT donner un rôle à ▸ **the director cast her in the role of the mother** le metteur en scène lui a attribué le rôle de la mère **3.** [vote] **: to cast one's vote** voter **4.** [metal] couler / [statue] mouler.
◆ ***cast about***, ***cast around*** **vi : to cast about for sthg** chercher qqch.
◆ ***cast aside*** **vt sep** *fig* écarter, rejeter.
◆ ***cast off*** ■ **vt sep** [old practices] se défaire de.
■ **vi** NAUT larguer les amarres.

castanets [ˌkæstə'nets] **npl** castagnettes *fpl*.

castaway ['kɑ:stəweɪ] **n** naufragé *m*, -e *f*.

caste [kɑ:st] **n** caste *f*.

caster ['kɑ:stər] **n** [wheel] roulette *f*.

caster sugar **n** *UK* sucre *m* en poudre.

castigate ['kæstɪgeɪt] **vt** *fml* châtier, punir.

casting ['kɑ:stɪŋ] **n** [for film, play] distribution *f*.

casting couch **n** *inf* **: she denied having got the part on the casting couch** elle a nié avoir couché avec le metteur en scène pour obtenir le rôle.

casting vote **n** voix *f* prépondérante.

cast iron **n** fonte *f*.
◆ ***cast-iron*** **adj** **1.** [made of cast iron] en *OR* de fonte **2.** [will] de fer / [alibi] en béton.

castle ['kɑ:sl] **n** **1.** [building] château *m* **2.** CHESS tour *f*.

castoff ['kɑ:stɒf] **n** *(usu pl)* *UK* [piece of clothing] vieux vêtement *m* / *fig* [person] laissé-pour-compte *m*, laissée-pour-compte *f*.
◆ ***cast-off*** **adj** *UK* dont personne ne veut ▸ **cast-off clothes** vieux vêtements *mpl*.

castor ['kɑ:stər] = ***caster***.

castor oil **n** huile *f* de ricin.

castor sugar = ***caster sugar***.

castrate [kæ'streɪt] **vt** châtrer.

castration [kæ'streɪʃn] **n** castration *f*.

casual ['kæʒʊəl] **adj** **1.** [relaxed, indifferent] désinvolte ▸ **to make casual conversation** parler de choses et d'autres, parler à bâtons rompus ▸ **casual sex** rapports *mpl* sexuels de rencontre **2.** [offhand] sans-gêne **3.** [chance] fortuit(e) **4.** [clothes] décontracté(e), sport *(inv)* **5.** [work, worker] temporaire.

casually ['kæʒʊəlɪ] **adv** [in a relaxed manner] avec désinvolture ▸ **casually dressed** habillé simplement.

casualty ['kæʒjʊəltɪ] **(pl -ies) n** **1.** [dead person] mort *m*, -e *f*, victime *f* / [injured person] blessé *m*, -e *f* / [of road accident] accidenté *m*, -e *f* **2.** *UK* = ***casualty department***.

casualty department **n** *UK* service *m* des urgences.

cat [kæt] **n** **1.** [domestic] chat *m* ▸ **to be like a cat on hot bricks** *UK* *OR* **on a hot tin roof** *US* être sur des charbons ardents ▸ **to let the cat out of the bag** vendre la mèche ▸ **to put the cat among the pigeons** *UK* jeter un pavé dans la mare ▸ **to rain cats and dogs** pleuvoir des cordes ▸ **the cat's whiskers** *UK* le nombril du monde **2.** [wild] fauve *m*.

CAT **n** **1.** *UK* (abbr of ***computer-aided teaching***) EAO *m* **2.** [kæt] (abbr of ***computerized axial tomography***) CAT *f* ▸ **CAT scan** scanographie *f*.

cataclysmic [ˌkætə'klɪzmɪk] **adj** catastrophique.

catacombs ['kætəku:mz] **npl** catacombes *fpl*.

Catalan ['kætəˌlæn] ■ **adj** catalan(e).
■ **n** **1.** [person] Catalan *m*, -e *f* **2.** [language] catalan *m*.

catalogue, *US* ***catalog*** ['kætəlɒg] ■ **n** [gen] catalogue *m* / [in library] fichier *m*.
■ **vt** cataloguer.

Catalonia [ˌkætə'ləʊnɪə] **n** Catalogne *f* ▸ **in Catalonia** en Catalogne.

Catalonian [ˌkætə'ləʊnɪən] ■ **adj** catalan(e).
■ **n** [person] Catalan *m*, -e *f*.

catalyst ['kætəlɪst] **n** *lit* & *fig* catalyseur *m*.

catalytic convertor, ***catalytic converter*** [ˌkætə'lɪtɪkkən'vɜ:tər] **n** pot *m* catalytique.

catamaran [ˌkætəmə'ræn] **n** catamaran *m*.

catapult ['kætəpʌlt] ■ **n** **1.** *UK* [hand-held] lance-pierres *m inv* **2.** HIST [machine] catapulte *f*.
■ **vt** *lit* & *fig* catapulter.

cataract ['kætərækt] **n** cataracte *f*.

catarrh [kə'tɑ:r] **n** catarrhe *m*.

catastrophe [kə'tæstrəfɪ] **n** catastrophe *f*.

catastrophic [ˌkætə'strɒfɪk] **adj** catastrophique.

catatonic [ˌkætə'tɒnɪk] **adj** catatonique.

cat burglar **n** *UK* monte-en-l'air *m inv*.

catcall ['kætkɔ:l] **n** sifflet *m*.

catch [kætʃ] ■ **vt** (pt & pp **caught**) **1.** [gen] attraper ▸ **to catch hold of sthg** attraper qqch ▸ **to catch sb's arm** saisir *OR* prendre qqn par le bras ▸ **to catch sight *OR* a glimpse of** apercevoir ▸ **to catch sb's attention** attirer l'attention de qqn ▸ **to catch sb's imagination** séduire qqn ▸ **to catch (a) cold** attraper un rhume, s'enrhumer ▸ **to catch cold** attraper *OR* prendre froid ▸ **to catch the post** *UK* arriver à temps pour la levée ▸ **I just caught the end of the film** j'ai juste vu la fin du film
2. [discover, surprise] prendre, surprendre ▸ **to catch sb doing sthg** surprendre qqn à faire qqch ▸ **you won't catch me doing the washing-up!** aucun danger de me surprendre en train de faire la vaisselle! ▸ **don't let me catch you at it again!** que je ne t'y reprenne pas!
3. [hear clearly] saisir, comprendre ▸ **I didn't quite catch what you said** je n'ai pas bien entendu ce que vous avez dit
4. [trap] **: he got caught by the police** il s'est fait attraper par la police ▸ **we got caught in a thunderstorm** nous avons été surpris par l'orage ▸ **I caught my finger in the door** je me suis pris le doigt dans la porte ▸ **he caught his coat on the brambles** son manteau s'est accroché aux ronces
5. [strike] frapper ▸ **he fell and caught his head on the radiator** il est tombé et s'est cogné la tête contre le radiateur.
■ **vi** (pt & pp **caught**) **1.** [become hooked, get stuck] se prendre ▸ **her skirt caught on a nail** sa jupe s'est accrochée à un clou
2. [fire] prendre, partir.
■ **n 1.** [of ball, thing caught] prise *f* ▸ **good catch!** SPORT bien rattrapé! ▸ **he's a good catch** c'est une belle prise ▸ **to play catch** jouer à la balle
2. [fastener - of box] fermoir *m* / [- of window] loqueteau *m* / [- of door] loquet *m*
3. [snag] hic *m*, entourloupette *f* ▸ **where's *OR* what's the catch?** qu'est-ce que ça cache?, où est le piège?
◆ ***catch at*** **vt insep** attraper, essayer d'attraper.
◆ ***catch on*** **vi 1.** [become popular] prendre
2. *inf* [understand] **: to catch on (to sthg)** piger (qqch).
◆ ***catch out*** **vt sep** *UK* [trick] prendre en défaut, coincer
▸ **I won't be caught out like that again!** on ne m'y prendra plus!
◆ ***catch up*** ■ **vt sep** rattraper ▸ **the material got caught up in the machinery** le tissu s'est pris dans la machine ▸ **to get caught up in a wave of enthusiasm** être gagné par une vague d'enthousiasme ▸ **he was too caught up in the film to notice what was happening** il était trop absorbé par le film pour remarquer ce qui se passait.
■ **vi : to catch up on sthg** rattraper qqch ▸ **to catch up on *OR* with one's work** rattraper le retard qu'on a pris dans son travail ▸ **I need to catch up on some sleep** j'ai du sommeil à rattraper.
◆ ***catch up with*** **vt insep** rattraper ▸ **his past will catch up with him one day** il finira par être rattrapé par son passé.

catch-22 [-twentɪ'tu:] **n : it's a catch-22 situation** on ne peut pas s'en sortir.

catch-all **adj** fourre-tout *(inv)*.

catching ['kætʃɪŋ] **adj** contagieux(euse).

catchment area ['kætʃmənt-] **n** *UK* [of school] secteur *m* de recrutement scolaire / [of hospital] circonscription *f* hospitalière.

catchphrase ['kætʃfreɪz] **n** rengaine *f*.

catchword ['kætʃwɜ:d] **n** slogan *m*.

catchy ['kætʃɪ] (comp **-ier**, superl **-iest**) **adj** facile à retenir, entraînant(e).

catechism ['kætəkɪzm] **n** catéchisme *m*.

categorical [ˌkætɪ'gɒrɪkl] **adj** catégorique.

categorically [ˌkætɪ'gɒrɪklɪ] **adv** catégoriquement.

categorize, *UK* ***-ise*** ['kætəgəraɪz] **vt** [classify] **: to categorize sb (as sthg)** cataloguer qqn (en tant que *OR* comme).

category ['kætəgərɪ] (pl **-ies**) **n** catégorie *f*.

category leader **n** chef *m* de file dans sa catégorie.

cater ['keɪtəʳ] **vi** [provide food] s'occuper de la nourriture, prévoir les repas.
◆ ***cater for*** **vt insep** *UK* **1.** [tastes, needs] pourvoir à, satisfaire / [customers] s'adresser à **2.** [anticipate] prévoir.
◆ ***cater to*** **vt insep** satisfaire.

caterer ['keɪtərəʳ] **n** traiteur *m*.

catering ['keɪtərɪŋ] **n** [trade] restauration *f*.

caterpillar ['kætəpɪləʳ] **n** chenille *f*.

caterpillar tracks **npl** chenille *f*.

cat flap **n** *UK* chatière *f*.

catharsis [kə'θɑ:sɪs] (pl **-ses** [-si:z]) **n** catharsis *f*.

cathartic [kə'θɑ:tɪk] ■ **adj** cathartique.
■ **n** MED purgatif *m*, cathartique *m*.

cathedral [kə'θi:drəl] **n** cathédrale *f*.

catheter ['kæθɪtəʳ] **n** cathéter *m*.

cathode ray tube **n** tube *m* cathodique.

Catholic ['kæθlɪk] ■ **adj** catholique.
■ **n** catholique *mf*.
◆ ***catholic*** **adj** [tastes] éclectique.

Catholicism [kə'θɒlɪsɪzm] **n** catholicisme *m*.

catkin ['kætkɪn] **n** chaton *m*.

catnap ['kætnæp] *inf* ■ **n** (petit) somme *m* ▸ **to have a catnap** faire un petit somme.
■ **vi** sommeiller, faire un petit somme.

Catseyes® ['kætsaɪz] **npl** *UK* catadioptres *mpl*.

catsuit ['kætsu:t] **n** *UK* combinaison-pantalon *f*.

catsup ['kætsəp] **n** *esp US* ketchup *m*.

cattle ['kætl] **npl** bétail *m*.

cattle grid **n** *UK* *grille incluse dans le sol empêchant le bétail mais non les véhicules de passer.*

catty ['kætɪ] (comp **-ier**, superl **-iest**) **adj** *inf pej* [spiteful] rosse, vache.

catwalk ['kætwɔ:k] **n** passerelle *f*.

Caucasian [kɔ:'keɪzjən] ■ **adj** caucasien(enne).
■ **n 1.** GEOG Caucasien *m*, -enne *f* **2.** [white person] Blanc *m* Blanche *f*.

Caucasus ['kɔ:kəsəs] **n : the Caucasus** le Caucase.

caucus ['kɔ:kəs] **n 1.** *US* POL comité *m* électoral *(d'un parti)* **2.** *UK* POL comité *m (d'un parti).*

CULTURE

Caucus

Aux États Unis, les **caucus** sont d'importantes rencontres politiques organisées entre les membres d'un même parti politique, démocrate ou républicain. Le système de sélection des candidats à des postes politiques repose sur un système de **conventions.** Les conventions de niveau local désignent les délégués aux conventions de niveau supérieur et les candidats aux postes politiques de leur ressort. Les délégués de la Convention du comté élisent ceux de la Convention de l'État qui, eux-mêmes, élisent les délégués pour la Convention nationale. Lors de la Convention de l'État sont choisis les candidats à l'élection au poste de gouverneur d'un État fédéral (**State Governor**), lors de la Convention nationale ceux à l'élection présidentielle. Les premiers caucus de l'Iowa sont déterminants : si un candidat obtient de bons résultats dans cet État, sa campagne est largement avantagée. Depuis 1972, les caucus sont ainsi très révélateurs, mais de nos jours la plupart des candidats sont sélectionnés lors des élections primaires (**primaries**).

caught [kɔ:t] **pt & pp** ➤ ***catch***.

cauliflower ['kɒlɪ,flaʊər] **n** chou-fleur *m*.

causal ['kɔ:zl] **adj** causal(e).

cause [kɔ:z] ■ **n** cause *f* ▸ **I have no cause for complaint** je n'ai pas à me plaindre, je n'ai pas lieu de me plaindre ▸ **to have cause to do sthg** avoir lieu *OR* des raisons de faire qqch.
■ **vt** causer ▸ **to cause sb to do sthg** faire faire qqch à qqn ▸ **to cause sthg to be done** faire faire qqch ▸ **to cause a sensation** faire sensation.

causeway ['kɔ:zweɪ] **n** chaussée *f*.

caustic ['kɔ:stɪk] **adj** caustique.

caustic soda **n** soude *f* caustique.

cauterize, *UK* ***-ise*** ['kɔ:təraɪz] **vt** MED cautériser.

caution ['kɔ:ʃn] ■ **n 1.** *(U)* [care] précaution *f*, prudence *f* ▸ **to proceed with caution** [gen] agir avec circonspection *OR* avec prudence / [in car] avancer lentement **2.** [warning] avertissement *m* **3.** *UK* LAW réprimande *f*.
■ **vt 1.** [warn] **: to caution sb against doing sthg** déconseiller à qqn de faire qqch **2.** *UK* [subj: police officer] *informer un suspect que tout ce qu'il dira peut être retenu contre lui* ▸ **to caution sb for sthg** réprimander qqn pour qqch.
■ **vi : to caution against sthg** déconseiller qqch.

cautionary ['kɔ:ʃənərɪ] **adj** [tale] édifiant(e).

cautious ['kɔ:ʃəs] **adj** prudent(e).

cautiously ['kɔ:ʃəslɪ] **adv** avec prudence, prudemment.

cautiousness ['kɔ:ʃəsnɪs] **n** prudence *f*, circonspection *f*.

cavalier [,kævə'lɪər] **adj** [offhand] cavalier(ère).

cavalry ['kævlrɪ] **n** cavalerie *f*.

cave [keɪv] **n** caverne *f*, grotte *f*.
◆ ***cave in*** **vi 1.** [roof, ceiling] s'affaisser **2.** [yield] **: to cave in (to sthg)** capituler *OR* céder (devant qqch).

caveat ['kævɪæt] **n** avertissement *m* / LAW notification *f* d'opposition.

caveman ['keɪvmæn] (**pl -men** [-men]) **n** homme *m* des cavernes.

cavern ['kævən] **n** caverne *f*.

cavernous ['kævənəs] **adj** [room, building] immense.

caviar(e) ['kævɪɑ:r] **n** caviar *m*.

caving ['keɪvɪŋ] **n** *UK* spéléologie *f* ▸ **to go caving** faire de la spéléologie.

cavity ['kævətɪ] (**pl -ies**) **n** cavité *f*.

cavity wall insulation **n** *UK* isolation *f* des murs creux.

cavort [kə'vɔ:t] **vi** gambader.

cayenne (pepper) [keɪ'en-] **n** poivre *m* de cayenne.

CB **n 1.** (abbr of ***citizens' band***) CB *f* **2.** (abbr of ***Companion of (the Order of) the Bath***) *distinction honorifique britannique*.

CBC (abbr of ***Canadian Broadcasting Corporation***) **n** *office national canadien de radiodiffusion*.

CBE (abbr of ***Companion of (the Order of) the British Empire***) **n** *distinction honorifique britannique*.

CBI **n** abbr of ***Confederation of British Industry***.

CBS (abbr of ***Columbia Broadcasting System***) **n** *chaîne de télévision américaine*.

cc **n 1.** (abbr of ***cubic centimetre***) cm^3 **2.** (abbr of ***carbon copy***) pcc.

CC **n** abbr of ***county council***.

CCTV **n** abbr of ***closed circuit television***.

CD ■ **n** (abbr of ***compact disc***) CD *m*.
■ **1.** abbr of ***civil defence*** **2.** (abbr of ***Corps Diplomatique***) CD.

CD burner **n** COMPUT graveur *m* de CD.

CDI (abbr of ***compact disc interactive***) **n** CDI *m*.

CD player **n** lecteur *m* de CD.

CD-R [,si:di:'ɑ:r] (abbr of ***compact disc recordable***) **n** CD(-R) *m*.

Cdr. abbr of ***commander***.

CD-R drive [,si:di:'ɑ:,draɪv] **n** lecteur-graveur *m* de CD.

CD-ROM [,si:di:'rɒm] (abbr of ***compact disc read only memory***) **n** CD-ROM *m*, CD-Rom *m*.

CD-ROM drive **n** lecteur *m* de CD-ROM *OR* de disque optique.

CD-RW [,si:di:ɑ:'dʌblju:] (abbr of ***compact disc rewriteable***) **n** CD-RW *m*.

CDT (abbr of ***Central Daylight Time***) **n** *heure d'été du centre des États-Unis*.

CD tower **n** colonne *f* (de rangement) pour CD.

CDV (abbr of ***compact disc video***) **n** CD vidéo *m*.

CDW abbr of ***collision damage waiver***.

CD writer n graveur *m* de CD.

CE abbr of ***Church of England***.

cease [si:s] *fml* ■ vt cesser ▸ **to cease doing** *OR* **to do sthg** cesser de faire qqch.
■ vi cesser.

cease-fire n cessez-le-feu *m inv*.

ceaseless ['si:slɪs] adj *fml* incessant(e), continuel(elle).

ceaselessly ['si:slɪslɪ] adv *fml* sans arrêt *OR* cesse, continuellement.

cedar (tree) ['si:dər-] n cèdre *m*.

cede [si:d] vt céder.

cedilla [sɪ'dɪlə] n cédille *f*.

CEEB (abbr of ***College Entrance Examination Board***) n *commission d'admission dans l'enseignement supérieur aux États-Unis*.

Ceefax® ['si:fæks] n *UK* télétexte *m* de la BBC.

ceilidh ['keɪlɪ] n *manifestations informelles avec chants, contes et danses en Écosse et en Irlande*.

ceiling ['si:lɪŋ] n *lit* & *fig* plafond *m*.

ceiling price n ECON prix *m* plafond.

celebrate ['selɪbreɪt] ■ vt **1.** [gen] célébrer, fêter **2.** RELIG célébrer.
■ vi faire la fête.

celebrated ['selɪbreɪtɪd] adj célèbre.

celebration [ˌselɪ'breɪʃn] n **1.** *(U)* [activity, feeling] fête *f*, festivités *fpl* **2.** [event] festivités *fpl*.

celebrity [sɪ'lebrətɪ] (pl -ies) n célébrité *f*.

celeriac [sɪ'lerɪæk] n céleri-rave *m*.

celery ['selərɪ] n céleri *m* (en branches).

celestial [sɪ'lestjəl] adj céleste.

celibacy ['selɪbəsɪ] n célibat *m*.

celibate ['selɪbət] adj célibataire.

cell [sel] n [gen & COMPUT] cellule *f*.

cellar ['selər] n cave *f*.

cellist ['tʃelɪst] n violoncelliste *mf*.

cello ['tʃeləʊ] (pl -s) n violoncelle *m*.

Cellophane® ['seləfeɪn] n Cellophane® *f*.

cellphone ['selfəʊn], ***cellular phone*** ['seljʊlər-] n téléphone *m* cellulaire.

cellulite ['seljʊlaɪt] n cellulite *f*.

Celluloid® ['seljʊlɔɪd] n celluloïd® *m*.

cellulose ['seljʊləʊs] n cellulose *f*.

Celsius ['selsɪəs] adj Celsius *(inv)*.

Celt [kelt] n Celte *mf*.

Celtic ['keltɪk] ■ adj celte.
■ n [language] celte *m*.

cement [sɪ'ment] ■ n ciment *m*.
■ vt *lit* & *fig* cimenter.

cement mixer n bétonnière *f*.

cemetery ['semɪtrɪ] (pl -ies) n cimetière *m*.

cenotaph ['senətɑ:f] n cénotaphe *m*.

censor ['sensər] ■ n censeur *m*.
■ vt censurer.

censorship ['sensəʃɪp] n censure *f*.

censure ['senʃər] ■ n blâme *m*, critique *f*.
■ vt blâmer, critiquer.

census ['sensəs] (pl -es [-i:z]) n recensement *m*.

cent [sent] n **1.** [pour le dollar] cent *m* **2.** [pour l'euro] centime *m*, (euro) cent *m offic*.

centenary *UK* [sen'ti:nərɪ] (pl -ies), ***centennial*** *US* [sen'tenjəl] n centenaire *m*.

center *US* = ***centre*** etc.

centigrade ['sentɪgreɪd] adj centigrade.

centigram(me) ['sentɪgræm] n centigramme *m*.

centilitre *UK*, ***centiliter*** *US* ['sentɪˌli:tər] n centilitre *m*.

centimetre *UK*, ***centimeter*** *US* ['sentɪˌmi:tər] n centimètre *m*.

centipede ['sentɪpi:d] n mille-pattes *m inv*.

central ['sentrəl] adj central(e) ▸ **central to** essentiel(elle) à.

Central African ■ adj centrafricain(e).
■ n Centrafricain *m*, -e *f*.

Central African Republic n : **the Central African Republic** la République centrafricaine ▸ **in the Central African Republic** en République centrafricaine.

Central America n Amérique *f* centrale ▸ **in Central America** en Amérique centrale.

Central American ■ adj centraméricain(e).
■ n Centraméricain *m*, -e *f*.

Central Asia n Asie *f* centrale ▸ **in Central Asia** en Asie centrale.

Central Europe n Europe *f* centrale.

Central European ■ n habitant *m*, -e *f* de l'Europe centrale.
■ adj d'Europe centrale.

central government n l'État *m (par opposition aux pouvoirs régionaux)*.

central heating n chauffage *m* central.

centralism ['sentrəlɪzm] n centralisme *m*.

centralization [ˌsentrəlaɪ'zeɪʃn] n centralisation *f*.

centralize, *UK* ***-ise*** ['sentrəlaɪz] vt centraliser.

centralized ['sentrəlaɪzd] adj centralisé(e).

central locking [-'lɒkɪŋ] n AUT verrouillage *m* centralisé.

centrally ['sentrəlɪ] adv centralement.

centrally heated adj équipé(e) du chauffage central

central nervous system n système *m* nerveux central.

central processing unit n COMPUT unité *f* centrale (de traitement).

central purchasing department n [in company] centrale *f* d'achat(s).

central reservation n *UK* AUT terre-plein *m* central

centre *UK*, ***center*** *US* ['sentəʳ] ■ **n** centre *m* ▸ **in the centre** au centre ▸ **centre of attention** centre d'attraction, point *m* de mire ▸ **centre of gravity** centre de gravité ▸ **a sports/health centre** un centre sportif/médical.
■ **adj 1.** [middle] central(e) ▸ **a centre parting** une raie au milieu **2.** POL du centre, centriste.
■ **vt** centrer.
◆ ***centre around***, ***centre on*** **vt insep** se concentrer sur.

centre back *UK*, ***center back*** *US* **n** FOOTBALL arrière *m* central.

centrefold *UK*, ***centerfold*** *US* ['sentəfəʊld] **n** [poster] photo *f* de pin-up.

centre forward *UK*, ***center forward*** *US* **n** FOOTBALL avant-centre *m inv*.

centre half *UK*, ***center half*** *US* **n** FOOTBALL arrière *m* central.

centreline *UK*, ***centerline*** *US* ['sentəlaɪn] **n** axe *m*, ligne *f* médiane.

centrepiece *UK*, ***centerpiece*** *US* ['sentəpi:s] **n 1.** [decoration] milieu *m* de table **2.** *fig* [principal element] élément *m* principal.

centre-spread *UK*, ***center spread*** *US* **n** double page *f* centrale.

centrifugal force [sentrɪ'fju:gl-] **n** force *f* centrifuge.

century ['sentʃʊrɪ] (pl **-ies**) **n** siècle *m*.

CEO (abbr of ***chief executive officer***) **n** *US* P-DG *m inv*.

ceramic [sɪ'ræmɪk] **adj** en céramique.
◆ ***ceramics*** **npl** [objects] objets *mpl* en céramique.

cereal ['sɪərɪəl] **n** céréale *f*.

cerebral ['serɪbrəl] **adj** cérébral(e).

cerebral palsy **n** paralysie *f* cérébrale.

ceremonial [ˌserɪ'məʊnjəl] ■ **adj** [dress] de cérémonie / [duties] honorifique.
■ **n** cérémonial *m*.

ceremonious [ˌserɪ'məʊnjəs] **adj** solennel(elle).

ceremoniously [ˌserɪ'məʊnjəslɪ] **adv** solennellement, avec cérémonie / [mock-solemnly] cérémonieusement.

ceremony ['serɪmənɪ] (pl **-ies**) **n 1.** [event] cérémonie *f* **2.** *(U)* [pomp, formality] cérémonies *fpl* ▸ **without ceremony** sans cérémonie ▸ **to stand on ceremony** faire des cérémonies.

cert [sɜ:t] **n** *UK inf* **: it's a (dead) cert** c'est tout ce qu'il y a de sûr, c'est couru.

cert. abbr of ***certificate***.

certain ['sɜ:tn] **adj 1.** [gen] certain(e) ▸ **he is certain to be late** il est certain qu'il sera en retard, il sera certainement en retard ▸ **to be certain of sthg/of doing sthg** être assuré de qqch/de faire qqch, être sûr de qqch/de faire qqch ▸ **to make certain** vérifier ▸ **to make certain of** s'assurer de ▸ **I know for certain that...** je suis sûr OR certain que... ▸ **to a certain extent** jusqu'à un certain point, dans une certaine mesure **2.** [named person] **: a certain...** un certain (une certaine)...

certainly ['sɜ:tnlɪ] **adv** certainement ▸ **can you help me? – certainly!** pouvez-vous m'aider? – bien sûr OR volontiers! ▸ **certainly not!** bien sûr que non!, certainement pas!

certainty ['sɜ:tntɪ] (pl **-ies**) **n** certitude *f*.

CertEd [sɜ:t'ed] (abbr of ***Certificate in Education***) **n** *diplôme universitaire en sciences de l'éducation*.

certifiable [ˌsɜ:tɪ'faɪəbl] **adj** [mad] bon (bonne) à enfermer.

certificate [sə'tɪfɪkət] **n** certificat *m*.

certification [ˌsɜ:tɪfɪ'keɪʃn] **n** certification *f*.

certified ['sɜ:tɪfaɪd] **adj** [teacher] diplômé(e) / [document] certifié(e).

certified mail **n** *US* envoi *m* recommandé.

certified public accountant **n** *US* expert-comptable *m*.

certify ['sɜ:tɪfaɪ] (pt & pp **-ied**) **vt 1.** [declare true] **: to certify (that)** certifier OR attester que **2.** [give certificate to] diplômer **3.** [declare insane] déclarer mentalement aliéné(e) ▸ **you should be certified!** on devrait t'enfermer!

cervical [sə'vaɪkl] **adj** [cancer] du col de l'utérus.

cervical smear **n** *UK* frottis *m* vaginal.

cervix ['sɜ:vɪks] (pl **-ices** [-ɪsi:z]) **n** col *m* de l'utérus.

cesarean (section) [sɪ'zeərɪən-] *US* = ***caesarean (section)***.

cessation [se'seɪʃn] **n** cessation *f*.

cesspit ['sespɪt], ***cesspool*** ['sespu:l] **n** fosse *f* d'aisance.

CET (abbr of ***Central European Time***) **n** *heure d'Europe centrale*.

cf. (abbr of ***confer***) cf.

c/f abbr of ***carried forward***.

CFC (abbr of ***chlorofluorocarbon***) **n** CFC *m*.

HOW TO ...

express certainty

Elle va réussir, j'en suis sûr et certain / I'm convinced she'll pass
Je suis persuadé qu'il va revenir / I'm sure he'll come back
Je suis convaincu de sa bonne foi / I'm sure he acted in good faith
Tu es sûr que c'était elle ? / Are you sure it was her?
On va les retrouver, c'est sûr / We'll definitely find them
Bien sûr qu'il va venir / Of course he'll come
Je sais pertinemment qu'il ne le fera pas / I know for a fact that he won't do it
Je t'assure, c'est quelqu'un de très bien / Believe me, he's/she's a really nice person
Il n'y a pas de doute, c'est bien lui / There's no doubt about it, it is him

cg (abbr of ***centigram***) cg.

CG n abbr of ***coastguard***.

CGA (abbr of ***colour graphics adapter***) n adapteur *m* graphique couleur CGA.

CGI n **1.** COMPUT (abbr of ***common gateway interface***) CGI *f*, interface *f* commune de passerelle **2.** COMPUT (abbr of ***computer-generated images***) images *fpl* de synthèse.

CGT n abbr of ***capital gains tax***.

ch (abbr of ***central heating***) ch. cent.

ch. (abbr of ***chapter***) chap.

CH (abbr of ***Companion of Honour***) n *distinction honorifique britannique*.

Chad [tʃæd] n Tchad *m* ▸ **in Chad** au Tchad.

chafe [tʃeɪf] ■ vt [rub] irriter.
■ vi **1.** [skin] être irrité(e) **2.** [person] **: to chafe at** s'irriter OR s'énerver de.

chaff [tʃɑːf] *(U)* n balle *f*.

chaffinch ['tʃæfɪntʃ] n pinson *m*.

chagrin ['ʃægrɪn] ■ n *liter* (vif) dépit *m*, (vive) déception *f* OR contrariété *f* ▸ **much to my chagrin** à mon grand dépit.
■ vt contrarier, décevoir.

chain [tʃeɪn] ■ n chaîne *f* ▸ **chain of events** suite *f* OR série *f* d'événements ▸ **chain of office** chaîne *f (insigne de la fonction de maire)*.
■ vt [person, animal] enchaîner / [object] attacher avec une chaîne.

chain letter n chaîne *f*.

chain mail n *(U)* cotte *f* de mailles.

chain reaction n réaction *f* en chaîne.

chain saw n tronçonneuse *f*.

chain-smoke vi fumer cigarette sur cigarette.

chain-smoker n fumeur invétéré *m*, fumeuse invétérée *f*, gros fumeur *m*, grosse fumeuse *f*.

chain store n grand magasin *m (à succursales multiples)*.

chair [tʃeəʳ] ■ n **1.** [gen] chaise *f* / [armchair] fauteuil *m* **2.** [university post] chaire *f* **3.** [of meeting] présidence *f* ▸ **to take the chair** présider **4.** *inf US* **: the chair** la chaise électrique.
■ vt [meeting] présider / [discussion] diriger.

chairlift n télésiège *m*.

chairman ['tʃeəmən] (pl **-men** [-mən]) n président *m*, -e *f*.

chairmanship ['tʃeəmənʃɪp] n présidence *f*.

chairperson ['tʃeəˌpɜːsn] (pl -s) n président *m*, -e *f*.

chairwoman ['tʃeəˌwʊmən] (pl **-women** [-ˌwɪmɪn]) n présidente *f*.

chaise longue [ʃeɪz'lɒŋ] (pl **chaises longues** [ʃeɪz'lɒŋ]) n méridienne *f*.

chalet ['ʃæleɪ] n chalet *m*.

chalice ['tʃælɪs] n calice *m*.

chalk [tʃɔːk] n craie *f*.
◆ ***by a long chalk*** adv *UK* de loin.
◆ ***not by a long chalk*** adv *UK* loin s'en faut, loin de là.
◆ ***chalk up*** vt sep [victory, success] remporter.

chalkboard ['tʃɔːkbɔːd] n *US* tableau *m* (noir).

challenge ['tʃælɪndʒ] ■ n défi *m* ▸ **to take up the challenge** relever le défi ▸ **he needs a job that presents more of a challenge** il a besoin d'un emploi plus stimulant.
■ vt **1.** [to fight, competition] **: she challenged me to a race/a game of chess** elle m'a défié à la course/aux échecs ▸ **to challenge sb to do sthg** défier qqn de faire qqch ▸ **she needs a job that really challenges her** elle a besoin d'un travail qui soit pour elle une gageure OR un challenge **2.** [question] mettre en question OR en doute.

challenger ['tʃælɪndʒəʳ] n challenger *m*.

challenging ['tʃælɪndʒɪŋ] adj **1.** [task, job] stimulant(e) **2.** [look, tone of voice] provocateur(trice).

chamber ['tʃeɪmbəʳ] n [gen] chambre *f*.
◆ ***chambers*** npl [of barrister, judge] cabinet *m*.

chambermaid ['tʃeɪmbəmeɪd] n femme *f* de chambre.

chamber music n musique *f* de chambre.

chamber of commerce n chambre *f* de commerce.

chamber orchestra n orchestre *m* de chambre.

chameleon [kə'miːljən] n caméléon *m*.

chamois[1] ['ʃæmwɑː] (pl **chamois**) n [animal] chamois *m*.

chamois[2] ['ʃæmɪ] n **: chamois (leather)** peau *f* de chamois.

champ [tʃæmp] ■ n *inf* champion *m*, -onne *f*.
■ vi [horse] ronger, mâchonner.

champagne [ˌʃæm'peɪn] n champagne *m*.

champion ['tʃæmpjən] n champion *m*, -onne *f*.

championship ['tʃæmpjənʃɪp] n championnat *m*.

chance [tʃɑːns] ■ n **1.** *(U)* [luck] hasard *m* ▸ **it was pure chance that I found it** je l'ai trouvé tout à fait par hasard ▸ **by chance** par hasard ▸ **if by any chance** si par hasard ▸ **is there any chance of seeing you again?** serait-il possible de vous revoir? ▸ **to leave things to chance** laisser faire les choses ▸ **to leave nothing to chance** ne rien laisser au hasard
2. [likelihood] chance *f* ▸ **we have an outside chance of success** nous avons une très faible chance de réussir ▸ **she's got a good OR strong chance of being accepted** elle a de fortes chances d'être acceptée OR reçue ▸ **to be in with a chance of doing sth** avoir une chance de faire qqch ▸ **she didn't stand a chance (of doing sthg)** elle n'avait aucune chance (de faire qqch) ▸ **on the off chance** à tout hasard
3. [opportunity] occasion *f* ▸ **I haven't had a chance to write to him** je n'ai pas trouvé l'occasion de lui écrire ▸ **give her a chance to defend herself** donnez-lui l'occasion de se défendre ▸ **I'm offering you the chance of a lifetime** je vous offre la chance de votre vie ▸ **this is your last chance** c'est votre dernière chance
4. [risk] risque *m* ▸ **to take a chance** risquer le coup ▸ **to take a chance on doing sthg** se risquer à faire qqch ▸ **I don't want to take the chance of losing** je ne veux pas prendre le risque de perdre.
■ adj fortuit(e), accidentel(elle).
■ vt **1.** [risk] risquer ▸ **to chance it** tenter sa chance

2. *liter* [happen] **: to chance to do sthg** faire qqch par hasard.
◆ ***chances*** **npl** chances *fpl* ▸ **(the) chances are (that) he'll never find out** il y a de fortes ***or*** grandes chances qu'il ne l'apprenne jamais ▸ **what are her chances of making a full recovery?** quelles sont ses chances de se rétablir complètement?

chancellor ['tʃɑ:nsələʳ] **n 1.** [chief minister] chancelier *m*, -ière *f* **2.** UNIV président *m*, -e *f* honoraire.

Chancellor of the Exchequer **n** *UK* Chancelier *m* de l'Échiquier, ≃ ministre *m* des Finances.

chancy ['tʃɑ:nsɪ] (comp **-ier**, superl **-iest**) **adj** *inf* [risky] risqué(e).

chandelier [,ʃændə'lɪəʳ] **n** lustre *m*.

change [tʃeɪndʒ] ■ **n 1.** [gen] **: change (in sb/in sthg)** changement *m* (en qqn/de qqch) ▸ **change of clothes** vêtements *mpl* de rechange ▸ **a change for the better/worse** un changement en mieux/pire, une amélioration/dégradation ▸ **to make a change** changer un peu ▸ **for a change** pour changer (un peu) ▸ **it'll be *or* make a nice change for them not to have the children in the house** cela les changera agréablement de ne pas avoir les enfants à la maison ▸ **I need a change of scene *or* scenery** j'ai besoin de changer de décor ***or*** d'air
2. [money] monnaie *f* ▸ **can you give me change for five pounds?** pouvez-vous me faire la monnaie de cinq livres? ▸ **I don't have any loose *or* small change** je n'ai pas de petite monnaie.
■ **vt 1.** [gen] changer ▸ **to change one's name** changer de nom ▸ **to change one's clothes** changer de vêtements, se changer ▸ **to change sthg into sthg** changer ***or*** transformer qqch en qqch ▸ **the illness completely changed his personality** la maladie a complètement transformé son caractère ▸ **to change one's mind** changer d'avis
2. [jobs, trains, sides] changer de ▸ **to change places with sb** changer de place avec qqn ▸ **the liquid/her hair has changed colour** le liquide a/ses cheveux ont changé de couleur ▸ **to change hands** COMM changer de main
3. [money] changer ▸ **I'd like to change my pounds into dollars** j'aimerais changer mes livres contre des ***or*** en dollars ▸ **can you change a ten-pound note?** [into coins] pouvez-vous me donner la monnaie d'un billet de dix livres?
■ **vi 1.** [gen] changer ▸ **to change for the better/worse** changer en mieux/pire ▸ **the wind has changed** le vent a changé ***or*** tourné ▸ **wait for the lights to change** attendez que le feu passe au vert
2. [change clothes] se changer ▸ **to change into another pair of trousers** changer de pantalon ▸ **they changed out of their uniforms** ils ont enlevé leurs uniformes
3. [be transformed] **: to change into** se changer en.
◆ ***change over*** **vi** [convert] **: to change over from/to** passer de/à.

changeable ['tʃeɪndʒəbl] **adj** [mood] changeable / [weather] variable.

changed [tʃeɪndʒd] **adj** changé(e).

change machine **n** distributeur *m* de monnaie.

change of life **n : the change of life** le retour *m* d'âge.

changeover ['tʃeɪndʒ,əʊvəʳ] **n : changeover (to)** passage *m* (à), changement *m* (pour).

change purse **n** *US* porte-monnaie *m inv*.

changing ['tʃeɪndʒɪŋ] **adj** changeant(e).

changing room **n** *UK* SPORT vestiaire *m* / [in shop] cabine *f* d'essayage.

channel ['tʃænl] ■ **n 1.** TV chaîne *f* / RADIO station *f* ▸ **the film is on Channel 2** le film est sur la deuxième chaîne **2.** [for irrigation] canal *m* / [duct] conduit *m* **3.** [on river, sea] chenal *m*.
■ **vt** (*UK* **-led**, cont **-ling**, *US* **-ed**, cont **-ing**) *lit* & *fig* canaliser.
◆ ***Channel*** **n : the (English) Channel** la Manche.
◆ ***channels*** **npl : to go through the proper channels** suivre ***or*** passer la filière.

channel-hop **vi** TV zapper.

channel-hopper **n** TV zappeur *m*, -euse *f*.

Channel Islands **npl : the Channel Islands** les îles *fpl* Anglo-Normandes ▸ **in the Channel Islands** dans les îles Anglo-Normandes.

channel of distribution **n** circuit *m* ***or*** canal *m* de distribution.

Channel tunnel **n : the Channel tunnel** le tunnel sous la Manche.

chant [tʃɑ:nt] ■ **n** chant *m*.
■ **vt 1.** RELIG chanter **2.** [words, slogan] scander.
■ **vi 1.** RELIG chanter **2.** [repeat words] scander des mots/des slogans.

chaos ['keɪɒs] **n** chaos *m*.

chaotic [keɪ'ɒtɪk] **adj** chaotique.

chap [tʃæp] **n** *UK inf* [man] type *m*.

chapat(t)i [tʃə'pætɪ] (pl **chapat(t)i(e)s**) **n** galette *f* de pain indienne.

chapel ['tʃæpl] **n** chapelle *f*.

chaperon(e) ['ʃæpərəʊn] ■ **n** chaperon *m*.
■ **vt** chaperonner.

chaplain ['tʃæplɪn] **n** aumônier *m*.

chapped [tʃæpt] **adj** [skin, lips] gercé(e).

chapter ['tʃæptəʳ] **n** chapitre *m*.

char [tʃɑ:ʳ] ■ **n** *UK* [cleaner] femme *f* de ménage.
■ **vt** (pt & pp **-red**, cont **-ring**) [burn] calciner.
■ **vi** (pt & pp **-red**, cont **-ring**) *UK* [work as cleaner] faire des ménages.

character ['kærəktəʳ] **n 1.** [gen] caractère *m* ▸ **her behaviour is out of character** ce comportement ne lui ressemble pas **2.** [in film, book, play] personnage *m* **3.** *inf* [eccentric] phénomène *m*, original *m*.

character actor **n** acteur *m* de genre.

character assassination **n** diffamation *f*.

character code **n** COMPUT code *m* de caractère.

characteristic [,kærəktə'rɪstɪk] ■ **adj** caractéristique.
■ **n** caractéristique *f*.

characteristically [,kærəktə'rɪstɪklɪ] **adv** de façon caractéristique.

characterization, *UK* ***-isation*** [,kærəktəraɪ'zeɪʃn] **n** caractérisation *f*.

characterize, *UK* ***-ise*** ['kærəktəraɪz] **vt** caractériser.

characterless ['kærəktəlɪs] adj sans caractère.

character sketch n portrait *m* OR description *f* rapide.

character witness n témoin *m* de moralité.

charade [ʃə'rɑːd] n farce *f*.

◆ ***charades*** n *(U)* charades *fpl*.

charcoal ['tʃɑːkəʊl] n [for drawing] charbon *m* / [for burning] charbon de bois.

chard [tʃɑːd] n bette *f*, blette *f*.

charge [tʃɑːdʒ] ■ n **1.** [cost] prix *m* ▸ **free of charge** gratuit ▸ **admission charge** prix d'entrée ▸ **delivery charge** frais *mpl* de port ▸ **postal/telephone charges** frais postaux/téléphoniques ▸ **there's a charge of one pound for use of the locker** il faut payer une livre pour utiliser la consigne automatique ▸ **there's no charge for children** c'est gratuit pour les enfants
2. LAW accusation *f*, inculpation *f* ▸ **to file charges against sb** déposer une plainte contre qqn ▸ **he was arrested on a charge of conspiracy** il a été arrêté sous l'inculpation d'association criminelle ▸ **he pleaded guilty to the charge of robbery** il a plaidé coupable à l'accusation de vol ▸ **the government rejected charges that it was mismanaging the economy** le gouvernement a rejeté l'accusation selon laquelle il gérait mal l'économie
3. [responsibility] **: to take charge of** se charger de ▸ **to be in charge of, to have charge of** être responsable de, s'occuper de ▸ **in charge** responsable ▸ **who's in charge here?** qui est-ce qui commande ici? ▸ **I was put in charge of the investigation** on m'a confié la responsabilité de l'enquête
4. ELEC & MIL charge *f*.
■ vt **1.** [customer, sum] faire payer ▸ **they charge £5 for admission** le prix d'entrée est 5 livres ▸ **the doctor charged her $90 for a visit** le médecin lui a fait payer OR lui a pris 90 dollars pour une consultation ▸ **how much do you charge?** vous prenez combien? ▸ **to charge sthg to sb** mettre qqch sur le compte de qqn ▸ **can I charge this jacket?** *US* [with a credit card] puis-je payer cette veste avec ma carte (de crédit)?
2. [suspect, criminal] **: to charge sb (with)** accuser qqn (de) ▸ **I'm charging you with the murder of X** je vous inculpe du meurtre de X
3. ELEC & MIL charger.
■ vi **1.** [ask in payment] **: do you charge for delivery?** est-ce que vous faites payer la livraison? ▸ **he doesn't charge** il ne demande OR prend rien
2. [rush] se précipiter, foncer ▸ **suddenly two policemen charged into the room** tout d'un coup deux policiers ont fait irruption dans la pièce.

chargeable ['tʃɑːdʒəbl] adj **1.** [costs] **: chargeable to** à la charge de **2.** [offence] qui entraîne une inculpation.

chargeable asset n FIN actif *m* imposable sur les plus-values.

chargeable expenses n FIN frais *mpl* facturables.

chargeable gain n FIN bénéfice *m* imposable.

charge account n compte *m* crédit.

charge card n carte *f* de compte crédit *(auprès d'un magasin)*.

charged [tʃɑːdʒd] adj [emotional] chargé(e).

chargé d'affaires [ˌʃɑːʒeɪdæ'feəʳ] (pl **chargés d'affaires**) n chargé *m* d'affaires.

charge hand n *UK* chef *m* d'équipe.

charge nurse n *UK* infirmier *m*, -ère *f* en chef.

charger ['tʃɑːdʒəʳ] n **1.** [for batteries] chargeur *m*, -euse *f* **2.** *liter* [soldier's horse] cheval *m* de bataille.

charge sheet n *UK* procès-verbal *m*.

chariot ['tʃærɪət] n char *m*.

charisma [kə'rɪzmə] n charisme *m*.

charismatic [ˌkærɪz'mætɪk] adj charismatique.

charitable ['tʃærətəbl] adj **1.** [person, remark] charitable **2.** [organization] de charité.

charitably ['tʃærətəblɪ] adv charitablement.

charity ['tʃærətɪ] (pl **-ies**) n charité *f*.

charlatan ['ʃɑːlətən] n charlatan *m*.

charm [tʃɑːm] ■ n charme *m*.
■ vt charmer.

charm bracelet n bracelet *m* à breloques.

charmer ['tʃɑːməʳ] n charmeur *m*, -euse *f*.

charming ['tʃɑːmɪŋ] adj charmant(e).

charmingly ['tʃɑːmɪŋlɪ] adv [attractive] de façon charmante / [smile, dressed] avec charme.

charred [tʃɑːd] adj calciné(e).

chart [tʃɑːt] ■ n **1.** [diagram] graphique *m*, diagramme *m* **2.** [map] carte *f* ▸ **weather chart** carte *f* météorologique.
■ vt **1.** [plot, map] porter sur une carte **2.** *fig* [record] retracer **3.** être au hit-parade.
◆ ***charts*** npl **: the charts** le hit-parade.

charter ['tʃɑːtəʳ] ■ n [document] charte *f*.
■ vt [plane, boat] affréter.

chartered accountant [ˌtʃɑːtəd-] n *UK* expert-comptable *m*.

charter flight n vol *m* charter.

charter member n *US* [founder] membre *m* fondateur.

charter plane n (avion *m*) charter *m*.

chart-topping adj qui est en tête du hit-parade.

chary ['tʃeərɪ] (comp **-ier**, superl **-iest**) adj **: to be chary of doing sthg** hésiter à faire qqch.

chase [tʃeɪs] ■ n [pursuit] poursuite *f*, chasse *f* ▸ **to give chase** poursuivre.
■ vt **1.** [pursue] poursuivre **2.** [drive away] chasser **3.** *fig* [money, jobs] faire la chasse à.
■ vi **: to chase after sb/sthg** courir après qqn/qqch.
◆ ***chase up*** vt sep *UK* [person, information] rechercher, faire la chasse à.

chaser ['tʃeɪsəʳ] n [drink] *verre d'alcool qu'on prend après une bière*.

chasm ['kæzm] n *lit & fig* abîme *m*.

chassis ['ʃæsɪ] (pl **chassis**) n châssis *m*.

chaste [tʃeɪst] adj chaste.

chasten ['tʃeɪsn] vt châtier.

chastise [tʃæ'staɪz] vt *fml* [scold] punir, châtier.

chastity ['tʃæstətɪ] n chasteté *f*.

chat [tʃæt] ■ n causerie *f*, bavardage *m* ◗ **to have a chat** causer, bavarder.
■ vi (pt & pp **-ted**, cont **-ting**) causer, bavarder.
◆ ***chat up*** vt sep *UK inf* baratiner.

chatline ['tʃætlaɪn] n [gen] réseau *m* téléphonique (payant) / [for sexual encounters] téléphone *m* rose.

chatroom ['tʃætrʊm] n salle *f* de chat.

chat show n *UK* talk-show *m*.

chatter ['tʃætəʳ] ■ n **1.** [of person] bavardage *m* **2.** [of animal, bird] caquetage *m*.
■ vi **1.** [person] bavarder **2.** [animal, bird] jacasser, caqueter **3.** [teeth] : **his teeth were chattering** il claquait des dents.

chatterbox ['tʃætəbɒks] n *inf* moulin *m* à paroles.

chatty ['tʃætɪ] (comp **-ier**, superl **-iest**) adj [person] bavard(e) / [letter] plein(e) de bavardages.

chauffeur ['ʃəʊfəʳ] ■ n chauffeur *m*.
■ vt conduire.

chauffeur-driven adj conduit(e) par un chauffeur.

chauvinism ['ʃəʊvɪnɪzm] n **1.** [sexism] machisme *m*, phallocratie *f* **2.** [nationalism] chauvinisme *m*.

chauvinist ['ʃəʊvɪnɪst] n **1.** [sexist] macho *m* **2.** [nationalist] chauvin *m*, -e *f*.

chauvinistic [ˌʃəʊvɪ'nɪstɪk] adj **1.** [sexist] macho, machiste **2.** [nationalistic] chauvin(e).

cheap [tʃi:p] ■ adj **1.** [inexpensive] pas cher (chère), bon marché *(inv)* ◗ **labour is cheaper in the Far East** la main-d'œuvre est moins chère en Extrême-Orient **2.** [at a reduced price - fare, rate] réduit(e) / [- ticket] à prix réduit **3.** [low-quality] de mauvaise qualité **4.** [joke, comment] facile.
■ adv (à) bon marché ◗ **I can get it for you cheaper** je peux vous le trouver pour moins cher.
■ n : **on the cheap** pour pas cher.

cheapen ['tʃi:pn] vt [degrade] rabaisser.

cheaply ['tʃi:plɪ] adv à bon marché, pour pas cher.

cheapness ['tʃi:pnɪs] n **1.** [low cost] bas prix *m* **2.** [low quality] mauvaise qualité *f* **3.** [of joke, comment] facilité *f*.

cheapo ['tʃi:pəʊ] adj *inf* pas cher (chère).

cheapskate ['tʃi:pskeɪt] n *inf* grigou *m*.

cheat [tʃi:t] ■ n tricheur *m*, -euse *f*.
■ vt tromper ◗ **to cheat sb out of sthg** escroquer qqch à qqn ◗ **to feel cheated** se sentir lésé *OR* frustré.
■ vi **1.** [in game, exam] tricher **2.** *inf* [be unfaithful] : **to cheat on sb** tromper qqn.

cheating ['tʃi:tɪŋ] n tricherie *f*.

cheat sheet n *US inf* antisèche *f*.

Chechen ['tʃetʃen] ■ adj tchétchène.
■ n Tchétchène *mf*.

Chechenia [ˌtʃetʃen'jɑ:], ***Chechnya*** [ˌtʃetʃ'njɑ:] n Tchétchénie *f* ◗ **in Chechenia** en Tchétchénie.

check [tʃek] ■ n **1.** [inspection, test] : **check (on)** contrôle *m* (de) ◗ **to do** *OR* **to run a check on sb** se renseigner sur qqn
2. [restraint] : **check (on)** frein *m* (à),, restriction *f* (sur) ◗ **to put a check on sthg** freiner qqch ◗ **to keep** *OR* **hold sthg in check** [emotions] maîtriser qqch
3. *US* [bill] note *f*
4. [pattern] carreaux *mpl*
5. *US* [mark, tick] coche *f*
6. *US* = ***cheque***.
■ vt **1.** [test, verify] vérifier ◗ **the doctor checked my blood pressure** le médecin a pris ma tension / [passport, ticket] contrôler
2. [restrain, stop] enrayer, arrêter ◗ **to check o.s.** se retenir.
■ vi : **to check (for sthg)** vérifier (qqch) ◗ **to check on sthg** vérifier *OR* contrôler qqch ◗ **I'll have to check with the accountant** je vais devoir vérifier auprès du comptable.
◆ ***check in*** ■ vt sep [luggage, coat] enregistrer.
■ vi **1.** [at hotel] signer le registre
2. [at airport] se présenter à l'enregistrement.
◆ ***check into*** vt insep : **to check into a hotel** descendre dans un hôtel.
◆ ***check off*** vt sep pointer, cocher.
◆ ***check out*** ■ vt sep **1.** [luggage, coat] retirer
2. [investigate] vérifier
3. *inf* : **check this out** [look] vise un peu ça / [listen] écoute-moi ça.
■ vi [from hotel] régler sa note.
◆ ***check up*** vi : **to check up on sb** prendre des renseignements sur qqn ◗ **to check up (on sthg)** vérifier (qqch).

CULTURE

Checks and Balances

Le système constitutionnel américain, basé sur la séparation des pouvoirs, fonctionne sur le mode des **checks and balances**, les contrôles et les équilibres. Le gouvernement fédéral est partagé entre le pouvoir exécutif (le président), le pouvoir législatif (le Congrès) et le pouvoir judiciaire (les cours de justice). Chaque branche peut ainsi contrôler le pouvoir des autres départements et l'empêcher de devenir trop puissant. Le Congrès peut destituer le président (cf. **impeachment**), les **Courts** peuvent considérer qu'une loi votée par le Congrès est anticonstitutionnelle et le président peut disposer d'un droit de veto contre le Congrès ou nommer des juges au sein des cours fédérales.

checkbook *US* = ***chequebook***.

checked [tʃekt] adj à carreaux.

checkerboard [tʃekəbɔ:d] n *US* damier.

checkered *US* = ***chequered***.

checkers ['tʃekəz] n *(U) US* jeu *m* de dames.

check guarantee card n *US* carte *f* bancaire.

check-in n enregistrement *m*.

checking account ['tʃekɪŋ-] n *US* compte *m* courant.

checklist ['tʃeklɪst] n liste *f* de contrôle.

checkmate ['tʃekmeɪt] n échec et mat *m*.

checkout ['tʃekaʊt] n [in supermarket] caisse *f*.

checkpoint ['tʃekpɔɪnt] n [place] (poste *m* de) contrôle *m*.

checkup ['tʃekʌp] n MED bilan *m* de santé, check-up *m*.

Cheddar (cheese) ['tʃedəʳ-] n (fromage *m* de) cheddar *m*.

cheek [tʃi:k] ■ **n** **1.** [of face] joue *f* **2.** *inf* [impudence] culot *m*.
■ **vt** *UK inf* être insolent(e) avec.

cheekbone ['tʃi:kbəʊn] **n** pommette *f*.

-cheeked [tʃi:kt] **suffix** aux joues... ▸ **rosy-cheeked** aux joues roses *or* rouges ▸ **round-cheeked** aux joues rebondies *or* rondes, joufflu.

cheekily ['tʃi:kɪlɪ] **adv** avec insolence.

cheekiness ['tʃi:kɪnɪs] **n** insolence *f*.

cheeky ['tʃi:kɪ] (comp **-ier**, superl **-iest**) **adj** insolent(e), effronté(e).

cheer [tʃɪəʳ] ■ **n** [shout] acclamation *f*.
■ **vt** **1.** [shout for] acclamer **2.** [gladden] réjouir.
■ **vi** applaudir.
◆ ***cheers*** **excl** **1.** [said before drinking] santé! **2.** *UK inf* [goodbye] salut!, ciao!, tchao! **3.** *UK inf* [thank you] merci.
◆ ***cheer on*** **vt sep** encourager.
◆ ***cheer up*** ■ **vt sep** remonter le moral à.
■ **vi** s'égayer.

cheerful ['tʃɪəfʊl] **adj** joyeux(euse), gai(e).

cheerfully ['tʃɪəfʊlɪ] **adv** **1.** [joyfully] joyeusement, gaiement **2.** [willingly] de bon gré *or* cœur.

cheerfulness ['tʃɪəfʊlnɪs] **n** gaieté *f*.

cheering ['tʃɪərɪŋ] ■ **adj** [news, story] réconfortant(e).
■ **n** *(U)* acclamations *fpl*.

cheerio [ˌtʃɪərɪ'əʊ] **excl** *UK inf* au revoir!, salut!

cheerleader ['tʃɪəˌli:dəʳ] **n** *majorette qui stimule l'enthousiasme des supporters des équipes sportives, surtout aux États-Unis*.

cheerless ['tʃɪəlɪs] **adj** morne, triste.

cheery ['tʃɪərɪ] (comp **-ier**, superl **-iest**) **adj** joyeux(euse).

cheese [tʃi:z] **n** fromage *m*.

cheeseboard ['tʃi:zbɔ:d] **n** plateau *m* à fromage.

cheeseburger ['tʃi:zˌbɜ:gəʳ] **n** cheeseburger *m*, hamburger *m* au fromage.

cheesecake ['tʃi:zkeɪk] **n** CULIN gâteau *m* au fromage blanc, cheesecake *m*.

cheesed off [tʃi:zd-] **adj** *UK inf* **: to be cheesed off** en avoir marre ▸ **I'm cheesed off with this job** j'en ai marre de ce boulot.

cheesy ['tʃi:zɪ] (comp **-ier**, superl **-iest**) **adj** [tasting of cheese] au goût de fromage.

cheetah ['tʃi:tə] **n** guépard *m*.

chef [ʃef] **n** chef *mf*.

chemical ['kemɪkl] ■ **adj** chimique.
■ **n** produit *m* chimique.

chemically ['kemɪklɪ] **adv** chimiquement.

chemical weapons **npl** armes *fpl* chimiques.

chemist ['kemɪst] **n** **1.** *UK* [pharmacist] pharmacien *m*, -enne *f* ▸ **chemist's (shop)** pharmacie *f* **2.** [scientist] chimiste *mf*.

chemistry ['kemɪstrɪ] **n** chimie *f*.

chemotherapy [ˌki:məʊ'θerəpɪ] **n** chimiothérapie *f*.

cheque *UK*, ***check*** *US* [tʃek] **n** chèque *m* ▸ **to pay by cheque** payer par chèque.

cheque account *UK*, ***checking account*** *US* **n** compte *m* chèques.

chequebook *UK*, ***checkbook*** *US* ['tʃekbʊk] **n** chéquier *m*, carnet *m* de chèques.

chequebook journalism *UK*, ***checkbook journalism*** *US* **n** *dans les milieux de la presse, pratique qui consiste à payer des sommes importantes pour le témoignage d'une personne impliquée dans une affaire.*

CULTURE

Chequebook Journalism (UK), Checkbook Journalism (US)

Ce terme qualifie les journaux, en particulier ceux qu'on appelle **tabloids** (publications de format réduit destinées à un lectorat populaire), qui offrent de grosses sommes d'argent contre des informations confidentielles sur la vie privée des stars, sur les scandales ou toutes sortes de crimes. Ces histoires, appréciées du grand public, sont extrêmement lucratives pour cette presse spécialisée, mais ce type de journalisme est assez méprisé.

cheque card **n** *UK* carte *f* bancaire.

chequered *UK*, ***checkered*** *US* ['tʃekəd] **adj** **1.** [patterned] à carreaux **2.** *fig* [career, life] mouvementé(e).

Chequers ['tʃekəz] **n** *(U) résidence secondaire officielle du Premier ministre britannique.*

cherish ['tʃerɪʃ] **vt** chérir / [hope] nourrir, caresser.

cherished ['tʃerɪʃt] **adj** cher (chère).

cherry ['tʃerɪ] (pl **-ies**) **n** [fruit] cerise *f* ▸ **cherry (tree)** cerisier *m*.

cherub ['tʃerəb] (pl **-s** *or* **-im** [-ɪm]) **n** chérubin *m*.

chervil ['tʃɜ:vɪl] **n** cerfeuil *m*.

Ches. (abbr of ***Cheshire***) *comté anglais.*

chess [tʃes] **n** *(U)* échecs *mpl*.

chessboard ['tʃesbɔ:d] **n** échiquier *m*.

chessman ['tʃesmæn] (pl **-men** [-men]) **n** pièce *f*.

chest [tʃest] **n** **1.** ANAT poitrine *f* ▸ **to get sthg off one's chest** *inf* déballer ce qu'on a sur le cœur **2.** [box] coffre *m*.

chesterfield ['tʃestəfi:ld] **n** canapé *m*.

chestnut ['tʃesnʌt] ■ **adj** [colour] châtain *(inv)*.
■ **n** [nut] châtaigne *f* ▸ **chestnut (tree)** châtaignier *m*.

chest of drawers (pl **chests of drawers**) **n** commode *f*.

chesty ['tʃestɪ] (comp **-ier**, superl **-iest**) **adj** [cough] de poitrine.

chevron ['ʃevrən] **n** chevron *m*.

chew [tʃu:] ■ **n** *UK* [sweet] bonbon *m* (à mâcher).
■ **vt** mâcher.
◆ ***chew over*** **vt sep** *fig* [think over] ruminer, remâcher.
◆ ***chew up*** **vt sep** mâchouiller.

chewing gum ['tʃu:ɪŋ-] **n** chewing-gum *m*.

chewy [tʃu:ɪ] (comp **-ier**, superl **-iest**) **adj** [food] difficile à mâcher.

chic [ʃi:k] ■ **adj** chic *(inv)*.
■ **n** chic *m*.

chicanery [ʃɪ'keɪnərɪ] **n** *(U)* chicane *f*.

chick [tʃɪk] **n** [bird] oisillon *m* / [chicken] poussin *m*.

chicken ['tʃɪkɪn] ■ **adj** *inf* [cowardly] froussard(e).
■ **n 1.** [bird, food] poulet *m* ▸ **it's a chicken and egg situation** c'est l'histoire de la poule et de l'œuf **2.** *inf* [coward] froussard *m*, -e *f*.
◆ ***chicken out*** **vi** *inf* se dégonfler.

chickenfeed ['tʃɪkɪnfi:d] **n** *(U) fig* bagatelle *f*.

chickenpox ['tʃɪkɪnpɒks] **n** *(U)* varicelle *f*.

chicken wire **n** grillage *m*.

chickpea ['tʃɪkpi:] **n** pois *m* chiche.

chicory ['tʃɪkərɪ] **n** *UK* [vegetable] endive *f*.

chide [tʃaɪd] (pt **chided** OR **chid** [tʃɪd], pp **chid** OR **chidden** ['tʃɪdn]) **vt** *liter* **: to chide sb (for sthg)** réprimander qqn (à propos de qqch).

chief [tʃi:f] ■ **adj 1.** [main - aim, problem] principal(e) **2.** [head] en chef.
■ **n** chef *m*.

chief constable **n** *UK* commissaire *m* de police divisionnaire.

chief executive **n** directeur général *m*, directrice générale *f*.
◆ ***Chief Executive*** **n** *US* **: the Chief Executive** le président des États-Unis.

chief executive officer **n** *US* président-directeur général *m*.

chief justice **n** président *m* de la Cour Suprême (des États-Unis).

chiefly ['tʃi:flɪ] **adv 1.** [mainly] principalement **2.** [above all] surtout.

chief of staff **n** chef *m* d'état-major.

chief superintendent **n** *UK* commissaire *m* de police principal.

chieftain ['tʃi:ftən] **n** chef *m*.

chiffon ['ʃɪfɒn] **n** mousseline *f*.

chihuahua [tʃɪ'wɑ:wə] **n** chihuahua *m*.

chilblain ['tʃɪlbleɪn] **n** engelure *f*.

child [tʃaɪld] (pl **children** ['tʃɪldrən]) **n** enfant *mf*.

childbearing ['tʃaɪld,beərɪŋ] **n** maternité *f*.

child benefit **n** *(U) UK* ≃ allocations *fpl* familiales.

childbirth ['tʃaɪldbɜ:θ] **n** *(U)* accouchement *m*.

child care **n 1.** *UK* ADMIN protection *f* de l'enfance **2.** *US* [day care] **: child care center** crèche *f*, garderie *f*.

child-friendly **adj** [area, city] aménagé(e) pour les enfants / [house, furniture] conçu(e) pour les enfants.

childhood ['tʃaɪldhʊd] **n** enfance *f*.

childish ['tʃaɪldɪʃ] **adj** *pej* puéril(e), enfantin(e).

childishly ['tʃaɪldɪʃlɪ] **adv** *pej* de façon puérile.

childless ['tʃaɪldlɪs] **adj** sans enfants.

childlike ['tʃaɪldlaɪk] **adj** enfantin(e), d'enfant.

childminder ['tʃaɪld,maɪndəʳ] **n** *UK* gardienne *f* d'enfants, nourrice *f*.

child prodigy **n** enfant *mf* prodige.

childproof ['tʃaɪldpru:f] **adj** [container] *qui ne peut pas être ouvert par les enfants* ▸ **childproof lock** verrouillage *m* de sécurité pour enfants.

children ['tʃɪldrən] **npl** ➤ ***child***.

children's home **n** maison *f* d'enfants.

child support **n** *US* LAW pension *f* alimentaire.

Chile ['tʃɪlɪ] **n** Chili *m* ▸ **in Chile** au Chili.

Chilean ['tʃɪlɪən] ■ **adj** chilien(enne).
■ **n** Chilien *m*, -enne *f*.

chili ['tʃɪlɪ] = ***chilli***.

chill [tʃɪl] ■ **adj** frais (fraîche).
■ **n 1.** [illness] coup *m* de froid **2.** [in temperature] **: there's a chill in the air** le fond de l'air est frais **3.** [feeling of fear] frisson *m*.
■ **vt 1.** [drink, food] mettre au frais **2.** [person] faire frissonner.
■ **vi** [drink, food] rafraîchir.

chilli ['tʃɪlɪ] (pl **-es**) **n** [vegetable] piment *m*.

chilling ['tʃɪlɪŋ] **adj 1.** [very cold] glacial(e) **2.** [frightening] qui glace le sang.

chilli powder **n** poudre *f* de piment.

chilly ['tʃɪlɪ] (comp **-ier**, superl **-iest**) **adj** froid(e) ▸ **to feel chilly** avoir froid ▸ **it's chilly** il fait froid.

chime [tʃaɪm] ■ **n** [of bell, clock] carillon *m*.
■ **vt** [time] sonner.
■ **vi** [bell, clock] carillonner.

chimney ['tʃɪmnɪ] **n** cheminée *f*.

chimneypot ['tʃɪmnɪpɒt] **n** mitre *f* de cheminée.

chimneysweep ['tʃɪmnɪswi:p] **n** ramoneur *m*.

chimp(anzee) [tʃɪmp(ən'zi:)] **n** chimpanzé *m*.

chin [tʃɪn] **n** menton *m*.

china ['tʃaɪnə] ■ **n** porcelaine *f*.
■ **comp** en porcelaine.

China ['tʃaɪnə] **n** Chine *f* ▸ **in China** en Chine ▸ **the People's Republic of China** la République populaire de Chine.

china clay **n** kaolin *m*.

China Sea **n : the China Sea** la mer de Chine.

Chinatown ['tʃaɪnətaʊn] **n** quartier *m* chinois.

chinchilla [tʃɪn'tʃɪlə] **n** chinchilla *m*.

Chinese [,tʃaɪ'ni:z] ■ **adj** chinois(e).
■ **n** [language] chinois *m*.
■ **npl : the Chinese** les Chinois *mpl*.

Chinese cabbage **n** chou *m* chinois.

Chinese lantern **n** lanterne *f* vénitienne.

Chinese leaves **npl** *UK* = ***Chinese cabbage***.

chink [tʃɪŋk] ■ **n 1.** [narrow opening] fente *f* **2.** [sound] tintement *m*.
■ **vi** tinter.

chinos ['tʃi:nəʊz] **npl** *pantalon de grosse toile beige porté à l'origine par les militaires de l'armée de l'air américaine*.

chintz [tʃɪnts] ■ **n** chintz *m*.
■ **comp** de chintz.

chinwag [ˈtʃɪnwæg] **n** *UK inf* **: to have a chinwag** tailler une bavette.

chip [tʃɪp] ■ **n 1.** *UK* [fried potato] frite *f* / *US* [potato crisp] chip *m* **2.** [of glass, metal] éclat *m* / [of wood] copeau *m* **3.** [flaw] ébréchure *f* **4.** [microchip] puce *f* **5.** [for gambling] jeton *m*

⏭ **when the chips are down** en cas de coup dur ▸ **to have a chip on one's shoulder** en avoir gros sur le cœur.

■ **vt** (**pt & pp -ped, cont -ping**) [cup, glass] ébrécher.

◆ ***chip in*** *inf* ■ **vt insep** [contribute] contribuer.

■ **vi 1.** [contribute] contribuer **2.** [interrupt] mettre son grain de sel.

◆ ***chip off*** **vt sep** enlever petit morceau par petit morceau.

chip-based [-beɪst] **adj** COMPUT à puce.

chipboard [ˈtʃɪpbɔːd] **n** aggloméré *m*.

chipmunk [ˈtʃɪpmʌŋk] **n** tamia *m*.

chipolata [ˌtʃɪpəˈlɑːtə] **n** chipolata *f*.

chipped [tʃɪpt] **adj** [flawed] ébréché(e).

chippings [ˈtʃɪpɪŋz] **npl** [on road] gravillons *mpl* / [of wood] copeaux *mpl* ▸ **'loose chippings'** 'attention gravillons'.

chip shop **n** *UK* friterie *f*.

chiropodist [kɪˈrɒpədɪst] **n** pédicure *mf*.

chiropody [kɪˈrɒpədɪ] **n** podologie *f*.

chirp [tʃɜːp] **vi** [bird] pépier / [cricket] chanter.

chirpy [ˈtʃɜːpɪ] (**comp -ier, superl -iest**) **adj** gai(e).

chisel [ˈtʃɪzl] ■ **n** [for wood] ciseau *m* / [for metal, rock] burin *m*.

■ **vt** (*UK* **-led, cont -ling,** *US* **-ed, cont -ing**) ciseler.

chit [tʃɪt] **n** [note] note *f*, reçu *m*.

chitchat [ˈtʃɪttʃæt] **n** *(U) inf* bavardage *m*.

chivalrous [ˈʃɪvlrəs] **adj** chevaleresque.

chivalry [ˈʃɪvlrɪ] **n** *(U)* **1.** *liter* [of knights] chevalerie *f* **2.** [good manners] galanterie *f*.

chives [tʃaɪvz] **npl** ciboulette *f*.

chiv(v)y [ˈtʃɪvɪ] (**pt & pp chivvied** *OR* **chivied**) **vt 1.** *inf* [nag] harceler ▸ **to chivvy sb into doing sthg** harceler qqn jusqu'à ce qu'il fasse qqch **2.** [hunt - game] chasser / [- criminal] pourchasser.

◆ ***chivvy up*** **vt sep** *inf* faire activer.

chloride [ˈklɔːraɪd] **n** chlorure *m*.

chlorinated [ˈklɔːrɪneɪtɪd] **adj** chloré(e).

chlorine [ˈklɔːriːn] **n** chlore *m*.

chlorofluorocarbon [ˈklɔːrəʊˌflɔːrəʊˈkɑːbən] **n** chlorofluorocarbone *m*.

chloroform [ˈklɒrəfɔːm] **n** chloroforme *m*.

chlorophyll [ˈklɒrəfɪl] **n** chlorophylle *f*.

choc-ice [ˈtʃɒkaɪs] **n** *UK* Esquimau® *m*.

chock [tʃɒk] **n** cale *f*.

chock-a-block, ***chock-full*** **adj** *inf* **: chock-a-block (with)** plein(e) à craquer (de).

chocolate [ˈtʃɒkələt] ■ **n** chocolat *m*.

■ **comp** au chocolat.

choice [tʃɔɪs] ■ **n** choix *m* ▸ **to make a choice** faire un choix ▸ **to have first choice** pouvoir choisir en premier ▸ **it's your choice** c'est à vous de choisir *OR* décider ▸ **we had no choice but to accept** nous ne pouvions pas faire autrement que d'accepter ▸ **by** *OR* **from choice** par choix ▸ **a wide choice of goods** un grand choix de marchandises.

■ **adj** de choix.

choir [ˈkwaɪəʳ] **n** chœur *m*.

choirboy [ˈkwaɪəbɔɪ] **n** jeune choriste *m*.

choke [tʃəʊk] ■ **n** AUT starter *m*.

■ **vt 1.** [strangle] étrangler, étouffer **2.** [block] obstruer, boucher.

■ **vi** s'étrangler.

◆ ***choke back*** **vt insep** [anger] étouffer / [tears] refouler.

choked [tʃəʊkt] **adj 1.** [cry, voice] étranglé(e) **2.** *UK inf* [person - moved] secoué(e) / [- sad] peiné(e), attristé(e) / [- annoyed] énervé(e), fâché(e).

cholera [ˈkɒlərə] **n** choléra *m*.

cholesterol [kəˈlestərɒl] **n** cholestérol *m*.

chomp [ˈtʃɒmp] *inf* ■ **vi & vt** mastiquer bruyamment.

■ **n** mastication *f* bruyante.

choose [tʃuːz] (**pt chose, pp chosen**) ■ **vt 1.** [select] choisir ▸ **there's little** *OR* **not much to choose between them** ils se valent **2.** [decide] **: to choose to do sthg** décider *OR* choisir de faire qqch.

■ **vi** [select] **: to choose (from)** choisir (parmi *OR* entre).

choos(e)y [ˈtʃuːzɪ] (**comp -ier, superl -iest**) **adj** difficile.

chop [tʃɒp] ■ **n 1.** CULIN côtelette *f* **2.** [blow] coup *m* (de hache *etc*) ▸ **he's for the chop** *UK fig* il va sûrement se faire saquer.

■ **vt** (**pt & pp -ped, cont -ping**) **1.** [wood] couper / [vegetables] hacher **2.** *inf fig* [funding, budget] réduire

⏭ **to chop and change** changer sans cesse d'avis.

◆ ***chops*** **npl** *inf* babines *fpl*.

◆ ***chop down*** **vt sep** [tree] abattre.

◆ ***chop up*** **vt sep** couper en morceaux.

chopper [ˈtʃɒpəʳ] **n 1.** [axe] couperet *m* **2.** *inf* [helicopter] hélico *m*.

chopping board [ˈtʃɒpɪŋ-] **n** hachoir *m*.

choppy [ˈtʃɒpɪ] (**comp -ier, superl -iest**) **adj** [sea] agité(e).

chopstick [ˈtʃɒpstɪk] **n** baguette *f (pour manger)*.

choral [ˈkɔːrəl] **adj** choral(e).

chord [kɔːd] **n** MUS accord *m* ▸ **to strike a chord with sb** toucher qqn.

chore [tʃɔːʳ] **n** corvée *f* ▸ **household chores** travaux *mpl* ménagers.

choreograph [ˈkɒrɪəgrɑːf] **vt** [ballet, dance] chorégraphier, faire la chorégraphie de / *fig* [meeting, party] organiser.

choreographer [ˌkɒrɪˈɒgrəfəʳ] **n** chorégraphe *mf*.

choreography [ˌkɒrɪˈɒgrəfɪ] **n** chorégraphie *f*.

chortle [ˈtʃɔːtl] **vi** glousser.

chorus [ˈkɔːrəs] ■ **n 1.** [part of song] refrain *m* **2.** [singers] chœur *m* **3.** *fig* [of praise, complaints] concert *m*.

■ **vt** répondre en chœur.

chose [tʃəʊz] **pt** ➤ ***choose***.

chosen ['tʃəʊzn] pp ➤ ***choose***.

choux pastry [ʃu:-] **n** pâte *f* à choux.

chow [tʃaʊ] **n** [dog] chow-chow *m*.

chowder ['tʃaʊdəʳ] **n** [of fish] soupe *f* de poisson / [of seafood] soupe *f* aux fruits de mer.

Christ [kraɪst] ■ **n** Christ *m*.
■ **excl** Seigneur!, bon Dieu!

christen ['krɪsn] **vt 1.** [baby] baptiser **2.** [name] nommer.

christening ['krɪsnɪŋ] ■ **n** baptême *m*.
■ **comp** de baptême.

Christian ['krɪstʃən] ■ **adj 1.** RELIG chrétien(enne) **2.** [kind] charitable.
■ **n** chrétien *m*, -enne *f*.

Christianity [,krɪstɪ'ænətɪ] **n** christianisme *m*.

Christian name **n** prénom *m*.

Christmas ['krɪsməs] ■ **n** Noël *m* ▸ **happy** OR **merry Christmas!** joyeux Noël!
■ **comp** de Noël.

Christmas cake **n** *UK* gâteau *m* de Noël.

Christmas card **n** carte *f* de Noël.

Christmas carol **n** chant *m* de Noël, noël *m* / RELIG cantique *m* de Noël.

Christmas cracker **n** *UK* diablotin *m*.

Christmas Day **n** jour *m* de Noël.

Christmas Eve **n** veille *f* de Noël.

Christmas Island **n** l'île *f* Christmas ▸ **on Christmas Island** à l'île Christmas.

Christmas pudding **n** *UK* pudding *m* (de Noël).

Christmas stocking **n** ≃ soulier *m* de Noël.

Christmastime ['krɪsməstaɪm] **n : at Christmastime** à Noël.

Christmas tree **n** arbre *m* de Noël.

chrome [krəʊm], ***chromium*** ['krəʊmɪəm] ■ **n** chrome *m*.
■ **comp** chromé(e).

chromosome ['krəʊməsəʊm] **n** chromosome *m*.

chronic ['krɒnɪk] **adj** [illness, unemployment] chronique / [liar, alcoholic] invétéré(e).

chronically ['krɒnɪklɪ] **adv** de façon chronique.

chronicle ['krɒnɪkl] ■ **n** chronique *f*.
■ **vt** faire la chronique de.

chronicler ['krɒnɪkləʳ] **n** chroniqueur *m*, -euse *f*.

chronological [,krɒnə'lɒdʒɪkl] **adj** chronologique.

chronologically [,krɒnə'lɒdʒɪklɪ] **adv** chronologiquement.

chronology [krə'nɒlədʒɪ] **n** chronologie *f*.

chrysalis ['krɪsəlɪs] (pl **-lises** [-lɪsi:z]) **n** chrysalide *f*.

chrysanthemum [krɪ'sænθəməm] (pl **-s**) **n** chrysanthème *m*.

chubbiness ['tʃʌbɪnɪs] **n** rondeur *f*.

chubby ['tʃʌbɪ] (comp **-bier**, superl **-biest**) **adj** [cheeks, face] joufflu(e) / [person, hands] potelé(e).

chuck [tʃʌk] **vt** *inf* **1.** [throw] lancer, envoyer **2.** [job, boyfriend] laisser tomber.
◆ ***chuck away***, ***chuck out*** **vt sep** *inf* jeter, balancer.

chuckle ['tʃʌkl] ■ **n** petit rire *m*.
■ **vi** glousser.

chuffed [tʃʌft] **adj** *UK inf* **: chuffed (with sthg/to do sthg)** ravi(e) (de qqch/de faire qqch).

chug [tʃʌg] (pt & pp **-ged**, cont **-ging**) **vi** [train] faire teuf-teuf.

chum [tʃʌm] **n** *inf* copain *m*, copine *f*.

chummy ['tʃʌmɪ] (comp **-mier**, superl **-miest**) **adj** *inf* **: to be chummy with sb** être copain (copine) avec qqn.

chump [tʃʌmp] **n** *inf* imbécile *mf*.

chunk [tʃʌŋk] **n** gros morceau *m*.

chunky ['tʃʌŋkɪ] (comp **-ier**, superl **-iest**) **adj** [person, furniture] trapu(e) / [sweater, jewellery] gros (grosse).

church [tʃɜ:tʃ] **n 1.** [building] église *f* ▸ **to go to church** aller à l'église / [Catholics] aller à la messe **2.** [organization] Église *f*.

churchgoer ['tʃɜ:tʃ,gəʊəʳ] **n** pratiquant *m*, -e *f*.

churchman ['tʃɜ:tʃmən] (pl **-men** [-mən]) **n** membre *m* du clergé, ecclésiastique *m*.

Church of England **n : the Church of England** l'Église d'Angleterre.

Church of Scotland **n : the Church of Scotland** l'Église *f* d'Écosse.

churchyard ['tʃɜ:tʃjɑ:d] **n** cimetière *m*.

churlish ['tʃɜ:lɪʃ] **adj** grossier(ère).

churn [tʃɜ:n] ■ **n 1.** [for making butter] baratte *f* **2.** [for milk] bidon *m*.
■ **vt** [stir up] battre.
■ **vi : my stomach was churning** j'avais l'estomac tout retourné.
◆ ***churn out*** **vt sep** *inf* produire en série.
◆ ***churn up*** **vt sep** battre.

chute [ʃu:t] **n** glissière *f* ▸ **rubbish** *UK* OR **garbage** *US* **chute** vide-ordures *m inv*.

chutney ['tʃʌtnɪ] **n** chutney *m*.

chutzpah ['hʊtspə] **n** *(esp) US inf* culot *m*.

CI abbr of ***Channel Islands***.

CIA (abbr of ***Central Intelligence Agency***) **n** CIA *f*.

ciabatta [tʃə'bɑ:tə] **n** ciabatta *m*.

CIB (abbr of ***Criminal Investigation Branch***) **n** *la police judiciaire américaine*.

cicada [sɪ'kɑ:də] **n** cigale *f*.

CID (abbr of ***Criminal Investigation Department***) **n** *la police judiciaire britannique*.

cider ['saɪdəʳ] **n** *UK* cidre *m* ▸ **hard cider** *US* cidre *m*.

CIF (abbr of ***cost, insurance and freight***) CAF, caf.

cigar [sɪ'gɑ:ʳ] **n** cigare *m*.

cigarette [,sɪgə'ret] **n** cigarette *f*.

cigarette butt, ***cigarette end*** *UK* **n** mégot *m*.

cigarette holder **n** fume-cigarette *m inv*.

cigarette lighter **n** briquet *m*.

cigarette paper **n** papier *m* à cigarettes.

ciggie ['sɪgɪ] **n** *inf* clope *m ou f*, sèche *f*.

C-in-C **n** abbr of ***commander-in-chief***.

cinch [sɪntʃ] **n** *inf* **: it's a cinch** c'est un jeu d'enfants.

cinder ['sɪndəʳ] **n** cendre *f*.

cinderblock ['sɪndəblɒk] **n** *US* parpaing *m*.

Cinderella [,sɪndə'relə] **n** Cendrillon *f*.

cine-camera ['sɪnɪ-] **n** caméra *f*.

cine-film ['sɪnɪ-] **n** *UK* film *m*.

cinema ['sɪnəmə] **n** *UK* cinéma *m*.

cinemagoer ['sɪnɪmə,gəʊəʳ] **n** personne *f* qui fréquente les cinémas.

cinematic [,sɪnɪ'mætɪk] **adj** cinématographique.

cinematography [,sɪnəmə'tɒgrəfɪ] **n** *UK* cinématographie *f*.

cinnamon ['sɪnəmən] **n** cannelle *f*.

cipher ['saɪfəʳ] **n** [secret writing] code *m*.

circa ['sɜ:kə] **prep** environ.

circle ['sɜ:kl] ■ **n** **1.** [gen] cercle *m* ▸ **to come full circle** revenir à son point de départ ▸ **to go round in circles** *fig* tourner en rond **2.** [in theatre, cinema] balcon *m*.
■ **vt** **1.** [draw a circle round] entourer (d'un cercle) **2.** [move round] faire le tour de.
■ **vi** [plane] tourner en rond.

circuit ['sɜ:kɪt] **n** **1.** [gen & ELEC] circuit *m* **2.** [lap] tour *m* / [movement round] révolution *f*.

circuit board **n** plaquette *f* (de circuits imprimés).

circuit breaker **n** disjoncteur *m*.

circuitous [sə'kju:ɪtəs] **adj** indirect(e).

circular ['sɜ:kjʊləʳ] ■ **adj** **1.** [gen] circulaire **2.** [argument] qui tourne en rond.
■ **n** [letter] circulaire *f* / [advertisement] prospectus *m*.

circulate ['sɜ:kjʊleɪt] ■ **vi** **1.** [gen] circuler **2.** [socialize] se mêler aux invités.
■ **vt** [rumour] propager / [document] faire circuler.

circulation [,sɜ:kjʊ'leɪʃn] **n** **1.** [gen] circulation *f* **2.** PRESS tirage *m*.

circumcise ['sɜ:kəmsaɪz] **vt** circoncire.

circumcision [,sɜ:kəm'sɪʒn] **n** circoncision *f*.

circumference [sə'kʌmfərəns] **n** circonférence *f*.

circumflex ['sɜ:kəmfleks] **n** **: circumflex (accent)** accent *m* circonflexe.

circumnavigate [,sɜ:kəm'nævɪgeɪt] **vt** **: to circumnavigate the world** faire le tour du monde en bateau.

circumscribe ['sɜ:kəmskraɪb] **vt** *fml* [restrict] limiter.

circumspect ['sɜ:kəmspekt] **adj** circonspect(e).

circumstances ['sɜ:kəmstənsɪz] **npl** circonstances *fpl* ▸ **under** OR **in no circumstances** en aucun cas ▸ **under** OR **in the circumstances** en de telles circonstances.

circumstantial [,sɜ:kəm'stænʃl] **adj** *fml* **: circumstantial evidence** preuve *f* indirecte.

circumvent [,sɜ:kəm'vent] **vt** *fml* [law, rule] tourner, contourner.

circumvention [,sɜ:kəm'venʃn] **n** [of law, rule] fait *m* de tourner OR contourner.

circus ['sɜ:kəs] **n** cirque *m*.

cirrhosis [sɪ'rəʊsɪs] **n** cirrhose *f*.

CIS (abbr of ***Commonwealth of Independent States***) **n** CEI *f*.

cissy ['sɪsɪ] (pl **-ies**) **n** *UK inf* femmelette *f*.

cistern ['sɪstən] **n** **1.** *UK* [inside roof] réservoir *m* d'eau **2.** [in toilet] réservoir *m* de chasse d'eau.

citation [saɪ'teɪʃn] **n** citation *f*.

cite [saɪt] **vt** citer.

citizen ['sɪtɪzn] **n** **1.** [of country] citoyen *m*, -enne *f* **2.** [of town] habitant *m*, -e *f*.

Citizens' Advice Bureau **n** *service britannique d'information et d'aide au consommateur.*

Citizens' Band **n** citizen band *f (fréquence radio réservée au public)*.

citizenship ['sɪtɪznʃɪp] **n** citoyenneté *f*.

citric acid ['sɪtrɪk-] **n** acide *m* citrique.

citrus fruit ['sɪtrəs-] **n** agrume *m*.

city ['sɪtɪ] (pl **-ies**) **n** ville *f*, cité *f*.
◆ ***City*** **n** *UK* **: the City** la City *(quartier financier de Londres)*.

city centre *UK* **n** centre-ville *m*.

city-dweller **n** citadin *m*, -e *f*.

city hall **n** *US* ≃ mairie *f*, ≃ hôtel *m* de ville.

city technology college **n** *UK établissement d'enseignement technique du secondaire subventionné par les entreprises.*

civic ['sɪvɪk] **adj** [leader, event] municipal(e) / [duty, pride] civique.

civic centre *UK*, ***civic center*** *US* **n** centre *m* administratif municipal.

civics ['sɪvɪks] **n** *(U)* instruction *f* civique.

civil ['sɪvl] **adj** **1.** [public] civil(e) **2.** [polite] courtois(e), poli(e).

civil defence *UK*, ***civile defense*** *US* **n** protection *f* civile.

civil disobedience **n** résistance *f* passive à la loi.

civil engineer **n** ingénieur *m* des travaux publics.

civil engineering **n** génie *m* civil.

civilian [sɪ'vɪljən] ■ **n** civil *m*, -e *f*.
■ **comp** civil(e).

civility [sɪ'vɪlətɪ] **n** politesse *f*.

civilization [,sɪvəlaɪ'zeɪʃn] **n** civilisation *f*.

civilize, *UK* ***-ise*** ['sɪvɪlaɪz] **vt** civiliser.

civilized ['sɪvəlaɪzd] **adj** civilisé(e).

civil law **n** droit *m* civil.

civil liberties **npl** libertés *fpl* civiques.

civil list **n** *UK* liste *f* civile *(allouée à la famille royale par le Parlement britannique)*.

civil rights **npl** droits *mpl* civils.

civil servant **n** fonctionnaire *mf*.

civil service n fonction *f* publique.

civil war n guerre *f* civile.

CJD n abbr of ***Creutzfeldt-Jakob disease***.

cl (abbr of ***centilitre***) cl.

clad [klæd] adj *liter* [dressed] **: clad in** vêtu(e) de.

cladding ['klædɪŋ] n *UK* revêtement *m*.

claim [kleɪm] ■ n **1.** [demand] demande *f* ◗ **she has many claims on her time** elle est très prise ◗ **he made too many claims on their generosity** il a abusé de leur générosité ◗ **pay claim** demande *f* d'augmentation (de salaire) **2.** [in insurance] demande *f* d'indemnité ◗ **to put in a claim for sthg** demander une indemnité pour qqch **3.** [right] droit *m* ◗ **to lay claim to sthg** revendiquer qqch ◗ **his only claim to fame is that he once appeared on TV** c'est à une apparition à la télévision qu'il doit d'être célèbre **4.** [assertion] affirmation *f* ◗ **I make no claims to understand why** je ne prétends pas comprendre pourquoi.
■ vt **1.** [ask for] réclamer ◗ **to claim damages** réclamer des dommages et intérêts **2.** [responsibility, credit] revendiquer ◗ **he claims all the credit** il s'attribue tout le mérite **3.** [maintain] prétendre ◗ **it is claimed that...** on dit *OR* prétend que... ◗ **to claim to be sthg** se faire passer pour qqch, prétendre être qqch.
■ vi **: to claim for sthg** faire une demande d'indemnité pour qqch ◗ **to claim (on one's insurance)** faire une déclaration de sinistre.

claimant ['kleɪmənt] n [to throne] prétendant *m*, -e *f* / [of state benefit] demandeur *m*, -eresse *f*, requérant *m*, -e *f*.

claim form n [for expenses] note *f* de frais / [for insurance] formulaire *m* de déclaration de sinistre.

clairvoyant [kleə'vɔɪənt] ■ adj [person] qui a des dons de double vue.
■ n voyant *m*, -e *f*.

clam [klæm] (pt & pp **-med**, cont **-ming**) n palourde *f*.
◆ ***clam up*** vi *inf* la boucler.

clamber ['klæmbəʳ] vi grimper.

clammy ['klæmɪ] (comp **-mier**, superl **-miest**) adj [skin] moite / [weather] lourd et humide.

clamor ['klæməʳ] *US* = ***clamour***.

clamorous ['klæmərəs] adj bruyant(e).

clamour *UK*, ***clamor*** *US* ['klæməʳ] ■ n *(U)* **1.** [noise] cris *mpl* **2.** [demand] revendication *f* bruyante.
■ vi **: to clamour for sthg** demander qqch à cor et à cri.

clamp [klæmp] ■ n **1.** [gen] pince *f*, agrafe *f* **2.** [for carpentry] serre-joint *m* **3.** MED clamp *m* **4.** AUT sabot *m* de Denver.
■ vt **1.** [gen] serrer **2.** AUT poser un sabot de Denver à.
◆ ***clamp down*** vi **: to clamp down (on)** sévir (contre).

clampdown ['klæmpdaʊn] n **: clampdown (on)** répression *f* (contre).

clan [klæn] n clan *m*.

clandestine [klæn'destɪn] adj clandestin(e).

clang [klæŋ] ■ n bruit *m* métallique.
■ vi émettre un bruit métallique.

clanger ['klæŋəʳ] n *UK inf* gaffe *f*.

clank [klæŋk] ■ n cliquetis *m*.
■ vi cliqueter.

clap [klæp] ■ n **1.** [of hands] applaudissement *m*, battement *m* (de main) **2.** [of thunder] coup *m*.
■ vt (pt & pp **-ped**, cont **-ping**) **1.** [hands] **: to clap one's hands** applaudir, taper des mains **2.** *inf* [place] mettre ◗ **to clap eyes on sb** apercevoir qqn.
■ vi (pt & pp **-ped**, cont **-ping**) applaudir, taper des mains.

clapboard ['klæpbɔːd] n *US* bardeau *m*.

clapped-out [klæpt-] adj *UK inf* déglingué(e).

clapperboard ['klæpəbɔːd] n claquette *f*.

clapping ['klæpɪŋ] n *(U)* applaudissements *mpl*.

claptrap ['klæptræp] n *(U) inf* sottises *fpl*.

claret ['klærət] n **1.** [wine] bordeaux *m* rouge **2.** [colour] bordeaux *m inv*.

clarification [ˌklærɪfɪ'keɪʃn] n [explanation] éclaircissement *m*, clarification *f*.

clarify ['klærɪfaɪ] (pt & pp **-ied**) vt [explain] éclaircir, clarifier.

clarinet [ˌklærə'net] n clarinette *f*.

clarity ['klærətɪ] n clarté *f*.

clash [klæʃ] ■ n **1.** [of interests, personalities] conflit *m* **2.** [fight, disagreement] heurt *m*, affrontement *m* **3.** [noise] fracas *m*.
■ vi **1.** [fight, disagree] se heurter **2.** [differ, conflict] entrer en conflit **3.** [coincide] **: to clash (with sthg)** tomber en même temps (que qqch) **4.** [colours] jurer **5.** [cymbals] résonner.

clasp [klɑːsp] ■ n [on necklace] fermoir *m* / [on belt] boucle *f*.
■ vt [hold tight] serrer ◗ **to clasp hands** se serrer la main.

class [klɑːs] ■ n **1.** [gen] classe *f* **2.** [lesson] cours *m*, classe *f* **3.** [category] catégorie *f* ◗ **to be in a class of one's own** être d'une tout autre classe.
■ comp de classe.
■ vt classer.

class-conscious adj *pej* snob *(inv)*.

classic ['klæsɪk] ■ adj classique.
■ n classique *m*.
◆ ***classics*** npl humanités *fpl*.

classical ['klæsɪkl] adj classique.

classical music n musique *f* classique.

classification [ˌklæsɪfɪ'keɪʃn] n classification *f*.

classified ['klæsɪfaɪd] adj [information, document] classé secret (classée secrète).

classified ad n petite annonce *f*.

classify ['klæsɪfaɪ] (pt & pp **-ied**) vt classifier, classer.

classless ['klɑːslɪs] adj sans distinctions sociales.

classmate ['klɑːsmeɪt] n camarade *mf* de classe.

classroom ['klɑːsrʊm] n (salle *f* de) classe *f*.

classroom assistant n SCH aide-éducateur *m*, -rice *f*.

classy ['klɑːsɪ] (comp **-ier**, superl **-iest**) adj *inf* chic *(inv)*.

clatter ['klætəʳ] ■ n cliquetis *m* / [louder] fracas *m*.
■ vi [metal object] cliqueter.

clause [klɔːz] n **1.** [in document] clause *f* **2.** GRAM proposition *f*.

claustrophobia [ˌklɔːstrə'fəʊbjə] n claustrophobie *f*.

claustrophobic [ˌklɔːstrəˈfəʊbɪk] **adj 1.** [atmosphere] qui rend claustrophobe **2.** [person] claustrophobe.

claw [klɔː] ■ **n 1.** [of cat, bird] griffe *f* **2.** [of crab, lobster] pince *f*.
■ **vt** griffer.
■ **vi** [person] **: to claw at** s'agripper à.
◆ ***claw back*** **vt sep** *UK* [money] récupérer.

clay [kleɪ] **n** argile *f*.

clay pigeon shooting **n** ball-trap *m*.

clean [kliːn] ■ **adj 1.** [not dirty] propre **2.** [sheet of paper, driving licence] vierge / [reputation] sans tache ▸ **clean living** une vie saine ▸ **to come clean about sthg** *inf* confesser qqch **3.** [joke] de bon goût **4.** [smooth] net (nette) ▸ **to make a clean break** couper net ▸ **we made a clean break with the past** nous avons rompu avec le passé, nous avons tourné la page.
■ **adv : the handle broke clean off** l'anse a cassé net ▸ **I clean forgot** j'ai complètement oublié.
■ **vt** nettoyer ▸ **I cleaned the mud from my shoes** j'ai enlevé la boue de mes chaussures ▸ **to clean one's teeth** se brosser OR laver les dents ▸ **to clean the windows** faire les vitres OR les carreaux.
■ **vi** [person] faire le ménage.
■ **n : to give sthg a clean** nettoyer qqch ▸ **the carpet needs a good clean** la moquette a grand besoin d'être nettoyée.
◆ ***clean out*** **vt sep 1.** [room, drawer] nettoyer à fond **2.** *inf fig* [person] nettoyer.
◆ ***clean up*** ■ **vt sep** [clear up] nettoyer ▸ **clean this mess up!** nettoyez-moi ce fouillis!
■ **vi** *inf* [make a profit] ramasser de l'argent.

clean-cut **adj 1.** [lines] net (nette) / [shape] bien délimité(e), net (nette) **2.** [person] propre (sur soi), soigné(e).

cleaner [ˈkliːnəʳ] **n 1.** [person] personne *f* qui fait le ménage ▸ **window cleaner** laveur *m*, -euse *f* de vitres **2.** [substance] produit *m* d'entretien **3.** [machine] appareil *m* de nettoyage **4.** [shop] **: cleaner's** pressing *m*.

cleaning [ˈkliːnɪŋ] **n** nettoyage *m*.

cleaning lady **n** femme *f* de ménage.

cleanliness [ˈklenlɪnɪs] **n** propreté *f*.

clean-living **adj** qui mène une vie saine.

cleanly [ˈkliːnlɪ] **adv** [cut] nettement.

cleanness [ˈkliːnnɪs] **n** propreté *f*.

cleanse [klenz] **vt 1.** [skin, wound] nettoyer **2.** *fig* [make pure] purifier ▸ **to cleanse sb/sthg of** délivrer qqn/qqch de.

cleanser [ˈklenzəʳ] **n** [detergent] détergent *m* / [for skin] démaquillant *m*.

clean-shaven [-ˈʃeɪvn] **adj** rasé(e) de près.

cleansing [ˈklenzɪŋ] ■ **n** nettoyage *m*.
■ **adj** [lotion] démaquillant(e) / [power, property] de nettoyage.

cleanup [ˈkliːnʌp] **n** nettoyage *m*.

clear [klɪəʳ] ■ **adj 1.** [gen] clair(e) / [glass, plastic] transparent(e) ▸ **clear honey** miel liquide ▸ **on a clear day** par temps clair
2. [easily understood] clair(e) / [voice, sound] qui s'entend nettement / [difference] net (nette) ▸ **to make sthg clear (to sb)** expliquer qqch clairement (à qqn) ▸ **to make it clear that** préciser que ▸ **to make o.s. clear** bien se faire comprendre ▸ **it's clear that he's lying** il est évident OR clair qu'il ment ▸ **it is a clear case of favouritism** c'est manifestement du favoritisme, c'est un cas de favoritisme manifeste ▸ **he is quite clear about what has to be done** il sait parfaitement ce qu'il y a à faire ▸ **they won by a clear majority** ils ont gagné avec une large majorité ▸ **a clear profit** un bénéfice net
3. [road, space] libre, dégagé(e) ▸ **the roads are clear of snow** les routes sont déblayées OR déneigées ▸ **we're clear of the traffic** nous sommes sortis des encombrements ▸ **his schedule is clear** il n'a rien de prévu sur son emploi du temps ▸ **we have two clear days to get there** on a deux jours entiers pour y aller
4. [not guilty] **: to have a clear conscience** avoir la conscience tranquille.
■ **adv : to stand clear** s'écarter ▸ **to stay clear of sb/sthg, to steer clear of sb/sthg** éviter qqn/qqch.
■ **n : in the clear** [out of danger] hors de danger / [free from suspicion] au-dessus de tout soupçon.
■ **vt 1.** [road, path] dégager / [table] débarrasser / [obstacle, fallen tree] enlever ▸ **she cleared the plates from the table** elle a débarrassé la table ▸ **to clear one's throat** s'éclaircir la voix ▸ **clear the room!** évacuez la salle! ▸ **the police cleared the way for the procession** la police a ouvert un passage au cortège ▸ **the talks cleared the way for a ceasefire** les pourparlers ont préparé le terrain OR ont ouvert la voie pour un cessez-le-feu ▸ **I went for a walk to clear my head** j'ai fait un tour pour m'éclaircir les idées
2. LAW innocenter ▸ **to clear sb of a charge** disculper qqn d'une accusation ▸ **give him a chance to clear himself** donnez-lui la possibilité de se justifier OR de prouver son innocence ▸ **to clear one's name** se justifier, défendre son honneur
3. [jump] sauter, franchir
4. [debt] s'acquitter de ▸ **he cleared the backlog of work** il a rattrapé le travail en retard
5. [pass through] **: to clear customs** [person] passer la douane / [shipment] être dédouané ▸ **the bill cleared the Senate** le projet de loi a été voté par le Sénat
6. [authorize] donner le feu vert à ▸ **you'll have to clear it with the boss** il faut demander l'autorisation OR l'accord OR le feu vert du patron
7. [cheque] compenser
8. SPORT **: to clear the ball** dégager le ballon.
■ **vi** [fog, smoke] se dissiper / [weather, sky] s'éclaircir ▸ **it takes three days for the cheque to clear** il y a trois jours de délai d'encaissement.
◆ ***clear away*** **vt sep** [plates] débarrasser ▸ **we cleared away the dishes** nous avons débarrassé (la table) OR desservi / [books] enlever.
◆ ***clear off*** **vi** *UK inf* dégager ▸ **clear off!** fiche le camp!
◆ ***clear out*** ■ **vt sep** [cupboard] vider / [room] ranger ▸ **to clear everyone out of a room** faire évacuer une pièce.
■ **vi** *inf* [leave] dégager.
◆ ***clear up*** ■ **vt sep 1.** [tidy] ranger
2. [mystery, misunderstanding] éclaircir.
■ **vi 1.** [weather] s'éclaircir ▸ **it's clearing up** le temps se lève
2. [tidy up] tout ranger.

clearance [ˈklɪərəns] **n 1.** [of rubbish] enlèvement *m* / [of land] déblaiement *m* **2.** [permission] autorisation *f* **3.** [free space] dégagement *m*.

clearance sale n soldes *mpl*.

clear-cut adj net (nette).

cleared cheque [klɪəd-] n chèque *m* compensé.

clear-headed [-'hedɪd] adj lucide.

clearing ['klɪərɪŋ] n [in wood] clairière *f*.

clearing bank n *UK* banque *f* de dépôt.

clearing house n **1.** [organization] bureau *m* central **2.** [bank] chambre *f* de compensation.

clearing-up n **1.** [of house] remise *f* en ordre **2.** [after earthquake, bombing] déblaiement *m*.

clearly ['klɪəlɪ] adv **1.** [distinctly, lucidly] clairement **2.** [obviously] manifestement.

clearout ['klɪəraʊt] n *esp UK inf* (grand) nettoyage *m*.

clear-sighted adj qui voit juste.

clearway ['klɪəweɪ] n *UK route où le stationnement n'est autorisé qu'en cas d'urgence.*

cleavage ['kli:vɪdʒ] n **1.** [between breasts] décolleté *m* **2.** [division] division *f*.

cleaver ['kli:vəʳ] n couperet *m*.

clef [klef] n clef *f*.

cleft [kleft] n fente *f*.

cleft palate n fente *f* de la voûte du palais.

clematis ['klemətɪs] n clématite *f*.

clemency ['klemənsɪ] n clémence *f*.

clementine ['kleməntaɪn] n clémentine *f*.

clench [klentʃ] vt serrer.

clergy ['klɜ:dʒɪ] npl : **the clergy** le clergé.

clergyman ['klɜ:dʒɪmən] (pl **-men** [-mən]) n membre *m* du clergé.

clergywoman ['klɜ:dʒɪ,wʊmən] (pl **-women** [-,wɪmɪn]) n (femme *f*) pasteur *m*.

cleric ['klerɪk] n membre *m* du clergé.

clerical ['klerɪkl] adj **1.** ADMIN de bureau **2.** RELIG clérical(e).

clerk [*UK* klɑ:k, *US* klɜ:rk] n **1.** [in office] employé *m*, -e *f* de bureau **2.** LAW clerc *mf* **3.** *US* [shop assistant] vendeur *m*, -euse *f*.

clever ['klevəʳ] adj **1.** [intelligent - person] intelligent(e) / [- idea] ingénieux(euse) **2.** [skilful] habile, adroit(e).

cleverly ['klevəlɪ] adv **1.** [intelligently] intelligemment **2.** [skilfully] habilement.

cleverness ['klevənɪs] n **1.** [intelligence] intelligence *f* **2.** [skill] habileté *f*.

cliché [*UK* 'kli:ʃeɪ, *US* kli:'ʃeɪ] n cliché *m*.

clichéd [*UK* 'kli:ʃeɪd, *US* kli:'ʃeɪd] adj banal(e) ▸ **a clichéd phrase** un cliché, une banalité, un lieu commun.

click [klɪk] ■ n [of lock] déclic *m* / [of tongue, heels] claquement *m*.

■ vt **1.** faire claquer **2.** COMPUT cliquer ▸ **to click on** cliquer sur.

■ vi **1.** [heels] claquer / [camera] faire un déclic **2.** *inf fig* [become clear] : **it clicked** cela a fait tilt **3.** COMPUT cliquer.

clickable image ['klɪkəbl-] n COMPUT image *f* cliquable.

clickable image map ['klɪkəbl-] n COMPUT image *f* cliquable.

client ['klaɪənt] n client *m*, -e *f*.

client account n compte *m* client.

client confidence n confiance *f* de la clientèle OR du client.

clientele [,kli:ən'tel] n clientèle *f*.

client list n liste *f* de clients.

client-server ■ n COMPUT client-serveur *m*.

■ comp COMPUT : **client-server database** base de données client-serveur.

cliff [klɪf] n falaise *f*.

cliffhanger ['klɪf,hæŋəʳ] n *inf* situation *f* à suspense.

climactic [klaɪ'mæktɪk] adj [point] culminant(e).

climate ['klaɪmɪt] n climat *m*.

climatic [klaɪ'mætɪk] adj climatique.

climax ['klaɪmæks] n [culmination] apogée *m*.

climb [klaɪm] ■ n ascension *f*, montée *f*.

■ vt [tree, rope] monter à / [stairs] monter / [wall, hill] escalader.

■ vi **1.** [person] monter, grimper ▸ **they climbed over the fence** ils passèrent par-dessus la barrière **2.** [plant] grimper / [road] monter / [plane] prendre de l'altitude **3.** [increase] augmenter.

◆ **climb down** vi *fig* reconnaître qu'on a tort.

climb-down n *UK* reculade *f*.

climber ['klaɪməʳ] n **1.** [person] alpiniste *mf*, grimpeur *m*, -euse *f* **2.** [plant] plante *f* grimpante.

climbing ['klaɪmɪŋ] n [rock climbing] escalade *f* / [mountain climbing] alpinisme *m*.

climbing frame n *UK* cage *f* à poules.

climes [klaɪmz] npl : **in sunnier climes** sous des cieux plus cléments.

clinch [klɪntʃ] vt [deal] conclure.

cling [klɪŋ] (pt & pp **clung**) vi **1.** [hold tightly] : **to cling (to)** s'accrocher (à), se cramponner (à) **2.** [clothes] : **to cling (to)** coller (à).

clingfilm ['klɪŋfɪlm] n *UK* film *m* alimentaire transparent.

clinging ['klɪŋɪŋ] adj *lit & fig* collant(e).

clingy ['klɪŋɪ] (comp **-ier**, superl **-iest**) adj [clothing] moulant(e) / *pej* [person] importun(e).

clinic ['klɪnɪk] n [building] centre *m* médical, clinique *f*.

clinical ['klɪnɪkl] adj **1.** MED clinique **2.** *fig* [attitude] froid(e).

clinically ['klɪnɪklɪ] adv MED cliniquement.

clink [klɪŋk] ■ n cliquetis *m*.

■ vi tinter.

clip [klɪp] ■ n **1.** [for paper] trombone *m* / [for hair] pince *f* / [of earring] clip *m* / TECH collier *m* **2.** [excerpt] extrait *m*.

■ vt (pt & pp **-ped**, cont **-ping**) **1.** [fasten] attacher **2.** [nails] couper / [hedge] tailler / [newspaper cutting] découper **3.** *inf* [hit] : **to clip sb round the ear** flanquer une gifle à qqn.

clipboard ['klɪpbɔ:d] **n** écritoire *f* à pince.

clip-on **adj** [badge] à pince ◗ **clip-on earrings** clips *mpl*.

clipped [klɪpt] **adj** [voice] saccadé(e).

clippers ['klɪpəz] **npl** [for hair] tondeuse *f* / [for nails] pince *f* à ongles / [for hedge] cisaille *f* à haie / [for pruning] sécateur *m*.

clipping ['klɪpɪŋ] **n** *US* [from newspaper] coupure *f*.

clique [kli:k] **n** clique *f*.

cliquey ['kli:kɪ], ***cliquish*** ['kli:kɪʃ] **adj** *pej* exclusif(ive), qui a l'esprit de clan.

cloak [kləʊk] ■ **n** **1.** [garment] cape *f* **2.** *fig* [for secret] couverture *f*.

■ **vt : to be cloaked in** être entouré(e) de.

cloak-and-dagger **adj : a cloak-and-dagger story** un roman d'espionnage.

cloakroom ['kləʊkrʊm] **n** **1.** [for clothes] vestiaire *m* **2.** *UK* [toilets] toilettes *fpl*.

clobber ['klɒbə^r] *inf* ■ **n** *(U) UK* **1.** [belongings] affaires *fpl* **2.** [clothes] vêtements *mpl*.

■ **vt** [hit] frapper, tabasser.

clock [klɒk] **n** **1.** [large] horloge *f* / [small] pendule *f* ◗ **(a)round the clock** [work, be open] 24 heures sur 24 ◗ **to put the clock back** retarder l'horloge / *fig* revenir en arrière ◗ **to put the clock forward** avancer l'horloge **2.** AUT [mileometer] compteur *m*.

◆ ***clock in***, ***clock on*** **vi** [at work] pointer *(à l'arrivée)*.

◆ ***clock off***, ***clock out*** **vi** [at work] pointer *(à la sortie)*.

◆ ***clock up*** **vt insep** [miles] faire, avaler.

clockwise ['klɒkwaɪz] **adj & adv** dans le sens des aiguilles d'une montre.

clockwork ['klɒkwɜ:k] ■ **n : to go like clockwork** *fig* aller *OR* marcher comme sur des roulettes.

■ **comp** [toy] mécanique.

clod [klɒd] **n** [of earth] motte *f*.

clog [klɒg] (pt & pp **-ged**, cont **-ging**) **vt** boucher.

◆ ***clogs*** **npl** sabots *mpl*.

◆ ***clog up*** ■ **vt sep** boucher.

■ **vi** se boucher.

clogged [klɒgd] **adj** bouché(e).

cloister ['klɔɪstə^r] **n** [passage] cloître *m*.

cloistered ['klɔɪstəd] **adj** cloîtré(e).

clone [kləʊn] ■ **n** [gen & COMPUT] clone *m*.

■ **vt** cloner.

cloning ['kləʊnɪŋ] **n** clonage *m*.

close[1] [kləʊs] ■ **adj** **1.** [near] **: close (to)** proche (de), près (de) ◗ **the library is close to the school** la bibliothèque est près de l'école ◗ **we are close to an agreement** nous sommes presque arrivés à un accord ◗ **close to tears** au bord des larmes ◗ **they're very close in age** ils ont presque le même âge ◗ **a close friend** un ami intime (une amie intime) ◗ **a close relative** un parent proche ◗ **close up, close to** de près ◗ **close by, close at hand** tout près ◗ **that was a close shave** *OR* **thing** *OR* **call** on l'a échappé belle **2.** [link, resemblance] fort(e) / [cooperation, connection] étroit(e) ◗ **they stay in close contact** ils restent en contact en permanence **3.** [questioning] serré(e) / [examination] minutieux(euse) ◗ **to keep a close watch on sb/sthg** surveiller qqn/qqch de près ◗ **to pay close attention** faire très attention ◗ **to have a close look at sb/sthg** regarder qqn/qqch de près **4.** *UK* [weather] lourd(e) / [air in room] renfermé(e) **5.** [result, contest, race] serré(e).

■ **adv : close (to)** près (de) ◗ **I live close to the river** j'habite près de la rivière ◗ **she lives close by** elle habite tout près ◗ **to come closer (together)** se rapprocher ◗ **don't come too close** n'approche pas *OR* ne t'approche pas trop ◗ **did you win? – no, we didn't even come close** avez-vous gagné? – non, loin de là.

■ **n** [street] cul-de-sac *m*.

◆ ***close on***, ***close to*** **prep** [almost] près de.

close[2] [kləʊz] ■ **vt** **1.** [gen] fermer ◗ **to close one's eyes (to something)** fermer les yeux (sur qqch) **2.** [end] clore ◗ **the subject is now closed** l'affaire est close **3.** COMPUT fermer ◗ **to close (a window)** fermer (une fenêtre) ◗ **to close (an application)** quitter (une application).

■ **vi** **1.** [shop, bank] fermer / [door, lid] (se) fermer ◗ **this window doesn't close properly** cette fenêtre ne ferme pas bien *OR* ferme mal ◗ **the door closed quietly behind them** la porte s'est refermée sans bruit derrière eux **2.** [end] se terminer, finir **3.** FIN **: the share index closed two points down** l'indice (boursier) a clôturé en baisse de deux points.

■ **n** fin *f* ◗ **to bring sthg to a close** mettre fin à qqch ◗ **the year drew to a close** l'année s'acheva.

◆ ***close down*** **vt sep & vi** fermer.

◆ ***close in*** **vi** [night, fog] descendre / [person] **: to close in (on)** approcher *OR* se rapprocher (de).

◆ ***close off*** **vt insep** [road] barrer ◗ **the area was closed off to the public** le quartier était fermé au public.

close-cropped [ˌkləʊs-] **adj** ras(e).

closed [kləʊzd] **adj** fermé(e).

closed circuit television **n** télévision *f* en circuit fermé.

closedown ['kləʊzdaʊn] **n** **1.** *UK* RADIO & TV fin *f* (des émissions) **2.** [of factory] fermeture *f*.

closed shop **n** *entreprise dans laquelle le monopole d'embauche est pratiqué*.

close-fitting [ˌkləʊs-] **adj** près du corps.

close-knit [ˌkləʊs-] **adj** (très) uni(e).

closely ['kləʊslɪ] **adv** [listen, examine, watch] de près / [resemble] beaucoup ◗ **to be closely related to** *OR* **with** être proche parent de ◗ **to work closely with sb** travailler en étroite collaboration avec qqn.

closeness ['kləʊsnɪs] **n** **1.** [nearness] proximité *f* **2.** [intimacy] intimité *f*.

closeout ['kləʊzaʊt] **n** *US* liquidation *f*.

close quarters [ˌkləʊs-] **npl : at close quarters** de près.

close-range [kləʊs-] **adj** à courte portée.

close-run ['kləʊs-] **adj** = ***close***[1] *(adj, sense 5)* .

close season [ˌkləʊs-] **n** *UK* fermeture *f* de la chasse *OR* de la pêche.

closet ['klɒzɪt] ■ **n** *US* [cupboard] placard *m*.
■ **adj** *inf* non avoué(e).
■ **vt : to be closeted with sb** être enfermé(e) avec qqn.

close-up ['kləʊs-] **n** gros plan *m*.

closing ['kləʊzɪŋ] **adj** [stages, remarks] final(e) / [speech] de clôture.

closing price **n** prix *m* de clôture.

closing time ['kləʊzɪŋ-] **n** heure *f* de fermeture.

closure ['kləʊʒəʳ] **n** fermeture *f*.

clot [klɒt] ■ **n 1.** [of blood, milk] caillot *m* **2.** *UK inf* [fool] empoté *m*, -e *f*.
■ **vi** (pt & pp **-ted**, cont **-ting**) [blood] coaguler.

cloth [klɒθ] **n 1.** *(U)* [fabric] tissu *m* **2.** [duster] chiffon *m* / [for drying] torchon *m*.

clothe [kləʊð] **vt** *fml* [dress] habiller ▸ **clothed in** habillé(e) de.

cloth-eared **adj** *UK inf* dur(e) de la feuille, sourdingue.

clothes [kləʊðz] **npl** vêtements *mpl*, habits *mpl* ▸ **to put one's clothes on** s'habiller ▸ **to take one's clothes off** se déshabiller.

clothes basket **n** panier *m* à linge.

clothes brush **n** brosse *f* à habits.

clothes hanger **n** cintre *m*.

clotheshorse ['kləʊðzhɔ:s] **n** séchoir *m* à linge.

clothesline ['kləʊðzlaɪn] **n** corde *f* à linge.

clothes peg *UK*, ***clothespin*** *US* ['kləʊðzpɪn] **n** pince *f* à linge.

clothing ['kləʊðɪŋ] **n** *(U)* vêtements *mpl*, habits *mpl*.

clotted cream ['klɒtɪd-] **n** *UK crème épaisse, spécialité de la Cornouailles*.

cloud [klaʊd] ■ **n** nuage *m* ▸ **to be under a cloud** être mal vu.
■ **vt 1.** [mirror] embuer **2.** *fig* [memory, happiness] gâcher ▸ **to cloud the issue** brouiller les cartes.
◆ ***cloud over*** **vi 1.** [sky] se couvrir **2.** [face] s'assombrir.

cloudburst ['klaʊdbɜ:st] **n** trombe *f* d'eau.

cloud-cuckoo-land **n** *UK inf* **: they are living in cloud-cuckoo-land** ils n'ont pas les pieds sur terre.

cloudless ['klaʊdlɪs] **adj** sans nuages.

cloudy ['klaʊdɪ] (comp **-ier**, superl **-iest**) **adj 1.** [sky, day] nuageux(euse) **2.** [liquid] trouble.

clout [klaʊt] *inf* ■ **n 1.** [blow] coup *m* **2.** *(U)* [influence] poids *m*, influence *f*.
■ **vt** donner un coup à.

clove [kləʊv] **n : a clove of garlic** une gousse d'ail.
◆ ***cloves*** **npl** [spice] clous *mpl* de girofle.

clover ['kləʊvəʳ] **n** trèfle *m*.

cloverleaf ['kləʊvəli:f] (pl **-leaves** [-li:vz]) **n** [plant] feuille *f* de trèfle.

clown [klaʊn] ■ **n 1.** [performer] clown *mf* **2.** [fool] pitre *m*.
■ **vi** faire le pitre.

cloying ['klɔɪɪŋ] **adj 1.** [smell] écœurant(e) **2.** [sentimentality] à l'eau de rose.

club [klʌb] ■ **n 1.** [organization, place] club *m* **2.** [weapon] massue *f* **3. : (golf) club** club *m* **4.** [playing card] trèfle *m*.
■ **comp** [member, fees] du club.
■ **vt** (pt & pp **-bed**, cont **-bing**) matraquer.
◆ ***clubs*** **npl** [playing cards] trèfle *m* ▸ **the six of clubs** le six de trèfle.
◆ ***club together*** **vi** se cotiser.

club car **n** *US* RAIL wagon-restaurant *m*.

club class **n** classe *f* club.

clubhouse ['klʌbhaʊs] (pl [-haʊzɪz]) **n** club *m*, pavillon *m*.

club sandwich **n** sandwich *m* mixte *(à trois étages)*.

cluck [klʌk] **vi** glousser.

clue [klu:] **n 1.** [in crime] indice *m* ▸ **I haven't (got) a clue (about)** je n'ai aucune idée (sur) **2.** [answer] **: the clue to sthg** la solution de qqch **3.** [in crossword] définition *f*.

clued-up [klu:d-] **adj** *UK inf* calé(e).

clueless ['klu:lɪs] **adj** *inf* qui n'a aucune idée.

clump [klʌmp] ■ **n 1.** [of trees, bushes] massif *m*, bouquet *m* **2.** [sound] bruit *m* sourd.
■ **vi : to clump about** marcher d'un pas lourd.

clumsily ['klʌmzɪlɪ] **adv 1.** [ungracefully] maladroitement **2.** [tactlessly] sans tact.

clumsiness ['klʌmzɪnɪs] **n 1.** [lack of coordination] maladresse *f*, gaucherie *f* **2.** [awkwardness - of tool] caractère *m* peu pratique / [- of design] lourdeur *f* **3.** [tactlessness] gaucherie *f*, manque *m* de tact.

clumsy ['klʌmzɪ] (comp **-ier**, superl **-iest**) **adj 1.** [ungraceful] maladroit(e), gauche **2.** [awkward - tool, object] peu pratique / [- design] lourd (e) **3.** [tactless] gauche, sans tact.

clung [klʌŋ] **pt & pp** ➤ ***cling***.

clunk [klʌŋk] ■ **n** [sound] bruit *m* sourd.
■ **vi** faire un bruit sourd.

cluster ['klʌstəʳ] ■ **n** [group] groupe *m*.
■ **vi** [people] se rassembler / [buildings] être regroupé(e).

cluster bomb **n** bombe *f* à fragmentation.

cluster sampling **n** échantillonnage *m* aréolaire ***OR*** par grappes.

clutch [klʌtʃ] ■ **n** AUT embrayage *m*.
■ **vt** agripper.
■ **vi : to clutch at** s'agripper à.
◆ ***clutches*** **npl : in the clutches of** dans les griffes de.

clutch bag **n** pochette *f*.

clutter ['klʌtəʳ] ■ **n** désordre *m* ▸ **in a clutter** en désordre.
■ **vt** mettre en désordre.

cm (abbr of ***centimetre***) **n** cm.

CNAA (abbr of ***Council for National Academic Awards***) **n** *organisme non universitaire délivrant des diplômes en Grande-Bretagne*.

CND (abbr of ***Campaign for Nuclear Disarmament***) **n** *mouvement pour le désarmement nucléaire*.

CNG [si:en'dʒi:] (abbr of ***compressed natural gas***) **n** GNC.

co- [kəʊ] **prefix** co-.

c/o (abbr of **care of**) a/s.

CO[1] n 1. abbr of **commanding officer** 2. (abbr of **Commonwealth Office**) *secrétariat d'État au Commonwealth* 3. abbr of **conscientious objector**.

CO[2] abbr of **Colorado**.

Co. 1. (abbr of **Company**) Cie 2. abbr of **County**.

coach [kəʊtʃ] ■ n 1. *UK* [bus] car *m*, autocar *m* 2. *UK* RAIL voiture *f* 3. [horsedrawn] carrosse *m* 4. SPORT entraîneur *m* 5. [tutor] répétiteur *m*, -trice *f*.
■ vt 1. SPORT entraîner 2. [tutor] donner des leçons (particulières) à.

coaching ['kəʊtʃɪŋ] n *(U)* 1. SPORT entraînement *m* 2. [tutoring] leçons *fpl* particulières.

coachload ['kəʊtʃləʊd] n : **a coachload of tourists** un autocar *OR* car plein de touristes.

coach party n *esp UK* excursion *f* en autocar.

coach trip n *UK* excursion *f* en autocar.

coagulate [kəʊ'ægjʊleɪt] vi coaguler.

coal [kəʊl] n charbon *m*.

coalesce [,kəʊə'les] vi s'unir.

coalface ['kəʊlfeɪs] n front *m* de taille.

coalfield ['kəʊlfi:ld] n bassin *m* houiller.

coal gas n gaz *m* de houille.

coalition [,kəʊə'lɪʃn] n coalition *f*.

coalition government n POL gouvernement *m* de coalition.

coalman ['kəʊlmæn] (pl **-men** [-men]) n *UK* charbonnier *m*.

coalmine ['kəʊlmaɪn] n mine *f* de charbon.

coalminer ['kəʊl,maɪnəʳ] n mineur *m*.

coalmining ['kəʊl,maɪnɪŋ] n charbonnage *m*.

coarse [kɔ:s] adj 1. [rough - cloth] grossier(ère) / [- hair] épais(aisse) / [- skin] granuleux(euse) 2. [vulgar] grossier(ère).

coarse fishing n *UK* pêche *f* en eau douce *(à l'exclusion du saumon)*.

coarsen ['kɔ:sn] ■ vt rendre grossier(ère).
■ vi devenir grossier(ère).

coast [kəʊst] ■ n côte *f*.
■ vi [in car, on bike] avancer en roue libre.

coastal ['kəʊstl] adj côtier(ère).

coaster ['kəʊstəʳ] n [small mat] dessous *m* de verre.

coastguard ['kəʊstgɑ:d] n 1. [person] garde-côte *m* 2. [organization] : **the coastguard** la gendarmerie maritime.

coastline ['kəʊstlaɪn] n côte *f*.

coast-to-coast adj [walk, route, race] d'un bout du pays à l'autre / [TV channel, network] national(e).

coat [kəʊt] ■ n 1. [garment] manteau *m* 2. [of animal] pelage *m* 3. [layer] couche *f*.
■ vt : **to coat sthg (with)** recouvrir qqch (de) / [with paint] enduire qqch (de).

coat hanger n cintre *m*.

coating ['kəʊtɪŋ] n couche *f* / CULIN glaçage *m*.

coat of arms (pl **coats of arms**) n blason *m*.

coat tails npl queue *f* de pie *(costume)* ▸ **to ride on sb's coat tails** profiter de l'influence *OR* de la position de qqn ▸ **she hangs on his coat tails** elle est pendue à ses basques.

coauthor [kəʊ'ɔ:θəʳ] n co-auteur *m*.

coax [kəʊks] vt : **to coax sb (to do *OR* into doing sthg)** persuader qqn (de faire qqch) à force de cajoleries.

coaxial cable [,kəʊ'æksɪəl-] n COMPUT câble *m* coaxial.

cob [kɒb] n ➤ ***corn***.

cobalt ['kəʊbɔ:lt] n cobalt *m*.

cobble ['kɒbl] ◆ **cobble together** vt sep [agreement, book] bricoler / [speech] improviser.

cobbled ['kɒbld] adj pavé(e).

cobbler ['kɒbləʳ] n cordonnier *m*, -ière *f*.

cobbles ['kɒblz], **cobblestones** ['kɒblstəʊnz] npl pavés *mpl*.

Cobol ['kəʊbɒl] (abbr of **Common Business Oriented Language**) n COBOL *m*.

cobra ['kəʊbrə] n cobra *m*.

co-branding n alliance *f* de marque, co-branding *m*.

cobweb ['kɒbweb] n toile *f* d'araignée.

Coca-Cola® [,kəʊkə'kəʊlə] n Coca-Cola® *m inv*.

cocaine [kəʊ'keɪn] n cocaïne *f*.

cock [kɒk] ■ n 1. [male chicken] coq *m* 2. [male bird] mâle *m*.
■ vt 1. [gun] armer 2. [head] incliner.
◆ **cock up** vt sep *UK v inf* faire merder.

cock-a-hoop adj *UK inf* ravi(e).

cock-and-bull story n histoire *f* à dormir debout.

cockatoo [,kɒkə'tu:] (pl -s) n cacatoès *m*.

cockerel ['kɒkrəl] n jeune coq *m*.

cocker spaniel n cocker *m*.

cockeyed ['kɒkaɪd] adj *inf* 1. [lopsided] de travers 2. [foolish] complètement fou (folle).

cockfight ['kɒkfaɪt] n combat *m* de coqs.

cockiness ['kɒkɪnɪs] n impertinence *f*.

cockle ['kɒkl] n [shellfish] coque *f*.

Cockney ['kɒknɪ] ■ n (pl **Cockneys**) 1. [person] Cockney *mf (personne issue des quartiers populaires de l'est de Londres)* 2. [dialect, accent] cockney *m*.
■ comp cockney *(inv)*.

cockpit ['kɒkpɪt] n [in plane] cockpit *m*.

cockroach ['kɒkrəʊtʃ] n cafard *m*.

cocksure [,kɒk'ʃɔ:ʳ] adj trop sûr(e) de soi.

cocktail ['kɒkteɪl] n cocktail *m*.

cocktail bar n bar *m (dans un hôtel, un aéroport)*.

cocktail dress n robe *f* de soirée.

cocktail lounge n bar *m (dans un hôtel, un aéroport)*.

cocktail party n cocktail *m (fête)*.

cocktail shaker [-,ʃeɪkəʳ] n shaker *m*.

cocktail stick n bâtonnet *m* à apéritif.

cock-up **n** *UK v inf* **: to make a cock-up** se planter.

cocky ['kɒkɪ] (comp **-ier**, superl **-iest**) **adj** *inf* suffisant(e).

cocoa ['kəʊkəʊ] **n** cacao *m*.

coconut ['kəʊkənʌt] **n** noix *f* de coco.

cocoon [kə'ku:n] ■ **n** *lit & fig* cocon *m*.
■ **vt** *fig* [person] couver.

cocooned [kə'ku:nd] **adj** enfermé(e), cloîtré(e).

cod [kɒd] (pl **cod**) **n** morue *f*.

COD abbr of ***cash on delivery, collect on delivery***.

code [kəʊd] ■ **n** code *m*.
■ **vt** coder.

coded ['kəʊdɪd] **adj** codé(e).

codeine ['kəʊdi:n] **n** codéine *f*.

code name **n** nom *m* de code.

code of practice **n** déontologie *f*.

codeword ['kəʊdwɜ:d] **n** [password] mot *m* de passe / [name] mot *m* codé.

cod-liver oil **n** huile *f* de foie de morue.

codswallop ['kɒdz,wɒləp] **n** *(U) UK inf* bêtises *fpl*.

co-ed [kəʊ'ed] ■ **adj** abbr of ***coeducational***.
■ **n 1.** (abbr of ***coeducational student***) *étudiante d'une université mixte américaine* **2.** (abbr of ***coeducational school***) *école mixte britannique*.

co-edition **n** coédition *f*.

coeducation [,kəʊedʒʊ'keɪʃn] **n** éducation *f* mixte.

coeducational [,kəʊedju:'keɪʃənl] **adj** mixte.

coefficient [,kəʊɪ'fɪʃnt] **n** coefficient *m*.

coerce [kəʊ'ɜ:s] **vt : to coerce sb (into doing sthg)** contraindre qqn (à faire qqch).

coercion [kəʊ'ɜ:ʃn] **n** coercition *f*.

coexist [,kəʊɪg'zɪst] **vi** coexister.

coexistence [,kəʊɪg'zɪstəns] **n** coexistence *f*.

coexistent [,kəʊɪg'zɪstənt] **adj** coexistant(e).

C. of C. (abbr of ***chamber of commerce***) **n** CC *f*.

C of E abbr of ***Church of England***.

coffee ['kɒfɪ] **n** café *m*.

coffee bar **n** *UK* café *m*.

coffee bean **n** grain *m* de café.

coffee break **n** pause-café *f*.

coffee cup **n** tasse *f* à café.

coffee grinder **n** moulin *m* à café.

coffee mill **n** moulin *m* à café.

coffee morning **n** *UK réunion matinale pour prendre le café*.

coffeepot ['kɒfɪpɒt] **n** cafetière *f*.

coffee shop **n 1.** *UK* [shop] café *m* **2.** *US* [restaurant] ≃ café-restaurant *m*.

coffee table **n** table *f* basse.

coffee-table book **n** beau livre *m (destiné à être feuilleté plutôt que véritablement lu)*.

coffers ['kɒfəz] **npl** coffres *mpl*.

coffin ['kɒfɪn] **n** cercueil *m*.

cog [kɒg] **n** [tooth on wheel] dent *f* / [wheel] roue *f* dentée ▸ **a cog in the machine** *fig* un simple rouage.

cogent ['kəʊdʒənt] **adj** convaincant(e).

cogitate ['kɒdʒɪteɪt] **vi** *fml* réfléchir.

cognac ['kɒnjæk] **n** cognac *m*.

cognitive ['kɒgnɪtɪv] **adj** cognitif(ive).

cognoscenti [,kɒnjə'ʃenti:] **npl** connaisseurs *mpl*.

cogwheel ['kɒgwi:l] **n** roue *f* dentée.

cohabit [,kəʊ'hæbɪt] **vi** *fml* cohabiter.

cohabitation [,kəʊhæbɪ'teɪʃn] **n** cohabitation *f*.

coherent [kəʊ'hɪərənt] **adj** cohérent(e).

coherently [kəʊ'hɪərəntlɪ] **adv** de façon cohérente.

cohesion [kəʊ'hi:ʒn] **n** cohésion *f*.

cohesive [kəʊ'hi:sɪv] **adj** cohésif(ive).

cohort ['kəʊhɔ:t] **n** cohorte *f*.

COHSE ['kəʊzɪ] (abbr of ***Confederation of Health Service Employees***) **n** *ancien syndicat britannique des employés des services de santé*.

COI (abbr of ***Central Office of Information***) **n** *service public britannique d'information en Grande-Bretagne*.

coil [kɔɪl] ■ **n 1.** [of rope] rouleau *m* / [one loop] boucle *f* **2.** ELEC bobine *f* **3.** *UK* [contraceptive device] stérilet *m*.
■ **vt** enrouler.
■ **vi** s'enrouler.
◆ ***coil up*** **vt sep** enrouler.

coiled [kɔɪld] **adj** enroulé(e).

coin [kɔɪn] ■ **n** pièce *f* (de monnaie).
■ **vt** [word] inventer ▸ **to coin a phrase** pour employer un lieu commun.

coinage ['kɔɪnɪdʒ] **n 1.** *(U)* [currency] monnaie *f* **2.** [new word] néologisme *m*.

coin-box **n** *UK* cabine *f* (publique) à pièces.

coincide [,kəʊɪn'saɪd] **vi** coïncider.

coincidence [kəʊ'ɪnsɪdəns] **n** coïncidence *f*.

coincidental [kəʊ,ɪnsɪ'dentl] **adj** de coïncidence.

coincidentally [kəʊ,ɪnsɪ'dentəlɪ] **adv** par hasard.

coin-operated [-'ɒpə,reɪtɪd] **adj** automatique.

coitus ['kəʊɪtəs] **n** coït *m*.

coke [kəʊk] **n 1.** [fuel] coke *m* **2.** *drug sl* coco *f*, coke *f*.

Coke® [kəʊk] **n** Coca® *m*.

Col. (abbr of ***colonel***) Col.

cola ['kəʊlə] **n** cola *m*.

COLA ['kəʊlə] (abbr of ***cost-of-living adjustment***) **n** *actualisation des salaires, indemnités, etc en fonction du coût de la vie*.

colander ['kʌləndə^r] **n** passoire *f*.

cold [kəʊld] ■ **adj** froid(e) ▸ **it's cold** il fait froid ▸ **to be cold** avoir froid ▸ **her hands are cold** elle a les mains froides ▸ **to get cold** [person] avoir froid / [hot food] refroidir ▸ **she was out cold** elle était sans connaissance.

■ **n 1.** [illness] rhume *m* ▸ **to have a cold** être enrhumé ▸ **to catch (a) cold** attraper un rhume, s'enrhumer **2.** [low temperature] froid *m* ▸ **come in out of the cold** entrez vous mettre au chaud.

CONFUSABLE / PARONYME

cold

When translating cold, note that *froid* and *froideur* are not interchangeable. *Froid* is used to describe temperature and by extension, people's emotions and attitudes, whereas *froideur* is restricted to the emotional sense.

cold-blooded [-'blʌdɪd] **adj 1.** [animal] à sang-froid **2.** *fig* [killer] sans pitié / [murder] de sang-froid.

cold calling **n** [on phone] démarchage *m* téléphonique / [at home] démarchage *m* à domicile.

cold cream **n** cold-cream *m*.

cold cuts **npl** *esp US* assiette *f* anglaise.

cold feet **npl : to have** *OR* **get cold feet** *inf* avoir la trouille.

cold-hearted [-'hɑːtɪd] **adj** insensible.

coldly ['kəʊldlɪ] **adv** froidement.

coldness ['kəʊldnɪs] **n** froideur *f*.

cold shoulder **n : to give sb the cold shoulder** *inf* être froid(e) avec qqn.

cold sore **n** bouton *m* de fièvre.

cold storage **n : to put sthg into cold storage** [food] mettre qqch en chambre froide.

cold sweat **n** sueur *f* froide.

cold war **n : the cold war** la guerre froide.

coleslaw ['kəʊlslɔː] **n** chou *m* cru mayonnaise.

colic ['kɒlɪk] **n** colique *f*.

collaborate [kə'læbəreɪt] **vi** collaborer.

collaboration [kəˌlæbə'reɪʃn] **n** collaboration *f*.

collaborative [kə'læbərətɪv] **adj** fait(e) en collaboration *OR* en commun.

collaborator [kə'læbəreɪtəʳ] **n** collaborateur *m*, -trice *f*.

collage ['kɒlɑːʒ] **n** collage *m*.

collagen ['kɒlədʒən] **n** collagène *m*.

collapse [kə'læps] ■ **n** [gen] écroulement *m*, effondrement *m* / [of marriage] échec *m*.
■ **vi 1.** [building, person] s'effondrer, s'écrouler / [marriage] échouer **2.** [fold up] être pliant(e).

collapsible [kə'læpsəbl] **adj** pliant(e).

collar ['kɒləʳ] ■ **n 1.** [on clothes] col *m* **2.** [for dog] collier *m* **3.** TECH collier *m*, bague *f*.
■ **vt** *inf* [detain] coincer.

collarbone ['kɒləbəʊn] **n** clavicule *f*.

collate [kə'leɪt] **vt** collationner.

collateral [kɒ'lætərəl] **n** *(U)* nantissement *m*.

collateralize [kɒˌlætərə'laɪz] **vt** *US* FIN garantir.

collation [kə'leɪʃn] **n** collation *f*.

colleague ['kɒliːg] **n** collègue *mf*.

collect [kə'lekt] ■ **vt 1.** [gather together - gen] rassembler, recueillir / [- wood] ramasser ▸ **to collect o.s.** se reprendre **2.** [as a hobby] collectionner **3.** [go to get] aller chercher, passer prendre **4.** [money] recueillir / [taxes] percevoir ▸ **to collect an order** COMM retirer une commande ▸ **collect on delivery** *US* paiement à la livraison.
■ **vi 1.** [crowd, people] se rassembler **2.** [dust, leaves, dirt] s'amasser, s'accumuler **3.** [for charity, gift] faire la quête.
■ **adv** *US* TELEC **: to call (sb) collect** téléphoner (à qqn) en PCV.
■ **adj** *US* **: a collect call** un (appel en) PCV.
◆ ***collect up*** **vt sep** ramasser.

collectable [kə'lektəbl] ■ **adj** prisé(e) (par les collectionneurs).
■ **n** objet *m* prisé par les collectionneurs.

collected [kə'lektɪd] **adj 1.** [calm] posé(e), maître (maîtresse) de soi **2.** LIT **: collected works** œuvres *fpl* complètes.

collecting [kə'lektɪŋ] **n** *(U)* [hobby] fait *m* de collectionner.

collection [kə'lekʃn] **n 1.** [of objects] collection *f* **2.** LIT recueil *m* **3.** [of rubbish] ramassage *m* / [of taxes] perception *f* **4.** [of money] quête *f* **5.** [of mail] levée *f*.

collective [kə'lektɪv] ■ **adj** collectif(ive).
■ **n** coopérative *f*.

collective bargaining **n** *(U) négociations de convention collective.*

collectively [kə'lektɪvlɪ] **adv** collectivement.

collective ownership **n** propriété *f* collective.

collector [kə'lektəʳ] **n 1.** [as a hobby] collectionneur *m*, -euse *f* **2.** [of debts, rent] encaisseur *m* ▸ **collector of taxes** percepteur *m*.

collector's item **n** pièce *f* de collection.

college ['kɒlɪdʒ] **n 1.** [gen] ≃ école *f* d'enseignement (technique) supérieur **2.** [of university] *maison communautaire d'étudiants sur un campus universitaire.*

college of education **n** ≃ institut *m* de formation de maîtres.

collide [kə'laɪd] **vi : to collide (with)** entrer en collision (avec).

collie ['kɒlɪ] **n** colley *m*.

colliery ['kɒljərɪ] (pl -ies) **n** *esp UK* mine *f*.

collision [kə'lɪʒn] **n 1.** [crash] **: collision (with/between)** collision *f* (avec/entre) ▸ **to be on a collision course (with)** *fig* aller au-devant de l'affrontement (avec) **2.** *fig* [conflict] conflit *m*.

collision damage waiver **n** rachat *m* de franchise.

colloquial [kə'ləʊkwɪəl] **adj** familier(ère).

colloquialism [kə'ləʊkwɪəlɪzm] **n** expression *f* familière.

collude [kə'luːd] **vi : to collude with sb** comploter avec qqn.

collusion [kə'luːʒn] **n : in collusion with** de connivence avec.

cologne [kə'ləʊn] **n** eau *f* de cologne.

Colombia [kə'lɒmbɪə] **n** Colombie *f* ▸ **in Colombia** en Colombie.

Colombian [kə'lɒmbɪən] ■ **adj** colombien(enne).
■ **n** Colombien *m*, -enne *f*.

Colombo [kə'lʌmbəʊ] **n** Colombo.

colon ['kəʊlən] **n 1.** ANAT côlon *m* **2.** [punctuation mark] deux-points *m inv*.

colonel ['kɜːnl] **n** colonel *m*.

colonial [kə'ləʊnjəl] **adj** colonial(e).

colonialism [kə'ləʊnjəlɪzm] **n** colonialisme *m*.

colonist ['kɒlənɪst] **n** colon *m*.

colonize, *UK* ***-ise*** ['kɒlənaɪz] **vt** coloniser.

colonnade [ˌkɒlə'neɪd] **n** colonnade *f*.

colony ['kɒlənɪ] (**pl -ies**) **n** colonie *f*.

color *US* = ***colour*** *etc*.

Colorado [ˌkɒlə'rɑːdəʊ] **n** Colorado *m* ▸ **in Colorado** dans le Colorado.

colorado beetle **n** doryphore *m*.

colossal [kə'lɒsl] **adj** colossal(e).

colostomy [kə'lɒstəmɪ] (**pl -ies**) **n** colostomie *f*.

colour *UK*, ***color*** *US* ['kʌləʳ] ■ **n** couleur *f* ▸ **in colour** en couleur.
■ **adj** en couleur.
■ **vt 1.** [food, liquid] colorer / [with pen, crayon] colorier **2.** [dye] teindre **3.** *fig* [judgment] fausser.
■ **vi** rougir.
◆ ***colours*** **npl** [flag, of team] couleurs *fpl*.
◆ ***colour in*** **vt sep** colorier.

colour bar *UK*, ***color bar*** *US* **n** discrimination *f* raciale.

colour barrier *UK*, ***color barrier*** *US* **n** discrimination *f* raciale.

colour-blind *UK*, ***color-blind*** *US* **adj** *lit* daltonien(enne) / *fig* qui ne fait pas de discrimination raciale.

colour blindness **n** *lit* daltonisme *m* / *fig* fait *m* de ne pas faire de discrimination raciale.

colour code *UK*, ***color code*** *US* **n** code *m* coloré.
◆ ***colour-code*** *UK*, ***color-code*** *US* **vt : to colour-code sthg** coder qqch avec des couleurs.

colour-coded *UK*, ***color-coded*** *US* **adj** codé(e) par couleur.

coloured *UK*, ***colored*** *US* ['kʌləd] **adj** de couleur ▸ **brightly coloured** de couleur vive.

-coloured *UK*, ***-colored*** *US* **suffix** (de) couleur... ▸ **rust-coloured** couleur de rouille.

colourfast *UK*, ***colorfast*** *US* ['kʌləfɑːst] **adj** grand teint *(inv)*.

colourful *UK*, ***colorful*** *US* ['kʌləfʊl] **adj 1.** [gen] coloré(e) **2.** [person, area] haut(e) en couleur.

colouring *UK*, ***coloring*** *US* ['kʌlərɪŋ] **n 1.** [dye] colorant *m* **2.** *(U)* [complexion] teint *m*.

colourless *UK*, ***colorless*** *US* ['kʌləlɪs] **adj 1.** [not coloured] sans couleur, incolore **2.** *fig* [uninteresting] terne.

colour scheme *UK*, ***color scheme*** *US* **n** combinaison *f* de couleurs.

colour supplement **n** *UK* supplément *m* illustré.

colt [kəʊlt] **n** [young horse] poulain *m*.

column ['kɒləm] **n 1.** [gen] colonne *f* **2.** PRESS [article] rubrique *f*.

column inch **n** *unité de mesure des espaces publicitaires équivalant à une colonne sur un pouce.*

columnist ['kɒləmnɪst] **n** chroniqueur *m*.

.com ['dotkɒm] COMPUT *abréviation désignant les entreprises commerciales dans les adresses électroniques*.

coma ['kəʊmə] **n** coma *m*.

comatose ['kəʊmətəʊs] **adj** comateux(euse).

comb [kəʊm] ■ **n** [for hair] peigne *m*.
■ **vt 1.** [hair] peigner **2.** [search] ratisser.

combat ['kɒmbæt] ■ **n** combat *m*.
■ **vt** combattre.

combat fatigue **n** psychose *f* traumatique, syndrome *m* commotionnel.

combative ['kɒmbətɪv] **adj** combatif(ive).

combination [ˌkɒmbɪ'neɪʃn] **n** combinaison *f*.

combination lock **n** serrure *f* à combinaison.

combination skin **n** peau *f* mixte.

combination therapy **n** thérapie *f* combinatoire, multithérapie *f*.

combine ■ **vt** [kəm'baɪn] [gen] rassembler / [pieces] combiner ▸ **to combine sthg with sthg** [two substances] mélanger qqch avec ***or*** à qqch / *fig* allier qqch à qqch.
■ **vi** [kəm'baɪn] COMM & POL **: to combine (with)** fusionner (avec).
■ **n** ['kɒmbaɪn] **1.** [group] cartel *m* **2.** = ***combine harvester***.

combined [kəm'baɪnd] **adj** combiné(e), conjugué(e) ▸ **a combined effort** un effort conjugué / MIL **: combined forces** forces alliées ▸ **combined operation** [by several nations] opération alliée / [by forces of one nation] opération interarmées.

combine harvester [-'hɑːvɪstəʳ] **n** moissonneuse-batteuse *f*.

combustible [kəm'bʌstəbl] **adj** combustible.

combustion [kəm'bʌstʃn] **n** combustion *f*.

come [kʌm] (**pt came, pp come**) **vi 1.** [move] venir / [arrive] arriver, venir ▸ **come here** venez ici ▸ **coming!** j'arrive! ▸ **come with me** [accompany] venez avec moi, accompagnez-moi / [follow] suivez-moi ▸ **would you like to come for lunch/dinner?** voulez-vous venir déjeuner/dîner? ▸ **I've got people coming** [short stay] j'ai des invités / [long stay] il y a des gens qui viennent ▸ **to come in time/late** arriver à temps/en retard ▸ **the news came as a shock** la nouvelle m'a/lui a *etc* fait un choc ▸ **the time has come** le moment est venu ▸ **fashions come and go** la mode change tout le temps ▸ **the computer industry has come a very long way since then** l'informatique a fait énormément de progrès depuis ce temps-là ▸ **to come running** arriver en courant ▸ **he doesn't know whether he's coming or going** il ne sait plus où il en est
2. [reach] **: to come up to** arriver à, monter jusqu'à ▸ **the water came up to my knees** l'eau m'arrivait aux genoux

▸ **to come down to** descendre *OR* tomber jusqu'à ▸ **her hair comes (down) to her waist** ses cheveux lui arrivent à la taille
3. [happen] arriver, se produire ▸ **such an opportunity only comes once in your life** une telle occasion ne se présente qu'une fois dans la vie ▸ **take life as it comes** prenez la vie comme elle vient ▸ **come what may** quoi qu'il arrive ▸ **how did you come to fail your exam?** comment as-tu fait pour échouer à ton examen?
4. [become] **: to come true** se réaliser ▸ **to come undone** se défaire ▸ **to come unstuck** se décoller
5. [begin gradually] **: to come to do sthg** en arriver à *OR* en venir à faire qqch ▸ **we have come to expect this kind of thing** nous nous attendons à ce genre de chose maintenant ▸ **(now that I) come to think of it** maintenant que j'y songe, réflexion faite
6. [be placed in order] venir, être placé(e) ▸ **P comes before Q** P vient avant Q, P précède Q ▸ **who came first?** qui a été placé premier? ▸ **she came second in the exam** elle était deuxième à l'examen ▸ **that speech comes in Act 3/on page 10** on trouve ce discours dans l'acte 3/à la page 10
7. [exist] exister ▸ **this table comes in two sizes** cette table existe *OR* se fait en deux dimensions ▸ **a house doesn't come cheap** une maison coûte *OR* revient cher ▸ **he's as silly as they come** il est sot comme pas un
8. *v inf* [sexually] jouir.

◆ ***to come*** **adv** à venir ▸ **in (the) days/years to come** dans les jours/années à venir.

◆ ***come about*** **vi** [happen] arriver, se produire.

◆ ***come across*** ■ **vt insep** tomber sur, trouver par hasard.
■ **vi** [speaker, message] faire de l'effet ▸ **you don't come across very well** tu présentes mal ▸ **to come across as being sincere** donner l'impression d'être sincère.

◆ ***come along*** **vi 1.** [arrive by chance] arriver
2. [improve - work] avancer / [- student] faire des progrès ▸ **the project is coming along nicely** le projet avance bien
▸▸ **come along!** [expressing encouragement] allez! / [hurry up] allez, dépêche-toi!

◆ ***come apart*** **vi 1.** [fall to pieces] tomber en morceaux
2. [come off] se détacher.

◆ ***come around***, ***come round*** *UK* **vi 1.** [change opinion] changer d'avis
2. [regain consciousness] reprendre connaissance, revenir à soi
3. [happen] venir, revenir ▸ **when the championships/elections come around** au moment des championnats/élections.

◆ ***come at*** **vt insep** [attack] attaquer.

◆ ***come back*** **vi 1.** [in talk, writing] **: to come back to sthg** revenir à qqch
2. [memory] **: to come back (to sb)** revenir (à qqn)
3. [become fashionable again] redevenir à la mode.

◆ ***come by*** **vt insep 1.** [get, obtain] trouver, dénicher
2. *US* [visit, drop in on] **: they came by the house** ils sont passés à la maison.

◆ ***come down*** **vi 1.** [decrease] baisser
2. [descend] descendre.

◆ ***come down to*** **vt insep** se résumer à, se réduire à.

◆ ***come down with*** **vt insep** [cold, flu] attraper.

◆ ***come forward*** **vi** se présenter.

◆ ***come from*** **vt insep** venir de.

◆ ***come in*** **vi 1.** [enter] entrer ▸ **come in!** entrez!
2. [arrive, be received] arriver
3. [be involved] jouer un rôle ▸ **I don't see where I come in** je ne vois pas quel rôle je vais jouer.

◆ ***come in for*** **vt insep** [criticism] être l'objet de.

◆ ***come into*** **vt insep 1.** [inherit] hériter de
2. [begin to be] **: to come into being** prendre naissance, voir le jour ▸ **to come into sight** apparaître.

◆ ***come of*** **vt insep** [result from] résulter de.

◆ ***come off*** **vi 1.** [button, label] se détacher / [stain] s'enlever
2. [joke, attempt] réussir
3. [person] **: to come off well/badly** bien/mal s'en tirer
▸▸ **come off it!** *inf* et puis quoi encore!, non mais sans blague!

◆ ***come on*** **vi 1.** [start] commencer, apparaître
2. [start working - light, heating] s'allumer
3. [progress, improve] avancer, faire des progrès
▸▸ **come on!** [expressing encouragement] allez! / [hurry up] allez, dépêche-toi! / [expressing disbelief] allons donc!

◆ ***come out*** **vi 1.** [exit] sortir ▸ **would you like to come out with me tonight?** est-ce que tu veux sortir avec moi ce soir?
2. [become known] être découvert(e)
3. [appear - product, book, film] sortir, paraître / [- sun, moon, stars] paraître
4. [in exam, race] finir, se classer
5. [go on strike] faire grève
6. [declare publicly] **: to come out for/against sthg** se déclarer pour/contre qqch
7. [photograph] réussir.

◆ ***come out in*** **vt insep : to come out in spots** avoir une éruption.

◆ ***come over*** ■ **vi** [move towards speaker] venir ▸ **do you want to come over this evening?** tu veux venir à la maison ce soir?
■ **vt insep** [subj: sensation, emotion] envahir ▸ **I don't know what's come over her** je ne sais pas ce qui lui a pris.

◆ ***come round*** *UK* **vi** = ***come around***.

◆ ***come through*** ■ **vt insep** survivre à.
■ **vi 1.** [arrive] arriver
2. [survive] s'en tirer.

◆ ***come to*** ■ **vt insep 1.** [reach] **: to come to an end** se terminer, prendre fin ▸ **to come to power** arriver au pouvoir ▸ **to come to a decision** arriver à *OR* prendre une décision
2. [concern] **: when it comes to physics, she's a genius** pour ce qui est de la physique, c'est un génie ▸ **when it comes to paying...** quand il faut payer...
3. [amount to] s'élever à.
■ **vi** [regain consciousness] revenir à soi, reprendre connaissance.

◆ ***come under*** **vt insep 1.** [be subjected to - authority, control] dépendre de / [- influence] tomber sous, être soumis à ▸ **the government is coming under pressure to lower taxes** le gouvernement subit des pressions visant à réduire les impôts ▸ **to come under attack (from)** être en butte aux attaques (de)
2. [heading] se trouver sous.

◆ ***come up*** **vi 1.** [be mentioned] survenir

2. [be imminent] approcher
3. [happen unexpectedly] se présenter
4. [sun] se lever.
◆ ***come up against*** **vt insep** se heurter à.
◆ ***come upon*** **vt insep** [find] tomber sur.
◆ ***come up to*** **vt insep 1.** [approach - in space] s'approcher de / [- in time] **: we're coming up to Christmas** Noël approche
2. [equal] répondre à.
◆ ***come up with*** **vt insep** [answer, idea] proposer.

comeback ['kʌmbæk] **n** come-back *m* ▸ **to make a comeback** [fashion] revenir à la mode / [actor] revenir à la scène.

Comecon ['kɒmɪkɒn] (abbr of ***Council for Mutual Economic Assistance***) **n** Comecon *m*.

comedian [kə'mi:djən] **n** [comic] comique *m* / THEAT comédien *m*.

comedienne [kə,mi:dɪ'en] **n** [comic] actrice *f* comique / THEAT comédienne *f*.

comedown ['kʌmdaʊn] **n** *inf* **: it was a comedown for her** elle est tombée bien bas pour faire ça.

comedy ['kɒmədɪ] (pl **-ies**) **n** comédie *f*.

come-hither **adj** *inf* aguichant(e) ▸ **a come-hither look** un regard aguichant.

comely ['kʌmlɪ] **adj** *liter* attrayant(e).

come-on **n : to give sb the come-on** *inf* essayer d'aguicher qqn.

comet ['kɒmɪt] **n** comète *f*.

come-uppance [,kʌm'ʌpəns] **n : to get one's come-uppance** *inf* recevoir ce qu'on mérite.

comfort ['kʌmfət] ■ **n 1.** *(U)* [ease] confort *m* ▸ **that was too close for comfort** c'était moins cinq **2.** [luxury] commodité *f* **3.** [solace] réconfort *m*, consolation *f*.
■ **vt** réconforter, consoler.

comfortable ['kʌmftəbl] **adj 1.** [gen] confortable **2.** *fig* [person - at ease, financially] à l'aise **3.** [after operation, accident] **: he's comfortable** son état est stationnaire.

comfortably ['kʌmftəblɪ] **adv 1.** [sit, sleep] confortablement **2.** [without financial difficulty] à l'aise ▸ **comfortably off** à l'aise **3.** [win] aisément.

comforter ['kʌmfətəʳ] **n 1.** [person] soutien *m* moral **2.** *US* [quilt] édredon *m*.

comforting ['kʌmfətɪŋ] **adj** [thought, words] réconfortant(e).

comfort station **n** *US dated* toilettes *fpl* publiques.

comfy ['kʌmfɪ] (comp **-ier**, superl **-iest**) **adj** *inf* confortable.

comic ['kɒmɪk] ■ **adj** comique, amusant(e).
■ **n 1.** [comedian] comique *m*, actrice *f* comique **2.** [magazine] bande *f* dessinée.
◆ ***comics*** **npl** *US* [in newspaper] bandes *fpl* dessinées.

comical ['kɒmɪkl] **adj** comique, drôle.

comic book **n** magazine *m* de bandes dessinées.

comic strip **n** bande *f* dessinée.

coming ['kʌmɪŋ] ■ **adj** [future] à venir, futur(e).
■ **n : comings and goings** allées et venues *fpl*.

coming of age **n** majorité *f*.

coming out **n** entrée *f* dans le monde *(d'une jeune fille)*.

comma ['kɒmə] **n** virgule *f*.

command [kə'mɑ:nd] ■ **n 1.** [order] ordre *m* ▸ **they are at your command** ils sont à vos ordres **2.** *(U)* [control] commandement *m* ▸ **who is in command here?** qui est-ce qui commande ici? ▸ **in command of** MIL à la tête de / *fig* en possession de **3.** [of language, subject] maîtrise *f* ▸ **she has a good command of two foreign languages** elle possède bien deux langues étrangères ▸ **to have at one's command** [language] maîtriser / [resources] avoir à sa disposition **4.** COMPUT commande *f*.
■ **vt 1.** [order] **: to command sb to do sthg** ordonner *OR* commander à qqn de faire qqch ▸ **she commanded that we leave immediately** elle nous a ordonné *OR* nous a donné l'ordre de partir immédiatement **2.** MIL [control] commander **3.** [deserve - respect] inspirer / [- attention, high price] mériter.

commandant [,kɒmən'dænt] **n** commandant *m*.

command economy **n** économie *f* planifiée.

commandeer [,kɒmən'dɪəʳ] **vt** réquisitionner.

commander [kə'mɑ:ndəʳ] **n 1.** [in army] commandant *m* **2.** [in navy] capitaine *m* de frégate.

commander-in-chief (pl **commanders-in-chief**) **n** commandant *m* en chef.

commanding [kə'mɑ:ndɪŋ] **adj 1.** [lead, position] dominant(e) **2.** [voice, manner] impérieux(euse).

commanding officer **n** commandant *m*.

commandment [kə'mɑ:ndmənt] **n** RELIG commandement *m*.

command module **n** module *m* de commande.

commando [kə'mɑ:ndəʊ] (pl **-s** *OR* **-es**) **n** commando *m*.

command performance **n** *représentation de gala organisée à la demande d'un chef d'État.*

commemorate [kə'memərext] **vt** commémorer.

commemoration [kə,memə'reɪʃn] **n** commémoration *f*.

commemorative [kə'memərətɪv] **adj** commémoratif(ive).

commence [kə'mens] *fml* ■ **vt** commencer, entamer ▸ **to commence doing sthg** commencer à faire qqch.
■ **vi** commencer.

commencement [kə'mensmənt] **n** *fml* commencement *m*, début *m*.

commend [kə'mend] **vt 1.** [praise] **: to commend sb (on** *OR* **for)** féliciter qqn (de) **2.** [recommend] **: to commend sthg (to sb)** recommander qqch (à qqn).

commendable [kə'mendəbl] **adj** louable.

commendably [kə'mendəblɪ] **adv** de façon louable ▸ **his speech was commendably brief** son discours avait le mérite de la brièveté.

commendation [,kɒmen'deɪʃn] **n : to get a commendation for sthg** être récompensé(e) pour qqch.

commensurate [kə'menʃərət] **adj** *fml* **: commensurate with** correspondant(e) à.

comment ['kɒment] ■ **n** commentaire *m*, remarque *f* ▸ **no comment!** sans commentaire! ▸ **teacher's comments** SCH appréciations *fpl* du professeur.
■ **vt : to comment that** remarquer que.
■ **vi : to comment (on)** faire des commentaires **OR** remarques (sur) ▸ **comment on the text** commentez le texte, faites le commentaire du texte.

commentary ['kɒməntrɪ] (pl **-ies**) **n** commentaire *m*.

commentate ['kɒmənteɪt] **vi** RADIO & TV **: to commentate (on)** faire un reportage (sur).

commentator ['kɒmənteɪtəʳ] **n** commentateur *m*, -trice *f*.

commerce ['kɒmɜːs] **n** *(U)* commerce *m*, affaires *fpl*.

commercial [kə'mɜːʃl] ■ **adj** commercial(e).
■ **n** publicité *f*, spot *m* publicitaire.

commercial bank **n** banque *f* commerciale **OR** de commerce.

commercial break **n** publicités *fpl*.

commercial college **n** école *f* de secrétariat.

commercialism [kə'mɜːʃəlɪzm] **n** mercantilisme *m*.

commercialization, *UK* ***-isation*** [kəˌmɜːʃəlaɪ'zeɪʃn] **n** commercialisation *f*.

commercialize, *UK* ***-ise*** [kə'mɜːʃəlaɪz] **vt** commercialiser.

commercialized, *UK* ***-ised*** [kə'mɜːʃəlaɪzd] **adj** commercial(e).

commercially [kə'mɜːʃəlɪ] **adv** commercialement.

commercial television **n** *UK* chaînes *fpl* (de télévision) privées **OR** commerciales.

commercial traveller **n** *UK dated* voyageur *m* **OR** représentant *m* de commerce.

commercial vehicle **n** *UK* véhicule *m* utilitaire.

commie ['kɒmɪ] *inf pej* ■ **adj** coco.
■ **n** coco *mf*.

commiserate [kə'mɪzəreɪt] **vi : to commiserate with sb** témoigner de la compassion pour qqn.

commiseration [kəˌmɪzə'reɪʃn] **n** compassion *f*.

commission [kə'mɪʃn] ■ **n 1.** [money, investigative body] commission *f* ▸ **commission of inquiry, fact-finding commission** commission d'enquête **2.** [order for work] commande *f* ▸ **work done on commission** travail fait sur commande.
■ **vt** [work] commander ▸ **to commission sb to do sthg** charger qqn de faire qqch.

commissionaire [kəˌmɪʃə'neəʳ] **n** *UK* portier *m (d'un hôtel, etc)*.

commissioned officer [kə'mɪʃənd-] **n** officier *m*.

commissioner [kə'mɪʃnəʳ] **n 1.** [in police] commissaire *mf* **2.** [commission member] membre *mf* d'une commission.

commit [kə'mɪt] (pt & pp **-ted**, cont **-ting**) **vt 1.** [crime, sin] commettre ▸ **to commit suicide** se suicider **2.** [promise - money, resources] allouer ▸ **to commit o.s. (to sthg/to doing sthg)** s'engager (à qqch/à faire qqch) **3.** [consign] **: to commit sb to prison** faire incarcérer qqn ▸ **to commit sthg to memory** apprendre qqch par cœur.

commitment [kə'mɪtmənt] **n 1.** *(U)* [dedication] engagement *m* **2.** [responsibility] obligation *f*.

committal [kə'mɪtl] **n 1.** [sending - gen] remise *f* / [- to prison] incarcération *f*, emprisonnement *m* / [- to mental hospital] internement *m* / [- to grave] mise *f* en terre **2.** LAW **: committal proceedings, committal for trial** ≃ mise *f* en accusation **3.** [of crime] perpétration *f*.

committed [kə'mɪtɪd] **adj** [writer, politician] engagé(e) / [Christian] convaincu(e) ▸ **he's committed to his work** il fait preuve d'engagement dans son travail.

committed costs **npl** coûts *mpl* engagés.

committee [kə'mɪtɪ] **n** commission *f*, comité *m*.

commode [kə'məʊd] **n** [with chamber pot] chaise *f* percée.

commodity [kə'mɒdətɪ] (pl **-ies**) **n** marchandise *f*.

commodity exchange **n** bourse *f* des matières premières.

commodity market **n** ECON marché *m* des matières premières.

commodity tax **n** ECON impôt *m* sur les denrées.

common ['kɒmən] ■ **adj 1.** [frequent] courant(e) ▸ **it's quite common** c'est courant **OR** tout à fait banal ▸ **a common occurrence** une chose fréquente **OR** qui arrive souvent ▸ **a common expression** une expression courante ▸ **in common use** d'usage courant **2.** [shared] **: common (to)** commun(e) (à) ▸ **by common consent** d'un commun accord **3.** [ordinary] banal(e) ▸ **the common people** le peuple, les gens du commun ▸ **the common man** Monsieur *m* tout-le-monde **4.** *UK pej* [vulgar] vulgaire.
■ **n** [land] terrain *m* communal.
◆ ***in common*** **adv** en commun ▸ **to have sthg in common with sb** avoir qqch en commun avec qqn ▸ **we have nothing in common** nous n'avons rien en commun.

common cold **n** rhume *m*.

common currency **n** ECON monnaie *f* commune.

common denominator **n** *fig* & MATHS dénominateur *m* commun.

Common Entrance **n** *UK* SCH *examen de fin d'études primaires permettant d'entrer dans une "public school"*.

commoner ['kɒmənəʳ] **n** roturier *m*, -ère *f*.

common factor **n** facteur *m* commun.

common gateway interface **n** COMPUT interface *f* commune de passerelle.

common good **n : for the common good** dans l'intérêt général.

common ground **n** [in interests] intérêt *m* commun / [for discussion] terrain *m* d'entente.

common knowledge **n : it is common knowledge that...** tout le monde sait que..., il est de notoriété publique que...

common land **n** *(U)* terrain *m* communal.

common law **n** droit *m* coutumier.
◆ ***common-law*** **adj : common-law wife** concubine *f*.

commonly ['kɒmənlɪ] **adv** [generally] d'une manière générale, généralement.

Common Market **n** *dated* **: the Common Market** le Marché commun.

common-or-garden **adj** *UK inf* **: the common-or-garden variety** le modèle standard *OR* ordinaire.

commonplace ['kɒmənpleɪs] **adj** banal(e), ordinaire.

common room **n** [staffroom] salle *f* des professeurs / [for students] salle commune.

Commons ['kɒmənz] **npl** *UK* **: the Commons** les Communes *fpl*, la Chambre des Communes.

common sense **n** *(U)* bon sens *m*.

Commonwealth ['kɒmənwelθ] **n : the Commonwealth** le Commonwealth.

Commonwealth of Independent States **n : the Commonwealth of Independent States** la Communauté des États Indépendants.

commotion [kə'məʊʃn] **n** remue-ménage *m*.

communal ['kɒmjʊnl] **adj** [kitchen, garden] commun(e) / [life] communautaire, collectif(ive).

communally ['kɒmjʊnəlɪ] **adv** collectivement, en commun.

commune ■ **n** ['kɒmju:n] communauté *f*.
■ **vi** [kə'mju:n] **: to commune with** communier avec.

communicate [kə'mju:nɪkeɪt] **vt & vi** communiquer.

communicating [kə'mju:nɪkeɪtɪŋ] **adj** [rooms] communicant(e) ▸ **communicating door** porte *f* de communication.

communication [kə,mju:nɪ'keɪʃn] **n** contact *m* / TELEC communication *f* ▸ **are you in communication with her?** êtes-vous en contact *OR* en relation avec elle? ▸ **to be good at communication, to have good communication skills** avoir des talents de communicateur, être un bon communicateur.
◆ ***communications*** **npl** moyens *mpl* de communication.

communication cord **n** *UK* sonnette *f* d'alarme.

communications satellite **n** satellite *m* de communication.

communicative [kə'mju:nɪkətɪv] **adj** [talkative] communicatif(ive).

communicator [kə'mju:nɪkeɪtə^r] **n : to be a good communicator** avoir le don de la communication ▸ **to be a bad communicator** avoir des difficultés de communication.

communion [kə'mju:njən] **n** communion *f*.
◆ ***Communion*** **n** *(U)* RELIG communion *f*.

communiqué [kə'mju:nɪkeɪ] **n** communiqué *m*.

Communism ['kɒmjʊnɪzm] **n** communisme *m*.

Communist ['kɒmjʊnɪst] ■ **adj** communiste.
■ **n** communiste *mf*.

community [kə'mju:nətɪ] (**pl -ies**) **n** communauté *f* ▸ **the business community** le monde des affaires ▸ **the international community** la communauté internationale.

community care **n** *système britannique d'assistance sociale au niveau local.*

community centre *UK*, ***community center*** *US* **n** foyer *m* municipal.

community charge **n** *UK* ≃ impôts *mpl* locaux.

community home **n** *UK* centre *m* d'éducation surveillée.

community policing **n** ≃ îlotage *m*.

community service **n** *(U)* travail *m* d'intérêt général.

community spirit **n** esprit *m* de groupe.

commutable [kə'mju:təbl] **adj** LAW commuable.

commutation ticket [,kɒmju:'teɪʃn] **n** *US* carte *f* de transport.

commute [kə'mju:t] ■ **vt** LAW commuer.
■ **vi** [to work] *faire la navette pour se rendre à son travail.*

commuter [kə'mju:tə^r] **n** *personne qui fait tous les jours la navette de banlieue en ville pour se rendre à son travail.*

commuting [kə'mju:tɪŋ] **n** *(U)* trajets *mpl* réguliers, migrations *fpl* quotidiennes *(entre le domicile, généralement en banlieue, et le lieu de travail).*

Comoro Islands, ***Comoros Islands***, ***Comoros*** **npl : the Comoro Islands** les îles *fpl* Comores ▸ **in the Comoro Islands** aux îles Comores.

compact ■ **adj** [kəm'pækt] compact(e).
■ **n** ['kɒmpækt] **1.** [for face powder] poudrier *m* **2.** *US* AUT **: compact (car)** petite voiture *f*.
■ **vt** [kəm'pækt] tasser, rendre compact.

compact disc **n** compact *m* (disc *m*), disque *m* compact.

compact disc player **n** lecteur *m* de disques compacts.

companion [kəm'pænjən] **n** [person] camarade *mf* ▸ **travelling** *UK* *OR* **traveling** *US* **companion** compagnon *m*, compagne *f* de voyage.

companionable [kəm'pænjənəbl] **adj** sociable.

companionship [kəm'pænjənʃɪp] **n** compagnie *f*.

company ['kʌmpənɪ] (**pl -ies**) **n 1.** [COMM - gen] société *f* / [- insurance, airline, shipping company] compagnie *f* ▸ **Jones &Company** Jones et Compagnie **2.** [companionship] compagnie *f* ▸ **we enjoy one another's company** nous aimons être ensemble ▸ **she's good company** elle est d'agréable compagnie ▸ **to keep sb company** tenir compagnie à qqn ▸ **to part company (with)** se séparer (de) **3.** [of actors] troupe *f*.

company car **n** voiture *f* de fonction.

company director **n** directeur *m*, -trice *f*.

company secretary **n** secrétaire général *m*, secrétaire générale *f*.

comparable ['kɒmprəbl] **adj : comparable (to** *OR* **with)** comparable (à).

comparative [kəm'pærətɪv] **adj 1.** [relative] relatif(ive) **2.** [study, in grammar] comparatif(ive).

comparatively [kəm'pærətɪvlɪ] **adv** [relatively] relativement.

comparative testing **n** *(U)* essais *mpl* comparatifs.

compare [kəm'peəʳ] ■ vt : **to compare sb/sthg (with** *OR* **to)** comparer qqn/qqch (avec), comparer qqn/qqch (à) ▸ **compared with** *OR* **to** par rapport à ▸ **to compare notes** échanger ses impressions.
■ **vi : to compare (with)** être comparable (à) ▸ **to compare favourably/unfavourably with** supporter/ne pas supporter la comparaison avec.

comparison [kəm'pærɪsn] n comparaison *f* ▸ **in comparison with** *OR* **to** en comparaison de, par rapport à.

compartment [kəm'pɑ:tmənt] n compartiment *m*.

compartmentalize, *UK* ***-ise*** [ˌkɒmpɑ:t'mentəlaɪz] vt compartimenter.

compass ['kʌmpəs] n [magnetic] boussole *f*.
◆ ***compasses*** npl : **(a pair of) compasses** un compas.

compassion [kəm'pæʃn] n compassion *f*.

compassionate [kəm'pæʃənət] adj compatissant(e).

compassionate leave n [gen & MIL] permission *f* exceptionnelle *(pour raisons personnelles)*.

compassion fatigue n *lassitude du public à l'égard des nécessiteux*.

compatibility [kəm,pætə'bɪlətɪ] n [gen & COMPUT] : **compatibility (with)** compatibilité *f* (avec).

compatible [kəm'pætəbl] adj [gen & COMPUT] : **compatible (with)** compatible (avec).

compatriot [kəm'pætrɪət] n compatriote *mf*.

compel [kəm'pel] (pt & pp -led, cont -ling) vt **1.** [force] : **to compel sb (to do sthg)** contraindre *OR* obliger qqn (à faire qqch) **2.** [cause - sympathy, attention] susciter.

compelling [kəm'pelɪŋ] adj [forceful] irrésistible.

compendium [kəm'pendɪəm] (pl **-diums** *OR* **-dia** [-dɪə]) n [book] abrégé *m*.

compensate ['kɒmpenseɪt] ■ vt : **to compensate sb for sthg** [financially] dédommager *OR* indemniser qqn de qqch.
■ **vi : to compensate for sthg** compenser qqch.

compensation [ˌkɒmpen'seɪʃn] n **1.** [money] : **compensation (for)** dédommagement *m* (pour) **2.** [way of compensating] : **compensation (for)** compensation *f* (pour).

compere ['kɒmpeəʳ] *UK* ■ n animateur *m*, -trice *f*.
■ vt présenter, animer.

compete [kəm'pi:t] vi **1.** [vie - people] : **to compete with sb for sthg** disputer qqch à qqn ▸ **to compete for sthg** se disputer qqch **2.** COMM : **to compete (with)** être en concurrence (avec) ▸ **to compete for sthg** se faire concurrence pour qqch ▸ **we have to compete on an international level** nous devons être à la hauteur de la concurrence sur le plan international **3.** [take part] être en compétition ▸ **to compete against sb for sthg** concourir *OR* être en compétition avec qqn pour qqch.

competence ['kɒmpɪtəns] n *(U)* [proficiency] compétence *f*, capacité *f*.

competent ['kɒmpɪtənt] adj compétent(e).

competently ['kɒmpɪtəntlɪ] adv avec compétence.

competing [kəm'pi:tɪŋ] adj [theories] opposé(e).

competition [ˌkɒmpɪ'tɪʃn] n **1.** *(U)* [rivalry] rivalité *f*, concurrence *f* **2.** *(U)* COMM concurrence *f* **3.** [race, contest] concours *m*, compétition *f*.

competitive [kəm'petətɪv] adj **1.** [person] qui a l'esprit de compétition / [match, sport] de compétition ▸ **competitive examination** concours *m* **2.** [COMM - goods] compétitif(ive) / [- manufacturer] concurrentiel(elle).

competitive advantage n avantage *m* concurrentiel.

competitive analysis n analyse *f* des concurrents.

competitively [kəm'petətɪvlɪ] adv **1.** [play] dans un esprit de compétition **2.** COMM : **competitively priced** à un prix compétitif.

competitive marketplace n marché *m* de concurrence.

competitiveness [kəm'petətɪvnɪs] n compétitivité *f*.

competitive pricing n fixation *f* des prix compétitifs.

competitor [kəm'petɪtəʳ] n concurrent *m*, -e *f*.

HOW TO ...

express comparison

Ils en ont eu autant que nous / They've had as much/as many as us
C'est comme l'an dernier / It's like last year
Cet appartement est plus cher/bien plus cher/encore plus cher que le nôtre / This flat is more expensive/much more expensive/even more expensive than ours
On a mis plus de temps que prévu / It's taken us longer than we thought
C'est mieux que l'an dernier / It's better than last year
Il est moins doué que ses parents / He's not as gifted as his parents
Il est loin d'être aussi rapide qu'elle / He's nowhere near as fast as she is
C'est pire que l'an dernier / It's worse than last year
Ils sont aussi paresseux l'un que l'autre / They're both as lazy as each other
Comparée à Londres, Toulouse est une petite ville / Compared with London, Toulouse is quite small
Contrairement à son frère, il comprend la plaisanterie / Unlike his brother, he can take a joke
Il adore l'opéra et la peinture, alors qu'elle est plutôt sportive / He loves opera and painting whereas she is more interested in sport
Autant son dernier spectacle était ennuyeux, autant celui-ci m'a passionné / I loved this show, whereas I found the last one boring

compilation [ˌkɒmpɪ'leɪʃn] **n** compilation *f.*

compile [kəm'paɪl] **vt** rédiger.

compiler [kəm'paɪlər] **n 1.** [gen] compilateur *m*, -trice *f* **2.** [of dictionary] rédacteur *m*, -trice *f* **3.** COMPUT compilateur *m*.

complacence [kəm'pleɪsns], ***complacency*** [kəm'pleɪsnsɪ] **n** autosatisfaction *f*.

complacent [kəm'pleɪsnt] **adj** satisfait(e) de soi.

complacently [kəm'pleɪsntlɪ] **adv** [act] d'un air suffisant / [say] d'un ton suffisant.

complain [kəm'pleɪn] **vi 1.** [make complaint] **: to complain (about)** se plaindre (de) ▸ **to complain to sb (about sthg)** se plaindre à *OR* auprès de qqn (au sujet de qqch) ▸ **she complained that he was always late** elle s'est plainte qu'il était toujours en retard **2.** MED **: to complain of** se plaindre de.

complainant [kəm'pleɪnənt] **n** demandeur *m*, demanderesse *f*.

complaining [kəm'pleɪnɪŋ] **adj** [customer] mécontent(e).

complaint [kəm'pleɪnt] **n 1.** [gen] plainte *f* / [in shop] réclamation *f* **2.** MED affection *f*, maladie *f*.

complement ■ **n** ['kɒmplɪmənt] **1.** [accompaniment] accompagnement *m* **2.** [number] effectif *m* ▸ **full complement** effectif complet **3.** GRAM complément *m*.
■ **vt** ['kɒmplɪˌment] aller bien avec.

complementary [ˌkɒmplɪ'mentərɪ] **adj** complémentaire.

complementary medicine **n** médecine *f* douce.

complete [kəm'pli:t] ■ **adj 1.** [gen] complet(ète) ▸ **the complete works of Shakespeare** les œuvres complètes de Shakespeare ▸ **he's a complete fool** c'est un crétin fini *OR* un parfait imbécile ▸ **complete with** doté(e) de, muni(e) de **2.** [finished] achevé(e).
■ **vt 1.** [make whole] compléter ▸ **to complete an order** COMM exécuter une commande **2.** [finish] achever, terminer **3.** [questionnaire, form] remplir.

completely [kəm'pli:tlɪ] **adv** complètement.

completeness [kəm'pli:tnɪs] **n** état *m* complet.

completion [kəm'pli:ʃn] **n** achèvement *m*.

complex ['kɒmpleks] ■ **adj** complexe.
■ **n** [mental, of buildings] complexe *m*.

complexion [kəm'plekʃn] **n** teint *m* ▸ **of all complexions** *fig* de tous bords.

complexity [kəm'pleksətɪ] (pl **-ies**) **n** complexité *f*.

compliance [kəm'plaɪəns] **n : compliance (with)** conformité *f* (à).

compliant [kəm'plaɪənt] **adj** [person] docile / [document, object] conforme.

complicate ['kɒmplɪkeɪt] **vt** compliquer.

complicated ['kɒmplɪkeɪtɪd] **adj** compliqué(e).

complication [ˌkɒmplɪ'keɪʃn] **n** complication *f*.

complicity [kəm'plɪsətɪ] **n : complicity (in)** complicité *f* (dans).

compliment ■ **n** ['kɒmplɪmənt] compliment *m*.
■ **vt** ['kɒmplɪˌment] **: to compliment sb (on)** féliciter qqn (de).
◆ ***compliments*** **npl** *fml* compliments *mpl*.

complimentary [ˌkɒmplɪ'mentərɪ] **adj 1.** [admiring] flatteur(euse) **2.** [free] gratuit(e).

complimentary ticket **n** billet *m* de faveur.

compliments slip **n** *esp UK* papillon *m (joint à un envoi etc)*.

comply [kəm'plaɪ] (pt & pp **-ied**) **vi : to comply with** se conformer à.

component [kəm'pəʊnənt] **n** composant *m*.

compose [kəm'pəʊz] **vt 1.** [gen] composer ▸ **to be composed of** se composer de, être composé de **2.** [calm] **: to compose o.s.** se calmer.

composed [kəm'pəʊzd] **adj** [calm] calme.

composer [kəm'pəʊzər] **n** compositeur *m*, -trice *f*.

composite ['kɒmpəzɪt] ■ **adj** composite.
■ **n** composite *m*.

composition [ˌkɒmpə'zɪʃn] **n** composition *f*.

HOW TO ...

complain

J'ai une réclamation à faire au sujet de l'ordinateur acheté chez vous / I've got a complaint about the computer I bought from you

Je ne suis pas très content/pas content du tout du service qui nous a été fourni / I am not very happy/not at all happy with the service we have received

J'estime que le travail a été effectué de façon déplorable / I am not at all happy with the way in which the work was done

Il y a un problème avec le chauffage, il ne marche plus du tout / There's a problem with the heating. It's not working

Nous avons été traités de façon inadmissible / The way we have been treated is quite unacceptable

Je pense que vous devriez me rembourser ou au moins me le remplacer / I think you should give me my money back or at least replace it

Je pense être en droit d'attendre un dédommagement / I think I am well within my rights to ask for compensation

J'exige le remboursement intégral de l'appareil photo/de mes frais / I expect the cost of the camera/my expenses to be fully reimbursed

Je voudrais voir le directeur, s'il vous plaît / I'd like to see the manager, please

J'aimerais que ce problème soit résolu le plus vite possible / I would appreciate (it) if this problem could be sorted out as quickly as possible

Je compte sur vous pour régler ce problème / I am relying on you to sort out this problem

compos mentis [ˌkɒmpəsˈmentɪs] **adj** sain d'esprit.

compost [*UK* ˈkɒmpɒst, *US* ˈkɒmpəʊst] **n** compost *m*.

composure [kəmˈpəʊʒəʳ] **n** sang-froid *m*, calme *m*.

compound ■ **adj** [ˈkɒmpaʊnd] composé(e).
■ **n** [ˈkɒmpaʊnd] **1.** CHEM & LING composé *m* **2.** [enclosed area] enceinte *f*.
■ **vt** [kəmˈpaʊnd] **1.** [mixture, substance] **: to be compounded of** se composer de, être composé(e) de **2.** [difficulties] aggraver.

compound fracture **n** fracture *f* multiple.

compound interest **n** FIN intérêts *mpl* composés.

comprehend [ˌkɒmprɪˈhend] **vt** [understand] comprendre.

comprehensible [ˌkɒmprɪˈhensəbl] **adj** compréhensible, intelligible.

comprehension [ˌkɒmprɪˈhenʃn] **n** compréhension *f*.

comprehensive [ˌkɒmprɪˈhensɪv] ■ **adj 1.** [account, report] exhaustif(ive), détaillé(e) **2.** [insurance] tous-risques *(inv)*.
■ **n** *UK* = ***comprehensive school***.

FALSE FRIENDS / FAUX AMIS
comprehensive

Compréhensif n'est pas la traduction du mot anglais *comprehensive*. Compréhensif se traduit par *understanding*.
▸ Elle a toujours été très compréhensive avec nous *She has always been very understanding with us*

comprehensively [ˌkɒmprɪˈhensɪvlɪ] **adv** [study, cover] exhaustivement.

comprehensive school **n** *établissement secondaire britannique d'enseignement général*.

compress [kəmˈpres] **vt 1.** [squeeze, press] comprimer **2.** [shorten - text] condenser.

compression [kəmˈpreʃn] **n 1.** [of air] compression *f* **2.** [of text] condensation *f*.

comprise [kəmˈpraɪz] **vt** comprendre ▸ **to be comprised of** consister en, comprendre.

compromise [ˈkɒmprəmaɪz] ■ **n** compromis *m*.
■ **vt** compromettre ▸ **to compromise o.s.** se compromettre.
■ **vi** transiger.

compromising [ˈkɒmprəmaɪzɪŋ] **adj** compromettant(e).

compulsion [kəmˈpʌlʃn] **n 1.** [strong desire] **: to have a compulsion to do sthg** ne pas pouvoir s'empêcher de faire qqch **2.** *(U)* [obligation] obligation *f*.

compulsive [kəmˈpʌlsɪv] **adj 1.** [smoker, liar etc] invétéré(e) **2.** [book, TV programme] captivant(e).

compulsively [kəmˈpʌlsɪvlɪ] **adv 1.** PSYCHOL [drink, steal, smoke] d'une façon compulsive **2.** *fig* irrésistiblement.

compulsory [kəmˈpʌlsərɪ] **adj** obligatoire.

compulsory purchase **n** *UK* expropriation *f (pour cause d'utilité publique)*.

compunction [kəmˈpʌŋkʃn] **n** *(U)* scrupule *m*, remords *m*.

computation [ˌkɒmpjuːˈteɪʃn] **n** calcul *m*.

computational [ˌkɒmpjuːˈteɪʃənl] **adj** quantitatif(ive), statistique ▸ **computational linguistics** linguistique *f* computationnelle.

compute [kəmˈpjuːt] **vt** calculer.

computer [kəmˈpjuːtəʳ] **n** ordinateur *m*.

computer-aided, ***computer-assisted*** **adj** assisté(e) par ordinateur.

computer-aided design **n** conception *f* assistée par ordinateur.

computer-aided learning **n** enseignement *m* assisté par ordinateur.

computer-aided translation **n** traduction *f* assistée par ordinateur.

computer crime **n** fraude *f* informatique.

computer dating **n** *(U) rencontres sélectionnées par ordinateur*.

computer game **n** jeu *m* électronique.

computer-generated [-ˈdʒenəreɪtɪd] **adj** créé(e) par ordinateur.

computer-generated image **n** image *f* de synthèse.

computer graphics **npl** infographie *f*.

computerization [kəmˌpjuːtəraɪˈzeɪʃn] **n** informatisation *f*.

computerize, *UK* ***-ise*** [kəmˈpjuːtəraɪz] **vt** informatiser.

computerized, *UK* ***-ised*** [kəmˈpjuːtəraɪzd] **adj** informatisé(e).

computerized accounts **n** comptabilité *f* informatisée.

computer language **n** langage *m* de programmation.

computer literacy **n** compétence *f* informatique.

computer-literate **adj** qui a des compétences en informatique.

computer program **n** programme *m* informatique.

computer programmer **n** programmeur *m*, -euse *f*.

computer programming **n** programmation *f*.

computer science **n** informatique *f*.

computer scientist **n** informaticien *m*, -enne *f*.

computer virus **n** virus *m* informatique.

computing [kəmˈpjuːtɪŋ] **n** informatique *f*.

comrade [ˈkɒmreɪd] **n** camarade *mf*.

comradeship [ˈkɒmreɪdʃɪp] **n** camaraderie *f*.

comsat [ˈkɒmsæt] **abbr of *communications satellite***.

con [kɒn] *inf* ■ **n 1.** [trick] escroquerie *f* **2.** *prison sl* taulard *m*.
■ **vt** (pt & pp -ned, cont -ning) [trick] **: to con sb (out of)** escroquer qqn (de) ▸ **to con sb into doing sthg** persuader qqn de faire qqch (en lui mentant).

con artist **n** *inf* arnaqueur *m*.

concave [ˌkɒn'keɪv] **adj** concave.

conceal [kən'siːl] **vt** cacher, dissimuler ▸ **to conceal sthg from sb** cacher qqch à qqn.

concealed [kən'siːld] **adj** [lighting] indirect(e) / [driveway, entrance] caché(e).

concede [kən'siːd] ■ **vt** concéder.
■ **vi** céder.

conceit [kən'siːt] **n** [arrogance] vanité *f*.

conceited [kən'siːtɪd] **adj** vaniteux(euse).

conceivable [kən'siːvəbl] **adj** concevable.

conceivably [kən'siːvəblɪ] **adv : they might conceivably win** il se peut qu'ils gagnent ▸ **I can't conceivably do that** il n'est pas question que je fasse ça.

conceive [kən'siːv] ■ **vt** concevoir.
■ **vi 1.** MED concevoir **2.** [imagine] **: to conceive of** concevoir.

concentrate ['kɒnsəntreɪt] ■ **vt** concentrer ▸ **it concentrates the mind** cela aide à se concentrer.
■ **vi : to concentrate (on)** se concentrer (sur) ▸ **the government should concentrate on improving the economy** le gouvernement devrait s'attacher à améliorer la situation économique.

concentrated ['kɒnsəntreɪtɪd] **adj** concentré(e) / [effort] intense.

concentrated marketing **n** marketing *m* concentré.

concentration [ˌkɒnsən'treɪʃn] **n** concentration *f*.

concentration camp **n** camp *m* de concentration.

concentric [kən'sentrɪk] **adj** concentrique.

concept ['kɒnsept] **n** concept *m*.

conception [kən'sepʃn] **n** [gen & MED] conception *f*.

concept testing **n** tests *mpl* de concept.

conceptual [kən'septʃʊəl] **adj** conceptuel(elle).

conceptualize, *UK* ***-ise*** [kən'septʃʊəlaɪz] **vt** conceptualiser.

concern [kən'sɜːn] ■ **n 1.** [worry, anxiety] souci *m*, inquiétude *f* ▸ **to show concern for** s'inquiéter de ▸ **there's no cause for concern** il n'y a pas de raison de s'inquiéter ▸ **this is a matter of great concern** c'est un sujet très inquiétant ▸ **my main concern is the price** ce qui m'inquiète surtout, c'est le prix
2. [matter of interest] **: it's no concern of mine** cela ne me regarde pas
3. COMM [company] affaire *f*.
■ **vt 1.** [worry] inquiéter ▸ **to be concerned (about)** s'inquiéter (de) ▸ **we were concerned to learn that...** nous avons appris avec inquiétude que...
2. [involve] concerner, intéresser ▸ **as far as I'm concerned** en ce qui me concerne ▸ **to be concerned with** [subj: person] s'intéresser à ▸ **to concern o.s. with sthg** s'intéresser à, s'occuper de
3. [subj: book, film] traiter de.

concerned [kən'sɜːnd] **adj 1.** [worried] inquiet(ète), soucieux(euse) ▸ **we were concerned for** *OR* **about his health** nous étions inquiets pour sa santé **2.** [involved] intéressé(e) ▸ **pass this request on to the department concerned** transmettez cette demande au service compétent ▸ **notify the person concerned** avisez qui de droit ▸ **the people concerned** [in question] les personnes en question *OR* dont il s'agit / [involved] les intéressés.

concerning [kən'sɜːnɪŋ] **prep** en ce qui concerne.

concert ['kɒnsət] **n** concert *m*.
◆ ***in concert*** **adv 1.** MUS à l'unisson **2.** *fml* [acting as one] de concert.

concerted [kən'sɜːtɪd] **adj** [effort] concerté(e).

concert hall **n** salle *f* de concert.

concertina [ˌkɒnsə'tiːnə] ■ **n** concertina *m*.
■ **vi** (pt & pp **-ed**, cont **-ing**) *UK* [cars] s'écraser en accordéon.

concerto [kən'tʃɜːtəʊ] (pl **-s**) **n** concerto *m*.

concession [kən'seʃn] **n 1.** [gen] concession *f* **2.** *UK* [special price] réduction *f*.

concessionaire [kənˌseʃə'neəʳ] **n** concessionnaire *mf*.

concessionary [kən'seʃnərɪ] **adj** *UK* [fare] à prix réduit.

conciliation [kənˌsɪlɪ'eɪʃn] **n** conciliation *f*.

conciliatory [kən'sɪlɪətrɪ] **adj** conciliant(e).

concise [kən'saɪs] **adj** concis(e).

concisely [kən'saɪslɪ] **adv** de façon concise, avec concision.

conclave ['kɒŋkleɪv] **n** conclave *m*.

conclude [kən'kluːd] ■ **vt** conclure.
■ **vi** [meeting] prendre fin / [speaker] conclure.

conclusion [kən'kluːʒn] **n** conclusion *f* ▸ **it was a foregone conclusion** c'était à prévoir ▸ **to jump to the wrong conclusion** tirer des conclusions trop hâtives.

conclusive [kən'kluːsɪv] **adj** concluant(e).

conclusively [kən'kluːsɪvlɪ] **adv** de façon concluante *OR* décisive, définitivement.

concoct [kən'kɒkt] **vt** préparer / *fig* concocter.

concoction [kən'kɒkʃn] **n** préparation *f*.

concord ['kɒŋkɔːd] **n** [harmony] concorde *f*.

concourse ['kɒŋkɔːs] **n** [hall] hall *m*.

concrete ['kɒŋkriːt] ■ **adj** [definite] concret(ète).

HOW TO ...

concede a point

Je dois reconnaître *ou* admettre que vous avez raison / I have to admit that you're right
Effectivement, c'est une manière de voir les choses / Well, that's one way of looking at things
Peut-être, effectivement / You may well be right
C'est possible, oui / I suppose so
Tu n'as pas tort / You're not wrong there
C'est très cher, je vous l'accorde / Granted, it's very expensive
C'est juste / You've got a point there

■ n *(U)* béton *m*.
■ comp [made of concrete] en béton.
■ vt bétonner.

concrete mixer n bétonnière *f*.

concubine ['kɒŋkjʊbaɪn] n concubine *f*.

concur [kən'kɜːʳ] (pt & pp **-red**, cont **-ring**) vi [agree] : **to concur (with)** être d'accord (avec).

concurrent [kən'kʌrənt] adj **1.** [simultaneous] concomitant(e), simultané(e) **2.** [acting together] concerté(e) **3.** [agreeing] concordant(e), d'accord **4.** MATHS & TECH [intersecting] concourant(e).

concurrently [kən'kʌrəntlɪ] adv simultanément.

concussed [kən'kʌst] adj commotionné(e).

concussion [kən'kʌʃn] n commotion *f*.

condemn [kən'dem] vt condamner.

condemnation [ˌkɒndem'neɪʃn] n condamnation *f*.

condemned [kən'demd] adj condamné(e).

condensation [ˌkɒnden'seɪʃn] n condensation *f*.

condense [kən'dens] ■ vt condenser.
■ vi se condenser.

condensed milk [kən'denst-] n lait *m* concentré ▸ **sweetened condensed milk** lait *m* concentré sucré.

condescend [ˌkɒndɪ'send] vi **1.** [talk down] : **to condescend to sb** se montrer condescendant(e) envers qqn **2.** [deign] : **to condescend to do sthg** daigner faire qqch, condescendre à faire qqch.

condescending [ˌkɒndɪ'sendɪŋ] adj condescendant(e).

condiment ['kɒndɪmənt] n condiment *m*.

condition [kən'dɪʃn] ■ n **1.** [gen] condition *f* ▸ **in (a) good/bad condition** en bon/mauvais état ▸ **out of condition** pas en forme ▸ **in working condition** en état de marche ▸ **to make a condition that** stipuler que **2.** MED maladie *f* ▸ **he has a heart condition** il a une maladie du cœur.
■ vt **1.** [gen] conditionner **2.** [hair] : **to condition one's hair** mettre de l'après-shampooing.
◆ ***conditions*** npl conditions *fpl*.

conditional [kən'dɪʃənl] adj conditionnel(elle) ▸ **to be conditional on** *OR* **upon** dépendre de.

conditionality [kənˌdɪʃə'nælətɪ] n conditionnalité *f*.

conditionally [kən'dɪʃnəlɪ] adv conditionnellement.

conditioned [kən'dɪʃnd] adj conditionné(e).

conditioner [kən'dɪʃnəʳ] n **1.** [for hair] après-shampooing *m* **2.** [for clothes] assouplissant *m*.

conditioning [kən'dɪʃnɪŋ] n PSYCHOL conditionnement *m*.

condo ['kɒndəʊ] n *US inf* abbr of ***condominium***.

condolences [kən'dəʊlənsɪz] npl condoléances *fpl*.

condom ['kɒndəm] n préservatif *m*.

condominium [ˌkɒndə'mɪnɪəm] n *US* **1.** [apartment] appartement *m* dans un immeuble en copropriété **2.** [apartment block] immeuble *m* en copropriété.

condone [kən'dəʊn] vt excuser.

condor ['kɒndɔːʳ] n condor *m*.

conducive [kən'djuːsɪv] adj : **to be conducive to sthg/to doing sthg** inciter à qqch/à faire qqch.

conduct ■ n ['kɒndʌkt] conduite *f* ▸ **her conduct towards me** son comportement envers moi *OR* à mon égard.
■ vt [kən'dʌkt] **1.** [carry out, transmit] conduire **2.** [behave] : **to conduct o.s. well/badly** se conduire bien/mal **3.** MUS diriger.
■ vi MUS diriger.

conducted tour [kən'dʌktɪd-] n *UK* visite *f* guidée.

conductor [kən'dʌktəʳ] n **1.** MUS chef *m* d'orchestre **2.** [on bus] receveur *m* **3.** *US* [on train] chef *m* de train.

conductress [kən'dʌktrɪs] n [on bus] receveuse *f*.

conduit ['kɒndɪt] n conduit *m*.

cone [kəʊn] n **1.** [shape] cône *m* **2.** [for ice cream] cornet *m* **3.** [from tree] pomme *f* de pin.
◆ ***cone off*** vt sep *UK* [road, lane] mettre des cônes de signalisation sur.

confectioner [kən'fekʃnəʳ] n confiseur *m* ▸ **confectioner's (shop)** confiserie *f*.

confectionery [kən'fekʃnərɪ] n confiserie *f*.

confederation [kənˌfedə'reɪʃn] n confédération *f*.

Confederation of British Industry n : **the Confederation of British Industry** ≃ le conseil du patronat.

confer [kən'fɜːʳ] (pt & pp **-red**, cont **-ring**) ■ vt : **to confer sthg (on sb)** conférer qqch (à qqn).
■ vi : **to confer (with sb on** *OR* **about sthg)** s'entretenir (avec qqn de qqch).

conference ['kɒnfərəns] n conférence *f* ▸ **in conference** en conférence.

conference call n téléconférence *f*.

conference centre *UK*, ***conference center*** *US* n centre *m* de conférences.

conference hall n salle *f* de conférence.

conferencing ['kɒnfərənsɪŋ] n *(U)* téléconférence *f*.

confess [kən'fes] ■ vt **1.** [admit] avouer, confesser ▸ **to confess one's guilt** *OR* **that one is guilty** avouer sa culpabilité, s'avouer coupable ▸ **I must** *OR* **I have to confess I was wrong** je dois reconnaître *OR* admettre que j'avais tort **2.** RELIG confesser.
■ vi : **to confess to sthg** avouer qqch.

confession [kən'feʃn] n confession *f* ▸ **I've a confession to make** j'ai un aveu à vous faire.

confessional [kən'feʃənl] n confessionnal *m*.

confetti [kən'fetɪ] n *(U)* confettis *mpl*.

confidant [ˌkɒnfɪ'dænt] n confident *m*.

confidante [ˌkɒnfɪ'dænt] n confidente *f*.

confide [kən'faɪd] ■ vt confier.
■ vi : **to confide in sb** se confier à qqn.

confidence ['kɒnfɪdəns] **n 1.** [self-assurance] confiance *f* en soi, assurance *f* ▸ **he lacks confidence** il n'est pas très sûr de lui **2.** [trust] confiance *f* ▸ **to have confidence in** avoir confiance en ▸ **I have every confidence that you'll succeed** je suis absolument certain que vous réussirez ▸ **to put one's confidence in sb/sthg** faire confiance à qqn/qqch **3.** [secrecy] **: in confidence** en confidence **4.** [secret] confidence *f.*

CONFUSABLE / PARONYME
confidence

When translating confidence, note that *confiance* and *confidence* are not interchangeable. *Confiance* means *trust*, while *confidence* is only used to refer to a *secret*.

confidence trick **n** abus *m* de confiance.

confident ['kɒnfɪdənt] **adj 1.** [self-assured] **: to be confident** avoir confiance en soi **2.** [sure] sûr(e).

confidential [ˌkɒnfɪ'denʃl] **adj** confidentiel(elle).

confidentiality ['kɒnfɪˌdenʃɪ'ælətɪ] **n** confidentialité *f.*

confidentially [ˌkɒnfɪ'denʃəlɪ] **adv** confidentiellement.

confidently ['kɒnfɪdəntlɪ] **adv** [speak, predict] avec assurance.

configuration [kənˌfɪgə'reɪʃn] **n** [gen & COMPUT] configuration *f.*

configure [kən'fɪgə] **vt** [gen & COMPUT] configurer.

confine [kən'faɪn] **vt 1.** [limit] limiter ▸ **to confine o.s. to** se limiter à **2.** [shut up] enfermer, confiner.

confined [kən'faɪnd] **adj** [space, area] restreint(e).

confinement [kən'faɪnmənt] **n 1.** [imprisonment] emprisonnement *m* **2.** *dated* & MED couches *fpl.*

confines ['kɒnfaɪnz] **npl** confins *mpl.*

confirm [kən'fɜ:m] **vt** confirmer.

confirmation [ˌkɒnfə'meɪʃn] **n** confirmation *f.*

confirmed [kən'fɜ:md] **adj** [habitual] invétéré(e) / [bachelor, spinster] endurci(e).

confiscate ['kɒnfɪskeɪt] **vt** confisquer.

confiscation [ˌkɒnfɪ'skeɪʃn] **n** confiscation *f.*

conflagration [ˌkɒnflə'greɪʃn] **n** conflagration *f.*

conflict ■ **n** ['kɒnflɪkt] conflit *m* ▸ **to be in conflict (with)** être en conflit (avec) ▸ **a conflict of interests** un conflit d'intérêts.
■ **vi** [kən'flɪkt] **: to conflict (with)** s'opposer (à), être en conflit (avec).

conflicting [kən'flɪktɪŋ] **adj** contradictoire.

conform [kən'fɔ:m] **vi : to conform (to** *OR* **with)** se conformer (à).

conformism [kən'fɔ:mɪzm] **n** conformisme *m.*

conformist [kən'fɔ:mɪst] ■ **adj** conformiste.
■ **n** conformiste *mf.*

conformity [kən'fɔ:mətɪ] **n : conformity (to** *OR* **with)** conformité *f* (à).

confound [kən'faʊnd] **vt** [confuse, defeat] déconcerter.

confounded [kən'faʊndɪd] **adj** *inf dated* sacré(e).

confront [kən'frʌnt] **vt 1.** [problem, enemy] affronter **2.** [challenge] **: to confront sb (with)** confronter qqn (avec).

confrontation [ˌkɒnfrʌn'teɪʃn] **n** affrontement *m.*

confuse [kən'fju:z] **vt 1.** [disconcert] troubler ▸ **to confuse the issue** brouiller les cartes **2.** [mix up] confondre.

confused [kən'fju:zd] **adj 1.** [not clear] compliqué(e) **2.** [disconcerted] troublé(e), désorienté(e) ▸ **I'm confused** je n'y comprends rien.

confusing [kən'fju:zɪŋ] **adj** pas clair(e).

confusingly [kən'fju:zɪŋlɪ] **adv** de façon embrouillée.

confusion [kən'fju:ʒn] **n** confusion *f.*

conga ['kɒŋgə] **n : the conga** la conga.

congeal [kən'dʒi:l] **vi** [blood] se coaguler.

congenial [kən'dʒi:njəl] **adj** sympathique, agréable.

congenital [kən'dʒenɪtl] **adj** MED congénital(e).

conger eel ['kɒŋgər-] **n** congre *m.*

congested [kən'dʒestɪd] **adj 1.** [street, area] encombré(e) **2.** MED congestionné(e).

congestion [kən'dʒestʃn] **n 1.** [of traffic] encombrement *m* **2.** MED congestion *f.*

conglomerate [ˌkən'glɒmərət] **n** COMM conglomérat *m.*

conglomeration [kənˌglɒmə'reɪʃn] **n** conglomération *f.*

HOW TO ...
confirm

La réunion a bien lieu aujourd'hui ? / Is the meeting really taking place today?
Vous êtes sur qu'ils pourront venir ? / Are you sure that they'll be able to come?
Je ne suis pas sûr d'avoir encore vos coordonnées / I'm not sure whether I still have your address and phone number
Il n'y a pas eu de difficultés avec notre devis ? / Did you have any problem with our estimate?
Je suis dans la bonne direction ? / Am I going the right way?
C'est bien à droite, puis à gauche ? / Is it right and then left?
Pourriez-vous me dire quand il faut descendre, s'il vous plaît ? / Could you tell me where to get off, please?
C'est bien l'arrêt pour... ? / Is this the right stop for...?

Congo ['kɒŋgəʊ] **n 1.** [country] **: the Congo** le Congo ▸ **in the Congo** au Congo **2.** [former Zaïre] **: the Democratic Republic of Congo** la République démocratique du Congo **3.** [river] **: the Congo** le fleuve Zaïre.

Congolese [ˌkɒŋgə'li:z] ■ **adj** congolais(e).
■ **n** Congolais *m*, -e *f*.

congrats [kən'græts] **excl** *inf* chapeau!

congratulate [kən'grætʃʊleɪt] **vt : to congratulate sb (on sthg/on doing sthg)** féliciter qqn (de qqch/d'avoir fait qqch).

congratulations [kənˌgrætʃʊ'leɪʃənz] **npl** félicitations *fpl*.

congratulatory [kən'grætʃʊlətrɪ] **adj** de félicitations.

congregate ['kɒŋgrɪgeɪt] **vi** se rassembler.

congregation [ˌkɒŋgrɪ'geɪʃn] **n** assemblée *f* des fidèles.

congress ['kɒŋgres] **n** [meeting] congrès *m*.
◆ ***Congress*** **n** *US* POL le Congrès.

CULTURE

Congress

Le Congrès, institué en 1789 par l'article 1 de la Constitution américaine, est composé de la « Chambre haute » (le Sénat) et de la « Chambre basse » (la Chambre des représentants). Le Sénat comprend cent sénateurs, à raison de deux sénateurs par État : ils ratifient les traités, corroborent les principales décisions du président et peuvent destituer le chef de l'État de ses fonctions en utilisant la procédure de l'**impeachment**. La Chambre des représentants est composée de 435 représentants, répartis parmi les États en fonction du nombre d'habitants qu'ils possèdent : ils conçoivent et votent toutes les lois afférentes au budget du gouvernement, mais toute nouvelle loi doit être approuvée par les deux chambres dont le pouvoir est égal en matière de législation.

congressional [kəŋ'greʃənl] **adj** *US* POL du Congrès.

congressman ['kɒŋgresmən] (**pl -men** [-mən]) **n** *US* POL membre *m* du Congrès.

congresswoman ['kɒŋgresˌwʊmən] (**pl -women** [-ˌwɪmɪn]) **n** *US* POL membre *m* (féminin) du Congrès.

conical ['kɒnɪkl] **adj** conique.

conifer ['kɒnɪfər] **n** conifère *m*.

coniferous [kə'nɪfərəs] **adj** [tree] conifère / [forest] de conifères.

conjecture [kən'dʒektʃər] ■ **n** conjecture *f*.
■ **vt & vi** conjecturer.

conjugal ['kɒndʒʊgl] **adj** conjugal(e).

conjugation [ˌkɒndʒʊ'geɪʃn] **n** GRAM conjugaison *f*.

conjunction [kən'dʒʌŋkʃn] **n 1.** GRAM conjonction *f* **2.** [combination] combinaison *f*, mélange *m* ▸ **in conjunction with** conjointement avec.

conjunctivitis [kənˌdʒʌŋktɪ'vaɪtɪs] **n** conjonctivite *f*.

conjure ■ **vt** [kən'dʒʊər] *fml* supplier.
■ **vi** ['kʌndʒər] [by magic] faire des tours de prestidigitation.
◆ ***conjure up*** **vt sep** évoquer.

conjurer ['kʌndʒərər] **n** prestidigitateur *m*, -trice *f*.

conjuring trick ['kʌndʒərɪŋ-] **n** tour *m* de prestidigitation.

conjuror ['kʌndʒərər] = ***conjurer***.

conk [kɒŋk] **n** *inf UK* pif *m*.
◆ ***conk out*** **vi** *inf* tomber en panne.

conker ['kɒŋkər] **n** *UK* marron *m*.

conman ['kɒnmæn] (**pl -men** [-men]) **n** escroc *m*.

connect [kə'nekt] ■ **vt 1.** [join] **: to connect sthg (to)** relier qqch (à) **2.** [on telephone] mettre en communication ▸ **I'm trying to connect you** j'essaie d'obtenir votre communication **3.** [associate] associer ▸ **to connect sb/sthg to, to connect sb/sthg with** associer qqn/qqch à **4.** ELEC [to power supply] **: to connect sthg to** brancher qqch à.
■ **vi** [train, plane, bus] **: to connect (with)** assurer la correspondance (avec).

connected [kə'nektɪd] **adj** [related] **: to be connected with** avoir un rapport avec ▸ **they are not connected** il n'y a aucun rapport entre eux.

Connecticut [kə'netɪkət] **n** Connecticut *m* ▸ **in Connecticut** dans le Connecticut.

connecting [kə'nektɪŋ] **adj : connecting flight/train** correspondance *f*.

connection [kə'nekʃn] **n 1.** [relationship] **: connection (between/with)** rapport *m* (entre/avec) ▸ **to make a connection between** *OR* **to** *OR* **with sthg** faire le lien avec qqch ▸ **in connection with** à propos de **2.** ELEC branchement *m*, connexion *f* **3.** [on telephone] communication *f*

HOW TO ...

congratulate someone

C'est formidable ! / That's wonderful!
Bravo ! / Well done!
Bien joué ! / Well done!
C'était très réussi ta soirée / It was a wonderful party
(Toutes mes) félicitations ! / Congratulations!
Félicitations pour votre promotion ! / Congratulations on your promotion!
Laissez-moi vous féliciter / Let me congratulate you
Je suis très content pour vous / I'm so happy for you
Ça m'a fait très plaisir d'apprendre que tu avais réussi ton concours / I was so pleased to hear that you'd passed your exam
Nous avons été ravis d'apprendre la bonne nouvelle / We were delighted to hear the good news
Ça, c'est une bonne nouvelle ! / That's great news!

▸ **it's a bad connection** la ligne est mauvaise **4.** [plane, train, bus] correspondance *f* ▸ **to miss one's connection** rater sa correspondance **5.** [professional acquaintance] relation *f*.

connective tissue [kə'nektɪv-] **n** tissu *m* conjonctif.

connexion [kə'nekʃn] *UK* = ***connection***.

connive [kə'naɪv] **vi 1.** [plot] comploter ▸ **to connive with sb** être de connivence avec qqn **2.** [allow to happen] : **to connive at sthg** fermer les yeux sur qqch.

conniving [kə'naɪvɪŋ] **adj** *pej* malhonnête.

connoisseur [ˌkɒnə'sɜːʳ] **n** connaisseur *m*, -euse *f*.

connotation [ˌkɒnə'teɪʃn] **n** connotation *f*.

connote [kə'nəʊt] **vt 1.** *fml* [imply - subj: word, phrase, name] évoquer **2.** LING connoter.

conquer ['kɒŋkəʳ] **vt 1.** [country etc] conquérir **2.** [fears, inflation etc] vaincre.

conqueror ['kɒŋkərəʳ] **n** conquérant *m*, -e *f*.

conquest ['kɒŋkwest] **n** conquête *f*.

cons [kɒnz] **npl 1.** *UK inf* : **all mod cons** tout confort **2.** ➤ ***pro***.

Cons. abbr of ***Conservative***.

conscience ['kɒnʃəns] **n** conscience *f* ▸ **to have a guilty conscience** avoir mauvaise conscience ▸ **in all conscience** en mon/votre *etc* âme et conscience.

conscientious [ˌkɒnʃɪ'enʃəs] **adj** consciencieux(euse).

conscientiously [ˌkɒnʃɪ'enʃəslɪ] **adv** consciencieusement.

conscientiousness [ˌkɒnʃɪ'enʃəsnɪs] **n** conscience *f*.

conscientious objector **n** objecteur *m* de conscience.

conscious ['kɒnʃəs] **adj 1.** [not unconscious] conscient(e) **2.** [aware] : **conscious of sthg** conscient(e) de qqch ▸ **fashion-conscious** qui suit la mode ▸ **money-conscious** qui fait attention à ses dépenses **3.** [intentional - insult] délibéré(e), intentionnel(elle) / [- effort] conscient(e).

-conscious **suffix** conscient de ▸ **clothes-conscious** qui fait attention à sa tenue ▸ **fashion-conscious** qui suit la mode ▸ **age-conscious** conscient de son âge ▸ **health-conscious** soucieux de sa santé ▸ **money-conscious** qui fait attention à ses dépenses.

consciously ['kɒnʃəslɪ] **adv** intentionnellement.

consciousness ['kɒnʃəsnɪs] **n** conscience *f*.

consciousness raising **n** sensibilisation *f*.
◆ ***consciousness-raising*** **comp** [group, session] de prise de conscience.

conscript ■ **n** ['kɒnskrɪpt] MIL conscrit *m*.
■ **vt** [kən'skrɪpt] MIL appeler sous les drapeaux.

conscription [kən'skrɪpʃn] **n** conscription *f*.

consecrate ['kɒnsɪkreɪt] **vt** consacrer.

consecration [ˌkɒnsɪ'kreɪʃn] **n** consécration *f*.

consecutive [kən'sekjʊtɪv] **adj** consécutif(ive).

consecutively [kən'sekjʊtɪvlɪ] **adv** consécutivement.

consensual [kən'sensjʊəl] **adj** LAW & MED [contract, agreement] consensuel(elle).

consensus [kən'sensəs] **n** consensus *m*.

consent [kən'sent] ■ **n** *(U)* **1.** [permission] consentement *m* **2.** [agreement] accord *m*.
■ **vi** : **to consent (to)** consentir (à).

consenting adult [kən'sentɪŋ-] **n** adulte *m* consentant.

consequence ['kɒnsɪkwəns] **n 1.** [result] conséquence *f* ▸ **as a consequence of** à la suite de ▸ **in consequence** par conséquent ▸ **to take** *OR* **to suffer the consequences** accepter *OR* subir les conséquences **2.** [importance] importance *f* ▸ **it's of no consequence** c'est sans conséquence, cela n'a pas d'importance.

consequent ['kɒnsɪkwənt] **adj** *fml* consécutif(ive) / [resulting] résultant(e).

consequential [ˌkɒnsɪ'kwenʃl] **adj** *fml* **1.** = ***consequent*** **2.** [important - decision] de conséquence, conséquent(e).

consequently ['kɒnsɪkwəntlɪ] **adv** par conséquent.

conservation [ˌkɒnsə'veɪʃn] **n** [of nature] protection *f* / [of buildings] conservation *f* / [of energy, water] économie *f*.

conservation area **n** secteur *m* sauvegardé.

conservationist [ˌkɒnsə'veɪʃənɪst] **n** écologiste *mf*.

conservatism [kən'sɜːvətɪzm] **n** conservatisme *m*.
◆ ***Conservatism*** **n** POL conservatisme *m*.

conservative [kən'sɜːvətɪv] ■ **adj 1.** [traditionalist] traditionaliste **2.** [cautious] prudent(e).
■ **n** traditionaliste *mf*.
◆ ***Conservative*** ■ **adj** POL conservateur(trice).
■ **n** POL conservateur *m*, -trice *f*.

conservatively [kən'sɜːvətɪvlɪ] **adv** [dress] de façon conventionnelle.

Conservative Party **n** : **the Conservative Party** le parti conservateur.

conservator [kən'sɜːvətəʳ] **n** gardien *m*, -enne *f*.

conservatory [kən'sɜːvətrɪ] **(pl -ies) n** [of house] jardin *m* d'hiver.

conserve ■ **n** ['kɒnsɜːv] confiture *f*.
■ **vt** [kən'sɜːv] [energy, supplies] économiser / [nature, wildlife] protéger.

consider [kən'sɪdəʳ] **vt 1.** [think about] examiner ▸ **I'll consider it** je verrai, je réfléchirai ▸ **have you ever considered becoming an actress?** avez-vous jamais songé à devenir actrice? ▸ **she's being considered for the post of manager** on pense à elle pour le poste de directeur **2.** [take into account] prendre en compte ▸ **all things considered** tout compte fait ▸ **he has a wife and family to consider** il a une femme et une famille à prendre en considération **3.** [judge] considérer ▸ **I've always considered her (as** *OR* **to be) a good friend** je l'ai toujours considérée comme une bonne amie ▸ **I consider myself lucky** je m'estime heureux.

considerable [kən'sɪdrəbl] **adj** considérable.

considerably [kən'sɪdrəblɪ] **adv** considérablement.

considerate [kən'sɪdərət] **adj** prévenant(e) ▸ **that's very considerate of you** c'est très gentil à vous *OR* de votre part.

considerately [kən'sɪdərətlɪ] **adv** avec des égards.

consideration [kənˌsɪdəˈreɪʃn] n **1.** *(U)* [careful thought] réflexion *f* ▸ **the matter needs careful consideration** le sujet demande une attention particulière ▸ **to take sthg into consideration** tenir compte de qqch, prendre qqch en considération ▸ **under consideration** à l'étude **2.** *(U)* [care] attention *f* ▸ **to show consideration for sb/sb's feelings** ménager qqn/la sensibilité de qqn **3.** [factor] facteur *m*.

considered [kənˈsɪdəd] adj **: it's my considered opinion that...** après mûre réflexion je pense que...

considering [kənˈsɪdərɪŋ] ■ prep étant donné.
■ conj étant donné que.

consign [kənˈsaɪn] vt **: to consign sb/sthg to** reléguer qqn/qqch à.

consignee [ˌkɒnsaɪˈniː] n destinataire *mf*.

consigner *US* = ***consignor***.

consignment [ˌkənˈsaɪnmənt] n [load] expédition *f*.

consignment note n *UK* bordereau *m* d'expédition.

consignor [kənˈsaɪnəʳ] n expéditeur *m*, -trice *f*.

consist [kənˈsɪst] ◆ ***consist in*** vt insep **: to consist in sthg** consister dans qqch ▸ **to consist in doing sthg** consister à faire qqch. ◆ ***consist of*** vt insep consister en.

consistency [kənˈsɪstənsɪ] (pl -ies) n **1.** [coherence] cohérence *f* **2.** [texture] consistance *f*.

consistent [kənˈsɪstənt] adj **1.** [regular - behaviour] conséquent(e) / [- improvement] régulier(ère) / [- supporter] constant(e) **2.** [coherent] cohérent(e) ▸ **to be consistent with** [with one's position] être compatible avec / [with the facts] correspondre avec.

FALSE FRIENDS / FAUX AMIS

consistent

Consistant n'est pas la traduction du mot anglais *consistent*. Consistant se traduit par *thick* ou *substantial*.

▸ Nous avons mangé un repas très consistant / *We had a really substantial meal*

▸ Ces pâtes sont meilleures avec une sauce consistante / *This type of pasta is best with a thick sauce*

consistently [kənˈsɪstəntlɪ] adv **1.** [without exception] invariablement **2.** [argue, reason] de manière cohérente.

consolation [ˌkɒnsəˈleɪʃn] n réconfort *m*.

consolation prize n prix *m* de consolation.

console ■ n [ˈkɒnsəʊl] tableau *m* de commande / COMPUT & MUS console *f*.
■ vt [kənˈsəʊl] consoler ▸ **he had to console himself with second place** il a dû se contenter de la deuxième place.

consolidate [kənˈsɒlɪdeɪt] ■ vt **1.** [strengthen] consolider **2.** [merge] fusionner.
■ vi fusionner.

consolidated [kənˈsɒlɪdeɪtɪd] adj [annuity, loan, loss] consolidé(e) / [in name of company] *désigne une société née de la fusion de deux entreprises* ▸ **consolidated accounts** comptes *mpl* consolidés OR intégrés.

consolidation [kənˌsɒlɪˈdeɪʃn] *(U)* n **1.** [strengthening] affermissement *m* **2.** [merging] fusion *f*.

consols [ˈkɒnsəlz] npl *UK* fonds *mpl* consolidés.

consommé [*UK* kənˈsɒmeɪ, *US* ˌkɒnsəˈmeɪ] n consommé *m*.

consonant [ˈkɒnsənənt] n consonne *f*.

consort ■ vi [kənˈsɔːt] *fml* **: to consort with sb** fréquenter qqn.
■ n [ˈkɒnsɔːt] **: prince consort** prince *m* consort.

consortium [kənˈsɔːtjəm] (pl **-tiums** OR **-tia** [-tjə]) n consortium *m*.

conspicuous [kənˈspɪkjʊəs] adj voyant(e), qui se remarque.

conspicuous consumption n ECON consommation *f* ostentatoire.

conspicuously [kənˈspɪkjʊəslɪ] adv [dressed] de manière voyante / [wealthy] ostensiblement.

conspiracy [kənˈspɪrəsɪ] (pl -ies) n conspiration *f*, complot *m*.

conspirator [kənˈspɪrətəʳ] n conspirateur *m*, -trice *f*.

conspiratorial [kənˌspɪrəˈtɔːrɪəl] adj de conspirateur.

conspiratorially [kənˌspɪrəˈtɔːrɪəlɪ] adv [smile, whisper, wink] d'un air de conspiration.

conspire [kənˈspaɪəʳ] ■ vt **: to conspire to do sthg** comploter de faire qqch / [subj: events] contribuer à faire qqch.
■ vi **: to conspire against/with sb** conspirer contre/avec qqn.

constable [ˈkʌnstəbl] n *UK* [policeman] agent *m* de police.

constabulary [kənˈstæbjʊlərɪ] (pl -ies) n *UK* police *f*.

constancy [ˈkɒnstənsɪ] n constance *f*.

constant [ˈkɒnstənt] adj **1.** [unvarying] constant(e) **2.** [recurring] continuel(elle) **3.** *liter* [faithful] fidèle.

constantly [ˈkɒnstəntlɪ] adv constamment.

constellation [ˌkɒnstəˈleɪʃn] n constellation *f*.

consternation [ˌkɒnstəˈneɪʃn] n consternation *f*.

constipated [ˈkɒnstɪpeɪtɪd] adj constipé(e).

constipation [ˌkɒnstɪˈpeɪʃn] n constipation *f*.

constituency [kənˈstɪtjʊənsɪ] (pl -ies) n [area] circonscription *f* électorale.

constituency party n *UK* section *f* locale du parti.

constituent [kənˈstɪtjʊənt] ■ adj constituant(e).
■ n **1.** [voter] électeur *m*, -trice *f* **2.** [element] composant *m*.

constitute ['kɒnstɪtju:t] **vt 1.** [form, represent] représenter, constituer **2.** [establish, set up] constituer.

constitution [ˌkɒnstɪ'tju:ʃn] **n** constitution *f*.
◆ ***Constitution*** **n : the (United States) Constitution** la Constitution américaine.

CULTURE
Constitution

Établie lors de la Convention constitutionnelle de Philadelphie en 1787, la Constitution américaine est un document qui réunit l'ensemble des principes fondamentaux du gouvernement fédéral. Elle entra en vigueur en 1789, avant l'instauration de la « Déclaration des droits des États-Unis » (**Bill of Rights**) en 1791 : les dix premiers amendements garantissaient la sauvegarde des libertés individuelles, puis dix-sept autres furent rajoutés ultérieurement, proclamant notamment l'abolition de l'esclavage ou le droit de vote aux femmes. À titre de comparaison, la Constitution britannique n'est pas un document écrit mais un ensemble de lois évoluant dans le temps par rapport au système juridique de base.

constitutional [ˌkɒnstɪ'tju:ʃənl] **adj** constitutionnel(elle).

constitutional law **n** droit *m* constitutionnel.

constitutionally [ˌkɒnstɪ'tju:ʃnəlɪ] **adv 1.** POL [act] constitutionnellement **2.** [strong, weak] de *OR* par nature.

constrain [kən'streɪn] **vt 1.** [coerce] forcer, contraindre ▸ **to constrain sb to do sthg** forcer qqn à faire qqch **2.** [restrict] limiter.

constrained [kən'streɪnd] **adj** [inhibited] contraint(e).

constraint [kən'streɪnt] **n 1.** [restriction] **: constraint (on)** limitation *f* (à) **2.** *(U)* [self-control] retenue *f*, réserve *f* **3.** [coercion] contrainte *f*.

constrict [kən'strɪkt] **vt 1.** [compress] serrer **2.** [limit] limiter.

constricting [kən'strɪktɪŋ] **adj 1.** [clothes] qui entrave les mouvements **2.** [circumstances, lifestyle] contraignant(e).

construct ■ **vt** [kən'strʌkt] construire.
■ **n** ['kɒnstrʌkt] *fml* [concept] concept *m*.

construction [kən'strʌkʃn] ■ **n** construction *f* ▸ **under construction** en construction.
■ **comp** [worker] du bâtiment ▸ **construction site** chantier *m*.

construction industry **n** industrie *f* du bâtiment.

constructive [kən'strʌktɪv] **adj** constructif(ive).

constructive dismissal **n** démission *f* provoquée (sous la pression de la direction).

constructively [kən'strʌktɪvlɪ] **adv** d'une manière constructive.

construe [kən'stru:] **vt** *fml* [interpret] **: to construe sthg as** interpréter qqch comme.

consul ['kɒnsəl] **n** consul *m*, -e *f*.

consular ['kɒnsjʊlər] **adj** consulaire.

consulate ['kɒnsjʊlət] **n** consulat *m*.

consult [kən'sʌlt] ■ **vt** consulter.
■ **vi : to consult with sb** s'entretenir avec qqn.

consultancy [kən'sʌltənsɪ] **(pl -ies) n** *UK* [company] cabinet *m* d'expert-conseil.

consultancy fee **n** *UK* honoraires *mpl* d'expert.

consultant [kən'sʌltənt] **n 1.** [expert] expert-conseil *m* **2.** *UK* [hospital doctor] spécialiste *mf*.

consultation [ˌkɒnsəl'teɪʃn] **n 1.** [meeting, discussion] entretien *m* **2.** [reference] consultation *f*.

consultative [kən'sʌltətɪv] **adj** consultatif(ive).

consulting [kən'sʌltɪŋ] **n** cabinet *m* d'expert.

consulting fee **n** honoraires *mpl* d'expert.

consulting room **n** MED cabinet *m* de consultation.

consumable goods [kən'sju:məbl-] **n** produits *mpl* de consommation.

consumables [kən'sju:məblz] **npl** produits *mpl* de consommation.

consume [kən'sju:m] **vt 1.** [food, fuel etc] consommer **2.** *liter* [fill] **: to be consumed by hatred/passion** être consumé(e) par la haine/la passion.

CONFUSABLE / PARONYME
consume

When translating to consume, note that the French verbs *consommer* and *consumer* are not interchangeable. *Consommer* always refers to consumer activity, while *consumer* is used to refer to emotions such as love or jealousy or to describe the destruction of something, especially by fire.

consumer [kən'sju:mər] ■ **n** consommateur *m*, -trice *f*.
■ **comp** du consommateur.

consumer behaviour **n** comportement *m* du consommateur.

consumer confidence index **n** indice *m* de confiance.

consumer credit **n** *(U)* crédit *m* à la consommation.

consumer demand **n** demande *f* des consommateurs.

consumer durables **npl** biens *mpl* de consommation durables.

consumer goods **npl** biens *mpl* de consommation.

consumerism [kən'sju:mərɪzm] **n** *(U)* **1.** [buying] (règne *m* de la) société *f* de consommation **2.** [protection of rights] consumérisme *m*.

consumer market **n** marché *m* de la consommation.

consumer preference **n** préférence *f* du consommateur.

consumer profile **n** profil *m* du consommateur.

consumer society **n** société *f* de consommation.

consumer spending **n** *(U)* dépenses *fpl* de consommation.

consumer testing n tests *mpl* auprès des consommateurs.

consumer trends n tendances *fpl* de la consommation.

consummate ■ adj [kən'sʌmət] consommé(e) / [liar] fieffé(e).
■ vt ['kɒnsəmeɪt] consommer.

consummation [,kɒnsə'meɪʃn] n **1.** [of marriage] consommation *f* **2.** [culmination] apogée *m*.

consumption [kən'sʌmpʃn] n **1.** [use] consommation *f* **2.** *dated* [tuberculosis] phtisie *f*.

cont. abbr of ***continued***.

contact ['kɒntækt] ■ n **1.** *(U)* [touch, communication] contact *m* ▸ **in contact (with sb)** en rapport OR contact (avec qqn) ▸ **to lose contact with sb** perdre le contact avec qqn ▸ **to come into contact with sb** entrer OR se mettre en contact OR en rapport avec qqn ▸ **to make contact with sb** prendre contact OR entrer en contact avec qqn **2.** [person] relation *f*, contact *m* ▸ **she has some useful business contacts** elle a quelques bons contacts (professionnels).
■ vt contacter, prendre contact avec / [by phone] joindre, contacter.

contactable [kɒn'tæktəbl] adj que l'on peut joindre OR contacter, joignable ▸ **I'm contactable at this number** on peut me contacter OR m'appeler à ce numéro.

contact lens n verre *m* OR lentille *f* de contact.

contact number n : **do you have a contact number?** tu as un numéro où on peut te joindre?

contacts ['kɒntækts] npl lentilles *fpl* (de contact).

contact sport n sport *m* de contact.

contagious [kən'teɪdʒəs] adj contagieux(euse).

contain [kən'teɪn] vt **1.** [hold, include] contenir, renfermer **2.** *fml* [control] contenir / [epidemic] circonscrire.

contained [kən'teɪnd] adj [person] maître (maîtresse) de soi.

container [kən'teɪnəʳ] n **1.** [box, bottle etc] récipient *m* **2.** [for transporting goods] conteneur *m*, container *m*.

containerize, *UK* ***-ise*** [kən'teɪnəraɪz] vt COMM [goods] conteneuriser / [port] convertir à la conteneurisation.

container ship n porte-conteneurs *m inv*.

containment [kən'teɪnmənt] n *(U)* **1.** [limitation] : **our efforts at the containment of this violence** nos efforts pour contenir cette violence **2.** POL : **policy of containment** politique *f* d'endiguement.

contaminate [kən'tæmɪneɪt] vt contaminer.

contaminated [kən'tæmɪneɪtɪd] adj contaminé(e).

contamination [kən,tæmɪ'neɪʃn] n contamination *f*.

cont'd abbr of ***continued***.

contemplate ['kɒntempleɪt] ■ vt **1.** [consider] envisager ▸ **to contemplate doing sthg** envisager de faire qqch **2.** *fml* [look at] contempler.
■ vi [consider] méditer.

contemplation [,kɒntem'pleɪʃn] n contemplation *f*.

contemplative [kən'templətɪv] adj contemplatif(ive).

contemporary [kən'tempərərɪ] ■ adj contemporain(e).
■ n (pl -ies) contemporain *m*, -e *f*.

contempt [kən'tempt] n **1.** [scorn] : **contempt (for)** mépris *m* (pour) ▸ **to hold sb in contempt** mépriser qqn **2.** LAW : **contempt (of court)** outrage *m* à la cour.

contemptible [kən'temptəbl] adj méprisable.

contemptuous [kən'temptʃʊəs] adj méprisant(e) ▸ **contemptuous of sthg** dédaigneux(euse) de qqch.

contend [kən'tend] ■ vi **1.** [deal] : **to contend with sthg** faire face à qqch ▸ **I've got enough to contend with** j'ai assez de problèmes comme ça **2.** [compete] : **to contend for** [subj: several people] se disputer / [subj: one person] se battre pour ▸ **to contend against** lutter contre.
■ vt *fml* [claim] : **to contend that...** soutenir OR prétendre que...

contender [kən'tendəʳ] n [in election] candidat *m*, -e *f* / [in competition] concurrent *m*, -e *f* / [in boxing etc] prétendant *m*, -e *f*.

content ■ adj [kən'tent] : **content (with)** satisfait(e) (de), content(e) (de) ▸ **to be content to do sthg** ne pas demander mieux que de faire qqch.
■ n ['kɒntent] **1.** [amount] teneur *f* ▸ **it has a high fibre content** c'est riche en fibres **2.** [subject matter] contenu *m*
■ vt [kən'tent] : **to content o.s. with sthg/with doing sthg** se contenter de qqch/de faire qqch.
◆ ***contents*** npl **1.** [of container, document] contenu *m* **2.** [at front of book] table *f* des matières.

contented [kən'tentɪd] adj satisfait(e).

contentedly [kən'tentɪdlɪ] adv avec contentement.

contention [kən'tenʃn] n *fml* **1.** [argument, assertion] assertion *f*, affirmation *f* **2.** *(U)* [disagreement] dispute *f*, contestation *f* **3.** [competition] : **to be in contention** être en lice.

contentious [kən'tenʃəs] adj contentieux(euse), contesté(e).

contentment [kən'tentmənt] n contentement *m*.

contest ■ n ['kɒntest] **1.** [competition] concours *m* **2.** [for power, control] combat *m*, lutte *f*.
■ vt [kən'test] **1.** [compete for] disputer **2.** [dispute] contester.

contestant [kən'testənt] n concurrent *m*, -e *f*.

context ['kɒntekst] n contexte *m* ▸ **out of context** [word] hors contexte / [remark] hors de son contexte.

context-sensitive adj COMPUT contextuel(le).

contextual [kɒn'tekstjʊəl] adj [criticism] contextuel(elle).

contextualize, ***-ise*** *UK* [kɒn'tekstjʊəlaɪz] vt [event, facts] contextualiser, remettre dans son contexte.

continent ['kɒntɪnənt] n continent *m*.
◆ ***Continent*** n *UK* : **the Continent** l'Europe *f* continentale.

continental [,kɒntɪ'nentl] ■ adj **1.** GEOG continental(e) **2.** *UK* [European - food] d'Europe continentale / [- holidays] en Europe continentale.
■ n *UK* Européen continental *m*, Européenne continentale *f*.

continental breakfast **n** petit déjeuner *m (par opposition à 'English breakfast').*

continental climate **n** climat *m* continental.

continental drift **n** dérive *f* des continents.

continental quilt **n** *UK* couette *f.*

continental shelf **n** plateau *m* continental.

contingency [kən'tɪndʒənsɪ] (pl -ies) **n** éventualité *f.*

contingency fee **n** LAW *aux États-Unis, principe permettant à un avocat de recevoir une part des sommes attribuées à son client si ce dernier gagne son procès.*

contingency fund **n** fonds *mpl* de prévoyance.

contingency plan **n** plan *m* d'urgence.

contingent [kən'tɪndʒənt] ■ **adj** *fml* **: to be contingent on** *OR* **upon** dépendre de.
■ **n** contingent *m.*

continual [kən'tɪnjʊəl] **adj** continuel(elle).

continually [kən'tɪnjʊəlɪ] **adv** continuellement.

continuation [kən,tɪnjʊ'eɪʃn] **n 1.** *(U)* [act] continuation *f* **2.** [sequel] suite *f.*

continue [kən'tɪnju:] ■ **vt 1.** [carry on] continuer, poursuivre ▸ **to continue doing** *OR* **to do sthg** continuer à *OR* de faire qqch **2.** [after an interruption] reprendre.
■ **vi 1.** [carry on] continuer ▸ **to continue with sthg** poursuivre qqch, continuer qqch **2.** [after an interruption] reprendre, se poursuivre.

continuity [,kɒntɪ'nju:ətɪ] **n** continuité *f.*

continuous [kən'tɪnjʊəs] **adj** continu(e).

continuous assessment **n** *UK* contrôle *m* continu des connaissances.

continuously [kən'tɪnjʊəslɪ] **adv** sans arrêt, continuellement.

contort [kən'tɔ:t] ■ **vt** tordre.
■ **vi** se tordre.

contortion [kən'tɔ:ʃn] **n 1.** *(U)* [twisting] torsion *f* **2.** [position] contorsion *f.*

contour ['kɒn,tʊəʳ] ■ **n 1.** [outline] contour *m* **2.** [on map] courbe *f* de niveau.
■ **comp** [map] avec courbes de niveau ▸ **contour line** courbe *f* de niveau.

contraband ['kɒntrəbænd] ■ **adj** de contrebande.
■ **n** contrebande *f.*

contraception [,kɒntrə'sepʃn] **n** contraception *f.*

contraceptive [,kɒntrə'septɪv] ■ **adj** [method, device] anticonceptionnel(elle), contraceptif(ive) ⁄ [advice] sur la contraception.
■ **n** contraceptif *m.*

contraceptive pill **n** pilule *f* anticonceptionnelle *OR* contraceptive.

contract ■ **n** ['kɒntrækt] contrat *m* ▸ **to be under contract** être sous contrat, avoir un contrat ▸ **to put work out to contract** sous-traiter du travail ▸ **contract of employment** contrat de travail.
■ **vt** [kən'trækt] **1.** [gen] contracter **2.** COMM **: to contract sb (to do sthg)** passer un contrat avec qqn (pour faire qqch) ▸ **to contract to do sthg** s'engager par contrat à faire qqch.
■ **vi** [decrease in size, length] se contracter.
◆ ***contract in*** **vi** *esp UK* s'engager par contrat.
◆ ***contract out*** ■ **vt sep** [work] sous-traiter.
■ **vi** *UK* **: to contract out (of)** se dégager (de).

contraction [kən'trækʃn] **n** contraction *f.*

contractor [kən'træktəʳ] **n** entrepreneur *m.*

contractual [kən'træktʃʊəl] **adj** contractuel(elle).

contractually [kən'træktʃʊəlɪ] **adv** [binding] par contrat.

contradict [,kɒntrə'dɪkt] **vt** contredire.

contradiction [,kɒntrə'dɪkʃn] **n** contradiction *f* ▸ **contradiction in terms** contradiction dans les termes.

contradictory [,kɒntrə'dɪktərɪ] **adj** contradictoire ⁄ [behaviour] incohérent(e).

contraflow ['kɒntrəfləʊ] **n** *UK* circulation *f* à contresens.

contralto [kən'træltəʊ] (pl -s) **n** contralto *m.*

contraption [kən'træpʃn] **n** machin *m*, truc *m.*

contrary ['kɒntrərɪ] ■ **adj 1.** [opposite] **: contrary (to)** contraire (à), opposé(e) (à) **2.** [kən'treərɪ] [awkward] contrariant(e).
■ **n** contraire *m* ▸ **on the contrary** au contraire ▸ **evidence to the contrary** preuves tendant à démontrer le contraire ▸ **his statements to the contrary** ses propos soutenant le contraire.
◆ ***contrary to*** **prep** contrairement à.

contrast ■ **n** ['kɒntrɑ:st] contraste *m* ▸ **by** *OR* **in contrast** par contraste ▸ **in contrast with** *OR* **to sthg** par contraste avec qqch.
■ **vt** [kən'trɑ:st] contraster.
■ **vi** [kən'trɑ:st] **: to contrast (with)** faire contraste (avec).

contrasting [kən'trɑ:stɪŋ] **adj** [colours] contrasté(e) ⁄ [personalities, views] opposé(e), contraire.

contravene [,kɒntrə'vi:n] **vt** enfreindre, transgresser.

contravention [,kɒntrə'venʃn] **n** *fml* infraction *f*, contravention *f.*

contribute [kən'trɪbju:t] ■ **vt 1.** [money] apporter ⁄ [help, advice, ideas] donner, apporter **2.** [write] **: to contribute an article to a magazine** écrire un article pour un magazine.
■ **vi 1.** [gen] **: to contribute (to)** contribuer (à) **2.** [write material] **: to contribute to** collaborer à.

contributing [kən'trɪbju:tɪŋ] **adj : to be a contributing factor in** contribuer à.

contribution [,kɒntrɪ'bju:ʃn] **n 1.** [of money] **: contribution (to)** cotisation *f* (à), contribution *f* (à) **2.** [to debate] **: his contribution to the discussion** ce qu'il a apporté à la discussion **3.** [article] article *m.*

contributor [kən'trɪbjʊtəʳ] **n 1.** [of money] donateur *m*, -trice *f* **2.** [to magazine, newspaper] collaborateur *m*, -trice *f.*

contributory [kən'trɪbjʊtərɪ] **adj : to be a contributory factor in** contribuer à.

contributory pension plan *US* = ***contributory pension scheme.***

contributory pension scheme **n** *UK* système *m* de retraite par répartition.

contrite ['kɒntraɪt] **adj** *liter* contrit(e), pénitent(e).

contrition [kən'trɪʃn] **n** *liter* contrition *f*, pénitence *f*.

contrivance [kən'traɪvns] **n** [contraption] machine *f*, appareil *m*.

contrive [kən'traɪv] **vt** *fml* **1.** [engineer] combiner **2.** [manage] **: to contrive to do sthg** se débrouiller pour faire qqch, trouver moyen de faire qqch.

contrived [kən'traɪvd] **adj** tiré(e) par les cheveux.

control [kən'trəʊl] ■ **n 1.** [gen] contrôle *m* / [of traffic] régulation *f* ▸ **to gain OR take control (of)** prendre le contrôle (de) ▸ **beyond OR outside sb's control** indépendant de la volonté de qqn ▸ **to get sb/sthg under control** maîtriser qqn/qqch ▸ **everything's under control** tout va bien, aucun problème, tout est au point ▸ **to be in control of sthg** [subj: boss, government] diriger qqch / [subj: army] avoir le contrôle de qqch / [of emotions, situation] maîtriser qqch ▸ **to have control of OR over sb** avoir de l'autorité sur qqn ▸ **to get out of control** [subj: crowd] devenir impossible à contrôler ▸ **his car went out of control** il a perdu le contrôle de sa voiture ▸ **her children are completely out of control** ses enfants sont intenables ▸ **to lose control** [of emotions] perdre le contrôle **2.** [in experiment] témoin *m* **3.** [restraint] contrôle *m* ▸ **price/wage controls** contrôle des prix/des salaires.
■ **vt** (pt & pp **-led**, cont **-ling**) **1.** [company, country] être à la tête de, diriger **2.** [operate] commander, faire fonctionner **3.** [restrict, restrain - disease] enrayer, juguler / [- inflation] mettre un frein à, contenir / [- children] tenir / [- crowd] contenir / [- traffic] régler / [- emotions] maîtriser, contenir ▸ **to control o.s.** se maîtriser, se contrôler.
■ **comp** [button, knob, switch] de commande.
◆ ***controls*** **npl** [of machine, vehicle] commandes *fpl*.

control code **n** COMPUT code *m* de commande.

control experiment **n** cas *m* témoin.

control group **n** groupe *m* témoin.

control key **n** COMPUT touche *f* "control".

controllable [kən'trəʊləbl] **adj** [animal, person, crowd] discipliné(e) / [emotions, situation] maîtrisable / [expenditure, inflation] contrôlable.

controllable costs **npl** coûts *mpl* maîtrisables.

controlled [kən'trəʊld] **adj** [person] maître (maîtresse) de soi.

controlled economy **n** ECON économie *f* dirigée OR planifiée.

controlled price **n** taxe *f* ▸ **to sell sth at the controlled price** vendre qqch à la taxe.

controller [kən'trəʊləʳ] **n** [person] contrôleur *m*.

controlling [kən'trəʊlɪŋ] **adj** [factor] déterminant(e).

controlling interest **n** participation *f* majoritaire.

control panel **n** tableau *m* de bord.

control room **n** salle *f* des commandes, centre *m* de contrôle.

control tower **n** tour *f* de contrôle.

controversial [ˌkɒntrə'vɜːʃl] **adj** [writer, theory] controversé(e) ▸ **to be controversial** donner matière à controverse.

controversy ['kɒntrəvɜːsɪ, *UK* kən'trɒvəsɪ] (pl **-ies**) **n** controverse *f*, polémique *f*.

conundrum [kə'nʌndrəm] (pl **-s**) **n** énigme *f*.

conurbation [ˌkɒnɜː'beɪʃn] **n** *fml* conurbation *f*.

convalesce [ˌkɒnvə'les] **vi** se remettre d'une maladie, relever de maladie.

convalescence [ˌkɒnvə'lesns] **n** convalescence *f*.

convalescent [ˌkɒnvə'lesnt] ■ **adj** [home] de convalescence.
■ **n** convalescent *m*, -e *f*.

convection [kən'vekʃn] **n** convection *f*.

convector [kən'vektəʳ] **n** radiateur *m* à convection.

convene [kən'viːn] ■ **vt** convoquer, réunir.
■ **vi** se réunir, s'assembler.

convener [kən'viːnəʳ] **n** *UK* président *m*, -e *f (d'une commission)*.

convenience [kən'viːnjəns] **n 1.** [usefulness] commodité *f* **2.** [personal comfort, advantage] agrément *m*, confort *m* ▸ **at your earliest convenience** *fml* dès que possible **3.** [facility] confort *m*.

convenience food **n** aliment *m* tout préparé.

convenience store **n** *US petit supermarché de quartier.*

convenient [kən'viːnjənt] **adj 1.** [suitable] qui convient **2.** [handy] pratique, commode.

conveniently [kən'viːnjəntlɪ] **adv** d'une manière commode ▸ **conveniently situated** bien situé.

convent ['kɒnvənt] **n** couvent *m*.

convention [kən'venʃn] **n 1.** [agreement, assembly] convention *f* **2.** [practice] usage *m*, convention *f*.

conventional [kən'venʃənl] **adj** conventionnel(elle) ▸ **it's conventional to...** l'usage veut que...

HOW TO ...
make conversation

Je me présente : Jean / Let me introduce myself, I'm Jean
Bonjour. Tu t'appelles Marie, c'est ça ? / Hi. It's Marie, isn't it?
Bonjour. Toi tu es Anne, non ? / Hello. You're Anne, aren't you?
Vous vous connaissez depuis longtemps ? / Have you known each other long?
Est-ce que nous ne nous sommes pas déjà rencontrés ? / Haven't we met before?
C'est la première fois que vous venez ? / Is this your first time here?
Ça fait longtemps que vous attendez ? / Have you been waiting long?
Il fait chaud aujourd'hui, hein ? / It's hot today, isn't it?

conventionally [kən'venʃnəlɪ] **adv** d'une manière conventionnelle.

convent school **n** couvent *m*.

converge [kən'vɜːdʒ] **vi : to converge (on)** converger (sur).

convergence criteria **npl** critères *mpl* de convergence.

conversant [kən'vɜːsənt] **adj** *fml* **: conversant with sthg** familiarisé(e) avec qqch, qui connaît bien qqch.

conversation [ˌkɒnvə'seɪʃn] **n** conversation *f* ▸ **to make conversation** faire la conversation.

conversational [ˌkɒnvə'seɪʃənl] **adj** de la conversation.

conversationalist [ˌkɒnvə'seɪʃnəlɪst] **n** causeur *m*, -euse *f*.

conversationally [ˌkɒnvə'seɪʃnəlɪ] **adv** [mention, say] sur le ton de la conversation.

conversation piece **n** **1.** [unusual object] curiosité *f* **2.** [play] *pièce au dialogue brillant*.

converse ■ **adj** ['kɒnvɜːs] *fml* opposé(e), contraire.
■ **n** ['kɒnvɜːs] [opposite] **: the converse** le contraire, l'inverse *m*.
■ **vi** [kən'vɜːs] *fml* converser.

conversely [kən'vɜːslɪ] **adv** *fml* inversement.

conversion [kən'vɜːʃn] **n** **1.** [changing, in religious beliefs] conversion *f* **2.** [in building] aménagement *m*, transformation *f* **3.** RUGBY transformation *f*.

conversion table **n** table *f* de conversion.

convert ■ **vt** [kən'vɜːt] **1.** [change] **: to convert sthg to** *OR* **into** convertir qqch en ▸ **to convert sb (to)** RELIG convertir qqn (à) **2.** [building, ship] **: to convert sthg to** *OR* **into** transformer qqch en, aménager qqch en **3.** RUGBY transformer.
■ **vi** [kən'vɜːt] **: to convert from sthg to sthg** passer de qqch à qqch.
■ **n** ['kɒnvɜːt] converti *m*, -e *f*.

converted [kən'vɜːtɪd] **adj** **1.** [building, ship] aménagé(e) **2.** RELIG converti(e).

convertible [kən'vɜːtəbl] ■ **adj** **1.** [bed, sofa] transformable, convertible **2.** [currency] convertible **3.** [car] décapotable.
■ **n** (voiture *f*) décapotable *f*.

convex [kɒn'veks] **adj** convexe.

convey [kən'veɪ] **vt** **1.** *fml* [transport] transporter **2.** [express] **: to convey sthg (to sb)** communiquer qqch (à qqn).

conveyancing [kən'veɪənsɪŋ] **n** *(U)* LAW procédure *f* translative de propriété.

conveyor belt [kən'veɪəʳ-] **n** tapis *m* roulant.

convict ■ **n** ['kɒnvɪkt] détenu *m*.
■ **vt** [kən'vɪkt] **: to convict sb of sthg** reconnaître qqn coupable de qqch.

convicted [kən'vɪktɪd] **adj : he's a convicted murderer** il a été reconnu coupable d'un meurtre.

conviction [kən'vɪkʃn] **n** **1.** [belief, fervour] conviction *f* **2.** LAW [of criminal] condamnation *f*.

convince [kən'vɪns] **vt** convaincre, persuader ▸ **to convince sb of sthg/to do sthg** convaincre qqn de qqch/de faire qqch, persuader qqn de qqch/de faire qqch.

convinced [kən'vɪnst] **adj : convinced (of)** convaincu(e) (de), persuadé(e) (de).

convincing [kən'vɪnsɪŋ] **adj** **1.** [persuasive] convaincant(e) **2.** [resounding - victory] retentissant(e), éclatant(e).

convincingly [kən'vɪnsɪŋlɪ] **adv** [argue, speak, pretend] de façon convaincante / [beat, win] de façon éclatante.

convivial [kən'vɪvɪəl] **adj** convivial(e), joyeux(euse).

convocation [ˌkɒnvə'keɪʃn] **n** **1.** [summoning] convocation *f* **2.** [meeting] assemblée *f* / RELIG synode *m*.

convoluted ['kɒnvəluːtɪd] **adj** [tortuous] compliqué(e).

convoy ['kɒnvɔɪ] **n** convoi *m* ▸ **in convoy** en convoi.

convulse [kən'vʌls] **vt** [person] **: to be convulsed with** se tordre de.

convulsion [kən'vʌlʃn] **n** MED convulsion *f*.

convulsive [kən'vʌlsɪv] **adj** convulsif(ive).

coo [kuː] **vi** [for a baby] roucouler.

cook [kʊk] ■ **n** cuisinier *m*, -ère *f* ▸ **she's a good cook** elle fait bien la cuisine.
■ **vt** **1.** [food] faire cuire / [meal] préparer **2.** *inf* [falsify] maquiller.
■ **vi** [person] cuisiner, faire la cuisine / [food] cuire.
◆ ***cook up*** **vt sep** [plan] combiner / [excuse] inventer.

cookbook ['kʊkˌbʊk] = ***cookery book***.

cooked [kʊkt] **adj** cuit(e).

cooker ['kʊkəʳ] **n** *UK* [stove] cuisinière *f*.

cookery ['kʊkərɪ] **n** cuisine *f*.

cookery book **n** *UK* livre *m* de cuisine.

cookie ['kʊkɪ] **n** **1.** *esp US* [biscuit] biscuit *m*, gâteau *m* sec **2.** COMPUT cookie *m*, mouchard *m offic*.

cooking ['kʊkɪŋ] ■ **n** cuisine *f* ▸ **do you like cooking?** tu aimes faire la cuisine?
■ **comp** de cuisine / [chocolate] à cuire ▸ **cooking oil** huile *f* de friture.

cooking apple **n** pomme *f* à cuire.

cookout ['kʊkaʊt] **n** *US* barbecue *m*.

cool [kuːl] ■ **adj** **1.** [not warm] frais (fraîche) / [dress] léger(ère) **2.** [calm] calme **3.** [unfriendly] froid(e) **4.** *inf* [excellent] génial(e) / [trendy] branché(e).
■ **vt** faire refroidir.
■ **vi** **1.** [become less warm] refroidir **2.** [abate] se calmer.
■ **n** [calm] **: to keep/lose one's cool** garder/perdre son sang-froid, garder/perdre son calme.
◆ ***cool down*** ■ **vt sep** **1.** [make less warm - food] faire refroidir / [- person] rafraîchir **2.** [make less angry] calmer, apaiser.
■ **vi** **1.** [become less warm - food, engine] refroidir / [- person] se rafraîchir **2.** [become less angry] se calmer.
◆ ***cool off*** **vi** **1.** [become less warm] refroidir / [person] se rafraîchir **2.** [become less angry] se calmer.

coolant ['kuːlənt] **n** agent *m* de refroidissement.

cool box **n** *UK* glacière *f*.

cooler **n** *US* glacière *f*.

cool-headed [-'hedɪd] **adj** calme.

cooling-off period ['ku:lɪŋ-] **n** délai *m* de réflexion.

cooling tower ['ku:lɪŋ-] **n** refroidisseur *m*.

coolly ['ku:lɪ] **adv** **1.** [calmly] calmement **2.** [in unfriendly way] froidement.

coolness ['ku:lnɪs] **n** **1.** [in temperature] fraîcheur *f* **2.** [calmness] calme *m*, sang-froid *m* **3.** [unfriendliness] froideur *f*.

coop [ku:p] **n** poulailler *m*.
◆ ***coop up*** **vt sep** *inf* confiner.

Co-op ['kəʊ,ɒp] (abbr of ***Co-operative society***) **n** Coop *f*.

cooperate [kəʊ'ɒpəreɪt] **vi : to cooperate (with sb/sthg)** coopérer (avec qqn/à qqch), collaborer (avec qqn/à qqch).

cooperation [kəʊ,ɒpə'reɪʃn] **n** *(U)* **1.** [collaboration] coopération *f*, collaboration *f* **2.** [assistance] aide *f*, concours *m*.

cooperative [kəʊ'ɒpərətɪv] ■ **adj** coopératif(ive).
■ **n** coopérative *f*.

co-opt **vt : to co-opt sb (into** ***OR*** **onto)** coopter qqn (à).

coordinate ■ **n** [kəʊ'ɔ:dɪnət] [on map, graph] coordonnée *f*.
■ **vt** [kəʊ'ɔ:dɪneɪt] coordonner.
◆ ***coordinates*** **npl** [clothes] coordonnés *mpl*.

coordination [kəʊ,ɔ:dɪ'neɪʃn] **n** coordination *f*.

coordinator [kəʊ'ɔ:dɪneɪtəʳ] **n** coordinateur *m*, coordonnateur *m*.

co-owner **n** copropriétaire *mf*.

co-ownership **n** copropriété *f*.

cop [kɒp] **n** *inf* flic *m*.
◆ ***cop out*** (pt & pp **-ped**, cont **-ping**) **vi** *inf* **: to cop out (of sthg)** se défiler ***OR*** se dérober (à qqch).

copartner [,kəʊ'pɑ:tnəʳ] **n** coassocié *m*, -e *f*.

cope [kəʊp] **vi** se débrouiller ▸ **to cope with** faire face à ▸ **I can't cope anymore** je n'en peux plus.

Copenhagen [,kəʊpən'heɪgən] **n** Copenhague.

copier ['kɒpɪəʳ] **n** copieur *m*, photocopieur *m*.

co-pilot ['kəʊ,paɪlət] **n** copilote *mf*.

copious ['kəʊpjəs] **adj** [notes] copieux(euse) / [supply] abondant(e).

cop-out **n** *inf* dérobade *f*, échappatoire *f*.

copper ['kɒpəʳ] **n** **1.** [metal] cuivre *m* **2.** *UK inf* [police officer] flic *m*.

coppice ['kɒpɪs], ***copse*** [kɒps] **n** taillis *m*, hallier *m*.

co-produce **vt** CIN & TV coproduire.

co-production **n** CIN & TV coproduction *f*.

copulate ['kɒpjʊleɪt] **vi : to copulate (with)** s'accoupler (à ***OR*** avec).

copulation [,kɒpjʊ'leɪʃn] **n** copulation *f*.

copy ['kɒpɪ] ■ **n** (pl **-ies**) **1.** [imitation] copie *f*, reproduction *f* **2.** [duplicate] copie *f* **3.** [of book] exemplaire *m* / [of magazine] numéro *m*.
■ **vt** (pt & pp **-ied**) **1.** [imitate] copier, imiter **2.** [photocopy] photocopier.
■ **vi** (pt & pp **-ied**) copier.
◆ ***copy down*** **vt sep** prendre des notes de.
◆ ***copy in*** **vt sep** mettre en copie ▸ **to copy sb in (on sth)** mettre qn en copie de qch.
◆ ***copy out*** **vt sep** recopier.

copycat ['kɒpɪkæt] ■ **n** *inf* copieur *m*, -euse *f*.
■ **comp** inspiré(e) par un autre (une autre).

copy editor **n** secrétaire *mf* de rédaction.

copy-protect **vt** protéger contre la copie.

copyreader ['kɒpɪ,ri:dəʳ] *US* = ***subeditor***.

copyright ['kɒpɪraɪt] **n** copyright *m*, droit *m* d'auteur.

copy typist **n** *UK* dactylo(graphe) *f*.

copywriter ['kɒpɪ,raɪtəʳ] **n** concepteur-rédacteur publicitaire *m*, conceptrice-rédactrice publicitaire *f*.

coral ['kɒrəl] ■ **n** corail *m*.
■ **comp** de corail.

coral reef **n** récif *m* de corail.

Coral Sea **n : the Coral Sea** la mer de Corail.

cord [kɔ:d] ■ **n** **1.** [string] ficelle *f* / [rope] corde *f* **2.** [electric] fil *m*, cordon *m* **3.** [fabric] velours *m* côtelé.
■ **comp** en velours côtelé.
◆ ***cords*** **npl** pantalon *m* en velours côtelé.

cordial ['kɔ:djəl] ■ **adj** cordial(e), chaleureux(euse).
■ **n** cordial *m*.

cordially ['kɔ:dɪəlɪ] **adv** cordialement.

cordless ['kɔ:dlɪs] **adj** [telephone] sans fil / [shaver] à piles.

Cordoba ['kɔ:dəbə] **n** Cordoue.

cordon ['kɔ:dn] **n** cordon *m*.
◆ ***cordon off*** **vt sep** barrer (par un cordon de police).

cordon bleu [-blɜ:] **adj** cordon bleu.

corduroy ['kɔ:dərɔɪ] ■ **n** velours *m* côtelé.
■ **comp** en velours côtelé.

core [kɔ:ʳ] ■ **n** **1.** [of apple] trognon *m*, cœur *m* **2.** [of cable, Earth] noyau *m* / [of nuclear reactor] cœur *m* **3.** *fig* [of people] noyau *m* / [of problem, policy] essentiel *m*.
■ **vt** enlever le cœur de.

CORE [kɔ:ʳ] (abbr of ***Congress of Racial Equality***) **n** *ligue américaine contre le racisme*.

core brand **n** marque *f* phare.

core business **n** activité *f* centrale.

core market **n** marché *m* principal ***OR*** de référence.

corer ['kɔ:rəʳ] **n** vide-pomme *m inv*.

corespondent [,kəʊrɪ'spɒndənt] **n** LAW codéfendeur *m*, -eresse *f*.

core time n *UK* plage *f* fixe.

Corfu [kɔː'fuː] n Corfou ▸ **in Corfu** à Corfou.

corgi ['kɔːgɪ] (pl **-s**) n corgi *m*.

coriander [ˌkɒrɪ'ændəʳ] n coriandre *f*.

cork [kɔːk] n **1.** [material] liège *m* **2.** [stopper] bouchon *m*.

corkage ['kɔːkɪdʒ] n *droit de débouchage sur un vin apporté par le consommateur.*

corked [kɔːkt] **adj** [wine] qui a le goût de bouchon.

corkscrew ['kɔːkskruː] n tire-bouchon *m*.

cormorant ['kɔːmərənt] n cormoran *m*.

corn [kɔːn] ■ n **1.** *UK* [wheat] grain *m* / *US* [maize] maïs *m* ▸ **corn on the cob** épi *m* de maïs cuit **2.** [on foot] cor *m*.
■ **comp : corn bread** pain *m* de farine de maïs ▸ **corn oil** huile *f* de maïs.

Corn (abbr of ***Cornwall***) *comté anglais.*

cornea ['kɔːnɪə] (pl **-s**) n cornée *f*.

corned beef [kɔːnd-] n *UK* corned-beef *m inv*.

corner ['kɔːnəʳ] ■ n **1.** [angle] coin *m*, angle *m* ▸ **to look at sb/sthg out of the corner of one's eye** regarder qqn/qqch du coin de l'œil ▸ **to cut corners** *fig* brûler les étapes **2.** [bend in road] virage *m*, tournant *m* ▸ **on** ***OR*** **at the corner** au coin ▸ **it's just around** ***OR*** ***UK*** **round the corner** [house, shop] c'est à deux pas d'ici / *fig* [event] c'est tout proche **3.** FOOTBALL corner *m*.
■ **vt 1.** [person, animal] acculer **2.** [market] accaparer.

corner flag n SPORT piquet *m* de coin.

corner kick n = ***corner***.

corner shop n magasin *m* du coin ***OR*** du quartier.

cornerstone ['kɔːnəstəʊn] n *fig* pierre *f* angulaire.

cornet ['kɔːnɪt] n **1.** [instrument] cornet *m* à pistons **2.** *UK* [ice-cream cone] cornet *m* de glace.

cornfield ['kɔːnfiːld] n **1.** *UK* [of wheat] champ *m* de blé **2.** *US* [of maize] champ *m* de maïs.

cornflakes ['kɔːnfleɪks] **npl** corn-flakes *mpl*.

cornflour *UK* ['kɔːnflaʊəʳ], ***cornstarch*** *US* ['kɔːnstɑːtʃ] n ≃ Maïzena® *f*, fécule *f* de maïs.

cornice ['kɔːnɪs] n corniche *f*.

Cornish ['kɔːnɪʃ] ■ **adj** de Cornouailles, cornouaillais(e).
■ **npl : the Cornish** les Cornouaillais *mpl*.

Cornishman ['kɔːnɪʃmən] (pl **-men** [-mən]) n Cornouaillais *m*.

Cornishwoman ['kɔːnɪʃˌwʊmən] (pl **-women** [-ˌwɪmɪn]) n Cornouaillaise *f*.

cornstarch ['kɔːnstɑːtʃ] *US* = ***cornflour***.

cornucopia [ˌkɔːnjʊ'kəʊpjə] n *liter* corne *f* d'abondance.

Cornwall ['kɔːnwɔːl] n Cornouailles *f* ▸ **in Cornwall** en Cornouailles.

corny ['kɔːnɪ] (comp **-ier**, superl **-iest**) **adj** *inf* [joke] peu original(e) / [story, film] à l'eau de rose.

corollary [kə'rɒlərɪ] (pl **-ies**) n corollaire *m*.

coronary ['kɒrənrɪ] (pl **-ies**), ***coronary thrombosis*** [-θrɒm'bəʊsɪs] (pl **-ses** [-siːz]) n infarctus *m* du myocarde.

coronation [ˌkɒrə'neɪʃn] n couronnement *m*.

coroner ['kɒrənəʳ] n coroner *m*.

Corp. (abbr of ***corporation***) Cie.

corpora ['kɔːpərə] **npl** ➤ ***corpus***.

corporal ['kɔːpərəl] n [gen] caporal *m* / [in artillery] brigadier *m*.

corporal punishment n châtiment *m* corporel.

corporate ['kɔːpərət] **adj 1.** [business] corporatif(ive), de société **2.** [collective] collectif(ive).

corporate assets n biens *mpl* sociaux.

corporate banking n banque *f* d'entreprise.

corporate body n LAW personne *f* morale.

corporate culture n culture *f* d'entreprise.

corporate entertainment n divertissement *m* fourni par la société.

corporate finance n finance *f* d'entreprise.

corporate hospitality n *(U) réceptions données par une société pour ses clients.*

corporate identity n image *f* de marque.

corporate image n image *f* de marque.

corporate institution n LAW personne *f* morale.

corporate law n droit *m* des sociétés ***OR*** des entreprises.

corporately ['kɔːpərətlɪ] **adv 1.** [as a corporation] **: I don't think we should involve ourselves corporately** je ne pense pas que nous devrions nous impliquer en tant que société **2.** [as a group] collectivement.

corporate sponsorship n sponsoring *m*, parrainage *m* d'entreprises.

corporate tax *US* = ***corporation tax***.

corporation [ˌkɔːpə'reɪʃn] n **1.** *UK* [town council] conseil *m* municipal **2.** [large company] compagnie *f*, société *f* enregistrée.

corporation tax n *UK* impôt *m* sur les sociétés.

corporatism ['kɔːpərətɪzm] n corporatisme *m*.

corps [kɔːʳ] (pl **corps**) n corps *m* ▸ **the press corps** la presse.

corpse [kɔːps] n cadavre *m*.

corpulent ['kɔːpjʊlənt] **adj** corpulent(e).

corpus ['kɔːpəs] (pl **-pora** [-pərə] ***OR*** **-puses** [-pəsiːz]) n corpus *m*, recueil *m*.

corpuscle ['kɔːpʌsl] n globule *m*.

corral [kɒ'rɑ:l] n corral *m*.

correct [kə'rekt] ■ adj **1.** [accurate] correct(e), exact(e) ▸ **that is correct** c'est exact ▸ **you're quite correct** tu as parfaitement raison **2.** [proper, socially acceptable] correct(e), convenable ▸ **the correct procedure** la procédure d'usage.
■ vt corriger ▸ **to correct sb on** *OR* **about sthg** corriger *OR* reprendre qqn sur qqch ▸ **to correct o.s.** se reprendre, se corriger.

correction [kə'rekʃn] n correction *f*.

correction fluid n liquide *m* correcteur.

correctly [kə'rektlɪ] adv **1.** [accurately] correctement, exactement **2.** [properly, acceptably] correctement, comme il faut.

correctness [kə'rektnɪs] n **1.** [of answer, prediction] exactitude *f*, justesse *f* **2.** [of behaviour, dress] correction *f*.

correlate ['kɒrəleɪt] ■ vt mettre en corrélation, corréler.
■ vi : **to correlate (with)** correspondre (à), être en corrélation (avec).

correlation [,kɒrə'leɪʃn] n corrélation *f*.

correspond [,kɒrɪ'spɒnd] vi **1.** [gen] : **to correspond (with** *OR* **to)** correspondre (à) **2.** [write letters] : **to correspond (with sb)** correspondre (avec qqn).

correspondence [,kɒrɪ'spɒndəns] n : **correspondence (with)** correspondance *f* (avec).

correspondence course n cours *m* par correspondance.

correspondent [,kɒrɪ'spɒndənt] n correspondant *m*, -e *f*.

corresponding [,kɒrɪ'spɒndɪŋ] adj correspondant(e).

corridor ['kɒrɪdɔ:ʳ] n [in building] couloir *m*, corridor *m*.

corroborate [kə'rɒbəreɪt] vt corroborer, confirmer.

corroboration [kə,rɒbə'reɪʃən] n corroboration *f*, confirmation *f*.

corroborative [kə'rɒbərətɪv] adj [evidence, statement] à l'appui.

corrode [kə'rəʊd] ■ vt corroder, attaquer.
■ vi se corroder.

corrosion [kə'rəʊʒn] n corrosion *f*.

corrosive [kə'rəʊsɪv] adj corrosif(ive).

corrugated ['kɒrəgeɪtɪd] adj ondulé(e).

corrugated iron n tôle *f* ondulée.

corrupt [kə'rʌpt] ■ adj [gen & COMPUT] corrompu(e) ▸ **corrupt practices** pratiques *fpl* malhonnêtes.
■ vt corrompre, dépraver.

corruptible [kə'rʌptəbl] adj corruptible.

corruption [kə'rʌpʃn] n corruption *f*.

corruptly [kə'rʌptlɪ] adv **1.** [dishonestly] de manière corrompue **2.** [in a depraved way] d'une manière dépravée *OR* corrompue.

corsage [kɔ:'sɑ:ʒ] n petit bouquet *m* de fleurs *(porté au corsage)*.

corset ['kɔ:sɪt] n corset *m*.

Corsica ['kɔ:sɪkə] n Corse *f* ▸ **in Corsica** en Corse.

Corsican ['kɔ:sɪkən] ■ adj corse.
■ n **1.** [person] Corse *mf* **2.** [language] corse *m*.

cortege, **cortège** [kɔ:'teɪʒ] n cortège *m*.

cortisone ['kɔ:tɪzəʊn] n cortisone *f*.

cos [1], *UK* **'cos**, *US* **cause** [kɒz] *inf* conj = ***because***.

cos [2] [kɒs] *UK* = ***cos lettuce***.

c.o.s. (abbr of ***cash on shipment***) paiement à l'expédition.

cosh [kɒʃ] *UK* ■ n matraque *f*, gourdin *m*.
■ vt frapper, matraquer.

cosignatory [,kəʊ'sɪgnətrɪ] (pl -ies) n cosignataire *mf*.

cosily *UK*, **cozily** *US* ['kəʊzɪlɪ] adv [furnished] confortablement.

cosine ['kəʊsaɪn] n cosinus *m*.

cos lettuce [kɒs-] n *UK* romaine *f*.

cosmetic [kɒz'metɪk] ■ n cosmétique *m*, produit *m* de beauté.
■ adj *fig* superficiel(elle).

cosmetic surgery n chirurgie *f* esthétique.

cosmic ['kɒzmɪk] adj cosmique.

cosmology [kɒz'mɒlədʒɪ] n cosmologie *f*.

cosmonaut ['kɒzmənɔ:t] n cosmonaute *mf*.

cosmopolitan [kɒzmə'pɒlɪtn] adj cosmopolite.

cosmos ['kɒzmɒs] n : **the cosmos** le cosmos.

Cossack ['kɒsæk] n cosaque *m*.

cosset ['kɒsɪt] vt dorloter, choyer.

cost [kɒst] ■ n *lit* & *fig* coût *m* ▸ **the cost of petrol has gone up** le prix de l'essence a augmenté ▸ **the firm cut its costs by 30%** l'entreprise a réduit ses frais de 30 % ▸ **th**

HOW TO ...

correct somebody

Je crois que ce n'est pas tout à fait ça / I don't think that's quite right
En fait, ce n'est pas tout à fait exact / Actually, that's not strictly true
Vous croyez ? Moi je dirais plutôt que... / Do you think so? I'd say...
Tu es sûr que ça se dit/s'écrit comme ça ? / Are you sure that's how you say/spell it?
Si je peux me permettre, je pense que ce n'est pas tout à fait ça / With all due respect, I don't think that's quite right
Vous vous trompez, il n'a rien à voir là-dedans / You're wrong, this has nothing to do with him
Non, c'est faux / No, that's wrong
Ce n'est pas ça du tout / That's totally wrong
Tu ne m'as pas compris / You've misunderstood me
Ah non, je n'ai pas dit ça ! / I didn't say that at all!

car was repaired at a cost of £500 la réparation de la voiture a coûté 500 livres ▸ **at no extra cost** sans frais supplémentaires ▸ **at the cost of her job/reputation/marriage** au prix de son travail/sa réputation/son mariage ▸ **to find out** *OR* **to learn** *OR* **to discover to one's cost** apprendre *OR* découvrir à ses dépens ▸ **at all costs** à tout prix, coûte que coûte.
■ vt **1.** (pt & pp **cost**) *lit* & *fig* coûter ▸ **how much does it cost?** combien ça coûte?, combien cela coûte-t-il? ▸ **did it cost much?** est-ce que cela a coûté cher? ▸ **it cost me £10** ça m'a coûté 10 livres ▸ **it costs nothing to join** l'inscription est gratuite ▸ **it cost us a lot of time and effort** ça nous a demandé beaucoup de temps et de travail ▸ **it cost him his job** cela lui a coûté son travail, cela lui a fait perdre son travail **2.** (pt & pp **-ed**) COMM [estimate] évaluer le coût de.
◆ ***costs*** **npl** LAW dépens *mpl*, frais *mpl* judiciaires ▸ **to be awarded costs** se voir accorder des frais et dépens ▸ **to be ordered to pay costs** être condamné aux dépens.

cost accountant **n** responsable *m* de la comptabilité analytique.

cost analysis **n** analyse *f* des coûts *OR* du prix de revient.

co-star ['kəʊ-] ■ **n** partenaire *mf*.
■ **vt** [subj: film] avoir comme vedettes.
■ **vi : to co-star with** partager la vedette avec.

Costa Rica [ˌkɒstə'ri:kə] **n** Costa Rica *m* ▸ **in Costa Rica** au Costa Rica.

Costa Rican [ˌkɒstə'ri:kən] ■ **adj** costaricien(enne).
■ **n** Costaricien *m*, -enne *f*.

cost-benefit analysis **n** analyse *f* coûts-bénéfices.

cost centre *UK*, ***cost center*** *US* **n** centre *m* de coût.

cost-conscious **adj : to be cost-conscious** contrôler ses dépenses ▸ **in these cost-conscious days** par les temps qui courent où tout le monde fait attention à *OR* surveille ses dépenses.

cost-cutting ■ **n** compression *f* *OR* réduction *f* des coûts.
■ **adj** de compression *OR* de réduction des coûts.

cost-effective **adj** rentable.

cost-effectiveness **n** rentabilité *f*.

cost factor **n** facteur *m* coût.

costing ['kɒstɪŋ] **n** évaluation *f* du coût.

costly ['kɒstlɪ] (comp **-ier**, superl **-iest**) **adj** *lit* & *fig* coûteux(euse).

cost management **n** gestion *f* des coûts.

cost of living **n** coût *m* de la vie.

cost-of-living index **n** *UK* indice *m* du coût de la vie.

cost of sales **n** coût *m* de revient des produits vendus.

cost-plus **adj : on a cost-plus basis** sur la base du prix de revient majoré.

cost price **n** prix *m* coûtant *OR* de revient.

costume ['kɒstju:m] **n 1.** [gen] costume *m* **2.** *UK* [swimming costume] maillot *m* (de bain).

costume jewellery *UK*, ***costume jewelry*** *US* **n** *(U)* bijoux *mpl* fantaisie.

cosy *UK*, ***cozy*** *US* ['kəʊzɪ] ■ **adj** (comp **-ier**, superl **-iest**) **1.** [house, room] douillet(ette) / [atmosphere] chaleureux(euse) ▸ **to feel cosy** se sentir bien au chaud **2.** [intimate] intime.
■ **n** (pl **-ies**) cosy *m*.

cot [kɒt] **n 1.** *UK* [for child] lit *m* d'enfant, petit lit **2.** *US* [folding bed] lit *m* de camp.

cot death **n** *UK* mort *f* subite du nourrisson.

coterie ['kəʊtərɪ] **n** cercle *m*, cénacle *m* / *pej* coterie *f*, clique *f*.

cottage ['kɒtɪdʒ] **n** cottage *m*, petite maison *f* (de campagne).

cottage cheese **n** fromage *m* blanc.

cottage hospital **n** *UK* petit hôpital *m* (en zone rurale).

cottage industry **n** industrie *f* artisanale.

cottage pie **n** *UK* ≃ hachis *m* Parmentier.

cotton ['kɒtn] ■ **n 1.** [gen] coton *m* **2.** [thread] fil *m* de coton.
■ **comp** de coton.
◆ ***cotton on*** **vi** *inf* **: to cotton on (to sthg)** piger (qqch), comprendre (qqch).

cotton bud *UK*, ***cotton swab*** *US* **n** coton-tige *m*.

cotton candy **n** *US* barbe *f* à papa.

cotton swab *US* = ***cotton bud***.

cotton wool **n** *UK* ouate *f*, coton *m* hydrophile.

couch [kaʊtʃ] ■ **n 1.** [sofa] canapé *m*, divan *m* **2.** [in doctor's surgery] lit *m*.
■ **vt** exprimer, formuler.

couchette [ku:'ʃet] **n** *UK* couchette *f*.

couch potato **n** *inf* flemmard *m*, -e *f (qui passe son temps devant la télé)*.

cougar ['ku:gə^r] (pl **cougar** *OR* **-s**) **n** cougouar *m*, couguar *m*.

cough [kɒf] ■ **n** toux *f* ▸ **I've got a cough** je tousse.
■ **vi** tousser.
■ **vt** [blood] cracher (en toussant).
◆ ***cough up*** **vt sep 1.** [bring up] cracher (en toussant) **2.** *v inf* [pay up] casquer, cracher.

cough drop *US*, ***cough sweet*** *UK* **n** pastille *f* pour la toux.

coughing ['kɒfɪŋ] **n** *(U)* toux *f*.

cough mixture **n** *UK* sirop *m* pour la toux.

cough syrup *US* = ***cough mixture***.

could [kʊd] **modal vb 1.** [be able to] **: I'd come if I could** je viendrais si je (le) pouvais ▸ **she could no longer walk** elle ne pouvait plus marcher ▸ **he could see her talking to her boss** il la voyait qui parlait avec son patron ▸ **she could read and write** elle savait lire et écrire ▸ **she could speak three languages** elle parlait trois langues **2.** [in polite requests and suggestions] **: could I borrow your sweater?** est-ce que je pourrais t'emprunter ton pull? ▸ **could you help me please?** pourriez-vous *OR* est-ce que vous pourriez m'aider, s'il vous plaît? ▸ **you could always complain to the director** tu pourrais toujours te plaindre au directeur ▸ **if I could just intervene here** est-ce que je peux me permettre d'intervenir ici? **3.** [indicating possibility] **: they**

could give up at any time ils pourraient abandonner n'importe quand ▸ could he be lying? se pourrait-il qu'il mente? ▸ they could have changed their plans ils ont peut-être changé leurs plans ▸ I couldn't possibly do it before tomorrow je ne pourrai vraiment pas le faire avant demain ▸ how could you say that? comment avez-vous pu dire ça OR une chose pareille? ▸ who on earth could that be? qui diable cela peut-il bien être?

couldn't ['kʊdnt] = ***could not***.

could've ['kʊdəv] = ***could have***.

council ['kaʊnsl] ■ n conseil *m*.
■ comp du conseil.

council estate n *UK* quartier *m* de logements sociaux.

council house n *UK* maison *f* qui appartient à la municipalité, ≃ H.L.M. *m ou f*

councillor *UK*, ***councilor*** *US* ['kaʊnsələr] n *UK* conseiller *m*, -ère *f*.

councilman *US* = ***councilor***.

Council of Europe n conseil *m* de l'Europe.

council of war n conseil *m* de guerre.

councilor *US* = ***councillor***.

council tax n *UK* ≃ impôts *mpl* locaux.

councilwoman *US* = ***councilor***.

counsel ['kaʊnsəl] ■ n 1. *(U) fml* [advice] conseil *m* 2. [lawyer] avocat *m*, -e *f*.
■ vt (*UK* -led, cont -ling, *US* -ed, cont -ing) : **to counsel sb to do sthg** *fml* conseiller à qqn de faire qqch.

counselling *UK*, ***counseling*** *US* ['kaʊnsəlɪŋ] n *(U)* conseils *mpl*.

counsellor *UK*, ***counselor*** *US* ['kaʊnsələr] n 1. [gen] conseiller *m*, -ère *f* 2. *US* [lawyer] avocat *m*.

count [kaʊnt] ■ n 1. [total] total *m* ▸ **to keep count of** tenir le compte de ▸ **to lose count of sthg** ne plus savoir qqch, ne pas se rappeler qqch ▸ **blood (cell) count** numération *f* globulaire
2. [point] : **I disagree with him on two counts** je ne suis pas d'accord avec lui sur deux points
3. LAW [charge] chef *m* d'accusation ▸ **guilty on three counts of murder** coupable de meurtre sur trois chefs d'accusation
4. [aristocrat] comte *m*.
■ vt 1. [gen] compter ▸ **there are five people, not counting me** sans moi, on est cinq ▸ **not counting public holidays** sans compter les jours fériés ▸ **don't count your chickens (before they're hatched)** *prov* il ne faut pas vendre la peau de l'ours (avant de l'avoir tué) *prov*
2. [consider] : **to count sb as sthg** considérer qqn comme qqch ▸ **student grants are not counted as taxable income** les bourses d'études ne sont pas considérées comme revenu imposable ▸ **count yourself lucky (that...)** estime-toi heureux (que...)
■ vi 1. [gen] compter ▸ **to count (up) to** compter jusqu'à ▸ **to count on one's fingers** compter sur ses doigts ▸ **counting from tomorrow** à partir de demain
2. [be considered] : **to count as** être considéré(e) comme ▸ **two children count as one adult** deux enfants comptent pour un adulte ▸ **this exam counts towards the final mark** cet examen compte dans la note finale ▸ **experience counts more than qualifications** l'expérience compte davantage que les diplômes ▸ **that/he doesn't count** ça/il ne compte pas.
◆ ***count against*** vt insep jouer contre.
◆ ***count in*** vt sep *inf* : **count me in!** je suis de la partie!
◆ ***count (up)on*** vt insep 1. [rely on] compter sur ▸ **we're counting on you** nous comptons sur toi ▸ **I wouldn't count on him turning up, if I were you** si j'étais vous, je ne m'attendrais pas à ce qu'il vienne
2. [expect] s'attendre à, prévoir ▸ **I wasn't counting on getting here so early** je ne comptais pas arriver si tôt.
◆ ***count out*** vt sep 1. [money] compter
2. *inf* [leave out] : **count me out!** ne comptez pas sur moi!
◆ ***count up*** vt insep compter.

countdown ['kaʊntdaʊn] n compte *m* à rebours.

countenance ['kaʊntənəns] ■ n *liter* [face] visage *m*.
■ vt approuver, admettre.

counter ['kaʊntər] ■ n 1. [in shop, bank] comptoir *m* 2. [in board game] pion *m*.
■ vt : **to counter sthg (with)** [criticism] riposter à qqch (par) ▸ **to counter sthg by doing sthg** s'opposer à qqch en faisant qqch.
■ vi : **to counter with sthg/by doing sthg** riposter par qqch/en faisant qqch.
◆ ***counter to*** adv contrairement à ▸ **to run counter to** aller à l'encontre de.

counteract [ˌkaʊntə'rækt] vt contrebalancer, compenser.

counterattack ['kaʊntərəˌtæk] ■ n contre-attaque *f*.
■ vt & vi contre-attaquer.

counterbalance [ˌkaʊntə'bæləns] vt *fig* contrebalancer, compenser.

counterbid ['kaʊntəbɪd] n FIN [during takeover] contre-OPA *f inv*.

counterblast ['kaʊntəblɑːst] n *inf* riposte *f*.

counterclaim ['kaʊntəkleɪm] n demande *f* reconventionnelle.

counterclockwise [ˌkaʊntə'klɒkwaɪz] adj & adv *US* dans le sens inverse des aiguilles d'une montre.

counterculture ['kaʊntəˌkʌltʃər] n contre-culture *f*.

counterespionage [ˌkaʊntər'espɪənɑːʒ] n contre-espionnage *m*.

counterfeit ['kaʊntəfɪt] ■ adj faux (fausse).
■ vt contrefaire.

counterfoil ['kaʊntəfɔɪl] n *UK* talon *m*, souche *f*.

counterintelligence [ˌkaʊntərɪn'telɪdʒəns] n contre-espionnage *m*.

countermand [ˌkaʊntə'mɑːnd] vt annuler.

countermeasure [ˌkaʊntə'meʒər] n contre-mesure *f*.

counteroffensive [ˌkaʊntərə'fensɪv] n contre-offensive *f*.

counteroffer [ˌkaʊntər'ɒfər] n offre *f* / [higher] surenchère *f*.

counterpane ['kaʊntəpeɪn] n *UK dated* couvre-lit *m*, dessus-de-lit *m inv*.

counterpart ['kaʊntəpɑːt] n [person] homologue *mf* / [thing] équivalent *m*, -e *f*.

counterpoint ['kaʊntəpɔɪnt] **n** MUS contrepoint *m*.

counterproductive [,kaʊntəprə'dʌktɪv] **adj** qui a l'effet inverse.

counter-revolution **n** contre-révolution *f*.

countersank ['kaʊntəsæŋk] **pt** ➤ ***countersink***.

countersign ['kaʊntəsaɪn] **vt** contresigner.

countersink ['kaʊntəsɪŋk] (**pt -sank, pp -sunk**) **vt** [hole] fraiser / [screw] noyer.

countess ['kaʊntɪs] **n** comtesse *f*.

countless ['kaʊntlɪs] **adj** innombrable.

countrified ['kʌntrɪfaɪd] **adj** *pej* campagnard(e), rustique.

country ['kʌntrɪ] ■ **n** (**pl -ies**) **1.** [nation] pays *m* **2.** [countryside] **: the country** la campagne ▸ **in the country** à la campagne **3.** [region] région *f* / [terrain] terrain *m* **4.** MUS = ***country and western***.
■ **comp** de la campagne, campagnard(e).

country and western ■ **n** country *m*.
■ **comp** country *(inv)*.

country club **n** club *m* de loisirs (à la campagne).

country dancing **n** *UK (U)* danse *f* folklorique.

country-dweller **n** campagnard *m*, -e *f*, habitant *m*, -e *f* de la campagne.

country house **n** manoir *m*.

countryman ['kʌntrɪmən] (**pl -men** [-mən]) **n** [from same country] compatriote *m*.

country music **n** = ***country and western***.

country park **n** *UK* parc *m* naturel.

countryside ['kʌntrɪsaɪd] **n** campagne *f*.

countrywoman ['kʌntrɪ,wʊmən] (**pl -women** [-,wɪmɪn]) **n** [from same country] compatriote *f*.

county ['kaʊntɪ] (**pl -ies**) **n** comté *m*.

county council **n** *UK* conseil *m* général.

county court **n** ≃ tribunal *m* de grande instance.

county town *UK*, ***county seat*** *US* **n** chef-lieu *m*.

coup [ku:] **n 1.** [rebellion] **: coup (d'état)** coup *m* d'État **2.** [success] coup *m* (de maître), beau coup *m*.

coupé, ***coupe*** ['ku:peɪ] **n** coupé *m*.

couple ['kʌpl] ■ **n 1.** [in relationship] couple *m* **2.** [small number] **: a couple (of)** [two] deux / [a few] quelques, deux ou trois.
■ **vt 1.** [join] **: to couple sthg (to)** atteler qqch (à) **2.** *fig* [associate] **: to couple sthg with** associer qqch à ▸ **coupled with** ajouté *OR* joint à.

couplet ['kʌplɪt] **n** couplet *m*.

coupling ['kʌplɪŋ] **n** RAIL attelage *m*.

coupon ['ku:pɒn] **n 1.** [voucher] bon *m* **2.** [form] coupon *m*.

courage ['kʌrɪdʒ] **n** courage *m* ▸ **to take courage (from sthg)** être encouragé (par qqch) ▸ **to have the courage of one's convictions** avoir le courage de ses opinions.

courageous [kə'reɪdʒəs] **adj** courageux(euse).

courageously [kə'reɪdʒəslɪ] **adv** courageusement, avec courage.

courgette [kɔ:'ʒet] **n** *UK* courgette *f*.

courier ['kʊrɪəʳ] **n 1.** *UK* [on holiday] guide *m*, accompagnateur *m*, -trice *f* **2.** [to deliver letters, packages] courrier *m*, messager *m*.

course [kɔ:s] ■ **n 1.** [gen] cours *m* ▸ **course of action** ligne *f* de conduite ▸ **your best course of action is to sue** la meilleure chose que vous ayez à faire est d'intenter un procès ▸ **in the course of** au cours de ▸ **in the course of the next few weeks** dans le courant des semaines qui viennent ▸ **in the normal** *OR* **ordinary course of events** normalement, en temps normal ▸ **to run** *OR* **take its course** [illness, event] suivre son cours
2. SCH & UNIV enseignement *m*, cours *mpl* ▸ **to take a course (in)** suivre un cours (de) ▸ **it's a five-year course** c'est un enseignement sur cinq ans ▸ **I'm taking** *OR* **doing a computer course** je suis des cours *OR* un stage d'informatique
3. MED [of injections] série *f* ▸ **course of treatment** traitement *m*
4. [of ship, plane] route *f* ▸ **to change course** [ship, plane, company] changer de cap *OR* de direction / *fig* [argument, discussion] changer de direction, dévier ▸ **to be on course** suivre le cap fixé / *fig* [on target] être dans la bonne voie ▸ **to be off course** faire fausse route
5. [of meal] plat *m* ▸ **a three/five course meal** un repas comprenant trois/cinq plats ▸ **first course** entrée *f* ▸ **there's a cheese course** il y a du fromage
6. SPORT terrain *m* ▸ **to stay the course** tenir le coup.
■ **vi** *liter* [flow] couler.
◆ ***of course*** **adv 1.** [inevitably, not surprisingly] évidemment, naturellement ▸ **no-one believed me, of course** évidemment *OR* bien sûr, personne ne m'a cru
2. [for emphasis] bien sûr ▸ **of course I believe you/she loves you** bien sûr que je te crois/qu'elle t'aime ▸ **of course not** bien sûr que non.

coursebook ['kɔ:sbʊk] **n** *UK* livre *m* de cours.

coursework ['kɔ:swɜ:k] **n** *(U)* travail *m* personnel.

court [kɔ:t] ■ **n 1.** [LAW - building, room] cour *f*, tribunal *m* / [- judge, jury] **: the court** la justice ▸ **silence in court!** silence dans la salle! ▸ **to appear in court** comparaître devant un tribunal ▸ **to go to court** aller en justice ▸ **to take sb to court** faire un procès à qqn ▸ **to settle sthg out of court** régler qqch à l'amiable **2.** [SPORT - gen] court *m* / [- for basketball, volleyball] terrain *m* ▸ **on court** sur le court **3.** [courtyard, of monarch] cour *f*.
■ **vt** [danger, disaster] aller au-devant de / [favour] rechercher ▸ **to court popularity** chercher à se rendre populaire.
■ **vi** *dated* sortir ensemble, se fréquenter.

court circular **n** *UK* bulletin *m* quotidien de la cour.

courteous ['kɜ:tjəs] **adj** courtois(e), poli(e).

courteously ['kɜ:tjəslɪ] **adv** [speak, reply] avec courtoisie, courtoisement.

courtesan [,kɔ:tɪ'zæn] **n** courtisane *f*.

courtesy ['kɜ:tɪsɪ] **n** courtoisie *f*, politesse *f*.
◆ ***(by) courtesy of*** **prep** avec la permission de.

courtesy car **n** voiture *f* mise gratuitement à la disposition du client.

courtesy coach **n** *UK* [at airport] navette *f* gratuite.

courtesy shuttle **n** [at airport] navette *f* gratuite.

courthouse ['kɔːthaʊs] (pl [-haʊzɪz]) **n** *US* palais *m* de justice, tribunal *m*.

courtier ['kɔːtjəʳ] **n** courtisan *m*.

court-martial ■ **n** (pl **court-martials** *OR* **courts-martial**) cour *f* martiale.
■ **vt** (*UK* **-led**, cont **-ling**, *US* **-ed**, cont **-ing**) traduire en cour *f* martiale.

Court of Appeal *UK*, ***Court of Appeals*** *US* **n** cour *f* d'appel.

court of inquiry **n** *UK* commission *f* d'enquête.

court of law **n** tribunal *m*, cour *f* de justice.

court order **n** ordonnance *f* du tribunal.

courtroom ['kɔːtrʊm] **n** salle *f* de tribunal.

courtship ['kɔːtʃɪp] **n 1.** [of people] cour *f* **2.** [of animals] parade *f*.

court shoe **n** *UK* escarpin *m*.

courtyard ['kɔːtjɑːd] **n** cour *f*.

cousin ['kʌzn] **n** cousin *m*, -e *f*.

couture [kuː'tʊəʳ] **n** haute couture *f*.

cove [kəʊv] **n** [bay] crique *f*.

coven ['kʌvən] **n** réunion *f* de sorcières.

covenant ['kʌvənənt] **n 1.** [of money] engagement *m* contractuel **2.** [agreement] convention *f*, contrat *m*.

Covent Garden [ˌkɒvənt-] **n** *ancien marché de Londres, aujourd'hui importante galerie marchande.*

Coventry ['kɒvəntrɪ] **n : to send sb to Coventry** *UK* mettre qqn en quarantaine.

cover ['kʌvəʳ] ■ **n 1.** [covering - of furniture] housse *f* / [- of pan] couvercle *m* / [- of book, magazine] couverture *f* ▸ **to read a book (from) cover to cover** lire un livre de la première à la dernière page *OR* d'un bout à l'autre
2. [blanket] couverture *f* ▸ **bed cover** couvre-lit *m*
3. [protection, shelter] abri *m* ▸ **to take cover** s'abriter, se mettre à l'abri ▸ **under cover** à l'abri, à couvert ▸ **under cover of darkness** à la faveur de la nuit ▸ **air cover** MIL couverture *f* aérienne ▸ **to break cover** [person] sortir à découvert *OR* de sa cachette
4. [concealment] couverture *f* ▸ **to work under cover** travailler clandestinement ▸ **your cover has been blown** *inf* vous avez été démasqué
5. *UK* [insurance] couverture *f*, garantie *f* ▸ **to have cover against sthg** être couvert *OR* assuré contre qqch
6. MUS = ***cover version***.
■ **vt 1.** [gen] **: to cover sthg (with)** couvrir qqch (de) ▸ **to cover one's eyes/ears** se couvrir les yeux/les oreilles ▸ **to be covered in dust/snow** être recouvert de poussière/neige ▸ **his face was covered in spots** son visage était couvert de boutons ▸ **water covers most of the earth's surface** l'eau recouvre la plus grande partie de la surface de la terre
2. [include, deal with] englober, comprendre ▸ **his interests cover a wide field** il a des intérêts très variés ▸ **there's one point we haven't covered** il y a un point que nous n'avons pas traité *OR* vu ▸ **the law doesn't cover that kind of situation** la loi ne prévoit pas ce genre de situation ▸ **£30 should cover it** 30 livres devraient suffire
3. [insure] **: to cover sb against** couvrir qqn en cas de
4. PRESS, RADIO & TV [report on] couvrir, faire la couverture de.
■ **vi : to cover for sb** [replace] remplacer qqn.
◆ ***cover up*** **vt sep 1.** [person, object, face] couvrir **2.** *fig* [scandal] dissimuler, cacher.

coverage ['kʌvərɪdʒ] **n** [of news] reportage *m* ▸ **radio/television coverage of the tournament** la retransmission radiophonique/télévisée du tournoi.

coveralls ['kʌvərɔːlz] **npl** *US* bleu *m* de travail.

cover charge **n** couvert *m*.

cover girl **n** cover-girl *f*.

covering ['kʌvərɪŋ] **n** [of floor] revêtement *m* / [of snow, dust] couche *f*.

covering letter *UK*, ***cover letter*** *US* **n** lettre *f* explicative *OR* d'accompagnement.

cover note **n** *UK* lettre *f* de couverture, attestation *f* provisoire d'assurance.

cover price **n** [of magazine] prix *m*.

cover story **n** article *m* principal (faisant la couverture).

covert ['kʌvət] **adj** [activity] clandestin(e) / [look, glance] furtif(ive).

cover-up **n** étouffement *m*, dissimulation *f*.

cover version **n** reprise *f*.

covet ['kʌvɪt] **vt** convoiter.

cow [kaʊ] ■ **n 1.** [farm animal] vache *f* **2.** [female elephant] femelle *f* **3.** *UK inf pej* [woman] vache *f*, chameau *m*.
■ **vt** intimider, effrayer.

coward ['kaʊəd] **n** lâche *mf*, poltron *m*, -onne *f*.

cowardice ['kaʊədɪs] **n** lâcheté.

cowardliness ['kaʊədlɪnɪs] **n** lâcheté *f*.

cowardly ['kaʊədlɪ] **adj** lâche.

cowboy ['kaʊbɔɪ] ■ **n 1.** [cattlehand] cow-boy *m* **2.** *UK inf* [dishonest workman] fumiste *m*.
■ **comp** de cow-boys.

cower ['kaʊəʳ] **vi** se recroqueviller.

cowhide ['kaʊhaɪd] **n** peau *f* de vache.

cowl neck [kaʊl-] **n** col *m* capuche.

co-worker **n** collègue *mf*.

cowpat ['kaʊpæt] **n** bouse *f* de vache.

cowshed ['kaʊʃed] **n** étable *f*.

cox [kɒks], ***coxswain*** ['kɒksən] **n** barreur *m*.

coy [kɔɪ] **adj** qui fait le/la timide.

coyly ['kɔɪlɪ] **adv** en faisant le/la timide.

coyness ['kɔɪnɪs] **n** [timidness] timidité *f* affectée *OR* feinte / [provocativeness] coquetteries *fpl*.

coyote [kɔɪ'əʊtɪ] **n** coyote *m*.

cozy *US* = ***cosy***.

cp. (abbr of ***compare***) cf.

c/p (abbr of ***carriage paid***) pp.

CP (abbr of ***Communist Party***) **n** PC *m*.

CPA **n** abbr of ***certified public accountant***.

CPI (abbr of ***Consumer Price Index***) **n** IPC *m*.

Cpl. (abbr of ***corporal***) C.

CP/M (abbr of ***control program for micro-computers***) **n** CP/M *m*.

c.p.s. (abbr of ***characters per second***) cps.

CPS (abbr of ***Crown Prosecution Service***) **n** ≃ ministère *m* public.

CPSA (abbr of ***Civil and Public Services Association***) **n** *syndicat britannique de la fonction publique.*

CPU **n abbr of** ***central processing unit***.

cr. **abbr of** ***credit, creditor***.

crab [kræb] **n** crabe *m*.

crab apple **n** pomme *f* sauvage.

crabby ['kræbɪ] (comp **-ier**, superl **-iest**) **adj** *inf* grognon(onne), ronchon(onne).

crack [kræk] ■ **n 1.** [in glass, pottery] fêlure *f* / [in wall, wood, ground] fissure *f* / [in skin] gerçure *f* **2.** [gap - in door] entrebâillement *m* / [- in curtains] interstice *m* ▸ **at the crack of dawn** au point du jour **3.** [noise - of whip] claquement *m* / [- of twigs] craquement *m* **4.** [joke] plaisanterie *f* **5.** *inf* [attempt] **: to have a crack at sthg** tenter qqch, essayer de faire qqch **6.** *drug sl* crack *m*.
■ **adj** [troops] de première classe ▸ **crack shot** tireur *m*, -euse *f* d'élite.
■ **vt 1.** [glass, plate] fêler / [wood, wall] fissurer **2.** [egg, nut] casser **3.** [whip] faire claquer ▸ **to crack the whip** faire le gendarme **4.** [bang, hit sharply] **: to crack one's head** se cogner la tête **5.** *inf* [bottle] **: to crack (open) a bottle** ouvrir une bouteille **6.** [solve - problem] résoudre / [- code] déchiffrer ▸ **the police have cracked the case** la police a résolu l'affaire ▸ **I think we've cracked it** je pense que nous y sommes arrivés **7.** *inf* [make - joke] faire.
■ **vi 1.** [glass, pottery] se fêler / [ground, wood, wall] se fissurer / [skin] se crevasser, se gercer **2.** [whip] claquer / [twigs] craquer **3.** [break down - person] craquer, s'effondrer / [- system, empire] s'écrouler / [- resistance] se briser ▸ **their marriage cracked under the strain** leur mariage s'est détérioré sous l'effet du stress **4.** *UK inf* [act quickly] **: to get cracking** s'y mettre ▸ **I'll get cracking on dinner/cleaning the windows** je vais me mettre à préparer le dîner/nettoyer les vitres.
◆ ***crack down*** **vi : to crack down (on)** sévir (contre).
◆ ***crack up*** ■ **vi 1.** [ice] se fissurer / [paint] se craqueler / [ground] se crevasser **2.** *inf* [person] craquer, s'effondrer ▸ **I must be cracking up** [going mad] je débloque **3.** *inf* [with laughter] se tordre de rire.
■ **vt sep 1.** [make laugh] faire se tordre de rire **2.** *(always passive)* [say good things about] **: he's not what he's cracked up to be** il n'est pas aussi fantastique qu'on le dit **OR** prétend.

crackbrained ['krækbreɪnd] **adj** *inf* débile, dingue.

crackdown ['krækdaʊn] **n : crackdown (on)** mesures *fpl* énergiques (contre).

cracked ['krækt] **adj 1.** [vase, glass] fêlé(e) / [wall] fissuré(e) / [paint, varnish] craquelé(e) **2.** [voice] fêlé(e) **3.** *inf* [mad] cinglé(e), toqué(e).

cracker ['krækəʳ] **n 1.** [biscuit] cracker *m*, craquelin *m* **2.** *UK* [for Christmas] diablotin *m*.

crackers ['krækəz] **adj** *UK inf* dingue, cinglé(e).

cracking ['krækɪŋ] **adj** *inf* **: to walk at a cracking pace** *UK* marcher à toute allure.

crackle ['krækl] ■ **n** [of fire] crépitement *m* / [of frying food, on radio] grésillement *m* / [on phone] friture *f*.
■ **vi** [fire] crépiter / [frying food, radio] grésiller.

crackling ['kræklɪŋ] **n** *(U)* **1.** [of fire] crépitement *m* / [of cooking, on radio] grésillement *m* / [on phone] friture *f* **2.** [pork skin] couenne *f* rissolée.

crackpot ['krækpɒt] *inf* ■ **adj** fou (folle).
■ **n** cinglé *m*, -e *f*, tordu *m*, -e *f*.

crack-up **n** *inf* **1.** [of person] dépression *f* (nerveuse) **2.** [of country, economy] effondrement *m*.

Cracow ['krækaʊ] **n** Cracovie.

cradle ['kreɪdl] ■ **n** berceau *m* / TECH nacelle *f*.
■ **vt** [baby] bercer / [object] tenir délicatement.

craft [krɑ:ft] (pl **craft**) **n 1.** [trade, skill] métier *m* **2.** [boat] embarcation *f*.

craftily ['krɑ:ftɪlɪ] **adv** astucieusement ▸ **to behave craftily** agir astucieusement **OR** habilement / *pej* agir avec ruse.

craftiness ['krɑ:ftɪnɪs] **n** habileté *f* / *pej* ruse *f*, roublardise *f*.

craftsman ['krɑ:ftsmən] (pl **-men** [-mən]) **n** artisan *m*, homme *m* de métier.

craftsmanship ['krɑ:ftsmənʃɪp] **n** *(U)* **1.** [skill] dextérité *f*, art *m* **2.** [skilled work] travail *m*, exécution *f*.

craftsmen **npl** ➤ ***craftsman***.

crafty ['krɑ:ftɪ] (comp **-ier**, superl **-iest**) **adj** [person, idea, scheme] malin(igne), astucieux(ieuse) / *pej* [person] rusé(e), roublard(e) / [idea, scheme] rusé(e).

crag [kræg] **n** rocher *m* escarpé.

craggy ['krægɪ] (comp **-ier**, superl **-iest**) **adj 1.** [rock] escarpé(e) **2.** [face] anguleux(euse).

Crakow ['krækaʊ] **n** Cracovie.

cram [kræm] (pt & pp **-med**, cont **-ming**) ■ **vt 1.** [stuff] fourrer **2.** [overfill] **: to cram sthg with** bourrer qqch de.
■ **vi** bachoter.

crammed ['kræmd] **adj** [full - bus, train, room, suitcase] bourré(e), bondé(e) ▸ **to be crammed with people** être bondé ▸ **to be crammed with sthg** être plein à craquer **OR** bourré de qqch ▸ **the encyclopedia is crammed with useful information** l'encyclopédie regorge d'informations utiles.

cramming ['kræmɪŋ] **n** bachotage *m*.

cramp [kræmp] ■ **n** crampe *f*.
■ **vt** gêner, entraver.

cramped [kræmpt] **adj** [room] exigu(ë) ▸ **it's a bit cramped in here** on est un peu à l'étroit ici.

crampon ['kræmpən] **n** crampon *m*.

cranberry ['krænbərɪ] (pl **-ies**) **n** canneberge *f*, airelle *f*.

crane [kreɪn] ■ **n** grue *f*.
■ **vt : to crane one's neck** tendre le cou.
■ **vi** tendre le cou.

crane fly **n** tipule *f*.

cranium ['kreɪnjəm] (pl **-niums** **OR** **-nia** [-njə]) **n** crâne *m*.

crank [kræŋk] ■ **n 1.** TECH manivelle *f* **2.** *inf* [person] excentrique *mf*.

■ vt 1. [wind - handle] tourner / [- mechanism] remonter (à la manivelle) 2. AUT faire démarrer à la manivelle.

crankshaft ['kræŋkʃɑ:ft] n vilebrequin *m*.

cranky ['kræŋkɪ] (comp -ier, superl -iest) adj *inf* 1. [odd] excentrique 2. *US* [bad-tempered] grognon(onne).

cranny ['krænɪ] (pl -ies) n ➤ ***nook***.

crap [kræp] n *(U) v inf* merde *f* ▸ **it's a load of crap** tout ça, c'est des conneries.

crappy ['kræpɪ] (comp -ier, superl -iest) adj *v inf* merdique.

crash [kræʃ] ■ n 1. [accident] accident *m* ▸ **car/plane/train crash** accident de voiture/d'avion/ferroviaire ▸ **to be (involved) in a crash** [person] avoir un accident 2. [noise] fracas *m* ▸ **a crash of thunder** un coup de tonnerre 3. FIN krach *m* 4. COMPUT panne *f*.

■ vt 1. : **I crashed the car** j'ai eu un accident avec la voiture ▸ **she crashed the car into a wall** elle est rentrée dans *OR* a percuté un mur (avec la voiture) 2. COMPUT planter 3. *inf* [attend without invitation] : **to crash a party** entrer dans une fête sans y être invité.

■ vi 1. [cars, trains] se percuter, se rentrer dedans / [car, train] avoir un accident / [plane] s'écraser ▸ **to crash into** [wall] rentrer dans, emboutir ▸ **we're going to crash** [plane] on va s'écraser / [car] on va lui rentrer dedans/rentrer dans le mur *etc* / [train] on va avoir un accident ▸ **the cars crashed (head on)** les voitures se sont embouties *OR* percutées (par l'avant) 2. [fall, hit loudly or violently] : **the tree came crashing down** l'arbre est tombé avec fracas ▸ **the vase crashed to the ground** le vase s'est écrasé au sol 3. [FIN - business, company] faire faillite / [- stock market] s'effondrer 4. COMPUT tomber en panne 5. *inf* [sleep] dormir / [fall asleep] s'endormir.

◆ ***crash out*** vi *inf* [fall asleep] s'endormir / [spend the night, sleep] roupiller.

crash barrier n glissière *f* de sécurité.

crash course n cours *m* intensif.

crash diet n régime *m* intensif.

crash-dive vi faire une plongée rapide.

crash helmet n casque *m* de protection.

crash-land ■ vt faire atterrir en catastrophe.

■ vi atterrir en catastrophe.

crash landing n atterrissage *m* en catastrophe.

crash pad n *v inf* piaule *f* de dépannage ▸ **he let me use this place as a crash pad** il m'a laissé crécher chez lui pour me dépanner.

crass [kræs] adj [comment, person] lourd(e) / [behaviour, stupidity] grossier(ère).

crassly ['kræslɪ] adv [behave, comment] lourdement.

crassness ['kræsnɪs] n [of comment, person] lourdeur *f*, manque *m* de finesse ▸ **the crassness of his behaviour** son manque de finesse.

crate [kreɪt] n cageot *m*, caisse *f*.

crater ['kreɪtəʳ] n cratère *m*.

cravat [krə'væt] n cravate *f*.

crave [kreɪv] ■ vt [affection, luxury] avoir soif de / [cigarette, chocolate] avoir un besoin fou *OR* maladif de.

■ vi : **to crave for** [affection, luxury] avoir soif de / [cigarette, chocolate] avoir un besoin fou *OR* maladif de.

craving ['kreɪvɪŋ] n : **craving for** [affection, luxury] soif *f* de / [cigarette, chocolate] besoin *m* fou *OR* maladif de.

crawl [krɔ:l] ■ vi 1. [baby] marcher à quatre pattes / [person] se traîner 2. [insect] ramper 3. [vehicle, traffic] avancer au pas 4. *inf* [place, floor] : **to be crawling with** grouiller de 5. *inf* [grovel] : **to crawl (to sb)** ramper (devant qqn).

■ n 1. [slow pace] : **at a crawl** au pas, au ralenti 2. [swimming stroke] : **the crawl** le crawl.

crawler lane n *UK* voie *f* pour véhicules lents.

crayfish ['kreɪfɪʃ] (pl **crayfish** *OR* -es) n écrevisse *f*.

crayon ['kreɪɒn] n crayon *m* de couleur.

craze [kreɪz] n engouement *m*.

crazed [kreɪzd] adj : **crazed (with)** rendu fou (rendue folle) (de).

-crazed suffix rendu fou par ▸ **drug-crazed** rendu fou par la drogue ▸ **power-crazed dictators** des dictateurs fous de pouvoir ▸ **he was half-crazed with fear** il était à moitié fou de peur.

crazily ['kreɪzɪlɪ] adv [behave] comme un fou.

craziness ['kreɪzɪnɪs] n folie *f*.

crazy ['kreɪzɪ] (comp -ier, superl -iest) adj *inf* 1. [mad] fou (folle) ▸ **to drive** *OR* **to send sb crazy** rendre qqn fou ▸ **like crazy** [work, drive, run, spend money] comme un fou 2. [enthusiastic] : **to be crazy about sb/sthg** être fou (folle) de qqn/qqch ▸ **he's football crazy** c'est un fana *OR* un cinglé de foot.

crazy paving n *UK* dallage *m* irrégulier.

CRB [ˌsi:ɑ:'bi:] (abbr of ***Criminal Records Bureau***) n *Organisme chargé de vérifier le casier judiciaire de personnels sensibles.*

CRE (abbr of ***Commission for Racial Equality***) n *commission contre la discrimination raciale.*

creak [kri:k] ■ n [of door, handle] craquement *m* / [of floorboard, bed] grincement *m*.

■ vi [door, handle] craquer / [floorboard, bed] grincer.

creaky ['kri:kɪ] (comp -ier, superl -iest) adj [door, handle] qui craque / [floorboard, bed] qui grince.

cream [kri:m] ■ adj [in colour] crème *(inv)*.

■ n 1. [gen] crème *f* 2. [colour] crème *m*.

■ vt *UK* [potatoes] mettre en purée.

◆ ***cream off*** vt sep *fig* écrémer.

cream cake n *UK* gâteau *m* à la crème.

cream cheese n fromage *m* frais.

cream cracker n *UK* biscuit *m* salé *(souvent mangé avec du fromage)*.

cream of tartar n crème *f* de tartre.

cream tea n *UK goûter se composant de thé et de scones servis avec de la crème et de la confiture.*

creamy ['kri:mɪ] (comp -ier, superl -iest) adj 1. [taste, texture] crémeux(euse) 2. [colour] crème *(inv)*.

crease [kri:s] ■ n [in fabric - deliberate] pli *m* / [- accidental] (faux) pli.

■ vt froisser.

■ vi 1. [fabric] se froisser 2. [face, forehead] se plisser.

creased [kri:st] **adj 1.** [fabric] froissé(e) **2.** [face] plissé(e).

crease-resistant **adj** infroissable.

create [kri:'eɪt] **vt** créer.

creation [kri:'eɪʃn] **n** création *f*.

creative [kri:'eɪtɪv] **adj** créatif(ive).

creatively [kri:'eɪtɪvlɪ] **adv** de manière créative ▸ **you're not thinking very creatively about your future** tu n'as pas d'idées très originales pour ton avenir.

creative marketing **n** créativité *f* commerciale.

creative team **n** équipe *f* de création.

creativity [ˌkri:eɪ'tɪvətɪ] **n** créativité *f*.

creator [kri:'eɪtəʳ] **n** créateur *m*, -trice *f*.

creature ['kri:tʃəʳ] **n** créature *f*.

creature comforts **npl** confort *m* matériel ▸ **I like my creature comforts** j'aime ***OR*** je suis attaché à mon (petit) confort.

crèche [kreʃ] **n** *UK* crèche *f*.

credence ['kri:dns] **n : to give *OR* lend credence to sthg** ajouter foi à qqch.

credentials [krɪ'denʃlz] **npl 1.** [papers] papiers *mpl* d'identité / *fig* [qualifications] capacités *fpl* **2.** [references] références *fpl*.

credibility [ˌkredə'bɪlətɪ] **n** crédibilité *f* ▸ **credibility rating** crédibilité *f*.

credibility gap **n** manque *m* de crédibilité.

credible ['kredəbl] **adj** crédible.

credibly ['kredəblɪ] **adv** [argue] de manière crédible.

credit ['kredɪt] ■ **n 1.** FIN crédit *m* ▸ **to be in credit** [person] avoir un compte approvisionné / [account] être approvisionné ▸ **on credit** à crédit ▸ **to give sb credit, to give credit to sb** [bank] accorder un découvert à qqn / [shop, pub] faire crédit à qqn ▸ **interest-free credit** crédit gratuit
2. *(U)* [praise] honneur *m*, mérite *m* ▸ **to take the credit for sthg/doing sthg** s'attribuer le mérite de qqch/d'avoir fait qqch ▸ **all the credit should go to the team** tout le mérite doit revenir à l'équipe ▸ **to be to sb's credit** [successfully completed] être à l'actif de qqn / [in sb's favour] être à l'honneur de qqn ▸ **to her credit she did finish the exam** il faut lui accorder qu'elle a fini l'examen ▸ **to be a credit to one's family/school, to do one's family/school credit** faire honneur à sa famille/son école, être l'honneur de sa famille/son école ▸ **to give sb credit for sthg** reconnaître que qqn a fait qqch ▸ **I gave you credit for more sense** je vous supposais plus de bon sens
3. UNIV unité *f* de valeur.
■ **comp** [boom] du crédit / [sales] à crédit ▸ **credit entry** écriture *f* au crédit ▸ **credit side** crédit *m*, avoir *m* ▸ **to run a credit check on sb** [to ensure enough money in account] vérifier la solvabilité de qqn, vérifier que le compte de qqn est approvisionné / [to ensure no record of bad debts] vérifier le passé bancaire de qqn.
■ **vt 1.** FIN **: to credit £10 to an account, to credit an account with £10** créditer un compte de 10 livres
2. *inf* [believe] croire
3. [give the credit to] **: to credit sb with sthg** accorder ***OR*** attribuer qqch à qqn ▸ **he's credited with inventing...** il a, dit-on, inventé...
◆ ***credits*** **npl** CIN générique *m*.

creditable ['kredɪtəbl] **adj** honorable.

credit account **n** *UK* compte *m* créditeur.

credit agreement **n** accord *m* ***OR*** convention *f* de crédit.

credit balance **n** solde *m* créditeur.

credit broker **n** courtier *m* en crédits ***OR*** en prêts.

credit card **n** carte *f* de crédit.

credit control **n** [on spending] encadrement *m* du crédit / [debt recovery] recouvrement *m* de créances.

credit facilities **npl** *UK* facilités *fpl* de paiement ***OR*** de crédit.

credit limit *UK*, ***credit line*** *US* **n** limite *f* de crédit.

credit note **n** avoir *m* / FIN note *f* de crédit.

creditor ['kredɪtəʳ] **n** créancier *m*, -ère *f*.

credit purchase **n** achat *m* à crédit.

credit rating **n** degré *m* de solvabilité.

CULTURE

Credit Rating

La « notation de crédit » est une information financière sur la situation budgétaire d'une personne désirant emprunter des fonds. Cette cote est attribuée selon le montant des dettes, la capacité à rembourser et le respect des délais de remboursement. Les organismes de crédit, les banques et les commerces peuvent ainsi vérifier les antécédents financiers de leurs clients avant de leur accorder un prêt : ils refuseront une demande de crédit si le montant de leurs dettes à court terme excède 20 % de leurs revenus annuels. Cependant, de plus en plus d'organismes de crédit en ligne vérifient les facilités de paiement de leurs clients, même s'ils ont obtenu une notation (on peut aussi consulter sa notation personnelle en ligne).

credit squeeze **n** restriction *f* de crédit.

credit terms **npl** modalités *fpl* de crédit.

credit transfer **n** virement *m* de crédits.

credit voucher **n** chèque *m* de caisse.

creditworthiness ['kredɪtˌwɜ:ðɪnɪs] **n** solvabilité *f*.

creditworthy ['kredɪtˌwɜ:ðɪ] **adj** solvable.

credulity [krɪ'dju:lətɪ] **n** crédulité *f*.

credulous ['kredjʊləs] **adj** crédule.

creed [kri:d] **n 1.** [belief] principes *mpl* **2.** RELIG croyance *f*.

creek [kri:k] **n 1.** [inlet] crique *f* **2.** *US* [stream] ruisseau *m*.

creep [kri:p] ■ **vi (pt & pp crept) 1.** [insect] ramper / [traffic] avancer au pas **2.** [move stealthily] se glisser **3.** *inf* [grovel] **: to creep (to sb)** ramper (devant qqn).
■ **n** *inf* [nasty person] sale type *m*.
◆ ***creeps*** **npl : to give sb the creeps** *inf* donner la chair de poule à qqn.
◆ ***creep in*** **vi** [appear] apparaître.
◆ ***creep up on*** **vt** surprendre.

creeper ['kri:pəʳ] **n** [plant] plante *f* grimpante.

◆ ***creepers*** npl chaussures *fpl* à semelles de crêpe.

creeping ['kri:pɪŋ] adj **1.** [plant - upwards] grimpant(e) / [- along the ground] rampant(e) **2.** [insect] rampant(e) **3.** *fig* [inflation] galopant(e) / [change] graduel(elle) ▸ **creeping paralysis** paralysie *f* progressive.

creepy ['kri:pɪ] (comp -ier, superl -iest) adj *inf* qui donne la chair de poule.

creepy-crawly [-'krɔ:lɪ] (pl **creepy-crawlies**) n *inf* bestiole *f* qui rampe.

cremate [krɪ'meɪt] vt incinérer.

cremation [krɪ'meɪʃn] n incinération *f*.

crematorium *UK* [,kremə'tɔ:rɪəm] (pl **-riums** *OR* **-ria** [-rɪə]), ***crematory*** *US* ['kremətrɪ] (pl **-ies**) n crématorium *m*.

crème de la crème ['kremdəlæ'krem] n : **the crème de la crème** le gratin, le dessus du panier.

creosote ['krɪəsəʊt] ■ n créosote *f*.
■ vt créosoter.

crepe [kreɪp] n **1.** [cloth, rubber] crêpe *m* **2.** [pancake] crêpe *f*.

crepe bandage n *UK* bande *f* Velpeau®.

crepe paper n *(U)* papier *m* crépon.

crepe-soled shoes npl *UK* chaussures *fpl* à semelles de crêpe.

crept [krept] pt & pp ➤ ***creep***.

Cres. abbr of ***Crescent***.

crescendo [krɪ'ʃendəʊ] (pl -s) n crescendo *m*.

crescent ['kresnt] ■ adj en forme de croissant ▸ **crescent moon** croissant *m* de lune.
■ n **1.** [shape] croissant **2.** *UK* [street] rue *f* en demi-cercle.

cress [kres] n cresson *m*.

crest [krest] n **1.** [of bird, hill] crête *f* **2.** [on coat of arms] timbre *m*.

crestfallen ['krest,fɔ:ln] adj découragé(e).

Crete [kri:t] n Crète *f* ▸ **in Crete** en Crète.

cretin ['kretɪn] n *inf* [idiot] crétin *m*, -e *f*.

cretinous ['kretɪnəs] adj *fig* & MED crétin(e).

Creutzfeldt-Jakob disease [,krɔɪtsfelt'jækɒb-] n maladie *f* de Creutzfeldt-Jakob.

crevasse [krɪ'væs] n crevasse *f*.

crevice ['krevɪs] n fissure *f*.

crew [kru:] n **1.** [of ship, plane] équipage *m* **2.** [team] équipe *f* ▸ **ambulance crew** ambulanciers *mpl*.

crew cut n coupe *f* en brosse.

crewman ['kru:mæn] (pl **-men** [-men]) n membre *m* d'équipage.

crew neck n col *m* ras le *OR* du cou, ras-le-cou *m*.

crib [krɪb] ■ n [cot] lit *m* d'enfant.
■ vt (pt & pp **-bed**, cont **-bing**) *inf* [copy] : **to crib sthg off** *OR* **from sb** copier qqch sur qqn.

cribbage ['krɪbɪdʒ] n *jeu de cartes dans lequel les points sont comptabilisés sur une tablette.*

crib death n *US* = ***cot death***.

crick [krɪk] ■ n [in neck] torticolis *m*.
■ vt : **to crick one's neck, to have a crick in one's neck** attraper un torticolis ▸ **to crick one's back** se faire un tour de reins.

cricket ['krɪkɪt] ■ n **1.** [game] cricket *m* **2.** [insect] grillon *m*.
■ comp de cricket.

cricketer ['krɪkɪtəʳ] n joueur *m* de cricket.

crikey ['kraɪkɪ] excl *UK inf dated* zut alors!

crime [kraɪm] ■ n crime *m* ▸ **a life of crime** une vie de criminel ▸ **crimes against humanity** crimes *mpl* contre l'humanité.
■ comp : **crime novel** roman *m* policier ▸ **crime prevention** lutte *f* contre le crime.

Crimea [kraɪ'mɪə] n : **the Crimea** la Crimée ▸ **in the Crimea** en Crimée.

crime wave n vague *f* de criminalité.

criminal ['krɪmɪnl] ■ adj criminel(elle).
■ n criminel *m*, -elle *f*.

criminal assault n agression *f* criminelle, voie *f* de fait.

criminal court n cour *f* d'assises.

criminal damage n *délit consistant à causer volontairement des dégâts matériels.*

criminality [,krɪmɪ'nælətɪ] n criminalité *f*.

criminalize, *UK* ***-ise*** ['krɪmɪnəlaɪz] vt criminaliser.

criminal law n droit *m* pénal.

criminal lawyer n avocat *m*, -e *f* au criminel, pénaliste *mf*.

criminally ['krɪmɪnəlɪ] adv criminellement ▸ **he's been criminally negligent** sa négligence est criminelle.

criminal offence n délit *m* ▸ **drink driving is a criminal offence** la conduite en état d'ivresse est un crime puni par la loi.

criminal record n casier *m* judiciaire ▸ **she hasn't got a criminal record** son casier judiciaire est vierge, elle n'a pas de casier judiciaire.

Criminal Records Bureau n *organisme chargé de vérifier le casier judiciaire de personnels sensibles.*

criminology [,krɪmɪ'nɒlədʒɪ] n criminologie *f*.

crimp [krɪmp] vt [hair] crêper.

crimson ['krɪmzn] ■ adj [in colour] rouge foncé *(inv)* / [with embarrassment] cramoisi(e).
■ n cramoisi *m*.

cringe [krɪndʒ] vi **1.** [in fear] avoir un mouvement de recul (par peur) **2.** *inf* [with embarrassment] : **to cringe (at sthg)** ne plus savoir où se mettre (devant qqch).

cringeworthy ['krɪndʒ,wɜ:ðɪ] adj *inf* hérissant(e), qui hérisse.

cringing ['krɪndʒɪŋ] adj [fearful] craintif(ive) / [servile] servile, obséquieux(euse).

crinkle ['krɪŋkl] ■ n [in paper] pli *m* / [in cloth] (faux) pli
■ vt [clothes] froisser.
■ vi [clothes] se froisser.

cripple ['krɪpl] ■ n *dated* & *offens* infirme *mf*.
■ vt **1.** MED [disable] estropier **2.** [country] paralyser / [ship, plane] endommager.

crippling ['krɪplɪŋ] **adj 1.** MED [disease] qui rend infirme **2.** [taxes, debts] écrasant(e).

crisis ['kraɪsɪs] (pl **crises** ['kraɪsi:z]) **n** crise *f.*

crisp [krɪsp] **adj 1.** [pastry] croustillant(e) / [apple, vegetables] croquant(e) / [snow] craquant(e) **2.** [weather, manner] vif (vive).

◆ ***crisps*** **npl** *UK* chips *fpl.*

crispbread ['krɪspbred] **n** *UK* pain *m* suédois.

crispy ['krɪspɪ] (comp **-ier**, superl **-iest**) **adj** [pastry] croustillant(e) / [apple, vegetables] croquant(e).

crisscross ['krɪskrɒs] ■ **adj** entrecroisé(e).

■ **vt** entrecroiser.

■ **vi** s'entrecroiser.

criterion [kraɪ'tɪərɪən] (pl **-rions** *OR* **-ria** [-rɪə]) **n** critère *m.*

critic ['krɪtɪk] **n 1.** [reviewer] critique *mf* **2.** [detractor] détracteur *m*, -trice *f.*

critical ['krɪtɪkl] **adj** critique ◗ **to be critical of sb/sthg** critiquer qqn/qqch.

critically ['krɪtɪklɪ] **adv 1.** [ill] gravement ◗ **critically important** d'une importance capitale **2.** [analytically] de façon critique.

critical path **n** [gen & COMPUT] chemin *m* critique.

critical path method **n** méthode *f* du chemin critique.

criticism ['krɪtɪsɪzm] **n** critique *f.*

criticize, *UK* ***-ise*** ['krɪtɪsaɪz] **vt & vi** critiquer.

critique [krɪ'ti:k] **n** critique *f.*

croak [krəʊk] ■ **n 1.** [of frog] coassement *m* / [of raven] croassement *m* **2.** [hoarse voice] voix *f* rauque.

■ **vi 1.** [frog] coasser / [raven] croasser **2.** [person] parler d'une voix rauque.

croaky ['krəʊkɪ] **adj** enroué(e).

Croat ['krəʊæt], ***Croatian*** [krəʊ'eɪʃn] ■ **adj** croate.

■ **n 1.** [person] Croate *mf* **2.** [language] croate *m.*

Croatia [krəʊ'eɪʃə] **n** Croatie *f* ◗ **in Croatia** en Croatie.

Croatian = ***Croat.***

crochet ['krəʊʃeɪ] ■ **n** crochet *m.*

■ **vt** faire au crochet.

crockery ['krɒkərɪ] **n** vaisselle *f.*

crocodile ['krɒkədaɪl] (pl **crocodile** *OR* **-s**) **n** crocodile *m.*

crocodile tears **npl** larmes *fpl* de crocodile.

crocus ['krəʊkəs] (pl **-es** [-i:z]) **n** crocus *m.*

croft [krɒft] **n** *UK* petite ferme *f (particulièrement en Écosse).*

croissant **n** croissant *m.*

crony ['krəʊnɪ] (pl **-ies**) **n** *inf* copain *m*, copine *f.*

cronyism ['krəʊnɪɪzm] **n** copinage *m.*

crook [krʊk] ■ **n 1.** [criminal] escroc *m* **2.** [of arm, elbow] pliure *f* **3.** [shepherd's staff] houlette *f.*

■ **vt** [finger, arm] plier.

crooked ['krʊkɪd] **adj 1.** [bent] courbé(e) **2.** [teeth, tie] de travers **3.** *inf* [dishonest] malhonnête.

croon [kru:n] **vt & vi** chantonner.

crop [krɒp] ■ **n 1.** [kind of plant] culture *f* **2.** [harvested produce] récolte *f* **3.** [whip] cravache *f.*

■ **vt** (pt & pp **-ped**, cont **-ping**) **1.** [hair] couper très court **2.** [subj: cows, sheep] brouter.

◆ ***crop up*** **vi** survenir.

cropper ['krɒpə^r] **n** *inf* **: to come a cropper** [fall over] se casser la figure / [make mistake] se planter.

crop spraying **n** pulvérisation *f* des cultures.

croquet ['krəʊkeɪ] **n** croquet *m.*

croquette [krɒ'ket] **n** croquette *f.*

cross [krɒs] ■ **adj** [person] fâché(e) / [look] méchant(e) ◗ **to get cross (with sb)** se fâcher (contre qqn) ◗ **she's cross with me** elle est fâchée contre moi ◗ **he makes me so cross!** qu'est-ce qu'il peut m'agacer!

■ **n 1.** [gen] croix *f* ◗ **he signed with a cross** il a signé d'une croix ◗ **the Cross** la Croix **2.** [hybrid] croisement *m* ◗ **a cross between a horse and a donkey** un croisement d'un cheval et d'une ânesse ◗ **a cross between a thriller and a comedy** un mélange de policier et de comédie.

■ **vt 1.** [gen] traverser ◗ **the bridge crosses the river at Orléans** le pont franchit *OR* enjambe le fleuve à Orléans ◗ **it crossed my mind that...** j'ai pensé *OR* l'idée m'a effleuré que... **2.** [arms, legs] croiser ◗ **to cross one's arms/one's legs** croiser les bras/les jambes ◗ **cross your fingers** *OR* **keep your fingers crossed for me** pense à moi et croise les doigts **3.** RELIG **: to cross o.s.** faire le signe de croix, se signer **4.** *UK* [cheque] barrer.

■ **vi 1.** [go across] traverser ◗ **she crossed (over) to the other side of the road** elle a traversé la route ◗ **they crossed from Dover to Boulogne** ils ont fait la traversée de Douvres à Boulogne **2.** [intersect] se croiser ◗ **our letters crossed in the post** nos lettres se sont croisées.

◆ ***cross off***, ***cross out*** **vt sep** rayer.

crossbar ['krɒsbɑ:^r] **n 1.** SPORT barre *f* transversale **2.** [on bicycle] barre *f.*

crossbow ['krɒsbəʊ] **n** arbalète *f.*

crossbreed ['krɒsbri:d] **n** hybride *m.*

cross-Channel **adj** trans-Manche.

cross-check ■ **n** contre-vérification *f.*

■ **vt** faire une contre-vérification de.

cross-country ■ **adj : cross-country running** cross *m* ◗ **cross-country skiing** ski *m* de fond.

■ **adv** à travers champs.

■ **n** cross-country *m*, cross *m.*

cross-cultural **adj** interculturel(elle).

cross-dressing **n** travestisme *m.*

crossed line **n** TELEC **: we've got a crossed line** il y a des interférences.

cross-examination **n** LAW contre-interrogatoire *m.*

cross-examine **vt** LAW faire subir un contre-interrogatoire à / *fig* questionner de près.

cross-eyed [-aɪd] **adj** qui louche.

cross-fertilization **n** croisement *m* / *fig* osmose *f.*

cross-fertilize **vt** [plants] croiser.

crossfire ['krɒs,faɪə^r] **n** *(U)* feu *m* croisé.

crosshead ['krɒs,hed] **adj : crosshead screw** vis *m* cruciforme ◗ **crosshead screwdriver** tournevis *m* cruciforme.

crossing ['krɒsɪŋ] **n 1.** [on road] passage *m* clouté / [on railway line] passage *m* à niveau **2.** [sea journey] traversée *f*.

cross-legged [-legd] **adv** en tailleur.

crossly ['krɒslɪ] **adv** [say] d'un air fâché.

crossover ['krɒs,əʊvəʳ] ■ **n 1.** [of roads] (croisement *m* par) pont *m* routier / [for pedestrians] passage *m* clouté / RAIL voie *f* de croisement **2.** BIOL croisement *m*.
■ **adj** MUS [style] hybride.

cross-party **adj** POL **: cross-party agreement** accord *m* entre partis.

cross-platform **adj** multiplateforme.

crossply ['krɒsplaɪ] ■ **adj** [tyre] à carcasse diagonale.
■ **n** (pl -ies) pneu *m* à carcasse diagonale.

cross-post **vt** COMPUT faire un envoi multiple de.

cross-posting **n** COMPUT envoi *m* multiple.

cross-purposes **npl : to talk at cross-purposes** ne pas parler de la même chose ▸ **to be at cross-purposes** ne pas être sur la même longueur d'ondes.

cross-question ■ **n** contre-interrogatoire *m*.
■ **vt** faire subir un contre-interrogatoire à.

cross-refer **vt & vi** renvoyer.

cross-reference **n** renvoi *m*.

crossroads ['krɒsrəʊdz] (pl **crossroads**) **n** croisement *m* ▸ **to be at a crossroads** *fig* se trouver à un point critique.

cross-section **n 1.** [drawing] coupe *f* transversale **2.** [sample] échantillon *m*.

crosswalk ['krɒswɔ:k] **n** *US* passage *m* clouté, passage *m* pour piétons.

crossways ['krɒsweɪz] = ***crosswise***.

crosswind ['krɒswɪnd] **n** vent *m* de travers.

crosswise ['krɒswaɪz] **adv** en travers.

crossword (puzzle) ['krɒswɜ:d-] **n** mots croisés *mpl*.

crotch [krɒtʃ] **n** entrejambe *m*.

crotchet ['krɒtʃɪt] **n** *UK* MUS noire *f*.

crotchety ['krɒtʃɪtɪ] **adj** *UK inf* grognon(onne).

crouch [kraʊtʃ] **vi** s'accroupir.

croup [kru:p] **n 1.** [illness] croup *m* **2.** [of horse] croupe *f*.

croupier ['kru:pɪəʳ] **n** croupier *m*.

crouton ['kru:tɒn] **n** croûton *m*.

crow [krəʊ] ■ **n** corbeau *m* ▸ **as the crow flies** à vol d'oiseau.
■ **vi 1.** [cock] chanter **2.** *inf* [person] frimer.

crowbar ['krəʊbɑ:ʳ] **n** pied-de-biche *m*.

crowd [kraʊd] ■ **n 1.** [mass of people] foule *f* ▸ **she stands out in a crowd** elle se distingue de la masse ▸ **the crowd** la foule, la masse du peuple **2.** [particular group] bande *f*, groupe *m*.
■ **vi** s'amasser ▸ **to crowd round sb/sthg** se presser autour de qqn/qqch.
■ **vt 1.** [streets, town] remplir **2.** [force into small space] entasser.

crowded ['kraʊdɪd] **adj : crowded (with)** bondé(e) (de), plein(e) (de).

crowdpuller ['kraʊd,pʊləʳ] **n** *UK inf* **: his play is a real crowdpuller** sa pièce attire les foules.

crown [kraʊn] ■ **n 1.** [of king, on tooth] couronne *f* **2.** [of head, hill] sommet *m* / [of hat] fond *m*.
■ **vt** couronner.
◆ ***Crown*** ■ **n : the Crown** [monarchy] la Couronne.
■ **comp** de la Couronne.

crown court **n** *UK* [in England, Wales] tribunal *m* de grande instance.

crowning ['kraʊnɪŋ] **adj** *fig* suprême ▸ **the crowning glory of her career** le couronnement de sa carrière.

crown jewels **npl** joyaux *mpl* de la Couronne.

crown prince **n** prince *m* héritier.

crow's feet **npl** pattes *fpl* d'oie.

crow's nest **n** nid *m* de pie.

CRT [si:ɑ:'ti:] (abbr of ***cathode ray tube***) **n** tube *m* cathodique.

crucial ['kru:ʃl] **adj** crucial(e).

crucially ['kru:ʃlɪ] **adv** de façon cruciale ▸ **crucially important** d'une importance cruciale.

crucible ['kru:sɪbl] **n** creuset *m*.

crucifix ['kru:sɪfɪks] **n** crucifix *m*.

Crucifixion [,kru:sɪ'fɪkʃn] **n : the Crucifixion** la Crucifixion.

crucify ['kru:sɪfaɪ] (pt & pp **-ied**) **vt** crucifier.

crude [kru:d] ■ **adj 1.** [material] brut(e) **2.** [joke, drawing] grossier(ère).
■ **n** *(U)* **: crude (oil)** brut *m*.

crudely ['kru:dlɪ] **adv 1.** [joke, remark] grossièrement crûment **2.** [draw, sketch] grossièrement, sommairement.

crude oil **n** *(U)* brut *m*.

cruel [krʊəl] (comp **-ler**, superl **-lest**) **adj** cruel(elle).

cruelly ['krʊəlɪ] **adv** cruellement.

cruelty ['krʊəltɪ] **n** *(U)* cruauté *f*.

cruet ['kru:ɪt] **n** service *m* à condiments.

cruise [kru:z] ■ **n** croisière *f*.
■ **vi 1.** [sail] croiser **2.** [car] rouler / [plane] voler.

cruise missile **n** missile *m* de croisière.

cruiser ['kru:zəʳ] **n 1.** [warship] croiseur *m* **2.** [cabin cruiser] yacht *m* de croisière.

crumb [krʌm] **n 1.** [of food] miette *f* **2.** *fig* [of information] bribe *f*.

crumble ['krʌmbl] ■ **n** crumble *m* (aux fruits).
■ **vt** émietter.
■ **vi 1.** [bread, cheese] s'émietter / [building, wall] s'écrouler / [cliff] s'ébouler / [plaster] s'effriter **2.** *fig* [society, relationship] s'effondrer.

crumbly ['krʌmblɪ] (comp **-ier**, superl **-iest**) **adj** friable.

crummy ['krʌmɪ] (comp **-mier**, superl **-miest**) **adj** *inf* minable.

crumpet ['krʌmpɪt] **n** CULIN petite crêpe *f* épaisse.

crumple ['krʌmpl] ■ **vt** [crease] froisser.
■ **vi** [clothes] se froisser / [car, bodywork] se mettre en accordéon.
◆ ***crumple up*** **vt sep** chiffonner.

crunch [krʌntʃ] ■ **n** crissement *m* ▸ **when it comes to the crunch** *inf* au moment crucial *OR* décisif ▸ **if it comes to the crunch** *inf* s'il le faut.
■ **vt 1.** [with teeth] croquer **2.** [underfoot] crisser.
■ **vi** [feet, tyres] crisser.

crunchy ['krʌntʃɪ] (comp **-ier**, superl **-iest**) **adj 1.** [food] croquant(e) **2.** [snow, gravel] qui crisse.

crusade [kru:'seɪd] ■ **n** *liter & fig* croisade *f*.
■ **vi : to crusade for/against** faire campagne pour/contre.

crusader [kru:'seɪdəʳ] **n 1.** HIST croisé *m* **2.** [campaigner] militant *m*, -e *f*.

crush [krʌʃ] ■ **n 1.** [crowd] foule *f* **2.** *inf* [infatuation] **: to have a crush on sb** avoir le béguin pour qqn **3.** *UK* [drink] **: orange crush** orange *f* pressée.
■ **vt 1.** [gen] écraser / [seeds, grain] broyer / [ice] piler **2.** *fig* [hopes] anéantir ▸ **she felt crushed by the news** elle a été accablée *OR* atterrée par la nouvelle.

crush barrier **n** *UK* barrière *f* de sécurité.

crushing ['krʌʃɪŋ] **adj 1.** [defeat, blow] écrasant(e) **2.** [remark] humiliant(e).

crust [krʌst] **n** croûte *f*.

crustacean [krʌ'steɪʃn] **n** crustacé *m*.

crusty ['krʌstɪ] (comp **-ier**, superl **-iest**) **adj 1.** [food] croustillant(e) **2.** [person] grincheux(euse).

crutch [krʌtʃ] **n 1.** [stick] béquille *f* / *fig* soutien *m* **2.** *UK* [crotch] entrejambe *m*.

crux [krʌks] **n** nœud *m*.

cry [kraɪ] ■ **n** (pl **cries**) **1.** [weep] **: to have a good cry** pleurer un bon coup **2.** [of person, bird] cri *m* ▸ **he heard a cry for help** il a entendu crier au secours ▸ **a far cry from** loin de.
■ **vt** (pt & pp **cried**) [tears] pleurer ▸ **to cry o.s. to sleep** s'endormir à force de pleurer ▸ **to cry wolf** crier au loup.
■ **vi 1.** [weep] pleurer ▸ **she cried in** *OR* **with frustration** elle pleurait d'impuissance **2.** [shout] crier ▸ **to cry for help** crier au secours.
◆ ***cry off*** **vi** *UK* se dédire.
◆ ***cry out*** ■ **vt** crier.
■ **vi** crier / [in pain, dismay] pousser un cri.
◆ ***cry out for*** **vt insep** [demand] réclamer à grands cris ▸ **the room is crying out for...** la pièce a bien besoin de...

crybaby ['kraɪˌbeɪbɪ] (pl **-ies**) **n** *inf pej* pleurnicheur *m*, -euse *f*.

crying ['kraɪɪŋ] ■ **adj** *inf* **: it's a crying shame** c'est scandaleux ▸ **a crying need for sthg** un grand besoin de qqch, un besoin urgent de qqch.
■ **n** *(U)* pleurs *mpl*.

cryogenics [ˌkraɪə'dʒenɪks] **n** *(U)* cryogénie *f*.

cryonics [kraɪ'ɒnɪks] **n** *(U)* cryogénisation *f*.

cryopreservation [ˌkraɪəprezə'veɪʃn] **n** *(U)* cryoconservation *f*.

crypt [krɪpt] **n** crypte *f*.

cryptic ['krɪptɪk] **adj** mystérieux(euse), énigmatique.

crypto- [krɪptəʊ] **prefix** crypto-.

crystal ['krɪstl] ■ **n** cristal *m*.
■ **comp** en cristal.

crystal ball **n** boule *f* de cristal.

crystal clear **adj 1.** [transparent] de cristal **2.** [obvious] clair(e) comme de l'eau de roche.

crystal-gazing **n** *(U)* [in ball] (art *m* de la) voyance *f* / *fig* prédictions *fpl*, prophéties *fpl*.

crystallize, *UK* ***-ise*** ['krɪstəlaɪz] ■ **vi** *lit & fig* se cristalliser.
■ **vt 1.** [make clear] cristalliser, concrétiser **2.** [preserve in sugar] **: crystallized fruit** fruits *mpl* confits.

CSC (abbr of ***Civil Service Commission***) **n** *commission de recrutement des fonctionnaires*.

CSE (abbr of ***Certificate of Secondary Education***) **n** *ancien brevet de l'enseignement secondaire en Grande-Bretagne*.

CS gas **n** *(U)* gaz *m* lacrymogène.

CST (abbr of ***Central Standard Time***) **n** *heure du centre des États-Unis*.

CSU (abbr of ***Civil Service Union***) **n** *syndicat de la fonction publique*.

ct abbr of ***carat***.

CT abbr of ***Connecticut***.

CTC abbr of ***city technology college***.

cu. abbr of ***cubic***.

cub [kʌb] **n 1.** [young animal] petit *m* **2.** [boy scout] louveteau *m*.

Cuba ['kju:bə] **n** Cuba ▸ **in Cuba** à Cuba.

Cuban ['kju:bən] ■ **adj** cubain(e).
■ **n** Cubain *m*, -e *f*.

cubbyhole ['kʌbɪhəʊl] **n** cagibi *m*.

cube [kju:b] ■ **n** cube *m*.
■ **vt** MATHS élever au cube.

cube root **n** racine *f* cubique.

cubic ['kju:bɪk] **adj** cubique.

cubicle ['kju:bɪkl] **n** cabine *f*.

cubism ['kju:bɪzm] **n** cubisme *m*.

cubist ['kju:bɪst] **n** cubiste *mf*.

cub reporter **n** jeune reporter *m*.

Cub Scout **n** louveteau *m*.

cuckoo ['kʊku:] **n** coucou *m*.

cuckoo clock **n** coucou *m*.

cucumber ['kju:kʌmbəʳ] **n** concombre *m*.

cud [kʌd] **n : to chew the cud** *lit & fig* ruminer.

cuddle ['kʌdl] ■ **n** caresse *f*, câlin *m*.
■ **vt** caresser, câliner.
■ **vi** se faire un câlin, se câliner.
◆ ***cuddle up*** **vi : to cuddle up (to sb)** se pelotonner (contre qqn).

cuddly ['kʌdlɪ] (comp **-ier**, superl **-iest**) **adj** [person] câlin(e).

cuddly toy **n** jouet *m* en peluche.

cudgel ['kʌdʒəl] ■ **n** trique *f* ▸ **to take up the cudgels for sb/sthg** prendre fait et cause pour qqn/qqch.
■ **vt** (*UK* **-led**, cont **-ling**, *US* **-ed**, cont **-ing**) frapper à coups de trique.

cue [kju:] **n 1.** RADIO, THEAT & TV signal *m* ▸ **on cue** au bon moment ▸ **to take one's cue from sb** emboîter le pas à qqn **2.** *fig* [stimulus] signe *m* ▸ **this could be the cue for a recovery** cela pourrait marquer le début d'une amélioration **3.** [in snooker, pool] queue *f* (de billard).

cuff [kʌf] ■ **n 1.** [of sleeve] poignet *m* ▸ **off the cuff** au pied levé **2.** *US* [of trouser] revers *m inv* **3.** [blow] gifle *f*.
■ **vt** gifler.

cuff link **n** bouton *m* de manchette.

cu. in. abbr of ***cubic inch(es)***.

cuisine [kwɪ'zi:n] **n** cuisine *f*.

cul-de-sac ['kʌldəsæk] **n** cul-de-sac *m*.

culinary ['kʌlɪnərɪ] **adj** culinaire.

cull [kʌl] ■ **n** massacre *m*.
■ **vt 1.** [kill] massacrer **2.** [gather] recueillir.

culminate ['kʌlmɪneɪt] **vi : to culminate in sthg** se terminer par qqch, aboutir à qqch.

culmination [ˌkʌlmɪ'neɪʃn] **n** apogée *m*.

culottes [kju:'lɒts] **npl** jupe-culotte *f*.

culpable ['kʌlpəbl] **adj** coupable.

culprit ['kʌlprɪt] **n** coupable *mf*.

cult [kʌlt] ■ **n** culte *m*.
■ **comp** culte.

cultivate ['kʌltɪveɪt] **vt** cultiver.

cultivated ['kʌltɪveɪtɪd] **adj** cultivé(e).

cultivation [ˌkʌltɪ'veɪʃn] **n** *(U)* [farming] culture *f*.

cultural ['kʌltʃərəl] **adj** culturel(elle).

culturally ['kʌltʃərəlɪ] **adv** culturellement.

culture ['kʌltʃəʳ] **n** culture *f*.

cultured ['kʌltʃəd] **adj** [educated] cultivé(e).

cultured pearl **n** perle *f* de culture.

culture gap **n** fossé *m* culturel.

culture shock **n** choc *m* culturel.

culture vulture **n** *inf hum* fana *mf* de culture.

culvert ['kʌlvət] **n** conduit *m*.

cumbersome ['kʌmbəsəm] **adj 1.** [object] encombrant(e) **2.** [system] lourd(e).

cumin ['kʌmɪn] **n** cumin *m*.

cumulative ['kju:mjʊlətɪv] **adj** cumulatif(ive).

cunning ['kʌnɪŋ] ■ **adj 1.** [shrewd] astucieux(euse), malin(igne) ⁄ *pej* rusé(e), fourbe **2.** [skilful] habile, astucieux(euse).
■ **n** *(U)* **1.** [guile] finesse *f*, astuce *f* ⁄ *pej* ruse *f*, fourberie *f* **2.** [skill] habileté *f*, adresse *f*.

cunningly ['kʌnɪŋlɪ] **adv 1.** [shrewdly] astucieusement, finement ⁄ *pej* avec ruse OR fourberie **2.** [skilfully] habilement, astucieusement.

cup [kʌp] ■ **n 1.** [container, unit of measurement] tasse *f* ▸ **a cup of coffee** une tasse de café **2.** [prize, competition] coupe *f* **3.** [of bra] bonnet *m*.
■ **vt** (pt & pp **-ped**, cont **-ping**) [hands] mettre en coupe ▸ **to cup one's hands around sthg** mettre ses mains autour de qqch.

cupboard ['kʌbəd] **n** placard *m*.

cup final **n** SPORT finale *f* de la coupe ▸ **the Cup Final** *UK* la finale de la Coupe de Football.

cup finalist **n** SPORT finaliste *mf* de la coupe.

cup holder **n** SPORT détenteur *m* de la coupe.

cupid ['kju:pɪd] **n** [figure] amour *m*.

cupola ['kju:pələ] (pl **-s**) **n** coupole *f*.

cup tie **n** *UK* match *m* de coupe.

curable ['kjʊərəbl] **adj** curable, guérissable.

curate ['kjʊərət] **n** *UK* vicaire *m*.

curator [ˌkjʊə'reɪtəʳ] **n** conservateur *m*, -trice *f*.

curb [kɜ:b] ■ **n 1.** [control] **: curb (on)** frein *m* (à) **2.** *US* [of road] bord *m* du trottoir.
■ **vt** mettre un frein à.

curd cheese **n** *UK* ≃ fromage *m* blanc.

curdle ['kɜ:dl] **vi** cailler.

cure [kjʊəʳ] ■ **n : cure (for)** MED remède *m* (contre) ⁄ *fig* remède *m* (à).
■ **vt 1.** MED guérir **2.** [solve - problem] éliminer **3.** [rid] **: to cure sb of sthg** guérir qqn de qqch, faire perdre l'habitude de qqch à qqn **4.** [preserve - by smoking] fumer ⁄ [- by salting] saler ⁄ [- tobacco, hide] sécher.

cure-all **n** panacée *f*.

curfew ['kɜ:fju:] **n** couvre-feu *m*.

curio ['kjʊərɪəʊ] (pl **-s**) **n** bibelot *m*.

curiosity [ˌkjʊərɪ'ɒsətɪ] **n** curiosité *f*.

curious ['kjʊərɪəs] **adj : curious (about)** curieux(euse) (à propos de).

curiously ['kjʊərɪəslɪ] **adv 1.** [inquisitively] avec curiosité **2.** [strangely] curieusement ▸ **curiously enough** curieusement, chose curieuse.

curl [kɜ:l] ■ **n 1.** [of hair] boucle *f* **2.** [of smoke] volute *f*.
■ **vt 1.** [hair] boucler **2.** [roll up] enrouler.
■ **vi 1.** [hair] boucler **2.** [roll up] s'enrouler ▸ **to curl into a ball** se mettre en boule.
◆ ***curl up*** **vi** [person, animal] se mettre en boule, se pelotonner.

curler ['kɜ:ləʳ] **n** bigoudi *m*.

curling ['kɜ:lɪŋ] **n** curling *m*.

curling iron **n** *US* fer *m* à friser.

curling tongs **npl** *UK* fer *m* à friser.

curly ['kɜ:lɪ] (comp **-ier**, superl **-iest**) **adj** [hair] bouclé(e).

currant ['kʌrənt] **n** [dried grape] raisin *m* de Corinthe, raisin sec.

currency ['kʌrənsɪ] (pl **-ies**) **n 1.** [type of money] monnaie *f* **2.** *(U)* [money] devise *f* **3.** *fml* [acceptability] **: to gain currency** s'accréditer.

current ['kʌrənt] ■ **adj** [price, method] actuel(elle) ⁄ [year, week] en cours ⁄ [boyfriend, girlfriend] du moment ▸ **current issue** dernier numéro.
■ **n 1.** [of water, air, electricity] courant *m* ▸ **alternating/direct current** courant *m* alternatif/continu **2.** [trend] tendance *f*.

current account **n** *UK* compte *m* courant.

current affairs **npl** actualité *f*, questions *fpl* d'actualité.

current assets **npl** actif *m* circulant.

current liabilities **npl** passif *m* exigible à court terme.

currently ['kʌrəntlɪ] **adv** actuellement.

curricular [kə'rɪkjələr] **adj** au programme.

curriculum [kə'rɪkjələm] (pl **-lums** *OR* **-la** [-lə]) **n** programme *m* d'études.

curriculum vitae [-'vi:taɪ] (pl **curricula vitae**) **n** curriculum vitae *m*.

curried ['kʌrɪd] **adj** au curry.

curry ['kʌrɪ] (pl **-ies**) **n** curry *m*.

curry powder **n** poudre *f* de curry.

curse [kɜ:s] ■ **n 1.** [evil spell] malédiction *f* / *fig* fléau *m* **2.** [swearword] juron *m*.
■ **vt** maudire.
■ **vi** jurer.

cursor ['kɜ:sər] **n** COMPUT curseur *m*.

cursory ['kɜ:sərɪ] **adj** superficiel(elle).

curt [kɜ:t] **adj** brusque.

curtail [kɜ:'teɪl] **vt 1.** [visit] écourter **2.** [rights, expenditure] réduire.

curtailment [kɜ:'teɪlmənt] **n** [of rights, expenditure] réduction *f*.

curtain ['kɜ:tn] **n** rideau *m*.
◆ ***curtain off*** **vt sep** [bed] cacher derrière un rideau / [room] diviser par un rideau.

curtain call **n** rappel *m*.

curtain raiser **n** *fig* lever *m* de rideau.

curts(e)y ['kɜ:tsɪ] (pt & pp **curtsied**) ■ **n** révérence *f*.
■ **vi** faire une révérence.

curvaceous [kɜ:'veɪʃəs] **adj** *inf* bien roulé(e).

curvature ['kɜ:vətjər] **n** courbure *f* / MED [of spine] déviation *f*.

curve [kɜ:v] ■ **n** courbe *f*.
■ **vi** faire une courbe.

curved [kɜ:vd] **adj** courbe.

curvy ['kɜ:vɪ] (comp **-ier**, superl **-iest**) **adj** [line] courbé(e) / [woman] bien roulée.

cushion ['kʊʃn] ■ **n** coussin *m*.
■ **vt** [fall, blow, effects] amortir ▸ **to be cushioned against** [inflation, reality] être paré contre.

cushy ['kʊʃɪ] (comp **-ier**, superl **-iest**) **adj** *inf* pépère, peinard(e).

custard ['kʌstəd] **n** *UK* crème *f* anglaise.

custard pie **n** tarte *f* à la crème.

custard powder **n** *UK* crème *f* anglaise instantanée en poudre.

custodial [kʌ'stəʊdjəl] **adj 1.** LAW de prison ▸ **custodial sentence** peine *f* de prison **2.** [guarding] **: custodial staff** personnel *m* de surveillance.

custodian [kʌ'stəʊdjən] **n** [of building] gardien *m*, -enne *f* / [of museum] conservateur *m*.

custody ['kʌstədɪ] **n 1.** [of child] garde *f* ▸ **to be given** *OR* **awarded custody of a child** LAW obtenir la garde d'un enfant **2.** LAW **: in custody** en garde à vue ▸ **he was taken into (police) custody** il a été mis en état d'arrestation.

custom ['kʌstəm] **n 1.** [tradition, habit] coutume *f* **2.** COMM clientèle *f* ▸ **thank you for your custom** merci de nous avoir honorés de votre commande.
◆ ***customs*** **n** [place] douane *f* ▸ **to go through customs** passer (à) la douane.

customary ['kʌstəmrɪ] **adj** [behaviour] coutumier(ère) / [way, time] habituel(elle).

custom-built **adj** fait(e) sur commande *OR* mesure.

customer ['kʌstəmər] **n 1.** [client] client *m*, -e *f* **2.** *inf* [person] type *m*.

customer base **n** base *f* de clientèle *OR* de consommateurs.

customer care **n** *qualité du service fourni à la clientèle.*

customer database **n** base *f* de données de consommateurs.

customer loyalty **n** fidélité *f* de la clientèle.

customer profile **n** profil *m* de la clientèle.

customer services **npl** service *m* (à la) clientèle.

customize, *UK* ***-ise*** ['kʌstəmaɪz] **vt** [make] fabriquer *OR* assembler sur commande / [modify] modifier sur commande.

custom-made **adj** fait(e) sur mesure.

Customs and Excise **n** *UK* ≃ service *m* des contributions indirectes.

customs duty **n** droit *m* de douane.

customs officer **n** douanier *m*, -ère *f*.

cut [kʌt] ■ **n 1.** [in wood] entaille *f* / [in skin] coupure *f* ▸ **to make a cut in sthg** [with knife, scissors] faire une entaille dans qqch ▸ **she had a nasty cut on her leg** elle s'était fait une vilaine entaille à la jambe
2. [of meat] morceau *m*
3. [reduction] **: cut (in)** [taxes, salary, personnel] réduction *f* (de) / [film, article] coupure *f* (dans) ▸ **a cut in government spending** une réduction *OR* diminution des dépenses publiques ▸ **budget cuts** FIN compressions *fpl* budgétaires
4. *inf* [share] part *f*
5. [of suit, hair] coupe *f*
▸▸ **a cut above (the rest)** *inf* supérieur(e) aux autres.
■ **vt** (pt & pp **cut**, cont **-ting**) **1.** [gen] couper ▸ **to cut one's finger** se couper le doigt ▸ **cut the box open with the knife** ouvrez la boîte avec le couteau ▸ **she cut articles from the paper** elle découpait des articles dans le journal ▸ **cut the cake in half/in three pieces** coupez le gâteau en deux/en trois ▸ **I cut my nails/my hair** je me suis coupé les ongles/les cheveux ▸ **you've had your hair cut** vous vous êtes fait couper les cheveux
2. [taxes, costs, workforce] réduire ▸ **to cut prices** casser les prix ▸ **the athlete cut 5 seconds off the world record** *OR* **cut the world record by 5 seconds** l'athlète a amélioré le record mondial de 5 secondes
3. [interrupt] interrompre, couper ▸ **to cut sb short** couper la parole à qqn ▸ **we had to cut our visit short** nous avons dû écourter notre visite ▸ **to cut a long story short, I left** bref *OR* en deux mots, je suis parti

4. [subj: baby] **: he's cutting a tooth** il fait ses dents
5. *inf* [lecture, class] sécher.
■ vi (pt & pp cut, cont -ting) **1.** [gen] couper ▸ **cut around the edge** découpez *OR* coupez en suivant le bord ▸ **she cut into the bread** elle a entamé le pain
2. [intersect] se couper
3. COMPUT couper
4. CIN & TV [stop filming] couper / [change scenes] **: the film cuts straight from the love scene to the funeral** l'image passe directement de la scène d'amour à l'enterrement.
◆ ***cut across*** vt insep **1.** [as short cut] couper à travers ▸ **this path cuts across the swamp** ce sentier traverse *OR* coupe à travers le marécage
2. [transcend] ne pas tenir compte de.
◆ ***cut back*** ■ vt sep **1.** [prune] tailler
2. [reduce] réduire.
■ **vi : to cut back on** réduire, diminuer.
◆ ***cut down*** ■ vt sep **1.** [chop down] couper
2. [reduce] réduire, diminuer.
■ **vi : to cut down on smoking/eating/spending** fumer/manger/dépenser moins.
◆ ***cut in*** vi **1.** [interrupt] **: to cut in (on sb)** interrompre (qqn)
2. AUT & SPORT se rabattre.
◆ ***cut off*** vt sep **1.** [piece, crust] couper
2. [finger, leg - subj: surgeon] amputer
3. [power, telephone, funding] couper
4. [separate] **: to be cut off (from)** [person] être coupé(e) (de) / [village] être isolé(e) (de).
◆ ***cut out*** ■ vt sep **1.** [photo, article] découper / [sewing pattern] couper / [dress] tailler ▸ **to be cut out for sthg** *fig* [person] être fait pour qqch
2. [stop] **: to cut out smoking/chocolates** arrêter de fumer/de manger des chocolats ▸ **cut it out!** *inf* ça suffit!
3. [exclude] exclure.
■ vi [stall] caler.
◆ ***cut up*** vt sep [chop up] couper, hacher.

cut-and-dried adj tout fait (toute faite).

cut-and-paste vt & vi COMPUT couper-coller.

cut and thrust n **: the cut and thrust of parliamentary debate** les joutes oratoires des débats parlementaires ▸ **it's cut and thrust** la lutte est acharnée.

cutback ['kʌtbæk] **n : cutback (in)** réduction *f* (de).

cute [kju:t] adj [appealing] mignon(onne).

cut glass ■ n cristal *m* taillé.
■ comp en cristal taillé.

cuticle ['kju:tɪkl] n envie *f*.

cutlery ['kʌtlərɪ] n *(U)* couverts *mpl*.

cutlet ['kʌtlɪt] n côtelette *f*.

cutoff (point) ['kʌtof-] n [limit] point *m* de limite.

cutout ['kʌtaʊt] n **1.** [on machine] disjoncteur *m* **2.** [shape] découpage *m*.

cut-price *UK*, ***cut-rate*** *US* adj à prix réduit.

cutter ['kʌtəʳ] n [tool] coupoir *m*.

cutthroat ['kʌtθrəʊt] adj [ruthless] acharné(e).

cutting ['kʌtɪŋ] ■ adj [sarcastic - remark] cinglant(e) / [- wit] acerbe.
■ n **1.** [of plant] bouture *f* **2.** *UK* [from newspaper] coupure *f* **3.** *UK* [for road, railway] tranchée *f*.

cutting board n *US* planche *f* à découper.

cuttlefish ['kʌtlfɪʃ] (pl **cuttlefish**) n seiche *f*.

cut up adj *UK inf* [upset] affligé(e).

CV (abbr of ***curriculum vitae***) n CV *m*.

cwo (abbr of ***cash with order***) *payable à la commande*.

cwt. abbr of ***hundredweight***.

cyanide ['saɪənaɪd] n cyanure *m*.

cybercafé ['saɪbə,kæfeɪ] n cybercafé *m*.

cybercrime ['saɪbə,kraɪm] n délinquance *f* informatique.

cyberculture ['saɪbə,kʌltʃəʳ] n cyberculture *f*.

cybernaut ['saɪbə,nɔ:t] n cybernaute *mf*.

cybernetics [,saɪbə'netɪks] n *(U)* cybernétique *f*.

cyberpet ['saɪbə,pet] n animal *m* virtuel.

cyberpunk ['saɪbə,pʌnk] n cyberpunk *m*.

cyberspace ['saɪbəspeɪs] n cyberespace *m*.

cybersquatting ['saɪbəskwɒtɪŋ] n COMPUT cybersquatting *m*.

cybersurfer ['saɪbə,sɜ:fəʳ] n cybernaute *mf*.

cyborg ['saɪbɔ:g] n cyborg *m*.

cyclamen ['sɪkləmən] (pl **cyclamen**) n cyclamen *m*.

cycle ['saɪkl] ■ n **1.** [of events, songs] cycle *m* **2.** [bicycle] bicyclette *f*.
■ comp [path, track] cyclable / [race] cycliste / [shop] de cycles.
■ vi faire de la bicyclette.

cyclic(al) ['saɪklɪk(l)] adj cyclique.

cycling ['saɪklɪŋ] n cyclisme *m*.

cyclist ['saɪklɪst] n cycliste *mf*.

cyclone ['saɪkləʊn] n cyclone *m*.

cygnet ['sɪgnɪt] n jeune cygne *m*.

cylinder ['sɪlɪndəʳ] n cylindre *m*.

cylinder block n bloc-cylindres *m*.

cylinder head n culasse *f*.

cylinder-head gasket n joint *m* de culasse.

cylindrical [sɪ'lɪndrɪkl] adj cylindrique.

cymbal ['sɪmbl] n cymbale *f*.

cynic ['sɪnɪk] n cynique *mf*.

cynical ['sɪnɪkl] adj cynique.

cynically ['sɪnɪklɪ] adv cyniquement.

cynicism ['sɪnɪsɪzm] n cynisme *m*.

CYO (abbr of ***Catholic Youth Organization***) n *aux États-Unis, association de jeunes catholiques*.

cypher ['saɪfəʳ] *UK* = ***cipher***.

cypress ['saɪprəs] n cyprès *m*.

Cypriot ['sɪprɪət] ■ **adj** chypriote.
■ **n** Chypriote *mf* ▶ **Greek/Turkish Cypriot** Chypriote grec (grecque)/turc (turque).

Cyprus ['saɪprəs] **n** Chypre *f* ▶ **in Cyprus** à Chypre.

cyst [sɪst] **n** kyste *m*.

cystic fibrosis [ˌsɪstɪkfaɪ'brəʊsɪs] **n** mucoviscidose *f*.

cystitis [sɪs'taɪtɪs] **n** cystite *f*.

cytology [saɪ'tɒlədʒɪ] **n** cytologie *f*.

CZ (abbr of ***canal zone***) *zone du canal de Panama*.

czar [zɑːʳ] **n** [sovereign] tsar *m* / [top person] éminence *f* grise, ponte *m*.

Czech [tʃek] ■ **adj** tchèque.
■ **n 1.** [person] Tchèque *mf* **2.** [language] tchèque *m*.

Czechoslovak [ˌtʃekə'sləʊvæk] = ***Czechoslovakian***.

Czechoslovakia [ˌtʃekəslə'vækɪə] **n** Tchécoslovaquie *f* ▶ **in Czechoslovakia** en Tchécoslovaquie.

Czechoslovakian [ˌtʃekəslə'vækɪən] ■ **adj** tchécoslovaque.
■ **n** Tchécoslovaque *mf*.

Czech Republic **n** République *f* tchèque.

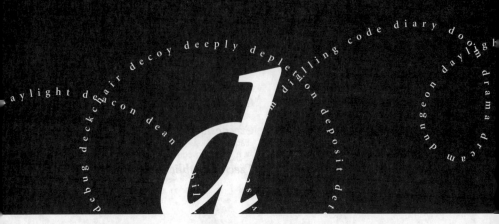

d[1] [diː] (pl **d's** *OR* **ds**), ***D***[1] (pl **D's** *OR* **Ds**) **n** [letter] d *m inv*, D *m inv*.

◆ ***D*** **n 1.** MUS ré *m* **2.** SCH [mark] D *m inv*.

d[2] [diː] (abbr of ***penny***) *symbole du penny anglais jusqu'en 1971*.

D[2] *US* abbr of ***Democrat***, ***Democratic***.

d. (abbr of ***died***) **: d. 1913** mort en 1913.

DA abbr of ***district attorney***.

dab [dæb] ■ **n** [of cream, powder, ointment] petit peu *m* / [of paint] touche *f*.
■ **vt** (pt & pp **-bed**, cont **-bing**) **1.** [skin, wound] tamponner **2.** [apply - cream, ointment] **: to dab sthg on** *OR* **onto** appliquer qqch sur.
■ **vi** (pt & pp **-bed**, cont **-bing**) **: to dab at sthg** tamponner qqch.

dabble ['dæbl] ■ **vt** tremper dans l'eau.
■ **vi : to dabble in** toucher un peu à.

dabbler ['dæbləʳ] **n** dilettante *mf*.

dab hand **n** *UK* **: to be a dab hand (at sthg)** être doué(e) (pour qqch).

Dacca ['dækə] **n** Dacca.

dachshund ['dækshʊnd] **n** teckel *m*.

dad [dæd], ***daddy*** ['dædɪ] (pl **-ies**) **n** *inf* papa *m*.

daddy longlegs [-'lɒŋlegz] (pl **daddy longlegs**) **n** faucheur *m*.

daffodil ['dæfədɪl] **n** jonquille *f*.

daft [dɑːft] **adj** *UK inf* stupide, idiot(e).

dagger ['dægəʳ] **n** poignard *m*.

dahlia ['deɪljə] **n** dahlia *m*.

daily ['deɪlɪ] ■ **adj 1.** [occurrence] quotidien(enne) ▸ **a daily paper** un quotidien ▸ **to be paid on a daily basis** être payé à la journée **2.** [rate, output] journalier(ère).
■ **adv** [happen, write] quotidiennement ▸ **twice daily** deux fois par jour.
■ **n** (pl **-ies**) **1.** [newspaper] quotidien *m* **2.** *UK* [cleaning woman] femme *f* de ménage.

daintily ['deɪntɪlɪ] **adv** [eat, walk] délicatement / [dressed] coquettement.

dainty ['deɪntɪ] (comp **-ier**, superl **-iest**) **adj** délicat(e).

dairy ['deərɪ] (pl **-ies**) **n 1.** [on farm] laiterie *f* **2.** [shop] crémerie *f*.

dairy cattle **npl** vaches *fpl* laitières.

dairy farm **n** ferme *f* laitière.

dairy products **npl** produits *mpl* laitiers.

dais ['deɪɪs] **n** estrade *f*.

daisy ['deɪzɪ] (pl **-ies**) **n** [weed] pâquerette *f* / [cultivated] marguerite *f*.

daisy wheel **n** marguerite *f*.

daisy-wheel printer **n** imprimante *f* à marguerite.

Dakar ['dækɑːʳ] **n** Dakar.

Dakota [də'kəʊtə] **n** Dakota *m* ▸ **in Dakota** dans le Dakota.

dal [dɑːl] = ***dhal***.

dale [deɪl] **n** vallée *f*.

dalmatian [dæl'meɪʃn] **n** [dog] dalmatien *m*.

dam [dæm] ■ **n** [across river] barrage *m*.
■ **vt** (pt & pp **-med**, cont **-ming**) construire un barrage sur
◆ ***dam up*** **vt sep** endiguer.

damage ['dæmɪdʒ] ■ **n 1.** [physical harm] dommage *m* dégât *m* ▸ **damage to property** dégâts *mpl* matériel **2.** [harmful effect] tort *m*.
■ **vt 1.** [harm physically] endommager, abîmer **2.** [hav harmful effect on] nuire à.
◆ ***damages*** **npl** LAW dommages et intérêts *mpl* ▸ **t award damages to sb for sthg** accorder des dommage et intérêts à qqn pour qqch.

damaging ['dæmɪdʒɪŋ] **adj : damaging (to)** préjudiciable (à).

Damascus [də'mæskəs] **n** Damas.

Dame [deɪm] **n** *UK titre accordé aux femmes titulaires d certaines décorations*.

dammit ['dæmɪt] **excl** *inf* mince ▸ **as near as dammi** *UK* à un cheveu près.

damn [dæm] ■ **adj** *inf* fichu(e), sacré(e).
■ **adv** *inf* sacrément.
■ **n** *inf* : **not to give** OR **care a damn (about sthg)** se ficher pas mal (de qqch).
■ **vt 1.** RELIG [condemn] damner **2.** *inf* [curse] : **damn you!** va au diable! ▸ **damn it!** zut!
■ **excl** *inf* zut!

damnable ['dæmnəbl] **adj** *dated* [appalling] détestable.

damnation [dæm'neɪʃn] **n** RELIG damnation *f*.

damned [dæmd] *inf* ■ **adj** fichu(e), sacré(e) ▸ **I'm damned if...** si tu crois que... ▸ **well I'll be** *US* OR **I'm damned!** *UK* c'est trop fort!, elle est bien bonne celle-là!
■ **adv** sacrément.

damnedest ['dæmdəst] *inf* ■ **n** [utmost] : **he did his damnedest to ruin the party** il a vraiment fait tout ce qu'il pouvait pour gâcher la soirée.
■ **adj** *US* incroyable.

damn-fool **adj** *inf* crétin(e), idiot(e).

damning ['dæmɪŋ] **adj** accablant(e).

damp [dæmp] ■ **adj** humide.
■ **n** humidité *f*.
■ **vt** [make wet] humecter.
◆ ***damp down*** **vt sep** [restrain - unrest, violence] contenir, maîtriser / [- enthusiasm] refroidir.

damp course **n** *UK* couche *f* d'étanchéité.

dampen ['dæmpən] **vt 1.** [make wet] humecter **2.** *fig* [emotion] abattre.

damper ['dæmpəʳ] **n 1.** MUS étouffoir *m* **2.** [for fire] registre *m*
▸▸ **to put a damper on sthg** jeter un froid sur qqch.

dampness ['dæmpnɪs] **n** humidité *f*.

damp-proof **adj** protégé(e) contre l'humidité, hydrofuge ▸ **damp-proof course** CONSTR couche *f* d'étanchéité.

damp squib **n** *UK inf* déception *f*.

damson ['dæmzn] **n** prune *f* de Damas.

dance [dɑːns] ■ **n 1.** [gen] danse *f* **2.** [social event] bal *m*.
■ **vi** danser ▸ **to dance with sb** danser avec qqn.

dance floor **n** piste *f* de danse.

dancer ['dɑːnsəʳ] **n** danseur *m*, -euse *f*.

dancing ['dɑːnsɪŋ] **n** *(U)* danse *f*.

D and C (abbr of ***dilation and curettage***) **n** *dilatation et curetage*.

dandelion ['dændɪlaɪən] **n** pissenlit *m*.

dandruff ['dændrʌf] **n** *(U)* pellicules *fpl*.

dandy ['dændɪ] (pl **-ies**) **n** dandy *m*.

Dane [deɪn] **n** Danois *m*, -e *f*.

danger ['deɪndʒəʳ] **n 1.** *(U)* [possibility of harm] danger *m* ▸ **'danger, keep out!'** 'danger, entrée interdite!' ▸ **in danger** en danger ▸ **out of danger** hors de danger **2.** [hazard, risk] : **danger (to)** risque *m* (pour) ▸ **to be in danger of doing sthg** risquer de faire qqch.

danger list **n** *UK* : **to be on the danger list** être dans un état critique.

danger money **n** *(U) UK* prime *f* de risque.

dangerous ['deɪndʒərəs] **adj** dangereux(euse).

dangerous driving **n** *UK* LAW conduite *f* dangereuse.

dangerously ['deɪndʒərəslɪ] **adv** dangereusement ▸ **dangerously ill** gravement malade.

danger zone **n** zone *f* dangereuse.

dangle ['dæŋgl] ■ **vt** laisser pendre.
■ **vi** pendre.

Danish ['deɪnɪʃ] ■ **adj** danois(e).
■ **n 1.** [language] danois *m* **2.** *US* = ***Danish pastry***.
■ **npl** : **the Danish** les Danois *mpl*.

Danish blue **n** [cheese] bleu *m* danois.

Danish pastry **n** *gâteau feuilleté fourré aux fruits*.

dank [dæŋk] **adj** humide et froid(e).

Danube ['dænjuːb] **n** : **the Danube** le Danube.

dapper ['dæpəʳ] **adj** pimpant(e).

dappled ['dæpld] **adj 1.** [light] tacheté(e) **2.** [horse] pommelé(e).

Dardanelles [ˌdɑːdə'nelz] **npl** : **the Dardanelles** les Dardanelles *fpl*.

dare [deəʳ] ■ **vt 1.** [be brave enough] : **to dare to do sthg** oser faire qqch ▸ **don't you dare!** je te le déconseille! **2.** [challenge] : **to dare sb to do sthg** défier qqn de faire qqch ▸ **I dare you!** chiche!
▸▸ **I dare say** je suppose, sans doute.
■ **vi** oser ▸ **how dare you!** comment osez-vous!
■ **n** défi *m* ▸ **to do sthg for a dare** faire qqch par défi.

daredevil ['deəˌdevl] **n** casse-cou *m inv*.

daren't [deənt] *UK* = ***dare not***.

Dar es-Salaam [ˌdɑːressə'lɑːm] **n** Dar es-Salaam.

daring ['deərɪŋ] ■ **adj** audacieux(euse).
■ **n** audace *f*.

daringly ['deərɪŋlɪ] **adv** audacieusement, hardiment ▸ **a daringly low neckline** un décolleté audacieux OR provocant.

dark [dɑːk] ■ **adj 1.** [room, night] sombre ▸ **it's getting dark** il commence à faire nuit **2.** [in colour] foncé(e) ▸ **dark chocolate** chocolat *m* noir **3.** [dark-haired] brun(e) / [dark-skinned] basané(e) ▸ **to have dark hair** avoir les cheveux bruns, être brun **4.** *fig* [days, thoughts] sombre, triste / [look] noir(e).
■ **n 1.** [darkness] : **the dark** l'obscurité *f* ▸ **to see in the dark** voir dans le noir ▸ **to be afraid of the dark** avoir peur du noir ▸ **to be in the dark about sthg** ignorer tout de qqch **2.** [night] : **before/after dark** avant/après la tombée de la nuit.

Dark Ages **npl** : **the Dark Ages** le haut Moyen Âge.

darken ['dɑːkn] ■ **vt** assombrir.
■ **vi** s'assombrir.

dark glasses **npl** lunettes *fpl* noires.

dark horse **n** *fig* quantité *f* inconnue.

darkish ['dɑːkɪʃ] **adj** [colour, sky, wood] plutôt OR assez sombre / [hair, skin] plutôt brun(e) OR foncé(e) / [person] plutôt brun(e).

darkly ['dɑːklɪ] **adv** [hint] énigmatiquement / [say] sur un ton sinistre.

darkness ['dɑːknɪs] **n** obscurité *f*.

darkroom ['dɑ:krʊm] **n** chambre *f* noire.

dark-skinned **adj** à la peau foncée.

darling ['dɑ:lɪŋ] ■ **adj 1.** [dear] chéri(e) **2.** *inf* [cute] adorable.
■ **n 1.** [loved person, term of address] chéri *m*, -e *f* **2.** [idol] chouchou *m*, idole *f*.

darn [dɑ:n] ■ **n** reprise *f*.
■ **vt** repriser.
■ **adj** *inf* sacré(e), satané(e).
■ **adv** *inf* sacrément.
■ **excl** *inf* zut!

darning ['dɑ:nɪŋ] **n** [work] reprisage *m*.

darning needle **n** aiguille *f* à repriser.

dart [dɑ:t] ■ **n 1.** [arrow] fléchette *f* **2.** SEW pince *f*.
■ **vt** darder.
■ **vi** se précipiter.
◆ ***darts*** **n** [game] jeu *m* de fléchettes.

dartboard ['dɑ:tbɔ:d] **n** cible *f* de jeu de fléchettes.

dash [dæʃ] ■ **n 1.** [of milk, wine] goutte *f* / [of cream] soupçon *m* / [of salt] pincée *f* / [of colour, paint] touche *f* **2.** [in punctuation] tiret *m* **3.** AUT tableau *m* de bord **4.** [rush] : **to make a dash for** se ruer vers.
■ **vt** [throw] jeter avec violence ▶ **several boats were dashed against the cliffs** plusieurs bateaux ont été projetés *OR* précipités contre les falaises ▶ **to dash sb's hopes** réduire les espoirs de qqn à néant.
■ **vi** se précipiter ▶ **I must dash!** je dois me sauver!
◆ ***dash off*** **vt sep** [write quickly] écrire en vitesse.

dashboard ['dæʃbɔ:d] **n** tableau *m* de bord.

dashing ['dæʃɪŋ] **adj** fringant(e).

dastardly ['dæstədlɪ] **adj** *dated* odieux, infâme.

DAT [dæt] (abbr of ***digital audio tape***) **n** DAT *m*.

data ['deɪtə] **n** *(U)* données *fpl*.

data bank **n** banque *f* de données.

database ['deɪtəbeɪs] **n** base *f* de données.

data capture **n** saisie *f* de données.

dataglove ['deɪtəglʌv] **n** gant *m* numérique.

data processing **n** traitement *m* de données.

data protection **n** protection *f* de l'information.

Data Protection Act **n** loi *f* sur la protection de l'information *(en Grande-Bretagne)*.

data transmission **n** transmission *f* de données.

date [deɪt] ■ **n 1.** [in time] date *f* ▶ **what's the date today?, what's today's date?** quelle est la date aujourd'hui?, le combien sommes-nous aujourd'hui? ▶ **today's date is the 20th January** nous sommes le 20 janvier ▶ **would you be free on that date?** est-ce que vous seriez libre ce jour-là *OR* à cette date? ▶ **to set a date** fixer une date / [engaged couple] fixer la date de son mariage ▶ **at a later *OR* some future date** plus tard, ultérieurement *fml* ▶ **to date** à ce jour **2.** [appointment] rendez-vous *m inv* ▶ **let's make a date for lunch** prenons rendez-vous pour déjeuner ensemble ▶ **to go out on a date** sortir en compagnie de quelqu'un **3.** [person] petit ami *m*, petite amie *f* ▶ **who's your date tonight?** avec qui sors-tu ce soir? **4.** [fruit] datte *f*.
■ **vt 1.** [gen] dater ▶ **a fax dated May 6th** un fax daté du 6 mai **2.** [go out with] sortir avec.
■ **vi 1.** [go out of fashion] dater **2.** [go out on dates] sortir avec des garçons/filles ▶ **how long have you two been dating?** ça fait combien de temps que vous sortez ensemble *OR* que vous vous voyez?
◆ ***date back to, date from*** **vt insep** dater de.

datebook ['deɪtbʊk] **n** *US* agenda *m*.

dated ['deɪtɪd] **adj** qui date.

date line **n** ligne *f* de changement de date.

date of birth **n** date *f* de naissance.

date rape **n** *viol commis par une personne connue de la victime.*

datestamp ['deɪtstæmp] ■ **n** tampon *m* dateur / [used for cancelling] oblitérateur *m*, timbre *m* à date / [postmark] cachet *m* de la poste.
■ **vt** [book] tamponner, mettre le cachet de la date sur / [letter] oblitérer.

dating ['deɪtɪŋ] **n** [of building, artefact] datation *f*.

daub [dɔ:b] **vt : to daub sthg with sthg** barbouiller qqch de qqch.

daughter ['dɔ:təʳ] **n** fille *f*.

daughter-in-law (pl **daughters-in-law**) **n** belle-fille *f*.

daunt [dɔ:nt] **vt** intimider.

daunting ['dɔ:ntɪŋ] **adj** intimidant(e).

dauntless ['dɔ:ntlɪs] **adj** déterminé(e).

dawdle ['dɔ:dl] **vi** flâner.

dawdler ['dɔ:dləʳ] **n** lambin *m*, -e *f*, traînard *m*, -e *f*.

dawdling ['dɔ:dlɪŋ] ■ **n : stop all this dawdling!** arrête de traînasser!
■ **adj** traînard.

dawn [dɔ:n] ■ **n** *liter & fig* aube *f* ▶ **at dawn** à l'aube ▶ **from dawn to dusk** du matin au soir.
■ **vi 1.** [day] poindre **2.** [era, period] naître.
◆ ***dawn (up)on*** **vt insep** venir à l'esprit de.

dawn chorus **n** *esp UK* concert *m* des oiseaux à l'aube.

dawn raid **n** descente *f* à l'aube / [by police] descente *OR* rafle *f* à l'aube / FIN attaque *f* à l'ouverture.

day [deɪ] **n 1.** jour *m* / [duration] journée *f* ▶ **it's a nice *OR* fine day** c'est une belle journée, il fait beau aujourd'hu[i] ▶ **what day is it (today)?** quel jour sommes-nous (aujourd'hui)? ▶ **(on) that day** ce jour-là ▶ **(on) the day (that *OR* when) she was born** le jour où elle est née ▶ **the day before** la veille ▶ **the day after** le lendemain ▶ **the day before yesterday** avant-hier ▶ **the day after tomorrow** après-demain ▶ **all day (long)** toute la journée ▶ **any day now** d'un jour à l'autre ▶ **one day, some day, one of these days** un jour (ou l'autre), un de ces jours ▶ **day after day, day in day out** jour après jour ▶ **day and night** jour et nui[t] ▶ **to call it a day** laisser tomber ▶ **to make sb's day** réchauffer le cœur de qqn ▶ **to save money for a rainy day** mettre de l'argent de côté en cas de besoin **2.** *(often p[l])* [lifetime, era] époque *f* ▶ **in days to come** à l'avenir ▶ **i[n] days gone by** par le passé ▶ **in the good old days** dans l[e] temps ▶ **in my/our day** de mon/notre temps ▶ **the happiest/worst days of my life** les plus beaux/les pires jours d[e] ma vie ▶ **what are you up to these days?** qu'est-ce qu[e] tu fais de beau ces temps-ci? ▶ **honestly, teenagers these days!** vraiment, les adolescents d'aujourd'hui! ▶ **thos[e]**

were the days c'était le bon temps ▸ **his days are numbered** ses jours sont comptés ▸ **it's early days yet** ce n'est que le début.
◆ ***days*** **adv** le jour.

CONFUSABLE / PARONYME
day
When translating **day**, note that *jour* and *journée* are not interchangeable. *Jour* is used to refer to a day as a distinct unit of time, while *journée* emphasises duration.

daybook ['deɪbʊk] **n** main *f* courante, journal *m*.

dayboy ['deɪbɔɪ] **n** *UK* SCH externe *m*.

daybreak ['deɪbreɪk] **n** aube *f* ▸ **at daybreak** à l'aube.

day care **n** [for elderly, disabled] service *m* d'accueil de jour / [for children] service *m* de garderie.
◆ ***day-care*** **adj** [facilities - for elderly, disabled] d'accueil de jour / [- for children] de garderie.

day-care centre *UK*, ***day-care center*** *US* **n** **1.** *UK centre d'animation et d'aide sociale* **2.** *US* garderie *f*.

day centre *UK*, ***day center*** *US* **n** *centre d'animation et d'aide sociale*.

daydream ['deɪdri:m] ■ **n** rêverie *f*.
■ **vi** rêvasser.

daydreamer ['deɪdri:mər] **n** rêveur *m*, -euse *f*.

daygirl ['deɪgɜ:l] **n** *UK* SCH externe *f*.

Day-Glo® ['deɪgləʊ] **adj** fluorescent(e).

daylight ['deɪlaɪt] **n** **1.** [light] lumière *f* du jour **2.** [dawn] aube *f*
▸▸ **to scare the (living) daylights out of sb** *inf* faire une peur bleue à qqn.

daylight robbery **n** : **that's daylight robbery** *UK inf* c'est du vol manifeste.

daylight saving time **n** heure *f* d'été.

day nursery **n** *UK* garderie *f*, crèche *f*.

day off (pl **days off**) **n** jour *m* de congé.

day pupil **n** *UK* SCH externe *mf*.

day release **n** *UK jour de formation*.

day return **n** *UK billet aller et retour valable pour une journée*.

dayroom ['deɪru:m] **n** salle *f* commune.

day school **n** externat *m*.

day shift **n** équipe *f* de jour.

daytime ['deɪtaɪm] ■ **n** jour *m*, journée *f*.
■ **comp** [job, flight] de jour.

daytime television **n** émissions *fpl* télévisées pendant la journée.

day-to-day **adj** [routine, life] journalier(ère) ▸ **on a day-to-day basis** au jour le jour.

day trip **n** excursion *f* d'une journée.

day tripper **n** excursionniste *mf*.

daze [deɪz] ■ **n** : **in a daze** hébété(e), ahuri(e).
■ **vt** **1.** [subj: blow] étourdir **2.** *fig* [subj: shock, event] abasourdir, sidérer.

dazed [deɪzd] **adj** **1.** [by blow] étourdi(e) **2.** *fig* [by shock, event] abasourdi(e), sidéré(e).

dazzle ['dæzl] ■ **n** *(U)* éblouissement *m*.
■ **vt** éblouir.

dazzling ['dæzlɪŋ] **adj** éblouissant(e).

DBE (abbr of ***Dame Commander of the Order of the British Empire***) **n** *distinction honorifique britannique pour les femmes*.

DBS (abbr of ***direct broadcasting by satellite***) **n** *télédiffusion directe par satellite*

DC[1] **n** (abbr of ***direct current***) courant *m* continu.

DC[2] abbr of ***District of Columbia***.

dd. abbr of ***delivered***.

DD (abbr of ***Doctor of Divinity***) **n** *UK docteur en théologie*.

D/D abbr of ***direct debit***.

D-day, ***D-Day*** ['di:deɪ] **n** *fig* & HIST le jour J.

DDS (abbr of ***Doctor of Dental Science***) **n** *UK docteur en dentisterie*.

DDT (abbr of ***dichlorodiphenyltrichloroethane***) **n** DDT *m*.

DE abbr of ***Delaware***.

DEA (abbr of ***Drug Enforcement Administration***) **n** *agence américaine de lutte contre la drogue*.

deacon ['di:kn] **n** diacre *m*.

deaconess [ˌdi:kə'nes] **n** diaconesse *f*.

deactivate [ˌdi:'æktɪveɪt] **vt** désamorcer.

dead [ded] ■ **adj** **1.** [not alive, not lively] mort(e) ▸ **dead or alive** mort ou vif ▸ **half dead with hunger/exhaustion** à demi mort de faim/d'épuisement ▸ **dead and buried** mort et enterré ▸ **the dead woman's husband** le mari de la défunte ▸ **to drop (down)** *OR* **to fall down dead** tomber mort ▸ **to shoot sb dead** abattre qqn ▸ **he wouldn't be seen dead doing that** il ne ferait cela pour rien au monde
2. [numb] engourdi(e)
3. [not operating - battery] à plat ▸ **the telephone's dead** il n'y a pas de tonalité
4. [complete - silence] de mort ▸ **dead calm** NAUT calme *m* plat ▸ **to come to a dead stop** s'arrêter net
5. [lacking activity - town] mort / [- business, market] très calme.
■ **adv** **1.** [directly, precisely] : **dead ahead** droit devant soi ▸ **dead on time** pile à l'heure ▸ **you're dead right** *UK inf* tu as entièrement raison
2. *inf* [completely] tout à fait ▸ **to be dead set against sthg** être tout à fait opposé à qqch ▸ **to be dead set on sthg** vouloir faire qqch à tout prix
3. [suddenly] : **to stop dead** s'arrêter net.
■ **n** : **in the dead of night/winter** au cœur de la nuit/de l'hiver.
■ **npl** : **the dead** les morts *mpl*.

dead beat **adj** *fig* crevé(e), mort(e).

deadbeat ['dedbi:t] **n** *US inf* flemmard *m*, -e *f*.

dead centre *UK*, ***dead center*** *US* **n** plein milieu *m*.

dead duck n : **it's a dead duck** *inf* c'est foutu, c'est fichu.

deaden ['dedn] vt [sound] assourdir / [pain] calmer.

dead end n impasse *f*.

dead-end job n travail *m* sans débouchés.

deadhead ['dedhed] vt enlever les fleurs fanées de.

dead heat n arrivée *f* ex-aequo.

dead letter n *fig* [rule, law] lettre *f* morte.

deadline ['dedlaɪn] n dernière limite *f*.

deadliness ['dedlɪnɪs] n [of poison, snake] caractère *m* mortel / [of weapon] caractère *m* meurtrier.

deadlock ['dedlɒk] n impasse *f*.

deadlocked ['dedlɒkt] adj dans une impasse.

dead loss n *UK inf* : **to be a dead loss** [person, thing] être complètement nul (nulle) à rien.

deadly ['dedlɪ] ■ adj (comp -ier, superl -iest) **1.** [poison, enemy] mortel(elle) **2.** [accuracy] imparable ▸ **in deadly earnest** [say] avec le plus grand sérieux.
■ adv [boring, serious] tout à fait ▸ **deadly pale** d'une pâleur mortelle.

deadly nightshade n *UK* belladone *f*.

deadpan ['dedpæn] ■ adj pince-sans-rire *(inv)*.
■ adv impassiblement.

dead ringer n *inf* sosie *m* ▸ **to be a dead ringer for sb** être le sosie de qqn.

Dead Sea n : **the Dead Sea** la mer Morte.

dead weight n *lit* & *fig* poids *m* mort.

dead wood *UK*, ***deadwood*** *US* ['dedwʊd] n *(U) fig* [people] personnes *fpl* improductives / [things, material] choses *fpl* inutiles.

deaf [def] ■ adj sourd(e) ▸ **to be deaf to sthg** être sourd à qqch.
■ npl : **the deaf** les sourds *mpl*.

deaf-and-dumb adj sourd-muet (sourde-muette).

deafen ['defn] vt assourdir.

deafening ['defnɪŋ] adj assourdissant(e).

deafeningly ['defnɪŋlɪ] adv : **deafeningly loud** assourdissant.

deaf-mute ■ adj sourd-muet (sourde-muette).
■ n sourd-muet *m*, sourde-muette *f*.

deafness ['defnɪs] n surdité *f*.

deal [di:l] ■ n **1.** [quantity] : **a good** *OR* **great deal** beaucoup ▸ **a good** *OR* **great deal of** beaucoup de, bien de/des ▸ **he thinks a great deal of her** il l'estime énormément ▸ **big deal!** *inf iro* tu parles d'un coup!, la belle affaire! ▸ **he made a big deal out of it** *inf* il en a fait tout un plat *OR* tout un cinéma
2. [business agreement] marché *m*, affaire *f* ▸ **to do** *OR* **strike a deal with sb** conclure un marché avec qqn ▸ **the deal is off** l'affaire est annulée, le marché est rompu ▸ **the government does not do deals with terrorists** le gouvernement ne traite pas avec les terroristes
3. *inf* [treatment] : **to get a bad deal** ne pas faire une affaire ▸ **to give sb a fair deal** traiter loyalement avec qqn.
■ vt (pt & pp dealt) **1.** [strike] : **to deal sb/sthg a blow, to deal a blow to sb/sthg** porter un coup à qqn/qqch
2. [cards] donner, distribuer
3. [drugs] revendre.
■ vi (pt & pp **dealt**) **1.** [at cards] donner, distribuer
2. [in drugs] faire le trafic (de drogues).
◆ ***deal in*** vt insep COMM faire le commerce de.
◆ ***deal out*** vt sep distribuer.
◆ ***deal with*** vt insep **1.** [handle] s'occuper de ▸ **a difficult child to deal with** un enfant difficile ▸ **I can't deal with all the work I've got** je ne me sors pas de tout le travail que j'ai ▸ **the management dealt with the situation promptly** la direction a réagi immédiatement
2. [be about] traiter de ▸ **in my lecture, I shall deal with...** dans mon cours, je traiterai de...
3. [do business with] traiter *OR* négocier avec.

dealer ['di:lər] n **1.** [trader] négociant *m* / [in drugs] trafiquant *m* **2.** [cards] donneur *m*.

dealership ['di:ləʃɪp] n concession *f*.

dealing ['di:lɪŋ] n commerce *m*.
◆ ***dealings*** npl relations *fpl*, rapports *mpl*.

dealt [delt] pt & pp ➤ ***deal***.

dean [di:n] n doyen *m*.

dear [dɪər] ■ adj : **dear (to)** cher (chère) (à) ▸ **Dear Sir** [in letter] Cher Monsieur ▸ **Dear Madam** Chère Madame ▸ **Dear Mrs Baker** Madame / [less formal] Chère Madame / [informal] Chère Madame Baker.
■ n chéri *m*, -e *f*.
■ excl : **oh dear!** mon Dieu!

dearly ['dɪəlɪ] adv [love, wish] de tout son cœur.

dearth [dɜ:θ] n pénurie *f*.

death [deθ] n mort *f* ▸ **to freeze/to starve to death** mourir de froid/de faim ▸ **to meet one's death** trouver la mort ▸ **to be put to death** être mis à mort, être exécuté ▸ **to frighten sb to death** faire une peur bleue à qqn ▸ **to worry sb to death** rendre qqn fou d'inquiétude ▸ **to be sick to death of sthg/of doing sthg** en avoir marre de qqch/de faire qqch ▸ **to be at death's door** être à l'article de la mort.

deathbed ['deθbed] n lit *m* de mort.

deathblow ['deθbləʊ] n *fig* coup *m* fatal *OR* mortel ▸ **to be the deathblow for sthg** porter un coup fatal *OR* mortel à qqch.

death certificate n acte *m* de décès.

death duty *UK*, ***death tax*** *US* n droits *mpl* de succession.

death knell n glas *m*.

deathly ['deθlɪ] ■ adj (comp -ier, superl -iest) de mort.
■ adv comme la mort.

death penalty n peine *f* de mort.

death rate n taux *m* de mortalité.

death row n *US* quartier *m* des condamnés à mort.

death sentence n condamnation *f* à mort.

death squad n escadron *m* de la mort.

death tax *US* = ***death duty***.

death throes [-ˌrəʊz] **npl** agonie *f* / [painful] affres *fpl* de la mort / *fig* agonie *f* ▸ **to be in one's death throes** agoniser, être agonisant / [suffering] connaître les affres de la mort ▸ **to be in its death throes** *fig* [project, business] agoniser, être agonisant.

death toll **n** nombre *m* de morts.

death trap **n** *inf* véhicule *m*/bâtiment *m* dangereux.

Death Valley **n** la Vallée de la Mort.

deathwatch beetle **n** vrillette *f*.

death wish **n** désir *m* de mort.

deb [deb] **n** *inf* débutante *f*.

débâcle, ***debacle*** [de'bɑ:kl] **n** débâcle *f*.

debar [di:'bɑ:ʳ] (pt & pp -red, cont -ring) **vt : to debar sb (from)** [place] exclure qqn (de) ▸ **to debar sb from doing sthg** interdire à qqn de faire qqch.

debase [dɪ'beɪs] **vt** dégrader ▸ **to debase o.s.** s'avilir.

debasement [dɪ'beɪsmənt] **n** dégradation *f* / [of person] avilissement *m*.

debatable [dɪ'beɪtəbl] **adj** discutable, contestable.

debate [dɪ'beɪt] ■ **n** débat *m* ▸ **there's been a lot of debate about it** cela a été très OR longuement débattu ▸ **open to debate** discutable.
■ **vt** débattre, discuter ▸ **to debate whether** s'interroger pour savoir si.
■ **vi** débattre.

debating society [dɪ'beɪtɪŋ-] **n** *UK* club *m* de débats.

debauched [dɪ'bɔ:tʃt] **adj** débauché(e).

debauchery [dɪ'bɔ:tʃərɪ] **n** débauche *f*.

debenture [dɪ'bentʃəʳ] **n** obligation *f* (sans garantie).

debenture stock **n** *UK* capital *m* obligations.

debilitate [dɪ'bɪlɪteɪt] **vt** débiliter, affaiblir.

debilitating [dɪ'bɪlɪteɪtɪŋ] **adj** débilitant(e).

debility [dɪ'bɪlətɪ] **n** débilité *f*, faiblesse *f*.

debit ['debɪt] ■ **n** débit *m*.
■ **vt** débiter.

debit account **n** compte *m* débiteur.

debit card **n** carte *f* de paiement à débit immédiat.

debit note **n** note *f* de débit.

debonair [ˌdebə'neəʳ] **adj** fringant(e).

debrief [ˌdi:'bri:f] **vt** faire faire un compte-rendu de mission à.

debriefing [ˌdi:'bri:fɪŋ] **n** compte-rendu *m* (de mission).

debris ['deɪbri:] **n** *(U)* débris *mpl*.

debt [det] **n** dette *f* ▸ **to be in debt** avoir des dettes, être endetté(e) ▸ **to get** OR **to run into debt** s'endetter ▸ **to be in sb's debt** être redevable à qqn ▸ **bad debt** mauvaise créance ▸ **outstanding debt** dette OR créance à recouvrer.

debt burden **n** surendettement *m*, fardeau *m* de la dette.

debt collector **n** agent *m* de recouvrements.

debtor ['detəʳ] **n** débiteur *m*, -trice *f*.

debt rescheduling, ***debt restructuring*** **n** rééchelonnement *m* des dettes.

debt-ridden **adj** criblé(e) de dettes.

debt trap **n** piège *m* de la dette.

debug [ˌdi:'bʌg] (pt & pp -ged, cont -ging) **vt 1.** [room] enlever les micros cachés dans **2.** COMPUT [program] mettre au point, déboguer.

debunk [ˌdi:'bʌŋk] **vt** démentir.

debut ['deɪbju:] **n** débuts *mpl*.

debutante ['debjʊtɑ:nt] **n** débutante *f*.

Dec. (abbr of ***December***) déc.

decade ['dekeɪd] **n** décennie *f*.

decadence ['dekədəns] **n** décadence *f*.

decadent ['dekədənt] **adj** décadent(e).

decaf(f) ['di:kæf] **n** *inf* déca *m*.

decaffeinated [dɪ'kæfɪneɪtɪd] **adj** décaféiné(e).

decal ['di:kæl] **n** *US* décalcomanie *f*.

decamp [dɪ'kæmp] **vi** *inf* décamper, filer.

decant [dɪ'kænt] **vt** décanter.

decanter [dɪ'kæntəʳ] **n** carafe *f*.

decapitate [dɪ'kæpɪteɪt] **vt** décapiter.

decathlete [dɪ'kæθli:t] **n** décathlonien *m*.

decathlon [dɪ'kæθlɒn] **n** décathlon *m*.

decay [dɪ'keɪ] ■ **n 1.** [of body, plant] pourriture *f*, putréfaction *f* / [of tooth] carie *f* **2.** *fig* [of building] délabrement *m* / [of society] décadence *f*.
■ **vi 1.** [rot] pourrir / [tooth] se carier **2.** *fig* [building] se délabrer, tomber en ruines / [society] tomber en décadence.

deceased [dɪ'si:st] ■ **adj** décédé(e).
■ **n** (pl **deceased**) **: the deceased** le défunt, la défunte.

deceit [dɪ'si:t] **n** tromperie *f*, supercherie *f*.

deceitful [dɪ'si:tfʊl] **adj** trompeur(euse), fourbe.

deceitfully [dɪ'si:tfʊlɪ] **adv** trompeusement, avec duplicité.

deceive [dɪ'si:v] **vt** [person] tromper, duper / [subj: memory, eyes] jouer des tours à ▸ **to deceive o.s.** se leurrer, s'abuser.

decelerate [ˌdi:'seləreɪt] **vi** ralentir.

December [dɪ'sembəʳ] **n** décembre *m* ; see also ***September***.

decency ['di:snsɪ] **n** décence *f*, bienséance *f* ▸ **to have the decency to do sthg** avoir la décence de faire qqch.

decent ['di:snt] **adj 1.** [behaviour, dress] décent(e) **2.** [wage, meal] correct(e), décent(e) **3.** [person] gentil(ille), brave.

decently ['di:sntlɪ] **adv 1.** [properly] décemment, convenablement **2.** [adequately] correctement.

decentralization [di:ˌsentrəlaɪ'zeɪʃn] **n** décentralisation *f*.

decentralize, *UK* ***-ise*** [ˌdi:'sentrəlaɪz] **vt** décentraliser.

deception [dɪ'sepʃn] **n 1.** [lie, pretence] tromperie *f*, duperie *f* **2.** *(U)* [lying] supercherie *f*.

deceptive [dɪ'septɪv] **adj** trompeur(euse).

deceptively [dɪ'septɪvlɪ] **adv** en apparence.

decibel ['desɪbel] **n** décibel *m*.

decide [dɪ'saɪd] ■ **vt** décider ▸ **to decide to do sthg** décider de faire qqch.
■ **vi** se décider ▸ **I can't decide** je n'arrive pas à me décider ▸ **to decide against/in favour of doing sthg** décider de ne pas/de faire qqch.
◆ ***decide (up)on*** **vt insep** se décider pour, choisir.

decided [dɪ'saɪdɪd] **adj 1.** [definite] certain(e), incontestable **2.** [resolute] décidé(e), résolu(e).

decidedly [dɪ'saɪdɪdlɪ] **adv 1.** [clearly] manifestement, incontestablement **2.** [resolutely] résolument.

decider [dɪ'saɪdəʳ] **n** [goal] but *m* décisif / [point] point *m* décisif / [match] match *m* décisif, rencontre *f* décisive / [factor] facteur *m* décisif.

deciding [dɪ'saɪdɪŋ] **adj : deciding vote** vote *m* décisif.

deciduous [dɪ'sɪdjʊəs] **adj** à feuilles caduques.

decimal ['desɪml] ■ **adj** décimal(e).
■ **n** décimale *f*.

decimal currency **n** monnaie *f* décimale.

decimalize, *UK* ***-ise*** ['desɪməlaɪz] **vt** *UK* décimaliser.

decimal place **n** décimale *f*.

decimal point **n** virgule *f*.

decimate ['desɪmeɪt] **vt** décimer.

decimation [ˌdesɪ'meɪʃn] **n** décimation *f*.

decipher [dɪ'saɪfəʳ] **vt** déchiffrer.

decision [dɪ'sɪʒn] **n** décision *f* ▸ **to make a decision** prendre une décision ▸ **to come to** *OR* **to arrive at** *OR* **to reach a decision** parvenir à une décision ▸ **to make the right/wrong decision** faire le bon/mauvais choix ▸ **it's your decision** c'est toi qui décides.

decision-maker **n** décideur *m*, -euse *f*, décisionnaire *mf*.

decision-making **n** prise *f* de décisions.

decisive [dɪ'saɪsɪv] **adj 1.** [person] déterminé(e), résolu(e) **2.** [factor, event] décisif(ive).

decisively [dɪ'saɪsɪvlɪ] **adv 1.** [speak] d'un ton décidé / [act] avec décision **2.** [considerably, definitely] nettement, bien.

decisiveness [dɪ'saɪsɪvnɪs] **n** fermeté *f*, résolution *f*.

deck [dek] ■ **n 1.** [of ship] pont *m* **2.** [of bus] étage *m* ▸ **top** *OR* **upper deck** impériale *f* **3.** [of cards] jeu *m* **4.** *US* [of house] véranda *f*.
■ **vt** [decorate] **: to deck sthg with** parer *OR* orner qqch de.
◆ ***deck out*** **vt sep** agrémenter, parer.

deckchair ['dektʃeəʳ] **n** chaise longue *f*, transat *m*.

deckhand ['dekhænd] **n** matelot *m*.

declamation [ˌdeklə'meɪʃn] **n** déclamation *f*.

declaration [ˌdeklə'reɪʃn] **n** déclaration *f*.

Declaration of Independence **n : the Declaration of Independence** *la Déclaration d'Indépendance des États-Unis d'Amérique (1776).*

declare [dɪ'kleəʳ] **vt** déclarer.

declared [dɪ'kleəd] **adj** [intention, supporter] avoué(e), déclaré(e).

declassified [ˌdi:'klæsɪfaɪd] **adj** [information] déclassé(e).

declassify [ˌdi:'klæsɪfaɪ] (**pt & pp -ied**) **vt** [information] déclasser.

decline [dɪ'klaɪn] ■ **n** déclin *m* ▸ **to be in decline** être en déclin ▸ **on the decline** en baisse.
■ **vt** décliner ▸ **to decline to do sthg** refuser de faire qqch.
■ **vi 1.** [deteriorate] décliner **2.** [refuse] refuser.

declutch [dɪ'klʌtʃ] **vi** *UK* débrayer.

decode [ˌdi:'kəʊd] **vt** décoder.

decoder [ˌdi:'kəʊdəʳ] **n** décodeur *m*.

decommission [ˌdi:kə'mɪʃn] **vt** mettre hors service.

decompose [ˌdi:kəm'pəʊz] **vi** se décomposer.

decomposition [ˌdi:kɒmpə'zɪʃn] **n** décomposition *f*.

decompress [ˌdi:kəm'pres] **vt** [gas, air] décomprimer / [diver] faire passer en chambre de décompression.

decompression [ˌdi:kəm'preʃn] **n** décompression *f*.

decompression chamber [ˌdi:kəm'preʃn-] **n** chambre *f* de décompression.

decompression sickness [ˌdi:kəm'preʃn-] **n** maladie *f* des caissons.

decongestant [ˌdi:kən'dʒestənt] **n** décongestionnant *m*.

deconstruct [ˌdi:kən'strʌkt] **vt** déconstruire.

deconstruction [ˌdi:kən'strʌkʃn] **n** déconstruction *f*.

decontaminate [ˌdi:kən'tæmɪneɪt] **vt** décontaminer.

decontamination ['di:kənˌtæmɪ'neɪʃn] ■ **n** décontamination *f*.
■ **comp** [equipment, team] de décontamination / [expert] en décontamination.

decor, ***décor*** ['deɪkɔ:ʳ] **n** décor *m*.

decorate ['dekəreɪt] **vt** décorer.

decoration [ˌdekə'reɪʃn] **n** décoration *f*.

decorative ['dekərətɪv] **adj** décoratif(ive).

decorator ['dekəreɪtəʳ] **n** décorateur *m*, -trice *f*.

decorous ['dekərəs] **adj** bienséant(e), convenable.

decorum [dɪ'kɔ:rəm] **n** décorum *m*.

decoy ■ **n** ['di:kɔɪ] [for hunting] appât *m*, leurre *m* / [person] compère *m*.
■ **vt** [dɪ'kɔɪ] attirer dans un piège.

decrease ■ **n** ['di:kri:s] **: decrease (in)** diminution *f* (de) baisse *f* (de).
■ **vt** [dɪ'kri:s] diminuer, réduire.
■ **vi** [dɪ'kri:s] diminuer, décroître.

decreasing [di:'kri:sɪŋ] **adj** qui diminue, décroissant(e)

decree [dɪ'kri:] ■ **n 1.** [order, decision] décret *m* **2.** *US* LAW arrêt *m*, jugement *m*.
■ **vt** décréter, ordonner.

decree absolute (**pl decrees absolute**) **n** *UK* jugement *m* définitif.

decree nisi [-'naɪsaɪ] (**pl decrees nisi**) **n** *UK* jugement *m* provisoire.

decrepit [dɪ'krepɪt] **adj** [person] décrépit(e) / [house] délabré(e).

decrepitude [dɪ'krepɪtju:d] **n** décrépitude *f*.

decriminalization [di:ˌkrɪmɪnəlaɪ'zeɪʃn] **n** dépénalisation *f*.

decriminalize**, UK **-ise [di:'krɪmɪnəˌlaɪz] **vt** dépénaliser.

decry [dɪ'kraɪ] (pt & pp **-ied**) **vt** décrier, dénigrer.

dedicate ['dedɪkeɪt] **vt** **1.** [book] dédier **2.** [life, career] consacrer ▸ **to dedicate o.s. to sthg** se consacrer à qqch.

dedicated ['dedɪkeɪtɪd] **adj** **1.** [person] dévoué(e) **2.** COMPUT spécialisé(e).

dedication [ˌdedɪ'keɪʃn] **n** **1.** [commitment] dévouement *m* **2.** [in book] dédicace *f*.

deduce [dɪ'dju:s] **vt** déduire, conclure.

deducible [dɪ'dju:səbl] **adj** qui peut se déduire.

deduct [dɪ'dʌkt] **vt** déduire, retrancher.

deductible [dɪ'dʌktəbl] **adj** déductible.

deduction [dɪ'dʌkʃn] **n** déduction *f*.

deed [di:d] **n** **1.** [action] action *f*, acte *m* **2.** LAW acte *m* notarié.

deed poll (pl **deed polls** *OR* **deeds poll**) **n** *UK* **: to change one's name by deed poll** changer de nom légalement *OR* officiellement.

deem [di:m] **vt** juger, considérer ▸ **to deem it wise to do sthg** juger prudent de faire qqch.

de-emphasize**, UK **-ise [di:'emfəsaɪz] **vt** [need, claim, feature] moins insister sur, se montrer moins insistant sur.

deep [di:p] ■ **adj** profond(e) ▸ **the water/hole is five metres deep** l'eau/le trou a cinq mètres de profondeur ▸ **the deep blue sea** le vaste océan ▸ **deep in the forest** au (fin) fond de la forêt ▸ **the crowd stood 15 deep** la foule se tenait sur 15 rangées ▸ **to be in a deep sleep** être profondément endormi ▸ **a deep breath** une inspiration profonde ▸ **we're in deep trouble** nous sommes dans de sales draps ▸ **with deepest sympathy** avec mes plus sincères condoléances ▸ **the deep end** [of swimming pool] le grand bain ▸ **to be thrown in at the deep end** *fig* recevoir le baptême du feu.

■ **adv** profondément ▸ **they went deep into the forest** ils se sont enfoncés dans la forêt ▸ **feelings were running deep** les sentiments se sont exacerbés ▸ **deep down** [fundamentally] au fond ▸ **to be deep in thought** être perdu(e) dans ses pensées ▸ **don't go in too deep** [in water] n'allez pas où c'est profond, n'allez pas trop loin ▸ **don't get in too deep** [involved] ne t'implique pas trop.

-deep **suffix : she was knee-/waist-deep in water** elle avait de l'eau jusqu'aux genoux/jusqu'à la taille ▸ **the water is only ankle-deep** l'eau ne monte *OR* n'arrive qu'aux chevilles.

deepen ['di:pn] ■ **vt** [hole, channel] approfondir.

■ **vi** **1.** [river, sea] devenir profond(e) **2.** [crisis, recession, feeling] s'aggraver **3.** [darkness] augmenter.

deepening ['di:pnɪŋ] **adj** [crisis, recession] qui s'aggrave.

deep freeze **n** congélateur *m*.

◆ ***deep-freeze*** **vt** congeler.

deep-fried **adj** frit(e).

deep-fry **vt** faire frire.

deep-heat treatment **n** MED thermothérapie *f*.

deeply ['di:plɪ] **adv** profondément.

deepness ['di:pnɪs] **n** [of ocean, voice, writer, remark] profondeur *f* / [of note, sound] gravité *f*.

deep-rooted **adj** [prejudice] ancré(e), enraciné(e) / [hatred] vivace, tenace / [affection] profond(e).

deep-sea **adj : deep-sea diving** plongée *f* sous-marine ▸ **deep-sea fishing** pêche *f* hauturière.

deep-seated ['si:tɪd] **adj** [belief, fear] profond(e), enraciné(e).

deep-set **adj** [eyes] enfoncé(e).

deer [dɪəʳ] (pl **deer**) **n** cerf *m*.

deerstalker ['dɪəˌstɔ:kəʳ] **n** [hat] chapeau *m* à la Sherlock Holmes.

de-escalate [ˌdi:'eskəleɪt] ■ **vt** faire diminuer.

■ **vi** diminuer.

deface [dɪ'feɪs] **vt** barbouiller.

de facto [deɪ'fæktəʊ] **adv** & **adj** de facto, de fait.

defamation [ˌdefə'meɪʃn] **n** diffamation *f*.

defamatory [dɪ'fæmətrɪ] **adj** diffamatoire, diffamant(e).

default [dɪ'fɔ:lt] ■ **n** **1.** [failure] défaillance *f* ▸ **by default** par défaut **2.** COMPUT valeur *f* par défaut ▸ **drive C is the default** C est l'unité de disque par défaut.

■ **comp** COMPUT implicite, par défaut.

■ **vi** **1.** manquer à ses engagements ▸ **to default on** manquer à **2.** COMPUT prendre une sélection par défaut ▸ **the computer automatically defaults to drive C** l'ordinateur sélectionne l'unité de disque C par défaut.

defaulter [dɪ'fɔ:ltəʳ] **n** partie *f* défaillante.

default setting **n** COMPUT configuration *f* par défaut.

default value **n** COMPUT valeur *f* par défaut.

defeat [dɪ'fi:t] ■ **n** défaite *f* ▸ **to admit defeat** s'avouer battu(e) *OR* vaincu(e).

■ **vt** **1.** [team, opponent] vaincre, battre **2.** [motion, proposal] rejeter **3.** [plans] faire échouer.

defeatism [dɪ'fi:tɪzm] **n** défaitisme *m*.

defeatist [dɪ'fi:tɪst] ■ **adj** défaitiste.

■ **n** défaitiste *mf*.

defecate ['defəkeɪt] **vi** déféquer.

defect ■ **n** ['di:fekt] défaut *m*.

■ **vi** [dɪ'fekt] **: to defect to** passer à.

defection [dɪ'fekʃn] **n** défection *f*.

defective [dɪ'fektɪv] **adj** défectueux(euse).

defector [dɪ'fektəʳ] **n** transfuge *mf*.

***defence** UK, **defense** US* [dɪ'fens] ■ **n** **1.** [gen] défense *f* ▸ **to come to sb's defence** venir à la défense de qqn ▸ **to act/to speak in defence of sthg** [following attack] agir/parler en défense de qqch / [in support of] agir/parler en faveur de qqch **2.** [protective device, system] protection *f* ▸ **to use sthg as a defence against sthg** se servir de qqch comme défense *OR* protection contre qqch, se servir de qqch pour se défendre *OR* se protéger de qqch **3.** LAW **: the defence** la défense ▸ **witness for the defence** témoin *m* à décharge, témoin de la défense ▸ **the case for the defence** la défense ▸ **he said in defence that...** il a répondu pour sa défense que... **4.** SPORT défense *f*.

■ comp **1.** MIL [forces] de défense / [cuts, minister, spending] de la défense **2.** LAW [lawyer] de la défense / [witness] à décharge.
◆ ***defences*** **npl** [of country] moyens *mpl* de défense.

defenceless UK, ***defenseless*** US [dɪ'fenslɪs] **adj** sans défense.

defence mechanism UK, ***defense mechanism*** US **n** mécanisme *m* de défense.

defend [dɪ'fend] ■ **vt** défendre ▸ **to defend o.s.** se défendre.
■ **vi** SPORT défendre.

defendant [dɪ'fendənt] **n** défendeur *m*, -eresse *f* / [in trial] accusé *m*, -e *f*.

defender [dɪ'fendər] **n** défenseur *m*.

defense US = ***defence***.

defenseless US = ***defenceless***.

defensible [dɪ'fensəbl] **adj** [idea, opinion] défendable.

defensive [dɪ'fensɪv] ■ **adj** défensif(ive).
■ **n : on the defensive** sur la défensive.

defensively [dɪ'fensɪvlɪ] **adv : they played very defensively** SPORT ils ont eu un jeu très défensif ▸ **"it's not my fault" she said, defensively** "ce n'est pas de ma faute" dit-elle, sur la défensive.

defer [dɪ'fɜːr] (pt & pp **-red**, cont **-ring**) ■ **vt** différer.
■ **vi : to defer to sb** s'en remettre à (l'opinion de) qqn.

deference ['defərəns] **n** déférence *f*.

deferential [ˌdefə'renʃl] **adj** respectueux(euse).

deferred [dɪ'fɜːd] **adj** [gen] ajourné(e), retardé(e) / [payment, charges, shares] différé(e) / [annuity] à paiement différé, à jouissance différée ▸ **deferred sentence** LAW jugement *m* dont le prononcé est suspendu, jugement ajourné.

defiance [dɪ'faɪəns] **n** défi *m* ▸ **in defiance of** au mépris de.

defiant [dɪ'faɪənt] **adj** [person] intraitable, intransigeant(e) / [action] de défi.

defiantly [dɪ'faɪəntlɪ] **adv** [say] d'un ton de défi.

defibrillator [diː'fɪbrɪleɪtər] **n** MED défibrillateur *m*.

deficiency [dɪ'fɪʃnsɪ] (pl **-ies**) **n 1.** [lack] manque *m* / [of vitamins] carence *f* **2.** [inadequacy] imperfection *f*, défaut *m*.

deficient [dɪ'fɪʃnt] **adj 1.** [lacking] **: to be deficient in** manquer de **2.** [inadequate] insuffisant(e), médiocre.

deficit ['defɪsɪt] **n** déficit *m*.

defile [dɪ'faɪl] **vt** souiller, salir.

define [dɪ'faɪn] **vt** définir.

defining [dɪ'faɪnɪŋ] **adj** restrictif(ive).

definite ['defɪnɪt] **adj 1.** [plan] bien déterminé(e) / [date] certain(e) **2.** [improvement, difference] net (nette), marqué(e) **3.** [answer] précis(e), catégorique **4.** [confident - person] assuré(e).

definite article **n** article *m* défini.

definitely ['defɪnɪtlɪ] **adv 1.** [without doubt] sans aucun doute, certainement **2.** [for emphasis] catégoriquement ▸ **are you going to the show? – definitely!** est-ce que tu vas au spectacle? – absolument!

definition [ˌdefɪ'nɪʃn] **n 1.** [gen] définition *f* **2.** [clarity] clarté *f*, précision *f*.

definitive [dɪ'fɪnɪtɪv] **adj** définitif(ive).

definitively [dɪ'fɪnɪtɪvlɪ] **adv** définitivement.

deflate [dɪ'fleɪt] ■ **vt 1.** [balloon, tyre] dégonfler **2.** *fig* [person] rabaisser, humilier **3.** ECON [prices] faire baisser ▸ **to deflate the economy** pratiquer une politique déflationniste ▸ **this measure is intended to deflate the economy** cette mesure est destinée à faire de la déflation.
■ **vi** [balloon, tyre] se dégonfler.

deflation [dɪ'fleɪʃn] **n** ECON déflation *f*.

deflationary [dɪ'fleɪʃnərɪ] **adj** [policy] de déflation / [measure] déflationniste.

deflect [dɪ'flekt] **vt** [ball, bullet] dévier / [stream] détourner, dériver / [criticism] détourner.

deflection [dɪ'flekʃn] **n** [of ball, bullet] déviation *f* / [of stream] détournement *m*, dérivation *f*.

defog [ˌdiː'fɒg] **vt** *US* AUT désembuer.

defogger [ˌdiː'fɒgər] **n** *US* AUT dispositif *m* antibuée.

deforest [ˌdiː'fɒrɪst] **vt** déboiser.

deforestation [diːˌfɒrɪ'steɪʃn] **n** déforestation *f*, déboisement *m*.

deform [dɪ'fɔːm] **vt** déformer.

deformed [dɪ'fɔːmd] **adj** difforme.

deformity [dɪ'fɔːmətɪ] (pl **-ies**) **n** difformité *f*, malformation *f*.

Defra ['defrə] (abbr of ***Department for Environment, Food & Rural Affairs***) **n** *UK* ADMIN ministère *m* de l'Agriculture britannique *m*.

defragment [ˌdiːfræg'ment] **vt** COMPUT défragmenter

defraud [dɪ'frɔːd] **vt** [person] escroquer / [Inland Revenue] frauder.

defray [dɪ'freɪ] **vt** [costs] couvrir / [expenses] rembourser

defrost [ˌdiː'frɒst] ■ **vt 1.** [fridge] dégivrer / [frozen food] décongeler **2.** *US* [AUT - de-ice] dégivrer / [- demist] désembuer.
■ **vi** [fridge] dégivrer / [frozen food] se décongeler.

deft [deft] **adj** adroit(e).

deftly ['deftlɪ] **adv** adroitement.

defunct [dɪ'fʌŋkt] **adj** qui n'existe plus / [person] défunt(e).

defuse [ˌdiː'fjuːz] **vt** désamorcer.

defy [dɪ'faɪ] (pt & pp **-ied**) **vt 1.** [gen] défier ▸ **to defy sb to do sthg** mettre qqn au défi de faire qqch **2.** [efforts] résister à, faire échouer.

degenerate ■ **adj** [dɪ'dʒenərət] dégénéré(e).
■ **n** [dɪ'dʒenərət] dégénéré *m*, -e *f*.
■ **vi** [dɪ'dʒenəreɪt] **: to degenerate (into)** dégénérer (en)

degenerative [dɪ'dʒenərətɪv] **adj** dégénératif(ive).

degradation [ˌdegrə'deɪʃn] **n** [of person] déchéance *f* [of place] dégradation *f*.

degrade [dɪ'greɪd] **vt** [person] avilir.

degrading [dɪ'greɪdɪŋ] **adj** dégradant(e), avilissant(e).

degree [dɪ'gri:] **n 1.** [measurement] degré *m* ▸ **the temperature is 28 degrees in New York** la température est de 28 degrés à New York ▸ **it's three degrees outside** il fait trois degrés dehors ▸ **a 90 degree angle** GEOM un angle de 90 degrés
2. UNIV diplôme *m* universitaire ▸ **she has a degree in economics** elle est diplômée en sciences économiques ▸ **he's taking *OR* doing a degree in biology** il fait une licence de biologie
3. [amount] **: to a certain degree** jusqu'à un certain point, dans une certaine mesure ▸ **a degree of risk** un certain risque ▸ **a degree of truth** une certaine part de vérité ▸ **by degrees** progressivement, petit à petit
4. *US* LAW **: murder in the first degree** homicide *m* volontaire.

-degree **suffix : first/second/third-degree burns** brûlures *fpl* au premier/deuxième/troisième degré ▸ **first-degree murder** *US* LAW ≃ homicide *m* volontaire.

dehumanize, *UK* ***-ise*** [di:'hju:mənaɪz] **vt** déshumaniser.

dehumidify [ˌdi:hju:'mɪdɪfaɪ] **vt** déshumidifier.

dehydrate [ˌdi:haɪ'dreɪt] **vt** déshydrater.

dehydrated [ˌdi:haɪ'dreɪtɪd] **adj** déshydraté(e).

dehydration [ˌdi:haɪ'dreɪʃn] **n** déshydratation *f*.

de-ice [di:'aɪs] **vt** dégivrer.

de-icer [di:'aɪsər] **n** dégivreur *m*.

deification [ˌdi:ɪfɪ'keɪʃn] **n** déification *f*.

deify ['di:ɪfaɪ] **vt** déifier.

deign [deɪn] **vt : to deign to do sthg** daigner faire qqch.

deity ['di:ɪtɪ] (**pl -ies**) **n** dieu *m*, déesse *f*, divinité *f*.

déjà vu [ˌdeʒɑ:'vju:] **n** déjà vu *m*.

dejected [dɪ'dʒektɪd] **adj** abattu(e), découragé(e).

dejectedly [dɪ'dʒektɪdlɪ] **adv** [speak] d'un ton abattu / [look] d'un air abattu.

dejection [dɪ'dʒekʃn] **n** abattement *m*, découragement *m*.

del. (abbr of ***delete***) [on keyboard] suppr.

Del. abbr of ***Delaware***.

Delaware ['deləweər] **n** Delaware *m* ▸ **in Delaware** dans le Delaware.

delay [dɪ'leɪ] ■ **n** retard *m*, délai *m* ▸ **there's a three to four hour delay on all international flights** il y a trois à quatre heures de retard sur tous les vols internationaux ▸ **without delay** sans délai.
■ **vt 1.** [cause to be late] retarder ▸ **the flight was delayed (for) three hours** le vol a été retardé de trois heures **2.** [defer] différer ▸ **to delay doing sthg** tarder à faire qqch.
■ **vi : to delay (in doing sthg)** tarder (à faire qqch).

delayed [dɪ'leɪd] **adj : to be delayed** [person, train] être retardé(e).

delayed-action [dɪ'leɪd-] **adj** [response] après coup ▸ **delayed-action shutter** PHOT dispositif *m* à retardement.

delaying [dɪ'leɪɪŋ] **adj** dilatoire ▸ **delaying action** manœuvres *fpl* dilatoires.

delectable [dɪ'lektəbl] **adj** délicieux(euse).

delectation [ˌdi:lek'teɪʃn] **n** *liter* & *hum* délectation *f* ▸ **for your delectation** pour votre plus grand plaisir.

delegate ■ **n** ['delɪgət] délégué *m*, -e *f*.
■ **vt** ['delɪgeɪt] déléguer ▸ **to delegate sb to do sthg** déléguer qqn pour faire qqch ▸ **to delegate sthg to sb** déléguer qqch à qqn.
■ **vi** ['delɪgeɪt] déléguer.

delegation [ˌdelɪ'geɪʃn] **n** délégation *f*.

delete [dɪ'li:t] **vt** supprimer, effacer.

delete key **n** COMPUT touche *f* effacer.

deletion [dɪ'li:ʃn] **n** suppression *f*, effacement *m*.

Delhi ['delɪ] **n** Delhi.

Delhi belly **n** *inf hum* tourista *f*.

deli ['delɪ] **n** *inf* abbr of ***delicatessen***.

deliberate ■ **adj** [dɪ'lɪbərət] **1.** [intentional] voulu(e), délibéré(e) **2.** [slow] lent(e), sans hâte.
■ **vi** [dɪ'lɪbəreɪt] délibérer.

deliberately [dɪ'lɪbərətlɪ] **adv 1.** [on purpose] exprès, à dessein **2.** [slowly] posément, sans se presser.

deliberation [dɪˌlɪbə'reɪʃn] **n 1.** [consideration] délibération *f* **2.** [slowness] mesure *f*.
◆ ***deliberations*** **npl** délibérations *fpl*, discussions *fpl*.

delicacy ['delɪkəsɪ] (**pl -ies**) **n 1.** [gen] délicatesse *f* **2.** [food] mets *m* délicat.

delicate ['delɪkət] **adj** délicat(e) / [movement] gracieux(euse).

delicately ['delɪkətlɪ] **adv 1.** [gen] délicatement / [move] gracieusement, avec grâce **2.** [tactfully] avec délicatesse, subtilement.

delicatessen [ˌdelɪkə'tesn] **n** épicerie *f* fine.

delicious [dɪ'lɪʃəs] **adj** délicieux(euse).

deliciously [dɪ'lɪʃəslɪ] **adv** délicieusement.

delight [dɪ'laɪt] ■ **n 1.** [great pleasure] délice *m* ▸ **to take delight in doing sthg** prendre grand plaisir à faire qqch **2.** [wonderful thing, person] **: she's a delight to work with** c'est un plaisir de travailler avec elle ▸ **a delight to the eyes** un régal pour les yeux.
■ **vt** enchanter, charmer.
■ **vi : to delight in sthg/in doing sthg** prendre grand plaisir à qqch/à faire qqch.

delighted [dɪ'laɪtɪd] **adj : delighted (by *OR* with)** enchanté(e) (de), ravi(e) (de) ▸ **to be delighted that** être enchanté *OR* ravi que ▸ **to be delighted to do sthg** être enchanté *OR* ravi de faire qqch.

delightful [dɪ'laɪtfʊl] **adj** ravissant(e), charmant(e) / [meal] délicieux(euse).

delightfully [dɪ'laɪtfʊlɪ] **adv** d'une façon charmante.

delimit [di:'lɪmɪt] **vt** délimiter.

delineate - 162 ...eɪt] **vt** **1.** [outline, sketch] tracer **2.** [de-...] définir, décrire.

delineation [dɪ,lɪnɪ'eɪʃn] **n** **1.** [sketch] tracé *m* **2.** [definition] définition *f*, description *f*.

delinquency [dɪ'lɪŋkwənsɪ] **n** délinquance *f*.

delinquent [dɪ'lɪŋkwənt] ■ **adj** délinquant(e).
■ **n** délinquant *m*, -e *f*.

delirious [dɪ'lɪrɪəs] **adj** *liter* & *fig* délirant(e).

deliriously [dɪ'lɪrɪəslɪ] **adv** de façon délirante, frénétiquement ▸ **deliriously happy** follement heureux.

delirium [dɪ'lɪrɪəm] **n** délire *m*.

deliver [dɪ'lɪvəʳ] ■ **vt** **1.** [distribute] **: to deliver sthg (to sb)** [mail, newspaper] distribuer qqch (à qqn) / COMM livrer qqch (à qqn) ▸ **what time is the post *OR* mail delivered?** le courrier est distribué à quelle heure? ▸ **can he deliver the goods?** *inf* est-ce qu'il peut tenir parole? **2.** [speech] faire / [warning] donner / [message] remettre / [blow, kick] donner, porter **3.** [baby] mettre au monde **4.** [free] délivrer **5.** *US* POL [votes] obtenir.
■ **vi** **1.** COMM livrer **2.** [fulfil promise] tenir sa promesse.

deliverance [dɪ'lɪvərəns] **n** délivrance *f*.

delivery [dɪ'lɪvərɪ] (**pl -ies**) **n** **1.** COMM livraison *f* **2.** [way of speaking] élocution *f* **3.** [birth] accouchement *m*.

delivery note **n** bulletin *m* de livraison.

delivery van *UK*, ***delivery truck*** *US* **n** camionnette *f* de livraison.

delphinium [del'fɪnɪəm] (**pl -s**) **n** delphinium *m*, pied-d'alouette *m*.

delta ['deltə] (**pl -s**) **n** delta *m*.

delude [dɪ'lu:d] **vt** tromper, induire en erreur ▸ **to delude o.s.** se faire des illusions.

deluded [dɪ'lu:dɪd] **adj** **1.** [mistaken, foolish] **: a poor deluded young man** un pauvre jeune homme qu'on a trompé *OR* induit en erreur **2.** PSYCHOL sujet à des délires.

deluge ['delju:dʒ] ■ **n** déluge *m* / *fig* avalanche *f*.
■ **vt : to be deluged with** être débordé(e) *OR* submergé(e) de.

delusion [dɪ'lu:ʒn] **n** illusion *f* ▸ **delusions of grandeur** folie *f* des grandeurs.

deluxe, ***de luxe*** [də'lʌks] **adj** de luxe.

delve [delv] **vi : to delve into** [past] fouiller / [bag etc] fouiller dans.

Dem. abbr of ***Democrat***, ***Democratic***.

demagogue *UK*, ***demagog*** *US* ['deməgɒg] **n** démagogue *m*.

demand [dɪ'mɑ:nd] ■ **n** **1.** [claim, firm request] revendication *f*, exigence *f* ▸ **wage demand** revendication salariale ▸ **on demand** sur demande **2.** [obligation, requirement] exigence *f* ▸ **to make demands on sb** exiger beaucoup de qqn **3.** ECON & COMM **: demand (for)** demande *f* (de) ▸ **in demand** demandé(e), recherché(e) ▸ **due to public demand** à la demande du public.
■ **vt** **1.** [ask for - justice, money] réclamer / [- explanation, apology] exiger ▸ **to demand to do sthg** exiger de faire qqch **2.** [require] demander, exiger.

FALSE FRIENDS / FAUX AMIS

demand

Demander n'est pas la traduction du mot anglais *demand*. Demander se traduit par *to ask*.
▸ **Je vais demander un renseignement à l'accueil /** ***I'll ask for information at reception***

demanding [dɪ'mɑ:ndɪŋ] **adj** **1.** [exhausting] astreignant(e) **2.** [not easily satisfied] exigeant(e).

demand-led **adj** ECON tiré(e) par la demande.

demarcate ['di:mɑ:keɪt] **vt** *fml* délimiter.

demarcation [,di:mɑ:'keɪʃn] **n** démarcation *f*.

demarcation dispute **n** *UK* conflit *m* de compétence.

dematerialize, *UK* ***-ise*** [di:mə'tɪərɪəlaɪz] **vi** se volatiliser.

demean [dɪ'mi:n] **vt** avilir, déshonorer ▸ **to demean o.s.** s'abaisser.

demeaning [dɪ'mi:nɪŋ] **adj** avilissant(e), dégradant(e).

demeanour *UK*, ***demeanor*** *US* [dɪ'mi:nəʳ] **n** *(U)* *fml* comportement *m*.

demented [dɪ'mentɪd] **adj** fou (folle), dément(e).

dementia [dɪ'menʃə] **n** démence *f*.

demerara sugar [,demə'reərə-] **n** *UK* cassonade *f*.

demerger [,di:'mɜ:dʒəʳ] **n** scission *f*.

demerit [di:'merɪt] **n** **1.** *fml* [flaw] démérite *m*, faute *f* **2.** *US* SCH & MIL blâme *m*.

demigod ['demɪgɒd] **n** demi-dieu *m*.

demijohn ['demɪdʒɒn] **n** dame-jeanne *f*, bonbonne *f*.

demilitarize, ***-ise*** *UK* [,di:'mɪlɪtəraɪz] **vt** démilitariser.

demilitarized zone, *UK* ***demilitarised zone*** [,di:'mɪlɪtəraɪzd-] **n** zone *f* démilitarisée.

demimonde [,demɪ'mɒnd] **n** demi-monde *m*.

demise [dɪ'maɪz] **n** *(U)* décès *m* / *fig* mort *f*, fin *f*.

demist [,di:'mɪst] **vt** *UK* désembuer.

demister [,di:'mɪstəʳ] **n** *UK* dispositif *m* antibuée.

demo ['deməʊ] (abbr of ***demonstration***) **n** *UK* *inf* manif *f*.

demob [,di:'mɒb] (**pt & pp -bed**, **cont -bing**) *UK* *inf* ■ **vt** démobiliser.
■ **n** **1.** [demobilization] démobilisation *f* **2.** [soldier] soldat *m* démobilisé.
■ **comp : demob suit** ≃ tenue *f* civile.

demobilization [diːˌməʊbɪlaɪˈzeɪʃn] **n** démobilisation *f*.

demobilize, *UK* ***-ise*** [ˌdiːˈməʊbɪlaɪz] **vt** démobiliser.

democracy [dɪˈmɒkrəsɪ] (pl **-ies**) **n** démocratie *f*.

democrat [ˈdeməkræt] **n** démocrate *mf*.
◆ ***Democrat*** **n** *US* démocrate *mf*.

democratic [ˌdeməˈkrætɪk] **adj** démocratique.
◆ ***Democratic*** **adj** *US* démocrate.

democratically [ˌdeməˈkrætɪklɪ] **adv** démocratiquement.

Democratic Party **n** *US* **: the Democratic Party** le Parti démocrate.

democratize, *UK* ***-ise*** [dɪˈmɒkrətaɪz] **vt** démocratiser.

demographic [ˌdeməˈgræfɪk] **adj** démographique.

demographic profile **n** profil *m* démographique.

demographics [ˌdeməˈgræfɪks] **n** statistiques *fpl* démographiques.

demographic segmentation **n** segmentation *f* démographique.

demolish [dɪˈmɒlɪʃ] **vt 1.** [destroy] démolir **2.** *inf* [eat] engloutir, engouffrer.

demolition [ˌdeməˈlɪʃn] **n** démolition *f*.

demon [ˈdiːmən] ■ **n** [evil spirit] démon *m*.
■ **comp** *inf* **: demon driver/chess player** as du volant/des échecs.

demonic [diːˈmɒnɪk] **adj** diabolique.

demonstrable [dɪˈmɒnstrəbl] **adj** démontrable.

demonstrably [dɪˈmɒnstrəblɪ] **adv** manifestement.

demonstrate [ˈdemənstreɪt] ■ **vt 1.** [prove] démontrer, prouver **2.** [machine, computer] faire une démonstration de.
■ **vi : to demonstrate (for/against)** manifester (pour/contre).

demonstration [demənˈstreɪʃn] **n 1.** [of machine, emotions] démonstration *f* **2.** [public meeting] manifestation *f*.

demonstrative [dɪˈmɒnstrətɪv] **adj** expansif(ive), démonstratif(ive).

demonstrator [ˈdemənstreɪtəʳ] **n 1.** [in march] manifestant *m*, -e *f* **2.** [of machine, product] démonstrateur *m*, -trice *f*.

demoralization [dɪˌmɒrəlaɪˈzeɪʃn] **n** démoralisation *f*.

demoralize, *UK* ***-ise*** [dɪˈmɒrəlaɪz] **vt** démoraliser.

demoralized [dɪˈmɒrəlaɪzd] **adj** démoralisé(e).

demoralizing [dɪˈmɒrəlaɪzɪŋ] **adj** démoralisant(e).

demote [ˌdiːˈməʊt] **vt** rétrograder.

demotion [ˌdiːˈməʊʃn] **n** rétrogradation *f*.

demotivate [ˌdiːˈməʊtɪveɪt] **vt** démotiver.

demo version **n** COMPUT version *f* de démonstration ***OR*** d'évaluation.

demure [dɪˈmjʊəʳ] **adj** modeste, réservé(e).

demutualize, *UK* ***-ise*** [ˌdiːˈmuːtʃʊəlaɪz] **vi** FIN *passer d'un statut de société mutuelle à un statut de société par actions.*

demystify [ˌdiːˈmɪstɪfaɪ] (pt & pp **-ied**) **vt** démystifier.

den [den] **n** [of animal] antre *m*, tanière *f*.

denationalization [ˈdiːˌnæʃnəlaɪˈzeɪʃn] **n** dénationalisation *f*.

denationalize, *UK* ***-ise*** [ˌdiːˈnæʃnəlaɪz] **vt** dénationaliser.

deniable [dɪˈnaɪəbl] **adj** niable.

denial [dɪˈnaɪəl] **n** [of rights, facts, truth] dénégation *f* / [of accusation] démenti *m* ▸ **in denial** en déni.

denier [ˈdenɪəʳ] **n** denier *m*.

denigrate [ˈdenɪgreɪt] **vt** dénigrer.

denim [ˈdenɪm] **n** jean *m*.
◆ ***denims*** **npl : a pair of denims** un jean.

denim jacket **n** veste *f* en jean.

denizen [ˈdenɪzn] **n** *liter* & *hum* habitant *m*, -e *f*.

Denmark [ˈdenmɑːk] **n** Danemark *m* ▸ **in Denmark** au Danemark.

denomination [dɪˌnɒmɪˈneɪʃn] **n 1.** RELIG confession *f* **2.** [money] valeur *f*.

denominator [dɪˈnɒmɪneɪtəʳ] **n** dénominateur *m*.

denote [dɪˈnəʊt] **vt** dénoter.

denounce [dɪˈnaʊns] **vt** dénoncer.

dense [dens] **adj 1.** [crowd, forest] dense / [fog] dense, épais(aisse) **2.** *inf* [stupid] bouché(e).

densely [ˈdenslɪ] **adv : densely packed** [hall etc] complètement bondé(e) ▸ **densely populated** très peuplé(e) ▸ **densely wooded** couvert(e) de forêts épaisses.

density [ˈdensətɪ] (pl **-ies**) **n** densité *f*.

dent [dent] ■ **n** bosse *f*.
■ **vt** cabosser.

dental [ˈdentl] **adj** dentaire ▸ **dental appointment** rendez-vous *m* chez le dentiste.

dental floss **n** fil *m* dentaire.

dental hygienist **n** = ***hygienist***.

dental plate **n** prothèse *f* dentaire.

dental surgeon **n** chirurgien-dentiste *m*.

dental treatment **n** traitement *m* dentaire.

dented [ˈdentɪd] **adj** cabossé(e).

dentist [ˈdentɪst] **n** dentiste *mf*.

dentistry [ˈdentɪstrɪ] **n** dentisterie *f*.

dentures ['dentʃəz] **npl** dentier *m*.

denude [dɪ'nju:d] **vt** *fml* **: to denude sthg (of)** dépouiller qqch (de).

denunciation [dɪˌnʌnsɪ'eɪʃn] **n** dénonciation *f*.

deny [dɪ'naɪ] (pt & pp **-ied**) **vt 1.** [refute] nier ▸ **to deny doing or having done sth** nier avoir faire qch **2.** *fml* [refuse] nier, refuser ▸ **to deny sb sthg** refuser qqch à qqn.

deodorant [di:'əʊdərənt] **n** déodorant *m*.

depart [dɪ'pɑ:t] **vi** *fml* **1.** [leave] **: to depart (from)** partir (de) **2.** [differ] **: to depart from sthg** s'écarter de qqch.

department [dɪ'pɑ:tmənt] **n 1.** [in organization] service *m* **2.** [in shop] rayon *m* **3.** SCH & UNIV département *m* **4.** [in government] département *m*, ministère *m*.

departmental [ˌdi:pɑ:t'mentl] **adj** de service.

department store **n** grand magasin *m*.

departure [dɪ'pɑ:tʃəʳ] **n 1.** [leaving] départ *m* **2.** [change] nouveau départ *m* ▸ **a departure from tradition** un écart par rapport à la tradition.

departure lounge **n** salle *f* d'embarquement.

depend [dɪ'pend] **vi : to depend on** [be dependent on] dépendre de / [rely on] compter sur / [emotionally] se reposer sur ▸ **it depends on you/the weather** cela dépend de vous/du temps ▸ **it depends** cela dépend ▸ **depending on** selon.

dependable [dɪ'pendəbl] **adj** [person] sur qui on peut compter / [source of income] sûr(e) / [car] fiable.

dependant [dɪ'pendənt] **n** personne *f* à charge.

dependence [dɪ'pendəns] **n : dependence (on)** dépendance *f* (de).

dependency [dɪ'pendənsɪ] (pl **-ies**) **n** dépendance *f*.

dependency culture **n** ECON *situation d'une société dont les membres ont une mentalité d'assistés*.

dependent [dɪ'pendənt] **adj 1.** [reliant] **: dependent (on)** dépendant(e) (de) ▸ **to be dependent on sb/sthg** dépendre de qqn/qqch ▸ **the economy is dependent on oil** l'économie repose sur le pétrole **2.** [addicted] dépendant(e), accro **3.** [contingent] **: to be dependent on** dépendre de.

depersonalize, ***-ise*** *UK* [ˌdi:'pɜ:snəlaɪz] **vt** dépersonnaliser.

depict [dɪ'pɪkt] **vt 1.** [show in picture] représenter **2.** [describe] **: to depict sb/sthg as** dépeindre qqn/qqch comme.

depiction [dɪ'pɪkʃn] **n 1.** [description] description *f* **2.** [picture] représentation *f*.

depilatory [dɪ'pɪlətrɪ] **adj** dépilatoire.

deplete [dɪ'pli:t] **vt** épuiser.

depletion [dɪ'pli:ʃn] **n** épuisement *m*.

deplorable [dɪ'plɔ:rəbl] **adj** déplorable.

deplore [dɪ'plɔ:ʳ] **vt** déplorer.

deploy [dɪ'plɔɪ] **vt** déployer.

deployment [dɪ'plɔɪmənt] **n** déploiement *m*.

depoliticize, ***-ise*** *UK* [ˌdi:pə'lɪtɪsaɪz] **vt** dépolitiser.

depopulate [ˌdi:'pɒpjʊleɪt] **vt** dépeupler.

depopulated [ˌdi:'pɒpjʊleɪtɪd] **adj** dépeuplé(e).

depopulation [di:ˌpɒpjʊ'leɪʃn] **n** dépeuplement *m*.

deport [dɪ'pɔ:t] **vt** expulser.

deportation [ˌdi:pɔ:'teɪʃn] **n** expulsion *f*.

deportation order **n** arrêt *m* d'expulsion.

deportee [ˌdi:pɔ:'ti:] **n** expulsé *m*, -e *f* / HIST [prisoner] déporté *m*, -e *f*.

deportment [dɪ'pɔ:tmənt] **n** *fml* & *dated* [behaviour] comportement *m* / [carriage, posture] maintien *m*.

depose [dɪ'pəʊz] **vt** déposer.

deposit [dɪ'pɒzɪt] ■ **n 1.** [gen] dépôt *m* ▸ **to make a deposit** [into bank account] déposer de l'argent **2.** [payment - as guarantee] caution *f* / [- as instalment] acompte *m* / [- on bottle] consigne *f* ▸ **a £50 deposit** 50 livres d'acompte **OR** d'arrhes.

■ **vt** déposer ▸ **I'd like to deposit £500** j'aimerais faire un versement de 500 livres.

deposit account **n** *UK* compte *m* sur livret.

deposition [ˌdepə'zɪʃn] **n 1.** LAW déposition *f* **2.** [of minerals] dépôt *m* **3.** [removal of leader] déposition *f*.

depositor [də'pɒzɪtəʳ] **n** déposant *m*, -e *f*.

depot ['depəʊ] **n 1.** [gen] dépôt *m* **2.** *US* [station] gare *f*.

depravation [ˌdeprə'veɪʃn] **n** dépravation *f*.

depraved [dɪ'preɪvd] **adj** dépravé(e).

depravity [dɪ'prævətɪ] **n** dépravation *f*.

deprecate ['deprɪkeɪt] **vt** *fml* désapprouver.

deprecating ['deprɪkeɪtɪŋ] **adj** désapprobateur(trice).

depreciate [dɪ'pri:ʃɪeɪt] **vi** se déprécier.

depreciation [dɪˌpri:ʃɪ'eɪʃn] **n** dépréciation *f*.

depress [dɪ'pres] **vt 1.** [sadden, discourage] déprimer **2.** [weaken - economy] affaiblir / [- prices] faire baisser.

depressant [dɪ'presənt] **n** dépresseur *m*.

depressed [dɪ'prest] **adj 1.** [sad] déprimé(e) **2.** [rundown - area] en déclin.

depressing [dɪ'presɪŋ] **adj** déprimant(e).

depressingly [dɪ'presɪŋlɪ] **adv** [say, speak] de manière déprimante ▸ **unemployment is depressingly high** le taux de chômage est déprimant.

depression [dɪ'preʃn] **n 1.** [gen] dépression *f* **2.** [sadness] tristesse *f*.

◆ ***Depression*** **n** ECON **: the (Great) Depression** la crise (économique) de 1929.

depressive [dɪ'presɪv] **adj** dépressif(ive).

deprivation [ˌdeprɪ'veɪʃn] **n** privation *f*.

deprive [dɪ'praɪv] **vt : to deprive sb of sthg** priver qqn de qqch.

deprived [dɪ'praɪvd] **adj** défavorisé(e).

dept. abbr of ***department***.

depth [depθ] **n** profondeur *f* ▸ **the canal is about 12 metres in depth** le canal a environ 12 mètres de profondeur ▸ **depth of field/focus** PHOT profondeur *f* de champ/foyer ▸ **in depth** [study, analyse] en profondeur ▸ **to be out of one's depth** [in water] ne pas avoir pied / *fig* avoir perdu pied, être dépassé.
◆ ***depths*** **npl : the depths** [of seas] les profondeurs *fpl* / [of memory, archives] le fin fond ▸ **in the depths of winter** au cœur de l'hiver ▸ **to be in the depths of despair** toucher le fond du désespoir.

depth charge **n** grenade *f* sous-marine.

deputation [ˌdepjʊ'teɪʃn] **n** délégation *f*.

deputize, *UK* ***-ise*** ['depjʊtaɪz] **vi : to deputize for sb** assurer les fonctions de qqn, remplacer qqn.

deputy ['depjʊtɪ] ■ **adj** adjoint(e) ▸ **deputy chairman** vice-président *m* ▸ **deputy head** SCH directeur *m* adjoint ▸ **deputy leader** POL vice-président *m*.
■ **n** (**pl -ies**) **1.** [second-in-command] adjoint *m*, -e *f* **2.** *US* [deputy sheriff] shérif *m* adjoint.

derail [dɪ'reɪl] **vt** [train] faire dérailler.

derailment [dɪ'reɪlmənt] **n** déraillement *m*.

deranged [dɪ'reɪndʒd] **adj** dérangé(e).

derby [*UK* 'dɑːbɪ, *US* 'dɜːbɪ] (**pl -ies**) **n 1.** SPORT derby *m* **2.** *US* [hat] chapeau *m* melon.

deregulate [ˌdiː'regjʊleɪt] **vt** déréglementer.

deregulation [ˌdiːregjʊ'leɪʃn] **n** déréglementation *f*.

derelict ['derəlɪkt] **adj** en ruines.

dereliction [ˌderə'lɪkʃn] **n 1.** [abandonment] abandon *m* **2.** *UK* [negligence] négligence *f* ▸ **dereliction of duty** manquement *m* au devoir.

deride [dɪ'raɪd] **vt** railler.

derision [dɪ'rɪʒn] **n** dérision *f*.

derisive [dɪ'raɪsɪv] **adj** moqueur(euse).

derisively [dɪ'raɪsɪvlɪ] **adv** avec dérision / [say, speak] d'un ton moqueur.

derisory [də'raɪzərɪ] **adj 1.** [puny, trivial] dérisoire **2.** [derisive] moqueur(euse).

derivation [ˌderɪ'veɪʃn] **n** [of word] dérivation *f*.

derivative [dɪ'rɪvətɪv] ■ **adj** *pej* pas original(e).
■ **n** dérivé *m*.

derive [dɪ'raɪv] ■ **vt 1.** [draw, gain] **: to derive sthg from sthg** tirer qqch de qqch **2.** [originate] **: to be derived from** venir de.
■ **vi : to derive from** venir de.

dermatitis [ˌdɜːmə'taɪtɪs] **n** dermatite *f*.

dermatologist [ˌdɜːmə'tɒlədʒɪst] **n** dermatologue *mf*.

dermatology [ˌdɜːmə'tɒlədʒɪ] **n** dermatologie *f*.

derogatory [dɪ'rɒgətrɪ] **adj** [comment, remark] désobligeant(e) / [word] péjoratif(ive).

derrick ['derɪk] **n 1.** [crane] mât *m* de charge **2.** [over oil well] derrick *m*.

derv [dɜːv] **n** *UK* gas-oil *m*.

desalination [diːˌsælɪ'neɪʃn] **n** dessalement *m*, dessalaison *f*.

descant ['deskænt] **n** [tune] déchant *m*.

descend [dɪ'send] ■ **vt** *fml* [go down] descendre.
■ **vi 1.** *fml* [go down] descendre **2.** [fall] **: to descend (on)** [enemy] s'abattre (sur) / [subj: silence, gloom] tomber (sur) **3.** [arrive] **: to descend on** [a town] arriver en nombre dans, envahir / [subj: in-laws etc] arriver à l'improviste chez **4.** [stoop] **: to descend to sthg/to doing sthg** s'abaisser à qqch/à faire qqch.

descendant [dɪ'sendənt] **n** descendant *m*, -e *f*.

descended [dɪ'sendɪd] **adj : to be descended from sb** descendre de qqn.

descending [dɪ'sendɪŋ] **adj : in descending order** en ordre décroissant.

descent [dɪ'sent] **n 1.** [downwards movement] descente *f* **2.** *(U)* [origin] origine *f*.

describe [dɪ'skraɪb] **vt** décrire.

description [dɪ'skrɪpʃn] **n 1.** [account] description *f* ▸ **a man answering the police description** un homme correspondant au signalement donné par la police **2.** [type] sorte *f*, genre *m*.

descriptive [dɪ'skrɪptɪv] **adj** descriptif(ive).

desecrate ['desɪkreɪt] **vt** profaner.

desecration [ˌdesɪ'kreɪʃn] **n** profanation *f*.

desegregate [ˌdiː'segrɪgeɪt] **vt** pratiquer la déségrégation dans.

deselect [ˌdiːsɪ'lekt] **vt** *UK* ne pas resélectionner pour une réélection.

desensitize, ***-ise*** *UK* [ˌdiː'sensɪtaɪz] **vt** désensibiliser.

desert ■ **n** ['dezət] désert *m*.
■ **vt** [dɪ'zɜːt] **1.** [place] déserter **2.** [person, group] déserter, abandonner.
■ **vi** [dɪ'zɜːt] MIL déserter.
◆ ***deserts*** **npl** [dɪ'zɜːts] **: to get one's just deserts** recevoir ce que l'on mérite.

deserted [dɪ'zɜːtɪd] **adj** désert(e).

deserter [dɪ'zɜːtəʳ] **n** déserteur *m*.

desertion [dɪ'zɜːʃn] **n 1.** MIL désertion *f* **2.** [of person] abandon *m*.

desert island ['dezət-] **n** île *f* déserte.

deserve [dɪ'zɜːv] **vt** mériter ▸ **to deserve to do sthg** mériter de faire qqch ▸ **she deserves wider recognition** elle mérite d'être plus largement reconnue.

deserved [dɪ'zɜːvd] **adj** mérité(e).

deservedly [dɪ'zɜːvɪdlɪ] **adv** à juste titre.

deserving [dɪ'zɜːvɪŋ] **adj** [person] méritant(e) / [cause, charity] méritoire ▸ **to be deserving of sthg** *fml* mériter qqch.

desiccated ['desɪkeɪtɪd] **adj** séché(e).

design [dɪ'zaɪn] ■ **n 1.** [plan, drawing] plan *m*, étude *f* **2.** *(U)* [art] design *m* **3.** [pattern] motif *m*, dessin *m* **4.** [shape] ligne *f* / [of dress] style *m* **5.** *fml* [intention] dessein *m* ▸ **by design** à dessein ▸ **to have designs on sb/sthg** avoir des desseins sur qqn/qqch.
■ **vt 1.** [draw plans for - building, car] faire les plans de, dessiner / [- dress] créer **2.** [plan] concevoir, mettre au point ▸ **to be designed for sthg/to do sthg** être conçu pour qqch/pour faire qqch.

designate ■ **adj** ['dezɪgnət] désigné(e).
■ **vt** ['dezɪgneɪt] désigner ▸ **to designate sb as sthg/to do sthg** désigner qqn à qqch/pour faire qqch.

designation [ˌdezɪg'neɪʃn] **n** *fml* [name] appellation *f*.

designer [dɪ'zaɪnəʳ] ■ **adj** de marque.
■ **n** INDUST concepteur *m*, -trice *f* / ARCHIT dessinateur *m*, -trice *f* / [of dresses etc] styliste *mf* / THEAT décorateur *m*, -trice *f*.

designer stubble **n** *hum* barbe *f* de deux jours.

desirability [dɪˌzaɪərə'bɪlətɪ] **n** *(U)* **1.** [benefits] intérêt *m*, avantage *m*, opportunité *f* ▸ **no one questions the desirability of lowering interest rates** personne ne conteste les avantages d'une baisse des taux d'intérêts **2.** [attractiveness] charmes *mpl*, attraits *mpl*.

desirable [dɪ'zaɪərəbl] **adj 1.** [enviable, attractive] désirable **2.** *fml* [appropriate] désirable, souhaitable.

desire [dɪ'zaɪəʳ] ■ **n** désir *m* ▸ **desire for sthg/to do sthg** désir de qqch/de faire qqch.
■ **vt** désirer ▸ **it leaves a lot to be desired** ça laisse beaucoup à désirer.

desirous [dɪ'zaɪərəs] **adj** *fml* **: desirous of sthg/of doing sthg** désireux(euse) de qqch/de faire qqch.

desist [dɪ'zɪst] **vi** *fml* **: to desist (from doing sthg)** cesser (de faire qqch).

desk [desk] **n** bureau *m* ▸ **reception desk** réception *f* ▸ **information desk** bureau *m* de renseignements.

deskbound ['deskbaʊnd] **adj** sédentaire ▸ **she hates being deskbound** elle déteste faire un travail sédentaire.

desk clerk **n** *US* réceptionniste *mf*.

desk editor **n** rédacteur *m*, -trice *f*.

deskill [ˌdi:'skɪl] **vt** déqualifier.

desk lamp **n** lampe *f* de bureau.

desktop ['desktɒp] ■ **adj** [computer] de bureau.
■ **n** COMPUT bureau *m*, poste *m* de travail.

desktop publishing **n** publication *f* assistée par ordinateur.

desolate ['desələt] **adj 1.** [place] abandonné(e) **2.** [person] désespéré(e), désolé(e).

desolation [ˌdesə'leɪʃn] **n** désolation *f*.

despair [dɪ'speəʳ] ■ **n** *(U)* désespoir *m* ▸ **to be in despair** être au désespoir.
■ **vi** désespérer ▸ **to despair of** désespérer de ▸ **to despair of doing sthg** désespérer de faire qqch.

despairing [dɪ'speərɪŋ] **adj** de désespoir.

despairingly [dɪ'speərɪŋlɪ] **adv** avec désespoir.

despatch [dɪ'spætʃ] *UK* = ***dispatch***.

desperate ['desprət] **adj** désespéré(e) ▸ **to be desperate for sthg** avoir absolument besoin de qqch.

desperately ['desprətlɪ] **adv** désespérément ▸ **desperately ill** gravement malade.

desperation [ˌdespə'reɪʃn] **n** désespoir *m* ▸ **he agreed in desperation** en désespoir de cause, il a accepté.

despicable [dɪ'spɪkəbl] **adj** ignoble.

despicably [dɪ'spɪkəblɪ] **adv** [behave] bassement, d'une façon indigne.

despise [dɪ'spaɪz] **vt** [person] mépriser / [racism] exécrer.

despite [dɪ'spaɪt] **prep** malgré.

despondent [dɪ'spɒndənt] **adj** abattu(e), consterné(e).

despondently [dɪ'spɒndəntlɪ] **adv** d'un air consterné / [say, speak] d'un ton consterné.

despot ['despɒt] **n** despote *m*.

despotic [de'spɒtɪk] **adj** despotique.

dessert [dɪ'zɜ:t] **n** dessert *m*.

dessertspoon [dɪ'zɜ:tspu:n] **n 1.** [spoon] cuillère *f* à dessert **2.** [spoonful] cuillerée *f* à dessert.

dessert wine **n** vin *m* doux.

destabilization, *UK* ***-isation*** [di:ˌsteɪbɪlaɪ'zeɪʃn] **n** déstabilisation *f*.

destabilize, *UK* ***-ise*** [ˌdi:'steɪbɪlaɪz] **vt** déstabiliser.

destination [ˌdestɪ'neɪʃn] **n** destination *f*.

destined ['destɪnd] **adj 1.** [intended] **: destined for** destiné(e) à ▸ **destined to do sthg** destiné à faire qqch **2.** [bound] **: destined for** à destination de.

destiny ['destɪnɪ] (pl -ies) **n** destinée *f*.

destitute ['destɪtju:t] **adj** indigent(e).

destitution [ˌdestɪ'tju:ʃn] **n** misère *f*, indigence *f*.

de-stress [di:'stres] **n** dé-stresser *inf*.

destroy [dɪ'strɔɪ] **vt 1.** [ruin] détruire ▸ **to destroy sb's life** briser la vie de qqn **2.** [put down - animal] faire piquer.

destroyer [dɪ'strɔɪəʳ] **n 1.** [ship] destroyer *m* **2.** [person, thing] destructeur *m*, -trice *f*.

destruction [dɪ'strʌkʃn] **n** destruction *f*.

destructive [dɪ'strʌktɪv] **adj** [harmful] destructeur(trice).

destructively [dɪ'strʌktɪvlɪ] **adv** de façon destructrice.

destructiveness [dɪ'strʌktɪvnɪs] **n** [of bomb, weapon] capacité *f* destructrice / [of criticism] caractère *m* destructeur / [of person] penchant *m* destructeur.

desultory ['desəltrɪ] **adj** *fml* [conversation] décousu(e) / [attempt] peu enthousiaste.

Det. abbr of ***Detective***.

detach [dɪ'tætʃ] **vt 1.** [pull off] détacher ▸ **to detach sthg from sthg** détacher qqch de qqch **2.** [dissociate] **: to detach o.s. from sthg** [from reality] se détacher de qqch / [from proceedings, discussions] s'écarter de qqch.

detachable [dɪ'tætʃəbl] **adj** détachable, amovible.

detached [dɪ'tætʃt] **adj** [unemotional] détaché(e).

detached house **n** *UK* maison *f* individuelle.

detachment [dɪ'tætʃmənt] **n** détachement *m*.

detail ['di:teɪl] ■ **n 1.** [small point] détail *m* ▸ **to go into detail** entrer dans les détails ▸ **in detail** en détail ▸ **attention to detail is important** il faut être minutieux OR méticuleux **2.** MIL détachement *m*.
■ **vt** [list] détailler.
◆ ***details*** **npl** [personal information] coordonnées *fpl*.

detailed ['di:teɪld] **adj** détaillé(e).

detain [dɪ'teɪn] **vt 1.** [in police station] détenir / [in hospital] garder **2.** [delay] retenir.

detainee [ˌdi:teɪ'ni:] **n** détenu *m*, -e *f*.

detect [dɪ'tekt] **vt 1.** [subj: person] déceler **2.** [subj: machine] détecter.

detectable [dɪ'tektəbl] **adj** [gen] détectable / [illness] que l'on peut dépister.

detection [dɪ'tekʃn] **n** *(U)* **1.** [of crime] dépistage *m* **2.** [of aircraft, submarine] détection *f*.

detective [dɪ'tektɪv] **n** détective *mf*.

detective novel **n** roman *m* policier.

detector [dɪ'tektəʳ] **n** détecteur *m*.

detector van **n** *UK voiture-radar utilisée pour la détection des postes de télévision non déclarés.*

détente [deɪ'tɒnt] **n** POL détente *f*.

detention [dɪ'tenʃn] **n 1.** [of suspect, criminal] détention *f* ▸ **in detention** en détention **2.** SCH retenue *f* ▸ **in detention** en retenue.

detention centre **n** *UK* centre *m* de détention.

deter [dɪ'tɜːʳ] (pt & pp **-red**, cont **-ring**) **vt** dissuader ▸ **to deter sb from doing sthg** dissuader qqn de faire qqch.

detergent [dɪ'tɜːdʒənt] **n** détergent *m*.

deteriorate [dɪ'tɪərɪəreɪt] **vi** se détériorer.

deterioration [dɪˌtɪərɪə'reɪʃn] **n** détérioration *f*.

determination [dɪˌtɜːmɪ'neɪʃn] **n** détermination *f*.

determine [dɪ'tɜːmɪn] **vt 1.** [establish, control] déterminer **2.** *fml* [decide] **: to determine to do sthg** décider de faire qqch.

determined [dɪ'tɜːmɪnd] **adj 1.** [person] déterminé(e) ▸ **determined to do sthg** déterminé à faire qqch **2.** [effort] obstiné(e).

determining [dɪ'tɜːmɪnɪŋ] **adj** déterminant(e).

deterrent [dɪ'terənt] ■ **adj** de dissuasion, dissuasif(ive).
■ **n** moyen *m* de dissuasion.

detest [dɪ'test] **vt** détester.

detestable [dɪ'testəbl] **adj** détestable.

dethrone [dɪ'θrəʊn] **vt** détrôner.

detonate ['detəneɪt] ■ **vt** faire détoner.
■ **vi** détoner.

detonator ['detəneɪtəʳ] **n** détonateur *m*.

detour ['diːˌtʊəʳ] ■ **n** détour *m*.
■ **vi** faire un détour.
■ **vt** (faire) dévier.

detox ['diːtɒks] **n** *inf* désintoxication *f* ▸ **detox centre** centre *m* de désintoxication.

detoxification [diːˌtɒksɪfɪ'keɪʃn] **n** [of person] désintoxication *f*.

detoxify [ˌdiː'tɒksɪfaɪ] (pt & pp **-ied**) **vt** [person] désintoxiquer.

detract [dɪ'trækt] **vi : to detract from** diminuer.

detraction [dɪ'trækʃn] **n** critique *f*, dénigrement *m*.

detractor [dɪ'træktəʳ] **n** détracteur *m*, -trice *f*.

detriment ['detrɪmənt] **n : to the detriment of** au détriment de.

detrimental [ˌdetrɪ'mentl] **adj** préjudiciable.

detritus [dɪ'traɪtəs] **n** *(U)* détritus *m*.

deuce [djuːs] **n** TENNIS égalité *f*.

Deutschmark ['dɔɪtʃˌmɑːk] **n** mark *m* allemand.

devaluation [ˌdiːvæljʊ'eɪʃn] **n** dévaluation *f*.

devalue [ˌdiː'væljuː] **vt** dévaluer.

devastate ['devəsteɪt] **vt 1.** [destroy - area, city] dévaster **2.** *fig* [person] accabler.

devastated ['devəsteɪtɪd] **adj 1.** [area, city] dévasté(e) **2.** *fig* [person] accablé(e).

devastating ['devəsteɪtɪŋ] **adj 1.** [hurricane, remark] dévastateur(trice) **2.** [upsetting] accablant(e) **3.** [attractive] irrésistible.

devastatingly ['devəsteɪtɪŋlɪ] **adv** de manière dévastatrice / [as intensifier] **: devastatingly beautiful** d'une beauté irrésistible.

devastation [ˌdevə'steɪʃn] **n** dévastation *f*.

develop [dɪ'veləp] ■ **vt 1.** [gen] développer **2.** [land, area] aménager, développer **3.** [illness, fault, habit] contracter **4.** [resources] développer, exploiter.
■ **vi 1.** [grow, advance] se développer ▸ **to develop into sthg** devenir qqch **2.** [appear - problem, trouble] se déclarer **3.** PHOT se développer.

developer [dɪ'veləpəʳ] **n 1.** [of land] promoteur *m* immobilier **2.** [person] **: to be an early/a late developer** être en avance/en retard sur son âge **3.** PHOT [chemical] développateur *m*, révélateur *m*.

developing country [dɪ'veləpɪŋ-] **n** pays *m* en voie de développement.

development [dɪ'veləpmənt] **n 1.** [gen] développement *m* ▸ **a surprise development** un rebondissement ▸ **there are no new developments** il n'y a rien de nouveau ▸ **development grant** subvention *f* pour le développement **2.** *(U)* [of land, area] exploitation *f* **3.** [land being developed] zone *f* d'aménagement / [developed area] zone aménagée **4.** [group of buildings] lotissement *m* **5.** *(U)* [of illness, fault] évolution *f*.

developmental [dɪˌveləp'mentl] **adj** de développement.

development area **n** *UK* zone *f* d'aménagement.

deviance ['diːvjəns], ***deviancy*** ['diːvjənsɪ] **n** [gen & PSYCHOL] déviance *f* ▸ **deviance from the norm** écart *m* par rapport à la norme.

deviant ['diːvjənt] ■ **adj** déviant(e).
■ **n** déviant *m*, -e *f*.

deviate ['diːvɪeɪt] **vi : to deviate (from)** dévier (de), s'écarter (de).

deviation [ˌdiːvɪ'eɪʃn] **n 1.** [abnormality] déviance *f* **2.** [departure - from rule, plan] écart *m* / *pej* déviation *f*.

device [dɪ'vaɪs] **n 1.** [apparatus] appareil *m*, dispositif *m* **2.** [plan, method] moyen *m* ▸ **to leave sb to their own devices** laisser qqn se débrouiller tout seul.

devil ['devl] **n 1.** [evil spirit] diable *m* ▸ **speak** *OR* **talk of the devil (and he appears)!** quand on parle du loup (on en voit la queue)! ▸ **better the devil you know than the devil you don't** *prov* on sait ce qu'on perd, on ne sait pas ce qu'on trouve ▸ **the devil finds** *OR* **makes work for idle hands** *prov* l'oisiveté est (la) mère de tous les vices *prov* **2.** *inf* [person] type *m* ▸ **you little devil!** petit monstre! ▸ **you lucky devil!** veinard! ▸ **poor devil!** pauvre diable! **3.** [for emphasis] **: who/where/why the devil...?** qui/où/pourquoi diable...? ▸ **how the devil should I know?** comment voulez-vous que je sache?

◆ ***Devil*** **n** [Satan] **: the Devil** le Diable.

devilish ['devlɪʃ] **adj** diabolique.

devil-may-care **adj** insouciant(e).

devil's advocate **n** avocat *m* du diable ▸ **to play devil's advocate** se faire l'avocat du diable.

devious ['di:vjəs] **adj 1.** [dishonest - person] retors(e), sournois(e) / [- scheme, means] détourné(e) **2.** [tortuous] tortueux(euse).

deviously ['di:vjəslɪ] **adv** sournoisement.

deviousness ['di:vjəsnɪs] **n** [dishonesty] sournoiserie *f*.

devise [dɪ'vaɪz] **vt** concevoir.

deviser [dɪ'vaɪzəʳ] **n** [of plan] inventeur *m*, -trice *f* / [of scheme] auteur *m*.

devoid [dɪ'vɔɪd] **adj** *fml* **: devoid of** dépourvu(e) de, dénué(e) de.

devolution [ˌdi:və'lu:ʃn] **n** POL dévolution *f*, décentralisation *f*.

> CULTURE
> ## Devolution
> Après les réformes de décentralisation du gouvernement travailliste britannique, de nouvelles institutions politiques ont été mises en place : le Parlement écossais et l'Assemblée nationale galloise. La **dévolution** (ou autonomie) de l'Écosse et du pays de Galles a été établie le 1er juillet 1999, après un vote massif par référendum en 1997. L'Écosse a obtenu le pouvoir de légiférer dans les domaines non réservés au Parlement britannique, tels que la santé, l'éducation, les transports, l'agriculture, la pêche, le sport, la culture ou les affaires régionales. En revanche, les lois votées par le Parlement de Westminster s'appliquent toujours au pays de Galles, l'Assemblée galloise ne disposant d'aucun pouvoir législatif.

devolve [dɪ'vɒlv] **vi** *fml* **: to devolve on** *OR* **upon sb** incomber à qqn.

devote [dɪ'vəʊt] **vt : to devote sthg to sthg** consacrer qqch à qqch ▸ **to devote o.s. to sthg** se vouer *OR* se consacrer à qqch.

devoted [dɪ'vəʊtɪd] **adj** dévoué(e) ▸ **a devoted mother** une mère dévouée à ses enfants.

devotee [ˌdevə'ti:] **n** [fan] passionné *m*, -e *f*.

devotion [dɪ'vəʊʃn] **n 1.** [commitment] **: devotion (to)** dévouement *m* (à) **2.** RELIG dévotion *f*.

> CONFUSABLE / PARONYME
> ## devotion
> When translating **devotion**, note that ***dévotion*** and ***dévouement*** are not interchangeable. ***Dévotion*** usually refers to religious fervour and ***dévouement*** expresses the idea of dedication.

devour [dɪ'vaʊəʳ] **vt** *liter & fig* dévorer.

devout [dɪ'vaʊt] **adj** dévot(e).

dew [dju:] **n** rosée *f*.

dexterity [dek'sterətɪ] **n** dextérité *f*.

dext(e)rous ['dekstrəs] **adj** habile.

dextrose ['dekstrəʊs] **n** dextrose *m*.

DFE (abbr of ***Department for Education***) **n** *ministère britannique de l'éducation nationale.*

DG **n abbr of *director-general*.**

dhal [dɑ:l] **n** dal *m*.

DHSS (abbr of ***Department of Health and Social Security***) **n** *ancien nom du ministère britannique de la santé et de la sécurité sociale.*

DHTML [ˌdi:eɪtʃti:em'el] (abbr of ***Dynamic Hypertext Markup Language***) **n** COMPUT DHTML *m*.

diabetes [ˌdaɪə'bi:ti:z] **n** diabète *m*.

diabetic [ˌdaɪə'betɪk] ■ **adj 1.** [person] diabétique **2.** [jam, chocolate] pour diabétiques.

■ **n** diabétique *mf*.

diabolic(al) [ˌdaɪə'bɒlɪk(l)] **adj 1.** [evil] diabolique **2.** *inf* [very bad] atroce.

diaeresis *UK*, ***dieresis*** *US* [daɪ'erɪsɪs] (pl **-ses** [-si:z]) **n** tréma *m*.

diagnose ['daɪəgnəʊz] **vt** diagnostiquer.

diagnosis [ˌdaɪəg'nəʊsɪs] (pl **-ses** [-si:z]) **n** diagnostic *m*.

diagnostic [ˌdaɪəg'nɒstɪk] **adj** diagnostique.

diagnostics [ˌdaɪəg'nɒstɪks] **n** *(U)* COMPUT & MED diagnostic *m*.

diagonal [daɪ'ægənl] ■ **adj** [line] diagonal(e).

■ **n** diagonale *f*.

diagonally [daɪ'ægənəlɪ] **adv** en diagonale.

diagram ['daɪəgræm] **n** diagramme *m*.

diagrammatic [ˌdaɪəgrə'mætɪk] **adj** en forme de diagramme.

dial ['daɪəl] ■ **n** cadran *m* / [of radio] cadran de fréquences.

■ **vt** (*UK* **-led**, cont **-ling**, *US* **-ed**, cont **-ing**) [number] composer.

dialect ['daɪəlekt] **n** dialecte *m.*

dialling code ['daɪəlɪŋ-] **n** *UK* indicatif *m.*

dialling tone *UK* ['daɪəlɪŋ-], ***dial tone*** *US* **n** tonalité *f.*

dialogue *UK*, ***dialog*** *US* ['daɪəlɒg] **n** dialogue *m.*

dialogue box *UK*, ***dialog box*** *US* **n** COMPUT boîte *f* de dialogue.

dial tone *US* = ***dialling tone.***

dial-up access **n** COMPUT accès *m* commuté.

dialysis [daɪ'ælɪsɪs] **n** dialyse *f.*

diamanté [dɪə'mɒnteɪ] **adj** diamanté(e).

diameter [daɪ'æmɪtə^r] **n** diamètre *m.*

diametrically [ˌdaɪə'metrɪklɪ] **adv : diametrically opposed** diamétralement opposé(e).

diamond ['daɪəmənd] **n 1.** [gem] diamant *m* **2.** [shape] losange *m* **3.** [playing card] carreau *m.*
◆ ***diamonds*** **npl** carreau *m* ▸ **the six of diamonds** le six de carreau.

diamond wedding **n** noces *fpl* de diamant.

diaper ['daɪəpə^r] **n** *US* couche *f.*

diaphanous [daɪ'æfənəs] **adj** diaphane.

diaphragm ['daɪəfræm] **n** diaphragme *m.*

diarist ['daɪərɪst] **n** [private] auteur *m* d'un journal intime / [of public affairs] chroniqueur *m.*

diarrhoea *UK*, ***diarrhea*** *US* [ˌdaɪə'rɪə] **n** diarrhée *f.*

diary ['daɪərɪ] (pl **-ies**) **n 1.** [appointment book] agenda *m* **2.** [journal] journal *m.*

diatribe ['daɪətraɪb] **n** diatribe *f.*

dice [daɪs] ■ **n** (pl **dice**) [for games] dé *m* ▸ **no dice** *US inf* pas question.
■ **vt** couper en dés.

dicey ['daɪsɪ] (comp **-ier**, superl **-iest**) **adj** *esp UK inf* risqué(e).

dichotomy [daɪ'kɒtəmɪ] (pl **-ies**) **n** dichotomie *f.*

dickens ['dɪkɪnz] **n** *UK inf dated* **: who/what/where the dickens...?** qui/que/où diable...?

dickhead ['dɪkhed] **n** *v inf* con *m.*

dickybird ['dɪkɪbɜ:d] **n** *inf* petit oiseau *m.*

Dictaphone® ['dɪktəfəʊn] **n** Dictaphone® *m.*

dictate ■ **vt** [dɪk'teɪt] dicter ▸ **to dictate sthg to sb** dicter qqch à qqn.
■ **vi** [dɪk'teɪt] **1.** [read aloud] **: to dictate to sb** dicter à qqn **2.** [give orders] **: to dictate to sb** commander à qqn, donner des ordres à qqn.
■ **n** ['dɪkteɪt] ordre *m.*

dictation [dɪk'teɪʃn] **n** dictée *f.*

dictator [dɪk'teɪtə^r] **n** dictateur *m.*

dictatorial [ˌdɪktə'tɔ:rɪəl] **adj** dictatorial(e).

dictatorship [dɪk'teɪtəʃɪp] **n** dictature *f.*

diction ['dɪkʃn] **n** diction *f.*

dictionary ['dɪkʃənrɪ] (pl **-ies**) **n** dictionnaire *m.*

dictum ['dɪktəm] (pl **dicta** ['dɪktə] *OR* **dictums**) **n** *fml* **1.** [statement] affirmation *f* / LAW remarque *f* superfétatoire **2.** [maxim] dicton *m*, maxime *f.*

did [dɪd] **pt** ➤ ***do.***

didactic [dɪ'dæktɪk] **adj** didactique.

didactically [dɪ'dæktɪklɪ] **adv** didactiquement.

diddle ['dɪdl] **vt** *inf* escroquer, rouler.

didn't ['dɪdnt] = ***did not.***

die [daɪ] ■ **vi** (pt & pp **died**, cont **dying**) mourir ▸ **to be dying** se mourir ▸ **to be dying to do sthg** mourir d'envie de faire qqch ▸ **to be dying for a drink/cigarette** mourir d'envie de boire un verre/de fumer une cigarette.
■ **n 1.** [for shaping metal] matrice *f* **2.** (pl **dice** [daɪs]) [dice] dé *m.*
◆ ***die away*** **vi** [sound] s'éteindre / [wind] tomber.
◆ ***die down*** **vi** [sound] s'affaiblir / [wind] tomber / [fire] baisser.
◆ ***die out*** **vi** s'éteindre, disparaître.

diehard ['daɪhɑ:d] **n : to be a diehard** être coriace / [reactionary] être réactionnaire.

dieresis [daɪ'erɪsɪs] *US* = ***diaeresis.***

diesel ['di:zl] **n** diesel *m.*

diesel engine **n** AUT moteur *m* diesel / RAIL locomotive *f* diesel.

diesel fuel, ***diesel oil*** **n** diesel *m.*

diet ['daɪət] ■ **n 1.** [eating pattern] alimentation *f* **2.** [to lose weight] régime *m* ▸ **to be on a diet** être au régime ▸ **to go on a diet** faire *OR* suivre un régime.
■ **comp** [low-calorie] de régime.
■ **vi** faire *OR* suivre un régime.

dietary ['daɪətrɪ] **adj** diététique.

dietary fibre *UK*, ***dietary fiber*** *US* **n** *(U)* fibres *fpl* alimentaires.

dieter ['daɪətə^r] **n** personne *f* qui suit un régime.

dietician [ˌdaɪə'tɪʃn] **n** diététicien *m*, -enne *f.*

differ ['dɪfə^r] **vi 1.** [be different] être différent(e), différer / [people] être différent ▸ **to differ from** être différent de **2.** [disagree] **: to differ with sb (about sthg)** ne pas être d'accord avec qqn (à propos de qqch).

difference ['dɪfrəns] **n** différence *f* ▸ **I can't tell the difference between the two** je ne vois pas la différence entre les deux ▸ **it doesn't make any difference** cela ne change rien ▸ **to make all the difference** faire toute la différence ▸ **a difference of opinion** une différence *OR* divergence d'opinion.

different ['dɪfrənt] **adj : different (from)** différent(e) (de) ▸ **that's quite a different matter** ça, c'est une autre affaire *OR* histoire.

differential [ˌdɪfə'renʃl] ■ **adj** différentiel(elle).
■ **n 1.** [between pay scales] écart *m* **2.** TECH différentielle *f.*

differentiate [ˌdɪfə'renʃɪeɪt] ■ **vt : to differentiate sthg from sthg** différencier qqch de qqch, faire la différence entre qqch et qqch.
■ **vi : to differentiate (between)** faire la différence (entre).

differently ['dɪfrəntlɪ] **adv** différemment, autrement ▸ **to think differently** ne pas être d'accord.

differently abled **adj** [in politically correct language] handicapé(e).

difficult ['dɪfɪkəlt] **adj** difficile.

difficulty ['dɪfɪkəltɪ] (pl **-ies**) **n** difficulté *f* ▶ **to have difficulty in doing sthg** avoir de la difficulté *OR* du mal à faire qqch.

diffidence ['dɪfɪdəns] **n** manque *m* d'assurance.

diffident ['dɪfɪdənt] **adj** [person] qui manque d'assurance / [manner, voice, approach] hésitant(e).

diffuse ■ **adj** [dɪ'fju:s] **1.** [vague] diffus(e) **2.** [spread out - city] étendu(e) / [- company] éparpillé(e).
■ **vt** [dɪ'fju:z] diffuser, répandre.
■ **vi** [dɪ'fju:z] **1.** [light] se diffuser, se répandre **2.** [information] se répandre.

diffusion [dɪ'fju:ʒn] **n** diffusion *f*.

dig [dɪg] ■ **vi** (pt & pp **dug**, cont **digging**) **1.** [in ground] creuser **2.** [subj: belt, strap] **: his elbow was digging into my side** son coude me rentrait dans les côtes ▶ **to dig into sb** couper qqn.
■ **vt** (pt & pp **dug**, cont **digging**) **1.** [hole] creuser **2.** [garden] bêcher **3.** [press] **: to dig sthg into sthg** enfoncer qqch dans qqch.
■ **n 1.** *fig* [unkind remark] pique *f* **2.** ARCHEOL fouilles *fpl*.
◆ ***dig out*** **vt sep 1.** [rescue] dégager **2.** *inf* [find] dénicher.
◆ ***dig up*** **vt sep 1.** [from ground] déterrer / [potatoes] arracher **2.** *inf* [information] dénicher.

digest ■ **n** ['daɪdʒest] résumé *m*, digest *m*.
■ **vt** [dɪ'dʒest] *lit* & *fig* digérer.

digestible [dɪ'dʒestəbl] **adj** digeste.

digestion [dɪ'dʒestʃn] **n** digestion *f*.

digestive [dɪ'dʒestɪv] **adj** digestif(ive).

digestive biscuit [daɪ'dʒestɪv-] **n** *UK* ≃ sablé *m* (à la farine complète).

digit ['dɪdʒɪt] **n 1.** [figure] chiffre *m* **2.** [finger] doigt *m* / [toe] orteil *m*.

digital ['dɪdʒɪtl] **adj** numérique.

digital audio tape = ***DAT***.

digital broadcasting **n** diffusion *f* numérique.

digital camcorder **n** Caméscope® *m* numérique.

digital camera **n** appareil *m* photo numérique.

digital computer **n** calculateur *m* numérique.

digital display **n** affichage *m* numérique.

digitally remastered ['dɪdʒɪtəlɪri:'mɑ:stəd] **adj** remixé(e) en numérique.

digital radio **n** radio *f* numérique.

digital recording **n** enregistrement *m* numérique.

digital signature **n** signature *f* électronique.

digital television **n** [technique] télévision *f* numérique.

digital watch **n** montre *f* à affichage digital.

digitization [,dɪdʒɪtaɪ'zeɪʃn] **n** numérisation *f*.

digitize, *UK* ***-ise*** ['dɪdʒɪtaɪz] **vt** numériser.

dignified ['dɪgnɪfaɪd] **adj** digne, plein(e) de dignité.

dignify ['dɪgnɪfaɪ] (pt & pp **-ied**) **vt** [place, appearance] donner de la grandeur à.

dignitary ['dɪgnɪtrɪ] (pl **-ies**) **n** dignitaire *m*.

dignity ['dɪgnətɪ] **n** dignité *f*.

digress [daɪ'gres] **vi : to digress (from)** s'écarter (de).

digression [daɪ'greʃn] **n** digression *f*.

digs [dɪgz] **npl** *UK inf* piaule *f*.

dike [daɪk] **n 1.** [wall, bank] digue *f* **2.** *inf offens* [lesbian] gouine *f*.

diktat ['dɪktɑ:t] **n** diktat *m*.

dilapidated [dɪ'læpɪdeɪtɪd] **adj** délabré(e).

dilapidation [dɪ,læpɪ'deɪʃn] **n** [of building] délabrement *m*, dégradation *f*.

dilate [daɪ'leɪt] ■ **vt** dilater.
■ **vi** se dilater.

dilated [daɪ'leɪtɪd] **adj** dilaté(e).

dilemma [dɪ'lemə] **n** dilemme *m*.

dilettante [,dɪlɪ'tæntɪ] (pl **-tes** *OR* **-ti** [-tɪ]) **n** dilettante *mf*.

diligence ['dɪlɪdʒəns] **n** application *f*.

diligent ['dɪlɪdʒənt] **adj** appliqué(e).

diligently ['dɪlɪdʒəntlɪ] **adv** avec assiduité *OR* soin *OR* application, assidûment.

dill [dɪl] **n** aneth *m*.

dilly-dally ['dɪlɪdælɪ] (pt & pp **dilly-dallied**) **vi** *inf* [dawdle] lanterner, lambiner / [hesitate] hésiter, tergiverser.

dilute [daɪ'lu:t] ■ **adj** dilué(e).
■ **vt : to dilute sthg (with)** diluer qqch (avec).

dilution [daɪ'lu:ʃn] **n** dilution *f*.

dim [dɪm] ■ **adj** (comp **-mer**, superl **-mest**) **1.** [dark - light] faible / [- room] sombre **2.** [indistinct - memory, outline] vague **3.** [weak - eyesight] faible **4.** *inf* [stupid] borné(e).
■ **vt** & **vi** (pt & pp **-med**, cont **-ming**) baisser.

dime [daɪm] **n** *US* (pièce *f* de) dix cents *mpl* ▶ **they're a dime a dozen** [common] il y en a à la pelle.

dimension [dɪ'menʃn] **n** dimension *f*.

-dimensional [dɪ'menʃənl] **suffix : two/four-dimensional** à deux/quatre dimensions.

dime store **n** *US* supérette *f* de quartier.

diminish [dɪ'mɪnɪʃ] **vt** & **vi** diminuer.

diminished [dɪ'mɪnɪʃt] **adj** diminué(e).

diminished responsibility **n** LAW responsabilité *f* atténuée.

diminishing [dɪ'mɪnɪʃɪŋ] ■ **adj** [influence, number, speed] décroissant(e), qui va en diminuant / [price, quality] qui baisse, en baisse ▶ **the law of diminishing returns** la loi des rendements décroissants.
■ **n** diminution *f*, baisse *f*.

diminution [,dɪmɪ'nju:ʃn] **n 1.** [in number, value] diminution *f*, baisse *f* / [in speed] réduction *f* / [in intensity, importance, strength] diminution *f*, affaiblissement *m* / [in temperature] baisse *f*, abaissement *m* / [in authority, price] baisse *f* ▸ **there has been no diminution in** *OR* **of our enthusiasm** notre enthousiasme n'a en rien faibli **2.** MUS diminution *f*.

diminutive [dɪ'mɪnjʊtɪv] *fml* ▪ **adj** minuscule.
▪ **n** GRAM diminutif *m*.

dimly ['dɪmlɪ] **adv** [lit] faiblement / [remember] vaguement.

dimmers ['dɪmərz] **npl** *US* [dipped headlights] phares *mpl* code *(inv)* / [parking lights] feux *mpl* de position.

dimmer (switch) ['dɪməʳ-] **n 1.** variateur *m* de lumière **2.** *US* = ***dipswitch***.

dimple ['dɪmpl] **n** fossette *f*.

dimwit ['dɪmwɪt] **n** *inf* crétin *m*, -e *f*.

dim-witted [-'wɪtɪd] **adj** *inf* crétin(e).

din [dɪn] **n** *inf* barouf *m*.

dine [daɪn] **vi** *fml* dîner.
◆ ***dine out*** **vi** dîner dehors.

diner ['daɪnəʳ] **n 1.** [person] dîneur *m*, -euse *f* **2.** *US* [café] petit restaurant *m* sans façon.

dingbat ['dɪŋbæt] **n** *inf* **1.** *US* [thing] truc *m*, machin *m* **2.** [fool] crétin *m*, -e *f*, gourde *f*.

dingdong [ˌdɪŋ'dɒŋ] ▪ **adj** *inf* [battle, argument] acharné(e).
▪ **n 1.** [of bell] ding dong *m* **2.** *UK inf* [quarrel] engueulade *f* / [fight] bagarre *f*.

dinghy ['dɪŋgɪ] (pl **-ies**) **n** [for sailing] dériveur *m* / [for rowing] (petit) canot *m*.

dinginess ['dɪndʒɪnɪs] **n** [shabbiness] aspect *m* miteux *OR* douteux / [drabness] couleur *f* terne.

dingo ['dɪŋgəʊ] (pl **-es**) **n** dingo *m*.

dingy ['dɪndʒɪ] (comp **-ier**, superl **-iest**) **adj** [shabby] miteux(euse) / [dirty] douteux(euse) / [colour] terne.

dining car ['daɪnɪŋ-] **n** wagon-restaurant *m*.

dining room ['daɪnɪŋ-] **n 1.** [in house] salle *f* à manger **2.** [in hotel] restaurant *m*.

dining table ['daɪnɪŋ-] **n** table *f (de salle à manger)*.

dinkie ['dɪŋkɪ] (abbr of ***double income no kids***) **n** *inf personne mariée aisée et sans enfants*.

dinner ['dɪnəʳ] **n** dîner *m*.

dinner dance **n** dîner *m* dansant.

dinner jacket **n** smoking *m*.

dinner party **n** dîner *m (sur invitation)*.

dinner service **n** service *m* de table.

dinner table **n** table *f (de salle à manger)*.

dinnertime ['dɪnətaɪm] **n** heure *f* du dîner.

dinosaur ['daɪnəsɔːʳ] **n** dinosaure *m*.

dint [dɪnt] **n** *fml* **: by dint of** à force de.

diocese ['daɪəsɪs] **n** diocèse *m*.

diode ['daɪəʊd] **n** diode *f*.

dioxin [daɪ'ɒksɪn] **n** dioxine *f*.

dip [dɪp] ▪ **n 1.** [in road, ground] déclivité *f* **2.** [sauce] sauce *f*, dip *m* **3.** [swim] baignade *f* (rapide) ▸ **to go for a dip** aller se baigner en vitesse, aller faire trempette.
▪ **vt** (pt & pp **-ped**, cont **-ping**) **1.** [into liquid] **: to dip sthg in** *OR* **into** tremper *OR* plonger qqch dans **2.** *UK* AUT **: to dip one's headlights** se mettre en code.
▪ **vi** (pt & pp **-ped**, cont **-ping**) **1.** [sun] baisser, descendre à l'horizon / [wing] plonger **2.** [road, ground] descendre.

Dip. *UK* abbr of ***diploma***.

diphtheria [dɪf'θɪərɪə] **n** diphtérie *f*.

diphthong ['dɪfθɒŋ] **n** diphtongue *f*.

diploma [dɪ'pləʊmə] (pl **-s**) **n** diplôme *m*.

diplomacy [dɪ'pləʊməsɪ] **n** diplomatie *f*.

diplomat ['dɪpləmæt] **n** diplomate *m*.

diplomatic [ˌdɪplə'mætɪk] **adj 1.** [service] diplomatique **2.** [tactful] diplomate.

diplomatically [ˌdɪplə'mætɪklɪ] **adv** POL diplomatiquement / *fig* avec diplomatie, diplomatiquement.

diplomatic bag **n** valise *f* diplomatique.

diplomatic corps **n** corps *m* diplomatique.

diplomatic immunity **n** immunité *f* diplomatique.

diplomatic relations **npl** relations *fpl* diplomatiques.

dippy ['dɪpɪ] (comp **-ier**, superl **-iest**) **adj** *inf* écervelé(e).

dipsomaniac [ˌdɪpsə'meɪnɪæk] **n** dipsomane *mf*.

dipstick ['dɪpstɪk] **n** AUT jauge *f (de niveau d'huile)*.

dipswitch ['dɪpswɪtʃ] **n** *UK* AUT manette *f* des codes.

dire ['daɪəʳ] **adj** [need, consequences] extrême / [warning] funeste ▸ **in dire straits** dans une situation désespérée.

direct [dɪ'rekt] ▪ **adj** direct(e) / [challenge] manifeste ▸ **direct flight/route** vol *m*/chemin *m* direct ▸ **he's a direct descendant of the King** il descend du roi en ligne directe ▸ **she asked some very direct questions** elle a posé des questions parfois très directes ▸ **it's the direct opposite of what I said** c'est exactement le contraire de ce que j'ai dit.
▪ **vt 1.** [gen] diriger ▸ **can you direct me to the train station?** pourriez-vous m'indiquer le chemin de la gare?
2. [aim] **: to direct sthg at sb** [question, remark] adresser qqch à qqn ▸ **the campaign is directed at teenagers** cette campagne vise les adolescents ▸ **we should direct all our efforts towards improving our education service** nous devrions consacrer tous nos efforts à améliorer notre système scolaire
3. CIN, RADIO & TV [film, programme] réaliser / [actors] diriger / THEAT [play] mettre en scène
4. [order] **: to direct sb to do sthg** ordonner à qqn de faire qqch ▸ **to direct the jury** instruire le jury.
▪ **adv** directement.

direct access **n** accès *m* direct.

direct action **n** action *f* directe.

direct advertising **n** publicité *f* directe.

direct costs **n** charges *fpl* directes, frais *mpl* directs.

direct current **n** courant *m* continu.

direct debit **n** *UK* prélèvement *m* automatique.

direct dialling *UK*, ***direct dialing*** *US* **n** automatique *m*.

direct hit **n** coup *m* au but *OR* de plein fouet.

direction [dɪ'rekʃn] **n** direction *f* ▸ **under the direction of** sous la direction de.
◆ ***directions*** **npl** **1.** [to find a place] indications *fpl* **2.** [for use] instructions *fpl*.

directive [dɪ'rektɪv] **n** directive *f*.

directly [dɪ'rektlɪ] **adv** **1.** [in straight line] directement **2.** [honestly, clearly] sans détours **3.** [exactly - behind, above] exactement **4.** [immediately] immédiatement **5.** [very soon] tout de suite.

direct mail **n** publipostage *m*.

direct marketing **n** marketing *m* direct.

direct memory access **n** COMPUT accès *m* direct à la mémoire.

directness [dɪ'rektnɪs] **n** **1.** [of person, reply] franchise *f* / [of remark] absence *f* d'ambiguïté **2.** [of attack] caractère *m* direct.

direct object **n** complément *m* (d'objet) direct.

director [dɪ'rektəʳ] **n** **1.** [of company] directeur *m*, -trice *f* **2.** THEAT metteur *m* en scène / CIN & TV réalisateur *m*, -trice *f*.

directorate [dɪ'rektərət] **n** conseil *m* d'administration.

director-general (pl **directors-general** *OR* **director-generals**) **n** directeur *m* général.

directorial [ˌdaɪrek'tɔːrɪəl] **adj** de mise en scène.

Director of Public Prosecutions **n** *UK* ≃ procureur *m* général.

director's chair **n** fauteuil *m* régisseur.

directorship [dɪ'rektəʃɪp] **n** **1.** [position] poste *m* de directeur **2.** [period] direction *f*.

directory [dɪ'rektərɪ] (pl **-ies**) **n** **1.** [annual publication] annuaire *m* **2.** COMPUT répertoire *m*.

directory enquiries *UK*, ***directory assistance*** *US* **n** (service *m* des) renseignements *mpl* téléphoniques.

direct rule **n** centralisation *f* de pouvoir.

direct selling **n** *(U)* vente *f* directe.

direct speech *UK*, ***direct discourse*** *US* **n** discours *m* direct.

direct taxation **n** imposition *f* directe.

dirge [dɜːdʒ] **n** chant *m* funèbre.

dirt [dɜːt] **n** *(U)* **1.** [mud, dust] saleté *f* **2.** [earth] terre *f*.

dirt-cheap *inf* ■ **adv** pour rien ▸ **I bought it dirt-cheap** je l'ai payé trois fois rien.
■ **adj** très bon marché.

dirt track **n** chemin *m* de terre.

dirty ['dɜːtɪ] ■ **adj** (**comp -ier, superl -iest**) **1.** [not clean, not fair] sale ▸ **he got his shirt dirty** il a sali sa chemise ▸ **to give sb a dirty look** regarder qqn de travers *OR* d'un sale œil **2.** [smutty - language, person] grossier(ère) / [- book, joke] cochon(onne) ▸ **to have a dirty mind** avoir l'esprit mal tourné.
■ **vt** (**pt & pp -ied**) salir.

dirty money **n** argent *m* mal acquis *OR* sale.

dirty trick **n** [malicious act] sale tour *m* ▸ **to play a dirty trick on sb** jouer un sale tour *OR* un tour de cochon à qqn.
◆ ***dirty tricks*** **npl : they've been up to their dirty tricks again** ils ont encore fait des leurs ▸ **dirty tricks campaign** POL *manœuvres déloyales visant à discréditer un adversaire politique*.

disability [ˌdɪsə'bɪlətɪ] (pl **-ies**) **n** infirmité *f* ▸ **people with disabilities** les handicapés.

disable [dɪs'eɪbl] **vt** **1.** [injure] rendre infirme **2.** [put out of action - guns, vehicle] mettre hors d'action.

disabled [dɪs'eɪbld] ■ **adj** [person] handicapé(e), infirme.
■ **npl : the disabled** les handicapés, les infirmes.

disablement [dɪs'eɪblmənt] **n** invalidité *f*.

disabuse [ˌdɪsə'bjuːz] **vt** *fml* **: to disabuse sb (of)** détromper qqn (sur).

disadvantage [ˌdɪsəd'vɑːntɪdʒ] **n** désavantage *m*, inconvénient *m* ▸ **to be at a disadvantage** être désavantagé ▸ **to be to sb's disadvantage** être au désavantage de qqn.

disadvantaged [ˌdɪsəd'vɑːntɪdʒd] **adj** défavorisé(e).

disadvantageous [ˌdɪsædvɑːn'teɪdʒəs] **adj** désavantageux(euse).

disaffected [ˌdɪsə'fektɪd] **adj** mécontent(e).

disaffection [ˌdɪsə'fekʃn] **n** mécontentement *m*.

disagree [ˌdɪsə'griː] **vi** **1.** [have different opinions] **: to disagree (with)** ne pas être d'accord (avec) **2.** [differ] ne pas concorder **3.** [subj: food, drink] **: to disagree with sb** ne pas réussir à qqn.

disagreeable [ˌdɪsə'griːəbl] **adj** désagréable.

disagreement [ˌdɪsə'griːmənt] **n** **1.** [in opinion] désaccord *m* **2.** [argument] différend *m* **3.** [dissimilarity] différence *f*.

disallow [ˌdɪsə'laʊ] **vt** **1.** *fml* [appeal, claim] rejeter **2.** [goal] refuser.

disappear [ˌdɪsə'pɪəʳ] **vi** disparaître.

disappearance [ˌdɪsə'pɪərəns] **n** disparition *f*.

HOW TO ...
express disagreement

Je ne suis absolument pas *ou* pas du tout d'accord / I totally disagree
Je ne suis pas de cet *ou* de votre avis / I don't agree with you
Désolé, mais je ne suis pas d'accord / I'm sorry, but I don't agree
Je ne suis pas convaincu du tout / I'm not at all convinced
Oui, mais cela ne veut pas dire pour autant que... / Yes, but that doesn't mean to say that...
Je ne pense pas qu'il s'agisse de ça / I don't think that's what it's about
Je ne partage pas votre opinion / I do not share your opinion

disappoint [ˌdɪsəˈpɔɪnt] **vt** décevoir.

disappointed [ˌdɪsəˈpɔɪntɪd] **adj : disappointed (in** *OR* **with)** déçu(e) (par).

disappointing [ˌdɪsəˈpɔɪntɪŋ] **adj** décevant(e).

disappointingly [ˌdɪsəˈpɔɪntɪŋlɪ] **adv : disappointingly low grades** des notes d'une faiblesse décevante ▸ **he did disappointingly badly in the exam** ses résultats à l'examen ont été très décevants.

disappointment [ˌdɪsəˈpɔɪntmənt] **n** déception *f*.

disapproval [ˌdɪsəˈpruːvl] **n** désapprobation *f*.

disapprove [ˌdɪsəˈpruːv] **vi : to disapprove of sb/sthg** désapprouver qqn/qqch ▸ **do you disapprove?** est-ce que tu as quelque chose contre?

disapproving [ˌdɪsəˈpruːvɪŋ] **adj** désapprobateur(trice).

disapprovingly [ˌdɪsəˈpruːvɪŋlɪ] **adv** [look] d'un air désapprobateur / [speak] d'un ton désapprobateur, avec désapprobation.

disarm [dɪsˈɑːm] **vt & vi** *lit & fig* désarmer.

disarmament [dɪsˈɑːməmənt] **n** désarmement *m*.

disarming [dɪsˈɑːmɪŋ] **adj** désarmant(e).

disarmingly [dɪsˈɑːmɪŋlɪ] **adv** de façon désarmante ▸ **disarmingly honest/friendly** d'une honnêteté/amabilité désarmante.

disarray [ˌdɪsəˈreɪ] **n : in disarray** en désordre / [government] en pleine confusion.

disassemble [ˌdɪsəˈsembl] **vt** démonter, désassembler.

disassociate [ˌdɪsəˈsəʊʃɪeɪt] **vt : to disassociate o.s. from** se dissocier de.

disaster [dɪˈzɑːstəʳ] **n 1.** [damaging event] catastrophe *f* ▸ **air disaster** catastrophe aérienne **2.** *(U)* [misfortune] échec *m*, désastre *m* **3.** *inf* [failure] désastre *m*.

disaster area **n** [after natural disaster] zone *f* sinistrée.

disastrous [dɪˈzɑːstrəs] **adj** désastreux(euse).

disastrously [dɪˈzɑːstrəslɪ] **adv** de façon désastreuse.

disavow [ˌdɪsəˈvaʊ] **vt** *fml* [child, opinion] désavouer / [responsibility, faith] renier.

disavowal [ˌdɪsəˈvaʊəl] **n** *fml* [of child, opinion] désaveu *m* / [of responsibility, faith] reniement *m*.

disband [dɪsˈbænd] ■ **vt** [army, club] disperser / [organization] disperser, dissoudre.
■ **vi** [army] se disperser / [organization] se dissoudre.

disbar [dɪsˈbɑːʳ] **(pt & pp -ed, cont -ing) vt** LAW rayer du barreau *OR* du tableau de l'ordre *(des avocats)*.

disbelief [ˌdɪsbɪˈliːf] **n : in** *OR* **with disbelief** avec incrédulité.

disbelieve [ˌdɪsbɪˈliːv] **vt** ne pas croire.

disc *UK*, ***disk*** *US* [dɪsk] **n** disque *m*.

disc. abbr of ***discount***.

discard [dɪˈskɑːd] **vt** mettre au rebut.

discarded [dɪˈskɑːdɪd] **adj** mis(e) au rebut.

disc brake *UK*, ***disk brake*** *US* **n** frein *m* à disque.

discern [dɪˈsɜːn] **vt** discerner, distinguer.

discernible [dɪˈsɜːnəbl] **adj 1.** [visible] visible **2.** [noticeable] sensible.

discernibly [dɪˈsɜːnəblɪ] **adv** [visibly] visiblement / [noticeably] perceptiblement, sensiblement.

discerning [dɪˈsɜːnɪŋ] **adj** judicieux(euse).

discernment [dɪˈsɜːnmənt] **n** discernement *m*.

discharge ■ **n** [ˈdɪstʃɑːdʒ] **1.** [of patient] autorisation *f* de sortie, décharge *f* / LAW relaxe *f* ▸ **to get one's discharge** MIL être rendu à la vie civile **2.** *fml* [fulfilment - of duties] accomplissement *m* **3.** [emission - of smoke] émission *f* / [- of sewage] déversement *m* / MED écoulement *m* **4.** [payment] acquittement *m*.
■ **vt** [dɪsˈtʃɑːdʒ] **1.** [allow to leave - patient] signer la décharge de / [- prisoner, defendant] relaxer / [- soldier] rendre à la vie civile **2.** *fml* [fulfil] assumer **3.** [emit - smoke] émettre / [- sewage, chemicals] déverser **4.** [pay] acquitter, régler.

discharged bankrupt **n** *esp UK* failli *m* réhabilité.

disciple [dɪˈsaɪpl] **n** disciple *m*.

disciplinarian [ˌdɪsɪplɪˈneərɪən] **n** *personne impitoyable en matière de discipline.*

disciplinary [ˈdɪsɪplɪnərɪ] **adj** disciplinaire ▸ **to take disciplinary action against sb** prendre des mesures disciplinaires contre qqn.

discipline [ˈdɪsɪplɪn] ■ **n** discipline *f*.
■ **vt 1.** [control] discipliner **2.** [punish] punir.

disciplined [ˈdɪsɪplɪnd] **adj** discipliné(e).

disc jockey **n** disc-jockey *m*.

disclaim [dɪsˈkleɪm] **vt** *fml* nier.

disclaimer [dɪsˈkleɪməʳ] **n** dénégation *f*, désaveu *m*.

disclose [dɪsˈkləʊz] **vt** révéler, divulguer.

disclosure [dɪsˈkləʊʒəʳ] **n** révélation *f*, divulgation *f*.

disco [ˈdɪskəʊ] **(pl -s) (abbr of *discotheque*) n** discothèque *f*.

HOW TO ...

express disapproval

Je désapprouve totalement son attitude / I don't approve of his attitude at all
Ça ne me plaît pas qu'il fréquente ces gens / I don't like him mixing with those people
Elle a eu tort de lui parler comme ça / She had no right to speak to him like that
Ce ne sont pas des façons (de faire) / That's no way to behave
Mais qu'est-ce qui lui a pris ! / What's his problem?
Je ne peux pas dire que j'approuve son attitude / I can't say that I approve of his attitude
Je ne sais pas si elle a bien fait de lui en parler / I'm not sure she did the right thing by telling him
C'est inadmissible ! / It's just not on!

discography [dɪs'kɒgrəfɪ] **n** discographie *f*.

discoloration [dɪsˌkʌlə'reɪʃn] **n** décoloration *f*.

discolour *UK*, ***discolor*** *US* ■ **vt** décolorer / [teeth] jaunir.
■ **vi** se décolorer / [teeth] jaunir.

discoloured *UK*, ***discolored*** *US* **adj** décoloré(e) / [teeth] jauni(e).

discomfort [dɪs'kʌmfət] **n** **1.** *(U)* [physical pain] douleur *f* ▸ **to be in some discomfort** ne pas se sentir très bien ▸ **to cause sb discomfort** gêner qqn **2.** *(U)* [anxiety, embarrassment] malaise *m* **3.** [uncomfortable condition] inconfort *m*.

disconcert [ˌdɪskən'sɜ:t] **vt** déconcerter.

disconcerting [ˌdɪskən'sɜ:tɪŋ] **adj** déconcertant(e).

disconcertingly [ˌdɪskən'sɜ:tɪŋlɪ] **adv** de façon déconcertante.

disconnect [ˌdɪskə'nekt] **vt** **1.** [detach] détacher **2.** [from gas, electricity - appliance] débrancher / [- house] couper **3.** TELEC couper.

disconnected [ˌdɪskə'nektɪd] **adj** [thoughts] sans suite / [events] sans rapport.

disconsolate [dɪs'kɒnsələt] **adj** triste, inconsolable.

disconsolately [dɪs'kɒnsələtlɪ] **adv** tristement, inconsolablement.

discontent [ˌdɪskən'tent] **n** : **discontent (with)** mécontentement *m* (à propos de).

discontented [ˌdɪskən'tentɪd] **adj** mécontent(e).

discontentment [ˌdɪskən'tentmənt] **n** : **discontentment (with)** mécontentement *m* (à propos de).

discontinue [ˌdɪskən'tɪnju:] **vt** cesser, interrompre.

discontinued line [ˌdɪskən'tɪnju:d-] **n** COMM fin *f* de série.

discontinuous [ˌdɪskən'tɪnjʊəs] **adj** [gen, LING & MATHS] discontinu(e).

discord ['dɪskɔ:d] **n** **1.** *(U)* [disagreement] discorde *f*, désaccord *m* **2.** MUS dissonance *f*.

discordant [dɪ'skɔ:dənt] **adj** **1.** [conflicting] discordant(e) / [relationship] plein(e) de discordance **2.** MUS dissonant(e).

discotheque ['dɪskəʊtek] **n** discothèque *f*.

discount ■ **n** ['dɪskaʊnt] remise *f* ▸ **I bought it at a discount** je l'ai acheté au rabais ▸ **she got a discount** on lui a fait une remise ▸ **'discount for cash'** 'escompte au comptant' ▸ **shares offered at a discount** des actions offertes en dessous du pair.
■ **vt** [*UK* dɪs'kaʊnt, *US* 'dɪskaʊnt] [report, claim] ne pas tenir compte de.

discounted rate [dɪs'kaʊntɪd-] **n** taux *m* d'escompte.

discount house **n** **1.** FIN maison *f* d'escompte **2.** [store] magasin *m* de vente au rabais.

discount rate **n** taux *m* d'escompte.

discount store **n** COMM magasin *m* de vente au rabais.

discourage [dɪs'kʌrɪdʒ] **vt** décourager ▸ **to discourage sb from doing sthg** dissuader qqn de faire qqch.

discouraged [dɪs'kʌrɪdʒd] **adj** découragé(e) ▸ **don't be discouraged** ne te laisse pas abattre OR décourager.

discouragement [dɪ'skʌrɪdʒmənt] **n** **1.** [attempt to discourage] : **I met with discouragement on all sides** tout le monde a essayé de me décourager ▸ **my plans met with discouragement** on a essayé de me dissuader de poursuivre mes projets **2.** [deterrent] : **the metal shutters act as a discouragement to vandals** les rideaux métalliques servent à décourager les vandales.

discouraging [dɪ'skʌrɪdʒɪŋ] **adj** décourageant(e).

discourse ['dɪskɔ:s] **n** *fml* : **discourse (on)** discours *m* (sur).

discourse analysis **n** LING analyse *f* du discours.

discourteous [dɪs'kɜ:tjəs] **adj** discourtois(e).

discourtesy [dɪs'kɜ:tɪsɪ] **n** manque *m* de courtoisie.

discover [dɪ'skʌvər] **vt** découvrir.

discoverer [dɪ'skʌvərər] **n** : **the discoverer of sthg** la personne qui a découvert qqch.

discovery [dɪ'skʌvərɪ] (pl -ies) **n** découverte *f*.

discredit [dɪs'kredɪt] ■ **n** discrédit *m*.
■ **vt** discréditer.

discredited [dɪs'kredɪtɪd] **adj** discrédité(e).

discreet [dɪ'skri:t] **adj** discret(ète).

discreetly [dɪ'skri:tlɪ] **adv** discrètement.

discrepancy [dɪ'skrepənsɪ] (pl -ies) **n** : **discrepancy (in/between)** divergence *f* (entre).

discrete [dɪs'kri:t] **adj** *fml* séparé(e), bien distinct(e).

discretion [dɪ'skreʃn] **n** *(U)* **1.** [tact] discrétion *f* **2.** [judgment] jugement *m*, discernement *m* ▸ **use your own discretion** à vous de juger ▸ **at the discretion of** à la discrétion de.

discretionary [dɪ'skreʃənrɪ] **adj** discrétionnaire.

discriminate [dɪ'skrɪmɪneɪt] **vi** **1.** [distinguish] différencier, distinguer ▸ **to discriminate between** faire la distinction entre **2.** [be prejudiced] : **to discriminate against sb** faire de la discrimination envers qqn.

discriminating [dɪ'skrɪmɪneɪtɪŋ] **adj** judicieux(ieuse).

discrimination [dɪˌskrɪmɪ'neɪʃn] **n** **1.** [prejudice] discrimination *f* **2.** [judgment] discernement *m*, jugement *m*.

discriminatory [dɪ'skrɪmɪnətrɪ] **adj** [treatment, proposals] discriminatoire ▸ **the company is being discriminatory** la société pratique la discrimination.

discursive [dɪ'skɜ:sɪv] **adj** *fml* [essay, report, person] discursif(ive).

discus ['dɪskəs] (pl -es [-i:z]) **n** disque *m*.

discuss [dɪ'skʌs] **vt** discuter (de) ▸ **to discuss sthg with sb** discuter de qqch avec qqn.

discussion [dɪ'skʌʃn] **n** discussion *f* ▸ **to come up for discussion** [report, proposal] être discuté ▸ **under discussion** en discussion.

disdain [dɪs'deɪn] ■ **n** : **disdain (for)** dédain *m* (pour).
■ **vt** dédaigner ▸ **to disdain to do sthg** dédaigner de faire qqch.

disdainful [dɪs'deɪnfʊl] **adj** dédaigneux(euse).

disease [dɪ'zi:z] **n 1.** [illness] maladie *f* **2.** *fig* [unhealthy attitude, habit] mal *m*.

diseased [dɪ'zi:zd] **adj** [plant, body] malade.

disembark [ˌdɪsɪm'bɑ:k] **vi** débarquer.

disembarkation [ˌdɪsembɑ:'keɪʃn] **n** débarquement *m*.

disembodied [ˌdɪsɪm'bɒdɪd] **adj** désincarné(e).

disembowel [ˌdɪsɪm'baʊəl] (*UK* **-led**, cont **-ling**, *US* **-ed**, cont **-ing**) **vt** éviscérer.

disenchanted [ˌdɪsɪn'tʃɑ:ntɪd] **adj : disenchanted (with)** désenchanté(e) (de).

disenchantment [ˌdɪsɪn'tʃɑ:ntmənt] **n** désillusion *f*, désenchantement *m*.

disenfranchise [ˌdɪsɪn'fræntʃaɪz] = ***disfranchise***.

disengage [ˌdɪsɪn'geɪdʒ] **vt 1.** [release] **: to disengage sthg (from)** libérer *OR* dégager qqch (de) ▸ **to disengage o.s. from** se libérer *OR* se dégager de **2.** TECH déclencher ▸ **to disengage the gears** débrayer.

disengagement [ˌdɪsɪn'geɪdʒmənt] **n** désengagement *m*.

disentangle [ˌdɪsɪn'tæŋgl] **vt : to disentangle sthg from** enlever qqch de ▸ **to disentangle o.s. from** se dégager de.

disfavour *UK*, ***disfavor*** *US* [dɪs'feɪvər] **n 1.** [dislike, disapproval] désapprobation *f* **2.** [state of disapproval] **: to be in disfavour with sb** être mal vu de qqn.

disfigure [dɪs'fɪgər] **vt** défigurer.

disfigured [dɪs'fɪgəd] **adj** défiguré(e).

disfigurement [dɪs'fɪgəmənt] **n** défigurement *m*.

disfranchise [ˌdɪs'fræntʃaɪz] **vt** priver du droit électoral.

disgorge [dɪs'gɔ:dʒ] **vt 1.** *fml* [from stomach] vomir **2.** *liter* [emit] déverser.

disgrace [dɪs'greɪs] ■ **n 1.** [shame] honte *f* ▸ **to bring disgrace on sb** jeter la honte sur qqn ▸ **in disgrace** en défaveur **2.** [cause of shame - thing] honte *f*, scandale *m* / [- person] honte *f*.

■ **vt** faire honte à ▸ **to disgrace o.s.** se couvrir de honte.

disgraceful [dɪs'greɪsfʊl] **adj** honteux(euse), scandaleux(euse).

disgracefully [dɪs'greɪsfʊlɪ] **adv** honteusement.

disgruntled [dɪs'grʌntld] **adj** mécontent(e).

disguise [dɪs'gaɪz] ■ **n** déguisement *m* ▸ **in disguise** déguisé(e).

■ **vt 1.** [person, voice] déguiser ▸ **to disguise o.s. as** se déguiser en **2.** [hide - fact, feelings] dissimuler.

disgust [dɪs'gʌst] ■ **n : disgust (at)** [behaviour, violence] dégoût *m* (pour) / [decision] dégoût (devant) ▸ **in disgust** dégoûté(e), écœuré(e).

■ **vt** dégoûter, écœurer.

disgusted [dɪs'gʌstɪd] **adj** [displeased] écœuré(e) / [sick] écœuré(e), dégoûté(e).

disgusting [dɪs'gʌstɪŋ] **adj** dégoûtant(e).

disgustingly [dɪs'gʌstɪŋlɪ] **adv : a disgustingly bad meal** un repas épouvantable ▸ **she is disgustingly clever/successful** *inf* elle est intelligente/elle réussit au point que c'en est écœurant.

dish [dɪʃ] **n** plat *m* / *US* [plate] assiette *f*.

◆ ***dishes*** **npl** vaisselle *f* ▸ **to do** *OR* **wash the dishes** faire la vaisselle.

◆ ***dish out*** **vt sep** *inf* distribuer.

◆ ***dish up*** **vt sep** *inf* servir.

dish aerial *UK*, ***dish antenna*** *US* **n** antenne *f* parabolique.

disharmony [ˌdɪs'hɑ:mənɪ] **n** désaccord *m*, mésentente *f*.

dishcloth ['dɪʃklɒθ] **n** lavette *f*.

dishearten [dɪs'hɑ:tn] **vt** décourager, abattre, démoraliser ▸ **don't get disheartened** ne te décourage pas, ne te laisse pas abattre.

disheartened [dɪs'hɑ:tnd] **adj** découragé(e).

disheartening [dɪs'hɑ:tnɪŋ] **adj** décourageant(e).

dishevelled *UK*, ***disheveled*** *US* [dɪ'ʃevəld] **adj** [person] échevelé(e) / [hair] en désordre.

dishonest [dɪs'ɒnɪst] **adj** malhonnête.

dishonesty [dɪs'ɒnɪstɪ] **n** malhonnêteté *f*.

dishonour *UK*, ***dishonor*** *US* [dɪs'ɒnər] ■ **n** déshonneur *m*.

■ **vt** déshonorer.

dishonourable *UK*, ***dishonorable*** *US* [dɪs'ɒnərəbl] **adj** [person] peu honorable / [behaviour] déshonorant(e).

dish rack **n** égouttoir *m* (à vaisselle).

dishtowel ['dɪʃtaʊəl] **n** torchon *m*.

dishwasher ['dɪʃˌwɒʃər] **n** [machine] lave-vaisselle *m inv*.

dish(washing) soap **n** *US* liquide *m* pour la vaisselle.

dishy ['dɪʃɪ] (comp **-ier**, superl **-iest**) **adj** *UK inf* mignon(onne), sexy *(inv)*.

disillusion [ˌdɪsɪ'lu:ʒn] ■ **vt** faire perdre ses illusions à, désillusionner.

■ **n** = ***disillusionment***.

disillusioned [ˌdɪsɪ'lu:ʒnd] **adj** désillusionné(e), désenchanté(e) ▸ **to become disillusioned** perdre ses illusions ▸ **to be disillusioned with** ne plus avoir d'illusions sur.

disillusionment [ˌdɪsɪ'lu:ʒnmənt] **n : disillusionment (with)** désillusion *f* *OR* désenchantement *m* (en ce qui concerne).

disincentive [ˌdɪsɪn'sentɪv] **n : to be a disincentive** avoir un effet dissuasif / [in work context] être démotivant(e).

disinclination [ˌdɪsɪnklɪ'neɪʃn] **n** [of person] peu *m* d'inclination ▸ **her disinclination to believe him** sa tendance à ne pas le croire ▸ **the West's disinclination to go on lending** le peu d'enthousiasme dont fait preuve l'Occident pour continuer à prêter de l'argent.

disinclined [ˌdɪsɪn'klaɪnd] **adj : to be disinclined to do sthg** être peu disposé(e) à faire qqch.

disinfect [ˌdɪsɪn'fekt] **vt** désinfecter.

disinfectant [ˌdɪsɪn'fektənt] **n** désinfectant *m*.

disinfection [ˌdɪsɪn'fekʃn] **n** désinfection *f*.

disinformation [ˌdɪsɪnfə'meɪʃn] **n** désinformation *f*.

disingenuous [ˌdɪsɪn'dʒenjʊəs] **adj** peu sincère.

disingenuously [ˌdɪsɪn'dʒenjʊəslɪ] **adv** avec peu de sincérité.

disingenuousness [ˌdɪsɪn'dʒenjʊəsnɪs] **n** manque *m* de sincérité.

disinherit [ˌdɪsɪn'herɪt] **vt** déshériter.

disintegrate [dɪs'ɪntɪgreɪt] **vi 1.** [object] se désintégrer, se désagréger **2.** *fig* [project] s'écrouler / [marriage] se désagréger.

disintegration [dɪsˌɪntɪ'greɪʃn] **n 1.** [of object] désintégration *f*, désagrégation *f* **2.** *fig* [of project, marriage] effondrement *m*.

disinterest [ˌdɪs'ɪntərest] **n 1.** [objectivity] **: his disinterest was the reason we chose him** on l'a choisi parce qu'il n'avait aucun intérêt dans l'affaire **2.** [lack of interest] manque *m* d'intérêt.

disinterested [ˌdɪs'ɪntrəstɪd] **adj 1.** [objective] désintéressé(e) **2.** [uninterested] **: disinterested (in)** indifférent(e) (à).

disinvestment [ˌdɪsɪn'vestmənt] **n** désinvestissement *m*.

disjointed [dɪs'dʒɔɪntɪd] **adj** décousu(e).

disk [dɪsk] **n 1.** COMPUT disque *m*, disquette *f* **2.** *US* = *disc*.

disk crash **n** COMPUT atterrissage *m* de tête.

disk drive **n** COMPUT lecteur *m* de disques ***OR*** de disquettes.

diskette [dɪs'ket] **n** COMPUT disquette *f*.

disk operating system **n** COMPUT système *m* d'exploitation (à disques).

dislike [dɪs'laɪk] ■ **n : dislike (of)** aversion *f* (pour) ▸ **her likes and dislikes** ce qu'elle aime et ce qu'elle n'aime pas ▸ **to take a dislike to sb/sthg** prendre qqn/qqch en grippe.
■ **vt** ne pas aimer.

dislocate ['dɪsləkeɪt] **vt 1.** MED se démettre **2.** [disrupt - plans] désorganiser, perturber.

dislocation [ˌdɪslə'keɪʃn] **n 1.** [of shoulder, knee] luxation *f*, déboîtement *m* **2.** [disruption - of plans] perturbation *f*.

dislodge [dɪs'lɒdʒ] **vt : to dislodge sthg (from)** déplacer qqch (de) / [free] décoincer qqch (de) ▸ **to dislodge sb from a position** déloger qqn d'un poste.

disloyal [ˌdɪs'lɔɪəl] **adj : disloyal (to)** déloyal(e) (envers).

disloyalty [ˌdɪs'lɔɪəltɪ] **n** déloyauté *f* ▸ **an act of disloyalty** un acte déloyal.

dismal ['dɪzml] **adj 1.** [gloomy, depressing] lugubre **2.** [unsuccessful - attempt] infructueux(euse) / [- failure] lamentable.

dismantle [dɪs'mæntl] **vt** démanteler.

dismay [dɪs'meɪ] ■ **n** consternation *f* ▸ **to sb's dismay** à la consternation de qqn.
■ **vt** consterner.

dismayed [dɪs'meɪd] **adj** consterné(e), effondré(e).

dismember [dɪs'membər] **vt** démembrer.

dismiss [dɪs'mɪs] **vt 1.** [from job] **: to dismiss sb (from)** congédier qqn (de) **2.** [refuse to take seriously - idea, person] écarter / [- plan, challenge] rejeter ▸ **police dismissed the warning as a hoax** la police n'a pas tenu compte de l'avertissement et l'a pris pour une mauvaise plaisanterie **3.** [allow to leave - class] laisser sortir / [- troops] faire rompre les rangs à ▸ **class dismissed!** vous pouvez sortir! **4.** LAW [hung jury] dissoudre ▸ **to dismiss a charge** [judge] rendre une ordonnance de non-lieu ▸ **case dismissed!** affaire classée!

dismissal [dɪs'mɪsl] **n 1.** [from job] licenciement *m*, renvoi *m* **2.** [refusal to take seriously] rejet *m*.

dismissive [dɪs'mɪsɪv] **adj** [tone of voice, gesture] méprisant(euse) ▸ **to be dismissive of** ne faire aucun cas de.

dismissively [dɪs'mɪsɪvlɪ] **adv** [offhandedly] d'un ton dédaigneux / [in final tone of voice] d'un ton sans appel.

dismount [ˌdɪs'maʊnt] **vi : to dismount (from)** descendre (de).

disobedience [ˌdɪsə'bi:djəns] **n** désobéissance *f*.

disobedient [ˌdɪsə'bi:djənt] **adj** désobéissant(e).

disobediently [ˌdɪsə'bi:djəntlɪ] **adv** de manière désobéissante.

disobey [ˌdɪsə'beɪ] ■ **vt** désobéir à.
■ **vi** désobéir.

disorder [dɪs'ɔ:dər] **n 1.** [disarray] **: in disorder** en désordre **2.** *(U)* [rioting] troubles *mpl* **3.** MED trouble *m*.

disordered [dɪs'ɔ:dəd] **adj 1.** [in disarray] en désordre **2.** MED **: mentally disordered** déséquilibré(e).

HOW TO ...

express dislikes

Je déteste conduire la nuit / I hate driving at night
Je ne supporte pas qu'on me parle comme ça / I will not be spoken to like that
Ça m'agace qu'elle s'invite sans prévenir / It annoys me the way she comes round without any warning
Il me tape sur le système *inf* / He gets on my nerves
Je ne peux pas le voir (en peinture) *inf* / I can't stand him
Je ne l'aime pas trop / I don't really like him/her/it
Je ne suis pas très branché sport *inf* / I'm not really into sport
L'informatique, c'est pas vraiment mon truc *inf* / Computers aren't really my thing
Les films de science-fiction, ce n'est pas ma tasse de thé / Science fiction films aren't really my cup of tea
Ses tableaux ne m'emballent pas *inf* / I don't think much of his paintings

disorderly [dɪs'ɔːdəlɪ] **adj** **1.** [untidy - room] en désordre / [- appearance] désordonné(e) **2.** [unruly] indiscipliné(e).

disorderly conduct **n** LAW trouble *m* de l'ordre public.

disorganization [dɪsˌɔːgənaɪ'zeɪʃn] **n** désorganisation *f*.

disorganized, *UK* ***-ised*** [dɪs'ɔːgənaɪzd] **adj** [person] désordonné(e), brouillon(onne) / [system] mal conçu(e).

disorient [dɪs'ɔːrɪənt], ***disorientate*** *UK* [dɪs'ɔːrɪənteɪt] **vt** désorienter ▶ **to be disoriented** être désorienté ▶ **it's easy to become disoriented** c'est facile de perdre son sens de l'orientation / *fig* on a vite fait d'être désorienté.

disoriented [dɪs'ɔːrɪəntɪd], ***disorientated*** *UK* [dɪs'ɔːrɪənteɪtɪd] **adj** désorienté(e).

disorientation [dɪsˌɔːrɪən'teɪʃn] **n** désorientation *f*.

disown [dɪs'əʊn] **vt** désavouer.

disparage [dɪ'spærɪdʒ] **vt** dénigrer.

disparaging [dɪ'spærɪdʒɪŋ] **adj** désobligeant(e).

disparagingly [dɪ'spærɪdʒɪŋlɪ] **adv** [say, look at] d'un air désobligeant.

disparate ['dɪspərət] **adj** disparate.

disparity [dɪ'spærətɪ] (**pl -ies**) **n : disparity (between** *OR* **in)** disparité *f* (entre).

dispassionate [dɪ'spæʃnət] **adj** impartial(e).

dispassionately [dɪ'spæʃnətlɪ] **adv** [unemotionally] sans émotion, calmement / [objectively] objectivement, impartialement.

dispatch [dɪ'spætʃ] ■ **n** [message] dépêche *f*.
■ **vt** [send] envoyer, expédier.

dispatch box **n** *UK* POL [box] valise *f* officielle / [in House of Commons] *tribune d'où parlent les membres du gouvernement et leurs homologues du cabinet fantôme*.

dispatch rider **n** MIL estafette *f* / [courier] coursier *m*.

dispel [dɪ'spel] (**pt & pp -led, cont -ling**) **vt** [feeling] dissiper, chasser.

dispensable [dɪ'spensəbl] **adj** [person] dont on peut se passer / [expenses, luxury] superflu(e).

dispensary [dɪ'spensərɪ] (**pl -ies**) **n** officine *f*.

dispensation [ˌdɪspen'seɪʃn] **n** [permission] dispense *f*.

dispense [dɪ'spens] **vt** [justice, medicine] administrer.
◆ ***dispense with*** **vt insep** **1.** [do without] se passer de **2.** [make unnecessary] rendre superflu(e) ▶ **to dispense with the need for sthg** rendre qqch superflu.

dispenser [dɪ'spensəʳ] **n** distributeur *m*.

dispensing chemist [dɪ'spensɪŋ-] **n** *UK* pharmacien *m*, -enne *f*.

dispersal [dɪ'spɜːsl] **n** dispersion *f*.

disperse [dɪ'spɜːs] ■ **vt** **1.** [crowd] disperser **2.** [knowledge, news] répandre, propager.
■ **vi** se disperser.

dispirited [dɪ'spɪrɪtɪd] **adj** découragé(e), abattu(e).

dispiriting [dɪ'spɪrɪtɪŋ] **adj** décourageant(e).

displace [dɪs'pleɪs] **vt** **1.** [cause to move] déplacer **2.** [supplant] supplanter.

displaced person [dɪs'pleɪst-] **n** personne *f* déplacée.

displacement [dɪs'pleɪsmənt] **n** déplacement *m*.

displacement activity **n** PSYCHOL déplacement *m*.

display [dɪ'spleɪ] ■ **n** **1.** [arrangement] exposition *f* / [of goods, merchandise] étalage *m*, exposition *f* ▶ **on display** exposé ▶ **to put sthg on display** exposer qqch ▶ **the exam results were on display** les résultats des examens étaient affichés **2.** [demonstration] manifestation *f* **3.** [public event] spectacle *m* ▶ **a fireworks display** un feu d'artifice **4.** [COMPUT - device] écran *m* / [- information displayed] affichage *m*, visualisation *f*.
■ **vt** **1.** [arrange] exposer **2.** [show] faire preuve de, montrer.

display advertisement **n** encadré *m*.

display advertising **n** *(U)* publicité *f* par affichage.

displease [dɪs'pliːz] **vt** déplaire à, mécontenter.

displeased [dɪs'pliːzd] **adj** mécontent(e) ▶ **to be displeased with** *OR* **at** être mécontent de.

displeasure [dɪs'pleʒəʳ] **n** mécontentement *m*.

disposable [dɪ'spəʊzəbl] **adj** [throw away] jetable.

disposable camera **n** appareil *m* photo jetable.

disposable income **n** surplus *m*, revenu *m* disponible.

disposal [dɪ'spəʊzl] **n** **1.** [removal] enlèvement *m* **2.** [availability] **: at sb's disposal** à la disposition de qqn.

dispose [dɪ'spəʊz] ◆ ***dispose of*** **vt insep** [get rid of] se débarrasser de / [problem] résoudre.

disposed [dɪ'spəʊzd] **adj** **1.** [willing] **: to be disposed to do sthg** être disposé(e) à faire qqch **2.** [friendly] **: to be well disposed to** *OR* **towards sb** être bien disposé(e) envers qqn.

disposition [ˌdɪspə'zɪʃn] **n** **1.** [temperament] caractère *m*, tempérament *m* **2.** [tendency] **: disposition to do sthg** tendance *f* à faire qqch.

dispossess [ˌdɪspə'zes] **vt** *fml* **: to dispossess sb of sthg** déposséder qqn de qqch.

dispossessed [ˌdɪspə'zest] ■ **npl : the dispossessed** les dépossédés *mpl*.
■ **adj** dépossédé(e).

disproportion [ˌdɪsprə'pɔːʃn] **n** disproportion *f*.

disproportionate [ˌdɪsprə'pɔːʃnət] **adj : disproportionate (to)** disproportionné(e) (à).

disproportionately [ˌdɪsprə'pɔːʃnətlɪ] **adv** d'une façon disproportionnée ▶ **a disproportionately large sum** une somme disproportionnée.

disprove [ˌdɪs'pruːv] **vt** réfuter.

disputable [dɪ'spjuːtəbl] **adj** discutable, contestable.

dispute [dɪ'spjuːt] ■ **n** **1.** [quarrel] dispute *f* **2.** *(U)* [disagreement] désaccord *m* ▶ **in dispute** [people] en désaccord / [matter] en discussion ▶ **open to dispute** contestable **3.** INDUST conflit *m*.
■ **vt** contester ▶ **I would dispute that** je ne suis pas d'accord.

disputed [dɪ'spju:tɪd] **adj** **1.** [decision, fact, claim] contesté(e) **2.** [fought over] **: this is a much disputed territory** ce territoire fait l'objet de beaucoup de conflits.

disqualification [dɪs,kwɒlɪfɪ'keɪʃn] **n** disqualification *f*.

disqualify [,dɪs'kwɒlɪfaɪ] (**pt & pp -ied**) **vt** **1.** [subj: authority] **: to disqualify sb (from doing sthg)** interdire à qqn (de faire qqch) ▸ **to disqualify sb from driving** *UK* retirer le permis de conduire à qqn **2.** [subj: illness, criminal record] **: to disqualify sb (from doing sthg)** rendre qqn incapable (de faire qqch) **3.** SPORT disqualifier.

disquiet [dɪs'kwaɪət] **n** inquiétude *f*.

disquieting [dɪs'kwaɪətɪŋ] **adj** *fml* inquiétant(e), troublant(e).

disregard [,dɪsrɪ'gɑ:d] ■ **n** *(U)* **: disregard (for)** [money, danger] mépris *m* (pour) / [feelings] indifférence *f* (à).
■ **vt** [fact] ignorer / [danger] mépriser / [warning] ne pas tenir compte de.

disrepair [,dɪsrɪ'peə^r] **n** délabrement *m* ▸ **to fall into disrepair** se délabrer.

disreputable [dɪs'repjʊtəbl] **adj** peu respectable.

disreputably [dɪs'repjʊtəblɪ] **adv** [behave] d'une manière honteuse.

disrepute [,dɪsrɪ'pju:t] **n : to bring sthg into disrepute** discréditer qqch ▸ **to fall into disrepute** acquérir une mauvaise réputation.

disrespect [,dɪsrɪ'spekt] **n** irrespect *m*, irrévérence *f* ▸ **she has a healthy disrespect for authority** elle porte un irrespect *OR* une irrévérence salutaire à toute forme d'autorité ▸ **I meant no disrespect (to your family)** je ne voulais pas me montrer irrespectueux *OR* irrévérencieux (envers votre famille) ▸ **to show disrespect towards sb/sthg** manquer de respect à qqn/qqch ▸ **to treat sb/sthg with disrespect** traiter qqn/qqch irrespectueusement.

disrespectful [,dɪsrɪ'spektfʊl] **adj** irrespectueux(euse).

disrupt [dɪs'rʌpt] **vt** perturber.

disruption [dɪs'rʌpʃn] **n** perturbation *f*.

disruptive [dɪs'rʌptɪv] **adj** perturbateur(trice).

diss [dɪs] **vt** *v inf* **: to diss sb** se foutre de qn.

dissatisfaction ['dɪs,sætɪs'fækʃn] **n** mécontentement *m*.

dissatisfied [,dɪs'sætɪsfaɪd] **adj : dissatisfied (with)** mécontent(e) (de), pas satisfait(e) (de).

dissect [dɪ'sekt] **vt** *lit & fig* disséquer.

dissection [dɪ'sekʃn] **n** *lit & fig* dissection *f*.

dissemble [dɪ'sembl] *liter* ■ **vi** dissimuler.
■ **vt** [feelings, motives] dissimuler.

disseminate [dɪ'semɪneɪt] **vt** disséminer.

dissemination [dɪ,semɪ'neɪʃn] **n** dissémination *f*.

dissension [dɪ'senʃn] **n** discorde *f*, dissension *f*.

dissent [dɪ'sent] ■ **n** dissentiment *m*.
■ **vi : to dissent (from)** être en désaccord (avec).

dissenter [dɪ'sentə^r] **n** dissident *m*, -e *f*.

dissenting [dɪ'sentɪŋ] **adj : dissenting voice** opinion *f* contraire.

dissertation [,dɪsə'teɪʃn] **n** dissertation *f*.

disservice [,dɪs'sɜ:vɪs] **n : to do sb a disservice** rendre un mauvais service à qqn.

dissidence ['dɪsɪdəns] **n** [disagreement] désaccord *m* / POL dissidence *f*.

dissident ['dɪsɪdənt] **n** dissident *m*, -e *f*.

dissimilar [,dɪ'sɪmɪlə^r] **adj : dissimilar (to)** différent(e) (de).

dissimilarity [,dɪsɪmɪ'lærətɪ] (**pl -ies**) **n** différence *f*.

dissimulate [dɪ'sɪmjʊleɪt] *fml* ■ **vt** dissimuler, cacher.
■ **vi** dissimuler.

dissimulation [dɪ,sɪmjʊ'leɪʃn] **n** *fml* dissimulation *f*.

dissipate ['dɪsɪpeɪt] ■ **vt** **1.** PHYS [heat, energy] dissiper **2.** [cloud, fears] dissiper / [fortune] dilapider, gaspiller / [energies] disperser, gaspiller.
■ **vi** se dissiper.

dissipated ['dɪsɪpeɪtɪd] **adj** [person, life] dissolu(e).

dissipation [,dɪsɪ'peɪʃn] **n** **1.** [of cloud, fears, hopes] dissipation *f* / [of fortune] dilapidation *f* / [of energies] dispersion *f*, gaspillage *m* / PHYS [of heat, energy] dissipation *f* **2.** [debauchery] débauche *f*.

dissociate [dɪ'səʊʃɪeɪt] **vt** dissocier ▸ **to dissociate o.s. from** se dissocier de.

dissolute ['dɪsəlu:t] **adj** dissolu(e).

dissoluteness ['dɪsəlu:tnɪs] **n** débauche *f*.

dissolution [,dɪsə'lu:ʃn] **n** dissolution *f*.

dissolve [dɪ'zɒlv] ■ **vt** dissoudre.
■ **vi** **1.** [substance] se dissoudre **2.** *fig* [disappear] disparaître.
◆ ***dissolve in(to)*** **vt insep : to dissolve into tears** fondre en larmes.

dissonance ['dɪsənəns] **n** MUS dissonance *f* / *fig* discordance *f*.

dissonant ['dɪsənənt] **adj** MUS dissonant(e) / *fig* [colours, opinions] discordant(e).

dissuade [dɪ'sweɪd] **vt : to dissuade sb (from)** dissuader qqn (de).

distance ['dɪstəns] ■ **n** distance *f* ▸ **at a distance of 50 metres** à (une distance de) 50 mètres ▸ **is it within walking distance?** peut-on y aller à pied? ▸ **a short distance away** tout près ▸ **from a distance** de loin ▸ **in the distance** au loin ▸ **to keep sb at a distance** tenir qqn à distance (respectueuse) ▸ **to keep one's distance (from sb)** garder ses distances (par rapport à qqn).
■ **vt : to distance o.s. from** se distancier de.

distance learning **n** télé-enseignement *m*.

distant ['dɪstənt] **adj** **1.** [gen] **: distant (from)** éloigné(e) (de) **2.** [reserved - person, manner] distant(e).

distantly ['dɪstəntlɪ] **adv** **1.** [in the distance] au loin **2.** [resemble] vaguement ▸ **to be distantly related** [people] avoir un lien de parenté éloigné / [ideas, concepts] avoir un rapport éloigné **3.** [speak, behave, look] froidement, d'un air distant *OR* froid.

distaste [dɪs'teɪst] **n : distaste (for)** dégoût *m* (pour).

distasteful [dɪs'teɪstfʊl] **adj** répugnant(e), déplaisant(e).

distastefully [dɪs'teɪstfʊlɪ] **adv** [with repugnance - look] d'un air dégoûté / [with bad taste - presented, portrayed] avec mauvais goût.

Dist. Atty. abbr of ***district attorney***.

distemper [dɪ'stempəʳ] **n** *(U)* **1.** [paint] détrempe *f* **2.** [disease] maladie *f* de Carré.

distend [dɪ'stend] ■ **vt** gonfler.
■ **vi** [stomach] se ballonner, se gonfler / [sails] se gonfler.

distended [dɪ'stendɪd] **adj** [stomach] ballonné(e) gonflé(e).

distil *UK* (pt & pp **-led**, cont **-ling**), ***distill*** *US* [dɪ'stɪl] **vt 1.** [liquid] distiller **2.** *fig* [information] tirer.

distillation [ˌdɪstɪ'leɪʃn] **n** *lit* & *fig* distillation *f*.

distiller [dɪ'stɪləʳ] **n** distillateur *m*.

distillery [dɪ'stɪlərɪ] (pl **-ies**) **n** distillerie *f*.

distinct [dɪ'stɪŋkt] **adj 1.** [different] **: distinct (from)** distinct(e) (de), différent(e) (de) ▸ **as distinct from** par opposition à **2.** [definite - improvement] net (nette) ▸ **a distinct possibility** une forte chance.

distinction [dɪ'stɪŋkʃn] **n 1.** [difference] distinction *f*, différence *f* ▸ **to draw *or* make a distinction between** faire une distinction entre **2.** *(U)* [excellence] distinction *f* **3.** [exam result] mention *f* très bien.

distinctive [dɪ'stɪŋktɪv] **adj** distinctif(ive).

distinctively [dɪ'stɪŋktɪvlɪ] **adv** [coloured] de manière distinctive.

distinctly [dɪ'stɪŋktlɪ] **adv** [see, remember] clairement.

distinguish [dɪ'stɪŋgwɪʃ] **vt 1.** [tell apart] **: to distinguish sthg from sthg** distinguer qqch de qqch, faire la différence entre qqch et qqch **2.** [perceive] distinguer **3.** [characterize] caractériser **4.** [excel] **: to distinguish o.s.** se distinguer.

distinguishable [dɪ'stɪŋgwɪʃəbl] **adj 1.** [visible] visible **2.** [recognizable] reconnaissable ▸ **to be easily distinguishable from** se distinguer facilement de, être facile à distinguer de ▸ **the male is distinguishable by his red legs** le mâle est reconnaissable à *or* se distingue par ses pattes rouges.

distinguished [dɪ'stɪŋgwɪʃt] **adj** distingué(e).

distinguishing [dɪ'stɪŋgwɪʃɪŋ] **adj** [feature, mark] distinctif(ive) ▸ **distinguishing features** [on passport] signes *m* particuliers.

distort [dɪ'stɔ:t] **vt** déformer.

distorted [dɪ'stɔ:tɪd] **adj** déformé(e).

distortion [dɪ'stɔ:ʃn] **n** déformation *f*.

distract [dɪ'strækt] **vt : to distract sb (from)** distraire qqn (de).

distracted [dɪ'stræktɪd] **adj** [preoccupied] distrait(e).

distracting [dɪ'stræktɪŋ] **adj 1.** [disruptive] gênant(e) ▸ **I find it distracting** ça m'empêche de me concentrer ▸ **it's very distracting having so many people in the office** c'est très difficile de se concentrer (sur son travail) avec autant de gens dans le bureau **2.** [amusing] distrayant(e).

distraction [dɪ'strækʃn] **n 1.** [interruption, diversion] distraction *f* **2.** [state of mind] confusion *f* ▸ **to drive sb to distraction** rendre qqn fou.

distraught [dɪ'strɔ:t] **adj** éperdu(e).

distress [dɪ'stres] ■ **n** [anxiety] détresse *f* / [pain] douleur *f*, souffrance *f*.
■ **vt** affliger.

distressed [dɪ'strest] **adj** [anxious, upset] affligé(e).

distressing [dɪ'stresɪŋ] **adj** [news, image] pénible.

distress signal **n** signal *m* de détresse.

distribute [dɪ'strɪbju:t] **vt 1.** [gen] distribuer **2.** [spread out] répartir.

distribution [ˌdɪstrɪ'bju:ʃn] **n 1.** [gen] distribution *f* **2.** [spreading out] répartition *f*.

distribution channel **n** canal *m* de distribution.

distributor [dɪ'strɪbjʊtəʳ] **n** AUT & COMM distributeur *m*.

district ['dɪstrɪkt] **n 1.** [area - of country] région *f* / [- of town] quartier *m* **2.** ADMIN district *m*.

district attorney **n** *US* ≃ procureur *m* de la République.

district council **n** *UK* ≃ conseil *m* général.

district court **n** *US* ≃ tribunal *m* d'instance (fédéral).

district nurse **n** *UK* infirmière *f* visiteuse *or* à domicile.

District of Columbia **n** district *m* de Columbia ▸ **in the District of Columbia** dans le district de Columbia.

distrust [dɪs'trʌst] ■ **n** méfiance *f*.
■ **vt** se méfier de.

distrustful [dɪs'trʌstfʊl] **adj** méfiant(e).

disturb [dɪ'stɜ:b] **vt 1.** [interrupt] déranger **2.** [upset, worry] inquiéter **3.** [sleep, surface] troubler.

disturbance [dɪ'stɜ:bəns] **n 1.** POL troubles *mpl* / [fight] tapage *m* ▸ **disturbance of the peace** LAW trouble *m* de l'ordre public **2.** [interruption] dérangement *m* **3.** [of mind, emotions] trouble *m*.

disturbed [dɪ'stɜ:bd] **adj 1.** [emotionally, mentally] perturbé(e) **2.** [worried] inquiet(ète).

disturbing [dɪ'stɜ:bɪŋ] **adj** [image] bouleversant(e) / [news] inquiétant(e).

disturbingly [dɪ'stɜ:bɪŋlɪ] **adv : the level of pollution is disturbingly high** la pollution a atteint un niveau inquiétant.

disunity [ˌdɪs'ju:nətɪ] **n** désunion *f*.

disuse [ˌdɪs'ju:s] **n : to fall into disuse** [word, custom, law] tomber en désuétude.

disused [ˌdɪs'ju:zd] **adj** désaffecté(e).

ditch [dɪtʃ] ■ **n** fossé *m*.
■ **vt** *inf* [boyfriend, girlfriend] plaquer / [old car, clothes] se débarrasser de / [plan] abandonner.

dither ['dɪðəʳ] **vi** hésiter.

ditherer ['dɪðərəʳ] **n** *inf* **: he's such a terrible ditherer** il est toujours à hésiter sur tout.

ditsy ['dɪtsɪ] (comp **-ier**, superl **-iest**) **adj** *US inf* écervelé(e).

ditto ['dɪtəʊ] **adv** idem.

diuretic [ˌdaɪjʊ'retɪk] **n** diurétique *m*.
diva ['diːvə] (pl -s) **n** diva *f*.
divan [dɪ'væn] **n** divan *m*.
divan bed **n** *UK* divan-lit *m*.
dive [daɪv] ■ **vi** (*UK* -d, *US* -d *OR* dove) plonger / [bird, plane] piquer ▸ **she dived into the crowd** elle se jeta dans la foule.
■ **n 1.** [gen] plongeon *m* **2.** [of plane] piqué *m* **3.** *inf pej* [bar, restaurant] bouge *m*.
dive-bomb **vt** bombarder en piqué.
diver ['daɪvəʳ] **n** plongeur *m*, -euse *f*.
diverge [daɪ'vɜːdʒ] **vi : to diverge (from)** diverger (de).
divergence [daɪ'vɜːdʒəns] **n** divergence *f*.
divergent [daɪ'vɜːdʒənt] **adj** divergent(e).
diverse [daɪ'vɜːs] **adj** divers(e).
diversification [daɪˌvɜːsɪfɪ'keɪʃn] **n** diversification *f*.
diversify [daɪ'vɜːsɪfaɪ] (pt & pp -ied) ■ **vt** diversifier.
■ **vi** se diversifier.
diversion [daɪ'vɜːʃn] **n 1.** [amusement] distraction *f* / [tactical] diversion *f* **2.** *UK* [of traffic] déviation *f* **3.** [of river, funds] détournement *m*.
diversionary [daɪ'vɜːʃnrɪ] **adj** [tactics] de diversion.
diversity [daɪ'vɜːsətɪ] **n** diversité *f*.
divert [daɪ'vɜːt] **vt 1.** *UK* [traffic] dévier **2.** [river, funds] détourner **3.** [person - amuse] distraire / [- tactically] détourner.
divest [daɪ'vest] **vt** *fml* **: to divest sb of** dépouiller qqn de ▸ **to divest o.s. of** se défaire de.
divide [dɪ'vaɪd] ■ **vt 1.** [separate] séparer **2.** [share out] diviser, partager ▸ **to divide sthg between** *OR* **among** partager qqch entre **3.** [split up] **: to divide sthg (into)** diviser qqch (en) **4.** MATHS **: 89 divided by 3** 89 divisé par 3 **5.** [people - in disagreement] diviser.
■ **vi** se diviser.
■ **n** [difference] division *f*.
◆ ***divide up*** **vt sep 1.** [split up] diviser **2.** [share out] partager.
divided [dɪ'vaɪdɪd] **adj** [nation] divisé(e) / [opinions, loyalties] partagé(e).
dividend ['dɪvɪdend] **n** dividende *m* ▸ **to pay dividends** *fig* porter ses fruits.
divider [dɪ'vaɪdəʳ] **n** [in room] meuble *m* de séparation.
◆ ***dividers*** **npl** MATHS **: (a pair of) dividers** un compas à pointes sèches.
dividers [dɪ'vaɪdəz] **npl** *UK* compas *m* à pointes sèches.
dividing line [dɪ'vaɪdɪŋ-] **n** ligne *f* de démarcation.
divine [dɪ'vaɪn] ■ **adj** divin(e).
■ **vt 1.** [truth, meaning] deviner / [future] prédire **2.** [water] découvrir, détecter.
diving ['daɪvɪŋ] **n** *(U)* plongeon *m* / [with breathing apparatus] plongée *f* (sous-marine).
diving board **n** plongeoir *m*.
diving suit **n** combinaison *f* de plongée.
divinity [dɪ'vɪnətɪ] (pl -ies) **n 1.** [godliness, god] divinité *f* **2.** [study] théologie *f*.
divisible [dɪ'vɪzəbl] **adj : divisible (by)** divisible (par).
division [dɪ'vɪʒn] **n 1.** [gen] division *f* **2.** [separation] séparation *f*.
divisional [dɪ'vɪʒənl] **adj** de la division, de division ▸ **the divisional manager** le directeur de la division ▸ **there were six divisional managers there** il y avait six directeurs de division.
division sign **n** signe *m* de division.
divisive [dɪ'vaɪsɪv] **adj** qui sème la division *OR* la discorde.
divisiveness [dɪ'vaɪsɪvnɪs] **n : the divisiveness of this policy is evident to everyone** il apparaît clairement à tout le monde que cette politique crée des *OR* est source de divisions.
divorce [dɪ'vɔːs] ■ **n** divorce *m* ▸ **he asked his wife for a divorce** il a demandé à sa femme de divorcer, il a demandé le divorce à sa femme ▸ **her first marriage ended in divorce** son premier mariage s'est soldé par un divorce ▸ **they're getting a divorce** ils divorcent.
■ **vt 1.** [husband, wife] divorcer ▸ **they got divorced a few years ago** ils ont divorcé il y a quelques années **2.** [separate] **: to divorce sthg from** séparer qqch de.
divorcé [dɪ'vɔːseɪ] **n** divorcé *m*.
divorced [dɪ'vɔːst] **adj** divorcé(e).
divorcée [dɪvɔː'siː] **n** divorcée *f*.
divulge [daɪ'vʌldʒ] **vt** divulguer.
DIY (abbr of ***do-it-yourself***) **n** *UK* bricolage *m*.
dizzily ['dɪzɪlɪ] **adv 1.** [walk] avec une sensation de vertige **2.** [behave] étourdiment.
dizziness ['dɪzɪnɪs] **n** vertige *m*.
dizzy ['dɪzɪ] (comp -ier, superl -iest) **adj 1.** [giddy] **: to feel dizzy** avoir la tête qui tourne **2.** *fig* [height] vertigineux(euse).
DJ, ***deejay*** **n 1.** (abbr of ***disc jockey***) disc-jockey *m* **2.** (abbr of ***dinner jacket***) smoking *m*.
Djakarta [dʒə'kɑːtə] = ***Jakarta***.
DJIA (abbr of ***Dow Jones Industrial Average***) **n** *US indice Dow Jones*.
Djibouti [dʒɪ'buːtɪ] **n** Djibouti ▸ **in Djibouti** à Djibouti.
dl (abbr of ***decilitre***) dl.
DLit(t) [ˌdiː'lɪt] (abbr of ***Doctor of Letters***) **n** *docteur ès lettres*.
DLO (abbr of ***dead-letter office***) **n** *centre de recherche du courrier*.
dm (abbr of ***decimetre***) dm.
DM (abbr of ***Deutsche Mark***) DM.
DMA (abbr of ***direct memory access***) **n** *accès direct à la mémoire*.
DMus ['diː'mjuːz] (abbr of ***Doctor of Music***) **n** *UK docteur en musique*.
DMZ (abbr of ***demilitarized zone***) **n** *zone démilitarisée*.
DNA (abbr of ***deoxyribonucleic acid***) **n** ADN *m*.
D-notice **n** *UK censure imposée à la presse pour sécurité d'État*.

DNS [ˌdiːen'es] (abbr of ***Domain Name System***) n COMPUT DNS *m*, système *m* de nom de domaine.

do [1] [duː] ■ **aux vb** (pt **did**, pp **done**) **1.** *(in negatives)* **: I don't believe you** je ne te crois pas ▸ **don't leave it there** ne le laisse pas là ▸ **I didn't want to see him** je ne voulais pas le voir
2. *(in questions)* **: what did he want?** qu'est-ce qu'il voulait? ▸ **do you know her?** est-ce que tu la connais?, la connais-tu? ▸ **do you think she'll come?** tu crois qu'elle viendra?
3. *(referring back to previous verb)* **: she reads more than I do** elle lit plus que moi ▸ **I like reading – so do I** j'aime lire – moi aussi ▸ **neither do I/does she** moi/elle non plus ▸ **I'll talk to her about it – please do/don't!** je lui en parlerai – oh, oui/non s'il vous plaît! ▸ **yes it does – no it doesn't** mais si – mais non
4. *(in question tags)* **: you know her, don't you?** tu la connais, n'est-ce pas? ▸ **I upset you, didn't I?** je t'ai fait de la peine, n'est-ce pas? ▸ **so you think you can dance, do you?** alors tu t'imagines que tu sais danser, c'est ça? ▸ **you didn't sign it, did you?** [disbelief, horror] tu ne l'as pas signé, quand même?
5. [for emphasis] **: I did tell you but you've forgotten** je te l'avais bien dit, mais tu l'as oublié ▸ **do come in** entrez donc ▸ **if you do decide to buy it** si tu décides finalement de l'acheter.
■ **vt** (pt **did**, pp **done**) **1.** [perform an activity, a service] faire
▸ **what are you doing?** qu'est-ce que tu fais?, que fais-tu?, qu'es-tu en train de faire? ▸ **to do aerobics/gymnastics** faire de l'aérobic/de la gymnastique ▸ **he did a good job** il a fait du bon travail ▸ **they do gourmet dinners** ils font OR préparent des repas gastronomiques ▸ **what can I do for you?** que puis-je (faire) pour vous? ▸ **shall we do lunch?** *inf* et si on allait déjeuner ensemble? ▸ **to do the cooking/housework** faire la cuisine/le ménage ▸ **to do one's hair** se coiffer ▸ **to do one's teeth** se laver OR se brosser les dents
2. [take action] faire ▸ **to do something about sthg** trouver une solution pour qqch ▸ **somebody do something!** que quelqu'un fasse quelque chose! ▸ **I don't know what to do with him!** je ne sais vraiment pas que faire de lui! ▸ **what do you want me to do with this?** que veux-tu que je fasse de ça?
3. [have particular effect] faire ▸ **to do more harm than good** faire plus de mal que de bien ▸ **who did this to you?** qui est-ce qui t'a fait ça? ▸ **what have you done to your hair?** qu'est-ce que tu as fait à tes cheveux?
4. [referring to job] **: what do you do?** qu'est-ce que vous faites dans la vie?
5. [study] faire ▸ **I did physics at school** j'ai fait de la physique à l'école
6. [travel at a particular speed] faire, rouler ▸ **the car can do 110 mph** ≃ la voiture peut faire du 180 à l'heure
7. [be good enough for] **: that'll do me nicely** cela m'ira très bien, cela fera très bien mon affaire.
■ **vi** (pt **did**, pp **done**) **1.** [act] faire ▸ **do as I tell you** fais comme je te dis ▸ **do as you're told!** fais ce qu'on te dit! ▸ **you would do well to reconsider** tu ferais bien de reconsidérer la question
2. [perform in a particular way] **: they're doing really well** leurs affaires marchent bien ▸ **he could do better** il pourrait mieux faire ▸ **the company's not doing too badly** l'entreprise ne se débrouille pas trop mal ▸ **how did you do in the exam?** comment ça a marché à l'examen? ▸ **well done!** bien joué!, bravo!
3. [be good enough, be sufficient] suffire, aller ▸ **will £6 do?** est-ce que 6 livres suffiront?, 6 livres, ça ira? ▸ **that will do** ça suffit ▸ **this won't do** ça ne peut pas continuer comme ça.
■ **n** (pl **dos** OR **do's**) [party] fête *f*, soirée *f*.
◆ ***dos*** **npl : dos and don'ts** ce qu'il faut faire et ne pas faire.
◆ ***do away with*** **vt insep** supprimer.
◆ ***do down*** **vt sep** *UK inf* dire du mal de.
◆ ***do for*** **vt insep** *UK inf* **: these kids will do for me** ces gosses vont me tuer ▸ **I'm done for** je suis fichu OR foutu.
◆ ***do in*** **vt sep 1.** *inf* [murder, kill] supprimer, assassiner
2. [injure] **: to do one's back/one's knee in** se bousiller le dos/le genou.
◆ ***do out of*** **vt sep** *inf* **: to do sb out of sthg** escroquer OR carotter qqch à qqn.
◆ ***do up*** **vt sep 1.** [fasten - shoelaces, shoes] attacher / [- buttons, coat] boutonner ▸ **your shirt's not done up** ta chemise est déboutonnée
2. [decorate - room, house] refaire
3. [wrap up] emballer.
◆ ***do with*** **vt insep 1.** [need] avoir besoin de ▸ **I could have done with some help** j'aurais eu bien besoin d'aide
2. [have connection with] **: it has to do with your missing car** c'est au sujet de votre voiture volée ▸ **that has nothing to do with it** ça n'a rien à voir, ça n'a aucun rapport ▸ **what's that got to do with it?** et alors, quel rapport?, qu'est-ce que ça a à voir? ▸ **I had nothing to do with it** je n'y étais pour rien ▸ **it's nothing to do with me** je n'y suis pour rien ▸ **I want nothing to do with it/you** je ne veux rien avoir à faire là-dedans/avec toi.
◆ ***do without*** ■ **vt insep** se passer de.
■ **vi** s'en passer.

do [2] (abbr of ***ditto***) do.

DOA (abbr of ***dead on arrival***) **adj** mort(e) pendant son transport à l'hôpital.

doable ['duːəbl] **adj** *inf* faisable.

d.o.b., ***DOB*** abbr of ***date of birth***.

Doberman ['dəubəmən] (pl **-s**) **n** doberman *m*.

doc [dɒk] **n** *inf* [doctor] toubib *m* ▸ **morning, doc** bonjour docteur.

docile [*UK* 'dəusaɪl, *US* 'dɒsəl] **adj** docile.

docility [də'sɪlətɪ] **n** docilité *f*.

dock [dɒk] ■ **n 1.** [in harbour] docks *mpl* **2.** LAW banc *m* des accusés.
■ **vt** [wages] faire une retenue sur.
■ **vi** [ship] arriver à quai.

docker ['dɒkəʳ] **n** docker *mf*.

docket ['dɒkɪt] **n** *UK* fiche *f* (descriptive).

docklands ['dɒkləndz] **npl** *UK* docks *mpl*.

dockworker ['dɒkwɜːkəʳ] = ***docker***.

dockyard ['dɒkjɑːd] **n** chantier *m* naval.

doctor ['dɒktər] ■ n **1.** MED docteur *m*, médecin *m* ▸ **he/she is a doctor** il/elle est docteur *OR* médecin ▸ **to go to the doctor('s)** aller chez le docteur ▸ **doctor's note** certificat *m* médical **2.** UNIV docteur *m*.
■ vt **1.** [results, report] falsifier / [text, food] altérer **2.** *UK* [cat] châtrer.

doctorate ['dɒktərət], **doctor's degree** n doctorat *m*.

doctrinaire [,dɒktrɪ'neər] adj doctrinaire.

doctrine ['dɒktrɪn] n doctrine *f*.

docudrama [,dɒkjʊ'drɑːmə] (pl -s) n TV docudrame *m*.

document ■ n ['dɒkjʊmənt] document *m* ▸ **to draw up a document** rédiger un document ▸ **may I have a look at your travel documents, sir?** pourrais-je voir votre titre de transport, monsieur?
■ vt ['dɒkjʊment] documenter.

documentary [,dɒkjʊ'mentərɪ] ■ adj documentaire.
■ n (pl -ies) documentaire *m*.

documentation [,dɒkjʊmen'teɪʃn] n documentation *f*.

document case n porte-documents *m inv*.

DOD (abbr of ***Department of Defense***) n *ministère américain de la défense.*

doddering ['dɒdərɪŋ], **doddery** ['dɒdərɪ] adj *inf* branlant(e).

doddle ['dɒdl] n *UK inf* **: it was a doddle** c'était du gâteau.

Dodecanese [,dəʊdɪkə'niːz] npl **: the Dodecanese** le Dodécanèse ▸ **in the Dodecanese** dans le Dodécanèse.

dodge [dɒdʒ] ■ n *inf* combine *f*.
■ vt éviter, esquiver.
■ vi s'esquiver.

Dodgems® ['dɒdʒəmz] npl *UK* autos *fpl* tamponneuses.

dodgy ['dɒdʒɪ] adj *UK inf* [plan, deal] douteux(euse).

dodo ['dəʊdəʊ] (pl -s *OR* -es) n **1.** [extinct bird] dronte *m*, dodo *m* **2.** *inf* [fool] andouille *f*.

doe [dəʊ] n **1.** [deer] biche *f* **2.** [rabbit] lapine *f*.

DOE n **1.** (abbr of ***Department of the Environment***) *ministère britannique de l'environnement* **2.** (abbr of ***Department of Energy***) *ministère américain de l'énergie.*

doer ['duːər] n *inf* personne *f* dynamique.

does *(weak form* [dəz], *strong form* [dʌz]) ➤ ***do***.

doesn't ['dʌznt] = ***does not***.

dog [dɒg] ■ n **1.** [animal] chien *m*, chienne *f* ▸ **'beware of the dog'** 'attention, chien méchant' ▸ **it's a dog's life** c'est une vie de chien ▸ **it's (a case of) dog eat dog** c'est la loi de la jungle ▸ **you can't teach an old dog new tricks** *prov* les vieilles habitudes ont la vie dure ▸ **this country is going to the dogs** ce pays va à vau-l'eau **2.** *US* [hot dog] hot dog *m* **3.** *US* [product, company] catastrophe *f* / [thing] **: it's a dog** c'est nul.
■ vt (pt & pp -ged, cont -ging) **1.** [subj: person - follow] suivre de près **2.** [subj: problems, bad luck] poursuivre ▸ **to be dogged by bad health/problems** ne pas arrêter d'avoir des ennuis de santé/des problèmes.

dog biscuit n biscuit *m* pour chien.

dog collar n **1.** [of dog] collier *m* de chien **2.** [of priest] col *m* d'ecclésiastique.

dog-eared [-ɪəd] adj écorné(e).

dog-end n *UK inf* [of cigarette] mégot *m*.

dogfight ['dɒgfaɪt] n **1.** [between dogs] combat *m* de chiens **2.** [between aircraft] combat *m* aérien.

dog food n nourriture *f* pour chiens.

dogged ['dɒgɪd] adj tenace.

doggedly ['dɒgɪdlɪ] adv [fight, persist] avec ténacité *OR* persévérance / [refuse] obstinément.

doggedness ['dɒgɪdnɪs] n [of person] ténacité *f*, persévérance *f* / [of courage] ténacité *f*.

doggone ['dɒgɒn] excl *US inf* fichu(e) ▸ **doggone it!** zut!

doggy, **doggie** ['dɒgɪ] (pl -ies) n toutou *m*.

doggy bag, **doggie bag** n *sac pour emporter les restes d'un repas au restaurant.*

doghouse ['dɒghaʊs] (pl [-haʊzɪz]) n **1.** *US* [kennel] chenil *m*, niche *f* **2.** *inf phr* **: to be in the doghouse (with sb)** ne pas être en odeur de sainteté *OR* être en disgrâce (auprès de qqn).

dog licence n *UK permis de posséder un chien.*

dogma ['dɒgmə] n dogme *m*.

dogmatic [dɒg'mætɪk] adj dogmatique.

dogmatism ['dɒgmətɪzm] n dogmatisme *m*.

do-gooder [-'gʊdər] n *pej* bonne âme *f*.

dog paddle n nage *f* du chien.

dogs n *inf* [feet] pannards *mpl*.

dogsbody ['dɒgz,bɒdɪ] (pl -ies) n *UK inf* [woman] bonne *f* à tout faire / [man] factotum *m*.

dog tag n MIL plaque *f* d'identification.

dog-tired adj *inf* épuisé(e).

doing ['duːɪŋ] n **: is this your doing?** c'est toi qui est cause de tout cela?
◆ ***doings*** npl actions *fpl*.

do-it-yourself n *(U)* bricolage *m*.

doldrums ['dɒldrəmz] npl **: to be in the doldrums** *fig* être dans le marasme.

dole [dəʊl] n *UK* [unemployment benefit] allocation *f* de chômage ▸ **to be on the dole** être au chômage.
◆ ***dole out*** vt sep [food, money] distribuer au compte-gouttes.

doleful ['dəʊlfʊl] adj morne.

doll [dɒl] n poupée *f*.

dollar ['dɒlər] n dollar *m*.

dollar area n zone *f* dollar.

dollarization [dɒləraɪ'zeɪʃn] n dollarisation *f*.

dollar rate n cours *m* du dollar.

dollar sign n signe *m* dollar.

dolled up [dɒld-] adj *inf* pomponné(e).

dollhouse *US* = ***doll's house***.

dollop ['dɒləp] n *inf* bonne cuillerée *f*.

doll's house *UK*, **dollhouse** [dɒlhaʊs] *US* n maison *f* de poupée.

dolly ['dɒlɪ] (pl **-ies**) **n** **1.** [doll] poupée *f* **2.** [for TV or film camera] travelling *m*.

dolly bird **n** *UK inf dated* poupée *f*.

Dolomites ['dɒləmaɪts] **npl : the Dolomites** les Dolomites *fpl*.

dolphin ['dɒlfɪn] **n** dauphin *m*.

domain [də'meɪn] **n** *lit* & *fig* & COMPUT domaine *m*.

domain name **n** COMPUT nom *m* de domaine.

Domain Name System **n** COMPUT système *m* de nom de domaine.

dome [dəʊm] **n** dôme *m*.

domestic [də'mestɪk] ■ **adj** **1.** [policy, politics, flight, market] intérieur(e) **2.** [chores, animal] domestique **3.** [home-loving] casanier(ère).
■ **n** domestique *mf*.

domestically [də'mestɪklɪ] **adv** ECON & POL **: to be produced domestically** être produit à l'intérieur du pays ***OR*** au niveau national.

domestic appliance **n** appareil *m* ménager.

domesticate [də'mestɪkeɪt] **vt** [animal] domestiquer, apprivoiser / *hum* [person] habituer aux tâches ménagères.

domesticated [də'mestɪkeɪtɪd] **adj** **1.** [animal] domestiqué(e) **2.** *hum* [person] popote *(inv)*.

domestication [də,mestɪ'keɪʃn] **n** [of animal] domestication *f*, apprivoisement *m*.

domesticity [,dəʊme'stɪsətɪ] **n** *(U)* vie *f* de famille.

domicile ['dɒmɪsaɪl] **n** domicile *m*.

domiciliary [,dɒmɪ'sɪljərɪ] **adj** ADMIN [visit] domiciliaire / [care, services] à domicile.

dominance ['dɒmɪnəns] **n** prédominance *f* / [of person] supériorité *f*.

dominant ['dɒmɪnənt] **adj** dominant(e) / [personality, group] dominateur(trice).

dominant brand **n** marque *f* dominante.

dominate ['dɒmɪneɪt] **vt** dominer.

dominating ['dɒmɪneɪtɪŋ] **adj** [person] dominateur(trice).

domination [,dɒmɪ'neɪʃn] **n** domination *f*.

domineer [,dɒmɪ'nɪəʳ] **vi** se montrer autoritaire ▸ **to domineer over sb** se montrer autoritaire avec qqn.

domineering [,dɒmɪ'nɪərɪŋ] **adj** autoritaire.

Dominica [də'mɪnɪkə] **n** la Dominique ▸ **in Dominica** à la Dominique.

Dominican Republic [də'mɪnɪkən-] **n : the Dominican Republic** la République Dominicaine ▸ **in the Dominican Republic** en République Dominicaine.

dominion [də'mɪnjən] **n** **1.** *(U)* [power] domination *f* **2.** [land] territoire *m*.

domino ['dɒmɪnəʊ] (pl **-es**) **n** domino *m*.
◆ ***dominoes*** **npl** dominos *mpl*.

domino effect **n** effet *m* d'entraînement.

don [dɒn] ■ **n** *UK* UNIV professeur *m* d'université.
■ **vt** (pt & pp **-ned**, cont **-ning**) *fml* [clothing] revêtir.

donate [də'neɪt] **vt** faire don de.

donation [də'neɪʃn] **n** don *m*.

done [dʌn] ■ **pp** ➤ ***do***.
■ **adj** **1.** [job, work] achevé(e) ▸ **I'm nearly done** j'ai presque fini **2.** [cooked] cuit(e) **3.** [socially acceptable] **: that's not the done thing** ça ne se fait pas.
■ **excl** [to conclude deal] tope!

donkey ['dɒŋkɪ] (pl **-s**) **n** âne *m*, ânesse *f*.

donkey jacket **n** *UK veste longue en tissu épais, généralement bleu foncé.*

donkeywork ['dɒŋkɪwɜːk] **n** *UK inf* **: to do the donkeywork** faire le sale boulot.

donor ['dəʊnəʳ] **n** **1.** MED donneur *m*, -euse *f* **2.** [to charity] donateur *m*, -trice *f*.

donor card **n** carte *f* de donneur.

don't [dəʊnt] = ***do not***.

don't know **n** [on survey] sans opinion *mf inv* / [voter] indécis *m*, -e *f*.

donut ['dəʊnʌt] *US* = ***doughnut***.

doodah ['duːdɑː] **n** *inf* truc *m*, bidule *m*.

doodle ['duːdl] ■ **n** griffonnage *m*.
■ **vi** griffonner.

doom [duːm] **n** [fate] destin *m*.

doomed [duːmd] **adj** condamné(e) ▸ **they were doomed to die** ils étaient condamnés à mourir ▸ **the plan was doomed to failure** le plan était voué à l'échec.

door [dɔːʳ] **n** porte *f* / [of vehicle] portière *f* ▸ **she walked through the door** elle franchit la porte ▸ **can someone answer the door?** est-ce que quelqu'un peut aller ouvrir? ▸ **to open the door to sthg** *fig* ouvrir la voie à qqch.

doorbell ['dɔːbel] **n** sonnette *f*.

do-or-die **adj** [chance, effort] désespéré(e), ultime / [attitude, person] jusqu'au-boutiste.

door drop **n** distribution *f* à domicile.

doorhandle ['dɔːhændl] **n** poignée *f* de porte.

doorknob ['dɔːnɒb] **n** bouton *m* de porte.

doorknocker ['dɔː,nɒkəʳ] **n** heurtoir *m*.

doorman ['dɔːmən] (pl **-men** [-mən]) **n** portier *m*.

doormat ['dɔːmæt] **n** *lit* & *fig* paillasson *m*.

doorstep ['dɔːstep] **n** pas *m* de la porte.

doorstepping ['dɔːstepɪŋ] *UK* ■ **n** [by politician] démarchage *m* électoral / [by journalists] *pratique journalistique qui consiste à harceler les gens jusque chez eux.*
■ **adj** [politician] *qui fait du démarchage électoral* / [journalist] *qui harcèle les gens jusque chez eux.*

doorstop ['dɔːstɒp] **n** butoir *m* de porte.

door-to-door **adj** [salesman, selling] à domicile.

doorway ['dɔːweɪ] **n** embrasure *f* de la porte.

dope [dəʊp] ■ **n** *inf* **1.** *drug sl* dope *f* **2.** [for athlete, horse] dopant *m* **3.** *inf* [fool] imbécile *mf*.
■ **vt** [horse] doper.

dope test **n** contrôle *m* anti-dopage.

dopey, dopy ['dəʊpɪ] (comp **-ier**, superl **-iest**) **adj** **1.** *inf* [silly] idiot(e), abruti(e) **2.** [drugged] drogué(e), dopé(e) / [sleepy] (à moitié) endormi(e).

doppelgänger ['dɒpl,gæŋər] **n** double *m (d'une personne vivante)*, sosie *m*.

dopy **adj** = ***dopey***.

dorm *inf* **n** *US* = ***dormitory***.

dormant ['dɔːmənt] **adj** **1.** [volcano] endormi(e) **2.** [law] inappliqué(e).

dormer (window) ['dɔːmər-] **n** lucarne *f*.

dormice ['dɔːmaɪs] **npl** ➤ ***dormouse***.

dormitory ['dɔːmətrɪ] (**pl -ies**) **n** **1.** [gen] dortoir *m* **2.** *US* [in university] ≃ cité *f* universitaire.

Dormobile® ['dɔːmə,biːl] **n** *UK* camping-car *m*.

dormouse ['dɔːmaʊs] (**pl -mice** ['-maɪs]) **n** loir *m*.

Dors (abbr of ***Dorset***) *comté anglais*.

DOS [dɒs] (abbr of ***disk operating system***) **n** DOS *m*.

dosage ['dəʊsɪdʒ] **n** dosage *m*.

dose [dəʊs] ■ **n** **1.** MED dose *f* **2.** *fig* [amount] **: a dose of the measles** la rougeole.
■ **vt : to dose sb with sthg** administrer qqch à qqn.

dosh [dɒʃ] **n** *UK v inf* fric *m*.

doss [dɒs] ◆ ***doss down*** **vi** *UK inf* crécher.

dosser ['dɒsər] **n** *UK inf* clochard *m*, -e *f*.

dosshouse ['dɒshaʊs] (**pl** [-haʊzɪz]) **n** *UK inf* asile *m* de nuit.

dossier ['dɒsɪeɪ] **n** dossier *m*.

dot [dɒt] ■ **n** point *m* ▸ **on the dot** à l'heure pile.
■ **vt** (**pt & pp -ted, cont -ting**) **: dotted with** parsemé(e) de.

DOT (abbr of ***Department of Transportation***) **n** *ministère américain du transport*.

dotage ['dəʊtɪdʒ] **n : to be in one's dotage** être gâteux(euse).

dote [dəʊt] ◆ ***dote (up)on*** **vt insep** adorer.

doting ['dəʊtɪŋ] **adj : she has a doting grandfather** elle a un grand-père qui l'adore.

dot-matrix printer **n** imprimante *f* matricielle.

dotted line ['dɒtɪd-] **n** ligne *f* pointillée ▸ **to sign on the dotted line** *fig* donner formellement son accord.

dotty ['dɒtɪ] (**comp -ier, superl -iest**) **adj** *UK inf* toqué(e).

double ['dʌbl] ■ **adj** double ▸ **double thickness** double épaisseur ▸ **"ally" is spelt "a", double "l", "y"** "ally" s'écrit "a", deux "l", "y" ▸ **a word with a double meaning** un mot à double sens ▸ **double doors** porte *f* à deux battants.
■ **adv** **1.** [twice] **: double the amount** deux fois plus ▸ **to see double** voir double **2.** [in two] en deux ▸ **to bend double** se plier en deux.
■ **n** **1.** [twice as much] **: I earn double what I used to** je gagne le double de ce que je gagnais auparavant ▸ **at** *OR* **on the double** au pas de course **2.** [drink, look-alike] double *m* **3.** CIN doublure *f*.
■ **vt** doubler.
■ **vi** **1.** [increase twofold] doubler **2.** [have second purpose] **: to double as** faire office de.
◆ ***doubles*** **npl** TENNIS double *m*.
◆ ***double back*** **vi insep** [animal, person, road] tourner brusquement ▸ **the path doubles back on itself** le sentier te ramène sur tes pas.
◆ ***double up*** ■ **vt sep : to be doubled up** être plié(e) en deux.
■ **vi** [bend over] se plier en deux.

double act **n** *esp UK* duo *m*.

double agent **n** agent *m* double.

double-barrelled *UK*, ***double-barreled*** *US* [-'bærəld] **adj** **1.** [shotgun] à deux coups **2.** *UK* [name] à rallonge.

double bass [-beɪs] **n** contrebasse *f*.

double bed **n** lit *m* pour deux personnes, grand lit.

double bill **n** double programme *m*.

double-blind **adj** [experiment, test] en double aveugle / [method] à double insu, à double anonymat.

double-breasted [-'brestɪd] **adj** [jacket] croisé(e).

double-check **vt & vi** revérifier.

double chin **n** double menton *m*.

double click **n** COMPUT double-clic *m*.
◆ ***double-click*** ■ **vi** faire un double-clic, cliquer deux fois.
■ **vt** double-cliquer ▸ **to double-click on sthg** double-cliquer sur qqch.

double cream **n** *UK* crème *f* fraîche épaisse.

double-cross **vt** trahir.

double-crosser [-'krɒsər] **n** traître *m*, -esse *f*, faux jeton *m*.

double date **n** sortie *f* à quatre *(deux couples)*.
◆ ***double-date*** **vi** sortir à quatre *(deux couples)*.

double-dealer **n : to be a double-dealer** jouer double jeu.

double-dealing ■ **n** *(U)* fourberie *f*, double jeu *m*.
■ **adj** fourbe, faux(fausse) comme un jeton.

double-decker [-'dekər] **n** *UK* [bus] autobus *m* à impériale.

double-declutch [-diː'klʌtʃ] **vi** *UK* AUT faire un double débrayage.

double-density **adj** COMPUT [disk] double-densité *(inv)*.

double digits *US* = ***double figures***.

double Dutch **n** *UK* charabia *m*, baragouin *m* ▸ **it's all double Dutch to me!** c'est de l'hébreu pour moi!

double-edged [-'edʒd] **adj** *lit & fig* à double tranchant.

double entendre [,duːblɑ̃'tɑ̃dr] **n** allusion *f* grivoise.

double fault **n** double faute *f*.

double figures **npl** *UK* **: to be in(to) double figures** être au-dessus de dix, dépasser la dizaine.

double first **n** *UK* ≃ mention *f* très bien *(dans deux disciplines à la fois)*.

double-glazing [-'gleɪzɪŋ] **n** double vitrage *m*.

double indemnity **n** *US* indemnité *f* double.

double-jointed [-'dʒɔɪntɪd] **adj** désarticulé(e).

double-lock **vt** fermer à double tour.

double-page spread **n** PRESS & TYPO double page *f*.

double-park **vi** se garer en double file.

double parking **n** stationnement *m* en double file.

double-quick **adj & adv** *UK inf* en deux temps trois mouvements.

double room **n** chambre *f* pour deux personnes.

double-sided **adj** COMPUT [disk] double-face.

double spacing **n** double interligne *m* ▸ **in double spacing** à double interligne.

double standard **n : to have double standards** avoir deux poids *OR* deux mesures.

double take **n : to do a double take** marquer un temps d'arrêt.

double-talk **n** *(U)* propos *mpl* ambigus.

double taxation **n** double imposition *f*.

doublethink ['dʌbl,θɪŋk] **n** *(U) raisonnement de mauvaise foi qui contient des contradictions flagrantes* ▸ **it's another case of doublethink** c'est encore un raisonnement pervers.

double time **n** tarif *m* double.

double vision **n** vue *f* double.

double whammy [-'wæmɪ] **n** double malédiction *f*.

doubly ['dʌblɪ] **adv** doublement.

doubt [daʊt] ■ **n** doute *m* ▸ **there is no doubt that** il n'y a aucun doute que ▸ **I have no doubt *OR* doubts about it** je n'en doute pas ▸ **without (a) doubt** sans aucun doute ▸ **beyond all doubt** indubitablement ▸ **to be in doubt** [person] ne pas être sûr(e) / [outcome] être incertain(e) ▸ **if *OR* when in doubt** s'il y a un doute, en cas de doute ▸ **to cast doubt on sthg** mettre qqch en doute ▸ **no doubt** sans aucun doute ▸ **I have my doubts about him** j'ai des doutes sur lui *OR* à son sujet.

■ **vt** douter ▸ **to doubt whether *OR* if** douter que ▸ **I doubt (whether) she'll be there** je doute qu'elle soit là ▸ **I doubt it** j'en doute ▸ **there was no doubting their sincerity** on ne pouvait pas mettre en doute leur sincérité.

doubtful ['daʊtfʊl] **adj 1.** [decision, future] incertain(e) **2.** [unsure] **: to be doubtful about *OR* of** douter de **3.** [person, value] douteux(euse).

doubtfully ['daʊtfʊlɪ] **adv** [uncertainly] avec doute, d'un air de doute / [indecisively] avec hésitation, de façon indécise.

doubtfulness ['daʊtfʊlnɪs] **n 1.** [uncertainty] incertitude *f* / [hesitation] indécision *f* **2.** [dubiousness] caractère *m* équivoque *OR* douteux.

doubtless ['daʊtlɪs] **adv** sans aucun doute.

dough [dəʊ] **n** *(U)* **1.** CULIN pâte *f* **2.** *v inf* [money] fric *m*.

doughnut ['dəʊnʌt] **n** beignet *m*.

dour [dʊəʳ] **adj** austère.

douse [daʊs] **vt 1.** [fire, flames] éteindre **2.** [drench] tremper.

dove¹ [dʌv] **n** [bird] colombe *f*.

dove² [dəʊv] *US* **pt** ➤ ***dive***.

dovecot(e) ['dʌvkɒt] **n** colombier *m*.

Dover ['dəʊvəʳ] **n** Douvres.

dovetail ['dʌvteɪl] *fig* ■ **vt** faire coïncider.

■ **vi** coïncider.

dovetail joint **n** assemblage *m* à queue d'aronde.

dowager ['daʊədʒəʳ] **n** douairière *f*.

dowdy ['daʊdɪ] (comp **-ier**, superl **-iest**) **adj** sans chic.

Dow-Jones average [,daʊ'dʒəʊnz-] **n : the Dow-Jones average** le Dow-Jones, l'indice *m* Dow-Jones.

down [daʊn] ■ **adv 1.** [downwards] en bas, vers le bas ▸ **to bend down** se pencher ▸ **to climb down** descendre ▸ **to fall down** tomber (par terre) ▸ **to pull down** tirer vers le bas ▸ **down and down** de plus en plus bas ▸ **down at the bottom of the hill/page** en bas de la colline/de la page ▸ **I'll be down in a minute** [downstairs] je descends dans un instant

2. [along] **: we went down to have a look** on est allé jeter un coup d'œil ▸ **I'm going down to the shop** je vais au magasin

3. [southwards] **: we travelled down to London** on est descendu à Londres ▸ **we're going down south** nous descendons vers le sud

4. [lower in amount] **: prices are coming down** les prix baissent ▸ **down to the last detail** jusqu'au moindre détail

5. [in written form] **: to write sthg down** noter qqch ▸ **get it down in writing *OR* on paper** mettez-le par écrit ▸ **it's down in my diary/on the calendar** c'est dans mon agenda/sur le calendrier.

■ **prep 1.** [downwards] **: they ran down the hill/stairs** ils ont descendu la colline/l'escalier en courant ▸ **a line down the middle of the page** une ligne verticale au milieu de la page ▸ **tears ran down her face** des larmes coulaient le long de son visage ▸ **to go down the plughole** passer par le trou (de l'évier/de la baignoire) ▸ **it's down the stairs** c'est en bas de l'escalier

2. [along] **: to walk down the street** descendre la rue ▸ **they live down the street** ils habitent plus loin *OR* plus bas dans la rue.

■ **adj 1.** *inf* [depressed] **: to feel down** avoir le cafard

2. [behind] **: they're two goals down** ils perdent de deux buts

3. [lower in amount] **: prices are down again** les prix ont encore baissé ▸ **the pound is down against the dollar** FIN la livre a baissé par rapport au dollar

4. [computer, telephones] en panne.

■ **n** *(U)* duvet *m*.

■ **vt 1.** [knock over] abattre

2. [drink] avaler d'un trait.

◆ ***downs*** **npl** *UK* collines *fpl*.

down-and-out ■ **adj** indigent(e).

■ **n** personne *f* dans le besoin.

down-at-heel, *US* ***down-at-the-heels*** **adj** déguenillé(e).

downbeat ['daʊnbi:t] **adj** *inf* pessimiste.

downcast ['daʊnkɑ:st] **adj 1.** [sad] démoralisé(e) **2.** [eyes] baissé(e).

downer ['daʊnəʳ] **n** *inf* **1.** [drug] tranquillisant *m* **2.** [depressing event or person] **: he's/it's a real downer** il est/c'est flippant.

downfall ['daʊnfɔ:l] **n** *(U)* ruine *f*.

downgrade ['daʊngreɪd] **vt** [job] déclasser / [employee] rétrograder.

downhearted [ˌdaʊn'hɑːtɪd] **adj** découragé(e).

downhill [ˌdaʊn'hɪl] ■ **adj 1.** [downward] en pente ▸ **it's downhill all the way now** *fig* ça va être du gâteau maintenant **2.** [skiing] **: downhill skier** descendeur *m*, -euse *f*.
■ **n** [race in skiing] descente *f*.
■ **adv : to walk downhill** descendre la côte ▸ **her career is going downhill** *fig* sa carrière est sur le déclin.

Downing Street ['daʊnɪŋ-] **n** *rue du centre de Londres où réside le Premier ministre.*

CULTURE
Downing Street

Le numéro 10 **Downing Street**, à Westminster, est la résidence officielle du Premier ministre à Londres. C'est là que se tiennent les réunions protocolaires du Conseil des ministres et que sont reçus les chefs d'État et les dignitaires étrangers. Tony Blair est le premier chef d'État à avoir préféré s'installer au numéro 11 de la même rue, la résidence habituelle du ministre des Finances, considérant que l'endroit était plus confortable. Le terme **Downing Street** désigne plus largement le gouvernement britannique ou le Premier ministre anglais.

down-in-the-mouth **adj : to be down-in-the-mouth** être abattu(e).

download [ˌdaʊn'ləʊd] **vt** COMPUT télécharger.

downloadable [ˌdaʊn'ləʊdəbl] **adj** COMPUT téléchargeable.

downloading [ˌdaʊn'ləʊdɪŋ] **n** COMPUT téléchargement *m*.

down-market **adj** [product] bas de gamme / [book] grande diffusion *(inv)* ▸ **it's a rather down-market area** ce n'est pas un quartier très chic.

down payment **n** acompte *m*.

downplay ['daʊnpleɪ] **vt** minimiser.

downpour ['daʊnpɔː] **n** pluie *f* torrentielle.

downright ['daʊnraɪt] ■ **adj** [lie] effronté(e).
■ **adv** franchement.

downscale [ˌdaʊn'skeɪl] **adj** *US* = ***downmarket***.

downshift [ˌdaʊn'ʃɪft] **vi** *US* rétrograder.

downside ['daʊnsaɪd] **n** désavantage *m*.

downsize ['daʊnsaɪz] **vt 1.** [company] réduire les effectifs de **2.** COMPUT [application] réduire l'échelle de.

downsizing ['daʊnsaɪzɪŋ] **n** INDUST réduction *f* des effectifs / COMPUT réduction *f* d'échelle.

Down's syndrome **n** trisomie *f* 21.

downstairs [ˌdaʊn'steəz] ■ **adj** du bas / [on floor below] à l'étage en-dessous.
■ **adv** en bas / [on floor below] à l'étage en-dessous ▸ **to come** *OR* **go downstairs** descendre.

downstream [ˌdaʊn'striːm] **adv** en aval.

downswing ['daʊnswɪŋ] **n 1.** [trend] tendance *f* à la baisse, baisse *f* **2.** GOLF mouvement *m* descendant.

downtime ['daʊntaɪm] **n** temps *m* improductif.

down-to-earth **adj** terre-à-terre *(inv)*.

downtown [ˌdaʊn'taʊn] *esp US* ■ **adj : downtown Paris** le centre de Paris.
■ **adv** en ville.

downtrodden ['daʊnˌtrɒdn] **adj** opprimé(e).

downturn ['daʊntɜːn] **n : downturn (in)** baisse *f* (de).

down under **adv** en Australie/Nouvelle-Zélande.

downward ['daʊnwəd] ■ **adj 1.** [towards ground] vers le bas **2.** [trend] à la baisse.
■ **adv** = ***downwards***.

downward-compatible **adj** COMPUT compatible vers le bas.

downward mobility **n** ECON régression *f* sociale.

downwards ['daʊnwədz] **adv 1.** [look, move] vers le bas **2.** [in hierarchy] **: from the president downwards** du président jusqu'au bas de la hiérarchie.

downward trend **n** ECON tendance *f* à la baisse *OR* baissière.

downwind [ˌdaʊn'wɪnd] **adv** dans le sens du vent.

dowry ['daʊərɪ] (**pl -ies**) **n** dot *f*.

doz. (abbr of ***dozen***) douz.

doze [dəʊz] ■ **n** somme *m*.
■ **vi** sommeiller.
◆ ***doze off*** **vi** s'assoupir.

dozen ['dʌzn] ■ **num adj : a dozen eggs** une douzaine d'œufs.
■ **n** douzaine *f* ▸ **50p a dozen** 50p la douzaine ▸ **dozens of** *inf* des centaines de.

dozy ['dəʊzɪ] (**comp -ier, superl -iest**) **adj 1.** [sleepy] somnolent(e) **2.** *UK inf* [stupid] lent(e).

DP (abbr of ***data processing***) **n** informatique *f*.

DPh, ***DPhil*** [ˌdiː'fɪl] (abbr of ***Doctor of Philosophy***) **n** *UK docteur en philosophie*.

DPP *UK* abbr of ***Director of Public Prosecutions***.

DPT (abbr of ***diphtheria, pertussis, tetanus***) **n** DCT *m*.

DPW (abbr of ***Department of Public Works***) **n** *UK ministère de l'équipement*.

dr abbr of ***debtor***.

Dr. **1.** (abbr of ***Drive***) av **2.** (abbr of ***Doctor***) Dr.

drab [dræb] (**comp -ber, superl -best**) **adj** [colour] terne, fade / [surroundings] morne, triste.

drabness ['dræbnɪs] **n** [of colour] caractère *m* *OR* aspect *m* terne, fadeur *f* / [of surroundings] caractère *m* *OR* aspect *m* morne, tristesse *f*, grisaille *f*.

draconian [drə'kəʊnjən] **adj** draconien(enne).

draft [drɑːft] ■ **n 1.** [early version] premier jet *m*, ébauche *f* / [of letter] brouillon *m* ▸ **draft treaty** projet *m* de convention **2.** [money order] traite *f* **3.** *US* MIL **: the draft** la conscription *f* **4.** *US* = ***draught***.
■ **vt 1.** [speech] ébaucher, faire le plan de / [letter] faire le brouillon de **2.** *US* MIL appeler **3.** [staff] muter.

draft dodger [-dɒdʒəʳ] **n** *US* insoumis *m*.

draftee [ˌdrɑːf'tiː] **n** *US* appelé *m*.

draft-proof *US* = ***draught-proof***.

draft-proofing *US* = ***draught-proofing***.

draft quality n [of printout] qualité *f* brouillon OR listing, qualité *f* liste rapide.

draftsman *US* = ***draughtsman***.

draftsmanship *US* = ***draughtsmanship***.

drafty *US* = ***draughty***.

drag [dræg] ■ vt (pt & pp -ged, cont -ging) **1.** [gen] traîner ▸ **to drag sthg on** OR **along the ground** traîner qqch par terre ▸ **to drag one's feet** traîner les pieds ▸ **I couldn't drag him away from his work** je ne pouvais pas l'arracher à son travail ▸ **don't drag me into this!** ne me mêlez pas à vos histoires! **2.** [lake, river] draguer **3.** COMPUT faire glisser ▸ **to drag and drop** glisser-lâcher.
■ vi (pt & pp -ged, cont -ging) **1.** [dress, coat] traîner **2.** *fig* [time, action] traîner en longueur.
■ n **1.** *inf* [bore] plaie *f* ▸ **he's a real drag!** c'est un vrai casse-pieds! ▸ **what a drag!** quelle barbe!, c'est la barbe! **2.** *inf* [on cigarette] bouffée *f* **3.** [wind resistance] coefficient *m* de pénétration (dans l'air) **4.** [cross-dressing] **: in drag** en travesti.
◆ ***drag down*** vt sep *fig* **: they dragged him down with them** ils l'ont entraîné dans leur chute.
◆ ***drag in*** vt sep [include - person] mêler / [- subject] faire allusion à.
◆ ***drag on*** vi [meeting, time] s'éterniser, traîner en longueur ▸ **don't let the matter drag on** ne laissez pas traîner l'affaire.
◆ ***drag out*** vt sep **1.** [protract] prolonger, faire traîner **2.** [facts] tirer, arracher ▸ **to drag sthg out of sb** soutirer qqch à qqn.

drag-and-drop n COMPUT glisser-lâcher *m*.

dragnet ['drægnet] n **1.** [net] drège *f* **2.** *fig* [to catch criminal] piège *m*.

dragon ['drægən] n *lit* & *fig* dragon *m*.

dragonfly ['drægnflaɪ] (pl -ies) n libellule *f*.

dragoon [drə'gu:n] ■ n dragon *m*.
■ vt **: to dragoon sb into doing sthg** contraindre qqn à faire qqch.

drag racing n course *f* de dragster.

dragster ['drægstəʳ] n dragster *m*.

drain [dreɪn] ■ n **1.** [pipe] égout *m* ▸ **down the drain** [money] jeté par les fenêtres **2.** [depletion - of resources, funds] **: drain on** épuisement *m* de.
■ vt **1.** [vegetables] égoutter / [land] assécher, drainer **2.** [strength, resources] épuiser ▸ **to feel drained** être vidé(e) **3.** [drink, glass] boire.
■ vi [dishes] égoutter ▸ **the blood drained from his face** il blêmit.

drainage ['dreɪnɪdʒ] n **1.** [pipes, ditches] (système *m* du) tout-à-l'égout *m* **2.** [draining - of land] drainage *m*.

drained [dreɪnd] adj [of strength, resources] épuisé(e), éreinté(e).

draining board *UK* ['dreɪnɪŋ-], ***drainboard*** *US* ['dreɪnbɔ:rd] n égouttoir *m*.

drainpipe ['dreɪnpaɪp] n tuyau *m* d'écoulement.

drainpipes, ***drainpipe trousers*** npl *UK* pantalon-cigarette *m*.

drake [dreɪk] n canard *m*.

dram [dræm] n *Scot* goutte *f* (de whisky).

drama ['drɑ:mə] ■ n **1.** [play, excitement] drame *m* **2.** *(U)* [art] théâtre *m*.
■ comp [school] d'art dramatique / [critic] dramatique.

dramatic [drə'mætɪk] adj **1.** [gen] dramatique **2.** [sudden, noticeable] spectaculaire.

dramatically [drə'mætɪklɪ] adv **1.** [noticeably] de façon spectaculaire **2.** [theatrically] de façon théâtrale.

dramatics [drə'mætɪks] ■ n *(U)* THEAT art *m* dramatique, dramaturgie *f*.
■ npl *fig* [behaviour] comédie *f*, cirque *m*.

dramatist ['dræmətɪst] n dramaturge *mf*.

dramatization [,dræmətaɪ'zeɪʃn] n adaptation *f* pour la télévision/la scène/l'écran.

dramatize, *UK* ***-ise*** ['dræmətaɪz] vt **1.** [rewrite as play, film] adapter pour la télévision/la scène/l'écran **2.** *pej* [make exciting] dramatiser.

drank [dræŋk] pt ➤ ***drink***.

drape [dreɪp] vt draper ▸ **to be draped with** OR **in** être drapé(e) de.
◆ ***drapes*** npl *US* rideaux *mpl*.

draper ['dreɪpəʳ] n *UK dated* marchand *m*, -e *f* de tissus.

drapery ['dreɪpərɪ] n *UK* mercerie *f*.

drastic ['dræstɪk] adj **1.** [measures] drastique, radical(e) **2.** [improvement, decline] spectaculaire.

drastically ['dræstɪklɪ] adv [change, decline] de façon spectaculaire.

drat [dræt] excl *inf* **: drat!** diable!, bon sang!

dratted ['drætɪd] adj *inf* sacré(e).

draught *UK*, ***draft*** *US* [drɑ:ft] n **1.** [air current] courant *m* d'air **2.** *liter* [gulp] gorgée *f* **3.** [from barrel] **: on draught** [beer] à la pression.
◆ ***draughts*** n *UK* jeu *m* de dames.

draught beer *UK*, ***draft beer*** *US* n bière *f* à la pression.

draughtboard ['drɑ:ftbɔ:d] n *UK* damier *m*.

draught excluder [-ɪk'sklu:dəʳ] n *UK* bourrelet *m* (de porte).

draught-proof *UK*, ***draft-proof*** *US* ■ vt calfeutrer.
■ adj calfeutré(e).

draught-proofing *UK*, ***draft-proofing*** *US* [-,pru:fɪŋ] n calfeutrage *m*.

draughtsman *UK*, ***draftsman*** *US* ['drɑ:ftsmən] n (pl -men [-mən]) dessinateur *m*, -trice *f*.

draughtsmanship *UK*, ***draftsmanship*** *US* ['drɑ:ftsmənʃɪp] n [skill] talent *m* de dessinateur.

draughty *UK*, ***drafty*** *US* ['drɑ:ftɪ] adj (comp -ier, superl -iest) plein(e) de courants d'air.

draw [drɔː] ■ vt (pt drew, pp drawn) **1.** [pull, take] tirer ▸ **to draw the curtains** [open] tirer OR ouvrir les rideaux / [shut] tirer OR fermer les rideaux ▸ **he drew his knife from** OR **out of his pocket** il a tiré son couteau de sa poche ▸ **to draw a sword** dégainer une épée ▸ **to draw water from a well** puiser de l'eau dans un puits ▸ **to draw money from the bank** retirer de l'argent à la banque ▸ **to draw lots** tirer au sort ▸ **to draw breath** *fig* souffler
2. [sketch] dessiner ▸ **to draw a picture of sb** faire le portrait de qqn ▸ **she drew a vivid picture of village life** elle (nous) a fait une description vivante de la vie de village ▸ **to draw the line at sthg** ne pas admettre qqch, se refuser à qqch
3. [comparison, distinction] établir, faire
4. [attract, lead] attirer, entraîner ▸ **to draw sb's attention to** attirer l'attention de qqn sur ▸ **to be** OR **feel drawn to** être OR se sentir attiré(e) par.
■ vi (pt drew, pp drawn) **1.** [sketch] dessiner
2. [move] **: to draw near** [person] s'approcher / [time] approcher ▸ **to draw away** reculer ▸ **the crowd drew to one side** la foule s'est rangée sur le côté OR s'est écartée ▸ **to draw to an end** OR **a close** tirer à sa fin ▸ **to draw to a halt** s'arrêter
3. SPORT faire match nul ▸ **Italy drew against Spain** l'Italie et l'Espagne ont fait match nul ▸ **to be drawing** être à égalité.
■ n **1.** SPORT [result] match *m* nul
2. [lottery] tirage *m*
3. [attraction] attraction *f*.
◆ ***draw in*** vi **1.** [move] **: the train drew in** le train est entré en gare
2. [days] raccourcir.
◆ ***draw into*** vt sep **: to draw sb into sthg** mêler qqn à qqch ▸ **I got drawn into the project** je me suis laissé impliquer dans le projet.
◆ ***draw on*** vt insep **1.** = ***draw upon***
2. [cigarette] tirer sur.
◆ ***draw out*** vt sep **1.** [encourage - person] faire sortir de sa coquille
2. [prolong] prolonger
3. [money] faire un retrait de, retirer.
◆ ***draw up*** ■ vt sep [contract, plan] établir, dresser.
■ vi [vehicle] s'arrêter.
◆ ***draw upon*** vt insep [information] utiliser, se servir de / [reserves, resources] puiser dans.

drawback ['drɔːbæk] n inconvénient *m*, désavantage *m*.

drawbridge ['drɔːbrɪdʒ] n pont-levis *m*.

drawdown ['drɔːdaʊn] n tirage *m*.

drawer [drɔːʳ] n [in desk, chest] tiroir *m*.

drawing ['drɔːɪŋ] n dessin *m*.

drawing board n planche *f* à dessin ▸ **back to the drawing board** *inf* retour à la case départ.

drawing pin n *UK* punaise *f*.

drawing room n salon *m*.

drawl [drɔːl] ■ n voix *f* traînante.
■ vt dire d'une voix traînante.

drawn [drɔːn] ■ pp ➤ ***draw***.
■ adj **1.** [curtains] tiré(e) **2.** [face] fatigué(e), tiré(e).

drawn-out adj prolongé(e).

drawstring ['drɔːstrɪŋ] n cordon *m*.

dread [dred] ■ n *(U)* épouvante *f*.
■ vt appréhender ▸ **to dread doing sthg** appréhender de faire qqch ▸ **I dread to think** je n'ose pas imaginer.

dreaded ['dredɪd] adj redouté(e).

dreadful ['dredfʊl] adj affreux(euse), épouvantable.

dreadfully ['dredfʊlɪ] adv **1.** [badly] terriblement **2.** [extremely] extrêmement ▸ **I'm dreadfully sorry** je regrette infiniment.

dreadlocks ['dredlɒks] npl coiffure *f* rasta.

dream [driːm] ■ n **1.** rêve *m* ▸ **I had a dream about my mother** j'ai rêvé de ma mère ▸ **the child had a bad dream** l'enfant a fait un mauvais rêve OR un cauchemar ▸ **sweet dreams!** faites de beaux rêves!
2. [wish, fantasy] rêve *m*, désir *m* ▸ **the woman of his dreams** la femme de ses rêves ▸ **her dream was to become a pilot** elle rêvait de devenir pilote ▸ **a job beyond my wildest dreams** un travail comme je n'ai jamais osé imaginer OR qui dépasse tous mes rêves ▸ **the American dream** le rêve américain ▸ **the holiday was like a dream come true** les vacances étaient comme un rêve devenu réalité ▸ **in your dreams!** *inf* tu peux toujours rêver!
■ adj de rêve ▸ **the dream ticket** POL [policies] le programme utopique OR à faire rêver / [candidates] le couple idéal.
■ vt (pt & pp -ed OR dreamt) rêver ▸ **he dreamt a dream** il a fait un rêve ▸ **you must have dreamt it** vous avez dû le rêver ▸ **to dream (that)...** rêver que... ▸ **I never dreamed this would happen** je n'aurais jamais pensé que cela puisse arriver.
■ vi (pt & pp -ed OR dreamt) **: to dream (of** OR **about)** rêver (de) ▸ **it can't be true – I must be dreaming** ce n'est pas vrai, je rêve ▸ **I wouldn't dream of it** cela ne me viendrait même pas à l'idée ▸ **dream on!** *inf* on peut toujours rêver!
◆ ***dream up*** vt sep inventer.

dreamboat ['driːmbəʊt] n *inf dated* homme *m*, femme *f* de rêve.

dreamer ['driːməʳ] n [unrealistic person] utopiste *mf*.

dreamily ['driːmɪlɪ] adv rêveusement.

dreamlike ['driːmlaɪk] adj comme dans un rêve.

dreamt [dremt] pt & pp ➤ ***dream***.

dream world n monde *m* imaginaire.

dreamy ['driːmɪ] (comp -ier, superl -iest) adj **1.** [distracted] rêveur(euse) **2.** [dreamlike] de rêve.

dreariness ['drɪərɪnɪs] n [of surroundings] aspect *m* morne OR terne, monotonie *f* / [of life] monotonie *f*, tristesse *f*.

dreary ['drɪərɪ] (comp -ier, superl -iest) adj **1.** [weather] morne / [surroundings] morne, triste / [life] morne, monotone **2.** [person] ennuyeux(euse).

dredge [dredʒ] ■ n = ***dredger***.
■ vt draguer.
◆ ***dredge up*** vt sep **1.** [with dredger] draguer **2.** *fig* [from past] déterrer.

dredger ['dredʒəʳ] n [ship] dragueur *m* / [machine] drague *f*.

dregs [dregz] npl *lit* & *fig* lie *f*.

drench [drentʃ] vt tremper ▸ **to be drenched in** OR **with** être inondé(e) de.

drenching ['drentʃɪŋ] ■ **n** trempage *m*.
■ **adj : drenching rain** pluie *f* battante *OR* diluvienne.

Dresden ['drezdən] **n** Dresde.

dress [dres] ■ **n 1.** [woman's garment] robe *f* **2.** *(U)* [clothing] costume *m*, tenue *f*.
■ **vt 1.** [clothe] habiller ▸ **to be dressed** être habillé(e) ▸ **to be dressed in** être vêtu(e) de ▸ **to get dressed** s'habiller **2.** [bandage] panser **3.** CULIN [salad] assaisonner.
■ **vi** s'habiller.
◆ ***dress up*** ■ **vt sep** [facts] maquiller.
■ **vi 1.** [in costume] se déguiser **2.** [in best clothes] s'habiller (élégamment).

dressage ['dresɑːʒ] **n** dressage *m*.

dress circle **n** *UK* premier balcon *m*.

dresser ['dresəʳ] **n 1.** [for dishes] vaisselier *m* **2.** *US* [chest of drawers] commode *f* **3.** [person] **: a smart dresser** une personne qui s'habille avec chic.

dressing ['dresɪŋ] **n 1.** [bandage] pansement *m* **2.** [for salad] assaisonnement *m* **3.** *US* [for turkey] farce *f*.

dressing-down **n** *UK inf* réprimande *f*, semonce *f* ▸ **to give sb a dressing-down** passer un savon à qqn.

dressing gown *UK* **n** robe *f* de chambre.

dressing room **n 1.** THEAT loge *f* **2.** SPORT vestiaire *m*.

dressing table **n** coiffeuse *f*.

dressing-up **n** [children's game] déguisement *m*.

dressmaker ['dres,meɪkəʳ] **n** couturier *m*, -ère *f*.

dressmaking ['dres,meɪkɪŋ] **n** couture *f*.

dress rehearsal **n** générale *f*.

dress sense **n : to have good dress sense** savoir s'habiller ▸ **she's got no dress sense** elle ne sait pas s'habiller.

dress shirt **n** chemise *f* de soirée.

dressy ['dresɪ] (**comp -ier**, **superl -iest**) **adj** habillé(e).

drew [druː] **pt** ➤ ***draw***.

dribble ['drɪbl] ■ **n 1.** [saliva] bave *f* **2.** [trickle] traînée *f*.
■ **vt** SPORT dribbler.
■ **vi 1.** [drool] baver **2.** [liquid] tomber goutte à goutte, couler.

dribs [drɪbz] **npl : in dribs and drabs** peu à peu, petit à petit.

dried [draɪd] ■ **pp** ➤ ***dry***.
■ **adj** [milk, eggs] en poudre / [fruit] sec (sèche) / [flowers] séché(e).

dried-up **adj** asséché(e).

drier ['draɪəʳ] = ***dryer***.

drift [drɪft] ■ **n 1.** [movement] mouvement *m* / [direction] direction *f*, sens *m* **2.** [meaning] sens *m* général ▸ **I get your drift** je vois ce que vous voulez dire **3.** [of snow] congère *f* / [of sand, leaves] amoncellement *m*, entassement *m*.
■ **vi 1.** [boat] dériver **2.** [snow, sand, leaves] s'amasser, s'amonceler **3.** [person] errer ▸ **to drift into sthg** se retrouver dans qqch ▸ **to drift apart** se détacher l'un de l'autre.
◆ ***drift off*** **vi** [person] s'assoupir.

drifter ['drɪftəʳ] **n** [person] personne *f* sans but dans la vie.

driftwood ['drɪftwʊd] **n** bois *m* flottant.

drill [drɪl] ■ **n 1.** [tool] perceuse *f* / [dentist's] fraise *f* / [in mine] perforatrice *f* **2.** [exercise, training] exercice *m*.
■ **vt 1.** [wood, hole] percer / [tooth] fraiser / [well] forer **2.** [soldiers] entraîner ▸ **to drill sthg into sb** faire rentrer qqch dans la tête de qqn.
■ **vi 1.** [bore] **: to drill into** [wood] percer dans / [tooth] fraiser dans **2.** [excavate] **: to drill for oil** forer à la recherche de pétrole.

drilling platform ['drɪlɪŋ-] **n** plate-forme *f* pétrolière *OR* de forage.

drily ['draɪlɪ] = ***dryly***.

drink [drɪŋk] ■ **n 1.** [gen] boisson *f* / [alcoholic] verre *m* ▸ **would you like something to drink?** voulez-vous boire quelque chose? ▸ **may I have a drink?** puis-je boire quelque chose? ▸ **a drink of water** un verre d'eau ▸ **we invited them in for a drink** nous les avons invités à prendre un verre ▸ **there's plenty of food and drink** il y a tout ce qu'on veut à boire et à manger
2. *(U)* [alcohol] alcool *m* ▸ **to be the worse for drink** être en état d'ébriété ▸ **to smell of drink** sentir l'alcool.
■ **vt** (**pt drank**, **pp drunk**) boire ▸ **the water is not fit to drink** l'eau n'est pas potable.
■ **vi** (**pt drank**, **pp drunk**) boire ▸ **she drank out of** *OR* **from the bottle** elle a bu à la bouteille ▸ **to drink to sb/ to sb's success** boire à qqn/à la réussite de qqn ▸ **'don't drink and drive'** 'boire ou conduire, il faut choisir'.

drinkable ['drɪŋkəbl] **adj 1.** [water] potable **2.** [palatable] buvable.

drink-driving *UK*, ***drunk driving*** *US*, ***drunken driving*** *US* **n** conduite *f* en état d'ivresse.

drinker ['drɪŋkəʳ] **n** buveur *m*, -euse *f*.

drinking ['drɪŋkɪŋ] ■ **adj : I'm not a drinking man** je ne bois pas.
■ **n** *(U)* boisson *f*.

drinking fountain **n** fontaine *f* d'eau potable.

drinking-up time **n** *UK moment où les clients doivent finir leur verre avant la fermeture du bar.*

drinking water **n** eau *f* potable.

drinks machine *UK*, ***drink machine*** *US* **n** distributeur *m* de boissons.

drip [drɪp] ■ **n 1.** [drop] goutte *f* **2.** MED goutte-à-goutte *m inv* **3.** *inf* [wimp] femmelette *f*.
■ **vt** (**pt & pp -ped**, **cont -ping**) laisser tomber goutte à goutte.
■ **vi** (**pt & pp -ped**, **cont -ping**) **1.** [gen] goutter, tomber goutte à goutte **2.** [person] **: to be dripping with** *lit & fig* être ruisselant(e) de.

drip-dry **adj** qui ne se repasse pas.

drip-feed ■ **n** goutte-à-goutte *m inv*.
■ **vt** alimenter par perfusion.

dripping ['drɪpɪŋ] ■ **adj : dripping (wet)** dégoulinant(e).
■ **n** *(U)* graisse *f*.

drippy ['drɪpɪ] (**comp -ier**, **superl -iest**) **adj 1.** *inf pej* [person] mou *(before vowel or silent 'h'* **mol***)* (molle) **2.** [tap] qui fuit *OR* goutte.

drive [draɪv] ■ n **1.** [in car] trajet *m* (en voiture) ▸ **to go for a drive** faire une promenade (en voiture) ▸ **it's an hour's drive from here** c'est à une heure d'ici en voiture
2. [urge] désir *m*, besoin *m*
3. [campaign] campagne *f* ▸ **the company is having a sales drive** la compagnie fait une campagne de vente
4. *(U)* [energy] dynamisme *m*, énergie *f* ▸ **we need someone with drive** il nous faut quelqu'un de dynamique
5. [road to house] allée *f*
6. SPORT drive *m*.
■ vt (pt **drove**, pp **driven**) **1.** [vehicle, passenger] conduire ▸ **he drives a taxi/lorry** il est chauffeur de taxi/camionneur ▸ **I drive a Volvo** j'ai une Volvo ▸ **he drove her into town** il l'a conduite *OR* emmenée en voiture en ville ▸ **she drove the car into a tree** elle a heurté un arbre avec la voiture
2. TECH entraîner, actionner ▸ **driven by electricity** marchant à l'électricité
3. [animals, people] pousser ▸ **to drive sb out of the house/of the country** chasser qqn de la maison/du pays
4. [motivate, push] pousser ▸ **he drives himself too hard** il exige trop de lui-même
5. [force] **: to drive sb to sthg/to do sthg** pousser qqn à qqch/à faire qqch, conduire qqn à qqch/à faire qqch ▸ **he was driven to it** on lui a forcé la main ▸ **to drive sb mad** *OR* **crazy** rendre qqn fou ▸ **his performance drove the audience wild** *inf* son spectacle a mis le public en délire
6. [nail, stake] enfoncer
7. SPORT driver.
■ vi (pt **drove**, pp **driven**) [driver] conduire / [travel by car] aller en voiture ▸ **do you** *OR* **can you drive?** savez-vous conduire? ▸ **I was driving at 100 mph** je roulais à 160 km/h ▸ **we drove home/down to the coast** nous sommes rentrés/descendus sur la côte en voiture ▸ **they drove all night** ils ont roulé toute la nuit ▸ **drive on the right** roulez à droite, tenez votre droite.
◆ ***drive at*** vt insep **: what are you driving at?** où voulez-vous en venir?
◆ ***drive down*** vt sep ECON [prices, inflation] faire baisser.
◆ ***drive up*** vt sep ECON [prices, inflation] faire monter.

drive-by (pl **drive-bys**) n *inf* **: drive-by shooting** fusillade *f* en voiture.

drive-in *esp US* ■ n drive-in *m*, ciné-parc *m offic*.
■ adj [retaurant, movie theather] drive-in *(inv)*.

drivel ['drɪvl] n *(U) inf* foutaises *fpl*, idioties *fpl*.

driven ['drɪvn] pp ➤ ***drive***.

-driven suffix **1.** TECH (fonctionnant) à ▸ **electricity/steam-driven engine** machine électrique/à vapeur **2.** *fig* déterminé par ▸ **market/consumer-driven** déterminé par les contraintes du marché/les exigences du consommateur **3.** COMPUT contrôlé par ▸ **menu-driven** contrôlé par menu.

driver ['draɪvər] n **1.** [of vehicle - gen] conducteur *m*, -trice *f* / [- of taxi] chauffeur *m* **2.** COMPUT pilote *m*.

driver's license *US* = ***driving licence***.

drive shaft n arbre *m* de transmission.

drive-through ■ adj où l'on reste dans sa voiture.
■ n drive-in *m inv*, ciné-parc *m offic*.

driveway ['draɪvweɪ] n allée *f*.

driving ['draɪvɪŋ] ■ adj [rain] battant(e) / [wind] cinglant(e).
■ n *(U)* conduite *f*.

driving force n force *f* motrice.

driving instructor n moniteur *m*, -trice *f* d'auto-école.

driving lesson n leçon *f* de conduite.

driving licence *UK*, ***driver's license*** *US* n permis *m* de conduire.

driving mirror n rétroviseur *m*.

driving school n auto-école *f*.

driving seat n place *f* du conducteur ▸ **she's in the driving seat** *fig* c'est elle qui mène l'affaire *OR* qui tient les rênes.

driving test n (examen *m* du) permis *m* de conduire.

drizzle ['drɪzl] ■ n bruine *f*.
■ impers vb bruiner.

drizzly ['drɪzlɪ] (comp **-ier**, superl **-iest**) adj bruineux(euse).

droll [drəʊl] adj drôle.

dromedary ['drɒmədrɪ] (pl **-ies**) n dromadaire *m*.

drone [drəʊn] ■ n **1.** [of traffic, voices] ronronnement *m* / [of insect] bourdonnement *m* **2.** [male bee] abeille *f* mâle, faux-bourdon *m*.
■ vi [engine] ronronner / [insect] bourdonner.
◆ ***drone on*** vi parler d'une voix monotone ▸ **to drone on about sthg** rabâcher qqch.

drool [dru:l] vi baver ▸ **to drool over** *fig* baver (d'admiration) devant.

droop [dru:p] vi **1.** [head] pencher / [shoulders, eyelids] tomber **2.** *fig* [spirits] faiblir.

droopy ['dru:pɪ] (comp **-ier**, superl **-iest**) adj [moustache, shoulders] qui tombe / [flowers] qui commence à se faner.

drop [drɒp] ■ n **1.** [of liquid] goutte *f* ▸ **drop by drop** goutte à goutte ▸ **it's just a drop in the ocean** ce n'est qu'une goutte d'eau dans la mer **2.** [decrease] baisse *f*, chute *f* ▸ **a drop in prices** une baisse *OR* une chute des prix **3.** [distance down] dénivellation *f* ▸ **it was a long drop from the top of the wall** ça faisait haut depuis le haut du mur ▸ **sheer drop** à-pic *m inv* **4.** [delivery] livraison *f* / [from plane] parachutage *m*, droppage *m* ▸ **to make a drop** déposer un colis **5.** [sweet] pastille *f*.
■ vt (pt & pp **-ped**, cont **-ping**) **1.** [let fall] laisser tomber ▸ **they dropped soldiers/supplies by parachute** ils ont parachuté des soldats/du ravitaillement ▸ **to drop anchor** NAUT mouiller, jeter l'ancre **2.** [voice, speed, price] baisser **3.** [abandon] abandonner ▸ **I've dropped the idea of going** j'ai renoncé à y aller ▸ **let's drop the subject** ne parlons plus de cela, parlons d'autre chose / [player] exclure **4.** [let out of car] déposer ▸ **could you drop me at the corner please?** pouvez-vous me déposer au coin s'il vous plaît? **5.** [utter] **: to drop a hint that** laisser entendre que ▸ **she let (it) drop that she had been there** [accidentally] elle a laissé échapper qu'elle y était allée / [deliberately] elle a fait comprendre qu'elle y était allée **6.** TENNIS [game, set] perdre **7.** [send] **: to drop sb a note** *OR* **line** écrire un petit mot à qqn ▸ **I'll drop it in the post** *OR* **mail** je la mettrai à la poste.

■ vi (pt & pp -ped, cont -ping) **1.** [fall] tomber ▸ **she dropped to her knees** elle est tombée à genoux ▸ **I'm ready to drop** [from fatigue] je tombe de fatigue, je ne tiens plus sur mes jambes / [from sleepiness] je tombe de sommeil ▸ **she dropped dead** elle est tombée raide morte ▸ **the road drops into the valley** la route plonge vers la vallée **2.** [temperature, demand] baisser / [voice, wind] tomber **3.** [end] cesser ▸ **there the matter dropped** l'affaire en est restée là.

◆ ***drops*** **npl** MED gouttes *fpl.*

◆ ***drop by*** vi *inf* passer.

◆ ***drop in*** vi *inf* **: to drop in (on sb)** passer (chez qqn).

◆ ***drop off*** ■ vt sep déposer.

■ vi **1.** [fall asleep] s'endormir **2.** [interest, sales] baisser.

◆ ***drop out*** vi **: she dropped out of the race** elle s'est retirée de la course ▸ **he dropped out of school** il a abandonné ses études ▸ **to drop out of society** vivre en marge de la société.

drop-dead adv *inf* vachement ▸ **he's drop-dead gorgeous** il est craquant.

drop-down adj COMPUT [menu] déroulant(e).

drop goal n drop-goal *m*, drop *m*.

drop-in centre n *UK centre d'assistance sociale permanente.*

drop kick n coup *m* de pied tombé.

droplet ['drɒplɪt] n gouttelette *f.*

drop-off n **1.** [decrease] baisse *f*, diminution *f* ▸ **a drop-off in sales** une baisse des ventes **2.** *US* [descent] à-pic *m inv* ▸ **there's a sharp drop-off in the road** la rue descend en pente très raide.

dropout ['drɒpaʊt] n [from society] marginal *m*, -e *f* / [from college] étudiant *m*, -e *f* qui abandonne ses études.

dropper ['drɒpəʳ] n compte-gouttes *m inv.*

droppings ['drɒpɪŋz] npl [of bird] fiente *f* / [of animal] crottes *fpl.*

drop shot n amorti *m*.

dross [drɒs] n *(U) UK* déchets *mpl* / *fig* rebut *m*.

drought [draʊt] n sécheresse *f.*

drove [drəʊv] ■ pt ➤ ***drive***.

■ n [of animals] troupeau *m* en marche / [of people] foule *f.*

drown [draʊn] ■ vt **1.** [in water] noyer **2.** [sound] **: to drown (out)** couvrir.

■ vi se noyer.

drowsily ['draʊzɪlɪ] adv d'un air somnolent.

drowsiness ['draʊzɪnɪs] n *(U)* somnolence *f* ▸ **'may cause drowsiness'** [medication] 'peut provoquer des somnolences'.

drowsy ['draʊzɪ] (comp -ier, superl -iest) adj assoupi(e), somnolent(e).

drudge [drʌdʒ] n homme *m* de peine, femme *f* de peine.

drudgery ['drʌdʒərɪ] n *(U)* corvée *f.*

drug [drʌg] ■ n **1.** [medicine] médicament *m* ▸ **to be on drugs** prendre des médicaments **2.** [narcotic] drogue *f* ▸ **to be on drugs** se droguer ▸ **drug user** drogué *m*, -e *f.*

■ vt (pt & pp -ged, cont -ging) droguer.

drug abuse n usage *m* de stupéfiants.

drug addict n drogué *m*, -e *f*, toxicomane *mf.*

drug addiction n toxicomanie *f.*

druggist ['drʌgɪst] n *US* pharmacien *m*, -enne *f.*

drug peddler, drug pedlar n = ***drug peddler***.

drug pusher n revendeur *m*, -euse *f* de drogue.

drugstore ['drʌgstɔːʳ] n *US* drugstore *m*.

drug test n [of athlete, horse] contrôle *m* antidopage.

druid ['dru:ɪd] n druide *m*.

drum [drʌm] ■ n **1.** MUS tambour *m* **2.** [container] bidon *m*.

■ vt & vi (pt & pp -med, cont -ming) tambouriner.

◆ ***drums*** npl batterie *f.*

◆ ***drum into*** vt sep **: to drum sthg into sb** enfoncer qqch dans la tête de qqn.

◆ ***drum up*** vt sep [support, business] rechercher, solliciter.

drumbeat ['drʌmbi:t] n roulement *m* de tambour.

drum brake n frein *m* à tambour.

drum kit n batterie *f.*

drummer ['drʌməʳ] n [gen] (joueur *m*, -euse *f* de) tambour *m* / [in pop group] batteur *m*, -euse *f.*

drumming ['drʌmɪŋ] n [of rain, fingers] tambourinage *m*.

drum roll n roulement *m* de tambour.

drumstick ['drʌmstɪk] n **1.** [for drum] baguette *f* de tambour **2.** [of chicken] pilon *m*.

drunk [drʌŋk] ■ pp ➤ ***drink***.

■ adj **1.** [on alcohol] ivre, soûl(e) ▸ **to get drunk** se soûler, s'enivrer ▸ **drunk and disorderly** en état d'ivresse sur la voie publique **2.** *fig* [excited, carried away] **: to be drunk with** *OR* **on** être enivré(e) *OR* grisé(e) par.

■ n soûlard *m*, -e *f.*

drunkard ['drʌŋkəd] n alcoolique *mf.*

drunk driving *US* = ***drink-driving***.

drunken ['drʌŋkn] adj [person] ivre / [quarrel] d'ivrognes.

drunken driving *US* = ***drink-driving***.

drunkenly ['drʌŋkənlɪ] adv [speak, sing, shout] comme un ivrogne.

drunkenness ['drʌŋkənɪs] n ivresse *f.*

dry [draɪ] ■ adj (comp -ier, superl -iest) **1.** [gen] sec (sèche) / [day] sans pluie **2.** [river, earth] asséché(e) **3.** [wry] pince-sans-rire *(inv)* **4.** [dull] aride.

■ vt (pt & pp **dried**) [gen] sécher / [with cloth] essuyer.

■ vi (pt & pp **dried**) sécher.

◆ ***dry out*** vt sep & vi sécher.

◆ ***dry up*** ■ vt sep [dishes] essuyer.

■ vi **1.** [river, lake] s'assécher **2.** [supply] se tarir **3.** [actor, speaker] avoir un trou, sécher **4.** *UK* [dry dishes] essuyer.

dry battery n batterie *f* sèche.

dry-clean vt nettoyer à sec.

dry cleaner n **: dry cleaner's** pressing *m*.

dry-cleaning n nettoyage *m* à sec.

dry dock n cale *f* sèche.

dryer ['draɪəʳ] n [for clothes] séchoir *m*.

dry ginger n *boisson gazeuse au gingembre.*

dry goods **npl** *US* [clothes] mercerie *f* / [food] aliments *mpl* secs.

dry ice **n** neige *f* carbonique.

dry land **n** terre *f* ferme.

dryly ['draılı] **adv** [wryly] sèchement.

dryness ['draınıs] **n** *(U)* **1.** [of ground] sécheresse *f* / [of humour] causticité *f* **2.** [dullness] aridité *f*.

dry-roasted **adj** [peanuts] grillé(e) à sec.

dry rot **n** pourriture *f* sèche.

dry run **n** répétition *f*.

dry ski slope **n** *esp UK* piste *f* de ski artificielle.

dry-stone wall **n** mur *m* de pierres sèches.

drysuit ['draısu:t] **n** combinaison de plongée (étanche) *f*.

DSc (abbr of ***Doctor of Science***) **n** *UK docteur en sciences.*

DSS (abbr of ***Department of Social Security***) **n** *ministère britannique de la sécurité sociale.*

DST (abbr of ***daylight saving time***) *heure d'été aux États-Unis.*

DT abbr of ***data transmission***.

DTI (abbr of ***Department of Trade and Industry***) **n** *ministère britannique du commerce et de l'industrie.*

DTP (abbr of ***desktop publishing***) **n** PAO *f*.

DT's [,di:'ti:z] (abbr of ***delirium tremens***) **npl** *inf* **: to have the DT's** avoir une crise de délirium tremens.

dual ['dju:əl] **adj** double.

dual-branded **adj** sous marque double.

dual carriageway **n** *UK* route *f* à quatre voies.

dual control **n** double commande *f*.

dual-currency **adj** [system] bi-monétaire.

dual economy **n** économie *f* duale.

dual nationality **n** double nationalité *f*.

dual-purpose **adj** à double emploi.

Dubai [,du:'baı] **n** Dubayy.

dubbed [dʌbd] **adj 1.** CIN doublé(e) **2.** [nicknamed] surnommé(e).

dubious ['dju:bjəs] **adj 1.** [suspect] douteux(euse) **2.** [uncertain] hésitant(e), incertain(e) ▸ **to be dubious about doing sthg** hésiter à faire qqch.

dubiously ['dju:bjəslı] **adv 1.** [doubtfully] d'un air de doute **2.** [in suspect manner] d'une manière douteuse.

Dublin ['dʌblın] **n** Dublin.

Dubliner ['dʌblınər] **n** Dublinois *m*, -e *f*.

duchess ['dʌtʃıs] **n** duchesse *f*.

duchy ['dʌtʃı] (pl -ies) **n** duché *m*.

duck [dʌk] ■ **n** canard *m* ▸ **she took to it like a duck to water** elle était comme un poisson dans l'eau.
■ **vt 1.** [head] baisser **2.** [responsibility] esquiver, se dérober à **3.** [submerge] **: to duck sb** mettre la tête de qqn sous l'eau.
■ **vi 1.** [lower head] se baisser **2.** [dive] **: he ducked behind the wall** il se cacha derrière le mur.
◆ ***duck out*** **vi : to duck out (of sthg)** se soustraire (à qqch).

duckling ['dʌklıŋ] **n** caneton *m*.

duct [dʌkt] **n 1.** [pipe] canalisation *f* **2.** ANAT canal *m*.

dud [dʌd] ■ **adj** [bomb] non éclaté(e) / [cheque] sans provision, en bois.
■ **n** obus *m* non éclaté.

dude [dju:d] **n** *US inf* [man] gars *m*, type *m*.

dude ranch **n** *aux États-Unis, ranch qui propose des activités touristiques.*

due [dju:] ■ **adj 1.** [expected] **: to be due to do sthg** devoir faire qqch ▸ **the book is due out in May** le livre doit sortir en mai ▸ **she's due back shortly** elle devrait rentrer sous peu ▸ **when is the train due?** à quelle heure le train doit-il arriver? ▸ **her baby is** OR **she's due any day now** elle doit accoucher d'un jour à l'autre
2. [appropriate] dû (due), qui convient ▸ **to give sthg due consideration** accorder mûre réflexion à qqch ▸ **to fail to exercise due care and attention** ne pas prêter l'attention nécessaire ▸ **in due course** [at the appropriate time] en temps voulu / [eventually] à la longue ▸ **with (all) due respect...** avec tout le respect que je vous dois..., sauf votre respect...
3. [owed, owing] dû (due) ▸ **when's the next instalment due?** quand le prochain versement doit-il être fait? ▸ **repayment due on December 1st** remboursement à effectuer le 1er décembre ▸ **she's due a pay rise** elle devrait recevoir une augmentation ▸ **to be due an apology** avoir droit à des excuses ▸ **to be due a bit of luck/some good weather** mériter un peu de chance/du beau temps ▸ **(to give) credit where credit's due** pour dire ce qui est, pour être juste.
■ **adv : due west** droit vers l'ouest.
■ **n** dû *m* ▸ **to give him his due** il faut lui rendre cette justice.
◆ ***dues*** **npl** cotisation *f*.
◆ ***due to*** **prep** [owing to] dû à / [because of] provoqué par, à cause de ▸ **due to bad weather they arrived late** ils sont arrivés en retard à cause du mauvais temps ▸ **it's all due to you** c'est grâce à toi.

due date **n** jour *m* de l'échéance.

duel ['dju:əl] ■ **n** duel *m*.
■ **vi** (*UK* **-led**, cont **-ling**, *US* **-ed**, cont **-ing**) se battre en duel.

duet [dju:'et] **n** duo *m*.

duff [dʌf] **adj** *UK inf* [useless] nul (nulle).
◆ ***duff up*** **vt sep** *UK inf* tabasser.

duffel bag ['dʌfl-] **n** sac *m* marin.

duffel coat ['dʌfl-] **n** duffel-coat *m*.

duffle bag ['dʌfl-] = ***duffel bag***.

duffle coat ['dʌfl-] = ***duffel coat***.

dug [dʌg] **pt & pp** ➤ ***dig***.

dugout ['dʌgaʊt] **n 1.** [canoe] pirogue *f* **2.** SPORT abri *m* de touche.

duke [dju:k] **n** duc *m*.

Duke of Edinburgh's Award Scheme **n** *bourse du duc d'Édimbourg.*

dull [dʌl] ■ adj **1.** [boring - book, conversation] ennuyeux(euse) / [- person] terne **2.** [colour, light] terne **3.** [weather] maussade **4.** [sound, ache] sourd(e).
■ vt **1.** [pain] atténuer / [senses] émousser **2.** [make less bright] ternir.

dullness ['dʌlnɪs] n **1.** [slow-wittedness] lenteur *f* OR lourdeur *f* d'esprit **2.** [tedium - of book, speech] caractère *m* ennuyeux **3.** [dimness - of light] faiblesse *f* / [- of weather] caractère *m* maussade **4.** [of sound, pain] caractère *m* sourd / [of blade] manque *m* de tranchant **5.** [listlessness] apathie *f*.

dully ['dʌlɪ] adv **1.** [listlessly] d'un air déprimé **2.** [tediously] de manière ennuyeuse **3.** [dimly] faiblement **4.** [not sharply] sourdement.

duly ['dju:lɪ] adv **1.** [properly] dûment **2.** [as expected] comme prévu.

dumb [dʌm] adj **1.** [unable to speak] muet(ette) **2.** *inf* [stupid] idiot(e).

dumbbell ['dʌmbel] n [weight] haltère *m*.

dumbfound [dʌm'faʊnd] vt abasourdir, interloquer.

dumbfounded [dʌm'faʊndɪd] adj [person] abasourdi(e), interloqué(e) / [silence] stupéfait(e) ▸ **to be dumbfounded at** OR **by sthg** être abasourdi OR interloqué par qqch.

dumbing down ['dʌmɪŋ-] n nivellement *m* par le bas.

dumbstruck ['dʌmstrʌk] adj muet(ette) de stupeur.

dumbwaiter [ˌdʌm'weɪtəʳ] n [lift] monte-plats *m inv*.

dumdum (bullet) ['dʌmdʌm-] n dum-dum *f*.

dummy ['dʌmɪ] ■ adj faux (fausse).
■ n (pl -ies) **1.** [of tailor] mannequin *m* **2.** [mock-up] maquette *f* **3.** *UK* [for baby] sucette *f*, tétine *f* **4.** SPORT feinte *f*.
■ vt & vi SPORT feinter.

dummy run n essai *m*.

dump [dʌmp] ■ n **1.** [for rubbish] décharge *f* **2.** MIL dépôt *m* **3.** *inf* [ugly place] taudis *m*.
■ vt **1.** [put down] déposer **2.** [dispose of] jeter **3.** COMPUT vider **4.** *inf* [boyfriend, girlfriend] laisser tomber, plaquer.
■ vi *inf* ▸ **to dump on sb** mettre qn dans la merde *vulg*.
◆ ***dumps*** npl : **to be (down) in the dumps** avoir le cafard.

dumper (truck) *UK* ['dʌmpəʳ-], ***dump truck*** *US* n tombereau *m*, dumper *m*.

dumping ['dʌmpɪŋ] n décharge *f* ▸ **'no dumping'** 'décharge interdite'.

dumping ground n décharge *f*.

dumpling ['dʌmplɪŋ] n boulette *f* de pâte.

dump truck *US* = ***dumper (truck)***.

dumpy ['dʌmpɪ] (comp -ier, superl -iest) adj *inf* boulot(otte).

dunce [dʌns] n cancre *m*.

dune [dju:n] n dune *f*.

dung [dʌŋ] n fumier *m*.

dungarees [ˌdʌŋgə'ri:z] npl **1.** *UK* [for work] bleu *m* de travail / [fashion garment] salopette *f* **2.** *US* [heavy jeans] jean *m* épais.

dungeon ['dʌndʒən] n cachot *m*.

dunk [dʌŋk] vt *inf* tremper.

Dunkirk [dʌn'kɜ:k] n Dunkerque.

dunno [də'nəʊ] *inf* = ***I don't know***.

duo ['dju:əʊ] n duo *m*.

duodenal ulcer [ˌdju:əʊ'di:nl-] n ulcère *m* duodénal.

dupe [dju:p] ■ n dupe *f*.
■ vt [trick] duper ▸ **to dupe sb into doing sthg** amener qqn à faire qqch en le dupant.

duplex ['dju:pleks] n *US* **1.** [apartment] duplex *m* **2.** [house] maison *f* jumelée.

duplicate ■ adj ['dju:plɪkət] [key, document] en double.
■ n ['dju:plɪkət] double *m* ▸ **in duplicate** en double.
■ vt ['dju:plɪkeɪt] **1.** [copy - gen] faire un double de / [- on photocopier] photocopier **2.** [repeat] : **to duplicate work** faire double emploi.

duplication [ˌdju:plɪ'keɪʃn] *(U)* n **1.** [copying] copie *f* **2.** [repetition] répétition *f*.

duplicity [dju:'plɪsətɪ] n duplicité *f*.

Dur (abbr of ***Durham***) comté anglais.

durability [ˌdjʊərə'bɪlətɪ] n [of product] solidité *f*.

durable ['djʊərəbl] adj solide, résistant(e).

durable goods n biens *mpl* (de consommation) durables.

durables ['djʊərəblz] npl biens *mpl* (de consommation) durables.

duration [djʊ'reɪʃn] n durée *f* ▸ **for the duration of** jusqu'à la fin de.

duress [djʊ'res] n : **under duress** sous la contrainte.

Durex® ['djʊəreks] n préservatif *m*.

during ['djʊərɪŋ] prep pendant, au cours de.

dusk [dʌsk] n crépuscule *m*.

dusky ['dʌskɪ] (comp -ier, superl -iest) adj *liter* mordoré(e).

dust [dʌst] ■ n *(U)* poussière *f* ▸ **to gather dust** [get dusty] se couvrir de poussière / *fig* tomber dans l'oubli.
■ vt **1.** [clean] épousseter **2.** [cover with powder] : **to dust sthg (with)** saupoudrer qqch (de).
■ vi faire la poussière.
◆ ***dust off*** vt sep épousseter / *fig* dépoussiérer.

dustbin ['dʌstbɪn] n *UK* poubelle *f*.

dustbin man *UK* = ***dustman***.

dustbowl ['dʌstbəʊl] n désert *m* de poussière.

dustcart ['dʌstkɑ:t] n *UK* camion *m* des boueux.

dust cover n [on book] jaquette *f*.

duster ['dʌstəʳ] n **1.** [cloth] chiffon *m* (à poussière) **2.** *US* [overall] blouse *f*, tablier *m*.

dustiness ['dʌstɪnɪs] n état *m* poussiéreux.

dusting ['dʌstɪŋ] n **1.** [of room, furniture] époussetage *m*, dépoussiérage *m* ▸ **to do the dusting** épousseter, enlever OR faire la poussière **2.** [with sugar, insecticide] saupoudrage *m*.

dust jacket n [on book] jaquette *f*.

dustman ['dʌstmən] (pl -men [-mən]) n *UK* éboueur *m*, -se *f*.

dustpan ['dʌstpæn] **n** pelle *f* à poussière.

dustproof ['dʌstpru:f] **adj** imperméable ***OR*** étanche à la poussière.

dustsheet ['dʌstʃi:t] **n** *UK* housse *f* de protection.

dust storm **n** tempête *f* de poussière.

dust-up **n** *inf* accrochage *m*, prise *f* de bec.

dusty ['dʌstɪ] (comp **-ier**, superl **-iest**) **adj** poussiéreux(euse).

Dutch [dʌtʃ] ■ **adj** néerlandais(e), hollandais(e).
■ **n** [language] néerlandais *m*, hollandais *m*.
■ **npl : the Dutch** les Néerlandais, les Hollandais.
■ **adv : to go Dutch** partager les frais.

Dutch auction **n** *UK* enchères *fpl* au rabais.

Dutch barn **n** *UK* hangar *m* à récoltes.

Dutch cap **n** *UK* diaphragme *m*.

Dutch courage **n : he had a drink to give himself some Dutch courage** il but un verre pour se donner du courage.

Dutch elm disease **n** maladie *f* des ormes.

Dutchman ['dʌtʃmən] (pl **-men** [-mən]) **n** Néerlandais *m*, Hollandais *m*.

Dutchwoman ['dʌtʃ,wʊmən] (pl **-women** [-,wɪmɪn]) **n** Néerlandaise *f*, Hollandaise *f*.

dutiable ['dju:tjəbl] **adj** [goods] taxable.

dutiful ['dju:tɪfʊl] **adj** obéissant(e).

dutifully ['dju:tɪflɪ] **adv** consciencieusement.

duty ['dju:tɪ] (pl **-ies**) **n 1.** *(U)* [responsibility] devoir *m* ▸ **to do one's duty** faire son devoir ▸ **to fail in one's duty** manquer à son devoir **2.** [work] **: to be on/off duty** être/ne pas être de service **3.** [tax] droit *m*.
◆ ***duties*** **npl** fonctions *fpl* ▸ **in the course of one's duties** dans l'exercice de ses fonctions.

duty bound **adj : to be duty bound (to do sthg)** être tenu(e) (de faire qqch).

duty-free **adj** hors taxe.

duty-free shop **n** boutique *f* hors taxe.

duty officer **n** préposé *m*, -e *f* de service.

duvet ['du:veɪ] **n** *UK* couette *f*.

duvet cover **n** *UK* housse *f* de couette.

DVD (abbr of ***Digital Video*** ***OR*** ***Versatile Disc***) **n** DVD *m*.

DVD player **n** lecteur *m* de DVD.

DVD-ROM (abbr of ***Digital Video*** ***OR*** ***Versatile Disc read only memory***) **n** DVD-ROM *m*.

DVLC (abbr of ***Driver and Vehicle Licensing Centre***) **n** *service des immatriculations et des permis de conduire en Grande-Bretagne*.

DVM (abbr of ***Doctor of Veterinary Medicine***) **n** *UK docteur vétérinaire*.

dwarf [dwɔ:f] ■ **adj** [plant, animal] nain(e).
■ **n** (pl **-s** ***OR*** **dwarves** [dwɔ:vz]) nain *m*, -e *f*.
■ **vt** [tower over] écraser.

dweeb [dwi:b] **n** *US inf* crétin *m*, -e *f*.

dwell [dwel] (pt & pp **dwelt** ***OR*** **-ed**) **vi** *liter* habiter.
◆ ***dwell on*** **vt insep** s'étendre sur.

-dweller ['dweləʳ] **suffix : city-dweller** habitant *m*, -e *f* de la ville.

dwelling ['dwelɪŋ] **n** *liter* habitation *f*.

dwelt [dwelt] **pt & pp** ➤ ***dwell***.

dwindle ['dwɪndl] **vi** diminuer.

dwindling ['dwɪndlɪŋ] **adj** en diminution.

dye [daɪ] ■ **n** teinture *f*.
■ **vt** teindre.

dyed [daɪd] **adj** teint(e).

dyed-in-the-wool [daɪd-] **adj** bon teint *(inv)*.

dying ['daɪɪŋ] ■ **cont** ➤ ***die***.
■ **adj** [person] mourant(e), moribond(e) / [plant, language, industry] moribond.
■ **npl : the dying** les mourants *mpl*.

dyke [daɪk] = ***dike***.

dynamic [daɪ'næmɪk] **adj** dynamique.
◆ ***dynamics*** **npl** dynamique *f*.

dynamism ['daɪnəmɪzm] **n** dynamisme *m*.

dynamite ['daɪnəmaɪt] ■ **n** *(U) lit & fig* dynamite *f*.
■ **vt** dynamiter, faire sauter.

dynamo ['daɪnəməʊ] (pl **-s**) **n** dynamo *f*.

dynasty [*UK* 'dɪnəstɪ, *US* 'daɪnəstɪ] (pl **-ies**) **n** dynastie *f*.

dysentery ['dɪsntrɪ] **n** dysenterie *f*.

dysfunction [dɪs'fʌŋkʃn] **n** MED dysfonction *f*, dysfonctionnement *m*.

dysfunctional [dɪs'fʌŋkʃənəl] **adj** dysfonctionnel(elle) ▸ **dysfunctional family** famille *f* disfonctionnelle.

dyslexia [dɪs'leksɪə] **n** dyslexie *f*.

dyslexic [dɪs'leksɪk] **adj** dyslexique.

dyspepsia [dɪs'pepsɪə] **n** dyspepsie *f*.

dystrophy ['dɪstrəfɪ] **n** ➤ ***muscular dystrophy***.

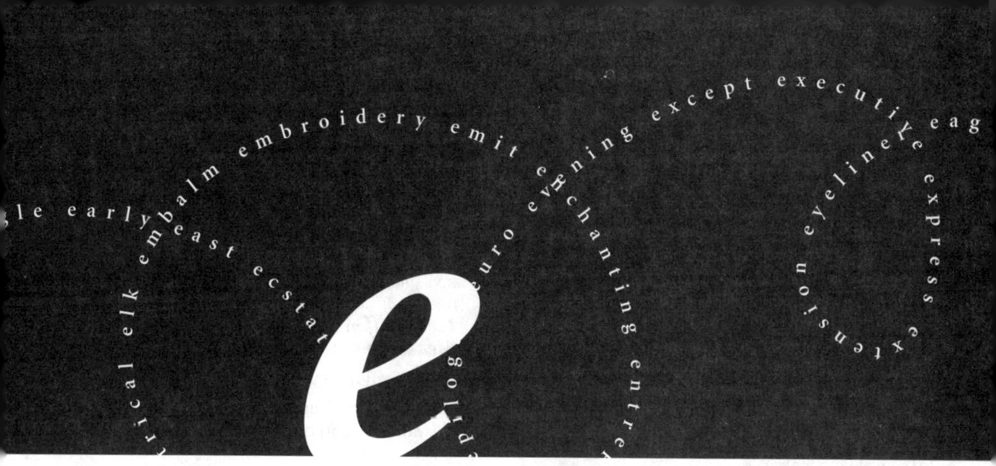

e [iː] (pl e's OR es), ***E*** (pl E's OR Es) n [letter] e *m inv*, E *m inv*.
◆ ***E*** n **1.** MUS mi *m* **2.** (abbr of ***east***) E.

ea. (abbr of ***each***) **: £3.00 ea.** 3 livres pièce.

e-account n compte *m* bancaire électronique.

each [iːtʃ] ■ adj chaque.
■ pron chacun(e) ▸ **the books cost £10.99 each** les livres coûtent 10,99 livres (la) pièce ▸ **each other** l'un l'autre (l'une l'autre), les uns les autres (les unes les autres) ▸ **they love each other** ils s'aiment ▸ **we've known each other for years** nous nous connaissons depuis des années.

eager ['iːgəʳ] adj passionné(e), avide ▸ **to be eager for** être avide de ▸ **to be eager to do sthg** être impatient de faire qqch.

eager beaver n *inf* travailleur *m* acharné, travailleuse *f* acharnée, mordu *m*, -e *f* du travail.

eagerly ['iːgəlɪ] adv [talk, plan] avec passion, avidement / [wait] avec impatience.

eagerness ['iːgənɪs] n [to know, see, find out] impatience *f* / [to help] empressement *m* / [in eyes, voice] excitation *f*, enthousiasme *m* ▸ **his eagerness to please** sa volonté de plaire.

eagle ['iːgl] n [bird] aigle *m*.

eagle-eyed [-aɪd] adj qui a des yeux d'aigle.

eaglet ['iːglɪt] n aiglon *m*, -onne *f*.

E and OE (abbr of ***errors and omissions excepted***) s. e & o.

ear [ɪəʳ] n **1.** [gen] oreille *f* ▸ **by ear** MUS à l'oreille ▸ **to have an ear for** [music, languages] avoir (de) l'oreille pour ▸ **to go in one ear and out the other** *inf* entrer par une oreille et ressortir par l'autre ▸ **to have OR keep one's ear to the ground** *inf* être aux écoutes ▸ **to play it by ear** *fig* improviser, voir sur le moment **2.** [of corn] épi *m*.

earache ['ɪəreɪk] n **: to have earache, to have an earache** *US* avoir mal à l'oreille.

earbuds npl oreillettes *fpl*.

eardrum ['ɪədrʌm] n tympan *m*.

-eared [ɪəd] suffix **: long/short-eared** à oreilles longues/courtes ▸ **pointy-eared** *inf* aux oreilles en pointe.

earful ['ɪəfʊl] n **: to get an earful of water** prendre de l'eau plein l'oreille
▸▸ **to give sb an earful** *inf* [tell off] passer un savon à qqn ▸ **to give sb an earful about sthg** *US* [say a lot to] raconter qqch à qqn en long, en large et en travers.

earl [ɜːl] n comte *m*.

earlier ['ɜːlɪəʳ] ■ adj [previous] précédent(e) / [more early] plus tôt.
■ adv plus tôt ▸ **as I mentioned earlier** comme je l'ai signalé tout à l'heure ▸ **earlier on** plus tôt.

earliest ['ɜːlɪəst] ■ adj [first] premier(ère) / [most early] le plus tôt.
■ n **: at the earliest** au plus tôt.

earlobe ['ɪələʊb] n lobe *m* de l'oreille.

early ['ɜːlɪ] ■ adj (comp -ier, superl -iest) **1.** [before expected time] en avance ▸ **to be early** [person, train, flight, winter] être en avance ▸ **you're too early** vous arrivez trop tôt, vous êtes en avance ▸ **let's have an early lunch** déjeunons de bonne heure
2. [in day] de bonne heure ▸ **the early train** le premier train ▸ **to make an early start** partir de bonne heure ▸ **I need an early night** je dois me coucher de bonne heure
3. [at beginning] **: in the early sixties** au début des années soixante ▸ **the early chapters** les premiers chapitres ▸ **he's in his early twenties** il a une vingtaine d'années.
■ adv **1.** [before expected time] en avance ▸ **I was ten minutes early** j'étais en avance de dix minutes
2. [in day] tôt, de bonne heure ▸ **as early as** dès ▸ **early on** tôt ▸ **early in the evening/in the afternoon** tôt le soir/(dans) l'après-midi
3. [at beginning] **: early in her life** dans sa jeunesse ▸ **early in the year/winter** au début de l'année/de l'hiver.

early bird n **: to be an early bird** *inf* être matinal
▸▸ **it's the early bird that catches the worm** *prov* [it's good to get up early] le monde appartient à ceux qui se lèvent tôt *prov* / [it's good to arrive early] les premiers arrivés sont les mieux servis.

early closing n *UK* COMM *jour où l'on ferme tôt.*

early retirement n retraite *f* anticipée.

early warning system n système *m* de première alerte.

earmark ['ɪəmɑːk] **vt : to be earmarked for** être réservé(e) à.

earmuffs ['ɪəmʌfs] **npl** cache-oreilles *m inv*.

earn [ɜːn] **vt 1.** [as salary] gagner **2.** COMM rapporter **3.** *fig* [respect, praise] gagner, mériter.

earned income [ɜːnd-] **n** revenus *mpl* salariaux.

earner ['ɜːnəʳ] **n 1.** [person] salarié *m*, -e *f* **2.** *UK inf* [deal] **: a nice little earner** une affaire juteuse.

earnest ['ɜːnɪst] **adj** sérieux(euse).
◆ ***in earnest*** ■ **adj** sérieux(euse).
■ **adv** pour de bon, sérieusement.

earnestly ['ɜːnɪstlɪ] **adv** sérieusement.

earnestness ['ɜːnɪstnɪs] **n** sérieux *m*, gravité *f*.

earnings ['ɜːnɪŋz] **npl** [of person] salaire *m*, gains *mpl* / [of company] bénéfices *mpl*.

earnings-related **adj** [pension, payment] proportionnel(elle) au salaire.

ear, nose and throat specialist **n** oto-rhino-laryngologiste *mf*, oto-rhino *mf*.

earphones ['ɪəfəʊnz] **npl** casque *m*.

earpiece ['ɪəpiːs] **n** [of telephone receiver, personal stereo] écouteur *m*.

earplugs ['ɪəplʌgz] **npl** boules *fpl* Quiès®.

earring ['ɪərɪŋ] **n** boucle *f* d'oreille.

earshot ['ɪəʃɒt] **n : within earshot** à portée de voix ▸ **out of earshot** hors de portée de voix.

ear-splitting **adj** assourdissant(e).

earth [ɜːθ] ■ **n** [gen & ELEC] terre *f* ▸ **how/what/where/why on earth...?** mais comment/que/où/pourquoi donc...? ▸ **there's nothing on earth I'd like better** il n'y a rien au monde dont j'aie plus envie ▸ **to bring sb down to earth (with a bump)** ramener qqn sur terre (brutalement) ▸ **to come back down to earth again** revenir *OR* redescendre sur terre ▸ **to cost the earth** *UK* coûter les yeux de la tête.
■ **vt** *UK* ELEC **: to be earthed** être à la masse.

earthenware ['ɜːθnweəʳ] ■ **adj** en terre cuite.
■ **n** *(U)* poteries *fpl*.

earthling ['ɜːθlɪŋ] **n** terrien *m*, -enne *f*.

earthly ['ɜːθlɪ] **adj** terrestre ▸ **what earthly reason could she have for doing that?** *inf* pourquoi diable a-t-elle fait ça?

earth mother **n 1.** MYTH déesse *f* de la Terre **2.** *inf fig* mère *f* nourricière.

earthquake ['ɜːθkweɪk] **n** tremblement *m* de terre.

earth sciences **npl** sciences *fpl* de la terre.

earth-shaking, ***earth-shattering*** **adj** *UK inf* [news] renversant(e).

earth tremor **n** secousse *f* tellurique.

earthward(s) ['ɜːθwəd(z)] **adv** vers la terre.

earthworks ['ɜːθwɜːks] **npl** ARCHEOL fortifications *fpl* en terre.

earthworm ['ɜːθwɜːm] **n** ver *m* de terre.

earthy ['ɜːθɪ] (comp -ier, superl -iest) **adj 1.** *fig* [humour, person] truculent(e) **2.** [taste, smell] de terre, terreux(euse).

earwax ['ɪəwæks] **n** cérumen *m*.

earwig ['ɪəwɪg] **n** perce-oreille *m*.

ease [iːz] ■ **n** *(U)* **1.** [lack of difficulty] facilité *f* ▸ **to do sthg with ease** faire qqch sans difficulté *OR* facilement **2.** [comfort] **: a life of ease** une vie facile ▸ **at ease** à l'aise ▸ **ill at ease** mal à l'aise.
■ **vt 1.** [pain] calmer / [restrictions] modérer **2.** [move carefully] **: to ease sthg in/out** faire entrer/sortir qqch délicatement.
■ **vi** [problem] s'arranger / [pain] s'atténuer / [rain] diminuer.
◆ ***ease off*** **vi** [pain] s'atténuer / [rain] diminuer.
◆ ***ease up*** **vi 1.** [rain] diminuer **2.** [relax] se détendre.

easel ['iːzl] **n** chevalet *m*.

easily ['iːzɪlɪ] **adv 1.** [without difficulty] facilement **2.** [without doubt] de loin **3.** [in a relaxed manner] tranquillement.

easiness ['iːzɪnɪs] **n** [lack of difficulty] facilité *f*.

east [iːst] ■ **n 1.** [direction] est *m* **2.** [region] **: the east** l'est *m*.
■ **adj** est *(inv)* / [wind] d'est.
■ **adv** à l'est, vers l'est ▸ **east of** à l'est de.
◆ ***East*** **n : the East** [gen & POL] l'Est *m* / [Asia] l'Orient *m*.

eastbound ['iːstbaʊnd] **adj** en direction de l'est.

East End **n : the East End** *les quartiers est de Londres*.

Easter ['iːstəʳ] **n** Pâques *m*.

Easter bunny **n** [gen] lapin *m* de Pâques / [imaginary creature] *personnage imaginaire qui distribue des friandises aux enfants*.

Easter egg **n** œuf *m* de Pâques.

Easter Island **n** l'île *f* de Pâques ▸ **in *OR* on Easter Island** à l'île de Pâques.

easterly ['iːstəlɪ] **adj** à l'est, de l'est / [wind] de l'est ▸ **in an easterly direction** vers l'est.

eastern ['iːstən] **adj** de l'est.
◆ ***Eastern*** **adj** [gen & POL] de l'Est / [from Asia] oriental(e).

Eastern bloc [-blɒk] **n : the Eastern bloc** le bloc de l'Est.

Easterner ['iːstənəʳ] **n** *personne qui vient de l'est* / *US* habitant(e) de la partie Est des Etats-Unis.

Easter Sunday **n** dimanche *m* de Pâques.

East German ■ **adj** d'Allemagne de l'Est.
■ **n** Allemand *m*, -e *f* de l'Est.

East Germany **n : (former) East Germany** (l'ex-) Allemagne *f* de l'Est ▸ **in East Germany** en Allemagne de l'Est.

east-northeast ■ **n** est-nord-est *m*.
■ **adj** [direction] est-nord-est / [wind] d'est-nord-est.
■ **adv** en direction de l'est-nord-est / [blow] d'est-nord-est.

east-southeast ■ **n** est-sud-est *m*.
■ **adj** [direction] est-sud-est / [wind] d'est-sud-est.
■ **adv** en direction de l'est-sud-est / [blow] d'est-sud-est.

eastward ['iːstwəd] ■ **adj** à l'est, vers l'est.
■ **adv** = ***eastwards***.

eastwards ['iːstwədz] **adv** vers l'est.

easy ['iːzɪ] ■ **adj** (comp -ier, superl -iest) **1.** [not difficult comfortable] facile ▸ **it's easy to see why/that...** on voi bien pourquoi/que... ▸ **it's an easy mistake to make** c'es

une erreur qui est facile à faire ▸ **the easy way out** *OR* **option** la solution facile *OR* de facilité ▸ **in easy stages** [travel] par petites étapes / [learn] sans peine ▸ **it's easy money** *inf* c'est de l'argent gagné facilement *OR* sans se fatiguer **2.** [relaxed - manner] naturel(elle) / [- person, atmosphere] décontracté(e) ▸ **I'm easy** *inf* [I don't mind] ça m'est égal ▸ **easy to get on with** facile à vivre.
■ **adv : to go easy on** *inf* y aller doucement avec ▸ **to take it** *OR* **things easy** *inf* ne pas se fatiguer ▸ **easier said than done** plus facile à dire qu'à faire.

easy-care **adj** *UK* [garment] d'entretien facile.

easy chair **n** fauteuil *m*.

easygoing [ˌiːzɪˈɡəʊɪŋ] **adj** [person] facile à vivre / [manner] complaisant(e).

easy listening **n** MUS variété *f*.

easy-peasy **n** *inf hum* fastoche, facile.

eat [iːt] (**pt ate, pp eaten**) **vt & vi** manger.
◆ ***eat away, eat into*** **vt insep 1.** [subj: acid, rust] ronger **2.** [deplete] grignoter.
◆ ***eat out*** **vi** manger au restaurant.
◆ ***eat up*** **vt sep 1.** [food] manger **2.** *fig* [use up] **: to eat up money** revenir très cher ▸ **to eat up time** demander beaucoup de temps.

eatable [ˈiːtəbl] **adj** [palatable] mangeable.

eaten [ˈiːtn] **pp** ➤ ***eat***.

eater [ˈiːtəʳ] **n** mangeur *m*, -euse *f*.

eatery [ˈiːtərɪ] **n** *US inf* restaurant *m*.

eating apple [ˈiːtɪŋ-] **n** pomme *f* à couteau.

eau de Cologne [ˌəʊdəkəˈləʊn] **n** eau *f* de Cologne.

eaves [ˈiːvz] **npl** avant-toit *m*.

eavesdrop [ˈiːvzdrɒp] (**pt & pp -ped, cont -ping**) **vi : to eavesdrop (on sb)** écouter (qqn) de façon indiscrète.

e-banking **n** cyberbanque *f*.

ebb [eb] ■ **n** reflux *m* ▸ **the ebb and flow** *fig* les hauts et les bas ▸ **to be at a low ebb** *fig* aller mal.
■ **vi 1.** [tide, sea] se retirer, refluer **2.** *liter* [strength] **: to ebb (away)** décliner.

ebb tide **n** marée *f* descendante.

Ebola (virus) [ɪˈbəʊlə-] **n** MED (virus *m*) Ebola *m*.

ebony [ˈebənɪ] ■ **adj** [colour] noir(e) d'ébène.
■ **n** ébène *f*.

e-book **n** livre *m* électronique.

e-broker **n** FIN courtier *m*, -ère *f* électronique.

e-broking **n** FIN courtage *m* électronique.

ebullient [ɪˈbʊljənt] **adj** exubérant(e).

e-business **n 1.** [company] cyberentreprise *f* **2.** *(U)* [trade] cybercommerce *m*, commerce *m* électronique.

EC (abbr of ***European Community***) **n** CE *f*.

e-cash **n** argent *m* virtuel *OR* électronique.

ECB (abbr of ***European Central bank***) **n** BCE *f*.

eccentric [ɪkˈsentrɪk] ■ **adj** [odd] excentrique, bizarre.
■ **n** [person] excentrique *mf*.

eccentrically [ɪkˈsentrɪklɪ] **adv 1.** [dress, talk] de manière excentrique **2.** ASTRON, MATHS & TECH excentriquement.

eccentricity [ˌeksenˈtrɪsətɪ] (**pl -ies**) **n** [oddity] excentricité *f*, bizarrerie *f*.

ecclesiastic(al) [ɪˌkliːzɪˈæstɪk(l)] **adj** ecclésiastique.

ECG **n 1.** (abbr of ***electrocardiogram***) ECG *m* **2.** (abbr of ***electrocardiograph***) ECG *m*.

ECGD (abbr of ***Export Credits Guarantee Department***) **n** *organisme britannique d'assurance pour le commerce extérieur,* ≃ COFACE *f*.

ECH *UK* (abbr of ***electric central heating***) *chauffage central électrique*.

echelon [ˈeʃəlɒn] **n** échelon *m*.

echo [ˈekəʊ] ■ **n** (**pl -es**) *lit & fig* écho *m*.
■ **vt** (**pt & pp -ed, cont -ing**) [words] répéter / [opinion] faire écho à.
■ **vi** (**pt & pp -ed, cont -ing**) retentir, résonner.

éclair [eɪˈkleəʳ] **n** éclair *m*.

eclectic [eˈklektɪk] **adj** éclectique.

eclipse [ɪˈklɪps] ■ **n** *lit & fig* éclipse *f*.
■ **vt** *fig* éclipser.

ECM *US* (abbr of ***European Common Market***) **n** *Marché commun européen*.

eco- [ˌiːkəʊ-] **prefix** éco-.

eco-friendly **adj** qui respecte l'environnement.

eco-label **n** écolabel *m*.

E-coli [ˌiːˈkəʊlaɪ] **n** E-coli *m*, bactérie *f* Escherischia coli.

ecological [ˌiːkəˈlɒdʒɪkl] **adj** écologique.

ecologically [ˌiːkəˈlɒdʒɪklɪ] **adv** du point de vue écologique.

ecologist [ɪˈkɒlədʒɪst] **n** écologiste *mf*.

ecology [ɪˈkɒlədʒɪ] **n** écologie *f*.

e-commerce **n** *(U)* commerce *m* électronique, cybercommerce *m*.

economic [ˌiːkəˈnɒmɪk] **adj 1.** ECON économique **2.** [profitable] rentable.

economical [ˌiːkəˈnɒmɪkl] **adj 1.** [cheap] économique **2.** [person] économe.

economically [ˌiːkəˈnɒmɪklɪ] **adv 1.** ECON économiquement **2.** [live] de manière économe / [write] avec sobriété / [use] de manière économe, avec parcimonie.

Economic and Monetary Union **n** Union *f* économique et monétaire.

economic climate **n** climat *m* économique.

economic migrant **n** émigrant *m*, -e *f* de la faim *OR* pour des raisons économiques.

economics [ˌiːkəˈnɒmɪks] ■ **n** *(U)* économie *f* (politique), sciences *fpl* économiques.
■ **npl** [of plan, business] aspect *m* financier.

economist [ɪˈkɒnəmɪst] **n** économiste *mf*.

economize, *UK* ***-ise*** [ɪˈkɒnəmaɪz] **vi** économiser.

economy [ɪˈkɒnəmɪ] (**pl -ies**) **n** économie *f* ▸ **false economy** fausse économie ▸ **economies of scale** économies d'échelle.

economy class **n** classe *f* touriste.

economy-class syndrome n syndrome *m* de la classe économique.

economy drive n campagne *f* de restrictions.

economy-size(d) adj [pack, jar] taille économique *(inv)*.

ecorefill [ˌiːkəʊ'riːfɪl] n écorecharge *f*.

ecosystem ['iːkəʊˌsɪstəm] n écosystème *m*.

ecotax ['iːkəʊtæks] n écotaxe *f*.

ecoterrorist ['iːkəʊˌterərɪst] n écoterroriste *mf*.

ecotourism ['iːkəʊˌtʊərɪzm] n écotourisme *m*, tourisme *m* vert.

eco-warrior n éco-guerrier *m*, -ère *f*.

ECSC (abbr of ***European Coal &Steel Community***) n CECA *f*.

ecstasy ['ekstəsɪ] (pl **-ies**) n **1.** [pleasure] extase *f*, ravissement *m* ▸ **to go into ecstasies about sthg** s'extasier sur qqch **2.** [drug] ecstasy *m ou f*.

ecstatic [ek'stætɪk] adj [person] en extase / [feeling] extatique.

ecstatically [ek'stætɪklɪ] adv [say, shout] d'un air extasié ▸ **to be ecstatically happy** être au comble du bonheur.

ECT (abbr of ***electroconvulsive therapy***) n électrochocs *mpl*.

ectoplasm ['ektəplæzm] n ectoplasme *m*.

ECU, ***Ecu*** ['ekjuː] (abbr of ***European Currency Unit***) n ECU *m*, écu *m*.

Ecuador ['ekwədɔːr] n Équateur *m* ▸ **in Ecuador** en Équateur.

Ecuadoran [ˌekwə'dɔːrən], ***Ecuadorian*** [ˌekwə'dɔːrɪən] ■ adj équatorien(enne).
■ n Équatorien *m*, -enne *f*.

ecumenical [iːkjʊ'menɪkl] adj œcuménique.

eczema ['eksɪmə] n eczéma *m*.

ed. **1.** (abbr of ***edited***) sous la dir. de, coll. **2.** abbr of ***edition*** **3.** abbr of ***editor***.

Edam ['iːdæm] n édam *m*.

eddy ['edɪ] ■ n (pl **-ies**) tourbillon *m*.
■ vi (pt & pp **-ied**) tourbillonner.

Eden ['iːdn] n : **(the Garden of) Eden** le jardin *m* d'Éden, l'Éden *m*.

edge [edʒ] ■ n **1.** [gen] bord *m* / [of coin, book] tranche *f* / [of knife] tranchant *m* ▸ **to be on the edge of** *fig* être à deux doigts de **2.** [advantage] **: to have an edge over** *OR* **the edge on** avoir un léger avantage sur **3.** *fig* [in voice] note *f* tranchante.
■ vi : **to edge forward** avancer tout doucement.
◆ ***on edge*** adj contracté(e), tendu(e).

edged [edʒd] adj : **edged with** bordé(e) de.

edgeways *UK* ['edʒweɪz], ***edgewise*** *US* ['edʒwaɪz] adv latéralement, de côté.

edginess ['edʒɪnɪs] n nervosité *f*.

edging ['edʒɪŋ] n [of cloth] liseré *m* / [of paper] bordure *f*.

edgy ['edʒɪ] (comp **-ier**, superl **-iest**) adj contracté(e), tendu(e).

edible ['edɪbl] adj [safe to eat] comestible.

edict ['iːdɪkt] n décret *m*.

edifice ['edɪfɪs] n édifice *m*.

edify ['edɪfaɪ] (pt & pp **-ied**) vt édifier.

edifying ['edɪfaɪɪŋ] adj édifiant(e).

Edinburgh ['edɪnbrə] n Édimbourg.

Edinburgh Festival n : **the Edinburgh Festival** le Festival d'Édimbourg.

edit ['edɪt] vt **1.** [correct - text] corriger **2.** CIN monter / RADIO & TV réaliser **3.** [magazine] diriger / [newspaper] être le rédacteur en chef de.
◆ ***edit out*** vt sep couper.

editing ['edɪtɪŋ] n [of newspaper, magazine] rédaction *f* / [initial corrections] révision *f*, correction *f* / [in preparation for publication] édition *f*, préparation *f* à la publication / [of film, tape] montage *m* / COMPUT [of file] édition *f*.

edition [ɪ'dɪʃn] n édition *f*.

editor ['edɪtər] n **1.** [of magazine] directeur *m*, -trice *f* / [of newspaper] rédacteur *m*, -trice *f* en chef **2.** [of text] correcteur *m*, -trice *f* **3.** CIN monteur *m*, -euse *f* / RADIO & TV réalisateur *m*, -trice *f*.

editorial [ˌedɪ'tɔːrɪəl] ■ adj [department, staff] de la rédaction / [style, policy] éditorial(e) / [freedom] des rédacteurs.
■ n éditorial *m*.

editor-in-chief n rédacteur *m*, -trice *f* en chef.

EDP (abbr of ***electronic data processing***) n *traitement électronique de données*.

EDT (abbr of ***Eastern Daylight Time***) n *heure d'été de l'Est des États-Unis*.

educate ['edʒʊkeɪt] vt **1.** SCH & UNIV instruire **2.** [inform] informer, éduquer.

educated ['edʒʊkeɪtɪd] adj [person] instruit(e) ▸ **to make an educated guess** faire une supposition bien informée.

education [ˌedʒʊ'keɪʃn] n **1.** [gen] éducation *f* ▸ **the education system** le système éducatif ▸ **standards of education** niveau *m* scolaire ▸ **primary/secondary education** (enseignement *m*) primaire *m*/secondaire *m* ▸ **tertiary education** enseignement *m* supérieur **2.** [teaching] enseignement *m*, instruction *f*.

educational [ˌedʒʊ'keɪʃənl] adj **1.** [establishment, policy] pédagogique **2.** [toy, experience] éducatif(ive).

educationalist [ˌedʒʊ'keɪʃnəlɪst] n pédagogue *mf*.

educationally [ˌedʒʊ'keɪʃnəlɪ] adv d'un point de vue éducatif ▸ **educationally deprived child** *enfant qui n'a pas suivi une scolarité normale*.

educative ['edʒʊkətɪv] adj éducatif(ive).

educator ['edʒʊkeɪtər] n éducateur *m*, -trice *f*.

edutainment [edʒʊ'teɪnmənt] ■ n apprentissage *m* par le jeu, édutainment *m*.
■ adj ludo-éducatif(ive).

Edwardian [ed'wɔːdɪən] adj de l'époque 1900.

EEC (abbr of ***European Economic Community***) n CEE *f*.

e-economy n économie *f* en ligne.

EEG n **1.** (abbr of ***electroencephalogram***) EEG *m* **2.** (abbr of ***electroencephalograph***) EEG *m*.

eek [i:k] excl *inf* hi!

eel [i:l] n anguille *f*.

EENT (abbr of ***eye, ear, nose and throat***) n ophtalmologie *f* et ORL *f*.

eerie ['ɪərɪ] (comp **-ier**, superl **-iest**) **adj** inquiétant(e), sinistre.

eerily ['ɪərəlɪ] **adv** sinistrement, d'une manière sinistre ▸ **it was eerily quiet in the house** un calme inquiétant régnait dans la maison.

eery ['ɪərɪ] (comp **-ier**, superl **-iest**) **adj** inquiétant(e), sinistre.

EET (abbr of ***Eastern European Time***) **n** *heure d'Europe orientale*.

efface [ɪ'feɪs] **vt** effacer.

effect [ɪ'fekt] ■ **n 1.** [gen] effet *m* ▸ **to have an effect on** avoir ***OR*** produire un effet sur ▸ **for effect** pour attirer l'attention, pour se faire remarquer ▸ **to take effect** [law] prendre effet, entrer en vigueur ▸ **to put sthg into effect** [policy, law] mettre qqch en application ▸ **with immediate effect** à compter d'aujourd'hui ▸ **to no *OR* little effect** en vain **2.** [meaning] **: a statement to the effect that...** une déclaration selon laquelle... ▸ **or words to that effect** ou quelque chose de ce genre.
■ **vt** [repairs, change] effectuer / [reconciliation] amener.
◆ ***effects*** **npl : (special) effects** effets *mpl* spéciaux ▸ **personal effects** *fml* effets *mpl* personnels.

effective [ɪ'fektɪv] **adj 1.** [successful] efficace **2.** [actual, real] effectif(ive).

effectively [ɪ'fektɪvlɪ] **adv 1.** [successfully] efficacement **2.** [in fact] effectivement.

effectiveness [ɪ'fektɪvnɪs] **n** efficacité *f*.

effeminate [ɪ'femɪnət] **adj** efféminé(e).

effervesce [ˌefə'ves] **vi** pétiller.

effervescence [ˌefə'vesəns] **n** [of liquid] effervescence *f* / [of wine] pétillement *m* / *fig* [of person] vitalité *f*, pétulance *f* / [of personality] pétulance *f*.

effervescent [ˌefə'vesənt] **adj** [liquid] effervescent(e) / [drink] gazeux(euse).

effete [ɪ'fi:t] **adj** *fml* [person, gesture] veule.

efficacious [efɪ'keɪʃəs] **adj** *fml* efficace.

efficacy ['efɪkəsɪ] **n** efficacité *f*.

efficiency [ɪ'fɪʃənsɪ] **n** [of person, method] efficacité *f* / [of factory, system] rendement *m*.

efficient [ɪ'fɪʃənt] **adj** efficace.

efficiently [ɪ'fɪʃəntlɪ] **adv** efficacement.

effigy ['efɪdʒɪ] (pl **-ies**) **n** effigie *f*.

effing ['efɪŋ] *UK v inf* ■ **adj** de merde.
■ **adv** foutrement.
■ **n : there was a lot of effing and blinding** on a eu droit à un chapelet de jurons.

effluent ['efluənt] **n** effluent *m*.

effort ['efət] n effort *m* ▸ **to be worth the effort** valoir la peine ▸ **with effort** avec peine ▸ **to make the effort to do sthg** s'efforcer de faire qqch ▸ **to make an/no effort to do sthg** faire un effort/ne faire aucun effort pour faire qqch.

effortless ['efətlɪs] **adj** [easy] facile / [natural] aisé(e).

effortlessly ['efətlɪslɪ] **adv** sans effort, facilement.

effrontery [ɪ'frʌntərɪ] **n** effronterie *f*.

effusive [ɪ'fju:sɪv] **adj** [person] démonstratif(ive) / [welcome] plein(e) d'effusions.

effusively [ɪ'fju:sɪvlɪ] **adv** avec effusion.

EFL ['efəl] (abbr of ***English as a foreign language***) **n** *anglais langue étrangère*.

EFT (abbr of ***electronic funds transfer***) **n** COMPUT transfert *m* de fonds électronique.

EFTA ['eftə] (abbr of ***European Free Trade Association***) **n** AELE *f*, AEL-E *f*.

EFTPOS ['eftpɒs] (abbr of ***electronic funds transfer at point of sale***) **n** COMPUT transfert *m* de fonds électronique au point de vente.

EFTS [efts] (abbr of ***electronic funds transfer system***) **n** *système électronique de transferts de fonds*.

e.g. (abbr of ***exempli gratia***) **adv** par exemple.

EGA (abbr of ***enhanced graphics adapter***) **n** adapteur *m* graphique couleur EGA.

egalitarian [ɪˌgælɪ'teərɪən] **adj** égalitaire.

egg [eg] **n** œuf *m*.
◆ ***egg on*** **vt sep** pousser, inciter.

eggcup ['egkʌp] **n** coquetier *m*.

egghead ['eghed] **n** *inf* intello *mf*.

eggplant ['egplɑ:nt] **n** *US* aubergine *f*.

eggshell ['egʃel] **n** coquille *f* d'œuf.

egg timer **n** [with sand] sablier *m* / [mechanical] minuteur *m*.

egg whisk **n** fouet *m*.

egg white **n** blanc *m* d'œuf.

egg yolk **n** jaune *m* d'œuf.

egis **n** *US* = ***aegis***.

ego ['i:gəʊ] (pl **-s**) **n** moi *m*.

egocentric [ˌi:gəʊ'sentrɪk] **adj** égocentrique.

egocentricity [ˌi:gəʊsen'trɪsətɪ], ***egocentrism*** [ˌi:gəʊ'sentrɪzm] **n** égocentrisme *m*.

egoism ['i:gəʊɪzm] **n** égoïsme *m*.

egoist ['i:gəʊɪst] **n** égoïste *mf*.

egoistic [ˌi:gəʊ'ɪstɪk] **adj** égoïste.

egoistically [ˌi:gəʊ'ɪstɪklɪ] **adv** égoïstement.

egotism ['i:gətɪzm] **n** égotisme *m*.

egotist ['i:gətɪst] **n** égotiste *mf*.

egotistic(al) [ˌi:gə'tɪstɪk(l)] **adj** égotiste.

egotistically [ˌi:gə'tɪstɪklɪ] **adv** de manière égotiste.

ego trip **n** *inf* **: she's just on an ego trip** c'est par vanité qu'elle le fait.

Egypt ['i:dʒɪpt] **n** Égypte *f* ▸ **in Egypt** en Égypte.

Egyptian [ɪ'dʒɪpʃn] ■ **adj** égyptien(enne).
■ **n** Égyptien *m*, -enne *f*.

eh [eɪ] **excl** *UK inf* hein?

eiderdown ['aɪdədaʊn] **n** *esp UK* [bed cover] édredon *m*.

eight [eɪt] **num** huit ; see also ***six***.

eighteen [ˌeɪ'tiːn] **num** dix-huit ; see also ***six***.

eighteenth [ˌeɪ'tiːnθ] **num** dix-huitième ; see also ***sixth***.

eighth [eɪtθ] **num** huitième ; see also ***sixth***.

eightieth ['eɪtɪɪθ] **num** quatre-vingtième ; see also ***sixth***.

eighty ['eɪtɪ] (pl **-ies**) **num** quatre-vingts ; see also ***sixty***.

Eire ['eərə] **n** République *f* d'Irlande.

EIS (abbr of ***Educational Institute of Scotland***) **n** *syndicat écossais d'enseignants*.

either ['aɪðəʳ OR 'iːðəʳ] ■ **adj 1.** [one or the other] l'un ou l'autre (l'une ou l'autre) (des deux) ▸ **she couldn't find either jumper** elle ne trouva ni l'un ni l'autre des pulls ▸ **either way** de toute façon **2.** [each] chaque ▸ **on either side** de chaque côté.
■ **pron : either (of them)** l'un ou l'autre *m*, l'une ou l'autre *f* ▸ **I don't like either (of them)** je n'aime aucun des deux, je n'aime ni l'un ni l'autre.
■ **adv** *(in negatives)* non plus ▸ **I don't either** moi non plus.
■ **conj : either... or** soit... soit, ou... ou ▸ **either you stop complaining or I go home!** ou tu arrêtes de te plaindre, ou je rentre chez moi ▸ **I'm not fond of either him or his wife** je ne les aime ni lui ni sa femme.

ejaculate [ɪ'dʒækjʊleɪt] ■ **vt** *fml* [exclaim] s'écrier.
■ **vi** [have orgasm] éjaculer.

ejaculation [ɪˌdʒækjʊ'leɪʃn] **n 1.** [physiological] éjaculation *f* **2.** *fml* [exclamation] exclamation *f*.

eject [ɪ'dʒekt] **vt 1.** [troublemaker] expulser **2.** [cartridge, pilot] éjecter / [lava] projeter.

ejection [ɪ'dʒekʃn] **n 1.** [of troublemaker] expulsion *f* **2.** [of cartridge, pilot] éjection *f* / [of lava] projection *f*.

ejector seat *UK* [ɪ'dʒektəʳ-], ***ejection seat*** *US* [ɪ'dʒekʃn-] **n** siège *m* éjectable.

eke [iːk] ◆ ***eke out*** **vt sep** [make last] faire durer / [scrape] **: to eke out a living** gagner tout just sa vie.

EKG (abbr of ***electrocardiogram***) **n** *US* ECG *m*.

el [el] (abbr of ***elevated railroad***) **n** *US inf* chemin *m* de fer aérien.

elaborate ■ **adj** [ɪ'læbrət] [ceremony, procedure] complexe / [explanation, plan] détaillé(e), minutieux(euse).
■ **vi** [ɪ'læbəreɪt] **: to elaborate (on)** donner des précisions (sur).

elaborately [ɪ'læbərətlɪ] **adv** [planned] minutieusement / [decorated] avec recherche.

elaboration [ɪˌlæbə'reɪʃn] **n** [working out - of scheme, plan] élaboration *f* / [details] exposé *m* minutieux.

élan [eɪ'læn] **n** vigueur *f*, énergie *f*.

elapse [ɪ'læps] **vi** s'écouler.

elastic [ɪ'læstɪk] ■ **adj** *lit* & *fig* élastique.
■ **n** *(U)* élastique *m*.

elasticated *UK* [ɪ'læstɪkeɪtɪd], ***elasticized*** *US* [ɪ'læstɪsaɪzd] **adj** élastique.

elastic band **n** *UK* élastique *m*, caoutchouc *m*.

elasticity [ˌelæ'stɪsətɪ] **n** élasticité *f*.

Elastoplast® [ɪ'læstəplɑːst] **n** *UK* pansement *m* adhésif.

elated [ɪ'leɪtɪd] **adj** transporté(e) (de joie).

elation [ɪ'leɪʃn] **n** exultation *f*, joie *f*.

elbow ['elbəʊ] ■ **n** coude *m*.
■ **vt : to elbow sb aside** écarter qqn du coude.

elbow grease **n** *inf* huile *f* de coude.

elbowroom ['elbəʊrʊm] **n** *inf* **: to have some elbowroom** avoir ses coudées franches.

elder ['eldəʳ] ■ **adj** aîné(e).
■ **n 1.** [older person] aîné *m*, -e *f* **2.** [of tribe, church] ancien *m* **3. : elder (tree)** sureau *m*.

elderberry ['eldəˌberɪ] (pl **-ies**) **n** [fruit] baie *f* de sureau / [tree] sureau *m*.

elderflower ['eldəˌflaʊəʳ] **n** fleur *f* de sureau.

elderly ['eldəlɪ] ■ **adj** âgé(e).
■ **npl : the elderly** les personnes *fpl* âgées.

elder statesman **n** vétéran *m* de la politique.

eldest ['eldɪst] **adj** aîné(e).

Eldorado [ˌeldɒ'rɑːdəʊ] **n** Eldorado *m*.

elect [ɪ'lekt] ■ **adj** élu(e).
■ **vt 1.** [by voting] élire **2.** *fml* [choose] **: to elect to do sthg** choisir de faire qqch.

elected [ɪ'lektɪd] **adj** élu(e).

election [ɪ'lekʃn] **n** élection *f* ▸ **to have OR hold an election** procéder à une élection ▸ **local elections** élections locales.

election campaign **n** campagne *f* électorale.

electioneering [ɪˌlekʃə'nɪərɪŋ] **n** *(U) pej* propagande *f* électorale.

election promise **n** promesse *f* électorale.

elective [ɪ'lektɪv] **n** *US* SCH cours *m* facultatif.

elector [ɪ'lektəʳ] **n** électeur *m*, -trice *f*.

electoral [ɪ'lektərəl] **adj** électoral(e).

electoral college **n** *US* POL collège *m* électoral.

electoral register, ***electoral roll*** **n** *UK* **: the electoral register** la liste électorale.

electorate [ɪ'lektərət] **n : the electorate** l'électorat *m*.

electric [ɪ'lektrɪk] **adj** *lit* & *fig* électrique.
◆ ***electrics*** **npl** *UK inf* [in car, machine] installation *f* électrique.

electrical [ɪ'lektrɪkl] **adj** électrique.

electrical engineer **n** ingénieur *m* électricien.

electrical engineering **n** électrotechnique *f*.

electrically [ɪ'lektrɪklɪ] **adv** [heated] à l'électricité / [charged, powered] électriquement.

electrical shock = ***electric shock***.

electric blanket **n** couverture *f* chauffante.

electric blue ■ n bleu *m* électrique.
■ adj bleu électrique.

electric chair n : **the electric chair** la chaise électrique.

electric cooker n cuisinière *f* électrique.

electric current n courant *m* électrique.

electric eel n anguille *f* électrique.

electric fence n clôture *f* électrique.

electric fire n radiateur *m* électrique.

electric guitar n guitare *f* électrique.

electrician [ˌɪlek'trɪʃn] n électricien *m*, -enne *f*.

electricity [ˌɪlek'trɪsətɪ] n électricité *f*.

electric light n lumière *f* électrique.

electric shock n décharge *f* électrique.

electric shock therapy n *(U)* électrochocs *mpl*.

electric storm n orage *m* magnétique.

electrification [ɪˌlektrɪfɪ'keɪʃn] n électrification *f*.

electrify [ɪ'lektrɪfaɪ] (pt & pp **-ied**) vt **1.** TECH électrifier **2.** *fig* [excite] galvaniser, électriser.

electrifying [ɪ'lektrɪfaɪŋ] adj [exciting] galvanisant(e), électrisant(e).

electro- [ɪ'lektrəʊ] prefix électro-.

electrocardiogram [ɪˌlektrəʊ'kɑːdɪəgræm] n électrocardiogramme *m*.

electrocardiograph [ɪˌlektrəʊ'kɑːdɪəgrɑːf] n électrocardiographe *m*.

electrocute [ɪ'lektrəkjuːt] vt électrocuter.

electrode [ɪ'lektrəʊd] n électrode *f*.

electroencephalogram [ɪˌlektrəʊen'sefələgræm] n électro-encéphalogramme *m*.

electroencephalograph [ɪˌlektrəʊen'sefələgrɑːf] n électro-encéphalographe *m*.

electrolysis [ˌɪlek'trɒləsɪs] n électrolyse *f*.

electrolyte [ɪ'lektrəʊlaɪt] n électrolyte *m*.

electromagnet [ɪˌlektrəʊ'mægnɪt] n électro-aimant *m*.

electromagnetic [ɪˌlektrəʊmæg'netɪk] adj électromagnétique.

electron [ɪ'lektrɒn] n électron *m*.

electronic [ˌɪlek'trɒnɪk] adj électronique.
◆ ***electronics*** ■ n *(U)* [technology, science] électronique *f*.
■ npl [equipment] (équipement *m*) électronique *f*.

electronically [ˌɪlek'trɒnɪklɪ] adv électroniquement / [operated] par voie électronique.

electronic banking n opérations *fpl* bancaires électroniques.

electronic data processing n traitement *m* électronique de données.

electronic funds transfer n COMPUT transfert *m* de fonds électronique.

electronic mail n courrier *m* électronique.

electronic mailbox n boîte *f* aux lettres (électronique).

electronic media n médias *mpl* électroniques.

electronic news gathering n journalisme *m* électronique.

electronic organizer, ***electronic organiser*** *UK* n agenda *m* électronique.

electronic publishing n *(U)* édition *f* électronique.

electronic tag n bracelet *m* électronique.

electronic tagging n *(U)* étiquetage *m* électronique.

electronic trading n transactions *fpl* boursières electroniques.

electron microscope n microscope *m* électronique.

electroplated [ɪ'lektrəʊpleɪtɪd] adj métallisé(e) par galvanoplastie.

elegance ['elɪgəns] n élégance *f*.

elegant ['elɪgənt] adj élégant(e).

elegantly ['elɪgəntlɪ] adv élégamment.

elegiac [elɪ'dʒaɪək] ■ adj élégiaque.
■ n élégie *f*.

elegy ['elɪdʒɪ] (pl **-ies**) n élégie *f*.

element ['elɪmənt] n **1.** [gen] élément *m* ▸ **an element of truth** une part de vérité **2.** [in heater, kettle] résistance *f* ▸▸ **to be in one's element** être dans son élément.
◆ ***elements*** npl **1.** [basics] rudiments *mpl* **2.** [weather] : **the elements** les éléments *mpl*.

elementary [ˌelɪ'mentərɪ] adj élémentaire.

elementary school n *US* école *f* primaire.

elephant ['elɪfənt] (pl **elephant** OR **-s**) n éléphant *m*.

elevate ['elɪveɪt] vt **1.** [give importance to] : **to elevate sb/sthg (to)** élever qqn/qqch (à) **2.** [raise] soulever.

elevated ['elɪveɪtɪd] adj **1.** [important] important(e) **2.** [lofty] élevé(e) **3.** [raised] surélevé(e).

elevation [ˌelɪ'veɪʃn] n **1.** [promotion] élévation *f* **2.** [height] hauteur *f*.

elevator ['elɪveɪtəʳ] n *US* ascenseur *m*.

eleven [ɪ'levn] num onze ; see also ***six***.

elevenses [ɪ'levnzɪz] n *(U)* *UK* ≃ pause-café *f*.

eleventh [ɪ'levnθ] num onzième ; see also ***sixth***.

eleventh hour n *fig* : **the eleventh hour** la onzième heure, la dernière minute.

elf [elf] (pl **elves** [elvz]) n elfe *m*, lutin *m*.

elfin ['elfɪn] adj *fig* [face, features] délicat(e).

elicit [ɪ'lɪsɪt] vt *fml* : **to elicit sthg (from sb)** arracher qqch (à qqn).

elide [ɪ'laɪd] vt élider.

eligibility [ˌelɪdʒə'bɪlətɪ] n **1.** [suitability] admissibilité *f* **2.** *dated* [of bachelor] acceptabilité *f*.

eligible ['elɪdʒəbl] adj **1.** [suitable, qualified] admissible ▸ **to be eligible for sthg** avoir droit à qqch ▸ **to be eligible to do sthg** avoir le droit de faire qqch **2.** *dated* [bachelor] : **to be eligible** être un bon parti.

eliminate [ɪ'lɪmɪneɪt] vt : **to eliminate sb/sthg (from)** éliminer qqn/qqch (de).

elimination [ɪˌlɪmɪ'neɪʃn] n élimination *f*.

elimination competition n *US* = ***knockout competition***.

elision [ɪ'lɪʒn] n élision *f*.

elite [ɪ'li:t] ■ **adj** d'élite.
■ **n** élite *f*.

elitism [ɪ'li:tɪzm] **n** élitisme *m*.

elitist [ɪ'li:tɪst] ■ **adj** élitiste.
■ **n** élitiste *mf*.

elixir [ɪ'lɪksəʳ] **n 1.** [magic drink] élixir *m* **2.** *fig* [magic cure] panacée *f*.

Elizabethan [ɪˌlɪzə'bi:θn] ■ **adj** élisabéthain(e).
■ **n** Élisabéthain *m*, -e *f*.

elk [elk] (pl **elk** *OR* **-s**) **n** élan *m*.

ellipse [ɪ'lɪps] **n** ellipse *f*.

ellipsis [ɪ'lɪpsɪs] (pl **-ses** [-si:z]) **n** GRAM ellipse *f*.

elliptical [ɪ'lɪptɪkl] **adj 1.** [in shape] en ellipse **2.** *fml* [indirect, cryptic] elliptique.

elm [elm] **n : elm (tree)** orme *m*.

elocution [ˌelə'kju:ʃn] **n** élocution *f*, diction *f*.

elongate ['i:lɒŋgeɪt] ■ **vt** allonger / [line] prolonger.
■ **vi** s'allonger, s'étendre.

elongated ['i:lɒŋgeɪtɪd] **adj** allongé(e) / [fingers] long (longue).

elope [ɪ'ləʊp] **vi : to elope (with)** s'enfuir (avec).

elopement [ɪ'ləʊpmənt] **n** fugue *f* (amoureuse).

eloquence ['eləkwəns] **n** éloquence *f*.

eloquent ['eləkwənt] **adj** éloquent(e).

eloquently ['eləkwəntlɪ] **adv** avec éloquence.

El Salvador [ˌel'sælvədɔ:ʳ] **n** Salvador *m* ▸ **in El Salvador** au Salvador.

else [els] **adv : anything else** n'importe quoi d'autre ▸ **anything else?** [in shop] et avec ça?, ce sera tout? ▸ **he doesn't need anything else** il n'a besoin de rien d'autre ▸ **everyone else** tous les autres ▸ **nothing else** rien d'autre ▸ **someone else** quelqu'un d'autre ▸ **something else** quelque chose d'autre ▸ **somewhere else** autre part ▸ **who/what else?** qui/quoi d'autre? ▸ **where else?** (à) quel autre endroit? ▸ **if all else fails** en dernier recours ▸ **it'll teach him a lesson, if nothing else** au moins, ça lui servira de leçon.
◆ ***or else*** **conj 1.** [or if not] sinon, sans quoi **2.** [as threat] ou alors...!, sinon...!

elsewhere [els'weəʳ] **adv** ailleurs, autre part.

ELT (abbr of ***English language teaching***) **n** *enseignement de l'anglais*.

elucidate [ɪ'lu:sɪdeɪt] *fml* ■ **vt** élucider.
■ **vi** expliquer.

elude [ɪ'lu:d] **vt** échapper à.

elusive [ɪ'lu:sɪv] **adj** insaisissable / [success] qui échappe.

elusively [ɪ'lu:sɪvlɪ] **adv** [answer] de manière élusive / [move] de manière insaisissable.

elves [elvz] **npl** ➤ ***elf***.

'em [əm] *inf* **pron abbr of** ***them***.

EMA (abbr of ***European Monetary Agreement***) **n** AME *m (Accord monétaire européen)*.

emaciated [ɪ'meɪʃɪeɪtɪd] **adj** [face] émacié(e) / [person, limb] décharné(e).

e-mail, ***email*** (abbr of ***electronic mail***) **n** [message] (e-)mail *m*, courrier *m* électronique ▸ **to send an e-mail** envoyer un mail / [address] e-mail *m*, adresse *f* électronique, courriel *m* ***Québec***.

e-mail account **n** compte *m* de courrier électronique.

e-mail address **n** adresse *f* électronique.

emanate ['emənеɪt] *fml* ■ **vt** dégager.
■ **vi : to emanate from** émaner de.

emancipate [ɪ'mænsɪpeɪt] **vt : to emancipate sb (from)** affranchir *OR* émanciper qqn (de).

emancipated [ɪ'mænsɪpeɪtɪd] **adj** affranchi(e), émancipé(e).

emancipation [ɪˌmænsɪ'peɪʃn] **n : emancipation (from)** affranchissement *m* (de), émancipation *f* (de).

emasculate [ɪ'mæskjʊleɪt] **vt** *fml* [weaken] émasculer.

emasculation [ɪˌmæskjʊ'leɪʃn] **n** *fml* [weakening] émasculation *f*.

embalm [ɪm'bɑ:m] **vt** embaumer.

embalmer [ɪm'bɑ:məʳ] **n** embaumeur *m*, thanatopracteur *m*.

embankment [ɪm'bæŋkmənt] **n** [of river] berge *f* / [of railway] remblai *m* / [of road] banquette *f*.

embargo [em'bɑ:gəʊ] ■ **n** (pl **-es**) **: embargo (on)** embargo *m* (sur).
■ **vt** (pt & pp **-ed**, cont **-ing**) mettre l'embargo sur.

embark [ɪm'bɑ:k] **vi 1.** [board ship] **: to embark (on)** embarquer (sur) **2.** [start] **: to embark on** *OR* **upon sthg** s'embarquer dans qqch.

embarkation [ˌembɑ:'keɪʃn] **n** embarquement *m*.

embarkation card **n** *UK* carte *f* d'embarquement.

embarrass [ɪm'bærəs] **vt** embarrasser.

embarrassed [ɪm'bærəst] **adj** embarrassé(e).

embarrassing [ɪm'bærəsɪŋ] **adj** embarrassant(e).

embarrassingly [ɪm'bærəsɪŋlɪ] **adv** de manière embarrassante ▸ **it was embarrassingly obvious** c'était évident au point d'en être embarrassant.

embarrassment [ɪm'bærəsmənt] **n** embarras *m* ▸ **to be an embarrassment** [person] causer de l'embarras / [thing] être embarrassant.

embassy ['embəsɪ] (pl **-ies**) **n** ambassade *f*.

embattled [ɪm'bætld] **adj** [troubled] en difficulté.

embed [ɪm'bed] (pt & pp **-ded**, cont **-ding**) **vt** [in wood] enfoncer / [in rock] sceller / [in cement] sceller, noyer / [jewels] enchâsser, incruster.

embedded [ɪm'bedɪd] **adj** [in wood] enfoncé(e) / [in rock] scellé(e) / [in cement] scellé(e), noyé(e) / [jewels] enchâssé(e), incrusté(e).

embellish [ɪm'belɪʃ] **vt 1.** [decorate] **: to embellish sthg (with)** [room, house] décorer qqch (de) / [dress] orner qqch (de) **2.** [story] enjoliver.

embers ['embəz] **npl** braises *fpl*.

embezzle [ɪm'bezl] **vt** détourner.

embezzlement [ɪm'bezlmənt] **n** détournement *m* de fonds.

embezzler [ɪm'bezləʳ] **n** escroc *m*.

embittered [ɪm'bɪtəd] **adj** aigri(e).

emblazoned [ɪm'bleɪznd] **adj** **1.** [design, emblem] : **emblazoned (on)** blasonné(e) (sur) **2.** [flag, garment] : **to be emblazoned with** arborer l'insigne *OR* le blason de.

emblem ['embləm] **n** emblème *m*.

emblematic [,emblə'mætɪk] **adj** emblématique.

embodiment [ɪm'bɒdɪmənt] **n** incarnation *f*.

embody [ɪm'bɒdɪ] (pt & pp **-ied**) **vt** incarner ▸ **to be embodied in sthg** être exprimé dans qqch.

embolism ['embəlɪzm] **n** embolie *f*.

emboss [ɪm'bɒs] **vt** [metal] repousser, estamper / [leather] estamper, gaufrer / [cloth, paper] gaufrer.

embossed [ɪm'bɒst] **adj** **1.** [heading, design] : **embossed (on)** inscrit(e) (sur), gravé(e) en relief (sur) **2.** [wallpaper, leather] gaufré(e).

embrace [ɪm'breɪs] ■ **n** étreinte *f*.
■ **vt** embrasser.
■ **vi** s'embrasser, s'étreindre.

embrocation [,embrə'keɪʃn] **n** *esp UK* embrocation *f*.

embroider [ɪm'brɔɪdəʳ] ■ **vt** **1.** SEW broder **2.** *pej* [embellish] enjoliver.
■ **vi** SEW broder.

embroidered [ɪm'brɔɪdəd] **adj** SEW brodé(e).

embroidery [ɪm'brɔɪdərɪ] **n** *(U)* broderie *f*.

embroil [ɪm'brɔɪl] **vt** : **to be embroiled (in)** être mêlé(e) (à).

embryo ['embrɪəʊ] (pl **-s**) **n** embryon *m* ▸ **in embryo** *fig* à l'état embryonnaire.

embryonic [,embrɪ'ɒnɪk] **adj** embryonnaire.

emcee [,em'si:] *US* abbr of ***master of ceremonies***.

emend [ɪ'mend] **vt** corriger.

emerald ['emərəld] ■ **adj** [colour] émeraude *(inv)*.
■ **n** [stone] émeraude *f*.

emerge [ɪ'mɜ:dʒ] ■ **vi** **1.** [come out] : **to emerge (from)** émerger (de) **2.** [from experience, situation] : **to emerge from** sortir de **3.** [become known] apparaître **4.** [come into existence - poet, artist] percer / [- movement, organization] émerger.
■ **vt** : **it emerges that...** il ressort *OR* il apparaît que...

emergence [ɪ'mɜ:dʒəns] **n** émergence *f*.

emergency [ɪ'mɜ:dʒənsɪ] ■ **adj** d'urgence.
■ **n** (pl **-ies**) urgence *f* ▸ **in an emergency, in emergencies** en cas d'urgence.

emergency brake **n** [generally] frein *m* de secours / *US* [handbrake] frein *m* à main.

emergency exit **n** sortie *f* de secours.

emergency landing **n** atterrissage *m* forcé.

emergency room **n** *US* salle *f* des urgences.

emergency services **npl** ≃ police-secours *f*.

emergency stop **n** *UK* arrêt *m* d'urgence.

emergency tax **n** impôt *m* extraordinaire.

emergent [ɪ'mɜ:dʒənt] **adj** qui émerge.

emerging market **n** ECON marché *m* émergeant.

emery board ['emərɪ-] **n** lime *f* à ongles.

emetic [ɪ'metɪk] ■ **adj** émétique.
■ **n** émétique *m*.

emigrant ['emɪgrənt] **n** émigré *m*, -e *f*.

emigrate ['emɪgreɪt] **vi** : **to emigrate (to)** émigrer (en/à).

emigration [,emɪ'greɪʃn] **n** émigration *f*.

émigré, ***emigré*** ['emɪgreɪ] **n** émigré *m*, -e *f*.

eminence ['emɪnəns] **n** *(U)* [prominence] renom *m*.

eminent ['emɪnənt] **adj** éminent(e).

eminently ['emɪnəntlɪ] **adv** *fml* éminemment.

emir [e'mɪəʳ] **n** émir *m*.

emirate ['emərət] **n** émirat *m*.

emissary ['emɪsərɪ] (pl **-ies**) **n** émissaire *m*.

emission [ɪ'mɪʃn] **n** émission *f*.

emit [ɪ'mɪt] (pt & pp **-ted**, cont **-ting**) **vt** émettre.

Emmental, ***Emmenthal*** ['emən,tɑ:l] **n** Emmental *m*.

emollient [ɪ'mɒlɪənt] **n** **1.** *fml* émollient *m* **2.** [cream] crème *f* *OR* lotion *f* hydratante.

emolument [ɪ'mɒljʊmənt] **n** *UK fml* émoluments *mpl*.

emoticon [ɪ'məʊtɪkɒn] **n** émoticon *m*, souriant *m*.

emotion [ɪ'məʊʃn] **n** **1.** *(U)* [strength of feeling] émotion *f* **2.** [particular feeling] sentiment *m*.

emotional [ɪ'məʊʃənl] **adj** **1.** [sensitive, demonstrative] émotif(ive) **2.** [moving] émouvant(e) **3.** [psychological] émotionnel(elle).

emotional intelligence **n** intelligence *f* émotionnelle.

emotionally [ɪ'məʊʃnəlɪ] **adv** **1.** [with strong feeling] avec émotion **2.** [psychologically] émotionnellement.

emotional purchase **n** achat *m* d'émotion.

emotionless [ɪ'məʊʃnlɪs] **adj** impassible.

emotive [ɪ'məʊtɪv] **adj** qui enflamme l'esprit.

empathize, *UK* ***-ise*** ['empəθaɪz] **vt** : **to empathize with** s'identifier à.

empathy ['empəθɪ] **n** *(U)* : **empathy (with)** empathie *f* (envers), communion *f* de sentiments (avec).

emperor ['empərəʳ] **n** empereur *m*.

emphasis ['emfəsɪs] (pl **-ses** [-si:z]) **n** : **emphasis (on)** accent *m* (sur) ▸ **with great emphasis** avec insistance ▸ **to lay** *OR* **place emphasis on sthg** insister sur *OR* souligner qqch.

emphasize, *UK* ***-ise*** ['emfəsaɪz] **vt** insister sur.

emphatic [ɪm'fætɪk] **adj** [forceful] catégorique.

emphatically [ɪm'fætɪklɪ] **adv** **1.** [with emphasis] catégoriquement **2.** [certainly] absolument.

emphysema [,emfɪ'si:mə] **n** emphysème *m*.

empire ['empaɪəʳ] **n** empire *m*.

empire-building **n** édification *f* d'empires ▸ **there's too much empire-building going on** on joue trop les bâtisseurs d'empires.

empirical [ɪm'pɪrɪkl] **adj** empirique.

empirically [ɪm'pɪrɪklɪ] **adv** empiriquement.

empiricism [ɪm'pɪrɪsɪzm] **n** empirisme *m*.

employ [ɪm'plɔɪ] **vt** employer ▸ **they employ 245 staff** ils ont 245 employés ▸ **he has been employed with the firm for twenty years** il travaille pour cette entreprise depuis vingt ans ▸ **to be employed as** être employé comme ▸ **to employ sthg as sthg/to do sthg** employer qqch comme qqch/pour faire qqch.

employable [ɪm'plɔɪəbl] **adj** qui peut être employé(e).

employed [ɪm'plɔɪd] ■ **adj** employé(e) ▸ **I am not employed at the moment** je n'ai pas de travail en ce moment.

■ **npl** personnes *fpl* qui ont un emploi ▸ **employers and employed** patronat *m* et salariat *m*.

employee [ɪm'plɔɪiː] **n** employé *m*, -e *f*.

employee's contributions **npl** [to benefits] cotisations *fpl* salariales, charges *fpl* sociales salariales.

employer [ɪm'plɔɪəʳ] **n** employeur *m*, -euse *f*.

employer's contributions **npl** [to employee benefits] cotisations *fpl* patronales, charges *fpl* sociales patronales.

employment [ɪm'plɔɪmənt] **n** emploi *m*, travail *m*.

employment agency **n** bureau *m* *OR* agence *f* de placement.

employment office **n** ≃ Agence *f* Nationale pour l'Emploi.

emporium [em'pɔːrɪəm] **n** [shop] grand magasin *m*.

empower [ɪm'paʊəʳ] **vt** *fml* **: to be empowered to do sthg** être habilité(e) à faire qqch.

empowering [ɪm'paʊərɪŋ] **adj** qui donne un sentiment de pouvoir.

empress ['emprɪs] **n** impératrice *f*.

emptiness ['emptɪnɪs] *(U)* **n** vide *m*.

empty ['emptɪ] ■ **adj** (comp **-ier**, superl **-iest**) **1.** [containing nothing] vide **2.** *pej* [meaningless] vain(e) **3.** *liter* [tedious] morne.

■ **vt** vider ▸ **to empty sthg into/out of** vider qqch dans/de.

■ **vi** (pt & pp **-ied**) se vider.

■ **n** (pl **-ies**) *inf* bouteille *f* vide.

empty-handed [-'hændɪd] **adj** les mains vides.

empty-headed [-'hedɪd] **adj** sans cervelle.

EMS (abbr of ***European Monetary System***) **n** SME *m*.

EMT (abbr of ***emergency medical technician***) **n** *technicien médical des services d'urgence*.

emu ['iːmjuː] (pl **emu** *OR* **-s**) **n** émeu *m*.

EMU (abbr of ***Economic and Monetary Union***) **n** UEM *f*.

emulate ['emjʊleɪt] **vt** imiter.

emulsify [ɪ'mʌlsɪfaɪ] **vt** émulsionner, émulsifier.

emulsion [ɪ'mʌlʃn] ■ **n** *UK* **1. : emulsion (paint)** peinture *f* mate *OR* à émulsion **2.** PHOT émulsion *f*.

■ **vt** *UK* peindre.

emulsion paint = ***emulsion*** *(n sense 1)*.

enable [ɪ'neɪbl] **vt : to enable sb to do sthg** permettre à qqn de faire qqch.

enact [ɪ'nækt] **vt 1.** LAW promulguer **2.** THEAT jouer.

enactment [ɪ'næktmənt] **n** LAW promulgation *f*.

enamel [ɪ'næml] **n 1.** [material] émail *m* **2.** [paint] peinture *f* laquée.

enamelled *UK*, ***enameled*** *US* [ɪ'næmld] **adj** en émail.

enamel paint **n** peinture *f* laquée.

enamoured *UK*, ***enamored*** *US* [ɪ'næməd] **adj : enamoured of** amoureux(euse) de.

en bloc [ɒn'blɒk] **adv** *fml* en bloc.

enc. abbr of ***enclosure***, ***enclosed***.

encamp [ɪn'kæmp] **vi** camper.

encampment [ɪn'kæmpmənt] **n** campement *m*.

encapsulate [ɪn'kæpsjʊleɪt] **vt : to encapsulate sthg (in)** résumer qqch (en).

encase [ɪn'keɪs] **vt : to be encased in** [armour] être enfermé(e) dans / [leather] être bardé(e) de.

encash [ɪn'kæʃ] **vt** *UK* encaisser.

enchant [ɪn'tʃɑːnt] **vt 1.** [delight] enchanter, ravir **2.** [put spell on] enchanter, ensorceler.

enchanted [ɪn'tʃɑːntɪd] **adj : enchanted (by/with)** enchanté(e) (par/de).

enchanting [ɪn'tʃɑːntɪŋ] **adj** enchanteur(eresse).

enchantingly [ɪn'tʃɑːntɪŋlɪ] **adv** [sing, play] merveilleusement bien ▸ **enchantingly pretty** ravissant.

enchantment [ɪn'tʃɑːntmənt] **n 1.** [delight] enchantement *m*, ravissement *m* ▸ **to fill sb with enchantment** enchanter *OR* ravir qqn **2.** [casting of spell] enchantement *m*, ensorcellement *m*.

enchilada [ˌentʃɪ'lɑːdə] **n** *plat mexicain consistant en une galette de maïs frite, farcie à la viande et servie avec une sauce piquante*.

encircle [ɪn'sɜːkl] **vt** entourer / [subj: troops] encercler.

encl. = ***enc.***

enclave ['enkleɪv] **n** enclave *f*.

enclose [ɪn'kləʊz] **vt 1.** [surround, contain] entourer **2.** [put in envelope] joindre ▸ **please find enclosed...** veuillez trouver ci-joint...

enclosure [ɪn'kləʊʒəʳ] **n 1.** [place] enceinte *f* **2.** [in letter] pièce *f* jointe.

encode [en'kəʊd] **vt** coder, chiffrer / COMPUT encoder.

encoding [en'kəʊdɪŋ] **n** codage *m* / COMPUT encodage *m*.

encompass [ɪn'kʌmpəs] **vt** *fml* **1.** [include] contenir **2.** [surround] entourer / [subj: troops] encercler.

encore ['ɒŋkɔːʳ] ■ **n** rappel *m*.

■ **excl** bis!

encounter [ɪn'kaʊntər] ■ **n** rencontre *f*.
■ **vt** *fml* rencontrer.

encourage [ɪn'kʌrɪdʒ] **vt 1.** [give confidence to] **: to encourage sb (to do sthg)** encourager qqn (à faire qqch) **2.** [promote] encourager, favoriser.

encouragement [ɪn'kʌrɪdʒmənt] **n** encouragement *m*.

encouraging [ɪn'kʌrɪdʒɪŋ] **adj** encourageant(e).

encroach [ɪn'krəʊtʃ] **vi : to encroach on** *OR* **upon** empiéter sur.

encrusted [ɪn'krʌstɪd] **adj : encrusted with** incrusté(e) de / [with mud] encroûté(e) de.

encrypt [en'krɪpt] **vt 1.** COMPUT crypter **2.** TV coder.

encryption [en'krɪpʃn] **n** *(U)* **1.** COMPUT cryptage *m* **2.** TV codage *m*, encodage *m*.

encumber [ɪn'kʌmbər] **vt** *fml* **: to be encumbered with** être encombré(e) de / [with debts] être grevé(e) de.

encyclop(a)edia [ɪn,saɪklə'pi:djə] **n** encyclopédie *f*.

encyclop(a)edic [ɪn,saɪkləʊ'pi:dɪk] **adj** encyclopédique.

end [end] ■ **n 1.** [gen] fin *f* ▸ **at an end** terminé, fini ▸ **to come to an end** se terminer, s'arrêter ▸ **to put an end to sthg** mettre fin à qqch ▸ **at the end of the day** *fig* en fin de compte ▸ **in the end** [finally] finalement ▸ **an end in itself** une fin en soi ▸ **to achieve** *OR* **to attain one's end** atteindre son but
2. [of rope, path, garden, table] bout *m*, extrémité *f* / [of box] côté *m* ▸ **end to end** bout à bout ▸ **to change ends** SPORT changer de côté ▸ **this is the end of the road** *OR* **line** c'est fini ▸ **to make (both) ends meet** [financially] joindre les deux bouts
3. [leftover part - of cigarette] mégot *m* / [- of pencil] bout *m*.
■ **vt** mettre fin à / [meeting, discussion] clore / [day] finir ▸ **to end sthg with** terminer *OR* finir qqch par ▸ **he decided to end it all** [life, relationship] il décida d'en finir.
■ **vi** se terminer ▸ **to end in** se terminer par ▸ **it'll end in tears** ça va mal finir ▸ **to end with** se terminer par *OR* avec.
◆ ***on end*** **adv 1.** [upright] debout
2. [continuously] d'affilée ▸ **for hours/days on end** pendant des heures entières/des jours entiers.
◆ ***no end*** **adv** *inf* [pleased, worried] vachement.
◆ ***no end of*** **prep** *inf* énormément de.
◆ ***end up*** **vi** finir ▸ **to end up doing sthg** finir par faire qqch.

endanger [ɪn'deɪndʒər] **vt** mettre en danger.

endangered species [ɪn'deɪndʒəd-] **n** espèce *f* en voie de disparition.

endear [ɪn'dɪər] **vt : to endear sb to sb** faire aimer *OR* apprécier qqn de qqn ▸ **to endear o.s. to sb** se faire aimer de qqn, plaire à qqn.

endearing [ɪn'dɪərɪŋ] **adj** [personality, person] attachant(e) / [smile] engageant(e).

endearingly [ɪn'dɪərɪŋlɪ] **adv** de manière attachante / [smile] de manière engageante.

endearment [ɪn'dɪəmənt] **n** paroles *fpl* affectueuses.

endeavour *UK*, ***endeavor*** *US fml* [ɪn'devər] ■ **n** effort *m*, tentative *f*.
■ **vt : to endeavour to do sthg** s'efforcer *OR* tenter de faire qqch.

endemic [en'demɪk] **adj** endémique.

endgame ['endgeɪm] **n** CHESS fin *m* de partie.

ending ['endɪŋ] **n** fin *f*, dénouement *m*.

endive ['endaɪv] **n 1.** *US* [salad vegetable] endive *f* **2.** *UK* [chicory] chicorée *f*.

endless ['endlɪs] **adj 1.** [unending] interminable / [patience, possibilities] infini(e) / [resources] inépuisable **2.** [vast] infini(e).

endlessly ['endlɪslɪ] **adv** sans arrêt, continuellement / [stretch] à perte de vue ▸ **endlessly patient/kind** d'une patience/gentillesse infinie.

end-of-month **adj** [balance, payments, settlement, statement] de fin de mois.

end-of-year **adj 1.** [gen] de fin d'année **2.** FIN de fin d'exercice ▸ **end-of-year balance sheet** bilan *m* de l'exercice.

endorphin [en'dɔ:fɪn] **n** MED endorphine *f*.

endorse [ɪn'dɔ:s] **vt 1.** [approve] approuver **2.** [cheque] endosser **3.** *UK* [driving licence] porter une contravention à.

endorsement [ɪn'dɔ:smənt] **n 1.** [approval] approbation *f* **2.** [of cheque] endossement *m* **3.** *UK* [on driving licence] *contravention portée au permis de conduire*.

endoscope ['endəskəʊp] **n** MED endoscope *m*.

endow [ɪn'daʊ] **vt 1.** [equip] **: to be endowed with sthg** être doté(e) de qqch **2.** [donate money to] faire des dons à.

endowment [ɪn'daʊmənt] **n 1.** *fml* [ability] capacité *f*, qualité *f* **2.** [donation] don *m*.

endowment insurance **n** *UK* assurance *f* à capital différé.

HOW TO ...

express encouragement

Je trouve tout cela très positif / I have a good feeling about this
Tout ça m'a l'air très bien / That all seems fine to me
Vous tenez le bon bout / You're on the right track
Encore un effort. Vous y êtes presque / Come on, you're almost there
Tu ne vas pas laisser tomber maintenant ! / You can't give up now!
Vas-y, demande-lui ! / Go on, ask her!
Allez, tu sais bien que ça va te plaire / Oh, go on - you know you'll enjoy it
Tu es très bien comme ça / You look just fine

endowment mortgage **n** *UK prêt-logement lié à une assurance-vie.*

endowment policy **n** assurance *f* mixte.

end product **n** produit *m* fini.

end result **n** résultat *m* final.

endurable [ɪn'djʊərəbl] **adj** supportable.

endurance [ɪn'djʊərəns] **n** endurance *f*.

endurance test **n** épreuve *f* d'endurance.

endure [ɪn'djʊər] ■ **vt** supporter, endurer.
■ **vi** perdurer.

enduring [ɪn'djʊərɪŋ] **adj** durable.

end user **n** utilisateur final *m*, utilisatrice finale *f*.

endways *UK* ['endweɪz], ***endwise*** *US* ['endwaɪz] **adv** **1.** [not sideways] en long **2.** [with ends touching] bout à bout.

enema ['enɪmə] **n** lavement *m*.

enemy ['enɪmɪ] ■ **n** (**pl -ies**) ennemi *m*, -e *f*.
■ **comp** ennemi(e).

energetic [,enə'dʒetɪk] **adj** énergique / [person] plein(e) d'entrain.

energetically [,enə'dʒetɪklɪ] **adv** énergiquement.

energize, *UK* ***-ise*** ['enədʒaɪz] **vt** [person] donner de l'énergie à, stimuler / ELEC exciter, envoyer de l'électricité dans.

energy ['enədʒɪ] (**pl -ies**) **n** énergie *f* ▸ **to be/to feel full of energy** être/se sentir plein d'énergie ▸ **to save** *OR* **to conserve energy** faire des économies d'énergie ▸ **energy crisis** crise *f* énergétique *OR* de l'énergie.

energy-saving **adj** d'économie d'énergie.

enervate ['enəveɪt] **vt** *fml* débiliter.

enervating ['enəveɪtɪŋ] **adj** *fml* débilitant(e).

enfold [ɪn'fəʊld] **vt** *liter* **1.** [embrace] **: to enfold sb/sthg (in)** envelopper qqn/qqch (dans) ▸ **to enfold sb in one's arms** étreindre qqn **2.** [engulf] envelopper.

enforce [ɪn'fɔ:s] **vt** appliquer, faire respecter.

enforceable [ɪn'fɔ:səbl] **adj** applicable.

enforced [ɪn'fɔ:st] **adj** forcé(e).

enforcement [ɪn'fɔ:smənt] **n** application *f*.

enfranchise [ɪn'fræntʃaɪz] **vt** **1.** [give vote to] accorder le droit de vote à **2.** [set free] affranchir.

ENG (abbr of ***electronic news gathering***) **n** journalisme *m* électronique.

engage [ɪn'geɪdʒ] ■ **vt** **1.** [attention, interest] susciter, éveiller ▸ **to engage sb in conversation** engager la conversation avec qqn **2.** TECH engager **3.** *fml* [employ] engager ▸ **to be engaged in** *OR* **on sthg** prendre part à qqch.
■ **vi** [be involved] **: to engage in** s'occuper de.

engaged [ɪn'geɪdʒd] **adj** **1.** *UK* [to be married] **: engaged (to sb)** fiancé(e) (à qqn) ▸ **to get engaged** se fiancer **2.** [busy] occupé(e) ▸ **engaged in sthg** engagé dans qqch **3.** *UK* [telephone, toilet] occupé(e).

engaged tone **n** *UK* tonalité *f* 'occupé'.

engagement [ɪn'geɪdʒmənt] **n** **1.** [to be married] fiançailles *fpl* **2.** [appointment] rendez-vous *m inv*.

engagement ring **n** bague *f* de fiançailles.

engaging [ɪn'geɪdʒɪŋ] **adj** engageant(e) / [personality] attirant(e).

engender [ɪn'dʒendər] **vt** *fml* engendrer, susciter.

engine ['endʒɪn] **n** **1.** [of vehicle] moteur *m* **2.** RAIL locomotive *f*.

engine driver **n** *UK* mécanicien *m*.

engineer [,endʒɪ'nɪər] ■ **n** **1.** [of roads] ingénieur *m*, -e *f* / [of machinery, on ship] mécanicien *m*, -ienne *f* / [of electrical equipment] technicien *m*, -ienne *f* **2.** *US* [train driver] mécanicien *m*, -ienne *f*.
■ **vt** **1.** [construct] construire **2.** [contrive] manigancer.

engineering [,endʒɪ'nɪərɪŋ] **n** ingénierie *f*.

England ['ɪŋglənd] **n** Angleterre *f* ▸ **in England** en Angleterre.

English ['ɪŋglɪʃ] ■ **adj** anglais(e).
■ **n** [language] anglais *m*.
■ **npl : the English** les Anglais.

English breakfast **n** petit déjeuner *m* anglais traditionnel.

English Channel **n : the English Channel** la Manche.

Englishman ['ɪŋglɪʃmən] (**pl -men** [-mən]) **n** Anglais *m*.

English muffin **n** *US sorte de gaufre.*

English-speaking **adj** [as native language] anglophone / [as learned language] parlant anglais.

Englishwoman ['ɪŋglɪʃ,wʊmən] (**pl -women** [-wɪmɪn]) **n** Anglaise *f*.

engrave [ɪn'greɪv] **vt : to engrave sthg (on stone/in one's memory)** graver qqch (sur la pierre/dans sa mémoire).

engraver [ɪn'greɪvər] **n** graveur *m*.

engraving [ɪn'greɪvɪŋ] **n** gravure *f*.

engrossed [ɪn'grəʊst] **adj : to be engrossed (in sthg)** être absorbé(e) (par qqch).

engrossing [ɪn'grəʊsɪŋ] **adj** absorbant(e).

engulf [ɪn'gʌlf] **vt** engloutir.

enhance [ɪn'hɑ:ns] **vt** améliorer.

enhancement [ɪn'hɑ:nsmənt] **n** amélioration *f*.

enigma [ɪ'nɪgmə] **n** énigme *f*.

enigmatic [,enɪg'mætɪk] **adj** énigmatique.

enigmatically [,enɪg'mætɪklɪ] **adv** [smile, speak] d'un air énigmatique / [worded] d'une manière énigmatique.

enjoy [ɪn'dʒɔɪ] ■ **vt** **1.** [like] aimer ▸ **to enjoy doing sthg** avoir plaisir à *OR* aimer faire qqch ▸ **to enjoy life** aimer la vie ▸ **to enjoy o.s.** s'amuser ▸ **enjoy your meal!** bon appétit! **2.** *fml* [possess] jouir de.
■ **vi** *US* **: enjoy!** [enjoy yourself] amuse-toi bien! / [before meal] bon appétit!

enjoyable [ɪn'dʒɔɪəbl] **adj** agréable.

enjoyably [ɪn'dʒɔɪəblɪ] **adv** de manière agréable.

enjoyment [ɪn'dʒɔɪmənt] **n** **1.** [gen] plaisir *m* **2.** *fml* [possession] jouissance *f*.

enlarge [ɪn'lɑ:dʒ] **vt** agrandir.
◆ ***enlarge (up)on*** **vt insep** développer.

enlargement [ɪn'lɑ:dʒmənt] **n 1.** [expansion] extension *f* **2.** PHOT agrandissement *m*.

enlighten [ɪn'laɪtn] **vt** éclairer.

enlightened [ɪn'laɪtnd] **adj** éclairé(e).

enlightening [ɪn'laɪtnɪŋ] **adj** édifiant(e).

enlightenment [ɪn'laɪtnmənt] **n** *(U)* éclaircissement *m*.
◆ ***Enlightenment*** **n : the Enlightenment** le siècle des Lumières.

enlist [ɪn'lɪst] ■ **vt 1.** MIL enrôler **2.** [recruit] recruter **3.** [obtain] s'assurer.
■ **vi** MIL **: to enlist (in)** s'enrôler (dans).

enlisted man [ɪn'lɪstɪd-] **n** *US* simple soldat *m*.

enliven [ɪn'laɪvn] **vt** animer / [book, film] égayer.

en masse [ɒn'mæs] **adv** en masse, massivement.

enmeshed [ɪn'meʃt] **adj : enmeshed in** empêtré(e) dans.

enmity ['enmətɪ] (pl **-ies**) **n** hostilité *f*.

ennoble [ɪ'nəʊbl] **vt 1.** [elevate to nobility] anoblir **2.** [dignify] ennoblir.

enormity [ɪ'nɔ:mətɪ] **n** [extent] étendue *f*.

enormous [ɪ'nɔ:məs] **adj** énorme / [patience, success] immense.

enormously [ɪ'nɔ:məslɪ] **adv** énormément / [long, pleased] immensément.

enough [ɪ'nʌf] ■ **adj** assez de ▸ **enough money/time** assez d'argent/de temps.
■ **pron** assez ▸ **more than enough** largement, bien assez ▸ **enough is enough** trop c'est trop ▸ **that's enough (of that)!** ça suffit maintenant! ▸ **to have had enough (of sthg)** en avoir assez (de qqch).
■ **adv 1.** [sufficiently] assez ▸ **big enough for sthg/to do sthg** assez grand pour qqch/pour faire qqch ▸ **to be good enough to do sthg** *fml* être assez gentil pour ***or*** de faire qqch, être assez aimable pour ***or*** de faire qqch **2.** [rather] plutôt ▸ **strangely enough** bizarrement, c'est bizarre.

en passant [ɑ̃'pæsɑ̃] **adv** en passant.

enquire [ɪn'kwaɪər] ■ **vt** *UK* **: to enquire when/whether/how...** demander quand/si/comment...
■ **vi : to enquire (about)** se renseigner (sur).

enquiry [ɪn'kwaɪərɪ] (pl **-ies**) **n 1.** [question] demande *f* de renseignements ▸ **'Enquiries'** 'renseignements' **2.** [investigation] enquête *f*.

enquiry desk, enquiry office **n** accueil *m*.

enrage [ɪn'reɪdʒ] **vt** rendre furieux, mettre en rage.

enraged [ɪn'reɪdʒd] **adj** [person] furieux(ieuse) / [animal] enragé(e).

enrich [ɪn'rɪtʃ] **vt** enrichir.

enriching [ɪn'rɪtʃɪŋ] **adj** enrichissant(e).

enrol *UK* (pt & pp **-led**, cont **-ling**), ***enroll*** *US* (pt & pp **-ed**, cont **-ing**) [ɪn'rəʊl] ■ **vt** inscrire.
■ **vi : to enrol (in)** s'inscrire (à).

enrolment *UK*, ***enrollment*** *US* [ɪn'rəʊlmənt] **n 1.** *(U)* [registration] inscription *f* **2.** [person enrolled] inscrit *m*.

en route [ɒn'ru:t] **adv : en route (to)** en route (vers) ▸ **en route from** en provenance de.

ensconced [ɪn'skɒnst] **adj** *liter* **: ensconced (in)** bien installé(e) (dans).

ensemble [ɒn'sɒmbl] **n** [gen & MUS] ensemble *m*.

enshrine [ɪn'ʃraɪn] **vt : to be enshrined in** être garanti(e) par.

ensign ['ensaɪn] **n 1.** [flag] pavillon *m* **2.** *US* [sailor] enseigne *m*.

enslave [ɪn'sleɪv] **vt** asservir.

enslavement [ɪn'sleɪvmənt] **n** *lit* asservissement *m* / *fig* sujétion *f*, asservissement *m*.

ensue [ɪn'sju:] **vi** s'ensuivre.

ensuing [ɪn'sju:ɪŋ] **adj** qui s'ensuit.

en suite [ˌɒn'swi:t] **adj & adv : with en suite bathroom, with bathroom en suite** avec salle de bain particulière.

ensure [ɪn'ʃʊər] **vt** assurer ▸ **to ensure (that)...** s'assurer que...

ENT (abbr of ***Ear, Nose & Throat***) **n** ORL *f*.

entail [ɪn'teɪl] **vt** entraîner ▸ **what does the work entail?** en quoi consiste le travail?

entangled [ɪn'tæŋgld] **adj 1.** [caught] **: to be entangled in** être emmêlé(e) ***or*** enchevêtré(e) dans **2.** [in problem, difficult situation] **: to be entangled in** être empêtré(e) dans **3.** *fig* [with person] **: to be entangled with** avoir une liaison avec.

entanglement [ɪn'tæŋglmənt] **n** liaison *f* (amoureuse).

entente cordiale **n** entente *f* cordiale.

CULTURE

Entente Cordiale

Le 8 avril 1904 à Londres, l'Angleterre et la France signaient le traité de « l'Entente cordiale », dont le but était de dissiper les différends qui divisaient les deux pays au Maroc, en Égypte, au Siam, à Madagascar, aux Nouvelles-Hébrides, en Afrique centrale et occidentale, et à Terre-Neuve. Cet accord marqua le passage d'une époque assombrie par les conflits et les rivalités à une histoire faite de réconciliations, et joua un rôle décisif en ouvrant la voie à la coopération diplomatique et militaire qui précéda la Première Guerre mondiale. L'Entente cordiale, les alliances anglo-russe et franco-russe ont formé la « Triple Entente » entre la France, l'Angleterre et la Russie.

enter ['entər] ■ **vt 1.** [room, vehicle] entrer dans ▸ **the ship entered the harbour** le navire est entré au ***or*** dans le port **2.** [university, army] entrer à / [school] s'inscrire à, s'inscrire dans **3.** [competition, race] s'inscrire à / [politics] se lancer dans **4.** [register] **: to enter sb/sthg for sthg** inscrire qqn/qqch à qqch **5.** [write down] inscrire **6.** COMPUT entrer **7.** [submit] présenter ▸ **to enter an appeal** LAW interjeter appel.

■ vi 1. [come or go in] entrer 2. [register] : **to enter (for)** s'inscrire (à).
◆ ***enter into*** vt insep [negotiations, correspondence] entamer ▸ **to enter into an agreement with sb** conclure un accord avec qqn.

enteritis [ˌentə'raɪtɪs] n entérite *f*.

enter key n COMPUT (touche *f*) entrée *f*.

enterprise ['entəpraɪz] n entreprise *f*.

enterprise culture n ECON *attitude favorable à l'essor de l'esprit d'entreprise.*

enterprise zone n *UK zone dans une région défavorisée qui bénéficie de subsides de l'État.*

enterprising ['entəpraɪzɪŋ] adj qui fait preuve d'initiative.

entertain [ˌentə'teɪn] ■ vt 1. [amuse] divertir 2. [invite - guests] recevoir 3. *fml* [thought, proposal] considérer 4. *fml* [hopes] nourrir.
■ vi [have guests] recevoir.

FALSE FRIENDS / FAUX AMIS

entertain

Entretenir n'est pas la traduction du mot anglais *to entertain*. Entretenir se traduit par *to maintain* ou *to look after*.
▸ Cette voiture a été très bien entretenue / *This car has been very well maintained*
▸ Elle sait entretenir son jardin / *She knows how to look after her garden*

entertainer [ˌentə'teɪnəʳ] n fantaisiste *mf*.

entertaining [ˌentə'teɪnɪŋ] ■ adj divertissant(e).
■ n : **to do a lot of entertaining** recevoir beaucoup.

entertainment [ˌentə'teɪnmənt] ■ n 1. *(U)* [amusement] divertissement *m* 2. [show] spectacle *m*.
■ comp du spectacle.

entertainment allowance n *UK* frais *mpl* de représentation.

enthral *UK* (pt & pp -led, cont -ling), ***enthrall*** *US* (pt & pp -ed, cont -ing) [ɪn'θrɔːl] vt captiver.

enthralling [ɪn'θrɔːlɪŋ] adj captivant(e).

enthrone [ɪn'θrəʊn] vt introniser.

enthuse [ɪn'θjuːz] vi : **to enthuse (over)** s'enthousiasmer (pour).

enthusiasm [ɪn'θjuːzɪæzm] n 1. [passion, eagerness] : **enthusiasm (for)** enthousiasme *m* (pour) 2. [interest] passion *f*.

enthusiast [ɪn'θjuːzɪæst] n enthousiaste *mf*.

enthusiastic [ɪnˌθjuːzɪ'æstɪk] adj enthousiaste.

enthusiastically [ɪnˌθjuːzɪ'æstɪklɪ] adv avec enthousiasme.

entice [ɪn'taɪs] vt séduire.

enticing [ɪn'taɪsɪŋ] adj alléchant(e) / [smile] séduisant(e).

enticingly [ɪn'taɪsɪŋlɪ] adv de façon séduisante ▸ **delicious smells wafted enticingly from the kitchen** de délicieuses odeurs de cuisine mettaient l'eau à la bouche.

entire [ɪn'taɪəʳ] adj entier(ère).

entirely [ɪn'taɪəlɪ] adv entièrement, totalement.

entirety [ɪn'taɪrətɪ] n : **in its entirety** en entier.

entitle [ɪn'taɪtl] vt 1. [allow] : **to entitle sb to sthg** donner droit à qqch à qqn ▸ **to entitle sb to do sthg** autoriser qqn à faire qqch ▸ **to be entitled to do sthg** [by status] avoir qualité pour *OR* être habilité à faire qqch / [by rules] avoir le droit *OR* être en droit de faire qqch 2. [film, painting] intituler ▸ **the book is entitled...** le livre s'intitule...

entitled [ɪn'taɪtld] adj 1. [allowed] autorisé(e) ▸ **to be entitled to sthg** avoir droit à qqch ▸ **to be entitled to do sthg** avoir le droit de faire qqch 2. [called] intitulé(e).

entitlement [ɪn'taɪtlmənt] n droit *m*.

entity ['entətɪ] (pl -ies) n entité *f*.

entomology [ˌentə'mɒlədʒɪ] n entomologie *f*.

entourage [ˌɒntʊ'rɑːʒ] n entourage *m*.

entrails ['entreɪlz] npl entrailles *fpl*.

entrance ■ n ['entrəns] 1. [way in] : **entrance (to)** entrée *f* (de) 2. [arrival] entrée *f* 3. [entry] : **to gain entrance to** [building] obtenir l'accès à / [society, university] être admis(e) dans.
■ vt [ɪn'trɑːns] ravir, enivrer.

entrance examination n examen *m* d'entrée.

entrance fee n 1. [to cinema, museum] droit *m* d'entrée 2. [for club] droit *m* d'inscription.

entrance hall ['entrəns-] n [in house] vestibule *m* / [in hotel] hall *m*.

entrancing [ɪn'trɑːnsɪŋ] adj enchanteur(eresse).

entrant ['entrənt] n [in race, competition] concurrent *m*, -e *f*.

entrapment [ɪn'træpmənt] n *incitation au délit par un policier afin de justifier une arrestation.*

entreat [ɪn'triːt] vt : **to entreat sb (to do sthg)** supplier qqn (de faire qqch).

entreaty [ɪn'triːtɪ] (pl -ies) n prière *f*, supplication *f*.

entrée ['ɒntreɪ] n 1. [right of entry] entrée *f* 2. CULIN [course preceding main dish] entrée *f* / *US* [main dish] plat *m* principal *OR* de résistance.

entrenched [ɪn'trentʃt] adj ancré(e).

entrepreneur [ˌɒntrəprə'nɜːʳ] n entrepreneur *m*.

entrepreneurial [ˌɒntrəprə'nɜːrɪəl] adj [person] qui a l'esprit d'entreprise / [skill] d'entrepreneur.

entrust [ɪn'trʌst] vt : **to entrust sthg to sb, to entrust sb with sthg** confier qqch à qqn.

entry ['entrɪ] (pl -ies) n 1. [gen] entrée *f* ▸ **she was refused entry to the country** on lui a refusé l'entrée dans le pays ▸ **to gain entry to** avoir accès à ▸ **'no entry'** 'défense d'entrer' / AUT 'sens interdit' 2. [in competition] inscription *f* 3. [in dictionary] entrée *f* / [in diary, ledger] inscription *f*.

entry fee n entrée *f*.

entry form n formulaire *m OR* feuille *f* d'inscription.

Entryphone® ['entrɪ,fəʊn] **n** *UK* Interphone® *m (à l'entrée d'un immeuble ou de bureaux).*

entry visa **n** visa *m* d'entrée.

entryway ['entrɪ,weɪ] **n** *US* entrée *f.*

entwine [ɪn'twaɪn] ■ **vt** entrelacer.
■ **vi** s'entrelacer.

E number **n** additif *m* E.

enumerate [ɪ'nju:məreɪt] **vt** énumérer.

enunciate [ɪ'nʌnsɪeɪt] ■ **vt 1.** [word] articuler **2.** [idea, plan] énoncer, exposer.
■ **vi** articuler.

envelop [ɪn'veləp] **vt** envelopper.

envelope ['envələʊp] **n** enveloppe *f.*

enviable ['envɪəbl] **adj** enviable.

envious ['envɪəs] **adj** envieux(euse).

enviously ['envɪəslɪ] **adv** avec envie.

environment [ɪn'vaɪərənmənt] **n 1.** [surroundings] milieu *m*, cadre *m* **2.** [natural world] **: the environment** l'environnement *m* ▸ **Department of the Environment** *UK* ≃ ministère *m* de l'Environnement **3.** COMPUT environnement *m.*

environment agency **n** agence *f* pour la protection de l'environnement.

environmental [ɪn,vaɪərən'mentl] **adj** [pollution, awareness] de l'environnement / [impact] sur l'environnement.

Environmental Heath Officer **n** *UK* inspecteur *m* sanitaire.

environmentalist [ɪn,vaɪərən'mentəlɪst] **n** écologiste *mf*, environnementaliste *mf.*

environmentally [ɪn,vaɪərən'mentəlɪ] **adv** [damaging] pour l'environnement ▸ **to be environmentally aware** être sensible aux problèmes de l'environnement.

Environmental Protection Agency **n** *US* ≃ ministère *m* de l'Environnement.

environment-friendly **adj** [policy] respectueux (euse) de l'environnement / [product] non polluant(e).

environs [ɪn'vaɪərənz] **npl** environs *mpl.*

envisage [ɪn'vɪzɪdʒ], ***envision*** *US* [ɪn'vɪʒn] **vt** envisager.

envoy ['envɔɪ] **n** émissaire *m.*

envy ['envɪ] ■ **n** envie *f*, jalousie *f* ▸ **to be the envy of** faire envie à ▸ **to be green with envy** être malade de jalousie.
■ **vt** (pt & pp **-ied**) envier ▸ **to envy sb sthg** envier qqch à qqn.

enzyme ['enzaɪm] **n** enzyme *f.*

EOC abbr of ***Equal Opportunities Commission.***

eon *US* = ***aeon.***

EP (abbr of ***European Parliament***) **n** Parlement *m* européen.

EPA abbr of ***Environmental Protection Agency.***

epaulet(te) ['epəlet] **n** épaulette *f.*

ephemeral [ɪ'femərəl] **adj** éphémère.

epic ['epɪk] ■ **adj** épique.
■ **n** épopée *f.*

epicentre *UK*, ***epicenter*** *US* ['epɪsentər] **n** épicentre *m.*

epidemic [,epɪ'demɪk] **n** épidémie *f.*

epidural [,epɪ'djʊərəl] **n** péridurale *f.*

epigram ['epɪɡræm] **n** épigramme *f.*

epigraph ['epɪɡrɑ:f] **n** épigraphe *f.*

epilepsy ['epɪlepsɪ] **n** épilepsie *f.*

epileptic [,epɪ'leptɪk] ■ **adj** épileptique.
■ **n** épileptique *mf.*

epilogue ['epɪlɒɡ] **n** épilogue *m.*

Epiphany [ɪ'pɪfənɪ] **n** Épiphanie *f.*

episcopal [ɪ'pɪskəpl] **adj** épiscopal(e).

episode ['epɪsəʊd] **n** épisode *m.*

episodic [,epɪ'sɒdɪk] **adj** [story, play] en épisodes.

epistle [ɪ'pɪsl] **n** épître *f.*

epitaph ['epɪtɑ:f] **n** épitaphe *f.*

epithet ['epɪθet] **n** épithète *f.*

epitome [ɪ'pɪtəmɪ] **n : the epitome of** le modèle de.

epitomize, *UK* ***-ise*** [ɪ'pɪtəmaɪz] **vt** incarner.

epoch ['i:pɒk] **n** époque *f.*

epoch-making [-'meɪkɪŋ] **adj** qui fait date.

eponymous [ɪ'pɒnɪməs] **adj** éponyme.

EPOS ['i:pɒs] (abbr of ***electronic point of sale***) **n** *point de vente électronique.*

EQ [i:'kju:] (abbr of ***emotional intelligence quotient***) **n** QE *m*, quotient *m* émotionnel.

equable ['ekwəbl] **adj** [character, person] égal(e), placide / [climate] égal(e), constant(e).

equably ['ekwəblɪ] **adv** tranquillement, placidement.

equal ['i:kwəl] ■ **adj 1.** [gen] **: equal (to)** égal(e) (à) ▸ **equal in number** égal en nombre ▸ **on equal terms** d'égal à égal **2.** [capable] **: equal to sthg** à la hauteur de qqch.
■ **n** égal *m*, -e *f* ▸ **to talk to sb as an equal** parler à qqn d'égal à égal.
■ **vt** (*UK* **-led**, cont **-ling**, *US* **-ed**, cont **-ing**) égaler ▸ **2 and 2 equal(s) 4** 2 et 2 égalent ***or*** font 4 ▸ **let x equal y** si x égale y.

equality [i:'kwɒlətɪ] **n** égalité *f.*

equalize, *UK* ***-ise*** ['i:kwəlaɪz] ■ **vt** niveler.
■ **vi** *UK* SPORT égaliser.

equalizer ['i:kwəlaɪzər] **n** *UK* SPORT but *m* égalisateur.

equally ['i:kwəlɪ] **adv 1.** [important, stupid] tout aussi ▸ **I like them equally** je les apprécie de la même façon **2.** [in amount] en parts égales **3.** [also] en même temps.

equal opportunities **npl** égalité *f* des chances.

Equal Opportunities Commission **n** *commission britannique pour l'égalité des chances dans le travail.*

equal(s) sign **n** signe *m* d'égalité.

equanimity [,ekwə'nɪmətɪ] **n** sérénité *f*, égalité *f* d'âme.

equate [ɪ'kweɪt] **vt : to equate sthg with sthg** assimiler qqch à qqch.

equation [ɪ'kweɪʒn] **n** équation *f.*

equator [ɪ'kweɪtəʳ] **n : the equator** l'équateur *m.*

equatorial [ˌekwə'tɔ:rɪəl] **adj** équatorial(e).

Equatorial Guinea **n** Guinée *f* équatoriale.

equestrian [ɪ'kwestrɪən] **adj** équestre.

equidistant [ˌi:kwɪ'dɪstənt] **adj : equidistant (from)** équidistant(e) (de).

equilateral triangle [ˌi:kwɪ'lætərəl-] **n** triangle *m* équilatéral.

equilibrium [ˌi:kwɪ'lɪbrɪəm] **n** équilibre *m.*

equine ['ekwaɪn] **adj** chevalin(e).

equinox ['i:kwɪnɒks] **n** équinoxe *m.*

equip [ɪ'kwɪp] (pt & pp **-ped**, cont **-ping**) **vt** équiper ▸ **to equip sb/sthg with** équiper qqn/qqch de, munir qqn/qqch de ▸ **he's well equipped for the job** il est bien préparé pour ce travail.

equipment [ɪ'kwɪpmənt] **n** *(U)* équipement *m*, matériel *m.*

equitable ['ekwɪtəbl] **adj** équitable.

equitably ['ekwɪtəblɪ] **adv** équitablement, avec justice.

equities ['ekwətɪz] **npl** FIN actions *fpl* ordinaires.

equity ['ekwətɪ] (pl **-ies**) **n 1.** [fairness] équité *f* **2.** LAW [system] équité *f* / [right] droit *m* équitable **3.** FIN [market value] fonds *mpl* ***or*** capitaux *mpl* propres.
◆ ***Equity*** **n** *principal syndicat britannique des gens du spectacle.*

equivalence [ɪ'kwɪvələns] **n** équivalence *f.*

equivalent [ɪ'kwɪvələnt] ■ **adj** équivalent(e) ▸ **to be equivalent to** être équivalent à, équivaloir à.
■ **n** équivalent *m.*

equivocal [ɪ'kwɪvəkl] **adj** équivoque.

equivocally [ɪ'kwɪvəklɪ] **adv 1.** [ambiguously] de manière équivoque ***or*** ambiguë **2.** [dubiously] de manière douteuse.

equivocate [ɪ'kwɪvəkeɪt] **vi** parler de façon équivoque.

equivocation [ɪˌkwɪvə'keɪʃn] **n** *(U) fml* [words] paroles *fpl* équivoques / [prevarication] tergiversation *f.*

er [ɜ:ʳ] **excl** euh!

ER (abbr of ***Elizabeth Regina***) *emblème de la reine Elizabeth.*

era ['ɪərə] (pl **-s**) **n** ère *f*, période *f.*

ERA ['ɪərə] (abbr of ***Equal Rights Amendment***) **n** *US projet d'amendement constitutionnel pour l'égalité des droits des femmes.*

eradicate [ɪ'rædɪkeɪt] **vt** éradiquer.

eradication [ɪˌrædɪ'keɪʃn] **n** éradication *f.*

erase [ɪ'reɪz] **vt 1.** [rub out] gommer **2.** *fig* [memory] effacer / [hunger, poverty] éliminer.

eraser [ɪ'reɪzəʳ] **n** gomme *f.*

erect [ɪ'rekt] ■ **adj 1.** [person, posture] droit(e) **2.** [penis] en érection.
■ **vt 1.** [statue] ériger / [building] construire **2.** [tent] dresser.

erection [ɪ'rekʃn] **n 1.** *(U)* [of statue] érection *f* / [of building] construction *f* **2.** [erect penis] érection *f.*

ergonomic [ˌɜ:gəʊ'nɒmɪk] **adj** ergonomique.

ergonomically [ˌɜ:gəʊ'nɒmɪkəlɪ] **adv** du point de vue ergonomique.

ergonomics [ˌɜ:gə'nɒmɪks] **n** ergonomie *f.*

ERISA [ə'ri:sə] (abbr of ***Employee Retirement Income Security Act***) **n** *loi américaine sur les pensions de retraite.*

Eritrea [ˌerɪ'treɪə] **n** Érythrée *f* ▸ **in Eritrea** en Érythrée.

Eritrean [ˌerɪ'treɪən] ■ **adj** érythréen(enne).
■ **n** Érythréen *m*, -enne *f.*

ERM (abbr of ***Exchange Rate Mechanism***) **n** mécanisme *m* des changes (du SME).

ermine ['ɜ:mɪn] **n** [fur] hermine *f.*

ERNIE ['ɜ:nɪ] (abbr of ***Electronic Random Number Indicator Equipment***) **n** *UK dispositif de tirage des numéros gagnants des 'Premium Bonds'.*

erode [ɪ'rəʊd] ■ **vt 1.** [rock, soil] éroder **2.** *fig* [confidence, rights] réduire.
■ **vi 1.** [rock, soil] s'éroder **2.** *fig* [confidence] diminuer / [rights] se réduire.

erogenous zone [ɪ'rɒdʒɪnəs-] **n** zone *f* érogène.

erosion [ɪ'rəʊʒn] **n 1.** [of rock, soil] érosion *f* **2.** *fig* [of confidence] baisse *f* / [of rights] diminution *f.*

erotic [ɪ'rɒtɪk] **adj** érotique.

erotica [ɪ'rɒtɪkə] **npl** ART art *m* érotique / LIT littérature *f* érotique.

erotically [ɪ'rɒtɪklɪ] **adv** érotiquement.

eroticism [ɪ'rɒtɪsɪzm] **n** érotisme *m.*

err [ɜ:ʳ] **vi** se tromper ▸ **to err is human** l'erreur est humaine ▸ **to err on the side of** pécher par excès de.

errand ['erənd] **n** course *f*, commission *f* ▸ **to go on** ***or*** **run an errand** faire une course.

errata [e'rɑ:tə] ■ **npl** ➤ ***erratum***.
■ **npl** [list] errata *m inv.*

erratic [ɪ'rætɪk] **adj** irrégulier(ère).

erratically [ɪ'rætɪklɪ] **adv** [act, behave] de manière fantasque ***or*** capricieuse / [move, work] irrégulièrement, par à-coups ▸ **he drives erratically** il conduit de façon déconcertante.

erratum [e'rɑ:təm] (pl **errata**) **n** erratum *m.*

erroneous [ɪ'rəʊnjəs] **adj** *fml* erroné(e).

error ['erəʳ] **n** erreur *f* ▸ **a spelling/typing error** une faute d'orthographe/de frappe ▸ **an error of judgment** une erreur de jugement ▸ **in error** par erreur.

error message **n** COMPUT message *m* d'erreur.

erstwhile ['ɜ:stwaɪl] **adj** *liter* d'autrefois.

erudite ['eru:daɪt] **adj** savant(e).

erupt [ɪ'rʌpt] **vi 1.** [volcano] entrer en éruption **2.** *fig* [violence, war] éclater.

eruption [ɪ'rʌpʃn] n 1. [of volcano] éruption *f* 2. [of violence] explosion *f* / [of war] déclenchement *m*.

ESA (abbr of ***European Space Agency***) n ESA *f*, ASE *f*.

escalate ['eskəleɪt] vi 1. [conflict] s'intensifier 2. [costs] monter en flèche.

escalation [ˌeskə'leɪʃn] n 1. [of conflict, violence] intensification *f* 2. [of costs] montée *f* en flèche.

escalator ['eskəleɪtəʳ] n escalier *m* roulant.

escalator clause n clause *f* d'indexation.

escalope ['eskəˌlɒp] n escalope *f*.

escapade [ˌeskə'peɪd] n aventure *f*, exploit *m*.

escape [ɪ'skeɪp] ■ n 1. [gen] fuite *f*, évasion *f* ▸ **to make one's escape** s'échapper ▸ **to have a lucky escape** l'échapper belle 2. [leakage - of gas, water] fuite *f*.
■ vt échapper à ▸ **to escape doing sthg** éviter de faire qqch ▸ **to escape notice** échapper à l'attention.
■ vi 1. [gen] s'échapper, fuir / [from prison] s'évader ▸ **to escape from** [place] s'échapper de / [danger, person] échapper à ▸ **he escaped to Italy** il s'est enfui en Italie 2. [survive] s'en tirer.

escape artist *US* = ***escapologist***.

escape clause n clause *f* échappatoire.

escaped [ɪ'skeɪpt] adj échappé(e) ▸ **an escaped prisoner** un évadé.

escape key n COMPUT touche *f* d'échappement.

escape route n 1. [from prison] moyen *m* d'évasion 2. [from fire] *itinéraire d'évacuation en cas d'incendie*.

escapism [ɪ'skeɪpɪzm] n *(U)* évasion *f* (de la réalité).

escapist [ɪ'skeɪpɪst] adj [literature, film] d'évasion.

escapologist [ˌeskə'pɒlədʒɪst], **escape artist** *US* n virtuose *mf* de l'évasion.

escarpment [ɪ'skɑːpmənt] n escarpement *m*.

eschew [ɪs'tʃuː] vt *fml* s'abstenir de.

escort ■ n ['eskɔːt] 1. [guard] escorte *f* ▸ **under escort** sous escorte 2. [companion - male] cavalier *m* / [- female] hôtesse *f*.
■ vt [ɪ'skɔːt] escorter, accompagner.

escort agency n agence *f* d'hôtesses.

ESF [iːes'ef] (abbr of ***European Social Fund***) n FSE *m*.

e-shopping n *(U)* cyberachat *m*.

Eskimo ['eskɪməʊ] ■ adj esquimau(aude).
■ n (pl -s) 1. [person] Esquimau *m*, -aude *f* *(attention: le terme 'Eskimo', comme son équivalent français, est souvent considéré comme injurieux en Amérique du Nord. On préférera le terme 'Inuit')* 2. [language] esquimau *m*.

ESL (abbr of ***English as a Second Language***) n *anglais deuxième langue*.

esophagus *US* = ***oesophagus***.

esoteric [ˌesə'terɪk] adj ésotérique.

esp. abbr of ***especially***.

ESP n 1. (abbr of ***extrasensory perception***) perception *f* extrasensorielle 2. (abbr of ***English for special purposes***) *anglais à usage professionnel*.

espadrille [ˌespə'drɪl] n espadrille *f*.

especial [ɪ'speʃl] adj *fml* spécial(e), particulier(ère).

especially [ɪ'speʃəlɪ] adv 1. [in particular] surtout 2. [more than usually] particulièrement 3. [specifically] spécialement.

Esperanto [ˌespə'ræntəʊ] n espéranto *m*.

espionage ['espɪəˌnɑːʒ] n espionnage *m*.

esplanade [ˌesplə'neɪd] n esplanade *f*.

espouse [ɪ'spaʊz] vt épouser.

espresso [e'spresəʊ] (pl -s) n express *m inv*.

Esq. abbr of ***Esquire***.

Esquire [ɪ'skwaɪəʳ] n : **G. Curry Esquire** Monsieur G. Curry.

essay ['eseɪ] n 1. SCH & UNIV dissertation *f* 2. LIT essai *m*.

essayist ['eseɪɪst] n essayiste *mf*.

essence ['esns] n 1. [nature] essence *f*, nature *f* ▸ **in essence** par essence 2. CULIN extrait *m*.

essential [ɪ'senʃl] adj 1. [absolutely necessary] : **essential (to** *OR* **for)** indispensable (à) 2. [basic] essentiel(elle), de base.
◆ ***essentials*** npl 1. [basic commodities] produits *mpl* de première nécessité 2. [most important elements] essentiel *m*.

essentially [ɪ'senʃəlɪ] adv essentiellement, fondamentalement.

est. abbr of ***established***, ***estimated***, ***estimate***.

EST (abbr of ***Eastern Standard Time***) n *heure d'hiver de la côte est des États-Unis*.

establish [ɪ'stæblɪʃ] vt 1. [gen] établir ▸ **to establish contact with** établir le contact avec ▸ **it has been established that there is no case against the defendant** il a été démontré qu'il n'y a pas lieu de poursuivre l'accusé 2. [organization, business] fonder, créer.

established [ɪ'stæblɪʃt] adj 1. [custom] établi(e) 2. [business, company] fondé(e).

establishment [ɪ'stæblɪʃmənt] n 1. [gen] établissement *m* 2. [of organization, business] fondation *f*, création *f*.
◆ ***Establishment*** n [status quo] : **the Establishment** l'ordre *m* établi, l'Establishment *m*.

estate [ɪ'steɪt] n 1. [land, property] propriété *f*, domaine *m* 2. : **(housing) estate** lotissement *m* 3. *US* : **(industrial) estate** zone *f* industrielle 4. LAW [inheritance] biens *mpl*.

estate agency n *UK* agence *f* immobilière.

estate agent n *UK* agent *m* immobilier.

estate car n *UK* break *m*.

estd., **est'd.** abbr of ***established***.

esteem [ɪ'stiːm] ■ n estime *f* ▸ **to hold sb/sthg in high esteem** tenir qqn/qqch en haute estime.
■ vt estimer.

esthetic *US* = ***aesthetic*** etc.

estimate ■ n ['estɪmət] 1. [calculation, judgment] estimation *f*, évaluation *f* 2. COMM devis *m*.
■ vt ['estɪmeɪt] estimer, évaluer.
■ vi ['estɪmeɪt] COMM : **to estimate for** faire *OR* établir un devis pour.

estimated ['estɪmeɪtɪd] adj estimé(e).

estimation [ˌestɪ'meɪʃn] **n** **1.** [opinion] opinion *f* **2.** [calculation] estimation *f*, évaluation *f*.

Estonia [e'stəʊnɪə] **n** Estonie *f* ▸ **in Estonia** en Estonie.

Estonian [e'stəʊnɪən] ■ **adj** estonien(enne).
■ **n** **1.** [person] Estonien *m*, -enne *f* **2.** [language] estonien *m*.

estranged [ɪ'streɪndʒd] **adj** [couple] séparé(e) / [husband, wife] dont on s'est séparé.

estrogen *US* = ***oestrogen***.

estuary ['estjʊərɪ] (**pl -ies**) **n** estuaire *m*.

ETA (abbr of ***estimated time of arrival***) **n** HPA *f*.

e-tailer **n** détaillant *m* en ligne.

et al. ['etæl] (abbr of ***et alii***) et coll., et al.

etc. (abbr of ***et cetera***) etc.

etcetera [ɪt'setərə] **adv** et cetera.

etch [etʃ] **vt** graver à l'eau forte ▸ **to be etched on sb's memory** être gravé dans la mémoire de qqn.

etching ['etʃɪŋ] **n** gravure *f* à l'eau forte.

ETD (abbr of ***estimated time of departure***) **n** HPD *f*.

eternal [ɪ'tɜ:nl] **adj** **1.** [life] éternel(elle) **2.** *fig* [complaints, whining] sempiternel(elle) **3.** [truth, value] immuable.

eternally [ɪ'tɜ:nəlɪ] **adv** éternellement.

eternity [ɪ'tɜ:nətɪ] **n** éternité *f*.

eternity ring **n** *UK* bague *f* de fidélité.

ether ['i:θər] **n** éther *m*.

ethereal [i:'θɪərɪəl] **adj** éthéré(e).

ethic ['eθɪk] **n** éthique *f*, morale *f*.
◆ ***ethics*** ■ **n** *(U)* [study] éthique *f*, morale *f*.
■ **npl** [morals] morale *f*.

ethical ['eθɪkl] **adj** moral(e).

Ethiopia [ˌi:θɪ'əʊpɪə] **n** Éthiopie *f* ▸ **in Ethiopia** en Éthiopie.

Ethiopian [ˌi:θɪ'əʊpɪən] ■ **adj** éthiopien(enne).
■ **n** Éthiopien *m*, -enne *f*.

ethnic ['eθnɪk] **adj** **1.** [traditions, groups] ethnique **2.** [clothes] folklorique.

ethnic cleansing [-'klenzɪŋ] **n** purification *f* ethnique.

ethnicity ['eθnɪsɪtɪ] **n** appartenance *f* ethnique.

ethnic minority **n** minorité *f* ethnique.

ethnocentric [ˌeθnəʊ'sentrɪk] **adj** ethnocentrique.

ethnology [eθ'nɒlədʒɪ] **n** ethnologie *f*.

ethos ['i:θɒs] **n** éthos *m*.

etiquette ['etɪket] **n** convenances *fpl*, étiquette *f*.

e-trade **n** *(U)* cybercommerce *m*, commerce *m* électronique.

ETV (abbr of ***educational television***) **n** *télévision scolaire*.

etymological [ˌetɪmə'lɒdʒɪkl] **adj** étymologique.

etymologist [ˌetɪ'mɒlədʒist] **n** étymologiste *mf*.

etymology [ˌetɪ'mɒlədʒɪ] (**pl -ies**) **n** étymologie *f*.

EU (abbr of ***European Union***) **n** UE *f* ▸ **EU policy** la politique de l'Union Européenne, la politique communautaire.

eucalyptus [ˌju:kə'lɪptəs] **n** eucalyptus *m*.

eulogize, *UK* ***-ise*** ['ju:lədʒaɪz] **vt** faire le panégyrique de.

eulogy ['ju:lədʒɪ] (**pl -ies**) **n** panégyrique *m*.

eunuch ['ju:nək] **n** eunuque *m*.

euphemism ['ju:fəmɪzm] **n** euphémisme *m*.

euphemistic [ˌju:fə'mɪstɪk] **adj** euphémique.

euphemistically [ˌju:fə'mɪstɪklɪ] **adv** par euphémisme, euphémiquement *fml*.

euphoria [ju:'fɔ:rɪə] **n** euphorie *f*.

euphoric [ju:'fɒrɪk] **adj** euphorique.

Eurasia [jʊə'reɪʒə] **n** Eurasie *f*.

Eurasian [jʊə'reɪʒən] ■ **adj** eurasien(enne).
■ **n** Eurasien *m*, -enne *f*.

eureka [jʊə'ri:kə] **excl** eurêka!

euro ['jʊərəʊ] **n** euro *m*.

Euro- **prefix** euro-.

euro area **n** zone *f* euro.

Eurobabble ['jʊərəʊbæbl] **n** *inf pej* jargon *m* de Bruxelles.

euro cent **n** centime *m*, (euro) cent *m offic*.

Eurocentric ['jʊərəʊˌsentrɪk] **adj** européocentrique.

Eurocheque ['jʊərəʊˌtʃek] **n** *UK* eurochèque *m*.

Eurocrat ['jʊərəˌkræt] **n** eurocrate *mf*.

Eurocurrency ['jʊ:rəʊˌkʌrənsɪ] (**pl -ies**) **n** eurodevise *f* ▸ **Eurocurrency market** marché *m* des eurodevises.

Eurodollar ['jʊərəʊˌdɒlər] **n** eurodollar *m*.

Euro MP (abbr of ***European Member of Parliament***) **n** député *m* OR parlementaire *m* européen, eurodéputé *m*.

Europe ['jʊərəp] **n** Europe *f*.

European [ˌjʊərə'pi:ən] ■ **adj** européen(enne).
■ **n** Européen *m*, -enne *f*.

European Central Bank **n** Banque *f* centrale européenne.

European Commission **n** Commission *f* des communautés européennes.

European Community **n** Communauté *f* européenne.

European Court of Human Rights **n** Cour *f* européenne des droits de l'homme.

European Court of Justice **n** Cour *f* européenne de justice.

European Currency Unit **n** unité *f* monétaire européenne.

European Economic Community **n** Communauté *f* économique européenne.

Europeanism [ˌjʊərə'pi:ənɪzm] **n** européanisme *m*.

Europeanize, *UK* ***-ise*** [ˌjʊərə'pi:ənaɪz] **vt** européaniser.

European Monetary System n Système *m* monétaire européen.

European Parliament n Parlement *m* européen.

European Single Market n Marché *m* unique européen.

European Social Fund n Fonds *m* social européen.

European Standards Commission n comité *m* européen de normalisation.

European Union n Union *f* européenne.

Europhile ['jʊərəʊˌfaɪl] n partisan *m* de l'Europe unie.

Euro-rebel n POL *politicien qui s'oppose à la ligne pro-européenne de son parti.*

Eurosceptic ['jʊərʊəˌskeptɪk] n *UK* eurosceptique *mf.*

Eurostar® ['jʊərəʊstɑːʳ] n Eurostar® *m.*

Eurotunnel® ['jʊərəʊˌtʌnl] n Eurotunnel *m.*

Eurovision® ['jʊərəʊˌvɪʒn] n Eurovision® *f* ▸ **the Eurovision Song Contest** le concours Eurovision de la chanson.

euro zone n zone *f* euro.

Eustachian tube [juː'steɪʃən-] n trompe *f* d'Eustache.

euthanasia [ˌjuːθə'neɪzjə] n euthanasie *f.*

evacuate [ɪ'vækjʊeɪt] vt évacuer.

evacuation [ɪˌvækjʊ'eɪʃn] n évacuation *f.*

evacuee [ɪˌvækjuː'iː] n évacué *m*, -e *f.*

evade [ɪ'veɪd] vt **1.** [gen] échapper à **2.** [issue, question] esquiver, éluder.

evaluate [ɪ'væljʊeɪt] vt évaluer.

evaluation [ɪˌvæljʊ'eɪʃn] n évaluation *f.*

evangelical [ˌiːvæn'dʒelɪkl] adj évangélique.

evangelism [ɪ'vændʒəlɪzm] n évangélisation *f.*

evangelist [ɪ'vændʒəlɪst] n évangéliste *mf.*

evangelize, *UK* ***-ise*** [ɪ'vændʒəlaɪz] vt évangéliser.

evaporate [ɪ'væpəreɪt] vi **1.** [liquid] s'évaporer **2.** *fig* [hopes, fears] s'envoler / [confidence] disparaître.

evaporated milk [ɪ'væpəreɪtɪd-] n lait *m* condensé (non sucré).

evaporation [ɪˌvæpə'reɪʃn] n évaporation *f.*

evasion [ɪ'veɪʒn] n **1.** [of responsibility] dérobade *f* ▸ **tax evasion** évasion *f* fiscale **2.** [lie] faux-fuyant *m.*

evasive [ɪ'veɪsɪv] adj évasif(ive) ▸ **to take evasive action** faire une manœuvre d'évitement.

evasively [ɪ'veɪsɪvlɪ] adv évasivement ▸ **he replied evasively** il a répondu en termes évasifs.

evasiveness [ɪ'veɪsɪvnɪs] n caractère *m* évasif.

eve [iːv] n veille *f.*

even ['iːvn] ■ adj **1.** [speed, rate] régulier(ère) / [temperature, temperament] égal(e) **2.** [flat, level] plat(e), régulier(ère) **3.** [equal - contest] équilibré(e) / [- teams, players] de la même force / [- scores] à égalité ▸ **to get even with sb** se venger de qqn ▸ **now we're even** nous voilà quittes, nous sommes quittes maintenant **4.** [not odd - number] pair(e).

■ adv **1.** [gen] même ▸ **even now** encore maintenant ▸ **even then** même alors ▸ **not even** même pas **2.** [in comparisons] : **even bigger/better/more stupid** encore plus grand/mieux/plus bête.

◆ ***even as*** conj au moment même où.

◆ ***even if*** conj même si.

◆ ***even so*** adv quand même.

◆ ***even though*** conj bien que *(+ subjunctive).*

◆ ***even out*** ■ vt sep égaliser.

■ vi s'égaliser.

even-handed [-'hændɪd] adj impartial(e).

evening ['iːvnɪŋ] n soir *m* / [duration, entertainment] soirée *f* ▸ **(good) evening!** bonsoir! ▸ **in the evening** le soir ▸ **it is 8 o'clock in the evening** il est 8 h du soir ▸ **this evening** ce soir ▸ **that evening** ce soir-là ▸ **tomorrow evening** demain soir.

◆ ***evenings*** adv *US* le soir.

CONFUSABLE / PARONYME

evening

When translating evening, note that *soir* and *soirée* are not interchangeable. *Soir* is used to refer to evening as part of the day, as opposed to morning or afternoon. With *soirée* the emphasis is on the duration of the evening.

evening class n cours *m* du soir.

evening dress n [worn by man] habit *m* de soirée / [worn by woman] robe *f* du soir.

evening star n étoile *f* du berger.

evening wear n *(U)* = ***evening dress.***

evenly ['iːvnlɪ] adv **1.** [breathe, distributed] régulièrement **2.** [equally - divided] également ▸ **to be evenly matched** être de la même force **3.** [calmly] calmement, sur un ton égal.

evenness ['iːvnnɪs] n **1.** [of breathing] régularité *f* **2.** [equality] bon équilibre *m.*

evensong ['iːvnsɒŋ] n vêpres *fpl.*

event [ɪ'vent] n **1.** [happening] événement *m* **2.** SPORT épreuve *f* **3.** [case] : **in the event of** en cas de ▸ **in the event that** au cas où.

◆ ***in any event*** adv en tout cas, de toute façon.

◆ ***in the event*** adv *UK* en l'occurrence, en réalité.

even-tempered [-'tempəd] adj d'humeur égale.

eventful [ɪ'ventfʊl] adj mouvementé(e).

eventide home ['iːvntaɪd-] n *UK euph* hospice *m* de vieillards.

eventing [ɪ'ventɪŋ] n *UK* SPORT : **(three-day) eventing** concours *m* complet.

eventual [ɪ'ventʃʊəl] adj final(e) ▸ **the eventual winner was X** finalement, le vainqueur a été X.

eventuality [ɪˌventʃʊ'ælətɪ] (pl **-ies**) n éventualité *f.*

eventually [ɪ'ventʃʊəlɪ] **adv** finalement, en fin de compte.

FALSE FRIENDS / FAUX AMIS
eventually

Éventuellement n'est pas la traduction du mot anglais *eventually*. Éventuellement se traduit par *possibly*.
▸ Je pourrais éventuellement revenir demain / *I could possibly come back tomorrow*

ever ['evəʳ] **adv 1.** [at any time] jamais ▸ **have you ever been to Paris?** êtes-vous déjà allé à Paris? ▸ **I hardly ever see him** je ne le vois presque jamais ▸ **if ever** si jamais ▸ **all they ever do is work** ils ne font que travailler / [with comparatives] **: lovelier/more slowly than ever** plus joli/plus lentement que jamais ▸ **he's as sarcastic as ever** il est toujours aussi sarcastique / [with superlatives] **: the first/biggest ever** le tout premier/plus grand qu'on ait jamais vu **2.** [all the time] toujours ▸ **as ever** comme toujours ▸ **for ever** pour toujours **3.** [for emphasis] **: ever so** *UK* tellement ▸ **ever such** *UK* vraiment ▸ **why/how ever?** pourquoi/comment donc? ▸ **is he ever stupid!** *US* ce qu'il est bête! ▸ **they lived happily ever after** ils vécurent heureux jusqu'à la fin de leurs jours.
◆ ***ever since*** ■ **adv** depuis (ce moment-là).
■ **conj** depuis que.
■ **prep** depuis.

Everest ['evərɪst] **n** l'Everest *m*.

Everglades ['evə,gleɪdz] **npl : the Everglades** les Everglades *mpl*.

evergreen ['evəgri:n] ■ **adj** à feuilles persistantes.
■ **n** arbre *m* à feuilles persistantes.

everlasting [,evə'lɑ:stɪŋ] **adj** éternel(elle).

every ['evrɪ] **adj** chaque ▸ **every morning** chaque matin, tous les matins ▸ **there's every chance she'll pass the exam** elle a toutes les chances de réussir à son examen ▸ **every (single) one of these pencils is broken** tous ces crayons (sans exception) sont cassés ▸ **once every month** une fois par mois.
◆ ***every now and then, every so often*** **adv** de temps en temps, de temps à autre.
◆ ***every other*** **adj : every other day** tous les deux jours, un jour sur deux ▸ **every other street** une rue sur deux.
◆ ***every which way*** **adv** *US* partout, de tous côtés.

everybody ['evrɪ,bɒdɪ] = ***everyone***.

everyday ['evrɪdeɪ] **adj** quotidien(enne).

everyone ['evrɪwʌn] **pron** chacun, tout le monde.

everyplace *inf US* = ***everywhere***.

everything ['evrɪθɪŋ] **pron** tout.

everywhere ['evrɪweəʳ] **adv** partout.

evict [ɪ'vɪkt] **vt** expulser.

eviction [ɪ'vɪkʃn] **n** expulsion *f*.

eviction notice **n** avis *m* d'expulsion.

evidence ['evɪdəns] **n** *(U)* **1.** [proof] preuve *f* **2.** LAW [of witness] témoignage *m* ▸ **to give evidence** témoigner.
◆ ***in evidence*** **adj** [noticeable] en évidence.

evident ['evɪdənt] **adj** évident(e), manifeste.

evidently ['evɪdəntlɪ] **adv 1.** [seemingly] apparemment **2.** [obviously] de toute évidence, manifestement.

evil ['i:vl] ■ **adj** [person] mauvais(e), malveillant(e).
■ **n** mal *m*.

evil eye **n : the evil eye** le mauvais œil ▸ **to give sb the evil eye** jeter le mauvais œil à qqn.

evil-minded [-'maɪndɪd] **adj** malveillant(e), malintentionné(e).

evince [ɪ'vɪns] **vt** *fml* faire montre de.

evocation [,evəʊ'keɪʃn] **n** évocation *f*.

evocative [ɪ'vɒkətɪv] **adj** évocateur(trice).

evoke [ɪ'vəʊk] **vt** [memory] évoquer / [emotion, response] susciter.

evolution [,i:və'lu:ʃn] **n** évolution *f*.

evolutionary [,i:və'lu:ʃnərɪ] **adj** évolutionniste.

evolve [ɪ'vɒlv] ■ **vt** développer.
■ **vi : to evolve (into/from)** se développer (en/à partir de).

ewe [ju:] **n** brebis *f*.

ex [eks] ■ **prep 1.** COMM départ, sortie ▸ **price ex works** prix *m* départ ***OR*** sortie usine **2.** FIN sans.
■ **n** *inf* [gen] ex *mf* / [husband] ex-mari *m* / [wife] ex-femme *f* ▸ **my ex** [girlfriend] mon ancienne petite amie / [boyfriend] mon ancien petit ami.

ex- [eks] **prefix** ex-.

exacerbate [ɪg'zæsəbeɪt] **vt** [feeling] exacerber / [problems] aggraver.

exact [ɪg'zækt] ■ **adj** exact(e), précis(e) ▸ **to be exact** pour être exact ***OR*** précis, exactement.
■ **vt : to exact sthg (from)** exiger qqch (de).

exacting [ɪg'zæktɪŋ] **adj** [job, standards] astreignant(e) / [person] exigeant(e).

exactitude [ɪg'zæktɪtju:d] **n** exactitude *f*.

exactly [ɪg'zæktlɪ] ■ **adv** exactement ▸ **it's not exactly what I expected** ce n'est pas tout à fait ce que j'attendais.
■ **excl** exactement!, parfaitement!

exaggerate [ɪg'zædʒəreɪt] **vt & vi** exagérer.

exaggerated [ɪg'zædʒəreɪtɪd] **adj** [sigh, smile] forcé(e).

exaggeratedly [ɪg'zædʒəreɪtɪdlɪ] **adv** d'une manière exagérée, exagérément.

exaggeration [ɪg,zædʒə'reɪʃn] **n** exagération *f*.

exalted [ɪg'zɔ:ltɪd] **adj** haut placé(e).

exam [ɪg'zæm] **n** examen *m* ▸ **to take *OR* sit *UK* an exam** passer un examen ▸ **to pass/to fail an exam** réussir à/échouer à un examen.

examination [ɪg,zæmɪ'neɪʃn] **n** examen *m*.

examination board **n** comité *m* d'examen.

examine [ɪg'zæmɪn] **vt 1.** [gen] examiner / [passport] contrôler **2.** LAW, SCH & UNIV interroger.

examiner [ɪg'zæmɪnəʳ] **n** *UK* examinateur *m*, -trice *f* ▸ **internal/external examiner** UNIV examinateur *m* de l'établissement/de l'extérieur.

examining body [ɪg'zæmɪnɪŋ-] **n** jury *m* d'examen.

exam paper **n** *UK* [test] sujet *m* (d'examen) / [answers] copie *f*.

example [ɪg'zɑ:mpl] **n** exemple *m* ▸ **for example** par exemple ▸ **to follow sb's example** suivre l'exemple de qqn ▸ **to set an example** montrer l'exemple ▸ **to make an example of sb** punir qqn pour l'exemple.

exam room *US* = ***consulting room***.

exasperate [ɪg'zæspəreɪt] **vt** exaspérer.

exasperating [ɪg'zæspəreɪtɪŋ] **adj** énervant(e), exaspérant(e).

exasperatingly [ɪg'zæspəreɪtɪŋlɪ] **adv : the service is exasperatingly slow in this restaurant** le service est d'une lenteur exaspérante *OR* désespérante dans ce restaurant.

exasperation [ɪg,zæspə'reɪʃn] **n** exaspération *f*.

excavate ['ekskəveɪt] **vt 1.** [land] creuser **2.** [object] déterrer.

excavation [,ekskə'veɪʃn] **n 1.** [gen] excavation *f* **2.** ARCHEOL fouilles *fpl*.

excavator ['ekskə,veɪtə'] **n** *UK* [machine] pelleteuse *f*.

exceed [ɪk'si:d] **vt 1.** [amount, number] excéder **2.** [limit, expectations] dépasser.

exceedingly [ɪk'si:dɪŋlɪ] **adv** extrêmement.

excel [ɪk'sel] (pt & pp **-led**, cont **-ling**) **vi : to excel (in** *OR* **at)** exceller (dans) ▸ **to excel o.s.** *UK* se surpasser.

excellence ['eksələns] **n** excellence *f*, supériorité *f*.

Excellency ['eksələnsɪ] (pl **-ies**) **n** Excellence *f*.

excellent ['eksələnt] **adj** excellent(e).

except [ɪk'sept] ■ **prep & conj : except (for)** à part, sauf ▸ **except weekends** à part *OR* excepté *OR* sauf le week-end ▸ **except if** sauf *OR* à part si.
■ **vt : to except sb (from)** exclure qqn (de).

excepted [ɪk'septɪd] **adj** à part, excepté(e) ▸ **present company excepted** à l'exception des personnes présentes.

excepting [ɪk'septɪŋ] *fml* **prep & conj** = ***except***.

exception [ɪk'sepʃn] **n 1.** [exclusion] **: exception (to)** exception *f* (à) ▸ **with the exception of** à l'exception de ▸ **without exception** sans exception **2.** [offence] **: to take exception to** s'offenser de, se froisser de.

exceptional [ɪk'sepʃənl] **adj** exceptionnel(elle).

exceptionally [ɪk'sepʃnəlɪ] **adv** exceptionnellement.

excerpt ['eksɜ:pt] **n : excerpt (from)** extrait *m* (de), passage *m* (de).

excess [ɪk'ses] *(before nouns* ['ekses]*)* ■ **adj** excédentaire.
■ **n** excès *m* ▸ **to be in excess of** dépasser ▸ **to excess** à l'excès.

excess baggage **n** excédent *m* de bagages.

excess fare **n** *UK* supplément *m*.

excessive [ɪk'sesɪv] **adj** excessif(ive).

excessively [ɪk'sesɪvlɪ] **adv** excessivement.

excess luggage = ***excess baggage***.

exchange [ɪks'tʃeɪndʒ] ■ **n 1.** [gen] échange *m* ▸ **in exchange (for)** en échange (de) **2.** TELEC **: (telephone) exchange** central *m* (téléphonique) **3.** FIN change *m* ▸ **foreign exchange office** bureau *m* de change.
■ **vt** [swap] échanger ▸ **to exchange sthg for sthg** échanger qqch contre qqch ▸ **to exchange sthg with sb** échanger qqch avec qqn.

exchange rate **n** FIN taux *m* de change.

Exchange Rate Mechanism **n** mécanisme *m* (des taux) de change (du SME).

Exchequer [ɪks'tʃekə'] **n** *UK* **: the Exchequer** ≃ le ministère des Finances.

excise ['eksaɪz] ■ **n** *(U)* contributions *fpl* indirectes.
■ **vt** *fml* [tumour] exciser / [passage from book] supprimer.

excise duties **npl** droits *mpl* de régie.

excise duty ['eksaɪz-] **n** [taxation] contribution *f* indirecte.

excitable [ɪk'saɪtəbl] **adj** excitable.

excite [ɪk'saɪt] **vt** exciter.

excited [ɪk'saɪtɪd] **adj** excité(e).

excitedly [ɪk'saɪtɪdlɪ] **adv** [behave, watch] avec agitation / [say] sur un ton animé / [wait] fébrilement.

excitement [ɪk'saɪtmənt] **n 1.** [state] excitation *f* **2.** [exciting thing] sensation *f*, émotion *f*.

exciting [ɪk'saɪtɪŋ] **adj** passionnant(e) / [prospect] excitant(e).

excl. **1.** (abbr of ***excluding***) ▸ **excl. taxes** HT **2.** abbr of ***exclude(d)***.

exclaim [ɪk'skleɪm] ■ **vt** s'écrier.
■ **vi** s'exclamer.

exclamation [,ekskləˈmeɪʃn] **n** exclamation *f*.

exclamation mark *UK*, ***exclamation point*** *US* **n** point *m* d'exclamation.

exclude [ɪk'sklu:d] **vt : to exclude sb/sthg (from)** exclure qqn/qqch (de).

excluding [ɪk'sklu:dɪŋ] **prep** sans compter, à l'exclusion de.

exclusion [ɪk'sklu:ʒn] **n : exclusion (from)** exclusion *f* (de) ▸ **to the exclusion of** à l'exclusion de.

exclusion clause **n** clause *f* d'exclusion.

exclusive [ɪk'sklu:sɪv] ■ **adj 1.** [high-class] fermé(e) **2.** [unique - use, news story] exclusif(ive) ▸ **to have an exclusive contract with a company** avoir un contrat exclusif avec une société.
■ **n** PRESS exclusivité *f*.
◆ ***exclusive of*** **prep : exclusive of interest** intérêts non compris.

exclusive licence **n** licence *f* exclusive.

exclusively [ɪk'sklu:sɪvlɪ] **adv** exclusivement.

exclusiveness [ɪk'sklu:sɪvnɪs], ***exclusivity*** [,eksklu:'sɪvətɪ] **n 1.** [of restaurant, address, district] chic *m* **2.** [of contract] nature *f* exclusive.

exclusive rights **n** droits *mpl* exclusifs, exclusivité *f*.

excommunicate [,ekskə'mju:nɪkeɪt] **vt** excommunier.

excommunication ['ekskə,mju:nɪ'keɪʃn] **n** excommunication *f*.

excrement ['ekskrɪmənt] **n** excrément *m*.

excrete [ɪk'skri:t] **vt** excréter.

excruciating [ɪk'skru:ʃieɪtɪŋ] **adj** atroce.

excruciatingly [ɪk'skru:ʃieɪtɪŋlɪ] **adv** [painful, boring] atrocement, affreusement.

excursion [ɪk'skɜ:ʃn] **n** [trip] excursion *f*.

excusable [ɪk'skju:zəbl] **adj** excusable.

excuse ■ **n** [ɪk'skju:s] excuse *f* ▸ **I'm not making excuses for them** je ne les excuse pas ▸ **to make one's excuses** s'excuser, présenter ses excuses.
■ **vt** [ɪk'skju:z] **1.** [gen] excuser ▸ **to excuse sb for sthg/for doing sthg** excuser qqn de qqch/de faire qqch ▸ **to excuse o.s. (for doing sthg)** s'excuser (de faire qqch) ▸ **I'll excuse your lateness (just) this once** je te pardonne ton retard pour cette fois ▸ **excuse me** [to attract attention] excusez-moi / [forgive me] pardon, excusez-moi / *US* [sorry] pardon **2.** [let off] **: to excuse sb (from)** dispenser qqn (de).

ex-directory **adj** *UK* sur la liste rouge.

exec [ɪg'zek] **abbr of** ***executive***.

execrable ['eksɪkrəbl] **adj** exécrable.

execute ['eksɪkju:t] **vt** exécuter.

execution [ˌeksɪ'kju:ʃn] **n** exécution *f*.

executioner [ˌeksɪ'kju:ʃnər] **n** bourreau *m*.

executive [ɪg'zekjʊtɪv] ■ **adj 1.** [power, board] exécutif(ive) **2.** [desk, chair] de cadre, spécial(e) cadre / [washroom] de la direction.
■ **n 1.** COMM cadre *m* **2.** [of government] exécutif *m* / [of political party] comité *m* central, bureau *m*.

executive director **n** cadre *m* supérieur.

executive toy **n** gadget *m* pour cadres.

executor [ɪg'zekjʊtər] **n** exécuteur *m* testamentaire.

exemplary [ɪg'zemplərɪ] **adj** exemplaire.

exemplify [ɪg'zemplɪfaɪ] (pt & pp -ied) **vt 1.** [typify] exemplifier **2.** [give example of] exemplifier, illustrer.

exempt [ɪg'zempt] ■ **adj : exempt (from)** exempt(e) (de).
■ **vt : to exempt sb (from)** exempter qqn (de).

exemption [ɪg'zempʃn] **n** exemption *f*.

exercise ['eksəsaɪz] ■ **n** exercice *m* ▸ **to take exercise** prendre de l'exercice ▸ **piano exercises** exercices de piano ▸ **it was a pointless exercise** cela n'a servi absolument à rien ▸ **they're on exercises** MIL ils sont à l'exercice.
■ **vt 1.** [gen] exercer / [dog, horse] donner de l'exercice à / [troops] entraîner **2.** [trouble] **: to exercise sb's mind** préoccuper qqn.
■ **vi** prendre de l'exercice.

exercise bike **n** vélo *m* d'appartement.

exercise book **n** *UK* [notebook] cahier *m* d'exercices / [published book] livre *m* d'exercices.

exercise yard **n** [in prison] cour *f*, préau *m*.

exert [ɪg'zɜ:t] **vt** exercer / [strength] employer ▸ **to exert o.s.** se donner du mal.

exertion [ɪg'zɜ:ʃn] **n** effort *m*.

exfoliate [eks'fəʊlɪeɪt] ■ **vi** s'exfolier.
■ **vt** exfolier.

ex gratia [eks'greɪʃə] **adj** [payment] à titre gracieux.

exhale [eks'heɪl] ■ **vt** exhaler.
■ **vi** expirer.

exhaust [ɪg'zɔ:st] ■ **n 1.** *(U)* [fumes] gaz *mpl* d'échappement **2. : exhaust (pipe)** pot *m* OR tuyau *m* d'échappement.
■ **vt** épuiser.

exhausted [ɪg'zɔ:stɪd] **adj** épuisé(e).

exhausting [ɪg'zɔ:stɪŋ] **adj** épuisant(e).

exhaustion [ɪg'zɔ:stʃn] **n** épuisement *m*.

exhaustive [ɪg'zɔ:stɪv] **adj** complet(ète), exhaustif(ive).

exhaustively [ɪg'zɔ:stɪvlɪ] **adv** exhaustivement.

exhaust pipe **n** pot *m* OR tuyau *m* d'échappement.

exhibit [ɪg'zɪbɪt] ■ **n 1.** ART objet *m* exposé **2.** LAW pièce *f* à conviction.
■ **vt 1.** [demonstrate - feeling] montrer / [- skill] faire preuve de **2.** ART exposer.
■ **vi** ART exposer.

exhibition [ˌeksɪ'bɪʃn] **n 1.** ART exposition *f* **2.** [of feeling] démonstration *f*
▸▸ **to make an exhibition of o.s.** *UK* se donner en spectacle.

exhibitionism [ˌeksɪ'bɪʃnɪzm] **n 1.** [gen] besoin *m* OR volonté *f* de se faire remarquer **2.** PSYCHOL exhibitionnisme *m*.

exhibitionist [ˌeksɪ'bɪʃnɪst] **n** exhibitionniste *mf*.

exhibitor [ɪg'zɪbɪtər] **n** exposant *m*, -e *f*.

exhilarate [ɪg'zɪləreɪt] **vt** exalter, griser.

exhilarated [ɪg'zɪləreɪtɪd] **adj** [mood, laugh] exalté(e).

exhilarating [ɪg'zɪləreɪtɪŋ] **adj** [experience] grisant(e) / [walk] vivifiant(e).

exhilaration [ɪgˌzɪlə'reɪʃn] **n** exaltation *f*, griserie *f*.

exhort [ɪg'zɔ:t] **vt : to exhort sb to do sthg** exhorter qqn à faire qqch.

exhume [eks'hju:m] **vt** exhumer.

ex-husband **n** ex-mari *m*.

exile ['eksaɪl] ■ **n 1.** [condition] exil *m* ▸ **in exile** en exil **2.** [person] exilé *m*, -e *f*.
■ **vt : to exile sb (from/to)** exiler qqn (de/vers).

exiled ['eksaɪld] **adj** exilé(e).

exist [ɪg'zɪst] **vi** exister.

existence [ɪg'zɪstəns] **n** existence *f* ▸ **in existence** qui existe, existant(e) ▸ **to come into existence** naître.

existential [ˌegzɪ'stenʃl] **adj** existentiel(elle).

existentialism [ˌegzɪ'stenʃəlɪzm] **n** existentialisme *m*.

existentialist [ˌegzɪ'stenʃəlɪst] ■ **adj** existentialiste.
■ **n** existentialiste *mf*.

existing [ɪg'zɪstɪŋ] **adj** existant(e).

exit ['eksɪt] ■ **n** sortie *f* ▸ **to make one's exit** sortir / THEAT faire sa sortie.
■ **vi** sortir.

exit charge(s) **n** frais *mpl* de sortie.

exit poll **n** *sondage effectué à la sortie des bureaux de vote*.

exit visa **n** visa *m* de sortie.

exodus ['eksədəs] **n** exode *m*.

ex officio [eksə'fɪʃɪəʊ] **adj & adv** ex officio.

exonerate [ɪg'zɒnəreɪt] **vt : to exonerate sb (from)** disculper qqn (de).

exorbitant [ɪg'zɔːbɪtənt] **adj** exorbitant(e).

exorbitantly [ɪg'zɔːbɪtəntlɪ] **adv** [priced] excessivement, démesurément.

exorcism ['eksɔːsɪzm] **n** exorcisme *m* ▸ **to carry out** *OR* **to perform an exorcism** pratiquer un exorcisme.

exorcist ['eksɔːsɪst] **n** exorciste *mf*.

exorcize, *UK* ***-ise*** ['eksɔːsaɪz] **vt** exorciser.

exotic [ɪg'zɒtɪk] **adj** exotique.

exotically [ɪg'zɒtɪklɪ] **adv** [dressed, decorated] avec exotisme ▸ **exotically perfumed** [flower] aux senteurs exotiques / [person] au parfum exotique.

expand [ɪk'spænd] ■ **vt** [production, influence] accroître / [business, department, area] développer.
■ **vi** [population, influence] s'accroître / [business, department, market] se développer / [metal] se dilater.
◆ ***expand (up)on*** **vt insep** développer.

expandable [ɪk'spændɪbl] **adj** [gas, material] expansible / [idea, theory] qui peut être développé / [basic set] qui peut être complété / COMPUT [memory] extensible.

expanding [ɪk'spændɪŋ] **adj 1.** [company, empire, gas, metal] en expansion / [influence] grandissant(e) / [industry, market] en expansion, qui se développe ▸ **the expanding universe theory** la théorie de l'expansion de l'univers **2.** [extendable] **: expanding suitcase/briefcase** valise/serviette extensible.

expanse [ɪk'spæns] **n** étendue *f*.

expansion [ɪk'spænʃn] **n** [of production, population] accroissement *m* / [of business, department, area] développement *m* / [of metal] dilatation *f*.

expansion card **n** COMPUT carte *f* d'extension.

expansionism [ɪk'spænʃənɪzm] **n** expansionnisme *m*.

expansionist [ɪk'spænʃənɪst] **adj** expansionniste.

expansion slot **n** COMPUT créneau *m* pour carte d'extension.

expansive [ɪk'spænsɪv] **adj** expansif(ive).

expansively [ɪk'spænsɪvlɪ] **adv** [talk, gesture] de manière expansive.

expat [ˌeks'pæt] (abbr of ***expatriate***) *inf* ■ **n** expatrié *m*, -e *f*.
■ **adj** [Briton, American] expatrié(e) / [bar, community] des expatriés.

expatriate [eks'pætrɪət] ■ **adj** expatrié(e).
■ **n** expatrié *m*, -e *f*.

expect [ɪk'spekt] ■ **vt 1.** [anticipate] s'attendre à / [event, letter, baby] attendre ▸ **when do you expect it to be ready?** quand pensez-vous que cela sera prêt? ▸ **to expect sb to do sthg** s'attendre à ce que qqn fasse qqch ▸ **(at) what time should we expect you then?** à quelle heure devons-nous vous attendre alors? ▸ **to expect the worst** s'attendre au pire ▸ **I expected as much!** je m'en doutais!, c'est bien ce que je pensais! ▸ **she is as well as can be expected** elle va aussi bien que sa condition le permet **2.** [count on] compter sur **3.** [demand] exiger, demander ▸ **to expect sb to do sthg** attendre de qqn qu'il fasse qqch ▸ **to expect sthg from sb** exiger qqch de qqn ▸ **I'm expected to write all his speeches** je suis censé *OR* supposé rédiger tous ses discours **4.** *UK* [suppose] supposer ▸ **I expect so** je crois que oui ▸ **I expect you're right** tu dois avoir raison.
■ **vi 1.** [anticipate] **: to expect to do sthg** compter faire qqch
2. [be pregnant] **: to be expecting** être enceinte, attendre un bébé.

expectancy ➤ ***life expectancy***.

expectant [ɪk'spektənt] **adj** qui est dans l'expectative.

expectantly [ɪk'spektəntlɪ] **adv** dans l'expectative.

expectant mother **n** femme *f* enceinte.

expectation [ˌekspek'teɪʃn] **n 1.** [hope] espoir *m*, attente *f* ▸ **to have high expectations of sb/sthg** attendre beaucoup de qqn/qqch ▸ **to exceed sb's expectations** dépasser l'attente *OR* les espérances de qqn **2.** [belief] **: it's my expectation that...** à mon avis,... ▸ **against all expectation** *OR* **expectations, contrary to all expectation** *OR* **expectations** contre toute attente.

expected [ɪk'spektɪd] **adj** attendu(e).

expectorant [ɪk'spektərənt] **n** expectorant *m*.

expedient [ɪk'spiːdjənt] *fml* ■ **adj** indiqué(e).
■ **n** expédient *m*.

expedite ['ekspɪdaɪt] **vt** *fml* accélérer / [arrival, departure] hâter.

expedition [ˌekspɪ'dɪʃn] **n** expédition *f*.

expeditionary force ['ekspɪ'dɪʃnərɪ-] **n** corps *m* expéditionnaire.

expel [ɪk'spel] (pt & pp **-led**, cont **-ling**) **vt 1.** [gen] expulser **2.** SCH renvoyer.

expend [ɪk'spend] **vt : to expend time/money (on)** consacrer du temps/de l'argent (à).

expendability [ɪkˌspendə'bɪlətɪ] **n** [of people, workforce, equipment] superfluité *f* / [of troops, spies] caractère *m* sacrifiable.

expendable [ɪk'spendəbl] **adj** [person, workforce, equipment] superflu(e) / [troops, spies] qui peut être sacrifié(e).

expenditure [ɪk'spendɪtʃər] **n** *(U)* dépense *f*.

expense [ɪk'spens] **n 1.** [amount spent] dépense *f* **2.** *(U)* [cost] frais *mpl* ▸ **to go to great expense (to do sthg)** faire beaucoup de frais (pour faire qqch) ▸ **at the expense of** au prix de ▸ **at sb's expense** [financial] aux frais de qqn / *fig* aux dépens de qqn.
◆ ***expenses*** **npl** COMM frais *mpl* ▸ **on expenses** sur la note de frais.

expense account **n** frais *mpl* de représentation.

expenses-paid **adj** [trip, holiday] tous frais payés.

expensive [ɪk'spensɪv] **adj 1.** [financially - gen] cher (chère), coûteux(euse) / [- tastes] dispendieux(euse) **2.** [mistake] qui coûte cher.

expensively [ɪk'pensɪvlɪ] **adv** à grands frais.

experience [ɪk'spɪərɪəns] ■ **n** expérience *f* ▸ **do you have any experience of working with animals?** avez-vous déjà travaillé avec des animaux? ▸ **to speak from**

experience parler en connaissance de cause ▸ **to put sthg down to experience** tirer un enseignement *OR* une leçon de qqch.
▪ **vt** [difficulty] connaître / [disappointment] éprouver, ressentir / [loss, change] subir.

experienced [ɪk'spɪərɪənst] **adj** expérimenté(e) ▸ **to be experienced at** *OR* **in sthg** avoir de l'expérience en *OR* en matière de qqch.

experiment [ɪk'sperɪmənt] ▪ **n** expérience *f* ▸ **to carry out an experiment** faire une expérience.
▪ **vi : to experiment (with sthg)** expérimenter (qqch) ▸ **to experiment on** faire une expérience sur.

experimental [ɪk,sperɪ'mentl] **adj** expérimental(e).

experimentally [ɪk,sperɪ'mentəlɪ] **adv** [by experimenting] expérimentalement / [as an experiment] à titre expérimental.

experimentation [ɪk,sperɪmen'teɪʃn] **n** expérimentation *f.*

expert ['ekspɜ:t] ▪ **adj** expert(e) / [advice] d'expert ▸ **expert at sthg/at doing sthg** expert en qqch/à faire qqch.
▪ **n** expert *m*, -e *f.*

expertise [,ekspɜ:'ti:z] **n** *(U)* compétence *f.*

expertly ['ekspɜ:tlɪ] **adv** d'une manière experte, expertement.

expert system **n** COMPUT système *m* expert.

expiate ['ekspɪeɪt] **vt** expier.

expiration *US* = ***expiry.***

expiration date *US* = ***expiry date.***

expire [ɪk'spaɪər] **vi** expirer.

expiry [ɪk'spaɪərɪ] **n** *UK* expiration *f.*

expiry date **n** *UK* date *f* de péremption.

explain [ɪk'spleɪn] ▪ **vt** expliquer ▸ **to explain sthg to sb** expliquer qqch à qqn.
▪ **vi** s'expliquer ▸ **to explain to sb (about sthg)** expliquer (qqch) à qqn.
◆ ***explain away*** **vt sep** justifier.

explanation [,eksplə'neɪʃn] **n : explanation (for)** explication *f* (de).

explanatory [ɪk'splænətrɪ] **adj** explicatif(ive).

expletive [ɪk'spli:tɪv] **n** *fml* juron *m.*

explicit [ɪk'splɪsɪt] **adj** explicite ▸ **sexually explicit** à teneur sexuelle explicite.

explicitly [ɪk'splɪsɪtlɪ] **adv** explicitement.

explode [ɪk'spləʊd] ▪ **vt 1.** [bomb] faire exploser **2.** *fig* [theory] discréditer.
▪ **vi** *lit* & *fig* exploser.

exploit ▪ **n** ['eksplɔɪt] exploit *m.*
▪ **vt** [ɪk'splɔɪt] exploiter.

exploitation [,eksplɔɪ'teɪʃn] **n** *(U)* exploitation *f.*

exploitative [ɪk'splɔɪtətɪv] **adj** [practices] relevant de l'exploitation ▸ **the company's exploitative attitude towards the workforce** la manière dont l'entreprise exploite la main-d'œuvre.

exploration [,eksplə'reɪʃn] **n** exploration *f.*

exploratory [ɪk'splɒrətrɪ] **adj** exploratoire.

explore [ɪk'splɔ:r] **vt** & **vi** explorer.

explorer [ɪk'splɔ:rər] **n** explorateur *m*, -trice *f.*

explosion [ɪk'spləʊʒn] **n** explosion *f* / [of interest, emotion] débordement *m.*

explosive [ɪk'spləʊsɪv] ▪ **adj** *lit* & *fig* explosif(ive).
▪ **n** explosif *m.*

explosive device **n** engin *m* explosif.

exponent [ɪk'spəʊnənt] **n** [of theory] défenseur *m.*

exponential [,ekspə'nenʃl] **adj** exponentiel(elle).

export ▪ **n** ['ekspɔ:t] exportation *f.*
▪ **comp** ['ekspɔ:t] d'exportation.
▪ **vt** [ɪk'spɔ:t] exporter.
◆ ***exports*** **npl** exportations *fpl.*

exportable [ɪk'spɔ:təbl] **adj** exportable.

exportation [,ekspɔ:'teɪʃn] **n** exportation *f.*

export ban **n** interdiction *f* d'exporter.

exporter [ek'spɔ:tər] **n** exportateur *m*, -trice *f.*

export licence *UK*, ***export license*** *US* **n** permis *m* d'exportation.

expose [ɪk'spəʊz] **vt 1.** [uncover] exposer, découvrir ▸ **to be exposed to sthg** être exposé à qqch **2.** [unmask - corruption] révéler / [- person] démasquer.

exposé [eks'pəʊzeɪ] **n** exposé *m.*

exposed [ɪk'spəʊzd] **adj** [land, house, position] exposé(e).

exposition [,ekspə'zɪʃn] **n 1.** *fml* [explanation] exposé *m* **2.** [exhibition] exposition *f.*

HOW TO ...

ask for and give explanations

Asking for explanations

Qu'est-ce que tu veux dire, exactement ? / What do you mean exactly?
C'est-à-dire ? / Meaning?
Pourriez-vous être plus précis ? / Could you be a little more specific?
Qu'entendez-vous par là ? / What do you mean by that?
Où est-ce que tu veux en venir, au juste ? / Where exactly are you heading with that?
Comment ça ? / How do you mean?

Giving explanations

Je veux/voulais dire que... / I mean/meant that...
Je vais tâcher d'être plus clair... / Let me try to explain a little more clearly...
Je m'explique : ... / Let me explain:...
Ce que j'essaie de dire, c'est... / What I'm trying to say is...

exposure [ɪk'spəʊʒəʳ] **n 1.** [to light, radiation] exposition *f* **2.** MED **: to die of exposure** mourir de froid **3.** [unmasking - of corruption] révélation *f* / [- of person] dénonciation *f* **4.** [PHOT - time] temps *m* de pose / [- photograph] pose *f* **5.** *(U)* [publicity] publicité *f* / [coverage] couverture *f*.

exposure meter **n** posemètre *m*.

expound [ɪk'spaʊnd] *fml* ■ **vt** exposer.
■ **vi : to expound on** faire un exposé sur.

express [ɪk'spres] ■ **adj 1.** *UK* [letter, delivery] exprès *(inv)* **2.** [train, coach] express *(inv)* **3.** *fml* [specific] exprès(esse).
■ **adv** exprès.
■ **n** [train] rapide *m*, express *m*.
■ **vt** exprimer ▸ **to express o.s.** s'exprimer.

expression [ɪk'spreʃn] **n** expression *f*.

expressionism [ɪk'spreʃənɪzm] **n** expressionnisme *m*.

expressionist [ɪk'spreʃənɪst] ■ **adj** expressionniste.
■ **n** expressionniste *mf*.

expressionistic [ɪk,spreʃə'nɪstɪk] **adj** ART expressionniste.

expressionless [ɪk'spreʃənlɪs] **adj** [voice] sans expression / [face] impassible.

expressive [ɪk'spresɪv] **adj** expressif(ive).

expressively [ɪk'spresɪvlɪ] **adv** de façon expressive.

expressiveness [ɪk'spresɪvnɪs] **n** [of face, gesture, smile] expressivité *f*.

expressly [ɪk'spreslɪ] **adv** expressément.

expressway [ɪk'spresweɪ] **n** *US* voie *f* express.

expropriate [eks'prəʊprɪeɪt] **vt** exproprier.

expropriation [eks,prəʊprɪ'eɪʃn] **n** expropriation *f*.

expulsion [ɪk'spʌlʃn] **n 1.** [gen] expulsion *f* **2.** SCH renvoi *m*.

exquisite [ɪk'skwɪzɪt] **adj** exquis(e).

exquisitely [ɪk'skwɪzɪtlɪ] **adv** de façon exquise.

ex-serviceman **n** *UK* ancien combattant *m*.

ex-servicewoman **n** *UK* ancienne combattante *f*.

ext., ***extn.*** (abbr of ***extension***) **: ext. 4174** p. 4174.

extant [ek'stænt] **adj** qui existe encore.

extemporize, *UK* ***-ise*** [ɪk'stempəraɪz] **vi** *fml* improviser.

extend [ɪk'stend] ■ **vt 1.** [enlarge - building] agrandir **2.** [make longer - gen] prolonger / [- visa] proroger / [- deadline] repousser **3.** [expand - rules, law] étendre (la portée de) / [- power] accroître ▸ **the company decided to extend its activities into the export market** la société a décidé d'étendre ses activités au marché de l'exportation **4.** [stretch out - arm, hand] étendre **5.** [offer - help] apporter, offrir / [- credit] accorder ▸ **to extend an invitation to sb** faire une invitation à qqn ▸ **to extend a welcome to sb** souhaiter la bienvenue à qqn.
■ **vi 1.** [stretch - in space] s'étendre / [- in time] continuer **2.** [rule, law] **: to extend to sb/sthg** inclure qqn/qqch.

extendable [ɪk'stendəbl] **adj** [contract] qui peut être prolongé(e).

extended family **n** famille *f* élargie.

extended-play [ɪk'stendɪd-] **adj** [record] double-durée.

extension [ɪk'stenʃn] **n 1.** [to building] agrandissement *m* **2.** [lengthening - gen] prolongement *m* / [- of visit] prolongation *f* / [- of visa] prorogation *f* / [- of deadline] report *m* **3.** [of power] accroissement *m* / [of law] élargissement *m* **4.** TELEC poste *m* **5.** ELEC prolongateur *m* **6.** COMPUT **: filename extension** extension *m* de nom de fichier.

extension cable **n** rallonge *f*.

extension cord *US* **n** = ***extension lead***.

extension lead **n** *UK* prolongateur *m*, rallonge *f*.

extensive [ɪk'stensɪv] **adj 1.** [in amount] considérable **2.** [in area] vaste **3.** [in range - discussions] approfondi(e) / [- changes, use] considérable.

extensively [ɪk'stensɪvlɪ] **adv 1.** [in amount] considérablement **2.** [in range] abondamment, largement.

extent [ɪk'stent] **n 1.** [of land, area] étendue *f*, superficie *f* / [of problem, damage] étendue **2.** [degree] **: to what extent...?** dans quelle mesure...? ▸ **to the extent that** [in so far as] dans la mesure où / [to the point where] au point que ▸ **to a certain extent** jusqu'à un certain point ▸ **to a large** ***or*** **great extent** en grande partie ▸ **to some extent** en partie.

extenuating circumstances [ɪk'stenjʊeɪtɪŋ-] **npl** circonstances *fpl* atténuantes.

exterior [ɪk'stɪərɪəʳ] ■ **adj** extérieur(e).
■ **n 1.** [of house, car] extérieur *m* **2.** [of person] dehors *m*, extérieur *m*.

exterminate [ɪk'stɜːmɪneɪt] **vt** exterminer.

extermination [ɪk,stɜːmɪ'neɪʃn] **n** extermination *f*.

external [ɪk'stɜːnl] **adj** externe.
◆ ***externals*** **npl** apparences *fpl*.

external debt **n** ECON dette *f* extérieure.

externalize, ***-ise*** *UK* [ɪk'stɜːnəlaɪz] **vt** extérioriser.

externally [ɪk'stɜːnəlɪ] **adv** extérieurement.

extinct [ɪk'stɪŋkt] **adj 1.** [species] disparu(e) **2.** [volcano] éteint(e).

extinction [ɪk'stɪŋkʃn] **n** [of species] extinction *f*, disparition *f*.

extinguish [ɪk'stɪŋgwɪʃ] **vt 1.** [fire, cigarette] éteindre **2.** *fig* [memory, feeling] anéantir.

extinguisher [ɪk'stɪŋgwɪʃəʳ] **n** = ***fire extinguisher***.

extn. = ***ext***.

extol (pt & pp -led, cont -ling), *US* ***extoll*** (pt & pp -ed, cont -ing) [ɪk'stəʊl] **vt** louer.

extort [ɪk'stɔːt] **vt : to extort sthg from sb** extorquer qqch à qqn.

extortion [ɪk'stɔːʃn] **n** extorsion *f*.

extortionate [ɪk'stɔːʃnət] **adj** *pej* exorbitant(e).

extortionately [ɪk'stɔːʃnətlɪ] **adv** démesurément, excessivement.

extra ['ekstrə] ■ **adj** supplémentaire ▸ **no extra charge/cost** aucun supplément de prix/frais supplémentaire ▸ **service/VAT is extra** le service/la TVA est en supplément ▸ **she asked for an extra £2** elle a demandé 2 livres de plus.

■ n 1. [addition] supplément *m* ▸ **optional extra** option *f* ▸ **a car with many extras** une voiture avec de nombreux accessoires en option 2. CIN & THEAT figurant *m*, -e *f*.
■ adv [hard, big] extra / [pay, charge] en plus.

extra- ['ekstrə] prefix extra-.

extract ■ n ['ekstrækt] extrait *m*.
■ vt [ɪk'strækt] 1. [take out - tooth] arracher ▸ **to extract sthg from** tirer qqch de 2. [confession, information] : **to extract sthg (from sb)** arracher qqch (à qqn), tirer qqch (de qqn) 3. [coal, oil] extraire.

extraction [ɪk'strækʃn] *(U)* n 1. [origin] origine *f* 2. [of coal, tooth] extraction *f*.

extractor [ɪk'stræktəʳ] n [machine, tool] extracteur *m* / [fan] ventilateur *m*, aérateur *m* ▸ **juice extractor** *UK* presse-fruits *m inv*.

extracurricular [ˌekstrəkə'rɪkjʊləʳ] adj en dehors du programme.

extradite ['ekstrədaɪt] vt : **to extradite sb (from/to)** extrader qqn (de/vers).

extradition [ˌekstrə'dɪʃn] ■ n extradition *f*.
■ comp d'extradition.

extramarital [ˌekstrə'mærɪtl] adj extraconjugal(e).

extramural [ˌekstrə'mjʊərəl] adj UNIV hors faculté.

extraneous [ɪk'streɪnjəs] adj 1. [irrelevant] superflu(e) 2. [outside] extérieur(e).

extraordinarily [ɪk'strɔ:dnrəlɪ] adv 1. [as intensifier] extraordinairement, incroyablement 2. [unusually] extraordinairement, d'une manière inhabituelle.

extraordinary [ɪk'strɔ:dnrɪ] adj *UK* extraordinaire.

extraordinary general meeting n *UK* assemblée *f* générale extraordinaire.

extrapolate [ɪk'stræpəleɪt] vt & vi extrapoler.

extrasensory perception [ˌekstrə'sensərɪ-] n perception *f* extrasensorielle.

extraterrestrial [ˌekstrətə'restrɪəl] adj extraterrestre.

extra time n *UK* SPORT prolongation *f*.

extravagance [ɪk'strævəgəns] n 1. *(U)* [excessive spending] gaspillage *m*, prodigalités *fpl* 2. [luxury] extravagance *f*, folie *f*.

extravagant [ɪk'strævəgənt] adj 1. [wasteful - person] dépensier(ère) / [- use, tastes] dispendieux(euse) 2. [elaborate, exaggerated] extravagant(e).

extravagantly [ɪk'strævəgəntlɪ] adv 1. [wastefully] : **to live extravagantly** vivre sur un grand pied ▸ **an extravagantly furnished room** une pièce meublée à grands frais OR luxueusement meublée 2. [exaggeratedly - behave, act, talk] de manière extravagante / [- praise] avec excès ▸ **extravagantly worded claims** des affirmations exagérées OR excessives.

extravaganza [ɪkˌstrævə'gænzə] n folie *f*, fantaisie *f*.

extreme [ɪk'stri:m] ■ adj extrême ▸ **on the extreme right of the screen** à l'extrême droite de l'écran ▸ **extreme sports** sports *mpl* extrêmes.
■ n extrême *m* ▸ **extremes of temperature** extrêmes de température ▸ **to extremes** à l'extrême ▸ **to take sthg to extremes** mener qqch à l'extrême ▸ **in the extreme** à l'extrême.

extremely [ɪk'stri:mlɪ] adv extrêmement.

extremism [ɪk'stri:mɪzm] n extrémisme *m*.

extremist [ɪk'stri:mɪst] ■ adj extrémiste.
■ n extrémiste *mf*.

extremity [ɪk'stremətɪ] (pl -ies) n extrémité *f*.

extricate ['ekstrɪkeɪt] vt : **to extricate sthg (from)** dégager qqch (de) ▸ **to extricate o.s. (from)** [from seat belt] s'extirper (de) / [from difficult situation] se tirer (de).

extrovert ['ekstrəvɜ:t] ■ adj extraverti(e).
■ n extraverti *m*, -e *f*.

extruded [ɪk'stru:dɪd] adj extrudé(e).

exuberance [ɪg'zju:bərəns] n exubérance *f*.

exuberant [ɪg'zju:bərənt] adj exubérant(e).

exuberantly [ɪg'zju:bərəntlɪ] adv avec exubérance.

exude [ɪg'zju:d] vt 1. [liquid, smell] exsuder 2. *fig* [confidence] respirer / [charm] déborder de.

exult [ɪg'zʌlt] vi exulter ▸ **to exult at** OR **in** se réjouir de.

exultant [ɪg'zʌltənt] adj triomphant(e).

exultation [ˌegzʌl'teɪʃn] n exultation *f*.

ex-wife n ex-femme *f*.

eye [aɪ] ■ n 1. [gen] œil *m* ▸ **before my *(etc)* (very) eyes** juste sous mes *(etc)* yeux ▸ **to cast** OR **run one's eye over sthg** jeter un coup d'œil sur qqch ▸ **to catch one's eye** attirer le regard ▸ **to catch sb's eye** attirer l'attention de qqn ▸ **the children were all eyes** les enfants n'en perdaient pas une miette ▸ **to clap** OR **lay** OR **set eyes on sb** poser les yeux sur qqn ▸ **to cry one's eyes out** pleurer toutes les larmes de son corps ▸ **to feast one's eyes on sthg** se délecter à regarder qqch ▸ **to have an eye for sthg** avoir le coup d'œil pour qqch, s'y connaître en qqch ▸ **he has eyes in the back of his head** il a des yeux derrière la tête ▸ **to have one's eye on sb** avoir qqn à l'œil ▸ **to have one's eye on sthg** avoir repéré qqch ▸ **in my *(etc)* eyes** à mes *(etc)* yeux ▸ **to keep one's eyes open** avoir l'œil ▸ **to keep one's eyes open for sthg** [try to find] essayer de repérer qqch ▸ **to keep an eye on sthg** surveiller qqch, garder l'œil sur qqch ▸ **there is more to this than meets the eye** ce n'est pas aussi simple que cela OR qu'il y paraît ▸ **to open sb's eyes (to sthg)** ouvrir les yeux de qqn (sur qqch) ▸ **not to see eye to eye with sb** ne pas partager la même opinion que qqn ▸ **to close** OR **shut one's eyes to sthg** fermer les yeux sur qqch ▸ **to turn a blind eye to sthg** ignorer qqch ▸ **I'm up to my eyes in work** *UK* j'ai du travail jusque par-dessus la tête ▸ **with an eye to sthg/to doing sthg** en vue de qqch/de faire qqch 2. [of needle] chas *m*.
■ vt (cont eyeing, cont eying) regarder, reluquer.
◆ ***eye up*** vt sep *UK* reluquer.

eyeball ['aɪbɔ:l] ■ n globe *m* oculaire.
■ vt *inf* fixer.

eyebath ['aɪbɑ:θ] n œillère *f (pour bains d'œil)*.

eyebrow ['aɪbraʊ] n sourcil *m* ▸ **to raise one's eyebrows** tiquer, sourciller.

eyebrow pencil n crayon *m* à sourcils.

eye candy **n** *(U) inf* tape *m* à l'oeil *hum & pej*.

eye-catching **adj** voyant(e).

eye contact **n : to make eye contact with sb** regarder qqn dans les yeux ▸ **to avoid eye contact with sb** éviter le regard de qqn.

-eyed [aɪd] **suffix** aux yeux... ▸ **blue-eyed** aux yeux bleus ▸ **she stared at him, wide-eyed** elle le regardait, les yeux écarquillés ▸ **one-eyed** borgne, qui n'a qu'un œil.

eye drops **npl** gouttes *fpl* (pour les yeux).

eyeful ['aɪfʊl] **n 1.** [of dirt, dust] **: I got an eyeful of sand** j'ai reçu du sable plein les yeux **2.** *inf* [look] regard *m* ▸ **get an eyeful of that!** visez un peu ça! **3.** *inf* [woman] belle fille *f*.

eyelash ['aɪlæʃ] **n** cil *m*.

eyelet ['aɪlɪt] **n** œillet *m*.

eye-level **adj** qui est au niveau ***OR*** à la hauteur de l'œil.

eyelid ['aɪlɪd] **n** paupière *f* ▸ **she didn't bat an eyelid** *inf* elle n'a pas sourcillé ***OR*** bronché.

eyeliner ['aɪˌlaɪnəʳ] **n** eye-liner *m*.

eye-opener **n** *inf* révélation *f*.

eyepatch ['aɪpætʃ] **n** cache *m*.

eye shadow **n** fard *m* à paupières.

eyesight ['aɪsaɪt] **n** vue *f*.

eyesore ['aɪsɔːʳ] **n** *pej* horreur *f*.

eyestrain ['aɪstreɪn] **n** fatigue *f* des yeux.

eyetooth ['aɪtuːθ] (pl -teeth [-tiːθ]) **n** *UK* **: to give one's eyeteeth for sthg/to do sthg** donner n'importe quoi pour qqch/pour faire qqch.

eyewash ['aɪwɒʃ] **n** *(U) UK inf dated* [nonsense] fadaises *fpl*.

eyewitness [ˌaɪ'wɪtnɪs] **n** témoin *mf* oculaire.

eyrie ['aɪərɪ] **n** aire *f (d'un aigle)*.

e-zine ['iːziːn] **n** magazine *m* électronique.

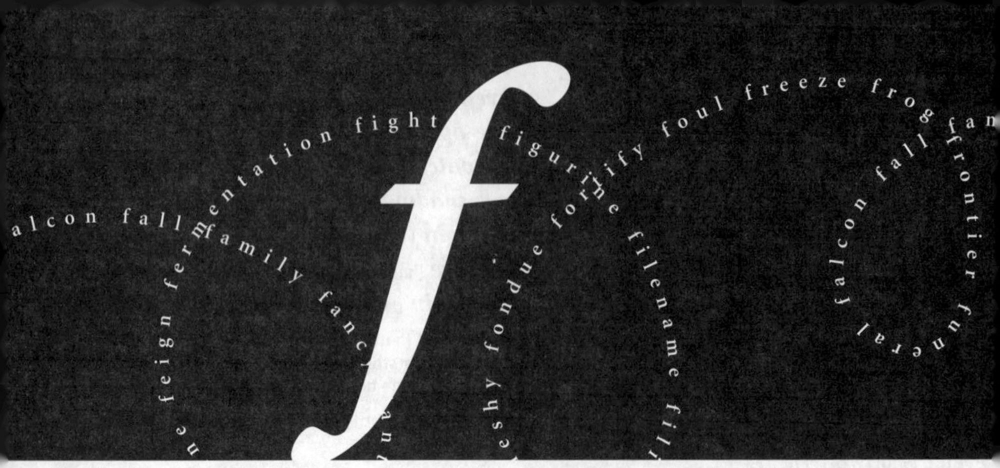

f [ef] (pl f's *OR* fs), ***F*** (pl F's *OR* Fs) **n** [letter] f *m inv*, F *m inv*.
◆ ***F*** **n 1.** MUS fa *m* **2.** (abbr of ***Fahrenheit***) F.

FA (abbr of ***Football Association***) **n** *fédération britannique de football.*

FAA (abbr of ***Federal Aviation Administration***) **n** *direction fédérale de l'aviation civile américaine.*

fab [fæb] **adj** *inf* super.

fable ['feɪbl] **n** fable *f*.

fabled ['feɪbld] **adj** fabuleux(euse), légendaire.

fabric ['fæbrɪk] **n 1.** [cloth] tissu *m* **2.** [of building, society] structure *f*.

FALSE FRIENDS / FAUX AMIS

fabric

Fabrique n'est pas la traduction du mot anglais *fabric*. Fabrique se traduit par *factory*.
▸ Une fabrique de chaussures / *A shoe factory*

fabricate ['fæbrɪkeɪt] **vt** fabriquer.

fabrication [,fæbrɪ'keɪʃn] **n 1.** [lie, lying] fabrication *f*, invention *f* **2.** [manufacture] fabrication *f*.

fabric conditioner **n** assouplissant *m* (textile).

fabulous ['fæbjʊləs] **adj 1.** [gen] fabuleux(euse) **2.** *inf* [excellent] sensationnel(elle), fabuleux(euse).

fabulously ['fæbjʊləslɪ] **adv** fabuleusement.

facade, façade [fə'sɑ:d] **n** façade *f*.

face [feɪs] ■ **n 1.** [of person] visage *m*, figure *f* ▸ **face to face** face à face ▸ **to look sb in the face** regarder qqn dans les yeux ▸ **to say sthg to sb's face** dire qqch à qqn en face ▸ **to show one's face** se montrer
2. [expression] visage *m*, mine *f* ▸ **to make *OR* pull a face** faire la grimace ▸ **her face fell** son visage s'est assombri ▸ **she put on a brave face** elle a fait bon visage *OR* bonne contenance
3. [of cliff, mountain] face *f*, paroi *f* / [of building] façade *f* / [of clock, watch] cadran *m* / [of coin, shape] face
4. [surface - of planet] surface *f* ▸ **she has vanished off the face of the earth** *fig* elle a complètement disparu de la circulation
5. [respect] **: to save/lose face** sauver/perdre la face
▸▸▸ **to fly in the face of sthg** être en contradiction avec qqch ▸ **it flies in the face of logic** ce n'est pas logique ▸ **on the face of it** à première vue.
■ **vt 1.** [look towards - subj: person, building] faire face à ▸ **the house faces the sea/south** la maison donne sur la mer/est orientée vers le sud ▸ **she was facing him** elle était en face de lui / [turn towards] faire face à ▸ **face the wall** tournez-vous vers le mur
2. [decision, crisis] être confronté(e) à / [problem, danger] faire face à ▸ **I was faced with having to pay for the damage** j'ai été obligé *OR* dans l'obligation de payer les dégâts ▸ **we'll just have to face the music** *inf* il va falloir affronter la tempête *OR* faire front
3. [truth] faire face à, admettre ▸ **we must face facts** il faut voir les choses comme elles sont ▸ **let's face it, we're lost** admettons-le, nous sommes perdus
4. *inf* [cope with] affronter ▸ **I can't face telling her** je n'ai pas le courage de le lui dire.
◆ ***face down*** **adv** [person] face contre terre / [object] à l'envers / [card] face en dessous.
◆ ***face up*** **adv** [person] sur le dos / [object] à l'endroit / [card] face en dessus.
◆ ***in the face of*** **prep** devant.
◆ ***face up to*** **vt insep** faire face à.

facecloth ['feɪsklɒθ] **n** *UK* gant *m* de toilette.

face cream **n** crème *f* pour le visage.

-faced [feɪst] **suffix** au visage... ▸ **round-faced** au visage rond ▸ **white-faced** blême.

faceless ['feɪslɪs] **adj** anonyme.

facelift ['feɪslɪft] **n** lifting *m* / *fig* restauration *f*, rénovation *f*.

face mask **n** [cosmetic] masque *m* de beauté / SPORT masque *m*.

face-off **n** SPORT remise *f* en jeu / *fig* confrontation *f*.

face pack **n** *UK* masque *m* de beauté.

face powder **n** poudre *f* de riz, poudre pour le visage.

face-saving [-,seɪvɪŋ] **adj** qui sauve la face.

facet ['fæsɪt] **n** facette *f*.

facetious [fə'si:ʃəs] **adj** facétieux(euse).

facetiously [fə'si:ʃəslɪ] **adv** facétieusement.

face-to-face adj face à face.

face value n [of coin, stamp] valeur *f* nominale ▸ **to take sthg at face value** prendre qqch au pied de la lettre.

facial [ˈfeɪʃl] ■ adj facial(e).
■ n nettoyage *m* de peau.

facial mask, facial masque *US* = ***face mask***.

facile [*UK* ˈfæsaɪl, *US* ˈfæsl] adj *pej* facile.

facilitate [fəˈsɪlɪteɪt] vt faciliter.

facilitator [fəˈsɪlɪteɪtəʳ] n animateur *m*, -trice *f* de groupe.

facility [fəˈsɪlətɪ] (pl -ies) n **1.** [ability] **: to have a facility for sthg** avoir de la facilité *OR* de l'aptitude pour qqch **2.** [feature] fonction *f* ▸ **the clock also has a radio facility** ce réveil fait aussi radio ▸ **an overdraft facility** *UK* une autorisation de découvert.
◆ ***facilities*** npl [amenities] équipement *m*, aménagement *m* ▸ **there are facilities for cooking** il y a ce qu'il faut pour faire la cuisine ▸ **washing facilities** installations sanitaires.

facing [ˈfeɪsɪŋ] adj d'en face / [sides] opposé(e).

facsimile [fækˈsɪmɪlɪ] n **1.** [fax] télécopie *f*, fax *m* **2.** [copy] fac-similé *m*.

facsimile machine = ***fax machine***.

fact [fækt] n **1.** [true piece of information] fait *m* ▸ **the fact is** le fait est ▸ **the fact remains that...** toujours est-il que... ▸ **I'll give you all the facts and figures** je vous donnerai tous les détails voulus ▸ **to know sthg for a fact** savoir pertinemment qqch ▸ **I know for a fact that they're friends** je sais pertinemment qu'ils sont amis **2.** *(U)* [truth] faits *mpl*, réalité *f* ▸ **fact and fiction** le réel et l'imaginaire.
◆ ***in fact*** adv en fait ▸ **he claims to be a writer, but in (actual) fact he's a journalist** il prétend être écrivain mais en fait c'est un journaliste.

fact-finding [-ˈfaɪndɪŋ] adj d'enquête.

faction [ˈfækʃn] n faction *f*.

factional [ˈfækʃənl] adj [dispute] de factions.

fact of life n fait *m*, réalité *f* ▸ **the facts of life** *euph* les choses *fpl* de la vie.

factor [ˈfæktəʳ] n facteur *m*, -trice *f*.

factoring [ˈfæktərɪŋ] n FIN affacturage *m*, factoring *m*.

factoring agent n FIN agent *m* d'affacturage.

factoring charges n FIN commission *f* d'affacturage.

factoring company n FIN société *f* d'affacturage.

factorize, -ise *UK* [ˈfæktəraɪz] vt mettre en facteurs.

factory [ˈfæktərɪ] (pl -ies) n fabrique *f*, usine *f*.

factory farming n élevage *m* industriel.

factory price n prix *m* usine *OR* sortie usine.

factory ship n navire-usine *m*.

factotum [fækˈtəʊtəm] (pl -s) n *inf* factotum *m*, intendant *m*, -e *f*.

fact sheet n résumé *m*, brochure *f*.

factual [ˈfæktʃʊəl] adj factuel(elle), basé(e) sur les faits.

faculty [ˈfækltɪ] (pl -ies) n **1.** [gen] faculté *f* **2.** *US* [of college] **: the faculty** le corps enseignant.

FA Cup n *en Angleterre, championnat de football dont la finale se joue à Wembley*.

fad [fæd] n engouement *m*, mode *f* / [personal] marotte *f*.

faddy [ˈfædɪ] (comp -ier, superl -iest) adj *UK inf pej* capricieux(euse).

fade [feɪd] ■ vt [jeans, curtains, paint] décolorer.
■ vi **1.** [jeans, curtains, paint] se décolorer / [colour] passer / [flower] se flétrir, faner **2.** [light] baisser, diminuer **3.** [sound] diminuer, s'affaiblir **4.** [memory] s'effacer / [feeling, interest] diminuer **5.** [smile] s'effacer, s'évanouir.
◆ ***fade away, fade out*** vi [sound, anger] diminuer / [image] s'effacer.

faded [ˈfeɪdɪd] adj [colour] passé(e).

faeces *UK*, ***feces*** *US* [ˈfi:si:z] npl fèces *fpl*.

Faeroe, Faroe [ˈfeərəʊ] n **: the Faeroe Islands, the Faeroes** les îles *fpl* Féroé ▸ **in the Faeroe Islands** aux îles Féroé.

faff [fæf] ◆ ***faff about, faff around*** vi *UK inf* glander.

fag [fæg] n *inf* **1.** *UK* [cigarette] clope *m* **2.** *UK* [chore] corvée *f* **3.** *US offens* [homosexual] pédé *m*.

fag end n *UK inf* mégot *m*.

fagged out [fægd-] adj *UK inf* crevé(e).

faggot [ˈfægət] n **1.** *UK* CULIN boulette *f* de viande **2.** *US inf offens* [homosexual] pédé *m*.

Fahrenheit [ˈfærənhaɪt] adj Fahrenheit *(inv)*.

fail [feɪl] ■ n SCH & UNIV échec *m*.
■ vt **1.** [exam, test] rater, échouer à ▸ **he failed his driving test** il n'a pas eu son permis
2. [not succeed] **: to fail to do sthg** ne pas arriver à faire qqch ▸ **I fail to see how I can help** je ne vois pas comment je peux aider
3. [neglect] **: to fail to do sthg** manquer *OR* omettre de faire qqch ▸ **he failed to mention he was married** il a omis de signaler qu'il était marié ▸ **they never fail to call** ils ne manquent jamais d'appeler
4. [candidate] refuser
5. [subj: courage] manquer à / [subj: friend, memory] lâcher ▸ **words fail me** je ne sais pas quoi dire.
■ vi **1.** [not succeed] ne pas réussir *OR* y arriver ▸ **her attempt was bound to fail** sa tentative était vouée à l'échec ▸ **it never fails** ça ne rate jamais ▸ **if all else fails** en désespoir de cause
2. [not pass exam] échouer ▸ **I failed in maths** j'ai été collé *OR* recalé en maths
3. [stop functioning] lâcher ▸ **his heart failed** son cœur s'est arrêté ▸ **the power failed** il y a eu une panne d'électricité
4. [be insufficient] manquer, faire défaut ▸ **their crops failed** ils ont perdu les récoltes ▸ **she failed in her duty** elle a manqué *OR* failli à son devoir
5. [weaken - health, daylight] décliner / [- eyesight] baisser.
◆ ***without fail*** adv [for certain] sans faute, à coup sûr / [always] inévitablement, immanquablement.

failed [feɪld] adj [singer, writer] raté(e).

failing [ˈfeɪlɪŋ] ■ n [weakness] défaut *m*, point *m* faible.
■ prep à moins de ▸ **failing that** à défaut.

fail-safe adj [device] à sûreté intégrée.

failure ['feɪljəʳ] **n 1.** [lack of success, unsuccessful thing] échec *m* ▸ **her failure to attend** le fait qu'elle ne soit pas venue ▸ **the play was a dismal failure** la pièce a été *OR* a fait un four noir **2.** [person] raté *m*, -e *f* ▸ **I feel a complete failure** je me sens vraiment nulle **3.** [of engine, brake] défaillance *f* / [of crop] perte *f* ▸ **heart failure** arrêt *m* cardiaque ▸ **a power failure** une panne d'électricité.

faint [feɪnt] ■ **adj 1.** [smell] léger(ère) / [memory] vague / [sound, hope] faible **2.** [slight - chance] petit(e), faible ▸ **I haven't the faintest idea** je n'en ai pas la moindre idée **3.** [dizzy] **: I'm feeling a bit faint** je ne me sens pas bien ▸ **he was faint with exhaustion** la tête lui tournait de fatigue.
■ **vi** s'évanouir ▸ **to be fainting from** *OR* **with hunger** défaillir de faim.

faint-hearted [-'hɑːtɪd] **adj** timoré(e), timide.

faintly ['feɪntlɪ] **adv 1.** [recall] vaguement / [shine] faiblement / [smile - indifferently] vaguement / [- sadly] faiblement **2.** [rather, slightly] légèrement.

faintness ['feɪntnɪs] **n 1.** [dizziness] étourdissement *m*, étourdissements *mpl* **2.** [of image] flou *m* **3.** [of smell, sound, hope] faiblesse *f* / [of memory] imprécision *f*.

fair [feəʳ] ■ **adj 1.** [just – person] juste, équitable / [contest, match] correct / [criticism] justifié, mérité ▸ **it's not fair!** ce n'est pas juste! ▸ **to be fair...** il faut dire que... ▸ **she's had more than her fair share of problems** elle a largement eu sa part de problèmes ▸ **fair's fair: it's her turn now** il faut être juste, c'est son tour maintenant **2.** [quite large] grand(e), important(e) ▸ **she reads a fair amount** elle lit pas mal **3.** [quite good] assez bon (assez bonne) ▸ **to have a fair idea of sthg** avoir sa petite idée sur qqch **4.** [hair] blond(e) **5.** [skin, complexion] clair(e) **6.** [weather] beau (belle).
■ **n 1.** *UK* [funfair] fête *f* foraine **2.** [trade fair] foire *f*.
■ **adv** [fairly] loyalement ▸ **he told us fair and square** il nous l'a dit sans détours *OR* carrément ▸ **to play fair** jouer franc jeu.
◆ ***fair enough*** **adv** *inf* OK, d'accord.

fair copy **n** copie *f* au propre.

fair game **n** proie *f* rêvée.

fairground ['feəgraʊnd] **n** champ *m* de foire.

fair-haired [-'heəd] **adj** [person] blond(e).

fairly ['feəlɪ] **adv 1.** [rather] assez ▸ **fairly certain** presque sûr **2.** [justly] équitablement / [describe] avec impartialité / [fight, play] loyalement.

fair-minded [-'maɪndɪd] **adj** impartial(e), équitable.

fairness ['feənɪs] **n** [justness] équité *f* ▸ **in fairness (to sb)** pour être juste (envers qqn).

fair play **n** fair-play *m inv*.

fair sex **n : the fair sex** le beau sexe.

fair-sized **adj** assez grand(e).

fair-skinned **adj** blanc (blanche), de peau.

fairway ['feəweɪ] **n** fairway *m*, allée *f* ***Québec***.

fair-weather **adj** [clothing, vessel] qui convient seulement au beau temps ▸ **a fair-weather friend** un ami des beaux *OR* bons jours.

fairy ['feərɪ] (**pl -ies**) **n** [imaginary creature] fée *f* / *inf offens* pédé *m*.

fairy godmother **n** *fig* & LIT bonne fée *f*.

fairy lights **npl** *UK* guirlande *f* électrique.

fairy story **n** LIT conte *m* de fées / [untruth] histoire *f* à dormir debout.

fairy tale **n** conte *m* de fées.

fait accompli [ˌfeɪtə'kɒmpliː] (**pl faits accomplis** [ˌfeɪzə'kɒmpliː]) **n** fait *m* accompli.

faith [feɪθ] **n 1.** [belief] foi *f*, confiance *f* ▸ **faith in sb/sthg** confiance en qqn/qqch ▸ **in bad faith** de mauvaise foi ▸ **in good faith** en toute bonne foi **2.** RELIG foi *f*.

faithful ['feɪθfʊl] ■ **adj 1.** [person] fidèle **2.** [account, translation] exact(e).
■ **npl** RELIG **: the faithful** les fidèles *mpl*.

faithfully ['feɪθfʊlɪ] **adv** [loyally] fidèlement ▸ **to promise faithfully that...** donner sa parole que... ▸ **Yours faithfully** *UK* [in letter] je vous prie d'agréer mes salutations distinguées.

faithfulness ['feɪθfʊlnɪs] **n 1.** [loyalty] fidélité *f* **2.** [truth - of account, translation] exactitude *f*.

faith healer **n** guérisseur *m*, -euse *f*.

faithless ['feɪθlɪs] **adj** déloyal(e).

fake [feɪk] ■ **adj** faux (fausse).
■ **n 1.** [object, painting] faux *m* **2.** [person] imposteur *m*.
■ **vt 1.** [results] falsifier / [signature] imiter **2.** [illness, emotions] simuler.
■ **vi** [pretend] simuler, faire semblant.

falcon ['fɔːlkən] **n** faucon *m*.

Falkland Islands ['fɔːklənd-], ***Falklands*** ['fɔːkləndz] **npl : the Falkland Islands** les îles *fpl* Falkland, les Malouines *fpl* ▸ **in the Falkland Islands** aux îles Falkland, aux Malouines.

fall [fɔːl] ■ **vi** (**pt fell, pp fallen**) **1.** [gen] tomber ▸ **she fell off the stool/out of the window** elle est tombée du tabouret/par la fenêtre ▸ **they fell into one another's arms** ils sont tombés dans les bras l'un de l'autre ▸ **to fall flat** [joke] tomber à plat ▸ **as night fell** à la tombée de la nuit **2.** [decrease] baisser
3. [become] **: to fall asleep** s'endormir ▸ **to fall ill** tomber malade ▸ **to fall in love** tomber amoureux(euse) ▸ **to fall open** s'ouvrir ▸ **to fall silent** se taire ▸ **to fall vacant** se libérer
4. [belong, be classed] **: to fall into two groups** se diviser en deux groupes ▸ **the matter falls under our jurisdiction** cette question relève de notre juridiction
5. [disintegrate] **: to fall to bits** *OR* **pieces** tomber en morceaux
6. [be captured - city] **: to fall (to sb)** tomber (aux mains de qqn)
7. *UK* POL [constituency] **: to fall to sb** passer à qqn.
■ **n 1.** [gen] **: fall (in)** chute (de)
2. *US* [autumn] automne *m*.
◆ ***falls*** **npl** chutes *fpl*.
◆ ***fall about*** **vi** *UK inf* **: to fall about (laughing)** se tordre (de rire).
◆ ***fall apart*** **vi 1.** [disintegrate - book, chair] tomber en morceaux / *fig* **: their marriage is falling apart** leur mariage est en train de se briser *OR* va à vau-l'eau
2. *fig* [country] tomber en ruine / [person] s'effondrer.

◆ ***fall away*** **vi** [land] descendre, s'abaisser.
◆ ***fall back*** **vi** [person, crowd] reculer.
◆ ***fall back on*** **vt insep** [resort to] se rabattre sur.
◆ ***fall behind*** **vi 1.** [in race] se faire distancer
2. [with rent] être en retard ▸ **to fall behind with** *UK* OR **in** *US* **one's work** avoir du retard dans son travail.
◆ ***fall down*** **vi** [fail] échouer ▸ **the plan falls down on three points** ce plan pèche sur trois points.
◆ ***fall for*** **vt insep 1.** *inf* [fall in love with] tomber amoureux(euse) de
2. [trick, lie] se laisser prendre à ▸ **to fall for it** tomber dans le panneau.
◆ ***fall in*** **vi 1.** [roof, ceiling] s'écrouler, s'affaisser
2. MIL former les rangs.
◆ ***fall in with*** **vt insep** [go along with] accepter.
◆ ***fall off*** **vi 1.** [branch, handle] se détacher, tomber
2. [demand, numbers] baisser, diminuer.
◆ ***fall on*** **vt insep 1.** [subj: eyes, gaze] tomber sur
2. [attack] se jeter sur.
◆ ***fall out*** **vi 1.** [hair, tooth] tomber
2. [friends] se brouiller
3. MIL rompre les rangs.
◆ ***fall over*** ■ **vt insep : to fall over sthg** trébucher sur qqch et tomber ▸ **to be falling over o.s. to do sthg** *inf* se mettre en quatre pour faire qqch.
■ **vi** [person, chair] tomber.
◆ ***fall through*** **vi** [plan, deal] échouer.
◆ ***fall to*** **vt insep** [subj: duty] incomber à, revenir à ▸ **it falls to me to...** c'est à moi de...

fallacious [fəˈleɪʃəs] **adj** *fml* fallacieux(euse).

fallacy [ˈfæləsɪ] (pl **-ies**) **n** erreur *f*, idée *f* fausse.

fallen [ˈfɔːln] **pp** ➤ *fall*.

fall guy **n** *US inf* [scapegoat] bouc *m* émissaire.

fallible [ˈfæləbl] **adj** faillible.

falling [ˈfɔːlɪŋ] **adj** [decreasing] en baisse.

falling off **n** diminution *f*, baisse *f* ▸ **there has been a recent falling-off in sales** les ventes ont accusé une baisse ces derniers temps.

Fallopian tube [fəˈləʊpɪən-] **n** trompe *f* de Fallope.

fallout [ˈfɔːlaʊt] **n** *(U)* [radiation] retombées *fpl*.

fallout shelter **n** abri *m* antiatomique.

fallow [ˈfæləʊ] **adj : to lie fallow** être en jachère.

false [fɔːls] **adj 1.** [generally] faux (fausse) **2.** [insincere] perfide, fourbe / [disloyal] déloyal (e).

false alarm **n** fausse alerte *f*.

falsehood [ˈfɔːlshʊd] **n** *fml* **1.** [lie] mensonge *m* **2.** *(U)* [lack of truth] fausseté *f*.

falsely [ˈfɔːlslɪ] **adv** à tort / [smile, laugh] faussement.

falseness [ˈfɔːlsnɪs] **n 1.** [of belief, statement] fausseté *f* **2.** [of friend, lover] infidélité *f* **3.** [insincerity] fausseté *f*, manque *m* de sincérité.

false start **n** *lit & fig* faux départ *m*.

false teeth **npl** dentier *m*.

falsetto [fɔːlˈsetəʊ] ■ **n** (pl **-s**) [singer] fausset *m*.
■ **adv** [sing] en fausset.

falsification [ˌfɔːlsɪfɪˈkeɪʃn] **n** falsification *f*.

falsify [ˈfɔːlsɪfaɪ] (pt & pp **-ied**) **vt** falsifier.

falter [ˈfɔːltəʳ] **vi 1.** [move unsteadily] chanceler **2.** [steps, voice] devenir hésitant(e) **3.** [hesitate, lose confidence] hésiter.

faltering [ˈfɔːltərɪŋ] **adj** [steps, voice] hésitant(e).

fame [feɪm] **n** gloire *f*, renommée *f*.

famed [feɪmd] **adj** célèbre, renommé(e) ▸ **famed for his generosity** connu OR célèbre pour sa générosité.

familiar [fəˈmɪljəʳ] **adj** familier(ère) ▸ **familiar to sb** connu de qqn ▸ **his name is familiar** j'ai déjà entendu son nom (quelque part), son nom me dit quelque chose ▸ **a familiar feeling** un sentiment bien connu ▸ **familiar with sthg** familiarisé(e) avec qqch ▸ **to be on familiar terms with sb** être en termes familiers avec qqn.

familiarity [fəˌmɪlɪˈærətɪ] **n** *(U)* **1.** [knowledge] **: familiarity with sthg** connaissance *f* de qqch, familiarité *f* avec qqch **2.** [normality] caractère *m* familier **3.** *pej* [excessive informality] familiarité *f*.

familiarization, *UK* ***-isation*** [fəˌmɪljəraɪˈzeɪʃn] **n** familiarisation *f*.

familiarize, *UK* ***-ise*** [fəˈmɪljəraɪz] **vt : to familiarize o.s. with sthg** se familiariser avec qqch ▸ **to familiarize sb with sthg** familiariser qqn avec qqch.

family [ˈfæmlɪ] ■ **n** (pl **-ies**) famille *f* ▸ **have you any family?** [relatives] avez-vous de la famille? / [children] avez-vous des enfants? ▸ **to start a family** avoir un (premier) enfant.
■ **comp 1.** [belonging to family] de famille **2.** [suitable for all ages] familial(e).

family business **n** entreprise *f* familiale.

family credit **n** *(U) UK* ≃ complément *m* familial.

family doctor **n** médecin *m* de famille.

family life **n** vie *f* de famille.

family man **n : he's a family man** il aime la vie de famille, c'est un bon père de famille.

family name **n** nom *m* de famille.

family planning **n** planning *m* familial ▸ **family planning clinic** centre *m* de planning familial.

family tree **n** arbre *m* généalogique.

famine [ˈfæmɪn] **n** famine *f*.

famished [ˈfæmɪʃt] **adj** *inf* [very hungry] affamé(e) ▸ **I'm famished!** je meurs de faim!

famous [ˈfeɪməs] **adj : famous (for)** célèbre (pour).

famously [ˈfeɪməslɪ] **adv** *dated* **: to get on** OR **along famously** s'entendre comme larrons en foire.

fan [fæn] ■ **n 1.** [of paper, silk] éventail *m* **2.** [electric or mechanical] ventilateur *m* **3.** [enthusiast] fan *mf*.
■ **vt** (pt & pp **-ned**, cont **-ning**) **1.** [face] éventer ▸ **to fan o.s.** s'éventer **2.** [fire, feelings] attiser.
◆ ***fan out*** **vi** se déployer.

fanatic [fəˈnætɪk] **n** fanatique *mf*.

fanatical [fəˈnætɪkl] **adj** fanatique.

fanatically [fəˈnætɪkəlɪ] **adv** fanatiquement.

fanaticism [fəˈnætɪsɪzm] **n** fanatisme *m*.

fan belt **n** courroie *f* de ventilateur.

fanciable ['fænsɪəbl] adj *UK inf* plutôt bien, pas mal du tout.

fanciful ['fænsɪfʊl] adj **1.** [odd] bizarre, fantasque **2.** [elaborate] extravagant(e).

fancily ['fænsɪlɪ] adv d'une façon recherchée *OR* raffinée.

fan club n fan-club *m*.

fancy ['fænsɪ] ■ adj (comp -ier, superl -iest) **1.** [elaborate - hat, clothes] extravagant(e) / [- food, cakes] raffiné(e) **2.** [expensive - restaurant, hotel] de luxe / [- prices] fantaisiste.
■ n (pl -ies) **1.** *UK* [desire, liking] envie *f*, lubie *f* ▸ **to take a fancy to sb** se prendre d'affection pour qqn ▸ **to take a fancy to sthg** se mettre à aimer qqch ▸ **to take sb's fancy** faire envie à qqn, plaire à qqn **2.** [fantasy] rêve *m*.
■ vt (pt & pp -ied) **1.** *UK inf* [want] avoir envie de ▸ **to fancy doing sthg** avoir envie de faire qqch **2.** *UK inf* [like] : **I fancy her** elle me plaît ▸ **to fancy o.s.** ne pas se prendre pour rien *OR* n'importe qui ▸ **to fancy o.s. as sthg** se prendre pour qqch **3.** [imagine] : **fancy meeting you here!** tiens, c'est toi! je n'aurais jamais pensé te rencontrer ici! ▸ **fancy that!** ça alors! **4.** *dated* [think] penser.

fancy dress n *(U)* déguisement *m*.

fancy-dress party n fête *f* déguisée.

fancy-free adj sans souci.

fancy goods npl articles *mpl* fantaisie.

fanfare ['fænfeəʳ] n fanfare *f*.

fang [fæŋ] n [of wolf] croc *m* / [of snake] crochet *m*.

fan heater n radiateur *m* soufflant.

fanlight ['fænlaɪt] n *UK* imposte *f*.

fan mail n courrier *m* de fans.

fanny ['fænɪ] n *US inf* [buttocks] fesses *fpl*.

fanny pack n *US* banane *f (sac)*.

fantasize, *UK* ***-ise*** ['fæntəsaɪz] vi : **to fantasize (about sthg/about doing sthg)** fantasmer (sur qqch/sur le fait de faire qqch).

fantastic [fæn'tæstɪk] adj **1.** *inf* [wonderful] fantastique, formidable **2.** [incredible] extraordinaire, incroyable **3.** [exotic] fabuleux(euse).

fantastically [fæn'tæstɪklɪ] adv **1.** [extremely] extrêmement **2.** [exotically] fabuleusement, extraordinairement.

fantasy ['fæntəsɪ] ■ n (pl -ies) **1.** [dream, imaginary event] rêve *m*, fantasme *m* **2.** *(U)* [fiction] fiction *f* **3.** [imagination] fantaisie *f*.
■ comp imaginaire.

fantasy football n *jeu où chaque participant se constitue une équipe virtuelle avec les noms de footballeurs réels, chaque but marqué par ceux-ci dans la réalité valant un point dans le jeu.*

fanzine ['fænzi:n] n fanzine *m*.

fao (abbr of ***for the attention of***) à l'attention de.

FAO (abbr of ***Food and Agriculture Organization***) n FAO *f*.

FAQ [fak *OR* ɛfeɪ'kju:] ■ n COMPUT (abbr of ***frequently asked questions***) foire *f* aux questions, FAQ *f*.
■ adj & adv (abbr of ***free alongside quay***) FLQ.

far [fɑ:ʳ] ■ adv **1.** [in distance] loin ▸ **how far is it?** c'est à quelle distance?, (est-ce que) c'est loin? ▸ **have you come far?** vous venez de loin? ▸ **far away** *OR* **off** loin ▸ **far and wide** partout ▸ **as far as** jusqu'à ▸ **as far as the eye can see** à perte de vue
2. [in time] : **far away** *OR* **off** loin ▸ **he's not far off sixty** il n'a pas loin de la soixantaine ▸ **as far back as** [be founded] dès / [remember, go] jusqu'à ▸ **so far** jusqu'à maintenant, jusqu'ici
3. [in degree or extent] bien ▸ **I wouldn't trust him very far** je ne lui ferais pas tellement confiance ▸ **she is far more intelligent than I am** elle est bien *OR* beaucoup plus intelligente que moi ▸ **he's not far wrong** *OR* **out** *OR* **off** il n'est pas loin ▸ **as far as** autant que ▸ **as far as I know** (pour) autant que je sache ▸ **as far as I'm concerned** en ce qui me concerne ▸ **as far as possible** autant que possible, dans la mesure du possible ▸ **it's all right as far as it goes** pour ce qui est de ça, pas de problème ▸ **in so far as** dans la mesure où ▸ **far and away, by far** de loin ▸ **far from it** loin de là, au contraire ▸ **so far so good** jusqu'ici tout va bien ▸ **£5 doesn't go far nowadays** on ne va pas loin avec 5 livres de nos jours ▸ **to go so far as to do sthg** aller jusqu'à faire qqch ▸ **to go too far** aller trop loin.
■ adj (comp **farther** *OR* **further**, superl **farthest** *OR* **furthest**) **1.** [extreme] : **the far end of the street** l'autre bout de la rue ▸ **the far right of the party** l'extrême droite du parti ▸ **the door on the far left** la porte la plus à gauche **2.** *liter* [remote] lointain(e).

faraway ['fɑ:rəweɪ] adj lointain(e).

farce [fɑ:s] n **1.** THEAT farce *f* **2.** *fig* [disaster] pagaille *f*, vaste rigolade *f*.

farcical ['fɑ:sɪkl] adj grotesque.

fare [feəʳ] ■ n **1.** [payment] prix *m*, tarif *m* **2.** *dated* [food] nourriture *f*.
■ vi [manage] : **to fare well/badly** bien/mal se débrouiller.

Far East n : **the Far East** l'Extrême-Orient *m*.

Far Eastern adj extrême-oriental.

fare stage n *UK* section *f*.

farewell [ˌfeə'wel] ■ n adieu *m*.
■ excl *liter* adieu!

far-fetched [-'fetʃt] adj bizarre, farfelu ▸ **a far-fetched alibi** un alibi tiré par les cheveux ▸ **a far-fetched story** une histoire à dormir debout.

far-flung adj [widespread] étendu(u), vaste / [far] lointain(e).

farm [fɑ:m] ■ n ferme *f*.
■ vt cultiver.
■ vi être cultivateur.
◆ ***farm out*** vt sep confier en sous-traitance.

farmer ['fɑ:məʳ] n fermier *m*, -ière *f*.

farmhand ['fɑ:mhænd] n ouvrier *m*, -ère *f* agricole.

farmhouse ['fɑ:mhaʊs] (pl [-haʊzɪz]) n ferme *f*.

farming ['fɑ:mɪŋ] n *(U)* agriculture *f* / [of animals] élevage *m*.

farm labourer *UK*, ***farm laborer*** *US* = ***farmhand***.

farmland ['fɑ:mlænd] n *(U)* terres *fpl* cultivées *OR* arables.

farmstead ['fɑ:msted] **n** *US* ferme *f*.

farm worker = ***farmhand***.

farmyard ['fɑ:mjɑ:d] **n** cour *f* de ferme.

Faroe = ***Faeroe***.

Faroese [ˌfeərəʊ'i:z] ■ **adj** féroïen(ne).
■ **n 1.** GEOG Féroïen *m*, -ne *f* **2.** LING féroïen *m*.

far-off **adj 1.** [days] lointain(e) / [time] reculé(e) **2.** [in distance] lointain(e).

far-reaching [-'ri:tʃɪŋ] **adj** d'une grande portée.

farrier ['færɪəʳ] **n** maréchal *m* ferrant.

farsighted [ˌfɑ:'saɪtɪd] **adj 1.** [person] prévoyant(e) / [plan] élaboré(e) avec clairvoyance **2.** *US* [longsighted] hypermétrope.

farsightedness [ˌfɑ:'saɪtɪdnɪs] **n 1.** [of person] prévoyance *f*, perspicacité *f* / [of act, decision] clairvoyance *f* **2.** *US* MED hypermétropie *f*, presbytie *f*.

fart [fɑ:t] *v inf* ■ **n 1.** [air] pet *m* **2.** [person] con *m*, conne *f* ▶ **an old fart** un vieux con.
■ **vi** péter.

farther ['fɑ:ðəʳ] **compar** ➤ ***far***.

farthest ['fɑ:ðəst] **superl** ➤ ***far***.

FAS (abbr of ***free alongside ship***) FLB.

fascia ['feɪʃə] **n** [on shop] enseigne *f* / *dated* [in car] tableau *m* de bord.

fascinate ['fæsɪneɪt] **vt** fasciner.

fascinating ['fæsɪneɪtɪŋ] **adj** [person, country] fascinant(e) / [job] passionnant(e) / [idea, thought] très intéressant(e).

fascinatingly ['fæsɪneɪtɪŋlɪ] **adv** d'une façon fascinante ***OR*** passionnante.

fascination [ˌfæsɪ'neɪʃn] **n** fascination *f*.

fascism ['fæʃɪzm] **n** fascisme *m*.

fascist ['fæʃɪst] ■ **adj** fasciste.
■ **n** fasciste *mf*.

fashion ['fæʃn] ■ **n 1.** [clothing, style] mode *f* ▶ **to be in/out of fashion** être/ne plus être à la mode ▶ **fashion model** mannequin *m* (de mode) **2.** [manner] manière *f*.
■ **vt** *fml* façonner, fabriquer.

fashionable ['fæʃnəbl] **adj** à la mode.

fashionably ['fæʃnəblɪ] **adv** élégamment, à la mode ▶ **her hair is fashionably short** elle a les cheveux coupés court selon la mode.

fashion-conscious **adj** qui suit la mode.

fashion designer **n** styliste *mf*.

fashion show **n** défilé *m* de mode.

fashion victim **n** *hum* victime *f* de la mode.

fast [fɑ:st] ■ **adj 1.** [rapid] rapide ▶ **fast train** rapide *m* **2.** [clock, watch] en avance ▶ **my watch is (three minutes) fast** ma montre avance (de trois minutes).
■ **adv 1.** [rapidly] vite ▶ **how fast does this car go?** à quelle vitesse va cette voiture? ▶ **she ran off as fast as her legs would carry her** elle s'est sauvée à toutes jambes, elle a pris ses jambes à son cou **2.** [firmly] solidement ▶ **shut fast** bien fermé ▶ **to hold fast to sthg** *lit* & *fig* s'accrocher à qqch ▶ **fast asleep** profondément endormi.
■ **n** jeûne *m*.
■ **vi** jeûner.

fast breeder reactor **n** surrégénérateur *m*.

fasten ['fɑ:sn] ■ **vt** [jacket, bag] fermer / [seat belt] attacher ▶ **to fasten sthg to sthg** attacher qqch à qqch.
■ **vi : to fasten on to sb/sthg** se cramponner à qqn/qqch.

fastener ['fɑ:snəʳ] **n** [of bag, necklace] fermoir *m* / [of dress] fermeture *f*.

fastening ['fɑ:snɪŋ] **n** fermeture *f*.

fast food **n** fast-food *m*, restauration *f* rapide.

fast-forward ■ **n** avance *f* rapide.
■ **vt** mettre en avance rapide.
■ **vi** mettre la bande en avance rapide.

fastidious [fə'stɪdɪəs] **adj** [fussy] méticuleux(euse).

fast lane **n** [on motorway] voie *f* rapide ▶ **life in the fast lane** *fig* la vie à cent à l'heure.

fast-moving **adj** [film] plein(e) d'action ▶ **fast-moving events** des évènements rapides.

fast-track **adj : fast-track executives** *des cadres qui gravissent rapidement les échelons*.

fat [fæt] ■ **adj** (comp **-ter**, superl **-test**) **1.** [overweight] gros (grosse), gras (grasse) ▶ **to get fat** grossir **2.** [not lean - meat] gras (grasse) **3.** [thick - file, wallet] gros (grosse), épais(aisse) **4.** [large - profit, cheque] gros (grosse) **5.** *iro* [small] **: a fat lot of good that did you!** ça t'a bien avancé! ▶ **I reckon you'll get it back – fat chance!** je pense qu'on te le rendra – tu parles !
■ **n 1.** [flesh, on meat, in food] graisse *f* **2.** *(U)* [for cooking] matière *f* grasse ▶ **margarine low in fat** margarine pauvre en matières grasses ***OR*** allégée ▶ **pork fat** saindoux *m*.

fatal ['feɪtl] **adj 1.** [serious - mistake] fatal(e) / [- decision, words] fatidique **2.** [accident, illness] mortel(elle).

fatalism ['feɪtəlɪzm] **n** fatalisme *m*.

fatalist ['feɪtəlɪst] ■ **adj** fataliste.
■ **n** fataliste *mf*.

fatalistic [ˌfeɪtə'lɪstɪk] **adj** fataliste.

fatality [fə'tælətɪ] (pl **-ies**) **n 1.** [accident victim] mort *m* **2.** = ***fatalism***.

fatally ['feɪtəlɪ] **adv 1.** [seriously] sérieusement, gravement **2.** [wounded] mortellement ▶ **fatally ill** dans un état désespéré.

fat cat **n** *inf pej* richard *m*, huile *f*.

fate [feɪt] **n 1.** [destiny] destin *m* ▶ **to tempt fate** tenter le diable **2.** [result, end] sort *m*.

fated ['feɪtɪd] **adj** fatal(e), marqué(e) par le destin ▶ **to be fated to do sthg** être voué ***OR*** destiné à faire qqch.

fateful ['feɪtfʊl] **adj** fatidique.

fat-free **adj** sans matières grasses.

fathead ['fæthed] **n** *inf* imbécile *mf*, patate *f*.

father ['fɑ:ðəʳ] ■ **n** père *m*.
■ **vt** engendrer.
◆ ***Father*** **n 1.** [priest] Père *m* **2.** [God] Dieu le Père *m* ▶ **Our Father** notre Père.

Father Christmas **n** *UK* le Père Noël.

father figure **n** personne *f* qui joue le rôle du père ▸ **he was a father figure for all the employees** le personnel le considérait un peu comme un père.

fatherhood ['fɑːðəhʊd] **n** *(U)* paternité *f*.

father-in-law (pl **fathers-in-law**) **n** beau-père *m*.

fatherly ['fɑːðəlɪ] **adj** paternel(elle).

Father's Day **n** fête *f* des Pères.

fathom ['fæðəm] ■ **n** brasse *f*.
■ **vt : to fathom sb/sthg (out)** comprendre qqn/qqch.

fatigue [fə'tiːg] ■ **n 1.** [exhaustion] épuisement *m* **2.** [in metal] fatigue *f*.
■ **vt** épuiser.
◆ ***fatigues*** **npl** tenue *f* de corvée, treillis *m*.

fatless ['fætlɪs] **adj** sans matières grasses.

fatness ['fætnɪs] **n** [of person] embonpoint *m*.

fatten ['fætn] **vt** engraisser.
◆ ***fatten up*** **vt sep** engraisser.

fattening ['fætnɪŋ] **adj** qui fait grossir.

fatty ['fætɪ] ■ **adj** (comp **-ier**, superl **-iest**) gras (grasse).
■ **n** (pl **-ies**) *inf pej* gros *m*, grosse *f*.

fatuous ['fætjʊəs] **adj** *fml* stupide, niais(e).

fatuously ['fætjʊəslɪ] **adv** *fml* stupidement, niaisement.

fatwa ['fætwə] **n** RELIG fatwa *f*.

faucet ['fɔːsɪt] **n** *US* robinet *m*.

fault ['fɔːlt] ■ **n 1.** [responsibility, in tennis] faute *f* ▸ **it's my fault** c'est de ma faute **2.** [mistake, imperfection] défaut *m* ▸ **to find fault with sb/sthg** critiquer qqn/qqch ▸ **at fault** fautif(ive) **3.** GEOL faille *f*.
■ **vt : to fault sb (on sthg)** prendre qqn en défaut (sur qqch).

faultless ['fɔːltlɪs] **adj** impeccable.

faulty ['fɔːltɪ] (comp **-ier**, superl **-iest**) **adj** défectueux(euse).

fauna ['fɔːnə] **n** faune *f*.

faux pas [ˌfəʊ'pɑː] (pl **faux pas**) **n** faux-pas *m*.

favour *UK*, ***favor*** *US* ['feɪvər] ■ **n 1.** [approval] faveur *f*, approbation *f* ▸ **to look with favour on sb** considérer qqn favorablement ▸ **in sb's favour** en faveur de qqn ▸ **to be in/out of favour with sb** avoir/ne pas avoir les faveurs de qqn, avoir/ne pas avoir la cote avec qqn ▸ **to curry favour with sb** chercher à gagner la faveur de qqn **2.** [kind act] service *m* ▸ **to do sb a favour** rendre (un) service à qqn **3.** [favouritism] favoritisme *m* **4.** [advantage] **: to rule in sb's favour** décider OR statuer en faveur de qqn ▸ **the odds are in his favour** il est (donné) favori.
■ **vt 1.** [prefer] préférer, privilégier **2.** [treat better, help] favoriser **3.** *iro* [honour] **: to favour sb with sthg** faire à qqn l'honneur de qqch.
◆ ***in favour*** **adv** [in agreement] pour, d'accord.
◆ ***in favour of*** **prep 1.** [in preference to] au profit de **2.** [in agreement with] **: to be in favour of sthg/of doing sthg** être partisan(e) de qqch/de faire qqch.

favourable *UK*, ***favorable*** *US* ['feɪvrəbl] **adj** [positive] favorable.

favourably *UK*, ***favorably*** *US* ['feɪvrəblɪ] **adv** favorablement / [placed] bien.

favoured *UK*, ***favored*** *US* ['feɪvəd] **adj** favorisé(e).

favourite *UK*, ***favorite*** *US* ['feɪvrɪt] ■ **adj** favori(ite).
■ **n** [person] favori *m*, -ite *f*.
◆ ***favorites*** **npl** COMPUT favoris *mpl*, signets *mpl*.

favouritism *UK*, ***favoritism*** *US* ['feɪvrɪtɪzm] **n** favoritisme *m*.

fawn [fɔːn] ■ **adj** fauve *(inv)*.
■ **n** [animal] faon *m*.
■ **vi : to fawn on sb** flatter qqn servilement.

fax [fæks] ■ **n** fax *m*, télécopie *f*.
■ **vt 1.** [person] envoyer un fax à **2.** [document] envoyer en fax.

fax machine **n** fax *m*, télécopieur *m*.

fax modem **n** modem *m* fax.

fax number **n** numéro *m* de fax.

faze [feɪz] **vt** *inf* démonter, déconcerter.

FBI (abbr of ***Federal Bureau of Investigation***) **n** *US* FBI *m*.

FCC (abbr of ***Federal Communications Commission***) **n** *conseil fédéral de l'audiovisuel aux États-Unis,* ≃ CSA *m*.

FCO (abbr of ***Foreign and Commonwealth Office***) **n** *ministère britannique des affaires étrangères et du Commonwealth*.

FD (abbr of ***Fire Department***) **n** *US* & *Can* *sapeurs-pompiers*.

FDA **n 1.** (abbr of ***Food and Drug Administration***) *administration délivrant l'autorisation de mise sur le marché des médicaments et des produits alimentaires aux États-Unis* **2.** (abbr of ***Association of First Division Civil Servants***) *syndicat britannique des hauts fonctionnaires*.

FDD [ˌefdiː'diː] (abbr of ***floppy disk drive***) **n** COMPUT lecteur *m* de disquettes.

HOW TO ...
express fear

J'ai peur des araignées / I'm scared of spiders
J'ai peur dans le noir/de tomber / I'm afraid of the dark/of falling
J'ai peur qu'il se perde / I'm worried that he'll get lost
J'étais mort de peur *inf* / I was petrified
J'ai une peur bleue des serpents / I'm terrified of snakes
Je m'inquiète pour sa santé / I'm worried about his health
Il se fait beaucoup de souci pour son travail / He really worries about his work
Je crains sa réaction quand il l'apprendra / I'm dreading his reaction when he finds out
J'appréhende son retour / I'm dreading him coming back

FE n *UK* & *Aus* abbr of ***Further Education***.

fear [fɪəʳ] ■ n **1.** *(U)* [feeling] peur *f* ▸ **have no fear** ne craignez rien, soyez sans crainte **2.** [object of fear] crainte *f* ▸ **he expressed his fears about their future** il a exprimé son inquiétude en ce qui concerne leur avenir **3.** [risk] risque *m* ▸ **for fear of** de peur de *(+ infin)*, de peur que *(+ subjunctive)* ▸ **there is no fear of her leaving** elle ne risque pas de partir, il est peu probable qu'elle parte.
■ vt **1.** [be afraid of] craindre, avoir peur de ▸ **never fear, fear not** ne craignez rien, soyez tranquille **2.** [anticipate] craindre ▸ **to fear (that)...** craindre que..., avoir peur que...
■ vi [be afraid] **: to fear for sb/sthg** avoir peur pour qqn/qqch, craindre pour qqn/qqch.

fearful ['fɪəfʊl] adj **1.** *fml* [frightened] peureux(euse) ▸ **to be fearful of sthg** avoir peur de qqch **2.** [frightening] effrayant(e).

fearfully ['fɪəfʊlɪ] adv **1.** [look, say] peureusement, craintivement **2.** *inf dated* [as intensifier] affreusement, horriblement.

fearless ['fɪəlɪs] adj intrépide.

fearlessly ['fɪəlɪslɪ] adv avec intrépidité.

fearlessness ['fɪəlɪsnɪs] n audace *f*, absence *f* de peur.

fearsome ['fɪəsəm] adj [temper] effroyable.

feasibility [ˌfiːzə'bɪlətɪ] n *(U)* possibilité *f*.

feasibility study n étude *f* de faisabilité.

feasible ['fiːzəbl] adj faisable, possible.

feast [fiːst] ■ n [meal] festin *m*, banquet *m*.
■ vi **: to feast on** *OR* **off sthg** se régaler de qqch.

feat [fiːt] n exploit *m*, prouesse *f*.

feather ['feðəʳ] n plume *f*.

feather bed n lit *m* de plume.

featherbed ['feðəbed] vt ECON [industry, business] subventionner excessivement.

featherbedding ['feðəbedɪŋ] n ECON [of industry, business] subventionnement *m* excessif.

featherbrained ['feðəbreɪnd] adj [person] écervelé(e) / [idea, scheme] inconsidéré(e).

feathered ['feðəd] adj [headdress] de plumes ▸ **our feathered friends** *hum* nos amis les oiseaux.

featherweight ['feðəweɪt] n [boxer] poids *m* plume.

feathery ['feðərɪ] adj **1.** [bird] à plumes **2.** *fig* [light and soft - snowflake] doux et léger comme la plume.

feature ['fiːtʃəʳ] ■ n **1.** [characteristic] caractéristique *f* ▸ **the novel has just one redeeming feature** le roman est sauvé par un seul élément **2.** GEOG particularité *f* **3.** [article] article *m* de fond **4.** RADIO & TV émission *f* spéciale, spécial *m* **5.** CIN long métrage *m*.
■ vt **1.** [subj: film, exhibition] mettre en vedette ▸ **featuring James Dean** avec, dans le rôle principal, James Dean **2.** PRESS [display prominently] **: the story/the picture is featured on the front page** le récit/la photo est en première page **3.** [comprise] présenter, comporter.
■ vi **: to feature (in)** figurer en vedette (dans).
◆ ***features*** npl [of face] traits *mpl*.

feature film n long métrage *m*.

feature-length adj CIN **: a feature-length film** un long métrage ▸ **a feature-length cartoon** un film d'animation.

featureless ['fiːtʃəlɪs] adj sans trait distinctif.

feature writer n journaliste *mf*.

Feb. [feb] (abbr of ***February***) févr.

February ['februərɪ] n février *m* ; see also ***September***.

feces *US* = ***faeces***.

feckless ['feklɪs] adj inepte.

fecklessness ['feklɪsnɪs] n [ineffectuality] manque *m* d'efficacité / [irresponsibility] irresponsabilité *f*.

fed [fed] ■ pt & pp ➤ ***feed***.
■ n *US inf* agent *m*, -e *f* du FBI.

Fed [fed] n **1.** *US inf* (abbr of ***Federal Reserve Board***) *organe de contrôle de la Banque centrale américaine* **2.** abbr of ***federal*** **3.** abbr of ***federation***.

fed. abbr of ***federal***, ***federation***, ***federated***.

federal ['fedrəl] adj fédéral(e).

Federal Bureau of Investigation n FBI *m*, ≃ police *f* judiciaire.

federalism ['fedrəlɪzm] n fédéralisme *m*.

federalist ['fedrəlɪst] ■ adj fédéraliste.
■ n fédéraliste *mf*.

federalize, *UK* ***-ise*** ['fedrəlaɪz] ■ vt fédéraliser.
■ vi se fédéraliser.

federally ['fedrəlɪ] adv **: to be federally funded** être financé par le gouvernement fédéral.

Federal Reserve n *US* Réserve *f* fédérale.

CULTURE

Federal Reserve

La Banque centrale des États-Unis ou Banque fédérale américaine fut créée par le Congrès en 1913. Elle est chargée de quatre obligations principales : diriger la politique monétaire du pays en fixant les taux d'intérêt, superviser et réglementer les institutions bancaires tout en protégeant les droits aux crédits des consommateurs, maintenir la stabilité du système financier et, enfin, fournir certains services budgétaires au gouvernement, aux citoyens américains, aux institutions financières et aux organismes financiers étrangers.

federation [ˌfedə'reɪʃn] n fédération *f*.

fedora [fɪ'dɔːrə] n [hat] chapeau *m* mou.

fed up adj **: to be fed up (with)** en avoir marre (de).

fee [fiː] n [of school] frais *mpl* / [of doctor] honoraires *mpl* / [for membership] cotisation *f* / [for entrance] tarif *m*, prix *m*.

feeble ['fiːbəl] adj faible.

feeble-minded adj faible d'esprit.

feebleness ['fiːblnɪs] n faiblesse *f*.

feebly ['fiːblɪ] adv faiblement.

feed [fiːd] ■ vt (pt & pp **fed**) **1.** [give food to] nourrir ▸ **to feed sthg to sb, to feed sb sthg** donner qqch à manger à

qqn **2.** [fire, fears] alimenter ▸ **to feed a parking meter** mettre des pièces dans un parcmètre **3.** [put, insert] **: to feed sthg into sthg** mettre *OR* insérer qqch dans qqch ▸ **to feed data into a computer** entrer des données dans un ordinateur.
■ **vi** (pt & pp **fed**) **1.** [take food] **: to feed (on *OR* off)** se nourrir (de) **2.** [be strengthened] **: to feed on *OR* off** s'appuyer sur.
■ **n 1.** [for baby] repas *m* **2.** [animal food] nourriture *f*.

feedback ['fi:dbæk] **n** *(U)* **1.** [reaction] réactions *fpl* ▸ **we haven't had much feedback from them** nous n'avons pas eu beaucoup de réactions *OR* d'échos de leur part ▸ **we welcome feedback from customers** nous sommes toujours heureux d'avoir les impressions *OR* les réactions de nos clients **2.** ELEC réaction *f*, rétroaction *f*.

feedbag ['fi:dbæg] **n** *US* musette *f* (mangeoire).

feeder ['fi:dər] ■ **n** [eater] mangeur *m*, -euse *f*.
■ **comp** [road, railway line] secondaire.

feeding bottle ['fi:dɪŋ-] **n** *UK* biberon *m*.

feeding frenzy **n** frénésie *f* alimentaire / **: to have a feeding frenzy** avoir un comportement agressif.

feel [fi:l] ■ **vt** (pt & pp **felt**) **1.** [touch] toucher ▸ **feel the quality of this cloth** apprécie la qualité de ce tissu ▸ **to feel one's way** avancer à tâtons / [in new job, difficult situation] avancer avec précaution
2. [sense, experience, notice] sentir / [emotion] ressentir ▸ **to feel o.s. doing sthg** se sentir faire qqch
3. [believe] **: to feel (that)...** croire que..., penser que... ▸ **she feels very strongly that...** elle est tout à fait convaincue que...
▸▸ **I'm not feeling myself today** je ne suis pas dans mon assiette aujourd'hui.
■ **vi** (pt & pp **felt**) **1.** [have sensation] **: to feel cold/hot/sleepy** avoir froid/chaud/sommeil ▸ **my hands/feet feel cold** j'ai froid aux mains/pieds ▸ **to feel safe** se sentir en sécurité ▸ **to feel like sthg/like doing sthg** [be in mood for] avoir envie de qqch/de faire qqch
2. [have emotion] se sentir ▸ **to feel angry** être en colère ▸ **to feel (like) a fool** se sentir bête ▸ **if that's how you feel...** si c'est comme ça que tu vois les choses...
3. [seem] sembler ▸ **it feels good to be alive/home** c'est bon d'être en vie/chez soi ▸ **it feels strange** ça fait drôle
4. [by touch] **: to feel hard/soft/smooth/rough** être dur/doux/lisse/rêche (au toucher) ▸ **your forehead feels hot** ton front est brûlant ▸ **it feels like leather** on dirait du cuir ▸ **to feel for sthg** chercher qqch.
■ **n 1.** [sensation, touch] toucher *m*, sensation *f*
2. [atmosphere] atmosphère *f* ▸ **his music has a really Latin feel (to it)** il y a vraiment une influence latine dans sa musique
▸▸ **to get the feel of sthg** s'habituer à qqch ▸ **to have a feel for sthg** avoir l'instinct pour qqch.

feeler ['fi:lər] **n** antenne *f*.

feelgood ['fi:lgud] **adj** *inf* qui donne la pêche ▸ **the feel-good factor** l'optimisme *m* ambiant.

feeling ['fi:lɪŋ] **n 1.** [emotion] sentiment *m* ▸ **I know the feeling** je sais ce que c'est ▸ **bad feeling** animosité *f*, hostilité *f* ▸ **the feeling is mutual** c'est réciproque **2.** [physical sensation] sensation *f* **3.** [intuition, sense] sentiment *m*, impression *f* / [opinion] avis *m*, opinion *f* ▸ **I had a feeling he would write** j'avais le pressentiment qu'il allait écrire ▸ **she has very strong feelings about it** elle a des opinions très arrêtées là-dessus **4.** [understanding] sensibilité *f* ▸ **to have a feeling for sthg** comprendre *OR* apprécier qqch.
◆ ***feelings*** **npl** sentiments *mpl* ▸ **to hurt sb's feelings** blesser (la sensibilité de) qqn ▸ **no hard feelings!** sans rancune!

fee-paying [-'peɪɪŋ] **adj** *UK* [pupil] d'un établissement privé / [school] privé(e).

feet [fi:t] **npl** ➤ ***foot***.

feign [feɪn] **vt** *fml* feindre.

feint [feɪnt] ■ **n** feinte *f*.
■ **vi** feinter.

feisty ['faɪstɪ] (comp **-ier**, superl **-iest**) **adj** *inf* [lively] plein(e) d'entrain / [combative] qui a du cran.

felicitous [fɪ'lɪsɪtəs] **adj** *fml* heureux(euse).

feline ['fi:laɪn] ■ **adj** félin(e).
■ **n** félin *m*.

fell [fel] ■ **pt** ➤ ***fall***.
■ **vt** [tree, person] abattre.
◆ ***fells*** **npl** GEOG lande *f*.

fella ['felə] **n** *inf* [man] mec *m*, type *m*.

feller ['felər] *inf UK* = ***fella***.

fellow ['feləʊ] ■ **n 1.** *dated* [man] homme *m* **2.** [comrade, peer] camarade *m*, compagnon *m* **3.** [of society, college] membre *m*, associé *m*.
■ **adj : one's fellow men** ses semblables ▸ **fellow feeling** sympathie *f* ▸ **fellow passenger** compagnon *m*, compagne *f* (de voyage) ▸ **fellow student** camarade *mf* (d' tudes,

fellowship ['feləʊʃɪp] **n 1.** [comradeship] amitié *f*, camaraderie *f* **2.** [society] association *f*, corporation *f* **3.** [of society, college] titre *m* de membre *OR* d'associé **4.** UNIV [scholarship] bourse *f* d'études dans l'enseignement supérieur / [status] poste *m* de chercheur(euse).

felony ['felənɪ] (pl **-ies**) **n** LAW crime *m*, forfait *m*.

felt [felt] ■ **pt** & **pp** ➤ ***feel***.
■ **n** *(U)* feutre *m*.

felt-tip pen **n** stylo-feutre *m*.

female ['fi:meɪl] ■ **adj** [person] de sexe féminin / [animal, plant] femelle / [sex, figure] féminin(e) ▸ **female student** étudiante *f* ▸ **female worker** travailleuse *f*, ouvrière *f*.
■ **n** femelle *f*.

feminine ['femɪnɪn] ■ **adj** féminin(e).
■ **n** GRAM féminin *m*.

femininity [femɪ'nɪnətɪ] **n** *(U)* féminité *f*.

feminism ['femɪnɪzm] **n** féminisme *m*.

feminist ['femɪnɪst] **n** féministe *mf*.

fence [fens] ■ **n** [barrier] clôture *f* ▸ **to sit on the fence** *fig* ménager la chèvre et le chou.
■ **vt** clôturer, entourer d'une clôture.
◆ ***fence off*** **vt sep** séparer par une clôture.

fencing ['fensɪŋ] **n 1.** SPORT escrime *f* **2.** [material] clôture *f*.

fend [fend] **vi : to fend for o.s.** se débrouiller tout seul.
◆ ***fend off*** **vt sep** [blows] parer / [questions, reporters] écarter.

fender ['fendəʳ] **n 1.** [around fireplace] pare-feu *m inv* **2.** [on boat] défense *f* **3.** *US* [on car] aile *f*.

fennel ['fenl] **n** fenouil *m*.

fens [fenz] **npl** *UK* marais *mpl*.

fenugreek ['fenjʊˌgri:k] **n** fenugrec *m*.

feral ['ferəl] **adj** sauvage.

ferment ■ **n** ['fɜ:ment] *(U)* [unrest] agitation *f*, effervescence *f* ▸ **in ferment** en effervescence.
■ **vi** [fə'ment] [wine, beer] fermenter.

fermentation [ˌfɜ:mən'teɪʃn] **n** fermentation *f*.

fermented [fə'mentɪd] **adj** fermenté(e).

fern [fɜ:n] **n** fougère *f*.

ferocious [fə'rəʊʃəs] **adj** [animal, criticism] féroce / [heat] terrible, intense / [climate] rude.

ferociously [fə'rəʊʃəslɪ] **adv** férocement, avec férocité.

ferociousness [fə'rəʊʃəsnɪs], ***ferocity*** [fə'rɒsətɪ] **n** [of person, animal, attack, criticism] férocité *f* / [of heat] intensité *f*, caractère *m* torride / [of climate] rudesse *f*.

ferret ['ferɪt] **n** furet *m*.
◆ ***ferret about***, ***ferret around*** **vi** *inf* fureter un peu partout.
◆ ***ferret out*** **vt sep** *inf* dénicher.

Ferris wheel ['ferɪs-] **n** *esp US* grande roue *f*.

ferry ['ferɪ] ■ **n** ferry *m*, ferry-boat *m* / [smaller] bac *m*.
■ **vt** transporter.

ferryboat ['ferɪbəʊt] **n** = ***ferry***.

ferryman ['ferɪmən] (pl **-men** [-mən]) **n** passeur *m*.

fertile ['fɜ:taɪl] **adj 1.** [land, imagination] fertile, fécond(e) **2.** [person] fécond(e).

fertility [fɜ:'tɪlətɪ] **n 1.** [of land, imagination] fertilité *f* **2.** [of person] fécondité *f*.

fertility drug **n** traitement *m* contre la stérilité.

fertilization, *UK* ***-isation*** [ˌfɜ:tɪlaɪ'zeɪʃn] **n 1.** [of soil] fertilisation *f* **2.** [of egg] fécondation *f*.

fertilize, *UK* ***-ise*** ['fɜ:tɪlaɪz] **vt 1.** [soil] fertiliser, amender **2.** [egg] féconder.

fertilizer, *UK* ***-iser*** ['fɜ:tɪlaɪzəʳ] **n** engrais *m*.

fervent ['fɜ:vənt] **adj** fervent(e).

fervently ['fɜ:vəntlɪ] **adv** [beg, desire, speak] avec ferveur / [believe] ardemment.

fervour *UK*, ***fervor*** *US* ['fɜ:vəʳ] **n** ferveur *f*.

fess up **vi insep** *inf* cracher le morceau.

fester ['festəʳ] **vi 1.** [wound, sore] suppurer **2.** [emotion, quarrel] s'aigrir.

festival ['festəvl] **n 1.** [event, celebration] festival *m* **2.** [holiday] fête *f*.

festive ['festɪv] **adj** de fête.

festive season **n** *UK* **: the festive season** la période des fêtes.

festivity [fes'tɪvətɪ] (pl **-ies**) **n** [merriness] fête *f*.
◆ ***festivities*** **npl** festivités *fpl* ▸ **the Christmas festivities** les fêtes *fpl* de Noël.

festoon [fe'stu:n] **vt** décorer de guirlandes ▸ **to be festooned with** être décoré de.

feta ['fetə] **n : feta (cheese)** feta *f*.

fetal ['fi:tl] *US* = ***foetal***.

fetch [fetʃ] **vt 1.** [go and get] aller chercher ▸ **go/run and fetch him** va/va vite le chercher **2.** [raise - money] rapporter ▸ **the painting fetched £8,000** le tableau a atteint la somme de 8 000 livres.
◆ ***fetch up*** *inf* **vi insep** [end up] se retrouver ▸ **to fetch up in hospital/in a ditch** se retrouver à l'hôpital/dans un fossé.

fetching ['fetʃɪŋ] **adj** séduisant(e).

fetchingly ['fetʃɪŋlɪ] **adv** [smile] d'un air séduisant ▸ **with his hat balanced fetchingly on his head** avec son chapeau élégamment posé sur la tête.

fete, ***fête*** [feɪt] ■ **n** fête *f*, kermesse *f*.
■ **vt** fêter, faire fête à.

fetid ['fetɪd] **adj** fétide.

fetish ['fetɪʃ] **n 1.** [sexual obsession] objet *m* de fétichisme **2.** [mania] manie *f*, obsession *f*.

fetishism ['fetɪʃɪzm] **n** fétichisme *m*.

fetishistic [ˌfetɪ'ʃɪstɪk] **adj** PSYCHOL fétichiste.

fetlock ['fetlɒk] **n** boulet *m*.

fetter ['fetəʳ] **vt** [person] enchaîner / [movements] entraver.
◆ ***fetters*** **npl** fers *mpl*, chaînes *fpl*.

fettle ['fetl] **n** *inf dated* **: in fine fettle** en pleine forme.

fetus ['fi:təs] *US* = ***foetus***.

feud [fju:d] ■ **n** querelle *f*.
■ **vi** se quereller.

feudal ['fju:dl] **adj** féodal(e).

feudalism ['fju:dəlɪzm] **n** féodalisme *m*.

feuding ['fju:dɪŋ] **n** *(U)* querelle *f*, querelles *fpl* / [more aggressive] vendetta *f*.

fever ['fi:vəʳ] **n** fièvre *f*.

fevered ['fi:vəd] **adj** fiévreux(euse).

feverish ['fi:vərɪʃ] **adj** fiévreux(euse).

fever pitch **n** comble *m*.

few [fju:] ■ **adj** peu de ▸ **the first few pages** les toutes premières pages ▸ **in the past/next few days** pendant les deux ou trois derniers/prochains jours ▸ **he has a few more friends than I have** il a un peu plus d'amis que moi ▸ **quite a few, a good few** pas mal de, un bon nombre de ▸ **few and far between** rares ▸ **he's had a few (too many)** *inf* [drinks] il a bu un coup (de trop).
■ **pron** peu ▸ **how many of them are there? – very few** combien sont-ils? – très peu nombreux ▸ **a few** quelques-uns *mpl*, quelques-unes *f*.

fewer ['fju:əʳ] ■ **adj** moins (de) ▸ **no fewer than** pas moins de.
■ **pron** moins.

fewest ['fju:əst] **adj** le moins (de).

fez [fez] **n** fez *m*.

FH *UK* abbr of ***fire hydrant***.

FHA (abbr of ***Federal Housing Administration***) **n** *organisme de gestion des logements sociaux aux États-Unis*.

fiancé [fɪ'ɒnseɪ] **n** fiancé *m*.

fiancée [fɪ'ɒnseɪ] **n** fiancée *f*.

fiasco [fɪ'æskəʊ] (*UK* -s, *esp US* -es) **n** fiasco *m*.

fiat money ['faɪæt-] **n** *US* monnaie *f* fiduciaire.

fib [fɪb] *inf* ■ **n** bobard *m*, blague *f*.
■ **vi** (pt & pp **-bed**, cont **-bing**) raconter des bobards *OR* des blagues.

fibber ['fɪbər] **n** *inf* menteur *m*, -euse *f*.

fibre *UK*, ***fiber*** *US* ['faɪbər] **n** fibre *f*.

fibreboard *UK*, ***fiberboard*** *US* ['faɪbəbɔːd] **n** *(U)* panneau *m* de fibres.

fibreglass *UK*, ***fiberglass*** *US* ['faɪbəglɑːs] ■ **n** *(U)* fibre *f* de verre.
■ **comp** en fibre de verre.

fibre optic *UK*, ***fiber optic*** *US* **adj** [cable] en fibres optiques.

fibre optics *UK*, ***fiber optics*** *US* **n** *(U)* fibre *f* optique, fibres *fpl* optiques.

fibre-tip (pen) *UK* = ***felt-tip pen***.

fibroid ['faɪbrɔɪd] **n** fibrome *m*.

fibrositis [,faɪbrə'saɪtɪs] **n** fibrosite *f*.

fibrous ['faɪbrəs] **adj** fibreux(euse).

FICA (abbr of ***Federal Insurance Contributions Act***) **n** *loi américaine régissant les cotisations sociales*.

fickle ['fɪkl] **adj** versatile.

fiction ['fɪkʃn] **n** fiction *f*.

fictional ['fɪkʃənl] **adj** fictif(ive).

fictionalize, *UK* ***-ise*** ['fɪkʃənəlaɪz] **vt** romancer.

fictitious [fɪk'tɪʃəs] **adj** [false] fictif(ive).

fiddle ['fɪdl] ■ **vi** [play around] **: to fiddle with sthg** tripoter qqch.
■ **vt** *UK inf* truquer.
■ **n 1.** [violin] violon *m* ▸ **to be (as) fit as a fiddle** se porter comme un charme ▸ **to play second fiddle (to sb)** jouer un rôle secondaire (auprès de qqn), passer au second plan (auprès de qqn) **2.** *UK inf* [fraud] combine *f*, escroquerie *f*.
◆ ***fiddle about***, ***fiddle around*** **vi 1.** [fidget] ne pas se tenir tranquille, s'agiter ▸ **to fiddle about with sthg** tripoter qqch **2.** [waste time] perdre son temps.

fiddler ['fɪdlər] **n** joueur *m*, -euse *f* de violon.

fiddly ['fɪdlɪ] (comp **-ier**, superl **-iest**) **adj** *UK inf* délicat(e).

fidelity [fɪ'delətɪ] **n 1.** [loyalty] fidélité *f* **2.** [accuracy - of report] fidélité *f*.

fidget ['fɪdʒɪt] **vi** remuer.

fidgety ['fɪdʒɪtɪ] **adj** *inf* remuant(e).

fiduciary [fɪ'djuːʃɪərɪ] ■ **adj** fiduciaire.
■ **n** (pl **-ies**) fiduciaire *mf*.

field [fiːld] ■ **n 1.** [gen & COMPUT] champ *m* ▸ **field of vision** champ de vision **2.** [for sports] terrain *m* ▸ **to lead the field** [in race] mener la course, être en tête / *fig* [in sales, area of study] être en tête **3.** [of knowledge] domaine *m* ▸ **what's your field?, what field are you in?** quel est ton domaine? **4.** [real environment] **: in the field** sur le terrain.
■ **vi** tenir le champ.

field day **n : to have a field day** s'en donner à cœur joie.

fielder ['fiːldər] **n** joueur *m* qui tient le champ.

field event **n** compétition *f* d'athlétisme *(hormis la course)*.

field glasses **npl** jumelles *fpl*.

field hockey **n** *US* hockey *m* (sur gazon).

field marshal **n** ≃ maréchal *m* (de France).

fieldmouse ['fiːldmaʊs] (pl **fieldmice** [-maɪs]) **n** mulot *m*.

field study **n** étude *f* sur le terrain.

field trip **n** SCH voyage *m* d'étude.

fieldwork ['fiːldwɜːk] **n** *(U)* recherches *fpl* sur le terrain.

fieldworker ['fiːldwɜːkər] **n** chercheur *m*, -euse *f* *OR* enquêteur *m*, -trice *f* sur le terrain.

fiend [fiːnd] **n 1.** [cruel person] monstre *m* **2.** *inf* [fanatic] fou *m*, folle *f*, mordu *m*, -e *f*.

fiendish ['fiːndɪʃ] **adj 1.** [evil] diabolique **2.** *inf* [very difficult, complex] abominable, atroce.

fiendishly ['fiːndɪʃlɪ] **adv 1.** [cruelly] diaboliquement **2.** *inf* [extremely] **: fiendishly difficult** abominablement *OR* atrocement difficile.

fierce [fɪəs] **adj** féroce / [heat] torride / [storm, temper] violent(e).

fiercely ['fɪəslɪ] **adv** férocement / [attack] violemment / [defend] avec acharnement.

fierceness ['fɪəsnɪs] **n 1.** [of animal, look, person] férocité *f* **2.** [of desire] violence *f* / [of sun] ardeur *f* / [of resistance] acharnement *m* / [of criticism] férocité *f*.

fiery ['faɪərɪ] (comp **-ier**, superl **-iest**) **adj 1.** [burning] ardent(e) **2.** [spicy] très piquant(e) **3.** [volatile - speech] enflammé(e) / [- temper, person] fougueux(euse) **4.** [bright red] flamboyant(e).

fiesta [fɪ'estə] **n** fiesta *f*.

FIFA ['fiːfə] (abbr of ***Fédération Internationale de Football Association***) **n** FIFA *f*.

fifteen [fɪf'tiːn] **num** quinze ; see also ***six***.

fifteenth [,fɪf'tiːnθ] **num** quinzième ; see also ***sixth***.

fifth [fɪfθ] **num** cinquième ; see also ***sixth***.

Fifth Amendment **n : the Fifth Amendment** le Cinquième Amendement *(qui garantit les droits des inculpés, aux États-Unis)*.

fifth column **n** cinquième colonne *f*.

fiftieth ['fɪftɪəθ] **num** cinquantième ; see also ***sixth***.

fifty ['fɪftɪ] **num** cinquante ; see also ***sixty***.

fifty-fifty ■ **adj** moitié-moitié, fifty-fifty ▸ **to have a fifty-fifty chance** avoir cinquante pour cent de chances.
■ **adv** moitié-moitié, fifty-fifty.

fig [fɪg] **n** figue *f*.

fight [faɪt] ■ **n 1.** [physical] bagarre *f* ▸ **to have a fight (with sb)** se battre (avec qqn), se bagarrer (avec qqn) ▸ **to pick a fight (with sb)** chercher la bagarre (avec qqn) ▸ **to put up a fight** se battre, se défendre ▸ **are you going to the fight?** [boxing match] est-ce que tu vas voir le combat? **2.** *fig* [battle, struggle] lutte *f*, combat *m*

3. [argument] dispute *f* ▸ **to have a fight (with sb)** se disputer (avec qqn).
■ **vt** (pt & pp **fought**) **1.** [physically] se battre contre *OR* avec
2. [conduct - war] mener ▸ **to fight a battle** livrer (une) bataille ▸ **to fight a court case** [- subj: lawyer] défendre une cause / [- subj: plaintiff, defendant] être en procès ▸ **to fight an election** [politician] se présenter à une élection
3. [enemy, racism] combattre.
■ **vi** (pt & pp **fought**) **1.** [in war, punch-up] se battre ▸ **he fought in the war** il a fait la guerre
2. *fig* [struggle] **: to fight for/against sthg** lutter pour/contre qqch ▸ **to fight for one's rights/to clear one's name** lutter pour ses droits/pour prouver son innocence
3. [argue] **: to fight (about *OR* over)** se battre *OR* se disputer (à propos de).
◆ ***fight back*** ■ **vt insep** refouler.
■ **vi** riposter.
◆ ***fight off*** **vt sep** **1.** [attacker] repousser
2. [illness, desire] venir à bout de.
◆ ***fight out*** **vt sep : leave them to fight it out** laisse-les se bagarrer et régler cela entre eux.

fighter ['faɪtəʳ] **n** **1.** [plane] avion *m* de chasse, chasseur *m* **2.** [soldier] combattant *m* **3.** [combative person] battant *m*, -e *f*.

fighter-bomber **n** MIL chasseur *m* bombardier.

fighting ['faɪtɪŋ] **n** *(U)* [punch-up] bagarres *fpl* / [in war] conflits *mpl*.

fighting chance **n : to have a fighting chance** avoir de bonnes chances.

fig leaf **n** BOT feuille *f* de figuier / [on statue, in painting] feuille *f* de vigne / *fig* camouflage *m*.

figment ['fɪgmənt] **n : a figment of sb's imagination** le fruit de l'imagination de qqn.

figurative ['fɪgərətɪv] **adj** **1.** [meaning] figuré(e) **2.** ART figuratif(ive).

figuratively ['fɪgərətɪvlɪ] **adv** au figuré.

figure [*UK* 'fɪgəʳ, *US* 'fɪgjər] ■ **n** **1.** [statistic, number] chiffre *m* ▸ **in round figures** en chiffres ronds ▸ **to put a figure on sthg** chiffrer qqch ▸ **to be in double figures** [inflation, unemployment] dépasser la barre *OR* le seuil des 10 % ▸ **she's good at figures** elle est bonne en calcul **2.** [human shape, outline] silhouette *f*, forme *f* **3.** [personality, diagram] figure *f* **4.** [shape of body] ligne *f*.
■ **vt** *esp US* [suppose] penser, supposer.
■ **vi** [feature] figurer, apparaître ▸ **she figured prominently in the scandal** elle a été très impliquée dans le scandale.
◆ ***figure out*** **vt sep** [understand] comprendre / [find] trouver ▸ **she still hasn't figured out how to do it** elle n'a toujours pas trouvé comment faire ▸ **we couldn't figure it out** nous n'arrivions pas à comprendre *OR* saisir.

figurehead ['fɪgəhed] **n** **1.** [on ship] figure *f* de proue **2.** *fig & pej* [leader] homme *m* de paille.

figure-hugging [-ˌhʌgɪŋ] **adj** [dress] moulant(e).

figure of eight *UK & Aus*, ***figure eight*** *US* **n** huit *m inv*.

figure of speech **n** figure *f* de rhétorique.

figure skating **n** patinage *m* artistique.

figurine [*UK* 'fɪgəriːn, *US* ˌfɪgjə'riːn] **n** figurine *f*.

Fiji ['fiːdʒiː] **n** Fidji *fpl* ▸ **in Fiji** à Fidji.

Fijian [ˌfiː'dʒiːən] ■ **adj** fidjien(enne).
■ **n** Fidjien *m*, -enne *f*.

filament ['fɪləmənt] **n** [in light bulb] filament *m*.

filch [fɪltʃ] **vt** *inf* chiper.

file [faɪl] ■ **n** **1.** [folder, report] dossier *m* ▸ **on file, on the files** répertorié dans les dossiers **2.** COMPUT fichier *m* **3.** [tool] lime *f* **4.** [line] **: in single file** en file indienne.
■ **vt** **1.** [document] classer ▸ **to be filed under a letter/subject** être classé sous une lettre/dans une catégorie **2.** [LAW - accusation, complaint] porter, déposer / [- lawsuit] intenter ▸ **to file a suit against sb** intenter un procès à qqn ▸ **to file an appeal** *US* interjeter *OR* faire appel **3.** [fingernails, wood] limer ▸ **to file one's fingernails** se limer les ongles.
■ **vi** **1.** [classify documents] faire du classement **2.** [walk in single file] marcher en file indienne ▸ **the troops filed past the general** les troupes ont défilé devant le général **3.** LAW **: to file for divorce** demander le divorce.

file clerk *US* = ***filing clerk***.

file management **n** COMPUT gestion *f* de fichiers.

file manager **n** COMPUT gestionnaire *m* de fichiers.

filename ['faɪlˌneɪm] **n** COMPUT nom *m* de fichier.

file-sharing **adj** d'échange de fichiers.

filet *US* = ***fillet***.

filibuster ['fɪlɪbʌstəʳ] **vi** *esp US* POL faire de l'obstruction parlementaire.

filigree ['fɪlɪgriː] ■ **adj** en filigrane.
■ **n** filigrane *m*.

filing ['faɪlɪŋ] **n** **1.** [of documents] classement *m* ▸ **I still have a lot of filing to do** j'ai encore beaucoup de choses à classer **2.** LAW [of complaint, claim] dépôt *m*.

filing cabinet ['faɪlɪŋ-] **n** classeur *m*, fichier *m*.

filing clerk ['faɪlɪŋ-] **n** *UK* documentaliste *mf*.

Filipino [ˌfɪlɪ'piːnəʊ] ■ **adj** philippin(e).
■ **n** (pl -s) Philippin *m*, -e *f*.

fill [fɪl] ■ **vt** **1.** [gen] remplir ▸ **to fill sthg with sthg** remplir qqch de qqch ▸ **she filled his head with nonsense** elle lui a bourré le crâne de bêtises **2.** [gap, hole] boucher ▸ **the product filled a gap in the market** le produit a comblé un vide sur le marché **3.** [vacancy - subj: employer] pourvoir à / [- subj: employee] prendre.
■ **n : to eat one's fill** manger à sa faim ▸ **to have had one's fill of sthg** en avoir assez de qqch.
◆ ***fill in*** ■ **vt sep** **1.** [form] remplir **2.** [inform] **: to fill sb in (on)** mettre qqn au courant (de).
■ **vt insep : I'm just filling in time** je fais ça en attendant.
■ **vi** [substitute] **: to fill in for sb** remplacer qqn.
◆ ***fill out*** ■ **vt sep** [form] remplir.
■ **vi** [get fatter] prendre de l'embonpoint.
◆ ***fill up*** ■ **vt sep** remplir.
■ **vi** se remplir ▸ **to fill up with petrol** faire le plein d'essence.

filled [fɪld] **adj** **1.** [roll] garni(e) **2.** [with emotion] **: filled (with)** plein(e) (de).

filler ['fɪləʳ] **n** [for cracks] mastic *m*.

filler cap n *UK* bouchon *m* du réservoir d'essence.

fillet *UK*, ***filet*** *US* ['fɪlɪt] n filet *m*.

fillet steak n filet *m* de bœuf.

fill-in n *inf* pis-aller *m inv*.

filling ['fɪlɪŋ] ■ adj très nourrissant(e).
■ n **1.** [in tooth] plombage *m* **2.** [in cake, sandwich] garniture *f*.

filling station n station-service *f*.

fillip ['fɪlɪp] n coup *m* de fouet.

filly ['fɪlɪ] (pl -ies) n pouliche *f*.

film [fɪlm] ■ n **1.** [movie] film *m* **2.** [layer, for camera] pellicule *f* **3.** [footage] images *fpl*.
■ vt & vi filmer.

film buff n *inf* cinéphile *mf*.

film crew n équipe *f* de tournage.

film festival n festival *m* cinématographique *OR* du cinéma.

filmgoer ['fɪlm,gəʊəʳ] n amateur *m* de cinéma, cinéphile *mf* ▸ **she is a regular filmgoer** elle va régulièrement au cinéma.

film industry n industrie *f* cinématographique *OR* du cinéma.

filming ['fɪlmɪŋ] n *(U)* tournage *m*.

film noir n CIN film *m* noir.

film rights n droits *mpl* cinématographiques.

film star n vedette *f* de cinéma.

filmstrip ['fɪlmstrɪp] n film *m* fixe.

film studio n studio *m* (de cinéma).

filmy ['fɪlmɪ] adj [material] léger(ère), vaporeux(euse), aérien(enne).

filo ['fi:ləʊ] n CULIN : **filo (pastry)** *pâte feuilletée très fine utilisée dans les pâtisseries moyen-orientales*.

Filofax® ['faɪləʊfæks] n Filofax® *m*.

filter ['fɪltəʳ] ■ n filtre *m*.
■ vt [coffee] passer / [water, oil, air] filtrer.
■ vi [people] : **to filter in** entrer par petits groupes.
◆ ***filter out*** vt sep filtrer.
◆ ***filter through*** vi filtrer.

filter coffee n café *m* filtre.

filter lane n *UK* ≃ voie *f* de droite.

filter paper n papier *m* filtre.

filter-tipped [-'tɪpt] adj à bout filtre.

filth [fɪlθ] n *(U)* **1.** [dirt] saleté *f*, crasse *f* **2.** [obscenity] obscénités *fpl*.

filthy ['fɪlθɪ] (comp -ier, superl -iest) adj **1.** [very dirty] dégoûtant(e), répugnant(e) **2.** [obscene] obscène.

filtration [fɪl'treɪʃn] n filtrage *m*, filtration *f*.

filtration plant [fɪl'treɪʃn-] n station *f* d'épuration.

Fimbra ['fɪmbrə] (abbr of ***Financial Intermediaries, Managers and Brokers Regulatory Association***) n *organisme britannique contrôlant les activités des courtiers d'assurances*.

fin [fɪn] n **1.** [of fish] nageoire *f* **2.** *US* [for swimmer] palme *f*.

final ['faɪnl] ■ adj **1.** [last] dernier(ère) **2.** [at end] final(e) **3.** [definitive] définitif(ive) ▸ **the referee's decision is final** la décision de l'arbitre est sans appel ▸ **that's my final offer** c'est ma dernière offre ▸ **I'm not moving, and that's final!** je ne bouge pas, un point c'est tout!
■ n finale *f*.
◆ ***finals*** npl UNIV examens *mpl* de dernière année.

final cut n CIN final cut *m*, montage *m* définitif.

final demand n dernier avertissement *m*.

finale [fɪ'nɑ:lɪ] n finale *m*.

finalist ['faɪnəlɪst] n finaliste *mf*.

finality [faɪ'nælətɪ] n [of decision, death] irrévocabilité *f*, caractère *m* définitif ▸ **there was a note of finality in his voice** il y avait quelque chose d'irrévocable dans sa voix.

finalization, *UK* ***-isation*** [,faɪnəlaɪ'zeɪʃn] n [of details, plans, arrangements] mise *f* au point / [of deal, agreement] conclusion *f*.

finalize, *UK* ***-ise*** ['faɪnəlaɪz] vt [details, plans] mettre au point / [deal, decision, agreement] mener à bonne fin.

finally ['faɪnəlɪ] adv enfin.

final offer n dernier prix *m*.

finance ■ n ['faɪnæns] *(U)* finance *f*.
■ vt [faɪ'næns] financer.
◆ ***finances*** npl finances *fpl*.

finance company n établissement *m* de crédit.

financial [fɪ'nænʃl] adj financier(ère).

financial adviser *UK*, ***financial advisor*** *US* n conseiller financier *m*, conseillère financière *f*.

financially [fɪ'nænʃəlɪ] adv financièrement.

financial services npl services *mpl* financiers.

financial year *UK*, ***fiscal year*** *US* n exercice *m*.

CULTURE

Financial Year (UK), Fiscal Year (US)

En Angleterre, l'année fiscale débute le 6 avril pour les particuliers et le 1er avril pour les organismes publics. Les travailleurs indépendants reçoivent au mois d'avril leur déclaration d'impôts, où ils doivent inscrire leurs revenus pour l'année fiscale en cours. Les redevances fiscales sont ensuite transmises deux fois par an, fin janvier et fin juillet. Aux États-Unis en revanche, l'année fiscale débute le 1er octobre pour les organismes publics et coïncide avec le calendrier annuel pour les salariés. Les compagnies nouvellement créées peuvent choisir les dates de début et de fin de leur année fiscale et respecter ultérieurement ce calendrier.

financier [fɪ'nænsɪəʳ] n *UK* financier *m*.

finch [fɪntʃ] n fringillidé *m*.

find [faɪnd] ■ vt (pt & pp found) **1.** [gen] trouver ▸ **to find one's way** trouver son chemin ▸ **I find her very pretty** je la trouve très jolie ▸ **he finds it very hard/impossible to make friends** il a beaucoup de mal à/il n'arrive pas à se faire des amis ▸ **go and find me a pair of scissors** va me

chercher une paire de ciseaux ▸ **to find one's feet** [in new job, situation] prendre ses repères **2.** [realize] **: to find (that)...** s'apercevoir que... / [discover, learn] constater ▸ **they came back to find the house had been burgled** à leur retour, ils ont constaté que la maison avait été cambriolée **3.** LAW **: to be found guilty/not guilty (of)** être déclaré(e) coupable/non coupable (de).
■ **n** trouvaille *f.*
◆ ***find out*** ■ **vi** se renseigner.
■ **vt insep 1.** [information] se renseigner sur **2.** [truth] découvrir, apprendre.
■ **vt sep** démasquer.

findings ['faɪndɪŋz] **npl** conclusions *fpl.*

fine [faɪn] ■ **adj 1.** [good - work] excellent(e) / [- building, weather] beau (belle) ▸ **a fine day** une belle journée ▸ **of the finest quality** de première qualité **2.** [perfectly satisfactory] très bien ▸ **I'm fine** ça va bien ▸ **I'll be back in about an hour or so – fine** je serai de retour d'ici environ une heure – d'accord *OR* entendu *OR* très bien ▸ **that sounds fine** [suggestion, idea] très bien, parfait **3.** [thin, smooth] fin(e) ▸ **to cut it fine** calculer juste **4.** [minute - detail, distinction] subtil(e) / [- adjustment, tuning] délicat(e).
■ **adv** [very well] très bien.
■ **n** amende *f* ▸ **a parking fine** une contravention *OR* amende pour stationnement interdit.
■ **vt** condamner à une amende.

fine art **n** *(U)* beaux-arts *mpl*
▸▸▸ **he's got it down to a fine art** *inf* il est expert en la matière.

fine arts **npl** beaux-arts *mpl.*

finely ['faɪnlɪ] **adv 1.** [chopped, ground] fin **2.** [tuned, balanced] délicatement.

fineness ['faɪnnɪs] **n** finesse *f.*

finery ['faɪnərɪ] **n** *(U)* parure *f.*

finesse [fɪ'nes] **n** finesse *f.*

fine-tooth(ed) comb **n : to go over sthg with a fine-toothed comb** passer qqch au peigne fin.

fine-tune **vt** [mechanism] régler avec précision / *fig* [plan] peaufiner / [economy] *régler grâce à des mesures fiscales et monétaires.*

fine-tuning [-'tju:nɪŋ] **n** [of machine, engine, radio] réglage *m* fin / *fig* [of plan] peaufinage *m* / [of economy] *réglage obtenu par des mesures fiscales et monétaires.*

finger ['fɪŋgəʳ] ■ **n** doigt *m* ▸ **to be all fingers and thumbs** avoir des mains de beurre, avoir deux mains gauches ▸ **to keep one's fingers crossed** croiser les doigts ▸ **she didn't lay a finger on him** elle n'a pas touché un cheveu de sa tête ▸ **he didn't lift a finger to help** il n'a pas levé le petit doigt ▸ **to point a** *OR* **the finger at sb** [accuse] accuser qqn ▸ **to put one's finger on sthg** mettre le doigt sur qqch ▸ **something has changed but I can't put my finger on it** il y a quelque chose de changé mais je n'arrive pas à dire ce que c'est ▸ **to twist sb round one's little finger** faire ce qu'on veut de qqn ▸ **to have one's finger on the pulse** [person] être très au fait de ce qui se passe / [magazine, TV programme] être à la pointe de l'actualité.
■ **vt** [feel] palper.

finger buffet **n** *buffet où sont servis des petits sandwiches, des petits fours et des légumes crus.*

finger food **n** [savoury] amuse-gueules *mpl* / [sweet] petits-fours *mpl.*

fingering ['fɪŋgərɪŋ] **n 1.** MUS [technique, numerals] doigté *m* **2.** *pej* [touching] tripotage *m* **3.** [knitting wool] laine *f* fine à tricoter.

fingerless ['fɪŋgələs] **adj : fingerless glove** mitaine *f.*

fingermark ['fɪŋgəmɑ:k] **n** trace *f* de doigt.

fingernail ['fɪŋgəneɪl] **n** ongle *m (de la main).*

fingerprint ['fɪŋgəprɪnt] **n** empreinte *f* (digitale) ▸ **to take sb's fingerprints** prendre les empreintes de qqn.

fingertip ['fɪŋgətɪp] **n** bout *m* du doigt ▸ **at one's fingertips** sur le bout des doigts.

finicky ['fɪnɪkɪ] **adj** *pej* [eater, task] difficile / [person] tatillon(onne).

finish ['fɪnɪʃ] ■ **n 1.** [end] fin *f* / [of race] arrivée *f* **2.** [texture] finition *f.*
■ **vt** finir, terminer / [exhaust] achever, tuer ▸ **to finish doing sthg** finir *OR* terminer de faire qqch.
■ **vi** finir, terminer / [school, film] se terminer ▸ **to finish first/third** [in race] arriver premier/troisième.
◆ ***finish off*** **vt sep** finir, terminer.
◆ ***finish up*** **vi** finir ▸ **they finished up arguing** ils ont fini par se disputer.
◆ ***finish with*** **vt insep** [want no more contact with] en finir avec / [boyfriend, girlfriend] rompre avec / [have no further use for] ne plus avoir besoin de.

finished ['fɪnɪʃt] **adj 1.** [ready, done, over] fini(e), terminé(e) **2.** [no longer interested] **: to be finished with sthg** en avoir fini avec qqch **3.** *inf* [done for] fichu(e).

finishing line ['fɪnɪʃɪŋ-] *UK*, ***finish line*** *US* **n** ligne *f* d'arrivée.

finishing school ['fɪnɪʃɪŋ-] **n** *école privée pour jeunes filles surtout axée sur l'enseignement des bonnes manières.*

finishing touch **n : to put the finishing touches to sthg** mettre la dernière touche *OR* la dernière main à qqch.

finite ['faɪnaɪt] **adj** fini(e).

Finland ['fɪnlənd] **n** Finlande *f* ▸ **in Finland** en Finlande.

Finn [fɪn] **n** Finlandais *m*, -e *f.*

Finnish ['fɪnɪʃ] ■ **adj** finlandais(e), finnois(e).
■ **n** [language] finnois *m.*

fiord [fjɔ:d] = ***fjord.***

fir [fɜ:ʳ] **n** sapin *m.*

fire ['faɪəʳ] ■ **n 1.** [gen] feu *m* ▸ **on fire** en feu ▸ **his forehead/he is on fire** *fig* [because of fever] son front/il est brûlant ▸ **to lay a fire** préparer un feu ▸ **to catch fire** prendre feu ▸ **to set fire to sthg** mettre le feu à qqch ▸ **open fire** feu de cheminée
2. [out of control] incendie *m* ▸ **fire!** au feu! ▸ **to cause** *OR* **to start a fire** [person, faulty wiring] provoquer un incendie ▸ **the building/village was set on fire** le bâtiment/village a été incendié
3. *UK* [heater] appareil *m* de chauffage
4. *(U)* [shooting] coups *mpl* de feu ▸ **to open fire (on)** ouvrir le feu (sur) ▸ **to return (sb's) fire** riposter (au tir de qqn).
■ **vt 1.** [shoot] tirer
2. *fig* [questions, accusations] lancer
3. *esp US* [dismiss] renvoyer.

■ **vi : to fire (on** *OR* **at)** faire feu (sur), tirer (sur) ▸ **fire!** MIL feu! ▸ **fire away!** allez-y!

fire alarm **n** avertisseur *m* d'incendie.

firearm ['faɪərɑ:m] **n** arme *f* à feu.

fireball ['faɪəbɔ:l] **n** boule *f* de feu.

firebomb ['faɪəbɒm] ■ **n** bombe *f* incendiaire.

■ **vt** lancer des bombes incendiaires à.

firebrand ['faɪəbrænd] **n** *fig* exalté *m*, -e *f*.

firebreak ['faɪəbreɪk] **n** pare-feu *m inv*.

fire brigade *UK*, ***fire department*** *US* **n** sapeurs-pompiers *mpl*.

fire chief *US* = ***fire master***.

firecracker ['faɪəˌkrækəʳ] **n** pétard *m*.

-fired ['faɪəd] **suffix** chauffé à ▸ **oil-fired/gas-fired central heating** chauffage central au mazout/gaz.

fire-damaged **adj** endommagé(e) par le feu.

fire department *US* = ***fire brigade***.

fire door **n** porte *f* coupe-feu.

fire drill **n** exercice *m* d'évacuation en cas d'incendie.

fire-eater **n** [performer] avaleur *m* de feu.

fire engine **n** voiture *f* de pompiers.

fire escape **n** escalier *m* de secours.

fire exit **n** sortie *f* de secours.

fire extinguisher **n** extincteur *m* d'incendie.

firefight ['faɪəfaɪt] **n** bataille *f* armée.

firefighter ['faɪəfaɪtəʳ] **n** pompier *m*, -ière *f*.

fire-fighting ■ **n** lutte *f* contre les incendies.

■ **comp** [equipment, techniques] de lutte contre les incendies.

firefly ['faɪəflaɪ] (**pl -flies**) **n** luciole *f*.

fireguard ['faɪəgɑ:d] **n** garde-feu *m inv*.

fire hazard **n : to be a fire hazard** présenter un risque d'incendie.

firehouse *US* = ***fire station***.

fire hydrant [-'haɪdrənt] **n** bouche *f* d'incendie.

firelight ['faɪəlaɪt] **n** *(U)* lueur *f* du feu.

firelighter ['faɪəlaɪtəʳ] **n** allume-feu *m inv*.

fireman ['faɪəmən] (**pl -men** [-mən]) **n** pompier *m*, -ière *f*.

fire master *UK*, ***fire chief*** *US* **n** capitaine *m* des pompiers.

fireplace ['faɪəpleɪs] **n** cheminée *f*.

fireplug *US* ['faɪəplʌg] = ***fire hydrant***.

firepower ['faɪəˌpaʊəʳ] **n** puissance *f* de feu.

fireproof ['faɪəpru:f] **adj** ignifugé(e).

fire-raiser [-ˌreɪzəʳ] **n** *UK* pyromane *mf*.

fire regulations **npl** consignes *fpl* en cas d'incendie.

fire service **n** *UK* sapeurs-pompiers *mpl*.

fireside ['faɪəsaɪd] **n : by the fireside** au coin du feu.

fire station **n** caserne *f* des pompiers.

fire truck *US* = ***fire engine***.

firewall ['faɪəwɔ:l] **n** COMPUT pare-feu *m*.

fire warden **n** [in forest] guetteur *m* d'incendie.

firewood ['faɪəwʊd] **n** bois *m* de chauffage.

firework ['faɪəwɜ:k] **n** pièce *f* d'artifice.

◆ ***fireworks*** **npl** [outburst of anger] étincelles *fpl* / [display] feu *m* d'artifice.

firework(s) display **n** feu *m* d'artifice.

firing ['faɪərɪŋ] **n** *(U)* MIL tir *m*, fusillade *f*.

firing line **n** MIL ligne *f* de tir ▸ **to be in the firing line** *fig* être dans la ligne de tir.

firing squad **n** peloton *m* d'exécution.

firm [fɜ:m] ■ **adj 1.** [gen] ferme ▸ **to stand firm** tenir bon **2.** [support, structure] solide **3.** [evidence, news] certain(e).

■ **n** firme *f*, société *f*.

◆ ***firm up*** ■ **vt sep 1.** [prices, trade] renforcer **2.** [agreement] rendre définitif(ive).

■ **vi** [prices, trade] se renforcer.

firmly ['fɜ:mlɪ] **adv** fermement.

firmness ['fɜ:mnɪs] **n 1.** [gen] fermeté *f* **2.** [discipline] rigueur *f* **3.** [of beliefs] force *f*.

first [fɜ:st] ■ **adj** premier(ère) ▸ **for the first time** pour la première fois ▸ **first thing in the morning** tôt le matin ▸ **the first six months** les six premiers mois ▸ **first things first** commençons par le plus important ▸ **I don't know the first thing about it** je ne sais absolument rien là-dessus, je n'y connais rien du tout.

■ **adv 1.** [before anyone else] en premier ▸ **I saw it first!** c'est moi qui l'ai vu le premier *OR* en premier! ▸ **women and children first** les femmes et les enfants d'abord **2.** [before anything else] d'abord ▸ **first of all** tout d'abord **3.** [for the first time] (pour) la première fois.

■ **n 1.** [person] premier *m*, -ère *f* **2.** [unprecedented event] première *f* **3.** *UK* UNIV *diplôme universitaire avec mention très bien*.

◆ ***at first*** **adv** d'abord.

◆ ***at first hand*** **adv** de première main.

first aid **n** *(U)* premiers secours *mpl*.

first-aider [-'eɪdəʳ] **n** *UK* secouriste *mf*.

first-aid kit **n** trousse *f* de premiers secours.

First Amendment **n** *US* **: the First Amendment** le Premier Amendement *(de la Constitution des États-Unis garantissant les libertés individuelles du citoyen américain, notamment la liberté d'expression)*.

first-born ■ **adj** premier-né (première-née).

■ **n** premier-né *m*, première-née *f*.

first-class **adj 1.** [excellent] excellent(e) **2.** *UK* UNIV avec mention très bien **3.** [ticket, compartment] de première classe / [stamp, letter] tarif normal.

first-class mail **n** courrier *m* tarif normal.

first cousin **n** cousin germain *m*, cousine germaine *f*.

first-day cover **n** émission *f* du premier jour.

first-degree **adj 1.** MED **: first-degree burn** brûlure *f* au premier degré **2.** *US* LAW **: first-degree murder** ≃ homicide *m* volontaire.

first floor **n** *UK* premier étage *m* / *US* rez-de-chaussée *m inv*.

first-generation **adj** de première génération.

firsthand [fɜːstˈhænd] **adj** & **adv** de première main.

first lady **n** première dame *f* du pays, femme *f* du Président.

first language **n** langue *f* maternelle.

first lieutenant **n** lieutenant *m*.

firstly [ˈfɜːstlɪ] **adv** premièrement.

first mate **n** second *m*.

First Minister **n** [in Scottish Parliament] président *m* du Parlement écossais.

first name **n** prénom *m*.
◆ ***first-name*** **adj : to be on first-name terms with sb** appeler qqn par son prénom.

first night **n** première *f*.

first offender **n** délinquant *m* primaire.

first officer = ***first mate***.

first-past-the-post **adj** *UK* POL [system] majoritaire à un tour.

first-rate **adj** excellent(e).

first refusal **n** priorité *f*.

First Secretary **n** [in Welsh Assembly] président *m* de l'Assemblée galloise.

first-time buyer **n** [of property] *personne achetant un logement pour la première fois*.

First World War **n : the First World War** la Première Guerre Mondiale.

firtree [ˈfɜːtriː] = ***fir***.

FIS (abbr of ***Family Income Supplement***) **n** *complément familial en Grande-Bretagne*.

fiscal [ˈfɪskl] **adj** fiscal(e).

fiscal year *US* = ***financial year***.

fish [fɪʃ] ■ **n** (pl **fish**) poisson *m*.
■ **vt** [river, sea] pêcher dans.
■ **vi 1.** [fisherman] **: to fish (for sthg)** pêcher (qqch) **2.** [try to obtain] **: to fish for** [compliments] essayer de s'attirer / [information] essayer d'obtenir.
◆ ***fish out*** **vt sep** *inf* sortir, extirper.

fish and chips **npl** *UK* poisson *m* frit avec frites.

fish-and-chip shop **n** *UK magasin vendant du poisson frit et des frites*.

fishbowl [ˈfɪʃbəʊl] **n** bocal *m* (à poissons).

fishcake [ˈfɪʃkeɪk] **n** croquette *f* de poisson.

fisherman [ˈfɪʃəmən] (pl **-men** [-mən]) **n** pêcheur *m*, -se *f*.

fishery [ˈfɪʃərɪ] (pl **-ies**) **n** pêcherie *f*.

fish-eye lens **n** objectif *m* ultra-grand angle.

fish factory **n** usine *f* piscicole.

fish farm **n** centre *m* de pisciculture.

fish farming **n** pisciculture *f*.

fish finger *UK*, ***fish stick*** *US* **n** CULIN bâtonnet *m* de poisson pané.

fishhook [ˈfɪʃhʊk] **n** hameçon *m*.

fishing [ˈfɪʃɪŋ] **n** pêche *f* ▸ **to go fishing** aller à la pêche.

fishing boat **n** bateau *m* de pêche.

fishing ground **n** zone *f* de pêche.

fishing line **n** ligne *f* de pêche.

fishing rod **n** canne *f* à pêche.

fishmonger [ˈfɪʃˌmʌŋgəʳ] **n** *UK* poissonnier *m*, -ère *f* ▸ **fishmonger's (shop)** poissonnerie *f*.

fishnet [ˈfɪʃnet] **n 1.** [for fishing] filet *m* **2.** [material] **: fishnet stockings/tights** bas *mpl*/collant *m* résille.

fish slice **n** *UK* pelle *f* à poisson.

fish stick *US* = ***fish finger***.

fish tank **n** [in house] aquarium *m* / [on fish farm] vivier *m*.

fishwife [ˈfɪʃwaɪf] (pl **-wives** [-waɪvz]) **n** *dated* & *pej* mégère *f*.

fishy [ˈfɪʃɪ] (comp **-ier**, superl **-iest**) **adj 1.** [smell, taste] de poisson **2.** [suspicious] louche.

fission [ˈfɪʃn] **n** fission *f*.

fissure [ˈfɪʃəʳ] **n** fissure *f*.

fist [fɪst] **n** poing *m*.

fistfight [ˈfɪstfaɪt] **n** bagarre *f* aux poings ▸ **to have a fistfight with sb** se battre aux poings contre qqn.

fisticuffs [ˈfɪstɪkʌfs] **n** *(U) hum* bagarre *f*.

fit [fɪt] ■ **adj 1.** [suitable] convenable ▸ **fit to eat** [edible] mangeable / [not poisonous] comestible ▸ **fit to drink** [water] potable ▸ **to be fit for sthg** être bon (bonne) à qqch ▸ **a meal fit for a king** un repas digne d'un roi ▸ **to be fit to do sthg** être apte à faire qqch ▸ **she's not a fit mother** c'est une mère indigne ▸ **to be fit to drop** être mort de fatigue ▸ **to see OR think fit (to do sthg)** juger bon (de faire qqch) **2.** [healthy] en forme ▸ **to keep fit** se maintenir en forme ▸ **to be as fit as a fiddle** se porter comme un charme.
■ **n 1.** [of clothes, shoes] ajustement *m* ▸ **it's a tight fit** c'est un peu juste ▸ **it's a good fit** c'est la bonne taille **2.** [epileptic seizure] crise *f* ▸ **to have a fit** avoir une crise / *fig* piquer une crise **3.** [bout - of crying] crise *f* / [- of rage] accès *m* / [- of sneezing] suite *f* ▸ **to get a fit of the giggles** être pris d'un *OR* piquer un fou rire ▸ **in fits and starts** par à-coups.
■ **vt** (pt & pp **-ted**, cont **-ting**) **1.** [be correct size for] aller à ▸ **those trousers fit you better than the other ones** ce pantalon te va mieux que l'autre ▸ **the lid doesn't fit the pot very well** ce couvercle n'est pas très bien adapté à la casserole **2.** [place] **: to fit sthg into sthg** insérer qqch dans qqch **3.** [provide] **: to fit sthg with sthg** équiper *OR* munir qqch de qqch **4.** [be suitable for] correspondre à ▸ **to make the punishment fit the crime** adapter le châtiment au crime **5.** [for clothes] **: to be fitted for** essayer.
■ **vi** (pt & pp **-ted**, cont **-ting**) [be correct size, go] aller / [into container] entrer ▸ **we won't all fit round one table** nous ne tiendrons pas tous autour d'une table.
◆ ***fit in*** ■ **vt sep** [find time for - patient] prendre / [- friend] trouver du temps pour ▸ **could you fit in this translation by the end of the week?** est-ce que vous pourriez faire cette traduction d'ici la fin de la semaine?
■ **vi** s'intégrer ▸ **to fit in with sthg** correspondre à qqch ▸ **to fit in with sb** s'accorder à qqn.

fitful [ˈfɪtfʊl] **adj** [sleep] agité(e) / [wind, showers] intermittent(e).

fitfully ['fɪtfʊlɪ] **adv** [work] par à-coups / [attend] irrégulièrement / [sleep] de manière intermittente.

fitment ['fɪtmənt] **n** *UK* meuble *m* encastré.

fitness ['fɪtnɪs] **n** *(U)* **1.** [health] forme *f* **2.** [suitability] : **fitness (for)** aptitude *f* (pour).

fitted ['fɪtəd] **adj 1.** [suited] : **fitted for** *OR* **to** apte à ▸ **to be fitted to do sthg** être apte à faire qqch **2.** [tailored - shirt, jacket] ajusté(e) ▸ **fitted sheet** drap-housse *m* **3.** *UK* [built-in] encastré(e).

fitted carpet [ˌfɪtəd-] **n** *UK* moquette *f*.

fitted kitchen [ˌfɪtəd-] **n** *UK* cuisine *f* intégrée *OR* équipée.

fitter ['fɪtər] **n** [mechanic] monteur *m*.

fitting ['fɪtɪŋ] ■ **adj** *fml* approprié(e).
■ **n 1.** [part] appareil *m* **2.** [for clothing] essayage *m*.
◆ ***fittings*** **npl** *UK* installations *fpl*.

-fitting **suffix : close-fitting, tight-fitting** [item of clothing] moulant / [screwtop lid] qui ferme bien / [lid of saucepan] adapté ▸ **loose-fitting** [item of clothing] ample.

fittingly ['fɪtɪŋlɪ] **adv** [dressed] convenablement ▸ **fittingly, the government has agreed to ratify the treaty** comme il le fallait, le gouvernement a accepté de ratifier le traité.

fitting room **n** cabine *f* d'essayage.

fit-up **n** *v inf UK crime sl* coup *m* monté.

five [faɪv] **num** cinq ; see also ***six***.

five and dime **n** *US* bazar *m*, supérette *f*.

five-a-side *UK* ■ **n** SPORT football *m* à dix.
■ **comp** SPORT : **five-a-side football** football *m* à dix.

five-day week **n** semaine *f* de cinq jours.

fivefold ['faɪvfəʊld] ■ **adj** [increase] au quintuple.
■ **adv** par cinq, au quintuple.

fiver ['faɪvər] **n** *inf* **1.** *UK* [amount] cinq livres *fpl* / [note] billet *m* de cinq livres **2.** *US* [amount] cinq dollars *mpl* / [note] billet *m* de cinq dollars.

five-star **adj** [hotel] cinq étoiles / [treatment] exceptionnel(elle).

Five-Year Plan **n** ECON Plan *m* quinquennal.

fix [fɪks] ■ **vt 1.** [gen] fixer ▸ **to fix sthg to sthg** fixer qqch à qqch ▸ **have you (got) anything fixed for Friday?** as-tu quelque chose de prévu pour vendredi? **2.** [arrange, sort out] s'occuper de ▸ **I'll fix it** je vais m'en occuper ▸ **try to fix it so you don't have to stay overnight** essaye de t'arranger pour que tu ne sois pas obligé de passer la nuit là-bas **3.** [in memory] graver **4.** [repair] réparer **5.** *inf* [rig] truquer **6.** [food, drink] préparer.
■ **n 1.** *inf* [difficult situation] : **to be in a fix** être dans le pétrin **2.** *drug sl* piqûre *f* **3.** *inf* [unfair arrangement] : **the result was a fix** le résultat avait été truqué.
◆ ***fix up*** **vt sep 1.** [provide] : **to fix sb up with sthg** obtenir qqch pour qqn **2.** [arrange] arranger ▸ **to fix sb up with a date** trouver un/une partenaire à qqn **3.** [room, house] refaire.

fixated [fɪk'seɪtɪd] **adj** fixé(e) ▸ **to be fixated on sthg** être fixé sur qqch.

fixation [fɪk'seɪʃn] **n : fixation (on** *OR* **about)** obsession *f* (de).

fixed [fɪkst] **adj 1.** [attached] fixé(e) **2.** [set, unchanging] fixe / [smile] figé(e).

fixed assets **npl** immobilisations *fpl*.

fixedly ['fɪksɪdlɪ] **adv** [stare] fixement.

fixed rate **n** FIN taux *m* fixe.

fixer ['fɪksər] **n 1.** *inf* [person] combinard *m*, -e *f* **2.** PHOT fixateur *m* **3.** [adhesive] adhésif *m*.

fixture ['fɪkstʃər] **n 1.** [furniture] installation *f* **2.** [permanent feature] tradition *f* bien établie **3.** *UK* SPORT rencontre *f* (sportive).

fizz [fɪz] ■ **vi** [lemonade, champagne] pétiller / [fireworks] crépiter.
■ **n** [of drink] pétillement *m*.

fizziness ['fɪzɪnɪs] **n** [of drink] pétillement *m*.

fizzle ['fɪzl] ◆ ***fizzle out*** **vi** [fire] s'éteindre / [firework] se terminer / [interest, enthusiasm] se dissiper.

fizzy ['fɪzɪ] (**comp -ier, superl -iest**) **adj** pétillant(e).

fjord [fjɔːd] **n** fjord *m*.

FL abbr of ***Florida***.

flab [flæb] **n** *inf pej* graisse *f*.

flabbergasted ['flæbəgɑːstɪd] **adj** sidéré(e).

flabby ['flæbɪ] (**comp -ier, superl -iest**) **adj** mou (molle).

flaccid ['flæsɪd] **adj** flasque.

flag [flæg] ■ **n** drapeau *m*.
■ **vi** (**pt & pp -ged, cont -ging**) [person, enthusiasm, energy] faiblir / [conversation] traîner.
◆ ***flag down*** **vt sep** [taxi] héler ▸ **to flag sb down** faire signe à qqn de s'arrêter.

flag day **n 1.** [in UK] *jour de quête d'une œuvre de charité* **2.** [in US] : **Flag Day** *le 14 juin, jour férié qui commémore la création du drapeau américain.*

flagged [flægd] **adj** dallé(e).

flagging ['flægɪŋ] **adj** [enthusiasm, spirits] qui baisse / [conversation] qui tombe *OR* s'épuise.

flag of convenience **n** *UK* pavillon *m* de complaisance.

flagon ['flægən] **n** *dated* **1.** [bottle] bonbonne *f* **2.** [jug] cruche *f*.

flagpole ['flægpəʊl] **n** mât *m*.

flagrant ['fleɪgrənt] **adj** flagrant(e).

flagrantly ['fleɪgrəntlɪ] **adv** [abuse, disregard, defy] d'une manière flagrante.

flagship ['flægʃɪp] **n 1.** [ship] vaisseau *m* amiral **2.** *fig* [product] produit *m* vedette / [company] fleuron *m*.

flagship store **n** magasin *m* vitrine.

flagstaff = ***flagpole***.

flagstone ['flægstəʊn] **n** dalle *f*.

flag-waving **n** *(U) inf fig* discours *mpl* cocardiers.

flail [fleɪl] **vi** battre l'air.

flair [fleər] **n 1.** [talent] don *m* ▸ **to have a flair for sthg** avoir un don pour qqch **2.** *(U)* [stylishness] style *m*.

flak [flæk] **n** *(U)* **1.** [gunfire] tir *m* antiaérien **2.** *inf* [criticism] critiques *fpl* sévères.

flake [fleɪk] ■ **n** [of paint, plaster] écaille *f* / [of snow] flocon *m* / [of skin] petit lambeau *m*.
■ **vi** [paint, plaster] s'écailler / [skin] peler.
◆ ***flake out*** **vi** *inf* s'écrouler de fatigue.

flaky ['fleɪkɪ] (comp **-ier**, superl **-iest**) **adj** **1.** [flaking - skin] qui pèle / [- paintwork] écaillé(e) / [- texture] floconneux(euse) **2.** *inf* [person] barjo.

flaky pastry **n** *(U)* pâte *f* feuilletée.

flambé ['flɑ:mbeɪ] ■ **adj** flambé(e).
■ **vt** (pt & pp **-ed**, cont **-ing**) flamber.

flamboyance [flæm'bɔɪəns] **n** [of style, dress, behaviour] extravagance *f*.

flamboyant [flæm'bɔɪənt] **adj** **1.** [showy, confident] extravagant(e) **2.** [brightly coloured] flamboyant(e).

flamboyantly [flæm'bɔɪəntlɪ] **adv** de manière extravagante.

flame [fleɪm] ■ **n** flamme *f* ▸ **in flames** en flammes ▸ **to burst into flames** s'enflammer ▸ **old flame** ancien béguin *m*.
■ **vi** **1.** [be on fire] flamber **2.** [redden] s'empourprer.

flamenco [flə'meŋkəʊ] ■ **n** flamenco *m*.
■ **comp** [dancer] de flamenco ▸ **flamenco music** flamenco *m*.

flameproof ['fleɪmpru:f] **adj** [dish] allant au feu.

flame-retardant [-rɪ'tɑ:dənt] **adj** qui ralentit la propagation des flammes.

flame-thrower [-,θrəʊə^r] **n** lance-flammes *m inv*.

flaming ['fleɪmɪŋ] **adj** **1.** [fire-coloured] flamboyant(e) **2.** *UK* [very angry] furibond(e) **3.** *UK inf* [expressing annoyance] foutu(e), fichu(e).

flamingo [flə'mɪŋgəʊ] (pl **-s** *OR* **-es**) **n** flamant *m* rose.

flammable ['flæməbl] **adj** inflammable.

flan [flæn] **n** *UK* tarte *f* / *US* flan *m*.

Flanders ['flɑ:ndəz] **n** Flandre *f*, Flandres *fpl*.

flange [flændʒ] **n** bride *f*.

flank [flæŋk] ■ **n** flanc *m*.
■ **vt** : **to be flanked by** être flanqué(e) de.

flannel ['flænl] **n** **1.** [fabric] flanelle *f* **2.** *UK* [facecloth] gant *m* de toilette.
◆ ***flannels*** **npl** *UK* pantalon *m* de flanelle.

flannelette [flænə'let] **n** pilou *m*.

flap [flæp] ■ **n** **1.** [of envelope, pocket] rabat *m* / [of skin] lambeau *m* **2.** *UK inf* [panic] : **in a flap** paniqué(e).
■ **vt** & **vi** (pt & pp **-ped**, cont **-ping**) battre.

flapjack ['flæpdʒæk] **n** **1.** *UK* [biscuit] biscuit *m* à l'avoine **2.** *US* [pancake] crêpe *f* épaisse.

flare [fleə^r] ■ **n** [distress signal] fusée *f* éclairante.
■ **vi** **1.** [burn brightly] : **to flare (up)** s'embraser **2.** [intensify] : **to flare (up)** [war, revolution] s'intensifier soudainement / [person] s'emporter **3.** [widen - trousers, skirt] s'évaser / [- nostrils] se dilater.
◆ ***flares*** **npl** *UK* pantalon *m* à pattes d'éléphant.

flared [fleəd] **adj** [trousers] à pattes d'éléphant / [skirt] évasé(e).

flare gun **n** pistolet *m* de détresse, lance-fusées *m inv*.

flash [flæʃ] ■ **adj** **1.** PHOT au flash **2.** *inf* [expensive-looking] tape-à-l'œil *(inv)*.
■ **n** **1.** [of light, colour] éclat *m* ▸ **flash of lightning** éclair *m* **2.** PHOT flash *m* **3.** [sudden moment] éclair *m* ▸ **in a flash** en un rien de temps ▸ **quick as a flash** rapide comme l'éclair.
■ **vt** **1.** [shine] projeter ▸ **to flash one's headlights** faire un appel de phares **2.** [send out - signal, smile] envoyer / [- look] jeter ▸ **to flash a smile at sb** *fig* lancer *OR* adresser un sourire à qqn **3.** [show] montrer ▸ **to flash a message up on the screen** faire apparaître un message sur l'écran ▸ **to flash one's money around** [to impress] dépenser son argent avec ostentation.
■ **vi** **1.** [torch] briller **2.** [light - on and off] clignoter / [eyes] jeter des éclairs ▸ **lightning flashed directly overhead** il y a eu des éclairs juste au-dessus ▸ **to flash at sb** AUT faire un appel de phares à qqn **3.** [rush] : **to flash by** *OR* **past** passer comme un éclair **4.** [thought] : **to flash into one's mind** venir soudainement à l'esprit ▸ **my life flashed before me** ma vie a défilé devant mes yeux **5.** [appear] surgir.

flashback ['flæʃbæk] **n** flash-back *m*, retour *m* en arrière.

flashbulb ['flæʃbʌlb] **n** ampoule *f* de flash.

flash card **n** *carte portant un mot, une image, etc utilisée comme aide à l'apprentissage.*

flashcube ['flæʃkju:b] **n** flash *m* en forme de cube.

flasher ['flæʃə^r] **n** **1.** *UK* [light] clignotant *m* **2.** *UK inf* [man] exhibitionniste *m*.

flash flood **n** crue *f* subite.

flashgun ['flæʃgʌn] **n** flash *m*.

flashily ['flæʃɪlɪ] **adv** *inf pej* d'une manière tapageuse *OR* tape-à-l'œil, tapageusement.

flashlight ['flæʃlaɪt] **n** *esp US* [torch] lampe *f* électrique.

flash photography **n** photographie *f* au flash.

flash point **n** **1.** [moment] moment *m* critique **2.** [place] point *m* chaud.

flashy ['flæʃɪ] (comp **-ier**, superl **-iest**) **adj** *inf* tape-à-l'œil *(inv)*.

flask [flɑ:sk] **n** **1.** [thermos flask] Thermos® *m ou f* **2.** CHEM ballon *m* **3.** [hip flask] flasque *f*.

flat [flæt] ■ **adj** (comp **-ter**, superl **-test**) **1.** [gen] plat(e) ▸ **he was lying flat on his back** il était allongé à plat sur le dos ▸ **to fall flat** [joke] tomber à plat **2.** [tyre] crevé(e) **3.** [refusal, denial] catégorique **4.** [business, trade] calme **5.** [dull - voice, tone] monotone / [- performance, writing] terne ▸ **to feel flat** *fig* se sentir vidé *OR* à plat **6.** [MUS - person] qui chante trop grave / [- note] bémol **7.** [fare, price] fixe **8.** [beer, lemonade] éventé(e) ▸ **to go flat** [beer, soft drink] s'éventer, perdre ses bulles **9.** [battery] à plat.
■ **adv** **1.** [level] à plat **2.** [absolutely] : **flat broke** complètement fauché(e) ▸ **she turned me down flat** elle m'a opposé un refus catégorique **3.** [exactly] : **two hours flat** deux heures pile **4.** MUS faux.
■ **n** **1.** *UK* [apartment] appartement *m* ▸ **(block of) flats** immeuble *m* (d'habitation) **2.** [of hand, blade] plat *m* **3.** MUS bémol *m*.
◆ ***flat out*** **adv** [work] d'arrache-pied / [travel - subj: vehicle] le plus vite possible.

flat cap **n** *UK* casquette *f*.

flat-chested [-'tʃestɪd] **adj** plat(e) comme une limande.

flatfish ['flætfɪʃ] (pl **flatfish**) **n** poisson *m* plat.

flat-footed [-'fʊtɪd] **adj** aux pieds plats.

flat-hunt **vi** *(usu in progressive) UK* chercher un appartement.

flatlet ['flætlɪt] **n** *UK* studio *m*.

flatly ['flætlɪ] **adv** **1.** [absolutely] catégoriquement **2.** [dully - say] avec monotonie / [- perform] de façon terne.

flatmate ['flætmeɪt] **n** *UK personne avec laquelle on partage un appartement.*

flat racing **n** *(U)* courses *fpl* de plat.

flat rate **n** tarif *m* forfaitaire.

flat-screen **adj** TV & COMPUT à écran plat.

flatten ['flætn] **vt** **1.** [make flat - steel, paper] aplatir / [- wrinkles, bumps] aplanir ▸ **to flatten o.s. against sthg** s'aplatir contre qqch **2.** [destroy] raser **3.** *inf* [knock out] assommer.
◆ ***flatten out*** ■ **vi** s'aplanir.
■ **vt sep** aplanir.

flatter ['flætəʳ] **vt** flatter ▸ **to flatter o.s. (that)** se flatter *(de + infin)*.

flatterer ['flætərəʳ] **n** flatteur *m*, -euse *f*.

flattering ['flætərɪŋ] **adj** **1.** [complimentary] flatteur (euse) **2.** [clothes] seyant(e).

flattery ['flætərɪ] **n** flatterie *f*.

flatulence ['flætjʊləns] **n** flatulence *f*.

flatulent ['flætjʊlənt] **adj** flatulent.

flatware ['flætweəʳ] **n** *(U) US* couverts *mpl*.

flaunt [flɔːnt] **vt** faire étalage de.

flautist *UK* ['flɔːtɪst], ***flutist*** *US* ['fluːtɪst] **n** flûtiste *mf*.

flavour *UK*, ***flavor*** *US* ['fleɪvəʳ] ■ **n** **1.** [of food] goût *m* / [of ice cream, yoghurt] parfum *m* **2.** *fig* [atmosphere] atmosphère *f*.
■ **vt** parfumer.

-flavoured *UK*, ***-flavored*** *US* ['fleɪvəd] **suffix : chocolate-flavoured** au chocolat ▸ **vanilla-flavoured** à la vanille.

flavouring *UK*, ***flavoring*** *US* ['fleɪvərɪŋ] **n** *(U)* parfum *m*.

flavourless *UK*, ***flavorless*** *US* ['fleɪvəlɪs] **adj** sans goût, insipide.

flaw [flɔː] **n** [in material, character] défaut *m* / [in plan, argument] faille *f*.

flawed [flɔːd] **adj** [material, character] qui présente des défauts / [plan, argument] qui présente des failles.

flawless ['flɔːlɪs] **adj** parfait(e).

flax [flæks] **n** lin *m*.

flay [fleɪ] **vt** [skin] écorcher.

flea [fliː] **n** puce *f* / *UK inf* **: to send sb away with a flea in his/her ear** envoyer promener qqn.

fleabite ['fliːbaɪt] **n** piqûre *f* OR morsure *f* de puce / *fig* [trifle] broutille *f*.

flea-bitten **adj** couvert(e) de puces / *fig* [shabby] miteux(euse).

flea collar **n** collier *m* anti-puces.

flea market **n** marché *m* aux puces.

fleapit ['fliːpɪt] **n** *inf* cinéma *m* OR théâtre *m* miteux ▸ **the local fleapit** *hum* le cinéma du coin.

fleck [flek] ■ **n** moucheture *f*, petite tache *f*.
■ **vt : flecked with** moucheté(e) de.

fled [fled] **pt & pp** ➤ ***flee***.

fledg(e)ling ['fledʒlɪŋ] ■ **adj** [industry] nouveau(elle) / [doctor, democracy] jeune.
■ **n** oisillon *m*.

flee [fliː] (pt & pp **fled**) **vt & vi** fuir.

fleece [fliːs] ■ **n** [animal] toison *f* / [fabric] polaire *f*.
■ **vt** *inf* escroquer.

fleecy ['fliːsɪ] **adj** [material] laineux(euse) / [clouds] cotonneux(euse).

fleet [fliːt] **n** **1.** [of ships] flotte *f* **2.** [of cars, buses] parc *m*.

fleeting ['fliːtɪŋ] **adj** [moment] bref (brève) / [look] fugitif(ive) / [visit] éclair *(inv)*.

fleetingly ['fliːtɪŋlɪ] **adv** [glimpse] rapidement.

Fleet Street **n** *rue de Londres dont le nom est utilisé pour désigner la presse britannique.*

CULTURE

Fleet Street

L'appellation de **Fleet Street**, (du nom d'une rivière londonienne, la Fleet), est directement associée à l'industrie de la presse anglaise. En 1500, un pionnier de l'imprimerie, Wynkyn de Worde, fut le premier à éditer plus de 800 livres situés dans ses locaux près de Shoe Lane, puis les sociétés d'édition se multiplièrent dans l'avenue. Avec l'impression du premier journal en 1702, la rue fut investie par des centaines de titres nationaux et locaux, et devint le cœur géographique de la presse britannique. Quand on est passé à l'impression électronique, la plupart des publications se sont déplacées dans les Docklands.

Fleming ['flemɪŋ] **n** Flamand *m*, -e *f*.

Flemish ['flemɪʃ] ■ **adj** flamand(e).
■ **n** [language] flamand *m*.
■ **npl : the Flemish** les Flamands *mpl*.

flesh [fleʃ] **n** chair *f* ▸ **his/her flesh and blood** [family] les siens ▸ **in the flesh** en chair et en os.
◆ ***flesh out*** **vt sep** étoffer.

flesh-coloured *UK*, ***flesh-colored*** *US* **adj** [tights] couleur chair.

flesh wound **n** blessure *f* superficielle.

fleshy ['fleʃɪ] (comp **-ier**, superl **-iest**) **adj** [arms] charnu(e) / [person] bien en chair / [cheeks] joufflu(e).

flew [fluː] **pt** ➤ ***fly***.

flex [fleks] ■ **n** ELEC fil *m*.
■ **vt** [bend] fléchir.

flexibility ['fleksə'bɪlətɪ] **n** flexibilité *f*.

flexible ['fleksəbl] **adj** flexible.

flexitime ['fleksɪtaɪm], *US* ***flextime*** ['flekstaɪm] **n** *(U)* horaire *m* à la carte ***OR*** flexible.

flick [flɪk] ■ **n 1.** [of whip, towel] petit coup *m* **2.** [with finger] chiquenaude *f* **3.** *inf* [cinema] film *m*.
■ **vt 1.** [whip, towel] donner un petit coup de **2.** [with finger - remove] enlever d'une chiquenaude / [- throw] envoyer d'une chiquenaude **3.** [switch] appuyer sur.
◆ ***flicks*** **npl** *UK inf dated* **: the flicks** le ciné.
◆ ***flick through*** **vt insep** feuilleter.

flicker ['flɪkəʳ] ■ **n 1.** [of light, candle] vacillement *m* **2.** [of hope, interest] lueur *f*.
■ **vi 1.** [candle, light] vaciller **2.** [shadow] trembler / [eyelids] ciller.

flick knife **n** *UK* couteau *m* à cran d'arrêt.

flier ['flaɪəʳ] **n 1.** [pilot] aviateur *m*, -trice *f* **2.** [aircraft passenger] passager *m*, -ère *f* **3.** [advertising leaflet] prospectus *m*.

flies [flaɪz] **npl 1.** = ***fly*** *(n sense 2)* **2.** THEAT dessus *mpl*, cintres *mpl*.

flight [flaɪt] **n 1.** [gen] vol *m* ▸ **flight BA 314 to Paris** le vol BA 314 à destination de Paris ▸ **how was your flight?** as-tu fait bon voyage? ▸ **flight of fancy *OR* of the imagination** envolée *f* de l'imagination **2.** [of steps, stairs] volée *f* ▸ **it's another three flights up** c'est trois étages plus haut **3.** [escape] fuite *f* ▸ **to take flight** prendre la fuite.

flight attendant **n** steward *m*, hôtesse *f* de l'air.

flight crew **n** équipage *m*.

flight deck **n 1.** [of aircraft carrier] pont *m* d'envol **2.** [of plane] cabine *f* de pilotage.

flight path **n** trajectoire *f*.

flight recorder **n** enregistreur *m* de vol.

flight simulator **n** simulateur *m* de vol.

flighty ['flaɪtɪ] (**comp -ier**, **superl -iest**) **adj** frivole.

flimsily ['flɪmzɪlɪ] **adv** [built, constructed] d'une manière peu solide, peu solidement.

flimsy ['flɪmzɪ] (**comp -ier**, **superl -iest**) **adj** [dress, material] léger(ère) / [building, bookcase] peu solide / [excuse] piètre.

flinch [flɪntʃ] **vi** tressaillir ▸ **to flinch from sthg/from doing sthg** reculer devant qqch/à l'idée de faire qqch.

fling [flɪŋ] ■ **n** *inf* [affair] aventure *f*, affaire *f*.
■ **vt** (**pt & pp flung**) lancer ▸ **to fling o.s. into an armchair/onto the ground** se jeter dans un fauteuil/par terre.

flint [flɪnt] **n 1.** [rock] silex *m* **2.** [in lighter] pierre *f*.

flinty ['flɪntɪ] (**comp -ier**, **superl -iest**) **adj** [rocks, soil] siliceux(euse) / *fig* [heart] de pierre.

flip [flɪp] ■ **vt** (**pt & pp -ped**, **cont -ping**) **1.** [turn - pancake] faire sauter / [- record] tourner **2.** [switch] appuyer sur **3.** [flick] envoyer d'une chiquenaude ▸ **to flip a coin** jouer à pile ou face.
■ **vi** (**pt & pp -ped**, **cont -ping**) *inf* [lose control] flipper / [become angry] piquer une colère.
■ **n 1.** [flick] chiquenaude *f* **2.** [somersault] saut *m* périlleux.
◆ ***flip through*** **vt insep** feuilleter.

flip chart **n** tableau *m* à feuilles.

flip-flop **n** [shoe] tong *f*.

flippant ['flɪpənt] **adj** désinvolte.

flippantly ['flɪpəntlɪ] **adv** avec désinvolture.

flipper ['flɪpəʳ] **n 1.** [of animal] nageoire *f* **2.** [for swimmer, diver] palme *f*.

flipping ['flɪpɪŋ] *UK inf* ■ **adj** fichu(e).
■ **adv** sacrément.

flip side **n 1.** *fig* [disadvantage of] inconvénient *m* **2.** [of record] face *f* B.

flip top **n** [of packet] couvercle *m* à rabat.

flirt [flɜːt] ■ **n** flirt *m*.
■ **vi 1.** [with person] **: to flirt (with sb)** flirter (avec qqn) **2.** [with idea] **: to flirt with sthg** caresser qqch.

flirtation [flɜː'teɪʃn] **n 1.** [gen] flirt *m* **2.** [brief interest] **: to have a flirtation with sthg** caresser qqch.

flirtatious [flɜː'teɪʃəs] **adj** flirteur(euse).

flit [flɪt] (**pt & pp -ted**, **cont -ting**) **vi 1.** [bird] voleter **2.** [expression, idea] **: to flit across** traverser.

float [fləʊt] ■ **n 1.** [for buoyancy] flotteur *m* **2.** [in procession] char *m* **3.** [money] petite caisse *f*.
■ **vt 1.** [on water] faire flotter **2.** [idea, project] lancer.
■ **vi** [on water] flotter / [through air] glisser.

floater ['fləʊtəʳ] **n** *US* [floating voter] (électeur *m*) indécis *m*, électrice *f* indécise.

floating ['fləʊtɪŋ] **adj 1.** [on water] flottant(e) **2.** [transitory] instable.

floating rate **n** FIN taux *m* flottant.

floating voter **n** *UK* (électeur *m*) indécis *m*, électrice *f* indécise.

flock [flɒk] ■ **n 1.** [of birds] vol *m* / [of sheep] troupeau *m* **2.** *fig* [of people] foule *f*.
■ **vi : to flock to** aller en masse à.

floe [fləʊ] **n** banquise *f*.

flog [flɒg] (**pt & pp -ged**, **cont -ging**) **vt 1.** [whip] flageller **2.** *UK inf* [sell] refiler.

flogging ['flɒgɪŋ] **n** [beating] flagellation *f* / LAW supplice *m* du fouet ***OR*** de la flagellation.

flood [flʌd] ■ **n 1.** [of water] inondation *f* **2.** [great amount] déluge *m*, avalanche *f*.
■ **vt 1.** [with water, light] inonder **2.** [overwhelm] **: to flood sthg (with)** inonder qqch (de) ▸ **to flood the market** inonder le marché.
■ **vi 1.** [river] déborder **2.** [street, land] être inondé(e) **3.** [arrive in great amounts] **: applications have flooded in** on a été inondé de demandes ▸ **to flood back** revenir en foule.
◆ ***floods*** **npl 1.** [of water] inondations *fpl* **2.** *fig* [of tears] torrents *mpl*.

flood-damaged **adj** abîmé(e) ***OR*** endommagé(e) par les eaux.

floodgates ['flʌdgeɪts] **npl : to open the floodgates** ouvrir les vannes.

flooding ['flʌdɪŋ] **n** *(U)* inondations *fpl*.

floodlight ['flʌdlaɪt] **n** projecteur *m*.

floodlit ['flʌdlɪt] **adj** [match, ground] éclairé(e) *(avec des projecteurs)* / [building] illuminé(e).

flood tide n marée *f* haute.

floor [flɔːʳ] ■ n **1.** [of room - gen] sol *m* / [- wooden] plancher *m* / [of club, disco] piste *f* ▸ **to put sthg/to sit on the floor** poser qqch/s'asseoir par terre **2.** [of valley, sea, forest] fond *m* **3.** [storey] étage *m* **4.** [at meeting, debate] auditoire *m* ▸ **to have/to take the floor** [speaker] avoir/prendre la parole **5.** FIN corbeille *f*.
■ vt **1.** [knock down] terrasser **2.** [baffle] dérouter.

floor area n [of room, office] surface *f*.

floorboard ['flɔːbɔːd] n plancher *m*.

floor cloth n *UK* serpillière *f*.

floor covering n [linoleum, fitted carpet] revêtement *m* de sol / [rug] tapis *m*.

flooring ['flɔːrɪŋ] n planchéiage *m*.

floor lamp n *US* lampadaire *m*.

floor plan n plan *m*.

floor show n spectacle *m* de cabaret.

floorspace ['flɔːspeɪs] n espace *m*.

floorwalker ['flɔːˌwɔːkəʳ] n surveillant *m*, -e *f* de magasin.

floozy ['fluːzɪ] (pl **-ies**) n *dated* & *pej* pouffiasse *f*.

flop [flɒp] *inf* ■ n [failure] fiasco *m*.
■ vi (pt & pp **-ped**, cont **-ping**) **1.** [fail] être un fiasco **2.** [fall - subj: person] s'affaler.

floppy ['flɒpɪ] (comp **-ier**, superl **-iest**) adj [ears, flower] tombant(e) / [collar] lâche.

floppy (disk) n disquette *f*, disque *m* souple.

flora ['flɔːrə] n flore *f* ▸ **flora and fauna** la flore et la faune.

floral ['flɔːrəl] adj floral(e) / [pattern, dress] à fleurs.

Florence ['flɒrəns] n Florence.

floret ['flɒrɪt] n [of cauliflower, broccoli] bouquet *m*.

florid ['flɒrɪd] adj **1.** [red] rougeaud(e) **2.** [extravagant] fleuri(e).

Florida ['flɒrɪdə] n Floride *f* ▸ **in Florida** en Floride.

florist ['flɒrɪst] n fleuriste *mf* ▸ **florist's (shop)** magasin *m* de fleuriste.

floss [flɒs] ■ n *(U)* **1.** [silk] bourre *f* de soie **2.** [dental floss] fil *m* dentaire.
■ vt : **to floss one's teeth** se nettoyer les dents au fil dentaire.

flotation [fləʊ'teɪʃn] n COMM lancement *m*.

flotilla [flə'tɪlə] n flottille *f*.

flotsam ['flɒtsəm] n *(U)* : **flotsam and jetsam** débris *mpl* / *fig* épaves *fpl*.

flounce [flaʊns] ■ n volant *m*.
■ vi : **to flounce out/off** sortir/partir dans un mouvement d'humeur.

flounced [flaʊnst] adj [skirt] à volants.

flounder ['flaʊndəʳ] ■ n (pl **flounder** *OR* **-s**) flet *m*.
■ vi **1.** [in water, mud, snow] patauger **2.** [in conversation] bredouiller.

flour ['flaʊəʳ] n farine *f*.

flourish ['flʌrɪʃ] ■ vi [plant, flower] bien pousser / [children] être en pleine santé / [company, business] prospérer / [arts] s'épanouir.
■ vt brandir.
■ n grand geste *m*.

flourishing ['flʌrɪʃɪŋ] adj [plant, garden] florissant(e) / [children] resplendissant(e) de santé / [company, arts] prospère.

floury ['flaʊərɪ] adj **1.** [covered in flour - hands] enfariné(e) / [- clothes] couvert(e) de farine **2.** [potatoes] farineux(euse).

flout [flaʊt] vt bafouer.

flow [fləʊ] ■ n **1.** [movement - of water, information] circulation *f* / [- of funds] mouvement *m* / [- of words] flot *m* ▸ **to be in full flow** [orator] être en plein discours **2.** [of tide] flux *m*.
■ vi **1.** [gen] couler ▸ **the river flows into the sea** la rivière se jette dans la mer ▸ **the whisky flowed freely** le whisky a coulé à flots **2.** [traffic,] s'écouler ▸ **new measures designed to enable the traffic to flow more freely** de nouvelles mesures destinées à rendre la circulation plus fluide **3.** [tide] monter **4.** [hair, clothes] flotter **5.** [result] : **to flow from** découler de **6.** [days, weeks] : **to flow by** s'écouler.

flow chart, flow diagram n organigramme *m*.

flower ['flaʊəʳ] ■ n fleur *f*.
■ comp [pattern] floral(e).
■ vi **1.** [bloom] fleurir **2.** *fig* [flourish] s'épanouir.

flower arrangement n art *m* floral / [actual arrangement] composition *f* florale.

flowerbed ['flaʊəbed] n parterre *m*.

flowered ['flaʊəd] adj à fleurs.

flower girl n **1.** [selling flowers] marchande *f* de fleurs **2.** *US* & *Scot* [at wedding] *petite fille qui porte des fleurs dans un mariage*, ≃ demoiselle *f* d'honneur.

flowering ['flaʊərɪŋ] ■ adj à fleurs.
■ n épanouissement *m*.

flowerpot ['flaʊəpɒt] n pot *m* de fleurs.

flower power n *pacifisme prôné par les hippies, surtout dans les années soixante*.

flower-seller n vendeur *m*, -euse *f* de fleurs.

flowery ['flaʊərɪ] (comp **-ier**, superl **-iest**) adj **1.** [dress, material] à fleurs **2.** *pej* [style] fleuri(e).

flowing ['fləʊɪŋ] adj [water, writing] coulant(e) / [hair, robes] flottant(e).

flown [fləʊn] pp ➤ ***fly***.

fl. oz. abbr of ***fluid ounce***.

flu [fluː] n *(U)* grippe *f* ▸ **to have (the) flu** avoir la grippe.

fluctuate ['flʌktʃʊeɪt] vi [rate, temperature, results] fluctuer / [interest, enthusiasm, support] être fluctuant *OR* variable.

fluctuating ['flʌktʃʊeɪtɪŋ] adj [rate, figures, prices] fluctuant(e) / [enthusiasm, support] fluctuant(e), variable / [needs, opinions] fluctuant(e), changeant(e).

fluctuation [ˌflʌktʃʊ'eɪʃn] n fluctuation *f*.

flue [fluː] n conduit *m*, tuyau *m*.

fluency ['flu:ənsɪ] **n** aisance *f* ▸ **fluency in French** aisance à s'exprimer en français.

fluent ['flu:ənt] **adj 1.** [in foreign language] **: to speak fluent French** parler couramment le français ▸ **to be fluent (in French)** parler couramment (le français) **2.** [writing, style] coulant(e), aisé(e).

fluently ['flu:əntlɪ] **adv 1.** [speak - in foreign language] couramment **2.** [read, speak, write] avec aisance.

fluff [flʌf] ■ **n** *(U)* **1.** [down] duvet *m* **2.** [dust] moutons *mpl*.
■ **vt 1.** [puff up] faire bouffer **2.** *inf* [do badly] rater.

fluffy ['flʌfɪ] (comp **-ier**, superl **-iest**) **adj** duveteux(euse) / [toy] en peluche.

fluid ['flu:ɪd] ■ **n** fluide *m* / [in diet, for cleaning] liquide *m*.
■ **adj 1.** [flowing] fluide **2.** [unfixed] changeant(e).

fluidity [flu:'ɪdətɪ] **n 1.** [of substance] fluidité *f* **2.** [of style, play] fluidité *f* **3.** [liability to change - of situation, plans] indétermination *f*.

fluid ounce **n** = *0,03 litre*.

fluke [flu:k] **n** *inf* [chance] coup *m* de bol.

fluky ['flu:kɪ] **adj** *inf* [lucky - shot, guess] heureux(euse) / **what a fluky goal!** quel coup de bol, ce but!

flummox ['flʌməks] **vt** désarçonner.

flummoxed ['flʌməkst] **adj : I was completely flummoxed** ça m'a complètement démonté.

flung [flʌŋ] **pt & pp** ➤ ***fling***.

flunk [flʌŋk] *esp US inf* ■ **vt 1.** [exam, test] rater **2.** [student] recaler.
■ **vi** se faire recaler.

fluorescent [flʊə'resənt] **adj** fluorescent(e).

fluorescent light **n** lumière *f* fluorescente.

fluoridate ['flʊərɪdeɪt] **vt** fluorurer.

fluoride ['flʊəraɪd] **n** fluorure *m*.

fluorine ['flʊəri:n] **n** fluor *m*.

flurry ['flʌrɪ] (pl **-ies**) **n 1.** [of snow] rafale *f*, averse *f* **2.** *fig* [of objections] concert *m* / [of activity, excitement] débordement *m*.

flush [flʌʃ] ■ **adj 1.** [level] **: flush with** de niveau avec **2.** *inf* [rich] plein(e) aux as.
■ **n 1.** [in lavatory] chasse *f* d'eau **2.** [blush] rougeur *f* **3.** [sudden feeling] accès *m* ▸ **in the first flush of sthg** *liter* dans la première ivresse de qqch.
■ **vt 1.** [toilet] **: to flush the toilet** tirer la chasse d'eau ▸ **to flush sthg down the toilet** faire partir qqch en tirant la chasse d'eau **2.** [force out of hiding] **: to flush sb out** déloger qqn.
■ **vi** [blush] rougir.

flushed [flʌʃt] **adj 1.** [red-faced] rouge **2.** [excited] **: flushed with** exalté(e) par.

fluster ['flʌstəʳ] ■ **n** trouble *m*.
■ **vt** troubler.

flustered ['flʌstəd] **adj** troublé(e).

flute [flu:t] **n** MUS flûte *f*.

fluted ['flu:tɪd] **adj** cannelé(e).

flutist *US* = ***flautist***.

flutter ['flʌtəʳ] ■ **n 1.** [of wings] battement *m* **2.** [of heart] palpitation *f* **3.** *inf* [of excitement] émoi *m*.
■ **vt** battre.
■ **vi 1.** [bird, insect] voleter / [wings] battre **2.** [flag, dress] flotter **3.** [heart] palpiter.

flux [flʌks] **n** [change] **: to be in a state of flux** être en proie à des changements permanents.

fly [flaɪ] ■ **n** (pl **flies**) **1.** [insect] mouche *f* ▸ **I wouldn't mind being a fly on the wall** *inf* j'aimerais bien être une petite souris ▸ **a fly in the ointment** *fig* un ennui, un hic ▸ **there are no flies on him** *inf* il n'est pas fou
2. [of trousers] braguette *f*.
■ **vt** (pt **flew**, pp **flown**) **1.** [kite, plane] faire voler
2. [passengers, supplies] transporter par avion
3. [flag] faire flotter.
■ **vi** (pt **flew**, pp **flown**) **1.** [bird, insect, plane] voler
2. [pilot] faire voler un avion
3. [passenger] voyager en avion
4. [move fast, pass quickly] filer ▸ **I really must fly!** *inf* il faut vraiment que je file OR que je me sauve! ▸ **time flies** comme le temps passe ▸ **to knock** OR **to send sb flying** envoyer qqn rouler à terre
5. [rumours, stories] se répandre comme une traînée de poudre
6. [attack] **: to fly at sb** sauter sur qqn ▸ **to let fly** [physically] envoyer OR décocher un coup / [verbally] s'emporter
7. [flag] flotter.
◆ ***fly away*** **vi** s'envoler.
◆ ***fly in*** ■ **vt sep** envoyer par avion.
■ **vi** [plane] arriver / [person] arriver par avion.
◆ ***fly into*** **vt insep : to fly into a rage/temper** s'emporter.
◆ ***fly out*** ■ **vt sep** envoyer par avion.
■ **vi** [plane] partir / [person] partir en avion ▸ **I'll fly out to join you next Monday** je prendrai l'avion pour te rejoindre lundi prochain.

flyaway ['flaɪəˌweɪ] **adj 1.** [hair] fin(e), difficile **2.** [person] frivole, étourdi(e) / [idea] frivole.

flyblown ['flaɪbləʊn] **adj** *lit* couvert(e) OR plein(e) de chiures de mouches / [meat] avarié(e) / *fig* très défraîchi(e).

flyby ['flaɪˌbaɪ] *US* = ***flypast***.

fly-by-night *inf* ■ **adj 1.** [unreliable] peu fiable, sur qui on ne peut pas compter / [firm, operation] véreux, louche **2.** [passing] éphémère.
■ **n 1.** [person - irresponsible] écervelé *m*, -e *f* / [- in debt] débiteur *m*, -trice *f* qui décampe en douce **2.** [nightclubber] fêtard *m*, -e *f*, couche-tard *mf*.

fly-fishing **n** pêche *f* à la mouche.

fly half **n** *UK* demi *m* d'ouverture.

flying ['flaɪɪŋ] ■ **adj** volant(e).
■ **n** aviation *f* ▸ **to like flying** aimer prendre l'avion.

flying colours *UK*, ***flying colors*** *US* **npl : to pass (sthg) with flying colours** réussir (qqch) haut la main.

flying doctor **n** médecin *m* volant.

flying fish **n** poisson *m* volant, exocet *m*.

flying officer **n** *UK* lieutenant *m* de l'armée de l'air.

flying picket **n** piquet *m* de grève volant.

flying saucer **n** soucoupe *f* volante.

flying squad n *UK force d'intervention rapide de la police.*

flying start n : **to get off to a flying start** prendre un départ sur les chapeaux de roue.

flying visit n visite *f* éclair.

flyleaf ['flaɪli:f] (pl -leaves [-li:vz]) n page *f* de garde.

fly-on-the-wall adj [documentary] pris(e) sur le vif.

flyover ['flaɪ,əʊvər] n *UK* saut-de-mouton *m*.

flypast ['flaɪ,pɑ:st] n *UK* défilé *m* aérien.

flysheet ['flaɪʃi:t] n *UK* auvent *m*.

fly spray n insecticide *m*.

fly-tipping n dépôt *m* d'ordures illégal.

flyweight ['flaɪweɪt] n poids *m* mouche.

flywheel ['flaɪwi:l] n volant *m*.

FM n **1.** (abbr of ***frequency modulation***) FM *f* **2.** abbr of ***field marshal***.

FMB (abbr of ***Federal Maritime Board***) n *conseil supérieur de la marine marchande américaine.*

FMCS (abbr of ***Federal Mediation and Conciliation Services***) n *organisme américain de conciliation des conflits du travail.*

FMD [,efem'di:] (abbr of ***foot and mouth disease***) n fièvre *f* aphteuse.

FO (abbr of ***Foreign Office***) n *ministère britannique des affaires étrangères.*

foal [fəʊl] n poulain *m*.

foam [fəʊm] ■ n *(U)* **1.** [bubbles] mousse *f* **2.** : **foam (rubber)** caoutchouc *m* Mousse®.
■ vi [water, champagne] mousser.

foaming ['fəʊmɪŋ] = ***foamy***.

foam rubber n caoutchouc *m* Mousse®.

foamy ['fəʊmɪ] (comp -ier, superl -iest) adj [with bubbles] mousseux(euse).

fob [fɒb] (pt & pp -bed, cont -bing) ◆ ***fob off*** vt sep repousser ▸ **to fob sthg off on sb** refiler qqch à qqn ▸ **to fob sb off with sthg** se débarrasser de qqn à l'aide de qqch.

FOB, f.o.b. (abbr of ***free on board***) FOB, F.o.b.

fob watch n montre *f* de gousset.

foc (abbr of ***free of charge***) Fco.

focaccia [,fə'kætʃjə] n focacce *f (sorte de pain italien).*

focal ['fəʊkl] adj *lit* & *fig* focal(e).

focal length n distance *f* focale, focale *f*.

focal point n foyer *m* / *fig* point *m* central.

foci ['fəʊsaɪ] npl ➤ ***focus***.

focus ['fəʊkəs] ■ n (pl -cuses [-kəsi:z] OR -ci [-saɪ]) **1.** PHOT mise *f* au point ▸ **in focus** net ▸ **out of focus** flou **2.** [centre - of rays] foyer *m* / [- of earthquake] centre *m* ▸ **focus of attention** centre d'attention.
■ vt [lens, camera] mettre au point ▸ **to focus sthg on** [lens, camera, eyes] ajuster qqch sur / [attention] concentrer qqch sur ▸ **all eyes were focused on him** tous les regards étaient rivés sur lui.
■ vi **1.** [with camera, lens] se fixer / [eyes] accommoder ▸ **to focus on sthg** [with camera, lens] se fixer sur qqch / [with eyes] fixer qqch **2.** [attention] : **to focus on sthg** se concentrer sur qqch ▸ **the debate focussed on unemployment** le débat était centré sur le problème du chômage ▸ **his speech focussed on the role of the media** son discours a porté principalement sur le rôle des médias.

focus group n groupe-témoin *m*.

fodder ['fɒdər] n *(U)* fourrage *m*.

foe [fəʊ] n *liter* ennemi *m*.

FOE n **1.** (abbr of ***Friends of the Earth***) AT *mpl* **2.** (abbr of ***Fraternal Order of Eagles***) *organisation caritative américaine.*

foetal *UK*, ***fetal*** *US* ['fi:tl] adj [position] fœtal(e) / [death] du fœtus.

foetus *UK*, ***fetus*** *US* ['fi:təs] n fœtus *m*.

fog [fɒg] n *(U)* brouillard *m*.

fogbound ['fɒgbaʊnd] adj bloqué(e) par le brouillard.

fogey ['fəʊgɪ] = ***fogy***.

foggiest ['fɒgɪəst] n *inf* : **I haven't the foggiest** je n'en ai pas la moindre idée.

foggy ['fɒgɪ] (comp -ier, superl -iest) adj [misty] brumeux(euse).

foghorn ['fɒghɔ:n] n sirène *f* de brume.

fog lamp *UK*, ***fog light*** *US* n feu *m* de brouillard.

fogy ['fəʊgɪ] (pl -ies) n *inf* : **old fogy** vieux machin *m*.

foible ['fɔɪbl] n marotte *f*.

foil [fɔɪl] ■ n **1.** *(U)* [metal sheet - of tin, silver] feuille *f* / CULIN papier *m* d'aluminium **2.** [contrast] : **to be a foil to** OR **for** servir de repoussoir à.
■ vt déjouer.

foist [fɔɪst] vt : **to foist sthg on sb** imposer qqch à qqn.

fold [fəʊld] ■ vt **1.** [bend, close up] plier ▸ **to fold one's arms** croiser les bras **2.** [wrap] envelopper.
■ vi **1.** [close up - table, chair] se plier / [- petals, leaves] se refermer **2.** *inf* [company, project] échouer / THEAT quitter l'affiche.
■ n **1.** [in material, paper] pli *m* **2.** [for animals] parc *m* **3.** *fig* [spiritual home] : **the fold** le bercail.
◆ ***fold up*** ■ vt sep plier.
■ vi **1.** [close up - table, map] se plier / [- petals, leaves] se refermer **2.** [company, project] échouer.

-fold suffix : **a ten-fold increase** une multiplication par dix ▸ **your investment should multiply six-fold** votre investissement devrait vous rapporter six fois plus.

foldaway ['fəʊldə,weɪ] adj pliant(e).

folder ['fəʊldər] n **1.** [for papers - wallet] chemise *f* / [- binder] classeur *m* **2.** COMPUT dossier *m*, répertoire *m*.

folding ['fəʊldɪŋ] adj [table, umbrella] pliant(e) / [doors] en accordéon.

foldout ['fəʊldaʊt] n encart *m*.

foliage ['fəʊlɪɪdʒ] n feuillage *m*.

folic acid ['fəʊlɪk-] n acide *m* folique.

folk [fəʊk] ■ **adj** [art, dancing] folklorique / [medicine] populaire.
■ **npl** [people] gens *mpl*.
■ **n** [music] musique *f* folk.
◆ ***folks*** **npl** *inf* **1.** [relatives] famille *f* **2.** [everyone] **: hi there, folks!** bonjour tout le monde!

folklore ['fəʊklɔːʳ] **n** folklore *m*.

folk music **n** musique *f* folk.

folk singer **n** chanteur *m*, -euse *f* folk.

folk song **n** chanson *f* folk.

folksy ['fəʊksɪ] (comp **-ier**, superl **-iest**) **adj** *esp US inf* sympa *(inv)*, décontract *(inv)*.

follicle ['fɒlɪkl] **n** follicule *m*.

follow ['fɒləʊ] ■ **vt** suivre ▸ **(to be) followed by sthg** (être) suivi de qqch ▸ **to follow sb in/out** entrer/sortir à la suite de qqn ▸ **his eyes followed her everywhere** il la suivait partout du regard *OR* des yeux ▸ **he followed his father into politics** il est entré en politique sur les traces de son père.
■ **vi 1.** [gen] suivre ▸ **as follows** comme suit **2.** [be logical] tenir debout ▸ **it follows that...** il s'ensuit que...
◆ ***follow up*** **vt sep 1.** [pursue - idea, suggestion] prendre en considération / [- advertisement] donner suite à **2.** [complete] **: to follow sthg up with** faire suivre qqch de.

follower ['fɒləʊəʳ] **n** [believer] disciple *mf*.

following ['fɒləʊɪŋ] ■ **adj** suivant(e).
■ **n** groupe *m* d'admirateurs.
■ **prep** après.

follow-my-leader *UK*, ***follow-the-leader*** *US* **n** *jeu où tout le monde doit imiter tous les mouvements d'un joueur désigné*.

follow-through **n 1.** [of plan] suite *f*, continuation *f* **2.** [in ball games] accompagnement *m (d'un coup)* / [in billiards] coulé *m*.

follow-up ■ **adj** complémentaire.
■ **n** suite *f*.

folly ['fɒlɪ] **n** *(U)* [foolishness] folie *f*.

foment [fəʊ'ment] **vt** *fml* fomenter.

fond [fɒnd] **adj 1.** [affectionate] affectueux(euse) ▸ **to be fond of** aimer beaucoup **2.** *liter* [hope, wish] naïf (naïve).

fondant ['fɒndənt] **n** fondant *m*.

fondle ['fɒndl] **vt** caresser.

fondly ['fɒndlɪ] **adv 1.** [affectionately - gaze, smile] affectueusement / [- remember] avec tendresse **2.** *liter* [believe, wish] naïvement.

fondness ['fɒndnɪs] **n** [for person] affection *f* / [for thing] penchant *m*.

fondue ['fɒndjuː] **n** fondue *f*.

font [fɒnt] **n 1.** [in church] fonts *mpl* baptismaux **2.** COMPUT & TYPO police *f* (de caractères).

food [fuːd] **n** nourriture *f* ▸ **that's food for thought** cela donne à réfléchir.

food chain **n** chaîne *f* alimentaire.

food court **n** *partie d'un centre commercial où se trouvent les restaurants*.

foodie ['fuːdɪ] **n** *inf* fin gourmet *m*.

food mixer **n** mixer *m*.

food poisoning [-ˌpɔɪznɪŋ] **n** intoxication *f* alimentaire.

food processor [-ˌprəʊsesəʳ] **n** robot *m* ménager.

food stamp **n** *US* bon *m* alimentaire *(accordé aux personnes sans ressources)*.

foodstuffs ['fuːdstʌfs] **npl** denrées *fpl* alimentaires.

fool [fuːl] ■ **n 1.** [idiot] idiot *m*, -e *f* ▸ **I felt such a fool** je me suis senti bête ▸ **to make a fool of sb** tourner qqn en ridicule ▸ **to make a fool of o.s.** se rendre ridicule ▸ **to act** *OR* **play the fool** faire l'imbécile **2.** *UK* [dessert] ≃ mousse *f*.
■ **vt** duper ▸ **your excuses don't fool me** vos excuses ne prennent pas avec moi ▸ **to fool sb into doing sthg** amener qqn à faire qqch en le dupant.
■ **vi** faire l'imbécile.
◆ ***fool about, fool around*** **vi 1.** [behave foolishly] faire l'imbécile ▸ **I'm only fooling around** je ne fais que plaisanter, c'est pour rire **2.** *inf* [be unfaithful] être infidèle.

foolhardy ['fuːlˌhɑːdɪ] **adj** téméraire.

foolish ['fuːlɪʃ] **adj** idiot(e), stupide.

foolishly ['fuːlɪʃlɪ] **adv** stupidement, bêtement.

foolishness ['fuːlɪʃnɪs] **n** *(U)* bêtise *f*.

foolproof ['fuːlpruːf] **adj** infaillible.

foolscap ['fuːlzkæp] **n** *(U)* papier *m* ministre.

foot [fʊt] ■ **n 1.** (pl **feet** [fiːt]) [gen] pied *m* / [of animal] patte *f* / [of page, stairs] bas *m* ▸ **to be on one's feet** être debout ▸ **the children are always under my feet** les enfants sont toujours dans mes jambes ▸ **to get to one's feet** se mettre debout, se lever ▸ **on foot** à pied ▸ **to be back on one's feet** être remis (d'une maladie) ▸ **he claims he's divorced – divorced, my foot!** *inf* il prétend être divorcé – divorcé, mon œil ! ▸ **to get** *OR* **to start off on the right/wrong foot** être bien/mal parti ▸ **to have itchy feet** avoir la bougeotte ▸ **to have two left feet** *inf* être pataud *OR* empoté ▸ **to put one's foot down** mettre le holà ▸ **to put one's foot in it** mettre les pieds dans le plat ▸ **to put one's feet up** se reposer ▸ **to be rushed off one's feet** ne pas avoir le temps de souffler ▸ **to set foot in** mettre le pied en ▸ **to stand on one's own two feet** se débrouiller (par soi-même) **2.** (pl **foot** *OR* **feet**) [unit of measurement] = *30,48 cm*, ≃ pied *m*.
■ **vt** *inf* **: to foot the bill** payer la note.

footage ['fʊtɪdʒ] **n** *(U)* séquences *fpl*.

foot-and-mouth disease **n** fièvre *f* aphteuse.

football ['fʊtbɔːl] **n 1.** [game - soccer] football *m*, foot *m* / [- American football] football américain **2.** [ball] ballon *m* de football *OR* foot.

football club **n** *UK* club *m* de football.

footballer ['fʊtbɔːləʳ] **n** *UK* joueur *m*, -euse *f* de football, footballeur *m*, -euse *f*.

football field **n** *US* terrain *m* de football américain.

football game **n** *US* match *m* de football américain.

football ground **n** *UK* terrain *m* de football.

football match **n** *UK* match *m* de football.

football player = ***footballer***.

football pools **npl** *UK* ≃ loto *m* sportif.

football supporter **n** *esp UK* supporter *m* (de football).

footbath ['fʊtbɑːθ] (pl [-bɑːðz]) **n** bain *m* de pieds.

footbrake ['fʊtbreɪk] **n** frein *m* (à pied).

footbridge ['fʊtbrɪdʒ] **n** passerelle *f*.

footer ['fʊtər] **n** COMPUT titre *m* en bas de page.

-footer **suffix : the boat is a 15-footer** le bateau mesure 15 pieds *OR* environ 4,50 mètres.

footfall ['fʊtfɔːl] **n 1.** [sound] bruit *m* de pas **2.** COMM fréquentation *f*.

foot fault **n** faute *f* de pied.

foothills ['fʊthɪlz] **npl** contreforts *mpl*.

foothold ['fʊthəʊld] **n** prise *f* (de pied) ▸ **to get a foothold** trouver une prise (de pied) / *fig* prendre pied, s'imposer.

footing ['fʊtɪŋ] **n 1.** [foothold] prise *f* ▸ **to lose one's footing** trébucher **2.** *fig* [basis] position *f* ▸ **on an equal footing (with)** sur un pied d'égalité (avec).

footlights ['fʊtlaɪts] **npl** THEAT rampe *f*.

footling ['fuːtlɪŋ] **adj** *dated* & *pej* futile.

footloose ['fʊtluːs] **adj : footloose and fancy-free** libre comme l'air.

footman ['fʊtmən] (pl **-men** [-mən]) **n** valet *m* de pied.

footmark ['fʊtmɑːk] = ***footprint***.

footnote ['fʊtnəʊt] **n** note *f* en bas de page.

footpath ['fʊtpɑːθ] (pl [-pɑːðz]) **n** sentier *m*.

footprint ['fʊtprɪnt] **n** empreinte *f* (de pied), trace *f* (de pas).

footrest ['fʊtrest] **n** [gen] repose-pieds *m* / [stool] tabouret *m*.

footsie ['fʊtsɪ] **n** *inf* **: to play footsie with sb** *UK* faire du pied à qqn / *US* être le complice de qqn.

Footsie ['fʊtsɪ] **n** *inf nom familier de l'indice boursier du Financial Times*.

footsore ['fʊtsɔːr] **adj : to be footsore** avoir mal aux pieds.

footstep ['fʊtstep] **n 1.** [sound] bruit *m* de pas **2.** [footprint] empreinte *f* (de pied) ▸ **to follow in sb's footsteps** marcher sur *OR* suivre les traces de qqn.

footstool ['fʊtstuːl] **n** tabouret *m*.

footwear ['fʊtweər] **n** *(U)* chaussures *fpl*.

footwork ['fʊtwɜːk] **n** *(U)* SPORT jeu *m* de jambes.

fop [fɒp] **n** dandy *m*.

foppish ['fɒpɪʃ] **adj** [man] dandy / [dress, manner] de dandy.

for [fɔːr] ■ **prep 1.** [referring to intention, destination, purpose] pour ▸ **this is for you** c'est pour vous ▸ **the plane for Paris** l'avion à destination de Paris ▸ **I'm going for the papers** je vais prendre *OR* acheter les journaux ▸ **let's meet for a drink** retrouvons-nous pour prendre un verre ▸ **we did it for a laugh** *OR* **for fun** on l'a fait pour rire ▸ **what's it for?** ça sert à quoi? ▸ **what for?** pourquoi? ▸ **I don't know what she said that for** je ne sais pas pourquoi elle a dit ça ▸ **'for sale'** 'à vendre' ▸ **these books are for reference only** ces livres sont à consulter sur place
2. [representing, on behalf of] pour ▸ **the MP for Barnsley** le député de Barnsley ▸ **let me do that for you** laissez-moi faire, je vais vous le faire ▸ **I'll go to the meeting for you** j'irai à la réunion à votre place
3. [because of] pour, en raison de ▸ **for various reasons** pour plusieurs raisons ▸ **the town is famous for its cathedral** la ville est célèbre pour sa cathédrale ▸ **a prize for swimming** un prix de natation ▸ **he couldn't speak for laughing** il ne pouvait pas parler tellement il riait ▸ **for fear of being ridiculed** de *OR* par peur d'être ridiculisé
4. [with regard to] pour ▸ **to be ready for sthg** être prêt à *OR* pour qqch ▸ **it's not for me to say** ce n'est pas à moi à le dire ▸ **to be young for one's age** être jeune pour son âge ▸ **to feel sorry for sb** plaindre qqn
5. [indicating amount of time, space] **: there's no time for that now** on n'a pas le temps de faire cela *OR* de s'occuper de cela maintenant ▸ **there's room for another person** il y a de la place pour encore une personne
6. [indicating period of time] **: she'll be away for a month** elle sera absente (pendant) un mois ▸ **we talked for hours** on a parlé pendant des heures ▸ **I've lived here for 3 years** j'habite ici depuis 3 ans, cela fait 3 ans que j'habite ici ▸ **I can do it for you for tomorrow** je peux vous le faire pour demain
7. [indicating distance] pendant, sur ▸ **for 50 kilometres** pendant *OR* sur 50 kilomètres ▸ **I walked for miles** j'ai marché (pendant) des kilomètres
8. [indicating particular occasion] pour ▸ **for Christmas** pour Noël ▸ **the meeting scheduled for the 30th** la réunion prévue pour le 30
9. [indicating amount of money, price] **: they're 50p for ten** cela coûte 50p les dix ▸ **I bought/sold it for £10** je l'ai acheté/vendu 10 livres ▸ **I wrote a cheque for £15** j'ai fait un chèque de 15 livres
10. [in favour of, in support of] pour ▸ **to vote for sthg** voter pour qqch ▸ **to be all for sthg** être tout à fait pour *OR* en faveur de qqch
11. [in ratios] pour
12. [indicating meaning, exchange] **: P for Peter** P comme Peter ▸ **what's the Greek for 'mother'?** comment dit-on 'mère' en grec? ▸ **do you have change for a pound?** vous avez la monnaie d'une livre? ▸ **he exchanged the bike for another model** il a échangé le vélo contre *OR* pour un autre modèle.
■ **conj** *fml* [as, since] car.
◆ ***for all*** ■ **prep** malgré ▸ **for all his money...** malgré tout son argent...
■ **conj : for all I know** pour autant que je sache ▸ **for all I care** pour ce que cela me fait.
◆ ***for ever*** **adv** = ***forever***.

FOR (abbr of ***free on rail***) franco wagon.

forage ['fɒrɪdʒ] **vi : to forage (for)** fouiller (pour trouver).

foray ['fɒreɪ] **n : foray (into)** *liter* incursion *f* (dans).

forbad [fə'bæd], ***forbade*** [fə'beɪd] **pt** ➤ ***forbid***.

forbearance [fɔː'beərəns] **n 1.** [patience] patience *f*, tolérance *f* **2.** [restraint] abstention *f*.

forbearing [fɔː'beərɪŋ] **adj** tolérant(e).

forbid [fə'bɪd] (pt **-bade** *OR* **-bad**, pp **forbid** *OR* **-bidden**, cont **-bidding**) **vt** interdire, défendre ▸ **to forbid sb to do sthg** interdire *OR* défendre à qqn de faire qqch ▸ **God** *OR* **Heaven forbid!** pourvu que non!

forbidden [fə'bɪdn] ■ **pp** ➤ ***forbid***.
■ **adj** interdit(e), défendu(e).

forbidding [fə'bɪdɪŋ] **adj** [severe, unfriendly] austère / [threatening] sinistre.

force [fɔ:s] ■ **n 1.** [gen] force *f* ▸ **force of habit** force de l'habitude ▸ **force of circumstances** force *f* des choses ▸ **by force** de force ▸ **the force of gravity** la pesanteur
2. [group] **: sales force** représentants *mpl* de commerce ▸ **security forces** forces *fpl* de sécurité ▸ **in force** en force ▸ **the students were there in force** les étudiants étaient venus en force *OR* en grand nombre
3. [effect] **: to be in/to come into force** être/entrer en vigueur.
■ **vt 1.** [gen] forcer ▸ **to force sb to do sthg** forcer qqn à faire qqch ▸ **the car forced us off the road** la voiture nous a forcés à quitter la route ▸ **to force sthg open** forcer qqch (pour l'ouvrir) ▸ **to force one's way through** se frayer un chemin à travers ▸ **to force one's way into** entrer de force dans
2. [press] **: to force sthg on sb** imposer qqch à qqn.
◆ ***forces*** **npl : the forces** les forces *fpl* armées ▸ **to join forces** joindre ses efforts.
◆ ***by force of*** **prep** à force de.
◆ ***force back*** **vt sep** [crowd] repousser / [emotion, tears] refouler.
◆ ***force down*** **vt sep 1.** [food] se forcer à manger
2. [aeroplane] forcer à atterrir.

forced [fɔ:st] **adj** forcé(e).

forced landing **n** atterrissage *m* forcé.

force-feed **vt** nourrir de force.

forceful ['fɔ:sfʊl] **adj** [person] énergique / [speech] vigoureux(euse).

forcefully ['fɔ:sfʊlɪ] **adv** avec force.

forcemeat ['fɔ:smi:t] **n** *esp UK* farce *f*.

forceps ['fɔ:seps] **npl** forceps *m*.

forcible ['fɔ:səbl] **adj 1.** [using physical force] par (la) force **2.** [powerful] fort(e).

forcibly ['fɔ:səblɪ] **adv 1.** [using physical force] de force **2.** [powerfully] avec vigueur.

ford [fɔ:d] ■ **n** gué *m*.
■ **vt** traverser à gué.

fore [fɔ:ʳ] ■ **adj** NAUT à l'avant.
■ **n : to come to the fore** s'imposer.

forearm ['fɔ:rɑ:m] **n** avant-bras *m inv*.

forebears ['fɔ:beəz] **npl** aïeux *mpl*.

foreboding [fɔ:'bəʊdɪŋ] **n** pressentiment *m*.

forecast ['fɔ:kɑ:st] ■ **n** prévision *f* ▸ **(weather) forecast** prévisions météorologiques.
■ **vt** (pt & pp **forecast** *OR* **-ed**) prévoir.

forecaster ['fɔ:kɑ:stəʳ] **n 1.** [analyst] prévisionniste *mf* **2.** [of weather] présentateur *m*, -trice *f* de la météo.

foreclose [fɔ:'kləʊz] ■ **vt** saisir.
■ **vi : to foreclose on sb** saisir les biens de qqn.

foreclosure [fɔ:'kləʊʒəʳ] **n** saisie *f*.

forecourt ['fɔ:kɔ:t] **n** [of petrol station] devant *m* / [of building] avant-cour *f*.

forefathers ['fɔ:ˌfɑ:ðəz] = ***forebears***.

forefinger ['fɔ:ˌfɪŋgəʳ] **n** index *m*.

forefront ['fɔ:frʌnt] **n : in** *OR* **at the forefront of** au premier plan de.

forego [fɔ:'gəʊ] = ***forgo***.

foregoing [fɔ:'gəʊɪŋ] ■ **adj** précédent(e).
■ **n** *fml* **: the foregoing** ce qui précède.

foregone conclusion ['fɔ:gɒn-] **n : it's a foregone conclusion** c'est couru.

foreground ['fɔ:graʊnd] **n** premier plan *m* ▸ **in the foreground** au premier plan.

forehand ['fɔ:hænd] **n** TENNIS coup *m* droit.

forehead ['fɔ:hed] **n** front *m*.

foreign ['fɒrən] **adj 1.** [gen] étranger(ère) / [correspondent] à l'étranger **2.** [policy, trade] extérieur(e).

foreign affairs **npl** affaires *fpl* étrangères.

foreign aid **n** aide *f* extérieure.

foreign body **n** corps *m* étranger.

foreign competition **n** concurrence *f* étrangère.

foreign currency **n** *(U)* devises *fpl* étrangères.

foreigner ['fɒrənəʳ] **n** étranger *m*, -ère *f*.

foreign exchange **n** change *m* ▸ **foreign exchange markets** marchés *mpl* des devises ▸ **foreign exchange rates** taux *mpl* de change.

foreign investment **n** *(U)* investissement *m* étranger.

foreign minister **n** ministre *m* des Affaires étrangères.

Foreign Office **n** *UK* **: the Foreign Office** ≃ le ministère des Affaires étrangères.

Foreign Secretary **n** *UK* ≃ ministre *m* des Affaires étrangères.

foreleg ['fɔ:leg] **n** [of horse] membre *m* antérieur / [of other animals] patte *f* de devant.

foreman ['fɔ:mən] (pl **-men** [-mən]) **n 1.** [of workers] contremaître *m*, -esse *f* **2.** LAW président *m* du jury.

foremost ['fɔ:məʊst] ■ **adj** principal(e).
■ **adv : first and foremost** tout d'abord.

forename ['fɔ:neɪm] **n** prénom *m*.

forensic [fə'rensɪk] **adj** [department, investigation] médico-légal(e).

forensic medicine, forensic science **n** médecine *f* légale.

foreplay ['fɔ:pleɪ] **n** *(U)* préliminaires *mpl*.

forerunner ['fɔ:ˌrʌnəʳ] **n** précurseur *m*.

foresee [fɔ:'si:] (pt **-saw** [-'sɔ:], pp **-seen**) **vt** prévoir.

foreseeable [fɔ:'si:əbl] **adj** prévisible ▸ **for the foreseeable future** pour tous les jours/mois *(etc)* à venir ▸ **in the foreseeable future** dans un futur proche.

foreseen [fɔ:'si:n] **pp** ➤ ***foresee***.

foreshadow [fɔ:'ʃædəʊ] **vt** présager.

foreshortened [fɔ:'ʃɔ:tnd] **adj** raccourci(e).

foresight **[ˈfɔːsaɪt] n** *(U)* prévoyance *f*.

foreskin **[ˈfɔːskɪn] n** prépuce *m*.

forest **[ˈfɒrɪst] n** forêt *f*.

forestall **[fɔːˈstɔːl] vt** [attempt, discussion] prévenir / [person] devancer.

forestry **[ˈfɒrɪstrɪ] n** sylviculture *f*.

Forestry Commission **n** *UK* **: the Forestry Commission** ≃ les Eaux et Forêts *fpl*.

foretaste **[ˈfɔːteɪst] n** avant-goût *m*.

foretell **[fɔːˈtel] (pt & pp -told) vt** prédire.

forethought **[ˈfɔːθɔːt] n** prévoyance *f*.

foretold **[fɔːˈtəʊld] pt & pp** ➤ ***foretell***.

forever **[fəˈrevəʳ] adv 1.** [eternally] (pour) toujours **2.** *inf* [long time] **: don't take forever about it!** et ne mets pas des heures!

forewarn **[fɔːˈwɔːn] vt** avertir.

foreword **[ˈfɔːwɜːd] n** avant-propos *m inv*.

forfeit **[ˈfɔːfɪt] ■ n** amende *f* / [in game] gage *m*.
■ **vt** perdre.

forfeiture **[ˈfɔːfɪtʃəʳ] n 1.** LAW [loss] perte *f* par confiscation / *fig* [surrender] renonciation *f* ▶ **forfeiture of rights** renonciation aux droits **2.** [penalty] prix *m*, peine *f* / COMM [sum] amende *f*, dédit *m*.

forgave **[fəˈgeɪv] pt** ➤ ***forgive***.

forge **[fɔːdʒ] ■ n** forge *f*.
■ **vt 1.** *fig* & INDUST forger **2.** [signature, money] contrefaire / [passport] falsifier.
◆ ***forge ahead*** **vi** prendre de l'avance.

forger **[ˈfɔːdʒəʳ] n** faussaire *mf*.

forgery **[ˈfɔːdʒərɪ] (pl -ies) n 1.** *(U)* [crime] contrefaçon *f* **2.** [forged article] faux *m*.

forget **[fəˈget] (pt -got, pp -gotten, cont -getting) ■ vt** oublier ▶ **let's forget the whole business** n'en parlons plus ▶ **to forget to do sthg** oublier de faire qqch ▶ **forget it!** laisse tomber! ▶ **to forget o.s.** perdre le contrôle de soi.
■ **vi : to forget (about sthg)** oublier (qqch).

forgetful **[fəˈgetfʊl] adj** distrait(e), étourdi(e).

forgetfulness **[fəˈgetfʊlnɪs] n** étourderie *f*.

forget-me-not **n** myosotis *m*.

forgettable **[fəˈgetəbl] adj** qui ne présente pas d'intérêt.

forgivable **[fəˈgɪvəbl] adj** pardonnable.

forgivably **[fəˈgɪvəblɪ] adv : she was, quite forgivably, rather annoyed with him!** elle était plutôt en colère contre lui, et on la comprend!

forgive **[fəˈgɪv] (pt -gave, pp -given [-ˈgɪvən]) vt** pardonner ▶ **to forgive sb for sthg/for doing sthg** pardonner qqch à qqn/à qqn d'avoir fait qqch.

forgiveness **[fəˈgɪvnɪs] n** *(U)* pardon *m*.

forgiving **[fəˈgɪvɪŋ] adj** indulgent(e).

forgo **[fɔːˈgəʊ] (pt -went, pp -gone [-ˈgɒn]) vt** *fml* renoncer à.

forgot **[fəˈgɒt] pt** ➤ ***forget***.

forgotten **[fəˈgɒtn] pp** ➤ ***forget***.

fork **[fɔːk] ■ n 1.** [for eating] fourchette *f* **2.** [for gardening] fourche *f* **3.** [in road] bifurcation *f* / [of river] embranchement *m*.
■ **vi** bifurquer.
◆ ***fork out*** *inf* ■ **vt insep** allonger, débourser ▶ **to fork out money on** *UK* **OR for** *US* allonger **OR** débourser de l'argent pour.
■ **vi : to fork out (for)** casquer (pour).

CONFUSABLE / PARONYME

fork

When translating **fork**, note that *fourchette* and *fourche* are not interchangeable. *Fourchette* is an item of cutlery, whereas *fourche* is an agricultural tool.

forked **[fɔːkt] adj** [tongue] fourchu(e) / [river, road] à bifurcation.

forklift truck **[ˈfɔːklɪft-] n** chariot *m* élévateur.

forlorn **[fəˈlɔːn] adj 1.** [person, face] malheureux(euse), triste **2.** [place, landscape] désolé(e) **3.** [hope, attempt] désespéré(e).

form **[fɔːm] ■ n 1.** [shape, fitness, type] forme *f* ▶ **we studied three different forms of government** nous avons examiné trois systèmes de gouvernement **OR** trois régimes différents ▶ **form of address** formule de politesse ▶ **on form** *UK*, **in form** *US* en pleine forme ▶ **off form** *esp UK* pas en forme ▶ **in the form of** sous forme de ▶ **to take the form of** prendre la forme de ▶ **what form should my questions take?** comment devrais-je formuler mes questions? **2.** [questionnaire] formulaire *m* ▶ **printed form** imprimé *m* **3.** *UK* SCH classe *f* **4.** [usual behaviour] **: true to form** typiquement.
■ **vt** former ▶ **form a queue** *UK* **OR line** *US* **please** faites la queue, s'il vous plaît ▶ **to form the basis of sthg** constituer la base de **OR** servir de base à qqch.
■ **vi** se former ▶ **doubts began to form in his mind** des doutes commencèrent à prendre forme dans son esprit, il commença à avoir des doutes.

formal **[ˈfɔːml] adj 1.** [official, conventional] officiel(elle) ▶ **formal agreement/contract** accord *m*/contrat *m* en bonne et due forme ▶ **a formal dinner** un dîner officiel ▶ **formal dress** [for ceremony] tenue *f* de cérémonie / [for evening] tenue *f* de soirée ▶ **we gave him a formal warning** nous l'avons averti officiellement **OR** dans les règles **2.** [person] formaliste / [language] soutenu(e).

formality **[fɔːˈmælətɪ] (pl -ies) n** formalité *f*.

formalize, *UK* ***-ise*** **[ˈfɔːməlaɪz] vt** organiser de façon formelle.

formally **[ˈfɔːməlɪ] adv 1.** [correctly, seriously] de façon correcte **2.** [not casually] **: to be formally dressed** être en tenue de cérémonie **3.** [officially] officiellement.

format **[ˈfɔːmæt] ■ n** [gen & COMPUT] format *m*.
■ **vt (pt & pp -ted, cont -ting)** COMPUT formater.

formation **[fɔːˈmeɪʃn] n 1.** [gen] formation *f* **2.** [of idea, plan] élaboration *f*.

formative **[ˈfɔːmətɪv] adj** formateur(trice).

formatting **[ˈfɔːmætɪŋ] n** COMPUT formatage *m*.

former ['fɔːməʳ] ■ **adj 1.** [previous] ancien(enne) ▸ **former husband** ex-mari *m* ▸ **former pupil** ancien élève *m*, ancienne élève *f* **2.** [first of two] premier(ère).
■ **n : the former** le premier (la première), celui-là (celle-là).

formerly ['fɔːməlɪ] **adv** autrefois.

form feed **n** changement *m* de page.

Formica® [fɔː'maɪkə] **n** Formica® *m*.

formidable ['fɔːmɪdəbl] **adj** redoutable, terrible.

FALSE FRIENDS / FAUX AMIS
formidable

Formidable n'est pas la traduction du mot anglais *formidable*. Formidable se traduit par *tremendous*.
▸ **Elle a une volonté formidable, elle réussira !** / *She has tremendous willpower, she'll succeed!*

formidably ['fɔːmɪdəblɪ] **adv** redoutablement, terriblement.

formless ['fɔːmlɪs] **adj** informe.

Formosa [fɔː'məʊsə] **n** Formose ▸ **in Formosa** à Formose.

formula ['fɔːmjʊlə] (**pl -as** *OR* **-ae** [-iː]) **n** formule *f*.

formulaic [ˌfɔːmjʊ'leɪɪk] **adj : formulaic expression** formule *f*.

formulate ['fɔːmjʊleɪt] **vt** formuler.

formulation [ˌfɔːmjʊ'leɪʃn] **n** formulation *f*.

fornicate ['fɔːnɪkeɪt] **vi** *fml* forniquer.

forsake [fə'seɪk] (**pt forsook**, **pp forsaken**) **vt** *liter* [person] abandonner / [habit] renoncer à.

forsaken [fə'seɪkn] **adj** abandonné(e).

forsook [fə'sʊk] **pt** ➤ ***forsake***.

forsythia [fɔː'saɪθjə] **n** forsythia *m*.

fort [fɔːt] **n** fort *m* ▸ **to hold (down) the fort** [at office, shop] garder la boutique.

CULTURE
Fort Knox

Fort Knox est une importante base militaire américaine située au sud de Louisville, dans l'État du Kentucky. Célèbre pour ses réserves nationales de lingots et de pièces d'or, le dépôt servit également à protéger les biens des pays occupés durant la Seconde Guerre mondiale (comme la **Magna Carta**, la Grande Charte britannique, ou les joyaux de la couronne d'Angleterre), ainsi que des documents historiques américains (la Constitution et la Déclaration d'indépendance). En raison de cette attribution, le terme **Fort Knox** désigne désormais un lieu sous haute protection ou quelque chose hors de prix.

forte ['fɔːtɪ] **n** point *m* fort.

forth [fɔːθ] **adv** *liter* en avant ▸ **from that day forth** dorénavant.

forthcoming [fɔːθ'kʌmɪŋ] **adj 1.** [imminent] à venir **2.** [available] **: no answer was forthcoming** on n'a pas eu de réponse **3.** [helpful] communicatif(ive).

forthright ['fɔːθraɪt] **adj** franc (franche), direct(e).

forthwith [ˌfɔːθ'wɪθ] **adv** *fml* aussitôt.

fortieth ['fɔːtɪɪθ] **num** quarantième ; see also ***sixth***.

fortification [ˌfɔːtɪfɪ'keɪʃn] **n** fortification *f*.

fortified wine ['fɔːtɪfaɪd-] **n** vin *m* de liqueur.

fortify ['fɔːtɪfaɪ] (**pt & pp -ied**) **vt 1.** MIL fortifier **2.** *fig* [resolve] renforcer.

fortitude ['fɔːtɪtjuːd] **n** courage *m*.

fortnight ['fɔːtnaɪt] **n** *UK* quinze jours *mpl*, quinzaine *f*.

fortnightly ['fɔːtˌnaɪtlɪ] ■ **adj** *UK* bimensuel(elle).
■ **adv** tous les quinze jours.

fortress ['fɔːtrɪs] **n** forteresse *f*.

fortuitous [fɔː'tjuːɪtəs] **adj** *fml* fortuit(e).

fortunate ['fɔːtʃnət] **adj** heureux(euse) ▸ **to be fortunate** avoir de la chance.

fortunately ['fɔːtʃnətlɪ] **adv** heureusement.

fortune ['fɔːtʃuːn] **n 1.** [wealth] fortune *f* **2.** [luck] fortune *f*, chance *f* **3.** [future] **: to tell sb's fortune** dire la bonne aventure à qqn.
◆ ***fortunes*** **npl** fortune *f*.

fortune cookie **n** *US biscuit chinois dans lequel est caché un horoscope*.

fortune-teller [-ˌteləʳ] **n** diseuse *f* de bonne aventure.

fortune-telling **n** [gen] *fait de dire la bonne aventure* / [with cards] cartomancie *f*.

forty ['fɔːtɪ] **num** quarante ; see also ***sixty***.

forty winks **npl** *inf* petit somme *m*.

forum ['fɔːrəm] (**pl -s**) **n 1.** [gén] forum *m*, tribune *f* **2.** COMPUT forum *m*.

forward ['fɔːwəd] ■ **adj 1.** [movement] en avant ▸ **the seat is too far forward** le siège est trop avancé *OR* en avant **2.** [planning] à long terme **3.** [impudent] effronté(e).
■ **adv 1.** [ahead] en avant ▸ **to go** *OR* **move forward** avancer ▸ **three witnesses came forward** *fig* trois témoins se sont présentés **2.** [in time] **: to bring a meeting forward** avancer la date d'une réunion ▸ **to put a watch forward** avancer une montre.
■ **n** SPORT avant *m*.
■ **vt 1.** [letter] faire suivre / [goods] expédier **2.** [career] faire avancer.

forwarding address ['fɔːwədɪŋ-] **n** adresse *f* où faire suivre le courrier.

forward-looking [-'lʊkɪŋ] **adj** tourné(e) vers le futur.

forwardness ['fɔːwədnɪs] **n** [boldness] effronterie *f*.

forward roll **n** cabriole *f*, culbute *f*.

forwards ['fɔːwədz] **adv** = ***forward***.

forward slash **n** COMPUT barre *f* oblique.

forwent [fɔː'went] **pt** ➤ ***forgo***.

fossil ['fɒsl] **n** fossile *m*.

fossil fuel **n** combustible *m* fossile.

fossilized, ***-ised*** *UK* ['fɒsɪlaɪzd] **adj** fossilisé(e).

foster ['fɒstəʳ] ■ **adj** [family] d'accueil.
■ **vt 1.** [child] accueillir **2.** *fig* [nurture] nourrir, entretenir.

foster child **n** enfant *m* placé en famille d'accueil.

foster parent **n** parent *m* nourricier.

fought [fɔ:t] **pt & pp** ➤ ***fight***.

foul [faʊl] ■ **adj 1.** [gen] infect(e) / [water] croupi(e) ▸ **to fall foul of sb** se mettre qqn à dos **2.** [language] grossier(ère), ordurier(ère).
■ **n** SPORT faute *f*.
■ **vt** *fml* **1.** [make dirty] souiller, salir **2.** SPORT commettre une faute contre **3.** [mechanism, propeller] entraver.
◆ ***foul up*** **vt sep** *inf* gâcher.

foul-mouthed [-'maʊðd] **adj** au langage grossier.

foul play **n** *(U)* **1.** SPORT antijeu *m* **2.** [crime] acte *m* malveillant.

foul-up **n** *inf* [mix-up] cafouillage *m* / [mechanical difficulty] problème *m* ***OR*** difficulté *f* mécanique.

found [faʊnd] ■ **pt & pp** ➤ ***find***.
■ **vt 1.** [hospital, town] fonder **2.** [base] **: to found sthg on** fonder ***OR*** baser qqch sur.

foundation [faʊn'deɪʃn] **n 1.** [creation, organization] fondation *f* **2.** [basis] fondement *m*, base *f* **3. : foundation (cream)** fond *m* de teint.
◆ ***foundations*** **npl** CONSTR fondations *fpl*.

foundation course **n** cours *m* introductif.

foundation stone **n** première pierre *f*.

founder ['faʊndəʳ] ■ **n** fondateur *m*, -trice *f*.
■ **vi 1.** [ship] sombrer **2.** *fig* [plan, hopes] s'effondrer, s'écrouler.

founder member **n** membre *m* fondateur.

founding ['faʊndɪŋ] **n** [of hospital] fondation *f*, création *f*.

founding father **n** père *m* fondateur.

foundling ['faʊndlɪŋ] **n** *fml* enfant *mf* trouvé ▸ **foundling hospital** hospice *m* pour enfants trouvés.

foundry ['faʊndrɪ] (**pl -ies**) **n** fonderie *f*.

fount [faʊnt] **n** [origin] source *f* / *UK* TYPO police *f*.

fountain ['faʊntɪn] **n** fontaine *f*.

fountain pen **n** stylo *m* à encre.

four [fɔ:ʳ] **num** quatre ▸ **on all fours** à quatre pattes ; see also ***six***.

four-by-four **n** AUT quatre-quatre *m*.

four-door **adj** à quatre portes.

four-leaved clover [-li:vd-] *UK*, ***four-leaf clover*** [-li:f-] *US* **n** trèfle *m* à quatre feuilles.

four-letter word **n** mot *m* grossier.

four-ply **adj** [wool] à quatre fils / [wood] contreplaqué(e) *(à quatre plis)*.

four-poster (bed) **n** lit *m* à baldaquin.

foursome ['fɔ:səm] **n** groupe *m* de quatre.

four-star **adj** [hotel] quatre étoiles.

fourteen [,fɔ:'ti:n] **num** quatorze ; see also ***six***.

fourteenth [,fɔ:'ti:nθ] **num** quatorzième ; see also ***sixth***.

fourth [fɔ:θ] **num** quatrième ; see also ***sixth***.

fourth estate **n : the fourth estate** le quatrième pouvoir, la presse.

fourthly ['fɔ:θlɪ] **adv** quatrièmement, en quatrième lieu.

Fourth of July **n : the Fourth of July** *Fête de l'Indépendance américaine, célébrée le 4 juillet.*

CULTURE

Fourth of July

Le 4 juillet 1776 à Philadelphie dans l'État de Pennsylvanie, le Congrès continental signait la Déclaration d'indépendance des États-Unis. Cette date du « jour de l'Indépendance » (**Independence Day**), devenue la fête nationale américaine, est largement célébrée par de grandes manifestations patriotiques. La date en elle-même n'a jamais été modifiée, et toute tentative pour la déplacer au samedi précédent ou au lundi suivant quand le 4 tombe un dimanche est toujours décriée. La plupart des villes américaines organisent des parades et des feux d'artifice. Un long week-end de trois jours est également accordé et beaucoup d'Américains en profitent pour voyager.

Fourth World **n : the Fourth World** le quart-monde.

four-way stop **n** *US* carrefour *m* à quatre stops.

four-wheel drive **n : with four-wheel drive** à quatre roues motrices.

fowl [faʊl] (**pl fowl** ***OR*** **-s**) **n** volaille *f*.

fox [fɒks] ■ **n** renard *m*.
■ **vt** laisser perplexe.

foxed [fɒkst] **adj** [paper] marqué(e) ***OR*** taché(e) de rousseurs.

foxglove ['fɒksglʌv] **n** digitale *f*.

foxhole ['fɒkshəʊl] **n** terrier *m* de renard.

foxhound ['fɒkshaʊnd] **n** fox-hound *m*.

foxhunt ['fɒkshʌnt] **n** chasse *f* au renard.

foxhunting ['fɒks,hʌntɪŋ] **n** *(U)* chasse *f* au renard.

foxy ['fɒksɪ] **adj** *inf* [sexy] sexy *(inv)*.

foyer ['fɔɪeɪ] **n 1.** [of hotel, theatre] foyer *m* **2.** *US* [of house] hall *m* d'entrée.

FPA (abbr of ***Family Planning Association***) **n** *association britannique pour le planning familial.*

fr. (abbr of ***franc***) F.

Fr. (abbr of ***father***) P.

fracas ['frækɑ:, *US* 'freɪkəs] (*UK* **fracas**, *US* **-ses** [-si:z]) **n** bagarre *f*.

fraction ['frækʃn] **n** fraction *f* ▸ **a fraction too big** légèrement ***OR*** un petit peu trop grand.

fractionally ['frækʃnəlɪ] **adv** un tout petit peu.

fractious ['frækʃəs] **adj** grincheux(euse).

fracture ['fræktʃəʳ] ■ **n** fracture *f.*
■ **vt** fracturer.

fragile ['frædʒaɪl] **adj** fragile.

fragility [frə'dʒɪlətɪ] **n** fragilité *f.*

fragment ■ **n** ['frægmənt] fragment *m.*
■ **vi** [fræg'ment] se fragmenter.

fragmentary ['frægməntrɪ] **adj** fragmentaire.

fragmentation [ˌfrægmen'teɪʃn] **n** [breaking] fragmentation *f* / [division] fragmentation *f*, morcellement *m* ▸ **fragmentation bomb** bombe *f* à fragmentation ▸ **fragmentation grenade** grenade *f* offensive.

fragmented [fræg'mentɪd] **adj** fragmenté(e).

fragrance ['freɪgrəns] **n** parfum *m.*

fragrant ['freɪgrənt] **adj** parfumé(e).

frail [freɪl] **adj** fragile.

frailty ['freɪltɪ] (pl **-ies**) **n 1.** [gen] fragilité *f* **2.** [moral weakness] faiblesse *f.*

frame [freɪm] ■ **n 1.** [gen] cadre *m* / [of glasses] monture *f* / [of door, window] encadrement *m* / [of boat] carcasse *f* **2.** [physique] charpente *f.*
■ **vt 1.** [gen] encadrer **2.** [express] formuler **3.** *inf* [set up] monter un coup contre.

frame of mind **n** état *m* d'esprit.

framework ['freɪmwɜːk] **n 1.** [structure] armature *f*, carcasse *f* **2.** *fig* [basis] structure *f*, cadre *m.*

franc [fræŋk] **n** franc *m.*

France [frɑːns] **n** France *f* ▸ **in France** en France.

franchise ['fræntʃaɪz] **n 1.** POL droit *m* de vote **2.** COMM franchise *f.*

franchisee [ˌfræntʃaɪ'ziː] **n** franchisé *m.*

franchisor ['fræntʃaɪzəʳ] **n** franchiseur *m.*

Francophile ['fræŋkəfaɪl] ■ **adj** francophile.
■ **n** francophile *mf.*

Francophobe ['fræŋkəfəʊb] ■ **adj** francophobe.
■ **n** francophobe *mf.*

Francophone ['fræŋkəfəʊn] ■ **adj** francophone.
■ **n** francophone *mf.*

Franglais ['frɒŋgleɪ] **n** franglais *m.*

frank [fræŋk] ■ **adj** franc (franche).
■ **vt** *UK* affranchir.

Frankfurt ['fræŋkfət] **n : Frankfurt (am Main)** Francfort (-sur-le-Main).

frankfurter ['fræŋkfɜːtəʳ] **n** saucisse *f* de Francfort.

frankincense ['fræŋkɪnsens] **n** encens *m.*

franking machine ['fræŋkɪŋ-] **n** *UK* machine *f* à affranchir.

frankly ['fræŋklɪ] **adv** franchement.

frankness ['fræŋknɪs] **n** franchise *f.*

frantic ['fræntɪk] **adj** frénétique ▸ **to be frantic (with worry)** être fou (folle) d'inquiétude.

frantically ['fræntɪklɪ] **adv** frénétiquement, avec frénésie.

frappe [*UK* 'fræpeɪ, *US* fræ'peɪ] **n** [drink] milk-shake *m* *(épais).*

fraternal [frə'tɜːnl] **adj** fraternel(elle).

fraternally [frə'tɜːnəlɪ] **adv** fraternellement.

fraternity [frə'tɜːnətɪ] (pl **-ies**) **n 1.** [community] confrérie *f* **2.** *(U)* [friendship] fraternité *f* **3.** *US* [of students] club *m* d'étudiants *(de sexe masculin).*

fraternize, *UK* ***-ise*** ['frætənaɪz] **vi** fraterniser.

fraud [frɔːd] **n 1.** *(U)* [crime] fraude *f* **2.** *pej* [impostor] imposteur *m.*

fraudulence ['frɔːdjʊləns] **n** caractère *m* frauduleux.

fraudulent ['frɔːdjʊlənt] **adj** frauduleux(euse).

fraudulently ['frɔːdjʊləntlɪ] **adv** frauduleusement.

fraught [frɔːt] **adj 1.** [full] **: fraught with** plein(e) de **2.** *UK* [person] tendu(e) / [time, situation] difficile.

fray [freɪ] ■ **vt** *fig* **: my nerves were frayed** j'étais extrêmement tendu(e), j'étais à bout de nerfs.
■ **vi** [material, sleeves] s'user ▸ **tempers frayed** *fig* l'atmosphère était tendue OR électrique.
■ **n** *liter* bagarre *f.*

frayed [freɪd] **adj** [jeans, collar] élimé(e).

frazzled ['fræzld] **adj** *inf* **1.** [person] éreinté(e) **2.** [by cooking] desséché(e).

FRB (abbr of ***Federal Reserve Board***) **n** *organe de contrôle de la Banque centrale américaine.*

FRCP (abbr of ***Fellow of the Royal College of Physicians***) *membre de l'académie de médecine britannique.*

FRCS (abbr of ***Fellow of the Royal College of Surgeons***) *membre de l'académie de chirurgie britannique.*

freak [friːk] ■ **adj** bizarre, insolite.
■ **n 1.** [strange creature] monstre *m*, phénomène *m* **2.** [unusual event] accident *m* bizarre **3.** *inf* [fanatic] fana *mf.*
◆ ***freak out*** *inf* ■ **vi** [get angry] exploser (de colère) / [panic] paniquer.
■ **vt sep : to freak sb out** faire sauter qqn au plafond.

freakish ['friːkɪʃ] **adj** bizarre, insolite.

freaky ['friːkɪ] **adj** *inf* bizarre, insolite.

freckle ['frekl] **n** tache *f* de rousseur.

freckled ['frekld] **adj** taché(e) de son, marqué(e) de taches de rousseur ▸ **a freckled face/nose** un visage/nez couvert de taches de rousseur.

free [friː] ■ **adj** (comp **freer**, superl **freest**) **1.** [gen] libre ▸ **to be free to do sthg** être libre de faire qqch ▸ **feel free!** je t'en prie! ▸ **the hostage managed to get free** l'otage a réussi à se libérer ▸ **to set free** libérer ▸ **free from** OR **of worry** sans souci ▸ **she doesn't have a free moment** elle n'a pas un moment de libre
2. [not paid for] gratuit(e)
3. [generous] **: to be free with money** dépenser sans compter ▸ **she's very free with her criticism** elle ne ménage pas ses critiques.
■ **adv 1.** [without payment] gratuitement ▸ **free of charge** gratuitement ▸ **for free** gratuitement ▸ **children travel (for) free** les enfants voyagent gratuitement
2. [run, live] librement.
■ **vt** (pt & pp **freed**) **1.** [gen] libérer
2. [trapped person, object] dégager ▸ **she tried to free herself from his grasp** elle essaya de se libérer OR dégager de son étreinte.

-free [fri:] **suffix** sans.

freebie ['fri:bɪ] **n** *inf* faveur *f*.

freedom ['fri:dəm] **n 1.** [gen] liberté *f* ▸ **freedom of information** liberté d'information ▸ **freedom of speech** liberté d'expression **2.** [exception] **: freedom (from)** exemption *f* (de).

freedom fighter **n** partisan *m*, -e *f*.

free enterprise **n** *(U)* libre entreprise *f*.

free-fall **n** *(U)* chute *f* libre.

Freefone® ['fri:fəʊn] **n** *(U) UK* ≃ numéro *m* vert.

free-for-all **n** mêlée *f* générale.

free gift **n** prime *f*.

freehand ['fri:hænd] **adj & adv** à main levée.

freehold ['fri:həʊld] ■ **adv** en propriété inaliénable.
■ **n** propriété *f* foncière inaliénable.

freeholder ['fri:həʊldəʳ] **n** propriétaire foncier *m*, propriétaire foncière *f*.

free house **n** *UK* pub *m* en gérance libre.

free kick **n** coup *m* franc.

freelance ['fri:lɑ:ns] ■ **adj** indépendant(e), free-lance *(inv)*.
■ **adv** en free-lance.
■ **n** indépendant *m*, -e *f*, free-lance *mf inv*.
■ **vi** travailler en indépendant *OR* en free-lance.

freelancer ['fri:lɑ:nsəʳ] **n** travailleur *m* indépendant, travailleuse *f* indépendante, free-lance *mf inv*.

freeloader ['fri:ləʊdəʳ] **n** *inf* parasite *m*.

freely ['fri:lɪ] **adv 1.** [gen] librement **2.** [generously] sans compter.

freeman ['fri:mən] (pl **-men** [-mən]) **n** *UK* citoyen *m*, -enne *f* d'honneur.

free-market economy **n** économie *f* de marché.

Freemason ['fri:ˌmeɪsn] **n** franc-maçon *m*.

Freemasonry ['fri:ˌmeɪsnrɪ] **n** franc-maçonnerie *f*.

freemen ['fri:mən] **npl** *UK* ➤ ***freeman***.

Freepost® ['fri:pəʊst] **n** *UK* port *m* payé.

free-range **adj** de ferme.

free sample **n** échantillon *m* gratuit.

freesia ['fri:zjə] **n** freesia *m*.

free speech **n** liberté *f* d'expression.

free spirit **n** non-conformiste *mf*.

freestanding [ˌfri:'stændɪŋ] **adj** [furniture] non-encastré(e).

freestyle ['fri:staɪl] **n** [in swimming] nage *f* libre.

freethinker [fri:'θɪŋkəʳ] **n** libre-penseur *m*, -euse *f*.

Freetown ['fri:taʊn] **n** Freetown.

free trade **n** *(U)* libre-échange *m*.

free-trade agreement **n** accord *m* de libre-échange.

freeware ['fri:weəʳ] **n** COMPUT logiciel *m* public, logiciel *m* libre.

freeway ['fri:weɪ] **n** *US* autoroute *f*.

freewheel [ˌfri:'wi:l] **vi** [on bicycle] rouler en roue libre / [in car] rouler au point mort.

freewheeling [ˌfri:'wi:lɪŋ] **adj** *inf* sans contrainte.

free will **n** *(U)* libre arbitre *m* ▸ **to do sthg of one's own free will** faire qqch de son propre gré.

free world **n** *dated* **: the free world** les pays *mpl* non-communistes.

freeze [fri:z] ■ **vt** (pt **froze**, pp **frozen**) **1.** [gen] geler / [food] congeler **2.** [wages, prices] bloquer.
■ **vi** (pt **froze**, pp **frozen**) **1.** [gen] geler **2.** [stop moving] s'arrêter.
■ **n 1.** [cold weather] gel *m* **2.** [of wages, prices] blocage *m*.
◆ ***freeze over*** **vi** geler.
◆ ***freeze up*** **vi** geler, se bloquer.

freeze-dried [-'draɪd] **adj** lyophilisé(e).

freeze-dry **vt** lyophiliser.

freeze-frame **n** CIN arrêt *m* sur image.

freezer ['fri:zəʳ] **n** congélateur *m*.

freezing ['fri:zɪŋ] ■ **adj** glacé(e) ▸ **I'm freezing** je gèle.
■ **n** = ***freezing point***.

freezing point **n** point *m* de congélation.

freight [freɪt] **n** [goods] fret *m*.

freight train **n** *US* train *m* de marchandises.

French [frentʃ] ■ **adj** français(e).
■ **n** [language] français *m*.
■ **npl : the French** les Français *mpl*.

French bean **n** *UK* haricot *m* vert.

French bread **n** *(U)* baguette *f*.

French Canadian ■ **adj** canadien français (canadienne française).
■ **n** Canadien français *m*, Canadienne française *f*.

French chalk **n** *(U)* craie *f* de tailleur.

French doors = ***French windows***.

French dressing **n** [in UK] vinaigrette *f* / [in US] *sauce-salade à base de mayonnaise et de ketchup*.

French fries **npl** *esp US* frites *fpl*.

French horn **n** cor *m* d'harmonie.

French kiss ■ **n** baiser *m* profond.
■ **vt** embrasser sur la bouche *(avec la langue)*.
■ **vi** s'embrasser sur la bouche *(avec la langue)*.

Frenchman ['frentʃmən] (pl **-men** [-mən]) **n** Français *m*.

French polish **n** *(U) UK* vernis *m* à l'alcool.

French Riviera **n : the French Riviera** la Côte d'Azur.

French stick **n** *UK* baguette *f*.

French toast **n** pain *m* perdu.

French windows **npl** porte-fenêtre *f*.

Frenchwoman ['frentʃˌwʊmən] (pl **-women** [-ˌwɪmɪn]) **n** Française *f*.

frenetic [frə'netɪk] **adj** frénétique.

frenetically [frə'netɪklɪ] **adv** frénétiquement.

frenzied ['frenzɪd] **adj** [haste, activity] frénétique / [attack] déchaîné(e) / [mob] en délire.

frenzy ['frenzɪ] (pl **-ies**) **n** frénésie *f*.

frequency ['fri:kwənsɪ] (pl **-ies**) **n** fréquence *f*.

frequency modulation **n** modulation *f* de fréquence.

frequent ■ **adj** ['fri:kwənt] fréquent(e).
■ **vt** [frɪ'kwent] fréquenter.

frequently ['fri:kwəntlɪ] **adv** fréquemment.

frequent user card **n** carte *f* de fidélité.

fresco ['freskəʊ] (pl **-es** *OR* **-s**) **n** fresque *f*.

fresh [freʃ] ■ **adj 1.** [gen] frais (fraîche) ▸ **I need some fresh air** j'ai besoin de prendre l'air ▸ **fresh from** [the oven] qui sort de / [university] frais émoulu (fraîche émoulue) de ▸ **as fresh as a daisy** frais comme une rose **2.** [not salty] doux (douce) **3.** [new - drink, piece of paper] autre / [- look, approach] nouveau(elle) ▸ **start on a fresh page** prenez une nouvelle page ▸ **to make a fresh start** repartir à zéro **4.** *inf dated* [cheeky] familier(ère) ▸ **to get fresh with sb** se montrer osé(e) avec qqn.
■ **adv : fresh-ground/made** qui vient juste d'être moulu(e) / fait(e) ▸ **to be fresh out of sthg** *inf* ne plus avoir de qqch.

freshen ['freʃn] ■ **vt** rafraîchir.
■ **vi** [wind] devenir plus fort(e).
◆ ***freshen up*** ■ **vt sep 1.** [wash] **: to freshen o.s. up** faire un brin de toilette **2.** [smarten up] rafraîchir.
■ **vi** faire un brin de toilette.

fresher ['freʃəʳ] **n** *UK* UNIV bizut *m*, étudiant *m*, -e *f* de première année.

freshly ['freʃlɪ] **adv** [squeezed, ironed] fraîchement.

freshman ['freʃmən] (pl **-men** [-mən]) **n** *US* UNIV bizut *m*, étudiant *m*, -e *f* de première année.

freshness ['freʃnɪs] **n** *(U)* **1.** [gen] fraîcheur *f* **2.** [originality] nouveauté *f*.

freshwater ['freʃ,wɔ:təʳ] **adj** d'eau douce.

fret [fret] (pt & pp **-ted**, cont **-ting**) **vi** [worry] s'inquiéter.

fretful ['fretfʊl] **adj** [baby] grognon(onne) / [night, sleep] agité(e).

fretfully ['fretfʊlɪ] **adv** [anxiously - ask, say] avec inquiétude.

fretsaw ['fretsɔ:] **n** scie *f* à découper.

Freudian slip ['frɔɪdɪən-] **n** lapsus *m*.

FRG (abbr of ***Federal Republic of Germany***) **n** RFA *f*.

Fri. (abbr of ***Friday***) ven.

friar ['fraɪəʳ] **n** frère *m*.

fricassee ['frɪkəsi:] ■ **n** fricassée *f*.
■ **vt** fricasser.

friction ['frɪkʃn] **n** *(U)* friction *f*.

friction tape **n** *US & Can* chatterton *m*.

Friday ['fraɪdɪ] **n** vendredi *m* ; see also ***Saturday***.

fridge [frɪdʒ] **n** frigo *m*.

fridge-freezer **n** *UK* réfrigérateur-congélateur *m*.

fried [fraɪd] ■ **pt & pp** ➤ ***fry***.
■ **adj** frit(e) ▸ **fried egg** œuf *m* au plat.

friend [frend] **n** ami *m*, -e *f* ▸ **Bill's a good friend of mine** Bill est un grand ami à moi ▸ **to be friends** être amis ▸ **to be friends with sb** être ami avec qqn ▸ **we're just good friends** nous sommes bons amis sans plus ▸ **to make friends (with sb)** se lier d'amitié (avec qqn).

friendless ['frendlɪs] **adj** sans amis.

friendliness ['frendlɪnɪs] **n** gentillesse *f*.

friendly ['frendlɪ] ■ **adj** (comp **-ier**, superl **-iest**) [person, manner, match] amical(e) / [nation] ami(e) / [argument] sans conséquence ▸ **to be friendly with sb** être ami avec qqn.
■ **n** (pl **-ies**) *esp UK* match *m* amical.

friendly society **n** *UK* mutuelle *f*.

friendly takeover bid **n** OPA *f* amicale.

friendship ['frendʃɪp] **n** amitié *f*.

fries [fraɪz] = ***French fries***.

Friesian (cow) ['fri:zjən-] **n** *esp UK* (vache *f*) frisonne *f*.

frieze [fri:z] **n** frise *f*.

frigate ['frɪgət] **n** frégate *f*.

frigging ['frɪgɪŋ] **adj** *v inf* **: move your frigging car!** enlève-moi cette foutue bagnole!

fright [fraɪt] **n** peur *f* ▸ **to give sb a fright** faire peur à qqn ▸ **to take fright** prendre peur.

frighten ['fraɪtn] **vt** faire peur à, effrayer ▸ **to frighten sb into doing sthg** forcer qqn à faire qqch sous la menace.
◆ ***frighten away*** **vt sep** chasser en faisant peur à.
◆ ***frighten off*** **vt sep** chasser en faisant peur à.

frightened ['fraɪtnd] **adj** apeuré(e) ▸ **to be frightened of sthg/of doing sthg** avoir peur de qqch/de faire qqch.

frightening ['fraɪtnɪŋ] **adj** effrayant(e).

frighteningly ['fraɪtnɪŋlɪ] **adv** à faire peur ▸ **the story was frighteningly true to life** l'histoire était d'un réalisme effrayant.

frightful ['fraɪtfʊl] **adj** *dated* effroyable.

frightfully ['fraɪtfʊlɪ] **adv** *UK dated* **: he's a frightfully good dancer** il danse remarquablement bien ▸ **I'm frightfully sorry** je suis absolument désolé.

frigid ['frɪdʒɪd] **adj 1.** [sexually] frigide **2.** [very cold] glacial, glacé(e).

frigidity [frɪ'dʒɪdətɪ] **n 1.** [sexual] frigidité *f* **2.** [coldness] froideur *f*.

frill [frɪl] **n 1.** [decoration] volant *m* **2.** *inf* [extra] supplément *m*.

frilly ['frɪlɪ] (comp **-ier**, superl **-iest**) **adj** à fanfreluches.

fringe [frɪndʒ] ■ **n 1.** [gen] frange *f* **2.** [edge - of village] bordure *f* / [- of wood, forest] lisière *f*.
■ **vt** [edge] border.

fringe benefit **n** avantage *m* extrasalarial.

fringe group **n** groupe *m* marginal.

fringe theatre **n** *UK* théâtre *m* d'avant-garde.

Frisbee® ['frɪzbɪ] **n** Frisbee *m inv*.

Frisian Islands ['frɪʒən-] **npl : the Frisian Islands** l'archipel *m* frison.

frisk [frɪsk] ■ **vt** fouiller.
■ **vi** gambader.

frisky ['frɪskɪ] (comp **-ier**, superl **-iest**) **adj** *inf* vif (vive).

fritter ['frɪtəʳ] **n** beignet *m*.
◆ ***fritter away*** **vt sep** gaspiller ▸ **to fritter money/time away on sthg** gaspiller son argent/son temps en qqch.

frivolity [frɪ'vɒlətɪ] (pl **-ies**) **n** frivolité *f*.

frivolous ['frɪvələs] **adj** frivole.

frizz [frɪz] ■ **n : she had a frizz of blond hair** elle avait des cheveux blonds tout frisés.
■ **vt** faire friser.
■ **vi** friser.

frizzy ['frɪzɪ] (comp **-ier**, superl **-iest**) **adj** crépu(e).

fro [frəʊ] ➤ ***to***.

frock [frɒk] **n** *dated* robe *f*.

frog [frɒg] **n** [animal] grenouille *f* ▸ **to have a frog in one's throat** avoir un chat dans la gorge.

frogman ['frɒgmən] (pl **-men** [-mən]) **n** homme-grenouille *m*.

frogmarch ['frɒgmɑ:tʃ] **vt** *esp UK emmener quelqu'un de force en lui tenant les bras dans le dos.*

frogmen ['frɒgmən] **npl** ➤ ***frogman***.

frogspawn ['frɒgspɔ:n] **n** *(U)* œufs *mpl* de grenouille.

frolic ['frɒlɪk] ■ **n** ébats *mpl*.
■ **vi** (pt & pp **-ked**, cont **-king**) folâtrer.

from *(weak form* [frəm]*, strong form* [frɒm]*)* **prep 1.** [indicating source, origin, removal] de ▸ **where are you from?** d'où venez-vous?, d'où êtes-vous? ▸ **I've just come back from there** j'en reviens ▸ **I got a letter from her today** j'ai reçu une lettre d'elle aujourd'hui ▸ **a flight from Paris** un vol en provenance de Paris ▸ **to translate from Spanish into English** traduire d'espagnol en anglais ▸ **to drink from a glass** boire dans un verre ▸ **he's not back from work yet** il n'est pas encore rentré de son travail ▸ **he took a notebook from his pocket** il a sorti un carnet de sa poche ▸ **to take sthg (away) from sb** prendre qqch à qqn ▸ **I bought my piano from a neighbour** j'ai acheté mon piano à un voisin
2. [indicating a deduction] de ▸ **to deduct sthg from sthg** retrancher qqch de qqch
3. [indicating escape, separation] de ▸ **he ran away from home** il a fait une fugue, il s'est sauvé de chez lui ▸ **we sheltered from the rain in a cave** nous nous sommes abrités de la pluie dans une caverne
4. [indicating position] de ▸ **seen from above/below** vu(e) d'en haut/d'en bas
5. [indicating distance] de ▸ **it's 60 km from here** c'est à 60 km d'ici ▸ **how far is it from Paris to Lyons?** combien y a-t-il de Paris à Lyon?
6. [indicating material object is made out of] en ▸ **it's made from wood/plastic** c'est en bois/plastique ▸ **Calvados is made from apples** le calvados est fait avec des pommes
7. [starting at a particular time] de ▸ **from 2 pm to** *OR* **till 6 pm** de 14 h à 18 h ▸ **from birth** de naissance ▸ **from the age of four** à partir de quatre ans ▸ **from the moment I saw him** dès que *OR* dès l'instant où je l'ai vu ▸ **from now on** désormais, dorénavant
8. [indicating difference] de ▸ **to be different from sb/sthg** être différent de qqn/qqch
9. [indicating change] **: from... to** de... à ▸ **the price went up from £100 to £150** le prix est passé *OR* monté de 100 livres à 150 livres
10. [because of, as a result of] de ▸ **to suffer from cold/hunger** souffrir du froid/de la faim ▸ **I guessed she was Australian from the way she spoke** j'ai deviné qu'elle était australienne à sa façon de parler
11. [on the evidence of] d'après, à ▸ **to speak from personal experience** parler par expérience *OR* d'après son expérience personnelle ▸ **from what you're saying...** d'après ce que vous dites... ▸ **from the way she talks you'd think she were the boss** à l'entendre, on croirait que c'est elle le patron
12. [indicating lowest amount] depuis, à partir de ▸ **prices start from £50** le premier prix est de 50 livres.

frond [frɒnd] **n** fronde *f*.

front [frʌnt] ■ **n 1.** [most forward part - gen] avant *m* / [- of dress, envelope, house] devant *m* / [- of class] premier rang *m* / [of queue] début *m* ▸ **I'll be at the front of the train** je serai en tête de *OR* à l'avant du train **2.** METEOR & MIL front *m* ▸ **to present a united front (on sthg)** *fig* faire front commun (devant qqch) **3.** [issue, area] plan *m* ▸ **on the domestic/employment front** sur le plan intérieur/du travail ▸ **the Prime Minister is being attacked on all fronts** on s'en prend au Premier ministre de tous côtés **4. : (sea)front** front *m* de mer ▸ **a walk along** *OR* **on the front** une promenade au bord de la mer **5.** [outward appearance - of person] contenance *f* / *pej* [- of business] façade *f* ▸ **to put on a bold** *OR* **brave front** faire preuve de courage.
■ **adj** [tooth, garden] de devant / [row, page] premier(ère) ▸ **front seat/wheel** AUT siège *m*/roue *f* avant ▸ **front cover** couverture *f*.
■ **vt 1.** [be opposite] être en face de **2.** [TV programme] présenter.
■ **vi : to front onto sthg** donner sur qqch.
◆ ***in front*** **adv 1.** [further forward - walk, push] devant / [- people] à l'avant **2.** [winning] **: to be in front** mener.
◆ ***in front of*** **prep** devant.

frontage ['frʌntɪdʒ] **n** [of house] façade *f* / [of shop] devanture *f*.

frontal ['frʌntl] **adj 1.** [attack] de front **2.** [view] de face.

frontbench [ˌfrʌnt'bentʃ] **n** *UK à la chambre des Communes, bancs occupés respectivement par les ministres du gouvernement en exercice et ceux du gouvernement fantôme.*

frontbencher [ˌfrʌnt'bentʃəʳ] **n** *UK* [member of the government] ministre *m* / [member of the opposition] membre *m* du cabinet fantôme.

front desk **n** réception *f*.

front door **n** porte *f* d'entrée.

frontier ['frʌnˌtɪəʳ, *US* frʌn'tɪər] **n** [border] frontière *f* / *fig* limite *f*.

frontispiece ['frʌntɪspi:s] **n** frontispice *m*.

front line **n : the front line** le front.

front-loading **adj** [washing machine] à chargement frontal.

front man **n 1.** [of company, organization] porte-parole *m inv* **2.** TV présentateur *m*.

front of house **n** THEAT *partie d'un théâtre où peuvent circuler les spectateurs.*

front-page **adj** [article] de première page.

front room **n** salon *m*.

front-runner **n** favori *m*, -ite *f*.

front-wheel drive **n** traction *f* avant.

frost [frɒst] ■ **n** gel *m*.
■ **vi : to frost over** *OR* **up** geler.

frostbite ['frɒstbaɪt] **n** *(U)* gelure *f*.

frostbitten ['frɒst,bɪtn] **adj** [toe, finger] gelé(e).

frosted ['frɒstɪd] **adj** **1.** [glass] dépoli(e) **2.** *US* CULIN glacé(e).

frostily ['frɒstɪlɪ] **adv** de manière glaciale, froidement.

frosting ['frɒstɪŋ] **n** *US (U)* glaçage *m*.

frosty ['frɒstɪ] (comp **-ier**, superl **-iest**) **adj** **1.** [weather, welcome] glacial(e) **2.** [field, window] gelé(e).

froth [frɒθ] ■ **n** [on beer] mousse *f* / [on sea] écume *f*.
■ **vi** [beer] mousser / [sea] écumer.

frothy ['frɒθɪ] (comp **-ier**, superl **-iest**) **adj** [beer] mousseux(euse) / [sea] écumeux(euse).

frown [fraʊn] ■ **n** froncement *m* de sourcils.
■ **vi** froncer les sourcils.
◆ ***frown (up)on*** **vt insep** désapprouver.

froze [frəʊz] **pt** ➤ ***freeze***.

frozen [frəʊzn] ■ **pp** ➤ ***freeze***.
■ **adj** [generally] gelé(e) / [food] congelé(e) ▸ **frozen with fear** *fig* mort(e) de peur.

frozen assets **npl** capitaux *mpl* gelés.

FRS **n** **1.** (abbr of ***Fellow of the Royal Society***) *membre de l'académie des sciences britannique* **2.** (abbr of ***Federal Reserve System***) *banque centrale américaine*.

frugal ['fru:gl] **adj** **1.** [meal] frugal(e) **2.** [person, life] économe.

frugally ['fru:gəlɪ] **adv** [live] simplement, frugalement / [distribute, give] parcimonieusement.

fruit [fru:t] ■ **n** (pl **fruit** *OR* **-s**) fruit *m* ▸ **to bear fruit** *fig* porter ses fruits.
■ **comp** [flan] aux fruits ▸ **fruit tree** arbre *m* fruitier.
■ **vi** donner des fruits.

fruitcake ['fru:tkeɪk] **n** cake *m*.

fruit cocktail **n** macédoine *f* de fruits.

fruiterer ['fru:tərəʳ] **n** *UK dated* fruitier *m*.

fruit fly **n** mouche *f* du vinaigre, drosophile *f*.

fruitful ['fru:tfʊl] **adj** [successful] fructueux(euse).

fruitfully ['fru:tfʊlɪ] **adv** fructueusement.

fruition [fru:'ɪʃn] **n : to come to fruition** se réaliser.

fruit juice **n** jus *m* de fruits.

fruitless ['fru:tlɪs] **adj** vain(e).

fruitlessly ['fru:tlɪslɪ] **adv** en vain, vainement.

fruit machine **n** *UK* machine *f* à sous.

fruit salad **n** salade *f* de fruits, macédoine *f*.

fruity ['fru:tɪ] (comp **-ier**, superl **-iest**) **adj** **1.** [flavour, sauce] fruité(e), de fruit / [perfume, wine] fruité(e) **2.** [voice] étoffé(e), timbré(e) **3.** *inf* [joke, story] corsé(e), salé(e).

frump [frʌmp] **n** femme *f* mal habillée.

frumpish ['frʌmpɪʃ] = ***frumpy***.

frumpy ['frʌmpɪ] (comp **-ier**, superl **-iest**) **adj** mal habillé(e).

frustrate [frʌ'streɪt] **vt** **1.** [annoy, disappoint] frustrer **2.** [prevent] faire échouer.

frustrated [frʌ'streɪtɪd] **adj** **1.** [person, artist] frustré(e) **2.** [effort, love] vain(e).

frustrating [frʌ'streɪtɪŋ] **adj** frustrant(e).

frustration [frʌ'streɪʃn] **n** frustration *f*.

fry [fraɪ] (pt & pp **fried**) **vt** & **vi** frire.

fryer ['fraɪəʳ] **n** **1.** [pan] poêle *f* (à frire) / [for deep-fat frying] friteuse *f* **2.** [chicken] poulet *m* à frire.

frying pan ['fraɪɪŋ-] **n** poêle *f* à frire ▸ **to jump out of the frying pan into the fire** tomber de Charybde en Scylla.

fry-up **n** *UK inf plat constitué de plusieurs aliments frits ensemble*.

FSA [,efes'eɪ] (abbr of ***Food Standards Agency***) *UK agence pour la sécurité alimentaire*.

ft. abbr of ***foot***, ***feet***.

FT (abbr of ***Financial Times***) **n** *quotidien britannique d'information financière* ▸ **the FT index** l'indice *m* boursier du FT, ≃ le Cac 40.

FTC (abbr of ***Federal Trade Commission***) **n** *organisme américain chargé de faire respecter les lois anti-trust*.

FTP (abbr of ***file transfer protocol***) **n** FTP *m*.

fuchsia ['fju:ʃə] **n** fuchsia *m*.

fuck [fʌk] *vulg* ■ **vt** & **vi** baiser.
■ **excl** putain de merde!
◆ ***fuck off*** **vi** *vulg* foutre le camp ▸ **fuck off!** fous le camp!

fucker ['fʌkəʳ] **n** *vulg* **: you stupid fucker!** mais qu'est-ce que tu peux être con!

fucking ['fʌkɪŋ] **adj** *vulg* putain de.

fuddled ['fʌdld] **adj** confus(e).

fuddy-duddy ['fʌdɪ,dʌdɪ] (pl **-ies**) **n** *inf pej* personne *f* vieux jeu.

fudge [fʌdʒ] ■ **n** *(U)* [sweet] caramel *m* (mou).
■ **vt** *inf* [figures] truquer / [issue] esquiver.

fuel [fjʊəl] ■ **n** combustible *m* / [for engine] carburant *m* ▸ **to add fuel to** *fig* alimenter.
■ **vt** (*UK* **-led**, cont **-ling**, *US* **-ed**, cont **-ing**) **1.** [supply with fuel] alimenter (en combustible/carburant) **2.** *fig* [speculation] nourrir.

fuel-efficient **adj** économique, qui ne consomme pas beaucoup.

fuel pump **n** pompe *f* d'alimentation.

fuel tank **n** réservoir *m* à carburant.

fug [fʌg] **n** *UK* renfermé *m*.

fugitive ['fju:dʒətɪv] **n** fugitif *m*, -ive *f*.

fugue [fju:g] **n** fugue *f*.

fulcrum ['fʊlkrəm] (pl **-crums** *OR* **-cra** [-krə]) **n** pivot *m*.

fulfil *UK* (pt & pp **-led**, cont **-ling**), ***fulfill*** *US* [fʊl'fɪl] **vt** **1.** [duty, role] remplir / [hope] répondre à / [ambition, prophecy] réaliser **2.** [satisfy - need] satisfaire ▸ **to fulfil o.s.** s'épanouir.

fulfilled [fʊl'fɪld] **adj** [life] épanoui(e), heureux(euse) / [person] épanoui(e), comblé(e).

fulfilling [fʊl'fɪlɪŋ] **adj** épanouissant(e).

fulfilment *UK*, ***fulfillment*** *US* [fʊl'fɪlmənt] **n** *(U)* **1.** [satisfaction] grande satisfaction *f* **2.** [of ambition, dream] réalisation *f* / [of role, promise] exécution *f* / [of need] satisfaction *f*.

full [fʊl] ■ **adj 1.** [gen] plein(e) / [bus, car park] complet(ète) / [with food] gavé(e), repu(e) ▸ **her parents were full of hope** ses parents étaient remplis d'espoir ▸ **her letters are full of spelling mistakes** ses lettres sont truffées de fautes d'orthographe ▸ **to be full of o.s.** être plein(e) de soi-même *OR* imbu(e) de sa personne
2. [complete - recovery, control] total(e) / [- explanation, day] entier(ère) / [- volume] maximum *(inv)* ▸ **the house is a full 10 miles from town** la maison est à 15 bons kilomètres de la ville ▸ **in full uniform** en grande tenue ▸ **I didn't get the full story** je n'ai pas entendu tous les détails de l'histoire
3. [busy - life] rempli(e) / [- timetable, day] chargé(e) ▸ **I've got a full week ahead of me** j'ai une semaine chargée devant moi
4. [flavour] riche
5. [plump - figure] rondelet(ette) / [- mouth] charnu(e)
6. [skirt, sleeve] ample.
■ **adv 1.** [directly] **: full in the face** en plein (dans le) visage **2.** [very] **: you know full well that...** tu sais très bien que...
3. [at maximum] au maximum ▸ **I turned the heat full on** *UK* *OR* **on full** j'ai mis le chauffage à fond.
■ **n : in full** complètement, entièrement ▸ **she paid in full** elle a tout payé ▸ **to the full** pleinement ▸ **to enjoy life to the full** *UK* profiter de la vie au maximum.

fullback ['fʊlbæk] **n** SPORT arrière *m*.

full-blooded [-'blʌdɪd] **adj 1.** [pure-blooded] de race pure **2.** [strong, complete] robuste.

full-blown [-'bləʊn] **adj** général(e) ▸ **to have full-blown AIDS** avoir le Sida avéré.

full board **n** pension *f* complète.

full-bodied [-'bɒdɪd] **adj** qui a du corps.

full cream milk **n** *UK* lait *m* entier.

full dress **n** *(U)* tenue *f* de cérémonie.

full-face **adj** de face.

full-fashioned *US* = ***fully-fashioned***.

full-fledged *US* = ***fully-fledged***.

full-frontal **adj** de face.

full-grown **adj** adulte.

full house **n** [at show, event] représentation *f* à bureaux fermés.

full-length ■ **adj 1.** [portrait, mirror] en pied **2.** [dress, novel] long (longue) ▸ **full-length film** long métrage.
■ **adv** de tout son long.

full monty [- 'mɒntɪ] **n** *inf* **: the full monty** la totale.

full moon **n** pleine lune *f*.

fullness ['fʊlnɪs] **n** [of voice] ampleur *f* / [of life] richesse *f* ▸ **in the fullness of time** avec le temps.

full-on **adj** *inf* [documentary, film - hard-hitting] dur(e) / [- sexually explicit] cru(e) ▸ **he's full-on** [- gen] il en fait trop / [- making sexual advances] il est entreprenant.

full-page **adj** sur toute une page.

full-scale **adj 1.** [life-size] grandeur nature *(inv)* **2.** [complete] de grande envergure.

full-size(d) **adj 1.** [life-size] grandeur nature *(inv)* **2.** [adult] adulte **3.** *US* AUT **: full-sized car** grande berline.

full stop *UK* ■ **n** point *m*.
■ **adv** un point c'est tout.

full time **n** *UK* SPORT fin *f* de match.
◆ ***full-time*** **adj & adv** [work, worker] à temps plein.

full up **adj** [bus, train] complet(ète) / [with food] gavé(e), repu(e).

fully ['fʊlɪ] **adv** [understand, satisfy] tout à fait / [train, describe] entièrement.

fully-fashioned *UK*, ***full-fashioned*** *US* [-'fæʃnd] **adj** moulant(e).

fully-fledged *UK*, ***full-fledged*** *US* [-'fledʒd] **adj** diplômé(e).

fulness ['fʊlnɪs] = ***fullness***.

fulsome ['fʊlsəm] **adj** excessif(ive).

fumble ['fʌmbl] ■ **vt** [catch] mal attraper.
■ **vi** fouiller, tâtonner ▸ **to fumble for** fouiller pour trouver.

fume [fju:m] **vi** [with anger] rager.
◆ ***fumes*** **npl** [from paint] émanations *fpl* / [from smoke] fumées *fpl* / [from car] gaz *mpl* d'échappement.

fumigate ['fju:mɪgeɪt] **vt** fumiger.

fun [fʌn] ■ **n** *(U)* **1.** [pleasure, amusement] **: the game is great fun** ce jeu est très amusant ▸ **to have fun** s'amuser ▸ **for fun, for the fun of it** pour s'amuser **2.** [playfulness] **: to be full of fun** être plein(e) d'entrain **3.** [ridicule] **: to make fun of** *OR* **poke fun at sb** se moquer de qqn.
■ **adj** amusant(e).

function ['fʌŋkʃn] ■ **n 1.** [gen] fonction *f* **2.** [formal social event] réception *f* officielle **3.** [software] fonctionnalité *f*.
■ **vi** fonctionner ▸ **to function as** servir de.

functional ['fʌŋkʃnəl] **adj 1.** [practical] fonctionnel (elle) **2.** [operational] en état de marche.

functionality [fʌŋkʃ'nælətɪ] **n** fonctionnalité *f*.

functionary ['fʌŋkʃnərɪ] (pl -ies) **n** fonctionnaire *mf*.

function key **n** COMPUT touche *f* de fonction.

function room **n** salle *f* de réception.

fund [fʌnd] ■ **n** [generally] fonds *m* / *fig* [of knowledge] puits *m*.
■ **vt** financer.
◆ ***funds*** **npl** fonds *mpl*.

fundamental [ˌfʌndə'mentl] **adj : fundamental (to)** fondamental(e) (à).
◆ ***fundamentals*** **npl** principes *mpl* de base.

fundamentalism [ˌfʌndə'mentəlɪzm] **n** [generally] fondamentalisme *m* / [Muslim] intégrisme *m*.

fundamentalist [ˌfʌndə'mentəlɪst] ■ **adj** [gen] fondamentaliste / [Muslim] intégriste.
■ **n** [gen] fondamentaliste *mf* / [Muslim] intégriste *mf*.

fundamentally [ˌfʌndə'mentəlɪ] **adv** fondamentalement.

fundholder ['fʌndhəʊldəʳ] **n** *cabinet médical ayant obtenu le droit de gérer son propre budget auprès du système de sécurité sociale britannique.*

funding ['fʌndɪŋ] **n** *(U)* financement *m.*

fund management **n** gestion *f* de fonds.

fundraiser ['fʌnd,reɪzəʳ] **n** [person] collecteur *m*, -trice *f* de fonds / [event] *projet organisé pour collecter des fonds.*

fund-raising [-,reɪzɪŋ] ■ **n** *(U)* collecte *f* de fonds.
■ **comp** [event, campaign] organisé(e) pour collecter des fonds.

funeral ['fju:nərəl] **n** obsèques *fpl.*

funeral director **n** entrepreneur *m* de pompes funèbres.

funeral home *US* = ***funeral parlour.***

funeral march **n** marche *f* funèbre.

funeral parlour *UK*, ***funeral home*** *US* **n** entreprise *f* de pompes funèbres.

funeral pyre **n** bûcher *m* (funéraire).

funeral service **n** service *m* funèbre.

funereal [fju:'nɪərɪəl] **adj** funèbre.

funfair ['fʌnfeəʳ] **n** *UK* fête *f* foraine.

fungal ['fʌŋgl] **adj** fongique.

fungi ['fʌŋgaɪ] **npl** ➤ ***fungus.***

fungicide ['fʌndʒɪsaɪd] **n** fongicide *m.*

fungus ['fʌŋgəs] (pl **-gi** [-gaɪ] *OR* **-guses** [-gəsi:z]) **n** champignon *m.*

funk [fʌŋk] **n** *(U)* **1.** MUS funk *m* **2.** *UK inf dated* [fear] frayeur *f* ▸ **to be in a (blue) funk** avoir une peur bleue **3.** *esp US inf dated* [depression] découragement *m.*

funky ['fʌŋkɪ] (comp **-ier**, superl **-iest**) **adj** MUS funky *(inv).*

fun-loving **adj** qui aime s'amuser *OR* rire.

funnel ['fʌnl] ■ **n 1.** [tube] entonnoir *m* **2.** [of ship] cheminée *f.*
■ **vt** (*UK* **-led**, cont **-ling**, *US* **-ed**, cont **-ing**) [crowd] canaliser / [money, food] diriger.
■ **vi** (*UK* **-led**, cont **-ling**, *US* **-ed**, cont **-ing**) se diriger.

funnily ['fʌnɪlɪ] **adv** [strangely] bizarrement ▸ **funnily enough** chose curieuse.

funny ['fʌnɪ] (comp **-ier**, superl **-iest**) **adj 1.** [amusing, odd] drôle ▸ **she didn't see the funny side of it** elle n'a pas vu le côté comique de la situation **2.** [odd] bizarre, drôle ▸ **the wine tastes funny** le vin a un drôle de goût ▸ **I think it's funny that he should turn up now** je trouve (ça) bizarre qu'il arrive maintenant ▸ **I feel a bit funny** [ill] je ne suis pas dans mon assiette, je suis un peu patraque.

funny bone **n** petit juif *m.*

funny farm **n** *inf hum* maison *f* de fous.

fun run **n** *course à pied organisée pour collecter des fonds.*

fur [fɜ:ʳ] **n** fourrure *f.*

fur coat **n** (manteau *m* de) fourrure *f.*

furious ['fjʊərɪəs] **adj 1.** [very angry] furieux(euse) **2.** [wild - effort, battle] acharné(e) / [- temper] déchaîné(e).

furiously ['fjʊərɪəslɪ] **adv 1.** [angrily] furieusement **2.** [wildly - fight, try] avec acharnement / [- run] à une allure folle.

furled [fɜ:ld] **adj** [umbrella, flag] roulé(e) / [sail] serré(e).

furlong ['fɜ:lɒŋ] **n** = *201,17 mètres.*

furnace ['fɜ:nɪs] **n** [fire] fournaise *f.*

furnish ['fɜ:nɪʃ] **vt 1.** [fit out] meubler **2.** *fml* [provide] fournir ▸ **to furnish sb with sthg** fournir qqch à qqn.

furnished ['fɜ:nɪʃt] **adj** meublé(e).

furnishings ['fɜ:nɪʃɪŋz] **npl** mobilier *m.*

furniture ['fɜ:nɪtʃəʳ] **n** *(U)* meubles *mpl* ▸ **a piece of furniture** un meuble.

furniture polish **n** encaustique *m*, produit *m* d'entretien des meubles.

furore *UK* ['fjʊərɔ:rɪ], ***furor*** *US* ['fjʊrɔ:r] **n** scandale *m.*

furrier ['fʌrɪəʳ] **n** fourreur *m.*

furrow ['fʌrəʊ] **n 1.** [in field] sillon *m* **2.** [on forehead] ride *f.*

furrowed ['fʌrəʊd] **adj 1.** [field, land] labouré(e) **2.** [brow] ridé(e).

furry ['fɜ:rɪ] (comp **-ier**, superl **-iest**) **adj 1.** [animal] à fourrure **2.** [material] recouvert(e) de fourrure.

further ['fɜ:ðəʳ] ■ **compar** ➤ ***far.***
■ **adv 1.** [gen] plus loin ▸ **how much further is it?** combien de kilomètres y a-t-il? ▸ **further on** plus loin ▸ **she's further on than the rest of the students** *fig* elle est en avance sur les autres étudiants ▸ **further forward** plus en avant ▸ **further (to the) south** plus au sud ▸ **this mustn't go any further** ceci doit rester entre nous
2. [more - complicate, develop] davantage / [- enquire] plus avant
3. [in addition] de plus ▸ **I have nothing further to say** je n'ai rien d'autre *OR* rien de plus à dire.
■ **adj** nouveau(elle), supplémentaire ▸ **for further information, phone this number** pour tout renseignement complémentaire, appelez ce numéro ▸ **do you have any further questions?** avez-vous d'autres questions à poser? ▸ **until further notice** jusqu'à nouvel ordre.
■ **vt** [career, aims] faire avancer / [cause] encourager.
◆ ***further to*** **prep** *fml* suite à.

further education **n** *UK* & *Aus* éducation *f* postscolaire.

furthermore [,fɜ:ðə'mɔ:ʳ] **adv** de plus.

furthermost ['fɜ:ðəməʊst] **adj** le plus éloigné (la plus éloignée).

furthest ['fɜ:ðɪst] ■ **superl** ➤ ***far.***
■ **adj** le plus éloigné (la plus éloignée).
■ **adv** le plus loin.

furtive ['fɜ:tɪv] **adj** [person] sournois(e) / [glance] furtif(ive).

furtively ['fɜ:tɪvlɪ] **adv** furtivement.

fury ['fjʊərɪ] **n** fureur *f* ▸ **in a fury** en fureur.

fuse **[fju:z]** ■ **n 1.** ELEC fusible *m*, plomb *m* **2.** [of bomb] détonateur *m* / [of firework] amorce *f*.
■ **vt 1.** [join by heat] réunir par la fusion **2.** [combine] fusionner.
■ **vi 1.** ELEC **: the lights have fused** les plombs ont sauté **2.** [join by heat] fondre **3.** [combine] fusionner.

fuse-box **n** boîte *f* à fusibles.

fused **[fju:zd] adj** [plug] avec fusible incorporé.

fuselage **['fju:zəlɑ:ʒ] n** fuselage *m*.

fuse wire **n** fusible *m*.

fusillade **[,fju:zə'leɪd] n** fusillade *f*.

fusion **['fju:ʒn] n** fusion *f*.

fuss **[fʌs]** ■ **n 1.** [excitement, anxiety] agitation *f* ▸ **to make a fuss** faire des histoires **2.** *(U)* [complaints] protestations *fpl* ▸ **what a lot of fuss about nothing!** que d'histoires pour rien! ▸ **you should have made a fuss about it** tu n'aurais pas dû laisser passer ça
▸▸ **to make a fuss of sb** *UK* être aux petits soins pour qqn.
■ **vi** faire des histoires.
◆ ***fuss over*** **vt insep** être aux petits soins pour.

fussbudget **['fʌs,bʌdʒət]** *US* = ***fusspot***.

fussily **['fʌsɪlɪ] adv 1.** [fastidiously] de façon méticuleuse *OR* tatillonne / [nervously] avec anxiété **2.** [over-ornate] de façon tarabiscotée.

fussiness **['fʌsɪnɪs] n 1.** [fastidiousness] côté *m* tatillon **2.** [ornateness - of decoration] tarabiscotage *m*.

fusspot *UK* **['fʌspɒt]**, ***fussbudget*** *US* **['fʌs,bʌdʒət] n** *inf* tatillon *m*, -onne *f*.

fussy **['fʌsɪ] (comp -ier, superl -iest) adj 1.** [fastidious - person] tatillon(onne) / [- eater] difficile **2.** [over-decorated] tarabiscoté(e).

fusty **['fʌstɪ] (comp -ier, superl -iest) adj 1.** *UK* [room] qui sent le moisi **2.** [scent] qui sent le renfermé **3.** [idea] vieillot(otte).

futile **['fju:taɪl] adj** vain(e).

futility **[fju:'tɪlətɪ] n** futilité *f*.

futon **['fu:tɒn] n** futon *m*.

future **['fju:tʃər]** ■ **n 1.** [gen] avenir *m* ▸ **in future** à l'avenir ▸ **in the future** dans le futur, à l'avenir **2.** GRAM futur *m*.
■ **adj** futur(e).
◆ ***futures*** **npl** FIN transactions *fpl* à terme.

future perfect **n** futur *m* antérieur.

future tense **n** future *m*.

futuristic **[,fju:tʃə'rɪstɪk] adj** futuriste.

fuze *US* = ***fuse*** *(n sense 2)* .

fuzz **[fʌz] n 1.** [hair] cheveux *mpl* crépus **2.** *inf dated* [police] **: the fuzz** les flics *mpl*.

fuzzy **['fʌzɪ] (comp -ier, superl -iest) adj 1.** [hair] crépu(e) **2.** [photo, image] flou(e) **3.** [thoughts, mind] confus(e).

fwd. abbr of ***forward***.

f-word **n** *euph* **: the f-word** le mot 'fuck'.

fwy abbr of ***freeway***.

FY **n** abbr of ***fiscal year***.

FYI abbr of ***for your information***.

g [1] [dʒi:] (pl g's *or* gs), ***G*** (pl G's *or* Gs) **n** [letter] g *m inv*, G *m inv*.
◆ ***G*** ■ **n** MUS sol *m*.
■ **1.** (abbr of ***good***) B **2.** *US* (abbr of ***general (audience)***) *tous publics*.

g [2] **1.** (abbr of ***gram***) g **2.** (abbr of ***gravity***) g.

G7 **n** ECON & POL le G7, le groupe des 7.

G8 **n** ECON & POL le G8, le groupe des 8.

GA abbr of ***Georgia***.

gab [gæb] ➤ ***gift***.

gabardine [ˌgæbə'di:n] **n** gabardine *f*.

gabble ['gæbl] ■ **vt** & **vi** baragouiner.
■ **n** charabia *m*.

gable ['geɪbl] **n** pignon *m*.

Gabon [gæ'bɒn] **n** Gabon *m* ▸ **in Gabon** au Gabon.

Gabonese [ˌgæbɒ'ni:z] ■ **adj** gabonais(e).
■ **npl : the Gabonese** les Gabonais.

gad [gæd] (pt & pp **-ded**, cont **-ding**) ◆ ***gad about*** **vi** *inf dated* partir en vadrouille.

gadabout ['gædəbaʊt] **n** *inf dated* vadrouilleur *m*, -euse *f*.

gadget ['gædʒɪt] **n** gadget *m*.

gadgetry ['gædʒɪtrɪ] **n** *(U)* gadgets *mpl*.

Gaelic ['geɪlɪk] ■ **adj** gaélique.
■ **n** gaélique *m*.

gaffe [gæf] **n** gaffe *f*.

gaffer ['gæfəʳ] **n** *UK inf* [boss] patron *m*.

gag [gæg] ■ **n 1.** [for mouth] bâillon *m* **2.** *inf* [joke] blague *f*, gag *m*.
■ **vt** (pt & pp **-ged**, cont **-ging**) [put gag on] bâillonner.
■ **vi** (pt & pp **-ged**, cont **-ging**) [choke] s'étrangler.

gaga ['gɑ:gɑ:] **adj** *inf* [senile, crazy] gaga ▸ **he's absolutely gaga about her** il est complètement fou d'elle.

gage *US* = ***gauge***.

gaggle ['gægl] ■ **n** *lit* & *fig* troupeau *m*.
■ **vi** cacarder.

gaiety ['geɪətɪ] **n** gaieté *f*.

gaily ['geɪlɪ] **adv 1.** [cheerfully] gaiement **2.** [thoughtlessly] allègrement.

gain [geɪn] ■ **n 1.** [gen] profit *m* **2.** [improvement] augmentation *f*.
■ **vt 1.** [acquire] gagner ▸ **to gain experience** acquérir de l'expérience **2.** [increase in - speed, weight] prendre / [- confidence] gagner en / [- quantity, time] gagner **3.** [subj: watch, clock] **: to gain 10 minutes** avancer de 10 minutes.
■ **vi 1.** [advance] **: to gain in sthg** gagner en qqch **2.** [benefit] **: to gain from *or* by sthg** tirer un avantage de qqch ▸ **who stands to gain by this deal?** qui y gagne dans cette affaire? **3.** [watch, clock] avancer.
◆ ***gain on*** **vt insep** rattraper.

gainful ['geɪnfʊl] **adj** *fml* lucratif(ive).

gainfully ['geɪnfʊlɪ] **adv** *fml* lucrativement.

gainsay [ˌgeɪn'seɪ] (pt & pp **-said**) **vt** *fml* contredire.

gait [geɪt] **n** démarche *f*.

gaiters ['geɪtəz] **npl** guêtres *fpl*.

gal., ***gall.*** abbr of ***gallon***.

gala ['gɑ:lə] ■ **n** [celebration] gala *m*.
■ **comp** de gala.

galactic [gə'læktɪk] **adj** galactique.

Galapagos Islands [gə'læpəgəs-] **npl : the Galapagos Islands** les (îles *fpl*) Galapagos *fpl* ▸ **in the Galapagos Islands** aux (îles) Galapagos.

galaxy ['gæləksɪ] (pl **-ies**) **n** galaxie *f*.

gale [geɪl] **n** [wind] grand vent *m*.

Galicia [gə'lɪʃɪə] **n 1.** [in Central Europe] Galicie *f* ▸ **in Galicia** en Galicie **2.** [in Spain] Galice *f* ▸ **in Galicia** en Galice.

gall [gɔ:l] ■ **n** [nerve] **: to have the gall to do sthg** avoir le toupet de faire qqch.
■ **vt** contrarier.

gall. abbr of ***gallon***.

gallant ['gælənt *or* gə'lænt] **adj 1.** ['gælənt] [courageous] courageux(euse) **2.** [gə'lænt *or* 'gælənt] [polite to women] galant.

gallantly **['gæləntlı] adv 1.** [bravely] courageusement, vaillamment **2.** [chivalrously] galamment.

gallantry **['gæləntrı] n 1.** [courage] bravoure *f* **2.** [politeness to women] galanterie *f*.

gall bladder **n** vésicule *f* biliaire.

galleon **['gælıən] n** galion *m*.

gallery **['gælərı] (pl -ies) n 1.** [gen] galerie *f* **2.** [for displaying art] musée *m* **3.** [in theatre] paradis *m*.

galley **['gælı] (pl -s) n 1.** [ship] galère *f* **2.** [kitchen] coquerie *f*.

Gallic **['gælık] adj** français(e).

galling **['gɔ:lıŋ] adj** humiliant(e).

gallivant **[,gælı'vænt] vi** *inf* mener une vie de patachon.

gallon **['gælən] n** = *4,546 litres* gallon *m*.

gallop **['gæləp] ■ n** galop *m*.
■ **vi** galoper.

galloping **['gæləpıŋ] adj** [inflation] galopant(e).

gallows **['gæləʊz] (pl gallows) n** gibet *m*.

gallstone **['gɔ:lstəʊn] n** calcul *m* biliaire.

Gallup poll **['gæləp-] n** *UK* sondage *m* d'opinion.

galore **[gə'lɔ:ʳ] adj** en abondance.

galoshes **[gə'lɒʃız]** *UK* **npl** caoutchoucs *mpl*, claques *fpl Québec*.

galvanize, *UK* ***-ise*** **['gælvənaız] vt 1.** TECH galvaniser **2.** [impel] **: to galvanize sb into action** pousser qqn à agir.

Gambia **['gæmbıə] n : (the) Gambia** la Gambie ▸ **in (the) Gambia** en Gambie.

Gambian **['gæmbıən] ■ adj** gambien(enne).
■ **n** Gambien *m*, -enne *f*.

gambit **['gæmbıt] n** entrée *f* en matière.

gamble **['gæmbl] ■ n** [calculated risk] risque *m* ▸ **to take a gamble** prendre un risque.
■ **vi 1.** [bet] jouer ▸ **to gamble on** jouer de l'argent sur **2.** [take risk] **: to gamble on** miser sur.

gambler **['gæmbləʳ] n** joueur *m*, -euse *f*.

gambling **['gæmblıŋ] n** *(U)* jeu *m*.

gambol **['gæmbl]** (*UK* **-led, cont -ling,** *US* **-ed, cont -ing) vi** gambader.

game **[geım] ■ n 1.** [gen] jeu *m* ▸ **do you fancy a game of chess?** ça te dit de faire une partie d'échecs? ▸ **game, set and match** jeu, set et match **2.** [match] match *m* **3.** *(U)* [hunted animals] gibier *m*
⏭ **to beat sb at their own game** battre qqn sur son propre terrain ▸ **the game's up** tout est perdu ▸ **to give the game away** vendre la mèche ▸ **what's your game?** *inf* à quoi joues-tu?
■ **adj 1.** [brave] courageux(euse) **2.** [willing] **: game (for sthg/to do sthg)** partant(e) (pour qqch/pour faire qqch).
◆ ***games*** **■ n** *(U) UK* SCH éducation *f* physique.
■ **npl** [sporting contest] jeux *mpl*.

gamekeeper **['geım,ki:pəʳ] n** garde-chasse *m*.

gamely **['geımlı] adv 1.** [bravely] courageusement **2.** [willingly] volontairement.

game plan **n** stratégie *f*, plan *m* d'attaque.

game reserve **n** réserve *f* (de chasse).

games console **[geımz -] n** COMPUT console *f* de jeux.

game show **n** jeu *m* télévisé.

gamesmanship **['geımzmənʃıp] n** *art de gagner habilement*.

game theory **n** théorie *f* des jeux.

gamey **[geımı] (comp -ier, superl -iest) =** ***gamy***.

gaming **['geımıŋ] n** *(U)* jeux *mpl* informatiques.

gamma **['gæmə] n** gamma *m*.

gamma rays **npl** rayons *mpl* gamma.

gammon **['gæmən] n** *esp UK* jambon *m* fumé.

gammy **['gæmı] (comp -ier, superl -iest) adj** *UK inf* boiteux(euse).

gamut **['gæmət] n** gamme *f* ▸ **to run the gamut of** passer par toute la gamme de.

gamy **['geımı] (comp -ier, superl -iest) adj** [meat] faisandé(e).

gander **['gændəʳ] n** [male goose] jars *m*.

gang **[gæŋ] n 1.** [of criminals] gang *m* **2.** [of young people] bande *f*.
◆ ***gang up*** **vi** *inf* **: to gang up (on)** se liguer (contre).

gang-bang **n** *vulg* viol *m* collectif.

Ganges **['gændʒi:z] n : the (River) Ganges** le Gange.

gangland **['gæŋlænd] n** *(U)* milieu *m*.

gangling **['gæŋglıŋ],** ***gangly*** **['gæŋglı] (comp -ier, superl -iest) adj** dégingandé(e).

ganglion **['gæŋglıən] (pl ganglia ['gæŋglıə]) n 1.** ANAT ganglion *m* **2.** [centre, focus] centre *m*, foyer *m*.

gangplank **['gæŋplæŋk] n** passerelle *f*.

gangrene **['gæŋgri:n] n** gangrène *f*.

gangrenous **['gæŋgrınəs] adj** gangreneux(euse).

gangster **['gæŋstəʳ] n** gangster *m*.

gangway **['gæŋweı] n 1.** *UK* [aisle] allée *f* **2.** [gangplank] passerelle *f*.

gannet **['gænıt] (pl gannet** *OR* **-s) n** [bird] fou *m* (de Bassan).

gantry **['gæntrı] (pl -ies) n** portique *m*.

GAO **(abbr of *General Accounting Office*) n** *Cour des comptes américaine*.

gaol **[dʒeıl]** *UK dated* **=** ***jail***.

gap **[gæp] n 1.** [empty space] trou *m* / [in text] blanc *m* / *fig* [in knowledge, report] lacune *f* ▸ **he has a gap between his front teeth** il a les dents de devant écartées ▸ **I could see through a gap in the curtains** je voyais par la fente entre les rideaux ▸ **a gap in the market** un créneau sur le marché **2.** [interval of time] période *f* ▸ **she returned to work after a gap of six years** elle s'est remise à travailler après une interruption de six ans **3.** *fig* [great difference] fossé *m*.

gape **[geıp] vi 1.** [person] rester bouche bée **2.** [hole, shirt] bâiller.

gaping **['geıpıŋ] adj 1.** [open-mouthed] bouche bée *(inv)* **2.** [wide-open] béant(e) / [shirt] grand ouvert (grande ouverte).

gappy ['gæpɪ] (comp **-ier**, superl **-iest**) **adj** **1.** [account, knowledge] plein(e) de lacunes **2. : gappy teeth** des dents écartées.

gap year **n** *année d'interruption volontaire des études, avant l'entrée à l'université.*

garage [*UK* 'gærɑ:ʒ *OR* 'gærɪdʒ, *US* gə'rɑ:ʒ] **n** **1.** [gen] garage *m* **2.** *UK* [for fuel] station-service *f.*

garage sale [gə'rɑ:ʒ] **n** *US vente d'occasion chez un particulier,* ≃ vide-grenier *m.*

garb [gɑ:b] **n** *(U) fml* tenue *f.*

garbage ['gɑ:bɪdʒ] **n** *(U)* **1.** *esp US* [refuse] détritus *mpl* **2.** *inf* [nonsense] idioties *fpl.*

garbage bag **n** *US* sac-poubelle *m.*

garbage can **n** *US* poubelle *f.*

garbage collector **n** *US* éboueur *m*, -euse *f.*

garbage disposal unit **n** *US* broyeur *m* d'ordures.

garbage man *US* = ***garbage collector.***

garbage truck **n** *US* camion-poubelle *m.*

garble ['gɑ:bl] **vt** [involuntarily - story, message] embrouiller / [- quotation] déformer / [deliberately - facts] dénaturer, déformer.

garbled ['gɑ:bld] **adj** [story, message, explanation - involuntarily] embrouillé(e), confus(e) / [- deliberately] déformé(e), dénaturé(e).

garden ['gɑ:dn] ■ **n** jardin *m.*
■ **comp** de jardin.
■ **vi** jardiner.
◆ ***gardens*** **npl** jardins *mpl* (publics).

garden centre *UK*, ***garden center*** *US* **n** jardinerie *f.*

garden city **n** *UK* cité-jardin *f.*

gardener ['gɑ:dnəʳ] **n** [professional] jardinier *m*, -ère *f* / [amateur] personne *f* qui aime jardiner, amateur *m*, -rice *f* de jardinage.

garden flat **n** *UK* rez-de-jardin *m inv.*

gardenia [gɑ:'di:njə] **n** gardénia *m.*

gardening ['gɑ:dnɪŋ] ■ **n** jardinage *m.*
■ **comp** [gloves, equipment, book] de jardinage / [expert] en jardinage.

garden party **n** garden-party *f.*

garden shed **n** abri *m* de jardin.

garden-variety **adj** *US* ordinaire.

gargantuan [gɑ:'gæntjʊən] **adj** gargantuesque.

gargle ['gɑ:gl] **vi** se gargariser.

gargoyle ['gɑ:gɔɪl] **n** gargouille *f.*

garish ['geərɪʃ] **adj** [colour] criard(e) / [clothes] tapageur(euse).

garishly ['geərɪʃlɪ] **adv : garishly dressed** vêtu de manière tapageuse.

garishness ['geərɪʃnɪs] **n** [of appearance] tape-à-l'œil *m inv* / [of colour] crudité *f*, violence *f.*

garland ['gɑ:lənd] **n** guirlande *f* de fleurs.

garlic ['gɑ:lɪk] **n** ail *m.*

garlic bread **n** pain *m* à l'ail.

garlicky ['gɑ:lɪkɪ] **adj** *inf* qui sent l'ail.

garment ['gɑ:mənt] **n** *fml* vêtement *m.*

garner ['gɑ:nəʳ] **vt** *fml* recueillir.

garnet ['gɑ:nɪt] **n** [red stone] grenat *m.*

garnish ['gɑ:nɪʃ] ■ **n** garniture *f.*
■ **vt** garnir.

garret ['gærət] **n** mansarde *f.*

garrison ['gærɪsn] ■ **n** [soldiers] garnison *f.*
■ **vt** tenir en garnison.

garrulous ['gærələs] **adj** volubile.

garter ['gɑ:təʳ] **n** **1.** [for socks] support-chaussette *m* / [for stockings] jarretière *f* **2.** *US* [suspender] jarretelle *f.*

garter belt **n** *US* porte-jarretelles *m inv.*

gas [gæs] ■ **n** (pl **gases** *OR* **gasses** ['gæsi:z]) **1.** [gen] gaz *m inv* **2.** *US* [for vehicle] essence *f.*
■ **vt** (pt & pp **-sed**, cont **-sing**) gazer.

gasbag ['gæsbæg] **n** *UK inf pej* moulin *m* à paroles, pie *f.*

gas chamber **n** chambre *f* à gaz.

Gascony ['gæskənɪ] **n** Gascogne *f* ▸ **in Gascony** en Gascogne.

gas cooker **n** *UK* cuisinière *f* à gaz.

gas cylinder **n** bouteille *f* de gaz.

gaseous ['gæsɪəs] **adj** gazeux(euse).

gas fire **n** *UK* appareil *m* de chauffage à gaz.

gas-fired **adj** *UK* **: gas-fired central heating** chauffage *m* central au gaz.

gas fitter *UK* **n** ajusteur *m* gazier.

gas gauge **n** *US* jauge *f* d'essence.

gas guzzler **n** *US* **: to be a gas guzzler** consommer beaucoup (d'essence).

gash [gæʃ] ■ **n** entaille *f.*
■ **vt** entailler.

gas heater **n** [radiator] radiateur *m* à gaz / [for water] chauffe-eau *m inv* à gaz.

gas jet **n** brûleur *m.*

gasket ['gæskɪt] **n** joint *m* d'étanchéité.

gas lighter **n** [for cooker] allume-gaz *m* / [for cigarettes] briquet *m* à gaz.

gas main **n** conduite *f* de gaz.

gasman ['gæsmæn] (pl **-men** [-men]) **n** [who reads meter] employé *m* du gaz / [for repairs] installateur *m* de gaz.

gas mask **n** masque *m* à gaz.

gas meter **n** compteur *m* à gaz.

gasoline ['gæsəli:n] **n** *US* essence *f.*

gasometer [gæ'sɒmɪtəʳ] **n** réservoir *m* collecteur de gaz.

gas oven **n** **1.** [for cooking] four *m* à gaz **2.** [gas chamber] chambre *f* à gaz.

gasp [gɑ:sp] ■ **n** halètement *m.*
■ **vi** **1.** [breathe quickly] haleter **2.** [in shock, surprise] avoir le souffle coupé.

gas pedal **n** *US* accélérateur *m.*

gasping ['gɑ:spɪŋ] **adj** *UK inf* mort(e) de soif.

gas ring n [part of cooker] brûleur *m* / [small cooker] réchaud *m* à gaz.

gas station n *US* station-service *f*.

gas stove = ***gas cooker***.

gassy ['gæsɪ] (comp -ier, superl -iest) adj *pej* gazeux(euse).

gas tank n *US* réservoir *m*.

gas tap n [for mains supply] robinet *m* de gaz / [on gas fire] prise *f* de gaz.

gastric ['gæstrɪk] adj gastrique.

gastric ulcer n ulcère *m* gastrique.

gastritis [gæs'traɪtɪs] n gastrite *f*.

gastroenteritis ['gæstrəʊˌentə'raɪtɪs] n gastro-entérite *f*.

gastronomic [ˌgæstrə'nɒmɪk] adj gastronomique.

gastronomy [gæs'trɒnəmɪ] n gastronomie *f*.

gasworks ['gæswɜːks] (pl **gasworks**) n usine *f* à gaz.

gate [geɪt] n [of garden, farm] barrière *f* / [of town, at airport] porte *f* / [of park] grille *f*.

CULTURE

–gate

Le suffixe -gate est utilisé à la fin de certains mots anglais pour dénoncer d'importants scandales ayant défrayé la chronique. Sa première apparition date de 1972, avec le scandale du **Watergate**, qui provoqua la première démission d'un président américain : Richard Nixon. D'autres exemples font référence à **l'Irangate** (où les États-Unis furent accusés d'avoir vendu illégalement des armes à l'Iran dans les années 1980), au **Monicagate** (scandale dans lequel le président Clinton et une ex-stagiaire de la Maison-Blanche furent impliqués à la fin des années 1990), ou encore au **Dianagate** (polémique autour des circonstances de la mort de la princesse Diana).

gateau ['gætəʊ] (pl **-teaux** [-təʊz]) n *esp UK* gros gâteau *m (décoré et fourré à la crème)*.

gatecrash ['geɪtkræʃ] *inf* ■ vi [at party] s'inviter, jouer les pique-assiette / [at paying event] resquiller.
■ vt : **to gatecrash a party** aller à une fête sans invitation.

gatecrasher ['geɪtkræʃəʳ] n *inf* [at party] pique-assiette *mf* / [at paying event] resquilleur *m*, -euse *f*.

gatehouse ['geɪthaʊs] n (pl [-haʊzɪz]) loge *f* du gardien.

gatekeeper ['geɪtˌkiːpəʳ] n **1.** [gen] gardien *m*, -enne *f* **2.** [in purchasing department] contrôleur *m*, relais *m*, filtre *m*.

gatepost ['geɪtpəʊst] n montant *m* de barrière.

gateway ['geɪtweɪ] n **1.** [entrance] entrée *f* **2.** [means of access] : **gateway to** [generally] porte *f* de / *fig* clé *f* de.

gather ['gæðəʳ] ■ vt **1.** [collect] ramasser / [flowers] cueillir / [information] recueillir / [courage, strength] rassembler ▸ **to gather together** rassembler ▸ **to gather one's thoughts** se concentrer ▸ **to gather dust** ramasser la poussière **2.** [increase - speed, force] prendre **3.** [understand] : **to gather (that)...** croire comprendre que... ▸ **I gather he isn't coming then** j'en déduis qu'il ne vient pas, donc il ne vient pas **4.** [cloth - into folds] plisser ▸ **the dress is gathered at the waist** la robe est froncée à la taille.
■ vi [come together] se rassembler / [clouds] s'amonceler.
◆ ***gather up*** vt sep rassembler.

gathering ['gæðərɪŋ] n [meeting] rassemblement *m*.

GATT [gæt] (abbr of ***General Agreement on Tariffs and Trade***) n GATT *m*.

gauche [gəʊʃ] adj gauche.

gaudy ['gɔːdɪ] (comp -ier, superl -iest) adj voyant(e).

gauge, *US* ***gage*** [geɪdʒ] ■ n **1.** [for rain] pluviomètre *m* / [for fuel] jauge *f* (d'essence) / [for tyre pressure] manomètre *m* **2.** [of gun, wire] calibre *m* **3.** RAIL écartement *m*.
■ vt **1.** [measure] mesurer **2.** [evaluate] jauger.

Gaul [gɔːl] n **1.** [country] Gaule *f* **2.** [person] Gaulois *m*, -e *f*.

gaunt [gɔːnt] adj **1.** [thin] hâve **2.** [bare, grim] désolé(e).

gauntlet ['gɔːntlɪt] n gant *m* (de protection) ▸ **to run the gauntlet of sthg** endurer qqch ▸ **to throw down the gauntlet (to sb)** jeter le gant (à qqn).

gauze [gɔːz] n gaze *f*.

gave [geɪv] pt ➤ ***give***.

gawk [gɔːk], ***gawp*** *UK* [gɔːp] vi *inf* : **to gawk (at)** rester bouche bée (devant).

gawky ['gɔːkɪ] (comp -ier, superl -iest) adj *inf* [person] dégingandé(e) / [movement] désordonné(e).

gawp *UK* = ***gawk***.

gay [geɪ] ■ adj **1.** [gen] gai(e) **2.** [homosexual] homo *(inv)*, gay *(inv)*.
■ n homo *mf*, gay *mf*.

Gaza Strip ['gɑːzə-] n : **the Gaza Strip** la bande de Gaza.

gaze [geɪz] ■ n regard *m* (fixe).
■ vi : **to gaze at sb/sthg** regarder qqn/qqch (fixement).

gazebo [gə'ziːbəʊ] (pl -s) n belvédère *m*.

gazelle [gə'zel] (pl **gazelle** OR **-s**) n gazelle *f*.

gazette [gə'zet] n [newspaper] gazette *f*.

gazetteer [ˌgæzɪ'tɪəʳ] n index *m* géographique.

gazump [gə'zʌmp] vt *UK inf* : **to be gazumped** être victime d'une suroffre.

GB[1] (abbr of ***Great Britain***) n G-B *f*.

GB[2] ***Gb*** (abbr of ***gigabyte***), n gigabyte *m*.

GBH (abbr of ***grievous bodily harm***) n LAW coups *mpl* et blessures *fpl*.

GC (abbr of ***George Cross***) n *distinction honorifique britannique*.

GCH *UK* (abbr of ***gas central heating***) n *chauffage central à gaz*.

GCHQ (abbr of ***Government Communications Headquarters***) n *en Grande-Bretagne, centre d'interception des télécommunications étrangères*.

GCSE (abbr of ***General Certificate of Secondary Education***) **n** *examen de fin d'études secondaires en Grande-Bretagne.*

Gdns abbr of ***Gardens***.

GDP (abbr of ***gross domestic product***) **n** PIB *m*.

GDR (abbr of ***German Democratic Republic***) **n** RDA *f*.

gear [gɪəʳ] ■ **n** **1.** TECH [mechanism] embrayage *m* **2.** [speed - of car, bicycle] vitesse *f* ▸ **to change gear** changer de vitesse ▸ **to be in/out of gear** être en prise/au point mort ▸ **to be in first/second gear** être en première/seconde **3.** *(U)* [equipment, clothes] équipement *m*.
■ **vt : to gear sthg to sb/sthg** destiner qqch à qqn/qqch ▸ **the government's policies were not geared to cope with an economic recession** la politique mise en place par le gouvernement n'était pas prévue pour faire face à une récession économique.
◆ ***gear up*** **vi : to gear up for sthg/to do sthg** se préparer pour qqch/à faire qqch.

gearbox ['gɪəbɒks] **n** *UK* boîte *f* de vitesses.

gearing ['gɪərɪŋ] **n** TECH engrenage *m*.

gearknob ['gɪənɒb] **n** AUT boule *f* du levier de vitesse.

gear lever *UK*, ***gear stick*** *UK*, ***gear shift*** *US* **n** levier *m* de vitesse.

gearwheel **n** pignon *m*, roue *f* d'engrenage.

gee [dʒiː] **excl** *esp US inf* [expressing surprise, excitement] **: gee (whiz)!** ça alors!

geek ['giːk] **n** *inf* débile *mf* ▸ **a movie/computer geek** un dingue de cinéma/d'informatique.

geese [giːs] **npl** ➤ ***goose***.

gee up ■ **excl** [to horse] hue!
■ **vt sep** *UK inf* faire avancer.

geezer ['giːzəʳ] **n** *UK inf* bonhomme *m*, coco *m*.

Geiger counter ['gaɪgəʳ-] **n** compteur *m* Geiger.

geisha (girl) ['geɪʃə-] **n** geisha *f*.

gel [dʒel] ■ **n** [for hair] gel *m*.
■ **vi** (**pt & pp -led**, **cont -ling**) **1.** [thicken] prendre **2.** *fig* [take shape] prendre tournure.

gelatin ['dʒelətɪn], ***gelatine*** [ˌdʒelə'tiːn] **n** gélatine *f*.

gelatinous [dʒə'lætɪnəs] **adj** gélatineux(euse).

gelding ['geldɪŋ] **n** hongre *m*.

gelignite ['dʒelɪgnaɪt] **n** gélignite *f*.

gem [dʒem] **n** **1.** [jewel] pierre *f* précieuse, gemme *f* **2.** *fig* [person, thing] perle *f*.

Gemini ['dʒemɪnaɪ] **n** Gémeaux *mpl* ▸ **to be (a) Gemini** être Gémeaux.

gemstone ['dʒemstəʊn] **n** pierre *f* précieuse.

gen [dʒen] **n** *(U) UK inf dated* info *f*.
◆ ***gen up*** (**pt & pp -ned up**, **cont -ning up**) **vi** *UK inf dated* **: to gen up (on sthg)** se rancarder (sur qqch).

gen. (abbr of ***general, generally***) gén.

Gen. (abbr of ***General***) Gal.

gender ['dʒendəʳ] **n** **1.** [sex] sexe *m* **2.** GRAM genre *m*.

gene [dʒiːn] **n** gène *m*.

genealogical [ˌdʒiːnjə'lɒdʒɪkl] **adj** généalogique.

genealogist [ˌdʒiːnɪ'ælədʒɪst] **n** généalogiste *mf*.

genealogy [ˌdʒiːnɪ'ælədʒɪ] (**pl -ies**) **n** généalogie *f*.

genera ['dʒenərə] **npl** ➤ ***genus***.

general ['dʒenərəl] ■ **adj** général(e) ▸ **I get the general idea** je vois en gros ▸ **this book is for the general reader** ce livre est destiné au lecteur moyen ▸ **to be in general use** être d'usage courant OR répandu ▸ **to go in the general direction of sthg** se diriger plus ou moins vers qqch ▸ **in the general interest** dans l'intérêt de tous.
■ **n** général *m*.
◆ ***in general*** **adv** en général.

general anaesthetic, ***general anesthetic*** *US* **n** anesthésie *f* générale.

General Assembly **n** [of UN] Assemblée *f* générale.

general delivery **n** *US* poste *f* restante.

general election **n** élections *fpl* législatives.

general headquarters **n** (grand) quartier *m* général.

general hospital **n** centre *m* hospitalier.

generalist ['dʒenərəlɪst] **n** non-spécialiste *mf*, généraliste *mf*.

generality [ˌdʒenə'rælətɪ] (**pl -ies**) **n** généralité *f*.

generalization, *UK* ***-isation*** [ˌdʒenərəlaɪ'zeɪʃn] **n** généralisation *f*.

generalize, *UK* ***-ise*** ['dʒenərəlaɪz] **vi : to generalize (about)** généraliser (au sujet de OR sur).

generalized, *UK* ***-ised*** ['dʒenərəlaɪzd] **adj** **1.** [involving many] généralisé(e) **2.** [non-specific] général(e).

general knowledge **n** culture *f* générale.

generally ['dʒenərəlɪ] **adv** **1.** [usually, in most cases] généralement **2.** [unspecifically] en général / [describe] en gros.

general manager **n** directeur général *m*, directrice générale *f*.

general meeting **n** assemblée *f* générale.

general practice **n** **1.** [branch of medicine] médecine *f* générale **2.** [place] cabinet *m* de généraliste.

general practitioner **n** (médecin *m*) généraliste *m*.

general public **n : the general public** le grand public.

general-purpose **adj** polyvalent(e).

general strike **n** grève *f* générale.

generate ['dʒenəreɪt] **vt** [energy, jobs] générer / [electricity, heat] produire / [interest, excitement] susciter.

generation [ˌdʒenə'reɪʃn] **n** **1.** [gen] génération *f* ▸ **first/second generation** première/deuxième génération **2.** [creation - of jobs] création *f* / [- of electricity] production *f* / [- of interest, excitement] induction *f*.

generation gap **n** fossé *m* des générations.

generator ['dʒenəreɪtəʳ] **n** ELEC génératrice *f*, générateur *m*.

generic [dʒɪ'nerɪk] **adj** générique.

generic brand **n** marque *f* générique.

generic product **n** produit *m* générique.

generosity [ˌdʒenə'rɒsətɪ] **n** générosité *f*.

generous ['dʒenərəs] **adj** généreux(euse).

generously ['dʒenərəslɪ] **adv** généreusement.

genesis ['dʒenəsɪs] (pl **-ses** [-si:z]) **n** [origin] genèse *f.*

genetic [dʒɪ'netɪk] **adj** génétique.
◆ ***genetics*** **n** *(U)* génétique *f.*

genetically [dʒɪ'netɪklɪ] **adv** génétiquement ▸ **genetically modified** génétiquement modifié(e) ▸ **genetically modified organism** organisme *m* génétiquement modifié.

genetic code **n** code *m* génétique.

genetic engineering *(U)* **n** manipulation *f* génétique.

genetic fingerprinting [-'fɪŋgəprɪntɪŋ] **n** *(U)* empreinte *f* génétique.

geneticist [dʒɪ'netɪsɪst] **n** généticien *m*, -enne *f.*

Geneva [dʒɪ'ni:və] **n** Genève.

Geneva convention **n : the Geneva convention** la Convention de Genève.

genial ['dʒi:njəl] **adj 1.** [person] aimable, affable / [expression] cordial(e), chaleureux(euse) **2.** *liter* [weather] clément(e).

FALSE FRIENDS / FAUX AMIS
genial
Génial n'est pas la traduction du mot anglais *genial*. Génial se traduit par *brilliant*.
▸ Ce fut une invention géniale / *It was a brilliant invention*

geniality [,dʒi:nɪ'ælətɪ] **n 1.** [of person, expression] cordialité *f*, amabilité *f* **2.** *liter* [of weather] clémence *f.*

genially ['dʒi:njəlɪ] **adv** cordialement, chaleureusement.

genie ['dʒi:nɪ] (pl **genies** *OR* **genii** ['dʒi:nɪaɪ]) **n** génie *m.*

genital ['dʒenɪtl] **adj** génital(e).

genitalia [,dʒenɪ'teɪlɪə] **npl** *fml* organes *mpl* génitaux, parties *fpl* génitales.

genitals ['dʒenɪtlz] **npl** organes *mpl* génitaux.

genitive ['dʒenɪtɪv] ■ **n** génitif *m* ▸ **in the genitive** au génitif.
■ **adj** du génitif ▸ **the genitive case** le génitif.

genius ['dʒi:njəs] (pl **-es** [-i:z]) **n** génie *m* ▸ **genius for sthg/for doing sthg** génie de qqch/pour faire qqch.

Genoa ['dʒenəʊə] **n** Gênes.

genocide ['dʒenəsaɪd] **n** génocide *m.*

genome ['dʒi:nəʊm] **n** génome *m.*

genre ['ʒɑ̃rə] **n** genre *m.*

gent [dʒent] **n** *UK inf dated* gentleman *m.*
◆ ***gents*** **n** *UK* [toilets] toilettes *fpl* pour hommes / [sign on door] messieurs.

genteel [dʒen'ti:l] **adj 1.** [refined] distingué(e) **2.** [affected - speech] maniéré(e), affecté(e) / [- manner] affecté(e) / [- language] précieux(euse).

FALSE FRIENDS / FAUX AMIS
genteel
Gentil n'est pas la traduction du mot anglais *genteel*. Gentil se traduit par *kind* ou *nice*.
▸ Ils sont gentils avec moi / *They're kind ou nice to me*
▸ Merci, c'est très gentil / *Thanks, that's very kind of you*

gentile ['dʒentaɪl] ■ **adj** gentil(ille).
■ **n** gentil *m*, -ille *f.*

gentility [dʒen'tɪlətɪ] **n 1.** [good breeding] distinction *f* **2.** [gentry] petite noblesse *f* **3.** *(U)* [affected politeness] manières *fpl* affectées.

gentle ['dʒentl] **adj** doux (douce) / [tap, telling-off] léger(ère) ▸ **we gave him a gentle hint** nous l'avons discrètement mis sur la voie.

gentleman ['dʒentlmən] (pl **-men** [-mən]) **n 1.** [well-behaved man] gentleman *m* **2.** [man] monsieur *m.*

gentlemanly ['dʒentlmənlɪ] **adj** courtois(e).

gentleman's agreement **n** gentleman's agreement *m*, accord *m* qui repose sur l'honneur.

gentlemen [-mən] **npl** ➤ ***gentleman.***

gentleness ['dʒentlnɪs] **n** douceur *f.*

gentlewoman ['dʒentl,wʊmən] (pl **-women** [-,wɪmɪn]) **n 1.** [of noble birth] dame *f* **2.** [refined] femme *f* du monde **3.** [lady-in-waiting] dame *f* d'honneur *OR* de compagnie.

gently ['dʒentlɪ] **adv** [gen] doucement / [speak, smile] avec douceur.

gentrification [,dʒentrɪfɪ'keɪʃn] **n** embourgeoisement *m.*

gentry ['dʒentrɪ] **n** petite noblesse *f.*

genuflect ['dʒenju:flekt] **vi** *fml* faire une génuflexion.

genuine ['dʒenjʊɪn] **adj** [generally] authentique / [interest, customer] sérieux(euse) / [person, concern] sincère.

genuinely ['dʒenjʊɪnlɪ] **adv** réellement.

genus ['dʒi:nəs] (pl **genera** ['dʒenərə]) **n** genre *m.*

geographer [dʒɪ'ɒgrəfəʳ] **n** géographe *mf.*

geographical [dʒɪə'græfɪkl] **adj** géographique.

geography [dʒɪ'ɒgrəfɪ] **n** géographie *f.*

geological [,dʒɪə'lɒdʒɪkl] **adj** géologique.

geologist [dʒɪ'ɒlədʒɪst] **n** géologue *mf.*

geology [dʒɪ'ɒlədʒɪ] **n** géologie *f.*

geometric(al) [,dʒɪə'metrɪk(l)] **adj** géométrique.

geometrically [,dʒɪə'metrɪklɪ] **adv** géométriquement.

geometry [dʒɪ'ɒmətrɪ] **n** géométrie *f*.

geophysics [,dʒi:əʊ'fɪzɪks] **n** *(U)* géophysique *f*.

Geordie ['dʒɔ:dɪ] **n** *personne originaire de Tyneside*.

George Cross ['dʒɔ:dʒ-] **n** *UK décoration décernée pour actes de bravoure*.

Georgia ['dʒɔ:dʒjə] **n** [in US, in Europe] Géorgie *f* ▶ **in Georgia** en Géorgie.

Georgian ['dʒɔ:dʒjən] ■ **adj 1.** *UK* [house, furniture] ≃ style XVIIIe (siècle) **2.** GEOG géorgien(enne).
■ **n** Géorgien *m*, -enne *f*.

geranium [dʒɪ'reɪnjəm] (pl **-s**) **n** géranium *m*.

gerbil ['dʒɜ:bɪl] **n** gerbille *f*.

geriatric [,dʒerɪ'ætrɪk] **adj 1.** MED gériatrique **2.** *pej* [person] décrépit(e) / [object] vétuste.

geriatrics [,dʒerɪ'ætrɪks] **n** *(U)* gériatrie *f*.

germ [dʒɜ:m] **n 1.** [bacterium] germe *m*, microbe *m* **2.** *fig* [of idea, plan] embryon *m*.

German ['dʒɜ:mən] ■ **adj** allemand(e).
■ **n 1.** [person] Allemand *m*, -e *f* **2.** [language] allemand *m*.

Germanic [dʒɜ:'mænɪk] **adj** germanique.

German measles **n** *(U)* rubéole *f*.

German shepherd (dog) **n** berger *m* allemand.

Germany ['dʒɜ:mənɪ] (pl **-ies**) **n** Allemagne *f* ▶ **in Germany** en Allemagne.

germ-free **adj** stérilisé(e), aseptisé(e).

germicide ['dʒɜ:mɪsaɪd] **n** germicide *m*.

germinate ['dʒɜ:mɪneɪt] ■ **vt 1.** [seed] faire germer **2.** *fig* [idea, feeling] faire naître.
■ **vi** *lit* & *fig* germer.

germination [,dʒɜ:mɪ'neɪʃn] **n 1.** [of seed] germination *f* **2.** *fig* [of idea, feeling] développement *m*.

germ warfare **n** *(U)* guerre *f* bactériologique.

gerontology [,dʒerɒn'tɒlədʒɪ] **n** gérontologie *f*.

gerrymandering ['dʒerɪmændərɪŋ] *(U)* **n** charcutage *m* électoral.

gerund ['dʒerənd] **n** gérondif *m*.

gestation [dʒe'steɪʃn] **n** gestation *f*.

gestation period **n** *fig* & *fig* période *f* de gestation.

gesticulate [dʒes'tɪkjʊleɪt] **vi** *fml* gesticuler.

gesticulation [dʒe,stɪkjʊ'leɪʃn] **n** *fml* gesticulation *f*.

gesture ['dʒestʃər] ■ **n** geste *m*.
■ **vi : to gesture to** *OR* **towards sb** faire signe à qqn.

get [get] (*UK* **got**, cont **-ting**, *US* **got**, pp **gotten**, cont **-ting**) ■ **vt 1.** [cause to do] **: to get sb to do sthg** faire faire qqch à qqn ▶ **we couldn't get her to leave** on n'a pas pu la faire partir ▶ **I'll get my sister to help** je vais demander à ma sœur de nous aider ▶ **I got it to work** *OR* **working** j'ai réussi à le faire marcher
2. [cause to be done] **: to get sthg done** faire faire qqch ▶ **I got the car fixed** j'ai fait réparer la voiture ▶ **to get one's hair cut** se faire couper les cheveux
3. [cause to become] **: to get sb pregnant** rendre qqn enceinte ▶ **I can't get the car started** je n'arrive pas à mettre la voiture en marche ▶ **get the suitcases ready** préparez les bagages ▶ **to get things going** faire avancer les choses
4. [cause to move] **: to get sb/sthg through sthg** faire passer qqn/qqch par qqch ▶ **to get sb/sthg out of sthg** faire sortir qqn/qqch de qqch ▶ **how are you going to get this package to them?** comment allez-vous leur faire parvenir ce paquet?
5. [bring, fetch] aller chercher ▶ **can I get you something to eat/drink?** est-ce que je peux vous offrir quelque chose à manger/boire ? ▶ **I'll get my coat** je vais chercher mon manteau
6. [answer - door, telephone] répondre ▶ **the doorbell's ringing – I'll get it!** quelqu'un sonne à la porte – j'y vais!
7. [obtain - gen] obtenir / [- job, house] trouver ▶ **I'm going out to get a breath of fresh air** je sors prendre l'air ▶ **get plenty of exercise** faites plein d'exercice ▶ **she gets her shyness from her father** elle tient sa timidité de son père
8. [receive] recevoir, avoir ▶ **what did you get for your birthday?** qu'est-ce que tu as eu pour ton anniversaire? ▶ **she gets a good salary** elle touche un bon traitement ▶ **when did you get the news?** quand as-tu reçu la nouvelle? ▶ **he got 5 years for smuggling** il a écopé de *OR* il a pris 5 ans (de prison) pour contrebande
9. [offer as gift] offrir, donner ▶ **I don't know what to get Jill for her birthday** je ne sais pas quoi acheter à Jill pour son anniversaire
10. [experience a sensation] avoir ▶ **do you get the feeling he doesn't like us?** tu n'as pas l'impression qu'il ne nous aime pas? ▶ **I get a real thrill out of driving fast** cela me donne des sensations fortes de conduire vite
11. [bcome infected with, start to suffer from] avoir, attraper ▶ **to get a cold** attraper un rhume ▶ **I get a headache when I drink red wine** le vin rouge me donne mal à la tête
12. [understand] comprendre, saisir ▶ **I don't get it** *inf* je ne comprends pas, je ne saisis pas ▶ **he didn't seem to get the point** il ne semblait pas comprendre *OR* piger
13. [hear correctly] entendre, saisir ▶ **I didn't get his name** je n'ai pas saisi son nom
14. [catch - bus, train, plane] prendre
15. [capture] prendre, attraper
16. *inf* [annoy] **: what really gets me is his smugness** c'est sa suffisance qui m'agace *OR* qui m'énerve
17. [find] **: you get a lot of artists here** on trouve *OR* il y a beaucoup d'artistes ici.
■ **vi 1.** [become] devenir ▶ **to get suspicious** devenir méfiant ▶ **to get fat** grossir ▶ **I'm getting cold/bored** je commence à avoir froid/à m'ennuyer ▶ **it's getting late** il se fait tard
2. [go] aller, se rendre / [arrive] arriver ▶ **he never got there** il n'est jamais arrivé ▶ **I only got back yesterday** je suis rentré hier seulement ▶ **how do you get to the museum?** comment est-ce qu'on fait pour aller au musée?
3. [eventually succeed in] **: to get to do sthg** parvenir à *OR* finir par faire qqch ▶ **did you get to see him?** est-ce que tu as réussi à le voir? ▶ **she got to enjoy the classes** elle a fini par aimer les cours ▶ **I never got to visit Beijing** je n'ai jamais pu aller à Beijing ▶ **to get to know sb** apprendre à connaître qqn

4. [progress] **: how far have you got?** où en es-tu? ▸ **we got as far as buying the paint** on est allé jusqu'à acheter la peinture ▸ **I got to the point where I didn't care any more** j'en suis arrivé à m'en ficher complètement ▸ **now we're getting somewhere** enfin on avance ▸ **we're getting nowhere** on n'arrive à rien.
■ aux vb **: to get excited** s'exciter ▸ **to get hurt** se faire mal ▸ **to get married** se marier ▸ **to get divorced** divorcer ▸ **to get beaten up, to get beat up** *esp US* se faire tabasser ▸ **to get used to (doing) sthg** s'habituer à (faire) qqch ▸ **let's get going** *OR* **moving** allons-y / see also ***have***.

◆ ***get about*** *UK*, ***get around*** vi [move from place to place] se déplacer ▸ **she gets about on crutches/in a wheelchair** elle se déplace avec des béquilles/en chaise roulante ▸ **he certainly gets about** *fig* il connaît beaucoup de monde / see also ***get around***, ***get round***.

◆ ***get across*** vt sep [idea, policy] communiquer ▸ **to get one's message across** se faire comprendre.

◆ ***get ahead*** vi avancer ▸ **to get ahead in life** *OR* **in the world** réussir dans la vie.

◆ ***get along*** vi **1.** [manage] se débrouiller ▸ **how are you getting along?** comment vas-tu?, comment ça va?
2. [progress] avancer, faire des progrès
3. [have a good relationship] s'entendre ▸ **she's easy to get along with** elle est facile à vivre.

◆ ***get around***, ***get round*** *UK* ■ vt insep [overcome] venir à bout de, surmonter.
■ vi **1.** [circulate - news, rumour] circuler, se répandre
2. [eventually do] **: to get around to (doing) sthg** trouver le temps de faire qqch ▸ **she won't get around to reading it before tomorrow** elle n'arrivera pas à (trouver le temps de) le lire avant demain / see also ***get about***, ***get round***.

◆ ***get at*** vt insep **1.** [reach] parvenir à
2. [imply] vouloir dire ▸ **what are you getting at?** où veux-tu en venir?
3. *UK inf* [criticize] critiquer, dénigrer.

◆ ***get away*** vi **1.** [leave] partir, s'en aller
2. [go on holiday] partir en vacances ▸ **to get away from it all** partir se détendre loin de tout
3. [escape] s'échapper, s'évader ▸ **the thief got away with all the jewels** le voleur est parti *OR* s'est sauvé avec tous les bijoux.

◆ ***get away with*** vt insep **: he got away with cheating on his taxes** personne ne s'est aperçu qu'il avait fraudé le fisc ▸ **to let sb get away with sthg** passer qqch à qqn ▸ **she just lets him get away with it** elle le laisse tout faire, elle lui passe tout.

◆ ***get back*** ■ vt sep [recover, regain] retrouver, récupérer ▸ **he got his job back** il a été repris ▸ **you'll have to get your money back from the shop** il faut que vous vous fassiez rembourser par le magasin ▸ **to get one's own back (on sb)** *inf* se venger (de qqn).
■ vi **1.** [return] rentrer ▸ **I got back in the car/on the bus** je suis remonté dans la voiture/dans le bus
2. [move away] s'écarter.

◆ ***get back to*** vt insep **1.** [return to previous state, activity] revenir à ▸ **to get back to sleep** se rendormir ▸ **things are getting back to normal** la situation redevient normale ▸ **to get back to work** [after pause] se remettre au travail / [after illness] reprendre son travail
2. *inf* [phone back] rappeler ▸ **I'll get back to you on that** je te reparlerai de ça plus tard.

◆ ***get by*** vi se débrouiller, s'en sortir.

◆ ***get down*** vt sep **1.** [depress] déprimer ▸ **don't let it get you down** ne te laisse pas abattre
2. [fetch from higher level] descendre.

◆ ***get down to*** vt insep s'attaquer à ▸ **to get down to doing sthg** se mettre à faire qqch ▸ **to get down to work** se mettre au travail.

◆ ***get in*** ■ vi **1.** [enter - gen] entrer / [- to vehicle] monter ▸ **a car pulled up and she got in** une voiture s'est arrêtée et elle est montée dedans
2. [arrive] arriver / [arrive home] rentrer ▸ **what time does your plane get in?** à quelle heure ton avion arrive-t-il?
3. [be elected] être élu(e)
4. [be admitted - to school, university] entrer, être admis *OR* reçu ▸ **he applied to Oxford but he didn't get in** il voulait entrer à Oxford mais il n'a pas pu.
■ vt sep **1.** [bring in] rentrer ▸ **to get in supplies** s'approvisionner
2. [call in - doctor, plumber] faire venir
3. [hand in, submit] rendre, remettre
4. [interject] **: to get a word in** placer un mot.

◆ ***get in on*** vt insep se mêler de, participer à ▸ **to get in on a deal** prendre part à un marché.

◆ ***get into*** vt insep **1.** [car] monter dans
2. [become involved in] se lancer dans ▸ **he wants to get into politics** il veut se lancer dans la politique ▸ **to get into an argument with sb** se disputer avec qqn
3. [enter into a particular situation, state] **: to get into a panic** s'affoler ▸ **to get into trouble** s'attirer des ennuis ▸ **to get into the habit of doing sthg** prendre l'habitude de faire qqch
4. [be accepted as a student at] être admis(e) *OR* accepté(e) à
5. *inf* [affect] **: what's got into you?** qu'est-ce qui te prend?

◆ ***get off*** ■ vt sep **1.** [remove] enlever ▸ **get your hands off me!** ne me touche pas!
2. [free from punishment] tirer d'affaire / [in court] faire acquitter ▸ **he'll need a good lawyer to get him off** il lui faudra un bon avocat pour se tirer d'affaire.
■ vt insep **1.** [go away from] partir de ▸ **get off my property** fichez le camp de chez moi
2. [train, bus etc] descendre de.
■ vi **1.** [leave bus, train] descendre
2. [escape punishment] s'en tirer ▸ **he got off lightly** il s'en est tiré à bon compte ▸ **the students got off with a fine/warning** les étudiants en ont été quittes pour une amende/un avertissement
3. [depart] partir ▸ **the project got off to a bad/good start** *fig* le projet a pris un mauvais/bon départ.

◆ ***get off with*** vt insep *UK inf* avoir une touche avec ▸ **did you get off with anyone last night?** est-ce que tu as fait des rencontres hier soir?

◆ ***get on*** ■ vt sep [put on] mettre.
■ vt insep **1.** [bus, train, plane] monter dans
2. [horse] monter sur ▸ **get on your feet** levez-vous, mettez-vous debout ▸ **it took the patient a while to get (back) on his feet** *fig* le patient a mis longtemps à se remettre sur pied.
■ vi **1.** [enter bus, train] monter

2. [have good relationship] s'entendre, s'accorder ▸ **my mother and I get on well** je m'entends bien avec ma mère ▸ **to be difficult/easy to get on with** être difficile/facile à vivre
3. [progress] avancer, progresser ▸ **how are you getting on?** comment ça va? ▸ **John is getting on very well in maths** John se débrouille très bien en maths
4. [proceed] **: to get on (with sthg)** continuer (qqch), poursuivre (qqch) ▸ **they got on with the job** ils se sont remis au travail ▸ **get on with it!** [continue speaking] continuez! / [continue working] allez! au travail!
5. [be successful professionally] réussir
6. [grow old] **: to be getting on** se faire vieux (vieille)
7. [grow late - time] **: time's getting on** il se fait tard.

◆ ***get on for*** vt insep *UK inf* [be approximately] **: to be getting on for** approcher de ▸ **the president is getting on for sixty** le président approche la soixantaine ***or*** a presque soixante ans ▸ **there were getting on for 5,000 people at the concert** il y avait près de 5 000 personnes au concert.

◆ ***get on to*** vt insep **1.** [talk about] se mettre à parler de ▸ **to get onto a subject *or* onto a topic** aborder un sujet **2.** *UK* [contact] contacter.

◆ ***get out*** ■ vt sep **1.** [take out] sortir
2. [remove] enlever.
■ vi **1.** [leave - of building, room] sortir / [- of car, train] descendre ▸ **he was lucky to get out alive** il a eu de la chance de s'en sortir vivant
2. [news] s'ébruiter.

◆ ***get out of*** ■ vt insep **1.** [car] descendre de ▸ **to get out of bed** se lever, sortir de son lit
2. [escape from] s'évader de, s'échapper de
3. [avoid] éviter, se dérober à ▸ **to get out of doing sthg** se dispenser de faire qqch ▸ **we have to go: there's no getting out of it** il faut qu'on y aille, il n'y a pas moyen d'y échapper.
■ vt sep **1.** [cause to escape from or avoid] **: to get sb out of jail** faire sortir qqn de prison ▸ **my confession got him out of trouble** ma confession l'a tiré d'affaire
2. [gain from] gagner, retirer ▸ **to get a lot out of sthg** tirer (un) grand profit de qqch.

◆ ***get over*** ■ vt insep **1.** [recover from] se remettre de ▸ **I can't get over it!** je n'en reviens pas! ▸ **I'll never get over her** je ne l'oublierai jamais
2. [overcome] surmonter, venir à bout de ▸ **they soon got over their shyness** ils ont vite oublié ***or*** surmonté leur timidité.
■ vt sep *UK* [communicate] communiquer.

◆ ***get over with*** vt sep **: to get sthg over with** en finir avec qqch ▸ **let's get it over (with)** finissons-en.

◆ ***get round*** vt insep & vi *UK* = ***get around***.

◆ ***get through*** ■ vt insep **1.** [job, task] arriver au bout de ▸ **I got through an enormous amount of work** j'ai abattu beaucoup de travail
2. [exam] réussir à
3. [food, drink] consommer
4. [unpleasant situation] endurer, supporter ▸ **he got through it alive** il s'en est sorti (vivant).
■ vi **1.** [make o.s. understood] **: to get through (to sb)** se faire comprendre (de qqn)
2. TELEC obtenir la communication ▸ **I can't get through to his office** je n'arrive pas à avoir son bureau.

◆ ***get to*** vt insep *inf* [annoy] taper sur les nerfs à ▸ **don't let it get to you!** ne t'énerve pas pour ça!

◆ ***get together*** ■ vt sep [organize - team, belongings] rassembler / [- project, report] préparer.
■ vi se réunir ▸ **can we get together after the meeting?** on peut se retrouver après la réunion?

◆ ***get up*** ■ vi se lever ▸ **get up off the floor!** relève-toi!
■ vt insep [petition, demonstration] organiser.

◆ ***get up to*** vt insep *inf* faire ▸ **I wonder what they are getting up to** *UK* je me demande ce qu'ils fabriquent ***or*** ce qu'ils sont encore en train de faire.

getaway ['getəweɪ] n fuite *f*.

getaway car n *voiture qui sert à la fuite des gangsters*.

get-rich-quick adj *inf* **: a get-rich-quick scheme** un projet pour faire fortune rapidement.

get-together n *inf* réunion *f*.

getup ['getʌp] n *inf* **1.** *inf* [outfit] accoutrement *m* / [disguise] déguisement *m* **2.** [of book, product] présentation *f*.

get-up-and-go n *(U) inf* tonus *m*.

get-well card n carte *f* de vœux de prompt rétablissement.

geyser ['giːzəʳ] n **1.** [hot spring] geyser *m* **2.** *UK* [water heater] chauffe-eau *m inv*.

Ghana ['gɑːnə] n Ghana *m* ▸ **in Ghana** au Ghana.

Ghan(a)ian [gɑː'neɪən] ■ adj ghanéen(enne).
■ n Ghanéen *m*, -enne *f*.

ghastly ['gɑːstlɪ] (comp -ier, superl -iest) adj **1.** *inf* [very bad, unpleasant] épouvantable ▸ **to feel/look ghastly** être dans un état/avoir une mine épouvantable **2.** [horrifying, macabre] effroyable.

gherkin ['gɜːkɪn] n cornichon *m*.

ghetto ['getəʊ] (pl -s ***or*** -es) n ghetto *m*.

ghetto blaster [-ˌblɑːstəʳ] n *inf* grand radiocassette *m* portatif.

ghettoization, *UK* ***-isation*** [getəʊaɪ'zeɪʃn] n ghettoïsation *f*.

ghost [gəʊst] ■ n [spirit] spectre *m* ▸ **he doesn't have a ghost of a chance** il n'a pas l'ombre d'une chance.
■ vt = ***ghostwrite***.

ghostly ['gəʊstlɪ] (comp -ier, superl -iest) adj spectral(e).

ghost town n ville *f* fantôme.

ghostwrite ['gəʊstraɪt] (pt -wrote, pp -written) vt écrire à la place de l'auteur.

ghostwriter ['gəʊstˌraɪtəʳ] n nègre *m*.

ghostwritten ['gəʊstˌrɪtn] pp ➤ ***ghostwrite***.

ghostwrote ['gəʊstrəʊt] pt ➤ ***ghostwrite***.

ghoul [guːl] n **1.** [spirit] goule *f* **2.** *pej* [ghoulish person] personne *f* macabre.

ghoulish ['guːlɪʃ] adj macabre.

GHQ (abbr of ***general headquarters***) n GQG *m*.

GHz (abbr of ***gigahertz***) n GHz *m*.

GI (abbr of ***government issue***) n GI *m*.

giant ['dʒaɪənt] ■ adj géant *m*, -e *f*.
■ n géant *m*, -e *f*.

giantess ['dʒaɪəntes] n géante *f*.

giantkiller ['dʒaɪənt,kɪləʳ] **n** SPORT *petite équipe victorieuse d'une équipe plus forte.*

giant panda **n** panda *m* géant.

giant-size(d) **adj** géant(e).

gibber ['dʒɪbəʳ] **vi** bredouiller.

gibbering ['dʒɪbərɪŋ] **adj : I was a gibbering wreck!** j'étais dans un de ces états! ▸ **he's a gibbering idiot** *inf* c'est un sacré imbécile.

gibberish ['dʒɪbərɪʃ] **n** *(U)* charabia *m*, inepties *fpl*.

gibbon ['gɪbən] **n** gibbon *m*.

gibe [dʒaɪb] ■ **n** insulte *f*.
■ **vi : to gibe at sb/sthg** insulter qqn/qqch.

giblets ['dʒɪblɪts] **npl** abats *mpl*.

Gibraltar [dʒɪ'brɔːltəʳ] **n** Gibraltar *m* ▸ **in Gibraltar** à Gibraltar ▸ **the Rock of Gibraltar** le rocher de Gibraltar.

Gibraltarian [,dʒɪbrɔːl'teərɪən] **n** Gibraltarien *m*, -ne *f*.

giddily ['gɪdɪlɪ] **adv 1.** [dizzily] vertigineusement **2.** [frivolously] à la légère, avec insouciance.

giddiness ['gɪdɪnɪs] **n** *(U)* **1.** [dizziness] vertiges *mpl*, étourdissements *mpl* **2.** [frivolousness] légèreté *f*, étourderie *f*.

giddy ['gɪdɪ] (comp **-ier**, superl **-iest**) **adj 1.** [dizzy] **: to feel giddy** avoir la tête qui tourne **2.** [frivolous - person, behaviour] frivole, écervelé(e).

giddy up **excl** [to horse] **: giddy up!** hue!

gift [gɪft] **n 1.** [present] cadeau *m* ▸ **to make sb a gift of sthg** offrir qqch à qqn, faire cadeau de qqch à qqn / **: he thinks he's God's gift to mankind/to women** il se prend pour le Messie/pour Don Juan **2.** [talent] don *m* ▸ **to have a gift for sthg/for doing sthg** avoir un don pour qqch/pour faire qqch ▸ **the gift of the gab** le bagou **3.** *inf* [bargain] affaire *f* ▸ **at £5, it's a gift** 5 livres, c'est donné.

GIFT [gɪft] (abbr of ***gamete in fallopian transfer***) **n** fivete *f*.

gift certificate *US* = ***gift token***.

gifted ['gɪftɪd] **adj** doué(e).

gift horse **n**
▸▸ **don't** *OR* **never look a gift horse in the mouth** *prov* à cheval donné on ne regarde pas la bouche.

gift token, **gift voucher** **n** *UK* chèque-cadeau *m*.

gift-wrap **vt** faire un paquet cadeau de.

gift-wrapped [-ræpt] **adj** sous emballage-cadeau.

gig [gɪg] **n** *inf* [concert] concert *m*.

gigabyte ['gaɪgəbaɪt] **n** COMPUT giga-octet *m*.

gigahertz ['gɪgəhɜːts] **n** gigahertz *m*.

gigantic [dʒaɪ'gæntɪk] **adj** énorme, gigantesque.

giggle ['gɪgl] ■ **n 1.** [laugh] fou rire *m* **2.** *UK inf* [fun] **: to be a giggle** être marrant(e) *OR* tordant(e) ▸ **to have a giggle** bien s'amuser.
■ **vi** [laugh] rire bêtement.

giggly ['gɪglɪ] (comp **-ier**, superl **-iest**) **adj** qui rit bêtement.

GIGO ['gaɪgəʊ] (abbr of ***garbage in, garbage out***) COMPUT *qualité à l'entrée = qualité à la sortie.*

gigolo ['ʒɪgələʊ] (pl **-s**) **n** *pej* gigolo *m*.

gigot ['ʒiːgəʊ] **n** gigot *m*.

gild [gɪld] ■ **n** = ***guild***.
■ **vt** (pt **-ed**, pp **-ed** *OR* **gilt** [gɪlt]) dorer ▸ **it would be gilding the lily** ce serait du peaufinage.

gilded ['gɪldɪd] **adj** = ***gilt***.

gill [dʒɪl] **n** [unit of measurement] quart *m* de pinte *(= 0,142 litre)*.

gills [gɪlz] **npl** [of fish] branchies *fpl*.

gilt [gɪlt] ■ **adj** [covered in gold] doré(e).
■ **n** *(U)* [gold layer] dorure *f*.
◆ ***gilts*** **npl** *UK* FIN valeurs *fpl* de père de famille.

gilt-edged [-edʒd] **adj** FIN de père de famille.

gimme ['gɪmɪ] *inf* = ***give me***.

gimmick ['gɪmɪk] **n** astuce *f*.

gimmicky ['gɪmɪkɪ] **adj** *inf* qui relève du procédé.

gin [dʒɪn] **n** gin *m* ▸ **gin and tonic** gin-tonic *m*.

ginger ['dʒɪndʒəʳ] ■ **n 1.** [root] gingembre *m* **2.** [powder] gingembre *m* en poudre.
■ **adj** *UK* [colour] roux (rousse).

ginger ale **n** *boisson gazeuse au gingembre.*

ginger beer **n** *boisson britannique non-alcoolisée au gingembre.*

gingerbread ['dʒɪndʒəbred] **n** pain *m* d'épice.

ginger group **n** *UK* groupe *m* de pression.

ginger-haired [-'heəd] **adj** *UK* roux (rousse).

gingerly ['dʒɪndʒəlɪ] **adv** avec précaution.

ginger nut **n** biscuit *m* au gingembre.

ginger snap = ***ginger nut***.

gingham ['gɪŋəm] **n** [cloth] vichy *m*.

gingivitis [,dʒɪndʒɪ'vaɪtɪs] **n** gingivite *f*.

ginormous [,dʒaɪ'nɔːməs] **adj** *inf* gigantesque.

ginseng ['dʒɪnseŋ] **n** ginseng *m*.

gipsy *UK*, **gypsy** ['dʒɪpsɪ] ■ **adj** gitan(e).
■ **n** (pl **-ies**) [generally] gitan *m*, -e *f* / *pej* bohémien *m*, -enne *f*.

giraffe [dʒɪ'rɑːf] (pl **giraffe** *OR* **-s**) **n** girafe *f*.

gird [gɜːd] (pt & pp **-ed** *OR* **girt**) **vt** ➤ ***loin***.

girder ['gɜːdəʳ] **n** poutrelle *f*.

girdle ['gɜːdl] **n** [corset] gaine *f*.

girl [gɜːl] **n 1.** [gen] fille *f* **2.** [girlfriend] petite amie *f*.

girl Friday **n** *dated* aide *f*.

girlfriend ['gɜːlfrend] **n 1.** [female lover] petite amie *f* **2.** [female friend] amie *f*.

girl guide *UK*, **girl scout** *US* **n** *dated* éclaireuse *f*, guide *f*.
◆ ***Girl Guides*** **n : the Girl Guides** *UK* les Guides *fpl*.

girlhood ['gɜːlhʊd] **n** [as child] enfance *f* / [as adolescent] adolescence *f*.

girlie magazine ['gɜːlɪ] **n** *inf* magazine *m* érotique *OR* déshabillé.

girlish ['gɜːlɪʃ] **adj** de petite fille.

girl scout *US* = ***girl guide***.

giro ['dʒaɪrəʊ] (pl -s) **n** *UK* **1.** *(U)* [system] virement *m* postal **2. : giro (cheque)** chèque *m* d'indemnisation *f* (chômage **OR** maladie).

girt [gɜːt] **pt & pp** ➤ ***gird***.

girth [gɜːθ] **n 1.** [circumference - of tree] circonférence *f* / [- of person] tour *m* de taille **2.** [of horse] sangle *f*.

gist [dʒɪst] **n** substance *f* ▸ **to get the gist of sthg** comprendre **OR** saisir l'essentiel de qqch.

give [gɪv] ■ **vt** (pt **gave**, pp **given**) **1.** [gen] donner / [message] transmettre / [attention, time] consacrer ▸ **to give sb/sthg sthg** donner qqch à qqn/qqch ▸ **to give sb pleasure/a fright/a smile** faire plaisir/peur/un sourire à qqn ▸ **to give sb a look** jeter un regard à qqn ▸ **to give a shrug** hausser les épaules ▸ **to give a sigh** pousser un soupir ▸ **to give a speech** faire un discours ▸ **to give sb a message** communiquer un message à qqn ▸ **just give me time!** sois patient! ▸ **I hope I don't give you my cold** j'espère que je ne vais pas te passer mon rhume ▸ **the children can wash up; it will give them something to do** les enfants peuvent faire la vaisselle, ça les occupera **2.** [as present] **: to give sb sthg, to give sthg to sb** donner qqch à qqn, offrir qqch à qqn **3.** *UK* [pay] **: how much did you give for it?** combien l'avez-vous payé?
▸▸ **I was given to believe OR understand that...** *fml* on m'a fait comprendre que... ▸ **I'd give anything OR my right arm to do that** je donnerais n'importe quoi **OR** très cher pour faire ça.
■ **vi** (pt **gave**, pp **given**) [collapse, break] céder, s'affaisser.
■ **n** [elasticity] élasticité *f*, souplesse *f*.
◆ ***give or take*** **prep : give or take a day/£10** à un jour/10 livres près.
◆ ***give away*** **vt sep 1.** [get rid of] donner **2.** [reveal] révéler ▸ **he didn't give anything away** il n'a rien dit.
◆ ***give back*** **vt sep** [return] rendre ▸ **the store gave him his money back** le magasin l'a remboursé.
◆ ***give in*** **vi 1.** [admit defeat] abandonner, se rendre **2.** [agree unwillingly] **: to give in to sthg** céder à qqch.
◆ ***give off*** **vt insep** [smell] exhaler / [smoke] faire / [heat] produire.
◆ ***give out*** ■ **vt sep** [distribute] distribuer.
■ **vi** [supplies] s'épuiser / [car] lâcher ▸ **her strength was giving out** elle était à bout de forces, elle n'en pouvait plus.
◆ ***give over*** ■ **vt sep** [dedicate] **: to be given over to** [subj: time] être consacré(e) à / [subj: building] être réservé(e) à.
■ **vi** *UK inf* [stop] **: give over!** arrête!
◆ ***give up*** ■ **vt sep 1.** [stop] renoncer à ▸ **to give up drinking/smoking** arrêter de boire/de fumer **2.** [surrender] **: to give o.s. up (to sb)** se rendre (à qqn).
■ **vi** abandonner, se rendre ▸ **I give up** [in game, project] je renonce.
◆ ***give up on*** **vt insep** [abandon] laisser tomber.

give-and-take **n** *(U)* [compromise] concessions *fpl* de part et d'autre.

giveaway ['gɪvəˌweɪ] ■ **adj 1.** [tell-tale] révélateur(trice) **2.** [very cheap] dérisoire.
■ **n** [tell-tale sign] signe *m* révélateur.

given ['gɪvn] ■ **pp** ➤ ***give***.
■ **adj 1.** [set, fixed] convenu(e), fixé(e) ▸ **at any given time** à un moment donné **2.** [prone] **: to be given to sthg/to doing sthg** être enclin(e) à qqch/à faire qqch.
■ **prep** étant donné ▸ **given that** étant donné que.

given name **n** *esp US* prénom *m*.

giver ['gɪvər] **n** donneur *m*, -euse *f*.

gizmo ['gɪzməʊ] (pl -s) **n** *inf* gadget *m*, truc *m*.

gizzard ['gɪzəd] **n** gésier *m* ▸ **it sticks in my gizzard** *fig* ça me reste en travers de la gorge.

glacé ['glæseɪ] **adj 1.** [cherry] glacé(e), confit(e) ▸ **glacé icing** glaçage *m (d'un gâteau)* **2.** [leather, silk] glacé(e).

glacial ['gleɪsjəl] **adj 1.** [of glacier] glaciaire **2.** [unfriendly] glacial(e).

glacier ['glæsjər] **n** glacier *m*.

glad [glæd] (comp **-der**, superl **-dest**) **adj 1.** [happy, pleased] content(e) ▸ **to be glad about sthg** être content de qqch ▸ **to be glad that** être content que **2.** [willing] **: to be glad to do sthg** faire qqch volontiers **OR** avec plaisir **3.** [grateful] **: to be glad of sthg** être content(e) de qqch.

gladden ['glædn] **vt** *liter* réjouir.

glade [gleɪd] **n** *liter* clairière *f*.

glad-hand ['glædhænd] **vt** *inf pej* accueillir avec de grandes démonstrations d'amitié.

gladiator ['glædɪeɪtər] **n** gladiateur *m*.

gladioli [ˌglædɪ'əʊlaɪ] **npl** glaïeuls *mpl*.

gladly ['glædlɪ] **adv 1.** [happily, eagerly] avec joie **2.** [willingly] avec plaisir.

glad rags **npl** *inf* vêtements *mpl* chic ▸ **to put on one's glad rags** se mettre sur son trente et un, se saper.

glam [glæm] *UK inf* ■ **adj** = ***glamorous***.
■ **n** = ***glamour***.
◆ ***glam up*** **vt sep** (pt & pp **-ed up**, cont **-ming up**) *inf* **1.** [person] **: to get glammed up** [with clothes] mettre ses belles fringues, se saper / [with make-up] se faire une beauté, se faire toute belle **2.** [building] retaper / [town] embellir.

glamor *US* = ***glamour***.

glamorize, *UK* ***-ise*** ['glæməraɪz] **vt** faire apparaître sous un jour séduisant.

glamorous ['glæmərəs] **adj** [person] séduisant(e) / [appearance] élégant(e) / [job, place] prestigieux(euse).

glamorously ['glæmərəslɪ] **adv** brillamment, de manière éblouissante.

glamour *UK*, ***glamor*** *US* ['glæmər] **n** [of person] charme *m* / [of appearance] élégance *f*, chic *m* / [of job, place] prestige *m*.

glance [glɑːns] ■ **n** [quick look] regard *m*, coup d'œil *m* ▸ **to cast OR take a glance at sthg** jeter un coup d'œil à qqch ▸ **at a glance** d'un coup d'œil ▸ **at first glance** au premier coup d'œil.
■ **vi** [look quickly] **: to glance at sb/sthg** jeter un coup d'œil à qqn/qqch ▸ **to glance at OR through sthg** jeter un coup d'œil à **OR** sur qqch.
◆ ***glance off*** **vt insep** [subj: ball, bullet] ricocher sur.

glancing ['glɑːnsɪŋ] **adj** de côté, oblique.

gland [glænd] **n** glande *f*.

glandular ['glændjʊləʳ] **adj** glandulaire, glanduleux(euse).

glandular fever [,glændjʊləʳ-] **n** *UK* mononucléose *f* infectieuse.

glare [gleəʳ] ■ **n** **1.** [scowl] regard *m* mauvais **2.** *(U)* [of headlights, publicity] lumière *f* aveuglante.
■ **vi** **1.** [scowl] jeter un regard mauvais ▸ **to glare at sb/sthg** regarder qqn/qqch d'un œil mauvais **2.** [sun, lamp] briller d'une lumière éblouissante.

glaring ['gleərɪŋ] **adj** **1.** [very obvious] flagrant(e) **2.** [blazing, dazzling] aveuglant(e).

glaringly ['gleərɪŋlɪ] **adv** : **it's glaringly obvious** ça crève les yeux.

glasnost ['glæznɒst] **n** glasnost *f*, transparence *f*.

glass [glɑːs] ■ **n** **1.** [gen] verre *m* **2.** *(U)* [glassware] verrerie *f*.
■ **comp** [bottle, jar] en *OR* de verre / [door, partition] vitré(e).
◆ ***glasses*** **npl** [spectacles] lunettes *fpl*.

glassblowing ['glɑːs,bləʊɪŋ] **n** soufflage *m* du verre.

glassblower ['glɑːs,bləʊəʳ] **n** souffleur *m (de verre)*.

glass ceiling **n** *terme désignant le "plafond" qui empêche la progression dans la hiérarchie*.

glass fibre *UK*, ***glass fiber*** *US* **n** *(U)* *UK* fibre *f* de verre.

glasshouse ['glɑːshaʊs] (pl [-haʊzɪz]) **n** *UK* serre *f*.

glassware ['glɑːsweəʳ] **n** *(U)* verrerie *f*.

glassy ['glɑːsɪ] (comp **-ier**, superl **-iest**) **adj** **1.** [smooth, shiny] lisse comme un miroir **2.** [blank, lifeless] vitreux(euse).

glassy-eyed **adj** à l'œil terne *OR* vitreux ▸ **to be glassy-eyed** avoir le regard vitreux *OR* terne.

Glaswegian [glæz'wiːdʒjən] ■ **adj** de Glasgow.
■ **n** **1.** habitant *m*, -e *f* de Glasgow **2.** [dialect] dialecte *m* de Glasgow.

glaucoma [glɔː'kəʊmə] **n** glaucome *m*.

glaze [gleɪz] ■ **n** [on pottery] vernis *m* / [on pastry, flan] glaçage *m*.
■ **vt** [pottery, tiles, bricks] vernisser / [pastry, flan] glacer.
◆ ***glaze over*** **vi** devenir terne *OR* vitreux(euse).

glazed [gleɪzd] **adj** **1.** [dull, bored] terne, vitreux(euse) **2.** [covered with shiny layer - pottery] vernissé(e) / [- pastry, flan] glacé(e) **3.** [with glass] vitré(e).

glazier ['gleɪzjəʳ] **n** vitrier *m*, -ière *f*.

glazing ['gleɪzɪŋ] **n** **1.** [of pottery] vernissage *m* / [of floor, tiles] vitrification *f* / [of leather, silk] glaçage *m* **2.** CULIN [process] glaçage *m* / [substance] glace *f*.

GLC (abbr of ***Greater London Council***) **n** *ancien organe administratif du grand Londres*.

gleam [gliːm] ■ **n** [of gold] reflet *m* / [of fire, sunset, disapproval] lueur *f*.
■ **vi** **1.** [surface, object] luire **2.** [light, eyes] briller.

gleaming ['gliːmɪŋ] **adj** brillant(e).

glean [gliːn] **vt** [gather] glaner.

glee [gliː] **n** *(U)* [joy] joie *f*, jubilation *f*.

gleeful ['gliːfʊl] **adj** joyeux(euse).

gleefully ['gliːfʊlɪ] **adv** joyeusement, avec allégresse *OR* joie.

glen [glen] **n** *Scot* vallée *f*.

glib [glɪb] (comp **-ber**, superl **-best**) **adj** *pej* [salesman, politician] qui a du bagout / [promise, excuse] facile.

glibly ['glɪblɪ] **adv** *pej* trop facilement.

glide [glaɪd] **vi** **1.** [move smoothly - dancer, boat] glisser sans effort / [- person] se mouvoir sans effort **2.** [to fly] planer.

glider ['glaɪdəʳ] **n** [plane] planeur *m*.

gliding ['glaɪdɪŋ] **n** [sport] vol *m* à voile.

glimmer ['glɪməʳ] ■ **n** [faint light] faible lueur *f* / *fig* signe *m*, lueur ▸ **a glimmer of hope** une lueur d'espoir.
■ **vi** luire *OR* briller faiblement.

glimpse [glɪmps] ■ **n** **1.** [look, sight] aperçu *m* ▸ **to catch a glimpse of sb/sthg** apercevoir qqn/qqch, entrevoir qqn/qqch **2.** [idea, perception] idée *f*.
■ **vt** **1.** [catch sight of] apercevoir, entrevoir **2.** [perceive] pressentir.

glint [glɪnt] ■ **n** **1.** [flash] reflet *m* **2.** [in eyes] éclair *m*.
■ **vi** étinceler.

glisten ['glɪsn] **vi** luire.

glistening ['glɪsnɪŋ] **adj** luisant(e).

glitch [glɪtʃ] **n** *inf* [in plan] pépin *m* / ELEC saute *f* de tension.

glitter ['glɪtəʳ] ■ **n** *(U)* scintillement *m*.
■ **vi** **1.** [object, light] scintiller **2.** [eyes] briller.

glitterati [,glɪtə'rɑːtiː] **npl** *inf* : **the glitterati** *hum* le beau monde *m inv*.

glittering ['glɪtərɪŋ] **adj** scintillant(e), brillant(e).

glittery ['glɪtərɪ] **adj** **1.** [light] scintillant(e), brillant(e) **2.** *pej* [jewellery] clinquant(e) / [make-up, décor] voyant(e), tape-à-l'œil *(inv)*.

glitz [glɪts] **n** *inf* tape-à-l'œil *m*, clinquant *m* ▸ **Hollywood glitz** le clinquant de Hollywood.

glitzy ['glɪtsɪ] (comp **-ier**, superl **-iest**) **adj** *inf* [glamorous] tape-à-l'œil *(inv)*.

gloat [gləʊt] **vi** : **to gloat (over sthg)** se réjouir (de qqch).

global ['gləʊbl] **adj** [worldwide] mondial(e).

globalism ['gləʊbəlɪzm] **n** mondialisme *m*.

globalization, *UK* ***-isation*** [,gləʊbəlaɪ'zeɪʃn] **n** mondialisation *f*.

globalize, *UK* ***-ise*** ['gləʊbəlaɪz] **vt** **1.** [make worldwide] rendre mondial(e) ▸ **a globalized conflict** un conflit mondial **2.** [generalize] globaliser.

globally ['gləʊbəlɪ] **adv** à l'échelle mondiale, mondialement.

global market **n** COMM marché *m* global *OR* international.

global marketplace **n** COMM marché *m* global *OR* international.

global strategy **n** stratégie *f* globale.

global village **n** village *m* planétaire.

global warming [-'wɔ:mɪŋ] **n** réchauffement *m* de la planète.

globe [gləʊb] **n 1.** [Earth] **: the globe** la terre **2.** [spherical map] globe *m* terrestre **3.** [spherical object] globe *m*.

globe artichoke **n** artichaut *m*.

globetrotter ['gləʊb,trɒtər] **n** *inf* globe-trotter *m*.

globetrotting ['gləʊb,trɒtɪŋ] **n** *(U)* voyages *mpl* aux quatre coins du monde.

globule ['glɒbju:l] **n** gouttelette *f*.

gloom [glu:m] **n** *(U)* **1.** [darkness] obscurité *f* **2.** [unhappiness] tristesse *f*.

gloomily ['glu:mɪlɪ] **adv** sombrement, mélancoliquement, tristement.

gloomy ['glu:mɪ] (comp **-ier**, superl **-iest**) **adj 1.** [room, sky, prospects] sombre **2.** [person, atmosphere, mood] triste, lugubre.

glorification [,glɔ:rɪfɪ'keɪʃn] **n** glorification *f*.

glorified ['glɔ:rɪfaɪd] **adj** *pej* **: it's just a glorified swimming pool** il ne s'agit que d'une vulgaire piscine.

glorify ['glɔ:rɪfaɪ] (pt & pp **-ied**) **vt** exalter.

glorious ['glɔ:rɪəs] **adj 1.** [beautiful, splendid] splendide **2.** [very enjoyable] formidable **3.** [successful, impressive] magnifique.

gloriously ['glɔ:rɪəslɪ] **adv** glorieusement.

glory ['glɔ:rɪ] (pl **-ies**) **n 1.** *(U)* [fame, admiration] gloire *f* ▸ **to have one's moment of glory** avoir son heure de gloire **2.** *(U)* [beauty] splendeur *f* ▸ **in all her glory** dans toute sa splendeur ***OR*** gloire **3.** [best feature] merveille *f* ▸ **the palace is one of the greatest glories of the age** le palais est un des joyaux ***OR*** des chefs-d'œuvre de cette époque.

◆ ***glories*** **npl** [triumphs] triomphes *mpl*.

◆ ***glory in*** **vt insep** [relish] savourer.

Glos (abbr of ***Gloucestershire***) *comté anglais*.

gloss [glɒs] **n 1.** *(U)* [shine] brillant *m*, lustre *m* **2.** [paint] peinture *f* brillante.

◆ ***gloss over*** **vt insep** passer sur.

glossary ['glɒsərɪ] (pl **-ies**) **n** glossaire *m*.

gloss paint **n** peinture *f* brillante.

glossy ['glɒsɪ] (comp **-ier**, superl **-iest**) **adj 1.** [hair, surface] brillant(e) **2.** [book, photo] sur papier glacé.

glossy (magazine) **n** *UK* magazine *m* de luxe.

glove [glʌv] **n** gant *m*.

glove box, glove compartment **n** boîte *f* à gants.

glove puppet **n** *UK* marionnette *f* (à gaine).

glow [gləʊ] ■ **n** *(U)* **1.** [of fire, light, sunset] lueur *f* **2.** [of skin - because of heat, exercise] rougeur *f* / [- because of health] teint *m* rose et frais **3.** [feeling - of pride] sensation *f* / [- of anger] élan *m* / [- of shame, pleasure] sentiment *m*.

■ **vi 1.** [shine out - fire] rougeoyer / [light, stars, eyes] flamboyer **2.** [shine in light] briller **3.** [with colour] flamboyer **4.** [flush] **: to glow (with)** [heat] être rouge (de) / [pleasure, health] rayonner (de).

glower ['glaʊər] **vi : to glower (at)** lancer des regards noirs (à).

glowing ['gləʊɪŋ] **adj** [very favourable] dithyrambique.

glowingly ['gləʊɪŋlɪ] **adv : to speak glowingly of sb/sthg** parler de qqn/qqch en termes enthousiastes ***OR*** chaleureux.

glow-worm **n** ver *m* luisant.

glucose ['glu:kəʊs] **n** glucose *m*.

glue [glu:] ■ **n** *(U)* colle *f*.

■ **vt** (cont **glueing** ***OR*** **gluing**) [stick with glue] coller ▸ **to glue sthg to sthg** coller qqch à ***OR*** avec qqch ▸ **to be glued to the TV** *fig* être rivé(e) à la télé.

glue-sniffer [-,snɪfər] **n : to be a glue-sniffer** inhaler ***OR*** sniffer (de la colle).

glue-sniffing [-,snɪfɪŋ] **n** inhalation *f* de colle.

glum [glʌm] (comp **-mer**, superl **-mest**) **adj** [unhappy] triste, morose.

glumly ['glʌmlɪ] **adv** tristement, avec morosité.

glut [glʌt] **n** surplus *m*.

gluten ['glu:tən] **n** gluten *m*.

gluten-free **adj** sans gluten.

glutinous ['glu:tɪnəs] **adj** glutineux(euse).

glutton ['glʌtn] **n** [greedy person] glouton *m*, -onne *f* ▸ **to be a glutton for punishment** être maso, être masochiste.

gluttonous ['glʌtənəs] **adj** glouton(onne), goulu(e).

gluttony ['glʌtənɪ] **n** gloutonnerie *f*.

glycerin *esp US* ['glɪsərɪn], ***glycerine*** ['glɪsəri:n] **n** glycérine *f*.

gm (abbr of ***gram***) g.

GM (abbr of ***genetically modified***) **adj** génétiquement modifié(e).

GMAT (abbr of ***Graduate Management Admissions Test***) **n** *test d'admission aux programmes de MBA*.

GMB **n** *important syndicat ouvrier britannique*.

GMO (abbr of ***genetically modified organism***) **n** OGM *m*.

GMT (abbr of ***Greenwich Mean Time***) **n** GMT *m*.

gnarled [nɑ:ld] **adj** [tree, hands] noueux(euse).

gnash [næʃ] **vt : to gnash one's teeth** grincer des dents.

gnat [næt] **n** moucheron *m*.

gnaw [nɔ:] ■ **vt** [chew] ronger.

■ **vi** [worry] **: to gnaw (away) at sb** ronger qqn.

gnawing ['nɔ:ɪŋ] **adj 1.** [pain] lancinant(e), tenaillant(e) / [hunger] tenaillant(e) **2.** [anxiety, doubt] tenaillant(e), torturant(e).

gnome [nəʊm] **n** gnome *m*, lutin *m*.

GNP (abbr of ***gross national product***) **n** PNB *m*.

gnu [nuː] (pl gnu *OR* -s) n gnou *m*.

GNVQ *UK* (abbr of **general national vocational qualification**) n *diplôme sanctionnant deux années d'études professionnelles à la fin du secondaire*, ≃ baccalauréat *m* professionnel.

go [gəʊ] ■ vi (pt **went**, pp **gone**) **1.** [move, travel] aller ▸ **where are you going?** où vas-tu? ▸ **he's gone to Portugal** il est allé au Portugal ▸ **to go to the doctor** aller voir *OR* aller chez le médecin ▸ **we went by bus/train** nous sommes allés en bus/par le train ▸ **where does this path go?** où mène ce chemin? ▸ **to go and do sthg** aller faire qqch ▸ **to go swimming/shopping/jogging** aller nager/faire les courses/faire du jogging ▸ **to go for a walk** aller se promener, faire une promenade ▸ **to go to church/school/university** aller à l'église/l'école/l'université ▸ **to go to work** aller travailler *OR* à son travail ▸ **where do we go from here?** *fig* qu'est-ce qu'on fait maintenant?
2. [depart] partir, s'en aller ▸ **I must go** *esp UK*, **I have to go** il faut que je m'en aille ▸ **what time does the bus go?** *UK* à quelle heure part le bus? ▸ **let's go!** allons-y! ▸ **go!** partez!
3. [be or remain in a particular state] : **to go hungry** souffrir de la faim ▸ **we went in fear of our lives** nous craignions pour notre vie ▸ **to go unpunished** rester impuni(e)
4. [become] devenir ▸ **to go grey** *UK OR* **gray** *US* grisonner, devenir gris(e) ▸ **to go mad** *OR* **crazy** devenir fou(folle)
5. [pass - time] passer ▸ **the time went slowly/quickly** le temps a passé lentement/a vite passé
6. [progress] marcher, se dérouler ▸ **the conference went very smoothly** la conférence s'est déroulée sans problème *OR* s'est très bien passée ▸ **to go well/badly** aller bien/mal ▸ **how's it going?** *inf* comment ça va?
7. [function, work] marcher ▸ **the clock's stopped going** la pendule s'est arrêtée ▸ **her daughter kept the business going** sa fille a continué à faire marcher l'affaire ▸ **the car won't go** *esp UK* la voiture ne veut pas démarrer
8. [indicating intention, expectation] : **to be going to do sthg** aller faire qqch ▸ **what are you going to do now?** qu'est-ce que tu vas faire maintenant? ▸ **he said he was going to be late** il a prévenu qu'il allait arriver en retard ▸ **we're going (to go) to America in June** on va (aller) en Amérique en juin ▸ **it's going to rain/snow** il va pleuvoir/neiger ▸ **she's going to have a baby** elle attend un bébé ▸ **it's not going to be easy** cela ne va pas être facile
9. [bell, alarm] sonner
10. [be spent] passer, partir ▸ **all my money goes on** *OR* **toward** *US* **food and rent** tout mon argent est passé *OR* parti en nourriture et en loyer
11. [be given] : **to go to** aller à, être donné(e) à
12. [be disposed of] : **he'll have to go** il va falloir le congédier *OR* le mettre à la porte ▸ **'everything must go'** 'tout doit disparaître' ▸ **the necklace went for £350** le collier s'est vendu 350 livres ▸ **going, going, gone!** une fois, deux fois, adjugé!
13. [stop working, break - light bulb, fuse] sauter / [- rope] céder ▸ **the battery's going** la pile commence à être usée
14. [deteriorate - hearing, sight] baisser ▸ **her mind has started to go** elle n'a plus toute sa tête *OR* toutes ses facultés
15. [match, be compatible] : **to go (with)** aller (avec) ▸ **this blouse goes well with the skirt** ce chemisier va bien avec la jupe ▸ **those colours don't really go (well together)** ces couleurs ne vont pas bien ensemble ▸ **red wine goes well with meat** le vin rouge se marie bien avec la viande
16. [fit] aller ▸ **that goes at the bottom** ça va au fond ▸ **the piano barely goes through the door** le piano entre *OR* passe de justesse par la porte
17. [belong] aller, se mettre ▸ **the plates go in the cupboard** les assiettes vont *OR* se mettent dans le placard
18. [in division] : **three into two won't go, three won't go into two** deux divisé par trois n'y va pas
19. [when referring to saying, story or song] : **how does that tune/song go?** c'est quoi déjà l'air/la chanson? ▸ **as the saying goes** comme on dit, comme dit le proverbe
20. *inf* [with negative - in giving advice] : **now, don't go catching cold** ne va pas attraper froid surtout
21. *inf* [expressing irritation, surprise] : **now what's he gone and done?** qu'est-ce qu'il a fait encore? ▸ **she's gone and bought a new car!** elle a été s'acheter une nouvelle voiture! ▸ **you've gone and done it now!** eh bien cette fois-ci, on peut dire que tu en as fait une belle!
▸▸ **it just goes to show** c'est bien vrai, vous voyez bien ▸ **it just goes to show that none of us is perfect** cela prouve bien que personne n'est parfait.
■ vt (pt **went**, pp **gone**) [make noise of] faire ▸ **the dog went 'woof'** le chien a fait 'oua-oua'.
■ n (pl **goes**) **1.** *UK* [turn] tour *m* ▸ **it's my go** c'est à moi (de jouer)
2. *inf* [attempt] : **to have a go (at sthg)** essayer (de faire qqch) ▸ **have a go!** tente le coup!, vas-y!
3. *inf* [success] : **to make a go of sthg** réussir qqch
▸▸ **to have a go at sb** *UK inf* s'en prendre à qqn, engueuler qqn ▸ **to be on the go** *inf* être sur la brèche ▸ **it's all go** ça n'arrête pas!

◆ ***to go*** adv **1.** [remaining] : **there are only three days to go** il ne reste que trois jours
2. *US* [to take away] à emporter.

◆ ***go about*** ■ vt insep **1.** [perform] : **to go about one's business** vaquer à ses occupations
2. [tackle] : **how do you intend going about it?** comment comptes-tu faire *OR* t'y prendre?
■ vi = ***go around***.

◆ ***go after*** vt insep [person] courir après / [prize] viser / [job] essayer d'obtenir.

◆ ***go against*** vt insep **1.** [conflict with] heurter, aller à l'encontre de
2. [act contrary to] contrarier, s'opposer à ▸ **she went against my advice** elle n'a pas suivi mon conseil
3. [decision, public opinion] être défavorable à.

◆ ***go ahead*** vi **1.** [proceed] : **to go ahead with sthg** mettre qqch à exécution ▸ **go ahead!** allez-y!
2. [take place] avoir lieu.

◆ ***go along*** vi [proceed] avancer ▸ **as you go along** au fur et à mesure ▸ **he makes it up as he goes along** il invente au fur et à mesure.

◆ ***go along with*** vt insep [suggestion, idea] appuyer, soutenir / [person] suivre ▸ **he went along with his father's wishes** il s'est conformé aux *OR* a respecté les désirs de son père.

◆ ***go around*** vi **1.** [behave in a certain way] : **she goes around putting everyone's back up** *UK* elle n'arrête pas

de prendre les gens à rebrousse-poil ▸ **there's no need to go around telling everyone** tu n'as pas besoin d'aller le crier sur les toits
2. [frequent] **: to go around with sb** fréquenter qqn
3. [spread] circuler, courir ▸ **there's a rumour going around about her** il court un bruit sur elle.

◆ ***go away*** vi insep partir, s'en aller ▸ **go away!** va-t-en! ▸ **I'm going away for a few days** je pars pour quelques jours.

◆ ***go back on*** vt insep [one's word, promise] revenir sur.

◆ ***go back to*** vt insep **1.** [return to activity] reprendre, se remettre à ▸ **to go back to sleep** se rendormir
2. [return to previous topic] revenir à
3. [date from] remonter à, dater de.

◆ ***go before*** vi **: her new paintings were unlike anything that had gone before** ses nouveaux tableaux étaient complètement différents de ses précédents ▸ **we wanted to forget what had gone before** nous voulions oublier ce qui s'était passé avant.

◆ ***go by*** ■ vi [time] s'écouler, passer ▸ **in days** *OR* **in times** *OR* **in years gone by** autrefois, jadis.
■ **vt insep 1.** [be guided by] suivre
2. [judge from] juger d'après ▸ **going by her accent, I'd say she's from New York** si j'en juge d'après son accent, je dirais qu'elle vient de New York.

◆ ***go down*** ■ vi **1.** [get lower - prices] baisser
2. [be accepted] être accepté(e) ▸ **to go down well/badly** être bien/mal accueilli(e) ▸ **a cup of coffee would go down nicely** une tasse de café serait la bienvenue
3. [sun] se coucher
4. [sink] couler
5. [tyre, balloon] se dégonfler
6. COMPUT tomber en panne.
■ **vt insep** descendre.

◆ ***go down with*** vt insep [illness] attraper.

◆ ***go for*** vt insep **1.** [choose] choisir
2. [be attracted to] être attiré(e) par
3. [attack] tomber sur, attaquer
4. [try to obtain - job, record] essayer d'obtenir ▸ **go for it!** *inf* vas-y!
5. [be valid] s'appliquer à ▸ **does that go for me too?** est-ce que cela vaut pour *OR* s'applique à moi aussi?

◆ ***go in*** vi entrer.

◆ ***go in for*** vt insep **1.** [competition] prendre part à / [exam] se présenter à
2. [take up as a profession] entrer dans ▸ **he thought about going in for teaching** il a pensé devenir enseignant
3. [activity - enjoy] aimer / [- participate in] faire, s'adonner à.

◆ ***go into*** vt insep **1.** [discuss, describe in detail] **: I'd rather not go into that now** je préférerais ne pas en parler pour le moment ▸ **to go into detail** *OR* **details** entrer dans le détail *OR* les détails
2. [investigate] étudier, examiner
3. [take up as a profession] entrer dans ▸ **to go into the army** [as profession] devenir militaire de carrière
4. [be put into] **: a lot of hard work went into that book** ce livre a demandé *OR* nécessité beaucoup de travail
5. [begin] **: to go into a rage** se mettre en rage ▸ **to go into a spin** [plane] tomber en vrille.

◆ ***go off*** ■ vi **1.** [explode] exploser
2. [alarm] sonner
3. *UK* [go bad - food] se gâter
4. [lights, heating] s'éteindre ▸ **the electricity went off** l'électricité a été coupée
5. *UK* [happen] se passer, se dérouler
6. *US inf* [person] s'emporter.
■ **vt insep** [lose interest in] ne plus aimer.

◆ ***go off with*** vt insep prendre.

◆ ***go on*** ■ vi **1.** [take place, happen] se passer
2. [heating] se mettre en marche
3. [continue] **: to go on (doing)** continuer (à faire) ▸ **I can't go on!** je n'en peux plus! ▸ **go on** [continue talking] allez-y ▸ **their affair has been going on for years** leur liaison dure depuis des années
4. [proceed to further activity] **: to go on to sthg** passer à qqch ▸ **to go on to do sthg** faire qqch après ▸ **he went on to explain why** il a ensuite expliqué pourquoi
5. [proceed to another place] **: are you going on to Richard's?** *UK* vous allez chez Richard après?
6. [go in advance] partir devant
7. [talk for too long] parler à n'en plus finir ▸ **she does go on!** elle n'arrête pas de parler! ▸ **to go on about sthg** ne pas arrêter de parler de qqch
8. [pass - time] passer.
■ **vt insep** [be guided by] se fonder sur.
■ **excl** allez ▸ **go on, treat yourself** allez, fais-toi plaisir.

◆ ***go on at*** vt insep *UK inf* [nag] harceler.

◆ ***go out*** vi **1.** [leave] sortir ▸ **she goes out to work** elle travaille en dehors de la maison
2. [socially] **: to go out (with sb)** sortir (avec qqn)
3. [light, fire, cigarette] s'éteindre
4. [stop being fashionable] passer de mode.

◆ ***go over*** vt insep **1.** [examine] examiner, vérifier
2. [repeat, review] repasser ▸ **let's go over it again** reprenons, récapitulons.

◆ ***go over to*** vt insep **1.** [change to] adopter, passer à ▸ **I've gone over to another brand of washing powder** je viens de changer de marque de lessive
2. [change sides to] passer à ▸ **to go over to the other side** changer de parti
3. RADIO & TV passer l'antenne à.

◆ ***go round*** vi *UK* **1.** [be enough for everyone] suffire ▸ **there's just enough to go round** il y en a juste assez pour tout le monde
2. [revolve] tourner ; see also ***go around***.

◆ ***go through*** ■ vt insep **1.** [experience] subir, souffrir ▸ **we've gone through a lot together** nous avons vécu beaucoup de choses ensemble
2. [spend] dépenser
3. [study, search through] examiner ▸ **she went through his pockets** elle lui a fait les poches, elle a fouillé dans ses poches
4. [list - reading] lire / [- speaking] lire à haute voix.
■ **vi** [be approved] passer, être accepté(e).

◆ ***go through with*** vt insep [action, threat] aller jusqu'au bout de.

◆ ***go toward(s)*** vt insep contribuer à.

◆ ***go under*** vi *lit* & *fig* couler.

◆ ***go up*** ■ vi **1.** [gen] monter

2. [prices] augmenter ▸ **rents are going up** les loyers sont en hausse
3. [be built] se construire
4. [explode] exploser, sauter
5. [burst into flames] **: to go up (in flames)** prendre feu, s'enflammer
6. [be uttered] **: a cheer went up** on a applaudi.
■ **vt insep** monter.
◆ ***go with*** **vt insep** aller avec.
◆ ***go without*** ■ **vt insep** se passer de.
■ **vi** s'en passer.

goad [gəʊd] **vt** [provoke] talonner ▸ **to goad sb into doing sthg** talonner qqn jusqu'à ce qu'il fasse qqch.

go-ahead ■ **adj** [dynamic] dynamique.
■ **n** *(U)* [permission] feu *m* vert ▸ **to give sb the go-ahead (for sthg)** donner à qqn le feu vert (pour qqch).

goal [gəʊl] **n** but *m* ▸ **to score a goal** SPORT marquer un but.

goal difference **n** différence *f* de buts.

goalie ['gəʊlɪ] **n** *inf* gardien *m* (de but).

goalkeeper ['gəʊl,ki:pəʳ] **n** gardien *m* de but.

goalkeeping ['gəʊl,ki:pɪŋ] **n** jeu *m* du gardien de but ▸ **we saw some great goalkeeping on both sides** les deux gardiens de but ont très bien joué.

goal kick **n** coup *m* de pied de but, dégagement *m* aux six mètres.

goalless ['gəʊllɪs] **adj : goalless draw** match *m* sans but marqué.

goal line **n** ligne *f* de but.

goalmouth ['gəʊlmaʊθ] (**pl** [-maʊðz]) **n** but *m*.

goalpost ['gəʊlpəʊst] **n** poteau *m* de but.

goat [gəʊt] **n** chèvre *f* ▸ **to act the goat** *UK inf* faire l'imbécile.

goatee [gəʊ'ti:] **n** barbiche *f*, bouc *m*.

gob [gɒb] *inf* ■ **n** *UK* [mouth] gueule *f*.
■ **vi** (**pt & pp -bed, cont -bing**) [spit] mollarder.

gobble ['gɒbl] **vt** engloutir.
◆ ***gobble down***, ***gobble up*** **vt sep** engloutir.

gobbledegook, ***gobbledygook*** ['gɒbldɪgu:k] **n** **1.** [pompous official language] jargon *m* **2.** *inf* [nonsense] charabia *m*.

go-between **n** intermédiaire *mf*.

Gobi ['gəʊbɪ] **n : the Gobi Desert** le désert de Gobi.

goblet ['gɒblɪt] **n** verre *m* à pied.

goblin ['gɒblɪn] **n** lutin *m*, farfadet *m*.

gobsmacked ['gɒbsmækt] **adj** *UK inf* bouche bée *(inv)*.

go-cart = ***go-kart***.

god [gɒd] **n** dieu *m*, divinité *f*.
◆ ***God*** ■ **n** Dieu *m* ▸ **God knows** Dieu seul le sait ▸ **for God's sake** pour l'amour de Dieu ▸ **thank God** Dieu merci.
■ **excl : (my) God!** mon Dieu!
◆ ***gods*** **npl** *UK inf* [in theatre] **: the gods** le poulailler.

god-awful **adj** *inf* atroce, affreux(euse).

godchild ['gɒdtʃaɪld] (**pl -children** [-,tʃɪldrən]) **n** filleul *m*, -e *f*.

goddam(n) ['gɒdæm] *esp US v inf* ■ **adj** foutu(e).
■ **excl** bordel!

goddamned ['gɒdæmd] *v inf* = ***goddam(n)*** *(adj)*.

goddaughter ['gɒd,dɔ:təʳ] **n** filleule *f*.

goddess ['gɒdɪs] **n** déesse *f*.

godfather ['gɒd,fɑ:ðəʳ] **n** parrain *m*.

god-fearing **adj** croyant(e), pieux(euse).

godforsaken ['gɒdfə,seɪkn] **adj** morne, désolé(e).

godless ['gɒdlɪs] **adj** irréligieux(euse), impie.

godlike ['gɒdlaɪk] **adj** divin(e), céleste.

godmother ['gɒd,mʌðəʳ] **n** marraine *f*.

godparents ['gɒd,peərənts] **npl** parrain et marraine *mpl*.

godsend ['gɒdsend] **n** aubaine *f*.

godson ['gɒdsʌn] **n** filleul *m*.

goer ['gəʊəʳ] **n** *UK inf* **1.** [fast person, vehicle, animal] fonceur *m*, -euse *f* **2.** [sexually active person] **: he's/she's a real goer** il/elle n'y va pas par quatre chemins *(pour séduire qqn)*.

goes [gəʊz] ➤ ***go***.

gofer ['gəʊfəʳ] **n** *inf* larbin *m*.

go-getter [-'getəʳ] **n** *inf* battant *m*, -e *f*.

goggle ['gɒgl] **vi : to goggle (at sb/sthg)** regarder (qqn/qqch) avec des yeux ronds.

goggles ['gɒglz] **npl** lunettes *fpl*.

go-go dancer **n** danseur *m*, -euse *f* de cabaret.

going ['gəʊɪŋ] ■ **n** *(U)* **1.** [rate of advance] allure *f* ▸ **that was good going** ça a été vite **2.** [travel conditions] conditions *fpl*.
■ **adj 1.** *UK* [available] disponible ▸ **you've got a lot going for you** vous avez beaucoup d'atouts **2.** [rate, salary] en vigueur.

going concern **n** affaire *f* qui marche.

going-over (**pl goings-over**) **n** *inf* **1.** [checkup] révision *f*, vérification *f* / [cleanup] nettoyage *m* ▸ **the house needs a good going-over** il faudrait nettoyer la maison à fond **2.** *fig* **: to give sb a (good) going-over** [scolding] passer un savon à qqn / [beating] passer qqn à tabac.

goings-on **npl** événements *mpl*, histoires *fpl*.

go-kart [-kɑ:t] **n** kart *m*.

Golan Heights ['gəʊ,læn-] **npl : the Golan Heights** le plateau du Golan.

gold [gəʊld] ■ **n 1.** *(U)* [metal, jewellery] or *m* ▸ **to be as good as gold** [person] être sage comme une image, être mignon(onne) tout plein / [worth] de très bonne qualité **2.** [medal] médaille *f* d'or.
■ **comp** [made of gold] en or.
■ **adj** [gold-coloured] doré(e).

gold card **n** carte *f* Gold.

gold-digger **n** [prospector] chercheur *m* d'or / *fig* aventurier *m*, -ère *f*.

gold dust **n** poudre *f* d'or ▸ **jobs are like gold dust around here** *fig* le travail est rare **OR** ne court pas les rues par ici.

golden ['gəʊldən] **adj 1.** [made of gold] en or **2.** [gold-coloured] doré(e).

golden age **n** âge *m* d'or.

golden eagle **n** aigle *m* royal.

golden handcuffs **npl** *inf* primes *fpl (versées à un cadre à intervalles réguliers pour le dissuader de partir).*

golden handshake **n** prime *f* de départ.

golden hello **n** *inf* gratification *f* de début de service.

golden jubilee **n** (fête *f* du) cinquantième anniversaire *m*.

golden oldie **n** *inf* vieux tube *m*.

golden opportunity **n** occasion *f* en or.

golden retriever **n** (golden) retriever *m*.

golden rule **n** règle *f* d'or.

golden syrup **n** *UK* mélasse *f* raffinée.

golden wedding **n** noces *fpl* d'or.

goldfinch ['gəʊldfɪntʃ] **n** chardonneret *m*.

goldfish ['gəʊldfɪʃ] (pl **goldfish**) **n** poisson *m* rouge.

goldfish bowl **n** bocal *m* (à poissons).

gold leaf **n** *(U)* feuille *f* d'or.

gold medal **n** médaille *f* d'or.

goldmine ['gəʊldmaɪn] **n** *lit* & *fig* mine *f* d'or.

gold plate **n 1.** [utensils] orfèvrerie *f*, vaisselle *f* d'or **2.** [plating] plaque *f* d'or.

gold-plated [-'pleɪtɪd] **adj** plaqué(e) or.

gold-rimmed **adj : gold-rimmed spectacles** lunettes *fpl* à montures en or.

goldsmith ['gəʊldsmɪθ] **n** orfèvre *mf*.

gold standard **n : the gold standard** l'étalon-or *m*.

golf [gɒlf] **n** golf *m*.

golf ball **n 1.** [for golf] balle *f* de golf **2.** [for typewriter] boule *f*.

golf club **n** [stick, place] club *m* de golf.

golf course **n** terrain *m* de golf.

golfer ['gɒlfəʳ] **n** golfeur *m*, -euse *f*.

golly ['gɒlɪ] **excl** *inf dated* mince!

gondola ['gɒndələ] **n** [boat] gondole *f*.

gondolier [ˌgɒndə'lɪəʳ] **n** gondolier *m*.

gone [gɒn] ■ **pp** ➤ ***go***.
■ **adj** [no longer here] parti(e).
■ **prep** *UK* **: it's gone ten (o'clock)** il est dix heures passées.

goner ['gɒnəʳ] **n** *inf* **: to be a goner** être fichu, -e *f* OR cuit, -e *f*.

gong [gɒŋ] **n** gong *m*.

gonna ['gɒnə] *inf* = ***going to***.

gonorrhoea *UK*, ***gonorrhea*** *US* [ˌgɒnə'rɪə] **n** blennorragie *f*.

goo [gu:] **n** *(U) inf* truc *m* poisseux.

good [gʊd] ■ **adj** (comp **better**, superl **best**) **1.** [gen] bon (bonne) ▸ **it's good to see you again** ça fait plaisir de te revoir ▸ **it feels good to be outside** ça fait du bien d'être dehors ▸ **to be good at sthg** être bon en qqch ▸ **to be good with** [animals, children] savoir y faire avec / [one's hands] être habile de ▸ **it's good for you** c'est bon pour toi OR pour la santé ▸ **to feel good** [person] se sentir bien ▸ **it's good that...** c'est bien que... ▸ **good!** très bien! ▸ **have a good day!** bonne journée! ▸ **he speaks good English** il parle bien anglais ▸ **we're good friends** nous sommes très amis
2. [kind - person] gentil(ille) ▸ **to be good to sb** être très attentionné(e) envers qqn ▸ **to be good enough to do sthg** avoir l'amabilité de faire qqch
3. [well-behaved - child] sage / [- behaviour] correct(e) ▸ **be good!** sois sage!, tiens-toi tranquille!
4. [attractive - legs, figure] joli(e) ▸ **that colour looks good on him** cette couleur lui va bien
5. [ample, considerable] bon(bonne), considérable ▸ **a good deal of money** beaucoup d'argent ▸ **a good thirty years ago** il y a bien trente ans ▸ **the trip will take you a good two hours** il vous faudra deux bonnes heures pour faire le voyage
▸▸ **it's a good job** *UK* OR **thing (that)...,** c'est très bien que..., c'est une bonne chose que... ▸ **good for you!** très bien! ▸ **to give as good as one gets** rendre la pareille ▸ **to make good** réussir ▸ **to make sthg good** réparer qqch.
■ **n 1.** *(U)* [benefit] bien *m* ▸ **for the good of** pour le bien de ▸ **for your own good** pour ton bien ▸ **it will do him good** ça lui fera du bien
2. [use] utilité *f* ▸ **what's the good of** OR **in** *esp US* **doing that?** à quoi bon faire ça? ▸ **it's no good** ça ne sert à rien ▸ **it's no good crying/worrying** ça ne sert à rien de pleurer/de s'en faire ▸ **will this be** OR **do any good?** cela peut-il faire l'affaire?
3. *(U)* [morally correct behaviour] bien *m* ▸ **to be up to no good** préparer un sale coup.
◆ ***goods*** **npl** [merchandise] marchandises *fpl*, articles *mpl* ▸ **to come up with** OR **deliver the goods** *UK inf* tenir ses promesses.
◆ ***as good as*** **adv** pratiquement, pour ainsi dire ▸ **it's as good as new** c'est comme neuf.
◆ ***for good*** **adv** [forever] pour de bon, définitivement.
◆ ***good afternoon*** **excl** bonjour!
◆ ***good day*** **excl** *dated* bonjour!
◆ ***good evening*** **excl** bonsoir!
◆ ***good morning*** **excl** bonjour!
◆ ***good night*** **excl** bonsoir! / [at bedtime] bonne nuit!

HOW TO ...
say goodbye

Au revoir, Aurélie / Goodbye, Aurélie
Au revoir, et merci encore ! / Goodbye, and thanks again!
Bonsoir ! / Good night!
À bientôt / See you soon OR Speak to you soon
À tout à l'heure / See you later
À la prochaine ! *inf* / See you!
Salut ! *inf* / Bye!

goodbye [ˌgʊd'baɪ] ■ **excl** au revoir!
■ **n** au revoir *m*.

good-for-nothing ■ **adj** bon (bonne) à rien.
■ **n** bon *m* à rien, bonne *f* à rien.

Good Friday **n** Vendredi *m* saint.

good-hearted **adj** [person] bon(bonne), généreux (euse) / [action] fait(e) avec les meilleures intentions.

good-humoured *UK*, ***good-humored*** *US* [-'hjuːməd] **adj** [person] de bonne humeur / [smile, remark, rivalry] bon enfant *(inv)*.

goodie ['gʊdɪ] *inf* = ***goody***.

good-looker **n** *inf* [man] bel homme *m* / [younger] beau garçon *m* / [woman] belle femme *f* / [younger] belle fille *f*.

good-looking [-'lʊkɪŋ] **adj** [person] beau (belle).

good looks **npl** [attractive appearance] beauté *f*.

good-natured [-'neɪtʃəd] **adj** [person] d'un naturel aimable / [rivalry, argument] bon enfant *(inv)*.

goodness ['gʊdnɪs] ■ **n** *(U)* **1.** [kindness] bonté *f* **2.** [nutritive quality] valeur *f* nutritive.
■ **excl : (my) goodness!** mon Dieu!, Seigneur! ▸ **for goodness' sake!** par pitié!, pour l'amour de Dieu! ▸ **thank goodness!** grâce à Dieu!

good Samaritan **n** bon Samaritain *m*, bonne Samaritaine *f* ▸ **she's a real good Samaritan** elle a tout du bon Samaritain ▸ **the good Samaritan laws** *US* LAW *lois qui protègent un sauveteur de toutes poursuites éventuelles engagées par le blessé*.
◆ ***Good Samaritan*** **n** [in Bible] **: the Good Samaritan** le bon Samaritain.

goods train **n** *UK* train *m* de marchandises.

good-tempered [-'tempəd] **adj** [meeting, discussion] agréable / [person] qui a bon caractère.

good turn **n : to do sb a good turn** rendre un service à qqn.

goodwill [ˌgʊd'wɪl] **n** bienveillance *f*.

goody ['gʊdɪ] *inf* ■ **n** (pl **-ies**) *UK* [person] bon *m*.
■ **excl** chouette!
◆ ***goodies*** **npl** *inf* **1.** [delicious food] friandises *fpl* **2.** [desirable objects] merveilles *fpl*, trésors *mpl*.

gooey ['guːɪ] (comp **gooier**, superl **gooiest**) **adj** *inf* [sticky] qui colle / *pej* poisseux(euse).

goof [guːf] *US inf* ■ **n** [mistake] gaffe *f*.
■ **vi** faire une gaffe.
◆ ***goof off*** **vi** *US inf* tirer au flanc.

goofy ['guːfɪ] (comp **-ier**, superl **-iest**) **adj** *US inf* [silly] dingue.

goolies ['guːlɪ] **npl** *UK v inf* roupettes *fpl*.

goon [guːn] **n** *inf* **1.** [fool] abruti *m*, -e *f* **2.** *US* [hired thug] casseur *m (au service de quelqu'un)* ▸ **goon squad** [strikebreakers] milice *f* patronale.

goose [guːs] (pl **geese** [giːz]) **n** [bird] oie *f*.

gooseberry ['gʊzbərɪ] (pl **-ies**) **n** **1.** [fruit] groseille *f* à maquereau **2.** *UK inf* [third person] **: to play gooseberry** tenir la chandelle.

goose bumps *esp US inf* **npl** = ***gooseflesh***.

gooseflesh ['guːsfleʃ] **n** chair *f* de poule.

goose pimples *UK* **npl** = ***gooseflesh***.

goose-step ['guːsˌstep] ■ **n** pas *m* de l'oie.
■ **vi** (pt & pp **-ped**, cont **-ping**) faire le pas de l'oie.

GOP (abbr of ***Grand Old Party***) **n** *le parti républicain aux États-Unis*.

gopher ['gəʊfər] **n** geomys *m*.

gore [gɔːr] ■ **n** *(U) liter* [blood] sang *m*.
■ **vt** encorner.

gorge [gɔːdʒ] ■ **n** gorge *f*, défilé *m*.
■ **vt : to gorge o.s. on** *OR* **with sthg** se bourrer *OR* se goinfrer de qqch.
■ **vi** se goinfrer.

gorgeous ['gɔːdʒəs] **adj** [generally] divin(e) / *inf* [good-looking] magnifique, splendide.

gorilla [gə'rɪlə] **n** gorille *m*.

gormless ['gɔːmlɪs] **adj** *UK inf* bêta (bêtasse).

gorse [gɔːs] **n** *(U)* ajonc *m*.

gory ['gɔːrɪ] (comp **-ier**, superl **-iest**) **adj** sanglant(e).

gosh [gɒʃ] **excl** *inf* ça alors!

gosling ['gɒzlɪŋ] **n** oison *m*.

go-slow **n** *UK* grève *f* du zèle.

gospel ['gɒspl] ■ **n** [doctrine] évangile *m* ▸ **gospel (truth)** parole *f* d'évangile.
■ **comp** [singer] de gospel ▸ **gospel songs** *OR* **music** gospel *m*.
◆ ***Gospel*** **n** Évangile *m*.

gossamer ['gɒsəmər] **n** *(U)* **1.** [spider's thread] fils *mpl* de la Vierge **2.** [material] étoffe *f* légère.

gossip ['gɒsɪp] ■ **n** **1.** [conversation] bavardage *m* / *pej* commérage *m* **2.** [person] commère *f*.
■ **vi** [talk] bavarder, papoter / *pej* cancaner.

gossip column **n** échos *mpl*.

gossip columnist **n** échotier *m*, -ère *f*.

gossipy ['gɒsɪpɪ] **adj** *inf* [person] bavard(e) / [letter] plein(e) de bavardages / *pej* cancanier(ère) / [style] anecdotique.

got [gɒt] **pt & pp** ➤ ***get***.

Goth [gɒθ] **n : the Goths** les Goths *mpl*.

Gothic ['gɒθɪk] **adj** gothique.

gotta ['gɒtə] *inf* = ***got to***.

gotten ['gɒtn] *US* **pp** ➤ ***get***.

gouge [gaʊdʒ] ◆ ***gouge out*** **vt sep** [hole] creuser / [eyes] arracher.

goulash ['guːlæʃ] **n** goulache *m*.

gourd [gʊəd] **n** gourde *f*.

gourmand ['gʊəmənd] **n** [glutton] gourmand *m*, -e *f* / [gourmet] gourmet *m*.

gourmet ['gʊəmeɪ] ■ **n** gourmet *m*.
■ **comp** [food, restaurant] gastronomique / [cook] gastronome.

gout [gaʊt] **n** *(U)* MED goutte *f*.

govern ['gʌvən] ■ **vt** **1.** [gen] gouverner **2.** [control] régir.
■ **vi** POL gouverner.

governable ['gʌvnəbl] **adj** gouvernable.

governess ['gʌvənɪs] **n** gouvernante *f*.

governing ['gʌvənɪŋ] **adj** gouvernant(e).

governing body **n** conseil *m* d'administration.

government ['gʌvnmənt] ■ **n** gouvernement *m* ▸ **the art of government** l'art de gouverner ▸ **democratic government** la démocratie.
■ **comp** [minister, policy] du gouvernement / [borrowing, expenditure] de l'État, public ▸ **a government-funded project** un projet subventionné par l'État.

government aid **n** aide *f* gouvernementale ***OR*** de l'État.

governmental [,gʌvn'mentl] **adj** gouvernemental(e).

government grant **n** subvention *f* de l'État.

government handouts **n** subventions *fpl* gouvernementales.

government spending **n** *(U)* dépenses *fpl* publiques.

government stock *(U)* **n** fonds *mpl* publics ***OR*** d'État.

government subsidy **n** subvention *f* d'État.

governor ['gʌvənəʳ] **n 1.** POL gouverneur *m* **2.** *UK* [of school] ≃ membre *m* du conseil d'établissement / [of bank] gouverneur *m* **3.** *UK* [of prison] directeur *m*.

governor-general (pl **governor-generals** ***OR*** **governors-general**) **n** gouverneur *m* général.

governorship ['gʌvənəʃɪp] **n** fonctions *fpl* de gouverneur.

govt (abbr of ***government***) gvt.

gown [gaʊn] **n 1.** [for woman] robe *f* **2.** [for surgeon] blouse *f* / [for judge, academic, graduate] robe *f*, toge *f*.

GP **n** *UK* abbr of ***general practitioner***.

GPMU (abbr of ***Graphical, Paper and Media Union***) **n** *syndicat britannique des ouvriers du livre*.

GPO (abbr of ***General Post Office***) **n 1.** [in UK] *ancien nom des services postaux britanniques* **2.** [in US] *la poste centrale d'une ville*.

GPS [,dʒi:pi:'es] (abbr of ***Global Positioning System***) **n** GPS *m*.

gr. abbr of ***gross***.

grab [græb] ■ **vt** (pt & pp **-bed**, cont **-bing**) **1.** [seize] saisir **2.** *inf* [sandwich] avaler en vitesse ▸ **to grab a few hours' sleep** dormir quelques heures **3.** *inf* [appeal to] emballer.
■ **vi** (pt & pp **-bed**, cont **-bing**) **: to grab at sthg** faire un geste pour attraper qqch.
■ **n : to make a grab at *OR* for sthg** faire un geste pour attraper qqch.

grace [greɪs] ■ **n 1.** [elegance] grâce *f* **2.** [graciousness] **: to do sthg with good grace** faire qqch de bonne grâce ▸ **to have the grace to do sthg** avoir la bonne grâce de faire qqch **3.** *(U)* [extra time] répit *m* **4.** [prayer] grâces *fpl*.
■ **vt** *fml* **1.** [honour] honorer de sa présence **2.** [decorate] orner, décorer.

graceful ['greɪsfʊl] **adj** gracieux(euse), élégant(e).

gracefully ['greɪsfʊlɪ] **adv** [dance, move] avec grâce, gracieusement / [apologize] avec élégance.

graceless ['greɪslɪs] **adj 1.** [ugly] sans attrait **2.** [ill-mannered] grossier(ère), peu élégant(e).

gracious ['greɪʃəs] ■ **adj 1.** [polite] courtois(e) **2.** [elegant] élégant(e).
■ **excl : (good) gracious!** *dated* juste ciel!

graciously ['greɪʃəslɪ] **adv** [politely] poliment.

graciousness ['greɪʃəsnɪs] **n** [of person] bienveillance *f*, générosité *f*, gentillesse *f* / [of action] grâce *f*, élégance *f* / [of lifestyle, surroundings] élégance *f*, raffinement *m* / RELIG miséricorde *f*, clémence *f*.

gradable ['greɪdəbl] **adj 1.** [capable of being graded] qui peut être classé(e) **2.** LING comparatif(ive).

gradation [grə'deɪʃn] **n** gradation *f*.

grade [greɪd] ■ **n 1.** [quality - of worker] catégorie *f* / [- of wool, paper] qualité *f* / [- of petrol] type *m* / [- of eggs] calibre *m* ▸ **to make the grade** y arriver, être à la hauteur **2.** *US* [class] classe *f* **3.** *US* [mark] note *f*.
■ **vt 1.** [classify] classer **2.** [mark, assess] noter.

grade crossing **n** *US* passage *m* à niveau.

grade school **n** *US* école *f* primaire.

gradient ['greɪdjənt] **n** pente *f*, inclinaison *f*.

gradual ['grædʒʊəl] **adj** graduel(elle), progressif(ive).

gradually ['grædʒʊəlɪ] **adv** graduellement, petit à petit.

graduate ■ **n** ['grædʒʊət] **1.** [from university] diplômé *m*, -e *f* **2.** *US* [of high school] ≃ titulaire *mf* du baccalauréat.
■ **comp** *US* [postgraduate] de troisième cycle.
■ **vi** ['grædʒʊeɪt] **1.** [from university] **: to graduate (from)** ≃ obtenir son diplôme (à) **2.** *US* [from high school] **: to graduate (from)** ≃ obtenir son baccalauréat (à) **3.** [progress] **: to graduate from sthg (to sthg)** passer de qqch (à qqch).

graduated ['grædjʊeɪtɪd] **adj** [ruler] gradué(e) / [tax] progressif(ive) ▸ **graduated pension scheme** *UK* régime *m* de retraite proportionnelle.

graduate school **n** *US* troisième cycle *m* d'université.

graduation [,grædʒʊ'eɪʃn] **n** *(U)* **1.** [ceremony] remise *f* des diplômes **2.** [completion of course] obtention *f* de son diplôme.

graffiti [grə'fi:tɪ] **n** *(U)* graffiti *mpl*.

graft [grɑ:ft] ■ **n 1.** [from plant] greffe *f*, greffon *m* **2.** MED greffe *f* **3.** *UK* [hard work] boulot *m* **4.** *US inf* [corruption] graissage *m* de patte.
■ **vt 1.** [plant, skin] greffer ▸ **to graft sthg onto sthg** greffer qqch sur qqch **2.** *fig* [idea, system] incorporer, intégrer ▸ **to graft sthg onto sthg** incorporer qqch à qqch, intégrer qqch dans qqch.

grain [greɪn] **n 1.** [gen] grain *m* **2.** *(U)* [crops] céréales *fpl* **3.** *(U)* [pattern - in wood] fil *m* / [- in material] grain *m* / [- in stone, marble] veines *fpl* ▸ **it goes against the grain (for me)** cela va à l'encontre de mes principes.

grainy ['greɪnɪ] (comp **-ier**, superl **-iest**) **adj** [surface, texture - of wood] veineux(euse) / [- of stone] grenu(e), granuleux(euse) / [- of leather, paper] grenu(e), grené(e) / PHOT qui a du grain.

gram [græm] **n** gramme *m*.

grammar ['græməʳ] **n** grammaire *f*.

grammar checker **n** COMPUT vérificateur *m* grammatical.

grammar school **n** [in UK] ≃ lycée *m* / [in US] école *f* primaire.

grammatical [grəˈmætɪkl] **adj** grammatical(e).

grammatically [grəˈmætɪklɪ] **adv** grammaticalement, du point de vue grammatical.

gramme [græm] *UK* = ***gram***.

gramophone [ˈgræməfəʊn] **n** *dated* gramophone *m*, phonographe *m*.

gran [græn] **n** *UK inf* mamie *f*, mémé *f*.

Granada [grəˈnɑːdə] **n** Grenade.

granary [ˈgrænərɪ] (pl **-ies**) **n** grenier *m (à grain)*.

grand [grænd] ■ **adj 1.** [impressive] grandiose, imposant(e) **2.** [ambitious] grand(e) **3.** [important] important(e) / [socially] distingué(e) **4.** *inf dated* [excellent] sensationnel(elle), formidable.
■ **n** (pl **grand**) *inf* [thousand pounds] mille livres *fpl* / [thousand dollars] mille dollars *mpl*.

Grand Canyon **n : the Grand Canyon** le Grand Canyon.

grandchild [ˈgræntʃaɪld] (pl **-children** [-ˌtʃɪldrən]) **n** [boy] petit-fils *m* / [girl] petite-fille *f*.
◆ ***grandchildren*** **npl** petits-enfants *mpl*.

grand(d)ad [ˈgrændæd] **n** *inf* papi *m*, pépé *m*.

granddaughter [ˈgrænˌdɔːtəʳ] **n** petite-fille *f*.

grand duke **n** grand duc *m*.

grandeur [ˈgrændʒəʳ] **n 1.** [splendour] splendeur *f*, magnificence *f* **2.** [status] éminence *f*.

grandfather [ˈgrændˌfɑːðəʳ] **n** grand-père *m*.

grandfather clock **n** horloge *f*, pendule *f* de parquet.

grand finale **n** apothéose *f*.

grandiloquence [grænˈdɪləkwəns] **n** *fml* grandiloquence *f*.

grandiloquent [grænˈdɪləkwənt] **adj** *fml* grandiloquent(e).

grandiose [ˈgrændɪəʊz] **adj** *pej* [building] prétentieux(euse) / [plan] extravagant(e).

grand jury **n** *US* tribunal *m* d'accusation.

grand larceny **n** *US* vol *m* qualifié.

grandly [ˈgrændlɪ] **adv** [behave, say] avec grandeur / [live] avec faste / [dress] avec panache.

grandma [ˈgrænmɑː] **n** *inf* mamie *f*, mémé *f*.

grand master **n** grand maître *m*.

grandmother [ˈgrænˌmʌðəʳ] **n** grand-mère *f*.

Grand National **n : the Grand National** *la plus importante course d'obstacles de Grande-Bretagne, se déroulant à Aintree dans la banlieue de Liverpool.*

grandness [ˈgrændnɪs] **n** [of behaviour] grandeur *f*, noblesse *f* / [of lifestyle] faste *m* / [of appearance] panache *m*.

grandpa [ˈgrænpɑː] **n** *inf* papi *m*, pépé *m*.

grandparents [ˈgrænˌpeərənts] **npl** grands-parents *mpl*.

grand piano **n** piano *m* à queue.

grand prix [ˌgrɒnˈpriː] (pl **grands prix** [ˌgrɒnˈpriː]) **n** grand prix *m*.

grand slam **n** SPORT grand chelem *m*.

grandson [ˈgrænsʌn] **n** petit-fils *m*.

grandstand [ˈgrændstænd] **n** tribune *f*.

grand total **n** somme *f* globale, total *m* général.

granite [ˈgrænɪt] **n** granit *m*.

granny [ˈgrænɪ] (pl **-ies**) **n** *inf* mamie *f*, mémé *f*.

granny flat **n** *UK appartement indépendant dans une maison, pour y loger un parent âgé.*

granola [grəˈnəʊlə] **n** *US* muesli *m*.

grant [grɑːnt] ■ **n** subvention *f* / [for study] bourse *f*.
■ **vt 1.** [wish, appeal] accorder / [request] accéder à **2.** [admit] admettre, reconnaître ▸ **I grant (that)...** je reconnais *OR* j'admets que... **3.** [give] accorder ▸ **to take sb for granted** [not appreciate sb's help] penser que tout ce que qqn fait va de soi / [not value sb's presence] penser que qqn fait partie des meubles ▸ **to take sthg for granted** [result, sb's agreement] considérer qqch comme acquis ▸ **it is taken for granted that...** cela semble aller de soi que..., cela paraît normal *OR* tout naturel que...

grant-maintained [-meɪnˈteɪnd] **adj** *UK* SCH subventionné(e) *(par l'État)*.

granular [ˈgrænjʊləʳ] **adj** [surface] granuleux(euse), granulaire / [structure] grenu(e).

granulated sugar [ˈgrænjʊleɪtɪd-] **n** sucre *m* cristallisé.

granule [ˈgrænjuːl] **n** [generally] granule *m* / [of sugar] grain *m*.

grape [greɪp] **n** (grain *m* de) raisin *m* ▸ **some grapes** du raisin ▸ **a bunch of grapes** une grappe de raisin.

grapefruit [ˈgreɪpfruːt] (pl **grapefruit** *OR* **-s**) **n** pamplemousse *m*.

grape picking [-ˈpɪkɪŋ] **n** *(U)* vendange *f*, vendanges *fpl*.

grapevine [ˈgreɪpvaɪn] **n** vigne *f* ▸ **on the grapevine** *fig* par le téléphone arabe.

graph [grɑːf] **n** graphique *m*.

graphic [ˈgræfɪk] **adj 1.** [vivid] vivant(e) **2.** ART graphique.
◆ ***graphics*** **npl** graphique *f* ▸ **computer graphics** infographie *f*.

graphically [ˈgræfɪklɪ] **adv 1.** MATHS graphiquement **2.** [vividly] de façon très imagée.

graphic artist **n** graphiste *mf*.

graphic arts **npl** arts *mpl* graphiques.

graphic design **n** design *m* graphique.

graphic designer **n** graphiste *mf*.

graphic equalizer **n** égaliseur *m* graphique.

graphic novel **n** bande *f* dessinée.

graphics card [ˈgræfɪks-] **n** COMPUT carte *f* graphique.

graphite [ˈgræfaɪt] **n** *(U)* graphite *m*, mine *f* de plomb.

graphology [græˈfɒlədʒɪ] **n** graphologie *f*.

graph paper **n** *(U)* papier *m* millimétré.

grapple [ˈgræpl] ◆ ***grapple with*** **vt insep 1.** [person, animal] lutter avec **2.** [problem] se débattre avec, se colleter avec.

grappling iron ['græplɪŋ-] **n** grappin *m*.

grasp [grɑ:sp] ■ **n 1.** [grip] prise *f* ▸ **in** *OR* **within one's grasp** *fig* à portée de la main **2.** [understanding] compréhension *f* ▸ **to have a good grasp of sthg** avoir une bonne connaissance de qqch.
■ **vt 1.** [grip, seize] saisir, empoigner **2.** [understand] saisir, comprendre **3.** [opportunity] saisir.

grasping ['grɑ:spɪŋ] **adj** *pej* avide, cupide.

grass [grɑ:s] ■ **n 1.** *drug sl* & BOT herbe *f* **2.** *UK crime sl* mouchard *m*, indic *m*.
■ **vi** *UK crime sl* moucharder ▸ **to grass on sb** dénoncer qqn.

grasshopper ['grɑ:s,hɒpəʳ] **n** sauterelle *f*.

grassland ['grɑ:slænd] **n** prairie *f*.

grass roots ■ **npl** *fig* base *f*.
■ **comp** du peuple.

grass snake **n** couleuvre *f*.

grassy ['grɑ:sɪ] (comp **-ier**, superl **-iest**) **adj** herbeux (euse), herbu(e).

grate [greɪt] ■ **n** grille *f* de foyer.
■ **vt** râper.
■ **vi** grincer, crisser ▸ **to grate on sb's nerves** taper sur les nerfs de qqn.

grateful ['greɪtfʊl] **adj : to be grateful to sb (for sthg)** être reconnaissant(e) à qqn (de qqch).

gratefully ['greɪtfʊlɪ] **adv** avec reconnaissance.

grater ['greɪtəʳ] **n** râpe *f*.

gratification [,grætɪfɪ'keɪʃn] **n 1.** [pleasure] plaisir *m*, satisfaction *f* **2.** [satisfaction - of wish] assouvissement *m*, satisfaction *f*.

gratify ['grætɪfaɪ] (pt & pp **-ied**) **vt 1.** [please - person] : **to be gratified** être content(e), être satisfait(e) **2.** [satisfy - wish] satisfaire, assouvir.

gratifying ['grætɪfaɪɪŋ] **adj** gratifiant(e).

grating ['greɪtɪŋ] ■ **adj** grinçant(e) / [voix] de crécelle.
■ **n** [grille] grille *f*.

gratis ['grætɪs] ■ **adj** gratuit(e).
■ **adv** gratuitement.

gratitude ['grætɪtju:d] **n** *(U)* **: gratitude (to sb for sthg)** gratitude *f OR* reconnaissance *f* (envers qqn de qqch).

gratuitous [grə'tju:ɪtəs] **adj** *fml* gratuit(e).

gratuitously [grə'tju:ɪtəslɪ] **adv** *fml* gratuitement, sans motif.

gratuity [grə'tju:ɪtɪ] (pl **-ies**) **n** *fml* [tip] pourboire *m*, gratification *f*.

grave[1] [greɪv] ■ **adj** [generally] grave / [concern] sérieux(euse).
■ **n** tombe *f* ▸ **to turn (over) in one's grave** se retourner dans sa tombe.

grave[2] [grɑ:v] **adj** LING **: e grave** e *m* accent grave.

grave accent [grɑ:v-] **n** accent *m* grave.

gravedigger ['greɪv,dɪgəʳ] **n** fossoyeur *m*, -euse *f*.

gravel ['grævl] ■ **n** *(U)* gravier *m*.
■ **comp** de gravier.

gravelled *UK*, ***graveled*** *US* ['grævld] **adj** couvert(e) de gravier.

gravelly ['grævəlɪ] **adj 1.** [like or containing gravel] graveleux(euse) / [road] de gravier / [riverbed] caillouteux (euse) **2.** [voice] rauque, râpeux(euse).

gravestone ['greɪvstəʊn] **n** pierre *f* tombale.

graveyard ['greɪvjɑ:d] **n** cimetière *m*.

graveyard slot **n 1.** RADIO & TV [late in the evening] tranche *f* nocturne **2.** [at the same time as another programme] *tranche horaire pendant laquelle est diffusée une émission à taux de grande écoute sur une chaîne ou une station rivale.*

gravitate ['grævɪteɪt] **vi : to gravitate towards** être attiré(e) par.

gravitational [,grævɪ'teɪʃənl] **adj** gravitationnel(elle), de gravitation.

gravity ['grævətɪ] **n 1.** [force] gravité *f*, pesanteur *f* **2.** [seriousness] gravité *f*.

gravy ['greɪvɪ] **n 1.** *(U)* [meat juice] jus *m* de viande **2.** *US v inf* [easy money] bénef *m*.

gravy boat **n** saucière *f*.

gravy train **n** *inf* **: the gravy train** le fromage, l'assiette *f* au beurre.

gray *US* = ***grey***.

grayscale *US* = ***greyscale***.

graze [greɪz] ■ **vt 1.** [subj: cows, sheep] brouter, paître **2.** [subj: farmer] faire paître **3.** [skin] écorcher, égratigner **4.** [touch lightly] frôler, effleurer.
■ **vi** [cows, sheep] brouter, paître.
■ **n** écorchure *f*, égratignure *f*.

grease [gri:s] ■ **n** graisse *f* ▸ **grease stains** des traces de gras.
■ **vt** graisser.

grease gun **n** pistolet *m* graisseur.

greasepaint ['gri:speɪnt] **n** fard *m* gras.

greaseproof paper [,gri:spru:f-] **n** *(U) UK* papier *m* sulfurisé.

greasy ['gri:sɪ] (comp **-ier**, superl **-iest**) **adj 1.** [covered in grease] graisseux(euse) / [clothes] taché(e) de graisse **2.** [food, skin, hair] gras (grasse).

greasy spoon **n** *inf* gargote *f*.

great [greɪt] ■ **adj 1.** [gen] grand(e) ▸ **great big** énorme ▸ **a great big coward/layabout** un gros lâche/fainéant ▸ **a great friend** un grand ami ▸ **with great pleasure** avec grand plaisir ▸ **a great number of** un grand nombre de **2.** *inf* [splendid] génial(e), formidable ▸ **to feel great** se sentir en pleine forme ▸ **great!** super!, génial! ▸ **she has a great voice** elle a une voix magnifique ▸ **you look great tonight!** tu es magnifique ce soir!
■ **n** grand *m*, -e *f*.

great-aunt **n** grand-tante *f*.

Great Barrier Reef **n : the Great Barrier Reef** la Grande Barrière.

Great Bear **n : the Great Bear** la Grande Ourse.

Great Britain n Grande-Bretagne *f* ▸ **in Great Britain** en Grande-Bretagne.

greatcoat ['greɪtkəʊt] n pardessus *m*.

Great Dane n danois *m*.

Greater ['greɪtər] adj **: Greater Manchester/New York** l'agglomération *f* de Manchester/New York.

great-grandchild n [boy] arrière-petit-fils *m* / [girl] arrière-petite-fille *f*.
◆ ***great-grandchildren*** npl arrière-petits-enfants *mpl*.

great-granddaughter n arrière-petite-fille *f*.

great-grandfather n arrière-grand-père *m*.

great-grandmother n arrière-grand-mère *f*.

great-grandparents npl arrière-grands-parents *mpl*.

great-grandson n arrière-petit-fils *m*.

Great Lakes npl **: the Great Lakes** les Grands Lacs *mpl*.

greatly ['greɪtlɪ] adv [generally] beaucoup / [different] très.

great-nephew n petit-neveu *m*.

greatness ['greɪtnɪs] n grandeur *f*.

great-niece n petite-nièce *f*.

great-uncle n grand-oncle *m*.

Great Wall of China n **: the Great Wall of China** la Grande Muraille (de Chine).

Great War n **: the Great War** la Grande Guerre, la guerre de 1914-18.

Grecian ['gri:ʃn] adj grec (grecque).

Greece [gri:s] n Grèce *f* ▸ **in Greece** en Grèce.

greed [gri:d] n *(U)* **1.** [for food] gloutonnerie *f* **2.** [for money, power] **: greed (for)** avidité *f* (de).

greedily ['gri:dɪlɪ] adv [generally] gloutonnement / [look at food] avec gourmandise.

greediness ['gri:dɪnɪs] = ***greed***.

greedy ['gri:dɪ] (comp -ier, superl -iest) adj **1.** [for food] glouton(onne) **2.** [for money, power] **: greedy for sthg** avide de qqch.

Greek [gri:k] ■ adj grec (grecque) ▸ **the Greek Islands** les îles *fpl* grecques.
■ n **1.** [person] Grec *m*, Grecque *f* **2.** [language] grec *m*.

green [gri:n] ■ adj **1.** [in colour, unripe] vert(e) **2.** [ecological - issue, politics] écologique / [- person] vert(e) **3.** *inf* [inexperienced] inexpérimenté(e), jeune **4.** *inf* [jealous] **: green (with envy)** malade de jalousie.
■ n **1.** [colour] vert *m* ▸ **in green** en vert **2.** GOLF green *m* **3. : village green** pelouse *f* communale.
◆ ***Green*** n POL vert *m*, -e *f*, écologiste *mf* ▸ **the Greens** les Verts, les Écologistes.
◆ ***greens*** npl [vegetables] légumes *mpl* verts.

greenback ['gri:nbæk] n *US inf* billet *m* vert.

green bean n haricot *m* vert.

green belt n *UK* ceinture *f* verte.

Green Beret n *US inf* **: the Green Berets** les bérets *mpl* verts.

green card n **1.** *UK* [for vehicle] carte *f* verte **2.** *US* [residence permit] carte *f* verte, ≃ carte *f* de séjour.

CULTURE

Green Card

La « carte verte » est un document que doit posséder tout citoyen étranger désireux de vivre et de travailler aux États-Unis (il n'est plus de couleur verte aujourd'hui). La procédure d'obtention, longue et compliquée, concerne les proches directs des citoyens américains, notamment les épouses (chaque année, des milliers d'Américains se marient avec des étrangères), les personnes pouvant prouver qu'elles ont un emploi permanent (leurs employeurs peuvent les parrainer), les réfugiés politiques souhaitant changer de statut (ils doivent résider depuis plus d'un an aux États-Unis) et ceux qui investissent dans le pays. Les personnes venant de pays dont le taux d'immigration aux États-Unis est faible peuvent s'inscrire à la « Loterie de la carte verte » : 50 000 cartes sont ainsi délivrées chaque année.

Green Cross Code n *UK code de sécurité routière destiné aux enfants*.

greenery ['gri:nərɪ] n verdure *f*.

greenfield ['gri:nfi:ld] comp **: greenfield site** *terrain non construit à l'extérieur d'une ville*.

greenfinch ['gri:nfɪntʃ] n verdier *m*.

green-fingered [-'fɪŋgəd] adj *UK* qui a la main verte.

green fingers npl *UK* **: to have green fingers** avoir la main verte.

greenfly ['gri:nflaɪ] (pl **greenfly** OR **-ies**) n puceron *m*.

greengage ['gri:ngeɪdʒ] n reine-claude *f*.

greengrocer ['gri:n,grəʊsər] n *esp UK* marchand *m*, -e *f* de légumes ▸ **greengrocer's (shop)** magasin *m* de fruits et légumes.

greenhorn ['gri:nhɔ:n] n *US* **1.** [newcomer] immigrant *m*, -e *f* **2.** [novice] novice *mf*.

greenhouse ['gri:nhaʊs] (pl [-haʊzɪz]) n serre *f*.

greenhouse effect n **: the greenhouse effect** l'effet *m* de serre.

greening ['gri:nɪŋ] n **1.** [attitude] prise *f* de conscience écologique **2.** [politics] politique *f* d'amélioration des espaces verts.

greenish ['gri:nɪʃ] adj verdâtre, qui tire sur le vert.

greenkeeper ['gri:n,ki:pər] n *UK personne chargée de l'entretien d'un terrain de golf ou de bowling*.

Greenland ['gri:nlənd] n Groenland *m* ▸ **in Greenland** au Groenland.

Greenlander ['gri:nləndər] n Groenlandais *m*, -e *f*.

green light n *fig* **: to give sb/sthg the green light** donner le feu vert à qqn/qqch.

green onion n *US* ciboule *f*, cive *f*.

green paper n *UK* POL ≃ livre *m* blanc.

Green Party n : **the Green Party** le Parti écologiste.

green pound n ECON livre *f* verte.

green salad n salade *f* verte.

greenskeeper ['gri:nz,ki:pər] n *US personne chargée de l'entretien d'un terrain de golf ou de bowling.*

green tea n thé *m* vert.

green thumb n *US* : **to have a green thumb** avoir la main verte.

green-thumbed [-'θʌmd] *US* = ***green-fingered***.

greet [gri:t] vt **1.** [say hello to] saluer **2.** [receive] accueillir **3.** [subj: sight, smell] s'offrir à.

greeting ['gri:tɪŋ] n salutation *f*, salut *m*.
◆ ***greetings*** npl : **Christmas/birthday greetings** vœux *mpl* de Noël/d'anniversaire.

greetings card *UK*, ***greeting card*** *US* n carte *f* de vœux.

gregarious [grɪ'geərɪəs] adj sociable.

gremlin ['gremlɪn] n *inf* lutin *m*.

Grenada [grə'neɪdə] n Grenade *f* ▸ **in Grenada** à la Grenade.

grenade [grə'neɪd] n : **(hand) grenade** grenade *f* (à main).

Grenadian [grə'neɪdɪən] ■ adj grenadin(e).
■ n Grenadin *m*, -e *f*.

grenadier [,grenə'dɪər] n grenadier *m*.

grenadine ['grenədi:n] n grenadine *f*.

grew [gru:] pt ➤ ***grow***.

grey *UK*, ***gray*** *US* [greɪ] ■ adj **1.** [in colour] gris(e) **2.** [grey-haired] : **to go grey** grisonner **3.** [unhealthily pale] blême **4.** [dull, gloomy] morne, triste.
■ n gris *m* ▸ **in grey** en gris.

grey area *UK*, ***gray area*** *US* n *fig* zone *f* d'ombre.

grey-haired *UK*, ***gray-haired*** *US* [-'heəd] adj aux cheveux gris.

greyhound ['greɪhaʊnd] n lévrier *m*.

Greyhound® n : **Greyhound buses** *réseau d'autocars couvrant tous les États-Unis.*

greying *UK*, ***graying*** *US* ['greɪɪŋ] adj grisonnant(e).

grey matter *UK*, ***gray matter*** *US* n matière *f* grise.

greyscale *UK*, ***grayscale*** *US* ['greɪskeɪl] n COMPUT échelle *f* de gris.

grey squirrel *UK*, ***gray squirrel*** *US* n écureuil *m* gris.

grid [grɪd] n **1.** [grating] grille *f* **2.** [system of squares] quadrillage *m*.

griddle ['grɪdl] n plaque *f* à cuire.

gridiron ['grɪd,aɪən] n **1.** [in cooking] gril *m* **2.** *US* [game] football *m* américain / [field] terrain *m* de football américan.

gridlock ['grɪdlɒk] n embouteillage *m*.

grief [gri:f] n *(U)* **1.** [sorrow] chagrin *m*, peine *f* **2.** *inf* [trouble] ennuis *mpl*
⏭ **to come to grief** [person] avoir de gros problèmes / [project] échouer, tomber à l'eau ▸ **good grief!** Dieu du ciel!, mon Dieu!

grief-stricken adj accablé(e) de douleur.

grievance ['gri:vns] n grief *m*, doléance *f*.

grieve [gri:v] ■ vt *fml* : **it grieves me to...** cela me peine OR me consterne de...
■ vi [at death] être en deuil ▸ **to grieve for sb/sthg** pleurer qqn/qqch.

grieving ['gri:vɪŋ] n deuil *m*.

grievous ['gri:vəs] adj *fml* [generally] grave / [shock] cruel(elle).

grievous bodily harm n *(U)* coups *mpl* et blessures *fpl*.

grievously ['gri:vəslɪ] adv *fml* [generally] gravement / [wounded] grièvement.

griffin ['grɪfɪn] n MYTH griffon *m*.

grill [grɪl] ■ n **1.** [on cooker, fire] gril *m* **2.** [food] grillade *f*.
■ vt **1.** [cook on grill] griller, faire griller **2.** *inf* [interrogate] cuisiner.

grille [grɪl] n grille *f*.

grim [grɪm] (comp **-mer**, superl **-mest**) adj **1.** [stern - face, expression] sévère / [- determination] inflexible **2.** [cheerless - truth, news] sinistre / [- room, walls] lugubre / [- day] morne, triste.

grimace [grɪ'meɪs] ■ n grimace *f*.
■ vi grimacer, faire la grimace.

grime [graɪm] n *(U)* crasse *f*, saleté *f*.

grimly ['grɪmlɪ] adv sévèrement.

grimness ['grɪmnɪs] n **1.** [sternness] sévérité *f*, gravité *f* **2.** [of story] côté *m* sinistre OR macabre / [of prospects, situation] côté *m* difficile.

grimy ['graɪmɪ] (comp **-ier**, superl **-iest**) adj sale, encrassé(e).

HOW TO ...
express greetings

Bon anniversaire ! / Happy birthday!
Joyeux anniversaire ! / Happy anniversary!
Joyeux Noël ! / Merry Christmas!
Joyeuses Pâques ! / Happy Easter!
Bonne année ! / Happy New Year!
Meilleurs vœux ! / Best wishes!
Toutes mes félicitations ! / Congratulations!
À la tienne OR À la vôtre ! / Cheers!
Bon appétit ! / Enjoy your meal!
Je te souhaite bonne chance dans ton nouveau travail / Here's wishing you all the best in your new job

grin [grɪn] ■ n (large) sourire *m*.
■ vi (pt & pp **-ned**, cont **-ning**) sourire ▸ **to grin at sb/sthg** adresser un large sourire à qqn/qqch ▸ **to grin and bear it** en prendre son parti.

grind [graɪnd] ■ vt (pt & pp **ground**) **1.** [crush] moudre **2.** [press] **: to grind sthg into sthg** [generally] enfoncer qqch dans qqch / [cigarette] écraser qqch dans qqch.
■ vi (pt & pp **ground**) [scrape] grincer.
■ n **1.** [hard, boring work] corvée *f* ▸ **the daily grind** le train-train quotidien **2.** *US inf* [hard worker] bûcheur *m*, -euse *f*, bosseur *m*, -euse *f*.
◆ ***grind down*** vt sep [oppress] opprimer.
◆ ***grind up*** vt sep pulvériser.

grinder ['graɪndəʳ] n moulin *m*.

grinding ['graɪndɪŋ] adj écrasant(e) ▸ **grinding poverty** misère *f* noire.

grindstone ['graɪndstəʊn] n meule *f*.

grinning ['grɪnɪŋ] adj souriant(e).

grip [grɪp] ■ n **1.** [grasp, hold] prise *f* ▸ **to release one's grip on sb/sthg** lâcher qqn/qqch ▸ **to have a good grip on sb/sthg** bien tenir qqn/qqch **2.** [control] contrôle *m* ▸ **he's got a good grip on the situation** il a la situation bien en main ▸ **in the grip of sthg** en proie à qqch ▸ **to get to grips with sthg** s'attaquer à qqch ▸ **to get a grip on o.s.** se ressaisir ▸ **to lose one's grip** perdre les pédales **3.** [adhesion] adhérence *f* **4.** [handle] poignée *f* **5.** [bag] sac *m* (de voyage).
■ vt (pt & pp **-ped**, cont **-ping**) **1.** [grasp] saisir / [subj: tyres] adhérer à **2.** *fig* [imagination, country] captiver.

gripe [graɪp] *inf* ■ n [complaint] plainte *f*.
■ vi **: to gripe (about sthg)** râler OR rouspéter (contre qqch).

griping ['graɪpɪŋ] n *(U) inf* ronchonnements *mpl*, rouspétance *f*.

gripping ['grɪpɪŋ] adj passionnant(e).

grisly ['grɪzlɪ] (comp **-ier**, superl **-iest**) adj [horrible, macabre] macabre.

grist [grɪst] n **: it's all grist to the mill** OR *Can* **for his mill** cela apporte de l'eau à son moulin.

gristle ['grɪsl] n *(U)* nerfs *mpl*.

gristly ['grɪslɪ] (comp **-ier**, superl **-iest**) adj nerveux(euse).

grit [grɪt] ■ n **1.** [stones] gravillon *m* / [in eye] poussière *f* **2.** *inf* [courage] cran *m*.
■ vt (pt & pp **-ted**, cont **-ting**) sabler.
◆ ***grits*** npl *US* gruau *m* de maïs.

gritter ['grɪtəʳ] n *UK* camion *m* de sablage.

gritty ['grɪtɪ] (comp **-ier**, superl **-iest**) adj **1.** [stony] couvert(e) de gravillon **2.** *inf* [brave - person] qui a du cran / [- performance, determination] courageux(euse).

grizzle ['grɪzl] vi *UK inf* [cry fretfully] pleurnicher, geindre.

grizzled ['grɪzld] adj grisonnant(e).

grizzly ['grɪzlɪ] (pl **-ies**) n **: grizzly (bear)** ours *m* gris, grizzli *m*.

groan [grəʊn] ■ n gémissement *m*.
■ vi **1.** [moan] gémir **2.** [creak] grincer, gémir.

grocer ['grəʊsəʳ] n épicier *m*, -ère *f* ▸ **grocer's (shop)** *UK* épicerie *f*.

groceries ['grəʊsərɪz] npl [foods] provisions *fpl*.

grocery ['grəʊsərɪ] (pl **-ies**) n [shop] épicerie *f*.

groggily ['grɒgɪlɪ] adv **1.** [weakly] faiblement **2.** [unsteadily - from exhaustion, from blows] de manière chancelante OR groggy.

groggy ['grɒgɪ] (comp **-ier**, superl **-iest**) adj **1.** [weak] faible, affaibli(e) **2.** [from exhaustion, from blows] groggy *(inv)*.

groin [grɔɪn] n aine *f*.

groom [gru:m] ■ n **1.** [of horses] palefrenier *m*, -ière *f*, garçon *m* d'écurie **2.** [bridegroom] marié *m*.
■ vt **1.** [brush] panser **2.** *fig* [prepare] **: to groom sb (for sthg)** préparer OR former qqn (pour qqch).

grooming ['gru:mɪŋ] n **1.** [of person] toilette *f* / [neat appearance] présentation *f* **2.** [of horse] pansage *m* / [of dog] toilettage *m*.

groove [gru:v] n [in metal, wood] rainure *f* / [in record] sillon *m*.

groovy ['gru:vɪ] adj *inf dated* **1.** [excellent] super, génial(e) **2.** [fashionable] branché(e).

grope [grəʊp] ■ vt **1.** [woman] peloter **2.** [try to find] **: to grope one's way** avancer à tâtons.
■ vi **: to grope (about** *UK* OR **around) for sthg** chercher qqch à tâtons.

gross [grəʊs] ■ adj **1.** [total] brut(e) **2.** *fml* [serious - negligence] coupable / [- misconduct] choquant(e) / [- inequality] flagrant(e) **3.** [coarse, vulgar] grossier(ère) **4.** *inf* [obese] obèse, énorme.
■ n (pl **gross** OR **-es** [-i:z]) grosse *f*, douze douzaines *fpl*.
■ vt gagner brut, faire une recette brute de.

gross domestic product n produit *m* intérieur brut.

gross income n [in accounts] produit *m* brut.

grossly ['grəʊslɪ] adv [seriously] extrêmement, énormément ▸ **grossly overweight** obèse ▸ **grossly unjust** d'une injustice criante.

gross margin n marge *f* brute.

gross national product n produit *m* national brut.

gross profit n bénéfice *m* brut.

grotesque [grəʊ'tesk] adj grotesque.

grotesquely [grəʊ'tesklɪ] adv grotesquement, absurdement.

grotto ['grɒtəʊ] (pl **-es** OR **-s**) n grotte *f*.

grotty ['grɒtɪ] (comp **-ier**, superl **-iest**) adj *UK inf* minable.

grouch [graʊtʃ] *inf* ■ vi rouspéter, ronchonner, grogner ▸ **to grouch about sthg** rouspéter OR ronchonner après qqch, grogner contre qqch.
■ n rouspéteur *m*, -euse *f*.

grouchy ['graʊtʃɪ] (comp **-ier**, superl **-iest**) adj *inf* grognon(onne), maussade.

ground [graʊnd] ■ pt & pp ➤ ***grind***.
■ n **1.** *(U)* [surface of earth] sol *m*, terre *f* ▸ **above ground** en surface ▸ **below ground** sous terre ▸ **on the ground** par terre, au sol ▸ **to be thin on the ground** *UK* être rare

▸ **to get sthg off the ground** *fig* faire démarrer qqch ▸ **to break fresh** *OR* **new ground** *fig* innover, faire œuvre de pionnier ▸ **it suits him down to the ground** ça lui va à merveille, ça lui convient parfaitement ▸ **to cut the ground from under sb's feet** couper l'herbe sous les pieds de qqn ▸ **to go to ground** se terrer ▸ **to run sb/sthg to ground** traquer qqn/qqch ▸ **to stand one's ground** tenir bon, rester sur ses positions ▸ **to drive/to work o.s. into the ground** se tuer au travail ▸ **you're on dangerous ground** vous êtes sur un terrain glissant
2. *(U)* [area of land] terrain *m*
3. [for sport etc] terrain *m*
4. [advantage] **: to gain/lose ground** gagner/perdre du terrain.
■ **vt 1.** [base] **: to be grounded on** *OR* **in sthg** être fondé(e) sur qqch
2. [train] former ▸ **the students are well grounded in computer sciences** les étudiants ont une bonne formation *OR* de bonnes bases en informatique
3. [aircraft, pilot] interdire de vol
4. *inf* [child] priver de sortie
5. *US* ELEC **: to be grounded** être à la masse.
◆ ***grounds*** **npl 1.** [reason] motif *m*, raison *f* ▸ **on the grounds of** pour raison de ▸ **on the grounds that** en raison du fait que ▸ **grounds for sthg** motifs de qqch ▸ **grounds for doing sthg** raisons de faire qqch ▸ **on medical/moral grounds** pour (des) raisons médicales/morales / LAW **: grounds for appeal** voies *fpl* de recours ▸ **grounds for divorce** motif *m* de divorce
2. [land round house] parc *m* / [around block of flats, hospital] terrain *m*
3. [of coffee] marc *m*
4. [area] **: hunting grounds** terrain *m* de chasse ▸ **fishing grounds** lieux *mpl* de pêche.

ground beef **n** *US* steak *m* haché.

ground-breaking **adj** révolutionnaire ▸ **this is ground-breaking technology** c'est une véritable percée technologique.

ground control **n** contrôle *m* au sol.

ground cover **n** *(U)* sous-bois *mpl*.

ground crew **n** personnel *m* au sol.

ground floor **n** rez-de-chaussée *m inv*.

ground-in **adj** [dirt] incrusté(e).

grounding ['graʊndɪŋ] **n : grounding (in)** connaissances *fpl* de base (en).

groundless ['graʊndlɪs] **adj** sans fondement.

ground level **n : at ground level** au rez-de-chaussée, au niveau du sol.

groundnut *UK* ['graʊndnʌt] **n** arachide *f*.

ground plan **n 1.** [of building] plan *m* horizontal **2.** [course of action] plan *m* d'action.

ground rent **n** *UK* redevance *f* foncière.

ground rules **npl** règles *fpl* de base.

groundsheet ['graʊndʃiːt] **n** tapis *m* de sol.

groundskeeper *US* [graʊndz'kiːpə], ***groundsman*** *UK* ['graʊndzmən] (pl **-men** [-mən]) **n** *personne chargée de l'entretien d'un terrain de sport.*

ground staff **n 1.** [at sports ground] personnel *m* d'entretien *(d'un terrain de sport)* **2.** *UK* = ***ground crew***.

groundswell ['graʊndswel] **n** vague *f* de fond.

groundwork ['graʊndwɜːk] **n** *(U)* travail *m* préparatoire.

ground zero **n** hypocentre *m*, point *m* zéro.

group [gruːp] ■ **n** groupe *m*.
■ **vt** grouper, réunir.
■ **vi : to group (together)** se grouper.

group captain **n** *UK* colonel *m* de l'armée de l'air.

groupie ['gruːpɪ] **n** *inf* groupie *f*.

grouping ['gruːpɪŋ] **n** groupement *m*.

group practice **n** cabinet *m* de groupe.

group therapy **n** thérapie *f* de groupe.

grouse [graʊs] ■ **n** (pl **grouse** *OR* **-s**) **1.** [bird] grouse *f*, coq *m* de bruyère **2.** *inf* [complaint] plainte *f*.
■ **vi** *inf* râler, rouspéter.

grout [graʊt] ■ **n** coulis *m* au ciment.
■ **vt** jointoyer.

grove [grəʊv] **n** [group of trees] bosquet *m* ▸ **orange grove** orangerie *f*.

grovel ['grɒvl] (*UK* **-led**, cont **-ling**, *US* **-ed**, cont **-ing**) **vi : to grovel (to sb)** ramper (devant qqn).

grow [grəʊ] (pt **grew**, pp **grown**) ■ **vi 1.** [gen] pousser / [person, animal] grandir / [company, city] s'agrandir / [fears, influence, traffic] augmenter, s'accroître / [problem, idea, plan] prendre de l'ampleur / [economy] se développer ▸ **our love/friendship grew over the years** notre amour/amitié a grandi au fil des ans ▸ **the town grew in importance** la ville a gagné en importance
2. [become] devenir ▸ **to grow bigger** grandir, s'agrandir ▸ **to grow old** vieillir ▸ **to grow tired of sthg** se fatiguer de qqch
3. [do eventually] **: to grow to like sb/sthg** finir par aimer qqn/qqch ▸ **to grow to hate sb/sthg** finir par détester qqn/qqch ▸ **I've grown to respect him** j'ai appris à le respecter.
■ **vt 1.** [plants] faire pousser
2. [hair, beard] laisser pousser ▸ **he's trying to grow a beard** il essaie de se laisser pousser la barbe.
◆ ***grow apart*** **vi** [friends] s'éloigner / [family] se défaire.
◆ ***grow into*** **vt insep** [clothes, shoes] devenir assez grand(e) pour mettre ▸ **he'll soon grow into those shoes** il pourra bientôt mettre ces chaussures, bientôt ces chaussures lui iront.
◆ ***grow on*** **vt insep** *inf* plaire de plus en plus à ▸ **it'll grow on you** cela finira par te plaire.
◆ ***grow out*** **vi** [perm, dye] disparaître.
◆ ***grow out of*** **vt insep 1.** [clothes, shoes] devenir trop grand(e) pour ▸ **he's grown out of most of his clothes** la plupart de ses vêtements ne lui vont plus, il ne rentre plus dans la plupart de ses vêtements
2. [habit] perdre.
◆ ***grow up*** **vi 1.** [become adult] grandir, devenir adulte ▸ **grow up!** ne fais pas l'enfant! ▸ **what do you want to be when you grow up?** que veux-tu faire quand tu seras grand?
2. [develop] se développer.

grow bag **n** *UK* *sac plastique rempli d'engrais dans lequel on fait pousser une plante.*

grower ['grəʊəʳ] n cultivateur *m*, -trice *f*.

growing ['grəʊɪŋ] ■ adj **1.** [plant] croissant(e) / [child] grandissant(e) **2.** [increasing - debt, number, amount] qui augmente / [- friendship, impatience] grandissant(e) ▸ **there are growing fears of a nuclear war** on craint de plus en plus une guerre nucléaire.
■ comp : **wine growing region** région vinicole.

growl [graʊl] ■ n [of animal, engine] grondement *m* / [of person] grognement *m*.
■ vi [animal] grogner, gronder / [engine] vrombir, gronder / [person] grogner.

grown [grəʊn] ■ pp ➤ ***grow***.
■ adj adulte.

grown-up ■ adj **1.** [fully grown] adulte, grand(e) **2.** [mature] mûr(e).
■ n adulte *mf*, grande personne *f*.

growth [grəʊθ] n **1.** [increase - gen] croissance *f* / [- of opposition, company] développement *m* / [- of population] augmentation *f*, accroissement *m* ▸ **intellectual/spiritual growth** développement intellectuel/spirituel ▸ **economic growth** développement *m* OR croissance *f* économique **2.** MED [lump] tumeur *f*, excroissance *f*.

growth area n secteur *m* en expansion.

growth industry n industrie *f* en plein essor OR de pointe.

growth market n marché *m* porteur.

growth rate n taux *m* de croissance.

GRSM (abbr of ***Graduate of the Royal Schools of Music***) n *diplômé du conservatoire de musique britannique*.

grub [grʌb] n **1.** [insect] larve *f* **2.** *inf* [food] bouffe *f*.

grubby ['grʌbɪ] (comp -ier, superl -iest) adj sale, malpropre.

grudge [grʌdʒ] ■ n rancune *f* ▸ **to bear sb a grudge, to bear a grudge against sb** garder rancune à qqn.
■ vt : **to grudge sb sthg** [generally] donner qqch à qqn à contrecœur / [success] en vouloir à qqn à cause de qqch ▸ **to grudge doing sthg** faire qqch à contrecœur.

grudging ['grʌdʒɪŋ] adj peu enthousiaste.

grudgingly ['grʌdʒɪŋlɪ] adv à contrecœur, de mauvaise grâce.

gruel [grʊəl] n bouillie *f* d'avoine.

gruelling *UK*, **grueling** *US* ['grʊəlɪŋ] adj épuisant(e), exténuant(e).

gruesome ['gru:səm] adj horrible, effroyable.

gruff [grʌf] adj **1.** [hoarse] gros (grosse) **2.** [rough, unfriendly] brusque, bourru(e).

gruffly ['grʌflɪ] adv **1.** [of manner] avec brusquerie **2.** [of speech, voice] : **to speak gruffly** parler d'un ton bourru.

gruffness ['grʌfnɪs] n **1.** [of manner] brusquerie *f* **2.** [of speech, voice] ton *m* bourru.

grumble ['grʌmbl] ■ n **1.** [complaint] ronchonnement *m*, grognement *m* **2.** [rumble - of thunder, train] grondement *m* / [- of stomach] gargouillement *m*.
■ vi **1.** [complain] : **to grumble about sthg** rouspéter OR grommeler contre qqch **2.** [rumble - thunder, train] gronder / [- stomach] gargouiller.

grumbling ['grʌmblɪŋ] n **1.** [complaining] rouspétance *f* **2.** [rumbling] grondement *m*.

grump [grʌmp] n *inf* bougon *m*, -onne *f*, ronchon *m*, -onne *f* ▸ **to have the grumps** être de mauvais poil.

grumpily ['grʌmpɪlɪ] adv *inf* en ronchonnant, d'un ton OR air ronchon.

grumpiness ['grʌmpɪnɪs] n *inf* mauvaise humeur *f*, maussaderie *f*, caractère *m* désagréable.

grumpy ['grʌmpɪ] (comp -ier, superl -iest) adj *inf* renfrogné(e).

grunge [grʌndʒ] n **1.** *inf* [dirt] crasse *f* **2.** [music, fashion] grunge *m*.

grungy ['grʌndʒɪ] adj *inf* **1.** [dirty] crasseux(euse) **2.** [style, fashion] grunge *(inv)*.

grunt [grʌnt] ■ n grognement *m*.
■ vi grogner.

GSM (abbr of ***global system for mobile communication***) n TELEC GSM *m*.

G-string n cache-sexe *m inv*.

GU abbr of ***Guam***.

Guadeloupe [,gwɑ:də'lu:p] n la Guadeloupe ▸ **in Guadeloupe** à la Guadeloupe.

Guam [gwɑ:m] n Guam *f*.

guarantee [,gærən'ti:] ■ n garantie *f* ▸ **there's no guarantee that he'll arrive on time** ce n'est pas sûr OR certain qu'il arrivera à l'heure ▸ **this cooker has a five-year guarantee** cette cuisinière est garantie cinq ans ▸ **money-back guarantee** remboursement *m* garanti ▸ **under guarantee** sous garantie.
■ comp : **guarantee agreement** garantie *f*.
■ vt garantir.

guarantor [,gærən'tɔ:ʳ] n *fml* garant *m*, -e *f*, caution *f*.

guard [gɑ:d] ■ n **1.** [person] garde *m* / [in prison] gardien *m*
2. [group of guards] garde *f*
3. [defensive operation] garde *f* ▸ **to stand guard** monter la garde ▸ **to be on guard** être de garde OR de faction ▸ **to be on (one's) guard (against)** se tenir OR être sur ses gardes (contre) ▸ **to catch sb off guard** prendre qqn au dépourvu ▸ **to drop OR to lower one's guard** relâcher sa surveillance ▸ **to keep a prisoner under guard** garder un prisonnier sous surveillance ▸ **the military kept guard over the town** les militaires gardaient la ville ▸ **the prisoners were taken under guard to the courthouse** les prisonniers furent emmenés sous escorte au palais de justice
4. *UK* RAIL chef *m* de train
5. [protective device - for body] protection *f* / [- for fire] garde-feu *m inv*.
■ vt **1.** [protect - building] protéger, garder / [- person] protéger ▸ **the house was heavily guarded** la maison était étroitement surveillée ▸ **to guard sb against danger** protéger qqn d'un danger ▸ **guard the letter with your life** veille bien sur cette lettre
2. [prisoner] garder, surveiller

3. [hide - secret] garder.
◆ ***guard against*** **vt insep** se protéger contre ▸ **to guard against doing sthg** se garder de faire qqch ▸ **how can we guard against such accidents (happening)?** comment éviter OR empêcher (que) de tels accidents (arrivent)?

guard dog **n** chien *m* de garde.

guarded ['gɑ:dɪd] **adj** prudent(e) ▸ **he's always very guarded** il surveille toujours ses paroles.

guardedly ['gɑ:dɪdlɪ] **adv** avec réserve, prudemment.

guardian ['gɑ:djən] **n 1.** [of child] tuteur *m*, -trice *f* **2.** [protector] gardien *m*, -enne *f*, protecteur *m*, -trice *f*.

guardian angel **n** ange *m* gardien.

guardianship ['gɑ:djənʃɪp] **n** tutelle *f*.

guardrail ['gɑ:dreɪl] **n** [on road] barrière *f* de sécurité.

guardroom ['gɑ:drʊm] **n 1.** MIL [for guards] corps *m* de garde **2.** [for prisoners] salle *f* de garde.

guardsman ['gɑ:dzmən] (pl **-men** [-mən]) **n** *UK* soldat *m* de la garde royale / *US* soldat *m* de la garde nationale.

guard's van **n** *UK* wagon *m* du chef de train.

Guatemala [ˌgwɑ:tə'mɑ:lə] **n** Guatemala *m* ▸ **in Guatemala** au Guatemala.

Guatemalan [ˌgwɑ:tə'mɑ:lən] ■ **adj** guatémaltèque.
■ **n** Guatémaltèque *mf*.

guava ['gwɑ:və] [fruit] goyave *f* / [tree] goyavier *m*.

gubernatorial [ˌgu:bənə'tɔ:rɪəl] **adj** *US* de OR du gouverneur ▸ **gubernatorial elections** élections des gouverneurs.

guerilla [gə'rɪlə] = ***guerrilla***.

Guernsey ['gɜ:nzɪ] **n 1.** [place] Guernesey *f* ▸ **in Guernsey** à Guernesey **2.** [sweater] jersey *m* **3.** [cow] vache *f* de Guernesey.

guerrilla [gə'rɪlə] **n** guérillero *m* ▸ **urban guerrilla** guérillero *m* des villes.

guerrilla warfare **n** *(U)* guérilla *f*.

guess [ges] ■ **n** conjecture *f* ▸ **to take a guess** essayer de deviner ▸ **at a (rough) guess, I'd say 200** à vue de nez, je dirais 200 ▸ **it's anybody's guess** Dieu seul le sait, qui sait? ▸ **I'll give you three guesses** devine un peu.
■ **vt** deviner ▸ **guess what?** tu sais quoi? ▸ **guess who I saw in town** devine (un peu) qui j'ai vu en ville.
■ **vi 1.** [conjecture] deviner ▸ **the police guessed right** la police a deviné OR vu juste ▸ **to guess at sthg** deviner qqch ▸ **to keep sb guessing** laisser qqn dans le doute
2. [suppose] **: I guess (so)** je suppose (que oui).

guesstimate ['gestɪmət] **n** *inf* calcul *m* au pif.

guesswork ['geswɜ:k] **n** *(U)* conjectures *fpl*, hypothèses *fpl*.

guest [gest] **n 1.** [gen] invité *m*, -e *f* **2.** [at hotel] client *m*, -e *f*
▸▸ **be my guest!** je t'en prie!

guesthouse ['gesthaʊs] (pl [-haʊzɪz]) **n** pension *f* de famille.

guest of honour *UK*, ***guest of honor*** *US* **n** invité *m*, -e *f* d'honneur.

guestroom ['gestrʊm] **n** chambre *f* d'amis.

guest star **n** invité-vedette *m*, invitée-vedette *f*.

guest worker **n** travailleur immigré *m*, travailleuse immigrée *f*.

guff [gʌf] **n** *(U) inf* bêtises *fpl*, idioties *fpl*.

guffaw [gʌ'fɔ:] ■ **n** gros rire *m*.
■ **vi** rire bruyamment.

GUI (abbr of ***graphical user interface***) **n** COMPUT interface *f* utilisateur graphique.

Guiana [gaɪ'ænə] **n** Guyane *f* ▸ **in Guiana** en Guyane.

guidance ['gaɪdəns] **n** *(U)* **1.** [help] conseils *mpl* **2.** [leadership] direction *f* ▸ **under the guidance of** sous la houlette de.

guide [gaɪd] ■ **n 1.** [person, book] guide *m* **2.** [indication] indication *f* ▸ **as a rough guide** en gros, approximativement ▸ **conversions are given as a guide** les conversions sont données à titre indicatif.
■ **vt 1.** [show by leading] guider **2.** [control] diriger ▸ **he guided the country through some difficult times** il a su conduire le pays durant des périodes difficiles **3.** [influence] **: to be guided by sb/sthg** se laisser guider par qqn/qqch.
◆ ***Guide*** **n** éclaireuse *f*, guide *f*.

guide book, ***guidebook*** ['gaɪdbʊk] **n** guide *m*.

guided missile ['gaɪdɪd-] **n** missile *m* guidé.

guide dog **n** chien *m* d'aveugle.

guided tour ['gaɪdɪd-] **n** visite *f* guidée.

guidelines ['gaɪdlaɪnz] **npl** directives *fpl*, lignes *fpl* directrices.

guiding ['gaɪdɪŋ] **adj** qui sert de guide / [principle] directeur(trice).

guild [gɪld] **n 1.** HIST corporation *f*, guilde *f* **2.** [association] association *f*.

guildhall ['gɪldhɔ:l] **n** salle *f* de réunion d'une corporation.

guile [gaɪl] **n** *(U) liter* ruse *f*, astuce *f*.

guileless ['gaɪllɪs] **adj** *liter* franc (franche).

guillemot ['gɪlɪmɒt] **n** guillemot *m*.

guillotine ['gɪləˌti:n] ■ **n 1.** [for executions] guillotine *f* **2.** [for paper] massicot *m* **3.** *UK* POL *limite de temps fixée pour le vote d'une loi au Parlement*.
■ **vt** [execute] guillotiner.

guilt [gɪlt] **n** culpabilité *f*.

guiltily ['gɪltɪlɪ] **adv** d'un air coupable / [behave] d'une façon coupable.

guilty ['gɪltɪ] (comp **-ier**, superl **-iest**) **adj** coupable ▸ **to be guilty of sthg** être coupable de qqch ▸ **to be found guilty/not guilty** LAW être reconnu coupable/non coupable ▸ **to have a guilty conscience** avoir mauvaise conscience.

guinea ['gɪnɪ] **n** guinée *f*.

Guinea ['gɪnɪ] **n** Guinée *f* ▶ **in Guinea** en Guinée.

Guinea-Bissau [-bɪ'səʊ] **n** Guinée-Bissau *f*.

guinea fowl **n** pintade *f*.

guinea pig **n** cobaye *m*.

guise [gaɪz] **n** *fml* apparence *f*.

guitar [gɪ'tɑːr] **n** guitare *f*.

guitarist [gɪ'tɑːrɪst] **n** guitariste *mf*.

gulag ['guːlæg] **n** goulag *m*.

gulch [gʌltʃ] **n** *US* ravin *m*.

gulf [gʌlf] **n** **1.** [sea] golfe *m* **2.** [breach, chasm] **: gulf (between)** abîme *m* (entre).
◆ ***Gulf*** **n : the Gulf** le Golfe.

Gulf States **npl : the Gulf States** [in US] les États du golfe du Mexique / [around Persian Gulf] les États du Golfe.

Gulf Stream **n : the Gulf Stream** le Gulf Stream.

gull [gʌl] **n** mouette *f*.

gullet ['gʌlɪt] **n** [of person] œsophage *m* / [of bird] gosier *m*.

gulley ['gʌlɪ] (pl -s) = ***gully***.

gullibility [ˌgʌlə'bɪlətɪ] **n** crédulité *f*.

gullible ['gʌləbl] **adj** crédule.

gully ['gʌlɪ] (pl **-ies**) **n** **1.** [valley] ravine *f* **2.** [ditch] rigole *f*.

gulp [gʌlp] ■ **n** [of drink] grande gorgée *f* / [of food] grosse bouchée *f*.
■ **vt** avaler.
■ **vi** avoir la gorge nouée.
◆ ***gulp down*** **vt sep** avaler.

gum [gʌm] ■ **n** **1.** [chewing gum] chewing-gum *m* **2.** [adhesive] colle *f*, gomme *f* **3.** ANAT gencive *f*.
■ **vt** (pt & pp **-med**, cont **-ming**) coller.

gumboil ['gʌmbɔɪl] **n** abcès *m* à la gencive.

gumboots ['gʌmbuːts] **npl** *UK dated* bottes *fpl* de caoutchouc.

gumption ['gʌmpʃn] **n** *inf* **1.** [common sense] jugeote *f* **2.** [determination] cran *m*.

gumshield ['gʌmʃiːld] **n** protège-dents *m inv*.

gumshoe ['gʌmʃuː] **n** *US crime sl* privé *m*.

gun [gʌn] (pt & pp **-ned**, cont **-ning**) **n** **1.** [weapon - small] revolver *m* / [- rifle] fusil *m* / [- large] canon *m* ▶ **to stick to one's guns** tenir bon, ne pas en démordre **2.** [starting pistol] pistolet *m* ▶ **to jump the gun** agir prématurément **3.** [tool] pistolet *m* / [for staples] agrafeuse *f*.
◆ ***gun down*** **vt sep** abattre.

gunboat ['gʌnbəʊt] **n** canonnière *f*.

gundog ['gʌndɒg] **n** chien *m* de chasse.

gunfight ['gʌnfaɪt] **n** fusillade *f*.

gunfire ['gʌnfaɪər] **n** *(U)* coups *mpl* de feu.

gunge [gʌndʒ] **n** *(U) UK inf* matière *f* poisseuse.

gung-ho [ˌgʌŋ'həʊ] **adj** *inf* trop enthousiaste.

gunk [gʌŋk] **n** *inf* matière *f* poisseuse.

gunman ['gʌnmən] (pl **-men** [-mən]) **n** personne *f* armée.

gunner ['gʌnər] **n** artilleur *m*.

gunpoint ['gʌnpɔɪnt] **n : at gunpoint** sous la menace d'un fusil OR pistolet.

gunpowder ['gʌnˌpaʊdər] **n** poudre *f* à canon.

gunrunning ['gʌnˌrʌnɪŋ] **n** trafic *m* d'armes.

gunshot ['gʌnʃɒt] **n** [firing of gun] coup *m* de feu.

gunsmith ['gʌnsmɪθ] **n** armurier *m*, -ière *f*.

gurgle ['gɜːgl] ■ **vi** **1.** [water] glouglouter **2.** [baby] gazouiller.
■ **n** **1.** [of water] glouglou *m* **2.** [of baby] gazouillis *m*.

guru ['gʊruː] **n** gourou *mf*, guru *mf*.

gush [gʌʃ] ■ **n** jaillissement *m*.
■ **vt** [blood] répandre / [oil] cracher.
■ **vi** **1.** [flow out] jaillir **2.** *pej* [enthuse] s'exprimer de façon exubérante.

gushing ['gʌʃɪŋ] **adj** *pej* trop exubérant(e).

gusset ['gʌsɪt] **n** gousset *m*.

gust [gʌst] ■ **n** rafale *f*, coup *m* de vent.
■ **vi** souffler par rafales.

gusto ['gʌstəʊ] **n : with gusto** avec enthousiasme.

gusty ['gʌstɪ] (comp **-ier**, superl **-iest**) **adj** venteux(euse), de grand vent / [wind] qui souffle par rafales.

gut [gʌt] ■ **n** MED intestin *m*.
■ **vt** (pt & pp **-ted**, cont **-ting**) **1.** [remove organs from] vider **2.** [destroy] éventrer.
◆ ***guts*** **npl** *inf* **1.** [intestines] intestins *mpl* ▶ **to hate sb's guts** ne pas pouvoir piffer qqn, ne pas pouvoir voir qqn en peinture **2.** [courage] cran *m* ▶ **to have guts** avoir du cran.

gut reaction **n** réaction *f* viscérale.

gutsy ['gʌtsɪ] (comp **-ier**, superl **-iest**) **adj** *inf* **1.** [courageous] qui a du cran **2.** [powerful - film, language, novel] qui a du punch, musclé(e) ▶ **a gutsy singer** un chanteur qui a des tripes.

gutted ['gʌtɪd] **adj** *UK v inf* **: to be** OR **to feel gutted** en être malade.

gutter ['gʌtər] **n** **1.** [ditch] rigole *f* **2.** [on roof] gouttière *f*.

guttering ['gʌtərɪŋ] **n** *(U) esp UK* gouttières *fpl*.

gutter press **n** *UK pej* presse *f* à sensation.

guttural ['gʌtərəl] **adj** guttural(e).

guv [gʌv] **n** *UK inf* chef *m*.

guy [gaɪ] **n** **1.** *inf* [man] type *m* **2.** [person] copain *m*, copine *f* **3.** *UK* [dummy] *effigie de Guy Fawkes*.

Guyana [gaɪ'ænə] **n** Guyana *m* ▶ **in Guyana** au Guyana.

Guy Fawkes' Night [-'fɔːks-] **n** *fête célébrée le 5 novembre en Grande-Bretagne*.

guyline *US* ['gaɪlaɪn], **guy rope** **n** corde *f* de tente.

guzzle ['gʌzl] ■ **vt** [food] bâfrer / [drink] lamper.
■ **vi** s'empiffrer.

gym [dʒɪm] **n** *inf* **1.** [gymnasium] gymnase *m* **2.** [exercises] gym *f*.

gymkhana [dʒɪm'kɑːnə] **n** *esp UK* gymkhana *m*.

gymnasium [dʒɪm'neɪzjəm] (pl **-iums** *OR* **-ia** [-jə]) **n** gymnase *m*.

gymnast ['dʒɪmnæst] **n** gymnaste *mf*.

gymnastic [dʒɪm'næstɪk] **adj** [exercises] de gymnastique / [ability] de gymnaste.

gymnastics [dʒɪm'næstɪks] **n** *(U)* gymnastique *f*.

gym shoes **npl** (chaussures *fpl* de) tennis *mpl*.

gymslip ['dʒɪm,slɪp] **n** *UK* tunique *f*.

gynaecological *UK*, ***gynecological*** *US* [,gaɪnəkə'lɒdʒɪkl] **adj** gynécologique.

gynaecologist *UK*, ***gynecologist*** *US* [,gaɪnə'kɒlədʒɪst] **n** gynécologue *mf*.

gynaecology *UK*, ***gynecology*** *US* [,gaɪnə'kɒlədʒɪ] **n** gynécologie *f*.

gyp [dʒɪp] *US* ■ **vt** escroquer.
■ **n** escroc.

gypsy ['dʒɪpsɪ] (pl **-ies**) = ***gipsy***.

gyrate [dʒaɪ'reɪt] **vi** tournoyer.

gyration [dʒaɪ'reɪʃn] **n** mouvement *m* giratoire.

gyroscope ['dʒaɪrəskəʊp] **n** gyroscope *m*.

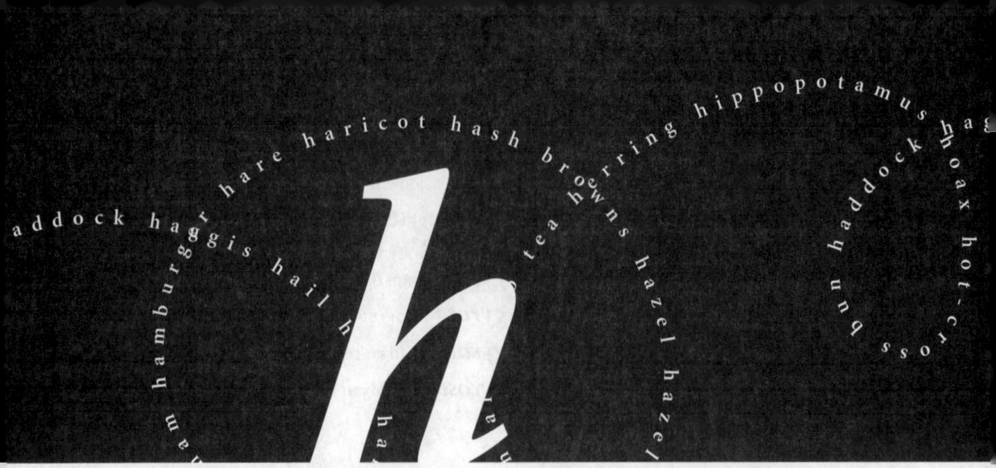

h [eɪtʃ] (pl h's *or* hs), ***H*** (pl H's *or* Hs) **n** [letter] h *m inv*, H *m inv*.

h & c abbr of ***hot and cold (water)***.

ha [hɑ:] **excl** ha!

habeas corpus [ˌheɪbjəsˈkɔ:pəs] **n** habeas corpus *m*.

haberdashery [ˈhæbədæʃərɪ] (pl -ies) **n** *UK* mercerie *f*.

habit [ˈhæbɪt] **n 1.** [customary practice] habitude *f* ▸ **out of habit** par habitude ▸ **to be in/get into the habit of doing sthg** avoir/prendre l'habitude de faire qqch ▸ **to make a habit of doing sthg** avoir l'habitude de faire qqch **2.** [garment] habit *m*.

habitable [ˈhæbɪtəbl] **adj** habitable.

habitat [ˈhæbɪtæt] **n** habitat *m*.

habitation [hæbɪˈteɪʃn] **n** habitation *f*.

habit-forming [-ˌfɔ:mɪŋ] **adj** qui crée une accoutumance.

habitual [həˈbɪtʃʊəl] **adj 1.** [usual, characteristic] habituel(elle) **2.** [regular] invétéré(e).

habitually [həˈbɪtʃʊəlɪ] **adv** habituellement.

habituate [həˈbɪtʃʊeɪt] **vt** *fml* **: to habituate o.s./sb to sthg** s'habituer/habituer qqn à qqch.

hack [hæk] ■ **n 1.** [writer] écrivailleur *m*, -euse *f* **2.** *US inf* [taxi] taxi *m*.
■ **vt 1.** [cut] tailler **2.** COMPUT pirater.
■ **vi** [cut] taillader.
◆ ***hack into*** **vt insep** COMPUT pirater.
◆ ***hack through*** **vt insep : to hack through sthg** se frayer un chemin dans qqch à coups de hache.

hacker [ˈhækəʳ] **n : (computer) hacker** pirate *m* informatique.

hackie [ˈhækɪ] **n** *US inf* chauffeur *m* de taxi.

hacking [ˈhækɪŋ] **n** COMPUT piratage *f* informatique.

hacking cough **n** toux *f* sèche et douloureuse.

hacking jacket **n** veste *f* de cheval.

hackles [ˈhæklz] **npl** [on animal] plumes *fpl* du cou ▸ **to make sb's hackles rise, to get sb's hackles up** hérisser qqn.

hackney cab *UK*, ***hackney carriage*** [ˈhæknɪ-] **n** *fml* [taxi] taxi *m*.

hackneyed [ˈhæknɪd] **adj** rebattu(e).

hacksaw [ˈhæksɔ:] **n** scie *f* à métaux.

had (*weak form* [həd], *strong form* [hæd]) **pt & pp** ➤ ***have***.

haddock [ˈhædək] (pl **haddock**) **n** églefin *m*, aiglefin *m*.

hadn't [ˈhædnt] = ***had not***.

haematology *UK*, ***hematology*** *US* [ˌhi:məˈtɒlədʒɪ] **n** hématologie *f*.

haemoglobin *UK*, ***hemoglobin*** *US* [ˌhi:məˈgləʊbɪn] **n** hémoglobine *f*.

haemophilia *UK*, ***hemophilia*** *US* [ˌhi:məˈfɪlɪə] **n** hémophilie *f*.

haemophiliac *UK*, ***hemophiliac*** *US* [ˌhi:məˈfɪlɪæk] **n** hémophile *mf*.

haemorrhage *UK*, ***hemorrhage*** *US* [ˈhemərɪdʒ]
■ **n** hémorragie *f*.
■ **vi** faire une hémorragie.

haemorrhoids *UK*, ***hemorrhoids*** *US* [ˈhemərɔɪdz] **npl** hémorroïdes *fpl*.

hag [hæg] **n** *pej* vieille sorcière *f*.

haggard [ˈhægəd] **adj** [face] défait(e) / [person] abattu(e).

haggis [ˈhægɪs] **n** *plat typique écossais fait d'une panse de brebis farcie, le plus souvent servie avec des navets et des pommes de terre.*

haggle [ˈhægl] **vi** marchander ▸ **to haggle over** *or* **about sthg** marchander qqch ▸ **to haggle with sb** marchander avec qqn.

haggling [ˈhæglɪŋ] **n** marchandage *m*.

Hague [heɪg] **n : The Hague** La Haye.

hail [heɪl] ■ **n** METEOR grêle *f* / *fig* pluie *f*.
■ **vt 1.** [call] héler **2.** [acclaim] **: to hail sb/sthg as sthg** acclamer qqn/qqch comme qqch.
■ **impers vb** grêler.

hailstone [ˈheɪlstəʊn] **n** grêlon *m*.

hailstorm [ˈheɪlstɔ:m] **n** averse *f* de grêle.

hair [heəʳ] **n 1.** *(U)* [on human head] cheveux *mpl* ▸ **to do one's hair** se coiffer ▸ **I like the way you've done your hair** j'aime bien la façon dont tu t'es coiffé ▸ **to let one's hair down** se défouler ▸ **to make sb's hair stand on end**

faire dresser les cheveux sur la tête à qqn ▸ **to wash one's hair** se laver les cheveux *OR* la tête ▸ **she put her hair up** elle a relevé ses cheveux ▸ **keep him out of my hair** *inf* fais en sorte que je ne l'aie pas dans les jambes ▸ **she didn't turn a hair** elle n'a pas cillé **2.** *(U)* [on animal, human skin] poils *mpl* **3.** [individual hair - on head] cheveu *m* / [- on skin] poil *m* ▸ **to split hairs** couper les cheveux en quatre.

hairband ['heəbænd] **n** bandeau *m*.

hairbrush ['heəbrʌʃ] **n** brosse *f* à cheveux.

hairclip ['heəklɪp] **n** barrette *f*.

haircut ['heəkʌt] **n** coupe *f* de cheveux.

hairdo ['heədu:] (pl -s) **n** *inf dated* coiffure *f*.

hairdresser ['heə,dresəʳ] **n** coiffeur *m*, -euse *f* ▸ **hairdresser's (salon)** salon *m* de coiffure.

hairdressing ['heə,dresɪŋ] ■ **n** coiffure *f*.
■ **comp** de coiffure.

hairdryer ['heə,draɪəʳ] **n** [handheld] sèche-cheveux *m inv* / [over the head] casque *m*.

-haired [heəd] **suffix : long/short-haired** [person] aux cheveux longs/courts / [animal] à poil(s) long(s)/court(s) ▸ **wire-haired** [dog] à poil(s) dur(s).

hair gel **n** gel *m* coiffant.

hairgrip ['heəgrɪp] **n** *UK* pince *f* à cheveux.

hairless ['heəlɪs] **adj** [head] chauve, sans cheveux / [face] glabre / [body] peu poilu(e) / [animal] sans poils / [leaf] glabre.

hairline ['heəlaɪn] **n** naissance *f* des cheveux.

hairline fracture **n** fêlure *f*.

hairnet ['heənet] **n** filet *m* à cheveux.

hairpiece ['heəpi:s] **n** postiche *m*.

hairpin ['heəpɪn] **n** épingle *f* à cheveux.

hairpin bend *UK*, ***hairpin turn*** *US* **n** virage *m* en épingle à cheveux.

hair-raising [-,reɪzɪŋ] **adj** à faire dresser les cheveux sur la tête / [journey] effrayant(e).

hair remover [-rɪ,mu:vəʳ] **n** (crème *f*) dépilatoire *m*.

hair restorer **n** lotion *f* capillaire régénératrice.

hair's breadth **n : by a hair's breadth** d'un cheveu, de justesse.

hair slide **n** *UK* barrette *f*.

hair splitting **n** ergotage *m*.

hairspray ['heəspreɪ] **n** laque *f*.

hairstyle ['heəstaɪl] **n** coiffure *f*.

hairstylist ['heə,staɪlɪst] **n** coiffeur *m*, -euse *f*.

hairy ['heərɪ] (comp **-ier**, superl **-iest**) **adj 1.** [covered in hair] velu(e), poilu(e) **2.** *inf* [frightening] à faire dresser les cheveux sur la tête.

Haiti ['heɪtɪ] **n** Haïti *m* ▸ **in Haiti** à Haïti.

Haitian ['heɪʃn] ■ **adj** haïtien(enne).
■ **n** Haïtien *m*, -enne *f*.

hake [heɪk] (pl **hake** *OR* **-s**) **n** colin *m*, merluche *f*.

halal [hə'lɑ:l] = ***hallal***.

halcyon ['hælsɪən] **adj** paradisiaque.

hale [heɪl] **adj : hale and hearty** en pleine forme.

half [*UK* hɑ:f, *US* hæf] ■ **adj** demi(e) ▸ **half a dozen** une demi-douzaine ▸ **half an hour** une demi-heure ▸ **half a pound** une demi-livre ▸ **half my life** la moitié de ma vie ▸ **to travel half fare** voyager à demi-tarif ▸ **to have half a mind to do sthg** *inf* avoir bien envie de faire qqch.
■ **adv 1.** [gen] à moitié ▸ **to be half full of sthg** être à moitié rempli de qqch ▸ **half English** à moitié anglais(e) ▸ **half-and-half** moitié-moitié ▸ **not half!** *UK inf* tu parles! ▸ **it's not half cold today!** il fait rudement *OR* sacrément froid aujourd'hui!
2. [by half] de moitié ▸ **to be half as big/fast as sb/sthg** être moitié moins grand(e)/rapide que qqn/qqch ▸ **to be half as big again (as sb/sthg)** être moitié plus grand(e) (que qqn/qqch)
3. [in telling the time] **: half past ten** *UK*, **half after ten** *US* dix heures et demie ▸ **it's half past** il est la demie.
■ **n** (pl **halves** *(senses 1 and 2)* [*UK* hɑ:vz, *US* hævz] **halves** *OR* **halfs** *(pl senses 3, 4 and 5)*) **1.** [gen] moitié *f* ▸ **three and a half years** trois ans et demi ▸ **it cuts the journey time in half** cela réduit de moitié la durée du voyage ▸ **by half** de moitié ▸ **in half** en deux ▸ **to be too clever by half** *UK* être un peu trop malin(igne) ▸ **he doesn't do things by halves** *UK* il ne fait pas les choses à moitié ▸ **to go halves (with sb)** partager (avec qqn) ▸ **that was a walk and a half!** *inf* c'était une sacrée promenade!
2. SPORT [of match] mi-temps *f*
3. SPORT [halfback] demi *m*
4. *UK* [of beer] demi *m*
5. *UK* [child's ticket] demi-tarif *m*, tarif *m* enfant ▸ **two and two halves, please** [on bus, train] deux billets tarif normal et deux billets demi-tarif, s'il vous plaît.
■ **pron** la moitié ▸ **half of them** la moitié d'entre eux ▸ **I wrote half of it** j'en ai écrit la moitié.

halfback ['hɑ:fbæk] **n** SPORT demi *m*.

half-baked [-'beɪkt] **adj** *inf fig* [idea] à la noix / [project] mal conçu(e).

half board **n** *esp UK* demi-pension *f*.

half-breed ■ **adj** métis(isse).
■ **n** métis *m*, -isse *f (attention: le terme 'half-breed' est considéré comme raciste)*.

half-brother **n** demi-frère *m*.

half-caste [-kɑ:st] ■ **adj** métis(isse).
■ **n** métis *m*, -isse *f (attention: le terme 'half-caste' est considéré comme raciste)*.

half cock **n : to go off (at) half cock** *UK* mal partir.

half-day **n** demi-journée *f*.

half-dozen **n** demi-douzaine *f* ▸ **a half-dozen eggs** une demi-douzaine d'œufs.

half-eaten **adj** à moitié mangé(e).

half-full **adj** à moitié *OR* à demi plein(e).

half-hearted [-'hɑ:tɪd] **adj** sans enthousiasme.

half-heartedly [-'hɑ:tɪdlɪ] **adv** sans enthousiasme.

half hour **n** demi-heure *f*.
◆ ***half-hour*** **adj** = ***half-hourly***.

half-hourly **adj** de toutes les demi-heures.
◆ ***half-hourly*** **adv** toutes les demi-heures.

half-joking **adj** mi-figue, mi-raisin.

half-jokingly **adv** d'un air mi-figue, mi-raisin.

half-length **adj** [coat, jacket] court(e).
half-light **n** pénombre *f*.
half-marathon **n** semi-marathon *m*.
half-mast **n : at half-mast** [flag] en berne.
half measure **n** demi-mesure *f*.
half moon **n** demi-lune *f*.
half-naked **adj** à moitié nu(e).
half note **n** *US* MUS blanche *f*.
half-open ■ **adj** [eyes, door, window] entrouvert(e).
■ **vt** [eyes, door, window] entrouvrir.
halfpenny ['heɪpnɪ] (pl **-pennies** *OR* **-pence** [-pens]) **n** *UK* demi-penny *m*.
half-price **adj** à moitié prix.
◆ ***half price*** **adv** moitié prix.
half-shut **adj** [eyes, door, window] mi-clos(e), à moitié fermé(e).
half-sister **n** demi-sœur *f*.
half step **n** *US* MUS demi-ton *m*.
half term **n** *UK* congé *m* de mi-trimestre.
half-time **n** *(U)* mi-temps *f*.
halftone **n** *US* MUS demi-ton *m*.
half-truth **n** demi-vérité *f*.
half-volley ■ **n** [in tennis] demi-volée *f*.
■ **vt** [in tennis] **: he half-volleyed the ball to the baseline** d'une demi-volée, il a envoyé la balle sur la ligne de fond.
halfway [hɑ:f'weɪ] ■ **adj** à mi-chemin.
■ **adv 1.** [in space] à mi-chemin **2.** [in time] à la moitié ▸▸ **to meet sb halfway** arriver à un compromis avec qqn.
halfway house **n 1.** [on journey] (auberge *f*) relais *m* **2.** [for rehabilitation] centre *m* de réadaptation *(pour anciens détenus, malades mentaux, drogués etc)* **3.** *fig* [halfway stage] (stade *m* de) transition *f* / [compromise] compromis *m*.
half-wit **n** *pej* faible *mf* d'esprit.
half-yearly *UK* **adj** semestriel(elle).
◆ ***half yearly*** **adv** tous les six mois.
halibut ['hælɪbət] (pl **halibut** *OR* **-s**) **n** flétan *m*.
halitosis [ˌhælɪ'təʊsɪs] **n** mauvaise haleine *f*.
hall [hɔ:l] **n 1.** [in house] vestibule *m*, entrée *f* **2.** [meeting room, building] salle *f* **3.** *UK* UNIV [hall of residence] résidence *f* universitaire ▸ **to live in hall** loger en cité universitaire **4.** [country house] manoir *m*.
hallal [hə'lɑ:l] ■ **adj** hallal *(inv)*.
■ **n** viande *f* hallal.
halleluja [ˌhælɪ'lu:jə] **excl** alléluia!
hallmark ['hɔ:lmɑ:k] **n 1.** [typical feature] marque *f* **2.** [on metal] poinçon *m*.
hallo [hə'ləʊ] *UK* = ***hello***.
hall of residence (pl **halls of residence**) **n** *UK* UNIV résidence *f* universitaire.
hallowed ['hæləʊd] **adj** [respected] consacré(e).
Hallowe'en, ***Halloween*** [ˌhæləʊ'i:n] **n** Halloween *f* *(fête des sorcières et des fantômes)*.
hallstand ['hɔ:lstænd] **n** portemanteau *m*.
hallucinate [hə'lu:sɪneɪt] **vi** avoir des hallucinations.
hallucination [ˌhəlu:sɪ'neɪʃn] **n** hallucination *f*.
hallucinatory [hə'lu:sɪnətrɪ] **adj** hallucinatoire.
hallucinogenic [həˌlu:sɪnə'dʒenɪk] **adj** hallucinogène.
hallway ['hɔ:lweɪ] **n** vestibule *m*.
halo ['heɪləʊ] (pl **-es** *OR* **-s**) **n** [of saint] nimbe *m* / ASTRON halo *m*.
halo effect **n** effet *m* de halo.
halogen ['hælədʒen] ■ **n** halogène *m*.
■ **comp** halogène.
halt [hɔ:lt] ■ **n** [stop] **: to come to a halt** [vehicle] s'arrêter, s'immobiliser / [activity] s'interrompre ▸ **to grind to a halt** [stop moving] s'arrêter / [stop working] péricliter ▸ **to call a halt to sthg** mettre fin à qqch.
■ **vt** arrêter.
■ **vi** s'arrêter.
halter ['hɔ:ltəʳ] **n** [for horse] licou *m*.
halterneck ['hɔ:ltənek], *US* ***halter top*** **adj** dos nu *(inv)*.
halting ['hɔ:ltɪŋ] **adj** hésitant(e).
haltingly ['hɔ:ltɪŋlɪ] **adv** [say, speak] de façon hésitante.
halva, ***halwa*** ['hælvə] **n** *(U)* halva *m*.
halve [*UK* hɑ:v, *US* hæv] **vt 1.** [reduce by half] réduire de moitié **2.** [divide] couper en deux.
halves [*UK* hɑ:vz, *US* hævz] **npl** ➤ ***half***.
ham [hæm] ■ **n 1.** [meat] jambon *m* **2.** *pej* [actor] cabotin *m*, -e *f* **3.** [radio fanatic] **: (radio) ham** radioamateur *m*.
■ **comp** au jambon.
■ **vt** (pt & pp **-med**, cont **-ming**) **: to ham it up** cabotiner.
Hamburg ['hæmbɜ:g] **n** Hambourg.
hamburger ['hæmbɜ:gəʳ] **n 1.** [burger] hamburger *m* **2.** *(U)* *US* [mince] viande *f* hachée.
ham-fisted [-'fɪstɪd] **adj** maladroit(e).
hamlet ['hæmlɪt] **n** hameau *m*.
hammer ['hæməʳ] ■ **n** marteau *m*.
■ **vt 1.** [with tool] marteler / [nail] enfoncer à coups de marteau **2.** *fig* [with fist] marteler du poing **3.** *inf* [defeat] battre à plates coutures.
■ **vi 1.** [with tool] frapper au marteau **2.** [with fist] **: to hammer (on)** cogner du poing (à) **3.** *fig* **: to hammer away at** [task] s'acharner à.
◆ ***hammer into*** **vt sep** *fig* **: to hammer sthg into sb** faire entrer qqch dans la tête de qqn.
◆ ***hammer out*** ■ **vt insep** [agreement, solution] parvenir finalement à.
■ **vt sep** [dent] enlever à coups de marteau.
hammock ['hæmək] **n** hamac *m*.
hammy ['hæmɪ] (comp **-ier**, superl **-iest**) **adj** *inf* cabotin(e).
hamper ['hæmpəʳ] ■ **n 1.** *UK* [for food] panier *m* d'osier **2.** *US* [for laundry] panier *m* à linge sale.
■ **vt** gêner.
hamster ['hæmstəʳ] **n** hamster *m*.
hamstring ['hæmstrɪŋ] ■ **n** tendon *m* du jarret.
■ **vt** paralyser.

hand [hænd] ■ **n 1.** [part of body] main *f* ▸ **to hold hands** se tenir la main ▸ **she's asked me to go along and hold her hand** *fig* elle m'a demandé de l'accompagner pour lui donner du courage ▸ **hand in hand** [people] main dans la main ▸ **hands off!** bas les pattes!, pas touche! ▸ **hands up!** haut les mains! ▸ **by hand** à la main ▸ **to ask for sb's hand in marriage** demander la main de qqn, demander qqn en mariage ▸ **at the hands of** aux mains de ▸ **with one's bare hands** à mains nues ▸ **to be on one's hands and knees** être à quatre pattes ▸ **to change hands** [car, house] changer de propriétaire ▸ **to force sb's hand** forcer la main à qqn ▸ **to get** ***OR*** **lay one's hands on** mettre la main sur ▸ **to get out of hand** échapper à tout contrôle ▸ **to give sb a free hand** donner carte blanche à qqn ▸ **to go hand in hand** [things] aller de pair ▸ **to be good with one's hands** être adroit de ses mains ▸ **to be in good** ***OR*** **safe hands** être en de bonnes mains ▸ **can I leave this in your hands?** puis-je te demander de t'en occuper? ▸ **to have a hand in sthg** être impliqué dans qqch ▸ **to have a hand in doing sthg** contribuer à faire qqch ▸ **my hands are tied** *fig* j'ai les mains liées ▸ **to have a situation in hand** avoir une situation en main ▸ **to have one's hands full** avoir du pain sur la planche ▸ **to have time in hand** avoir du temps libre ▸ **to live from hand to mouth** arriver tout juste à joindre les deux bouts ▸ **to make money hand over fist** gagner de l'argent par millions ▸ **to need a firm hand** avoir besoin d'être sérieusement pris(e) en main ▸ **to take sb in hand** prendre qqn en main ▸ **to try one's hand at sthg** s'essayer à qqch ▸ **to wait on sb hand and foot** être aux petits soins pour qqn ▸ **to wash one's hands of sthg** se laver les mains de qqch **2.** [help] coup *m* de main ▸ **do you need a hand (with that)?** as-tu besoin d'un coup de main? ▸ **to give** ***OR*** **lend sb a hand (with sthg)** donner un coup de main à qqn (pour faire qqch) **3.** [worker] ouvrier *m*, -ère *f* ▸ **old hand** expert *m*, vieux *m* de la vieille ▸ **to be an old hand at sthg** avoir une vaste expérience de qqch **4.** [of clock, watch] aiguille *f* **5.** [handwriting] écriture *f* **6.** [of cards] jeu *m*, main *f* ▸ **to overplay one's hand** *fig* trop présumer de ses capacités ▸ **to show** ***OR*** **to reveal one's hand** *fig* dévoiler son jeu.

■ **vt : to hand sthg to sb, to hand sb sthg** passer qqch à qqn.

◆ ***(close) at hand*** **adv** proche.

◆ ***on hand*** **adv** disponible.

◆ ***on the other hand*** **conj** d'autre part.

◆ ***out of hand*** **adv** [completely] d'emblée.

◆ ***to hand*** **adv** à portée de la main, sous la main.

◆ ***hand down*** **vt sep** transmettre ▸ **the necklace has been handed down from mother to daughter for six generations** le collier s'est transmis de mère en fille depuis six générations.

◆ ***hand in*** **vt sep** remettre ▸ **to hand in one's resignation** remettre sa démission.

◆ ***hand on*** **vt sep** transmettre.

◆ ***hand out*** **vt sep** distribuer.

◆ ***hand over*** ■ **vt sep 1.** [baton, money] remettre ▸ **he was handed over to the French police** il a été livré à la ***OR*** aux mains de la police française **2.** [responsibility, power] transmettre.

■ **vi : to hand over (to)** passer le relais (à).

handbag ['hændbæg] **n** sac *m* à main.

handball ['hændbɔːl] **n** [game] handball *m*.

handbill ['hændbɪl] **n** prospectus *m*.

handbook ['hændbʊk] **n** [for car, machine] manuel *m* / *UK* [for tourist] guide *m*.

handbrake ['hændbreɪk] **n** frein *m* à main.

handclap ['hændklæp] **n** *UK* **: to give the slow handclap** *taper des mains lentement pour manifester sa désapprobation.*

handcrafted ['hændkrɑːftɪd] **adj** fait(e) (à la) main.

handcuff ['hændkʌf] **vt** mettre ***OR*** passer les menottes à.

handcuffs ['hændkʌfs] **npl** menottes *fpl*.

hand-drier **n** sèche-mains *m inv*.

-handed ['hændɪd] **suffix : right-handed** droitier ▸ **single-handed** tout seul (toute seule) ▸ **empty-handed** les mains vides, bredouille ▸ **one-handed catch** interception *f* à une main.

handful ['hændfʊl] **n 1.** [of sand, grass, people] poignée *f* **2.** *inf* [person] **: to be a handful** être difficile.

handgun ['hændgʌn] **n** revolver *m*, pistolet *m*.

hand-held **adj** [appliance] à main / [camera] portatif(ive).

hand-held PC **n** (ordinateur *m*) portable *m*.

handicap ['hændɪkæp] ■ **n** handicap *m*.

■ **vt** (pt & pp **-ped**, cont **-ping**) handicaper / [progress, work] entraver.

handicapped ['hændɪkæpt] ■ **adj** handicapé(e).

■ **npl : the handicapped** les handicapés *mpl*.

handicraft ['hændɪkrɑːft] **n** activité *f* artisanale.

handiwork ['hændɪwɜːk] **n** *(U)* ouvrage *m*.

handkerchief ['hæŋkətʃɪf] (pl **-chiefs** ***OR*** **-chieves** [-tʃiːvz]) **n** mouchoir *m*.

hand-knitted **adj** tricoté(e) main, tricoté(e) à la main.

handle ['hændl] ■ **n** [generally] poignée *f* / [of jug, cup] anse *f* / [of knife, pan] manche *m* ▸ **to fly off the handle** sortir de ses gonds.

■ **vt 1.** [with hands] manipuler / [without permission] toucher à ▸ **'handle with care!'** 'manipuler avec précaution' ▸ **to handle the ball** [in football] faire une main ▸ **to handle stolen goods** receler des objets volés

2. [deal with, be responsible for] s'occuper de / [difficult situation] faire face à ▸ **you handled that very well** tu as très bien réglé les choses ▸ **do you think you can handle the job?** penses-tu être capable de faire le travail? ▸ **how is she handling it?** comment s'en sort-elle?

3. [treat] traiter, s'y prendre avec ▸ **he's good at handling people** il sait s'y prendre avec les gens.

■ **vi** [car] **: to handle well/badly** être maniable/peu maniable.

handlebars ['hændlbɑːz] **npl** guidon *m*.

handler ['hændlər] **n 1.** [of dog] maître-chien *m* **2.** [at airport] **: (baggage) handler** bagagiste *m*.

handling charges ['hændlɪŋ-] **npl** [at bank] frais *mpl* de gestion.

hand lotion **n** lotion *f* pour les mains.

hand luggage **n** *(U)* *UK* bagages *mpl* à main.

handmade [ˌhænd'meɪd] **adj** fait(e) (à la) main.

hand-me-down **n** *inf* vêtement *m* usagé.

handout ['hændaʊt] **n 1.** [gift] don *m* **2.** [leaflet] prospectus *m*.

handover ['hændəʊvəʳ] **n** [of hostage, prisoner] remise *f* / [of power] passation *f* / [in relay race] passage *m*.

handpick [hænd'pɪk] **vt 1.** [fruit, vegetables] cueillir à la main **2.** *fig* [people] sélectionner avec soin, trier sur le volet.

handpicked [ˌhænd'pɪkt] **adj** trié(e) sur le volet.

hand puppet **n** *US* marionnette *f* (à gaine).

handrail ['hændreɪl] **n** rampe *f*.

handset ['hændset] **n** combiné *m*.

hand-sewn **adj** cousu(u) main, cousu(u) à la main.

hands-free kit ['hændz-] **n** kit *m* mains libres.

handshake ['hændʃeɪk] **n** serrement *m* ***or*** poignée *f* de main.

hands-off ['hændz-] **adj** non-interventionniste.

handsome ['hænsəm] **adj 1.** [good-looking] beau (belle) **2.** [reward, profit] beau (belle) / [gift] généreux(euse).

handsomely ['hænsəmlɪ] **adv** généreusement.

hands-on ['hændz-] **adj** [training] pratique / [manager] qui s'implique.

handstand ['hændstænd] **n** équilibre *m (sur les mains)*.

hand-stitched **adj** cousu(e) main, cousu(e) à la main.

hand-to-hand **adj & adv** au corps à corps.

hand-to-mouth **adj** précaire.
◆ ***hand to mouth*** **adv** au jour le jour.

handwash ['hændwɒʃ] ■ **vt** laver à la main.
■ **n : to do a handwash** faire une lessive à la main.

handwriting ['hændˌraɪtɪŋ] **n** écriture *f*.

handwritten ['hændˌrɪtn] **adj** écrit(e) à la main, manuscrit(e).

handy ['hændɪ] (**comp -ier, superl -iest**) **adj** *inf* **1.** [useful] pratique ▸ **to come in handy** être utile **2.** [skilful] adroit(e) **3.** [near] tout près, à deux pas ▸ **to keep sthg handy** garder qqch à portée de la main.

handyman ['hændɪmæn] (**pl -men** [-men]) **n** bricoleur *m*.

hang [hæŋ] ■ **vt 1.** (**pp hung**) [suspend - curtains, coat, decoration, picture] accrocher, suspendre / [- door] fixer, monter / [- wallpaper] coller, poser ▸ **to hang sthg from** ***or*** **on sthg** accrocher qqch à qqch ▸ **to hang one's head (in shame)** baisser la tête (de honte) ▸ **hang it (all)!** *UK inf dated* ras le bol!
2. (**pp hung** ***or*** **hanged**) [execute] pendre ▸ **to hang o.s.** se pendre.
■ **vi 1.** (**pp hung**) [be suspended] pendre, être accroché(e) ▸ **to hang from sthg** être accroché(e) ***or*** suspendu(e) à qqch ▸ **her pictures are now hanging in several art galleries** ses tableaux sont maintenant exposés dans plusieurs galeries d'art ▸ **his suit hangs well** son costume tombe bien ▸ **time hangs heavy on my hands** le temps me semble long
2. (**pp hung** ***or*** **hanged**) [be executed] être pendu(e)
3. (**pp hung**) COMPUT planter.
■ **n : to get the hang of sthg** *inf* saisir le truc ***or*** attraper le coup pour faire qqch ▸ **you'll soon get the hang of it** tu vas bientôt t'y faire.
◆ ***hang about*** *UK*, ***hang around*** **vi** [be idle, waste time] traîner ▸ **she doesn't hang about** ***or*** **around** [soon gets what she wants] elle ne perd pas de temps / [wait] attendre ▸ **he kept me hanging about** ***or*** **around for half an hour** il m'a fait poireauter pendant une demi-heure.
◆ ***hang on*** ■ **vt insep** [depend on] dépendre de.
■ **vi 1.** [keep hold] **: to hang on (to)** s'accrocher ***or*** se cramponner (à)
2. *inf* [continue waiting] attendre ▸ **hang on!** [wait] attends! / [indicating astonishment, disagreement] une minute! ▸ **hang on and I'll get him for you** [on phone] ne quitte pas, je te le passe
3. [persevere] tenir bon ▸ **hang on in there!** *inf* [don't give up] tiens bon!, tiens le coup!
◆ ***hang onto*** **vt insep 1.** [keep hold of] se cramponner à, s'accrocher à
2. [keep] garder.
◆ ***hang out*** ■ **vt sep** [washing] étendre.
■ **vi** *inf* [spend time] traîner ▸ **to let it all hang out** *dated* [person] se relâcher complètement, se laisser aller.
◆ ***hang round*** **vt insep** *UK* = ***hang about***.
◆ ***hang together*** **vi** [alibi, argument] se tenir.
◆ ***hang up*** ■ **vt sep** pendre.
■ **vi 1.** [on telephone] raccrocher
2. [hanging] être accroché(e), pendre.
◆ ***hang up on*** **vt insep** TELEC raccrocher au nez de.

hangar ['hæŋəʳ] **n** hangar *m*.

hangdog ['hæŋdɒg] **adj** de chien battu.

hanger ['hæŋəʳ] **n** cintre *m*.

hanger-on (**pl hangers-on**) **n** *pej* parasite *m*.

hang glider **n** [apparatus] deltaplane *m*.

hang gliding **n** *(U)* deltaplane *m*, vol *m* libre.

hanging ['hæŋɪŋ] **n 1.** [execution] pendaison *f* **2.** [drapery] tenture *f*.

hangman ['hæŋmən] (**pl -men** [-mən]) **n** bourreau *m*.

hangover ['hæŋˌəʊvəʳ] **n 1.** [from drinking] gueule *f* de bois **2.** [from past] **: hangover (from)** reliquat *m* (de).

hang-up **n** *inf* complexe *m*.

hank [hæŋk] **n** écheveau *m*.

hanker ['hæŋkəʳ] ◆ ***hanker after***, ***hanker for*** **vt insep** convoiter.

hankering ['hæŋkərɪŋ] **n : hankering after** ***or*** **for** envie *f* de.

hankie, ***hanky*** ['hæŋkɪ] (**pl -ies**) (**abbr of** ***handkerchief***) **n** *inf* mouchoir *m*.

hanky-panky [-'pæŋkɪ] **n** *(U) inf* **1.** [sexual activity] galipettes *fpl* **2.** [mischief] entourloupettes *fpl*, blagues *fpl*.

Hanoi [hæ'nɔɪ] **n** Hanoi.

Hansard ['hænsɑːd] **n** *compte-rendu officiel des débats parlementaires en Grande-Bretagne*.

Hants [hænts] (**abbr of** ***Hampshire***) *comté anglais*.

haphazard [ˌhæp'hæzəd] **adj** fait(e) au hasard.

haphazardly [ˌhæp'hæzədlɪ] **adv** au hasard.

hapless ['hæplɪs] **adj** *liter* infortuné(e).

happen ['hæpən] **vi 1.** [occur] arriver, se passer ▸ **where did the accident happen?** où l'accident s'est-il produit *OR* est-il arrivé *OR* a-t-il eu lieu ? ▸ **these things happen** ce sont des choses qui arrivent ▸ **don't let it happen again** faites en sorte que cela ne se reproduise pas ▸ **to happen to sb** arriver à qqn ▸ **if anything happens** *OR* **should happen to me** s'il m'arrivait quelque chose **2.** [chance] **: do you happen to have his address?** auriez-vous son adresse, par hasard? ▸ **I just happened to meet him** je l'ai rencontré par hasard ▸ **it happens to be right** il se trouve que c'est juste ▸ **as it happens** en fait ▸ **if you happen to see him** si jamais tu le vois.

happening ['hæpənɪŋ] **n** événement *m*.

happily ['hæpɪlɪ] **adv 1.** [with pleasure] de bon cœur **2.** [contentedly] **: to be happily doing sthg** être bien tranquillement en train de faire qqch **3.** [fortunately] heureusement.

happiness ['hæpɪnɪs] **n** bonheur *m*.

happy ['hæpɪ] (**comp -ier, superl -iest**) **adj 1.** [gen] heureux(euse) ▸ **to be happy to do sthg** être heureux de faire qqch ▸ **I would be happy to do it** je le ferais volontiers ▸ **happy birthday!** joyeux anniversaire! ▸ **happy Christmas** *UK* joyeux Noël ▸ **happy New Year!** bonne année! ▸ **happy ending** [in book, film] fin *f* heureuse, dénouement *m* heureux ▸ **to have a happy ending** [book, film] bien finir ▸ **those were happy days** c'était le bon temps **2.** [satisfied] heureux(euse), content(e) ▸ **to be happy with** *OR* **about sthg** être heureux de qqch ▸ **I'm not at all happy about your decision** je ne suis pas du tout content de votre décision ▸ **that should keep the kids happy** cela devrait occuper les enfants.

happy event **n** heureux événement *m*.

happy-go-lucky **adj** décontracté(e).

happy hour **n** *inf moment dans la journée où les boissons sont vendues moins cher dans les bars.*

happy medium **n** juste milieu *m*.

harangue [hə'ræŋ] ■ **n** harangue *f*.
■ **vt** haranguer.

Harare [hə'rɑ:rɪ] **n** Harare.

harass ['hærəs] **vt** harceler.

harassed ['hærəst] **adj** harcelé(e), tourmenté(e).

harassment ['hærəsmənt] **n** harcèlement *m*.

harbinger ['hɑ:bɪndʒə^r] **n** *liter* signe *m* avant-coureur.

harbour *UK*, ***harbor*** *US* ['hɑ:bə^r] ■ **n** port *m*.
■ **vt 1.** [feeling] entretenir / [doubt, grudge] garder **2.** [person] héberger.

harbour master *UK*, ***harbor master*** *US* **n** capitaine *m* de port.

hard [hɑ:d] ■ **adj 1.** [gen] dur(e) ▸ **life is hard** c'est dur, la vie ▸ **it's hard work** c'est dur ▸ **it's hard to say** c'est difficile à dire ▸ **to be hard on sb/sthg** être dur avec qqn/pour qqch ▸ **to give sb a hard time** en faire voir de dures à qqn ▸ **he's hard to get on with** il n'est pas facile à vivre ▸ **I find it hard to understand/believe that...** je n'arrive pas à comprendre/croire que... ▸ **hard luck!** pas de chance!, pas de veine!, pas de bol!
2. [winter, frost] rude
3. [water] calcaire
4. [fact] concret(ète) / [news] sûr(e), vérifié(e)
5. *UK* POL **: hard left/right** extrême gauche/droite.
■ **adv 1.** [strenuously - work] dur / [- listen, concentrate] avec effort ▸ **to try hard (to do sthg)** faire de son mieux (pour faire qqch) ▸ **you'll have to try harder** il faudra que tu fasses plus d'efforts ▸ **to work hard at improving one's service/French** beaucoup travailler pour améliorer son service/français ▸ **as hard as possible, as hard as one can** [work, try] le plus qu'on peut / [push, hit, squeeze] de toutes ses forces
2. [forcefully] fort ▸ **to be hard hit by sthg** être durement touché(e) par qqch
3. [heavily - rain] à verse / [- snow] dru
4. [solid] **: the ground was frozen hard** le gel avait complètement durci la terre ▸ **to set hard** [concrete] prendre
▸▸ **to be hard pushed** *OR* **put** *OR* **pressed to do sthg** avoir bien de la peine à faire qqch ▸ **to feel hard done by** avoir l'impression d'avoir été traité(e) injustement ▸ **to play hard to get** se faire désirer.

hard-and-fast **adj** [rule] absolu(e).

hardback ['hɑ:dbæk] ■ **adj** relié(e).
■ **n** livre *m* relié.

hardball ['hɑ:dbɔ:l] **n : to play hardball** *inf fig* employer les grands moyens.

hard-bitten **adj** dur(e) à cuire.

hardboard ['hɑ:dbɔ:d] **n** panneau *m* de fibres.

hard-boiled **adj 1.** CULIN **: hard-boiled egg** œuf *m* dur **2.** [person] dur(e) à cuire.

hard cash **n** *(U)* espèces *fpl*.

hard cider **n** *US* cidre *m*.

hard copy **n** COMPUT sortie *f* papier.

hard-core **adj 1.** [criminal] endurci(e) **2.** [pornography] hard *(inv)*.
◆ ***hard core*** **n** [of group] noyau *m* (dur).

hard court **n** court *m* en dur.

hardcover ['hɑ:d,kʌvə^r] = ***hardback***.

hard currency **n** devise *f* forte.

hard disk **n** COMPUT disque *m* dur.

hard-disk drive **n** COMPUT unité *f* de disque dur.

hard drugs **npl** drogues *fpl* dures.

hard-earned [-'ɜ:nd] **adj** [money] durement gagné(e) / [victory] durement *OR* difficilement remporté(e) / [reputation] durement acquis(e) / [holiday, reward] bien mérité(e).

harden ['hɑ:dn] ■ **vt** [arteries] durcir / [steel] tremper.
■ **vi 1.** [glue, concrete] durcir **2.** [person] s'endurcir **3.** [attitude, opposition] se durcir.

hardened ['hɑ:dnd] **adj** [criminal] endurci(e).

hardening ['hɑ:dnɪŋ] **n** durcissement *m*.

hard-faced [-'feɪst] **adj** au visage dur.

hard-fought [-'fɔ:t] **adj** [game, battle] rudement disputé(e).

hard hat **n 1.** [of construction worker] casque *m* **2.** *US inf* [construction worker] ouvrier *m* du bâtiment.

hard-headed [-'hedɪd] **adj** [decision] pragmatique ▸ **to be hard-headed** [person] avoir la tête froide.

hard-hearted [-'hɑ:tɪd] **adj** insensible, impitoyable.

hard-hitting [-'hɪtɪŋ] **adj** [report] sans indulgence.

hardiness ['hɑ:dɪnɪs] **n** [of person] résistance *f*, robustesse *f* / [of plant, tree] résistance *f*.

hard labour *UK*, ***hard labor*** *US* **n** *(U)* travaux *mpl* forcés.

hard line **n : to take a hard line on sthg** adopter une position ferme vis-à-vis de qqch.
◆ ***hard-line*** **adj** convaincu(e).
◆ ***hard lines*** **npl** *UK inf* **: hard lines!** pas de chance!

hard-liner **n** partisan *m* de la manière forte.

hardly ['hɑ:dlɪ] **adv** **1.** [scarcely] à peine, ne... guère ▸ **this is hardly the time for complaints** ce n'est guère le moment de se plaindre ▸ **hardly ever/anything** presque jamais/rien ▸ **I can hardly move/wait** je peux à peine bouger/attendre **2.** [only just] à peine.

hard margin **n** *Ir* = ***hard shoulder***.

hardness ['hɑ:dnɪs] **n** **1.** [firmness] dureté *f* **2.** [difficulty] difficulté *f*.

hard-nosed [-nəʊzd] **adj** [businessman] à la tête froide / [approach] pragmatique.

hard of hearing ■ **npl : the hard of hearing** les malentendants *mpl*.
■ **adj : to be hard of hearing** être dur(e) d'oreille.

hard-pressed [-'prest], ***hard-pushed*** [-'pʊʃt] **adj : to be hard-pressed for money/ideas/suggestions** être à court d'argent/d'idées/de suggestions ▸ **to be hard-pressed for time** manquer de temps ▸ **to be hard-pressed to do sthg** avoir du mal à faire qqch.

hard sell **n** vente *f* agressive ▸ **to give sb the hard sell** y aller à la vente agressive avec qqn.

hardship ['hɑ:dʃɪp] **n** **1.** *(U)* [difficult conditions] épreuves *fpl* **2.** [difficult circumstance] épreuve *f*.

hard shoulder **n** *UK* AUT bande *f* d'arrêt d'urgence.

hard up **adj** *inf* fauché(e) ▸ **hard up for sthg** à court de qqch.

hardware ['hɑ:dweəʳ] **n** *(U)* **1.** [tools, equipment] quincaillerie *f* **2.** COMPUT hardware *m*, matériel *m*.

hardware shop *UK*, ***hardware store*** *US* **n** quincaillerie *f*.

hardwearing [ˌhɑ:d'weərɪŋ] **adj** *UK* résistant(e).

hard-wired [-'waɪəd] **adj** COMPUT câblé(e).

hard-won [-'wʌn] **adj** [victory, trophy, independence] durement gagné(e) / [reputation] durement acquis(e).

hardwood ['hɑ:dwʊd] **n** bois *m* dur.

hardworking [ˌhɑ:d'wɜ:kɪŋ] **adj** travailleur(euse).

hardy ['hɑ:dɪ] (comp -ier, superl -iest) **adj** **1.** [person, animal] vigoureux(euse), robuste **2.** [plant] résistant(e), vivace.

hare [heəʳ] ■ **n** lièvre *m*.
■ **vi** *UK inf* **: to hare off** partir à fond de train.

harebrained ['heəˌbreɪnd] **adj** *inf* [person] écervelé(e) / [scheme, idea] insensé(e).

harelip [ˌheə'lɪp] **n** bec-de-lièvre *m*.

harem [*UK* hɑ:'ri:m, *US* 'hærəm] **n** harem *m*.

haricot (bean) ['hærɪkəʊ-] **n** haricot *m* blanc.

hark [hɑ:k] ◆ ***hark back*** **vi : to hark back to** revenir à.

harlequin ['hɑ:ləkwɪn] **n** arlequin *m*.

Harley Street ['hɑ:lɪ-] **n** *rue du centre de Londres célèbre pour ses spécialistes en médecine.*

harlot ['hɑ:lət] **n** *dated* prostituée *f*.

harm [hɑ:m] ■ **n** **1.** [injury] mal *m* **2.** [damage - to clothes, plant] dommage *m* / [- to reputation] tort *m* ▸ **to do harm to sb, to do sb harm** faire du tort à qqn ▸ **to do harm to sthg, to do sthg harm** endommager qqch ▸ **to mean no harm by sthg** ne pas faire qqch méchamment ▸ **there's no harm in it** il n'y a pas de mal à cela ▸ **to be out of harm's way** [person] être en sûreté OR lieu sûr / [thing] être en lieu sûr ▸ **she/it came to no harm** il ne lui est rien arrivé.
■ **vt** **1.** [injure] faire du mal à **2.** [damage - clothes, plant] endommager / [- reputation] faire du tort à.

harmful ['hɑ:mfʊl] **adj** nuisible, nocif(ive).

harmless ['hɑ:mlɪs] **adj** **1.** [not dangerous] inoffensif(ive) **2.** [inoffensive] innocent(e).

harmlessly ['hɑ:mlɪslɪ] **adv** [generally] sans faire de mal / [explode] sans faire de dégâts.

harmonic [hɑ:'mɒnɪk] **adj** harmonique.

harmonica [hɑ:'mɒnɪkə] **n** harmonica *m*.

harmonics [hɑ:'mɒnɪks] **n** *(U)* harmoniques *mpl*.

harmonious [hɑ:'məʊnjəs] **adj** harmonieux(euse).

harmoniously [hɑ:'məʊnjəslɪ] **adv** harmonieusement.

harmonium [hɑ:'məʊnjəm] (pl -s) **n** harmonium *m*.

harmonize, *UK* ***-ise*** ['hɑ:mənaɪz] ■ **vt** harmoniser.
■ **vi** s'harmoniser.

harmony ['hɑ:mənɪ] (pl -ies) **n** harmonie *f* ▸ **in harmony with** [in agreement] en harmonie OR en accord avec.

harness ['hɑ:nɪs] ■ **n** [for horse, child] harnais *m*.
■ **vt** **1.** [horse] harnacher **2.** [energy, resources] exploiter.

harp [hɑ:p] **n** harpe *f*.
◆ ***harp on*** **vi : to harp on (about sthg)** rabâcher (qqch).

harpist ['hɑ:pɪst] **n** harpiste *mf*.

harpoon [hɑ:'pu:n] ■ **n** harpon *m*.
■ **vt** harponner.

harpsichord ['hɑ:psɪkɔ:d] **n** clavecin *m*.

harpy ['hɑ:pɪ] (pl -ies) **n** *fig* & *pej* harpie *f*, mégère *f*.

harridan ['hærɪdn] **n** *pej* harpie *f*, vieille sorcière *f*.

harrowing ['hærəʊɪŋ] **adj** [experience] éprouvant(e) / [report, film] déchirant(e).

harry ['hærɪ] (pt & pp -ied) **vt** *fml* **: to harry sb (for sthg)** harceler qqn (pour obtenir qqch).

harsh [hɑ:ʃ] **adj** **1.** [life, conditions] rude / [criticism, treatment] sévère **2.** [to senses - sound] discordant(e) / [- light, voice] criard(e) / [- surface] rugueux(euse), rêche / [- taste] âpre.

harshly ['hɑ:ʃlɪ] **adv** **1.** [punish, treat, criticize] sévèrement / [speak] durement **2.** [to senses - shine] de façon criarde.

harshness ['hɑːʃnɪs] **n 1.** [of life, conditions] rigueur *f* / [of criticism, treatment] sévérité *f*, dureté *f* **2.** [to senses - of sound] discordance *f* / [- of texture] rugosité *f*, dureté *f* / [- of light, colour] aspect *m* criard.

harvest ['hɑːvɪst] ■ **n** [of cereal crops] moisson *f* / [of fruit] récolte *f* / [of grapes] vendange *f*, vendanges *fpl*.
■ **vt** [cereals] moissonner / [fruit] récolter / [grapes] vendanger.

harvest festival **n** fête *f* de la moisson.

has *(weak form* [həz], *strong form* [hæz]*)* ➤ ***have***.

has-been **n** *inf pej* ringard *m*, -e *f*.

hash [hæʃ] **n 1.** [food] hachis *m* **2.** *UK inf* [mess] **: to make a hash of sthg** faire un beau gâchis de qqch **3.** *drug sl* hasch *m*.
◆ ***hash up*** **vt sep** *UK inf* faire un beau gâchis de.

hash browns **npl** pommes de terre *fpl* sautées.

hashish ['hæʃiːʃ] **n** haschich *m*.

hash mark **n** *symbole typographique ressemblant au dièse servant à indiquer un espace ou, aux États-Unis, par exemple, un numéro de téléphone.*

hasn't ['hæznt] = ***has not***.

hassle ['hæsl] *inf* ■ **n** [annoyance] tracas *m*, embêtement *m* ▸ **it can be a real hassle** ça peut être vraiment l'horreur.
■ **vt** tracasser.

haste [heɪst] **n** hâte *f* ▸ **to do sthg in haste** faire qqch à la hâte ▸ **to make haste** *dated* se hâter.

hasten ['heɪsn] *fml* ■ **vt** hâter, accélérer.
■ **vi** se hâter, se dépêcher ▸ **to hasten to do sthg** s'empresser de faire qqch.

hastily ['heɪstɪlɪ] **adv 1.** [quickly] à la hâte **2.** [rashly] sans réfléchir.

hasty ['heɪstɪ] (comp **-ier**, superl **-iest**) **adj 1.** [quick] hâtif(ive) **2.** [rash] irréfléchi(e).

hat [hæt] **n** chapeau *m* ▸ **keep it under your hat** gardez-le pour vous ▸ **to be talking through one's hat** dire n'importe quoi ▸ **old hat** vieux jeu *(inv)*, dépassé(e).

hatbox ['hæt,bɒks] **n** carton *m* à chapeau.

hatch [hætʃ] ■ **vt 1.** [chick] faire éclore / [egg] couver **2.** *fig* [scheme, plot] tramer.
■ **vi** [chick, egg] éclore.
■ **n : (serving) hatch** passe-plats *m inv*.

hatchback ['hætʃ,bæk] **n** voiture *f* avec hayon.

hatchet ['hætʃɪt] **n** hachette *f* ▸ **to bury the hatchet** enterrer la hache de guerre.

hatchet-faced **adj** au visage en lame de couteau.

hatchet job **n** *inf* **: to do a hatchet job on sb** démolir qqn.

hatchway ['hætʃ,weɪ] **n** passe-plats *m inv*, guichet *m*.

hate [heɪt] ■ **n** *(U)* haine *f*.
■ **vt 1.** [detest] haïr **2.** [dislike] détester ▸ **I hate to bother you, but...** je suis désolé de vous déranger, mais... ▸ **to hate doing sthg** avoir horreur de faire qqch.

hateful ['heɪtfʊl] **adj** odieux(euse).

hate mail **n** lettres *fpl* d'injures.

hatred ['heɪtrɪd] **n** *(U)* haine *f*.

hat trick **n** SPORT **: to score a hat trick** marquer trois buts.

haughtily ['hɔːtɪlɪ] **adv** avec arrogance, de manière hautaine.

haughtiness ['hɔːtɪnɪs] **n** arrogance *f*, caractère *m* hautain.

haughty ['hɔːtɪ] (comp **-ier**, superl **-iest**) **adj** hautain(e).

haul [hɔːl] ■ **n 1.** [of drugs, stolen goods] prise *f*, butin *m* **2.** [distance] **: long haul** long voyage *m* ***OR*** trajet *m* / [period of time] **: on the long haul** à long terme.
■ **vt 1.** [pull] traîner, tirer **2.** *UK* [transport by lorry] camionner.

haulage ['hɔːlɪdʒ] **n** transport *m* routier ***OR*** ferroviaire, camionnage *m*.

haulage contractor **n** *UK* entrepreneur *m* de transports routiers.

haulier *UK* ['hɔːlɪəʳ], ***hauler*** *US* ['hɔːlər] **n** entrepreneur *m* de transports routiers.

haunch [hɔːntʃ] **n** [of person] hanche *f* / [of animal] derrière *m*, arrière-train *m* ▸ **a haunch of venison** un cuissot de chevreuil.

haunt [hɔːnt] ■ **n** repaire *m*.
■ **vt** hanter.

haunted ['hɔːntɪd] **adj 1.** [house, castle] hanté(e) **2.** [look] égaré(e).

haunting ['hɔːntɪŋ] **adj** obsédant(e).

Havana [hə'vænə] **n** La Havane.

have [hæv] (pt & pp **had**) ■ **aux vb** [to form perfect tenses - gen] avoir / [- with many intransitive verbs] être ▸ **to have eaten** avoir mangé ▸ **to have left** être parti(e) ▸ **to have sat down** s'être assis(e) ▸ **she hasn't gone yet, has she?** elle n'est pas encore partie, si? ▸ **no, she hasn't** non ▸ **yes, she has** oui ▸ **I was out of breath, having run all the way** j'étais essoufflé d'avoir couru tout le long du chemin ▸ **after** ***OR*** **when you have finished, you may leave** quand vous aurez fini, vous pourrez partir ▸ **I have been thinking** j'ai réfléchi ▸ **I have known her for three years/since childhood** je la connais depuis trois ans/depuis mon enfance ▸ **we had gone to bed early** nous nous étions couchés de bonne heure.
■ **vt 1.** [possess, receive] **: to have (got)** avoir ▸ **she has (got) red hair** elle a les cheveux roux, elle est rousse ▸ **he's got loads of imagination** il a plein d'imagination ▸ **I don't have any money, I have no money, I haven't got any money** je n'ai pas d'argent ▸ **do you have any experience of teaching?** avez-vous déjà enseigné? ▸ **I don't have time** ***OR*** **I haven't got time to stop for lunch** je n'ai pas le temps de m'arrêter pour déjeuner ▸ **I've got things to do** j'ai (des choses) à faire ▸ **she has a baker's shop/bookshop** elle tient une boulangerie/librairie ▸ **I've got it!** ça y est, j'ai trouvé ***OR*** j'y suis!
2. [experience illness] avoir ▸ **to have flu** *UK* ***OR*** **the flu** avoir la grippe
3. *(referring to an action, instead of another verb)* **: to have a read** *UK* lire ▸ **to have a swim** nager ▸ **to have a bath/shower** *UK* prendre un bain/une douche ▸ **to have a cigarette** fumer une cigarette ▸ **to have a meeting** tenir une

réunion ▸ **to have a bad day** passer une mauvaise journée ▸ **to have a good time** s'amuser ▸ **have a nice day!** bonne journée!
4. [give birth to] avoir ▸ **to have a baby** avoir un bébé
5. [cause to be done] **: to have sb do sthg** faire faire qqch à qqn ▸ **he soon had them all laughing** il eut tôt fait de les faire tous rire ▸ **to have sthg done** faire faire qqch ▸ **I'm having the house decorated** je fais décorer la maison ▸ **to have one's hair cut** se faire couper les cheveux ▸ **I love having my back rubbed** j'adore qu'on me frotte le dos
6. [be treated in a certain way] **: I had my car stolen** je me suis fait voler ma voiture, on m'a volé ma voiture
7. *inf* [cheat] **: to be had** se faire avoir ▸ **you've been had!** tu t'es fait avoir!
▸▸ **to have it in for sb** en avoir après qqn, en vouloir à qqn ▸ **to have had it** [car, machine, clothes] avoir fait son temps ▸ **I've had it!** je n'en peux plus! ▸ **who won? – you've got me there** [bewilder, perplex] qui a gagné? – là, tu me poses une colle.
■ **modal vb 1.** [be obliged] **: to have (got) to do sthg** devoir faire qqch, être obligé(e) de faire qqch ▸ **do you have to go?, have you got to go?** *esp UK* est-ce que tu dois partir?, est-ce que tu es obligé de partir? ▸ **I've got to go to work** il faut que j'aille travailler ▸ **I hate having to get up early** j'ai horreur de devoir me lever tôt ▸ **you've got to be joking!** vous plaisantez!, c'est une plaisanterie!
2. [need] devoir ▸ **you have (got) to get some rest** il faut que vous vous reposiez, vous devez vous reposer.
◆ ***haves*** **npl : the haves and the have–nots** les riches et les pauvres.
◆ ***have on*** **vt sep 1.** [be wearing] porter ▸ **to have nothing on** être tout nu (toute nue)
2. *UK* [tease] faire marcher
3. *UK* [have to do] **: to have (got) a lot on** être très pris(e).
◆ ***have out*** **vt sep 1.** [have removed] **: to have one's appendix/tonsils out** se faire opérer de l'appendicite/des amygdales ▸ **to have a tooth out** se faire arracher une dent
2. [discuss frankly] **: to have it out with sb** s'expliquer avec qqn.
◆ ***have up*** **vt sep** *UK inf* **: to have sb up for sthg** traduire qqn en justice pour qqch ▸ **they were had up by the police for vandalism** ils ont été arrêtés pour vandalisme.

haven ['heɪvn] **n** havre *m.*

have-nots **npl : the have-nots** les démunis *mpl*, les défavorisés *mpl.*

haven't ['hævnt] = ***have not.***

haversack ['hævəsæk] **n** *UK dated* sac *m* à dos.

havoc ['hævək] **n** *(U)* dégâts *mpl* ▸ **to play havoc with** [gen] abîmer / [with health] détraquer / [with plans] ruiner.

Hawaii [hə'waiː] **n** Hawaii *m* ▸ **in Hawaii** à Hawaii.

Hawaiian [hə'waɪjən] ■ **adj** hawaiien(enne).
■ **n** Hawaiien *m*, -enne *f.*

hawk [hɔːk] ■ **n** faucon *m* ▸ **to watch sb like a hawk** ne pas lâcher qqn des yeux.
■ **vt** colporter.

hawker ['hɔːkər] **n** colporteur *m*, -euse *f.*

hawk-eyed **adj 1.** [keen-sighted] au regard d'aigle **2.** *fig* [vigilant] qui a l'œil partout.

hawthorn ['hɔːθɔːn] **n** aubépine *f.*

hay [heɪ] **n** foin *m.*

hay fever **n** *(U)* rhume *m* des foins.

haymaking ['heɪˌmeɪkɪŋ] **n** fenaison *f.*

haystack ['heɪˌstæk] **n** meule *f* de foin.

haywire ['heɪˌwaɪər] **adj** *inf* **: to go haywire** [person] perdre la tête / [machine] se détraquer.

hazard ['hæzəd] ■ **n** hasard *m.*
■ **vt** hasarder.

FALSE FRIENDS / FAUX AMIS
hazard

Hasard n'est pas la traduction du mot anglais *hazard.* Hasard se traduit par *chance* ou *luck.*
▸ Ils n'ont rien laissé au hasard / *They left nothing to chance*

hazardous ['hæzədəs] **adj** hasardeux(euse).

hazard (warning) lights **npl** AUT feux *mpl* de détresse.

haze [heɪz] **n** brume *f.*

hazel ['heɪzl] ■ **adj** noisette *(inv).*
■ **n** [tree] noisetier *m.*

hazelnut ['heɪzlˌnʌt] **n** noisette *f.*

haziness ['heɪzɪnɪs] **n 1.** [of sky, weather] état *m* brumeux **2.** [of memory, thinking] flou *m*, imprécision *f* **3.** PHOT flou *m.*

hazy ['heɪzɪ] (**comp -ier, superl -iest**) **adj 1.** [misty] brumeux(euse) **2.** [memory, ideas] flou(e), vague.

H-bomb **n** bombe *f* H.

HDD (**abbr of *hard disk drive***) **n** COMPUT disque *m* dur.

he [hiː] ■ **pers pron 1.** *(unstressed)* il ▸ **he's tall** il est grand ▸ **he who** *fml* (celui) qui ▸ **there he is** le voilà **2.** *(stressed)* lui ▸ **HE can't do it** lui ne peut pas le faire.
■ **n** *inf* [referring to animal, baby] **: it's a he** [animal] c'est un mâle / [baby] c'est un garçon.
■ **comp** mâle ▸ **he-goat** bouc *m.*

HE **1.** abbr of ***high explosive*** **2.** (abbr of ***His (or Her) Excellency***) S.Exc., S.E.

head [hed] ■ **n 1.** [of person, animal] tête *f* ▸ **a** *OR* **per head** par tête, par personne ▸ **off the top of my head, I'd say...** comme ça je dirais... ▸ **I couldn't make head nor** *OR* **or tail of it** je n'y comprenais rien ▸ **on your own head be it** à vos risques et périls ▸ **I'm banging my head against a brick wall** *inf* je me tape la tête contre les murs ▸ **to bite** *OR* **snap sb's head off** rembarrer qqn ▸ **to laugh one's head off** rire à gorge déployée ▸ **to sing/shout one's head off** chanter/crier à tue-tête ▸ **to be off one's head** *UK*, **to be out of one's head** *US* être dingue ▸ **to be soft in the head** *UK inf* être débile ▸ **to go to one's head** [alcohol, praise] monter à la tête ▸ **to keep one's head** garder son sang-froid ▸ **to lose one's head** perdre la tête ▸ **we put our heads together** nous avons conjugué nos efforts ▸ **to take it into one's head to do sthg** se mettre en tête de faire qqch ▸ **the idea never entered my head** ça ne m'est jamais venu à l'esprit ▸ **she has no head for business** elle n'a pas le sens des affaires ▸ **he went over my head to the president** il est allé voir le président sans me consulter **2.** [of table, bed, hammer] tête *f* / [of stairs, page] haut *m* ▸ **at**

the head of the procession/queue en tête de (la) procession/de (la) queue **3.** [of flower] tête *f* / [of cabbage] pomme *f* **4.** [leader] chef *m* ▸ **head of state** chef *m* d'État **5.** *UK* [head teacher] directeur *m*, -trice *f*
▸▸ *UK* **to come to a head** atteindre un point critique.
■ **vt 1.** [procession, list] être en tête de **2.** [be in charge of] être à la tête de **3.** FOOTBALL **: to head the ball** faire une tête ▸ **he headed the ball into the goal** il a marqué de la tête.
■ **vi : where are you heading?** où allez-vous? ▸ **we headed back to the office** nous sommes retournés au bureau.
◆ ***heads*** **npl** [on coin] face *f* ▸ **heads or tails?** pile ou face?
◆ ***head for*** **vt insep 1.** [place] se diriger vers ▸ **she headed for home** elle rentra (à la maison) **2.** *fig* [trouble, disaster] aller au devant de ▸ **to be heading for a fall** courir à l'échec.
◆ ***head off*** **vt sep 1.** [intercept] intercepter **2.** *fig* [threat, disaster] parer à.

headache ['hedeɪk] **n** mal *m* de tête ▸ **to have a headache** avoir mal à la tête.

headachy ['hedeɪkɪ] **adj** *inf* **: I'm feeling a bit headachy** j'ai un peu mal à la tête.

headband ['hedbænd] **n** bandeau *m*.

headboard ['hed,bɔ:d] **n** dosseret *m*.

head boy **n** *UK élève chargé de la discipline et qui siège aux conseils de son école.*

headbutt ['hedbʌt] ■ **n** coup *m* de tête, coup *m* de boule.
■ **vt** donner un coup de tête ***OR*** de boule à.

head case **n** *inf* dingue *mf*.

head cold **n** rhume *m* de cerveau.

head count **n** compte *m*.

headdress ['hed,dres] **n** coiffe *f*.

-headed ['hedɪd] **suffix** à tête... ▸ **a silver-headed cane** une canne à pommeau d'argent ▸ **a three-headed dragon** un dragon à trois têtes.

header ['hedəʳ] **n** FOOTBALL tête *f*.

headfirst [,hed'fɜ:st] **adv** (la) tête la première.

headgear ['hed,gɪəʳ] **n** *(U)* couvre-chef *m*.

head girl **n** *UK élève chargée de la discipline et qui siège aux conseils de son école.*

headhunt ['hedhʌnt] **vt** recruter (chez la concurrence).

headhunter ['hed,hʌntəʳ] **n** chasseur *m* de têtes.

heading ['hedɪŋ] **n** titre *m*, intitulé *m*.

headlamp ['hedlæmp] **n** *UK* phare *m*.

headland ['hedlənd] **n** cap *m*.

headless ['hedlɪs] **adj 1.** [arrow, body, screw] sans tête ▸ **he was running around like a headless chicken** *hum* il courait dans tous les sens **2.** [company, commission] sans chef.

headlight ['hedlaɪt] **n** phare *m*.

headline ['hedlaɪn] **n** [in newspaper] gros titre *m* / TV & RADIO grand titre *m*.

headlock ['hedlɒk] **n** cravate *f*.

headlong ['hedlɒŋ] ■ **adv 1.** [quickly] à toute allure **2.** [unthinkingly] tête baissée **3.** [headfirst] (la) tête la première.
■ **adj** [unthinking] irréfléchi(e).

headmaster [,hed'mɑ:stəʳ] **n** *UK* directeur *m* (d'une école).

headmistress [,hed'mɪstrɪs] **n** *UK* directrice *f* (d'une école).

head office **n** siège *m* social.

head-on ■ **adj** [collision] de plein fouet / [confrontation] de front.
■ **adv** de plein fouet.

headphones ['hedfəʊnz] **npl** casque *m*.

headquarter [hed'kwɔ:təʳ] **vt : to be headquartered in** avoir son siège à.

headquarters [,hed'kwɔ:təz] **npl** [of business, organization] siège *m* / [of armed forces] quartier *m* général.

headrest ['hedrest] **n** appui-tête *m*.

headroom ['hedrʊm] **n** *(U)* hauteur *f*.

headscarf ['hedskɑ:f] (pl **-scarves** [-skɑ:vz] ***OR*** **-scarfs**) **n** foulard *m*.

headset ['hedset] **n** casque *m*.

headship ['hedʃɪp] **n** *UK* direction *f* (d'une école).

headstand ['hedstænd] **n** poirier *m*.

head start **n** avantage *m* au départ ▸ **head start on** ***OR*** **over** avantage sur.

headstone ['hedstəʊn] **n** pierre *f* tombale.

headstrong ['hedstrɒŋ] **adj** volontaire, têtu(e).

head teacher **n** *UK* directeur *m*, -trice *f* (d'une école).

head-up **adj** [in aeroplane, car] **: head-up display** affichage *m* tête-haute.

head waiter **n** maître *m* d'hôtel.

headway ['hedweɪ] **n : to make headway** faire des progrès.

headwind ['hedwɪnd] **n** vent *m* contraire.

heady ['hedɪ] (comp **-ier**, superl **-iest**) **adj 1.** [exciting] grisant(e) **2.** [causing giddiness] capiteux(euse).

heal [hi:l] ■ **vt 1.** [cure] guérir **2.** *fig* [troubles, discord] apaiser.
■ **vi** se guérir.
◆ ***heal up*** **vi** se cicatriser, se refermer.

healer ['hi:ləʳ] **n** guérisseur *m*, -euse *f*.

healing ['hi:lɪŋ] ■ **adj** curatif(ive).
■ **n** *(U)* guérison *f*.

health [helθ] **n** santé *f* ▸ **to be in good/poor health** être en bonne/mauvaise santé ▸ **to drink (to) sb's health** boire à la santé de qqn.

health care **n** *(U)* services *mpl* médicaux.

health centre **n** *UK* ≃ centre *m* médico-social.

health-conscious **adj** soucieux(euse) de sa santé.

health farm **n** établissement *m* de cure.

health food **n** *(U)* produits *mpl* diététiques ***OR*** naturels ***OR*** biologiques.

health-food shop n magasin *m* de produits diététiques.

health hazard n danger *m* OR risque *m* pour la santé.

healthily ['helθɪlɪ] adv [eat, live] sainement.

health service n *UK* ≃ sécurité *f* sociale.

health visitor n *UK* infirmière *f* visiteuse.

healthy ['helθɪ] (comp -ier, superl -iest) adj **1.** [gen] sain(e) **2.** [well] en bonne santé, bien portant(e) **3.** *fig* [economy, company] qui se porte bien **4.** [profit] bon (bonne).

heap [hi:p] ■ n tas *m* ▸ **in a heap** en tas.
■ vt **1.** [pile up] entasser **2.** *fig* [give] **: to heap gifts on sb** couvrir qqn de cadeaux ▸ **to heap praise on sb** combler qqn d'éloges ▸ **to heap scorn on sb** accabler qqn de mépris.
◆ ***heaps*** npl *inf* **: heaps of** [people, objects] des tas de / [time, money] énormément de.

heaped [hi:pt] *UK*, ***heaping*** ['hi:pɪŋ] *US* adj gros (grosse) ▸ **a heaped teaspoonful** une cuiller à café bombée OR pleine.

hear [hɪəʳ] (pt & pp **heard** [hɜ:d]) ■ vt **1.** [gen & LAW] entendre ▸ **can you hear me?** m'entendez-vous (bien)? ▸ **he could hear someone crying** il entendait (quelqu'un) pleurer ▸ **I've heard it said that...** j'ai entendu dire que... ▸ **you're hearing things** tu t'imagines des choses ▸ **the case will be heard in March** l'affaire se plaidera au mois de mars
2. [learn of] apprendre ▸ **to hear (that)...** apprendre que... ▸ **I hear you're leaving** j'ai appris que tu partais.
■ vi **1.** [perceive sound] entendre
2. [know] **: haven't you heard? he's dead** vous n'êtes pas au courant? il est mort ▸ **to hear about** entendre parler de ▸ **did you hear about her husband?** tu es au courant, pour son mari? ▸ **I've heard so much about you** j'ai tellement entendu parler de vous
3. [receive news] **: to hear about** avoir des nouvelles de ▸ **I hear about her through her sister** j'ai de ses nouvelles par sa sœur ▸ **have you heard about your blood test yet?** as-tu déjà reçu des nouvelles à propos de ta prise de sang? ▸ **to hear from sb** recevoir des nouvelles de qqn ▸ **looking forward to hearing from you** [in letters] dans l'attente de vous lire
▸▸ **to have heard of** avoir entendu parler de ▸ **I've never heard of her** je ne la connais pas ▸ **I won't hear of it!** je ne veux pas en entendre parler!
◆ ***hear out*** vt sep écouter jusqu'au bout.

hearing ['hɪərɪŋ] ■ n **1.** [sense] ouïe *f* ▸ **Joe was in** OR **within Jim's hearing** Jim était à portée de voix de Joe ▸ **hard of hearing** dur(e) d'oreille **2.** [trial] audience *f* ▸ **to get a fair hearing** [generally] pouvoir défendre sa cause / LAW être jugé(e) équitablement.
■ adj entendant(e).

hearing aid n audiophone *m*.

hearing impaired npl **: the hearing impaired** les malentendants *mpl*.

hearsay ['hɪəseɪ] n ouï-dire *m*.

hearse [hɜ:s] n corbillard *m*.

heart [hɑ:t] n *lit & fig* cœur *m* ▸ **from the heart** du fond du cœur ▸ **to lose heart** perdre courage ▸ **to have a change of heart** changer d'avis ▸ **she opened** OR **poured out her heart to me** elle m'a dévoilé son cœur ▸ **he didn't have the heart to refuse** il n'a pas eu le courage OR le cœur de refuser ▸ **her heart's in the right place** elle a bon cœur ▸ **there's a woman/a man after my own heart** voilà une femme/un homme selon mon cœur ▸ **the heart of the matter** le fond du problème ▸ **my heart leapt** j'ai bondi de joie ▸ **my heart sank** je me suis senti abattu ▸ **it's a subject close to my heart** c'est un sujet qui me tient à cœur ▸ **from the bottom of my heart** du fond du cœur ▸ **his heart isn't in it** il n'a pas le cœur à cela ▸ **in one's heart of hearts** au plus profond de son cœur ▸ **to do sthg to one's heart's content** faire qqch à souhait ▸ **to break sb's heart** briser le cœur à qqn ▸ **to set one's heart on sthg/on doing sthg** désirer absolument qqch/faire qqch, vouloir à tout prix qqch/faire qqch ▸ **to take sthg to heart** prendre qqch à cœur ▸ **to have a heart of gold** avoir un cœur d'or ▸ **to wear one's heart on one's sleeve** montrer OR laisser paraître ses sentiments.
◆ ***hearts*** npl [cards] cœur *m* ▸ **the six of hearts** le six de cœur.
◆ ***at heart*** adv au fond (de soi).
◆ ***by heart*** adv par cœur ▸ **to learn/to know sthg by heart** apprendre/savoir qqch par cœur.

heartache ['hɑ:teɪk] n *fig* peine *f* de cœur.

heart attack n crise *f* cardiaque.

heartbeat ['hɑ:tbi:t] n [generally] battement *m* de cœur / MED pulsation *f* cardiaque.

heartbreak ['hɑ:tbreɪk] n [grief - gen] (immense) chagrin *m*, déchirement *m* / [- in love] chagrin *m* d'amour.

heartbreaking ['hɑ:tˌbreɪkɪŋ] adj à fendre le cœur.

heartbroken ['hɑ:tˌbrəʊkn] adj qui a le cœur brisé.

heartburn ['hɑ:tbɜ:n] n *(U)* brûlures *fpl* d'estomac.

heart condition n **: to have a heart condition** souffrir du cœur, être cardiaque.

heart disease n maladie *f* de cœur.

hearten ['hɑ:tn] vt encourager, donner du courage à ▸ **we were heartened to learn of the drop in interest rates** nous avons été contents d'apprendre que les taux d'intérêt avaient baissé.

heartening ['hɑ:tnɪŋ] adj encourageant(e).

heart failure n [end of heart beat] arrêt *m* cardiaque / [condition] défaillance *f* cardiaque.

heartfelt ['hɑ:tfelt] adj sincère.

hearth [hɑ:θ] n foyer *m*.

heartily ['hɑ:tɪlɪ] adv **1.** [enthusiastically - joke, laugh] de tout son cœur / [- say, thank, welcome] chaleureusement, de tout cœur / [- eat] de bon appétit **2.** [thoroughly] **: I heartily recommend it** je vous le conseille vivement ▸ **to be heartily disgusted with sthg** être on ne peut plus dégoûté de qqch.

heartiness ['hɑ:tɪnɪs] n **1.** [of thanks, welcome] cordialité *f*, chaleur *f* / [of agreement] sincérité *f* / [of appetite] vigueur *f* / [of dislike] ardeur *f* **2.** [enthusiasm] zèle *m*, empressement *m*.

heartland ['hɑ:tlænd] **n** centre *m*, cœur *m*.

heartless ['hɑ:tlɪs] **adj** sans cœur.

heartlessly ['hɑ:tlɪslɪ] **adv** sans pitié.

heartlessness ['hɑ:tlɪsnɪs] **n** [of person] manque *m* de cœur, caractère *m* impitoyable.

heartrending ['hɑ:t,rendɪŋ] **adj** déchirant(e), qui fend le cœur.

heart-searching **n : after a lot of heart-searching** après s'être beaucoup interrogé(e).

heart-stopping **adj** terrifiant(e).

heartstrings ['hɑ:tstrɪŋz] **npl : to play on** *OR* **to pull on** *OR* **to tug at sb's heartstrings** faire vibrer *OR* toucher la corde sensible de qqn ▸ **that song always tugs at my heartstrings** cette chanson me serre toujours le cœur.

heartthrob ['hɑ:tθrɒb] **n** *inf* idole *f*, coqueluche *f*.

heart-to-heart ■ **adj** à cœur ouvert.
■ **n** conversation *f* à cœur ouvert.

heart transplant **n** greffe *f* du cœur.

heartwarming ['hɑ:t,wɔ:mɪŋ] **adj** réconfortant(e).

hearty ['hɑ:tɪ] (comp **-ier**, superl **-iest**) **adj** **1.** [greeting, person] cordial(e) **2.** [substantial - meal] copieux(euse) / [- appetite] gros (grosse).

heat [hi:t] ■ **n** **1.** *(U)* [warmth] chaleur *f* ▸ **body heat** chaleur *f* animale ▸ **the radiator gives off a lot of heat** le radiateur chauffe bien ▸ **cook at a high/low heat** faire cuire à feu vif/doux ▸ **in the heat of the moment** dans l'agitation *OR* l'excitation du moment **2.** *(U) fig* [pressure] pression *f* ▸ **the mafia turned the heat on the mayor** la mafia a fait pression sur le maire **3.** [eliminating round] éliminatoire *f* **4.** ZOOL **: on** *UK* *OR* **in** *US* **heat** en chaleur.
■ **vt** chauffer.
◆ ***heat up*** ■ **vt sep** réchauffer.
■ **vi** chauffer.

heated ['hi:tɪd] **adj** [argument, discussion, person] animé(e) / [issue] chaud(e).

heatedly ['hi:tɪdlɪ] **adv** [debate, talk] avec passion / [argue, deny, refuse] avec passion *OR* emportement, farouchement.

heater ['hi:təʳ] **n** appareil *m* de chauffage.

heat exhaustion **n** épuisement *m* dû à la chaleur.

heath [hi:θ] **n** lande *f*.

heathen ['hi:ðn] ■ **adj** païen(enne).
■ **n** païen *m*, -enne *f*.

heather ['heðəʳ] **n** bruyère *f*.

heating ['hi:tɪŋ] **n** chauffage *m*.

heatproof ['hi:tpru:f] **adj** [gen] résistant(e) à la chaleur / [dish] qui va au four.

heat rash **n** boutons *mpl* de chaleur.

heat-resistant **adj** résistant(e) à la chaleur.

heat-seeking [-,si:kɪŋ] **adj** guidé(e) par la chaleur.

heatstroke ['hi:tstrəʊk] **n** *(U)* coup *m* de chaleur.

heat wave **n** canicule *f*, vague *f* de chaleur.

heave [hi:v] ■ **vt** **1.** [pull] tirer (avec effort) / [push] pousser (avec effort) **2.** *inf* [throw] lancer.
■ **vi** **1.** [pull] tirer **2.** [rise and fall] se soulever **3.** [retch] avoir des haut-le-cœur.
■ **n : to give sthg a heave** [pull] tirer qqch (avec effort) / [push] pousser qqch (avec effort).

heaven ['hevn] **n** paradis *m* ▸ **it was heaven** *fig* c'était divin *OR* merveilleux ▸ **heaven (alone) knows!** Dieu seul le sait!
◆ ***heavens*** ■ **npl : the heavens** *liter* les cieux *mpl*.
■ **excl : (good) heavens!** juste ciel!

heavenly ['hevnlɪ] **adj** **1.** *inf* [delightful] délicieux(euse), merveilleux(euse) **2.** *liter* [of the skies] céleste.

heaven-sent **adj** providentiel(elle) ▸ **a heaven-sent opportunity** une occasion providentielle *OR* qui tombe à pic.

heavily ['hevɪlɪ] **adv** **1.** [booked, in debt] lourdement / [rain, smoke, drink] énormément **2.** [solidly - built] solidement **3.** [breathe, sigh] péniblement, bruyamment **4.** [fall, sit down] lourdement.

heavily-built **adj** solidement bâti(e) ▸ **a heavily-built man** un homme costaud *OR* bien charpenté.

heaviness ['hevɪnɪs] **n** **1.** [gen] lourdeur *f* **2.** [intensity] intensité *f*.

heavy ['hevɪ] (comp **-ier**, superl **-iest**) **adj** **1.** [gen] lourd(e) ▸ **how heavy is it?** ça pèse combien? ▸ **the branches were heavy with fruit** les branches étaient chargées *OR* lourdes de fruits ▸ **with a heavy heart** [sad] le cœur gros
2. [traffic] dense / [rain] battant(e) / [fighting] acharné(e) / [casualties, corrections] nombreux(euses) / [smoker, drinker] gros (grosse) ▸ **she has a heavy cold** elle a un gros rhume, elle est fortement enrhumée ▸ **heavy fighting is reported in the Gulf** on signale des combats acharnés dans le Golfe ▸ **to be heavy on petrol** *UK* consommer beaucoup (d'essence)
3. [noisy - breathing] bruyant(e)
4. [schedule] chargé(e)
5. [physically exacting - work, job] pénible ▸ **I found his last novel very heavy going** j'ai trouvé son dernier roman très indigeste ▸ **to make heavy weather of sthg** faire une montagne de qqch.

heavy cream **n** *US* crème *f* fraîche épaisse.

heavy-duty **adj** solide, robuste.

heavy goods vehicle **n** *UK* poids lourd *m*.

heavy-handed [-'hændɪd] **adj** maladroit(e).

heavy-hearted [-'hɑ:tɪd] **adj** abattu(e), découragé(e).

heavy industry **n** industrie *f* lourde.

heavy metal **n** MUS heavy metal *m*.

heavyweight ['hevɪweɪt] ■ **adj** SPORT poids lourd.
■ **n** SPORT poids lourd *m*.

Hebrew ['hi:bru:] ■ **adj** hébreu, hébraïque.
■ **n** **1.** [person] Hébreu *m*, Israélite *mf* **2.** [language] hébreu *m*.

Hebrides ['hebrɪdi:z] **npl : the Hebrides** les (îles *fpl*) Hébrides *fpl* ▸ **in the Hebrides** aux Hébrides.

heck [hek] excl *inf* : **what/where/why the heck...?** que/où/pourquoi diable...? ▸ **a heck of a nice guy** un type vachement sympa ▸ **a heck of a lot of people** un tas de gens.

heckle ['hekl] ■ **vt** interpeller, interrompre.
■ **vi** interrompre bruyamment.

heckler ['heklər] **n** perturbateur *m*, -trice *f*.

heckling ['heklɪŋ] ■ **n** *(U)* harcèlement *m*, interpellations *fpl*.
■ **adj** qui fait du harcèlement, qui interpelle.

hectare ['hekteər] **n** hectare *m*.

hectic ['hektɪk] **adj** [meeting, day] agité(e), mouvementé(e).

hector ['hektər] *pej* ■ **vt** rudoyer.
■ **vi** agir de façon autoritaire.

hectoring ['hektərɪŋ] ■ **n** *(U)* harcèlement *m*, torture *f*.
■ **adj** [behaviour] tyrannique / [tone, voice] impérieux (euse), autoritaire.

he'd [hi:d] = ***he had, he would***.

hedge [hedʒ] ■ **n** haie *f*.
■ **vi** [prevaricate] répondre de façon détournée.

hedgehog ['hedʒhɒg] **n** hérisson *m*.

hedgerow ['hedʒrəʊ] **n** bordure *f* d'arbres.

hedonism ['hi:dənɪzm] **n** hédonisme *m*.

hedonist ['hi:dənɪst] **n** hédoniste *mf*.

hedonistic [ˌhi:də'nɪstɪk] **adj** hédoniste.

heebie-jeebies [ˌhi:bɪ'dʒi:bɪz] **npl** *inf* : **to have the heebie-jeebies** avoir la frousse *OR* les chocottes ▸ **the film gave me the heebie-jeebies** [revulsion] le film m'a donné la chair de poule / [fright] le film m'a donné la trouille *OR* la frousse ▸ **he gives me the heebie-jeebies** il me met mal à l'aise.

heed [hi:d] ■ **n** : **to pay heed to sb** prêter attention à qqn ▸ **to take heed of sthg** tenir compte de qqch.
■ **vt** *fml* tenir compte de.

heedless ['hi:dlɪs] **adj** : **to be heedless of sthg** ne pas tenir compte de qqch.

heedlessly ['hi:dlɪslɪ] **adv 1.** [without thinking] sans faire attention, à la légère **2.** [inconsiderately] avec insouciance, négligemment.

heel [hi:l] **n** talon *m* ▸ **to dig one's heels in** *fig* se buter ▸ **to follow hard on the heels of sb** être sur les talons de qqn ▸ **to follow hard on the heels of sthg** arriver immédiatement après qqch ▸ **to take to one's heels** prendre ses jambes à son cou ▸ **to turn on one's heel** tourner les talons.

heel bar **n** talon-minute *m*, réparations-minute *fpl*.

heels [hi:lz] = ***high heels***.

hefty ['heftɪ] (comp -ier, superl -iest) **adj 1.** [well-built] costaud(e) **2.** [large] gros (grosse).

heifer ['hefər] **n** génisse *f*.

height [haɪt] **n 1.** [of building, mountain] hauteur *f* / [of person] taille *f* ▸ **5 metres in height** 5 mètres de haut ▸ **what height is it?** ça fait quelle hauteur? ▸ **what height are you?** combien mesurez-vous? **2.** [above ground - of aircraft] altitude *f* ▸ **to gain/lose height** gagner/perdre de l'altitude ▸ **at shoulder height** à hauteur de l'épaule **3.** [zenith] : **at the height of the summer/season** au cœur de l'été/de la saison ▸ **at the height of his fame** au sommet de sa gloire.
◆ ***heights*** **npl** [high places] hauteurs *fpl* ▸ **to be afraid of heights** avoir le vertige.

heighten ['haɪtn] **vt** & **vi** augmenter.

heightened ['haɪtnd] **adj 1.** [building, ceiling, shelf] relevé(e), rehaussé(e) **2.** [fear, pleasure] intensifié(e) / [colour] plus vif(vive).

heinous ['heɪnəs] **adj** *fml* odieux(euse).

heir [eər] **n** héritier *m*.

heir apparent (pl **heirs apparent**) **n** héritier *m* présomptif.

heiress ['eərɪs] **n** héritière *f*.

heirloom ['eəlu:m] **n** [piece of furniture] meuble *m* de famille / [piece of jewellery] bijou *m* de famille.

heist [haɪst] **n** *inf* casse *m*.

held [held] **pt** & **pp** ➤ ***hold***.

helices ['helɪsi:z] **npl** ➤ ***helix***.

helicopter ['helɪkɒptər] **n** hélicoptère *m*.

helipad ['helɪpæd] **n** héliport *m*.

heliport ['helɪpɔ:t] **n** héliport *m*.

helium ['hi:lɪəm] **n** hélium *m*.

helix ['hi:lɪks] (pl **-lixes** [-lɪksi:z] *OR* **-lices** [-lɪsi:z]) **n** hélice *f*.

hell [hel] ■ **n 1.** *lit* & *fig* enfer *m* ▸ **he made her life hell** il lui a fait mener une vie infernale ▸ **working there was hell on earth** c'était l'enfer de travailler là-bas **2.** *inf* [for emphasis] : **he's a hell of a nice guy** c'est un type vachement sympa ▸ **what/where/why the hell...?** que/où/pourquoi..., bon sang? ▸ **what the hell are you doing?** qu'est-ce que tu fous? ▸ **a hell of a mess** un sacré bazar ▸ **a hell of a lot of books** tout un tas *OR* un paquet de livres ▸ **they had a hell of a time getting the car started** ils en ont bavé pour faire démarrer la voiture ▸ **from hell** *inf* cauchemardesque ▸ **it was a journey from hell!** *inf* ce voyage, c'était l'horreur! ▸ **to hurt like hell** faire vachement mal ▸ **like hell you will!** il n'y a pas de danger! ▸ **to get the hell out (of)** foutre le camp (de)
▸▸ **all hell broke loose** *inf* il y a eu de l'orage ▸ **to do sthg for the hell of it** *inf* faire qqch pour le plaisir, faire qqch juste comme ça ▸ **I went along just for the hell of it** *inf* j'y suis allé histoire de rire *OR* de rigoler ▸ **to give sb hell** *inf* [verbally] engueuler qqn ▸ **go to hell!** *v inf* va te faire foutre! ▸ **he ran off hell for leather** *inf* il est parti ventre à terre ▸ **there'll be hell to pay when he finds out** *inf* ça va barder *OR* chauffer quand il l'apprendra ▸ **to play hell with sthg** *inf* foutre qqch en l'air ▸ **to hell with him!** *inf* il peut aller se faire voir! ▸ **to hell with the expense!** *inf* au diable l'avarice! ▸ **hell's bells!, hell's teeth!** *inf* mince alors!
■ **excl** *inf* merde!, zut!

he'll [hi:l] = ***he will***.

hell-bent **adj** : **to be hell-bent on sthg/on doing sthg** vouloir à tout prix qqch/faire qqch.

hellhole ['helhəʊl] **n** *inf* bouge *m*.

hellish ['helɪʃ] **adj** infernal(e).

hellishly ['helɪʃlɪ] **adv** *UK inf* atrocement, épouvantablement.

hello [hə'ləʊ] **excl 1.** [as greeting] bonjour! / [on phone] allô! **2.** [to attract attention] hé!

Hell's Angels **npl** *nom d'un groupe de motards au comportement violent.*

helluva ['heləvə] **adj** *inf* **: he's a helluva guy** c'est un type vachement bien ▸ **I had a helluva time** [awful] je me suis emmerdé / [wonderful] je me suis vachement marré.

helm [helm] **n** *lit & fig* barre *f* ▸ **at the helm** à la barre.

helmet ['helmɪt] **n** casque *m*.

helmsman ['helmzmən] (pl **-men** [-mən]) **n** NAUT timonier *m*, -ière *f*.

help [help] ■ **n 1.** *(U)* [assistance] aide *f* ▸ **he gave me a lot of help** il m'a beaucoup aidé ▸ **she needs help going upstairs** il faut qu'elle se fasse aider pour *OR* elle a besoin qu'on l'aide à monter l'escalier ▸ **with the help of sthg** à l'aide de qqch ▸ **with sb's help** avec l'aide de qqn ▸ **to be of help** rendre service ▸ **'help wanted'** *US* 'cherchons employés'
2. *(U)* [emergency aid] secours *m* ▸ **he went to get help** il est allé chercher du secours
3. [useful person or object] **: to be a help** aider, rendre service ▸ **you've been a great help** vous m'avez été d'un grand secours, vous m'avez beaucoup aidé.
■ **vi** aider ▸ **is there anything I can do to help?** puis-je être utile? ▸ **losing your temper isn't going to help** ça ne sert à rien de perdre ton calme.
■ **vt 1.** [assist] aider ▸ **to help sb (to) do sthg** aider qqn à faire qqch ▸ **he helped me on/off with my coat** il m'a aidé à mettre/enlever mon manteau ▸ **to help sb with sthg** aider qqn à faire qqch ▸ **may I help you?** [in shop] que désirez-vous? ▸ **crying won't help anyone** cela ne sert à rien *OR* n'arrange rien de pleurer
2. [avoid] **: I can't help it** je n'y peux rien ▸ **I can't help thinking that we could have done more** je ne peux pas m'empêcher de penser qu'on aurait pu faire plus ▸ **I couldn't help laughing** je ne pouvais pas m'empêcher de rire ▸ **it can't be helped** tant pis! on n'y peut rien *OR* on ne peut pas faire autrement ▸ **are they coming? – not if I can help it!** est-ce qu'ils viennent? – pas si j'ai mon mot à dire!
▸▸ **to help o.s. (to sthg)** se servir (de qqch) ▸ **I helped myself to the cheese** je me suis servi en fromage.
■ **excl** au secours!, à l'aide!
◆ ***help out*** **vt sep & vi** aider.

help button **n** COMPUT case *f* d'aide.

help desk **n** service *m* d'assistance technique.

helper ['helpəʳ] **n 1.** [gen] aide *mf* **2.** *US* [to do housework] femme *f* de ménage.

helpful ['helpfʊl] **adj 1.** [person] serviable ▸ **you've been very helpful** vous (nous) avez bien rendu service **2.** [advice, suggestion] utile.

helpfully ['helpfʊlɪ] **adv** avec obligeance, obligeamment.

helpfulness ['helpfʊlnɪs] **n 1.** [of person] obligeance *f*, serviabilité *f* **2.** [of gadget, map] utilité *f*.

helping ['helpɪŋ] **n** portion *f* / [of cake, tart] part *f*.

helping hand **n** coup *m* de main.

helpless ['helplɪs] **adj** impuissant(e) / [look, gesture] d'impuissance.

helplessly ['helplɪslɪ] **adv 1.** [stand by, watch] sans rien pouvoir faire **2.** [uncontrollably] **: to laugh helplessly** avoir le fou rire.

helplessness ['helplɪsnɪs] **n 1.** [defencelessness] incapacité *f* de se défendre, vulnérabilité *f* **2.** [physical] incapacité *f*, impotence *f* / [mental] incapacité *f* **3.** [powerlessness - of person] impuissance *f*, manque *m* de moyens / [- of anger, feeling] impuissance *f* ▸ **a feeling of helplessness** un sentiment d'impuissance.

helpline ['helplaɪn] **n** ligne *f* d'assistance téléphonique.

help menu **n** COMPUT menu *m* d'aide.

Helsinki [hel'sɪŋkɪ] **n** Helsinki.

helter-skelter ['heltə'skeltəʳ] ■ **n** *UK* toboggan *m*.
■ **adv** pêle-mêle.

hem [hem] ■ **n** ourlet *m*.
■ **vt** (pt & pp **-med**, cont **-ming**) ourler
▸▸ **to hem and haw** *US* bredouiller, bafouiller.
◆ ***hem in*** **vt sep** encercler.

he-man **n** *inf hum* vrai mâle *m*.

hematology [ˌhi:mə'tɒlədʒɪ] *US* = ***haematology***.

hemisphere ['hemɪˌsfɪəʳ] **n** hémisphère *m*.

hemline ['hemlaɪn] **n** ourlet *m*.

hemlock ['hemlɒk] **n** [poison & BOT] ciguë *f*.

hemoglobin [ˌhi:mə'gləʊbɪn] *US* = ***haemoglobin***.

hemophilia [ˌhi:mə'fɪlɪə] *US* = ***haemophilia***.

hemophiliac [ˌhi:mə'fɪlɪæk] *US* = ***haemophiliac***.

hemorrhage ['hemərɪdʒ] *US* = ***haemorrhage***.

hemorrhoids ['hemərɔɪdz] *US* = ***haemorrhoids***.

hemp [hemp] **n** [plant, fibre] chanvre *m*.

hen [hen] **n 1.** [female chicken] poule *f* **2.** [female bird] femelle *f*.

hence [hens] **adv** *fml* **1.** [therefore] d'où **2.** [from now] d'ici.

henceforward [ˌhens'fɔ:wəd], ***henceforth*** [ˌhens'fɔ:θ] **adv** dorénavant, désormais.

henchman ['hentʃmən] (pl **-men** [-mən]) **n** *pej* acolyte *m*.

henna ['henə] ■ **n** henné *m*.
■ **vt** [hair] appliquer du henné sur.

hen night, ***hen party*** **n** *inf* [gen] soirée entre copines / *UK* [before wedding] **: she's having her hen night** elle enterre sa vie de célibataire.

henpecked ['henpekt] **adj** *pej* dominé(e) par sa femme.

hepatitis [ˌhepə'taɪtɪs] **n** hépatite *f*.

heptagon ['heptəgən] **n** heptagone *m*.

heptathlon [hep'tæθlɒn] **n** heptathlon *m*.

her [hɜ:ʳ] ■ **pers pron 1.** [direct - unstressed] la, l' *(+ vowel or silent 'h')* / [- stressed] elle ▸ **I know/like her** je la connais/l'aime (bien) ▸ **it's her** c'est elle ▸ **if I were** *OR* **was her** si j'étais elle, à sa place ▸ **you can't expect her to do it** tu ne peux pas exiger que ce soit elle qui le fasse
2. [referring to animal, car, ship] *follow the gender of your translation*

3. *(indirect)* lui ▸ **we spoke to her** nous lui avons parlé ▸ **he sent her a letter** il lui a envoyé une lettre
4. *(after prep, in comparisons etc)* elle ▸ **I'm shorter than her** je suis plus petit qu'elle.
■ **poss adj** son (sa), ses *(pl)* ▸ **her coat** son manteau ▸ **her bedroom** sa chambre ▸ **her children** ses enfants ▸ **her name is Sarah** elle s'appelle Sarah ▸ **it was her fault** c'était de sa faute à elle.

herald ['herəld] ■ **vt** *fml* annoncer.
■ **n 1.** [messenger] héraut *m* **2.** [sign] signe *m*.

heraldic [he'rældɪk] **adj** héraldique.

heraldry ['herəldrɪ] **n** héraldique *f*.

herb [*UK* hɜ:b, *US* ɜ:rb] **n** herbe *f*.

herbaceous [*UK* hɜ:'beɪʃəs, *US* ɜ:r'beɪʃəs] **adj** herbacé(e).

herbaceous border **n** bordure *f* de plantes herbacées.

herbal [*UK* 'hɜ:bl, *US* 'ɜ:rbl] **adj** à base de plantes.

herbalist [*UK* 'hɜ:bəlɪst, *US* 'ɜ:rbəlɪst] **n** herboriste *mf*.

herb(al) tea **n** tisane *f*.

herbicide [*UK* 'hɜ:bɪsaɪd, *US* 'ɜ:rbɪsaɪd] **n** herbicide *m*.

herbivore [*UK* 'hɜ:bɪvɔ:ʳ, *US* 'ɜ:rbɪvɔ:r] **n** herbivore *m*.

herbivorous [hɜ:'bɪvərəs, *US* ɜ:r'bɪvərəs] **adj** herbivore.

herd [hɜ:d] ■ **n** troupeau *m*.
■ **vt 1.** [cattle, sheep] mener **2.** *fig* [people] conduire, mener / [into confined space] parquer.

herdsman ['hɜ:dzmən] (pl **-men** [-mən]) **n** gardien *m* de troupeau.

here [hɪəʳ] **adv 1.** [in this place] ici ▸ **around here** par ici ▸ **winter is here** c'est l'hiver, l'hiver est arrivé ▸ **here he is/they are** le/les voici ▸ **here it is** le/la voici ▸ **here is/are** voici ▸ **here's a man who knows what he wants** voilà un homme qui sait ce qu'il veut ▸ **here and there** çà et là **2.** [present] là ▸ **he's not here today** il n'est pas là aujourd'hui ▸ **it's this one here that I want** c'est celui-ci que je veux **3.** [in toasts] **: here's to Paul** à la santé de Paul ▸ **here's to you, Paul** à ta santé, Paul.

hereabouts *UK* [ˌhɪərə'baʊts], ***hereabout*** *US* [ˌhɪərə'baʊt] **adv** par ici.

hereafter [ˌhɪər'ɑ:ftəʳ] ■ **adv** *fml* ci-après.
■ **n : the hereafter** l'au-delà *m*.

hereby [ˌhɪə'baɪ] **adv** *fml* par la présente.

hereditary [hɪ'redɪtrɪ] **adj** héréditaire.

heredity [hɪ'redətɪ] **n** hérédité *f*.

heresy ['herəsɪ] (pl **-ies**) **n** hérésie *f*.

heretic ['herətɪk] **n** hérétique *mf*.

herewith [ˌhɪə'wɪð] **adv** *fml* [with letter] ci-joint, ci-inclus.

heritage ['herɪtɪdʒ] **n** héritage *m*, patrimoine *m*.

heritage centre **n** *UK* musée *m*.

hermaphrodite [hɜ:'mæfrədaɪt] ■ **adj** hermaphrodite.
■ **n** hermaphrodite *m*.

hermetic [hɜ:'metɪk] **adj** hermétique.

hermetically [hɜ:'metɪklɪ] **adv : hermetically sealed** fermé(e) hermétiquement.

hermit ['hɜ:mɪt] **n** ermite *m*.

hermitage ['hɜ:mɪtɪdʒ] **n** ermitage *m*.

hermit crab **n** bernard-l'ermite *m inv*, pagure *m*.

hernia ['hɜ:njə] **n** hernie *f*.

hero ['hɪərəʊ] (pl **-es**) **n** héros *m*.

heroic [hɪ'rəʊɪk] **adj** héroïque.

heroically [hɪ'rəʊɪklɪ] **adv** héroïquement.

heroics [hɪ'rəʊɪks] **npl** [language] emphase *f*, déclamation *f* / [behaviour] affectation *f*, emphase *f*.

heroin ['herəʊɪn] **n** héroïne *f*.

heroine ['herəʊɪn] **n** héroïne *f*.

heroism ['herəʊɪzm] **n** héroïsme *m*.

heron ['herən] (pl **heron** *OR* **-s**) **n** héron *m*.

hero worship **n** culte *m* du héros.

herpes ['hɜ:pi:z] **n** herpès *m*.

herring ['herɪŋ] (pl **herring** *OR* **-s**) **n** hareng *m*.

herringbone ['herɪŋbəʊn] **n** [pattern] chevrons *mpl*.

hers [hɜ:z] **poss pron** le sien (la sienne), les siens (les siennes) *(pl)* ▸ **that money is hers** cet argent est à elle *OR* est le sien ▸ **it wasn't his fault, it was hers** ce n'était pas de sa faute à lui, c'était de sa faute à elle ▸ **a friend of hers** un ami à elle, un de ses amis.

herself [hɜ:'self] **pron 1.** *(reflexive)* se / *(after prep)* elle **2.** *(for emphasis)* elle-même ▸ **she did it herself** elle l'a fait toute seule.

Herts [hɑ:ts] (abbr of **Hertfordshire**) *comté anglais*.

hertz [hɜ:ts] (pl **hertz**) **n** hertz *m*.

he's [hi:z] = ***he is, he has***.

hesitance ['hezɪtəns], ***hesitancy*** ['hezɪtənsɪ] **n** hésitation *f*, indécision *f*.

hesitant ['hezɪtənt] **adj** hésitant(e) ▸ **to be hesitant about doing sthg** hésiter à faire qqch.

hesitantly ['hezɪtəntlɪ] **adv** [act, try] avec hésitation, timidement / [answer, speak] d'une voix hésitante.

hesitate ['hezɪteɪt] **vi** hésiter ▸ **to hesitate to do sthg** hésiter à faire qqch.

hesitation [ˌhezɪ'teɪʃn] **n** hésitation *f* ▸ **to have no hesitation in doing sthg** ne pas hésiter à faire qqch.

hessian ['hesɪən] **n** *UK* jute *m*.

heterogeneous [ˌhetərə'dʒi:njəs] **adj** *fml* hétérogène.

heterosexual [ˌhetərəʊ'sekʃʊəl] ■ **adj** hétérosexuel(elle).
■ **n** hétérosexuel *m*, -elle *f*.

het up [het-] **adj** *inf dated* excité(e), énervé(e).

hew [hju:] (pt **-ed**, pp **-ed** *OR* **hewn** [hju:n]) **vt** *liter* [stone] tailler / [wood] couper.

hex [heks] **n** *US* [curse] sort *m*.

hexagon ['heksəgən] **n** hexagone *m*.

hexagonal [hek'sægənl] **adj** hexagonal(e).

hey [heɪ] **excl** hé!

heyday ['heɪdeɪ] **n** âge *m* d'or.

hey presto [-'prestəʊ] **excl** *UK* passez muscade!

HF (abbr of ***high frequency***) HF.

HGV (abbr of ***heavy goods vehicle***) **n** PL *m* ▸ **an HGV licence** un permis PL.

hi [haɪ] **excl** *inf* salut!

HI abbr of ***Hawaii***.

hiatal hernia [haɪ'eɪtl-] = ***hiatus hernia***.

hiatus [haɪ'eɪtəs] (pl **-es** [-i:z]) **n** *fml* pause *f*.

hiatus hernia **n** hernie *f* hiatale.

hibernate ['haɪbəneɪt] **vi** hiberner.

hibernation [,haɪbə'neɪʃn] **n** hibernation *f*.

hiccup, hiccough ['hɪkʌp] ■ **n** hoquet *m* / *fig* [difficulty] accroc *m* ▸ **to have (the) hiccups** avoir le hoquet.
■ **vi** (pt & pp **-ped**, cont **-ping**) hoqueter.

hick [hɪk] **n** *esp US inf pej* péquenaud *m*, -e *f*.

hickey [hɪkɪ] **n** *US* suçon *m*.

hickory ['hɪkərɪ] ■ **n** (pl **-ies**) [tree] hickory *m*, noyer *m* blanc d'Amérique / [wood] (bois *m* de) hickory *m*.
■ **comp** en (bois de) hickory ▸ **hickory nut** fruit *m* du hickory, noix *f* d'Amérique.

hid [hɪd] **pt** ➤ ***hide***.

hidden ['hɪdn] ■ **pp** ➤ ***hide***.
■ **adj** caché(e).

hidden camera **n** caméra *f* cachée *OR* invisible.

hidden economy **n** économie *f* noire.

hide [haɪd] ■ **vt** (pt **hid**, pp **hidden**) **: to hide sthg (from sb)** cacher qqch (à qqn) / [information] taire qqch (à qqn) ▸ **to hide the truth (from sb)** taire *OR* dissimuler la vérité (à qqn).
■ **vi** (pt **hid**, pp **hidden**) se cacher ▸ **the ambassador hid behind his diplomatic immunity** *fig* l'ambassadeur s'est réfugié derrière son immunité diplomatique.
■ **n 1.** [animal skin] peau *f* **2.** *UK* [for watching birds, animals] cachette *f*.

hide-and-seek **n** cache-cache *m*.

hideaway ['haɪdəweɪ] **n** cachette *f*.

hidebound ['haɪdbaʊnd] **adj** *pej* [person] borné(e) / [institution] rigide.

hideous ['hɪdɪəs] **adj** [ugly] hideux(euse) / [error, conditions] abominable.

hideously ['hɪdɪəslɪ] **adv 1.** [deformed, wounded] hideusement, atrocement, affreusement **2.** *fig* [as intensifier] terriblement, horriblement.

hideout ['haɪdaʊt] **n** cachette *f*.

hidey-hole ['haɪdɪhəʊl] **n** *inf* planque *f*.

hiding ['haɪdɪŋ] **n 1.** [concealment] **: to be in hiding** se tenir caché(e) **2.** *inf* [beating] **: to give sb a (good) hiding** donner une (bonne) raclée *OR* correction à qqn.

hiding place **n** cachette *f*.

hierarchical [,haɪə'rɑ:kɪkl] **adj** hiérarchique.

hierarchically [,haɪə'rɑ:kɪklɪ] **adv** hiérarchiquement.

hierarchy ['haɪərɑ:kɪ] (pl **-ies**) **n** hiérarchie *f*.

hieroglyphics [,haɪərə'glɪfɪks] **npl** hiéroglyphes *mpl*.

hi-fi ['haɪfaɪ] **n** hi-fi *f inv*.

higgledy-piggledy [,hɪgldɪ'pɪgldɪ] *inf* ■ **adj** pêle-mêle *(inv)*.
■ **adv** pêle-mêle.

high [haɪ] ■ **adj 1.** [gen] haut(e) ▸ **it's 3 feet/6 metres high** cela fait 3 pieds/6 mètres de haut ▸ **how high is it?** cela fait combien de haut? ▸ **the building is eight storeys high** c'est un immeuble de *OR* à huit étages ▸ **the sun was high in the sky** le soleil était haut ▸ **to have a high opinion of sb/sthg** avoir une haute opinion de qqn/qqch
2. [speed, figure, altitude, office] élevé(e) ▸ **built to withstand high temperatures** conçu(e) pour résister à des températures élevées ▸ **high winds** des vents violents, de grands vents ▸ **she suffers from high blood pressure** elle a de la tension ▸ **areas of high unemployment** des régions à fort taux de chômage
3. [high-pitched] aigu(uë)
4. *drug sl* qui plane, défoncé(e)
5. *inf* [drunk] bourré(e).
■ **adv** haut ▸ **up high** en haut ▸ **we looked high and low for him** nous l'avons cherché partout.
■ **n** [highest point] maximum *m* ▸ **prices are at an all-time high** les prix ont atteint leur maximum ▸ **to reach a new high** atteindre un nouveau record *OR* maximum.

-high **suffix** à la hauteur de... ▸ **shoulder-high** à la hauteur de l'épaule.

high-and-mighty **adj** arrogant(e), impérieux(euse) ▸ **to be high-and-mighty** se donner de grands airs ▸ **don't act so high-and-mighty** ne prends pas tes airs de grand seigneur/grande dame.

highball ['haɪbɔ:l] **n** *US* whisky *m* à l'eau avec de la glace.

highbrow ['haɪbraʊ] **adj** *pej* intellectuel(elle).

high chair **n** chaise *f* haute *(d'enfant)*.

high-class **adj** de premier ordre / [hotel, restaurant] de grande classe.

high command **n** haut commandement *m*.

high commissioner **n** haut commissaire *m*.

high court **n** *US* LAW Cour *f* suprême.

High Court **n** *UK* LAW Cour *f* d'appel.

high-definition **adj** à haute définition.

high-density **adj** COMPUT haute densité *(inv)*.

high-end **adj** [computer, market] haut(e) de gamme.

higher ['haɪəʳ] **adj** [exam, qualification] supérieur(e).
◆ ***Higher*** **n : Higher (Grade)** SCH *examen de fin d'études secondaires en Écosse*.

higher education **n** *(U)* études *fpl* supérieures.

high explosive **n** explosif *m* puissant.

highfalutin [,haɪfə'lu:tɪn] **adj** *inf* affecté(e), prétentieux(euse).

high-fidelity **adj** haute-fidélité *(inv)*.

high-five **n** *inf geste que font deux personnes pour se féliciter ou se dire bonjour et qui consiste à se taper dans la main*.

high-flier, high-flyer **n** ambitieux *m*, -euse *f*.

high-flying **adj** [ambitious] ambitieux(euse).

high gear **n** *US* AUT quatrième/cinquième vitesse *f* / *fig* **: to move into high gear** passer la surmultipliée.

high-handed [-'hændɪd] **adj** [overbearing] autoritaire, despotique / [inconsiderate] cavalier(ère).

high-handedness [-'hændɪdnɪs] **n** [overbearing attitude - of person] caractère *m* autoritaire, despotisme *m* / [- of behaviour] caractère *m* arbitraire / [lack of consideration] jugement *m* cavalier.

high-heeled [-hi:ld] **adj** à talons hauts.

high heels **npl** talons *mpl* aiguilles.

high horse **n** *inf* **: to get on one's high horse** monter sur ses grands chevaux.

high jinks **npl** *inf* chahut *m*.

high jump **n** saut *m* en hauteur ▸ **to be for the high jump** *UK inf* être bon(bonne) pour une engueulade.

high jumper **n** sauteur *m (qui fait du saut en hauteur)*.

highlander ['haɪləndər] **n** [mountain dweller] montagnard *m*, -e *f*.
◆ ***Highlander*** **n** habitant *m*, -e *f* des Highlands, Highlander *m*.

Highland fling **n** *danse des Highlands traditionnellement exécutée en solo.*

Highland Games ['haɪlənd-] **npl** jeux *mpl* écossais.

Highlands ['haɪləndz] **npl : the Highlands** les Highlands *fpl (région montagneuse du nord de l'Écosse)*.

high-level **adj** [talks, discussions] à haut niveau / [diplomats, officials] de haut niveau.

high life **n : the high life** la grande vie.

highlight ['haɪlaɪt] ■ **n** [of event, occasion] moment *m* OR point *m* fort.
■ **vt** souligner / [with highlighter & COMPUT] surligner.
◆ ***highlights*** **npl** [in hair] reflets *mpl*, mèches *fpl*.

highlighter (pen) ['haɪlaɪtər-] **n** surligneur *m*.

highly ['haɪlɪ] **adv** **1.** [very] extrêmement, très **2.** [very well] très bien ▸ **very highly paid** très bien payé(e) **3.** [in important position] **: highly placed** haut placé(e) **4.** [favourably] **: to think highly of sb/sthg** penser du bien de qqn/qqch ▸ **to speak highly of sb/sthg** dire du bien de qqn/qqch ▸ **I highly recommend it** je vous le conseille vivement OR chaudement.

highly-strung **adj** *UK* nerveux(euse).

high mass, High Mass **n** grand-messe *f*.

high-minded [-'maɪndɪd] **adj** au caractère noble.

Highness ['haɪnɪs] **n : His/Her/Your (Royal) Highness** Son/Votre Altesse (Royale) ▸ **their (Royal) Highnesses** leurs Altesses (Royales).

high-octane **adj** à indice d'octane élevé.

high-performance **adj** performant(e).

high-pitched [-'pɪtʃt] **adj** aigu(uë).

high point **n** [of occasion] point *m* fort.

high-powered [-'paʊəd] **adj** **1.** [powerful] de forte puissance **2.** [prestigious - activity, place] de haut niveau / [- job, person] très important(e).

high-pressure **adj** **1.** [air, gas] à haute pression ▸ **high-pressure area** METEOR zone *f* de hautes pressions **2.** [selling] agressif(ive).

high priest **n** RELIG grand prêtre *m*.

high profile **n : to have a high profile** être très en vue.
◆ ***high-profile*** **adj** [job, position] qui est très en vue / [campaign] qui fait beaucoup de bruit.

high-ranking [-'ræŋkɪŋ] **adj** de haut rang.

high resolution ■ **n** COMPUT haute résolution *f*.
■ **adj** à haute résolution.

high rise **n** tour *f (immeuble)*.
◆ ***high-rise*** **adj : high-rise block of flats** *UK* tour *f*.

high-risk **adj** à haut risque.

high school **n** *UK établissement d'enseignement secondaire* / *US* ≃ lycée *m*.

high seas **npl : the high seas** la haute mer *f*.

high season **n** haute saison *f*.

high-speed **adj** **1.** [train] à grande vitesse **2.** PHOT à obturation rapide.

high-spirited **adj** [person] plein(e) d'entrain.

high spot **n** point *m* fort.

high street **n** *UK* rue *f* principale.

high-strung *US* = ***highly-strung***.

hightail ['haɪteɪl] **vt** *esp US inf* **: to hightail it out** filer.

high tea **n** *UK repas tenant lieu de goûter et de dîner, pris en fin d'après-midi.*

high-tech [-'tek] **adj** [method, industry] de pointe.

high technology **n** technologie *f* de pointe.

high-tension **adj** à haute tension.

high tide **n** marée *f* haute.

high treason **n** haute trahison *f*.

high water **n** *(U)* marée *f* haute.

highway ['haɪweɪ] **n** **1.** *US* [motorway] autoroute *f* **2.** [main road] grande route *f*.

Highway Code **n** *UK* **: the Highway Code** le code de la route.

high wire **n** corde *f* raide.

hijack ['haɪdʒæk] ■ **n** détournement *m*.
■ **vt** détourner.

hijacker ['haɪdʒækər] **n** [of aircraft] pirate *m* de l'air / [of vehicle] pirate *m* de la route.

hijacking ['haɪdʒækɪŋ] **n** **1.** [of car, plane, train] détournement *m* **2.** [robbery] vol *m*.

hike [haɪk] ■ **n** [long walk] randonnée *f*.
■ **vi** faire une randonnée.

hiker ['haɪkər] **n** randonneur *m*, -euse *f*.

hiking ['haɪkɪŋ] **n** marche *f*.

hilarious [hɪ'leərɪəs] **adj** hilarant(e).

hilariously [hɪ'leərɪəslɪ] **adv** joyeusement, gaiement ▸ **the film's hilariously funny** le film est à se tordre de rire.

hilarity [hɪ'lærətɪ] **n** hilarité *f*.

hill [hɪl] **n** **1.** [mound] colline *f* **2.** [slope] côte *f*.

hillbilly ['hɪl,bɪlɪ] (pl **-ies**) **n** *US inf pej* péquenaud *m*, -e *f*.

hillock ['hɪlək] **n** petite colline *f* / [smaller] petite élévation *f*.

hillside ['hɪlsaɪd] **n** coteau *m*.

hill start **n** *UK* & *Aus* démarrage *m* en côte.

hilltop ['hɪltɒp] ■ **adj** au sommet de la colline.
■ **n** sommet *m*.

hilly ['hɪlɪ] (comp **-ier**, superl **-iest**) **adj** vallonné(e).

hilt [hɪlt] **n** garde *f* ▸ **to the hilt** jusqu'au cou ▸ **to support/defend sb to the hilt** soutenir/défendre qqn à fond.

him [hɪm] **pers pron 1.** [direct - unstressed] le, l' *(+ vowel or silent 'h')* / [- stressed] lui ▸ **I know/like him** je le connais/l'aime (bien) ▸ **it's him** c'est lui ▸ **if I were** ***OR*** **was him** si j'étais lui, à sa place ▸ **you can't expect him to do it** tu ne peux pas exiger que ce soit lui qui le fasse **2.** *(indirect)* lui ▸ **we spoke to him** nous lui avons parlé ▸ **she sent him a letter** elle lui a envoyé une lettre **3.** *(after prep, in comparisons etc)* lui ▸ **I'm shorter than him** je suis plus petit que lui.

Himalayan [ˌhɪmə'leɪən] **adj** himalayen(enne).

Himalayas [ˌhɪmə'leɪəz] **npl : the Himalayas** l'Himalaya *m* ▸ **in the Himalayas** dans l'Himalaya.

himself [hɪm'self] **pron 1.** *(reflexive)* se / *(after prep)* lui **2.** *(for emphasis)* lui-même ▸ **he did it himself** il l'a fait tout seul.

hind [haɪnd] ■ **adj** de derrière.
■ **n** (pl **hind** ***OR*** **-s**) *esp UK* biche *f*.

hinder ['hɪndəʳ] **vt** gêner, entraver.

Hindi ['hɪndɪ] **n** hindi *m*.

hindmost ['haɪndməʊst] **adj** arrière.

hindquarters ['haɪndkwɔːtəz] **npl** arrière-train *m*.

hindrance ['hɪndrəns] **n** obstacle *m*.

hindsight ['haɪndsaɪt] **n : with the benefit of hindsight** avec du recul.

Hindu ['hɪnduː] ■ **adj** hindou(e).
■ **n** (pl **-s**) Hindou *m*, -e *f*.

Hinduism ['hɪnduːɪzm] **n** hindouisme *m*.

hinge [hɪndʒ] **n** [whole fitting] charnière *f* / [pin] gond *m*.
◆ ***hinge (up)on*** (cont **hingeing**) **vt insep** [depend on] dépendre de.

hinged [hɪndʒd] **adj** à charnière ***OR*** charnières ▸ **hinged flap** [of counter] abattant *m*.

hint [hɪnt] ■ **n 1.** [indication] allusion *f* ▸ **to drop a hint** faire une allusion ▸ **you could try dropping a hint that if his work doesn't improve...** tu pourrais essayer de lui faire comprendre que si son travail ne s'améliore pas... ▸ **to take the hint** saisir l'allusion **2.** [piece of advice] conseil *m*, indication *f* **3.** [small amount] soupçon *m*.
■ **vi : to hint at sthg** faire allusion à qqch ▸ **what are you hinting at?** qu'est-ce que tu insinues? / [in neutral sense] à quoi fais-tu allusion?
■ **vt : to hint that...** insinuer que...

hinterland ['hɪntəlænd] **n** arrière-pays *m*.

hip [hɪp] ■ **n** hanche *f*.
■ **adj** *inf* [fashionable] branché.

hipbath ['hɪpbɑːθ] **n** *esp UK* bain *m* de siège.

hipbone, hip bone ['hɪpbəʊn] **n** os *m* de la hanche, os *m* iliaque.

hip flask **n** flasque *f*.

hip-hop **n** [music] hip-hop *m*.

hippie ['hɪpɪ] = ***hippy***.

hippo ['hɪpəʊ] (pl **-s**) **n** hippopotame *m*.

hippopotamus [ˌhɪpə'pɒtəməs] (pl **-muses** [-məsiːz] ***OR*** **-mi** [-maɪ]) **n** hippopotame *m*.

hippy ['hɪpɪ] (pl **-ies**) **n** hippie *mf*.

hipsters ['hɪpstəz] **npl** *UK* pantalon *m* à taille basse.

hire ['haɪəʳ] ■ **n** *(U)* *UK* [of car, equipment] location *f* ▸ **for hire** [bicycles] à louer / [taxi] libre ▸ **on hire** en location.
■ **vt 1.** *UK* [rent] louer **2.** [employ] employer les services de ▸ **a hired killer** un tueur à gages.
◆ ***hire out*** **vt sep** *UK* louer.

hire car **n** *UK* voiture *f* de location.

hire purchase **n** *(U)* *UK* achat *m* à crédit ***OR*** à tempérament ▸ **to buy sthg on hire purchase** acheter qqch à crédit ***OR*** à tempérament.

hiring ['haɪərɪŋ] **n 1.** *UK* [of car] location *f* **2.** [of employee] embauche *f*.

his [hɪz] ■ **poss adj** son (sa), ses *(pl)* ▸ **his house** sa maison ▸ **his money** son argent ▸ **his children** ses enfants ▸ **his name is Joe** il s'appelle Joe ▸ **it wasn't his fault** ce n'était pas de sa faute à lui.
■ **poss pron** le sien (la sienne), les siens (les siennes) *(pl)* ▸ **that money is his** cet argent est à lui ***OR*** est le sien ▸ **it wasn't her fault, it was his** ce n'était pas de sa faute à elle, c'était de sa faute à lui ▸ **a friend of his** un ami à lui, un de ses amis.

Hispanic [hɪ'spænɪk] ■ **adj** hispanique.
■ **n** *esp US* Hispano-américain *m*, -e *f*.

hiss [hɪs] ■ **n** [of animal, gas] sifflement *m* / [of crowd] sifflet *m*.
■ **vt** [speaker, speech] siffler.
■ **vi** [animal, gas] siffler.

histogram ['hɪstəgræm] **n** histogramme *m*.

historian [hɪ'stɔːrɪən] **n** historien *m*, -enne *f*.

historic [hɪ'stɒrɪk] **adj** historique.

historical [hɪ'stɒrɪkəl] **adj** historique.

historically [hɪ'stɒrɪklɪ] **adv** historiquement / [traditionally] traditionnellement.

history ['hɪstərɪ] (pl **-ies**) **n 1.** [gen] histoire *f* ▸ **to go down in history** entrer dans l'histoire ▸ **to make history** faire l'histoire **2.** [past record] antécédents *mpl* ▸ **medical history** passé *m* médical **3.** COMPUT historique *m*.

histrionics [hɪstrɪ'ɒnɪks] **npl** *pej* drame *m*.

hit [hɪt] ■ **n 1.** [blow] coup *m*
2. [successful strike] coup *m* ***OR*** tir *m* réussi / [in fencing] touche *f* ▸ **to score a hit on sthg** toucher qqch
3. [success] succès *m* ▸ **to be a hit with** plaire à
4. COMPUT visite *f* (d'un site Internet).
■ **comp** à succès ▸ **hit single** ***OR*** **song** succès *m*, hit *m*, tube *m*.
■ **vt** (pt & pp **hit**, cont **-ting**) **1.** [strike] frapper / [nail] taper sur ▸ **to hit sb in the face/on the head** frapper qqn au visage/sur la tête ▸ **to hit one's head/knee (against sthg)** se cogner la tête/le genou (contre qqch) ▸ **to hit a ball over the net** envoyer un ballon par-dessus le filet

2. [crash into] heurter, percuter ▸ **the car hit a tree** la voiture a heurté OR est rentrée dans un arbre
3. [reach] atteindre ▸ **the bullet hit him in the shoulder** la balle l'a atteint OR touché à l'épaule ▸ **it suddenly hit me that...** *fig* il m'est soudain venu à l'esprit que... ▸ **to hit a problem** se heurter à un problème OR une difficulté
4. [affect badly] toucher, affecter ▸ **the region worst hit by the earthquake** la région la plus sévèrement touchée par le tremblement de terre ▸ **the child's death has hit them all very hard** la mort de l'enfant les a tous durement touchés OR frappés
▸▸ **to hit it off (with sb)** bien s'entendre (avec qqn).
◆ ***hit back*** vi *esp UK* **: our army hit back with a missile attack** notre armée a riposté en envoyant des missiles ▸ **to hit back (at)** répondre (à).
◆ ***hit on*** vt insep **1.** = ***hit upon***
2. *US inf* [chat up] draguer.
◆ ***hit out*** vi *esp UK* **: to hit out at** [physically] envoyer un coup à / [criticize] attaquer.
◆ ***hit upon*** vt insep [think of] trouver.

hit-and-miss = ***hit-or-miss***.

hit-and-run adj [accident] avec délit de fuite ▸ **hit-and-run driver** chauffard *m (qui a commis un délit de fuite)*.

hitch [hɪtʃ] ■ n [problem, snag] ennui *m* ▸ **without a hitch** OR **any hitches** sans anicroche.
■ vt **1.** [catch] **: to hitch a lift** OR **a ride** faire du stop
2. [fasten] **: to hitch sthg on** OR **onto** accrocher OR attacher qqch à ▸ **to get hitched** [one person] se caser / [couple] passer devant Monsieur le Maire.
■ vi [hitchhike] faire du stop.
◆ ***hitch up*** vt sep [pull up] remonter.

hitchhike ['hɪtʃhaɪk] vi faire de l'auto-stop.

hitchhiker ['hɪtʃhaɪkər] n auto-stoppeur *m*, -euse *f*.

hitchhiking ['hɪtʃhaɪkɪŋ], ***hitching*** ['hɪtʃɪŋ] n auto-stop *m*, stop *m*.

hi-tech [,haɪ'tek] = ***high-tech***.

hither ['hɪðər] adv *liter* ici ▸ **hither and thither** çà et là.

hitherto [,hɪðə'tu:] adv *fml* jusqu'ici.

hit list n liste *f* noire.

hit man n tueur *m (à gages)*.

hit-or-miss adj aléatoire.

hit parade n *dated* hit-parade *m*.

hit squad n *inf* commando *m* de tueurs.

HIV (abbr of ***human immunodeficiency virus***) n VIH *m*, HIV *m* ▸ **to be HIV-positive** être séropositif(ive).

hive [haɪv] n ruche *f* ▸ **a hive of activity** une véritable ruche.
◆ ***hive off*** vt sep *UK* [assets] séparer.

hiya ['haɪjə] excl salut *inf*.

hl (abbr of ***hectolitre***) hl.

HM (abbr of ***His (or Her) Majesty***) SM.

HMG (abbr of ***His (or Her) Majesty's Government***) *expression utilisée sur des documents officiels en Grande-Bretagne*.

HMI (abbr of ***His (or Her) Majesty's Inspector***) n *inspecteur de l'éducation nationale en Grande-Bretagne*.

HMO (abbr of ***health maintenance organization***) n *organisme américain pour la santé publique*.

HMS (abbr of ***His (or Her) Majesty's Ship***) *expression précédant le nom d'un bâtiment de la marine britannique*.

HMSO (abbr of ***His (or Her) Majesty's Stationery Office***) n *service officiel des publications en Grande-Bretagne*, ≃ Imprimerie *f* nationale.

HNC (abbr of ***Higher National Certificate***) n *brevet de technicien en Grande-Bretagne*.

HND (abbr of ***Higher National Diploma***) n *brevet de technicien supérieur en Grande-Bretagne*.

hoard [hɔ:d] ■ n [store] réserves *fpl* / [of useless items] tas *m*.
■ vt amasser / [food, petrol] faire des provisions de.

hoarder ['hɔ:də] n [gen] *personne ou animal qui fait des réserves* / [of money] thésauriseur *m*, -euse *f* ▸ **you're such a hoarder!** quel conservateur tu fais!

hoarding ['hɔ:dɪŋ] n *UK* [for advertisements] panneau *m* d'affichage publicitaire.

hoarfrost ['hɔ:frɒst] n gelée *f* blanche.

hoarse [hɔ:s] adj [person, voice] enroué(e) / [shout, whisper] rauque.

hoarsely ['hɔ:slɪ] adv d'une voix rauque OR enrouée.

hoax [həʊks] ■ n canular *m*.
■ comp **: hoax (telephone) call** canular *m* téléphonique.

hoaxer ['həʊksər] n mauvais plaisant *m*.

hob [hɒb] n *UK* [on cooker] rond *m*, plaque *f*.

hobble ['hɒbl] vi [limp] boitiller.

hobby ['hɒbɪ] (pl -ies) n passe-temps *m inv*, hobby *m*, violon *m* d'Ingres.

hobbyhorse ['hɒbɪhɔ:s] n **1.** [toy] cheval *m* à bascule **2.** *fig* [favourite topic] dada *m*.

hobnob ['hɒbnɒb] (pt & pp -bed, cont -bing) vi *pej* **: to hobnob with sb** frayer avec qqn.

hobo ['həʊbəʊ] (pl -es OR -s) n *US dated* clochard *m*, -e *f*.

Ho Chi Minh City ['həʊ,tʃi:'mɪn-] n Hô Chi Minh-Ville.

hock [hɒk] n *esp UK* [wine] vin *m* du Rhin.

hockey ['hɒkɪ] n **1.** *esp UK* [on grass] hockey *m* **2.** *US* [ice hockey] hockey *m* sur glace.

hocus-pocus ['həʊkəs'pəʊkəs] n [trickery] supercherie *f*, tromperie *f*.

hod [hɒd] n hotte *f*.

hodgepodge *US* = ***hotchpotch***.

hoe [həʊ] ■ n houe *f*.
■ vt biner.

hog [hɒg] ■ n **1.** *US* [pig] cochon *m* **2.** *inf* [greedy person] goinfre *m*
▸▸ **to go the whole hog** *inf* aller jusqu'au bout.
■ vt (pt & pp -ged, cont -ging) *inf* [monopolize] accaparer, monopoliser.

Hogmanay ['hɒgməneɪ] n *la Saint-Sylvestre en Écosse*.

hoi polloi [,hɔɪpə'lɔɪ] npl *pej* **: the hoi polloi** la populace.

hoist [hɔɪst] ■ **n** [device] treuil *m*.
■ **vt** hisser.

hoity-toity [ˌhɔɪtɪ'tɔɪtɪ] **adj** *inf pej* prétentieux(euse), péteux(euse) ▸ **she's very hoity-toity** c'est une vraie bêcheuse.

hokum ['həʊkəm] **n** *(U) US inf* niaiseries *fpl*.

hold [həʊld] ■ **vt** (**pt & pp held**) **1.** [gen] tenir ▸ **to hold sthg in one's hand** [book, clothing, guitar] avoir qqch à la main / [key, money] tenir qqch dans la main ▸ **to hold sb close** *OR* **tight** serrer qqn contre soi
2. [keep in position] maintenir
3. [carry on, engage in - conversation, meeting] tenir / [- party] donner / [organize] organiser ▸ **to hold an election/elections** procéder à une élection/à des élections
4. [as prisoner] détenir ▸ **to hold sb prisoner/hostage** détenir qqn prisonnier/comme otage ▸ **the police are holding him for questioning** la police l'a gardé à vue pour l'interroger
5. [have, possess - degree, permit, ticket] avoir, posséder / [- job, position] avoir, occuper
6. *fml* [consider] considérer, estimer ▸ **to hold (that)...** considérer que..., estimer que... ▸ **to hold sb responsible for sthg** rendre qqn responsable de qqch, tenir qqn pour responsable de qqch ▸ **to hold sthg dear** tenir à qqch
7. [on telephone] **: please hold (the line)** ne quittez pas, je vous prie
8. [keep, maintain] retenir ▸ **we have held costs to a minimum** nous avons limité nos frais au minimum ▸ **will the restaurant hold the table for us?** est-ce que le restaurant va nous garder la table?
9. [sustain, support] supporter
10. [contain] contenir ▸ **the main hall holds 500** on peut tenir à 500 dans la grande salle ▸ **what does the future hold for him?** que lui réserve l'avenir?
▸▸ **hold it!, hold everything!** attendez!, arrêtez! ▸ **to hold one's own** se défendre.
■ **vi** (**pt & pp held**) **1.** [cling] se tenir, s'accrocher ▸ **hold tight!** accrochez-vous bien!
2. [remain unchanged - gen] tenir / [- luck] persister / [- weather] se maintenir ▸ **to hold still** *OR* **steady** ne pas bouger, rester tranquille
3. [on phone] patienter.
■ **n 1.** [grasp, grip] prise *f*, étreinte *f* ▸ **to take** *OR* **lay hold of sthg** saisir qqch ▸ **to get hold of sthg** [obtain] se procurer qqch ▸ **to get hold of sb** [find] joindre ▸ **I've been trying to get hold of you all week!** je t'ai cherché toute la semaine!
2. [control, influence] prise *f* ▸ **to have a hold over sb** avoir de l'influence sur qqn ▸ **to take hold** [fire] prendre
3. [of ship, aircraft] cale *f*
4. [delay, pause] pause *f*, arrêt *m* ▸ **on hold** [gen & TELEC] en attente ▸ **we've put the project on hold** nous avons mis le projet en attente.
◆ ***hold against*** **vt sep : to hold sthg against sb** *fig* en vouloir à qqn de qqch.
◆ ***hold back*** ■ **vi** [hesitate] se retenir ▸ **to hold back from doing sthg** se retenir de faire qqch.
■ **vt sep 1.** [restrain, prevent] retenir / [anger] réprimer ▸ **to hold sb back from doing sthg** retenir qqn de faire qqch
2. [keep secret] cacher.
◆ ***hold down*** **vt sep** [job] garder.
◆ ***hold off*** ■ **vt sep** [fend off] tenir à distance / [delay] reporter.
■ **vi : the rain held off** il n'a pas plu.
◆ ***hold on*** **vi 1.** [wait] attendre / [on phone] ne pas quitter
2. [grip] **: to hold on (to sthg)** se tenir (à qqch).
◆ ***hold onto*** **vt insep** [power, job] garder.
◆ ***hold out*** ■ **vt sep** [hand, arms] tendre.
■ **vi 1.** [last] durer
2. [resist] **: to hold out (against sb/sthg)** résister (à qqn/ qqch).
◆ ***hold out for*** **vt insep** continuer à réclamer.
◆ ***hold up*** **vt sep 1.** [raise] lever
2. [delay] retarder ▸ **the accident held up traffic for an hour** l'accident a bloqué la circulation pendant une heure
3. *inf* [rob] faire un hold-up dans.
◆ ***hold with*** **vt insep** *fml* [approve of] approuver.

holdall ['həʊldɔːl] **n** *UK* fourre-tout *m inv*.

holder ['həʊldə^r] **n 1.** [for cigarette] porte-cigarettes *m inv* **2.** [owner] détenteur *m*, -trice *f* / [of position, title] titulaire *mf*.

holding ['həʊldɪŋ] ■ **n 1.** [investment] effets *mpl* en portefeuille **2.** [farm] ferme *f*.
■ **adj** [action, operation] *mené en vue de maintenir le statu quo*.

holding company **n** holding *m*.

hold-up ['həʊldʌp] **n 1.** [robbery] hold-up *m* **2.** [delay] retard *m*.

hole [həʊl] **n 1.** [gen] trou *m* ▸ **hole in one** GOLF trou réussi en un coup ▸ **to pick holes in sthg** [criticize] trouver à redire à qqch **2.** *UK inf* [predicament] pétrin *m*.
◆ ***hole up*** **vi** [hide, take shelter] se terrer.

holiday ['hɒlɪdeɪ] ■ **n 1.** *UK* [vacation] vacances *fpl* ▸ **to be/go on holiday** être/partir en vacances ▸ **everyone is getting ready for the Christmas holidays** tout le monde prépare les fêtes **2.** [public holiday] jour *m* férié ▸ **tomorrow is a holiday** demain c'est férié.
■ **comp** [mood, feeling, destination] de vacances ▸ **the holiday traffic** la circulation des départs en vacances.
■ **vi** *UK* passer les vacances.

CULTURE

Holidays

Au Royaume-Uni, les jours saints ne sont pas des fêtes nationales, à l'exception du Vendredi saint et du jour de Noël. D'autres jours fériés jalonnent le calendrier britannique : le 1er de l'An, la Saint-Patrick en Irlande du Nord, le lundi de Pâques, le 1er mai, les congés de printemps et d'été, et le 26 décembre, le **Boxing Day**. Aux États-Unis, et particulièrement sur la côte Est, la plupart des congés sont dédiés à des personnages célèbres (Martin Luther King, Christophe Colomb, les présidents Lincoln et Washington), aux victimes de guerre (**Memorial Day**) et aux vétérans en général (**Veterans' Day**), sans oublier la fête nationale **Independence Day**, la fête du Travail **Labor Day** et **Thanksgiving**.

holiday camp **n** *UK* camp *m* de vacances.
holiday home **n** *UK* maison *f* de vacances, résidence *f* secondaire.
holidaymaker ['hɒlɪdɪ,meɪkəʳ] **n** *UK* vacancier *m*, -ère *f*.
holiday pay **n** *UK salaire payé pendant les vacances.*
holiday resort **n** *UK* lieu *m* de vacances.
holiday season **n** *UK* saison *f* des vacances.
holiness ['həʊlɪnɪs] **n** [holy quality] sainteté *f*.
◆ ***Holiness*** **n** [in titles] **: His/Your Holiness** Sa/Votre Sainteté.
holistic [həʊ'lɪstɪk] **adj** holistique.
Holland ['hɒlənd] **n** Hollande *f* ▸ **in Holland** en Hollande.
hollandaise sauce [,hɒlən'deɪz-] **n** sauce *f* hollandaise.
holler ['hɒləʳ] **vi & vt** *inf* gueuler, brailler.
hollow ['hɒləʊ] ■ **adj** [tree, container] creux (creuse) / [eyes] cave / [promise, victory] faux (fausse) / [laugh] qui sonne faux.
■ **n** creux *m*.
◆ ***hollow out*** **vt sep** creuser, évider.
hollow-eyed **adj** aux yeux caves *OR* enfoncés.
holly ['hɒlɪ] **n** houx *m*.
Hollywood ['hɒlɪwʊd] ■ **n** [film industry] Hollywood.
■ **comp** hollywoodien(enne).
holocaust ['hɒləkɔːst] **n** [destruction] destruction *f*, holocauste *m*.
◆ ***Holocaust*** **n : the Holocaust** l'holocauste *m*.
hologram ['hɒləgræm] **n** hologramme *m*.
hols [hɒlz] **npl** *UK inf dated* vacances *fpl*.
Holstein ['hɒlstain] *esp US* = ***Friesian***.
Holstein-Friesian [hɒlstaɪn'friːzən] *esp UK* = ***Friesian***.
holster ['həʊlstəʳ] **n** étui *m*.
holy ['həʊlɪ] (**comp -ier, superl -iest**) **adj** saint(e) / [ground] sacré(e).
Holy Bible **n : the Holy Bible** la Sainte Bible.
Holy Communion **n** Sainte Communion *f*.
Holy Ghost **n : the Holy Ghost** le Saint-Esprit.
Holy Grail [-'greɪl] **n : the Holy Grail** le Saint-Graal.
Holy Land **n : the Holy Land** la Terre sainte.
holy orders **npl** ordres *mpl* sacrés.
Holy Spirit **n : the Holy Spirit** le Saint-Esprit.
holy war **n** guerre *f* sainte.
homage ['hɒmɪdʒ] *(U) fml* **n** hommage *m* ▸ **to pay homage to sb/sthg** rendre hommage à qqn/qqch.
home [həʊm] ■ **n 1.** [house, institution] maison *f* ▸ **to give sb a home** recueillir qqn chez soi ▸ **to have a home of one's own** avoir un foyer *OR* un chez-soi ▸ **to make one's home** s'établir, s'installer ▸ **New York will always be home for me!** c'est toujours à New York que je me sentirai chez moi! ▸ **it's a home from home** *UK OR* **home away from home** *US* on est ici comme chez soi **2.** [country] patrie *f* / [city] ville *f* natale **3.** [family] foyer *m* ▸ **to leave home** quitter la maison **4.** [for old people] maison *f* de retraite / [for children] foyer *m* pour enfants **5.** *fig* [place of origin] berceau *m* ▸ **the home of jazz** le berceau du jazz.
■ **adj 1.** [not foreign - gen] intérieur(e) / [- product] national(e) **2.** [in one's own home - life] de famille / [- improvements] domestique ▸ **home comforts** confort *m* du foyer **3.** [to house] **: home visit/delivery** visite *f*/livraison *f* à domicile **4.** [SPORT - game] sur son propre terrain / [- team] qui reçoit.
■ **adv** [to or at one's house] chez soi, à la maison ▸ **to go** *OR* **to get home** rentrer (chez soi *OR* à la maison) ▸ **to see sb home** raccompagner qqn jusque chez lui/elle
▸▸ **to bring sthg home (to sb)** faire prendre conscience de qqch (à qqn) ▸ **to drive** *OR* **hammer sthg home to sb** enfoncer *OR* faire rentrer qqch dans la tête de qqn.
◆ ***at home*** **adv 1.** [in one's house, flat] chez soi, à la maison **2.** [comfortable] à l'aise ▸ **at home with sthg** à l'aise dans qqch ▸ **to make o.s. at home** faire comme chez soi **3.** [in one's own country] chez nous **4.** SPORT **: to play at home** jouer sur son propre terrain.
◆ ***home in*** **vi : to home in on sthg** viser qqch, se diriger vers qqch / *fig* pointer sur qqch.
home address **n** adresse *f* du domicile.
home banking **n** *opérations bancaires effectuées à domicile par ordinateur.*
homeboy ['həʊmbɔɪ] **n** *US* **: he's a homeboy** [from our town] c'est un gars de chez nous / [in our gang] c'est un des nôtres.
home brew **n** *(U)* [beer] bière *f* faite à la maison.
homecoming ['həʊm,kʌmɪŋ] **n 1.** [return] retour *m* au foyer *OR* à la maison **2.** *US* SCH & UNIV *fête donnée en l'honneur de l'équipe de football et à laquelle sont invités les anciens élèves.*
home computer **n** ordinateur *m* domestique.
home cooking **n** cuisine *f* familiale.
Home Counties **npl : the Home Counties** *les comtés entourant Londres.*
home economics **n** *(U)* économie *f* domestique.
home fries **npl** *US* pommes de terre *fpl* sautées.
home ground **n 1.** [familiar territory] **: to be on home ground** *lit & fig* être sur son terrain **2.** SPORT terrain *m* du club.
homegrown [,həʊm'grəʊn] **adj** du jardin.
home help **n** *UK* aide *f* ménagère.
homeland ['həʊmlænd] **n 1.** [country of birth] patrie *f* **2.** [formerly in South Africa] homeland *m*, bantoustan *m*.
homeless ['həʊmlɪs] ■ **adj** sans abri.
■ **npl : the homeless** les sans-abri *mpl*.
homelessness ['həʊmlɪsnəs] **n** *fait d'être sans abri.*
home loan **n** prêt *m* d'accession à la propriété.
home-loving **adj** casanier(ère).
homely ['həʊmlɪ] **adj 1.** *UK* [simple] simple **2.** *US* [unattractive] ordinaire.
homemade [,həʊm'meɪd] **adj** fait(e) (à la) maison.
homemaker ['həʊm,meɪkə] **n** femme *f* au foyer.

home market **n** marché *m* intérieur.

home movie **n** film *m* amateur.

Home Office **n** *UK* **: the Home Office** ≃ le ministère de l'Intérieur.

homeopath [ˌhəʊmɪ'ɒpəθ] **n** *UK* homéopathe *mf.*

homeopathic [ˌhəʊmɪəʊ'pæθɪk] **adj** homéopathique.

homeopathy [ˌhəʊmɪ'ɒpəθɪ] **n** homéopathie *f.*

home owner, *US* ***homeowner*** ['həʊmˌəʊnə^r] **n** propriétaire *mf* (d'une maison/d'un appartement).

home page **n** COMPUT page *f* d'accueil.

homer *inf* **n** *US* = ***home run.***

home rule **n** autonomie *f.*

home run **n** *US* coup *m* de circuit.

home sales **n** ECON ventes *fpl* sur le marché intérieur.

Home Secretary **n** *UK* ≃ ministre *m* de l'Intérieur.

home shopping **n** [by telephone, computer] téléachat *m* / [by post] achat *m* par correspondance.

homesick ['həʊmsɪk] **adj** qui a le mal du pays.

homesickness ['həʊmˌsɪknɪs] **n** mal *m* du pays.

homespun ['həʊmspʌn] **adj** *fig* simple.

homestead ['həʊmsted] **n** *US* ferme *f* (avec dépendances).

home straight *UK*, ***home stretch*** *US* **n : the home straight** [of race] la dernière ligne droite / [of task] le dernier stade.

home town **n 1.** [of birth] ville *f* natale **2.** [of upbringing] **: his home town** la ville où il a grandi.

home truth **n** *esp UK* **: to tell sb a few home truths** dire ses quatre vérités à qqn.

homeward ['həʊmwəd] ■ **adj** de retour.
■ **adv** vers la maison.

homewards ['həʊmwədz] **adv** *UK* = ***homeward.***

homework ['həʊmwɜːk] **n** *(U)* **1.** SCH devoirs *mpl* **2.** *inf* [preparation] boulot *m.*

homeworker ['həʊmˌwɜːkə^r] **n** travailleur *m*, -euse *f* à domicile.

homey, ***homy*** ['həʊmɪ] **adj** *US* confortable, agréable.

homicidal [ˌhɒmɪ'saɪdl] **adj** homicide.

homicide ['hɒmɪsaɪd] **n** homicide *m.*

homily ['hɒmɪlɪ] (pl **-ies**) **n** [lecture] homélie *f.*

homing ['həʊmɪŋ] **adj** de retour au gîte / MIL **: homing device** tête *f* chercheuse.

homing pigeon **n** pigeon *m* voyageur.

homo ['həʊməʊ] *inf offens* ■ **n** pédé *m*, homo *mf.*
■ **adj** pédé, homo.

homoeopath [ˌhəʊmɪ'ɒpəθ] *UK* = ***homeopath.***

homoeopathic [ˌhəʊmɪəʊ'pæθɪk] *UK* = ***homeopathic.***

homoeopathy [ˌhəʊmɪ'ɒpəθɪ] *UK* = ***homeopathy.***

homogeneous [ˌhɒmə'dʒiːnjəs] **adj** homogène.

homogenize, *UK* ***-ise*** [hə'mɒdʒənaɪz] **vt** homogénéiser.

homophobia [ˌhəʊməʊ'fəʊbjə] **n** homophobie *f.*

homophobic [ˌhəʊməʊ'fəʊbɪk] **adj** homophobe.

homosexual [ˌhɒmə'sekʃʊəl] ■ **adj** homosexuel(elle).
■ **n** homosexuel *m*, -elle *f.*

homosexuality [ˌhɒməˌseksjʊ'ælətɪ] **n** homosexualité *f.*

homy = ***homey.***

hon **abbr of *honourable UK, honorable US, honorary.***

Hon. **abbr of *Honourable UK, Honorable US.***

Honduran [hɒn'djʊərən] ■ **adj** hondurien(enne).
■ **n** Hondurien *m*, -enne *f.*

Honduras [hɒn'djʊərəs] **n** Honduras *m* ▸ **in Honduras** au Honduras.

hone [həʊn] **vt** aiguiser.

honest ['ɒnɪst] ■ **adj 1.** [trustworthy] honnête, probe **2.** [frank] franc (franche), sincère ▸ **to be honest...** pour dire la vérité..., à dire vrai... ▸ **the honest truth** la pure vérité ▸ **give me your honest opinion** dites-moi sincèrement ce que vous en pensez **3.** [legal] légitime ▸ **to earn an honest living** gagner honnêtement sa vie.
■ **adv** *inf* = ***honestly*** *(sense 2).*

honestly ['ɒnɪstlɪ] ■ **adv 1.** [truthfully] honnêtement **2.** [expressing sincerity] je vous assure.
■ **excl** [expressing impatience, disapproval] franchement!

honesty ['ɒnɪstɪ] **n** honnêteté *f*, probité *f.*

honey ['hʌnɪ] **n 1.** [food] miel *m* **2.** [dear] chéri *m*, -e *f.*

honeybee ['hʌnɪbiː] **n** abeille *f.*

honeycomb ['hʌnɪkəʊm] **n** gâteau *m* de miel.

honeyed ['hʌnɪd] **adj** *fig* mielleux(euse).

honeymoon ['hʌnɪmuːn] ■ **n** *lit* & *fig* lune *f* de miel.
■ **vi** aller en voyage de noces, passer sa lune de miel.

honeymooner ['hʌnɪmuːnə^r] **n** nouveau **OR** jeune marié *m*, nouvelle **OR** jeune mariée *f.*

honeymoon period **n** [of prime minister, president] lune *f* de miel, état *m* de grâce.

honeysuckle ['hʌnɪˌsʌkl] **n** chèvrefeuille *m.*

Hong Kong [ˌhɒŋ'kɒŋ] **n** Hongkong, Hong Kong ▸ **in Hong Kong** à Hongkong.

honk [hɒŋk] ■ **vi 1.** [motorist] klaxonner **2.** [goose] cacarder.
■ **vt : to honk the horn** klaxonner.
■ **n 1.** [of horn] coup *m* de Klaxon® **2.** [of goose] cri *m.*

honky ['hɒŋkɪ] (pl **-ies**) **n** *US v inf terme injurieux désignant un Blanc.*

Honolulu [ˌhɒnə'luːluː] **n** Honolulu.

honor *US* = ***honour.***

honorable *US* = ***honourable.***

honorably *US* = ***honourably.***

honor bound *US* = ***honour bound.***

honorary [*UK* 'ɒnərərɪ, *US* ɒnə'reərɪ] **adj** honoraire.

honor roll **n** *US* & *Aus* tableau *m* d'honneur.

honors **npl** *US* = ***honours*** *(sense 1).*

honour *UK*, ***honor*** *US* ['ɒnər] ■ n honneur *m* ▸ **on my honour!** parole d'honneur! ▸ **he's on his honour to behave himself** il s'est engagé sur l'honneur *OR* sur son honneur à bien se tenir ▸ **in honour of sb/sthg** en l'honneur de qqn/qqch.
■ vt honorer.
◆ ***Honour*** n : **His/Your Honour** Son/Votre Honneur.
◆ ***honours*** npl **1.** [tokens of respect] honneurs *mpl* **2.** *UK* [of university degree] ≃ licence *f*
▸▸ **to do the honours** [serve food] servir / [introduce people] faire les présentations.

honourable *UK*, ***honorable*** *US* ['ɒnrəbl] adj honorable.
◆ ***Honourable*** adj [in titles] : **the Honourable...** l'honorable...

honourably *UK*, ***honorably*** *US* ['ɒnərəblɪ] adv honorablement.

honour bound *UK*, ***honor bound*** *US* adj : **to be honour bound to do sthg** être tenu(e) (par l'honneur) de faire qqch.

honours list n *UK liste des personnes qui doivent recevoir des titres honorifiques (conférés par la reine).*

Hons. (abbr of **honours degree**) *licence.*

hooch, ***hootch*** [hu:tʃ] n *inf* [drink] gnôle *f*.

hood [hʊd] n **1.** [on cloak, jacket] capuchon *m* **2.** [of cooker] hotte *f* **3.** [of pram, convertible car] capote *f* **4.** *US* [car bonnet] capot *m* **5.** *US inf* [gangster] gangster *m*.

hooded ['hʊdɪd] adj **1.** [wearing a hood] encapuchonné(e) **2.** [eyes] aux paupières tombantes.

hoodlum ['hu:dləm] n *inf dated* gangster *m*, truand *m*.

hoodwink ['hʊdwɪŋk] vt tromper, berner.

hooey ['hu:ɪ] n *(U) US inf* salades *fpl*.

hoof [hu:f *OR* hʊf] (pl -s *OR* **hooves** [hu:vz]) n sabot *m*.

hoo-ha ['hu:ˌhɑ:] n *inf* **1.** [noise] boucan *m*, potin *m* / [chaos] pagaille *f*, tohu-bohu *m* / [fuss] bruit *m*, histoires *fpl* **2.** *US* [party] fête *f* charivarique.

hook [hʊk] ■ n **1.** [for hanging things on] crochet *m* **2.** [for catching fish] hameçon *m* ▸ **he swallowed the story hook, line and sinker** *inf* il a gobé tout le paquet **3.** [fastener] agrafe *f* **4.** [of telephone] : **off the hook** décroché
▸▸ **to get sb off the hook** tirer qqn d'affaire.
■ vt **1.** [attach with hook] accrocher **2.** [catch with hook] prendre **3.** [arm, leg] : **to hook one's arm around sthg** passer son bras autour de qqch.
◆ ***hook up*** ■ vt sep : **to hook sthg up to sthg** connecter qqch à qqch.
■ vi insep *inf* [meet] se rencontrer / [work together] faire équipe.

hook and eye (pl **hooks and eyes**) n agrafe *f*.

hooked [hʊkt] adj **1.** [shaped like a hook] crochu(e) **2.** *inf* [addicted] : **to be hooked (on)** [drugs] être accro (à) / [music, art] être mordu(e) (de).

hooker ['hʊkər] n *US inf* putain *f*.

hook(e)y ['hʊkɪ] n *US inf* : **to play hookey** faire l'école buissonnière.

hook-nosed adj au nez recourbé *OR* crochu.

hooligan ['hu:lɪgən] n hooligan *m*, vandale *m*.

hooliganism ['hu:lɪgənɪzm] n hooliganisme *m*, vandalisme *m*.

hoop [hu:p] n **1.** [circular band] cercle *m* **2.** [toy] cerceau *m*.

hoopla ['hu:plɑ:] n **1.** *UK* [funfair game] jeu *m* d'anneaux *(dans les foires)* **2.** *US inf* [excitement] tohu-bohu *m* **3.** *US inf* [advertising] publicité *f* tapageuse.

hooray [hʊ'reɪ] = ***hurray***.

hoot [hu:t] ■ n **1.** [of owl] hululement *m* **2.** *UK* [of horn] coup *m* de Klaxon® **3.** [of person] : **a hoot of laughter** un hurlement de rire **4.** *UK inf* [something amusing] : **to be a hoot** être tordant(e).
■ vi **1.** [owl] hululer **2.** *UK* [horn] klaxonner **3.** *inf* [person] : **to hoot with laughter** hurler de rire, rire aux éclats.
■ vt *UK* : **to hoot the horn** klaxonner.

hootch = ***hooch***.

hooter ['hu:tər] n *UK* **1.** [horn] Klaxon® *m* **2.** *inf* [nose] pif *m*.

Hoover® *UK* ['hu:vər] n aspirateur *m*.
◆ ***hoover*** ■ vt [room] passer l'aspirateur dans / [carpet] passer à l'aspirateur.
■ vi passer l'aspirateur.

hooves [hu:vz] npl ➤ ***hoof***.

hop [hɒp] ■ n saut *m* / [on one leg] saut à cloche-pied.
■ vi (pt & pp **-ped**, cont **-ping**) sauter / [on one leg] sauter à cloche-pied / [bird] sautiller.
■ vt (pt & pp **-ped**, cont **-ping**) *US inf* [bus, train] sauter dans.
◆ ***hops*** npl houblon *m*.

hope [həʊp] ■ vi espérer ▸ **to hope for sthg** espérer qqch ▸ **I hope so** j'espère bien ▸ **I hope not** j'espère bien que non ▸ **to hope for the best** espérer que tout aille pour le mieux.
■ vt : **to hope (that)** espérer que ▸ **to hope to do sthg** espérer faire qqch.
■ n espoir *m* ▸ **in the hope of** dans l'espoir de ▸ **I don't hold out much hope** je n'ai pas beaucoup d'espoir, je n'y compte pas trop ▸ **to pin one's hopes on sthg** mettre tous ses espoirs dans qqch ▸ **to raise sb's hopes** donner de l'espoir à qqn.

hope chest n *US* trousseau *m*.

hopeful ['həʊpfʊl] ■ adj **1.** [optimistic] plein(e) d'espoir ▸ **to be hopeful of doing sthg** avoir l'espoir de faire qqch ▸ **to be hopeful of sthg** espérer qqch **2.** [promising] encourageant(e), qui promet.
■ n aspirant *m*.

hopefully ['həʊpfəlɪ] adv **1.** [in a hopeful way] avec bon espoir, avec optimisme **2.** [with luck] : **hopefully,...** espérons que...

hopeless ['həʊplɪs] adj **1.** [gen] désespéré(e) / [tears] de désespoir **2.** *inf* [useless] nul (nulle).

hopelessly ['həʊplɪslɪ] adv **1.** [despairingly] avec désespoir **2.** [completely] complètement.

hopper ['hɒpər] n [funnel] trémie *f*.

hopping ['hɒpɪŋ] adv *inf dated* : **to be hopping mad** être fou (folle) de colère.

hopscotch ['hɒpskɒtʃ] n marelle *f*.

horde [hɔ:d] **n** horde *f*, foule *f*.
◆ ***hordes*** **npl : hordes of** une foule de.

horizon [həˈraɪzn] **n** horizon *m* ▸ **on the horizon** *lit & fig* à l'horizon.
◆ ***horizons*** **npl** horizons *mpl*.

horizontal [ˌhɒrɪˈzɒntl] ■ **adj** horizontal(e).
■ **n : the horizontal** l'horizontale *f*.

horizontally [ˌhɒrɪˈzɒntəlɪ] **adv** horizontalement ▸ **extend your arms horizontally** tendez vos bras à l'horizontale ▸ **to move sb horizontally (to)** ADMIN & COMM muter qqn (à).

hormonal [hɔ:ˈməʊnl] **adj** hormonal(e).

hormone [ˈhɔ:məʊn] **n** hormone *f*.

hormone replacement therapy **n** traitement *m* hormonal substitutif.

horn [hɔ:n] **n 1.** [of animal] corne *f* **2.** MUS [instrument] cor *m* **3.** [on car] Klaxon® *m* / [on ship] sirène *f*.

hornet [ˈhɔ:nɪt] **n** frelon *m*.

hornpipe [ˈhɔ:npaɪp] **n** matelote *f (danse)*.

horn-rimmed [-ˈrɪmd] **adj** à monture d'écaille.

horny [ˈhɔ:nɪ] (comp **-ier**, superl **-iest**) **adj 1.** [hard] corné(e) / [hand] calleux(euse) **2.** *v inf* [sexually excited] excité(e) (sexuellement).

horoscope [ˈhɒrəskəʊp] **n** horoscope *m*.

horrendous [hɒˈrendəs] **adj** horrible.

horrendously [hɒˈrendəslɪ] **adv** horriblement.

horrible [ˈhɒrəbl] **adj** horrible.

horribly [ˈhɒrəblɪ] **adv** horriblement.

horrid [ˈhɒrɪd] **adj** [unpleasant] horrible.

horridly [ˈhɒrɪdlɪ] **adv** [as intensifier] atrocement, affreusement.

horrific [hɒˈrɪfɪk] **adj** horrible.

horrifically [hɒˈrɪfɪklɪ] **adv 1.** [gruesomely] atrocement **2.** [as intensifier] **: horrifically expensive** affreusement cher.

horrify [ˈhɒrɪfaɪ] (pt & pp **-ied**) **vt** horrifier.

horrifying [ˈhɒrɪfaɪɪŋ] **adj** horrifiant(e).

horror [ˈhɒrəʳ] **n** horreur *f* ▸ **to have a horror of sthg** avoir horreur de qqch ▸ **to my/his horror** à ma/sa grande horreur.

horror film *esp UK*, ***horror movie*** *esp US* **n** film *m* d'épouvante.

horror-stricken, ***horror-struck*** **adj** glacé(e) OR frappé(e) d'horreur.

hors d'oeuvre [ɔ:ˈdɜ:vr] (pl **hors d'oeuvres** [ɔ:ˈdɜ:vr]) **n** hors-d'œuvre *m inv*.

horse [hɔ:s] **n** [animal] cheval *m*.

horseback [ˈhɔ:sbæk] ■ **adj** à cheval ▸ **horseback riding** *US* équitation *f*.
■ **n : on horseback** à cheval.

horsebox *UK* [ˈhɔ:sbɒks], ***horsecar*** *US* [ˈhɔ:skɑ:ʳ] **n** van *m*.

horse chestnut **n** [nut] marron *m* d'Inde ▸ **horse chestnut (tree)** marronnier *m* d'Inde.

horse-drawn **adj** tiré(e) par des chevaux.

horsefly [ˈhɔ:sflaɪ] (pl **-flies**) **n** taon *m*.

horsehair [ˈhɔ:sheəʳ] **n** crin *m*.

horseman [ˈhɔ:smən] (pl **-men** [-mən]) **n** cavalier *m*.

horsemanship [ˈhɔ:smənʃɪp] **n 1.** [activity] équitation *f* **2.** [skill] talent *m* de cavalier.

horsemeat [ˈhɔ:smi:t] **n** viande *f* de cheval.

horse opera **n** *US hum* western *m*.

horseplay [ˈhɔ:spleɪ] **n** chahut *m*.

horsepower [ˈhɔ:sˌpaʊəʳ] **n** puissance *f* en chevaux.

horse racing **n** *(U)* courses *fpl* de chevaux.

horseradish [ˈhɔ:sˌrædɪʃ] **n** [plant] raifort *m*.

horserider [ˈhɔ:sraɪdəʳ] **n** *esp US* cavalier *m*, -ère *f*.

horse riding **n** *UK* équitation *f*.

horseshoe [ˈhɔ:sʃu:] **n** fer *m* à cheval.

horse show **n** concours *m* hippique.

horse trader **n** *fig & pej* maquignon *m*, -ne *f*.

horse trading **n** *fig & pej* maquignonnage *m*.

horsetrailer [ˈhɔ:sˌtreɪləʳ] *US* = ***horse box***.

horse trials **npl** concours *m* hippique.

horsewhip [ˈhɔ:swɪp] (pt & pp **-ped**, cont **-ping**) **vt** cravacher.

horsewoman [ˈhɔ:sˌwʊmən] (pl **-women** [-ˌwɪmɪn]) **n** cavalière *f*.

horsey, ***horsy*** [ˈhɔ:sɪ] **adj** *inf* **1.** [horse-like] chevalin(e) **2.** *UK* [fond of horses] féru(e) de cheval.

horticultural [ˌhɔ:tɪˈkʌltʃərəl] **adj** d'horticulture.

horticulture [ˈhɔ:tɪkʌltʃəʳ] **n** horticulture *f*.

hosanna [həʊˈzænə] ■ **n** hosanna *m*.
■ **excl : hosanna!** hosanna!

hose [həʊz] ■ **n** [hosepipe] tuyau *m*.
■ **vt** arroser au jet.
◆ ***hose down*** **vt sep** laver au jet.

hosepipe [ˈhəʊzpaɪp] **n** = ***hose***.

hosiery [ˈhəʊzɪərɪ] **n** bonneterie *f*.

hospice [ˈhɒspɪs] **n** hospice *m*.

hospitable [hɒˈspɪtəbl] **adj** hospitalier(ère), accueillant(e).

hospital [ˈhɒspɪtl] **n** hôpital *m*.

hospitality [ˌhɒspɪˈtælətɪ] **n** hospitalité *f*.

hospitality suite **n** *salon privé où sont offerts des rafraîchissements (lors d'une conférence etc).*

hospitalize, *UK* ***-ise*** [ˈhɒspɪtəlaɪz] **vt** hospitaliser.

host [həʊst] ■ **n 1.** [gen] hôte *m* **2.** [compere] animateur *m*, -trice *f* **3.** [large number] **: a host of** une foule de.
■ **comp 1.** [cell] hôte **2.** [team] qui reçoit ▸ **host city/country** ville *f*/pays *m* d'accueil.
■ **vt 1.** *fig* [meeting] présenter, animer **2.** [website] héberger.

hostage [ˈhɒstɪdʒ] **n** otage *m* ▸ **to be taken hostage** être pris(e) en otage ▸ **to be held hostage** être détenu(e) comme otage.

hostel ['hɒstl] **n** **1.** [basic accommodation] foyer *m* **2.** [youth hostel] auberge *f* de jeunesse.

hostelry ['hɒstəlrɪ] (pl **-ries**) **n** *hum* hostellerie *f*.

hostess ['həʊstes] **n** hôtesse *f*.

host family **n** famille *f* d'accueil.

hostile [*UK* 'hɒstaɪl, *US* 'hɒstl] **adj : hostile (to)** hostile (à).

hostile takeover bid **n** OPA *f* hostile.

hostility [hɒ'stɪlətɪ] **n** [antagonism, unfriendliness] hostilité *f*.

◆ ***hostilities*** **npl** hostilités *fpl*.

hosting ['həʊstɪŋ] **n** COMPUT [of web site] hébergement *m*.

hot [hɒt] (comp **-ter**, superl **-test**) **adj** **1.** [gen] chaud(e) ▸ **I'm hot** j'ai chaud ▸ **keep the meat hot** tenez la viande au chaud ▸ **it's hot** il fait chaud ▸ **in (the) hot weather** pendant les chaleurs ▸ **the books were selling like hot cakes** les livres se vendaient comme des petits pains **2.** [spicy] épicé(e) **3.** *inf* [expert] fort(e), calé(e) ▸ **to be hot on** *OR* **at sthg** être fort *OR* calé en qqch **4.** [recent] de dernière heure *OR* minute ▸ **the news is hot off the presses** ce sont des informations de toute dernière minute **5.** [close, following closely] **: the police were hot on their heels** *OR* **on their trail** la police les talonnait *OR* était à leurs trousses ▸ **he fled with the police in hot pursuit** il s'est enfui avec la police à ses trousses **6.** [temper] colérique ▸ **she has a hot temper** elle s'emporte facilement ▸ **to be** *OR* **to get hot under the collar (about sthg)** *inf* être en colère *OR* en rogne au sujet de qqch.

◆ ***hot up*** (pt & pp **-ted**, cont **-ting**) **vi** *inf UK* chauffer.

hot air **n** *inf* **: he's full of hot air** c'est une grande gueule ▸ **all her promises are just a lot of hot air** toutes ses promesses ne sont que des paroles en l'air.

hot-air balloon **n** montgolfière *f*.

hotbed ['hɒtbed] **n** foyer *m*.

hot-blooded **adj** **1.** [person - passionate] fougueux(euse), au sang chaud **2.** [horse - thoroughbred] de sang pur.

hotchpotch *UK* ['hɒtʃpɒtʃ], ***hodgepodge*** *US* ['hɒdʒpɒdʒ] **n** *inf* fouillis *m*, méli-mélo *m*.

hot cross bun **n** *petit pain sucré que l'on mange le vendredi saint.*

hot-desking **n** bureau *m* tournant.

hot dog **n** hot dog *m*.

hotel [həʊ'tel] ■ **n** hôtel *m*.

■ **comp** d'hôtel.

hotelier [həʊ'telɪəʳ] **n** hôtelier *m*, -ère *f*.

hotelkeeper [həʊ'tel,kiːpəʳ] **n** hôtelier *m*, -ère *f*.

hot flush *UK*, ***hot flash*** *US* **n** bouffée *f* de chaleur.

hotfoot ['hɒt,fʊt] **adv** à toute vitesse.

hothead ['hɒthed] **n** tête *f* brûlée, exalté *m*, -e *f*.

hotheaded [,hɒt'hedɪd] **adj** impulsif(ive).

hothouse ['hɒthaʊs] ■ **n** (pl [-haʊzɪz]) [greenhouse] serre *f*.

■ **comp** de serre.

hot key **n** COMPUT raccourci *m* clavier.

hot line **n** **1.** [between government heads] téléphone *m* rouge **2.** [special line] hot line *f*, assistance *f* téléphonique.

hotly ['hɒtlɪ] **adv** **1.** [passionately] avec véhémence **2.** [closely] de près.

hot pants **npl** mini-short *m (très court et moulant)*.

hotplate ['hɒtpleɪt] **n** plaque *f* chauffante.

hotpot ['hɒtpɒt] **n** *UK type de ragoût*.

hot potato **n** *inf fig* affaire *f* brûlante.

hot rod **n** voiture *f* gonflée.

hot seat **n** *inf* **: to be in the hot seat** être sur la sellette.

hotshot ['hɒtʃɒt] *inf* ■ **n** [expert] as *m*, crack *m* / [VIP] gros bonnet *m*.

■ **adj** super ▸ **they've hired some hotshot lawyer** ils ont pris un as du barreau.

hot spot **n** **1.** [exciting place] endroit *m* à la mode **2.** [politically unsettled area] point *m* chaud.

hot-tempered [-'tempəd] **adj** colérique.

hot water **n** *fig* **: to get into hot water** s'attirer des ennuis ▸ **to be in hot water** être dans le pétrin.

hot-water bottle **n** bouillotte *f*.

hot-wire **vt** *inf faire démarrer en court-circuitant l'allumage.*

houmous, ***houmus*** ['hʊmʊs] = ***hummus***.

hound [haʊnd] ■ **n** [dog] chien *m*.

■ **vt** **1.** [persecute] poursuivre, pourchasser **2.** [drive] **: to hound sb out (of)** chasser qqn (de).

hour ['aʊəʳ] **n** heure *f* ▸ **half an hour** une demi-heure ▸ **70 miles per** *OR* **an hour** 110 km à l'heure ▸ **on the hour** à l'heure juste ▸ **in the small hours** au petit matin *OR* jour.

◆ ***hours*** **npl** **1.** [of business] heures *fpl* d'ouverture ▸ **after hours** après l'heure de fermeture, après la fermeture **2.** [routine] **: to keep late hours** se coucher très tard ▸ **to keep regular hours** avoir une vie réglée.

hourglass ['aʊəglɑːs] ■ **n** sablier *m*.

■ **adj** en forme d'amphore ▸ **an hourglass figure** une taille de guêpe.

hourly ['aʊəlɪ] ■ **adj** **1.** [happening every hour] toutes les heures **2.** [per hour] à l'heure.

■ **adv** **1.** [every hour] toutes les heures **2.** [per hour] à l'heure **3.** *fig* [constantly] sans cesse, constamment.

house ■ **n** [haʊs] (pl ['haʊzɪz]) **1.** [gen] maison *f* ▸ **at** *OR* **to his house** chez lui ▸ **to clean the house** faire le ménage ▸ **to set up house** monter son ménage, s'installer ▸ **on the house** aux frais de la maison ▸ **to put** *OR* **set one's house in order** balayer devant sa porte **2.** POL chambre *f* **3.** [in debates] assistance *f* ▸ **this house believes...** la motion à débattre est la suivante... **4.** THEAT [audience] auditoire *m*, salle *f* ▸ **to have a full house** jouer à guichets fermés *OR* à bureaux fermés ▸ **to bring the house down, to bring down the house** *inf* faire crouler la salle sous les applaudissements **5.** MUS = ***house music*** **6.** *UK* SCH *au sein d'une école, répartition des élèves en groupes concurrents.*

■ **vt** [haʊz] [accommodate] loger, héberger / [department, store] abriter ▸ **this wing houses a laboratory/five families** cette aile abrite un laboratoire/cinq familles.

■ **adj** [haʊs] [within business] d'entreprise / [style] de la maison.

house arrest **n : under house arrest** en résidence surveillée.

houseboat ['hausbəut] **n** péniche *f* aménagée.

housebound ['hausbaund] **adj** confiné(e) chez soi.

housebreaking ['haus,breɪkɪŋ] **n** *(U)* cambriolage *m*.

housebroken ['haus,brəukn] **adj** *US* [pet] propre.

housecoat ['hauskəut] **n** peignoir *m*.

houseful ['hausful] **n : a houseful of guests** une pleine maisonnée d'invités ▸ **we've got a real houseful this weekend** la maison est vraiment pleine (de monde) ce week-end.

houseguest ['hausgest] **n** invité *m*, -e *f*.

household ['haushəuld] ■ **adj 1.** [domestic] ménager(ère) **2.** [word, name] connu(e) de tous.
■ **n** maison *f*, ménage *m*.

householder ['haus,həuldər] **n** propriétaire *mf (d'une maison)*.

household name **n : we want to make our brand a household name** nous voulons que notre marque soit connue de tous ▸ **she's a household name** tout le monde la connaît ***OR*** sait qui elle est.

house-hunt **vi** chercher un ***OR*** être à la recherche d'un logement.

househunting ['haus,hʌntɪŋ] **n** recherche *f* d'un logement.

house husband **n** homme *m* au foyer.

housekeeper ['haus,ki:pər] **n** gouvernante *f*.

housekeeping ['haus,ki:pɪŋ] **n** *(U)* **1.** [work] ménage *m* **2. : housekeeping (money)** argent *m* du ménage.

houseman ['hausmən] (pl **-men** [-mən]) **n** *UK* [medicine] ≃ interne *m*.

housemaster ['haus,mɑ:stər] **n** *UK* SCH *professeur responsable d'une "house"*.

housemen ['hausmən] **npl** ➤ ***houseman***.

housemistress ['haus,mɪstrɪs] **n** *UK* SCH *professeur responsable d'une "house"*.

house music **n** house music *f*.

House of Commons **n** *UK* **: the House of Commons** la Chambre des communes.

CULTURE

House of Commons

La Chambre des communes (ou « Chambre basse ») constitue, avec la Chambre des lords, l'une des deux chambres du Parlement britannique. Elle se compose de 659 membres, élus au suffrage universel direct pour un mandat de cinq ans, et a plus de pouvoir que la Chambre des lords. Elle joue un rôle majeur dans la procédure d'édiction de nouvelles lois et a un droit de regard sur les opérations financières du gouvernement, en approuvant notamment sa fiscalité et ses dépenses. Les membres du Parlement dont le parti est majoritaire lors d'une élection générale forment le gouvernement.

House of Lords **n** *UK* **: the House of Lords** la Chambre des lords.

CULTURE

House of Lords

La Chambre des lords (ou « Chambre haute »), l'une des deux chambres du Parlement britannique, se compose de divers membres : des « pairs héréditaires » (**Hereditary Peers**), qui héritent de leur titre (la plupart de ces derniers ont perdu depuis l'an 2000 le droit de siéger à la Chambre), des « pairs à vie » (**Life Peers**), qui sont nommés à vie par la Reine (la Chambre compte de plus en plus de membres de sexe féminin et de professions multiples), et des évêques (**Bishops**). Même si cette Chambre doit s'incliner devant les décisions de la Chambre des communes, elle participe activement à la législation : elle dispose d'un veto suspensif d'un an en cas de conflit sur une loi et peut retarder l'adoption d'un texte en matière budgétaire.

House of Representatives **n** *US* **: the House of Representatives** la Chambre des représentants.

CULTURE

House of Representatives

La Chambre des représentants (ou « Chambre basse ») compose, avec le Sénat (ou « Chambre haute »), le Congrès américain, qui a le pouvoir législatif. Elle compte 435 représentants, élus par les citoyens pour un mandat de deux ans : ils doivent être âgés de 25 ans minimum, détenir la citoyenneté américaine depuis au moins sept ans et résider dans l'État qu'ils représentent. En effet, chacun d'eux représente un district de son propre État, le nombre des districts étant déterminé par un recensement reconduit tous les dix ans. Les États très peuplés ont droit à plus de représentants ; les plus petits n'en ont qu'un seul.

house-owner **n** propriétaire *mf* d'une maison.

houseplant ['hausplɑ:nt] **n** plante *f* d'appartement.

house-proud **adj** qui a la manie d'astiquer.

houseroom ['hausrum] **n** *UK* place *f (pour loger qqn ou qqch)* ▸ **I wouldn't give that table houseroom!** je ne voudrais pas de cette table chez moi!

house-sit **vi : to house-sit for sb** *s'occuper de la maison de qqn pendant son absence*.

Houses of Parliament **npl : the Houses of Parliament** le Parlement britannique *(où se réunissent la Chambre des communes et la Chambre des lords)*.

house-to-house **adj** de porte en porte, maison par maison.

house-train **vt** *UK* [animal] dresser à être propre.

housewarming (party) ['haʊs,wɔ:mɪŋ-] n pendaison *f* de crémaillère.

housewife ['haʊswaɪf] (pl **-wives** [-waɪvz]) n femme *f* au foyer.

housewifely ['haʊs,waɪflɪ] adj de ménagère.

house wine n vin *m* de la maison.

housework ['haʊswɜ:k] n *(U)* ménage *m*.

housing ['haʊzɪŋ] ■ n **1.** *(U)* [accommodation] logement *m* **2.** [TECH - gen] boîtier *m* / [- of engine] coquille *f*.
■ comp [policy] du logement / [conditions] de logement / [shortage] de logements.

housing association n *UK* association *f* d'aide au logement.

housing benefit n *(U) UK* allocation *f* logement.

housing development n *US* ensemble *m* immobilier.

housing estate *UK*, ***housing project*** *US* n cité *f*.

hovel ['hɒvl] n masure *f*, taudis *m*.

hover ['hɒvəʳ] vi **1.** [fly] planer **2.** [person] **: to hover around sb** tourner *OR* rôder autour de qqn **3.** [hesitate] hésiter.

hovercraft ['hɒvəkrɑ:ft] (pl **hovercraft** *OR* **-s**) n aéroglisseur *m*, hovercraft *m*.

hoverport ['hɒvəpɔ:t] n hoverport *m*.

how [haʊ] adv **1.** [gen] comment ▸ **how do you do it?** comment fait-on? ▸ **how did you like** *OR* **how was the film?** comment as-tu trouvé le film? ▸ **how are you?** comment allez-vous? ▸ **how are things?** ça marche? ▸ **how do you do?** enchanté(e) (de faire votre connaissance) ▸ **how come?** comment ça se fait?
2. [referring to degree, amount] **: how high is it?** combien cela fait-il de haut?, quelle en est la hauteur? ▸ **how long have you been waiting?** cela fait combien de temps que vous attendez? ▸ **how many people came?** combien de personnes sont venues? ▸ **how old are you?** quel âge as-tu? ▸ **how far is it from here to the sea?** combien y a-t-il d'ici à la mer?
3. [in exclamations] **: how nice!** que c'est bien! ▸ **how awful!** quelle horreur! ▸ **how pretty you look!** que tu es jolie!
4. [expressing surprise] **: how can you be so rude?** comment peux-tu être aussi grossier?
◆ ***how about*** adv **: how about a drink?** si on prenait un verre? ▸ **how about you?** et toi?
◆ ***how much*** ■ pron combien ▸ **how much does it cost?** combien ça coûte?
■ adj combien de ▸ **how much bread?** combien de pain?

howdy ['haʊdɪ] excl *US inf* salut!

however [haʊ'evəʳ] ■ adv **1.** [nevertheless] cependant, toutefois **2.** [no matter how] quelque... que *(+ subjunctive)*, si... que *(+ subjunctive)* ▸ **however many/much** peu importe la quantité de **3.** [how] comment.
■ conj [in whatever way] de quelque manière que *(+ subjunctive)*.

howl [haʊl] ■ n hurlement *m* / [of laughter] éclat *m*.
■ vi hurler / [with laughter] rire aux éclats.

howler ['haʊləʳ] n *inf* bourde *f*, gaffe *f*.

howling ['haʊlɪŋ] adj *inf* [success] fou (folle).

hp (abbr of ***horsepower***) n CV *m*.

HP n **1.** *UK* (abbr of ***hire purchase***) ▸ **to buy sthg on HP** acheter qqch à crédit **2.** = ***hp***.

HQ (abbr of ***headquarters***) n QG *m*.

hr (abbr of ***hour***) h.

HRH (abbr of ***His (or Her) Royal Highness***) SAR.

HRT n abbr of ***hormone replacement therapy***.

HS abbr of ***high school***.

HST (abbr of ***Hawaiian Standard Time***) *heure de Hawaii*.

ht (abbr of ***height***) haut.

HT (abbr of ***high tension***) HT.

HTML (abbr of ***hypertext markup language***) n COMPUT HTML.

hub [hʌb] n **1.** [of wheel] moyeu *m* **2.** [of activity] centre *m*.

hub airport n *US* aéroport *m* important.

hubbub ['hʌbʌb] n vacarme *m*, brouhaha *m*.

hubcap ['hʌbkæp] n enjoliveur *m*.

huckleberry ['hʌklbərɪ] (pl **-ies**) n airelle *f*, myrtille *f*.

HUD (abbr of ***Department of Housing and Urban Development***) n *ministère américain de l'urbanisme et du logement*.

huddle ['hʌdl] ■ vi se blottir.
■ n petit groupe *m*.

hue [hju:] n [colour] teinte *f*, nuance *f*.

huff [hʌf] ■ n **: in a huff** froissé(e).
■ vi **: to huff and puff** souffler et haleter.

huffily ['hʌfɪlɪ] adv [reply] d'un ton vexé *OR* fâché / [behave] avec (mauvaise) humeur.

huffy ['hʌfɪ] (comp **-ier**, superl **-iest**) adj *inf* **1.** [offended] froissé(e) **2.** [touchy] susceptible.

hug [hʌg] ■ n étreinte *f* ▸ **to give sb a hug** serrer qqn dans ses bras.
■ vt (pt & pp **-ged**, cont **-ging**) **1.** [embrace] étreindre, serrer dans ses bras **2.** [hold] tenir ▸ **to hug sthg to o.s.** serrer qqch contre soi **3.** [stay close to] serrer.

huge [hju:dʒ] adj énorme / [subject] vaste / [success] fou (folle).

hugely ['hju:dʒlɪ] adv [increase] énormément / [as intensifier] énormément, extrêmement ▸ **the project has been hugely successful/expensive** le projet a été un succès complet/a coûté extrêmement cher.

huh [hʌ] excl **1.** [gen] hein? **2.** [expressing scorn] berk!

hulk [hʌlk] n **1.** [of ship] carcasse *f* **2.** [person] malabar *m*, mastodonte *m*.

hulking ['hʌlkɪŋ] adj énorme.

hull [hʌl] n coque *f*.

hullabaloo [,hʌləbə'lu:] n *inf* tintamarre *m*, raffut *m*.

hullo [hə'ləʊ] excl *UK* = ***hello***.

hum [hʌm] ■ vi (pt & pp **-med**, cont **-ming**) **1.** [audience, bees, wires] bourdonner / [machine] vrombir, ronfler **2.** [sing] fredonner, chantonner **3.** [be busy] être en pleine activité
▸▸ **to hum and haw** *UK* bredouiller, bafouiller.

■ vt (pt & pp **-med**, cont **-ming**) fredonner, chantonner.
■ n *(U)* [of bees, voices] bourdonnement *m* / [of machine] vrombissement *m*, ronflement *m* / [of conversation] brouhaha *m*.

human ['hju:mən] ■ **adj** humain(e).
■ **n : human (being)** être *m* humain.

humane [hju:'meɪn] **adj** humain(e).

humanely [hju:'meɪnlɪ] **adv** humainement.

human error **n** erreur *f* humaine.

Human Genome Project **n : the Human Genome Project** le projet génome humain.

human interest **n** PRESS dimension *f* humaine ▸ **a human interest story** un reportage à caractère social.

humanism ['hju:mənɪzm] **n** humanisme *m*.

humanist ['hju:mənɪst] **n** humaniste *mf*.

humanitarian [hju:ˌmænɪ'teərɪən] ■ **adj** humanitaire.
■ **n** humanitaire *mf*.

humanity [hju:'mænətɪ] **n** humanité *f*.
◆ ***humanities*** **npl : the humanities** les humanités *fpl*, les sciences *fpl* humaines.

humankind [ˌhju:mən'kaɪnd] **n** l'humanité *f*, le genre humain.

humanly ['hju:mənlɪ] **adv : humanly possible** humainement possible.

human nature **n** nature *f* humaine.

human race **n : the human race** la race humaine.

human resources **npl** ressources *fpl* humaines ▸ **department of human resources, human resources department** direction des ressources humaines.

human rights **npl** droits *mpl* de l'homme.

human shield **n** bouclier *m* humain.

humble ['hʌmbl] ■ **adj** humble / [origins, employee] modeste.
■ **vt** humilier ▸ **to humble o.s.** s'abaisser, s'humilier.

humbly ['hʌmblɪ] **adv** **1.** [not proudly] humblement **2.** [live, begin] modestement.

humbug ['hʌmbʌg] **n** **1.** *dated* [hypocrisy] hypocrisie *f* **2.** *UK* [sweet] *type de bonbon dur*.

humdinger [ˌhʌm'dɪŋəʳ] **n** *inf* **1.** [person] **: she's a real humdinger!** elle est vraiment extra *OR* sensass *OR* terrible ! **2.** [thing] **: that was a humdinger of a game!** quel match extraordinaire! ▸ **they had a real humdinger of a row!** ils se sont engueulés, quelque chose de bien!

humdrum ['hʌmdrʌm] **adj** monotone.

humid ['hju:mɪd] **adj** humide.

humidifier [hju:'mɪdɪfaɪəʳ] **n** humidificateur *m*.

humidity [hju:'mɪdətɪ] **n** humidité *f*.

humiliate [hju:'mɪlɪeɪt] **vt** humilier.

humiliating [hju:'mɪlɪeɪtɪŋ] **adj** humiliant(e).

humiliation [hju:ˌmɪlɪ'eɪʃn] **n** humiliation *f*.

humility [hju:'mɪlətɪ] **n** humilité *f*.

hummingbird ['hʌmɪŋbɜ:d] **n** colibri *m*, oiseau-mouche *m*.

hummus ['hʊmʊs] **n** houmous *m*.

humor *US* = ***humour***.

humorist ['hju:mərɪst] **n** humoriste *mf*.

humorous ['hju:mərəs] **adj** humoristique / [person] plein(e) d'humour.

humour *UK*, ***humor*** *US* ['hju:məʳ] ■ **n** **1.** [sense of fun] humour *m* **2.** [of situation, remark] côté *m* comique **3.** *dated* [mood] humeur *f*.
■ **vt** se montrer conciliant(e) envers.

humourless *UK*, ***humorless*** *US* ['hju:məlɪs] **adj** [person] qui manque d'humour / [book, situation, speech] sans humour.

hump [hʌmp] ■ **n** bosse *f*.
■ **vt** *UK inf* [carry] porter, coltiner.

humpbacked bridge ['hʌmpbækt-], ***humpback bridge*** ['hʌmpbæk-] **n** *UK* pont *m* en dos d'âne.

humpback whale ['hʌmpbæk-] **n** baleine *f* à bosse.

humungous [hju:'mʌŋgəs] **adj** *inf* [huge] énorme / [great] super, génial(e) ▸ **the book was a humungous success** le livre a eu un méga succès.

humus ['hju:məs] **n** humus *m*.

hunch [hʌntʃ] ■ **n** *inf* pressentiment *m*, intuition *f*.
■ **vt** voûter.
■ **vi** se pencher.

hunchback ['hʌntʃbæk] **n** *offens* bossu *m*, -e *f*.

hunchbacked ['hʌntʃbækt] **adj** *offens* bossu(e).

hunched [hʌntʃt] **adj** voûté(e).

hundred ['hʌndrəd] **num** cent ▸ **a** *OR* **one hundred** cent ▸ **about a hundred pupils** une centaine d'élèves ; see also ***six***.
◆ ***hundreds*** **npl** des centaines.

hundreds and thousands **npl** *UK paillettes de sucre colorées servant à décorer les gâteaux*.

hundredth ['hʌndrətθ] **num** centième ; see also ***sixth***.

hundredweight ['hʌndrədweɪt] **n** [in UK] poids *m* de 112 livres = *50,8 kg* / [in US] poids *m* de 100 livres = *45,3 kg*.

hung [hʌŋ] ■ **pt & pp** ➤ ***hang***.
■ **adj** [parliament, jury] sans majorité.

Hungarian [hʌŋ'geərɪən] ■ **adj** hongrois(e).
■ **n** **1.** [person] Hongrois *m*, -e *f* **2.** [language] hongrois *m*.

Hungary ['hʌŋgərɪ] **n** Hongrie *f* ▸ **in Hungary** en Hongrie.

hunger ['hʌŋgəʳ] **n** **1.** [gen] faim *f* **2.** [strong desire] soif *f*.
◆ ***hunger after***, ***hunger for*** **vt insep** *fig* avoir faim de, avoir soif de.

hunger strike **n** grève *f* de la faim.

hung over **adj** *inf* **: to be hung over** avoir la gueule de bois.

hungrily ['hʌŋgrəlɪ] **adv** [eat] voracement, avidement / *fig* [read, listen] avidement.

hungry ['hʌŋgrɪ] (comp **-ier**, superl **-iest**) **adj** **1.** [for food] **: to be hungry** avoir faim / [starving] être affamé(e) ▸ **to go hungry** souffrir de la faim **2.** [eager] **: to be hungry for** être avide de.

hung up **adj** *inf* **: to be hung up (on** *OR* **about)** être obsédé(e) (par).

hunk [hʌŋk] **n 1.** [large piece] gros morceau *m* **2.** *inf* [man] beau mec *m*.

hunky-dory [ˌhʌŋkɪ'dɔːrɪ] **adj** *inf* au poil.

hunt [hʌnt] ■ **n** chasse *f* / [for missing person] recherches *fpl*.
■ **vi 1.** [chase animals, birds] chasser ▸ **they hunt by night/in packs** ils chassent la nuit/en bande **2.** *UK* [chase foxes] chasser le renard ▸ **to go hunting** aller à la chasse **3.** [search] **: to hunt (for sthg)** chercher partout (qqch) ▸ **I've hunted all over town for a linen jacket** j'ai parcouru *OR* fait toute la ville pour trouver une veste en lin.
■ **vt 1.** [animals, birds] chasser **2.** [person] poursuivre, pourchasser.
◆ ***hunt down*** **vt sep** traquer.

hunter ['hʌntəʳ] **n 1.** [of animals, birds] chasseur *m*, -euse *f* **2.** [of things] **: bargain hunter** dénicheur *m*, -euse *f* d'occasions ▸ **autograph hunter** collectionneur *m*, -euse *f* d'autographes.

hunter-gatherer **n** chasseur-cueilleur *m*.

hunting ['hʌntɪŋ] ■ **n 1.** [of animals] chasse *f* **2.** *UK* [of foxes] chasse *f* au renard.
■ **comp** de chasse.

huntsman ['hʌntsmən] (pl **-men** [-mən]) **n** chasseur *m*.

hurdle ['hɜːdl] ■ **n 1.** [in race] haie *f* **2.** [obstacle] obstacle *m*.
■ **vt** [jump over] sauter.

hurdler ['hɜːdləʳ] **n** coureur *m*, -euse *f* *(qui fait des courses de haies)*.

hurl [hɜːl] **vt 1.** [throw] lancer avec violence **2.** [shout] lancer.

hurly-burly ['hɜːlɪˌbɜːlɪ] *UK* ■ **n** tohu-bohu *m* ▸ **the hurly-burly of city life** le tourbillon de la vie urbaine.
■ **adj** turbulent(e).

hurrah [hʊ'rɑː] **excl** *dated* hourra!

hurray [hʊ'reɪ] **excl** hourra!

hurricane ['hʌrɪkən] **n** ouragan *m*.

hurried ['hʌrɪd] **adj** [hasty] précipité(e).

hurriedly ['hʌrɪdlɪ] **adv** précipitamment / [eat, write] vite, en toute hâte.

hurry ['hʌrɪ] ■ **vt** (pt & pp **-ied**) [person] faire se dépêcher / [process] hâter ▸ **to hurry to do sthg** se dépêcher *OR* se presser de faire qqch.
■ **vi** (pt & pp **-ied**) se dépêcher, se presser.
■ **n** hâte *f*, précipitation *f* ▸ **to be in a hurry** être pressé(e) ▸ **to do sthg in a hurry** faire qqch à la hâte ▸ **to be in no hurry to do sthg** [unwilling] ne pas être pressé(e) de faire qqch.
◆ ***hurry up*** ■ **vi** se dépêcher.
■ **vt sep** faire se dépêcher.

hurt [hɜːt] ■ **vt** (pt & pp **hurt**) **1.** [physically, emotionally] blesser / [one's leg, arm] se faire mal à ▸ **is your back hurting you today?** est-ce que tu as mal au dos aujourd'hui? ▸ **to hurt o.s.** se faire mal ▸ **to hurt sb's feelings** blesser *OR* froisser qqn
2. *fig* [harm] faire du mal à.
■ **vi** (pt & pp **hurt**) **1.** [gen] faire mal ▸ **my leg hurts** ma jambe me fait mal
2. *fig* [do harm] faire du mal.
■ **adj** [physically] blessé(e) / [voice] offensé(e) ▸ **he's more frightened than hurt** il a eu plus de peur que de mal ▸ **a hurt expression** un regard meurtri *OR* blessé ▸ **don't feel hurt** ne le prends pas mal.
■ **n** *(U)* [emotional pain] peine *f*.

hurtful ['hɜːtfʊl] **adj** blessant(e).

hurtle ['hɜːtl] **vi** aller à toute allure.

husband ['hʌzbənd] **n** mari *m*.

husbandry ['hʌzbəndrɪ] **n** *fml* agriculture *f*.

hush [hʌʃ] ■ **n** silence *m*.
■ **excl** silence!, chut!

hushed [hʌʃt] **adj** [whisper, voice] étouffé(e) / [silence] profond(e), grand(e) ▸ **to speak in hushed tones** parler à voix basse.

hush-hush **adj** *inf* secret(ète), archi-secret(ète).

hush money **n** *(U) inf* pot-de-vin *m (pour acheter le silence de qqn)*.

husk [hʌsk] **n** [of seed, grain] enveloppe *f*.

huskily ['hʌskɪlɪ] **adv** [speak] d'une voix rauque / [sing] d'une voix voilée.

husky ['hʌskɪ] ■ **adj** (**comp -ier, superl -iest**) [hoarse] rauque.
■ **n** husky *m*.

hussy ['hʌsɪ] (pl **-ies**) **n** *dated* & *hum* [shameless woman] garce *f*, gourgandine *f dated* ▸ **you brazen hussy!** espèce de garce!

hustings ['hʌstɪŋz] **npl** *UK* plate-forme *f* électorale.

hustle ['hʌsl] ■ **vt 1.** [hurry] pousser, bousculer **2.** *US* [persuade] **: to hustle sb into doing sthg** forcer la main à qqn pour qu'il fasse qqch.
■ **n** agitation *f*.

hut [hʌt] **n 1.** [rough house] hutte *f* **2.** [shed] cabane *f*.

hutch [hʌtʃ] **n** clapier *m*.

hyacinth ['haɪəsɪnθ] **n** jacinthe *f*.

hybrid ['haɪbrɪd] ■ **adj** hybride.
■ **n 1.** [plant, animal] hybride *m* **2.** [mixture] entité *f* hybride.

hydrangea [haɪ'dreɪndʒə] **n** hortensia *m*.

hydrant ['haɪdrənt] **n** bouche *f* d'incendie.

hydraulic [haɪ'drɔːlɪk] **adj** hydraulique.
◆ ***hydraulics*** **npl** hydraulique *f*.

hydrocarbon [ˌhaɪdrə'kɑːbən] **n** hydrocarbure *m*.

hydrochloric acid [ˌhaɪdrə'klɔːrɪk-] **n** acide *m* chlorhydrique.

hydroelectric [ˌhaɪdrəʊɪ'lektrɪk] **adj** hydro-électrique.

hydroelectricity [ˌhaɪdrəʊɪlek'trɪsətɪ] **n** hydro-électricité *f*.

hydrofoil ['haɪdrəfɔɪl] **n** hydroptère *m*.

hydrogen ['haɪdrədʒən] **n** hydrogène *m*.

hydrogen bomb **n** bombe *f* à hydrogène.

hydrogen peroxide **n** eau *f* oxygénée.

hydrophobia [ˌhaɪdrə'fəʊbjə] **n** hydrophobie *f*.

hydroplane ['haɪdrəpleɪn] **n** **1.** [speedboat] hydroglisseur *m* **2.** [hydrofoil] hydroptère *m*.

hydrotherapy [ˌhaɪdrə'θerəpɪ] **n** hydrothérapie *f*.

hyena [haɪ'i:nə] **n** hyène *f*.

hygiene ['haɪdʒi:n] **n** hygiène *f*.

hygienic [haɪ'dʒi:nɪk] **adj** hygiénique.

hygienically [haɪ'dʒi:nɪklɪ] **adv** de façon hygiénique.

hygienist [haɪ'dʒi:nɪst] **n** *personne qui se charge du détartrage des dents.*

hymn [hɪm] **n** hymne *m*, cantique *m*.

hymn book, hymnbook ['hɪmbuk] **n** livre *m* de cantiques.

hype [haɪp] *inf* ■ **n** *(U)* battage *m* publicitaire. ■ **vt** faire un battage publicitaire autour de.

hyped up [haɪpt-] **adj** *inf* [person] excité(e).

hyper ['haɪpər] **adj** *inf* qui a la bougeotte.

hyperactive [ˌhaɪpər'æktɪv] **adj** hyperactif(ive).

hyperactivity [ˌhaɪpəræk'tɪvətɪ] **n** hyperactivité *f*.

hyperbole [haɪ'pɜ:bəlɪ] **n** hyperbole *f*.

hypercritical [ˌhaɪpə'krɪtɪkl] **adj** hypercritique.

hyperinflation [ˌhaɪpərɪn'fleɪʃn] **n** hyperinflation *f*.

hyperlink ['haɪpəlɪŋk] **n** lien *m* hypertexte, hyperlien *m*.

hypermarket ['haɪpəˌmɑ:kɪt] **n** *esp UK* hypermarché *m*.

hypersensitive [ˌhaɪpə'sensɪtɪv] **adj** hypersensible.

hypersensitivity ['haɪpəˌsensɪ'tɪvətɪ] **n** hypersensibilité *f*.

hypertension [ˌhaɪpə'tenʃn] **n** hypertension *f*.

hypertext ['haɪpətekst] ■ **n** COMPUT hypertexte *m*. ■ **comp** COMPUT **: hypertext link** lien *m* hypertexte.

hyperventilate [ˌhaɪpə'ventɪleɪt] **vi** faire de l'hyperventilation.

hyphen ['haɪfn] **n** trait *m* d'union.

hyphenate ['haɪfəneɪt] **vt** mettre un trait d'union à.

hypnosis [hɪp'nəʊsɪs] **n** hypnose *f* ▸ **under hypnosis** sous hypnose, en état d'hypnose.

hypnotherapy [ˌhɪpnəʊ'θerəpɪ] **n** hypnothérapie *f*.

hypnotic [hɪp'nɒtɪk] **adj** hypnotique.

hypnotism ['hɪpnətɪzm] **n** hypnotisme *m*.

hypnotist ['hɪpnətɪst] **n** hypnotiseur *m*.

hypnotize, *UK* ***-ise*** ['hɪpnətaɪz] **vt** hypnotiser.

hypoallergenic ['haɪpəʊˌælə'dʒenɪk] **adj** hypoallergénique.

hypochondria [ˌhaɪpə'kɒndrɪə] **n** hypocondrie *f*.

hypochondriac [ˌhaɪpə'kɒndrɪæk] **n** hypocondriaque *mf*.

hypocrisy [hɪ'pɒkrəsɪ] **n** hypocrisie *f*.

hypocrite ['hɪpəkrɪt] **n** hypocrite *mf*.

hypocritical [ˌhɪpə'krɪtɪkl] **adj** hypocrite.

hypodermic needle [ˌhaɪpə'dɜ:mɪk-] **n** aiguille *f* hypodermique.

hypodermic syringe [ˌhaɪpə'dɜ:mɪk-] **n** seringue *f* hypodermique.

hypothermia [ˌhaɪpəʊ'θɜ:mɪə] **n** hypothermie *f*.

hypothesis [haɪ'pɒθɪsɪs] (pl **-theses** [-θɪsi:z]) **n** hypothèse *f*.

hypothesize, *UK* ***-ise*** [haɪ'pɒθɪsaɪz] ■ **vt** émettre une hypothèse *OR* des hypothèses sur. ■ **vi** émettre une hypothèse *OR* des hypothèses.

hypothetical [ˌhaɪpə'θetɪkl] **adj** hypothétique.

hypothetically [ˌhaɪpə'θetɪklɪ] **adv** hypothétiquement.

hysterectomy [ˌhɪstə'rektəmɪ] (pl **-ies**) **n** hystérectomie *f*.

hysteria [hɪs'tɪərɪə] **n** hystérie *f*.

hysterical [hɪs'terɪkl] **adj** **1.** [gen] hystérique **2.** *inf* [very funny] désopilant(e).

hysterically [hɪs'terɪklɪ] **adv** hystériquement ▸ **it was hysterically funny!** c'était super drôle!

hysterics [hɪs'terɪks] **npl** **1.** [panic, excitement] crise *f* de nerfs **2.** *inf* [laughter] fou rire *m*.

Hz (abbr of ***hertz***) Hz.

i [aɪ] (pl i's), ***I***[1] (pl I's ***or*** Is) **n** [letter] i *m inv*, I *m inv*.

I[2] [aɪ] **pers pron 1.** *(unstressed)* je, j' *(before vowel or silent 'h')* ▸ **I like skiing** j'aime skier ▸ **he and I are leaving for Paris** lui et moi (nous) partons pour Paris ▸ **it is I** *fml* c'est moi **2.** *(stressed)* moi ▸ **I can't do it** moi je ne peux pas le faire.

I[3] abbr of ***Island***, ***Isle***.

IA abbr of ***Iowa***.

IAEA (abbr of ***International Atomic Energy Agency***) **n** AIEA *f*.

IAP (abbr of ***Internet Access Provider***) **n** fournisseur *m* d'accès à l'Internet.

ib = ***ibid***.

IBA (abbr of ***Independent Broadcasting Authority***) **n** *organisme d'agrément et de coordination des stations de radio et chaînes de télévision du secteur privé en Grande-Bretagne.*

Iberian [aɪ'bɪərɪən] ■ **adj** ibérique.
■ **n** Ibère *mf*.

Iberian peninsula **n : the Iberian peninsula** la péninsule Ibérique.

ibex ['aɪbeks] (pl **ibex** ***or*** **-es**) **n** bouquetin *m*.

ibid, ***ib*** (abbr of ***ibidem***) ibid.

i/c abbr of ***in charge (of)***.

ICA (abbr of ***Institute of Contemporary Art***) **n** *centre d'art moderne à Londres.*

ICBM (abbr of ***intercontinental ballistic missile***) **n** ICBM *m*.

ICC **n 1.** (abbr of ***International Chamber of Commerce***) CCI *f* **2.** HIST (abbr of ***Interstate Commerce Commission***) *commission fédérale américaine réglementant le commerce entre les États.*

ice [aɪs] ■ **n 1.** [frozen water, ice cream] glace *f* ▸ **to break the ice** *fig* rompre ***or*** briser la glace ▸ **her feet were like ice** elle avait les pieds gelés ▸ **to put sthg on ice : the reforms have been put on ice** les réformes ont été gelées ▸ **to walk** ***or*** **to be on thin ice** avancer en terrain miné **2.** *(U)* [on road] verglas *m* **3.** *(U)* [ice cubes] glaçons *mpl*.
■ **vt** CULIN glacer.
◆ ***ice over***, ***ice up*** **vi** [lake, pond] geler / [window, windscreen] givrer / [road] se couvrir de verglas.

ice age **n** période *f* glaciaire.

iceberg ['aɪsbɜːg] **n** iceberg *m*.

iceberg lettuce **n** laitue *f* iceberg.

icebox ['aɪsbɒks] **n 1.** *UK* [in refrigerator] freezer *m* **2.** *US dated* [refrigerator] réfrigérateur *m*.

icebreaker ['aɪsˌbreɪkəʳ] **n** [ship] brise-glace *m inv*.

ice bucket **n** seau *m* à glace.

ice cap **n** calotte *f* glaciaire.

ice-cold **adj** glacé(e).

ice cream **n** glace *f*.

ice-cream cone, ***ice-cream cornet*** *UK dated* **n** cornet *m* de glace.

ice-cream soda **n** soda *m* avec de la glace.

ice cream truck *US*, ***ice cream van*** *UK* **n** camionnette *f* de vendeur de glaces.

ice cube **n** glaçon *m*.

iced [aɪst] **adj** glacé(e).

ice dancing **n** *(U)* danse *f* sur glace.

ice floe **n** banc *m* de glace, glaciel *m* ***Québec***.

ice hockey **n** *UK* hockey *m* sur glace.

Iceland ['aɪslənd] **n** Islande *f* ▸ **in Iceland** en Islande.

Icelander ['aɪsləndəʳ] **n** Islandais *m*, -e *f*.

Icelandic [aɪs'lændɪk] ■ **adj** islandais(e).
■ **n** [language] islandais *m*.

ice lolly **n** *UK* sucette *f* glacée.

ice pack **n 1.** [pack ice] banquise *f* **2.** [ice bag] sac *m* à glaçons / MED poche *f* à glace.

ice pick **n** pic *m* à glace.

ice rink **n** patinoire *f*.

ice skate **n** patin *m* à glace.
◆ ***ice-skate*** **vi** faire du patin (à glace).

ice-skater **n** patineur *m*, -euse *f*.

ice-skating **n** patinage *m* (sur glace).

icicle ['aɪsɪkl] **n** glaçon *m* (naturel).

icily ['aɪsɪlɪ] **adv** [behave] d'une manière glaciale / [say, reply] d'un ton glacial.

icing ['aɪsɪŋ] n *(U)* glaçage *m*, glace *f* ▸ **the icing on the cake** *fig* un plus, la cerise sur le gâteau.

icing sugar n *UK* sucre *m* glace.

ICJ (abbr of ***International Court of Justice***) n CIJ *f*.

icon ['aɪkɒn] n [gen & COMPUT] icône *f*.

iconoclast [aɪ'kɒnəklæst] n iconoclaste *mf*.

iconoclastic [aɪˌkɒnə'klæstɪk] adj iconoclaste.

ICR (abbr of ***Institute for Cancer Research***) n *institut de recherche contre le cancer*.

ICU (abbr of ***intensive care unit***) n *unité de soins intensifs*.

icy ['aɪsɪ] (comp -ier, superl -iest) adj **1.** [weather, manner] glacial(e) **2.** [covered in ice] verglacé(e).

id [ɪd] n ça *m*.

ID[1] n *(U)* (abbr of ***identification***) papiers *mpl*.

ID[2] abbr of ***Idaho***.

I'd [aɪd] = ***I would, I had***.

Idaho ['aɪdəˌhəʊ] n Idaho *m* ▸ **in Idaho** dans l'Idaho.

ID card = ***identity card***.

IDD (abbr of ***international direct dialling***) n automatique *m* international.

idea [aɪ'dɪə] n idée *f* / [intention] intention *f* ▸ **I've had an idea** j'ai une idée ▸ **what a good idea!** quelle bonne idée! ▸ **it was a nice idea to phone** c'est gentil d'avoir pensé à téléphoner ▸ **it wasn't my idea!** l'idée n'était pas de moi! ▸ **to have an idea of** avoir une idée de ▸ **to have an idea (that)...** avoir idée que... ▸ **to have no idea** n'avoir aucune idée ▸ **you've no idea of the conditions in which they lived** tu ne peux pas t'imaginer les conditions dans lesquelles ils vivaient ▸ **no idea!** aucune idée! ▸ **to get the idea** *inf* piger ▸ **don't get the idea (that)...** ne va pas croire *OR* t'imaginer que... ▸ **the idea is to...** l'idée est de..., l'intention est de... ▸ **this is not my idea of fun** je ne trouve pas ça drôle *OR* ça ne m'amuse pas ▸ **don't put ideas into his head** ne va pas lui fourrer *OR* lui mettre des idées dans la tête.

ideal [aɪ'dɪəl] ■ adj idéal(e) ▸ **to be ideal for** être idéal *OR* parfait pour.
■ n idéal *m*.

idealism [aɪ'dɪəlɪzm] n idéalisme *m*.

idealist [aɪ'dɪəlɪst] n idéaliste *mf*.

idealistic [aɪˌdɪə'lɪstɪk] adj idéaliste.

idealize, *UK* ***-ise*** [aɪ'dɪəlaɪz] vt idéaliser.

ideally [aɪ'dɪəlɪ] adv idéalement / [suited] parfaitement.

identical [aɪ'dentɪkl] adj identique.

identically [aɪ'dentɪklɪ] adv identiquement ▸ **to be identically dressed** être habillé exactement de la même façon.

identical twins npl vrais jumeaux *mpl*, vraies jumelles *fpl*.

identifiable [aɪ'dentɪfaɪəbl] adj identifiable, reconnaissable.

identification [aɪˌdentɪfɪ'keɪʃn] n *(U)* **1.** [gen] : **identification (with)** identification *f* (à) **2.** [documentation] pièce *f* d'identité.

identification parade n *UK séance d'identification d'un suspect dans un échantillon de plusieurs personnes*.

identify [aɪ'dentɪfaɪ] (pt & pp -ied) ■ vt **1.** [recognize] identifier **2.** [subj: document, card] permettre de reconnaître **3.** [associate] : **to identify sb with sthg** associer qqn à qqch.
■ vi [empathize] : **to identify with** s'identifier à.

Identikit® ***picture*** [aɪ'dentɪkɪt-] n portrait-robot *m*.

identity [aɪ'dentətɪ] (pl -ies) n identité *f*.

identity card n carte *f* d'identité.

ideological [ˌaɪdɪə'lɒdʒɪkl] adj idéologique.

ideologically [ˌaɪdɪə'lɒdʒɪklɪ] adv du point de vue idéologique, idéologiquement ▸ **ideologically sound** [idea] défendable sur le plan idéologique / [person] dont les idées sont défendables sur le plan idéologique.

ideology [ˌaɪdɪ'ɒlədʒɪ] (pl -ies) n idéologie *f*.

idiocy ['ɪdɪəsɪ] n [stupidity] stupidité *f*, idiotie *f*.

idiom ['ɪdɪəm] n **1.** [phrase] expression *f* idiomatique **2.** *fml* [style] langue *f*.

idiomatic [ˌɪdɪə'mætɪk] adj idiomatique.

idiomatically [ˌɪdɪə'mætɪklɪ] adv de manière idiomatique.

idiosyncrasy [ˌɪdɪə'sɪŋkrəsɪ] (pl -ies) n particularité *f*, caractéristique *f*.

idiosyncratic [ˌɪdɪəsɪŋ'krætɪk] adj [style, behaviour] caractéristique.

idiot ['ɪdɪət] n idiot *m*, -e *f*, imbécile *mf*.

idiotic [ˌɪdɪ'ɒtɪk] adj idiot(e).

idiot-proof *inf* ■ adj COMPUT à l'épreuve de toute fausse manœuvre.
■ vt rendre infaillible.

idle ['aɪdl] ■ adj **1.** [lazy] oisif(ive), désœuvré(e) **2.** [not working - machine, factory] arrêté(e) / [- worker] qui chôme, en chômage **3.** [threat] vain(e) **4.** [curiosity] simple, pur(e).
■ vi tourner au ralenti.
◆ ***idle away*** vt sep [time] perdre à ne rien faire.

idleness ['aɪdlnɪs] n oisiveté *f*, désœuvrement *m*.

idler ['aɪdləʳ] n paresseux *m*, -euse *f*.

idly ['aɪdlɪ] adv **1.** [lazily] paresseusement **2.** [without purpose] négligemment.

idol ['aɪdl] n idole *f*.

idolatry [aɪ'dɒlətrɪ] n idolâtrie *f*.

idolize, *UK* ***-ise*** ['aɪdəlaɪz] vt idolâtrer, adorer.

idyll ['ɪdɪl] n idylle *f*.

idyllic [ɪ'dɪlɪk] adj idyllique.

i.e. (abbr of ***id est***) c-à-d.

if [ɪf] ■ conj **1.** [gen] si ▸ **if he comes, we'll ask him** s'il vient, on lui demandera ▸ **if I was older, I'd leave home** si j'étais plus âgé, je quitterais la maison ▸ **if you ever come** *OR* **if ever you come to London, do visit us** si jamais tu passes à Londres, viens nous voir ▸ **would you mind if I invited Angie too?** ça te dérangerait si j'invitais aussi Angie? ▸ **if possible** si (c'est) possible ▸ **if I were you** à ta place, si j'étais toi ▸ **to ask/to know/to wonder if** demander/savoir/se demander si ▸ **it doesn't matter if he comes or not** peu importe qu'il vienne ou (qu'il ne vienne) pas **2.** [though] bien que ▸ **he was intelligent if a little arrogant** il était intelligent, mais quelque peu arrogant **3.** [introducing comments, requests] **: if I could just come in here...** si je puis me permettre d'intervenir... ▸ **it's rather good, if I say so myself** c'est assez bon, sans fausse modestie ▸ **if you could all just wait in the hall, I'll be back in a second** si vous pouviez tous attendre dans l'entrée, je reviens tout de suite.

■ **n : no ifs and buts** *UK* *OR* **no ifs, ands or buts** *US* pas de si ni de mais *mpl.*

◆ ***if anything*** **adv** plutôt ▸ **he doesn't look any slimmer, if anything, he's put on weight** il n'a pas l'air plus mince, il a même plutôt grossi.

◆ ***if not*** **conj** sinon ▸ **did you finish on time? and if not, why not?** avez-vous terminé à temps? sinon, pourquoi? ▸ **hundreds, if not thousands** des centaines, voire des milliers.

◆ ***if only*** ■ **conj 1.** [naming a reason] ne serait-ce que **2.** [expressing regret] si seulement.

■ **excl** si seulement!

IFA (abbr of ***independent financial adviser***) **n** conseiller financier indépendant *m*, conseillère financière indépendante *f.*

iffy ['ɪfɪ] (comp **-ier**, superl **-iest**) **adj** *inf* incertain(e).

igloo ['ɪglu:] (pl **-s**) **n** igloo *m*, iglou *m.*

ignite [ɪg'naɪt] ■ **vt** mettre le feu à, enflammer ∕ [firework] tirer.

■ **vi** prendre feu, s'enflammer.

ignition [ɪg'nɪʃn] **n 1.** [act of igniting] ignition *f* **2.** AUT allumage *m* ▸ **to switch on the ignition** mettre le contact.

ignition key **n** clef *f* de contact.

ignoble [ɪg'nəubl] **adj** *fml* infâme.

ignominious [,ɪgnə'mɪnɪəs] **adj** *fml* ignominieux(euse).

ignominiously [,ɪgnə'mɪnɪəslɪ] **adv** *fml* ignominieusement.

ignominy ['ɪgnəmɪnɪ] **n** *fml* ignominie *f.*

ignoramus [,ɪgnə'reɪməs] (pl **-es** [-i:z]) **n** ignare *mf.*

ignorance ['ɪgnərəns] **n** ignorance *f.*

ignorant ['ɪgnərənt] **adj 1.** [uneducated, unaware] ignorant(e) ▸ **to be ignorant of sthg** être ignorant de qqch **2.** [rude] mal élevé(e).

ignore [ɪg'nɔ:r] **vt** [advice, facts] ne pas tenir compte de ∕ [person] faire semblant de ne pas voir ▸ **ignore him and he'll go away** fais comme s'il n'était pas là et il te laissera tranquille ▸ **they can no longer ignore what is going on here** il ne leur est plus possible d'ignorer *OR* de fermer les yeux sur ce qui se passe ici ▸ **the report ignores certain crucial facts** le rapport passe sous silence des faits cruciaux.

iguana [ɪ'gwɑ:nə] (pl **iguana** *OR* **-s**) **n** iguane *m.*

ikon ['aɪkɒn] = ***icon***.

IL abbr of ***Illinois***.

ILEA ['ɪlɪə] (abbr of ***Inner London Education Authority***) **n** *anciens services londoniens de l'enseignement*.

ileum ['ɪlɪəm] (pl **ilea** ['ɪlɪə]) **n** iléon *m.*

ilk [ɪlk] **n : of that ilk** [of that sort] de cet acabit, de ce genre.

ill [ɪl] ■ **adj 1.** [unwell] malade ▸ **to feel ill** se sentir malade *OR* souffrant ▸ **to be taken ill** *esp UK*, **to fall ill** tomber malade **2.** [bad] mauvais(e) ▸ **ill luck** malchance *f.*

■ **adv** mal ▸ **to speak/think ill of sb** dire/penser du mal de qqn.

◆ ***ills*** **npl** maux *mpl*, malheurs *mpl.*

ill. (abbr of ***illustration***) ill.

I'll [aɪl] = ***I will***, ***I shall***.

ill-advised [-əd'vaɪzd] **adj** *fml* [remark, action] peu judicieux(euse) ∕ [person] malavisé(e) ▸ **to be ill-advised to do sthg** être malavisé de faire qqch.

ill at ease **adj** mal à l'aise.

ill-bred **adj** mal élevé(e).

ill-considered **adj** irréfléchi(e).

ill-disposed **adj : to be ill-disposed towards sb** être mal disposé(e) *OR* malintentionné(e) envers qqn.

illegal [ɪ'li:gl] **adj** illégal(e).

illegal immigrant **n** immigré clandestin *m*, immigrée clandestine *f.*

illegality [,ɪli:'gælətɪ] (pl **-ies**) **n** illégalité *f.*

illegally [ɪ'li:gəlɪ] **adv** illégalement, d'une manière illégale.

illegible [ɪ'ledʒəbl] **adj** illisible.

illegitimacy [,ɪlɪ'dʒɪtɪməsɪ] **n** illégitimité *f.*

illegitimate [,ɪlɪ'dʒɪtɪmət] **adj** illégitime.

ill-equipped [-ɪ'kwɪpt] **adj : to be ill-equipped to do sthg** être mal placé(e) pour faire qqch.

ill-fated [-'feɪtɪd] **adj** fatal(e), funeste.

ill feeling **n** animosité *f.*

ill-founded [-'faundɪd] **adj** [confidence, trust] mal fondé(e) ∕ [doubts] sans fondement.

ill-gotten gains [-'gɒtən-] **npl** *hum* biens *mpl* mal acquis.

ill health **n** mauvaise santé *f.*

illicit [ɪ'lɪsɪt] **adj** illicite.

illicitly [ɪ'lɪsɪtlɪ] **adv** illicitement.

ill-informed **adj** mal renseigné(e).

Illinois [,ɪlɪ'nɔɪ] **n** Illinois *m* ▸ **in Illinois** dans l'Illinois.

illiteracy [ɪ'lɪtərəsɪ] **n** analphabétisme *m*, illettrisme *m.*

illiterate [ɪ'lɪtərət] ■ **adj** analphabète, illettré(e).

■ **n** analphabète *mf*, illettré *m*, -e *f.*

ill-mannered **adj** [person] mal élevé(e) ∕ [behaviour] grossier(ère).

illness ['ɪlnɪs] **n** maladie *f.*

illogical [ɪ'lɒdʒɪkl] **adj** illogique.

ill-suited **adj** mal assorti(e) ▸ **to be ill-suited for sthg** être inapte à qqch.

ill-tempered **adj** *fml* qui a mauvais caractère.

ill-timed [-'taɪmd] **adj** déplacé(e), mal à propos.

ill-treat **vt** maltraiter.

ill-treatment **n** mauvais traitement *m.*

illuminate [ɪ'lu:mɪneɪt] **vt** éclairer.

illuminated [ɪ'lu:mɪneɪtɪd] **adj 1.** [lit up] lumineux (euse) **2.** [book, manuscript] enluminé(e).

illuminating [ɪ'lu:mɪneɪtɪŋ] **adj** éclairant(e).

illumination [ɪˌlu:mɪ'neɪʃn] **n** *fml* [lighting] éclairage *m.*
◆ ***illuminations*** **npl** *UK* illuminations *fpl.*

illusion [ɪ'lu:ʒn] **n** illusion *f* ▸ **to have no illusions about** ne se faire OR n'avoir aucune illusion sur ▸ **to be under the illusion that** croire OR s'imaginer que, avoir l'illusion que.

illusionist [ɪ'lu:ʒənɪst] **n** prestidigitateur *m*, -euse *f*, illusionniste *mf.*

illusory [ɪ'lu:sərɪ] **adj** illusoire.

illustrate ['ɪləstreɪt] **vt** illustrer.

illustration [ˌɪlə'streɪʃn] **n** illustration *f.*

illustrative ['ɪləstrətɪv] **adj** [picture, diagram] qui illustre, explicatif(ive) / [action, event, fact] qui démontre, qui illustre ▸ **the demonstrations are illustrative of the need for reform** les manifestations montrent que des réformes sont nécessaires ▸ **illustrative examples** des exemples illustratifs.

illustrator ['ɪləstreɪtə^r] **n** illustrateur *m*, -trice *f.*

illustrious [ɪ'lʌstrɪəs] **adj** illustre, célèbre.

ill will **n** animosité *f.*

ill wind **n : it's an ill wind (that blows nobody any good)** *prov* à quelque chose malheur est bon.

ILO (abbr of ***International Labour Organization***) **n** OIT *f.*

ILWU (abbr of ***International Longshoremen's and Warehousemen's Union***) **n** *syndicat international de dockers et de magasiniers.*

I'm [aɪm] = ***I am.***

image ['ɪmɪdʒ] **n 1.** [gen] image *f* ▸ **I still have an image of her as a child** je la vois encore enfant ▸ **to be the image of sb** *fig* être tout le portrait de qqn, être qqn tout craché **2.** [of company, politician] image *f* de marque ▸ **the party tried to change its image** le parti a essayé de changer son image de marque.

image-conscious **adj** soucieux(euse) de son image.

imagery ['ɪmɪdʒrɪ] **n** *(U)* images *fpl.*

imaginable [ɪ'mædʒɪnəbl] **adj** imaginable.

imaginary [ɪ'mædʒɪnrɪ] **adj** imaginaire.

imagination [ɪˌmædʒɪ'neɪʃn] **n 1.** [ability] imagination *f* **2.** [fantasy] invention *f.*

imaginative [ɪ'mædʒɪnətɪv] **adj** [person] imaginatif(ive) / [solution] plein(e) d'imagination.

imaginatively [ɪ'mædʒɪnətɪvlɪ] **adv** avec imagination.

imagine [ɪ'mædʒɪn] **vt** imaginer ▸ **imagine (that) you've won** imagine que tu as gagné, suppose que tu aies gagné ▸ **to imagine doing sthg** s'imaginer OR se voir faisant qqch ▸ **I'd imagined him to be a much smaller man** je l'imaginais plus petit ▸ **you can't imagine how awful it was** vous ne pouvez pas (vous) imaginer OR vous figurer combien c'était horrible ▸ **you're imagining things** tu te fais des idées ▸ **imagine (that)!** tu t'imagines!

imaginings [ɪ'mædʒɪnɪŋz] **npl** imaginations *fpl.*

imam [ɪ'mɑ:m] **n** imam *m.*

imbalance [ˌɪm'bæləns] **n** déséquilibre *m.*

imbecile ['ɪmbɪsi:l] **n** imbécile *mf*, idiot *m*, -e *f.*

imbue [ɪm'bju:] **vt : to be imbued with** *fml* être imbu(e) de.

IMF (abbr of ***International Monetary Fund***) **n** FMI *m.*

IMHO (abbr of ***in my humble opinion***) **adv** *inf* à mon humble avis.

imitate ['ɪmɪteɪt] **vt** imiter.

imitation [ˌɪmɪ'teɪʃn] ■ **n** imitation *f.*
■ **adj** [jewellery] en toc ▸ **imitation leather** imitation *f* cuir.

imitator ['ɪmɪteɪtə^r] **n** imitateur *m*, -trice *f.*

immaculate [ɪ'mækjʊlət] **adj** impeccable.

immaculately [ɪ'mækjʊlətlɪ] **adv** impeccablement.

immaterial [ˌɪmə'tɪərɪəl] **adj** [unimportant] sans importance.

immature [ˌɪmə'tjʊə^r] **adj 1.** [lacking judgment] qui manque de maturité **2.** [not fully grown] jeune, immature.

immaturity [ˌɪmə'tjʊərətɪ] **n** immaturité *f.*

immeasurable [ɪ'meʒrəbl] **adj** incommensurable.

immeasurably [ɪ'meʒrəblɪ] **adv 1.** [long, high] incommensurablement **2.** [extremely] infiniment.

immediacy [ɪ'mi:djəsɪ] **n** caractère *m* immédiat.

immediate [ɪ'mi:djət] **adj 1.** [urgent] immédiat(e) / [problem, meeting] urgent(e) **2.** [very near] immédiat(e) / [family] le plus proche (la plus proche).

immediately [ɪ'mi:djətlɪ] ■ **adv 1.** [at once] immédiatement **2.** [directly] directement.
■ **conj** dès que.

immemorial [ˌɪmɪ'mɔ:rɪəl] **adj** immémorial(e) ▸ **from time immemorial** de temps immémorial.

immense [ɪ'mens] **adj** immense / [improvement, change] énorme.

immensely [ɪ'menslɪ] **adv** extrêmement, immensément.

immensity [ɪ'mensətɪ] **n** immensité *f.*

immerse [ɪ'mɜ:s] **vt : to immerse sthg in sthg** immerger OR plonger qqch dans qqch ▸ **to immerse o.s. in sthg** *fig* se plonger dans qqch.

immersion [ɪ'mɜ:ʃn] **n 1.** [in liquid] immersion *f* **2.** *fig* [in reading, work] absorption *f* ▸ **immersion course** stage *m* intensif **3.** ASTRON & RELIG immersion *f.*

immersion heater [ɪ'mɜ:ʃn-] **n** *UK* chauffe-eau *m* électrique.

immigrant ['ɪmɪgrənt] ■ **n** immigré *m*, -e *f.*
■ **comp** d'immigrés.

immigration [ˌɪmɪ'greɪʃn] ■ **n** immigration *f.*
■ **comp** de l'immigration.

imminence ['ɪmɪnəns] **n** imminence *f.*

imminent ['ɪmɪnənt] **adj** imminent(e).

immobile [ɪ'məʊbaɪl] **adj** immobile.

immobility [,ɪmə'bɪlətɪ] **n** immobilité *f*.

immobilization, *UK* ***-isation*** [ɪ,məʊbɪlaɪ'zeɪʃn] **n** immobilisation *f*.

immobilize, *UK* ***-ise*** [ɪ'məʊbɪlaɪz] **vt** immobiliser.

immobilizer [ɪ'məʊbɪlaɪzəʳ] **n** AUT système *m* antidémarrage.

immoderate [ɪ'mɒdərət] **adj** immodéré(e), excessif(ive).

immodest [ɪ'mɒdɪst] **adj 1.** [vain] vaniteux(euse), présomptueux(euse) **2.** [indecent] impudique.

immoral [ɪ'mɒrəl] **adj** immoral(e).

immorality [,ɪmə'rælətɪ] **n** immoralité *f*.

immortal [ɪ'mɔːtl] ■ **adj** immortel(elle).
■ **n** immortel *m*, -elle *f*.

immortality [,ɪmɔː'tælətɪ] **n** immortalité *f*.

immortalize, *UK* ***-ise*** [ɪ'mɔːtəlaɪz] **vt** immortaliser.

immov(e)able [ɪ'muːvəbl] **adj 1.** [fixed] fixe / [impossible to move] impossible à déplacer ▸ **immov(e)able feast** RELIG fête *f* fixe **2.** [determined - person] inébranlable **3.** LAW **: immov(e)able property** biens *mpl* immeubles *OR* immobiliers.
◆ ***immov(e)ables*** **npl** LAW biens *mpl* immobiliers.

immune [ɪ'mjuːn] **adj 1.** MED **: immune (to)** immunisé(e) (contre) **2.** *fig* [protected] **: to be immune to** *OR* **from** être à l'abri de.

immune system **n** système *m* immunitaire.

immunity [ɪ'mjuːnətɪ] **n 1.** MED **: immunity (to)** immunité *f* (contre) **2.** *fig* [protection] **: immunity to** *OR* **from** immunité *f* contre.

immunization, *UK* ***-isation*** [,ɪmjuːnaɪ'zeɪʃn] **n** immunisation *f*.

immunize, *UK* ***-ise*** ['ɪmjuːnaɪz] **vt : to immunize sb (against)** immuniser qqn (contre).

immunodeficiency [,ɪmjuːnəʊdɪ'fɪʃənsɪ] **n** immunodéficience *f*.

immunology [,ɪmjuː'nɒlədʒɪ] **n** immunologie *f*.

immutable [ɪ'mjuːtəbl] **adj** *fml* immuable.

imp [ɪmp] **n 1.** [creature] lutin *m* **2.** [naughty child] petit diable *m*, coquin *m*, -e *f*.

impact ■ **n** ['ɪmpækt] impact *m* ▸ **to make an impact on** *OR* **upon sb** faire une forte impression sur qqn ▸ **to make an impact on** *OR* **upon sthg** avoir un impact sur qqch ▸ **on impact** au moment de l'impact.
■ **vt** [ɪm'pækt] **1.** [collide with] entrer en collision avec **2.** [influence] avoir un impact sur.

impair [ɪm'peəʳ] **vt** affaiblir, abîmer / [efficiency] réduire.

impaired [ɪm'peəd] **adj** affaibli(e) / [efficiency] réduit(e).

impairment [ɪm'peəmənt] **n 1.** [weakening] affaiblissement *m*, diminution *f* **2.** [damage] détérioration *f*.

impale [ɪm'peɪl] **vt : to impale sb/sthg (on)** empaler qqn/qqch (sur).

impart [ɪm'pɑːt] **vt** *fml* **1.** [information] **: to impart sthg (to sb)** communiquer *OR* transmettre qqch (à qqn) **2.** [feeling, quality] **: to impart sthg (to)** donner qqch (à).

impartial [ɪm'pɑːʃl] **adj** impartial(e).

impartiality [ɪm,pɑːʃɪ'ælətɪ] **n** impartialité *f*.

impartially [ɪm'pɑːʃəlɪ] **adv** impartialement.

impassable [ɪm'pɑːsəbl] **adj** impraticable.

impasse [æm'pɑːs] **n** impasse *f* ▸ **to reach an impasse** aboutir à une impasse.

impassioned [ɪm'pæʃnd] **adj** passionné(e).

impassive [ɪm'pæsɪv] **adj** impassible.

impassively [ɪm'pæsɪvlɪ] **adv** impassiblement ▸ **to look at sb/sthg impassively** regarder qqn/qqch d'un air impassible.

impatience [ɪm'peɪʃns] **n 1.** [gen] impatience *f* **2.** [irritability] irritation *f*.

impatient [ɪm'peɪʃnt] **adj 1.** [gen] impatient(e) ▸ **to be impatient to do sthg** être impatient de faire qqch ▸ **to be impatient for sthg** attendre qqch avec impatience **2.** [irritable] **: to become** *OR* **get impatient** s'impatienter ▸ **she's impatient with her children** elle n'a aucune patience avec ses enfants.

impatiently [ɪm'peɪʃntlɪ] **adv** avec impatience.

impeach [ɪm'piːtʃ] **vt** *esp US* [official] mettre en accusation / [president] entamer la procédure d'impeachment contre.

impeachment [ɪm'piːtʃmənt] **n** [of president] procédure *f* de l'impeachment.

CULTURE

Impeachment

La procédure de l'**impeachment** permet au Congrès américain de destituer le président ou tout membre de l'Administration de ses fonctions, en cas de trahison, de trafic d'influence ou de crimes graves. La Chambre des représentants décide en premier lieu de destituer le haut fonctionnaire en votant sa mise en accusation, puis elle saisit le Sénat : la majorité des deux tiers suffit pour démettre l'élu. Seuls deux présidents ont été confrontés à cette procédure : Andrew Johnson, en 1868, qui refusa une loi votée par le Congrès, et Bill Clinton, en 1998, mêlé au scandale de l'affaire Monica Lewinsky. En 1974, Richard Nixon préféra démissionner pour éviter sa destitution après le scandale du Watergate.

impeccable [ɪm'pekəbl] **adj** impeccable.

impeccably [ɪm'pekəblɪ] **adv** impeccablement.

impecunious [,ɪmpɪ'kjuːnjəs] **adj** *fml* impécunieux(euse).

impede [ɪm'piːd] **vt** entraver, empêcher / [person] gêner.

impediment [ɪm'pedɪmənt] **n 1.** [obstacle] obstacle *m* **2.** [disability] défaut *m*.

impel [ɪm'pel] (pt & pp **-led**, cont **-ling**) **vt : to impel sb to do sthg** inciter qqn à faire qqch.

impending [ɪm'pendɪŋ] **adj** imminent(e).
impenetrable [ɪm'penɪtrəbl] **adj** impénétrable.
imperative [ɪm'perətɪv] ■ **adj** [essential] impératif(ive), essentiel(elle).
■ **n** impératif *m*.
imperceptible [ˌɪmpə'septəbl] **adj** imperceptible.
imperceptibly [ˌɪmpə'septəblɪ] **adv** imperceptiblement.
imperfect [ɪm'pɜːfɪkt] ■ **adj** imparfait(e).
■ **n** GRAM **: imperfect (tense)** imparfait *m*.
imperfection [ˌɪmpə'fekʃn] **n 1.** [gen] imperfection *f* **2.** [failing] défaut *m*.
imperfectly [ɪm'pɜːfɪktlɪ] **adv** imparfaitement.
imperial [ɪm'pɪərɪəl] **adj 1.** [of empire] impérial(e) **2.** [system of measurement] *qui a cours légal dans le Royaume-Uni*.
imperialism [ɪm'pɪərɪəlɪzm] **n** impérialisme *m*.
imperialist [ɪm'pɪərɪəlɪst] ■ **adj** impérialiste.
■ **n** impérialiste *mf*.
imperil [ɪm'perɪl] (*UK* **-led**, cont **-ling**, *US* **-ed**, cont **-ing**) **vt** mettre en péril *OR* en danger / [project] compromettre.
imperious [ɪm'pɪərɪəs] **adj** impérieux(euse).
imperiously [ɪm'pɪərɪəslɪ] **adv** impérieusement, autoritairement.
impermeable [ɪm'pɜːmɪəbl] **adj** [soil, cell, wall] imperméable / [container] étanche.
impersonal [ɪm'pɜːsnl] **adj** impersonnel(elle).
impersonally [ɪm'pɜːsnəlɪ] **adv** de façon impersonnelle.
impersonate [ɪm'pɜːsəneɪt] **vt** se faire passer pour.
impersonation [ɪmˌpɜːsə'neɪʃn] **n** usurpation *f* d'identité / [by mimic] imitation *f*.
impersonator [ɪm'pɜːsəneɪtəʳ] **n** imitateur *m*, -trice *f*.
impertinence [ɪm'pɜːtɪnəns] **n** impertinence *f*.
impertinent [ɪm'pɜːtɪnənt] **adj** impertinent(e).
impertinently [ɪm'pɜːtɪnəntlɪ] **adv** avec impertinence.
imperturbable [ˌɪmpə'tɜːbəbl] **adj** imperturbable.
impervious [ɪm'pɜːvjəs] **adj** [not influenced] **: impervious to** indifférent(e) à.
impetuous [ɪm'petʃʊəs] **adj** impétueux(euse).
impetus ['ɪmpɪtəs] **n** *(U)* **1.** [momentum] élan *m* **2.** [stimulus] impulsion *f*.
impinge [ɪm'pɪndʒ] **vi : to impinge on sb/sthg** affecter qqn/qqch.
impish ['ɪmpɪʃ] **adj** espiègle.
implacable [ɪm'plækəbl] **adj** implacable.
implant ■ **n** ['ɪmplɑːnt] implant *m*.
■ **vt** [ɪm'plɑːnt] **: to implant sthg in** *OR* **into sb** implanter qqch dans qqn.
implausible [ɪm'plɔːzəbl] **adj** peu plausible.
implement ■ **n** ['ɪmplɪmənt] outil *m*, instrument *m*.
■ **vt** ['ɪmplɪment] exécuter, appliquer.
implementation [ˌɪmplɪmen'teɪʃn] **n** application *f*, exécution *f*.
implicate ['ɪmplɪkeɪt] **vt : to implicate sb in sthg** impliquer qqn dans qqch.
implication [ˌɪmplɪ'keɪʃn] **n** implication *f* ▸ **I don't think you understand the implications of what you are saying** je ne suis pas sûr que vous mesuriez la portée de vos propos ▸ **the implication was that we would be punished** tout portait à croire que nous serions punis ▸ **by implication** par voie de conséquence.
implicit [ɪm'plɪsɪt] **adj 1.** [inferred] implicite **2.** [belief, faith] absolu(e).
implicitly [ɪm'plɪsɪtlɪ] **adv 1.** [by inference] implicitement **2.** [believe] absolument.
implied [ɪm'plaɪd] **adj** implicite.
implode [ɪm'pləʊd] **vi** imploser.
implore [ɪm'plɔːʳ] **vt : to implore sb (to do sthg)** implorer qqn (de faire qqch).
imploring [ɪm'plɔːrɪŋ] **adj** suppliant(e).
imply [ɪm'plaɪ] (pt & pp **-ied**) **vt 1.** [suggest] sous-entendre, laisser supposer *OR* entendre **2.** [involve] impliquer.
impolite [ˌɪmpə'laɪt] **adj** impoli(e).
impolitely [ˌɪmpə'laɪtlɪ] **adv** impoliment.
imponderable [ɪm'pɒndrəbl] **adj** impondérable.
◆ ***imponderables*** **npl** impondérables *mpl*.
import ■ **n** ['ɪmpɔːt] **1.** [product, action] importation *f* **2.** *fml* [meaning] teneur *f* **3.** *fml* [importance] importance *f*.
■ **vt** [ɪm'pɔːt] [gen & COMPUT] importer.
importance [ɪm'pɔːtns] **n** importance *f*.
important [ɪm'pɔːtnt] **adj** important(e) ▸ **to be important to sb** importer à qqn.
importantly [ɪm'pɔːtntlɪ] **adv : more importantly** ce qui est plus important.
importation [ˌɪmpɔː'teɪʃn] **n** importation *f*.
import ban **n** interdiction *f* d'importation.
imported [ɪm'pɔːtɪd] **adj** importé(e).
importer [ɪm'pɔːtəʳ] **n** importateur *m*, -trice *f*.
import-export **n** import-export *m*.
impose [ɪm'pəʊz] ■ **vt** [force] **: to impose sthg (on)** imposer qqch (à).
■ **vi** [cause trouble] **: to impose (on sb)** abuser (de la gentillesse de qqn).
imposing [ɪm'pəʊzɪŋ] **adj** imposant(e).
imposition [ˌɪmpə'zɪʃn] **n 1.** [of tax, limitations] imposition *f* **2.** [cause of trouble] **: it's an imposition** c'est abuser de ma gentillesse.
impossibility [ɪmˌpɒsə'bɪlətɪ] (pl **-ies**) **n** impossibilité *f*.
impossible [ɪm'pɒsəbl] ■ **adj** impossible.
■ **n : to do the impossible** faire l'impossible.
impossibly [ɪm'pɒsəblɪ] **adv 1.** [extremely] extrêmement ▸ **the film is impossibly long** le film n'en finit pas **2.** [unbearably] insupportablement ▸ **they behave impossibly** ils sont totalement insupportables.
impostor, ***imposter*** [ɪm'pɒstəʳ] **n** imposteur *m*.

impotence ['ɪmpətəns] **n** impuissance *f*.

impotent ['ɪmpətənt] **adj** impuissant(e).

impound [ɪm'paʊnd] **vt** confisquer.

impoverish [ɪm'pɒvərɪʃ] **vt** appauvrir.

impoverished [ɪm'pɒvərɪʃt] **adj** appauvri(e).

impoverishment [ɪm'pɒvərɪʃmənt] **n** appauvrissement *m*.

impracticable [ɪm'præktɪkəbl] **adj** irréalisable.

impractical [ɪm'præktɪkl] **adj** pas pratique.

imprecation [ˌɪmprɪ'keɪʃn] **n** imprécation *f*.

imprecise [ɪmprɪ'saɪs] **adj** imprécis(e).

impregnable [ɪm'pregnəbl] **adj 1.** [fortress, defences] imprenable **2.** *fig* [person] inattaquable.

impregnate ['ɪmpregneɪt] **vt 1.** [introduce substance into] **: to impregnate sthg with** imprégner qqch de **2.** *fml* [fertilize] féconder.

impresario [ˌɪmprɪ'sɑːrɪəʊ] (pl **-s**) **n** impresario *mf*.

impress [ɪm'pres] **vt 1.** [person] impressionner **2.** [stress] **: to impress sthg on sb** faire bien comprendre qqch à qqn.

impression [ɪm'preʃn] **n 1.** [gen] impression *f* ▸ **to be under the impression (that)...** avoir l'impression que... ▸ **I was under the impression that you were unable to come** j'étais persuadé que vous ne pouviez pas venir ▸ **to make an impression** faire impression ▸ **he always tries to make an impression** il essaie toujours d'impressionner les gens ▸ **my words made no impression on him whatsoever** mes paroles n'ont eu absolument aucun effet sur lui **2.** [impersonation] imitation *f* ▸ **she does a very good impression of the Queen** elle imite très bien la reine **3.** [of stamp, book] impression *f*, empreinte *f*.

impressionable [ɪm'preʃnəbl] **adj** impressionnable.

Impressionism [ɪm'preʃənɪzm] **n** impressionnisme *m*.

impressionist [ɪm'preʃənɪst] **n** imitateur *m*, -trice *f*.
◆ ***Impressionist*** ■ **adj** impressionniste.
■ **n** impressionniste *mf*.

impressionistic [ɪmˌpreʃə'nɪstɪk] **adj** [vague] vague, imprécis(e).

impressive [ɪm'presɪv] **adj** impressionnant(e).

impressively [ɪm'presɪvlɪ] **adv** remarquablement.

imprint ['ɪmprɪnt] **n 1.** [mark] empreinte *f* **2.** [publisher's name] nom *m* de l'éditeur.

imprinted [ɪm'prɪntɪd] **adj** imprimé(e).

imprison [ɪm'prɪzn] **vt** emprisonner.

imprisonment [ɪm'prɪznmənt] **n** emprisonnement *m*.

improbable [ɪm'prɒbəbl] **adj 1.** [story, excuse] improbable **2.** [hat, contraption] bizarre.

improbably [ɪm'prɒbəblɪ] **adv** invraisemblablement.

impromptu [ɪm'prɒmptjuː] **adj** impromptu(e).

improper [ɪm'prɒpəʳ] **adj 1.** [unsuitable] impropre **2.** [incorrect, illegal] incorrect(e) **3.** [rude] indécent(e).

improperly [ɪm'prɒpəlɪ] **adv 1.** [indecently] de manière déplacée **2.** [unsuitably] **: he was improperly dressed** il n'était pas habillé comme il faut **3.** [dishonestly] malhonnêtement **4.** [incorrectly] incorrectement, de manière incorrecte.

impropriety [ɪmprə'praɪətɪ] **n** inconvenance *f*.

improve [ɪm'pruːv] ■ **vi** s'améliorer / [patient] aller mieux ▸ **your maths has improved** vous avez fait des progrès en maths ▸ **to improve on** OR **upon sthg** améliorer qqch.
■ **vt** améliorer ▸ **to improve one's chances** augmenter ses chances ▸ **to improve one's mind** se cultiver l'esprit.

improved [ɪm'pruːvd] **adj** amélioré(e).

improvement [ɪm'pruːvmənt] **n : improvement (in/on)** amélioration *f* (de/par rapport à) ▸ **this is a great improvement on her previous work** c'est bien mieux que ce qu'elle faisait jusqu'à présent ▸ **there's room for improvement** ça pourrait être mieux ▸ **(home) improvements** travaux *mpl* de rénovation.

improvisation [ˌɪmprəvaɪ'zeɪʃn] **n** improvisation *f*.

improvise ['ɪmprəvaɪz] **vt & vi** improviser.

imprudent [ɪm'pruːdənt] **adj** imprudent(e).

impudence ['ɪmpjʊdəns] **n** effronterie *f*, impudence *f*.

impudent ['ɪmpjʊdənt] **adj** impudent(e).

impugn [ɪm'pjuːn] **vt** *fml* contester.

impulse ['ɪmpʌls] **n** impulsion *f* ▸ **on impulse** par impulsion.

impulse buy **n** achat *m* spontané OR d'impulsion OR impulsif.

impulse buyer **n** acheteur impulsif *m*, acheteuse impulsive *f*.

impulse buying [-'baɪɪŋ] **n** *(U)* achats *mpl* impulsifs.

impulsive [ɪm'pʌlsɪv] **adj** impulsif(ive).

impulsively [ɪm'pʌlsɪvlɪ] **adv** par OR sur impulsion, impulsivement.

impulsiveness [ɪm'pʌlsɪvnɪs] **n** caractère *m* impulsif.

impunity [ɪm'pjuːnətɪ] **n : with impunity** avec impunité.

impure [ɪm'pjʊəʳ] **adj** impur(e).

impurity [ɪm'pjʊərətɪ] (pl **-ies**) **n** impureté *f*.

IMRO ['ɪmrəʊ] (abbr of ***Investment Management Regulatory Organization***) *organisme britannique contrôlant les activités de banques d'affaires et de gestionnaires de fonds de retraite*.

IMS (abbr of ***International Monetary System***) **n** ECON SMI *m (Système monétaire international)*.

in [ɪn] ■ **prep 1.** [indicating place, position] dans ▸ **in a box/bag/drawer** dans une boîte/un sac/un tiroir ▸ **in the room/garden/lake** dans la pièce/le jardin/le lac ▸ **in Catherine's house** chez Catherine ▸ **in Paris** à Paris ▸ **in Belgium** en Belgique ▸ **in Canada** au Canada ▸ **in the United States** aux États-Unis ▸ **in the country** à la campagne ▸ **he's still in bed/in the bath** il est encore au lit/dans son bain ▸ **to be in hospital** *UK*, **to be in the hospital** *US* être à l'hôpital ▸ **throw the letter in the bin** jette la lettre à la poubelle ▸ **in here** ici ▸ **in there** là

2. [wearing] en ▸ **she was still in her nightclothes** elle était encore en chemise de nuit ▸ **dressed in a suit** vêtu(e) d'un costume ▸ **who's that woman in the hat?** qui est la femme avec le *OR* au chapeau?
3. [appearing in, included in] dans ▸ **there's a mistake in this paragraph** il y a une erreur dans ce paragraphe ▸ **in chapter six** au sixième chapitre ▸ **who's that man in the photo?** qui est cet homme sur la photo?
4. [at a particular time, season] **: in 2004** en 2004 ▸ **in April** en avril ▸ **in (the) spring** au printemps ▸ **in (the) winter** en hiver ▸ **at two o'clock in the afternoon** à deux heures de l'après-midi ▸ **he doesn't work in the afternoon/morning** il ne travaille pas l'après-midi/le matin ▸ **in the past** autrefois
5. [period of time - within] en / [- after] dans ▸ **he learned to type in two weeks** il a appris à taper à la machine en deux semaines ▸ **I'll be ready in five minutes** je serai prêt dans 5 minutes
6. [during] **: it's my first decent meal in weeks** c'est mon premier repas correct depuis des semaines ▸ **I hadn't seen her in years** ça faisait des années que je ne l'avais pas vue ▸ **in my absence** en *OR* pendant mon absence
7. [indicating situation, circumstances] **: in the sun** au soleil ▸ **in the rain** sous la pluie ▸ **in these circumstances** dans ces circonstances, en de telles circonstances ▸ **to live/die in poverty** vivre/mourir dans la misère ▸ **in danger/difficulty** en danger/difficulté ▸ **in love** amoureux
8. [indicating manner, condition] **: in cash** en liquide ▸ **in a loud/soft voice** d'une voix forte/douce ▸ **to write in pencil/ink** écrire au crayon/à l'encre ▸ **to speak in English/French** parler (en) anglais/français
9. [indicating cause] **: in anger** sous le coup de la colère ▸ **he charged the door in an effort to get free** dans un effort pour se libérer, il donna un grand coup dans la porte ▸ **he looked at me in amazement/horror** il me regarda stupéfait/horrifié ▸ **in reply** *OR* **response to your letter...** en réponse à votre lettre...
10. [specifying area of activity] dans ▸ **he's in computers** il est dans l'informatique ▸ **to be in the army/navy** être dans l'armée/la marine ▸ **advances in science** des progrès en science ▸ **our days were spent in swimming and sailing** nous passions nos journées à nager et à faire de la voile
11. [among] chez ▸ **a disease common in five-year-olds** une maladie très répanduc chez les enfants de cinq ans
12. [referring to quantity, numbers, age] **: in large/small quantities** en grande/petite quantité ▸ **in (their) thousands** par milliers ▸ **she's in her sixties** elle a la soixantaine
13. [describing arrangement] **: in twos** par deux ▸ **in a line/row/circle** en ligne/rang/cercle
14. [as regards] **: to be three metres in length/width** faire trois mètres de long/large ▸ **a change in direction** un changement de direction ▸ **a rise in prices** une augmentation des prix ▸ **she has no confidence in him** elle n'a aucune confiance en lui ▸ **in my opinion** *OR* **view** à mon avis
15. [in ratios] **: 5 pence in the pound** *UK* 5 pence par livre sterling ▸ **one in ten** un sur dix
16. *(after superl)* de ▸ **the longest river in the world** le fleuve le plus long du monde
17. *(+ present participle)* **: in doing sthg** en faisant qqch.
■ **adv 1.** [inside] dedans, à l'intérieur ▸ **put the clothes in** mets les vêtements dedans ▸ **he jumped in** il sauta dedans ▸ **to go in** entrer ▸ **do come in!** entrez donc!
2. [at home, work] là ▸ **I'm staying in tonight** je reste à la maison *OR* chez moi ce soir ▸ **is Judith in?** est-ce que Judith est là?
3. [arrived] **: what time does your train get in?** quand est-ce que votre train arrive? ▸ **entries must be in by May 1st** les bulletins doivent nous parvenir avant le 1er mai
4. [of tide] **: the tide's in** c'est la marée haute
5. POL [elected] **: he failed to get in at the last election** il n'a pas été élu aux dernières élections
▸▸ **we're in for some bad weather** nous allons avoir du mauvais temps ▸ **you're in for a shock** tu vas avoir un choc ▸ **to be in on sthg** être au courant de qqch.
■ **adj 1.** SPORT [within area of court] **: the umpire said that the ball was in** l'arbitre a dit que la balle était bonne
2. *inf* à la mode ▸ **short skirts are in this year** les jupes courtes sont à la mode cette année.
◆ ***ins*** **npl : the ins and outs** les tenants et les aboutissants *mpl*.
◆ ***in all*** **adv** en tout ▸ **there are 30 in all** il y en a 30 en tout.
◆ ***in between*** ■ **adv 1.** [in intermediate position] **: a row of bushes with little clumps of flowers in between** une rangée d'arbustes séparés par des petites touffes de fleurs ▸ **she plays either very well or very badly, never in between** elle joue très bien ou très mal, jamais entre les deux
2. [in time] entre-temps, dans l'intervalle.
■ **prep** entre.
◆ ***in that*** **conj** étant donné que ▸ **we are lucky in that there are only a few of us** nous avons de la chance d'être si peu nombreux.

in. abbr of ***inch***.

IN abbr of ***Indiana***.

inability [ˌɪnəˈbɪlətɪ] **n : inability (to do sthg)** incapacité *f* (à faire qqch).

inaccessibility [ˈɪnəkˌsesɪˈbɪlətɪ] **n** inaccessibilité *f*.

inaccessible [ˌɪnəkˈsesəbl] **adj** inaccessible.

inaccuracy [ɪnˈækjʊrəsɪ] (pl **-ies**) **n** inexactitude *f*.

inaccurate [ɪnˈækjʊrət] **adj** inexact(e).

inaction [ɪnˈækʃn] **n** inaction *f*.

inactive [ɪnˈæktɪv] **adj** inactif(ive).

inactivity [ˌɪnækˈtɪvətɪ] **n** inactivité *f*.

inadequacy [ɪnˈædɪkwəsɪ] (pl **-ies**) **n** insuffisance *f*.

inadequate [ɪnˈædɪkwət] **adj** insuffisant(e) ▸ **their response to the problem was inadequate** ils n'ont pas su trouver de réponse satisfaisante au problème ▸ **our machinery is inadequate for this type of work** notre outillage n'est pas adapté à ce genre de travail ▸ **being unemployed often makes people feel inadequate** les gens au chômage se sentent souvent inutiles ▸ **he's socially inadequate** c'est un inadapté.

inadequately [ɪnˈædɪkwətlɪ] **adv** de manière inadéquate / [fund, invest] insuffisamment.

inadmissible [ˌɪnədˈmɪsəbl] **adj** inadmissible / [evidence] irrecevable.

inadvertent [ˌɪnədˈvɜːtnt] **adj** commis(e) par inadvertance.

inadvertently [ˌɪnədˈvɜːtəntlɪ] **adv** par inadvertance.

inadvisability [ˈɪnəd,vaɪzəˈbɪlətɪ] **n** inopportunité *f*.

inadvisable [,ɪnədˈvaɪzəbl] **adj** déconseillé(e).

inalienable [ɪnˈeɪljənəbl] **adj** inaliénable.

inane [ɪˈneɪn] **adj** [behaviour, remark] inepte / [person] stupide.

inanely [ɪˈneɪnlɪ] **adv** stupidement.

inanimate [ɪnˈænɪmət] **adj** inanimé(e).

inanity [ɪˈnænətɪ] **n** [stupid remark] ineptie *f* / [of person] stupidité *f*.

inapplicable [ɪnˈæplɪkəbl] **adj** inapplicable.

inappropriate [ɪnəˈprəʊprɪət] **adj** [action, remark] inopportun(e) / [expression, word] impropre / [clothing] peu approprié(e).

inappropriately [,ɪnəˈprəʊprɪətlɪ] **adv** de manière peu convenable OR appropriée ▸ **she was inappropriately dressed** elle n'était pas vêtue pour la circonstance.

inarticulate [,ɪnɑːˈtɪkjʊlət] **adj** inarticulé(e), indistinct(e) / [person] qui s'exprime avec difficulté / [explanation] mal exprimé(e).

inasmuch [,ɪnəzˈmʌtʃ] ◆ ***inasmuch as*** **conj** *fml* attendu que.

inattention [,ɪnəˈtenʃn] **n : inattention (to)** inattention *f* (à).

inattentive [,ɪnəˈtentɪv] **adj : inattentive (to)** inattentif(ive) (à).

inattentively [,ɪnəˈtentɪvlɪ] **adv** sans prêter OR faire attention.

inaudible [ɪˈnɔːdɪbl] **adj** inaudible.

inaudibly [ɪˈnɔːdɪblɪ] **adv** indistinctement.

inaugural [ɪˈnɔːgjʊrəl] **adj** inaugural(e).

inaugural address, inaugural speech **n** *US* POL discours *m* inaugural.

inaugurate [ɪˈnɔːgjʊreɪt] **vt** [leader, president] investir / [building, system] inaugurer.

inauguration [ɪ,nɔːgjʊˈreɪʃn] **n** [of leader, president] investiture *f* / [of building, system] inauguration *f*.

inauspicious [,ɪnɔːˈspɪʃəs] **adj** *fml* peu propice.

in-basket *US* = ***in-tray***.

in-between **adj** intermédiaire.

inboard [ˈɪnbɔːd] **adj** in-bord *(inv)*.

inborn [,ɪnˈbɔːn] **adj** inné(e).

inbound [ˈɪnbaʊnd] **adj** qui arrive.

inbox [ˈɪnbɒks] **n** COMPUT boîte *f* de réception.

in-box *US* = ***in-tray***.

inbred [,ɪnˈbred] **adj 1.** [closely related] consanguin(e) / [animal] croisé(e) **2.** [inborn] inné(e).

inbreeding [ˈɪn,briːdɪŋ] **n** consanguinité *f* / [of animals] croisement *m*.

inbuilt [,ɪnˈbɪlt] **adj** [inborn] inné(e).

inc. (abbr of ***inclusive***) **: 12-15 April inc.** du 12 au 15 avril inclus.

Inc. [ɪŋk] (abbr of ***incorporated***) *US* ≃ SARL.

Inca [ˈɪŋkə] **n** Inca *mf*.

incalculable [ɪnˈkælkjʊləbl] **adj** incalculable.

incandescent [,ɪnkænˈdesnt] **adj** incandescent(e).

incantation [,ɪnkænˈteɪʃn] **n** incantation *f*.

incapable [ɪnˈkeɪpəbl] **adj** incapable ▸ **to be incapable of sthg/of doing sthg** être incapable de qqch/de faire qqch.

incapacitate [,ɪnkəˈpæsɪteɪt] **vt** rendre inapte physiquement.

incapacitated [,ɪnkəˈpæsɪteɪtɪd] **adj** inapte physiquement ▸ **incapacitated for work** mis(e) dans l'incapacité de travailler.

incapacity [,ɪnkəˈpæsətɪ] **n : incapacity (for)** incapacité *f* (de).

in-car **adj** AUT **: in-car stereo** autoradio *f* (à cassette).

incarcerate [ɪnˈkɑːsəreɪt] **vt** *fml* incarcérer.

incarceration [ɪn,kɑːsəˈreɪʃn] **n** *fml* incarcération *f*.

incarnate [ɪnˈkɑːneɪt] **adj** *fml* incarné(e).

incarnation [,ɪnkɑːˈneɪʃn] **n** *fml* incarnation *f*.

incendiary device [ɪnˈsendjərɪ-] **n** dispositif *m* incendiaire.

incense ■ **n** [ˈɪnsens] encens *m*.
■ **vt** [ɪnˈsens] [anger] mettre en colère.

incentive [ɪnˈsentɪv] **n 1.** [encouragement] motivation *f* **2.** COMM récompense *f*, prime *f*.

incentive program *US*, ***incentive scheme*** *UK* **n** programme *m* d'encouragement.

incentivize, *UK* ***-ise*** [ɪnˈsentɪvaɪz] **vt** motiver.

inception [ɪnˈsepʃn] **n** *fml* commencement *m*.

incessant [ɪnˈsesnt] **adj** incessant(e).

incessantly [ɪnˈsesntlɪ] **adv** sans cesse.

incest [ˈɪnsest] **n** inceste *m*.

incestuous [ɪnˈsestjʊəs] **adj 1.** [sexual] incestueux (euse) **2.** *fig* [too close] très fermé(e) / [relationship] en vase clos.

inch [ɪntʃ] ■ **n** = *2,5 cm*, ≃ pouce *m*.
■ **vi : to inch forward** avancer petit à petit.

incidence [ˈɪnsɪdəns] **n** *fml* [of disease, theft] fréquence *f*.

incident [ˈɪnsɪdənt] **n** incident *m*.

incidental [,ɪnsɪˈdentl] **adj** accessoire.

incidentally [,ɪnsɪˈdentəlɪ] **adv** à propos.

incidental music **n** musique *f* de fond.

incident room **n** *UK* [in police station] salle *f* des opérations.

incinerate [ɪnˈsɪnəreɪt] **vt** incinérer.

incinerator [ɪnˈsɪnəreɪtəʳ] **n** incinérateur *m*.

incipient [ɪnˈsɪpɪənt] **adj** *fml* naissant(e).

incision [ɪnˈsɪʒn] **n** incision *f*.

incisive [ɪnˈsaɪsɪv] **adj** incisif(ive).

incisively [ɪnˈsaɪsɪvlɪ] **adv** [think] de façon incisive / [ask, remark] de manière perspicace OR pénétrante.

incisor [ɪnˈsaɪzəʳ] **n** incisive *f*.

incite [ɪn'saɪt] **vt** inciter ▸ **to incite sb to do sthg** inciter qqn à faire qqch.

incitement [ɪn'saɪtmənt] **n** *(U)* **: incitement (to sthg/ to do sthg)** incitation *f* (à qqch/à faire qqch).

incl. abbr of ***including***. abbr of ***inclusive***.

inclement [ɪn'klemənt] **adj** *fml* inclément(e).

inclination [ˌɪnklɪ'neɪʃn] **n 1.** *(U)* [liking, preference] inclination *f*, goût *m* **2.** [tendency] **: inclination to do sthg** inclination *f* à faire qqch.

incline ■ **n** ['ɪnklaɪn] inclinaison *f*.
■ **vt** [ɪn'klaɪn] [head] incliner.

inclined [ɪn'klaɪnd] **adj 1.** [tending] **: to be inclined to sthg/to do sthg** avoir tendance à qqch/à faire qqch **2.** [wanting] **: to be inclined to do sthg** être enclin(e) à faire qqch **3.** [sloping] incliné(e).

include [ɪn'klu:d] **vt** inclure.

included [ɪn'klu:dɪd] **adj** inclus(e).

including [ɪn'klu:dɪŋ] **prep** y compris.

inclusion [ɪn'klu:ʒn] **n** inclusion *f*.

inclusive [ɪn'klu:sɪv] **adj** inclus(e) / [including all costs] tout compris (toute comprise) ▸ **inclusive of VAT** TVA incluse *OR* comprise.

inclusively [ɪn'klu:sɪvlɪ] **adv** inclusivement.

inclusivity [ˌɪnklu:'sɪvɪtɪ] **n** inclusion *f*, politique *f* d'inclusion.

incognito [ˌɪnkɒg'ni:təʊ] **adv** incognito.

incoherence [ˌɪnkəʊ'hɪərəns] **n** incohérence *f*.

incoherent [ˌɪnkəʊ'hɪərənt] **adj** incohérent(e).

incoherently [ˌɪnkəʊ'hɪərəntlɪ] **adv** de manière incohérente ▸ **to mutter incoherently** marmonner des paroles incohérentes.

income ['ɪŋkʌm] **n** revenu *m*.

income bracket **n** tranche *f* de salaire *OR* de revenu.

income group **n** tranche *f* de salaire *OR* de revenu.

incomes policy **n** *UK* politique *f* salariale *OR* des revenus.

income support **n** *(U) UK allocations supplémentaires accordées aux personnes ayant un faible revenu.*

income tax **n** impôt *m* sur le revenu.

incoming ['ɪnˌkʌmɪŋ] **adj 1.** [tide, wave] montant(e) **2.** [plane, passengers, mail] qui arrive / [phone call] de l'extérieur **3.** [government, official] nouveau(nouvelle).

incomings ['ɪnˌkʌmɪŋz] **npl** recettes *fpl*, revenus *mpl* ▸ **incomings and outgoings** dépenses *fpl* et recettes *fpl*.

incommunicado [ˌɪnkəmju:nɪ'kɑ:dəʊ] **adv : to be held incommunicado** être tenu(e) au secret.

incomparable [ɪn'kɒmpərəbl] **adj** incomparable.

incomparably [ɪn'kɒmpərəblɪ] **adv** incomparablement, infiniment.

incompatibility ['ɪnkəmˌpætə'bɪlətɪ] **n** incompatibilité *f* / [grounds for divorce] incompatibilité *f* d'humeur.

incompatible [ˌɪnkəm'pætɪbl] **adj : incompatible (with)** incompatible (avec).

incompetence [ɪn'kɒmpɪtəns] **n** incompétence *f*.

incompetent [ɪn'kɒmpɪtənt] **adj** incompétent(e).

incomplete [ˌɪnkəm'pli:t] **adj** incomplet(ète).

incompletely [ˌɪnkəm'pli:tlɪ] **adv** incomplètement.

incomprehensible [ɪnˌkɒmprɪ'hensəbl] **adj** incompréhensible.

inconceivable [ˌɪnkən'si:vəbl] **adj** inconcevable.

inconclusive [ˌɪnkən'klu:sɪv] **adj** peu concluant(e).

incongruous [ɪn'kɒŋgrʊəs] **adj** incongru(e).

inconsequential [ˌɪnkɒnsɪ'kwenʃl] **adj** sans importance.

inconsiderable [ˌɪnkən'sɪdərəbl] **adj : not inconsiderable** non négligeable.

inconsiderate [ˌɪnkən'sɪdərət] **adj** inconsidéré(e) / [person] qui manque de considération.

inconsiderately [ˌɪnkən'sɪdərətlɪ] **adv** sans aucune considération.

inconsistency [ˌɪnkən'sɪstənsɪ] (pl **-ies**) **n** inconsistance *f*.

inconsistent [ˌɪnkən'sɪstənt] **adj 1.** [not agreeing, contradictory] contradictoire / [person] inconséquent(e) ▸ **inconsistent with sthg** en contradiction avec qqch **2.** [erratic] inconsistant(e).

inconsolable [ˌɪnkən'səʊləbl] **adj** inconsolable.

inconsolably [ˌɪnkən'səʊləblɪ] **adv** de façon inconsolable.

inconspicuous [ˌɪnkən'spɪkjʊəs] **adj** qui passe inaperçu(e).

incontinence [ɪn'kɒntɪnəns] **n** incontinence *f*.

incontinent [ɪn'kɒntɪnənt] **adj** incontinent(e).

incontrovertible [ˌɪnkɒntrə'vɜ:təbl] **adj** *fml* indéniable, irréfutable.

inconvenience [ˌɪnkən'vi:njəns] ■ **n** désagrément *m*.
■ **vt** déranger.

inconvenient [ˌɪnkən'vi:njənt] **adj** inopportun(e).

inconveniently [ˌɪnkən'vi:njəntlɪ] **adv 1.** [happen, arrive] au mauvais moment, inopportunément **2.** [be situated] de façon malcommode, mal.

incorporate [ɪn'kɔ:pəreɪt] ■ **vt 1.** [integrate] **: to incorporate sb/sthg (into)** incorporer qqn/qqch (dans) **2.** [comprise] contenir, comprendre.
■ **vi** COMM [to form a corporation] se constituer en société commerciale.

incorporated [ɪn'kɔ:pəreɪtɪd] **adj** COMM constitué(e) en société commerciale.

incorporation [ɪnˌkɔ:pə'reɪʃn] **n 1.** [integration] incorporation *f* **2.** COMM [of company] constitution *f* en société commerciale.

incorrect [ˌɪnkə'rekt] **adj** incorrect(e).

incorrectly [ˌɪnkə'rektlɪ] **adv 1.** [wrongly] **: I was incorrectly quoted** j'ai été cité de façon incorrecte ▸ **the illness was incorrectly diagnosed** il y a eu erreur de diagnostic **2.** [improperly] incorrectement.

incorrigible [ɪn'kɒrɪdʒəbl] **adj** incorrigible.

incorruptible [ˌɪnkə'rʌptəbl] **adj** incorruptible.

increase ■ **n** ['ɪnkri:s] **: increase (in)** augmentation *f* (de) ▸ **to be on the increase** aller en augmentant.
■ **vt & vi** [ɪn'kri:s] augmenter.

increased [ɪn'kri:st] **adj** accru(e).

increasing [ɪn'kri:sɪŋ] **adj** croissant(e).

increasingly [ɪn'kri:sɪŋlɪ] **adv** de plus en plus.

increasing returns **npl** ECON rendement *m* croissant.

incredible [ɪn'kredəbl] **adj** incroyable.

incredibly [ɪn'kredəblɪ] **adv 1.** [amazingly] **: incredibly, we were on time** aussi incroyable que cela puisse paraître, nous étions à l'heure **2.** [extremely] incroyablement.

incredulity [ˌɪnkrɪ'dju:lətɪ] **n** incrédulité *f*.

incredulous [ɪn'kredjʊləs] **adj** incrédule.

incredulously [ɪn'kredjʊləslɪ] **adv** avec incrédulité.

increment ['ɪnkrɪmənt] **n** augmentation *f*.

incriminate [ɪn'krɪmɪneɪt] **vt** incriminer ▸ **to incriminate o.s.** se compromettre.

incriminating [ɪn'krɪmɪneɪtɪŋ] **adj** compromettant(e).

in-crowd **n** *inf* coterie *f* ▸ **to be in with the in-crowd** être branché(e).

incrusted [ɪn'krʌstɪd] = ***encrusted***.

incubate ['ɪnkjʊbeɪt] ■ **vt** incuber.
■ **vi** être en incubation.

incubation [ˌɪnkjʊ'beɪʃn] **n** incubation *f*.

incubator ['ɪnkjʊbeɪtəʳ] **n** [for baby] incubateur *m*, couveuse *f*.

inculcate ['ɪnkʌlkeɪt] **vt** *fml* **: to inculcate sthg in** *OR* **into sb** inculquer qqch à qqn.

incumbent [ɪn'kʌmbənt] *fml* ■ **adj : to be incumbent on** *OR* **upon sb to do sthg** incomber à qqn de faire qqch.
■ **n** [of post] titulaire *m*.

incur [ɪn'kɜ:ʳ] (pt & pp **-red**, cont **-ring**) **vt** encourir.

incurable [ɪn'kjʊərəbl] **adj** [disease] incurable.

incurably [ɪn'kjʊərəblɪ] **adv : to be incurably ill** avoir une maladie incurable ▸ **to be incurably lazy** *fig* être irrémédiablement paresseux(euse).

incurred expenditure [ɪn'kəd-] **n** FIN dépenses *fpl* engagées.

incurred expenses [ɪn'kəd-] **npl** = ***incurred expenditure***.

incursion [*UK* ɪn'kɜ:ʃn, *US* ɪn'kɜ:ʒn] **n** incursion *f*.

indebted [ɪn'detɪd] **adj** [grateful] **: indebted to sb** redevable à qqn.

indecency [ɪn'di:snsɪ] **n** indécence *f*.

indecent [ɪn'di:snt] **adj 1.** [improper] indécent(e) **2.** [unreasonable] malséant(e).

indecent assault **n** attentat *m* à la pudeur.

indecent exposure **n** outrage *m* public à la pudeur.

indecently [ɪn'di:sntlɪ] **adv** indécemment.

indecipherable [ˌɪndɪ'saɪfərəbl] **adj** indéchiffrable.

indecision [ˌɪndɪ'sɪʒn] **n** indécision *f*.

indecisive [ˌɪndɪ'saɪsɪv] **adj** indécis(e).

indecisively [ˌɪndɪ'saɪsɪvlɪ] **adv 1.** [hesitatingly] de manière indécise, avec hésitation **2.** [inconclusively] de manière peu convaincante *OR* concluante.

indeed [ɪn'di:d] **adv 1.** [certainly, to express surprise] vraiment ▸ **indeed I am, yes indeed** certainement **2.** [in fact] en effet **3.** [for emphasis] **: very big/bad indeed** extrêmement *OR* vraiment grand(e)/mauvais(e).

indefatigable [ˌɪndɪ'fætɪgəbl] **adj** *fml* infatigable.

indefatigably [ˌɪndɪ'fætɪgəblɪ] **adv** *fml* infatigablement, sans se fatiguer, inlassablement.

indefensible [ˌɪndɪ'fensəbl] **adj** indéfendable.

indefinable [ˌɪndɪ'faɪnəbl] **adj** indéfinissable.

indefinite [ɪn'defɪnɪt] **adj 1.** [not fixed] indéfini(e) **2.** [imprecise] vague.

indefinite article **n** article *m* indéfini.

indefinitely [ɪn'defɪnətlɪ] **adv 1.** [for unfixed period] indéfiniment **2.** [imprecisely] vaguement.

indelible [ɪn'deləbl] **adj** indélébile.

indelibly [ɪn'deləblɪ] **adv** de manière indélébile ▸ **her face remained indelibly fixed in his memory** son visage resta à jamais gravé dans sa mémoire.

indelicate [ɪn'delɪkət] **adj** indélicat(e).

indemnify [ɪn'demnɪfaɪ] (pt & pp **-ied**) **vt : to indemnify sb for** *OR* **against sthg** indemniser qqn de qqch.

indemnity [ɪn'demnətɪ] **n** indemnité *f*.

indent [ɪn'dent] **vt 1.** [dent] entailler **2.** [text] mettre en retrait.

indentation [ˌɪnden'teɪʃn] **n 1.** [dent] découpure *f*, entaille *f* **2.** [in text] alinéa *m*.

indenture [ɪn'dentʃəʳ] **n** contrat *m* d'apprentissage.

independence [ˌɪndɪ'pendəns] **n** indépendance *f*.

Independence Day **n** *fête de l'indépendance américaine, le 4 juillet.*

independent [ˌɪndɪ'pendənt] **adj : independent (of)** indépendant(e) (de) ▸ **to become independent** [country]

HOW TO ...

express indifference

Ça m'est égal / I don't mind either way
Ça m'est parfaitement égal / It makes absolutely no difference to me
De toute manière, ça ne porte pas à conséquence / In any case, it doesn't matter
Ça n'a pas d'importance / It doesn't matter
Peu importe, choisis / I don't mind, you choose
Cela revient au même / It all comes down to the same thing

accéder à l'indépendance ▸ **a man of independent means** un rentier ▸ **he is incapable of independent thought** il est incapable de penser par lui-même.

independently [ˌɪndɪ'pendəntlɪ] **adv** de façon indépendante ▸ **independently of sb/sthg** indépendamment de qqn/qqch.

independent school **n** *UK* école *f* privée.

in-depth **adj** approfondi(e).

indescribable [ˌɪndɪ'skraɪbəbl] **adj** indescriptible.

indescribably [ˌɪndɪ'skraɪbəblɪ] **adv** incroyablement.

indestructible [ˌɪndɪ'strʌktəbl] **adj** indestructible.

indeterminate [ˌɪndɪ'tɜːmɪnət] **adj** indéterminé(e).

index ['ɪndeks] ■ **n 1.** (pl **-dexes** [-deksiːz]) [of book] index *m* **2.** (pl **-dexes** [-deksiːz]) [in library] répertoire *m*, fichier *m* **3.** (pl **-dexes** [-deksiːz] ***OR*** **-dices** [-dɪsiːz]) ECON indice *m*.
■ **vt** [book] faire l'index de.

index card **n** fiche *f*.

index finger **n** index *m*.

index-linked *UK* [-ˌlɪŋkt], ***indexed*** *US* ['ɪndekst] **adj** ECON indexé(e).

index page **n** index *m*, page *f* d'accueil.

India ['ɪndjə] **n** Inde *f* ▸ **in India** en Inde.

India ink *US* = ***Indian ink***.

Indian ['ɪndjən] ■ **adj** indien(enne).
■ **n** Indien *m*, -enne *f*.

Indiana [ˌɪndɪ'ænə] **n** Indiana *m* ▸ **in Indiana** dans l'Indiana.

Indian ink *UK*, ***India ink*** *US* **n** encre *f* de Chine.

Indian Ocean **n : the Indian Ocean** l'océan *m* Indien.

Indian summer **n** été *m* indien.

india rubber, ***India rubber*** **n** caoutchouc *m*.

indicate ['ɪndɪkeɪt] ■ **vt** indiquer ▸ **he indicated his willingness to help** il nous a fait savoir qu'il était prêt à nous aider ▸ **as I have already indicated** comme je l'ai déjà signalé ***OR*** fait remarquer ▸ **to indicate(that one is turning) left/right** *UK* AUT mettre son clignotant à gauche/à droite (pour tourner).
■ **vi** *UK* AUT mettre son clignotant.

indication [ˌɪndɪ'keɪʃn] **n 1.** [suggestion] indication *f* **2.** [sign] signe *m*.

indicative [ɪn'dɪkətɪv] ■ **adj : indicative of** indicatif(ive) de.
■ **n** GRAM indicatif *m*.

indicator ['ɪndɪkeɪtəʳ] **n 1.** [sign] indicateur *m* **2.** *UK* AUT clignotant *m*.

indices ['ɪndɪsiːz] **npl** ➤ ***index***.

indict [ɪn'daɪt] **vt : to indict sb (for)** accuser qqn (de), mettre qqn en examen (pour).

indictable [ɪn'daɪtəbl] **adj** [person] qui peut être traduit(e) en justice / [offence] punissable.

indictment [ɪn'daɪtmənt] **n** [LAW - bill] acte *m* d'accusation / [- process] mise *f* en examen.

indie ['ɪndɪ] **adj** *inf* indépendant(e).

indifference [ɪn'dɪfrəns] **n** indifférence *f*.

indifferent [ɪn'dɪfrənt] **adj 1.** [uninterested] **: indifferent (to)** indifférent(e) (à) **2.** [mediocre] médiocre.

indigenous [ɪn'dɪdʒɪnəs] **adj** indigène.

indigestible [ˌɪndɪ'dʒestəbl] **adj** indigeste.

indigestion [ˌɪndɪ'dʒestʃn] **n** *(U)* indigestion *f*.

indignant [ɪn'dɪgnənt] **adj : indignant (at)** indigné(e) (de).

indignantly [ɪn'dɪgnəntlɪ] **adv** avec indignation.

indignation [ˌɪndɪg'neɪʃn] **n** indignation *f*.

indignity [ɪn'dɪgnətɪ] (pl **-ies**) **n** indignité *f*.

indigo ['ɪndɪgəʊ] ■ **adj** indigo *(inv)*.
■ **n** indigo *m*.

indirect [ˌɪndɪ'rekt] **adj** indirect(e).

indirect costs **npl** coûts *mpl* indirects.

indirect discourse *US*, ***indirect speech*** *UK* **n** discours *m* indirect.

indirect lighting **n** éclairage *m* indirect.

indirectly [ˌɪndɪ'rektlɪ] **adv** indirectement.

indirect object **n** objet *m* indirect.

indirect taxation **n** *(U)* contributions *fpl* indirectes, impôts *mpl* indirects.

indiscreet [ˌɪndɪ'skriːt] **adj** indiscret(ète).

indiscreetly [ˌɪndɪ'skriːtlɪ] **adv** indiscrètement.

indiscretion [ˌɪndɪ'skreʃn] **n** indiscrétion *f*.

indiscriminate [ˌɪndɪ'skrɪmɪnət] **adj** [person] qui manque de discernement / [treatment] sans distinction / [killing] commis au hasard.

indiscriminately [ˌɪndɪ'skrɪmɪnətlɪ] **adv** [admire] aveuglément / [treat] sans faire de distinction / [kill] au hasard.

indispensable [ˌɪndɪ'spensəbl] **adj** indispensable.

HOW TO ...
express indignation

(Mais) c'est une honte *ou* un scandale ! / That's outrageous!
On aura tout vu ! / I don't believe it!
Je n'ai jamais vu une chose pareille ! / I've never seen anything like it!
Regardez-moi ça ! / Just look at that!
Non mais je rêve ! *inf* / I don't believe it!
Non mais, tu te rends compte ! / Honestly!
Vous voulez répéter ! / Say that again!
Non mais, vous vous prenez pour qui ? / Just who do you think you are?
Quel culot ! / What a cheek!
Ça va pas, non ? *inf* / Are you out of your mind?

indisposed [ˌɪndɪ'spəʊzd] **adj** *fml* & *euph* [unwell] indisposé(e).

indisposition [ˌɪndɪspə'zɪʃn] **n** *fml euph* [illness] indisposition *f*.

indisputable [ˌɪndɪ'spju:təbl] **adj** indiscutable.

indistinct [ˌɪndɪ'stɪŋkt] **adj** indistinct(e) / [memory] vague.

indistinctly [ˌɪndɪ'stɪŋktlɪ] **adv** indistinctement.

indistinguishable [ˌɪndɪ'stɪŋgwɪʃəbl] **adj : indistinguishable (from)** que l'on ne peut distinguer (de).

individual [ˌɪndɪ'vɪdʒʊəl] ■ **adj 1.** [separate, for one person] individuel(elle) **2.** [distinctive] personnel(elle).
■ **n** individu *m*.

individualism [ˌɪndɪ'vɪdʒʊəlɪzm] **n** individualisme *m*.

individualist [ˌɪndɪ'vɪdʒʊəlɪst] **n** individualiste *mf*.

individualistic ['ɪndɪˌvɪdʒʊə'lɪstɪk] **adj** individualiste.

individuality ['ɪndɪˌvɪdʒʊ'ælətɪ] **n** individualité *f*.

individually [ˌɪndɪ'vɪdʒʊəlɪ] **adv** individuellement.

indivisible [ˌɪndɪ'vɪzəbl] **adj** indivisible.

Indochina [ˌɪndəʊ'tʃaɪnə] **n** Indochine *f* ▸ **in Indochina** en Indochine.

indoctrinate [ɪn'dɒktrɪneɪt] **vt** endoctriner.

indoctrination [ɪnˌdɒktrɪ'neɪʃn] **n** endoctrinement *m*.

indolence ['ɪndələns] **n 1.** *fml* [laziness] paresse *f*, indolence *f* **2.** MED indolence *f*.

indolent ['ɪndələnt] **adj** *fml* indolent(e).

indomitable [ɪn'dɒmɪtəbl] **adj** indomptable.

Indonesia [ˌɪndə'ni:zjə] **n** Indonésie *f* ▸ **in Indonesia** en Indonésie.

Indonesian [ˌɪndə'ni:zjən] ■ **adj** indonésien(enne).
■ **n 1.** [person] Indonésien *m*, -enne *f* **2.** [language] indonésien *m*.

indoor ['ɪndɔ:ʳ] **adj** [clothing] d'intérieur / [swimming pool] couvert(e) / [sports] en salle.

indoors [ˌɪn'dɔ:z] **adv** à l'intérieur.

indubitably [ɪn'dju:bɪtəblɪ] **adv** indubitablement.

induce [ɪn'dju:s] **vt 1.** [persuade] **: to induce sb to do sthg** inciter *OR* pousser qqn à faire qqch **2.** MED [labour] provoquer / [woman] provoquer l'accouchement de **3.** [bring about] provoquer.

-induced [ɪn'dju:st] **suffix : work-induced injury** accident *m* du travail ▸ **drug-induced sleep** sommeil *m* provoqué par des médicaments.

inducement [ɪn'dju:smənt] **n** [incentive] incitation *f*, encouragement *m*.

induction [ɪn'dʌkʃn] **n 1.** [into official position] **: induction (into)** installation *f* (à) **2.** [introduction] introduction *f* **3.** ELEC induction *f*.

induction course **n** *UK* stage *m* d'initiation.

indulge [ɪn'dʌldʒ] ■ **vt 1.** [whim, passion] céder à **2.** [child, person] gâter ▸ **to indulge o.s.** se faire plaisir.
■ **vi : to indulge in sthg** se permettre qqch.

indulgence [ɪn'dʌldʒəns] **n 1.** [act of indulging] indulgence *f* **2.** [special treat] gâterie *f*.

indulgent [ɪn'dʌldʒənt] **adj** indulgent(e).

indulgently [ɪn'dʌldʒəntlɪ] **adv** avec indulgence.

Indus ['ɪndəs] **n : the (River) Indus** l'Indus *m*.

industrial [ɪn'dʌstrɪəl] **adj** [gen] industriel(elle) / [unrest] social.

industrial accident **n** accident *m* du travail.

industrial action *esp UK*, ***job action*** *US* **n** *esp UK* **: to take industrial action** se mettre en grève.

industrial dispute **n** conflit *m* social, conflit *m* du travail.

industrial estate *UK*, ***industrial park*** *US* **n** zone *f* industrielle.

industrial injury **n** accident *m* du travail.

industrialist [ɪn'dʌstrɪəlɪst] **n** industriel *m*, -elle *f*.

industrialization, *UK* ***-isation*** [ɪnˌdʌstrɪəlaɪ'zeɪʃn] **n** industrialisation *f*.

industrialize, *UK* ***-ise*** [ɪn'dʌstrɪəlaɪz] ■ **vt** industrialiser.
■ **vi** s'industrialiser.

industrialized, *UK* ***-ised*** [ɪn'dʌstrɪəlaɪzd] **adj** industrialisé(e).

industrialized countries **n** pays *mpl* industrialisés.

industrial park *US* = ***industrial estate***.

industrial relations **npl** relations *fpl* patronat-syndicats.

industrial revolution **n** révolution *f* industrielle.

industrial tribunal **n** *UK* ≃ conseil *m* de prud'hommes.

industrious [ɪn'dʌstrɪəs] **adj** industrieux(euse).

industry ['ɪndəstrɪ] (**pl -ies**) **n 1.** [gen] industrie *f* **2.** *(U)* [hard work] assiduité *f*, application *f*.

inebriated [ɪ'ni:brɪeɪtɪd] **adj** *fml* ivre.

inedible [ɪn'edɪbl] **adj 1.** [meal, food] immangeable **2.** [plant, mushroom] non comestible.

ineffective [ˌɪnɪ'fektɪv] **adj** inefficace.

ineffectual [ˌɪnɪ'fektʃʊəl] **adj** *fml* inefficace / [person] incapable, incompétent(e).

inefficiency [ˌɪnɪ'fɪʃnsɪ] **n** inefficacité *f* / [of person] incapacité *f*, incompétence *f*.

inefficient [ˌɪnɪ'fɪʃnt] **adj** inefficace / [person] incapable, incompétent(e).

inefficiently [ˌɪnɪ'fɪʃntlɪ] **adv** inefficacement.

inelegant [ɪn'elɪgənt] **adj** inélégant(e), sans élégance.

inelegantly [ɪn'elɪgəntlɪ] **adv** de façon peu élégante.

ineligibility [ɪnˌelɪdʒə'bɪlətɪ] **n 1.** [gen] **: his ineligibility for unemployment benefit** le fait qu'il n'ait pas droit aux allocations de chômage ▸ **the ineligibility of most of the applications** l'irrecevabilité *f* de la plupart des demandes **2.** [for election] inéligibilité *f*.

ineligible [ɪn'elɪdʒəbl] **adj** inéligible ▸ **to be ineligible for sthg** ne pas avoir droit à qqch.

inept [ɪ'nept] **adj** inepte / [person] stupide.

ineptitude [ɪ'neptɪtju:d] **n** ineptie *f* / [of person] stupidité *f*.

ineptly [ɪ'neptlɪ] **adv** absurdement, stupidement.

inequality [,ɪnɪ'kwɒlətɪ] (pl **-ies**) **n** inégalité *f*.

inequitable [ɪn'ekwɪtəbl] **adj** *fml* inéquitable.

ineradicable [,ɪnɪ'rædɪkəbl] **adj** *fml* tenace, dont on ne peut se débarrasser.

inert [ɪ'nɜ:t] **adj** inerte.

inertia [ɪ'nɜ:ʃə] **n** inertie *f*.

inertia-reel seat belt **n** ceinture *f* de sécurité à enrouleur.

inertia selling **n** vente *f* forcée.

inescapable [,ɪnɪ'skeɪpəbl] **adj** inéluctable.

inessential [,ɪnɪ'senʃl] **adj** superflu(e).

inestimable [ɪn'estɪməbl] **adj** inestimable.

inevitability [ɪn,evɪtə'bɪlətɪ] **n** inévitabilité *f*.

inevitable [ɪn'evɪtəbl] ■ **adj** inévitable ▸ **it's inevitable that someone will feel left out** il est inévitable *OR* on ne pourra empêcher que quelqu'un se sente exclu ▸ **the inevitable cigarette in his mouth** l'éternelle *OR* l'inévitable cigarette au coin des lèvres.
■ **n : the inevitable** l'inévitable *m*.

inevitably [ɪn'evɪtəblɪ] **adv** inévitablement.

inexact [,ɪnɪg'zækt] **adj** inexact(e).

inexcusable [,ɪnɪk'skju:zəbl] **adj** inexcusable, impardonnable.

inexhaustible [,ɪnɪg'zɔ:stəbl] **adj** inépuisable.

inexorable [ɪn'eksərəbl] **adj** inexorable.

inexorably [ɪn'eksərəblɪ] **adv** inexorablement.

inexpensive [,ɪnɪk'spensɪv] **adj** bon marché *(inv)*, pas cher(chère).

inexpensively [,ɪnɪk'spensɪvlɪ] **adv** [sell] (à) bon marché, à bas prix / [live] à peu de frais.

inexperience [,ɪnɪk'spɪərɪəns] **n** inexpérience *f*.

inexperienced [,ɪnɪk'spɪərɪənst] **adj** inexpérimenté(e), qui manque d'expérience.

inexpert [ɪn'ekspɜ:t] **adj** inexpert(e).

inexplicable [,ɪnɪk'splɪkəbl] **adj** inexplicable.

inexplicably [,ɪnɪk'splɪkəblɪ] **adv** inexplicablement.

inextricably [ɪn'ekstrɪkəblɪ] **adv** inextricablement.

infallibility [ɪn,fælə'bɪlətɪ] **n** infaillibilité *f*.

infallible [ɪn'fæləbl] **adj** infaillible.

infamous ['ɪnfəməs] **adj** infâme.

infamy ['ɪnfəmɪ] **n** infamie *f*.

infancy ['ɪnfənsɪ] **n** petite enfance *f* ▸ **in its infancy** *fig* à ses débuts.

infant ['ɪnfənt] **n** **1.** [baby] nouveau-né *m*, nouveau-née *f*, nourrisson *m* **2.** [young child] enfant *mf* en bas âge.

infanticide [ɪn'fæntɪsaɪd] **n** **1.** [act] infanticide *m* **2.** [person] infanticide *mf*.

infantile ['ɪnfəntaɪl] **adj** *lit* & *pej* infantile.

infant industry **n** ECON industrie *f* naissante.

infant mortality **n** mortalité *f* infantile.

infantry ['ɪnfəntrɪ] **n** infanterie *f*.

infantryman ['ɪnfəntrɪmən] (pl **-men** [-mən]) **n** fantassin *m*.

infant school **n** *UK* école *f* maternelle *(de 5 à 7 ans)*.

infatuated [ɪn'fætjʊeɪtɪd] **adj : infatuated (with)** entiché(e) (de).

infatuation [ɪn,fætjʊ'eɪʃn] **n : infatuation (with)** béguin *m* (pour).

infect [ɪn'fekt] **vt** **1.** MED infecter **2.** *fig* [subj: enthusiasm] se propager à.

infected [ɪn'fektɪd] **adj : infected (with)** infecté(e) (par).

infection [ɪn'fekʃn] **n** infection *f*.

infectious [ɪn'fekʃəs] **adj** **1.** [disease] infectieux(euse) **2.** *fig* [feeling, laugh] contagieux(euse).

infer [ɪn'fɜ:ʳ] (pt & pp **-red**, cont **-ring**) **vt** [deduce] **: to infer sthg (from)** déduire qqch (de).

inference ['ɪnfrəns] **n** **1.** [conclusion] conclusion *f* **2.** [process of deduction] **: by inference** par déduction.

inferior [ɪn'fɪərɪəʳ] ■ **adj** **1.** [in status] inférieur(e) **2.** [product] de qualité inférieure / [work] médiocre.
■ **n** [in status] subalterne *mf*.

inferiority [ɪn,fɪərɪ'ɒrətɪ] **n** infériorité *f*.

inferiority complex **n** complexe *m* d'infériorité.

infernal [ɪn'fɜ:nl] **adj** *inf dated* infernal(e).

inferno [ɪn'fɜ:nəʊ] (pl **-s**) **n** brasier *m*.

infertile [ɪn'fɜ:taɪl] **adj** **1.** [woman] stérile **2.** [soil] infertile.

infertility [,ɪnfə'tɪlətɪ] **n** **1.** [of woman] stérilité *f* **2.** [of soil] infertilité *f*.

infestation [,ɪnfe'steɪʃn] **n** infestation *f*.

infested [ɪn'festɪd] **adj : infested with** infesté(e) de.

infidelity [,ɪnfɪ'delətɪ] **n** infidélité *f*.

infighting ['ɪn,faɪtɪŋ] **n** *(U)* querelles *fpl* intestines.

infiltrate ['ɪnfɪltreɪt] ■ **vt** infiltrer.
■ **vi : to infiltrate into** s'infiltrer dans.

infiltration [,ɪnfɪl'treɪʃn] **n** **1.** [of group] infiltration *f*, noyautage *m* **2.** [by liquid] infiltration *f*.

infiltrator ['ɪnfɪltreɪtəʳ] **n** agent *m* infiltré.

infinite ['ɪnfɪnət] **adj** infini(e).

infinitely ['ɪnfɪnətlɪ] **adv** infiniment.

infinitesimal [,ɪnfɪnɪ'tesɪml] **adj** infinitésimal(e).

infinitive [ɪn'fɪnɪtɪv] **n** infinitif *m*.

infinity [ɪn'fɪnətɪ] **n** infini *m*.

infirm [ɪn'fɜ:m] *fml* ■ **adj** infirme.
■ **npl : the infirm** les infirmes *mpl*.

infirmary [ɪn'fɜ:mərɪ] (pl **-ies**) **n** *UK* [in names] hôpital *m* / *US* SCH & UNIV infirmerie *f*.

infirmity [ɪn'fɜ:mətɪ] (pl **-ies**) **n** *fml* infirmité *f*.

inflamed [ɪn'fleɪmd] **adj** MED enflammé(e).

inflammable [ɪn'flæməbl] **adj** inflammable.

inflammation [,ɪnflə'meɪʃn] **n** MED inflammation *f*.

inflammatory [ɪn'flæmətrɪ] **adj** inflammatoire.

inflatable [ɪn'fleɪtəbl] **adj** gonflable.

inflate [ɪn'fleɪt] **vt 1.** [tyre, life jacket] gonfler **2.** ECON [prices, salaries] hausser, gonfler.

inflated [ɪn'fleɪtɪd] **adj 1.** [tyre, life jacket] gonflé(e) **2.** *pej* [exaggerated] **: he has an inflated opinion of himself** il a une haute opinion de lui-même **3.** ECON [salary, prices] exagéré(e), gonflé(e).

inflation [ɪn'fleɪʃn] **n** ECON inflation *f*.

inflationary [ɪn'fleɪʃnrɪ] **adj** ECON inflationniste.

inflationary gap **n** écart *m* inflationniste.

inflationary spiral **n** spirale *f* inflationniste.

inflation-proof **adj** protégé(e) contre les effets de l'inflation.

inflect [ɪn'flekt] ■ **vt 1.** LING [verb] conjuguer ⁄ [noun, pronoun, adjective] décliner ▸ **inflected form** forme *f* fléchie **2.** [tone, voice] moduler **3.** [curve] infléchir.
■ **vi** LING **: adjectives do not inflect in English** les adjectifs ne prennent pas de désinence en anglais.

inflection [ɪn'flekʃn] **n 1.** [of tone, voice] inflexion *f*, modulation *f* **2.** LING désinence *f*, flexion *f* **3.** [curve] flexion *f*, inflexion *f*, courbure *f* **4.** MATHS inflexion *f* ▸ **point of inflection** point *m* d'inflexion.

inflexibility [ɪnˌfleksə'bɪlətɪ] **n** inflexibilité *f*, rigidité *f*.

inflexible [ɪn'fleksəbl] **adj 1.** [material] rigide **2.** [person, arrangement] inflexible.

inflict [ɪn'flɪkt] **vt : to inflict sthg on sb** infliger qqch à qqn.

in-flight **adj** en vol *(inv)*.

inflow ['ɪnfləʊ] **n** afflux *m*.

influence ['ɪnflʊəns] ■ **n** influence *f* ▸ **to bring one's influence to bear on sthg** exercer son influence sur qqch ▸ **he is a bad influence on them** il a une mauvaise influence sur eux ▸ **under the influence of** [person, group] sous l'influence de ⁄ [alcohol, drugs] sous l'effet *OR* l'empire de.
■ **vt** influencer ▸ **he is easily influenced** il se laisse facilement influencer, il est très influençable.

influential [ˌɪnflʊ'enʃl] **adj** influent(e).

influenza [ˌɪnflʊ'enzə] **n** *(U)* grippe *f*.

influx ['ɪnflʌks] **n** afflux *m*.

info ['ɪnfəʊ] **n** *(U) inf* info *f*.

infomercial [ˌɪnfəʊ'mɜːʃl] **n** *US publicité télévisée sous forme de débat sur l'annonceur et son produit.*

inform [ɪn'fɔːm] **vt : to inform sb (of)** informer qqn (de) ▸ **to inform sb about** renseigner qqn sur.
◆ ***inform on*** **vt insep** dénoncer.

informal [ɪn'fɔːml] **adj 1.** [party, person] simple ⁄ [clothes] de tous les jours **2.** [negotiations, visit] officieux(euse) ⁄ [meeting] informel(elle).

informality [ˌɪnfɔː'mælətɪ] (**pl -ies**) **n 1.** [of gathering, meal] simplicité *f* ⁄ [of discussion, interview] absence *f* de formalité ⁄ [of manners] naturel *m* **2.** [of expression, language] familiarité *f*, liberté *f*.

informally [ɪn'fɔːməlɪ] **adv 1.** [talk, dress] simplement **2.** [meet, agree] officieusement.

informant [ɪn'fɔːmənt] **n** informateur *m*, -trice *f*.

informatics [ˌɪnfə'mætɪks] **n** *(U)* sciences *fpl* de l'information.

information [ˌɪnfə'meɪʃn] **n 1.** *(U)* **: information (on *OR* about)** renseignements *mpl OR* informations *fpl* (sur) ▸ **a piece of information** un renseignement ▸ **for your information** *fml* à titre d'information ▸ **for your information, it happened in 1938** je vous signale que cela s'est passé en 1938 **2.** COMPUT information *f*.

information desk **n** bureau *m* de renseignements.

information highway, ***information superhighway*** **n** autoroute *f* de l'information.

information office **n** bureau *m* de renseignements.

information retrieval **n** recherche *f* documentaire sur ordinateur.

information scientist **n** informaticien *m*, -enne *f*.

information superhighway = ***information highway***.

information technology **n** informatique *f*.

informative [ɪn'fɔːmətɪv] **adj** informatif(ive).

informed [ɪn'fɔːmd] **adj : well/badly informed** bien/mal renseigné(e) ▸ **he made an informed guess** il a essayé de deviner en s'aidant de ce qu'il savait.

informer [ɪn'fɔːmər] **n** indicateur *m*, -trice *f*.

infotainment ['ɪnfəʊteɪnmənt] **n** info-spectacle *m*, info-divertissement *m*.

infra dig [ˌɪnfrə-] **adj** *UK dated* dégradant(e).

infrared [ˌɪnfrə'red] **adj** infrarouge.

infrared mouse **n** COMPUT souris *f* infrarouge.

infrastructure ['ɪnfrəˌstrʌktʃər] **n** infrastructure *f*.

infrequent [ɪn'friːkwənt] **adj** peu fréquent(e).

infrequently [ɪn'friːkwəntlɪ] **adv** rarement, peu souvent.

infringe [ɪn'frɪndʒ] (**cont infringeing**) ■ **vt 1.** [right] empiéter sur **2.** [law, agreement] enfreindre.
■ **vi 1.** [on right] **: to infringe on** empiéter sur **2.** [on law, agreement] **: to infringe on** enfreindre.

infringement [ɪn'frɪndʒmənt] **n 1.** [of right] **: infringement (of)** atteinte *f* (à) **2.** [of law, agreement] transgression *f*.

infuriate [ɪn'fjʊərɪeɪt] **vt** rendre furieux(euse).

infuriating [ɪn'fjʊərɪeɪtɪŋ] **adj** exaspérant(e).

infuriatingly [ɪn'fjʊərɪeɪtɪŋlɪ] **adv : infuriatingly stubborn** d'un entêtement exaspérant.

infuse [ɪn'fjuːz] ■ **vt : to infuse sb/sthg with sthg** *fig* insuffler qqch à qqn/qqch.
■ **vi** [tea] infuser.

infusion [ɪn'fjuːʒn] **n 1.** [of enthusiasm, ideas] fait *m* d'insuffler ⁄ [of money] injection *f* **2.** [of tea, herbs] infusion *f*.

ingenious [ɪn'dʒiːnjəs] **adj** ingénieux(euse).

ingeniously [ɪn'dʒiːnjəslɪ] **adv** ingénieusement.

ingenuity [ˌɪndʒɪ'njuːətɪ] **n** ingéniosité *f*.

ingenuous [ɪn'dʒenjʊəs] **adj** ingénu(e), naïf(naïve).

ingest [ɪn'dʒest] **vt** ingérer.

ingot ['ɪŋgət] **n** lingot *m*.

ingrained [ˌɪn'greɪnd] **adj 1.** [dirt] incrusté(e) **2.** *fig* [belief, hatred] enraciné(e).

ingratiate [ɪn'greɪʃɪeɪt] **vt** *pej* **: to ingratiate o.s. with sb** se faire bien voir de qqn.

ingratiating [ɪn'greɪʃɪeɪtɪŋ] **adj** *pej* doucereux(euse), mielleux(euse).

ingratitude [ɪn'grætɪtju:d] **n** ingratitude *f.*

ingredient [ɪn'gri:djənt] **n** ingrédient *m* / *fig* élément *m.*

ingrowing ['ɪnˌgrəʊɪŋ], *US* ***ingrown*** ['ɪnˌgrəʊn] **adj : ingrowing toenail** ongle *m* incarné.

inhabit [ɪn'hæbɪt] **vt** habiter.

inhabitant [ɪn'hæbɪtənt] **n** habitant *m*, -e *f.*

inhalation [ˌɪnhə'leɪʃn] **n** inhalation *f.*

inhale [ɪn'heɪl] ■ **vt** inhaler, respirer.
■ **vi** [breathe in] respirer.

inhaler [ɪn'heɪlə^r] **n** MED inhalateur *m.*

inherent [ɪn'hɪərənt *OR* ɪn'herənt] **adj : inherent (in)** inhérent(e) (à).

inherently [ɪn'hɪərəntlɪ *OR* ɪn'herəntlɪ] **adv** fondamentalement, en soi.

inherit [ɪn'herɪt] ■ **vt** [property, right] hériter (de) / [title, peerage] accéder à ▸ **to inherit sthg (from sb)** hériter qqch (de qqn) ▸ **the problems inherited from the previous government** les problèmes hérités du gouvernement précédent ▸ **she inherited her father's intelligence** elle a hérité (de) l'intelligence de son père.
■ **vi** hériter.

inheritance [ɪn'herɪtəns] **n** héritage *m.*

inheritor [ɪn'herɪtə^r] **n** héritier *m*, -ère *f.*

inhibit [ɪn'hɪbɪt] **vt 1.** [prevent] empêcher **2.** PSYCHOL inhiber.

inhibited [ɪn'hɪbɪtɪd] **adj** [person] inhibé(e).

inhibiting [ɪn'hɪbɪtɪŋ] **adj** inhibant(e).

inhibition [ˌɪnhɪ'bɪʃn] **n** inhibition *f.*

inhospitable [ˌɪnhɒ'spɪtəbl] **adj** inhospitalier(ère).

in-house ■ **adj** interne / [staff] de la maison.
■ **adv** [produce, work] sur place.

inhuman [ɪn'hju:mən] **adj** inhumain(e).

inhumane [ˌɪnhju:'meɪn] **adj** inhumain(e).

inhumanity [ˌɪnhju:'mænətɪ] (**pl -ies**) **n 1.** [quality] inhumanité *f*, barbarie *f*, cruauté *f* ▸ **man's inhumanity to man** la cruauté de l'homme pour l'homme **2.** [act] atrocité *f*, brutalité *f.*

inimitable [ɪ'nɪmɪtəbl] **adj** inimitable.

iniquitous [ɪ'nɪkwɪtəs] **adj** *fml* inique.

iniquity [ɪ'nɪkwətɪ] (**pl -ies**) **n** *fml* iniquité *f.*

initial [ɪ'nɪʃl] ■ **adj** initial(e), premier(ère) ▸ **initial letter** initiale *f.*
■ **vt** (*UK* **-led**, **cont -ling**, *US* **-ed**, **cont -ing**) parapher.
◆ ***initials*** **npl** initiales *fpl.*

initialize, *UK* ***-ise*** [ɪ'nɪʃəlaɪz] **vt** COMPUT initialiser.

initially [ɪ'nɪʃəlɪ] **adv** initialement, au début.

initiate [ɪ'nɪʃɪeɪt] ■ **vt 1.** [talks] engager / [scheme] ébaucher, inaugurer **2.** [teach] **: to initiate sb into sthg** initier qqn à qqch.
■ **n** initié *m*, -e *f.*

initiation [ɪˌnɪʃɪ'eɪʃn] **n 1.** [of talks] commencement *m*, début *m* / [of scheme] ébauche *f*, inauguration *f* **2.** [teaching] initiation *f.*

initiative [ɪ'nɪʃətɪv] **n 1.** [gen] initiative *f* ▸ **on one's own initiative** de sa propre initiative ▸ **to take the initiative** prendre l'initiative ▸ **to use one's initiative** faire preuve d'initiative **2.** [advantage] **: to have the initiative** avoir l'avantage *m.*

initiator [ɪ'nɪʃɪeɪtə^r] **n** initiateur *m*, -trice *f*, instigateur *m*, -trice *f.*

inject [ɪn'dʒekt] **vt 1.** MED **: to inject sb with sthg, to inject sthg into sb** injecter qqch à qqn ▸ **to inject sb with penicillin** faire une piqûre de pénicilline à qqn **2.** *fig* [excitement] insuffler / [money] injecter ▸ **they've injected billions of dollars into the economy** ils ont injecté des milliards de dollars dans l'économie ▸ **he tried to inject some humour into the situation** *fig* il a tenté d'introduire un peu d'humour dans la situation.

injection [ɪn'dʒekʃn] **n** *lit* & *fig* injection *f.*

injudicious [ˌɪndʒu:'dɪʃəs] **adj** *fml* peu judicieux(euse).

injunction [ɪn'dʒʌŋkʃn] **n** LAW injonction *f.*

injure ['ɪndʒə^r] **vt 1.** [limb, person] blesser ▸ **to injure o.s.** se blesser ▸ **to injure one's arm** se blesser au bras **2.** *fig* [reputation, chances] compromettre.

injured [ɪn'dʒəd] ■ **adj 1.** [limb, person] blessé(e) **2.** *fig* [reputation] compromis(e) / [pride] froissé(e).
■ **npl : the injured** les blessés *mpl.*

injurious [ɪn'dʒʊərɪəs] **adj** *fml* **: injurious (to)** nuisible (à), néfaste (à).

injury ['ɪndʒərɪ] (**pl -ies**) **n 1.** [to limb, person] blessure *f* ▸ **to do o.s. an injury** se blesser **2.** *fig* [to reputation] coup *m*, atteinte *f.*

injury time **n** *(U)* *UK* arrêts *mpl* de jeu.

injustice [ɪn'dʒʌstɪs] **n** injustice *f* ▸ **to do sb an injustice** se montrer injuste envers qqn.

ink [ɪŋk] ■ **n** encre *f.*
■ **comp** [pen] à encre / [stain, blot] d'encre.
◆ ***ink in*** **vt sep** repasser à l'encre.

ink-jet printer **n** COMPUT imprimante *f* à jet d'encre.

inkling ['ɪŋklɪŋ] **n : to have an inkling of** avoir une petite idée de.

inkpad ['ɪŋkpæd] **n** tampon *m* encreur.

inkwell ['ɪŋkwel] **n** encrier *m.*

inky ['ɪŋkɪ] (**comp -ier**, **superl -iest**) **adj 1.** [inkstained] taché(e) d'encre **2.** [dark] noir(e) comme l'encre.

inlaid [ˌɪn'leɪd] **adj : inlaid (with)** incrusté(e) (de).

inland ■ **adj** ['ɪnlənd] intérieur(e).
■ **adv** [ɪn'lænd] à l'intérieur.

Inland Revenue **n** *UK* **: the Inland Revenue** ≃ le fisc.

in-laws **npl** *inf* [parents-in-law] beaux-parents *mpl* / [others] belle-famille *f.*

inlet ['ɪnlet] n **1.** [of lake, sea] avancée *f* **2.** TECH arrivée *f.*

in-line skates npl patins *mpl* en ligne, rollers *mpl.*

in-line skating n SPORT roller *m.*

inmate ['ɪnmeɪt] n [of prison] détenu *m*, -e *f* / [of mental hospital] interné *m*, -e *f.*

inmost ['ɪnməʊst] *liter* adj = ***innermost***.

inn [ɪn] n auberge *f.*

innards ['ɪnədz] npl entrailles *fpl.*

innate [ɪ'neɪt] adj inné(e).

innately [ɪ'neɪtlɪ] adv naturellement.

inner ['ɪnəʳ] adj **1.** [on inside] interne, intérieur(e) **2.** [feelings] intime.

inner circle n : **in the inner circles of power** dans les milieux proches du pouvoir ▸ **her inner circle of advisers** le cercle de ses conseillers les plus proches.

inner city ■ n : **the inner city** les quartiers *mpl* pauvres.
■ comp des quartiers pauvres.

innermost ['ɪnəməʊst] adj [secrets, thoughts] le plus profond(la plus profonde), le plus secret(la plus secrète).

inner tube n chambre *f* à air.

innings ['ɪnɪŋz] (pl **innings**) n *UK* CRICKET tour *m* de batte ▸ **to have had a good innings** *fig* avoir bien profité de l'existence.

innocence ['ɪnəsəns] n innocence *f.*

innocent ['ɪnəsənt] ■ adj innocent(e) ▸ **innocent of** [crime] non coupable de.
■ n innocent *m*, -e *f.*

innocently ['ɪnəsəntlɪ] adv innocemment.

innocuous [ɪ'nɒkjʊəs] adj inoffensif(ive).

innovation [,ɪnə'veɪʃn] n innovation *f.*

innovative ['ɪnəvətɪv] adj **1.** [idea, design] innovateur(trice) **2.** [person, company] novateur(trice).

innovator ['ɪnəveɪtəʳ] n innovateur *m*, -trice *f.*

innuendo [,ɪnju:'endəʊ] (pl -es *OR* -s) n insinuation *f.*

innumerable [ɪ'nju:mərəbl] adj innombrable.

innumerate [ɪ'nju:mərət] adj qui ne sait pas compter ▸ **he's completely innumerate** il est incapable d'additionner deux et deux.

inoculate [ɪ'nɒkjʊleɪt] vt : **to inoculate sb (with sthg)** inoculer (qqch à) qqn ▸ **to inoculate sb (against)** vacciner qqn (contre).

inoculation [ɪ,nɒkjʊ'leɪʃn] n inoculation *f.*

inoffensive [,ɪnə'fensɪv] adj inoffensif(ive).

inoperable [ɪn'ɒprəbl] adj **1.** MED inopérable **2.** [method] impossible à mettre en œuvre.

inoperative [ɪn'ɒprətɪv] adj **1.** [rule, tax] inopérant(e) **2.** [machine] qui ne marche pas.

inopportune [ɪn'ɒpətju:n] adj inopportun(e).

inordinate [ɪ'nɔ:dɪnət] adj *fml* excessif(ive), démesuré(e).

inordinately [ɪ'nɔ:dɪnətlɪ] adv *fml* excessivement.

inorganic [,ɪnɔ:'gænɪk] adj inorganique.

in-patient n malade hospitalisé *m*, malade hospitalisée *f.*

input ['ɪnpʊt] ■ n **1.** [contribution] contribution *f*, concours *m* **2.** COMPUT & ELEC entrée *f.*
■ vt (pt & pp **input** *OR* **-ted**, cont **-ting**) COMPUT entrer.

input/output n COMPUT entrée-sortie *f.*

inquest ['ɪnkwest] n enquête *f.*

inquire [ɪn'kwaɪəʳ] ■ vt : **to inquire when/whether/how...** demander quand/si/comment...
■ vi : **to inquire (about)** se renseigner (sur).
◆ ***inquire after*** vt insep s'enquérir de.
◆ ***inquire into*** vt insep enquêter sur.

inquiring [ɪn'kwaɪərɪŋ] adj **1.** [person, mind] curieux(euse) **2.** [look, tone] interrogateur(trice).

inquiry [ɪn'kwaɪərɪ] (pl -ies) n **1.** [question] demande *f* de renseignements ▸ **'Inquiries'** *UK* 'renseignements' **2.** [investigation] enquête *f* ▸ **to hold** *OR* **to conduct an inquiry into sthg** faire une enquête sur qqch ▸ **he is helping police with their inquiries** la police est en train de l'interroger ▸ **upon further inquiry** après vérification.

inquiry desk n *UK* bureau *m* de renseignements.

inquisition [,ɪnkwɪ'zɪʃn] n *fml* & *pej* inquisition *f.*
◆ ***Inquisition*** n HIST : **the Inquisition** l'Inquisition *f.*

inquisitive [ɪn'kwɪzətɪv] adj [curious] curieux(euse) / *pej* [nosy] indiscret(ète).

inquisitively [ɪn'kwɪzətɪvlɪ] adv [curiously] avec curiosité / *pej* [nosily] de manière indiscrète.

inquisitiveness [ɪn'kwɪzətɪvnɪs] n [curiosity] curiosité *f* / *pej* [nosiness] indiscrétion *f.*

inroads ['ɪnrəʊdz] npl : **to make inroads into** [savings] entamer.

insane [ɪn'seɪn] ■ adj fou(folle).
■ npl : **the insane** les malades *mpl* mentaux.

insanely [ɪn'seɪnlɪ] adv **1.** [crazily - laugh, behave, talk] comme un fou **2.** [as intensifier - funny, rich] follement ▸ **he was insanely jealous** il était fou de jalousie.

insanitary [ɪn'sænɪtrɪ] adj insalubre.

insanity [ɪn'sænətɪ] n folie *f.*

insatiable [ɪn'seɪʃəbl] adj insatiable.

inscribe [ɪn'skraɪb] vt **1.** [engrave] graver **2.** [write] inscrire.

inscription [ɪn'skrɪpʃn] n **1.** [engraved] inscription *f* **2.** [written] dédicace *f.*

inscrutable [ɪn'skru:təbl] adj impénétrable.

insect ['ɪnsekt] n insecte *m.*

insect bite n piqûre *f* d'insecte.

insecticide [ɪn'sektɪsaɪd] n insecticide *m.*

insect repellent n lotion *f* anti-moustiques.

insecure [,ɪnsɪ'kjʊəʳ] adj **1.** [person] anxieux(euse) **2.** [job, investment] incertain(e).

insecurely [,ɪnsɪ'kjʊəlɪ] adv : **insecurely balanced** en équilibre instable ▸ **insecurely closed/bolted/attached** mal fermé(e)/verrouillé(e)/attaché(e).

insecurity [,ɪnsɪ'kjʊərətɪ] n insécurité *f.*

insemination [ɪn,semɪ'neɪʃn] n insémination *f.*

insensible [ɪn'sensəbl] **adj** **1.** [unconscious] inconscient(e) **2.** [unaware, not feeling] **: insensible of/to** insensible à.

insensitive [ɪn'sensətɪv] **adj : insensitive (to)** insensible (à).

insensitively [ɪn'sensətɪvlɪ] **adj** avec un grand manque de tact.

insensitivity [ɪn,sensə'tɪvətɪ] **n** insensibilité *f*.

inseparable [ɪn'seprəbl] **adj** inséparable.

insert ■ **vt** [ɪn'sɜ:t] **: to insert sthg (in** ***OR*** **into)** insérer qqch (dans).
■ **n** ['ɪnsɜ:t] [in newspaper] encart *m*.

insertion [ɪn'sɜ:ʃn] **n** insertion *f*.

in-service training **n** formation *f* en cours d'emploi.

inset ['ɪnset] **n** encadré *m*.

inshore ■ **adj** ['ɪnʃɔ:ʳ] côtier(ère).
■ **adv** [ɪn'ʃɔ:ʳ] [be situated] près de la côte / [move] vers la côte.

inside [ɪn'saɪd] ■ **prep** **1.** [building, object] à l'intérieur de, dans / [group, organization] au sein de ▸ **inside the house** à l'intérieur de la maison ▸ **what goes on inside his head?** qu'est-ce qui se passe dans sa tête? ▸ **it's just inside the limit** c'est juste (dans) la limite
2. [time] **: inside (of) three weeks** en moins de trois semaines.
■ **adv** **1.** [gen] dedans, à l'intérieur ▸ **to go inside** entrer ▸ **come inside!** entrez! ▸ **bring the chairs inside** rentre les chaises ▸ **it's hollow inside** c'est creux à l'intérieur, l'intérieur est creux
2. *prison sl* en taule ▸ **he's been inside** il a fait de la taule.
■ **adj** **1.** intérieur(e) ▸ **the inside pages** [of newspaper] les pages intérieures ▸ **the inside lane** [in athletics] la corde / [driving on left] la voie de gauche / [driving on right] la voie de droite ▸ **inside leg measurement** hauteur *f* de l'entrejambe
2. FOOTBALL **: inside left/right** inter *m* gauche/droit.
■ **n** **1.** [interior] **: the inside** l'intérieur *m* ▸ **she has a scar on the inside of her wrist** elle a une cicatrice à l'intérieur du poignet ▸ **inside out** [clothes] à l'envers ▸ **he turned his pockets inside out** il a retourné ses poches ▸ **to know sthg inside out** connaître qqch à fond
2. AUT **: the inside** [in UK] la gauche / [in Europe, US] la droite ▸ **walk on the inside** marchez loin du bord
3. *fig* **: only someone on the inside would know that** seul quelqu'un de la maison saurait ça.
◆ ***insides*** **npl** *inf* tripes *fpl*.
◆ ***inside of*** **prep** *US* [building, object] à l'intérieur de, dans.

inside information **n** *(U)* renseignements *mpl* obtenus à la source.

inside job **n** *inf* coup *m* monté de l'intérieur.

insider [,ɪn'saɪdəʳ] **n** initié *m*, -e *f*.

insider dealing, insider trading **n** *(U)* délits *mpl* d'initiés.

inside story **n : I got the inside story from his wife** j'ai appris la vérité sur cette affaire par sa femme.

insidious [ɪn'sɪdɪəs] **adj** insidieux(euse).

insight ['ɪnsaɪt] **n** **1.** [wisdom] sagacité *f*, perspicacité *f* **2.** [glimpse] **: insight (into)** aperçu *m* (de).

insignia [ɪn'sɪgnɪə] (pl **insignia**) **n** insigne *m*.

insignificance [,ɪnsɪg'nɪfɪkəns] **n** insignifiance *f*.

insignificant [,ɪnsɪg'nɪfɪkənt] **adj** insignifiant(e).

insincere [,ɪnsɪn'sɪəʳ] **adj** pas sincère.

insincerely [,ɪnsɪn'sɪəlɪ] **adv** sans sincérité, de manière hypocrite.

insincerity [,ɪnsɪn'serətɪ] **n** manque *m* de sincérité.

insinuate [ɪn'sɪnjʊeɪt] **vt** insinuer, laisser entendre.

insinuation [ɪn,sɪnjʊ'eɪʃn] **n** insinuation *f*.

insipid [ɪn'sɪpɪd] **adj** insipide.

insist [ɪn'sɪst] ■ **vt** **1.** [claim] **: to insist (that)...** insister sur le fait que... ▸ **she insists that she locked the door** elle maintient qu'elle a fermé la porte à clef **2.** [demand] **: to insist (that)...** insister pour que *(+ subjunctive)*... ▸ **you should insist that you be paid** vous devriez exiger qu'on vous paye.
■ **vi : to insist (on sthg)** exiger (qqch) ▸ **to insist on doing sthg** tenir à faire qqch, vouloir absolument faire qqch ▸ **she insists on doing it her way** elle tient à le faire à sa façon ▸ **he insisted on my taking the money** il a tenu à ce que je prenne l'argent.

insistence [ɪn'sɪstəns] **n : insistence (on)** insistance *f* (à).

insistent [ɪn'sɪstənt] **adj** **1.** [determined] insistant(e) ▸ **to be insistent on** insister sur **2.** [continual] incessant(e).

insistently [ɪn'sɪstəntlɪ] **adv** [stare, knock] avec insistance / [ask, urge] avec insistance, instamment.

in situ [,ɪn'sɪtju:] **adv** in situ.

insofar [,ɪnsəʊ'fɑ:ʳ] ◆ ***insofar as*** **conj** *fml* dans la mesure où.

insole ['ɪnsəʊl] **n** semelle *f* intérieure.

insolence ['ɪnsələns] **n** insolence *f*.

insolent ['ɪnsələnt] **adj** insolent(e).

insolently ['ɪnsələntlɪ] **adv** insolemment, avec insolence.

insoluble [ɪn'sɒljʊbl], ***insolvable*** *US* [ɪn'sɒlvəbl] **adj** insoluble.

insolvency [ɪn'sɒlvənsɪ] **n** insolvabilité *f*.

insolvent [ɪn'sɒlvənt] **adj** insolvable.

insomnia [ɪn'sɒmnɪə] **n** insomnie *f*.

insomniac [ɪn'sɒmnɪæk] **n** insomniaque *mf*.

insomuch [,ɪnsəʊ'mʌtʃ] ◆ ***insomuch as*** **conj** *fml* d'autant que.

inspect [ɪn'spekt] **vt** **1.** [letter, person] examiner **2.** [factory, troops] inspecter.

inspection [ɪn'spekʃn] **n** **1.** [investigation] examen *m* **2.** [official check] inspection *f*.

inspector [ɪn'spektəʳ] **n** inspecteur *m*, -trice *f*.

inspector of taxes **n** *UK* inspecteur *m*, -trice *f* des impôts.

inspiration [,ɪnspə'reɪʃn] **n** inspiration *f*.

inspirational [ˌɪnspəˈreɪʃənl] **adj 1.** [inspiring] inspirant(e) **2.** [inspired] inspiré(e).

inspire [ɪnˈspaɪəʳ] **vt : to inspire sb to do sthg** pousser OR encourager qqn à faire qqch ▸ **to inspire sb with sthg, to inspire sthg in sb** inspirer qqch à qqn.

inspired [ɪnˈspaɪəd] **adj 1.** [artist, performance] inspiré(e) **2.** [guess, idea] brillant(e).

inspiring [ɪnˈspaɪərɪŋ] **adj** qui inspire.

inst. **1.** *dated* (abbr of ***instant***) ▸ **on the 4th inst.** le 4 courant **2.** abbr of ***institute*** / abbr of ***institution***.

instability [ˌɪnstəˈbɪlətɪ] **n** instabilité *f*.

install [ɪnˈstɔːl] **vt 1.** [fit & COMPUT] installer **2.** [appoint] **: to install sb (as sthg)** nommer qqn (qqch) **3.** [settle] **: to install o.s.** s'installer.

installation [ˌɪnstəˈleɪʃn] **n** installation *f*.

installment US = ***instalment***.

installment plan **n** US achat *m* à crédit.

instalment UK, ***installment*** US [ɪnˈstɔːlmənt] **n 1.** [payment] acompte *m* ▸ **in instalments** par acomptes **2.** [episode] épisode *m*.

instance [ˈɪnstəns] **n** exemple *m* ▸ **he agrees with me in most instances** la plupart du temps OR dans la plupart des cas il est d'accord avec moi ▸ **our policy, in that instance, was to raise interest rates** notre politique en la circonstance OR l'occurrence a consisté à augmenter les taux d'intérêt ▸ **for instance** par exemple ▸ **in the first instance** UK en premier lieu.

instant [ˈɪnstənt] ■ **adj 1.** [immediate] instantané(e), immédiat(e) **2.** [coffee] soluble / [food] à préparation rapide.
■ **n** instant *m* ▸ **the instant (that)...** dès OR aussitôt que... ▸ **this instant** tout de suite, immédiatement.

instant-access **adj** [bank account] à accès immédiat.

instantaneous [ˌɪnstənˈteɪnjəs] **adj** instantané(e).

instantaneously [ˌɪnstənˈteɪnjəslɪ] **adv** instantanément.

instantly [ˈɪnstəntlɪ] **adv** immédiatement.

instant replay **n** US = ***action replay***.

instead [ɪnˈsted] **adv** au lieu de cela.
◆ ***instead of*** **prep** au lieu de ▸ **instead of him** à sa place.

instep [ˈɪnstep] **n** cou-de-pied *m*.

instigate [ˈɪnstɪgeɪt] **vt** être à l'origine de, entreprendre.

instigation [ˌɪnstɪˈgeɪʃn] **n : at the instigation of** à l'instigation *f* de.

instigator [ˈɪnstɪgeɪtəʳ] **n** instigateur *m*, -trice *f*.

instil UK (pt & pp -led, cont -ling), ***instill*** US (pt & pp -ed, cont -ing) [ɪnˈstɪl] **vt : to instil sthg in** OR **into sb** instiller qqch à qqn.

instinct [ˈɪnstɪŋkt] **n 1.** [intuition] instinct *m* **2.** [impulse] réaction *f*, mouvement *m*.

instinctive [ɪnˈstɪŋktɪv] **adj** instinctif(ive).

instinctively [ɪnˈstɪŋktɪvlɪ] **adv** instinctivement.

institute [ˈɪnstɪtjuːt] ■ **n** institut *m*.
■ **vt** instituer.

institution [ˌɪnstɪˈtjuːʃn] **n** institution *f*.

institutional [ˌɪnstɪˈtjuːʃənl] **adj** institutionnel(elle) / *pej* [food] d'internat.

institutionalize, UK ***-ise*** [ˌɪnstɪˈtjuːʃənˌlaɪz] **vt 1.** [establish] institutionnaliser ▸ **to become institutionalized** s'institutionnaliser **2.** [place in a hospital, home] placer dans un établissement *(médical ou médico-social)* ▸ **to be institutionalized** être interné(e) ▸ **to become institutionalized** ne plus être capable de se prendre en charge *(après des années passées dans des établissements spécialisés)*.

institutional racism, ***institutionalized racism*** [ˌɪnstɪˈtjuːʃənˌlaɪzd-] **n** racisme *m* institutionnel.

in-store promotion **n** promotion *f* sur le lieu de vente.

instruct [ɪnˈstrʌkt] **vt 1.** [tell, order] **: to instruct sb to do sthg** charger qqn de faire qqch **2.** [teach] instruire ▸ **to instruct sb in sthg** enseigner qqch à qqn.

instruction [ɪnˈstrʌkʃn] **n** instruction *f*.
◆ ***instructions*** **npl** mode *m* d'emploi, instructions *fpl*.

instruction manual **n** manuel *m*.

instructive [ɪnˈstrʌktɪv] **adj** instructif(ive).

instructor [ɪnˈstrʌktəʳ] **n 1.** [gen] instructeur *m*, -trice *f*, moniteur *m*, -trice *f* **2.** US SCH enseignant *m*, -e *f*.

instructress [ɪnˈstrʌktrɪs] **n** instructrice *f*, monitrice *f*.

instrument [ˈɪnstrʊmənt] **n** *lit* & *fig* instrument *m*.

instrumental [ˌɪnstrʊˈmentl] ■ **adj 1.** [important, helpful] **: to be instrumental in** contribuer à **2.** [music] instrumental(e).
■ **n** morceau *m* instrumental.

instrumentalist [ˌɪnstrʊˈmentəlɪst] **n** instrumentiste *mf*.

instrument panel **n** tableau *m* de bord.

insubordinate [ˌɪnsəˈbɔːdɪnət] **adj** insubordonné(e).

insubordination [ˈɪnsəˌbɔːdɪˈneɪʃn] **n** insubordination *f*.

insubstantial [ˌɪnsəbˈstænʃl] **adj** [structure] peu solide / [meal] peu substantiel(elle).

insufferable [ɪnˈsʌfərəbl] **adj** *fml* insupportable.

insufficient [ˌɪnsəˈfɪʃnt] **adj** *fml* insuffisant(e).

insufficiently [ˌɪnsəˈfɪʃntlɪ] **adv** *fml* insuffisamment.

insular [ˈɪnsjʊləʳ] **adj** *pej* [outlook] borné(e) / [person] à l'esprit étroit.

insulate [ˈɪnsjʊleɪt] **vt 1.** [loft, cable] isoler / [hot water tank] calorifuger **2.** [protect] **: to insulate sb against** OR **from sthg** protéger qqn de qqch.

insulating tape [ˈɪnsjʊleɪtɪŋ-] **n** UK chatterton *m*.

insulation [ˌɪnsjʊˈleɪʃn] **n** isolation *f*.

insulator [ˈɪnsjʊleɪtəʳ] **n** [material] isolant *m* / [device] isolateur *m*.

insulin [ˈɪnsjʊlɪn] **n** insuline *f*.

insult ■ **vt** [ɪnˈsʌlt] insulter, injurier.
■ **n** [ˈɪnsʌlt] insulte *f*, injure *f* ▸ **to add insult to injury** aggraver les choses.

insulting [ɪnˈsʌltɪŋ] **adj** insultant(e), injurieux(euse).

insuperable [ɪn'suːprəbl] **adj** *fml* insurmontable.

insurable [ɪn'ʃɔːrəbl] **adj** assurable.

insurance [ɪn'ʃʊərəns] ■ **n 1.** [against fire, accident, theft] assurance *f* ▸ **to take out insurance (against sthg)** prendre ***OR*** contracter une assurance (contre qqch), s'assurer (contre qqch) ▸ **she got £2,000 in insurance** elle a reçu 2 000 livres de l'assurance **2.** *fig* [safeguard, protection] protection *f*, garantie *f* ▸ **take Sam with you, just as an insurance** emmenez Sam avec vous, on ne sait jamais ***OR*** au cas où.
■ **comp** [company, agent] d'assurances / [certificate] d'assurance.

insurance broker **n** courtier *m* d'assurances.

insurance policy **n** police *f* d'assurance.

insurance premium **n** prime *f* d'assurance.

insure [ɪn'ʃʊə^r] ■ **vt 1.** [against fire, accident, theft] **: to insure sb/sthg against sthg** assurer qqn/qqch contre qqch **2.** *US* [make certain] s'assurer.
■ **vi** [prevent] **: to insure against** se protéger de.

insured [ɪn'ʃʊəd] ■ **adj** [against fire, accident, theft] **: insured (against *OR* for sthg)** assuré(e) (contre qqch).
■ **n : the insured** l'assuré.

insurer [ɪn'ʃʊərə^r] **n** assureur *m*.

insurgent [ɪn'sɜːdʒənt] **n** insurgé *m*, -e *f*.

insurmountable [ˌɪnsə'maʊntəbl] **adj** *fml* insurmontable.

insurrection [ˌɪnsə'rekʃn] **n** insurrection *f*.

intact [ɪn'tækt] **adj** intact(e).

intake ['ɪnteɪk] **n 1.** [amount consumed] consommation *f* **2.** *UK* [people recruited] admission *f* **3.** [inlet] prise *f*, arrivée *f*.

intangible [ɪn'tændʒəbl] **adj** intangible, impalpable / [proof] non tangible.

integral ['ɪntɪgrəl] **adj** intégral(e) ▸ **to be integral to sthg** faire partie intégrante de qqch.

integrate ['ɪntɪgreɪt] ■ **vi** s'intégrer ▸ **to integrate with *OR* into sthg** s'intégrer dans qqch.
■ **vt** intégrer ▸ **to integrate sb/sthg with sthg, to integrate sb/sthg into sthg** intégrer qqn/qqch dans qqch.

integrated ['ɪntɪgreɪtɪd] **adj** intégré(e).

integrated circuit **n** circuit *m* intégré.

integration [ˌɪntɪ'greɪʃn] **n : integration (with/into)** intégration *f* (à/dans).

integrity [ɪn'tegrətɪ] **n 1.** [honour] intégrité *f*, honnêteté *f* **2.** *fml* [wholeness] intégrité *f*, totalité *f*.

intellect ['ɪntəlekt] **n 1.** [ability to think] intellect *m* **2.** [cleverness] intelligence *f*.

intellectual [ˌɪntə'lektjʊəl] ■ **adj** intellectuel(elle).
■ **n** intellectuel *m*, -elle *f*.

intellectualize, *UK* ***-ise*** [ˌɪntə'lektjʊəlaɪz] **vt** intellectualiser.

intellectually [ˌɪntə'lektjʊəlɪ] **adv** intellectuellement.

intelligence [ɪn'telɪdʒəns] **n** *(U)* **1.** [ability to think] intelligence *f* **2.** [information service] service *m* de renseignements **3.** [information] informations *fpl*, renseignements *mpl*.

intelligence quotient **n** quotient *m* intellectuel.

intelligence test **n** test *m* d'aptitude intellectuelle.

intelligent [ɪn'telɪdʒənt] **adj** intelligent(e).

intelligent card **n** carte *f* à puce ***OR*** à mémoire.

intelligently [ɪn'telɪdʒəntlɪ] **adv** intelligemment, avec intelligence.

intelligentsia [ɪnˌtelɪ'dʒentsɪə] **n : the intelligentsia** l'intelligentsia *f*.

intelligible [ɪn'telɪdʒəbl] **adj** intelligible.

intemperate [ɪn'tempərət] **adj** *fml* immodéré(e).

intend [ɪn'tend] **vt** [mean] avoir l'intention de ▸ **it was intended as advice** je voulais juste donner des conseils ▸ **it wasn't intended as criticism** il n'a pas dit pour critiquer ▸ **to be intended for** être destiné(e) à ▸ **to be intended to do sthg** être destiné(e) à faire qqch, viser à faire qqch ▸ **to intend doing *OR* to do sthg** avoir l'intention de faire qqch.

intended [ɪn'tendɪd] **adj** [result] voulu(e) / [victim] visé(e).

intense [ɪn'tens] **adj 1.** [gen] intense **2.** [serious - person] sérieux(euse).

intensely [ɪn'tenslɪ] **adv 1.** [irritating, boring] extrêmement / [suffer] énormément **2.** [look] intensément.

intensifier [ɪn'tensɪfaɪə^r] **n 1.** LING intensif *m* **2.** PHOT renforçateur *m*.

intensify [ɪn'tensɪfaɪ] (pt & pp **-ied**) ■ **vt** intensifier, augmenter.
■ **vi** s'intensifier.

intensity [ɪn'tensətɪ] **n** intensité *f*.

intensive [ɪn'tensɪv] **adj** intensif(ive).

-intensive **suffix** qui utilise beaucoup de... ▸ **labour-intensive** qui nécessitent une main-d'œuvre importante ▸ **energy-intensive** [appliance, industry] grand consommateur (grande consommatrice) d'énergie.

intensive care **n : to be in intensive care** être en réanimation.

intensive care unit **n** service *m* de réanimation, unité *f* de soins intensifs.

intensively [ɪn'tensɪvlɪ] **adv** intensivement.

intent [ɪn'tent] ■ **adj 1.** [absorbed] absorbé(e) **2.** [determined] **: to be intent on *OR* upon doing sthg** être résolu(e) ***OR*** décidé(e) à faire qqch.
■ **n** *fml* intention *f*, dessein *m* ▸ **to *OR* for all intents and purposes** pratiquement, virtuellement.

intention [ɪn'tenʃn] **n** intention *f*.

intentional [ɪn'tenʃənl] **adj** intentionnel(elle), voulu(e).

intentionally [ɪn'tenʃənəlɪ] **adv** intentionnellement ▸ **I didn't do it intentionally** je ne l'ai pas fait exprès.

intention to buy **n** intention *f* d'achat.

intently [ɪn'tentlɪ] **adv** avec attention, attentivement.

inter [ɪn'tɜː^r] (pt & pp **-red**, cont **-ring**) **vt** *fml* enterrer.

interact [ˌɪntər'ækt] **vi 1.** [communicate, work together] **: to interact (with sb)** communiquer (avec qqn) **2.** [react] **: to interact (with sthg)** interagir (avec qqch).

interaction [ˌɪntər'ækʃn] **n** interaction *f*.

interactive [ˌɪntər'æktɪv] **adj** COMPUT interactif(ive).

interactive television **n** télévision *f* interactive.

interactivity [ˌɪntəræk'tɪvɪtɪ] **n** interactivité *f*.

intercede [ˌɪntə'siːd] **vi** *fml* **: to intercede (with sb)** intercéder (auprès de qqn).

intercept [ˌɪntə'sept] **vt** intercepter.

interception [ˌɪntə'sepʃn] **n** interception *f*.

interchange ■ **n** ['ɪntətʃeɪndʒ] **1.** [exchange] échange *m* **2.** [road junction] échangeur *m*.
■ **vt** [ˌɪntə'tʃeɪndʒ] échanger.

interchangeable [ˌɪntə'tʃeɪndʒəbl] **adj : interchangeable (with)** interchangeable (avec).

intercity [ˌɪntə'sɪtɪ] ■ **adj** *UK* interurbain(e).
■ **n** *système de trains rapides reliant les grandes villes en Grande-Bretagne* ▸ **Intercity 125**® *train rapide pouvant rouler à 125 miles (200 km) à l'heure.*

intercom ['ɪntəkɒm] **n** Interphone® *m* ▸ **on** *OR* **over the intercom** à l'Interphone®.

intercommunicate [ˌɪntəkə'mjuːnɪkeɪt] **vi** communiquer.

interconnect [ˌɪntəkə'nekt] **vi : to interconnect (with)** être relié(e) (à), être connecté(e) (à).

intercontinental ['ɪntəˌkɒntɪ'nentl] **adj** intercontinental(e).

intercontinental ballistic missile **n** missile *m* balistique intercontinental.

intercourse ['ɪntəkɔːs] **n** *(U) UK* [sexual] rapports *mpl* (sexuels).

interdenominational ['ɪntədɪˌnɒmɪ'neɪʃənl] **adj** interconfessionnel(elle).

interdepartmental ['ɪntəˌdiːpɑːt'mentl] **adj** [in company, hospital] entre services / [in university, government] entre départements.

interdependence [ˌɪntədɪ'pendəns] **n** interdépendance *f*.

interdependent [ˌɪntədɪ'pendənt] **adj** interdépendant(e).

interdict ['ɪntədɪkt] **n** **1.** LAW interdiction *f* **2.** RELIG interdit *m*.

interest ['ɪntrəst] ■ **n** **1.** [gen] intérêt *m* ▸ **to have an interest in** s'intéresser à ▸ **she takes a great/an active interest in politics** elle s'intéresse beaucoup/activement à la politique ▸ **he has** *OR* **takes no interest whatsoever in music** il ne s'intéresse absolument pas à la musique ▸ **to show (an) interest in sthg** manifester de l'intérêt pour qqch ▸ **to hold sb's interest** retenir l'attention de qqn ▸ **politics has** *OR* **holds no interest for me** la politique ne présente aucun intérêt pour moi ▸ **to lose interest** se désintéresser ▸ **to be of interest to sb** intéresser qqn
2. [hobby] centre *m* d'intérêt ▸ **we share the same interests** nous avons les mêmes centres d'intérêt ▸ **his only interests are television and comic books** la télévision et les bandes dessinées sont les seules choses qui l'intéressent
3. [advantage, benefit] intérêt *m* ▸ **it's in your own interest** *OR* **interests** c'est dans votre propre intérêt ▸ **it's in all our interests to cut costs** nous avons tout intérêt à *OR* il est dans notre intérêt de réduire les coûts ▸ **I have your interests at heart** tes intérêts me tiennent à cœur ▸ **in the interest(s) of** dans l'intérêt de ▸ **big business interests** de gros intérêts commerciaux
4. *(U)* FIN intérêt *m*, intérêts *mpl* ▸ **to pay interest on a loan** payer des intérêts sur un prêt ▸ **the investment will bear 6% interest** le placement rapportera 6 %.
■ **vt** intéresser ▸ **to interest sb in sthg** [arouse interest] intéresser qqn à qqch ▸ **can I interest you in a drink?** je peux vous offrir un verre?

interested ['ɪntrəstɪd] **adj** intéressé(e) ▸ **to be interested in** s'intéresser à ▸ **I'm not interested in that** cela ne m'intéresse pas ▸ **to be interested in doing sthg** avoir envie de faire qqch.

interest-free **adj** FIN sans intérêt.

interest-free credit **n** crédit *m* gratuit.

interest-free loan **n** prêt *m* sans intérêt.

interesting ['ɪntrəstɪŋ] **adj** intéressant(e).

interestingly ['ɪntrəstɪŋlɪ] **adv** de façon intéressante ▸ **interestingly enough, they were out** chose intéressante, ils étaient sortis.

interest rate **n** taux *m* d'intérêt.

interface ■ **n** ['ɪntəfeɪs] **1.** COMPUT interface *f* **2.** *fig* [junction] rapports *mpl*, relations *fpl*.
■ **vt** [ˌɪntə'feɪs] COMPUT interfacer.

interfere [ˌɪntə'fɪəʳ] **vi** **1.** [meddle] **: to interfere in sthg** s'immiscer dans qqch, se mêler de qqch ▸ **don't interfere!** ne t'en mêle pas! ▸ **to interfere in sb's life** s'immiscer *OR* s'ingérer dans la vie de qqn **2.** [damage] **: to interfere with sthg** gêner *OR* contrarier qqch / [routine] déranger qqch ▸ **to interfere with the course of justice** entraver le cours de la justice ▸ **it interferes with my work** cela me gêne dans mon travail **3.** RADIO **: local radio sometimes interferes with police transmissions** la radio locale brouille *OR* perturbe parfois les transmissions de la police.

interference [ˌɪntə'fɪərəns] **n** *(U)* **1.** [meddling] **: interference (with** *OR* **in)** ingérence *f* (dans), intrusion *f* (dans) **2.** TELEC parasites *mpl*.

interfering [ˌɪntə'fɪərɪŋ] **adj** *pej* qui se mêle de tout.

intergalactic [ˌɪntəgə'læktɪk] **adj** intergalactique.

interim ['ɪntərɪm] ■ **adj** provisoire.
■ **n : in the interim** dans l'intérim, entre-temps.

interior [ɪn'tɪərɪəʳ] ■ **adj** **1.** [inner] intérieur(e) **2.** POL de l'Intérieur.
■ **n** intérieur *m*.

interior decorator **n** décorateur *m*, -trice *f*.

interior design **n** architecture *f* d'intérieurs.

interior designer **n** architecte *mf* d'intérieur.

interject [ˌɪntə'dʒekt] ■ **vt** **1.** *fml* [add] lancer **2.** [interrupt] interrompre.
■ **vi** interrompre, lancer une remarque.

interjection [ˌɪntə'dʒekʃn] **n** *fml* **1.** [remark] interruption *f* **2.** GRAM interjection *f*.

interlace [ˌɪntəˈleɪs] ■ **vt 1.** [entwine] entrelacer **2.** [intersperse] entremêler.
■ **vi** s'entrelacer, s'entrecroiser.

interleave [ˌɪntəˈliːv] **vt** TYPO **: to interleave sthg with sthg** interfolier qqch avec qqch.

interlock [ˌɪntəˈlɒk] ■ **vi** [gears] s'enclencher, s'engrener / [fingers] s'entrelacer.
■ **vt** [gears] enclencher, engrener / [fingers] entrelacer.

interlocutor [ˌɪntəˈlɒkjʊtəʳ] **n** interlocuteur *m*, -trice *f*.

interloper [ˈɪntələʊpəʳ] **n** *pej* intrus *m*, -e *f*.

interlude [ˈɪntəluːd] **n 1.** [pause] intervalle *m* **2.** [interval] interlude *m*.

intermarriage [ˌɪntəˈmærɪdʒ] **n 1.** [within family, clan] endogamie *f* **2.** [between different groups] mariage *m* mixte.

intermarry [ˌɪntəˈmærɪ] (pt & pp **-ied**) **vi : to intermarry (with)** se marier (avec).

intermediary [ˌɪntəˈmiːdjərɪ] (pl **-ies**) **n** intermédiaire *mf*.

intermediate [ˌɪntəˈmiːdjət] **adj 1.** [transitional] intermédiaire **2.** [post-beginner - level] moyen(enne) / [- student, group] de niveau moyen.

interment [ɪnˈtɜːmənt] **n** enterrement *m*, inhumation *f*.

interminable [ɪnˈtɜːmɪnəbl] **adj** interminable, sans fin.

interminably [ɪnˈtɜːmɪnəblɪ] **adv** interminablement ▸ **the play seemed interminably long** la pièce semblait interminable ▸ **the discussions dragged on interminably** les discussions s'éternisaient.

intermingle [ˌɪntəˈmɪŋgl] **vi : to intermingle with sb** se mêler à qqn ▸ **to intermingle with sthg** se mélanger avec qqch.

intermission [ˌɪntəˈmɪʃn] **n** entracte *m*.

intermittent [ˌɪntəˈmɪtənt] **adj** intermittent(e).

intermittently [ˌɪntəˈmɪtəntlɪ] **adv** par intervalles, par intermittence ▸ **the journal has been published only intermittently** la revue n'a connu qu'une parution irrégulière.

intern ■ **vt** [ɪnˈtɜːn] interner.
■ **n** [ˈɪntɜːn] *US* [gen] stagiaire *mf* / MED interne *mf*.

internal [ɪnˈtɜːnl] **adj 1.** [gen] interne **2.** [within country] intérieur(e).

internal affairs **n** POL affaires *fpl* intérieures.

internal-combustion engine **n** moteur *m* à combustion interne.

internalize, -ise *UK* [ɪnˈtɜːnəlaɪz] **vt 1.** [values, behaviour] intérioriser **2.** INDUST & FIN internaliser.

internally [ɪnˈtɜːnəlɪ] **adv 1.** [within the body] **: to bleed internally** faire une hémorragie interne **2.** [within country] à l'intérieur **3.** [within organization] intérieurement.

Internal Revenue Service **n** *US* **: the Internal Revenue Service** ≃ le fisc.

international [ˌɪntəˈnæʃənl] ■ **adj** international(e).
■ **n** *UK* **1.** SPORT [match] match *m* international **2.** SPORT [player] international *m*, -e *f*.

International Court of Justice **n : the International Court of Justice** la Cour internationale de justice.

international date line **n : the international date line** la ligne de changement de date.

internationalize, -ise *UK* [ˌɪntəˈnæʃnəlaɪz] **vt** internationaliser.

internationally [ˌɪntəˈnæʃnəlɪ] **adv** dans le monde entier.

International Monetary Fund **n : the International Monetary Fund** le Fonds monétaire international.

international money market **n** marché *m* monétaire international.

international relations **npl** relations *fpl* internationales.

International Standards Organization **n : the International Standards Organization** l'Organisation *f* internationale de normalisation.

International Trade Administration **n : the International Trade Administration** l'Administration *f* du commerce international.

CULTURE

International Trade Administration

La mission de l'Administration du commerce international (l'ITA) est de favoriser les exportations américaines, de contribuer à la compétitivité des entreprises américaines sur les marchés mondiaux et de les protéger des importations déloyales. Elle fournit aux entreprises du pays des informations pratiques pour les aider à choisir les meilleurs produits et marchés internationaux et leur permet de bénéficier des accords commerciaux passés avec les pays étrangers.

internecine [*UK* ˌɪntəˈniːsaɪn, *US* ɪntərˈniːsn] **adj** *fml* intestin(e).

internee [ˌɪntɜːˈniː] **n** interné *m*, -e *f* politique.

Internet [ˈɪntənet] **n : the Internet** l'Internet *m*.

Internet access **n** *(U)* accès à l'Internet *m*.

Internet Access Provider **n** fournisseur *m* d'accès à l'Internet.

Internet address **n** adresse *f* Internet.

Internet banking **n** *(U)* opérations *fpl* bancaires par l'Internet.

Internet café **n** cybercafé *m*.

Internet connection **n** connexion *f* Internet ***OR*** à l'Internet.

Internet Presence Provider **n** *fournisseur d'accès à l'Internet proposant l'hébergement de sites Web*.

Internet protocol **n** protocole *m* Internet.

Internet radio **n** radio *f* par Internet.

Internet Relay Chat **n** service *m* de bavardage Internet, canal *m* de dialogue en direct.

Internet Service Provider **n** fournisseur *m* d'accès.

Internet start-up, Internet start-up company **n** start-up *f*, jeune *f* pousse d'entreprise *offic*.

Internet television, Internet TV **n** *(U)* télévision *f* Internet.

Internet user **n** internaute *mf*.

internment [ɪn'tɜ:nmənt] **n** internement *m* politique.

internship ['ɪntɜ:nʃɪp] **n** [with firm] stage *m* en entreprise / *US* MED internat *m*.

interpersonal [ˌɪntə'pɜ:sənl] **adj** de personne à personne, entre personnes / [skills] de communication.

interplay ['ɪntəpleɪ] **n : interplay (of/between)** interaction *f* (de/entre).

Interpol ['ɪntəpɒl] **n** Interpol *m*.

interpolate [ɪn'tɜ:pəleɪt] **vt** *fml* **1.** [add] **: to interpolate sthg (into)** ajouter qqch (à) **2.** [interrupt] interrompre.

interpose [ˌɪntə'pəʊz] **vt** *fml* **1.** [add] ajouter **2.** [interrupt] interrompre.

interpret [ɪn'tɜ:prɪt] ■ **vt : to interpret sthg (as)** interpréter qqch (comme).
■ **vi** [translate] faire l'interprète.

interpretation [ɪnˌtɜ:prɪ'teɪʃn] **n** interprétation *f*.

interpreter [ɪn'tɜ:prɪtəʳ] **n** interprète *mf*.

interpreting [ɪn'tɜ:prɪtɪŋ] **n** [occupation] interprétariat *m*.

interracial [ˌɪntə'reɪʃl] **adj** entre des races différentes, racial(e).

interrelate [ˌɪntərɪ'leɪt] ■ **vt** mettre en corrélation.
■ **vi : to interrelate (with)** être lié(e) (à), être en corrélation (avec).

interrogate [ɪn'terəgeɪt] **vt** interroger.

interrogation [ɪnˌterə'geɪʃn] **n** [gen, LING & COMPUT] interrogation *f* / [by police] interrogatoire *m*.

CONFUSABLE / PARONYME

interrogation

When translating interrogation, note that *interrogatoire* and *interrogation* are not interchangeable. *Interrogatoire* is used to refer to a police interrogation, while *interrogation* is used to refer to computing queries.

interrogation mark *UK*, ***interrogation point*** **n** *US* point *m* d'interrogation.

interrogative [ˌɪntə'rɒgətɪv] ■ **adj** GRAM interrogatif(ive).
■ **n** GRAM interrogatif *m*.

interrogator [ɪn'terəgeɪtəʳ] **n** interrogateur *m*, -trice *f*.

interrogatory [ˌɪntə'rɒgətrɪ] **adj** interrogateur(trice).

interrupt [ˌɪntə'rʌpt] ■ **vt** interrompre / [calm] rompre.
■ **vi** interrompre.

interruption [ˌɪntə'rʌpʃn] **n** interruption *f*.

intersect [ˌɪntə'sekt] ■ **vi** s'entrecroiser, s'entrecouper.
■ **vt** croiser, couper.

intersection [ˌɪntə'sekʃn] **n** [in road] croisement *m*, carrefour *m*.

intersperse [ˌɪntə'spɜ:s] **vt : to be interspersed with** être émaillé(e) de, être entremêlé(e) de.

interstate ['ɪntəsteɪt] ■ **adj** [commerce, highway] entre États.
■ **n** *US* autoroute *f*.

intertwine [ˌɪntə'twaɪn] ■ **vt** entrelacer ▸ **their lives are inextricably intertwined** leurs vies sont inextricablement liées.
■ **vi** s'entrelacer.

interval ['ɪntəvl] **n 1.** [gen] intervalle *m* ▸ **at intervals** par intervalles ▸ **at monthly/yearly intervals** tous les mois/ans **2.** *UK* [at play, concert] entracte *m*.

intervene [ˌɪntə'vi:n] **vi 1.** [person, police] **: to intervene (in)** intervenir (dans), s'interposer (dans) **2.** [event, war, strike] survenir **3.** [time] s'écouler.

intervening [ˌɪntə'vi:nɪŋ] **adj** [period] qui s'est écoulé(e).

intervention [ˌɪntə'venʃn] **n** intervention *f*.

interventionist [ˌɪntə'venʃənɪst] ■ **adj** interventionniste.
■ **n** interventionniste *mf*.

interview ['ɪntəvju:] ■ **n 1.** [for job] entrevue *f*, entretien *m* ▸ **to invite** OR **to call sb for interview** convoquer qqn pour une entrevue **2.** PRESS interview *f* ▸ **she gave him an exclusive interview** elle lui a accordé une interview en exclusivité.
■ **vt 1.** [for job] faire passer une entrevue OR un entretien à / [for opinion poll] interroger, sonder ▸ **shortlisted applicants will be interviewed in March** les candidats sélectionnés seront convoqués pour un entretien en mars **2.** PRESS interviewer.

interviewee [ˌɪntəvju:'i:] **n 1.** [for job] candidat *m*, -e *f* **2.** PRESS interviewé *m*, -e *f*.

interviewer ['ɪntəvju:əʳ] **n 1.** [for job] personne *f* qui fait passer une entrevue **2.** PRESS interviewer *m*.

interweave [ˌɪntə'wi:v] (pt -wove, pp -woven) *fig* ■ **vt** entremêler.
■ **vi** s'entremêler.

intestate [ɪn'testeɪt] **adj : to die intestate** mourir intestat *(inv)*.

intestinal [ɪn'testɪnl] **adj** intestinal(e).

intestine [ɪn'testɪn] **n** intestin *m*.
◆ ***intestines*** **npl** intestins *mpl*.

intimacy ['ɪntɪməsɪ] (pl **-ies**) **n** **1.** [closeness] **: intimacy (between/with)** intimité *f* (entre/avec) **2.** [intimate remark] familiarité *f*.

intimate ■ **adj** ['ɪntɪmət] **1.** [gen] intime **2.** *fml* [sexually] **: to be intimate with sb** avoir des rapports intimes avec qqn **3.** [detailed - knowledge] approfondi(e).
■ **n** ['ɪntɪmət] *fml* intime *mf*.
■ **vt** ['ɪntɪmeɪt] *fml* faire savoir, faire connaître.

intimately ['ɪntɪmətlɪ] **adv** **1.** [very closely] étroitement **2.** [as close friends] intimement **3.** [in detail] à fond.

intimation [ˌɪntɪ'meɪʃn] **n** *fml* signe *m*, indication *f*.

intimidate [ɪn'tɪmɪdeɪt] **vt** intimider.

intimidating [ɪn'tɪmɪdeɪtɪŋ] **adj** intimidant(e).

intimidation [ɪnˌtɪmɪ'deɪʃn] **n** intimidation *f*.

into ['ɪntʊ] **prep** **1.** [inside] dans **2.** [against] **: to bump into sthg** se cogner contre qqch ▸ **to crash into** rentrer dans **3.** [referring to change in state] en ▸ **to translate sthg into Spanish** traduire qqch en espagnol **4.** [concerning] **: research/investigation into** recherche/enquête sur **5.** MATHS **: 3 into 2** 2 divisé par 3 **6.** *inf* [interested in] **: to be into sthg** être passionné(e) par qqch.

intolerable [ɪn'tɒlrəbl] **adj** intolérable, insupportable.

intolerably [ɪn'tɒlrəblɪ] **adv** intolérablement, insupportablement.

intolerance [ɪn'tɒlərəns] **n** intolérance *f*.

intolerant [ɪn'tɒlərənt] **adj** intolérant(e) ▸ **to be intolerant of** faire preuve d'intolérance à l'égard de.

intonation [ˌɪntə'neɪʃn] **n** intonation *f*.

intone [ɪn'təʊn] **vt** *fml* psalmodier.

intoxicated [ɪn'tɒksɪkeɪtɪd] **adj** **1.** [drunk] ivre **2.** *fig* [excited] **: to be intoxicated by** *OR* **with sthg** être grisé(e) *OR* enivré(e) par qqch.

intoxicating [ɪn'tɒksɪkeɪtɪŋ] **adj** **1.** [alcoholic] alcoolisé(e) **2.** *fig* [exciting] grisant(e), enivrant(e).

intoxication [ɪnˌtɒksɪ'keɪʃn] **n** **1.** [drunkenness] ivresse *f* **2.** [excitement] griserie *f*, ivresse *f*.

intractable [ɪn'træktəbl] **adj** **1.** [stubborn] intraitable **2.** [insoluble] insoluble.

intranet, Intranet ['ɪntrənɛt] **n** intranet *m*.

intransigence [ɪn'trænzɪdʒəns] **n** intransigeance *f*.

intransigent [ɪn'trænzɪdʒənt] **adj** intransigeant(e).

intransitive [ɪn'trænzətɪv] **adj** intransitif(ive).

intrastate [ˌɪntrə'steɪt] **adj** à l'intérieur d'un même État.

intrauterine contraceptive device [ˌɪntrə'ju:tərаɪn] **n** stérilet *m*, dispositif *m* anticonceptionnel intra-utérin.

intrauterine device [ˌɪntrə'ju:tərаɪn] **n** stérilet *m*, dispositif *m* anticonceptionnel intra-utérin.

intravenous [ˌɪntrə'vi:nəs] **adj** intraveineux(euse).

intravenously [ˌɪntrə'vi:nəslɪ] **adv** par voie intraveineuse ▸ **he's being fed intravenously** on l'alimente par perfusion.

in-tray *esp UK*, ***in-basket*** *US*, ***in-box*** *US* **n** casier *m* des affaires à traiter.

intrepid [ɪn'trepɪd] **adj** intrépide.

intricacy ['ɪntrɪkəsɪ] (pl **-ies**) **n** complexité *f*.

intricate ['ɪntrɪkət] **adj** compliqué(e).

intricately ['ɪntrɪkətlɪ] **adv** de façon complexe *OR* compliquée.

intrigue [ɪn'tri:g] ■ **n** intrigue *f*.
■ **vt** intriguer, exciter la curiosité de.
■ **vi : to intrigue against** intriguer *OR* comploter contre.

intriguing [ɪn'tri:gɪŋ] **adj** fascinant(e).

intriguingly [ɪn'tri:gɪŋlɪ] **adv** bizarrement, curieusement.

intrinsic [ɪn'trɪnsɪk] **adj** intrinsèque.

intrinsically [ɪn'trɪnsɪklɪ] **adv** intrinsèquement.

intro ['ɪntrəʊ] (pl **-s**) **n** *inf* introduction *f*.

introduce [ˌɪntrə'dju:s] **vt** **1.** [present] présenter ▸ **to introduce sb to sb** présenter qqn à qqn ▸ **let me introduce myself, I'm John** je me présente : John ▸ **has everyone been introduced?** les présentations ont été faites?

HOW TO ...

express oneself in a job interview

Comme vous pouvez voir sur mon CV... / As you can see from my CV...
Cela fait presque dix ans que je travaille dans l'édition / I have been in publishing for almost ten years
Je crois être doué pour les relations humaines / I think I'm good at dealing with people
J'aime beaucoup travailler en équipe / I love working as part of a team
En quoi consiste le travail ? / What does the job involve?
Qui serait mon supérieur direct ? / Who would I be reporting to?
S'agit-il d'un contrat à durée indéterminée ? / Is it a permanent contract?
Quels sont les horaires de travail habituels ? / What are the normal working hours?

2. [bring in] **: to introduce sthg (to** ***OR*** **into)** introduire qqch (dans) **3.** [allow to experience] **: to introduce sb to sthg** initier qqn à qqch, faire découvrir qqch à qqn **4.** [signal beginning of] annoncer.

introduction [ˌɪntrəˈdʌkʃn] **n 1.** [in book, of new method] introduction *f* **2.** [first experience] **: introduction to sthg** premier contact *m* avec qqch **3.** [of people] **: introduction (to sb)** présentation *f* (à qqn).

introductory [ˌɪntrəˈdʌktrɪ] **adj** d'introduction, préliminaire.

introductory offer **n** offre *f* de lancement.

introductory price **n** prix *m* de lancement.

introspection [ˌɪntrəˈspekʃn] **n** introspection *f*.

introspective [ˌɪntrəˈspektɪv] **adj** introspectif(ive).

introvert [ˈɪntrəvɜːt] **n** introverti *m*, -e *f*.

introverted [ˈɪntrəvɜːtɪd] **adj** introverti(e).

intrude [ɪnˈtruːd] **vi** faire intrusion ▸ **to intrude on sb** déranger qqn.

intruder [ɪnˈtruːdər] **n** intrus *m*, -e *f*.

intrusion [ɪnˈtruːʒn] **n** intrusion *f*.

intrusive [ɪnˈtruːsɪv] **adj** gênant(e), importun(e).

intuition [ˌɪntjuːˈɪʃn] **n** intuition *f*.

intuitive [ɪnˈtjuːɪtɪv] **adj** intuitif(ive).

Inuit [ˈɪnʊɪt] ■ **adj** inuit *(inv)*.
■ **n** Inuit *mf inv*.

inundate [ˈɪnʌndeɪt] **vt 1.** *fml* [flood] inonder **2.** [overwhelm] **: to be inundated with** être submergé(e) de.

inured [ɪˈnjʊəd] **adj** *fml* **: to be inured to sthg** être aguerri(e) à qqch, être endurci(e) à qqch ▸ **to become inured to sthg** s'aguerrir à qqch, s'endurcir à qqch.

invade [ɪnˈveɪd] **vt 1.** *fig* & MIL envahir **2.** [disturb - privacy] violer.

invader [ɪnˈveɪdər] **n** envahisseur *m*, -euse *f*.

invading [ɪnˈveɪdɪŋ] **adj** [troops] d'invasion.

invalid ■ **adj** [ɪnˈvælɪd] **1.** [illegal, unacceptable] non valide, non valable **2.** [not reasonable] non valable.
■ **n** [ˈɪnvəlɪd] invalide *mf*.
◆ ***invalid out*** **vt sep** [ˈɪnvəlɪd] *esp UK* **: to be invalided out of the army** être réformé(e) pour raisons de santé.

invalidate [ɪnˈvælɪdeɪt] **vt** invalider, annuler.

invalid chair [ˈɪnvəlɪd-] **n** *UK dated* fauteuil *m* roulant.

invalidity [ˌɪnvəˈlɪdətɪ] **n 1.** MED invalidité *f* **2.** [of contract, agreement] manque *m* de validité, nullité *f* **3.** [of argument] manque *m* de fondement.

invaluable [ɪnˈvæljʊəbl] **adj : invaluable (to)** [help, advice, person] précieux(euse) (pour) / [experience, information] inestimable (pour).

invariable [ɪnˈveərɪəbl] **adj** invariable.

invariably [ɪnˈveərɪəblɪ] **adv** invariablement, toujours.

invasion [ɪnˈveɪʒn] **n** *lit* & *fig* invasion *f*.

invasive [ɪnˈveɪsɪv] **adj** MED [surgery] invasif(ive) / *fig* envahissant(e).

invective [ɪnˈvektɪv] **n** *(U) fml* invectives *fpl*.

inveigle [ɪnˈveɪgl] **vt** *fml* **: to inveigle sb into sthg** attirer qqn dans qqch par la ruse ▸ **to inveigle sb into doing sthg** amener qqn à faire qqch (par la ruse), persuader qqn de faire qqch (par la ruse).

invent [ɪnˈvent] **vt** inventer.

invention [ɪnˈvenʃn] **n** invention *f*.

inventive [ɪnˈventɪv] **adj** inventif(ive).

inventor [ɪnˈventər] **n** inventeur *m*, -trice *f*.

inventory [ˈɪnvəntrɪ] (pl -ies) **n 1.** [list] inventaire *m* **2.** *US* [goods] stock *m*.

inventory control **n** gestion *f* du stock.

inverse [ɪnˈvɜːs] ■ **adj** inverse.
■ **n** inverse *m*, contraire *m*.

inversion [ɪnˈvɜːʃn] **n 1.** [gen] inversion *f* / [of roles, relations] renversement *m* **2.** MUS [of chord] renversement *m* / [in counterpoint] inversion *f* **3.** ANAT, ELEC & MATHS inversion *f*.

invert [ɪnˈvɜːt] **vt** retourner.

invertebrate [ɪnˈvɜːtɪbreɪt] **n** invertébré *m*.

inverted commas [ɪnˌvɜːtɪd-] **npl** *UK* guillemets *mpl*.

inverted snob [ɪnˈvɜːtɪd-] **n** *UK pej* snob *mf* à l'envers, personne *f* qui fait du snobisme à l'envers.

HOW TO ...

introduce oneself and other people

Introducing oneself

Je me présente, je m'appelle Michèle / Allow me to introduce myself, I'm Michèle

Bonjour, moi c'est Michèle / Hello, I'm Michèle

Nous ne nous connaissons pas ? / I don't think we've met, have we?

Introducing other people

Je vais faire les présentations / Let me do the introductions

J'aimerais vous présenter un vieil ami, Paul Darmont / I'd like you to meet an old friend of mine, Paul Darmont

Claude, je te présente M. Darmont / Claude, I'd like you to meet Mr Darmont

Tout le monde se connaît ? / Does everyone know each other?

Marc, (voici) Claude ; Claude, (voici) Marc / Marc, (this is) Claude; Claude, (this is) Marc

invest [ɪn'vest] ■ **vt** **1.** [money] **: to invest sthg (in)** investir qqch (dans) **2.** [time, energy] **: to invest sthg in sthg/in doing sthg** consacrer qqch à qqch/à faire qqch, employer qqch à qqch/à faire qqch **3.** *fml* [endow] **: to invest sb with sthg** investir qqn de qqch.
■ **vi** **1.** FIN **: to invest (in sthg)** investir (dans qqch) **2.** *fig* [buy] **: to invest in sthg** se payer qqch, s'acheter qqch.

investigate [ɪn'vestɪgeɪt] ■ **vt** enquêter sur, faire une enquête sur / [subj: scientist] faire des recherches sur.
■ **vi** faire une enquête.

investigation [ɪn,vestɪ'geɪʃn] **n** **1.** [enquiry] **: investigation (into)** enquête *f* (sur) / [scientific] recherches *fpl* (sur) **2.** *(U)* [investigating] investigation *f*.

investigative [ɪn'vestɪgətɪv] **adj** d'investigation.

investigative journalism **n** journalisme *m* d'investigation OR d'enquête.

investigative reporter **n** reporter *m* d'investigation OR d'enquête.

investigator [ɪn'vestɪgeɪtə^r] **n** investigateur *m*, -trice *f*.

investigatory [ɪn'vestɪgeɪtərɪ] **adj** d'investigation.

investiture [ɪn'vestɪtʃə^r] **n** investiture *f*.

investment [ɪn'vestmənt] **n** **1.** FIN investissement *m*, placement *m* **2.** [of energy] dépense *f*.

investment analyst **n** analyste *mf* en placements.

investment bank **n** banque *f* d'affaires.

investment trust **n** société *f* d'investissement.

investor [ɪn'vestə^r] **n** investisseur *m*.

inveterate [ɪn'vetərət] **adj** invétéré(e).

invidious [ɪn'vɪdɪəs] **adj** [task] ingrat(e) / [comparison] injuste.

invigilate [ɪn'vɪdʒɪleɪt] *UK* ■ **vi** surveiller les candidats (à un examen).
■ **vt** surveiller.

invigilator [ɪn'vɪdʒɪleɪtə^r] **n** *UK* surveillant *m*, -e *f*.

invigorating [ɪn'vɪgəreɪtɪŋ] **adj** tonifiant(e), vivifiant(e).

invincibility [ɪn,vɪnsɪ'bɪlətɪ] **n** invincibilité *f*.

invincible [ɪn'vɪnsɪbl] **adj** [army, champion] invincible / [record] imbattable.

inviolate [ɪn'vaɪələt] **adj** *liter* inviolé(e).

invisibility [ɪn,vɪzɪ'bɪlətɪ] **n** invisibilité *f*.

invisible [ɪn'vɪzɪbl] **adj** invisible.

invisible assets **npl** biens *mpl* incorporels.

invisible earnings **npl** revenus *mpl* invisibles.

invisible ink **n** encre *f* sympathique.

invitation [,ɪnvɪ'teɪʃn] **n** **1.** [request] invitation *f* **2.** [encouragement] **: an invitation to sthg/to do sthg** une incitation à qqch/à faire qqch, une invite à qqch/à faire qqch.

invite [ɪn'vaɪt] **vt** **1.** [ask to come] **: to invite sb (to)** inviter qqn (à) **2.** [ask politely] **: to invite sb to do sthg** inviter qqn à faire qqch **3.** [ask for] **: the chairman invited questions** le président a invité l'assistance à poser des questions **4.** [encourage] **: to invite trouble** aller au devant des ennuis ▸ **to invite gossip** faire causer.

inviting [ɪn'vaɪtɪŋ] **adj** attrayant(e), agréable / [food] appétissant(e).

in vitro fertilization [,ɪn'vi:trəʊ-] **n** fécondation *f* in vitro.

invoice ['ɪnvɔɪs] ■ **n** facture *f*.
■ **vt** **1.** [client] envoyer la facture à **2.** [goods] facturer.

invoke [ɪn'vəʊk] **vt** **1.** *fml* [law, act] invoquer **2.** [feelings] susciter, faire naître / [help] demander, implorer.

involuntarily [ɪn'vɒləntrəlɪ] **adv** involontairement.

involuntary [ɪn'vɒləntrɪ] **adj** involontaire.

involve [ɪn'vɒlv] **vt** **1.** [entail] nécessiter ▸ **what's involved?** de quoi s'agit-il? ▸ **to involve doing sthg** nécessiter de faire qqch ▸ **a job which involves meeting people** un travail où l'on est amené à rencontrer beaucoup de gens **2.** [concern, affect] toucher ▸ **to be involved in an accident** avoir un accident ▸ **several vehicles were involved in the accident** plusieurs véhicules étaient impliqués dans cet accident **3.** [person] **: to involve sb in sthg** impliquer qqn dans qqch ▸ **we try to involve the parents in the running of the school** nous essayons de faire participer les parents à la vie de l'école ▸ **to involve o.s. in sthg** s'impliquer dans qqch, prendre part à qqch.

involved [ɪn'vɒlvd] **adj** **1.** [complex] complexe, compliqué(e) **2.** [participating, implicated] **: the amount of work involved is enormous** la quantité de travail à fournir est énorme ▸ **he had no idea of the problems involved** il n'avait aucune idée des problèmes en jeu OR en cause ▸ **to be involved in sthg** participer OR prendre part à qqch ▸ **over 100 companies are involved in the scheme** plus de 100 sociétés sont associées à OR parties prenantes dans ce projet **3.** [in relationship] **: to be involved with sb** avoir des relations intimes avec qqn ▸ **he doesn't want to get involved** il ne veut pas s'attacher.

involvement [ɪn'vɒlvmənt] **n** **1.** [participation] **: involvement (in)** participation *f* (à) **2.** [concern, enthusiasm] **: involvement (in)** engagement *m* (dans).

HOW TO ...

invite somebody to do something

J'organise une fête pour mon anniversaire samedi 22. Vous viendrez, j'espère ? / I'm having a birthday party on Saturday 22. I hope you'll be able to come

Tu viens boire un verre après le travail ? / Why don't you come for a drink after work?

Tu es libre pour déjeuner un jour de la semaine prochaine ? / Are you free for lunch one day next week?

Je me demandais si tu aimerais venir dîner un soir avec Catherine ? / I was wondering if you and Catherine would like to come to dinner one evening?

Pourquoi ne viendrais-tu pas avec nous à Paris ? / Why don't you come to Paris with us?

Une partie de tennis, ça te tente ? / Do you fancy a game of tennis?

invulnerable [ɪn'vʌlnərəbl] **adj : invulnerable (to)** invulnérable (à).

inward ['ɪnwəd] ■ **adj 1.** [inner] intérieur(e) **2.** [towards the inside] vers l'intérieur.
■ adv *US* = ***inwards***.

inward investment **n** investissement *m* de l'étranger.

inward-looking **adj** [person] introverti(e), replié(e) sur soi / [group] replié(e) sur soi, fermé(e) / [philosophy] introspectif(ive) / *pej* nombriliste ▸ **he's become very inward-looking lately** il s'est beaucoup refermé *OR* replié sur lui-même ces derniers temps.

inwardly ['ɪnwədlɪ] **adv** intérieurement.

inwards ['ɪnwədz] **adv** vers l'intérieur.

in-your-face **adj** *inf* provocant(e).

I/O (abbr of ***input/output***) E/S.

IOC (abbr of ***International Olympic Committee***) **n** CIO *m*.

iodine [*UK* 'aɪədi:n, *US* 'aɪədaɪn] **n** iode *m*.

IOM abbr of ***Isle of Man***.

ion ['aɪən] **n** ion *m*.

Ionian Sea [aɪ'əʊnjən-] **n : the Ionian Sea** la mer Ionienne.

iota [aɪ'əʊtə] **n** brin *m*, grain *m*.

IOU (abbr of ***I owe you***) **n** reconnaissance *f* de dette.

IOW abbr of ***Isle of Wight***.

Iowa ['aɪəʊə] **n** Iowa *m* ▸ **in Iowa** dans l'Iowa.

IP (abbr of ***Internet Protocol***) **n : IP address** adress *f* IP ▸ **IP number** numéro *m* IP.

IPA (abbr of ***International Phonetic Alphabet***) **n** API *m*.

IPP (abbr of ***Internet Presence Provider***) **n** *fournisseur d'accès à l'Internet proposant l'hébergement de sites Web*.

IQ (abbr of ***intelligence quotient***) **n** QI *m*.

IRA **n 1.** (abbr of ***Irish Republican Army***) IRA *f* **2.** (abbr of ***individual retirement account***) *aux États-Unis, compte d'épargne retraite (à avantages fiscaux)*.

Iran [ɪ'rɑ:n] **n** Iran *m* ▸ **in Iran** en Iran.

Iranian [ɪ'reɪnjən] ■ **adj** iranien(enne).
■ **n** Iranien *m*, -enne *f*.

Iraq [ɪ'rɑ:k] **n** Iraq *m*, Irak *m* ▸ **in Iraq** en Iraq.

Iraqi [ɪ'rɑ:kɪ] ■ **adj** iraquien(enne), irakien(enne).
■ **n** Iraquien *m*, -enne *f*, Irakien *m*, -enne *f*.

irascible [ɪ'ræsəbl] **adj** *fml* irascible, coléreux(euse).

irate [aɪ'reɪt] **adj** furieux(euse).

IRC (abbr of ***Internet Relay Chat***) **n** IRC *m*, service *m* de bavardage Internet, dialogue *m* en direct.

IRC channel **n** canal *m* IRC, canal *m* de dialogue en direct.

Ireland ['aɪələnd] **n** Irlande *f* ▸ **in Ireland** en Irlande ▸ **the Republic of Ireland** la République d'Irlande.

iridescent [,ɪrɪ'desənt] **adj** *liter* irisé(e) / [silk] chatoyant(e).

iris ['aɪərɪs] (pl **-es** [-i:z]) **n** iris *m*.

Irish ['aɪrɪʃ] ■ **adj** irlandais(e).
■ **n** [language] irlandais *m*.
■ **npl : the Irish** les Irlandais.

Irish coffee **n** Irish coffee *m*.

Irishman ['aɪrɪʃmən] (pl **-men** [-mən]) **n** Irlandais *m*.

Irish Sea **n : the Irish Sea** la mer d'Irlande.

Irish stew **n** ragoût *m* de viande à l'irlandaise.

Irishwoman ['aɪrɪʃ,wʊmən] (pl **-women** [-,wɪmɪn]) **n** Irlandaise *f*.

irk [ɜ:k] **vt** ennuyer, contrarier.

irksome ['ɜ:ksəm] **adj** ennuyeux(euse), assommant(e).

IRN (abbr of ***Independent Radio News***) **n** *UK agence de presse radiophonique*.

IRO (abbr of ***International Refugee Organization***) **n** HIST *organisation humanitaire américaine pour les réfugiés*.

iron ['aɪən] ■ **adj 1.** [made of iron] de *OR* en fer **2.** *fig* [very strict] de fer.
■ **n 1.** [metal, golf club] fer *m* **2.** [for clothes] fer *m* à repasser.
■ **vt** repasser.
◆ ***iron out*** **vt sep** *fig* [difficulties] aplanir / [problems] résoudre.

Iron Age ■ **n : the Iron Age** l'âge de fer.
■ **comp** de l'âge de fer.

Iron Curtain **n : the Iron Curtain** le rideau de fer.

ironic(al) [aɪ'rɒnɪk(l)] **adj** ironique.

ironically [aɪ'rɒnɪklɪ] **adv** ironiquement.

ironing ['aɪənɪŋ] **n** repassage *m* ▸ **to do the ironing** faire le repassage.

ironing board **n** planche *f* *OR* table *f* à repasser.

iron lung **n** poumon *m* d'acier.

ironmonger ['aɪən,mʌŋgəʳ] **n** *UK dated* quincaillier *m* ▸ **ironmonger's (shop)** quincaillerie *f*.

ironworks ['aɪənwɜ:ks] (pl **ironworks**) **n** usine *f* sidérurgique.

irony ['aɪrənɪ] (pl **-ies**) **n** ironie *f*.

irradiate [ɪ'reɪdɪeɪt] **vt** irradier.

irrational [ɪ'ræʃənl] **adj** irrationnel(elle), déraisonnable / [person] non rationnel(elle).

irrationality [ɪ,ræʃə'nælətɪ] **n** irrationalité *f*.

irrationally [ɪ'ræʃnəlɪ] **adv** irrationnellement.

irreconcilable [ɪ,rekən'saɪləbl] **adj** inconciliable.

irrecoverable [,ɪrɪ'kʌvərəbl] **adj 1.** [thing lost] irrécupérable / [debt] irrécouvrable **2.** [loss, damage, wrong] irréparable.

irredeemable [,ɪrɪ'di:məbl] **adj** *fml* **1.** [irreplaceable] irréparable **2.** [hopeless] irrémédiable.

irrefutable [ɪ'refjʊtəbl] **adj** irréfutable.

irregular [ɪ'regjʊləʳ] **adj** irrégulier(ère).

irregularity [ɪ,regjʊ'lærətɪ] (pl **-ies**) **n** irrégularité *f*.

irregularly [ɪ'regjʊləlɪ] **adv** irrégulièrement.

irrelevance [ɪ'reləvəns], ***irrelevancy*** [ɪ'reləvənsɪ] (pl **-ies**) **n** manque *m* de pertinence.

irrelevant [ɪ'reləvənt] **adj** sans rapport.

irreligious [ˌɪrɪ'lɪdʒəs] **adj** irréligieux(euse).

irremediable [ˌɪrɪ'miːdjəbl] **adj** *fml* irrémédiable.

irreparable [ɪ'repərəbl] **adj** irréparable.

irreplaceable [ˌɪrɪ'pleɪsəbl] **adj** irremplaçable.

irrepressible [ˌɪrɪ'presəbl] **adj** [enthusiasm] que rien ne peut entamer ▸ **he's irrepressible** il est d'une bonne humeur à toute épreuve.

irreproachable [ˌɪrɪ'prəʊtʃəbl] **adj** irréprochable.

irresistible [ˌɪrɪ'zɪstəbl] **adj** irrésistible.

irresistibly [ˌɪrɪ'zɪstəblɪ] **adv** irrésistiblement.

irresolute [ɪ'rezəluːt] **adj** *fml* irrésolu(e), indécis(e).

irrespective [ˌɪrɪ'spektɪv] ◆ ***irrespective of*** **prep** sans tenir compte de.

irresponsible [ˌɪrɪ'spɒnsəbl] **adj** irresponsable.

irretrievable [ˌɪrɪ'triːvəbl] **adj** irréparable, irrémédiable.

irretrievably [ˌɪrɪ'triːvəblɪ] **adv** irréparablement, irrémédiablement ▸ **irretrievably lost** perdu(e) pour toujours ***OR*** à tout jamais.

irreverence [ɪ'revərəns] **n** irrévérence *f*.

irreverent [ɪ'revərənt] **adj** irrévérencieux(euse).

irreversible [ˌɪrɪ'vɜːsəbl] **adj** [judgement, decision] irrévocable / [change, damage] irréversible.

irrevocable [ɪ'revəkəbl] **adj** irrévocable.

irrigate ['ɪrɪgeɪt] **vt** irriguer.

irrigation [ˌɪrɪ'geɪʃn] ■ **n** irrigation *f*.
■ **comp** d'irrigation.

irritable ['ɪrɪtəbl] **adj** irritable.

irritable bowel syndrome **n** syndrome *m* du côlon irritable.

irritably ['ɪrɪtəblɪ] **adv** avec irritation.

irritant ['ɪrɪtənt] ■ **adj** irritant(e).
■ **n 1.** [irritating situation] source *f* d'irritation **2.** [substance] irritant *m*.

irritate ['ɪrɪteɪt] **vt** irriter.

irritated ['ɪrɪteɪtɪd] **adj 1.** [annoyed] irrité(e), agacé(e) ▸ **don't get irritated!** ne t'énerve pas! **2.** MED [eyes, skin] irrité(e).

irritating ['ɪrɪteɪtɪŋ] **adj** irritant(e).

irritation [ɪrɪ'teɪʃn] **n 1.** [anger, soreness] irritation *f* **2.** [cause of anger] source *f* d'irritation.

IRS (abbr of ***Internal Revenue Service***) **n** *US* **: the IRS** ≃ le fisc.

is [ɪz] ➤ ***be***.

ISA (abbr of ***individual savings account***) **n** *UK* ≃ PEA *m* *(plan d'épargne en actions)*.

ISBN (abbr of ***International Standard Book Number***) **n** ISBN *m*.

ISDN (abbr of ***integrated services digital network***) ■ **n** COMPUT RNIS *m (réseau numérique à intégration de services)*.
■ **vt : to ISDN sth** *inf* envoyer qch par RNIS.

ISDN card **n** COMPUT carte *f* RNIS.

ISDN line **n** COMPUT ligne *f* RNIS.

ISDN modem **n** COMPUT modem *m* RNIS ***OR*** Numéris.

Islam ['ɪzlɑːm] **n** islam *m*.

Islamabad [ɪz'lɑːməbæd] **n** Islamabad.

Islamic [ɪz'læmɪk] **adj** islamique.

Islamic fundamentalist **n** fondamentaliste *mf* islamiste.

Islamist ['ɪzləmɪst] **adj & n** islamiste *mf*.

island ['aɪlənd] **n 1.** [isle] île *f* **2.** AUT refuge *m* pour piétons.

islander ['aɪləndəʳ] **n** habitant *m*, -e *f* d'une île.

isle [aɪl] **n** île *f*.

Isle of Man **n : the Isle of Man** l'île *f* de Man ▸ **in *OR* on the Isle of Man** à l'île de Man.

Isle of Wight [-waɪt] **n : the Isle of Wight** l'île *f* de Wight ▸ **on the Isle of Wight** à l'île de Wight.

isn't ['ɪznt] = ***is not***.

ISO (abbr of ***International Standards Organisation***) **n** ISO *f*.

isobar ['aɪsəbɑːʳ] **n** isobare *f*.

isolate ['aɪsəleɪt] **vt : to isolate sb/sthg (from)** isoler qqn/qqch (de).

isolated ['aɪsəleɪtɪd] **adj** isolé(e).

isolation [aɪsə'leɪʃn] **n** isolement *m* ▸ **in isolation** [alone] dans l'isolement / [separately] isolément.

isolationism [ˌaɪsə'leɪʃənɪzm] **n** isolationnisme *m*.

isosceles triangle [aɪ'sɒsɪliːz-] **n** triangle *m* isocèle.

isotope ['aɪsətəʊp] **n** isotope *m*.

ISP **n** abbr of ***Internet Service Provider***.

Israel ['ɪzreɪəl] **n** Israël *m* ▸ **in Israel** en Israël.

Israeli [ɪz'reɪlɪ] ■ **adj** israélien(enne).
■ **n** Israélien *m*, -enne *f*.

Israelite ['ɪzˌrɪəlaɪt] ■ **adj** israélite.
■ **n** Israélite *mf*.

issue ['ɪʃuː] ■ **n 1.** [important subject] question *f*, problème *m* / *pej* **: to make an issue of sthg** faire toute une affaire de qqch ▸ **where do you stand on the abortion issue?** quel est votre point de vue sur (la question de) l'avortement? ▸ **that's not the issue** il ne s'agit pas de ça ▸ **the important issues of the day** les grands problèmes du moment ▸ **to cloud *OR* confuse the issue** brouiller les cartes ▸ **the subject has now become a real issue between us** ce sujet est maintenant source de désaccord entre nous ▸ **to take issue with sb/sthg** être en désaccord avec qqn/qqch ▸ **at issue** en question, en cause
2. [edition] numéro *m* ▸ **the latest issue of the magazine** le dernier numéro du magazine
3. [bringing out - of banknotes, shares] émission *f* ▸ **date of issue** date *f* de délivrance ▸ **army issue** modèle *m* de l'armée ▸ **standard issue** modèle *m* standard.
■ **vt 1.** [make public - decree, statement] faire / [- warning] lancer
2. [bring out - banknotes, shares] émettre / [- book] publier
3. [passport] délivrer ▸ **to issue sthg to sb, to issue sb with sthg** fournir qqch à qqn ▸ **we were all issued with rations** on nous a distribué à tous des rations.

■ vi 1. [smoke, steam] : **to issue from** sortir de, s'échapper de
2. [problems] : **to issue from** découler de.

Istanbul [ˌɪstæn'bʊl] n Istanbul.

ISTC (abbr of ***Iron and Steels Confederation***) n *syndicat britannique des ouvriers de la sidérurgie*.

isthmus ['ɪsməs] n isthme *m*.

it [ɪt] ■ **pron 1.** [referring to specific person or thing - subj] il (elle) / [- direct object] le (la), l' *(+ vowel or silent 'h')* / [- indirect object] lui ▸ **did you find it?** tu l'as trouvé(e) ? ▸ **give it to me at once** donne-moi ça tout de suite ▸ **give it a shake** secoue-le ▸ **is it a boy or a girl?** c'est un garçon ou une fille?
2. [with prepositions] : **he told me all about it** il m'a tout raconté ▸ **there was nothing inside it** il n'y avait rien dedans *OR* à l'intérieur ▸ **put the vegetables in it** mettez-y les légumes ▸ **on it** dessus ▸ **under it** dessous ▸ **beside it** à côté ▸ **from/of it** en ▸ **he's very proud of it** il en est très fier
3. [impersonal use] il, ce ▸ **it is cold today** il fait froid aujourd'hui ▸ **it's raining/snowing** il pleut/neige ▸ **it's 500 miles from here to Vancouver** Vancouver est à 800 kilomètres d'ici ▸ **it's two o'clock** il est deux heures ▸ **who is it? it's Mary/me** qui est-ce ? c'est Mary/moi ▸ **I like it here** je me plais beaucoup ici ▸ **I couldn't bear it if she left** je ne supporterais pas qu'elle parte ▸ **it's the children who worry me most** ce sont les enfants qui m'inquiètent le plus ▸ **it's a goal!** but!
■ n *inf* **1.** [in games] : **you're it!** c'est toi le chat!, c'est toi qui y es!
2. [most important person] : **he thinks he's it** il s'y croit.

IT n abbr of ***information technology***.

Italian [ɪ'tæljən] ■ **adj** italien(enne).
■ **n 1.** [person] Italien *m*, -enne *f* **2.** [language] italien *m*.

italic [ɪ'tælɪk] **adj** italique.
◆ ***italics*** **npl** italiques *fpl*.

italicize, -ise *UK* [ɪ'tælɪsaɪz] vt mettre en italique ▸ **the italicized words** les mots en italique.

Italy ['ɪtəlɪ] n Italie *f* ▸ **in Italy** en Italie.

itch [ɪtʃ] ■ n démangeaison *f*.
■ vi **1.** [be itchy] : **my arm itches** mon bras me démange **2.** *fig* [be impatient] : **to be itching to do sthg** mourir d'envie de faire qqch.

itching ['ɪtʃɪŋ] n démangeaison *f*.

itchy ['ɪtʃɪ] (comp -ier, superl -iest) **adj** qui démange.

it'd ['ɪtəd] = ***it would, it had***.

item ['aɪtəm] **n 1.** [gen] chose *f*, article *m* / [on agenda] question *f*, point *m* **2.** PRESS article *m*.

itemize, *UK* **-ise** ['aɪtəmaɪz] vt détailler.

itemized bill, *UK* **itemised bill** ['aɪtəmaɪzd-] n facture *f* détaillée.

itinerant [ɪ'tɪnərənt] **adj** [salesperson] ambulant(e) / [preacher] itinérant(e).

itinerary [aɪ'tɪnərərɪ] (pl **-ies**) n itinéraire *m*.

it'll [ɪtl] = ***it will***.

ITN (abbr of ***Independent Television News***) n *service britannique d'actualités télévisées pour les chaînes relevant de l'IBA*.

its [ɪts] **poss adj** son (sa), ses *(pl)*.

it's [ɪts] = ***it is, it has***.

itself [ɪt'self] **pron 1.** *(reflexive)* se / *(after prep)* soi **2.** *(for emphasis)* lui-même(elle-même) ▸ **in itself** en soi.

ITV (abbr of ***Independent Television***) n *sigle désignant les programmes diffusés par les chaînes relevant de l'IBA*.

IUCD (abbr of ***intrauterine contraceptive device***) n stérilet *m*.

IUD (abbr of ***intrauterine device***) n stérilet *m*.

I've [aɪv] = ***I have***.

IVF (abbr of ***in vitro fertilization***) n FIV *f*.

ivory ['aɪvərɪ] ■ **adj** [ivory-coloured] ivoire *(inv)*.
■ n ivoire *m*.
■ **comp** [made of ivory] en ivoire, d'ivoire.

Ivory Coast n : **(the) Ivory Coast** la Côte-d'Ivoire ▸ **in (the) Ivory Coast** en Côte-d'Ivoire.

ivory tower n *fig* tour *f* d'ivoire.

ivy ['aɪvɪ] n lierre *m*.

Ivy League n *US les huit grandes universités de l'est des États-Unis*.

CULTURE

Ivy League

Le terme **Ivy League** désigne les plus prestigieuses universités américaines : Harvard, Yale, Princeton, Columbia, Dartmouth, Cornell, Brown et Pennsylvanie. Très sélectives, elles attirent les étudiants les plus brillants en raison de leur excellence académique et se classent parmi les plus grandes universités mondiales en termes de dotations financières (ces institutions privées reçoivent également d'importants fonds de recherche de la part du gouvernement fédéral). La plupart des Américains rêvent de pouvoir y inscrire leurs enfants car, à l'image des présidents George W. Bush et Kennedy, le fait d'avoir été admis dans l'un de ces établissements prouve que l'on fait partie de l'élite.

j [dʒeɪ] (pl j's ***OR*** js), ***J*** (pl J's ***OR*** Js) **n** [letter] j *m inv*, J *m inv*.

J/A abbr of ***joint account***.

jab [dʒæb] ■ **n 1.** *UK inf* [injection] piqûre *f* **2.** [in boxing] direct *m*.
■ **vt** (pt & pp **-bed**, cont **-bing**) **: to jab sthg into** planter ***OR*** enfoncer qqch dans.
■ **vi** (pt & pp **-bed**, cont **-bing**) **: to jab at** [in boxing] envoyer un direct à.

jabber [ˈdʒæbəʳ] **vt** & **vi** baragouiner.

jack [dʒæk] **n 1.** [device] cric *m* **2.** [playing card] valet *m*.
◆ ***jack in*** **vt sep** *UK inf* laisser tomber, plaquer ▸ **he's jacked in his job** il a plaqué son boulot.
◆ ***jack up*** **vt sep 1.** [car] soulever avec un cric **2.** *fig* [prices] faire grimper.

jackal [ˈdʒækəl] **n** chacal *m*.

jackass [ˈdʒækæs] **n 1.** [donkey] âne *m*, baudet *m* **2.** *inf* [imbecile] imbécile *mf*.

jackdaw [ˈdʒækdɔː] **n** choucas *m*.

jacket [ˈdʒækɪt] **n 1.** [garment] veste *f* **2.** [of potato] peau *f*, pelure *f* **3.** [of book] jaquette *f* **4.** *US* [of record] pochette *f*.

jacket potato **n** *UK* pomme de terre *f* en robe de chambre.

jackhammer [ˈdʒækˌhæməʳ] **n** *US* marteau piqueur *m*.

jack-in-the-box **n** diable *m* qui sort de sa boîte.

jackknife [ˈdʒæknaɪf] ■ **n** (pl **jackknives** [-naɪvz]) couteau *m* de poche.
■ **vi : the truck jackknifed** le camion s'est mis en travers de la route.

jack-of-all-trades (pl **jacks-of-all-trades**) **n** touche-à-tout *m*.

jack plug **n** *UK* ELEC jack *m*.

jackpot [ˈdʒækpɒt] **n** gros lot *m*.

Jacobean [ˌdʒækəˈbɪən] **adj** de l'époque de Jacques Ier.

Jacobite [ˈdʒækəbaɪt] ■ **adj** jacobite.
■ **n** jacobite *mf*.

Jacuzzi® [dʒəˈkuːzɪ] **n** Jacuzzi® *m*, bain *m* à remous.

jade [dʒeɪd] ■ **adj** [jade-coloured] vert (de) jade *(inv)*.
■ **n 1.** [stone] jade *m* **2.** [colour] vert *m* jade.
■ **comp** [made of jade] de jade *(inv)*.

jaded [ˈdʒeɪdɪd] **adj** blasé(e).

jagged [ˈdʒægɪd] **adj** déchiqueté(e), dentelé(e).

jaguar [ˈdʒægjʊəʳ] **n** jaguar *m*.

jail [dʒeɪl] ■ **n** prison *f*.
■ **vt** emprisonner, mettre en prison.

jailbait [ˈdʒeɪlbeɪt] **n** *(U) US inf* mineur *m*, -e *f* ▸ **she's jailbait** c'est un coup à se retrouver en taule *(pour détournement de mineur)*.

jailbird [ˈdʒeɪlbɜːd] **n** *inf* taulard *m*, -e *f*.

jailbreak [ˈdʒeɪlbreɪk] **n** évasion *f* de prison.

jailer [ˈdʒeɪləʳ] **n** geôlier *m*, -ère *f*.

jailhouse [ˈdʒeɪlhaʊs] (pl [-haʊzɪz]) **n** *US* prison *f*.

Jakarta [dʒəˈkɑːtə] **n** Djakarta, Jakarta.

jalapeño [dʒæləˈpiːnəʊ] **n** petit piment *m* vert.

jam [dʒæm] ■ **n 1.** [preserve] confiture *f* **2.** [of traffic] embouteillage *m*, bouchon *m* **3.** *inf* [difficult situation] **: to get into/be in a jam** se mettre/être dans le pétrin.
■ **vt** (pt & pp **-med**, cont **-ming**) **1.** [mechanism, door] bloquer, coincer **2.** [push tightly] **: to jam sthg into** entasser ***OR*** tasser qqch dans ▸ **to jam sthg onto** enfoncer qqch sur **3.** [block - streets] embouteiller / [- switchboard] surcharger **4.** RADIO brouiller.
■ **vi** (pt & pp **-med**, cont **-ming**) [lever, door] se coincer / [brakes] se bloquer.

Jamaica [dʒəˈmeɪkə] **n** Jamaïque *f* ▸ **in Jamaica** à la Jamaïque.

Jamaican [dʒəˈmeɪkn] ■ **adj** jamaïcain(e), jamaïquain(e).
■ **n** Jamaïcain *m*, -e *f*, Jamaïquain *m*, -e *f*.

jamb [dʒæm] **n** chambranle *m*, montant *m*.

jamboree [ˌdʒæmbəˈriː] **n 1.** [celebration] fête *f*, festivités *fpl* **2.** [gathering of scouts] jamboree *m*.

jamjar [ˈdʒæmdʒɑːʳ] **n** pot *m* à confiture.

jamming [ˈdʒæmɪŋ] **n** RADIO brouillage *m*.

jammy [ˈdʒæmɪ] (comp **-ier**, superl **-iest**) **adj** *inf* **1.** [sticky with jam] poisseux(euse) ▸ **jammy fingers** des doigts poisseux de confiture **2.** *UK* [lucky] chanceux(euse) ▸ **you jammy beggar!** espèce de veinard!

jam-packed [-'pækt] **adj** *inf* plein(e) à craquer.

jam session **n** bœuf *m*, jam-session *f*.

Jan. ['dʒæn] (abbr of ***January***) janv.

jangle ['dʒæŋgl] ■ **n** [of keys] cliquetis *m* / [of bells] tintamarre *m*.
■ **vt** [keys] faire cliqueter / [bells] faire retentir.
■ **vi** [keys] cliqueter / [bells] retentir.

janitor ['dʒænɪtəʳ] **n** *US* & *Scot* concierge *mf*.

January ['dʒænjʊərɪ] **n** janvier *m* ; see also ***September***.

Japan [dʒə'pæn] **n** Japon *m* ▸ **in Japan** au Japon.

Japanese [ˌdʒæpə'ni:z] ■ **adj** japonais(e).
■ **n** (pl **Japanese**) [language] japonais *m*.
■ **npl** [people] **: the Japanese** les Japonais *mpl*.

jape [dʒeɪp] **n** *dated* tour *m*, farce *f*.

jar [dʒɑ:ʳ] ■ **n** pot *m*.
■ **vt** (pt & pp **-red**, cont **-ring**) [shake] secouer.
■ **vi** (pt & pp **-red**, cont **-ring**) **1.** [noise, voice] **: to jar (on sb)** irriter (qqn), agacer (qqn) **2.** [colours] jurer.

jargon ['dʒɑ:gən] **n** jargon *m*.

jarring ['dʒɑ:rɪŋ] **adj** [noise, colours] discordant(e).

Jas. (abbr of ***James***) Jacques.

jasmine ['dʒæzmɪn] **n** jasmin *m*.

jaundice ['dʒɔ:ndɪs] **n** jaunisse *f*.

jaundiced ['dʒɔ:ndɪst] **adj** *fig* [attitude, view] aigri(e).

jaunt [dʒɔ:nt] **n** balade *f*.

jauntily ['dʒɔ:ntɪlɪ] **adv** [cheerfully] joyeusement, jovialement / [in a sprightly way] lestement.

jaunty ['dʒɔ:ntɪ] (comp **-ier**, superl **-iest**) **adj** désinvolte, insouciant(e).

Java ['dʒɑ:və] **n** Java ▸ **in Java** à Java.

Java script **n** COMPUT (langage *m*) Javascript *m*.

javelin ['dʒævlɪn] **n** javelot *m*.

jaw [dʒɔ:] ■ **n** mâchoire *f*.
■ **vi** *inf* tailler une bavette.

jawbone ['dʒɔ:bəʊn] **n** (os *m*) maxillaire *m*.

jay [dʒeɪ] **n** geai *m*.

jaywalk ['dʒeɪwɔ:k] **vi** traverser en dehors des clous.

jaywalker ['dʒeɪwɔ:kəʳ] **n** piéton *m* qui traverse en dehors des clous.

jazz [dʒæz] **n** **1.** MUS jazz *m* **2.** *US inf* [insincere talk] baratin *m*.
◆ ***jazz up*** **vt sep** *inf* égayer.

jazz band **n** orchestre *m* de jazz.

jazz singer **n** chanteur *m*, -euse *f* de jazz.

jazzy ['dʒæzɪ] (comp **-ier**, superl **-iest**) **adj** *inf* [bright] voyant(e).

JCR (abbr of ***junior common room***) **n** *salle des étudiants*.

JCS **n** abbr of ***Joint Chiefs of Staff***.

JD (abbr of ***Justice Department***) **n** *ministère américain de la Justice*.

jealous ['dʒeləs] **adj** jaloux(ouse).

jealously ['dʒeləslɪ] **adv** jalousement.

jealousy ['dʒeləsɪ] **n** jalousie *f*.

jeans [dʒi:nz] **npl** jean *m*, blue-jean *m*.

Jedda ['dʒedə] **n** Djedda.

Jeep® [dʒi:p] **n** Jeep® *f*.

jeer [dʒɪəʳ] ■ **vt** huer, conspuer.
■ **vi : to jeer (at sb)** huer (qqn), conspuer (qqn).
◆ ***jeers*** **npl** huées *fpl*.

jeering ['dʒɪərɪŋ] **adj** moqueur(euse), railleur(euse).

Jehovah's Witness [dʒɪˌhəʊvəz-] **n** témoin *m* de Jéhovah.

Jell-O® ['dʒeləʊ] **n** *US* gelée *f*.

jelly ['dʒelɪ] **n** (pl **jellies**) **1.** *UK* gelée *f* **2.** *esp US* [jam] confiture *f*.

jelly baby **n** *UK bonbon à la gélatine en forme de bébé*.

jelly bean **n** *bonbon à la gélatine couvert de sucre*.

jellyfish ['dʒelɪfɪʃ] (pl **jellyfish** *OR* **-es** [-i:z]) **n** méduse *f*.

jelly roll **n** *US* gâteau *m* roulé.

jemmy *UK* ['dʒemɪ], ***jimmy*** *US* ['dʒɪmɪ] (pl **-ies**) **n** pince-monseigneur *f*.

jeopardize, *UK* ***-ise*** ['dʒepədaɪz] **vt** compromettre, mettre en danger.

jeopardy ['dʒepədɪ] **n : in jeopardy** en péril *OR* danger, menacé(e).

jerk [dʒɜ:k] ■ **n** **1.** [movement] secousse *f*, saccade *f* **2.** *inf* [fool] abruti *m*, -e *f*.
■ **vt : he jerked his head around** il tourna la tête brusquement ▸ **he jerked the door open** il ouvrit la porte d'un coup sec.
■ **vi** [person] sursauter / [vehicle] cahoter.

jerkily ['dʒɜ:kɪlɪ] **adv** par à-coups, par saccades.

jerkin ['dʒɜ:kɪn] **n** blouson *m*.

jerky ['dʒɜ:kɪ] (comp **-ier**, superl **-iest**) **adj** saccadé(e).

jerry-built ['dʒerɪ-] **adj** *inf pej* construit(e) à la va-vite.

jersey ['dʒɜ:zɪ] (pl **-s**) **n** **1.** [sweater] pull *m* **2.** [cloth] jersey *m*.

Jersey ['dʒɜ:zɪ] **n** **1.** *UK* Jersey *f* ▸ **in Jersey** à Jersey **2.** *US* New-Jersey *m*.

Jerusalem [dʒə'ru:sələm] **n** Jérusalem.

Jerusalem artichoke **n** topinambour *m*.

jest [dʒest] **n** *fml* plaisanterie *f* ▸ **in jest** pour rire.

jester ['dʒesteʳ] **n** bouffon *m*.

Jesuit ['dʒezjʊɪt] ■ **adj** jésuite.
■ **n** jésuite *m*.

Jesus (Christ) ['dʒi:zəs-] **n** Jésus *m*, Jésus-Christ *m*.

jet [dʒet] ■ **n** **1.** [plane] jet *m*, avion *m* à réaction **2.** [of fluid] jet *m* **3.** [nozzle, outlet] ajutage *m*.
■ **vi** (pt & pp **-ted**, cont **-ting**) [travel by jet] voyager en jet *OR* en avion.

jet-black **adj** noir(e) comme (du) jais.

jet engine **n** moteur *m* à réaction.

jetfoil ['dʒetfɔɪl] **n** hydroglisseur *m*.

jet lag **n** fatigue *f* due au décalage horaire.

jet-lagged [-lægd] **adj** fatigué(e) par le décalage horaire ▸ **I'm still a bit jet-lagged** je ne suis pas complètement remis du décalage horaire.

jet-propelled [-prəˈpeld] **adj** à réaction.

jetsam [ˈdʒetsəm] ➤ ***flotsam***.

jet set **n : the jet set** le jet-set.

jet-setter **n** *inf* membre *m* du jet-set.

jetski [ˈdʒetski] **n** scooter *m* de mer, jetski *m*.

jettison [ˈdʒetɪsən] **vt 1.** [cargo] jeter, larguer **2.** *fig* [ideas] abandonner, renoncer à.

jetty [ˈdʒetɪ] (pl **-ies**) **n** jetée *f*.

Jew [dʒuː] **n** Juif *m*, -ive *f*.

jewel [ˈdʒuːəl] ■ **n** bijou *m* / [in watch] rubis *m*.
■ **comp** [box, chest] à bijoux.

jewel case **n** boîte *f* de CD.

jewelled *UK*, ***jeweled*** *US* [ˈdʒuːəld] **adj** orné(e) de bijoux / [watch] à rubis.

jeweller *UK*, ***jeweler*** *US* [ˈdʒuːələʳ] **n** bijoutier *m*, -ière *f* ▸ **jeweller's (shop)** *UK* bijouterie *f*.

jewellery *UK*, ***jewelry*** *US* [ˈdʒuːəlrɪ] **n** *(U)* bijoux *mpl*.

jewelry store *US* **n** bijouterie *f*.

Jewess [ˈdʒuːɪs] **n** juive *f*.

Jewish [ˈdʒuːɪʃ] **adj** juif(ive).

JFK (abbr of ***John Fitzgerald Kennedy International Airport***) **n** *aéroport de New York*.

jib [dʒɪb] **n 1.** [of crane] flèche *f* **2.** [sail] foc *m*.
◆ ***jib at*** **vi** (pt & pp **-bed at**, cont **-bing at**) [person] **: to jib at sthg** [person] rechigner à faire qqch / [horse] regimber devant qqch.

jibe [dʒaɪb] **n** sarcasme *m*, moquerie *f*.

Jidda [ˈdʒɪdə] = ***Jedda***.

jiffy [ˈdʒɪfɪ] **n** *inf* **: in a jiffy** en un clin d'œil.

Jiffy bag® **n** *UK* enveloppe *f* matelassée.

jig [dʒɪg] ■ **n** gigue *f*.
■ **vi** (pt & pp **-ged**, cont **-ging**) danser la gigue ▸ **to jig around** se trémousser.

jiggle [ˈdʒɪgl] **vt** secouer.

jigsaw (puzzle) [ˈdʒɪgsɔː-] **n** puzzle *m*.

jihad [dʒɪˈhɑːd] **n** djihad *m*.

jilt [dʒɪlt] **vt** laisser tomber.

jimmy *US* = ***jemmy***.

jingle [ˈdʒɪŋgl] ■ **n 1.** [sound] cliquetis *m* **2.** [song] jingle *m*, indicatif *m*.
■ **vi** [bell] tinter / [coins, bracelets] cliqueter.

jingoism [ˈdʒɪŋgəʊɪzm] **n** *pej* chauvinisme *m*.

jingoistic [ˌdʒɪŋgəʊˈɪstɪk] **adj** *pej* chauvin(e), cocardier(ère).

jinx [dʒɪŋks] **n** poisse *f*.

jinxed [dʒɪŋkst] **adj** qui a la poisse.

JIT (abbr of ***just in time***) **adj** JAT, juste à temps.

JIT distribution **n** distribution *f* JAT.

JIT production **n** production *f* JAT.

JIT purchasing **n** achat *m* JAT.

jitters [ˈdʒɪtəz] **npl** *inf* **: the jitters** le trac.

jittery [ˈdʒɪtərɪ] **adj** *inf* nerveux(euse).

jiu-jitsu [dʒuːˈdʒɪtsuː] = ***jujitsu***.

jive [dʒaɪv] ■ **n 1.** [dance] rock *m* **2.** *US inf dated* [glib talk] baratin *m*.
■ **vi** danser le rock.

job [dʒɒb] **n 1.** [employment] emploi *m* ▸ **to find a job** trouver du travail OR un emploi ▸ **to look for a job** chercher un emploi OR du travail ▸ **to be out of a job** être sans emploi OR au chômage ▸ **a Saturday/summer job** un boulot OR un job pour le samedi/l'été ▸ **she's got a very good job** elle a une très bonne situation OR place ▸ **he took a job as a rep** il a pris un emploi de représentant ▸ **hundreds of jobs have been lost** des centaines d'emplois ont été supprimés, des centaines de personnes ont été licenciées
2. [task] travail *m*, tâche *f* ▸ **to do a good job** faire du bon travail ▸ **to make a good job of sthg** faire bien OR réussir qqch ▸ **try to do a better job next time** essayez de faire mieux la prochaine fois ▸ **it's not my job to...** ce n'est pas à moi de... ▸ **she had the job of breaking the bad news** c'est elle qui était chargée d'annoncer les mauvaises nouvelles ▸ **it's not perfect but it does the job** ce n'est pas parfait mais ça fera l'affaire
3. [difficult task] **: to have a job doing sthg** avoir du mal à faire qqch
4. [state of affairs] **: it's a good job they were home** heureusement qu'ils étaient à la maison ▸ **thanks for the map, it's just the job** merci pour la carte, c'est exactement ce qu'il me fallait ▸ **to give sb/sthg up as a bad job** laisser tomber qqn/qqch qui n'en vaut pas la peine ▸ **we decided to make the best of a bad job** nous avons décidé de faire avec ce que nous avions
5. *inf* [crime] coup *m* ▸ **to pull a job** faire un casse
6. COMPUT tâche *f*
7. *inf* [plastic surgery] **: to have a nose job** se faire refaire le nez.

job action **n** *US* = ***industrial action***.

jobbing [ˈdʒɒbɪŋ] **adj** *UK* qui travaille à la tâche.

job centre **n** *UK* agence *f* pour l'emploi.

job creation **n** création *f* d'emplois.

job creation scheme **n** *UK* plan *m* de création d'emplois.

job description **n** profil *m* du poste.

jobholder [ˈdʒɒbˌhəʊldəʳ] **n** salarié *m*, -e *f*.

jobhunter [ˈdʒɒbˌhʌntə] = ***jobseeker***.

job hunting **n** recherche *f* d'un emploi ▸ **to go/to be job hunting** aller/être à la recherche d'un emploi.

jobless [ˈdʒɒblɪs] ■ **adj** au chômage.
■ **npl : the jobless** les chômeurs *mpl*.

job lot **n** lot *m* de marchandises.

job satisfaction **n** satisfaction *f* dans le travail.

job security **n** sécurité *f* de l'emploi.

job seeker **n** *UK fml* demandeur *m* d'emploi.

Job Seekers Allowance **n** *UK* indemnité *f* de chômage.

jobsharing [ˈdʒɒbʃeərɪŋ] **n** partage *m* de l'emploi.

jobsworth ['dʒɒbzwəθ] **n** *UK inf* petit chef *m* *(qui invoque le règlement pour éviter toute initiative).*

Joburg, Jo'burg ['dʒəʊbɜːg] **n** *inf* Johannesburg.

jock [dʒɒk] **n** *inf* **1.** *US* [sporty type] sportif *m* **2.** [jockey] jockey *m* **3.** [disc jockey] disc-jockey *m.*

jockey ['dʒɒkɪ] (pl -s) ■ **n** jockey *mf.*
■ **vi : to jockey for position** manœuvrer pour devancer ses concurrents.

Jockey shorts® **npl** slip *m* kangourou.

jockstrap ['dʒɒkstræp] **n** suspensoir *m.*

jocular ['dʒɒkjʊlər] **adj** *fml* **1.** [cheerful] enjoué(e), jovial(e) **2.** [funny] amusant(e).

jodhpurs ['dʒɒdpəz] **npl** jodhpurs *mpl*, culotte *f* de cheval.

Joe Bloggs [-blɒgz] *UK*, ***Joe Blow*** *US & Aus* **n** *inf* Monsieur Tout le Monde.

Joe Public [dʒəʊ-] **n** *UK* l'homme *m* de la rue.

jog [dʒɒg] ■ **n : to go for a jog** faire du jogging.
■ **vt** (pt & pp **-ged**, cont **-ging**) pousser ▸ **to jog sb's memory** rafraîchir la mémoire de qqn.
■ **vi** (pt & pp **-ged**, cont **-ging**) faire du jogging, jogger.

jogger ['dʒɒgər] **n** joggeur *m*, -euse *f.*

jogging ['dʒɒgɪŋ] **n** jogging *m.*

joggle ['dʒɒgl] **vt** secouer.

Johannesburg [dʒə'hænɪsbɜːg] **n** Johannesburg.

john [dʒɒn] **n** *US inf* petit coin *m*, cabinets *mpl.*

John Hancock [-'hænkɒk] **n** *US inf* signature *f.*

join [dʒɔɪn] ■ **n** raccord *m*, joint *m.*
■ **vt 1.** [connect - gen] unir, joindre / [- towns] relier ▸ **the workmen joined the pipes (together)** les ouvriers ont raccordé les tuyaux ▸ **we camped where the stream joins the river** nous avons campé là où le ruisseau rejoint la rivière ▸ **to join hands** [- in prayer] joindre les mains / [- link hands] se donner la main ▸ **to be joined in marriage** *OR* **matrimony** être uni(e) par les liens du mariage ▸ **we must join forces (against the enemy)** nous devons unir nos forces (contre l'ennemi) **2.** [get together with] rejoindre, retrouver ▸ **they joined us for lunch** ils nous ont retrouvés pour déjeuner ▸ **will you join me for** *OR* **in a drink?** vous prendrez bien un verre avec moi? **3.** [political party] devenir membre de / [club] s'inscrire à / [army] s'engager dans ▸ **to join a queue** *UK*, **to join a line** *US* prendre la queue ▸ **so you've been burgled too? join the club!** alors, toi aussi tu as été cambriolé? bienvenue au club!
■ **vi 1.** [connect] se joindre **2.** [become a member - gen] devenir membre / [- of club] s'inscrire.
◆ ***join in*** ■ **vt insep** prendre part à, participer à ▸ **he joined in the protest** il s'associa aux protestations ▸ **all join in the chorus!** reprenez tous le refrain en chœur!
■ **vi** participer ▸ **she started singing and the others joined in** elle a commencé à chanter et les autres se sont mis à chanter avec elle.
◆ ***join up*** **vi 1.** MIL s'engager dans l'armée **2.** [meet] **: to join up with sb** rejoindre qqn.

joined-up [dʒɔɪnd-] **adj : can you do joined-up writing yet?** tu sais lier les lettres?

joiner ['dʒɔɪnər] **n** *UK* menuisier *m*, -ière *f.*

joinery ['dʒɔɪnərɪ] **n** *UK* menuiserie *f.*

joint [dʒɔɪnt] ■ **adj** [effort] conjugué(e) / [responsibility] collectif(ive) ▸ **to take joint action** mener une action commune ▸ **joint custody** LAW garde *f* conjointe.
■ **n 1.** [gen & TECH] joint *m* **2.** ANAT articulation *f* ▸ **to put one's shoulder out of joint** se démettre *OR* se déboîter l'épaule **3.** [of meat] rôti *m* **4.** *inf* [place] bouge *m* **5.** *drug sl* joint *m.*

joint account **n** compte *m* joint.

Joint Chiefs of Staff **npl : the Joint Chiefs of Staff** *l'organe consultatif du ministère américain de la Défense, composé des chefs d'état-major des trois armées.*

jointed ['dʒɔɪntɪd] **adj** articulé(e).

join-the-dots **n** *(U) UK jeu qui consiste à relier des points numérotés pour découvrir un dessin.*

jointly ['dʒɔɪntlɪ] **adv** conjointement.

joint ownership **n** copropriété *f.*

joint-stock company **n** *US* société *f* anonyme par actions.

joint venture **n** joint-venture *m.*

joist [dʒɔɪst] **n** poutre *f*, solive *f.*

jojoba [hə'həʊbə] **n** jojoba *m.*

joke [dʒəʊk] ■ **n** blague *f*, plaisanterie *f* ▸ **we did it for a joke** nous l'avons fait pour rire *OR* pour rigoler ▸ **he's just a joke** il est un objet de risée ▸ **to play a joke on sb** faire une blague à qqn, jouer un tour à qqn ▸ **it's gone beyond a joke** ça commence à bien faire ▸ **it's no joke** *inf* [not easy] ce n'est pas de la tarte ▸ **he can't take a joke** il n'a pas le sens de l'humour.
■ **vi** plaisanter, blaguer ▸ **Tom's passed his driving test – you're joking!** Tom a eu son permis de conduire – sans blague! *OR* tu veux rire? ▸ **to joke about sthg** plaisanter sur qqch, se moquer de qqch.

joker ['dʒəʊkər] **n 1.** [person] blagueur *m*, -euse *f* **2.** [playing card] joker *m.*

jokey ['dʒəʊkɪ] (comp **-ier**, superl **-iest**) **adj** *inf* comique.

jokingly ['dʒəʊkɪŋlɪ] **adv** en plaisantant, pour plaisanter.

jollity ['dʒɒlətɪ] **n** *fml* jovialité *f*, gaieté *f.*

jolly ['dʒɒlɪ] ■ **adj** (comp **-ier**, superl **-iest**) [person] jovial(e), enjoué(e) / *dated* [time, party] agréable.
■ **adv** *UK inf dated* drôlement, rudement.

FALSE FRIENDS / FAUX AMIS

jolly

Joli n'est pas la traduction du mot anglais *jolly*. Joli se traduit par *pretty* ou *lovely*.
▸ Cette petite fille est très jolie / *She is a very pretty little girl*
▸ Elle a acheté un joli coussin en soie / *She bought a lovely silk cushion*

jolt [dʒəʊlt] ■ **n 1.** [jerk] secousse *f*, soubresaut *m* **2.** [shock] choc *m.*
■ **vt** secouer ▸ **to jolt sb into doing sthg** inciter fortement qqn à faire qqch.
■ **vi** cahoter.

Joneses ['dʒəʊnzɪz] **npl : to keep up with the Joneses** essayer d'avoir le même standing que ses voisins.

Jordan ['dʒɔ:dn] **n** Jordanie *f* ▸ **in Jordan** en Jordanie ▸ **the Jordan (River)** le Jourdain.

Jordanian [dʒɔ:'deɪnjən] ■ **adj** jordanien(enne).
■ **n** Jordanien *m*, -enne *f*.

joss stick [dʒɒs-] **n** bâton *m* d'encens.

jostle ['dʒɒsl] ■ **vt** bousculer.
■ **vi** se bousculer.

jot [dʒɒt] **n** [of truth] grain *m*, brin *m*.
◆ ***jot down*** (pt & pp **-ted**, cont **-ting**) **vt sep** noter, prendre note de.

jotter ['dʒɒtəʳ] **n** *UK* [exercise book] cahier *m*, carnet *m* / [pad] bloc-notes *m*.

jottings ['dʒɒtɪŋz] **npl** notes *fpl*.

joule [dʒu:l] **n** joule *m*.

journal ['dʒɜ:nl] **n 1.** [magazine] revue *f* **2.** [diary] journal *m*.

journalese [,dʒɜ:nə'li:z] **n** *pej* jargon *m* journalistique.

journalism ['dʒɜ:nəlɪzm] **n** journalisme *m*.

journalist ['dʒɜ:nəlɪst] **n** journaliste *mf*.

journey ['dʒɜ:nɪ] (pl **-s**) **n** voyage *m*.

FALSE FRIENDS / FAUX AMIS
journey

Journée n'est pas la traduction du mot anglais *journey*. Journée se traduit par *day*.
▸ J'ai eu une journée fatigante / *I've had an exhausting day*

joust [dʒaʊst] **vi** jouter.

jovial ['dʒəʊvjəl] **adj** jovial(e).

jowls [dʒaʊlz] **npl** bajoues *fpl*.

joy [dʒɔɪ] **n** joie *f*.

joyful ['dʒɔɪfʊl] **adj** joyeux(euse).

joyfully ['dʒɔɪfʊlɪ] **adv** joyeusement, avec joie.

joyless ['dʒɔɪlɪs] **adj** [unhappy] triste, sans joie / [dull] morne, maussade.

joyous ['dʒɔɪəs] **adj** *liter* joyeux(euse).

joyously ['dʒɔɪəslɪ] **adv** *liter* avec joie, joyeusement.

joyride ['dʒɔɪraɪd] **n** virée *f (dans une voiture volée)*.

joyrider ['dʒɔɪraɪdəʳ] **n** *personne qui vole une voiture pour aller faire une virée*.

joystick ['dʒɔɪstɪk] **n** AERON manche *m* (à balai) / COMPUT manette *f*.

JP **n** abbr of ***Justice of the Peace***.

JPEG ['dʒeɪpeg] (abbr of ***Joint Photographic Experts Group***) **n** COMPUT (format *m*) JPEG *m*.

Jr. (abbr of ***Junior***) Jr.

JSA **n** *UK* abbr of ***Job Seekers Allowance***.

JTPA (abbr of ***Job Training Partnership Act***) **n** *programme gouvernemental américain de formation*.

jubilant ['dʒu:bɪlənt] **adj** [person] débordant(e) de joie, qui jubile / [shout] de joie.

jubilation [,dʒu:bɪ'leɪʃn] **n** joie *f*, jubilation *f*.

jubilee ['dʒu:bɪli:] **n** jubilé *m*.

Judaism [dʒu:'deɪɪzm] **n** judaïsme *m*.

judder ['dʒʌdəʳ] **vi** trembler violemment.

judge [dʒʌdʒ] ■ **n** juge *mf*.
■ **vt 1.** [gen] juger **2.** [estimate] évaluer, juger.
■ **vi** juger ▸ **to judge from** OR **by, judging from** OR **by** à en juger par.

judg(e)ment ['dʒʌdʒmənt] **n** jugement *m* ▸ **to pass judgement (on)** LAW prononcer OR rendre un jugement (sur) / *fig* [on person, situation] porter un jugement (sur) ▸ **to reserve judgement** s'abstenir de donner son avis OR de porter un jugement ▸ **against my better judgement** sachant pertinemment que j'avais tort.

judg(e)mental [dʒʌdʒ'mentl] **adj** *pej* qui critique, qui porte des jugements.

judicial [dʒu:'dɪʃl] **adj** judiciaire.

judiciary [dʒu:'dɪʃərɪ] **n : the judiciary** la magistrature.

judicious [dʒu:'dɪʃəs] **adj** judicieux(euse).

judo ['dʒu:dəʊ] **n** judo *m*.

jug [dʒʌg] **n** *UK* pot *m*, pichet *m*.

juggernaut ['dʒʌgənɔ:t] **n** *UK* poids *m* lourd.

juggle ['dʒʌgl] ■ **vt** *lit* & *fig* jongler avec.
■ **vi** jongler.

juggler ['dʒʌgləʳ] **n** jongleur *m*, -euse *f*.

jugular (vein) ['dʒʌgjʊləʳ-] **n** (veine *f*) jugulaire *f*.

juice [dʒu:s] **n** jus *m*.
◆ ***juices*** **npl** [in stomach] sucs *mpl*.

juicer ['dʒu:səʳ] **n** presse-fruits *m inv*.

juicy ['dʒu:sɪ] (comp **-ier**, superl **-iest**) **adj 1.** [fruit] juteux(euse) **2.** *inf* [story] croustillant(e) **3.** [role] séduisant(e), tentant(e).

jujitsu [dʒu:'dʒɪtsu:] **n** jiu-jitsu *m inv*.

jukebox ['dʒu:kbɒks] **n** juke-box *m*.

Jul. (abbr of ***July***) juill.

July [dʒu:'laɪ] **n** juillet *m* ; see also ***September***.

jumble ['dʒʌmbl] ■ **n** [mixture] mélange *m*, fatras *m*.
■ **vt : to jumble (up)** mélanger, embrouiller.

jumble sale **n** *UK* vente *f* de charité *(où sont vendus des articles d'occasion)*.

jumbo ['dʒʌmbəʊ] (pl **-s**) ■ **n 1.** *inf* [elephant] éléphant *m*, pachyderme *m* **2.** = ***jumbo jet***.
■ **adj** énorme, géant(e).

jumbo jet ['dʒʌmbəʊ-] **n** jumbo-jet *m*.

jumbo-sized [-saɪzd] **adj** énorme, géant(e).

jump [dʒʌmp] ■ **n 1.** [leap] saut *m*, bond *m* **2.** [fence] obstacle *m* **3.** [rapid increase] flambée *f*, hausse *f* brutale ▸▸ **to keep one jump ahead of sb** avoir une longueur d'avance sur qqn.
■ **vt 1.** [fence, stream] sauter, franchir d'un bond **2.** *inf* [attack] sauter sur, tomber sur **3.** *inf* [leave] **: to jump ship** *lit* & *fig* quitter le navire **4.** [not wait one's turn at] **: to jump**

the queue UK ne pas attendre son tour, resquiller ▸ **she jumped the lights** elle a grillé *OR* brûlé le feu (rouge) **5.** *US* [train, bus] prendre sans payer.
■ vi **1.** [gen] sauter, bondir / [in surprise] sursauter ▸ **to jump across sthg** traverser qqch d'un bond ▸ **to jump to conclusions** tirer des conclusions hâtives ▸ **to jump down sb's throat** *inf* houspiller *OR* enguirlander qqn **2.** [increase rapidly] grimper en flèche, faire un bond.
◆ ***jump at*** vt insep *fig* sauter sur.

jumped-up ['dʒʌmpt-] adj *UK inf pej* prétentieux(euse).

jumper ['dʒʌmpəʳ] n **1.** *UK* [pullover] pull *m*, sweat *m inf* **2.** *US* [dress] robe *f* chasuble.

jumper cables npl *US* = ***jump leads***.

jumper leads npl *UK* & *Aus* = ***jump leads***.

jumping-off point, ***jumping-off place*** n point *m* de départ, tremplin *m*.

jump jet n avion *m* à décollage vertical.

jump leads npl *UK* câbles *mpl* de démarrage.

jump rope n *US* corde *f* à sauter.

jump-start vt **: to jump-start a car** faire démarrer une voiture en la poussant.

jumpsuit ['dʒʌmpsu:t] n combinaison-pantalon *f*.

jumpy ['dʒʌmpɪ] (comp -ier, superl -iest) adj *inf* nerveux(euse).

Jun. abbr of ***June***.

junction ['dʒʌŋkʃn] n *UK* [of roads] carrefour *m* / RAIL embranchement *m*.

junction box n *UK* ELEC boîte *f* d'accouplement.

juncture ['dʒʌŋktʃəʳ] n *fml* **: at this juncture** à ce moment même.

June [dʒu:n] n juin *m* ; see also ***September***.

jungle ['dʒʌŋgl] n *lit* & *fig* jungle *f*.

jungle gym n *US* [in playground] cage *f* d'écureuil.

junior ['dʒu:njəʳ] ■ adj **1.** [gen] jeune **2.** [after name] junior.
■ n **1.** [in rank] subalterne *mf* **2.** [in age] cadet *m*, -ette *f* **3.** *US* SCH ≃ élève *mf* de première **4.** *US* UNIV ≃ étudiant *m*, -e *f* de troisième année / ≃ étudiant *m*, -e *f* en licence.

junior college n *US établissement d'enseignement supérieur où l'on obtient un diplôme en deux ans.*

junior doctor n interne *mf*.

junior high school n *US* ≃ collège *m* d'enseignement secondaire.

junior minister n *UK* secrétaire *mf* d'État.

junior school n *UK* école *f* primaire.

juniper ['dʒu:nɪpəʳ] n genièvre *m*.

junk [dʒʌŋk] ■ n [unwanted objects] bric-à-brac *m*.
■ vt balancer, se débarrasser de.

junk e-mail n *pej* messages *mpl* publicitaires.

junket ['dʒʌŋkɪt] n **1.** [pudding] lait *m* caillé **2.** *inf pej* [trip] voyage *m* aux frais de la princesse.

junk food n *(U) pej* **: to eat junk food** manger des cochonneries.

junkie ['dʒʌŋkɪ] n *drug sl* drogué *m*, -e *f*.

junk mail n *(U) pej* prospectus *mpl* publicitaires envoyés par la poste.

junk shop n boutique *f* de brocanteur.

junkyard ['dʒʌŋkjɑ:d] n **1.** [for scrap metal] entrepôt *m* de ferraille ▸ **at the junkyard** chez le ferrailleur **2.** [for discarded objects] dépotoir *m*.

Junr (abbr of ***Junior***) Jr.

junta [*UK* 'dʒʌntə, *US* 'hʊntə] n junte *f*.

Jupiter ['dʒu:pɪtəʳ] n [planet] Jupiter *f*.

jurisdiction [ˌdʒʊərɪs'dɪkʃn] n juridiction *f*.

jurisprudence [ˌdʒʊərɪs'pru:dəns] n jurisprudence *f*.

juror ['dʒʊərəʳ] n juré *m*, -e *f*.

jury ['dʒʊərɪ] (pl -ies) n jury *m*.

jury box n banc *m* des jurés.

jury duty *US*, ***jury service*** *UK* n participation *f* à un jury.

jury-rigging n LAW truquage *m* d'un jury.

just [dʒʌst] ■ adv **1.** [recently] **: he's just left** il vient de partir ▸ **just last week** pas plus tard que la semaine dernière ▸ **she's just this moment** *OR* **minute left the office** elle vient de sortir du bureau à l'instant ▸ **he's just been to Mexico** il revient *OR* rentre du Mexique
2. [at that moment] **: I was just going to phone you** j'allais juste *OR* justement te téléphoner, j'étais sur le point de te téléphoner ▸ **I was just about to go** j'allais juste partir, j'étais sur le point de partir ▸ **I'm just going to do it now** je vais le faire tout de suite *OR* à l'instant ▸ **she arrived just as I was leaving** elle est arrivée au moment même où je partais *OR* juste comme je partais ▸ **I'm just off** *inf* je m'en vais ▸ **just coming!** *inf* j'arrive tout de suite!
3. [only, simply] **: just a little** juste un peu ▸ **it was just a dream** ce n'était qu'un rêve ▸ **we're just friends** nous sommes amis, c'est tout ▸ **he was just trying to help** il voulait juste *OR* simplement rendre service ▸ **if he could just work a little harder!** si seulement il pouvait travailler un peu plus! ▸ **just add water** vous n'avez plus qu'à ajouter de l'eau ▸ **don't argue, just do it!** ne discute pas, fais-le, c'est tout! ▸ **just a minute** *OR* **moment** *OR* **second!** un (petit) instant! ▸ **this is not just any horse race, this is the Derby!** ça n'est pas n'importe quelle course de chevaux, c'est le Derby!
4. [almost not] tout juste, à peine ▸ **I could just make out what they were saying** je parvenais tout juste à entendre ce qu'ils disaient ▸ **I only just missed the train** j'ai manqué le train de peu ▸ **we have just enough time** on a juste assez de temps ▸ **I may** *OR* **might just be able to do it** il n'est pas impossible que je puisse le faire ▸ **it's just after/before two o'clock** il est un peu plus/moins de deux heures
5. [for emphasis] **: the coast is just marvellous** la côte est vraiment magnifique ▸ **everything is just fine** tout est parfait ▸ **just think what might have happened!** imagine un

peu ce qui aurait pu arriver! ▸ **just look at this mess!** non, mais regarde un peu ce désordre! ▸ **it just isn't good enough** c'est loin d'être satisfaisant, c'est tout
6. [exactly, precisely] tout à fait, exactement ▸ **just at that moment** juste à ce moment-là ▸ **it's just what I need** c'est tout à fait ce qu'il me faut ▸ **just what are you getting at?** où veux-tu en venir exactement? ▸ **he's just like his father** c'est son père tout craché ▸ **you speak French just as well as I do** ton français est tout aussi bon que le mien ▸ **don't come in just yet** n'entre pas tout de suite
7. [in requests] **: could you just move over please?** pourriez-vous vous pousser un peu s'il vous plaît?
■ **adj** juste, équitable.
◆ ***just about*** **adv** à peu près, plus ou moins ▸ **can you reach the shelf? – just about!** est-ce que tu peux atteindre l'étagère? – (tout) juste! ▸ **their plane should be taking off just about now** leur avion devrait être sur le point de décoller ▸ **I've just about had enough of your sarcasm!** j'en ai franchement assez de tes sarcasmes!
◆ ***just as*** **adv 1.** [in comparison] tout aussi ▸ **you're just as clever as he is** tu es tout aussi intelligent que lui
2. [exactly as] **: just as I thought/predicted** comme je le pensais/prévoyais
3. [at the same time as] juste au moment où.
◆ ***just in case*** ■ **conj** juste au cas où ▸ **just in case we don't see each other** juste au cas où nous ne nous verrions pas.
■ **adv** au cas où ▸ **take a coat, just in case** prends un manteau, on ne sait jamais *OR* au cas où.
◆ ***just now*** **adv 1.** [a short time ago] il y a un moment, tout à l'heure ▸ **I heard a noise just now** je viens juste d'entendre un bruit ▸ **when did this happen? – just now** quand cela s'est-il passé? – à l'instant
2. [at this moment] en ce moment ▸ **I'm busy just now** je suis occupé pour le moment.
◆ ***just then*** **adv** à ce moment-là.
◆ ***just the same*** **adv** [nonetheless] quand même.

justice ['dʒʌstɪs] **n 1.** [gen] justice *f* **2.** [of claim, cause] bien-fondé *m*
▸▸ **to do justice to sthg** [job] faire bien qqch, faire qqch comme il faut ▸ **to do justice to a meal** faire honneur à un repas.

Justice of the Peace (pl **Justices of the Peace**) **n** juge *m* de paix.

justifiable ['dʒʌstɪfaɪəbl] **adj** justifiable, défendable.

justifiable homicide **n** homicide *m* par légitime défense.

justifiably ['dʒʌstɪfaɪəblɪ] **adv** à juste titre.

justification [,dʒʌstɪfɪ'keɪʃn] **n** justification *f*.

justify ['dʒʌstɪfaɪ] (pt & pp **-ied**) **vt** [give reasons for] justifier.

just-in-time **adj** ECON juste à temps.

just-in-time distribution **n** ECON distribution *f* juste à temps.

just-in-time production **n** ECON production *f* juste à temps.

just-in-time purchasing **n** ECON achat *m* juste à temps.

justly ['dʒʌstlɪ] **adv** [act] avec justice / [deserved] à juste titre.

justness ['dʒʌstnɪs] **n** bien-fondé *m*.

jut [dʒʌt] (pt & pp **-ted**, cont **-ting**) **vi : to jut (out)** faire saillie, avancer.

jute [dʒu:t] **n** jute *m*.

juvenile ['dʒu:vənaɪl] ■ **adj 1.** LAW mineur(e), juvénile **2.** [childish] puéril(e).
■ **n** LAW mineur *m*, -e *f*.

juvenile court **n** tribunal *m* pour enfants.

juvenile delinquency **n** délinquance *f* juvénile.

juvenile delinquent **n** jeune délinquant *m*, -e *f*.

juxtapose [,dʒʌkstə'pəʊz] **vt** juxtaposer.

juxtaposition [,dʒʌkstəpə'zɪʃn] **n** juxtaposition *f*.

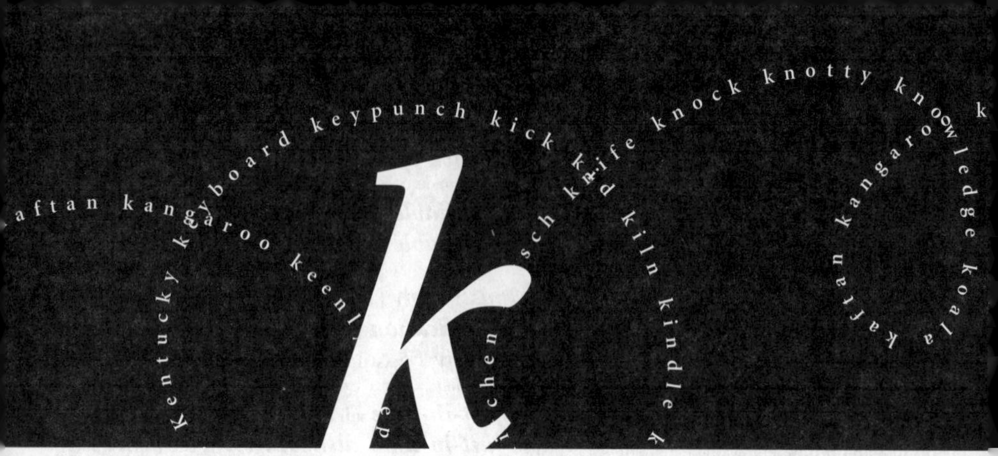

k (pl k's OR ks), ***K***[1] (pl K's OR Ks) [keɪ] n [letter] k *m inv*, K *m inv*.

K[2] **1.** (abbr of ***kilobyte***) Ko **2.** abbr of ***Knight*** **3.** (abbr of ***thousand***) K.

Kabul ['kɑ:bl] n Kaboul.

kaftan ['kæftæn] n = ***caftan***.

Kalahari Desert [ˌkælə'hɑ:rɪ-] n **: the Kalahari Desert** le (désert du) Kalahari.

kale [keɪl] n chou *m* frisé.

kaleidoscope [kə'laɪdəskəʊp] n kaléidoscope *m*.

kamikaze [ˌkæmɪ'kɑ:zɪ] n kamikaze *m*.

Kampala [kæm'pɑ:lə] n Kampala.

Kampuchea [ˌkæmpu:'tʃɪə] n Kampuchéa *m* ▸ **in Kampuchea** au Kampuchéa.

Kampuchean [ˌkæmpu:'tʃɪən] ■ adj cambodgien(enne).
■ n Cambodgien *m*, -enne *f*.

kangaroo [ˌkæŋgə'ru:] n kangourou *m*.

Kansas ['kænzəs] n Kansas *m* ▸ **in Kansas** dans le Kansas.

kaolin ['keɪəlɪn] n kaolin *m*.

kaput [kə'pʊt] adj *inf* fichu(e), foutu(e).

karaoke [ˌkærə'əʊkɪ] n karaoké *m*.

karat ['kærət] n *US* [for gold] carat *m*.

karate [kə'rɑ:tɪ] n karaté *m*.

karma ['kɑ:mə] n karma *m*, karman *m*.

Kashmir [kæʃ'mɪəʳ] n Cachemire *m* ▸ **in Kashmir** au Cachemire.

Katar [kæ'tɑ:ʳ] = ***Qatar***.

Kat(h)mandu [ˌkætmæn'du:] n Katmandou, Katmandu.

kayak ['kaɪæk] n kayak *m*.

Kazakhstan [ˌkæzæk'stɑ:n] n Kazakhstan *m* ▸ **in Kazakhstan** au Kazakhstan.

kB, KB (abbr of ***kilobyte(s)***) n COMPUT Ko *m*.

KC (abbr of ***King's Counsel***) n ≃ bâtonnier *m* de l'ordre.

kcal (abbr of ***kilocalorie***) Kcal.

kd (abbr of ***knocked down***) *livré en kit, à monter soi-même.*

kebab [kɪ'bæb] n *UK* brochette *f*.

kedgeree [ˌkedʒə'ri:] n *UK plat de riz, poisson et œufs durs mélangés.*

keel [ki:l] n quille *f* ▸ **on an even keel** stable.
◆ ***keel over*** vi [ship] chavirer / [person] tomber dans les pommes.

keen [ki:n] adj **1.** *UK* [enthusiastic] enthousiaste, passionné(e) ▸ **she's a keen gardener** c'est une passionnée de jardinage ▸ **he was keen to talk to her** il tenait à OR voulait absolument lui parler ▸ **to be keen on sthg** avoir la passion de qqch ▸ **I'm not so keen on the idea** l'idée ne m'enchante OR ne m'emballe pas vraiment ▸ **he's keen on her** elle lui plaît ▸ **to be keen to do OR on doing sthg** tenir à faire qqch **2.** [interest, desire, mind] vif (vive) / [competition] âpre, acharné(e) **3.** [sense of smell] fin(e) / [eyesight] perçant(e).

keenly ['ki:nlɪ] adv **1.** [contested, interested] vivement **2.** [listen, watch] attentivement.

keenness ['ki:nnɪs] n **1.** *UK* [enthusiasm] enthousiasme *m* **2.** [of competition] intensité *f* **3.** [of eyesight] acuité *f* / [of hearing] finesse *f*.

keep [ki:p] ■ vt (pt & pp **kept**) **1.** [retain, store] garder ▸ **keep the change!** gardez la monnaie! ▸ **please keep your seats** veuillez rester assis ▸ **we've kept some cake for you** on t'a gardé du gâteau ▸ **she keeps her money in the bank** elle met son argent à la banque ▸ **how long can you keep fish in the freezer?** combien de temps peut-on garder OR conserver du poisson au congélateur? ▸ **where do you keep the playing cards?** où est-ce que vous rangez les cartes à jouer? ▸ **if that's your idea of a holiday, you can keep it!** *inf* si c'est ça ton idée des vacances, tu peux te la garder!
2. [maintain in specified state] **: to keep sb quiet** faire tenir qqn tranquille ▸ **to keep sthg warm** garder qqch au chaud ▸ **the doors are kept locked** les portes sont toujours fermées à clef ▸ **to keep sthg up to date** tenir qqch à jour ▸ **the weather kept us indoors** le temps nous a empêchés de sortir ▸ **he kept his hands in his pockets** il a gardé les

mains dans les poches ▸ **keep the noise to a minimum** essayez de ne pas faire trop de bruit ▸ **keep the engine running** n'arrêtez pas le moteur ▸ **to keep sthg going** [organization, business] faire marcher qqch / [music, conversation] ne pas laisser qqch s'arrêter

3. [prevent] **: to keep sb/sthg from doing sthg** empêcher qqn/qqch de faire qqch ▸ **I couldn't keep myself from laughing** je n'ai pas pu m'empêcher de rire

4. [detain] retenir / [prisoner] détenir ▸ **I don't want to keep you** je ne voudrais pas vous retenir ▸ **I don't want to keep you from your work** je ne veux pas vous empêcher de travailler ▸ **what kept you?** qu'est-ce qui t'a retardé? ▸ **to keep sb waiting** faire attendre qqn ▸ **to keep sb in hospital/prison** garder qqn à l'hôpital/en prison

5. [promise] tenir / [appointment] aller à / [vow] être fidèle à ▸ **to keep order/the peace** maintenir l'ordre/la paix

6. [not disclose] **: to keep sthg from sb** cacher qqch à qqn ▸ **to keep sthg to o.s.** garder qqch pour soi

7. [diary, record, notes] tenir ▸ **my secretary keeps my accounts** ma secrétaire tient *OR* s'occupe de ma comptabilité

8. [support] **: he hardly earns enough to keep himself** il gagne à peine de quoi vivre ▸ **she has a husband and six children to keep** elle a un mari et six enfants à nourrir

9. [own - sheep, pigs] élever / [- shop] tenir / [- car] avoir, posséder

10. [guard] garder ▸ **to keep goal** être gardien de but

▸▸| **they keep themselves to themselves** ils restent entre eux, ils se tiennent à l'écart.

■ **vi** (pt & pp **kept**) **1.** [remain] **: to keep warm** se tenir au chaud ▸ **to keep quiet** garder le silence ▸ **keep quiet!** taisez-vous! ▸ **keep calm!** restez calmes!, du calme! ▸ **to keep in touch with sb** rester en contact avec qqn

2. [continue] **: he keeps interrupting me** il n'arrête pas de m'interrompre ▸ **letters keep pouring in** les lettres continuent d'affluer ▸ **to keep talking/walking** continuer à parler/à marcher ▸ **don't keep apologizing** arrête de t'excuser ▸ **she had several failures but kept trying** elle a essuyé plusieurs échecs mais elle a persévéré ▸ **with so few customers, it's a wonder the shop keeps going** avec si peu de clients, c'est un miracle que le magasin ne ferme pas

3. [continue moving] **: to keep left/right** garder sa gauche/sa droite ▸ **to keep north/south** continuer vers le nord/le sud ▸ **keep to the path** ne vous écartez pas du chemin

4. [food] se conserver ▸ **it will keep for a week in the refrigerator** vous pouvez le garder *OR* conserver au réfrigérateur pendant une semaine

5. *UK dated* [in health] **: how are you keeping?** comment allez-vous? ▸ **she's keeping well** elle va bien.

■ **n 1. : to earn one's keep** gagner sa vie ▸ **he gives his mother £50 a week for his keep** il donne 50 livres par semaine à sa mère pour sa pension

2. [in castle] donjon *m.*

◆ ***keeps*** **n : for keeps** pour toujours.

◆ ***keep at*** **vt insep : to keep at it** [work hard] travailler d'arrache-pied.

◆ ***keep away*** ■ **vt sep** tenir éloigné(e), empêcher d'approcher ▸ **spectators were kept away by the fear of violence** la peur de la violence tenait les spectateurs à distance.

■ **vi insep** ne pas s'approcher ▸ **keep away from those people** évitez ces gens-là.

◆ ***keep back*** **vt sep 1.** [keep at a distance - crowd, spectators] tenir éloigné, empêcher de s'approcher

2. [information] cacher, ne pas divulguer ▸ **I'm sure he's keeping something back (from us)** je suis sûr qu'il (nous) cache quelque chose

3. [retain, detain] retenir ▸ **to be kept back after school** être en retenue.

◆ ***keep down*** **vt sep 1.** [not raise] ne pas lever ▸ **keep your head down!** ne lève pas la tête!, garde la tête baissée! ▸ **keep your voices down!** parlez doucement!

2. [prices] empêcher de monter / [numbers, costs] restreindre, limiter

3. [food] garder ▸ **she can't keep solid foods down** son estomac ne garde aucun aliment solide.

◆ ***keep from*** **vt insep** s'empêcher de, se retenir de ▸ **I couldn't keep from laughing** je n'ai pas pu m'empêcher de rire.

◆ ***keep in with*** **vt insep : to keep in with sb** rester en bons termes avec qqn.

◆ ***keep off*** ■ **vt sep** [dogs, birds, trespassers] éloigner / [rain, sun] protéger de ▸ **this cream will keep the mosquitoes off** cette crème vous protégera contre les moustiques ▸ **keep your hands off!** pas touche!, bas les pattes!

■ **vt insep : 'keep off the grass'** '(il est) interdit de marcher sur la pelouse'.

◆ ***keep on*** **vi 1.** [continue] **: to keep on (doing sthg)** [without stopping] continuer (de *OR* à faire qqch) / [repeatedly] ne pas arrêter (de faire qqch) ▸ **they kept on talking** ils ont continué à parler ▸ **I keep on making the same mistakes** je fais toujours les mêmes erreurs

2. [talk incessantly] **: to keep on (about sthg)** ne pas arrêter de parler (de qqch) ▸ **don't keep on about it!** ça suffit, j'ai compris!

◆ ***keep on at*** **vt insep** *UK* harceler.

◆ ***keep out*** ■ **vt sep** empêcher d'entrer ▸ **a guard dog to keep intruders out** un chien de garde pour décourager les intrus ▸ **a scarf to keep the cold out** une écharpe pour vous protéger du froid.

■ **vi : 'keep out'** 'défense d'entrer' ▸ **to keep out of an argument** ne pas intervenir dans une discussion.

◆ ***keep to*** ■ **vt insep** [rules, deadline] respecter, observer ▸ **keep to the point** *OR* **the subject!** ne vous écartez pas du sujet!

■ **vt sep** [limit] **: we must keep spending to a minimum** il faut limiter les dépenses au minimum.

◆ ***keep up*** ■ **vt sep 1.** [prevent from falling - shelf, roof] maintenir ▸ **I need a belt to keep my trousers up** j'ai besoin d'une ceinture pour empêcher mon pantalon de tomber / **: it will keep prices up** ça empêchera les prix de baisser

2. [continue to do] continuer / [maintain] maintenir ▸ **you have to keep up the payments** on ne peut pas interrompre les versements ▸ **to keep up appearances** sauver les apparences ▸ **keep up the good work!** c'est du bon travail, continuez! ▸ **you're doing well, keep it up!** c'est bien, continuez!

■ **vi 1.** [continue] continuer ▸ **if this noise keeps up, I'll scream** si ce bruit continue, je crois que je vais hurler

2. [maintain pace, level] **: to keep up (with sb)** aller aussi vite (que qqn) ▸ **he's finding it hard to keep up in his new class** il a du mal à suivre dans sa nouvelle classe ▸ **to keep up with the news** suivre l'actualité

3. [remain in contact] **: to keep up with sb** rester en contact avec qqn.

keeper ['kiːpər] **n** gardien *m*, -enne *f*.

keep-fit *UK* ■ n *(U)* gymnastique *f*.
■ comp de gymnastique.

keeping ['ki:pɪŋ] n **1.** [care] garde *f* **2.** [conformity, harmony] **: to be in/out of keeping with** [rules] être/ne pas être conforme à / [subj: furniture] aller/ne pas aller avec.

keepsake ['ki:pseɪk] n souvenir *m*.

keg [keg] n tonnelet *m*, baril *m*.

kelp [kelp] n varech *m*.

ken [ken] n **: it's beyond my ken** ça dépasse mes compétences.

kennel ['kenl] n *UK* [place for dog to sleep] niche *f* / *US* [for breeding, looking after dogs] chenil *m*.
◆ ***kennels*** npl *UK* chenil *m*.

Kentucky [ken'tʌkɪ] n Kentucky *m* ▸ **in Kentucky** dans le Kentucky.

Kenya ['kenjə] n Kenya *m* ▸ **in Kenya** au Kenya.

Kenyan ['kenjən] ■ adj kenyan(e).
■ n Kenyan *m*, -e *f*.

kept [kept] pt & pp ➤ ***keep***.

kerb [kɜ:b] n *UK* bordure *f* du trottoir.

kerb crawler [-,krɔ:lər] n *UK* *homme en voiture qui accoste les prostituées*.

kerb crawling n *fait de longer le trottoir en voiture à la recherche d'une prostituée*.

kerbstone ['kɜ:bstəʊn] n *UK* (pierre *f* de) bordure *f* de trottoir.

kerfuffle [kə'fʌfl] n *UK inf* **: what a kerfuffle!** quelle histoire!

kernel ['kɜ:nl] n amande *f*.

kerosene ['kerəsi:n] n *US* [paraffin] paraffine *f*.

kestrel ['kestrəl] n crécerelle *f*.

ketch [ketʃ] n ketch *m*.

ketchup ['ketʃəp] n ketchup *m*.

kettle ['ketl] n bouilloire *f*.

kettledrum ['ketldrʌm] n timbale *f*.

key [ki:] ■ n **1.** [gen & MUS] clef *f*, clé *f* ▸ **the key (to sthg)** *fig* la clé (de qqch) **2.** [of typewriter, computer, piano] touche *f* **3.** MUS ton *m* ▸ **in the key of B minor** en si mineur **4.** [of map] légende *f*.
■ adj clé ▸ **key industries** industries clés, industries-clés ▸ **a key factor** un élément décisif.
◆ ***key in*** vt sep [text, data] saisir / [code] composer.

keyboard ['ki:bɔ:d] ■ n [gen & COMPUT] clavier *m*.
■ vt COMPUT [text, data] saisir.

keyboarder ['ki:bɔ:dər] n COMPUT claviste *mf*.

keyboard shortcut n raccourci *m* clavier.

key card n badge *m*.

keyed up [,ki:d-] adj *inf* tendu(e), énervé(e).

keyhole ['ki:həʊl] n trou *m* de serrure.

keyhole surgery n cœliochirurgie *f*.

keynote ['ki:nəʊt] ■ n note *f* dominante.
■ **comp : keynote speech** discours-programme *m*.

keypad ['ki:pæd] n COMPUT pavé *m* numérique.

keypunch ['ki:pʌntʃ] n *US* perforatrice *f* à clavier.

key ring n porte-clés *m inv*.

keystone ['ki:stəʊn] n *lit* & *fig* clef *f* de voûte.

keystroke ['ki:strəʊk] n COMPUT frappe *f* d'une touche.

kg (abbr of ***kilogram***) kg.

KGB n KGB *m*.

khaki ['kɑ:kɪ] ■ adj kaki *(inv)*.
■ n **1.** [colour] kaki *m* **2.** [cloth] toile *f* kaki.

Khmer [kmeər] ■ adj khmer (khmère).
■ n **1.** [person] Khmer *m*, -ère *f* ▸ **Khmer Rouge** Khmer rouge *m* **2.** [language] khmer *m*.

KHz (abbr of ***kilohertz***) n KHz *m*.

kibbutz [kɪ'bʊts] (pl **kibbutzim** [kɪbʊ'tsi:m] OR -es [-i:z]) n kibboutz *m*.

kibosh ['kaɪbɒʃ] n *inf* **: to put the kibosh on sthg** ficher qqch en l'air.

kick [kɪk] ■ n **1.** [with foot] coup *m* de pied ▸ **to aim a kick at sb/sthg** lancer OR donner un coup de pied en direction de qqn/qqch ▸ **it was a real kick in the teeth for him** *inf* ça lui a fait un sacré coup / *inf* **: she needs a kick up the backside** OR **in the pants** elle a besoin d'un coup de pied aux fesses
2. *inf* [excitement] **: to get a kick from** OR **out of sthg** trouver qqch excitant ▸ **to do sthg for kicks** faire qqch pour le plaisir.
■ vt **1.** [with foot] donner un coup de pied à ▸ **she kicked the ball over the wall** elle a envoyé la balle par-dessus le mur (d'un coup de pied) ▸ **I kicked the door open** j'ai ouvert la porte d'un coup de pied ▸ **the dancers kicked their legs in the air** les danseurs lançaient les jambes en l'air ▸ **to kick a penalty** [in rugby] marquer OR réussir une pénalité / [in football] tirer un penalty ▸ **to kick o.s.** *fig* se donner des gifles OR des claques ▸ **to kick the bucket** *inf* passer l'arme à gauche, casser sa pipe
2. *inf* [give up] **: to kick the habit** arrêter.
■ vi **1.** [person - repeatedly] donner des coups de pied / [- once] donner un coup de pied
2. [baby] gigoter
3. [animal] ruer.
◆ ***kick around***, ***kick about*** *UK* ■ vt sep **1. : to kick a ball around** jouer au ballon
2. *inf* [idea] débattre ▸ **we kicked a few ideas around** on a discuté à bâtons rompus.
■ vi *inf* traîner.
◆ ***kick in*** ■ vt sep défoncer à coups de pied ▸ **I'll kick his teeth in!** *inf* je vais lui casser la figure!
■ vi insep *inf* entrer en action.
◆ ***kick off*** vi **1.** FOOTBALL donner le coup d'envoi
2. *inf fig* [start] démarrer.
◆ ***kick out*** vt sep *inf* vider, jeter dehors.
◆ ***kick up*** vt insep *inf* **: to kick up a fuss** OR **a row** faire toute une histoire.

kickback ['kɪkbæk] **n 1.** *inf* [bribe] dessous-de-table *m inv*, pot-de-vin *m* **2.** TECH recul *m* **3.** [backlash] contre-coup *m*.

kickoff ['kɪkɒf] **n** engagement *m*.

kick-start **vt** faire démarrer à l'aide du pied / *fig* [economy] faire démarrer.

kid [kɪd] ■ **n 1.** *inf* [child] gosse *mf*, gamin *m*, -e *f* **2.** *inf* [young person] petit jeune *m*, petite jeune *f* **3.** [goat, leather] chevreau *m*.
■ **comp** *esp US inf* [brother, sister] petit(e).
■ **vt** (pt & pp **-ded**, cont **-ding**) *inf* **1.** [tease] faire marcher **2.** [delude] **: to kid o.s.** se faire des illusions.
■ **vi** (pt & pp **-ded**, cont **-ding**) *inf* **: to be kidding** plaisanter ▸ **no kidding!** sans blague!

kiddie, ***kiddy*** (pl **-ies**) ['kɪdɪ] **n** *inf* gosse *mf*, gamin *m*, -e *f*.

kid gloves **npl : to treat** OR **handle sb with kid gloves** prendre des gants avec qqn.

kidnap ['kɪdnæp] (pt & pp **-ped**, cont **-ping**) **vt** kidnapper, enlever.

kidnapper *UK* ['kɪdnæpəʳ] **n** kidnappeur *m*, -euse *f*, ravisseur *m*, -euse *f*.

kidnapping ['kɪdnæpɪŋ] **n** enlèvement *m*.

kidney ['kɪdnɪ] (pl **-s**) **n 1.** ANAT rein *m* **2.** CULIN rognon *m*.

kidney bean **n** haricot *m* rouge.

kidney machine **n** rein *m* artificiel.

Kilimanjaro [ˌkɪlɪmən'dʒɑːrəʊ] **n** Kilimandjaro *m*.

kill [kɪl] ■ **vt 1.** [cause death of] tuer ▸ **my feet are killing me** *fig* j'ai horriblement mal aux pieds ▸ **these shoes are killing me** ces chaussures me font souffrir le martyre ▸ **they were killing themselves laughing** OR **with laughter** ils étaient morts de rire ▸ **to kill time** tuer le temps **2.** *fig* [hope, chances] mettre fin à / [pain] supprimer.
■ **vi** tuer.
■ **n** mise *f* à mort ▸ **to be in at the kill** assister au coup de grâce.
◆ ***kill off*** **vt sep 1.** [species, animal] exterminer **2.** *fig* [hope, chances] mettre fin à.

killer ['kɪləʳ] **n** [person] meurtrier *m*, -ère *f* / [animal] tueur *m*, -euse *f*.

killer whale **n** épaulard *m*, orque *f*.

killing ['kɪlɪŋ] ■ **adj** *inf dated* [very funny] tordant(e).
■ **n** meurtre *m* ▸ **to make a killing** *inf* faire une bonne affaire, réussir un beau coup.

killjoy ['kɪldʒɔɪ] **n** *pej* rabat-joie *m inv*.

kiln [kɪln] **n** four *m*.

kilo ['kiːləʊ] (pl **-s**) (abbr of ***kilogram***) **n** kilo *m*.

kilo- ['kɪlə] **prefix** kilo-.

kilobyte ['kɪləbaɪt] **n** COMPUT kilo-octet *m*.

kilocalorie ['kɪləˌkælərɪ] **n** kilocalorie *f*.

kilogram, *esp UK* ***kilogramme*** ['kɪləgræm] **n** kilogramme *m*.

kilohertz ['kɪləhɜːtz] (pl **kilohertz**) **n** kilohertz *m*.

kilojoule ['kɪlədʒuːl] **n** kilojoule *m*.

kilometre *UK* ['kɪləˌmiːtəʳ], ***kilometer*** *US* [kɪ'lɒmɪtər] **n** kilomètre *m*.

kilowatt ['kɪləwɒt] **n** kilowatt *m*.

kilt [kɪlt] **n** kilt *m*.

kilter ['kɪltəʳ] ◆ ***out of kilter*** **adj** en dérangement, en panne.

kimono [kɪ'məʊnəʊ] (pl **-s**) **n** kimono *m*.

kin [kɪn] **n** ➤ ***kith***.

kind [kaɪnd] ■ **adj** gentil(ille), aimable ▸ **to be kind to sb** être gentil avec qqn ▸ **it's very kind of you to take an interest** c'est très gentil à vous de vous y intéresser ▸ **she was kind enough to say nothing** elle a eu la gentillesse de ne rien dire ▸ **would you be so kind as to...?** *fml* voulez-vous avoir la gentillesse OR l'amabilité de...?
■ **n** [sort, type] genre *m*, sorte *f* ▸ **hundreds of different kinds of books** des centaines de livres de toutes sortes ▸ **all kinds of people** toutes sortes de gens ▸ **it's a different kind of problem** c'est un tout autre problème, c'est un problème d'un autre ordre ▸ **I think he's some kind of specialist** OR **a specialist of some kind** je crois que c'est un genre de spécialiste ▸ **what kind of computer have you got?** qu'est-ce que vous avez comme (marque d')ordinateur? ▸ **an agreement of a kind** une sorte d'accord ▸ **they're two of a kind** ils se ressemblent ▸ **I said nothing of the kind!** je n'ai rien dit de pareil OR de tel!
▸▸ **a kind of** une sorte de, une espèce de ▸ **I had a kind of (a) feeling you'd come** j'avais comme l'impression que tu viendrais ▸ **kind of** *inf* plutôt ▸ **it's kind of big and round** c'est plutôt OR dans le genre grand et rond ▸ **I'm kind of sad about it** ça me rend un peu triste ▸ **did you hit him? – well, kind of** tu l'as frappé? – oui, si on veut.
◆ ***in kind*** **adv** [with goods, services] en nature ▸ **to pay sb in kind** payer qqn en nature.

kinda ['kaɪndə] *US inf* = ***kind of***.

kindergarten ['kɪndəˌgɑːtn] **n** *UK* jardin *m* d'enfants / *US* ≃ première classe de la maternelle.

kind-hearted [-'hɑːtɪd] **adj** qui a bon cœur, bon (bonne).

kindle ['kɪndl] **vt 1.** [fire] allumer **2.** *fig* [feeling] susciter.

kindling ['kɪndlɪŋ] **n** *(U)* petit bois *m*.

kindly ['kaɪndlɪ] ■ **adj** (comp **-ier**, superl **-iest**) **1.** [person] plein(e) de bonté, bienveillant(e) **2.** [gesture] plein(e) de gentillesse.
■ **adv 1.** [speak, smile] avec gentillesse ▸ **he has always treated me kindly** il a toujours été gentil avec moi ▸ **to look kindly on** *fig* être favorable à **2.** *fml* [please] **: kindly leave the room!** veuillez sortir, s'il vous plaît! ▸ **will you kindly...?** veuillez..., je vous prie de...
▸▸ **not to take kindly to sthg** mal prendre qqch ▸ **they don't take kindly to people arriving late** ils n'apprécient pas beaucoup OR tellement qu'on arrive en retard.

kindness ['kaɪndnɪs] **n** gentillesse *f*.

kindred ['kɪndrɪd] **adj** [similar] semblable, similaire ▸ **kindred spirit** âme *f* sœur.

kinetic [kɪ'netɪk] adj cinétique.

kinfolk(s) ['kɪnfəʊk(s)] *US* = **kinsfolk**.

king [kɪŋ] n roi *m*.

kingdom ['kɪŋdəm] n **1.** [country] royaume *m* **2.** [of animals, plants] règne *m*.

kingfisher ['kɪŋ,fɪʃər] n martin-pêcheur *m*.

kingpin ['kɪŋpɪn] n **1.** AUT pivot *m* de l'essieu avant **2.** *fig* [person] pilier *m*, cheville *f* ouvrière.

king prawn n (grosse) crevette *f*.

king-size(d) [-saɪz(d)] adj [cigarette] long(longue) / [pack] géant(e) ▸ **a king-sized bed** un grand lit *(de 195 cm)*.

kink [kɪŋk] n [in rope] entortillement *m*.

kinky ['kɪŋkɪ] (comp -ier, superl -iest) adj *inf* vicieux(euse).

kinsfolk ['kɪnzfəʊk] npl *US* famille *f*.

kinship ['kɪnʃɪp] n *(U)* **1.** [family relationship] parenté *f* **2.** [closeness] affinités *fpl*.

kinsman ['kɪnzmən] (pl **-men** [-mən]) n parent *m*.

kinswoman ['kɪnz,wʊmən] (pl **-women** [-,wɪmɪn]) n parente *f*.

kiosk ['ki:ɒsk] n **1.** [small shop] kiosque *m* **2.** *UK* [telephone box] cabine *f* (téléphonique).

kip [kɪp] *UK inf* ■ n somme *m*, roupillon *m*.
■ vi (pt & pp **-ped**, cont **-ping**) faire *OR* piquer un petit somme.

kipper ['kɪpər] n hareng *m* fumé *OR* saur.

Kirk [kɜ:k] n *Scot* : **the Kirk** l'Église *f* (presbytérienne) d'Écosse.

kirsch [kɪəʃ] n kirsch *m*.

kiss [kɪs] ■ n baiser *m* ▸ **to give sb a kiss** embrasser qqn, donner un baiser à qqn.
■ vt embrasser ▸ **to kiss sb's cheek** embrasser qqn sur la joue ▸ **to kiss sb goodbye** dire au revoir à qqn en l'embrassant.
■ vi s'embrasser.

kissagram ['kɪsəgræm] n *service de "télégramme parlé" comprenant un baiser, à l'occasion d'un anniversaire, par exemple.*

kiss-and-tell adj PRESS : **another kiss-and-tell story by an ex-girlfriend** encore des révélations intimes faites *OR* des secrets d'alcôve dévoilés par une ancienne petite amie.

kiss curl n *UK* accroche-cœur *m*.

kisser ['kɪsər] n **1.** [person] : **is he a good kisser?** est-ce qu'il embrasse bien? **2.** *inf dated* [face, mouth] tronche *f*.

kiss of life n *UK* : **the kiss of life** le bouche-à-bouche.

kit [kɪt] n **1.** [set] trousse *f* **2.** *(U)* SPORT affaires *fpl*, équipement *m* **3.** [to be assembled] kit *m*.
◆ ***kit out*** (pt & pp -ted, cont -ting) vt sep *UK* équiper.

kit bag n sac *m* de marin.

kitchen ['kɪtʃɪn] n cuisine *f*.

kitchenette [,kɪtʃɪ'net] n kitchenette *f*.

kitchen garden n (jardin *m*) potager *m*.

kitchen sink n évier *m*.

kitchen unit n élément *m* de cuisine.

kitchenware ['kɪtʃɪnweər] n *(U)* ustensiles *mpl* de cuisine.

kite [kaɪt] n **1.** [toy] cerf-volant *m* **2.** [bird] milan *m*.

Kite mark n *UK* ≃ NF *(conforme aux normes françaises de sécurité)*.

kith [kɪθ] n *dated* : **kith and kin** parents et amis *mpl*.

kitsch [kɪtʃ] n & adj kitsch *m inv*.

kitten ['kɪtn] n chaton *m*.

kitty ['kɪtɪ] (pl -ies) n **1.** [shared fund] cagnotte *f* **2.** *inf* [animal] chat(te).

kiwi ['ki:wi:] n **1.** [bird] kiwi *m*, aptéryx *m* **2.** *inf* [New Zealander] Néo-Zélandais *m*, -e *f*.

KKK abbr of ***Ku Klux Klan***.

klaxon ['klæksn] n sirène *f*.

Kleenex® ['kli:neks] n Kleenex® *m*.

kleptomania [,kleptə'meɪnɪə] n kleptomanie *f*, cleptomanie *f*.

kleptomaniac [,kleptə'meɪnɪæk] n kleptomane *mf*.

klutz [klʌts] n *inf* balourd *m*, -e *f*, godiche *f*.

km (abbr of ***kilometre***) km.

km/h (abbr of ***kilometres per hour***) km/h.

knack [næk] n : **to have a** *OR* **the knack (for doing sthg)** avoir le coup (pour faire qqch).

knacker ['nækər] *UK* ■ n [horse slaughterer] équarrisseur *m*.
■ vt *v inf* épuiser.

knackered ['nækəd] adj *UK v inf* crevé(e), claqué(e).

knapsack ['næpsæk] n sac *m* à dos.

knave [neɪv] n [in cards] valet *m*.

knead [ni:d] vt pétrir.

knee [ni:] n genou *m* ▸ **to be on one's knees** être à genoux / *fig* être sur les genoux ▸ **to bring someone to his/her knees** *fig* faire capituler qqn.

kneecap ['ni:kæp] n rotule *f*.

knee-deep adj : **we were knee-deep in snow/water** la neige/l'eau nous arrivait jusqu'aux genoux.

knee-high adj à hauteur de genou.

knee jerk n réflexe *m* rotulien.
◆ ***knee-jerk*** adj automatique ▸ **knee-jerk reaction** *fig & pej* réflexe *m*, automatisme *m*.

kneel [ni:l] (*UK* **knelt**, *US* **knelt** *OR* **-ed**) vi se mettre à genoux, s'agenouiller.
◆ ***kneel down*** vi se mettre à genoux, s'agenouiller.

knee-length adj [skirt] qui arrive aux genoux / [boots] qui montent jusqu'aux genoux.

knee pad n genouillère *f*.

knees-up n *UK inf dated* fête *f*.

knell [nel] **n** glas *m*.

knelt [nelt] **pt & pp** ➤ ***kneel***.

knew [nju:] **pt** ➤ ***know***.

knickers ['nɪkəz] **npl 1.** *UK* [underwear] culotte *f* **2.** *US* [trousers] pantalon *m* de golf.

knick-knack ['nɪknæk] **n** babiole *f*, bibelot *m*.

knife [naɪf] ■ **n** (pl **knives** [naɪvz]) couteau *m* ▸ **to be** *OR* **to go under the knife** *inf* passer sur le billard ▸ **the knives are out** ils sont à couteaux tirés *OR* en guerre ouverte.
■ **vt** donner un coup de couteau à, poignarder ▸ **he was knifed in the back** *fig* on lui a tiré dans le dos *OR* dans les pattes.

knife-edge **n** [blade] fil *m* d'un couteau ▸ **we were on a knife-edge** *fig* on était sur des charbons ardents ▸ **his decision was (balanced) on a knife-edge** sa décision ne tenait qu'à un fil.

knife-point **n : at knife-point** sous la menace du couteau.

knifing ['naɪfɪŋ] **n** bagarre *f* au couteau.

knight [naɪt] ■ **n 1.** [in history, member of nobility] chevalier *m* **2.** [in chess] cavalier *m*.
■ **vt** faire chevalier.

knighthood ['naɪthʊd] **n** titre *m* de chevalier.

knit [nɪt] ■ **adj : closely** *OR* **tightly knit** *fig* très uni(e).
■ **vt** (pt & pp **knit** *OR* **-ted**, cont **-ting**) tricoter.
■ **vi** (pt & pp **knit** *OR* **-ted**, cont **-ting**) **1.** [with wool] tricoter **2.** [broken bones] se souder.

knitted ['nɪtɪd] **adj** tricoté(e).

knitting ['nɪtɪŋ] **n** *(U)* tricot *m*.

knitting machine **n** machine *f* à tricoter.

knitting needle **n** aiguille *f* à tricoter.

knitting pattern **n** modèle *m* (de tricot).

knitwear ['nɪtweəʳ] **n** *(U)* tricots *mpl*.

knives [naɪvz] **npl** ➤ ***knife***.

knob [nɒb] **n 1.** [on door] poignée *f*, bouton *m* / [on drawer] poignée / [on bedstead] pomme *f* **2.** [on TV, radio] bouton *m*.

knobbly *UK* ['nɒblɪ] (comp -ier, superl -iest), ***knobby*** *US* ['nɒbɪ] (comp -ier, superl -iest) **adj** noueux (euse).

knock [nɒk] ■ **n 1.** [hit] coup *m* ▸ **there was a knock at the door/window** on a frappé à la porte/fenêtre ▸ **give it a knock with a hammer** donne un coup de marteau dessus
2. *inf* [setback] coup *m* dur ▸ **his reputation has taken a hard knock** sa réputation en a pris un sérieux coup.
■ **vt 1.** [hit] frapper, cogner ▸ **to knock a hole in a wall** faire un trou dans un mur ▸ **to knock a nail into a wall** enfoncer un clou dans un mur ▸ **to knock sb/sthg over** renverser qqn/qqch ▸ **the force of the explosion knocked us to the floor** la force de l'explosion nous a projetés à terre ▸ **I knocked my head on** *OR* **against the low ceiling** je me suis cogné la tête contre le *OR* au plafond ▸ **maybe it will knock some sense into him** cela lui mettra peut-être du plomb dans la cervelle, cela le ramènera peut-être à la raison
2. *inf* [criticize] critiquer, dire du mal de.
■ **vi 1.** [on door] **: to knock on** *OR* **at the door** frapper (à la porte) ▸ **they knock on the wall when we're too noisy** ils tapent *OR* cognent contre le mur quand on fait trop de bruit ▸ **to knock against** *OR* **into** heurter, cogner ▸ **she knocked into the desk** elle s'est heurtée *OR* cognée contre le bureau ▸ **his knees were knocking** *hum* ses genoux jouaient des castagnettes
2. [car engine] cogner, avoir des ratés.
◆ ***knock around, knock about*** *UK inf* ■ **vt sep** [beat] battre / [ill-treat] malmener ▸ **the old car's been knocked around a bit** la vieille voiture a pris quelques coups ici et là.
■ **vi 1.** [travel] bourlinguer
2. [spend time] **: to knock around with sb** fréquenter qqn.
◆ ***knock back*** **vt sep** *inf* [drink] s'enfiler.
◆ ***knock down*** **vt sep 1.** *UK* [subj: car, driver] renverser ▸ **she was knocked down by a bus** elle a été renversée par un bus
2. [building] démolir
3. [price] (faire) baisser ▸ **I managed to knock him down to $500** j'ai réussi à le faire baisser jusqu'à 500 dollars.
◆ ***knock off*** ■ **vt sep 1.** [from shelf, wall] faire tomber ▸ **he was knocked off his bicycle** le choc l'a fait tomber de sa bicyclette
2. [money] **: to knock £5 off** faire un rabais de 5 livres
3. *UK inf* [steal] chiper, piquer / [rob] dévaliser
4. *inf* [write rapidly] torcher ▸ **she can knock off an article in half an hour** elle peut pondre un article en une demi-heure
5. *inf* **: knock it off!** [stop] arrête ton char!
■ **vi** *inf* [stop working] finir son travail *OR* sa journée.
◆ ***knock out*** **vt sep 1.** [make unconscious] assommer
2. [from competition] éliminer.
◆ ***knock over*** **vt sep** renverser, faire tomber.
◆ ***knock up*** *UK* ■ **vt sep 1.** *UK* [meal, report] préparer *OR* faire en vitesse / [structure] construire à la va-vite
2. *v inf* [make pregnant] mettre en cloque.
■ **vi** *UK* TENNIS faire des balles.

knockabout ['nɒkəbaʊt] **adj** turbulent(e), violent(e) ▸ **a knockabout comedy** *OR* **farce** une grosse farce ▸ **a knockabout comedian** un clown.

knockdown ['nɒk,daʊn] ■ **adj 1.** [forceful] **: a knockdown blow** un coup à assommer un bœuf ▸ **a knockdown argument** un argument massue **2.** *inf* [reduced] **: for sale at knockdown prices** en vente à des prix imbattables *OR* défiant toute concurrence ▸ **I got it for a knockdown price** je l'ai eu pour trois fois rien **3.** [easy to dismantle] démontable.
■ **n** [in boxing] knock-down *m*.

knocker ['nɒkəʳ] **n** [on door] heurtoir *m*.

knocking ['nɒkɪŋ] **n** *(U)* **1.** [on door] coups *mpl* **2.** *inf* [criticism] critique *f*, critiques *fpl*.

knocking copy **n** publicité *f* comparative dénigrante.

knocking-off time n UK inf : **it's knocking-off time** c'est l'heure de se tirer.

knock-kneed [-'ni:d] adj cagneux(euse), qui a les genoux cagneux.

knock-on effect n UK réaction f en chaîne.

knockout ['nɒkaʊt] n knock-out m, K.-O. m

knockout competition n UK compétition f avec éliminatoires.

knock-up n UK TENNIS : **to have a knock-up** faire des balles.

knot [nɒt] ■ n 1. [gen] nœud m ▸ **to tie/untie a knot** faire/défaire un nœud ▸ **to tie sthg in a knot, to tie a knot in sthg** nouer qqch, faire un nœud à qqch ▸ **my stomach was in knots** j'avais l'estomac noué 2. [of people] petit attroupement m 3. NAUT nœud m ▸ **we are doing 15 knots** nous filons 15 nœuds ▸ **at a rate of knots** à toute allure, à un train d'enfer.
■ vt (pt & pp -ted, cont -ting) nouer, faire un nœud à ▸ **he knotted the rope around his waist** il s'est attaché OR noué la corde autour de la taille.

knotted ['nɒtɪd] adj noué(e).

knotty ['nɒtɪ] (comp -ier, superl -iest) adj fig épineux(euse).

know [nəʊ] ■ vt (pt knew, pp known) 1. [gen] savoir / [language] savoir parler ▸ **do you know her phone number?** vous connaissez son numéro de téléphone? ▸ **she knows a lot about politics** elle s'y connaît en politique ▸ **to know (that)...** savoir que... ▸ **I know for a fact that he's lying** je sais pertinemment qu'il ment ▸ **to know how to do sthg** savoir faire qqch ▸ **I know what I'm talking about** je sais de quoi je parle ▸ **she really knows her job/subject** elle connaît son boulot/sujet ▸ **to let sb know (about sthg)** faire savoir (qqch) à qqn, informer qqn (de qqch) ▸ **any problems, let me know** au moindre problème, n'hésitez pas ▸ **to get to know sthg** apprendre qqch ▸ **you know what I mean** tu vois ce que je veux dire
2. [person, place] connaître ▸ **to get to know sb** apprendre à mieux connaître qqn ▸ **to know sb by sight/by reputation** connaître qqn de vue/de réputation
3. [recognize] reconnaître ▸ **she knows a bargain when she sees one** elle sait reconnaître une bonne affaire ▸ **she doesn't know right from wrong** elle ne sait pas discerner le bien du mal OR faire la différence entre le bien et le mal
4. [nickname, call] : **Ian White, known as 'Chalky'** Ian White, connu sous le nom de 'Chalky' ▸ **they're known as June bugs in America** on les appelle des "June bugs" en Amérique.
■ vi (pt knew, pp known) savoir ▸ **to know of sthg** connaître qqch ▸ **not that I know (of)** pas que je sache ▸ **to know about** [be aware of] être au courant de / [be expert in] s'y connaître en ▸ **you never know** on ne sait jamais ▸ **God OR Heaven knows!** Dieu seul le sait! ▸ **he ought to have known better** il aurait dû réfléchir.
■ n : **to be in the know** être au courant.
◆ ***as far as I know*** adv (pour) autant que je sache ▸ **not as far as I know** pas que je sache.
◆ ***you know*** adv 1. [for emphasis] : **I was right, you know** j'avais raison, tu sais
2. [giving an opinion] : **he was just, you know, a bit boring** il était juste un peu ennuyeux, si tu vois ce que je veux dire ▸ **you know, sometimes I wonder why I do this** tu sais, parfois je me demande pourquoi je fais ça
3. [adding information] : **it was that blonde woman, you know, the one with the dog** c'était la femme blonde, tu sais, celle qui avait un chien.

CONFUSABLE / PARONYME

know

When translating **to know**, note that *savoir* and *connaître* are not interchangeable. *Savoir* means to know how to do something, while *connaître* means to know someone or be familiar with someone or something.

know-all UK, **know-it-all** US n (monsieur) je-sais-tout m, (madame) je-sais-tout f.

know-how n savoir-faire m, technique f.

knowing ['nəʊɪŋ] adj [smile, look] entendu(e).

knowingly ['nəʊɪŋlɪ] adv 1. [smile, look] d'un air entendu 2. [intentionally] sciemment.

know-it-all US = ***know-all***.

knowledge ['nɒlɪdʒ] n (U) 1. [gen] connaissance f ▸ **it's common knowledge that...** tout le monde sait que... ▸ **without my knowledge** à mon insu ▸ **to my knowledge** à ma connaissance ▸ **to the best of my knowledge** à ma connaissance, autant que je sache 2. [learning, understanding] savoir m, connaissances fpl.

knowledgeable ['nɒlɪdʒəbl] adj bien informé(e).

knowledgeably ['nɒlɪdʒəblɪ] adv en connaisseur ▸ **he speaks very knowledgeably about art** il parle d'art en connaisseur.

known [nəʊn] ■ pp ➤ ***know***.
■ adj connu(e).

knuckle ['nʌkl] n 1. ANAT articulation f OR jointure f du doigt 2. [of meat] jarret m.
◆ ***knuckle down*** vi s'y mettre, se mettre au travail ▸ **to knuckle down to sthg/to doing sthg** se mettre sérieusement à qqch/à faire qqch.
◆ ***knuckle under*** vi céder, capituler.

knuckle-duster n coup-de-poing m américain.

KO (abbr of ***knock-out***) n K.-O. m

koala (bear) [kəʊ'ɑ:lə-] n koala m.

kook [ku:k] n US inf fou m, folle f, dingue mf.

kooky ['ku:kɪ] (comp -ier, superl -iest) adj US inf fêlé(e), dingue.

Koran [kɒ'rɑ:n] n : **the Koran** le Coran.

Korea [kə'rɪə] n Corée f ▸ **in Korea** en Corée.

Korean [kə'rɪən] ■ adj coréen(enne).
■ n 1. [person] Coréen m, -enne f 2. [language] coréen m.

kosher ['kəʊʃəʳ] **adj 1.** [meat] kasher *(inv)* **2.** *inf* [reputable] O.K. *(inv)*, réglo *(inv)*.

Kosovan ['kɑsəvən], ***Kosovar*** ['kɑsəvər] ■ **n** Kosovar *m*, -e *f*.
■ **adj** kosovar.

Kosovo [kɑsəvɔ] **n** Kosovo *m*.

Koweit = ***Kuwait***.

kowtow [ˌkaʊ'taʊ] **vi : to kowtow (to sb)** faire des courbettes (à ***OR*** devant qqn).

kph (abbr of ***kilometres per hour***) km/h.

Krakow ['krækəʊ] = ***Cracow***.

Kremlin ['kremlɪn] **n : the Kremlin** le Kremlin.

krypton ['krɪptɒn] **n** krypton *m*.

KS abbr of ***Kansas***.

KT abbr of ***Knight***.

Kuala Lumpur [ˌkwɑ:lə'lʊmˌpʊəʳ] **n** Kuala Lumpur.

kudos ['kju:dɒs] **n** prestige *m*, gloire *f*.

Ku Klux Klan [ku:klʌks'klæn] **n : the Ku Klux Klan** le Ku Klux Klan.

kumquat ['kʌmkwɒt] **n** kumquat *m*.

kung fu [ˌkʌŋ'fu:] **n** kung-fu *m*.

Kurd [kɜ:d] **n** Kurde *mf*.

Kurdish ['kɜ:dɪʃ] **adj** kurde.

Kurdistan [ˌkɜ:dɪ'stɑ:n] **n** Kurdistan *m* ▸ **in Kurdistan** au Kurdistan.

Kuwait [kʊ'weɪt], ***Koweit*** [kəʊ'weɪt] **n 1.** [country] Koweït *m* ▸ **in Kuwait** au Koweït **2.** [city] Koweït City.

Kuwaiti [kʊ'weɪtɪ] ■ **adj** koweïtien(enne).
■ **n** Koweïtien *m*, -enne *f*.

kW (abbr of ***kilowatt***) kW.

KY abbr of ***Kentucky***.

l [1] [el] (pl l's *or* ls), ***L*** [1] (pl L's *or* Ls) **n** [letter] l *m inv*, L *m inv*.

l [2] (abbr of ***litre***) l.

L [2] **1.** abbr of ***lake*** **2.** abbr of ***large*** **3.** (abbr of ***left***) g **4.** abbr of ***learner***.

la [lɑ:] **n** MUS la *m*.

La abbr of ***Louisiana***.

LA abbr of ***Los Angeles, Louisiana***.

lab [læb] **n** *inf* labo *m*.

label ['leɪbl] ■ **n 1.** [identification] étiquette *f* **2.** [of record] label *m*, maison *f* de disques.
■ **vt** (*UK* **-led**, cont **-ling**, *US* **-ed**, cont **-ing**) **1.** [fix label to] étiqueter **2.** [describe] **: to label sb (as)** cataloguer *or* étiqueter qqn (comme).

labor *US* = ***labour*** *etc*.

laboratory [*UK* lə'bɒrətrɪ, *US* 'læbrə,tɔ:rɪ] ■ **n** (pl **-ies**) laboratoire *m*.
■ **comp** de laboratoire.

Labor Day **n** *fête du travail américaine (premier lundi de septembre).*

> CULTURE
> ## Labor Day
> Congé fédéral depuis 1894, le Labor Day (« fête du Travail »), l'équivalent français du 1er Mai, est célébré aux États-Unis en l'honneur de tous les salariés le premier lundi de septembre. Ce jour férié marque la fin de l'été – les plages et les stations balnéaires populaires sont très fréquentées durant ce dernier long week-end – ainsi que la rentrée scolaire : certaines écoles sont ouvertes dès la fin du mois d'août, mais la plupart des établissements rouvrent leurs portes la semaine suivant ce jour férié.

laborious [lə'bɔ:rɪəs] **adj** laborieux(euse).

laboriously [lə'bɔ:rɪəslɪ] **adv** laborieusement.

labor union **n** *US* syndicat *m*.

labour *UK*, ***labor*** *US* ['leɪbəʳ] ■ **n 1.** [gen & MED] travail *m* ▸ **she went into labour** MED le travail a commencé **2.** [workers, work carried out] main d'œuvre *f*.
■ **vt : there's no need to labour the point** pas besoin de s'appesantir là-dessus.
■ **vi** travailler dur ▸ **to labour at** *or* **over** peiner sur ▸ **to labour under a delusion** se faire des illusions *or* des idées ▸ **to labour under a misapprehension** être dans l'erreur.
◆ ***Labour*** *UK* ■ **adj** POL travailliste.
■ **n** *(U)* POL les travaillistes *mpl*.

labour camp *UK*, ***labor camp*** *US* **n** camp *m* de travaux forcés.

labour costs *UK*, ***labor costs*** *US* **npl** coûts *mpl* de la main-d'œuvre.

laboured *UK*, ***labored*** *US* ['leɪbəd] **adj** [breathing] pénible / [style] lourd(e), laborieux(euse).

labourer *UK*, ***laborer*** *US* ['leɪbərəʳ] **n** travailleur manuel *m*, travailleuse manuelle *f* / [agricultural] ouvrier agricole *m*, ouvrière agricole *f*.

labour force *UK*, ***labor force*** *US* **n** main-d'œuvre *f*.

labour-intensive *UK*, ***labor-intensive*** *US* **adj** à forte main d'œuvre.

labour laws, ***labor laws*** *US* **n** législation *f* du travail.

labour market *UK*, ***labor market*** *US* **n** marché *m* du travail.

labour of love *UK*, ***labor of love*** *US* **n** tâche *f* effectuée par plaisir.

labour pains *UK*, ***labor pains*** *US* **npl** douleurs *fpl* de l'accouchement.

Labour Party **n** *UK* **: the Labour Party** le parti travailliste.

labour relations *UK*, ***labor relations*** *US* **npl** relations *fpl* entre employeurs et employés.

laboursaving *UK*, ***laborsaving*** *US* ['leɪbə,seɪvɪŋ] **adj : laboursaving device** appareil *m* ménager.

labour shortage, ***labor shortage*** *US* **n** pénurie *f* de main-d'œuvre.

Labrador ['læbrədɔːʳ] **n** **1.** [dog] labrador *m* **2.** GEOG Labrador *m*.

labyrinth ['læbərɪnθ] **n** labyrinthe *m*.

lace [leɪs] ■ **n** **1.** [fabric] dentelle *f* **2.** [of shoe] lacet *m*.
■ **comp** en *OR* de dentelle.
■ **vt** **1.** [shoe] lacer **2.** [drink, food] verser de l'alcool *OR* une drogue dans.
◆ ***lace up*** **vt sep** lacer.

lacemaking ['leɪsˌmeɪkɪŋ] **n** fabrication *f* de (la) dentelle.

lacerate ■ **vt** ['læsəreɪt] lacérer ▸ **his hands were lacerated by the broken glass** il avait les mains lacérées par le verre brisé.
■ **adj** ['læsərət] BOT : **lacerate leaves** feuilles *fpl* dentées *OR* dentelées.

laceration [ˌlæsə'reɪʃn] **n** lacération *f*.

lace-up ■ **adj** [shoes] à lacets.
■ **n** *UK* chaussure *f* à lacets.

lack [læk] ■ **n** manque *m* ▸ **for** *OR* **through lack of** par manque de ▸ **no lack of** bien assez de.
■ **vt** manquer de.
■ **vi** : **to be lacking in sthg** manquer de qqch ▸ **to be lacking** manquer, faire défaut.

lackadaisical [ˌlækə'deɪzɪkl] **adj** *pej* nonchalant(e).

lackey ['lækɪ] (pl **-s**) **n** *pej* larbin *m*.

lacklustre *UK*, ***lackluster*** *US* ['lækˌlʌstəʳ] **adj** terne.

laconic [lə'kɒnɪk] **adj** *fml* laconique.

lacquer ['lækəʳ] ■ **n** [for wood] vernis *m*, laque *f* / *UK* [for hair] laque *f*.
■ **vt** laquer.

lacrosse [lə'krɒs] **n** crosse *f*.

lactic acid ['læktɪk-] **n** acide *m* lactique.

lactose ['læktəʊs] **n** lactose *m*.

lacy ['leɪsɪ] (comp **-ier**, superl **-iest**) **adj** de *OR* en dentelle.

lad [læd] **n** *UK* **1.** *inf* [boy] garçon *m*, gars *m* **2.** [stable boy] lad *m*.

ladder ['lædəʳ] ■ **n** **1.** [for climbing] échelle *f* **2.** *UK* [in tights] maille *f* filée, estafilade *f*.
■ **vt** & **vi** *UK* [tights] filer.

ladderproof ['lædəpruːf] **adj** *UK* indémaillable.

laden ['leɪdn] **adj** : **laden (with)** chargé(e) (de).

la-di-da [ˌlɑːdɪ'dɑː] **adj** *inf pej* maniéré(e).

ladies *UK* ['leɪdɪz], ***ladies' room*** *US* **n** toilettes *fpl* (pour dames).

ladies' man **n** don Juan *m*, homme *m* à femmes.

lading ['leɪdɪŋ] ➤ ***bill of lading***.

ladle ['leɪdl] ■ **n** louche *f*.
■ **vt** servir (à la louche).

lady ['leɪdɪ] ■ **n** (pl **-ies**) **1.** [gen] dame *f* **2.** *US inf* [to address woman] ma petite dame.
■ **comp** *dated* : **a lady doctor** une femme docteur.
◆ ***Lady*** **n** Lady *f* ▸ **Our Lady** Notre-Dame *f*.

ladybird *UK* ['leɪdɪbɜːd], ***ladybug*** *US* ['leɪdɪbʌg] **n** coccinelle *f*.

lady-in-waiting [-'weɪtɪŋ] (pl **ladies-in-waiting**) **n** dame *f* d'honneur.

ladykiller ['leɪdɪˌkɪləʳ] **n** *inf* bourreau *m* des cœurs.

ladylike ['leɪdɪlaɪk] **adj** distingué(e).

ladyship ['leɪdɪʃɪp] **n** : **Your** *OR* **Her Ladyship** *lit* Madame (la baronne/la vicomtesse/la comtesse) / *fig* & *hum* la maîtresse de ces lieux.

lag [læg] ■ **vi** (pt & pp **-ged**, cont **-ging**) : **to lag (behind)** [person, runner] traîner / [economy, development] être en retard, avoir du retard.
■ **vt** (pt & pp **-ged**, cont **-ging**) [roof, pipe] calorifuger.
■ **n** [timelag] décalage *m*.

lager ['lɑːgəʳ] **n** (bière *f*) blonde *f*.

lager lout **n** *UK jeune qui, sous l'influence de l'alcool, cherche la bagarre ou commet des actes de vandalisme*.

lagging ['lægɪŋ] **n** calorifuge *m*.

lagoon [lə'guːn] **n** lagune *f*.

Lagos ['leɪgɒs] **n** Lagos.

lah-di-dah = ***la-di-da***.

laid [leɪd] **pt** & **pp** ➤ ***lay***.

laid-back **adj** *inf* relaxe, décontracté(e).

lain [leɪn] **pp** ➤ ***lie***.

lair [leəʳ] **n** repaire *m*, antre *m*.

lairy ['leərɪ] **adj** tape à l'oeil *(inv) inf*, bruyant(e).

laissez-faire ['leɪseɪ'feəʳ] ■ **adj** non-interventionniste.
■ **n** non-interventionnisme *m*.

laity ['leɪətɪ] **n** RELIG : **the laity** les laïcs *mpl*.

lake [leɪk] **n** lac *m*.

Lake District **n** : **the Lake District** la région des lacs *(au nord-ouest de l'Angleterre)*.

Lake Geneva **n** le lac Léman *OR* de Genève.

lakeside ['leɪksaɪd] **adj** au bord de l'eau.

lama ['lɑːmə] (pl **-s**) **n** lama *m*.

lamb [læm] **n** agneau *m*.

lambast [læm'bæst], ***lambaste*** [læm'beɪst] **vt** démolir.

lamb chop **n** côtelette *f* d'agneau.

lambing ['læmɪŋ] **n** agnelage *m*.

lambskin ['læmskɪn] **n** agneau *m*, peau *f* d'agneau.

lambswool ['læmzwʊl] ■ **n** lambswool *m*.
■ **comp** en lambswool, en laine d'agneau.

lame [leɪm] **adj** *lit* & *fig* boiteux(euse).

lamé ['lɑːmeɪ] **n** lamé *m*.

lame duck **n** **1.** [person, business] canard *m* boiteux **2.** *US* [President] *président non réélu, pendant la période séparant l'élection de l'investiture de son successeur*.

lamely ['leɪmlɪ] **adv** [argue, lie] maladroitement.

lament [lə'ment] ■ **n** lamentation *f*.
■ **vt** se lamenter sur.

lamentable ['læməntəbl] **adj** lamentable.

laminate ['læmɪneɪt] ■ **vt** TECH [bond in layers] laminer / [veneer] plaquer.
■ **n** stratifié *m*.

laminated ['læmɪneɪtɪd] **adj** [wood] stratifié(e) / [glass] feuilleté(e) / [steel] laminé(e).

lamp [læmp] **n** lampe *f*.

lamplight ['læmplaɪt] **n** lumière *f* de la lampe.

lampoon [læm'pu:n] ■ **n** satire *f*.
■ **vt** faire la satire de.

lamppost ['læmppəʊst] **n** réverbère *m*.

lampshade ['læmpʃeɪd] **n** abat-jour *m*.

LAN (abbr of ***local area network***) **n** COMPUT réseau *m* local.

lance [lɑ:ns] ■ **n** lance *f*.
■ **vt** [boil] percer.

lance corporal **n** caporal *m*.

lancet ['lɑ:nsɪt] **n** bistouri *m*, lancette *f*.

Lancs [læŋks] (abbr of ***Lancashire***) *comté anglais*.

land [lænd] ■ **n 1.** [solid ground] terre *f* (ferme) / [farming ground] terre, terrain *m* ▸ **this is good farming land** c'est de la bonne terre ▸ **building land** terrain constructible ▸ **a piece of land** [for farming] un lopin de terre / [for building] un terrain (à bâtir) ▸ **to live off the land** vivre des ressources naturelles de la terre ▸ **we travelled by land to Cairo** nous sommes allés au Caire par la route
2. [property] terres *fpl*, propriété *f* ▸ **get off my land!** sortez de mes terres!
3. [nation] pays *m*.
■ **vt 1.** [from ship, plane] débarquer ▸ **they have succeeded in landing men on the moon** ils ont réussi à envoyer des hommes sur la Lune
2. [catch - fish] prendre
3. [plane] atterrir
4. *inf* [obtain] décrocher
5. *inf* [place] **: I landed him a blow** *OR* **landed him one on the nose** je lui ai flanqué *OR* collé mon poing dans la figure ▸ **to land sb in trouble** attirer des ennuis à qqn ▸ **to be landed with sthg** se coltiner qqch.
■ **vi 1.** [plane] atterrir ▸ **to land on the moon** atterrir sur la Lune, alunir ▸ **to land in the sea** amerrir
2. [fall] tomber ▸ **an apple landed on her head** elle a reçu une pomme sur la tête
3. [from ship] débarquer.
◆ ***land up*** **vi** *inf* atterrir ▸ **the car landed up in the ditch** la voiture a terminé sa course dans le fossé ▸ **you'll land up in jail!** tu finiras en prison!

CONFUSABLE / PARONYME
land

When translating land, note that *terre* and *terrain* are not interchangeable. *Terre* is used is used to refer to land in general whereas *terrain* is used when talking about the quality of the soil or to refer to a plot of land.

landed gentry ['lændɪd-] **npl** noblesse *f* de province.

landfall ['lændfɔ:l] **n** NAUT **: to make landfall** apercevoir la terre, arriver en vue d'une côte.

landfill ['lændfɪl] **n** ensevelissement *m* de déchets.

landing ['lændɪŋ] **n 1.** [of stairs] palier *m* **2.** AERON atterrissage *m* **3.** [of goods from ship] débarquement *m*.

landing card **n** carte *f* de débarquement.

landing craft **n** péniche *f* de débarquement.

landing gear **n** *(U)* train *m* d'atterrissage.

landing lights **npl** [on plane] phares *mpl* d'atterrissage / [at airport] balises *fpl* (d'atterrissage).

landing stage **n** débarcadère *m*.

landing strip **n** piste *f* d'atterrissage.

landlady ['lænd,leɪdɪ] (pl **-ies**) **n** [living in] logeuse *f* / [owner] propriétaire *f*.

landlocked ['lændlɒkt] **adj** sans accès à la mer.

landlord ['lændlɔ:d] **n 1.** [of rented property] propriétaire *m* **2.** *UK* [of pub] patron *m*.

landmark ['lændmɑ:k] **n** point *m* de repère / *fig* événement *m* marquant.

landmine ['lændmaɪn] **n** mine *f* (terrestre).

landowner ['lænd,əʊnər] **n** propriétaire foncier *m*, propriétaire foncière *f*.

land registry **n** *UK* cadastre *m*.

Land Rover® ['-rəʊvər] **n** Land Rover® *f*.

landscape ['lændskeɪp] ■ **n** paysage *m*.
■ **vt** concevoir les plans de, aménager.

landscape gardener **n** paysagiste *mf*, jardinier *m*, -ère *f* paysagiste.

landslide ['lændslaɪd] **n 1.** [of earth] glissement *m* de terrain / [of rocks] éboulement *m* **2.** *fig* [election victory] victoire *f* écrasante.

landslip ['lændslɪp] **n** glissement *m* de terrain.

lane [leɪn] **n 1.** [in country] petite route *f*, chemin *m* **2.** [in town] ruelle *f* **3.** [for traffic] voie *f* ▸ **'keep in lane'** 'ne changez pas de file' **4.** AERON & SPORT couloir *m* **5.** [for shipping] route *f* de navigation.

language ['læŋgwɪdʒ] **n 1.** [of people, country] langue *f* ▸ **to speak the same language** parler le même langage **2.** [terminology, ability to speak] langage *m* ▸ **medical/legal language** langage médical/juridique ▸ **a computer language** un langage machine ▸ **mind your language!** surveille ton langage!

CONFUSABLE / PARONYME
language

When translating language, note that *langue* and *langage* are not interchangeable. *Langue* is used when talking about a specific language used in a country or region, while *langage* refers to the concept of language in general or to a specific set of vocabulary or terminology.

language lab(oratory) **n** labo(ratoire) *m* de langues.

languid ['læŋgwɪd] **adj** *liter* langoureux(euse).

languidly ['læŋgwɪdlɪ] **adv** *liter* langoureusement.

languish ['læŋgwɪʃ] **vi** languir.

languorous ['læŋgərəs] **adj** *liter* langoureux(euse).

lank [læŋk] **adj** terne.

lanky ['læŋkɪ] (comp **-ier**, superl **-iest**) **adj** dégingandé(e).

lanolin(e) ['lænəlɪn] **n** lanoline *f*.

lantern ['læntən] **n** lanterne *f*.

Lao = ***Laotian***.

Laos [laʊs] **n** Laos *m* ▸ **in Laos** au Laos.

Laotian ['laʊʃn] ■ **adj** laotien(enne).
■ **n 1.** [person] Laotien *m*, -enne *f* **2.** [language] laotien *m*.

lap [læp] ■ **n 1.** [of person] **: on sb's lap** sur les genoux de qqn **2.** [of race] tour *m* de piste.
■ **vt** (pt & pp **-ped**, cont **-ping**) **1.** [subj: animal] laper **2.** [in race] prendre un tour d'avance sur.
■ **vi** (pt & pp **-ped**, cont **-ping**) [water, waves] clapoter.
◆ ***lap up*** **vt sep 1.** [drink] laper **2.** *fig* [compliments] se gargariser de / [lies] gober, avaler.

laparoscopy [,læpə'rɒskəpɪ] (pl **-ies**) **n** laparoscopie *f*.

La Paz [læ'pæz] **n** La Paz.

lap dance ■ **vi** danser *(pour les clients d'un bar)*.
■ **n** danse *f (pour les clients d'un bar)*.

lap dancer **n** danseur *m*, -euse *f* de bar.

lapdog ['læpdɒg] **n** [animal] petit chien *m* d'appartement / *fig & pej* [person] toutou *m*, caniche *m*.

lapel [lə'pel] **n** revers *m*.

lapis lazuli [,læpɪs'læzjʊlaɪ] **n** lapis *m*, lapis-lazuli *m inv*.

Lapland ['læplænd] **n** Laponie *f* ▸ **in Lapland** en Laponie.

Lapp [læp] ■ **adj** lapon(e).
■ **n 1.** [person] Lapon *m*, -e *f* **2.** [language] lapon *m*.

lapse [læps] ■ **n 1.** [failing] défaillance *f* ▸ **lapse in** OR **of concentration** moment *m* d'inattention **2.** [in behaviour] écart *m* de conduite **3.** [of time] intervalle *m*, laps *m* de temps ▸ **after a lapse of six months** au bout de six mois.
■ **vi 1.** [passport] être périmé(e) / [membership] prendre fin / [tradition] se perdre **2.** [person] **: to lapse into bad habits** prendre de mauvaises habitudes ▸ **to lapse into silence** se taire ▸ **she kept lapsing into Russian** elle se remettait sans cesse à parler russe.

lapsed [læpst] **adj** [Catholic] qui ne pratique plus.

laptop computer **n** (ordinateur *m*) portable *m*.

larceny ['lɑ:sənɪ] **n** *(U)* vol *m* (simple).

larch [lɑ:tʃ] **n** mélèze *m*.

lard [lɑ:d] **n** saindoux *m*.

larder ['lɑ:dər] **n** *dated* garde-manger *m inv*.

large [lɑ:dʒ] **adj** grand(e) / [person, animal, book] gros (grosse) ▸ **on a large scale** à grande échelle ▸ **she wrote him a large cheque** elle lui a fait un chèque pour une somme importante OR une grosse somme ▸ **he was standing there as large as life** il était là, en chair et en os.
◆ ***at large*** **adv 1.** [as a whole] dans son ensemble **2.** [prisoner, animal] en liberté.
◆ ***by and large*** **adv** dans l'ensemble.

largely ['lɑ:dʒlɪ] **adv** en grande partie.

larger-than-life ['lɑ:dʒər-] **adj** [character] exubérant(e).

large-scale **adj** à grande échelle.

largesse, *US* ***largess*** [lɑ:'dʒes] **n** *(U)* largesses *fpl*.

lark [lɑ:k] **n 1.** [bird] alouette *f* **2.** *inf* [joke] blague *f* ▸ **for a lark** pour rigoler.
◆ ***lark about*** **vi** *UK* s'amuser.

larva ['lɑ:və] (pl **-vae** [-vi:]) **n** larve *f*.

laryngitis [,lærɪn'dʒaɪtɪs] **n** *(U)* laryngite *f*.

larynx ['lærɪŋks] (pl **larynges** ['lærɪŋʒi:z] OR **larynxes** ['lærɪŋksi:z]) **n** larynx *m*.

lasagne, ***lasagna*** [lə'zænjə] **n** lasagnes *fpl*.

lascivious [lə'sɪvɪəs] **adj** *fml & pej* lascif(ive).

lasciviously [lə'sɪvɪəslɪ] **adv** *fml & pej* lascivement.

laser ['leɪzər] **n** laser *m*.

laser beam **n** rayon *m* laser.

laser disc **n** disque *m* laser.

laser printer **n** imprimante *f* (à) laser.

laser show **n** spectacle *m* laser.

lash [læʃ] ■ **n 1.** [eyelash] cil *m* **2.** [with whip] coup *m* de fouet.
■ **vt 1.** [gen] fouetter **2.** [tie] attacher.
◆ ***lash out*** **vi 1.** [physically] **: to lash out (at** OR **against)** envoyer un coup (à) **2.** *UK inf* [spend money] **: to lash out (on sthg)** faire une folie (en s'achetant qqch).

lass [læs] **n** *esp Scot* jeune fille *f*.

lassitude ['læsɪtju:d] **n** *fml* lassitude *f*.

lasso [læ'su:] ■ **n** (pl **-s**) lasso *m*.
■ **vt** (pt & pp **-ed**, cont **-ing**) attraper au lasso.

last [lɑ:st] ■ **adj** dernier(ère) ▸ **last Monday** lundi dernier ▸ **last week/year** la semaine/l'année dernière, la semaine/l'année passée ▸ **I've been here for the last five years** je suis ici depuis cinq ans, cela fait cinq ans que je suis ici ▸ **last night** hier soir ▸ **last July** en juillet dernier, l'année dernière au mois de juillet ▸ **that was the last time I saw him** c'était la dernière fois que je le voyais ▸ **you said that last time** c'est ce que tu as dis la dernière fois ▸ **at the last minute** OR **moment** à la dernière minute ▸ **I didn't like her last film** je n'ai pas aimé son dernier film ▸ **I'm down to my last cigarette** il ne me reste plus qu'une seule cigarette ▸ **down to the last detail/penny** jusqu'au moindre détail/dernier sou ▸ **last but one** avant-dernier (avant-dernière) ▸ **he's the last person I expected to see** c'est bien la dernière personne que je m'attendais à voir ▸ **that's the last thing I wanted** je n'avais vraiment pas besoin de ça ▸ **I'll get my money back if it's the last thing I do** je récupérerai mon argent coûte que coûte ▸ **I always clean my teeth last thing at night** je me brosse toujours les dents juste avant de me coucher.
■ **adv 1.** [most recently] la dernière fois ▸ **when did you last see him?** quand l'avez-vous vu pour la dernière fois? ▸ **they last came to see us in 1998** leur dernière visite remonte à 1998
2. [finally] en dernier, le dernier(la dernière) ▸ **she arrived last** elle est arrivée la dernière OR en dernier ▸**..., and last but not least...** ...et en dernier, mais non par ordre d'importance,...

■ **pron : she was the last to arrive** elle est arrivée la dernière ▸ **the Saturday before last** pas samedi dernier, mais le samedi d'avant ▸ **the year before last** il y a deux ans ▸ **the last but one** l'avant-dernier *m*, l'avant-dernière *f* ▸ **to leave sthg till last** faire qqch en dernier.
■ **n : we drank the last of the wine** on a bu ce qui restait de vin ▸ **the last I saw of him** la dernière fois que je l'ai vu ▸ **I hope that's the last we see of them** j'espère qu'on ne les reverra plus ▸ **you haven't heard the last of this!** vous aurez de mes nouvelles!
■ **vi** durer / [food] se garder, se conserver / [feeling] persister ▸ **it lasted (for) ten days** cela a duré dix jours ▸ **we've got enough food to last another week** nous avons assez à manger pour une semaine encore ▸ **how long can we last without water?** combien de temps tiendrons-nous sans eau? ▸ **he won't last long** [in job] il ne tiendra pas longtemps / [will soon die] il n'en a plus pour longtemps ▸ **built/made to last** construit(e)/fait(e) pour durer.
■ **vt : have we got enough to last us until tomorrow?** en avons-nous assez pour tenir *OR* aller jusqu'à demain? ▸ **that fountain pen will last you a lifetime** vous pourrez garder ce stylo plume toute votre vie.
◆ ***at last*** **adv** enfin ▸ **free at last** enfin libre ▸ **at long last** enfin.

last-ditch **adj** ultime, désespéré(e).

lasting ['lɑ:stɪŋ] **adj** durable.

lastly ['lɑ:stlɪ] **adv** pour terminer, finalement.

last-minute **adj** de dernière minute.

last name **n** nom *m* de famille.

last post **n** *UK* **1.** [postal collection] dernière levée *f* **2.** MIL extinction *f* des feux.

last rites **npl** derniers sacrements *mpl*.

last straw **n : it was the last straw** cela a été la goutte (d'eau) qui fait déborder le vase.

Last Supper **n : the Last Supper** la Cène.

last word **n : to have the last word** avoir le dernier mot.

Las Vegas [,læs'veɪgəs] **n** Las Vegas.

latch [lætʃ] ■ **n** loquet *m* ▸ **on the latch** *UK* qui n'est pas fermé à clef.
■ **vt** fermer au loquet.
◆ ***latch onto*** **vt insep** *inf* s'accrocher à.

latchkey ['lætʃki:] (pl -s) **n** clef *f* de la porte d'entrée.

latchkey kid **n** *enfant qui rentre seul après l'école et qui a la clé du domicile familial.*

late [leɪt] ■ **adj 1.** [not on time] **: to be late (for sthg)** être en retard (pour qqch) ▸ **to be 10 minutes late** avoir 10 minutes de retard ▸ **to make sb late** retarder qqn, mettre qqn en retard ▸ **we apologize for the late arrival of flight 906** nous vous prions d'excuser le retard du vol 906
2. [near end of] **: in late December, late in December** vers la fin décembre ▸ **in the late afternoon** tard dans l'après-midi, en fin d'après-midi ▸ **she's in her late fifties** elle approche la soixantaine ▸ **in the late seventies** à la fin des années soixante-dix ▸ **in late 1970** fin 1970 ▸ **at this late stage** à ce stade avancé
3. [later than normal] tardif(ive) ▸ **to have a late lunch** déjeuner tard ▸ **late booking** réservation *f* de dernière minute
4. [former] ancien(enne)
5. [dead] **: the late Mr Fox** le défunt M. Fox, feu M. Fox *fml* ▸ **her late husband** son défunt mari, feu son mari *fml*.
■ **adv 1.** [not on time] en retard ▸ **to arrive/to go to bed late** arriver/se coucher tard ▸ **to arrive 20 minutes late** arriver avec 20 minutes de retard
2. [later than normal] tard ▸ **to work/go to bed late** travailler/se coucher tard ▸ **it's getting late** il se fait tard ▸ **late in the afternoon** tard dans l'après-midi ▸ **late in the day** *lit* vers la fin de la journée ▸ **it's rather late in the day to be thinking about that** *fig* c'est un peu tard pour penser à ça.
◆ ***of late*** **adv** récemment, dernièrement.

late adopter **n** utilisateur tardif *m*, utilisatrice tardive *f*.

latecomer ['leɪt,kʌmər] **n** retardataire *mf*.

lately ['leɪtlɪ] **adv** ces derniers temps, dernièrement.

lateness ['leɪtnɪs] **n** *(U)* **1.** [of person, train] retard *m* **2.** [of meeting, event] heure *f* tardive.

late-night **adj** [TV programme] programmé(e) à une heure tardive / [shop] ouvert(e) en nocturne.

latent ['leɪtənt] **adj** latent(e).

late payment **n** retard *m* de paiement.

later ['leɪtər] ■ **adj** [date] ultérieur(e) / [edition] postérieur(e) ▸ **in later life** plus tard (dans la vie).
■ **adv : later (on)** plus tard.

lateral ['lætərəl] **adj** latéral(e).

lateral integration **n** ECON intégration *f* latérale.

lateral thinking **n** approche *f* originale.

latest ['leɪtɪst] ■ **adj** dernier(ère) ▸ **the latest date/time** la date/l'heure limite.
■ **n : have you heard the latest?** vous connaissez la dernière? ▸ **what's the latest on the trial?** qu'y a-t-il de nouveau sur le procès? ▸ **at the latest** au plus tard.

latex ['leɪteks] ■ **n** latex *m*.
■ **comp** en latex.

lath [lɑ:θ] **n** latte *f*.

lathe [leɪð] **n** tour *m*.

lather ['lɑ:ðər] ■ **n** mousse *f* (de savon).
■ **vt** savonner.
■ **vi** mousser.

Latin ['lætɪn] ■ **adj** latin(e).
■ **n** [language] latin *m*.

Latin America **n** Amérique *f* latine ▸ **in Latin America** en Amérique latine.

Latin American **n** [person] Latino-Américain *m*, -e *f*.

Latin-American **adj** latino-américain(e).

latitude ['lætɪtju:d] **n** latitude *f*.

latrine [lə'tri:n] **n** latrines *fpl*.

latter ['lætər] ■ **adj 1.** [later] dernier(ère) **2.** [second] deuxième.
■ **n : the latter** celui-ci (celle-ci), ce dernier (cette dernière).

latter-day **adj** moderne.

latterly ['lætəlɪ] **adv** *fml* récemment.

lattice ['lætɪs] **n** treillis *m*, treillage *m*.

lattice window **n** fenêtre *f* treillagée.

Latvia ['lætvɪə] **n** Lettonie *f* ▸ **in Latvia** en Lettonie.

Latvian ['lætvɪən] ■ **adj** letton(onne).
■ **n 1.** [person] Letton *m*, -onne *f* **2.** [language] letton *m*.

laudable ['lɔ:dəbl] **adj** louable.

laugh [lɑ:f] ■ **n** rire *m* ▸ **to give a laugh** rire ▸ **she left the room with a laugh** elle sortit en riant **OR** dans un éclat de rire ▸ **we had a good laugh** *inf* on a bien rigolé, on s'est bien amusé ▸ **to have (a bit of) a laugh** rigoler **OR** se marrer un peu ▸ **to do sthg for laughs OR a laugh** *inf* faire qqch pour rire **OR** rigoler ▸ **he's always good for a laugh** avec lui, on se marre bien ▸ **what a laugh!** qu'est-ce qu'on s'est marré! ▸ **they had the last laugh** finalement, ce sont eux qui ont bien ri.
■ **vi** rire ▸ **to burst out laughing** éclater de rire ▸ **to laugh aloud OR out loud** rire aux éclats ▸ **she was laughing about his gaffe all day** sa gaffe l'a fait rire toute la journée ▸ **we laughed about it afterwards** après coup, cela nous a fait bien rire, on en a ri après coup ▸ **they laughed in my face** ils m'ont ri au nez ▸ **once we get the contract, we're laughing** une fois qu'on aura empoché le contrat, on sera tranquilles.
■ **vt 1.** [in amusement] **: to laugh o.s. silly** se tordre de rire, être plié(e) en deux de rire
2. [in ridicule] **: he was laughed off the stage/out of the room** il a quitté la scène/la pièce sous les rires moqueurs ▸ **to laugh sthg out of court** tourner qqch en dérision.
◆ ***laugh at*** **vt insep 1.** [in amusement] **: we all laughed at the joke/the film** la blague/le film nous a tous fait rire **2.** [mock] se moquer de, rire de.
◆ ***laugh off*** **vt sep** tourner en plaisanterie ▸ **he tried to laugh off the defeat** il s'efforça de ne pas prendre sa défaite trop au sérieux.

laughable ['lɑ:fəbl] **adj** ridicule, risible.

laughing gas ['lɑ:fɪŋ-] **n** gaz *m* hilarant.

laughingly ['lɑ:fɪŋlɪ] **adv 1.** [cheerfully] en riant **2.** [inappropriately] **: this noise is laughingly called folk music** c'est ce bruit qu'on appelle le plus sérieusement du monde de la musique folk.

laughing stock **n** risée *f*.

laughter ['lɑ:ftəʳ] **n** *(U)* rire *m*, rires *mpl*.

launch [lɔ:ntʃ] ■ **n 1.** [gen] lancement *m* **2.** [boat] chaloupe *f* ▸ **(pleasure) launch** bateau *m* de plaisance.
■ **vt** lancer ▸ **that was the audition that launched me on my career** cette audition a donné le coup d'envoi de ma carrière ▸ **to launch a military offensive** déclencher **OR** lancer une attaque.
◆ ***launch into*** **vt insep** se lancer dans.

launcher ['lɔ:ntʃəʳ] **n** lanceur *m*.

launching ['lɔ:ntʃɪŋ] **n** lancement *m*.

launch(ing) pad, ***launchpad*** ['lɔ:ntʃ(ɪŋ)-] **n** pas *m* de tir.

launder ['lɔ:ndəʳ] **vt** *lit & fig* blanchir.

laundrette, *UK* ***Launderette***® [lɔ:n'dret], *US* ***Laundromat***® ['lɔ:ndrəmæt] **n** laverie *f* automatique.

laundry ['lɔ:ndrɪ] (pl **-ies**) **n 1.** *(U)* [clothes] lessive *f* **2.** [business] blanchisserie *f* **3.** [room] buanderie *f*.

laundry basket **n** *UK* panier *m* à linge.

laureate ['lɔ:rɪət] ➤ ***poet laureate***.

laurel ['lɒrəl] **n** laurier *m*.

laurels ['lɒrəlz] **npl : to rest on one's laurels** se reposer sur ses lauriers.

Lautro ['lautrəu] (abbr of ***Life Assurance and Unit Trust Regulatory Organization***) **n** *organisme britannique contrôlant les activités de compagnies d'assurance-vie et de SICAV*.

lava ['lɑ:və] **n** lave *f*.

lavatory ['lævətrɪ] (pl **-ies**) **n** *esp UK* toilettes *fpl*.

lavatory paper **n** *UK* papier *m* hygiénique.

lavender ['lævəndəʳ] ■ **adj** [colour] (bleu) lavande *(inv)*.
■ **n** [plant] lavande *f*.

lavish ['lævɪʃ] ■ **adj 1.** [generous] généreux(euse) ▸ **to be lavish with** être prodigue de **2.** [sumptuous] somptueux(euse).
■ **vt : to lavish sthg on sb** prodiguer qqch à qqn.

lavishly ['lævɪʃlɪ] **adv 1.** [generously] généreusement **2.** [sumptuously] somptueusement.

law [lɔ:] ■ **n 1.** [gen] loi *f* ▸ **a law against gambling** une loi qui interdit les jeux d'argent ▸ **against the law** contraire à la loi, illégal(e) ▸ **to break the law** enfreindre **OR** transgresser la loi ▸ **by law** selon la loi ▸ **in OR under British law** selon la loi britannique ▸ **the bill became law** le projet de loi a été voté **OR** adopté ▸ **law and order** ordre *m* public ▸ **to lay down the law** *inf* faire la loi ▸ **the law of the jungle** la loi de la jungle **2.** LAW droit *m* **3.** *inf* [police] **: the law** les flics *mpl* **4.** [scientific principle] loi *f* ▸ **the law of supply and demand** ECON la loi de l'offre et de la demande.
■ **comp** [student, degree] en droit / [faculty, school] de droit.

law-abiding [-ə,baɪdɪŋ] **adj** respectueux(euse) des lois.

law-breaker **n** personne *f* qui enfreint **OR** transgresse les lois.

law centre **n** bureau *m* d'aide judiciaire.

law court **n** tribunal *m*, cour *f* de justice.

law-enforcement **adj** *US* chargé(e) de faire respecter la loi ▸ **law-enforcement officer** *représentant d'un service chargé de faire respecter la loi*.

lawful ['lɔ:fʊl] **adj** légal(e), licite.

lawfully ['lɔ:fʊlɪ] **adv** légalement.

lawless ['lɔ:lɪs] **adj 1.** [illegal] contraire à la loi, illégal(e) **2.** [without laws] sans loi.

lawlessness ['lɔ:lɪsnɪs] **n** non-respect *m* de la loi / [anarchy] anarchie *f* / [illegality] illégalité *f*.

Law Lords **npl** *UK* LAW **: the Law Lords** les juges *mpl* de la Chambre des Lords.

lawmaker ['lɔ:,meɪkəʳ] **n** législateur *m*, -trice *f*.

lawn [lɔ:n] **n** pelouse *f*, gazon *m*.

lawnmower ['lɔ:n,məʊəʳ] **n** tondeuse *f* à gazon.

lawn party **n** *US* garden-party *f*.

lawn tennis **n** tennis *m* (sur gazon).

law school **n** faculté *f* de droit.

lawsuit ['lɔ:su:t] **n** procès *m*.

lawyer ['lɔ:jəʳ] **n** [in court] avocat *m* / [of company] conseiller *m*, -ère *f* juridique / [for wills, sales] notaire *m*.

CULTURE

Lawyer

Aux États-Unis comme en Angleterre, le terme **lawyer** désigne un avocat (les Américains utilisent formellement le synonyme **attorney**). Au Royaume-Uni, il existe deux acceptions différentes pour cette profession : le **solicitor** (« intermédiaire ») travaille dans un cabinet et représente ses clients devant certaines cours en cas de divorce ou de transferts de biens ; le **barrister** (« avocat ») défend son client à la Cour devant un juge. Aux États-Unis, un avocat membre du barreau d'un certain État n'est pas toujours autorisé à exercer en dehors de sa juridiction : toutefois, chaque citoyen peut être représenté par un avocat dans l'État où il réside.

lax [læks] **adj** relâché(e).

laxative ['læksətɪv] **n** laxatif *m*.

laxity ['læksətɪ], ***laxness*** ['læksnɪs] **n** relâchement *m*.

lay [leɪ] ■ **pt** ➤ ***lie***.
■ **vt** (pt & pp **laid**) **1.** [gen] poser, mettre / *fig* **: to lay the blame for sthg on sb** rejeter la responsabilité de qqch sur qqn ▸ **he laid the baby on the bed** il a couché l'enfant sur le lit ▸ **to lay sb to rest** *euph* enterrer qqn **2.** [trap, snare] tendre, dresser / [plans] faire ▸ **to lay the table** *UK* mettre la table *OR* le couvert **3.** [egg] pondre.
■ **adj 1.** RELIG laïque **2.** [untrained] profane.
◆ ***lay aside*** **vt sep** mettre de côté ▸ **you should lay aside any personal opinions you might have** *fig* vous devez faire abstraction de toute opinion personnelle.
◆ ***lay before*** **vt sep : to lay sthg before sb** [proposal] présenter *OR* soumettre qqch à qqn.
◆ ***lay down*** **vt sep 1.** [guidelines, rules] imposer, stipuler **2.** [put down] déposer ▸ **to lay down one's life** se sacrifier.
◆ ***lay into*** **vt insep** *inf* attaquer.
◆ ***lay off*** ■ **vt sep** [make redundant] licencier.
■ **vt insep** *inf* **1.** [leave alone] ficher la paix à **2.** [give up] arrêter.
◆ ***lay on*** **vt sep** *UK* [provide, supply] organiser ▸ **they had transport laid on for us** ils s'étaient occupés de nous procurer un moyen de transport ▸ **to lay it on thick** *inf fig* en rajouter.
◆ ***lay out*** **vt sep 1.** [arrange] arranger, disposer **2.** [design] concevoir **3.** [corpse] faire la toilette de.
◆ ***lay over*** **vi** *US* faire escale.

layabout ['leɪəbaʊt] **n** *UK inf* fainéant *m*, -e *f*.

lay-by (pl **lay-bys**) **n** *UK* aire *f* de stationnement.

lay days **npl** starie *f*, jours *mpl* de planche.

layer ['leɪəʳ] **n** couche *f* / *fig* [level] niveau *m*.

layered ['leɪəd] **adj** SEW **: a layered skirt** une jupe à volants.

layette [leɪ'et] **n** layette *f*.

layman ['leɪmən] (pl **-men** [-mən]) **n 1.** [untrained person] profane *m* **2.** RELIG laïc *m*.

lay-off **n** licenciement *m*.

layout ['leɪaʊt] **n** [of office, building] agencement *m* / [of garden] plan *m* / [of page] mise *f* en page.

layover ['leɪəʊvəʳ] **n** *US* escale *f*.

lay preacher **n** prédicateur *m* laïque.

laze [leɪz] **vi : to laze (around** *OR* **about)** *UK* paresser.

lazily ['leɪzɪlɪ] **adv** paresseusement, avec nonchalance.

laziness ['leɪzɪnɪs] **n** paresse *f*.

lazy ['leɪzɪ] (comp **-ier**, superl **-iest**) **adj** [person] paresseux(euse), fainéant(e) / [action] nonchalant(e).

lazybones ['leɪzɪbəʊnz] (pl **lazybones**) **n** *inf* paresseux *m*, -euse *f*, fainéant *m*, -e *f*.

lb (abbr of ***pound***) *livre (unité de poids)*.

LB abbr of ***Labrador***.

lbw (abbr of ***leg before wicket***) *au cricket, faute d'un joueur qui met une jambe devant le guichet*.

lc (abbr of ***lower case***) bdc.

L/C abbr of ***letter of credit***.

LCD (abbr of ***liquid crystal display***) **n** *affichage à cristaux liquides*.

Ld abbr of ***Lord***.

LDC (abbr of ***less-developed country***) **n** PMA *m (pays moins développé)*.

L-driver **n** *UK* conducteur débutant *m*, conductrice débutante *f (qui n'a pas encore son permis)*.

LDS **n** *UK* (abbr of ***Licentiate in Dental Surgery***) *diplômé en chirurgie dentaire*.

LEA (abbr of ***local education authority***) **n** direction *f* régionale de l'enseignement *(en Angleterre et aux pays de Galles)*.

lead[1] [li:d] ■ **n 1.** [winning position] **: to be in** *OR* **have the lead** mener, être en tête ▸ **to go into** *OR* **to take the lead** [in race] prendre la tête / [in match] mener ▸ **to have a 10-point/10-length lead** avoir 10 points/10 longueurs d'avance
2. [initiative, example] initiative *f*, exemple *m* ▸ **to take the lead** montrer l'exemple ▸ **take your lead from me** prenez exemple sur moi ▸ **to follow sb's lead** suivre l'exemple de qqn
3. THEAT **: the lead** le rôle principal
4. [clue] indice *m* ▸ **the police have several leads** la police tient plusieurs pistes
5. *UK* [for dog] laisse *f*
6. [wire, cable] câble *m*, fil *m*.
■ **adj** [role] principal(e) ▸ **lead singer** chanteur *m*, -euse *f*.
■ **vt** (pt & pp **led**) **1.** [be at front of] mener, être à la tête de ▸ **to lead an army into battle** mener une armée au combat
2. [guide] guider, conduire ▸ **to lead sb somewhere** mener *OR* conduire qqn quelque part ▸ **she led him down the stairs** elle lui fit descendre l'escalier ▸ **to lead the way** montrer le chemin ▸ **police motorcyclists led the way** des motards de la police ouvraient la route
3. [be in charge of] être à la tête de, diriger ▸ **to lead the prayers/singing** diriger la prière/les chants
4. [life] mener

5. [cause, bring] **: to lead sb to do sthg** inciter *OR* pousser qqn à faire qqch ▸ **he led me to believe (that) he was innocent** il m'a amené à croire qu'il était innocent ▸ **this leads me to my second point** ceci m'amène à ma seconde remarque ▸ **he is easily led** il se laisse facilement influencer.

■ **vi** (pt & pp **led**) **1.** [go] mener, conduire ▸ **to lead to/into** donner sur, donner accès à ▸ **where does this door lead to?** sur quoi ouvre cette porte? ▸ **the stairs lead to the cellar** l'escalier mène *OR* conduit à la cave ▸ **take the street that leads away from the station** prenez la rue qui part de la gare ▸ **that road leads nowhere** cette route ne mène nulle part

2. [be ahead] mener ▸ **to lead by 2 metres** avoir 2 mètres d'avance ▸ **to lead by 3 points to 1** mener par 3 points à 1 ▸ **if you lead, I'll follow** allez-y, je vous suis

3. [result in] **: to lead to sthg** aboutir à qqch, causer qqch ▸ **the decision led to panic on Wall Street** la décision a semé la panique à Wall Street ▸ **one thing led to another** une chose en amenait une autre ▸ **several factors led to his decision to leave** plusieurs facteurs le poussèrent *OR* l'amenèrent à décider de partir

4. *UK* PRESS **: to lead with sthg** mettre qqch à la une.

◆ ***lead off*** ■ **vt insep** [subj: door, room] donner sur ▸ **several avenues lead off the square** plusieurs avenues partent de la place.

■ **vi 1.** [road, corridor] **: to lead off (from)** partir (de)

2. [begin] commencer.

◆ ***lead on*** ■ **vi insep : lead on!** allez-y!

■ **vt sep 1.** [trick] **: to lead sb on** faire marcher qqn

2. [in progression] amener ▸ **this leads me on to my second point** ceci m'amène à mon deuxième point.

◆ ***lead up to*** **vt insep 1.** [precede] conduire à, aboutir à ▸ **the events leading up to the war** les événements qui devaient déclencher la guerre ▸ **in the months leading up to her death** pendant les mois qui précédèrent sa mort

2. [build up to] amener ▸ **what are you leading up to?** où voulez-vous en venir?

lead² [led] ■ **n** plomb *m* / [in pencil] mine *f*.

■ **comp** en *OR* de plomb.

leaded ['ledɪd] **adj** [petrol] au plomb / [window] à petits carreaux.

leaden ['ledn] **adj 1.** *liter* [sky] de plomb **2.** [very dull] mortellement ennuyeux(euse).

leader ['li:dəʳ] **n 1.** [head, chief] chef *mf* / POL leader *mf* **2.** [in race, competition] premier *m*, -ère *f* ▸ **she was up with the leaders** elle était parmi les premiers *OR* dans le peloton de tête ▸ **the institute is a world leader in cancer research** l'institut occupe une des premières places mondiales en matière de recherche contre le cancer **3.** *UK* PRESS éditorial *m*.

leadership ['li:dəʃɪp] **n 1.** [people in charge] **: the leadership** les dirigeants *mpl* **2.** [position of leader] direction *f* **3.** *(U)* [qualities of leader] qualités *fpl* de chef.

leadership battle, ***leadership contest*** **n** POL lutte *f* pour la position de leader.

leadership election **n** POL élections *fpl* pour la position de leader.

lead-free [led-] **adj** sans plomb.

lead guitar [li:d-] **n** première *f* guitare.

lead-in [li:d-] **n** *UK* **1.** [introductory remarks] introduction *f*, remarques *fpl* préliminaires **2.** [wire] descente *f* d'antenne.

leading ['li:dɪŋ] **adj 1.** [most important] principal(e) **2.** [main] **: leading part** *OR* **role** THEAT rôle *m* principal / *fig* rôle prépondérant **3.** [at front] de tête.

leading article **n** *UK* éditorial *m*.

leading lady **n** premier rôle *m* féminin.

leading light **n** personnage *m* très important *OR* influent.

leading man **n** premier rôle *m* masculin.

leading question **n** question *f* insidieuse.

lead pencil [led-] **n** crayon *m* à mine de plomb *OR* à papier.

lead poisoning [led-] **n** saturnisme *m*.

leads and lags [li:dz-] **npl** ECON termaillage *m*.

lead time [li:d-] **n** COMM délai *m* de livraison.

lead user [li:d-] **n** utilisateur *m*, -trice *f* pilote.

leaf [li:f] (pl **leaves** [li:vz]) **n 1.** [of tree, plant] feuille *f* **2.** [of table - hinged] abattant *m* / [- pull-out] rallonge *f* **3.** [of book] feuille *f*, page *f*.

◆ ***leaf through*** **vt insep** [magazine] parcourir, feuilleter.

leaflet ['li:flɪt] ■ **n** prospectus *m*.

■ **vt** [area] distribuer des prospectus dans.

leafy ['li:fɪ] (comp **-ier**, superl **-iest**) **adj** feuillu(e) / [suburb, lane] planté(e) d'arbres.

league [li:g] **n** ligue *f* / SPORT championnat *m* ▸ **to be in league with** être de connivence avec ▸ **United are league leaders at the moment** United est en tête du championnat en ce moment ▸ **he's not in the same league as his father** il n'a pas la classe de son père.

league table **n** *UK* classement *m* du championnat.

league standings **npl** *US* classement *m* du championnat.

leak [li:k] ■ **n** *lit* & *fig* fuite *f*.

■ **vt** [secret, information] divulguer.

■ **vi** [liquid] fuir.

◆ ***leak out*** **vi 1.** [liquid] fuir **2.** *fig* [secret, information] transpirer, être divulgué(e).

leakage ['li:kɪdʒ] **n** fuite *f*.

leakproof ['li:kpru:f] **adj** étanche.

leaky ['li:kɪ] (comp **-ier**, superl **-iest**) **adj** qui fuit.

lean [li:n] ■ **adj 1.** [slim] mince **2.** [meat] maigre **3.** *fig* [month, time] mauvais(e).

■ **vt** (pt & pp **leant** *OR* **-ed**) [rest] **: to lean sthg against** appuyer qqch contre, adosser qqch à.

■ **vi** (pt & pp **leant** *OR* **-ed**) **1.** [bend, slope] se pencher **2.** [rest] **: to lean on/against** s'appuyer sur/contre.

leaning ['li:nɪŋ] **n : leaning (towards)** penchant *m* (pour).

leant [lent] **pt & pp** ➤ ***lean***.

lean-to (pl **lean-tos**) **n** appentis *m*.

leap [li:p] ■ **n** *lit* & *fig* bond *m* ▸ **it's a great leap forward in medical research** c'est un grand bond en avant pour la recherche médicale ▸ **in leaps and bounds** à pas de géant.

■ vi (pt & pp **leapt** *OR* -ed) **1.** [gen] bondir ▸ **to leap to one's feet** se lever d'un bond ▸ **she leapt to the wrong conclusion** elle a conclu trop hâtivement **2.** *fig* [increase] faire un bond.
◆ ***leap at*** vt insep *fig* [opportunity] sauter sur.

leapfrog ['li:pfrɒg] ■ n saute-mouton *m inv*.
■ vt (pt & pp -ged, cont -ging) dépasser (d'un bond).
■ vi (pt & pp -ged, cont -ging) : **to leapfrog over** sauter par-dessus.

leapt [lept] pt & pp ➤ ***leap***.

leap year n année *f* bissextile.

learn [lɜ:n] (pt & pp -ed *OR* learnt) ■ vt : **to learn (that)...** apprendre que... ▸ **to learn (how) to do sthg** apprendre à faire qqch ▸ **he's learnt his lesson now** *fig* cela lui a servi de leçon.
■ vi : **to learn (of** *OR* **about sthg)** apprendre (qqch) ▸ **to learn from one's mistakes** tirer la leçon de ses erreurs ▸ **they learnt the hard way** ils ont été à dure école.

learned ['lɜ:nɪd] adj savant(e).

learner ['lɜ:nər] n débutant *m*, -e *f*.

learner (driver) n *UK* conducteur débutant *m*, conductrice débutante *f (qui n'a pas encore son permis)*.

learning ['lɜ:nɪŋ] n savoir *m*, érudition *f*.

learning curve n courbe *f* d'apprentissage.

learning difficulties, ***learning disabilities*** npl difficultés *fpl* d'apprentissage.

learnt [lɜ:nt] pt & pp ➤ ***learn***.

lease [li:s] ■ n bail *m* ▸ **a new lease of life** *UK*, **a new lease on life** *US* une seconde jeunesse.
■ vt louer ▸ **to lease sthg from sb** louer qqch à qqn ▸ **to lease sthg to sb** louer qqch à qqn.

leaseback ['li:sbæk] n cession *f* de bail, cession-bail *f*.

leasehold ['li:shəuld] ■ adj loué(e) à bail, tenu(e) à bail.
■ adv à bail.

leaseholder ['li:sˌhəuldər] n locataire *mf*.

leash [li:ʃ] n *US* laisse *f*.

leasing ['li:sɪŋ] n crédit-bail *m*, leasing *m*.

least [li:st] *(superl of* **little***)* ■ adj : **the least** le moindre(la moindre), le plus petit(la plus petite) ▸ **he earns the least money of any of us** de nous tous, c'est lui qui gagne le moins.
■ pron [smallest amount] : **the least** le moins ▸ **it's the least (that) he can do** c'est la moindre des choses qu'il puisse faire ▸ **not in the least** pas du tout, pas le moins du monde ▸ **to say the least** c'est le moins qu'on puisse dire.
■ adv : **(the) least** le moins(la moins).
◆ ***at least*** adv au moins ⁄ [to correct] du moins.
◆ ***least of all*** adv surtout pas, encore moins.
◆ ***not least*** adv *fml* notamment.

least-developed country n pays *m* parmi les moins avancés.

leather ['leðər] ■ n cuir *m*.
■ comp en cuir.

leatherbound ['leðəbaund] adj relié(e) (en) cuir.

leatherette® [ˌleðə'ret] n similicuir *m*.

leathery ['leðərɪ] adj [meat] coriace ⁄ [skin] parcheminé(e), tanné(e).

leave [li:v] ■ vt (pt & pp **left**) **1.** [gen] laisser ▸ **he's out: do you want to leave a message?** il n'est pas là, voulez-vous laisser un message? ▸ **I must have left my gloves at the café** j'ai dû oublier mes gants au café ▸ **can I leave my suitcase with you for a few minutes?** puis-je vous confier ma valise quelques instants? ▸ **if you don't like your dinner, then leave it** si tu n'aimes pas ton dîner, laisse-le ▸ **I left him to his reading** je l'ai laissé à sa lecture ▸ **can I leave you to deal with it, then?** vous vous en chargez, alors? ▸ **she leaves me to get on with things** elle me laisse faire ▸ **right then, I'll leave you to it** bon, eh bien, je te laisse ▸ **leave it with me** laissez-moi faire, je m'en charge ▸ **leave it to me!** je m'en occupe!, je m'en charge! ▸ **leave yourself an hour to get to the airport** prévoyez une heure pour aller à l'aéroport ▸ **don't leave things to the last minute** n'attendez pas la dernière minute (pour faire ce que vous avez à faire) ▸ **he left his work unfinished** il n'a pas terminé son travail ▸ **their behaviour leaves a lot to be desired** leur conduite laisse beaucoup à désirer ▸ **to leave sb alone** laisser qqn tranquille ▸ **it leaves me cold** ça me laisse froid
2. [go away from] quitter ▸ **he left the room** il est sorti de *OR* il a quitté la pièce ▸ **she left London yesterday** elle est partie de *OR* elle a quitté Londres hier ▸ **I left home at 18** je suis parti de chez moi *OR* de chez mes parents à 18 ans ▸ **she left him for another man** elle l'a quitté pour un autre ▸ **to leave school** quitter l'école ▸ **to leave the table** se lever de table
3. [bequeath] : **to leave sb sthg, to leave sthg to sb** léguer *OR* laisser qqch à qqn ▸ **she left all her money to charity** elle légua toute sa fortune à des œuvres de charité.
■ vi (pt & pp **left**) partir ▸ **when did you leave?** quand est-ce que vous êtes partis? ▸ **we're leaving for Mexico tomorrow** nous partons pour le Mexique demain ▸ **if you'd rather I left...** si vous voulez que je vous laisse...
■ n **1.** congé *m* ▸ **to be on leave** [from work] être en congé ⁄ [from army] être en permission
2. *fml* [permission] permission *f*, autorisation *f* ▸ **by** *OR* **with your leave** avec votre permission
3. [farewell] congé *m* ▸ **to take one's leave (of sb)** prendre congé (de qqn) ▸ **to take leave of one's senses** perdre la tête *OR* la raison ; see also ***left***.
◆ ***leave aside*** vt sep laisser de côté ▸ **leaving aside the question of cost** si on laisse de côté la question du coût.
◆ ***leave behind*** vt sep **1.** [go away from] abandonner, laisser ▸ **it's hard to leave all your friends and relations behind** c'est dur de laisser tous ses amis et sa famille derrière soi ▸ **she soon left the other runners behind** elle a vite distancé tous les autres coureurs ▸ **if you don't work harder, you'll get left behind** si tu ne travailles pas plus, tu vas te retrouver loin derrière les autres
2. [forget] oublier, laisser.
◆ ***leave off*** ■ vt sep **1.** [omit] : **to leave sthg off (sthg)** omettre qqch (de qqch)
2. [stop] : **to leave off doing sthg** s'arrêter de faire qqch.
■ vi s'arrêter ▸ **we'll carry on from where we left off** nous allons reprendre là où nous nous étions arrêtés.
◆ ***leave out*** vt sep omettre, exclure ▸ **leave out any reference to her husband in your article** dans votre article, évitez toute allusion à son mari ▸ **to feel left out** se sentir de trop, se sentir exclu(e)

▸▸ **leave it out!** *UK v inf* lâche-moi!
◆ ***leave over*** **vt sep** [allow or cause to remain] laisser ▸ **to be left over** rester ▸ **there are still one or two left over** il en reste encore un ou deux.

leave of absence **n** congé *m*.

leaves [li:vz] **npl** ➤ ***leaf***.

Lebanese [ˌlebəˈni:z] ■ **adj** libanais(e).
■ **n** (pl **Lebanese**) [person] Libanais *m*, -e *f*.

Lebanon [ˈlebənən] **n** Liban *m* ▸ **in (the) Lebanon** au Liban.

lech [letʃ] *inf* ■ **vi : he's always leching after my secretary** il n'arrête pas de reluquer ma secrétaire.
■ **n** obsédé *m* (sexuel).

lecher [ˈletʃəʳ] **n** obsédé *m* (sexuel).

lecherous [ˈletʃərəs] **adj** *pej* lubrique, libidineux(euse).

lecherously [ˈletʃərəslɪ] **adv** lubriquement, avec lubricité ▸ **to look at sb lecherously** regarder qqn d'un œil lubrique.

lechery [ˈletʃərɪ] **n** lubricité *f*.

lectern [ˈlektən] **n** lutrin *m*.

lecture [ˈlektʃəʳ] ■ **n 1.** [talk - gen] conférence *f* / UNIV cours *m* magistral ▸ **to give a lecture (on sthg)** faire une conférence (sur qqch) / UNIV faire un cours (sur qqch) **2.** [scolding] **: to give sb a lecture** réprimander qqn, sermonner qqn.
■ **vt** [scold] réprimander, sermonner.
■ **vi : to lecture on sthg** faire un cours sur qqch ▸ **to lecture in sthg** être professeur de qqch.

FALSE FRIENDS / FAUX AMIS
lecture

Lecture n'est pas la traduction du mot anglais *lecture*. Lecture se traduit par *reading*.
▸ N'oublie pas ton livre de lecture / *Don't forget your reading book*

lecture hall **n** amphithéâtre *m*.

lecturer [ˈlektʃərəʳ] **n** [speaker] conférencier *m*, -ère *f* / *UK* UNIV maître assistant *m*.

lecture room **n** salle *f* de cours *OR* de conférences.

lectureship [ˈlektʃəʃɪp] **n** UNIV poste *m* d'assistant ▸ **he got a lectureship at the University of Oxford** il a été nommé assistant à l'université d'Oxford
▸▸ **senior lectureship** ≃ poste de maître de conférences.

lecture theatre **n** *UK* amphithéâtre *m*.

led [led] **pt & pp** ➤ ***lead***[1].

LED (abbr of ***light-emitting diode***) **n** LED *f*.

ledge [ledʒ] **n 1.** [of window] rebord *m* **2.** [of mountain] corniche *f*.

ledger [ˈledʒəʳ] **n** grand livre *m*.

lee [li:] **n : in the lee of** à l'abri de.

leech [li:tʃ] **n** *lit & fig* sangsue *f*.

leek [li:k] **n** poireau *m*.

leer [lɪəʳ] ■ **n** regard *m* libidineux.
■ **vi : to leer at** reluquer.

Leeward Islands [ˈli:wəd-] **npl : the Leeward Islands** les îles *fpl* Sous-le-Vent.

leeway [ˈli:weɪ] **n 1.** [room to manoeuvre] marge *f* de manœuvre **2.** [time lost] **: to make up leeway** rattraper son retard.

left [left] ■ **pt & pp** ➤ ***leave***.
■ **adj 1.** [remaining] **: to be left** rester ▸ **have you** *OR* **do you have any money left?** il te reste de l'argent? **2.** [not right] gauche.
■ **adv** à gauche.
■ **n : on** *OR* **to the left** à gauche ▸ **keep to the left** gardez votre gauche.
◆ ***Left*** **n** POL **: the Left** la Gauche.

left-click ■ **vt** COMPUT cliquer avec le bouton gauche de la souris sur.
■ **vi** COMPUT cliquer avec le bouton gauche de la souris.

left-footed [-ˈfʊtɪd] **adj** gaucher(ère) (du pied).

left-hand **adj** de gauche ▸ **left-hand side** gauche *f*, côté *m* gauche.

left-hand drive ■ **adj** [car] avec la conduite à gauche.
■ **n** conduite *f* à gauche.

left-handed [-ˈhændɪd] ■ **adj 1.** [person] gaucher(ère) **2.** [implement] pour gaucher **3.** *US* [compliment] faux(fausse).
■ **adv** de la main gauche.

left-hander [-ˈhændəʳ] **n** gaucher *m*, -ère *f*.

Leftist [ˈleftɪst] ■ **adj** POL de gauche, gauchiste.
■ **n** POL gauchiste *mf*.

left luggage (office) **n** *UK* consigne *f*.

left-of-centre **adj** POL de centre-gauche ▸ **his views are slightly left-of-centre** ses opinions sont plutôt de centre-gauche.

leftover [ˈleftəʊvəʳ] **adj** qui reste, en surplus.
◆ ***leftovers*** **npl** restes *mpl*.

left wing **n** POL gauche *f*.
◆ ***left-wing*** **adj** POL de gauche.

left-winger **n** POL homme *m* de gauche, femme de gauche *f*.

lefty [ˈleftɪ] (pl **-ies**) **n 1.** *UK inf* POL gauchiste *mf*, gaucho *m* **2.** *US* [left-handed person] gaucher *m*, -ère *f*.

leg [leg] **n 1.** [of person, trousers] jambe *f* / [of animal] patte *f* ▸ **to be on one's last legs** être à bout de souffle ▸ **you don't have a leg to stand on!** ça ne tient pas debout! ▸ **to pull sb's leg** faire marcher qqn **2.** CULIN [of lamb] gigot *m* / [of pork, chicken] cuisse *f* **3.** [of furniture] pied *m* **4.** [of journey, match] étape *f* ▸ **away leg** *UK* FOOTBALL match *m* à l'extérieur *OR* sur terrain adverse.

legacy [ˈlegəsɪ] (pl **-ies**) **n** *lit & fig* legs *m*, héritage *m*.

legal [ˈli:gl] **adj 1.** [concerning the law] juridique ▸ **to take legal advice** consulter un juriste *OR* un avocat **2.** [lawful] légal(e) ▸ **they're below the legal age** ils n'ont pas atteint l'âge légal ▸ **to make sthg legal** légaliser qqch.

legal action **n : to take legal action against sb** intenter un procès à qqn, engager des poursuites contre qqn.

legal aid **n** assistance *f* judiciaire.

legal eagle **n** *inf hum* avocat *m*, -e *f*.

legality [li:ˈgælətɪ] **n** légalité *f*.

legalization, *UK* ***-isation*** [ˌli:gəlaɪ'zeɪʃn] **n** légalisation *f*.

legalize, *UK* ***-ise*** ['li:gəlaɪz] **vt** légaliser, rendre légal.

legally ['li:gəlɪ] **adv** légalement ▸ **legally binding** qui oblige en droit.

legal separation **n** LAW séparation *f* de corps.

legal tender **n** monnaie *f* légale.

legation [lɪ'geɪʃn] **n** légation *f*.

legend ['ledʒənd] **n** *lit* & *fig* légende *f*.

legendary ['ledʒəndrɪ] **adj** *lit* & *fig* légendaire.

leggings ['legɪŋz] **npl** jambières *fpl*, leggings *mpl* ***OU*** *fpl*.

leggy ['legɪ] (comp **-ier**, superl **-iest**) **adj** [woman] qui a des jambes interminables.

legibility [ˌledʒɪ'bɪlətɪ] **n** lisibilité *f*.

legible ['ledʒəbl] **adj** lisible.

legibly ['ledʒəblɪ] **adv** lisiblement.

legion ['li:dʒən] ■ **n** *lit* & *fig* légion *f*.
■ **adj** *fml* **: to be legion** être légion *(inv)*.

legionnaire's disease [ˌli:dʒə'neəz-] **n** maladie *f* du légionnaire, légionellose *f*.

legislate ['ledʒɪsleɪt] **vi : to legislate (for/against)** faire des lois (pour/contre).

legislation [ˌledʒɪs'leɪʃn] **n** législation *f*.

legislative ['ledʒɪslətɪv] **adj** législatif(ive).

legislative body **n** corps *m* législatif.

legislator ['ledʒɪsleɪtəʳ] **n** législateur *m*, -trice *f*.

legislature ['ledʒɪsleɪtʃəʳ] **n** corps *m* législatif.

legitimacy [lɪ'dʒɪtɪməsɪ] **n** légitimité *f*.

legitimate [lɪ'dʒɪtɪmət] **adj** légitime.

legitimately [lɪ'dʒɪtɪmətlɪ] **adv** légitimement.

legitimize, *UK* ***-ise*** [lɪ'dʒɪtəmaɪz] **vt** légitimer.

legless ['leglɪs] **adj** *UK inf* [drunk] bourré(e), rond(e).

leg-pull **n** *inf* canular *m*, farce *f*.

legroom ['legrʊm] **n** *(U)* place *f* pour les jambes.

leg-up **n : to give sb a leg-up** *lit* faire la courte échelle à qqn / *fig* donner un coup de main ***OR*** de pouce à qqn.

legwarmers [-ˌwɔ:məz] **npl** jambières *fpl*.

legwork ['legwɜ:k] **n : I had to do the legwork** *inf* j'ai dû beaucoup me déplacer.

Leics (abbr of **Leicestershire**) *comté anglais*.

leisure [*UK* 'leʒəʳ, *US* 'li:ʒər] **n** loisir *m*, temps *m* libre ▸ **at (one's) leisure** à loisir, tout à loisir.

leisure centre **n** *UK* centre *m* de loisirs.

leisurely [*UK* 'leʒəlɪ, *US* 'li:ʒərlɪ] ■ **adj** [pace] lent(e), tranquille.
■ **adv** [walk] sans se presser.

leisure time **n** *(U)* temps *m* libre, loisirs *mpl*.

leisurewear ['leʒəweəʳ] **n** *(U)* vêtements *mpl* de sport.

lemming ['lemɪŋ] **n** lemming *m* ▸ **like lemmings** *fig* comme les moutons de Panurge.

lemon ['lemən] **n** [fruit] citron *m*.

lemonade [ˌlemə'neɪd] **n 1.** *UK* [fizzy] limonade *f* **2.** *esp US* [flat] citronnade *f* **3.** *US* [juice] citron *m* pressé.

lemon curd **n** *UK* crème *f* au citron.

lemongrass ['lemənɡrɑ:s] **n** *(U)* citronnelle *f*.

lemon juice **n** jus *m* de citron.

lemon sole **n** limande-sole *f*.

lemon squash **n** *UK* citronnade *f*.

lemon squeezer [-'skwi:zəʳ] **n** presse-citron *m inv*.

lemon tea **n** thé *m* (au) citron.

lend [lend] (pt & pp **lent**) **vt 1.** [loan] prêter ▸ **to lend sb sthg, to lend sthg to sb** prêter qqch à qqn **2.** [offer] **: to lend support (to sb)** offrir son soutien (à qqn) ▸ **to lend assistance (to sb)** prêter assistance (à qqn) **3.** [add] **: to lend sthg to sthg** [quality] ajouter qqch à qqch.

lender ['lendəʳ] **n** prêteur *m*, -euse *f*.

lending library ['lendɪŋ-] **n** bibliothèque *f* de prêt.

lending rate ['lendɪŋ-] **n** taux *m* de crédit.

length [leŋθ] **n 1.** [gen] longueur *f* ▸ **what length is it?** ça fait quelle longueur? ▸ **it's five metres in length** cela fait cinq mètres de long ▸ **the length and breadth of** partout dans, dans tout ▸ **articles must be less than 5,000 words in length** les articles doivent faire moins de 5 000 mots ▸ **to win by a length** [in swimming, rowing] gagner d'une longueur **2.** [piece - of string, wood] morceau *m*, bout *m* / [- of cloth] coupon *m* **3.** [duration] durée *f* ▸ **bonuses are given for length of service** les primes sont accordées selon l'ancienneté
▸▸ **to go to great lengths to do sthg** tout faire pour faire qqch ▸ **he would go to any lengths to meet her** il ferait n'importe quoi pour la rencontrer.
◆ ***at length*** **adv 1.** [eventually] enfin **2.** [in detail] à fond.

-length **suffix** à hauteur de ▸ **knee-length socks** chaussettes *fpl* (montantes), mi-bas *mpl*.

lengthen ['leŋθən] ■ **vt** [dress] rallonger / [life] prolonger.
■ **vi** allonger.

lengthily ['leŋθɪlɪ] **adv** longuement.

lengthways ['leŋθweɪz], ***lengthwise*** ['leŋθwaɪz] **adv** dans le sens de la longueur.

lengthy ['leŋθɪ] (comp **-ier**, superl **-iest**) **adj** très long (longue).

leniency ['li:njənsɪ] **n** clémence *f*, indulgence *f*.

lenient ['li:njənt] **adj** [person] indulgent(e) / [laws] clément(e).

leniently ['li:njəntlɪ] **adv** avec clémence ***OR*** indulgence ▸ **the magistrate had treated him leniently** le magistrat s'était montré indulgent ***OR*** avait fait preuve d'indulgence à son égard.

lens [lenz] **n 1.** [of camera] objectif *m* / [of glasses] verre *m* **2.** [contact lens] verre *m* de contact, lentille *f* (cornéenne).

lent [lent] **pt** & **pp** ➤ ***lend***.

Lent [lent] **n** Carême *m*.

lentil ['lentɪl] **n** lentille *f*.

Leo ['li:əʊ] **n** Lion ▸ **to be (a) Leo** être Lion.

leopard ['lepəd] **n** léopard *m*.

leopardess ['lepədɪs] **n** léopard *m* femelle.

leopard skin ■ **n** peau *f* de léopard.
■ **adj** [coat, rug] en (peau de) léopard.

leotard ['li:ətɑ:d] **n** collant *m*.

leper ['lepər] **n** lépreux *m*, -euse *f*.

leprechaun ['leprəkɔ:n] **n** lutin *m (irlandais)*.

leprosy ['leprəsɪ] **n** lèpre *f*.

lesbian ['lezbɪən] ■ **adj** lesbien(enne).
■ **n** lesbienne *f*.

lesbianism ['lezbɪənɪzm] **n** lesbianisme *m*.

lesion ['li:ʒn] **n** lésion *f*.

Lesotho [lə'su:tu:] **n** Lesotho *m*.

less [les] *(compar of little)* ■ **adj** moins de ▸ **less money/time than me** moins d'argent/de temps que moi ▸ **of less importance/value** de moindre importance/valeur ▸ **I seem to have less and less energy** on dirait que j'ai de moins en moins d'énergie.
■ **pron** moins ▸ **there was less than I expected** il y en avait moins que je m'y attendais ▸ **it costs less than you think** ça coûte moins cher que tu ne le crois ▸ **no less than £50** pas moins de 50 livres ▸ **we found we had less and less to say to each other** nous nous sommes rendu compte que nous avions de moins en moins de choses à nous dire ▸ **let's hope we see less of them in future** espérons que nous les verrons moins souvent à l'avenir ▸ **the less... the less...** moins... moins...
■ **adv** moins ▸ **the blue dress costs less** la robe bleue coûte moins cher ▸ **less than five** moins de cinq ▸ **less and less** de moins en moins ▸ **I don't think any (the) less of her** OR **I think no less of her because of what happened** ce qui s'est passé ne l'a pas fait baisser dans mon estime.
■ **prep** [minus] moins ▸ **that's £300 less ten per cent for store card holders** ça fait 300 livres moins dix pour cent avec la carte du magasin.
◆ ***no less*** **adv** rien de moins ▸ **he won the Booker prize, no less!** il a obtenu le Booker prize, rien de moins que ça! ▸ **taxes rose by no less than 15%** les impôts ont augmenté de 15 %, ni plus ni moins.

less-developed country **n** pays *m* moins développé.

lessee [le'si:] **n** preneur *m*, -euse *f*, locataire *mf*.

lessen ['lesn] ■ **vt** [risk, chance] diminuer, réduire / [pain] atténuer.
■ **vi** [gen] diminuer / [pain] s'atténuer.

lesser ['lesər] **adj** moindre ▸ **to a lesser extent** OR **degree** à un degré moindre.

lesser-known **adj** moins connu(e).

lesson ['lesn] **n** leçon *f*, cours *m* ▸ **to give/take lessons (in)** donner/prendre des leçons (de) ▸ **to teach sb a lesson** *fig* donner une (bonne) leçon à qqn.

lessor [le'sɔ:r] **n** bailleur *m*, -eresse *f*.

lest [lest] **conj** *fml* de crainte que.

let [let] (**pt & pp let, cont -ting**) **vt 1.** [allow] **: to let sb do sthg** laisser qqn faire qqch ▸ **I couldn't come because my parents wouldn't let me** je ne suis pas venu parce que mes parents ne me l'ont pas permis ▸ **she let her hair grow** elle s'est laissé pousser les cheveux ▸ **we can't let this happen** on ne peut pas laisser faire ça ▸ **let me buy you a drink** laissez-moi vous offrir un verre ▸ **don't let me stop you going** je ne veux pas t'empêcher d'y aller ▸ **to let sb know sthg** dire qqch à qqn ▸ **to let sb have sthg** donner qqch à qqn ▸ **to let go of sb/sthg** lâcher qqn/qqch ▸ **to let sb go** [gen] laisser (partir) qqn / [prisoner] libérer qqn ▸ **let me go!, let go of me!** lâchez-moi! **2.** [in verb forms] **: let's go!** allons-y! ▸ **shall we have a picnic? – yes, let's!** si on faisait un pique-nique? – d'accord! ▸ **let me start by saying how pleased I am to be here** laissez-moi d'abord vous dire combien je suis ravi d'être ici ▸ **let me think** attends, voyons voir ▸ **let's see** voyons ▸ **don't let me catch you at it again!** que je ne t'y reprenne plus! ▸ **let them wait** qu'ils attendent ▸ **let the festivities begin!** que la fête commence! **3.** *esp UK* [rent out] louer ▸ **'to let'** 'à louer'.
◆ ***let alone*** **conj** encore moins, sans parler de.
◆ ***let down*** **vt sep 1.** *UK* [deflate] dégonfler **2.** [disappoint] décevoir ▸ **I felt really let down** j'étais vraiment déçu ▸ **our old car has never let us down** notre vieille voiture ne nous a jamais laissés tomber.
◆ ***let in*** **vt sep** [admit] laisser OR faire entrer ▸ **here's the key to let yourself in** voici la clé pour entrer ▸ **the roof lets the rain in** le toit laisse entrer OR passer la pluie.
◆ ***let in for*** **vt sep : you don't know what you're letting yourself in for** tu ne sais pas à quoi tu t'engages.
◆ ***let in on*** **vt sep : to let sb in on sthg** mettre qqn au courant de qqch.
◆ ***let off*** **vt sep 1.** *UK* [excuse] **: to let sb off sthg** dispenser qqn de qqch **2.** [not punish] ne pas punir **3.** [bomb] faire éclater / [gun, firework] faire partir.
◆ ***let on*** **vi : don't let on!** *UK* ne dis rien (à personne)!
◆ ***let out*** ■ **vt sep 1.** [allow to go out] laisser sortir ▸ **to let air out of sthg** dégonfler qqch **2.** [laugh, scream] laisser échapper.
■ **vi** *US* SCH finir.
◆ ***let up*** **vi 1.** [rain] diminuer **2.** [person] s'arrêter.

letdown ['letdaʊn] **n** *inf* déception *f*.

lethal ['li:θl] **adj** mortel(elle), fatal(e).

lethally ['li:θəlɪ] **adv** mortellement.

lethargic [lə'θɑ:dʒɪk] **adj** léthargique.

lethargy ['leθədʒɪ] **n** léthargie *f*.

let-out **n** *UK* [excuse] prétexte *m* / [way out] échappatoire *f*.

Letraset® ['letrəset] **n** Letraset®.

let's [lets] = ***let us***.

letter ['letər] **n** lettre *f* ▸ **the letter of the law** *fig* la lettre de la loi ▸ **she obeyed the instructions to the letter** elle a suivi les instructions à la lettre OR au pied de la lettre ▸ **the letters of D. H. Lawrence** la correspondance de D. H. Lawrence.

letter bomb **n** lettre *f* piégée.

letterbox ['letəbɒks] **n** *UK* boîte *f* aux OR à lettres.

letterhead ['letəhed] **n** en-tête *m*.

lettering ['letərɪŋ] **n** *(U)* caractères *mpl*.

letter of credit **n** lettre *f* de crédit.

letter opener **n** coupe-papier *m inv*.

letter-perfect **adj** *US* absolument parfait(e).

letter quality **n** COMPUT qualité *f* courrier.

letters patent **npl** lettres *fpl* patentes.

lettuce ['letɪs] **n** laitue *f*, salade *f*.

letup ['letʌp] **n** [in fighting] répit *m* / [in work] relâchement *m*.

leukaemia, *esp US* ***leukemia*** [lu:'ki:mɪə] **n** leucémie *f*.

levee ['levɪ] **n** *US* [embankment] digue *f*.

level ['levl] ■ **adj 1.** [equal in height] à la même hauteur / [horizontal] horizontal(e) ▸ **to be level with** être au niveau de ▸ **hold the tray level** tenez le plateau à l'horizontale *OR* bien à plat **2.** [equal in standard] à égalité ▸ **the leading cars are almost level** les voitures de tête sont presque à la même hauteur **3.** [flat] plat(e), plan(e) ▸ **to make sthg level** aplanir qqch ▸ **a level spoonful** une cuillerée rase.

■ **adv : to draw level with sb** arriver à la même hauteur que qqn, rejoindre qqn.

■ **n 1.** [gen] niveau *m* ▸ **at ground level** au niveau du sol ▸ **at cabinet/national level** à l'échelon ministériel/national ▸ **noise levels are far too high** le niveau sonore est bien trop élevé ▸ **check the oil level** [in car] vérifiez le niveau d'huile ▸ **inflation has reached new levels** l'inflation a atteint de nouveaux sommets ▸ **her level of English is poor** elle n'a pas un très bon niveau en anglais ▸ **to be on a level (with)** être du même niveau (que) ▸ **she's on a different level from the others** elle n'est pas au même niveau que les autres ▸ **on a practical level** du point de vue pratique ▸ **to come down to sb's level** se mettre au niveau de qqn ▸ **to be on the level** *inf* être réglo **2.** *US* [spirit level] niveau *m* à bulle.

■ **vt** (*UK* **-led**, cont **-ling**, *US* **-ed**, cont **-ing**) **1.** [make flat] niveler, aplanir **2.** [demolish] raser **3.** [aim] **: to level a gun at** pointer *OR* braquer un fusil sur ▸ **to level an accusation at** *OR* **against sb** lancer une accusation contre qqn.

◆ ***level off***, ***level out*** **vi 1.** [inflation] se stabiliser **2.** [aeroplane] se mettre en palier.

◆ ***level with*** **vt insep** *inf* être franc (franche) *OR* honnête avec.

level crossing **n** *UK* passage *m* à niveau.

level-headed [-'hedɪd] **adj** raisonnable.

level pegging [-'pegɪŋ] **adj** *UK* **: to be level pegging** être à égalité.

lever [*UK* 'li:vəʳ, *US* 'levər] **n** levier *m*.

leverage [*UK* 'li:vərɪdʒ, *US* 'levərɪdʒ] **n** *(U)* **1.** [force] **: to get leverage on sthg** avoir une prise sur qqch **2.** *fig* [influence] influence *f*.

leveraged buyout [*UK* 'li:vərɪdʒd-, *US* 'levərɪdʒd-] **n** rachat *m* d'entreprise financé par l'endettement.

leveraged management buyout [*UK* 'li:vərɪdʒd-, *US* 'levərɪdʒd-] **n** rachat *m* d'entreprise par les salariés.

leviathan [lɪ'vaɪəθn] **n** *fig* colosse *m*.

levitate ['levɪteɪt] ■ **vi** léviter.

■ **vt** faire léviter, soulever par lévitation.

levitation [,levɪ'teɪʃn] **n** lévitation *f*.

levity ['levətɪ] **n** légèreté *f*.

levy ['levɪ] ■ **n** prélèvement *m*, impôt *m*.

■ **vt** (pt & pp **-ied**) prélever, percevoir.

lewd [lju:d] **adj** obscène.

lexical ['leksɪkl] **adj** lexical(e).

lexicographer [,leksɪ'kɒgrəfəʳ] **n** lexicographe *mf*.

lexicography [,leksɪ'kɒgrəfɪ] **n** lexicographie *f*.

lexicon ['leksɪkən] **n** lexique *m*.

ley line **n** *ensemble de repères indiquant le tracé probable d'un chemin préhistorique.*

LI abbr of ***Long Island***.

liability [,laɪə'bɪlətɪ] (pl **-ies**) **n 1.** responsabilité *f* ▸ **liability for tax** assujettissement à l'impôt **2.** *fig* [person, thing] danger *m* public ▸ **the house he had inherited was a real liability** la maison dont il avait hérité lui coûtait une petite fortune *OR* lui revenait cher.

◆ ***liabilities*** **npl** FIN dettes *fpl*, passif *m* ▸ **to meet one's liabilities** faire face à ses engagements.

liable ['laɪəbl] **adj 1.** [likely] **: to be liable to do sthg** risquer de faire qqch, être susceptible de faire qqch ▸ **if you don't remind him, he's liable to forget** si on ne lui rappelle pas, il risque d'oublier **2.** [prone] **: to be liable to sthg** être sujet(ette) à qqch **3.** LAW **: to be liable (for)** être responsable (de) ▸ **to be liable for sb's debts** répondre des dettes de qqn ▸ **to be liable for tax** [person] être assujetti(e) à *OR* redevable de l'impôt / [goods] être assujetti(e) à une taxe ▸ **to be liable to** être passible de.

liaise [lɪ'eɪz] **vi** *UK* **: to liaise with** assurer la liaison avec.

liaison [lɪ'eɪzɒn] **n** liaison *f*.

liar ['laɪəʳ] **n** menteur *m*, -euse *f*.

Lib. [lɪb] abbr of ***Liberal***.

libel ['laɪbl] ■ **n** LAW diffamation *f* ▸ **the libel laws** la législation en matière de diffamation ▸ **libel suit** procès *m* en diffamation.

■ **vt** (*UK* **-led**, cont **-ling**, *US* **-ed**, cont **-ing**) diffamer.

libellous *UK*, ***libelous*** *US* ['laɪbələs] **adj** diffamatoire.

liberal ['lɪbərəl] ■ **adj 1.** [tolerant] libéral(e) **2.** [generous] généreux(euse).

■ **n** libéral *m*, -e *f*.

◆ ***Liberal*** ■ **adj** POL libéral(e).

■ **n** POL libéral *m*, -e *f*.

liberal arts **npl** *esp US* arts *mpl* libéraux.

Liberal Democrat **n** *adhérent du principal parti centriste britannique.*

liberalism ['lɪbərəlɪzm] **n** libéralisme *m*.

liberalize, *UK* ***-ise*** ['lɪbərəlaɪz] **vt** libéraliser.

liberally ['lɪbərəlɪ] **adv** libéralement ▸ **a liberally spiced dish** un plat généreusement épicé.

liberal-minded [-'maɪndɪd] **adj** large d'esprit.

Liberal Party **n** *esp UK* HIST **: the Liberal Party** le parti libéral.

liberate ['lɪbəreɪt] **vt** libérer.

liberated ['lɪbəreɪtɪd] **adj** libéré(e).

liberating ['lɪbəreɪtɪŋ] **adj** libérateur(trice).

liberation [,lɪbə'reɪʃn] **n** libération *f*.

liberator ['lɪbəreɪtəʳ] **n** libérateur *m*, -trice *f*.

Liberia [laɪ'bɪərɪə] **n** Liberia *m* ▸ **in Liberia** au Liberia.

Liberian [laɪ'bɪərɪən] ■ **adj** libérien(enne).

■ **n** Libérien *m*, -enne *f*.

libertine ['lɪbəti:n] **n** *liter* & *pej* libertin *m*.

liberty ['lɪbətɪ] (pl **-ies**) **n** liberté *f* ▸ **at liberty** en liberté ▸ **to be at liberty to do sthg** être libre de faire qqch ▸ **to take liberties (with sb)** prendre des libertés (avec qqn).

libido [lɪ'bi:dəʊ] (pl **-s**) **n** libido *f*.

Libra ['li:brə] **n** Balance *f* ▸ **to be (a) Libra** être Balance.

librarian [laɪ'breərɪən] **n** bibliothécaire *mf*.

librarianship [laɪ'breərɪənʃɪp] **n** *UK* **: diploma in librarianship** diplôme de bibliothécaire.

library ['laɪbrərɪ] (pl **-ies**) **n** bibliothèque *f*.

FALSE FRIENDS / FAUX AMIS
library

Librairie n'est pas la traduction du mot anglais *library*. Librairie se traduit par *bookshop*.
▸ Elle veut ouvrir une petite librairie / *She wants to open a little bookshop*

library book **n** livre *m* de bibliothèque.

libretto [lɪ'bretəʊ] (pl **-s**) **n** livret *m*.

Libya ['lɪbɪə] **n** Libye *f* ▸ **in Libya** en Libye.

Libyan ['lɪbɪən] ■ **adj** libyen(enne).
■ **n** Libyen *m*, -enne *f*.

lice [laɪs] **npl** ➤ ***louse***.

licence *UK*, ***license*** *US* ['laɪsəns] **n 1.** *UK* [gen] permis *m*, autorisation *f* ▸ **driving licence** *UK*, **driver's license** *US* permis *m* de conduire ▸ **TV licence** redevance *f* télé **2.** *UK* COMM licence *f* ▸ **under licence** sous licence.

licence number **n** *UK* [on vehicle] numéro *m* d'immatriculation / [on driving licence] numéro *m* de permis de conduire.

license ['laɪsəns] ■ **vt** autoriser.
■ **n** *US* = ***licence***.

licensed ['laɪsənst] **adj 1.** [person] **: to be licensed to do sthg** avoir un permis pour *OR* l'autorisation de faire qqch **2.** *UK* [premises] qui détient une licence de débit de boissons.

licensed brand name **n** nom *m* de marque sous licence.

licensed product **n** produit *m* sous licence.

licensee [ˌlaɪsən'si:] **n** *UK* [of pub] gérant *m*, -e *f*.

license plate **n** *US* plaque *f* d'immatriculation.

licensing agreement ['laɪsənsɪŋ-] **n** accord *m* de licence.

licensing hours ['laɪsənsɪŋ-] **npl** *UK* *heures d'ouverture des débits de boissons*.

licensing laws ['laɪsənsɪŋ-] **npl** *UK* *lois réglementant la vente d'alcool*.

licentious [laɪ'senʃəs] **adj** *fml* licencieux(euse).

lichen ['laɪkən] **n** lichen *m*.

lick [lɪk] ■ **n 1.** [act of licking] **: to give sthg a lick** lécher qqch **2.** *inf* [small amount] **: a lick of paint** un petit coup de peinture.
■ **vt 1.** [gen] lécher ▸ **to lick one's lips** se lécher les lèvres / *fig* se frotter les mains **2.** *inf* [defeat] écraser, battre à plates coutures.

licking ['lɪkɪŋ] **n** *inf* [thrashing] raclée *f*, dégelée *f* / [defeat] déculottée *f*.

licorice ['lɪkərɪs] *US* = ***liquorice***.

lid [lɪd] **n 1.** [cover] couvercle *m* **2.** [eyelid] paupière *f*.

lido ['li:dəʊ] (pl **-s**) **n 1.** *UK* [swimming pool] piscine *f* en plein air **2.** [beach] plage *f*.

lie [laɪ] ■ **n** mensonge *m* ▸ **to tell lies** mentir, dire des mensonges.
■ **vi** (pt **lay**, pp **lain**, cont **lying**) **1.** (pt & pp **lied**) [tell lie] **: to lie (to sb)** mentir (à qqn) ▸ **he lied about his age** il a menti sur son âge
2. [be horizontal] être allongé(e), être couché(e) ▸ **she lay on the beach all day** elle est restée allongée sur la plage toute la journée ▸ **she was lying on the couch** elle était couchée *OR* allongée sur le divan ▸ **she lay awake for hours** elle resta plusieurs heures sans pouvoir s'endormir ▸ **'here lies John Smith'** 'ci-gît John Smith'
3. [lie down] s'allonger, se coucher ▸ **lie on your back** couchez-vous sur le dos
4. [be situated] se trouver, être ▸ **a folder lay open on the desk before her** un dossier était ouvert devant elle sur le bureau ▸ **snow lay (thick) on the ground** il y avait une (épaisse) couche de neige ▸ **a vast desert lay before us** un immense désert s'étendait devant nous
5. [exist] **: the problem lies in getting them motivated** le problème, c'est de réussir à les motiver ▸ **where do our real interests lie?** qu'est-ce qui compte vraiment pour nous? ▸ **they didn't know what lay ahead of them** ils ne savaient pas ce qui les attendait
▸▸ **to lie low** *inf* se planquer, se tapir.
◆ ***lie about***, ***lie around*** **vi** *UK* traîner ▸ **don't leave your things lying about** ne laisse pas traîner tes affaires.
◆ ***lie down*** **vi** s'allonger, se coucher ▸ **he won't take it lying down** il ne va pas accepter ça sans rien dire.
◆ ***lie in*** **vi** *UK* rester au lit, faire la grasse matinée.

Liechtenstein ['lɪktənstaɪn] **n** Liechtenstein *m* ▸ **in Liechtenstein** au Liechtenstein.

lie detector **n** détecteur *m* de mensonges.

lie-down **n** *UK* **: to have a lie-down** faire une sieste *OR* un (petit) somme.

lie-in **n** *UK* **: to have a lie-in** faire la grasse matinée.

lieu [lju: *OR* lu:] ◆ ***in lieu*** **adv** *esp UK fml* à la place ▸ **in lieu of** au lieu de, à la place de.

Lieut. (abbr of ***lieutenant***) lieut.

lieutenant [*UK* lef'tenənt, *US* lu:'tenənt] **n** lieutenant *m*, -e *f*.

lieutenant colonel **n** lieutenant-colonel *m*.

life [laɪf] ■ **n** (pl **lives** [laɪvz]) **1.** [gen] vie *f* ▸ **I've worked hard all my life** j'ai travaillé dur toute ma vie ▸ **I've never eaten snails in my life** je n'ai jamais mangé d'escargots de ma vie ▸ **she's the only woman in his life** c'est la seule femme dans sa vie ▸ **they lead a strange life** ils mènent une drôle de vie ▸ **I want to live my own life** je veux vivre ma vie ▸ **we don't want to spend the rest of our lives here** on ne veut pas finir nos jours ici ▸ **hundreds lost their lives** des centaines de personnes ont trouvé la mort ▸ **it's a matter of life and death** c'est une question de vie ou de mort ▸ **is there life on Mars?** y a-t-il de la vie sur Mars? ▸ **life is hard** la vie est dure ▸ **just relax and enjoy life!**

profite donc un peu de la vie! ▸ **for life** à vie ▸ **how's life?** *inf* comment ça va? ▸ **that's life!** c'est la vie! ▸ **I can't for the life of me remember...** rien à faire, je n'arrive pas à me rappeler... ▸ **to lay down one's life** donner sa vie ▸ **to risk life and limb** risquer sa peau ▸ **to scare the life out of sb** faire une peur bleue à qqn ▸ **to take sb's life** tuer qqn ▸ **to take one's own life** se donner la mort
2. [liveliness] vie *f* ▸ **there's more life in Sydney than in Wellington** Sydney est plus animé que Wellington ▸ **to come to life** s'animer ▸ **to breathe life into** donner vie à ▸ **she was the life and soul of the party** c'est elle qui a mis de l'ambiance dans la soirée
3. ART nature *f* ▸ **to draw from life** dessiner d'après nature
4. LIT réalité *f* ▸ **his novels are very true to life** ses romans sont très réalistes
5. *(U) inf* [life imprisonment] emprisonnement *m* à perpétuité ▸ **the kidnappers got life** les ravisseurs ont été condamnés à perpétuité OR à la prison à vie ▸ **he's doing life** il purge une peine à perpétuité.
■ **comp** [member] à vie.

life-and-death adj extrêmement grave OR critique.

life annuity n rente *f* viagère.

life assurance esp *UK* = ***life insurance***.

lifebelt n bouée *f* de sauvetage.

lifeblood ['laɪfblʌd] n *fig* élément *m* vital, âme *f*.

lifeboat ['laɪfbəʊt] n canot *m* de sauvetage.

lifeboatman ['laɪfbəʊtmən] (pl **-men** [-mən]) n sauveteur *m* en mer.

life buoy n bouée *f* de sauvetage.

life cycle n cycle *m* de vie.

life expectancy n espérance *f* de vie.

life-giving adj qui insuffle la vie, vivifiant.

lifeguard ['laɪfgɑːd] n [at swimming pool] maître-nageur sauveteur *m* / [at beach] gardien *m* de plage.

life history n vie *f* ▸ **the organism takes on many different forms during its life history** l'organisme prend de nombreuses formes au cours de sa vie OR de son existence ▸ **she told me her whole life history** elle m'a raconté l'histoire de sa vie.

life imprisonment [-ɪm'prɪznmənt] n emprisonnement *m* à perpétuité.

life insurance n assurance-vie *f*.

life jacket n gilet *m* de sauvetage.

lifeless ['laɪflɪs] adj **1.** [dead] sans vie, inanimé(e) **2.** [listless - performance] qui manque de vie / [- voice] monotone.

lifelike ['laɪflaɪk] adj **1.** [statue, doll] qui semble vivant(e) **2.** [portrait] ressemblant(e).

lifeline ['laɪflaɪn] n corde *f* (de sauvetage) / *fig* lien *m* vital (avec l'extérieur).

lifelong ['laɪflɒŋ] adj de toujours.

life-or-death = ***life-and-death***.

life peer n *UK* pair *m* à vie.

life preserver [-prɪ,zɜːvər] n *US* [life belt] bouée *f* de sauvetage / [life jacket] gilet *m* de sauvetage.

lifer ['laɪfər] n *inf* condamné *m*, -e *f* à perpète.

life raft n canot *m* pneumatique (de sauvetage).

lifesaver ['laɪf,seɪvər] n [person] maître-nageur sauveteur *m*.

life sentence n condamnation *f* à perpétuité.

life-size(d) [-saɪz(d)] adj grandeur nature *(inv)*.

lifespan ['laɪfspæn] n **1.** [of person, animal] espérance *f* de vie **2.** [of product, machine] durée *f* de vie.

life story n biographie *f*.

lifestyle ['laɪfstaɪl] n mode *m* OR style *m* de vie.

life-support system n respirateur *m* artificiel.

life-threatening adj [illness] qui peut être mortel(elle).

lifetime ['laɪftaɪm] n vie *f* ▸ **in my lifetime** de mon vivant.

LIFFE (abbr of ***London International Financial Futures Exchange***) n ≃ MATIF *m (marché à terme d'instruments financiers)*.

lift [lɪft] ■ n **1.** [in car] **: to give sb a lift** emmener OR prendre qqn en voiture **2.** [in morale, energy] **: to give sb a lift** remonter le moral à qqn **3.** *UK* [elevator] ascenseur *m*.
■ vt **1.** [gen] lever / [weight] soulever ▸ **she lifted her eyes from her magazine** elle leva les yeux de sa revue ▸ **I feel as if a burden has been lifted from my shoulders** j'ai l'impression qu'on m'a enlevé un poids des épaules **2.** [spirits, heart] remonter **3.** [plagiarize] plagier **4.** *inf* [steal] voler.
■ vi **1.** [lid] s'ouvrir **2.** [fog] se lever.
◆ ***lift off*** vi insep [plane, rocket] décoller.

liftoff n décollage *m*.

ligament ['lɪgəmənt] n ligament *m*.

ligature ['lɪgətʃər] ■ n **1.** [gen, MED & TYPO] ligature *f* **2.** MUS liaison *f*.
■ vt ligaturer.

light [laɪt] ■ adj **1.** [not dark] clair(e) ▸ **light blue/green** bleu/vert clair *(inv)* ▸ **it isn't light enough to read** il n'y a pas assez de lumière pour lire ▸ **it's getting light already** il commence déjà à faire jour
2. [not heavy] léger(ère) ▸ **light clothes** vêtements *mpl* légers ▸ **a light rain was falling** il tombait une pluie fine ▸ **to be a light sleeper** avoir le sommeil léger
3. [not much, not intense - traffic] fluide / [- corrections] peu nombreux(euses) ▸ **I had a light lunch** j'ai mangé légèrement à midi, j'ai déjeuné léger
4. [not difficult] facile / [comedy, music] léger, facile ▸ **take some light reading** prends quelque chose de facile à lire ▸ **light entertainment** variétés *fpl*.
■ n **1.** *(U)* [brightness] lumière *f* ▸ **it looks brown in this light** on dirait que c'est marron avec cette lumière ▸ **by the light of our flashlamps** à la lumière de nos lampes de poche ▸ **to see the light** [understand] comprendre / [be converted] trouver le chemin de la vérité ▸ **to see the light of day** voir le jour
2. [device] lampe *f* ▸ **turn the light on/off** allume/éteins (la lumière) ▸ **to go out like a light** *inf* [fall asleep] s'endormir tout de suite / [faint] tomber dans les pommes
3. [AUT - gen] feu *m* / [- headlamp] phare *m* ▸ **the lights** le feu (de signalisation) ▸ **turn left at the lights** tournez à

gauche au feu rouge ▸ **the lights were (on) amber** le feu était à l'orange ▸ **parking/reversing lights** feux de stationnement/de recul
4. [for cigarette] feu *m* ▸ **have you got a light?** vous avez du feu? ▸ **to set light to sthg** mettre le feu à qqch
5. [perspective] **: in light of, in the light of** *UK* à la lumière de ▸ **in a good/bad light** sous un jour favorable/défavorable ▸ **to see sb/sthg in a different light** voir qqn/qqch sous un jour nouveau
▸▸| **to bring to light** mettre en lumière ▸ **to come to light** être découvert(e) *OR* dévoilé(e) ▸ **to see the light** [understand] comprendre ▸ **to throw** *OR* **cast** *OR* **shed light on sthg** clarifier qqch.
■ **vt** (pt & pp **lit** *OR* **-ed**) **1.** [lamp, cigarette] allumer ▸ **to light a fire** allumer un feu, faire du feu
2. [room, stage] éclairer.
■ **adv : to travel light** voyager léger.
◆ ***light out*** vi *US inf* se tirer.
◆ ***light up*** ■ vt sep **1.** [illuminate] éclairer
2. [cigarette] allumer.
■ vi **1.** [face] s'éclairer
2. *inf* [start smoking] allumer une cigarette.

light aircraft n avion *m* léger.

light ale n *UK bière blonde légère.*

lightbulb n ampoule *f*.

light cream n *US* crème *f* liquide.

lighted ['laɪtɪd] adj [room] éclairé(e).

light-emitting diode [-ɪ'mɪtɪŋ-] n diode *f* électroluminescente.

lighten ['laɪtn] ■ vt **1.** [give light to] éclairer / [make less dark] éclaircir **2.** [make less heavy] alléger.
■ vi [brighten] s'éclaircir.
◆ ***lighten up*** vi *inf* se dérider.

lighter ['laɪtə^r] n [cigarette lighter] briquet *m*.

light-fingered [-'fɪŋgəd] adj *inf* chapardeur(euse).

light fitting n applique *f* (électrique).

light-headed [-'hedɪd] adj **: to feel light-headed** avoir la tête qui tourne.

light-headedness [-'hedɪdnɪs] n [dizziness] vertige *m* / [tipsiness] ivresse *f*.

light-hearted [-'hɑ:tɪd] adj **1.** [cheerful] joyeux(euse), gai(e) **2.** [amusing] amusant(e).

lighthouse ['laɪthaʊs] (pl [-haʊzɪz]) n phare *m*.

light industry n industrie *f* légère.

lighting ['laɪtɪŋ] n éclairage *m*.

lighting-up time n *UK heure où les véhicules doivent allumer leurs phares.*

lightly ['laɪtlɪ] adv **1.** [gen] légèrement **2.** [frivolously] à la légère.

light meter n PHOT posemètre *m*, cellule *f* photoélectrique.

lightness ['laɪtnɪs] n **1.** [brightness, light] clarté *f* **2.** [of object, tone, step] légèreté *f*.

lightning ['laɪtnɪŋ] n *(U)* éclair *m*, foudre *f*.

lightning conductor *UK*, ***lightning rod*** *US* n paratonnerre *m*.

lightning strike n *UK* grève *f* surprise.

light opera n opérette *f*.

light pen n crayon *m* optique, photostyle *m*.

lightship ['laɪtʃɪp] n bateau-feu *m*, bateau-phare *m*.

lights-out n extinction *f* des feux.

lightweight ['laɪtweɪt] ■ adj **1.** [object] léger(ère) **2.** *fig & pej* [person] insignifiant(e).
■ n **1.** [boxer] poids *m* léger **2.** *fig & pej* [person] personne *f* insignifiante.

light year n année-lumière *f*.

likable ['laɪkəbl] adj sympathique.

like [laɪk] ■ prep **1.** [gen] comme ▸ **there's a car like ours** voilà une voiture comme la nôtre ▸ **to look like sb/sthg** ressembler à qqn/qqch ▸ **she's nothing like her sister** elle ne ressemble pas du tout à sa sœur ▸ **to taste like sthg** avoir un goût de qqch ▸ **it seemed like hours** c'était comme si des heures entières s'étaient écoulées ▸ **there's no place like home** rien ne vaut son chez-soi ▸ **like this/that** comme ci/ça ▸ **sorry to interrupt you like this, but...** désolé de vous interrompre ainsi, mais... ▸ **don't talk to me like that!** ne me parle pas sur ce ton!
2. [asking for opinion or description] **: what's your new boss like?** comment est ton nouveau patron? ▸ **what's the weather like?** quel temps fait-il? ▸ **what does it taste like?** quel goût ça a?
3. [typical of] **: that's just like him!** c'est bien de lui!, ça lui ressemble! ▸ **kids are like that: what do you expect?** les gosses sont comme ça, qu'est-ce que tu veux! ▸ **it's not like him to be rude** ça ne lui ressemble pas *OR* ce n'est pas son genre d'être impoli
4. [such as] tel que, comme ▸ **I'm useless at things like sewing** je ne suis bon à rien quand il s'agit de couture et de choses comme ça
5. [in approximations] **: it cost something like £200** ça a coûté dans les 200 livres ▸ **it was more like midnight when we got home** il était plus près de minuit quand nous sommes arrivés à la maison ▸ **that's more like it!** voilà qui est mieux!
■ vt **1.** [gen] aimer ▸ **I like her** elle me plaît ▸ **I like her, but I don't love her** je l'aime bien, mais je ne suis pas amoureux d'elle ▸ **I don't like him** je ne l'aime pas beaucoup, il ne me plaît pas ▸ **to like doing** *OR* **to do sthg** aimer faire qqch ▸ **I don't like being talked at** je n'aime pas qu'on me fasse des discours ▸ **I like people to be frank with me** j'aime qu'on soit franc avec moi ▸ **I don't like you swearing, I don't like it when you swear** je n'aime pas que tu dises des gros mots ▸ **do what you like** fais ce que tu veux *OR* ce qui te plaît ▸ **whether you like it or not!** que ça te plaise ou non! ▸ **how do you like my jacket?** comment trouves-tu ma veste? ▸ **how do you like your coffee, black or white?** vous prenez votre café noir ou avec du lait?
2. [in offers, requests] **: would you like some more cake?** vous prendrez encore du gâteau? ▸ **would you like to go out tonight?** ça te dirait de *OR* tu as envie de sortir ce soir? ▸ **would you like me to do it for you?** veux-tu que je le fasse à ta place? ▸ **I'd like to go** je voudrais bien *OR* j'aimerais y aller ▸ **I'd like you to come** je voudrais bien *OR* j'aimerais que vous veniez ▸ **I'd like your opinion on this wine** j'aimerais savoir ce que tu penses de ce vin ▸ **if you like** si vous voulez.

■ adj : **people of like mind** des gens qui pensent comme lui/moi *etc*.
■ n : **the like** une chose pareille ▸ **and the like** et d'autres choses du même genre ▸ **you can only compare like with like** on ne peut comparer que ce qui est comparable.
■ conj *inf* **1.** [as] comme ▸ **like I was saying** *inf* comme je disais ▸ **they don't make them like they used to!** ils/elles ne sont plus ce qu'ils/elles étaient! ▸ **tell it like it is** dis les choses comme elles sont
2. [as if] comme si ▸ **he acted like he was in charge** il se comportait comme si c'était lui le chef ▸ **she felt like she wanted to cry** elle avait l'impression qu'elle allait pleurer.
◆ ***likes*** npl : **likes and dislikes** goûts *mpl*
▸▸ **the likes of us/them** *etc inf* les gens comme nous/eux *etc*.

-like suffix : **dream-like** onirique, de rêve ▸ **ghost-like** fantomatique.

likeable ['laɪkəbl] = ***likable***.

likelihood ['laɪklɪhʊd] n *(U)* chances *fpl*, probabilité *f* ▸ **in all likelihood** selon toute probabilité.

likely ['laɪklɪ] adj **1.** [probable] probable ▸ **he's likely to get angry** il risque de se fâcher ▸ **they're likely to win** ils vont sûrement gagner ▸ **a likely story!** *iro* à d'autres! **2.** [candidate] prometteur(euse).

like-minded [-'maɪndɪd] adj de même opinion.

liken ['laɪkn] vt : **to liken sb/sthg to** assimiler qqn/qqch à.

likeness ['laɪknɪs] n **1.** [resemblance] : **likeness (to)** ressemblance *f* (avec) **2.** [portrait] portrait *m*.

likewise ['laɪkwaɪz] adv [similarly] de même ▸ **to do likewise** faire pareil ***OR*** de même.

liking ['laɪkɪŋ] n [for person] affection *f*, sympathie *f* / [for food, music] goût *m*, penchant *m* ▸ **to have a liking for sthg** avoir le goût de qqch ▸ **to be to sb's liking** être du goût de qqn, plaire à qqn.

lilac ['laɪlək] ■ adj [colour] lilas *(inv)*.
■ n lilas *m*.

Lilo® ['laɪləʊ] (pl -s) n *UK* matelas *m* pneumatique.

lilt [lɪlt] n rythme *m*, cadence *f*.

lilting ['lɪltɪŋ] adj [voice] mélodieux(euse), chantant(e).

lily ['lɪlɪ] (pl -ies) n lis *m*.

lily-livered [-'lɪvəd] adj *hum* froussard(e).

lily of the valley (pl lilies of the valley) n muguet *m*.

Lima ['li:mə] n Lima.

limb [lɪm] n **1.** [of body] membre *m* **2.** [of tree] branche *f*
▸▸ **to be out on a limb** être en mauvaise posture.

limber ['lɪmbəʳ] ◆ ***limber up*** vi s'échauffer.

limbo ['lɪmbəʊ] (pl -s) n **1.** *(U)* [uncertain state] : **to be in limbo** être dans les limbes **2.** [dance] : **the limbo** le limbo.

lime [laɪm] n **1.** [fruit] citron *m* vert **2.** [drink] : **lime (juice)** jus *m* de citron vert **3.** [linden tree] tilleul *m* **4.** [substance] chaux *f*.

lime cordial n sirop *m* de citron vert.

lime-green adj vert jaune *(inv)*.

limelight ['laɪmlaɪt] n : **to be in the limelight** être au premier plan.

limerick ['lɪmərɪk] n *poème humoristique en cinq vers*.

limestone ['laɪmstəʊn] n *(U)* pierre *f* à chaux, calcaire *m*.

limey ['laɪmɪ] (pl -s) n *US inf terme péjoratif désignant un Anglais*.

limit ['lɪmɪt] ■ n limite *f* ▸ **he's/she's the limit!** *inf* il/elle dépasse les bornes! ▸ **off limits** d'accès interdit ▸ **within limits** [to an extent] dans une certaine mesure.
■ vt limiter, restreindre ▸ **to limit o.s. to sthg** se limiter à qqch.

limitation [ˌlɪmɪ'teɪʃn] n limitation *f*, restriction *f* ▸ **to know one's limitations** connaître ses limites.

limited ['lɪmɪtɪd] adj limité(e), restreint(e).

limited edition n [of book] édition *f* à tirage limité.

limited (liability) company n *UK* société *f* anonyme.

limitless ['lɪmɪtlɪs] adj illimité(e).

limo ['lɪməʊ] *inf* n abbr of ***limousine***.

limousine ['lɪməzi:n] n limousine *f*.

limp [lɪmp] ■ adj mou (molle).
■ n : **to have a limp** boiter.
■ vi boiter ▸ **to go limp** s'affaisser.

limpet ['lɪmpɪt] n patelle *f*, bernique *f*.

limpid ['lɪmpɪd] adj *liter* limpide.

limply ['lɪmplɪ] adv mollement.

limp-wristed [-'rɪstɪd] adj *offens* efféminé(e).

linchpin, ***lynchpin*** ['lɪntʃpɪn] n *fig* cheville *f* ouvrière.

Lincs. [lɪŋks] (abbr of ***Lincolnshire***) *comté anglais*.

linctus ['lɪŋktəs] n *UK* sirop *m* pour la toux.

HOW TO ...
express likes

J'aime assez/J'aime vraiment beaucoup ce tableau / I quite like/I really love that painting
J'aime bien mon nouveau travail / I like my new job
J'adore me promener sur la plage / I love walking on the beach
C'est un vrai mordu de jazz / He's really into jazz
L'actualité me passionne / I have a passion for current affairs
Il me plaît énormément / I like him a lot
Je m'intéresse beaucoup à l'actualité / I'm very interested in current affairs
Je l'apprécie beaucoup / I like him/her a lot
Je la trouve très sympathique / I think she's very nice
J'ai un faible pour elle / I've a soft spot for her

line [laɪn] ■ **n 1.** [gen] ligne *f* ▸ **to draw a line** tracer ***OR*** tirer une ligne ▸ **to walk in a straight line** marcher en ligne droite ▸ **line of sight *OR* of vision** ligne de visée ▸ **there's been a mistake somewhere along the line** il s'est produit une erreur quelque part
2. [row] rangée *f* ▸ **stand in line, children** mettez-vous en rang, les enfants ▸ **to step into line** se mettre en rang
3. [queue] file *f*, queue *f* ▸ **to stand *OR* wait in line** faire la queue ▸ **he's in line for promotion** il devrait être promu bientôt ▸ **he's first in line for the throne** c'est l'héritier du trône
4. [RAIL - track] voie *f* / [- route] ligne *f* ▸ **there's a new coach line to London** il y a un nouveau service d'autocars pour Londres
5. NAUT **: shipping line** compagnie *f* de navigation
6. [of writing, text] ligne *f* / [of poem, song] vers *m* ▸ **he forgot his lines** il a oublié son texte ▸ **to drop sb a line** envoyer un mot à qqn ▸ **to read between the lines** lire entre les lignes
7. TELEC ligne *f* ▸ **the line went dead** la communication a été coupée ▸ **hold the line!** ne quittez pas! ▸ **a voice came on the other end of the line** une voix a répondu à l'autre bout du fil ▸ **on line** COMPUT en ligne
8. [conformity] **: it's in/out of line with company policy** c'est conforme/ce n'est pas conforme à la politique de la société ▸ **it's more or less in line with what we'd expected** cela correspond plus ou moins à nos prévisions ▸ **to bring wages into line with inflation** actualiser les salaires en fonction de l'inflation ▸ **to step out of line** faire cavalier seul
9. [approach] **: what line did you take?** quelle stratégie as-tu adoptée? ▸ **they took a hard *OR* tough line on terrorism** ils ont adopté une politique de fermeté envers le terrorisme ▸ **I don't follow your line of thinking** je ne suis pas ton raisonnement ▸ **to think along the same lines** partager la même opinion ▸ **another idea along the same lines** une autre idée dans le même genre ▸ **to be on the right lines** *UK* être sur la bonne voie
10. *inf* [work] **: she's in the same line (of work) as you** elle travaille dans la même branche que toi ▸ **what line (of business) are you in?, what's your line (of business)?** qu'est-ce que vous faites dans la vie?
11. [wrinkle] ride *f*
12. [string, wire] corde *f* ▸ **a fishing line** une ligne
13. [borderline, limit] frontière *f* ▸ **the line between frankness and rudeness** la limite entre la franchise et l'impolitesse ▸ **the population is split along religious lines** la population est divisée selon des critères religieux ▸ **they crossed the state line into Nevada** ils ont franchi la frontière du Nevada ▸ **to draw the line at sthg** refuser de faire ***OR*** d'aller jusqu'à faire qqch
14. [lineage] lignée *f* ▸ **he comes from a long line of doctors** il est issu d'une longue lignée de médecins
15. COMM gamme *f* ▸ **product line** gamme *f* ***OR*** ligne de produits.
■ **vt 1.** [form rows along] **: trees lined the streets** les rues étaient bordées d'arbres ▸ **crowds lined the streets** la foule était ***OR*** s'était massée sur les trottoirs
2. [drawer, box] tapisser / [clothes] doubler ▸ **lined with silk** doublé(e) de soie ▸ **to line one's pockets** *inf* s'en mettre plein les poches.

◆ ***lines*** **npl** SCH **: to be given 100 lines** avoir 100 lignes à faire.

◆ ***on the line*** **adv : to put sthg/to be on the line** mettre qqch/être en jeu.
◆ ***out of line*** **adj** [remark, behaviour] déplacé(e).
◆ ***line up*** ■ **vt sep 1.** [in rows] aligner
2. [organize] prévoir ▸ **I've got a treat lined up for the kids** j'ai préparé une surprise pour les gosses.
■ **vi** [in row] s'aligner / [in queue] faire la queue.

lineage ['lɪnɪɪdʒ] **n** lignée *f*.

linear ['lɪnɪəʳ] **adj** linéaire.

lined [laɪnd] **adj 1.** [paper] réglé(e) **2.** [wrinkled] ridé(e).

line dancing **n** line *m* dancing.

line drawing **n** dessin *m* au trait.

line feed **n** saut *m* de ligne

linen ['lɪnɪn] ■ **n** *(U)* **1.** [cloth] lin *m* **2.** [tablecloths, sheets] linge *m* (de maison).
■ **comp 1.** [suit] de ***OR*** en lin **2.** [cupboard] à linge.

linen basket **n** *UK* panier *m* à linge.

line-out **n** SPORT touche *f*, remise *f* en jeu.

line printer **n** imprimante *f* ligne par ligne.

liner ['laɪnəʳ] **n** [ship] paquebot *m*.

linesman ['laɪnzmən] (pl **-men** [-mən]) **n** TENNIS juge *m* de ligne / FOOTBALL juge de touche.

lineup ['laɪnʌp] **n 1.** SPORT équipe *f* **2.** *US* [identity parade] rangée *f* de suspects *(pour identification par un témoin)*.

linger ['lɪŋgəʳ] **vi 1.** [person] s'attarder **2.** [doubt, pain] persister.

lingerie ['lænʒərɪ] **n** *(U)* lingerie *f*.

lingering ['lɪŋgrɪŋ] **adj** [doubt] persistant(e) / [hope] faible / [illness] long (longue).

lingo ['lɪŋgəʊ] (pl **-es**) **n** *inf* jargon *m*.

linguist ['lɪŋgwɪst] **n** linguiste *mf*.

linguistic [lɪŋ'gwɪstɪk] **adj** linguistique.

linguistics [lɪŋ'gwɪstɪks] **n** *(U)* linguistique *f*.

liniment ['lɪnɪmənt] **n** liniment *m*.

lining ['laɪnɪŋ] **n 1.** [of coat, curtains, box] doublure *f* **2.** [of stomach] muqueuse *f* **3.** AUT [of brakes] garniture *f*.

link [lɪŋk] ■ **n 1.** [of chain] maillon *m* **2.** [connection] **: link (between/with)** lien *m* (entre/avec) ▸ **a rail/telephone link** une liaison ferroviaire/téléphonique **3.** COMPUT lien *m* ▸ **links to sthg** liens vers qqc.
■ **vt** [cities, parts] relier / [events] lier ▸ **to link arms** se donner le bras.
■ **vi** COMPUT avoir un lien vers ▸ **to link to sth** mettre un lien avec qch.
◆ ***link up*** **vt sep** relier ▸ **to link sthg up with sthg** relier qqch avec ***OR*** à qqch.

linkage ['lɪŋkɪdʒ] **n** *(U)* [relationship] lien *m*, relation *f*.

linked [lɪŋkt] **adj** lié(e).

link road **n** route *f* de jonction.

links [lɪŋks] (pl **links**) **n** terrain *m* de golf *(au bord de la mer)*.

linkup ['lɪŋkʌp] **n** liaison *f*.

lino *UK* ['laɪnəʊ], ***linoleum*** [lɪ'nəʊlɪəm] **n** lino *m*, linoléum *m*.

linseed oil ['lɪnsi:d-] **n** huile *f* de lin.

lint [lɪnt] **n** *(U)* **1.** *UK* [dressing] compresse *f* **2.** *esp US* [fluff] peluches *fpl*.

lintel ['lɪntl] **n** linteau *m*.

lion ['laɪən] **n** lion *m*.

lion cub **n** lionceau *m*.

lioness ['laɪənes] **n** lionne *f*.

lionize, *UK* ***-ise*** ['laɪənaɪz] **vt** porter aux nues.

lip [lɪp] **n 1.** [of mouth] lèvre *f* ▸ **my lips are sealed** je ne dirai rien **2.** [of container] bord *m*.

lip balm = ***lip salve***.

lip gloss **n** brillant *m* à lèvres.

liposuction ['lɪpəʊˌsʌkʃn] **n** liposuccion *f*.

-lipped [lɪpt] **suffix : thin-lipped** aux lèvres minces.

lippy ['lɪpɪ] (**comp -ier, superl -iest**) **adj** *inf* insolent(e), culotté(e).

lip-read **vi** lire sur les lèvres.

lip-reading **n** lecture *f* sur les lèvres.

lip salve *UK*, ***lip balm*** **n** pommade *f* pour les lèvres.

lip service **n : to pay lip service to sthg** approuver qqch pour la forme.

lipstick ['lɪpstɪk] **n** rouge *m* à lèvres.

lip-synch [-sɪŋk] ■ **vi** chanter en play-back.
■ **vt : to lip-synch a song** chanter une chanson en play-back.

liquefy ['lɪkwɪfaɪ] (**pt & pp -ied**) ■ **vt** liquéfier.
■ **vi** se liquéfier.

liqueur [lɪ'kjʊəʳ] **n** liqueur *f*.

liquid ['lɪkwɪd] ■ **adj** liquide.
■ **n** liquide *m*.

liquid assets **npl** liquidités *fpl*.

liquidate ['lɪkwɪdeɪt] **vt** liquider.

liquidation [ˌlɪkwɪ'deɪʃn] **n** liquidation *f*.

liquidator ['lɪkwɪdeɪtəʳ] **n** liquidateur *m*, -trice *f*.

liquid courage *US* = ***Dutch courage***.

liquid crystal display **n** affichage *m* à cristaux liquides.

liquidity [lɪ'kwɪdətɪ] **n** liquidité *f*.

liquidize, *UK* ***-ise*** ['lɪkwɪdaɪz] **vt** CULIN passer au mixer.

liquidizer, *UK* ***-iser*** ['lɪkwɪdaɪzəʳ] **n** mixer *m*.

liquor ['lɪkəʳ] **n** *(U)* alcool *m*, spiritueux *mpl*.

liquorice *UK*, ***licorice*** *US* ['lɪkərɪs] **n** réglisse *f*.

liquor store **n** *US* magasin *m* de vins et d'alcools.

lira ['lɪərə] **n** lire *f*.

Lisbon ['lɪzbən] **n** Lisbonne.

lisp [lɪsp] ■ **n** zézaiement *m*.
■ **vi** zézayer.

lissom(e) ['lɪsəm] **adj** *liter* gracile.

list [lɪst] ■ **n** liste *f*.
■ **vt** [in writing] faire la liste de / [in speech] énumérer.
■ **vi** NAUT donner de la bande, gîter.

listed building [ˌlɪstɪd-] **n** *UK* monument *m* classé.

listed company ['lɪstɪd-] **n** *UK* société *f* cotée en Bourse.

listen ['lɪsn] **vi : to listen to (sb/sthg)** écouter (qqn/qqch) ▸ **to listen for sthg** guetter qqch.
◆ ***listen in*** **vi 1.** RADIO être à l'écoute, écouter **2.** [eavesdrop] **: to listen in (on sthg)** écouter (qqch).
◆ ***listen up*** **vi** *esp US inf* écouter.

listener ['lɪsnəʳ] **n** auditeur *m*, -trice *f*.

listing ['lɪstɪŋ] **n** [COMPUT - action] listage *m* / [- result] listing *m*.
◆ ***listings*** **npl : the listings** le calendrier des spectacles.

listless ['lɪstlɪs] **adj** apathique, mou (molle).

listlessly ['lɪstlɪslɪ] **adv** [without energy] sans énergie *OR* vigueur, avec apathie / [weakly] mollement / [without interest] d'un air absent.

list price **n** prix *m* de catalogue.

lit [lɪt] **pt & pp** ➤ ***light***.

litany ['lɪtənɪ] (**pl -ies**) **n** litanie *f*.

liter *US* = ***litre***.

literacy ['lɪtərəsɪ] **n** fait *m* de savoir lire et écrire.

literal ['lɪtərəl] **adj** littéral(e).

literally ['lɪtərəlɪ] **adv** littéralement ▸ **to take sthg literally** prendre qqch au pied de la lettre.

literary ['lɪtərərɪ] **adj** littéraire.

literary agent **n** agent *m* littéraire.

literate ['lɪtərət] **adj 1.** [able to read and write] qui sait lire et écrire **2.** [well-read] cultivé(e).

-literate **suffix : to be computer-literate** avoir des connaissances en informatique.

literati [ˌlɪtə'rɑ:tɪ] **npl** *fml* gens *mpl* de lettres, lettrés *mpl*.

literature ['lɪtrətʃəʳ] **n** littérature *f* / [printed information] documentation *f*.

lithe [laɪð] **adj** souple, agile.

lithium ['lɪθɪəm] **n** lithium *m*.

lithograph ['lɪθəgrɑ:f] **n** lithographie *f*.

lithography [lɪ'θɒgrəfɪ] **n** lithographie *f*.

Lithuania [ˌlɪθjʊ'eɪnjə] **n** Lituanie *f* ▸ **in Lithuania** en Lituanie.

Lithuanian [ˌlɪθjʊ'eɪnjən] ■ **adj** lituanien(enne).
■ **n 1.** [person] Lituanien *m*, -enne *f* **2.** [language] lituanien *m*.

litigant ['lɪtɪgənt] **n** plaideur *m*, -euse *f*.

litigate ['lɪtɪgeɪt] **vi** plaider.

litigation [ˌlɪtɪ'geɪʃn] **n** litige *m* ▸ **to go to litigation** aller en justice.

litigious [lɪ'tɪdʒəs] **adj** *fml* & *pej* [fond of lawsuits] procédurier(ère).

litmus paper ['lɪtməs-] **n** papier *m* de tournesol.

litmus test ['lɪtməs-] **n** CHEM réaction *f* au tournesol / *fig* épreuve *f* de vérité.

litre *UK*, ***liter*** *US* ['li:təʳ] **n** litre *m*.

litter ['lɪtəʳ] ■ **n 1.** *(U)* [rubbish] ordures *fpl*, détritus *mpl* **2.** [of animals] portée *f*.
■ **vt : to be littered with** être couvert(e) de.

litterbin ['lɪtə,bɪn] **n** *UK* boîte *f* à ordures.

litterlout *UK* ['lɪtəlaʊt], ***litterbug*** ['lɪtəbʌg] **n** *personne qui jette des ordures n'importe où.*

litter tray **n** *UK* caisse *f* (pour litière).

little ['lɪtl] ■ **adj 1.** [not big] petit(e) ▸ **when I was little** quand j'étais petit ▸ **my little sister** ma petite sœur ▸ **the shop is a little way along the street** le magasin se trouve un peu plus loin dans la rue ▸ **a little chat** un brin de causette ▸ **a little while** un petit moment ▸ **they had a little argument** ils se sont un peu disputés
2. (**comp less, superl least**) [not much] peu de ▸ **little money** peu d'argent ▸ **very little time** très peu de temps ▸ **I'm afraid there's little hope left** je crains qu'il n'y ait plus beaucoup d'espoir.
■ **pron 1.** [small amount] pas grand-chose ▸ **very little is known about his childhood** on ne sait pas grand-chose *OR* on ne sait que très peu de choses sur son enfance ▸ **little of the money was left** il ne restait pas beaucoup d'argent, il restait peu d'argent ▸ **I see very little of him now** je ne le vois plus beaucoup, je ne le vois guère ▸ **there's little one can say** il n'y a pas grand-chose à dire ▸ **I gave her as little as possible** je lui ai donné le minimum
2. [certain amount] **: a little of everything** un peu de tout ▸ **the little I saw looked excellent** le peu que j'en ai vu paraissait excellent.
■ **adv** peu, pas beaucoup ▸ **we go there as little as possible** nous y allons le moins possible ▸ **it's little short of madness** ça frise la folie ▸ **little by little** peu à peu.
◆ ***a little*** ■ **n** un peu de ▸ **I speak a little French** je parle quelques mots de français ▸ **a little money** un peu d'argent.
■ **pron** un peu.
■ **adv** un peu ▸ **I'm a little tired** je suis un peu fatigué ▸ **I walked on a little** j'ai marché encore un peu.

little finger **n** petit doigt *m*, auriculaire *m*.

little-known **adj** peu connu(e).

little toe **n** petit orteil *m*.

liturgy ['lɪtədʒɪ] (**pl -ies**) **n** liturgie *f*.

live[1] [lɪv] ■ **vi 1.** [gen] vivre ▸ **as long as I live** tant que je vivrai, de mon vivant ▸ **was she still living when her grandson was born?** est-ce qu'elle était encore en vie quand son petit-fils est né? ▸ **I won't live to see them grow up** je ne vivrai pas assez vieux pour les voir grandir ▸ **to live to a ripe old age** vivre vieux (vieille) *OR* jusqu'à un âge avancé ▸ **to live dangerously** vivre dangereusement ▸ **they lived happily ever after** ils vécurent heureux jusqu'à la fin de leurs jours ▸ **to live in poverty/luxury** vivre dans la pauvreté/le luxe ▸ **she lives for her children/for skiing** elle ne vit que pour ses enfants/que pour le ski ▸ **let's live for the moment** *OR* **for today!** vivons l'instant présent! ▸ **she really knows how to live** elle sait vraiment profiter de la vie ▸ **long live the Queen!** vive la reine! ▸ **live and let live!** *prov* laisse faire! ▸ **well, you live and learn!** on en apprend tous les jours!
2. [have one's home] habiter, vivre ▸ **to live in Paris** habiter (à) Paris ▸ **to live in a flat/a castle** habiter (dans) un appartement/un château ▸ **I live in** *OR* **on Bank Street** j'habite Bank Street ▸ **do you live with your parents?** habitez-vous chez vos parents? ▸ **they have nowhere to live** ils sont à la rue
3. [support o.s.] vivre ▸ **they don't earn enough to live** ils ne gagnent pas de quoi vivre ▸ **he lives by teaching** il gagne sa vie en enseignant ▸ **how does she live on that salary?** comment s'en sort-elle avec ce salaire?
■ **vt : to live a quiet life** mener une vie tranquille ▸ **to live a life of poverty** vivre dans la pauvreté ▸ **she lived the life of a film star** elle a vécu comme une star de cinéma ▸ **to live it up** *inf* faire la noce.
◆ ***live down*** **vt sep** faire oublier ▸ **you'll never live this down!** [ridicule] tu n'as pas fini d'en entendre parler!
◆ ***live in*** **vi** [student] être interne.
◆ ***live off*** **vt insep** [savings, the land] vivre de / [family] vivre aux dépens de.
◆ ***live on*** ■ **vt insep** vivre de ▸ **his pension is all they have to live on** ils n'ont que sa retraite pour vivre.
■ **vi** [memory, feeling] rester, survivre ▸ **his memory lives on** son souvenir est encore vivant.
◆ ***live out*** ■ **vt insep : she lived out the rest of her life in Spain** elle a passé le reste de sa vie en Espagne ▸ **to live out one's fantasies** réaliser ses rêves.
■ **vi** [student] être externe.
◆ ***live through*** **vt insep** connaître ▸ **they've lived through war and famine** ils ont connu la guerre et la famine.
◆ ***live together*** **vi** vivre ensemble.
◆ ***live up to*** **vt insep : to live up to sb's expectations** répondre à l'attente de qqn ▸ **to live up to one's reputation** faire honneur à sa réputation.
◆ ***live with*** **vt insep 1.** [cohabit with] vivre avec
2. *inf* [accept] se faire à, accepter ▸ **she's not easy to live with** elle n'est pas facile à vivre ▸ **I don't like the situation, but I have to live with it** cette situation ne me plaît pas, mais je n'ai pas le choix.

live[2] [laɪv] ■ **adj 1.** [living] vivant(e) ▸ **a real live cowboy** *inf* un cowboy, un vrai de vrai ▸ **live births** naissances *fpl* viables ▸ **live yoghurt** yaourt *m* actif **2.** [coal] ardent(e) **3.** [bullet, bomb] non explosé(e) ▸ **live ammunition** munitions *fpl* de combat **4.** ELEC sous tension ▸ **live circuit** circuit *m* alimenté *OR* sous tension **5.** RADIO & TV en direct / [performance] en public ▸ **Sinatra live at the Palladium** Sinatra en concert au Palladium ▸ **recorded before a live audience** enregistré en public.
■ **adv** RADIO & TV en direct / [perform] en public ▸ **the match can be seen/is going out live at 3.30 p.m.** on peut suivre le match/le match est diffusé en direct à 15 h 30.

lived-in ['lɪvdɪn] **adj** [comfortable] confortable / [occupied] habité(e) ▸ **the room had a nice lived-in feel** on sentait que la pièce était habitée.

live-in [lɪv-] **adj** [housekeeper] logé(e) et nourri(e) ▸ **a live-in boyfriend/girlfriend** un petit ami/une petite amie avec qui on vit.

livelihood ['laɪvlɪhʊd] **n** gagne-pain *m inv*.

liveliness ['laɪvlɪnɪs] **n** vivacité *f*.

lively ['laɪvlɪ] (**comp -ier, superl -iest**) **adj 1.** [person] plein(e) d'entrain **2.** [debate, meeting] animé(e) **3.** [mind] vif (vive).

liven ['laɪvn] ◆ ***liven up*** ■ vt sep [person] égayer / [place] animer.
■ vi s'animer.

liver ['lɪvəʳ] n foie *m*.

Liverpudlian ■ adj de Liverpool.
■ n habitant *m*, -e *f* de Liverpool.

liver sausage *UK*, ***liverwurst*** *US* ['lɪvəwɜ:st] n saucisse *f* (au pâté) de foie.

livery ['lɪvərɪ] (pl -ies) n livrée *f*.

lives [laɪvz] npl ➤ ***life***.

livestock ['laɪvstɒk] n *(U)* bétail *m*.

live wire [laɪv-] n fil *m* sous tension / *inf fig* boute-en-train *m inv*.

livid ['lɪvɪd] adj **1.** *inf* [angry] furieux(euse) **2.** [bruise] violacé(e).

living ['lɪvɪŋ] ■ adj vivant(e), en vie.
■ n : **to earn** *OR* **make a living** gagner sa vie ▸ **what do you do for a living?** qu'est-ce que vous faites dans la vie?

living conditions npl conditions *fpl* de vie.

living expenses npl frais *mpl* de subsistance.

living room n salle *f* de séjour, living *m*.

living standards npl niveau *m* de vie.

living wage n minimum *m* vital.

lizard ['lɪzəd] n lézard *m*.

llama ['lɑ:mə] (pl **llama** *OR* **-s**) n lama *m*.

LLB (abbr of ***Bachelor of Laws***) n *titulaire d'une licence de droit*.

LLD (abbr of ***Doctor of Laws***) n *docteur en droit*.

LLDC (abbr of ***least-developed country***) n PMD *m (pays parmi les moins avancés)*.

LMBO (abbr of ***leveraged management buyout***) n rachat *m* d'entreprise par les salariés.

LMT (abbr of ***Local Mean Time***) n *heure solaire aux États-Unis*.

lo [ləʊ] excl : **lo and behold** et comme par miracle.

load [ləʊd] ■ n **1.** [burden, thing carried] chargement *m*, charge *f* ▸ **the reforms should lighten the load of classroom teachers** les réformes devraient faciliter la tâche des enseignants ▸ **hire somebody to share the load** embauchez quelqu'un pour vous faciliter la tâche ▸ **that's a load off my mind!** me voilà soulagé d'un poids! ▸ **get a load of this** *inf* [look] vise un peu ça / [listen] écoute-moi ça **2.** [large amount] : **loads of, a load of** *inf* des tas de, plein de ▸ **a load of rubbish** *esp UK OR* **of bull** *esp US inf* de la foutaise ▸ **it'll be loads of fun** ça va être super marrant ▸ **she's got loads of money** elle est bourrée de fric, elle a un fric monstre
3. [batch of laundry] machine *f*.
■ vt [gen & COMPUT] charger / [video recorder] mettre une vidéo-cassette dans ▸ **to load sb/sthg with** charger qqn/qqch de ▸ **load the bags into the car** chargez *OR* mettez les sacs dans la voiture ▸ **to load a gun/camera (with)** charger un fusil/un appareil (avec) ▸ **to load a film/tape** mettre une pellicule/une cassette ▸ **to load a program** COMPUT charger un programme ▸ **to load the dice** piper les dés.
■ vi **1.** [receive freight] charger ▸ **the ship is loading** le navire est en cours de chargement
2. [computer program] se charger.
◆ ***load down*** vt sep charger (lourdement) ▸ **he was loaded down with packages** il avait des paquets plein les bras ▸ **I'm loaded down with work** je suis surchargé de travail.
◆ ***load up*** vt sep & vi charger.

loaded ['ləʊdɪd] adj **1.** [question] insidieux(euse) **2.** *inf* [rich] plein(e) aux as **3.** *esp US* [drunk] ivre.

loading bay ['ləʊdɪŋ-] n aire *f* de chargement.

loads [ləʊdz] adv *inf* vachement ▸ **it'll cost loads** ça va coûter un max *OR* vachement cher.

loaf [ləʊf] (pl **loaves** [ləʊvz]) n : **a loaf (of bread)** un pain.

loafer ['ləʊfəʳ] n [shoe] mocassin *m*.

loam [ləʊm] n terreau *m*.

loan [ləʊn] ■ n prêt *m* ▸ **he asked me for a loan** il m'a demandé de lui prêter de l'argent ▸ **on loan** prêté(e) ▸ **the picture is on loan to an American museum** le tableau a été prêté à un musée américain ▸ **I have three books on loan from the library** j'ai emprunté trois livres à la bibliothèque.
■ vt prêter ▸ **to loan sthg to sb, to loan sb sthg** prêter qqch à qqn.

loan account n compte *m* d'avances.

loan capital n capital-obligations *m*.

loan shark n *inf pej* usurier *m*.

loath [ləʊθ] adj *fml* : **to be loath to do sthg** ne pas vouloir faire qqch, hésiter à faire qqch.

loathe [ləʊð] vt détester ▸ **to loathe doing sthg** avoir horreur de *OR* détester faire qqch.

loathing ['ləʊðɪŋ] n *fml* dégoût *m*, répugnance *f*.

loathsome ['ləʊðsəm] adj dégoûtant(e), répugnant(e).

loaves [ləʊvz] npl ➤ ***loaf***.

lob [lɒb] ■ n TENNIS lob *m*.
■ vt (pt & pp -bed, cont -bing) **1.** [throw] lancer **2.** TENNIS : **to lob a ball** lober, faire un lob.

lobby ['lɒbɪ] ■ n (pl -ies) **1.** [of hotel] hall *m* **2.** [pressure group] lobby *m*, groupe *m* de pression.
■ vt (pt & pp -ied) faire pression sur.

lobbying ['lɒbɪɪŋ] n *(U)* POL pressions *fpl* ▸ **there has been intense lobbying against the bill** il y a eu de fortes pressions pour que le projet de loi soit retiré.

lobbyist ['lɒbɪɪst] n membre *m* d'un groupe de pression.

lobe [ləʊb] n lobe *m*.

lobelia [lə'bi:ljə] n lobélie *f*.

lobotomy [lə'bɒtəmɪ] (pl -ies) n lobotomie *f*.

lobster ['lɒbstəʳ] n homard *m*.

local ['ləʊkl] ■ adj local(e).
■ n *inf* **1.** [person] : **the locals** les gens *mpl* du coin *OR* du pays **2.** *UK* [pub] café *m OR* bistro *m* du coin **3.** *US* [bus, train] omnibus *m*.

local anaesthetic, *US* ***local anesthetic*** n anesthésie *f* locale.

local area network n COMPUT réseau *m* local.

local authority n *UK* autorités *fpl* locales.

local call n communication *f* urbaine.

local colour *UK*, ***local color*** *US* n couleur *f* locale.

local derby n *UK* derby *m*.

locale [ləʊ'kɑːl] n *fml* lieu *m*, endroit *m*.

local education authority n direction *f* régionale de l'enseignement *(en Angleterre et au pays de Galles)*.

local government n administration *f* municipale.

locality [ləʊ'kælətɪ] (pl **-ies**) n endroit *m*.

localization, *UK* ***-isation*** *UK* [ˌləʊkəlaɪ'zeɪʃn] n COMPUT localisation *f*.

localize, *UK* ***-ise*** ['ləʊkəlaɪz] vt **1.** [pinpoint, locate] localiser, situer **2.** [confine] localiser, limiter ▸ **they have tried to localize the effect of the strike** ils ont essayé de limiter l'effet de la grève **3.** [concentrate - power, money] concentrer.

localized, *UK* ***-ised*** ['ləʊkəlaɪzd] adj localisé(e).

locally ['ləʊkəlɪ] adv **1.** [on local basis] localement **2.** [nearby] dans les environs, à proximité.

local time n heure *f* locale.

locate [*UK* ləʊ'keɪt, *US* 'ləʊkeɪt] ■ vt **1.** [find - position] trouver, repérer / [- source, problem] localiser **2.** [situate - business, factory] implanter, établir ▸ **to be located** être situé(e).
■ vi [settle] **: to locate in** s'installer dans.

location [ləʊ'keɪʃn] n **1.** [place] emplacement *m* **2.** CIN **: on location** en extérieur.

location shot n CIN extérieur *m*.

loc. cit. (abbr of ***loco citato***) loc. cit.

loch [lɒk OR lɒx] n *Scot* loch *m*, lac *m*.

lock [lɒk] ■ n **1.** [of door] serrure *f* ▸ **under lock and key** [object] sous clef / [person] sous les verrous **2.** [on canal] écluse *f* **3.** AUT [steering lock] angle *m* de braquage ▸ **on full lock** braqué(e) à fond **4.** [of hair] mèche *f* **5.** TECH [device - gen] verrou *m* / [- on gun] percuteur *m* / [- on keyboard] **: shift OR caps lock** touche *f* de verrouillage majuscule
▸▸ **lock, stock and barrel** en bloc.
■ vt **1.** [door, car, drawer] fermer à clef / [bicycle] cadenasser **2.** [immobilize] bloquer **3.** [hold firmly] **: to be locked in an embrace** être étroitement enlacé(e) ▸ **to lock arms** [police cordon] former un barrage ▸ **to be locked in combat** être engagé(e) dans un combat / *fig* être aux prises.
■ vi **1.** [door, suitcase] fermer à clef **2.** [become immobilized] se bloquer ▸ **push the lever back until it locks into place** pousse le levier jusqu'à ce qu'il s'enclenche.
◆ ***locks*** npl *liter* chevelure *f*, cheveux *mpl*.
◆ ***lock away*** vt sep [valuables] mettre sous clef / [criminal] incarcérer, mettre sous les verrous ▸ **we keep the alcohol locked away** nous gardons l'alcool sous clef.
◆ ***lock in*** vt sep enfermer (à clef) ▸ **he locked himself in** il s'est enfermé (à l'intérieur).
◆ ***lock out*** vt sep **1.** [accidentally] enfermer dehors, laisser dehors ▸ **to lock o.s. out** s'enfermer dehors **2.** [deliberately] empêcher d'entrer, mettre à la porte.
◆ ***lock up*** ■ vt sep **1.** [person - in prison] mettre en prison OR sous les verrous / [- in asylum] enfermer **2.** [house] fermer à clef **3.** [valuables] enfermer, mettre sous clef.
■ vi fermer (à clef) ▸ **the last to leave locks up** le dernier à partir ferme la porte à clef.

lockable ['lɒkəbl] adj qu'on peut fermer à clef.

locker ['lɒkəʳ] n casier *m*.

locker room n vestiaire *m*.

locket ['lɒkɪt] n médaillon *m*.

lockjaw ['lɒkdʒɔː] n *dated* tétanos *m*.

lockout ['lɒkaʊt] n lock-out *m inv*.

locksmith ['lɒksmɪθ] n serrurier *m*, -ière *f*.

lockup ['lɒkʌp] n **1.** [prison] prison *f* **2.** *UK* [garage] garage *m*, box *m*.

loco ['ləʊkəʊ] *inf* ■ adj *US* timbré(e).
■ n (pl **-s**) *UK* locomotive.

locomotive ['ləʊkəˌməʊtɪv] n locomotive *f*.

locum ['ləʊkəm] (pl **-s**) n *esp UK* remplaçant *m*, -e *f*.

locust ['ləʊkəst] n sauterelle *f*, locuste *f*.

lodge [lɒdʒ] ■ n **1.** [of caretaker, freemasons] loge *f* **2.** [of manor house] pavillon *m* (de gardien) **3.** [for hunting] pavillon *m* de chasse.
■ vi **1.** *fml* [stay] **: to lodge with sb** loger chez qqn **2.** [become stuck] se loger, se coincer **3.** *fig* [in mind] s'enraciner, s'ancrer.
■ vt [complaint] déposer ▸ **to lodge an appeal** interjeter OR faire appel.

lodger ['lɒdʒəʳ] n locataire *mf*.

lodging ['lɒdʒɪŋ] n ➤ ***board***.
◆ ***lodgings*** npl chambre *f* meublée.

loft [lɒft] n grenier *m*.

lofty ['lɒftɪ] (comp **-ier**, superl **-iest**) adj **1.** [noble] noble **2.** *pej* [haughty] hautain(e), arrogant(e) **3.** *liter* [high] haut(e), élevé(e).

log [lɒg] ■ n **1.** [of wood] bûche *f* **2.** [of ship] journal *m* de bord / [of plane] carnet *m* de vol.
■ vt (pt & pp **-ged**, cont **-ging**) consigner, enregistrer.
◆ ***log in***, ***log on*** vi COMPUT ouvrir une session.
◆ ***log off***, ***log out*** vi COMPUT fermer une session.

loganberry ['ləʊgənbərɪ] (pl **-ies**) n *sorte de framboise*.

logarithm ['lɒgərɪðm] n logarithme *m*.

logbook ['lɒgbʊk] n **1.** [of ship] journal *m* de bord / [of plane] carnet *m* de vol **2.** *UK* [of car] ≃ carte *f* grise.

log cabin n cabane *f* en rondins.

log fire n feu *m* de bois.

loggerheads ['lɒgəhedz] n **: at loggerheads** en désaccord.

logic ['lɒdʒɪk] n logique *f*.

logical ['lɒdʒɪkl] adj logique.

logically ['lɒdʒɪklɪ] adv logiquement.

login (name) ['lɒgɪn] n COMPUT nom *m* d'utilisateur OR de login.

logistical [lə'dʒɪstɪkl] adj logistique.

logistically [lə'dʒɪstɪklɪ] adv sur le plan logistique.

logistics [lə'dʒɪstɪks] ■ n *(U)* MIL logistique *f*.
■ npl *fig* organisation *f*.

logjam ['lɒgdʒæm] n *esp US* & *Can* impasse *f*.

logo ['ləʊgəʊ] (pl -s) n logo *m*.

logrolling ['lɒgrəʊlɪŋ] n *(U) US* échange *m* de faveurs.

logy ['ləʊgɪ] adj *US inf* patraque.

loin [lɔɪn] n filet *m*.

◆ ***loins*** npl reins *mpl* ▸ **to gird one's loins** prendre son courage à deux mains.

loincloth ['lɔɪnklɒθ] n pagne *m*.

loiter ['lɔɪtər] vi traîner.

loll [lɒl] vi **1.** [sit, lie around] se prélasser **2.** [hang down - head, tongue] pendre.

lollipop ['lɒlɪpɒp] n sucette *f*.

lollipop lady n *UK dame qui fait traverser la rue aux enfants à la sortie des écoles.*

lollipop man n *UK monsieur qui fait traverser la rue aux enfants à la sortie des écoles.*

lollop ['lɒləp] vi [person] marcher lourdement / [animal] galoper.

lolly ['lɒlɪ] (pl -ies) n *UK inf* **1.** [lollipop] sucette *f* **2.** [ice lolly] sucette *f* glacée **3.** [money] fric *m*, blé *m*.

London ['lʌndən] n Londres.

Londoner ['lʌndənər] n Londonien *m*, -enne *f*.

lone [ləʊn] adj solitaire.

loneliness ['ləʊnlɪnɪs] n [of person] solitude *f* / [of place] isolement *m*.

lonely ['ləʊnlɪ] (comp -ier, superl -iest) adj **1.** [person] solitaire, seul(e) ▸ **to feel lonely** se sentir seul **2.** [childhood] solitaire **3.** [place] isolé(e).

lonely hearts adj : **lonely hearts club** club *m* de rencontres ▸ **lonely hearts column** rubrique *f* rencontres *(des petites annonces)*.

lone parent n *UK* père *m*/mère *f* célibataire.

loner ['ləʊnər] n solitaire *mf*.

lonesome ['ləʊnsəm] adj *US inf* **1.** [person] solitaire, seul(e) **2.** [place] isolé(e).

long [lɒŋ] ■ adj **1.** [in space] long (longue) ▸ **the pool's 33 metres long** la piscine fait 33 mètres de long ▸ **how long is the pool?** quelle est la longueur de la piscine?, la piscine fait combien de long? ▸ **the article is 80 pages long** l'article fait 80 pages ▸ **is it a long way (away)?** est-ce loin (d'ici)? ▸ **it's a long way to the beach** la plage est loin ▸ **long trousers** *OR* **US pants** pantalon *m* long **2.** [in time] long (longue) ▸ **how long will the flight be/was the meeting?** combien de temps durera le vol/a duré la réunion? ▸ **her five-year-long battle with the authorities** sa lutte de cinq années contre les autorités ▸ **to have a long memory** avoir une bonne mémoire *OR* une mémoire d'éléphant ▸ **I've had a long day** j'ai eu une journée bien remplie ▸ **I've known her (for) a long time** *OR* **while** je la connais depuis longtemps, cela fait longtemps que je la connais ▸ **at long last!** enfin!

■ adv longtemps ▸ **they live longer than humans** ils vivent plus longtemps que les êtres humains ▸ **I haven't been here long** je viens d'arriver, j'arrive juste ▸ **how long will it take?** combien de temps cela va-t-il prendre? ▸ **how long will you be?** tu en as pour combien de temps? ▸ **please wait: she won't be long** attendez, s'il vous plaît, elle ne va pas tarder ▸ **don't be** *OR* **take too long** fais vite ▸ **how long does it take to get there?** combien de temps faut-il pour y aller? ▸ **this won't take long** ça va être vite fait ▸ **how long is it since we last visited them?** quand sommes-nous allés les voir pour la dernière fois? ▸ **long before you were born** bien avant que tu sois né ▸ **the decision had been taken long before** la décision avait été prise depuis longtemps ▸ **the longest-running TV series** le plus long feuilleton télévisé ▸ **all day/week long** toute la journée/la semaine ▸ **so long!** *inf* au revoir!, salut!

■ n : **the long and the short of it is that...** le fin mot de l'histoire, c'est que..., enfin bref...

■ vi : **to long** *OR* **to be longing to do sthg** être impatient(e) *OR* avoir hâte de faire qqch ▸ **I was longing to tell her the truth** je mourais d'envie de lui dire la vérité.

◆ ***as long as, so long as*** conj **1.** [during the time that] tant que ▸ **as long as he's in power, there will be no hope** tant qu'il sera au pouvoir, il n'y aura aucun espoir **2.** [providing] à condition que, pourvu que ▸ **you can have it as long as you give me it back** vous pouvez le prendre à condition que *OR* pourvu que vous me le rendiez.

◆ ***before long*** adv [soon] dans peu de temps, sous peu / [soon afterwards] peu (de temps) après.

◆ ***for long*** adv longtemps ▸ **he's still in charge here, but not for long** c'est encore lui qui s'en occupe, mais plus pour longtemps.

◆ ***no longer*** adv ne... plus ▸ **not any longer** plus maintenant ▸ **I no longer like him** je ne l'aime plus ▸ **I can't wait any longer** je ne peux pas attendre plus longtemps, je ne peux plus attendre.

◆ ***long for*** vt insep [want very much] désirer ardemment / [look forward to] attendre avec impatience ▸ **she was longing for a letter from you** elle attendait impatiemment que vous lui écriviez.

long. (abbr of ***longitude***) long.

long-awaited [-ə'weɪtɪd] adj tant attendu(e).

longboat ['lɒŋbəʊt] n chaloupe *f*.

long-distance adj [runner, race] de fond ▸ **long-distance lorry** *UK OR* **truck** *US* **driver** routier *m*.

long-distance call n communication *f* interurbaine.

long division n division *f* par écrit.

long-drawn-out adj interminable, qui n'en finit pas.

long drink n long drink *m*.

longed-for ['lɒŋd-] adj très attendu(e).

longevity [lɒn'dʒevətɪ] n longévité *f*.

long-forgotten adj oublié(e) depuis longtemps ▸ **a long-forgotten tradition** une tradition tombée en désuétude.

long-haired adj [person] aux cheveux longs / [animal] à longs poils.

longhand ['lɒŋhænd] n écriture *f* normale.

long-haul adj long-courrier.

longing ['lɒŋɪŋ] ■ adj plein(e) de convoitise.

■ n **1.** [desire] envie *f*, convoitise *f* ▸ **a longing for** un grand désir *OR* une grande envie de **2.** [nostalgia] nostalgie *f*, regret *m*.

longingly ['lɒŋɪŋlɪ] adv [with desire] avec envie / [nostalgically] avec nostalgie.

Long Island **n** Long Island ▸ **in Long Island** à Long Island.

longitude ['lɒndʒɪtju:d] **n** longitude *f*.

long johns **npl** caleçon *m* long.

long jump **n** saut *m* en longueur.

long-lasting **adj** qui dure longtemps, durable.

long-life **adj** [milk] longue conservation *(inv)* / [battery] longue durée *(inv)*.

longlist ['lɑŋlɪst] **n** première *f* liste.

long-lived [-lɪvd] **adj** [family, species] d'une grande longévité / [friendship] durable / [prejudice] tenace, qui a la vie dure.

long-lost **adj** [artefact] perdu(e) depuis longtemps / [relative] perdu(e) de vue depuis longtemps.

long-playing record [-'pleɪɪŋ-] **n** 33 tours *m*.

long-range **adj 1.** [missile, bomber] à longue portée **2.** [plan, forecast] à long terme.

long-running **adj** [TV programme] diffusé(e) depuis de nombreuses années / [play] qui tient depuis longtemps l'affiche / [dispute] qui dure depuis longtemps.

longshoreman ['lɒŋʃɔ:mən] (pl **-men** [-mən]) **n** *US* docker *m*.

long shot **n** [guess] coup *m* à tenter *(sans grand espoir de succès)*.

longsighted [,lɒŋ'saɪtɪd] **adj** *UK* presbyte.

longsightedness [,lɒŋ'saɪtɪdnɪs] **n** *UK* **1.** MED hypermétropie *f*, presbytie *f* **2.** *fig* [good judgement] prévoyance *f*, discernement *m*.

long-standing **adj** de longue date.

long-suffering **adj** [person] à la patience infinie.

long term **n : in the long term** à long terme.
◆ ***long-term*** **adj** à long terme.

long-term unemployment **n** chômage *m* structurel.

long vacation **n** *UK* grandes vacances *fpl*.

long wave **n** *(U)* grandes ondes *fpl*.

longways ['lɒŋweɪz] **adv** dans le sens de la longueur.

longwearing [,lɒŋ'weərɪŋ] **adj** *US* solide, résistant(e).

long weekend **n** long week-end *m*.

longwinded [,lɒŋ'wɪndɪd] **adj** [person] prolixe, verbeux(euse) / [speech] interminable, qui n'en finit pas.

loo [lu:] (pl **-s**) **n** *UK inf* cabinets *mpl*, petit coin *m*.

loofa(h) ['lu:fə] **n** luffa *m*, éponge *f*.

look [lʊk] ■ **n 1.** [with eyes] regard *m* ▸ **to take** *OR* **have a look (at sthg)** regarder (qqch), jeter un coup d'œil (à qqch) ▸ **to give sb a look** jeter un regard à qqn, regarder qqn de travers ▸ **she gave me a dirty look** elle m'a jeté un regard mauvais ▸ **it's worth a quick look** ça vaut le coup d'œil ▸ **do you mind if I take a look around?** ça vous gêne si je jette un coup d'œil?
2. [search] **: to have a look (for sthg)** chercher (qqch) ▸ **have another look** cherche encore
3. [appearance] aspect *m*, air *m* ▸ **he had a strange look in his eyes** il avait un drôle de regard ▸ **by the look** *OR* **looks of it, by the look** *OR* **looks of things** vraisemblablement, selon toute probabilité ▸ **I quite like the look of the next candidate** j'aime assez le profil du prochain candidat ▸ **I don't like the look of it** ça ne me dit rien de bon *OR* rien qui vaille.
■ **vi 1.** [with eyes] regarder ▸ **look, there's Brian!** regarde, voilà Brian! ▸ **what's happening outside? let me look** qu'est-ce qui se passe dehors? laissez-moi voir ▸ **they crept up on me while I wasn't looking** ils se sont approchés de moi pendant que j'avais le dos tourné ▸ **I'm just looking** [in shop] je jette un coup d'œil ▸ **she looked along the row/down the list** elle a parcouru la rangée/la liste du regard ▸ **he was looking out of the window/over the wall/up the chimney** il regardait par la fenêtre/par-dessus le mur/dans la cheminée
2. [search] chercher ▸ **you can't have looked hard enough** tu n'as pas dû beaucoup chercher
3. [seem] avoir l'air, sembler ▸ **you look** *OR* **are looking better today** tu as l'air (d'aller) mieux aujourd'hui ▸ **how do I look?** comment tu me trouves? ▸ **it looks all right to me** moi, je trouve ça bien ▸ **he looks good in jeans** les jeans lui vont bien ▸ **it'll look good on your CV** ça fera bien sur ton curriculum ▸ **it'll look bad if I don't contribute** ça fera mauvaise impression si je ne contribue pas ▸ **he looks as if he hasn't slept** il a l'air d'avoir mal dormi ▸ **it looks like rain** *OR* **as if it will rain** on dirait qu'il va pleuvoir ▸ **she looks like her mother** elle ressemble à sa mère ▸ **is this our room? – it looks like it** c'est notre chambre? – ça m'en a tout l'air ▸ **it doesn't look as if they're coming** on dirait qu'ils ne vont pas venir
4. [building, window] **: to look (out) onto** donner sur ▸ **to look north/west** être exposé(e) au nord/à l'ouest.
■ **vt 1.** [look at] **: look what you've done!** regarde ce que tu as fait! ▸ **look who's coming!** regarde qui arrive! ▸ **look who's talking!** tu peux parler, toi! ▸ **to look sb up and down** regarder qqn de haut en bas, toiser qqn du regard
2. [appear] **: to look one's age** faire *OR* porter son âge ▸ **he's 70, but he doesn't look it** il a 70 ans mais il n'en a pas l'air *OR* mais il ne les fait pas ▸ **to look one's best** être *OR* paraître à son avantage ▸ **I must have looked a fool** j'ai dû passer pour un imbécile ▸ **to make sb look a fool** *OR* **an idiot** tourner qqn en ridicule.
■ **excl : look!, look here!** dites donc! ▸ **look, I can't pay you back just yet** écoute, je ne peux pas te rembourser tout de suite.

◆ ***looks*** **npl** [attractiveness] beauté *f* ▸ **she's got everything, looks, intelligence, youth...** elle a tout pour elle, elle est belle, intelligente, jeune...

◆ ***look after*** **vt insep** s'occuper de ▸ **she has a sick mother to look after** elle a une mère malade à charge ▸ **Grandma can look after the children while we're away** Grand-mère peut garder les enfants pendant notre absence ▸ **you should look after your clothes more carefully** tu devrais prendre plus grand soin de tes vêtements ▸ **look after yourself!** fais bien attention à toi!

◆ ***look around***, ***look round*** *UK* ■ **vt insep** [house, shop, town] faire le tour de.
■ **vi 1.** [turn] se retourner
2. [browse] regarder.

◆ ***look at*** **vt insep 1.** [see, glance at] regarder ▸ **they looked at each other** ils ont échangé un regard
2. [examine] examiner ▸ **to have one's teeth looked at** se faire examiner les dents

3. [judge] considérer ▸ **that's not the way I look at it** ce n'est pas comme ça que je vois les choses.
◆ ***look back*** **vi** [reminisce] penser au passé, évoquer le passé ▸ **it seems funny now we look back on it** ça semble drôle quand on y pense aujourd'hui ▸ **she's never looked back** depuis, elle a accumulé les succès.
◆ ***look down on*** **vt insep** [condescend to] mépriser.
◆ ***look for*** **vt insep** chercher ▸ **are you looking for a fight?** tu cherches la bagarre? ▸ **it's not the result we were looking for** ce n'est pas le résultat que nous attendions.
◆ ***look forward to*** **vt insep** attendre avec impatience ▸ **to look forward to doing sthg** être impatient(e) de faire qqch ▸ **I look forward to hearing from you soon** [in letter] dans l'attente de votre réponse.
◆ ***look into*** **vt insep** examiner, étudier ▸ **it's a problem that needs looking into** c'est un problème qu'il faut examiner *OR* sur lequel il faut se pencher.
◆ ***look on*** ■ **vt insep** = ***look upon***.
■ **vi** regarder.
◆ ***look out*** **vi** prendre garde, faire attention ▸ **look out!** attention!
◆ ***look out for*** **vt insep** [person] guetter / [new book] être à l'affût de, essayer de repérer ▸ **you have to look out for snakes** il faut faire attention *OR* se méfier, il y a des serpents ▸ **to look out for o.s.** penser à soi.
◆ ***look round*** **vt insep** *UK* = ***look around***.
◆ ***look through*** **vt insep** [gen] examiner / [newspaper] parcourir.
◆ ***look to*** **vt insep 1.** [depend on] compter sur
2. [future] songer à.
◆ ***look up*** ■ **vt sep 1.** [in book] chercher
2. [visit - person] aller *OR* passer voir.
■ **vi** [improve - business] reprendre ▸ **things are looking up** ça va mieux, la situation s'améliore.
◆ ***look upon*** **vt insep : to look upon sb/sthg as** considérer qqn/qqch comme.
◆ ***look up to*** **vt insep** admirer.

look-alike **n** sosie *m*.

looker ['lʊkər] **n** *inf* canon *m* ▸ **she's/he's quite a looker** elle/il n'est pas mal (du tout).

look-in **n** *UK inf* **: I didn't get a look-in** je n'avais aucune chance / [in conversation] je n'ai pas pu en placer une.

lookout ['lʊkaʊt] **n 1.** [place] poste *m* de guet **2.** [person] guetteur *m* **3.** [search] **: to be on the lookout for** être à la recherche de.

look-up table **n** COMPUT table *f* de recherche.

loom [lu:m] ■ **n** métier *m* à tisser.
■ **vi** [building, person] se dresser / *fig* [date, threat] être imminent(e) ▸ **to loom large** être un sujet d'inquiétude *OR* de préoccupation.
◆ ***loom up*** **vi** surgir.

LOOM (abbr of **Loyal Order of Moose**) **n** *association caritative américaine*.

looming ['lu:mɪŋ] **adj** imminent(e).

loony ['lu:nɪ] *inf* ■ **adj** (comp **-ier**, superl **-iest**) cinglé(e), timbré(e).
■ **n** (pl **-ies**) cinglé *m*, -e *f*, fou *m*, folle *f*.

loony bin **n** *inf offens* asile *m*.

loop [lu:p] ■ **n 1.** [gen & COMPUT] boucle *f* **2.** [contraceptive] stérilet *m*.
■ **vt** faire une boucle à.
■ **vi** faire une boucle.

loophole ['lu:phəʊl] **n** faille *f*, échappatoire *f*.

loopy ['lu:pɪ] (comp **-ier**, superl **-iest**) **adj** *inf* [crazy] dingue, cinglé(e).

loo roll **n** *UK inf* rouleau *m* de papier hygiénique.

loose [lu:s] ■ **adj 1.** [not firm - joint] desserré(e) / [- handle, post] branlant(e) / [- tooth] qui bouge *OR* branle / [- knot] défait(e) ▸ **he prised a brick loose** il a réussi à faire bouger une brique ▸ **remove all the loose plaster** enlève tout le plâtre qui se détache ▸ **to work loose** [- nail] sortir / [- screw, bolt] se desserrer / [- knot] se défaire / [- tooth, slate] bouger / [- button] se détacher ▸ **loose connection** ELEC mauvais contact *m*
2. [unpackaged - sweets, nails] en vrac, au poids ▸ **loose coal** charbon *m* en vrac ▸ **I always buy vegetables loose** je n'achète jamais de légumes préemballés
3. [clothes] ample, large
4. [not restrained, fixed - hair] dénoué(e) / [- animal] en liberté, détaché(e) ▸ **a loose sheet of paper** une feuille volante ▸ **several pages have come loose** plusieurs pages se sont détachées ▸ **his arms hung loose at his sides** il avait les bras ballants
5. [vague, imprecise - translation] approximatif(ive) / [- connection, link] vague ▸ **they have loose ties with other political groups** ils sont vaguement liés à d'autres groupes politiques
6. *pej* & *dated* [woman] facile / [living] dissolu(e)
7. *US inf* [relaxed] **: to stay loose** rester cool.
■ **n : on the loose** en liberté.

loose change **n** petite *OR* menue monnaie *f*.

loose cover **n** *UK* [for armchair, sofa] housse *f*.

loose end **n** détail *m* inexpliqué ▸ **to be at a loose end** *UK*, **to be at loose ends** *US* être désœuvré(e), n'avoir rien à faire.

loose-fitting **adj** ample.

loose-leaf binder **n** classeur *m*.

loosely ['lu:slɪ] **adv 1.** [not firmly] sans serrer **2.** [inexactly] approximativement.

loosen ['lu:sn] ■ **vt** desserrer, défaire ▸ **loosen the cake from the sides of the tin** détachez le gâteau des bords du moule ▸ **the wine soon loosened his tongue** le vin eut vite fait de lui délier la langue ▸ **they have loosened their ties with Moscow** *fig* leurs liens avec Moscou se sont relâchés.
■ **vi** se desserrer.
◆ ***loosen up*** **vi 1.** [before game, race] s'échauffer **2.** *inf* [relax] se détendre **3.** [get less severe] se montrer moins sévère ▸ **to loosen up on discipline** relâcher la discipline.

loot [lu:t] ■ **n** butin *m*.
■ **vt** piller.

looter ['lu:tər] **n** pillard *m*, -e *f*.

looting ['lu:tɪŋ] **n** pillage *m*.

lop [lɒp] (pt & pp **-ped**, cont **-ping**) **vt** élaguer, émonder.
◆ ***lop off*** **vt sep** couper.

lope [ləʊp] **vi** courir en faisant des bonds.

lopsided [-'saɪdɪd] adj **1.** [table] bancal(e), boiteux(euse) / [picture] de travers **2.** *fig* [biased] tendancieux(euse).

lord [lɔ:d] n *UK* seigneur *m*.
◆ ***Lord*** n **1.** RELIG **: the Lord** [God] le Seigneur ▸ **good Lord!** Seigneur!, mon Dieu! **2.** *UK* [in titles] Lord *m* / [as form of address] **: my Lord** Monsieur le duc/comte *etc*.
◆ ***Lords*** npl *UK* POL **: the (House of) Lords** la Chambre des lords.

Lord Chancellor n *UK* Lord Chancelier *m*.

lordly ['lɔ:dlɪ] (comp -ier, superl -iest) adj **1.** [noble] noble **2.** *pej* [arrogant] arrogant(e), hautain(e).

Lord Mayor n *UK* Lord-Maire *m*.

Lordship ['lɔ:dʃɪp] n **: your/his Lordship** Monsieur le duc/comte *etc*.

Lord's Prayer n **: the Lord's Prayer** le Notre Père.

lore [lɔ:ʳ] n *(U)* traditions *fpl*.

lorry ['lɒrɪ] (pl -ies) n *UK* camion *m*.

lorry driver n *UK* camionneur *m*, conducteur *m* de poids lourd.

lorry-load n *UK* chargement *m*.

lose [lu:z] (pt & pp lost) ■ vt **1.** [gen] perdre ▸ **you've got nothing to lose** tu n'as rien à perdre ▸ **we haven't got a moment to lose** il n'y a pas une seconde à perdre ▸ **30 lives were lost in the fire** 30 personnes ont péri dans l'incendie, l'incendie a fait 30 morts ▸ **he lost four games to Karpov** il a perdu quatre parties contre Karpov ▸ **to lose one's appetite** perdre l'appétit ▸ **to lose one's balance** perdre l'équilibre ▸ **to lose consciousness** perdre connaissance ▸ **to lose one's head** perdre la tête ▸ **to lose sight of** *lit & fig* perdre de vue ▸ **to lose one's voice** avoir une extinction de voix ▸ **to lose one's way** se perdre, perdre son chemin / *fig* être un peu perdu(e) ▸ **to lose weight** perdre du poids **2.** [subj: clock, watch] retarder de ▸ **to lose time** retarder **3.** [pursuers] semer.
■ vi perdre ▸ **they lost by one goal** ils ont perdu d'un but ▸ **either way, I can't lose** je suis gagnant à tous les coups.
◆ ***lose out*** vi être perdant(e) ▸ **to lose out on a deal** être perdant dans une affaire.

loser ['lu:zəʳ] n **1.** [gen] perdant *m*, -e *f* ▸ **a good/bad loser** un bon/mauvais joueur *m*, une bonne/mauvaise joueuse *f* **2.** *inf pej* [unsuccessful person] raté *m*, -e *f*.

losing ['lu:zɪŋ] adj perdant(e).

loss [lɒs] n **1.** [gen] perte *f* ▸ **the closure will cause the loss of hundreds of jobs** la fermeture provoquera la disparition de centaines d'emplois **2.** COMM **: to make a loss** perdre de l'argent ▸ **the company announced losses of** OR **a loss of a million pounds** la société a annoncé un déficit d'un million de livres
▸▸ **to be at a loss** être perplexe, être embarrassé(e) ▸ **I'm at a loss to explain what happened** je n'arrive pas à expliquer comment cela a pu se produire ▸ **I was at a loss for words** je ne savais pas quoi dire, les mots me manquaient ▸ **to cut one's losses** faire la part du feu.

loss adjuster [-ə'dʒʌstəʳ] n *UK* responsable *m* de l'évaluation des sinistres.

loss leader n COMM *article vendu à perte dans le but d'attirer la clientèle*.

lossmaker ['lɒsmeɪkəʳ] n gouffre *m* financier.

lost [lɒst] ■ pt & pp ➤ ***lose***.
■ adj **1.** [gen] perdu(e) ▸ **can you help me, I'm lost** pouvez-vous m'aider, je me suis perdu OR égaré ▸ **they have discovered a lost masterpiece** ils ont découvert un chef-d'œuvre disparu ▸ **to get lost** se perdre ▸ **get lost!** *inf* fous/foutez le camp! ▸ **I'm lost for words** je ne sais pas quoi dire **2.** [ineffective] **: to be lost on sb** [advice, warning] être sans effet sur qqn, n'avoir aucun effet sur qqn ▸ **the allusion was lost on me** je n'ai pas compris OR saisi l'allusion **3.** [opportunity] perdu(e), manqué(e).

lost-and-found office n *US* bureau *m* des objets trouvés.

lost cause n cause *f* perdue.

lost property n *(U) UK* objets *mpl* trouvés.

lost property office n *UK* bureau *m* des objets trouvés.

lot [lɒt] n **1.** [large amount] **: a lot (of), lots (of)** beaucoup (de) ▸ **there's a lot still to be done** il y a encore beaucoup à faire ▸ **there's not a lot you can do about it** tu n'y peux pas grand-chose ▸ **what a lot of people!** quelle foule!, que de monde! ▸ **she takes a lot of care over her appearance** elle fait très attention à son apparence ▸ **do you need any paper/envelopes? I've got lots** est-ce que tu as besoin de papier/d'enveloppes? j'en ai plein ▸ **there are lots to choose from** il y a du choix
2. *UK inf* [entire amount] **: the lot** le tout ▸ **take all this lot and dump it in my office** prends tout ça et mets-le dans mon bureau
3. *UK inf* [group of people] **: they're a strange lot** ce sont des gens bizarres ▸ **this lot are leaving today and another lot are arriving tomorrow** ce groupe part aujourd'hui et un autre (groupe) arrive demain ▸ **come here, you lot!** venez ici, vous autres!
4. [at auction] lot *m*
5. [destiny] sort *m* ▸ **to be content with one's lot** être content de son sort
6. *US* [of land] terrain *m* / [car park] parking *m*
▸▸ **to draw lots** tirer au sort.
◆ ***a lot*** adv beaucoup ▸ **a lot better/more** beaucoup mieux/plus ▸ **thanks a lot!** merci beaucoup!

loth [ləʊθ] = ***loath***.

lotion ['ləʊʃn] n lotion *f*.

lottery ['lɒtərɪ] (pl -ies) n *lit & fig* loterie *f*.

lotto ['lɒtəʊ] n loto *m (jeu de société)*.

lotus ['ləʊtəs] n lotus *m*.

lotus position n position *f* du lotus.

loud [laʊd] ■ adj **1.** [not quiet, noisy - gen] fort(e) / [- person] bruyant(e) ▸ **he's a bit loud, isn't he?** ce n'est pas le genre discret! **2.** [colour, clothes] voyant(e).
■ adv fort ▸ **the music was turned up loud** on avait mis la musique à fond ▸ **loud and clear** clairement ▸ **to read out loud** lire à haute voix ▸ **I was thinking out loud** je pensais tout haut.

loudhailer [,laʊd'heɪləʳ] n *UK* mégaphone *m*, porte-voix *m inv*.

loudly ['laʊdlɪ] adv **1.** [noisily] fort **2.** [gaudily] de façon voyante.

loudmouth ['laʊdmaʊθ] (pl [-maʊðz]) n *inf* grande gueule *f*.

loudmouthed ['laʊdmaʊðd] adj *inf* 1. [noisy] fort(e) en gueule 2. [boastful] crâneur(euse) / [gossipy] bavard(e), frimeur(euse).

loudness ['laʊdnɪs] n force *f*, intensité *f* / [of TV, radio] bruit *m*.

loudspeaker [ˌlaʊd'spi:kəʳ] n haut-parleur *m*.

Louisiana [lu:ˌi:zɪ'ænə] n Louisiane *f* ▸ **in Louisiana** en Louisiane.

lounge [laʊndʒ] ■ n 1. *UK* [in house] salon *m* 2. [in airport] hall *m*, salle *f* 3. *UK* = ***lounge bar***.
■ vi (cont **loungeing**) se prélasser.
◆ ***lounge around***, ***lounge about*** *UK* vi flemmarder, traîner.

lounge bar n *UK l'une des deux salles d'un bar, la plus confortable*.

lounger ['laʊndʒəʳ] n 1. [sunbed] lit *m* de plage 2. [person] paresseux *m*, -euse *f*.

lounge suit n *UK* complet *m*, complet-veston *m*.

louse [laʊs] n 1. (pl **lice** [laɪs]) [insect] pou *m* 2. (pl -s) *inf pej* [person] salaud *m*.
◆ ***louse up*** vt sep *US v inf* foutre en l'air.

lousy ['laʊzɪ] (comp **-ier**, superl **-iest**) adj *inf* minable, nul(le) / [weather] pourri(e) ▸ **to feel lousy** être mal fichu(e).

lout [laʊt] n rustre *m*.

loutish ['laʊtɪʃ] adj [behaviour] grossier(ère) / [manners] de rustre, mal dégrossi(e).

louvre *UK*, ***louver*** *US* ['lu:vəʳ] n persienne *f*.

louvred *UK*, ***louvered*** *US* ['lu:vəd] adj à claire-voie.

lovable ['lʌvəbl] adj adorable.

love [lʌv] ■ n 1. [gen] amour *m* ▸ **a love of** *OR* **for football** une passion pour le football ▸ **he did it out of love for her** il l'a fait par amour pour elle ▸ **to be in love** être amoureux(euse) ▸ **to fall in love** tomber amoureux(euse) ▸ **it was love at first sight** ce fut le coup de foudre ▸ **she's the love of his life** c'est la femme de sa vie ▸ **to make love** faire l'amour ▸ **give her my love** embrasse-la pour moi ▸ **love from** [at end of letter] affectueusement, grosses bises ▸ **I wouldn't do it for love nor money** *inf* je ne le ferais pas pour tout l'or du monde, je ne le ferais pour rien au monde ▸ **there's no love lost between them** ils se détestent cordialement
2. *UK inf* [form of address] mon chéri (ma chérie) ▸ **thank you, (my) love** *inf* merci, mon chou
3. TENNIS zéro *m*.
■ vt aimer ▸ **I like you but I don't love you** je t'aime bien mais je ne suis pas amoureux de toi ▸ **to love to do sthg** *OR* **doing sthg** aimer *OR* adorer faire qqch ▸ **I'd love to come** j'aimerais beaucoup venir ▸ **I'd love you to come** j'aimerais beaucoup que *OR* cela me ferait très plaisir que tu viennes ▸ **would you like to come too? – I'd love to** voudriez-vous venir aussi? – avec grand plaisir.

love affair n liaison *f*.

lovebird ['lʌvbɜ:d] n 1. [bird] perruche *f* ▸ **lovebirds** inséparables *mpl* 2. *hum* [lover] amoureux *m*, -euse *f*.

lovebite ['lʌvbaɪt] n suçon *m*.

love-hate adj : **a love-hate relationship** une relation d'amour-haine.

loveless ['lʌvlɪs] adj sans amour.

love letter n lettre *f* d'amour.

love life n vie *f* amoureuse.

lovelorn ['lʌvlɔ:n] adj malheureux(euse) en amour.

lovely ['lʌvlɪ] (comp **-ier**, superl **-iest**) adj 1. [beautiful] très joli(e) 2. [pleasant] très agréable, excellent(e).

lovemaking ['lʌvˌmeɪkɪŋ] n *(U)* amour *m*, rapports *mpl*.

lover ['lʌvəʳ] n 1. [sexual partner] amant *m*, -e *f* 2. [enthusiast] passionné *m*, -e *f*, amoureux *m*, -euse *f*.

lovesick ['lʌvsɪk] adj qui languit d'amour.

love song n chanson *f* d'amour.

love story n histoire *f* d'amour.

lovey-dovey ['lʌvɪˌdʌvɪ] adj *inf pej* doucereux(euse).

loving ['lʌvɪŋ] adj [person, relationship] affectueux (euse) / [care] tendre.

lovingly ['lʌvɪŋlɪ] adv avec amour.

low [ləʊ] ■ adj 1. [not high - gen] bas (basse) / [- wall, building] peu élevé(e) / [- standard, quality] mauvais(e) / [- intelligence] faible / [- neckline] décolleté(e) ▸ **this room has a low ceiling** cette pièce est basse de plafond ▸ **'low bridge'** AUT 'hauteur limitée' ▸ **the temperature is in the low twenties** il fait un peu plus de vingt degrés ▸ **to have a low opinion of sb** avoir mauvaise opinion de qqn ▸ **old people are given very low priority** les personnes âgées ne sont absolument pas considérées comme prioritaires ▸ **to cook sthg over a low heat** faire cuire qqch à petit feu ▸ **a low pressure area** METEOR une zone de basse pression ▸ **attendance was low** il y avait peu de monde ▸ **low in calories** pauvre en calories
2. [little remaining] presque épuisé(e) ▸ **to be low on sthg** manquer de qqch
3. [not loud - voice] bas (basse) / [- whisper, moan] faible ▸ **turn the radio down low** mettez la radio moins fort ▸ **turn the lights down low** baissez les lumières
4. [depressed] déprimé(e) ▸ **I'm in rather low spirits, I feel rather low** je n'ai pas le moral, je suis assez déprimé
5. [not respectable] bas (basse).
■ adv 1. [not high] bas ▸ **lower down** plus bas ▸ **to fly low** [plane] voler à basse altitude ▸ **he bowed low** il s'inclina profondément ▸ **to lie low** [hide] se cacher / [keep low profile] adopter un profil bas
2. [not loudly - speak] à voix basse / [- whisper] faiblement
3. [in intensity] bas ▸ **stocks are running low** les réserves baissent ▸ **the batteries are running low** les piles sont usées.
■ n 1. [low point] niveau *m* *OR* point *m* bas ▸ **the heating is on low** le chauffage est au minimum ▸ **the dollar has reached a record low** le dollar a atteint son niveau le plus bas ▸ **relations between them are at an all-time low** leurs relations n'ont jamais été si mauvaises
2. METEOR dépression *f*.

low-alcohol adj à faible teneur en alcool.

lowbrow ['ləʊbraʊ] adj peu intellectuel(elle).

low-budget adj économique.

low-calorie adj à basses calories.

Low Church n Basse Église *f*.

low-cost adj (à) bon marché.

Low Countries **npl : the Low Countries** les Pays-Bas *mpl*.

low-cut **adj** décolleté(e).

lowdown *inf* **n : to give sb the lowdown (on sthg)** mettre qqn au parfum (de qqch).
◆ ***low-down*** **adj** méprisable.

low-end **adj** [goods] bas(basse) de gamme.

lower[1] ['ləʊəʳ] ■ **adj** inférieur(e).
■ **vt 1.** [gen] baisser / [flag] abaisser ▸ **supplies were lowered down to us on a rope** on nous a descendu des provisions au bout d'une corde ▸ **to lower one's guard** *fig* prêter le flanc **2.** [reduce - price, level] baisser / [- age of consent] abaisser / [- resistance] diminuer ▸ **lower your voice** parlez moins fort, baissez la voix **3.** [morally] **: she wouldn't lower herself to talk to them** elle ne s'abaisserait pas au point de leur adresser la parole.

lower[2] ['laʊəʳ] **vi 1.** [sky] se faire menaçant(e) **2.** [person] **: to lower at sb** regarder qqn d'un air menaçant.

lower-case ['ləʊəʳ-] ■ **adj** TYPO en bas de casse.
■ **n** bas *m* de casse.

Lower Chamber ['ləʊəʳ-] **n** *UK* POL Chambre *f* basse *OR* des communes.

lower class ['ləʊəʳ-] **n : the lower class** *OR* **lower classes** les classes populaires *fpl*.
◆ ***lower-class*** ['ləʊəʳ-] **adj** populaire.

Lower House ['ləʊəʳ-] **n** *UK* = ***Lower Chamber***.

lowest common denominator ['ləʊɪst-] **n** *fig* & MATHS **: the lowest common denominator** le plus petit dénominateur commun.

low-fat **adj** [yogurt, crisps] allégé(e) / [milk] demi-écrémé(e).

low-flying **adj** volant(e) à basse altitude.

low frequency **n** basse fréquence *f*.

low gear **n** première (vitesse) *f*.

low-heeled **adj** à talons plats.

low-key **adj** discret(ète).

lowland ['ləʊlənd] **n** plaine *f*, basse terre *f*.

Lowlands ['ləʊləndz] **npl : the Lowlands** [of Scotland] les Basses Terres *fpl* (d'Écosse).

low-level **adj** [talks] à bas niveau / [operation] de faible envergure ▸ **low-level flying** AERON vol *m* à basse altitude ▸ **low-level radiation** irradiation *f* de faible intensité.

low-level language **n** COMPUT langage *m* de bas niveau.

low life **n** *inf* pègre *f*.

low-loader [-'ləʊdəʳ] **n** *UK* **1.** AUT semi-remorque *m* à plate-forme surbaissée **2.** RAIL wagon *m* à plate-forme surbaissée.

lowly ['ləʊlɪ] (**comp -ier, superl -iest**) **adj** modeste, humble.

low-lying **adj** bas (basse).

Low Mass **n** messe *f* basse.

low-necked [-'nekt] **adj** décolleté(e).

low-paid **adj** mal payé(e).

low profile **n : to keep a low profile** garder un profil bas.
◆ ***low-profile*** **adj 1.** discret(ète) **2.** AUT **: low-profile tyre** pneu *m* à profil bas.

low-rise **adj** bas (basse).

low season **n** *UK* basse saison *f*.

low-tar **adj : low-tar cigarettes** cigarettes *fpl* à faible teneur en goudron.

low-tech [-'tek] **adj** rudimentaire.

low tide **n** marée *f* basse.

low water **n** *(U)* basses eaux *fpl*.

loyal ['lɔɪəl] **adj** loyal(e).

loyalist ['lɔɪəlɪst] **n** loyaliste *mf*.

loyally ['lɔɪəlɪ] **adv** loyalement, fidèlement.

loyalty ['lɔɪəltɪ] (**pl -ies**) **n** loyauté *f* ▸ **her loyalty to the cause is not in doubt** son dévouement à la cause n'est pas mis en doute ▸ **my loyalties are divided** je suis déchiré (entre les deux), entre les deux mon cœur balance.

loyalty card **n** carte *f* de fidélité.

lozenge ['lɒzɪndʒ] **n 1.** [tablet] pastille *f* **2.** [shape] losange *m*.

LP (**abbr of *long-playing record***) **n** 33 tours *m*.

LPG [ˌelpiː'dʒiː] (**abbr of *liquified petroleum gas***) **n** GPL *m*.

L-plate **n** *UK plaque signalant que le conducteur du véhicule est en conduite accompagnée.*

LPN (**abbr of *licensed practical nurse***) **n** *US aide infirmière diplômée.*

LRAM (**abbr of *Licentiate of the Royal Academy of Music***) **n** *membre de l'Académie de musique britannique.*

LSAT (**abbr of *Law School Admissions Test***) **n** *aux États-Unis, test d'admission aux études de droit.*

LSD[1] (**abbr of *lysergic acid diethylamide***) **n** LSD *m*.

LSD[2], ***L.S.D.***, ***£.s.d.***, ***l.s.d.*** (**abbr of *pounds, shillings and pence - librae, solidi, denarii***) **n** *système monétaire en usage en Grande-Bretagne jusqu'en 1971.*

LSE (**abbr of *London School of Economics***) **n** *grande école de sciences économiques et politiques à Londres.*

LSO (**abbr of *London Symphony Orchestra***) **n** *orchestre symphonique de Londres.*

LT **n 1.** (**abbr of *low tension***) BT **2.** (**abbr of *Local Time***) *heure locale aux États-unis.*

Lt. (**abbr of *lieutenant***) Lieut.

Ltd, ***ltd*** (**abbr of *limited***) *esp UK* ≃ SARL ▸ **Smith and Sons, Ltd** ≃ Smith &Fils, SARL.

lubricant ['luːbrɪkənt] **n** lubrifiant *m*.

lubricate ['luːbrɪkeɪt] **vt** lubrifier.

lubrication [ˌluːbrɪ'keɪʃn] **n** lubrification *f*.

lucid ['luːsɪd] **adj** lucide.

lucidity [luː'sɪdətɪ] **n 1.** [of mind] lucidité *f* **2.** [of style, account] clarté *f*, limpidité *f*.

lucidly ['luːsɪdlɪ] **adv** lucidement.

luck [lʌk] **n** chance *f* ▸ **good luck** chance ▸ **good luck!** bonne chance! ▸ **bad luck** malchance *f* ▸ **it's bad luck to spill salt** renverser du sel porte malheur ▸ **bad** *OR* **hard luck!** pas de chance! ▸ **as luck would have it I'd forgotten my keys** et comme par hasard, j'avais oublié mes clés ▸ **to be in luck** avoir de la chance ▸ **to be down on one's luck** avoir la poisse *OR* la guigne ▸ **to push one's luck** jouer avec le feu ▸ **to try one's luck at sthg** tenter sa chance à qqch ▸ **with (any) luck** avec un peu de chance.
◆ ***luck out*** **vi** *US inf* avoir un coup de pot.

luckily ['lʌkılı] **adv** heureusement.

luckless ['lʌklıs] **adj** malchanceux(euse).

lucky ['lʌkı] **(comp -ier, superl -iest) adj 1.** [fortunate - person] qui a de la chance / [- event] heureux(euse) ▸ **to have a lucky escape** l'échapper belle **2.** [bringing good luck] porte-bonheur *(inv)*.

lucky dip **n** *UK sac rempli de cadeaux, dans lequel on pioche sans regarder*.

lucrative ['lu:krətıv] **adj** lucratif(ive).

ludicrous ['lu:dıkrəs] **adj** ridicule.

ludicrously ['lu:dıkrəslı] **adv** ridiculement.

ludo ['lu:dəʊ] **n** *UK* jeu *m* des petits chevaux.

lug [lʌg] **(pt & pp -ged, cont -ging) vt** *inf* traîner.

luggage ['lʌgıdʒ] **n** *(U)* bagages *mpl*.

luggage rack **n** porte-bagages *m inv*.

luggage van **n** *UK* fourgon *m*.

lugubrious [lu:'gu:brıəs] **adj** *liter* lugubre.

lukewarm ['lu:kwɔ:m] **adj** *lit* & *fig* tiède.

lull [lʌl] ■ **n : lull (in)** [storm] accalmie *f* (de) / [fighting, conversation] arrêt *m* (de) ▸ **the lull before the storm** *fig* le calme avant la tempête.
■ **vt : to lull sb to sleep** endormir qqn en le berçant ▸ **to lull sb into a false sense of security** endormir les soupçons de qqn.

lullaby ['lʌləbaı] **(pl -ies) n** berceuse *f*.

lumbago [lʌm'beıgəʊ] **n** *(U)* lumbago *m*.

lumber ['lʌmbər] ■ **n** *(U)* **1.** *US* [timber] bois *m* de charpente **2.** *UK* [bric-a-brac] bric-à-brac *m inv*.
■ **vi** se traîner d'un pas lourd.
◆ ***lumber with*** **vt sep** *UK inf* **: to lumber sb with sthg** coller qqch à qqn.

lumbering ['lʌmbərıŋ] **adj** lourd(e), pesant(e).

lumberjack ['lʌmbədʒæk] **n** bûcheron *m*, -onne *f*.

lumber mill ['lʌmbə,mıl] **n** *US* scierie *f*.

lumber room **n** *UK* débarras *m*.

lumberyard ['lʌmbəjɑ:d] **n** *US* chantier *m* de bois.

luminosity [,lu:mı'nɒsətı] **n** luminosité *f*.

luminous ['lu:mınəs] **adj** [dial] lumineux(euse) / [paint, armband] phosphorescent(e).

lump [lʌmp] ■ **n 1.** [gen] morceau *m* / [of earth, clay] motte *f* / [in sauce] grumeau *m* **2.** [on body] grosseur *f*.
■ **vt : to lump sthg together** réunir qqch ▸ **to lump it** *inf* faire avec, s'en accommoder.

lumpectomy [,lʌm'pektəmı] **(pl -ies) n** ablation *f* d'une tumeur au sein.

lump sum **n** somme *f* globale.

lumpy ['lʌmpı] **(comp -ier, superl -iest) adj** [sauce] plein(e) de grumeaux / [mattress] défoncé(e).

lunacy ['lu:nəsı] **n** folie *f*.

lunar ['lu:nər] **adj** lunaire.

lunatic ['lu:nətık] ■ **adj** *pej* dément(e), démentiel(elle).
■ **n 1.** *pej* [fool] fou *m*, folle *f* **2.** *dated* [insane person] fou *m*, folle *f*, aliéné *m*, -e *f*.

lunatic asylum **n** asile *m* d'aliénés.

lunatic fringe **n** éléments *mpl* extrémistes.

lunch [lʌntʃ] ■ **n** déjeuner *m*.
■ **vi** déjeuner.

lunchbox ['lʌntʃbɒks] **n 1.** [for sandwiches] *boîte dans laquelle on transporte son déjeuner* **2.** *UK inf hum* bijoux *mpl* de famille.

luncheon ['lʌntʃən] **n** *fml* déjeuner *m*.

luncheonette [,lʌntʃə'net] **n** *US* = cafétéria *f*.

luncheon meat, *US* ***lunchmeat*** [,lʌntʃ'mi:t] **n** *sorte de saucisson*.

luncheon voucher **n** *UK* ticket-restaurant *m*.

lunch hour **n** pause *f* de midi.

lunchmeat *US* = ***luncheon meat***.

lunchpail ['lʌntʃpeıl] **n** *US* [for sandwiches] *boîte dans laquelle on transporte son déjeuner*.

lunchtime ['lʌntʃtaım] **n** heure *f* du déjeuner.

lung [lʌŋ] **n** poumon *m*.

lung cancer **n** cancer *m* du poumon.

lunge [lʌndʒ] **(cont lungeing) vi** faire un brusque mouvement (du bras) en avant ▸ **to lunge at sb** s'élancer sur qqn.

lungful ['lʌŋfʊl] **n : take a lungful of air** inspirez à fond.

lupin ['lu:pın], ***lupine*** *US* ['lu:paın] **n** lupin *m*.

lurch [lɜ:tʃ] ■ **n** [of person] écart *m* brusque / [of car] embardée *f* ▸ **to leave sb in the lurch** laisser qqn dans le pétrin.
■ **vi** [person] tituber / [car] faire une embardée.

lure [ljʊər] ■ **n** charme *m* trompeur.
■ **vt** attirer *OR* persuader par la ruse.

lurid ['ljʊərıd] **adj 1.** [outfit] aux couleurs criardes **2.** [story, details] affreux(euse).

lurk [lɜ:k] **vi 1.** [person] se cacher, se dissimuler **2.** [memory, danger, fear] subsister.

lurking ['lɜ:kıŋ] **adj** [doubts, fear] vague.

Lusaka [lu:'sɑ:kə] **n** Lusaka.

luscious ['lʌʃəs] **adj 1.** [delicious] succulent(e) **2.** *inf fig* [woman] appétissant(e).

lush [lʌʃ] ■ **adj 1.** [luxuriant] luxuriant(e) **2.** [rich] luxueux(euse).
■ **n** *US* & *Can inf* [drunkard] alcolo *mf*.

lust [lʌst] **n 1.** [sexual desire] désir *m* **2.** *fig* **: lust for sthg** soif *f* de qqch ▸ **lust for life** fureur *f* de vivre.
◆ ***lust after***, ***lust for*** **vt insep 1.** [wealth, power] être assoiffé(e) de **2.** [person] désirer.

luster *US* = ***lustre***.

lustful ['lʌstfʊl] **adj** lubrique.

lustily ['lʌstɪlɪ] **adv** [sing, shout] à pleine gorge, à pleins poumons.

lustre *UK*, ***luster*** *US* ['lʌstəʳ] **n** lustre *m*.

lusty ['lʌstɪ] (comp **-ier**, superl **-iest**) **adj** vigoureux(euse).

lute [lu:t] **n** luth *m*.

luv [lʌv] **n** *UK inf* chéri *m*, -e *f*.

luvvie ['lʌvɪ] **n** *UK inf* théâtreux prétentieux *m*, théâtreuse prétentieuse *f*.

Luxembourg ['lʌksəmbɜ:g] **n** **1.** [country] Luxembourg *m* ▸ **in Luxembourg** au Luxembourg **2.** [city] Luxembourg.

luxuriant [lʌg'ʒʊərɪənt] **adj** luxuriant(e).

luxuriate [lʌg'ʒʊərɪeɪt] **vi** *fml* **: to luxuriate in** s'abandonner aux plaisirs de.

luxurious [lʌg'ʒʊərɪəs] **adj** **1.** [expensive] luxueux(euse) **2.** [pleasurable] voluptueux(euse).

luxury ['lʌkʃərɪ] ■ **n** (pl **-ies**) luxe *m*.
■ **comp** de luxe.

luxury goods **npl** produits *mpl* de luxe.

LV *UK* abbr of ***luncheon voucher***.

LW (abbr of ***long wave***) GO.

lychee [ˌlaɪ'tʃi:] **n** litchi *m*.

Lycra® ['laɪkrə] ■ **n** Lycra® *m*.
■ **comp** en Lycra®.

lying ['laɪɪŋ] ■ **adj** [person] menteur(euse).
■ **n** *(U)* mensonges *mpl*.

lymph gland [lɪmf-] **n** ganglion *m* lymphatique.

lynch [lɪntʃ] **vt** lyncher.

lynching ['lɪntʃɪŋ] **n** lynchage *m*.

lynchpin ['lɪntʃpɪn] = ***linchpin***.

lynx [lɪŋks] (pl **lynx** *OR* **-es** [-i:z]) **n** lynx *m inv*.

Lyon(s) ['laɪən(z)] **n** Lyon.

lyre ['laɪəʳ] **n** lyre *f*.

lyric ['lɪrɪk] **adj** lyrique.

lyrical ['lɪrɪkl] **adj** lyrique.

lyricist ['lɪrɪsɪst] **n** [of poems] poète *m* lyrique / [of song, opera] parolier *m*, -ère *f*.

lyrics ['lɪrɪks] **npl** paroles *fpl*.

m [1] [em] (pl m's *OR* ms), ***M*** [1] (pl M's *OR* Ms) **n** [letter] m *m inv*, M *m inv*.

m [2] **1.** (abbr of ***metre***) m **2.** (abbr of ***million***) M **3.** abbr of ***mile***.

M [2] **1.** *UK* abbr of ***motorway*** **2.** (abbr of ***medium***) M.

ma [mɑ:] **n** *inf* maman *f*.

MA ■ **n** abbr of ***Master of Arts***.
■ abbr of ***Massachusetts***.

ma'am [mæm] **n** madame *f*.

mac [mæk] (abbr of ***mackintosh***) **n** *UK inf* [coat] imper *m*.

macabre [mə'kɑ:brə] **adj** macabre.

Macao [mə'kaʊ] **n** Macao *m* ▸ **in Macao** à Macao.

macaroni [ˌmækə'rəʊnɪ] **n** *(U)* macaronis *mpl*.

macaroni cheese *UK*, ***macaroni and cheese*** *US* **n** *(U)* macaronis *mpl* au gratin.

macaroon [ˌmækə'ru:n] **n** macaron *m*.

macaw [mə'kɔ:] **n** ara *m*.

Mace® [meɪs] ■ **n** [spray] gaz *m* lacrymogène.
■ **vt** *US inf* bombarder au gaz lacrymogène.

mace [meɪs] **n** **1.** [ornamental rod] masse *f* **2.** [spice] macis *m*.

Macedonia [ˌmæsɪ'dəʊnjə] **n** Macédoine *f* ▸ **in Macedonia** en Macédoine.

Macedonian [ˌmæsɪ'dəʊnjən] ■ **adj** macédonien(enne).
■ **n** Macédonien *m*, -enne *f*.

machete [mə'ʃetɪ] **n** machette *f*.

Machiavellian [ˌmækɪə'velɪən] **adj** machiavélique.

machinations [ˌmækɪ'neɪʃnz] **npl** machinations *fpl*.

machine [mə'ʃi:n] ■ **n** *lit* & *fig* machine *f*.
■ **vt** **1.** SEW coudre à la machine **2.** TECH usiner.

machine code **n** COMPUT code *m* machine.

machinegun [mə'ʃi:ngʌn] **n** mitrailleuse *f*.

machine-gun **vt** (pt & pp **-ned**, cont **-ning**) mitrailler.

machine language **n** COMPUT langage *m* machine.

machine-readable **adj** COMPUT en langage machine.

machinery [mə'ʃi:nərɪ] **n** *(U)* machines *fpl* / *fig* mécanisme *m*.

machine shop **n** atelier *m* d'usinage.

machine tool **n** machine-outil *f*.

machine translation **n** traduction *f* automatique.

machine-washable **adj** lavable à la *OR* en machine.

machinist [mə'ʃi:nɪst] **n** **1.** SEW mécanicienne *f* **2.** TECH machiniste *mf*, opérateur *m*, -trice *f*.

machismo [mə'tʃɪzməʊ] **n** machisme *m*.

macho ['mætʃəʊ] **adj** *inf* macho *(inv)*.

mackerel ['mækrəl] (pl **mackerel** *OR* **-s**) **n** maquereau *m*.

mackintosh ['mækɪntɒʃ] **n** *UK dated* imperméable *m*.

macramé [mə'krɑ:mɪ] **n** macramé *m*.

macro ['mækrəʊ] (abbr of ***macroinstruction***) **n** COMPUT macro-instruction *f*.

macrobiotic [ˌmækrəʊbaɪ'ɒtɪk] **adj** macrobiotique.

macroclimate ['mækrəʊˌklaɪmət] **n** macroclimat *m*.

macrocosm ['mækrəʊkɒzm] **n** macrocosme *m*.

macroeconomics ['mækrəʊˌi:kə'nɒmɪks] **n** *(U)* macroéconomie *f*.

macroinstruction [ˌmækrɪn'strʌkʃn] **n** COMPUT macro-instruction *f*.

macromarketing [ˌmækrəʊ'mɑ:kɪtɪŋ] **n** macromarketing *m*.

mad [mæd] (comp **-der**, superl **-dest**) **adj** **1.** [insane] fou (folle) ▸ **to go mad** devenir fou ▸ **to be mad with joy/grief** être fou de joie/douleur ▸ **to drive sb mad** rendre qqn fou ▸ **to be as mad as a hatter** *OR* **a March hare** être fou à lier

2. *esp UK inf* [foolish] insensé(e)

3. [furious] furieux(euse) ▸ **he went mad when he saw them** il s'est mis dans une colère noire en les voyant ▸ **to be mad at** *OR* **with sb** être en colère *OR* fâché(e) contre qqn ▸ **don't get mad** ne vous fâchez pas

4. [hectic - rush, pace] fou (folle) ▸ **there was a mad rush for the door** tous les gens se sont rués vers la porte comme des fous ▸ **I'm in a mad rush** *inf* je suis très pressé, je suis à la bourre ▸ **like mad** *inf* comme un fou
5. [very enthusiastic] **: to be mad about sb/sthg** *inf* être fou (folle) de qqn/qqch.

Madagascan [ˌmædəˈgæskn] ■ **adj** malgache.
■ **n 1.** [person] Malgache *mf* **2.** [language] malgache *m*.

Madagascar [ˌmædəˈgæskər] **n** Madagascar *m* ▸ **in Madagascar** à Madagascar.

madam [ˈmædəm] **n** madame *f*.

madcap [ˈmædkæp] **adj** risqué(e), insensé(e).

mad cow disease **n** *inf* maladie *f* de la vache folle.

madden [ˈmædn] **vt** exaspérer.

maddening [ˈmædnɪŋ] **adj** exaspérant(e).

made [meɪd] **pt & pp** ➤ ***make***.

-made [meɪd] **suffix** fait(e) ▸ **factory-made** fait(e) *OR* fabriqué(e) en usine ▸ **French-made** de fabrication française.

Madeira [məˈdɪərə] **n 1.** [wine] madère *m* **2.** GEOG Madère *f* ▸ **in Madeira** à Madère.

made-to-measure **adj** fait(e) sur mesure.

made-to-order **adj** (fait(e)) sur commande.

made-up **adj 1.** [with make-up] maquillé(e) **2.** [prepared] préparé(e) **3.** [invented] fabriqué(e).

madhouse [ˈmædhaʊs] (pl [-haʊzɪz]) **n** *fig* maison *f* de fous.

madly [ˈmædlɪ] **adv** [frantically] comme un fou ▸ **madly in love** follement amoureux(euse).

madman [ˈmædmən] (pl **-men** [-mən]) **n** fou *m*.

madness [ˈmædnɪs] **n** *lit & fig* folie *f*, démence *f*.

Madonna [məˈdɒnə] **n** Madone *f*.

Madrid [məˈdrɪd] **n** Madrid.

madrigal [ˈmædrɪgl] **n** madrigal *m*.

madwoman [ˈmædˌwʊmən] (pl **-women** [-ˌwɪmɪn]) **n** folle *f*.

maestro [ˈmaɪstrəʊ] (pl **-tros** *OR* **-tri** [-trɪ]) **n** maestro *m*.

Mafia [ˈmæfɪə] **n : the Mafia** la Mafia.

mag [mæg] (abbr of ***magazine***) **n** *inf* revue *f*, magazine *m*.

magazine [ˌmægəˈziːn] **n 1.** PRESS revue *f*, magazine *m* / RADIO & TV magazine **2.** [of gun] magasin *m*.

magazine rack **n** porte-revues *m*.

magenta [məˈdʒentə] ■ **adj** magenta *(inv)*.
■ **n** magenta *m*.

maggot [ˈmægət] **n** ver *m*, asticot *m*.

Maghreb [ˈmɑːgrəb] **n : the Maghreb** le Maghreb.

magic [ˈmædʒɪk] ■ **adj** magique ▸ **a magic spell** un sortilège.
■ **n** magie *f* ▸ **the medicine worked like magic** le remède a fait merveille ▸ **discover the magic of Greece** découvrez les merveilles de la Grèce.

magical [ˈmædʒɪkl] **adj** magique.

magically [ˈmædʒɪklɪ] **adv** magiquement ▸ **don't think it will just happen magically** ne t'imagine pas que cela va se produire comme par enchantement.

magic carpet **n** tapis *m* volant.

magic eye **n** *UK* cellule *f* photo-électrique, œil *m* électrique.

magician [məˈdʒɪʃn] **n** magicien *m*, -ienne *f*.

magic wand **n** baguette *f* magique.

magisterial [ˌmædʒɪˈstɪərɪəl] **adj 1.** [behaviour, manner] magistral(e) **2.** LAW de magistrat.

magistrate [ˈmædʒɪstreɪt] **n** magistrat *m*, -e *f*, juge *m*.

magistrates' court [ˈmædʒɪstreɪts↓] **n** *UK* ≃ tribunal *m* d'instance.

Magna Carta [ˈmægnəˈkɑːtə] **n : the Magna Carta** la Grande Charte d'Angleterre.

magna cum laude [ˌmægnəkʊmˈlaʊdeɪ] **adv** UNIV avec mention très bien.

magnanimity [ˌmægnəˈnɪmətɪ] **n** *fml* magnanimité *f*.

magnanimous [mægˈnænɪməs] **adj** *fml* magnanime.

magnanimously [mægˈnænɪməslɪ] **adv** *fml* avec magnanimité, magnanimement.

magnate [ˈmægneɪt] **n** magnat *m*.

magnesium [mægˈniːzɪəm] **n** magnésium *m*.

magnet [ˈmægnɪt] **n** aimant *m*.

magnetic [mægˈnetɪk] **adj** *lit & fig* magnétique.

magnetic disk **n** disque *m* magnétique.

magnetic field **n** champ *m* magnétique.

magnetic tape **n** bande *f* magnétique.

magnetism [ˈmægnɪtɪzm] **n** *lit & fig* magnétisme *m*.

magnification [ˌmægnɪfɪˈkeɪʃn] **n** grossissement *m*.

magnificence [mægˈnɪfɪsəns] **n** splendeur *f*.

magnificent [mægˈnɪfɪsənt] **adj** magnifique, superbe.

magnify [ˈmægnɪfaɪ] (**pt & pp -ied**) **vt** [in vision] grossir / [sound] amplifier / *fig* exagérer.

magnifying glass [ˈmægnɪfaɪɪŋ-] **n** loupe *f*.

magnitude [ˈmægnɪtjuːd] **n** envergure *f*, ampleur *f*.

magnolia [mægˈnəʊljə] **n 1.** [tree] magnolia *m* **2.** [flower] fleur *f* de magnolia.

magnum [ˈmægnəm] (pl **-s**) **n** magnum *m*.

magpie [ˈmægpaɪ] **n** pie *f*.

maharaja(h) [ˌmɑːhəˈrɑːdʒə] **n** maharaja *m*, maharajah *m*.

mahogany [məˈhɒgənɪ] **n** acajou *m*.

maid [meɪd] **n** [servant] domestique *f*.

maiden [ˈmeɪdn] ■ **adj** [flight] premier(ère).
■ **n** *liter* jeune fille *f*.

maiden aunt **n** *dated* tante *f* célibataire.

maiden name **n** nom *m* de jeune fille.

maiden over **n** *au cricket, série de balles où aucun point n'a été marqué.*

maiden speech **n** *UK* POL premier discours *m*.

maiden voyage **n** voyage *m* inaugural.

mail [meɪl] ■ n **1.** [letters, parcels] courrier *m* ▸ **the mail is only collected twice a week** il n'y a que deux levées par semaine **2.** [system] poste *f* ▸ **your cheque is in the mail** votre chèque a été posté.
■ vt *esp US* poster.

mailbag ['meɪlbæg] n sac *m* postal.

mail bomb n *US* [letter] lettre *f* piégée / [parcel] colis *m* piégé.

mailbox ['meɪlbɒks] n *US* boîte *f* à ***OR*** aux lettres.

mail carrier *US* = ***mailman***.

mail drop n *US* boîte *f* à ***OR*** aux lettres.

mailing ['meɪlɪŋ] n **1.** [posting] expédition *f*, envoi *m* par la poste **2.** COMM & COMPUT mailing *m*, publipostage *m*.

mailing list n liste *f* d'adresses.

mailing shot n COMPUT & COMM publipostage *m*, mailing *m*.

mailman ['meɪlmæn] (pl **-men** [-mən]) n *US* facteur *m*, -rice *f*.

mail merge n COMPUT publipostage *m*, mailing *m*.

mail order n vente *f* par correspondance.

mailroom ['meɪlru:m] n *US* service *m* du courrier.

mailshot ['meɪlʃɒt] n *UK* publipostage *m*.

mail train n train *m* postal.

mail truck n *US* fourgonnette *f* des postes.

mail van n *UK* **1.** AUT fourgonnette *f* des postes **2.** RAIL wagon-poste *m*.

maim [meɪm] vt estropier.

main [meɪn] ■ adj principal(e) ▸ **the main thing we have to consider is his age** la première chose à prendre en compte, c'est son âge ▸ **you're safe: that's the main thing** tu es sain et sauf, c'est le principal.
■ n [pipe] conduite *f*.
◆ ***mains*** npl *UK* **: the mains** le secteur.
◆ ***in the main*** adv dans l'ensemble.

main course n plat *m* principal.

Maine [meɪn] n le Maine ▸ **in Maine** dans le Maine.

mainframe (computer) ['meɪnfreɪm-] n gros ordinateur *m*, processeur *m* central.

mainland ['meɪnlənd] ■ adj continental(e).
■ n **: the mainland** le continent.

mainline ['meɪnlaɪn] ■ adj RAIL de grande ligne.
■ vt *drug sl* shooter.
■ vi *drug sl* se shooter.

main line n RAIL grande ligne *f*.

mainly ['meɪnlɪ] adv principalement.

main office n *esp US* siège *m* social.

main road n route *f* à grande circulation.

mainsail ['meɪnseɪl ***OR*** 'meɪnsəl] n grand-voile *f*.

mains-operated adj *UK* fonctionnant sur secteur.

mainstay ['meɪnsteɪ] n pilier *m*, élément *m* principal.

mainstream ['meɪnstri:m] ■ adj dominant(e).
■ n **: the mainstream** la tendance générale.

main street n **1.** *lit* rue *f* principale **2.** *US fig* **: Main Street** *les petits commerçants*.

maintain [meɪn'teɪn] vt **1.** [preserve, keep constant] maintenir ▸ **to maintain law and order** maintenir l'ordre ▸ **to maintain a position** *fig* & MIL tenir une position **2.** [provide for, look after] entretenir ▸ **they have two children at university to maintain** ils ont deux enfants à charge à l'université **3.** [assert] **: to maintain (that)...** maintenir que..., soutenir que...

maintainable [meɪn'teɪnəbl] adj [attitude, opinion, position] soutenable, défendable.

maintenance ['meɪntənəns] n **1.** [of public order] maintien *m* **2.** [care] entretien *m*, maintenance *f* **3.** *UK* LAW pension *f* alimentaire.

maintenance order n *UK* LAW obligation *f* alimentaire.

maisonette [ˌmeɪzə'net] n *UK* duplex *m*.

maître d' [ˌmetrə'di:] n maître *m* d'hôtel.

maize [meɪz] n *UK* maïs *m*.

Maj. (abbr of ***Major***) ≃ Cdt.

majestic [mə'dʒestɪk] adj majestueux(euse).

majestically [mə'dʒestɪklɪ] adv majestueusement.

majesty ['mædʒəstɪ] (pl **-ies**) n [grandeur] majesté *f*.
◆ ***Majesty*** n **: His/Her Majesty** Sa Majesté le roi/la reine.

major ['meɪdʒəʳ] ■ adj **1.** [important] majeur(e) ▸ **don't worry: it's not a major problem** ne t'inquiète pas, ce n'est pas très grave ▸ **of major importance** d'une grande importance, d'une importance capitale ▸ **a major role** [in play, film] un grand rôle / [in negotiations, reform] un rôle capital ***OR*** essentiel ▸ **she underwent major surgery** elle a subi une grosse opération **2.** [main] principal(e) ▸ **the major part of our research** l'essentiel de nos recherches **3.** MUS majeur(e) ▸ **a sonata in E major** une sonate en mi majeur ▸ **in a major key** en (mode) majeur.
■ n **1.** [in army] ≃ chef *m* de bataillon / [in air force] commandant *m* **2.** *US* UNIV [subject] matière *f* ▸ **Tina is a physics major** Tina fait des études de physique.
■ vi **: to major in** *US* se spécialiser en.

Majorca [mə'dʒɔ:kə ***OR*** mə'jɔ:kə] n Majorque *f* ▸ **in Majorca** à Majorque.

Majorcan [mə'dʒɔ:kn ***OR*** mə'jɔ:kn] ■ adj majorquin(e).
■ n Majorquin *m*, -e *f*.

majorette [ˌmeɪdʒə'ret] n majorette *f*.

major general n général *m* de division.

majority [mə'dʒɒrətɪ] (pl **-ies**) n majorité *f* ▸ **the majority of people** la plupart des gens ▸ **the vast majority of the tourists were Japanese** les touristes, dans leur très grande majorité, étaient des Japonais ▸ **in a *OR* the majority** dans la majorité ▸ **she was elected by a majority of 6** elle a été élue avec une majorité de 6 voix ***OR*** par 6 voix de majorité.

majority rule n POL gouvernement *m* à la majorité absolue, système *m* majoritaire.

majority shareholder n actionnaire *mf* majoritaire.

major league *US* ■ n **1.** [gen] première division *f* ▸ **major league team** grande équipe *(sportive)* **2.** [in base-ball] *une des deux principales divisions de base-ball professionnel aux États-Unis.*
■ **adj** [significant] de premier rang / [as intensifier] **: he's a major-league jerk** c'est un imbécile de première.

major road n route *f* principale *OR* à grande circulation, ≃ nationale *f.*

make [meɪk] ■ vt (pt & pp **made**) **1.** [gen - produce] faire / [- manufacture] faire, fabriquer ▸ **to make a meal** préparer un repas ▸ **'made in Japan'** 'fabriqué au Japon' ▸ **to make a film** *esp UK OR* **movie** *esp US* tourner *OR* réaliser un film ▸ **I don't make the rules** ce n'est pas moi qui fais les règlements
2. [perform an action] faire ▸ **to make an offer** faire une offre ▸ **to make a request** faire une demande ▸ **to make a mistake** faire une erreur, se tromper ▸ **to make a decision** prendre une décision ▸ **to make a note of sthg** prendre note de qqch ▸ **to make a phone call** passer un coup de fil
3. [cause to be] rendre ▸ **to make sb happy/sad** rendre qqn heureux/triste ▸ **it makes her tired** ça la fatigue ▸ **this will make things easier** cela facilitera les choses ▸ **I'd like to make it clear that it wasn't my fault** je voudrais qu'on comprenne bien que je n'y suis pour rien ▸ **to make o.s. heard** se faire entendre ▸ **the film made her (into) a star** le film a fait d'elle une vedette ▸ **he made her a manager** il l'a nommée directrice ▸ **he makes a joke of everything** il tourne tout en plaisanterie ▸ **the building has been made into offices** l'immeuble a été réaménagé *OR* converti en bureaux
4. [force, cause to do] **: to make sb do sthg** faire faire qqch à qqn, obliger qqn à faire qqch ▸ **what makes you think they're wrong?** qu'est-ce qui te fait penser qu'ils ont tort? ▸ **you made me jump** tu m'as fait sursauter ▸ **you make it look easy** à vous voir, on croirait que c'est facile ▸ **we were made to wait in the hall** on nous a fait attendre dans le vestibule ▸ **to make sb laugh** faire rire qqn ▸ **she made herself keep running** elle s'est forcée à continuer à courir
5. [be constructed] **: to be made of** être en ▸ **it's made of wood/metal/wool** c'est en bois/métal/laine ▸ **what's it made of?** c'est en quoi?
6. [add up to] faire ▸ **2 and 2 make 4** 2 et 2 font 4 ▸ **how old does that make him?** quel âge ça lui fait?
7. *UK* [calculate] **: I make it 50** d'après moi il y en a 50, j'en ai compté 50 ▸ **what time do you make it?** quelle heure as-tu? ▸ **I make it 6 o'clock** il est 6 heures (à ma montre)
8. [earn] gagner, se faire ▸ **she makes £30,000 a year** elle se fait *OR* elle gagne 30 000 livres par an ▸ **how much do you make a month?** combien gagnes-tu par mois? ▸ **to make a profit** faire des bénéfices ▸ **to make a loss** essuyer des pertes
9. [have the right qualities for] **: she'd make a good dancer** elle ferait une bonne danseuse ▸ **he'll make somebody a good husband** ce sera un excellent mari ▸ **books make excellent presents** les livres constituent de très beaux cadeaux
10. [reach] arriver à ▸ **we should make Houston/port by evening** nous devrions arriver à Houston/atteindre le port d'ici ce soir ▸ **did you make your train?** as-tu réussi à avoir ton train? ▸ **I won't be able to make lunch** je ne pourrai pas déjeuner avec toi ▸ **their first record made the top ten** leur premier disque est rentré au top ten ▸ **the story made the front page** l'histoire a fait la une des journaux
11. [cause to be a success] assurer *OR* faire le succès de ▸ **she really makes the play/film** c'est elle qui fait le succès de la pièce/du film ▸ **if this deal comes off we're made!** si ça marche, on touche le gros lot!
12. [gain - friend, enemy] se faire ▸ **to make friends (with sb)** se lier d'amitié (avec qqn)
13. *US* [in directions] **: make a right/left** tournez à droite/à gauche
▸▸ **to make it** [reach in time] arriver à temps / [be a success] réussir, arriver / [be able to attend] se libérer, pouvoir venir ▸ **to have it made** avoir trouvé le filon ▸ **to make do with** se contenter de ▸ **it's broken but we'll just have to make do** c'est cassé mais il faudra faire avec *OR* nous débrouiller avec.
■ **n 1.** [brand] marque *f* ▸ **what make is your car?** de quelle marque est votre voiture?
2. *inf pej* **: to be on the make** [act dishonestly, selfishly] être intéressé(e).

◆ ***make for*** vt insep **1.** [move towards] se diriger vers ▸ **he made for his gun** il fit un geste pour saisir son pistolet
2. [contribute to, be conducive to] rendre probable, favoriser ▸ **this typeface makes for easier reading** cette police permet une lecture plus facile.

◆ ***make of*** ■ vt sep **1.** [understand] comprendre ▸ **can you make anything of these instructions?** est-ce que tu comprends quelque chose à ce mode d'emploi?
2. [give importance to] **: I think you're making too much of a very minor problem** je pense que tu exagères l'importance de ce petit problème.
■ **vt insep** [think of] penser de ▸ **what do you make of the Smiths?** qu'est-ce que tu penses des Smith?

◆ ***make off*** vi *inf* filer.

◆ ***make off with*** vt insep *inf* filer avec.

◆ ***make out*** ■ vt sep **1.** [see, hear] discerner / [understand] comprendre ▸ **I can't make her out at all** je ne la comprends pas du tout
2. [fill out - cheque] libeller / [- bill, receipt] faire / [- form] remplir.
■ **vt insep** [pretend, claim] **: to make out (that)...** prétendre que... ▸ **she made out that she was busy** elle a fait semblant d'être occupée ▸ **don't make yourself out to be something you're not** ne prétends pas être ce que tu n'es pas.
■ **vi insep 1.** *inf* [manage] se débrouiller ▸ **how did you make out at work today?** comment ça s'est passé au boulot aujourd'hui?
2. *US v inf* [neck, pet] se peloter ▸ **to make out with sb** [have sex] s'envoyer qqn.

◆ ***make over*** vt sep **1.** [transfer] transférer, céder
2. [change appearance] transformer ▸ **the garage had been made over into a workshop** le garage a été transformé en atelier.

◆ ***make up*** ■ vt sep **1.** [compose, constitute] composer, constituer
2. [story, excuse] inventer
3. [apply cosmetics to] maquiller ▸ **to make o.s. up** se maquiller ▸ **he was heavily made up** il était très maquillé *OR* fardé

4. [prepare - gen] faire / [- prescription] préparer, exécuter **5.** [make complete] compléter **6.** [resolve - quarrel] **: to make it up (with sb)** se réconcilier (avec qqn).
■ **vi** [become friends again] se réconcilier.
◆ ***make up for*** **vt insep** compenser ▸ **to make up for lost time** rattraper le temps perdu.
◆ ***make up to*** **vt sep : to make it up to sb (for sthg)** se racheter auprès de qqn (pour qqch).

make-believe **n : it's all make-believe** c'est (de la) pure fantaisie.

makeover ['meɪkəʊvər] **n** transformation *f*.

maker ['meɪkər] **n** [of product] fabricant *m*, -e *f* / [of film] réalisateur *m*, -trice *f*.

-maker **suffix 1.** [manufacturer] fabricant *m*, -e *f* **2.** [machine] **: electric coffee-maker** cafetière *f* électrique ▸ **ice cream-maker** sorbetière *f*.

makeshift ['meɪkʃɪft] **adj** de fortune.

make-up **n 1.** [cosmetics] maquillage *m* ▸ **make-up bag** trousse *f* de maquillage ▸ **make-up remover** démaquillant *m* **2.** [person's character] caractère *m* **3.** [of team, group, object] constitution *f*.

makeweight ['meɪkweɪt] **n** complément *m* de poids.

making ['meɪkɪŋ] **n** fabrication *f* ▸ **to be the making of sb/sthg** être l'origine de la réussite de qqn/qqch ▸ **his problems are of his own making** ses problèmes sont de sa faute ▸ **in the making** en formation ▸ **history in the making** l'histoire en train de se faire ▸ **to have the makings of** avoir l'étoffe de.

maladjusted [ˌmælə'dʒʌstɪd] **adj** inadapté(e).

maladroit [ˌmælə'drɔɪt] **adj** *fml* maladroit(e), gauche, malhabile.

malady ['mælədɪ] (**pl -ies**) **n** *liter* maladie *f*, affection *f*, mal *m*.

malaise [mə'leɪz] **n** *fml* malaise *m*.

malaria [mə'leərɪə] **n** malaria *f*.

malarkey [mə'lɑːkɪ] **n** *(U) inf* bêtises *fpl*, sottises *fpl*.

Malawi [mə'lɑːwɪ] **n** Malawi *m* ▸ **in Malawi** au Malawi.

Malawian [mə'lɑːwɪən] ■ **adj** malawite.
■ **n** Malawite *mf*.

Malay [mə'leɪ] ■ **adj** malais(e).
■ **n 1.** [person] Malais *m*, -e *f* **2.** [language] malais *m*.

Malaya [mə'leɪə] **n** Malaisie *f*, Malaysia *f* occidentale ▸ **in Malaya** en Malaisie.

Malayan [mə'leɪən] ■ **adj** malais(e).
■ **n** Malais *m*, -e *f*.

Malaysia [mə'leɪzɪə] **n** Malaysia *f* ▸ **in Malaysia** en Malaysia.

Malaysian [mə'leɪzɪən] ■ **adj** malaysien(enne).
■ **n** Malaysien *m*, -enne *f*.

malcontent ['mælkənˌtent] **n** *fml* mécontent *m*, -e *f*.

Maldives ['mɔːldaɪvz] **npl : the Maldives** les (îles *fpl*) Maldives *fpl* ▸ **in the Maldives** aux Maldives.

male [meɪl] ■ **adj** [gen] mâle / [sex] masculin(e).
■ **n** mâle *m*.

male chauvinism **n** phallocratie *f*.

male chauvinist **n** phallocrate *m* ▸ **male chauvinist pig!** sale phallocrate!

male nurse **n** *dated* infirmier *m*.

malevolence [mə'levələns] **n** *fml* malveillance *f*.

malevolent [mə'levələnt] **adj** *fml* malveillant(e).

malevolently [mə'levələntlɪ] **adv** *fml* avec malveillance.

malfeasance [mæl'fiːzns] **n** LAW méfait *m*, malversation *f*.

malformation [ˌmælfɔː'meɪʃn] **n** malformation *f*.

malformed [mæl'fɔːmd] **adj** difforme.

malfunction [mæl'fʌŋkʃn] ■ **n** mauvais fonctionnement *m*.
■ **vi** mal fonctionner.

Mali ['mɑːlɪ] **n** Mali *m* ▸ **in Mali** au Mali.

malice ['mælɪs] **n** méchanceté *f*.

malicious [mə'lɪʃəs] **adj** méchant(e), malveillant(e).

maliciously [mə'lɪʃəslɪ] **adv 1.** [gen] méchamment, avec malveillance **2.** LAW avec préméditation, avec intention de nuire.

malign [mə'laɪn] ■ **adj** *fml* pernicieux(euse).
■ **vt** calomnier.

malignant [mə'lɪgnənt] **adj** MED malin(igne).

malinger [mə'lɪŋgər] **vi** *pej* simuler une maladie.

malingerer [mə'lɪŋgərər] **n** *pej* simulateur *m*, -trice *f*.

mall [mɔːl] **n** *esp US* **: (shopping) mall** centre *m* commercial.

malleable ['mælɪəbl] **adj** *lit* & *fig* malléable.

mallet ['mælɪt] **n** maillet *m*.

malnourished [ˌmæl'nʌrɪʃt] **adj** sous-alimenté(e).

malnutrition [ˌmælnjuː'trɪʃn] **n** malnutrition *f*.

malpractice [ˌmæl'præktɪs] **n** *(U)* LAW faute *f* professionnelle.

malpractice suit **n** *US* LAW *procès pour faute ou négligence professionnelle*.

malt [mɔːlt] **n** malt *m*.

Malta ['mɔːltə] **n** Malte *f* ▸ **in Malta** à Malte.

Maltese [ˌmɔːl'tiːz] ■ **adj** maltais(e).
■ **n** (**pl Maltese**) **1.** [person] Maltais *m*, -e *f* **2.** [language] maltais *m*.

maltreat [ˌmæl'triːt] **vt** maltraiter.

maltreatment [ˌmæl'triːtmənt] **n** mauvais traitement *m*.

malt whisky *UK*, ***malt whiskey*** *US* **n** whisky *m* pur, malt *m inv*.

mammal ['mæml] **n** mammifère *m*.

mammogram ['mæməgræm] **n** mammographie *f*.

Mammon ['mæmən] **n** *liter* le Veau d'or.

mammoth ['mæməθ] ■ **adj** gigantesque.
■ **n** mammouth *m*.

man [mæn] ■ **n** (**pl men** [men]) **1.** homme *m* ▸ **a young man** un jeune homme ▸ **an old man** un vieillard ▸ **he seems a nice man** il a l'air gentil ▸ **he's not a betting/**

drinking man ce n'est pas un homme qui parie/boit ▸ **he's not a man to make a mistake** il n'est pas homme à se tromper ▸ **a TV repair man** un réparateur télé ▸ **officers and men** [in army] officiers et hommes de troupe / [in navy] officiers et matelots ▸ **man and wife** mari et femme ▸ **what more can a man do?** qu'est-ce qu'on peut faire de plus? ▸ **one of the most deadly poisons known to man** un des plus dangereux poisons connus de l'homme ▸ **my old man** *inf* [husband] mon homme / [father] mon vieux ▸ **the man in the street** l'homme de la rue ▸ **to be man enough to do sthg** avoir le courage de faire qqch ▸ **it's every man for himself** c'est chacun pour soi **2.** *inf* [as form of address] mon vieux.

■ **vt** (pt & pp **-ned**, cont **-ning**) [ship, spaceship] fournir du personnel pour / [telephone] répondre au / [switchboard] assurer le service de ▸ **man the lifeboats!** mettez les canots à la mer!

■ **excl** *inf* **: man, was it big!** bon sang, qu'est-ce que c'était grand!

man-about-town (pl **men-about-town**) **n** *UK* homme *m* du monde, mondain *m*.

manacles ['mænəklz] **npl** [round wrists] menottes *fpl* / [round legs] chaînes *fpl*.

manage ['mænɪdʒ] ■ **vi 1.** [cope] se débrouiller, y arriver ▸ **can you manage?** ça ira? ▸ **give me a fork: I can't manage with chopsticks** donne-moi une fourchette, je ne m'en sors pas avec des baguettes ▸ **we had to manage without heating** nous avons dû nous passer de chauffage **2.** [get by financially] s'en sortir.

■ **vt 1.** [succeed, cope with] **: to manage to do sthg** arriver à faire qqch ▸ **you'll manage it** ça ira ▸ **she managed a smile** elle trouva la force de sourire ▸ **I can't manage all this extra work** je ne peux pas faire face à ce surcroît de travail ▸ **can you manage that rucksack?** pouvez-vous porter ce sac à dos? ▸ **he can't manage the stairs any more** il n'arrive plus à monter l'escalier

2. [be responsible for, control] gérer ▸ **I'm very bad at managing money** je suis incapable de gérer un budget ▸ **she's a difficult child to manage** c'est une enfant difficile, c'est une enfant dont on ne fait pas ce qu'on veut

3. [be available for] **: can you manage 9 o'clock/next Saturday?** pouvez-vous venir à 9 h/samedi prochain? ▸ **can you manage lunch tomorrow?** pouvez-vous déjeuner avec moi demain?

manageable ['mænɪdʒəbl] **adj** maniable.

managed fund ['mænɪdʒd↓] **n** fonds *m* géré.

management ['mænɪdʒmənt] **n 1.** [control, running] gestion *f* ▸ **she was praised for her management of the situation** on a applaudi la façon dont elle s'est comportée dans cette situation **2.** [people in control] direction *f* ▸ **'under new management'** 'changement de direction *OR* de propriétaire'.

management buy-in **n** apport *m* de gestion.

management buyout **n** rachat *m* d'une entreprise par les salariés.

management consultancy **n** [activity] conseil *m* en gestion (d'entreprise) / [firm] cabinet *m* (de) conseil.

management consultant **n** conseiller *m*, -ère *f* en gestion.

management information system **n** COMPUT système *m* intégré de gestion.

manager ['mænɪdʒəʳ] **n** [of organization] directeur *m*, -trice *f* / [of shop, restaurant, hotel] gérant *m*, -e *f* / [of football team, pop star] manager *m*.

manageress [ˌmænɪdʒə'res] **n** *dated UK* [of organization] directrice *f* / [of shop, restaurant, hotel] gérante *f*.

managerial [ˌmænɪ'dʒɪərɪəl] **adj** directorial(e).

managing director ['mænɪdʒɪŋ-] **n** directeur général *m*, directrice générale *f*.

managing editor **n** rédacteur *m*, -trice *f* en chef.

Managua [mə'nægwə] **n** Managua.

Mancunian [mæŋ'kju:njən] ■ **adj** de Manchester.
■ **n** [person] habitant *m*, -e *f* de Manchester.

mandarin ['mændərɪn] **n 1.** [fruit] mandarine *f* **2.** [civil servant] mandarin *m*.

mandate ['mændeɪt] **n** mandat *m*.

mandatory ['mændətrɪ] **adj** obligatoire.

man-day **n** *UK* jour-homme *m* ▸ **30 man-days** 30 journées *fpl* de travail.

mandolin [mændə'lɪn] **n** mandoline *f*.

mane [meɪn] **n** crinière *f*.

man-eater **n** [animal] anthropophage *m* / [cannibal] cannibale *m*, anthropophage *m* / *hum* [woman] dévoreuse *f* d'hommes, mante *f* religieuse.

man-eating [-ˌi:tɪŋ] **adj** mangeur(euse) d'hommes.

maneuver *US* = ***manoeuvre***.

maneuverable *US* = ***manoeuvrable***.

manful ['mænfʊl] **adj** [courageous] vaillant, ardent.

manfully ['mænfʊlɪ] **adv** courageusement, vaillamment.

manganese ['mæŋgəni:z] **n** manganèse *m*.

mange [meɪndʒ] **n** gale *f*.

manger ['meɪndʒəʳ] **n** mangeoire *f*.

mangetout (pea) [ˌmɑ̃ʒ'tu:-] **n** *UK* mange-tout *m inv*.

mangle ['mæŋgl] **vt** mutiler, déchirer.

mango ['mæŋgəʊ] (pl **-es** *OR* **-s**) **n** mangue *f*.

mangrove ['mæŋgrəʊv] **n** palétuvier *m*.

mangy ['meɪndʒɪ] (comp **-ier**, superl **-iest**) **adj** galeux(euse).

manhandle ['mænˌhændl] **vt** malmener.

manhole ['mænhəʊl] **n** regard *m*, trou *m* d'homme.

manhood ['mænhʊd] **n : to reach manhood** devenir un homme.

man-hour **n** FIN heure-homme *f*.

manhunt ['mænhʌnt] **n** chasse *f* à l'homme.

mania ['meɪnjə] **n : mania (for)** manie *f* (de).

maniac ['meɪnɪæk] **n** fou *m*, folle *f* ▸ **a sex maniac** un obsédé sexuel (une obsédée sexuelle).

maniacal [mə'naɪəkl] **adj 1.** [crazy] fou *(before vowel or silent 'h'* **fol***)* (folle) ▸ **maniacal laughter** rire *m* hystérique **2.** PSYCHOL maniaque.

manic ['mænɪk] adj *fig* [person] surexcité(e) / [behaviour] de fou.

manic depression n psychose *f* maniaco-dépressive.

manic-depressive ■ adj maniaco-dépressif (maniaco-dépressive).
■ n maniaco-dépressif *m*, maniaco-dépressive *f*.

manicure ['mænɪˌkjʊəʳ] ■ n manucure *f*.
■ vt [person] faire une manucure à ▸ **to manicure one's nails** se faire les ongles.

manicurist ['mænɪˌkjʊərɪst] n manucure *mf*.

manifest ['mænɪfest] *fml* ■ adj manifeste, évident(e).
■ vt manifester.

manifestation [ˌmænɪfes'teɪʃn] n *fml* manifestation *f*.

manifestly ['mænɪfestlɪ] adv *fml* manifestement.

manifesto [ˌmænɪ'festəʊ] (pl -s *OR* -es) n manifeste *m*.

manifold ['mænɪfəʊld] ■ adj *liter* nombreux(euse), multiple.
■ n AUT tubulure *f*, collecteur *m*.

manikin ['mænɪkɪn] = ***mannequin***.

Manila [mə'nɪlə] n Manille.

manil(l)a [mə'nɪlə] adj en papier kraft.

manipulate [mə'nɪpjʊleɪt] vt *lit* & *fig* manipuler.

manipulation [məˌnɪpjʊ'leɪʃn] n *lit* & *fig* manipulation *f*.

manipulative [mə'nɪpjʊlətɪv] adj [person] rusé(e) / [behaviour] habile, subtil(e).

Manitoba [ˌmænɪ'təʊbə] n Manitoba *m* ▸ **in Manitoba** dans le Manitoba.

mankind [mæn'kaɪnd] n humanité *f*, genre *m* humain.

manlike ['mænlaɪk] adj **1.** [virile] viril(e), masculin(e) **2.** [woman] masculin(e).

manliness ['mænlɪnɪs] n virilité *f*.

manly ['mænlɪ] (comp -ier, superl -iest) adj viril(e).

man-made adj [fabric, fibre] synthétique / [environment] artificiel(elle) / [problem] causé(e) par l'homme.

man management n *UK* gestion *f* des ressources humaines.

manna ['mænə] n manne *f*.

manned [mænd] adj [vehicle] doté(e) d'un équipage / [flight] habité(e).

mannequin ['mænɪkɪn] n mannequin *mf*.

manner ['mænəʳ] n **1.** [method] manière *f*, façon *f* ▸ **in a manner of speaking** pour ainsi dire ▸ **not by any manner of means** en aucune manière, aucunement **2.** [attitude] attitude *f*, comportement *m* ▸ **I don't like his manner** je n'aime pas ses façons ▸ **he has a good telephone manner** il fait bonne impression au téléphone **3.** [type, sort] **: all manner of** toutes sortes de.
◆ ***manners*** npl manières *fpl* ▸ **it's bad manners to talk with your mouth full** c'est mal élevé *OR* ce n'est pas poli de parler la bouche pleine.

mannered ['mænəd] adj *fml* maniéré(e), affecté(e).

mannerism ['mænərɪzm] n tic *m*, manie *f*.

mannikin ['mænɪkɪn] = ***mannequin***.

mannish ['mænɪʃ] adj masculin(e).

manoeuvrable *UK*, ***maneuverable*** *US* [mə'nu:vrəbl] adj facile à manœuvrer, maniable.

manoeuvre *UK*, ***maneuver*** *US* [mə'nu:vəʳ] ■ n manœuvre *f*.
■ vt & vi manœuvrer.
◆ ***manoeuvres*** npl MIL manœuvres *fpl*.

manor ['mænəʳ] n manoir *m*.

manpower ['mænˌpaʊəʳ] n main-d'œuvre *f*.

manservant ['mænsɜ:vənt] (pl **men-** [men-]) n *dated* valet *m* de chambre.

mansion ['mænʃn] n château *m*.

man-size(d) adj grand(e), de grande personne.

manslaughter ['mænˌslɔ:təʳ] n homicide *m* involontaire.

mantelpiece ['mæntlpi:s] n (dessus *m* de) cheminée *f*.

mantle ['mæntl] n **1.** *liter* [of snow] manteau *m* **2.** *fml* [of leadership, high office] responsabilité *f*.

man-to-man ■ adj d'homme à homme.
■ adv [talk] d'homme à homme.

mantra ['mæntrə] n mantra *m inv*.

manual ['mænjʊəl] ■ adj manuel(elle).
■ n manuel *m*.

manually ['mænjʊəlɪ] adv à la main, manuellement.

manual worker n travailleur manuel *m*, travailleuse manuelle *f*.

manufacture [ˌmænjʊ'fæktʃəʳ] ■ n fabrication *f* / [of cars] construction *f*.
■ vt fabriquer / [cars] construire.

manufacturer [ˌmænjʊ'fæktʃərəʳ] n fabricant *m* / [of cars] constructeur *m*.

manufacturing [ˌmænjʊ'fæktʃərɪŋ] n fabrication *f*.

manufacturing costs n frais *mpl* de fabrication.

manufacturing industries npl industries *fpl* de fabrication.

manure [mə'njʊəʳ] n fumier *m*.

manuscript ['mænjʊskrɪpt] n manuscrit *m*.

Manx [mæŋks] ■ adj de l'île de Man, manxois(e).
■ n [language] manx *m*.

many ['menɪ] ■ adj (comp **more**, superl **most**) beaucoup de ▸ **how many...?** combien de...? ▸ **too many** trop de ▸ **as many... as** autant de... que ▸ **so many** autant de ▸ **a good** *OR* **great many** un grand nombre de.
■ pron [a lot, plenty] beaucoup.

Maori ['maʊrɪ] ■ adj maori(e).
■ n Maori *m*, -e *f*.

map [mæp] n carte *f*.
◆ ***map out*** (pt & pp -ped, cont -ping) vt sep [plan] élaborer / [timetable] établir / [task] définir.

maple ['meɪpl] n érable *m*.

maple leaf n feuille *f* d'érable.

maple syrup n sirop *m* d'érable.

Maputo [mə'pu:təʊ] n Maputo.

mar [mɑ:ʳ] (pt & pp -red, cont -ring) vt gâter, gâcher.

Mar. abbr of ***March***.

marathon ['mærəθn] ■ adj marathon *(inv)*.
■ n marathon *m*.

marathon runner n marathonien *m*, -enne *f*.

marauder [mə'rɔ:dəʳ] n maraudeur *m*, -euse *f*.

marauding [mə'rɔ:dɪŋ] adj maraudeur(euse).

marble ['mɑ:bl] n **1.** [stone] marbre *m* **2.** [for game] bille *f*.
◆ ***marbles*** n *(U)* [game] billes *fpl*.

march [mɑ:tʃ] ■ n marche *f*.
■ vi **1.** [soldiers] marcher au pas **2.** [demonstrators] manifester, faire une marche de protestation **3.** [quickly] **: to march up to sb** s'approcher de qqn d'un pas décidé.
■ vt **: to march sb out the door** faire sortir qqn.

March [mɑ:tʃ] n mars *m* ; see also ***September***.

marcher ['mɑ:tʃəʳ] n [protester] marcheur *m*, -euse *f*.

marching orders ['mɑ:tʃɪŋ-] npl **: to get one's marching orders** se faire mettre à la porte.

marchioness ['mɑ:ʃənes] n marquise *f*.

march-past n défilé *m*.

Mardi Gras [ˌmɑ:dɪ'grɑ:] n mardi *m* gras, carnaval *m*.

mare [meəʳ] n jument *f*.

marg [mɑ:dʒ] n *UK inf* margarine *f*.

marg. [mɑ:dʒ] n = ***margin***.

margarine [ˌmɑ:dʒə'ri:n *OR* ˌmɑ:gə'ri:n] n margarine *f*.

marge [mɑ:dʒ] n *UK inf* margarine *f*.

margin ['mɑ:dʒɪn] n **1.** [gen] marge *f* ▸ **to win by a narrow margin** gagner de peu *OR* de justesse **2.** [edge - of an area] bord *m*.

marginal ['mɑ:dʒɪnl] adj marginal(e), secondaire.

marginalize, *UK* ***-ise*** ['mɑ:dʒɪnəlaɪz] vt marginaliser.

marginally ['mɑ:dʒɪnəlɪ] adv très peu.

marginal seat n POL *en Grande-Bretagne, circonscription électorale où la majorité passe facilement d'un parti à un autre*.

marigold ['mærɪgəʊld] n souci *m*.

marihuana, ***marijuana*** [ˌmærɪ'wɑ:nə] n marihuana *f*.

marina [mə'ri:nə] n marina *f*.

marinade [ˌmærɪ'neɪd] ■ n marinade *f*.
■ vt & vi mariner.

marinate ['mærɪneɪt] vt & vi mariner.

marine [mə'ri:n] adj marin(e).

Marine n marine *m*.

marionette [ˌmærɪə'net] n marionnette *f*.

marital ['mærɪtl] adj [sex, happiness] conjugal(e) / [problems] matrimonial(e).

marital status n situation *f* de famille.

maritime ['mærɪtaɪm] adj maritime.

Maritime Provinces, ***Maritimes*** npl **: the Maritime Provinces** les Provinces *fpl* Maritimes.

marjoram ['mɑ:dʒərəm] n marjolaine *f*.

mark [mɑ:k] ■ n **1.** [sign, symbol] marque *f* ▸ **to make a mark on sthg** faire une marque sur qqch, marquer qqch ▸ **a mark of affection** une marque d'affection ▸ **as a mark of respect** en signe de respect
2. [trace, stain] tache *f*, marque *f* ▸ **there wasn't a mark on the body** le corps ne portait aucune trace de coups ▸ **the years she spent in prison have left their mark** ses années en prison l'ont marquée
3. *esp UK* [in exam] note *f*, point *m* ▸ **the mark is out of 100** la note est sur 100 ▸ **to get full marks** obtenir la meilleure note (possible) ▸ **she deserves full marks for imagination** il faut saluer son imagination
4. [stage, level] barre *f* ▸ **to reach the half-way mark** arriver à mi-course ▸ **sales topped the 5 million mark** les ventes ont dépassé la barre des 5 millions
5. [currency] mark *m*
⏭ **to make one's mark** se faire un nom, réussir ▸ **to be quick off the mark in doing sthg** faire qqch sans perdre de temps ▸ **to be up to the mark** [be capable] être à la hauteur / [meet expectations] être satisfaisant ▸ **wide of the mark** à côté de la question.
■ vt **1.** [gen] marquer ▸ **the towels were marked with his name** les serviettes étaient à son nom, son nom était marqué sur les serviettes ▸ **mark the text with your initials** inscrivez vos initiales sur ce texte
2. [stain] marquer, tacher ▸ **the scandal marked him for life** [mentally] le scandale l'a marqué pour la vie
3. [distinguish] marquer ▸ **X marks the spot** l'endroit est marqué d'un X ▸ **let's have some champagne to mark the occasion** ouvrons une bouteille de champagne pour fêter l'événement ▸ **he has all the qualities that mark a good golfer** il possède toutes les qualités d'un bon golfeur
4. *esp UK* [exam, essay] noter, corriger ▸ **the exam was marked out of 100** l'examen a été noté sur 100 ▸ **to mark sthg wrong/right** marquer qqch comme étant faux/juste.
◆ ***mark down*** vt sep **1.** [COMM - prices] baisser / [- goods] baisser le prix de, démarquer ▸ **marked down shirts** chemises démarquées *OR* soldées
2. [downgrade] baisser la note de.
◆ ***mark off*** vt sep **1.** [divide, isolate] délimiter ▸ **one corner of the field had been marked off by a fence** un coin du champ avait été isolé par une barrière
2. [cross off] cocher.
◆ ***mark up*** vt sep **1.** [on notice] marquer ▸ **the menu is marked up on the blackboard** le menu est sur le tableau
2. [COMM - prices] augmenter / [- goods] augmenter le prix de
3. [annotate] annoter.

markdown ['mɑ:kdaʊn] n démarque *f*.

marked [mɑ:kt] adj [change, difference] marqué(e) / [improvement, deterioration] sensible.

markedly ['mɑ:kɪdlɪ] adv [different] d'une façon marquée / [worse, better] sensiblement, manifestement.

marker ['mɑ:kəʳ] n **1.** [sign] repère *m* **2.** [pen] marqueur *m*.

marker pen n marqueur *m*.

market ['mɑ:kɪt] ■ n **1.** [gen] marché *m* ▸ **to be on the market** être sur le marché *OR* en vente ▸ **he's unable to find a market for his products** il ne trouve pas de débouchés pour ses produits **2.** [clientele] marché *m*, clientèle *f* ▸ **this ad should appeal to the teenage market**

cette pub devrait séduire les jeunes **3.** FIN marché *m* / [index] indice *m* ▸ **the market has risen 10 points** l'indice est en hausse de 10 points.
■ **vt** commercialiser.
■ **vi** *US* [shop] **: to go marketing** aller faire ses courses.

marketability [,mɑːkɪtə'bɪlɪtɪ] **n** [of goods, product] possibilité *f* de commercialisation.

marketable ['mɑːkɪtəbl] **adj** commercialisable.

market analysis **n** analyse *f* de marché.

market conditions **npl** conditions *fpl* du marché.

market day **n** jour *m* de marché.

market demand **n** demande *f* du marché.

market-driven **adj** déterminé(e) par les contraintes du marché.

market-driven economy **n** économie *f* de marché.

market economy **n** économie *f* de marché OR libérale.

marketeer [,mɑːkə'tɪəʳ] **n 1. : black marketeer** trafiquant *m*, -e *f* (au marché noir) **2.** *UK* POL **: pro-marketeer** partisan *m*, -e *f* du Marché commun ▸ **anti-marketeer** adversaire *mf* du Marché commun.

market entry **n** lancement *m* sur le marché.

market forces **npl** forces *fpl* OR tendances *fpl* du marché.

market garden **n** *UK* jardin *m* maraîcher.

market growth **n** croissance *f* du marché.

market indicator **n** indicateur *m* de marché, signal *m* du marché.

marketing ['mɑːkɪtɪŋ] **n** marketing *m*.

marketing campaign **n** campagne *f* commerciale.

marketing concept **n** concept *m* de marketing.

marketing mix **n** marchéage *m*, marketing mix *m*.

marketing plan **n** plan *m* marketing.

marketing spend **n** dépenses *fpl* de marketing.

marketing strategy **n** stratégie *f* marketing.

marketing tool **n** outil *m* de marketing.

market leader **n** [product] premier produit *m* sur le marché / [firm] leader *m* du marché.

market maker **n** FIN teneur *m* de marché.

market penetration **n** pénétration *f* du marché.

marketplace ['mɑːkɪtpleɪs] **n 1.** [in a town] place *f* du marché **2.** COMM marché *m*.

market positioning **n** positionnement *m* sur le marché.

market price **n** prix *m* du marché.

market profile **n** profil *m* du marché.

market research **n** étude *f* de marché.

market researcher **n** *personne qui fait des études de marché.*

market segment **n** segment *m* de marché.

market share **n** part *f* de marché.

market survey **n** enquête *f* de marché.

market town **n** marché *m*.

market value **n** valeur *f* marchande.

marking ['mɑːkɪŋ] **n** SCH correction *f*.
◆ ***markings*** **npl** [on animal, flower] taches *fpl*, marques *fpl* / [on road] signalisation *f* horizontale.

marksman ['mɑːksmən] (pl **-men** [-mən]) **n** tireur *m* d'élite.

marksmanship ['mɑːksmənʃɪp] **n** adresse *f* au tir.

markswoman ['mɑːkswəmən] (pl **-women** [-,wɪmɪn]) **n** tireuse *f* d'élite.

markup ['mɑːkʌp] **n** majoration *f*.

marmalade ['mɑːməleɪd] **n** confiture *f* d'oranges amères.

maroon [mə'ruːn] **adj** bordeaux *(inv)*.

marooned [mə'ruːnd] **adj** abandonné(e).

marquee [mɑː'kiː] **n** *UK* grande tente *f*.

marquess ['mɑːkwɪs] = ***marquis***.

marquetry ['mɑːkɪtrɪ] **n** marqueterie *f*.

marquis ['mɑːkwɪs] **n** marquis *m*.

marriage ['mærɪdʒ] **n** mariage *m*.

marriage bureau **n** *UK* agence *f* matrimoniale.

marriage certificate **n** acte *m* de mariage.

marriage guidance *UK Aus*, ***marriage counseling*** *US* **n** conseil *m* conjugal.

marriage guidance counsellor *UK*, ***marriage counselor*** *US* **n** conseiller conjugal *m*, conseillère conjugale *f*.

marriage of convenience **n** mariage *m* de raison.

married ['mærɪd] **adj 1.** [person] marié(e) ▸ **to get married** se marier **2.** [life] conjugal(e).

marrow ['mærəʊ] **n 1.** *UK* [vegetable] courge *f* **2.** [in bones] moelle *f*.

marry ['mærɪ] (pt & pp **-ied**) ■ **vt 1.** [become spouse of] épouser, se marier avec **2.** [subj: priest, registrar] marier.
■ **vi** se marier.

Mars [mɑːz] **n** [planet] Mars *f*.

Marseille(s) [mɑː'seɪ(z)] **n** Marseille.

marsh [mɑːʃ] **n** marais *m*, marécage *m*.

marshal ['mɑːʃl] ■ **n 1.** MIL maréchal *m* **2.** [steward] membre *m* du service d'ordre **3.** *US* [law officer] officier *m* de police fédérale.
■ **vt** (*UK* **-led**, cont **-ling**, *US* **-ed**, cont **-ing**) *lit* & *fig* rassembler.

marshalling yard ['mɑːʃlɪŋ-] **n** *UK* gare *f* de triage.

marshland ['mɑːʃlænd] **n** terrain *m* marécageux.

marshmallow [*UK* ,mɑːʃ'mæləʊ, *US* 'mɑːrʃ,meləʊ] **n** guimauve *f*.

marshy ['mɑːʃɪ] (comp **-ier**, superl **-iest**) **adj** marécageux(euse).

marsupial [mɑː'suːpjəl] **n** marsupial *m*.

martial ['mɑːʃl] **adj** martial(e).

martial arts **npl** arts *mpl* martiaux.

martial law **n** loi *f* martiale.

Martian ['mɑːʃn] ■ **adj** martien(enne).
■ **n** Martien *m*, -enne *f*.

martin ['mɑːtɪn] **n** martinet *m*.

martini [mɑː'tiːnɪ] **n** [cocktail] martini *m*.

Martinique [ˌmɑːtɪ'niːk] **n** la Martinique *f* ▸ **in Martinique** à la Martinique.

martyr ['mɑːtəʳ] **n** martyr *m*, -e *f*.

martyrdom ['mɑːtədəm] **n** martyre *m*.

martyred ['mɑːtəd] **adj** de martyr.

marvel ['mɑːvl] ■ **n** merveille *f* ▸ **it's a marvel that...** c'est un miracle que... *(+ subjunctive)*.
■ **vt** (*UK* **-led**, cont **-ling**, *US* **-ed**, cont **-ing**) **: to marvel that** s'étonner de ce que.
■ **vi** (*UK* **-led**, cont **-ling**, *US* **-ed**, cont **-ing**) **: to marvel (at)** s'émerveiller (de), s'étonner (de).

marvellous *UK*, ***marvelous*** *US* ['mɑːvələs] **adj** merveilleux(euse).

marvellously *UK*, ***marvelously*** *US* ['mɑːvələslɪ] **adv** merveilleusement, à merveille.

Marxism ['mɑːksɪzm] **n** marxisme *m*.

Marxist ['mɑːksɪst] ■ **adj** marxiste.
■ **n** marxiste *mf*.

Maryland ['meərɪlænd] **n** Maryland *m* ▸ **in Maryland** dans le Maryland.

marzipan ['mɑːzɪpæn] **n** *(U)* pâte *f* d'amandes.

mascara [mæs'kɑːrə] **n** mascara *m*.

mascot ['mæskət] **n** mascotte *f*.

masculine ['mæskjʊlɪn] **adj** masculin(e).

masculinity [ˌmæskjʊ'lɪnətɪ] **n** masculinité *f*.

mash [mæʃ] **vt** *UK inf* faire une purée de.

MASH [mæʃ] (abbr of ***mobile army surgical hospital***) **n** *US hôpital militaire de campagne.*

mashed potato *UK* [mæʃt-] **n** purée *f* de pommes de terre.

mask [mɑːsk] *lit & fig* ■ **n** masque *m*.
■ **vt** masquer.

masked [mɑːskt] **adj** masqué(e).

masking tape ['mɑːskɪŋ-] **n** papier *m* cache.

masochism ['mæsəkɪzm] **n** masochisme *m*.

masochist ['mæsəkɪst] **n** masochiste *mf*.

masochistic [ˌmæsə'kɪstɪk] **adj** masochiste.

mason ['meɪsn] **n 1.** [stonemason] maçon *m* **2.** [freemason] franc-maçon *m*.

masonic [mə'sɒnɪk] **adj** maçonnique.

masonry ['meɪsnrɪ] **n** [stones] maçonnerie *f*.

masquerade [ˌmæskə'reɪd] **vi : to masquerade as** se faire passer pour ▸ **to masquerade under an assumed name** se cacher sous un faux nom.

mass [mæs] ■ **n** [gen & PHYS] masse *f* ▸ **the streets were a solid mass of people/traffic** les rues regorgeaient de monde/de voitures.
■ **adj** [protest, meeting] en masse, en nombre / [support] massif(ive) ▸ **mass grave** charnier *m* ▸ **mass hypnosis/hysteria** hypnose *f*/hystérie *f* collective ▸ **mass murderer** tueur *m* fou.
■ **vt** masser.
■ **vi** se masser.
◆ ***Mass*** **n** RELIG messe *f*.
◆ ***masses*** **npl 1.** *esp UK inf* [lots] **: masses (of)** des masses (de) / [food] des tonnes (de) **2.** [workers] **: the masses** les masses *fpl*.

Massachusetts [ˌmæsə'tʃuːsɪts] **n** Massachusetts *m* ▸ **in Massachusetts** dans le Massachusetts.

massacre ['mæsəkəʳ] ■ **n** massacre *m*.
■ **vt** massacrer.

massage [*UK* 'mæsɑːʒ, *US* mə'sɑːʒ] ■ **n** massage *m*.
■ **vt** masser.

massage parlour *UK*, ***massage parlor*** *US* **n** institut *m* de massage.

massed [mæst] **adj 1.** [crowds, soldiers] massé(e), regroupé(e) ▸ **massed bands** *UK* ensemble *m* de fanfares **2.** [collective] de masse ▸ **the massed weight of public opinion** le poids de l'opinion publique.

masseur [mæ'sɜːʳ] **n** masseur *m*.

masseuse [mæ'sɜːz] **n** masseuse *f*.

massive ['mæsɪv] **adj** massif(ive), énorme.

massively ['mæsɪvlɪ] **adv** massivement.

mass mailing **n** envoi *m* en nombre.

mass-market **adj** grand public *(inv)*.

mass media **n & npl : the mass media** les (mass) media *mpl*.

mass-produce **vt** fabriquer en série.

mass production **n** fabrication *f* ***or*** production *f* en série.

mass unemployment **n** chômage *m* sur une grande échelle.

mast [mɑːst] **n 1.** [on boat] mât *m* **2.** RADIO & TV pylône *m*.

mastectomy [mæs'tektəmɪ] (pl **-ies**) **n** mastectomie *f*.

master ['mɑːstəʳ] ■ **n 1.** [gen] maître *m* **2.** *UK* [SCH - in primary school] instituteur *m*, maître *m* / [- in secondary school] professeur *m* **3.** [original copy] original *m*.
■ **adj** maître ▸ **master chef/craftsman** maître chef *m*/artisan *m*.
■ **vt** maîtriser / [difficulty] surmonter, vaincre / [situation] se rendre maître de.

master bedroom **n** chambre *f* principale.

masterbrand ['mɑːstəbrænd] **n** marque *f* vedette.

master class **n** cours *m* de maître / MUS master class *m*.

master disk **n** COMPUT disque *m* d'exploitation.

master file **n** COMPUT fichier *m* principal ***or*** maître.

masterful ['mɑːstəfʊl] **adj** autoritaire.

master key **n** passe *m*, passe-partout *m inv*.

masterly ['mɑːstəlɪ] **adj** magistral(e).

mastermind ['mɑːstəmaɪnd] ■ **n** cerveau *m*.
■ **vt** organiser, diriger.

Master of Arts **(pl Masters of Arts) n 1.** [degree] maîtrise *f* ès lettres **2.** [person] titulaire *mf* d'une maîtrise ès lettres.

master of ceremonies **(pl masters of ceremonies) n** maître *m* de cérémonie.

Master of Science **(pl Masters of Science) n 1.** [degree] maîtrise *f* ès sciences **2.** [person] titulaire *mf* d'une maîtrise ès sciences.

masterpiece ['mɑːstəpiːs] **n** chef-d'œuvre *m*.

master plan **n** stratégie *f* globale.

master's degree **n** ≃ maîtrise *f*.

masterstroke ['mɑːstəstrəʊk] **n** coup *m* magistral ***OR*** de maître.

master switch **n** interrupteur *m* général ***OR*** principal.

masterwork ['mɑːstəwɜːk] **n** chef-d'œuvre *m*.

mastery ['mɑːstərɪ] **n** maîtrise *f*.

masthead ['mɑːsthed] **n 1.** NAUT tête *f* de mât **2.** PRESS titre *m*.

mastic ['mæstɪk] **n** mastic *m*.

masticate ['mæstɪkeɪt] **vt & vi** *fml* mastiquer, mâcher.

mastiff ['mæstɪf] **n** mastiff *m*.

masturbate ['mæstəbeɪt] **vi** se masturber.

masturbation [ˌmæstə'beɪʃn] **n** masturbation *f*.

mat [mæt] **n 1.** [on floor] petit tapis *m* / [at door] paillasson *m* **2.** [on table] set *m* (de table) / [coaster] dessous *m* de verre.

match [mætʃ] ■ **n 1.** [game] match *m* ▸ **a rugby/boxing match** un match de rugby/de boxe ▸ **to play a match** jouer un match **2.** [for lighting] allumette *f* ▸ **to light *OR* to strike a match** frotter ***OR*** craquer une allumette ▸ **a box/book of matches** une boîte/une pochette d'allumettes **3.** [equal] **: to be no match for sb** ne pas être de taille à lutter contre qqn ▸ **he's found *OR* met his match (in Pauline)** il a trouvé à qui parler (avec Pauline) **4.** [combination] **: they are *OR* make a good match** ils vont bien ensemble ▸ **the new paint's not quite a perfect match** la nouvelle peinture n'est pas exactement de la même couleur que la précédente.
■ **vt 1.** [be the same as, go with] correspondre à, s'accorder avec ▸ **the gloves match the scarf** les gants sont assortis à l'écharpe **2.** [pair off] faire correspondre ▸ **can you match the names with the photographs?** pouvez-vous attribuer à chaque photo le nom qui lui correspond? **3.** [be equal with] égaler, rivaliser avec ▸ **his arrogance is matched only by that of his father** son arrogance n'a d'égale que celle de son père **4.** [oppose] **: to match sb against sb** opposer qqn à qqn.
■ **vi 1.** [be the same] correspondre ▸ **I can't find two socks that match** je ne parviens pas à trouver deux chaussettes identiques **2.** [go together well] être assorti(e) ▸ **a red scarf with a bonnet to match** un foulard rouge avec un bonnet assorti.

matchbox ['mætʃbɒks] **n** boîte *f* à allumettes.

matched [mætʃt] **adj : to be well matched** [well suited] être bien assortis(es) / [equal in strength] être de force égale.

match-fit **adj** *UK* **: to be match-fit** être en état de jouer.

matching ['mætʃɪŋ] **adj** assorti(e).

matchless ['mætʃlɪs] **adj** *liter* sans pareil, incomparable.

matchmaker ['mætʃˌmeɪkəʳ] **n** marieur *m*, -euse *f*.

match play **n** GOLF match-play *m*.

match point **n** TENNIS balle *f* de match.

matchstick ['mætʃstɪk] **n** allumette *f*.

match-winner **n** atout *m* pour gagner, joker *m*.

mate [meɪt] ■ **n 1.** *UK inf* [friend] copain *m*, copine *f*, pote *m* **2.** *UK inf* [term of address] mon vieux **3.** [of female animal] mâle *m* / [of male animal] femelle *f* **4.** NAUT **: (first) mate** second *m*.
■ **vi** s'accoupler.

material [mə'tɪərɪəl] ■ **adj 1.** [goods, benefits, world] matériel(elle) **2.** [important] important(e), essentiel(elle).
■ **n 1.** [substance] matière *f*, substance *f* / [type of substance] matériau *m*, matière **2.** [fabric] tissu *m*, étoffe *f* / [type of fabric] tissu **3.** *(U)* [information - for book, article] matériaux *mpl* ▸ **background material** documentation de base **4.** [finished work] **: a comic who writes his own material** un comique qui écrit ses propres textes ***OR*** sketches **5.** [suitable person or persons] **: is he officer/university material?** a-t-il l'étoffe d'un officier/universitaire?
◆ ***materials*** **npl** matériaux *mpl* ▸ **teaching materials** SCH supports *mpl* pédagogiques.

> CONFUSABLE / PARONYME
> **material**
> When translating **material**, note that *matériau* and *matériel* are not interchangeable. *Matériau* refers to building material, while *matériel* is used for equipment for a specific activity.

materialism [mə'tɪərɪəlɪzm] **n** matérialisme *m*.

materialist [mə'tɪərɪəlɪst] **n** matérialiste *mf*.

materialistic [məˌtɪərɪə'lɪstɪk] **adj** matérialiste.

materialize, *UK* ***-ise*** [mə'tɪərɪəlaɪz] **vi 1.** [offer, threat] se concrétiser, se réaliser **2.** [person, object] apparaître.

materially [mə'tɪərɪəlɪ] **adv 1.** [benefit, suffer] matériellement **2.** [different] essentiellement.

maternal [mə'tɜːnl] **adj** maternel(elle).

maternity [mə'tɜːnətɪ] **n** maternité *f*.

maternity allowance **n** *allocation de maternité versée par l'État à une femme n'ayant pas droit à la "maternity pay"*.

maternity benefit **n** *(U) UK* allocations *fpl* (de) maternité.

maternity dress **n** robe *f* de grossesse.

maternity hospital **n** maternité *f*.

maternity leave **n** congé *m* (de) maternité.

maternity pay **n** *allocation de maternité versée par l'employeur*.

math *US* = ***maths***.

mathematical [ˌmæθəˈmætɪkl] **adj** mathématique.

mathematically [ˌmæθəˈmætɪklɪ] **adv** mathématiquement.

mathematician [ˌmæθəməˈtɪʃn] **n** mathématicien *m*, -enne *f*.

mathematics [ˌmæθəˈmætɪks] **n** *(U)* mathématiques *fpl*.

maths *UK* [mæθs], ***math*** *US* [mæθ] (abbr of ***mathematics***) ■ **n** *(U)* maths *fpl*.
■ **comp** de maths.

maths coprocessor *UK*, ***math coprocessor*** *US* [-ˌkəʊˈprəʊsesəʳ] **n** COMPUT coprocesseur *m* mathématique.

matinée, ***matinee*** [ˈmætɪneɪ] **n** matinée *f*.

matinée coat, ***matinée jacket*** **n** *UK* veste *f* de bébé.

mating [ˈmeɪtɪŋ] **n** accouplement *m*.

mating call **n** appel *m* du mâle.

mating instinct **n** instinct *m* sexuel.

mating season **n** saison *f* des amours.

matriarch [ˈmeɪtrɪɑːk] **n 1.** [of society] *femme ayant une autorité matriarcale* **2.** *liter* [of family] aïeule *f*, doyenne *f*.

matriarchal [ˌmeɪtrɪˈɑːkl] **adj** matriarcal.

matriarchy [ˈmeɪtrɪɑːkɪ] (pl **-ies**) **n** matriarcat *m*.

matrices [ˈmeɪtrɪsiːz] **npl** ➤ ***matrix***.

matriculate [məˈtrɪkjʊleɪt] **vi** s'inscrire.

matriculation [məˌtrɪkjʊˈleɪʃn] **n** inscription *f*.

matrimonial [ˌmætrɪˈməʊnjəl] **adj** *fml* matrimonial(e), conjugal(e).

matrimony [ˈmætrɪmənɪ] **n** *(U)* *fml* mariage *m*.

matrix [ˈmeɪtrɪks] (pl **matrices** [ˈmeɪtrɪsiːz] *OR* **-es** [-iːz]) **n 1.** [context, framework] contexte *m*, structure *f* **2.** MATHS & TECH matrice *f*.

matron [ˈmeɪtrən] **n 1.** *UK* [in hospital] infirmière *f* en chef **2.** *UK* [in school] infirmière *f* **3.** *US* [in prison] gardienne *f*.

matronly [ˈmeɪtrənlɪ] **adj** *euph* [woman] qui a l'allure d'une matrone / [figure] de matrone.

matt *UK*, ***matte*** *US* [mæt] **adj** mat(e).

matted [ˈmætɪd] **adj** emmêlé(e).

matter [ˈmætəʳ] ■ **n 1.** [question, situation] question *f*, affaire *f* ▸ **business matters** affaires *fpl* ▸ **money matters** questions *fpl* d'argent ▸ **a matter of life and death** une question de vie ou de mort ▸ **the fact** *OR* **truth of the matter is...** la vérité c'est que..., le fait est que... ▸ **that's another** *OR* **a different matter** c'est tout autre chose, c'est une autre histoire ▸ **I reported the matter to the police** j'ai rapporté les faits à la police ▸ **there's the small matter of the £100 you owe me** il y a ce petit problème des 100 livres que tu me dois ▸ **as a matter of course** automatiquement ▸ **to make matters worse** aggraver la situation ▸ **and to make matters worse...** pour tout arranger... ▸ **as a matter of principle** par principe ▸ **within a matter of hours** en l'affaire de quelques heures ▸ **that's a matter of opinion** c'est (une) affaire *OR* question d'opinion ▸ **a matter of time** une question de temps
2. [trouble, cause of pain] **: there's something the matter with my radio** il y a quelque chose qui cloche *OR* ne va pas dans ma radio ▸ **is there something** *OR* **is anything the matter?** il y a quelque chose qui ne va pas?, il y a un problème? ▸ **what's the matter?** qu'est-ce qu'il y a? ▸ **what's the matter with him?** qu'est-ce qu'il a? ▸ **what's the matter with your eyes?** qu'est-ce que vous avez aux yeux? ▸ **what's the matter with the way I dress?** qu'est-ce que vous reprochez à ma façon de m'habiller? ▸ **nothing's the** *OR* **there's nothing the matter** il n'y a rien, tout va bien ▸ **nothing's the matter with me** je vais parfaitement bien
3. PHYS matière *f*
4. *(U)* [material] matière *f* ▸ **reading matter** choses *fpl* à lire ▸ **printed matter** imprimés *mpl*.
■ **vi** [be important] importer, avoir de l'importance ▸ **it doesn't matter** cela n'a pas d'importance ▸ **what does it matter?** quelle importance est-ce que ça a?, qu'importe? ▸ **it matters a lot** cela a beaucoup d'importance, c'est très important ▸ **it doesn't matter to me what you do with your money** ce que tu fais de ton argent m'est égal ▸ **money is all that matters to him** il n'y a que l'argent qui l'intéresse.
◆ ***as a matter of fact*** **adv** en fait, à vrai dire.
◆ ***for that matter*** **adv** d'ailleurs.
◆ ***no matter*** **adv : no matter what** coûte que coûte, à tout prix ▸ **no matter what I do** quoi que je fasse ▸ **no matter how hard I try to explain...** j'ai beau essayer de lui expliquer... ▸ **no matter where I am** où que je sois.

Matterhorn [ˈmætəˌhɔːn] **n : the Matterhorn** le mont Cervin.

matter-of-fact **adj** terre-à-terre, neutre.

matting [ˈmætɪŋ] **n** *(U)* natte *f*.

mattress [ˈmætrɪs] **n** matelas *m*.

mature [məˈtjʊəʳ] ■ **adj 1.** [person, attitude] mûr(e) **2.** [cheese] fait(e) / [wine] arrivé(e) à maturité.
■ **vi 1.** [person] mûrir **2.** [cheese, wine] se faire.

mature economy **n** économie *f* en pleine maturité.

mature student **n** *UK* UNIV *étudiant qui a commencé ses études sur le tard*.

maturity [məˈtjʊərətɪ] **n** maturité *f*.

maudlin [ˈmɔːdlɪn] **adj** larmoyant(e).

maul [mɔːl] **vt** mutiler.

Maundy Thursday [ˈmɔːndɪ-] **n** RELIG jeudi *m* saint.

Mauritania [ˌmɒrɪˈteɪnjə] **n** Mauritanie *f* ▸ **in Mauritania** en Mauritanie.

Mauritanian [ˌmɒrɪˈteɪnjən] ■ **adj** mauritanien(enne).
■ **n** Mauritanien *m*, -enne *f*.

Mauritian [məˈrɪʃn] ■ **adj** mauricien(enne).
■ **n** Mauricien *m*, -enne *f*.

Mauritius [məˈrɪʃəs] **n** l'île *f* Maurice ▸ **in Mauritius** à l'île Maurice.

mausoleum [ˌmɔːsəˈlɪəm] (pl **-s**) **n** mausolée *m*.

mauve [məʊv] ■ **adj** mauve.
■ **n** mauve *m*.

maverick ['mævərɪk] n non-conformiste *mf*.

mawkish ['mɔːkɪʃ] adj d'une sentimentalité excessive.

max. [mæks] (abbr of ***maximum***) max.

maxim ['mæksɪm] (pl -s) n maxime *f*.

maxima ['mæksɪmə] npl ➤ ***maximum***.

maximal ['mæksɪml] adj maximal(e).

maximize, *UK* ***-ise*** ['mæksɪmaɪz] vt maximiser, porter au maximum.

maximum ['mæksɪməm] ■ adj maximum *(inv)*.
■ n (pl **maxima** ['mæksɪmə] *OR* -s) maximum *m*.

may [meɪ] modal vb **1.** [expressing possibility] **: it may rain** il se peut qu'il pleuve, il va peut-être pleuvoir ▸ **this may take some time** ça prendra peut-être *OR* il se peut que ça prenne du temps ▸ **you may well be right** il est fort possible *OR* il se peut bien que vous ayez raison ▸ **he may have been right** il avait peut-être raison ▸ **she may not have arrived yet** il se peut *OR* il se pourrait qu'elle ne soit pas encore arrivée ▸ **be that as it may** quoi qu'il en soit
2. [expressing permission] **: may I come in?** puis-je entrer? ▸ **may I make a suggestion?** puis-je me permettre de faire une suggestion? ▸ **you may sit down** vous pouvez vous asseoir ▸ **I will go home now, if I may** je vais rentrer chez moi, si vous me le permettez ▸ **if I may say so** si je peux *OR* puis me permettre cette remarque ▸ **may I say how pleased we are that you could come** permettez-moi de vous dire à quel point nous sommes ravis que vous ayez pu venir
3. [as contrast] **: it may be expensive but...** c'est peut-être cher, mais... ▸ **you may think I'm imagining things, but I think I'm being followed** tu vas croire que je divague mais je crois que je suis suivi
4. *fml* [can] pouvoir ▸ **on a clear day the coast may be seen** on peut voir la côte par temps clair
5. *fml* [expressing wish, hope] **: may she rest in peace** qu'elle repose en paix ▸ **may the best man win!** que le meilleur gagne! ▸ **may they be happy!** qu'ils soient heureux!
▸▸ **may as well : can I go home now? – you may as well** est-ce que je peux rentrer chez moi maintenant? – tu ferais aussi bien ▸ **we may as well have another drink** tant qu'à faire, autant prendre un autre verre ; see also ***might***.

May [meɪ] n mai *m* ; see also ***September***.

Maya ['maɪə] n **: the Maya** les Mayas *mpl*.

Mayan ['maɪən] adj maya.

maybe ['meɪbiː] adv peut-être ▸ **maybe I'll come** je viendrai peut-être.

Mayday ['meɪdeɪ] n [SOS] SOS *m* ▸ **to send out a Mayday signal** envoyer un signal de détresse *OR* un SOS.

May Day n le Premier mai.

mayfly ['meɪflaɪ] (pl **-flies**) n éphémère *m*.

mayhem ['meɪhem] n pagaille *f*.

mayn't [meɪnt] *UK* = ***may not***.

mayonnaise [ˌmeɪə'neɪz] n mayonnaise *f*.

mayor [meəʳ] n maire *m*.

mayoress ['meərɪs] n esp *UK* **1.** [female mayor] femme *f* maire **2.** [mayor's wife] femme *f* du maire.

maypole ['meɪpəʊl] n ≃ mai *m*.

may've ['meɪəv] = ***may have***.

maze [meɪz] n *lit* & *fig* labyrinthe *m*, dédale *m*.

MB **1.** (abbr of ***megabyte***) Mo **2.** abbr of ***Manitoba***.

MBA (abbr of ***Master of Business Administration***) n *(titulaire d'une) formation supérieure au management*.

MBBS (abbr of ***Bachelor of Medicine and Surgery***) n *(titulaire d'une) licence de médecine et de chirurgie*.

MBE (abbr of ***Member of the Order of the British Empire***) n *distinction honorifique britannique*.

MBI (abbr of ***management buy-in***) n apport *m* de gestion.

MC abbr of ***master of ceremonies***.

MCAT (abbr of ***Medical College Admissions Test***) n *US test d'admission aux études de médecine*.

MCC (abbr of ***Marylebone Cricket Club***) n *célèbre club de cricket de Londres*.

McCarthyism [mə'kɑːθɪɪzm] n Maccartisme *m*, Maccarthysme *m*.

McCoy [mə'kɔɪ] n *inf* **: the real McCoy** de l'authentique, du vrai de vrai.

MCP (abbr of ***male chauvinist pig***) n *inf* phallo *m*.

MD[1] n **1.** abbr of ***Doctor of Medicine*** **2.** *UK* abbr of ***managing director***.

MD[2] abbr of ***Maryland***.

MDT (abbr of ***Mountain Daylight Time***) n *heure d'été des montagnes Rocheuses*.

me [miː] pers pron **1.** [direct, indirect] me, m' *(+ vowel or silent 'h')* ▸ **can you see/hear me?** tu me vois/m'entends? ▸ **it's me** c'est moi ▸ **they spoke to me** ils m'ont parlé ▸ **she gave it to me** elle me l'a donné **2.** [stressed, after prep, in comparisons *etc*] moi ▸ **you can't expect me to do it** tu ne peux pas exiger que ce soit moi qui le fasse ▸ **she's shorter than me** elle est plus petite que moi.

ME ■ n (abbr of ***myalgic encephalomyelitis***) myélo-encéphalite *f*.
■ abbr of ***Maine***.

meadow ['medəʊ] n prairie *f*, pré *m*.

meagre *UK*, ***meager*** *US* ['miːgəʳ] adj maigre.

meal [miːl] n repas *m* ▸ **to make a meal of sthg** *UK fig* & *pej* faire toute une histoire *OR* tout un plat de qqch.

meals on wheels npl repas *mpl* à domicile *(pour personnes âgées ou handicapées)*.

meal ticket n **1.** *US* ticket *m* restaurant **2.** *inf* [source of income] gagne-pain *m inv*.

mealtime ['miːltaɪm] n heure *f* du repas ▸ **at mealtimes** aux heures des repas.

mealy-mouthed ['miːlɪ'maʊðd] adj *pej* mielleux (euse), patelin(e).

mean [mi:n] ■ **vt** (**pt** & **pp meant**) **1.** [signify] signifier, vouloir dire ▸ **what do you mean?** qu'est-ce que tu veux dire? ▸ **what do you mean by "wrong"?** qu'entendez-vous par "faux"? ▸ **do you mean** *OR* **you mean it's over already?** tu veux dire que c'est déjà fini? ▸ **does the name Heathcliff mean anything to you?** est-ce que le nom de Heathcliff vous dit quelque chose? ▸ **do you mean us?** tu veux dire nous?
2. [matter, be of value] compter ▸ **money means nothing to him** l'argent ne compte pas pour lui ▸ **this watch means a lot to me** je suis très attaché à cette montre ▸ **your friendship means a lot to her** votre amitié compte beaucoup pour elle ▸ **you mean everything to me** tu es tout pour moi
3. [intend] **: to mean to do sthg** vouloir faire qqch, avoir l'intention de faire qqch ▸ **I didn't mean to drop it** je n'ai pas fait exprès de le laisser tomber ▸ **I only meant to help** je voulais seulement me rendre utile ▸ **without meaning to** involontairement ▸ **to be meant for sb/sthg** être destiné(e) à qqn/qqch ▸ **to be meant to do sthg** être censé(e) faire qqch ▸ **they're meant for each other** ils sont faits l'un pour l'autre ▸ **it was meant to be** c'était écrit ▸ **to mean well** agir dans une bonne intention
4. [be serious about] **: I mean it** je suis sérieux(euse) ▸ **I didn't mean it!** [action] je ne l'ai pas fait exprès! / [words] je n'étais pas sérieux!
5. [entail] occasionner, entraîner ▸ **going to see a film means driving into town** pour voir un film, nous sommes obligés de prendre la voiture et d'aller en ville
▸▸ **I mean** [as explanation] c'est vrai / [as correction] je veux dire ▸ **why diet? I mean, you're not exactly fat** pourquoi te mettre au régime? on ne peut pas dire que tu sois grosse.
■ **adj 1.** *UK* [miserly] radin(e), chiche ▸ **to be mean with sthg** être avare de qqch
2. [unkind] mesquin(e), méchant(e) ▸ **to be mean to sb** être mesquin envers qqn ▸ **I feel mean about not inviting her** j'ai un peu honte de ne pas l'avoir invitée
3. [average] moyen(enne)
4. *iro* **: she's no mean singer** elle a de la voix ▸ **that's no mean feat** c'est un véritable exploit.
■ **n** [average] moyenne *f* ; see also ***means***.

meander [mɪ'ændəʳ] **vi** [river, road] serpenter / [person] errer.

meaning ['mi:nɪŋ] **n** sens *m*, signification *f*.

meaningful ['mi:nɪŋfʊl] **adj** [look] significatif(ive) / [relationship, discussion] important(e).

meaningfully ['mi:nɪŋfʊlɪ] **adv** de façon significative.

meaningless ['mi:nɪŋlɪs] **adj** [gesture, word] dénué(e) *OR* vide de sens / [proposal, discussion] sans importance.

meanness ['mi:nnɪs] **n 1.** [stinginess] avarice *f* **2.** [unkindness] mesquinerie *f*, méchanceté *f*.

means [mi:nz] ■ **n** [method, way] moyen *m* ▸ **a means to an end** un moyen d'arriver à ses fins ▸ **by means of** au moyen de.
■ **npl** [money] moyens *mpl*, ressources *fpl*.
◆ ***by all means*** **adv** mais certainement, bien sûr.
◆ ***by no means*** **adv** nullement, en aucune façon.

mean-spirited **adj** mesquin(e).

means test **n** *esp UK enquête sur les ressources d'une personne (qui demande une aide financière à l'État).*

meant [ment] **pt** & **pp** ➤ ***mean***.

meantime ['mi:n,taɪm] **n : in the meantime** en attendant.

meanwhile ['mi:n,waɪl] **adv 1.** [at the same time] pendant ce temps **2.** [between two events] en attendant.

measles ['mi:zlz] **n : (the) measles** la rougeole.

measly ['mi:zlɪ] (**comp -ier**, **superl -iest**) **adj** *inf* misérable, minable.

measurable ['meʒərəbl] **adj** [improvement, deterioration] sensible.

measurably ['meʒərəblɪ] **adv** sensiblement.

measure ['meʒəʳ] ■ **n 1.** [gen] mesure *f* ▸ **we have taken measures to correct the fault** nous avons pris des mesures pour rectifier l'erreur ▸ **to take** *OR* **to get the measure of sb** *fig* jauger qqn, se faire une opinion de qqn **2.** [amount] **: to achieve a measure of independence** parvenir à une certaine indépendance ▸ **for good measure** pour faire bonne mesure **3.** [indication] **: it is a measure of her success that...** la preuve de son succès, c'est que...
4. [ruler] mètre *m*, règle *f*.
■ **vt** & **vi** mesurer ▸ **to measure o.s. against sb** se mesurer à qqn.
◆ ***measure up*** **vi : to measure up (to)** être à la hauteur (de) ▸ **to measure up to sb's expectations** répondre aux espérances de qqn.

measured ['meʒəd] **adj** [steps, tone] mesuré(e).

measurement ['meʒəmənt] **n** mesure *f*.

measuring ['meʒərɪŋ] **n** mesurage *m*.

measuring jug **n** verre *m* gradué, doseur *m*.

measuring tape **n** mètre *m* (à ruban) / [in dressmaking] centimètre *m*.

meat [mi:t] **n** viande *f*.

meatball ['mi:tbɔ:l] **n** boulette *f* de viande.

meat-eater **n** carnivore *mf* ▸ **we aren't big meat-eaters** nous ne mangeons pas beaucoup de viande, nous ne sommes pas de gros mangeurs de viande.

meat-eating **adj** carnivore.

meat loaf (**pl meat loaves**) **n** pain *m* de viande.

meat pie **n** tourte *f* à la viande.

meaty ['mi:tɪ] (**comp -ier**, **superl -iest**) **adj** *fig* important(e).

Mecca ['mekə] **n** La Mecque ▸ **a Mecca for** *fig* la Mecque de.

mechanic [mɪ'kænɪk] **n** mécanicien *m*, -enne *f*.
◆ ***mechanics*** ■ **n** *(U)* [study] mécanique *f*.
■ **npl** *fig* mécanisme *m*.

mechanical [mɪ'kænɪkl] **adj 1.** [device] mécanique **2.** [person, mind] fort(e) en mécanique **3.** [routine, automatic] machinal(e).

mechanical engineer **n** ingénieur *m* mécanicien.

mechanical engineering **n** génie *m* mécanique.

mechanically [mɪ'kænɪklɪ] **adv** mécaniquement / *fig* machinalement, mécaniquement ▸ **mechanically recovered meat** viande *f* séparée mécaniquement.

mechanism ['mekənɪzm] **n** *lit* & *fig* mécanisme *m*.

mechanization, *UK* ***-isation*** [ˌmekənaɪ'zeɪʃn] **n** mécanisation *f*.

mechanize, *UK* ***-ise*** ['mekənaɪz] **vt** & **vi** mécaniser.

MEd [ˌem'ed] (abbr of ***Master of Education***) **n** *(titulaire d'une) maîtrise en sciences de l'éducation*.

medal ['medl] **n** médaille *f*.

medallion [mɪ'dæljən] **n** médaillon *m*.

medallist *UK*, ***medalist*** *US* ['medəlɪst] **n** médaillé *m*, -e *f*.

meddle ['medl] **vi** : **to meddle in** se mêler de.

meddler ['medləʳ] **n 1.** [busybody] : **she's such a meddler** il faut toujours qu'elle fourre son nez partout **2.** [tamperer] touche-à-tout *mf inv*.

meddlesome ['medlsəm] **adj** [person] qui met son nez partout.

media ['mi:djə] ■ **npl** ➤ ***medium***.
■ **n** & **npl** : **the media** les médias *mpl*.

media circus **n** cirque *m* médiatique.

media coverage **n** couverture *f* médiatique, médiatisation *f*.

mediaeval [ˌmedɪ'i:vl] = ***medieval***.

media event **n** événement *m* médiatique.

media hype **n** battage *m* médiatique.

media mix **n** mix média *m*.

median ['mi:djən] ■ **adj** MATHS médian(e).
■ **n** *US* [of road] bande *f* médiane *(qui sépare les deux côtés d'une grande route)*.

media studies **npl** études *fpl* de communication.

mediate ['mi:dɪeɪt] ■ **vt** négocier.
■ **vi** : **to mediate (for/between)** servir de médiateur (pour/entre).

mediation [ˌmi:dɪ'eɪʃn] **n** médiation *f*.

mediator ['mi:dɪeɪtəʳ] **n** médiateur *m*, -trice *f*.

medic ['medɪk] **n 1.** *UK inf* [medical student] carabin *m* **2.** *UK inf* [doctor] toubib *m* **3.** *US* MIL médecin *m* militaire.

Medicaid ['medɪkeɪd] **n** *US assistance médicale aux personnes sans ressources*.

medical ['medɪkl] ■ **adj** médical(e).
■ **n** *UK* examen *m* médical.

medical certificate **n** certificat *m* médical.

medical examination **n** visite *f* médicale.

medical insurance **n** assurance *f* maladie.

medically ['medɪklɪ] **adv** médicalement ▸ **medically approved** approuvé(e) par les autorités médicales.

medical officer **n** [in factory] médecin *m* du travail / MIL médecin militaire.

medical student **n** étudiant *m*, -e *f* en médecine.

medicament ['medɪkəmənt] **n** *fml* médicament *m*.

Medicare ['medɪkeəʳ] **n** *US programme fédéral d'assistance médicale pour personnes âgées et handicapées*.

CULTURE

Medicare/Medicaid

En 1965, deux programmes d'assurances santé sont instaurés aux États-Unis : le **Medicaid** (« la Sécurité sociale ») et le **Medicare** (« l'Aide médicale pour les plus démunis » : enfants, personnes âgées, invalides). Le premier est financé par les cotisations individuelles des assurés, déduites directement de leur salaire ; ceux–ci paient en complément 30 % de leurs frais de santé. Le deuxième système est entièrement subventionné par le gouvernement, qui de nos jours doit engager une réforme afin de pallier le déficit financier des deux systèmes : le nombre de bénéficiaires ne cesse d'augmenter, et d'ici 2011 près de 77 millions de citoyens issus du **baby-boom** devront être pris en charge.

medicated ['medɪkeɪtɪd] **adj** traitant(e).

medication [ˌmedɪ'keɪʃn] **n 1.** [use of medicines] médication *f* **2.** [medicine] médicament *m*.

medicinal [me'dɪsɪnl] **adj** médicinal(e).

medicine ['medsɪn] **n 1.** [subject, treatment] médecine *f* ▸ **Doctor of Medicine** UNIV docteur *m* en médecine **2.** [substance] médicament *m*.

medicine cabinet, ***medicine chest*** **n** (armoire *f* à) pharmacie *f*.

medicine man **n** sorcier *m*.

medieval [ˌmedɪ'i:vl] **adj** médiéval(e).

mediocre [ˌmi:dɪ'əʊkəʳ] **adj** médiocre.

mediocrity [ˌmi:dɪ'ɒkrətɪ] **n** médiocrité *f*.

HOW TO ...

arrange to meet somebody

On pourrait se voir quelque part la semaine prochaine ? / How about meeting up somewhere next week?
Tu es libre demain midi pour déjeuner ? / Are you free for lunch tomorrow?
Nous avons rendez-vous avec l'agent immobilier devant l'immeuble / We're meeting the estate agent in front of the building
On se retrouve à l'entrée du parc, d'accord ? / Let's meet at the entrance to the park. OK?
Mardi 10 h 30, ça vous va ? / Is Tuesday at 10.30 OK for you?
Disons demain, 20 h 30, devant le cinéma / Let's say tomorrow, 8.30, in front of the cinema
Je passerai te prendre chez toi à 8 heures / I'll pick you up at your place at 8 o'clock

meditate ['medɪteɪt] vi : **to meditate (on** *OR* **upon)** méditer (sur).

meditation [,medɪ'teɪʃn] n méditation *f*.

meditative ['medɪtətɪv] adj méditatif(ive).

Mediterranean [,medɪtə'reɪnjən] ■ n 1. [sea] : **the Mediterranean (Sea)** la (mer) Méditerranée 2. [person] Méditerranéen *m*, -enne *f*.
■ adj méditerranéen(enne).

medium ['mi:djəm] ■ adj moyen(enne).
■ n 1. (pl **media** ['mi:djə]) [way of communicating] moyen *m* ▸ **television is a powerful medium in education** la télévision est un très bon instrument éducatif 2. (pl **mediums**) [spiritualist] médium *m* 3. (pl **mediums**) [middle course] milieu *m* ▸ **the happy medium** le juste milieu.

medium-dry adj demi-sec.

medium-range adj : **medium-range missile** missile *m* à moyenne portée.

medium-rare adj CULIN [meat] entre saignant et à point.

medium-size(d) [-saɪz(d)] adj de taille moyenne.

medium-term adj à moyen terme.

medium wave n onde *f* moyenne.

medley ['medlɪ] (pl -s) n 1. [mixture] mélange *m* 2. MUS pot-pourri *m*.

meek [mi:k] adj docile.

meekly ['mi:klɪ] adv docilement.

meet [mi:t] ■ vt (pt & pp met) 1. [gen] rencontrer / [by arrangement] retrouver ▸ **to meet sb on the stairs** croiser qqn dans l'escalier ▸ **I'll meet you on the platform in 20 minutes** je te retrouve sur le quai dans 20 minutes ▸ **I'm meeting Gregory this afternoon** j'ai rendez-vous avec Gregory cet après-midi ▸ **fancy meeting you here!** je ne m'attendais pas à vous trouver ici! ▸ **my eyes met his** nos regards se croisèrent *OR* se rencontrèrent
2. [go to meet - person] aller/venir attendre, aller/venir chercher / [- train, plane] aller attendre ▸ **nobody was at the station to meet me** personne ne m'attendait à la gare ▸ **he'll meet us at the station** il viendra nous chercher à la gare ▸ **I'll be there to meet the bus** je serai là à l'arrivée du car
3. [make acquaintance of] rencontrer, faire la connaissance de ▸ **I met him last year** je l'ai rencontré *OR* j'ai fait sa connaissance l'année dernière ▸ **I'd like you to meet Mr Jones** j'aimerais vous présenter M. Jones ▸ **(I'm very) glad** *OR* **pleased to meet you** enchanté (de faire votre connaissance) ▸ **it's the first case of this sort I've met** c'est la première fois que je vois un cas semblable
4. [need, requirement] satisfaire, répondre à ▸ **supply isn't meeting demand** l'offre est inférieure à la demande
5. [problem] résoudre / [challenge] répondre à
6. [costs] payer ▸ **I couldn't meet the payments** je n'ai pas pu régler *OR* payer les échéances
7. [treat] accueillir ▸ **his suggestion was met with howls of laughter** sa proposition a été accueillie par des éclats de rire.
■ vi (pt & pp **met**) 1. [gen] se rencontrer / [by arrangement] se retrouver / [for a purpose] se réunir ▸ **we met on the stairs** nous nous sommes croisés dans l'escalier ▸ **shall we meet at the station?** on se retrouve *OR* on se donne rendez-vous à la gare? ▸ **we first met in 1989** nous nous sommes rencontrés pour la première fois en 1989 ▸ **have you two met?** est-ce que vous vous connaissez déjà?, vous vous êtes déjà rencontrés? ▸ **until we meet again!** à la prochaine! ▸ **the committee meets once a month** le comité se réunit une fois par mois
2. [join] se joindre ▸ **the cross stands where four roads meet** la croix se trouve à la jonction de quatre routes ▸ **their eyes met** leurs regards se rencontrèrent *OR* se croisèrent.
■ n *US* [meeting] meeting *m*.
◆ ***meet up*** vi se retrouver ▸ **to meet up with sb** rencontrer qqn, retrouver qqn.
◆ ***meet with*** vt insep 1. [encounter - disapproval] être accueilli(e) par / [- success] remporter / [- failure] essuyer ▸ **the agreement met with general approval** l'accord a reçu l'approbation générale
2. *US* [by arrangement] retrouver.

meeting ['mi:tɪŋ] n 1. [for discussions, business] réunion *f* 2. [by chance] rencontre *f* / [by arrangement] entrevue *f* 3. [people at meeting] : **the meeting** l'assemblée *f*.

meeting place n lieu *m* de réunion.

mega- ['megə] prefix méga-.

megabit ['megəbɪt] n COMPUT méga-bit *m*.

megabuck ['megəbʌk] n *US inf* million *m* de dollars.

megabyte ['megəbaɪt] n COMPUT méga-octet *m*.

megahertz ['megəhɜ:ts] n mégahertz *m*.

megalomania [,megələ'meɪnjə] n mégalomanie *f*.

HOW TO ...

chair a meeting

Bonjour à tous. Merci d'être venus / Good morning, everyone. Thank you for coming
Tout le monde est là ? / Is everyone here?
Est-ce qu'il y aura des retardataires ? / Are there going to be any latecomers?
Est-ce qu' on pourrait commencer maintenant ? / Could we make a start now?
Le premier point à l'ordre du jour est le lancement de notre nouveau produit / The first item on the agenda is our new product launch
Pouvons-nous passer au deuxième point ? / Can we move on to the second point?
Faisons la pause café maintenant / Let's break for coffee now
Quelqu'un a un commentaire à ajouter ? / Does anyone else have any further comments?
D'autres questions à l'ordre du jour ? / Any other business?
Si personne n'a plus rien à ajouter, la réunion est terminée / If no one has anything to add, I'll bring this meeting to a close

megalomaniac [ˌmegələ'meɪnɪæk] **n** mégalomane *mf*.

megaphone ['megəfəʊn] **n** mégaphone *m*, porte-voix *m inv*.

megastar ['megəstɑːr] **n** *inf* superstar *f*.

megaton ['megətʌn] **n** mégatonne *f*.

megawatt ['megəwɒt] **n** mégawatt *m*.

melamine ['meləmiːn] **n** mélamine *f*.

melancholic [ˌmelən'kɒlɪk] ■ **adj** mélancolique.
■ **n** mélancolique *mf*.

melancholy ['melənkəlɪ] ■ **adj** [person] mélancolique / [news, facts] triste.
■ **n** mélancolie *f*.

melanin ['melənɪn] **n** mélanine *f*.

melanoma [ˌmelə'nəʊmə] **n** mélanome *m*.

melee, ***mêlée*** ['meleɪ] **n** mêlée *f*.

mellifluous [me'lɪfluəs], ***mellifluent*** [me'lɪfluənt] **adj** *liter* mélodieux(euse).

mellow ['meləʊ] ■ **adj** [light, voice] doux (douce) / [taste, wine] moelleux(euse).
■ **vt** : **to be mellowed by age** s'assagir avec l'âge.
■ **vi** s'adoucir.

mellowing ['meləʊɪŋ] ■ **n 1.** [of fruit, wine] maturation *f* **2.** [of person, mood, light] adoucissement *m* / [of stone] patine *f*.
■ **adj** adoucissant(e).

mellowness ['meləʊnɪs] **n 1.** [of fruit] douceur *f* / [of wine] moelleux *m*, velouté *m* **2.** [of light, colour] douceur *f* / [of voice, music] douceur *f*, mélodie *f* **3.** [of person, mood] douceur *f*, sérénité *f*.

melodic [mɪ'lɒdɪk] **adj** mélodique.

melodious [mɪ'ləʊdjəs] **adj** mélodieux(euse).

melodrama ['melədrɑːmə] **n** mélodrame *m*.

melodramatic [ˌmelədrə'mætɪk] **adj** mélodramatique.

melodramatically [ˌmelədrə'mætɪklɪ] **adv** de façon mélodramatique.

melody ['melədɪ] (pl **-ies**) **n** mélodie *f*.

melon ['melən] **n** melon *m*.

melt [melt] ■ **vt** faire fondre.
■ **vi 1.** [become liquid] fondre **2.** *fig* : **his heart melted at the sight** il fut tout attendri devant ce spectacle **3.** [disappear] : **to melt (away)** fondre ▸ **to melt into the background** s'effacer.
◆ ***melt down*** **vt sep** fondre.

meltdown ['meltdaʊn] **n 1.** PHYS fusion *f* du cœur (du réacteur) **2.** *inf* ECON effondrement *m*.

melting ['meltɪŋ] ■ **adj 1.** *lit* fondant(e) ▸ **melting ice/snow** de la glace/neige qui fond **2.** *fig* attendrissant(e).
■ **n** [of ice, snow] fonte *f* / [of metal] fusion *f*, fonte *f*.

melting point ['meltɪŋ-] **n** point *m* de fusion.

melting pot ['meltɪŋ-] **n** *fig* creuset *m*.

member ['membər] ■ **n** membre *m* / [of club] adhérent *m*, -e *f* ▸ **he became a member of the party in 1985** il a adhéré au parti en 1985 ▸ **you're practically a member of the family now** tu fais presque partie de la famille maintenant.
■ **comp** membre ▸ **member country/state** pays *m*/état *m* membre.

Member of Congress (pl **Members of Congress**) **n** *US* membre *m* du Congrès.

Member of Parliament (pl **Members of Parliament**) **n** *UK* ≃ député *m*.

Member of the Scottish Parliament (pl **Members of the Scottish Parliament**) **n** membre *m* du Parlement écossais.

membership ['membəʃɪp] **n 1.** [of organization] adhésion *f* ▸ **they have applied for membership to the EU** ils ont demandé à entrer dans OR à faire partie de l'UE ▸ **membership fee** cotisation *f* **2.** [number of members] nombre *m* d'adhérents **3.** [members] : **the membership** les membres *mpl*.

membership card **n** carte *f* d'adhésion.

membrane ['membreɪn] **n** membrane *f*.

memento [mɪ'mentəʊ] (pl **-s**) **n** souvenir *m*.

memo ['meməʊ] (pl **-s**) **n** note *f* de service.

memoir ['memwɑːr] **n 1.** [biography] biographie *f* **2.** [essay, monograph] mémoire *m*.

memoirs ['memwɑːz] **npl** mémoires *mpl*.

memo pad **n** bloc-notes *m*.

memorabilia [ˌmemərə'bɪlɪə] **npl** souvenirs *mpl*.

memorable ['memərəbl] **adj** mémorable.

memorably ['memərəblɪ] **adv** : **a memorably hot summer** un été torride dont on se souvient encore.

memorandum [ˌmemə'rændəm] (pl **-da** [-də] OR **-dums**) **n** *fml* note *f* de service.

memorial [mɪ'mɔːrɪəl] ■ **adj** commémoratif(ive).
■ **n** monument *m*.

Memorial Day **n** *US dernier lundi du mois de mai (férié aux États-Unis en l'honneur des soldats américains morts pour la patrie).*

memorize, *UK* ***-ise*** ['meməraɪz] **vt** [phone number, list] retenir / [poem] apprendre par cœur.

memory ['memərɪ] (pl **-ies**) **n 1.** [gen & COMPUT] mémoire *f* ▸ **from memory** de mémoire ▸ **to lose one's memory** perdre la mémoire ▸ **I've got a very good/bad memory for names** j'ai/je n'ai pas une très bonne mémoire des noms ▸ **within living memory** de mémoire d'homme **2.** [event, experience] souvenir *m* ▸ **to have good/bad memories of sthg** garder un bon/mauvais souvenir de qqch ▸ **I have no memory of it** je n'en ai aucun souvenir ▸ **in memory of** en souvenir de.

memory bank **n** bloc *m* de mémoire.

memory card **n** COMPUT carte *f* d'extension mémoire.

men [men] **npl** ➤ ***man***.

menace ['menəs] ■ **n 1.** [gen] menace *f* **2.** *inf* [nuisance] plaie *f*.
■ **vt** menacer.

menacing ['menəsɪŋ] **adj** menaçant(e).

menacingly ['menəsɪŋlɪ] **adv** [speak] d'un ton menaçant / [look] d'un air menaçant.

menagerie [mɪ'nædʒərɪ] **n** ménagerie *f*.

mend [mend] ■ **n** *inf* **: to be on the mend** aller mieux.
■ **vt** réparer / [clothes] raccommoder / [sock, pullover] repriser ▸ **to mend one's ways** s'amender.

mendacity [men'dæsətɪ] (pl **-ies**) **n** *(U)* *fml* mensonge *m*, mensonges *mpl*.

mending ['mendɪŋ] **n : to do the mending** faire le raccommodage.

menfolk ['menfəʊk] **npl** *dated* hommes *mpl*.

menial ['mi:njəl] **adj** avilissant(e).

meningitis [ˌmenɪn'dʒaɪtɪs] **n** *(U)* méningite *f*.

meniscus [mə'nɪskəs] (pl **-es** *OR* **menisci** [-'nɪsaɪ]) **n** ménisque *m*.

menopausal [ˌmenə'pɔ:zl] **adj** ménopausique.

menopause ['menəpɔ:z] **n : the menopause** *UK*, **menopause** *US* la ménopause.

menservants ['mensɜ:vənts] **npl** ➤ ***manservant***.

men's room **n** *US* **: the men's room** les toilettes *fpl* pour hommes.

menstrual ['menstrʊəl] **adj** menstruel(elle).

menstruate ['menstrʊeɪt] **vi** avoir ses règles.

menstruation [ˌmenstrʊ'eɪʃn] **n** menstruation *f*.

menswear ['menzweəʳ] **n** *(U)* vêtements *mpl* pour hommes.

mental ['mentl] **adj** mental(e) / [image, picture] dans la tête.

mental age **n** âge *m* mental.

mental arithmetic **n** calcul *m* mental.

mental block **n** blocage *m* (psychologique).

mental health **n** santé *f* mentale.

mental hospital **n** hôpital *m* psychiatrique.

mentality [men'tælətɪ] **n** mentalité *f*.

mentally ['mentəlɪ] **adv** mentalement ▸ **to be mentally ill** être malade mental (malade mentale) ▸ **to be mentally retarded** être arriéré mental (arriérée mentale).

mentally handicapped ■ **npl : the mentally handicapped** les handicapés *mpl* mentaux.
■ **adj : to be mentally-handicapped** être handicapé mental (handicapée mentale).

mental note **n : to make a mental note to do sthg** prendre note mentalement de faire qqch.

menthol ['menθɒl] **n** menthol *m*.

mentholated ['menθəleɪtɪd] **adj** mentholé(e).

mention ['menʃn] ■ **vt** mentionner, signaler ▸ **I should mention that it was dark at the time** il faut signaler *OR* je tiens à faire remarquer qu'il faisait nuit ▸ **someone, without mentioning any names, has broken my hairdryer** je ne citerai personne, mais quelqu'un a cassé mon séchoir à cheveux ▸ **to mention sb in one's will** coucher qqn sur son testament ▸ **not to mention** sans parler de ▸ **don't mention it!** je vous en prie!
■ **n** mention *f*.

mentor ['mentɔ:ʳ] **n** mentor *m*.

menu ['menju:] **n** [gen & COMPUT] menu *m*.

menu bar **n** COMPUT barre *f* de menu.

menu-driven **adj** COMPUT dirigé(e) par menu.

meow *US* = ***miaow***.

MEP (abbr of ***Member of the European Parliament***) **n** parlementaire *m* européen.

mercantile ['mɜ:kəntaɪl] **adj** *fml* commercial(e).

mercenary ['mɜ:sɪnrɪ] ■ **adj** *pej* mercenaire.
■ **n** (pl **-ies**) mercenaire *m*.

merchandise ['mɜ:tʃəndaɪz] **n** *(U)* marchandises *fpl*.

merchandising ['mɜ:tʃəndaɪzɪŋ] **n** merchandising *m*, marchandisage *m*.

merchant ['mɜ:tʃənt] ■ **adj** marchand(e).
■ **n** marchand *m*, -e *f*, commerçant *m*, -e *f*.

merchant bank **n** banque *f* d'affaires.

merchant banker **n** banquier *m* d'affaires.

merchant navy *UK*, ***merchant marine*** *US* **n** marine *f* marchande.

merchant seaman **n** marin *m* de la marine marchande.

merciful ['mɜ:sɪfʊl] **adj** **1.** [person] clément(e) **2.** [death, release] qui est une délivrance.

mercifully ['mɜ:sɪfʊlɪ] **adv** [fortunately] par bonheur, heureusement.

merciless ['mɜ:sɪlɪs] **adj** impitoyable.

mercilessly ['mɜ:sɪlɪslɪ] **adv** impitoyablement.

mercurial [mɜ:'kjʊərɪəl] **adj** *liter* [temperament] changeant(e), inégal(e) / [person] d'humeur changeante.

mercury ['mɜ:kjʊrɪ] **n** mercure *m*.

Mercury ['mɜ:kjʊrɪ] **n** [planet] Mercure *f*.

mercy ['mɜ:sɪ] (pl **-ies**) **n** **1.** [kindness, pity] pitié *f* ▸ **at the mercy of** à la merci de **2.** [blessing] **: what a mercy that...** quelle chance que...

mercy killing **n** euthanasie *f*.

mere [mɪəʳ] **adj** seul(e) ▸ **she's a mere child** ce n'est qu'une enfant ▸ **it cost a mere £10** cela n'a coûté que 10 livres.

merely ['mɪəlɪ] **adv** seulement, simplement.

meretricious [ˌmerɪ'trɪʃəs] **adj** *fml* factice.

merge [mɜ:dʒ] ■ **vt** COMM & COMPUT fusionner.
■ **vi** **1.** COMM **: to merge (with)** fusionner (avec) **2.** [roads, lines] **: to merge (with)** se joindre (à) **3.** [colours] se fondre.
■ **n** COMPUT fusion *f*.

merger ['mɜ:dʒəʳ] **n** fusion *f*.

meridian [mə'rɪdɪən] **n** méridien *m*.

meringue [mə'ræŋ] **n** meringue *f*.

merino [mə'ri:nəʊ] **adj** de mérinos.

merit ['merɪt] ■ **n** [value] mérite *m*, valeur *f*.
■ **vt** *fml* mériter.
◆ ***merits*** **npl** [advantages] qualités *fpl* ▸ **to judge sthg on its merits** juger qqch selon ses qualités.

meritocracy [ˌmerɪ'tɒkrəsɪ] (pl **-ies**) **n** méritocratie *f*.

mermaid ['mɜːmeɪd] **n** sirène *f*.

merrily ['merɪlɪ] **adv** joyeusement / *iro* allègrement.

merriment ['merɪmənt] **n** hilarité *f*.

merry ['merɪ] (comp **-ier**, superl **-iest**) *UK* **adj 1.** [happy] joyeux(euse) ▸ **Merry Christmas!** joyeux Noël! **2.** *inf* [tipsy] gai(e), éméché(e).

merry-go-round **n** manège *m*.

merrymaking ['merɪˌmeɪkɪŋ] **n** *(U)* réjouissances *fpl*.

mesh [meʃ] ■ **n** maille *f* (du filet) ▸ **wire mesh** grillage *m*.
■ **vi** [gears] s'engrener.

mesmerize, *UK* ***-ise*** ['mezməraɪz] **vt : to be mesmerized by** être fasciné(e) par.

mess [mes] **n 1.** [untidy state] désordre *m* / *fig* gâchis *m* ▸ **to be (in) a mess** [room] être en désordre / [hair] être ébouriffé / *fig* [life] être sens dessus dessous **2.** MIL mess *m*.
◆ ***mess around***, ***mess about*** *UK inf* ■ **vt sep : to mess sb around** traiter qqn par-dessus *OR* par-dessous la jambe.
■ **vi 1.** [fool around] perdre *OR* gaspiller son temps **2.** [interfere] **: to mess around with sthg** s'immiscer dans qqch.
◆ ***mess up*** **vt sep** *inf* **1.** [room] mettre en désordre / [clothes] salir **2.** *fig* [spoil] gâcher.
◆ ***mess with*** **vt insep** *inf* **: don't mess with them** tiens-toi à l'écart.

message ['mesɪdʒ] **n** message *m* ▸ **to get one's message across** se faire comprendre ▸ **to get the message** *inf* piger.

message switching [-'swɪtʃɪŋ] **n** COMPUT commutation *f* de messages.

messenger ['mesɪndʒəʳ] **n** messager *m*, -ère *f* ▸ **by messenger** par porteur.

messiah [mɪ'saɪə] **n** messie *m*.
◆ ***Messiah*** **n : the Messiah** le Messie.

messianic [ˌmesɪ'ænɪk] **adj** messianique.

messily ['mesɪlɪ] **adv 1.** [untidily] mal, de façon peu soignée / [in a disorganized way] n'importe comment ▸ **the affair ended messily** *fig* l'affaire s'est mal terminée **2.** [dirtily] comme un cochon.

Messrs, ***Messrs.*** (abbr of ***messieurs***) ['mesəz] MM.

messy ['mesɪ] (comp **-ier**, superl **-iest**) **adj 1.** [dirty] sale / [untidy] désordonné(e) ▸ **a messy job** un travail salissant **2.** *inf* [divorce] difficile / [situation] embrouillé(e).

met [met] **pt** & **pp** ➤ ***meet***.

Met [met] **n 1.** (abbr of ***Metropolitan Opera***) ▸ **the Met** l'opéra *m* de New-York **2.** (abbr of ***Metropolitan Museum of Art (in New York)***) ▸ **the Met** le musée d'Art Moderne de New-York **3.** (abbr of ***Metropolitan Police***)) ▸ **the Met** la police de Londres.

metabolic [ˌmetə'bɒlɪk] **adj** métabolique.

metabolism [mɪ'tæbəlɪzm] **n** métabolisme *m*.

metabolize, *UK* ***-ise*** [mɪ'tæbəlaɪz] **vt** métaboliser.

metal ['metl] ■ **n** métal *m*.
■ **comp** en *OR* de métal.

metal detector **n** détecteur *m* de métaux.

metallic [mɪ'tælɪk] **adj 1.** [sound, ore] métallique **2.** [paint, finish] métallisé(e).

metallurgist [me'tælədʒɪst] **n** métallurgiste *m*.

metallurgy [me'tælədʒɪ] **n** métallurgie *f*.

metalwork ['metəlwɜːk] **n** [craft] ferronnerie *f*.

metalworker ['metəlˌwɜːkəʳ] **n** [craftsman] ferronnier *m* / [in industry] métallurgiste *m*.

metamorphose [ˌmetə'mɔːfəʊz] **vi : to metamorphose (into)** se métamorphoser (en).

metamorphosis [ˌmetə'mɔːfəsɪs *OR* ˌmetəmɔː'fəʊsɪs] (pl **-phoses** [-'fəʊsiːz]) **n** métamorphose *f*.

metaphor ['metəfəʳ] **n** métaphore *f*.

metaphorical [ˌmetə'fɒrɪkl] **adj** métaphorique.

metaphorically [ˌmetə'fɒrɪklɪ] **adv** métaphoriquement ▸ **metaphorically speaking** métaphoriquement.

metaphysical [ˌmetə'fɪzɪkl] **adj** métaphysique.

metaphysically [ˌmetə'fɪzɪklɪ] **adv** métaphysiquement.

metaphysics [ˌmetə'fɪzɪks] **n** *(U)* métaphysique *f*.

mete [miːt] ◆ ***mete out*** **vt sep** *fml* [punishment] infliger.

meteor ['miːtɪəʳ] **n** météore *m*.

meteoric [miːtɪ'ɒrɪk] **adj** météorique.

meteorite ['miːtjəraɪt] **n** météorite *m ou f*.

meteorological [ˌmiːtjərə'lɒdʒɪkl] **adj** météorologique.

meteorologist [miːtjə'rɒlədʒɪst] **n** météorologue *mf*, météorologiste *mf*.

meteorology [miːtjə'rɒlədʒɪ] **n** météorologie *f*.

meter ['miːtəʳ] ■ **n 1.** [device] compteur *m* ▸ **parking meter** parcmètre *m* **2.** *US* = ***metre***.
■ **vt** [gas, electricity] établir la consommation de.

metered ['miːtəd] **adj** décompté(e) à la minute.

methadon(e) ['meθədəʊn] **n** méthadone *f*.

methane ['miːθeɪn] **n** méthane *m*.

methinks [mɪ'θɪŋks] (pt **methought** [-'θɔːt]) **vb** *dated & hum* ce me semble.

method ['meθəd] **n** méthode *f*.

methodical [mɪ'θɒdɪkl] **adj** méthodique.

methodically [mɪ'θɒdɪklɪ] **adv** méthodiquement.

Methodist ['meθədɪst] ■ **adj** méthodiste.
■ **n** méthodiste *mf*.

methodological [ˌmeθədə'lɒdʒɪkl] **adj** *fml* méthodologique.

methodology [ˌmeθə'dɒlədʒɪ] (pl **-ies**) **n** *fml* méthodologie *f*.

meths [meθs] **n** *(U) UK inf* alcool *m* à brûler.

methyl alcohol **n** méthanol *m*, alcool *m* méthylique.

methylated spirits ['meθɪleɪtɪd-] **n** *(U)* alcool *m* à brûler.

meticulous [mɪ'tɪkjʊləs] **adj** méticuleux(euse).

meticulously [mɪ'tɪkjʊləslɪ] **adv** méticuleusement.

meticulousness [mɪ'tɪkjʊləsnɪs] **n** minutie *f*, méticulosité *f* ▸ **with great meticulousness** avec un soin tout particulier.

Met Office (abbr of ***Meteorological Office***) **n** *la météo britannique*.

metre *UK*, ***meter*** *US* ['miːtəʳ] **n** mètre *m*.

metric ['metrɪk] **adj** métrique.

metrical ['metrɪkl] **adj** LIT métrique.

metrication [ˌmetrɪ'keɪʃn] **n** *UK* adoption *f* du système métrique.

metric system **n : the metric system** le système métrique.

metric ton **n** tonne *f*.

metro ['metrəʊ] (pl -s) **n** métro *m*.

metronome ['metrənəʊm] **n** métronome *m*.

metropolis [mɪ'trɒpəlɪs] (pl -es [-iːz]) **n** métropole *f*.

metropolitan [ˌmetrə'pɒlɪtn] **adj** métropolitain(e).

Metropolitan Police **npl : the Metropolitan Police** la police de Londres.

mettle ['metl] **n : to be on one's mettle** être d'attaque ▸ **to show** *OR* **prove one's mettle** montrer ce dont on est capable.

mew [mjuː] = ***miaow***.

mews [mjuːz] (pl **mews**) **n** *UK* ruelle *f*.

Mexican ['meksɪkn] ■ **adj** mexicain(e).
■ **n** Mexicain *m*, -e *f*.

Mexican wave **n** ola *f*.

Mexico ['meksɪkəʊ] **n** Mexique *m* ▸ **in Mexico** au Mexique.

Mexico City **n** Mexico.

mezzanine ['metsəniːn] **n 1.** [floor] mezzanine *f* **2.** *US* [in theatre] corbeille *f*.

mezzo-soprano (pl **mezzo-sopranos**) **n 1.** [singer] mezzo-soprano *f* **2.** [voice] mezzo-soprano *m*.

MFA (abbr of ***Master of Fine Arts***) **n** *(titulaire d'une) maîtrise en beaux-arts*.

mfr abbr of ***manufacturer***.

mg (abbr of ***milligram***) mg.

Mgr **1.** (abbr of ***Monseigneur, Monsignor***) Mgr **2.** abbr of ***manager***.

MHR *US* & *Aus* abbr of ***Member of the House of Representatives***.

MHz (abbr of ***megahertz***) MHz.

MI5 (abbr of ***Military Intelligence 5***) **n** *service de contre-espionnage britannique*.

MI6 (abbr of ***Military Intelligence 6***) **n** *service de renseignements britannique*.

MIA (abbr of ***missing in action***) *expression indiquant qu'une personne a disparu lors d'un combat*.

miaow *UK* [miː'aʊ], ***meow*** *US* [mɪ'aʊ] ■ **n** miaulement *m*, miaou *m*.
■ **vi** miauler.

mice [maɪs] **npl** ➤ ***mouse***.

Mich. abbr of ***Michigan***.

Michigan ['mɪʃɪgən] **n** Michigan *m* ▸ **in Michigan** dans le Michigan.

mickey ['mɪkɪ] **n : to take the mickey out of sb** *UK inf* se payer la tête de qqn, faire marcher qqn.

MICR (abbr of ***magnetic ink character recognition***) **n** *reconnaissance magnétique de caractères*.

micro ['maɪkrəʊ] (pl -s) **n** micro *m*.

micro- ['maɪkrəʊ] **prefix** micro-.

microbe ['maɪkrəʊb] **n** microbe *m*.

microbiologist [ˌmaɪkrəʊbaɪ'ɒlədʒɪst] **n** microbiologiste *mf*.

microbiology [ˌmaɪkrəʊbaɪ'ɒlədʒɪ] **n** microbiologie *f*.

microchip ['maɪkrəʊtʃɪp] **n** COMPUT puce *f*.

microcircuit ['maɪkrəʊˌsɜːkɪt] **n** microcircuit *m*.

microcomputer [ˌmaɪkrəʊkəm'pjuːtəʳ] **n** micro-ordinateur *m*.

microcomputing [ˌmaɪkrəʊkəm'pjuːtɪŋ] **n** micro-informatique *f*.

microcosm ['maɪkrəkɒzm] **n** microcosme *m*.

microelectronics ['maɪkrəʊɪˌlek'trɒnɪks] **n** *(U)* microélectronique *f*.

microfiche ['maɪkrəʊfiːʃ] (pl **microfiche** *OR* -s) **n** microfiche *f*.

microfilm ['maɪkrəʊfɪlm] **n** microfilm *m*.

microlight ['maɪkrəlaɪt] **n** ULM *m*.

micromarketing [ˌmaɪkrəʊ'mɑːkɪtɪŋ] **n** micromarketing *m*.

micromesh ['maɪkrəʊmeʃ] **n** maille *f* super-fine.

micron ['maɪkrɒn] **n** micron *m*.

microorganism [ˌmaɪkrəʊ'ɔːgənɪzm] **n** micro-organisme *m*.

microphone ['maɪkrəfəʊn] **n** microphone *m*, micro *m*.

microprocessor ['maɪkrəʊˌprəʊsesəʳ] **n** COMPUT microprocesseur *m*.

microprogram ['maɪkrəʊˌprəʊgræm] **n** microprogramme *m*.

micro scooter **n** trottinette *f* pliante.

microscope ['maɪkrəskəʊp] **n** microscope *m*.

microscopic [ˌmaɪkrə'skɒpɪk] **adj** microscopique.

microscopically [ˌmaɪkrə'skɒpɪklɪ] **adv** [examine] au microscope ▸ **microscopically small** invisible à l'œil nu.

microsecond ['maɪkrəʊˌsekənd] **n** microseconde *m*.

microsurgery [ˌmaɪkrə'sɜːdʒərɪ] **n** microchirurgie *f*.

microwave ['maɪkrəweɪv] ■ **n 1.** PHYS micro-onde *f* **2.** = ***microwave oven***.
■ **vt** faire cuire au micro-ondes.

microwaveable ['maɪkrəʊˌweɪvəbl] **adj** micro-ondable.

microwave oven **n** four *m* à micro-ondes *m*.

mid [mɪd] ■ **adj 1.** [middle] **: in mid October** à la mi-octobre, au milieu du mois d'octobre ▸ **he's in his mid fifties** il a environ 55 ans ▸ **she stopped in mid sentence** elle s'est arrêtée au milieu de sa phrase, sa phrase est restée en suspens **2.** [half] **: mid green** vert ni clair ni foncé **3.** [central] central(e), du milieu ▸ **mid Wales** le centre *OR* la région centrale du pays de Galles.
■ **prep** *liter* = ***amid***.

mid- [mɪd] **prefix : mid-height** mi-hauteur ▸ **mid-morning** milieu de la matinée ▸ **mid-winter** plein hiver.

midair [mɪd'eəʳ] ■ **adj** en plein ciel.
■ **n : in midair** en plein ciel.

mid-Atlantic ■ **adj** [accent] américanisé(e).
■ **n : in (the) mid-Atlantic** au milieu de l'Atlantique.

midday [mɪd'deɪ] **n** midi *m*.

middle ['mɪdl] ■ **adj 1.** [centre] du milieu, du centre **2.** [in time] **: she was in her middle twenties** elle avait dans les 25 ans.
■ **n 1.** [centre] milieu *m*, centre *m* ▸ **in the middle (of)** au milieu (de) ▸ **in the middle of nowhere** en pleine cambrousse **2.** [in time] milieu *m* ▸ **to be in the middle of doing sthg** être en train de faire qqch ▸ **to be in the middle of a meeting** être en pleine réunion ▸ **in the middle of the night** au milieu de la nuit, en pleine nuit **3.** [waist] taille *f*.

middle age **n** âge *m* mûr.

middle-aged **adj** d'une cinquantaine d'années.

Middle Ages **npl : the Middle Ages** le Moyen Âge.

Middle America **n 1.** GEOG Amérique *f* centrale **2.** [sector of society] l'Amérique *f* moyenne ⁄ *pej* l'Amérique *f* bien pensante.

middlebrow ['mɪdlbraʊ] ■ **n** *pej* [reader] lecteur *m* moyen, lectrice *f* moyenne ⁄ [audience] spectateur *m* moyen, spectatrice *f* moyenne.
■ **adj** [reader, audience] moyen(enne) ▸ **their music's very middlebrow** leur musique s'adresse à un public moyen ▸ **middlebrow programmes** programmes s'adressant à un public moyen.

middle-class **adj** bourgeois(e).

middle classes **npl : the middle classes** la bourgeoisie.

middle distance **n : in the middle distance** au second plan.

middle ear **n** ANAT oreille *f* moyenne.

Middle East **n : the Middle East** le Moyen-Orient.

Middle Eastern **adj** du Moyen-Orient.

Middle England **n** l'Angleterre *f* moyenne.

middle finger **n** majeur *m*.

middle ground **n 1.** [in picture] second plan *m* **2.** *fig* terrain *m* neutre.

middleman ['mɪdlmæn] (**pl -men** [-men]) **n** intermédiaire *mf*.

middle management **n** *(U)* cadres *mpl* moyens.

middle name **n** second prénom *m*.

middle-of-the-road **adj** modéré(e).

middle school **n** *UK* ≃ premier cycle *m* du secondaire.

middleweight ['mɪdlweɪt] **n** poids *m* moyen.

middling ['mɪdlɪŋ] **adj** moyen(enne).

Middx (abbr of ***Middlesex***) *ancien comté anglais*.

Mideast [,mɪd'i:st] **n** *US* **: the Mideast** le Moyen-Orient.

midfield [,mɪd'fi:ld] **n** FOOTBALL milieu *m* de terrain.

midge [mɪdʒ] **n** moucheron *m*.

midget ['mɪdʒɪt] **n** *offens* nain *m*, -e *f*.

midi system, MIDI system ['mɪdɪ-] **n** *UK* chaîne *f* midi.

Midlands ['mɪdləndz] **npl : the Midlands** *les comtés du centre de l'Angleterre*.

midlife crisis **n : he's having** OR **going through a midlife crisis** il a du mal à passer le cap de la cinquantaine.

midnight ['mɪdnaɪt] ■ **n** minuit *m*.
■ **comp** de minuit.

midpoint ['mɪdpɔɪnt] **n** [in space, time] milieu *m*.

mid-range **adj** COMM [computer, car] de milieu de gamme.

midriff ['mɪdrɪf] **n** diaphragme *m*.

midst [mɪdst] **n** *fml* **1.** [in space] **: in the midst of** au milieu de ▸ **in our midst** parmi nous **2.** [in time] **: to be in the midst of doing sthg** être en train de faire qqch.

midstream [mɪd'stri:m] **n : in midstream** [in river] au milieu du courant ⁄ *fig* [when talking] en plein milieu.

midsummer ['mɪd,sʌməʳ] **n** cœur *m* de l'été.

Midsummer Day **n** 24 juin.

midterm [mɪd'tɜ:m] **n 1.** SCH & UNIV milieu *m* du trimestre **2.** MED [of pregnancy] milieu *m*.

mid-term election **n** *US* élection *f* de mi-mandat.

midway [,mɪd'weɪ] **adv 1.** [in space] **: midway (between)** à mi-chemin (entre) **2.** [in time] **: midway through the meeting** en pleine réunion.

midweek ■ **adj** ['mɪdwi:k] du milieu de la semaine.
■ **adv** [mɪd'wi:k] en milieu de semaine.

Midwest [,mɪd'west] **n : the Midwest** le Midwest.

Midwestern [,mɪd'westən] **adj** du Midwest.

midwife ['mɪdwaɪf] (**pl -wives** [-waɪvz]) **n** sage-femme *f*.

midwifery ['mɪd,wɪfərɪ] **n** obstétrique *f*.

midwinter [,mɪd'wɪntəʳ] **n** [solstice] solstice *m* d'hiver ▸ **in midwinter** au milieu de l'hiver.

miffed [mɪft] **adj** *inf* vexé(e).

might [maɪt] ■ **modal vb 1.** [expressing possibility] **: I might be home late tonight** je rentrerai peut-être tard ce soir ▸ **the criminal might be armed** il est possible que le criminel soit armé ▸ **why not come with us? – I might** pourquoi ne viens-tu pas avec nous? – peut-être ▸ **she might have decided not to go** il se peut qu'elle ait décidé de ne pas y aller ▸ **you might well be right** il se pourrait bien que vous ayez raison
2. [expressing suggestion] **: it might be better to wait** il vaut peut-être mieux attendre ▸ **you might try using a different approach altogether** vous pourriez adopter une approche entièrement différente
3. *fml* [asking permission] **: might I interrupt?** puis-je me permettre de vous interrompre? ▸ **might I** OR **if I might make a suggestion?** puis-je me permettre de suggérer quelque chose? ▸ **he asked if he might leave the room** il demanda s'il pouvait sortir de la pièce
4. [commenting on statement] **: that, I might add, was not my idea** cela n'était pas mon idée, soit dit en passant

5. [ought to] : **you might at least tidy up your room!** tu pourrais au moins ranger ta chambre! ▸ **you might have warned me!** tu aurais pu me prévenir! ▸ **I might have known** *OR* **guessed** j'aurais dû m'en douter
▸▸ **we might as well go home (as stay here)** nous ferions aussi bien de rentrer chez nous (plutôt que de rester ici).
■ **n** *(U)* force *f* ▸ **with all one's might** de toutes ses forces.

mightily ['maɪtɪlɪ] **adv 1.** [with vigour] avec vigueur, vigoureusement **2.** [extremely] extrêmement.

mightn't ['maɪtənt] = ***might not***.

might've ['maɪtəv] = ***might have***.

mighty ['maɪtɪ] *esp UK* ■ **adj** (comp **-ier**, superl **-iest**) **1.** [powerful] puissant(e) **2.** [very large] imposant(e).
■ **adv** *US inf* drôlement, vachement.

migraine ['mi:greɪn *OR* 'maɪgreɪn] **n** migraine *f*.

migrant ['maɪgrənt] ■ **adj** [bird, animal] migrateur(trice).
■ **n 1.** [bird, animal] migrateur *m* **2.** [person] émigré *m*, -e *f*.

migrant worker **n** [seasonal] travailleur *m* saissonnier, travailleuse saissonnière *f* / [foreign] travailleur *m* immigré, travailleuse immigrée *f*.

migrate [*UK* maɪ'greɪt, *US* 'maɪgreɪt] **vi 1.** [bird, animal] migrer **2.** [person] émigrer.

migration [maɪ'greɪʃn] **n** migration *f*.

migratory ['maɪgrətrɪ] **adj** [bird] migrateur(trice) / [journey] migratoire.

mike [maɪk] (abbr of ***microphone***) **n** *inf* micro *m*.

mild [maɪld] ■ **adj 1.** [disinfectant, reproach] léger(ère) **2.** [tone, weather] doux (douce) **3.** [illness] bénin(igne).
■ **n** *bière anglaise légère*.

mildew ['mɪldju:] **n** *(U)* moisissure *f*.

mildly ['maɪldlɪ] **adv 1.** [gently] doucement ▸ **that's putting it mildly** c'est le moins qu'on puisse dire **2.** [not strongly] légèrement **3.** [slightly] un peu.

mild-mannered **adj** mesuré(e), calme.

mildness ['maɪldnɪs] **n** *(U)* douceur *f*.

mile [maɪl] **n** mile *m* / NAUT mille *m* ▸ **you can see for miles** on peut voir sur des kilomètres ▸ **to walk for miles** marcher pendant des kilomètres ▸ **you can see it a mile off** ça se voit de loin ▸ **it's miles from anywhere** c'est un endroit complètement isolé ▸ **not a million miles from here** tout près d'ici, parmi nous ▸ **this is miles better** c'est cent fois mieux ▸ **to be miles away** *fig* être très loin.

mileage ['maɪlɪdʒ] **n** distance *f* en miles, ≃ kilométrage *m*.

mileage (allowance) **n** ≃ indemnité *f* kilométrique.

mil(e)ometer [maɪ'lɒmɪtəʳ] **n** *UK* compteur *m* de miles, ≃ compteur kilométrique.

milepost ['maɪlpəʊst] **n** ≃ borne *f* (kilométrique).

milestone ['maɪlstəʊn] **n** [marker stone] borne *f* / *fig* événement *m* marquant *OR* important.

milieu [*UK* 'mi:ljɜ:, *US* mi:l'ju:] (pl **-s** *OR* **-x** [-z]) **n** milieu *m*.

militancy ['mɪlɪtənsɪ] **n** militantisme *m*.

militant ['mɪlɪtənt] ■ **adj** militant(e).
■ **n** militant *m*, -e *f*.

militarism ['mɪlɪtərɪzm] **n** militarisme *m*.

militarist ['mɪlɪtərɪst] **n** militariste *mf*.

militaristic [ˌmɪlɪtə'rɪstɪk] **adj** militariste.

militarized zone, *UK* ***militarised zone*** ['mɪlɪtəraɪzd-] **n** zone *f* militarisée.

military ['mɪlɪtrɪ] ■ **adj** militaire.
■ **n** : **the military** les militaires *mpl*, l'armée *f*.

military police **n** police *f* militaire.

militate ['mɪlɪteɪt] **vi** *fml* : **to militate against** militer contre.

militia [mɪ'lɪʃə] **n** milice *f*.

militiaman [mɪ'lɪʃəmən] (pl **-men** [-mən]) **n** milicien *m*.

milk [mɪlk] ■ **n** lait *m*.
■ **vt 1.** [cow] traire **2.** *fig* [use to own ends] exploiter.

milk chocolate ■ **n** chocolat *m* au lait.
■ **comp** au chocolat au lait.

milk float *UK*, ***milk truck*** *US* **n** voiture *f* de laitier.

milking ['mɪlkɪŋ] **n** traite *f*.

milking machine **n** machine *f* à traire, trayeuse *f*.

milkman ['mɪlkmən] (pl **-men** [-mən]) **n** laitier *m*, -ière *f*.

milk powder **n** lait *m* en poudre.

milk round **n** *UK* [by milkman] tournée *f* du laitier.

milk shake **n** milk-shake *m*.

milk tooth **n** *UK* dent *m* de lait.

milk truck *US* = ***milk float***.

milky ['mɪlkɪ] (comp **-ier**, superl **-iest**) **adj 1.** [coffee] avec beaucoup de lait **2.** [pale white] laiteux(euse).

Milky Way **n** : **the Milky Way** la Voie lactée.

mill [mɪl] ■ **n 1.** [flourmill, grinder] moulin *m* **2.** [factory] usine *f*.
■ **vt** moudre.
◆ ***mill about***, ***mill around*** **vi** grouiller.

millenarian [ˌmɪlɪ'neərɪən] ■ **adj** millénariste.
■ **n** millénariste *mf*.

millennial [mɪ'lenɪəl] **adj** du millenium.

millennium [mɪ'lenɪəm] (pl **millennia** [mɪ'lenɪə]) **n** millénaire *m*.

millepede ['mɪlɪpi:d] = ***millipede***.

miller ['mɪləʳ] **n** meunier *m*, -ière *f*.

millet ['mɪlɪt] **n** millet *m*.

milli- ['mɪlɪ] **prefix** milli-.

millibar ['mɪlɪbɑ:ʳ] **n** millibar *m*.

milligram, *UK* ***milligramme*** ['mɪlɪgræm] **n** milligramme *m*.

millilitre *UK*, ***milliliter*** *US* ['mɪlɪˌli:təʳ] **n** millilitre *m*.

millimetre *UK*, ***millimeter*** *US* ['mɪlɪˌmi:təʳ] **n** millimètre *m*.

millinery ['mɪlɪnrɪ] **n** chapellerie *f* féminine.

million ['mɪljən] **n** million *m* ▸ **his secretary is one in a million** sa secrétaire est une perle rare ▸ **that man is**

worth several million cet homme est plusieurs fois milliardaire ▸ **a million, millions of** *fig* des milliers de, un million de ▸ **there were simply millions of people at the concert!** il y avait un monde fou au concert!

millionaire [ˌmɪljə'neər] **n** millionnaire *mf*.

millionairess [ˌmɪljə'neərɪs] **n** *dated* millionnaire *f*.

millionth ['mɪljənθ] ■ **num** millionième.
■ **n 1.** [ordinal] millionième *mf* **2.** [fraction] millionième *m*.

millipede ['mɪlɪpi:d] **n** mille-pattes *m inv*.

millisecond ['mɪlɪˌsekənd] **n** millième *m* de seconde.

millstone ['mɪlstəʊn] **n** meule *f* ▸ **he's like a millstone around my neck** c'est un boulet que je traîne.

millwheel ['mɪlwi:l] **n** roue *f* de moulin.

milometer [maɪ'lɒmɪtər] *UK* = ***mileometer***.

mime [maɪm] ■ **n** mime *m*.
■ **vt** & **vi** mimer.

mimic ['mɪmɪk] ■ **n** imitateur *m*, -trice *f*.
■ **vt** (**pt** & **pp -ked, cont -king**) imiter.

mimicry ['mɪmɪkrɪ] **n** imitation *f*.

mimosa [mɪ'məʊzə] **n** mimosa *m*.

min. [mɪn] **1.** (abbr of ***minute***) mn, min **2.** (abbr of ***minimum***) min.

Min. abbr of ***ministry***.

minaret [mɪnə'ret] **n** minaret *m*.

mince [mɪns] ■ **n** *UK* viande *f* hachée.
■ **vt** *UK* [garlic] hacher.
■ **vi** marcher à petits pas maniérés.

mincemeat ['mɪnsmi:t] **n 1.** [fruit] *mélange de pommes, raisins secs et épices utilisé en pâtisserie* **2.** *UK* [meat] viande *f* hachée.

mince pie **n** tartelette *f* de Noël.

mincer ['mɪnsər] **n** *UK* hachoir *m*.

mind [maɪnd] ■ **n 1.** [gen] esprit *m* ▸ **state of mind** état d'esprit ▸ **to be of sound mind** être sain(e) d'esprit ▸ **to bear sthg in mind** ne pas oublier qqch ▸ **to call sthg to mind** se rappeler qqch ▸ **to cast one's mind back to sthg** repenser à qqch ▸ **to come into/cross sb's mind** venir à/traverser l'esprit de qqn ▸ **to have sthg on one's mind** avoir l'esprit préoccupé, être préoccupé(e) par qqch ▸ **to keep an open mind** réserver son jugement ▸ **my mind has gone blank** j'ai un trou de mémoire ▸ **the trip took her mind off her worries** ce petit voyage lui a changé les idées ▸ **that's a load** *OR* **weight off my mind!** je me sens soulagé, quel soulagement! ▸ **it went clean** *OR* **right out of my mind** cela m'est complètement sorti de l'esprit *OR* de la tête ▸ **at the back of one's mind** au fond de soi-même ▸ **to put sthg to the back of one's mind** chasser qqch de son esprit ▸ **you must put the idea out of your mind** tu dois te sortir cette idée de la tête ▸ **to have sthg in mind** avoir qqch dans l'idée ▸ **no one in their right mind would do such a thing** aucune personne sensée n'agirait ainsi ▸ **to have one's mind set on sthg** vouloir qqch à tout prix ▸ **to have a mind to do sthg** avoir bien envie de faire qqch ▸ **to broaden one's mind** enrichir l'esprit ▸ **to make one's mind up** se décider ▸ **to put** *OR* **set sb's mind at rest** rassurer qqn
2. [attention] **: to put one's mind to sthg** s'appliquer à qqch ▸ **to keep one's mind on sthg** se concentrer sur qqch ▸ **I can't seem to apply my mind to the problem** je n'arrive pas à me concentrer sur le problème ▸ **to slip one's mind** sortir de l'esprit
3. [opinion] **: to change one's mind** changer d'avis ▸ **to my mind** à mon avis ▸ **to be of the same** *OR* **of like** *OR* **of one mind** être du même avis ▸ **to speak one's mind** parler franchement ▸ **to be in** *UK* *OR* **of** *US* **two minds (about sthg)** se tâter *OR* être indécis(e) (à propos de qqch)
4. [person] cerveau *m* ▸ **great minds think alike** les grands esprits se rencontrent.
■ **vi 1.** [be bothered] **: I don't mind** ça m'est égal ▸ **I hope you don't mind** j'espère que vous n'y voyez pas d'inconvénient ▸ **do you mind if I open the window?** cela vous dérange si j'ouvre la fenêtre? ▸ **would you mind if I opened the window?** est-ce que cela vous ennuierait si j'ouvrais la fenêtre? ▸ **I don't mind if people laugh at me – but you should mind!** je ne me soucie guère que les gens se moquent de moi – mais vous devriez! ▸ **do you mind!** *iro* [politely] vous permettez? / [indignantly] non mais! ▸ **never mind** [don't worry] ne t'en fais pas / [it's not important] ça ne fait rien
2. [be careful] **: mind out!** *UK* attention!
■ **vt 1.** [be bothered about, dislike] **: I don't mind waiting** ça ne me gêne *OR* dérange pas d'attendre ▸ **I really don't mind what he says/thinks** je me fiche de ce qu'il peut dire/penser ▸ **I don't mind him** il ne me dérange pas ▸ **do you mind me smoking?** cela ne vous ennuie *OR* dérange pas que je fume? ▸ **did you mind me inviting her?** tu aurais peut-être préféré que je ne l'invite pas?, ça t'ennuie que je l'aie invitée? ▸ **would you mind turning out the light, please?** [politely] pourriez-vous éteindre la lumière, s'il vous plaît? / [aggressively] est-ce que cela vous dérangerait beaucoup d'éteindre la lumière? ▸ **I wouldn't mind a beer** je prendrais bien une bière
2. *esp UK* [pay attention to] faire attention à, prendre garde à ▸ **mind your own business!** occupe-toi de ce qui te regarde!, mêle-toi de tes oignons! ▸ **mind your language!** surveille ton langage! ▸ **'mind the step'** 'attention à la marche' ▸ **mind you don't break it** fais bien attention de ne pas le casser ▸ **mind what you're doing!** regarde ce que tu fais! ▸ **never mind that now** [leave it] ne vous occupez pas de cela tout de suite / [forget it] ce n'est plus la peine de s'en occuper
3. *esp UK* [take care of - luggage] garder, surveiller / [- shop] tenir.
◆ ***mind you*** **adv** remarquez ▸ **mind you, I'm not surprised** remarque *OR* tu sais, cela ne m'étonne pas.

mind-bending [-ˌbendɪŋ] **adj** *inf* hallucinant(e).

mind-blowing **adj** *inf* [amazing] époustouflant(e).

mind-boggling **adj** extraordinaire, stupéfiant(e).

-minded [ˌmaɪndɪd] **suffix 1.** *(with adj)* **: simple-minded** simple d'esprit ▸ **they're so narrow-minded** ils sont tellement étroits d'esprit **2.** *(with adv)* **: to be politically-minded** s'intéresser beaucoup à la politique ▸ **to be scientifically-minded** avoir l'esprit scientifique **3.** *(with n)* **: to be very money-minded** avoir un faible pour l'argent *OR* être très porté(e) sur l'argent.

minder ['maɪndər] **n** *UK inf* [bodyguard] ange *m* gardien.

mindful ['maɪndfʊl] **adj : mindful of** [risks] attentif(ive) à / [responsibility] soucieux(euse) de.

mindless ['maɪndlɪs] **adj** stupide, idiot(e).

mind reader **n : I'm not a mind reader** *hum* je ne suis pas devin.

mindset ['maɪndset] **n** façon *f* de voir les choses.

mind's eye **n : in my mind's eye** dans mon imagination.

mine [1] [maɪn] **poss pron** le mien (la mienne), les miens (les miennes) *(pl)* ▸ **that money is mine** cet argent est à moi ▸ **it wasn't your fault, it was mine** ce n'était pas de votre faute, c'était de la mienne OR de ma faute à moi ▸ **a friend of mine** un ami à moi, un de mes amis.

mine [2] [maɪn] ■ **n** mine *f* ▸ **a mine of information** *fig* une mine de renseignements.
■ **vt 1.** [coal, gold] extraire **2.** [road, beach, sea] miner.

mine detector **n** détecteur *m* de mines.

minefield ['maɪnfi:ld] **n** champ *m* de mines / *fig* situation *f* explosive.

minelayer ['maɪn,leɪəʳ] **n** mouilleur *m* de mines.

miner ['maɪnəʳ] **n** mineur *m*, -euse *f*.

mineral ['mɪnərəl] ■ **adj** minéral(e).
■ **n** minéral *m*.

mineralogist [,mɪnə'rælədʒɪst] **n** minéralogiste *mf*.

mineralogy [,mɪnə'rælədʒɪ] **n** minéralogie *f*.

mineral water **n** eau *f* minérale.

mineshaft ['maɪnʃɑ:ft] **n** puits *m* de mine.

minestrone [,mɪnɪ'strəʊnɪ] **n** minestrone *m*.

minesweeper ['maɪn,swi:pəʳ] **n** dragueur *m* de mines.

mineworker ['maɪn,wɜ:kəʳ] **n** ouvrier *m*, -ère *f* de la mine, mineur *m*.

minging ['mɪŋɪŋ] **adj** *UK v inf* horrible.

mingle ['mɪŋgl] ■ **vt : to mingle sthg with sthg** mélanger qqch à qqch.
■ **vi : to mingle (with)** [sounds, fragrances] se mélanger (à) / [people] se mêler (à).

mini ['mɪnɪ] **n** [skirt] minijupe *f*.

mini- ['mɪnɪ] **prefix** mini-.

miniature ['mɪnətʃəʳ] ■ **adj** miniature.
■ **n 1.** [painting] miniature *f* **2.** [of alcohol] bouteille *f* miniature **3.** [small scale] **: in miniature** en miniature.

miniaturized, -ised *UK* ['mɪnətʃəraɪzd] **adj** miniaturisé(e).

minibus ['mɪnɪbʌs] (pl **-es**) **n** minibus *m*.

minicab ['mɪnɪkæb] **n** *UK* radiotaxi *m*.

minicomputer [,mɪnɪkəm'pju:təʳ] **n** mini-ordinateur *m*.

MiniDisc® ['mɪnɪdɪsk] **n** Minidisc® *m*.

minidish ['mɪnɪdɪʃ] **n** mini-parabole *f*.

minidress ['mɪnɪdres] **n** mini-robe *f*.

minim ['mɪnɪm] **n** *UK* MUS blanche *f*.

minima ['mɪnɪmə] **npl** ➤ ***minimum***.

minimal ['mɪnɪml] **adj** [cost] insignifiant(e) / [damage] minime.

minimalism ['mɪnɪməlɪzm] **n** minimalisme *m*.

minimalist ['mɪnɪməlɪst] **n** minimaliste *mf*.

minimally ['mɪnɪməlɪ] **adv** à peine.

minimize, *UK* ***-ise*** ['mɪnɪ,maɪz] **vt** minimiser.

minimum ['mɪnɪməm] ■ **adj** minimum *(inv)*.
■ **n** (pl **minima** ['mɪnɪmə] OR **-s**) minimum *m* ▸ **keep expenses to a minimum** limitez au minimum les dépenses, dépensez le moins possible ▸ **there was only the minimum of damage** il n'y a eu que des dégâts minimes ▸ **at the (very) minimum it will cost £2,000** (en mettant les choses) au mieux, cela coûtera 2 000 livres.

minimum charge **n** tarif *m* minimum.

minimum deposit **n** acompte *m* minimum.

minimum lending rate [-'lendɪŋ-] **n** *UK* taux *m* de base, taux *m* officiel d'escompte.

minimum payment **n** paiement *m* minimum.

minimum wage **n** salaire *m* minimum.

CULTURE

Minimum Wage

Introduit au Royaume-Uni en avril 1999, le **National Minimum Wage** (« salaire minimum national ») détermine le taux horaire minimal que l'employeur doit payer à ses employés. Il vise à faire valoir non plus la réduction des prix (souvent basés sur des salaires minimaux), mais la compétitivité des entreprises par rapport à la qualité des produits et des services qu'elles fournissent. Ces taux sont fixés par la **Low Pay Commission** (« Commission indépendante du salaire minimal ») pour trois catégories de salariés : les travailleurs de plus de 22 ans, les jeunes de 18 à 21 ans et les plus jeunes, âgés de 16 et 17 ans. Aux États-Unis, le **Federal Minimum Wage** (« Salaire Minimum Fédéral ») existe également, mais sa fourchette de rémunération varie suivant les États.

mining ['maɪnɪŋ] ■ **n** exploitation *f* minière.
■ **adj** minier(ère).

mining engineer **n** ingénieur *m* des mines.

minion ['mɪnjən] **n** larbin *m*, laquais *m*.

minipill ['mɪnɪpɪl] **n** minipilule *f*.

mini-series **n** TV mini-feuilleton *m*.

miniskirt ['mɪnɪskɜ:t] **n** minijupe *f*.

minister ['mɪnɪstəʳ] **n 1.** POL ministre *m* **2.** RELIG pasteur *m*.
◆ ***minister to*** **vt insep** [person] donner OR prodiguer ses soins à / [needs] pourvoir à.

ministerial [,mɪnɪ'stɪərɪəl] **adj** ministériel(elle).

minister of state **n** *UK* secrétaire *mf* d'État.

ministry ['mɪnɪstrɪ] (pl **-ies**) **n 1.** POL ministère *m* ▸ **Ministry of Defence** *UK* ministère *m* de la Défense **2.** RELIG **: the ministry** le saint ministère.

mink [mɪŋk] (pl **mink**) **n** vison *m*.

mink coat **n** manteau *m* de vison.

Minnesota [,mɪnɪ'səʊtə] **n** Minnesota *m* ▸ **in Minnesota** dans le Minnesota.

minnow ['mɪnəʊ] n vairon *m*.

minor ['maɪnə^r] ■ **adj** [gen & MUS] mineur(e) / [detail] petit(e) / [role] secondaire ▸ **minor offence** LAW délit *m* mineur ▸ **to have a minor operation** MED subir une petite intervention chirurgicale *OR* une intervention chirurgicale bénigne ▸ **in A minor** MUS en la mineur.
■ **n** mineur *m*, -e *f*.

minority [maɪ'nɒrətɪ] (pl **-ies**) **n** minorité *f* ▸ **to be in a** *OR* **the minority** être en minorité.

minority government **n** gouvernement *m* minoritaire.

minority shareholder *UK*, ***minority stockholder*** *US* **n** actionnaire *mf* minoritaire.

minor league ■ **n** *US* SPORT ≃ division *f* d'honneur.
■ **adj** *fig* secondaire, de peu d'importance ▸ **they're minor league compared with some American corporations** ils sont loin d'avoir l'envergure de certaines grandes sociétés américaines.

minster ['mɪnstə^r] **n** *UK* cathédrale *f*.

minstrel ['mɪnstrəl] **n** ménestrel *m*.

mint [mɪnt] ■ **n 1.** [herb] menthe *f* **2.** [sweet] bonbon *m* à la menthe **3.** [for coins] **: the Mint** l'hôtel de la Monnaie ▸ **in mint condition** en parfait état.
■ **vt** [coins] battre.

mint sauce n sauce *f* à la menthe.

minuet [ˌmɪnjʊ'et] **n** menuet *m*.

minus ['maɪnəs] ■ **prep** moins.
■ **adj** [answer, quantity] négatif(ive).
■ **n** (pl **-es** [-iːz]) **1.** MATHS signe *m* moins **2.** [disadvantage] handicap *m*.

minuscule ['mɪnəskjuːl] **adj** minuscule.

minus sign n signe *m* moins.

minute[1] ['mɪnɪt] ■ **n** minute *f* ▸ **at any minute** à tout moment, d'une minute à l'autre ▸ **at the last minute** au dernier moment, à la dernière minute ▸ **stop that this minute!** arrête tout de suite *OR* immédiatement! ▸ **wait a minute!** attendez une minute *OR* un instant!
■ **adj : up-to-the-minute** [news] de dernière heure ; [design] dernier cri *(inv)*.
◆ ***minutes*** **npl** procès-verbal *m*, compte rendu *m*.

minute[2] [maɪ'njuːt] **adj** minuscule ▸ **in minute detail** par le menu.

minute hand ['mɪnɪt-] **n** aiguille *f* des minutes.

minutely [maɪ'njuːtlɪ] **adv 1.** [carefully] minutieusement, avec un soin minutieux / [in detail] en détail, par le menu **2.** [fold] tout petit / [move] imperceptiblement, très légèrement.

minutiae [maɪ'njuːʃɪaɪ] **npl** menus détails *mpl*.

miracle ['mɪrəkl] **n** miracle *m*.

miraculous [mɪ'rækjʊləs] **adj** miraculeux(euse).

miraculously [mɪ'rækjʊləslɪ] **adv** miraculeusement, par miracle.

mirage [mɪ'rɑːʒ] **n** *lit* & *fig* mirage *m*.

mire [maɪə^r] **n** fange *f*, boue *f*.

mirror ['mɪrə^r] ■ **n** miroir *m*, glace *f*.
■ **vt** [subj: mirror, water] refléter / COMPUT donner un site miroir à.

mirror image n image *f* inversée.

mirror site n COMPUT site *m* miroir.

mirth [mɜːθ] **n** *liter* hilarité *f*, gaieté *f*.

mirthless ['mɜːθlɪs] **adj** *liter* triste, sombre, morne / [laugh] faux(fausse), forcé(e).

MIS (abbr of ***management information system***) n COMPUT système *m* intégré de gestion.

misadventure [ˌmɪsəd'ventʃə^r] **n** *UK* LAW **: death by misadventure** mort *f* accidentelle.

misaligned [ˌmɪsə'laɪnd] **adj** mal aligné(e).

misanthropic [ˌmɪsən'θrɒpɪk] **adj** [person] misanthrope / [thoughts] misanthropique.

misanthropist [mɪ'sænθrəpɪst] **n** misanthrope *mf*.

misanthropy [mɪ'sænθrəpɪ] **n** misanthropie *f*.

misapplication ['mɪsˌæplɪ'keɪʃn] **n** mauvaise application *f*, application erronée.

misapprehension ['mɪsˌæprɪ'henʃn] **n** idée *f* fausse.

misappropriate [ˌmɪsə'prəʊprɪeɪt] **vt** détourner.

misappropriation ['mɪsəˌprəʊprɪ'eɪʃn] **n** détournement *m*.

misbegotten [ˌmɪsbɪ'gɒtn] **adj** *fml* **1.** [plan] mal conçu(e), bâtard(e) / [child] bâtard(e), illégitime **2.** [illegally obtained] d'origine douteuse.

misbehave [ˌmɪsbɪ'heɪv] ■ **vi** se conduire mal ▸ **stop misbehaving!** sois sage! ▸ **he's misbehaving again!** il fait encore des siennes!
■ **vt : to misbehave oneself** se conduire mal.

misbehaviour *UK*, ***misbehaviour*** *US* [ˌmɪsbɪ'heɪvjə^r] **n** mauvaise conduite *f*.

misc, ***misc.*** [mɪsk] abbr of ***miscellaneous***.

miscalculate [ˌmɪs'kælkjʊleɪt] ■ **vt** mal calculer.
■ **vi** se tromper.

miscalculation [ˌmɪskælkjʊ'leɪʃn] **n** mauvais calcul *m*, erreur *f* de calcul.

miscarriage [ˌmɪs'kærɪdʒ] **n** MED fausse couche *f* ▸ **to have a miscarriage** faire une fausse couche.

miscarriage of justice n erreur *f* judiciaire.

miscarry [ˌmɪs'kærɪ] (pt & pp **-ied**) **vi 1.** [woman] faire une fausse couche **2.** [plan] échouer.

miscast [ˌmɪs'kɑːst] (pt & pp **miscast**) **vt** CIN & THEAT [play] se tromper dans la distribution de / [actor] mal choisir le rôle de ▸ **Jim was hopelessly miscast as Romeo** Jim n'était vraiment pas fait pour jouer le rôle de Roméo.

miscellaneous [ˌmɪsə'leɪnjəs] **adj** varié(e), divers(e).

miscellany [*UK* mɪ'selənɪ, *US* 'mɪsəleɪnɪ] (pl **-ies**) **n** recueil *m*.

mischance [ˌmɪs'tʃɑːns] **n** *fml* malchance *f* ▸ **by mischance** par malheur.

mischief ['mɪstʃɪf] **n** *(U)* **1.** [playfulness] malice *f*, espièglerie *f* **2.** [naughty behaviour] sottises *fpl*, bêtises *fpl* **3.** [harm] dégât *m*.

mischievous ['mɪstʃɪvəs] **adj** **1.** [playful] malicieux(euse) **2.** [naughty] espiègle, coquin(e).

mischievously ['mɪstʃɪvəslɪ] **adv** [naughtily, playfully] malicieusement / [nastily] méchamment, avec malveillance.

misconceived [ˌmɪskən'si:vd] **adj** [idea] mal conçu(e).

misconception [ˌmɪskən'sepʃn] **n** idée *f* fausse.

misconduct [ˌmɪs'kɒndʌkt] **n** inconduite *f*.

misconstruction [ˌmɪskən'strʌkʃn] **n** **1.** [gen] fausse interprétation *f* ▸ **the law is open to misconstruction** la loi peut prêter à des interprétations erronées **2.** GRAM mauvaise construction *f*.

misconstrue [ˌmɪskən'stru:] **vt** *fml* mal interpréter.

miscount [ˌmɪs'kaʊnt] **vt & vi** mal compter.

misdeed [ˌmɪs'di:d] **n** *fml* méfait *m*.

misdemeanour *UK*, ***misdemeanor*** *US* [ˌmɪsdɪ'mi:nəʳ] **n** LAW délit *m*.

misdirected [ˌmɪsdɪ'rektɪd] **adj** [letter] mal adressé(e) / [efforts, energy] mal dirigé(e).

miser ['maɪzəʳ] **n** avare *mf*.

miserable ['mɪzrəbl] **adj** **1.** [person] malheureux(euse), triste **2.** [conditions, life] misérable / [pay] dérisoire / [weather] maussade **3.** [failure] pitoyable, lamentable.

miserably ['mɪzrəblɪ] **adv** **1.** [reply, cry] pitoyablement **2.** [live] misérablement **3.** [fail] pitoyablement, lamentablement.

miserly ['maɪzəlɪ] **adj** avare.

misery ['mɪzərɪ] (**pl -ies**) **n** **1.** [of person] tristesse *f* **2.** [of conditions, life] misère *f*.

misfire [ˌmɪs'faɪəʳ] **vi** **1.** [gun, plan] rater **2.** [car engine] avoir des ratés.

misfit ['mɪsfɪt] **n** inadapté *m*, -e *f*.

misfortune [mɪs'fɔ:tʃu:n] **n** **1.** [bad luck] malchance *f* **2.** [piece of bad luck] malheur *m*.

misgiving [mɪs'gɪvɪŋ] **n** doute *m*, appréhension *f* ▸ **the whole idea fills me with misgiving** l'idée même me remplit d'appréhension.

misgivings [mɪs'gɪvɪŋz] **npl** craintes *fpl*, doutes *mpl* ▸ **to have misgivings about** avoir des doutes quant à, douter de.

misguided [ˌmɪs'gaɪdɪd] **adj** [person] malavisé(e) / [attempt] malencontreux(euse) / [opinion] peu judicieux(euse).

mishandle [ˌmɪs'hændl] **vt** **1.** [person, animal] manier sans précaution **2.** [negotiations] mal mener / [business] mal gérer.

mishap ['mɪshæp] **n** mésaventure *f* ▸ **without mishap** sans encombre *OR* incident.

mishear [ˌmɪs'hɪəʳ] (**pt & pp -heard** [-'hɜ:d]) **vt & vi** mal entendre.

mishit ■ **vt** [ˌmɪs'hɪt] (**pt & pp mishit**) SPORT [ball] mal frapper.
■ **vi** [ˌmɪs'hɪt] (**pt & pp mishit**) mal frapper la balle.
■ **n** ['mɪshɪt] mauvais coup *m*, coup *m* manqué.

mishmash ['mɪʃmæʃ] **n** *inf* méli-mélo *m*.

misinform [ˌmɪsɪn'fɔ:m] **vt** mal renseigner, mal informer.

misinformation [ˌmɪsɪnfə'meɪʃn] **n** désinformation *f*.

misinterpret [ˌmɪsɪn'tɜ:prɪt] **vt** mal interpréter.

misinterpretation ['mɪsɪnˌtɜ:prɪ'teɪʃn] **n** erreur *f* d'interprétation ▸ **the rules are open to misinterpretation** l'interprétation du règlement prête à confusion.

misjudge [ˌmɪs'dʒʌdʒ] **vt** **1.** [distance, time] mal évaluer **2.** [person, mood] méjuger, se méprendre sur.

misjudg(e)ment [ˌmɪs'dʒʌdʒmənt] **n** : **to make a misjudgement** faire une erreur de jugement.

miskick ■ **vt** [ˌmɪs'kɪk] SPORT : **he miskicked the ball** il a raté son coup de pied.
■ **vi** [ˌmɪs'kɪk] rater le ballon.
■ **n** ['mɪskɪk] coup *m* de pied raté.

mislay [ˌmɪs'leɪ] (**pt & pp -laid** [-'leɪd]) **vt** égarer.

mislead [ˌmɪs'li:d] (**pt & pp -led**) **vt** induire en erreur.

misleading [ˌmɪs'li:dɪŋ] **adj** trompeur(euse).

misled [ˌmɪs'led] **pt & pp** ➤ ***mislead***.

mismanage [ˌmɪs'mænɪdʒ] **vt** mal gérer, mal administrer.

mismanagement [ˌmɪs'mænɪdʒmənt] **n** mauvaise gestion *f* *OR* administration *f*.

mismatch [ˌmɪs'mætʃ] **vt** : **to be mismatched** être mal assorti(e).

misnomer [ˌmɪs'nəʊməʳ] **n** nom *m* mal approprié.

misogynist [mɪ'sɒdʒɪnɪst] **n** misogyne *mf*.

misogyny [mɪ'sɒdʒɪnɪ] **n** misogynie *f*.

misplace [ˌmɪs'pleɪs] **vt** mal placer.

misplaced [ˌmɪs'pleɪst] **adj** mal placé(e).

misprint ['mɪsprɪnt] **n** faute *f* d'impression.

mispronounce [ˌmɪsprə'naʊns] **vt** mal prononcer.

mispronunciation ['mɪsprəˌnʌnsɪ'eɪʃn] **n** faute *f* de prononciation.

misquotation [ˌmɪskwəʊ'teɪʃn] **n** citation *f* inexacte.

misquote [ˌmɪs'kwəʊt] **vt** citer de façon inexacte.

misread [ˌmɪs'ri:d] (**pt & pp -read** [-'red]) **vt** **1.** [read wrongly] mal lire **2.** [misinterpret] mal interpréter.

misrepresent ['mɪsˌreprɪ'zent] **vt** dénaturer.

misrepresentation ['mɪsˌreprɪzen'teɪʃn] **n** **1.** *(U)* [wrong interpretation] mauvaise interprétation *f* **2.** [false account] déformation *f*.

misrule [ˌmɪs'ru:l] **n** mauvais gouvernement *m*, mauvaise administration *f*.

miss [mɪs] ■ **vt** **1.** [gen] rater, manquer ▸ **you didn't miss much** vous n'avez pas manqué grand-chose ▸ **it's too good an opportunity to miss** c'est une occasion trop belle pour qu'on la manque ▸ **to miss school** manquer l'école ▸ **I'm sorry, I missed you in the crowd** désolé, je ne vous ai pas vu *OR* remarqué *OR* aperçu dans la foule ▸ **I missed the beginning of your question** je n'ai pas entendu le début de votre question ▸ **they've missed my name off the list** ils ont oublié mon nom sur la liste ▸ **you've missed** *OR* **you're missing the point!** vous

n'avez rien compris! **2.** [home, person] **: I miss my family/her** ma famille/elle me manque ▸ **you'll be missed when you retire** on vous regrettera *OR* vous nous manquerez quand vous serez à la retraite **3.** [avoid, escape] échapper à ▸ **I just missed being run over** j'ai failli me faire écraser **4.** [be short of, lack] manquer de ▸ **I'm missing two books from my collection** il me manque deux livres dans ma collection, deux livres de ma collection ont disparu.
■ **vi** rater ▸ **missed!** raté!
■ **n : to give sthg a miss** *UK inf* ne pas aller à qqch.
◆ ***miss out*** ■ **vt sep** *UK* [omit - by accident] oublier / [- deliberately] omettre.
■ **vi : to miss out on sthg** ne pas pouvoir profiter de qqch.

Miss [mɪs] **n** Mademoiselle *f*.

misshapen [ˌmɪs'ʃeɪpn] **adj** difforme.

missile [*UK* 'mɪsaɪl, *US* 'mɪsəl] **n 1.** [weapon] missile *m* **2.** [thrown object] projectile *m*.

missile launcher [-ˌlɔ:ntʃər] **n** lance-missiles *m inv*.

missing ['mɪsɪŋ] **adj 1.** [lost] perdu(e), égaré(e) **2.** [not present] manquant(e), qui manque.

missing link **n** maillon *m* qui manque à la chaîne.

missing person **n** personne *f* disparue.

mission ['mɪʃn] **n** mission *f*.

missionary ['mɪʃənrɪ] (pl **-ies**) **n** missionnaire *mf*.

mission control **n** centre *m* de contrôle.

missis ['mɪsɪz] *UK* = ***missus***.

Mississippi [ˌmɪsɪ'sɪpɪ] **1.** [river] **: the Mississippi (River)** le Mississippi **2.** [state] Mississippi *m* ▸ **in Mississippi** dans le Mississippi.

missive ['mɪsɪv] **n** *fml* missive *f*.

Missouri [mɪ'zʊərɪ] **n 1.** [river] **: the Missouri (River)** le Missouri **2.** Missouri *m* ▸ **in Missouri** dans le Missouri.

misspell [ˌmɪs'spel] (*UK* **-spelt** *OR* **-spelled**) **vt** mal orthographier.

misspelling [ˌmɪs'spelɪŋ] **n** faute *f* d'orthographe.

misspelt [ˌmɪs'spelt] **pt & pp** *UK* ➤ ***misspell***.

misspend [ˌmɪs'spend] (**pt & pp -spent** [-'spent]) **vt** gaspiller.

missus ['mɪsɪz] **n** *UK inf* **1.** [wife] bourgeoise *f* ▸ **I'll have to ask the missus** je dois demander à la patronne **2.** [woman] **: eh, missus!** dites, m'dame *OR* ma p'tite dame!

mist [mɪst] **n** brume *f*.
◆ ***mist over***, ***mist up*** **vi** s'embuer.

mistake [mɪ'steɪk] ■ **n** erreur *f* ▸ **by mistake** par erreur ▸ **there must be some mistake** il doit y avoir erreur *OR* un malentendu ▸ **to make a mistake** faire une erreur, se tromper ▸ **I made the mistake of losing my temper** j'ai commis l'erreur de *OR* j'ai eu le tort de me fâcher.
■ **vt** (**pt -took, pp -taken**) **1.** [misunderstand - meaning] mal comprendre / [- intention] se méprendre sur **2.** [fail to recognize] **: you can't mistake our house: it has green shutters** vous ne pouvez pas vous tromper, notre maison a des volets verts ▸ **to mistake sb/sthg for** prendre qqn/qqch pour, confondre qqn/qqch avec ▸ **I'm often mistaken for my sister** on me prend souvent pour ma sœur ▸ **there's no mistaking...** il est impossible de ne pas reconnaître...

mistaken [mɪ'steɪkn] ■ **pp** ➤ ***mistake***.
■ **adj 1.** [person] **: to be mistaken (about)** se tromper (en ce qui concerne *OR* sur) **2.** [belief, idea] erroné(e), faux (fausse).

mistaken identity **n : a case of mistaken identity** une erreur sur la personne.

mistakenly [mɪs'teɪknlɪ] **adv** par erreur.

mister ['mɪstər] **n** *inf* monsieur *m*.
◆ ***Mister*** **n** Monsieur *m*.

mistime [ˌmɪs'taɪm] **vt** [tackle, shot] mal calculer / [announcement] faire au mauvais moment.

mistletoe ['mɪsltəʊ] **n** gui *m*.

mistook [mɪ'stʊk] **pt** ➤ ***mistake***.

mistranslate [ˌmɪstræns'leɪt] ■ **vt** mal traduire.
■ **vi** faire des contresens.

mistranslation [ˌmɪstræns'leɪʃn] **n** erreur *f* de traduction.

mistreat [ˌmɪs'tri:t] **vt** maltraiter.

mistreatment [ˌmɪs'tri:tmənt] **n** mauvais traitement *m*.

mistress ['mɪstrɪs] **n** maîtresse *f*.

mistrial ['mɪstraɪəl] **n 1.** erreur *f* judiciaire **2.** *US procès annulé par manque d'unanimité parmi les jurés*.

mistrust [ˌmɪs'trʌst] ■ **n** méfiance *f*.
■ **vt** se méfier de.

mistrustful [ˌmɪs'trʌstfʊl] **adj : mistrustful (of)** méfiant(e) (à l'égard de).

misty ['mɪstɪ] (**comp -ier, superl -iest**) **adj** brumeux(euse).

misunderstand [ˌmɪsʌndə'stænd] (**pt & pp -stood**) **vt & vi** mal comprendre.

misunderstanding [ˌmɪsʌndə'stændɪŋ] **n** malentendu *m*.

misunderstood [ˌmɪsʌndə'stʊd] **pt & pp** ➤ ***misunderstand***.

misuse ■ **n** [ˌmɪs'ju:s] **1.** [of one's time, resources] mauvais emploi *m* **2.** [of power] abus *m* / [of funds] détournement *m*.
■ **vt** [ˌmɪs'ju:z] **1.** [one's time, resources] mal employer **2.** [power] abuser de / [funds] détourner.

MIT (abbr of ***Massachusetts Institute of Technology***) **n** *l'institut de technologie du Massachusetts*.

mite [maɪt] **n 1.** [insect] mite *f* **2.** *inf dated* [small amount] **: a mite** un brin, un tantinet **3.** [small child] petit *m*, -e *f*.

miter *US* = ***mitre***.

mitigate ['mɪtɪgeɪt] **vt** atténuer, mitiger.

mitigating ['mɪtɪgeɪtɪŋ] **adj : mitigating circumstances** circonstances *fpl* atténuantes.

mitigation [ˌmɪtɪ'geɪʃn] **n** atténuation *f*.

mitre *UK*, ***miter*** *US* ['maɪtər] **n 1.** [hat] mitre *f* **2.** [joint] onglet *m*.

mitt [mɪt] n **1.** *inf* = ***mitten*** **2.** [in baseball] gant *m*.

mitten ['mɪtn] n moufle *f*.

mix [mɪks] ■ vt **1.** [gen] mélanger **2.** [activities] **: to mix sthg with sthg** combiner *OR* associer qqch et qqch **3.** [drink] préparer / [cement] malaxer.
■ vi **1.** [gen] se mélanger **2.** [socially] **: to mix with** fréquenter.
■ n **1.** [gen] mélange *m* **2.** MUS mixage *m*.
◆ ***mix up*** vt sep **1.** [confuse] confondre **2.** [disorganize] mélanger.

mix-and-match adj [clothes] que l'on peut coordonner à volonté.

mixed [mɪkst] adj **1.** [assorted] assortis(ies) ▸ **to have mixed feelings** être partagé(e) **2.** [sexually, racially] mixte ▸ **mixed school** école *f* mixte ▸ **man of mixed race** métis *m* ▸ **woman of mixed race** métisse *f*.

mixed-ability adj *UK* [class] tous niveaux confondus.

mixed blessing n *quelque chose qui a du bon et du mauvais.*

mixed doubles n SPORT double *m* mixte.

mixed economy n économie *f* mixte.

mixed grill n *UK* assortiment *m* de grillades.

mixed marriage n mariage *m* mixte.

mixed-media adj multimédia *(inv)*.

mixed up adj **1.** [confused - person] qui ne sait plus où il en est, paumé(e) / [- mind] embrouillé(e) **2.** [involved] **: to be mixed up in sthg** être mêlé(e) à qqch.

mixer ['mɪksəʳ] n [for food] mixer *m*.

mixer tap n *UK* (robinet *m*) mélangeur *m*.

mixing ['mɪksɪŋ] n **1.** [gen] mélange *m* **2.** CIN, ELECTRON & MUS mixage *m* ▸ **mixing desk** table *f* de mixage.

mixing bowl n grand bol *m* de cuisine.

mixture ['mɪkstʃəʳ] n **1.** [gen] mélange *m* **2.** MED préparation *f*.

mix-up n *inf* confusion *f*.

MJPEG [em'dʒeɪpeg] (abbr of ***Moving Joint Photographic Expert Group***) n COMPUT (format *m*) MJPEG *m*.

mk, ***MK*** abbr of ***mark***.

mkt abbr of ***market***.

ml (abbr of ***millilitre***) ml.

MLitt [em'lɪt] (abbr of ***Master of Literature, Master of Letters***) n *(titulaire d'une) maîtrise de lettres.*

MLR *UK* abbr of ***minimum lending rate***.

mm (abbr of ***millimetre***) mm.

MMR (abbr of ***measles, mumps & rubella***) n MED ROR *m*.

MMX (abbr of ***multimedia extensions***) n COMPUT MMX *m*.

MN[1] n *UK* abbr of ***Merchant Navy***.

MN[2] abbr of ***Minnesota***.

mnemonic [nɪ'mɒnɪk] n mnémotechnique *f*.

m.o. abbr of ***money order***.

MO ■ n abbr of ***medical officer***.
■ abbr of ***Missouri***.

moan [məʊn] ■ n **1.** [of pain, sadness] gémissement *m* **2.** *inf* [complaint] plainte *f*.
■ vi **1.** [in pain, sadness] gémir **2.** *inf* [complain] **: to moan (about)** rouspéter *OR* râler (à propos de).

moaner ['məʊnəʳ] n *inf* grognon *m*, -onne *f*, râleur *m*, -euse *f*.

moaning ['məʊnɪŋ] n *(U)* [complaining] plaintes *fpl*, jérémiades *fpl*.

moat [məʊt] n douves *fpl*.

mob [mɒb] ■ n foule *f*.
■ vt (pt & pp **-bed**, cont **-bing**) assaillir.

mobile ['məʊbaɪl] ■ adj **1.** [gen] mobile **2.** [able to travel] motorisé(e).
■ n **1.** *UK* [telephone] téléphone *m* portable **2.** ART mobile *m*.

mobile home n auto-caravane *f*.

mobile library n *UK* bibliobus *m*.

mobile phone n esp *UK* téléphone *m* portable.

mobile shop n marchand *m* ambulant.

mobility [mə'bɪlətɪ] n mobilité *f*.

mobility allowance n *UK* allocation *f* de transport.

mobilization, *UK* ***-isation*** [ˌməʊbɪlaɪ'zeɪʃn] n mobilisation *f*.

mobilize, *UK* ***-ise*** ['məʊbɪlaɪz] vt & vi mobiliser.

moccasin ['mɒkəsɪn] n mocassin *m*.

mocha ['mɒkə] n moka *m*.

mock [mɒk] ■ adj faux (fausse) ▸ **mock exam** *UK* examen blanc.
■ vt se moquer de.
■ vi se moquer.

mockery ['mɒkərɪ] n moquerie *f* ▸ **to make a mockery of sthg** tourner qqch en dérision.

mocking ['mɒkɪŋ] adj moqueur(euse).

mockingbird ['mɒkɪŋbɜːd] n moqueur *m*.

mock-up n maquette *f*.

mod [mɒd] n *en Angleterre, membre d'un groupe de jeunes des années 60 qui s'opposaient aux rockers.*

MoD n *UK* abbr of ***Ministry of Defence***.

mod cons [ˌmɒd-] (abbr of ***modern conveniences***) npl *UK inf* **: all mod cons** tout confort, tt. conf.

mode [məʊd] n mode *m*.

model ['mɒdl] ■ n **1.** [gen] modèle *m* **2.** [fashion model] mannequin *m*.
■ adj **1.** [perfect] modèle **2.** [reduced-scale] (en) modèle réduit.
■ vt (*UK* **-led**, cont **-ling**, *US* **-ed**, cont **-ing**) **1.** [clay] modeler **2.** [clothes] **: to model a dress** présenter un modèle de robe **3.** [emulate] **: to model o.s. on sb** prendre modèle *OR* exemple sur qqn, se modeler sur qqn.
■ vi (*UK* **-led**, cont **-ling**, *US* **-ed**, cont **-ing**) être mannequin.

modelling *UK*, ***modeling*** *US* ['mɒdəlɪŋ] n **1.** [building models] modelage *m* / [as a hobby] construction *f* de maquettes **2.** [in fashion shows] **: modelling is extremely well-paid** le travail de mannequin est très bien payé, les mannequins sont très bien payés ▸ **to make a career in modelling** faire une carrière de mannequin **3.** MATHS modélisation *f*.

modem ['məʊdem] **n** COMPUT modem *m*.

moderate ■ **adj** ['mɒdərət] modéré(e).
■ **n** ['mɒdərət] POL modéré *m*, -e *f*.
■ **vt** ['mɒdəreɪt] modérer.
■ **vi** ['mɒdəreɪt] se modérer.

moderately ['mɒdərətlɪ] **adv** [not very] pas très, plus ou moins.

moderation [ˌmɒdə'reɪʃn] **n** modération *f* ▸ **in moderation** avec modération.

moderator ['mɒdəreɪtər] **n** **1.** *UK* [of exam] examinateur *m*, -trice *f* **2.** *US* [mediator] médiateur *m*, -trice *f* **3.** TV modérateur *m*, -trice *f*.

modern ['mɒdən] **adj** moderne.

modern-day **adj** moderne, d'aujourd'hui.

modernism ['mɒdənɪzm] **n** modernisme *m*.

modernist ['mɒdənɪst] ■ **adj** moderniste.
■ **n** moderniste *mf*.

modernity [mɒ'dɜːnətɪ] **n** modernité *f*.

modernization, *esp UK* ***-isation*** [ˌmɒdənaɪ'zeɪʃn] **n** modernisation *f*.

modernize, *UK* ***-ise*** ['mɒdənaɪz] ■ **vt** moderniser.
■ **vi** se moderniser.

modern languages **npl** langues *fpl* vivantes.

modest ['mɒdɪst] **adj** modeste.

modestly ['mɒdɪstlɪ] **adv** modestement.

modesty ['mɒdɪstɪ] **n** modestie *f*.

modicum ['mɒdɪkəm] **n** minimum *m*.

modification [ˌmɒdɪfɪ'keɪʃn] **n** modification *f*.

modify ['mɒdɪfaɪ] (pt & pp **-ied**) **vt** modifier.

modular ['mɒdjʊlər] **adj** modulaire.

modulate ['mɒdjʊleɪt] **vt** **1.** ELECTRON & MUS moduler / [voice] moduler **2.** [moderate, tone down] adapter, ajuster.

modulated ['mɒdjʊleɪtɪd] **adj** modulé(e).

modulation [ˌmɒdjʊ'leɪʃn] **n** modulation *f*.

module ['mɒdjuːl] **n** module *m*.

modus operandi ['məʊdəsˌɒpə'rændiː] **n** *fml* & *liter* méthode *f* (de travail), procédé *m*.

Mogadishu [ˌmɒgə'dɪʃuː] **n** Mogadishu.

moggy ['mɒgɪ] (pl **-ies**) **n** *UK inf* minou *m*.

mogul ['məʊgl] **n** *fig* magnat *m*.

MOH (abbr of ***Medical Officer of Health***) **n** *en Grande-Bretagne, direction de la santé publique*.

mohair ['məʊheər] ■ **n** mohair *m*.
■ **comp** en mohair.

Mohican [məʊ'hiːkən **OR** 'məʊɪkən] **n** Mohican *m*.

moist [mɔɪst] **adj** [soil, climate] humide / [cake] moelleux(euse).

moisten ['mɔɪsn] **vt** humecter.

moisture ['mɔɪstʃər] **n** humidité *f*.

moisturize, *UK* ***-ise*** ['mɔɪstʃəraɪz] **vt** hydrater.

moisturizer, *UK* ***-iser*** ['mɔɪstʃəraɪzər] **n** crème *f* hydratante, lait *m* hydratant.

molar ['məʊlər] **n** molaire *f*.

molasses [mə'læsɪz] **n** *(U)* mélasse *f*.

mold *US* = ***mould***.

Moldavia [mɒl'deɪvjə] **n** Moldavie *f* ▸ **in Moldavia** en Moldavie.

molding *US* = ***moulding***.

Moldova [mɒl'dəʊvə] **n : the Republic of Moldova** la république de Moldova.

moldy *US* = ***mouldy***.

mole [məʊl] **n** **1.** [animal, spy] taupe *f* **2.** [on skin] grain *m* de beauté.

molecular [mə'lekjʊlər] **adj** moléculaire.

molecule ['mɒlɪkjuːl] **n** molécule *f*.

molehill ['məʊlhɪl] **n** taupinière *f*.

moleskin ['məʊlskɪn] **n** **1.** [fur] (peau *f* de) taupe *f* **2.** [cotton] coton *m* sergé.

molest [mə'lest] **vt** **1.** [attack sexually] attenter à la pudeur de **2.** [attack] molester.

molestation [ˌməʊle'steɪʃn] **n** *(U)* brutalité *f*, violences *fpl* / [sexual] attentat *m* à la pudeur.

molester [mə'lestər] **n : child molester** *personne qui est coupable d'attentat à la pudeur sur des enfants*.

mollify ['mɒlɪfaɪ] (pt & pp **-ied**) **vt** apaiser, calmer.

mollusc *UK*, ***mollusk*** *US* ['mɒləsk] **n** mollusque *m*.

mollycoddle ['mɒlɪˌkɒdl] **vt** *inf* chouchouter.

Molotov cocktail ['mɒlətɒf-] **n** cocktail *m* Molotov.

molt *US* = ***moult***.

molten ['məʊltn] **adj** en fusion.

mom [mɒm] **n** *US inf* maman *f*.

moment ['məʊmənt] **n** moment *m*, instant *m* ▸ **to choose the right moment** choisir son moment ▸ **moment of truth** minute *f* de vérité ▸ **at any moment** d'un moment à l'autre ▸ **at the moment** en ce moment ▸ **at the last moment** au dernier moment ▸ **for the moment** pour le moment ▸ **for one moment** pendant un instant.

momentarily ['məʊməntərɪlɪ] **adv** **1.** [for a short time] momentanément **2.** *US* [soon] très bientôt.

momentary ['məʊməntrɪ] **adj** momentané(e), passager(ère).

momentous [mə'mentəs] **adj** capital(e), très important(e).

momentum [mə'mentəm] **n** *(U)* **1.** PHYS moment *m* **2.** *fig* [speed, force] vitesse *f* ▸ **to gather momentum** prendre de la vitesse.

momma ['mɒmə], ***mommy*** ['mɒmɪ] **n** *US inf* maman *f*.

Mon. (abbr of ***Monday***) lun.

Monaco ['mɒnəkəʊ] **n** Monaco.

monarch ['mɒnək] **n** monarque *m*.

monarchist ['mɒnəkɪst] **n** monarchiste *mf*.

monarchy ['mɒnəkɪ] (pl **-ies**) **n** monarchie *f*.

monastery ['mɒnəstrɪ] (pl **-ies**) **n** monastère *m*.

monastic [mə'næstɪk] **adj** monastique.

monasticism [mə'næstɪsɪzm] **n** monachisme *m*.

Monday ['mʌndɪ] **n** lundi *m* ; see also ***Saturday***.

monetarism ['mʌnɪtərɪzm] **n** monétarisme *m*.

monetarist ['mʌnɪtərɪst] **n** monétariste *mf*.

monetary ['mʌnɪtrɪ] **adj** monétaire.

monetary policy **n** politique *f* monétaire.

monetary reform **n** réforme *f* monétaire.

money ['mʌnɪ] **n** argent *m* ▸ **to make money** gagner de l'argent ▸ **to get one's money's worth** en avoir pour son argent ▸ **to put money into sthg** investir dans qqch ▸ **money is no object** peu importe le prix ▸ **there's no money in translating** la traduction ne rapporte pas OR ne paie pas.

money-back guarantee **n** garantie *f* de remboursement.

money-back offer **n** offre *f* de remboursement.

money belt **n** ceinture *f* portefeuille.

moneybox ['mʌnɪbɒks] **n** *UK* tirelire *f*.

moneyed ['mʌnɪd] **adj** *fml* riche, cossu(e).

money-grubbing [-,grʌbɪŋ] *inf pej* ■ **n** radinerie *f*.
■ **adj** radin(e).

moneylender ['mʌnɪ,lendəʳ] **n** prêteur *m*, -euse *f* sur gages.

moneymaker ['mʌnɪ,meɪkəʳ] **n** affaire *f* lucrative.

moneymaking ['mʌnɪ,meɪkɪŋ] **adj** lucratif(ive).

money market **n** marché *m* monétaire.

money order **n** mandat *m* postal.

money-spinner [-,spɪnəʳ] **n** *esp UK inf* mine *f* d'or.

money supply **n** masse *f* monétaire.

mongol ['mɒŋgəl] *dated & offens* ■ **adj** mongolien(enne).
■ **n** mongolien *m*, -ienne *f*.
◆ ***Mongol*** **n** = ***Mongolian***.

Mongolia [mɒŋ'gəʊlɪə] **n** Mongolie *f* ▸ **in Mongolia** en Mongolie.

Mongolian [mɒŋ'gəʊlɪən] ■ **adj** mongol(e).
■ **n 1.** [person] Mongol *m*, -e *f* **2.** [language] mongol *m*.

mongoose ['mɒŋgu:s] (pl **-s**) **n** mangouste *f*.

mongrel ['mʌŋgrəl] **n** [dog] bâtard *m*.

monitor ['mɒnɪtəʳ] ■ **n** COMPUT, MED & TV moniteur *m*.
■ **vt 1.** [check] contrôler, suivre de près **2.** [broadcasts, messages] être à l'écoute de.

monk [mʌŋk] **n** moine *m*.

monkey ['mʌŋkɪ] (pl **-s**) **n** singe *m*.

monkey nut **n** *UK* cacahuète *f*.

monkey wrench **n** clef *f* à molette.

monkfish ['mʌŋkfɪʃ] (pl **monkfish** OR **-es**) **n** [angler fish] baudroie *f*, lotte *f* / [angel shark] ange *m* de mer.

mono ['mɒnəʊ] ■ **adj** mono *(inv)*.
■ **n 1.** [sound] monophonie *f* **2.** *US inf* [glandular fever] mononucléose *f* (infectieuse).

monochrome ['mɒnəkrəʊm] **adj** monochrome.

monocle ['mɒnəkl] **n** monocle *m*.

monogamous [mɒ'nɒgəməs] **adj** monogame.

monogamy [mɒ'nɒgəmɪ] **n** monogamie *f*.

monogram ['mɒnəgræm] ■ **n** monogramme *m*.
■ **vt** (pt & pp **-med**, cont **-ming**) marquer d'un monogramme.

monogrammed ['mɒnəgræmd] **adj** marqué(é) d'un monogramme ▸ **monogrammed handkerchiefs** mouchoirs avec un monogramme brodé.

monograph ['mɒnəgrɑ:f] **n** monographie *f*.

monolingual [,mɒnə'lɪŋgwəl] **adj** monolingue.

monolith ['mɒnəlɪθ] **n** monolithe *m*.

monolithic [,mɒnə'lɪθɪk] **adj** monolithique.

monologue, *US* ***monolog*** ['mɒnəlɒg] **n** monologue *m*.

mononucleosis ['mɒnəʊ,nju:klɪ'əʊsɪs] **n** *US* mononucléose *f* (infectieuse).

monoplane ['mɒnəpleɪn] **n** monoplan *m*.

monopolistic [mə,nɒpə'lɪstɪk] **adj** monopoliste, monopolistique.

monopolization, *UK* ***-isation*** [mə,nɒpəlaɪ'zeɪʃn] **n** monopolisation *f*.

monopolize, *UK* ***-ise*** [mə'nɒpəlaɪz] **vt** monopoliser.

monopoly [mə'nɒpəlɪ] (pl **-ies**) **n : monopoly (on** OR **of)** monopole *m* (de) ▸ **the Monopolies and Mergers Commission** *UK organisme chargé de contrôler le fusionnement des entreprises*.

monorail ['mɒnəreɪl] **n** monorail *m*.

monosemic [,mɒnəʊ'si:mɪk] **adj** monosémique.

monosodium glutamate [,mɒnə'səʊdjəm-'glu:təmeɪt] **n** glutamate *m* (de sodium).

monosyllabic [,mɒnəsɪ'læbɪk] **adj** monosyllabique.

monosyllable ['mɒnə,sɪləbl] **n** monosyllabe *m*.

monotheism ['mɒnəθi:,ɪzm] **n** monothéisme *m*.

monotone ['mɒnətəʊn] **n** ton *m* monocorde.

monotonous [mə'nɒtənəs] **adj** monotone.

monotonously [mə'nɒtənəslɪ] **adv** de façon monotone.

monotony [mə'nɒtənɪ] **n** monotonie *f*.

monoxide [mɒ'nɒksaɪd] **n** monoxyde *m*.

Monrovia [mən'rəʊvɪə] **n** Monrovia.

Monsignor [,mɒn'si:njəʳ] **n** monsignor *m*.

monsoon [mɒn'su:n] **n** mousson *f*.

monster ['mɒnstəʳ] ■ **n 1.** [creature, cruel person] monstre *m* **2.** [huge thing, person] colosse *m*.
■ **adj** géant(e), monstre.

monstrosity [mɒn'strɒsətɪ] (pl **-ies**) **n** monstruosité *f*.

monstrous ['mɒnstrəs] **adj** monstrueux(euse).

monstrously ['mɒnstrəslɪ] **adv** affreusement.

montage ['mɒntɑ:ʒ] **n** montage *m*.

Montana [mɒn'tænə] **n** Montana *m* ▸ **in Montana** dans le Montana.

Mont Blanc [ˌmɔ̃'blɑ̃] **n** le mont Blanc.

Montenegro [ˌmɒntɪ'ni:grəʊ] **n** Monténégro *m*.

Montevideo [ˌmɒntɪvɪ'deɪəʊ] **n** Montevideo.

month [mʌnθ] **n** mois *m*.

monthly ['mʌnθlɪ] ■ **adj** mensuel(elle).
■ **adv** mensuellement.
■ **n** (**pl -ies**) [publication] mensuel *m*.

monthly instalment **n** mensualité *f*.

Montreal [ˌmɒntrɪ'ɔ:l] **n** Montréal.

monument ['mɒnjʊmənt] **n** monument *m*.

monumental [ˌmɒnjʊ'mentl] **adj** monumental(e).

monumentally [ˌmɒnjʊ'mentəlɪ] **adv** **1.** [build] de façon monumentale **2.** [extremely] extrêmement.

moo [mu:] ■ **n** (**pl -s**) meuglement *m*, beuglement *m*.
■ **vi** meugler, beugler.

mooch [mu:tʃ] ◆ ***mooch about*** *UK*, ***mooch around*** **vi** *inf* traîner.

mood [mu:d] **n** **1.** [generally] humeur *f* ▸ **in a (bad) mood** de mauvaise humeur ▸ **in a good mood** de bonne humeur ▸ **are you in the mood for a hamburger?** un hamburger, ça te dit? **2.** [bad temper, sulk] mauvaise humeur *f*, bouderie *f* **3.** [atmosphere] ambiance *f*, atmosphère *f* ▸ **the mood is one of cautious optimism** l'ambiance est à l'optimisme prudent.

moodily ['mu:dɪlɪ] **adv** [behave] maussadement, d'un air morose / [talk, reply] d'un ton maussade.

moodiness ['mu:dɪnɪs] **n** **1.** [sullenness] humeur *f* maussade, maussaderie *f* **2.** [volatility] humeur *f* changeante ▸ **it's his moodiness I can't stand** ce sont ses sautes d'humeur que je ne supporte pas.

mood swing **n** saute *f* d'humeur.

moody ['mu:dɪ] (**comp -ier, superl -iest**) **adj** **1.** [changeable] lunatique **2.** [bad-tempered] de mauvaise humeur, mal luné(e).

moon [mu:n] **n** lune *f* ▸ **to be over the moon** *UK inf* être aux anges.

moonbeam ['mu:nbi:m] **n** rayon *m* de lune.

moon landing **n** atterrissage *m* sur la lune, alunissage *m*.

moonlight ['mu:nlaɪt] ■ **n** clair *m* de lune.
■ **vi** (**pt & pp -ed**) travailler au noir.

moonlight flit **n** *UK inf* **: to do a moonlight flit** déménager à la cloche de bois.

moonlighting ['mu:nlaɪtɪŋ] **n** *(U)* travail *m* au noir.

moonlit ['mu:nlɪt] **adj** [countryside] éclairé(e) par la lune / [night] de lune.

moonscape ['mu:nskeɪp] **n** paysage *m* lunaire.

moonshine ['mu:nʃaɪn] **n** *(U)* **1.** clair *m* de lune **2.** *inf* [foolishness] sornettes *fpl*, sottises *fpl*, bêtises *fpl* **3.** *US* [illegally made spirits] alcool *m* de contrebande.

moon shot **n** tir *m* lunaire.

moonstone ['mu:nstəʊn] **n** pierre *f* de lune.

moonstruck ['mu:nstrʌk] **adj** *inf* fêlé(e).

moony ['mu:nɪ] (**comp -ier, superl -iest**) **adj** *inf* rêveur(euse).

moor [mɔ:ʳ] ■ **n** lande *f*.
■ **vt** amarrer.
■ **vi** mouiller.

Moor [mɔ:ʳ] **n** Maure *m*, Mauresque *f*.

moorhen ['mɔ:hen] **n** **1.** [waterfowl] poule *f* d'eau **2.** [female grouse] grouse *f* d'Écosse.

mooring ['mɔ:rɪŋ] **n** **1.** [act] amarrage *m*, mouillage *m* **2.** [place] mouillage *m*.

moorings ['mɔ:rɪŋz] **npl** [ropes, chains] amarres *fpl* / [place] mouillage *m* ▸ **the boat was (riding) at her moorings** le bateau tirait sur ses amarres.

Moorish ['mɔ:rɪʃ] **adj** mauresque.

moorland ['mɔ:lənd] **n** *esp UK* lande *f*.

moose [mu:s] (**pl moose**) **n** [North American] orignal *m*.

moot [mu:t] **vt** *fml* [question] soulever.

moot point **n** point *m* discutable.

mop [mɒp] ■ **n** **1.** [for cleaning] balai *m* à laver **2.** *inf* [hair] tignasse *f*.
■ **vt** (**pt & pp -ped, cont -ping**) **1.** [floor] laver **2.** [sweat] essuyer ▸ **to mop one's brow** s'essuyer le front.
◆ ***mop up*** **vt sep** [clean up] éponger.

mope [məʊp] **vi** broyer du noir.
◆ ***mope about*** *UK*, ***mope around*** **vi** traîner.

moped ['məʊped] **n** vélomoteur *m*.

mopping-up operation ['mɒpɪŋ-] **n** opération *f* de nettoyage.

moral ['mɒrəl] ■ **adj** moral(e) ▸ **moral support** soutien *m* moral.
■ **n** [lesson] morale *f*.
◆ ***morals*** **npl** moralité *f*.

morale [mə'rɑ:l] **n** *(U)* moral *m*.

morale-booster **n : it was a morale-booster** ça nous/leur *etc* a remonté le moral.

moralist ['mɒrəlɪst] **n** moraliste *mf*.

moralistic [ˌmɒrə'lɪstɪk] **adj** moralisateur(trice).

morality [mə'rælətɪ] (**pl -ies**) **n** moralité *f*.

moralize, *UK* ***-ise*** ['mɒrəlaɪz] **vi : to moralize (about** *OR* **on)** moraliser (sur).

moralizing, *UK* ***-ising*** ['mɒrəlaɪzɪŋ] ■ **adj** moralisateur(trice), moralisant(e).
■ **n** *(U)* leçons *fpl* de morale, prêches *mpl*.

morally ['mɒrəlɪ] **adv** moralement.

Moral Majority **n** *groupe de pression américain ultra-conservateur lié aux églises fondamentalistes.*

morass [mə'ræs] **n** [of detail, paperwork] fatras *m*.

moratorium [ˌmɒrə'tɔ:rɪəm] (**pl -ria** [-rɪə]) **n** moratoire *m*.

morbid ['mɔ:bɪd] **adj** morbide.

morbidly ['mɔ:bɪdlɪ] **adv** maladivement.

more [mɔ:ʳ] ■ **adv** **1.** *(with adj and adverbs)* plus ▸ **more important (than)** plus important (que) ▸ **more often/quickly (than)** plus souvent/rapidement (que)
2. [to a greater degree] plus, davantage ▸ **you should read more** tu devrais lire plus *OR* davantage ▸ **I like wine more than beer** je préfère le vin à la bière, j'aime mieux le vin

que la bière ▸ **she's more like a mother to me than a sister** elle est davantage une mère qu'une sœur pour moi ▸ **we were more hurt than angry** nous étions plus offensés que fâchés, nous étions offensés plutôt que fâchés
3. [another time] **: once/twice more** une fois/deux fois de plus, encore une fois/deux fois.
■ **adj 1.** [larger number, amount of] plus de, davantage de ▸ **there were more boys than girls** il y avait plus de garçons que de filles ▸ **there are more trains in the morning** il y a plus de trains le matin ▸ **more than 70 people died** plus de 70 personnes ont péri
2. [additional, further] encore (de) ▸ **you should eat more fish** tu devrais manger davantage de *OR* plus de poisson ▸ **three more people arrived** trois autres personnes sont arrivées ▸ **I finished two more chapters today** j'ai fini deux autres *OR* encore deux chapitres aujourd'hui ▸ **have some more tea** prends encore du thé ▸ **do you have any more stamps?** est-ce qu'il vous reste des timbres? ▸ **we need more money/time** il nous faut plus d'argent/de temps, il nous faut davantage d'argent/de temps ▸ **there'll be no more skiing this winter** le ski est fini pour cet hiver.
■ **pron 1.** [greater amount, number] plus, davantage ▸ **more than five** plus de cinq ▸ **he's got more than I have** il en a plus que moi ▸ **there are more of them than there are of us** ils sont plus nombreux que nous ▸ **I wish I could do more for her** j'aimerais pouvoir l'aider plus *OR* davantage ▸ **it's more of a problem now than it used to be** ça pose plus de problèmes maintenant qu'avant ▸ **she's more of a singer than a dancer** c'est une chanteuse plus qu'une danseuse ▸ **no more no less** ni plus ni moins
2. [additional amount] plus, encore ▸ **there's more if you want it** il y en a encore si tu veux ▸ **he asked for more** il en redemanda ▸ **I couldn't eat any more, thanks** je ne pourrais plus rien avaler, merci ▸ **she just can't take any more** elle n'en peut vraiment plus ▸ **something/nothing more** quelque chose/rien de plus ▸ **more of the same** la même chose ▸ **need I say more?** si tu vois ce que je veux dire ▸ **that's more like it!** voilà, c'est mieux! ▸ **there's plenty more where that came from** si vous en revoulez, il n'y a qu'à demander ▸ **(and) what's more** de plus, qui plus est.
◆ ***any more*** **adv : not... any more** ne... plus ▸ **we don't go there any more** nous n'y allons plus ▸ **he still works here, doesn't he? – not any more (he doesn't)** il travaille encore ici, n'est-ce pas? – non, plus maintenant.
◆ ***more and more*** ■ **adv & pron** de plus en plus ▸ **more and more depressed** de plus en plus déprimé(e).
■ **adj** de plus en plus de ▸ **there are more and more cars on the roads** il y a de plus en plus de voitures sur les routes.
◆ ***more or less*** **adv 1.** [almost] plus ou moins
2. [approximately] environ, à peu près.

morello [mə'reləʊ] (pl -s) **n : morello (cherry)** griotte *f.*

moreover [mɔː'rəʊvəʳ] **adv** de plus.

mores ['mɔːreɪz] **npl** *fml* mœurs *fpl.*

morgue [mɔːg] **n** morgue *f.*

MORI ['mɒrɪ] (abbr of ***Market & Opinion Research Institute***) **n** *institut de sondage.*

moribund ['mɒrɪbʌnd] **adj** moribond(e).

Mormon ['mɔːmən] **n** mormon *m*, -e *f.*

morn [mɔːn] **n 1.** *liter* [morning] matin *m* **2.** ***Scot*** **: the morn** [tomorrow] demain.

morning ['mɔːnɪŋ] **n** matin *m* / [duration] matinée *f* ▸ **I work in the morning** je travaille le matin ▸ **I'll do it tomorrow morning** *OR* **in the morning** je le ferai demain ▸ **I worked all morning** j'ai travaillé toute la matinée ▸ **when I awoke it was morning** quand je me suis réveillé il faisait jour.
◆ ***mornings*** **adv** le matin.

morning-after pill **n** pilule *f* du lendemain.

morning dress **n** *esp UK* habit *m*, frac *m.*

morning sickness **n** *(U)* nausées *fpl* (matinales).

morning star **n** étoile *f* du matin.

Moroccan [mə'rɒkən] ■ **adj** marocain(e).
■ **n** Marocain *m*, -e *f.*

Morocco [mə'rɒkəʊ] **n** Maroc *m* ▸ **in Morocco** au Maroc.

moron ['mɔːrɒn] **n** *inf* idiot *m*, -e *f*, crétin *m*, -e *f.*

moronic [mə'rɒnɪk] **adj** idiot(e), crétin(e).

morose [mə'rəʊs] **adj** morose.

morphine ['mɔːfiːn] **n** morphine *f.*

morris dancing ['mɒrɪs-] **n** *(U) danse folklorique anglaise.*

morrow ['mɒrəʊ] **n** *liter* **1.** [next day] lendemain *m* ▸ **on the morrow** le lendemain **2.** *dated* [morning] matin *m.*

Morse (code) [mɔːs-] **n** morse *m.*

morsel ['mɔːsl] **n** bout *m*, morceau *m.*

mortal ['mɔːtl] ■ **adj** mortel(elle).
■ **n** mortel *m*, -elle *f.*

mortality [mɔː'tælətɪ] **n** mortalité *f.*

mortality rate **n** taux *m* de mortalité.

mortally ['mɔːtəlɪ] **adv** mortellement.

mortar ['mɔːtəʳ] **n** mortier *m.*

mortarboard ['mɔːtəbɔːd] **n** mortier *m (chapeau).*

mortgage ['mɔːgɪdʒ] ■ **n** emprunt-logement *m.*
■ **vt** hypothéquer.

mortgage broker **n** courtier *m* en prêts hypothécaires.

mortgagee [ˌmɔːgɪ'dʒiː] **n** créancier *m*, -ère *f* hypothécaire.

mortgage lender **n** prêteur *m* hypothécaire.

mortgage rate **n** taux *m* de crédit immobilier.

mortgagor [ˌmɔːgɪ'dʒɔːʳ] **n** débiteur *m*, -trice *f* hypothécaire.

mortician [mɔː'tɪʃn] **n** *US* entrepreneur *m* de pompes funèbres.

mortification [ˌmɔːtɪfɪ'keɪʃn] **n** mortification *f.*

mortified ['mɔːtɪfaɪd] **adj** mortifié(e).

mortify ['mɔːtɪfaɪ] (pt & pp **-ied**) ■ **vt** mortifier.
■ **vi** MED [become gangrenous] se gangrener / [undergo tissue death] se nécroser, se mortifier.

mortise lock ['mɔːtɪs-] **n** serrure *f* encastrée.

mortuary ['mɔːtʃʊərɪ] (pl **-ies**) **n** morgue *f.*

mosaic [mə'zeɪɪk] **n** mosaïque *f.*

Moscow ['mɒskəʊ] n Moscou.

Moses basket n *UK* couffin *m*.

Moslem ['mɒzləm] *dated* = ***Muslim***.

mosque [mɒsk] n mosquée *f*.

mosquito [mə'ski:təʊ] (pl **-es** *OR* **-s**) n moustique *m*.

mosquito net n moustiquaire *f*.

moss [mɒs] n mousse *f*.

mossy ['mɒsɪ] (comp **-ier**, superl **-iest**) adj moussu(e), couvert(e) de mousse.

most [məʊst] *(superl of* **many***)* ■ adj **1.** [the majority of] la plupart de ▸ **most tourists here are German** la plupart des touristes ici sont allemands ▸ **I like most kinds of fruit** j'aime presque tous les fruits
2. [largest amount of] **: (the) most** le plus de ▸ **she's got (the) most money/sweets** c'est elle qui a le plus d'argent/de bonbons ▸ **which of your inventions gave you most satisfaction?** laquelle de vos inventions vous a procuré la plus grande satisfaction?
■ pron **1.** [the majority] la plupart ▸ **most of the tourists here are German** la plupart des touristes ici sont allemands ▸ **most of the snow has melted** presque toute la neige a fondu ▸ **most of them** la plupart d'entre eux
2. [largest amount] **: (the) most** le plus ▸ **which of the three applicants has (the) most to offer?** lequel des trois candidats a le plus à offrir? ▸ **at most** au maximum, tout au plus
▸▸ **to make the most of sthg** profiter de qqch au maximum.
■ adv **1.** [to greatest extent] **: (the) most** le plus ▸ **what worries you most?, what most worries you?** qu'est-ce qui vous inquiète le plus? ▸ **it's the most beautiful house I've ever seen** c'est la plus belle maison que j'aie jamais vue
2. *fml* [very] très, fort ▸ **a most interesting theory** une théorie fort intéressante
3. *US inf* [almost] presque.

most-favoured nation n nation *f* la plus favorisée ▸ **this country has most-favoured nation status** ce pays bénéficie de la clause de la nation la plus favorisée.

mostly ['məʊstlɪ] adv principalement, surtout.

MOT *UK* ■ n (abbr of ***Ministry of Transport (test)***) *contrôle technique annuel obligatoire pour les véhicules de plus de trois ans.*
■ vt **: to have one's car MOT'd** soumettre sa voiture au contrôle technique.

motel [məʊ'tel] n motel *m*.

moth [mɒθ] n papillon *m* de nuit / [in clothes] mite *f*.

mothball ['mɒθbɔ:l] n boule *f* de naphtaline.

moth-eaten adj mité(e).

mother ['mʌðəʳ] ■ n mère *f*.
■ vt [child] materner, dorloter.

motherboard ['mʌðəbɔ:d] n COMPUT carte *f* mère.

mother country n (mère) patrie *f*.

mother figure n figure *f* maternelle.

motherfucker ['mʌðə,fʌkəʳ] n *esp US vulg* [person] enculé *m*, -e *f* / [thing] saloperie *f*.

motherhood ['mʌðəhʊd] n maternité *f*.

Mothering Sunday ['mʌðərɪŋ-] n *UK* fête *f* des Mères.

mother-in-law (pl **mothers-in-law**) n belle-mère *f*.

motherland ['mʌðəlænd] n (mère) patrie *f*.

motherless ['mʌðəlɪs] adj orphelin(e) de mère.

motherly ['mʌðəlɪ] adj maternel(elle).

Mother Nature n la nature.

mother-of-pearl ■ n nacre *f*.
■ comp de nacre.

Mother's Day n fête *f* des Mères.

mother ship n ravitailleur *m*.

mother superior n mère *f* supérieure.

mother-to-be (pl **mothers-to-be**) n future maman *f*.

mother tongue n langue *f* maternelle.

motif [məʊ'ti:f] n motif *m*.

motion ['məʊʃn] ■ n **1.** [gen] mouvement *m* ▸ **to set sthg in motion** mettre qqch en branle ▸ **to go through the motions** [act insincerely] faire semblant de faire quelque chose **2.** [in debate] motion *f*.
■ vt **: to motion sb to do sthg** faire signe à qqn de faire qqch.
■ vi **: to motion to sb** faire signe à qqn.

motionless ['məʊʃənlɪs] adj immobile.

motion picture n *US* film *m*.

motion sickness n *US* mal *m* des transports.

motivate ['məʊtɪveɪt] vt **1.** [act, decision] motiver **2.** [student, workforce] **: to motivate sb (to do sthg)** pousser qqn (à faire qqch).

motivated ['məʊtɪveɪtɪd] adj motivé(e).

motivating ['məʊtɪviɪtɪŋ] adj motivant(e).

motivation [,məʊtɪ'veɪʃn] n motivation *f*.

motivational [,məʊtɪ'veɪʃənl] adj motivationnel(elle) ▸ **motivational research** études *fpl* de motivation.

motive ['məʊtɪv] n [reason] motif *m* / LAW mobile *m*.

motiveless ['məʊtɪvlɪs] adj immotivé(e), injustifié(e) ▸ **an apparently motiveless murder** un meurtre sans mobile apparent.

motley ['mɒtlɪ] adj *pej* hétéroclite.

motocross ['məʊtəkrɒs] n motocross *m*.

motor ['məʊtəʳ] ■ adj automobile.
■ n [engine] moteur *m*.
■ vi *UK dated* aller en automobile.

Motorail® ['məʊtəreɪl] n *UK* train *m* autocouchette *OR* autos-couchettes.

motorbike ['məʊtəbaɪk] n *UK inf* moto *f*.

motorboat ['məʊtəbəʊt] n canot *m* automobile.

motorcade ['məʊtəkeɪd] n cortège *m* de voitures.

motor car n *UK dated* automobile *f*, voiture *f*.

motorcycle ['məʊtə,saɪkl] n moto *f*.

motorcyclist ['məʊtə,saɪklɪst] n motocycliste *mf*.

motor home n camping-car *m*.

motoring ['məʊtərɪŋ] ■ adj *dated* [magazine, correspondent] automobile ▸ **a motoring offence** une infraction au code de la route.
■ n tourisme *m* automobile.

motorist ['məʊtərɪst] n automobiliste *mf*.

motorize, *UK* ***-ise*** ['məʊtəraɪz] vt motoriser.

motor lodge n *US* motel *m*.

motor mechanic n mécanicien *m*.

motor neurone disease n maladie *f* de Charcot.

motor racing n *(U) UK* course *f* automobile.

motor scooter n scooter *m*.

motorsport ['məʊtəspɔ:t] n sport *m* mécanique.

motor vehicle n *fml* véhicule *m* automobile.

motorway ['məʊtəweɪ] *UK* ■ n autoroute *f*.
■ comp d'autoroute.

mottled ['mɒtld] adj [leaf] tacheté(e) / [skin] marbré(e).

motto ['mɒtəʊ] (pl -s *OR* -es) n devise *f*.

mould *UK*, ***mold*** *US* [məʊld] ■ n **1.** [growth] moisissure *f* **2.** [shape] moule *m*.
■ vt **1.** [shape] mouler, modeler **2.** *fig* [influence] former, façonner.

moulding *UK*, ***molding*** *US* ['məʊldɪŋ] n **1.** [decoration] moulure *f* **2.** [moulded object] moulage *m*.

mouldy *UK*, ***moldy*** *US* (comp -ier, superl -iest) ['məʊldɪ] adj moisi(e).

moult *UK*, ***molt*** *US* [məʊlt] ■ vt perdre.
■ vi muer.

mound [maʊnd] n **1.** [small hill] tertre *m*, butte *f* **2.** [pile] tas *m*, monceau *m*.

mount [maʊnt] ■ n **1.** [support - for jewel] monture *f* / [- for photograph] carton *m* de montage / [- for machine] support *m* **2.** [horse] monture *f* **3.** [mountain] mont *m*.
■ vt monter ▸ **to mount a horse** monter sur un cheval ▸ **to mount a bike** monter sur *OR* enfourcher un vélo ▸ **to mount guard over** monter la garde auprès de.
■ vi **1.** [increase] monter, augmenter **2.** [climb on horse] se mettre en selle.

mountain ['maʊntɪn] n *lit* & *fig* montagne *f* ▸ **don't make a mountain out of a molehill** n'en fais pas une montagne.

mountain bike n VTT *m*.

mountaineer [ˌmaʊntɪ'nɪə^r] n alpiniste *mf*.

mountaineering [ˌmaʊntɪ'nɪərɪŋ] n alpinisme *m*.

mountain goat n chamois *m*.

mountain lion n puma *m*, cougouar *m*.

mountainous ['maʊntɪnəs] adj [region] montagneux(euse).

mountain range n chaîne *f* de montagnes.

mountain rescue n secours *m* en montagne.

mountainside ['maʊntɪnsaɪd] n flanc *m* *OR* versant *m* d'une montagne ▸ **a village perched on the mountainside** un village juché à flanc de montagne.

mounted ['maʊntɪd] adj monté(e), à cheval.

mounted police n : **the mounted police** la police montée.

Mountie ['maʊntɪ] n *inf membre de la police montée canadienne.*

mounting ['maʊntɪŋ] ■ n = ***mount*** *(sense 1).*
■ adj [pressure, anxiety] croissant(e).

mourn [mɔ:n] ■ vt pleurer.
■ vi : **to mourn (for sb)** pleurer (qqn).

mourner ['mɔ:nə^r] n [related] parent *m* du défunt / [unrelated] ami *m*, -e *f* du défunt.

mournful ['mɔ:nfʊl] adj [face] triste / [sound] lugubre.

mourning ['mɔ:nɪŋ] n deuil *m* ▸ **in mourning** en deuil.

mouse [maʊs] (pl **mice** [maɪs]) n COMPUT & ZOOL souris *f*.

mouse mat *UK*, ***mouse pad*** *US* n COMPUT tapis *m* de souris.

mouse potato n *inf personne passant le plus clair de son temps devant son ordinateur.*

mousetrap ['maʊstræp] n souricière *f*.

moussaka [mu:'sɑ:kə] n moussaka *f*.

mousse [mu:s] n mousse *f*.

moustache [mə'stɑ:ʃ], ***mustache*** *US* ['mʌstæʃ] n moustache *f*.

mousy ['maʊsɪ] (comp -ier, superl -iest) adj *pej* **1.** [shy] timide, effacé(e) **2.** [in colour - hair] châtain clair.

mouth ■ n [maʊθ] (pl [maʊðz]) **1.** [of person, animal] bouche *f* / [of dog, cat, lion] gueule *f* ▸ **to keep one's mouth shut** *inf* se taire **2.** [of cave] entrée *f* / [of river] embouchure *f*.
■ vt [maʊð] [words] former silencieusement (avec la bouche).

-mouthed [maʊðd] suffix : **open-mouthed** bouche bée ▸ **wide-mouthed** [bottle] à large goulot.

mouthful ['maʊθfʊl] n **1.** [of food] bouchée *f* / [of drink] gorgée *f* **2.** *inf* [difficult name] nom *m* à coucher dehors.

mouth organ ['maʊθˌɔ:gən] n harmonica *m*.

mouthpiece ['maʊθpi:s] n **1.** [of telephone] microphone *m* / [of musical instrument] bec *m* **2.** [spokesperson] porte-parole *m inv*.

mouth-to-mouth adj : **mouth-to-mouth resuscitation** bouche-à-bouche *m inv*.

mouth ulcer n aphte *m*.

mouthwash ['maʊθwɒʃ] n eau *f* dentifrice.

mouth-watering [-ˌwɔ:tərɪŋ] adj alléchant(e).

movable ['mu:vəbl] adj mobile.

move [mu:v] ■ n **1.** [movement] mouvement *m* ▸ **one move and you're dead!** un seul geste et tu es mort! ▸ **it's late, I ought to be making a move** il se fait tard, il faut que j'y aille ▸ **to be on the move** [person] être en déplacement / [troops] être en marche ▸ **to get a move on** *inf* se remuer, se grouiller
2. [change - of house] déménagement *m* / [- of job] changement *m* d'emploi
3. [step, measure] pas *m*, démarche *f* ▸ **she made the first move** elle a fait le premier pas ▸ **what do you think their next move will be?** selon vous, que vont-ils faire maintenant?
4. [in game - action] coup *m* / [- turn to play] tour *m*.

■ vt **1.** [shift] déplacer, bouger ▸ **we moved all the chairs indoors/outdoors** nous avons rentré/sorti toutes les chaises ▸ **move all those papers off the table!** enlève tous ces papiers de la table! ▸ **don't move anything on my desk** ne touche à rien sur mon bureau ▸ **move your head to the left** inclinez la tête vers la gauche
2. [change - job, office] changer de ▸ **to move house** *UK* déménager ▸ **she's been moved to the New York office/ to accounts** elle a été mutée au bureau de New York/affectée à la comptabilité ▸ **the meeting has been moved to Friday** [- postponed] la réunion a été remise à vendredi / [- brought forward] la réunion a été avancée à vendredi
3. [emotionally] émouvoir ▸ **I was deeply moved** j'ai été profondément ému OR touché
4. [cause] **: to move sb to do sthg** inciter qqn à faire qqch
5. [propose] **: to move sthg/that...** proposer qqch/que...
■ vi **1.** [shift] bouger ▸ **the handle won't move** la poignée ne bouge pas ▸ **I was so scared I couldn't move** j'étais pétrifié (de terreur) ▸ **she wouldn't move out of my way** elle ne voulait pas s'écarter de mon chemin ▸ **I jumped off while the train was still moving** j'ai sauté avant l'arrêt du train ▸ **the truck started moving backwards** le camion a commencé à reculer ▸ **the guests moved into/out of the dining room** les invités passèrent dans/sortirent de la salle à manger ▸ **the Earth moves around the Sun** la Terre tourne autour du Soleil
2. [to new house] déménager / [to new job] changer d'emploi ▸ **when are you moving to your new apartment?** quand est-ce que vous emménagez dans votre nouvel appartement? ▸ **the company has moved to more modern premises** la société s'est installée dans des locaux plus modernes ▸ **he's moved to a job in publishing** il travaille maintenant dans l'édition
3. [act] agir ▸ **the town council moved to have the school closed down** la municipalité a pris des mesures pour faire fermer l'école ▸ **to get things moving** faire avancer les choses.

◆ ***move about*** vi *UK* = ***move around***.

◆ ***move along*** ■ vt sep faire avancer.
■ vi se déplacer ▸ **the police asked him to move along** la police lui a demandé de circuler.

◆ ***move around*** vi **1.** [fidget] remuer
2. [travel] voyager.

◆ ***move away*** vi [leave] partir.

◆ ***move in*** ■ vt sep [troops] faire intervenir.
■ vi [to house] emménager ▸ **his mother-in-law has moved in with them** sa belle-mère s'est installée OR est venue habiter chez eux.

◆ ***move off*** vi [train, car] partir, s'ébranler.

◆ ***move on*** ■ vt sep faire circuler.
■ vi **1.** [after stopping] se remettre en route
2. [change, progress] **: she's moved on to better things** elle a trouvé une meilleure situation ▸ **can we move on to the second point?** pouvons-nous passer au deuxième point?
■ vi *US* [in life] se tourner vers l'avenir.

◆ ***move out*** ■ vt sep [troops] retirer.
■ vi [from house] déménager ▸ **his girlfriend has moved out** son amie l'a quitté.

◆ ***move over*** vi s'écarter, se pousser.

◆ ***move up*** vi **1.** [on bench] se déplacer
2. *fig* **: you've moved up in the world!** tu en as fait du chemin!

moveable ['mu:vəbl] = ***movable***.

movement ['mu:vmənt] n mouvement *m* ▸ **liberation movement** mouvement de libération ▸ **his movements are being watched** ses déplacements sont surveillés ▸ **his speeches over the last year show a movement towards the right** les discours qu'il a prononcés depuis un an font apparaître un glissement vers la droite.

mover ['mu:vəʳ] n **1.** [physical] **: she's a lovely mover** *inf* elle bouge bien ▸ **he's a fast mover** *inf* c'est un tombeur ▸ **the movers and the shakers** [key people] les hommes *mpl* et les femmes *fpl* d'action **2.** [of a proposal, motion] motionnaire *mf* **3.** *US* [removal company] déménageur *m*.

movie ['mu:vɪ] n *esp US* film *m*.

movie buff n *esp US inf* cinéphile *mf*.

movie camera n caméra *f*.

moviegoer ['mu:vɪˌgəʊəʳ] n *US* cinéphile *mf*.

movie house n *US dated* (salle *f* de) cinéma *m*.

movie industry n *esp US* industrie *f* cinématographique OR du cinéma.

movie rights n *US* droits *mpl* cinématographiques.

movie star n *esp US* star *f*, vedette *f* de cinéma.

movie theater n *US* cinéma *m*.

moving ['mu:vɪŋ] adj **1.** [emotionally] émouvant(e), touchant(e) **2.** [not fixed] mobile.

moving staircase n escalier *m* roulant.

mow [məʊ] (pt -ed, pp -ed OR mown) vt faucher / [lawn] tondre.

◆ ***mow down*** vt sep faucher.

mower ['məʊəʳ] n tondeuse *f* à gazon.

mown [məʊn] pp ➤ ***mow***.

Mozambican [ˌməʊzæm'bi:kn] ■ adj mozambicain(e).
■ n Mozambicain *m*, -e *f*.

Mozambique [ˌməʊzæm'bi:k] n Mozambique *m* ▸ **in Mozambique** au Mozambique.

MP n **1.** (abbr of ***Military Police***) PM **2.** *UK* (abbr of ***Member of Parliament***) ≃ député *m* **3.** *Can* abbr of ***Mounted Police***.

MP3 [ˌempi:'θri:] (abbr of ***MPEG-1 Audio Layer-3***) n COMPUT MP3 *m*.

MPEG ['empeg] (abbr of ***Moving Pictures Expert Group***) n COMPUT MPEG *m*.

mpg (abbr of ***miles per gallon***) n *miles au gallon*.

mph (abbr of ***miles per hour***) n *miles à l'heure*.

MPhil [ˌem'fɪl] (abbr of ***Master of Philosophy***) n *(titulaire d'une) maîtrise de lettres*.

MPS (abbr of ***Member of the Pharmaceutical Society***) n *membre de l'Académie de pharmacie britannique*.

Mr ['mɪstəʳ] n Monsieur *m* / [on letter] M.

MRC (abbr of ***Medical Research Council***) n *conseil de la recherche médicale en Grande-Bretagne*.

MRCP (abbr of ***Member of the Royal College of Physicians***) n *membre de l'Académie de médecine britannique*.

MRCS (abbr of ***Member of the Royal College of Surgeons***) **n** *membre de l'Académie de chirurgie britannique.*

MRCVS (abbr of ***Member of the Royal College of Veterinary Surgeons***) **n** *membre de l'Académie de chirurgie vétérinaire britannique.*

Mr Right **n** *inf* l'homme *m* idéal, le prince charmant ▸ **she's waiting for Mr Right** elle attend le prince charmant ***OR*** l'homme de ses rêves.

Mrs ['mɪsɪz] **n** Madame *f* / [on letter] Mme.

ms. (abbr of ***manuscript***) **n** ms.

MS ■ **n 1.** (abbr of ***manuscript***) ms **2.** (abbr of ***Master of Science***) *(titulaire d'une) maîtrise de sciences américaine* **3.** (abbr of ***multiple sclerosis***) SEP *f.*
■ abbr of ***Mississippi***.

Ms [mɪz] **n** *titre que les femmes peuvent utiliser au lieu de madame ou mademoiselle pour éviter la distinction entre les femmes mariées et les célibataires.*

MSA (abbr of ***Master of Science in Agriculture***) **n** *(titulaire d'une) maîtrise en sciences agricoles.*

MSB (abbr of ***most significant bit/byte***) **n** *bit/octet de poids fort.*

MSc (abbr of ***Master of Science***) **n** *(titulaire d'une) maîtrise de sciences.*

MSF (abbr of ***Manufacturing Science and Finance***) **n** *confédération syndicale britannique.*

msg **n** message *m.*

MSG abbr of ***monosodium glutamate***.

Msgr (abbr of ***Monsignor***) Mgr.

MSP **n** abbr of ***Member of the Scottish Parliament***.

MST (abbr of ***Mountain Standard Time***) **n** *heure d'hiver des montagnes Rocheuses.*

MSW (abbr of ***Master of Social Work***) **n** *(titulaire d'une) maîtrise en travail social.*

MT ■ **n** (abbr of ***machine translation***) TA *f.*
■ abbr of ***Montana***.

Mt (abbr of ***mount***) Mt.

much [mʌtʃ] ■ **adj** (comp **more**, superl **most**) beaucoup de ▸ **there isn't much rice left** il ne reste pas beaucoup de riz ▸ **the tablets didn't do much good** les comprimés n'ont pas servi à grand-chose ***OR*** n'ont pas fait beaucoup d'effet ▸ **as much money as...** autant d'argent que... ▸ **too much** trop de ▸ **how much...?** combien de...? ▸ **how much money do you earn?** tu gagnes combien? ▸ **however much money you give him, it won't be enough** vous pouvez lui donner autant d'argent que vous voulez, ça ne suffira pas.
■ **pron** beaucoup ▸ **is there any left? – not much** est-ce qu'il en reste? – pas beaucoup ▸ **I don't think much of his new house** sa nouvelle maison ne me plaît pas trop ▸ **there's not much anyone can do about it** personne n'y peut grand-chose ▸ **it costs as much as the Japanese model** ça coûte le même prix que le modèle japonais ▸ **too much** trop ▸ **how much do you want?** [gen] combien en voulez-vous? / [money] combien voulez-vous? ▸ **I agreed with much of what she said** j'étais d'accord avec presque tout ce qu'elle a dit ▸ **I'm not much of a cook** je suis un piètre cuisinier ▸ **so much for all my hard work** tout ce travail pour rien ▸ **I thought as much** c'est bien ce que je pensais ▸ **it's not up to much** *UK inf* ça ne vaut pas grand-chose ▸ **there's much to be said for the old-fashioned method** la vieille méthode a beaucoup d'avantages ▸ **there's not much to choose between them** ils se valent.
■ **adv** beaucoup ▸ **much happier/more slowly** beaucoup plus heureux/plus lentement ▸ **I don't go out much** je ne sors pas beaucoup ***OR*** souvent ▸ **thank you very much** merci beaucoup ▸ **without so much as...** sans même...
◆ ***much as*** **conj** bien que *(+ subjunctive).*
◆ ***so much*** ■ **pron** [such a lot] tant ▸ **I've learnt so much on this course** j'ai vraiment appris beaucoup (de choses) en suivant ces cours ▸ **there's still so much to do** il y a encore tant à faire.
■ **adv** tellement ▸ **thank you ever so much** merci infiniment ***OR*** mille fois.

muchness ['mʌtʃnɪs] **n** *UK* **: to be much of a muchness** être blanc bonnet et bonnet blanc.

muck [mʌk] *inf* **n** *(U)* **1.** [dirt] saletés *fpl* **2.** [manure] fumier *m.*
◆ ***muck about***, *UK* ***muck around*** *inf* ■ **vt sep : to muck sb about** traiter qqn par-dessus ***OR*** par-dessous la jambe.
■ **vi** traîner.
◆ ***muck in*** **vi** *UK inf* donner un coup de main.
◆ ***muck out*** **vt sep** [stable] nettoyer.
◆ ***muck up*** **vt sep** *inf* gâcher.

muckraking ['mʌkreɪkɪŋ] **n** *fig* mise *f* au jour de scandales.

mucky ['mʌkɪ] (comp **-ier**, superl **-iest**) **adj 1.** [gen] sale **2.** *UK inf* pornographique.

mucous ['mju:kəs] **adj** muqueux(euse) ▸ **mucous membrane** muqueuse *f.*

mucus ['mju:kəs] **n** mucus *m.*

mud [mʌd] **n** boue *f.*

muddle ['mʌdl] ■ **n** désordre *m*, fouillis *m* ▸ **to be in a muddle** [room, finances] être en désordre / [person] ne plus s'y retrouver ▸ **my finances are in an awful muddle** ma situation financière n'est pas claire du tout ***OR*** est complètement embrouillée ▸ **let's try to sort out this muddle** *fig* essayons de démêler cet écheveau.
■ **vt 1.** [papers] mélanger **2.** [person] embrouiller ▸ **now you've got me muddled** maintenant, je ne sais plus où j'en suis.
◆ ***muddle along*** **vi** se débrouiller tant bien que mal.
◆ ***muddle through*** **vi** se tirer d'affaire, s'en sortir tant bien que mal.
◆ ***muddle up*** **vt sep** mélanger.

muddle-headed [-ˌhedɪd] **adj** [thinking] confus(e) / [person] brouillon(onne).

muddy ['mʌdɪ] ■ **adj** (comp **-ier**, superl **-iest**) boueux(euse).
■ **vt** (pt & pp **-ied**) *fig* embrouiller.

mudflap ['mʌdflæp] **n** *UK* pare-boue *m inv.*

mudflat ['mʌdflæt] **n** laisse *f.*

mudguard ['mʌdgɑ:d] **n** garde-boue *m inv.*

mud hut **n** case *f* en pisé ***OR*** en terre.

mudpack ['mʌdpæk] **n** masque *m* de beauté.

mudslinging ['mʌdˌslɪŋɪŋ] **n** *(U) fig* attaques *fpl.*

muesli ['mju:zlɪ] **n** muesli *m*.
muezzin [mu:'ezɪn] **n** muezzin *m*.
muff [mʌf] ■ **n** manchon *m*.
■ **vt** *inf* louper.
muffin ['mʌfɪn] **n** muffin *m*.
muffle ['mʌfl] **vt** étouffer.
muffled ['mʌfld] **adj** **1.** [sound] sourd(e), étouffé(e) **2.** [person] **: muffled (up)** emmitouflé(e).
muffler ['mʌflər] **n** *US* [for car] silencieux *m*.
mug [mʌg] ■ **n** **1.** [cup] (grande) tasse *f* **2.** *UK inf* [fool] andouille *f*.
■ **vt** (pt & pp **-ged**, cont **-ging**) [attack] agresser.
mugger ['mʌgər] **n** agresseur *m*.
mugging ['mʌgɪŋ] **n** agression *f*.
muggy ['mʌgɪ] (comp **-ier**, superl **-iest**) **adj** lourd(e), moite.
mugshot ['mʌgʃɒt] **n** *inf* photo *f* (de criminel).
Muhammad [mə'hæmɪd] **n** Mohammed, Mahomet.
mujaheddin [ˌmu:dʒəhe'di:n] **npl** moudjahiddin *mpl*.
mulatto [mju:'lætəʊ] (pl **-s** *OR* **-es**) **n** *offens* mûlatre *m*, mûlatresse *f*.
mulberry ['mʌlbərɪ] (pl **-ies**) **n** **1.** [tree] mûrier *m* **2.** [fruit] mûre *f*.
mulch [mʌltʃ] ■ **n** paillis *m*.
■ **vt** pailler.
mule [mju:l] **n** mule *f*.
mull [mʌl] ◆ ***mull over*** **vt sep** ruminer, réfléchir à.
mullah ['mʌlə] **n** mollah *m*.
mulled [mʌld] **adj : mulled wine** vin *m* chaud.
mullet ['mʌlɪt] (pl **mullet** *OR* **-s**) **n** mulet *m*.
mulligatawny [ˌmʌlɪgə'tɔ:nɪ] **n** *soupe indienne au curry*.
mullioned ['mʌlɪənd] **adj** [window] à meneaux.
multi- ['mʌltɪ] **prefix** multi-.
multiaccess [ˌmʌltɪ'ækses] **adj** COMPUT multiaccès *(inv)*.
multichannel [ˌmʌltɪ'tʃænl] **adj** multicanal.
multicoloured *UK*, ***multicolored*** *US* ['mʌltɪˌkʌləd] **adj** multicolore.
multicultural [ˌmʌltɪ'kʌltʃərəl] **adj** multiculturel(elle).
multidisciplinary ['mʌltɪˌdɪsɪ'plɪnərɪ] **adj** *UK* pluridisciplinaire, multidisciplinaire.
multiethnic [ˌmʌltɪ'eθnɪk] **adj** pluriethnique.
multifaceted [ˌmʌltɪ'fæsɪtɪd] **adj** présentant de multiples facettes.
multifaith ['mʌltɪfeɪθ] **adj** multiconfessionnel(le) ▸ **multifaith organization** organisation multiconfessionnelle.
multifarious [ˌmʌltɪ'feərɪəs] **adj** *fml* divers(e), très varié(e).
multigym ['mʌltɪdʒɪm] **n** appareil *m* de musculation.
multilateral [ˌmʌltɪ'lætərəl] **adj** multilatéral(e).
multilingual [ˌmʌltɪ'lɪŋgwəl] **adj** multilingue.
multimedia [ˌmʌltɪ'mi:djə] **adj** multimédia *(inv)*.
multi-million **adj : a multi-million pound/dollar project** un projet de plusieurs millions de livres/dollars.
multimillionaire ['mʌltɪˌmɪljə'neər] **n** multimillionnaire *mf*.
multinational [ˌmʌltɪ'næʃənl] ■ **adj** multinational(e).
■ **n** multinationale *f*.
multiparty ['mʌltɪˌpɑ:tɪ] **adj** multipartite ▸ **the multiparty system** le pluripartisme.
multiple ['mʌltɪpl] ■ **adj** multiple.
■ **n** multiple *m*.
multiple-choice **adj** à choix multiple.
multiple crash *UK*, ***multiple-car crash*** **n** carambolage *m*.
multiple injuries **npl** lésions *fpl* multiples.
multiple sclerosis [-sklɪ'rəʊsɪs] **n** sclérose *f* en plaques.
multiplex ['mʌltɪpleks] ■ **n** **1.** TELEC multiplex *m* **2.** CIN complexe *m* multisalles.
■ **comp** TELEC multiplex.
■ **vt** TELEC multiplexer.
multiplex cinema *UK*, ***multiplex theater*** *US* **n** complexe *m* multisalles.
multiplication [ˌmʌltɪplɪ'keɪʃn] **n** multiplication *f*.
multiplication sign **n** signe *m* de multiplication.
multiplication table **n** table *f* de multiplication.
multiplicity [ˌmʌltɪ'plɪsətɪ] **n** multiplicité *f*.
multiplier ['mʌltɪplaɪər] **n** **1.** ECON, ELECTRON & MATHS multiplicateur *m* **2.** COMPUT multiplieur *m*.
multiply ['mʌltɪplaɪ] (pt & pp **-ied**) ■ **vt** multiplier.
■ **vi** se multiplier.
multiprocessing ['mʌltɪprəʊsesɪŋ] **n** COMPUT multitraitement *m*.
multiprocessor [ˌmʌltɪ'prəʊsesər] **n** COMPUT multiprocesseur *m*.
multiprogramming [ˌmʌltɪ'prəʊgræmɪŋ] **n** COMPUT multiprogrammation *f*.
multipurpose [ˌmʌltɪ'pɜ:pəs] **adj** polyvalent(e), à usages multiples.
multiracial [ˌmʌltɪ'reɪʃl] **adj** multiracial(e).
multistorey *UK*, ***multistory*** *US* [ˌmʌltɪ'stɔ:rɪ] ■ **adj** à étages.
■ **n** [car park] parking *m* à étages.
multitasking [ˌmʌltɪ'tɑ:skɪŋ] ■ **n** multitâche *f*.
■ **comp** multitâche.
multitude ['mʌltɪtju:d] **n** multitude *f*.
multitudinous [ˌmʌltɪ'tju:dɪnəs] **adj** *fml* [countless] innombrable.
multi-user **adj** COMPUT [system] multi-utilisateurs *(inv)*.
multivitamin [*UK* 'mʌltɪvɪtəmɪn, *US* 'mʌltɪvaɪtəmɪn] **n** multivitamine *f*.
mum [mʌm] *inf* ■ **n** *UK* maman *f*.
■ **adj : to keep mum** ne pas piper mot.
mumble ['mʌmbl] **vt & vi** marmotter.

mumbo jumbo ['mʌmbəʊ'dʒʌmbəʊ] **n** charabia *m*.

mummify ['mʌmɪfaɪ] (pt & pp **-ied**) **vt** momifier.

mummy ['mʌmɪ] (pl **-ies**) **n** **1.** *UK inf* [mother] maman *f* **2.** [preserved body] momie *f*.

mumps [mʌmps] **n** *(U)* oreillons *mpl*.

munch [mʌntʃ] **vt** & **vi** croquer.

mundane [mʌn'deɪn] **adj** banal(e), ordinaire.

mung bean [mʌŋ-] **n** mungo *m*.

municipal [mju:'nɪsɪpl] **adj** municipal(e).

municipality [mju:ˌnɪsɪ'pælətɪ] (pl **-ies**) **n** municipalité *f*.

munificent [mju:'nɪfɪsənt] **adj** *fml* munificent(e).

munitions [mju:'nɪʃnz] **npl** munitions *fpl*.

mural ['mju:ərəl] **n** peinture *f* murale.

murder ['mɜ:dər] ■ **n** meurtre *m* ▸ **to get away with murder** *fig* pouvoir faire n'importe quoi impunément.
■ **vt** assassiner.

murderer ['mɜ:dərər] **n** meurtrier *m*, assassin *m*.

murderess ['mɜ:dərɪs] **n** *dated* meurtrière *f*.

murderous ['mɜ:dərəs] **adj** meurtrier(ère).

murky ['mɜ:kɪ] (comp **-ier**, superl **-iest**) **adj** **1.** [place] sombre **2.** [water, past] trouble.

murmur ['mɜ:mər] ■ **n** murmure *m* / MED souffle *m* au cœur.
■ **vt** & **vi** murmurer.

murmuring ['mɜ:mərɪŋ] ■ **n** murmure *m*.
■ **adj** murmurant.
◆ ***murmurings*** **npl** murmures *mpl*.

Murphy's law ['mɜ:fɪz-] **n** loi *f* de l'emmerdement maximum.

MusB [mju:z'bi:], ***Musbac*** [mju:z'bæk] (abbr of ***Bachelor of Music***) **n** *(titulaire d'un) diplôme d'études musicales*.

muscle ['mʌsl] **n** muscle *m* / *fig* [power] poids *m*, impact *m*.
◆ ***muscle in*** **vi** intervenir, s'immiscer.

muscleman ['mʌslmən] (pl **-men** [-men]) **n** hercule *m*.

Muscovite ['mʌskəvaɪt] ■ **adj** moscovite.
■ **n** Moscovite *mf*.

muscular ['mʌskjʊlər] **adj** **1.** [spasm, pain] musculaire **2.** [person] musclé(e).

muscular dystrophy [-'dɪstrəfɪ] **n** myopathie *f* primitive progressive, dystrophie *f* musculaire.

MusD [mju:z'di:], ***MusDoc*** [mju:z'dɒk] (abbr of ***Doctor of Music***) **n** *(titulaire d'un) doctorat d'études musicales*.

muse [mju:z] ■ **n** muse *f*.
■ **vi** méditer, réfléchir.

museum [mju:'zi:əm] **n** musée *m*.

museum piece **n** *lit* & *fig* pièce *f* de musée.

mush [mʌʃ] **n** **1.** [food] bouillie *f* **2.** *inf* [sentimentality] sentimentalité *f*.

mushroom ['mʌʃrʊm] ■ **n** champignon *m*.
■ **vi** [organization, party] se développer, grandir / [houses] proliférer.

mushroom cloud **n** champignon *m* atomique.

mushy ['mʌʃɪ] (comp **-ier**, superl **-iest**) **adj** **1.** [food] en bouillie **2.** *inf* [over-sentimental] à l'eau de rose, à la guimauve.

music ['mju:zɪk] **n** musique *f*.

musical ['mju:zɪkl] ■ **adj** **1.** [event, voice] musical(e) **2.** [child] doué(e) pour la musique, musicien(enne).
■ **n** comédie *f* musicale.

musical box *UK*, ***music box*** *US* **n** boîte *f* à musique.

musical chairs **n** *(U)* chaises *fpl* musicales.

musical instrument **n** instrument *m* de musique.

musically ['mju:zɪklɪ] **adv** [in a musical way] musicalement / [from a musical viewpoint] musicalement, d'un point de vue musical.

music box *US* = ***musical box***.

music centre *UK*, ***music center*** *US* **n** chaîne *f* compacte.

music hall **n** *UK* music-hall *m*.

musician [mju:'zɪʃn] **n** musicien *m*, -enne *f*.

music piracy **n** piratage *m* musical.

music stand **n** pupitre *m* à musique.

music video **n** clip *m* (vidéo).

musing ['mju:zɪŋ] ■ **n** *(U)* songes *mpl*, rêverie *f*.
■ **adj** songeur(euse), rêveur(euse).

musk [mʌsk] **n** musc *m*.

musket ['mʌskɪt] **n** mousquet *m*.

muskrat ['mʌskræt] **n** rat *m* musqué, ondatra *m*.

musky ['mʌskɪ] (comp **-ier**, superl **-iest**) **adj** musqué(e).

Muslim ['mʊzlɪm] ■ **adj** musulman(e).
■ **n** Musulman *m*, -e *f*.

muslin ['mʌzlɪn] **n** mousseline *f*.

musquash ['mʌskwɒʃ] **n** rat *m* musqué, ondatra *m*.

muss [mʌs] **vt** *US* : **to muss (up)** [clothes] chiffonner, froisser / [hair] déranger.

mussel ['mʌsl] **n** moule *f*.

must [mʌst] ■ **modal vb** **1.** [expressing obligation] devoir ▸ **I must go** il faut que je m'en aille, je dois partir ▸ **if you must know, he's asked me out to dinner** si tu veux tout savoir, il m'a invitée à dîner ▸ **must you be so rude?** es-tu obligé d'être aussi grossier? ▸ **you must come and visit** il faut absolument que tu viennes nous voir **2.** [expressing likelihood] : **you must be Alison** vous devez être Alison ▸ **they must have known** ils devaient le savoir.
■ **n** *inf* : **a must** un must, un impératif ▸ **the film is a must** c'est un film à voir absolument.

mustache *US* = ***moustache***.

mustachioed [mə'stɑ:ʃɪəʊd] **adj** moustachu(e).

mustard ['mʌstəd] **n** moutarde *f* ▸ **mustard and cress** *UK* moutarde blanche et cresson alénois.

mustard gas n gaz *m* moutarde.

muster ['mʌstəʳ] ■ **vt** rassembler.
■ **vi** se réunir, se rassembler.
◆ ***muster up*** **vt insep** rassembler.

musn't [mʌsnt] = ***must not***.

must've ['mʌstəv] = ***must have***.

musty ['mʌstɪ] (comp **-ier**, superl **-iest**) **adj** [smell] de moisi / [room] qui sent le renfermé *OR* le moisi.

mutable ['mju:təbl] **adj** [gen] mutable / [in astrology] mutable, commun(e).

mutant ['mju:tənt] ■ **adj** mutant(e).
■ **n** mutant *m*.

mutate [mju:'teɪt] **vi** subir une mutation, muter ▸ **to mutate into sthg** se changer en qqch, se transformer en qqch.

mutation [mju:'teɪʃn] **n** mutation *f*.

mute [mju:t] ■ **adj** muet(ette).
■ **n** muet *m*, -ette *f*.
■ **vt** étouffer, assourdir.

muted ['mju:tɪd] **adj 1.** [colour] sourd(e) **2.** [reaction] peu marqué(e) / [protest] voilé(e).

mutely ['mju:tlɪ] **adv** [stare, gaze] en silence.

mutilate ['mju:tɪleɪt] **vt** mutiler.

mutilation [ˌmju:tɪ'leɪʃn] **n** mutilation *f*.

mutineer [ˌmju:tɪ'nɪəʳ] **n** mutiné *m*, mutin *m*.

mutinous ['mju:tɪnəs] **adj** [crew, soldiers] mutiné(e) / [person, attitude] rebelle.

mutiny ['mju:tɪnɪ] ■ **n** (pl **-ies**) mutinerie *f*.
■ **vi** (pt & pp **-ied**) se mutiner.

mutt [mʌt] **n** *inf* **1.** *UK* [fool] andouille *f*, crétin *m*, -e *f* **2.** [dog] clébard *m*.

mutter ['mʌtəʳ] ■ **vt** [threat, curse] marmonner.
■ **vi** marmotter, marmonner ▸ **to mutter to o.s.** marmotter, parler dans sa barbe.

muttering ['mʌtərɪŋ] **n 1.** [remark] marmonnement *m*, marmottement *m* **2.** [sound] murmure *m*.

mutton ['mʌtn] **n** mouton *m* ▸ **she's mutton dressed as lamb** *UK* c'est une vieille coquette.

mutual ['mju:tʃʊəl] **adj 1.** [feeling, help] réciproque, mutuel(elle) **2.** [friend, interest] commun(e).

mutual fund **n** *US* fonds *m* commun de placement.

mutually ['mju:tʃʊəlɪ] **adv** mutuellement, réciproquement ▸ **mutually exclusive** qui s'excluent l'un l'autre.

Muzak® ['mju:zæk] **n** musique *f* d'ambiance.

muzzle ['mʌzl] ■ **n 1.** [of dog - mouth] museau *m* / [- guard] muselière *f* **2.** [of gun] gueule *f*.
■ **vt** *lit* & *fig* museler.

muzzy ['mʌzɪ] (comp **-ier**, superl **-iest**) **adj** *UK inf* embrouillé(e), confus(e).

MVP (abbr of ***most valuable player***) **n** *US titre de meilleur joueur décerné à celui qui a réalisé la meilleure performance lors d'un match, d'une saison etc.*

MW (abbr of ***medium wave***) PO.

my [maɪ] **poss adj 1.** [referring to oneself] mon (ma), mes *(pl)* ▸ **my dog** mon chien ▸ **my house** ma maison ▸ **my children** mes enfants ▸ **my name is Joe/Sarah** je m'appelle Joe/Sarah ▸ **it wasn't MY fault** ce n'était pas de ma faute à moi **2.** [in titles] **: yes, my Lord** oui, monsieur le comte/duc *etc*.

Myanmar [ˌmaɪæn'mɑ:ʳ] **n** Myanmar *m* ▸ **in Myanmar** au Myanmar.

mynah (bird) ['maɪnə-] **n** mainate *m*.

myopic [maɪ'ɒpɪk] **adj** myope.

myriad ['mɪrɪəd] *liter* ■ **adj** innombrable.
■ **n** myriade *f*.

myrrh [mɜ:ʳ] **n** myrrhe *f*.

myrtle ['mɜ:tl] **n** myrte *m*.

myself [maɪ'self] **pron 1.** *(reflexive)* me / *(after prep)* moi **2.** *(for emphasis)* moi-même ▸ **I did it myself** je l'ai fait tout seul.

mysterious [mɪ'stɪərɪəs] **adj** mystérieux(euse) ▸ **to be mysterious about sthg** faire (un) mystère de qqch.

mysteriously [mɪ'stɪərɪəslɪ] **adv** mystérieusement.

mystery ['mɪstərɪ] ■ **n** (pl **-ies**) mystère *m* ▸ **it's a mystery to me why she came** la raison de sa venue est un mystère pour moi, je n'ai aucune idée de la raison pour laquelle elle est venue ▸ **his past is a mystery** son passé est bien mystérieux ▸ **she has a certain mystery about her** il se dégage de sa personne une impression de mystère.
■ **comp** mystérieux(euse).

mystery (story) **n** histoire *f* à suspense.

mystery tour **n** *UK* voyage *m* surprise *(dont la destination est inconnue)*.

mystic ['mɪstɪk] ■ **adj** [power] occulte / [rite] mystique, ésotérique.
■ **n** mystique *mf*.

mystical ['mɪstɪkl] **adj** mystique.

mysticism ['mɪstɪsɪzm] **n** mysticisme *m*.

mystification [ˌmɪstɪfɪ'keɪʃn] **n** mystification *f*.

mystified ['mɪstɪfaɪd] **adj** perplexe.

mystify ['mɪstɪfaɪ] (pt & pp **-ied**) **vt** [puzzle] déconcerter, laisser *OR* rendre perplexe / [deceive] mystifier.

mystifying ['mɪstɪfaɪɪŋ] **adj** inexplicable, déconcertant(e).

mystique [mɪ'sti:k] **n** mystique *f*.

myth [mɪθ] **n** mythe *m*.

mythic ['mɪθɪk] **adj** légendaire.

mythical ['mɪθɪkl] **adj** mythique.

mythological [ˌmɪθə'lɒdʒɪkl] **adj** mythologique.

mythology [mɪ'θɒlədʒɪ] (pl **-ies**) **n** mythologie *f*.

myxomatosis [ˌmɪksəmə'təʊsɪs] **n** myxomatose *f*.

n [en] (pl **n's** OR **ns**), ***N*** (pl **N's** OR **Ns**) **n** [letter] n *m inv*, N *m inv*.
◆ ***N*** (abbr of ***north***) N.

n/a, ***N/A*** (abbr of ***not applicable***) s.o.

NA (abbr of ***Narcotics Anonymous***) **n** *association américaine d'aide aux toxicomanes*.

NAACP (abbr of ***National Association for the Advancement of Colored People***) **n** *association nationale américaine pour la promotion de gens de couleur*.

NAAFI ['næfɪ] (abbr of ***Navy, Army & Air Force Institute***) **n** *organisme approvisionnant les forces armées britanniques en biens de consommation*.

nab [næb] (pt & pp **-bed**, cont **-bing**) **vt** *inf* **1.** [arrest] pincer **2.** [get quickly] attraper, accaparer.

NACU (abbr of ***National Association of Colleges and Universities***) **n** *association des établissements d'enseignement supérieur américains*.

nadir ['neɪˌdɪəʳ] **n** *fml* & ASTRON nadir *m* ▸ **to be at/reach a nadir** *fig* être/tomber au plus bas.

naff [næf] **adj** *UK inf* nul (nulle).

NAFTA (abbr of ***North American Free Trade Agreement***) **n** ALENA *m (Accord de libre-échange nord-américain)*.

CULTURE
NAFTA

Signé en 1992, le traité de l'ALENA entre le Canada, les États-Unis et le Mexique est entré en vigueur en janvier 1994. Il ouvre les frontières douanières, à la libre circulation des marchandises, des capitaux et des investissements privés, ce qui a nettement amélioré la croissance économique et le niveau de vie des trois pays. Certains syndicats américains dénoncent cependant une délocalisation excessive des emplois. De plus, cet accord pose de sérieux problèmes économiques aux ports francs caribéens, qui doivent faire face à la concurrence des exportations mexicaines.

nag [næg] ■ **vt** (pt & pp **-ged**, cont **-ging**) harceler.
■ **vi** (pt & pp **-ged**, cont **-ging**) **: to nag at sb** harceler qqn ▸ **stop nagging!** arrête de me casser les pieds!
■ **n** *inf* **1.** [person] enquiquineur *m*, -euse *f* **2.** [horse] canasson *m*.

nagging ['nægɪŋ] **adj** **1.** [doubt] persistant(e), tenace **2.** [husband, wife] enquiquineur(euse).

nail [neɪl] ■ **n** **1.** [for fastening] clou *m* ▸ **to hit the nail on the head** mettre le doigt dessus **2.** [of finger, toe] ongle *m*.
■ **vt** clouer.
◆ ***nail down*** **vt sep** **1.** [lid] clouer **2.** *fig* [person] **: to nail sb down to sthg** faire préciser qqch à qqn.
◆ ***nail up*** **vt sep** [notice] fixer avec des clous, clouer.

nail-biting **adj** plein(e) de suspense.

nailbrush ['neɪlbrʌʃ] **n** brosse *f* à ongles.

nail clippers **npl** = ***nail scissors***.

nail file **n** lime *f* à ongles.

nail polish **n** vernis *m* à ongles.

nail scissors **npl** ciseaux *mpl* à ongles.

nail varnish **n** *UK* vernis *m* à ongles.

nail varnish remover [-rɪ'muːvəʳ] **n** *UK* dissolvant *m*.

Nairobi [naɪ'rəʊbɪ] **n** Nairobi.

naive, ***naïve*** [naɪ'iːv] **adj** naïf(ïve).

naively, ***naïvely*** [naɪ'iːvlɪ] **adv** naïvement, avec naïveté.

naivety, ***naïvety*** [naɪ'iːvtɪ] **n** naïveté *f*.

naked ['neɪkɪd] **adj** **1.** [body, flame] nu(e) ▸ **with the naked eye** à l'œil nu **2.** [emotions] manifeste, évident(e) / [aggression] non déguisé(e) ▸ **the naked truth** la vérité toute nue.

nakedness ['neɪkɪdnɪs] **n** nudité *f*.

NALGO ['nælgəʊ] (abbr of ***National and Local Government Officers' Association***) **n** *ancien syndicat britannique de la fonction publique*.

Nam [næm] (abbr of ***Vietnam***) **n** *US inf* Vietnam *m*.

NAM (abbr of ***National Association of Manufacturers***) **n** *organisation patronale américaine*.

namby-pamby [ˌnæmbɪ'pæmbɪ] ■ adj *inf* [person] gnangnan *(inv)*, cucul *(inv)* / [style] à l'eau de rose, fadasse.
■ n lavette *f*, gnangnan *mf*.

name [neɪm] ■ n **1.** [identification] nom *m* ▸ **what's your name?** comment vous appelez-vous? ▸ **my name's Richard** je m'appelle Richard ▸ **have you put your name down for evening classes?** est-ce que vous vous êtes inscrit aux cours du soir? ▸ **to know sb by name** connaître qqn de nom ▸ **someone by** *OR* **of the name of Penn** quelqu'un du nom de *OR* qui s'appelle Penn ▸ **I know it by** *OR* **under a different name** je le connais sous un autre nom ▸ **in my/his name** à mon/son nom ▸ **in the name of peace** au nom de la paix ▸ **in God's name!, in the name of God!** pour l'amour de Dieu! ▸ **in name only** de nom seulement ▸ **to call sb names** traiter qqn de tous les noms, injurier qqn
2. [reputation] réputation *f* ▸ **to make a name for o.s.** se faire un nom ▸ **we have the company's (good) name to think of** il faut penser au renom de la société ▸ **to have a bad name** avoir (une) mauvaise réputation
3. [famous person] grand nom *m*, célébrité *f*.
■ vt **1.** [give name to] nommer ▸ **they named the baby Felix** ils ont appelé *OR* prénommé le bébé Felix ▸ **to name sb/sthg after, to name sb/sthg for** *US* donner à qqn/à qqch le nom de ▸ **the fellow named Chip** le dénommé Chip
2. [identify] désigner, nommer ▸ **the journalist refused to name his source** le journaliste a refusé de révéler *OR* de donner le nom de son informateur ▸ **whatever you need, just name it** vos moindres désirs seront exaucés ▸ **name the books of the Old Testament** citez les livres de l'Ancien Testament ▸ **to name names** donner des noms
3. [appoint] nommer, désigner ▸ **she has been named as president** elle a été nommée présidente ▸ **June 22nd has been named as the date of the elections** la date du 22 juin a été retenue *OR* choisie pour les élections ▸ **they've finally named the day** ils ont enfin fixé la date de leur mariage.

name-calling n *(U)* insultes *fpl*, injures *fpl*.

name-dropping n *allusion fréquente à des personnes connues dans le but d'impressionner* ▸ **I hate name-dropping** je déteste les gens qui veulent donner l'impression de connaître tous les grands de ce monde.

nameless ['neɪmlɪs] adj inconnu(e), sans nom / [author] anonyme.

namely ['neɪmlɪ] adv à savoir, c'est-à-dire.

nameplate ['neɪmpleɪt] n plaque *f*.

namesake ['neɪmseɪk] n homonyme *m*.

Namibia [nɑː'mɪbɪə] n Namibie *f* ▸ **in Namibia** en Namibie.

Namibian [nɑː'mɪbɪən] ■ adj namibien(enne).
■ n Namibien *m*, -enne *f*.

naming ['neɪmɪŋ] n **1.** [gen] attribution *f* d'un nom / [of ship] baptême *m* **2.** [citing] mention *f*, citation *f* **3.** [appointment] nomination *f*.

nan(a) [næn(ə)] n *UK inf* mamie *f*, mémé *f*.

nan (bread) n *(U)* pain *m* nan.

nanny ['nænɪ] (pl -ies) n *UK* nurse *f*, bonne *f* d'enfants.

nanny goat n chèvre *f*, bique *f*.

nanny state n État *m* paternaliste.

nanometre *UK*, ***nanometer*** *US* ['nænəʊˌmiːtə^r] n nanomètre *m*.

nanosecond ['nænəʊˌsekənd] n nanoseconde *f*.

nanotechnology ['nænəʊˌteknɒlədʒɪ] n nanotechnologie *f*.

nap [næp] ■ n : **to have** *OR* **take a nap** faire un petit somme.
■ vi (pt & pp **-ped**, cont **-ping**) faire un petit somme ▸ **to be caught napping** *inf fig* être pris(e) au dépourvu.

NAPA (abbr of ***National Association of Performing Artists***) n *syndicat américain des gens du spectacle*.

napalm ['neɪpɑːm] n napalm *m*.

nape [neɪp] n nuque *f*.

napkin ['næpkɪn] n serviette *f*.

nappy ['næpɪ] (pl -ies) n *UK* couche *f*.

nappy liner n *UK* change *m* (jetable).

nappy rash n *UK* érythème *m* fessier ▸ **babies often get nappy rash** les bébés ont souvent les fesses rouges et irritées.

narcissi [nɑː'sɪsaɪ] npl ➤ ***narcissus***.

narcissism ['nɑːsɪsɪzm] n narcissisme *m*.

narcissistic [ˌnɑːsɪ'sɪstɪk] adj narcissique.

narcissus [nɑː'sɪsəs] (pl **-cissuses** *OR* **-cissi** [-sɪsaɪ]) n narcisse *m*.

narcotic [nɑː'kɒtɪk] n stupéfiant *m*, narcotique *m*.

nark [nɑːk] *UK inf dated* ■ n [police] mouchard *m*, indic *m*.
■ vt mettre en rogne.

narky ['nɑːkɪ] (comp -ier, superl -iest) adj *UK inf dated* de mauvais poil.

narrate [*UK* nə'reɪt, *US* 'næreɪt] vt raconter, narrer.

narration [*UK* nə'reɪʃn, *US* næ'reɪʃn] n narration *f*.

narrative ['nærətɪv] ■ adj narratif(ive).
■ n **1.** [story] récit *m*, narration *f* **2.** [skill] art *m* de la narration.

narrator [*UK* nə'reɪtə^r, *US* 'næreɪtər] n narrateur *m*, -trice *f*.

narrow ['nærəʊ] ■ adj **1.** [gen] étroit(e) ▸ **to have a narrow escape** l'échapper belle **2.** [victory, majority] de justesse ▸ **it was another narrow victory/defeat for the French side** l'équipe française l'a encore emporté de justesse/a encore perdu de peu.
■ vt **1.** [reduce] réduire, limiter ▸ **the police have narrowed their search to a few streets in central Glasgow** la police concentre ses recherches sur quelques rues du centre de Glasgow **2.** [eyes] fermer à demi, plisser.
■ vi *lit & fig* se rétrécir.
◆ ***narrow down*** vt sep réduire, limiter.

narrow-band adj à bande étroite.

narrow boat n péniche *f* (étroite).

narrow gauge n voie *f* étroite.
◆ ***narrow-gauge*** adj [track, line] à voie étroite.

narrowly ['nærəʊlɪ] adv **1.** [win, lose] de justesse **2.** [miss] de peu.

narrow-minded [-'maɪndɪd] **adj** [person] à l'esprit étroit, borné(e) / [attitude] étroit(e), borné(e).

narrow-mindedness [-'maɪndɪdnɪs] **n** étroitesse *f* d'esprit.

narrowness ['nærəʊnɪs] **n** étroitesse *f*.

NAS (abbr of ***National Academy of Sciences***) **n** *académie américaine des sciences.*

NASA ['næsə] (abbr of ***National Aeronautics and Space Administration***) **n** NASA *f*.

nasal ['neɪzl] **adj** nasal(e).

nascent ['neɪsənt] **adj** *fml* naissant(e).

NASDAQ [næzdæk] (abbr of ***National Association of Securities Dealers Automated Quotation***) **n** [in US] NASDAQ *m*.

nastily ['nɑːstɪlɪ] **adv** **1.** [unkindly] méchamment **2.** [painfully] **: to fall nastily** faire une mauvaise chute.

nastiness ['nɑːstɪnɪs] **n** [unkindness] méchanceté *f*.

nasturtium [nəs'tɜːʃəm] (pl **-s**) **n** capucine *f*.

nasty ['nɑːstɪ] (comp **-ier**, superl **-iest**) **adj** **1.** [unpleasant - smell, feeling] mauvais(e) / [- weather] vilain(e), mauvais(e) ▸ **things started to turn nasty** la situation a pris une vilaine tournure ▸ **everything they sell is cheap and nasty** ils ne vendent que de la pacotille **2.** [unkind] méchant(e) ▸ **to be nasty to sb** être méchant(e) avec qqn **3.** [problem] difficile, délicat(e) **4.** [injury] vilain(e) / [accident] grave / [fall] mauvais(e).

NAS/UWT (abbr of ***National Association of Schoolmasters/Union of Women Teachers***) **n** *syndicat d'enseignants et de chefs d'établissement en Grande-Bretagne.*

Natal [nə'tæl] **n** Natal *m* ▸ **in Natal** au Natal.

nation ['neɪʃn] **n** nation *f*.

national ['næʃənl] ■ **adj** national(e) / [campaign, strike] à l'échelon national / [custom] du pays, de la nation.
■ **n** ressortissant *m*, -e *f*.

national anthem **n** hymne *m* national.

National Curriculum **n : the National Curriculum** *programme introduit en 1988 définissant au niveau national (Angleterre et pays de Galles) le contenu de l'enseignement primaire et secondaire.*

national debt **n** dette *f* publique.

national dress **n** costume *m* national.

national grid **n** *UK* réseau *m* électrique national.

National Guard **n : the National Guard** la Garde Nationale *(armée nationale américaine composée de volontaires).*

National Health Service **n : the National Health Service** *le service national de santé britannique.*

National Heritage Minister **n** *ministre britannique de la culture et des sports.*

National Insurance *UK* **n** *(U)* **1.** [system] *système de sécurité sociale (maladie, retraite) et d'assurance chômage* **2.** [payment] ≃ contributions *fpl* à la Sécurité sociale.

nationalism ['næʃnəlɪzm] **n** nationalisme *m*.

nationalist ['næʃnəlɪst] ■ **adj** nationaliste.
■ **n** nationaliste *mf*.

nationalistic [ˌnæʃnə'lɪstɪk] **adj** nationaliste.

nationality [ˌnæʃə'nælətɪ] (pl **-ies**) **n** nationalité *f*.

nationalization, *UK* ***-isation*** [ˌnæʃnəlaɪ'zeɪʃn] **n** nationalisation *f*.

nationalize, *UK* ***-ise*** ['næʃnəlaɪz] **vt** nationaliser.

nationalized, *UK* ***-ised*** ['næʃnəlaɪzd] **adj** nationalisé(e).

National League **n** *l'une des deux ligues professionnelles de base-ball aux États-Unis.*

National Lottery **n** Loto *m* britannique.

nationally ['næʃnəlɪ] **adv** nationalement.

national park **n** parc *m* national.

national press **n** presse *f* nationale.

national service **n** MIL service *m* national ***OR*** militaire.

national socialism **n** national-socialisme *m*.

national socialist ■ **adj** national-socialiste.
■ **n** national-socialiste *mf*.

National Trust **n** *UK* **: the National Trust** *organisme non gouvernemental assurant la conservation de certains sites et monuments historiques.*

nationhood ['neɪʃənhʊd] **n** statut *m* de nation.

nation-state **n** État-nation *m*.

nationwide ['neɪʃənwaɪd] ■ **adj** dans tout le pays / [campaign, strike] à l'échelon national.
■ **adv** à travers tout le pays.

native ['neɪtɪv] ■ **adj** **1.** [country, area] natal(e) **2.** [language] maternel(elle) ▸ **a native English speaker** une personne de langue maternelle anglaise **3.** [plant, animal] indigène ▸ **native to** originaire de.
■ **n** autochtone *mf* / [of colony] indigène *mf*.

Native American **n** Indien *m*, -enne *f* d'Amérique, Amérindien *m*, -enne *f*.

Native Australian **n** aborigène *mf*.

native speaker **n** LING locuteur *m* natif, locutrice *f* native ▸ **a native speaker of French/German, a French/German native speaker** un(e) francophone/germanophone, une personne de langue maternelle française/allemande.

nativity [nə'tɪvətɪ] (pl **nativities**) **n** **1.** RELIG **: the Nativity** la Nativité **2.** [birth] horoscope *m*.

Nativity play **n** *pièce jouée par des enfants et représentant l'histoire de la Nativité.*

NATO ['neɪtəʊ] (abbr of ***North Atlantic Treaty Organization***) **n** OTAN *f*.

natter ['nætər] *UK inf* ■ **n : to have a natter** tailler une bavette, bavarder.
■ **vi** bavarder.

natty ['nætɪ] (comp **-ier**, superl **-iest**) **adj** *inf dated* [smart] chic *(inv)*.

natural ['nætʃrəl] ■ **adj** **1.** [gen] naturel(elle) ▸ **it's only natural for her to be worried *OR* that she should be worried** il est tout à fait normal ***OR*** il est tout naturel qu'elle se fasse du souci ▸ **natural yoghurt** yaourt *m* nature ▸ **to die of natural causes** mourir de mort naturelle **2.** [instinct,

talent] inné(e) **3.** [footballer, musician] né(e) ▸ **she's a natural organizer** c'est une organisatrice née, elle a un sens inné de l'organisation **4.** [parent] vrai(e).
■ **n 1. : she's a natural at dancing** c'est une danseuse née **2.** MUS bécarre *m*.
natural childbirth **n** accouchement *m* naturel.
natural disaster **n** catastrophe *f* naturelle.
natural gas **n** gaz *m* naturel.
natural history **n** histoire *f* naturelle.
naturalism ['nætʃrəlɪzm] **n** naturalisme *m*.
naturalist ['nætʃrəlɪst] **n** naturaliste *mf*.
naturalistic [ˌnætʃrə'lɪstɪk] **adj** naturaliste.
naturalize, *UK* ***-ise*** ['nætʃrəlaɪz] **vt** naturaliser ▸ **to be naturalized** se faire naturaliser.
naturally ['nætʃrəlɪ] **adv 1.** [gen] naturellement ▸ **to come naturally to sb** être naturel(elle) chez qqn **2.** [unaffectedly] sans affectation, avec naturel.
naturalness ['nætʃrəlnɪs] **n** naturel *m*.
natural resources **npl** ressources *fpl* naturelles.
natural science **n** sciences *fpl* naturelles.
natural selection **n** sélection *f* naturelle.
natural wastage **n** *(U) UK* départs *mpl* volontaires.
nature ['neɪtʃər] **n** nature *f* ▸ **it's not in her nature to struggle** ce n'est pas dans sa nature de lutter ▸ **the nature-nurture debate** le débat sur l'inné et l'acquis *OR* sur la nature et la culture ▸ **by nature** [basically] par essence / [by disposition] de nature, naturellement ▸ **do you sell chocolates or anything of that nature?** est-ce que vous vendez des chocolats ou ce genre de choses?
-natured ['neɪtʃəd] **suffix** d'une nature..., d'un caractère... ▸ **she's good/ill-natured** elle a bon/mauvais caractère.
nature reserve **n** réserve *f* naturelle.
nature trail **n** sentier *m* signalisé pour amateurs de la nature.
naturism ['neɪtʃərɪzm] **n** naturisme *m*.
naturist ['neɪtʃərɪst] **n** naturiste *mf*.
naturopathy [ˌneɪtʃə'rɒpəθɪ] **n** naturopathie *f*.
naughtily ['nɔːtɪlɪ] **adv 1.** [mischievously] avec malice, malicieusement ▸ **you have behaved very naughtily** tu as été très vilain **2.** [suggestively] avec grivoiserie.
naughtiness ['nɔːtɪnɪs] **n 1.** [disobedience] désobéissance *f* / [mischievousness] malice *f* **2.** [indecency] grivoiserie *f*, gaillardise *f*.
naughty ['nɔːtɪ] (**comp -ier, superl -iest**) **adj 1.** [badly behaved] vilain(e), méchant(e) **2.** [indecent] grivois(e).
nausea ['nɔːzjə] **n** nausée *f*.
nauseam ['nɔːzɪæm] ➤ ***ad nauseam***.
nauseate ['nɔːsɪeɪt] **vt** *lit* & *fig* écœurer.
nauseating ['nɔːsɪeɪtɪŋ] **adj** *lit* & *fig* écœurant(e).
nauseatingly ['nɔːsɪeɪtɪŋlɪ] **adv** à vous donner la nausée, à vous écœurer.
nauseous ['nɔːsjəs] **adj 1.** MED **: to feel nauseous** avoir mal au cœur, avoir des nausées **2.** *fig* [revolting] écœurant(e), dégoutant(e).
nautical ['nɔːtɪkl] **adj** nautique.
nautical mile **n** mille *m* marin.
naval ['neɪvl] **adj** naval(e).
naval officer **n** officier *m* de marine.
nave [neɪv] **n** nef *f*.
navel ['neɪvl] **n** nombril *m*.
navigable ['nævɪgəbl] **adj** navigable.
navigate ['nævɪgeɪt] ■ **vt 1.** [plane] piloter / [ship] gouverner **2.** [seas, river] naviguer sur.
■ **vi** AERON & NAUT naviguer / AUT lire la carte.
navigation [ˌnævɪ'geɪʃn] **n** navigation *f*.
navigational [ˌnævɪ'geɪʃnl] **adj** de (la) navigation.
navigator ['nævɪgeɪtər] **n** navigateur *m*.
navvy ['nævɪ] (**pl -ies**) **n** *UK inf dated* terrassier *m*.
navy ['neɪvɪ] ■ **n** (**pl -ies**) marine *f*.
■ **adj** [in colour] bleu marine *(inv)*.
navy blue ■ **adj** bleu marine *(inv)*.
■ **n** bleu *m* marine.
Nazareth ['næzərɪθ] **n** Nazareth.
Nazi ['nɑːtsɪ] ■ **adj** nazi(e).
■ **n** (**pl -s**) Nazi *m*, -e *f*.
Nazism ['nɑːtsɪzm], ***Naziism*** ['nɑːtsɪˌɪzm] **n** nazisme *m*.
NB, ***N.B.*** **1.** (**abbr of *nota bene***) NB **2. abbr of *New Brunswick***.
NBA **n 1.** (**abbr of *National Basketball Association***) *fédération américaine de basket-ball* **2.** (**abbr of *National Boxing Association***) *fédération américaine de boxe*.
NBC (**abbr of *National Broadcasting Company***) **n** *chaîne de télévision américaine*.
NC **abbr of 1. *no charge* 2. abbr of *North Carolina***.
NCC (**abbr of *Nature Conservancy Council***) **n** *organisme britannique de protection de la nature*.
NCCL (**abbr of *National Council for Civil Liberties***) **n** *ligue britannique de défense des libertés civiles*.
NCO **n abbr of *noncommissioned officer***.
NCU (**abbr of *National Communications Union***) **n** *syndicat britannique des communications*.
ND **abbr of *North Dakota***.
NDP (**abbr of *net domestic product***) **n** ECON PIN *m (produit intérieur net)*.
NE **1. abbr of *Nebraska* 2. abbr of *New England* 3.** (**abbr of *northeast***) N.E.
Neanderthal [nɪ'ændətɑːl] ■ **adj : Neanderthal man** homme *m* de Néandertal.
■ **n** homme *m* de Néandertal.
neap tide [niːp-] **n** (marée *f* de) morte-eau *f*.
near [nɪər] ■ **adj** proche ▸ **the near edge** le bord le plus proche ▸ **a near disaster** une catastrophe évitée de justesse *OR* de peu ▸ **when the time is near** quand le moment approchera ▸ **in the near future** dans un proche

avenir, dans un avenir prochain ▸ **to the nearest £10** à 10 livres près ▸ **it was a near thing** *UK* il était moins cinq ▸ **your nearest and dearest** *hum* vos proches.

■ **adv 1.** [close] près ▸ **to draw near** s'approcher ▸ **Christmas is drawing near** Noël approche
2. [almost] **: near impossible** presque impossible ▸ **nowhere near ready/enough** loin d'être prêt(e)/assez ▸ **as near as makes no difference** à peu de chose près, à quelque chose près.

■ **prep : near (to)** [in space] près de / [in time] près de, vers ▸ **don't go near the fire** ne t'approche pas du feu ▸ **is there a chemist's near here?** est-ce qu'il y a une pharmacie près d'ici *OR* dans le coin? ▸ **near the end of the book** vers la fin du livre ▸ **it's getting near Christmas** c'est bientôt Noël ▸ **near (to) tears** au bord des larmes ▸ **near (to) death** sur le point de mourir ▸ **that would be nearer the truth** ce serait plus près de la vérité ▸ **profits were near the 30% mark** les bénéfices approchaient la barre des 30 %.

■ **vt** approcher de ▸ **to near completion** être près d'être fini ▸ **he was nearing 70 when he got married** il allait sur ses 70 ans quand il s'est marié.

■ **vi** approcher.

near- **suffix : near-perfect** pratiquement *OR* quasi parfait(e) ▸ **near-complete** pratiquement *OR* quasi complet(ète).

nearby [nɪə'baɪ] ■ **adj** proche.
■ **adv** tout près, à proximité.

Near East **n : the Near East** le Proche-Orient.

nearly ['nɪəlɪ] **adv** presque ▸ **I nearly fell** j'ai failli tomber ▸ **I nearly cried** j'étais sur le point de pleurer ▸ **not nearly enough/as good** loin d'être suffisant(e)/aussi bon(bonne).

near miss **n 1.** SPORT coup *m* qui a raté de peu **2.** [between planes, vehicles] quasi-collision *f*, collision *f* évitée de justesse.

nearness ['nɪənɪs] **n** proximité *f*.

nearside ['nɪəsaɪd] *UK* ■ **adj** [right-hand drive] de gauche / [left-hand drive] de droite.
■ **n** [right-hand drive] côté *m* gauche / [left-hand drive] côté droit.

nearsighted [ˌnɪə'saɪtɪd] **adj** *US* myope.

neat [ni:t] **adj 1.** [room, house] bien tenu(e), en ordre / [work] soigné(e) / [handwriting] net (nette) / [appearance] soigné(e), net (nette) **2.** [solution, manoeuvre] habile, ingénieux(euse) **3.** [alcohol] pur(e), sans eau **4.** *US inf* [very good] chouette, super *(inv)*.

neatly ['ni:tlɪ] **adv 1.** [arrange] avec ordre / [write] soigneusement / [dress] avec soin **2.** [skilfully] habilement, adroitement.

neatness ['ni:tnɪs] **n** [of room] bon ordre *m* / [of handwriting] netteté *f* / [of appearance] mise *f* soignée.

Nebraska [nɪ'bræskə] **n** Nebraska *m* ▸ **in Nebraska** dans le Nebraska.

nebula ['nebjʊlə] (**pl -s** *OR* **-lae** [-li:]) **n 1.** ASTRON nébuleuse *f* **2.** MED [of cornea] nébulosité *f* / [of urine] aspect *m* trouble.

nebulous ['nebjʊləs] **adj** nébuleux(euse).

NEC (abbr of ***National Exhibition Centre***) **n** *parc d'expositions près de Birmingham en Angleterre.*

necessarily [*UK* 'nesəsrəlɪ, ˌnesə'serɪlɪ] **adv** forcément, nécessairement.

necessary ['nesəsrɪ] **adj 1.** [required] nécessaire, indispensable ▸ **to make the necessary arrangements** faire le nécessaire **2.** [inevitable] inévitable, inéluctable.

necessitate [nɪ'sesɪteɪt] **vt** nécessiter, rendre nécessaire.

necessity [nɪ'sesətɪ] (**pl -ies**) **n** nécessité *f* ▸ **there's no real necessity for us to go** il n'est pas indispensable que nous y allions ▸ **of necessity** inévitablement, fatalement ▸ **in case of absolute necessity** en cas de force majeure ▸ **the basic** *OR* **bare necessities of life** les choses qui sont absolument essentielles *OR* indispensables à la vie.

neck [nek] ■ **n 1.** ANAT cou *m* ▸ **to be up to one's neck (in sthg)** *fig* être (dans qqch) jusqu'au cou ▸ **to breathe down sb's neck** *fig* talonner qqn, être sur le dos de qqn ▸ **to stick one's neck out** *fig* prendre des risques, se mouiller **2.** [of shirt, dress] encolure *f* **3.** [of bottle] col *m*, goulot *m*.
■ **vi** *inf dated* se bécoter.

neckerchief ['nekətʃɪf] (**pl -chiefs** *OR* **-chieves** [-tʃi:vz]) **n** *dated* foulard *m*.

necklace ['neklɪs] **n** collier *m*.

neckline ['neklaɪn] **n** encolure *f*.

necktie ['nektaɪ] **n** *US fml* cravate *f*.

nectar ['nektəʳ] **n** nectar *m*.

nectarine ['nektərɪn] **n** brugnon *m*, nectarine *f*.

NEDC (abbr of ***National Economic Development Council***) **n** *agence nationale britannique de développement économique.*

Neddy ['nedɪ] **n** *inf surnom de la NEDC.*

née [neɪ] **adj** née.

need [ni:d] ■ **n** besoin *m* ▸ **there's no need to get up** ce n'est pas la peine de te lever ▸ **there's no need to panic** *OR* **for any panic** inutile de paniquer ▸ **there's no need for such language** tu n'as pas besoin d'être grossier ▸ **need for sthg/to do sthg** besoin de qqch/de faire qqch ▸ **to be in** *OR* **have need of sthg** *fml* avoir besoin de qqch ▸ **I have no need of your sympathy** je n'ai que faire de votre sympathie ▸ **if need be** si besoin est, si nécessaire ▸ **should the need arise** si cela s'avérait nécessaire, si le besoin s'en faisait sentir ▸ **your need is greater than mine** vous en avez plus besoin que moi ▸ **he saw to her every need** il subvenait à ses moindres besoins ▸ **in need** dans le besoin.

■ **vt 1.** [require] **: to need sthg/to do sthg** avoir besoin de qqch/de faire qqch ▸ **I need a drink/a shower** j'ai besoin de boire quelque chose/de prendre une douche ▸ **I need to go to the doctor** il faut que j'aille chez le médecin ▸ **have you got everything you need?** est-ce que tu as tout ce qu'il te faut? ▸ **it's just what I need** c'est exactement ce qu'il me faut ▸ **that's all we need!** *iro* il ne nous manquait plus que ça! ▸ **you only need to ask** vous n'avez qu'à demander ▸ **you don't need me to tell you that** vous devez le savoir mieux que moi ▸ **he likes to feel needed** il aime se sentir indispensable ▸ **the carpet needs cleaning** la moquette a besoin d'être nettoyée ▸ **there are still a few points that need to be made** il reste encore quelques questions à soulever

2. [be obliged] **: to need to do sthg** être obligé(e) de faire qqch ▸ **I need to be home by ten** il faut que je sois rentré *OR* je dois être rentré pour 10 h ▸ **you need to try harder** tu vas devoir faire *OR* il va falloir que tu fasses un effort supplémentaire.
■ **modal vb : need we go?** faut-il qu'on y aille? ▸ **you needn't come if you don't want to** vous n'avez pas besoin de *OR* vous n'êtes pas obligé de venir si vous n'en avez pas envie ▸ **I needn't tell you how important it is** je n'ai pas besoin de vous dire *OR* vous savez à quel point c'est important ▸ **it need not happen** cela ne doit pas forcément se produire ▸ **the accident need never have happened** cet accident aurait pu être évité ▸ **I needn't have bothered** je me suis donné bien du mal pour rien, ce n'était pas la peine que je me donne autant de mal ▸ **no one else need ever know** ça reste entre nous ▸ **need I say more?** ai-je besoin d'en dire davantage *OR* plus?
◆ ***needs*** **adv : if needs must** s'il le faut.

needful ['ni:dfʊl] ■ **adj** *fml* nécessaire, requis(e).
■ **n** *UK inf* **: to do the needful** faire le nécessaire ∕ [money] **: to find the needful** trouver le fric.

needle ['ni:dl] ■ **n 1.** [gen] aiguille *f* ▸ **it's like looking for a needle in a haystack** c'est comme chercher une aiguille dans une botte de foin **2.** [stylus] saphir *m*.
■ **vt** *inf* [annoy] asticoter, lancer des piques à.

needlecord ['ni:dlkɔ:d] **n** velours *m* mille-raies.

needlepoint ['ni:dlpɔɪnt] **n** dentelle *f* à l'aiguille.

needless ['ni:dlɪs] **adj** [risk, waste] inutile ∕ [remark] déplacé(e) ▸ **needless to say...** bien entendu...

needlessly ['ni:dlɪslɪ] **adv** inutilement, sans raison.

needlework ['ni:dlwɜ:k] **n 1.** [embroidery] travail *m* d'aiguille **2.** *(U)* [activity] couture *f*.

needn't ['ni:dnt] = ***need not***.

needs-based **adj** fondé(e) sur les besoins.

needs identification **n** identification *f* des besoins.

needy ['ni:dɪ] ■ **adj** (comp **-ier**, superl **-iest**) nécessiteux(euse), indigent(e).
■ **npl : the needy** les nécessiteux *mpl*.

ne'er [neəʳ] *liter* = ***never***.

ne'er-do-well **n** *dated* bon *m* à rien, bonne *f* à rien.

nefarious [nɪ'feərɪəs] **adj** *fml* odieux(euse), abominable.

negate [nɪ'geɪt] **vt** *fml* [efforts, achievements] annuler, détruire.

negation [nɪ'geɪʃn] **n** *fml* [of efforts, achievements] destruction *f*.

negative ['negətɪv] ■ **adj** négatif(ive).
■ **n 1.** PHOT négatif *m* **2.** LING négation *f* ▸ **to answer in the negative** répondre négativement *OR* par la négative.

negative equity **n** *(U) situation où l'acquéreur d'un bien immobilier reste redevable de l'emprunt contracté alors que son logement enregistre une moins-value.*

negatively ['negətɪvlɪ] **adv** négativement.

negative sign **n** signe *m* moins *OR* négatif.

neglect [nɪ'glekt] ■ **n** [of garden] mauvais entretien *m* ∕ [of children] manque *m* de soins ∕ [of duty] manquement *m* ▸ **through neglect** par négligence *f* ▸ **to suffer from neglect** [person] souffrir d'un manque de soins ∕ [building, garden] être laissé(e) à l'abandon.
■ **vt** négliger ∕ [garden] laisser à l'abandon ▸ **you shouldn't neglect your health** vous devriez vous soucier un peu plus de votre santé ▸ **governments have neglected the needs of the disabled for long enough** il est temps que les gouvernements cessent d'ignorer les besoins des invalides ▸ **to neglect to do sthg** négliger *OR* omettre de faire qqch.

neglected [nɪ'glektɪd] **adj** [child] délaissé(e), abandonné(e) ∕ [garden] laissé(e) à l'abandon.

neglectful [nɪ'glektfʊl] **adj** négligent(e) ▸ **to be neglectful of sb/sthg** négliger qqn/qqch.

negligee ['neglɪʒeɪ] **n** déshabillé *m*, négligé *m*.

negligence ['neglɪdʒəns] **n** négligence *f*.

negligent ['neglɪdʒənt] **adj** négligent(e).

negligently ['neglɪdʒəntlɪ] **adv** avec négligence.

negligible ['neglɪdʒəbl] **adj** négligeable.

negotiable [nɪ'gəʊʃjəbl] **adj** négociable ∕ [price, conditions] à débattre.

negotiate [nɪ'gəʊʃɪeɪt] ■ **vt 1.** COMM & POL négocier **2.** [obstacle] franchir ∕ [bend] prendre, négocier.
■ **vi** négocier ▸ **to negotiate with sb (for sthg)** engager des négociations avec qqn (pour obtenir qqch).

negotiating table [nɪ'gəʊʃɪeɪtɪŋ-] **n** table *f* des négociations.

negotiation [nɪ,gəʊʃɪ'eɪʃn] **n** négociation *f*.

negotiator [nɪ'gəʊʃɪeɪtəʳ] **n** négociateur *m*, -trice *f*.

Negress ['ni:grɪs] **n** négresse *f (attention: le terme 'Negress' est considéré raciste)*.

Negro ['ni:grəʊ] ■ **adj** noir(e).
■ **n** (pl **-es**) Noir *m (attention: le terme 'Negro' est considéré raciste)*.

neigh [neɪ] **vi** [horse] hennir.

neighbour *UK*, ***neighbor*** *US* ['neɪbəʳ] **n** voisin *m*, -e *f*.

neighbourhood *UK*, ***neighborhood*** *US* ['neɪbəhʊd] **n 1.** [of town] voisinage *m*, quartier *m* ▸ **in the neighbourhood** à proximité **2.** [approximate figure] **: in the neighbourhood of £300** environ 300 livres, dans les 300 livres.

neighbourhood watch **n** *UK système de surveillance d'un quartier par tous ses habitants (pour prévenir les cambriolages et autres crimes).*

neighbouring *UK*, ***neighboring*** *US* ['neɪbərɪŋ] **adj** avoisinant(e).

neighbourly *UK*, ***neighborly*** *US* ['neɪbəlɪ] **adj** bon voisin (bonne voisine).

neither ['naɪðəʳ *OR* 'ni:ðəʳ] ■ **adv : neither good nor bad** ni bon(bonne) ni mauvais(e) ▸ **that's neither here nor there** cela n'a rien à voir.
■ **pron & adj** ni l'un ni l'autre (ni l'une ni l'autre).
■ **conj : neither do I** moi non plus.

nemesis ['neməsɪs] **n** *liter* **1.** [retribution] **: it's nemesis** c'est un juste retour des choses **2.** [agency of retribution] **: she saw the British press as her nemesis** elle vit dans la presse britannique l'instrument de sa vengeance.

neo- ['niːəʊ] **prefix** néo-.

neoclassic(al) [ˌniːəʊ'klæsɪk(l)] **adj** néo-classique.

neoclassicism [ˌniːəʊ'klæsɪsɪzm] **n** néoclassicisme *m*.

neofascism [ˌniːəʊ'fæʃɪzm] **n** néofascisme *m*.

neofascist [ˌniːəʊ'fæʃɪst] ■ **adj** néofasciste.
■ **n** néofasciste *mf*.

neolithic [ˌniːə'lɪθɪk] **adj** néolithique.

neologism [niː'ɒlədʒɪzm] **n** néologisme *m*.

neon ['niːɒn] **n** néon *m*.

neonatal [ˌniːəʊ'neɪtl] **adj** néonatal(e).

neo-Nazi [ˌniːəʊ'nɑːtsɪ] ■ **n** néonazi *m*, -e *f*.
■ **adj** néonazi(e).

neon light **n** néon *m*, lumière *f* au néon.

neon sign **n** enseigne *f* lumineuse au néon.

Nepal [nɪ'pɔːl] **n** Népal *m* ▸ **in Nepal** au Népal.

Nepalese [ˌnepə'liːz] ■ **adj** népalais(e).
■ **n** (pl **Nepalese**) Népalais *m*, -e *f*.

Nepali [nɪ'pɔːlɪ] **n** [language] népalais *m*, népali *m*.

nephew ['nefjuː] **n** neveu *m*.

nepotism ['nepətɪzm] **n** népotisme *m*.

Neptune ['neptjuːn] **n** [planet] Neptune *f*.

nerd [nɜːd] **n** *inf pej* binoclard *m* ▸ **computer nerd** accro *m* d'informatique.

nerdy ['nɜːdɪ] **adj** *inf pej* ringard(e).

nerve [nɜːv] **n 1.** ANAT nerf *m* ▸ **to touch a raw nerve** *fig* toucher une corde sensible **2.** [courage] courage *m*, sang-froid *m inv* ▸ **to lose one's nerve** se dégonfler, flancher ▸ **his nerve failed him, he lost his nerve** [backed down] le courage lui a manqué / [panicked] il a perdu son sang-froid **3.** [cheek] culot *m*, toupet *m* ▸ **to have the nerve to do sthg** avoir le culot ***OR*** le toupet de faire qqch ▸ **what a nerve!** *inf* quel culot ***OR*** toupet!
◆ ***nerves*** **npl** nerfs *mpl* ▸ **I need a drink to steady my nerves** il faut que je boive un verre pour me calmer ▸ **to get on sb's nerves** taper sur les nerfs ***OR*** le système de qqn.

nerve cell **n** cellule *f* nerveuse.

nerve centre *UK*, ***nerve center*** *US* **n** *lit & fig* centre *m* nerveux.

nerve ending **n** terminaison *f* nerveuse.

nerve gas **n** gaz *m* neurotoxique.

nerve-racking [-ˌrækɪŋ] **adj** angoissant(e), éprouvant(e).

nervous ['nɜːvəs] **adj 1.** [gen] nerveux(euse) **2.** [apprehensive - smile, person] inquiet(ète) / [- performer] qui a le trac ▸ **to be nervous about sthg** appréhender qqch.

nervous breakdown **n** dépression *f* nerveuse.

nervously ['nɜːvəslɪ] **adv 1.** [gen] nerveusement **2.** [apprehensively] avec inquiétude.

nervousness ['nɜːvəsnɪs] **n** *(U)* **1.** [apprehension - of voice] inquiétude *f* / [- of performer] trac *m* **2.** [tenseness] nervosité *f*, tension *f*.

nervous system **n** système *m* nerveux.

nervous wreck **n : to be a nervous wreck** être à bout de nerfs.

nervy ['nɜːvɪ] (comp **-ier**, superl **-iest**) **adj 1.** *UK inf* [nervous] énervé(e) **2.** *US* [cheeky] culotté(e).

nest [nest] ■ **n** nid *m* ▸ **nest of tables** table *f* gigogne.
■ **vi** [bird] faire son nid, nicher.

nest egg **n** pécule *m*, bas *m* de laine.

nesting ['nestɪŋ] ■ **n** nidification *f*.
■ **comp** [bird] nicheur / [time, instinct] de (la) nidification.

nestle ['nesl] **vi** se blottir.

nestling ['neslɪŋ] **n** oisillon *m*.

net[1] [net] ■ **adj** net (nette) ▸ **net result** résultat final.
■ **n 1.** [gen] filet *m* **2.** [fabric] voile *m*, tulle *m*.
■ **vt** (pt & pp **-ted**, cont **-ting**) **1.** [fish] prendre au filet **2.** [money - subj: person] toucher net, gagner net / [- subj: deal] rapporter net.

net[2], ***Net*** [net] **n : the net** le Net ▸ **to surf the net** surfer sur le Net.

.net ['dɒtnet] COMPUT *abréviation désignant les organismes officiels de l'Internet dans les adresses électroniques.*

netball ['netbɔːl] **n** netball *m*.

net curtains **npl** *UK* voilage *m*.

net domestic product **n** produit *m* intérieur net.

nethead ['nethed] **n** *inf* accro *mf* d'Internet.

Netherlands ['neðələndz] **npl : the Netherlands** les Pays-Bas *mpl* ▸ **in the Netherlands** aux Pays-Bas.

nethermost ['neðəməʊst] **adj** *liter* le plus bas(basse) ***OR*** profond(e).

netiquette, ***Netiquette*** ['netiket] **n** nétiquette *f*.

netizen ['netizɪn] **n** COMPUT internaute *mf*.

net profit **n** bénéfice *m* net.

net receipts **n** recettes *fpl* nettes.

net revenue **n** *US* chiffre *m* d'affaires.

netspeak ['netspiːk] **n** *inf* COMPUT langage *m* du Net, cyberjargon *m*.

net surfer, ***Net surfer*** **n** internaute *mf*.

nett [net] **adj** *UK* = ***net***[1].

netting ['netɪŋ] **n 1.** [metal, plastic] grillage *m* **2.** [fabric] voile *m*, tulle *m*.

nettle ['netl] ■ **n** ortie *f*.
■ **vt** piquer ***OR*** toucher au vif.

network ['netwɜːk] ■ **n** réseau *m*.
■ **vt 1.** RADIO & TV diffuser **2.** COMPUT interconnecter.

network computer **n** ordinateur *m* réseau.

networking ['netwɜːkɪŋ] **n 1.** COMPUT mise *f* en réseau **2.** [gen & COMM] établissement *m* d'un réseau de liens ***OR*** de contacts.

network software **n** COMPUT logiciel *m* de réseau.

network TV **n** réseau *m* (de télévision) national.

neural ['njʊərəl] **adj** neural(e).

neuralgia [njʊə'rældʒə] **n** névralgie *f*.

neurological [ˌnjʊərə'lɒdʒɪkl] **adj** neurologique.

neurologist [ˌnjʊə'rɒlədʒɪst] **n** neurologue *mf*.

neurology [ˌnjʊə'rɒlədʒɪ] **n** neurologie *f*.

neuron ['njʊərɒn], ***neurone*** ['njʊərəʊn] **n** neurone *m*.

neurosis [ˌnjʊə'rəʊsɪs] (pl **-ses** [-si:z]) **n** névrose *f*.

neurosurgeon ['njʊərəʊˌsɜ:dʒən] **n** neurochirurgien *m*, -enne *f*.

neurosurgery [ˌnjʊərəʊ'sɜ:dʒərɪ] **n** neurochirurgie *f*.

neurotic [ˌnjʊə'rɒtɪk] ■ **adj** névrosé(e).
■ **n** névrosé *m*, -e *f*.

neuter ['nju:tər] ■ **adj** neutre.
■ **vt** [cat, dog] châtrer.

neutral ['nju:trəl] ■ **adj 1.** [gen] neutre **2.** [face, eyes] inexpressif(ive), sans expression.
■ **n 1.** AUT point *m* mort **2.** [country] état *m* ***OR*** pays *m* neutre / [person] personne *f* neutre.

neutrality [nju:'trælətɪ] **n** neutralité *f*.

neutralization, *UK* ***-isation*** [ˌnju:trəlaɪ'zeɪʃn] **n** neutralisation *f*.

neutralize, *UK* ***-ise*** ['nju:trəlaɪz] **vt** neutraliser.

neutron ['nju:trɒn] **n** neutron *m*.

neutron bomb **n** bombe *f* à neutrons.

Nevada [nɪ'vɑ:də] **n** Nevada *m* ▸ **in Nevada** dans le Nevada.

never ['nevər] **adv** jamais... ne, ne... jamais ▸ **never ever** jamais, au grand jamais ▸ **well I never!** ça par exemple!

never-ending **adj** interminable.

never-never **n** *UK inf* **: on the never-never** à crédit, à tempérament.

nevertheless [ˌnevəðə'les] **adv** néanmoins, pourtant.

new **adj** [nju:] **1.** [gen] nouveau(elle) ▸ **to be new to** [place] être nouveau dans / [job] être neuf(neuve) dans ▸ **you're new here, aren't you?** vous êtes nouveau ici, n'est-ce pas? ▸ **there are new people in the flat next door** il y a de nouveaux occupants dans l'appartement d'à côté ▸ **'under new management'** 'changement de propriétaire' ▸ **the newest fashions** la dernière mode ▸ **is there anything new on the catastrophe?** est-ce qu'il y a du nouveau sur la catastrophe? ▸ **there's nothing new under the sun** *prov* (il n'y a) rien de nouveau sous le soleil ▸ **that's a new one on me!** *inf* [joke] celle-là, on ne me l'avait jamais faite! / [news] première nouvelle! / [experience] on en apprend tous les jours! ▸ **what's new?** quoi de neuf? **2.** [not used, fresh] neuf (neuve) ▸ **a new tablecloth** [brand new] une nouvelle nappe, une nappe neuve / [fresh] une nouvelle nappe, une nappe propre ▸ **she needs a new sheet of paper** il lui faut une autre feuille de papier ▸ **as good as new** comme neuf ▸ **to feel like a new woman/man** se sentir revivre.
◆ ***news*** **n** [nju:z] *(U)* **1.** [information] nouvelle *f* ▸ **a piece of news** une nouvelle ▸ **is there any more news about *OR* on the explosion?** est-ce qu'on a plus d'informations sur l'explosion? ▸ **that's good/bad news** c'est une bonne/mauvaise nouvelle ▸ **have you had any news of her?** avez-vous eu de ses nouvelles? ▸ **to be in the news, to make the news** défrayer la chronique, faire parler de soi ▸ **he's bad news** *inf* on a toujours des ennuis avec lui ▸ **to break the news to sb** annoncer ***OR*** apprendre la nouvelle à qqn ▸ **no news is good news** *prov* pas de nouvelles, bonnes nouvelles *prov* ▸ **that's news to me** première nouvelle **2.** TV journal *m* télévisé, actualités *fpl* ▸ **the sports/financial news** la page sportive/financière **3.** RADIO informations *fpl*.

New Age **n** New Age *m*.

New Age traveller **n** *UK* voyageur *m* New Age.

newbie ['nju:bɪ] **n** *inf* COMPUT internaute *mf* novice, cybernovice *mf*.

new blood **n** *fig* sang *m* neuf ***OR*** frais.

newborn ['nju:bɔ:n] **adj** nouveau-né(e).

New Brunswick [-'brʌnzwɪk] **n** Nouveau-Brunswick *m* ▸ **in New Brunswick** dans le Nouveau-Brunswick.

New Caledonia [-ˌkælɪ'dəʊnjə] **n** Nouvelle-Calédonie *f* ▸ **in New Caledonia** en Nouvelle-Calédonie.

New Caledonian [-ˌkælɪ'dəʊnjən] ■ **adj** néo-calédonien(enne).
■ **n** Néo-Calédonien *m*, -enne *f*.

newcomer ['nju:ˌkʌmər] **n : newcomer (to sthg)** nouveau-venu *m*, nouvelle-venue *f* (dans qqch).

New Deal **n : the New Deal** le New Deal.

CULTURE

New Deal

Élu en 1932 président des États-Unis, alors en pleine récession, Franklin D. Roosevelt propose un programme de redressement économique : le New Deal (« Nouvelle donne »). Celui-ci comporte deux phases : l'adoption de mesures pour résorber le chômage grâce à des réformes monétaires, à de grands travaux publics, à la réorganisation des entreprises et à une aide à l'agriculture (1933-1934), puis d'importantes réformes sociales (1935-1941), dont la création de la Sécurité sociale en 1935. Mais, à partir de 1937, ces réformes sont freinées au profit de la politique étrangère, devant certains signes précurseurs de la Seconde Guerre mondiale. Ce programme a néanmoins servi de fondation à la politique sociale américaine actuelle.

New Delhi **n** New Delhi.

New England **n** Nouvelle-Angleterre *f* ▸ **in New England** en Nouvelle-Angleterre.

newfangled [ˌnju:'fæŋgld] **adj** *inf pej* ultramoderne, trop moderne.

newfound **adj** récent(e), de fraîche date.

Newfoundland ['nju:fəndlənd] **n** Terre-Neuve *f* ▸ **in Newfoundland** à Terre-Neuve.

New Guinea **n** Nouvelle-Guinée *f* ▸ **in New Guinea** en Nouvelle-Guinée.

New Hampshire [-'hæmpʃər] **n** New Hampshire *m* ▸ **in New Hampshire** dans le New Hampshire.

New Hebrides **npl** Nouvelles-Hébrides *fpl* ▸ **in the New Hebrides** aux Nouvelles-Hébrides.

New Jersey **n** New Jersey *m* ▸ **in New Jersey** dans le New Jersey.

New Labour **n** [in UK] New Labour *m*.

newly ['nju:lɪ] **adv** récemment, fraîchement.

newlyweds ['nju:lɪwedz] **npl** nouveaux *OR* jeunes mariés *mpl*.

New Mexico **n** Nouveau-Mexique *m* ▸ **in New Mexico** au Nouveau-Mexique.

new moon **n** nouvelle lune *f*.

newness ['nju:nɪs] **n 1.** [of building] nouveauté *f* / [of shoes, carpet] état *m* neuf **2.** [of ideas, experience, fashion] nouveauté *f*, originalité *f*.

New Orleans [-'ɔ:lɪənz] **n** La Nouvelle-Orléans.

new product development **n** développement *m* de nouveaux produits.

New Quebec **n** Nouveau-Québec *m* ▸ **in New Quebec** au Nouveau-Québec.

news agency **n** agence *f* de presse.

newsagent *UK* ['nju:zeɪdʒənt], ***newsdealer*** *US* ['nju:zdi:lər] **n** marchand *m* de journaux.

news bulletin **n** bulletin *m* d'informations.

newscast ['nju:zkɑ:st] **n** *esp US* **1.** RADIO informations *fpl* **2.** TV actualités *fpl*.

newscaster ['nju:zkɑ:stər] **n** présentateur *m*, -trice *f*.

news conference **n** conférence *f* de presse.

newsdealer *US* = ***newsagent***.

newsflash ['nju:zflæʃ] **n** flash *m* d'information.

newsgroup ['nju:zgru:p] **n** [on Internet] newsgroup *m*, groupe *m* de discussion.

newshound ['nju:zhaʊnd] **n** reporter *m*.

newsletter ['nju:zˌletər] **n** bulletin *m*.

newsman ['nju:zmæn] (pl **-men** [-mən]) **n** journaliste *m*, reporter *m*.

New South Wales **n** Nouvelle-Galles du Sud *f* ▸ **in New South Wales** en Nouvelle-Galles du Sud.

newspaper ['nju:zˌpeɪpər] **n** journal *m*.

newspaperman ['nju:zˌpeɪpəmæn] (pl **-men** [-men]) **n** journaliste *m*.

newspaperwoman ['nju:zˌpeɪpəwʊmæn] (pl **-women** [wɪmɪn]) **n** journaliste *f*.

newsprint ['nju:zprɪnt] **n** papier *m* journal.

newsreader ['nju:zˌri:dər] **n** *UK* présentateur *m*, -trice *f*.

newsreel ['nju:zri:l] **n** actualités *fpl* filmées.

news report **n** bulletin *m* d'informations.

newsroom ['nju:zru:m] **n 1.** PRESS salle *f* de rédaction **2.** RADIO & TV studio *m*.

news service **n** *US agence de presse qui publie ses informations par le biais d'un syndicat de distribution*.

newssheet ['nju:zʃi:t] **n** *UK* feuille *f* d'informations.

newsstand ['nju:zstænd] **n** kiosque *m* à journaux.

newswoman ['nju:zˌwʊmæn] (pl **-women** [wɪmɪn]) **n** journaliste *f*.

newsworthy ['nju:zˌwɜ:ðɪ] **adj** qui vaut la peine d'être publié(e) *OR* qu'on en parle.

newt [nju:t] **n** triton *m*.

new technology **n** nouvelle technologie *f*, technologie de pointe.

New Testament **n : the New Testament** le Nouveau Testament.

new town **n** ville *f* nouvelle.

new wave **n** nouvelle vague *f*.

New World **n : the New World** le Nouveau Monde.

New Year **n** nouvel an *m*, nouvelle année *f* ▸ **Happy New Year!** bonne année!

New Year's Day **n** jour *m* de l'an, premier *m* de l'an.

New Year's Eve **n** la Saint-Sylvestre.

New York ['jɔ:k] **n 1.** [city] **: New York (City)** New York **2.** [state] **: New York (State)** l'État *m* de New York ▸ **in (the State of) New York, in New York (State)** dans l'État de New York.

New Yorker [-'jɔ:kər] **n** New-Yorkais *m*, -e *f*.

New Zealand [-'zi:lənd] **n** Nouvelle-Zélande *f* ▸ **in New Zealand** en Nouvelle-Zélande.

New Zealander [-'zi:ləndər] **n** Néo-Zélandais *m*, -e *f*.

next [nekst] ■ **adj** prochain(e) / [room] d'à côté / [page] suivant(e) ▸ **next Tuesday** mardi prochain ▸ **next time** la prochaine fois ▸ **(the) next time I see him** la prochaine fois que je le vois *OR* verrai ▸ **(the) next time I saw him** quand je l'ai revu ▸ **next week** la semaine prochaine ▸ **the next week** la semaine suivante *OR* d'après ▸ **next year** l'année prochaine ▸ **keep quiet about it for the next few days** n'en parlez pas pendant les quelques jours qui viennent ▸ **(the) next minute she was dashing off out again/** une minute après, elle repartait ▸ **and (the) next thing I knew, I woke up in hospital** et l'instant d'après je me suis réveillé à l'hôpital ▸ **next, please!** au suivant! ▸ **who's next?** à qui le tour? ▸ **I'm next** c'est (à) mon tour, c'est à moi ▸ **translate the next sentence** traduisez la phrase suivante ▸ **their next child was a girl** ensuite, ils eurent une fille ▸ **ask the next person you meet** demandez à la première personne que vous rencontrez ▸ **take the next street on the left** prenez la prochaine à gauche ▸ **the day after next** le surlendemain ▸ **the week after next** dans deux semaines.

■ **adv 1.** [afterwards] ensuite, après ▸ **what did you do with it next?** et ensuite, qu'en avez-vous fait? ▸ **next on the agenda is the question of finance** la question suivante à l'ordre du jour est celle des finances **2.** [again] la prochaine fois ▸ **when we next met** quand nous nous sommes revus **3.** *(with superlatives)* **: the next youngest/ oldest child** l'enfant le plus jeune/le plus âgé ensuite ▸ **he's the next biggest after Dan** c'est le plus grand après *OR* à part Dan.

■ **prep** *US* à côté de.

◆ ***next to*** **prep** à côté de ▸ **come and sit next to me** venez vous asseoir à côté de *OR* près de moi ▸ **next to last** avant-dernier(ère) ▸ **next to impossible** presque *OR* quasiment impossible ▸ **it cost next to nothing** cela a coûté une bagatelle *OR* trois fois rien ▸ **I know next to nothing** je ne sais presque *OR* pratiquement rien.

next door **adv** à côté.

◆ ***next-door*** **adj : next-door neighbour** voisin *m*, -e *f* d'à côté.

next of kin **n** plus proche parent *m*.

NF ■ n (abbr of ***National Front***) ≃ FN *m*.
■ abbr of ***Newfoundland***.

NFL (abbr of ***National Football League***) n *fédération nationale de football américain*.

NFU (abbr of ***National Farmers' Union***) n *syndicat britannique d'exploitants agricoles*.

NG abbr of ***National Guard***.

NGO (abbr of ***non-governmental organization***) n ONG *f*.

NH abbr of ***New Hampshire***.

NHL (abbr of ***National Hockey League***) n *fédération nationale américaine de hockey sur glace*.

NHS (abbr of ***National Health Service***) n *service national de santé en Grande-Bretagne*, ≃ sécurité sociale *f*.

CULTURE
NHS

Mis en place au Royaume-Uni en 1948, le **National Health Service** (« Service de santé national ») dispense des soins médicaux aux citoyens britanniques : il est financé par le contribuable et dirigé par le département de la santé. Les consultations chez les médecins généralistes et les soins hospitaliers sont gratuits, on paie seulement pour les ordonnances. Néanmoins, des réformes ont été engagées car on attendait trop longtemps pour pouvoir être opéré, et de nouvelles structures fonctionnant 24 heures sur 24 ont été créées (comme le **NHS Direct**, un service d'infirmières et d'information médicale, et les établissements **NHS Clinics**).

NI ■ n abbr of ***National Insurance***.
■ abbr of ***Northern Ireland***.

CULTURE
NI (National Insurance)

L'Assurance nationale britannique (**National Insurance**) est un système de cotisations obligatoires pour les employés et les employeurs. Son montant, proportionnel aux revenus, est déduit des fiches de paie (seuls les travailleurs indépendants paient d'avance une part importante, puis un reliquat est calculé par rapport à leurs revenus annuels). C'est l'équivalent britannique de l'affiliation à la Sécurité sociale française : pour pouvoir travailler légalement en Angleterre, il est indispensable d'avoir un numéro d'immatriculation individuel, composé de deux lettres, suivies de six chiffres. Cette assurance prend en charge les allocations, les frais de santé et les pensions de retraite.

Niagara [naɪ'ægrə] n **: Niagara Falls** les chutes *fpl* du Niagara.

nib [nɪb] n plume *f*.

nibble ['nɪbl] ■ vt grignoter, mordiller.
■ vi **: to nibble at sthg** grignoter qqch.

Nicaragua [ˌnɪkə'rægjʊə] n Nicaragua *m* ▸ **in Nicaragua** au Nicaragua.

Nicaraguan [ˌnɪkə'rægjʊən] ■ adj nicaraguayen(enne).
■ n Nicaraguayen *m*, -enne *f*.

nice [naɪs] ■ adj **1.** [holiday, food] bon (bonne) / [day, picture] beau (belle) / [dress] joli(e) ▸ **to taste nice** avoir bon goût ▸ **to smell nice** sentir bon ▸ **she always looks nice** elle est toujours bien habillée *OR* mise ▸ **we had a nice meal** on a bien mangé ▸ **she's very nice** elle est très sympa ▸ **have a nice time** amusez-vous bien ▸ **it's nice to be back again** cela fait plaisir d'être de retour ▸ **(it was) nice meeting you** (j'ai été) ravi de faire votre connaissance ▸ **nice one!** bravo!, chapeau! **2.** [person] gentil(ille), sympathique ▸ **to be nice to sb** être gentil *OR* aimable avec qqn ▸ **that's nice of her** c'est gentil *OR* aimable de sa part ▸ **it's nice of you to say so** vous êtes bien aimable de le dire.
■ adv [as intensifier] **: nice long holidays** des vacances longues et agréables ▸ **a nice cold drink** une boisson bien fraîche / [with 'and'] **: take it nice and easy** allez-y doucement ▸ **it's nice and warm in here** il fait bon ici.

nice-looking [-'lʊkɪŋ] adj joli(e), beau (belle).

nicely ['naɪslɪ] adv **1.** [make, manage] bien / [dressed] joliment ▸ **that will do nicely** cela fera très bien l'affaire **2.** [politely - ask] poliment, gentiment / [- behave] bien.

nicety ['naɪsətɪ] (pl **-ies**) n délicatesse *f*, subtilité *f*.

niche [ni:ʃ] n [in wall] niche *f* / *fig* bonne situation *f*, voie *f*.

niche market n niche *f*.

niche marketing n marketing *m* ciblé.

niche product n produit *m* ciblé.

niche publishing n *publication d'ouvrages destinés à un public restreint*.

nick [nɪk] ■ n **1.** [cut] entaille *f*, coupure *f* **2.** *UK prison sl* [jail] **: the nick** la taule *OR* tôle **3.** *UK inf* [condition] **: in good/bad nick** en bon/mauvais état
▸▸ **in the nick of time** juste à temps.
■ vt **1.** [cut] couper, entailler **2.** *UK inf* [steal] piquer, faucher **3.** *UK inf* [arrest] pincer, choper.

nickel ['nɪkl] n **1.** [metal] nickel *m* **2.** *US* [coin] pièce *f* de cinq cents.

nickname ['nɪkneɪm] ■ n sobriquet *m*, surnom *m*.
■ vt surnommer.

Nicosia [ˌnɪkə'si:ə] n Nicosie.

nicotine ['nɪkəti:n] n nicotine *f*.

nicotine patch n patch *m OR* timbre *m* antitabac.

niece [ni:s] n nièce *f*.

nifty ['nɪftɪ] (comp **-ier**, superl **-iest**) adj *inf* génial(e), super *(inv)*.

Niger ['naɪdʒəʳ] n **1.** [country] Niger *m* ▸ **in Niger** au Niger **2.** [river] **: the (River) Niger** le Niger.

Nigeria [naɪ'dʒɪərɪə] n Nigeria *m* ▸ **in Nigeria** au Nigeria.

Nigerian [naɪ'dʒɪərɪən] ■ adj nigérian(e).
■ n Nigérian *m*, -e *f*.

Nigerien [naɪ'dʒɪərɪən] ■ adj nigérien(enne).
■ n Nigérien *m*, -enne *f*.

niggardly ['nɪgədlɪ] **adj** [person] pingre, avare / [gift, amount] mesquin(e), chiche.

niggle ['nɪgl] ■ **n** *UK* [worry] souci *m*, tracas *m*.
■ **vt 1.** *UK* [worry] tracasser **2.** [criticize] faire des réflexions à, critiquer.
■ **vi 1.** [worry] **: to niggle at sb** tracasser qqn **2.** [criticize] faire des réflexions, critiquer.

niggling ['nɪglɪŋ] ■ **adj 1.** [petty - person] tatillon(onne) / [- details] insignifiant(e) **2.** [fastidious - job] fastidieux(euse) **3.** [nagging - pain, doubt] tenace.
■ **n** chicanerie *f*, pinaillerie *f*.

nigh [naɪ] **adv** *liter* près, proche ▶ **well nigh** presque.

night [naɪt] **n 1.** [not day] nuit *f* ▶ **at night** la nuit ▶ **night and day, day and night** nuit et jour **2.** [evening] soir *m* ▶ **at night** le soir
▶▶ **to have an early night** se coucher de bonne heure ▶ **to have a late night** veiller, se coucher tard.
◆ ***nights*** **adv 1.** *US* [at night] la nuit **2.** *UK* [nightshift] **: to work nights** travailler *OR* être de nuit.

nightcap ['naɪtkæp] **n 1.** [drink] *boisson alcoolisée prise avant de se coucher* **2.** [hat] bonnet *m* de nuit.

night class **n** *US* = ***evening class***.

nightclothes ['naɪtkləʊðz] **npl** vêtements *mpl* de nuit.

nightclub ['naɪtklʌb] **n** boîte *f* de nuit.

nightclubbing ['naɪtklʌbɪŋ] **n : to go nightclubbing** sortir en boîte.

nightdress ['naɪtdres] **n** chemise *f* de nuit.

nightfall ['naɪtfɔ:l] **n** tombée *f* de la nuit *OR* du jour.

nightgown ['naɪtgaʊn] **n** chemise *f* de nuit.

nightie ['naɪtɪ] **n** *inf* chemise *f* de nuit.

nightingale ['naɪtɪŋgeɪl] **n** rossignol *m*.

nightlife ['naɪtlaɪf] **n** vie *f* nocturne, activités *fpl* nocturnes.

nightlight ['naɪtlaɪt] **n** veilleuse *f*.

nightly ['naɪtlɪ] ■ **adj** (de) toutes les nuits *OR* tous les soirs.
■ **adv** toutes les nuits, tous les soirs.

nightmare ['naɪtmeəʳ] **n** *lit* & *fig* cauchemar *m*.

nightmarish ['naɪtmeərɪʃ] **adj** cauchemardesque, de cauchemar.

night owl **n** *fig* couche-tard *m inv*, noctambule *mf*.

night porter **n** *UK* veilleur *m* de nuit.

night safe **n** coffre *m* de nuit.

night school **n** *(U)* cours *mpl* du soir.

night shift **n** [period] poste *m* de nuit.

nightshirt ['naɪtʃɜ:t] **n** chemise *f* de nuit d'homme.

nightspot ['naɪtˌspɒt] **n** boîte *f* de nuit.

nightstick ['naɪtˌstɪk] **n** *US* matraque *f*.

nighttime ['naɪttaɪm] **n** nuit *f*.

night vision **n** vision *f* nocturne.

night watchman **n** gardien *m* de nuit.

nightwear ['naɪtweəʳ] **n** *(U)* vêtements *mpl* de nuit.

nihilism ['naɪəlɪzm] **n** nihilisme *m*.

nihilist ['naɪɪlɪst] ■ **adj** nihiliste.
■ **n** nihiliste *mf*.

nihilistic [ˌnaɪɪ'lɪstɪk] **adj** nihiliste.

nil [nɪl] **n** néant *m* / *UK* SPORT zéro *m*.

Nile [naɪl] **n : the Nile** le Nil.

nimble ['nɪmbl] **adj** agile, leste / *fig* [mind] vif (vive).

nimbly ['nɪmblɪ] **adv** agilement, lestement.

nimbus ['nɪmbəs] (pl **nimbi** ['nɪmbaɪ] *OR* **nimbuses**) **n 1.** METEOR nimbus *m* **2.** [halo] nimbe *m*, auréole *f*.

NIMBY (abbr of ***not in my back yard***) pas près de chez moi.

nincompoop ['nɪŋkəmpu:p] **n** *inf dated* cruche *f*

nine [naɪn] **num** neuf ; see also ***six***.

nineteen [ˌnaɪn'ti:n] **num** dix-neuf ; see also ***six***.

nineteenth [naɪn'ti:nθ] **num** dix-neuvième ; see also ***sixth***.

ninetieth ['naɪntɪəθ] **num** quatre-vingt-dixième ; see also ***sixth***.

nine-to-five ■ **adv** de neuf heures du matin à cinq heures du soir ▶ **to work nine-to-five** avoir des horaires de bureau.
■ **adj 1.** [job] routinier(ère) **2.** [mentality, attitude] de gratte-papier.

ninety ['naɪntɪ] **num** quatre-vingt-dix ; see also ***sixty***.

ninny ['nɪnɪ] (pl **-ies**) **n** *inf dated* nigaud *m*, -e *f*.

ninth [naɪnθ] **num** neuvième ; see also ***sixth***.

nip [nɪp] ■ **n 1.** [pinch] pinçon *m* / [bite] morsure *f* **2.** [of drink] goutte *f*, doigt *m*.
■ **vt** (pt & pp **-ped**, cont **-ping**) [pinch] pincer / [bite] mordre.
■ **vi** (pt & pp **-ped**, cont **-ping**) *UK inf* **: to nip down to the pub** faire un saut au pub.

nipper ['nɪpəʳ] **n** *inf dated* gamin *m*, -e *f*, gosse *mf*.

nipple ['nɪpl] **n 1.** ANAT bout *m* de sein, mamelon *m* **2.** *US* [of bottle] tétine *f*.

nippy ['nɪpɪ] (comp **-ier**, superl **-iest**) **adj** *inf* **1.** [cold] froid(e), frisquet(ette) **2.** *UK* [quick - person] vif (vive) / [- car] nerveux(euse).

Nissen hut ['nɪsn-] **n** *UK* hutte *f* préfabriquée en tôle.

NIST (abbr of ***National Institute of Standards and Technology***) **n** *service américain des poids et mesures*.

nit [nɪt] **n 1.** [in hair] lente *f* **2.** *UK inf* [idiot] idiot *m*, -e *f*, crétin *m*, -e *f*.

nitpick ['nɪtpɪk] **vi** *inf* couper les cheveux en quatre, chercher la petite bête, pinailler.

nitpicking ['nɪtpɪkɪŋ] **n** *inf* ergotage *m*, pinaillage *m*.

nitrate ['naɪtreɪt] **n** nitrate *m*.

nitric acid ['naɪtrɪk-] **n** acide *m* nitrique.

nitrogen ['naɪtrədʒən] **n** azote *m*.

nitroglycerin(e) [ˌnaɪtrəʊ'glɪsəri:n] **n** nitroglycérine *f*.

nitty-gritty [ˌnɪtɪ'grɪtɪ] **n** *inf* **: to get down to the nitty-gritty** en venir à l'essentiel *OR* aux choses sérieuses.

nitwit ['nɪtwɪt] **n** *inf* imbécile *mf*, idiot *m*, -e *f*.

nix [nɪks] *US inf* ■ **n** [nothing] rien.
■ **adv** non.
■ **vt** [say no to] mettre son veto à.

NJ abbr of ***New Jersey***.

NLF (abbr of ***National Liberation Front***) **n** FLN *m*.

NLQ (abbr of ***near letter quality***) *qualité quasi-courrier.*

NLRB (abbr of ***National Labor Relations Board***) **n** *commission américaine d'arbitrage en matière d'emploi.*

NM abbr of ***New Mexico***.

no [nəʊ] ■ **adv 1.** [gen] non / [expressing disagreement] mais non ▸ **do you like spinach? – no, I don't** aimez-vous les épinards? – non
2. [not any] **: no bigger/smaller** pas plus grand/petit ▸ **no better** pas mieux ▸ **I can go no further** je ne peux pas aller plus loin.
■ **adj** aucun(e), pas de ▸ **I have no family** je n'ai pas de famille ▸ **she has no intention of leaving** elle n'a aucune intention de partir ▸ **no sensible person would dispute this** quelqu'un de raisonnable ne discuterait pas ▸ **no other washing powder gets clothes so clean** aucune autre lessive ne laisse votre linge aussi propre ▸ **there's no telling what will happen** impossible de dire ce qui va se passer ▸ **I'm no expert, I'm afraid** malheureusement, je ne suis pas un expert ▸ **he's no friend of mine** je ne le compte pas parmi mes amis ▸ **'no smoking'** 'défense de fumer' ▸ **'no swimming'** 'baignade interdite'.
■ **n** (pl **noes** [nəʊz]) non *m* ▸ **she won't take no for an answer** elle n'accepte pas de refus OR qu'on lui dise non.

No., no. (abbr of ***number***) No, no.

Noah's ark ['nəʊəz-] **n** l'arche *f* de Noé.

no-ball **n** SPORT balle *f* nulle.

nobble ['nɒbl] **vt** *UK inf* **1.** [racehorse] droguer **2.** [bribe] soudoyer, acheter **3.** [detain - person] accrocher.

Nobel prize [nəʊ'bel-] **n** prix *m* Nobel.

nobility [nə'bɪlətɪ] **n** noblesse *f*.

noble ['nəʊbl] ■ **adj** noble.
■ **n** noble *m*.

nobleman ['nəʊblmən] (pl **-men** [-mən]) **n** noble *m*, aristocrate *m*.

noblewoman ['nəʊbl,wʊmən] (pl **-women** [-,wɪmɪn]) **n** (femme) noble *f*, aristocrate *f*.

nobly ['nəʊblɪ] **adv** noblement.

nobody ['nəʊbədɪ] ■ **pron** personne, aucun(e).
■ **n** (pl **-ies**) *pej* rien-du-tout *mf*, moins que rien *mf*.

no-claims bonus **n** *UK* bonus *m*.

nocturnal [nɒk'tɜːnl] **adj** nocturne.

nod [nɒd] ■ **n** signe *m* OR inclination *f* de la tête.
■ **vt** (pt & pp **-ded**, cont **-ding**) **: to nod one's head** incliner la tête, faire un signe de tête.
■ **vi** (pt & pp **-ded**, cont **-ding**) **1.** [in agreement] faire un signe de tête affirmatif, faire signe que oui **2.** [to indicate sthg] faire un signe de tête **3.** [as greeting] **: to nod to sb** saluer qqn d'un signe de tête.
◆ ***nod off*** **vi** *inf* somnoler, s'assoupir.

nodding ['nɒdɪŋ] **adj** *UK* **: to have a nodding acquaintance with sb** connaître qqn de vue OR vaguement ▸ **a nodding acquaintance with marketing techniques** *fig* quelques notions des techniques de marketing.

node [nəʊd] **n** nœud *m*.

nodule ['nɒdjuːl] **n** nodule *m*.

no-fly zone **n** zone *f* d'exclusion aérienne.

no-frills [-'frɪlz] **adj** [service] minimum *(inv)* / [airline] à bas prix.

no-go area **n** *UK* zone *f* interdite.

no-good *inf* ■ **adj** propre à rien.
■ **n** bon *m* à rien, bonne *f* à rien.

no-holds-barred **adj** [report, documentary] sans fard.

no-hoper [-'həʊpər] **n** *inf* raté *m*, -e *f*, minable *mf*.

noise [nɔɪz] **n** bruit *m* ▸ **to make a noise** faire du bruit ▸ **noise pollution** nuisances *fpl* sonores, pollution *f* sonore.
◆ ***noises*** **npl** *inf* [indications of intentions] **: she made vague noises about emigrating** elle a vaguement parlé d'émigrer.

noiseless ['nɔɪzlɪs] **adj** silencieux(euse).

noiselessly ['nɔɪzlɪslɪ] **adv** sans bruit, silencieusement.

noisily ['nɔɪzɪlɪ] **adv** bruyamment.

noisy ['nɔɪzɪ] (comp **-ier**, superl **-iest**) **adj** bruyant(e).

nomad ['nəʊmæd] **n** nomade *mf*.

nomadic [nə'mædɪk] **adj** nomade.

no-man's-land **n** no man's land *m*.

nomenclature [*UK* nəʊ'menklətʃər, *US* 'nəʊmənkleɪtʃər] **n** nomenclature *f*.

nominal ['nɒmɪnl] **adj 1.** [in name only] de nom seulement, nominal(e) **2.** [very small] nominal(e), insignifiant(e).

nominally ['nɒmɪnəlɪ] **adv** nominalement, de nom.

nominate ['nɒmɪneɪt] **vt 1.** [propose] **: to nominate sb (for/as sthg)** proposer qqn (pour/comme qqch) **2.** [appoint] **: to nominate sb (as sthg)** nommer qqn (qqch) ▸ **to nominate sb (to sthg)** nominer qqn (à qqch).

nomination [,nɒmɪ'neɪʃn] **n** nomination *f*.

nominee [,nɒmɪ'niː] **n** personne *f* nommée OR désignée.

non- [nɒn] **prefix** non-.

nonacceptance [,nɒnək'septəns] **n** non-acceptation *f*.

nonaddictive [,nɒnə'dɪktɪv] **adj** qui ne provoque pas d'accoutumance OR de dépendance.

non-adopter **n** *consommateur qui n'essaie jamais de nouveaux produits.*

nonaffiliated [,nɒnə'fɪlɪeɪtɪd] **adj** non affilié(e), indépendant(e).

nonaggression [,nɒnə'greʃn] **n** non-agression *f*.

nonalcoholic [,nɒnælkə'hɒlɪk] **adj** non-alcoolisé(e).

nonaligned [,nɒnə'laɪnd] **adj** non-aligné(e).

nonattendance [,nɒnə'tendəns] **n** absence *f*.

nonbeliever [,nɒnbɪ'liːvər] **n** incroyant *m*, -e *f*, athée *mf*.

nonbinding [,nɒn'baɪndɪŋ] **adj** sans obligation, non contraignant(e).

nonbiodegradable ['nɒn,baɪəʊdɪ'greɪdəbl] **adj** non biodégradable.

nonchalance [*UK* 'nɒnʃələns, *US* ,nɒnʃə'lɑːns] **n** nonchalance *f*.

nonchalant [*UK* 'nɒnʃələnt, *US* ,nɒnʃə'lɑːnt] **adj** nonchalant(e).

nonchalantly [*UK* 'nɒnʃələntlɪ, *US* ,nɒnʃə'lɑːntlɪ] **adv** nonchalamment.

noncombatant [*UK* ,nɒn'kɒmbətənt, *US* ,nɒnkəm'bætənt] **n** non-combattant *m*, -e *f*.

noncommissioned officer [,nɒnkə'mɪʃənd-] **n** sous-officier *m*.

noncommittal [,nɒnkə'mɪtl] **adj** évasif(ive).

noncompetitive [,nɒnkəm'petɪtɪv] **adj** qui n'est pas basé(e) sur la compétition.

noncompliance [,nɒnkəm'plaɪəns] **n** non-respect *m*, non-observation *f* ▸ **noncompliance with the treaty** le non-respect du traité.

non compos mentis [-,kɒmpəs'mentɪs] **adj : to be non compos mentis** ne pas avoir toute sa raison.

nonconformist [,nɒnkən'fɔːmɪst] ■ **adj** non-conformiste.
■ **n** non-conformiste *mf*.

nonconformity [,nɒnkən'fɔːmətɪ] **n** non-conformité *f*.

noncontributory [,nɒnkən'trɪbjʊtərɪ] **adj** sans versements de la part des bénéficiaires.

noncooperation ['nɒnkəʊ,ɒpə'reɪʃn] **n** refus *m* de coopération.

non-dairy **adj** qui ne contient aucun produit laitier ▸ **non-dairy cream** *US crème liquide d'origine végétale*.

nondeductible [,nɒndɪ'dʌktəbl] **adj** non déductible.

nondescript [*UK* 'nɒndɪskrɪpt, *US* ,nɒndɪ'skrɪpt] **adj** quelconque, terne.

nondrinker [,nɒn'drɪŋkər] **n** personne *f* qui ne boit pas d'alcool.

nondrip [,nɒn'drɪp] **adj** qui ne coule pas.

nondriver [,nɒn'draɪvər] **n** personne *f* qui n'a pas le permis de conduire.

none [nʌn] ■ **pron 1.** [gen] aucun(e) ▸ **there was none left** il n'y en avait plus, il n'en restait plus ▸ **I'll have none of your nonsense** je ne tolérerai pas de bêtises de ta part **2.** [nobody] personne, nul (nulle).
■ **adv : none the worse/wiser** pas plus mal/avancé(e) ▸ **none the better** pas mieux.
◆ ***none too*** **adv** pas tellement **OR** trop.

nonentity [nɒ'nentətɪ] (pl **-ies**) **n** nullité *f*, zéro *m*.

nonessential [,nɒnɪ'senʃl] **adj** non-essentiel(elle), peu important(e).

nonetheless [,nʌnðə'les] **adv** néanmoins, pourtant.

non-event **n** événement *m* raté **OR** décevant.

nonexecutive director [,nɒnɪgsekjətɪv-] **n** administrateur *m*, -trice *f*.

nonexistent [,nɒnɪg'zɪstənt] **adj** inexistant(e).

nonfat ['nɒnfæt] **adj** sans matière grasse **OR** matières grasses.

nonfattening [,nɒn'fætnɪŋ] **adj** qui ne fait pas grossir.

nonfiction [,nɒn'fɪkʃn] **n** *(U)* ouvrages *mpl* généraux.

nonflammable [,nɒn'flæməbl] **adj** ininflammable.

non-habit-forming [-,fɔːmɪŋ] **adj** qui ne crée pas de phénomène d'accoutumance.

noninfectious [,nɒnɪn'fekʃəs] **adj** qui n'est pas infectieux(euse).

noninflammable [,nɒnɪn'flæməbl] = ***nonflammable***.

noninterference [,nɒnɪntə'fɪərəns], ***nonintervention*** [,nɒnɪntə'venʃn] **n** non-ingérence *f*, non-intervention *f*.

noninterventionist [,nɒnɪntə'venʃənɪst] **adj** [policy] non interventionniste, de non-intervention.

non-iron **adj** qui ne se repasse pas.

nonmalignant [,nɒnmə'lɪgnənt] **adj** bénin(igne).

non-member **n** [of club] personne *f* qui n'est pas membre.

non-native **adj** non-indigène ▸ **non-native speaker** locuteur *m* étranger **OR** non natif, locutrice *f* étrangère **OR** non native.

non-negotiable **adj** qu'on ne peut pas négocier **OR** débattre.

no-no **n** *inf* **: it's a no-no** c'est interdit **OR** défendu.

no-nonsense **adj** direct(e), sérieux(euse).

nonoperational [,nɒnɒpə'reɪʃənl] **adj** non-opérationnel(elle).

nonparticipation [,nɒnpɑːtɪsə'peɪʃən] **n** non-participation *f*.

nonpayment [,nɒn'peɪmənt] **n** non-paiement *m*.

nonplussed, *US* ***nonplused*** [,nɒn'plʌst] **adj** déconcerté(e), perplexe.

non-profit, *UK* ***non-profit-making*** **adj** à but non lucratif.

nonproliferation ['nɒnprə,lɪfə'reɪʃn] **n** non-prolifération *f*.

nonrefundable [nɒnrɪ'fʌndəbl] **adj** non remboursable.

nonrenewable [,nɒnrɪ'njuːəbl] **adj** non renouvelable.

nonresident [,nɒn'rezɪdənt] **n 1.** [of country] non-résident *m*, -e *f* **2.** [of hotel] client *m*, -e *f* de passage.

nonreturnable [,nɒnrɪ'tɜːnəbl] **adj** [bottle] non consigné(e).

nonsectarian [,nɒnsek'teərɪən] **adj** tolérant(e), ouvert(e).

nonsense ['nɒnsəns] ■ **n** *(U)* **1.** [meaningless words] charabia *m* **2.** [foolish idea] **: his accusations are utter nonsense** ses accusations n'ont aucun sens ▸ **it was nonsense to suggest...** il était absurde de suggérer... **3.** [foolish behaviour] bêtises *fpl*, idioties *fpl* ▸ **to make (a) nonsense of**

sthg gâcher *OR* saboter qqch ▸ **she took no nonsense from her subordinates** elle ne tolérait aucun manquement de la part de ses subordonnés.
■ **excl** quelles bêtises *OR* foutaises!

nonsensical [nɒn'sensɪkl] **adj** absurde, qui n'a pas de sens.

non sequitur [-'sekwɪtəʳ] **n** remarque *f* qui manque de suite.

nonsexist [,nɒn'seksɪst] ■ **adj** non sexiste.
■ **n** non-sexiste *mf*.

nonshrink [,nɒn'ʃrɪŋk] **adj** irrétrécissable.

nonskid [,nɒn'skɪd] **adj** [tyre] antidérapant(e).

nonslip [,nɒn'slɪp] **adj** antidérapant(e).

nonsmoker [,nɒn'sməʊkəʳ] **n** non-fumeur *m*, -euse *f*, personne *f* qui ne fume pas.

nonsmoking [,nɒn'sməʊkɪŋ] **adj** [area] (pour les) non-fumeurs.

nonstandard [,nɒn'stændəd] **adj 1.** LING [use of word] critiqué(e) ▸ **in nonstandard English** [colloquial] en anglais familier *OR* populaire / [dialectal] en anglais dialectal **2.** [product, size, shape] non-standard *(inv)*.

nonstarter [,nɒn'stɑ:təʳ] **n 1.** *UK inf* [plan] **: this is a nonstarter** ceci n'a aucune chance de réussir **2.** [in race] non-partant *m*.

nonstick [,nɒn'stɪk] **adj** qui n'attache pas, téflonisé(e).

nonstop [,nɒn'stɒp] ■ **adj** [flight] direct(e), sans escale / [activity] continu(e) / [rain] continuel(elle).
■ **adv** [talk, work] sans arrêt / [rain] sans discontinuer.

nontaxable [,nɒn'tæksəbl] **adj** non imposable.

nontoxic [,nɒn'tɒksɪk] **adj** non toxique.

nontransferable [,nɒntrænz'fɜ:rəbl] **adj** non transmissible.

non-U **adj** *UK dated* qui n'est pas très distingué(e), vulgaire.

nonviolence [,nɒn'vaɪələns] **n** non-violence *f*.

nonviolent [,nɒn'vaɪələnt] **adj** non-violent(e).

nonvoter [,nɒn'vəʊtəʳ] **n** abstentionniste *mf*, personne *f* qui ne vote pas.

nonvoting [,nɒn'vəʊtɪŋ] **adj 1.** [person] abstentionniste, qui ne vote pas **2.** FIN [shares] sans droit de vote.

nonwhite [,nɒn'waɪt] ■ **adj** de couleur.
■ **n** personne *f* de couleur.

noodle ['nu:dl] **n 1.** CULIN **: chicken noodle soup** soupe *f* de poulet aux vermicelles **2.** *US inf* [head] tronche *f*.

noodles ['nu:dlz] **npl** nouilles *fpl*.

nook [nʊk] **n** [of room] coin *m*, recoin *m* ▸ **every nook and cranny** tous les coins, les coins et les recoins.

nookie, ***nooky*** **n** ['nʊkɪ] *inf hum* **: a bit of nookie** une partie de jambes en l'air.

noon [nu:n] ■ **n** midi *m*.
■ **comp** de midi.

noonday ['nu:ndeɪ] *liter* = ***noon***.

no one **pron** = ***nobody***.

noose [nu:s] **n** nœud *m* coulant.

nope [nəʊp] **adv** *inf* non.

noplace *US* ['nəʊpleɪs] = ***nowhere***.

nor [nɔ:ʳ] **conj : nor do I** moi non plus ➤ ***neither***.

Nordic ['nɔ:dɪk] **adj** nordique.

Norf (abbr of ***Norfolk***) *comté anglais*.

norm [nɔ:m] **n** norme *f*.

normal ['nɔ:ml] **adj** normal(e).

normality [nɔ:'mælɪtɪ], *US* ***normalcy*** ['nɔ:mlsɪ] **n** normalité *f*.

normalization, *UK* ***-isation*** [,nɔ:məlaɪ'zeɪʃn] **n** normalisation *f*.

normalize, *UK* ***-ise*** ['nɔ:məlaɪz] ■ **vt** normaliser.
■ **vi** se normaliser, redevenir normal(e).

normally ['nɔ:məlɪ] **adv** normalement.

Norman ['nɔ:mən] ■ **adj** normand(e).
■ **n** Normand *m*, -e *f*.

Normandy ['nɔ:məndɪ] **n** Normandie *f* ▸ **in Normandy** en Normandie.

Norse [nɔ:s] **adj** nordique, scandinave.

north [nɔ:θ] ■ **n 1.** [direction] nord *m* **2.** [region] **: the north** le nord.
■ **adj** nord *(inv)* / [wind] du nord.
■ **adv** au nord, vers le nord ▸ **north of** au nord de.

North Africa **n** Afrique *f* du Nord ▸ **in North Africa** en Afrique du Nord.

North African ■ **adj** nord-africain(e), d'Afrique du Nord.
■ **n** Nord-Africain *m*, -e *f*.

North America **n** Amérique *f* du Nord.

North American ■ **adj** nord-américain(e).
■ **n** Nord-Américain *m*, -e *f*.

Northants [nɔ:'θænts] (abbr of ***Northamptonshire***) *comté anglais*.

northbound ['nɔ:θbaʊnd] **adj** en direction du nord ▸ **northbound carriageway** *UK* chaussée (du) nord.

North Carolina [-,kærə'laɪnə] **n** Caroline *f* du Nord ▸ **in North Carolina** en Caroline du Nord.

North Country **n : the North Country** le Nord de l'Angleterre.

Northd (abbr of ***Northumberland***) *comté anglais*.

North Dakota [-də'kəʊtə] **n** Dakota *m* du Nord ▸ **in North Dakota** dans le Dakota du Nord.

northeast [,nɔ:θ'i:st] ■ **n 1.** [direction] nord-est *m* **2.** [region] **: the northeast** le nord-est.
■ **adj** nord-est *(inv)* / [wind] du nord-est.
■ **adv** au nord-est, vers le nord-est ▸ **northeast of** au nord-est de.

northeasterly [,nɔ:θ'i:stəlɪ] **adj** au nord-est, du nord-est ▸ **in a northeasterly direction** vers le nord-est.

northeastern [,nɔ:θ'i:stən] **adj** nord-est *(inv)*, du nord-est.

northerly ['nɔ:ðəlɪ] **adj** du nord ▸ **in a northerly direction** vers le nord, en direction du nord.

northern ['nɔ:ðən] **adj** du nord, nord *(inv)*.

Northerner ['nɔ:ðənəʳ] **n** habitant *m*, -e *f* du Nord.

northern hemisphere **n** hémisphère *m* nord *OR* boréal.

Northern Ireland **n** Irlande *f* du Nord ▸ **in Northern Ireland** en Irlande du Nord.

Northern Lights **npl : the Northern Lights** l'aurore *f* boréale.

northernmost ['nɔːðənməʊst] **adj** le plus au nord (la plus au nord), à l'extrême nord.

Northern Territory **n** Territoire *m* du Nord ▸ **in Northern Territory** dans le Territoire du Nord.

North Korea **n** Corée *f* du Nord.

North Korean ■ **adj** nord-coréen(enne).
■ **n** Nord-Coréen *m*, -enne *f*.

North Pole **n : the North Pole** le pôle Nord.

North Sea ■ **n : the North Sea** la mer du Nord.
■ **comp** de la mer du Nord.

North Star **n : the North Star** l'étoile *f* polaire.

North Vietnam **n** Nord Viêt-Nam *m* ▸ **in North Vietnam** au Nord Viêt-Nam.

North Vietnamese ■ **adj** nord-vietnamien(enne).
■ **n** Nord-Vietnamien *m*, -enne *f*.

northward ['nɔːθwəd] ■ **adj** au nord ▸ **in a northward direction** vers le nord.
■ **adv** = ***northwards***.

northwards ['nɔːθwədz] **adv** au nord, vers le nord.

northwest [ˌnɔːθ'west] ■ **n 1.** [direction] nord-ouest *m* **2.** [region] **: the northwest** le nord-ouest.
■ **adj** nord-ouest *(inv)* / [wind] du nord-ouest.
■ **adv** au nord-ouest, vers le nord-ouest ▸ **northwest of** au nord-ouest de.

northwesterly [ˌnɔːθ'westəlɪ] **adj** au nord-ouest, du nord-ouest ▸ **in a northwesterly direction** vers le nord-ouest.

northwestern [ˌnɔːθ'westən] **adj** nord-ouest *(inv)*, du nord-ouest.

Northwest Territories **npl** *Can* **: the Northwest Territories** les Territoires *mpl* du Nord-Ouest.

North Yemen **n** Yemen *m* du Nord ▸ **in North Yemen** au Yemen du Nord.

Norway ['nɔːweɪ] **n** Norvège *f* ▸ **in Norway** en Norvège.

Norwegian [nɔː'wiːdʒən] ■ **adj** norvégien(enne).
■ **n 1.** [person] Norvégien *m*, -enne *f* **2.** [language] norvégien *m*.

Nos., ***nos.*** (abbr of ***numbers***) no.

nose [nəʊz] **n** nez *m* ▸ **under one's nose** sous le nez ▸ **you're just cutting off your nose to spite your face** c'est toi qui en pâtis ▸ **to have a nose for sthg** flairer qqch, savoir reconnaître qqch ▸ **he gets up my nose** *UK inf* il me tape sur les nerfs ▸ **keep your nose out of my business** occupe-toi *OR* mêle-toi de tes affaires, occupe-toi *OR* mêle-toi de tes oignons ▸ **to look down one's nose at sb** *fig* traiter qqn de haut ▸ **to look down one's nose at sthg** *fig* considérer qqch avec mépris ▸ **on the nose** *US inf* dans le mille ▸ **to pay through the nose** payer les yeux de la tête ▸ **to poke** *OR* **stick one's nose into sthg** mettre *OR* fourrer son nez dans qqch ▸ **to turn up one's nose at sthg** dédaigner qqch.
◆ ***nose about*** *UK*, ***nose around*** **vi** fouiner, fureter.

nosebag ['nəʊzbæg] **n** musette *f* (mangeoire).

nosebleed ['nəʊzbliːd] **n : to have a nosebleed** saigner du nez.

nosecone ['nəʊzkəʊn] **n** [of rocket] coiffe *f* / [of plane] nez *m*.

-nosed [nəʊzd] **suffix** au nez... ▸ **red-nosed** au nez rouge.

nosedive ['nəʊzdaɪv] ■ **n** [of plane] piqué *m*.
■ **vi 1.** [plane] descendre en piqué, piquer du nez **2.** *fig* [prices] dégringoler / [hopes] s'écrouler.

nose job **n** *inf* intervention *f* de chirurgie esthétique sur le nez ▸ **she's had a nose job** elle s'est fait refaire le nez.

nosey ['nəʊzɪ] = ***nosy***.

nosh [nɒʃ] **n** *UK inf* [food] bouffe *f*.

nosh-up **n** *UK inf* gueuleton *m*, bouffe *f*.

nostalgia [nɒ'stældʒə] **n : nostalgia (for sthg)** nostalgie *f* (de qqch).

nostalgic [nɒ'stældʒɪk] **adj** nostalgique.

nostril ['nɒstrəl] **n** narine *f*.

nosy ['nəʊzɪ] (comp **-ier**, superl **-iest**) **adj** curieux(euse), fouinard(e).

not [nɒt] **adv** ne pas, pas ▸ **we are not** *OR* **aren't sure** nous ne sommes pas sûrs ▸ **do not** *OR* **don't believe her** ne la croyez pas ▸ **we hope not** nous espérons que non ▸ **I think not** je ne crois pas ▸ **I'm afraid not** je crains que non ▸ **not always** pas toujours ▸ **whether they like it or not** que ça leur plaise ou non *OR* ou pas ▸ **it's Thomas, not Jake** c'est Thomas, pas Jake ▸ **not all her books are good** ses livres ne sont pas tous bons, tous ses livres ne sont pas bons ▸ **not that...** ce n'est pas que..., non pas que... ▸ **it's not unusual for him to be late** il n'est pas rare qu'il soit en retard ▸ **she really has a nice dress – not!** *inf* quelle belle robe elle a – façon de parler! *OR* faut pas être difficile! ▸ **not at all** [no] pas du tout / [to acknowledge thanks] de rien, je vous en prie.

notable ['nəʊtəbl] ■ **adj** notable, remarquable ▸ **to be notable for sthg** être célèbre pour qqch.
■ **n** notable *m*.

notably ['nəʊtəblɪ] **adv 1.** [in particular] notamment, particulièrement **2.** [noticeably] sensiblement, nettement.

notary ['nəʊtərɪ] (pl **-ies**) **n : notary (public)** notaire *m*.

notation [nəʊ'teɪʃn] **n** notation *f*.

notch [nɒtʃ] **n 1.** [cut] entaille *f*, encoche *f* **2.** *fig* [on scale] cran *m*.
◆ ***notch up*** **vt insep** marquer.

note [nəʊt] ■ **n 1.** [gen] note *f* / [short letter] mot *m* ▸ **to take** *OR* **to make notes** prendre des notes ▸ **she spoke from/without notes** elle a parlé en s'aidant/sans s'aider de notes ▸ **make a note of everything you spend** notez toutes vos dépenses ▸ **to take note of sthg** prendre note de qqch ▸ **to compare notes** échanger ses impressions *OR* ses vues ▸ **a doctor's** *OR* **sick** *UK* **note** un certificat *OR* une attestation du médecin (traitant) / SCH un certificat (médical)
2. *UK* [money] billet *m* (de banque) ▸ **ten-pound note** billet de dix livres
3. [sound, tone] ton *m*, note *f* / [feeling, quality] note *f* ▸ **the piercing note of the siren** le son strident de la sirène ▸ **the meeting began on a promising note** la réunion débuta

sur une note optimiste ▸ **on a more serious/a happier note** pour parler de choses plus sérieuses/plus gaies ▸ **to strike the right/a false note** [speech] sonner juste/faux / [behaviour] être/ne pas être dans le ton
4. [importance] **: of note** de marque, éminent(e)
5. MUS note *f* ▸ **to hit a high note** sortir un aigu.
■ **vt 1.** [notice] remarquer, constater ▸ **please note that payment is now due** veuillez effectuer le règlement dans les plus brefs délais
2. [mention] mentionner, signaler.
◆ ***notes*** **npl** [in book] notes *fpl*.
◆ ***note down*** **vt sep** noter, inscrire.

notebook ['nəʊtbʊk] **n 1.** [for notes] carnet *m*, calepin *m* **2.** COMPUT ordinateur *m* portable compact.

noted ['nəʊtɪd] **adj** célèbre, éminent(e).

notepad ['nəʊtpæd] **n 1.** [for notes] bloc-notes *m* **2.** COMPUT ardoise *f* électronique.

notepaper ['nəʊtpeɪpəʳ] **n** papier *m* à lettres.

noteworthy ['nəʊt,wɜːðɪ] **(comp -ier, superl -iest) adj** remarquable, notable.

nothing ['nʌθɪŋ] ■ **pron** rien ▸ **I've got nothing to do** je n'ai rien à faire ▸ **there's nothing in it** ce n'est pas vrai du tout, il n'y a pas un brin de vérité là-dedans ▸ **there's nothing to it** c'est facile comme tout *OR* simple comme bonjour ▸ **for nothing** pour rien ▸ **nothing if not** avant tout, surtout ▸ **nothing but** ne... que, rien que ▸ **there's nothing for it (but to do sthg)** *UK* il n'y a rien d'autre à faire (que de faire qqch).
■ **adv : you're nothing like your brother** tu ne ressembles pas du tout *OR* en rien à ton frère ▸ **I'm nothing like finished** je suis loin d'avoir fini.

nothingness ['nʌθɪŋnɪs] **n** néant *m*.

notice ['nəʊtɪs] ■ **n 1.** [written announcement] affiche *f*, placard *m* ▸ **a notice was pinned to the door** il y avait une notice sur la porte
2. [attention] **: it has come to my notice that...** mon attention a été attirée par le fait que... ▸ **it escaped my notice** je ne l'ai pas remarqué, je ne m'en suis pas aperçu ▸ **to bring sthg to sb's notice** faire remarquer qqch à qqn, attirer l'attention de qqn sur qqch ▸ **to take notice (of sb/sthg)** faire *OR* prêter attention (à qqn/qqch) ▸ **to take no notice (of sb/sthg)** ne pas faire attention (à qqn/qqch) ▸ **he didn't take a blind bit of notice** *UK* il n'y a tenu aucun compte
3. [warning] avis *m*, avertissement *m* ▸ **legally, they must give you a month's notice** d'après la loi, ils doivent vous donner un préavis d'un mois *OR* un mois de préavis ▸ **give me a few days' notice** prévenez-moi quelques jours à l'avance ▸ **at short notice** dans un bref délai ▸ **at a moment's notice** sur-le-champ, immédiatement ▸ **until further notice** jusqu'à nouvel ordre
4. [at work] **: to be given one's notice** recevoir son congé, être renvoyé(e) ▸ **to hand in one's notice** donner sa démission, demander son congé.
■ **vt** remarquer, s'apercevoir de.

noticeable ['nəʊtɪsəbl] **adj** sensible, perceptible.

noticeably ['nəʊtɪsəblɪ] **adv** sensiblement, nettement.

notice board **n** *UK* panneau *m* d'affichage.

notifiable ['nəʊtɪfaɪəbl] **adj** [disease] à déclaration obligatoire.

notification [,nəʊtɪfɪ'keɪʃn] **n** notification *f*, avis *m*.

notify ['nəʊtɪfaɪ] **(pt & pp -ied) vt : to notify sb (of sthg)** avertir *OR* aviser qqn (de qqch).

notion ['nəʊʃn] **n** idée *f*, notion *f*.
◆ ***notions*** **npl** *US* mercerie *f*.

notional ['nəʊʃənl] **adj** imaginaire, fictif(ive).

notoriety [,nəʊtə'raɪətɪ] **n** mauvaise *OR* triste réputation *f*.

notorious [nəʊ'tɔːrɪəs] **adj** [criminal] notoire / [place] mal famé(e) ▸ **to be notorious for sthg** être réputé(e) pour qqch.

notoriously [nəʊ'tɔːrɪəslɪ] **adv** notoirement.

Notts [nɒts] **(abbr of *Nottinghamshire*)** *comté anglais*.

notwithstanding [,nɒtwɪð'stændɪŋ] *fml* ■ **prep** malgré, en dépit de.
■ **adv** néanmoins, malgré tout.

nougat ['nuːgɑː] **n** nougat *m*.

nought [nɔːt] **num** zéro *m* ▸ **noughts and crosses** *UK* morpion *m*.

noun [naʊn] **n** nom *m*.

nourish ['nʌrɪʃ] **vt** nourrir.

nourishing ['nʌrɪʃɪŋ] **adj** nourrissant(e).

nourishment ['nʌrɪʃmənt] **n** *(U)* nourriture *f*, aliments *mpl*.

Nov. **(abbr of *November*)** nov.

Nova Scotia [,nəʊvə'skəʊʃə] **n** Nouvelle-Écosse *f* ▸ **in Nova Scotia** en Nouvelle-Écosse.

Nova Scotian [,nəʊvə'skəʊʃn] ■ **n** Néo-Écossais *m*, -e *f*.
■ **adj** néo-écossais(e).

novel ['nɒvl] ■ **adj** nouveau (nouvelle), original(e).
■ **n** roman *m*.

novelist ['nɒvəlɪst] **n** romancier *m*, -ère *f*.

novelty ['nɒvltɪ] **(pl -ies) n 1.** [gen] nouveauté *f* **2.** [cheap object] gadget *m*.

November [nə'vembəʳ] **n** novembre *m* ; see also ***September***.

novice ['nɒvɪs] **n** novice *mf*.

Novocaine® ['nəʊvəkeɪn] **n** novocaïne® *f*.

now [naʊ] ■ **adv 1.** [at this time, at once] maintenant ▸ **any day/time now** d'un jour/moment à l'autre ▸ **it's now or never** c'est le moment ou jamais ▸ **now and then** *OR* **again** de temps en temps, de temps à autre
2. [in past] à ce moment-là, alors
3. [to introduce statement] **: now a Jaguar is a very fast car** or, la Jaguar est une voiture très rapide ▸ **now, what was I saying?** voyons, où en étais-je? ▸ **now let me see** voyons voir ▸ **now let's just calm down** bon, on se calme maintenant ▸ **there now** *OR* **now, now, you mustn't cry** allons, allons, il ne faut pas pleurer.
■ **conj : now (that)** maintenant que ▸ **now you come to mention it** maintenant que tu le dis.
■ **n : for now** pour le présent ▸ **that's all for now** c'est tout pour le moment ▸ **from now on** à partir de maintenant, désormais ▸ **in a few years from now** d'ici quelques années ▸ **up until now** jusqu'à présent ▸ **by now** déjà ▸ **by**

now we were all exhausted nous étions alors tous épuisés ▸ **between now and next August/next year** d'ici le mois d'août prochain/l'année prochaine ▸ **I'd never met them before now** je ne les avais jamais rencontrés auparavant.

NOW [naʊ] (abbr of ***National Organization for Women***) **n** *organisation féministe américaine.*

nowadays ['naʊədeɪz] **adv** actuellement, aujourd'hui.

nowhere ['nəʊweəʳ], ***noplace*** *US* ['nəʊpleɪs] **adv** nulle part ▸ **to appear out of** *OR* **from nowhere** apparaître tout d'un coup ▸ **nowhere near** loin de ▸ **we're getting nowhere** on n'avance pas, on n'arrive à rien ▸ **this is getting us nowhere** cela ne nous avance à rien.

no-win situation **n** impasse *f.*

noxious ['nɒkʃəs] **adj** toxique.

nozzle ['nɒzl] **n** ajutage *m*, buse *f.*

NP abbr of ***notary public.***

NPD (abbr of ***new product development***) **n** développement *m* de nouveaux produits.

nr abbr of ***near.***

NS abbr of ***Nova Scotia.***

NSC (abbr of ***National Security Council***) **n** *conseil national américain de sécurité.*

NSF¹ **n** (abbr of ***National Science Foundation***) *fondation nationale américaine pour la science.*

NSF² abbr of ***not sufficient funds.***

NSPCC (abbr of ***National Society for the Prevention of Cruelty to Children***) **n** *association britannique de protection de l'enfance.*

NSU (abbr of ***nonspecific urethritis***) **n** urétrite *f* non spécifique.

NSW abbr of ***New South Wales.***

NT **n 1.** (abbr of ***New Testament***) NT *m* **2.** abbr of ***National Trust.***

nth [enθ] **adj** *inf* énième.

nuance ['nju:ɒns] **n** nuance *f.*

nub [nʌb] **n** nœud *m*, fond *m*.

Nubian Desert ['nju:bjən-] **n : the Nubian Desert** le désert de Nubie.

nubile [*UK* 'nju:baɪl, *US* 'nu:bəl] **adj** nubile.

nuclear ['nju:klɪəʳ] **adj** nucléaire.

nuclear bomb **n** bombe *f* nucléaire.

nuclear capability **n** puissance *f* *OR* potentiel *m* nucléaire.

nuclear disarmament **n** désarmement *m* nucléaire.

nuclear energy **n** énergie *f* nucléaire.

nuclear family **n** famille *f* nucléaire.

nuclear fission **n** fission *f* nucléaire.

nuclear-free zone **n** zone *f* antinucléaire.

nuclear fusion **n** fusion *f* nucléaire.

nuclear physics **n** physique *f* nucléaire.

nuclear power **n** énergie *f* nucléaire.

nuclear-powered **adj** à propulsion nucléaire ▸ **nuclear-powered submarine** sous-marin *m* nucléaire.

nuclear reactor **n** réacteur *m* nucléaire.

nuclear winter **n** hiver *m* nucléaire.

nucleic acid [nju:'kli:ɪk-] **n** acide *m* nucléique.

nucleus ['nju:klɪəs] (pl **-lei** [-lɪaɪ]) **n** *lit* & *fig* noyau *m.*

NUCPS (abbr of ***National Union of Civil and Public Servants***) **n** *syndicat britannique des employés de la fonction publique.*

nude [nju:d] ■ **adj** nu(e).
■ **n** nu *m* ▸ **in the nude** nu(e).

nudge [nʌdʒ] ■ **n** coup *m* de coude / *fig* encouragement *m*, incitation *f.*
■ **vt** pousser du coude / *fig* encourager, pousser.

nudist ['nju:dɪst] ■ **adj** nudiste.
■ **n** nudiste *mf.*

nudity ['nju:dətɪ] **n** nudité *f.*

nugget ['nʌgɪt] **n** pépite *f* ▸ **nugget of information** *fig* information *f* précieuse.

nuisance ['nju:sns] **n** ennui *m*, embêtement *m* ▸ **he's such a nuisance** il est vraiment casse-pieds ▸ **it's a nuisance having to attend all these meetings** c'est pénible de devoir assister à toutes ces réunions ▸ **to make a nuisance of o.s.** embêter le monde ▸ **what a nuisance!** quelle plaie! ▸ **stop being a nuisance** arrête de nous embêter ▸ **nuisance call** appel *m* anonyme.

NUJ (abbr of ***National Union of Journalists***) **n** *syndicat britannique des journalistes.*

nuke [nju:k] *inf* ■ **n** bombe *f* nucléaire.
■ **vt** atomiser.

null [nʌl] **adj : null and void** nul(nulle) et non avenu(e).

nullify ['nʌlɪfaɪ] (pt & pp **-ied**) **vt** annuler.

NUM (abbr of ***National Union of Mineworkers***) **n** *syndicat britannique des mineurs.*

numb [nʌm] ■ **adj** engourdi(e) ▸ **to be numb with** [fear] être paralysé(e) par / [cold] être transi(e) de.
■ **vt** engourdir.

number ['nʌmbəʳ] ■ **n 1.** [numeral] chiffre *m* ▸ **a six-figure number** un nombre de six chiffres ▸ **in round numbers** en chiffres ronds ▸ **the winning number** le numéro gagnant
2. [of telephone, house, car] numéro *m* ▸ **have you got my work number?** avez-vous mon numéro (de téléphone) au travail? ▸ **we live at number 80** nous habitons au (numéro) 80 ▸ **did you get the car's (registration) number?** tu as relevé le numéro d'immatriculation de la voiture?
3. [quantity] nombre *m* ▸ **a number of** un certain nombre de, plusieurs ▸ **a large number of people** un grand nombre de gens, de nombreuses personnes ▸ **any number of** un grand nombre de, bon nombre de ▸ **any number can participate** le nombre de participants est illimité ▸ **they were eight in number** ils étaient (au nombre de) huit ▸ **in equal numbers** en nombre égal
4. [song] chanson *f* ▸ **a dance number** un numéro de danse
5. *inf* [thing, person] **: this number is a hot seller** ce modèle se vend comme des petits pains ▸ **she was wearing a little black number** elle portait une petite robe noire.

■ vt **1.** [amount to, include] compter ▸ **I'm glad to number her among my closest friends** je suis heureux de la compter parmi mes meilleurs amis ▸ **the crowd numbered 5,000** il y avait une foule de 5 000 personnes
2. [give number to] numéroter.
■ vi : **she numbers among the great writers of the century** elle compte parmi les grands écrivains de ce siècle.

number-crunching [-ˌkrʌntʃɪŋ] n *inf* calcul *m* numérique.

numbering ['nʌmbərɪŋ] n numérotation *f*, numérotage *m*.

numberless ['nʌmbəlɪs] adj sans nombre, innombrable.

number one ■ adj premier(ère), principal(e).
■ n **1.** [priority] priorité *f* **2.** *inf* [oneself] soi, sa pomme.

numberplate ['nʌmbəpleɪt] n *UK* plaque *f* d'immatriculation.

Number Ten n *la résidence officielle du premier ministre britannique.*

numbness ['nʌmnɪs] n engourdissement *m*.

numbskull ['nʌmskʌl] = ***numskull***.

numeracy ['nju:mərəsɪ] n compétence *f* en calcul.

numeral ['nju:mərəl] n chiffre *m*.

numerate ['nju:mərət] adj [person] qui sait compter.

numerical [nju:'merɪkl] adj numérique.

numerically [nju:'merɪklɪ] adv numériquement.

numeric keypad [nju:'merɪk] n COMPUT pavé *m* numérique.

numerous ['nju:mərəs] adj nombreux(euse).

numskull ['nʌmskʌl] n *inf* crétin(e), imbécile *mf*.

nun [nʌn] n religieuse *f*, sœur *f*.

NUPE ['nju:pɪ] (abbr of ***National Union of Public Employees***) n *ancien syndicat britannique des employés de la fonction publique.*

nuptial ['nʌpʃl] adj *fml* nuptial(e).

NURMTW (abbr of ***National Union of Rail, Maritime and Transport Workers***) n *syndicat britannique des transports.*

nurse [nɜ:s] ■ n infirmière *f* ▸ **(male) nurse** infirmier *m*.
■ vt **1.** [patient, cold] soigner **2.** *fig* [desires, hopes] nourrir **3.** [subj: mother] allaiter.

nursemaid ['nɜ:smeɪd] n gouvernante *f*, nurse *f*.

nursery ['nɜ:sərɪ] ■ adj de maternelle.
■ n (pl -ies) **1.** [for children] garderie *f* **2.** [for plants] pépinière *f*.

nursery nurse n *UK* puéricultrice *f*.

nursery rhyme n comptine *f*.

nursery school n (école *f*) maternelle *f*.

nursery slopes npl *UK* pistes *fpl* pour débutants.

nursing ['nɜ:sɪŋ] n métier *m* d'infirmière.

nursing home n [for old people] maison *f* de retraite privée / *UK* [for childbirth] maternité *f* privée.

nurture ['nɜ:tʃər] vt **1.** [children] élever / [plants] soigner **2.** *fig* [hopes] nourrir.

NUS (abbr of ***National Union of Students***) n *union nationale des étudiants de Grande-Bretagne.*

nut [nʌt] n **1.** [to eat] *terme générique désignant les fruits tels que les noix, noisettes etc* **2.** [of metal] écrou *m* ▸ **nuts and bolts** *fig* rudiments *mpl* **3.** *inf* [mad person] cinglé *m*, -e *f* **4.** *inf* [enthusiast] fana *mf*, mordu *m*, -e *f* **5.** *inf* [head] caboche *f*.
◆ ***nuts*** ■ adj *inf* : **to be nuts** être dingue.
■ excl *US inf* zut!

NUT (abbr of ***National Union of Teachers***) n *syndicat britannique d'enseignants.*

nutcase ['nʌtkeɪs] n *inf* cinglé *m*, -e *f*.

nutcrackers ['nʌtˌkrækəz] npl casse-noix *m inv*, casse-noisettes *m inv*.

nutmeg ['nʌtmeg] n (noix *f* de) muscade *f*.

nutrient ['nju:trɪənt] n élément *m* nutritif.

nutrition [nju:'trɪʃn] n nutrition *f*.

nutritional [nju:'trɪʃənl] adj nutritif(ive).

nutritionist [nju:'trɪʃənɪst] n nutritionniste *mf*.

nutritious [nju:'trɪʃəs] adj nourrissant(e).

nutshell ['nʌtʃel] n : **in a nutshell** en un mot.

nutter ['nʌtər] n *UK inf* cinglé *m*, -e *f*.

nutty ['nʌtɪ] (comp -ier, superl -iest) adj **1.** [tasting of or containing nuts] aux noix *(aux amandes, aux noisettes etc)* ▸ **a nutty flavour** un goût de noix *(de noisette etc)* **2.** *inf* [crazy] dingue, timbré(e)
▸▸ **as nutty as a fruitcake** complètement dingue.

nuzzle ['nʌzl] ■ vt frotter son nez contre.
■ vi : **to nuzzle (up) against** se frotter contre, frotter son nez contre.

NV abbr of ***Nevada***.

NVQ (abbr of ***National Vocational Qualification***) n *UK examen sanctionnant une formation professionnelle.*

NW (abbr of ***north-west***) N.O.

NWT abbr of ***Northwest Territories***.

NY abbr of ***New York***.

Nyasaland [naɪ'æsəlænd] n Nyassaland *m*.

NYC abbr of ***New York City***.

nylon ['naɪlɒn] ■ n Nylon® *m*.
■ comp en Nylon®.
◆ ***nylons*** npl *dated* [stockings] bas *mpl* Nylon®.

nymph [nɪmf] n nymphe *f*.

nymphomaniac [ˌnɪmfə'meɪnɪæk] n nymphomane *f*.

NYSE (abbr of ***New York Stock Exchange***) n *première place boursière des États-Unis.*

NZ abbr of ***New Zealand***.

o [əʊ] (pl o's *OR* os), ***O*** (pl O's *OR* Os) n **1.** [letter] o *m inv*, O *m inv* **2.** [zero] zéro *m*.

O & M (abbr of ***organization and method***) n O et M.

oaf [əʊf] n butor *m*.

oak [əʊk] ■ n chêne *m*.
■ comp de *OR* en chêne.

OAP (abbr of ***old age pensioner***) n *UK* retraité *m*, -e *f*.

oar [ɔːʳ] n rame *f*, aviron *m* ▸ **to put *OR* stick one's oar in** mettre son grain de sel.

oarlock ['ɔːlɒk] n *US* [rowlock] dame *f* de nage.

oarsman ['ɔːzmən] (pl **-men** [-mən]) n rameur *m*.

oarswoman ['ɔːzˌwʊmən] (pl **-women** [-ˌwɪmɪn]) n rameuse *f*.

OAS (abbr of ***Organization of American States***) n OEA *f*.

oasis [əʊ'eɪsɪs] (pl **oases** [əʊ'eɪsiːz]) n oasis *f*.

oat [əʊt] n [plant] avoine *f*.

oatcake ['əʊtkeɪk] n galette *f* d'avoine.

oath [əʊθ] n **1.** [promise] serment *m* ▸ **on *OR* under oath** sous serment **2.** [swearword] juron *m*.

oatmeal ['əʊtmiːl] ■ n *(U)* flocons *mpl* d'avoine.
■ comp d'avoine.

oats [əʊts] npl [grain] avoine *f* ▸ **is he getting his oats?** *inf* est-ce qu'il a ce qu'il lui faut au lit?

OAU (abbr of ***Organization of African Unity***) n OUA *f*.

OB *UK* abbr of ***outside broadcast***.

obdurate ['ɒbdjʊrət] adj *fml* opiniâtre.

OBE (abbr of ***Order of the British Empire***) n *distinction honorifique britannique*.

obedience [ə'biːdjəns] n obéissance *f*.

obedient [ə'biːdjənt] adj obéissant(e), docile.

obediently [ə'biːdjəntlɪ] adv docilement.

obelisk ['ɒbəlɪsk] n obélisque *m*.

obese [əʊ'biːs] adj *fml* obèse.

obesity [əʊ'biːsətɪ] n *fml* obésité *f*.

obey [ə'beɪ] ■ vt obéir à.
■ vi obéir.

obfuscate ['ɒbfʌskeɪt] vt *fml* obscurcir.

obituary [ə'bɪtʃʊərɪ] (pl **-ies**) n nécrologie *f*.

object ■ n ['ɒbdʒɪkt] **1.** [gen] objet *m* ▸ **an object of ridicule/interest** un objet de ridicule/d'intérêt **2.** [aim] objectif *m*, but *m* ▸ **with this object in mind** dans ce but, à cette fin **3.** GRAM complément *m* d'objet.
■ vt [ɒb'dʒekt] objecter.
■ vi [ɒb'dʒekt] protester ▸ **if you don't object** si vous n'y voyez pas d'inconvénient ▸ **to object to sthg** faire objection à qqch, s'opposer à qqch ▸ **he objects to her smoking** il désapprouve qu'elle fume ▸ **to object to doing sthg** se refuser à faire qqch.

objection [əb'dʒekʃn] n objection *f* ▸ **to have no objection to sthg/to doing sthg** ne voir aucune objection à qqch/à faire qqch.

objectionable [əb'dʒekʃənəbl] adj [person, behaviour] désagréable / [language] choquant(e).

objective [əb'dʒektɪv] ■ adj objectif(ive).
■ n objectif *m*.

objectively [əb'dʒektɪvlɪ] adv d'une manière objective.

objectivity [ˌɒbdʒek'tɪvətɪ] n objectivité *f*.

object lesson ['ɒbdʒɪkt-] n : **an object lesson in sthg** une illustration de qqch.

objector [əb'dʒektəʳ] n opposant *m*, -e *f*.

obligate ['ɒblɪgeɪt] vt *fml* obliger.

obligation [ˌɒblɪ'geɪʃn] **n** obligation *f.*

obligatory [ə'blɪgətrɪ] **adj** obligatoire.

oblige [ə'blaɪdʒ] ■ **vt 1.** [force] **: to oblige sb to do sthg** forcer OR obliger qqn à faire qqch **2.** *fml* [do a favour to] obliger ▸ **I would be obliged if you would refrain from smoking** vous m'obligeriez beaucoup en ne fumant pas ▸ **much obliged!** merci beaucoup! ▸ **to be obliged to sb for sthg** savoir gré à qqn de qqch.
■ **vi** rendre service.

obliging [ə'blaɪdʒɪŋ] **adj** obligeant(e).

obligingly [ə'blaɪdʒɪŋlɪ] **adv** aimablement, obligeamment ▸ **the letter you obligingly sent me** la lettre que vous avez eu l'obligeance de m'envoyer.

oblique [ə'bli:k] ■ **adj** oblique / [reference, hint] indirect(e).
■ **n** TYPO barre *f* oblique.

obliquely [ə'bli:klɪ] **adv** indirectement.

obliterate [ə'blɪtəreɪt] **vt** [destroy] détruire, raser.

obliteration [əˌblɪtə'reɪʃn] **n** destruction *f.*

oblivion [ə'blɪvɪən] **n** oubli *m.*

oblivious [ə'blɪvɪəs] **adj : to be oblivious to** OR **of** être inconscient(e) de.

oblong ['ɒblɒŋ] ■ **adj** rectangulaire.
■ **n** rectangle *m.*

obnoxious [əb'nɒkʃəs] **adj** [person] odieux(euse) / [smell] infect(e), fétide / [comment] désobligeant(e).

o.b.o. (abbr of ***or best offer***) à déb.

oboe ['əubəu] **n** hautbois *m.*

oboist ['əubəuɪst] **n** hautboïste *mf.*

obscene [əb'si:n] **adj** obscène.

obscenely [əb'si:nlɪ] **adv** d'une manière obscène ▸ **he's obscenely rich** *fig* il est tellement riche que c'en est dégoûtant.

obscenity [əb'senətɪ] (**pl -ies**) **n** obscénité *f.*

obscure [əb'skjʊəʳ] ■ **adj** obscur(e).
■ **vt 1.** [gen] obscurcir **2.** [view] masquer.

obscurely [əb'skjʊəlɪ] **adv** obscurément.

obscurity [əb'skjʊərətɪ] **n** obscurité *f.*

obsequious [əb'si:kwɪəs] **adj** *fml* & *pej* obséquieux(euse).

obsequiousness [əb'si:kwɪəsnɪs] **n** *fml* & *pej* obséquiosité *f.*

observable [əb'zɜ:vəbl] **adj** [appreciable] notable, sensible / [visible] qu'on peut observer.

observably [əb'zɜ:vəblɪ] **adv** sensiblement.

observance [əb'zɜ:vəns] **n** observation *f.*

observant [əb'zɜ:vnt] **adj** observateur(trice).

observation [ˌɒbzə'veɪʃn] **n** observation *f.*

observational [ˌɒbzə'veɪʃənl] **adj** [faculties, powers] d'observation / [technique, research] observationnel(elle).

observation post **n** poste *m* d'observation.

observatory [əb'zɜ:vətrɪ] (**pl -ies**) **n** observatoire *m.*

observe [əb'zɜ:v] **vt 1.** [gen] observer **2.** [remark] remarquer, faire observer.

observer [əb'zɜ:vəʳ] **n** observateur *m*, -trice *f.*

obsess [əb'ses] **vt** obséder ▸ **to be obsessed by** OR **with sb/sthg** être obsédé(e) par qqn/qqch.

obsession [əb'seʃn] **n** obsession *f.*

obsessional [əb'seʃənl] **adj** obsessionnel(elle).

obsessive [əb'sesɪv] **adj** [person] obsessionnel(elle) / [need] qui est une obsession.

obsessively [əb'sesɪvlɪ] **adv** d'une manière obsessionnelle ▸ **he's obsessively cautious** il est d'une prudence obsessionnelle ▸ **he is obsessively attached to the toy** il a un attachement maladif pour ce jouet ▸ **she is obsessively attached to her mother** elle fait une fixation sur sa mère.

obsolescence [ˌɒbsə'lesns] **n** obsolescence *f.*

obsolescent [ˌɒbsə'lesnt] **adj** [system] qui tombe en désuétude / [machine] obsolescent(e).

obsolete ['ɒbsəli:t] **adj** obsolète.

obstacle ['ɒbstəkl] **n** obstacle *m.*

obstacle course, ***obstacle race*** **n** course *f* d'obstacles.

obstetric [ɒb'stetrɪk] **adj** obstétrical(e) / [nurse] en obstétrique.

obstetrician [ˌɒbstə'trɪʃn] **n** obstétricien *m*, -enne *f.*

obstetrics [ɒb'stetrɪks] **n** *(U)* obstétrique *f.*

obstinacy ['ɒbstɪnəsɪ] **n** obstination *f.*

HOW TO ...

express obligation

Est-ce qu'il faut prendre rendez-vous ? / Do you have to make an appointment?
Faut-il faire une réservation ? / Do you have to make a reservation?
Est-ce que je dois vraiment y aller ? / Do I really have to go?
Il faut que tu y sois à 8 heures / You have to be there at 8 o'clock
Il lui faudra d'abord repasser chez lui / He'll have to go home first
Vous devez absolument avoir fini sous huit jours / You absolutely must finish within eight days
L'assurance est obligatoire pour les locations non meublées / Insurance is compulsory for unfurnished accommodation
Il est obligé d'y aller / He's obliged to go

obstinate ['ɒbstənət] **adj** **1.** [stubborn] obstiné(e) **2.** [cough] persistant(e) / [stain, resistance] tenace.

obstinately ['ɒbstənətlɪ] **adv** obstinément.

obstreperous [əb'strepərəs] **adj** turbulent(e).

obstruct [əb'strʌkt] **vt** **1.** [block] obstruer ▸ **her hat obstructed my view** son chapeau m'empêchait de voir **2.** [hinder] entraver, gêner ▸ **to obstruct progress/justice** entraver la marche du progrès/le cours de la justice.

obstruction [əb'strʌkʃn] **n** **1.** [in road] encombrement *m* / [in pipe] engorgement *m* **2.** SPORT obstruction *f.*

obstructive [əb'strʌktɪv] **adj** [tactics] d'obstruction / [person] contrariant(e).

obtain [əb'teɪn] **vt** obtenir.

obtainable [əb'teɪnəbl] **adj** que l'on peut obtenir.

obtrusive [əb'tru:sɪv] **adj** [behaviour] qui attire l'attention / [smell] fort(e).

obtrusively [əb'tru:sɪvlɪ] **adv** de façon indiscrète.

obtuse [əb'tju:s] **adj** obtus(e).

obverse ['ɒbvɜ:s] **n** **1.** [of coin] **: the obverse** la face **2.** [opposite] inverse *m.*

obviate ['ɒbvɪeɪt] **vt** *fml* parer à.

obvious ['ɒbvɪəs] ■ **adj** évident(e).
■ **n : to state the obvious** enfoncer des portes ouvertes.

obviously ['ɒbvɪəslɪ] **adv** **1.** [of course] bien sûr **2.** [clearly] manifestement.

obviousness ['ɒbvɪəsnɪs] **n** évidence *f.*

OCAS (abbr of ***Organization of Central American States***) **n** ODEAC *f.*

occasion [ə'keɪʒn] ■ **n** **1.** [gen] occasion *f* ▸ **on the occasion of her wedding** à l'occasion de son mariage ▸ **if the occasion arises, should the occasion arise** si l'occasion se présente, le cas échéant ▸ **on occasion** *fml* de temps en temps, quelquefois **2.** [important event] événement *m* ▸ **to have a sense of occasion** savoir marquer le coup ▸ **to rise to the occasion** se montrer à la hauteur de la situation.
■ **vt** *fml* [cause] provoquer, occasionner.

occasional [ə'keɪʒənl] **adj** [showers] passager(ère) / [visit] occasionnel(elle) ▸ **I have the occasional drink/cigarette** je bois un verre/je fume une cigarette de temps à autre.

occasionally [ə'keɪʒnəlɪ] **adv** de temps en temps, quelquefois.

occasional table **n** table *f* basse.

occidental [,ɒksɪ'dentl] **adj** *liter* occidental(e).
◆ ***Occidental*** ■ **adj** occidental(e).
■ **n** Occidental *m*, -e *f.*

occluded front [ə'klu:dɪd-] **n** METEOR front *m* occlus.

occult [ɒ'kʌlt] ■ **adj** occulte.
■ **n : the occult** le surnaturel.

occupancy ['ɒkjʊpənsɪ] **n** occupation *f.*

occupant ['ɒkjʊpənt] **n** occupant *m*, -e *f* / [of vehicle] passager *m.*

occupation [,ɒkjʊ'peɪʃn] **n** **1.** [job] profession *f* ▸ **raising a family is a full-time occupation** élever des enfants, c'est un travail à plein temps **2.** [pastime, by army] occupation *f* ▸ **the offices are ready for occupation** les bureaux sont prêts à être occupés ▸ **army of occupation** armée *f* d'occupation.

occupational [,ɒkjʊ'peɪʃənl] **adj** [accident, injury] du travail / [pension] professionnel(elle).

occupational hazard **n** risque *m* du métier.

occupational pension scheme **n** *UK* caisse *f* de retraite maison.

occupational therapist **n** ergothérapeute *mf.*

occupational therapy **n** thérapeutique *f* occupationnelle, ergothérapie *f.*

occupied ['ɒkjʊpaɪd] **adj** occupé(e).

occupier ['ɒkjʊpaɪə^r^] **n** occupant *m*, -e *f.*

occupy ['ɒkjʊpaɪ] (pt & pp **-ied**) **vt** occuper ▸ **is this seat occupied?** est-ce que cette place est prise? ▸ **try to keep them occupied for a few minutes** essaie de les occuper quelques minutes ▸ **to occupy o.s.** s'occuper ▸ **occupying army** armée *f* d'occupation.

occur [ə'kɜ:^r^] (pt & pp **-red**, cont **-ring**) **vi** **1.** [happen - gen] avoir lieu, se produire / [- difficulty] se présenter **2.** [be present] se trouver, être présent(e) ▸ **such phenomena often occur in nature** on rencontre souvent de tels phénomènes dans la nature **3.** [thought, idea] **: to occur to sb** venir à l'esprit de qqn ▸ **it occurred to me later that he was lying** j'ai réalisé plus tard qu'il mentait ▸ **it would never occur to me to use violence** il ne me viendrait jamais à l'idée d'avoir recours à la violence.

occurrence [ə'kʌrəns] **n** [event] événement *m*, circonstance *f.*

ocean ['əʊʃn] **n** océan *m* ▸ **oceans of** *inf fig* des tonnes de.

oceangoing ['əʊʃn,gəʊɪŋ] **adj** au long cours.

Oceania [,əʊʃɪ'eɪnɪə] **n** Océanie *f* ▸ **in Oceania** en Océanie.

Oceanian [,əʊʃɪ'eɪnɪən] ■ **adj** océanien(enne).
■ **n** Océanien *m*, -enne *f.*

ocean liner **n** paquebot *m.*

oceanography [,əʊʃə'nɒgrəfɪ] **n** océanographie *f.*

ochre *UK*, ***ocher*** *US* ['əʊkə^r^] **adj** ocre *(inv).*

o'clock [ə'klɒk] **adv : two o'clock** deux heures.

OCR **n** abbr of ***optical character reader***, ***optical character recognition***.

Oct. (abbr of **October**) oct.

octagon ['ɒktəgən] **n** octogone *m.*

octagonal [ɒk'tægənl] **adj** octogonal(e).

octane ['ɒkteɪn] **n** octane *m.*

octane number, ***octane rating*** **n** indice *m* d'octane.

octave ['ɒktɪv] **n** octave *f.*

octet [ɒk'tet] **n** octuor *m.*

October [ɒk'təʊbəʳ] n octobre *m* ; see also ***September***.

octogenarian [,ɒktəʊdʒɪ'neərɪən] n octogénaire *mf*.

octopus ['ɒktəpəs] (pl **-puses** *OR* **-pi** [-paɪ]) n pieuvre *f*.

oculist ['ɒkjʊlɪst] n *dated* oculiste *mf*.

OD abbr of ***overdose***, ***overdrawn***.

odd [ɒd] adj **1.** [strange] bizarre, étrange ▸ **he's an odd character** c'est un drôle d'individu ▸ **it felt odd seeing her again** ça m'a fait (tout) drôle de la revoir **2.** [occasional] **: at odd moments** de temps en temps ▸ **I play the odd game of tennis** je joue au tennis de temps en temps ▸ **we took the odd photo** nous avons pris deux ou trois photos **3.** [not part of pair] dépareillé(e) **4.** [number] impair(e) ▸▸ **twenty odd years** une vingtaine d'années ▸ **he must be forty-odd** il doit avoir la quarantaine *OR* dans les quarante ans ▸ **the odd one** *OR* **man** *OR* **woman out** l'exception *f* ▸ **which of these drawings is the odd one out?** parmi ces dessins, lequel est l'intrus?
◆ ***odds*** npl [probability] **: the odds** les chances *fpl* ▸ **the odds are that...** il y a des chances pour que... *(+ subjunctive)*, iil est probable que... *(+ subjunctive)*, ▸ **the odds are ten to one against** la cote est de dix contre un ▸ **against the odds** envers et contre tout ▸ **they won against overwhelming odds** ils ont gagné alors que tout était contre eux ▸▸ **odds and sods** *inf UK*, **odds and ends** [miscellaneous objects] objets *mpl* divers, bric-à-brac *m inv* / [leftovers] restes *mpl* ▸ **to be at odds with sb** être en désaccord avec qqn ▸ **to be at odds with sthg** ne pas concorder avec qqch.

oddball ['ɒdbɔːl] n *inf* excentrique *mf*.

oddity ['ɒdɪtɪ] (pl **-ies**) n **1.** [person] personne *f* bizarre / [thing] chose *f* bizarre **2.** [strangeness] étrangeté *f*.

odd-job man *UK*, ***odd jobber*** *US* n homme *m* à tout faire.

odd jobs npl petits travaux *mpl*.

oddly ['ɒdlɪ] adv curieusement ▸ **oddly enough** chose curieuse.

oddments ['ɒdmənts] npl fins *fpl* de série.

odds-on ['ɒdz-] adj *inf* **: odds-on favourite** grand favori.

ode [əʊd] n ode *f*.

odious ['əʊdjəs] adj odieux(euse).

odometer [əʊ'dɒmɪtəʳ] n odomètre *m*.

odor *US* = ***odour***.

odorless *US* = ***odourless***.

odour *UK*, ***odor*** *US* ['əʊdəʳ] n odeur *f*.

odourless *UK*, ***odorless*** *US* ['əʊdəlɪs] adj inodore.

odyssey ['ɒdɪsɪ] n odyssée *f*.

OECD (abbr of ***Organization for Economic Cooperation and Development***) n OCDE *f*.

oedema *UK* [iː'diːmə] (pl **oedemata** [-mətə]), ***edema*** *US* [iː'diːmə] (pl **edemata** [-mətə]) n oedème *m*.

Oedipal ['iːdɪpl] adj œdipien(enne).

o'er ['əʊəʳ] *liter* = ***over*** *(adv, prep)* .

oesophagus *UK*, ***esophagus*** *US* [ɪ'sɒfəgəs] n œsophage *m*.

oestrogen *UK*, ***estrogen*** *US* ['iːstrədʒən] n œstrogène *m*.

of *(stressed* [ɒv]*, unstressed* [əv]*)* prep **1.** [gen] de ▸ **the cover of a book** la couverture d'un livre ▸ **a map of Spain** une carte d'Espagne ▸ **the King of England** le roi d'Angleterre ▸ **she's head of department** elle est chef de service ▸ **I'm proud of it** j'en suis fier ▸ **I'm afraid of the dark** j'ai peur du noir ▸ **to die of cancer** mourir d'un cancer ▸ **he's a friend of mine** c'est un ami à moi ▸ **a friend of mine saw me** un de mes amis m'a vu ▸ **it was kind/mean of him** c'était gentil/méchant de sa part
2. [expressing quantity, amount, age] de ▸ **thousands of people** des milliers de gens ▸ **a piece of cake** un morceau de gâteau ▸ **a cup of coffee** une tasse de café ▸ **a pound of tomatoes** une livre de tomates ▸ **a gang of criminals** une bande de malfaiteurs ▸ **at the age of nineteen** à dix-neuf ans, à l'âge de dix-neuf ans ▸ **a child of five** un enfant de cinq ans ▸ **there are six of us** nous sommes six ▸ **some/many/few of us were present** quelques-uns/beaucoup/peu d'entre nous étaient présents
3. [made from] en ▸ **to be made of sthg** être en qqch ▸ **a ring of solid gold** une bague en or massif ▸ **a heart of stone** un cœur de pierre
4. [with dates, periods of time] **: the 12th of February** le 12 février ▸ **in the middle of August** à la mi-août ▸ **the night of the disaster** la nuit de la catastrophe.

off [ɒf] ■ adv **1.** [indicating movement or distance away in space or time] **: to run off** partir en courant ▸ **to get off** descendre ▸ **to jump off** sauter ▸ **the ball hit the wall and bounced off** la balle a heurté le mur et a rebondi ▸ **I knocked the glass off** j'ai fait tomber le verre ▸ **off we go!** c'est parti! ▸ **they're off!** SPORT ils sont partis! ▸ **I'm off!** *inf* j'y vais! ▸ **10 miles off** à 16 kilomètres ▸ **far off** au loin ▸ **to keep off** se tenir éloigné(e) ▸ **two days off** dans deux jours ▸ **a long time off** encore loin
2. [so as to remove] **: to take sthg off** enlever *OR* ôter qqch ▸ **to come off** [sticker, handle] se détacher / [lipstick, paint] partir ▸ **to cut sthg off** couper qqch ▸ **could you help me off with my coat?** pouvez-vous m'aider à enlever mon manteau?
3. [so as to complete] **: to finish off** terminer ▸ **to kill off** achever
4. [not at work, school] **: to take a week off** prendre une semaine de congé ▸ **Monday's my day off** le lundi est mon jour de congé
5. [so as to disconnect or separate] **: to put** *OR* **switch** *OR* **turn the light off** éteindre la lumière ▸ **to turn the tap off** fermer le robinet ▸ **to fence/curtain sthg off** séparer qqch par une clôture/un rideau
6. [discounted] **: £10 off** 10 livres de remise *OR* réduction ▸ **the salesman gave me $20/20% off** le vendeur m'a fait une remise de 20 dollars/20 %
7. [financially] **: to be well off** être aisé(e) *OR* riche ▸ **to be badly off** être pauvre.
■ prep **1.** [at a distance from, away from] de ▸ **to get off a bus** descendre d'un bus ▸ **to jump off a wall** sauter d'un mur ▸ **to take a book off a shelf** prendre un livre sur une étagère ▸ **she knocked the vase off the table** elle a fait tomber le vase de la table ▸ **off the coast** près de la côte ▸ **an alley off Oxford Street** une ruelle qui part d'Oxford Street
2. [so as to remove from] **: to cut a branch off a tree** couper une branche d'un arbre ▸ **take the top off the bottle** enlève le bouchon de la bouteille

3. [not attending] : **to be off work** ne pas travailler ▸ **off school** absent de l'école
4. [by means of] : **it runs off gas/electricity/solar power** ça marche au gaz/à l'électricité/à l'énergie solaire ▸ **to live off vegetables** vivre de légumes
5. [no longer liking] : **she's off her food** elle n'a pas d'appétit ▸ **I'm off him at the moment** j'en ai marre de lui en ce moment
6. [deducted from] sur ▸ **they'll knock** *inf* OR **take something off it if you pay cash** ils vous feront une remise si vous payez en liquide
7. *inf* [from] : **to buy sthg off sb** acheter qqch à qqn ▸ **can I borrow £5 off you?** je peux t'emprunter 5 livres?
■ **adj 1.** *UK* [food] avarié(e), gâté(e) / [milk] tourné(e) ▸ **it smells/tastes off** on dirait que ce n'est plus bon
2. [TV, light] éteint(e) / [engine] coupé(e) ▸ **'off'** 'arrêt' ▸ **the off button** le bouton d'arrêt
3. [cancelled] annulé(e) ▸ **if that's your attitude, the deal's off!** si c'est comme ça que vous le prenez, ma proposition ne tient plus!
4. [not at work, school] absent(e) ▸ **I'll be off next week** je serai absent la semaine prochaine
5. *UK inf* [offhand] : **he was a bit off with me** il n'a pas été sympa avec moi.

offal ['ɒfl] **n** *(U)* abats *mpl*.

off-balance **adv : to throw/push sb off-balance** faire perdre l'équilibre à qqn.

offbeat ['ɒfbi:t] **adj** *inf* original(e), excentrique.

off-centre *UK*, ***off-center*** *US* ■ **adj** décentré(e), décalé(e).
■ **adv** de côté.

off-chance **n : on the off-chance that...** au cas où...

off colour **adj** *UK* [ill] patraque.

offcut ['ɒfkʌt] **n** chute *f*.

off-day **n** *UK inf* **: I'm having an off-day today** je ne suis pas dans mon assiette aujourd'hui.

off duty **adj** qui n'est pas de service / [doctor, nurse] qui n'est pas de garde.

offence *UK*, ***offense*** *US* [ə'fens] **n 1.** [crime] délit *m* **2.** [upset] : **to cause sb offence** vexer qqn ▸ **to take offence** se vexer.

offend [ə'fend] ■ **vt** offenser.
■ **vi** commettre un délit ▸ **to offend against** enfreindre.

offended [ə'fendɪd] **adj** offensé(e), froissé(e).

offender [ə'fendəʳ] **n 1.** [criminal] criminel *m*, -elle *f* **2.** [culprit] coupable *mf*.

offending [ə'fendɪŋ] **adj** qui est la cause OR à l'origine du problème.

offense ['ɒfens] *US* **n 1.** = ***offence*** **2.** SPORT attaque *f*.

offensive [ə'fensɪv] ■ **adj 1.** [behaviour, comment] blessant(e) ▸ **to find sthg offensive** être choqué(e) par qqch ▸ **to be offensive to sb** [person] injurier OR insulter qqn ▸ **this advertisement is offensive to Muslims/women** cette publicité porte atteinte à la religion musulmane/à la dignité de la femme **2.** [weapon, action] offensif(ive).
■ **n** offensive *f* ▸ **to go on** OR **take the offensive** passer à OR prendre l'offensive.

offensively [ə'fensɪvlɪ] **adv 1.** [behave, speak] d'une manière offensante OR blessante **2.** MIL & SPORT offensivement.

offensiveness [ə'fensɪvnɪs] **n** caractère *m* choquant.

offer ['ɒfəʳ] ■ **n 1.** [gen] offre *f*, proposition *f* **2.** [price, bid] offre *f* **3.** [in shop] promotion *f* ▸ **on offer** [available] en vente / [at a special price] en réclame, en promotion.
■ **vt 1.** [gen] offrir ▸ **to offer sthg to sb, to offer sb sthg** offrir qqch à qqn ▸ **to offer to do sthg** proposer OR offrir de faire qqch **2.** [provide - services] proposer / [- hope] donner.
■ **vi** s'offrir.

OFFER ['ɒfəʳ] (abbr of ***Office of Electricity Regulation***) **n** *organisme britannique chargé de contrôler les activités des compagnies régionales de la distribution d'électricité*.

offering ['ɒfərɪŋ] **n** RELIG offrande *f*.

off-guard **adv** au dépourvu.

offhand [,ɒf'hænd] ■ **adj** [nonchalant] désinvolte, cavalier(ère) / [abrupt] brusque.
■ **adv** tout de suite.

offhanded [,ɒf'hændɪd] **adj** = ***offhand*** *(adj)*.

offhandedly [,ɒf'hændɪdlɪ] **adv** [nonchalantly] de façon désinvolte OR cavalière, avec désinvolture / [with abruptness] brusquement, sans ménagement.

office ['ɒfɪs] **n 1.** [place, staff] bureau *m* **2.** [department] département *m*, service *m* **3.** [position] fonction *f*, poste *m* ▸ **in office** en fonction ▸ **to take office** entrer en fonction ▸ **to resign/to leave office** se démettre de/quitter ses fonctions ▸ **to run for** OR **to seek office** se présenter aux élections.

office automation **n** bureautique *f*.

office block **n** *UK* immeuble *m* de bureaux.

office boy **n** garçon *m* de bureau.

officeholder ['ɒfɪs,həʊldəʳ] **n** POL titulaire *mf* d'une fonction.

office hours **npl** heures *fpl* de bureau.

office junior **n** *UK* employé *m*, -e *f* subalterne.

HOW TO ...

offer to do something

Je peux vous aider ? / Can I help you?
Tu veux que j'aille chercher les enfants ? / Do you want me to go and pick up the children?
Et si je passais vous prendre ? / Why don't I come and get you?
Est-ce que j'ouvre une autre bouteille de vin ? / Shall I open another bottle of wine?
Je peux vous loger pendant votre séjour à Paris / I can put you up when you come to Paris
Si vous voulez, nous ferons les vérifications ensemble / If you like, we can check things together

Office of Fair Trading n *UK organisme de défense des consommateurs.*

officer ['ɒfɪsəʳ] n **1.** [in armed forces] officier *m* **2.** [in organization] agent *mf*, fonctionnaire *mf* **3.** [in police force] officier *m* (de police).

office work n travail *m* de bureau.

office worker n employé *m*, -e *f* de bureau.

official [ə'fɪʃl] ■ adj officiel(elle) ▸ **to go through the official channels** suivre la filière (habituelle).
■ n fonctionnaire *mf* ▸ **a bank/club/union official** un représentant de la banque/du club/du syndicat.

officialdom [ə'fɪʃəldəm] n bureaucratie *f*.

officially [ə'fɪʃəlɪ] adv **1.** [formally] officiellement **2.** [supposedly] en principe.

official receiver n syndic *m* de faillite.

officiate [ə'fɪʃɪeɪt] vi officier ▸ **to officiate at a wedding** célébrer un mariage.

officious [ə'fɪʃəs] adj *pej* trop zélé(e).

offing ['ɒfɪŋ] n : **in the offing** en vue, en perspective.

off-key ■ adj faux (fausse).
■ adv faux.

off-licence n *UK magasin autorisé à vendre des boissons alcoolisées à emporter.*

off limits adj interdit(e).

off-line adj COMPUT non connecté(e).

offload [ɒf'ləʊd] vt *inf* : **to offload sthg (onto sb)** se décharger de qqch (sur qqn).

off-peak ■ adj [electricity] utilisé(e) aux heures creuses / [fare] réduit(e) aux heures creuses.
■ adv [travel] aux heures creuses.

off-piste adj & adv SPORT hors-piste.

off-putting [-ˌpʊtɪŋ] adj désagréable, rébarbatif(ive).

off-road vehicle n véhicule *m* tout terrain.

off sales npl *UK* vente *f* de boissons alcoolisées à emporter.

offscreen ■ adj ['ɒfskri:n] CIN & TV [out of sight] hors champ, off.
■ adv [ɒf'skri:n] **1.** CIN & TV hors champ, off **2.** [in private life] dans le privé ▸ **he's less handsome offscreen** il est moins séduisant dans la réalité.

off season n : **the off season** la morte-saison.
◆ ***off-season*** adj hors saison.

offset [ˌɒf'set] (pt & pp **offset**, cont **-ting**) vt [losses] compenser.

offshoot ['ɒfʃu:t] n : **to be an offshoot of sthg** être né(e) OR provenir de qqch.

offshore ['ɒfʃɔ:ʳ] ■ adj [oil rig] en mer, offshore *(inv)* / [island] proche de la côte / [fishing] côtier(ère).
■ adv au large.

offshore fund n fonds *m* offshore.

offshore investment n placement *m* offshore.

offside *UK* ■ adj [ˌɒf'saɪd] **1.** [right-hand drive] de droite / [left-hand drive] de gauche **2.** SPORT hors-jeu *(inv)*.
■ adv [ˌɒf'saɪd] SPORT hors-jeu.
■ n ['ɒfsaɪd] [right-hand drive] côté *m* droit / [left-hand drive] côté gauche.

offspring ['ɒfsprɪŋ] (pl **offspring**) n rejeton *m*.

offstage [ˌɒf'steɪdʒ] adj & adv dans les coulisses.

off-the-cuff ■ adj impromptu(e), improvisé(e).
■ adv au pied levé, à l'improviste.

off-the-peg *UK*, ***off-the-rack*** *US* adj de prêt-à-porter.

off-the-record ■ adj officieux(euse).
■ adv confidentiellement.

off-the-shelf adj [goods] prêt(e) à l'usage.

off-the-wall adj *inf* loufoque.

off-white adj blanc cassé *(inv)*.

OFGAS ['ɒfgæs] (abbr of ***Office of Gas Supply***) n *organisme britannique chargé de contrôler les activités des compagnies régionales de la distribution du gaz.*

OFLOT ['ɒflɒt] (abbr of ***Office of the National Lottery***) n *organisme britannique chargé de contrôler la loterie nationale.*

OFSTED ['ɒfsted] (abbr of ***Office for Standards in Education***) n *organisme britannique chargé de contrôler les établissements scolaires.*

oft- suffix : **oft-quoted** souvent cité(e).

OFT *UK* abbr of ***Office of Fair Trading***.

OFTEL ['ɒftel] (abbr of ***Office of Telecommunications***) n *organisme britannique chargé de contrôler les activités des compagnies de télécommunications.*

often ['ɒfn OR 'ɒftn] adv souvent, fréquemment ▸ **how often do you visit her?** vous la voyez tous les combien? ▸ **as often as not** assez souvent ▸ **every so often** de temps en temps ▸ **more often than not** le plus souvent, la plupart du temps.

OFWAT ['ɒfwɒt] (abbr of ***Office of Water Supply***) n *organisme britannique chargé de contrôler les activités des compagnies régionales de la distribution de l'eau.*

ogle ['əʊgl] vt reluquer.

ogre ['əʊgəʳ] n ogre *m*.

oh [əʊ] excl oh! / [expressing hesitation] euh!

OH abbr of ***Ohio***.

Ohio [əʊ'haɪəʊ] n Ohio *m* ▸ **in Ohio** dans l'Ohio.

ohm [əʊm] n ohm *m*.

OHMS (abbr of ***On His (or Her) Majesty's Service***) *expression indiquant le caractère officiel d'un document en Grande-Bretagne.*

oil [ɔɪl] ■ n **1.** [gen] huile *f* **2.** [for heating] mazout *m* **3.** [petroleum] pétrole *m*.
■ vt graisser, lubrifier.
◆ ***oils*** npl ART huiles *fpl*.

oilcan ['ɔɪlkæn] n burette *f* d'huile.

oil change n vidange *f*.

oilcloth ['ɔɪlklɒθ] n toile *f* cirée.

oiled [ɔɪld] **adj** **1.** [machine] lubrifié(e), graissé(e) / [hinge, silk] huilé(e) **2.** *UK inf* [drunk] **: to be well oiled** être complètement bourré(e).

oilfield ['ɔɪlfi:ld] **n** gisement *m* pétrolifère.

oil filter **n** filtre *m* à huile.

oil-fired [-ˌfaɪəd] **adj** au mazout.

oil gauge **n** [for measuring level] jauge *f* ***OR*** indicateur *m* de niveau d'huile / [for measuring pressure] indicateur *m* de pression d'huile.

oil industry **n : the oil industry** l'industrie *f* pétrolière.

oil lamp **n** [burning oil] lampe *f* à huile / [burning paraffin] lampe *f* à pétrole.

oilman ['ɔɪlmən] (pl **-men** [-mən]) **n** pétrolier *m*.

oil paint **n** peinture *f* à l'huile *(produit)*.

oil painting **n** peinture *f* à l'huile.

oil-producing country **n** pays *m* pétrolier.

oil refinery **n** raffinerie *f* de pétrole.

oilrig ['ɔɪlrɪg] **n** [at sea] plate-forme *f* de forage ***OR*** pétrolière / [on land] derrick *m*.

oilskins ['ɔɪlskɪnz] **npl** ciré *m*.

oil slick **n** marée *f* noire.

oil tanker **n** **1.** [ship] pétrolier *m*, tanker *m* **2.** [lorry] camion-citerne *m*.

oil well **n** puits *m* de pétrole.

oily ['ɔɪlɪ] (comp **-ier**, superl **-iest**) **adj** **1.** [rag] graisseux(euse) / [food] gras (grasse) **2.** *pej* [smarmy] onctueux(euse), mielleux(euse).

ointment ['ɔɪntmənt] **n** pommade *f*.

oiro (abbr of ***offers in the region of***) **: oiro £100** 100 livres à débattre.

OK¹, ***okay*** [ˌəʊ'keɪ] *inf* ■ **adj : is it OK with *OR* by you?** ça vous va?, vous êtes d'accord? ▸ **it's OK but it could be better** ce n'est pas mal, mais ça pourrait être mieux ▸ **are you OK?** ça va? ▸ **he's OK, he's an OK guy** c'est un type sympa.
■ **adv** *inf* bien ▸ **is the engine working OK?** le moteur, ça va? ▸ **everything is going OK** tout marche bien ***OR*** va bien.
■ **n** (pl **OKs**) **: to give (sb) the OK** donner le feu vert (à qqn).
■ **excl** **1.** [expressing agreement] d'accord, O.K. ▸ **in five minutes, OK?** dans cinq minutes, ça va? **2.** [to introduce new topic] **: OK, can we start now?** bon, on commence?
■ **vt** (pt & pp **-ed**, cont **-ing**) approuver, donner le feu vert à.

OK² abbr of ***Oklahoma***.

Oklahoma [ˌəʊklə'həʊmə] **n** Oklahoma *m* ▸ **in Oklahoma** dans l'Oklahoma.

okra ['əʊkrə] **n** gombo *m*.

old [əʊld] ■ **adj** **1.** [gen] vieux (vieille), âgé(e) ▸ **how old are you?** quel âge as-tu? ▸ **I'm 20 years old** j'ai 20 ans ▸ **they have a 14-year-old boy** ils ont un garçon de 14 ans ▸ **to be old enough to do sthg** être en âge de faire qqch ▸ **he's old enough to look after himself** il est (bien) assez grand pour se débrouiller tout seul ▸ **she's two years older than him** elle a deux ans de plus que lui ▸ **my older sister** ma sœur aînée ▸ **an old man** un vieil homme ▸ **an old woman** une vieille femme ▸ **to get *OR* grow old** vieillir ▸ **they're old friends** ce sont de vieux amis ***OR*** des amis de longue date **2.** [former] ancien(enne) ▸ **in the old days** dans le temps, autrefois ▸ **the good old days** le bon vieux temps **3.** *inf* [as intensifier] **: any old** n'importe quel (n'importe quelle) ▸ **any old how** n'importe comment.
■ **npl : the old** les personnes *fpl* âgées.

old age **n** vieillesse *f* ▸ **I've got a little money put aside for my old age** j'ai quelques économies de côté pour mes vieux jours.

old age pension **n** *UK* pension *f* de vieillesse.

old age pensioner **n** *UK* retraité *m*, -e *f*.

Old Bailey [-'beɪlɪ] **n : the Old Bailey** *la Cour d'assises de Londres*.

Old Bill **npl** *UK v inf* **: the Old Bill** les flics *mpl*.

olden ['əʊldn] **adj** *liter* **: in the olden days** au temps jadis.

old-fashioned [-'fæʃnd] **adj** **1.** [outmoded] démodé(e), passé(e) de mode **2.** [traditional] vieux jeu *(inv)*.

old flame **n** *fig* ancien flirt *m*.

Old Glory **n** *US surnom du drapeau américain*.

old hand **n** vieux routier *m*, vétéran *m* ▸ **he's an old hand at flying these planes** cela fait des années qu'il pilote ces avions.

old hat **adj** *inf pej* dépassé(e).

old maid **n** *pej* vieille fille *f*.

old master **n** **1.** [painter] maître *m* **2.** [painting] tableau *m* de maître.

old people's home **n** hospice *m* de vieillards.

old school **n : of the old school** de la vieille école.

Old Testament **n : the Old Testament** l'Ancien Testament *m*.

old-time **adj** d'autrefois.

old-timer **n** **1.** [veteran] vieux routier *m*, vétéran *m* **2.** *esp US* [old man] vieillard *m*.

old wives' tale **n** conte *m* de bonne femme.

Old World **n : the Old World** l'Ancien monde *m*.

O level **n** *UK examen optionnel destiné, jusqu'en 1988, aux élèves de niveau seconde ayant obtenu de bons résultats*.

oligarchy ['ɒlɪgɑ:kɪ] (pl **-ies**) **n** oligarchie *f*.

olive ['ɒlɪv] ■ **adj** olive *(inv)*.
■ **n** olive *f* ▸ **olive (tree)** olivier *m*.

olive branch **n** rameau *m* d'olivier ▸ **to hold out an olive branch to sb** proposer à qqn de faire la paix.

olive green **adj** vert olive *(inv)*.

olive oil **n** huile *f* d'olive.

Olympic [ə'lɪmpɪk] **adj** olympique.
◆ ***Olympics*** **npl : the Olympics** les Jeux *mpl* Olympiques.

Olympic Games **npl : the Olympic Games** les Jeux *mpl* Olympiques.

OM (abbr of ***Order of Merit***) **n** *distinction honorifique britannique*.

Oman [əʊ'mɑ:n] **n** Oman *m* ▸ **in Oman** à Oman.

OMB (abbr of ***Office of Management and Budget***) n *organisme fédéral américain chargé de préparer le budget.*

ombudsman ['ɒmbʊdzmən] (pl -men [-mən]) n ombudsman *m.*

omelette, omelet *US* ['ɒmlɪt] n omelette *f* ▸ **mushroom omelette** omelette aux champignons.

omen ['əʊmen] n augure *m*, présage *m*.

ominous ['ɒmɪnəs] adj [event, situation] de mauvais augure / [sign] inquiétant(e) / [look, silence] menaçant(e).

ominously ['ɒmɪnəslɪ] adv [speak] d'un ton menaçant / [happen, change] de façon inquiétante.

omission [ə'mɪʃn] n omission *f*.

omit [ə'mɪt] (pt & pp -ted, cont -ting) vt omettre ▸ **to omit to do sthg** oublier de faire qqch.

omnibus ['ɒmnɪbəs] n **1.** [book] recueil *m* **2.** *UK* RADIO & TV *diffusion groupée des épisodes de la semaine.*

omnipotence [ɒm'nɪpətəns] n omnipotence *f*.

omnipotent [ɒm'nɪpətənt] adj tout-puissant (toute-puissante), omnipotent(e).

omnipresent [ˌɒmnɪ'prezənt] adj omniprésent(e).

omniscience [ɒm'nɪsɪəns] n omniscience *f*.

omniscient [ɒm'nɪsɪənt] adj omniscient(e).

omnivorous [ɒm'nɪvərəs] adj omnivore.

on [ɒn] ■ prep **1.** [indicating position, location] sur ▸ **on a chair/the wall** sur une chaise/le mur ▸ **to stand on one leg** se tenir sur une jambe ▸ **on the floor** par terre ▸ **on the ceiling** au plafond ▸ **the information is on disk** l'information est sur disquette ▸ **he works on a building site** il travaille sur un chantier ▸ **they live on a farm** ils habitent une ferme ▸ **on the left/right** à gauche/droite ▸ **she had a strange look on her face** elle avait une drôle d'expression ▸ **I only had £10 on me** je n'avais que 10 livres sur moi

2. [indicating means] **: the car runs on petrol** la voiture marche à l'essence ▸ **to be shown on TV** passer à la télé ▸ **on the radio** à la radio ▸ **what's on the other channel** *OR* **side?** qu'est-ce qu'il y a sur l'autre chaîne? ▸ **on the telephone** au téléphone ▸ **to live on fruit** vivre *OR* se nourrir de fruits ▸ **to hurt o.s. on sthg** se faire mal avec qqch ▸ **everyone will be judged on their merits** chacun sera jugé selon ses mérites

3. [indicating mode of transport] **: to travel on a bus/train/ship** voyager en bus/par le train/en bateau ▸ **I was on the bus** j'étais dans le bus ▸ **on foot** à pied

4. [concerning] sur ▸ **a book on astronomy** un livre sur l'astronomie ▸ **we all agree on that point** nous sommes tous d'accord sur ce point ▸ **he's good on modern history** il excelle en histoire moderne

5. [indicating time] **: on Thursday** jeudi ▸ **on the 10th of February** le 10 février ▸ **on my birthday** le jour de mon anniversaire ▸ **on Christmas Day** le jour de Noël ▸ **I don't work on Mondays** je ne travaille pas le lundi ▸ **on my return** à mon retour ▸ **on hearing the news** en apprenant la nouvelle

6. [indicating activity] **: to be on strike** être en grève ▸ **on holiday** *UK OR* **vacation** *US* en vacances ▸ **he's off on a trip to Brazil** il part pour un voyage au Brésil ▸ **she was sent on a course** on l'a envoyée suivre des cours ▸ **to be on night shift** être de nuit

7. [indicating what or who is affected] sur ▸ **she spent £1,000 on her new stereo** elle a dépensé 1 000 livres pour acheter sa nouvelle chaîne hi-fi ▸ **what are you working on at the moment?** sur quoi travaillez-vous en ce moment? ▸ **the impact on the environment** l'impact sur l'environnement ▸ **it's unfair on women** c'est injuste envers les femmes

8. [indicating membership] **: to be on a committee** faire partie *OR* être membre d'un comité

9. [using, supported by] **: to be on social security** recevoir l'aide sociale ▸ **he's on tranquillizers** il prend des tranquillisants ▸ **I'm still on antibiotics** je suis toujours sous antibiotiques ▸ **to be on drugs** se droguer

10. [earning] **: to be on £25,000 a year** gagner 25 000 livres par an ▸ **to be on a low income** avoir un faible revenu

11. [obtained from] **: interest on investments** intérêts de placements ▸ **a tax on alcohol** une taxe sur l'alcool

12. [in ratios] **: 25 cents on the dollar** 25 cents par dollar

13. [referring to musical instrument] à ▸ **to play sthg on the violin/flute/guitar** jouer qqch au violon/à la flûte/à la guitare ▸ **who's on guitar/on drums?** qui est à la guitare/à la batterie?

14. *inf* [paid by] **: the drinks are on me** c'est moi qui régale, c'est ma tournée.

■ adv **1.** [indicating covering, clothing] **: put the lid on** mettez le couvercle ▸ **to put a sweater on** mettre un pull ▸ **what did she have on?** qu'est-ce qu'elle portait? ▸ **why have you got your gloves on?** pourquoi as-tu mis tes gants? ▸ **he had nothing on** il était tout nu

2. [taking place] **: when the war was on** quand c'était la guerre, pendant la guerre ▸ **I've got a lot on this week** je suis très occupé cette semaine

3. [working] **: turn on the power** mets le courant ▸ **put** *OR* **turn** *OR* **switch the television on** allume la télévision ▸ **turn the tap on** ouvre le robinet ▸ **the car had its headlights on** les phares de la voiture étaient allumés

4. [indicating continuing action] **: to work on** continuer à travailler ▸ **the car drove on** la voiture ne s'est pas arrêtée ▸ **we talked on into the night** nous avons parlé jusque tard dans la nuit ▸ **he kept on walking** il continua à marcher

5. [forward] **: send my mail on (to me)** faites suivre mon courrier ▸ **later on** plus tard ▸ **earlier on** plus tôt

6. [of transport] **: the train stopped and we all got on** le train s'est arrêté et nous sommes tous montés

7. *inf* **: to be** *OR* **go on about sthg** parler de qqch sans arrêt ▸ **to be** *OR* **go on at sb (to do sthg)** *UK* harceler qqn (pour qu'il fasse qqch).

■ adj **1.** [working - electricity, light, radio, TV] allumé(e) / [- gas, tap] ouvert(e) / [- engine, machine] en marche / [- handbrake] serré(e) ▸ **the radio was on very loud** la radio hurlait ▸ **the "on" button** le bouton de mise en marche

2. [happening] **: there's a conference on next week** il y a une conférence la semaine prochaine ▸ **it's on at the local cinema** ça passe au cinéma du quartier ▸ **your favourite TV programme is on tonight** il y a ton émission préférée à la télé ce soir ▸ **is our deal still on?** est-ce que notre affaire tient toujours?

3. *inf* [feasible, possible] **: we'll never be ready by tomorrow: it just isn't on** nous ne serons jamais prêts pour demain, c'est tout bonnement impossible

4. *inf* [in agreement] **: are you still on for dinner tonight?** ça marche toujours pour le dîner de ce soir? ▸ **shall we say £10? – you're on!** disons 10 livres? – d'accord *OR* tope là!

◆ ***from... on*** **adv : from now on** dorénavant, désormais ▸ **from then on** à partir de ce moment-là.

◆ ***on and on*** **adv : to go on and on (about)** parler sans arrêt (de) ▸ **the list goes on and on** la liste n'en finit plus.

◆ ***on and off*** **adv** de temps en temps ▸ **it happened on and off throughout the day** cela s'est produit par intervalles *OR* intermittence toute la journée.

◆ ***on to, onto*** **prep** *(written as onto in senses 4 and 5 only)*
1. [to a position on top of] sur ▸ **she jumped on to the chair** elle a sauté sur la chaise
2. [to a position on a vehicle] dans ▸ **she got on to the bus** elle est montée dans le bus ▸ **he jumped on to his bicycle** il a sauté sur sa bicyclette
3. [to a position attached to] **: stick the photo on to the page with glue** colle la photo sur la page
4. [aware of wrongdoing] **: to be onto sb** être sur la piste de qqn
5. *UK* [into contact with] **: get onto the factory** contactez l'usine.

ON abbr of ***Ontario***.

on-board **adj** COMPUT [built-in] intégré(e).

ONC (abbr of ***Ordinary National Certificate***) **n** *brevet de technicien en Grande-Bretagne.*

once [wʌns] ■ **adv 1.** [on one occasion] une fois ▸ **once a day** une fois par jour ▸ **once again** *OR* **more** encore une fois ▸ **once and for all** une fois pour toutes ▸ **once in a while** de temps en temps ▸ **once or twice** une ou deux fois ▸ **for once** pour une fois **2.** [previously] autrefois, jadis ▸ **once upon a time** il était une fois.
■ **conj** dès que.
◆ ***at once*** **adv 1.** [immediately] immédiatement **2.** [at the same time] en même temps ▸ **all at once** tout d'un coup.

once-over **n** *inf* **: to give sb the once-over** jauger qqn d'un coup d'œil ▸ **to give sthg the once-over** jeter un coup d'œil à qqch.

oncologist [ɒŋ'kɒlədʒɪst] **n** oncologue *mf*, oncologiste *mf.*

oncoming ['ɒn,kʌmɪŋ] **adj** [traffic] venant en sens inverse / [danger] imminent(e).

OND (abbr of ***Ordinary National Diploma***) **n** *brevet de technicien supérieur en Grande-Bretagne.*

one [wʌn] ■ **num** [the number 1] un (une) ▸ **one hundred** cent ▸ **one thousand** mille ▸ **one and a half kilos** un kilo et demi ▸ **at one o'clock** à une heure ▸ **he'll be one (year old) in June** il aura un an en juin ▸ **page one** page un ▸ **one of my friends** l'un de mes amis, un ami à moi ▸ **only one answer is correct** il n'y a qu'une seule bonne réponse ▸ **one fifth** un cinquième ▸ **in ones and twos** par petits groupes.
■ **adj 1.** [only, single] seul(e), unique ▸ **it's her one ambition/love** c'est son unique ambition/son seul amour ▸ **no one man should have that responsibility** c'est trop de responsabilité pour un seul homme
2. [indefinite] **: one day we went to Athens** un jour nous sommes allés à Athènes ▸ **one of these days** un de ces jours ▸ **one car looks much like another to me** pour moi, toutes les voitures se ressemblent
3. [a] **: if there's one thing I hate it's rudeness** s'il y a une chose que je n'aime pas, c'est bien la grossièreté ▸ **I've got one awful hangover!** *inf* j'ai une de ces gueules de bois! ▸ **one hell of a bang** *inf* une détonation de tous les diables.
■ **pron 1.** [referring to a particular thing or person] **: which one do you want?** lequel voulez-vous? ▸ **which ones?** lesquels ? *mpl*, lesquelles ? *fpl* ▸ **this one** celui-ci *m*, celle-ci *f* ▸ **that one** celui-là *m*, celle-là *f* ▸ **the other one** l'autre *mf* ▸ **the right one** le bon, la bonne *f* ▸ **the wrong one** le mauvais, la mauvaise *f* ▸ **she's the one I told you about** c'est celle dont je vous ai parlé ▸ **he's the one who did it** c'est lui qui l'a fait ▸ **that's a good one!** elle est bien bonne celle-là! ▸ **that's an easy one** c'est facile ▸ **I'm not** *OR* **I've never been one to gossip but...** je ne suis pas du genre à cancaner, mais...
2. *inf* [blow] coup *m* ▸ **she really thumped him one** elle lui a flanqué un de ces coups
3. *esp UK fml* [you, anyone] on ▸ **one can only do one's best** on fait ce qu'on peut ▸ **to do one's duty** faire son devoir ▸ **it certainly makes one think** ça fait réfléchir, c'est sûr ▸ **to wash one's hands** se laver les mains.
◆ ***at one*** **adv : to be at one with sb/sthg** être d'accord avec qqn/en accord avec qqch.
◆ ***for one*** **adv** pour ma/sa *etc* part ▸ **I for one remain unconvinced** pour ma part je ne suis pas convaincu.
◆ ***in one*** **adv 1.** [combined] **: all in one** à la fois
2. [at one attempt] du premier coup ▸ **he did it in one** il l'a fait en un seul coup ▸ **got it in one!** *inf* du premier coup!
◆ ***one another*** **pron** l'un l'autre *m*, l'une l'autre *f*, les uns les autres *mpl*, les unes les autres *fpl* ▸ **they didn't dare talk to one another** ils n'ont pas osé se parler ▸ **we love one another** nous nous aimons.
◆ ***one up on*** **adv : to be** *OR* **have one up on sb** avoir l'avantage sur qqn.

one-armed bandit **n** *inf* machine *f* à sous.

one-dimensional **adj** unidimensionnel(elle).

one-liner **n** bon mot *m.*

one-man **adj** [business] dirigé(e) par un seul homme ▸ **one-man show** one-man show *m inv*, spectacle solo *m.*

one-man band **n 1.** [musician] homme-orchestre *m* **2.** *fig* [business] entreprise *f* dirigée par un seul homme.

oneness ['wʌnnɪs] **n** *(U) fml* [harmony] accord *m*, harmonie *f.*

one-night stand **n 1.** THEAT représentation *f* unique **2.** *inf* [sexual relationship] aventure *f* d'un soir.

one-off *UK inf* ■ **adj** [offer, event, product] unique.
■ **n : a one-off** [product] un exemplaire unique / [event] un événement unique.

one-on-one *US* = ***one-to-one***.

one-parent family **n** famille *f* monoparentale.

one-party **adj** POL à parti unique.

one-piece **adj** [swimsuit] une pièce *(inv).*

onerous ['əʊnərəs] **adj** *fml* [task] pénible / [responsibility] lourd(e), pesant(e).

oneself [wʌn'self] **pron** *esp UK fml* **1.** *(reflexive)* se / *(after prep)* soi **2.** *(emphatic)* soi-même.

one-sided [-'saɪdɪd] **adj 1.** [unequal] inégal(e) **2.** [biased] partial(e).

one-stop buying **n** *(U)* achats *mpl* regroupés.

one-stop shop **n** magasin *m* où l'on trouve de tout.

one-stop shopping **n** *(U)* achats *mpl* regroupés.

one-time **adj** ancien(enne).

one-to-one *UK*, ***one-on-one*** *US* **adj** [discussion] en tête-à-tête ▸ **one-to-one tuition** cours *mpl* particuliers.

one-touch dialling *UK*, ***one-touch dialing*** *US* **n** numérotation *f* rapide.

one-two **n 1.** [in boxing] *direct suivi d'un crochet de l'autre main* **2.** FOOTBALL une-deux *m inv*.

one-upmanship [ˌwʌn'ʌpmənʃɪp] **n** art *m* de faire toujours mieux que les autres.

one-way **adj 1.** [street] à sens unique **2.** [ticket] simple.

ongoing ['ɒnˌgəʊɪŋ] **adj** en cours, continu(e).

onion ['ʌnjən] **n** oignon *m*.

online ['ɒnlaɪn] **adj & adv** COMPUT en ligne.

online banking **n** *(U)* banque *f* en ligne.

online retailer **n** société *f* de commerce en ligne.

online shopping **n** *(U)* achats *mpl* par Internet.

onlooker ['ɒnˌlʊkər] **n** spectateur *m*, -trice *f*.

only ['əʊnlɪ] ■ **adj** seul(e), unique ▸ **an only child** un enfant unique.
■ **adv 1.** [gen] ne... que, seulement ▸ **he only reads science fiction** il ne lit que de la science fiction ▸ **there are only two people I trust** il n'y a que deux personnes en qui j'aie confiance ▸ **he's only a child!** ce n'est qu'un enfant! ▸ **it's only a scratch** c'est juste une égratignure ▸ **it only cost me £5** ça ne m'a coûté que 5 livres ▸ **he left only a few minutes ago** il est parti il n'y a pas deux minutes
2. [for emphasis] **: I only wish I could** je voudrais bien ▸ **it's only natural (that)...** c'est tout à fait normal que... ▸ **I was only too willing to help** je ne demandais qu'à aider ▸ **not only... but also** non seulement... mais encore ▸ **I only just caught the train** j'ai eu le train de justesse ▸ **it seems like only yesterday** c'est comme si c'était hier.
■ **conj** seulement, mais ▸ **he looks like his brother, only smaller** il ressemble à son frère, mais en plus petit.

o.n.o., ***ono*** (abbr of ***or near(est) offer***) *UK* à déb.

onomatopoeia ['ɒnəˌmætə'pi:ə] **n** onomatopée *f*.

onomatopoeic ['ɒnəˌmætə'pi:ɪk], ***onomatopoetic*** ['ɒnəˌmætəpəʊ'etɪk] **adj** onomatopéique.

onrush ['ɒnrʌʃ] **n** [of emotion] vague *f*, montée *f*.

on-screen **adj & adv** COMPUT à l'écran.

onset ['ɒnset] **n** début *m*, commencement *m*.

onshore ['ɒnʃɔ:r] **adj & adv** [from sea] du large / [on land] à terre.

onside [ɒn'saɪd] **adj & adv** SPORT en jeu.

on-site **adj** sur place.

onslaught ['ɒnslɔ:t] **n** attaque *f*.

onstage ['ɒnsteɪdʒ] **adj & adv** sur scène.

Ont. abbr of ***Ontario***.

on-target earnings **npl** [of salesperson] salaire *m* de base plus commissions.

Ontario [ɒn'teərɪəʊ] **n** Ontario *m* ▸ **in Ontario** dans l'Ontario.

on-the-job **adj** [training] sur le tas.

on-the-spot **adj** [interview] sur place.

onto *(stressed* ['ɒntu:] *unstressed before consonant* ['ɒntə] *unstressed before vowel* ['ɒntʊ]*)* = ***on to***.

onus ['əʊnəs] **n** responsabilité *f*, charge *f*.

onward ['ɒnwəd] **adj & adv** en avant.

onwards ['ɒnwədz] **adv** en avant ▸ **from now onwards** dorénavant, désormais ▸ **from then onwards** à partir de ce moment-là.

onyx ['ɒnɪks] **n** onyx *m*.

oodles ['u:dlz] **npl** *inf* **: oodles of** plein de, un tas de.

oof [ʊf] **excl** *inf* ouïe!, ouille!, aïe!

ooh [u:] **excl** *inf* oh!

oops [ʊps ***or*** u:ps] **excl** *inf* houp!, hop là!

ooze [u:z] ■ **vt** *fig* [charm, confidence] respirer.
■ **vi : to ooze from *or* out of sthg** suinter de qqch.
■ **n** vase *f*.

op [ɒp] (abbr of ***operation***) **n** *inf* MED & MIL opération *f*.

opacity [ə'pæsətɪ] **n** opacité *f* / *fig* obscurité *f*.

opal ['əʊpl] **n** [gem] opale *f*.

opaque [əʊ'peɪk] **adj** opaque / *fig* obscur(e).

OPEC ['əʊpek] (abbr of ***Organization of Petroleum Exporting Countries***) **n** OPEP *f*.

open ['əʊpn] ■ **adj 1.** [gen] ouvert(e) ▸ **her eyes were slightly open/wide open** ses yeux étaient entrouverts/grands ouverts ▸ **his shirt was open to the waist** sa chemise était ouverte ***or*** déboutonnée jusqu'à la ceinture ▸ **he kicked the door open** il a ouvert la porte d'un coup de pied ▸ **there's a bottle already open in the fridge** il y a une bouteille entamée dans le frigo ▸ **the book lay open at page six** le livre était ouvert à la page six
2. [for business] ouvert(e) ▸ **are you open on Saturdays?** ouvrez-vous le samedi? ▸ **we're open for business as usual** nous sommes ouverts comme à l'habitude
3. [view, road, space] dégagé(e) ▸ **only one lane on the bridge is open** il n'y a qu'une voie ouverte à la circulation sur le pont ▸ **the shelter was open on three sides** l'abri était ouvert sur trois côtés ▸ **the wide open spaces of Texas** les grands espaces du Texas ▸ **in the open air** en plein air ▸ **the open sea** la haute mer, le large
4. [uncovered - car, wagon] découvert(e) ▸ **an open fire** un feu de cheminée
5. [unoccupied, available - job] vacant(e) / [- period of time] libre ▸ **we have two positions open** nous avons deux postes à pourvoir ▸ **it's the only course of action open to us** c'est la seule chose que nous puissions faire ▸ **he wants to keep his options open** il ne veut pas s'engager
6. [meeting] public(ique) / [competition] ouvert(e) à tous ▸ **club membership is open to anyone** aucune condition particulière n'est requise pour devenir membre du club
7. [receptive] **: to be open (to)** être réceptif(ive) (à) ▸ **I try to keep an open mind about such things** j'essaie de ne pas avoir de préjugés sur ces questions ▸ **to lay o.s. open to criticism** s'exposer aux critiques ▸ **the prices are not open to negotiation** les prix ne sont pas négociables

8. [disbelief, honesty] manifeste, évident(e) ▸ **they acted in open violation of the treaty** ce qu'ils ont fait constitue une violation flagrante du traité ▸ **it's an open admission of guilt** cela équivaut à un aveu
9. [unresolved] non résolu(e) ▸ **the election is still wide open** l'élection n'est pas encore jouée ▸ **he wanted to leave the date open** il n'a pas voulu fixer de date.
■ **n 1. : in the open** [sleep] à la belle étoile / [eat] au grand air ▸ **to bring sthg out into the open** divulguer qqch, exposer qqch au grand jour
2. SPORT **: the British Open** l'open *m* ***OR*** le tournoi open de Grande-Bretagne.
■ **vt 1.** [gen] ouvrir ▸ **she opened her eyes very wide** elle ouvrit grand les yeux, elle écarquilla les yeux ▸ **the agreement opens the way for peace** l'accord va mener à la paix
2. [inaugurate] inaugurer ▸ **to open fire (on *OR* at sb)** ouvrir le feu (sur qqn) ▸ **to open the betting** [in poker] lancer les enchères.
■ **vi 1.** [door, flower] s'ouvrir ▸ **the window opens outwards** la fenêtre (s')ouvre vers l'extérieur ▸ **open wide!** ouvrez grand!
2. [shop, library] ouvrir ▸ **what time do you open on Sundays?** à quelle heure ouvrez-vous le dimanche?
3. [meeting, play] commencer ▸ **the hunting season opens in September** la chasse ouvre en septembre ▸ **she opened with a statement of the association's goals** elle commença par une présentation des buts de l'association ▸ **the film opens next week** le film sort la semaine prochaine ▸ **the Dow Jones opened at 2461** le Dow Jones a ouvert à 2461.
◆ ***open onto*** **vt insep** [subj: room, door] donner sur.
◆ ***open out*** **vi** [road, river] s'élargir ▸ **the sofa opens out into a bed** le canapé est convertible en lit.
◆ ***open up*** ■ **vt sep 1.** [for business] ouvrir ▸ **he wants to open up a travel agency** il veut ouvrir une agence de voyages
2. [develop] exploiter, développer ▸ **a discovery which opens up new fields of research** une découverte qui crée de nouveaux domaines de recherche.
■ **vi 1.** [possibilities] s'offrir, se présenter
2. [door, building] ouvrir ▸ **open up or I'll call the police!** ouvrez, sinon j'appelle la police! ▸ **a new hotel opens up every week** un nouvel hôtel ouvre ses portes chaque semaine
3. [become less reserved - person] s'ouvrir / [- discussion] s'animer.

open-air **adj** en plein air.

open-and-shut **adj** clair(e), évident(e).

opencast ['əʊpnkɑːst] **adj** [mining] à ciel ouvert.

open day **n** journée *f* portes ouvertes.

open-door **adj** [policy] de la porte ouverte.

open-ended [-'endɪd] **adj** [meeting] sans limite de durée.

opener ['əʊpnəʳ] **n** [for cans] ouvre-boîtes *m inv* / [for bottles] ouvre-bouteilles *m inv*, décapsuleur *m*.

open-handed [-'hændɪd] **adj** généreux(euse).

openhearted [ˌəʊpn'hɑːtɪd] **adj** franc (franche).

open-heart surgery **n** chirurgie *f* à cœur ouvert.

open house **n 1.** *US* = ***open day*** **2.** *US* [party] grande fête *f*
▸▸ **to keep open house** *UK* tenir table ouverte.

opening ['əʊpnɪŋ] ■ **adj** [first] premier(ère) / [remarks] préliminaire ▸ **the play's opening scene** le début de la pièce.
■ **n 1.** [act of opening] ouverture *f* ▸ **at the play's New York opening** lors de la première de la pièce à New York **2.** [beginning] commencement *m*, début *m* **3.** [in fence] trou *m*, percée *f* / [in clouds] trouée *f*, déchirure *f* **4.** [opportunity - gen] occasion *f* / COMM débouché *m* ▸ **her remarks about the company gave me the opening I needed** ses observations au sujet de l'entreprise m'ont fourni le prétexte dont j'avais besoin **5.** [job vacancy] poste *m*.

opening balance **n** solde *m* d'ouverture.

opening hours **npl** heures *fpl* d'ouverture.

opening night **n** première *f*.

opening time **n** *UK* [of pub] heure *f* d'ouverture.

open letter **n** lettre *f* ouverte.

openly ['əʊpənlɪ] **adv** ouvertement, franchement.

open market **n** marché *m* libre.

open marriage **n** mariage *m* moderne *(où chacun est libre d'avoir des aventures)*.

open-minded [-'maɪndɪd] **adj** [person] qui a l'esprit large / [attitude] large.

open-mindedness [-'maɪndɪdnɪs] **n** ouverture *f* d'esprit.

open-mouthed [-'maʊðd] **adj & adv** bouche bée *(inv)*.

open-necked [-'nekt] **adj** à col ouvert.

openness ['əʊpənnɪs] **n** [frankness] franchise *f*.

open-plan **adj** non cloisonné(e).

open primary **n** *US* POL *élection primaire ouverte à tous les électeurs*.

open prison **n** prison *f* ouverte.

open sandwich **n** canapé *m*.

open season **n** saison *f* de la chasse.

open secret **n** secret *m* de Polichinelle.

open sesame ■ **excl : open sesame!** sésame, ouvre-toi!
■ **n** *UK* [means to success] sésame *m* ▸ **good A-level results aren't necessarily an open sesame to university** de bons résultats aux A-levels n'ouvrent pas forcément la porte de l'université.

open shop **n** *absence de monopole syndical*.

Open University **n** *UK* **: the Open University** ≃ centre *m* national d'enseignement à distance.

open verdict **n** *UK* LAW *jugement qui enregistre un décès sans en spécifier la cause*.

opera ['ɒpərə] **n** opéra *m*.

operable ['ɒprəbl] **adj** MED opérable.

opera glasses **npl** jumelles *fpl* de théâtre.

operagoer ['ɒprəˌgəʊəʳ] **n** amateur *m* d'opéra.

opera house **n** opéra *m*.

opera singer **n** chanteur *m*, -euse *f* d'opéra.

operate ['ɒpəreɪt] ■ **vt 1.** [machine] faire marcher, faire fonctionner ▸ **a circuit-breaker operates the safety mechanism** un disjoncteur actionne *OR* déclenche le système de sécurité **2.** COMM diriger.
■ **vi 1.** [rule, law, system] jouer, être appliqué(e) / [machine] fonctionner, marcher ▸ **the factory is operating at full capacity** l'usine tourne à plein rendement ▸ **the drug operates on the nervous system** le médicament agit sur le système nerveux **2.** COMM opérer, travailler ▸ **the company operates out of Chicago** le siège de la société est à Chicago **3.** MED opérer ▸ **to operate on sb/sthg** opérer qqn/de qqch.

operatic [ˌɒpə'rætɪk] **adj** d'opéra.

operating cost ['ɒpəreɪtɪŋ-] **n** charge *f* opérationnelle.

operating room ['ɒpəreɪtɪŋ-] **n** *US* = ***operating theatre***.

operating system ['ɒpəreɪtɪŋ-] **n** COMPUT système *m* d'exploitation.

operating table ['ɒpəreɪtɪŋ-] **n** table *f* d'opération.

operating theatre *UK*, ***operating room*** *US* ['ɒpəreɪtɪŋ-] **n** salle *f* d'opération.

operation [ˌɒpə'reɪʃn] **n 1.** [gen & MED] opération *f* ▸ **a police/rescue operation** une opération de police/de sauvetage ▸ **to have an operation (for)** se faire opérer (de) ▸ **to perform an operation** réaliser une intervention **2.** [of machine] marche *f*, fonctionnement *m* ▸ **to be in operation** [machine] être en marche *OR* en service / [law, system] être en vigueur ▸ **to come into operation** [machine, train service] entrer en service / [law] entrer en vigueur **3.** [COMM - company] exploitation *f* / [- management] administration *f*, gestion *f*.

operational [ˌɒpə'reɪʃənl] **adj 1.** [machine] en état de marche **2.** [difficulty, costs] d'exploitation.

operative ['ɒprətɪv] ■ **adj** en vigueur.
■ **n** ouvrier *m*, -ère *f*.

operator ['ɒpəreɪtəʳ] **n 1.** TELEC standardiste *mf* **2.** [of machine] opérateur *m*, -trice *f* **3.** COMM directeur *m*, -trice *f*.

operetta [ˌɒpə'retə] **n** opérette *f*.

ophthalmic [ɒf'θælmɪk] **adj** ANAT [nerve] ophtalmique / MED [surgery] ophtalmologique.

ophthalmic optician **n** opticien *m*, -enne *f*.

ophthalmologist [ˌɒfθæl'mɒlədʒɪst] **n** ophtalmologue *mf*, ophtalmologiste *mf*.

ophthalmology [ˌɒfθæl'mɒlədʒɪ] **n** ophtalmologie *f*.

opinion [ə'pɪnjən] **n** opinion *f*, avis *m* ▸ **to be of the opinion that** être d'avis que, estimer que ▸ **in my opinion** à mon avis ▸ **my personal opinion is that...** je suis d'avis que..., pour ma part, je pense que... ▸ **I have a rather low opinion of him** je n'ai pas beaucoup d'estime pour lui.

opinionated [ə'pɪnjəneɪtɪd] **adj** *pej* dogmatique.

opinion poll **n** sondage *m* d'opinion.

opium ['əupjəm] **n** opium *m*.

opponent [ə'pəunənt] **n** adversaire *mf*.

opportune ['ɒpətju:n] **adj** opportun(e).

opportunism [ˌɒpə'tju:nɪzm] **n** opportunisme *m*.

opportunist [ˌɒpə'tju:nɪst] **n** opportuniste *mf*.

opportunistic [ˌɒpətju:'nɪstɪk] **adj** opportuniste.

opportunities and threats **npl** COMM opportunités *fpl* et menaces *fpl*.

opportunity [ˌɒpə'tju:nətɪ] (pl **-ies**) **n** occasion *f* ▸ **to take the opportunity to do *OR* of doing sthg** profiter de l'occasion pour faire qqch ▸ **I took every opportunity of travelling** je n'ai manqué aucune occasion de *OR* j'ai saisi toutes les occasions de voyager ▸ **to get the opportunity** avoir l'occasion ▸ **you missed a golden opportunity** vous avez manqué *OR* laissé passer une occasion en or ▸ **at every opportunity** à la moindre occasion.

oppose [ə'pəuz] **vt** s'opposer à.

opposed [ə'pəuzd] **adj** opposé(e) ▸ **to be opposed to** être contre, être opposé à ▸ **as opposed to** par opposition à.

opposing [ə'pəuzɪŋ] **adj** opposé(e).

opposite ['ɒpəzɪt] ■ **adj** opposé(e) / [house] d'en face ▸ **'see illustration on opposite page'** 'voir illustration ci-contre' ▸ **his words had just the opposite effect** ses paroles eurent exactement l'effet contraire.
■ **adv** en face ▸ **the lady opposite** la dame qui habite en face.
■ **prep** en face de ▸ **they sat opposite each other** ils étaient assis l'un en face de l'autre.
■ **n** contraire *m* ▸ **Mary is the complete opposite of her sister** Mary est tout à fait l'opposé de sa sœur.

opposite number **n** homologue *mf*.

HOW TO ...
express opinions

Giving one's opinion
À mon avis, il ment / In my opinion, he's lying
Personnellement, je pense que ce n'est pas une bonne solution / Personally, I don't think that's a good solution
Moi, je dirais que c'est plutôt mal écrit / If you ask me, it's not very well written
J'estime qu'elle est trop jeune / I think that she's too young
Il me semble que nous devons intervenir maintenant / I think we should intervene now
J'ai l'impression qu'il n'est pas très content / I get the impression he's not very happy

Avoiding giving an opinion
Je préférerais ne rien dire / I'd rather not say anything
C'est difficile à dire / It's hard to say
Je ne sais pas trop / I'm not sure
Aucune idée ! / No idea!
Ça dépend / It depends

opposite sex **n : the opposite sex** le sexe opposé.

opposition [ˌɒpəˈzɪʃn] **n 1.** [gen] opposition *f* **2.** [opposing team] adversaire *mf*.
◆ ***Opposition*** **n** *UK* POL **: the Opposition** l'opposition.

oppress [əˈpres] **vt 1.** [persecute] opprimer **2.** [depress] oppresser.

oppressed [əˈprest] ■ **adj** opprimé(e).
■ **npl : the oppressed** les opprimés *mpl*.

oppression [əˈpreʃn] **n** oppression *f*.

oppressive [əˈpresɪv] **adj 1.** [unjust] oppressif(ive) **2.** [weather, heat] étouffant(e), lourd(e) **3.** [silence] oppressant(e).

oppressively [əˈpresɪvlɪ] **adv** d'une manière oppressante *OR* accablante ▸ **it was oppressively hot** il faisait une chaleur étouffante *OR* accablante.

oppressor [əˈpresəʳ] **n** oppresseur *m*.

opprobrium [əˈprəʊbrɪəm] **n** opprobre *m*.

opt [ɒpt] ■ **vt : to opt to do sthg** choisir de faire qqch.
■ **vi : to opt for** opter pour.
◆ ***opt in*** **vi : to opt in (to)** choisir de participer (à).
◆ ***opt out*** **vi : to opt out (of)** [gen] choisir de ne pas participer (à) / [of responsibility] se dérober (à) / *UK* [of NHS] ne plus faire partie (de).

optic [ˈɒptɪk] **adj** optique.

optical [ˈɒptɪkl] **adj** optique.

optical character reader **n** COMPUT lecteur *m* optique de caractères.

optical character recognition **n** COMPUT reconnaissance *f* optique de caractères.

optical fibre *UK*, ***optical fiber*** *US* **n** TELEC fibre *f* optique.

optical illusion **n** illusion *f* d'optique.

optician [ɒpˈtɪʃn] **n 1.** [who sells glasses] opticien *m*, -enne *f* **2.** [ophthalmologist] ophtalmologiste *mf*.

optics [ˈɒptɪks] **n** *(U)* optique *f*.

optimal [ˈɒptɪml] **adj** optimal(e).

optimal price **n** prix *m* optimum.

optimism [ˈɒptɪmɪzm] **n** optimisme *m*.

optimist [ˈɒptɪmɪst] **n** optimiste *mf*.

optimistic [ˌɒptɪˈmɪstɪk] **adj** optimiste ▸ **to be optimistic about** être optimiste pour.

optimistically [ˌɒptɪˈmɪstɪklɪ] **adv** avec optimisme, d'une manière optimiste.

optimize, *UK* ***-ise*** [ˈɒptɪmaɪz] **vt** optimaliser.

optimum [ˈɒptɪməm] **adj** optimum *(inv)*.

option [ˈɒpʃn] **n** option *f*, choix *m* ▸ **she had no option but to pay up** elle n'a pas pu faire autrement que de payer ▸ **to have the option to do** *OR* **of doing sthg** pouvoir faire qqch, avoir la possibilité de faire qqch.

optional [ˈɒpʃənl] **adj** facultatif(ive) ▸ **an optional extra** un accessoire.

optionally [ˈɒpʃənəlɪ] **adv** facultativement.

optometry [ɒpˈtɒmətrɪ] **n** optométrie *f*.

opt-out **n** *UK* POL [of school, hospital] *décision de choisir l'autonomie vis-à-vis des pouvoirs publics* ▸ **Britain's opt-out from the Social Chapter** la décision de la Grande-Bretagne de ne pas souscrire au chapitre social européen.

opt-out clause **n** POL clause *f* d'exemption.

opulence [ˈɒpjʊləns] **n 1.** [wealth] opulence *f* **2.** [sumptuousness] magnificence *f*.

opulent [ˈɒpjʊlənt] **adj 1.** [wealthy] opulent(e) **2.** [sumptuous] magnifique.

opus [ˈəʊpəs] (pl **-es** [-iːz] *OR* **opera** [ˈɒpərə]) **n** MUS opus *m*.

or [ɔːʳ] **conj 1.** [gen] ou **2.** [after negative] **: he can't read or write** il ne sait ni lire ni écrire **3.** [otherwise] sinon **4.** [as correction] ou plutôt.

OR abbr of ***Oregon***.

oracle [ˈɒrəkl] **n** [prophet] oracle *m*.

oral [ˈɔːrəl] ■ **adj 1.** [spoken] oral(e) **2.** [MED - medicine] par voie orale, par la bouche / [- hygiene] buccal(e).
■ **n** oral *m*, épreuve *f* orale.

orally [ˈɔːrəlɪ] **adv 1.** [in spoken form] oralement **2.** MED par voie orale.

orange [ˈɒrɪndʒ] ■ **adj** orange *(inv)*.
■ **n 1.** [fruit] orange *f* **2.** [colour] orange *m*.

orangeade [ˌɒrɪndʒˈeɪd] **n** orangeade *f*.

orange blossom **n** *(U)* fleur *f* d'oranger.

Orangeman [ˈɒrɪndʒmən] (pl **-men** [-mən]) **n** *UK* orangiste *m*.

orang-outang [ɔːˌræŋuːˈtæŋ] **n** orang-outang *m*.

oration [ɔːˈreɪʃn] **n** *fml* discours *m*.

orator [ˈɒrətəʳ] **n** orateur *m*, -trice *f*.

oratorical [ˌɒrəˈtɒrɪkl] **adj** oratoire.

oratorio [ˌɒrəˈtɔːrɪəʊ] (pl **-s**) **n** oratorio *m*.

oratory [ˈɒrətrɪ] **n** art *m* oratoire, éloquence *f*.

orb [ɔːb] **n** globe *m*.

orbit [ˈɔːbɪt] ■ **n** orbite *f* ▸ **to be in/go into orbit (around)** être/entrer sur *OR* en orbite (autour de).
■ **vt** décrire une orbite autour de.

orbital [ˈɔːbɪtl] **adj** orbital(e) ▸ **orbital motorway** *UK* (autoroute *f*) périphérique *m*.

orchard [ˈɔːtʃəd] **n** verger *m* ▸ **apple orchard** champ *m* de pommiers, pommeraie *f*.

orchestra [ˈɔːkɪstrə] **n** orchestre *m*.

orchestral [ɔːˈkestrəl] **adj** orchestral(e).

orchestra pit **n** fosse *f* d'orchestre.

orchestrate [ˈɔːkɪstreɪt] **vt** *lit & fig* orchestrer.

orchestration [ˌɔːkeˈstreɪʃn] **n** *lit & fig* orchestration *f*.

orchid [ˈɔːkɪd] **n** orchidée *f*.

ordain [ɔːˈdeɪn] **vt 1.** [decree] ordonner, décréter **2.** RELIG **: to be ordained** être ordonné prêtre.

ordeal [ɔːˈdiːl] **n** épreuve *f*.

order [ˈɔːdəʳ] ■ **n 1.** [gen] ordre *m* ▸ **to give sb orders to do sthg** ordonner à qqn de faire qqch ▸ **we have orders to wait here** on a reçu l'ordre d'attendre ici ▸ **to be under**

orders to do sthg avoir (reçu) l'ordre de faire qqch ▸ **I'm just following orders** je ne fais qu'exécuter les ordres ▸ **on doctor's orders** sur ordre du médecin
2. COMM commande *f* ▸ **to place an order with sb for sthg** passer une commande de qqch à qqn ▸ **on order** commandé ▸ **to order** sur commande ▸ **your order has now arrived** votre commande est arrivée ▸ **can I take your order?** [in restaurant] avez-vous choisi?
3. [sequence] ordre *m* ▸ **in order** dans l'ordre ▸ **in alphabetical/chronological order** par ordre alphabétique/chronologique ▸ **in order of importance** par ordre d'importance
4. [fitness for use] **: in working order** en état de marche ▸ **out of order** [machine] en panne / [behaviour] déplacé(e) ▸ **in order** [correct] en ordre
5. *(U)* [discipline - gen] ordre *m* / [- in classroom] discipline *f* ▸ **to keep order** maintenir l'ordre ▸ **to restore order** rétablir l'ordre ▸ **children need to be kept in order** les enfants ont besoin de discipline ▸ **to put one's affairs/books in order** mettre de l'ordre dans ses affaires/livres, ranger ses affaires/livres
6. FIN **: (money) order** mandat *m* ▸ **pay to the order of A. Jones** payez à l'ordre de A. Jones
7. *esp US* [portion] part *f*.
■ vt **1.** [command] ordonner ▸ **to order sb to do sthg** ordonner à qqn de faire qqch ▸ **the doctor ordered him to rest for three weeks** le médecin lui a prescrit trois semaines de repos ▸ **he was ordered to pay costs** LAW il a été condamné aux dépens ▸ **to order that** ordonner que ▸ **the government ordered an inquiry into the disaster** le gouvernement a ordonné l'ouverture d'une enquête sur la catastrophe
2. COMM commander
3. [organize - society] organiser / [- ideas, thoughts] mettre de l'ordre dans / [- affairs] régler, mettre en ordre.
■ vi commander ▸ **would you like to order now?** [in restaurant] voulez-vous commander maintenant?
◆ ***orders*** npl RELIG **: to take holy orders** entrer dans les ordres.
◆ ***in the order of*** *UK*, ***on the order of*** *US* adv environ, de l'ordre de.
◆ ***in order that*** conj pour que, afin que *(+ subjunctive)*.
◆ ***in order to*** conj pour, afin de ▸ **in order not to upset you** pour éviter de vous faire de la peine.
◆ ***order about*** *UK*, ***order around*** vt sep commander.

order book n carnet *m* de commandes.

order form n bulletin *m* de commande.

orderly ['ɔːdəlɪ] (pl -ies) ■ adj [person] ordonné(e) / [crowd] discipliné(e) / [office, room] en ordre.
■ n [in hospital] garçon *m* de salle.

order number n numéro *m* de commande.

ordinal ['ɔːdɪnl] ■ adj ordinal(e).
■ n nombre *m* ordinal.

ordinarily ['ɔːdənrəlɪ] adv d'habitude, d'ordinaire.

ordinary ['ɔːdənrɪ] ■ adj **1.** [normal] ordinaire **2.** *pej* [unexceptional] ordinaire, quelconque.
■ n **: out of the ordinary** qui sort de l'ordinaire, exceptionnel(elle).

ordinary level n *UK* ≃ brevet *m* des collèges.

ordinary seaman n *UK* simple matelot *m*.

ordinary shares npl *UK* FIN actions *fpl* ordinaires.

ordination [ˌɔːdɪ'neɪʃn] n ordination *f*.

ordnance ['ɔːdnəns] n *(U)* **1.** [supplies] matériel *m* militaire **2.** [artillery] artillerie *f*.

Ordnance Survey n *service cartographique national en Grande-Bretagne*, ≃ IGN *m*.

ore [ɔːʳ] n minerai *m*.

oregano [ˌɒrɪ'gɑːnəʊ] n origan *m*.

Oregon ['ɒrɪgən] n Oregon *m* ▸ **in Oregon** dans l'Oregon.

.org ['dɒtɔːg] COMPUT *abréviation désignant les organisations à but non lucratif dans les adresses électroniques*.

organ ['ɔːgən] n **1.** [gen] organe *m* **2.** MUS orgue *m*.

organic [ɔː'gænɪk] adj **1.** [of animals, plants] organique **2.** [farming, food] biologique, bio *(inv)* **3.** *fig* [development] naturel(elle).

organically [ɔː'gænɪklɪ] adv [farm, grow] sans engrais chimiques.

organic chemistry n chimie *f* organique.

organic farming n culture *f* biologique.

organism ['ɔːgənɪzm] n organisme *m*.

organist ['ɔːgənɪst] n organiste *mf*.

organization, *UK* ***-isation*** [ˌɔːgənaɪ'zeɪʃn] n organisation *f*.

organizational, *UK* ***-isational*** [ˌɔːgənaɪ'zeɪʃnl] adj **1.** [structure, links] organisationnel(elle) **2.** [skill] d'organisation.

organization chart n organigramme *m*.

organize, *UK* ***-ise*** ['ɔːgənaɪz] ■ vt organiser.
■ vi [workers] se syndiquer.

organized, *UK* ***-ised*** ['ɔːgənaɪzd] adj organisé(e).

organized crime n crime *m* organisé.

organized labour *UK*, ***organized labor*** *US* n main d'œuvre *f* syndiquée.

HOW TO ...
give orders

Sortez (d'ici) ! / Get out of here!
Un peu de silence, s'il vous plaît ! / Quiet, please!
Pose ça tout de suite, tu m'entends ! / Put that down now, do you hear!
Ne rentre pas dans la cuisine, le sol est mouillé / Don't go into the kitchen: the floor's wet
Tu m'appelles dès qu'il arrive, d'accord ? / You call me as soon as he arrives, OK?
Reculez un peu, s'il vous plaît / Move back a little, please
Tournez à gauche au feu rouge / Turn left at the lights

organizer, *UK* ***-iser*** [ˈɔːgənaɪzəʳ] **n 1.** [person] organisateur *m*, -trice *f* **2.** [diary] organiseur *m*.

organza [ɔːˈgænzə] **n** organza *m*.

orgasm [ˈɔːgæzm] **n** orgasme *m*.

orgasmic [ɔːˈgæzmɪk] **adj** orgasmique, orgastique.

orgy [ˈɔːdʒɪ] (pl **-ies**) **n** *lit & fig* orgie *f*.

orient [ˈɔːrɪənt], ***orientate*** *UK* [ˈɔːrɪenteɪt] **vt : to be oriented towards** viser, s'adresser à ▸ **to orient o.s.** s'orienter.

Orient [ˈɔːrɪənt] **n : the Orient** l'Orient *m*.

oriental [ˌɔːrɪˈentl] ■ **adj** oriental(e).
■ **n** Oriental *m*, -e *f (attention: le terme 'oriental' est considéré raciste)*.

orientate [ˈɔːrɪenteɪt] *UK* = ***orient***.

-orientated [ˈɔːrɪenteɪtɪd] *UK* = ***-oriented***.

orientation [ˌɔːrɪenˈteɪʃn] **n** orientation *f*.

-oriented [ˈɔːrɪəntɪd], ***-orientated*** *UK* [ˈɔːrɪenteɪtɪd] **suffix** orienté(e) vers..., axé(e) sur... ▸ **ours is a money-oriented society** c'est l'argent qui mène notre société ▸ **pupil-oriented teaching** enseignement adapté aux besoins des élèves.

orienteering [ˌɔːrɪənˈtɪərɪŋ] **n** *(U)* course *f* d'orientation.

orifice [ˈɒrɪfɪs] **n** *fml* orifice *m*.

origami [ˌɒrɪˈgɑːmɪ] **n** origami *m*.

origin [ˈɒrɪdʒɪn] **n 1.** [of river] source *f* / [of word, conflict] origine *f* **2.** [birth] **: country of origin** pays *m* d'origine.
◆ ***origins*** **npl** origines *fpl*.

original [ɒˈrɪdʒənl] ■ **adj** original(e) / [meaning] originel(elle) / [owner] premier(ère).
■ **n** original *m*.

CONFUSABLE / PARONYME
original

When translating **original**, note that ***original*** and ***originel*** are not interchangeable. ***Original*** refers to something new and innovative, whereas ***originel*** is only used in the sense of first.

originality [əˌrɪdʒəˈnælətɪ] **n** originalité *f*.

originally [əˈrɪdʒənəlɪ] **adv** à l'origine, au départ.

original sin **n** péché *m* originel.

originate [əˈrɪdʒəneɪt] ■ **vt** être l'auteur de, être à l'origine de.
■ **vi** [belief, custom] **: to originate (in)** prendre naissance (dans) ▸ **to originate from** provenir de.

origination [əˌrɪdʒəˈneɪʃn] **n** *(U)* origine *f*.

originator [əˈrɪdʒəneɪtəʳ] **n** auteur *m*, initiateur *m*, -trice *f*.

Orinoco [ˌɒrɪˈnəʊkəʊ] **n : the (River) Orinoco** l'Orénoque *m*.

Orkney Islands [ˈɔːknɪ-], ***Orkneys*** [ˈɔːknɪz] **npl : the Orkney Islands** les Orcades *fpl* ▸ **in the Orkney Islands** dans les Orcades.

ornament [ˈɔːnəmənt] **n 1.** [object] bibelot *m* **2.** *(U)* [decoration] ornement *m*.

ornamental [ˌɔːnəˈmentl] **adj** [garden, pond] d'agrément / [design] décoratif(ive).

ornamentation [ˌɔːnəmenˈteɪʃn] **n** décoration *f*.

ornate [ɔːˈneɪt] **adj** orné(e).

ornately [ɔːˈneɪtlɪ] **adv** avec beaucoup d'ornements.

ornery [ˈɔːnərɪ] **adj** *US inf* désagréable.

ornithologist [ˌɔːnɪˈθɒlədʒɪst] **n** ornithologue *mf*, ornithologiste *mf*.

ornithology [ˌɔːnɪˈθɒlədʒɪ] **n** ornithologie *f*.

orphan [ˈɔːfn] ■ **n** orphelin *m*, -e *f*.
■ **vt : to be orphaned** devenir orphelin(e).

orphanage [ˈɔːfənɪdʒ] **n** orphelinat *m*.

orthodontics [ˌɔːθəˈdɒntɪks] **n** *(U)* orthodontie *f*.

orthodontist [ˌɔːθəˈdɒntɪst] **n** orthodontiste *mf*.

orthodox [ˈɔːθədɒks] **adj 1.** [conventional] orthodoxe **2.** RELIG [traditional] traditionaliste.

Orthodox Church **n : the Orthodox Church** l'Église *f* orthodoxe.

orthodoxy [ˈɔːθədɒksɪ] **n** orthodoxie *f*.

orthopaedic *UK*, ***orthopedic*** *US* [ˌɔːθəˈpiːdɪk] **adj** orthopédique.

orthopaedics *UK*, ***orthopedics*** *US* [ˌɔːθəˈpiːdɪks] **n** *(U)* orthopédie *f*.

orthopaedist *UK*, ***orthopedist*** *US* [ˌɔːθəˈpiːdɪst] **n** orthopédiste *mf*.

OS[1] **n** *UK* (abbr of ***Ordnance Survey***) ≃ IGN *m*.

OS[2] abbr of ***outsize***.

O/S abbr of ***out of stock***.

Oscar [ˈɒskəʳ] **n** CIN Oscar *m*.

oscillate [ˈɒsɪleɪt] **vi** *lit & fig* osciller.

oscillation [ˌɒsɪˈleɪʃn] **n** *lit & fig* oscillation *f*.

oscilloscope [ɒˈsɪləskəʊp] **n** oscilloscope *m*.

OSD (abbr of ***optical scanning device***) **n** *lecteur optique*.

OSHA (abbr of ***Occupational Safety and Health Administration***) **n** *direction de la sécurité et de l'hygiène au travail aux États-Unis*.

Oslo [ˈɒzləʊ] **n** Oslo.

osmosis [ɒzˈməʊsɪs] **n** osmose *f*.

osprey [ˈɒsprɪ] (pl **-s**) **n** balbuzard *m*.

ossify [ˈɒsɪfaɪ] (pt & pp **-ied**) ■ **vt** ossifier.
■ **vi** s'ossifier.

Ostend [ɒsˈtend] **n** Ostende.

ostensible [ɒˈstensəbl] **adj** prétendu(e).

ostensibly [ɒˈstensəblɪ] **adv** en apparence, soi-disant.

ostentation [ˌɒstənˈteɪʃn] **n** ostentation *f*.

ostentatious [ˌɒstənˈteɪʃəs] **adj** ostentatoire.

ostentatiously [ˌɒstənˈteɪʃəslɪ] **adv** avec ostentation.

osteoarthritis [ˌɒstɪəʊɑːˈθraɪtɪs] **n** *(U)* ostéoarthrose *f*.

osteopath [ˈɒstɪəpæθ] **n** ostéopathe *mf*.

osteopathy [ˌɒstɪˈɒpəθɪ] **n** ostéopathie *f*.

osteoporosis [ˌɒstɪəpɔːˈrəʊsɪs] **n** ostéoporose *f.*

ostracism [ˈɒstrəsɪzm] **n** ostracisme *m.*

ostracize**, UK* ***-ise [ˈɒstrəsaɪz] **vt** frapper d'ostracisme, mettre au ban.

ostrich [ˈɒstrɪtʃ] **n** autruche *f.*

OT **n 1.** (abbr of ***Old Testament***) AT *m* **2.** abbr of ***occupational therapy***.

OTC (abbr of ***Officer Training Corps***) **n** *section de formation des officiers en Grande-Bretagne.*

other [ˈʌðəʳ] ■ **adj** autre ▸ **the other one** l'autre ▸ **the other day/week** l'autre jour/semaine.

■ **adv : there was nothing to do other than confess** il ne pouvait faire autrement que d'avouer ▸ **other than John** John à part.

■ **pron : the other** l'autre ▸ **others** d'autres ▸ **the others** les autres ▸ **one after the other** l'un après l'autre (l'une après l'autre) ▸ **one or other of you** l'un (l'une) de vous deux ▸ **none other than** nul (nulle) autre que.

◆ ***something or other*** **pron** quelque chose, je ne sais quoi.

◆ ***somehow or other*** **adv** d'une manière ou d'une autre.

otherwise [ˈʌðəwaɪz] ■ **adv** autrement ▸ **or otherwise** [or not] ou non.

■ **conj** sinon.

other world **n : the other world** l'au-delà *m.*

otherworldly [ˌʌðəˈwɜːldlɪ] **adj** détaché(e) des biens de ce monde.

OTT (abbr of ***over the top***) **adj** *UK inf* **: it's a bit OTT** c'est un peu trop.

Ottawa [ˈɒtəwə] **n** Ottawa.

otter [ˈɒtəʳ] **n** loutre *f.*

OU *UK* **abbr of *Open University*.**

ouch [aʊtʃ] **excl** aïe!, ouïe!

ought [ɔːt] **aux vb 1.** [sensibly] **: I really ought to go** il faut absolument que je m'en aille ▸ **you ought to see a doctor** tu devrais aller chez le docteur **2.** [morally] **: you ought not to have done that** tu n'aurais pas dû faire cela ▸ **you ought to look after your children better** tu devrais t'occuper un peu mieux de tes enfants **3.** [expressing probability] **: she ought to pass her exam** elle devrait réussir à son examen.

oughtn't [ˈɔːtnt] **abbr of *ought not*.**

Ouija board® [ˈwiːdʒə-] **n** oui-ja *m.*

ounce [aʊns] **n** once *f (= 28,35 g).*

our [ˈaʊəʳ] **poss adj** notre, nos *(pl)* ▸ **our money/house** notre argent/maison ▸ **our children** nos enfants ▸ **it wasn't our fault** ce n'était pas de notre faute à nous.

ours [ˈaʊəz] **poss pron** le nôtre (la nôtre), les nôtres *(pl)* ▸ **that money is ours** cet argent est à nous ***OR*** est le nôtre ▸ **it wasn't their fault, it was ours** ce n'était pas de leur faute, c'était de notre faute à nous ***OR*** de la nôtre ▸ **a friend of ours** un ami à nous, un de nos amis.

ourselves [aʊəˈselvz] **pron pl 1.** *(reflexive)* nous **2.** *(for emphasis)* nous-mêmes ▸ **we did it by ourselves** nous l'avons fait tout seuls.

oust [aʊst] **vt : to oust sb (from)** évincer qqn (de).

ouster [ˈaʊstəʳ] **n** *US* [from country] expulsion *f* / [from office] renvoi *m.*

out [aʊt] **adv 1.** [not inside, out of doors] dehors ▸ **we all got out** [of car] nous sommes tous sortis ▸ **I'm going out for a walk** je sors me promener ▸ **to run out** sortir en courant ▸ **I met her on my way out** je l'ai rencontrée en sortant ▸ **out here** ici ▸ **out there** là-bas ▸ **out you go!** sors!, file! ▸ **'keep out'** 'défense d'entrer', 'entrée interdite'

2. [not at home, office] sorti(e) ▸ **John's out at the moment** John est sorti, John n'est pas là en ce moment ▸ **don't stay out too late** ne rentre pas trop tard ▸ **to eat out** aller au restaurant ▸ **an afternoon out** une sortie l'après-midi ▸ **let's have an evening out** et si on sortait ce soir? ▸ **a search party is out looking for them** une équipe de secours est partie à leur recherche

3. [indicating position or movement away] **: on the trip out** à l'aller ▸ **they live a long way out** ils habitent loin du centre ▸ **hold your arms/your hand out** tendez les bras/la main

4. [extinguished] éteint(e) ▸ **put *OR* turn the lights out** éteignez les lumières ▸ **the lights went out** les lumières se sont éteintes

5. [public, available] **: the secret is out** le secret a été éventé ▸ **we must stop the news getting out** nous devons empêcher la nouvelle de s'ébruiter ▸ **the new model will be *OR* come out next month** le nouveau modèle sort le mois prochain ▸ **it's the best computer out** c'est le meilleur ordinateur qui existe

6. [at lower level] **: the tide is out** la marée est basse

7. [out of fashion] démodé(e), passé(e) de mode

8. [in flower] en fleur ▸ **the crocuses are out** les crocus sont sortis

9. [visible] **: the sun is out** il fait du soleil ▸ **the stars are out** les étoiles brillent ▸ **the moon is out** la lune s'est levée

10. [finished] **: before the year is out** avant la fin de l'année

11. [wrong] **: your calculations are (way) out, you're (way) out in your calculations** vous vous êtes (complètement) trompé dans vos calculs ▸ **it's only a few inches out** c'est bon à quelques centimètres près

12. *inf* [on strike] en grève

13. [not possible] **: sorry, that's out** désolé, cela ne va pas ***OR*** n'est pas possible

14. [determined] **: to be out to do sthg** être résolu(e) ***OR*** décidé(e) à faire qqch ▸ **to be out for sthg** vouloir qqch.

◆ ***out of*** **prep 1.** [outside] en dehors de ▸ **to go out of the room** sortir de la pièce ▸ **he ran/limped/strolled out of the office** il est sorti du bureau en courant/en boitant/sans se presser ▸ **I stared out of the window** je regardais par la fenêtre ▸ **what time do you get out of school?** à quelle heure sors-tu de l'école? ▸ **to be out of the country** être à l'étranger ▸ **he's out of town** il n'est pas en ville ▸ **stay out of the sun** ne restez pas au soleil ▸ **you keep out of this!** mêlez-vous de ce qui vous regarde!

2. [indicating cause] par ▸ **out of spite/love/boredom** par dépit/amour/ennui

3. [indicating origin, source] de, dans ▸ **a page out of a book** une page d'un livre ▸ **to drink out of a glass** boire dans un verre ▸ **to get information out of sb** arracher ***OR*** soutirer des renseignements à qqn ▸ **it's made out of plastic** c'est en plastique ▸ **we can pay for it out of petty cash** on peut le payer avec l'argent des dépenses courantes

4. [without] sans ▸ **out of petrol/money** à court d'essence/d'argent ▸ **we're out of sugar** nous n'avons plus de sucre ▸ **out of work** au chômage
5. [sheltered from] à l'abri de ▸ **we're out of the wind here** nous sommes à l'abri du vent ici
6. [to indicate proportion] sur ▸ **one out of ten people** une personne sur dix ▸ **ten out of ten** dix sur dix.

out-and-out **adj** [liar] fieffé(e) / [disgrace] complet(ète).

outback ['aʊtbæk] **n : the outback** l'intérieur *m* du pays *(en Australie)*.

outbid [aʊt'bɪd] (pt & pp **outbid**, cont **-ding**) **vt : to outbid sb (for)** enchérir sur qqn (pour).

outboard (motor) ['aʊtbɔːd-] **n** (moteur *m*) hors-bord *m*.

outbound ['aʊtbaʊnd] **adj** [train, flight] en partance.

out box **n 1.** [for e-mail] corbeille *f* de départ **2.** *US* [on deskl] corbeille *f* sortie.

outbreak ['aʊtbreɪk] **n** [of war, crime] début *m*, déclenchement *m* / [of spots] éruption *f*.

outbuildings ['aʊtbɪldɪŋz] **npl** dépendances *fpl*.

outburst ['aʊtbɜːst] **n** explosion *f*.

outcast ['aʊtkɑːst] **n** paria *m*.

outclass [ˌaʊt'klɑːs] **vt** surclasser.

outcome ['aʊtkʌm] **n** issue *f*, résultat *m*.

outcrop ['aʊtkrɒp] **n** affleurement *m*.

outcry ['aʊtkraɪ] (pl **-ies**) **n** tollé *m*.

outdated [ˌaʊt'deɪtɪd] **adj** démodé(e), vieilli(e).

outdid [ˌaʊt'dɪd] **pt** ➤ ***outdo***.

outdistance [ˌaʊt'dɪstəns] **vt** *lit* & *fig* distancer.

outdo [ˌaʊt'duː] (pt **-did**, pp **-done** [-'dʌn]) **vt** surpasser.

outdoor ['aʊtdɔːʳ] **adj** [life, swimming pool] en plein air / [activities] de plein air.

outdoors [aʊt'dɔːz] **adv** dehors.

outer ['aʊtəʳ] **adj** extérieur(e) ▸ **Outer London** la grande banlieue de Londres.

Outer Mongolia **n** Mongolie-Extérieure *f*.

outermost ['aʊtəməʊst] **adj** [area] le plus éloigné (la plus éloignée) / [layer] le plus (la plus) à l'extérieur.

outer space **n** cosmos *m*.

outfit ['aʊtfɪt] **n 1.** [clothes] tenue *f* **2.** *inf* [organization] équipe *f*.

outfitters ['aʊtˌfɪtəz] **n** *UK dated* [for clothes] magasin *m* spécialisé de confection pour hommes.

outflank [ˌaʊt'flæŋk] **vt** MIL déborder, prendre à revers / *fig* déjouer les manœuvres de.

outflow ['aʊtfləʊ] **n 1.** [of fluid] écoulement *m* / [place of outflow] décharge *f* **2.** [of capital] sorties *fpl*, fuite *f* / [of population] exode *m*, sorties *fpl*, fuite *f*.

outgoing ['aʊtˌgəʊɪŋ] **adj 1.** [chairman] sortant(e) / [mail] à expédier / [train] en partance **2.** [friendly, sociable] ouvert(e).
◆ ***outgoings*** **npl** *UK* dépenses *fpl*.

outgrow [ˌaʊt'grəʊ] (pt **-grew**, pp **-grown**) **vt 1.** [clothes] devenir trop grand(e) pour **2.** [habit] se défaire de.

outhouse ['aʊthaʊs] (pl [-haʊzɪz]) **n 1.** *UK* [outbuilding] remise *f* **2.** *US* [toilet] toilettes *fpl* extérieures.

outing ['aʊtɪŋ] **n 1.** [trip] sortie *f* **2.** [of gay person] *campagne destinée à dévoiler l'homosexualité d'une personne publique*.

outlandish [aʊt'lændɪʃ] **adj** bizarre.

outlast [ˌaʊt'lɑːst] **vt** survivre à.

outlaw ['aʊtlɔː] ■ **n** hors-la-loi *m inv*.
■ **vt 1.** [practice] proscrire **2.** [person] mettre hors la loi.

outlay ['aʊtleɪ] **n** dépenses *fpl*.

outlet ['aʊtlet] **n 1.** [for emotion] exutoire *m* **2.** [hole, pipe] sortie *f* **3.** [shop] **: retail outlet** point *m* de vente **4.** *US* ELEC prise *f* (de courant).

outline ['aʊtlaɪn] ■ **n 1.** [brief description] grandes lignes *fpl* ▸ **in outline** en gros **2.** [silhouette] silhouette *f* ▸ **to draw sthg in outline** faire un croquis de qqch.
■ **vt 1.** [describe briefly] exposer les grandes lignes de ▸ **he outlined the situation briefly** il dressa un bref bilan de la situation **2.** [silhouette] **: to be outlined against** se dessiner ***or*** se découper sur **3.** ART esquisser (les traits de), tracer ▸ **to outline sthg in pencil** faire le croquis de qqch.

outlive [ˌaʊt'lɪv] **vt 1.** [subj: person] survivre à **2.** [subj: idea, object] **: it's outlived its usefulness** cela a fait son temps.

outlook ['aʊtlʊk] **n 1.** [disposition] attitude *f*, conception *f* ▸ **she has a pessimistic outlook** elle voit les choses en noir ***or*** de manière pessimiste **2.** [prospect] perspective *f* ▸ **the outlook for the New Year is promising** cette nouvelle année s'annonce prometteuse ▸ **the outlook for March is cold and windy** pour mars, on prévoit un temps froid avec beaucoup de vent.

outlying ['aʊtˌlaɪɪŋ] **adj** [village] reculé(e) / [suburbs] écarté(e).

outmanoeuvre *UK*, ***outmaneuver*** *US* [ˌaʊtmə'nuːvəʳ] **vt** [competitor, rival] l'emporter sur.

outmoded [ˌaʊt'məʊdɪd] **adj** démodé(e).

outnumber [ˌaʊt'nʌmbəʳ] **vt** surpasser en nombre.

out-of-bounds **adj 1.** [barred] interdit(e) ▸ **out-of-bounds to civilians** interdit aux civils **2.** *US* SPORT hors (du) terrain.

out-of-court **adj : out-of-court settlement** arrangement *m* à l'amiable.

out-of-date **adj** [passport] périmé(e) / [clothes] démodé(e) / [belief] dépassé(e).

out of doors **adv** dehors.

out-of-pocket **adj : I'm £5 out of pocket** j'en suis pour 5 livres de ma poche
▸▸ **out-of-pocket expenses** frais *mpl*.

out-of-the-ordinary **adj** insolite.

out-of-the-way **adj** [village] perdu(e) / [pub] peu fréquenté(e).

out-of-work **adj** au chômage.

outpace [ˌaʊt'peɪs] **vt 1.** [subj: person] devancer **2.** *fig* [subj: technology] dépasser.

outpatient ['aʊt,peɪʃnt] **n** malade *mf* en consultation externe.

outperform [,aʊtpə'fɔːm] **vt** avoir de meilleures performances que, être plus performant(e) que.

outplacement ['aʊtpleɪsmənt] **n** reconversion *f* externe.

outplay [,aʊt'pleɪ] **vt** SPORT dominer.

outpost ['aʊtpəʊst] **n** avant-poste *m*.

outpouring [,aʊt'pɔːrɪŋ] **n** [of emotion] effusion *f*.

output ['aʊtpʊt] ■ **n 1.** [production] production *f* **2.** COMPUT sortie *f*.
■ **vt** COMPUT sortir.

outrage ['aʊtreɪdʒ] ■ **n 1.** [emotion] indignation *f* **2.** [act] atrocité *f*.
■ **vt** outrager.

outraged ['aʊtreɪdʒd] **adj** outré(e).

outrageous [aʊt'reɪdʒəs] **adj 1.** [offensive, shocking] scandaleux(euse), monstrueux(euse) **2.** [very unusual] choquant(e) **3.** *US inf* [extravagant] extravagant(e).

outrageously [aʊt'reɪdʒəslɪ] **adv 1.** [scandalously] de façon scandaleuse, scandaleusement / [atrociously] atrocement, monstrueusement ▸ **we have been treated outrageously** on nous a traités d'une façon scandaleuse **2.** [extravagantly] de façon extravagante ▸ **the shop is outrageously expensive** les prix pratiqués dans ce magasin sont exorbitants.

outran [,aʊt'ræn] **pt** ➤ ***outrun***.

outrank [aʊt'ræŋk] **vt** être le supérieur de / MIL avoir un grade supérieur à.

outreach ■ **vt** [,aʊt'riːtʃ] **1.** [exceed] dépasser **2.** [in arm length] avoir le bras plus long que / [in boxing] avoir l'allonge supérieure à.
■ **n** ['aʊtriːtʃ] ADMIN *recherche des personnes qui ne demandent pas l'aide sociale dont elles pourraient bénéficier* ▸ **outreach worker** *employé ou bénévole dans un bureau d'aide sociale*.

outrider ['aʊt,raɪdər] **n** [on motorcycle] motocycliste *m* d'escorte.

outright ■ **adj** ['aʊtraɪt] absolu(e), total(e).
■ **adv** [,aʊt'raɪt] **1.** [deny] carrément, franchement **2.** [win, fail] complètement, totalement ▸ **to be killed outright** être tué(e) sur le coup.

outrun [,aʊt'rʌn] (**pt -ran**, **pp -run**, **cont -ning**) **vt** distancer.

outsell [,aʊt'sel] (**pt & pp -sold**) **vt** dépasser les ventes de.

outset ['aʊtset] **n : at the outset** au commencement, au début ▸ **from the outset** depuis le commencement *OR* début.

outshine [,aʊt'ʃaɪn] (**pt & pp -shone** [-'ʃɒn]) **vt** *fig* éclipser, surpasser.

outside ■ **adj** ['aʊtsaɪd] **1.** [gen] extérieur(e) ▸ **the outside world** le monde extérieur ▸ **she has few outside interests** elle s'intéresse à peu de choses à part son travail ▸ **an outside toilet** des toilettes (situées) à l'extérieur ▸ **the outside edge** le bord extérieur ▸ **an outside opinion** une opinion indépendante **2.** [unlikely - chance, possibility] faible ▸ **she has only an outside chance of winning** elle n'a que très peu de chances de gagner.
■ **adv** [,aʊt'saɪd] dehors, à l'extérieur ▸ **it's cold outside** il fait froid dehors ▸ **to go/run/look outside** aller/courir/regarder dehors ▸ **seen from outside** vu(e) de l'extérieur.
■ **prep** ['aʊtsaɪd] **1.** [not inside] à l'extérieur de, en dehors de ▸ **nobody is allowed outside the house** personne n'a le droit de quitter la maison ▸ **nobody outside the office must know** personne ne doit être mis au courant en dehors du bureau ▸ **we live some way outside the town** nous habitons assez loin de la ville ▸ **I don't think anybody outside France has heard of him** je ne pense pas qu'il soit connu ailleurs qu'en France **2.** [beyond] **: it's outside his field** ce n'est pas son domaine ▸ **outside office hours** en dehors des heures de bureau.
■ **n** ['aʊtsaɪd] extérieur *m* ▸ **at the outside** *fig* au plus, au maximum ▸ **looking at the problem from (the) outside** *fig* quand on considère le problème de l'extérieur.
◆ ***outside of*** **prep** [apart from] à part.

outside broadcast **n** *UK* RADIO & TV émission *f* réalisée à l'extérieur.

outside lane **n** AUT [in UK] voie *f* de droite / [in Europe, US] voie *f* de gauche.

outside line **n** TELEC ligne *f* extérieure.

outsider [,aʊt'saɪdər] **n 1.** [in race] outsider *m* **2.** [from society] étranger *m*, -ère *f*.

outsize ['aʊtsaɪz], ***outsized*** ['aʊtsaɪzd] **adj 1.** [bigger than usual] énorme, colossal(e) **2.** [clothes] grande taille *(inv)*.

outskirts ['aʊtskɜːts] **npl : the outskirts** la banlieue.

outsmart [,aʊt'smɑːt] **vt** être plus malin(igne) que.

outsold [,aʊt'səʊld] **pt & pp** ➤ ***outsell***.

outsource ['aʊtsɔːs] **vt** COMM sous-traiter, externaliser.

outsourcing ['aʊtsɔːsɪŋ] **n** externalisation *f*, sous-traitance *f*.

CULTURE

Outsourcing

De plus en plus d'entreprises occidentales cèdent à la nouvelle tendance de l'**outsourcing** (« externalisation »), en confiant certaines prestations techniques à des sociétés situées dans les pays en développement, où les salaires sont bien plus bas (notamment en Inde). Les postes concernés varient entre les centres d'appels, chargés d'assister les utilisateurs en leur fournissant un support technique, et la gestion des programmations informatiques de haut niveau, particulièrement prisée en Angleterre.

outspoken [,aʊt'spəʊkn] **adj** franc (franche).

outspokenness [,aʊt'spəʊkənnɪs] **n** franc-parler *m*.

outspread [,aʊt'spred] **adj** [arms, legs] écarté(e) / [wings, newspaper] déployé(e).

outstanding [,aʊt'stændɪŋ] **adj 1.** [excellent] exceptionnel(elle), remarquable **2.** [example] marquant(e) **3.** [not paid] impayé(e) **4.** [unfinished - work, problem] en suspens

▸ **there is still one outstanding matter** il reste encore un problème à régler ▸ **there are about 20 pages outstanding** il reste environ 20 pages à faire.

outstanding balance **n** solde *m* à découvert.

outstandingly [ˌaʊtˈstændɪŋlɪ] **adv** exceptionnellement, remarquablement.

outstay [ˌaʊtˈsteɪ] **vt : I don't want to outstay my welcome** je ne veux pas abuser de votre hospitalité.

outstretched [ˌaʊtˈstretʃt] **adj** [arm, hand] tendu(e) / [wings] déployé(e).

outstrip [ˌaʊtˈstrɪp] (pt & pp **-ped**, cont **-ping**) **vt** devancer.

outtake [ˈaʊtteɪk] **n** CIN & TV coupure *f*, prise *f* ratée

out tray **n** *UK* corbeille *f* sortie.

outvote [ˌaʊtˈvəʊt] **vt : to be outvoted** ne pas obtenir la majorité.

outward [ˈaʊtwəd] ■ **adj 1.** [going away] **: outward journey** aller *m* **2.** [apparent, visible] extérieur(e).
■ **adv** = ***outwards***.

outward bound course **n** école *f* d'endurcissement (en plein air).

outwardly [ˈaʊtwədlɪ] **adv** [apparently] en apparence.

outwards [ˈaʊtwədz] **adv** vers l'extérieur.

outweigh [ˌaʊtˈweɪ] **vt** *fig* primer sur.

outwit [ˌaʊtˈwɪt] (pt & pp **-ted**, cont **-ting**) **vt** se montrer plus malin(igne) que.

outworker [ˈaʊtˌwɜːkəʳ] **n** travailleur *m*, -euse *f* à domicile.

oval [ˈəʊvl] ■ **adj** ovale.
■ **n** ovale *m*.

Oval Office **n : the Oval Office** *bureau du président des États-Unis à la Maison-Blanche.*

ovarian [əʊˈveərɪən] **adj** ovarien(enne).

ovary [ˈəʊvərɪ] (pl **-ies**) **n** ovaire *m*.

ovation [əʊˈveɪʃn] **n** ovation *f* ▸ **the audience gave her a standing ovation** le public l'a ovationnée.

oven [ˈʌvn] **n** [for cooking] four *m*.

oven glove **n** gant *m* de cuisine.

ovenproof [ˈʌvnpruːf] **adj** qui va au four.

oven-ready **adj** prêt(e) à cuire.

ovenware [ˈʌvnweəʳ] **n** *(U)* plats *mpl* qui vont au four.

over [ˈəʊvəʳ] ■ **prep 1.** [above] au-dessus de ▸ **an eagle flew over us** un aigle passa au-dessus de nous ▸ **he was watching me over his newspaper** il m'observait par-dessus son journal ▸ **I couldn't hear what she was saying over the music** la musique m'empêchait d'entendre ce qu'elle disait
2. [on top of] sur ▸ **she wore a cardigan over her dress** elle portait un gilet par-dessus sa robe ▸ **I put my hand over my mouth** j'ai mis ma main devant ma bouche ▸ **he had his jacket over his arm** il avait sa veste sur le bras
3. [across the surface of] **: to cross over the road** traverser la rue ▸ **he ran his eye over the article** il a parcouru l'article des yeux ▸ **we travelled for days over land and sea** nous avons voyagé pendant des jours par terre et par mer ▸ **a strange look came over her face** son visage prit une expression étrange
4. [to or on the far side of] par-dessus ▸ **they live over the road** ils habitent en face ▸ **to go over the border** franchir la frontière ▸ **the village over the hill** le village de l'autre côté de la colline
5. [more than] plus de ▸ **it took me well/just over an hour** j'ai mis bien plus/un peu plus d'une heure ▸ **children over (the age of) 7** les enfants (âgés) de plus de 7 ans ▸ **over and above** en plus de
6. [concerning] à propos de, au sujet de ▸ **a disagreement over working conditions** un conflit portant sur les conditions de travail ▸ **they're always quarrelling over money** ils se disputent sans cesse pour des questions d'argent
7. [during] pendant ▸ **I've got a job over the long vacation** je vais travailler pendant les grandes vacances ▸ **what are you doing over Easter?** qu'est-ce que tu fais pour Pâques? ▸ **over the next few decades** au cours des prochaines décennies
8. [recovered from] **: are you over your bout of flu?** est-ce que tu es guéri OR est-ce que tu t'es remis de ta grippe? ▸ **he's over the shock now** il s'en est remis maintenant ▸ **we'll soon be over the worst** le plus dur sera bientôt passé
9. [senior to] **: he's over me at work** il occupe un poste plus élevé que le mien.
■ **adv 1.** [movement or location across] **: they flew over to America** ils se sont envolés pour les États-Unis ▸ **she walked over to him and said hello** elle s'approcha de lui pour dire bonjour ▸ **we invited them over** nous les avons invités chez nous ▸ **he must have seen us: he's coming over** il a dû nous voir, il vient vers nous OR de notre côté ▸ **she glanced over at me** elle jeta un coup d'œil dans ma direction ▸ **over here** ici ▸ **come over here!** viens (par) ici! ▸ **over there** là-bas
2. [to the ground] **: I fell over** je suis tombé (par terre) ▸ **to lean over** se pencher ▸ **she pushed the pile of books over** elle a renversé la pile de livres
3. [more] plus ▸ **men of 30 and over** les hommes âgés de 30 ans et plus
4. [remaining] **: there's nothing (left) over** il ne reste rien ▸ **I had a few pounds (left) over** il me restait quelques livres
5. [to another person] **: they handed him over to the authorities** ils l'ont remis aux autorités / RADIO & TV **: and now over to David Smith in Paris** nous passons maintenant l'antenne à David Smith à Paris / TELEC **: over (to you)!** à vous! ▸ **over and out!** terminé!
6. [involving repetitions] **: (all) over again** (tout) au début ▸ **over and over again** à maintes reprises, maintes fois ▸ **to do sthg over** *US* recommencer qqch.
■ **adj** [finished] fini(e), terminé(e).
■ **n** over *m*.

◆ ***all over*** ■ **prep 1.** [covering] **: the child had chocolate all over her face** l'enfant avait du chocolat sur toute la figure
2. [throughout] partout, dans tout ▸ **all over the world** dans le monde entier.
■ **adv** [everywhere] partout.
■ **adj** [finished] fini(e).

over- [ˈəʊvəʳ] **prefix** sur-.

overabundance [ˌəʊvərəˈbʌndəns] **n** surabondance *f.*

overachiever [ˌəʊvərəˈtʃiːvəʳ] **n** surdoué *m*, -e *f.*

overact [ˌəʊvərˈækt] **vi** *pej* THEAT en faire trop.

overactive [ˌəʊvərˈæktɪv] **adj** trop actif(ive).

overall ■ **adj** [ˈəʊvərɔːl] [general] d'ensemble.
■ **adv** [ˌəʊvərˈɔːl] en général.
■ **n** [ˈəʊvərɔːl] **1.** *UK* [gen] tablier *m* **2.** *US* [for work] bleu *m* de travail.
◆ ***overalls*** **npl 1.** *UK* [for work] bleu *m* de travail **2.** *US* [dungarees] salopette *f.*

overambitious [ˌəʊvəræmˈbɪʃəs] **adj** trop ambitieux(euse).

overanxious [ˌəʊvərˈæŋkʃəs] **adj** trop inquiet(ète), trop anxieux(euse).

overarm [ˈəʊvərɑːm] **adj & adv** par en-dessus.

overate [ˌəʊvərˈet] **pt** ➤ ***overeat.***

overawe [ˌəʊvərˈɔː] **vt** impressionner.

overbalance [ˌəʊvəˈbæləns] **vi** basculer.

overbearing [ˌəʊvəˈbeərɪŋ] **adj** autoritaire.

overblown [ˌəʊvəˈbləʊn] **adj** *pej* exagéré(e).

overboard [ˈəʊvəbɔːd] **adv : to fall overboard** tomber par-dessus bord ▸ **to go overboard** *inf fig* en faire trop ▸ **to go overboard about** *inf fig* s'enthousiasmer pour.

overbook [ˌəʊvəˈbʊk] **vi** surréserver.

overbooking [ˌəʊvəˈbʊkɪŋ] **n** surréservation *f*, surbooking *m.*

overborrowing [ˌəʊvəˈɒrbəʊɪŋ] **n** [of company] surendettement *m.*

overburden [ˌəʊvəˈbɜːdn] **vt : to be overburdened with sthg** être surchargé(e) de qqch.

overcame [ˌəʊvəˈkeɪm] **pt** ➤ ***overcome.***

overcapitalize*, UK* ***-ise*** [ˌəʊvəˈkæpɪtəlaɪz] **vt & vi** FIN surcapitaliser.

overcast [ˌəʊvəˈkɑːst] **adj** couvert(e).

overcautious [ˌəʊvəˈkɔːʃəs] **adj** trop prudent(e), prudent(e) à l'excès.

overcharge [ˌəʊvəˈtʃɑːdʒ] ■ **vt : to overcharge sb (for sthg)** faire payer (qqch) trop cher à qqn.
■ **vi : to overcharge (for sthg)** demander un prix excessif (pour qqch).

overcoat [ˈəʊvəkəʊt] **n** pardessus *m.*

overcome [ˌəʊvəˈkʌm] (**pt -came, pp -come**) **vt 1.** [fears, difficulties] surmonter **2.** [overwhelm] **: to be overcome (by** *OR* **with)** [emotion] être submergé(e) (de) / [grief] être accablé(e) (de).

overcompensate [ˌəʊvəˈkɒmpənseɪt] **vi : to overcompensate (for sthg)** surcompenser (qqch).

overcomplicated [ˌəʊvəˈkɒmplɪkeɪtɪd] **adj** trop *OR* excessivement compliqué(e).

overconfident [ˌəʊvəˈkɒnfɪdənt] **adj** [too certain] trop sûr(e) de soi / [arrogant] suffisant(e).

overcook [ˌəʊvəˈkʊk] **vt** faire trop cuire.

overcrowded [ˌəʊvəˈkraʊdɪd] **adj** bondé(e).

overcrowding [ˌəʊvəˈkraʊdɪŋ] **n** surpeuplement *m.*

overdevelop [ˌəʊvədɪˈveləp] **vt** [gen & PHOT] surdévelopper ▸ **parts of the coastline have been overdeveloped** par endroits, le littoral est trop construit.

overdeveloped [ˌəʊvədɪˈveləpt] **adj** *fig* & PHOT trop développé(e).

overdevelopment [ˌəʊvədɪˈveləpmənt] **n** surdéveloppement *m.*

overdo [ˌəʊvəˈduː] (**pt -did** [-ˈdɪd], **pp -done**) **vt 1.** [exaggerate] exagérer **2.** [do too much] trop faire ▸ **to overdo it** se surmener **3.** [overcook] trop cuire.

overdone [ˌəʊvəˈdʌn] ■ **pp** ➤ ***overdo.***
■ **adj** [food] trop cuit(e).

overdose ■ **n** [ˈəʊvədəʊs] overdose *f.*
■ **vi** [ˌəʊvəˈdəʊs] **: to overdose on** prendre une dose excessive de.

overdraft [ˈəʊvədrɑːft] **n** découvert *m.*

overdraft facility **n** autorisation *f* de découvert, facilités *fpl* de caisse.

overdraft limit **n** plafond *m* de découvert.

overdrawn [ˌəʊvəˈdrɔːn] **adj** à découvert.

overdressed [ˌəʊvəˈdrest] **adj** habillé(e) avec trop de recherche ▸ **I felt overdressed in my dinner suit** j'avais la sensation d'être emprunté dans mon smoking.

overdrive [ˈəʊvədraɪv] **n** *fig* **: to go into overdrive** mettre les bouchées doubles.

overdue [ˌəʊvəˈdjuː] **adj 1.** [late] **: overdue (for)** en retard (pour) **2.** [change, reform] **: (long) overdue** attendu(e) (depuis longtemps) ▸ **this reform is long overdue** cette réforme aurait dû être appliquée il y a longtemps **3.** [unpaid] arriéré(e), impayé(e) ▸ **our repayments are two months overdue** nous avons un retard de deux mois dans nos remboursements.

overeager [ˌəʊvərˈiːgəʳ] **adj** trop zélé(e).

overeat [ˌəʊvərˈiːt] (**pt -ate, pp -eaten**) **vi** trop manger.

overeating [ˌəʊvərˈiːtɪŋ] **n** [habitual] suralimentation *f.*

overemphasize*, UK* ***-ise*** [ˌəʊvərˈemfəsaɪz] **vt** donner trop d'importance à.

overenthusiastic [ˈəʊvərɪnˌθjuːzɪˈæstɪk] **adj** trop enthousiaste.

overestimate [ˌəʊvərˈestɪmeɪt] **vt** surestimer.

overexcite [ˌəʊvərɪkˈsaɪt] **vt** surexciter.

overexcited [ˌəʊvərɪkˈsaɪtɪd] **adj** surexcité(e).

overexcitement [ˌəʊvərɪkˈsaɪtmənt] **n** surexcitation *f.*

overexpose [ˌəʊvərɪkˈspəʊz] **vt** *lit* & *fig* surexposer.

overexposure [ˌəʊvərɪkˈspəʊʒəʳ] **n** *lit* & *fig* surexposition *f.*

overfamiliar [ˌəʊvəfəˈmɪljəʳ] **adj 1.** [too intimate, disrespectful] trop familier(ère) **2.** [conversant] **: I'm not overfamiliar with the system** je ne connais pas très bien le système.

overfeed [ˌəʊvəˈfiːd] (**pt & pp -fed** [-fed]) **vt** suralimenter.

overfill [ˌəʊvəˈfɪl] **vt** trop remplir.

overflow ■ **vi** [ˌəʊvəˈfləʊ] **1.** [gen] déborder ▸ **the glass is full to overflowing** le verre est plein à ras bord ▸ **the river frequently overflows onto the surrounding plain** la rivière inonde souvent la plaine environnante **2.** [streets, box] **: to be overflowing (with)** regorger (de) ▸ **full to overflowing** plein à craquer.
■ **vt** [ˌəʊvəˈfləʊ] déborder de ▸ **the river overflowed its banks** la rivière a débordé.
■ **n** [ˈəʊvəfləʊ] [pipe, hole] trop-plein *m*.

overflow pipe **n** trop-plein *m*, tuyau *m* d'écoulement.

overground [ˈəʊvəgraʊnd] ■ **adj** à la surface du sol, en surface ▸ **an overground rail link** une voie ferrée à l'air libre *OR* aérienne.
■ **adv** à la surface du sol ▸ **the line goes overground when it reaches the suburbs** la ligne fait surface quand elle arrive en banlieue.

overgrown [ˌəʊvəˈgrəʊn] **adj** [garden] envahi(e) par les mauvaises herbes.

overhang ■ **n** [ˈəʊvəhæŋ] surplomb *m*.
■ **vt** (pt & pp **-hung** [ˌəʊvəˈhæŋ]) surplomber.
■ **vi** (pt & pp **-hung** [ˌəʊvəˈhæŋ]) être en surplomb.

overhanging [ˌəʊvəˈhæŋɪŋ] **adj 1.** [cliff, ledge, balcony] en surplomb, en saillie ▸ **we walked under the overhanging branches** nous marchions sous un dais *OR* une voûte de branches **2.** *fig* [threat] imminent(e).

overhaul ■ **n** [ˈəʊvəhɔːl] **1.** [of car, machine] révision *f* **2.** *fig* [of system] refonte *f*, remaniement *m*.
■ **vt** [ˌəʊvəˈhɔːl] **1.** [car, machine] réviser **2.** *fig* [system] refondre, remanier.

overhead ■ **adj** [ˈəʊvəhed] aérien(enne).
■ **adv** [ˌəʊvəˈhed] au-dessus.
■ **n** [ˈəʊvəhed] *(U) US* frais *mpl* généraux.
◆ ***overheads*** **npl** *UK* frais *mpl* généraux.

overhead projector **n** rétroprojecteur *m*.

overhear [ˌəʊvəˈhɪəʳ] (pt & pp **-heard** [-ˈhɜːd]) **vt** entendre par hasard.

overheat [ˌəʊvəˈhiːt] ■ **vt** surchauffer.
■ **vi** [engine] chauffer.

overheated [ˌəʊvəˈhiːtɪd] **adj 1.** [too hot - room] surchauffé(e), trop chauffé(e) / [- engine] qui chauffe **2.** *fig* [angry] passionné(e), violent(e), exalté(e).

overhung [ˌəʊvəˈhʌŋ] **pt** & **pp** ➤ ***overhang***.

overindulge [ˌəʊvərɪnˈdʌldʒ] ■ **vt** trop gâter.
■ **vi : to overindulge (in)** abuser (de).

overindulgence [ˌəʊvərɪnˈdʌldʒəns] **n 1.** [in food and drink] excès *m*, abus *m* **2.** [towards person] indulgence *f* excessive, complaisance *f*.

overindulgent [ˌəʊvərɪnˈdʌldʒənt] **adj 1.** [in food and drink] **: he's overindulgent** c'est un bon vivant ▸ **an overindulgent weekend** un week-end de bombance **2.** [towards person] trop indulgent(e), complaisant(e).

overjoyed [ˌəʊvəˈdʒɔɪd] **adj : overjoyed (at)** transporté(e) de joie (à).

overkill [ˈəʊvəkɪl] **n** [excess] **: that would be overkill** ce serait de trop.

overladen [ˌəʊvəˈleɪdn] ■ **pp** ➤ ***overload***.
■ **adj** surchargé(e).

overlaid [ˌəʊvəˈleɪd] **pt** & **pp** ➤ ***overlay***.

overland [ˈəʊvəlænd] **adj** & **adv** par voie de terre.

overlap ■ **n** [ˈəʊvəlæp] *lit* & *fig* chevauchement *m*.
■ **vt** [ˌəʊvəˈlæp] (pt & pp **-ped**, cont **-ping**) [edge] dépasser de.
■ **vi** [ˌəʊvəˈlæp] (pt & pp **-ped**, cont **-ping**) *lit* & *fig* se chevaucher.

overlay [ˌəʊvəˈleɪ] (pt & pp **-laid**) **vt : to be overlaid with** être recouvert(e) de.

overleaf [ˌəʊvəˈliːf] **adv** au verso, au dos.

overload [ˌəʊvəˈləʊd] (pp **-loaded** *OR* **-laden**) **vt** surcharger.

overlong [ˌəʊvəˈlɒŋ] ■ **adj** trop long (trop longue).
■ **adv** trop longtemps.

overlook [ˌəʊvəˈlʊk] **vt 1.** [subj: building, room] donner sur ▸ **'villa overlooking the sea'** 'villa avec vue sur la mer' **2.** [disregard, miss] oublier, négliger ▸ **he seems to have overlooked the fact that I might have difficulties** l'idée que je puisse avoir des difficultés semble lui avoir échappé ▸ **his work has been overlooked for centuries** cela fait des siècles que ses travaux sont ignorés **3.** [excuse] passer sur, fermer les yeux sur.

overlord [ˈəʊvəlɔːd] **n** suzerain *m*.

overly [ˈəʊvəlɪ] **adv** trop.

overmanning [ˌəʊvəˈmænɪŋ] **n** *(U)* sureffectifs *mpl*.

overnight ■ **adj** [ˈəʊvənaɪt] **1.** [journey, parking] de nuit / [stay] d'une nuit **2.** *fig* [sudden] **: overnight success** succès *m* immédiat.
■ **adv** [ˌəʊvəˈnaɪt] **1.** [stay, leave] la nuit **2.** [suddenly] du jour au lendemain.

overnight bag **n** sac *m OR* nécessaire *m* de voyage.

overpaid [ˌəʊvəˈpeɪd] ■ **pt** & **pp** ➤ ***overpay***.
■ **adj** trop payé(e), surpayé(e).

overpass [ˈəʊvəpɑːs] **n** *US* ≃ saut-de-mouton *m*.

overpay [ˌəʊvəˈpeɪ] (pt & pp **-paid**) **vt** trop payer.

overpayment [ˌəʊvəˈpeɪmənt] **n** trop-perçu *m*.

overplay [ˌəʊvəˈpleɪ] **vt** [exaggerate] exagérer.

overpopulated [ˌəʊvəˈpɒpjʊleɪtɪd] **adj** surpeuplé(e).

overpopulation [ˈəʊvəˌpɒpjʊˈleɪʃn] **n** surpeuplement *m*, surpopulation *f*.

overpower [ˌəʊvəˈpaʊəʳ] **vt 1.** [in fight] vaincre **2.** *fig* [overwhelm] accabler, terrasser.

overpowering [ˌəʊvəˈpaʊərɪŋ] **adj** [desire] irrésistible / [smell] entêtant(e).

overpriced [ˌəʊvəˈpraɪst] **adj** *pej* excessivement cher (chère).

overproduction [ˌəʊvəprəˈdʌkʃn] **n** surproduction *f*.

overprotective [ˌəʊvəprəˈtektɪv] **adj** protecteur(trice) à l'excès.

overqualified [ˌəʊvəˈkwɒlɪfaɪd] **adj** surqualifié(e).

overran [ˌəʊvəˈræn] **pt** ➤ ***overrun***.

overrate [ˌəʊvəˈreɪt] **vt** [person] surestimer / [book, film] surfaire.

overrated [ˌəʊvəˈreɪtɪd] **adj** surfait(e).

overreach [ˌəʊvəˈriːtʃ] **vt : to overreach o.s.** trop entreprendre.

overreact [ˌəʊvərɪ'ækt] **vi : to overreact (to sthg)** réagir (à qqch) de façon excessive.

overreaction [ˌəʊvərɪ'ækʃn] **n** réaction *f* disproportionnée OR excessive / [panic] affolement *m*.

override [ˌəʊvə'raɪd] (**pt -rode, pp -ridden**) **vt 1.** [be more important than] l'emporter sur, prévaloir sur **2.** [overrule - decision] annuler.

overriding [ˌəʊvə'raɪdɪŋ] **adj** [need, importance] primordial(e).

overripe [ˌəʊvə'raɪp] **adj** trop mûr(e).

overrode [ˌəʊvə'rəʊd] **pt** ➤ ***override***.

overrule [ˌəʊvə'ru:l] **vt** [person] prévaloir contre / [decision] annuler / [objection] rejeter.

overrun [ˌəʊvə'rʌn] (**pt -ran, pp -run, cont -running**) ■ **vt 1.** MIL [occupy] occuper **2.** *fig* [cover, fill] **: to be overrun with** [weeds] être envahi(e) de / [rats] être infesté(e) de.
■ **vi** [programme, speech] dépasser (le temps alloué) / [meeting] dépasser l'heure prévue ▸ **the speech overran by ten minutes** le discours a duré dix minutes de plus que prévu.

oversaw [ˌəʊvə'sɔ:] **pt** ➤ ***oversee***.

overseas ■ **adj** ['əʊvəsi:z] [sales, company] à l'étranger / [market] extérieur(e) / [visitor, student] étranger(ère) ▸ **overseas aid** aide *f* aux pays étrangers.
■ **adv** [ˌəʊvə'si:z] à l'étranger.

oversee [ˌəʊvə'si:] (**pt -saw, pp -seen** [-'si:n]) **vt** surveiller.

overseer ['əʊvəˌsi:ər] **n** contremaître *m*.

oversensitive [ˌəʊvə'sensɪtɪv] **adj** trop sensible OR susceptible, hypersensible.

overshadow [ˌəʊvə'ʃædəʊ] **vt** [subj: building, tree] dominer / *fig* éclipser.

overshoot [ˌəʊvə'ʃu:t] (**pt & pp -shot**) **vt** dépasser, rater.

oversight ['əʊvəsaɪt] **n** oubli *m* ▸ **through oversight** par mégarde.

oversimplification ['əʊvəˌsɪmplɪfɪ'keɪʃn] **n** simplification *f* excessive.

oversimplify [ˌəʊvə'sɪmplɪfaɪ] (**pt & pp -ied**) **vt & vi** trop simplifier.

oversleep [ˌəʊvə'sli:p] (**pt & pp -slept** [-'slept]) **vi** ne pas se réveiller à temps.

overspend [ˌəʊvə'spend] (**pt & pp -spent** [-'spent]) **vi** trop dépenser.

overspill ['əʊvəspɪl] **n** [of population] excédent *m*.

overstaffed [ˌəʊvə'stɑ:ft] **adj : to be overstaffed** avoir un excédent de personnel.

overstate [ˌəʊvə'steɪt] **vt** exagérer.

overstatement [ˌəʊvə'steɪtmənt] **n** exagération *f* ▸ **to say that he's a singer would be an overstatement** il ne mérite pas vraiment le titre de chanteur.

overstay [ˌəʊvə'steɪ] **vt : I don't want to overstay my welcome** je ne veux pas abuser de votre hospitalité.

overstep [ˌəʊvə'step] (**pt & pp -ped, cont -ping**) **vt** dépasser ▸ **to overstep the mark** dépasser la mesure.

overstock [ˌəʊvə'stɒk] **vt** stocker à l'excès.

overstrike ['əʊvəstraɪk] ■ **n** COMPUT surimpression *f*.
■ **vt** COMPUT surimprimer.

oversubscribed [ˌəʊvəsʌb'skraɪbd] **adj : to be oversubscribed** [concert, play] être en surlocation ▸ **the share issue was oversubscribed** la demande d'achats a dépassé le nombre de titres émis ▸ **the school trip is oversubscribed** il y a trop d'élèves inscrits à l'excursion organisée par l'école.

overt ['əʊvɜ:t] **adj** déclaré(e), non déguisé(e).

overtake [ˌəʊvə'teɪk] (**pt -took, pp -taken** [-'teɪkn]) ■ **vt 1.** *UK* AUT doubler, dépasser **2.** [subj: misfortune, emotion] frapper.
■ **vi** *UK* AUT doubler.

overtaking [ˌəʊvə'teɪkɪŋ] **n** *UK* dépassement *m* ▸ **'no overtaking'** 'défense de doubler'.

over-the-counter **adj 1.** [medicines] vendu(e) sans ordonnance, en vente libre **2.** FIN **: over-the-counter market** marché *m* hors-cote.

overthrow ■ **n** ['əʊvəθrəʊ] [of government] coup *m* d'État.
■ **vt** [ˌəʊvə'θrəʊ] (**pt -threw** [-'θru:], **pp -thrown** [-'θrəʊn]) **1.** [government] renverser **2.** [idea] rejeter, écarter.

overtime ['əʊvətaɪm] ■ **n** *(U)* **1.** [extra work] heures *fpl* supplémentaires **2.** *US* SPORT prolongations *fpl*.
■ **adv : to work overtime** faire des heures supplémentaires.

overtime pay **n** rémunération *f* des heures supplémentaires.

overtly [əʊ'vɜ:tlɪ] **adv** ouvertement.

overtones ['əʊvətəʊnz] **npl** notes *fpl*, accents *mpl*.

overtook [ˌəʊvə'tʊk] **pt** ➤ ***overtake***.

overture ['əʊvəˌtjʊər] **n** MUS ouverture *f*.
◆ ***overtures*** **npl : to make overtures to sb** faire des ouvertures à qqn.

overturn [ˌəʊvə'tɜ:n] ■ **vt 1.** [gen] renverser **2.** [decision] annuler.
■ **vi** [vehicle] se renverser / [boat] chavirer.

overuse [ˌəʊvə'ju:z] **vt** abuser de.

overview ['əʊvəvju:] **n** vue *f* d'ensemble.

overweening [ˌəʊvə'wi:nɪŋ] **adj** *fml* démesuré(e).

overweight [ˌəʊvə'weɪt] **adj** trop gros (grosse).

overwhelm [ˌəʊvə'welm] **vt 1.** [subj: grief, despair] accabler ▸ **to be overwhelmed with joy** être au comble de la joie **2.** MIL [gain control of] écraser.

overwhelming [ˌəʊvə'welmɪŋ] **adj 1.** [overpowering] irrésistible, irrépressible **2.** [defeat, majority] écrasant(e).

overwhelmingly [ˌəʊvə'welmɪŋlɪ] **adv 1.** [generous, happy] immensément **2.** [in large numbers] en masse.

overwork [ˌəʊvə'wɜ:k] ■ **n** surmenage *m*.
■ **vt 1.** [person, staff] surmener **2.** *fig* [idea] exploiter.
■ **vi** se surmener.

overwrite [ˌəʊvə'raɪt] (**pt -wrote** [-'rəʊt], **pp -written** [-'rɪtn]) ■ **vt 1.** [write on top of] écrire sur, repasser sur **2.** COMPUT [file] écraser.
■ **vi** écrire dans un style ampoulé.

overwrought [ˌəʊvəˈrɔːt] adj excédé(e), à bout.

overzealous [ˌəʊvəˈzeləs] adj trop zélé(e).

ovulate [ˈɒvjʊleɪt] vi ovuler.

ovulation [ˌɒvjʊˈleɪʃn] n ovulation *f*.

ovum [ˈəʊvəm] (pl **ova** [ˈəʊvə]) n BIOL ovule *m*.

ow [aʊ] excl aïe!

owe [əʊ] vt : **to owe sthg to sb, to owe sb sthg** devoir qqch à qqn ▸ **how much** *OR* **what do I owe you?** combien est-ce que *OR* qu'est-ce que je vous dois? ▸ **we owe them an apology** nous leur devons des excuses ▸ **I owe it all to my parents** je suis redevable de tout cela à mes parents.

owing [ˈəʊɪŋ] adj dû (due).
◆ ***owing to*** prep à cause de, en raison de.

owl [aʊl] n hibou *m*.

own [əʊn] ■ adj propre ▸ **my own car** ma propre voiture ▸ **I have my very own bedroom** j'ai une chambre pour moi tout seul ▸ **it's all my own work** c'est moi qui ai tout fait ▸ **she has her own style** elle a son style à elle ▸ **it's your own fault!** tu n'as à t'en prendre qu'à toi-même! ▸ **you'll have to make up your own mind** c'est à toi et à toi seul de décider, personne ne pourra prendre cette décision à ta place.
■ pron : **I've got my own** j'ai le mien ▸ **he has a house of his own** il a une maison à lui, il a sa propre maison ▸ **her opinions are identical to my own** nous partageons exactement les mêmes opinions ▸ **the town has a character of its own** *OR* **all (of) its own** la ville possède un charme qui lui est propre *OR* un charme bien à elle ▸ **on one's own** tout seul (toute seule) ▸ **you're on your own now!** à toi de jouer maintenant! ▸ **I'm trying to get him on his own** j'essaie de le voir seul à seul ▸ **to come into one's own** [show one's capabilities] montrer de quoi on est capable ▸ **to get one's own back** *inf* prendre sa revanche ▸ **to make sthg one's own** s'approprier qqch.
■ vt posséder ▸ **they own 51% of the shares** ils détiennent 51 % des actions ▸ **does she own the house?** est-elle propriétaire de la maison? ▸ **who owns this car?** à qui appartient cette voiture? ▸ **they walked in as if they owned the place** *inf* ils sont entrés comme (s'ils étaient) chez eux.
◆ ***own up*** vi : **to own up (to sthg)** avouer *OR* confesser (qqch) ▸ **he owned up to his mistake** il a reconnu son erreur.

own brand n *UK* COMM *produit qui porte la marque de la maison*.

owner [ˈəʊnəʳ] n propriétaire *mf*.

owner-occupier n *esp UK* occupant *m* propriétaire.

ownership [ˈəʊnəʃɪp] n propriété *f*.

own goal n *UK* **1.** FOOTBALL : **to score an own goal** marquer contre son camp **2.** *fig* [foolish mistake] gaffe *f*.

own label n *UK* = ***own brand***.

ox [ɒks] (pl **oxen** [ˈɒksn]) n bœuf *m*.

Oxbridge [ˈɒksbrɪdʒ] n *désignation collective des universités d'Oxford et de Cambridge*.

CULTURE

Oxbridge

Ce terme désigne les universités anglaises d'Oxford et de Cambridge, qui, depuis leur création au XIIIème siècle, sont les plus prestigieuses au Royaume-Uni : elles évoquent l'excellence de l'enseignement et l'élitisme britannique. Les conditions d'admission sont très difficiles et, bien que le gouvernement encourage les étudiants des écoles publiques à tenter leur chance, ce sont surtout les élèves des écoles privées qui sont reçus. Depuis la création de Cambridge par des étudiants dissidents d'Oxford, il y a une grande rivalité entre les deux universités : les deux établissements organisent plusieurs compétitions annuelles, dont la plus célèbre est une course d'aviron qui existe depuis 1829.

oxen [ˈɒksn] npl ➤ ***ox***.

Oxfam [ˈɒksfæm] n *association humanitaire contre la faim*.

oxide [ˈɒksaɪd] n oxyde *m*.

oxidize, *UK* ***-ise*** [ˈɒksɪdaɪz] vi s'oxyder.

Oxon (abbr of ***Oxfordshire***) *comté anglais*.

Oxon. (abbr of ***Oxoniensis***) *de l'université d'Oxford*.

oxtail soup [ˈɒksteɪl-] n soupe *f* à la queue de bœuf.

ox tongue n langue *f* de bœuf.

oxyacetylene [ˌɒksɪəˈsetɪliːn] ■ n mélange *m* d'oxygène et d'acétylène.
■ comp [torch] oxyacétylénique.

oxygen [ˈɒksɪdʒən] n oxygène *m*.

oxygenate [ˈɒksɪdʒəneɪt] vt oxygéner.

oxygenation [ˌɒksɪdʒəˈneɪʃn] n oxygénation *f*.

oxygen mask n masque *m* à oxygène.

oxygen tent n tente *f* à oxygène.

oxymoron [ˌɒksɪˈmɔːrɒn] (pl **-ra** [-rə]) n oxymoron *m*.

oyster [ˈɔɪstəʳ] n huître *f*.

oz. abbr of ***ounce***.

ozone [ˈəʊzəʊn] n ozone *m*.

ozone-friendly adj qui préserve la couche d'ozone.

ozone layer n couche *f* d'ozone.

p [1] (pl p's OR ps), ***P*** [1] (pl P's OR Ps) [piː] **n** [letter] p *m inv*, P *m inv*.

P [2] **1.** abbr of ***president*** **2.** (abbr of ***prince***) Pce.

p [2] **1.** (abbr of ***page***) p **2.** abbr of ***penny***, ***pence***.

p & h (abbr of ***postage and handling***) **n** *US frais de port*.

P & L (abbr of ***profit and loss***) **n** *pertes et profits*.

p & p *UK* abbr of ***postage and packing***.

pa [pɑː] **n** *esp US inf* papa *m*.

p.a. (abbr of ***per annum***) p.a.

PA ■ **n 1.** *UK* abbr of ***personal assistant*** **2.** (abbr of ***public address system***) sono *f* **3.** (abbr of ***Press Association***) *agence de presse britannique*.
■ abbr of ***Pennsylvania***.

PABX (abbr of ***private automatic branch exchange***) **n** autocommutateur *m* privé.

PAC (abbr of ***political action committee***) **n** *comité américain de promotion du recours à l'action politique*.

pace [peɪs] ■ **n 1.** [speed, rate] vitesse *f*, allure *f* ▸ **at one's own pace** à son propre rythme ▸ **she quickened her pace** elle pressa le pas ▸ **to keep pace (with sb)** marcher à la même allure (que qqn) ▸ **to keep pace (with sthg)** se maintenir au même niveau (que qqch) ▸ **he couldn't stand OR take the pace** il n'arrivait pas à suivre le rythme ▸ **to make OR to set the pace** SPORT donner l'allure, mener le train / *fig* donner le ton **2.** [step] pas *m*.
■ **vt** [room] arpenter.
■ **vi : to pace (up and down)** faire les cent pas.

pacemaker ['peɪsˌmeɪkəʳ] **n 1.** MED stimulateur *m* cardiaque **2.** SPORT meneur *m*, -euse *f*.

pacesetter ['peɪsˌsetəʳ] **n** *US* SPORT meneur *m*, -euse *f*.

pachyderm ['pækɪdɜːm] **n** pachyderme *m*.

Pacific [pə'sɪfɪk] ■ **adj** du Pacifique.
■ **n : the Pacific (Ocean)** l'océan *m* Pacifique, le Pacifique.

pacification [ˌpæsɪfɪ'keɪʃn] **n 1.** [of person, baby] apaisement *m* **2.** [of country] pacification *f*.

Pacific Rim **n : the Pacific Rim** *groupe de pays situés au bord du Pacifique, particulièrement les pays industrialisés d'Asie*.

pacifier ['pæsɪfaɪəʳ] **n** *US* [for child] tétine *f*, sucette *f*.

pacifism ['pæsɪfɪzm] **n** pacifisme *m*.

pacifist ['pæsɪfɪst] **n** pacifiste *mf*.

pacify ['pæsɪfaɪ] (pt & pp **-ied**) **vt 1.** [person, baby] apaiser **2.** [country] pacifier.

pack [pæk] ■ **n 1.** [bag] sac *m* **2.** *esp US* [packet] paquet *m* **3.** [of cards] jeu *m* **4.** [of dogs] meute *f* / [of wolves, thieves] bande *f* ▸ **that's a pack of lies!** *UK* c'est un tissu de mensonges! **5.** RUGBY pack *m*.
■ **vt 1.** [clothes, belongings] emballer ▸ **I've already packed the towels** j'ai déjà mis les serviettes dans la valise ▸ **to pack one's bags** faire ses bagages **2.** [fill] remplir ▸ **he packed his pockets with sweets, he packed sweets into his pockets** il a bourré ses poches de bonbons ▸ **to be packed into** être entassé(e) dans ▸ **we managed to pack a lot into a week's holiday** *fig* on a réussi à faire énormément de choses en une semaine de vacances.
■ **vi** [for journey] faire ses bagages OR sa valise.
◆ ***pack in*** *UK inf* ■ **vt sep** [stop] plaquer ▸ **pack it in!** [stop annoying me] arrête!, ça suffit maintenant! / [shut up] la ferme!
■ **vi** tomber en panne.
◆ ***pack off*** **vt sep** *inf* [send away] expédier ▸ **I packed the kids off to bed/school** j'ai envoyé les gosses au lit/à l'école.
◆ ***pack up*** ■ **vt** [clothes, belongings] mettre dans une valise.
■ **vi 1.** [for journey] faire sa valise **2.** *inf* [finish work] se casser ▸ **I'm packing up for today** j'arrête pour aujourd'hui **3.** *UK inf* [car, washing machine] tomber en panne.

package ['pækɪdʒ] ■ **n 1.** [of books, goods] paquet *m* **2.** *fig* [of proposals] ensemble *m*, série *f* **3.** COMPUT progiciel *m*.
■ **vt** [wrap up] conditionner.

package deal **n** forfait *m* global.

package holiday **n** *UK* vacances *fpl* organisées.

packager ['pækɪdʒəʳ] **n 1.** [person] emballeur *m*, -euse *f* **2.** COMM *maison d'édition qui crée des livres sur commande pour d'autres maisons*.

package tour **n** vacances *fpl* organisées.

packaging ['pækɪdʒɪŋ] **n** conditionnement *m*.

packed [pækt] adj **: packed (with)** bourré(e) (de).

packed lunch n *UK* panier-repas *m*.

packed-out adj *UK inf* bourré(e).

packer ['pækəʳ] n [worker] emballeur *m*, -euse *f*, conditionneur *m*, -euse *f* / [machine] emballeuse *f*, conditionneuse *f*.

packet ['pækɪt] n **1.** [gen] paquet *m* **2.** *UK inf* [lot of money] **: their new car cost a packet** leur nouvelle voiture leur a coûté un paquet OR très cher.

packet switching [-ˌswɪtʃɪŋ] n COMPUT commutation *f* par paquets.

packhorse ['pækhɔːs] n cheval *m* de charge.

pack ice n pack *m*.

packing ['pækɪŋ] n [material] emballage *m*.

packing case n *UK* caisse *f* d'emballage.

pact [pækt] n pacte *m*.

pad [pæd] ■ n **1.** [of cotton wool] morceau *m* ▶ **shin pad** FOOTBALL protège-tibia *m* ▶ **shoulder pads** épaulettes *fpl* **2.** [of paper] bloc *m* **3.** [for space shuttle] **: (launch) pad** pas *m* de tir **4.** [of cat, dog] coussinet *m* **5.** *inf* [home] pénates *mpl*.
■ vt (pt & pp **-ded**, cont **-ding**) [furniture, jacket] rembourrer / [wound] tamponner.
■ vi (pt & pp **-ded**, cont **-ding**) [walk softly] marcher à pas feutrés.
◆ ***pad out*** vt sep *fig* [speech, letter] délayer.

padded ['pædɪd] adj rembourré(e).

padded cell n cellule *f* matelassée.

padding ['pædɪŋ] n **1.** [material] rembourrage *m* **2.** *fig* [in speech, letter] délayage *m*.

paddle ['pædl] ■ n **1.** [for canoe] pagaie *f* **2.** *UK* [in sea] **: to have a paddle** faire trempette **3.** *US* [table-tennis bat] raquette *f* (de ping-pong).
■ vi **1.** [in canoe] avancer en pagayant **2.** [duck] barboter **3.** *UK* [in sea] faire trempette.

paddle steamer, ***paddle boat*** *US* n bateau *m* à aubes.

paddling pool ['pædlɪŋ-] n *UK* **1.** [in park] pataugeoire *f* **2.** [inflatable] piscine *f* gonflable.

paddock ['pædək] n **1.** [small field] enclos *m* **2.** [at racecourse] paddock *m*.

paddy field ['pædɪ-] n rizière *f*.

paddy wagon ['pædɪ-] n *US inf* [Black Maria] panier *m* à salade.

padlock ['pædlɒk] ■ n cadenas *m*.
■ vt cadenasser.

paederast *UK*, ***pederast*** *US* ['pedəræst] n pédéraste *m*.

paediatric *UK*, ***pediatric*** *US* [ˌpiːdɪ'ætrɪk] adj de pédiatrie.

paediatrician *UK*, ***pediatrician*** *US* [ˌpiːdɪə'trɪʃn] n pédiatre *mf*.

paediatrics *UK*, ***pediatrics*** *US* [ˌpiːdɪ'ætrɪks] n pédiatrie *f*.

paedophile *UK* ['piːdəfaɪl], ***pedophile*** *US* ['pedəfaɪl] n pédophile *m*.

paedophilia *UK* [ˌpiːdəʊ'fɪlɪə], ***pedophilia*** *US* [ˌpedəʊ'fɪlɪə] n pédophilie *f*.

paella [paɪ'elə] n paella *f*.

paeony *UK* = ***peony***.

pagan ['peɪgən] ■ adj païen(enne).
■ n païen *m*, -enne *f*.

paganism ['peɪgənɪzm] n paganisme *m*.

page [peɪdʒ] ■ n **1.** [of book] page *f* **2.** [sheet of paper] feuille *f*.
■ vt **1.** [using a pager] biper **2.** [in airport] appeler au micro.

pageant ['pædʒənt] n [show] spectacle *m* historique.

pageantry ['pædʒəntrɪ] n apparat *m*.

page boy n **1.** *UK* [at wedding] garçon *m* d'honneur **2.** [hairstyle] coiffure *f* à la page.

pager ['peɪdʒəʳ] n récepteur *m* de poche.

paginate ['pædʒɪneɪt] vt paginer.

pagination [ˌpædʒɪ'neɪʃn] n pagination *f*.

pagoda [pə'gəʊdə] n pagode *f*.

paid [peɪd] ■ pt & pp ➤ ***pay***.
■ adj [work, holiday, staff] rémunéré(e), payé(e) ▶ **badly/well paid** mal/bien payé.

paid-up adj *UK* qui a payé sa cotisation.

pail [peɪl] n *dated* seau *m*.

pain [peɪn] ■ n **1.** [hurt] douleur *f* ▶ **to be in pain** souffrir **2.** *inf* [nuisance] **: it's/he is such a pain** c'est/il est vraiment assommant ▶ **a pain in the neck** *inf* un enquiquineur, une enquiquineuse *f*, un casse-pieds *m inv*.
■ vt **: it pains me (to do sthg)** je suis peiné (de faire qqch).
◆ ***pains*** npl [effort, care] **: to be at pains to do sthg** vouloir absolument faire qqch ▶ **to take pains to do sthg** se donner beaucoup de mal OR peine pour faire qqch ▶ **for one's pains** pour sa peine.

pained [peɪnd] adj peiné(e).

painful ['peɪnfʊl] adj **1.** [physically] douloureux(euse) **2.** [emotionally] pénible.

painfully ['peɪnfʊlɪ] adv **1.** [fall, hit] douloureusement **2.** [remember, feel] péniblement.

painkiller ['peɪnˌkɪləʳ] n calmant *m*, analgésique *m*.

painless ['peɪnlɪs] adj **1.** [without hurt] indolore, sans douleur **2.** *fig* [changeover] sans heurt.

painlessly ['peɪnlɪslɪ] adv sans douleur.

painstaking ['peɪnzˌteɪkɪŋ] adj [worker] assidu(e) / [detail, work] soigné(e).

painstakingly ['peɪnzˌteɪkɪŋlɪ] adv assidûment, avec soin.

paint [peɪnt] ■ n peinture *f*.
■ vt **1.** [gen] peindre **2.** [with make-up] **: to paint one's nails** se vernir les ongles.

paintbox ['peɪntbɒks] n ART boîte *f* de couleurs.

paintbrush ['peɪntbrʌʃ] n pinceau *m*.

painted ['peɪntɪd] adj peint(e).

painter ['peɪntəʳ] n peintre *mf*.

painting ['peɪntɪŋ] n **1.** *(U)* [activity] peinture *f* **2.** [picture] peinture *f*, tableau *m*.

paint stripper **n** décapant *m*.

paintwork ['peɪntwɜ:k] **n** *(U)* surfaces *fpl* peintes.

pair [peəʳ] **n 1.** [of shoes, wings] paire *f* ▸ **a pair of trousers** un pantalon ▸ **a pair of compasses** un compas **2.** [couple] couple *m*.
◆ ***pair off*** ■ **vt sep** mettre par paires **OR** deux.
■ **vi** se mettre par paires **OR** deux par deux.

paisley (pattern) ['peɪzlɪ-] ■ **n** *(U)* (motif *m*) cachemire *m*.
■ **comp** cachemire.

pajama [pə'dʒɑ:mə] *US* = ***pyjama***.

pajamas [pə'dʒɑ:məz] *US* = ***pyjamas***.

Paki ['pækɪ] **n** *UK offens terme raciste désignant un Pakistanais.*

Pakistan [*UK* ,pɑ:kɪ'stɑ:n, *US* 'pækɪstæn] **n** Pakistan *m* ▸ **in Pakistan** au Pakistan.

Pakistani [*UK* ,pɑ:kɪ'stɑ:nɪ, *US* 'pækɪ'stænɪ] ■ **adj** pakistanais(e).
■ **n** Pakistanais *m*, -e *f*.

pal [pæl] **n** *inf* **1.** [friend] copain *m*, copine *f* **2.** [as term of address] mon vieux *m*.

PAL (abbr of ***phase alternation line***) **n** PAL *m*.

palace ['pælɪs] **n** palais *m*.

palaeontology, ***paleontology*** *US* [,pælɪɒn-'tɒlədʒɪ] **n** paléontologie *f*.

palatable ['pælətəbl] **adj 1.** [food] agréable au goût **2.** *fig* [idea] acceptable, agréable.

palate ['pælət] **n** palais *m*.

palatial [pə'leɪʃl] **adj** pareil(eille) à un palais.

palaver [pə'lɑ:vəʳ] **n** *(U) inf* **1.** [talk] palabres *fpl* **2.** [fuss] histoire *f*, affaire *f*.

pale [peɪl] ■ **adj** pâle.
■ **vi : to pale into insignificance (beside)** n'être rien (à côté de).

pale ale **n** *UK* pale-ale *f*.

paleness ['peɪlnɪs] **n** pâleur *f*.

paleontology *US* = ***palaeontology***.

Palestine ['pælə,staɪn] **n** Palestine *f*.

Palestinian [,pælə'stɪnɪən] ■ **adj** palestinien(enne).
■ **n** Palestinien *m*, -enne *f*.

palette ['pælət] **n** palette *f*.

palette knife **n** ART couteau *m* à palette / *UK* CULIN spatule *f* (en métal).

palimony ['pælɪmənɪ] **n** *pension alimentaire versée à un concubin.*

palindrome ['pælɪndrəʊm] **n** palindrome *m*.

palings ['peɪlɪŋz] **npl** palissade *f*.

pall [pɔ:l] ■ **n 1.** [of smoke] voile *m* **2.** [coffin] cercueil *m*.
■ **vi** perdre de son charme.

pallbearer ['pɔ:l,beərəʳ] **n** porteur *m* de cercueil.

pallet ['pælɪt] **n** palette *f*.

palliative ['pælɪətɪv] **n** palliatif *m*.

palliative care **n** *(U)* MED soins *mpl* palliatifs.

pallid ['pælɪd] **adj** pâle, blafard(e).

pallor ['pæləʳ] **n** pâleur *f*.

palm [pɑ:m] **n 1.** [tree] palmier *m* **2.** [of hand] paume *f*.
◆ ***palm off*** **vt sep** *inf* **: to palm sthg off on sb** refiler qqch à qqn ▸ **to palm sb off with sthg** se débarrasser de qqn avec qqch ▸ **to palm sthg off as** faire passer qqch pour.

palmistry ['pɑ:mɪstrɪ] **n** chiromancie *f*.

palm oil **n** huile *f* de palme.

Palm Sunday **n** dimanche *m* des Rameaux.

palmtop **n** COMPUT ordinateur *m* de poche.

palm tree **n** palmier *m*.

palomino [,pælə'mi:nəʊ] (pl **-s**) **n** *cheval doré à crinière et queue blanches.*

palpable ['pælpəbl] **adj** évident(e), manifeste.

palpably ['pælpəblɪ] **adv** de façon évidente, manifestement.

palpitate ['pælpɪteɪt] **vi** palpiter.

palpitations [,pælpɪ'teɪʃənz] **npl** palpitations *fpl*.

palsy ['pɔ:lzɪ] **n** *dated* paralysie *f*.

paltry ['pɔ:ltrɪ] (**comp -ier, superl -iest**) **adj** dérisoire.

pampas ['pæmpəz] **n : the pampas** la pampa.

pampas grass **n** herbe *f* de la pampa.

pamper ['pæmpəʳ] **vt** choyer, dorloter.

pamphlet ['pæmflɪt] ■ **n** brochure *f*.
■ **vi** distribuer des brochures.

pamphleteer [,pæmflə'tɪəʳ] **n** POL pamphlétaire *mf*.

pan [pæn] ■ **n 1.** [gen] casserole *f* **2.** *US* [for bread, cakes] moule *m*.
■ **vt** (**pt & pp -ned, cont -ning**) *inf* [criticize] démolir.
■ **vi** (**pt & pp -ned, cont -ning**) **1.** [prospect] **: to pan for gold** laver l'or **2.** CIN faire un panoramique.

panacea [,pænə'sɪə] **n** panacée *f*.

panache [pə'næʃ] **n** panache *m*.

panama [,pænə'mɑ:] **n : panama (hat)** panama *m*.

Panama ['pænəmɑ:] **n** Panama *m* ▸ **in Panama** au Panama.

Panama Canal **n : the Panama Canal** le canal de Panama.

Panama City **n** Panama.

Panamanian [,pænə'meɪnjən] ■ **adj** panaméen(enne).
■ **n** Panaméen *m*, -enne *f*.

pan-American **adj** panaméricain(e).

pancake ['pænkeɪk] **n** crêpe *f*.

Pancake Day **n** mardi gras *m*.

pancake roll **n** *UK* rouleau *m* de printemps.

Pancake Tuesday **n** mardi gras *m*.

pancreas ['pæŋkrɪəs] **n** pancréas *m*.

panda ['pændə] (pl **panda OR -s**) **n** panda *m*.

panda car **n** *UK inf dated* voiture *f* de patrouille.

pandemic [pæn'demɪk] ■ **adj 1.** MED pandémique **2.** [universal] universel(elle), général(e).
■ **n** MED pandémie *f*.

pandemonium [ˌpændɪˈməʊnjəm] **n** tohu-bohu *m inv*.

pander [ˈpændəʳ] **vi : to pander to sb** se prêter aux exigences de qqn ▸ **to pander to sthg** se plier à qqch.

pane [peɪn] **n** vitre *f*, carreau *m*.

panel [ˈpænl] **n 1.** TV & RADIO invités *mpl* / [of experts] comité *m* **2.** [of wood] panneau *m* **3.** [of machine] tableau *m* de bord.

panel beater **n** *UK* AUT carrossier *m*, tôlier *m*.

panel discussion **n** débat *m*, tribune *f*.

panel game **n** *UK jeu télévisé où rivalisent des équipes d'invités célèbres*.

panelling *UK*, ***paneling*** *US* [ˈpænəlɪŋ] **n** *(U)* lambris *m*.

panellist *UK*, ***panelist*** *US* [ˈpænəlɪst] **n** invité *m*, -e *f*.

panel pin **n** *UK* clou *m* sans tête.

pan-fry **vt** (faire) sauter ▸ **pan-fried potatoes** pommes *fpl* (de terre) sautées.

pang [pæŋ] **n** tiraillement *m*.

panic [ˈpænɪk] ■ **n 1.** [alarm, fear] panique *f* **2.** *inf* [rush] hâte *f* ▸ **there's no panic** il n'y a pas le feu.
■ **vi** (pt & pp **-ked**, cont **-king**) paniquer.

panic button **n** signal *m* d'alarme ▸ **to hit the panic button** *inf* perdre les pédales.

panic buying **n** *(U)* achats *mpl* en catastrophe ***OR*** de dernière minute.

panicky [ˈpænɪkɪ] **adj** [person] paniqué(e) / [feeling] de panique.

panic stations **n** *UK inf* **: it was panic stations** c'était la panique générale.

panic-stricken **adj** affolé(e), pris(e) de panique.

pannier [ˈpænɪəʳ] **n** [on horse] bât *m* / [on bicycle] sacoche *f*.

panoply [ˈpænəplɪ] **n** panoplie *f*.

panorama [ˌpænəˈrɑːmə] **n** panorama *m*.

panoramic [ˌpænəˈræmɪk] **adj** panoramique.

pansy [ˈpænzɪ] (pl **-ies**) **n 1.** [flower] pensée *f* **2.** *offens* [man] tante *f*, tapette *f*.

pant [pænt] **vi** haleter.

pantheon [ˈpænθɪən] **n** panthéon *m*.

panther [ˈpænθəʳ] (pl **panther** ***OR*** **-s**) **n** panthère *f*.

panties [ˈpæntɪz] **npl** *inf* culotte *f*.

pantihose [ˈpæntɪhəʊz] *US* = ***pantyhose***.

panto [ˈpæntəʊ] (pl **-s**) **n** *UK inf spectacle de Noël pour enfants, généralement inspiré de contes de fées*.

pantomime [ˈpæntəmaɪm] **n** *UK spectacle de Noël pour enfants, généralement inspiré de contes de fées* ▸ **pantomime dame** *rôle travesti outré et ridicule dans la 'pantomime'*.

pantry [ˈpæntrɪ] (pl **-ies**) **n** garde-manger *m inv*.

pants [pænts] **npl 1.** *UK* [underpants - for men] slip *m* / [- for women] culotte *f*, slip **2.** *US* [trousers] pantalon *m*.

pantyhose [ˈpæntɪhəʊz] **npl** *US* collant *m*.

panty liner **n** protège-slip *m*.

papa [*UK* pəˈpɑː, *US* ˈpæpə] **n** papa *m*.

papacy [ˈpeɪpəsɪ] (pl **-ies**) **n : the papacy** la papauté.

papadum [ˈpæpədəm] = ***popadum***.

papal [ˈpeɪpl] **adj** papal(e).

paparazzi [ˌpæpəˈrætsɪ] **npl** *pej* paparazzi *mpl*.

papaya [pəˈpaɪə] **n** papaye *f*.

paper [ˈpeɪpəʳ] ■ **n 1.** *(U)* [for writing on] papier *m* ▸ **a piece of paper** [sheet] une feuille de papier / [scrap] un bout de papier ▸ **on paper** [written down] par écrit / [in theory] sur le papier ▸ **don't put anything down on paper!** ne mettez rien par écrit! ▸ **on paper, they're by far the better side** sur le papier, c'est de loin la meilleure équipe **2.** [newspaper] journal *m* **3.** [in exam - test] épreuve *f* / [- answers] copie *f* **4.** [essay] **: paper (on)** essai *m* (sur).
■ **adj** [hat, bag] en papier / *fig* [profits] théorique.
■ **vt** tapisser.
◆ ***papers*** **npl** [official documents] papiers *mpl*.
◆ ***paper over*** **vt insep** *fig* dissimuler ▸ **they tried to paper over the cracks** ils ont essayé de masquer les désaccords.

paperback [ˈpeɪpəbæk] **n : paperback (book)** livre *m* de poche ▸ **in paperback** en poche.

paperboy [ˈpeɪpəbɔɪ] **n** livreur *m* de journaux.

paper clip **n** trombone *m*.

paper feed **n** COMPUT & TYPO alimentation *f* en papier.

papergirl [ˈpeɪpəgɜːl] **n** livreuse *f* de journaux.

paper handkerchief **n** mouchoir *m* en papier.

paper knife **n** coupe-papier *m inv*.

paperless [ˈpeɪpəlɪs] **adj** [electronic - communication, record-keeping] informatique ▸ **the paperless office** le bureau entièrement informatisé.

papermill [ˈpeɪpəmɪl] **n** papeterie *f*, usine *f* à papier.

paper money **n** *(U)* papier-monnaie *m*.

paper round *UK*, ***paper route*** *US* **n : to do a paper round** livrer les journaux à domicile.

paper shop **n** *UK* marchand *m* de journaux.

paper-thin **adj** extrêmement mince ***OR*** fin(e).

paper towel **n** serviette *f* en papier.

paper tray **n** COMPUT bac *m* à papier.

paperweight [ˈpeɪpəweɪt] **n** presse-papiers *m inv*.

paperwork [ˈpeɪpəwɜːk] **n** paperasserie *f*.

papier-mâché [ˌpæpjeɪˈmæʃeɪ] ■ **n** papier mâché *m*.
■ **comp** en papier mâché.

papist [ˈpeɪpɪst] **n** *offens* papiste *mf*.

paprika [ˈpæprɪkə] **n** paprika *m*.

Pap smear [pæp↓] *US* = ***cervical smear***.

Papua [ˈpæpjʊə] **n** Papouasie *f*.

Papuan [ˈpæpjʊən] ■ **adj** papou(e).
■ **n** Papou *m*, -e *f*.

Papua New Guinea **n** Papouasie-Nouvelle-Guinée *f* ▸ **in Papua New Guinea** en Papouasie-Nouvelle-Guinée.

par [pɑːʳ] n **1.** [parity] **: on a par with** à égalité avec **2.** GOLF par *m*, normale *f Québec* ▸ **under/over par** en-dessous/en-dessus du par **3.** [good health] **: below *OR* under par** pas en forme.

para ['pærə] n *UK inf* para *m*.

parable ['pærəbl] n parabole *f*.

parabola [pə'ræbələ] n parabole *f*.

parabolic [,pærə'bɒlɪk] adj parabolique.

paracetamol [,pærə'siːtəmɒl] n *UK* paracétamol *m*.

parachute ['pærəʃuːt] ■ n parachute *m*.
■ vi sauter en parachute.

parachutist ['pærəʃuːtɪst] n parachutiste *mf*.

parade [pə'reɪd] ■ n **1.** [celebratory] parade *f*, revue *f* **2.** MIL défilé *m* ▸ **to be on parade** défiler **3.** *UK* [street of shops] rangée *f* de magasins.
■ vt **1.** [people] faire défiler **2.** [object] montrer **3.** *fig* [flaunt] afficher.
■ vi défiler.

parade ground n terrain *m* de manœuvres.

paradigm ['pærədaɪm] n paradigme *m*.

paradigmatic [,pærədɪg'mætɪk] adj paradigmatique.

paradise ['pærədaɪs] n paradis *m*.
◆ ***Paradise*** n Paradis *m*.

paradox ['pærədɒks] n paradoxe *m*.

paradoxical [,pærə'dɒksɪkl] adj paradoxal(e).

paradoxically [,pærə'dɒksɪklɪ] adv paradoxalement.

paraffin ['pærəfɪn] n *UK* paraffine *f*.

paraffin wax n paraffine *f*.

paragliding ['pærə,glaɪdɪŋ] n parapente *m*.

paragon ['pærəgən] n modèle *m*, parangon *m*.

paragraph ['pærəgrɑːf] n paragraphe *m*.

Paraguay ['pærəgwaɪ] n Paraguay *m* ▸ **in Paraguay** au Paraguay.

Paraguayan [,pærə'gwaɪən] ■ adj paraguayen(enne).
■ n Paraguayen *m*, -enne *f*.

parakeet ['pærəkiːt] n perruche *f*.

paralegal ['pærə,liːgəl] n assistant *m*, -e *f (d'un avocat)*.

parallel ['pærəlel] ■ adj *lit* & *fig* **: parallel (to *OR* with)** parallèle (à) ▸ **to run parallel to sthg** longer qqch.
■ n **1.** GEOM parallèle *f* **2.** [similarity & GEOG] parallèle *m* ▸ **the two industries have developed in parallel** ces deux industries se sont développées en parallèle ▸ **to draw a parallel between** faire *OR* établir un parallèle entre **3.** *fig* [similar person, object] équivalent *m* ▸ **to have no parallel** ne pas avoir d'équivalent.
■ vt *fig* être semblable à.

parallel bars npl barres *fpl* parallèles.

parallel cable n câble *m* parallèle.

parallelogram [,pærə'leləgræm] n parallélogramme *m*.

parallel port n port *m* parallèle.

parallel turn n [in skiing] virage *m* parallèle.

paralyse *UK*, ***paralyze*** *US* ['pærəlaɪz] vt *lit* & *fig* paralyser.

paralysed *UK*, ***paralyzed*** *US* ['pærəlaɪzd] adj *lit* & *fig* paralysé(e).

paralysis [pə'rælɪsɪs] (pl **-lyses** [-lɪsiːz]) n *lit* & *fig* paralysie *f*.

paralytic [,pærə'lɪtɪk] ■ adj **1.** MED paralytique **2.** *UK inf* [drunk] ivre mort(e).
■ n paralytique *mf*.

paramedic [,pærə'medɪk] n auxiliaire médical *m*, auxiliaire médicale *f*.

paramedical [,pærə'medɪkl] adj paramédical(e).

parameter [pə'ræmɪtəʳ] n paramètre *m*.

paramilitary [,pærə'mɪlɪtrɪ] adj paramilitaire.

paramount ['pærəmaʊnt] adj primordial(e) ▸ **of paramount importance** d'une importance suprême.

paranoia [,pærə'nɔɪə] n paranoïa *f*.

paranoiac [,pærə'nɔɪæk] ■ adj paranoïaque.
■ n paranoïaque *mf*.

paranoid ['pærənɔɪd] adj paranoïaque.

paranormal [,pærə'nɔːml] adj paranormal(e).

parapet ['pærəpɪt] n parapet *m*.

paraphernalia [,pærəfə'neɪljə] n *(U)* attirail *m*, bazar *m*.

paraphrase ['pærəfreɪz] ■ n paraphrase *f*.
■ vt paraphraser.
■ vi faire une paraphrase.

paraplegia [,pærə'pliːdʒə] n paraplégie *f*.

paraplegic [,pærə'pliːdʒɪk] ■ adj paraplégique.
■ n paraplégique *mf*.

parapsychology [,pærəsaɪ'kɒlədʒɪ] n parapsychologie *f*.

Paraquat® ['pærəkwɒt] n *UK* Paraquat® *m*.

parasailing ['pærə,seɪlɪŋ] n parachute *m* ascensionnel *(tracté par bateau)*.

parascending ['pærə,sendɪŋ] n parachute *m* ascensionnel *(tracté par véhicule)*.

parasite ['pærəsaɪt] n *lit* & *fig* parasite *m*.

parasitic [,pærə'sɪtɪk] adj *lit* & *fig* parasite.

parasol ['pærəsɒl] n [above table] parasol *m* / [hand-held] ombrelle *f*.

paratrooper ['pærətruːpəʳ] n parachutiste *mf*.

parboil ['pɑːbɔɪl] vt faire bouillir *OR* cuire à demi.

parcel ['pɑːsl] *UK* n paquet *m*.
◆ ***parcel up*** vt sep (pt & pp **-led up**, cont **-ling up**) empaqueter.

parcel bomb n *UK* colis *m* piégé.

parcel post n **: to send sthg parcel post** envoyer qqch par colis postal.

parched [pɑːtʃt] adj **1.** [gen] desséché(e) **2.** *inf* [very thirsty] assoiffé(e), mort(e) de soif.

parchment ['pɑːtʃmənt] n parchemin *m*.

pardon ['pɑ:dn] ■ n **1.** LAW grâce *f* **2.** *(U)* [forgiveness] pardon *m* ▸ **I beg your pardon?** [showing surprise, asking for repetition] comment?, pardon? ▸ **I beg your pardon!** [to apologize] je vous demande pardon!
■ **vt 1.** [forgive] pardonner ▸ **to pardon sb for sthg** pardonner qqch à qqn ▸ **pardon me!** pardon!, excusez-moi! **2.** LAW gracier.
■ **excl** comment?

pardonable ['pɑ:dnəbl] **adj** pardonnable.

pare [peəʳ] **vt** [apple] peler, éplucher / [fingernails] couper.
◆ **pare down** **vt sep 1.** [stick, fingernails] couper **2.** *fig* [reduce] réduire.

parent ['peərənt] **n** père *m*, mère *f*.
◆ **parents** **npl** parents *mpl*.

parentage ['peərəntɪdʒ] **n** *(U)* naissance *f*.

parental [pə'rentl] **adj** parental(e).

parent company **n** société *f* mère.

parenthesis [pə'renθɪsɪs] (pl **-theses** [-θɪsi:z]) **n** parenthèse *f*.

parenthetical [,pærən'θetɪkl] **adj** entre parenthèses.

parenthood ['peərənthʊd] **n** condition *f* de parent.

parenting ['peərəntɪŋ] **n** art *m* d'être parent.

parent-teacher association **n** association *f* des parents d'élèves et des professeurs.

pariah [pə'raɪə] **n** paria *m*.

Paris ['pærɪs] **n** Paris.

parish ['pærɪʃ] **n 1.** RELIG paroisse *f* **2.** *UK* [area of local government] commune *f*.

parish council **n** *UK* conseil *m* municipal.

parishioner [pə'rɪʃənəʳ] **n** paroissien *m*, -enne *f*.

Parisian [pə'rɪzjən] ■ **adj** parisien(enne).
■ **n** Parisien *m*, -enne *f*.

parity ['pærətɪ] **n** égalité *f*.

park [pɑ:k] ■ **n** parc *m*, jardin *m* public.
■ **vt** garer.
■ **vi** se garer, stationner.

parka ['pɑ:kə] **n** parka *f*.

park-and-ride **n** *système de contrôle de la circulation qui consiste à garer les voitures à l'extérieur des grandes villes, puis à utiliser les transports en commun*.

parking ['pɑ:kɪŋ] **n** stationnement *m* ▸ **'no parking'** 'défense de stationner', 'stationnement interdit'.

parking attendant **n** [in car park] gardien *m*, -enne *f* / [at hotel] voiturier *m*.

parking brake **n** *US* frein *m* à main.

parking garage **n** *US* parking *m* couvert.

parking light **n** *US* feu *m* de position.

parking lot **n** *US* parking *m*.

parking meter **n** parcmètre *m*.

parking place **n** place *f* de stationnement.

parking ticket **n** contravention *f*, PV *m*.

Parkinson's disease ['pɑ:kɪnsnz-] **n** maladie *f* de Parkinson.

park keeper **n** *UK* gardien *m*, -enne *f* de parc.

parkland ['pɑ:klænd] **n** *(U)* parc *m*.

parkway ['pɑ:kweɪ] **n** *US* *large route divisée ou bordée d'arbres*.

parky ['pɑ:kɪ] (comp **-ier**, superl **-iest**) **adj** *UK* *inf* **: it's parky** il fait frisquet.

parlance ['pɑ:ləns] **n : in common/legal parlance** en langage courant/juridique.

parliament ['pɑ:ləmənt] **n** parlement *m*.

parliamentarian [,pɑ:ləmen'teərɪən] **n** parlementaire *mf*.

parliamentary [,pɑ:lə'mentərɪ] **adj** parlementaire.

parlour *UK*, **parlor** *US* ['pɑ:ləʳ] **n** *dated* salon *m*.

parlour game *UK*, **parlor game** *US* **n** *dated* jeu *m* de salon.

parlous ['pɑ:ləs] **adj** *fml* précaire.

Parmesan (cheese) [,pɑ:mɪ'zæn-] **n** parmesan *m*.

parochial [pə'rəʊkjəl] **adj** *pej* de clocher.

parochialism [pə'rəʊkjəlɪzm] **n** *pej* esprit *m* de clocher.

parody ['pærədɪ] ■ **n** (pl **-ies**) parodie *f*.
■ **vt** (pt & pp **-ied**) parodier.

parole [pə'rəʊl] ■ **n** *(U)* parole *f* ▸ **on parole** en liberté conditionnelle.
■ **vt** mettre en liberté conditionnelle.

parole board **n** ≃ comité *m* de probation et d'assistance aux libérés.

paroxysm ['pærəksɪzm] **n** [of rage] accès *m* ▸ **a paroxysm of laughter** un fou rire.

parquet ['pɑ:keɪ] **n** parquet *m*.

parrot ['pærət] **n** perroquet *m*.

parrot fashion **adv** comme un perroquet.

parry ['pærɪ] (pt & pp **-ied**) **vt 1.** [blow] parer **2.** [question] éluder.

parser ['pɑ:zəʳ] **n** COMPUT analyseur *m* syntaxique.

parsimonious [,pɑ:sɪ'məʊnjəs] **adj** *fml* & *pej* parcimonieux(euse).

parsley ['pɑ:slɪ] **n** persil *m*.

parsnip ['pɑ:snɪp] **n** panais *m*.

parson ['pɑ:sn] **n** pasteur *m*.

parson's nose **n** *UK* croupion *m*.

part [pɑ:t] ■ **n 1.** [gen] partie *f* ▸ **the best** OR **better part of** la plus grande partie de ▸ **for the most part** dans l'ensemble ▸ **in part** en partie ▸ **to be (a) part of sthg** faire partie de qqch ▸ **it's very much part of the game/of the process** ça fait partie du jeu/du processus ▸ **part and parcel of** partie intégrante de
2. [of TV serial] épisode *m*
3. [component] pièce *f*

4. [in proportions] mesure *f*
5. THEAT rôle *m*
6. [involvement] **: part in** participation *f* à ▸ **to play an important part in** jouer un rôle important dans ▸ **to take part in** participer à ▸ **he has no part in the running of the company** il ne participe pas à *OR* il n'intervient pas dans la gestion de la société ▸ **to want no part in** ne pas vouloir se mêler de ▸ **for my part** en ce qui me concerne ▸ **on my/his** *etc* **part** de ma/sa *etc* part
7. [area - of country, town] **: which part of England are you from?** vous êtes d'où en Angleterre?, de quelle région de l'Angleterre venez-vous? ▸ **it's a dangerous part of town** c'est un quartier dangereux
8. *US* [hair parting] raie *f*.
■ **adv** en partie.
■ **vt : to part one's hair** se faire une raie ▸ **her hair's parted in the middle** elle a la raie au milieu.
■ **vi 1.** [couple] se séparer
2. [curtains] s'écarter, s'ouvrir.
◆ ***parts*** **npl : in these parts** dans cette région.
◆ ***part with*** **vt insep** [money] débourser / [possession] se défaire de.

partake [pɑː'teɪk] (pt **-took**, pp **-taken**) **vi** *fml* **: to partake of** prendre.

part exchange **n** *UK* reprise *f* ▸ **to take sthg in part exchange** reprendre qqch.

partial ['pɑːʃl] **adj 1.** [incomplete] partiel(elle) **2.** [biased] partial(e) **3.** [fond] **: to be partial to** avoir un penchant pour.

CONFUSABLE / PARONYME

partial

When translating **partial**, note that the French words *partial* and *partiel* are not interchangeable. *Partial* means *biased*, while *partiel* is used to describe something that is only partly done or completed.

partial eclipse **n** éclipse *f* partielle.

partiality [,pɑːʃɪ'ælətɪ] **n 1.** [bias] partialité *f* **2.** [fondness] **: partiality for** prédilection *f* *OR* penchant *m* pour.

partially ['pɑːʃəlɪ] **adv** partiellement.

partially sighted ■ **adj** malvoyant(e).
■ **npl : the partially sighted** les malvoyants *mpl*.

participant [pɑː'tɪsɪpənt] **n** participant *m*, -e *f*.

participate [pɑː'tɪsɪpeɪt] **vi : to participate (in)** participer (à).

participating interest [pɑː,tɪsɪ'peɪtɪŋ] **n** intérêt *m* de participation.

participation [pɑː,tɪsɪ'peɪʃn] **n** participation *f*.

participatory [pɑː,tɪsɪ'peɪtərɪ] **adj** participatif(ive).

participle ['pɑːtɪsɪpl] **n** participe *m*.

particle ['pɑːtɪkl] **n** particule *f*.

particle accelerator **n** accélérateur *m* de particules.

particle physics **n** *(U)* physique *f* des particules.

parti-coloured *UK*, ***parti-colored*** *US* ['pɑːtɪ-] **adj** bariolé(e).

particular [pə'tɪkjʊlər] **adj 1.** [gen] particulier(ère) ▸ **for no particular reason** sans raison particulière ▸ **it's an issue of particular importance to us** c'est une question qui revêt une importance toute particulière à nos yeux **2.** [fussy] pointilleux(euse) ▸ **particular about** exigeant(e) à propos de.
◆ ***particulars*** **npl** renseignements *mpl*.
◆ ***in particular*** **adv** en particulier ▸ **what are you thinking about? – nothing in particular** à quoi pensestu? – à rien en particulier.

particularity [pə,tɪkjʊ'lærətɪ] (pl **-ies**) **n** particularité *f*.

particularly [pə'tɪkjʊləlɪ] **adv** particulièrement.

parting ['pɑːtɪŋ] **n 1.** [separation] séparation *f* **2.** *UK* [in hair] raie *f*.

parting shot **n** flèche *f* du Parthe.

partisan [,pɑːtɪ'zæn] ■ **adj** partisan(e).
■ **n** partisan *m*, -e *f*.

partition [pɑː'tɪʃn] ■ **n 1.** [wall, screen] cloison *f* **2.** [of country] partition *f*.
■ **vt 1.** [room] cloisonner **2.** [country] partager.

partly ['pɑːtlɪ] **adv** partiellement, en partie.

partner ['pɑːtnər] ■ **n 1.** [in game, dance] partenaire *mf* / [spouse] conjoint *m*, -e *f* / [not married] compagnon *m*, compagne *f* **2.** [in business, crime] associé *m*, -e *f*.
■ **vt** être le(la) partenaire de.

partnership ['pɑːtnəʃɪp] **n** association *f* ▸ **to enter into partnership (with)** s'associer (avec).

part of speech **n** partie *f* du discours.

partook [pɑː'teɪkn] **pt** ➤ ***partake***.

part payment **n** paiement *m* partiel.

partridge ['pɑːtrɪdʒ] **n** perdrix *f*.

part-time **adj & adv** à temps partiel.

part-timer **n** travailleur *m*, -euse *f* à temps partiel.

party ['pɑːtɪ] ■ **n** (pl **-ies**) **1.** POL parti *m* **2.** [social gathering] fête *f*, réception *f* ▸ **to have** *OR* **throw a party** donner une fête **3.** [group] groupe *m* **4.** LAW partie *f* ▸ **to be a party to** être complice de.
■ **vi** *inf* faire la fête.

party animal **n** *inf* fêtard *m* ▸ **she's a real party animal** elle adore faire la fête.

partygoer ['pɑːtɪgəʊə] **n** fêtard *m*, -e *f*.

partying ['pɑːtɪɪŋ] **n : she's a great one for partying** *inf* elle adore faire la fête.

party line **n 1.** POL ligne *f* du parti **2.** TELEC ligne commune à deux abonnés.

party piece **n** *inf* numéro *m* habituel.

party political broadcast **n** *UK* *moment d'antenne réservé à un parti politique*.

party politics **n** *(U)* politique *f* politicienne.

party pooper **n** *inf* rabat-joie *m inv*.

party wall n mur *m* mitoyen.

PASCAL [pæ'skæl] n PASCAL *m*.

pass [pɑ:s] ■ n 1. SPORT passe *f* 2. [document - for security] laissez-passer *m inv* / [- for travel] carte *f* d'abonnement 3. *UK* [in exam] mention *f* passable ▶ **to get a pass** avoir la moyenne 4. [between mountains] col *m*
▶▶ **to make a pass at sb** faire du plat à qqn.
■ vt 1. [object, time] passer ▶ **to pass sthg to sb, to pass sb sthg** passer qqch à qqn 2. [person in street] croiser ▶ **the ships passed each other in the fog** les navires se sont croisés dans le brouillard 3. [place] passer devant 4. AUT dépasser, doubler 5. [exceed] dépasser ▶ **we've passed the exit** nous avons dépassé la sortie 6. [exam] réussir (à) / [driving test] passer ▶ **he didn't pass his history exam** il a échoué OR il a été recalé à son examen d'histoire 7. [candidate] recevoir, admettre 8. [law, motion] voter 9. [opinion] émettre / [judgment] rendre, prononcer.
■ vi 1. [gen] passer ▶ **his life passed before his eyes** il a vu sa vie défiler devant ses yeux ▶ **the weekend passed without surprises** le week-end s'est passé sans surprises 2. AUT doubler, dépasser ▶ **the road was too narrow for two cars to pass** la route était trop étroite pour que deux voitures se croisent 3. SPORT faire une passe 4. [in exam] réussir, être reçu(e) 5. [occur] se dérouler, avoir lieu.
◆ ***pass around, pass round*** *UK* vt sep faire passer.
◆ ***pass as*** vt insep passer pour ▶ **don't try to pass as an expert** n'essaie pas de te faire passer pour un expert.
◆ ***pass away*** vi *euph* s'éteindre.
◆ ***pass by*** ■ vt sep : **the news passed him by** la nouvelle ne l'a pas affecté ▶ **she felt life had passed her by** elle avait le sentiment d'avoir raté sa vie.
■ vi passer à côté.
◆ ***pass for*** vt insep = ***pass as***.
◆ ***pass off*** vt sep : **to pass sb/sthg off as** faire passer qqn/qqch pour ▶ **he passes himself off as an actor** il se fait passer pour un acteur.
◆ ***pass on*** ■ vt sep : **to pass sthg on (to)** [object] faire passer qqch (à) / [tradition, information] transmettre qqch (à) ▶ **they pass the costs on to their customers** ils répercutent les coûts sur leurs clients.
■ vi 1. [move on] continuer son chemin 2. *euph* = ***pass away***.
◆ ***pass out*** vi 1. [faint] s'évanouir 2. *UK* MIL finir OR terminer les classes.
◆ ***pass over*** ■ vt sep [overlook - person] : **he was passed over for promotion** on ne lui a pas accordé la promotion qu'il attendait.
■ vt insep [problem, topic] passer sous silence.
◆ ***pass round*** vt insep *UK* = ***pass around***.
◆ ***pass to*** vt insep passer à, revenir à.
◆ ***pass up*** vt sep [opportunity] laisser passer ▶ **I'll have to pass up their invitation** je vais devoir décliner leur invitation.

passable ['pɑ:səbl] adj 1. [satisfactory] passable 2. [road] praticable / [river] franchissable.

passably ['pɑ:səblɪ] adv passablement.

passage ['pæsɪdʒ] n 1. [gen] passage *m* 2. [between rooms] couloir *m* 3. [sea journey] traversée *f*.

passageway ['pæsɪdʒweɪ] n [between houses] passage *m* / [between rooms] couloir *m*.

passbook ['pɑ:sbʊk] n *UK* livret *m* (d'épargne).

pass degree n *en Grande-Bretagne, licence obtenue avec mention passable (par opposition au "honours degree").*

passé [pæ'seɪ] adj *pej* démodé(e).

passenger ['pæsɪndʒəʳ] n passager *m*, -ère *f*.

passenger seat n AUT [in front] siège *m* du passager / [in back] siège *m* arrière.

passenger train n train *m* de voyageurs.

passerby [,pɑ:sə'baɪ] (pl **passersby** [,pɑ:səz'baɪ]) n passant *m*, -e *f*.

passing ['pɑ:sɪŋ] ■ adj [going by] qui passe / [remark] en passant / [trend] passager(ère) ▶ **with each passing day he grew more worried** son inquiétude croissait de jour en jour.
■ n : **with the passing of time** avec le temps.
◆ ***in passing*** adv en passant.

passing place n voie *f* de dépassement, aire *f* de croisement.

passion ['pæʃn] n passion *f* ▶ **to have a passion for** avoir la passion de.
◆ ***Passion*** n : **the Passion** la Passion.

passionate ['pæʃənət] adj passionné(e).

passionately ['pæʃənətlɪ] adv avec passion.

passion fruit n fruit *m* de la passion.

passive ['pæsɪv] ■ adj passif(ive).
■ n GRAM : **the passive** le passif.

passively ['pæsɪvlɪ] adv passivement.

passive resistance n résistance *f* passive.

passive smoking n tabagisme *m* passif.

passivity [pæ'sɪvətɪ] n passivité *f*.

passkey ['pɑ:ski:] n passe *m*.

pass mark n *UK* SCH moyenne *f*.

Passover ['pɑ:s,əʊvəʳ] n : **(the) Passover** la Pâque juive.

passport ['pɑ:spɔ:t] n 1. [document] passeport *m* 2. *fig* [means] : **passport to** clef *f* de.

passport control n contrôle *m* des passeports.

pass-the-parcel n *UK jeu où l'on se passe un colis contenant soit un gage, soit un cadeau.*

password ['pɑ:swɜ:d] n mot *m* de passe.

password-protected adj COMPUT protégé(e) par mot de passe.

past [pɑ:st] ■ adj 1. [former] passé(e) ▶ **for the past five years** ces cinq dernières années ▶ **the past week** la semaine passée OR dernière ▶ **in past times** OR **times past** autrefois, (au temps) jadis
2. [finished] fini(e).
■ adv 1. [in times] : **it's ten past** il est dix
2. [in front] : **to go past** passer ▶ **to drive past** passer (devant) en voiture ▶ **to run past** passer (devant) en courant.
■ n passé *m* ▶ **the great empires of the past** les grands empires de l'histoire ▶ **in the past** dans le temps ▶ **to live in the past** vivre dans le passé.

■ **prep 1.** [in times] **: it's half past eight** il est huit heures et demie ▸ **it's five past nine** il est neuf heures cinq ▸ **it's already past midnight** il est déjà plus de minuit ***or*** minuit passé
2. [in front of] devant ▸ **we drove past them** nous les avons dépassés en voiture
3. [beyond] après, au-delà de ▸ **it's a few miles past the lake** c'est quelques kilomètres après le lac ▸ **I'm past caring** ça ne me fait plus ni chaud ni froid ▸ **to be past it** *inf* être trop vieux(vieille) pour ça ▸ **I wouldn't put it past him** *inf pej* cela ne m'étonnerait pas de lui.

pasta ['pæstə] **n** *(U)* pâtes *fpl.*

paste [peɪst] ■ **n 1.** [gen] pâte *f* **2.** CULIN pâté *m* **3.** *(U)* [glue] colle *f* **4.** *(U)* [jewellery] strass *m.*
■ **vt** coller.

pastel ['pæstl] ■ **adj** pastel *(inv).*
■ **n** pastel *m.*

paste-up **n** TYPO collage *m.*

pasteurize, *UK* ***-ise*** ['pɑːstʃəraɪz] **vt** pasteuriser.

pasteurized, *UK* ***-ised*** ['pɑːstʃəraɪzd] **adj 1.** [milk, beer] pasteurisé(e) **2.** *pej* [version, description] édulcoré(e), aseptisé(e).

pastiche [pæ'stiːʃ] **n** pastiche *m.*

pastille ['pæstɪl] **n** pastille *f.*

pastime ['pɑːstaɪm] **n** passe-temps *m inv.*

pasting ['peɪstɪŋ] **n** *inf* [beating] rossée *f.*

pastor ['pɑːstəʳ] **n** pasteur *m.*

pastoral ['pɑːstərəl] **adj** pastoral(e).

past participle **n** participe *m* passé.

past perfect **n** plus-que-parfait *m.*

pastrami [pə'strɑːmɪ] **n** *viande de bœuf fumée et épicée.*

pastry ['peɪstrɪ] (pl **-ies**) **n 1.** [mixture] pâte *f* **2.** [cake] pâtisserie *f.*

past tense **n** passé *m.*

pasture ['pɑːstʃəʳ] **n** pâturage *m*, pré *m.*

pastureland ['pɑːstʃəlænd] **n** pâturage *m*, herbage *m.*

pasty[1] ['peɪstɪ] (comp **-ier**, superl **-iest**) **adj** blafard(e), terreux(euse).

pasty[2] ['pæstɪ] (pl **-ies**) **n** *UK* petit pâté *m*, friand *m.*

pasty-faced ['peɪstɪˌfeɪst] **adj** au teint blafard ***or*** terreux.

pat [pæt] ■ **adj** (comp **-ter**, superl **-test**) tout prêt (toute prête), tout fait (toute faite).
■ **n 1.** [light stroke] petite tape *f* / [to animal] caresse *f* **2.** [of butter] noix *f*, noisette *f.*
■ **vt** (pt & pp **-ted**, cont **-ting**) [person] tapoter, donner une tape à / [animal] caresser.

Patagonia [ˌpætə'gəʊnjə] **n** Patagonie *f* ▸ **in Patagonia** en Patagonie.

Patagonian [ˌpætə'gəʊnjən] ■ **adj** patagon(onne).
■ **n** Patagon *m*, -onne *f.*

patch [pætʃ] ■ **n 1.** [piece of material] pièce *f* / [to cover eye] bandeau *m* **2.** [small area - of snow, ice] plaque *f* **3.** [of land] parcelle *f*, lopin *m* ▸ **vegetable patch** carré *m* de légumes **4.** MED patch *m* **5.** [period of time] **: a difficult patch** une mauvaise passe
▸▸ **not to be a patch on sb** *UK inf* ne pas arriver ***or*** venir à la cheville de qqn ▸ **not to be a patch on sthg** *UK inf* ne pas valoir qqch.
■ **vt** rapiécer.
◆ ***patch together*** **vt sep** faire à la va-vite.
◆ ***patch up*** **vt sep 1.** [mend] rafistoler, bricoler **2.** *fig* [quarrel] régler, arranger ▸ **to patch up a relationship** se raccommoder.

patchwork ['pætʃwɜːk] ■ **adj** en patchwork.
■ **n** patchwork *m.*

patchy ['pætʃɪ] (comp **-ier**, superl **-iest**) **adj** [gen] inégal(e) / [knowledge] insuffisant(e), imparfait(e).

pâté ['pæteɪ] **n** pâté *m.*

patent [*UK* 'peɪtənt, *US* 'pætənt] ■ **adj** [obvious] évident(e), manifeste.
■ **n** brevet *m* (d'invention).
■ **vt** faire breveter.

patented [*UK* 'peɪtəntɪd, *US* 'pætəntɪd] **adj** breveté(e).

patentee [*UK* ˌpeɪtən'tiː, *US* ˌpætən'tiː] **n** titulaire *m* d'un brevet.

patent leather **n** cuir *m* verni.

patently [*UK* 'peɪtəntlɪ, *US* 'pætəntlɪ] **adv** manifestement.

Patent Office **n** bureau *m* des brevets.

paternal [pə'tɜːnl] **adj** paternel(elle).

paternalistic [pəˌtɜːnə'lɪstɪk] **adj** *pej* paternaliste.

paternally [pə'tɜːnəlɪ] **adv** paternellement.

paternity [pə'tɜːnətɪ] **n** paternité *f.*

paternity leave **n** congé *m* parental *(pour pères).*

paternity suit **n** LAW action *f* en recherche de paternité.

paternity test **n** test *m* de recherche de paternité.

path [pɑːθ] (pl [pɑːðz]) **n 1.** [track] chemin *m*, sentier *m* **2.** [way ahead, course of action] voie *f*, chemin *m* **3.** [trajectory] trajectoire *f* **4.** COMPUT chemin *m* (d'accès)
▸▸ **our paths had crossed before** nos chemins s'étaient déjà croisés.

pathetic [pə'θetɪk] **adj 1.** [causing pity] pitoyable, attendrissant(e) **2.** [useless - efforts, person] pitoyable, minable.

pathetically [pə'θetɪklɪ] **adv 1.** [cry, whimper] pitoyablement **2.** [inadequate, feeble] lamentablement.

pathname ['pɑːθneɪm] **n** chemin *m* (d'accès).

pathological [ˌpæθə'lɒdʒɪkl] **adj** pathologique.

pathologist [pə'θɒlədʒɪst] **n** pathologiste *mf.*

pathology [pə'θɒlədʒɪ] **n** pathologie *f.*

pathos ['peɪθɒs] **n** pathétique *m.*

pathway ['pɑːθweɪ] **n** chemin *m*, sentier *m.*

patience ['peɪʃns] **n 1.** [of person] patience *f* ▸ **to try sb's patience** mettre la patience de qqn à l'épreuve, éprouver la patience de qqn **2.** *UK* [card game] réussite *f.*

patient ['peɪʃnt] ■ **adj** patient(e).
■ **n** [in hospital] patient *m*, -e *f*, malade *mf* / [of doctor] patient.

patiently ['peɪʃntlɪ] **adv** patiemment.

patina ['pætɪnə] **n** patine *f.*

patio ['pætɪəʊ] (pl **-s**) **n** patio *m*.

patio doors **npl** *portes vitrées coulissantes*.

Patna rice ['pætnə-] **n** riz *m* Patna (à grains longs).

patois ['pætwɑː] (pl **patois**) **n** patois *m*.

patriarch ['peɪtrɪɑːk] **n** patriarche *m*.

patriarchal [ˌpeɪtrɪ'ɑːkl] **adj** patriarcal(e).

patriarchy ['peɪtrɪɑːkɪ] (pl **-ies**) **n** patriarcat *m*.

patrician [pə'trɪʃn] **n** patricien *m*, -enne *f*.

patrimony [*UK* 'pætrɪmənɪ, *US* 'pætrɪməʊnɪ] **n** *fml* patrimoine *m*, héritage *m*.

patriot [*UK* 'pætrɪət, *US* 'peɪtrɪət] **n** patriote *mf*.

patriotic [*UK* ˌpætrɪ'ɒtɪk, *US* ˌpeɪtrɪ'ɒtɪk] **adj** [gen] patriotique / [person] patriote.

patriotically [*UK* ˌpætrɪ'ɒtɪklɪ, *US* ˌpeɪtrɪ'ɒtɪklɪ] **adv** patriotiquement, en patriote.

patriotism [*UK* 'pætrɪətɪzm, *US* 'peɪtrɪətɪzm] **n** patriotisme *m*.

patrol [pə'trəʊl] ■ **n** patrouille *f* ▸ **to be on patrol** être de patrouille ▸ **to go on patrol** aller en patrouille.
■ **vt** (pt & pp **-led**, cont **-ling**) patrouiller dans, faire une patrouille dans.

patrol car **n** voiture *f* de police.

patrolman [pə'trəʊlmən] (pl **-men** [-mən]) **n** *US* agent *m* de police.

patrol wagon **n** *US* fourgon *m* cellulaire.

patrolwoman [pə'trəʊlˌwʊmən] (pl **-women** [-ˌwɪmɪn]) **n** *US* femme *f* agent de police.

patron ['peɪtrən] **n 1.** [of arts] mécène *m*, protecteur *m*, -trice *f* **2.** *fml* [customer] client *m*, -e *f*.

FALSE FRIENDS / FAUX AMIS

patron

Patron n'est pas la traduction du mot anglais *patron*. Patron se traduit par *owner*.
▸ **Il connaît bien le patron du bar** / *He knows the owner of the bar well*

patronage ['peɪtrənɪdʒ] **n** patronage *m*.

patronize, *UK* ***-ise*** ['pætrənaɪz] **vt 1.** [talk down to] traiter avec condescendance **2.** *fml* [back financially] patronner, protéger.

patronizing, *UK* ***-ising*** ['pætrənaɪzɪŋ] **adj** condescendant(e).

patronizingly, *UK* ***-isingly*** ['pætrənaɪzɪŋlɪ] **adv** [smile] avec condescendance / [say] d'un ton condescendant.

patron saint **n** saint patron *m*, sainte patronne *f*.

patter ['pætəʳ] ■ **n 1.** [sound - of rain] crépitement *m* **2.** [talk] baratin *m*, bavardage *m*.
■ **vi** [feet, paws] trottiner / [rain] frapper, fouetter.

pattern ['pætən] **n 1.** [design] motif *m*, dessin *m* **2.** [of distribution, population] schéma *m* / [of life, behaviour] mode *m* ▸ **there is a definite pattern to the burglaries** on observe une constante bien précise dans les cambriolages **3.** [diagram] **: (sewing) pattern** patron *m* **4.** [model] modèle *m* ▸ **to set a pattern (for)** [subj: company, method, work] servir de modèle (à) / [subj: person] instaurer un modèle (pour).

patterned ['pætənd] **adj** à motifs.

patterning ['pætənɪŋ] **n 1.** PSYCHOL acquisition *f* des structures de pensée **2.** ZOOL [markings] marques *fpl*, taches *fpl*.

patty ['pætɪ] (pl **-ies**) **n** *esp US* petit pâté *m*.

paucity ['pɔːsətɪ] **n** *fml* indigence *f*.

paunch [pɔːntʃ] **n** bedaine *f*.

paunchy ['pɔːntʃɪ] (comp **-ier**, superl **-iest**) **adj** ventru(e), ventripotent(e).

pauper ['pɔːpəʳ] **n** *dated* indigent *m*, -e *f*, nécessiteux *m*, -euse *f*.

pause [pɔːz] ■ **n 1.** [short silence] pause *f*, silence *m* ▸ **there was a long pause before she answered** elle garda longtemps le silence avant de répondre **2.** [break] pause *f*, arrêt *m* ▸ **without a pause** sans s'arrêter, sans interruption.
■ **vi 1.** [stop speaking] marquer un temps **2.** [stop moving, doing] faire une pause, s'arrêter ▸ **without pausing for breath** sans même reprendre son souffle.

pave [peɪv] **vt** paver ▸ **to pave the way for sb/sthg** ouvrir la voie à qqn/qqch.

paved [peɪvd] **adj** pavé(e).

pavement ['peɪvmənt] **n 1.** *UK* [at side of road] trottoir *m* **2.** *US* [roadway] chaussée *f*.

pavement artist **n** *UK* artiste *mf* des rues.

pavilion [pə'vɪljən] **n** pavillon *m*.

paving ['peɪvɪŋ] **n** *(U)* pavé *m*.

paving stone **n** pavé *m*.

paw [pɔː] ■ **n** patte *f*.
■ **vt 1.** [subj: animal] donner des coups de patte à **2.** *pej* [subj: person] tripoter, peloter.

pawn [pɔːn] ■ **n** *lit & fig* pion *m*.
■ **vt** mettre en gage.

pawnbroker ['pɔːnˌbrəʊkəʳ] **n** prêteur *m*, -euse *f* sur gages.

pawnshop ['pɔːnʃɒp] **n** boutique *f* de prêteur sur gages.

pawpaw ['pɔːpɔː] **n** papaye *f*.

pay [peɪ] ■ **vt** (pt & pp **paid**) **1.** [gen] payer ▸ **to pay sb for sthg** payer qqn pour qqch, payer qqch à qqn ▸ **I paid £20 for that shirt** j'ai payé cette chemise 20 livres ▸ **to pay money into an account** verser de l'argent sur un compte ▸ **to pay a cheque into an account** déposer un chèque sur un compte ▸ **to pay one's way** payer sa part
2. [be profitable to] rapporter à ▸ **it will pay you not to say anything** *fig* tu as intérêt OR tu gagneras à ne rien dire **3.** [give, make] **: to pay attention (to sb/sthg)** prêter attention (à qqn/qqch) ▸ **to pay sb a compliment** faire un compliment à qqn ▸ **to pay sb a visit** rendre visite à qqn.
■ **vi** (pt & pp **paid**) payer ▸ **to pay dearly for sthg** *fig* payer qqch cher.
■ **n** salaire *m*, traitement *m*.
◆ ***pay back*** **vt sep 1.** [return loan of money] rembourser

2. [revenge oneself on] revaloir ▸ **I'll pay you back for that** tu me le paieras, je te le revaudrai.

◆ ***pay off*** ■ **vt sep 1.** [repay - debt] s'acquitter de, régler / [- loan] rembourser
2. [dismiss] licencier, congédier
3. [bribe] soudoyer, acheter.
■ **vi** [course of action] être payant(e).

◆ ***pay out*** ■ **vt sep 1.** [money] dépenser, débourser
2. [rope] laisser filer, lâcher.
■ **vi** dépenser, débourser.

◆ ***pay up*** **vi** payer.

payable ['peɪəbl] **adj 1.** [gen] payable **2.** [on cheque] : **payable to** à l'ordre de.

pay-and-display **adj : pay-and-display car park** parking *m* à horodateur ▸ **pay-and-display machine** horodateur *m*.

pay-as-you-earn *UK* **n** prélèvement *m* de l'impôt à la source.

pay-as-you-go **n** système *m* sans forfait.

payback ['peɪbæk] **n** FIN rapport *m (d'un investissement)*.

paybed ['peɪbed] **n** *UK* lit *m* privé.

paycheck ['peɪtʃek] **n** *US* paie *f*.

payday ['peɪdeɪ] **n** jour *m* de paie.

PAYE (abbr of ***pay-as-you-earn***) **n** *UK* prélèvement *m* de l'impôt à la source.

payee [peɪ'iː] **n** bénéficiaire *mf*.

pay envelope **n** *US* salaire *m*.

payer ['peɪəʳ] **n** payeur *m*, -euse *f*.

paying ['peɪɪŋ] ■ **n** paiement *m*.
■ **adj 1.** [who pays] payant(e) **2.** [profitable] payant(e), rentable.

paying guest **n** hôte *m* payant.

paying-in book **n** *UK* carnet *m* de versements.

paying-in slip **n** *UK* bordereau *m* de versement.

payload ['peɪləʊd] **n** charge *f* utile.

paymaster ['peɪˌmɑːstəʳ] **n** intendant *m*.

paymaster general **n** trésorier-payeur *m*.

payment ['peɪmənt] **n** paiement *m*.

payment facilities **n** facilités *fpl* de paiement.

payment schedule **n** échéancier *m* (de paiement).

payoff ['peɪɒf] **n 1.** [result] résultat *m* **2.** [redundancy payment] indemnité *f* de licenciement.

payola [peɪ'əʊlə] **n** *esp US inf* pot-de-vin *m*, dessous *m* de table.

pay packet **n** *UK* **1.** [envelope] enveloppe *f* de paie **2.** [wages] paie *f*.

pay-per-view ■ **n** TV système *m* de télévison à la carte *OR* à la séance.
■ **adj** à la carte, à la séance.

pay-per-view channel **n** chaîne *f* à la carte *OR* à la séance.

pay-per-view television **n** télévision *f* à la carte *OR* à la séance.

pay phone, *US* ***pay station*** **n** téléphone *m* public, cabine *f* téléphonique.

pay rise *UK*, ***pay raise*** *US* **n** augmentation *f* de salaire.

payroll ['peɪrəʊl] **n** registre *m* du personnel ▸ **they have 100 people on the payroll** ils ont 100 employés *OR* salariés.

payslip ['peɪslɪp] **n** *UK* feuille *f OR* bulletin *m* de paie.

pay station *US* = ***pay phone***.

pay television, ***pay TV*** **n** chaîne *f* à péage.

PBS (abbr of ***Public Broadcasting Service***) **n** *société américaine de production télévisuelle*.

PBX (abbr of ***private branch exchange***) **n** autocommutateur *m* privé.

pc ■ **n** abbr of ***postcard***.
■ (abbr of ***per cent***) p. cent.

p/c abbr of ***petty cash***.

PC ■ **n 1.** (abbr of ***personal computer***) PC *m*, micro *m* **2.** *UK* abbr of ***police constable*** **3.** *UK* (abbr of ***privy councillor***) *membre du conseil privé*.
■ **adj** abbr of ***politically correct***.

PCB (abbr of ***printed circuit board***) **n** plaquette *f* à circuits imprimés.

PCC (abbr of ***Press Complaints Commission***) **n** *organisme britannique de contrôle de la presse*.

PC card **n** carte *f* PC.

PC-compatible **adj** COMPUT compatible PC.

PCV (abbr of ***passenger carrying vehicle***) **n** *véhicule de transport en commun (en Grande-Bretagne)*.

pd abbr of ***paid***.

PD *US* abbr of ***police department***.

PDF (abbr of ***portable document format***) **n** COMPUT PDF *m*.

pdq (abbr of ***pretty damn quick***) **adv** *inf* illico presto.

PDSA (abbr of ***People's Dispensary for Sick Animals***) **n** *association britannique de soins aux animaux malades*.

PDT (abbr of ***Pacific Daylight Time***) **n** *heure d'été du Pacifique*.

PE (abbr of ***physical education***) **n** EPS *f*.

pea [piː] **n** pois *m*.

peace [piːs] **n** *(U)* paix *f* / [quiet, calm] calme *m*, tranquillité *f* ▸ **to be at peace with sthg/sb/o.s.** être en paix *OR* en accord avec qqch/qqn/soi-même ▸ **to make (one's) peace with sb** faire la paix avec qqn ▸ **we haven't had a moment's peace all morning** nous n'avons pas eu un moment de tranquillité de toute la matinée ▸ **all I want is a bit of peace and quiet** tout ce que je veux, c'est un peu de tranquillité ▸ **to have peace of mind** avoir l'esprit tranquille.

peaceable ['piːsəbl] **adj** paisible, pacifique.

peaceably ['piːsəblɪ] **adv** paisiblement, pacifiquement.

peace agreement **n** accord *m* de paix.

Peace Corps **n** *organisation américaine de coopération avec les pays en voie de développement*.

peaceful ['pi:sfʊl] **adj 1.** [quiet, calm] paisible, calme **2.** [not aggressive - person] pacifique / [- demonstration] non-violent(e).

peacefully ['pi:sfʊlɪ] **adv** paisiblement.

peacefulness ['pi:sfʊlnɪs] **n** paix *f*, calme *m*.

peacekeeper ['pi:sˌki:pəʳ] **n** [soldier] soldat *m* de la paix / [of United Nations] casque *m* bleu.

peacekeeping ['pi:sˌki:pɪŋ] ■ **n** maintien *m* de la paix. ■ **adj** de maintien de la paix ▸ **a United Nations peacekeeping force** des forces des Nations unies pour le maintien de la paix.

peacemaker ['pi:sˌmeɪkəʳ] **n** pacificateur *m*, -trice *f*.

peace negotiations **npl** négociations *fpl* pour la paix.

peace offering **n** *inf* gage *m* de paix, cadeau *m* (pour faire la paix).

peace talks **npl** pourparlers *mpl* de paix.

peacetime ['pi:staɪm] **n** temps *m* de paix.

peach [pi:tʃ] ■ **adj** couleur pêche *(inv)*.
■ **n** pêche *f*.

peach Melba [-'melbə] **n** pêche *f* Melba.

peacock ['pi:kɒk] **n** paon *m*.

peahen ['pi:hen] **n** paonne *f*.

peak [pi:k] ■ **n 1.** [mountain top] sommet *m*, cime *f* **2.** *fig* [of career, success] apogée *m*, sommet *m* **3.** [of cap] visière *f*.
■ **adj** [condition] optimum *(inv)*.
■ **vi** atteindre un niveau maximum.

peaked [pi:kt] **adj** [cap] à visière.

peak hours **npl** heures *fpl* d'affluence *OR* de pointe.

peak period **n** période *f* de pointe.

peak rate **n** tarif *m* normal.

peak viewing time **n** heures *fpl* de grande écoute.

peaky ['pi:kɪ] (comp **-ier**, superl **-iest**) **adj** *UK inf* souffrant(e), fatigué(e).

peal [pi:l] ■ **n** [of bells] carillonnement *m* / [of laughter] éclat *m* / [of thunder] coup *m*.
■ **vi** [bells] carillonner.

peanut ['pi:nʌt] **n** cacahuète *f*.

peanut butter **n** beurre *m* de cacahuètes.

pear [peəʳ] **n** poire *f*.

pearl [pɜ:l] **n** perle *f*.

pearly ['pɜ:lɪ] (comp **-ier**, superl **-iest**) **adj** nacré(e).

pear-shaped **adj** en forme de poire, piriforme.

peasant ['peznt] **n 1.** [in countryside] paysan *m*, -anne *f* **2.** *pej* [ignorant person] péquenaud *m*, -e *f*.

peasantry ['pezntrɪ] **n : the peasantry** la paysannerie, les paysans *mpl*.

peashooter ['pi:ˌʃu:təʳ] **n** sarbacane *f*.

peat [pi:t] **n** tourbe *f*.

peaty ['pi:tɪ] (comp **-ier**, superl **-iest**) **adj** tourbeux(euse).

pebble ['pebl] **n** galet *m*, caillou *m*.

pebbledash [ˌpebl'dæʃ] **n** *UK* crépi *m*.

pecan [*UK* 'pi:kən, *US* pɪ'kæn] ■ **n** [nut] (noix *f* de) pecan *m*, (noix *f* de) pacane *f* / [tree] pacanier *m*.
■ **adj** [pie, ice cream] à la noix de pecan.

peck [pek] ■ **n 1.** [with beak] coup *m* de bec **2.** [kiss] bise *f*.
■ **vt 1.** [with beak] picoter, becqueter **2.** [kiss] **: to peck sb on the cheek** faire une bise à qqn.

pecking order ['pekɪŋ-] **n** hiérarchie *f*.

peckish ['pekɪʃ] **adj** *UK inf* **: to feel peckish** avoir un petit creux.

pecs [peks] **npl** *inf* [pectorals] pectoraux *mpl*.

pectin ['pektɪn] **n** pectine *f*.

pectoral ['pektərəl] **adj** pectoral(e).

peculiar [pɪ'kju:ljəʳ] **adj 1.** [odd] bizarre, curieux(euse) **2.** [slightly ill] **: to feel peculiar** se sentir tout drôle (toute drôle) *OR* tout chose (toute chose) **3.** [characteristic] **: peculiar to** propre à, particulier(ère) à.

peculiarity [pɪˌkju:lɪ'ærətɪ] (pl **-ies**) **n 1.** [oddness] bizarrerie *f*, singularité *f* **2.** [characteristic] particularité *f*, caractéristique *f*.

peculiarly [pɪ'kju:ljəlɪ] **adv 1.** [especially] particulièrement **2.** [oddly] curieusement, bizarrement **3.** [characteristically] typiquement.

pecuniary [pɪ'kju:njərɪ] **adj** pécuniaire.

pedagogical [ˌpedə'gɒdʒɪkl] **adj** pédagogique.

pedagogy ['pedəgɒdʒɪ] **n** pédagogie *f*.

pedal ['pedl] ■ **n** pédale *f*.
■ **vi** (*UK* **-led**, cont **-ling**, *US* **-ed**, cont **-ing**) pédaler.

pedal bin **n** *UK* poubelle *f* à pédale.

pedal boat **n** pédalo *m*.

pedal car **n** voiture *f* à pédales.

pedalo ['pedələʊ] **n** *UK* pédalo *m*.

pedal pushers **npl** (pantalon *m*) corsaire *m*.

pedant ['pedənt] **n** *pej* pédant *m*, -e *f*.

pedantic [pɪ'dæntɪk] **adj** *pej* pédant(e).

pedantically [pɪ'dæntɪklɪ] **adv** *pej* de manière pédante, avec pédantisme.

pedantry ['pedəntrɪ] **n** *pej* pédantisme *m*, pédanterie *f*.

peddle ['pedl] **vt 1.** [drugs] faire le trafic de **2.** [gossip, rumour] colporter, répandre.

peddler ['pedləʳ] **n 1.** [drug dealer] trafiquant *m* de drogue **2.** *US* = ***pedlar***.

pederast ['pedəræst] *US* = ***paederast***.

pedestal ['pedɪstl] **n** piédestal *m* ▸ **to put sb on a pedestal** mettre qqn sur un piédestal.

pedestrian [pɪ'destrɪən] ■ **adj** *pej* médiocre, dépourvu(e) d'intérêt.
■ **n** piéton *m*.

pedestrian crossing **n** *UK* passage *m* pour piétons, passage clouté.

pedestrianization, *UK* ***-isation*** [pəˌdestrɪənaɪ'zeɪʃn] **n** transformation *f* en zone piétonne *OR* piétonnière.

pedestrianize, *UK* ***-ise*** [pɪ'destrɪənaɪz] **vt** transformer en zone piétonne *OR* piétonnière.

pedestrian precinct *UK*, ***pedestrian zone*** *US* n zone *f* piétonne *OR* piétonnière.

pediatric [ˌpi:dɪ'ætrɪk] *US* = ***paediatric***.

pediatrician [ˌpi:dɪə'trɪʃn] *US* = ***paediatrician***.

pediatrics [ˌpi:dɪ'ætrɪks] *US* = ***paediatrics***.

pedicure ['pedɪˌkjʊəʳ] **n** pédicurie *f*.

pedigree ['pedɪgri:] ■ **adj** [animal] de race.
■ **n 1.** [of animal] pedigree *m* **2.** [of person] ascendance *f*, généalogie *f*.

pedlar *UK*, ***peddler*** *US* ['pedləʳ] **n** colporteur *m*.

pedophile ['pedəfaɪl] *US* = ***paedophile***.

pedophilia [ˌpedəʊ'fɪlɪə] *US* = ***paedophilia***.

pee [pi:] *inf* ■ **n** pipi *m*, pisse *f* ▸ **to go for a pee** aller pisser un coup.
■ **vi** faire pipi, pisser.

peek [pi:k] *inf* ■ **n** coup *m* d'œil furtif.
■ **vi** jeter un coup d'œil furtif.

peel [pi:l] ■ **n** [of apple, potato] peau *f* / [of orange, lemon] écorce *f*.
■ **vt** éplucher, peler.
■ **vi 1.** [paint] s'écailler **2.** [wallpaper] se décoller **3.** [skin] peler.
◆ ***peel off*** **vt sep** [gen] enlever / [label] décoller, détacher.

peeler ['pi:ləʳ] **n** couteau-éplucheur *m*.

peelings ['pi:lɪŋz] **npl** épluchures *fpl*.

peep [pi:p] ■ **n 1.** [look] coup *m* d'œil *OR* regard *m* furtif **2.** *inf* [sound] bruit *m*.
■ **vi** jeter un coup d'œil furtif.
◆ ***peep out*** **vi** apparaître, se montrer.

peephole ['pi:phəʊl] **n** judas *m*.

peeping Tom [ˌpi:pɪŋ'tɒm] **n** voyeur *m*.

peep show **n** visionneuse *f*.

peer [pɪəʳ] ■ **n** pair *m*.
■ **vi** scruter, regarder attentivement.

peerage ['pɪərɪdʒ] **n** [rank] pairie *f* ▸ **the peerage** les pairs *mpl*.

peeress ['pɪərɪs] **n** pairesse *f*.

peer group **n** pairs *mpl*.

peerless ['pɪəlɪs] **adj** *fml* sans pareil.

peer pressure **n** influence *f* de ses pairs.

peeve [pi:v] **vt** *inf* mettre en rogne.

peeved [pi:vd] **adj** *inf* fâché(e), irrité(e).

peevish ['pi:vɪʃ] **adj** grincheux(euse).

peevishly ['pi:vɪʃlɪ] **adv** [say, refuse] d'un ton irrité / [behave] de façon désagréable ▸ **to complain peevishly** ronchonner.

peg [peg] ■ **n 1.** [hook] cheville *f* **2.** *UK* [for clothes] pince *f* à linge **3.** [for tent] piquet *m*.
■ **vt** (pt & pp **-ged**, cont **-ging**) *fig* [prices] bloquer.
◆ ***peg out*** **vi** *UK inf* casser sa pipe.

pegboard ['pegbɔ:d] **n** tableau *m* à trous.

PEI **abbr of *Prince Edward Island***.

pejorative [pɪ'dʒɒrətɪv] **adj** péjoratif(ive).

pekinese [ˌpi:kə'ni:z], ***pekingese*** [ˌpi:kɪŋ'i:z] **n** (pl **pekinese**) [dog] pékinois *m*.
◆ ***Pekinese***, ***Pekingese*** ■ **adj** pékinois(e).
■ **n** [person] Pékinois *m*, -e *f*.

Peking [pi:'kɪŋ] **n** Pékin.

pekingese = ***pekinese***.

pelican ['pelɪkən] (pl **pelican** *OR* **-s**) **n** pélican *m*.

pelican crossing **n** *UK passage pour piétons avec feux de circulation*.

pellet ['pelɪt] **n 1.** [small ball] boulette *f* **2.** [for gun] plomb *m*.

pell-mell [ˌpel'mel] **adv** à la débandade.

pelmet ['pelmɪt] **n** *UK* lambrequin *m*.

Peloponnese [ˌpeləpə'ni:z] **n : the Peloponnese** le Péloponnèse.

pelt [pelt] ■ **n 1.** [animal skin] peau *f*, fourrure *f* **2.** [speed] **: at full pelt** à fond de train, à toute vitesse.
■ **vt : to pelt sb (with sthg)** bombarder qqn (de qqch).
■ **vi** [run fast] **: to pelt along** courir ventre à terre ▸ **to pelt down the stairs** dévaler l'escalier.
◆ ***pelt down*** **impers vb** [rain] **: it's pelting down** il pleut à verse.

pelvic ['pelvɪk] **adj** pelvien(enne).

pelvis ['pelvɪs] (pl **-vises** *OR* **-ves** [-vi:z]) **n** pelvis *m*, bassin *m*.

pen [pen] ■ **n 1.** [for writing] stylo *m* **2.** [enclosure] parc *m*, enclos *m* **3.** *US inf* (abbr of ***penitentiary***) taule *f*.
■ **vt** (pt & pp **-ned**, cont **-ning**) **1.** *liter* [write] écrire **2.** [enclose] parquer.

penal ['pi:nl] **adj** pénal(e).

penal code **n** code *m* pénal.

penalization, *UK* ***-isation*** [ˌpi:nəlaɪ'zeɪʃn] **n** pénalisation *f*, sanction *f*.

penalize, *UK* ***-ise*** ['pi:nəlaɪz] **vt 1.** [gen] pénaliser **2.** [put at a disadvantage] désavantager.

penal settlement **n** colonie *f* pénitentiaire.

penalty ['penltɪ] (pl **-ies**) **n 1.** [punishment] pénalité *f* ▸ **to pay the penalty (for sthg)** *fig* supporter *OR* subir les conséquences (de qqch) **2.** [fine] amende *f* **3.** [in hockey] pénalité *f* ▸ **penalty (kick)** FOOTBALL penalty *m* / RUGBY (coup *m* de pied de) pénalité *f*.

penalty area **n** FOOTBALL surface *f* de réparation.

penalty box **n 1.** FOOTBALL = ***penalty area*** **2.** [in hockey] banc *m* des pénalités.

penalty clause **n** clause *f* pénale.

penalty goal **n** RUGBY but *m* de pénalité.

penalty kick ➤ ***penalty***.

penalty points **npl** [in quiz, game] gage *m* / [for drivers] points *mpl* de pénalité *(dans le système du permis à points).*

penalty spot **n** FOOTBALL point *m* de penalty.

penance ['penəns] **n** **1.** RELIG pénitence *f* **2.** *fig* [punishment] corvée *f*, pensum *m.*

pen-and-ink **adj** à la plume.

pence [pens] *UK* **npl** ➤ ***penny***.

penchant [*UK* pɑ̃ʃɑ̃, *US* 'pentʃənt] **n : to have a penchant for sthg** avoir un faible pour qqch ▸ **to have a penchant for doing sthg** avoir tendance à *OR* bien aimer faire qqch.

pencil ['pensl] ■ **n** crayon *m* ▸ **in pencil** au crayon.
■ **vt** (*UK* **-led**, cont **-ling**, *US* **-ed**, cont **-ing**) griffonner au crayon, crayonner.

pencil case **n** trousse *f (d'écolier).*

pencil sharpener **n** taille-crayon *m.*

pendant ['pendənt] **n** [jewel on chain] pendentif *m.*

pending ['pendɪŋ] *fml* ■ **adj** **1.** [imminent] imminent(e) **2.** [court case] en instance.
■ **prep** en attendant.

pending tray **n** *UK* (corbeille *f* des) affaires *fpl* en attente *OR* à traiter.

pendulum ['pendjʊləm] (pl **-s**) **n** balancier *m.*

penetrate ['penɪtreɪt] ■ **vt** **1.** [gen] pénétrer dans / [subj: light] percer / [subj: rain] s'infiltrer dans **2.** [subj: spy] infiltrer.
■ **vi** *inf* [be understood] **: it didn't penetrate** c'est resté sans effet sur lui.

penetrating ['penɪtreɪtɪŋ] **adj** pénétrant(e) / [scream, voice] perçant(e).

penetratingly ['penɪtreɪtɪŋlɪ] **adv** **1.** [loudly] **: to scream penetratingly** pousser un cri perçant **2.** *fig* avec perspicacité ▸ **she looked at him penetratingly** elle lui lança un regard pénétrant *OR* aigu.

penetration [ˌpenɪ'treɪʃn] **n** pénétration *f.*

penetrative ['penɪtrətɪv] **adj** [force] de pénétration ▸ **penetrative sex** pénétration *f.*

pen friend **n** *UK* correspondant *m*, -e *f.*

penguin ['peŋgwɪn] **n** manchot *m.*

penicillin [ˌpenɪ'sɪlɪn] **n** pénicilline *f.*

peninsula [pə'nɪnsjʊlə] (pl **-s**) **n** péninsule *f.*

penis ['pi:nɪs] (pl **penises** ['pi:nɪsɪz]) **n** pénis *m.*

penitence ['penɪtəns] **n** pénitence *f.*

penitent ['penɪtənt] **adj** repentant(e), contrit(e).

penitential [ˌpenɪ'tenʃl] ■ **adj** pénitentiel(elle).
■ **n** [book] pénitentiel *m.*

penitentiary [ˌpenɪ'tenʃərɪ] (pl **-ies**) **n** *US* prison *f.*

penknife ['pennaɪf] (pl **-knives** [-naɪvz]) **n** canif *m.*

pen name **n** pseudonyme *m.*

pennant ['penənt] **n** fanion *m*, flamme *f.*

penniless ['penɪlɪs] **adj** sans le sou.

Pennines ['penaɪnz] **npl : the Pennines** les Pennines, la chaîne Pennine.

Pennsylvania [ˌpensɪl'veɪnjə] **n** Pennsylvanie *f* ▸ **in Pennsylvania** en Pennsylvanie.

penny ['penɪ] **n** **1.** (pl **-ies**) *UK* [coin] penny *m* / *US* cent *m* **2.** (pl **pence** [pens]) *UK* [value] pence *m* ▸ **it was expensive, but it was worth every penny** c'était cher, mais j'en ai vraiment eu pour mon argent ▸ **it won't cost you a penny** ça ne vous coûtera pas un centime *OR* un sou
⏭ **they haven't got a penny to their name** *OR* **two pennies to rub together** ils n'ont pas un sou vaillant ▸ **a penny for your thoughts** à quoi penses-tu? ▸ **the penny dropped** *UK inf* j'ai compris *OR* pigé, ça a fait tilt ▸ **to spend a penny** *UK* aller au petit coin ▸ **they are two** *OR* **ten a penny** *UK inf* il y en a à la pelle.

penny-pincher [-ˌpɪntʃər] **n** pingre *mf*, radin *m*, -e *f.*

penny-pinching [-ˌpɪntʃɪŋ] ■ **adj** [person] radin(e), pingre / [attitude] mesquin(e).
■ **n** *(U)* économies *fpl* de bouts de chandelle.

penny whistle **n** pipeau *m.*

pen pal **n** *inf* correspondant *m*, -e *f.*

pension ['penʃn] **n** **1.** [on retirement] retraite *f* **2.** [from disability] pension *f* **3.** ['pɑ̃sjɔ̃] [small hotel] pension *f* de famille.
◆ ***pension off*** **vt sep** mettre à la retraite.

CULTURE

Pension

Divers régimes de retraite existent au Royaume-Uni : l'État verse une pension publique (**old age pension** ou **retirement pension**), d'un montant unique peu élevé, à partir de 60 ans aux femmes et à 65 ans aux hommes. La **State pension** (**retraite d'État**) est calculée sur les revenus et le paiement de cotisations auprès de l'Assurance nationale. De nos jours, peu d'entreprises britanniques proposent un régime de retraite, qu'il soit financé par cotisation partagée entre l'employé et l'employeur, ou entièrement pris en charge par l'employeur. Afin d'épargner pour leur retraite, les gens sont donc contraints d'investir dans des fonds de pensions privés, en bénéficiant de modes de paiement flexibles.

pensionable ['penʃənəbl] **adj : to be of pensionable age** avoir l'âge de la retraite.

pension book **n** *UK* livret *m* de retraite.

pensioner ['penʃənər] **n** *UK* **: (old-age) pensioner** retraité *m*, -e *f.*

pension fund **n** caisse *f* de retraite.

pension plan, pension scheme *UK* **n** plan *m OR* régime *m* de retraite.

pensive ['pensɪv] **adj** songeur(euse).

pentagon ['pentəgən] **n** pentagone *m*.
◆ ***Pentagon*** **n** *US* **: the Pentagon** le Pentagone *(siège du ministère américain de la Défense)*.

CULTURE
Pentagon

Situé près de la capitale Washington, le Pentagone regroupe les quartiers généraux du département de la Défense américain : c'est l'un des plus vastes bâtiments administratifs du monde. Le 11 septembre 2001, un avion percute une portion de l'édifice, qui vient d'être rénové et qui n'est fort heureusement occupé qu'en partie : 189 personnes périssent dans l'attentat mais le nombre de victimes aurait pu être bien plus élevé si tous les employés s'étaient trouvés sur la zone. Les réparations, qui ont coûté 501 millions de dollars, ont été achevées un an après le drame.

pentagonal [pen'tægənl] **adj** pentagonal(e).

pentathlon [pen'tæθlən] (pl **-s**) **n** pentathlon *m*.

Pentecost ['pentɪkɒst] **n** Pentecôte *f*.

penthouse ['penthaʊs] (pl [-haʊzɪz]) **n** appartement *m* de luxe (au dernier étage).

pent-up ['pent-] **adj** [emotions] refoulé(e) / [energy] contenu(e).

penultimate [pe'nʌltɪmət] **adj** avant-dernier(ère).

penury ['penjʊrɪ] **n** *fml* indigence *f*, misère *f*.

peony ['pɪənɪ] (pl **-ies**) **n** pivoine *f*.

people ['pi:pl] ■ **n** [nation, race] nation *f*, peuple *m*.
■ **npl 1.** [persons] personnes *fpl* ▸ **few/a lot of people** peu/beaucoup de monde, peu/beaucoup de gens ▸ **there were a lot of people present** il y avait beaucoup de monde
2. [in general] gens *mpl* ▸ **people won't like it** les gens ne vont pas aimer ça ▸ **rich/poor/blind people** les riches/pauvres/aveugles ▸ **young people** les jeunes ▸ **old people** les personnes âgées ▸ **people say that...** on dit que... ▸ **people say it's impossible** on dit que c'est impossible
3. [inhabitants] habitants *mpl* ▸ **Danish people** les Danois ▸ **the people of Brazil** les Brésiliens ▸ **the people of Glasgow** les habitants de Glasgow
4. POL **: the people** le peuple.
■ **vt : to be peopled by** *OR* **with** être peuplé(e) de.

people carrier **n** *UK* monospace *m*.

People's Republic of China **n : the People's Republic of China** la République populaire de Chine.

pep [pep] **n** *(U) inf* entrain *m*, pep *m*.
◆ ***pep up*** (pt & pp **-ped**, cont **-ping**) **vt sep** *inf* **1.** [person] remonter, requinquer **2.** [party, event] animer.

PEP (abbr of ***personal equity plan***) **n** *en Grande-Bretagne, plan d'épargne en actions exonéré d'impôt*.

pepper ['pepər] **n 1.** [spice] poivre *m* ▸ **black/white pepper** poivre noir/blanc **2.** [vegetable] poivron *m* ▸ **red/green pepper** poivron *m* rouge/vert.

pepperbox ['pepəbɒks] **n** *US* = ***pepper pot***.

peppercorn ['pepəkɔ:n] **n** grain *m* de poivre.

peppered ['pepəd] **adj 1.** [essay, speech] **: peppered (with)** truffé(e) (de) **2.** [walls] **: peppered (with)** criblé(e) (de).

pepper mill **n** moulin *m* à poivre.

peppermint ['pepəmɪnt] **n 1.** [sweet] bonbon *m* à la menthe **2.** [herb] menthe *f* poivrée.

pepper pot *UK*, ***pepperbox*** *US* ['pepəbɒks] **n** poivrier *m*.

peppery ['pepərɪ] **adj** poivré(e).

pep talk **n** *inf* paroles *fpl* *OR* discours *m* d'encouragement.

peptic ulcer ['peptɪk-] **n** ulcère *m* gastro-duodénal.

per [pɜ:r] **prep : per person** par personne ▸ **to be paid £10 per hour** être payé 10 livres de l'heure ▸ **per kilo** le kilo ▸ **as per instructions** conformément aux instructions.

per annum **adv** par an.

P-E ratio (abbr of ***price-earnings ratio***) **n** *indice de rentabilité d'une valeur*.

per capita [pə'kæpɪtə] **adj & adv** par personne.

perceive [pə'si:v] **vt 1.** [notice] percevoir **2.** [understand, realize] remarquer, s'apercevoir de **3.** [consider] **: to perceive sb/sthg as** considérer qqn/qqch comme.

perceived quality [pə'si:vd-] **n** qualité *f* perçue.

perceived value [pə'si:vd-] **n** valeur *f* perçue.

percent [pə'sent] **adv** pour cent.

percentage [pə'sentɪdʒ] **n** pourcentage *m*.

perceptible [pə'septəbl] **adj** sensible.

perceptibly [pə'septəblɪ] **adv** [diminish, change] sensiblement / [move] de manière perceptible ▸ **she was perceptibly thinner** elle avait sensiblement maigri.

perception [pə'sepʃn] **n 1.** [aural, visual] perception *f* **2.** [insight] perspicacité *f*, intuition *f* **3.** [opinion] opinion *f*.

perceptive [pə'septɪv] **adj** perspicace.

perceptively [pə'septɪvlɪ] **adv** de manière perspicace.

perceptiveness [pə'septɪvnɪs] **n** perspicacité *f*, pénétration *f*.

perch [pɜ:tʃ] ■ **n 1.** *lit* & *fig* [position] perchoir *m* **2.** (pl **perch** *OR* **-es**) [fish] perche *f*.
■ **vi** se percher.

percolate ['pɜ:kəleɪt] **vi 1.** [coffee] passer **2.** *fig* [news] s'infiltrer, filtrer.

percolator ['pɜ:kəleɪtər] **n** cafetière *f* à pression.

percussion [pə'kʌʃn] **n** MUS percussion *f* ▸ **the percussion (section)** la batterie, la percussion.

percussion instrument **n** MUS instrument *m* à percussion.

percussionist [pəˈkʌʃənɪst] **n** percussionniste *mf*.

peremptory [pəˈremptərɪ] **adj** péremptoire.

perennial [pəˈrenjəl] ■ **adj** permanent(e), perpétuel(elle) / BOT vivace.
■ **n** BOT plante *f* vivace.

perestroika [ˌperəˈstrɔɪkə] **n** perestroïka *f*.

perfect ■ **adj** [ˈpɜːfɪkt] parfait(e) ▸ **Monday is perfect for me** lundi me convient parfaitement ▸ **you have a perfect right to be here** vous avez parfaitement *OR* tout à fait le droit d'être ici ▸ **nobody's perfect** personne n'est parfait ▸ **he's a perfect nuisance** il est absolument insupportable.
■ **n** [ˈpɜːfɪkt] GRAM **: perfect (tense)** parfait *m*.
■ **vt** [pəˈfekt] parfaire, mettre au point.

perfect competition [ˈpɜːfɪkt-] **n** ECON concurrence *f* parfaite.

perfection [pəˈfekʃn] **n** perfection *f* ▸ **to perfection** parfaitement (bien).

perfectionism [pəˈfekʃənɪzm] **n** perfectionnisme *m*.

perfectionist [pəˈfekʃənɪst] **n** perfectionniste *mf*.

perfectly [ˈpɜːfɪktlɪ] **adv** parfaitement ▸ **you know perfectly well** tu sais très bien.

perfect pitch **n** MUS **: to have perfect pitch** avoir l'oreille absolue.

perfidious [pəˈfɪdɪəs] **adj** *liter* perfide.

perfidy [ˈpɜːfɪdɪ] (pl **-ies**) **n** *liter* perfidie *f*.

perforate [ˈpɜːfəreɪt] **vt** perforer.

perforated [ˈpɜːfəreɪtɪd] **adj** perforé(e), percé(e) ▸ **to have a perforated eardrum** avoir un tympan perforé *OR* crevé ▸ **tear along the perforated line** détacher suivant les pointillés.

perforation [ˌpɜːfəˈreɪʃn] **n** perforation *f*.

perforations [ˌpɜːfəˈreɪʃnz] **npl** [in paper] pointillés *mpl*.

perform [pəˈfɔːm] ■ **vt 1.** [carry out - gen] exécuter / [- function] remplir ▸ **to perform an operation** MED opérer **2.** [play, concert] jouer.
■ **vi 1.** [machine] marcher, fonctionner / [team, person] **: to perform well/badly** avoir de bons/mauvais résultats ▸ **the car performs well/badly in wet conditions** cette voiture a une bonne/mauvaise tenue de route par temps de pluie ▸ **the Miami branch is not performing well** les résultats de la succursale de Miami ne sont pas très satisfaisants ▸ **how does she perform under pressure?** comment réagit-elle lorsqu'elle est sous pression? **2.** [actor] jouer / [singer] chanter.

performance [pəˈfɔːməns] **n 1.** [carrying out] exécution *f* **2.** [show] représentation *f* **3.** [by actor, singer] interprétation *f* **4.** [by sportsman, politician] performance *f*, prestation *f* ▸ **the country's poor economic performance** les mauvais résultats économiques du pays ▸ **sterling's performance on the Stock Exchange** le comportement en bourse de la livre sterling **5.** [of car, engine] performance *f*.

performance appraisal **n** [system] système *m* d'évaluation / [individual] évaluation *f*.

performance art **n** art *m* de représentation.

performance car **n** voiture *f* à hautes performances *OR* très performante.

performance-related **adj** en fonction du mérite *OR* résultat ▸ **performance-related pay** salaire *m* au mérite.

performer [pəˈfɔːməʳ] **n** artiste *mf*, interprète *mf*.

performing [pəˈfɔːmɪŋ] **adj** [bear, dog] savant(e).

performing arts **npl : the performing arts** les arts *mpl* du spectacle.

perfume [ˈpɜːfjuːm] **n** parfum *m*.

perfumed [*UK* ˈpɜːfjuːmd, *US* pərˈfjuːmd] **adj** parfumé(e).

perfumery [pəˈfjuːmərɪ] (pl **-ies**) **n** parfumerie *f*.

perfunctory [pəˈfʌŋktərɪ] **adj** rapide, superficiel(elle).

perhaps [pəˈhæps] **adv** peut-être ▸ **perhaps so/not** peut-être que oui/non.

peril [ˈperɪl] **n** danger *m*, péril *m* ▸ **at one's peril** à ses risques et périls.

perilous [ˈperələs] **adj** dangereux(euse), périlleux(euse).

perilously [ˈperələslɪ] **adv** dangereusement.

perimeter [pəˈrɪmɪtəʳ] **n** périmètre *m* ▸ **perimeter fence** clôture *f* ▸ **perimeter wall** mur *m* d'enceinte.

period [ˈpɪərɪəd] ■ **n 1.** [gen] période *f* ▸ **within a period of a few months** en l'espace de quelques mois ▸ **we have a two-month period in which to do it** nous avons un délai de deux mois pour le faire ▸ **at that period in her life** à cette époque de sa vie **2.** SCH ≃ heure *f* **3.** [menstruation] règles *fpl* **4.** *US* [full stop] point *m*.
■ **comp** [dress, house] d'époque.

periodic [ˌpɪərɪˈɒdɪk] **adj** périodique.

periodical [ˌpɪərɪˈɒdɪkl] ■ **adj** = ***periodic***.
■ **n** [magazine] périodique *m*.

periodically [ˌpɪərɪˈɒdɪklɪ] **adv** périodiquement, de temps en temps.

periodic table **n** tableau *m* de Mendéleïev.

period pains **npl** règles *fpl* douloureuses.

period piece **n** [furniture] meuble *m* d'époque.

peripatetic [ˌperɪpəˈtetɪk] **adj** [salesman] itinérant(e) / [teacher] qui enseigne dans plusieurs écoles.

peripheral [pəˈrɪfərəl] ■ **adj 1.** [unimportant] secondaire **2.** [at edge] périphérique.
■ **n** COMPUT périphérique *m*.

periphery [pəˈrɪfərɪ] (pl **-ies**) **n** [edge] périphérie *f*.

periphrasis [pə'rɪfrəsɪs] (pl -ses [-si:z]) **n** périphrase *f*, circonlocution *f*.

periscope ['perɪskəʊp] **n** périscope *m*.

perish ['perɪʃ] **vi 1.** [die] périr, mourir **2.** [food] pourrir, se gâter / [rubber] se détériorer.

perishable ['perɪʃəbl] **adj** périssable.
◆ ***perishables*** **npl** denrées *fpl* périssables.

perishing ['perɪʃɪŋ] **adj** *UK inf* **1.** [cold] très froid(e) **2.** [damn] sacré(e).

peritonitis [,perɪtə'naɪtɪs] **n** *(U)* péritonite *f*.

perjure ['pɜ:dʒəʳ] **vt** LAW **: to perjure o.s.** se parjurer.

perjurer ['pɜ:dʒərəʳ] **n** faux témoin *m*.

perjury ['pɜ:dʒərɪ] **n** *(U)* LAW parjure *m*, faux témoignage *m*.

perk [pɜ:k] **n** *inf* à-côté *m*, avantage *m*.
◆ ***perk up*** **vi** se ragaillardir.

perky ['pɜ:kɪ] (comp **-ier**, superl **-iest**) **adj** *inf* [cheerful] guilleret(ette) / [lively] plein(e) d'entrain.

perm [pɜ:m] ■ **n** permanente *f*.
■ **vt : to have one's hair permed** se faire faire une permanente.

permanence ['pɜ:mənəns] **n** permanence *f*.

permanent ['pɜ:mənənt] ■ **adj** permanent(e) ▸ **are you here on a permanent basis?** êtes-vous ici à titre définitif? ▸ **permanent staff** [gen] personnel *m* permanent / [in public service] personnel *m* titulaire ▸ **a permanent post** [gen] un emploi permanent / [in public service] un poste de titulaire.
■ **n** *US* [perm] permanente *f*.

permanently ['pɜ:mənəntlɪ] **adv 1.** [blind, damaged] définitivement, de manière permanente **2.** [closed, available] en permanence.

permeable ['pɜ:mjəbl] **adj** perméable.

permeate ['pɜ:mɪeɪt] **vt 1.** [subj: liquid, smell] s'infiltrer dans, pénétrer **2.** [subj: feeling, idea] se répandre dans.

permissible [pə'mɪsəbl] **adj** *fml* acceptable, admissible.

permission [pə'mɪʃn] **n** permission *f*, autorisation *f* ▸ **to give sb permission to do sthg** donner à qqn la permission de faire qqch ▸ **who gave them permission?** qui le leur a permis ? ▸ **to ask for permission to do sthg** demander la permission OR l'autorisation de faire qqch ▸ **to have permission to do sthg** avoir la permission OR l'autorisation de faire qqch.

permissive [pə'mɪsɪv] **adj** permissif(ive).

permissiveness [pə'mɪsɪvnɪs] **n** permissivité *f*.

permit ■ **vt** (pt & pp **-ted**, cont **-ting** [pə'mɪt]) permettre ▸ **to permit sb to do sthg** permettre à qqn de faire qqch, autoriser qqn à faire qqch ▸ **you are not permitted to enter the building** vous n'avez pas le droit de pénétrer dans l'immeuble ▸ **to permit sb sthg** permettre qqch à qqn ▸ **smoking is not permitted upstairs** il est interdit de fumer à l'étage ▸ **weather permitting** si le temps le permet.
■ **n** ['pɜ:mɪt] permis *m*.

permutation [,pɜ:mju:'teɪʃn] **n** permutation *f*.

pernicious [pə'nɪʃəs] **adj** *fml* [harmful] pernicieux(euse).

pernickety [pə'nɪkətɪ] **adj** *UK inf* [fussy] tatillon(onne), pointilleux(euse).

peroxide [pə'rɒksaɪd] **n** peroxyde *m*.

peroxide blonde **n** blonde *f* décolorée.

perpendicular [,pɜ:pən'dɪkjʊləʳ] ■ **adj** perpendiculaire.
■ **n** perpendiculaire *f*.

perpetrate ['pɜ:pɪtreɪt] **vt** perpétrer, commettre.

perpetration [,pɜ:pɪ'treɪʃn] **n** perpétration *f*.

perpetrator ['pɜ:pɪtreɪtəʳ] **n** auteur *m*.

perpetual [pə'petʃʊəl] **adj 1.** *pej* [continuous] continuel(elle), incessant(e) **2.** [long-lasting] perpétuel(elle).

perpetually [pə'petʃʊəlɪ] **adv 1.** *pej* [continuously] sans cesse, continuellement **2.** [for ever] toujours, constamment.

perpetual motion **n** mouvement *m* perpétuel.

perpetuate [pə'petʃʊeɪt] **vt** perpétuer.

perpetuation [pə,petʃʊ'eɪʃn] **n** perpétuation *f*.

perpetuity [,pɜ:pɪ'tju:ətɪ] **n : in perpetuity** *fml* à perpétuité.

perplex [pə'pleks] **vt** rendre perplexe.

perplexed [pə'plekst] **adj** perplexe.

perplexing [pə'pleksɪŋ] **adj** déroutant(e), déconcertant(e).

perplexity [pə'pleksətɪ] **n** perplexité *f*.

perquisite ['pɜ:kwɪzɪt] **n** *fml* à-côté *m*, avantage *m*.

HOW TO ...
ask for permission

Est-ce que je peux me servir de l'ordinateur ? / Can I use the computer?
Est-ce que je peux m'asseoir ? / May I sit here?
J'emprunte ta voiture, d'accord ? / Is it OK if I borrow your car?
Ça te dérange si je fume ? / Do you mind if I smoke?
Je peux vous prendre cette chaise ? / Can I take this chair?

per se [pɜː'seɪ] **adv** *fml* en tant que tel (telle), en soi.

persecute ['pɜːsɪkjuːt] **vt** persécuter, tourmenter.

persecution [ˌpɜːsɪ'kjuːʃn] **n** persécution *f*.

persecutor ['pɜːsɪkjuːtəʳ] **n** persécuteur *m*, -trice *f*.

perseverance [ˌpɜːsɪ'vɪərəns] **n** persévérance *f*, ténacité *f*.

persevere [ˌpɜːsɪ'vɪəʳ] **vi 1.** [with difficulty] persévérer, persister ▸ **to persevere with** persévérer *OR* persister dans **2.** [with determination] **: to persevere in doing sthg** persister à faire qqch.

Persia ['pɜːʃə] **n** Perse *f* ▸ **in Persia** en Perse.

Persian ['pɜːʃn] ■ **adj** persan(e) / HIST perse.
■ **n 1.** [person] Persan *m*, -e *f* / HIST Perse *mf* **2.** [language] persan *m*.

Persian cat **n** chat *m* persan.

Persian Gulf **n : the Persian Gulf** le golfe Persique.

persist [pə'sɪst] **vi : to persist (in doing sthg)** persister *OR* s'obstiner (à faire qqch).

persistence [pə'sɪstəns] **n** persistance *f*.

persistent [pə'sɪstənt] **adj 1.** [noise, rain] continuel(elle) / [problem] constant(e) **2.** [determined] tenace, obstiné(e).

persistently [pə'sɪstəntlɪ] **adv 1.** [constantly] continuellement, constamment **2.** [determinedly] obstinément, avec persévérance.

persnickety [pə'snɪkɪtɪ] **adj** *US* tatillon(onne), pointilleux(euse).

person ['pɜːsn] (pl **people** ['piːpl] *OR* **persons**) *fml* **n 1.** [man or woman] personne *f* ▸ **in person** en personne ▸ **in the person of** en la personne de **2.** *fml* [body] **: about one's person** sur soi.

persona [pə'səʊnə] (pl **-s** *OR* **-ae** [-iː]) **n** personnage *m*.

personable ['pɜːsnəbl] **adj** sympathique, agréable.

personage ['pɜːsənɪdʒ] **n** personnage *m*.

personal ['pɜːsənl] ■ **adj 1.** [gen] personnel(elle) ▸ **personal belongings** *OR* **possessions** objets *mpl* personnels ▸ **just a few personal friends** rien que quelques amis intimes ▸ **my personal opinion is that he drowned** personnellement, je crois qu'il s'est noyé ▸ **the boss made a personal visit to the scene** le patron est venu lui-même *OR* en personne sur les lieux **2.** *pej* [rude] désobligeant(e) ▸ **there's no need to be so personal!** ce n'est pas la peine de t'en prendre à moi! ▸ **nothing personal!** ne le prenez pas pour vous!, n'y voyez rien de personnel!
■ **n** *US* petite annonce *f* (pour rencontres).

personal account **n** compte *m* personnel.

personal ad **n** *inf* petite annonce *f (pour rencontres)*.

personal allowance **n** *UK* [tax] abattement *m*.

personal assistant **n** secrétaire *mf* de direction.

personal call **n** communication *f* téléphonique privée.

personal column **n** petites annonces *fpl*.

personal computer **n** ordinateur *m* personnel *OR* individuel.

personal estate **n** *(U)* biens *mpl* personnels.

personal hygiene **n** hygiène *f* corporelle.

personality [ˌpɜːsə'nælətɪ] (pl **-ies**) **n** personnalité *f*.

personality disorder **n** trouble *m* de la personnalité.

personalize, *UK* ***-ise*** ['pɜːsənəlaɪz] **vt 1.** [mark with name] personnaliser **2.** [make too personal] rendre trop personnel(elle).

personalized, *UK* ***-ised*** ['pɜːsənəlaɪzd] **adj 1.** [marked with name] personnalisé(e) **2.** [for one person] personnel(elle).

personal loan **n** prêt *m* personnel *OR* personnalisé.

personally ['pɜːsnəlɪ] **adv** personnellement ▸ **personally (speaking), I think it's a silly idea** pour ma part *OR* en ce qui me concerne, je trouve que c'est une idée stupide ▸ **I was not personally involved in the project** je n'ai pas participé directement au projet ▸ **deliver the letter to the director personally** remettez la lettre en mains propres au directeur ▸ **to take sthg personally** se sentir visé(e) par qqch.

personal organizer, ***-iser*** *UK* **n** organiseur *m*.

personal pension plan **n** retraite *f* personnelle.

personal pronoun **n** pronom *m* personnel.

personal property **n** *(U)* LAW biens *mpl* personnels.

personal stereo **n** baladeur *m*, Walkman® *m*.

persona non grata [-'grɑːtə] (pl **personae non gratae** [-'grɑːtiː]) **n** persona non grata.

person-hour **n** = ***man-hour***.

personification [pəˌsɒnɪfɪ'keɪʃn] **n** personnification *f* ▸ **he is the personification of evil** c'est le mal personnifié *OR* en personne.

personify [pə'sɒnɪfaɪ] (pt & pp **-ied**) **vt** personnifier.

personnel [ˌpɜːsə'nel] ■ **n** *(U)* [department] service *m* du personnel.
■ **npl** [staff] personnel *m*.

personnel department **n** service *m* du personnel.

personnel officer **n** responsable *mf* du personnel.

person-to-person **adj** *esp US* avec préavis.

perspective [pə'spektɪv] **n 1.** ART perspective *f* ▸ **to draw sthg in perspective** dessiner qqch en perspective ▸ **the houses are out of perspective** la perspective des maisons est fausse ▸ **to get sthg in perspective** *fig* mettre qqch dans son contexte ▸ **to get things out of perspective** perdre le sens des proportions **2.** [view, judgment] point *m* de vue, optique *f* ▸ **it gives you a different perspective on the problem** cela vous permet de voir le problème sous un angle *OR* un jour différent.

Perspex® ['pɜːspeks] **n** *UK* ≃ Plexiglas® *m*.

perspicacious [ˌpɜːspɪˈkeɪʃəs] **adj** *fml* perspicace.

perspicacity [ˌpɜːspɪˈkæsətɪ] **n** *fml* perspicacité *f*.

perspiration [ˌpɜːspəˈreɪʃn] **n 1.** [sweat] sueur *f* **2.** [act of perspiring] transpiration *f*.

perspire [pəˈspaɪər] **vi** transpirer, suer.

persuade [pəˈsweɪd] **vt : to persuade sb to do sthg** persuader *OR* convaincre qqn de faire qqch ▸ **to persuade sb that** convaincre qqn que ▸ **to persuade sb of** convaincre qqn de.

persuasion [pəˈsweɪʒn] **n 1.** [act of persuading] persuasion *f* **2.** [belief - religious] confession *f* / [- political] opinion *f*, conviction *f*.

persuasive [pəˈsweɪsɪv] **adj** [person] persuasif(ive) / [argument] convaincant(e).

persuasively [pəˈsweɪsɪvlɪ] **adv** d'un ton persuasif, d'une manière convaincante.

persuasiveness [pəˈsweɪsɪvnəs] **n** force *f* de persuasion.

pert [pɜːt] **adj** mutin(e), coquin(e).

pertain [pəˈteɪn] **vi** *fml* **: pertaining to** concernant, relatif(ive) à.

pertinence [ˈpɜːtɪnəns] **n** pertinence *f*.

pertinent [ˈpɜːtɪnənt] **adj** pertinent(e), approprié(e).

pertly [ˈpɜːtlɪ] **adv** [reply] avec effronterie / [dress] coquettement.

perturb [pəˈtɜːb] **vt** inquiéter, troubler.

perturbed [pəˈtɜːbd] **adj** inquiet(ète), troublé(e).

perturbing [pəˈtɜːbɪŋ] **adj** inquiétant(e), troublant(e).

Peru [pəˈruː] **n** Pérou *m* ▸ **in Peru** au Pérou.

perusal [pəˈruːzl] **n** *fml* lecture *f* attentive.

peruse [pəˈruːz] **vt** *fml* lire attentivement.

Peruvian [pəˈruːvjən] ■ **adj** péruvien(enne).
■ **n** [person] Péruvien *m*, -enne *f*.

perv [pɜːv] **n** *UK inf* détraqué *m* (sexuel), détraquée *f* (sexuelle).

pervade [pəˈveɪd] **vt** *fml* [subj: smell] se répandre dans / [subj: feeling, influence] envahir.

pervasive [pəˈveɪsɪv] **adj** *fml* pénétrant(e), envahissant(e).

perverse [pəˈvɜːs] **adj** [contrary - person] contrariant(e) / [- enjoyment] malin(igne).

perversely [pəˈvɜːslɪ] **adv** [contrarily] par esprit de contradiction.

perverseness [pəˈvɜːsnɪs] **n** [stubbornness] entêtement *m*, obstination *f* / [unreasonableness, contrariness] esprit *m* de contradiction.

perversion [*UK* pəˈvɜːʃn, *US* pəˈvɜːrʒn] **n 1.** [sexual] perversion *f* **2.** [of truth] travestissement *m*.

perversity [pəˈvɜːsətɪ] **n** [contrariness] caractère *m* contrariant, esprit *m* de contradiction.

pervert ■ **n** [ˈpɜːvɜːt] pervers *m*, -e *f*.
■ **vt** [pəˈvɜːt] **1.** [truth, meaning] travestir, déformer / [course of justice] entraver **2.** [sexually] pervertir.

perverted [pəˈvɜːtɪd] **adj 1.** [sexually] pervers(e) **2.** [reasoning] tordu(e).

peseta [pəˈseɪtə] **n** peseta *f*.

pesky [ˈpeskɪ] (comp **-ier**, superl **-iest**) **adj** *esp US inf* fichu(e).

peso [ˈpeɪsəʊ] (pl **-s**) **n** peso *m*.

pessary [ˈpesərɪ] (pl **-ies**) **n** [medicine] ovule *m*.

pessimism [ˈpesɪmɪzm] **n** pessimisme *m*.

pessimist [ˈpesɪmɪst] **n** pessimiste *mf*.

pessimistic [ˌpesɪˈmɪstɪk] **adj** pessimiste.

pest [pest] **n 1.** [insect] insecte *m* nuisible / [animal] animal *m* nuisible **2.** *inf* [nuisance] casse-pieds *mf inv*.

pester [ˈpestər] **vt** harceler, importuner.

pesticide [ˈpestɪsaɪd] **n** pesticide *m*.

pestilence [ˈpestɪləns] **n** *liter* peste *f*, pestilence *f*.

pestle [ˈpesl] **n** pilon *m*.

pet [pet] ■ **adj** [favourite] **: pet subject** dada *m* ▸ **pet hate** bête *f* noire.
■ **n 1.** [animal] animal *m* (familier) **2.** [favourite person] chouchou *m*, -oute *f*.
■ **vt** (pt & pp **-ted**, cont **-ting**) caresser, câliner.
■ **vi** (pt & pp **-ted**, cont **-ting**) se peloter, se caresser.

petal [ˈpetl] **n** pétale *m*.

peter [ˈpiːtər] ◆ ***peter out*** **vi** [path] s'arrêter, se perdre / [interest] diminuer, décliner.

pethidine [ˈpeθɪdiːn] **n** péthidine *f*.

HOW TO ...

express persuasion

Persuading someone to do something

S'il te plaît, fais un effort, parle lui / Go on, make an effort and talk to him
Allez, sois gentille, prête-moi ta voiture / Oh go on, do me a favour and lend me your car
Vas-y, appelle-le ! / Go on, give him a ring!
Allez, viens, tu es sûr que tu ne veux pas venir ? / Come on, are you sure you don't want to come?
Je vous assure, vous ne regretterez pas / I promise you, you won't regret it

Persuading someone not to do something

Tu as bien réfléchi ? Tu es sûr de vouloir y aller ? / Have you thought carefully about this? Are you sure you want to go?
Si j'étais toi, je n'irais pas / If I were you, I wouldn't go
N'y va pas, ça ne va pas te plaire / Don't go: you won't like it
À ta place, j'y réfléchirais à deux fois avant d'accepter / If I were you, I'd think twice about it before accepting

petit bourgeois [pəˌti:ˈbʊəʒwɑ:] ■ **adj** petit-bourgeois (petite-bourgeoise).
■ **n** (pl **petits bourgeois** [pəˌti:ˈbʊəʒwɑ:]) petit-bourgeois *m*, petite-bourgeoise *f*.

petite [pəˈti:t] **adj** menu(e).

petit four [ˌpetiˈfɔ:] (pl **petits fours** [petiˈfɔ:z]) **n** petit-four *m*.

petition [pɪˈtɪʃn] ■ **n** pétition *f*.
■ **vt** adresser une pétition à.
■ **vi 1.** [campaign] **: to petition for/against** faire une pétition en faveur de/contre **2.** LAW **: to petition for divorce** faire une demande en divorce.

petitioner [pɪˈtɪʃənəʳ] **n** pétitionnaire *mf*.

pet name **n** petit nom *m*.

petrified [ˈpetrɪfaɪd] **adj** [terrified] paralysé(e) ***OR*** pétrifié(e) de peur.

petrify [ˈpetrɪfaɪ] (pt & pp **-ied**) **vt** [terrify] paralyser ***OR*** pétrifier de peur.

petrochemical [ˌpetrəʊˈkemɪkl] **adj** pétrochimique.

petrodollar [ˈpetrəʊˌdɒləʳ] **n** FIN pétrodollar *m*.

petrol [ˈpetrəl] **n** *UK* essence *f*.

petrolatum [ˌpetrəˈleɪtəm] **n** *US* vaseline *f*.

petrol bomb **n** *UK* cocktail *m* Molotov.

petrol can **n** *UK* bidon *m* à essence.

petrol cap **n** *UK* bouchon *m* d'essence.

petrol-driven **adj** *UK* [engine] à essence.

petrol engine **n** *UK* moteur *m* à essence.

petroleum [pɪˈtrəʊljəm] **n** pétrole *m*.

petroleum jelly **n** vaseline *f*.

petrol gauge **n** *UK* jauge *f* à essence.

petrol pump **n** *UK* pompe *f* à essence.

petrol station **n** *UK* station-service *f*.

petrol tank **n** *UK* réservoir *m* d'essence.

petrol tanker **n** *UK* **1.** [lorry] camion-citerne *m* **2.** [ship] pétrolier *m*, tanker *m*.

pet shop **n** animalerie *f*.

petticoat [ˈpetɪkəʊt] **n** jupon *m*.

pettiness [ˈpetɪnɪs] **n** [small-mindedness] mesquinerie *f*, étroitesse *f* d'esprit.

petty [ˈpetɪ] (comp **-ier**, superl **-iest**) **adj 1.** [small-minded] mesquin(e) **2.** [trivial] insignifiant(e), sans importance.

petty cash **n** *(U)* caisse *f* des dépenses courantes.

petty larceny **n** *US* larcin *m*.

petty-minded **adj** borné(e), mesquin(e).

petty officer **n** second maître *m*.

petulance [ˈpetjʊləns] **n** irritabilité *f*.

petulant [ˈpetjʊlənt] **adj** irritable.

petulantly [ˈpetjʊləntlɪ] **adv** [act, speak - irritably] avec irritation / [- sulkily] avec mauvaise humeur ▸ **"no!", she said petulantly** "non ! ", dit-elle avec mauvaise humeur.

pew [pju:] **n** banc *m* d'église.

pewter [ˈpju:təʳ] **n** étain *m*.

PG (abbr of ***parental guidance***) *en Grande-Bretagne, désigne un film pour lequel l'avis des parents est recommandé.*

PGA (abbr of ***Professional Golfers' Association***) **n** *association de joueurs de golf professionnels.*

pH **n** pH *m*.

PH (abbr of ***Purple Heart***) **n** *distinction militaire américaine.*

PHA (abbr of ***Public Housing Administration***) **n** *services du logement social aux États-Unis.*

phalanx [ˈfælæŋks] (pl **-es** ***OR*** **phalanges** [-lændʒi:z]) **n 1.** [in ancient armies] phalange *f* **2.** ANAT phalange *f* **3.** POL phalange *f*.

phallic [ˈfælɪk] **adj** phallique ▸ **phallic symbol** symbole *m* phallique.

phallus [ˈfæləs] (pl **-es** [-i:z] ***OR*** **phalli** [ˈfælaɪ]) **n** phallus *m*.

phantasm [ˈfæntæzm] **n** fantasme *m*.

phantom [ˈfæntəm] ■ **adj** fantomatique, spectral(e).
■ **n** [ghost] fantôme *m*.

phantom pregnancy **n** grossesse *f* nerveuse, fausse grossesse.

pharaoh [ˈfeərəʊ] **n** pharaon *m*.

Pharisee [ˈfærɪsi:] **n** Pharisien *m*, -enne *f*.

pharmaceutical [ˌfɑ:məˈsju:tɪkl] **adj** pharmaceutique.
◆ ***pharmaceuticals*** **npl** produits *mpl* pharmaceutiques.

pharmacist [ˈfɑ:məsɪst] **n** pharmacien *m*, -enne *f*.

pharmacological [ˌfɑ:məkəˈlɒdʒɪkl] **adj** pharmacologique.

pharmacologist [ˌfɑ:məˈkɒlədʒɪst] **n** pharmacologiste *mf*, pharmacologue *mf*.

pharmacology [ˌfɑ:məˈkɒlədʒɪ] **n** pharmacologie *f*.

pharmacy [ˈfɑ:məsɪ] (pl **-ies**) **n** pharmacie *f*.

pharyngitis [ˌfærɪnˈdʒaɪtɪs] **n** *(U)* pharyngite *f*.

pharynx [ˈfærɪŋks] (pl **-es** ***OR*** **pharynges** [fæˈrɪndʒi:z]) **n** pharynx *m*.

phase [feɪz] ■ **n** phase *f* ▸ **don't worry: it's just a phase she's going through** ne vous inquiétez pas, ça lui passera.
■ **vt** faire progressivement.
◆ ***phase in*** **vt sep** introduire progressivement ▸ **the increases will be phased in over five years** les augmentations seront échelonnées sur cinq ans.
◆ ***phase out*** **vt sep** supprimer progressivement.

phased [feɪzd] **adj** [withdrawal, development] progressif(ive), par étapes.

phase-out **n** suppression *f* progressive.

PhD (abbr of ***Doctor of Philosophy***) **n** *(titulaire d'un) doctorat de 3e cycle.*

pheasant [ˈfeznt] (pl **pheasant** ***OR*** **-s**) **n** faisan *m*.

phenobarbitone *UK* [ˌfi:nəʊˈbɑ:bɪtəʊn], ***phenobarbitol*** *US* [ˌfi:nəʊˈbɑ:bɪtl] **n** phénobarbital *m*.

phenomena [fɪˈnɒmɪnə] **npl** ➤ ***phenomenon***.

phenomenal [fɪˈnɒmɪnl] **adj** phénoménal(e), extraordinaire.

phenomenally [fɪˈnɒmɪnəlɪ] **adv** phénoménalement.

phenomenon [fɪ'nɒmɪnən] (pl **-mena** [-mɪnə]) **n** phénomène *m*.

pheromone ['ferəməʊn] **n** phéromone *f*, phérormone *f*.

phew [fju:] **excl** ouf!

phial ['faɪəl] **n** fiole *f*.

Philadelphia [ˌfɪlə'delfjə] **n** Philadelphie ▸ **in Philadelphia** à Philadelphie.

philanderer [fɪ'lændərəʳ] **n** coureur *m*, don Juan *m*.

philandering [fɪ'lændərɪŋ] **n** donjuanisme *m*.

philanthropic [ˌfɪlən'θrɒpɪk] **adj** philanthropique.

philanthropist [fɪ'lænθrəpɪst] **n** philanthrope *mf*.

philanthropy [fɪ'lænθrəpɪ] **n** philanthropie *f*.

philatelist [fɪ'lætəlɪst] **n** philatéliste *mf*.

philately [fɪ'lætəlɪ] **n** philatélie *f*.

philharmonic [ˌfɪlɑ:'mɒnɪk] **adj** philharmonique.

Philippine ['fɪlɪpi:n] **adj** philippin(e) ▸ **the Philippine Islands** les Philippines *fpl*.
◆ ***Philippines*** **npl : the Philippines** les Philippines *fpl*.

philistine [*UK* 'fɪlɪstaɪn, *US* 'fɪlɪsti:n] **n** philistin *m*, béotien *m*, -enne *f*.

Phillips® ['fɪlɪps] **comp : Phillips screw** vis *f* cruciforme ▸ **Phillips screwdriver** tournevis *m* cruciforme.

philologist [fɪ'lɒlədʒɪst] **n** philologue *mf*.

philology [fɪ'lɒlədʒɪ] **n** philologie *f*.

philosopher [fɪ'lɒsəfəʳ] **n** philosophe *mf*.

philosophical [ˌfɪlə'sɒfɪkl] **adj 1.** [gen] philosophique **2.** [stoical] philosophe.

philosophically [ˌfɪlə'sɒfɪklɪ] **adv 1.** [in philosophy] philosophiquement **2.** [calmly] philosophiquement, avec philosophie.

philosophize, *UK* ***-ise*** [fɪ'lɒsəfaɪz] **vi** philosopher.

philosophy [fɪ'lɒsəfɪ] (pl **-ies**) **n** philosophie *f*.

phlegm [flem] **n** flegme *m*.

phlegmatic [fleg'mætɪk] **adj** flegmatique.

Phnom Penh [ˌnɒm'pen] **n** Phnom Penh.

phobia ['fəʊbjə] **n** phobie *f* ▸ **to have a phobia about** avoir la phobie de.

phobic ['fəʊbɪk] ■ **adj** phobique.
■ **n** phobique *mf*.

phoenix ['fi:nɪks] **n** phénix *m*.

phone [fəʊn] ■ **n** téléphone *m* ▸ **to be on the phone** [speaking] être au téléphone / *UK* [connected to network] avoir le téléphone.
■ **comp** téléphonique.
■ **vt** téléphoner à, appeler.
■ **vi** téléphoner.
◆ ***phone up*** **vt sep & vi** téléphoner.

phone book **n** annuaire *m* (du téléphone).

phone booth, ***phone box*** *UK* **n** cabine *f* téléphonique.

phone call **n** coup *m* de téléphone *OR* fil ▸ **to make a phone call** passer *OR* donner un coup de fil.

phonecard ['fəʊnkɑ:d] **n** ≃ Télécarte® *f*.

phone-in **n** *UK* RADIO & TV programme *m* à ligne ouverte.

phone line **n 1.** [wire] câble *m* téléphonique **2.** [connection] ligne *f* téléphonique.

phone number **n** numéro *m* de téléphone.

phone-tapping [-ˌtæpɪŋ] **n** écoute *f* téléphonique.

phonetic [fə'netɪk] **adj** phonétique.

phonetically [fə'netɪklɪ] **adv** phonétiquement.

phonetic alphabet **n** alphabet *m* phonétique.

phonetics [fə'netɪks] **n** *(U)* phonétique *f*.

phoney, ***phony*** ['fəʊnɪ] *inf* ■ **adj** (comp **-ier**, superl **-iest**) **1.** [passport, address] bidon *(inv)* **2.** [person] hypocrite, pas franc (pas franche).
■ **n** (pl **-ies**) poseur *m*, -euse *f*.

phoney war **n** drôle de guerre *f*.

phony = ***phoney***.

phosphate ['fɒsfeɪt] **n** phosphate *m*.

phosphorescent [ˌfɒsfə'resnt] **adj** phosphorescent(e).

phosphorus ['fɒsfərəs] **n** phosphore *m*.

photo ['fəʊtəʊ] **n** photo *f* ▸ **to take a photo of sb/sthg** photographier qqn/qqch, prendre qqn/qqch en photo.

photo album **n** album *m* de photos.

photobooth ['fəʊtəʊbu:ð] **n** Photomaton®.

photocall ['fəʊtəʊkɔ:l] **n** *UK* séance *f* de photos.

photocopier ['fəʊtəʊˌkɒpɪəʳ] **n** photocopieur *m*, copieur *m*.

photocopy ['fəʊtəʊˌkɒpɪ] ■ **n** (pl **-ies**) photocopie *f*.
■ **vt** (pt & pp **-ied**) photocopier.

photocopying ['fəʊtəʊˌkɒpɪɪŋ] **n** *(U)* reprographie *f*, photocopie *f* ▸ **there's some photocopying to do** il y a des photocopies à faire.

photoelectric cell [ˌfəʊtəʊɪ'lektrɪk-] **n** cellule *f* photoélectrique.

photo finish **n** SPORT photo-finish *f*.

Photofit® ['fəʊtəʊfɪt] **n** *UK* **: Photofit (picture)** portrait-robot *m*, photo-robot *f*.

photogenic [ˌfəʊtəʊ'dʒenɪk] **adj** photogénique.

photograph ['fəʊtəgrɑ:f] ■ **n** photographie *f* ▸ **to take a photograph (of sb/sthg)** prendre (qqn/qqch) en photo, photographier (qqn/qqch).
■ **vt** photographier, prendre en photo.

photograph album **n** album *m* de photos.

photographer [fə'tɒgrəfəʳ] **n** photographe *mf*.

photographic [ˌfəʊtə'græfɪk] **adj** photographique.

photographically [ˌfəʊtə'græfɪklɪ] **adv** photographiquement.

photographic memory **n** mémoire *f* photographique.

photography [fə'tɒgrəfɪ] **n** photographie *f*.

photojournalism [ˌfəʊtəʊ'dʒɜ:nəlɪzm] **n** photojournalisme *m*.

photon ['fəʊtɒn] **n** photon *m*.

photo opportunity **n** séance *f* photoprotocolaire.

photosensitive [ˌfəʊtəʊ'sensɪtɪv] **adj** photosensible.

photoshoot ['fəʊtəʊʃuːt] **n** prise *f* de vue.

Photostat® ['fəʊtəstæt] (pt & pp **-ted**, cont **-ting**) **n** photostat *m*, photocopie *f*.
◆ ***photostat*** **vt** photocopier, faire un photostat de.

photosynthesis [ˌfəʊtəʊ'sɪnθəsɪs] **n** photosynthèse *f*.

photosynthesize, *UK* ***-ise*** [ˌfəʊtəʊ'sɪnθəsaɪz] **vt** fabriquer par photosynthèse.

phrasal verb ['freɪzl-] **n** verbe *m* à postposition.

phrase [freɪz] ■ **n** expression *f*.
■ **vt** exprimer, tourner.

phrasebook ['freɪzbʊk] **n** guide *m* de conversation *(pour touristes)*.

phraseology [ˌfreɪzɪ'ɒlədʒɪ] **n** phraséologie *f*.

phrasing ['freɪzɪŋ] **n** **1.** [expressing] choix *m* des mots **2.** MUS phrasé *m*.

phreaker ['friːkər] **n** *inf* TELEC pirate *m* du téléphone.

phreaking ['friːkɪŋ] **n** *inf* TELEC piratage *m* du téléphone.

phylum ['faɪləm] (pl **phyla** [-lə]) **n** phylum *m*.

Phys Ed ['fɪzed] (abbr of ***physical education***) **n** *US inf* éducation *f* physique.

physiatrics [ˌfɪzɪ'ætrɪks] **n** *(U) US* kinésithérapie *f*.

physiatrist [ˌfɪzɪ'ætrɪst] **n** *US* kinésithérapeute *mf*.

physical ['fɪzɪkl] ■ **adj** **1.** [gen] physique **2.** [world, objects] matériel(elle).
■ **n** [examination] visite *f* médicale.

physical chemistry **n** chimie *f* physique.

physical education **n** éducation *f* physique.

physical examination **n** visite *f* médicale.

physical geography **n** géographie *f* physique.

physical jerks **npl** *UK dated* exercices *mpl*, gymnastique *f*.

physically ['fɪzɪklɪ] **adv** physiquement.

physically handicapped ■ **adj : to be physically handicapped** être handicapé(e) physique.
■ **npl : the physically handicapped** les handicapés *mpl* physiques.

physical science **n** science *f* physique.

physical therapist **n** *US* kinésithérapeute *mf*.

physical therapy **n** *US* kinésithérapie *f* / [after accident or illness] rééducation *f*.

physical training **n** éducation *f* physique.

physician [fɪ'zɪʃn] **n** *fml* médecin *m*.

physicist ['fɪzɪsɪst] **n** physicien *m*, -enne *f*.

physics ['fɪzɪks] **n** *(U)* physique *f*.

physio ['fɪzɪəʊ] (pl **-s**) **n** *UK inf* **1.** (abbr of ***physiotherapist***) kiné *mf* **2.** (abbr of ***physiotherapy***) kiné *f*.

physiognomy [ˌfɪzɪ'ɒnəmɪ] (pl **-ies**) **n** *fml* physionomie *f*.

physiological [ˌfɪzɪə'lɒdʒɪkl] **adj** physiologique.

physiologist [ˌfɪzɪ'ɒlədʒɪst] **n** physiologiste *mf*.

physiology [ˌfɪzɪ'ɒlədʒɪ] **n** physiologie *f*.

physiotherapist [ˌfɪzɪəʊ'θerəpɪst] **n** *UK* kinésithérapeute *mf*.

physiotherapy [ˌfɪzɪəʊ'θerəpɪ] **n** *UK* kinésithérapie *f*.

physique [fɪ'ziːk] **n** physique *m*.

pi [paɪ] ■ **n** MATHS pi *m*.
■ **adj** *UK inf pej & dated* **1.** [pious] bigot(e) **2.** [self-satisfied] suffisant(e).

pianist ['pɪənɪst] **n** pianiste *mf*.

piano [pɪ'ænəʊ] (pl **-s**) **n** piano *m*.

piano accordion **n** accordéon *m* à clavier.

pic [pɪk] (pl **-s** *OR* **pix** [pɪks]) **n** *inf* [photograph] photo *f* / [picture] illustration *f*.

Picardy ['pɪkədɪ] **n** Picardie *f* ▸ **in Picardy** en Picardie.

piccalilli [ˌpɪkə'lɪlɪ] **n** piccalilli *f*.

piccolo ['pɪkələʊ] (pl **-s**) **n** piccolo *m*.

pick [pɪk] ■ **n** **1.** [tool] pioche *f*, pic *m* **2.** [selection] **: to take one's pick** choisir, faire son choix **3.** [best] **: the pick of** le meilleur (la meilleure) de.
■ **vt** **1.** [select, choose] choisir, sélectionner ▸ **to pick one's way across** *OR* **through sthg** traverser avec précaution **2.** [gather] cueillir **3.** [remove] enlever **4.** [nose] **: to pick one's nose** se décrotter le nez ▸ **to pick one's teeth** se curer les dents **5.** [fight, quarrel] chercher ▸ **to pick a fight (with sb)** chercher la bagarre (à qqn) **6.** [lock] crocheter.
■ **vi : to pick and choose** faire le/la difficile.
◆ ***pick at*** **vt insep** [food] picorer.
◆ ***pick on*** **vt insep** s'en prendre à, être sur le dos de.
◆ ***pick out*** **vt sep** **1.** [recognize] repérer, reconnaître **2.** [select, choose] choisir, désigner.
◆ ***pick up*** ■ **vt sep** **1.** [lift up] ramasser ▸ **to pick up the pieces** *fig* recoller les morceaux, recommencer comme avant **2.** [collect] aller chercher, passer prendre **3.** [collect in car] prendre, chercher **4.** [skill, language] apprendre / [habit] prendre / [bargain] découvrir ▸ **to pick up speed** prendre de la vitesse **5.** [subj: police] **: to pick sb up for sthg** arrêter *OR* cueillir qqn pour qqch **6.** *inf* [sexually - woman, man] draguer **7.** RADIO & TELEC [detect, receive] capter, recevoir **8.** [conversation, work] reprendre, continuer.
■ **vi** [improve, start again] reprendre.

pickaxe *UK*, ***pickax*** *US* ['pɪkæks] **n** pioche *f*, pic *m*.

picker ['pɪkər] **n** cueilleur *m*, -euse *f*.

picket ['pɪkɪt] ■ **n** piquet *m* de grève.
■ **vt** mettre un piquet de grève devant.

picket fence **n** clôture *f* de piquets, palissade *f*.

picketing ['pɪkətɪŋ] **n** *(U)* piquets *mpl* de grève.

picket line **n** piquet *m* de grève.

picking ['pɪkɪŋ] **n** **1.** [selection - of object] choix *m* / [- of team] sélection *f* **2.** [of fruit, vegetables] cueillette *f*, ramassage *m* ▸ **cherry-/strawberry-picking** cueillette des cerises/des fraises ▸ **mushroom-/potato-picking** ramassage des champignons/des pommes de terre **3.** [of lock] crochetage *m*.

pickings ['pɪkɪŋz] **npl : there are rich** *OR* **easy pickings to be had** on pourrait se faire pas mal d'argent, ça pourrait rapporter gros.

pickle ['pɪkl] ■ n *UK* pickles *mpl* / *US* cornichon *m* / **: to be in a pickle** *inf dated* être dans le pétrin.
■ vt conserver dans du vinaigre, de la saumure *etc*.

pickled ['pɪkld] adj **1.** [food] au vinaigre **2.** *inf dated* [drunk] rond(e), pompette.

pick-me-up n *inf* remontant *m*.

pickpocket ['pɪk,pɒkɪt] n pickpocket *m*, voleur *m* à la tire.

pick-up n **1.** [of record player] pick-up *m* **2.** [truck] camionnette *f*.

pick-up truck n camionnette *f*.

picky ['pɪkɪ] (comp -ier, superl -iest) adj *inf* difficile.

picnic ['pɪknɪk] ■ n pique-nique *m*.
■ vi (pt & pp -ked, cont -king) pique-niquer.

picnic basket, picnic hamper n panier *m* à pique-nique.

picnicker ['pɪknɪkəʳ] n pique-niqueur *m*, -euse *f*.

Pict [pɪkt] n **: the Picts** les Pictes *mpl*.

pictorial [pɪk'tɔːrɪəl] adj illustré(e).

picture ['pɪktʃəʳ] ■ n **1.** [painting] tableau *m*, peinture *f* / [drawing] dessin *m* **2.** [photograph] photo *f*, photographie *f* ▸ **to take a picture of sb, to take sb's picture** prendre une photo de qqn, prendre qqn en photo **3.** TV image *f* **4.** CIN film *m* **5.** [in mind] tableau *m*, image *f* **6.** *fig* [situation] tableau *m* ▸ **the economic picture is bleak** la situation économique est inquiétante **7.** [epitome] **: she's the picture of health** elle respire la santé
▸▸ **to get the picture** *inf* piger ▸ **to be in/out of the picture** être/ne pas être au courant ▸ **to put sb in the picture** mettre qqn au courant ▸ **the big picture** [overview] une vue d'ensemble.
■ vt **1.** [in mind] imaginer, s'imaginer, se représenter **2.** [in photo] photographier **3.** [in painting] représenter, peindre.
◆ ***pictures*** npl *UK dated* **: the pictures** le cinéma.

picture book n livre *m* d'images.

picture frame n cadre *m* (pour tableaux).

picture rail n cimaise *f*.

picturesque [,pɪktʃə'resk] adj pittoresque.

picture window n fenêtre *f* panoramique.

piddling ['pɪdlɪŋ] adj *inf pej* dérisoire, insignifiant(e).

pidgin ['pɪdʒɪn] ■ n pidgin *m*.
■ comp **: pidgin English** pidgin english *m* ▸ **pidgin French** petit nègre *m*.

pie [paɪ] n [savoury] tourte *f* / [sweet] tarte *f* ▸ **it's just pie in the sky** ce ne sont que des projets en l'air.

piebald ['paɪbɔːld] adj pie *(inv)*.

piece [piːs] n **1.** [gen] morceau *m* / [of string] bout *m* ▸ **a piece of furniture** un meuble ▸ **a piece of clothing** un vêtement ▸ **a piece of advice** un conseil ▸ **a piece of information** un renseignement ▸ **a piece of work** un travail ▸ **that was a real piece of luck** cela a vraiment été un coup de chance ▸ **to fall to pieces** tomber en morceaux ▸ **to be smashed to pieces** être cassé(e) en mille morceaux ▸ **to take sthg to pieces** démonter qqch ▸ **in pieces** en morceaux ▸ **in one piece** [intact] intact(e) / [unharmed] sain et sauf (saine et sauve) ▸ **to go to pieces** *fig* s'effondrer, craquer ▸ **to pull sthg to pieces** *lit* [doll, garment, book] mettre qqch en morceaux / [flower] effeuiller qqch / *fig* [argument, suggestion, idea] démolir qqch ▸ **to pull sb to pieces** *fig* descendre qqn en flammes **2.** [coin, item, in chess] pièce *f* / [in draughts] pion *m* **3.** PRESS article *m*.
◆ ***piece together*** vt sep [facts] coordonner.

pièce de résistance [,pjesdərezɪs'tɑ̃ːs] (pl **pièces de résistance** [,pjesdərezɪs'tɑ̃ːs]) n pièce *f* de résistance.

piecemeal ['piːsmiːl] ■ adj fait(e) petit à petit.
■ adv petit à petit, peu à peu.

piecework ['piːswɜːk] n *(U)* travail *m* à la pièce OR aux pièces.

pieceworker ['piːswɜːkəʳ] n travailleur *m*, -euse *f* à la pièce.

pie chart n camembert *m*, graphique *m* rond.

pied-à-terre [,pɪeɪdæ'teəʳ] (pl **pieds-à-terre** [,pɪeɪdæ'teəʳ]) n pied-à-terre *m inv*.

pie-eyed [-'aɪd] adj *inf dated* rond(e), gris(e).

pie plate n *US* moule *m* à tarte.

pier [pɪəʳ] n [at seaside] jetée *f*.

pierce [pɪəs] vt percer, transpercer ▸ **to have one's ears pierced** se faire percer les oreilles.

pierced [pɪəst] adj percé(e).

piercing ['pɪəsɪŋ] adj **1.** [sound, look] perçant(e) **2.** [wind] pénétrant(e).

piety ['paɪətɪ] n piété *f*.

piffle ['pɪfl] n *(U) inf* bêtises *fpl*, balivernes *fpl*.

piffling ['pɪflɪŋ] adj *inf* insignifiant(e).

pig [pɪg] n **1.** [animal] porc *m*, cochon *m* **2.** *inf pej* [greedy eater] goinfre *m*, glouton *m* ▸ **to make a pig of o.s.** se goinfrer **3.** *inf pej* [unkind person] sale type *m*.
◆ ***pig out*** (pt & pp -ged, cont -ging) vi *inf* s'empiffrer.

pigeon ['pɪdʒɪn] (pl **pigeon** OR **-s**) n pigeon *m*.

pigeon-chested [-,tʃestɪd] adj à la poitrine bombée.

pigeonhole ['pɪdʒɪnhəʊl] ■ n [compartment] casier *m*.
■ vt [classify] étiqueter, cataloguer.

pigeon-toed [-,təʊd] adj qui a les pieds en dedans.

piggish ['pɪgɪʃ] adj *inf* cochon(onne), dégoûtant(e).

piggy ['pɪgɪ] ■ adj (comp -ier, superl -iest) de cochon.
■ n (pl -ies) *inf* cochon *m*.

piggyback ['pɪgɪbæk] n **: to give sb a piggyback** porter qqn sur son dos.

piggybacking ['pɪgɪbækɪŋ] n FIN portage *m*.

piggy bank ['pɪgɪbæŋk] n tirelire *f*.

pigheaded [,pɪg'hedɪd] adj têtu(e).

piglet ['pɪglɪt] n porcelet *m*.

pigment ['pɪgmənt] n pigment *m*.

pigmentation [,pɪgmən'teɪʃn] n pigmentation *f*.

pigmy ['pɪgmɪ] (pl -ies) = ***pygmy***.

pigpen *US* = ***pigsty***.

pigskin ['pɪgskɪn] ■ n (peau *f* de) porc *m*.
■ comp en peau de porc.

pigsty ['pɪgstaɪ] (pl -ies), *US* **pigpen** ['pɪgpen] n *lit & fig* porcherie *f*.

pigswill ['pɪgswɪl] **n** *UK lit & fig* pâtée *f* pour les porcs.

pigtail ['pɪgteɪl] **n** natte *f*.

pike [paɪk] (pl -s) **n 1.** (pl **pike**) [fish] brochet *m* **2.** [spear] pique *f*.

pikestaff ['paɪkstɑ:f] **n** manche *m* d'une pique.

pilaster [pɪ'læstəʳ] **n** pilastre *m*.

Pilates [pɪ'lɑ:ti:z] **n** [gymnastics] Pilates *f*.

pilchard ['pɪltʃəd] **n** pilchard *m*.

pile [paɪl] ■ **n 1.** [heap] tas *m* ▸ **a pile of, piles of** un tas *OR* des tas de ▸ **to have piles of money** avoir plein d'argent, être plein aux as ▸ **I've got piles of work to do** j'ai un tas de boulot *OR* un boulot dingue **2.** [neat stack] pile *f* **3.** [of carpet] poil *m*.
■ **vt** empiler ▸ **the table was piled high with papers** il y avait une grosse pile de papiers sur la table.
◆ ***piles*** **npl** MED hémorroïdes *fpl*.
◆ ***pile in*** **vi** *inf* s'empiler.
◆ ***pile into*** **vt insep** *inf* s'entasser dans, s'empiler dans.
◆ ***pile out*** **vi** *inf* sortir en se bousculant.
◆ ***pile up*** ■ **vt sep** empiler, entasser.
■ **vi 1.** [form a heap] s'entasser **2.** *fig* [work, debts] s'accumuler.

pile driver **n** sonnette *f*.

pileup ['paɪlʌp] **n** AUT carambolage *m*.

pilfer ['pɪlfəʳ] ■ **vt** chaparder.
■ **vi : to pilfer (from)** faire du chapardage (dans).

pilgrim ['pɪlgrɪm] **n** pèlerin *m*.

pilgrimage ['pɪlgrɪmɪdʒ] **n** pèlerinage *m*.

pill [pɪl] **n 1.** [gen] pilule *f* **2.** [contraceptive] **: the pill** la pilule ▸ **to be on the pill** prendre la pilule.

pillage ['pɪlɪdʒ] ■ **n** pillage *m*.
■ **vt** piller.

pillar ['pɪləʳ] **n** *lit & fig* pilier *m*.

pillar box **n** *UK* boîte *f* aux lettres.

pillbox ['pɪlbɒks] **n 1.** [box for pills] boîte *f* à pilules **2.** MIL casemate *f*.

pillion ['pɪljən] **n** siège *m* arrière ▸ **to ride pillion** monter derrière.

pillock ['pɪlək] **n** *UK inf* imbécile *mf*.

pillory ['pɪlərɪ] ■ **n** (pl **-ies**) pilori *m*.
■ **vt** (pt & pp **-ied**) **: to be pilloried** être mis(e) au pilori.

pillow ['pɪləʊ] **n 1.** [for bed] oreiller *m* **2.** *US* [on sofa, chair] coussin *m*.

pillowcase ['pɪləʊkeɪs], ***pillowslip*** ['pɪləʊslɪp] **n** taie *f* d'oreiller.

pilot ['paɪlət] ■ **n 1.** AERON & NAUT pilote *mf* **2.** TV émission *f* pilote.
■ **comp** pilote.
■ **vt** piloter.

pilot burner, pilot light **n** veilleuse *f*.

pilot scheme **n** *UK* projet-pilote *m*.

pilot study **n** étude *f* pilote *OR* expérimentale.

pimento [pɪ'mentəʊ] (pl **pimento** *OR* **-s**) **n** piment *m*.

pimp [pɪmp] **n** *inf* maquereau *m*, souteneur *m*.

pimple ['pɪmpl] **n** bouton *m*.

pimply ['pɪmplɪ] (comp **-ier**, superl **-iest**) **adj** boutonneux(euse).

pin [pɪn] ■ **n 1.** [for sewing] épingle *f* **2.** *US* [brooch] broche *f* **3.** *UK* [drawing pin] punaise *f* **4.** [safety pin] épingle *f* de nourrice *OR* de sûreté **5.** [of plug] fiche *f* **6.** TECH goupille *f*, cheville *f* **7.** [in grenade] goupille *f* **8.** GOLF **: the pin** le drapeau de trou.
■ **vt** (pt & pp **-ned**, cont **-ning**) **: to pin sthg to/on sthg** épingler qqch à/sur qqch ▸ **to pin sb against** *OR* **to** clouer qqn contre ▸ **to pin sthg on sb** [blame] mettre *OR* coller qqch sur le dos de qqn ▸ **to pin one's hopes on sb/sthg** mettre tous ses espoirs en qqn/dans qqch.
◆ ***pin down*** **vt sep 1.** [identify] définir, identifier **2.** [force to make a decision] **: to pin sb down** obliger qqn à prendre une décision.
◆ ***pin up*** **vt sep** épingler.

PIN [pɪn] (abbr of ***personal identification number***) **n** code *m* confidentiel.

pinafore ['pɪnəfɔ:ʳ] **n 1.** [apron] tablier *m* **2.** *UK* [dress] chasuble *f*.

pinball ['pɪnbɔ:l] **n** flipper *m*.

pinball machine **n** flipper *m*.

pincer movement ['pɪnsəʳ-] **n** mouvement *m* de tenailles.

pincers ['pɪnsəz] **npl 1.** [tool] tenailles *fpl* **2.** [of crab] pinces *fpl*.

pinch [pɪntʃ] ■ **n 1.** [nip] pincement *m* ▸ **to feel the pinch** tirer le diable par la queue **2.** [of salt] pincée *f*.
■ **vt 1.** [nip] pincer **2.** [subj: shoes] serrer **3.** *UK inf* [steal] piquer, faucher.
◆ ***at a pinch*** *UK*, ***in a pinch*** *US* **adv** à la rigueur.

pinched [pɪntʃt] **adj** [features] tiré(e) ▸ **to be pinched for time/money** être à court de temps/d'argent ▸ **pinched with cold** transi de froid.

pinch-hit **vi** *US* **1.** [gen] effectuer un remplacement **2.** SPORT remplacer un joueur.

pincushion ['pɪn,kʊʃn] **n** pelote *f* à épingles.

pine [paɪn] ■ **n** pin *m*.
■ **comp** en pin.
■ **vi : to pine for** désirer ardemment.
◆ ***pine away*** **vi** languir.

pineapple ['paɪnæpl] **n** ananas *m*.

pine cone **n** pomme *f* de pin.

pine needle **n** aiguille *f* de pin.

pine nut **n** pignon *m*, pigne *f*.

pinetree ['paɪntri:] **n** pin *m*.

pinewood ['paɪnwʊd] **n 1.** [forest] pinède *f* **2.** *(U)* [material] bois *m* de pin.

ping [pɪŋ] ■ **n** [of bell] tintement *m* / [of metal] bruit *m* métallique.
■ **vi** [bell] tinter / [metal] faire un bruit métallique.

Ping-Pong® [-pɒŋ] **n** ping-pong *m*.

pinhole ['pɪnhəʊl] **n** trou *m* d'épingle.

pinion ['pɪnjən] ■ **n** pignon *m*.
■ **vt** [person] clouer.

pink [pɪŋk] ■ adj rose ▸ **to go** *OR* **turn pink** rosir, rougir. ■ n **1.** [colour] rose *m* ▸ **in pink** en rose **2.** [flower] mignardise *f*.

pink economy n *activités économiques générées par le pouvoir d'achat des homosexuels*.

pinkeye *US* = ***conjunctivitis***.

pink gin n *UK boisson alcoolisée contenant du gin et de l'angusture*.

pinkie ['pɪŋkɪ] n *US* & *Scot* petit doigt *m*.

pinking ['pɪŋkɪŋ] n *UK* AUT cliquettement *m*.

pinking scissors, **pinking shears** npl ciseaux *mpl* à cranter.

pink pound n *UK* : **the pink pound** *le pouvoir d'achat des homosexuels*.

pin money n *inf* argent *m* de poche.

pinnacle ['pɪnəkl] n **1.** [mountain peak, spire] pic *m*, cime *f* **2.** *fig* [high point] apogée *m*.

pin number n code *m* confidentiel.

pinny ['pɪnɪ] (pl -ies) n *UK inf* tablier *m*.

pinpoint ['pɪnpɔɪnt] vt **1.** [cause, problem] définir, mettre le doigt sur **2.** [position] localiser.

pinprick ['pɪnprɪk] n piqûre *f* d'épingle / *fig* petit désagrément *m*.

pins and needles n *(U) inf* fourmillements *mpl* ▸ **I've got pins and needles in my arm** j'ai des fourmis dans le bras, je ne sens plus mon bras
⏭ **to be on pins and needles** *US* trépigner d'impatience, ronger son frein.

pin-striped [-,straɪpt] adj à très fines rayures.

pint [paɪnt] n **1.** *UK* [unit of measurement] = *0,568 litre*, ≃ demi-litre *m* **2.** *US* [unit of measurement] = *0,473 litre*, ≃ demi-litre *m* **3.** *UK* [beer] ≃ demi *m*.

pintable ['pɪnteɪbl] n *UK* flipper *m*.

pinto ['pɪntəʊ] *US* ■ adj pie *(inv)*.
■ n (pl -s *OR* -es) cheval *m* pie.

pint-size(d) adj *inf* minuscule.

pinup ['pɪnʌp] n pin-up *f inv*.

pioneer [,paɪə'nɪər] ■ n *lit* & *fig* pionnier *m*.
■ vt : **to pioneer sthg** être un des premiers (une des premières) à faire qqch.

pioneering [,paɪə'nɪərɪŋ] adj [work, research] de pionnier.

pious ['paɪəs] adj **1.** RELIG pieux (pieuse) **2.** *pej* [sanctimonious] moralisateur(trice).

piously ['paɪəslɪ] adv pieusement.

pip [pɪp] n **1.** [seed] pépin *m* **2.** *UK* RADIO top *m*.

pipe [paɪp] ■ n **1.** [for gas, water] tuyau *m* **2.** [for smoking] pipe *f*.
■ vt acheminer par tuyau.
◆ **pipes** npl MUS cornemuse *f*.
◆ **pipe down** vi *inf* se taire, la fermer.
◆ **pipe up** vi *inf* se faire entendre.

pipe cleaner n cure-pipe *m*.

piped music n *UK* musique *f* de fond.

pipe dream n projet *m* chimérique.

pipeline ['paɪplaɪn] n [for gas] gazoduc *m* / [for oil] oléoduc *m*, pipeline *m* ▸ **to be in the pipeline** *fig* être imminent(e) *OR* proche.

piper ['paɪpər] n joueur *m*, -euse *f* de cornemuse.

piping hot ['paɪpɪŋ-] adj bouillant(e).

pipsqueak ['pɪpskwi:k] n *pej* & *dated* moins *m* que rien.

piquant ['pi:kənt] adj piquant(e).

pique [pi:k] n dépit *m* ▸ **a fit of pique** un accès de dépit.

piracy ['paɪrəsɪ] n **1.** [at sea] piraterie *f* **2.** [of video, program] piratage *m*.

piranha [pɪ'rɑ:nə] n piranha *m*.

pirate ['paɪrət] ■ adj [video, program] pirate.
■ n pirate *m*.
■ vt [video, program] pirater.

pirate radio n *UK* radio *f* pirate.

pirouette [,pɪrʊ'et] ■ n pirouette *f*.
■ vi pirouetter.

Pisces ['paɪsi:z] n Poissons *mpl* ▸ **to be (a) Pisces** être Poissons.

piss [pɪs] *vulg* ■ n [urine] pisse *f* ▸ **to have a piss** pisser
⏭ **to take the piss out of** *UK* se foutre de.
■ vi pisser.
◆ **piss down** impers vb *UK vulg* pleuvoir comme vache qui pisse.
◆ **piss off** *vulg* ■ vt sep emmerder.
■ vi *UK* foutre le camp ▸ **piss off!** fous le camp!

pissed [pɪst] adj *vulg* **1.** *UK* [drunk] bourré(e) **2.** *US* [annoyed] en rogne.

pissed off adj *vulg* en rogne.

pisshead ['pɪshed] n *vulg* **1.** *UK* [drunkard] poivrot *m*, -e *f*, soûlard *m*, -e *f* **2.** *US* [mean person] salaud *m*, salope *f* / [bore] emmerdeur *m*, -euse *f*.

piss-take n *UK vulg* [mockery] mise *f* en boîte / [of book, film] parodie *f*.

piss-up n *UK v inf* : **to go on** *OR* **to have a piss-up** se biturer, se soûler la gueule
⏭ **he couldn't organise a piss-up in a brewery** il n'est pas foutu d'organiser quoi que ce soit.

pistachio [pɪ'stɑ:ʃɪəʊ] (pl -s) n pistache *f*.

piste [pi:st] n piste *f* (de ski).

pistol ['pɪstl] n pistolet *m*.

pistol-whip vt frapper avec un pistolet.

piston ['pɪstən] n piston *m*.

pit [pɪt] ■ n **1.** [hole] trou *m* / [in road] petit trou / [on face] marque *f* **2.** [for orchestra] fosse *f* **3.** [mine] mine *f* **4.** [quarry] carrière *f* **5.** *US* [of fruit] noyau *m*
⏭ **the pit of one's stomach** le creux de l'estomac.
■ vt (pt & pp -ted, cont -ting) : **to pit sb against sb** opposer qqn à qqn ▸ **to pit one's wits against sb** se mesurer avec qqn.
◆ **pits** npl **1.** [in motor racing] : **the pits** les stands *mpl* **2.** *inf* [awful] : **the pits** l'horreur *f* complète *OR* totale.

pita bread ['pɪtə-] *US* = ***pitta bread***.

pit bull (terrier) n pitbull *m*, pit-bull *m*.

pitch [pɪtʃ] ■ **n 1.** *UK* SPORT terrain *m* **2.** MUS ton *m* **3.** [level, degree] degré *m* **4.** *UK* [selling place] place *f* **5.** *inf* [sales talk] baratin *m* **6.** AERON & NAUT tangage *m* **7.** [throw] lancement *m*.
■ **vt 1.** [throw] lancer ▸ **to be pitched into sthg** être catapulté(e) dans qqch **2.** [set - price] fixer / [- speech] adapter **3.** [tent] dresser / [camp] établir.
■ **vi 1.** [ball] rebondir **2.** [fall] **: to pitch forward** être projeté(e) en avant **3.** AERON & NAUT tanguer.
◆ ***pitch in*** **vi** s'y mettre ▸ **everybody is expected to pitch in** on attend de chacun qu'il mette la main à la pâte.

pitch-black **adj : it's pitch-black in here** il fait noir comme dans un four.

pitched [pɪtʃt] **adj** [sloping] penché(e).

pitched battle **n** bataille *f* rangée.

pitcher ['pɪtʃər] **n 1.** *US* [jug] cruche *f* **2.** [in baseball] lanceur *m*.

pitchfork ['pɪtʃfɔːk] **n** fourche *f*.

piteous ['pɪtɪəs] **adj** pitoyable.

piteously ['pɪtɪəslɪ] **adv** pitoyablement.

pitfall ['pɪtfɔːl] **n** piège *m*.

pith [pɪθ] **n 1.** [in plant] moelle *f* **2.** [of fruit] peau *f* blanche **3.** *fig* [crux] essence *f*.

pithead ['pɪthed] **n** carreau *m* de mine.

pith helmet **n** casque *m* colonial.

pithy ['pɪθɪ] (comp **-ier**, superl **-iest**) **adj** [brief] concis(e) / [terse] piquant(e).

pitiable ['pɪtɪəbl] **adj** pitoyable.

pitiful ['pɪtɪfʊl] **adj** [condition] pitoyable / [excuse, effort] lamentable.

pitifully ['pɪtɪfʊlɪ] **adv** [look, cry] pitoyablement / [poor] lamentablement.

pitiless ['pɪtɪlɪs] **adj** sans pitié, impitoyable.

pitilessly ['pɪtɪlɪslɪ] **adv** impitoyablement, sans pitié.

pitman ['pɪtmən] (pl **-men** [-mən]) **n** mineur *m* de fond.

pit pony **n** *UK* cheval *m* de mine.

pit prop **n** poteau *m* de mine.

pit stop **n 1.** [in motor racing] arrêt *m* aux stands **2.** *esp US hum* arrêt *m* pipi.

pitta bread ['pɪtə-] **n** *UK* pain *m* grec, pita *m*.

pittance ['pɪtəns] **n** [wage] salaire *m* de misère.

pitted ['pɪtɪd] **adj : pitted (with)** [face] grêlé(e) (par) / [metal] piqué(e) (de).

pitter-patter ['pɪtəˌpætər] **n** [of rain] crépitement *m*.

pituitary [pɪ'tjuːɪtrɪ] (pl **-ies**) **n : pituitary (gland)** glande *f* pituitaire.

pity ['pɪtɪ] ■ **n** pitié *f* ▸ **what a pity!** quel dommage! ▸ **it's a pity** c'est dommage ▸ **to take pity on sb** prendre qqn en pitié ▸ **to have pity on sb** avoir pitié de qqn.
■ **vt** (pt & pp **-ied**) plaindre.

pitying ['pɪtɪɪŋ] **adj** compatissant(e).

pityingly ['pɪtɪɪŋlɪ] **adv** avec compassion, avec pitié.

pivot ['pɪvət] ■ **n** *lit & fig* pivot *m*.
■ **vi : to pivot (on)** pivoter (sur).

pivotal ['pɪvətl] **adj** [crucial] crucial(e), central(e).

pixel ['pɪksl] **n** COMPUT pixel *m*.

pixie, pixy (pl **-ies**) ['pɪksɪ] **n** lutin *m*.

pizza ['piːtsə] **n** pizza *f*.

pizzazz [pɪ'zæz] **n** *inf* vitalité *f*, énergie *f*.

pl abbr of ***plural***.

Pl. (abbr of ***Place***) *rue*.

placard ['plækɑːd] **n** placard *m*, affiche *f*.

placate [plə'keɪt] **vt** calmer, apaiser.

placatory [plə'keɪtərɪ] **adj** apaisant(e).

place [pleɪs] ■ **n 1.** [location] endroit *m*, lieu *m* ▸ **place of birth** lieu de naissance ▸ **'store in a cool place'** 'à conserver au frais' **2.** [proper position, seat, vacancy, rank] place *f* ▸ **save me a place** garde-moi une place ▸ **the team is in fifth place** l'équipe est en cinquième position ▸ **what would you do (if you were) in my place?** que feriez-vous (si vous étiez) à ma place? ▸ **everything fell into place** *fig* tout s'éclaircit ▸ **to know one's place** savoir se tenir à sa place ▸ **to put sb in their place** remettre qqn à sa place **3.** [home] **: nice place you've got here** c'est joli chez vous ▸ **at/to my place** chez moi **4.** [in book] **: to lose one's place** perdre sa page **5.** MATHS **: decimal place** décimale *f* ▸ **to 3 decimal places, to 3 places of decimals** jusqu'à la troisième décimale **6.** [instance] **: in the first place** tout de suite ▸ **in the first place... and in the second place...** premièrement... et deuxièmement...
▸▸ **to take place** avoir lieu ▸ **to take the place of** prendre la place de, remplacer.
■ **vt 1.** [position, put] placer, mettre ▸ **he placed an ad in the local paper** il a fait passer *OR* mis une annonce dans le journal local **2.** [apportion] **: to place the responsibility for sthg on sb** tenir qqn pour responsable de qqch **3.** [identify] remettre ▸ **I can't place him** je n'arrive pas à (me) le remettre **4.** [an order] passer ▸ **to place a bet** parier ▸ **place your bets!** [in casino] faites vos jeux! **5.** [in race] **: to be placed** être placé(e).
◆ ***all over the place*** **adv** [everywhere] partout.
◆ ***in place*** **adv 1.** [in proper position] à sa place **2.** [established] mis(e) en place.
◆ ***in place of*** **prep** à la place de.
◆ ***out of place*** **adv** pas à sa place / *fig* déplacé(e).

placebo [plə'siːbəʊ] (pl **-s** *OR* **-es**) **n** placebo *m*.

place card **n** carte *f* marque-place.

placed [pleɪst] **adj** *inf* **: how are we placed for time?** est-ce qu'on a assez de temps? ▸ **how are you placed for money?** qu'est-ce que tu as comme argent?

place kick **n** SPORT coup *m* de pied placé.

place mat **n** set *m* (de table).

placement ['pleɪsmənt] **n** placement *m*.

place name **n** nom *m* de lieu ▸ **the study of place names** la toponymie.

placenta [plə'sentə] (pl **-s** *OR* **-tae** [-tiː]) **n** placenta *m*.

place setting **n** couvert *m*.

placid ['plæsɪd] **adj 1.** [person] placide **2.** [sea, place] calme.

placidly ['plæsɪdlɪ] **adv** avec placidité.

placing ['pleɪsɪŋ] **n** [act of putting] placement *m* / [situation, position] situation *f*, localisation *f* / [arrangement] disposition *f*.

plagiarism ['pleɪdʒərɪzm] **n** plagiat *m*.

plagiarist ['pleɪdʒərɪst] **n** plagiaire *mf*.

plagiarize, *UK* ***-ise*** ['pleɪdʒəraɪz] **vt** plagier.

plague [pleɪg] ■ **n 1.** MED peste *f* ▸ **to avoid sb/sthg like the plague** fuir qqn/qqch comme la peste **2.** *fig* [nuisance] fléau *m*.

■ **vt : to be plagued by** [bad luck] être poursuivi(e) par / [doubt] être rongé(e) par ▸ **to plague sb with questions** harceler qqn de questions.

plaice [pleɪs] (pl **plaice**) **n** carrelet *m*.

plaid [plæd] **n** plaid *m*.

Plaid Cymru [,plaɪd'kʌmrɪ] **n** *parti nationaliste gallois.*

plain [pleɪn] ■ **adj 1.** [not patterned] uni(e) **2.** [simple] simple **3.** [clear] clair(e), évident(e) ▸ **to make sthg plain to sb** (bien) faire comprendre qqch à qqn ▸ **I thought I'd made myself plain** je croyais avoir été assez clair **4.** [blunt] carré(e), franc (franche) ▸ **the time has come for plain speaking** le moment est venu de parler franchement **5.** [absolute] pur(e) (et simple) **6.** [not pretty] quelconque, ordinaire.

■ **adv** *inf* complètement.

■ **n** GEOG plaine *f*.

plain chocolate **n** *UK* chocolat *m* à croquer.

plain-clothes **adj** en civil.

plain flour **n** *UK* farine *f* (sans levure).

plainly ['pleɪnlɪ] **adv 1.** [obviously] manifestement **2.** [distinctly] clairement **3.** [frankly] carrément, sans détours **4.** [simply] simplement.

plainness ['pleɪnnɪs] **n 1.** [of clothes, cooking] simplicité *f* **2.** [clarity, obviousness] clarté *f* **3.** [unattractiveness] physique *m* quelconque *OR* ingrat.

plain sailing **n : it should be plain sailing from now on** ça devrait aller comme sur des roulettes maintenant.

plainspoken [,pleɪn'spəʊkən] **adj** au franc-parler.

plaintiff ['pleɪntɪf] **n** LAW demandeur *m*, -eresse *f*.

plaintive ['pleɪntɪv] **adj** plaintif(ive).

plait [plæt] ■ **n** natte *f*.

■ **vt** natter, tresser.

plan [plæn] ■ **n** plan *m*, projet *m* ▸ **the plan is to meet up at John's** l'idée, c'est de se retrouver chez John ▸ **to draw up** *OR* **to make a plan** dresser *OR* établir un plan ▸ **to go according to plan** se passer *OR* aller comme prévu(e) ▸ **to put a plan into operation** mettre un plan en œuvre.

■ **vt** (pt & pp **-ned**, cont **-ning**) **1.** [organize] préparer ▸ **they're planning a new venture** ils ont en projet une nouvelle entreprise ▸ **everything went as planned** tout s'est déroulé comme prévu **2.** [intend] **: to plan to do sthg** projeter de faire qqch, avoir l'intention de faire qqch ▸ **plan to finish it in about four hours** comptez environ quatre heures pour le terminer **3.** [design] concevoir.

■ **vi** (pt & pp **-ned**, cont **-ning**) **: it is important to plan ahead** il est important de faire des projets pour l'avenir ▸ **to plan (for sthg)** faire des projets (pour qqch).

◆ ***plans*** **npl** plans *mpl*, projets *mpl* ▸ **have you any plans for tonight?** avez-vous prévu quelque chose pour ce soir?

◆ ***plan on*** **vt insep : to plan on doing sthg** prévoir de faire qqch.

◆ ***plan out*** **vt sep** préparer dans le détail.

plane [pleɪn] ■ **adj** plan(e).

■ **n 1.** [aircraft] avion *m* **2.** GEOM plan *m* **3.** *fig* [level] niveau *m* **4.** [tool] rabot *m* **5.** [tree] platane *m*.

■ **vt** raboter.

planet ['plænɪt] **n** planète *f*.

planetarium [,plænɪ'teərɪəm] (pl **-riums** *OR* **-ria** [-rɪə]) **n** planétarium *m*.

planetary ['plænɪtrɪ] **adj** planétaire.

plane tree **n** platane *m*.

plangent ['plændʒənt] **adj** *liter* retentissant(e).

plank [plæŋk] **n 1.** [of wood] planche *f* **2.** POL [policy] point *m*.

plankton ['plæŋktən] **n** plancton *m*.

planned [plænd] **adj** [crime] prémédité(e) / [economy] planifié(e), dirigé(e).

planner ['plænəʳ] **n 1.** [designer] **: town** *UK* *OR* **city** *US* **planner** urbaniste *mf* **2.** [strategist] planificateur *m*, -trice *f*.

planning ['plænɪŋ] **n 1.** [designing] planification *f* **2.** [preparation] préparation *f*, organisation *f*.

planning permission **n** *UK* permis *m* de construire.

plan of action **n** plan *m* d'action.

plant [plɑ:nt] ■ **n 1.** BOT plante *f* **2.** [factory] usine *f* **3.** *(U)* [heavy machinery] matériel *m*.

■ **vt 1.** [gen] planter ▸ **fields planted with wheat** des champs (plantés) de blé ▸ **she planted herself in the doorway** elle se planta *OR* se campa dans l'entrée **2.** [bomb] poser ▸ **to plant sthg on sb** cacher qqch sur qqn.

◆ ***plant out*** **vt sep** repiquer.

plantain ['plæntɪn] **n** plantain *m*.

plantation [plæn'teɪʃn] **n** plantation *f*.

planter ['plɑ:ntəʳ] **n** [farmer] planteur *m*, -euse *f*.

plant pot **n** pot *m* de fleurs.

plaque [plɑ:k] **n 1.** [commemorative sign] plaque *f* **2.** *(U)* [on teeth] plaque *f* dentaire.

plasma ['plæzmə] **n** plasma *m*.

plasma screen **n** TV écran *m* (à) plasma.

plasma TV **n** télévision *f* à plasma.

plaster ['plɑ:stəʳ] ■ **n 1.** [material] plâtre *m* ▸ **in plaster** dans le plâtre **2.** *UK* [bandage] pansement *m* adhésif.

■ **vt 1.** [wall, ceiling] plâtrer **2.** [cover] **: to plaster sthg (with)** couvrir qqch (de).

plasterboard ['plɑ:stəbɔ:d] **n** placoplâtre® *m*.

plaster cast **n 1.** [for broken bones] plâtre *m* **2.** [model, statue] moule *m*.

plastered ['plɑ:stəd] **adj** *inf* [drunk] bourré(e).

plasterer ['plɑ:stərəʳ] **n** plâtrier *m*.

plastering ['plɑ:stərɪŋ] **n** plâtrage *m*.

plaster of Paris **n** plâtre *m* de moulage.

plastic ['plæstɪk] ■ **adj** plastique.
■ **n 1.** [material] plastique *m* **2.** *inf* [credit cards] cartes *fpl* de crédit ▸ **to put sthg on plastic** payer qqch avec une carte de crédit ▸ **do they take plastic?** est-ce qu'ils acceptent les cartes de crédit?

plastic bullet **n** balle *f* de plastique.

plastic explosive **n** plastic *m*.

Plasticine® *UK* ['plæstɪsi:n] **n** pâte *f* à modeler.

plasticity [plæs'tɪsətɪ] **n** *fml* plasticité *f*.

plasticize, *UK* ***-ise*** ['plæstɪsaɪz] **vt** plastifier.

plastic money **n** *(U)* cartes *fpl* de crédit.

plastic surgeon **n** spécialiste *mf* en chirurgie esthétique *OR* plastique.

plastic surgery **n** chirurgie *f* esthétique *OR* plastique.

plastic wrap **n** *US* film *m* alimentaire.

plate [pleɪt] ■ **n 1.** [dish] assiette *f* ▸ **to have a lot on one's plate** *fig* avoir du pain sur la planche ▸ **you can't expect everything to be handed to you on a plate** *fig* on ne peut pas tout t'apporter sur un plateau **2.** [sheet of metal, plaque] tôle *f* **3.** *(U)* [metal covering] **: gold/silver plate** plaqué *m* or/argent **4.** [in book] planche *f* **5.** [in dentistry] dentier *m*.
■ **vt : to be plated (with)** être plaqué(e) (de).

Plate **n : the River Plate** le Rio de la Plata.

plateau ['plætəʊ] (pl **-s** *OR* **-x** [-z]) **n** plateau *m* / *fig* phase *f* *OR* période *f* de stabilité.

plateful ['pleɪtfʊl] **n** assiettée *f*.

plate-glass **adj** vitré(e).

plate rack **n** égouttoir *m*.

platform ['plætfɔ:m] **n 1.** [stage] estrade *f* / [for speaker] tribune *f* **2.** [raised structure, of bus, of political party] plateforme *f* **3.** RAIL quai *m*.

platform shoes **npl** chaussures *fpl* à semelle compensée.

platform soles **npl** semelles *fpl* compensées.

platform ticket **n** *UK* ticket *m* de quai.

plating ['pleɪtɪŋ] **n** placage *m*.

platinum ['plætɪnəm] ■ **adj** [hair] platiné(e).
■ **n** platine *m*.
■ **comp** en platine.

platinum blonde **n** blonde *f* platinée.

platitude ['plætɪtju:d] **n** platitude *f*.

platonic [plə'tɒnɪk] **adj** platonique.

platoon [plə'tu:n] **n** section *f*.

platter ['plætəʳ] **n** [dish] plat *m*.

platypus ['plætɪpəs] (pl **-es** [-i:z]) **n** ornithorynque *m*.

plaudits ['plɔ:dɪts] **npl** *fml* louanges *fpl*, éloges *mpl*.

plausibility [ˌplɔ:zə'bɪlətɪ] **n** plausibilité *f*.

plausible ['plɔ:zəbl] **adj** plausible.

plausibly ['plɔ:zəblɪ] **adv** de façon plausible.

play [pleɪ] ■ **n 1.** *(U)* [amusement] jeu *m*, amusement *m* **2.** THEAT pièce *f* (de théâtre) ▸ **to be in a play** jouer dans une pièce ▸ **a radio play** une pièce radiophonique
3. SPORT **: play was interrupted by a shower** le match a été interrompu par une averse ▸ **in/out of play** en/hors jeu
4. [consideration] **: to come into play** *fig* entrer en jeu ▸ **to bring sthg into play** mettre qqch en jeu
5. [game] **: play on words** jeu *m* de mots ▸ **he is making a play for the presidency** il se lance dans la course à la présidence
6. TECH jeu *m*.
■ **vt 1.** [gen] jouer ▸ **to play a part** *OR* **role in** *fig* jouer un rôle dans ▸ **to play a trick/joke on sb** jouer un tour/faire une farce à qqn ▸ **to play the fool** faire l'idiot *OR* l'imbécile
2. [game, sport] jouer à ▸ **to play tennis/poker/dominoes** jouer au tennis/au poker/aux dominos ▸ **to play spades/trumps** jouer pique/atout ▸ **to play a match against sb** disputer un match avec *OR* contre qqn
3. [team, opponent] jouer contre ▸ **I played him at chess** j'ai joué aux échecs avec lui
4. MUS [instrument] jouer de
▸▸ **to play it cool** *inf* ne pas s'énerver, garder son calme ▸ **to play it safe** ne pas prendre de risques.
■ **vi** jouer ▸ **to play in a tournament** participer à un tournoi.

◆ ***play along*** **vi : to play along (with sb)** entrer dans le jeu (de qqn).

◆ ***play at*** **vt insep** jouer à ▸ **what's he playing at?** *inf* à quoi joue-t-il?

◆ ***play back*** **vt sep** [tape] réécouter / [film] repasser.

◆ ***play down*** **vt sep** minimiser.

◆ ***play off*** ■ **vt sep : to play sb/sthg off against** monter qqn/qqch contre.
■ **vi** SPORT jouer la belle.

◆ ***play (up)on*** **vt insep** jouer sur.

◆ ***play up*** ■ **vt sep** [emphasize] insister sur.
■ **vi 1.** [machine] faire des siennes
2. *UK* [child] ne pas être sage.

playable ['pleɪəbl] **adj** [pitch] praticable.

play-act **vi** jouer la comédie.

play-acting **n 1.** [pretence] (pure) comédie *f*, cinéma *m* **2.** [acting in play] théâtre *m*.

playback ['pleɪbæk] **n 1.** [replay] enregistrement *m* **2.** [function] lecture *f* ▸ **put it on playback** mettez-le en position lecture
▸▸ **playback head** tête *f* de lecture.

playbill ['pleɪbɪl] **n** affiche *f*.

playboy ['pleɪbɔɪ] **n** playboy *m*.

Play-Doh® *US* pâte *f* à modeler.

player ['pleɪəʳ] **n 1.** [gen] joueur *m*, -euse *f* **2.** THEAT acteur *m*, -trice *f*.

playfellow ['pleɪˌfeləʊ] **n** camarade *mf*.

playful ['pleɪfʊl] **adj 1.** [person, mood] taquin(e) **2.** [kitten, puppy] joueur(euse).

playfully ['pleɪfʊlɪ] **adv** en badinant.

playfulness ['pleɪfʊlnɪs] **n** enjouement *m*, espièglerie *f*.

playgoer ['pleɪ,gəʊəʳ] **n** amateur *m* de théâtre.

playground ['pleɪgraʊnd] **n 1.** *UK* cour *f* de récréation **2.** [in park] aire *f* de jeu.

playgroup ['pleɪgruːp] **n** *UK* jardin *m* d'enfants.

playhouse ['pleɪhaʊs] (pl [-haʊzɪz]) **n** *US* maison *f* en modèle réduit *(pour jouer)*.

playing ['pleɪɪŋ] **n** MUS **: the pianist's playing was excellent** le pianiste jouait merveilleusement bien ▸ **guitar playing is becoming more popular** de plus en plus de gens jouent de la guitare.

playing card **n** carte *f* à jouer.

playing field **n** terrain *m* de sport.

playlist ['pleɪlɪst] **n** *UK* liste *f* de disques à passer *(à la radio)*.

playmate ['pleɪmeɪt] **n** camarade *mf*.

playoff ['pleɪɒf] **n 1.** SPORT belle *f* **2.** *US* finale *f* de championnat.

playpen ['pleɪpen] **n** parc *m*.

playroom ['pleɪrʊm] **n** salle *f* de jeu.

playschool ['pleɪskuːl] **n** *UK* jardin *m* d'enfants.

plaything ['pleɪθɪŋ] **n** *lit* & *fig* jouet *m*.

playtime ['pleɪtaɪm] **n** récréation *f*.

playwright ['pleɪraɪt] **n** dramaturge *m*.

plaza ['plɑːzə] **n** [square] place *f* ▸ **shopping plaza** *esp US* centre *m* commercial.

plc *UK* abbr of ***public limited company***.

plea [pliː] **n 1.** [for forgiveness, mercy] supplication *f* / [for help, quiet] appel *m* **2.** LAW **: to enter a plea of not guilty** plaider non coupable.

plea bargaining **n** *possibilité pour un inculpé de se voir notifier un chef d'inculpation moins grave s'il accepte de plaider coupable*.

plead [pliːd] (pt & pp **-ed** *OR* **pled**) ■ **vt 1.** LAW plaider **2.** [give as excuse] invoquer.
■ **vi 1.** [beg] **: to plead with sb (to do sthg)** supplier qqn (de faire qqch) ▸ **to plead for sthg** implorer qqch **2.** LAW plaider.

pleading ['pliːdɪŋ] ■ **adj** suppliant(e).
■ **n** *(U)* supplications *fpl*.

pleadingly ['pliːdɪŋlɪ] **adv** [look] d'un air suppliant *OR* implorant / [ask] d'un ton suppliant *OR* implorant.

pleasant ['pleznt] **adj** agréable.

pleasantly ['plezntlɪ] **adv** [smile, speak] aimablement / [surprised] agréablement.

pleasantry ['plezntrɪ] (pl **-ies**) **n : to exchange pleasantries** échanger des propos aimables.

please [pliːz] ■ **vt** plaire à, faire plaisir à ▸ **you can't please everybody** on ne peut pas faire plaisir à tout le monde ▸ **to please o.s.** faire comme on veut ▸ **please yourself!** comme vous voulez!
■ **vi** plaire, faire plaisir ▸ **to be eager to please** chercher à faire plaisir ▸ **to do as one pleases** faire comme on veut ▸ **if you please** s'il vous plaît.
■ **adv** s'il vous plaît ▸ **please, make yourselves at home** faites comme chez vous, je vous en prie.

pleased [pliːzd] **adj 1.** [satisfied] **: to be pleased (with)** être content(e) (de) **2.** [happy] **: to be pleased (about)** être heureux(euse) (de) ▸ **pleased to meet you!** enchanté(enchanté) !

pleasing ['pliːzɪŋ] **adj** plaisant(e).

pleasingly ['pliːzɪŋlɪ] **adv** agréablement.

pleasurable ['pleʒərəbl] **adj** agréable.

pleasure ['pleʒəʳ] **n** plaisir *m* ▸ **with pleasure** avec plaisir, volontiers ▸ **it's a pleasure, my pleasure** je vous en prie ▸ **it's a great pleasure (to meet you)** ravi de faire votre connaissance ▸ **to take** *OR* **to find pleasure in doing sthg** prendre plaisir *OR* éprouver du plaisir à faire qqch.

pleat [pliːt] ■ **n** pli *m*.
■ **vt** plisser.

pleated ['pliːtɪd] **adj** plissé(e).

plebiscite ['plebɪsaɪt] **n** plébiscite *m*.

plectrum ['plektrəm] (pl **-s**) **n** plectre *m*.

pled [pled] **pt** & **pp** ➤ ***plead***.

pledge [pledʒ] ■ **n 1.** [promise] promesse *f* ▸ **pledge of allegiance** serment *m* de fidélité **2.** [token] gage *m*.
■ **vt 1.** [promise] promettre **2.** [make promise] **: to pledge o.s. to** s'engager à ▸ **to pledge sb to secrecy** faire promettre le secret à qqn **3.** [pawn] mettre en gage.

CULTURE

Pledge of Allegiance

Le « Serment de fidélité » (Pledge of Allegiance) est un bref discours que tout citoyen américain a appris par cœur, dans lequel il fait une promesse solennelle de loyauté envers son pays. De nos jours, il est encore récité quotidiennement par des millions d'écoliers. Lors de la cérémonie de naturalisation les personnes qui obtiennent la citoyenneté américaine doivent réciter un « serment d'allégeance » (Oath of Allegiance), différent de l'engagement originel. En juin 2004, la Cour suprême invalide une décision émanant de la Cour de justice, qui déclarait les termes « devant Dieu » (contenus dans le serment) anticonstitutionnels dans le cadre des écoles publiques ; elle avait déjà statué sur le fait qu'aucun élève n'avait « l'obligation » de réciter le serment à l'école.

plenary ['pliːnərɪ] ■ **adj** [meeting] plénier(ère).
■ **n** [plenary meeting] réunion *f* plénière / [plenary session] séance *f* plénière.

plenary powers **npl** POL pleins pouvoirs *mpl*.

plenary session **n** séance *f* plénière ▸ **in plenary session** en séance plénière.

plenitude ['plenɪtjuːd] **n** plénitude *f*.

plentiful ['plentɪfʊl] **adj** abondant(e).

plenty ['plentɪ] ■ n *(U)* abondance *f*.
■ pron : **plenty of** beaucoup de ▸ **we've got plenty of time** nous avons largement le temps.
■ adv **1.** [a lot] beaucoup ▸ **there's plenty more food in the fridge** il y a encore plein de choses à manger dans le frigo **2.** *US* [very] très.

plethora ['pleθərə] n pléthore *f*.

pleurisy ['plʊərəsɪ] n pleurésie *f*.

Plexiglas® ['pleksɪglɑ:s] n *US* Plexiglas® *m*.

pliability [ˌplaɪə'bɪlətɪ] n **1.** [of material] flexibilité *f* **2.** [of person] malléabilité *f*, docilité *f*.

pliable ['plaɪəbl], ***pliant*** ['plaɪənt] adj **1.** [material] pliable, souple **2.** *fig* [person] docile.

pliers ['plaɪəz] npl tenailles *fpl*, pinces *fpl*.

plight [plaɪt] n condition *f* critique.

plimsoll ['plɪmsəl] n *UK* tennis *m*.

Plimsoll line n ligne *f* de flottaison en charge.

plinth [plɪnθ] n socle *m*.

PLO (abbr of ***Palestine Liberation Organization***) n OLP *f*.

plod [plɒd] (pt & pp **-ded**, cont **-ding**) vi **1.** [walk slowly] marcher lentement *OR* péniblement **2.** [work slowly] peiner.

plodder ['plɒdəʳ] n *inf pej* bûcheur *m*, -euse *f*.

plodding ['plɒdɪŋ] adj *pej* [walk, rhythm, style] lourd(e), pesant(e) / [worker] lent(e).

plonk [plɒŋk] *UK inf* n *(U)* [wine] pinard *m*, vin *m* ordinaire.
◆ ***plonk down*** vt sep poser brutalement.

plonker ['plonkəʳ] n *UK* **1.** *vulg* [penis] quéquette *f* **2.** *v inf* [fool] andouille *f*.

plop [plɒp] ■ n ploc *m*.
■ vi (pt & pp **-ped**, cont **-ping**) faire ploc.

plot [plɒt] ■ n **1.** [plan] complot *m*, conspiration *f* **2.** [story] intrigue *f* **3.** [of land] (parcelle *f* de) terrain *m*, lopin *m* **4.** *US* [house plan] plan *m*.
■ vt (pt & pp **-ted**, cont **-ting**) **1.** [plan] comploter ▸ **to plot to do sthg** comploter de faire qqch **2.** [chart] déterminer, marquer **3.** MATHS tracer, marquer.
■ vi (pt & pp **-ted**, cont **-ting**) comploter.

plotter ['plɒtəʳ] n [schemer] conspirateur *m*, -trice *f*.

plotting ['plɒtɪŋ] n *(U)* **1.** [conspiring] complots *mpl*, conspirations *fpl* **2.** COMPUT & MATHS traçage *m*.

plough *UK*, ***plow*** *US* [plaʊ] ■ n charrue *f*.
■ vt [field] labourer.
◆ ***plough into*** ■ vt sep [money] investir.
■ vt insep [subj: car] rentrer dans.
◆ ***plough on*** vi continuer péniblement *OR* laborieusement.
◆ ***plough up*** vt sep [field] labourer.

ploughback *UK*, ***plowback*** *US* ['plaʊbæk] n FIN bénéfices *mpl* réinvestis.

ploughman *UK* (pl **-men**), ***plowman*** *US* ['plaʊmən] (pl **-men** [-mən]) n laboureur *m*.

ploughman's ['plaʊmənz] (pl **ploughman's**) n *UK* : **ploughman's (lunch)** *repas de pain, fromage et pickles*.

ploughshare *UK*, ***plowshare*** *US* ['plaʊʃeəʳ] n soc *m* de charrue.

plow *US* = ***plough*** *etc*.

ploy [plɔɪ] n stratagème *m*, ruse *f*.

PLR (abbr of ***Public Lending Right***) n *droit d'auteur versé pour les ouvrages prêtés par les bibliothèques*.

pls (abbr of ***please***) adv [in an email] svp.

pluck [plʌk] ■ vt **1.** [flower, fruit] cueillir **2.** [pull sharply] arracher **3.** [chicken, turkey] plumer **4.** [eyebrows] épiler **5.** MUS pincer.
■ n *(U)* courage *m*, cran *m*.
◆ ***pluck up*** vt insep : **to pluck up the courage to do sthg** rassembler son courage pour faire qqch.

pluckily ['plʌkɪlɪ] adv courageusement.

plucky ['plʌkɪ] (comp **-ier**, superl **-iest**) adj qui a du cran, courageux(euse).

plug [plʌg] ■ n **1.** ELEC prise *f* de courant **2.** *US* TELEC jack *m* **3.** [for bath, sink] bonde *f* **4.** *inf* [for new book, film] pub *f*, publicité *f* ▸ **to pull the plug on sb** *inf* couper l'herbe sous le pied de qqn.
■ vt (pt & pp **-ged**, cont **-ging**) **1.** [hole] boucher, obturer **2.** *inf* [new book, film] faire de la publicité pour.
◆ ***plug away*** vi insep travailler dur.
◆ ***plug in*** vt sep brancher.

plug-and-play ■ n COMPUT plug-and-play *m*.
■ adj COMPUT plug-and-play.

plughole ['plʌghəʊl] n *UK* bonde *f*, trou *m* d'écoulement.

plug-in ■ adj [radio] qui se branche sur le secteur / [accessory for computer, stereo] qui se branche sur l'appareil.
■ n COMPUT périphérique *m* prêt à brancher.

plum [plʌm] ■ adj **1.** [colour] prune *(inv)* **2.** [very good] : **a plum job** un poste en or.
■ n [fruit] prune *f*.

plumage ['plu:mɪdʒ] n plumage *m*.

plumb [plʌm] ■ adv **1.** *UK* [exactly] exactement, en plein **2.** *US* [completely] complètement.
■ vt : **to plumb the depths of** toucher le fond de.
◆ ***plumb in*** vt sep *UK* raccorder.

plumber ['plʌməʳ] n plombier *m*.

plumbing ['plʌmɪŋ] n *(U)* **1.** [fittings] plomberie *f*, tuyauterie *f* **2.** [work] plomberie *f*.

plumb line n fil *m* à plomb.

plume [plu:m] n **1.** [feather] plume *f* **2.** [on hat] panache *m* **3.** [column] : **a plume of smoke** un panache de fumée.

plummet ['plʌmɪt] vi **1.** [bird, plane] plonger **2.** *fig* [decrease] dégringoler.

plummy ['plʌmɪ] (comp **-ier**, superl **-iest**) adj *UK pej* [voice] de la haute, snob.

plump [plʌmp] adj bien en chair, grassouillet(ette).
◆ ***plump for*** vt insep opter pour, choisir.
◆ ***plump up*** vt sep [cushion] secouer.

plumpness ['plʌmpnɪs] n corpulence *f*, embonpoint *m*.

plum pudding n *UK dated* pudding *m* de Noël.

plunder ['plʌndəʳ] ■ **n** *(U)* **1.** [stealing, raiding] pillage *m* **2.** [stolen goods] butin *m*.
■ **vt** piller.

plunderer ['plʌndərəʳ] **n** pillard *m*, -e *f*.

plundering ['plʌndərɪŋ] ■ **n** *(U)* pillage *m*.
■ **adj** pillard(e).

plunge [plʌndʒ] ■ **n 1.** [dive] plongeon *m* ▸ **to take the plunge** se jeter à l'eau **2.** *fig* [decrease] dégringolade *f*, chute *f* ▸ **prices have taken a plunge** les prix ont chuté *OR* se sont effondrés.
■ **vt : to plunge sthg into** plonger qqch dans ▸ **the office was plunged into darkness** le bureau fut plongé dans l'obscurité.
■ **vi 1.** [dive] plonger, tomber **2.** *fig* [decrease] dégringoler ▸ **sales have plunged by 30%** les ventes ont chuté de 30 %.

plunger ['plʌndʒəʳ] **n** déboucheur *m* à ventouse.

plunging ['plʌndʒɪŋ] **adj** [neckline] plongeant(e).

pluperfect [,plu:'pɜ:fɪkt] **n : pluperfect (tense)** plus-que-parfait *m*.

plural ['plʊərəl] ■ **adj 1.** GRAM pluriel(elle) **2.** [not individual] collectif(ive) **3.** [multicultural] multiculturel(elle).
■ **n** pluriel *m*.

pluralism ['plʊərəlɪzm] **n** *fml* **1.** [gen] pluralisme *m* **2.** [holding of several offices] cumul *m*.

pluralist ['plʊərəlɪst] **n** *fml* [gen] pluraliste *mf*.

pluralistic [,plʊərə'lɪstɪk] **adj** *fml* pluraliste.

plurality [plʊ'rælətɪ] **n 1.** *fml* [large number] **: a plurality of** une multiplicité de **2.** *US* [majority] majorité *f*.

plus [plʌs] ■ **adj : 30 plus** 30 ou plus.
■ **n** (pl **pluses** *OR* **plusses** [plʌsi:z]) **1.** MATHS signe *m* plus **2.** *inf* [bonus] plus *m*, atout *m*.
■ **prep** et.
■ **conj** [moreover] de plus.

plus fours npl pantalon *m* de golf.

plush [plʌʃ] **adj** luxueux(euse), somptueux(euse).

plus sign n signe *m* plus.

Pluto ['plu:təʊ] **n** [planet] Pluton *f*.

plutocrat ['plu:təkræt] **n** ploutocrate *m*.

plutonium [plu:'təʊnɪəm] **n** plutonium *m*.

ply [plaɪ] ■ **adj : four ply** [wool] à quatre fils / [wood] à quatre plis.
■ **n** [of wool] fil *m* / [of wood] pli *m*.
■ **vt** (pt & pp **plied**) **1.** [trade] exercer **2.** [supply] **: to ply sb with drink** ne pas arrêter de remplir le verre de qqn.
■ **vi** (pt & pp **plied**) [ship] faire la navette.

plywood ['plaɪwʊd] **n** contreplaqué *m*.

p.m., pm (abbr of ***post meridiem***) **: at 3 p.m.** à 15 h.

PM abbr of ***prime minister***.

PMS abbr of ***premenstrual syndrome***.

PMT *UK* abbr of ***premenstrual tension***.

pneumatic [nju:'mætɪk] **adj** pneumatique.

pneumatic drill n *UK* marteau piqueur *m*.

pneumonia [nju:'məʊnjə] **n** *(U)* pneumonie *f*.

po abbr of ***postal order***.

Po [pəʊ] **n : the (River) Po** le Pô.

PO[1] abbr of ***Post Office***.

PO[2], **po** abbr of ***postal order***.

POA (abbr of ***Prison Officers' Association***) **n** *syndicat des agents pénitentiaires en Grande-Bretagne*.

poach [pəʊtʃ] ■ **vt 1.** [fish] pêcher sans permis / [deer] chasser sans permis **2.** *fig* [idea] voler **3.** CULIN pocher.
■ **vi** braconner.

poacher ['pəʊtʃəʳ] **n** braconnier *m*.

poaching ['pəʊtʃɪŋ] **n** braconnage *m*.

PO Box (abbr of ***Post Office Box***) **n** BP *f*.

pocket ['pɒkɪt] ■ **n** *lit & fig* poche *f* ▸ **we have prices to suit all pockets** nous avons des prix pour toutes les bourses ▸ **to be out of pocket** *UK* en être de sa poche ▸ **to live in each other's pockets** être trop ensemble ▸ **to pick sb's pocket** faire les poches à qqn ▸ **to have sb in one's pockets** avoir qqn dans sa poche ▸ **we had the deal in our pocket** le marché était dans la poche.
■ **adj** de poche.
■ **vt** empocher.

pocketbook ['pɒkɪtbʊk] **n 1.** [notebook] carnet *m* **2.** *US* [handbag] sac *m* à main.

pocket calculator n calculatrice *f* de poche, calculette *f*.

pocketful ['pɒkɪtfʊl] **n** pleine poche *f*.

pocket-handkerchief n *dated* mouchoir *m* de poche.

pocketknife ['pɒkɪtnaɪf] (pl **-knives** [-naɪvz]) **n** canif *m*.

pocket money n *UK* argent *m* de poche.

pocket-size(d) adj de poche.

pockmark ['pɒkmɑ:k] **n** marque *f* de la petite vérole.

pockmarked ['pɒkmɑ:kt] **adj** [face] grêlé(e) / [surface] criblé(e) de petits trous ▸ **pockmarked with rust** piqué(e) par la rouille.

pod [pɒd] **n 1.** [of plants] cosse *f* **2.** [of spacecraft] nacelle *f*.

podgy ['pɒdʒɪ] (comp **-ier**, superl **-iest**) **adj** *UK inf* boulot(otte), rondelet(ette).

podiatrist [pə'daɪətrɪst] **n** *US* pédicure *mf*.

podiatry [pə'daɪətrɪ] **n** *US* pédicure *f*.

podium ['pəʊdɪəm] (pl **-s** *OR* **-dia** [-dɪə]) **n** podium *m*.

POE (abbr of ***port of entry***) **n** *port d'arrivée*.

poem ['pəʊɪm] **n** poème *m*.

poet ['pəʊɪt] **n** poète *m*.

poetic [pəʊ'etɪk] **adj** poétique.

poetically [pəʊ'etɪklɪ] **adv** poétiquement.

poetic justice n justice *f* immanente.

poetic licence *UK*, ***poetic license*** *US* n licence *f* poétique.

poet laureate n poète *m* lauréat.

poetry ['pəʊɪtrɪ] n poésie *f*.

po-faced ['pəʊfeɪst] adj *UK inf* à l'air pincé.

pogo stick ['pəʊgəʊ-] n échasse *f* à ressort.

pogrom ['pɒgrəm] n pogrom *m*, pogrome *m*.

poignancy ['pɔɪnjənsɪ] n caractère *m* poignant.

poignant ['pɔɪnjənt] adj poignant(e).

poignantly ['pɔɪnjəntlɪ] adv de façon poignante.

poinsettia [pɔɪn'setɪə] n poinsettia *m*.

point [pɔɪnt] ■ n **1.** [tip] pointe *f*
2. [place] endroit *m*, point *m*
3. [time] stade *m*, moment *m* ▸ **the country is at a critical point in its development** le pays traverse une période *OR* phase critique de son développement ▸ **at one point, I thought the roof was going to cave in** à un moment (donné), j'ai cru que le toit allait s'effondrer ▸ **to be at the point of death** être sur le point de mourir ▸ **point of no return** point *m* de non-retour
4. [detail, argument] question *f*, détail *m* ▸ **you have a point** il y a du vrai dans ce que vous dites ▸ **to make a point** faire une remarque ▸ **to make one's point** dire ce qu'on a à dire, dire son mot ▸ **to prove his point he showed us a photo** pour prouver ses affirmations, il nous a montré une photo ▸ **point taken!** c'est juste ! ▸ **it's a sore point with her** *fig* elle est très sensible sur ce point
5. [main idea] point *m* essentiel ▸ **to get** *OR* **come to the point** en venir au fait ▸ **I'll come straight to the point** je serai bref ▸ **to miss the point** ne pas comprendre ▸ **beside the point** à côté de la question ▸ **to the point** pertinent(e), approprié(e)
6. [feature] **: good point** qualité *f* ▸ **bad point** défaut *m* ▸ **it's my weak/strong point** c'est mon point faible/fort
7. [purpose] **: what's the point in buying a new car?** à quoi bon acheter une nouvelle voiture ? ▸ **there's no point in having a meeting** cela ne sert à rien d'avoir une réunion
8. [on scale, in scores] point *m*
9. [in decimals] **: two point six** deux virgule six
10. [of compass] aire *f* du vent
11. *UK* ELEC prise *f* (de courant)
12. [punctuation mark] point *m*
▸▸ **to make a point of doing sthg** ne pas manquer de faire qqch.
■ vt **: to point sthg (at)** [gun, camera] braquer qqch (sur) / [finger, hose] pointer qqch (sur).
■ vi **1.** [indicate with finger] **: to point (at sb/sthg), to point (to sb/sthg)** montrer (qqn/qqch) du doigt, indiquer (qqn/qqch) du doigt ▸ **she pointed left** elle fit un signe vers la gauche
2. [face] **: to point north/south** indiquer le nord/le sud ▸ **insert the disk with the arrow pointing right** insérez la disquette, la flèche pointée vers la droite
3. *fig* [suggest] **: to point to sthg** suggérer qqch, laisser supposer qqch.
◆ ***points*** npl *UK* RAIL aiguillage *m*.
◆ ***up to a point*** adv jusqu'à un certain point, dans une certaine mesure.
◆ ***on the point of*** prep sur le point de ▸ **I was on the point of admitting everything** j'étais sur le point de tout avouer.
◆ ***point out*** vt sep [person, place] montrer, indiquer / [fact, mistake] signaler ▸ **I'd like to point out that it was my idea in the first place** je vous ferai remarquer que l'idée est de moi.

point-blank ■ adj [refusal] catégorique / [question] de but en blanc ▸ **at point-blank range** à bout portant.
■ adv **1.** [refuse] catégoriquement / [ask] de but en blanc **2.** [shoot] à bout portant.

point duty n *UK* service *m* de la circulation.

pointed ['pɔɪntɪd] adj **1.** [sharp] pointu(e) **2.** *fig* [remark] mordant(e), incisif(ive).

pointedly ['pɔɪntɪdlɪ] adv d'un ton mordant.

pointer ['pɔɪntəʳ] n **1.** *inf* [piece of advice] tuyau *m*, conseil *m* **2.** [needle] aiguille *f* **3.** [stick] baguette *f* **4.** COMPUT pointeur *m*.

pointing ['pɔɪntɪŋ] n [on wall] jointoiement *m*.

pointless ['pɔɪntlɪs] adj [gen] inutile, vain(e) / [crime, violence, vandalism] gratuit(e).

pointlessly ['pɔɪntlɪslɪ] adv [gen] inutilement, vainement / [hurt, murder, vandalize] gratuitement.

pointlessness ['pɔɪntlɪsnɪs] n [gen] inutilité *f* / [of remark] manque *m* d'à-propos / [of crime, violence, vandalism] gratuité *f*.

point of order (pl **points of order**) n question *f* de procédure *OR* de droit.

point-of-purchase advertising n publicité *f* sur le lieu de vente, PLV *f*.

point-of-purchase display n exposition *f* sur le lieu de vente.

point-of-purchase information n informations *fpl* sur le lieu de vente.

point-of-purchase material n matériel *m* de publicité sur le lieu de vente, matériel *m* de PLV.

point-of-purchase promotion n promotion *f* sur le lieu de vente.

point of sale (pl **points of sale**) n point *m* de vente.

point-of-sale promotion n promotion *f* sur le lieu de vente.

point of view (pl **points of view**) n point *m* de vue.

point-to-point n *UK* steeple-chase *m* pour cavaliers amateurs.

poise [pɔɪz] n calme *m*, sang-froid *m inv*.

poised [pɔɪzd] adj **1.** [ready] **: poised (for)** prêt(e) (pour) ▸ **to be poised to do sthg** se tenir prêt à faire qqch **2.** *fig* [calm] calme, posé(e).

poison ['pɔɪzn] ■ n poison *m*.
■ vt **1.** [gen] empoisonner **2.** [pollute] polluer.

poisoning ['pɔɪznɪŋ] **n** empoisonnement *m* ▸ **food poisoning** intoxication *f* alimentaire.

poisonous ['pɔɪznəs] **adj** **1.** [fumes] toxique **2.** [plant] vénéneux(euse) **3.** [snake] venimeux(euse) **4.** *fig* [rumours, influence] pernicieux(euse).

CONFUSABLE / PARONYME
poisonous

When translating **poisonous**, note that *vénéneux* and *venimeux* are not interchangeable. *Vénéneux* applies to plants, whereas *venimeux* applies to animals.

poison-pen letter **n** lettre *f* anonyme venimeuse.

poke [pəʊk] ■ **n** [prod, jab] coup *m*.
■ **vt** **1.** [prod] pousser, donner un coup de coude à **2.** [put] fourrer **3.** [fire] attiser, tisonner **4.** [stretch] **: he poked his head round the door** il a passé la tête dans l'embrasure de la porte.
■ **vi** [protrude] sortir, dépasser.
◆ ***poke about*** *UK*, ***poke around*** **vi** *inf* fouiller, fourrager.
◆ ***poke at*** **vt insep** [with finger] pousser (du doigt) / [with stick] pousser (avec un bâton).

poker ['pəʊkər] **n** **1.** [game] poker *m* **2.** [for fire] tisonnier *m*.

poker-faced [-ˌfeɪst] **adj** au visage impassible.

poky ['pəʊkɪ] (comp **-ier**, superl **-iest**) **adj** *pej* [room] exigu(ë), minuscule.

Poland ['pəʊlənd] **n** Pologne *f* ▸ **in Poland** en Pologne.

polar ['pəʊlər] **adj** polaire.

polar bear **n** ours *m* polaire *OR* blanc.

polarity [pəʊ'lærətɪ] **n** polarité *f*.

polarization, *UK* ***-isation*** [ˌpəʊləraɪ'zeɪʃn] **n** polarisation *f*.

polarize, *UK* ***-ise*** ['pəʊləraɪz] **vt** polariser.

Polaroid® ['pəʊlərɔɪd] **n** **1.** [camera] Polaroïd® *m* **2.** [photograph] photo *f* polaroïd.

Polaroids® ['pəʊlərɔɪdz] **npl** lunettes *fpl* polaroïd.

pole [pəʊl] **n** **1.** [rod, post] perche *f*, mât *m* **2.** ELEC & GEOG pôle *m* ▸ **poles apart** aux antipodes (l'un de l'autre).

Pole [pəʊl] **n** Polonais *m*, -e *f*.

poleaxed ['pəʊlækst] **adj** *UK inf* assommé(e).

polecat ['pəʊlkæt] **n** putois *m*.

polemic [pə'lemɪk] **n** *fml* polémique *f*.

polemicist [pə'lemɪsɪst] **n** *fml* polémiste *mf*.

pole position **n** pole position *f*.

Pole Star **n : the Pole Star** l'Étoile *f* Polaire.

pole vault **n : the pole vault** le saut à la perche.
◆ ***pole-vault*** **vi** sauter à la perche.

pole-vaulter [-ˌvɔːltər] **n** sauteur *m*, -euse *f* à la perche.

police [pə'liːs] ■ **npl** **1.** [police force] **: the police** la police **2.** [police officers] agents *mpl* de police ▸ **the police are on their way** la police arrive, les gendarmes arrivent ▸ **a man is helping police with their enquiries** un homme est entendu par les policiers dans le cadre de leur enquête.
■ **vt** maintenir l'ordre dans ▸ **the match was heavily policed** d'importantes forces de police étaient présentes lors du match.

police academy **n** *US* école *f* de police.

police car **n** voiture *f* de police.

police chief **n** ≃ préfet *m* de police.

police commissioner **n** commissaire *m* de police.

police constable **n** *UK* agent *m* de police.

police department **n** *US* service *m* de police.

police dog **n** chien *m* policier.

police force **n** police *f*.

police inspector **n** *UK* inspecteur *m*, -trice *f* de police.

policeman [pə'liːsmən] (pl **-men** [-mən]) **n** agent *m* de police.

police officer **n** policier *m*.

police record **n** casier *m* judiciaire.

police state **n** état *m* policier.

police station **n** commissariat *m* (de police).

policewoman [pə'liːsˌwʊmən] (pl **-women** [-ˌwɪmɪn]) **n** femme *f* agent de police.

policy ['pɒləsɪ] (pl **-ies**) **n** **1.** [plan] politique *f* **2.** [document] police *f*.

policy-holder **n** assuré *m*, -e *f*.

polio ['pəʊlɪəʊ] **n** polio *f*.

polish ['pɒlɪʃ] ■ **n** **1.** [for shoes] cirage *m* / [for floor] cire *f*, encaustique *f* **2.** [shine] brillant *m*, lustre *m* **3.** *fig* [refinement] raffinement *m*.
■ **vt** [shoes, floor] cirer / [car] astiquer / [cutlery, glasses] faire briller.
◆ ***polish off*** **vt sep** *inf* expédier.
◆ ***polish up*** **vt sep** [maths, language] perfectionner / [travail] peaufiner.

Polish ['pəʊlɪʃ] ■ **adj** polonais(e).
■ **n** [language] polonais *m*.
■ **npl : the Polish** les Polonais *mpl*.

polished ['pɒlɪʃt] **adj** **1.** [refined] raffiné(e) **2.** [accomplished] accompli(e), parfait(e).

polite [pə'laɪt] **adj** **1.** [courteous] poli(e) **2.** [refined] bien élevé(e), qui a du savoir-vivre.

politely [pə'laɪtlɪ] **adv** poliment.

politeness [pə'laɪtnɪs] **n** *(U)* politesse *f*.

politic ['pɒlətɪk] **adj** *fml* politique.

political [pə'lɪtɪkl] **adj** politique.

political asylum **n** droit *m* d'asile (politique).

political correctness **n** le politiquement correct.

political establishment **n** classe *f* politique dirigeante.

political football **n : the abortion issue has become a political football** les partis politiques se renvoient la balle au sujet de l'avortement.

political geography **n** géographie *f* politique.

politically [pə'lɪtɪklɪ] **adv** politiquement.
politically correct [pə,lɪtɪklɪ-] **adj** *conforme au mouvement qui préconise de remplacer les termes jugés discriminants par d'autres 'politiquement corrects'.*
political prisoner **n** prisonnier *m* politique.
political science **n** *(U)* sciences *fpl* politiques.
politician [,pɒlɪ'tɪʃn] **n** homme *m* politique, femme *f* politique.
politicization**, UK **-isation [pə,lɪtɪsaɪ'zeɪʃn] **n** politisation *f*.
politicize**, UK **-ise [pə'lɪtɪsaɪz] **vt** politiser.
politics ['pɒlətɪks] ■ **n** *(U)* politique *f*.
■ **npl 1.** [personal beliefs] **: what are his politics?** de quel bord est-il? **2.** [of group, area] politique *f*.
polka ['pɒlkə] **n** polka *f*.
polka dot **n** pois *m*.
poll [pəʊl] ■ **n 1.** [vote] vote *m*, scrutin *m* **2.** [survey - of opinion, intentions] sondage *m* ▸ **to conduct a poll on** *OR* **about sthg** faire un sondage d'opinion sur qqch, effectuer un sondage auprès de la population concernant qqch.
■ **vt 1.** [people] interroger, sonder **2.** [votes] obtenir.
◆ ***polls*** **npl : to go to the polls** aller aux urnes ▸ **the party is likely to be defeated at the polls** le parti sera probablement battu aux élections.
pollen ['pɒlən] **n** pollen *m*.
pollen count **n** taux *m* de pollen.
pollinate ['pɒləneɪt] **vt** féconder avec du pollen.
pollination [,pɒlɪ'neɪʃn] **n** pollinisation *f*.
polling ['pəʊlɪŋ] **n** *(U)* élections *fpl*.
polling booth **n** *UK* isoloir *m*.
polling day **n** *UK* jour *m* du scrutin *OR* des élections.
polling station **n** bureau *m* de vote.
pollster ['pəʊlstər] **n** enquêteur *m*, -euse *f*.
poll tax **n** *UK* ≃ impôts *mpl* locaux.
pollutant [pə'lu:tnt] **n** polluant *m*.
pollute [pə'lu:t] **vt** polluer.
polluter [pə'lu:tər] **n** pollueur *m*, -euse *f*.
pollution [pə'lu:ʃn] **n** pollution *f*.
polo ['pəʊləʊ] **n** polo *m*.
polo neck **n** *UK* **1.** [neck] col *m* roulé **2.** [jumper] pull *m* à col roulé.
◆ ***polo-neck*** **adj** *UK* à col roulé.
poltergeist ['pɒltəgaɪst] **n** esprit *m* frappeur.
poly ['pɒlɪ] (pl -s) **n** *UK inf* abbr of ***polytechnic***.
polyanthus [,pɒlɪ'ænθəs] (pl **-thuses** [-θəsi:z] *OR* **-thi** [-θaɪ]) **n** primevère *f*.
poly bag **n** *UK inf* sac *m* en plastique.
polyester [,pɒlɪ'estər] **n** polyester *m*.
polyethylene *US* = ***polythene***.
polygamist [pə'lɪgəmɪst] **n** polygame *mf*.
polygamous [pə'lɪgəməs] **adj** polygame.
polygamy [pə'lɪgəmɪ] **n** polygamie *f*.
polygon ['pɒlɪgɒn] **n** polygone *m*.
polymer ['pɒlɪmər] **n** polymère *m*.
Polynesia [,pɒlɪ'ni:zjə] **n** Polynésie *f* ▸ **in Polynesia** en Polynésie ▸ **French Polynesia** Polynésie française.
Polynesian [,pɒlɪ'ni:zjən] ■ **adj** polynésien(enne).
■ **n 1.** [person] Polynésien *m*, -enne *f* **2.** [language] polynésien *m*.
polyp ['pɒlɪp] **n** polype *m*.
polyphony [pə'lɪfənɪ] **n** *fml* polyphonie *f*.
polysemous [pə'lɪsɪməs] **adj** polysémique.
polystyrene [,pɒlɪ'staɪri:n] **n** polystyrène *m*.
polytechnic [,pɒlɪ'teknɪk] **n** *UK établissement d'enseignement supérieur; en 1993, les 'polytechnics' ont été transformés en universités.*
polythene *UK* ['pɒlɪθi:n], ***polyethylene*** *US* [,pɒlɪ'eθɪli:n] **n** polyéthylène *m*.
polythene bag **n** *UK* sac *m* en plastique.
polyunsaturated [,pɒlɪʌn'sætʃəreɪtɪd] **adj** polyinsaturé(e).
polyurethane [,pɒlɪ'jʊərəθeɪn] **n** polyuréthane *m*.
pom [pɒm] **n** *Aus inf terme péjoratif désignant un Anglais.*
pomander [pə'mændər] **n** diffuseur *m* de parfum.
pomegranate ['pɒmɪ,grænɪt] **n** grenade *f*.
pommel ['pɒml] **n** pommeau *m*.
pomp [pɒmp] **n** pompe *f*, faste *m*.
pompom ['pɒmpɒm] **n** pompon *m*.
pomposity [pɒm'pɒsətɪ] (pl **-ies**) **n 1.** *(U)* [of manner] comportement *m* pompeux, manières *fpl* pompeuses **2.** [of ceremony] apparat *m*, pompe *f* / [of style] caractère *m* pompeux.
pompous ['pɒmpəs] **adj 1.** [person] fat(e), suffisant(e) **2.** [style, speech] pompeux(euse).
pompously ['pɒmpəslɪ] **adv** pompeusement.
ponce [pɒns] **n** *UK v inf offens* **1.** [effeminate man] homme *m* efféminé **2.** [pimp] maquereau *m*.
poncho ['pɒntʃəʊ] (pl -s) **n** poncho *m*.
pond [pɒnd] **n** étang *m*, mare *f*.
ponder ['pɒndər] ■ **vt** considérer, peser.
■ **vi : to ponder (on** *OR* **over)** réfléchir (sur).
ponderous ['pɒndərəs] **adj 1.** [dull] lourd(e) **2.** [large, heavy] pesant(e).
pong [pɒŋ] *UK inf* ■ **n** puanteur *f*.
■ **vi** puer, schlinguer.
pontiff ['pɒntɪf] **n** souverain *m* pontife.
pontificate [pɒn'tɪfɪkeɪt] **vi** *pej* **: to pontificate (on)** pontifier (sur).
pontoon [pɒn'tu:n] **n 1.** [bridge] ponton *m* **2.** *UK* [game] vingt-et-un *m*.
pony ['pəʊnɪ] (pl **-ies**) **n** poney *m*.
ponytail ['pəʊnɪteɪl] **n** queue-de-cheval *f*.
pony-trekking [-,trekɪŋ] **n** *UK* randonnée *f* à cheval *OR* en poney.
pooch [pu:tʃ] **n** *inf* toutou *m*.
poodle ['pu:dl] **n** caniche *m*.

poof [pʊf] n *UK offens* tapette *f*, pédé *m*.

pooh [pu:] excl berk!, pouah!

pooh-pooh vt *inf* dédaigner.

pool [pu:l] ■ n **1.** [pond, of blood] mare *f* / [of rain, light] flaque *f* **2.** [swimming pool] piscine *f* **3.** SPORT billard *m* américain.
■ vt [resources] mettre en commun.
◆ ***pools*** npl *UK* **: the pools** ≃ le loto sportif.

pool table n (table *f* de) billard *m*.

pooped [pu:pt] adj *inf* crevé(e).

poor [pɔːʳ] ■ adj **1.** [gen] pauvre ▸ **they're too poor to own a car** ils n'ont pas les moyens d'avoir une voiture ▸ **you poor thing!** mon pauvre! **2.** [not very good] médiocre, mauvais(e) ▸ **my spelling/French is poor** je ne suis pas fort en orthographe/en français ▸ **she has very poor taste in clothes** elle s'habille avec un goût douteux ▸ **to be in poor health** être en mauvaise santé.
■ npl **: the poor** les pauvres *mpl*.

poorhouse ['pɔ:haʊs] (pl [-haʊzɪz]) n HIST hospice *m* des pauvres.

poorly ['pɔ:lɪ] ■ adj *UK inf* souffrant(e).
■ adv mal, médiocrement.

poorness ['pɔ:nɪs] n médiocrité *f*.

poor relation n *fig* parent *m* pauvre.

pop [pɒp] ■ n **1.** *(U)* [music] pop *m* **2.** *(U) inf* [fizzy drink] boisson *f* gazeuse **3.** *esp US inf* [father] papa *m* **4.** [sound] pan *m*.
■ vt (pt & pp -ped, cont -ping) **1.** [burst] faire éclater, crever **2.** [put quickly] mettre, fourrer.
■ vi (pt & pp -ped, cont -ping) **1.** [balloon] éclater, crever / [cork, button] sauter **2.** [eyes] **: his eyes popped** il a écarquillé les yeux **3.** [go quickly] **: I'm just popping to the newsagent's** je fais un saut chez le marchand de journaux.
◆ ***pop in*** vi faire une petite visite.
◆ ***pop up*** vi surgir.

POP (abbr of ***point of purchase***) n lieu *m* d'achat OR de vente.

popadum ['pɒpədəm] n poppadum *m*.

pop art n pop art *m*.

pop concert n concert *m* pop.

popcorn ['pɒpkɔ:n] n pop-corn *m*.

pope [pəʊp] n pape *m*.

pop group n groupe *m* pop.

poplar ['pɒpləʳ] n peuplier *m*.

poplin ['pɒplɪn] n popeline *f*.

popper ['pɒpəʳ] n *UK* pression *f*.

poppy ['pɒpɪ] (pl -ies) n coquelicot *m*, pavot *m*.

poppycock ['pɒpɪkɒk] n *(U) inf pej* & *dated* idioties *fpl*, bêtises *fpl*.

Poppy Day n *UK* anniversaire *m* de l'armistice.

Popsicle® ['pɒpsɪkl] n *US* sucette *f* glacée.

pop singer n chanteur *m*, -euse *f* pop.

populace ['pɒpjʊləs] n *fml* **: the populace** le peuple.

popular ['pɒpjʊləʳ] adj **1.** [gen] populaire ▸ **it's very popular with the customers** les clients l'apprécient beaucoup ▸ **a popular line** un article qui se vend bien ▸ **on** OR **by popular demand** à la demande générale **2.** [name, holiday resort] à la mode.

popularity [,pɒpjʊ'lærətɪ] n popularité *f*.

popularization, *UK* ***-isation*** [,pɒpjʊləraɪ'zeɪʃn] n **1.** [of trend, activity] popularisation *f* / [of science, philosophy] vulgarisation *f* **2.** [book] œuvre *f* de vulgarisation.

popularize, *UK* ***-ise*** ['pɒpjʊləraɪz] vt **1.** [make popular] populariser **2.** [simplify] vulgariser.

popularly ['pɒpjʊləlɪ] adv communément.

popular unrest n mécontentement *m* populaire.

populate ['pɒpjʊleɪt] vt peupler.

populated ['pɒpjʊleɪtɪd] adj peuplé(e).

population [,pɒpjʊ'leɪʃn] n population *f*.

population explosion n explosion *f* démographique.

populism ['pɒpjʊlɪzm] n populisme *m*.

populist ['pɒpjʊlɪst] n populiste *mf*.

pop-up adj **1.** [toaster] automatique **2.** [book] dont les images se déplient.

pop-up menu n COMPUT menu *m* local.

porcelain ['pɔ:səlɪn] n porcelaine *f*.

porch [pɔ:tʃ] n **1.** *UK* [entrance] porche *m* **2.** *US* [verandah] véranda *f*.

porcupine ['pɔ:kjʊpaɪn] n porc-épic *m*.

pore [pɔːʳ] n pore *m*.
◆ ***pore over*** vt insep examiner de près.

pork [pɔ:k] n porc *m*.

pork chop n côtelette *f* de porc.

pork pie n *UK* pâté *m* de porc en croûte.

porn [pɔ:n] (abbr of ***pornography***) n *(U) inf* porno *m* ▸ **hard porn** porno *m* hard, hard *m* ▸ **soft porn** porno *m* soft, soft *m*.

porno ['pɔ:nəʊ] adj *inf* porno.

pornographer [pɔ:'nɒgrəfəʳ] n pornographe *mf*.

pornographic [,pɔ:nə'græfɪk] adj pornographique.

pornography [pɔ:'nɒgrəfɪ] n pornographie *f*.

porosity [pɔ:'rɒsɪtɪ] (pl -ies) n *fml* porosité *f*.

porous ['pɔ:rəs] adj poreux(euse).

porpoise ['pɔ:pəs] n marsouin *m*.

porridge ['pɒrɪdʒ] n porridge *m*.

port [pɔ:t] ■ n **1.** [town, harbour] port *m* **2.** NAUT [left-hand side] bâbord *m* ▸ **to port** à bâbord **3.** [drink] porto *m* **4.** COMPUT port *m*.
■ comp **1.** [of a port] portuaire, du port **2.** NAUT [left-hand] de bâbord.

portable ['pɔ:təbl] adj portatif(ive).

Portacrib® ['pɔ:tə,krɪb] n *US* lit *m* pliant.

portal ['pɔ:tl] n **1.** COMPUT portal *m* **2.** [entrance] portail *m*.

Port-au-Prince [,pɔ:təʊ'prɪns] n Port-au-Prince.

portcullis [ˌpɔːtˈkʌlɪs] **n** herse *f*.

portend [pɔːˈtend] **vt** présager, augurer.

portent [ˈpɔːtənt] **n** présage *m*.

porter [ˈpɔːtəʳ] **n 1.** *UK* [doorman] concierge *m*, portier *m* **2.** [for luggage] porteur *m* **3.** *US dated* [on train] employé *m*, -e *f* des wagons-lits.

portfolio [ˌpɔːtˈfəʊljəʊ] (pl -s) **n 1.** [case] serviette *f* **2.** [sample of work] portfolio *m* **3.** FIN portefeuille *m*.

porthole [ˈpɔːthəʊl] **n** hublot *m*.

portion [ˈpɔːʃn] **n 1.** [section] portion *f*, part *f* **2.** [of food] portion *f*.

portly [ˈpɔːtlɪ] (comp **-ier**, superl **-iest**) **adj** corpulent(e).

port of call **n 1.** NAUT port *m* d'escale **2.** *fig* [on journey] endroit *m*.

Port of Spain **n** Port of Spain.

portrait [ˈpɔːtreɪt] **n** portrait *m*.

portraitist [ˈpɔːtreɪtɪst] **n** portraitiste *mf*.

portray [pɔːˈtreɪ] **vt 1.** CIN & THEAT jouer, interpréter **2.** [describe] dépeindre **3.** [paint] faire le portrait de.

portrayal [pɔːˈtreɪəl] **n 1.** CIN & THEAT interprétation *f* **2.** [painting, photograph] portrait *m* **3.** [description] description *f*.

Portugal [ˈpɔːtʃʊgl] **n** Portugal *m* ▶ **in Portugal** au Portugal.

Portuguese [ˌpɔːtʃʊˈgiːz] ■ **adj** portugais(e).
■ **n** [language] portugais *m*.
■ **npl : the Portuguese** les Portugais *mpl*.

Portuguese man-of-war **n** galère *f*.

POS (abbr of ***point of sale***) **n** PDV *m (point de vente)*.

pose [pəʊz] ■ **n 1.** [stance] pose *f* **2.** *pej* [affectation] pose *f*, affectation *f*.
■ **vt 1.** [danger] présenter **2.** [problem, question] poser.
■ **vi 1.** *pej* & ART poser **2.** [pretend to be] **: to pose as** se faire passer pour.

poser [ˈpəʊzəʳ] **n** *inf* **1.** *pej* [person] poseur *m*, -euse *f* **2.** [hard question] question *f* difficile, colle *f*.

poseur [pəʊˈzɜːʳ] **n** *inf pej* poseur *m*, -euse *f*.

posh [pɒʃ] **adj** *inf* **1.** [hotel, clothes] chic *(inv)* **2.** *UK* [accent, person] de la haute.

posit [ˈpɒzɪt] **vt** *fml* énoncer, poser en principe.

position [pəˈzɪʃn] ■ **n 1.** [gen] position *f* ▶ **they're in tenth position in the championship** ils sont à la dixième place OR ils occupent la dixième place du championnat ▶ **to change OR to shift position** changer de place ▶ **in position** en place, en position ▶ **take up your positions!, get into position!** [actors, dancers] à vos places! / [soldiers, guards] à vos postes! **2.** [job] poste *m*, emploi *m* **3.** [state] situation *f* ▶ **put yourself in my position** mettez-vous à ma place ▶ **to be in a/no position to do sthg** être/ne pas être à même de faire qqch.
■ **vt** placer, mettre en position ▶ **to position o.s.** se placer, se mettre ▶ **he positioned himself on the roof** il a pris position sur le toit.

positioning [pəˈzɪʃənɪŋ] **n** [of product] positionnement *m*.

positioning map **n** carte *f* de positionnement.

positioning strategy **n** stratégie *f* de positionnement.

positioning study **n** étude *f* de positionnement.

positive [ˈpɒzətɪv] **adj 1.** [gen] positif(ive) **2.** [sure] sûr(e), certain(e) ▶ **to be positive about sthg** être sûr de qqch **3.** [optimistic] positif(ive), optimiste ▶ **to be positive about sthg** avoir une attitude positive au sujet de qqch **4.** [definite] formel(elle), précis(e) ▶ **his intervention was a positive factor in the release of the hostages** son intervention a efficacement contribué à la libération des otages **5.** [evidence] irréfutable, indéniable ▶ **we have positive evidence of his involvement** nous avons des preuves irréfutables de son implication **6.** [downright] véritable ▶ **a positive pleasure** un véritable plaisir.

positive discrimination **n** discrimination *f* positive.

positively [ˈpɒzətɪvlɪ] **adv 1.** [optimistically] avec optimisme, de façon positive **2.** [definitely] formellement **3.** [favourably] favorablement **4.** [irrefutably] d'une manière irréfutable **5.** [completely] absolument, complètement.

positive thinking **n** idées *fpl* constructives.

positive vetting **n** *UK enquête sur une personne pour des raisons de sécurité.*

positivism [ˈpɒzɪtɪvɪzm] **n** positivisme *m*.

posse [ˈpɒsɪ] **n** *US* détachement *m*, troupe *f*.

possess [pəˈzes] **vt** posséder.

possessed [pəˈzest] **adj** [mad] possédé(e).

possession [pəˈzeʃn] **n** possession *f*.
◆ ***possessions*** **npl** possessions *fpl*, biens *mpl*.

possessive [pəˈzesɪv] ■ **adj** possessif(ive).
■ **n** GRAM possessif *m*.

possessively [pəˈzesɪvlɪ] **adv** d'une manière possessive.

possessiveness [pəˈzesɪvnɪs] **n** caractère *m* possessif, possessivité *f*.

possessor [pəˈzesəʳ] **n** possesseur *m*, propriétaire *mf*.

possibility [ˌpɒsəˈbɪlətɪ] (pl **-ies**) **n 1.** [chance, likelihood] possibilité *f*, chances *fpl* ▶ **there's no possibility of that happening** il n'y a aucune chance OR aucun risque que cela se produise ▶ **there's little possibility of any changes being made to the budget** il est peu probable que le budget soit modifié ▶ **there is a possibility that...** il se peut que... *(+ subjunctive)* ▶ **they hadn't even considered the possibility that he might leave** ils n'avaient même pas envisagé qu'il puisse partir **2.** [option] possibilité *f*, option *f*.

possible [ˈpɒsəbl] ■ **adj** possible ▶ **possible risks** des risques éventuels ▶ **it's possible (that) he won't come** il se peut qu'il ne vienne pas ▶ **the grant made it possible for me to continue my research** la bourse m'a permis de poursuivre mes recherches ▶ **as far as possible** [within one's competence] dans la mesure du possible / [at maximum distance] aussi loin que possible ▶ **as much as possible** autant que possible ▶ **as soon as possible** dès que possible ▶ **the best/worst possible** le(la) meilleur/pire possible.
■ **n** possible *m*.

possibly ['pɒsəblɪ] **adv 1.** [perhaps] peut-être **2.** [within one's power] **: I'll do all I possibly can** je ferai tout mon possible **3.** [expressing surprise] **: how could he possibly have known?** mais comment a-t-il pu le savoir? **4.** [for emphasis] **: I can't possibly accept your money** je ne peux vraiment pas accepter cet argent.

possum ['pɒsəm] (pl **possum** *OR* -s) **n** opossum *m*.

post [pəʊst] ■ **n 1.** *UK* [service] **: the post** la poste ▸ **the letter is in the post** la lettre a été postée ▸ **by post** par la poste **2.** *UK* [letters, delivery] courrier *m* **3.** *UK* [collection] levée *f* **4.** [pole] poteau *m* **5.** [position, job] poste *m*, emploi *m* **6.** MIL poste *m*

⏭ **to pip sb at the post** *UK* coiffer qqn au poteau.

■ **vt 1.** *UK* [by mail] poster, mettre à la poste **2.** [employee] muter **3.** COMPUT [message, question, advertisement] envoyer sur Internet

⏭ **to keep sb posted** tenir qqn au courant.

post- [pəʊst] **prefix** post-.

postage ['pəʊstɪdʒ] **n** affranchissement *m* ▸ **postage and packing** *UK* frais *mpl* de port et d'emballage.

postage stamp **n** *fml* timbre-poste *m*.

postal ['pəʊstl] **adj** postal(e).

postal order **n** *UK* mandat *m* postal.

postbag ['pəʊstbæg] **n** *UK* **1.** [bag] sac *m* postal **2.** *inf* [letters received] courrier *m*, lettres *fpl*.

postbox ['pəʊstbɒks] **n** *UK* boîte *f* aux lettres.

postcard ['pəʊstkɑːd] **n** carte *f* postale.

postcode ['pəʊstkəʊd] **n** *UK* code *m* postal.

postdate [,pəʊst'deɪt] **vt** postdater.

poster ['pəʊstər] **n** [for advertising] affiche *f* / [for decoration] poster *m*.

poster campaign **n** campagne *f* d'affichage.

poste restante [,pəʊst'restɑːnt] **n** *UK* poste *f* restante.

posterior [pɒ'stɪərɪər] ■ **adj** postérieur(e).

■ **n** *hum* postérieur *m*, derrière *m*.

posterity [pɒ'sterətɪ] **n** postérité *f*.

poster paint **n** *UK* gouache *f*.

post-feminism **n** postféminisme *m*.

post-feminist **adj** & **n** postféministe *mf*.

post-free **adj** *esp UK* franco (de port) *(inv)*.

postgraduate [,pəʊst'grædʒʊət] ■ **adj** de troisième cycle.

■ **n** étudiant *m*, -e *f* de troisième cycle.

posthaste [,pəʊst'heɪst] **adv** *liter* très vite, en toute hâte.

posthumous ['pɒstjʊməs] **adj** posthume.

posthumously ['pɒstjʊməslɪ] **adv** à titre posthume.

postimpressionism [,pəʊstɪm'preʃnɪzm] **n** postimpressionnisme *m*.

postimpressionist [,pəʊstɪm'preʃnɪst] ■ **n** postimpressionniste *mf*.

■ **adj** postimpressionniste.

post-industrial **adj** post-industriel(elle).

posting ['pəʊstɪŋ] **n** [assignment] affectation *f*.

Post-it (note)® **n** Post-it® *m*, becquet *m*.

postman ['pəʊstmən] (pl **-men** [-mən]) **n** *UK* facteur *m*, -rice *f*.

postmark ['pəʊstmɑːk] ■ **n** cachet *m* de la poste.

■ **vt** timbrer, tamponner.

postmaster ['pəʊst,mɑːstər] **n** receveur *m* des postes.

Postmaster General (pl **Postmasters General**) **n** ≃ ministre *m* des Postes et Télécommunications.

postmistress ['pəʊst,mɪstrɪs] **n** *dated* receveuse *f* des postes.

post-modern **adj** postmoderne.

post-modernism **n** postmodernisme *m*.

post-modernist ■ **n** postmoderniste *mf*.

■ **adj** postmoderniste.

postmortem [,pəʊst'mɔːtəm] ■ **adj : postmortem examination** autopsie *f*.

■ **n** *lit* & *fig* autopsie *f*.

postnatal [,pəʊst'neɪtl] **adj** post-natal(e).

post office **n 1.** [organization] **: the Post Office** les Postes et Télécommunications *fpl* **2.** [building] (bureau *m* de) poste *f*.

post-office box **n** boîte *f* postale.

postoperative [,pəʊst'ɒpərətɪv] **adj** postopératoire.

postpaid [,pəʊst'peɪd] **adj** port payé.

postpone [,pəʊst'pəʊn] **vt** reporter, remettre.

postponement [,pəʊst'pəʊnmənt] **n** renvoi *m*, report *m*.

postscript ['pəʊstskrɪpt] **n** post-scriptum *m inv* / *fig* supplément *m*, addenda *m inv*.

post-traumatic stress disorder **n** *(U)* névrose *f* post-traumatique.

postulate *fml* ■ **n** ['pɒstjʊlət] postulat *m*.

■ **vt** ['pɒstjʊleɪt] [theory] avancer.

posture ['pɒstʃər] ■ **n 1.** *(U)* [pose] position *f*, posture *f* **2.** *fig* [attitude] attitude *f*.

■ **vi** poser, prendre des attitudes.

posturing ['pɒstʃərɪŋ] **n** pose *f*, affectation *f*.

postviral syndrome [,pəʊst'vaɪərl-] **n** syndrome *m* de fatigue chronique.

postwar [,pəʊst'wɔːr] **adj** d'après-guerre.

posy ['pəʊzɪ] (pl **-ies**) **n** petit bouquet *m* de fleurs.

pot [pɒt] ■ **n 1.** [for cooking] marmite *f*, casserole *f* **2.** [for tea] théière *f* / [for coffee] cafetière *f* **3.** [for paint, jam, plant] pot *m* **4.** *(U) inf* [cannabis] herbe *f*.

■ **vt** (pt & pp **-ted**, cont **-ting**) [plant] mettre en pot.

potash ['pɒtæʃ] **n** potasse *f*.

potassium [pə'tæsɪəm] **n** potassium *m*.

potato [pə'teɪtəʊ] (pl **-es**) **n** pomme *f* de terre.

potato crisps *UK*, ***potato chips*** *US* **npl** (pommes *fpl*) chips *fpl*.

potato peeler [-,piːlər] **n** (couteau *m*) éplucheur *m*.

pot-bellied [-,belɪd] **adj** [from overeating] ventru(e) / [from malnutrition] au ventre gonflé.

potboiler ['pɒt,bɔɪlər] **n** œuvre *f* alimentaire.

potbound ['pɒtbaʊnd] **adj : a potbound plant** *une plante qui est devenue trop grande pour son pot.*

potency ['pəʊtənsɪ] *(U)* **n 1.** [power, influence] puissance *f* **2.** [of drink] teneur *f* en alcool **3.** [of man] virilité *f.*

potent ['pəʊtənt] **adj 1.** [powerful, influential] puissant(e) **2.** [drink] fort(e) **3.** [man] viril(e).

potentate ['pəʊtənteɪt] **n** potentat *m.*

potential [pə'tenʃl] ■ **adj** [energy, success] potentiel(elle) / [uses, danger] possible / [enemy] en puissance ▸ **we mustn't discourage potential investors** il ne faut pas décourager les investisseurs éventuels *OR* potentiels.
■ **n** *(U)* [of person] capacités *fpl* latentes ▸ **to have potential** [person] promettre / [company] avoir de l'avenir / [scheme] offrir des possibilités ▸ **to fulfil one's potential** donner toute sa mesure ▸ **he never achieved his full potential** il n'a jamais exploité pleinement ses capacités.

potentially [pə'tenʃəlɪ] **adv** potentiellement.

pothole ['pɒthəʊl] **n 1.** [in road] nid-de-poule *m* **2.** [underground] caverne *f,* grotte *f.*

potholer ['pɒt,həʊləʳ] **n** *UK* spéléologue *mf.*

potholing ['pɒt,həʊlɪŋ] **n** *UK* spéléologie *f* ▸ **to go potholing** faire de la spéléologie.

potion ['pəʊʃn] **n** [magic] breuvage *m* ▸ **love potion** philtre *m.*

potluck [,pɒt'lʌk] **n : to take potluck** [gen] choisir au hasard / [at meal] manger à la fortune du pot.

pot plant **n** *UK* plante *f* d'appartement.

potpourri [,pəʊ'pʊərɪ] **n 1.** *(U)* [dried flowers] fleurs *fpl* séchées **2.** [medley] pot-pourri *m.*

pot roast **n** rôti *m* braisé.

potshot ['pɒt,ʃɒt] **n : to take a potshot (at sthg)** tirer (sur qqch) sans viser.

potted ['pɒtɪd] **adj** *UK* **1.** [food] conservé(e) en pot **2.** *fig* [condensed] condensé(e), abrégé(e).

potted plant **n** plante *f* d'appartement.

potter ['pɒtəʳ] **n** potier *m*, -ière *f.*
◆ ***potter about, potter around*** **vi** *UK* bricoler.

Potteries ['pɒtərɪz] **npl : the Potteries** *la région des poteries dans le Staffordshire, en Angleterre.*

potter's wheel **n** tour *m* de potier.

pottery ['pɒtərɪ] **(pl -ies) n** poterie *f* ▸ **a piece of pottery** une poterie.

potting compost ['pɒtɪŋ-] **n** terreau *m.*

potty ['pɒtɪ] *inf* ■ **adj (comp -ier, superl -iest) : potty (about)** toqué(e) (de).
■ **n (pl -ies)** *UK* pot *m* (de chambre).

potty-train **vt : to potty-train a child** apprendre à un enfant à aller sur son pot.

potty-trained **adj** propre.

pouch [paʊtʃ] **n 1.** [small bag] petit sac *m* ▸ **tobacco pouch** blague *f* à tabac **2.** [of kangaroo] poche *f* ventrale.

pouffe [pu:f] **n** *UK* [seat] pouf *m.*

poultice ['pəʊltɪs] **n** cataplasme *m.*

poultry ['pəʊltrɪ] ■ **n** *(U)* [meat] volaille *f.*
■ **npl** [birds] volailles *fpl.*

pounce [paʊns] **vi : to pounce (on)** [bird] fondre (sur) / [person] se jeter (sur) ▸ **to pounce on** *fig* sauter sur.

pound [paʊnd] ■ **n 1.** *UK* [money] livre *f* **2.** [weight] = *453,6 grammes,* ≃ livre *f* **3.** [for cars, dogs] fourrière *f.*
■ **vt 1.** [strike loudly] marteler ▸ **they pounded the enemy positions with mortar fire** ils ont bombardé les positions ennemies au mortier **2.** [crush] piler, broyer.
■ **vi 1.** [strike loudly] **: the waves pounded against the rocks** les vagues venaient s'écraser sur *OR* fouettaient les rochers ▸ **to pound on** donner de grands coups à ▸ **the rain was pounding on the roof** la pluie tambourinait sur le toit **2.** [heart] battre fort ▸ **my head is pounding** j'ai des élancements dans la tête.

-pounder ['paʊndəʳ] **suffix : a fifteen-pounder** [fish] un poisson de 15 livres ▸ **a six-pounder** [gun] un canon *OR* une pièce de six.

pounding ['paʊndɪŋ] **n** *(U)* **1.** [of fists] martèlement *m* **2.** [of heart] battement *m* violent ▸ **to get** *OR* **take a pounding** [city] être pilonné(e) / [team] être battu(e) à plate couture *OR* à plates coutures.

pound sign **n** symbole *m* de la livre sterling.

pound sterling **n** livre *f* sterling.

pour [pɔ:ʳ] ■ **vt** verser ▸ **shall I pour you a drink?** je te sers quelque chose à boire? ▸ **to pour money into sthg** *fig* investir beaucoup d'argent dans qqch.
■ **vi 1.** [liquid] couler à flots ▸ **water poured from the gutters** l'eau débordait des gouttières ▸ **tears poured down her face** elle pleurait à chaudes larmes ▸ **smoke poured out of the blazing building** des nuages de fumée s'échappaient de l'immeuble en flammes **2.** *fig* [rush] **: to pour in/out** entrer/sortir en foule.
■ **impers vb** [rain hard] pleuvoir à verse.
◆ ***pour in*** **vi** [letters, news] affluer.
◆ ***pour out*** **vt sep 1.** [empty] vider **2.** [serve - drink] verser, servir **3.** *fig* [emotions] épancher ▸ **to pour out one's heart to sb** parler à qqn à cœur ouvert.

pouring ['pɔ:rɪŋ] **adj** [rain] torrentiel(elle).

pout [paʊt] ■ **n** moue *f.*
■ **vi** faire la moue.

POV abbr of ***point of view.***

poverty ['pɒvətɪ] **n** pauvreté *f* / *fig* [of ideas] indigence *f,* manque *m.*

poverty line **n** seuil *m* de pauvreté.

poverty-stricken **adj** [person] dans la misère / [area] misérable, très pauvre.

poverty trap **n** *UK situation dans laquelle, du fait d'une augmentation d'un revenu faible, on ne peut plus toucher les prestations sociales.*

pow [paʊ] **excl** *inf* pan!, paf!

POW abbr of ***prisoner of war.***

powder ['paʊdəʳ] ■ **n** poudre *f.*
■ **vt** [face, body] poudrer.

powder compact **n** poudrier *m.*

powdered ['paʊdəd] **adj 1.** [milk, eggs] en poudre **2.** [face] poudré(e).

powdered sugar **n** *US* sucre *m* en poudre.

powder puff **n** houppette *f.*

powder room n *dated* toilettes *fpl* pour dames.

powdery ['paʊdərɪ] adj [snow] poudreux(euse).

power ['paʊər] ■ n **1.** *(U)* [authority, ability] pouvoir *m* ▸ **it's beyond** *OR* **outside my power** cela dépasse ma compétence ▸ **to have power over sb** avoir de l'autorité sur qqn ▸ **to take power** prendre le pouvoir ▸ **to come to power** parvenir au pouvoir ▸ **to be in power** être au pouvoir ▸ **to be in** *OR* **within one's power to do sthg** être en son pouvoir de faire qqch ▸ **to have great powers of persuasion** avoir un grand pouvoir *OR* une grande force de persuasion ▸ **power of speech** parole *f* ▸ **the powers that be** les autorités *fpl* **2.** [strength, powerful person] puissance *f*, force *f* ▸ **economic and industrial power** la puissance économique et industrielle **3.** *(U)* [energy] énergie *f* ▸ **nuclear/solar power** énergie nucléaire/solaire **4.** [electricity] courant *m*, électricité *f*.

■ vt faire marcher, actionner ▸ **powered by solar energy** fonctionnant à l'énergie solaire.

power-assisted adj assisté(e).

power base n support *m* politique.

powerboat ['paʊəbəʊt] n hors-bord *m inv*.

power brand n marque *f* forte.

power broker n négociateur *m*, -trice *f*.

power cut n *UK* coupure *f* de courant.

-powered ['paʊəd] suffix : **high/low-powered** de haute/faible puissance ▸ **a high-powered executive** un cadre très haut placé ▸ **steam/wind-powered** mû (mue) par la vapeur/le vent.

power failure n panne *f* de courant.

powerful ['paʊəfʊl] adj **1.** [gen] puissant(e) **2.** [smell, voice] fort(e) **3.** [speech, novel] émouvant(e).

powerfully ['paʊəfʊlɪ] adv puissamment ▸ **he's powerfully built** il est d'une stature imposante.

powerhouse ['paʊəhaʊs] (pl [-haʊzɪz]) n *fig* personne *f* dynamique *OR* énergique.

powerless ['paʊəlɪs] adj impuissant(e) ▸ **to be powerless to do sthg** être dans l'impossibilité de faire qqch, ne pas pouvoir faire qqch.

power line n ligne *f* à haute tension.

power of attorney n procuration *f*.

power plant n centrale *f* électrique.

power point n *UK* prise *f* de courant.

power-sharing [-ˌʃeərɪŋ] n partage *m* du pouvoir.

power station n *UK* centrale *f* électrique.

power steering n direction *f* assistée.

power tool n outil *m* électrique.

power worker n employé *m*, -e *f* de l'électricité.

pp (abbr of ***per procurationem***) pp.

PPE (abbr of ***philosophy, politics and economics***) n *UK philosophie, science politique et science économique (cours à l'université).*

ppm (abbr of ***parts per million***) ppm.

PPS [1] n (abbr of ***parliamentary private secretary***) *parlementaire britannique assurant la liaison entre un ministre et les députés de son parti.*

PPS [2] (abbr of ***post postscriptum***) PPS.

PPV, ***ppv*** (abbr of ***pay-per-view***) n système *m* de télévison à la carte *OR* à la séance.

PQ abbr of ***Province of Quebec***.

PR ■ n **1.** abbr of ***proportional representation*** **2.** abbr of ***public relations***.

■ n abbr of ***Puerto Rico***.

Pr. (abbr of ***Prince***) Pce.

practicability [ˌpræktɪkə'bɪlətɪ] n *fml* **1.** [of plan, action] faisabilité *f*, viabilité *f* **2.** [of road] praticabilité *f*.

practicable ['præktɪkəbl] adj *fml* réalisable, faisable.

practical ['præktɪkl] ■ adj **1.** [gen] pratique ▸ **now, be practical, we can't afford a new car** allons, un peu de bon sens, nous n'avons pas les moyens de nous offrir une nouvelle voiture ▸ **for all practical purposes** en fait, en réalité **2.** [plan, solution] réalisable.

■ n épreuve *f* pratique.

practicality [ˌpræktɪ'kælətɪ] n *(U)* aspect *m* pratique.

◆ ***practicalities*** npl détails *mpl* pratiques.

practical joke n farce *f*.

practical joker n farceur *m*, -euse *f*.

practically ['præktɪklɪ] adv **1.** [in a practical way] d'une manière pratique **2.** [almost] presque, pratiquement.

practice ['præktɪs] ■ n **1.** *(U)* [at sport] entraînement *m* / [at music] répétition *f* ▸ **it's good practice for your interview** c'est un bon entraînement pour votre entrevue ▸ **to be out of practice** être rouillé(e) **2.** [training session - at sport] séance *f* d'entraînement / [- at music] répétition *f* **3.** [act of doing] **: to put sthg into practice** mettre qqch en pratique ▸ **in practice** [in fact] en réalité, en fait **4.** [habit] pratique *f*, coutume *f* ▸ **it's normal practice among most shopkeepers** c'est une pratique courante chez les commerçants **5.** *(U)* [of profession] exercice *m* ▸ **to be in practice as a doctor** exercer en tant que médecin **6.** [of doctor] cabinet *m* / [of lawyer] étude *f*.

■ vt & vi *US* = ***practise***.

practiced *US* = ***practised***.

practicing *US* = ***practising***.

practise *UK*, ***practice*** *US* ['præktɪs] ■ vt **1.** [sport] s'entraîner à / [piano] s'exercer à **2.** [custom] suivre, pratiquer / [religion] pratiquer ▸ **to practise what one preaches** prêcher par l'exemple **3.** [profession] exercer.

■ vi **1.** SPORT s'entraîner / MUS s'exercer **2.** [doctor, lawyer] exercer.

practised *UK*, ***practiced*** *US* ['præktɪst] adj [teacher, nurse] expérimenté(e) / [liar] fieffé(e) ▸ **to be practised at doing sthg** être expert(e) à faire qqch ▸ **a practised eye** un œil exercé.

practising *UK*, ***practicing*** *US* ['præktɪsɪŋ] adj [doctor, lawyer] en exercice / [Christian] pratiquant(e) / [homosexual] déclaré(e).

practitioner [præk'tɪʃnər] n praticien *m*, -enne *f* ▸ **medical practitioner** médecin *m*.

pragmatic [præg'mætɪk] adj pragmatique.

pragmatics [præg'mætɪks] n *(U)* LING pragmatique *f*.

pragmatism ['prægmətɪzm] n pragmatisme *m*.

pragmatist ['prægmətɪst] n pragmatiste *mf*.

Prague [prɑːg] **n** Prague.

prairie ['preərɪ] **n** prairie *f*.

praise [preɪz] ■ **n** louange *f*, louanges *fpl*, éloge *m*, éloges *mpl* ▸ **to sing sb's praises** chanter les louanges de qqn.
■ **vt** louer, faire l'éloge de.

praiseworthy ['preɪz,wɜːðɪ] **adj** louable, méritoire.

praline ['prɑːliːn] **n** praline *f*.

pram [præm] **n** *UK* landau *m*.

PRAM [præm] (abbr of ***programmable random access memory***) **n** RAM *f* programmable.

prance [prɑːns] **vi 1.** [person] se pavaner **2.** [horse] caracoler.

prang [præŋ] *UK inf dated* ■ **n** [of car] accrochage *m* / [of plane] collision *f*.
■ **vt** emboutir, bousiller.

prank [præŋk] **n** tour *m*, niche *f*.

prat [præt] **n** *UK v inf pej* crétin *m*, -e *f*.

prattle ['prætl] *pej* ■ **n** *(U)* bavardage *m*, babillage *m*.
■ **vi** babiller ▸ **to prattle on about sthg** parler sans fin de qqch.

prawn [prɔːn] **n** crevette *f* rose.

prawn cocktail **n** *UK* crevettes *fpl* mayonnaise.

prawn cracker **n** *genre de chips au goût de crevette*.

pray [preɪ] **vi : to pray (to sb)** prier (qqn) ▸ **to pray for rain** prier pour qu'il pleuve.

prayer [preəʳ] **n** *lit & fig* prière *f* ▸ **to say one's prayers** faire sa prière.
◆ ***prayers*** **npl** [service] office *m*.

prayer book **n** livre *m* de messe.

prayer mat **n** tapis *m* de prière.

prayer meeting **n** réunion *f* pour dire des prières.

praying mantis ['preɪɪŋ-] **n** mante *f* religieuse.

pre- [priː] **prefix** pré-.

preach [priːtʃ] ■ **vt** [gen] prêcher / [sermon] prononcer.
■ **vi 1.** RELIG **: to preach (to sb)** prêcher (qqn) **2.** *pej* [pontificate] **: to preach (at sb)** sermonner (qqn).

preacher ['priːtʃəʳ] **n** prédicateur *m*, -trice *f*, pasteur *m*, -(e) *f*.

preamble [priː'æmbl] **n** préambule *m*, avant-propos *m inv*.

prearrange [,priːə'reɪndʒ] **vt** organiser OR fixer à l'avance.

precancerous [,priː'kænsərəs] **adj** précancéreux(euse).

precarious [prɪ'keərɪəs] **adj** précaire.

precariously [prɪ'keərɪəslɪ] **adv** d'une manière précaire.

precariousness [prɪ'keərɪəsnɪs] **n** précarité *f*.

precast [,priː'kɑːst] **adj : precast concrete** béton *m* précoulé.

precaution [prɪ'kɔːʃn] **n** précaution *f* ▸ **as a precaution (against)** par précaution (contre).

precautionary [prɪ'kɔːʃənərɪ] **adj** de précaution, préventif(ive).

precede [prɪ'siːd] **vt** précéder.

precedence ['presɪdəns] **n : to take precedence over sthg** avoir la priorité sur qqch ▸ **to have** OR **take precedence over sb** avoir la préséance sur qqn.

precedent ['presɪdənt] **n** précédent *m*.

preceding [prɪ'siːdɪŋ] **adj** précédent(e).

precept ['priːsept] **n** précepte *m*.

precinct ['priːsɪŋkt] **n 1.** *UK* [area] **: pedestrian precinct** zone *f* piétonne ▸ **shopping precinct** centre *m* commercial **2.** *US* [district] circonscription *f* (administrative).
◆ ***precincts*** **npl** [of institution] enceinte *f*.

precious ['preʃəs] **adj 1.** [gen] précieux(euse) **2.** *inf iro* [damned] sacré(e) ▸ **precious little** très peu, bien peu **3.** [affected] affecté(e).

precious metal **n** métal *m* précieux.

precious stone **n** pierre *f* précieuse.

precipice ['presɪpɪs] **n** précipice *m*, paroi *f* à pic.

precipitate *fml* ■ **adj** [prɪ'sɪpɪtət] hâtif(ive).
■ **vt** [prɪ'sɪpɪteɪt] [hasten] hâter, précipiter.

precipitation [prɪ,sɪpɪ'teɪʃn] **n** précipitation *f*.

precipitous [prɪ'sɪpɪtəs] **adj 1.** [very steep] escarpé(e), à pic **2.** [hasty] hâtif(ive).

precipitously [prɪ'sɪpɪtəslɪ] **adv 1.** [steeply] à pic, abruptement **2.** [hastily] précipitamment.

précis [*UK* 'preɪsiː, *US* 'presiː] **n** résumé *m*.

precise [prɪ'saɪs] **adj** précis(e) / [measurement, date] exact(e) ▸ **49.5 to be precise** 49,5 pour être exact.

precisely [prɪ'saɪslɪ] **adv** précisément, exactement.

precision [prɪ'sɪʒn] ■ **n** précision *f*, exactitude *f*.
■ **comp** de précision.

preclude [prɪ'kluːd] **vt** *fml* empêcher / [possibility] écarter ▸ **to preclude sb from doing sthg** empêcher qqn de faire qqch.

precocious [prɪ'kəʊʃəs] **adj** précoce.

precocity [prɪ'kɒsətɪ] **n** *fml* précocité *f*.

precognition [,priːkɒg'nɪʃn] **n** *fml* connaissance *f* anticipée.

preconceived [,priːkən'siːvd] **adj** préconçu(e).

preconception [,priːkən'sepʃn] **n** préjugé *m*, idée *f* préconçue.

precondition [,priːkən'dɪʃn] **n** *fml* condition *f* sine qua non.

precooked [priː'kʊkt] **adj** précuit(e).

precursor [,priː'kɜːsəʳ] **n** *fml* précurseur *m*.

predate [priː'deɪt] **vt** précéder.

predator ['predətəʳ] **n 1.** [animal, bird] prédateur *m*, rapace *m* **2.** *fig* [person] corbeau *m*.

predatory ['predətrɪ] **adj 1.** [animal, bird] prédateur(trice) **2.** *fig* [person] rapace.

predatory pricing **n** fixation *f* des prix prédateurs.

predecease [,priːdɪ'siːs] **vt** décéder avant.

predecessor ['priːdɪsesəʳ] **n 1.** [person] prédécesseur *m* **2.** [thing] précédent *m*, -e *f*.

predestination [priː,destɪ'neɪʃn] **n** prédestination *f*.

predestine [,priː'destɪn] **vt : to be predestined to sthg/to do sthg** être prédestiné(e) à qqch/à faire qqch.

predetermination ['priːdɪ,tɜːmɪ'neɪʃn] **n** prédétermination *f*.

predetermine [,priːdɪ'tɜːmɪn] **vt 1.** [predestine] déterminer d'avance **2.** [prearrange] organiser *OR* fixer à l'avance.

predetermined [,priːdɪ'tɜːmɪnd] **adj 1.** [predestined] déterminé(e) d'avance **2.** [prearranged] organisé(e) *OR* fixé(e) à l'avance.

predicament [prɪ'dɪkəmənt] **n** situation *f* difficile ▸ **to be in a predicament** être dans de beaux draps.

predict [prɪ'dɪkt] **vt** prédire.

predictability [prɪ,dɪktə'bɪlətɪ] **n** prévisibilité *f*.

predictable [prɪ'dɪktəbl] **adj** prévisible.

predictably [prɪ'dɪktəblɪ] **adv** [react, behave] d'une manière prévisible ▸ **predictably, he was late** comme c'était à prévoir, il est arrivé en retard.

prediction [prɪ'dɪkʃn] **n** prédiction *f*.

predictor [prɪ'dɪktəʳ] **n** indicateur *m*.

predigest [,priːdaɪ'dʒest] **vt** *fig* prédigérer.

predilection [,priːdɪ'lekʃn] **n : predilection for sthg** prédilection *f* pour qqch.

predispose [,priːdɪs'pəʊz] **vt : to be predisposed to sthg/to do sthg** être prédisposé(e) à qqch/à faire qqch.

predisposition ['priː,dɪspə'zɪʃn] **n : predisposition to sthg/to do sthg, predisposition towards sthg/towards doing sthg** prédisposition *f* à qqch/à faire qqch.

predominance [prɪ'dɒmɪnəns] **n** prédominance *f*.

predominant [prɪ'dɒmɪnənt] **adj** prédominant(e).

predominantly [prɪ'dɒmɪnəntlɪ] **adv** principalement, surtout.

predominate [prɪ'dɒmɪneɪt] **vi** prédominer.

preeminence [,priː'emɪnəns] **n** prééminence *f*.

preeminent [priː'emɪnənt] **adj** le plus en vue (la plus en vue).

preeminently [,priː'emɪnəntlɪ] **adv** de façon prépondérante, avant tout.

preempt [,priː'empt] **vt 1.** [action, decision] devancer, prévenir **2.** [land] acquérir par droit de préemption.

preemptive [,priː'emptɪv] **adj** préventif(ive).

preemptive strike **n** attaque *f* préventive.

preen [priːn] **vt 1.** [subj: bird] lisser, nettoyer **2.** *fig* [subj: person] **: to preen o.s.** se faire beau (belle).

preexist [,priːɪg'zɪst] **vi** préexister.

prefab ['priːfæb] **n** *UK inf* maison *f* préfabriquée.

prefabricate [,priː'fæbrɪkeɪt] **vt** préfabriquer.

prefabricated [,priː'fæbrɪkeɪtɪd] **adj : prefabricated houses** maisons *fpl* en préfabriqué.

preface ['prefɪs] ■ **n : preface (to)** préface *f* (de), préambule *m* (de).

■ **vt : to preface sthg with sthg** faire précéder qqch de qqch.

prefect ['priːfekt] **n** *UK* [pupil] *élève de terminale qui aide les professeurs à maintenir la discipline.*

prefer [prɪ'fɜːʳ] (pt & pp **-red**, cont **-ring**) **vt** préférer ▸ **to prefer sb/sthg to sb/sthg** préférer qqn/qqch à qqn/qqch, aimer mieux qqn/qqch que qqn/qqch ▸ **to prefer to do sthg** préférer faire qqch, aimer mieux faire qqch.

preferable ['prefrəbl] **adj : preferable (to)** préférable (à).

preferably ['prefrəblɪ] **adv** de préférence.

preference ['prefərəns] **n** préférence *f*.

preference shares *UK* **npl** *(U)* actions *fpl* privilégiées *OR* de priorité.

preferential [,prefə'renʃl] **adj** préférentiel(elle).

preferential rate **n** tarif *m* préférentiel.

preferred [prɪ'fɜːd] **adj** préféré(e).

preferred stock *US* = ***preference shares***.

prefigure [priː'fɪgəʳ] **vt** annoncer, préfigurer.

prefix ['priːfɪks] **n** préfixe *m*.

pregnancy ['pregnənsɪ] (pl **-ies**) **n** grossesse *f*.

pregnancy test **n** test *m* de grossesse.

pregnant ['pregnənt] **adj 1.** [woman] enceinte / [animal] pleine, gravide **2.** *fig* [pause] lourd(e) de sens.

preheat [,priː'hiːt] **vt** préchauffer.

preheated [,priː'hiːtɪd] **adj** préchauffé(e).

prehistoric [,priːhɪ'stɒrɪk] **adj** préhistorique.

prehistory [,priː'hɪstərɪ] **n** préhistoire *f*.

pre-industrial **adj** préindustriel(elle).

pre-installed **adj** [software] préinstallé(e).

prejudge [,priː'dʒʌdʒ] **vt** [situation, issue] préjuger de / [person] juger d'avance.

HOW TO ...

express preferences

Je préfère de loin le cinéma à la télévision / I much prefer the cinema to television

Je préférerais que tu y ailles à ma place / I'd rather you went instead of me

J'aime mieux le vin rouge que le vin blanc / I prefer red wine to white wine

Plutôt que d'y aller en train, j'aimerais mieux y aller en avion / I'd rather fly than go by train

Samedi me conviendrait davantage / Saturday would suit me better

prejudice ['predʒʊdɪs] ■ **n 1.** [biased view] **: prejudice (in favour of/against)** préjugé *m* (en faveur de/contre), préjugés *mpl* (en faveur de/contre) **2.** *(U)* [harm] préjudice *m*, tort *m*.
■ **vt 1.** [bias] **: to prejudice sb (in favour of/against)** prévenir qqn (en faveur de/contre), influencer qqn (en faveur de/contre) **2.** [harm] porter préjudice à.

prejudiced ['predʒʊdɪst] **adj** [person] qui a des préjugés / [opinion] préconçu(e) ▸ **to be prejudiced in favour of/against** avoir des préjugés en faveur de/contre.

prejudicial [ˌpredʒʊ'dɪʃl] **adj : prejudicial (to)** préjudiciable (à), nuisible (à).

prelate ['prelɪt] **n** prélat *m*.

preliminary [prɪ'lɪmɪnərɪ] (pl **-ies**) **adj** préliminaire.
◆ ***preliminaries*** **npl** préliminaires *mpl*.

prelims ['pri:lɪmz] **npl** *UK* [exams] examens *mpl* préliminaires.

prelude ['prelju:d] **n** [event] **: prelude to sthg** prélude *m* de qqch.

premarital [ˌpri:'mærɪtl] **adj** avant le mariage.

premature ['preməˌtjʊər] **adj** prématuré(e).

prematurely ['preməˌtjʊəlɪ] **adv** prématurément.

premeditate [ˌpri:'medɪteɪt] **vt** préméditer.

premeditated [ˌpri:'medɪteɪtɪd] **adj** prémédité(e).

premeditation [pri:ˌmedɪ'teɪʃn] **n** préméditation *f* ▸ **without premeditation** sans préméditation.

premenstrual [pri:'menstrʊəl] **adj** prémenstruel(elle).

premenstrual syndrome, ***premenstrual tension*** *UK* [pri:'menstrʊəl-] **n** syndrome *m* prémenstruel.

premier ['premjər] ■ **adj** primordial(e), premier(ère).
■ **n** premier ministre *m*.

premiere ['premɪeər] **n** première *f*.

Premier League **n** *en Angleterre, ligue indépendante regroupant les meilleurs clubs de football.*

premiership ['premɪəʃɪp] **n** fonction *f* de premier ministre.

premise ['premɪs] **n** prémisse *f* ▸ **on the premise that** en partant du principe que.
◆ ***premises*** **npl** local *m*, locaux *mpl* ▸ **on the premises** sur place, sur les lieux.

premium ['pri:mjəm] **n** prime *f* ▸ **at a premium** [above usual value] à prix d'or / [in great demand] très recherché(e) *OR* demandé(e) ▸ **to put *OR* place a high premium on sthg** accorder *OR* attacher beaucoup d'importance à qqch.

premium bond **n** *UK* ≃ billet *m* de loterie.

premium price **n** prix *m* de prestige.

premium product **n** produit *m* de prestige.

premonition [ˌpremə'nɪʃn] **n** prémonition *f*, pressentiment *m*.

prenatal [ˌpri:'neɪtl] **adj** prénatal(e).

prenatal clinic **n** service *m* de consultation prénatale.

pre-nup **n** *inf* contrat *m* de mariage.

prenuptial [ˌpri:'nʌpʃl] **adj** prénuptial(e) ▸ **prenuptial agreement *OR* contract** contrat *m* de mariage.

preoccupation [pri:ˌɒkjʊ'peɪʃn] **n** préoccupation *f* ▸ **preoccupation with sthg** souci *m* de qqch.

preoccupied [pri:'ɒkjʊpaɪd] **adj : preoccupied (with)** préoccupé(e) (de).

preoccupy [pri:'ɒkjʊpaɪ] (pt & pp **-ied**) **vt** préoccuper.

preordain [ˌpri:ɔ:'deɪn] **vt** décider *OR* déterminer d'avance ▸ **to be preordained to do sthg** être prédestiné(e) à faire qqch.

prep [prep] **n** *(U) UK inf* devoirs *mpl*.

pre-packaged **adj** préconditionné(e), préemballé(e).

prepacked [ˌpri:'pækt] **adj** préconditionné(e).

prepaid ['pri:peɪd] **adj** payé(e) d'avance / [envelope] affranchi(e).

preparation [ˌprepə'reɪʃn] **n** préparation *f* ▸ **in preparation for** en vue de.
◆ ***preparations*** **npl** préparatifs *mpl* ▸ **to make preparations for** faire des préparatifs pour, prendre ses dispositions pour.

> CONFUSABLE / PARONYME
>
> **preparation**
>
> When translating **preparation**, note that ***préparatifs*** and ***préparation*** are not interchangeable. ***Préparatifs*** refers to the arrangements that are made for something, whereas ***préparation*** is used to describe the process of getting something ready, such as a meal.

preparatory [prɪ'pærətrɪ] **adj** [work, classes] préparatoire / [actions, measures] préliminaire.

preparatory school **n** [in UK] école *f* primaire privée / [in US] *école privée qui prépare à l'enseignement supérieur.*

prepare [prɪ'peər] ■ **vt** préparer.
■ **vi : to prepare for sthg/to do sthg** se préparer à qqch/à faire qqch.

prepared [prɪ'peəd] **adj 1.** [done beforehand] préparé(e) d'avance **2.** [willing] **: to be prepared to do sthg** être prêt(e) *OR* disposé(e) à faire qqch **3.** [ready] **: to be prepared for sthg** être prêt(e) pour qqch.

preparedness [prɪ'peədnɪs] **n : preparedness for war** préparation *f* à la guerre.

preponderance [prɪ'pɒndərəns] **n** *fml* majorité *f*.

preponderantly [prɪ'pɒndərəntlɪ] **adv** *fml* surtout, pour la plupart.

preposition [ˌprepə'zɪʃn] **n** préposition *f*.

prepossessing [ˌpri:pə'zesɪŋ] **adj** *fml* agréable, attrayant(e).

preposterous [prɪ'pɒstərəs] **adj** ridicule, absurde.

preposterously [prɪ'pɒstərəslɪ] **adv** absurdement, ridiculement.

preppie, ***preppy*** ['prepɪ] *esp US inf* ■ **n** (pl **-ies**) **: he's a preppie** il est BCBG.
■ **adj** BCBG.

preprogrammed [ˌpri:'prəʊgræmd] **adj** préprogrammé(e).

prep school abbr of ***preparatory school***.

prequel ['pri:kwəl] n *film ou roman racontant une histoire antérieure à une histoire principale, traitée dans un autre film ou roman.*

Pre-Raphaelite [ˌpri:'ræfəlaɪt] ■ adj préraphaélite.
■ n préraphaélite *mf*.

prerecord [ˌpri:rɪ'kɔ:d] vt préenregistrer.

prerecorded [ˌpri:rɪ'kɔ:dɪd] adj enregistré(e) à l'avance, préenregistré(e).

prerequisite [ˌpri:'rekwɪzɪt] n condition *f* préalable.

prerogative [prɪ'rɒgətɪv] n prérogative *f*, privilège *m*.

Pres. abbr of ***president***.

presage ['presɪdʒ] vt *fml* présager.

Presbyterian [ˌprezbɪ'tɪərɪən] ■ adj presbytérien(enne).
■ n presbytérien *m*, -enne *f*.

presbytery ['prezbɪtrɪ] n [residence] presbytère *m*.

preschool [ˌpri:'sku:l] ■ adj préscolaire.
■ n *US* école *f* maternelle.

prescient ['presɪənt] adj *fml* prescient(e).

prescribe [prɪ'skraɪb] vt **1.** MED prescrire **2.** [order] ordonner, imposer.

prescription [prɪ'skrɪpʃn] n [MED - written form] ordonnance *f* / [- medicine] médicament *m* ▸ **on prescription** sur ordonnance.

prescription charge n *UK prix (fixe) à payer pour chaque médicament figurant sur une ordonnance.*

prescriptive [prɪ'skrɪptɪv] adj normatif(ive).

preselect [ˌpri:sə'lekt] vt [tracks, channels] prérégler.

presence ['prezns] n présence *f* ▸ **to be in sb's presence** *OR* **in the presence of sb** être en présence de qqn ▸ **your presence is requested at Saturday's meeting** vous êtes prié d'assister à la réunion de samedi ▸ **there was a large student/police presence at the demonstration** il y avait un nombre important d'étudiants/un important service d'ordre à la manifestation ▸ **to have presence** avoir de la présence.

presence of mind n présence *f* d'esprit.

present ■ adj ['preznt] **1.** [current] actuel(elle) ▸ **at the present time** actuellement, à l'époque actuelle **2.** [in attendance] présent(e) ▸ **to be present at** assister à.
■ n ['preznt] **1.** [current time] **: the present** le présent ▸ **at present** actuellement, en ce moment ▸ **for the present** pour le moment ▸ **up to the present** jusqu'à présent, jusqu'à maintenant **2.** [gift] cadeau *m* ▸ **it's for a present** [in shop] c'est pour offrir **3.** GRAM **: present (tense)** présent *m*.
■ vt [prɪ'zent] **1.** [gen] présenter / [opportunity] donner ▸ **to present a bill in Parliament** présenter *OR* introduire un projet de loi au parlement **2.** [give] donner, remettre ▸ **to present sb with sthg, to present sthg to sb** donner *OR* remettre qqch à qqn **3.** [portray] représenter, décrire **4.** [arrive] **: to present o.s.** se présenter ▸ **if the opportunity presents itself** si l'occasion se présente.

presentable [prɪ'zentəbl] adj présentable.

presentation [ˌprezn'teɪʃn] n **1.** [gen] présentation *f* ▸ **on presentation of this voucher** sur présentation de ce bon **2.** [ceremony] remise *f* (de récompense/prix) **3.** [talk] exposé *m* ▸ **he made a very clear presentation of the case** il a très clairement présenté l'affaire **4.** [of play] représentation *f*.

presentation copy n exemplaire *m* offert gracieusement.

presentation pack n paquet *m* de présentation.

present day n **: the present day** aujourd'hui.
◆ ***present-day*** adj d'aujourd'hui, contemporain(e).

presenter [prɪ'zentər] n *UK* présentateur *m*, -trice *f*.

presentiment [prɪ'zentɪmənt] n *fml* pressentiment *m*.

presently ['prezəntlɪ] adv **1.** [soon] bientôt, tout à l'heure **2.** [at present] actuellement, en ce moment.

present perfect n passé *m* composé ▸ **in the present perfect** au passé composé.

present tense n présent *m* ▸ **in the present tense** au présent.

preservation [ˌprezə'veɪʃn] n *(U)* **1.** [maintenance] maintien *m* **2.** [protection] protection *f*, conservation *f*.

preservation order n esp *UK décret ordonnant la conservation d'un monument, édifice etc.*

preservative [prɪ'zɜ:vətɪv] n conservateur *m*.

preserve [prɪ'zɜ:v] ■ vt **1.** [maintain] maintenir **2.** [protect] conserver **3.** [food] conserver, mettre en conserve.
■ n [jam] confiture *f*.
◆ ***preserves*** npl [jam] confiture *f* / [vegetables] pickles *mpl*, condiments *mpl*.

preserved [prɪ'zɜ:vd] adj conservé(e).

preset [ˌpri:'set] (pt & pp **preset**, cont **-ting**) vt prérégler.

preshrunk [ˌpri:'ʃrʌŋk] adj irrétrécissable.

preside [prɪ'zaɪd] vi **: to preside (over *OR* at sthg)** présider (qqch).

presidency ['prezɪdənsɪ] (pl **-ies**) n présidence *f*.

president ['prezɪdənt] n **1.** [gen] président *m* **2.** *US* [company chairman] P-DG *m*.

president-elect n *titre du président des États-Unis nouvellement élu (en novembre) jusqu'à la cérémonie d'investiture présidentielle (le 20 janvier).*

presidential [ˌprezɪ'denʃl] adj présidentiel(elle).

press [pres] ■ n **1.** [push] pression *f*
2. [journalism] **: the press** [newspapers] la presse, les journaux *mpl* / [reporters] les journalistes *mpl* ▸ **they advertised in the press** ils ont fait passer une annonce dans les journaux ▸ **to get a good/bad press** avoir bonne/mauvaise presse
3. [printing machine] presse *f* / [for wine] pressoir *m*.
■ vt **1.** [push] appuyer sur ▸ **to press sthg against sthg** appuyer qqch sur qqch ▸ **I pressed myself against the wall** je me suis collé contre le mur ▸ **he pressed the lid shut** il a fermé le couvercle (en appuyant dessus) ▸ **to press sthg flat** aplatir qqch
2. [squeeze] serrer
3. [iron] repasser, donner un coup de fer à

4. [urge] **: to press sb (to do sthg *OR* into doing sthg)** presser qqn (de faire qqch) ▸ **to press sb for sthg** demander qqch à qqn avec insistance ▸ **to press sb for an answer** presser qqn de répondre
5. [force] **: to press sthg on *OR* upon sb** offrir qqch à qqn avec insistance
6. [pursue - claim] insister sur ▸ **to press (home) an advantage** profiter d'un avantage
7. LAW **: to press charges (against sb)** porter plainte (contre qqn).
■ **vi 1.** [push] **: to press (on sthg)** appuyer (sur qqch)
2. [squeeze] **: to press (on sthg)** serrer (qqch)
3. [crowd] se presser ▸ **they pressed forward to get a better view** ils poussaient pour essayer de mieux voir.
◆ ***press for*** **vt insep** demander avec insistance.
◆ ***press on*** **vi** [continue] **: to press on (with sthg)** continuer (qqch), ne pas abandonner (qqch) ▸ **we pressed on regardless** nous avons continué malgré tout.

press agency **n** agence *f* de presse.

press agent **n** agent *m* de publicité.

press baron **n** *UK* baron *m* ***OR*** magnat *m* de la presse.

press box **n** tribune *f* de la presse.

press campaign **n** campagne *f* de presse.

press clipping **n** *US* = ***press cutting***.

Press Complaints Commission **n** *organisme britannique de contrôle de la presse.*

press conference **n** conférence *f* de presse.

press corps **n** journalistes *mpl*.

press coverage **n** couverture *f* presse.

press cutting *UK*, ***press clipping*** *US* **n** coupure *f* de journal.

pressed [prest] **adj : to be pressed for time/money** être à court de temps/d'argent.

press fastener **n** *UK* pression *f*.

press gallery **n** tribune *f* de la presse.

pressgang ['presgæŋ] ■ **n** enrôleurs *mpl*, racoleurs *mpl*.
■ **vt** *UK* **: to pressgang sb into doing sthg** forcer la main à qqn pour qu'il fasse qqch.

pressing ['presɪŋ] **adj** urgent(e).

press kit **n** dossier *m* de presse *(distribué aux journalistes)*.

pressman ['presmæn] (pl -men [-men]) **n** *UK dated* journaliste *m*.

press officer **n** attaché *m* de presse.

press release **n** communiqué *m* de presse.

press secretary **n** POL ≃ porte-parole *m inv* du gouvernement.

press stud **n** *UK* pression *f*.

press-up **n** *UK* pompe *f*, traction *f*.

pressure ['preʃər] ■ **n** *(U)* **1.** [gen] pression *f* ▸ **to put pressure on sb (to do sthg)** faire pression sur qqn (pour qu'il fasse qqch) ▸ **we're under pressure to finish on time** on nous presse de respecter les délais ▸ **the pressure of work is too much for me** la charge de travail est trop lourde pour moi ▸ **she's under a lot of pressure just now** elle est vraiment sous pression en ce moment **2.** [stress] tension *f*.
■ **vt : to pressure sb to do *OR* into doing sthg** forcer qqn à faire qqch.

pressure cooker **n** Cocotte-Minute® *f*, autocuiseur *m*.

pressure gauge **n** manomètre *m*.

pressure group **n** groupe *m* de pression.

pressurization, *UK* ***-isation*** [ˌpreʃəraɪ'zeɪʃn] **n** pressurisation *f*.

pressurize, *UK* ***-ise*** ['preʃəraɪz] **vt 1.** TECH pressuriser **2.** *UK* [force] **: to pressurize sb to do *OR* into doing sthg** forcer qqn à faire qqch.

pressurized, *UK* ***-ised*** ['preʃəraɪzd] **adj** [container] pressurisé(e) / [liquid, gas] sous pression.

Prestel® ['prestel] **n** *UK* ≃ Télétel® *m*.

prestige [pre'stiːʒ] ■ **n** prestige *m*.
■ **comp** de prestige.

prestigious [pre'stɪdʒəs] **adj** prestigieux(euse).

presto [prestəʊ] **excl : (hey) presto!** passez muscade!

prestressed concrete [ˌpriː'strest-] **n** béton *m* précontraint.

presumably [prɪ'zjuːməblɪ] **adv** vraisemblablement.

presume [prɪ'zjuːm] **vt** présumer ▸ **to presume (that)...** supposer que... ▸ **presuming they agree** à supposer qu'ils soient d'accord ▸ **missing, presumed dead** MIL manque à l'appel ***OR*** porté disparu, présumé mort.

presumption [prɪ'zʌmpʃn] **n 1.** [assumption] supposition *f*, présomption *f* **2.** *(U)* [audacity] présomption *f*.

presumptuous [prɪ'zʌmptʃʊəs] **adj** présomptueux(euse).

presuppose [ˌpriːsə'pəʊz] **vt** présupposer.

pretax [ˌpriː'tæks] **adj** avant impôts.

pretence *UK*, ***pretense*** *US* [prɪ'tens] **n** prétention *f* ▸ **to make a pretence of doing sthg** faire semblant de faire qqch ▸ **under false pretences** sous des prétextes fallacieux.

pretend [prɪ'tend] ■ **vt : to pretend to do sthg** faire semblant de faire qqch ▸ **he pretended to be *OR* that he was their uncle** il s'est fait passer pour leur oncle ▸ **she pretends that everything is all right** elle fait comme si tout allait bien.
■ **vi** faire semblant ▸ **there's no point in pretending (to me)** inutile de faire semblant (avec moi) ▸ **I'm only pretending!** c'est juste pour rire!

FALSE FRIENDS / FAUX AMIS
pretend
Prétendre n'est pas la traduction du mot anglais *to pretend*. Prétendre se traduit par *to claim*.
▸ **Elle prétend que son enfant sait déjà marcher** / *She claims her child can already walk*

pretense *US* = ***pretence***.

pretension [prɪ'tenʃn] **n** prétention *f* ▸ **to have pretensions to sthg** avoir des prétentions à qqch.

pretentious [prɪ'tenʃəs] **adj** prétentieux(euse).

pretentiously [prɪ'tenʃəslɪ] **adv** de façon prétentieuse.

pretentiousness [prɪ'tenʃəsnɪs] n *(U)* prétention *f*.

preterite ['pretərət] n prétérit *m*.

pretext ['pri:tekst] n prétexte *m* ▸ **on OR under the pretext that...** sous prétexte que... ▸ **on OR under the pretext of doing sthg** sous prétexte de faire qqch.

Pretoria [prɪ'tɔ:rɪə] n Pretoria.

prettify ['prɪtɪfaɪ] (pt & pp -ied) vt enjoliver.

prettily ['prɪtɪlɪ] adv joliment.

prettiness ['prɪtɪnɪs] n **1.** [of appearance] beauté *f* **2.** *pej* [of style] mièvrerie *f*.

pretty ['prɪtɪ] ■ adj (comp -ier, superl -iest) **1.** [clothes, girl, place] joli(e) **2.** *pej* [style] précieux(euse).
■ adv [quite] plutôt ▸ **pretty much OR well** pratiquement, presque.

pretzel ['pretsl] n bretzel *m*.

prevail [prɪ'veɪl] vi **1.** [be widespread] avoir cours, régner **2.** [triumph] **: to prevail (over)** prévaloir (sur), l'emporter (sur) **3.** [persuade] **: to prevail on OR upon sb to do sthg** persuader qqn de faire qqch.

prevailing [prɪ'veɪlɪŋ] adj **1.** [current] actuel(elle) **2.** [wind] dominant(e).

prevalence ['prevələns] n *(U)* fréquence *f*.

prevalent ['prevələnt] adj courant(e), répandu(e).

prevaricate [prɪ'værɪkeɪt] vi *fml* tergiverser.

prevarication [prɪˌværɪ'keɪʃn] n *fml* tergiversation *f*, faux-fuyant *m*, faux-fuyants *mpl*.

prevent [prɪ'vent] vt **: to prevent sb/sthg (from doing sthg)** empêcher qqn/qqch (de faire qqch).

preventable [prɪ'ventəbl] adj qui peut être évité(e).

preventative [prɪ'ventətɪv] = ***preventive***.

prevention [prɪ'venʃn] n *(U)* prévention *f*.

preventive [prɪ'ventɪv] adj préventif(ive).

preview ['pri:vju:] n avant-première *f*.

previous ['pri:vjəs] adj **1.** [earlier] antérieur(e) ▸ **on a previous occasion** auparavant ▸ **I have a previous engagement** j'ai déjà un rendez-vous, je suis déjà pris ▸ **do you have any previous experience of this kind of work?** avez-vous déjà une expérience de ce genre de travail? **2.** [preceding] précédent(e).

previously ['pri:vjəslɪ] adv avant, auparavant.

prewar [ˌpri:'wɔ:r] adj d'avant-guerre.

prey [preɪ] n proie *f* ▸ **to fall prey to** devenir la proie de.
◆ ***prey on*** vt insep **1.** [live off] faire sa proie de **2.** [trouble] **: to prey on sb's mind** ronger qqn, tracasser qqn.

price [praɪs] ■ n **1.** [cost] prix *m* ▸ **prices are rising/falling** les prix sont en hausse/baisse ▸ **at any price** à tout prix ▸ **she achieved fame, but at a price** elle est devenue célèbre, mais ça lui a coûté cher ▸ **he puts a high price on loyalty** il attache beaucoup d'importance OR il accorde beaucoup de valeur à la loyauté **2.** [penalty] **: that's the price of fame** c'est la rançon de la gloire ▸ **to pay the price for sthg** payer le prix pour qqch ▸ **it's a small price to pay for peace of mind** c'est bien peu de chose pour avoir l'esprit tranquille.
■ vt fixer le prix de ▸ **his paintings are rather highly priced** le prix de ses tableaux est un peu élevé ▸ **the book is priced at £17** le livre coûte 17 livres.
◆ ***price down*** vt sep baisser le prix de, démarquer.
◆ ***price up*** vt sep augmenter le prix de.

price bid n offre *f* de prix.

price ceiling n plafond *m* de prix.

price cut n rabais *m*, réduction *f* (de prix).

price-cutting n *(U)* réductions *fpl* de prix.

-priced [praɪst] suffix **: high-priced** à prix élevé, (plutôt) cher(chère) ▸ **low-priced** à bas prix, peu cher(chère) ▸ **over-priced** trop cher(chère).

price differential n écart *m* de prix.

price-fixing [-fɪksɪŋ] n *(U)* contrôle *m* des prix.

price freeze n gel *m* des prix.

price increase n hausse *f* OR augmentation *f* des prix.

price index n indice *m* des prix.

priceless ['praɪslɪs] adj sans prix, inestimable.

price list n tarif *m*.

price tag n [label] étiquette *f*.

price war n guerre *f* des prix.

pricey ['praɪsɪ] (comp -ier, superl -iest) adj *inf* chérot *(inv)*.

prick [prɪk] ■ n **1.** [scratch, wound] piqûre *f* **2.** *vulg* [penis] bite *f* **3.** *vulg* [stupid person] con *m*, conne *f*.
■ vt piquer.
◆ ***prick up*** vt insep **: to prick up one's ears** [animal] dresser les oreilles / [person] dresser OR tendre l'oreille.

prickle ['prɪkl] ■ n **1.** [thorn] épine *f* **2.** [sensation on skin] picotement *m*.
■ vi picoter.

prickly ['prɪklɪ] (comp -ier, superl -iest) adj **1.** [plant, bush] épineux(euse) **2.** *fig* [person] irritable.

prickly heat n *(U)* boutons *mpl* de chaleur.

pride [praɪd] ■ n *(U)* **1.** [satisfaction] fierté *f* ▸ **to take pride in sthg/in doing sthg** être fier de qqch/de faire qqch ▸ **it was his pride and joy** c'était sa fierté ▸ **to have pride of place** avoir la place d'honneur **2.** [self-esteem] orgueil *m*, amour-propre *m* ▸ **to swallow one's pride** ravaler son orgueil **3.** *pej* [arrogance] orgueil *m*.
■ vt **: to pride o.s. on sthg** être fier (fière) de qqch.

priest [pri:st] n prêtre *m*.

priestess ['pri:stɪs] n prêtresse *f*.

priesthood ['pri:sthud] n **1.** [position, office] **: the priesthood** le sacerdoce **2.** [priests] **: the priesthood** le clergé.

prig [prɪg] n *pej* petit saint *m*, petite sainte *f*.

prim [prɪm] (comp -mer, superl -mest) adj *pej* guindé(e).

primacy ['praɪməsɪ] n *fml* primauté *f*.

prima donna [,priːmə'dɒnə] (pl -s) **n** prima donna *f inv* ▸ **to be a prima donna** *fig & pej* se prendre pour le nombril du monde.

primaeval [praɪ'miːvəl] *UK* = ***primeval***.

prima facie [,praɪmə'feɪʃiː] **adj** *fml* : **prima facie evidence** commencement *m* de preuve ▸ **prima facie case** affaire *f* qui, de prime abord, paraît fondée.

primal ['praɪml] **adj** *fml* **1.** [original] primitif(ive) **2.** [most important] primordial(e).

primarily ['praɪmərɪlɪ] **adv** principalement.

primary ['praɪmərɪ] ■ **adj 1.** [main] premier(ère), principal(e) **2.** SCH primaire.
■ **n** (pl **-ies**) *US* POL primaire *f.*

CULTURE

Primaries

Aux États-Unis, les « primaires » sont des assemblées locales organisées l'année de l'élection présidentielle, qui peuvent être tenues à tous les niveaux du gouvernement durant l'été : elles ont pour but de désigner les candidats de chaque parti (démocrate ou républicain), ainsi que les délégués de la Convention nationale qui soutiendront leur candidat unique à la présidence et à la vice-présidence. Au fur et à mesure de la campagne, les postulants sont éliminés au profit d'un favori : s'il se démarque dans chaque État et obtient l'adhésion des délégués, il a toutes les chances d'être élu en tant que représentant du parti. Il est officiellement désigné lors des conventions nationales, qui visent à promouvoir l'unité d'un parti et son programme politique.

primary colour *UK*, ***primary color*** *US* **n** couleur *f* primaire.

primary election **n** *US* primaire *f.*

primary market **n** marché *m* primaire.

primary school **n** école *f* primaire.

primary sector **n** secteur *m* primaire.

primate ['praɪmeɪt] **n 1.** ZOOL primate *m* **2.** RELIG primat *m.*

prime [praɪm] ■ **adj 1.** [main] principal(e), primordial(e) ▸ **of prime importance** de la plus haute importance, d'une importance primordiale **2.** [excellent] excellent(e) ▸ **it's a prime example of what I mean** c'est un excellent exemple de ce que je veux dire ▸ **prime quality** première qualité ▸ **prime cut of meat** morceau de premier choix.
■ **n** : **to be in one's prime** être dans la fleur de l'âge ▸ **to be past one's prime** être sur le retour.
■ **vt 1.** [gun, pump] amorcer **2.** [paint] apprêter **3.** [inform] : **to prime sb about sthg** mettre qqn au courant de qqch ▸ **to prime sb for a meeting** préparer qqn à une réunion.

prime minister **n** premier ministre *m.*

prime ministership, prime ministry **n** fonctions *fpl* de Premier ministre ▸ **during her prime ministership** pendant qu'elle était Premier ministre.

prime mover [-'muːvər] **n** instigateur *m*, -trice *f.*

prime number **n** nombre *m* premier.

primer ['praɪmər] **n 1.** [paint] apprêt *m* **2.** [textbook] introduction *f.*

prime time **n** *(U)* RADIO & TV heures *fpl* de grande écoute.
◆ ***prime-time*** **adj** aux heures de grande écoute.

prime-time advertising **n** publicité *f* au prime time.

primeval [praɪ'miːvl] **adj** [ancient] primitif(ive).

primitive ['prɪmɪtɪv] **adj** primitif(ive).

primly ['prɪmlɪ] **adv** *pej* d'une manière guindée OR collet monté ▸ **to be primly dressed** être habillé très comme il faut ▸ **she sat primly in the corner** elle se tenait assise très sagement dans le coin.

primordial [praɪ'mɔːdjəl] **adj** primordial(e).

primrose ['prɪmrəʊz] **n** primevère *f.*

Primus stove® ['praɪməs-] **n** *UK* réchaud *m* de camping.

prince [prɪns] **n** prince *m.*
◆ ***Prince*** **n** : **Prince of Wales** Prince de Galles.

Prince Charming **n** prince *m* charmant.

Prince Edward Island [-'edwəd-] **n** l'île *f* du Prince-Édouard.

princely ['prɪnslɪ] (comp **-ier**, superl **-iest**) **adj** princier(ère).

prince regent **n** prince *m* régent.

princess [prɪn'ses] **n** princesse *f.*
◆ ***Princess*** **n** : **the Princess Royal** la princesse royale.

principal ['prɪnsəpl] ■ **adj** principal(e).
■ **n 1.** *esp UK* SCH directeur *m*, -trice *f* **2.** UNIV doyen *m*, -enne *f.*

principal boy **n** *jeune héros d'une pantomime dont le rôle est traditionnellement joué par une femme.*

principality [,prɪnsɪ'pælətɪ] (pl **-ies**) **n** principauté *f.*

principally ['prɪnsəplɪ] **adv** principalement.

principle ['prɪnsəpl] **n** principe *m* ▸ **on principle, as a matter of principle** par principe ▸ **she has high principles** elle a des principes ▸ **she was a woman of principle** c'était une femme de principes OR qui avait des principes ▸ **it's against my principles to eat meat** j'ai pour principe de ne pas manger de viande.
◆ ***in principle*** **adv** en principe.

principled ['prɪnsəpld] **adj** [behaviour] dicté(e) par des principes / [person] qui a des principes.

print [prɪnt] ■ **n 1.** *(U)* [type] caractères *mpl* ▸ **in large print** en gros caractères ▸ **to appear in print** être publié(e) OR imprimé(e) ▸ **to be in print** être disponible ▸ **to be out of print** être épuisé(e) ▸ **the small** OR **fine print on a**

contract les lignes en petits caractères en bas d'un contrat **2.** ART gravure *f* **3.** [photograph] épreuve *f* **4.** [fabric] imprimé *m* **5.** [mark] empreinte *f*.
■ **vt 1.** [produce by printing] imprimer **2.** [publish] publier **3.** [write in block letters] écrire en caractères d'imprimerie.
■ **vi** [printer] imprimer.
◆ ***print out*** **vt sep** COMPUT imprimer.

printed ['prɪntɪd] **adj 1.** [gen] imprimé(e) ▸ **printed matter** imprimés *mpl* ▸ **the printed word** l'écrit *m* **2.** [notepaper] à en-tête.

printed circuit ['prɪntɪd-] **n** circuit *m* imprimé.

printed matter ['prɪntɪd-] **n** *(U)* imprimés *mpl*.

printer ['prɪntəʳ] **n 1.** [person, firm] imprimeur *mf* **2.** COMPUT imprimante *f*.

printing ['prɪntɪŋ] **n** *(U)* **1.** [act of printing] impression *f* **2.** [trade] imprimerie *f*.

printing press **n** presse *f* typographique.

printout ['prɪntaʊt] **n** COMPUT sortie *f* d'imprimante, listing *m*.

print run **n** tirage *m*.

prior ['praɪəʳ] ■ **adj** antérieur(e), précédent(e).
■ **n** [monk] prieur *m*.
◆ ***prior to*** **prep** avant ▸ **prior to doing sthg** avant de faire qqch.

prioritize, *UK* ***-ise*** [praɪ'ɒrɪtaɪz] **vt** donner la priorité à.

priority [praɪ'ɒrətɪ] ■ **adj** prioritaire.
■ **n** (pl **-ies**) priorité *f* ▸ **to have** *OR* **take priority (over)** avoir la priorité (sur) ▸ **to give priority to** donner *OR* accorder la priorité à ▸ **to do sthg as a (matter of) priority** faire qqch en priorité ▸ **the matter has top priority** l'affaire a la priorité absolue *OR* est absolument prioritaire.
◆ ***priorities*** **npl** priorités *fpl*.

priory ['praɪərɪ] (pl **-ies**) **n** prieuré *m*.

prise [praɪz] **vt : to prise sthg away from sb** arracher qqch à qqn ▸ **to prise sthg open** forcer qqch.

prism ['prɪzm] **n** prisme *m*.

prison ['prɪzn] **n** prison *f*.

prison camp **n** camp *m* de prisonniers.

prisoner ['prɪznəʳ] **n** prisonnier *m*, -ère *f* ▸ **to be taken prisoner** être fait prisonnier.

prisoner of war (pl **prisoners of war**) **n** prisonnier *m*, -ère *f* de guerre.

prissy ['prɪsɪ] (comp **-ier**, superl **-iest**) **adj** *pej* prude, guindé(e).

pristine ['prɪsti:n] **adj** [condition] parfait(e) / [clean] immaculé(e).

privacy [*UK* 'prɪvəsɪ, *US* 'praɪvəsɪ] **n** intimité *f*.

private ['praɪvɪt] ■ **adj 1.** [not public] privé(e) ▸ **private road** voie *f* privée ▸ **'private'** 'privé', 'interdit au public' ▸ **they want a private wedding** ils veulent se marier dans l'intimité **2.** [confidential] confidentiel(elle) ▸ **a private conversation** une conversation privée *OR* à caractère privé **3.** [personal] personnel(elle) ▸ **my private address** mon adresse personnelle, mon domicile **4.** [unsociable - person] secret(ète) ▸ **he's a very private person** c'est quelqu'un de très réservé.
■ **n 1.** [soldier] (simple) soldat *m* **2.** [secrecy] **: in private** en privé.
◆ ***privates*** **npl** *inf* parties *fpl*.

CULTURE
Private Education

Au Royaume-Uni, plus de 2 000 écoles échappent au contrôle gouvernemental et dispensent une éducation traditionnelle agrémentée d'activités sportives. Ces établissements, mixtes ou non, que l'on qualifie d'écoles privées en raison des frais de scolarité, accueillent des élèves qui peuvent être pensionnaires. Ils sont supervisés par des administrateurs, un intendant chargé de la gestion financière et un proviseur qui nomme le personnel, inscrit les élèves et prend certaines décisions. Les élèves brillants peuvent bénéficier de bourses d'études, dont le montant varie mais ne couvre que très rarement les frais de scolarité : ils sont récompensés après un examen pour leurs facultés intellectuelles ou artistiques.

private company **n** société *f* privée.

private detective **n** détective *m* privé.

private enterprise **n** *(U)* entreprise *f* privée.

private eye **n** détective *m* privé.

private income **n** revenu *m* personnel.

private investigator **n** détective *m* privé.

private life **n** vie *f* privée ▸ **in (his) private life** dans sa vie privée, en privé.

privately ['praɪvɪtlɪ] **adv 1.** [not by the state] **: privately owned** du secteur privé ▸ **to be privately educated** [at school] faire ses études dans une école privée / [with tutor] avoir un précepteur **2.** [confidentially] en privé ▸ **we met privately** nous avons eu une entrevue privée ▸ **can I see you privately?** puis-je vous voir en privé *OR* en tête-à-tête? **3.** [personally] intérieurement, dans son for intérieur.

private member **n** *UK* simple député *m*.

private parts **npl** *inf* parties *fpl*.

private pension **n** retraite *f* complémentaire.

private practice **n** *(U)* *UK* cabinet *m* de médecin non conventionné.

private property **n** propriété *f* privée.

private school **n** école *f* privée.

private screening, ***private showing*** **n** CIN projection *OR* séance *f* privée.

private sector **n : the private sector** le secteur privé.

privation [praɪ'veɪʃn] **n** *fml* privation *f*.

privatization, *UK* ***-isation*** [,praɪvɪtaɪ'zeɪʃn] **n** privatisation *f*.

privatize, *UK* ***-ise*** ['praɪvɪtaɪz] **vt** privatiser.

privet ['prɪvɪt] **n** troène *m*.

privilege ['prɪvɪlɪdʒ] **n** privilège *m*.

privileged ['prɪvɪlɪdʒd] **adj** privilégié(e).

privy ['prɪvɪ] **adj : to be privy to sthg** être dans le secret de qqch.

Privy Council **n** *UK* **: the Privy Council** le Conseil privé.

Privy Purse **n** *UK* **: the Privy Purse** la cassette du souverain.

prize [praɪz] ■ **adj** [possession] très précieux(euse) / [animal] primé(e) / [idiot, example] parfait(e).
■ **n** prix *m*.
■ **vt** priser.

prize day **n** *UK* jour *m* de la distribution des prix.

prizefight ['praɪzfaɪt] **n** combat *m* professionnel.

prizefighter ['praɪzfaɪtəʳ] **n** boxeur *m* professionnel.

prizefighting ['praɪzfaɪtɪŋ] **n** boxe *f* professionnelle.

prize-giving [-ˌgɪvɪŋ] **n** *UK* distribution *f* des prix.

prize money **n** prix *m* en argent.

prizewinner ['praɪzˌwɪnəʳ] **n** gagnant *m*, -e *f*.

prizewinning ['praɪzwɪnɪŋ] **adj** [novel, entry] primé(e) / [ticket, number, contestant] gagnant(e).

pro [prəʊ] (pl -s) **n 1.** *inf* [professional] pro *mf* **2.** [advantage] **: the pros and cons** le pour et le contre.

pro- [prəʊ] **prefix** pro-.

PRO (abbr of ***public relations officer***) **n** *responsable des relations publiques.*

proactive [prəʊ'æktɪv] **adj** [firm, industry, person] dynamique / PSYCHOL proactif(ive).

pro-am ['prəʊ'æm] ■ **adj** pro-am.
■ **n** tournoi *m* pro-am.

probability [ˌprɒbə'bɪlətɪ] (pl -ies) **n** probabilité *f* ▸ **in all probability** selon toute probabilité.

probability sample **n** échantillon *m* probabiliste.

probable ['prɒbəbl] **adj** probable.

probably ['prɒbəblɪ] **adv** probablement ▸ **probably not** probablement pas ▸ **will he write to you? – very probably** il t'écrira? – c'est très probable ▸ **she's probably left already** elle est probablement déjà partie, il est probable qu'elle soit déjà partie.

probate ['prəʊbeɪt] ■ **n** LAW homologation *f*.
■ **vt** *US* LAW homologuer.

probation [prə'beɪʃn] **n** *(U)* **1.** LAW mise *f* à l'épreuve ▸ **to put sb on probation** mettre qqn en sursis avec mise à l'épreuve **2.** [trial period] essai *m* ▸ **to be on probation** être à l'essai.

probationary [prə'beɪʃnrɪ] **adj** [teacher, nurse] à l'essai / [period, year] d'essai.

probationer [prə'beɪʃnəʳ] **n 1.** [employee] stagiaire *mf* **2.** LAW sursitaire *mf* avec mise à l'épreuve.

probation officer **n** agent *m* de probation.

probe [prəʊb] ■ **n 1.** [investigation] **: probe (into)** enquête *f* (sur) **2.** MED & TECH sonde *f*.
■ **vt** sonder.
■ **vi : to probe for** *OR* **into sthg** chercher à découvrir qqch.

probing ['prəʊbɪŋ] **adj** [question] pénétrant(e) / [look] inquisiteur(trice).

probity ['prəʊbətɪ] **n** *fml* probité *f*.

problem ['prɒbləm] ■ **n** problème *m* ▸ **to cause problems for sb** causer des ennuis *OR* poser des problèmes à qqn ▸ **that's going to be a bit of a problem** ça va poser un petit problème ▸ **I don't see what the problem is** je ne vois pas où est le problème ▸ **no problem!** *inf* pas de problème!
■ **comp** difficile.

problematic(al) [ˌprɒblə'mætɪk(l)] **adj** problématique, incertain(e).

problem page **n** *UK* courrier *m* du cœur.

problem-solving [-ˌsɒlvɪŋ] **n** résolution *f* de problèmes.

procedural [prə'siːdʒərəl] **adj** *fml* de procédure.

procedure [prə'siːdʒəʳ] **n** procédure *f*.

proceed ■ **vt** [prə'siːd] [do subsequently] **: to proceed to do sthg** se mettre à faire qqch.
■ **vi** [prə'siːd] **1.** [continue] **: before I proceed** avant d'aller plus loin ▸ **proceed with caution** agissez avec prudence ▸ **let's proceed to item 32** passons à la question 32 ▸ **to proceed (with sthg)** continuer (qqch), poursuivre (qqch) ▸ **to proceed with charges against sb** LAW poursuivre qqn en justice, intenter un procès contre qqn **2.** *fml* [advance] avancer ▸ **they are proceeding towards Calais** ils se dirigent vers Calais.
◆ ***proceeds*** **npl** ['prəʊsiːdz] recette *f* ▸ **all proceeds will go to charity** tout l'argent recueilli sera versé aux œuvres de charité.

proceedings [prə'siːdɪŋz] **npl 1.** [of meeting] débats *mpl* **2.** LAW poursuites *fpl*.

process ['prəʊses] ■ **n 1.** [series of actions] processus *m* ▸ **in the process** ce faisant ▸ **to be in the process of doing sthg** être en train de faire qqch **2.** [method] procédé *m*.
■ **vt** [raw materials, food, data] traiter, transformer / [application] s'occuper de.

processed ['prəʊsest] **adj** [food] traité(e), industriel(elle) *pej* ▸ **processed cheese** [for spreading] fromage *m* à tartiner / [in slices] fromage *m* en tranches.

processing ['prəʊsesɪŋ] **n** traitement *m*, transformation *f*.

procession [prə'seʃn] **n** cortège *m*, procession *f*.

processor ['prəʊsesəʳ] **n 1.** COMPUT processeur *m* **2.** CULIN robot *m* ménager *OR* de cuisine.

pro-choice **adj** pour le droit d'avortement.

proclaim [prə'kleɪm] **vt** proclamer.

proclamation [ˌprɒklə'meɪʃn] **n** proclamation *f*.

proclivity [prə'klɪvətɪ] (pl -ies) **n** *fml* **: proclivity to** *OR* **towards sthg** propension *f* à qqch.

procrastinate [prə'kræstɪneɪt] **vi** *fml* faire traîner les choses.

procrastination [prəˌkræstɪ'neɪʃn] **n** *fml* procrastination *f*.

procreate ['prəʊkrɪeɪt] **vi** *fml* procréer.

procreation [ˌprəʊkrɪ'eɪʃn] **n** *fml* procréation *f*.

proctor ['prɒktəʳ] *US* ■ **n** = ***invigilator***.
■ **vb** = ***invigilate***.

procurator fiscal ['prɒkjʊreɪtəʳ-] **n** *Scot* ≃ procureur *m*.

procure [prə'kjʊəʳ] vt *fml* [for oneself] se procurer / [for someone else] procurer / [release] obtenir.

procurement [prə'kjʊəmənt] n *fml* obtention *f*.

prod [prɒd] ■ n petit coup *m* ▸ **to give sb a prod** *fig* faire rappeler à qqn.
■ vt (pt & pp **-ded**, cont **-ding**) **1.** [push, poke] pousser doucement **2.** [remind, prompt] **: to prod sb (into doing sthg)** pousser OR inciter qqn (à faire qqch).

prodigal ['prɒdɪgl] adj *fml* prodigue.

prodigious [prə'dɪdʒəs] adj prodigieux(euse).

prodigy ['prɒdɪdʒɪ] (pl **-ies**) n prodige *m*.

produce ■ n ['prɒdju:s] *(U)* produits *mpl* ▸ **agricultural/dairy produce** produits agricoles/laitiers ▸ **produce of Spain** produit en Espagne.
■ vt [prə'dju:s] **1.** [gen] produire ▸ **halogen lamps produce a lot of light** les lampes halogènes donnent beaucoup de lumière **2.** [cause] provoquer, causer **3.** [show] présenter ▸ **he produced a £5 note from his pocket** il a sorti un billet de 5 livres de sa poche ▸ **the defendant was unable to produce any proof** l'accusé n'a pu fournir OR apporter aucune preuve **4.** *UK* THEAT mettre en scène.

producer [prə'dju:səʳ] n **1.** [of film, manufacturer] producteur *m*, -trice *f* **2.** *UK* THEAT metteur *m* en scène.

-producing [prə,dju:sɪŋ] suffix producteur(trice) de ▸ **oil-producing** producteur de pétrole.

product ['prɒdʌkt] n produit *m* ▸ **to be a product of sthg** être le produit OR le résultat de qqch.

product awareness n notoriété *f* OR mémorisation *f* du produit.

product bundling n groupage *m* de produits.

production [prə'dʌkʃn] n **1.** *(U)* [manufacture, of film] production *f* ▸ **to go into production** entrer en production ▸ **to put sthg into production** entreprendre la fabrication de qqch **2.** *(U)* [output] rendement *m* **3.** *UK (U)* THEAT [of play] mise *f* en scène **4.** [show - gen] production *f* / THEAT pièce *f*.

production line n chaîne *f* de fabrication.

production manager n directeur *m*, -trice *f* de la production.

productive [prə'dʌktɪv] adj **1.** [land, business, workers] productif(ive) **2.** [meeting, experience] fructueux(euse).

productively [prə'dʌktɪvlɪ] adv **1.** [operate, use] de façon productive **2.** [spend time] de façon fructueuse.

productivity [,prɒdʌk'tɪvətɪ] n productivité *f*.

productivity deal n accord *m* de productivité.

product life cycle n cycle *m* de vie du produit.

product management n gestion *f* de produits.

product manager n chef *m* de produit, directeur *m*, -trice *f* de produit.

product mix n assortiment *m* OR mix *m* de produits.

product placement n CIN & TV placement *m* de produits.

product range n gamme *f* de produits.

product testing n essais *mpl* de produits.

Prof. (abbr of ***Professor***) Pr.

profane [prə'feɪn] adj *fml* impie.

profanity [prə'fænətɪ] (pl **-ies**) n *fml* impiété *f*.

profess [prə'fes] vt *fml* professer ▸ **to profess to do/be** prétendre faire/être.

professed [prə'fest] adj *fml* déclaré(e).

profession [prə'feʃn] n profession *f* ▸ **by profession** de son métier ▸ **she's a lawyer by profession** elle exerce la profession d'avocat, elle est avocate (de profession) ▸ **the teaching profession** le corps enseignant, les enseignants *mpl*.

professional [prə'feʃənl] ■ adj **1.** [gen] professionnel(elle) ▸ **to take** OR **to get professional advice** [gen] consulter un professionnel / [from doctor/lawyer] consulter un médecin/un avocat ▸ **a professional soldier/diplomat** un militaire/diplomate de carrière ▸ **she is very professional in her approach to the problem** elle aborde le problème de façon très professionnelle **2.** [of high standard] de (haute) qualité.
■ n professionnel *m*, -elle *f*.

professional foul n faute *f* délibérée.

professionalism [prə'feʃnəlɪzm] n professionnalisme *m*.

professionally [prə'feʃnəlɪ] adv **1.** [as professional] en professionnel ▸ **professionally qualified** diplômé(e) **2.** [skilfully] de façon professionnelle.

professor [prə'fesəʳ] n **1.** *UK* UNIV professeur *m*, -(e) *f* (de faculté) **2.** *US* & *Can* [teacher] professeur *m*.

professorship [prə'fesəʃɪp] n chaire *f*.

proffer ['prɒfəʳ] vt *fml* **: to proffer sthg (to sb)** offrir qqch (à qqn) ▸ **to proffer one's hand (to sb)** tendre la main (à qqn).

proficiency [prə'fɪʃənsɪ] n **: proficiency (in)** compétence *f* (en).

proficient [prə'fɪʃənt] adj **: proficient (in** OR **at sthg)** compétent(e) (en qqch).

profile ['prəʊfaɪl] n profil *m* ▸ **in profile** de profil ▸ **to keep a low profile** adopter un profil bas.

profit ['prɒfɪt] ■ n **1.** [financial] bénéfice *m*, profit *m* ▸ **to make a profit** faire un bénéfice ▸ **to sell sthg at a profit** vendre qqch à profit **2.** [advantage] profit *m*.
■ vi [financially] être le (la) bénéficiaire / [gain advantage] tirer avantage OR profit.

profitability [,prɒfɪtə'bɪlətɪ] n rentabilité *f*.

profitable ['prɒfɪtəbl] adj **1.** [financially] rentable, lucratif(ive) **2.** [beneficial] fructueux(euse), profitable.

profitably ['prɒfɪtəblɪ] adv **1.** [at a profit] de façon rentable **2.** [spend time] utilement.

profit centre *UK*, ***profit center*** *US* n centre *m* de profit.

profiteering [,prɒfɪ'tɪərɪŋ] n affairisme *m*, mercantilisme *m*.

profit-making ■ adj à but lucratif.
■ n réalisation *f* de bénéfices.

profit margin n marge *f* bénéficiaire.

profit motive n motivation *f* par le profit.

profit-related pay n salaire *m* lié aux bénéfices.

profit-sharing n participation *f* **OR** intéressement *m* aux bénéfices ▸ **we have a profit-sharing agreement/ scheme** nous avons un accord/un système de participation (aux bénéfices).

profligate ['prɒflɪgɪt] adj *fml* **1.** [extravagant] prodigue **2.** [immoral] débauché(e).

pro forma [-'fɔːmə] adj pro forma.

profound [prə'faʊnd] adj profond(e).

profoundly [prə'faʊndlɪ] adv profondément.

profundity [prə'fʌndətɪ] (pl -ies) n *fml* profondeur *f*.

profuse [prə'fjuːs] adj [apologies, praise] profus(e) / [bleeding] abondant(e).

profusely [prə'fjuːslɪ] adv [sweat, bleed] abondamment ▸ **to apologize profusely** se confondre en excuses.

profusion [prə'fjuːʒn] n *fml* profusion *f*.

progeny ['prɒdʒənɪ] (pl -ies) n *fml* progéniture *f*.

progesterone [prə'dʒestərəʊn] n progestérone *f*.

prognosis [prɒg'nəʊsɪs] (pl -ses [-siːz]) n pronostic *m*.

prognostication [prɒg,nɒstɪ'keɪʃn] n *fml* pronostic *m*.

program ['prəʊgræm] ■ n **1.** COMPUT programme *m* **2.** *US* = ***programme***.
■ vt (pt & pp -med **OR** -ed, cont -ming, cont -ing) **1.** COMPUT programmer **2.** *US* = ***programme***.

programmable [prəʊ'græməbl] adj programmable.

programme *UK*, ***program*** *US* ['prəʊgræm] ■ n **1.** [schedule, booklet] programme *m* **2.** RADIO & TV émission *f*.
■ vt programmer ▸ **to programme sthg to do sthg** programmer qqch pour faire qqch.

programmer ['prəʊgræmər] n COMPUT programmeur *m*, -euse *f*.

programming ['prəʊgræmɪŋ] n programmation *f*.

programming language n langage *m* de programmation.

progress ■ n ['prəʊgres] progrès *m* ▸ **to make progress** [improve] faire des progrès ▸ **to make progress in sthg** avancer dans qqch ▸ **in progress** en cours.
■ vi [prə'gres] **1.** [improve - gen] progresser, avancer / [- person] faire des progrès **2.** [continue] avancer **3.** [move on] **: to progress to sthg** passer à qqch.

progression [prə'greʃn] n progression *f*.

progressive [prə'gresɪv] adj **1.** [enlightened] progressiste **2.** [gradual] progressif(ive).

progressively [prə'gresɪvlɪ] adv progressivement.

progress report n [on patient] bulletin *m* de santé / [on student] bulletin scolaire / [on work] compte-rendu *m*.

prohibit [prə'hɪbɪt] vt prohiber ▸ **to prohibit sb from doing sthg** interdire **OR** défendre à qqn de faire qqch.

prohibition [,prəʊɪ'bɪʃn] n **1.** [law, rule] prohibition *f* **2.** *(U)* [act of prohibiting] interdiction *f*, défense *f*.

prohibitive [prə'hɪbətɪv] adj prohibitif(ive).

prohibitively [prə'hɪbətɪvlɪ] adv **: prohibitively expensive** d'un coût prohibitif.

project ■ n ['prɒdʒekt] **1.** [plan, idea] projet *m*, plan *m* / [enterprise, undertaking] opération *f*, entreprise *f* ▸ **they're working on a new building project** ils travaillent sur un nouveau projet de construction ▸ **the start of the project has been delayed** le début de l'opération a été retardé **2.** SCH [study] **: project (on)** dossier *m* (sur), projet *m* (sur).
■ vt [prə'dʒekt] **1.** [gen] projeter ▸ **two new airports are projected for the next decade** il est prévu de construire deux nouveaux aéroports durant la prochaine décennie ▸ **the missile was projected into space** le missile a été envoyé dans l'espace **2.** [estimate] prévoir.
■ vi [prə'dʒekt] [jut out] faire saillie.

projected [prə'dʒektɪd] adj **1.** [planned - undertaking, visit] prévu(e) ▸ **they are opposed to the projected building scheme** ils sont contre le projet de construction **2.** [forecast - figures, production] prévu(e).

projectile [prə'dʒektaɪl] n projectile *m*.

projection [prə'dʒekʃn] n **1.** [estimate] prévision *f* **2.** [protrusion] saillie *f* **3.** *(U)* [display, showing] projection *f*.

projectionist [prə'dʒekʃənɪst] n projectionniste *mf*.

projection room n cabine *f* de projection.

project manager n [gen] chef *m* de projet / CONSTR maître *m* d'œuvre.

projector [prə'dʒektər] n projecteur *m*.

proletarian [,prəʊlɪ'teərɪən] adj prolétarien(enne).

proletariat [,prəʊlɪ'teərɪət] n prolétariat *m*.

pro-life adj pour le respect de la vie.

proliferate [prə'lɪfəreɪt] vi *fml* proliférer.

proliferation [prə,lɪfə'reɪʃn] n *fml* **1.** [rapid increase] prolifération *f* **2.** [large amount or number] grande quantité *f*.

prolific [prə'lɪfɪk] adj prolifique.

prologue, *US* ***prolog*** ['prəʊlɒg] n *lit* & *fig* prologue *m*.

prolong [prə'lɒŋ] vt prolonger.

HOW TO ...

express prohibition

Il est interdit de fumer dans les salles de cours / Smoking is not permitted in the classroom
Tu n'as pas le droit de conduire, tu es trop jeune / You're not allowed to drive: you're too young
Je te défends d'en parler à qui que ce soit / I forbid you to tell anyone about this
Et ne t'avise pas de recommencer ! / There'll be trouble if you do that again!
Pas question que tu ailles à ce concert ! / There's no way you're going to that concert!
Nous ne sommes pas censés quitter les bureaux avant 18 heures / We're not supposed to leave the office before 6pm

prolongation [ˌprəʊlɒŋˈgeɪʃn] **n** *fml* [in time] prolongation *f* / [in space] prolongement *m*, extension *f*.

prolonged [prəˈlɒŋd] **adj** long (longue).

prom [prɒm] **n 1.** *UK inf* (abbr of ***promenade***) promenade *f*, front *m* de mer **2.** *US* [ball] bal *m* d'étudiants **3.** *UK inf* (abbr of ***promenade concert***) concert *m* promenade.

promenade [ˌprɒməˈnɑːd] **n** *UK* [road by sea] promenade *f*, front *m* de mer.

promenade concert **n** *UK* concert *m* promenade.

prominence [ˈprɒmɪnəns] **n 1.** [importance] importance *f* **2.** [conspicuousness] proéminence *f*.

prominent [ˈprɒmɪnənt] **adj 1.** [important] important(e) ▸ **to play a prominent part** *OR* **role in sthg** jouer un rôle important *OR* de tout premier plan dans qqch **2.** [noticeable] proéminent(e).

prominently [ˈprɒmɪnəntlɪ] **adv** au premier plan, bien en vue.

promiscuity [ˌprɒmɪsˈkjuːətɪ] **n** promiscuité *f*.

promiscuous [prɒˈmɪskjʊəs] **adj** [person] aux mœurs légères / [behaviour] immoral(e).

promise [ˈprɒmɪs] ■ **n** promesse *f* ▸ **to make (sb) a promise** faire une promesse (à qqn) ▸ **she always keeps her promises** elle tient toujours ses promesses, elle tient toujours (sa) parole ▸ **to break one's promise** manquer à sa parole, ne pas tenir ses promesses ▸ **to show promise** avoir de l'avenir, promettre.

■ **vt : to promise (sb) to do sthg** promettre (à qqn) de faire qqch ▸ **to promise sb sthg** promettre qqch à qqn ▸ **I can't promise (you) anything** je ne peux rien vous promettre.

■ **vi** promettre.

promising [ˈprɒmɪsɪŋ] **adj** prometteur(euse).

promisingly [ˈprɒmɪsɪŋlɪ] **adv** d'une façon prometteuse ▸ **France started the match promisingly** la France a bien débuté la partie.

promissory note [ˈprɒmɪsərɪ-] **n** billet *m* à ordre.

promo [ˈprəʊməʊ] (pl -s) (abbr of ***promotion***) **n** *inf* promo *f*.

promontory [ˈprɒməntrɪ] (pl -ies) **n** promontoire *m*.

promote [prəˈməʊt] **vt 1.** [foster] promouvoir **2.** [push, advertise] promouvoir, lancer **3.** [in job] promouvoir.

promoter [prəˈməʊtəʳ] **n 1.** [organizer] organisateur *m*, -trice *f* **2.** [supporter] promoteur *m*, -trice *f*.

promotion [prəˈməʊʃn] **n** promotion *f*, avancement *m* ▸ **to get** *OR* **be given promotion** être promu(e), obtenir de l'avancement.

promotional [prəˈməʊʃənl] **adj** promotionnel(elle), publicitaire.

promotional material **n** matériel *m* de promotion.

promotional offer **n** offre *f* promotionnelle.

promotional price **n** prix *m* promotionnel.

promotional sample **n** échantillon *m* promotionnel.

prompt [prɒmpt] ■ **adj** rapide, prompt(e).

■ **adv : at nine o'clock prompt** à neuf heures précises *OR* tapantes.

■ **vt 1.** [motivate, encourage] **: to prompt sb (to do sthg)** pousser *OR* inciter qqn (à faire qqch) **2.** THEAT souffler sa réplique à.

■ **n** THEAT réplique *f*.

prompter [ˈprɒmptəʳ] **n** THEAT souffleur *m*, -euse *f*.

prompting [ˈprɒmptɪŋ] **n 1.** [persuasion] incitation *f* ▸ **no amount of prompting will induce me to go there** rien ne pourra me décider à y aller ▸ **she needed no prompting** elle ne s'est pas fait prier, elle l'a fait d'elle-même ▸ **at his mother's prompting, he wrote a letter of thanks** à l'instigation *OR* sur l'insistance de sa mère, il a écrit une lettre de remerciement **2.** THEAT **: some actors need frequent prompting** certains acteurs ont souvent recours au souffleur.

promptly [ˈprɒmptlɪ] **adv 1.** [immediately] rapidement, promptement **2.** [punctually] ponctuellement.

promptness [ˈprɒmptnɪs] **n 1.** [speediness] promptitude *f* **2.** [punctuality] ponctualité *f*.

promulgate [ˈprɒmlgeɪt] **vt** *fml* promulguer.

prone [prəʊn] **adj 1.** [susceptible] **: to be prone to sthg** être sujet(ette) à qqch ▸ **to be prone to do sthg** avoir tendance à faire qqch **2.** [lying flat] étendu(e) face contre terre.

prong [prɒŋ] **n** [of fork] dent *f*.

pronoun [ˈprəʊnaʊn] **n** pronom *m*.

pronounce [prəˈnaʊns] ■ **vt** prononcer.

■ **vi : to pronounce on** se prononcer sur.

pronounced [prəˈnaʊnst] **adj** prononcé(e).

pronouncement [prəˈnaʊnsmənt] **n** déclaration *f*.

pronunciation [prəˌnʌnsɪˈeɪʃn] **n** prononciation *f*.

proof [pruːf] **n 1.** [evidence] preuve *f* ▸ **do you have any proof?** vous en avez la preuve *OR* des preuves? ▸ **you need proof of identity** vous devez fournir une pièce d'identité ▸ **proof of purchase** reçu *m* **2.** [of book] épreuve *f* **3.** [of alcohol] teneur *f* en alcool.

-proof [pruːf] **suffix** à l'épreuve de ▸ **acid-proof** à l'épreuve des acides ▸ **an idiot-proof mechanism** un mécanisme (totalement) indéréglable.

proofread [ˈpruːfriːd] (pt & pp -read [-red]) **vt** corriger les épreuves de.

proofreader [ˈpruːfˌriːdəʳ] **n** correcteur *m*, -trice *f* d'épreuves.

proofreading [ˈpruːfˌriːdɪŋ] **n** correction *f* (d'épreuves).

prop [prɒp] ■ **n 1.** [physical support] support *m*, étai *m* **2.** *fig* [supporting thing, person] soutien *m* **3.** RUGBY pilier *m*.

■ **vt** (pt & pp **-ped**, cont **-ping**) **: to prop sthg against** appuyer qqch contre *OR* à.

◆ ***props*** **npl** accessoires *mpl*.

◆ ***prop up*** **vt sep 1.** [physically support] soutenir, étayer **2.** *fig* [sustain] soutenir.

Prop. abbr of ***proprietor***.

propaganda [ˌprɒpəˈgændə] **n** propagande *f*.

propagate ['prɒpəgeɪt] ■ **vt** propager.
■ **vi** se propager.

propagation [ˌprɒpə'geɪʃn] **n** propagation *f*.

propane ['prəʊpeɪn] **n** propane *m*.

propel [prə'pel] (pt & pp **-led**, cont **-ling**) **vt** propulser / *fig* pousser.

propellant, propellent [prə'pelənt] ■ **n** [for rocket] propergol *m* / [for gun] poudre *f* propulsive / [in aerosol] (agent *m*) propulseur *m*.
■ **adj** propulsif(ive), propulseur(euse).

propeller [prə'pelər] **n** hélice *f*.

propelling pencil [prə'pelɪŋ-] **n** *UK* porte-mine *m*.

propensity [prə'pensətɪ] (pl **-ies**) **n : propensity (for** *OR* **to)** propension *f* (à).

proper ['prɒpər] **adj 1.** [real] vrai(e) ▸ **he's not a proper doctor** ce n'est pas un vrai docteur **2.** [correct] correct(e), bon (bonne) ▸ **John wasn't waiting at the proper place** John n'attendait pas au bon endroit *OR* là où il fallait ▸ **you must go through the proper channels** il faut suivre la filière officielle ▸ **I don't have the proper tools for this engine** je n'ai pas les outils appropriés pour *OR* qui conviennent pour ce moteur **3.** [decent - behaviour] convenable **4.** *UK inf* [for emphasis] **: he's a proper idiot!** c'est un imbécile fini!

FALSE FRIENDS / FAUX AMIS

proper

Propre n'est pas la traduction du mot anglais *proper*. Propre se traduit par *neat* ou *tidy*.
▸ Chez eux, c'est bien propre / *Their house is neat and tidy*

properly ['prɒpəlɪ] **adv 1.** [satisfactorily, correctly] correctement, comme il faut ▸ **the engine isn't working properly** le moteur ne marche pas bien **2.** [decently] convenablement, comme il faut ▸ **I haven't thanked you properly** je ne vous ai pas remercié comme il faut *OR* comme il convient.

proper name, proper noun **n** nom *m* propre.

property ['prɒpətɪ] (pl **-ies**) **n 1.** *(U)* [possessions] biens *mpl*, propriété *f* **2.** [building] bien *m* immobilier / [land] terres *fpl* **3.** [quality] propriété *f*.

property developer **n** promoteur *m* immobilier.

property owner **n** propriétaire *m* (foncier).

property tax **n** impôt *m* foncier.

prophecy ['prɒfɪsɪ] (pl **-ies**) **n** prophétie *f*.

prophesy ['prɒfɪsaɪ] (pt & pp **-ied**) **vt** prédire.

prophet ['prɒfɪt] **n** prophète *m*.

prophetic [prə'fetɪk] **adj** prophétique.

propitious [prə'pɪʃəs] **adj** *fml* propice, favorable.

proponent [prə'pəʊnənt] **n** adepte *mf*, partisan *m*, -e *f*.

proportion [prə'pɔːʃn] **n 1.** [part] part *f*, partie *f* **2.** [ratio] rapport *m*, proportion *f* ▸ **in proportion to** proportionnellement à ▸ **out of all proportion to** sans commune mesure avec **3.** ART **: in proportion** proportionné(e) ▸ **out of proportion** mal proportionné ▸ **to get sthg out of proportion** *fig* exagérer qqch ▸ **a sense of proportion** *fig* le sens de la mesure.

proportional [prə'pɔːʃənl] **adj** proportionnel(elle).

proportionally [prə'pɔːʃnəlɪ] **adv** proportionnellement.

proportional representation **n** représentation *f* proportionnelle.

proportionate [prə'pɔːʃnət] **adj** proportionnel(elle).

proportionately [prə'pɔːʃnətlɪ] **adv** proportionnellement, en proportion.

proposal [prə'pəʊzl] **n 1.** [suggestion] proposition *f*, offre *f* **2.** [offer of marriage] demande *f* en mariage.

propose [prə'pəʊz] ■ **vt 1.** [suggest] proposer **2.** [intend] **: to propose to do** *OR* **doing sthg** avoir l'intention de faire qqch, se proposer de faire qqch **3.** [toast] porter.
■ **vi** faire une demande en mariage ▸ **to propose to sb** demander qqn en mariage.

proposed [prə'pəʊzd] **adj** proposé(e).

proposition [ˌprɒpə'zɪʃn] ■ **n** proposition *f* ▸ **to make sb a proposition** faire une proposition à qqn.
■ **vt** faire des propositions à.

propound [prə'paʊnd] **vt** *fml* soumettre, proposer.

proprietary [prə'praɪətrɪ] **adj** de marque déposée ▸ **proprietary brand** marque *f* déposée.

proprietor [prə'praɪətər] **n** propriétaire *mf*.

propriety [prə'praɪətɪ] *fml* **n** *(U)* bienséance *f*.

propulsion [prə'pʌlʃn] **n** propulsion *f*.

pro rata [-'rɑːtə] ■ **adj** proportionnel(elle).
■ **adv** au prorata.

prosaic [prəʊ'zeɪɪk] **adj** prosaïque, banal(e).

prosaically [prəʊ'zeɪɪklɪ] **adv** prosaïquement.

Pros. Atty *US* (abbr of ***prosecuting attorney***) *avocat général*.

proscenium [prə'siːnjəm] (pl **-niums** *OR* **-nia** [-njə]) **n : proscenium (arch)** proscenium *m*.

proscribe [prəʊ'skraɪb] **vt** *fml* proscrire.

prose [prəʊz] ■ **n** *(U)* prose *f*.
■ **comp** en prose.

prosecute ['prɒsɪkjuːt] ■ **vt** poursuivre (en justice).
■ **vi** [police] engager des poursuites judiciaires / [lawyer] représenter la partie plaignante.

prosecuting attorney ['prɒsɪkjuːtɪŋ-] **n** *US* ≃ procureur *m* (de la République).

prosecution [ˌprɒsɪ'kjuːʃn] **n** poursuites *fpl* judiciaires, accusation *f* ▸ **the prosecution** la partie plaignante / [in Crown case] ≃ le ministère public.

prosecutor ['prɒsɪkjuːtər] **n** *esp US* plaignant *m*, -e *f*.

prospect ■ **n** ['prɒspekt] **1.** [hope] possibilité *f*, chances *fpl* ▸ **there's little prospect of their winning the match** ils ont peu de chances de remporter le match **2.** [probability] perspective *f* ▸ **I don't relish the prospect of working for him** la perspective de travailler pour lui ne m'enchante guère ▸ **what are the weather prospects for tomorrow?** quelles sont les prévisions météorologiques pour demain?
■ **vi** [prə'spekt] **: to prospect (for sthg)** prospecter (pour chercher qqch) ▸ **to prospect for oil** chercher du pétrole ▸ **to prospect for new customers** rechercher *OR* démarcher de nouveaux clients.
◆ ***prospects*** **npl : prospects (for)** chances *fpl* (de), perspectives *fpl* (de) ▸ **good promotion prospects** de réelles possibilités d'avancement ▸ **the prospects for the automobile industry** les perspectives d'avenir de l'industrie automobile.

prospecting [prə'spektɪŋ] **n** prospection *f*.

prospective [prə'spektɪv] **adj** éventuel(elle).

prospector [prə'spektəʳ] **n** prospecteur *m*, -trice *f*.

prospectus [prə'spektəs] **(pl -es) n** prospectus *m*.

prosper ['prɒspəʳ] **vi** prospérer.

prosperity [prɒ'sperətɪ] **n** prospérité *f*.

prosperous ['prɒspərəs] **adj** prospère.

prostate (gland) ['prɒsteɪt-] **n** prostate *f*.

prosthesis [prɒs'θi:sɪs] **(pl -ses** [-si:z]**) n** prothèse *f*.

prosthetic [prɒs'θetɪk] **adj 1.** MED prothétique **2.** LING prosthétique.

prostitute ['prɒstɪtju:t] **n** prostituée *f* ▸ **male prostitute** prostitué *m*.

prostitution [,prɒstɪ'tju:ʃn] **n** prostitution *f*.

prostrate ■ **adj** ['prɒstreɪt] **1.** [lying down] à plat ventre **2.** [with grief] prostré(e).
■ **vt** [prɒ'streɪt] **: to prostrate o.s. (before sb)** se prosterner (devant qqn).

protagonist [prə'tægənɪst] **n** protagoniste *mf*.

protect [prə'tekt] **vt : to protect sb/sthg (against** *OR* **from),** protéger qqn/qqch (contre *OR* de).

protected [prə'tektɪd] **adj** protégé(e) ▸ **protected species** espèce *f* protégée.

protection [prə'tekʃn] **n : protection (from** *OR* **against)** protection *f* (contre), défense *f* (contre).

protectionism [prə'tekʃənɪzm] **n** protectionnisme *m*.

protectionist [prə'tekʃənɪst] **adj** protectionniste.

protection money **n** *argent versé par les victimes d'un racket.*

protective [prə'tektɪv] **adj 1.** [layer, clothing] de protection **2.** [person, feelings] protecteur(trice) ▸ **to feel protective towards sb** se montrer protecteur envers qqn.

protective custody **n** *détention d'une personne pour sa propre sécurité.*

protectively [prə'tektɪvlɪ] **adv** [behave, act] de façon protectrice ⁄ [speak] d'un ton protecteur, d'une voix protectrice ⁄ [look] d'un œil protecteur.

protectiveness [prə'tektɪvnɪs] **n** attitude *f* protectrice.

protector [prə'tektəʳ] **n 1.** [person] protecteur *m*, -trice *f* **2.** [object] dispositif *m* de protection.

protectorate [prə'tektərət] **n** protectorat *m*.

protégé ['prɒteʒeɪ] **n** protégé *m*.

protégée ['prɒteʒeɪ] **n** protégée *f*.

protein ['prəʊti:n] **n** protéine *f*.

protest ■ **n** ['prəʊtest] protestation *f*.
■ **vt** [prə'test] **1.** [innocence, love] protester de **2.** *US* [protest against] protester contre.
■ **vi** [prə'test] **: to protest (about/against)** protester (à propos de/contre).

Protestant ['prɒtɪstənt] ■ **adj** protestant(e).
■ **n** protestant *m*, -e *f*.

Protestantism ['prɒtɪstəntɪzm] **n** protestantisme *m*.

protestation [,prɒte'steɪʃn] **n** *fml* protestation *f*.

protester [prə'testəʳ] **n** [on march, at demonstration] manifestant *m*, -e *f*.

protest march **n** manifestation *f*, marche *f* de protestation.

protocol ['prəʊtəkɒl] **n** protocole *m*.

proton ['prəʊtɒn] **n** proton *m*.

prototype ['prəʊtətaɪp] **n** prototype *m*.

protracted [prə'træktɪd] **adj** prolongé(e).

protractor [prə'træktəʳ] **n** rapporteur *m*.

protrude [prə'tru:d] **vi** avancer, dépasser.

protruding [prə'tru:dɪŋ] **adj** [ledge] en saillie ⁄ [chin, ribs] saillant(e) ⁄ [eyes] globuleux(euse) ⁄ [teeth] proéminent(e), protubérant(e) ⁄ [belly] protubérant(e).

protrusion [prə'tru:ʒn] **n** *fml* avancée *f*, saillie *f*.

protuberance [prə'tju:bərəns] **n** *fml* protubérance *f*.

protuberant [prə'tju:bərənt] **adj** *fml* protubérant(e).

proud [praʊd] **adj 1.** [satisfied, dignified] fier (fière) ▸ **to be proud to do sthg** être fier de faire qqch **2.** *pej* [arrogant] orgueilleux(euse), fier (fière).

proudly ['praʊdlɪ] **adv 1.** [with satisfaction, dignity] fièrement, avec fierté **2.** *pej* [arrogantly] orgueilleusement.

provable ['pru:vəbl] **adj** qui peut être prouvé(e), prouvable.

prove [pru:v] **(pp -d** *OR* **proven)** ■ **vt** [show] prouver ▸ **I think I've proved my point** je crois avoir apporté la preuve de ce que j'avançais ▸ **to prove sb right/wrong** donner raison/tort à qqn ▸ **the accused is innocent until proved** *OR* **proven guilty** l'accusé est innocent jusqu'à preuve du contraire *OR* tant que sa culpabilité n'est pas prouvée ▸ **to prove o.s. to be sthg** se révéler être qqch.
■ **vi** [turn out] **: to prove (to be) false/useful** s'avérer faux(fausse)/utile.

proven ['pru:vn *OR* 'prəʊvn] ■ **pp** ➤ ***prove***.
■ **adj** [fact] avéré(e), établi(e) ⁄ [liar] fieffé(e).

provenance ['prɒvənəns] **n** *fml* provenance *f*.

Provençal [,prɒvɒn'sɑ:l] ■ **adj** provençal(e).
■ **n 1.** [person] Provençal *m*, -e *f* **2.** [language] Provençal *m*.

Provence [prɒ'vɑ:ns] **n** Provence *f* ▸ **in Provence** en Provence.

proverb ['prɒvɜ:b] **n** proverbe *m*.

proverbial [prə'vɜ:bjəl] **adj** proverbial(e).

provide [prə'vaɪd] **vt** fournir ▸ **to provide sb with sthg** fournir qqch à qqn ▸ **to provide sthg for sb** fournir qqch à qqn ▸ **write the answers in the spaces provided** écrivez les réponses dans les blancs prévus à cet effet ▸ **the new plant will provide 2,000 jobs** la nouvelle usine créera 2 000 emplois.
◆ ***provide for*** **vt insep 1.** [support] subvenir aux besoins de ▸ **I have a family to provide for** j'ai une famille à nourrir **2.** *fml* [make arrangements for] prévoir.

provided [prə'vaɪdɪd] ◆ ***provided (that)*** **conj** à condition que *(+ subjunctive)*, pourvu que *(+ subjunctive)*.

providence ['prɒvɪdəns] **n** providence *f*.

provident ['prɒvɪdənt] **adj** *fml* [foresighted] prévoyant(e) / [thrifty] économe.

providential [,prɒvɪ'denʃl] **adj** *fml* providentiel(elle).

providently ['prɒvɪdəntlɪ] **adv** *fml* avec prévoyance, prudemment.

provider [prə'vaɪdər] **n** pourvoyeur *m*, -euse *f*.

providing [prə'vaɪdɪŋ] ◆ ***providing (that)*** **conj** à condition que *(+ subjunctive)*, pourvu que *(+ subjunctive)*.

province ['prɒvɪns] **n 1.** [part of country] province *f* **2.** [speciality] domaine *m*, compétence *f*.
◆ ***provinces*** **npl : the provinces** la province.

provincial [prə'vɪnʃl] **adj 1.** [town, newspaper] de province **2.** *pej* [narrow-minded] provincial(e).

provision [prə'vɪʒn] **n 1.** *(U)* [act of supplying] **: provision (of)** approvisionnement *m* (en), fourniture *f* (de) ▸ **the provision of new jobs** la création d'emplois **2.** [supply] provision *f*, réserve *f* **3.** *(U)* [arrangements] **: to make provision for** [the future] prendre des mesures pour / [one's family] pourvoir aux besoins de **4.** [in agreement, law] clause *f*, disposition *f* ▸ **under the provisions of the UN charter/his will** selon les dispositions de la charte de l'ONU/de son testament.
◆ ***provisions*** **npl** [supplies] provisions *fpl* ▸ **the US sent medical provisions** les États-Unis envoyèrent des stocks de médicaments.

provisional [prə'vɪʒənl] **adj** provisoire.

Provisional IRA **n** *branche de l'IRA qui pratique le terrorisme.*

provisional licence **n** *UK* permis *m* de conduire provisoire *(jusqu'à l'obtention du permis de conduire).*

provisionally [prə'vɪʒnəlɪ] **adv** provisoirement, à titre provisoire.

proviso [prə'vaɪzəʊ] (**pl -s**) **n** condition *f*, stipulation *f* ▸ **with the proviso that** à (la) condition que *(+ subjunctive)*.

provisory [prə'vaɪzərɪ] **adj 1.** [conditional] conditionnel(elle) **2.** = ***provisional***.

Provo ['prəʊvəʊ] (**pl -s**) (abbr of ***Provisional***) **n** *inf membre de la branche de l'IRA pratiquant le terrorisme.*

provocation [,prɒvə'keɪʃn] **n** provocation *f*.

provocative [prə'vɒkətɪv] **adj** provocant(e).

provocatively [prə'vɒkətɪvlɪ] **adv** d'une manière provocante.

provoke [prə'vəʊk] **vt 1.** [annoy] agacer, contrarier **2.** [cause - fight, argument] provoquer / [- reaction] susciter.

provoking [prə'vəʊkɪŋ] **adj** agaçant(e), énervant(e).

provost ['prɒvəst] **n 1.** *UK* UNIV doyen *m* **2.** *Scot* [head of town council] maire *m*.

prow [praʊ] **n** proue *f*.

prowess ['praʊɪs] **n** prouesse *f*.

prowl [praʊl] ■ **n : to be on the prowl** rôder.
■ **vt** [streets] rôder dans.
■ **vi** rôder.

prowl car **n** *US* voiture *f* de police en patrouille.

prowler ['praʊlər] **n** rôdeur *m*, -euse *f*.

proximity [prɒk'sɪmətɪ] **n : proximity (to)** proximité *f* (de) ▸ **in the proximity of** à proximité de.

proxy ['prɒksɪ] (**pl -ies**) **n : by proxy** par procuration.

Prozac® ['prəuzæk] **n** Prozac® *m*.

prude [pru:d] **n** *pej* prude *f*.

prudence ['pru:dns] **n** prudence *f*.

prudent ['pru:dnt] **adj** prudent(e).

prudently ['pru:dntlɪ] **adv** prudemment, avec prudence.

prudish ['pru:dɪʃ] **adj** *pej* prude, pudibond(e).

prudishness ['pru:dɪʃnɪs] **n** *pej* pruderie *f*, pudibonderie *f*.

prune [pru:n] ■ **n** [fruit] pruneau *m*.
■ **vt** [tree, bush] tailler.

pruning ['pru:nɪŋ] **n** [of hedge, tree] taille *f* / [of branches] élagage *m* / *fig* [of budget, staff] élagage *m*.

prurient ['prʊərɪənt] **adj** *fml* lascif(ive).

Prussian ['prʌʃn] ■ **adj** prussien(enne).
■ **n** Prussien *m*, -enne *f*.

pry [praɪ] (**pt & pp pried**) **vi** se mêler de ce qui ne vous regarde pas ▸ **to pry into sthg** chercher à découvrir qqch.

prying ['praɪɪŋ] **adj** indiscret (ète) ▸ **away from prying eyes** à l'abri des regards indiscrets.

PS (abbr of ***postscript***) **n** PS *m*.

psalm [sɑ:m] **n** psaume *m*.

PSBR (abbr of ***public sector borrowing requirement***) **n** *partie du budget de l'État non couverte par les impôts en Grande-Bretagne.*

pseud [sju:d] **n** *UK inf* frimeur *m*, -euse *f*.

pseudo- [,sju:dəʊ] **prefix** pseudo-.

pseudonym ['sju:dənɪm] **n** pseudonyme *m*.

psi (abbr of ***pounds per square inch***) *livres au pouce carré (mesure de pression).*

psoriasis [sɒ'raɪəsɪs] **n** psoriasis *m*.

psst [pst] **excl** psitt!

PST (abbr of ***Pacific Standard Time***) **n** *heure du Pacifique.*

psych [saɪk] ◆ ***psych up*** **vt sep** *inf* préparer psychologiquement ▸ **to psych o.s. up** se préparer psychologiquement.

psyche ['saɪkɪ] **n** psyché *f*.

psychedelic [ˌsaɪkɪ'delɪk] **adj** psychédélique.

psychiatric [ˌsaɪkɪ'ætrɪk] **adj** psychiatrique.

psychiatric nurse **n** infirmier *m*, -ère *f* en psychiatrie.

psychiatrist [saɪ'kaɪətrɪst] **n** psychiatre *mf*.

psychiatry [saɪ'kaɪətrɪ] **n** psychiatrie *f*.

psychic ['saɪkɪk] ■ **adj 1.** [clairvoyant - person] doué(e) de seconde vue / [- powers] parapsychique **2.** MED psychique. ■ **n** médium *m*.

psycho ['saɪkəʊ] *inf* ■ **n** (pl **-s**) psychopathe *mf*. ■ **adj** psychopathe.

psychoanalyse *UK*, ***-yze*** *US* [ˌsaɪkəʊ'ænəlaɪz] **vt** psychanalyser.

psychoanalysis [ˌsaɪkəʊə'næləsɪs] **n** psychanalyse *f*.

psychoanalyst [ˌsaɪkəʊ'ænəlɪst] **n** psychanalyste *mf*.

psycholinguistics [ˌsaɪkəʊlɪŋ'gwɪstɪks] **n** *(U)* psycholinguistique *f*.

psychological [ˌsaɪkə'lɒdʒɪkl] **adj** psychologique.

psychological block **n** blocage *m* psychologique.

psychologically [ˌsaɪkə'lɒdʒɪklɪ] **adv** psychologiquement.

psychological profile **n** profil *m* psychologique.

psychological warfare **n** *(U)* guerre *f* psychologique.

psychologist [saɪ'kɒlədʒɪst] **n** psychologue *mf*.

psychology [saɪ'kɒlədʒɪ] **n** psychologie *f*.

psychopath ['saɪkəpæθ] **n** psychopathe *mf*.

psychopathic [ˌsaɪkə'pæθɪk] **adj** [person] psychopathe / [disorder, personality] psychopathique.

psychosis [saɪ'kəʊsɪs] (pl **-ses** [-si:z]) **n** psychose *f*.

psychosomatic [ˌsaɪkəʊsə'mætɪk] **adj** psychosomatique.

psychotherapist [ˌsaɪkəʊ'θerəpɪst] **n** psychothérapeute *mf*.

psychotherapy [ˌsaɪkəʊ'θerəpɪ] **n** psychothérapie *f*.

psychotic [saɪ'kɒtɪk] ■ **adj** psychotique. ■ **n** psychotique *mf*.

pt **abbr of** ***pint, point***.

PT (**abbr of** ***physical training***) **n** *UK* EPS *f*.

Pt. (**abbr of** ***Point***) [on map] Pte.

PTA (**abbr of** ***parent-teacher association***) **n** *association de parents d'élèves et de professeurs*.

Pte. **abbr of** ***Private***.

PTO[1] **n** (**abbr of** ***parent-teacher organization***) *aux États-Unis, association de parents d'élèves et de professeurs*.

PTO[2] (**abbr of** ***please turn over***) TSVP.

PTV **n 1.** (**abbr of** ***pay television***) *télévision payante* **2.** (**abbr of** ***public television***) *programmes télévisés éducatifs*.

pub [pʌb] **n** pub *m*.

pub. **abbr of** ***published***.

pub-crawl **n** *UK inf* **: to go on a pub-crawl** faire la tournée des pubs.

puberty ['pju:bətɪ] **n** puberté *f*.

pubescent [pju:'besnt] **adj** pubescent(e).

pubic ['pju:bɪk] **adj** du pubis.

public ['pʌblɪk] ■ **adj** public(ique) / [library] municipal(e) ▸ **built at public expense** construit(e) avec des fonds publics ▸ **in the public interest** dans l'intérêt général ▸ **let's talk somewhere less public** allons discuter dans un endroit plus tranquille ▸ **to restore public confidence** regagner la confiance de la population ▸ **public library** bibliothèque *f* municipale ▸ **she's active in public life** elle prend une part active aux affaires publiques ▸ **it's public knowledge that...** tout le monde sait que..., il est de notoriété publique que... ▸ **to make sthg public** rendre qqch public ▸ **to go public** COMM émettre des actions dans le public. ■ **n : the public** le public ▸ **in public** en public.

public-address system **n** système *m* de sonorisation.

publican ['pʌblɪkən] **n** *UK* & *Aus* gérant *m*, -e *f* d'un pub.

public assistance **n** *US* aide *f* sociale.

publication [ˌpʌblɪ'keɪʃn] **n** publication *f*.

public bar **n** *UK* bar *m*.

public company **n** société *f* anonyme *(cotée en Bourse)*.

public convenience **n** *UK* toilettes *fpl* publiques.

public debt **n** dette *f* publique OR de l'État.

public domain **n : in the public domain** dans le domaine public ▸ **public domain software** logiciel *m* (du domaine) public.

public health **n** santé *f* publique ▸ **public health hazard** risque *m* pour la santé publique ▸ **the public health authorities** *administration régionale des services publics de santé* ▸ **public health inspector** *dated* inspecteur *m* sanitaire.

public holiday **n** *UK* jour *m* férié.

public house **n** *UK* pub *m*.

public inquiry **n** enquête *f* officielle ▸ **to hold a public inquiry** faire une enquête officielle.

publicist ['pʌblɪsɪst] **n** agent *m* de publicité.

publicity [pʌb'lɪsɪtɪ] ■ **n** *(U)* publicité *f*. ■ **comp** de publicité.

publicity campaign **n** campagne *f* publicitaire OR de publicité.

publicity-seeking [-si:kɪŋ] **adj** [person] qui cherche à se faire de la publicité / [operation, manœuvre] publicitaire.

publicity stunt **n** coup *m* publicitaire.

publicize, *UK* ***-ise*** ['pʌblɪsaɪz] **vt** faire connaître au public.

public limited company **n** *UK* société *f* anonyme *(cotée en Bourse)*.

publicly ['pʌblɪklɪ] **adv** publiquement, en public.

public office **n** fonctions *fpl* officielles.

public opinion **n** *(U)* opinion *f* publique.

public ownership **n** nationalisation *f*.

public prosecutor **n** *UK* ≃ procureur *m* de la République.

public relations ■ **n** *(U)* relations *fpl* publiques.
■ **npl** relations *fpl* publiques.

public relations officer **n** responsable *mf* des relations publiques.

public school **n** **1.** *UK* [private school] école *f* privée **2.** *US* & *Scot* [state school] école *f* publique.

public sector **n** secteur *m* public.

public servant **n** fonctionnaire *mf*.

public service vehicle **n** *UK* autobus *m*.

public speaking **n** art *m* oratoire ▸ **unaccustomed as I am to public speaking** *hum* bien que je n'aie pas l'habitude de prendre la parole en public.

public spending **n** *(U)* dépenses *fpl* publiques *OR* de l'État.

public-spirited **adj** qui fait preuve de civisme.

public transport *UK*, ***public transportation*** *US* **n** *(U)* transports *mpl* en commun.

public utility **n** service *m* public.

public works **npl** travaux *mpl* publics.

publish ['pʌblɪʃ] **vt** publier.

publishable ['pʌblɪʃəbl] **adj** publiable.

publisher ['pʌblɪʃəʳ] **n** éditeur *m*, -trice *f*.

publishing ['pʌblɪʃɪŋ] **n** *(U)* [industry] édition *f*.

publishing company, ***publishing house*** **n** société *f* *OR* maison *f* d'édition.

pub lunch **n** *UK* *repas de midi servi dans un pub*.

puce [pju:s] **adj** puce *(inv)*.

puck [pʌk] **n** [in hockey] palet *m*, rondelle *f* *Québec*.

pucker ['pʌkəʳ] ■ **vt** plisser.
■ **vi** se plisser.

pudding ['pʊdɪŋ] **n** **1.** [food - sweet] entremets *m* / [- savoury] pudding *m* **2.** *(U)* *UK* [course] dessert *m*.

puddle ['pʌdl] **n** flaque *f*.

pudgy ['pʌdʒɪ] = ***podgy***.

puerile ['pjʊəraɪl] **adj** puéril(e).

Puerto Rican [ˌpwɜ:təʊ'ri:kən] ■ **adj** portoricain(e).
■ **n** Portoricain *m*, -e *f*.

Puerto Rico [ˌpwɜ:təʊ'ri:kəʊ] **n** Porto Rico, Puerto Rico.

puff [pʌf] ■ **n** **1.** [of cigarette, smoke] bouffée *f* **2.** [gasp] souffle *m*.
■ **vt** [cigarette] tirer sur.
■ **vi** **1.** [smoke] **: to puff at** *OR* **on sthg** fumer qqch **2.** [pant] haleter.
◆ ***puff out*** **vt sep** [cheeks, chest] gonfler.
◆ ***puff up*** **vi** se gonfler.

puffed [pʌft] **adj** **1.** [swollen] **: puffed (up)** gonflé(e) **2.** *UK inf* [out of breath] **: puffed (out)** essoufflé(e).

puffed sleeve **n** manche *f* ballon.

puffin ['pʌfɪn] **n** macareux *m*.

puffiness ['pʌfɪnɪs] **n** gonflement *m*, bouffissure *f*.

puff pastry **n** *(U)* pâte *f* feuilletée.

puffy ['pʌfɪ] (comp **-ier**, superl **-iest**) **adj** gonflé(e), bouffi(e).

pug [pʌg] **n** carlin *m*.

pugnacious [pʌg'neɪʃəs] **adj** *fml* querelleur(euse), batailleur(euse).

puke [pju:k] **vi** *inf* dégobiller.

pukka ['pʌkə] **adj** *UK inf* **1.** [genuine] vrai(e), authentique, véritable **2.** [done well] bien fait(e), très correct(e) / [excellent] de premier ordre **3.** [socially acceptable] (très) comme il faut.

Pulitzer Prize [pʊlɪtsə-] **n** [in US] prix *m* Pulitzer.

pull [pʊl] ■ **vt** **1.** [gen] tirer ▸ **pull the rope taut** tendez la corde ▸ **he pulled himself onto the riverbank** il se hissa sur la berge ▸ **pull the trigger** [of gun] appuyez *OR* pressez sur la détente ▸ **to pull sthg to bits** *OR* **pieces** *lit* démonter qqch / *fig* démolir qqch **2.** [strain - muscle, hamstring] se froisser ▸ **she pulled a muscle** elle s'est déchiré un muscle, elle s'est fait un claquage **3.** [tooth] arracher ▸ **to have a tooth pulled** *US* se faire arracher une dent **4.** [attract] attirer ▸ **the festival pulled a big crowd** le festival a attiré beaucoup de monde **5.** [gun] sortir ▸ **he pulled a gun on me** il a braqué un revolver sur moi.
■ **vi** tirer ▸ **the steering pulls to the right** la direction tire à droite.
■ **n** **1.** [tug with hand] **: to give sthg a pull** tirer sur qqch **2.** *(U)* [influence] influence *f*.
◆ ***pull ahead*** **vi : to pull ahead (of)** prendre la tête (devant).
◆ ***pull apart*** **vt sep** [separate] séparer.
◆ ***pull at*** **vt insep** tirer sur ▸ **I pulled at his sleeve** je l'ai tiré par la manche.
◆ ***pull away*** **vi** **1.** AUT démarrer **2.** [in race] prendre de l'avance.
◆ ***pull back*** **vi** reculer.
◆ ***pull down*** **vt sep** [building] démolir.
◆ ***pull in*** **vi** AUT se ranger ▸ **I pulled in for petrol** je me suis arrêté pour prendre de l'essence.
◆ ***pull off*** **vt sep** **1.** [take off] enlever, ôter **2.** [succeed in] réussir ▸ **will she (manage to) pull it off?** est-ce qu'elle va y arriver?
◆ ***pull on*** **vt sep** [clothes] mettre, enfiler.
◆ ***pull out*** ■ **vt sep** **1.** [remove - tooth, hair, weeds] arracher / [- cork, nail] enlever / [produce - wallet, weapon] sortir, tirer ▸ **she pulled a map out of her bag** elle sortit une carte de son sac **2.** [troops] retirer.
■ **vi** **1.** RAIL partir, démarrer **2.** AUT déboîter ▸ **he pulled out to overtake** il a déboîté pour doubler ▸ **to pull out into traffic** s'engager dans la circulation **3.** [withdraw] se retirer ▸ **they've pulled out of the deal** ils se sont retirés de l'affaire.
◆ ***pull over*** **vi** AUT se ranger.
◆ ***pull through*** ■ **vi** s'en sortir, s'en tirer.
■ **vt sep** tirer d'affaire.
◆ ***pull together*** ■ **vt sep : to pull o.s. together** se ressaisir, se reprendre ▸ **pull yourself together!** ressaisissez-vous!
■ **vi** *fig* faire un effort.
◆ ***pull up*** ■ **vt sep** **1.** [raise] remonter **2.** [chair] avancer **3.** [stop] **: to pull sb up short** arrêter qqn court.
■ **vi** s'arrêter.

pull-down menu **n** COMPUT menu *m* déroulant.

pulley ['pʊlɪ] (pl -s) **n** poulie *f*.

pullout ['pʊlaʊt] **n** supplément *m* détachable.

pullover ['pʊl,əʊvəʳ] **n** pull *m*.

pulp [pʌlp] ■ **adj** [fiction, novel] de quatre sous.
■ **n 1.** [for paper] pâte *f* à papier **2.** [of fruit] pulpe *f*.
■ **vt** [food] réduire en pulpe.

pulpit ['pʊlpɪt] **n** chaire *f*.

pulsar ['pʌlsɑːr] **n** pulsar *m*.

pulsate [pʌl'seɪt] **vi** [heart] battre fort / [air, music] vibrer.

pulse [pʌls] ■ **n 1.** MED pouls *m* ▸ **to take sb's pulse** prendre le pouls de qqn **2.** TECH impulsion *f*.
■ **vi** battre, palpiter.
◆ ***pulses*** **npl** [food] légumes *mpl* secs.

pulverize, *UK* ***-ise*** ['pʌlvəraɪz] **vt 1.** [crush] pulvériser **2.** *fig* [destroy - town] détruire / [- person] démolir.

puma ['pjuːmə] (pl **puma** OR **-s**) **n** puma *m*.

pumice (stone) ['pʌmɪs-] **n** pierre *f* ponce.

pummel ['pʌml] (*UK* **-led**, **cont -ling**, *US* **-ed**, **cont -ing**) **vt** bourrer de coups.

pump [pʌmp] ■ **n** pompe *f*.
■ **vt 1.** [water, gas] pomper **2.** *inf* [invest] **: to pump money into sthg** injecter des capitaux dans qqch **3.** *inf* [interrogate] essayer de tirer les vers du nez à.
■ **vi** [heart] battre fort.
◆ ***pumps*** **npl** [shoes] escarpins *mpl*.

pumpernickel ['pʌmpənɪkl] **n** pain *m* de seigle noir.

pumpkin ['pʌmpkɪn] **n** potiron *m*.

pumpkin pie **n** tarte *f* au potiron *(dessert achevant traditionnellement le dîner de Thanksgiving)*.

pun [pʌn] **n** jeu *m* de mots, calembour *m*.

punch [pʌntʃ] ■ **n 1.** [blow] coup *m* de poing **2.** [tool] poinçonneuse *f* **3.** [drink] punch *m*.
■ **vt 1.** [hit - once] donner un coup de poing à / [- repeatedly] donner des coups de poing à ▸ **to punch a hole in sthg** faire un trou dans qqch **2.** [ticket] poinçonner / [paper] perforer.
◆ ***punch in*** **vi** *US* pointer (en arrivant).
◆ ***punch out*** **vi** *US* pointer (en partant).

Punch-and-Judy show [-'dʒuːdɪ-] **n** guignol *m*.

punch bag *UK*, ***punch ball*** *UK*, ***punching bag*** *US* ['pʌntʃɪŋ-] **n** punching-ball *m*.

punch bowl **n** coupe *f* à punch.

punch-drunk **adj** sonné(e), groggy *(inv)*.

punch(ed) card [pʌntʃ(t)-] **n** carte *f* perforée.

punching bag *US* = ***punch bag***.

punch line **n** chute *f*.

punch-up **n** *UK inf* bagarre *f*.

punchy ['pʌntʃɪ] (**comp -ier**, **superl -iest**) **adj** *inf* [style] incisif(ive).

punctilious [pʌŋk'tɪlɪəs] **adj** *fml* pointilleux(euse).

punctual ['pʌŋktʃʊəl] **adj** ponctuel(elle).

punctuality [,pʌŋktʃʊ'ælətɪ] **n** ponctualité *f*, exactitude *f*.

punctually ['pʌŋktʃʊəlɪ] **adv** à l'heure.

punctuate ['pʌŋktʃʊeɪt] **vt** ponctuer.

punctuation [,pʌŋktʃʊ'eɪʃn] **n** ponctuation *f*.

punctuation mark **n** signe *m* de ponctuation.

puncture ['pʌŋktʃəʳ] ■ **n** crevaison *f*.
■ **vt** [tyre, ball] crever / [skin] piquer.

pundit ['pʌndɪt] **n** pontife *m*.

pungent ['pʌndʒənt] **adj 1.** [smell] âcre / [taste] piquant(e) **2.** *fig* [criticism] caustique, acerbe.

punish ['pʌnɪʃ] **vt** punir ▸ **to punish sb for sthg/for doing sthg** punir qqn pour qqch/pour avoir fait qqch.

punishable ['pʌnɪʃəbl] **adj** punissable.

punishing ['pʌnɪʃɪŋ] **adj** [schedule, work] épuisant(e), éreintant(e) / [defeat] cuisant(e).

punishment ['pʌnɪʃmənt] **n** punition *f*, châtiment *m* ▸ **to take a lot of punishment** [car, furniture] être malmené(e).

punitive ['pjuːnətɪv] **adj** [action] punitif(ive) / [tax] très lourd(e).

Punjab [,pʌn'dʒɑːb] **n : the Punjab** le Pendjab ▸ **in the Punjab** au Pendjab.

Punjabi [,pʌn'dʒɑːbɪ] ■ **adj** du Pendjab.
■ **n 1.** [person] habitant *m*, -e *f* du Pendjab **2.** [language] pendjabi *m*.

punk [pʌŋk] ■ **adj** punk *(inv)*.
■ **n 1.** *(U)* [music] **: punk (rock)** punk *m* **2. : punk (rocker)** punk *mf* **3.** *inf* [lout] loubard *m*.

punnet ['pʌnɪt] **n** *UK* barquette *f*.

punt [pʌnt] ■ **n** [boat] bateau *m* à fond plat.
■ **vi** [in boat] se promener en bateau à fond plat.

punter ['pʌntəʳ] **n** *UK* **1.** [gambler] parieur *m*, -euse *f* **2.** *inf* [customer] client *m*, -e *f*.

puny ['pjuːnɪ] (**comp -ier**, **superl -iest**) **adj** chétif(ive).

pup [pʌp] **n 1.** [young dog] chiot *m* **2.** [young seal] bébé phoque *m*.

pupil ['pjuːpl] **n 1.** [student] élève *mf* **2.** [of eye] pupille *f*.

puppet ['pʌpɪt] **n 1.** [toy] marionnette *f* **2.** *pej* [person, country] fantoche *m*, pantin *m*.

puppet government **n** gouvernement *m* fantoche.

puppetry ['pʌpɪtrɪ] **n** [art - of making] fabrication *f* de marionnettes / [- of manipulating] art *m* du marionnettiste.

puppet show **n** spectacle *m* de marionnettes.

puppy ['pʌpɪ] (pl **-ies**) **n** chiot *m*.

puppy fat **n** *(U) inf* rondeurs *fpl* d'adolescence.

purchase ['pɜːtʃəs] ■ **n** achat *m*.
■ **vt** acheter.

purchase order **n** bon *m* de commande OR d'achat.

purchase price **n** prix *m* d'achat.

purchaser ['pɜːtʃəsəʳ] **n** acheteur *m*, -euse *f*.

purchase tax **n** *UK* taxe *f* à l'achat.

purchasing behaviour ['pɜːtʃəsɪŋ-] **n** comportement *m* d'achat.

purchasing decision ['pɜːtʃəsɪŋ-] **n** décision *f* d'achat.

purchasing department ['pɜːtʃəsɪŋ-] n service *m* des achats.

purchasing power ['pɜːtʃəsɪŋ-] n pouvoir *m* d'achat.

purdah ['pɜːdə] n *système qui oblige les femmes musulmanes à vivre à l'écart du monde.*

pure [pjʊəʳ] adj pur(e).

purebred ['pjʊəbred] adj de race.

puree ['pjʊəreɪ] ■ n purée *f.*
■ vt écraser en purée.

purely ['pjʊəlɪ] adv purement.

pureness ['pjʊənɪs] n pureté *f.*

purgative ['pɜːgətɪv] n purgatif *m.*

purgatory ['pɜːgətrɪ] *(U)* n [suffering] purgatoire *m.*
◆ **Purgatory** n [place] purgatoire *m.*

purge [pɜːdʒ] ■ n POL purge *f.*
■ vt **1.** POL purger **2.** [rid] débarrasser, purger.

purification [ˌpjʊərɪfɪ'keɪʃn] n purification *f*, épuration *f.*

purifier ['pjʊərɪfaɪəʳ] n épurateur *m.*

purify ['pjʊərɪfaɪ] (pt & pp **-ied**) vt purifier, épurer.

purist ['pjʊərɪst] n puriste *mf.*

puritan ['pjʊərɪtən] ■ adj puritain(e).
■ n puritain *m*, -e *f.*

puritanical [ˌpjʊərɪ'tænɪkl] adj *pej* puritain(e).

purity ['pjʊərətɪ] n pureté *f.*

purl [pɜːl] ■ n maille *f* à l'envers.
■ vt tricoter à l'envers.

purloin [pɜː'lɔɪn] vt *fml* voler, dérober.

purple ['pɜːpl] ■ adj violet(ette).
■ n violet *m.*

purport [pə'pɔːt] vi *fml* : **to purport to do/be sthg** prétendre faire/être qqch.

purportedly [pə'pɔːtɪdlɪ] adv *fml* prétendument.

purpose ['pɜːpəs] n **1.** [reason] raison *f*, motif *m* **2.** [aim] but *m*, objet *m* ▸ **for this purpose** dans ce but, à cet effet ▸ **for our purposes** pour ce que nous voulons faire ▸ **to no purpose** en vain, pour rien **3.** [determination] détermination *f* ▸ **to have a sense of purpose** avoir un but dans la vie.
◆ **on purpose** adv exprès.

purpose-built adj *UK* construit(e) spécialement.

purposeful ['pɜːpəsfʊl] adj résolu(e), déterminé(e).

purposefully ['pɜːpəsfʊlɪ] adv [for a reason] dans un but précis, délibérément / [determinedly] d'un air résolu.

purposeless ['pɜːpəslɪs] adj [life] sans but, vide de sens / [act, violence] gratuit(e).

purposely ['pɜːpəslɪ] adv exprès.

purr [pɜːʳ] ■ n ronronnement *m.*
■ vi ronronner.

purse [pɜːs] ■ n **1.** [for money] porte-monnaie *m inv*, bourse *f* **2.** *US* [handbag] sac *m* à main.
■ vt [lips] pincer.

purser ['pɜːsəʳ] n commissaire *m* de bord.

purse snatcher [-ˌsnætʃər] n *US* voleur *m*, -euse *f* à la tire.

purse strings npl : **to hold the purse strings** tenir les cordons de la bourse.

pursue [pə'sjuː] vt **1.** [follow] poursuivre, pourchasser **2.** [policy, aim] poursuivre / [question] continuer à débattre / [matter] approfondir / [project] donner suite à ▸ **to pursue an interest in sthg** se livrer à qqch.

pursuer [pə'sjuːəʳ] n poursuivant *m*, -e *f.*

pursuit [pə'sjuːt] n **1.** *(U)* [attempt to obtain] recherche *f*, poursuite *f* **2.** [chase, in sport] poursuite *f* ▸ **in pursuit of** à la poursuite de ▸ **in hot pursuit** aux trousses **3.** [occupation] occupation *f*, activité *f.*

purvey [pə'veɪ] vt *fml* **1.** [sell] vendre, fournir ▸ **to purvey sthg to sb** fournir qqch à qqn, approvisionner qqn en qqch **2.** [communicate - information, news] communiquer / [- lies, rumours] colporter.

purveyor [pə'veɪəʳ] n *fml* fournisseur *m.*

pus [pʌs] n pus *m.*

push [pʊʃ] ■ vt **1.** [press, move - gen] pousser / [- button] appuyer sur ▸ **she pushed the cork into the bottle** elle enfonça le bouchon dans la bouteille ▸ **it will push inflation upwards** cela va relancer l'inflation **2.** [encourage] **: their coach doesn't push them hard enough** leur entraîneur ne les pousse pas assez ▸ **to push sb (to do sthg)** inciter *OR* pousser qqn (à faire qqch) **3.** [force] **: you're still weak, so don't push yourself** tu es encore faible, vas-y doucement ▸ **to push sb (into doing sthg)** forcer *OR* obliger qqn (à faire qqch) **4.** *inf* [promote] faire de la réclame pour **5.** *drug sl* vendre, fournir.
■ vi **1.** [gen] pousser / [on button] appuyer ▸ **people were pushing to get in** les gens se bousculaient pour entrer **2.** [campaign] **: to push for sthg** faire pression pour obtenir qqch.
■ n **1.** [with hand] poussée *f* ▸ **to give sb/sthg a push** pousser qqn/qqch **2.** [forceful effort] effort *m*
▸▸ **to give sb the push** *UK inf* [end relationship] plaquer qqn / [dismiss] ficher qqn à la porte ▸ **I can do it at a push** *inf* je peux le faire si c'est vraiment nécessaire.
◆ **push ahead** vi continuer, persévérer ▸ **to push ahead with sthg** persévérer dans qqch, continuer (à faire) qqch.
◆ **push around** vt sep *inf fig* marcher sur les pieds de.
◆ **push in** vi [in queue] resquiller.
◆ **push off** vi *inf* filer, se sauver.
◆ **push on** vi continuer.
◆ **push over** vt sep faire tomber.
◆ **push through** vt sep [law, reform] faire accepter.

pushbike ['pʊʃbaɪk] n *UK* vélo *m.*

push button n bouton *m.*
◆ **push-button** adj [telephone] à touches / [car window] à commande automatique ▸ **push-button controls** commandes *fpl* automatiques.

pushcart ['pʊʃkɑːt] n charrette *f* à bras.

pushchair ['pʊʃtʃeəʳ] n *UK* poussette *f.*

pushed [pʊʃt] adj *inf* : **to be pushed for sthg** être à court de qqch ▸ **to be hard pushed to do sthg** avoir du mal *OR* de la peine à faire qqch.

pusher ['pʊʃəʳ] n *drug sl* dealer *m.*

pushing ['pʊʃɪŋ] prep *inf* : **he's pushing 40** il frise la quarantaine.

pushover ['pʊʃ,əʊvər] n *inf* : **it's a pushover** c'est un jeu d'enfant.

push-start vt faire démarrer en poussant.

push technology n COMPUT technologie *f* du push de données.

push-up n *esp US* pompe *f*, traction *f*.

pushy ['pʊʃɪ] (comp -ier, superl -iest) adj *pej* qui se met toujours en avant.

puss [pʊs], ***pussy (cat)*** ['pʊsɪ-] n *inf* minet *m*, minou *m*.

pussyfoot ['pʊsɪfʊt] vi *inf* atermoyer, tergiverser.

pussy willow n saule *m*.

put [pʊt] (pt & pp put, cont -ting) vt **1.** [gen] mettre ▸ **music always puts him in a good mood** la musique le met toujours de bonne humeur ▸ **we put a lot of emphasis on creativity** nous mettons beaucoup l'accent sur la créativité ▸ **to put responsibility on sb** donner des responsabilités à qqn
2. [place] mettre, poser, placer ▸ **put the chairs nearer the table** approche les chaises de la table ▸ **he put his arm around my shoulders** il passa son bras autour de mes épaules ▸ **to put the children to bed** coucher les enfants
3. [express] dire, exprimer ▸ **to put one's thoughts into words** exprimer sa pensée, s'exprimer ▸ **to put it briefly** *OR* **simply, they refused** bref *OR* en un mot, ils ont refusé ▸ **he put his case very well** il a très bien présenté son cas
4. [question] poser ▸ **to put it to sb that...** suggérer à qqn que...
5. [estimate] estimer, évaluer
6. [invest] : **to put money into** investir de l'argent dans ▸ **I've put a lot of time into this work** j'ai passé beaucoup de temps à faire ce travail.

◆ ***put across*** vt sep [ideas] faire comprendre ▸ **she's good at putting herself across** elle sait se mettre en valeur.

◆ ***put aside*** vt sep **1.** [place on one side] mettre de côté, poser
2. *fig* [money] mettre de côté / [differences] ne pas tenir compte de ▸ **we have a little money put aside** nous avons un peu d'argent de côté.

◆ ***put away*** vt sep **1.** [tidy away] ranger
2. *inf* [lock up] enfermer.

◆ ***put back*** vt sep **1.** [replace] remettre (à sa place *OR* en place)
2. [postpone] remettre
3. [clock, watch] retarder.

◆ ***put by*** vt sep [money] mettre de côté.

◆ ***put down*** vt sep **1.** [lay down] poser, déposer ▸ **to put the phone down** raccrocher
2. [quell - rebellion] réprimer
3. *inf* [criticize] humilier
4. [write down] inscrire, noter ▸ **I can put it down as expenses** je peux le faire passer dans mes notes de frais
5. *UK* [kill] : **to have a dog/cat put down** faire piquer un chien/chat.

◆ ***put down to*** vt sep attribuer à.

◆ ***put forward*** vt sep **1.** [propose] proposer, avancer ▸ **she put her name forward for the post of treasurer** elle a posé sa candidature au poste de trésorière
2. [meeting, clock, watch] avancer.

◆ ***put in*** vt sep **1.** [time, effort] passer ▸ **I've put in a lot of work on that car** j'ai beaucoup travaillé sur cette voiture
2. [submit] présenter ▸ **to put in an application for a job** déposer sa candidature pour *OR* se présenter pour un emploi.

◆ ***put off*** vt sep **1.** [postpone] remettre (à plus tard) ▸ **the meeting has been put off until tomorrow** la réunion a été renvoyée *OR* remise à demain ▸ **I kept putting off telling him the truth** je continuais à repousser le moment de lui dire la vérité
2. [cause to wait] décommander
3. [discourage] dissuader
4. [disturb] déconcerter, troubler
5. [cause to dislike] dégoûter ▸ **it put me off skiing for good** ça m'a définitivement dégoûté du ski ▸ **don't be put off by his weird sense of humour** ne te laisse pas rebuter par son humour un peu particulier ▸ **it put me off my dinner** ça m'a coupé l'appétit
6. [switch off - radio, TV] éteindre.

◆ ***put on*** vt sep **1.** [clothes] mettre, enfiler
2. [arrange - exhibition] organiser / [- play] monter ▸ **they have put on 20 extra trains** ils ont ajouté 20 trains
3. [gain] : **to put on weight** prendre du poids, grossir
4. [switch on - radio, TV] allumer, mettre ▸ **to put the light on** allumer (la lumière) ▸ **to put the brake on** freiner
5. [CD, tape] passer, mettre
6. [start cooking] mettre à cuire ▸ **I've put the kettle on for tea** j'ai mis de l'eau à chauffer pour le thé
7. [pretend - gen] feindre / [- accent] prendre
8. [bet] parier, miser
9. [add] ajouter
10. *inf* [tease] faire marcher.

◆ ***put onto*** vt sep : **to put sb onto sb/sthg** indiquer qqn/qqch à qqn ▸ **I'll put you onto a good solicitor** je vous donnerai le nom d'un *OR* je vous indiquerai un bon avocat.

◆ ***put out*** vt sep **1.** [place outside] mettre dehors ▸ **I'll put the washing out (to dry)** je vais mettre le linge (dehors) à sécher
2. [book, statement] publier / [CD] sortir
3. [fire, cigarette] éteindre ▸ **to put the light out** éteindre (la lumière)
4. [extend - hand] tendre
5. *inf* [injure] : **to put one's back/hip out** se démettre le dos/la hanche
6. [annoy, upset] : **to be put out** être contrarié(e)
7. [inconvenience] déranger ▸ **to put o.s. out** se donner du mal.

◆ ***put over*** vt sep [ideas] faire comprendre.

◆ ***put through*** vt sep TELEC passer ▸ **put the call through to my office** passez-moi la communication dans mon bureau ▸ **I'll put you through to Mrs Powell** je vous passe Mme Powell.

◆ ***put together*** vt sep **1.** [assemble - machine, furniture] monter, assembler / [- team] réunir / [- report] composer ▸ **to put sthg (back) together again** remonter qqch
2. [combine] mettre ensemble ▸ **more than all the others put together** plus que tous les autres réunis
3. [organize] monter, organiser.

◆ ***put up*** ■ vt sep **1.** [build - gen] ériger / [- tent] dresser
2. [umbrella] ouvrir / [flag] hisser
3. [fix to wall] accrocher
4. [provide - money] fournir ▸ **who's putting the money up for the new business?** qui finance la nouvelle entreprise?
5. [propose - candidate] proposer
6. *UK* [increase] augmenter
7. [provide accommodation for] loger, héberger ▸ **to put sb up for the night** coucher qqn.
■ **vt insep : to put up a fight** se défendre.
◆ ***put upon*** vt insep : **to be put upon** se laisser faire.
◆ ***put up to*** vt sep : **to put sb up to sthg** pousser *OR* inciter qqn à faire qqch.
◆ ***put up with*** vt insep supporter.

putative ['pju:tətɪv] adj *fml* putatif(ive).

put-down n *inf* rebuffade *f*.

put-on ■ adj affecté(e), simulé(e).
■ n *inf* **1.** [pretence] simulacre *m* **2.** [hoax] canular *m* **3.** *US* [charlatan] charlatan *m*.

putrefaction [,pju:trɪ'fækʃn] n putréfaction *f*.

putrefy ['pju:trɪfaɪ] (pt & pp **-ied**) vi se putréfier.

putrid ['pju:trɪd] adj putride.

putsch [pʊtʃ] n putsch *m*.

putt [pʌt] ■ n putt *m*.
■ vt & vi putter.

putter ['pʌtə^r] n [club] putter *m*.
◆ ***putter about, putter around*** vi *US* bricoler.

putting green ['pʌtɪŋ-] n green *m*.

putty ['pʌtɪ] n mastic *m*.

put-up job n *inf* coup *m* monté.

put-upon adj *inf* exploité(e).

puzzle ['pʌzl] ■ n **1.** [toy] puzzle *m* / [mental] devinette *f* **2.** [mystery] mystère *m*, énigme *f*.
■ vt rendre perplexe.
■ **vi : to puzzle over sthg** essayer de comprendre qqch.
◆ ***puzzle out*** vt sep comprendre.

puzzled ['pʌzld] adj perplexe.

puzzling ['pʌzlɪŋ] adj curieux(euse).

PVC (abbr of ***polyvinyl chloride***) n PVC *m*.

Pvt. abbr of ***Private***.

pw (abbr of ***per week***) p.sem.

PWR (abbr of ***pressurized-water reactor***) n REP *m*.

PX (abbr of ***post exchange***) n *magasin de l'armée*.

pygmy ['pɪgmɪ] (pl **-ies**) n pygmée *m*.

pyjama [pə'dʒɑ:mə] comp *UK* de pyjama.

pyjamas [pə'dʒɑ:məz] npl *UK* pyjama *m* ▸ **a pair of pyjamas** un pyjama.

pylon ['paɪlən] n pylône *m*.

pyramid ['pɪrəmɪd] n pyramide *f*.

pyramid selling n vente *f* en pyramide.

pyre ['paɪə^r] n bûcher *m* funéraire.

Pyrenean [,pɪrə'ni:ən] adj pyrénéen(enne).

Pyrenees [,pɪrə'ni:z] npl : **the Pyrenees** les Pyrénées *fpl*.

Pyrex® ['paɪreks] ■ n Pyrex® *m*.
■ comp en Pyrex®.

pyromaniac [,paɪrə'meɪnɪæk] n pyromane *mf*.

pyrotechnics [,paɪrəʊ'teknɪks] *fml* ■ n *(U)* pyrotechnie *f*.
■ npl *fig* [skill] feu *m* d'artifice.

python ['paɪθn] (pl **python** *OR* **-s**) n python *m*.

q [kju:] (pl q's *OR* qs), ***Q*** (pl Q's *OR* Qs) **n** [letter] q *m inv*, Q *m inv*.

Qatar [kæ'tɑ:r] Qatar *m*, Katar *m* ▸ **in Qatar** au Qatar.

QC (abbr of ***Queen's Counsel***) **n** *UK* ≃ bâtonnier *m* de l'ordre.

QED (abbr of ***quod erat demonstrandum***) CQFD.

QM abbr of ***quartermaster***.

q.t., ***QT*** (abbr of ***quiet***) *inf* **: on the q.t.** en douce.

Q-tip® **n** *US* Coton-Tige® *m*.

qty (abbr of ***quantity***) qté.

quack [kwæk] ■ **n 1.** [noise] coin-coin *m inv* **2.** *inf pej* [doctor] charlatan *m*.
■ **vi** faire coin-coin.

quad [kwɒd] abbr of ***quadruple***, ***quadruplet***, ***quadrangle***.

quadrangle ['kwɒdræŋgl] **n 1.** [figure] quadrilatère *m* **2.** [courtyard] cour *f*.

quadrant ['kwɒdrənt] **n** quadrant *m*.

quadraphonic [,kwɒdrə'fɒnɪk] **adj** quadriphonique.

quadrilateral [,kwɒdrɪ'lætərəl] ■ **adj** quadrilatéral(e).
■ **n** quadrilatère *m*.

quadriplegic [,kwɒdrɪ'pli:dʒɪk] ■ **adj** tétraplégique.
■ **n** tétraplégique *mf*.

quadrophonic [,kwɒdrə'fɒnɪk] = ***quadraphonic***.

quadruped ['kwɒdrʊped] **n** *fml* quadrupède *m*.

quadruple [kwɒ'dru:pl] ■ **adj** quadruple.
■ **vt** & **vi** quadrupler.

quadruplet ['kwɒdrʊplɪt] **n** quadruplé *m*, -e *f*.

quaff [kwɒf] **vt** *liter* boire (à longs traits).

quagmire ['kwægmaɪəʳ] **n** bourbier *m*.

quail [kweɪl] ■ **n** (pl **quail** *OR* **-s**) caille *f*.
■ **vi** *liter* reculer.

quaint [kweɪnt] **adj 1.** [picturesque] pittoresque / [old-fashioned] au charme désuet **2.** [odd] bizarre, étrange.

quaintly ['kweɪntlɪ] **adv 1.** [picturesquely] de façon pittoresque / [in an old-fashioned way] **: they dress very quaintly** ils s'habillent à l'ancienne (mode) **2.** [oddly] bizarrement, étrangement.

quaintness ['kweɪntnɪs] **n 1.** [picturesqueness] pittoresque *m* / [old-fashioned charm] charme *m* vieillot *OR* désuet **2.** [oddness] bizarrerie *f*, étrangeté *f*.

quake [kweɪk] ■ **n** *inf* (abbr of ***earthquake***) tremblement *m* de terre.
■ **vi** trembler.

Quaker ['kweɪkəʳ] **n** quaker *m*, -eresse *f*.

qualification [,kwɒlɪfɪ'keɪʃn] **n 1.** [certificate] diplôme *m* **2.** [quality, skill] compétence *f* **3.** [qualifying statement] réserve *f*.

qualified ['kwɒlɪfaɪd] **adj 1.** [trained] diplômé(e) **2.** [able] **: to be qualified to do sthg** avoir la compétence nécessaire pour faire qqch **3.** [limited] restreint(e), modéré(e).

qualifier ['kwɒlɪfaɪəʳ] **n 1.** SPORT [person] qualifié *m*, -e *f* / [contest] (épreuve *f*) éliminatoire *f* **2.** GRAM qualificatif *m*.

qualify ['kwɒlɪfaɪ] (pt & pp -ied) ■ **vt 1.** [modify] apporter des réserves à **2.** [entitle] **: to qualify sb to do sthg** qualifier qqn pour faire qqch ▸ **her experience qualifies her for the post** son expérience lui permet de prétendre à ce poste.
■ **vi 1.** [pass exams] obtenir un diplôme ▸ **to qualify as an accountant/a vet** obtenir son diplôme de comptable/vétérinaire **2.** [be entitled] **: to qualify (for sthg)** avoir droit (à qqch), remplir les conditions requises (pour qqch) ▸ **none of the candidates really qualifies for the post** aucun candidat ne répond véritablement aux conditions requises pour ce poste **3.** SPORT se qualifier.

qualifying ['kwɒlɪfaɪɪŋ] **adj 1.** [modifying] nuancé(e) **2.** [entitling] **: qualifying exam** examen *m* d'entrée **3.** SPORT [time] qui permet de se qualifier ▸ **qualifying round** série *f* éliminatoire.

qualitative ['kwɒlɪtətɪv] **adj** qualitatif(ive).

qualitatively ['kwɒlɪtətɪvlɪ] **adv** qualitativement.

qualitative research **n** études *fpl* qualitatives.

quality ['kwɒlətɪ] ■ **n** (pl **-ies**) qualité *f* ▸ **we have a reputation for quality** nous sommes réputés pour la qualité de nos produits ▸ **I don't doubt her intellectual qualities** je ne doute pas de ses capacités intellectuelles.
■ **comp** de qualité.

quality control **n** contrôle *m* de qualité.

quality press **n** *UK* **: the quality press** la presse sérieuse.

quality time **n : I only spend an hour in the evening with my kids, but it's quality time** je ne passe qu'une heure avec mes gosses le soir, mais je profite bien d'eux.

qualms [kwɑ:mz] **npl** doutes *mpl.*

quandary ['kwɒndərɪ] (pl **-ies**) **n** embarras *m* ▸ **to be in a quandary about** *OR* **over sthg** être bien embarrassé(e) à propos de qqch.

quango ['kwæŋgəʊ] (pl **-s**) **n** *UK pej* (abbr of ***quasiautonomous non-governmental organization***) *commission indépendante financée par l'État.*

quantifiable [kwɒntɪ'faɪəbl] **adj** quantifiable.

quantify ['kwɒntɪfaɪ] (pt & pp **-ied**) **vt** quantifier.

quantitative ['kwɒntɪtətɪv] **adj** quantitatif(ive).

quantitative research **n** études *fpl* quantitatives.

quantity ['kwɒntətɪ] (pl **-ies**) **n** quantité *f* ▸ **in quantity** en quantité ▸ **an unknown quantity** une inconnue.

quantity surveyor **n** *UK* métreur *m*, -euse *f.*

quantum leap ['kwɒntəm-] **n** *fig* bond *m* en avant.

quantum theory ['kwɒntəm-] **n** théorie *f* des quanta.

quarantine ['kwɒrənti:n] ■ **n** quarantaine *f* ▸ **to be in quarantine** être en quarantaine.
■ **vt** mettre en quarantaine.

quark [kwɑ:k] **n** quark *m.*

quarrel ['kwɒrəl] ■ **n** querelle *f*, dispute *f* ▸ **I have no quarrel with her** je n'ai rien contre elle.
■ **vi** (*UK* **-led**, cont **-ling**, *US* **-ed**, cont **-ing**) **: to quarrel (with)** se quereller (avec), se disputer (avec).

quarrelling *UK*, ***quarreling*** *US* ['kwɒrəlɪŋ] **n** *(U)* disputes *fpl*, querelles *fpl.*

quarrelsome ['kwɒrəlsəm] **adj** querelleur(euse).

quarry ['kwɒrɪ] ■ **n** (pl **-ies**) **1.** [place] carrière *f* **2.** [prey] proie *f.*
■ **vt** (pt & pp **-ied**) extraire.

quarry tile **n** carreau *m.*

quart [kwɔ:t] **n** *UK = 1,136 litre / US = 0,946 litre,* ≃ litre *m.*

quarter ['kwɔ:tər] **n 1.** [fraction, weight] quart *m* ▸ **it's a quarter/three quarters empty** c'est au quart/aux trois quarts vide ▸ **a quarter past two, a quarter after two** *US* deux heures et quart ▸ **a quarter to two, a quarter of two** *US* deux heures moins le quart **2.** [of year] trimestre *m* **3.** *US* [coin] pièce *f* de 25 cents **4.** [area in town] quartier *m* **5.** [direction] **: from all quarters** de tous côtés.
◆ ***quarters*** **npl** [rooms] quartiers *mpl* ▸ **the servants' quarters** les appartements des domestiques.
◆ ***at close quarters*** **adv** de près.

quarterback ['kwɔ:təbæk] **n** SPORT quarterback *m*, quart-arrière *mf Québec.*

quarterdeck ['kwɔ:tədek] **n** gaillard *m* d'arrière.

quarterfinal [ˌkwɔ:tə'faɪnl] **n** quart *m* de finale.

quarterfinalist ['kwɔ:təfaɪnəlɪst] **n** quart-de-finaliste *mf.*

quarter-hour **adj** [intervals] d'un quart d'heure.

quarterlight **n** *UK* AUT déflecteur *m.*

quarterly ['kwɔ:təlɪ] ■ **adj** trimestriel(elle).
■ **adv** trimestriellement.
■ **n** (pl **-ies**) publication *f* trimestrielle.

quartermaster ['kwɔ:təˌmɑ:stər] **n** MIL intendant *m.*

quarter note **n** *US* MUS noire *f.*

quarter sessions **npl** [in UK] tribunal *m* de grande instance / [in US] *dans certains États, tribunal local à compétence criminelle, pouvant avoir des fonctions administratives.*

quartet [kwɔ:'tet] **n** quatuor *m.*

quarto ['kwɔ:təʊ] (pl **-s**) **n** in-quarto *m inv.*

quartz [kwɔ:ts] **n** quartz *m.*

quartz watch **n** montre *f* à quartz.

quasar ['kweɪzɑ:r] **n** quasar *m.*

quash [kwɒʃ] **vt 1.** [sentence] annuler, casser **2.** [rebellion] réprimer.

quasi- ['kweɪzaɪ] **prefix** quasi-.

quaver ['kweɪvər] ■ **n 1.** *UK* MUS croche *f* **2.** [in voice] tremblement *m*, chevrotement *m.*
■ **vi** trembler, chevroter.

quavering ['kweɪvərɪŋ] **adj** tremblant(e), chevrotant(e).

quay [ki:] **n** quai *m.*

quayside ['ki:saɪd] **n** bord *m* du quai.

queasiness ['kwi:zɪnɪs] **n** *(U)* **1.** [nausea] nausée *f* **2.** [uneasiness] scrupules *mpl.*

queasy ['kwi:zɪ] (comp **-ier**, superl **-iest**) **adj : to feel queasy** avoir mal au cœur.

Quebec [kwɪ'bek] **n 1.** [province] Québec *m* ▸ **in Quebec** au Québec **2.** [city] Québec.

Quebecer, ***Quebecker*** [kwɪ'bekər] **n** Québécois *m*, -e *f.*

queen [kwi:n] **n 1.** [gen] reine *f* **2.** [playing card] dame *f.*

queen bee **n** reine *f* des abeilles ▸ **she's the queen bee around here** *inf fig* c'est elle la patronne ici.

Queen Mother **n : the Queen Mother** la reine mère.

Queen's Counsel **n** *UK* avocat *m* de la Couronne.

Queen's English **n** *UK* **: the Queen's English** l'anglais *m* correct.

queen's evidence **n** *UK* **: to turn queen's evidence** témoigner contre ses complices.

queer [kwɪər] ■ **adj** [odd] étrange, bizarre ▸ **I'm feeling a bit queer** je ne me sens pas très bien.
■ **n** *offens* pédé *m*, homosexuel *m.*

queer-bashing [-ˌbæʃɪŋ] **n** *UK offens* chasse *f* aux pédés.

quell [kwel] **vt** réprimer, étouffer.

quench [kwentʃ] **vt : to quench one's thirst** se désaltérer.

querulous ['kwerʊləs] **adj** *fml* [child] ronchon-neur(euse) / [voice] plaintif(ive).

query ['kwɪərɪ] ■ **n** (pl **-ies**) question *f*.
■ **vt** (pt & pp **-ied**) mettre en doute, douter de.

query language **n** COMPUT langage *m* d'interrogation.

quest [kwest] **n** *liter* : **quest (for)** quête *f* (de).

question ['kwestʃn] ■ **n** **1.** [gen] question *f* ▸ **to ask (sb) a question** poser une question (à qqn) ▸ **it raises the question of how much teachers should be paid** cela soulève *OR* pose le problème du salaire des enseignants ▸ **it's only a question of money/time** ce n'est qu'une question d'argent/de temps
2. [doubt] doute *m* ▸ **to call** *OR* **bring sthg into question** mettre qqch en doute ▸ **it's open to question whether...** on peut se demander si... ▸ **without question** incontestablement, sans aucun doute ▸ **beyond question** [know] sans aucun doute
▸▸ **there's no question of...** il n'est pas question de...
■ **vt** **1.** [interrogate] questionner
2. [express doubt about] mettre en question *OR* doute.
◆ ***in question*** **adv** : **the... in question** le/la/les... en question.
◆ ***out of the question*** **adv** hors de question.

questionable ['kwestʃənəbl] **adj** **1.** [uncertain] discutable **2.** [not right, not honest] douteux(euse).

questioner ['kwestʃənəʳ] **n** personne *f* qui pose une question.

questioning ['kwestʃənɪŋ] ■ **adj** interrogateur(trice).
■ **n** *(U)* interrogation *f*.

questioningly ['kwestʃənɪŋlɪ] **adv** de manière interrogative.

question mark **n** point *m* d'interrogation.

question master *UK*, ***quizmaster*** *esp US* ['kwɪz,mɑ:stəʳ] **n** meneur *m* de jeu.

questionnaire [,kwestʃə'neəʳ] **n** questionnaire *m*.

question time **n** *UK* POL *heure réservée aux questions des députés*.

queue [kju:] *UK* ■ **n** queue *f*, file *f* ▸ **to jump the queue** resquiller, passer avant son tour.
■ **vi** faire la queue.

queue-jump **vi** *UK* resquiller.

quibble ['kwɪbl] *pej* ■ **n** chicane *f*.
■ **vi** : **to quibble (over** *OR* **about)** chicaner (à propos de).

quiche [ki:ʃ] **n** quiche *f*.

quick [kwɪk] ■ **adj** **1.** [gen] rapide ▸ **be quick (about it)!** faites vite!, dépêchez-vous! ▸ **to have a quick look** jeter un rapide coup d'œil **2.** [response, decision] prompt(e), rapide ▸ **he has a quick temper** il s'emporte facilement ▸ **she's quick on the uptake** elle comprend vite ▸ **they were very quick off the mark** *UK inf* ils n'ont pas perdu de temps.
■ **adv** *inf* vite, rapidement.

quicken ['kwɪkn] ■ **vt** accélérer, presser.
■ **vi** s'accélérer.

quickly ['kwɪklɪ] **adv** **1.** [rapidly] vite, rapidement **2.** [without delay] promptement, immédiatement.

quickness ['kwɪknɪs] **n** [speed] rapidité *f*.

quicksand ['kwɪksænd] **n** sables *mpl* mouvants.

quicksilver ['kwɪk,sɪlvəʳ] **n** vif-argent *m*, mercure *m*.

quickstep ['kwɪkstep] **n** quickstep *m*.

quick-tempered **adj** emporté(e).

quick-witted [-'wɪtɪd] **adj** [person] à l'esprit vif.

quid [kwɪd] (pl **quid**) **n** *UK inf* livre *f*.

quid pro quo [-'kwəʊ] (pl **quid pro quos** [-'kwəʊz]) **n** contrepartie *f*.

quiescent [kwaɪ'esnt] **adj** *fml* immobile.

quiet ['kwaɪət] ■ **adj** **1.** [not noisy] tranquille / [voice] bas (basse) / [engine] silencieux(euse) ▸ **be quiet!** taisez-vous! ▸ **quiet please!** silence, s'il vous plaît! ▸ **to have a quiet drink** boire un verre tranquillement **2.** [not busy] calme ▸ **anything for a quiet life** tout pour avoir la paix **3.** [silent] silencieux(euse) ▸ **to keep quiet about sthg** ne rien dire à propos de qqch, garder qqch secret ▸ **it was as quiet as the grave** il régnait un silence de mort **4.** [intimate] intime ▸ **to have a quiet word with sb** dire deux mots en particulier à qqn **5.** [colour] discret(ète), sobre.
■ **n** tranquillité *f* ▸ **on the quiet** *inf* en douce.
■ **vt** *US* calmer, apaiser.
◆ ***quiet down*** ■ **vt sep** calmer, apaiser.
■ **vi** se calmer.

quieten ['kwaɪətn] *UK* **vt** calmer, apaiser.
◆ ***quieten down*** ■ **vt sep** calmer, apaiser.
■ **vi** se calmer.

quietly ['kwaɪətlɪ] **adv** **1.** [without noise] sans faire de bruit, silencieusement / [say] doucement **2.** [without excitement] tranquillement, calmement **3.** [without fuss - leave] discrètement.

quietness ['kwaɪətnɪs] *(U)* **n** **1.** [silence] silence *m* **2.** [peacefulness] calme *m*, tranquillité *f*.

quiff [kwɪf] **n** *UK* mèche *f*.

quill (pen) [kwɪl-] **n** plume *f* d'oie.

quilt [kwɪlt] **n** [padded] édredon *m* ▸ **(continental) quilt** *UK* couette *f*.

quilted ['kwɪltɪd] **adj** matelassé(e).

quince [kwɪns] **n** coing *m*.

quinine [kwɪ'ni:n] **n** quinine *f*.

quins *UK* [kwɪnz], ***quints*** *US* [kwɪnts] **npl** *inf* quintuplés *mpl*.

quintessence [kwɪn'tesns] **n** quintessence *f*.

quintessential [kwɪntə'senʃl] **adj** typique.

quintet [kwɪn'tet] **n** quintette *m*.

quints *US* = ***quins***.

quintuplets [kwɪn'tju:plɪts] **npl** quintuplés *mpl*.

quip [kwɪp] ■ **n** raillerie *f*.
■ **vi** (pt & pp **-ped**, cont **-ping**) railler.

quire ['kwaɪəʳ] **n** cahier *m*.

quirk [kwɜ:k] **n** bizarrerie *f* ▸ **a quirk of fate** un caprice du sort.

quirky ['kwɜ:kɪ] (comp **-ier**, superl **-iest**) **adj** étrange, bizarre.

quit [kwɪt] (*UK* quit *OR* -ted, cont -ting, *US* quit, cont -ting) ■ vt **1.** [resign from] quitter **2.** [stop] **: to quit smoking** arrêter de fumer **3.** COMPUT quitter ▸ **to quit an application** quitter une application.
■ vi **1.** [resign] démissionner **2.** [give up] abandonner **3.** COMPUT quitter.

quite [kwaɪt] adv **1.** [completely] tout à fait, complètement ▸ **I quite agree** je suis entièrement d'accord ▸ **not quite** pas tout à fait ▸ **I don't quite understand** je ne comprends pas bien ▸ **you've had quite enough** vous en avez eu largement assez
2. [fairly, a little] assez, plutôt ▸ **quite a lot of people seem to believe it** un bon nombre de gens semblent le croire ▸ **I'd quite like to go** ça me plairait assez d'y aller ▸ **he was in France for quite some time** il a passé pas mal de temps en France
3. [for emphasis] **: she's quite a singer** c'est une chanteuse formidable ▸ **it was quite a surprise** c'était une drôle de surprise
4. *UK* [to express agreement] **: quite (so)!** exactement!

Quito ['ki:təʊ] n Quito.

quits [kwɪts] adj *inf* **: to be quits (with sb)** être quitte (envers qqn) ▸ **to call it quits** en rester là.

quitter ['kwɪtə^r] n *inf pej* dégonflé *m*, -e *f*.

quiver ['kwɪvə^r] ■ n **1.** [shiver] frisson *m* **2.** [for arrows] carquois *m*.
■ vi frissonner.

quivering ['kwɪvərɪŋ] adj frissonnant(e).

quixotic [kwɪk'sɒtɪk] adj *liter* chevaleresque.

quiz [kwɪz] ■ n (pl quizzes) **1.** [gen] quiz *m*, jeu-concours *m* **2.** *US* SCH interrogation *f*.
■ vt (pt & pp -zed, cont -zing) **: to quiz sb (about sthg)** interroger qqn (au sujet de qqch).

quizmaster *esp US* = ***question master***.

quizzical ['kwɪzɪkl] adj [questioning] interrogateur(trice) / [ironical] ironique, narquois(e).

quizzically ['kwɪzɪklɪ] adv [questioningly] d'un air interrogateur / [ironically] d'un air ironique *OR* narquois.

quoits [kwɔɪts] n *(U)* jeu *m* de palet.

Quonset hut ['kwɒnsɪt-] n *US* hutte *f* préfabriquée en tôle.

quorate ['kwɔ:reɪt] adj *UK* dont le quorum est atteint.

Quorn® [kwɔ:n] n *UK aliment aux protéines végétales servant de substitut à la viande.*

quorum ['kwɔ:rəm] n quorum *m*.

quota ['kwəʊtə] n quota *m*.

quotable ['kwəʊtəbl] adj **1.** [worth quoting] digne d'être cité **2.** [on the record] que l'on peut citer ▸ **what he said is not quotable** ce qu'il a dit ne peut être répété **3.** FIN cotable.

quotation [kwəʊ'teɪʃn] n **1.** [citation] citation *f* **2.** COMM devis *m*.

quotation marks npl guillemets *mpl* ▸ **in quotation marks** entre guillemets.

quote [kwəʊt] ■ n **1.** [citation] citation *f* **2.** COMM devis *m*.
■ vt **1.** [cite] citer **2.** COMM indiquer, spécifier.
■ vi **1.** [cite] **: to quote (from sthg)** citer (qqch) **2.** COMM **: to quote for sthg** établir un devis pour qqch.
◆ ***quotes*** npl *inf* guillemets *mpl*.

quoted company ['kwəʊtɪd-] n *UK* société *f* cotée en Bourse.

quotient ['kwəʊʃnt] n quotient *m*.

qv (abbr of ***quod vide***) *expression renvoyant le lecteur à une autre entrée dans une encyclopédie.*

QWERTY keyboard ['kwɜ:tɪ-] n clavier *m* QWERTY.

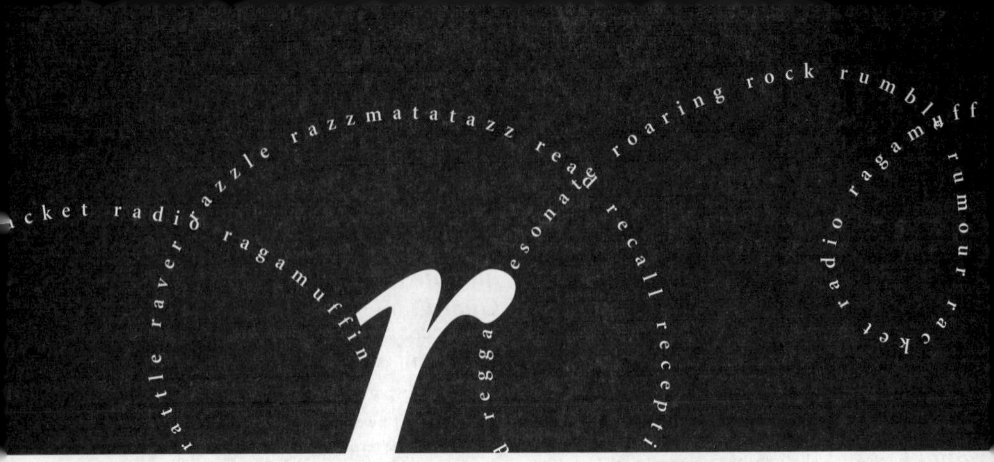

r [ɑːʳ] (pl **r's** *OR* **rs**), ***R*** [1] (pl **R's** *OR* **Rs**) **n** [letter] r *m inv*, R *m inv*.

R [2] **1.** (abbr of ***right***) dr. **2.** abbr of ***River*** **3.** (abbr of ***Réaumur***) R **4.** (abbr of ***restricted***) *aux États-Unis, indique qu'un film est interdit aux moins de 17 ans* **5.** *US* abbr of ***Republican*** **6.** *UK* (abbr of ***Rex***) *suit le nom d'un roi* **7.** *UK* (abbr of ***Regina***) *suit le nom d'une reine.*

R & B (abbr of ***rhythm and blues***) **n** R &B *m*.

R & D (abbr of ***research and development***) **n** R-D *f*.

RA (abbr of ***Royal Academy***) **n** *académie britannique des beaux-arts (organisant notamment un salon annuel).*

RAAF (abbr of ***Royal Australian Air Force***) **n** *armée de l'air australienne.*

Rabat [rəˈbɑːt] **n** Rabat.

rabbi [ˈræbaɪ] **n** rabbin *m*.

rabbit [ˈræbɪt] **n** lapin *m*.

rabbit hole **n** terrier *m*.

rabbit hutch **n** clapier *m*.

rabbit warren **n** garenne *f*.

rabble [ˈræbl] **n** cohue *f*.

rabble-rousing **adj** [speech] qui incite à la violence.

rabid [ˈræbɪd *OR* ˈreɪbɪd] **adj** *lit* & *fig* enragé(e).

rabies [ˈreɪbiːz] **n** rage *f*.

RAC (abbr of ***Royal Automobile Club***) **n** *club automobile britannique*, ≃ TCF *m*, ≃ ACF *m*.

raccoon [rəˈkuːn] **n** raton *m* laveur, chat *m* sauvage *Québec*.

race [reɪs] ■ **n 1.** [competition] course *f* ▸ **the race for the Presidency** la course à la présidence **2.** [people, ethnic background] race *f*.
■ **vt 1.** [compete against] faire la course avec **2.** [horse] faire courir.
■ **vi 1.** [compete] courir ▸ **to race against sb** faire la course avec qqn **2.** [rush] **: to race in/out** entrer/sortir à toute allure ▸ **a thousand ideas raced through her mind** mille idées lui sont passées par la tête **3.** [pulse] être très rapide **4.** [engine] s'emballer.

race car *US* = ***racing car***.

racecourse [ˈreɪskɔːs] **n** champ *m* de courses.

race driver *US* = ***racing driver***.

racehorse [ˈreɪshɔːs] **n** cheval *m* de course.

race meeting **n** *UK* courses *fpl*.

racer [ˈreɪsəʳ] **n** [runner] coureur *m*, -euse *f* / [horse] cheval *m* de course / [car] voiture *f* de course / [cycle] vélo *m* de course.

race relations **npl** relations *fpl* interraciales.

race riot **n** émeute *f* raciale.

racetrack [ˈreɪstræk] **n** piste *f* / *US* [racecourse] champ *m* de course.

racewalking [ˈreɪswɔːkɪŋ] **n** marche *f* athlétique.

racial [ˈreɪʃl] **adj 1.** [concerning a race] racial(e), ethnique **2.** [between races] racial(e).

racial discrimination [ˈreɪʃl-] **n** discrimination *f* raciale.

racialism [ˈreɪʃəlɪzm] **n** *UK dated* racisme *m*.

racialist [ˈreɪʃəlɪst] *UK dated* ■ **adj** raciste.
■ **n** raciste *mf*.

racially [ˈreɪʃəlɪ] **adv** du point de vue racial ▸ **a racially motivated attack** une agression raciste ▸ **racially prejudiced** raciste.

racing [ˈreɪsɪŋ] **n** *(U)* **: (horse) racing** les courses *fpl*.

racing car *UK*, ***race car*** *US* **n** voiture *f* de course.

racing driver *UK*, ***race driver*** *US* **n** coureur *m* automobile, pilote *m* de course.

racism [ˈreɪsɪzm] **n** racisme *m*.

racist [ˈreɪsɪst] ■ **adj** raciste.
■ **n** raciste *mf*.

rack [ræk] ■ **n 1.** [shelf - for bottles] casier *m* / [- for luggage] porte-bagages *m inv* / [- for plates] égouttoir *m* ▸ **toast rack** porte-toasts *m inv* **2.** CULIN **: rack of lamb** carré *m* d'agneau.
■ **vt** *liter* **: to be racked by** *OR* **with sthg** être tenaillé(e) par qqch.

racket [ˈrækɪt] **n 1.** *inf* [noise] boucan *m* **2.** [illegal activity] racket *m* **3.** SPORT raquette *f*.

racketeering [ˌrækəˈtɪərɪŋ] **n** *(U)* racket *m*.

raconteur [ˌrækɒnˈtɜːʳ] **n** conteur *m*, -euse *f*.

racquet ['rækɪt] **n** *UK* raquette *f*.

racy ['reɪsɪ] (comp **-ier**, superl **-iest**) **adj** [novel, style] osé(e).

RADA ['rɑːdə] (abbr of ***Royal Academy of Dramatic Art***) **n** *conservatoire britannique d'art dramatique*.

radar ['reɪdɑːʳ] **n** radar *m*.

radar trap **n** piège *m* radar.

radial ['reɪdjəl] ■ **adj** radial(e) ▸ **radial roads** routes *fpl* en étoile.
■ **n 1.** [tyre] pneu *m* radial ***OR*** à carcasse radiale **2.** [line] rayon *m*.

radian ['reɪdjən] **n** radian *m*.

radiance ['reɪdjəns] **n** *(U)* rayonnement *m*, éclat *m*.

radiant ['reɪdjənt] **adj 1.** [happy] radieux(euse) **2.** *liter* [brilliant] rayonnant(e) **3.** TECH radiant(e).

radiantly ['reɪdjəntlɪ] **adv** [shine, glow] avec éclat / [smile] d'un air radieux ▸ **radiantly beautiful** d'une beauté éclatante.

radiate ['reɪdɪeɪt] ■ **vt 1.** [heat, light] émettre, dégager **2.** [confidence, health] respirer.
■ **vi 1.** [heat, light] irradier **2.** [roads, lines] rayonner.

radiation [ˌreɪdɪ'eɪʃn] **n** [radioactive] radiation *f*.

radiation sickness **n** mal *m* des rayons.

radiator ['reɪdɪeɪtəʳ] **n** radiateur *m*.

radiator grille **n** calandre *f*.

radical ['rædɪkl] ■ **adj** radical(e).
■ **n** POL radical *m*, -e *f*.

radicalism ['rædɪkəlɪzm] **n** radicalisme *m*.

radically ['rædɪklɪ] **adv** radicalement.

radii ['reɪdɪaɪ] **npl** ➤ ***radius***.

radio ['reɪdɪəʊ] ■ **n** (pl **-s**) radio *f* ▸ **on the radio** à la radio.
■ **comp** de radio.
■ **vt** [person] appeler par radio / [information] envoyer par radio.

radioactive [ˌreɪdɪəʊ'æktɪv] **adj** radioactif(ive).

radioactive waste **n** *(U)* déchets *mpl* radioactifs.

radioactivity [ˌreɪdɪəʊæk'tɪvətɪ] **n** radioactivité *f*.

radio alarm **n** radio-réveil *m*.

radio cassette **n** radiocassette *f*.

radio-controlled [-kən'trəʊld] **adj** téléguidé(e).

radio frequency **n** radiofréquence *f*.

radiogram ['reɪdɪəʊˌgræm] **n** [message] radiogramme *m*.

radiographer [ˌreɪdɪ'ɒgrəfəʳ] **n** radiologue *mf*.

radiography [ˌreɪdɪ'ɒgrəfɪ] **n** radiographie *f*.

radiologist [ˌreɪdɪ'ɒlədʒɪst] **n** radiologue *mf*, radiologiste *mf*.

radiology [ˌreɪdɪ'ɒlədʒɪ] **n** radiologie *f*.

radiopaging ['reɪdɪəʊˌpeɪdʒɪŋ] **n** *système d'appel par récepteur de poche*.

radio station **n** station *f* de radio.

radiotelephone [ˌreɪdɪəʊ'telɪfəʊn] **n** radiotéléphone *m*.

radiotherapist [ˌreɪdɪəʊ'θerəpɪst] **n** radiothérapeute *mf*.

radiotherapy [ˌreɪdɪəʊ'θerəpɪ] **n** radiothérapie *f*.

radio wave **n** onde *f* hertzienne ***OR*** radioélectrique.

radish ['rædɪʃ] **n** radis *m*.

radium ['reɪdɪəm] **n** radium *m*.

radius ['reɪdɪəs] (pl **radii** ['reɪdɪaɪ]) **n 1.** MATHS rayon *m* **2.** ANAT radius *m*.

radon ['reɪdɒn] **n** radon *m*.

RAF **n** *UK* abbr of ***Royal Air Force***.

raffia ['ræfɪə] **n** raphia *m*.

raffish ['ræfɪʃ] **adj** *liter* dissolu(e).

raffle ['ræfl] ■ **n** tombola *f*.
■ **vt** mettre en tombola.

raft [rɑːft] **n 1.** [of wood] radeau *m* **2.** [large number] tas *m* ▸ **a raft of policies** POL un train de mesures.

rafter ['rɑːftəʳ] **n** chevron *m*.

rag [ræg] **n 1.** [piece of cloth] chiffon *m* ▸ **it's like a red rag to a bull** c'est comme la couleur rouge pour le taureau **2.** *pej* [newspaper] torchon *m*.
◆ ***rags*** **npl** [clothes] guenilles *fpl* ▸ **from rags to riches** de la misère à la richesse.

ragamuffin ['rægəˌmʌfɪn] **n** *liter* galopin *m*.

rag-and-bone man **n** *UK* chiffonnier *m*.

ragbag ['rægbæg] **n** *fig* ramassis *m*.

rag doll **n** poupée *f* de chiffon.

rage [reɪdʒ] ■ **n 1.** [fury] rage *f*, fureur *f* **2.** *inf* [fashion] **: to be (all) the rage** faire fureur.
■ **vi 1.** [person] être furieux(euse) **2.** [storm, argument] faire rage.

ragged ['rægɪd] **adj 1.** [person] en haillons / [clothes] en lambeaux **2.** [line, edge, performance] inégal(e).

raging ['reɪdʒɪŋ] **adj** [thirst, headache] atroce / [storm] déchaîné(e).

ragout ['rægu:] **n** ragoût *m*.

ragtime ['rægtaɪm] **n** ragtime *m*.

rag trade **n** *inf* **: the rag trade** la confection.

rag week **n** *UK semaine de carnaval organisée par des étudiants afin de collecter des fonds pour des œuvres charitables*.

raid [reɪd] ■ **n 1.** MIL raid *m* **2.** [by criminals] hold-up *m inv* / [by police] descente *f*.
■ **vt 1.** MIL faire un raid sur **2.** [subj: criminals] faire un hold-up dans / [subj: police] faire une descente dans.

raider ['reɪdəʳ] **n 1.** [attacker] agresseur *m* **2.** [thief] braqueur *m*.

rail [reɪl] ■ **n 1.** [on ship] bastingage *m* / [on staircase] rampe *f* / [on walkway] garde-fou *m* **2.** [bar] barre *f* **3.** RAIL rail *m* ▸ **by rail** en train.
■ **comp** [transport, travel] par le train / [strike] des cheminots.

railcard ['reɪlkɑːd] **n** *UK carte donnant droit à des tarifs préférentiels sur les chemins de fer*.

railing ['reɪlɪŋ] **n** [fence] grille *f* / [on ship] bastingage *m* / [on staircase] rampe *f* / [on walkway] garde-fou *m*.

railway *UK* ['reɪlweɪ], ***railroad*** *US* ['reɪlrəud] **n** [system, company] chemin *m* de fer / [track] voie *f* ferrée.

railway carriage **n** *UK* wagon *m*, voiture *f*.

railway crossing **n** *UK* passage *m* à niveau.

railway engine *UK*, ***railroad engine*** *US* **n** locomotive *f*.

railway line *UK*, ***railroad line*** *US* **n** [route] ligne *f* de chemin de fer / [track] voie *f* ferrée.

railwayman ['reɪlweɪmən] (pl **-men** [-mən]) **n** *UK* cheminot *m*.

railway station *UK*, ***railroad station*** *US* **n** gare *f*.

railway track *UK*, ***railroad track*** *US* **n** voie *f* ferrée.

rain [reɪn] ■ **n** pluie *f*.
■ **impers vb** METEOR pleuvoir ▸ **it's raining** il pleut.
■ **vi** [fall like rain] pleuvoir.
◆ ***rain down*** **vi** pleuvoir.
◆ ***rain off*** *UK*, ***rain out*** *US* **vt sep** annuler à cause de la pluie.

rainbow ['reɪnbəu] **n** arc-en-ciel *m*.

rainbow trout **n** truite *f* arc-en-ciel.

rain check **n** *US* **: I'll take a rain check (on that)** une autre fois peut-être.

raincoat ['reɪnkəut] **n** imperméable *m*.

raindrop ['reɪndrɒp] **n** goutte *f* de pluie.

rainfall ['reɪnfɔ:l] **n** [shower] chute *f* de pluie / [amount] précipitations *fpl*.

rain forest **n** forêt *f* tropicale humide.

rain gauge **n** pluviomètre *m*.

rainproof ['reɪnpru:f] **adj** imperméable.

rainstorm ['reɪnstɔ:m] **n** trombe *f* d'eau, pluie *f* torrentielle.

rainwater ['reɪn,wɔ:təʳ] **n** eau *f* de pluie.

rainy ['reɪnɪ] (comp **-ier**, superl **-iest**) **adj** pluvieux(euse).

raise [reɪz] ■ **vt 1.** [lift up] lever ▸ **to raise o.s.** se lever **2.** [increase - gen] augmenter / [- standards] élever ▸ **to raise one's voice** élever la voix ▸ **the age limit has been raised to 18** la limite d'âge a été repoussée à 18 ans ▸ **to raise sb's hopes** donner des espoirs à qqn **3.** [obtain - money] obtenir / [- support] réunir / [- taxes] lever ▸ **to raise money** [- from donations] collecter des fonds / [- by selling, borrowing] se procurer de l'argent **4.** [subject, doubt] soulever / [memories] évoquer **5.** [children, cattle] élever **6.** [crops] cultiver **7.** [build] ériger, élever.
■ **n** *US* augmentation *f* (de salaire).

raised [reɪzd] **adj 1.** [ground, platform, jetty] surélevé(e) / [pattern] en relief **2.** CULIN levé(e), à la levure **3.** LING [vowel] haut(e) **4.** [fabric] lainé(e), gratté(e).

raisin ['reɪzn] **n** raisin *m* sec.

Raj [rɑ:dʒ] **n : the Raj** l'empire britannique aux Indes.

rajah ['rɑ:dʒə] **n** raja *m*, rajah *m*.

rake [reɪk] ■ **n 1.** [implement] râteau *m* **2.** *dated & liter* [immoral man] débauché *m*.
■ **vt** [path, lawn] ratisser / [leaves] râteler.
◆ ***rake in*** **vt sep** *inf* amasser.
◆ ***rake up*** **vt sep** [past] fouiller dans.

rake-off **n** *inf* pourcentage *m*, commission *f*.

rakish ['reɪkɪʃ] **adj 1.** [dissolute] dissolu(e) **2.** [jaunty] désinvolte.

rally ['rælɪ] ■ **n** (pl **-ies**) **1.** [meeting] rassemblement *m* **2.** [car race] rallye *m* **3.** SPORT [exchange of shots] échange *m*.
■ **vt** (pt & pp **-ied**) rallier.
■ **vi** (pt & pp **-ied**) **1.** [supporters] se rallier **2.** [patient] aller mieux / [prices] remonter.
◆ ***rally around***, ***rally round*** *UK* ■ **vt insep** apporter son soutien à.
■ **vi** *inf* venir en aide.

rallying ['rælɪɪŋ] **n** *(U)* rallye *m*.

rallying cry **n** cri *m* de ralliement.

rallying point **n** point *m* de rassemblement.

ram [ræm] ■ **n** bélier *m*.
■ **vt** (pt & pp **-med**, cont **-ming**) **1.** [crash into] percuter contre, emboutir **2.** [force] tasser
⏭ **to ram sthg home** beaucoup insister sur qqch.

RAM [ræm] (abbr of ***random access memory***) **n** RAM *f*.

Ramadan [,ræmə'dæn] **n** ramadan *m*.

ramble ['ræmbl] ■ **n** randonnée *f*, promenade *f* à pied.
■ **vi 1.** [walk] faire une promenade à pied **2.** *pej* [talk] radoter.
◆ ***ramble on*** **vi** *pej* radoter.

rambler ['ræmbləʳ] **n** [walker] randonneur *m*, -euse *f*.

rambling ['ræmblɪŋ] **adj 1.** [house] plein(e) de coins et recoins **2.** [speech] décousu(e).

RAMC (abbr of ***Royal Army Medical Corps***) **n** *service de santé des armées britanniques*.

ramekin ['ræmɪkɪn] **n** ramequin *m*.

ramification [,ræmɪfɪ'keɪʃn] **n** ramification *f*.

ramp [ræmp] **n 1.** [slope] rampe *f* **2.** *UK* AUT [to slow traffic down] ralentisseur *m* ▸ **'ramp'** 'dénivellation' **3.** *US* AUT [to or from highway] bretelle *f*.

rampage [ræm'peɪdʒ] ■ **n : to go on the rampage** tout saccager.
■ **vi** se déchaîner.

rampant ['ræmpənt] **adj** qui sévit.

ramparts ['ræmpɑ:ts] **npl** rempart *m*.

ramraid ['ræmreɪd] **n** pillage *m*.

ramraider ['ræm,reɪdəʳ] **n** *personne qui pille les magasins en fracassant les vitrines avec sa voiture*.

ramshackle ['ræm,ʃækl] **adj** branlant(e).

ran [ræn] **pt** ➤ ***run***.

RAN (abbr of ***Royal Australian Navy***) **n** *marine de guerre australienne*.

ranch [rɑ:ntʃ] **n** ranch *m*.

rancher ['rɑ:ntʃəʳ] **n** propriétaire *mf* de ranch.

ranch house **n** *US* ranch *m*.

rancid ['rænsɪd] **adj** rance.

rancour *UK*, ***rancor*** *US* ['ræŋkəʳ] **n** *fml* rancœur *f*.

R and B **n** abbr of ***rhythm and blues***.

R and D **n** abbr of ***research and development***.

random ['rændəm] ■ **adj** fait(e) au hasard / [number] aléatoire.
■ **n : at random** au hasard.

random access memory **n** COMPUT mémoire *f* vive.

randomly ['rændəmlɪ] **adv** au hasard.

random sampling **n** échantillonnage *m* aléatoire.

R and R (abbr of ***rest and recreation***) **n** *esp US* permission *f*.

randy ['rændɪ] (comp **-ier**, superl **-iest**) **adj** *esp UK inf* excité(e).

rang [ræŋ] **pt** ➤ ***ring***.

range [reɪndʒ] ■ **n 1.** [of plane, telescope] portée *f* ◗ **at close range** à bout portant ◗ **to be out of range** être hors de portée ◗ **to be within range of** être à portée de
2. [of subjects, goods] gamme *f* ◗ **this car is the top/bottom of the range** cette voiture est le modèle haut/bas de gamme ◗ **the new autumn range** [of clothes] la nouvelle collection d'automne ◗ **that is beyond the range of the present inquiry** cela ne relève pas de cette enquête ◗ **price range** éventail *m* des prix ◗ **it's within my price range** c'est dans mes prix ◗ **children in the same age range** les enfants dans la même tranche d'âge
3. [of mountains] chaîne *f*
4. [shooting area] champ *m* de tir
5. MUS [of voice] tessiture *f*.
■ **vt** (cont **rangeing**) [place in row] mettre en rang.
■ **vi** (cont **rangeing**) **1.** [vary] **: to range between... and...** varier entre... et... ◗ **to range from... to...** varier de... à... ◗ **their ages range from 5 to 12** ils ont de 5 à 12 ans
2. [include] **: to range over sthg** couvrir qqch ◗ **our conversation ranged over a large number of topics** nous avons discuté d'un grand nombre de sujets.

ranger ['reɪndʒəʳ] **n** garde *m* forestier.

Rangoon [ræŋ'gu:n] **n** Rangoon.

rangy ['reɪndʒɪ] (comp **-ier**, superl **-iest**) **adj** élancé(e).

rank [ræŋk] ■ **adj 1.** [absolute - disgrace, stupidity] complet(ète) / [- injustice] flagrant(e) ◗ **he's a rank outsider** il n'a aucune chance
2. [smell] fétide.
■ **n 1.** [in hierarchy] grade *m* ◗ **the rank of manager** le titre de directeur ◗ **promoted to the rank of colonel** promu (au rang de *OR* au grade de) colonel ◗ **to pull rank** user de sa supériorité hiérarchique (pour faire faire qqch à qqn)
2. [social class] rang *m* ◗ **the lower ranks of society** les couches inférieures de la société
3. [row] rangée *f* ◗ **taxi rank** *UK* station *f* de taxis ◗ **to close ranks** serrer les rangs ◗ **to break ranks** MIL rompre les rangs / *fig* se désolidariser
▶▶ **the rank and file** la masse / [of union] la base.
■ **vt 1.** [classify] classer ◗ **I rank this as one of our finest performances** je considère que c'est une de nos meilleures représentations ◗ **he is ranked number 3** il est classé numéro 3
2. *US* [outrank] avoir un grade supérieur à.
■ **vi : to rank among** compter parmi ◗ **to rank as** être aux rangs de.
◆ ***ranks*** **npl 1.** MIL **: the ranks** le rang ◗ **to come up through** *OR* **to rise from the ranks** sortir du rang
2. *fig* [members] rangs *mpl* ◗ **to join the ranks of the opposition/unemployed** rejoindre les rangs de l'opposition/des chômeurs.

-rank **suffix : top-rank** grand(e), majeur(e) ◗ **second-rank** petit(e), mineur(e).

ranking ['ræŋkɪŋ] ■ **n** [rating] classement *m*.
■ **adj** *US* [high-ranking] du plus haut rang.

-ranking **suffix : high-ranking** de haut rang *OR* grade ◗ **low-ranking** de bas rang *OR* grade.

rankle ['ræŋkl] **vi : it rankled with him** ça lui est resté sur l'estomac *OR* le cœur.

ransack ['rænsæk] **vt** [search through] mettre tout sens dessus dessous dans / [damage] saccager.

ransom ['rænsəm] **n** rançon *f* ◗ **to hold sb to ransom** [keep prisoner] mettre qqn à rançon / *fig* exercer un chantage sur qqn.

rant [rænt] **vi** déblatérer.

ranting ['ræntɪŋ] **n** *(U)* invectives *fpl*.

rap [ræp] ■ **n 1.** [knock] coup *m* sec **2.** MUS rap *m*
▶▶ **to take the rap** *inf* trinquer, payer les pots cassés.
■ **vt** (pt & pp **-ped**, cont **-ping**) [table] frapper sur / [knuckles] taper sur.
■ **vi** (pt & pp **-ped**, cont **-ping**) **1.** [knock] **: to rap on** [door] frapper à / [table] frapper sur **2.** MUS rapper.

rapacious [rə'peɪʃəs] **adj** *fml* rapace.

rapaciousness [rə'peɪʃəsnɪs], ***rapacity*** [rə'pæsətɪ] **n** *fml* rapacité *f*.

rape [reɪp] ■ **n 1.** [crime, attack] viol *m* **2.** *fig* [of countryside] destruction *f* **3.** [plant] colza *m*.
■ **vt** violer.

rapeseed ['reɪpsi:d] **n** graine *f* de colza.

rapid ['ræpɪd] **adj** rapide.
◆ ***rapids*** **npl** rapides *mpl*.

rapid eye movement **n** *mouvement des globes oculaires pendant le sommeil paradoxal*.

rapid-fire **adj** [gun] à tir rapide ◗ **rapid-fire questions** un feu roulant de questions.

rapidity [rə'pɪdətɪ] **n** rapidité *f*.

rapidly ['ræpɪdlɪ] **adv** rapidement.

rapidness ['ræpɪdnɪs] = ***rapidity***.

rapist ['reɪpɪst] **n** violeur *m*.

rapper ['ræpəʳ] **n** rappeur *m*, -euse *f*.

rapport [ræ'pɔ:ʳ] **n** rapport *m*.

rapprochement [ræ'prɒʃmɑ̃] **n** *fml* rapprochement *m*.

rapt [ræpt] **adj** *liter* [interest, attention] profond(e) ◗ **to be rapt in thought** être plongé dans ses pensées.

rapture ['ræptʃəʳ] **n** *liter* ravissement *m* ◗ **to go into raptures over** *OR* **about** s'extasier sur.

rapturous ['ræptʃərəs] **adj** [applause, welcome] enthousiaste.

rapturously ['ræptʃərəslɪ] **adv** [watch] d'un air ravi, avec ravissement / [praise, applaud] avec enthousiasme.

rare [reəʳ] **adj 1.** [gen] rare **2.** [meat] saignant(e).

rarefied ['reərɪfaɪd] **adj 1.** [air] raréfié(e) **2.** *fig* [place, atmosphere] raffiné(e).

rarely ['reəlɪ] **adv** rarement.

rareness ['reənɪs] **n** rareté *f.*

raring ['reərɪŋ] **adj : to be raring to go** être impatient(e) de commencer.

rarity ['reərətɪ] (pl **-ies**) **n** rareté *f.*

rascal ['rɑ:skl] **n** polisson *m*, -onne *f.*

rash [ræʃ] ■ **adj** irréfléchi(e), imprudent(e).
■ **n 1.** MED éruption *f* **2.** [spate] succession *f*, série *f.*

rasher ['ræʃəʳ] **n** tranche *f.*

rashly ['ræʃlɪ] **adv** sans réfléchir.

rashness ['ræʃnɪs] **n** imprudence *f.*

rasp [rɑ:sp] ■ **n** [harsh sound] grincement *m.*
■ **vi** dire d'une voix âpre.

raspberry ['rɑ:zbərɪ] (pl **-ies**) **n 1.** [fruit] framboise *f* **2.** *inf* [rude sound] **: to blow a raspberry** faire pfft.

rasping ['rɑ:spɪŋ] **adj** [voice] âpre / [sound] grinçant(e).

Rasta ['ræstə] ■ **n** (abbr of ***Rastafarian***) rasta *mf.*
■ **adj** rasta *(inv).*

Rastafarian [,ræstə'feərɪən] ■ **n** rastafari *mf.*
■ **adj** rastafari *(inv).*

rat [ræt] **n 1.** [animal] rat *m* ▸ **to smell a rat** soupçonner anguille sous roche **2.** *inf pej* [person] ordure *f*, salaud *m.*

rat-arsed ['rætɑ:st] **adj** *UK vulg* bourré(e).

ratbag ['rætbæg] **n** *UK inf pej* salope *f.*

ratchet ['rætʃɪt] **n** rochet *m.*

rate [reɪt] ■ **n 1.** [speed] vitesse *f* / [of pulse] fréquence *f* ▸ **rate of flow** débit *m* ▸ **at this rate** à ce train-là ▸ **at the rate we're going** ***OR*** **at this rate we'll never get there** au rythme où nous allons, nous n'y arriverons jamais ▸ **any rate** *inf* enfin bref
2. [ratio, proportion] taux *m*
3. [price] tarif *m* ▸ **his rates have gone up** ses prix ont augmenté.
■ **vt 1.** [consider] **: I rate her very highly** je la tiens en haute estime ▸ **to rate sb/sthg as** considérer qqn/qqch comme ▸ **to rate sb/sthg among** classer qqn/qqch parmi
2. [deserve] mériter
3. *inf* [have high opinion of] **: I don't rate him as an actor** à mon avis, ce n'est pas un bon acteur.
◆ ***rates*** **npl** *UK dated* impôts *mpl* locaux.
◆ ***at any rate*** **adv** en tout cas.

-rate **suffix : first-rate** de premier ordre ▸ **second-rate** de deuxième ordre.

rateable value ['reɪtəbl-] **n** *UK dated* valeur *f* locative imposable.

rate of exchange **n** taux *m* ***OR*** cours *m* du change.

rate of return **n** [on investment] taux *m* de rendement.

ratepayer ['reɪt,peɪəʳ] **n** *UK dated* contribuable *mf.*

rather ['rɑ:ðəʳ] **adv 1.** [somewhat, more exactly] plutôt **2.** [to small extent] un peu **3.** [preferably] **: I'd rather wait** je préférerais attendre ▸ **she'd rather not go** elle préférerait ne pas y aller **4.** [on the contrary] **: (but) rather...** au contraire...
◆ ***rather than*** **conj** plutôt que.

ratification [,rætɪfɪ'keɪʃn] **n** ratification *f.*

ratify ['rætɪfaɪ] (pt & pp **-ied**) **vt** ratifier, approuver.

rating ['reɪtɪŋ] **n 1.** [of popularity] cote *f* **2.** *UK* [sailor] matelot *m.*
◆ ***ratings*** **npl** RADIO & TV indice *m* d'écoute.

ratings war **n** TV course *f* à l' Audimat®.

ratio ['reɪʃɪəʊ] (pl **-s**) **n** rapport *m.*

ration ['ræʃn] ■ **n** ration *f.*
■ **vt** rationner.
◆ ***rations*** **npl** vivres *mpl.*

rational ['ræʃənl] **adj** rationnel(elle).

rationale [,ræʃə'nɑ:l] **n** logique *f.*

rationalist ['ræʃənəlɪst] ■ **adj** rationaliste.
■ **n** rationaliste *mf.*

rationalistic [,ræʃənə'lɪstɪk] **adj** rationaliste.

rationality [,ræʃə'nælətɪ] **n 1.** [of belief, system] rationalité *f* **2.** [faculty] raison *f.*

rationalization*, UK* ***-isation*** [,ræʃənəlaɪ'zeɪʃn] **n** rationalisation *f.*

rationalize*, UK* ***-ise*** ['ræʃənəlaɪz] **vt** rationaliser.

rationally ['ræʃənəlɪ] **adv** rationnellement.

rationing ['ræʃənɪŋ] **n** rationnement *m.*

rat race **n** jungle *f.*

rattle ['rætl] ■ **n 1.** [of bottles, typewriter keys] cliquetis *m* / [of engine] bruit *m* de ferraille **2.** [toy] hochet *m.*
■ **vt 1.** [bottles] faire s'entrechoquer / [keys] faire cliqueter **2.** [unsettle] secouer.
■ **vi** [bottles] s'entrechoquer / [keys, machine] cliqueter / [engine] faire un bruit de ferraille.
◆ ***rattle off*** **vt sep** réciter à toute vitesse.
◆ ***rattle on*** **vi : to rattle on (about sthg)** parler sans arrêt (de qqch).
◆ ***rattle through*** **vt insep** [work] expédier / [speech, list] lire à toute allure.

rattlesnake ['rætlsneɪk], *US* ***rattler*** ['rætləʳ] *inf* **n** serpent *m* à sonnettes.

rattling ['rætlɪŋ] ■ **n** = ***rattle*** *(sense 1).*
■ **adj 1.** [sound] **: there was a rattling noise** on entendait un cliquetis **2.** [fast] rapide ▸ **at a rattling pace** à vive allure.
■ **adv** *inf dated* **: this book is a rattling good read** ce livre est vraiment formidable.

ratty ['rætɪ] (comp **-ier**, superl **-iest**) **adj** *inf* **1.** *UK* [in bad mood] de mauvais poil **2.** *US* [in bad condition] pourri(e).

raucous ['rɔ:kəs] **adj** [voice, laughter] rauque / [behaviour] bruyant(e).

raucously ['rɔ:kəslɪ] **adv 1.** [noisily] bruyamment **2.** [hoarsely] d'une voix rauque.

raunchy ['rɔ:ntʃɪ] (comp **-ier**, superl **-iest**) **adj** d'un sensualité brute.

ravage ['rævɪdʒ] **vt** ravager.
◆ ***ravages*** **npl** ravages *mpl.*

ravaged ['rævɪdʒd] **adj** ravagé(e).

rave [reɪv] ■ **adj** [review] élogieux(euse).
■ **n** *UK inf* [party] rave *f.*
■ **vi 1.** [talk angrily] **: to rave at** *OR* **against** tempêter *OR* fulminer contre **2.** [talk enthusiastically] **: to rave about** parler avec enthousiasme de.

raven ['reɪvn] ■ **adj** [hair] de jais.
■ **n** corbeau *m.*

ravenous ['rævənəs] **adj** [person] affamé(e) / [animal, appetite] vorace.

raver ['reɪvəʳ] **n** *inf* **1.** *dated* [enjoying social life] fêtard *m*, -e *f* **2.** [going to raves] raver *m*

rave-up **n** *UK inf dated* fête *f.*

ravine [rə'vi:n] **n** ravin *m.*

raving ['reɪvɪŋ] **adj** *inf* **: raving lunatic** fou furieux (folle furieuse).
◆ ***ravings*** **npl** délire *m.*

ravioli [ˌrævɪ'əʊlɪ] **n** *(U)* ravioli *mpl.*

ravish ['rævɪʃ] **vt** *liter* [delight] ravir, enchanter.

ravishing ['rævɪʃɪŋ] **adj** *liter* ravissant(e), enchanteur(eresse).

ravishingly ['rævɪʃɪŋlɪ] **adv** *liter* de façon ravissante / [as intensifier] **: ravishingly beautiful** d'une beauté éblouissante.

raw [rɔ:] **adj 1.** [uncooked] cru(e) **2.** [untreated] brut(e) **3.** [painful] à vif **4.** [inexperienced] novice ▸ **raw recruit** bleu *m* **5.** [weather] froid(e) / [wind] âpre.

raw deal **n : to get a raw deal** être défavorisé(e).

raw material **n** matière *f* première.

ray [reɪ] **n** [beam] rayon *m* / *fig* [of hope] lueur *f.*

rayon ['reɪɒn] **n** rayonne *f.*

raze [reɪz] **vt** raser.

razor ['reɪzəʳ] **n** rasoir *m.*

razor blade **n** lame *f* de rasoir.

razor-sharp **adj** coupant(e) comme un rasoir / *fig* [person, mind] vif (vive).

razzle ['ræzl] **n** *UK inf* **: to go on the razzle** faire les quatre cents coups.

razzmatazz ['ræzmətæz] **n** *inf* tape-à-l'œil *m inv.*

RC abbr of ***Roman Catholic.***

RCA (abbr of ***Royal College of Art***) **n** *école de beaux-arts à Londres.*

RCAF (abbr of ***Royal Canadian Air Force***) **n** *armée de l'air canadienne.*

RCMP (abbr of ***Royal Canadian Mounted Police***) **n** *police montée canadienne.*

RCN **n 1.** (abbr of ***Royal College of Nursing***) *syndicat britannique des infirmières et des infirmiers* **2.** (abbr of ***Royal Canadian Navy***) *marine de guerre canadienne.*

Rd abbr of ***Road.***

RDC (abbr of ***rural district council***) **n** *municipalité en zone rurale en Grande-Bretagne.*

re [ri:] **prep** COMM concernant.

RE **n 1.** (abbr of ***religious education***) instruction *f* religieuse **2.** (abbr of ***Royal Engineers***) *le génie militaire britannique.*

reach [ri:tʃ] ■ **vt 1.** [gen] atteindre ▸ **can you reach the top shelf?** est-ce que tu peux atteindre la dernière étagère? ▸ **the water reached (up to) my knees** l'eau m'arrivait aux genoux ▸ **her skirt reached down to her ankles** sa jupe lui descendait jusqu'aux chevilles ▸ **to reach the age of 80** atteindre l'âge de 80 ans
2. [destination] arriver à ▸ **they reached port** ils arrivèrent au *OR* gagnèrent le port ▸ **the letter hasn't reached him yet** la lettre ne lui est pas encore parvenue ▸ **the sound of laughter reached their ears** des rires parvenaient à leurs oreilles
3. [agreement, decision] parvenir à
4. [contact] joindre, contacter.
■ **vi 1.** [with hand] tendre la main ▸ **to reach out** tendre le bras ▸ **to reach down to pick sthg up** se pencher pour ramasser qqch
2. [land] s'étendre
3. [be long enough] **: it won't reach** ce n'est pas assez long.
■ **n 1.** [range] portée *f*, atteinte *f* ▸ **within reach** [object] à portée / [place] à proximité ▸ **the house is within easy reach of the shops** la maison est à proximité des magasins ▸ **within everyone's reach** [affordable by all] à la portée de toutes les bourses ▸ **out of** *OR* **beyond sb's reach** [object] hors de portée / [place] d'accès difficile, difficilement accessible
2. [of arm, boxer] allonge *f.*
◆ ***reaches*** **npl** étendue *f* ▸ **the upper/the lower reaches of a river** l'amont/l'aval d'une rivière.

reachable ['ri:tʃəbl] **adj 1.** [place] accessible / [object] à portée **2.** [contactable] joignable.

react [rɪ'ækt] **vi 1.** [gen] réagir **2.** MED **: to react to sthg** avoir une réaction à qqch.

reaction [rɪ'ækʃn] **n** réaction *f.*

reactionary [rɪ'ækʃənrɪ] ■ **adj** réactionnaire.
■ **n** réactionnaire *mf.*

reactivate [rɪ'æktɪveɪt] **vt** réactiver.

reactive [rɪ'æktɪv] **adj** [gen, CHEM & PHYS] réactif(ive) / PSYCHOL réactionnel(elle).

reactor [rɪ'æktəʳ] **n** réacteur *m.*

read [ri:d] ■ **vt** (pt & pp **read** [red]) **1.** [gen] lire ▸ **can you read music/braille/Italian?** savez-vous lire la musique/le braille/l'italien? ▸ **I can read him like a book!** je sais comment il fonctionne! ▸ **he reads the game very well** SPORT il a un bon sens du jeu ▸ **to read sb's lips** *lit* lire sur les lèvres de qqn ▸ **to take sthg as read** considérer qqch comme allant de soi
2. [subj: sign, letter] dire
3. [interpret, judge] interpréter
4. [subj: meter, thermometer] indiquer
5. *UK* UNIV étudier.
■ **vi** (pt & pp **read** [red]) lire ▸ **to read to sb** faire la lecture à qqn ▸ **the book reads well** le livre se lit bien ▸ **the book reads like a translation** à la lecture, on sent que ce roman est une traduction ▸ **to read between the lines** lire entre les lignes.

■ **n : to have a read** lire ▸ **to be a good read** être un bon livre, être d'une lecture agréable.

◆ ***read into*** **vt sep : to read a lot into sthg** attacher beaucoup d'importance à qqch ▸ **you shouldn't read too much into their silence** vous ne devriez pas accorder trop d'importance à leur silence.

◆ ***read out*** **vt sep** lire à haute voix.

◆ ***read up on*** **vt insep** étudier.

readable ['ri:dəbl] **adj** agréable à lire.

readdress [ˌri:ə'dres] **vt** [mail] faire suivre.

reader ['ri:dəʳ] **n** [of book, newspaper] lecteur *m*, -trice *f*.

readership ['ri:dəʃɪp] **n** [of newspaper] nombre *m* de lecteurs.

readily ['redɪlɪ] **adv 1.** [willingly] volontiers **2.** [easily] facilement.

readiness ['redɪnɪs] **n 1.** [preparation] **: to be in readiness** être prêt(e) **2.** [willingness] empressement *m*.

reading ['ri:dɪŋ] **n 1.** *(U)* [gen] lecture *f* **2.** [interpretation] interprétation *f* **3.** [on thermometer, meter] indications *fpl*.

reading age **n** *UK* niveau *m* de lecture ▸ **she has a reading age of 11** elle a le niveau de lecture d'un enfant de 11 ans.

reading lamp **n** lampe *f* de lecture ***OR*** de bureau.

reading list **n** [syllabus] liste *f* des ouvrages au programme / [for further reading] liste *f* des ouvrages recommandés.

reading room **n** salle *f* de lecture.

readjust [ˌri:ə'dʒʌst] ■ **vt** [instrument] régler (de nouveau) / [mirror] rajuster / [policy] rectifier.

■ **vi** [person] **: to readjust (to)** se réadapter (à).

readjustment [ˌri:ə'dʒʌstmənt] **n 1.** [readaptation] réadaptation *f* **2.** [alteration] rajustement *m*, réajustement *m*.

read-me file **n** COMPUT fichier *m* ouvrez-moi ***OR*** lisez-moi.

readmit [ˌri:əd'mɪt] **vt** réadmettre.

read-only [ri:d-] **adj** [disk, file] en lecture seule.

read-only memory [ri:d-] **n** mémoire *f* morte.

readout ['ri:daʊt] **n** COMPUT affichage *m*.

read-through [ri:d-] **n : to have a read-through of sthg** parcourir qqch.

readvertise [ˌri:'ædvətaɪz] ■ **vt** repasser une annonce de.

■ **vi** repasser une annonce.

ready ['redɪ] ■ **adj 1.** [prepared] prêt(e) ▸ **to be ready for anything** être prêt à tout ▸ **to be ready to do sthg** être prêt à faire qqch ▸ **are you ready to order?** vous avez choisi? ▸ **to get ready** se préparer ▸ **to get sthg ready** préparer qqch ▸ **ready, steady, go!** à vos marques, prêts, partez! **2.** [willing] **: to be ready to do sthg** être prêt(e) ***OR*** disposé(e) à faire qqch ▸ **you know me: I'm ready for anything** tu me connais, je suis toujours partant.

■ **vt** (**pt & pp -ied**) préparer.

ready cash **n** liquide *m*.

ready-made **adj** *lit* & *fig* tout fait (toute faite).

ready meal **n** *UK* plat *m* préparé.

ready money **n** liquide *m*.

ready-to-wear **adj** prêt-à-porter.

reaffirm [ˌri:ə'fɜ:m] **vt** réaffirmer.

reafforest [ˌri:ə'fɒrɪst] **vt** *UK* reboiser.

reafforestation ['ri:əˌfɒrɪ'steɪʃn] **n** *UK* reboisement *m*.

real ['rɪəl] ■ **adj 1.** [gen] vrai(e), véritable ▸ **they're real silver** ils sont en argent véritable ▸ **it was a real surprise** ce fut une vraie surprise ▸ **real life** réalité *f* ▸ **for real** pour de vrai ▸ **this is the real thing** [object] c'est de l'authentique / [situation] c'est pour de vrai ***OR*** de bon **2.** [actual] réel(elle) ▸ **the real world** le monde réel ▸ **in real terms** dans la pratique.

■ **adv** *US inf* très.

real ale **n** *UK* ale *f* véritable.

real estate **n** *(U)* biens *mpl* immobiliers.

realign [ˌri:ə'laɪn] **vt** POL regrouper.

realignment [ˌri:ə'laɪnmənt] **n** POL regroupement *m*.

realism ['rɪəlɪzm] **n** réalisme *m*.

realist ['rɪəlɪst] **n** réaliste *mf*.

realistic [ˌrɪə'lɪstɪk] **adj** réaliste.

realistically [ˌrɪə'lɪstɪklɪ] **adv** d'une manière réaliste, avec réalisme.

reality [rɪ'ælətɪ] (**pl -ies**) **n** réalité *f* ▸ **in reality** en réalité.

reality TV **n** *(U)* télévision *f* réalité.

realization, *UK* ***-isation*** [ˌrɪəlaɪ'zeɪʃn] **n** réalisation *f*.

realize, *UK* ***-ise*** ['rɪəlaɪz] **vt 1.** [understand] se rendre compte de, réaliser **2.** [sum of money, idea, ambition] réaliser.

real-life **adj** vrai(e) ▸ **the real-life drama of her battle against illness** le drame affreux de sa lutte contre la maladie.

reallocate [ˌri:'æləkeɪt] **vt** réattribuer.

really ['rɪəlɪ] ■ **adv 1.** [gen] vraiment ▸ **it really doesn't matter** ce n'est vraiment pas important **2.** [in fact] en réalité ▸ **he's quite nice, really** il est plutôt sympa, en fait.

■ **excl 1.** [expressing doubt] vraiment? **2.** [expressing surprise] pas possible! **3.** [expressing disapproval] franchement!, ça alors! ▸ **(well) really!** enfin!

realm [relm] **n 1.** *fig* [subject area] domaine *m* **2.** [kingdom] royaume *m*.

Real Player **n** COMPUT lecteur *m* Real Media.

real-time **adj** COMPUT en temps réel.

realtor ['rɪəltər] **n** *US* agent *m* immobilier.

realty ['rɪəltɪ] **n** *(U)* *US* biens *mpl* immobiliers.

ream [ri:m] **n** *UK* [of papers] rame *f*.

◆ ***reams*** **npl** *inf* des pages et des pages.

reap [ri:p] **vt 1.** [harvest] moissonner **2.** *fig* [obtain] récolter.

reappear [ˌri:ə'pɪəʳ] **vi** réapparaître, reparaître.

reappearance [ˌri:ə'pɪərəns] **n** réapparition *f*.

reapply [ˌri:ə'plaɪ] (**pt & pp -ied**) **vi : to reapply (for a job)** postuler de nouveau (à un emploi).

reappoint [ˌriːəˈpɔɪnt] **vt** réengager, rengager.

reappraisal [ˌriːəˈpreɪzl] **n** réévaluation *f*.

reappraise [ˌriːəˈpreɪz] **vt** réévaluer.

rear [rɪəʳ] ■ **adj** arrière *(inv)*, de derrière.
■ **n 1.** [back] arrière *m* ▸ **to bring up the rear** fermer la marche **2.** *inf* [bottom] derrière *m*.
■ **vt** [children, animals] élever.
■ **vi** [horse] **: to rear (up)** se cabrer.

rear admiral **n** vice-amiral *m*.

rearguard action [ˈrɪəgɑːd-] **n** combat *m* d'arrière-garde.

rear light **n** feu *m* arrière.

rearm [riːˈɑːm] **vt & vi** réarmer.

rearmament [rɪˈɑːməmənt] **n** réarmement *m*.

rearmost [ˈrɪəməʊst] **adj** dernier(ère).

rearrange [ˌriːəˈreɪndʒ] **vt 1.** [furniture, room] réarranger ∕ [plans] changer **2.** [meeting - to new time] changer l'heure de ∕ [- to new date] changer la date de.

rearrangement [ˌriːəˈreɪndʒmənt] **n 1.** [of furniture] réarrangement *m* **2.** [of meeting - to new time] changement *m* de l'heure ∕ [- to new date] changement de la date.

rearview mirror [ˈrɪəvjuː-] **n** rétroviseur *m*.

rear-wheel drive **n** AUT traction *f* arrière.

reason [ˈriːzn] ■ **n 1.** [cause] **: reason (for)** raison *f* (de) ▸ **by reason of** *fml* en raison de ▸ **for some reason** pour une raison ou pour une autre ▸ **why do you ask? – oh, no particular reason** pourquoi est-ce que tu me demandes ça? – oh, comme ça
2. *(U)* [justification] **: to have reason to do sthg** avoir de bonnes raisons de faire qqch ▸ **I have reason to believe (that)...** j'ai lieu de croire que... ▸ **they were upset, and with (good) reason** ils étaient bouleversés, et à juste titre **3.** [common sense] bon sens *m* ▸ **he won't listen to reason** on ne peut pas lui faire entendre raison ▸ **it stands to reason** c'est logique ▸ **within reason** dans la limite du raisonnable.
■ **vt** déduire.
■ **vi** raisonner.
◆ ***reason with*** **vt insep** raisonner (avec).

reasonable [ˈriːznəbl] **adj** raisonnable.

reasonably [ˈriːznəblɪ] **adv 1.** [quite] assez **2.** [sensibly] raisonnablement.

reasoned [ˈriːznd] **adj** raisonné(e).

reasoning [ˈriːznɪŋ] **n** raisonnement *m*.

reassemble [ˌriːəˈsembl] ■ **vt 1.** [reconstruct] remonter **2.** [regroup] rassembler.
■ **vi** se rassembler.

reassert [ˌriːəˈsɜːt] **vt** [authority] réaffirmer ▸ **you'll have to reassert yourself** vous devrez imposer à nouveau *OR* réaffirmer votre autorité.

reassess [ˌriːəˈses] **vt** réexaminer.

reassessment [ˌriːəˈsesmənt] **n** réexamen *m*.

reassign [ˌriːəˈsaɪn] **vt** réaffecter.

reassurance [ˌriːəˈʃʊərəns] **n 1.** [comfort] réconfort *m* **2.** [promise] assurance *f*.

reassure [ˌriːəˈʃʊəʳ] **vt** rassurer.

reassuring [ˌriːəˈʃʊərɪŋ] **adj** rassurant(e).

reassuringly [ˌriːəˈʃɔːrɪŋlɪ] **adv** d'une manière rassurante ▸ **reassuringly simple** d'une grande simplicité.

reawaken [ˌriːəˈweɪkn] **vt** [interest] faire renaître.

reawakening [ˌriːəˈweɪknɪŋ] **n** [of sleeper] réveil *m* ∕ [of interest, concern] réveil *m*.

rebate [ˈriːbeɪt] **n** [on product] rabais *m* ▸ **tax rebate** ≃ dégrèvement *m* fiscal.

rebel ■ **n** [ˈrebl] rebelle *mf*.
■ **adj** [ˈrebl] [soldier] rebelle ∕ [camp, territory] des rebelles ∕ [attack] de rebelles ▸ **rebel MP** *UK* parlementaire *mf* rebelle.
■ **vi** [rɪˈbel] (pt & pp **-led**, cont **-ling**) **: to rebel (against)** se rebeller (contre).

rebellion [rɪˈbeljən] **n** rébellion *f*.

rebellious [rɪˈbeljəs] **adj** rebelle.

rebirth [ˌriːˈbɜːθ] **n** renaissance *f*.

reboot [ˌriːˈbuːt] **vi** COMPUT redémarrer, réamorcer *offic*.

reborn [ˌriːˈbɔːn] **adj** réincarné(e) ▸ **to be reborn** renaître ▸ **I feel reborn** je me sens renaître.

rebound ■ **n** [ˈriːbaʊnd] [of ball] rebond *m* ▸ **to be on the rebound** [person] être sous le coup d'une déception sentimentale.
■ **vi** [rɪˈbaʊnd] **1.** [ball] rebondir **2.** *fig* [action, joke] **: to rebound on *OR* upon sb** se retourner contre qqn.

rebrand [ˌriːˈbrænd] **vt** effectuer le rebranding de.

rebranding [ˌriːˈbrændɪŋ] **n** rebranding *m*, changement *m* de marque.

rebuff [rɪˈbʌf] ■ **n** rebuffade *f*.
■ **vt** repousser.

rebuild [ˌriːˈbɪld] (pt & pp **rebuilt** [ˌriːˈbɪlt]) **vt** reconstruire.

rebuke [rɪˈbjuːk] *fml* ■ **n** réprimande *f*.
■ **vt** réprimander.

rebut [riːˈbʌt] (pt & pp **-ted**, cont **-ting**) **vt** *fml* réfuter.

rebuttal [riːˈbʌtl] **n** *fml* réfutation *f*.

rec. abbr of ***received***.

recalcitrant [rɪˈkælsɪtrənt] **adj** *fml* récalcitrant(e).

recall [rɪˈkɔːl] ■ **n 1.** [memory] rappel *m* **2.** [change] **: beyond recall** irrévocable.
■ **vt 1.** [remember] se rappeler, se souvenir de **2.** [summon back] rappeler ▸ **to recall Parliament** convoquer le Parlement.

recall rate **n** taux *m* de mémorisation.

recant [rɪˈkænt] ■ **vt 1.** *fml* [statement] rétracter **2.** RELIG abjurer.
■ **vi 1.** *fml* se rétracter **2.** RELIG abjurer.

recap [ˈriːkæp] ■ **n** récapitulation *f*.
■ **vt** (pt & pp **-ped**, cont **-ping**) **1.** [summarize] récapituler **2.** *US* [tyre] rechaper.
■ **vi** (pt & pp **-ped**, cont **-ping**) récapituler.

recapitulate [ˌriːkəˈpɪtjʊleɪt] **vt & vi** *fml* récapituler.

recapture [ˌriːˈkæptʃəʳ] ■ **n** reprise *f*.
■ **vt 1.** [feeling] retrouver **2.** [territory, prisoner] reprendre.

recd, ***rec'd*** abbr of ***received***.

recede [riː'siːd] **vi 1.** [person, car] s'éloigner / [hopes] s'envoler **2.** [hair] **: his hair is receding** son front se dégarnit.

receding [rɪ'siːdɪŋ] **adj** [hairline] dégarni(e) / [chin, forehead] fuyant(e).

receipt [rɪ'siːt] **n 1.** [piece of paper] reçu *m* **2.** *(U)* [act of receiving] réception *f*.
◆ ***receipts*** **npl** recettes *fpl*.

receivable [rɪ'siːvəbl] **adj 1.** [able to be received] recevable **2.** FIN à recevoir.

receive [rɪ'siːv] ■ **vt 1.** [gen] recevoir / [news] apprendre ▶ **to receive treatment (for sthg)** se faire soigner (pour qqch) ▶ **I'm receiving you loud and clear** RADIO je vous reçois cinq sur cinq **2.** [welcome] accueillir, recevoir ▶ **to be well/badly received** [film, speech] être bien/mal accueilli(e) ▶ **their offer was not well received** leur proposition n'a pas reçu un accueil favorable ▶ **to be received into the Church** être reçu(e) *OR* admis(e) dans le sein de l'Église.
■ **vi** [in tennis] recevoir le service.

Received Pronunciation [rɪ'siːvd-] **n** *UK* prononciation *f* standard (de l'anglais).

Received Standard [rɪ'siːvd-] **n** *US* prononciation *f* standard (de l'américain).

receiver [rɪ'siːvə^r] **n 1.** [of telephone] récepteur *m*, combiné *m* **2.** [radio, TV set] récepteur *m* **3.** [criminal] receleur *m*, -euse *f* **4.** FIN [official] administrateur *m*, -trice *f* judiciaire.

receivership [rɪ'siːvəʃɪp] **n : to go into receivership** être mis(e) en liquidation.

receiving end [rɪ'siːvɪŋ-] **n : to be on the receiving end (of sthg)** faire les frais (de qqch).

recent ['riːsnt] **adj** récent(e).

recently ['riːsntlɪ] **adv** récemment ▶ **until recently** jusqu'à ces derniers temps.

receptacle [rɪ'septəkl] **n** *fml* récipient *m*.

reception [rɪ'sepʃn] **n 1.** [gen] réception *f* **2.** [welcome] accueil *m*, réception *f*.

reception centre **n** *UK* centre *m* d'accueil.

reception class **n** *UK* cours *m* préparatoire.

reception desk **n** réception *f*.

receptionist [rɪ'sepʃənɪst] **n** réceptionniste *mf*.

reception room **n** *UK* salon *m*.

receptive [rɪ'septɪv] **adj** réceptif(ive).

receptiveness [rɪ'septɪvnɪs] **n** réceptivité *f*.

recess ['riːses *OR* rɪ'ses] **n 1.** [alcove] niche *f* **2.** [secret place] recoin *m* **3.** POL **: to be in recess** être en vacances **4.** *US* SCH récréation *f*.

recessed ['riːsest *OR* rɪ'sest] **adj** [window] dans un renfoncement / [door handle, light] encastré(e).

recession [rɪ'seʃn] **n** récession *f*.

recessionary [rɪ'seʃənrɪ] **adj** de récession.

recessive [rɪ'sesɪv] **adj** BIOL récessif(ive).

recharge [ˌriː'tʃɑːdʒ] **vt** recharger.

rechargeable [ˌriː'tʃɑːdʒəbl] **adj** rechargeable.

recipe ['resɪpɪ] **n** *lit* & *fig* recette *f*.

recipient [rɪ'sɪpɪənt] **n** [of letter] destinataire *mf* / [of cheque] bénéficiaire *mf* / [of award] récipiendaire *mf*.

FALSE FRIENDS / FAUX AMIS

recipient

Récipient n'est pas la traduction du mot anglais *recipient*. Récipient se traduit par *container*.
▶ Versez la soupe dans un récipient et congelez-la / *Put the soup in a container and freeze it*

reciprocal [rɪ'sɪprəkl] **adj** réciproque.

reciprocate [rɪ'sɪprəkeɪt] *fml* ■ **vt** rendre, retourner.
■ **vi** en faire autant.

reciprocity [ˌresɪ'prɒsətɪ] **n** *fml* réciprocité *f*.

recital [rɪ'saɪtl] **n** récital *m*.

recitation [ˌresɪ'teɪʃn] **n** récitation *f*.

recite [rɪ'saɪt] **vt 1.** [say aloud] réciter **2.** [list] énumérer.

reckless ['reklɪs] **adj 1.** [rash] imprudent(e) ▶ **reckless driving** conduite *f* imprudente **2.** [thoughtless] irréfléchi / [fearless] téméraire.

recklessly ['reklɪslɪ] **adv** [rashly] imprudemment / [thoughtlessly] sans réfléchir / [fearlessly] avec témérité ▶ **to spend recklessly** dépenser sans compter ▶ **he drives very recklessly** il conduit dangereusement.

recklessness ['reklɪsnɪs] **n** [rashness] imprudence *f* / [thoughtlessness] insouciance *f*, étourderie *f* / [fearlessness] témérité *f*.

reckon ['rekn] **vt 1.** *inf* [think] penser **2.** [consider, judge] considérer **3.** [expect] **: to reckon to do sthg** compter faire qqch **4.** [calculate] calculer.
◆ ***reckon on*** **vt insep** compter sur.
◆ ***reckon with*** **vt insep** [expect] s'attendre à ▶ **he's a person to be reckoned with** il faut compter avec lui.
◆ ***reckon without*** **vt insep** compter sans.

reckoning ['rekənɪŋ] **n** *(U)* [calculation] calculs *mpl* ▶ **day of reckoning** jour *m* de vérité.

reclaim [rɪ'kleɪm] **vt 1.** [claim back] réclamer **2.** [land] assécher.

reclamation [ˌreklə'meɪʃn] **n** [of land] assèchement *m*.

reclassify [ˌriː'klæsɪfaɪ] **(pt & pp -ied) vt** reclasser.

recline [rɪ'klaɪn] **vi** [person] être allongé(e).

reclining [rɪ'klaɪnɪŋ] **adj** [chair] à dossier réglable.

recluse [rɪ'kluːs] **n** reclus *m*, -e *f*.

reclusive [rɪ'kluːsɪv] **adj** reclus(e).

recognition [ˌrekəg'nɪʃn] **n** reconnaissance *f* ▶ **in recognition of** en reconnaissance de ▶ **the town has changed beyond** *OR* **out of all recognition** la ville est méconnaissable.

recognizable ['rekəgnaɪzəbl], *UK* ***-isable*** ['rekəgnaɪzəbl] **adj** reconnaissable.

recognizably ['rekəgnaɪzəblɪ], *UK* ***-isablly*** ['rekəgnaɪzəblɪ] **adv** d'une manière *OR* façon reconnaissable ▶ **the car was not recognizably Japanese** on n'aurait pas dit une voiture japonaise, cette voiture ne ressemblait pas à une voiture japonaise.

recognize, *UK* ***-ise*** ['rekəgnaɪz] **vt** reconnaître.

recognized, *UK* ***-ised*** ['rekəgnaɪzd] **adj 1.** [acknowledged] reconnu(e), admis(e) ▶ **she's a recognized authority on medieval history** c'est une autorité en histoire médiévale **2.** [identified] reconnu(e) **3.** [official] officiel (elle), attitré(e).

recoil ■ **vi** [rɪ'kɔɪl] **: to recoil (from)** reculer (devant).
■ **n** ['ri:kɔɪl] [of gun] recul *m*.

recollect [,rekə'lekt] **vt** se rappeler.

recollection [,rekə'lekʃn] **n** souvenir *m*.

recommence [,ri:kə'mens] **vt & vi** recommencer.

recommend [,rekə'mend] **vt 1.** [commend] **: to recommend sb/sthg (to sb)** recommander qqn/qqch (à qqn) ▶ **I'll recommend you to the Minister** j'appuyerai votre candidature auprès du ministre ▶ **the town has little to recommend it** la ville est sans grand intérêt **2.** [advise] conseiller, recommander ▶ **not (to be) recommended** à déconseiller.

recommendable [,rekə'mendəbl] **adj** recommandable.

recommendation [,rekəmen'deɪʃn] **n** recommandation *f*.

recommended retail price [,rekə'mendɪd-] **n** prix *m* de vente conseillé.

recompense ['rekəmpens] *fml* ■ **n** dédommagement *m*.
■ **vt** dédommager.

reconcilable ['rekənsaɪləbl] **adj** [opinions] conciliable, compatible / [people] compatible.

reconcile ['rekənsaɪl] **vt 1.** [beliefs, ideas] concilier **2.** [people] réconcilier ▶ **to be reconciled with sb** se réconcilier avec qqn **3.** [accept] **: to reconcile o.s. to sthg** se faire à l'idée de qqch.

CONFUSABLE / PARONYME

reconcile

When translating **to reconcile**, note that the French verbs ***concilier*** and ***réconcilier*** are not interchangeable. ***Concilier*** is used when referring to opinions or facts, whereas ***réconcilier*** refers to people.

reconciliation [,rekənsɪlɪ'eɪʃn] **n 1.** [of beliefs, ideas] conciliation *f* **2.** [of people] réconciliation *f*.

recondite ['rekəndaɪt] **adj** *fml* obscur(e).

reconditioned [,ri:kən'dɪʃnd] **adj** remis(e) en état.

reconfigure [,ri:kən'fɪgəʳ] **vt** COMPUT reconfigurer.

reconnaissance [rɪ'kɒnɪsəns] **n** reconnaissance *f*.

reconnect [,ri:kə'nekt] **vt** rebrancher.

reconnoitre *UK*, ***reconnoiter*** *US* [,rekə'nɔɪtəʳ] ■ **vt** reconnaître.
■ **vi** aller en reconnaissance.

reconsider [,ri:kən'sɪdəʳ] ■ **vt** reconsidérer.
■ **vi** reconsidérer la question.

reconsideration ['ri:kən,sɪdə'reɪʃn] **n** [reexamination] nouvel examen *m*, nouveau regard *m* / [of judgment] révision *f*.

reconstitute [,ri:'kɒnstɪtju:t] **vt** reconstituer.

reconstituted [,ri:'kɒnstɪtju:tɪd] **adj** reconstitué(e).

reconstruct [,ri:kən'strʌkt] **vt 1.** [gen] reconstruire **2.** [crime, event] reconstituer.

reconstruction [,ri:kən'strʌkʃn] **n 1.** [gen] reconstruction *f* **2.** [of crime, event] reconstitution *f*.

reconvene [,ri:kən'vi:n] **vt** convoquer de nouveau.

record ■ **n** ['rekɔ:d] **1.** [written account] rapport *m* / [file] dossier *m* ▶ **there is no record of their visit** il n'existe aucune trace de leur visite ▶ **the plane has a good safety record** l'avion est réputé pour sa sécurité ▶ **they keep a record of all deposits** ils enregistrent tous les versements ▶ **to keep sthg on record** archiver qqch ▶ **to go on record as saying (that)...** déclarer publiquement que... ▶ **(police) record** casier *m* judiciaire ▶ **service** *OR* **army record** MIL états *mpl* de service ▶ **off the record** non officiel ▶ **to set** *OR* **put the record straight** mettre les choses au clair **2.** [vinyl disc] disque *m* ▶ **to make** *OR* **to cut a record** faire *OR* graver un disque **3.** [best achievement] record *m* ▶ **to set/to break a record** établir/battre un record.
■ **adj** ['rekɔ:d] record *(inv)* ▶ **to reach record levels** atteindre un niveau record.
■ **vt** [rɪ'kɔ:d] **1.** [write down] noter ▶ **temperatures of 50° were recorded** on a relevé des températures de 50° ▶ **a photograph was taken to record the event** une photographie a été prise pour rappeler cet événement **2.** [put on tape] enregistrer.

record-breaker **n** personne *f* qui bat le record.

record-breaking **adj** qui bat tous les records.

recorded [rɪ'kɔ:dɪd] **adj 1.** [music, message, tape] enregistré(e) / [programme] préenregistré(e) / [broadcast] transmis(e) en différé **2.** [fact] attesté(e), noté(e) / [history] écrit(e) / [votes] exprimé(e) ▶ **throughout recorded history** pendant toute la période couverte par les écrits historiques.

recorded delivery **n : to send sthg by recorded delivery** envoyer qqch en recommandé.

recorder [rɪ'kɔ:dəʳ] **n** [musical instrument] flûte *f* à bec.

record holder **n** détenteur *m*, -trice *f* du record.

recording [rɪ'kɔ:dɪŋ] **n** enregistrement *m*.

recording studio **n** studio *m* d'enregistrement.

record library **n** discothèque *f*.

record player **n** tourne-disque *m*.

recount ■ **n** ['ri:kaʊnt] [of vote] deuxième dépouillement *m* du scrutin.
■ **vt 1.** [rɪ'kaʊnt] [narrate] raconter **2.** [,ri:'kaʊnt] [count again] recompter.

recoup [rɪ'ku:p] **vt** récupérer.

recourse [rɪ'kɔ:s] **n : to have recourse to** avoir recours à.

recover [rɪ'kʌvəʳ] ■ **vt 1.** [retrieve] récupérer ▶ **to recover sthg from sb** reprendre qqch à qqn ▶ **to recover damages** LAW obtenir des dommages-intérêts **2.** [one's balance] retrouver / [consciousness] reprendre ▶ **to recover o.s.** se ressaisir ▶ **to recover one's strength** reprendre des forces.
■ **vi 1.** [from illness] se rétablir / [from shock, divorce] se remettre ▶ **to be fully recovered** être complètement

guéri(e) OR rétabli(e) ▸ **I still haven't recovered from the shock** je ne me suis pas encore remis du choc **2.** *fig* [economy] se redresser / [trade] reprendre.

recoverable [ri:'kʌvrəbl] **adj** FIN récupérable.

recovery [rɪ'kʌvərɪ] (pl **-ies**) **n 1.** [from illness] guérison *f*, rétablissement *m* **2.** *fig* [of economy] redressement *m*, reprise *f* **3.** [retrieval] récupération *f*.

recovery position **n** MED position *f* latérale de sécurité.

recovery vehicle **n** *UK* dépanneuse *f*.

recreate [ˌri:krɪ'eɪt] **vt** recréer.

recreation [ˌrekrɪ'eɪʃn] **n** *(U)* [leisure] récréation *f*, loisirs *mpl*.

recreational [ˌrekrɪ'eɪʃənl] **adj** de récréation.

recreational vehicle *US* = ***RV***.

recreation ground **n** *UK* terrain *m* de jeux.

recreation room **n** salle *f* de récréation / *US* [in house] salle de jeu.

recrimination [rɪˌkrɪmɪ'neɪʃn] **n** récrimination *f*.

recrudescence [ˌri:kru:'desns] **n** *fml* recrudescence *f*.

recruit [rɪ'kru:t] ■ **n** recrue *f*.
■ **vt** recruter ▸ **to recruit sb to do sthg** *fig* embaucher qqn pour faire qqch.
■ **vi** recruter.

recruiting [rɪ'kru:tɪŋ] **n** recrutement *m*.

recruitment [rɪ'kru:tmənt] **n** recrutement *m*.

rectangle ['rekˌtæŋgl] **n** rectangle *m*.

rectangular [rek'tæŋgjʊlər] **adj** rectangulaire.

rectification [ˌrektɪfɪ'keɪʃn] **n** *fml* rectification *f*.

rectify ['rektɪfaɪ] (pt & pp **-ied**) **vt** *fml* [mistake] rectifier.

rectitude ['rektɪtju:d] **n** *fml* rectitude *f*.

rector ['rektər] **n 1.** [priest] pasteur *m* **2.** *Scot* [head - of school] directeur *m* / [- of college, university] *président élu par les étudiants*.

rectory ['rektərɪ] (pl **-ies**) **n** presbytère *m*.

rectum ['rektəm] **n** ANAT rectum *m*.

recuperate [rɪ'ku:pəreɪt] **vi** se rétablir.

recuperation [rɪˌku:pə'reɪʃn] **n** rétablissement *m*.

recur [rɪ'kɜ:r] (pt & pp **-red**, cont **-ring**) **vi** [error, problem] se reproduire / [dream] revenir / [pain] réapparaître.

recurrence [rɪ'kʌrəns] **n** répétition *f*.

recurrent [rɪ'kʌrənt] **adj** [error, problem] qui se reproduit souvent / [dream] qui revient souvent.

recurring [rɪ'kɜ:rɪŋ] **adj 1.** [error, problem] qui se reproduit souvent / [dream] qui revient souvent **2.** MATHS périodique.

recyclable [ˌri:'saɪkləbl] **adj** recyclable.

recycle [ˌri:'saɪkl] **vt** recycler.

recycle bin **n** COMPUT poubelle *f*, corbeille *f*.

recycled [ˌri:'saɪkld] **adj** [materials] recyclé(e).

recycling [ˌri:'saɪklɪŋ] **n** recyclage *m*.

red [red] ■ **adj** (comp **-der**, superl **-dest**) rouge / [hair] roux (rousse).
■ **n** rouge *m* ▸ **to be in the red** *inf* être à découvert ▸ **to see red** voir rouge.
◆ ***Red*** *pej* ■ **adj** rouge.
■ **n** rouge *mf*.

red alert **n** alerte *f* maximale ▸ **to be on red alert** être en état d'alerte maximale.

red blood cell **n** globule *m* rouge.

red-blooded [-'blʌdɪd] **adj** *hum* viril(e).

red-brick **adj** *UK* [building] en brique rouge.

redbrick university ['redbrɪk-] **n** *en Angleterre, ce terme désigne les universités de création relativement récente par opposition à Oxford et Cambridge*.

red card **n** FOOTBALL **: to be shown the red card, to get a red card** recevoir un carton rouge.

red carpet **n : to roll out the red carpet for sb** dérouler le tapis rouge pour qqn.
◆ ***red-carpet*** **adj : to give sb the red-carpet treatment** recevoir qqn en grande pompe.

red corpuscle **n** globule *m* rouge, hématie *f*.

Red Crescent **n : the Red Crescent** le Croissant Rouge.

Red Cross **n : the Red Cross** la Croix-Rouge.

redcurrant ['redˌkʌrənt] **n** [fruit] groseille *f* / [bush] groseillier *m*.

red deer **n** cerf *m*.

redden ['redn] **vt & vi** rougir.

redecorate [ˌri:'dekəreɪt] ■ **vt** [repaint] refaire les peintures de / [re-wallpaper] retapisser.
■ **vi** [repaint] refaire les peintures / [re-wallpaper] refaire les papiers peints.

redecoration [ri:ˌdekə'reɪʃn] **n** [painting] remise *f* à neuf des peintures / [wallpapering] remise *f* à neuf des papiers peints.

redeem [rɪ'di:m] **vt 1.** [save, rescue] racheter ▸ **to redeem o.s.** se racheter **2.** [from pawnbroker] dégager.

redeemable [rɪ'di:məbl] **adj 1.** [voucher] remboursable / [debt] remboursable, amortissable ▸ **the stamps are not redeemable for cash** les timbres ne peuvent être échangés contre des espèces **2.** [error] réparable / [sin, crime] expiable, rachetable / [sinner] rachetable.

redeeming [rɪ'di:mɪŋ] **adj** qui rachète (les défauts).

redefine [ˌri:dɪ'faɪn] **vt** redéfinir.

redemption [rɪ'dempʃn] **n** rédemption *f* ▸ **beyond** OR **past redemption** *fig* irrémédiable.

redeploy [ˌri:dɪ'plɔɪ] **vt** MIL redéployer / [staff] réorganiser, réaffecter.

redeployment [ˌri:dɪ'plɔɪmənt] **n** MIL redéploiement *m* / [of staff] réorganisation *f*, réaffectation *f*.

redesign [ˌri:dɪ'zaɪn] **vt** [room] redessiner / [system] réorganiser.

redevelop [ˌri:dɪ'veləp] **vt** réaménager.

redevelopment [ˌri:dɪ'veləpmənt] **n** réaménagement *m*.

redeye ['redaɪ] **n** *inf* [night flight] vol *m* de nuit.

red-eyed adj aux yeux rouges.

red-faced [-'feɪst] adj rougeaud(e), rubicond(e) / [with embarrassment] rouge de confusion.

red-haired [-'heəd] adj roux (rousse).

red-handed [-'hændɪd] adj : **to catch sb red-handed** prendre qqn en flagrant délit *OR* la main dans le sac.

redhead ['redhed] n roux *m*, rousse *f*.

red-headed = ***red-haired***.

red herring n *fig* fausse piste *f*.

red-hot adj **1.** [extremely hot] brûlant(e) / [metal] chauffé(e) au rouge **2.** [very enthusiastic] ardent(e).

redial [ˌri:'daɪəl] ■ vt : **to redial a number** refaire un numéro.
■ n : **automatic redial** système *m* de rappel du dernier numéro.

redid [ˌri:'dɪd] pt ➤ ***redo***.

residence hall *US* = ***hall of residence***.

Red Indian ■ adj de Peau-Rouge.
■ n Peau-Rouge *mf (attention: le terme 'Red Indian' est considéré comme raciste)*.

redirect [ˌri:dɪ'rekt] vt **1.** [energy, money] réorienter **2.** [traffic] détourner **3.** *UK* [letters] faire suivre.

rediscover [ˌri:dɪ'skʌvəʳ] vt redécouvrir.

rediscovery [ˌri:dɪ'skʌvrɪ] (pl -ies) n redécouverte *f*.

redistribute [ˌri:dɪ'strɪbju:t] vt redistribuer.

redistribution ['ri:ˌdɪstrɪ'bju:ʃn] n redistribution *f*.

red-letter day n jour *m* mémorable, jour à marquer d'une pierre blanche.

red light n [traffic signal] feu *m* rouge.

red-light district n quartier *m* chaud.

red meat n viande *f* rouge.

redneck ['rednek] *US inf pej* n *Américain d'origine modeste qui a des idées réactionnaires et des préjugés racistes*.

redness ['rednɪs] n rougeur *f*.

redo [ˌri:'du:] (pt -did, pp -done) vt refaire.

redolent ['redələnt] adj *liter* **1.** [reminiscent] : **redolent of** qui rappelle, évocateur(trice) de **2.** [smelling] : **redolent of** qui sent.

redone [ˌri:'dʌn] pp ➤ ***redo***.

redouble [ˌri:'dʌbl] vt : **to redouble one's efforts (to do sthg)** redoubler d'efforts (pour faire qqch).

redoubtable [rɪ'daʊtəbl] adj *liter* redoutable, formidable.

redraft [ˌri:'drɑ:ft] vt rédiger à nouveau.

redraw [ˌri:'drɔ:] (pt -drew, pp -drawn ['drɔ:n]) vt dessiner à nouveau.

redress [rɪ'dres] ■ n *(U) fml* réparation *f*.
■ vt : **to redress the balance** rétablir l'équilibre.

redrew [ˌri:'dru:] pt ➤ ***redraw***.

Red Sea n : **the Red Sea** la mer Rouge.

Red Square n la place Rouge.

red squirrel n écureuil *m*.

red tape n *fig* paperasserie *f* administrative.

reduce [rɪ'dju:s] ■ vt réduire ▸ **to be reduced to doing sthg** en être réduit(e) à faire qqch ▸ **to reduce sb to tears** faire pleurer qqn.
■ vi *US* [diet] suivre un régime amaigrissant.

reduced [rɪ'dju:st] adj réduit(e) ▸ **in reduced circumstances** dans la gêne.

reduction [rɪ'dʌkʃn] n **1.** [decrease] : **reduction (in)** réduction *f* (de), baisse *f* (de) **2.** [discount] rabais *m*, réduction *f*.

reductive [rɪ'dʌktɪv] adj *fml* réducteur(trice).

redundancy [rɪ'dʌndənsɪ] (pl -ies) n *UK* [dismissal] licenciement *m* / [unemployment] chômage *m*.

redundancy payment n *UK* indemnité *f* de licenciement.

redundant [rɪ'dʌndənt] adj **1.** *UK* [jobless] : **to be made redundant** être licencié(e) **2.** [not required] superflu(e).

redwood ['redwʊd] n : **redwood (tree)** séquoia *m*.

reecho [ˌri:'ekəʊ] ■ vt [repeat] répéter.
■ vi [echo again] retentir.

reed [ri:d] ■ n **1.** [plant] roseau *m* **2.** MUS anche *f*.
■ comp [basket] en roseau.

reeducate [ˌri:'edjʊkeɪt] vt rééduquer.

reedy ['ri:dɪ] (comp -ier, superl -iest) adj [voice] flûté(e), aigu(ë).

reef [ri:f] n récif *m*, écueil *m*.

reek [ri:k] ■ n relent *m*.
■ vi : **to reek (of sthg)** puer (qqch), empester (qqch).

reel [ri:l] ■ n **1.** [roll] bobine *f* **2.** [on fishing rod] moulinet *m*.
■ vi **1.** [stagger] chanceler **2.** [whirl] : **my mind was reeling** j'avais la tête qui tournait.
◆ ***reel in*** vt sep remonter.
◆ ***reel off*** vt sep [list] débiter.

reelect [ˌri:ɪ'lekt] vt : **to reelect sb (as) sthg** réélire qqn qqch.

reelection [ˌri:ɪ'lekʃn] n réélection *f*.

reemerge [ˌri:ɪ'mɜ:dʒ] vi [new facts] ressortir / [idea, clue] réapparaître / [problem, question] se reposer / [from hiding, tunnel] ressortir, ressurgir.

reemergence [ˌri:ɪ'mɜ:dʒəns] n réapparition *f*.

reemphasize, -ise *UK* [ˌri:'emfəsaɪz] vt souligner de nouveau.

reenact [ˌri:ɪ'nækt] vt [play] reproduire / [event] reconstituer.

reenter [ˌri:'entəʳ] vt [room, Earth's atmosphere] rentrer dans / [country] retourner dans.

reentry [ˌri:'entrɪ] n [into Earth's atmosphere] rentrée *f* / [into country] retour *m*.

reestablish [ˌri:ɪ'stæblɪʃ] vt **1.** [order] rétablir / [practice] restaurer / [law] remettre en vigueur **2.** [person] réhabiliter, réintégrer ▸ **the team have reestablished themselves as the best in the country** l'équipe s'est imposée de nouveau comme la meilleure du pays.

reexamination [ˌri:ɪg'zæmɪneɪʃn] n [of question] réexamen *m* / LAW nouvel interrogatoire *m*.

reexamine [ˌriːɪg'zæmɪn] **vt** examiner de nouveau.

reexport [ˌriː'ekspɔːt] ■ **n** COMM réexportation *f.*
■ **vt** COMM réexporter.

ref [ref] **n 1.** *inf* (abbr of ***referee***) arbitre *m* **2.** ADMIN (abbr of ***reference***) réf. *f*

refectory [rɪ'fektərɪ] (pl **-ies**) **n** réfectoire *m.*

refer [rɪ'fɜːʳ] (pt & pp **-red**, cont **-ring**) **vt 1.** [person] **: to refer sb to** [hospital] envoyer qqn à / [specialist] adresser qqn à / ADMIN renvoyer qqn à **2.** [report, decision] **: to refer sthg to** soumettre qqch à ▸ **to refer a case to a higher court** renvoyer *OR* déférer une affaire à une instance supérieure.
◆ ***refer to*** **vt insep 1.** [speak about] parler de, faire allusion à *OR* mention de ▸ **the revolutionaries are referred to as Mantras** ces révolutionaires sont connus sous le nom de Mantras **2.** [apply to] s'appliquer à, concerner ▸ **the numbers refer to footnotes** les chiffres renvoient à des notes en bas de page ▸ **these measures only refer to taxpayers** ses mesures ne s'appliquent qu'aux contribuables **3.** [consult] se référer à, se reporter à ▸ **I shall have to refer to my boss** je dois en référer à *OR* consulter mon patron.

referee [ˌrefə'riː] ■ **n 1.** SPORT arbitre *mf* **2.** *UK* [for job application] répondant *m*, -e *f.*
■ **vt** SPORT arbitrer.
■ **vi** SPORT être arbitre.

reference ['refrəns] **n 1.** [mention] **: reference (to)** allusion *f* (à), mention *f* (de) ▸ **with reference to** comme suite à **2.** *(U)* [for advice, information] **: reference (to)** consultation *f* (de), référence *f* (à) ▸ **for future reference** à titre d'information **3.** COMM référence *f* **4.** [in book] renvoi *m* ▸ **map reference** coordonnées *fpl* **5.** [for job application - letter] référence *f* / [- person] répondant *m*, -e *f.*

reference book **n** ouvrage *m* de référence.

reference library **n** bibliothèque *f* d'ouvrages à consulter.

reference number **n** numéro *m* de référence.

referendum [ˌrefə'rendəm] (pl **-s** *OR* **-da** [-də]) **n** référendum *m.*

referral [rɪ'fɜːrəl] **n** *fml* **1.** *(U)* [act of referring] envoi *m* **2.** [patient referred] malade envoyé *m*, malade envoyée *f.*

refill ■ **n** ['riːfɪl] **1.** [for pen] recharge *f* **2.** *inf* [drink] **: would you like a refill?** vous voulez encore un verre?
■ **vt** [ˌriː'fɪl] remplir à nouveau.

refillable [ˌriː'fɪləbl] **adj** [pen] rechargeable / [bottle] qu'on peut faire remplir à nouveau.

refinance [ˌriːfaɪ'næns] ■ **vt** [loan] refinancer.
■ **vi** [of company] se refinancer.

refinancing [ˌriːfaɪ'nænsɪŋ] **n** refinancement *m.*

refine [rɪ'faɪn] **vt** raffiner / *fig* peaufiner.

refined [rɪ'faɪnd] **adj** raffiné(e) / [system, theory] perfectionné(e).

refinement [rɪ'faɪnmənt] **n 1.** [improvement] perfectionnement *m* **2.** *(U)* [gentility] raffinement *m.*

refinery [rɪ'faɪnərɪ] (pl **-ies**) **n** raffinerie *f.*

refit ■ **n** ['riːfɪt] [of ship] réparation *f*, remise *f* en état.
■ **vt** [ˌriː'fɪt] (pt & pp **-ted**, cont **-ting**) [ship] réparer, remettre en état.

reflate [ˌriː'fleɪt] ■ **vt** ECON relancer.
■ **vi** ECON effectuer une relance (de l'économie).

reflation [ˌriː'fleɪʃn] **n** ECON relance *f.*

reflationary [riː'fleɪʃənrɪ] **adj** ECON de relance.

reflect [rɪ'flekt] ■ **vt 1.** [be a sign of] refléter **2.** [light, image] réfléchir, refléter / [heat] réverbérer ▸ **to be reflected in** se refléter dans **3.** [think] **: to reflect that...** se dire que...
■ **vi** [think] **: to reflect (on** *OR* **upon)** réfléchir (sur), penser (à).

reflection [rɪ'flekʃn] **n 1.** [sign] indication *f*, signe *m* **2.** [criticism] **: reflection on** critique *f* de **3.** [image] reflet *m* **4.** *(U)* [of light, heat] réflexion *f* **5.** [thought] réflexion *f* ▸ **on reflection** réflexion faite.

reflective [rɪ'flektɪv] **adj 1.** [surface, material] réfléchissant(e) **2.** [thoughtful] pensif(ive).

reflector [rɪ'flektəʳ] **n** réflecteur *m.*

reflex ['riːfleks] **n : reflex (action)** réflexe *m.*
◆ ***reflexes*** **npl** réflexes *mpl.*

reflex camera **n** appareil *m* reflex.

reflexive [rɪ'fleksɪv] **adj** GRAM [pronoun] réfléchi(e).

reflexively [rɪ'fleksɪvlɪ] **adv** GRAM [in meaning] au sens réfléchi / [in form] à la forme réfléchie.

reflexive verb **n** verbe *m* réfléchi.

reflexology [ˌriːflek'sɒlədʒɪ] **n** réflexothérapie *f.*

reforest [ˌriː'fɒrɪst] *US* = ***reafforest.***

reforestation [riːˌfɒrɪ'steɪʃn] *US* = ***reafforestation.***

reform [rɪ'fɔːm] ■ **n** réforme *f.*
■ **vt** [gen] réformer / [person] corriger.
■ **vi** [behave better] se corriger, s'amender.

re-form [riː'fɔːm] ■ **vt 1.** MIL [ranks] remettre en rang, reformer / [men] rallier **2.** [return to original form] rendre sa forme primitive *OR* originale à / [in new form] donner une nouvelle forme à / [form again] reformer.
■ **vi 1.** MIL [men] se remettre en rangs / [ranks] se reformer **2.** [group, band] se reformer.

reformat [ˌriː'fɔːmæt] (pt & pp **-ted**, cont **-ting**) **vt** COMPUT reformater.

Reformation [ˌrefə'meɪʃn] **n : the Reformation** la Réforme.

reformatory [rɪ'fɔːmətrɪ] **n** *US* centre *m* d'éducation surveillée (pour jeunes délinquants).

reformed [rɪ'fɔːmd] **adj** [better behaved] qui s'est corrigé(e) *OR* amendé(e).

reformer [rɪ'fɔːməʳ] **n** réformateur *m*, -trice *f.*

reformist [rɪ'fɔːmɪst] ■ **adj** réformiste.
■ **n** réformiste *mf.*

refract [rɪ'frækt] *fml* ■ **vt** réfracter.
■ **vi** se réfracter.

refraction [rɪ'frækʃn] **n** *fml* [phenomenon] réfraction *f* / [property] réfringence *f.*

refractive [rɪ'fræktɪv] **adj** *fml* réfringent(e).

refrain [rɪ'freɪn] ■ **n** refrain *m*.
■ **vi : to refrain from doing sthg** s'abstenir de faire qqch.

refresh [rɪ'freʃ] **vt** rafraîchir, revigorer ▸ **to refresh sb's memory** rafraîchir la mémoire de qqn.

refreshed [rɪ'freʃt] **adj** reposé(e).

refresher course [rɪ'freʃər-] **n** cours *m* de recyclage *OR* remise à niveau.

refreshing [rɪ'freʃɪŋ] **adj 1.** [pleasantly different] agréable, réconfortant(e) **2.** [drink, swim] rafraîchissant(e).

refreshingly [rɪ'freʃɪŋlɪ] **adv : it's refreshingly different** c'est un changement agréable.

refreshments [rɪ'freʃmənts] **npl** rafraîchissements *mpl*.

refrigerate [rɪ'frɪdʒəreɪt] **vt** réfrigérer.

refrigeration [rɪˌfrɪdʒə'reɪʃn] **n** réfrigération *f*.

refrigerator [rɪ'frɪdʒəreɪtər] **n** réfrigérateur *m*, Frigidaire® *m*.

refrigerator-freezer *US* = *fridge-freezer*.

refuel [ˌriː'fjʊəl] (*UK* **-led**, cont **-ling**, *US* **-ed**, cont **-ing**)
■ **vt** ravitailler.
■ **vi** se ravitailler en carburant.

refuelling *UK*, ***refueling*** *US* [ˌriː'fjʊəlɪŋ] ■ **n** ravitaillement *m* (en carburant).
■ **comp** [boom, tanker] de ravitaillement ▸ **to make a refuelling stop** AUT s'arrêter pour prendre de l'essence / AERON faire une escale technique.

refuge ['refjuːdʒ] **n** *lit* & *fig* refuge *m*, abri *m* ▸ **to take refuge in** se réfugier dans.

refugee [ˌrefjʊ'dʒiː] **n** réfugié *m*, -e *f*.

refugee camp **n** camp *m* de réfugiés.

refund ■ **n** ['riːfʌnd] remboursement *m*.
■ **vt** [rɪ'fʌnd] **: to refund sthg to sb, to refund sb sthg** rembourser qqch à qqn.

refundable [riː'fʌndəbl] **adj** remboursable.

refurbish [ˌriː'fɜːbɪʃ] **vt** remettre à neuf, rénover.

refurbishment [ˌriː'fɜːbɪʃmənt] **n** rénovation *f*.

refurnish [ˌriː'fɜːnɪʃ] **vt** remeubler.

refusal [rɪ'fjuːzl] **n : refusal (to do sthg)** refus *m* (de faire qqch).

refuse[1] [rɪ'fjuːz] ■ **vt** refuser ▸ **to refuse to do sthg** refuser de faire qqch.
■ **vi** refuser.

refuse[2] ['refjuːs] **n** *(U) fml* [rubbish] ordures *fpl*, détritus *mpl*.

refuse collection ['refjuːs-] **n** *UK fml* enlèvement *m* des ordures ménagères.

refuse collector ['refjuːs-] **n** *UK fml* éboueur *m*.

refuse dump ['refjuːs-] **n** *UK fml* décharge *f* (publique).

refutation [ˌrefjuː'teɪʃn] **n** *fml* réfutation *f*.

refute [rɪ'fjuːt] **vt** *fml* réfuter.

reg., ***regd.*** (abbr of ***registered***) **: reg. trademark** marque *f* déposée.

regain [rɪ'geɪn] **vt** [composure, health] retrouver / [leadership] reprendre.

regal ['riːgl] **adj** majestueux(euse), royal(e).

regale [rɪ'geɪl] **vt : to regale sb with sthg** divertir qqn en lui racontant qqch.

regalia [rɪ'geɪljə] **n** *(U)* insignes *mpl*.

regard [rɪ'gɑːd] ■ **n 1.** *(U)* [respect] estime *f*, respect *m* ▸ **I hold them in high regard** je les tiens en grande estime ▸ **out of regard for** par égard pour ▸ **without due regard to** sans tenir compte de ▸ **to have regard for sb** avoir de la considération pour qqn ▸ **they have no regard for your feelings** ils ne se soucient pas de vos sentiments **2.** [aspect] **: in this/that regard** à cet égard.
■ **vt** considérer ▸ **I regard their conclusions as correct** *OR* **to be correct** je tiens leurs conclusions pour correctes ▸ **to regard o.s. as** se considérer comme ▸ **to be highly regarded** être tenu(e) en haute estime.
◆ ***regards*** **npl : (with best) regards** bien amicalement ▸ **give her my regards** faites-lui mes amitiés ▸ **he sends his regards** vous avez le bonjour de sa part.
◆ ***as regards*** **prep** en ce qui concerne.
◆ ***in regard to***, ***with regard to*** **prep** en ce qui concerne, relativement à.

FALSE FRIENDS / FAUX AMIS

regard

Regarder n'est pas la traduction du mot anglais *to regard*. Regarder se traduit par *to look at*.
▸ Regarde-moi ça ! / *Just look at that!*

regarding [rɪ'gɑːdɪŋ] **prep** concernant, en ce qui concerne.

regardless [rɪ'gɑːdlɪs] **adv** quand même.
◆ ***regardless of*** **prep** sans tenir compte de, sans se soucier de.

regatta [rɪ'gætə] **n** régate *f*.

regd. = ***reg.***

Regency ['riːdʒənsɪ] **adj** Régence (anglaise).

regenerate [rɪ'dʒenəreɪt] **vt** [economy, project] relancer.

HOW TO ...

express refusal

Certainement pas ! / Certainly not!
Il n'en est pas question ! / It's out of the question!
Non, je regrette / No, sorry
Je ne peux pas accepter vos conditions / I can't accept your conditions
Je n'irai pas, un point c'est tout *ou* point final ! / I'm not going and that's final!
Alors là, tu peux toujours courir ! *inf* / Forget it!
Je m'y oppose catégoriquement / I'm completely against it

regeneration [rɪˌdʒenə'reɪʃn] n [of economy, project] relance *f*.

regent ['ri:dʒənt] n régent *m*, -e *f*.

reggae ['regeɪ] n reggae *m*.

regime [reɪ'ʒi:m] n régime *m*.

regiment ['redʒɪmənt] n régiment *m*.

regimental [ˌredʒɪ'mentl] adj du régiment.

regimented ['redʒɪmentɪd] adj [organization] trop rigide / [life] strict(e).

region ['ri:dʒən] n région *f* ▸ **in the region of** environ.

regional ['ri:dʒənl] adj régional(e).

regionalism ['ri:dʒənəlɪzm] n régionalisme *m*.

regionally ['ri:dʒnəlɪ] adv à l'échelle régionale.

register ['redʒɪstəʳ] ■ n [record] registre *m* ▸ **register of births, deaths and marriages** registre *m* de l'état civil ▸ **to call** *OR* **to take the register** SCH faire l'appel.
■ vt **1.** [record - name] (faire) enregistrer / [- birth, death] déclarer / [- vehicle] (faire) immatriculer / [- trademark] déposer / [- on list] inscrire ▸ **to register a complaint** déposer une plainte ▸ **to register one's vote** exprimer son vote, voter **2.** [show, measure] indiquer, montrer **3.** [express] exprimer ▸ **her face registered disbelief** l'incrédulité se lisait sur son visage.
■ vi **1.** [on official list] s'inscrire, se faire inscrire ▸ **to register with a GP/on the electoral roll** se faire inscrire auprès d'un médecin traitant/sur les listes électorales **2.** [at hotel] signer le registre **3.** *inf* [advice, fact] **: it didn't register** je n'ai pas compris ▸ **the truth slowly began to register (with me)** petit à petit, la vérité m'est apparue.

registered ['redʒɪstəd] adj **1.** [person] inscrit(e) / [car] immatriculé(e) / [charity] agréé(e) par le gouvernement **2.** [letter, parcel] recommandé(e).

Registered Nurse n infirmier *m* diplômé *OR* infirmière *f* diplômée d'État.

registered post *UK*, ***registered mail*** *US* n **: to send sthg by registered post** envoyer qqch en recommandé.

Registered Trademark n marque *f* déposée.

registered user n COMPUT utilisateur *m*, -trice *f* disposant d'une licence.

register office *UK* = ***registry office***.

registrar [ˌredʒɪ'strɑ:ʳ] n **1.** [keeper of records] officier *m* de l'état civil **2.** UNIV secrétaire *m* général **3.** *UK* [doctor] chef *m* de clinique.

registration [ˌredʒɪ'streɪʃn] n **1.** [gen] enregistrement *m*, inscription *f* **2.** AUT = ***registration number***.

registration document n *UK* AUT ≃ carte *f* grise.

registration number n AUT numéro *m* d'immatriculation.

registry ['redʒɪstrɪ] (pl **-ies**) n *UK* bureau *m* de l'enregistrement.

registry office n *UK* bureau *m* de l'état civil.

regress [rɪ'gres] vi **: to regress (to)** régresser (au stade de).

regression [rɪ'greʃn] n régression *f*.

regressive [rɪ'gresɪv] adj régressif(ive).

regret [rɪ'gret] ■ n regret *m* ▸ **much to our regret** à notre grand regret ▸ **I have no regrets** je n'ai pas de regrets, je ne regrette rien.
■ vt (pt & pp **-ted**, cont **-ting**) [be sorry about] **: to regret sthg/doing sthg** regretter qqch/d'avoir fait qqch ▸ **the airline regrets any inconvenience caused to passengers** la compagnie s'excuse pour la gêne occasionnée ▸ **we regret to announce...** nous sommes au regret d'annoncer...

regretful [rɪ'gretfʊl] adj [person] plein(e) de regrets / [look] de regret.

regretfully [rɪ'gretfʊlɪ] adv à regret.

regrettable [rɪ'gretəbl] adj regrettable, fâcheux(euse).

regrettably [rɪ'gretəblɪ] adv malheureusement.

regroup [ˌri:'gru:p] vi se regrouper.

regt abbr of ***regiment***.

regular ['regjʊləʳ] ■ adj **1.** [gen] régulier(ère) / [customer] fidèle **2.** [usual] habituel(elle) **3.** [normal - size] standard *(inv)* **4.** *US* [pleasant] sympa *(inv)*.
■ n [at pub] habitué *m*, -e *f* / [at shop] client *m*, -e *f* fidèle.

regular army n armée *f* de métier.

regularity [ˌregjʊ'lærətɪ] n régularité *f*.

regularly ['regjʊləlɪ] adv régulièrement.

regulate ['regjʊleɪt] vt régler.

regulation [ˌregjʊ'leɪʃn] ■ adj [standard] réglementaire.
■ n **1.** [rule] règlement *m* **2.** *(U)* [control] réglementation *f*.

regulatory ['regjʊlətrɪ] adj réglementaire.

regurgitate [rɪ'gɜ:dʒɪteɪt] vt *fml* régurgiter / *fig* & *pej* ressortir, répéter.

rehab ['ri:hæb] n *US inf* **: to be in rehab** faire une cure de désintoxication ▸ **rehab center** centre *m* de désintoxication.

rehabilitate [ˌri:ə'bɪlɪteɪt] vt [criminal] réinsérer, réhabiliter / [patient] rééduquer.

HOW TO ...

express regret

Malheureusement, nous n'avons pas pu arriver à temps / Unfortunately, we couldn't get there in time
Je regrette vraiment que vous n'ayez pas pu venir / I'm really sorry you couldn't make it
Je regrette ce que j'ai dit / I regret what I said
Si seulement je lui en avais parlé plus tôt ! / If only I'd told her sooner!
(Quel) dommage que je ne l'aie pas rencontré avant ! / What a pity I didn't meet him sooner!
Dire que je ne le reverrai probablement jamais ! / To think I'll probably never see him again!

rehabilitation [ˈriːəˌbɪlɪˈteɪʃn] **n** [of criminal] réinsertion *f*, réhabilitation *f* / [of patient] rééducation *f*.

rehash [ˌriːˈhæʃ] **vt** *inf pej* remanier.

rehearsal [rɪˈhɜːsl] **n** répétition *f*.

rehearse [rɪˈhɜːs] **vt & vi** répéter.

reheat [ˌriːˈhiːt] **vt** réchauffer.

rehouse [ˌriːˈhaʊz] **vt** reloger.

reign [reɪn] ■ **n** règne *m*.
■ **vi : to reign (over)** *lit & fig* régner (sur).

reigning [ˈreɪnɪŋ] **adj** [champion] actuel(elle).

reimburse [ˌriːɪmˈbɜːs] **vt : to reimburse sb (for)** rembourser qqn (de).

reimbursement [ˌriːɪmˈbɜːsmənt] **n** *fml* remboursement *m*.

Reims [riːmz] **n** Reims.

rein [reɪn] **n** *fig* **: to give (a) free rein to sb, to give sb free rein** laisser la bride sur le cou à qqn ▸ **to keep a tight rein on sb** tenir la bride haute à qqn ▸ **to keep a tight rein on sthg** contrôler étroitement qqch.
◆ ***reins*** **npl 1.** [for horse] rênes *fpl* **2.** *UK* [for child] laisse *f*.
◆ ***rein in*** **vt sep** [horse] serrer la bride à / *fig* modérer.

reincarnate ■ **vt** [riːˈɪnkɑːneɪt] réincarner.
■ **adj** [ˌriːɪnˈkɑːnɪt] réincarné(e).

reincarnation [ˌriːɪnkɑːˈneɪʃn] **n** réincarnation *f*.

reindeer [ˈreɪnˌdɪəʳ] (**pl reindeer**) **n** renne *m*.

reinforce [ˌriːɪnˈfɔːs] **vt 1.** [strengthen] renforcer **2.** [back up, confirm] appuyer, étayer.

reinforced concrete [ˌriːɪnˈfɔːst-] **n** béton *m* armé.

reinforcement [ˌriːɪnˈfɔːsmənt] **n 1.** *(U)* [strengthening] renforcement *m* **2.** [strengthener] renfort *m*.
◆ ***reinforcements*** **npl** renforts *mpl*.

reinstall **vt** COMPUT réinstaller.

reinstate [ˌriːɪnˈsteɪt] **vt** [employee] rétablir dans ses fonctions, réintégrer / [policy, method] rétablir.

reinstatement [ˌriːɪnˈsteɪtmənt] **n** [of employee] réintégration *f* / [of policy, method] rétablissement *m*.

reintegrate [ˌriːˈɪntɪgreɪt] **vt** réintégrer.

reintegration [ˈriːˌɪntɪˈgreɪʃn] **n** réintégration *f*.

reinterpret [ˌriːɪnˈtɜːprɪt] **vt** réinterpréter.

reintroduce [ˈriːˌɪntrəˈdjuːs] **vt** réintroduire.

reintroduction [ˌriːɪntrəˈdʌkʃn] **n** réintroduction *f*.

reissue [riːˈɪʃuː] ■ **n** [of book] réédition *f* / [of film] rediffusion *f*.
■ **vt** [book] rééditer / [film, record] ressortir.

reiterate [riːˈɪtəreɪt] **vt** *fml* réitérer, répéter.

reiteration [riːˌɪtəˈreɪʃn] **n** *fml* réitération *f*.

reject ■ **n** [ˈriːdʒekt] [product] article *m* de rebut.
■ **vt** [rɪˈdʒekt] **1.** [not accept] rejeter **2.** [candidate, coin] refuser.

rejection [rɪˈdʒekʃn] **n 1.** [non-acceptance] rejet *m* **2.** [of candidate] refus *m*.

rejig [ˌriːˈdʒɪg] (**pt & pp -ged, cont -ging**) **vt** *UK inf* réorganiser.

rejoice [rɪˈdʒɔɪs] **vi : to rejoice (at** OR **in)** se réjouir (de).

rejoicing [rɪˈdʒɔɪsɪŋ] **n** *(U)* réjouissance *f*.

rejoin[1] [ˌriːˈdʒɔɪn] **vt** rejoindre / [club] adhérer de nouveau à.

rejoin[2] [rɪˈdʒɔɪn] **vt** [reply] répondre, répliquer.

rejoinder [rɪˈdʒɔɪndəʳ] **n** réplique *f*, riposte *f*.

rejuvenate [rɪˈdʒuːvəneɪt] **vt** rajeunir.

rejuvenation [rɪˌdʒuːvəˈneɪʃn] **n** rajeunissement *m*.

rekindle [ˌriːˈkɪndl] **vt** *fig* ranimer, raviver.

relapse [rɪˈlæps] ■ **n** rechute *f* ▸ **to have a relapse** faire une rechute, rechuter.
■ **vi : to relapse into** retomber dans.

relate [rɪˈleɪt] ■ **vt 1.** [connect] **: to relate sthg to sthg** établir un lien OR rapport entre qqch et qqch **2.** [tell] raconter.
■ **vi 1.** [be connected] **: to relate to** avoir un rapport avec **2.** [concern] **: to relate to** se rapporter à **3.** [empathize] **: to relate (to sb)** s'entendre (avec qqn).
◆ ***relating to*** **prep** concernant.

related [rɪˈleɪtɪd] **adj 1.** [people] apparenté(e) ▸ **she is related to the president** elle est parente du président ▸ **to be related by marriage to sb** être parent(e) de qqn par alliance **2.** [issues, problems] lié(e) ▸ **problems related to health** problèmes qui se rattachent OR qui touchent à la santé ▸ **the two events are not related** les deux événements n'ont aucun rapport.

-related **suffix** lié(e) à ▸ **business-related activities** des activités liées OR ayant rapport aux affaires ▸ **performance-related bonus** prime *f* d'encouragement.

relation [rɪˈleɪʃn] **n 1.** [connection] **: relation (to/between)** rapport *m* (avec/entre) ▸ **in relation to** par rapport à **2.** [person] parent *m*, -e *f*.
◆ ***relations*** **npl** [relationship] relations *fpl*, rapports *mpl*.

relational [rɪˈleɪʃənl] **adj** COMPUT relationnel(elle).

relational database **n** COMPUT base *f* de données relationnelle.

relationship [rɪˈleɪʃnʃɪp] **n 1.** [between people, countries] relations *fpl*, rapports *mpl* / [romantic] liaison *f* **2.** [connection] rapport *m*, lien *m*.

relationship marketing **n** marketing *m* relationnel.

relative [ˈrelətɪv] ■ **adj** relatif(ive) ▸ **the relative qualities of the two candidates** les qualités respectives des deux candidats.
■ **n** parent *m*, -e *f* ▸ **she has relatives in Canada** elle a de la famille au Canada.
◆ ***relative to*** **prep** [compared with] relativement à / [connected with] se rapportant à, relatif(ive) à ▸ **taxation is relative to income** l'imposition est proportionnelle au revenu.

relatively [ˈrelətɪvlɪ] **adv** relativement.

relativism [ˈrelətɪvɪzm] **n** relativisme *m*.

relativist [ˈrelətɪvɪst] ■ **adj** relativiste.
■ **n** relativiste *mf*.

relativity [ˌreləˈtɪvətɪ] **n** relativité *f*.

relax [rɪ'læks] ■ **vt 1.** [person] détendre, relaxer **2.** [muscle, body] décontracter, relâcher / [one's grip] desserrer **3.** [rule] relâcher.
■ **vi 1.** [person] se détendre, se décontracter **2.** [muscle, body] se relâcher, se décontracter **3.** [one's grip] se desserrer.

relaxation [ˌriːlæk'seɪʃn] **n 1.** [of person] relaxation *f*, détente *f* **2.** [of rule] relâchement *m*.

relaxed [rɪ'lækst] **adj** détendu(e), décontracté(e).

relaxing [rɪ'læksɪŋ] **adj** relaxant(e), qui détend.

relay ['riːleɪ] ■ **n 1.** SPORT **: relay (race)** course *f* de relais ▸ **in relays** *fig* en se relayant **2.** RADIO & TV [broadcast] retransmission *f*.
■ **vt 1.** (pt & pp **-ed**) RADIO & TV [broadcast] relayer **2.** (pt & pp **-ed**) [message, information] transmettre, communiquer **3.** (pt & pp **relaid**) [carpet, tiles] poser à nouveau, reposer.

release [rɪ'liːs] ■ **n 1.** [from prison, cage] libération *f* ▸ **release on bail** mise en liberté provisoire (sous caution) **2.** [from pain, misery] délivrance *f* **3.** [statement] communiqué *m* **4.** [of gas, heat] échappement *m* **5.** *(U)* [of film, record] sortie *f* ▸ **to be on release** CIN passer dans les salles de cinéma **6.** [film] nouveau film *m* / [record] nouveau disque *m*.
■ **vt 1.** [set free] libérer ▸ **to release sb from captivity** libérer qqn ▸ **to be released on bail** LAW être libéré(e) sous caution **2.** [lift restriction on] **: to release sb from** dégager qqn de **3.** [make available - supplies] libérer / [- funds] débloquer **4.** [let go of] lâcher ▸ **he released his grip on my hand** il m'a lâché la *OR* il a lâché ma main **5.** [TECH - brake, handle] desserrer / [- mechanism] déclencher ▸ **to release the clutch** AUT débrayer **6.** [gas, heat] **: to be released (from/into)** se dégager (de/dans), s'échapper (de/dans) **7.** [film, record] sortir / [statement, report] publier.

relegate ['relɪgeɪt] **vt** reléguer ▸ **to be relegated** *UK* SPORT être relégué(e) à la division inférieure.

relegation [ˌrelɪ'geɪʃn] **n** relégation *f*.

relent [rɪ'lent] **vi** [person] se laisser fléchir / [wind, storm] se calmer.

relentless [rɪ'lentlɪs] **adj** implacable.

relentlessly [rɪ'lentlɪslɪ] **adv** implacablement.

relevance ['reləvəns] *(U)* **n 1.** [connection] **: relevance (to)** rapport *m* (avec) **2.** [significance] **: relevance (to)** importance *f* (pour).

relevant ['reləvənt] **adj 1.** [connected] **: relevant (to)** qui a un rapport (avec) **2.** [significant] **: relevant (to)** important(e) (pour) **3.** [appropriate - information] utile / [- document] justificatif(ive).

reliability [rɪˌlaɪə'bɪlətɪ] **n** fiabilité *f*.

reliable [rɪ'laɪəbl] **adj** [person] sur qui on peut compter, fiable / [device] fiable / [company, information] sérieux(euse).

reliably [rɪ'laɪəblɪ] **adv** de façon fiable ▸ **to be reliably informed (that)...** savoir de source sûre que...

reliance [rɪ'laɪəns] **n : reliance (on)** dépendance *f* (de).

reliant [rɪ'laɪənt] **adj : to be reliant on** être dépendant(e) de.

relic ['relɪk] **n** relique *f* / [of past] vestige *m*.

relief [rɪ'liːf] **n 1.** [comfort] soulagement *m* ▸ **to our great relief, much to our relief** à notre grand soulagement ▸ **to bring relief to sb** soulager qqn, apporter un soulagement à qqn ▸ **she reads detective novels for light relief** elle lit des romans policiers pour se distraire **2.** [for poor, refugees] aide *f*, assistance *f* ▸ **famine relief** aide *f* alimentaire **3.** *US* [social security] aide *f* sociale ▸ **to be on relief** recevoir des aides sociales *OR* des allocations.

relief map **n** carte *f* en relief.

relief road **n** *UK* route *f* de délestage.

relieve [rɪ'liːv] **vt 1.** [pain, anxiety] soulager ▸ **to relieve sb of sthg** [take away from] délivrer qqn de qqch **2.** [take over from] relayer **3.** [give help to] secourir, venir en aide à.

relieved [rɪ'liːvd] **adj** soulagé(e).

religion [rɪ'lɪdʒn] **n** religion *f*.

religious [rɪ'lɪdʒəs] **adj** religieux(euse) / [book] de piété.

religiously [rɪ'lɪdʒəslɪ] **adv** *lit* & *fig* religieusement.

reline [ˌriː'laɪn] **vt** [clothes, bag] redoubler / [brakes] changer les garnitures de.

relinquish [rɪ'lɪŋkwɪʃ] **vt** [power] abandonner / [claim, plan] renoncer à / [post] quitter.

relish ['relɪʃ] ■ **n 1.** [enjoyment] **: with (great) relish** avec délectation **2.** [pickle] condiment *m*.
■ **vt** [enjoy] prendre plaisir à ▸ **I don't relish the thought *OR* idea *OR* prospect of seeing him** la perspective de le voir ne m'enchante *OR* ne me sourit guère.

relive [ˌriː'lɪv] **vt** revivre.

reload [ˌriː'ləʊd] **vt** recharger.

relocate [ˌriːləʊ'keɪt] ■ **vt** installer ailleurs, transférer.
■ **vi** s'installer ailleurs, déménager.

relocation [ˌrɪləʊ'keɪʃn] **n** transfert *m*, déménagement *m*.

relocation expenses **npl** frais *mpl* de déménagement.

reluctance [rɪ'lʌktəns] **n** répugnance *f*.

reluctant [rɪ'lʌktənt] **adj** peu enthousiaste ▸ **to be reluctant to do sthg** rechigner à faire qqch, être peu disposé(e) à faire qqch.

reluctantly [rɪ'lʌktəntlɪ] **adv** à contrecœur, avec répugnance.

rely [rɪ'laɪ] (pt & pp **-ied**) ◆ ***rely on*** **vt insep 1.** [count on] compter sur ▸ **to rely on sb to do sthg** compter sur qqn *OR* faire confiance à qqn pour faire qqch **2.** [be dependent on] dépendre de.

REM (abbr of ***rapid eye movement***) **n** *activité oculaire intense durant le sommeil paradoxal.*

remain [rɪ'meɪn] ■ **vt** rester ▸ **to remain to be done** rester à faire ▸ **it remains to be seen...** reste à savoir... ▸ **the fact remains that we can't afford this house** il n'en reste pas moins que *OR* toujours est-il que nous ne pouvons pas nous offrir cette maison.
■ **vi** rester ▸ **to remain silent** garder le silence, rester silencieux ▸ **the real reasons were to remain a secret** les véritables raisons devaient demeurer secrètes.
◆ ***remains*** **npl 1.** [remnants] restes *mpl* **2.** [antiquities] ruines *fpl*, vestiges *mpl*.

remainder [rɪ'meɪndə^{r}] **n** reste *m*.

remaining [rɪ'meɪnɪŋ] adj qui reste ▸ **last remaining** dernier(ère).

remake ■ n ['ri:meɪk] CIN remake *m*.
■ vt [,ri:'meɪk] CIN refaire.

remand [rɪ'mɑ:nd] ■ n LAW : **on remand** en détention préventive.
■ vt LAW : **to remand sb (in custody)** placer qqn en détention préventive.

remand centre n *UK* maison *f* de détention préventive.

remark [rɪ'mɑ:k] ■ n [comment] remarque *f*, observation *f*.
■ vt [comment] : **to remark that...** faire remarquer que...
■ vi : **to remark on** faire des remarques sur.

remarkable [rɪ'mɑ:kəbl] adj remarquable.

remarkably [rɪ'mɑ:kəblɪ] adv remarquablement.

remarket [,ri:'mɑ:kɪt] vt recommercialiser.

remarketing [,ri:'mɑ:kɪtɪŋ] n marketing *m* de relance.

remarriage [,ri:'mærɪdʒ] n remariage *m*.

remarry [,ri:'mærɪ] (pt & pp **-ied**) vi se remarier.

remedial [rɪ'mi:djəl] adj **1.** [pupil, class] de rattrapage **2.** [exercise] correctif(ive) / [action] de rectification.

remedy ['remədɪ] ■ n (pl **-ies**) : **remedy (for)** MED remède *m* (pour ***OR*** contre) / *fig* remède (à ***OR*** contre).
■ vt (pt & pp **-ied**) remédier à.

remember [rɪ'membəʳ] ■ vt **1.** [gen] se souvenir de, se rappeler ▸ **don't you remember me?** [in memory] vous ne vous souvenez pas de moi? / [recognize] vous ne me reconnaissez pas? ▸ **I can't remember her name** son nom m'échappe, je ne me souviens pas de son nom ▸ **remember my advice** n'oubliez pas mes conseils ▸ **to remember to do sthg** ne pas oublier de faire qqch, penser à faire qqch ▸ **remember to close the door** n'oubliez pas de ***OR*** pensez à fermer la porte ▸ **to remember doing sthg** se souvenir d'avoir fait qqch, se rappeler avoir fait qqch ▸ **I remember locking the door** je me rappelle avoir ***OR*** je me souviens d'avoir fermé la porte à clé ▸ **we have nothing to remember him by** nous n'avons aucun souvenir de lui **2.** [as greeting] : **to remember sb to sb** rappeler qqn au bon souvenir de qqn ▸ **remember me to your parents** rappelez-moi au bon souvenir de vos parents.
■ vi se souvenir, se rappeler ▸ **if I remember rightly** si je me ***OR*** si je m'en souviens bien, si j'ai bonne mémoire.

remembrance [rɪ'membrəns] n : **in remembrance of** en souvenir ***OR*** mémoire de.

Remembrance Day n *UK* & *Can* l'Armistice *m*.

remind [rɪ'maɪnd] vt **1.** [tell] : **to remind sb of *OR* about sthg** rappeler qqch à qqn ▸ **to remind sb to do sthg** rappeler à qqn de faire qqch, faire penser à qqn à faire qqch ▸ **that reminds me!** à propos!, pendant que j'y pense! **2.** [be reminiscent of] : **she reminds me of my sister** elle me rappelle ma sœur.

reminder [rɪ'maɪndəʳ] n **1.** [to jog memory] : **to give sb a reminder (to do sthg)** faire penser à qqn (à faire qqch) **2.** [letter, note] rappel *m*.

reminisce [,remɪ'nɪs] vi évoquer des souvenirs ▸ **to reminisce about sthg** évoquer qqch.

reminiscences [,remɪ'nɪsənsɪz] npl souvenirs *mpl*.

reminiscent [,remɪ'nɪsnt] adj : **reminiscent of** qui rappelle, qui fait penser à.

remiss [rɪ'mɪs] adj négligent(e).

remission [rɪ'mɪʃn] n *(U)* **1.** LAW remise *f* **2.** MED rémission *f*.

remit[1] [rɪ'mɪt] (pt & pp **-ted**, cont **-ting**) vt [money] envoyer, verser.

remit[2] ['ri:mɪt] n *UK* [responsibility] attributions *fpl*.

remittance [rɪ'mɪtns] n **1.** [amount of money] versement *m* **2.** COMM règlement *m*, paiement *m*.

remnant ['remnənt] n **1.** [remaining part] reste *m*, restant *m* **2.** [of cloth] coupon *m*.

remodel [,ri:'mɒdl] (*UK* **-led**, cont **-ling**, *US* **-ed**, cont **-ing**) vt remodeler.

remonstrate ['remənstreɪt] vi *fml* : **to remonstrate (with sb about sthg)** faire des remontrances (à qqn au sujet de qqch).

remorse [rɪ'mɔ:s] n *(U)* remords *m*.

remorseful [rɪ'mɔ:sfʊl] adj plein(e) de remords.

remorsefully [rɪ'mɔ:sfʊlɪ] adv avec remords.

remorseless [rɪ'mɔ:slɪs] adj implacable.

remorselessly [rɪ'mɔ:slɪslɪ] adv implacablement.

remortgage [,ri:'mɔ:gɪdʒ] vt [house, property] hypothéquer de nouveau, prendre une nouvelle hypothèque sur.

remote [rɪ'məʊt] adj **1.** [far-off - place] éloigné(e) / [- time] lointain(e) **2.** [person] distant(e) **3.** [possibility, chance] vague.

remote access n COMPUT accès *m* à distance.

remote control n télécommande *f*.

remote-controlled [-kən'trəʊld] adj télécommandé(e).

remotely [rɪ'məʊtlɪ] adv **1.** [in the slightest] : **not remotely** pas le moins du monde, absolument pas **2.** [far off] au loin.

remoteness [rɪ'məʊtnɪs] n **1.** [of place] éloignement *m*, isolement *m* **2.** [of person] attitude *f* distante.

remould ['ri:məʊld] n *UK* pneu *m* rechapé.

removable [rɪ'mu:vəbl] adj [detachable] détachable, amovible.

removal [rɪ'mu:vl] n **1.** *(U)* [act of removing] enlèvement *m* **2.** *UK* [change of house] déménagement *m*.

removal man n *UK* déménageur *m*.

removal van n *UK* camion *m* de déménagement.

remove [rɪ'mu:v] vt **1.** [take away - gen] enlever / [- stain] faire partir, enlever / [- problem] résoudre / [- suspicion] dissiper ▸ **his name has been removed from the list** son nom ne figure plus sur la liste ▸ **the child must be removed from its mother** il faut retirer l'enfant à sa mère **2.** [clothes] ôter, enlever **3.** [employee] renvoyer ▸ **his opponents had him removed from office** ses opposants l'ont fait révoquer.

removed [rɪ'mu:vd] adj : **to be far removed from** être très éloigné(e) ***OR*** différent(e) de.

remover [rɪ'mu:vəʳ] n [for paint] décapant *m* / [for stains] détachant *m* / [for nail polish] dissolvant *m*.

remunerate [rɪ'mju:nəreɪt] **vt** *fml* rémunérer.

remuneration [rɪ,mju:nə'reɪʃn] **n** *fml* rémunération *f*.

remuneration package **n** *fml salaire et avantages complémentaires.*

remunerative [rɪ'mju:nərətɪv] **adj** *fml* rémunérateur(trice).

renaissance [rə'neɪsns] **n** renaissance *f*.

◆ ***Renaissance*** ■ **n : the Renaissance** ART & HIST la Renaissance.

■ **comp** [art, painter] de la Renaissance / [palace, architecture, style] Renaissance *(inv)*.

renal ['ri:nl] **adj** rénal(e).

rename [,ri:'neɪm] **vt 1.** [person] rebaptiser **2.** [file] changer le nom de, renommer.

rend [rend] (pt & pp **rent**) **vt** *liter* déchirer.

render ['rendəʳ] **vt** rendre / [assistance] porter / FIN [account] présenter.

rendering ['rendərɪŋ] **n** [of play, music] interprétation *f*.

rendezvous ['rɒndɪvu:] (pl **rendezvous**) **n** rendez-vous *m inv*.

rendition [ren'dɪʃn] **n** interprétation *f*.

renegade ['renɪgeɪd] **n** renégat *m*, -e *f*.

renege [rɪ'ni:g] **vi** *fml* **: to renege on** manquer à, revenir sur.

renegotiate [,ri:nɪ'gəʊʃɪeɪt] ■ **vt** renégocier.

■ **vi** négocier à nouveau.

renew [rɪ'nju:] **vt 1.** [gen] renouveler / [negotiations, strength] reprendre / [interest] faire renaître ▶ **to renew acquaintance with sb** renouer connaissance avec qqn **2.** [replace] remplacer.

renewable [rɪ'nju:əbl] **adj** renouvelable.

renewable resource **n** ressource *f* renouvelable.

renewal [rɪ'nju:əl] **n 1.** [of activity] reprise *f* **2.** [of contract, licence] renouvellement *m*.

rennet ['renɪt] **n** présure *f*.

renounce [rɪ'naʊns] **vt** renoncer à.

renovate ['renəveɪt] **vt** rénover.

renovation [,renə'veɪʃn] **n** rénovation *f*.

renown [rɪ'naʊn] **n** renommée *f*, renom *m*.

renowned [rɪ'naʊnd] **adj : renowned (for)** renommé(e) (pour).

rent [rent] ■ **pt & pp** ➤ ***rend***.

■ **n** [for house] loyer *m*.

■ **vt** louer.

◆ ***rent out*** **vt sep** louer.

rental ['rentl] ■ **adj** de location.

■ **n** [for car, television, video] prix *m* de location / [for house] loyer *m*.

rental car **n** *US* voiture *f* de location.

rent book **n** carnet *m* de quittances de loyer.

rent boy **n** *UK inf* jeune garçon *m* qui se prostitue.

rented ['rentɪd] **adj** loué(e).

rent-free ■ **adj** gratuit(e).

■ **adv** sans payer de loyer.

renumber [,ri:'nʌmbəʳ] **vt** renuméroter.

renunciation [rɪ,nʌnsɪ'eɪʃn] **n** renonciation *f*.

reoccupy [,ri:'ɒkjʊpaɪ] (pt & pp **-ied**) **vt** réoccuper.

reoccurrence [,ri:ə'kʌrəns] **n : if there's a reoccurrence...** si cela se reproduit...

reopen [,ri:'əʊpn] ■ **vt** rouvrir / [negotiations] reprendre.

■ **vi** rouvrir / [negotiations] reprendre / [wound] se rouvrir.

reopening [,ri:'əʊpnɪŋ] **n** [of shop] réouverture *f* / [of negotiations] reprise *f*.

reorder ■ **vt** [,ri:'ɔ:dər] **1.** COMM [goods, supplies] commander de nouveau, faire une nouvelle commande de **2.** [rearrange - numbers, statistics, objects] reclasser, réorganiser.

■ **n** ['ri:ɔ:dər] COMM nouvelle commande *f*.

reorganization, *UK* ***-isation*** ['ri:,ɔ:gənaɪ'zeɪʃn] **n** réorganisation *f*.

reorganize, *UK* ***-ise*** [,ri:'ɔ:gənaɪz] ■ **vt** réorganiser.

■ **vi** se réorganiser.

rep [rep] **n** *inf* **1.** (abbr of ***representative***) VRP *m* **2.** abbr of ***repertory*** **3.** abbr of ***repertory company***.

Rep. *US* abbr of ***Representative***, ***Republican***.

repackage [,ri:'pækɪdʒ] **vt 1.** [goods] remballer **2.** [public image] redorer *fig*.

repaid [ri:'peɪd] **pt & pp** ➤ ***repay***.

repaint [,ri:'peɪnt] **vt** repeindre.

repair [rɪ'peəʳ] ■ **n** réparation *f* ▶ **in good/bad repair** en bon/mauvais état.

■ **vt** réparer.

repair kit **n** trousse *f* à outils.

repairman [rɪ'peəmən] (pl **-men** [-mən]) **n** réparateur *m*.

repaper [,ri:'peɪpəʳ] **vt** retapisser.

reparations [,repə'reɪʃnz] **npl** réparations *fpl*.

repartee [,repɑ:'ti:] **n** repartie *f*.

repatriate [,ri:'pætrɪeɪt] **vt** rapatrier.

repatriation [,ri:pætrɪ'eɪʃn] **n** rapatriement *m*.

repay [ri:'peɪ] (pt & pp **repaid**) **vt 1.** [money] **: to repay sb sthg, to repay sthg to sb** rembourser qqch à qqn **2.** [favour] payer de retour, récompenser ▶ **to repay sb for sthg** récompenser qqn de *OR* pour qqch ▶ **how can I ever repay you (for your kindness)?** comment pourrai-je jamais vous remercier (pour votre gentillesse)? ▶ **to repay good for evil** rendre le bien pour le mal.

repayment [ri:'peɪmənt] **n** remboursement *m*.

repayment mortgage **n** prêt-logement *m*.

repayment options **n** formules *fpl* de remboursement.

repeal [rɪ'pi:l] ■ **n** abrogation *f*.

■ **vt** abroger.

repeat [rɪ'pi:t] ■ **vt 1.** [gen] répéter ▶ **to repeat o.s.** se répéter **2.** RADIO & TV rediffuser.

■ **n** RADIO & TV reprise *f*, rediffusion *f*.

repeated [rɪ'pi:tɪd] **adj** répété(e).

repeatedly [rɪ'pi:tɪdlɪ] **adv** à maintes reprises, très souvent.

repeat order n commande *f* renouvelée.

repeat sale n vente *f* répétée.

repel [rɪ'pel] (pt & pp **-led**, cont **-ling**) **vt** repousser.

repellent [rɪ'pelənt] ■ **adj** répugnant(e), repoussant(e).
■ **n : insect repellent** crème *f* anti-insecte.

repent [rɪ'pent] ■ **vt** se repentir de.
■ **vi : to repent (of)** se repentir (de).

repentance [rɪ'pentəns] **n** *(U)* repentir *m*.

repentant [rɪ'pentənt] **adj** repentant(e).

repercussions [ˌri:pə'kʌʃnz] **npl** répercussions *fpl*.

repertoire ['repətwɑ:ʳ] **n** répertoire *m*.

repertory ['repətrɪ] **n** répertoire *m*.

repertory company **n** compagnie *f* **OR** troupe *f* de répertoire.

repetition [ˌrepɪ'tɪʃn] **n** répétition *f*.

repetitious [ˌrepɪ'tɪʃəs], ***repetitive*** [rɪ'petɪtɪv] **adj** [action, job] répétitif(ive) / [article, speech] qui a des redites.

repetitive strain injury, ***repetitive stress injury*** ➤ *RSI*.

rephrase [ˌri:'freɪz] **vt** réécrire, tourner autrement.

replace [rɪ'pleɪs] **vt 1.** [gen] remplacer **2.** [put back] replacer, remettre (à sa place).

CONFUSABLE / PARONYME

replace

When translating **to replace**, note that the French verbs ***replacer*** and ***remplacer*** are not interchangeable. ***Replacer*** means ***to put back***, while ***remplacer*** means ***to take the place of***.

replacement [rɪ'pleɪsmənt] **n 1.** [substituting] remplacement *m* / [putting back] replacement *m* **2.** [new person] **: replacement (for sb)** remplaçant *m*, -e *f* (de qqn).

replacement part **n** pièce *f* de rechange.

replay ■ **n** ['ri:pleɪ] match *m* rejoué.
■ **vt** [ˌri:'pleɪ] **1.** [match, game] rejouer **2.** [film, tape] repasser.

replenish [rɪ'plenɪʃ] **vt : to replenish one's supply of sthg** se réapprovisionner en qqch.

replete [rɪ'pli:t] **adj** *fml* rempli(e) / [person] rassasié(e).

replica ['replɪkə] **n** copie *f* exacte, réplique *f*.

replicate ['replɪkeɪt] **vt** *fml* reproduire.

replication [ˌreplɪ'keɪʃn] **n** *fml* reproduction *f*.

reply [rɪ'plaɪ] ■ **n** (pl **-ies**) **: reply (to)** réponse *f* (à) ▸ **in reply (to)** en réponse (à).
■ **vt & vi** (pt & pp **-ied**) répondre.

reply coupon **n** coupon-réponse *m*.

reply-paid **adj** réponse payée.

report [rɪ'pɔ:t] ■ **n 1.** [account] rapport *m*, compte *m* rendu ▸ **he gave an accurate report of the situation** il a fait un rapport précis sur la situation ▸ **his report on the meeting** son compte rendu de la réunion ▸ **sales report** rapport *m* **OR** bilan *m* commercial
2. PRESS reportage *m* ▸ **according to newspaper/intelligence reports** selon les journaux/les services de renseignements ▸ **we have had reports of several burglaries in city stores** on nous a signalé plusieurs cambriolages dans les magasins du centre-ville
3. *UK* SCH bulletin *m* (scolaire).
■ **vt 1.** [news, crime] rapporter, signaler ▸ **the newspapers report heavy casualties** les journaux font état de nombreuses victimes ▸ **to report sb missing (to the police)** signaler la disparition de qqn (à la police) ▸ **to be reported missing/dead** être porté(e) disparu(e)/au nombre des morts ▸ **it is reported that a woman drowned** [unconfirmed news] une femme se serait noyée
2. [make known] **: to report that...** annoncer que... ▸ **the doctors report his condition as comfortable** les médecins déclarent son état satisfaisant
3. [complain about] **: to report sb (to)** dénoncer qqn (à) ▸ **they were reported to the police for vandalism** on les a dénoncés à la police pour vandalisme.
■ **vi 1.** [give account] **: to report (on)** faire un rapport (sur) / PRESS faire un reportage (sur)
2. [present oneself] **: to report (to sb/for sthg)** se présenter (à qqn/pour qqch) ▸ **to report for duty** prendre son service, se présenter au travail
3. [in hierarchy] **: to report to sb** être sous les ordres de qqn ▸ **I report directly to the sales manager** je dépends directement du chef des ventes.
◆ ***report back*** **vi : to report back (to)** présenter son rapport (à) ▸ **can you report back on what was discussed?** pouvez-vous rapporter ce qui a été dit?

reportage [ˌrepɔ:'tɑ:ʒ] *(U)* **n** reportage *m*.

report card **n** *US* bulletin *m* (scolaire).

reported [rɪ'pɔ:tɪd] **adj : there have been reported sightings of dolphins off the coast** on aurait vu des dauphins près des côtes ▸ **what was their last reported position?** où ont-ils été signalés pour la dernière fois?

reportedly [rɪ'pɔ:tɪdlɪ] **adv** à ce qu'il paraît.

reported speech **n** style *m* indirect.

reporter [rɪ'pɔ:təʳ] **n** reporter *m*.

repose [rɪ'pəʊz] **n** *liter* repos *m*.

reposition [ˌri:pə'zɪʃn] **vt** [brand, product] repositionner.

repositioning [ˌri:pə'zɪʃnɪŋ] **n** [of brand, product] repositionnement *m*.

repository [rɪ'pɒzɪtrɪ] (pl **-ies**) **n** dépôt *m*.

repossess [ˌri:pə'zes] **vt** saisir.

repossession [ˌri:pə'zeʃn] **n** saisie *f*.

repossession order **n** ordre *m* de saisie.

reprehensible [ˌreprɪ'hensəbl] **adj** *fml* répréhensible.

reprehensibly [ˌreprɪ'hensəblɪ] **adv** *fml* de façon répréhensible.

represent [ˌreprɪ'zent] **vt 1.** [gen] représenter ▸ **to be well OR strongly represented** être bien représenté(e) **2.** [describe] **: to represent sb/sthg as** décrire qqn/qqch comme.

representation [ˌreprɪzen'teɪʃn] **n** [gen] représentation *f*.
◆ ***representations*** **npl : to make representations to sb** faire une démarche auprès de qqn.

representational **[ˌreprɪzen'teɪʃənl] adj** [gen] représentatif(ive) / ART figuratif(ive).

representative **[ˌreprɪ'zentətɪv] ■ adj** représentatif(ive).
■ **n** représentant *m*, -e *f*.

representative sample **n** échantillon *m* type.

repress **[rɪ'pres] vt** réprimer.

repressed **[rɪ'prest] adj 1.** [person - sexually] refoulé(e) **2.** [feelings] réprimé(e), contenu(e).

repression **[rɪ'preʃn] n** répression *f* / [sexual] refoulement *m*.

repressive **[rɪ'presɪv] adj** répressif(ive).

reprieve **[rɪ'pri:v] ■ n 1.** [delay] sursis *m*, répit *m* **2.** LAW sursis *m*.
■ **vt** accorder un sursis à.

reprimand **['reprɪmɑ:nd] ■ n** réprimande *f*.
■ **vt** réprimander.

reprint **■ n ['ri:prɪnt]** réimpression *f*.
■ **vt [ˌri:'prɪnt]** réimprimer.

reprisal **[rɪ'praɪzl] n** représailles *fpl*.

reproach **[rɪ'prəʊtʃ] ■ n** reproche *m*.
■ **vt : to reproach sb for** *OR* **with sthg** reprocher qqch à qqn.

reproachful **[rɪ'prəʊtʃful] adj** [voice, look, attitude] réprobateur(trice) / [tone, words] de reproche, réprobateur(trice).

reproachfully **[rɪ'prəʊtʃfʊlɪ] adv** avec reproche ▸ **to look at sb reproachfully** lancer des regards réprobateurs à qqn.

reprobate **['reprəbeɪt] n** *hum* dépravé *m*, -e *f*.

reprocess **[ˌri:'prəʊses] vt** retraiter.

reprocessing **[ˌri:'prəʊsesɪŋ] n** retraitement *m* ▸ **nuclear reprocessing** retraitement des déchets nucléaires.

reproduce **[ˌri:prə'dju:s] ■ vt** reproduire.
■ **vi** se reproduire.

reproduction **[ˌri:prə'dʌkʃn] n** reproduction *f*.

reproductive **[ˌri:prə'dʌktɪv] adj** reproducteur(trice).

reprogram **[ˌri:'prəʊgræm]** (pt & pp **-med**, cont **-ming**) **vt** reprogrammer.

reproof **[rɪ'pru:f] n** *fml* reproche *m*, blâme *m*.

reprove **[rɪ'pru:v] vt** *fml* **: to reprove sb (for)** blâmer qqn (pour *OR* de), réprimander qqn (pour).

reproving **[rɪ'pru:vɪŋ] adj** *fml* réprobateur(trice).

reprovingly **[rɪ'pru:vɪŋlɪ] adv** *fml* [look] d'un air réprobateur *OR* de reproche / [say] d'un ton réprobateur *OR* de reproche.

reptile **['reptaɪl] n** reptile *m*.

Repub. *US* abbr of ***Republican***.

republic **[rɪ'pʌblɪk] n** république *f*.

republican **[rɪ'pʌblɪkən] ■ adj** républicain(e).
■ **n** républicain *m*, -e *f*.
◆ ***Republican*** **■ adj** républicain(e) ▸ **the Republican Party** *US* le parti républicain.
■ **n** républicain *m*, -e *f*.

republicanism **[rɪ'pʌblɪkənɪzm] n** républicanisme *m*.

repudiate **[rɪ'pju:dɪeɪt] vt** *fml* [offer, suggestion] rejeter / [friend] renier.

repudiation **[rɪˌpju:dɪ'eɪʃn] n** *fml* [of offer, suggestion] rejet *m* / [of friend] reniement *m*.

repugnance **[rɪ'pʌgnəns] n** *fml* répugnance *f*.

repugnant **[rɪ'pʌgnənt] adj** *fml* répugnant(e).

repulse **[rɪ'pʌls] vt** repousser.

repulsion **[rɪ'pʌlʃn] n** répulsion *f*.

repulsive **[rɪ'pʌlsɪv] adj** repoussant(e).

repulsively **[rɪ'pʌlsɪvlɪ] adv** de façon repoussante *OR* répugnante ▸ **repulsively ugly** d'une laideur repoussante.

reputable **['repjʊtəbl] adj** de bonne réputation.

reputation **[ˌrepjʊ'teɪʃn] n** réputation *f* ▸ **to have a reputation for sthg** être réputé(e) pour qqch ▸ **to have a reputation for being...** avoir la réputation d'être...

repute **[rɪ'pju:t] n : of repute** de renom ▸ **of good repute** de bonne réputation.

reputed **[rɪ'pju:tɪd] adj** réputé(e) ▸ **to be reputed to be sthg** être réputé pour être qqch, avoir la réputation d'être qqch.

reputedly **[rɪ'pju:tɪdlɪ] adv** à *OR* d'après ce qu'on dit.

reqd abbr of ***required***.

request **[rɪ'kwest] ■ n : request (for)** demande *f* (de) ▸ **on request** sur demande ▸ **at sb's request** sur *OR* à la demande de qqn ▸ **by popular request** à la demande générale ▸ **any last requests?** quelles sont vos dernières volontés?
■ **vt** demander ▸ **I enclose a postal order for £5, as requested** selon votre demande, je joins un mandat postal

HOW TO ...

make a request

Tu peux me donner un coup de main ? / Could you give me a hand?

Est-ce que vous pourriez m'aider à attraper ma valise, s'il vous plaît ? / Could you help me get my case down, please?

Vous voulez bien m'aider à descendre les colis ? / Could you help me take these parcels down, please?

Tu n'aurais pas le temps de relire cette lettre, par hasard ? / You wouldn't have the time to read this letter through for me, would you?

Je me demandais si tu ne pourrais pas me prêter dix euros ? / I was wondering whether you could lend me ten euros ?

Écoute, j'ai vraiment besoin de ta voiture / Listen, I really need to borrow your car

Merci de me rappeler dès que possible / Please phone me back as soon as possible

Tu me passes le sel, s'il te plaît ? / Can you pass me the salt, please?

de 5 livres ▸ **Mr and Mrs Booth request the pleasure of your company** M. et Mme Booth vous prient de leur faire l'honneur de votre présence ▸ **to request sb to do sthg** demander à qqn de faire qqch.

request stop n *UK* arrêt *m* facultatif.

requiem (mass) ['rekwɪəm-] n messe *f* de requiem.

require [rɪ'kwaɪər] vt [subj: person] avoir besoin de / [subj: situation] nécessiter ▸ **is that all you require?** c'est tout ce qu'il vous faut?, c'est tout ce dont vous avez besoin? ▸ **extreme caution is required** une extrême vigilance s'impose ▸ **to require sb to do sthg** exiger de qqn qu'il fasse qqch ▸ **candidates are required to provide three photographs** les candidats doivent fournir trois photographies.

required [rɪ'kwaɪəd] adj exigé(e), requis(e).

requirement [rɪ'kwaɪəmənt] n besoin *m* ▸ **energy requirements** besoins énergétiques ▸ **this doesn't meet our requirements** ceci ne répond pas à nos exigences ▸ **she doesn't fulfil the requirements for the job** elle ne remplit pas les conditions requises pour le poste.

requisite ['rekwɪzɪt] adj *fml* requis(e).

requisition [ˌrekwɪ'zɪʃn] vt réquisitionner.

reran [ˌri:'ræn] pt ➤ ***rerun***.

reread [ˌri:'ri:d] (pt & pp **reread** [ˌri:'red]) vt relire.

rerecord [ˌri:'rɪkɔ:d] vt réenregistrer.

rerelease [ˌri:rɪ'li:s] ■ vt [film, record] ressortir.
■ n [film, record] reprise *f*.

reroute [ˌri:'ru:t] vt dérouter.

rerun ■ n ['ri:rʌn] [of TV programme] rediffusion *f*, reprise *f* / *fig* répétition *f*.
■ vt [ˌri:'rʌn] (pt **-ran**, pp **-run**, cont **-ning**) **1.** [race] réorganiser **2.** [TV programme] rediffuser / [tape] passer à nouveau, repasser.

resale ['ri:seɪl] n revente *f*.

resale price maintenance n *UK prix imposé aux distributeurs par le fabricant*.

resale value n valeur *f* à la revente.

resat [ˌri:'sæt] pt & pp ➤ ***resit***.

reschedule [*UK* ˌri:'ʃedjʊl, *US* ˌri:'skedʒʊl] vt [to new date] changer la date de / [to new time] changer l'heure de / FIN rééchelonner.

rescind [rɪ'sɪnd] vt *fml* [contract] annuler / [law] abroger.

rescue ['reskju:] ■ n **1.** *(U)* [help] secours *mpl* ▸ **to go/come to sb's rescue** aller/venir au secours de qqn **2.** [successful attempt] sauvetage *m*.
■ vt sauver, secourir.

rescue operation n opération *f* de sauvetage.

rescuer ['reskjʊər] n sauveteur *m*, -euse *f*.

reseal [ˌri:'si:l] vt [letter] recacheter.

resealable [ˌri:'si:ləbl] adj [envelope] qui peut être recacheté(e).

research [ˌrɪ'sɜ:tʃ] ■ n : **research (on** *OR* **into)** recherche *f* (sur), recherches *fpl* (sur) ▸ **research and development** recherche et développement *m*.
■ vt faire des recherches sur.
■ vi : **to research (into)** faire des recherches (sur).

researcher [rɪ'sɜ:tʃər] n chercheur *m*, -euse *f*.

research work n *(U)* recherches *fpl*.

resell [ˌri:'sel] (pt & pp **resold**) vt revendre.

resemblance [rɪ'zembləns] n : **resemblance (to)** ressemblance *f* (avec).

resemble [rɪ'zembl] vt ressembler à.

resent [rɪ'zent] vt être indigné(e) par ▸ **I resent that!** je n'apprécie pas (ça) du tout!

resentful [rɪ'zentfʊl] adj plein(e) de ressentiment.

resentfully [rɪ'zentfʊlɪ] adv avec ressentiment.

resentment [rɪ'zentmənt] n ressentiment *m*.

reservation [ˌrezə'veɪʃn] n **1.** [booking] réservation *f* ▸ **to make a reservation** [on train] réserver une *OR* sa place / [in hotel] réserver *OR* retenir une chambre / [in restaurant] réserver une table **2.** [uncertainty] **: without reservation** sans réserve ▸ **to have reservations about sthg** faire *OR* émettre des réserves sur qqch **3.** *US* [for Native Americans] réserve *f* indienne.

reserve [rɪ'zɜ:v] ■ n **1.** [gen] réserve *f* ▸ **cash reserves** réserves de caisse ▸ **to draw on one's reserves** puiser dans ses réserves ▸ **to break through sb's reserve** amener qqn à sortir de sa réserve ▸ **to call up the reserve** *OR* **reserves** MIL faire appel à la réserve *OR* aux réservistes ▸ **in reserve** en réserve ▸ **luckily, they have some money in reserve** heureusement, ils ont (mis) un peu d'argent de côté **2.** SPORT remplaçant *m*, -e *f*.
■ vt **1.** [save] garder, réserver **2.** [book] réserver **3.** [retain] **: to reserve the right to do sthg** se réserver le droit de faire qqch.

reserve bank n *US* banque *f* de réserve.

reserve currency n monnaie *f* de réserve.

reserved [rɪ'zɜ:vd] adj réservé(e).

reserve price n prix *m* minimum.

reserve team n *UK* deuxième équipe *f*.

reservist [rɪ'zɜ:vɪst] n réserviste *m*.

reservoir ['rezəvwɑ:r] n réservoir *m*.

reset [ˌri:'set] (pt & pp **reset**, cont **-ting**) ■ vt **1.** [clock, watch] remettre à l'heure / [meter, controls] remettre à zéro **2.** [bone] remettre **3.** COMPUT réinitialiser.
■ vi COMPUT réinitialiser.

reset button n COMPUT bouton *m* de réinitialisation.

resettle [ˌri:'setl] ■ vt [land] repeupler / [people] établir, implanter.
■ vi [people] se fixer (ailleurs), s'établir (ailleurs).

resettlement [ˌri:'setlmənt] n [of land] repeuplement *m* / [of people] établissement *m*, implantation *f*.

reshape [ˌri:'ʃeɪp] vt [policy, thinking] réorganiser.

reshuffle [ˌri:'ʃʌfl] ■ n remaniement *m* ▸ **cabinet reshuffle** remaniement ministériel.
■ vt remanier.

reside [rɪ'zaɪd] vi *fml* résider.

residence ['rezɪdəns] n résidence *f* ▸ **in residence** en résidence ▸ **to take up residence** s'installer.

residence permit n permis *m* de séjour.

resident ['rezɪdənt] ■ **adj** résidant(e) / [chaplain, doctor] à demeure.
■ **n** résident *m*, -e *f*.

residential [,rezɪ'denʃl] **adj : residential course** *stage ou formation avec logement sur place* ▸ **residential institution** internat *m*.

residential area **n** quartier *m* résidentiel.

residents' association **n** association *f* de quartier.

residual [rɪ'zɪdjʊəl] **adj** restant(e) / CHEM résiduel(elle).

residue ['rezɪdju:] **n** reste *m* / CHEM résidu *m*.

resign [rɪ'zaɪn] ■ **vt 1.** [job] démissionner de **2.** [accept calmly] **: to resign o.s. to** se résigner à.
■ **vi : to resign (from)** démissionner (de).

resignation [,rezɪg'neɪʃn] **n 1.** [from job] démission *f* **2.** [calm acceptance] résignation *f*.

resigned [rɪ'zaɪnd] **adj : resigned (to)** résigné(e) (à).

resilience [rɪ'zɪlɪəns] **n** [of material] élasticité *f* / [of person] ressort *m*.

resilient [rɪ'zɪlɪənt] **adj** [material] élastique / [person] qui a du ressort.

resin ['rezɪn] **n** résine *f*.

resist [rɪ'zɪst] **vt** résister à.

resistance [rɪ'zɪstəns] **n** résistance *f*.

resistant [rɪ'zɪstənt] **adj 1.** [opposed] **: to be resistant to** [gen] résister à / [change] s'opposer à **2.** [immune] **: resistant (to)** rebelle (à).

-resistant **suffix : heat-resistant** qui résiste à la chaleur ▸ **water-resistant** résistant(e) à l'eau ▸ **flame-resistant** ignifugé(e).

resistor [rɪ'zɪstə^r] **n** ELEC résistance *f*.

resit *UK* ■ **n** ['ri:sɪt] deuxième session *f*.
■ **vt** [,ri:'sɪt] (**pt & pp -sat, cont -ting**) repasser, se représenter à.

resold [,ri:'səʊld] **pt & pp** ➤ ***resell***.

resolute ['rezəlu:t] **adj** résolu(e).

resolutely ['rezəlu:tlɪ] **adv** résolument.

resolution [,rezə'lu:ʃn] **n** résolution *f*.

resolve [rɪ'zɒlv] ■ **n** *(U)* [determination] résolution *f*.
■ **vt 1.** [decide] **: to resolve (that)...** décider que... ▸ **to resolve to do sthg** résoudre *OR* décider de faire qqch **2.** [solve] résoudre.

resonance ['rezənəns] **n** résonance *f*.

resonant ['rezənənt] **adj** résonnant(e).

resonate ['rezəneɪt] **vi** résonner.

resort [rɪ'zɔ:t] **n 1.** [for holidays] lieu *m* de vacances ▸ **ski resort** station de sports d'hiver **2.** [recourse] recours *m* ▸ **without resort to threats** sans avoir recours aux menaces ▸ **as a last resort, in the last resort** en dernier ressort *OR* recours.
◆ ***resort to*** **vt insep** recourir à, avoir recours à ▸ **you resorted to lying to your wife** vous en êtes venu à mentir à votre femme.

resound [rɪ'zaʊnd] **vi 1.** [noise] résonner **2.** [place] **: to resound with** retentir de.

resounding [rɪ'zaʊndɪŋ] **adj 1.** [loud - noise, blow, wail] retentissant(e) / [- voice] sonore, claironnant(e) / [- explosion] violent(e) **2.** [unequivocal] retentissant(e), éclatant(e).

resoundingly [rɪ'zaʊndɪŋlɪ] **adv 1.** [loudly] bruyamment **2.** [unequivocally - win] d'une manière retentissante *OR* décisive / [- criticize, condemn] sévèrement ▸ **the team was resoundingly beaten** l'équipe a été battue à plate couture.

resource [rɪ'sɔ:s] **n** ressource *f* ▸ **there's a limit to the resources we can invest** il y a une limite à la somme que nous pouvons investir ▸ **left to their own resources, they're likely to mess everything up** livrés à eux-mêmes, ils risquent de tout gâcher.

resourceful [rɪ'sɔ:sfʊl] **adj** plein(e) de ressources, débrouillard(e).

resourcefully [rɪ'sɔ:sfʊlɪ] **adv** ingénieusement.

resourcefulness [rɪ'sɔ:sfʊlnɪs] **n** *(U)* ressource *f*.

respect [rɪ'spekt] ■ **n 1.** [gen] **: respect (for)** respect *m* (pour) ▸ **to have respect for sb** avoir du respect à *OR* pour qqn ▸ **he has no respect for authority/money** il méprise l'autorité/l'argent ▸ **to do sthg out of respect for sb/sthg** faire qqch par respect pour qqn/qqch ▸ **I stood up in respect** je me suis levé respectueusement ▸ **to show respect for sb** témoigner du respect à *OR* pour qqn ▸ **you have to gain the children's respect** il faut savoir se faire respecter par les enfants ▸ **with respect** avec respect ▸ **with respect,...** sauf votre respect,... **2.** [aspect] **: in this *OR* that respect** à cet égard ▸ **in every respect** à tous égards ▸ **in some respects** à certains égards.
■ **vt** respecter ▸ **to respect sb for sthg** respecter qqn pour qqch.
◆ ***respects*** **npl** respects *mpl*, hommages *mpl* ▸ **to pay one's respects to sb** présenter ses respects *OR* ses hommages à qqn ▸ **to pay one's last respects to sb** rendre un dernier hommage à qqn.
◆ ***with respect to*** **prep** en ce qui concerne, quant à.

respectability [rɪ,spektə'bɪlətɪ] **n** respectabilité *f*.

respectable [rɪ'spektəbl] **adj 1.** [morally correct] respectable **2.** [adequate] raisonnable, honorable.

respectably [rɪ'spektəblɪ] **adv** [correctly] convenablement.

respected [rɪ'spektɪd] **adj** respecté(e).

respecter [rɪ'spektə^r] **n : she is no respecter of tradition** elle ne fait pas partie de ceux qui respectent la tradition ▸ **disease is no respecter of class** nous sommes tous égaux devant la maladie.

respectful [rɪ'spektfʊl] **adj** respectueux(euse).

respectfully [rɪ'spektfʊlɪ] **adv** avec respect, respectueusement.

respective [rɪ'spektɪv] **adj** respectif(ive).

respectively [rɪ'spektɪvlɪ] **adv** respectivement.

respiration [,respə'reɪʃn] **n** respiration *f*.

respirator ['respəreɪtə^r] **n** respirateur *m*.

respiratory [*UK* rɪ'spɪrətrɪ, *US* 'respərətɔ:rɪ] **adj** respiratoire.

respire [rɪ'spaɪə^r] **vi** MED respirer.

respite ['respaɪt] n répit *m*.

resplendent [rɪ'splendənt] adj *liter* resplendissant(e).

respond [rɪ'spɒnd] ■ vt répondre.
■ vi : **the patient is responding** le malade réagit positivement ▸ **to respond (to)** répondre (à) ▸ **her condition isn't responding to treatment** le traitement ne semble pas agir sur sa maladie ▸ **to respond to flattery** être sensible à la flatterie.

response [rɪ'spɒns] n réponse *f* ▸ **in response** en réponse.

response time n COMPUT temps *m* de réponse / MED & PSYCHOL temps *m* de réaction.

responsibility [rɪˌspɒnsə'bɪlətɪ] (pl -ies) n : **responsibility (for)** responsabilité *f* (de) ▸ **to accept *OR* take responsibility for sthg** prendre *OR* accepter la responsabilité de qqch.

responsible [rɪ'spɒnsəbl] adj **1.** [gen] : **it wasn't very responsible of him** ce n'était pas très sérieux de sa part ▸ **responsible (for sthg)** responsable (de qqch) ▸ **who's responsible for research?** qui est chargé de la recherche? ▸ **human error/a malfunction was responsible for the disaster** la catastrophe était due à une erreur humaine/à une défaillance technique ▸ **to be responsible to sb** être responsable devant qqn **2.** [job, position] qui comporte des responsabilités.

responsibly [rɪ'spɒnsəblɪ] adv de façon responsable.

responsive [rɪ'spɒnsɪv] adj **1.** [quick to react] qui réagit bien **2.** [aware] : **responsive (to)** attentif(ive) (à).

respray ■ n ['ri:spreɪ] : **to give a car a respray** repeindre une voiture.
■ vt [ˌri:'spreɪ] repeindre.

rest [rest] ■ n **1.** [remainder] : **the rest (of)** le reste (de) ▸ **the rest (of them)** les autres *mf pl / inf* : **and all the rest (of it), and the rest** et tout le reste *OR* tout le tralala
2. [relaxation, break] repos *m* ▸ **(a) rest will do him good** un peu de repos lui fera du bien ▸ **to have a rest** se reposer ▸ **try to get some rest** essayez de vous reposer (un peu) ▸ **he needs a rest from the pressure/the children** il a besoin de se détendre/d'un peu de temps sans les enfants ▸ **you'd better give the skiing a rest** vous feriez mieux de ne pas faire de ski pendant un certain temps ▸ **to put *OR* to set sb's mind at rest** tranquilliser *OR* rassurer qqn
3. [support] support *m*, appui *m*
4. MUS silence *m* ▸ **minim** *UK* ***OR*** **half** *US* **rest** demi-pause *f*
▸▸ **to come to rest** s'arrêter.
■ vt **1.** [relax] faire *OR* laisser reposer ▸ **sit down and rest your legs** assieds-toi et repose-toi les jambes
2. [support] : **to rest sthg on/against** appuyer qqch sur/contre.
■ vi **1.** [relax] se reposer ▸ **'rest in peace'** *euph* 'repose en paix'
2. [be supported] : **to rest on/against** s'appuyer sur/contre ▸ **his arm rested on the back of the sofa** son bras reposait sur le dossier du canapé
3. *fig* [argument, result] : **to rest on** reposer sur ▸ **the responsibility rests with you** c'est vous qui êtes responsable ▸ **the decision rests with you** il vous appartient de décider ▸ **can't you let the matter rest?** ne pouvez-vous pas abandonner cette idée?
▸▸ **rest assured** soyez certain(e).

rest area n *US* & *Aus* aire *f* de repos.

restart [ˌri:'stɑ:t] ■ vt [engine] remettre en marche / [work] reprendre, recommencer / [computer] reprendre, recommencer.
■ vi **1.** [play, film] reprendre **2.** [engine] se remettre en marche.

restate [ˌri:'steɪt] vt répéter.

restaurant ['restərɒnt] n restaurant *m*.

restaurant car n *UK* wagon-restaurant *m*.

rest cure n cure *f* de repos.

rested ['restɪd] adj reposé(e).

restful ['restfʊl] adj reposant(e).

rest home n maison *f* de repos.

resting place ['restɪŋ-] n lieu *m* de repos.

restitution [ˌrestɪ'tju:ʃn] n *fml* [returning] restitution *f* / [compensation] réparation *f*.

restive ['restɪv] adj agité(e).

restless ['restlɪs] adj agité(e).

restlessly ['restlɪslɪ] adv avec agitation.

restlessness ['restlɪsnɪs] n [fidgeting, nervousness] nervosité *f*, agitation *f* / [impatience] impatience *f*.

restock [ˌri:'stɒk] ■ vt réapprovisionner.
■ vi se réapprovisionner.

restoration [ˌrestə'reɪʃn] n **1.** [of law and order, monarchy] rétablissement *m* **2.** [renovation] restauration *f*.

restorative [rɪ'stɒrətɪv] adj *fml* fortifiant(e).

restore [rɪ'stɔ:ʳ] vt **1.** [law and order, monarchy] rétablir / [confidence] redonner **2.** [renovate] restaurer **3.** [give back] rendre, restituer.

restorer [rɪ'stɔ:rəʳ] n [person] restaurateur *m*, -trice *f*.

restrain [rɪ'streɪn] vt [person, crowd] contenir, retenir / [emotions] maîtriser, contenir ▸ **to restrain o.s. from doing sthg** se retenir de faire qqch.

restrained [rɪ'streɪnd] adj [tone] mesuré(e) / [person] qui se domine.

restraint [rɪ'streɪnt] n **1.** [restriction] restriction *f*, entrave *f* **2.** *(U)* [self-control] mesure *f*, retenue *f*.

restrict [rɪ'strɪkt] vt restreindre, limiter ▸ **to restrict o.s. to** se limiter à.

restricted [rɪ'strɪktɪd] adj **1.** [limited, small] limité(e) **2.** [not public - document] confidentiel(elle) / [- area] interdit(e).

restriction [rɪ'strɪkʃn] n restriction *f*, limitation *f* ▸ **to place restrictions on sthg** apporter des restrictions à qqch.

restrictive [rɪ'strɪktɪv] adj restrictif(ive).

restrictive practices npl pratiques *fpl* restrictives.

rest room n *US* toilettes *fpl*.

restructure [ˌriːˈstrʌktʃəʳ] **vt** restructurer.

restyle [ˌriːˈstaɪl] **vt** [car] changer le design de / [hair, clothes] changer de style de / [magazine] changer la présentation de.

result [rɪˈzʌlt] ■ **n** résultat *m* ▸ **our policy is beginning to get *OR* show results** notre politique commence à porter ses fruits ▸ **these problems are the result of a misunderstanding** ces problèmes sont dus à un malentendu ▸ **as a result** en conséquence ▸ **as a result of** [as a consequence of] à la suite de / [because of] à cause de.
■ **vi 1.** [cause] **: to result in** aboutir à ▸ **the dispute resulted in her resigning** la dispute a entraîné sa démission **2.** [be caused] **: a price rise would inevitably result** il en résulterait *OR* il s'ensuivrait inévitablement une augmentation des prix ▸ **to result (from)** résulter (de).

resultant [rɪˈzʌltənt] **adj** *fml* qui (en) résulte.

resume [rɪˈzjuːm] **vt & vi** reprendre.

> FALSE FRIENDS / FAUX AMIS
> **resume**
> Résumer n'est pas la traduction du mot anglais *to resume*. Résumer se traduit par *to summarize*.
> ▸ Veuillez résumer ce texte en dix lignes / *Please summarize this text in ten lines*

résumé [ˈrezjuːmeɪ] **n 1.** [summary] résumé *m* **2.** *US* [curriculum vitae] curriculum vitae *m inv*, CV *m*.

resumption [rɪˈzʌmpʃn] **n** reprise *f*.

resurface [ˌriːˈsɜːfɪs] ■ **vt** [road] regoudronner.
■ **vi** [rivalries, problems] réapparaître.

resurgence [rɪˈsɜːdʒəns] **n** réapparition *f*.

resurgent [rɪˈsɜːdʒənt] **adj** renaissant(e).

resurrect [ˌrezəˈrekt] **vt** *fig* ressusciter.

resurrection [ˌrezəˈrekʃn] **n** *fig* résurrection *f*.
◆ ***Resurrection*** **n : the Resurrection** la Résurrection.

resuscitate [rɪˈsʌsɪteɪt] **vt** réanimer.

resuscitation [rɪˌsʌsɪˈteɪʃn] **n** réanimation *f*.

retail [ˈriːteɪl] ■ **n** *(U)* détail *m*.
■ **adv** au détail.

retailer [ˈriːteɪləʳ] **n** détaillant *m*, -e *f*.

retail outlet **n** magasin *m* *OR* point *m* de (vente au) détail.

retail park **n** zone *f* commerciale.

retail price **n** prix *m* de détail.

retail price index **n** *UK* indice *m* des prix.

retain [rɪˈteɪn] **vt** conserver.

retainer [rɪˈteɪnəʳ] **n 1.** [fee] provision *f* **2.** [servant] serviteur *m*.

retaining wall [rɪˈteɪnɪŋ-] **n** mur *m* de soutènement.

retake ■ **vt** [ˌriːˈteɪk] (pt **-took** [-ˈtʊk], pp **-taken** [-ˈteɪkn]) **1.** [town, fortress] reprendre **2.** [exam] repasser **3.** CIN [shot] reprendre, refaire / [scene] refaire une prise (de vues) de.
■ **n** [ˈriːteɪk] **1.** [of exam] nouvelle session *f* **2.** CIN nouvelle prise *f* (de vues).

retaliate [rɪˈtælɪeɪt] **vi** rendre la pareille, se venger.

retaliation [rɪˌtælɪˈeɪʃn] **n** *(U)* vengeance *f*, représailles *fpl*.

retaliatory [rɪˈtælɪətrɪ] **adj** de représailles, de rétorsion ▸ **a retaliatory attack** une riposte.

retardant [rɪˈtɑːdnt] ■ **n** TECH retardateur *m*.
■ **adj** TECH retardateur(trice).

retarded [rɪˈtɑːdɪd] **adj** *offens* retardé(e).

retch [retʃ] **vi** avoir des haut-le-cœur.

retention [rɪˈtenʃn] **n** maintien *m*, conservation *f* / MED rétention *f*.

retentive [rɪˈtentɪv] **adj** [memory] fidèle.

rethink ■ **n** [ˈriːθɪŋk] **: to have a rethink (on *OR* about sthg)** repenser (qqch).
■ **vt & vi** [ˌriːˈθɪŋk] (pt & pp **-thought** [-ˈθɔːt]) repenser.

reticence [ˈretɪsəns] **n** réticence *f*.

reticent [ˈretɪsənt] **adj** peu communicatif(ive) ▸ **to be reticent about sthg** ne pas beaucoup parler de qqch.

retina [ˈretɪnə] (pl **-nas** *OR* **-nae** [-niː]) **n** rétine *f*.

retinue [ˈretɪnjuː] **n** suite *f*.

retire [rɪˈtaɪəʳ] **vi 1.** [from work] prendre sa retraite **2.** [withdraw] se retirer **3.** *fml* [to bed] (aller) se coucher.

retired [rɪˈtaɪəd] **adj** à la retraite, retraité(e).

retirement [rɪˈtaɪəmənt] **n** retraite *f*.

retirement age **n** âge *m* de la retraite.

> CULTURE
> **Retirement Age**
> Actuellement, l'âge officiel du départ en retraite au Royaume-Uni est de 65 ans pour les hommes et de 60 ans pour les femmes : il est cependant question de le mettre aussi à 65 ans pour les femmes (aux États-Unis, il est à 65 ans pour les deux sexes). De plus en plus de personnes décident d'arrêter de travailler dès 50 ans, parfois même plus tôt, en prenant une retraite anticipée, en particulier si elles bénéficient de pensions intéressantes.

retirement pension **n** retraite *f*.

retirement plan **n** *US* régime *m* de retraite.

retiring [rɪˈtaɪərɪŋ] **adj 1.** [shy] réservé(e) **2.** [from work] sur le point de prendre sa retraite.

retort [rɪˈtɔːt] ■ **n** [sharp reply] riposte *f*.
■ **vt** riposter.

retouch [ˌriːˈtʌtʃ] **vt** retoucher.

retrace [rɪˈtreɪs] **vt : to retrace one's steps** revenir sur ses pas.

retract [rɪˈtrækt] ■ **vt 1.** [statement] rétracter **2.** [undercarriage] rentrer, escamoter / [claws] rentrer.
■ **vi** [undercarriage] rentrer, s'escamoter.

retractable [rɪˈtræktəbl] **adj** escamotable.

retraction [rɪˈtrækʃn] **n** [of statement] rétractation *f*.

retrain [ˌriːˈtreɪn] ■ **vt** recycler.
■ **vi** se recycler.

retraining [ˌriːˈtreɪnɪŋ] **n** recyclage *m*.

retread ■ **n** [ˈriːtred] pneu *m* rechapé.
■ **vt** [ˌriːˈtred] rechaper.

retreat [rɪˈtriːt] ■ **n** retraite *f* ▸ **to beat a hasty retreat** partir en vitesse.
■ **vi** [move away] se retirer / MIL battre en retraite.

retrenchment [riːˈtrentʃmənt] **n** [of spending] réduction *f*.

retrial [ˌriːˈtraɪəl] **n** nouveau procès *m*.

retribution [ˌretrɪˈbjuːʃn] **n** châtiment *m*.

retrieval [rɪˈtriːvl] **n** *(U)* COMPUT recherche *f* et extraction *f*.

retrieve [rɪˈtriːv] **vt 1.** [get back] récupérer **2.** COMPUT rechercher et extraire **3.** [situation] sauver.

retriever [rɪˈtriːvəʳ] **n** [dog] retriever *m*.

retro [ˈretrəʊ] **adj** rétro *(inv)* ▸ **retro fashions** la mode rétro.

retroactive [ˌretrəʊˈæktɪv] **adj** *fml* rétroactif(ive).

retrograde [ˈretrəgreɪd] **adj** *fml* rétrograde.

retrogressive [ˌretrəˈgresɪv] **adj** *fml* rétrograde.

retrospect [ˈretrəspekt] **n : in retrospect** après coup.

retrospective [ˌretrəˈspektɪv] ■ **adj 1.** [mood, look] rétrospectif(ive) **2.** LAW [law, pay rise] rétroactif(ive).
■ **n** rétrospective *f*.

retrospectively [ˌretrəˈspektɪvlɪ] **adv 1.** [looking back] rétrospectivement **2.** LAW rétroactivement.

retry [ˌriːˈtraɪ] (pt & pp **-ied**) **vt** LAW refaire le procès de, juger à nouveau.

return [rɪˈtɜːn] ■ **n 1.** [arrival back, giving back] retour *m* ▸ **on her return** à son retour ▸ **by return (of post)** *UK* par retour du courrier ▸ **a return to normal** un retour à la normale ▸ **the strikers' return to work** la reprise du travail par les grévistes
2. TENNIS renvoi *m*
3. *UK* [ticket] aller et retour *m*
4. [profit] rapport *m*, rendement *m* ▸ **a 10% return on investment** un rendement de 10 % sur la somme investie.
■ **comp** [journey] de retour.
■ **vt 1.** [gen] rendre / [loan] rembourser / [library book] rapporter
2. [send back] renvoyer ▸ **'return to sender'** 'retour à l'expéditeur' ▸ **the soldiers returned our fire** les soldats répondirent à notre tir
3. [replace] remettre ▸ **she returned the file to the drawer** elle remit le dossier dans le tiroir
4. POL élire.
■ **vi** [come back] revenir / [go back] retourner ▸ **let's return to your question** revenons à votre question ▸ **to return to work** reprendre le travail ▸ **the situation should return to normal next week** la situation devrait redevenir normale la semaine prochaine.
◆ ***returns*** **npl** COMM recettes *fpl* ▸ **many happy returns (of the day)!** bon anniversaire!
◆ ***in return*** **adv** en retour, en échange.
◆ ***in return for*** **prep** en échange de.

returnable [rɪˈtɜːnəbl] **adj** [bottle] consigné(e).

returning officer [rɪˈtɜːnɪŋ-] **n** *UK* responsable *mf* du scrutin.

return key **n** COMPUT touche *f* entrée.

return match **n** match *m* retour.

return ticket **n** *UK* aller et retour *m*.

reunification [ˌriːjuːnɪfɪˈkeɪʃn] **n** réunification *f*.

reunify [ˌriːˈjuːnɪfaɪ] (pt & pp **-ied**) **vt** réunifier.

reunion [ˌriːˈjuːnjən] **n** réunion *f*.

Reunion [ˌriːˈjuːnjən] **n : Reunion (Island)** (l'île *f* de) la Réunion ▸ **in Reunion** à la Réunion.

reunite [ˌriːjuːˈnaɪt] **vt : to be reunited with sb** retrouver qqn.

reupholster [ˌriːʌpˈhəʊlstəʳ] **vt** recouvrir.

reusable [riːˈjuːzəbl] **adj** réutilisable.

reuse ■ **n** [ˌriːˈjuːs] réutilisation *f*.
■ **vt** [ˌriːˈjuːz] réutiliser.

rev [rev] *inf* ■ **n** (abbr of ***revolution***) tour *m*.
■ **vt** (pt & pp **-ved**, cont **-ving**) **: to rev the engine (up)** emballer le moteur.
■ **vi** (pt & pp **-ved**, cont **-ving**) **: to rev (up)** s'emballer.

revalue [ˌriːˈvæljuː] **vt** FIN réévaluer.

revamp [ˌriːˈvæmp] **vt** *inf* [system, department] réorganiser / [house] retaper.

rev counter **n** compte-tours *m inv*.

reveal [rɪˈviːl] **vt** révéler.

revealing [rɪˈviːlɪŋ] **adj 1.** [clothes - low-cut] décolleté(e) / [- transparent] qui laisse deviner le corps **2.** [comment] révélateur(trice).

revealingly [rɪˈviːlɪŋlɪ] **adv 1.** [significantly] **: revealingly, not one of them speaks a foreign language** il est révélateur qu'aucun d'entre eux ne parle une langue étrangère **2.** [exposing the body] **: a revealingly short dress** une robe courte qui laisse tout voir.

reveille [*UK* rɪˈvælɪ, *US* ˈrevəlɪ] **n** réveil *m*.

revel [ˈrevl] (*UK* **-led**, cont **-ling**, *US* **-ed**, cont **-ing**) **vi : to revel in sthg** se délecter de qqch.

revelation [ˌrevəˈleɪʃn] **n** révélation *f*.

reveller *UK*, ***reveler*** *US* [ˈrevələʳ] **n** fêtard *m*, -e *f*.

revelry [ˈrevəlrɪ] **n** *(U)* festivités *fpl*.

revenge [rɪˈvendʒ] ■ **n** vengeance *f* ▸ **to take revenge (on sb)** se venger (de qqn).
■ **comp** [killing, attack] suscité(e) par la vengeance.
■ **vt** venger ▸ **to revenge o.s. on sb** se venger de qqn.

revenue [ˈrevənjuː] **n** revenu *m*.

reverberate [rɪˈvɜːbəreɪt] **vi** retentir, se répercuter / *fig* avoir des répercussions.

reverberations [rɪˌvɜːbəˈreɪʃnz] **npl** réverbérations *fpl* / *fig* répercussions *fpl*.

revere [rɪˈvɪəʳ] **vt** révérer, vénérer.

reverence [ˈrevərəns] **n** révérence *f*, vénération *f*.

Reverend [ˈrevərənd] **n** révérend *m*.

Reverend Mother **n** révérende mère *f*.

reverent [ˈrevərənt] **adj** respectueux(euse).

reverential [ˌrevəˈrenʃl] **adj** révérencieux(euse).

reverently [ˈrevərəntlɪ] **adv** avec révérence, révérencieusement *liter*.

reverie ['revərɪ] **n** *liter* rêverie *f*.

revers [rɪ'vɪə] (pl **revers**) **n** revers *m*.

reversal [rɪ'vɜːsl] **n 1.** [of policy, decision] revirement *m* **2.** [ill fortune] revers *m* de fortune.

reverse [rɪ'vɜːs] ■ **adj** [order, process] inverse ▸ **in reverse order** en ordre inverse.
■ **n 1.** AUT **: reverse (gear)** marche *f* arrière ▸ **to be in reverse** être en marche arrière ▸ **to go into reverse** faire marche arrière
2. [opposite] **: the reverse** le contraire ▸ **did you enjoy it? – quite the reverse** cela vous a-t-il plu? – pas du tout ▸ **try to do the same thing in reverse** essayez de faire la même chose dans l'ordre inverse
3. [back] **: the reverse** [of paper] le verso, le dos / [of coin] le revers.
■ **vt 1.** [order, positions] inverser / [decision, trend] renverser ▸ **this could reverse the effects of all our policies** ceci pourrait annuler les effets de toute notre politique
2. [turn over] retourner
3. *UK* TELEC **: to reverse the charges** téléphoner en PCV.
■ **vi** AUT faire marche arrière ▸ **to reverse into a wall** rentrer dans un mur en faisant marche arrière ▸ **the driver in front reversed into me** la voiture qui était devant moi m'est rentrée dedans en marche arrière.

reverse-charge call **n** *UK* appel *m* en PCV.

reversed-out [rɪ'vɜːsd-] **adj** PRESS & TYPO inversé(e) (en noir au blanc).

reversible [rɪ'vɜːsəbl] **adj** réversible.

reversing light [rɪ'vɜːsɪŋ-] **n** *UK* feu *m* de marche arrière.

reversion [rɪ'vɜːʃn] **n** *(U) fml* retour *m*.

revert [rɪ'vɜːt] **vi : to revert to** retourner à.

review [rɪ'vjuː] ■ **n 1.** [of salary, spending] révision *f* / [of situation] examen *m* ▸ **salaries come up for review in December** les salaires doivent être révisés en décembre ▸ **the situation is under review** on est en train d'examiner la situation **2.** [of book, play] critique *f*, compte rendu *m*.
■ **vt 1.** [salary] réviser / [situation] examiner **2.** [book, play] faire la critique de **3.** [troops] passer en revue **4.** *US* [study again] réviser.

review copy **n** exemplaire *m* de service de presse.

reviewer [rɪ'vjuːəʳ] **n** critique *mf*.

revile [rɪ'vaɪl] **vt** injurier.

revise [rɪ'vaɪz] ■ **vt 1.** [reconsider] modifier **2.** [rewrite] corriger **3.** *UK* [study again] réviser.
■ **vi** *UK* **: to revise (for)** réviser (pour).

revised [rɪ'vaɪzd] **adj** [estimate, figure] nouveau(elle) / [version] revu(e) et corrigé(e).

revision [rɪ'vɪʒn] **n** révision *f*.

revisionism [rɪ'vɪʒnɪzm] **n** révisionnisme *m*.

revisionist [rɪ'vɪʒnɪst] ■ **adj** révisionniste.
■ **n** révisionniste *mf*.

revisit [ˌriː'vɪzɪt] **vt** visiter de nouveau.

revitalize, *UK* ***-ise*** [ˌriː'vaɪtəlaɪz] **vt** revitaliser.

revival [rɪ'vaɪvl] **n** [of economy, trade] reprise *f* / [of interest] regain *m*.

revive [rɪ'vaɪv] ■ **vt 1.** [person] ranimer **2.** [economy] relancer / [interest] faire renaître / [tradition] rétablir / [musical, play] reprendre / [memories] ranimer, raviver.
■ **vi 1.** [person] reprendre connaissance **2.** [economy] repartir, reprendre / [hopes] renaître.

revocation [ˌrevə'keɪʃn] **n** [of decision] annulation *f* / [of measure, law] abrogation *f*, annulation *f*, révocation *f* / [of will] révocation *f*, annulation *f* / [of title, diploma, permit] retrait *m*.

revoke [rɪ'vəʊk] **vt** [decision, order] annuler / [measure, law] abroger, annuler, révoquer / [will] révoquer, annuler / [licence, permit, right] retirer.

revolt [rɪ'vəʊlt] ■ **n** révolte *f*.
■ **vt** révolter, dégoûter.
■ **vi** se révolter.

revolting [rɪ'vəʊltɪŋ] **adj** dégoûtant(e) / [smell] infect(e).

revoltingly [rɪ'vəʊltɪŋlɪ] **adv** de façon dégoûtante ▸ **he's revoltingly ugly/dirty** il est d'une laideur/d'une saleté repoussante / [as intensifier] **: she's so revoltingly clever!** ça m'écœure qu'on puisse être aussi intelligent!

revolution [ˌrevə'luːʃn] **n 1.** [gen] révolution *f* **2.** TECH tour *m*, révolution *f*.

revolutionary [ˌrevə'luːʃnərɪ] ■ **adj** révolutionnaire.
■ **n** (pl **-ies**) révolutionnaire *mf*.

revolutionize, *UK* ***-ise*** [ˌrevə'luːʃənaɪz] **vt** révolutionner.

revolve [rɪ'vɒlv] **vi : to revolve (around)** tourner (autour de).

revolver [rɪ'vɒlvəʳ] **n** revolver *m*.

revolving [rɪ'vɒlvɪŋ] **adj** tournant(e) / [chair] pivotant(e).

revolving door **n** tambour *m*.

revue [rɪ'vjuː] **n** revue *f*.

revulsion [rɪ'vʌlʃn] **n** répugnance *f*.

reward [rɪ'wɔːd] ■ **n** récompense *f*.
■ **vt : to reward sb (for/with sthg)** récompenser qqn (de/par qqch).

rewarding [rɪ'wɔːdɪŋ] **adj** [job] qui donne de grandes satisfactions / [book] qui vaut la peine d'être lu(e).

rewind [ˌriː'waɪnd] (pt & pp **rewound**) **vt** [tape] rembobiner.

rewire [ˌriː'waɪəʳ] **vt** [house] refaire l'installation électrique de.

reword [ˌriː'wɜːd] **vt** reformuler.

rework [ˌriː'wɜːk] **vt** retravailler.

reworking [ˌriː'wɜːkɪŋ] **n** reprise *f* ▸ **the film is a reworking of the "doppelgänger" theme** le film reprend le thème du double.

rewound [ˌriː'waʊnd] **pt & pp** ➤ ***rewind***.

rewrite [ˌriː'raɪt] (pt **rewrote** [ˌriː'rəʊt], pp **rewritten** [ˌriː'rɪtn]) **vt** récrire.

REX (abbr of ***real-time executive routine***) **n** *superviseur en temps réel*.

Reykjavik ['rekjəvɪk] **n** Reykjavik.

RFC (abbr of ***Rugby Football Club***) n *fédération de rugby*.

RGN (abbr of ***registered general nurse***) n *en Grande-Bretagne, infirmier ou infirmière diplômé(e) d'État*.

Rh (abbr of ***rhesus***) Rh.

rhapsody ['ræpsədɪ] (pl -ies) n rhapsodie *f* ▸ **to go into rhapsodies about sthg** s'extasier sur qqch.

Rheims = ***Reims***.

rhesus ['ri:səs] n : **rhesus positive/negative** rhésus *m* positif/négatif.

rhesus factor n facteur *m* Rhésus.

rhetoric ['retərɪk] n rhétorique *f*.

rhetorically [rɪ'tɒrɪklɪ] adv en rhétoricien ▸ **"who knows?" she asked rhetorically** "qui sait?", demanda-t-elle sans vraiment attendre de réponse ▸ **I was only asking rhetorically** je demandais ça simplement pour la forme.

rhetorical question [rɪ'tɒrɪkl-] n question *f* pour la forme.

rheumatic [ru:'mætɪk] adj [pain, joint] rhumatismal(e) / [person] rhumatisant(e).

rheumatism ['ru:mətɪzm] n *(U)* rhumatisme *m*.

rheumatoid arthritis ['ru:mətɔɪd-] n polyarthrite *f* rhumatoïde.

Rhine [raɪn] n : **the (River) Rhine** le Rhin.

Rhineland ['raɪnlænd] n Rhénanie *f*.

rhinestone ['raɪnstəʊn] n faux diamant *m*.

rhino ['raɪnəʊ] (pl **rhino** OR **-s**), ***rhinoceros*** [raɪ'nɒsərəs] (pl **rhinoceros** OR **-es**) n rhinocéros *m*.

Rhode Island [rəʊd-] n Rhode Island *m* ▸ **in Rhode Island** dans le Rhode Island.

Rhodes [rəʊdz] n Rhodes ▸ **in Rhodes** à Rhodes.

Rhodesia [rəʊ'di:ʃə] n Rhodésie *f* ▸ **in Rhodesia** en Rhodésie.

rhododendron [ˌrəʊdə'dendrən] n rhododendron *m*.

rhombus ['rɒmbəs] (pl **-es** OR **-bi** [-baɪ]) n losange *m*.

Rhône [rəʊn] n : **the (River) Rhône** le Rhône.

rhubarb ['ru:bɑ:b] n rhubarbe *f*.

rhyme [raɪm] ■ n **1.** [word, technique] rime *f* ▸ **in rhyme** en vers **2.** [poem] poème *m*.
■ vi : **to rhyme (with)** rimer (avec).

rhyming slang ['raɪmɪŋ-] n *UK sorte d'argot traditionnellement employé par les Cockneys qui consiste à remplacer un mot par un groupe de mots choisis pour la rime*.

rhythm ['rɪðm] n rythme *m*.

rhythm and blues n rhythm and blues *m*.

rhythm guitar n guitare *f* rythmique.

rhythmic(al) ['rɪðmɪk(l)] adj rythmique.

rhythmically ['rɪðmɪklɪ] adv rythmiquement.

RI[1] n (abbr of ***religious instruction***) instruction *f* religieuse.

RI[2] abbr of ***Rhode Island***.

rib [rɪb] n **1.** ANAT côte *f* **2.** [of umbrella] baleine *f* / [of structure] membrure *f*.

ribald ['rɪbəld] adj paillard(e).

ribbed [rɪbd] adj [jumper, fabric] à côtes.

ribbing ['rɪbɪŋ] n **1.** *(U)* [fabric] côtes *fpl* **2.** *inf dated* [teasing] taquinerie *f*, mise *f* en boîte.

ribbon ['rɪbən] n ruban *m*.

rib cage n cage *f* thoracique.

rice [raɪs] n riz *m*.

rice field n rizière *f*.

rice paper n papier *m* de riz.

rice pudding n riz *m* au lait.

rice wine n alcool *m* de riz, saké *m*.

rich [rɪtʃ] ■ adj riche / [clothes, fabrics] somptueux(euse) ▸ **they want to get rich quick** ils veulent s'enrichir très vite ▸ **to be rich in** être riche en.
■ npl : **the rich** les riches *mpl*.
◆ ***riches*** npl richesses *fpl*, richesse *f*.

-rich suffix riche en... ▸ **vitamin-rich foods** aliments *mpl* riches en vitamines.

richly ['rɪtʃlɪ] adv **1.** [rewarded] largement / [provided] très bien ▸ **richly deserved** bien mérité **2.** [sumptuously] richement.

richness ['rɪtʃnɪs] n *(U)* richesse *f*.

Richter scale ['rɪktər-] n : **the Richter scale** l'échelle *f* de Richter.

rickets ['rɪkɪts] n *(U)* rachitisme *m*.

rickety ['rɪkətɪ] adj branlant(e).

rickshaw ['rɪkʃɔ:] n pousse-pousse *m inv*.

ricochet ['rɪkəʃeɪ] ■ n ricochet *m*.
■ vi (pt & pp **-ed** OR **-ted**, cont **-ing**, cont **-ting**) : **to ricochet (off)** ricocher (sur).

rid [rɪd] ■ adj : **to be rid of** être débarrassé(e) de.
■ vt (pt **rid** OR **-ded**, pp **rid**, cont **-ding**) : **to rid sb/sthg of** débarrasser qqn/qqch de ▸ **to get rid of** se débarrasser de.

riddance ['rɪdəns] n *inf* : **good riddance!** bon débarras!

ridden ['rɪdn] pp ➤ ***ride***.

-ridden suffix : **flea-ridden** infesté(e) de puces ▸ **disease-ridden** infesté(e) de maladies ▸ **debt-ridden** criblé(e) de dettes.

riddle ['rɪdl] n énigme *f*.

riddled ['rɪdld] adj : **to be riddled with** être criblé(e) de.

ride [raɪd] ■ n **1.** [trip] promenade *f*, tour *m* ▸ **she has a long car/bus ride to work** elle doit faire un long trajet en voiture/en bus pour aller travailler ▸ **it's a 30-minute ride by bus/train/car** il faut 30 minutes en bus/train/voiture ▸ **to go for a ride** [on horse] faire une promenade à cheval / [on bike] faire une promenade à vélo / [in car] faire un tour en voiture ▸ **to take sb for a ride** *inf fig* faire marcher qqn
2. *esp US* [lift - in car] : **can you give me a ride to the station?** peux-tu me conduire à la gare? ▸ **don't accept rides from strangers** ne montez pas dans la voiture de quelqu'un que vous ne connaissez pas
3. [in fairground - attraction] manège *m* / [- turn] tour *m* ▸ **it's 50p a ride** c'est 50 pence le tour.

■ vt (pt **rode**, pp **ridden**) **1.** [travel on] **: to ride a horse/a bicycle** monter à cheval/à bicyclette ▸ **he rides his bike to work** il va travailler à vélo, il va au travail à vélo ▸ **to ride the rapids** descendre les rapides ▸ **she was riding on a wave of popularity** elle était portée par une vague de popularité
2. *US* [travel in - bus, train, elevator] prendre
3. [distance] parcourir, faire.
■ vi (pt **rode**, pp **ridden**) [on horseback] monter à cheval, faire du cheval / [on bicycle] faire de la bicyclette *OR* du vélo ▸ **to ride in a car/bus** aller en voiture/bus ▸ **to ride off** [leave] partir / [move away] s'éloigner.
◆ ***ride up*** vi remonter.

rider ['raɪdəʳ] n [of horse] cavalier *m*, -ère *f* / [of bicycle] cycliste *mf* / [of motorbike] motocycliste *mf*.

ridge [rɪdʒ] n **1.** [of mountain, roof] crête *f*, arête *f* **2.** [on surface] strie *f*.

ridicule ['rɪdɪkju:l] ■ n ridicule *m*.
■ vt ridiculiser.

ridiculous [rɪ'dɪkjʊləs] adj ridicule.

ridiculously [rɪ'dɪkjʊləslɪ] adv ridiculement.

ridiculousness [rɪ'dɪkjʊləsnɪs] n ridicule *m* ▸ **the ridiculousness of the situation** le (côté) ridicule de la situation.

riding ['raɪdɪŋ] ■ n équitation *f* ▸ **to go riding** faire de l'équitation *OR* du cheval.
■ comp d'équitation.

riding crop n cravache *f*.

riding habit n habit *m* d'amazone.

riding school n école *f* d'équitation.

rife [raɪf] adj répandu(e) ▸ **the city was rife with rumours** des bruits couraient dans toute la ville.

riffraff ['rɪfræf] n racaille *f*.

rifle ['raɪfl] ■ n fusil *m*.
■ vt [drawer, bag] vider.
◆ ***rifle through*** vt insep fouiller dans.

rifle range n [indoor] stand *m* de tir / [outdoor] champ *m* de tir.

rift [rɪft] n **1.** GEOL fissure *f* **2.** [quarrel] désaccord *m*.

Rift Valley n **: the Rift Valley** le Rift Valley.

rig [rɪg] ■ n **1. : (oil) rig** [on land] derrick *m* / [at sea] plate-forme *f* de forage **2.** *US* [truck] semi-remorque *m*.
■ vt (pt & pp **-ged**, cont **-ging**) [match, election] truquer.
◆ ***rig up*** vt sep installer avec les moyens du bord.

rigging ['rɪgɪŋ] n [of ship] gréement *m*.

right [raɪt] ■ adj **1.** [correct - answer, time] juste, exact(e) / [- decision, direction, idea] bon (bonne) ▸ **that's right** c'est juste, oui ▸ **he didn't give me the right change** il ne m'a pas rendu la monnaie exacte ▸ **the clock is right** l'horloge est juste *OR* à l'heure ▸ **I owe you $5, right?** je te dois 5 dollars, c'est (bien) ça? ▸ **to be right (about)** avoir raison (au sujet de) ▸ **to get a question right** donner la bonne réponse ▸ **to get one's facts right** être sûr(e) de ce qu'on avance
2. [morally correct] bien *(inv)* ▸ **I only want to do what is right** je ne cherche qu'à bien faire ▸ **to be right to do sthg** avoir raison de faire qqch
3. [appropriate] qui convient ▸ **she's the right woman for the job** c'est la femme qu'il faut pour ce travail ▸ **when the time is right** au bon moment, au moment voulu ▸ **the colour is just right** la couleur est parfaite
4. [not left] droit(e) ▸ **raise your right hand** levez la main droite ▸ **take the next right (turn)** prenez la prochaine à droite
5. *UK inf* [complete] véritable ▸ **I felt like a right idiot** je me sentais vraiment bête.
■ n **1.** *(U)* [moral correctness] bien *m* ▸ **to be in the right** avoir raison
2. [entitlement, claim] droit *m* ▸ **you have every right to be angry** tu as toutes les raisons d'être en colère ▸ **by rights** en toute justice ▸ **in one's own right** soi-même
3. [not left] droite *f*.
■ adv **1.** [correctly] correctement ▸ **he can't do anything right** il ne peut rien faire correctement *OR* comme il faut
2. [not left] à droite ▸ **the party is moving further right** le parti est en train de virer plus à droite
3. [emphatic use] **: it's right in front of/behind you** c'est droit devant vous/juste derrière vous ▸ **right down/up** tout en bas/en haut ▸ **right here** ici (même) ▸ **right in the middle** en plein milieu ▸ **go right to the end of the street** allez tout au bout de la rue ▸ **to turn right around** se retourner ▸ **right after Christmas** tout de suite après Noël ▸ **I'll be right over** je viens tout de suite ▸ **right now** tout de suite ▸ **right away** immédiatement.
■ vt **1.** [injustice, wrong] réparer
2. [ship] redresser.
■ excl bon!
◆ ***Right*** n POL **: the Right** la droite.

right angle n angle *m* droit ▸ **to be at right angles (to)** faire un angle droit (avec).

right-angled triangle n *UK* triangle *m* rectangle.

right-click ■ vt COMPUT cliquer avec le bouton droit de la souris sur.
■ vi COMPUT cliquer avec le bouton droit de la souris.

righteous ['raɪtʃəs] adj *fml* [person] droit(e) / [indignation] justifié(e).

righteousness ['raɪtʃəsnɪs] n *fml* vertu *f*.

rightful ['raɪtfʊl] adj *fml* légitime.

rightfully ['raɪtfʊlɪ] adv *fml* légitimement.

right-hand adj de droite ▸ **right-hand side** droite *f*, côté *m* droit.

right-hand drive adj avec conduite à droite.

right-handed [-'hændɪd] adj [person] droitier(ère).

right-hand man n bras *m* droit.

Right Honourable adj *UK titre utilisé pour s'adresser à certains hauts fonctionnaires ou à quelqu'un ayant un titre de noblesse.*

rightly ['raɪtlɪ] adv **1.** [answer, believe] correctement **2.** [behave] bien **3.** [angry, worried] à juste titre.

right-minded [-'maɪndɪd] adj sensé(e).

rightness ['raɪtnɪs] n **1.** [correctness] justesse *f* **2.** [moral correctness] droiture *f*.

righto ['raɪtəʊ] excl *UK inf dated* d'accord!

right of asylum n POL droit *m* d'asile.

right-of-centre *UK*, ***right-of-center*** *US* **adj** centre droit.

right of way **n 1.** AUT priorité *f* **2.** [access] droit *m* de passage.

right-on **adj** *UK inf* idéologiquement correct(e).

rights issue [raɪts↓] **n** émission *f* de droits de souscription.

right-thinking [-'θɪŋkɪŋ] **adj** sensé(e).

right-to-life **adj** [movement, candidate] antiavortement *(inv)*.

right triangle *US* = ***right-angled triangle***.

right wing **n : the right wing** la droite.
◆ ***right-wing*** **adj** de droite.

right-winger **n** POL personne *f* qui est de droite.

rigid ['rɪdʒɪd] **adj 1.** [gen] rigide **2.** [harsh] strict(e).

rigidity [rɪ'dʒɪdətɪ] **n** rigidité *f*.

rigidly ['rɪdʒɪdlɪ] **adv 1.** [gen] rigidement **2.** [harshly] strictement.

rigmarole ['rɪgmərəʊl] **n** *pej* **1.** [process] comédie *f* **2.** [story] galimatias *m*.

rigor *US* = ***rigour***.

rigor mortis [-'mɔ:tɪs] **n** rigidité *f* cadavérique.

rigorous ['rɪgərəs] **adj** rigoureux(euse).

rigorously ['rɪgərəslɪ] **adv** rigoureusement.

rigour *UK*, ***rigor*** *US* ['rɪgəʳ] **n** rigueur *f*.

rig-out **n** *UK inf dated* accoutrement *m*.

rile [raɪl] **vt** agacer.

rim [rɪm] **n** [of container] bord *m* / [of wheel] jante *f* / [of spectacles] monture *f*.

rimless ['rɪmlɪs] **adj** [spectacles] sans monture.

-rimmed [rɪmd] **suffix : gold/steel-rimmed spectacles** lunettes *fpl* à monture en or/d'acier.

rind [raɪnd] **n** [of fruit] peau *f* / [of cheese] croûte *f* / [of bacon] couenne *f*.

ring [rɪŋ] ■ **n 1.** *UK* [telephone call] **: to give sb a ring** donner *OR* passer un coup de téléphone à qqn **2.** [sound of bell] sonnerie *f* ▸ **there was a ring at the door** on a sonné (à la porte) ▸ **the name has a familiar ring** ce nom me dit quelque chose **3.** [circular object] anneau *m* / [on finger] bague *f* / [for napkin] rond *m* **4.** [of people, trees] cercle *m* **5.** [for boxing] ring *m* **6.** [of criminals, spies] réseau *m*.
■ **vt (pt rang, pp rung) 1.** *UK* [make phone call to] téléphoner à, appeler **2.** [bell] (faire) sonner ▸ **to ring the doorbell** sonner à la porte ▸ **the name/title rings a bell** ce nom/titre me dit quelque chose **3.** (pt & pp **ringed**) [draw a circle round, surround] entourer.
■ **vi (pt rang, pp rung) 1.** *UK* [make phone call] téléphoner **2.** [bell, telephone, person] sonner ▸ **the doorbell rang** on a sonné (à la porte) ▸ **to ring for sb** sonner qqn **3.** [resound] **: my ears are ringing** j'ai les oreilles qui bourdonnent ▸ **to ring with** résonner de ▸ **the theatre rang with applause** la salle retentissait d'applaudissements
▸▸ **to ring true** sonner juste.
◆ ***ring back*** **vt sep & vi** *UK* rappeler.
◆ ***ring off*** **vi** *UK* raccrocher.
◆ ***ring out*** **vi 1.** [sound] retentir **2.** *UK* TELEC téléphoner à l'extérieur.
◆ ***ring up*** **vt sep** *UK* téléphoner à, appeler.

ring binder **n** classeur *m* à anneaux.

ringer ['rɪŋəʳ] **n : to be a dead ringer for sb** *inf* être le sosie de qqn.

ring-fence **vt** *UK* [money] allouer *(à des fins pré-établies par le gouvernement)*.

ring finger **n** annulaire *m*.

ringing ['rɪŋɪŋ] ■ **adj** retentissant(e).
■ **n** [of bell] sonnerie *f* / [in ears] tintement *m*.

ringing tone **n** sonnerie *f*.

ringleader ['rɪŋ,li:dəʳ] **n** chef *m*.

ringlet ['rɪŋlɪt] **n** anglaise *f*.

ringmaster ['rɪŋ,mɑ:stəʳ] **n** présentateur *m*.

ring-pull **n** *UK* anneau *m*, bague *f (sur une boîte de boisson)*.

ring road **n** *UK* (route *f*) périphérique *m*.

ringside ['rɪŋsaɪd] ■ **n : the ringside** le premier rang.
■ **comp** [seat] au premier rang.

ring tone **n** sonnerie *f*.

ringway ['rɪŋweɪ] **n** *UK* (route *f*) périphérique *m*.

ringworm ['rɪŋwɜ:m] **n** teigne *f*.

rink [rɪŋk] **n** [for ice skating] patinoire *f* / [for roller-skating] skating *m*.

rinse [rɪns] ■ **n : to give sthg a rinse** rincer qqch.
■ **vt** rincer ▸ **to rinse one's mouth out** se rincer la bouche.

Rio (de Janeiro) [,ri:əʊ(dədʒə'nɪərəʊ)] **n** Rio de Janeiro.

Rio Grande [,ri:əʊ'grændɪ] **n : the Rio Grande** le Rio Grande.

Rio Negro [,ri:əʊ'neɪgrəʊ] **n : the Rio Negro** le Rio Negro.

riot ['raɪət] ■ **n** émeute *f* ▸ **to run riot** se déchaîner.
■ **vi** participer à une émeute.

rioter ['raɪətəʳ] **n** émeutier *m*, -ère *f*.

rioting ['raɪətɪŋ] **n** *(U)* émeutes *fpl*.

riotous ['raɪətəs] **adj** [crowd] tapageur(euse) / [behaviour] séditieux(euse) / [party] bruyant(e).

riotously ['raɪətəslɪ] **adv 1.** [seditiously] de façon séditieuse **2.** [noisily] bruyamment **3.** [as intensifier] **: it's riotously funny** *inf* c'est à mourir *OR* à hurler de rire.

riot police **npl** ≃ CRS *mpl*.

riot shield **n** bouclier *m* antiémeute.

riot squad **n** brigade *f* antiémeutes.

rip [rɪp] ■ **n** déchirure *f*, accroc *m*.
■ **vt (pt & pp -ped, cont -ping) 1.** [tear] déchirer **2.** [remove violently] arracher.
■ **vi (pt & pp -ped, cont -ping)** se déchirer.
◆ ***rip off*** **vt sep** *inf* **1.** [person] arnaquer **2.** [product, idea] copier.
◆ ***rip up*** **vt sep** déchirer.

RIP (abbr of ***rest in peace***) qu'il/elle repose en paix.

ripcord ['rɪpkɔ:d] **n** poignée *f* d'ouverture.

ripe [raɪp] adj mûr(e).

ripen ['raɪpn] vt & vi mûrir.

ripeness ['raɪpnɪs] n maturité *f*.

rip-off n *inf* **: that's a rip-off!** c'est de l'escroquerie *OR* de l'arnaque!

ripple ['rɪpl] ■ n ondulation *f*, ride *f* ▸ **a ripple of applause** des applaudissements discrets.
■ vt rider.

rip-roaring adj *inf* [party] de tous les diables / [success] monstre.

rise [raɪz] ■ n **1.** [increase] augmentation *f*, hausse *f* ▸ **there has been a steep rise in house prices** les prix de l'immobilier ont beaucoup augmenté **2.** [in temperature] élévation *f*, hausse **3.** *UK* [increase in salary] augmentation *f* (de salaire) ▸ **to be given a rise** être augmenté **4.** [to power, fame] ascension *f* ▸ **the rise and fall of the fascist movement** la montée et la chute du mouvement fasciste **5.** [slope] côte *f*, pente *f*
▸▸ **to give rise to** donner lieu à.
■ vi (pt **rose**, pp **risen** ['rɪzn]) **1.** [move upwards] s'élever, monter ▸ **to rise to power** arriver au pouvoir ▸ **to rise to fame** devenir célèbre ▸ **to rise to a challenge/to the occasion** se montrer à la hauteur d'un défi/de la situation **2.** [from chair, bed] se lever ▸ **to rise to one's feet** se lever, se mettre debout **3.** [increase - gen] monter, augmenter / [- voice, level] s'élever **4.** [rebel] se soulever ▸ **to rise in revolt (against sb/sthg)** se révolter (contre qqn/qqch).
◆ ***rise above*** vt insep [problem] surmonter / [argument] ne pas faire cas de.

riser ['raɪzəʳ] n **: early riser** lève-tôt *mf inv* ▸ **late riser** lève-tard *mf inv*.

risible ['rɪzəbl] adj *fml* risible.

rising ['raɪzɪŋ] ■ adj **1.** [ground, tide] montant(e) **2.** [prices, inflation, temperature] en hausse **3.** [star, politician] à l'avenir prometteur.
■ n [revolt] soulèvement *m*.

rising damp n *UK* humidité *f (qui monte du sol)*.

risk [rɪsk] ■ n risque *m*, danger *m* ▸ **it's not worth the risk** c'est trop risqué ▸ **at one's own risk** à ses risques et périls ▸ **to run the risk of doing sthg** courir le risque de faire qqch ▸ **to take a risk** prendre un risque ▸ **at risk** en danger ▸ **all our jobs are at risk** tous nos emplois sont menacés ▸ **at the risk of** au risque de ▸ **at the risk of one's life** au péril de sa vie.
■ vt [health, life] risquer ▸ **to risk doing sthg** courir le risque de faire qqch ▸ **to risk it** tenter *OR* risquer le coup.

risk assessment n évaluation *f* des risques.

risk capital n capital *m* à risque.

risk-taking n *(U) le fait de prendre des risques*.

risky ['rɪskɪ] (comp **-ier**, superl **-iest**) adj risqué(e).

risotto [rɪ'zɒtəʊ] (pl **-s**) n risotto *m*.

risqué ['ri:skeɪ] adj risqué(e), osé(e).

rissole ['rɪsəʊl] n rissole *f*.

rite [raɪt] n rite *m*.

ritual ['rɪtʃʊəl] ■ adj rituel(elle).
■ n rituel *m*.

ritualistic [,rɪtʃʊə'lɪstɪk] adj ritualiste.

rival ['raɪvl] ■ adj rival(e), concurrent(e).
■ n rival *m*, -e *f*.
■ vt (*UK* **-led**, cont **-ling**, *US* **-ed**, cont **-ing**) rivaliser avec.

rivalry ['raɪvlrɪ] n rivalité *f*.

river ['rɪvəʳ] n rivière *f*, fleuve *m*.

river bank n berge *f*, rive *f*.

riverbed ['rɪvəbed] n lit *m* (de rivière *OR* de fleuve).

riverside ['rɪvəsaɪd] n **: the riverside** le bord de la rivière *OR* du fleuve.

rivet ['rɪvɪt] ■ n rivet *m*.
■ vt **1.** [fasten with rivets] river, riveter **2.** *fig* [fascinate] **: to be riveted by** être fasciné(e) par.

riveting ['rɪvɪtɪŋ] adj *fig* fascinant(e).

Riviera [,rɪvɪ'eərə] n **: the French Riviera** la Côte d'Azur ▸ **the Italian Riviera** la Riviera italienne.

Riyadh ['ri:æd] n Riyad, Riad.

RN n abbr of ***Royal Navy, registered nurse***.

RNA (abbr of ***ribonucleic acid***) n ARN *m*.

RNLI (abbr of ***Royal National Lifeboat Institution***) n *société britannique de sauvetage en mer*.

RNZAF (abbr of ***Royal New Zealand Air Force***) n *armée de l'air néo-zélandaise*.

RNZN (abbr of ***Royal New Zealand Navy***) n *marine de guerre néo-zélandaise*.

roach [rəʊtʃ] n *US* [cockroach] cafard *m*.

road [rəʊd] n route *f* / [small] chemin *m* / [in town] rue *f* ▸ **are we on the right road?** sommes-nous sur la bonne route? ▸ **by road** par la route ▸ **on the road** sur la route ▸ **we've been on the road for two days** on voyage depuis deux jours ▸ **to be on the road** [pop star, troupe] être en tournée ▸ **his car shouldn't be on the road** sa voiture devrait être retirée de la circulation ▸ **on the road to** *fig* sur le chemin de.

road atlas n atlas *m* routier.

roadblock ['rəʊdblɒk] n barrage *m* routier.

road-fund licence n *UK* ≃ vignette *f*.

road hog n *inf pej* chauffard *m*.

roadholding ['rəʊd,həʊldɪŋ] n AUT tenue *f* de route.

roadie ['rəʊdɪ] n *inf membre de l'équipe technique d'un groupe en tournée*.

roadkill ['rəʊdkɪl] n *(U)* animal *m* tué sur une route.

road manager n responsable *m* de tournée *(d'un chanteur ou d'un groupe pop)*.

road map n carte *f* routière.

road rage n *accès de colère de la part d'un automobiliste, se traduisant parfois par un acte de violence*.

road roller [-,rəʊləʳ] n rouleau *m* compresseur.

road safety n sécurité *f* routière.

road sense n [of driver] notion *f* de la conduite / [of pedestrian] **: children have to be taught road sense** on doit apprendre aux enfants à faire attention à la circulation.

roadshow ['rəʊdʃəʊ] n spectacle *m* de tournée.

roadside ['rəʊdsaɪd] ■ n **: the roadside** le bord de la route.

■ **comp** au bord de la route.

road sign **n** panneau *m* routier *OR* de signalisation.

roadsweeper ['rəʊd,swi:pəʳ] **n** **1.** [person] balayeur *m*, -euse *f* **2.** [vehicle] balayeuse *f*.

road tax **n** *UK* ≃ vignette *f*.

road test **n** essai *m* sur route.
◆ ***road-test*** **vt** essayer sur route.

road transport *UK*, ***road transportation*** *US* **n** transport *m* routier.

road-user **n** usager *m*, -ère *f* de la route.

roadway ['rəʊdweɪ] **n** chaussée *f*.

roadwork ['rəʊdwɜ:k] **n** *US* travaux *mpl* (de réfection des routes).

roadworks ['rəʊdwɜ:ks] **npl** *UK* travaux *mpl* (de réfection des routes).

roadworthy ['rəʊd,wɜ:ðɪ] **adj** en bon état de marche.

roam [rəʊm] ■ **vt** errer dans.
■ **vi** errer.

roar [rɔ:ʳ] ■ **vi** [person, lion] rugir / [wind] mugir / [car] gronder / [plane] vrombir ▸ **to roar with laughter** se tordre de rire.
■ **vt** hurler.
■ **n** [of person, lion] rugissement *m* / [of wind] mugissement *m* / [of traffic] grondement *m* / [of plane, engine] vrombissement *m*.

roaring ['rɔ:rɪŋ] **adj : a roaring fire** une belle flambée ▸ **roaring drunk** complètement saoul(e) ▸ **a roaring success** *UK* un succès monstre *OR* fou ▸ **to do a roaring trade** faire des affaires en or.

roast [rəʊst] ■ **adj** rôti(e).
■ **n** rôti *m*.
■ **vt** **1.** [meat, potatoes] rôtir **2.** [coffee, nuts] griller.

roast beef **n** rôti *m* de bœuf, rosbif *m*.

roasting ['rəʊstɪŋ] *inf* ■ **adj** torride.
■ **adv : a roasting hot day** une journée torride.

roasting tin **n** *UK* plat *m* à rôtir.

rob [rɒb] (pt & pp **-bed**, cont **-bing**) **vt** [person] voler / [bank] dévaliser ▸ **to rob sb of sthg** [money, goods] voler *OR* dérober qqch à qqn / [opportunity, glory] enlever qqch à qqn.

robber ['rɒbəʳ] **n** voleur *m*, -euse *f*.

robbery ['rɒbərɪ] (pl **-ies**) **n** vol *m*.

robe [rəʊb] **n** **1.** [gen] robe *f* **2.** *esp US* [dressing gown] peignoir *m*.

robin ['rɒbɪn] **n** rouge-gorge *m*.

robot ['rəʊbɒt] **n** robot *m*.

robotic [rəʊ'bɒtɪk] **adj** robotique.

robotics [rəʊ'bɒtɪks] **n** *(U)* robotique *f*.

robust [rəʊ'bʌst] **adj** robuste.

robustly [rəʊ'bʌstlɪ] **adv** robustement.

rock [rɒk] ■ **n** **1.** *(U)* [substance] roche *f* **2.** [boulder] rocher *m* ▸ **the boat struck the rocks** le bateau a été jeté sur les rochers **3.** *US* [pebble] caillou *m* **4.** [music] rock *m* **5.** *UK* [sweet] sucre *m* d'orge.
■ **comp** [music, band] de rock.
■ **vt** **1.** [baby] bercer ▸ **to rock a baby to sleep** bercer un bébé pour l'endormir **2.** [cradle, boat] balancer ▸ **the boat was rocked by the waves** [gently] le bateau était bercé par les flots / [violently] le bateau était ballotté par les vagues ▸ **to rock the boat** jouer les trouble-fête, semer le trouble **3.** [shock] secouer.
■ **vi** (se) balancer.
◆ ***on the rocks*** **adv** **1.** [drink] avec de la glace *OR* des glaçons **2.** [marriage, relationship] près de la rupture.

CONFUSABLE / PARONYME

rock

When translating **rock**, note that the French words *rocher* and *roche* are not interchangeable. *Rocher* describes an individual piece of rock, whereas with *roche* the emphasis is on the substance or the type of rock.

rockabilly ['rɒkə,bɪlɪ] **n** rockabilly *m*.

rock and roll **n** rock *m*, rock and roll *m*.

rock bottom **n : at rock bottom** au plus bas ▸ **to hit rock bottom** toucher le fond.
◆ ***rock-bottom*** **adj** [price] sacrifié(e).

rock cake **n** *UK* rocher *m*.

rock climber **n** varappeur *m*, -euse *f*.

rock climbing **n** varappe *f* ▸ **to go rock climbing** faire de la varappe.

rock dash **n** *US* crépi *m*.

rocker ['rɒkəʳ] **n** [chair] fauteuil *m* à bascule, rocking-chair *m*
▸▸ **to be off one's rocker** *inf* être fêlé.

rockery ['rɒkərɪ] (pl **-ies**) **n** *UK* rocaille *f*.

rocket ['rɒkɪt] ■ **n** **1.** [gen] fusée *f* **2.** MIL fusée *f*, roquette *f*.
■ **vi** monter en flèche.

rocket launcher [-,lɔ:ntʃəʳ] **n** lance-fusées *m inv*, lance-roquettes *m inv*.

rock face **n** paroi *f* rocheuse.

rockfall ['rɒkfɔ:l] **n** chute *f* de pierres.

rock-hard **adj** dur(e) comme de la pierre.

Rockies ['rɒkɪz] **npl : the Rockies** les Rocheuses *fpl*.

rocking ['rɒkɪŋ] **n** **1.** [of chair, boat] balancement *m* / [of baby] bercement *m* / [of head - to rhythm] balancement *m* **2.** TECH oscillation *f*.

rocking chair **n** fauteuil *m* à bascule, rocking-chair *m*.

rocking horse **n** cheval *m* à bascule.

rock music **n** rock *m*.

rock'n'roll [,rɒkən'rəʊl] = ***rock and roll***.

rock pool **n** mare *f* dans les rochers.

rock salt **n** sel *m* gemme.

rock-solid **adj** inébranlable.

rocky ['rɒkɪ] (comp **-ier**, superl **-iest**) **adj** **1.** [ground, road] rocailleux(euse), caillouteux(euse) **2.** [economy, marriage] précaire.

Rocky Mountains **npl : the Rocky Mountains** les montagnes *fpl* Rocheuses.

rococo [rəˈkəʊkəʊ] **adj** rococo *(inv)*.

rod [rɒd] **n** [metal] tige *f* / [wooden] baguette *f* ▸ **(fishing) rod** canne *f* à pêche.

rode [rəʊd] **pt** ➤ ***ride***.

rodent [ˈrəʊdənt] **n** rongeur *m*.

rodeo [ˈrəʊdɪəʊ] (pl -s) **n** rodéo *m*.

roe [rəʊ] **n** *(U)* œufs *mpl* de poisson.

roe deer **n** chevreuil *m*.

rogue [rəʊg] ■ **adj 1.** [animal] solitaire **2.** [person] dissident(e).
■ **n 1.** [likeable rascal] coquin *m*, -e *f* **2.** *dated* [dishonest person] filou *m*, crapule *f*.

roguish [ˈrəʊgɪʃ] **adj** espiègle.

role [rəʊl] **n** rôle *m*.

roll [rəʊl] ■ **n 1.** [of material, paper] rouleau *m*
2. [of bread] petit pain *m*
3. [list] liste *f*
4. [of drums, thunder] roulement *m* / [of dice] lancement *m* ▸ **to be on a roll** *inf* avoir le vent en poupe.
■ **vt** rouler / [log, ball] faire rouler ▸ **to roll sthg in** *OR* **between one's fingers** rouler qqch entre ses doigts ▸ **to roll one's r's** rouler les r ▸ **to roll one's eyes** [in fear, despair] rouler les yeux ▸ **rolled into one** tout à la fois ▸ **to roll one's own** *UK* [cigarettes] rouler ses cigarettes.
■ **vi** rouler ▸ **tears rolled down her face** des larmes roulaient sur ses joues ▸ **to be rolling in money** *OR* **rolling in it** *inf* rouler sur l'or, être plein aux as ▸ **to get** *OR* **to start things rolling** mettre les choses en marche.
◆ ***roll around***, ***roll about*** *UK* **vi** [person] se rouler ▸ **to roll around on the floor/grass** se rouler par terre/dans l'herbe / [object] rouler çà et là.
◆ ***roll back*** **vt sep** [prices] baisser.
◆ ***roll in*** **vi** *inf* [money] couler à flots.
◆ ***roll over*** **vi** se retourner ▸ **to roll over and over** [car] faire une série de tonneaux.
◆ ***roll up*** ■ **vt sep 1.** [carpet, paper] rouler
2. [sleeves] retrousser ▸ **he rolled his sleeves up above his elbows** il a roulé *OR* retroussé ses manches au-dessus du coude.
■ **vi** *inf* [arrive] s'amener, se pointer ▸ **roll up! roll up!** approchez!

roll bar **n** arceau *m* de sécurité.

roll call **n** appel *m*.

rolled [rəʊld] **adj 1.** [paper] en rouleau / [carpet] roulé(e) **2.** [iron, steel] laminé(e) **3.** [tobacco] en carotte ▸ **rolled oats** flocons *mpl* d'avoine.

rolled gold [rəʊld-] **n** *UK* plaqué *m* or.

rolled-up **adj** roulé(e), enroulé(e).

roller [ˈrəʊlər] **n** rouleau *m*.

rollerblade [ˈrəʊləbleɪd] **vi** SPORT faire du roller.

Rollerblades® [ˈrəʊləbleɪd] **n** rollers *mpl*, patins *mpl* en ligne.

rollerblading [ˈrəʊləbleɪdɪŋ] **n** roller *m* ▸ **to go rollerblading** faire du roller.

roller blind **n** *UK* store *m*.

roller coaster **n** montagnes *fpl* russes.

roller skate **n** patin *m* à roulettes.
◆ ***roller-skate*** **vi** faire du patin à roulettes.

roller-skating **n** patinage *m* à roulettes.

roller towel **n** essuie-main *m* à rouleau.

rollicking [ˈrɒlɪkɪŋ] **adj : we had a rollicking good time** on s'est amusé comme des (petits) fous.

rolling [ˈrəʊlɪŋ] **adj** [hills] onduleux(euse).

rolling credits, ***rolling titles*** **npl** CIN & TV générique *m* déroulant.

rolling mill **n** laminoir *m*.

rolling pin **n** rouleau *m* à pâtisserie.

rolling stock **n** matériel *m* roulant.

rollneck [ˈrəʊlnek] **adj** *UK* à col roulé.

roll of honour **n** *UK* liste *f* des combattants morts au champ d'honneur.

roll-on **adj** [deodorant] à bille.

roll-on roll-off **adj** *UK* **: roll-on roll-off ferry** roll on-roll off *m inv*, roulier *m*.

roly-poly [ˌrəʊlɪˈpəʊlɪ] (pl -ies) **n** *UK* **: roly-poly (pudding)** roulé *m* à la confiture.

ROM [rɒm] (abbr of ***read only memory***) **n** ROM *f*.

romaine lettuce [rəʊˈmeɪn-] **n** *esp US* romaine *f* *(laitue)*.

Roman [ˈrəʊmən] ■ **adj** romain(e).
■ **n** Romain *m*, -e *f*.

Roman alphabet **n** alphabet *m* romain.

Roman candle **n** chandelle *f* romaine.

Roman Catholic ■ **adj** catholique.
■ **n** catholique *mf*.

romance [rəʊˈmæns] **n 1.** *(U)* [romantic quality] charme *m* **2.** [love affair] idylle *f* **3.** [book] roman *m* (d'amour).

Romanesque [ˌrəʊməˈnesk] **adj** roman(e).

Romani [ˈrəʊmənɪ] = ***Romany***.

Romania [ruːˈmeɪnjə] **n** Roumanie *f* ▸ **in Romania** en Roumanie.

Romanian [ruːˈmeɪnjən] ■ **adj** roumain(e).
■ **n 1.** [person] Roumain *m*, -e *f* **2.** [language] roumain *m*.

Roman numeral **n** chiffre *m* romain.

romantic [rəʊˈmæntɪk] **adj** romantique.

CONFUSABLE / PARONYME

romantic

When translating **romantic**, note that the French words ***romantique*** and ***romanesque*** are not interchangeable. ***Romantique*** has to do with sentiment and romance, whereas ***romanesque*** is used to describe people or situations that one could expect to find in a novel.

romantically [rəʊˈmæntɪklɪ] **adv** de manière romantique, romantiquement *liter* ▸ **we're romantically involved** nous avons une liaison amoureuse.

romanticism [rəʊ'mæntɪsɪzm] **n** romantisme *m*.

romanticize, *UK* ***-ise*** [rəʊ'mæntɪsaɪz] **vt & vi** romancer.

Romany ['rəʊmənɪ] ■ **adj** de bohémien.
■ **n** (pl **-ies**) **1.** [person] bohémien *m*, -enne *f* **2.** [language] romani *m*.

Rome [rəʊm] **n** Rome.

romp [rɒmp] ■ **n** ébats *mpl*.
■ **vi** s'ébattre.

rompers ['rɒmpəz] **npl** barboteuse *f*.

romper suit ['rɒmpə^r-] **n** *UK* = ***rompers***.

roof [ru:f] **n** toit *m* / [of cave, tunnel] plafond *m* ▸ **the roof of the mouth** la voûte du palais ▸ **to have a roof over one's head** avoir OR posséder un toit ▸ **to go through** OR **hit the roof** *fig* exploser.

roof garden **n** jardin *m* sur le toit.

roofing ['ru:fɪŋ] **n** toiture *f*.

roof rack **n** *UK* galerie *f*.

rooftop ['ru:ftɒp] **n** toit *m*.

rook [rʊk] **n** **1.** [bird] freux *m* **2.** [chess piece] tour *f*.

rookie ['rʊkɪ] **n** *esp US inf* bleu *m*.

room [ru:m OR rʊm] **n** **1.** [in building] pièce *f* **2.** [bedroom] chambre *f* **3.** *(U)* [space] place *f* ▸ **there is room for improvement** on peut faire mieux ▸ **room to** OR **for manoeuvre** marge *f* de manœuvre.

-roomed [ru:md] **suffix : a five-roomed flat** un appartement de cinq pièces, un cinq-pièces.

roomer ['ru:mə^r] **n** *US* locataire *mf* de rapport.

roomful ['ru:mfʊl] **n** pleine salle *f* OR pièce *f* ▸ **a roomful of furniture** une pièce pleine de meubles.

rooming house ['ru:mɪŋ-] **n** *US* maison *f* de rapport.

roommate ['ru:mmeɪt] **n** **1.** [sharing room] camarade *mf* de chambre **2.** *US* [sharing house, flat] *personne avec qui l'on partage un logement*.

room service **n** service *m* dans les chambres.

room temperature **n** température *f* ambiante.

roomy ['ru:mɪ] (comp **-ier**, superl **-iest**) **adj** spacieux(euse).

roost [ru:st] ■ **n** perchoir *m*, juchoir *m* ▸ **to rule the roost** faire la loi.
■ **vi** se percher, se jucher.

rooster ['ru:stə^r] **n** *esp US* coq *m*.

root [ru:t] ■ **adj** [fundamental] principal(e), fondamental(e).
■ **n** racine *f* / *fig* [of problem] origine *f* ▸ **to take root** *lit & fig* prendre racine ▸ **to get at** OR **to the root of the problem** aller au fond du problème.
■ **vi : to root through** fouiller dans.
◆ ***roots*** **npl** racines *fpl* ▸ **their actual roots are in Virginia** en fait, ils sont originaires de Virginie ▸ **to put down roots** [person] s'enraciner.
◆ ***root about*** *UK*, ***root around*** **vi insep** fouiller ▸ **to root about for sthg** fouiller pour trouver qqch.
◆ ***root for*** **vt insep** *inf* encourager.
◆ ***root out*** **vt sep** [eradicate] extirper.

root beer **n** *esp US boisson gazeuse à base de racines de plantes*.

root crop **n** racine *f*.

rooted ['ru:tɪd] **adj : to be rooted to the spot** être cloué(e) sur place.

rootless ['ru:tlɪs] **adj** sans racines.

root vegetable **n** racine *f*.

rope [rəʊp] ■ **n** corde *f* ▸ **to know the ropes** *inf* connaître son affaire, être au courant.
■ **vt** corder / [climbers] encorder.
◆ ***rope in*** **vt sep** *inf* enrôler.
◆ ***rope off*** **vt sep** délimiter par une corde.

rope ladder **n** échelle *f* de corde.

rop(e)y ['rəʊpɪ] (comp **-ier**, superl **-iest**) **adj** *UK inf* **1.** [poor-quality] pas fameux(euse), pas brillant(e) **2.** [unwell] **: I feel a bit ropey today** je me sens un peu patraque aujourd'hui.

rosary ['rəʊzərɪ] (pl **-ies**) **n** rosaire *m*.

rose [rəʊz] ■ **pt** ➤ ***rise***.
■ **adj** [pink] rose.
■ **n** [flower] rose *f*.

rosé ['rəʊzeɪ] **n** rosé *m*.

rosebed ['rəʊzbed] **n** massif *m* de rosiers.

rosebud ['rəʊzbʌd] **n** bouton *m* de rose.

rose bush **n** rosier *m*.

rose hip **n** gratte-cul *m*.

rosemary ['rəʊzmərɪ] **n** romarin *m*.

rose-tinted **adj** teinté(e) en rose.

rosette [rəʊ'zet] **n** rosette *f*.

rosewater ['rəʊz,wɔ:tə^r] **n** eau *f* de rose.

rose window **n** rosace *f*.

rosewood ['rəʊzwʊd] **n** bois *m* de rose.

ROSPA ['rɒspə] (abbr of ***Royal Society for the Prevention of Accidents***) **n** *association britannique pour la prévention des accidents*.

roster ['rɒstə^r] **n** liste *f*, tableau *m*.

rostrum ['rɒstrəm] (pl **-trums** OR **-tra** [-trə]) **n** tribune *f*.

rosy ['rəʊzɪ] (comp **-ier**, superl **-iest**) **adj** rose.

rot [rɒt] ■ **n** *(U)* **1.** [decay] pourriture *f* **2.** *UK inf dated* [nonsense] bêtises *fpl*, balivernes *fpl*.
■ **vt & vi** (pt & pp **-ted**, cont **-ting**) pourrir.

rota ['rəʊtə] **n** *UK* liste *f*, tableau *m*.

rotary ['rəʊtərɪ] ■ **adj** rotatif(ive).
■ **n** *US* [roundabout] rond-point *m*.

Rotary Club **n : the Rotary Club** le Rotary Club.

rotate [rəʊ'teɪt] ■ **vt** **1.** [turn] faire tourner **2.** [alternate - jobs] faire à tour de rôle / [- crops] alterner.
■ **vi** [turn] tourner.

rotating [rəʊ'teɪtɪŋ] **adj** **1.** [turning] tournant(e), rotatif(ive) **2.** AGRIC **: rotating crops** cultures *fpl* alternantes OR en rotation.

rotation [rəʊ'teɪʃn] **n** **1.** [turning movement] rotation *f* **2.** [alternation] alternance *f* ▸ **in rotation** à tour de rôle.

rote [rəʊt] **n : by rote** de façon machinale, par cœur.

rote learning n apprentissage *m* machinal OR par cœur.

rotor ['rəʊtəʳ] n rotor *m*.

rotten ['rɒtn] adj 1. [decayed] pourri(e) 2. *inf* [bad] moche ▸ **he's a rotten goalkeeper** il est nul OR il ne vaut rien comme gardien de but ▸ **what a rotten trick!** quel sale tour! 3. *inf* [unwell] : **to feel rotten** se sentir mal fichu(e) 4. [unhappy, unfriendly] : **I feel rotten about it** ça me contrarie ▸ **to be rotten to sb** être dur(e) avec qqn.

rotting ['rɒtɪŋ] adj qui pourrit, pourri(e).

rotund [rəʊ'tʌnd] adj *fml* rondelet(ette).

rouble ['ru:bl] n rouble *m*.

rouge [ru:ʒ] n rouge *m* à joues.

rough [rʌf] ■ adj 1. [not smooth - surface] rugueux(euse), rêche / [- road] accidenté(e) / [- sea] agité(e), houleux(euse) / [- crossing] mauvais(e)
2. [person, treatment] brutal(e) / [manners, conditions] rude / [area] mal fréquenté(e) ▸ **they came in for some rough treatment** ils ont été malmenés ▸ **to give sb the rough edge of one's tongue** réprimander qqn, ne pas ménager ses reproches à qqn
3. [guess] approximatif(ive) ▸ **rough copy, rough draft** brouillon *m* ▸ **rough sketch** ébauche *f* ▸ **I only need a rough estimate** je n'ai pas besoin d'une réponse précise ▸ **at a rough guess** grosso modo, approximativement ▸ **rough paper** papier *m* brouillon
4. [harsh - voice, wine] âpre / [- life] dur(e) ▸ **to have a rough time** en baver ▸ **she's had a rough time of it** elle en a vu des dures OR de toutes les couleurs ▸ **to make things rough for sb** mener la vie dure à qqn
5. *UK inf* [tired, ill] mal fichu(e) ▸ **I'm feeling a bit rough** je ne suis pas dans mon assiette.
■ adv : **to sleep rough** *UK* coucher à la dure.
■ n 1. GOLF rough *m* ▸ **to take the rough with the smooth** prendre les choses comme elles viennent
2. [undetailed form] : **in rough** au brouillon.
■ vt
▸▸ **to rough it** vivre à la dure.
◆ ***rough out*** vt sep ébaucher.
◆ ***rough up*** vt sep *inf* [person] tabasser, passer à tabac.

roughage ['rʌfɪdʒ] n *(U)* fibres *fpl* alimentaires.

rough-and-ready adj rudimentaire.

rough-and-tumble n *(U)* bagarre *f*.

roughcast ['rʌfkɑ:st] n crépi *m*.

rough diamond n *UK fig* : **he's a rough diamond** sous ses dehors frustes, il a beaucoup de qualités.

roughen ['rʌfn] vt rendre rugueux(euse) OR rêche.

rough justice n justice *f* sommaire.

roughly ['rʌflɪ] adv 1. [approximately] approximativement 2. [handle, treat] brutalement 3. [built, made] grossièrement.

roughneck ['rʌfnek] n *inf* 1. *US inf* [ruffian] dur *m* 2. [oil-rig worker] *personne travaillant sur une plate-forme pétrolière*.

roughness ['rʌfnɪs] n 1. [of skin, surface] rugosité *f* 2. [of treatment, person] brutalité *f*.

roughshod ['rʌfʃɒd] adv : **to ride roughshod over sthg** passer outre à qqch ▸ **to ride roughshod over sb** traiter qqn cavalièrement.

roulette [ru:'let] n roulette *f*.

round [raʊnd] ■ adj rond(e) ▸ **500, in round numbers** 500 tout rond.
■ prep *UK* autour de ▸ **to sit round the fire/table** s'asseoir autour du feu/de la table ▸ **he put his arm round her shoulders/waist** il a passé son bras autour de ses épaules/de sa taille ▸ **round here** par ici ▸ **all round the country** dans tout le pays ▸ **just round the corner** au coin de la rue / *fig* tout près ▸ **to go round sthg** [obstacle] contourner qqch ▸ **there must be a way round the problem** *fig* il doit y avoir un moyen de contourner ce problème ▸ **to go round a museum** visiter un musée.
■ adv *UK* 1. [surrounding] : **all round** tout autour
2. [near] : **round about** dans le coin
3. [in measurements] : **10 metres round** 10 mètres de diamètre
4. [to other side] : **to go round** faire le tour ▸ **we drove round to the back** nous avons fait le tour (par derrière) ▸ **to turn round** se retourner ▸ **to look round** se retourner (pour regarder) ▸ **turn the wheel right round** OR **all the way round** faites faire un tour complet à la roue ▸ **we'll have to turn the car round** on va devoir faire demi-tour ▸ **to go round and round** tourner ▸ **we drove round and round for hours** on a tourné en rond pendant des heures
5. [at or to nearby place] : **come round and see us** venez OR passez nous voir ▸ **he's round at her house** il est chez elle ▸ **I'm just going round to the shop** je vais juste faire une course ▸ **can I have a look round?** je peux jeter un coup d'œil? ▸ **we had to take the long way round** on a dû faire le grand tour OR un grand détour
6. [from one person to another] : **hand the sweets round, hand round the sweets** faites passer les bonbons ▸ **there wasn't enough to go round** il n'y en avait pas assez pour tout le monde
7. [approximately] : **round (about)** vers, environ ▸ **round about midnight** vers minuit.
■ n 1. [of talks] série *f* ▸ **a round of applause** une salve d'applaudissements
2. [of competition] manche *f* ▸ **she's through to the final round** elle participera à la finale
3. [of doctor] visites *fpl* / [of postman, milkman] tournée *f*
4. [of ammunition] cartouche *f*
5. [of drinks] tournée *f* ▸ **it's my round** c'est ma tournée
6. [in boxing] reprise *f*, round *m*
7. [in golf] partie *f*.
■ vt [corner] tourner / [bend] prendre.
◆ ***rounds*** npl [of doctor] visites *fpl* ▸ **to go on one's rounds** faire ses visites ▸ **to do** OR **go the rounds** [story, joke] circuler / [illness] faire des ravages.
◆ ***round down*** vt sep arrondir au chiffre inférieur.
◆ ***round off*** vt sep terminer, conclure ▸ **he rounded off his meal with a glass of brandy** il a terminé son repas par un verre de cognac.
◆ ***round up*** vt sep 1. [gather together] rassembler
2. MATHS arrondir au chiffre supérieur.

roundabout ['raʊndəbaʊt] ■ adj détourné(e).
■ n *UK* 1. [on road] rond-point *m* 2. [at fairground] manège *m* 3. [at playground] tourniquet *m*.

rounded ['raʊndɪd] adj arrondi(e).

rounders ['raʊndəz] n *UK sorte de baseball.*

round-eyed adj *lit* aux yeux ronds / *fig* [surprised] avec des yeux ronds.

Roundhead ['raʊndhed] n Tête *f* ronde.

roundly ['raʊndlɪ] adv [beat] complètement / [condemn] franchement, carrément.

round-shouldered [-'ʃəʊldəd] adj voûté(e).

round-table adj : **round-table talks** table *f* ronde.

round the clock adv vingt-quatre heures sur vingt-quatre.
◆ ***round-the-clock*** adj vingt-quatre heures sur vingt-quatre.

round trip ■ adj aller-retour.
■ n aller et retour *m*.

roundup ['raʊndʌp] n [summary] résumé *m*.

rouse [raʊz] vt **1.** [wake up] réveiller **2.** [impel] : **to rouse o.s. to do sthg** se forcer à faire qqch ▸ **to rouse sb to action** pousser OR inciter qqn à agir **3.** [emotions] susciter, provoquer.

rousing ['raʊzɪŋ] adj [speech] vibrant(e), passionné(e) / [welcome] enthousiaste.

rout [raʊt] ■ n déroute *f*.
■ vt mettre en déroute.

route [*UK* ru:t, *US* raʊt] ■ n **1.** [gen] itinéraire *m* ▸ **a large crowd lined the route** il y avait une foule nombreuse sur tout le parcours ▸ **we need a map of the bus routes** il nous faut un plan des lignes d'autobus **2.** *fig* [way] chemin *m*, voie *f* ▸ **the route to success** *fig* le chemin de la réussite.
■ vt [goods] acheminer.

route map n [for journey] croquis *m* d'itinéraire / [for buses, trains] carte *f* du réseau.

route march n marche *f* d'entraînement.

router ['ru:tə, *US* 'raʊtər] n COMPUT routeur *m*.

routine [ru:'ti:n] ■ adj **1.** [normal] habituel(elle), de routine **2.** *pej* [uninteresting] de routine.
■ n routine *f*.

routinely [ru:'ti:nlɪ] adv de façon systématique.

roux [ru:] (pl **roux** [ru:]) n CULIN roux *m*.

rove [rəʊv] *liter* ■ vt errer dans.
■ vi : **to rove around** errer.

roving ['rəʊvɪŋ] adj itinérant(e).

row¹ [rəʊ] ■ n **1.** [line] rangée *f* / [of seats] rang *m* **2.** *fig* [of defeats, victories] série *f* ▸ **in a row** d'affilée, de suite.
■ vt [boat] faire aller à la rame / [person] transporter en canot OR bateau.
■ vi ramer.

row² [raʊ] *UK* ■ n **1.** [quarrel] dispute *f*, querelle *f* **2.** *inf* [noise] vacarme *m*, raffut *m*.
■ vi [quarrel] se disputer, se quereller.

rowboat ['rəʊbəʊt] n *US* canot *m*.

rowdiness ['raʊdɪnɪs] n chahut *m*, tapage *m*.

rowdy ['raʊdɪ] (comp -ier, superl -iest) adj chahuteur(euse), tapageur(euse).

rower ['rəʊər] n rameur *m*, -euse *f*.

row house [rəʊ-] n *US maison attenante aux maisons voisines.*

rowing ['rəʊɪŋ] n SPORT aviron *m*.

rowing boat n *UK* canot *m*.

rowing machine n machine *f* à ramer.

royal ['rɔɪəl] ■ adj royal(e).
■ n *inf* membre *m* de la famille royale.

Royal Air Force n : **the Royal Air Force** l'armée *f* de l'air britannique.

royal blue adj bleu roi *(inv)*.

royal family n famille *f* royale.

Royal Highness n : **His Royal Highness, the Prince of Wales** Son Altesse Royale, le prince de Galles.

royalist ['rɔɪəlɪst] n royaliste *mf*.

royal jelly n gelée *f* royale.

royally ['rɔɪəlɪ] adv *lit & fig* royalement / [like a king] en roi / [like a queen] en reine.

Royal Mail n : **the Royal Mail** *la Poste britannique.*

Royal Marines n *UK* : **the Royal Marines** les Marines *mpl* (britanniques).

Royal Navy n : **the Royal Navy** la marine de guerre (britannique).

royalty ['rɔɪəltɪ] n royauté *f*.
◆ ***royalties*** npl droits *mpl* d'auteur.

RP (abbr of ***received pronunciation***) n *UK prononciation standard de l'anglais britannique.*

RPI (abbr of ***retail price index***) n *UK* IPC *m*.

rpm npl (abbr of ***revolutions per minute***) tours *mpl* par minute, tr/min.

RR *US* abbr of ***railroad***.

RRP n abbr of ***recommended retail price***.

RSA (abbr of ***Royal Society of Arts***) n *société britannique pour la promotion des arts, de l'industrie et du commerce.*

RSC (abbr of ***Royal Shakespeare Company***) n *compagnie de théâtre britannique.*

RSI (abbr of ***repetitive strain*** OR ***stress injury***) n *douleur de poignet provoquée par les mouvements effectués au clavier d'un ordinateur.*

RSPB (abbr of ***Royal Society for the Protection of Birds***) n *ligue britannique pour la protection des oiseaux.*

RSPCA (abbr of ***Royal Society for the Prevention of Cruelty to Animals***) n *société britannique protectrice des animaux,* ≃ SPA *f*.

RST (abbr of ***Royal Shakespeare Theatre***) n *célèbre théâtre à Stratford-upon-Avon.*

RSVP (abbr of ***répondez s'il vous plaît***) RSVP.

Rt Hon (abbr of ***Right Honourable***) *expression utilisée pour des titres nobiliaires.*

Rt Rev (abbr of ***Right Reverend***) *expression utilisée pour un évêque de l'Église anglicane.*

rub [rʌb] (pt & pp -bed, cont -bing) ■ vt frotter ▸ **to rub one's eyes/hands** se frotter les yeux/les mains ▸ **to rub sthg in** [cream] faire pénétrer qqch (en frottant) ▸ **to rub it in** *inf fig* remuer le couteau dans la plaie ▸ **to rub sb up**

the wrong way *UK*, **to rub sb the wrong way** *US* prendre qqn à rebrousse-poil ▸ **to rub shoulders with sb** côtoyer *OR* coudoyer qqn.
■ vi frotter ▸ **my shoe is rubbing** ma chaussure me fait mal.
◆ ***rub off on*** vt insep [subj: quality] déteindre sur ▸ **with a bit of luck, her common sense will rub off on him** avec un peu de chance, son bon sens déteindra sur lui.
◆ ***rub out*** vt sep [erase] effacer.

rubber ['rʌbər] ■ adj en caoutchouc.
■ n **1.** [substance] caoutchouc *m* **2.** *UK* [eraser] gomme *f* **3.** *inf* [condom] préservatif *m* **4.** [in bridge] robre *m*, rob *m* **5.** *US* [overshoe] caoutchouc *m*.

rubber band n élastique *m*.

rubber boot n *US* botte *f* de caoutchouc.

rubber cheque *UK*, ***rubber check*** *US* n *inf* chèque *m* en bois.

rubber dinghy n canot *m* pneumatique.

rubberize, *UK* ***-ise*** ['rʌbəraɪz] vt caoutchouter.

rubberneck ['rʌbənek] vi *inf* faire le badaud.

rubber plant n caoutchouc *m*.

rubber ring n anneau *m* en caoutchouc / [for swimmer] bouée *f*.

rubber stamp n tampon *m*.
◆ ***rubber-stamp*** vt *fig* approuver sans discussion.

rubber tree n hévéa *m*.

rubbery ['rʌbərɪ] adj caoutchouteux(euse).

rubbing ['rʌbɪŋ] n [of brass] décalque *m*.

rubbish ['rʌbɪʃ] *esp UK* ■ n *(U)* **1.** [refuse] détritus *mpl*, ordures *fpl* **2.** *inf fig* [worthless objects] camelote *f* ▸ **the play was rubbish** la pièce était nulle **3.** *inf* [nonsense] bêtises *fpl*, inepties *fpl*.
■ vt *inf* débiner.

rubbish bin n *UK* poubelle *f*.

rubbish dump n *UK* dépotoir *m*.

rubbishy ['rʌbɪʃɪ] adj *UK inf* qui ne vaut rien, nul (nulle).

rubble ['rʌbl] n *(U)* décombres *mpl*.

rubella [ru:'belə] n MED rubéole *f*.

rubric ['ru:brɪk] n rubrique *f*.

ruby ['ru:bɪ] (pl -ies) n rubis *m*.

RUC (abbr of ***Royal Ulster Constabulary***) n *corps de police d'Irlande du Nord*.

ruched [ru:ʃt] adj garni(e) d'un ruché.

ruck [rʌk] n **1.** *UK inf* [fight] bagarre *f* **2.** RUGBY mêlée *f* ouverte.

rucksack ['rʌksæk] n sac *m* à dos.

ructions ['rʌkʃnz] npl *inf* grabuge *m*.

rudder ['rʌdər] n gouvernail *m*.

ruddy ['rʌdɪ] (comp -ier, superl -iest) adj **1.** [complexion, face] coloré(e) **2.** *UK inf dated* [damned] sacré(e).

rude [ru:d] adj **1.** [impolite - gen] impoli(e) / [- word] grossier(ère) / [- noise] incongru(e) **2.** [sudden] **: it was a rude awakening** le réveil fut pénible **3.** *liter* [primitive] grossier(ère), rudimentaire.

rudely ['ru:dlɪ] adv **1.** [impolitely] impoliment **2.** [suddenly] brusquement.

rudeness ['ru:dnɪs] n [impoliteness] impolitesse *f* / [of joke] grossièreté *f*.

rudimentary [ˌru:dɪ'mentərɪ] adj rudimentaire.

rudiments ['ru:dɪmənts] npl rudiments *mpl*.

rue [ru:] vt regretter (amèrement).

rueful ['ru:fʊl] adj triste.

ruefully ['ru:fʊlɪ] adv [sadly] tristement / [regretfully] avec regret.

ruff [rʌf] n fraise *f*.

ruffian ['rʌfjən] n *dated* voyou *m*.

ruffle ['rʌfl] vt **1.** [hair] ébouriffer / [water] troubler **2.** [person] froisser / [composure] faire perdre.

ruffled ['rʌfld] adj **1.** [flustered] décontenancé(e) **2.** [rumpled - sheets] froissé(e) / [- hair] ébouriffé(e) **3.** [decorated with frill] ruché(e), plissé(e).

rug [rʌg] n **1.** [carpet] tapis *m* **2.** [blanket] couverture *f*.

rugby ['rʌgbɪ] n rugby *m*.

Rugby League n rugby *m* à treize.

rugby tackle n plaquage *m*.
◆ ***rugby-tackle*** vt plaquer.

Rugby Union n rugby *m* à quinze.

rugged ['rʌgɪd] adj **1.** [landscape] accidenté(e) / [features] rude **2.** [vehicle] robuste.

ruggedness ['rʌgɪdnɪs] n [of landscape] aspect *m* accidenté.

rugger ['rʌgər] n *UK inf* rugby *m*.

ruin ['ru:ɪn] ■ n ruine *f*.
■ vt ruiner / [clothes, shoes] abîmer.
◆ ***in ruin(s)*** adv *lit & fig* en ruine.

ruination [ru:ɪ'neɪʃn] n ruine *f*.

ruined ['ru:ɪnd] adj **1.** [house, reputation, health] en ruine, ruiné(e) / [clothes] abîmé(e) **2.** [person - financially] ruiné(e).

ruinous ['ru:ɪnəs] adj [expensive] ruineux(euse).

ruinously ['ru:ɪnəslɪ] adv de façon ruineuse ▸ **ruinously expensive** ruineux(euse).

rule [ru:l] ■ n **1.** [gen] règle *f* ▸ **the rules of chess/grammar** les règles du jeu d'échecs/de la grammaire ▸ **to break the rules** ne pas respecter les règles ▸ **to bend the rules** faire une entorse au règlement ▸ **smoking is against the rules, it's against the rules to smoke** le règlement interdit de fumer ▸ **as a rule** en règle générale
2. [regulation] règlement *m* ▸ **the rules and regulations** le règlement
3. *(U)* [control] autorité *f* ▸ **the territories under French rule** les territoires sous autorité française ▸ **the rule of law** (l'autorité de) la loi.
■ vt **1.** [control] dominer ▸ **their lives are ruled by fear** leur vie est dominée par la peur
2. [govern] gouverner ▸ **if I ruled the world** si j'étais maître du monde
3. [decide] **: to rule (that)...** décider que...

■ **vi 1.** [give decision - gen] décider / LAW statuer ▶ **to rule against/in favour of sb** décider *OR* prononcer contre/en faveur de qqn
2. *fml* [be paramount] prévaloir
3. [king, queen] régner / POL gouverner.
◆ ***rule out*** **vt sep** exclure, écarter.

rulebook ['ru:lbʊk] **n : the rulebook** le règlement.

ruled [ru:ld] **adj** [paper] réglé(e).

ruler ['ru:ləʳ] **n 1.** [for measurement] règle *f* **2.** [leader] chef *m* d'État.

ruling ['ru:lɪŋ] ■ **adj** au pouvoir.
■ **n** décision *f*.

ruling body **n** instances *fpl* (dirigeantes).

rum [rʌm] ■ **n** rhum *m*.
■ **adj** (comp **-mer**, superl **-mest**) *UK inf dated* bizarre.

Rumania [ru:'meɪnjə] = ***Romania***.

Rumanian [ru:'meɪnjən] = ***Romanian***.

rumba ['rʌmbə] **n** rumba *f*.

rumble ['rʌmbl] ■ **n 1.** [of thunder, traffic] grondement *m* / [in stomach] gargouillement *m* **2.** *US inf* [fight] bagarre *f*.
■ **vt** *UK inf dated* **: to rumble sb** voir clair dans le jeu de qqn.
■ **vi** [thunder, traffic] gronder / [stomach] gargouiller.

rumbling ['rʌmblɪŋ] **n** [of thunder, traffic, cannons] grondement *m* / [of stomach] borborygmes *mpl*, gargouillis *mpl*, gargouillements *mpl*.
◆ ***rumblings*** **npl** [of discontent] grondement *m*, grondements *mpl* / [omens] présages *mpl*.

rumbustious [rʌm'bʌstɪəs] **adj** *UK* bruyant(e).

ruminate ['ru:mɪneɪt] **vi** *fml* **: to ruminate (about** *OR* **on sthg)** ruminer (qqch).

ruminative ['ru:mɪnətɪv] **adj** *fml* [person] pensif(ive), méditatif(ive) / [look, mood] pensif(ive).

rummage ['rʌmɪdʒ] **vi** fouiller.

rummage sale **n** *US* vente *f* de charité.

rummy ['rʌmɪ] **n** rami *m*.

rumour *UK*, ***rumor*** *US* ['ru:məʳ] **n** rumeur *f*.

rumoured *UK*, ***rumored*** *US* ['ru:məd] **adj : he is rumoured to be very wealthy** le bruit court *OR* on dit qu'il est très riche.

rump [rʌmp] **n 1.** [of animal] croupe *f* **2.** *inf* [of person] derrière *m* **3.** POL restant *m*.

rumple ['rʌmpl] **vt** froisser, chiffonner.

rump steak **n** romsteck *m*.

rumpus ['rʌmpəs] **n** *inf* chahut *m*.

rumpus room **n** *US* salle *f* de jeu.

run [rʌn] ■ **n 1.** [on foot] course *f* ▶ **to go for a run** faire un petit peu de course à pied ▶ **to break into a run** se mettre à courir ▶ **on the run** en fuite, en cavale ▶ **we've got them on the run!** MIL & SPORT nous les avons mis en déroute! ▶ **to make a run for it** se sauver ▶ **we have the run of the house while the owners are away** nous disposons de toute la maison pendant l'absence des propriétaires
2. [in car - for pleasure] tour *m* / [- journey] trajet *m* ▶ **she took me for a run in her new car** elle m'a emmené faire un tour dans sa nouvelle voiture
3. [series] suite *f*, série *f* ▶ **a run of bad luck** une période de déveine ▶ **in the short/long run** à court/long terme
4. THEAT **: to have a long run** tenir longtemps l'affiche
5. [great demand] **: run on** ruée *f* sur ▶ **a run on the banks** une panique bancaire
6. [in tights] échelle *f*
7. [in cricket, baseball] point *m*
8. [track - for skiing, bobsleigh] piste *f*.
■ **vt** (pt **ran**, pp **run**, cont **-ning**) **1.** [race, distance] courir ▶ **to run errands (for sb)** faire des courses *OR* commissions (pour qqn) ▶ **to be run off one's feet** être débordé(e) ▶ **to run the risk of doing sthg** courir le risque de faire qqch
2. [manage - business] diriger / [- shop, hotel] tenir / [- course] organiser ▶ **a badly run organization** une organisation mal gérée
3. [operate] faire marcher / COMPUT [program] exécuter
4. [car] avoir, entretenir
5. [water, bath] faire couler
6. [publish] publier ▶ **to run an ad (in the newspaper)** passer *OR* faire passer une annonce (dans le journal)
7. *inf* [drive] **: can you run me to the station?** tu peux m'amener *OR* me conduire à la gare?
8. [move] **: to run sthg along/over sthg** passer qqch le long de/sur qqch / [lay] **: it would be better to run the wires under the floorboards** ce serait mieux de faire passer les fils sous le plancher.
■ **vi** (pt **ran**, pp **run**, cont **-ning**) **1.** [on foot] courir ▶ **to run in a race** [horse, person] participer à une course ▶ **to run for it** se sauver ▶ **run for your lives!** sauve qui peut!
2. [pass - road, river, pipe] passer ▶ **to run through sthg** traverser qqch / [- hand, fingers] **: her eyes ran down the list** elle parcourut la liste des yeux ▶ **a shiver ran down my spine** un frisson me parcourut le dos
3. [in election] **: to run (for)** être candidat (à)
4. [operate - machine, factory] marcher / [- engine] tourner ▶ **everything is running smoothly** tout va comme sur des roulettes, tout va bien ▶ **to run on sthg** marcher à qqch ▶ **to run off sthg** marcher sur qqch
5. [bus, train] faire le service ▶ **trains run every hour** il y a un train toutes les heures ▶ **to be running late** [person] être en retard / [bus, train] avoir du retard
6. [flow] couler ▶ **my nose is running** j'ai le nez qui coule ▶ **the water's run cold** l'eau est froide au robinet ▶ **the Jari runs into the Amazon** le Jari se jette dans l'Amazone ▶ **to run dry** se tarir
7. [colour] déteindre / [ink] baver
8. [continue - contract, insurance policy] être valide / THEAT se jouer ▶ **output is running at 100 units a day** la production est de 100 unités par jour.
◆ ***run across*** **vt insep** [meet] tomber sur.
◆ ***run along*** **vi** *dated* **: run along now!** filez maintenant!
◆ ***run away*** **vi 1.** [flee] **: to run away (from)** s'enfuir (de) ▶ **to run away from home** faire une fugue
2. *fig* [avoid] **: to run away from sthg** éviter qqch.
◆ ***run away with*** **vt insep : don't let your enthusiasm run away with you!** ne t'emballe pas trop!

◆ ***run down*** ■ vt sep **1.** [in vehicle] renverser **2.** [criticize] dénigrer ▸ **stop running yourself down all the time** cesse de te rabaisser constamment
3. [production] restreindre / [industry] réduire l'activité de ▸ **the government was accused of running down the steel industry** le gouvernement a été accusé de laisser dépérir la sidérurgie.
■ vi [clock] s'arrêter / [battery] se décharger.
◆ ***run into*** vt insep **1.** [encounter - problem] se heurter à / [- person] tomber sur ▸ **to run into debt** s'endetter, faire des dettes
2. [in vehicle] rentrer dans
3. [amount to] se monter à, s'élever à.
◆ ***run off*** ■ vt sep [a copy] tirer ▸ **run me off five copies of this report** faites-moi cinq copies de ce rapport.
■ vi : **to run off (with)** s'enfuir (avec).
◆ ***run on*** vi [meeting] durer ▸ **time is running on** le temps passe.
◆ ***run out*** vi **1.** [food, supplies] s'épuiser ▸ **time is running out** il ne reste plus beaucoup de temps
2. [licence, contract] expirer.
◆ ***run out of*** vt insep manquer de ▸ **he's run out of money** il n'a plus d'argent ▸ **to run out of petrol** tomber en panne d'essence, tomber en panne sèche.
◆ ***run over*** vt sep renverser.
◆ ***run through*** vt insep **1.** [practise] répéter
2. [read through] parcourir.
◆ ***run to*** vt insep **1.** [amount to] monter à, s'élever à
2. *UK* [afford] : **I think I could run to a new suit** je crois bien que je pourrais me payer *OR* m'offrir un nouveau costume.
◆ ***run up*** vt insep [bill, debt] laisser accumuler ▸ **I've run up a huge overdraft** j'ai un découvert énorme.
◆ ***run up against*** vt insep se heurter à.

run-around n *inf* : **to give sb the run-around** faire des réponses de Normand à qqn.

runaway ['rʌnəweɪ] ■ adj [train, lorry] fou (folle) / [horse] emballé(e) / [victory] haut(e) la main / [inflation] galopant(e).
■ n fuyard *m*, fugitif *m*, -ive *f*.

rundown ['rʌndaʊn] n **1.** [report] bref résumé *m* **2.** [of industry] réduction *f* délibérée.
◆ ***run-down*** adj **1.** [building] délabré(e) **2.** [person] épuisé(e).

rung [rʌŋ] ■ pp ➤ ***ring***.
■ n échelon *m*, barreau *m*.

run-in n *inf* prise *f* de bec.

runnel ['rʌnl] n ruisseau *m*.

runner ['rʌnəʳ] n **1.** [athlete] coureur *m*, -euse *f* **2.** [of guns, drugs] contrebandier *m*, -ière *f* **3.** [of sledge] patin *m* / [for car seat] glissière *f* / [for drawer] coulisseau *m*.

runner bean n *UK* haricot *m* à rames.

runner-up (pl **runners-up**) n second *m*, -e *f*.

running ['rʌnɪŋ] ■ adj **1.** [argument, battle] continu(e) **2.** [consecutive] : **three weeks running** trois semaines de suite **3.** [water] courant(e) **4.** [working, operating] : **in running order** en état de marche
▸▸ **to be up and running** être opérationnel(elle).
■ n **1.** *(U)* SPORT course *f* ▸ **to go running** faire de la course **2.** [management] direction *f*, administration *f* **3.** [of machine] marche *f*, fonctionnement *m*
▸▸ **to be in the running (for)** avoir des chances de réussir (dans) ▸ **to be out of the running (for)** n'avoir aucune chance de réussir (dans) ▸ **to make the running** [in race] mener la course / [in relationship] prendre l'initiative.
■ **comp** de course.

running commentary n commentaire *m* suivi.

running costs npl frais *mpl* d'exploitation.

running mate n *US* candidat *m* à la vice-présidence.

running order n ordre *m* de passage.

running repairs npl réparations *fpl* courantes.

running time n durée *f*.

runny ['rʌnɪ] (comp -ier, superl -iest) adj **1.** [food] liquide **2.** [nose] qui coule.

run-off n **1.** SPORT [final] finale *f* / [after tie] belle *f* **2.** [water] trop-plein *m*.

run-of-the-mill adj banal(e), ordinaire.

run-on n **1.** [in printed matter] texte *m* composé à la suite *(sans alinéa)* **2.** [in dictionary] sous-entrée *f*.

runt [rʌnt] n avorton *m*.

run-through n répétition *f*.

run-up n **1.** [preceding time] : **in the run-up to sthg** dans la période qui précède qqch **2.** SPORT course *f* d'élan.

runway ['rʌnweɪ] n piste *f*.

rupture ['rʌptʃəʳ] n rupture *f*.

rural ['rʊərəl] adj rural(e).

ruse [ru:z] n ruse *f*.

rush [rʌʃ] ■ n **1.** [hurry] hâte *f* ▸ **to do sthg in a rush** faire qqch à la hâte ▸ **there's no rush** ça ne presse pas, ce n'est pas pressé
2. [surge] ruée *f*, bousculade *f* ▸ **to make a rush for sthg** se ruer *OR* se précipiter vers qqch ▸ **a rush of air** une bouffée d'air ▸ **a rush of blood to the head** un coup de sang
3. [demand] : **rush (on *OR* for)** ruée *f* (sur).
■ vt **1.** [hurry - work] faire à la hâte / [- person] bousculer / [- meal] expédier ▸ **don't rush your food** ne mange pas trop vite ▸ **to rush sb into doing sthg** forcer qqn à faire qqch à la hâte
2. [send quickly] transporter *OR* envoyer d'urgence
3. [attack suddenly] prendre d'assaut.
■ vi **1.** [hurry] se dépêcher ▸ **there's no need to rush** pas besoin de se presser ▸ **to rush into sthg** faire qqch sans réfléchir
2. [move quickly, suddenly] se précipiter, se ruer ▸ **he rushed in/out/past** il est entré précipitamment/sorti précipitamment/passé à toute allure ▸ **passers-by rushed to help the injured man** des passants se sont précipités au secours du blessé ▸ **the blood rushed to her head** le sang lui monta à la tête.
◆ ***rushes*** npl **1.** BOT joncs *mpl*
2. CIN épreuves *fpl* de tournage, rushes *mpl*.

rushed [rʌʃt] adj [person] pressé(e) / [work] fait(e) à la hâte.

rush hour n heures *fpl* de pointe *OR* d'affluence.

rush job n travail *m* d'urgence.

rusk [rʌsk] **n** *UK* biscotte *f*.

russet ['rʌsɪt] **adj** feuille-morte *(inv)*.

Russia ['rʌʃə] **n** Russie *f* ▸ **in Russia** en Russie.

Russian ['rʌʃn] ■ **adj** russe.
■ **n 1.** [person] Russe *mf* **2.** [language] russe *m*.

Russian Federation **n : the Russian Federation** la Fédération de Russie.

Russian roulette **n** roulette *f* russe.

rust [rʌst] ■ **n** rouille *f*.
■ **vi** se rouiller.

rusted ['rʌstɪd] **adj** rouillé(e).

rustic ['rʌstɪk] **adj** rustique.

rustle ['rʌsl] ■ **n** [of leaves] bruissement *m* / [of papers] froissement *m*.
■ **vt 1.** [paper] froisser **2.** *US* [cattle] voler.
■ **vi** [leaves] bruire / [papers] produire un froissement.

rustproof ['rʌstpru:f] **adj** inoxydable.

rusty ['rʌstɪ] (comp **-ier**, superl **-iest**) **adj** *lit* & *fig* rouillé(e).

rut [rʌt] **n** ornière *f* ▸ **to get into a rut** s'encroûter ▸ **to be in a rut** être prisonnier(ère) de la routine.

rutabaga [ˌru:tə'beɪgə] **n** *US* rutabaga *m*.

ruthless ['ru:θlɪs] **adj** impitoyable.

ruthlessly ['ru:θlɪslɪ] **adv** de façon impitoyable.

ruthlessness ['ru:θlɪsnɪs] **n** caractère *m* impitoyable.

rutted ['rʌtɪd] **adj** sillonné(e) ▸ **a badly rutted road** une route complètement défoncée.

RV **n 1.** (abbr of ***revised version***) *traduction de la Bible de 1611 révisée entre 1881 et 1895* **2.** *US* (abbr of ***recreational vehicle***) camping-car *m*.

Rwanda [rʊ'ændə] **n** Ruanda *m*, Rwanda *m* ▸ **in Rwanda** au Ruanda.

Rwandan [rʊ'ændən] ■ **adj** ruandais(e).
■ **n** Ruandais *m*, -e *f*.

rye [raɪ] **n 1.** [grain] seigle *m* **2.** [bread] pain *m* de seigle.

rye bread **n** pain *m* de seigle.

rye grass **n** ivraie *f*.

rye whiskey **n** *US* whisky *m* à base de seigle.

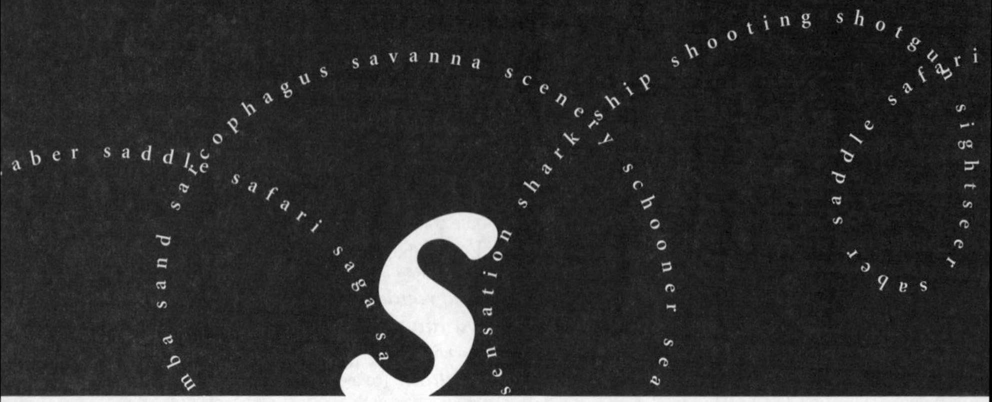

s (pl ss OR s's), ***S***[1] (pl Ss OR S's) [es] **n** [letter] s *m inv*, S *m inv*.

S[2] (abbr of ***south***) S.

S & M **n** abbr of ***sadomasochism***.

SA abbr of ***South Africa***, ***South America***.

Saar [sɑːʳ] **n : the Saar** la Sarre.

Sabbath ['sæbəθ] **n : the Sabbath** le sabbat.

sabbatical [sə'bætɪkl] **n** année *f* sabbatique ▸ **to be on sabbatical** faire une année sabbatique.

saber *US* = ***sabre***.

sabotage ['sæbətɑːʒ] ■ **n** sabotage *m*.
■ **vt** saboter.

saboteur [ˌsæbə'tɜːʳ] **n** saboteur *m*, -euse *f*.

sabre *UK*, ***saber*** *US* ['seɪbəʳ] **n** sabre *m*.

sabre-toothed tiger *UK*, ***saber-toothed tiger*** *US* **n** machairodonte *m*.

saccharin(e) ['sækərɪn] **n** saccharine *f*.

sachet ['sæʃeɪ] **n** sachet *m*.

sack [sæk] ■ **n 1.** [bag] sac *m* **2.** *UK inf* [dismissal] **: to get OR be given the sack** être renvoyé(e), se faire virer.
■ **vt** *UK inf* [dismiss] renvoyer, virer.

sackful ['sækfʊl] **n** sac *m*.

sacking ['sækɪŋ] **n 1.** [fabric] toile *f* à sac **2.** *UK inf* [dismissal] licenciement *m*.

sacrament ['sækrəmənt] **n** sacrement *m*.

sacred ['seɪkrɪd] **adj** sacré(e).

sacred cow **n** *fig* vache *f* sacrée.

sacrifice ['sækrɪfaɪs] *lit & fig* ■ **n** sacrifice *m*.
■ **vt** sacrifier.

sacrificial [ˌsækrɪ'fɪʃl] **adj** [rite, dagger] sacrificiel(elle) / [victim] du sacrifice.

sacrilege ['sækrɪlɪdʒ] **n** *lit & fig* sacrilège *m*.

sacrilegious [ˌsækrɪ'lɪdʒəs] **adj** *lit & fig* sacrilège.

sacrosanct ['sækrəʊsæŋkt] **adj** *lit & fig* sacro-saint(e).

sad [sæd] (comp **-der**, superl **-dest**) **adj** triste.

SAD **n** abbr of ***seasonal affective disorder***.

sadden ['sædn] **vt** attrister, affliger.

saddle ['sædl] ■ **n** selle *f*.
■ **vt 1.** [horse] seller **2.** *fig* [burden] **: to saddle sb with sthg** coller qqch à qqn.
◆ ***saddle up*** ■ **vt insep** seller.
■ **vi** seller son cheval.

saddlebag ['sædlbæg] **n** sacoche *f (de selle ou de bicyclette)*.

saddler ['sædləʳ] **n** sellier *m*.

sadism ['seɪdɪzm] **n** sadisme *m*.

sadist ['seɪdɪst] **n** sadique *mf*.

sadistic [sə'dɪstɪk] **adj** sadique.

sadly ['sædlɪ] **adv 1.** [unhappily] tristement **2.** [unfortunately] malheureusement.

sadness ['sædnɪs] **n** tristesse *f*.

sadomasochism [ˌseɪdəʊ'mæsəkɪzm] **n** sadomasochisme *m*.

sadomasochist [ˌseɪdəʊ'mæsəkɪst] **n** sadomasochiste *mf*.

sadomasochistic ['seɪdəʊˌmæsə'kɪstɪk] **adj** sadomasochiste.

s.a.e., ***sae*** abbr of ***stamped addressed envelope***.

safari [sə'fɑːrɪ] **n** safari *m* ▸ **to go on safari** aller en safari.

safari park **n** réserve *f*.

safe [seɪf] ■ **adj 1.** [not dangerous - gen] sans danger / [- driver, play, guess] prudent(e) ▸ **it's not safe** c'est dangereux ▸ **it's safe to say (that)...** on peut dire à coup sûr que... ▸ **in safe hands** en bonnes mains ▸ **I played it safe and arrived an hour early** pour ne pas prendre de risques, je suis arrivé une heure en avance
2. [not in danger] hors de danger, en sécurité ▸ **the money's safe in the bank** l'argent est en sécurité à la banque ▸ **your secret is safe with me** je saurai garder votre secret ▸ **(have a) safe journey!** bon voyage! ▸ **safe and sound** sain et sauf (saine et sauve)
3. [not risky - bet, method] sans risque / [- investment] sûr(e) ▸ **to be on the safe side** par précaution ▸ **it's as safe as houses** cela ne présente pas le moindre risque.
■ **n** coffre-fort *m*.

safebreaker ['seɪfˌbreɪkəʳ] **n** perceur *m* de coffre-fort.

safe-conduct **n** sauf-conduit *m*.

safe-deposit box *esp US* = ***safety-deposit box***.

safeguard ['seɪfgɑ:d] ■ **n : safeguard (against)** sauvegarde *f* (contre).

■ **vt : to safeguard sb/sthg (against)** sauvegarder qqn/qqch (contre), protéger qqn/qqch (contre).

safe haven **n** zone *f* protégée.

safe house **n** lieu *m* sûr.

safekeeping [ˌseɪf'ki:pɪŋ] **n** bonne garde *f*.

safely ['seɪflɪ] **adv** **1.** [not dangerously] sans danger **2.** [not in danger] en toute sécurité, à l'abri du danger **3.** [arrive - person] à bon port, sain et sauf (saine et sauve) / [- parcel] à bon port **4.** [for certain] **: I can safely say (that)...** je peux dire à coup sûr que...

safe seat **n** *UK* POL *siège de député qui traditionnellement va toujours au même parti*.

safe sex **n** sexe *m* sans risques, S.S.R. *m*

safety ['seɪftɪ] ■ **n** sécurité *f*.

■ **comp** de sécurité.

safety belt **n** ceinture *f* de sécurité.

safety catch **n** cran *m* de sûreté.

safety curtain **n** rideau *m* de fer.

safety-deposit box **n** *esp UK* coffre-fort *m*.

safety glass **n** verre *m* de sécurité.

safety helmet **n** casque *m* (de protection).

safety island **n** *US* refuge *m*.

safety match **n** allumette *f* de sûreté.

safety net **n** filet *m* (de protection).

safety pin **n** épingle *f* de sûreté ***OR*** de nourrice.

safety valve **n** soupape *f* de sûreté.

saffron ['sæfrən] **n** safran *m*.

sag [sæg] (**pt & pp -ged, cont -ging**) **vi** **1.** [sink downwards] s'affaisser, fléchir **2.** *fig* [decrease] baisser.

saga ['sɑ:gə] **n** saga *f* / *fig & pej* histoire *f*.

sage [seɪdʒ] ■ **adj** sage.

■ **n** **1.** *(U)* [herb] sauge *f* **2.** [wise man] sage *m*.

sagging ['sægɪŋ] **adj** **1.** [rope] détendu(e) / [bed, roof, bridge] affaissé(e) / [shelf, beam] qui ploie / [hemline] qui pend / [jowls, cheeks] pendant(e) / [breasts] tombant(e) **2.** [prices, demand] en baisse / [spirits] abattu(e), découragé(e).

saggy ['sægɪ] (**comp -gier, superl -giest**) **adj** [bed] affaissé(e) / [breasts] tombant(e).

Sagittarius [ˌsædʒɪ'teərɪəs] **n** Sagittaire *m* ▸ **to be (a) Sagittarius** être Sagittaire.

Sahara [sə'hɑ:rə] **n : the Sahara (Desert)** le (désert du) Sahara.

Saharan [sə'hɑ:rən] **adj** saharien(enne).

said [sed] **pt & pp** ➤ ***say***.

sail [seɪl] ■ **n** **1.** [of boat] voile *f* ▸ **in full sail** toutes voiles dehors ▸ **to set sail** faire voile, prendre la mer **2.** [journey] tour *m* en bateau ▸ **to go for a sail** faire un tour en bateau ▸ **it's a few hours' sail from here** c'est à quelques heures d'ici en bateau **3.** [of windmill] aile *f*.

■ **vt** **1.** [boat] piloter, manœuvrer ▸ **she sailed the boat into port** elle a manœuvré ***OR*** piloté le bateau jusque dans le port **2.** [sea] parcourir.

■ **vi** **1.** [person - gen] aller en bateau / SPORT faire de la voile **2.** [boat - move] naviguer / [- leave] partir, prendre la mer ▸ **the boat sailed up/down the river** le bateau remonta/descendit le fleuve ▸ **the ship sailed into harbour** le bateau est entré au port **3.** *fig* [through air] voler / [move quickly] **: a sports car sailed past me** une voiture de sport m'a doublé à toute vitesse ▸ **the ball sailed over the wall** la balle est passée par-dessus le mur.

◆ ***sail through*** **vt insep** *fig* réussir les doigts dans le nez.

sailboard ['seɪlbɔ:d] **n** planche *f* à voile.

sailboarder ['seɪlˌbɔ:dər] **n** véliplanchiste *mf*.

sailboarding ['seɪlˌbɔ:dɪŋ] **n** planche *f* à voile *(activité)*.

sailboat *US* = ***sailing boat***.

sailcloth ['seɪlklɒθ] **n** toile *f* à voile.

sailing ['seɪlɪŋ] **n** **1.** *(U)* SPORT voile *f* ▸ **to go sailing** faire de la voile **2.** [departure] départ *m*.

sailing boat *UK*, ***sailboat*** *US* ['seɪlbəʊt] **n** bateau *m* à voiles, voilier *m*.

sailing ship **n** voilier *m*.

sailor ['seɪlər] **n** marin *m*, matelot *m* ▸ **to be a good sailor** avoir le pied marin.

sailor suit **n** costume *m* marin.

saint [seɪnt] **n** saint *m*, -e *f*.

Saint Helena [-ɪ'li:nə] **n** Sainte-Hélène *f* ▸ **on Saint Helena** à Sainte-Hélène.

sainthood ['seɪnthʊd] **n** sainteté *f*.

Saint Lawrence [-'lɒrəns] **n : the Saint Lawrence (River)** le Saint-Laurent.

Saint Lucia [-'lu:ʃə] **n** Sainte-Lucie.

saintly ['seɪntlɪ] (**comp -ier, superl -iest**) **adj** [person] saint(e) / [life] de saint.

Saint Patrick's Day [-'pætrɪks-] **n** la Saint-Patrick.

saint's day **n** fête *f (d'un saint)*.

sake [seɪk] **n : for the sake of sb** par égard pour qqn, pour (l'amour de) qqn ▸ **for the children's sake** pour les enfants ▸ **for the sake of my health** pour ma santé ▸ **for the sake of argument** à titre d'exemple ▸ **to do sthg for its own sake** faire qqch pour le plaisir ▸ **for God's** ***OR*** **heaven's sake** pour l'amour de Dieu ***OR*** du ciel.

salacious [sə'leɪʃəs] **adj** *fml* [joke, book, look] salace, grivois(e), obscène.

salad ['sæləd] **n** salade *f*.

salad bar **n** [restaurant] *restaurant où l'on mange des salades* / [area] salad bar *m*.

salad bowl **n** saladier *m*.

salad cream **n** *UK sorte de mayonnaise douce*.

salad dressing **n** vinaigrette *f*.

salad oil **n** huile *f* de table.

salamander ['sæləˌmændər] **n** salamandre *f*.

salami [sə'lɑ:mɪ] **n** salami *m*.

salaried ['sælərɪd] **adj** salarié(e).

salary ['sælərɪ] (**pl -ies**) **n** salaire *m*, traitement *m*.

salary scale n échelle *f* des salaires.

sale [seɪl] n **1.** [gen] vente *f* ▸ **on sale** *UK*, **for sale** *US* en vente ▸ **(up) for sale** à vendre **2.** [at reduced prices] soldes *mpl* ▸ **the shop is having a sale** le magasin fait des soldes ▸ **in a sale** *UK*, **on sale** *US* en solde.
◆ ***sales*** ■ npl **1.** [quantity sold] ventes *fpl* **2.** [at reduced prices] : **the sales** les soldes *mpl*.
■ comp [figures, department] des ventes.

saleability [seɪlə'bɪlɪtɪ] n facilité *f* de vente OR d'écoulement.

saleroom *UK* ['seɪlrʊm], ***salesroom*** *US* ['seɪlzrʊm] n salle *f* des ventes.

sales assistant ['seɪlz-] *UK*, ***salesclerk*** ['seɪlzklɜːrk] *US* n vendeur *m*, -euse *f*.

sales conference n conférence *f* du personnel des ventes.

sales drive n campagne *f* de vente.

sales figures n chiffre *m* de ventes.

sales force n force *f* de vente.

sales forecast n prévision *f* des ventes.

salesman ['seɪlzmən] (pl **-men** [-mən]) n [in shop] vendeur *m* / [travelling] représentant *m* de commerce.

sales manager n directeur *m* commercial, directrice *f* commerciale.

salesmanship ['seɪlzmənʃɪp] n art *m* de la vente, technique *f* de vente.

salesperson ['seɪlzˌpɜːsn] (pl **-people** [-ˌpiːpl]) n [in shop] vendeur *m*, -euse *f* / [rep] représentant *m*, -e *f* (de commerce).

sales pitch n boniment *m*.

sales rep n *inf* représentant *m* de commerce.

sales representative n représentant *m* de commerce.

salesroom *US* = ***saleroom***.

sales slip n *US* [receipt] ticket *m* de caisse.

sales tax n taxe *f* à l'achat.

sales team n équipe *f* de vente.

saleswoman ['seɪlzˌwʊmən] (pl **-women** [-ˌwɪmɪn]) n [in shop] vendeuse *f* / [travelling] représentante *f* de commerce.

salient ['seɪljənt] adj *fml* qui ressort.

saline ['seɪlaɪn] adj salin(e) ▸ **saline drip** perfusion *f* de sérum artificiel.

saliva [sə'laɪvə] n salive *f*.

salivate ['sælɪveɪt] vi saliver.

sallow ['sæləʊ] adj cireux(euse).

sally ['sælɪ] n (pl **-ies**) [sortie] sortie *f*.
◆ ***sally forth*** vi (pt & pp **-ied**) *liter* sortir.

salmon ['sæmən] (pl **salmon** OR **-s**) n saumon *m*.

salmonella [ˌsælmə'nelə] n salmonelle *f*.

salmon pink ■ adj rose saumon *(inv)*.
■ n rose *m* saumon.

salon ['sælɒn] n salon *m*.

saloon [sə'luːn] n **1.** *UK* [car] berline *f* **2.** *US* [bar] saloon *m* **3.** *UK* [in pub] : **saloon (bar)** bar *m* **4.** [in ship] salon *m*.

salopettes [ˌsælə'pets] npl combinaison *f* de ski.

salt [sɔːlt OR sɒlt] ■ n sel *m* ▸ **the salt of the earth** le sel de la terre ▸ **to rub salt into sb's wounds** remuer OR retourner le couteau dans la plaie ▸ **take what he says with a pinch of salt** ne prenez pas ce qu'il dit au pied de la lettre.
■ comp [food] salé(e).
■ vt [food] saler / [roads] mettre du sel sur.
◆ ***salt away*** vt sep mettre de côté.

SALT [sɔːlt] (abbr of ***Strategic Arms Limitation Talks/Treaty***) n SALT *m négociations américano-soviétiques sur la limitation des armes stratégiques*.

saltcellar *UK* [ˌsɔːlt'selə], ***saltshaker*** *US* [ˌsɔːlt'ʃeɪkəʳ] n salière *f*.

salted ['sɔːltɪd] adj salé(e).

saltpetre *UK*, ***saltpeter*** *US* [ˌsɔːlt'piːtəʳ] n salpêtre *m*.

saltshaker *US* = ***saltcellar***.

saltwater ['sɔːltˌwɔːtəʳ] ■ n eau *f* de mer.
■ adj de mer.

salty ['sɔːltɪ] (comp **-ier**, superl **-iest**) adj [food] salé(e) / [water] saumâtre.

salubrious [sə'luːbrɪəs] adj *fml* salubre.

salutary ['sæljʊtrɪ] adj *fml* salutaire.

salute [sə'luːt] ■ n salut *m*.
■ vt saluer.
■ vi faire un salut.

Salvadorean, ***Salvadorian*** [ˌsælvə'dɔːrɪən] ■ adj salvadorien(enne).
■ n Salvadorien *m*, -enne *f*.

salvage ['sælvɪdʒ] ■ n *(U)* **1.** [rescue of ship] sauvetage *m* **2.** [property rescued] biens *mpl* sauvés.
■ vt sauver.

salvage vessel n bateau *m* de sauvetage.

salvation [sæl'veɪʃn] n salut *m*.

Salvation Army n : **the Salvation Army** l'Armée *f* du Salut.

salve [sælv] vt : **to do sthg to salve one's conscience** faire qqch pour avoir la conscience en paix.

salver ['sælvəʳ] n plateau *m*.

salvo ['sælvəʊ] (pl **-s** OR **-es**) n salve *f*.

Samaritan [sə'mærɪtn] n : **good Samaritan** bon Samaritain *m*.

samba ['sæmbə] n samba *f*.

same [seɪm] ■ adj même ▸ **she was wearing the same jumper as I was** elle portait le même pull que moi ▸ **at the same time** en même temps ▸ **one and the same** un seul et même (une seule et même).
■ pron : **the same** le même (la même), les mêmes *(pl)* ▸ **I'll have the same as you** je prendrai la même chose que toi ▸ **she earns the same as I do** elle gagne autant que moi ▸ **to do the same** faire de même, en faire autant ▸ **all** OR

just the same [anyway] quand même, tout de même ▸ **it's all the same to me** ça m'est égal ▸ **it's not the same** ce n'est pas pareil.
■ **adv : the same** [treat, spell] de la même manière.

same-day **adj** COMM [processing, delivery] dans la journée.

sameness ['seɪmnɪs] **n** *pej* monotonie *f*.

Samoa [sə'məʊə] **n** Samoa *m* ▸ **in Samoa** à Samoa ▸ **American Samoa** les Samoa américaines *fpl*.

Samoan [sə'məʊən] ■ **adj** samoan(e).
■ **n** Samoan *m*, -e *f*.

samosa [sə'məʊsə] **n** *petit pâté indien à la viande ou aux légumes*.

sample ['sɑːmpl] ■ **n** échantillon *m*
■ **vt 1.** [taste] goûter **2.** MUS faire le sampling de.

sampler ['sɑːmpləʳ] **n** SEW modèle *m* de broderie.

sampling ['sɑːmplɪŋ] **n** [gen & COMPUT] échantillonnage *m* / MUS échantillonnage *m*, sampling *m*.

sanatorium, US ***sanitorium*** (pl **-riums** *OR* **-ria** [-rɪə]) [ˌsænə'tɔːrɪəm] **n** sanatorium *m*.

sanctify ['sæŋktɪfaɪ] (pt & pp **-ied**) **vt** sanctifier.

sanctimonious [ˌsæŋktɪ'məʊnjəs] **adj** moralisateur(trice).

sanction ['sæŋkʃn] ■ **n** sanction *f*.
■ **vt** sanctionner.
◆ ***sanctions*** **npl** sanctions *fpl*.

sanctity ['sæŋktətɪ] **n** sainteté *f*.

sanctuary ['sæŋktʃʊərɪ] (pl **-ies**) **n 1.** [for birds, wildlife] réserve *f* **2.** [refuge] asile *m* **3.** [holy place] sanctuaire *m*.

sanctum ['sæŋktəm] (pl -s) **n** *fig* [private place] retraite *f*.

sand [sænd] ■ **n** sable *m*.
■ **vt** [wood] poncer.
◆ ***sands*** **npl** plage *f* de sable.

sandal ['sændl] **n** sandale *f*.

sandalwood ['sændlwʊd] **n** (bois *m* de) santal *m*.

sandbag ['sændbæg] **n** sac *m* de sable.

sandbank ['sændbæŋk] **n** banc *m* de sable.

sandblast ['sændblɑːst] **vt** décaper à la sableuse, sabler.

sandbox US = ***sandpit***.

sandcastle ['sændˌkɑːsl] **n** château *m* de sable.

sand dune **n** dune *f*.

sander ['sændəʳ] **n 1.** [tool] ponceuse *f* **2.** [truck] camion *m* de sablage.

S and M **n** *inf* sadomasochisme *m*.

sandpaper ['sændˌpeɪpəʳ] ■ **n** *(U)* papier *m* de verre.
■ **vt** poncer (au papier de verre).

sandpit UK ['sændpɪt], ***sandbox*** US ['sændbɒks] **n** bac *m* à sable.

sandstone ['sændstəʊn] **n** grès *m*.

sandstorm ['sændstɔːm] **n** tempête *f* de sable.

sand trap **n** US & Can GOLF bunker *m*, fosse *f* de sable *Québec*.

sandwich ['sænwɪdʒ] ■ **n** sandwich *m*.
■ **vt** *fig* **: to be sandwiched between** être (pris(e)) en sandwich entre.

sandwich bar **n** UK ≃ snack *m (où on vend des sandwiches)*.

sandwich board **n** panneau *m* publicitaire *(d'homme sandwich ou posé comme un tréteau)*.

sandwich course **n** UK stage *m* de formation professionnelle.

sandy ['sændɪ] (comp **-ier**, superl **-iest**) **adj 1.** [beach] de sable / [earth] sableux(euse) **2.** [sand-coloured] sable *(inv)*.

sane [seɪn] **adj 1.** [not mad] sain(e) d'esprit **2.** [sensible] raisonnable, sensé(e).

sanely ['seɪnlɪ] **adv** raisonnablement.

sang [sæŋ] **pt** ➤ ***sing***.

sangfroid [ˌsɒŋ'frwɑː] **n** sang-froid *m*.

sanguine ['sæŋgwɪn] **adj** *fml* optimiste.

sanitary ['sænɪtrɪ] **adj 1.** [method, system] sanitaire **2.** [clean] hygiénique, salubre.

sanitary inspector **n** inspecteur *m* de la santé publique.

sanitary towel UK, ***sanitary napkin*** US **n** serviette *f* hygiénique.

sanitation [ˌsænɪ'teɪʃn] **n** *(U)* [in house] installations *fpl* sanitaires.

sanitation worker **n** US *fml* éboueur *m*.

sanitize, UK ***-ise*** ['sænɪtaɪz] **vt** *fig* expurger.

sanitorium US = ***sanatorium***.

sanity ['sænətɪ] **n** *(U)* **1.** [saneness] santé *f* mentale, raison *f* **2.** [good sense] bon sens *m*.

sank [sæŋk] **pt** ➤ ***sink***.

San Marino [ˌsænmə'riːnəʊ] **n** Saint-Marin *m* ▸ **in San Marino** à Saint-Marin.

San Salvador [ˌsæn'sælvədɔːʳ] **n** San Salvador.

Sanskrit ['sænskrɪt] **n** sanskrit *m*, sanscrit *m*.

Santa (Claus) ['sæntə(ˌklɔːz)] **n** le père Noël.

São Paulo [ˌsaʊ'paʊləʊ] **n 1.** [city] São Paulo **2.** [state] **: São Paulo (State)** São Paulo *m*, l'État *m* de São Paulo ▸ **in São Paulo** dans le São Paulo.

sap [sæp] ■ **n 1.** [of plant] sève *f* **2.** *inf dated* [gullible person] nigaud *m*, -e *f*.
■ **vt** (pt & pp **-ped**, cont **-ping**) [weaken] saper.

sapling ['sæplɪŋ] **n** jeune arbre *m*.

sapphire ['sæfaɪəʳ] **n** saphir *m*.

Sarajevo [ˌsærə'jeɪvəʊ] **n** Sarajevo.

sarcasm ['sɑːkæzm] **n** sarcasme *m*.

sarcastic [sɑː'kæstɪk] **adj** sarcastique.

sarcastically [sɑː'kæstɪklɪ] **adv** d'un ton sarcastique.

sarcophagus [sɑː'kɒfəgəs] (pl **-gi** [-gaɪ] *OR* **-guses** [-gəsiːz]) **n** sarcophage *m*.

sardine [sɑː'diːn] **n** sardine *f*.

Sardinia [sɑː'dɪnjə] **n** Sardaigne *f* ▸ **in Sardinia** en Sardaigne.

sardonic [sɑː'dɒnɪk] **adj** sardonique.

sardonically [sɑː'dɒnɪklɪ] **adv** sardoniquement.

Sargasso Sea [sɑː'gæsəʊ-] **n : the Sargasso Sea** la mer des Sargasses.

sari ['sɑːrɪ] **n** sari *m*.

sarky ['sɑːkɪ] (**comp -ier**, **superl -iest**) **adj** *UK inf* sarcastique.

sarong [sə'rɒŋ] **n** sarong *m*.

sarsaparilla [ˌsɑːspə'rɪlə] **n** salsepareille *f*.

sartorial [sɑː'tɔːrɪəl] **adj** *fml* vestimentaire.

SAS (abbr of ***Special Air Service***) **n** *commando d'intervention spéciale de l'armée britannique*.

SASE *US* **abbr of *self-addressed stamped envelope*.**

sash [sæʃ] **n** [of cloth] écharpe *f*.

sash window **n** fenêtre *f* à guillotine.

Saskatchewan [ˌsæs'kætʃɪˌwən] **n** Saskatchewan *m*.

sassy ['sæsɪ] **adj** *US inf* culotté(e).

sat [sæt] **pt & pp** ➤ ***sit***.

SAT [sæt] **n 1.** (abbr of ***Standard Assessment Test***) *examen national en Grande-Bretagne pour les élèves de 7 ans, 11 ans et 13 ans* **2.** (abbr of ***Scholastic Aptitude Test***) *examen d'entrée à l'université aux États-Unis*.

CULTURE

SAT

Aux États-Unis, les étudiants souhaitant entrer à l'université doivent réussir un « test d'aptitude scolaire » (**Scholastic Aptitude Test**), comportant une épreuve mathématique et un oral (compréhension de la lecture, test d'analogie et analyse de phrases), qu'ils peuvent recommencer plusieurs fois pour améliorer leurs chances d'admission. D'autres passent l'ACT (**American College Test**), un examen très prisé par certaines universités du Middle West, qui permet de tester le niveau en mathématiques, la lecture en anglais et le raisonnement scientifique. L'inscription dans les facultés dépend de cette évaluation finale, des notes obtenues durant leur scolarité, des activités extrascolaires et des recommandations des professeurs. L'examen se compose de tests de rédaction, de lectures critiques et de mathématiques. Au Royaume-Uni, le « Test de curriculum national », qui porte sur l'écriture, l'orthographe, les mathématiques et les sciences, évalue le niveau scolaire des écoliers à 7, 11 et 13 ans.

Sat. (abbr of ***Saturday***) sam.

Satan ['seɪtn] **n** Satan *m*.

satanic [sə'tænɪk] **adj** satanique.

satanism ['seɪtənɪzm] **n** satanisme *m*.

satanist ['seɪtənɪst] ■ **adj** sataniste.
■ **n** sataniste *mf*.

satchel ['sætʃəl] **n** cartable *m*.

sated ['seɪtɪd] **adj** *liter* **: sated (with)** rassasié(e) (de).

satellite ['sætəlaɪt] ■ **n** satellite *m*.
■ **comp** [country, company] satellite.

satellite broadcast **n** émission *f* retransmise par satellite.

satellite dish **n** antenne *f* parabolique.

satellite link **n** liaison *f* par satellite.

satellite TV **n** télévision *f* par satellite.

satiate ['seɪʃɪeɪt] **vt** *liter* rassasier.

satin ['sætɪn] ■ **n** satin *m*.
■ **comp** [sheets, pyjamas] de *OR* en satin / [wallpaper, finish] satiné(e).

satire ['sætaɪəʳ] **n** satire *f*.

satirical [sə'tɪrɪkl] **adj** satirique.

satirically [sə'tɪrɪklɪ] **adv** satiriquement.

satirist ['sætərɪst] **n** satiriste *mf*.

satirize, *UK* ***-ise*** ['sætəraɪz] **vt** faire la satire de.

satisfaction [ˌsætɪs'fækʃn] **n** satisfaction *f* ▸ **is everything to your satisfaction?** est-ce que tout est à votre convenance? ▸ **the plan was agreed to everyone's satisfaction** le projet fut accepté à la satisfaction générale.

satisfactorily [ˌsætɪs'fæktərəlɪ] **adv** de façon satisfaisante.

satisfactory [ˌsætɪs'fæktərɪ] **adj** satisfaisant(e).

satisfied ['sætɪsfaɪd] **adj 1.** [happy] **: satisfied (with)** satisfait(e) (de) ▸ **a satisfied customer** un client satisfait ▸ **are you satisfied now you've made her cry?** tu es content de l'avoir fait pleurer? **2.** [convinced] **: to be satisfied that** être sûr(e) que.

satisfy ['sætɪsfaɪ] (**pt & pp -ied**) **vt 1.** [gen] satisfaire **2.** [convince] convaincre, persuader ▸ **to satisfy sb that** convaincre qqn que ▸ **to satisfy o.s. that** s'assurer que.

satisfying ['sætɪsfaɪɪŋ] **adj** satisfaisant(e).

satsuma [ˌsæt'suːmə] **n** satsuma *f*.

saturate ['sætʃəreɪt] **vt : to saturate sthg (with)** saturer qqch (de).

saturated fat ['sætʃəreɪtɪd-] **n** matière *f* grasse saturée.

saturation [ˌsætʃə'reɪʃn] **n** saturation *f*.

saturation bombing **n** bombardement *m* intensif.

saturation point **n : to reach saturation point** arriver à saturation *f*.

Saturday ['sætədɪ] ■ **n** samedi *m* ▸ **it's Saturday** on est samedi ▸ **are you going Saturday?** *inf* tu y vas samedi? ▸ **see you Saturday!** *inf* à samedi! ▸ **on Saturday** samedi ▸ **on Saturdays** le samedi ▸ **last Saturday** samedi dernier ▸ **this Saturday** ce samedi ▸ **next Saturday** samedi prochain ▸ **every Saturday** tous les samedis ▸ **every other Saturday** un samedi sur deux ▸ **the Saturday before** l'autre samedi ▸ **the Saturday before last** pas samedi dernier, mais le samedi d'avant ▸ **the Saturday after next, Saturday week** *UK*, **a week on Saturday** *UK* samedi en huit ▸ **to work Saturdays** travailler le samedi.
■ **comp** [paper] du *OR* de samedi ▸ **I have a Saturday appointment** j'ai un rendez-vous samedi ▸ **Saturday**

morning/afternoon/evening samedi matin/après-midi/soir ▸ **a Saturday job** un petit boulot *(le samedi pour gagner de l'argent de poche).*

Saturn ['sætən] **n** [planet] Saturne *f.*

sauce [sɔːs] **n 1.** CULIN sauce *f* **2.** *UK inf dated* [cheek] toupet *m.*

sauce boat **n** saucière *f.*

saucepan ['sɔːspən] **n** casserole *f.*

saucer ['sɔːsəʳ] **n** sous-tasse *f*, soucoupe *f.*

saucy ['sɔːsɪ] (comp **-ier**, superl **-iest**) **adj** *inf* coquin(e).

Saudi Arabia ['saʊdɪ-] **n** Arabie *f* Saoudite ▸ **in Saudi Arabia** en Arabie Saoudite.

Saudi (Arabian) ['saʊdɪ-] ■ **adj** saoudien(enne).
■ **n** [person] Saoudien *m*, -enne *f.*

sauna ['sɔːnə] **n** sauna *m.*

saunter ['sɔːntəʳ] **vi** flâner.

sausage ['sɒsɪdʒ] **n** saucisse *f.*

sausage meat **n** chair *f* à saucisse.

sausage roll **n** *UK* feuilleté *m* à la saucisse.

sauté [*UK* 'səʊteɪ, *US* səʊ'teɪ] ■ **adj** sauté(e).
■ **vt** (pt & pp **sautéed** OR **sautéd**) [potatoes] faire sauter / [onions] faire revenir.

savage ['sævɪdʒ] ■ **adj** [fierce] féroce.
■ **n** sauvage *mf.*
■ **vt** attaquer avec férocité.

savagely ['sævɪdʒlɪ] **adv** sauvagement, brutalement.

savageness ['sævɪdʒnɪs], ***savagery*** ['sævɪdʒrɪ] **n** férocité *f.*

savanna(h) [sə'vænə] **n** savane *f.*

save [seɪv] ■ **vt 1.** [rescue] sauver ▸ **to save sb's life** sauver la vie à OR de qqn **2.** [money - set aside] mettre de côté / [- spend less] économiser ▸ **we saved £10 by buying in bulk** on a économisé 10 livres en achetant en grosses quantités **3.** [time] gagner / [strength] économiser / [food] garder **4.** [avoid] éviter, épargner ▸ **to save sb sthg** épargner qqch à qqn ▸ **to save sb from doing sthg** éviter à qqn de faire qqch **5.** SPORT arrêter **6.** COMPUT sauvegarder.
■ **vi** [save money] mettre de l'argent de côté.
■ **n** SPORT arrêt *m.*
■ **prep** *fml* **: save (for)** sauf, à l'exception de.
◆ ***save up*** **vi** mettre de l'argent de côté.

save as you earn **n** *UK plan d'épargne national par prélèvements mensuels.*

saveloy ['sævəlɔɪ] **n** *UK* cervelas *m.*

saver ['seɪvəʳ] **n 1.** [person] épargnant *m*, -e *f* **2.** [product] bonne affaire *f* ▸ **super saver (ticket)** billet *m* à tarif réduit.

-saver **suffix : it's a real money-saver** ça permet d'économiser de l'argent OR de faire des économies.

saving ['seɪvɪŋ] ■ **n 1.** [thrift] épargne *f* **2.** [money saved] économie *f* ▸ **to make a saving** faire une économie.
■ **prep** *fml* sauf, hormis.

-saving **suffix : energy-saving** [device] d'économie, d'énergie ▸ **time-saving** qui fait gagner du temps.

saving grace **n : its saving grace was...** ce qui le rachetait, c'était...

savings ['seɪvɪŋz] **npl** économies *fpl.*

savings account **n** compte *m* d'épargne.

savings and loan association **n** *US* société *f* de crédit immobilier.

savings bank **n** caisse *f* d'épargne.

saviour *UK*, ***savior*** *US* ['seɪvjəʳ] **n** sauveur *m.*
◆ ***Saviour*** **n : the Saviour** le Sauveur.

savoir-faire [ˌsævwɑː'feəʳ] **n** savoir-vivre *m.*

savour *UK*, ***savor*** *US* ['seɪvəʳ] **vt** *lit & fig* savourer.

savoury *UK*, ***savory*** *US* ■ **adj 1.** *esp UK* [food] salé(e) **2.** [respectable] recommandable.
■ **n** (pl **-ies** ['seɪvərɪ]) *UK* petit plat *m* salé.

Savoy [sə'vɔɪ] **n** Savoie *f* ▸ **in Savoy** en Savoie.

savoy cabbage **n** chou *m* frisé de Milan.

saw [sɔː] ■ **pt** ➤ ***see.***
■ **n** scie *f.*
■ **vt** (*UK* **-ed**, pp **sawn**, *US* **-ed**) scier.

sawdust ['sɔːdʌst] **n** sciure *f* (de bois).

sawed-off shotgun *US* = ***sawn-off shotgun.***

sawmill ['sɔːmɪl] **n** scierie *f*, moulin *m* à scie *Québec.*

sawn [sɔːn] *UK* **pp** ➤ ***saw.***

sawn-off shotgun *UK*, ***sawed-off shotgun*** ['sɔːd-] *US* **n** carabine *f* à canon scié.

sax [sæks] **n** *inf* saxo *m.*

Saxon ['sæksn] ■ **adj** saxon(onne).
■ **n** Saxon *m*, -onne *f.*

saxophone ['sæksəfəʊn] **n** saxophone *m.*

saxophonist [*UK* sæk'sɒfənɪst, *US* 'sæksəfəʊnɪst] **n** saxophoniste *mf.*

say [seɪ] ■ **vt** (pt & pp **said**) **1.** [gen] dire ▸ **could you say that again?** vous pouvez répéter ce que vous venez de dire? ▸ **(let's) say you won the lottery...** supposons que tu gagnes le gros lot... ▸ **it says a lot about him** cela en dit long sur lui ▸ **she's said to be...** on dit qu'elle est... ▸ **I have nothing more to say on the matter** je n'ai rien à ajouter là-dessus ▸ **let's say no more about it** n'en parlons plus ▸ **say no more** n'en dis pas plus ▸ **enough said** [I understand] je vois ▸ **who can say?** qui sait? ▸ **to say the least** c'est le moins qu'on puisse dire ▸ **to say one's piece** dire ce qu'on a à dire ▸ **to say one's prayers** faire sa prière ▸ **to say to o.s.** se dire ▸ **to say nothing of** sans parler de ▸ **that goes without saying** cela va sans dire ▸ **I'll say this for him...** je dois lui rendre cette justice que... ▸ **it has a lot to be said for it** cela a beaucoup d'avantages ▸ **she didn't have much to say for herself** *inf* elle n'avait pas grand-chose à dire ▸ **say when** dis-moi stop **2.** [subj: clock, label] indiquer ▸ **it says "shake well"** c'est marqué "bien agiter".
■ **n : to have a/no say** avoir/ne pas avoir voix au chapitre ▸ **to have a say in sthg** avoir son mot à dire sur qqch ▸ **to have one's say** dire ce que l'on a à dire, dire son mot.
◆ ***that is to say*** **adv** c'est-à-dire.

SAYE **n abbr of *save as you earn.***

saying ['seɪɪŋ] **n** dicton *m.*

say-so **n** *inf* [permission] autorisation *f.*

SBNA (abbr of ***Small Business Administration***) **n** *organisme fédéral américain d'aide aux petites entreprises.*

s/c abbr of ***self-contained.***

SC ■ n abbr of ***supreme court***.
■ abbr of ***South Carolina***.

S/C abbr of ***self contained***.

scab [skæb] n **1.** [of wound] croûte *f* **2.** *inf pej* [non-striker] jaune *m*.

scabby ['skæbɪ] (comp **-ier**, superl **-iest**) **adj** couvert(e) de croûtes.

scabies ['skeɪbi:z] n *(U)* gale *f*.

scaffold ['skæfəʊld] n échafaud *m*.

scaffolding ['skæfəldɪŋ] n échafaudage *m*.

scalawag *US* = ***scallywag***.

scald [skɔ:ld] ■ n brûlure *f*.
■ vt ébouillanter ▸ **to scald one's arm** s'ébouillanter le bras.

scalding ['skɔ:ldɪŋ] **adj** bouillant(e).

scale [skeɪl] ■ n **1.** [gen] échelle *f* ▸ **the scale of the map is 1 to 50,000** la carte est au 50 millième ▸ **the scale of the devastation** l'étendue des dégâts ▸ **the sheer scale of the problem** l'ampleur même du problème ▸ **to do sthg on a large scale** faire qqch sur une grande échelle ▸ **to scale** [map, drawing] à l'échelle **2.** [of ruler, thermometer] graduation *f* **3.** MUS gamme *f* **4.** [of fish, snake] écaille *f* ▸ **the scales fell from her eyes** *fig* les écailles lui sont tombées des yeux **5.** *US* = ***scales***.
■ vt **1.** [cliff, mountain, fence] escalader **2.** [fish] écailler.
◆ ***scales*** npl balance *f* ▸ **(a pair of) bathroom scales** un pèse-personne.
◆ ***scale down*** vt insep réduire.

scale diagram n plan *m* à l'échelle.

scale model n modèle *m* réduit.

scallion ['skæljən] n *US* [spring onion] ciboule *f*.

scallop ['skɒləp] ■ n [shellfish] coquille *f* Saint-Jacques.
■ vt [edge, garment] festonner.

scallywag *UK* ['skælɪwæg], **scalawag** *US* ['skæləwæg] n *inf* polisson *m*, -onne *f*.

scalp [skælp] ■ n **1.** ANAT cuir *m* chevelu **2.** [trophy] scalp *m*.
■ vt scalper.

scalpel ['skælpəl] n scalpel *m*.

scalper ['skælpər] n *US* revendeur *m* de billets.

scam [skæm] n *inf* arnaque *f*.

scamp [skæmp] n *inf* coquin *m*, -e *f*.

scamper ['skæmpəʳ] vi trottiner.

scampi ['skæmpɪ] n *(U)* *UK* scampi *mpl*.

scan [skæn] ■ n MED scanographie *f* / [during pregnancy] échographie *f*.
■ vt (pt & pp **-ned**, cont **-ning**) **1.** [examine carefully] scruter **2.** [glance at] parcourir **3.** TECH balayer **4.** COMPUT faire un scannage de.
■ vi (pt & pp **-ned**, cont **-ning**) **1.** LIT se scander **2.** COMPUT scanner.

scandal ['skændl] n **1.** [gen] scandale *m* **2.** [gossip] médisance *f*.

scandalize, *UK* **-ise** ['skændəlaɪz] vt scandaliser.

scandalous ['skændələs] **adj** scandaleux(euse).

scandalously ['skændələslɪ] **adv** **1.** [act] scandaleusement **2.** [speak, write] de manière diffamatoire.

Scandinavia [,skændɪ'neɪvjə] n Scandinavie *f* ▸ **in Scandinavia** en Scandinavie.

Scandinavian [,skændɪ'neɪvjən] ■ **adj** scandinave.
■ n [person] Scandinave *mf*.

scanner ['skænəʳ] n [gen & COMPUT] scanner *m*.

scant [skænt] **adj** insuffisant(e).

scantily ['skæntɪlɪ] **adv** [furnished] pauvrement, chichement / [dressed] légèrement.

scanty ['skæntɪ] (comp **-ier**, superl **-iest**) **adj** [amount, resources] insuffisant(e) / [income] maigre / [dress] minuscule.

scapegoat ['skeɪpgəʊt] n bouc *m* émissaire.

scar [skɑ:ʳ] ■ n cicatrice *f*.
■ vt (pt & pp **-red**, cont **-ring**) **1.** [skin, face] marquer d'une cicatrice / [landscape] défigurer **2.** *fig* [mentally] marquer.

scarce ['skeəs] **adj** rare, peu abondant(e) ▸ **to make o.s. scarce** s'esquiver.

scarcely ['skeəslɪ] **adv** à peine ▸ **scarcely anyone** presque personne ▸ **I scarcely ever go there now** je n'y vais presque ***or*** pratiquement plus jamais ▸ **he scarcely spoke to me** c'est tout juste s'il m'a adressé la parole ▸ **I could scarcely tell his mother, now could I?** je ne pouvais quand même pas le dire à sa mère, non?

scarcity ['skeəsətɪ] n manque *m*.

scare [skeəʳ] ■ n **1.** [sudden fear] : **to give sb a scare** faire peur à qqn **2.** [public fear] panique *f* ▸ **bomb scare** alerte *f* à la bombe.
■ vt faire peur à, effrayer.
◆ ***scare away***, ***scare off*** vt sep faire fuir.

scarecrow ['skeəkrəʊ] n épouvantail *m*.

scared ['skeəd] **adj** apeuré(e) ▸ **to be scared** avoir peur ▸ **to be scared stiff *or* to death** être mort(e) de peur.

scaremongering ['skeə,mʌŋgrɪŋ] n alarmisme *m*.

scarey ['skeərɪ] = ***scary***.

scarf [skɑ:f] (pl **-s *or* scarves** [skɑ:vz]) n [wool] écharpe *f* / [silk] foulard *m*.

scarlet ['skɑ:lət] ■ **adj** écarlate.
■ n écarlate *f*.

scarlet fever n scarlatine *f*.

scarves [skɑ:vz] npl ➤ ***scarf***.

scary [skeərɪ] (comp **-ier**, superl **-iest**) **adj** *inf* qui fait peur.

scathing ['skeɪðɪŋ] **adj** [criticism] acerbe / [reply] cinglant(e) ▸ **to be scathing about sb/sthg** critiquer qqn/qqch de manière acerbe.

scathingly ['skeɪðɪŋlɪ] **adv** [retort, criticize] de manière cinglante.

scatter ['skætəʳ] ■ vt [clothes, paper] éparpiller / [seeds] semer à la volée.
■ vi se disperser.

scatterbrained ['skætəbreɪnd] **adj** *inf* écervelé(e).

scattered ['skætəd] **adj** [wreckage, population] dispersé(e) / [paper] éparpillé(e) / [showers] intermittent(e).

scatter-gun n fusil *m* de chasse.

scattering ['skætərɪŋ] n [small number] petit nombre *m* / [small amount] petite quantité *f*.

scatty ['skætɪ] (comp **-ier**, superl **-iest**) adj *UK inf* écervelé(e).

scavenge ['skævɪndʒ] ■ vt [object] récupérer.
■ vi [person] **: to scavenge for sthg** faire les poubelles pour trouver qqch.

scavenger ['skævɪndʒəʳ] n **1.** [animal] animal *m* nécrophage **2.** [person] personne *f* qui fait les poubelles.

SCE (abbr of ***Scottish Certificate of Education***) n *certificat de fin d'études secondaires en Écosse.*

scenario [sɪ'nɑːrɪəʊ] (pl -s) n **1.** [possible situation] hypothèse *f*, scénario *m* **2.** [of film, play] scénario *m*.

scene [siːn] n **1.** [in play, film, book] scène *f* ▸ **the scene is set** *OR* **takes place in Bombay** la scène se passe *OR* l'action se déroule à Bombay ▸ **to make a scene** *fig* faire une scène ▸ **behind the scenes** dans les coulisses
2. [sight] spectacle *m*, vue *f* / [picture] tableau *m* ▸ **scenes of horror/violence** scènes d'horreur/de violence ▸ **just picture the scene** essayez de vous représenter la scène
3. [location] lieu *m*, endroit *m* ▸ **the scene of the crime** le lieu du crime ▸ **on the scene** sur les lieux ▸ **the police were soon on the scene** la police est rapidement arrivée sur les lieux *OR* sur place ▸ **a change of scene** un changement de décor
4. [area of activity] **: the political scene** la scène politique ▸ **the music scene** le monde de la musique ▸ **it's not my scene** *inf* ce n'est pas mon truc ▸ **he disappeared from the scene for a few years** il a disparu de la circulation *OR* de la scène pendant quelques années
▸▸ **to set the scene for sb** mettre qqn au courant de la situation ▸ **to set the scene for sthg** préparer la voie à qqch.

scenery ['siːnərɪ] n *(U)* **1.** [of countryside] paysage *m* **2.** THEAT décor *m*, décors *mpl*.

scenic ['siːnɪk] adj [tour] touristique ▸ **a scenic view** un beau panorama.

scenic route n route *f* touristique.

scent [sent] ■ n **1.** [smell - of flowers] senteur *f*, parfum *m* / [- of animal] odeur *f*, fumet *m* **2.** *fig* [track] piste *f* **3.** *(U)* [perfume] parfum *m*.
■ vt *lit* & *fig* sentir.

scented ['sentɪd] adj parfumé(e).

scepter *US* = ***sceptre***.

sceptic *UK*, ***skeptic*** *US* ['skeptɪk] n sceptique *mf*.

sceptical *UK*, ***skeptical*** *US* ['skeptɪkl] adj **: sceptical (about)** sceptique (sur).

scepticism *UK*, ***skepticism*** *US* ['skeptɪsɪzm] n scepticisme *m*.

sceptre *UK*, ***scepter*** *US* ['septəʳ] n sceptre *m*.

SCF (abbr of ***Save the Children Fund***) n *association caritative britannique s'occupant des enfants.*

schedule [*UK* 'ʃedjuːl, *US* 'skedʒʊl] ■ n **1.** [plan] programme *m*, plan *m* ▸ **(according) to schedule** selon le programme, comme prévu(e) ▸ **the work was carried out according to schedule** le travail a été effectué selon les prévisions ▸ **on schedule** [at expected time] à l'heure (prévue) / [on expected day] à la date prévue ▸ **ahead of/behind schedule** en avance/en retard (sur le programme) ▸ **to fall behind schedule** prendre du retard sur les prévisions de travail
2. [list - of times] horaire *m* / [- of prices] tarif *m*
3. *US* [calendar] calendrier *m* / [timetable] emploi *m* du temps.
■ vt **: to schedule sthg (for)** prévoir qqch (pour) ▸ **the meeting was scheduled for 3 o'clock/Wednesday** la réunion était prévue pour 15 heures/mercredi ▸ **it's scheduled as a topic for the next meeting** c'est inscrit à l'ordre du jour de la prochaine réunion.

scheduled [*UK* 'ʃedjuːld, *US* 'skedʒʊld] adj **1.** [planned] prévu (e) ▸ **at the scheduled time** à l'heure prévue ▸ **we announce a change to our scheduled programmes** TV nous annonçons une modification de nos programmes **2.** [regular - stop, change] habituel(elle) **3.** [official - prices] tarifé(e) **4.** *UK* ADMIN **: scheduled building** bâtiment *m* classé (monument historique) ▸ **the scheduled territories** la zone sterling.

scheduled flight n vol *m* régulier.

schematic [skɪ'mætɪk] adj schématique.

scheme [skiːm] ■ n **1.** [plan] plan *m*, projet *m* **2.** *pej* [dishonest plan] combine *f* **3.** [arrangement] arrangement *m* ▸ **colour scheme** combinaison *f* de couleurs ▸ **the scheme of things** l'ordre des choses.
■ vt *pej* **: to scheme to do sthg** conspirer pour faire qqch.
■ vi *pej* conspirer.

scheming ['skiːmɪŋ] adj intrigant(e).

schism ['sɪzm *OR* 'skɪzm] n schisme *m*.

schizophrenia [ˌskɪtsə'friːnjə] n schizophrénie *f*.

schizophrenic [ˌskɪtsə'frenɪk] ■ adj schizophrène.
■ n schizophrène *mf*.

schlepp [ʃlep] *inf* ■ vt trimbaler.
■ vi **: to schlepp (around)** se trimbaler.

schmal(t)z [ʃmɔːlts] n *inf* sentimentalité *f* à la guimauve.

schmuck [ʃmʌk] n *US vulg* connard *m*.

scholar ['skɒləʳ] n **1.** [expert] érudit *m*, -e *f*, savant *m*, -e *f* **2.** *dated* [student] écolier *m*, -ère *f*, élève *mf* **3.** [holder of scholarship] boursier *m*, -ère *f*.

scholarly ['skɒləlɪ] adj **1.** [person] érudit(e), cultivé(e) **2.** [article, work] savant(e) **3.** [approach] rigoureux(euse), scientifique **4.** [circle] universitaire.

scholarship ['skɒləʃɪp] n **1.** [grant] bourse *f* (d'études) **2.** [learning] érudition *f*.

scholastic [skə'læstɪk] adj *fml* scolaire.

school [skuːl] n **1.** [gen] école *f* / [secondary school] lycée *m*, collège *m* ▸ **to be at** *OR* **in school** être à l'école *OR* en classe ▸ **I was at school with him** j'étais en classe avec lui, c'était un de mes camarades de classe ▸ **the whole school is** *OR* **are invited** toute l'école est invitée ▸ **to go back to school** [after illness] reprendre l'école / [after holidays] rentrer ▸ **school starts back next week** c'est la rentrée (scolaire *OR* des classes) la semaine prochaine **2.** [university department] faculté *f* **3.** *US* [university] université *f* **4.** [of fish] banc *m*.

school age n âge *m* scolaire.

schoolbag ['sku:lbæg] **n** cartable *m*.

schoolbook ['sku:lbʊk] **n** livre *m* scolaire *OR* de classe.

schoolboy ['sku:lbɔɪ] **n** écolier *m*, élève *m*.

school bus **n** car *m* de ramassage scolaire.

schoolchild ['sku:ltʃaɪld] (pl **-children** [-tʃɪldrən]) **n** écolier *m*, -ère *f*, élève *mf*.

schooldays ['sku:ldeɪz] **npl** années *fpl* d'école.

school district **n** *US aux États-Unis, autorité locale décisionnaire dans le domaine de l'enseignement primaire et secondaire.*

school friend **n** camarade *mf* d'école.

schoolgirl ['sku:lgɜ:l] **n** écolière *f*, élève *f*.

school holiday **n** *UK* jour *m* de congé scolaire ▸ **during the school holidays** pendant les vacances *OR* congés scolaires.

school hours **npl** heures *fpl* de classe *OR* d'école ▸ **in school hours** pendant les heures de classe ▸ **out of school hours** en dehors des heures de classe.

schooling ['sku:lɪŋ] **n** instruction *f*.

schoolkid ['sku:lkɪd] **n** *inf* écolier *m*, -ère *f*, élève *mf*.

school-leaver [-ˌli:vəʳ] **n** *UK élève qui a fini ses études secondaires.*

school-leaving age [-'li:vɪŋ-] **n** *UK* âge *m* de fin de scolarité.

schoolmarm ['sku:lmɑ:m] **n** *US* institutrice *f*.

schoolmaster ['sku:lˌmɑ:stəʳ] **n** *dated* [primary] instituteur *m*, maître *m* d'école / [secondary] professeur *m*.

schoolmate ['sku:lmeɪt] **n** camarade *mf* d'école.

schoolmistress ['sku:lˌmɪstrɪs] **n** *dated* [primary] institutrice *f*, maîtresse *f* d'école / [secondary] professeur *m*.

school of thought **n** école *f* (de pensée).

school report **n** *UK* bulletin *m*.

schoolroom ['sku:lrʊm] **n** salle *f* de classe.

schoolteacher ['sku:lˌti:tʃəʳ] **n** [primary] instituteur *m*, -trice *f* / [secondary] professeur *m*.

school uniform **n** uniforme *m* scolaire.

schoolwork ['sku:lwɜ:k] **n** *(U)* travail *m* scolaire *OR* de classe.

schoolyard **n** *US* cour *f* de récréation.

school year **n** année *f* scolaire.

schooner ['sku:nəʳ] **n 1.** [ship] schooner *m*, goélette *f* **2.** *UK* [sherry glass] grand verre *m* à xérès.

sciatica [saɪ'ætɪkə] **n** sciatique *f*.

science ['saɪəns] ■ **n** science *f*.
■ **comp** [student] en sciences / [degree] de *OR* ès sciences / [course] de sciences.

science fiction **n** science-fiction *f*.

science park **n** parc *m* scientifique.

scientific [ˌsaɪən'tɪfɪk] **adj** scientifique.

scientifically [ˌsaɪən'tɪfɪklɪ] **adv** scientifiquement, de manière scientifique ▸ **scientifically speaking** d'un *OR* du point de vue scientifique.

scientist ['saɪəntɪst] **n** scientifique *mf*.

sci-fi [ˌsaɪ'faɪ] (abbr of ***science fiction***) **n** *inf* science-fiction *f*, S.F. *f*

Scilly Isles ['sɪlɪ-], ***Scillies*** ['sɪlɪz] **npl : the Scilly Isles** les îles *fpl* Sorlingues ▸ **in the Scilly Isles** aux îles Sorlingues.

scintillating ['sɪntɪleɪtɪŋ] **adj** brillant(e).

scissors ['sɪzəz] **npl** ciseaux *mpl* ▸ **a pair of scissors** une paire de ciseaux.

sclerosis [sklɪ'rəʊsɪs] ➤ ***multiple sclerosis***.

scoff [skɒf] ■ **vt** *UK inf* bouffer, boulotter.
■ **vi : to scoff (at)** se moquer (de).

scold [skəʊld] **vt** gronder, réprimander.

scone [skɒn] **n** scone *m*.

scoop [sku:p] ■ **n 1.** [for sugar] pelle *f* à main / [for ice cream] cuiller *f* à glace **2.** [of ice cream] boule *f* **3.** [news report] exclusivité *f*, scoop *m*.
■ **vt** [with hands] prendre avec les mains / [with scoop] prendre avec une pelle à main.
◆ ***scoop out*** **vt sep** évider.

scoop neck **n** décolleté *m*.

scoot [sku:t] **vi** *inf* filer.

scooter ['sku:təʳ] **n 1.** [toy] trottinette *f* **2.** [motorcycle] scooter *m*.

scope [skəʊp] **n** *(U)* **1.** [opportunity] occasion *f*, possibilité *f* **2.** [of report, inquiry] étendue *f*, portée *f*.

scorch [skɔ:tʃ] ■ **vt** [clothes] brûler légèrement, roussir / [skin] brûler / [land, grass] dessécher.
■ **vi** roussir.

scorched earth policy [skɔ:tʃt-] **n** politique *f* de la terre brûlée.

scorcher ['skɔ:tʃəʳ] **n** *inf* [day] journée *f* torride.

scorching ['skɔ:tʃɪŋ] **adj** *inf* [day] torride / [sun] brûlant(e).

score [skɔ:ʳ] ■ **n 1.** SPORT score *m* ▸ **there was still no score at half-time** à la mi-temps, aucun but n'avait encore été marqué ▸ **what's the score?** FOOTBALL quel est le score? / [in tennis] où en est le jeu? / *fig* on en est où? ▸ **to know the score** *inf* connaître le topo **2.** [in test] note *f* **3.** *dated* [twenty] vingt **4.** MUS partition *f* ▸ **Cleo wrote the (film) score** Cleo est l'auteur de la musique (du film) **5.** [subject] **: on that score** à ce sujet, sur ce point.
■ **vt 1.** [goal, point] marquer ▸ **to score 100%** avoir 100 sur 100 ▸ **the bomber scored a direct hit** le bombardier a visé en plein sur la cible **2.** [success, victory] remporter **3.** [cut] entailler.
■ **vi 1.** SPORT marquer (un but/point) ▸ **the team didn't score** l'équipe n'a pas marqué **2.** [succeed] **: to score over sb** marquer un point contre qqn ▸ **that's where we score** c'est là que nous l'emportons, c'est là que nous avons l'avantage.
◆ ***scores*** **npl : scores of** des tas de, plein de ▸ **scores of people** beaucoup de gens.
◆ ***score out*** **vt sep** *UK* barrer, rayer.

scoreboard ['skɔ:bɔ:d] **n** tableau *m*.

scorecard ['skɔ:kɑ:d] **n** carte *f* de score.

score draw n FOOTBALL match *m* nul *(où chaque équipe a marqué).*

scoreline ['skɔ:laɪn] n score *m.*

scorer ['skɔ:rəʳ] n marqueur *m.*

scoring ['skɔ:rɪŋ] n *(U)* **1.** [of goals] marquage *m* d'un but / [number scored] buts *mpl* (marqués) **2.** [scorekeeping] marquage *m* des points, marque *f* / [points scored] points *mpl* marqués ▸ **I'm not sure about the scoring** je ne suis pas sûr de la manière dont on marque les points **3.** [scratching] rayures *fpl*, éraflures *fpl* / [notching] entaille *f*, entailles *fpl* / GEOL striage *m* **4.** MUS [orchestration] orchestration *f* / [arrangement] arrangement *m* / [composition] écriture *f.*

scorn [skɔ:n] ■ n *(U)* mépris *m*, dédain *m* ▸ **to pour scorn on sb** accabler qqn de mépris.
■ vt **1.** [person, attitude] mépriser **2.** [help, offer] rejeter, dédaigner.

scornful ['skɔ:nfʊl] adj méprisant(e) ▸ **to be scornful of sthg** mépriser qqch, dédaigner qqch.

scornfully ['skɔ:nfʊlɪ] adv avec mépris, dédaigneusement ▸ **"of course not", he said scornfully** "bien sûr que non", dit-il d'un ton méprisant.

Scorpio ['skɔ:pɪəʊ] (pl -s) n Scorpion *m* ▸ **to be (a) Scorpio** être Scorpion.

scorpion ['skɔ:pjən] n scorpion *m.*

Scot [skɒt] n Écossais *m*, -e *f.*

scotch [skɒtʃ] vt [rumour] étouffer / [plan] faire échouer.

Scotch [skɒtʃ] ■ adj écossais(e).
■ n scotch *m*, whisky *m.*

Scotch egg n *UK œuf dur enrobé de chair à saucisse et recouvert de chapelure.*

Scotch (tape)® n *US* Scotch® *m.*

scot-free adj *inf* : **to get off scot-free** s'en tirer sans être puni(e).

Scotland ['skɒtlənd] n Écosse *f* ▸ **in Scotland** en Écosse.

Scotland Yard n *ancien nom du siège de la police à Londres (aujourd'hui New Scotland Yard).*

Scots [skɒts] ■ adj écossais(e).
■ n [dialect] écossais *m.*

Scotsman ['skɒtsmən] (pl -men [-mən]) n Écossais *m.*

Scotswoman ['skɒtswʊmən] (pl -women [-ˌwɪmɪn]) n Écossaise *f.*

Scottish ['skɒtɪʃ] adj écossais(e).

Scottish National Party n *parti nationaliste écossais.*

Scottish Parliament n Parlement *m* écossais.

scoundrel ['skaʊndrəl] n *dated* gredin *m.*

scour [skaʊəʳ] vt **1.** [clean] récurer **2.** [search - town] parcourir / [- countryside] battre.

scourer ['skaʊrəʳ] n *UK* [pad] tampon *m* à récurer / [powder] poudre *f* à récurer.

scourge [skɜ:dʒ] n *fml* fléau *m.*

scouring pad ['skaʊərɪŋ-] n tampon *m* à récurer.

Scouse [skaʊs] n *UK inf* **1.** [person] habitant *m*, -e *f* de Liverpool **2.** [accent] accent *m* de Liverpool.

scout [skaʊt] n MIL éclaireur *m.*
◆ ***Scout*** n [boy scout] Scout *m.*
◆ ***scout around*** vi : **to scout around (for)** aller à la recherche (de).

scoutmaster ['skaʊtˌmɑ:stəʳ] n chef *m* scout.

scowl [skaʊl] ■ n regard *m* noir, air *m* renfrogné.
■ vi se renfrogner, froncer les sourcils ▸ **to scowl at sb** jeter des regards noirs à qqn.

scowling ['skaʊlɪŋ] adj [face] renfrogné(e), hargneux(euse).

SCR (abbr of ***senior common room***) n *UK salle des étudiants de 3e cycle.*

Scrabble® ['skræbl] n Scrabble® *m.*

scrabble ['skræbl] vi **1.** [scrape] : **to scrabble at sthg** gratter qqch **2.** [feel around] : **to scrabble around for sthg** tâtonner pour trouver qqch.

scraggy ['skrægɪ] (comp -ier, superl -iest) adj décharné(e), maigre.

scram [skræm] (pt & pp -med, cont -ming) vi *inf* filer, ficher le camp.

scramble ['skræmbl] ■ n [rush] bousculade *f*, ruée *f* ▸ **there was a scramble for the door** tout le monde s'est rué vers la porte ▸ **a scramble for profits/for jobs** une course effrénée au profit/à l'emploi.
■ vi **1.** [climb] : **to scramble up a hill** grimper une colline en s'aidant des mains *OR* à quatre pattes ▸ **to scramble over rocks** escalader des rochers en s'aidant des mains **2.** [compete] : **everyone was scrambling to get to the telephones** tout le monde se ruait vers les téléphones ▸ **to scramble for sthg** se disputer qqch ▸ **young people are having to scramble for jobs** les jeunes doivent se battre *OR* se démener pour trouver un boulot.
■ vt RADIO, TELEC & CULIN brouiller.

scrambled eggs ['skræmbld-] npl œufs *mpl* brouillés.

scrambler ['skræmbləʳ] n COMPUT brouilleur *m.*

scrambling ['skræmblɪŋ] n **1.** *UK* SPORT trial *m* **2.** [in rock climbing] grimpée *f* à quatre pattes.

scrap [skræp] ■ n **1.** [of paper, material] bout *m* / [of information] fragment *m* / [of conversation] bribe *f* ▸ **it won't make a scrap of difference** cela ne changera absolument rien ▸ **there isn't a scrap of truth in the story** il n'y a pas une parcelle de vérité *OR* il n'y a absolument rien de vrai dans cette histoire **2.** [metal] ferraille *f* ▸ **we sold the car for scrap** on a vendu la voiture à la ferraille *OR* à la casse **3.** *inf* [fight, quarrel] bagarre *f.*
■ vt (pt & pp -ped, cont -ping) [car] mettre à la ferraille / [plan, system] abandonner, laisser tomber.
◆ ***scraps*** npl [food] restes *mpl.*

scrapbook ['skræpbʊk] n album *m (de coupures de journaux).*

scrap dealer n ferrailleur *m*, marchand *m* de ferraille.

scrape [skreɪp] ■ n **1.** [scraping noise] raclement *m*, grattement *m* **2.** *inf dated* [difficult situation] : **to get into a scrape** se fourrer dans le pétrin.

■ **vt 1.** [clean, rub] gratter, racler ▸ **to scrape sthg off sthg** enlever qqch de qqch en grattant *OR* raclant **2.** [surface, car, skin] érafler.
■ **vi** gratter.
◆ ***scrape through*** **vt insep** réussir de justesse.
◆ ***scrape together***, ***scrape up*** **vt sep : to scrape some money together** réunir de l'argent en raclant les fonds de tiroirs.

scraper ['skreɪpəʳ] **n** grattoir *m*, racloir *m*.

scrap heap **n** tas *m* de ferraille ▸ **on the scrap heap** *fig* au rebut, au placard.

scrapings ['skreɪpɪŋz] **npl** raclures *fpl*.

scrap merchant **n** *UK* ferrailleur *m*, marchand *m* de ferraille.

scrap metal **n** ferraille *f*.

scrap paper, ***scratch paper*** *US* **n** (papier *m*) brouillon *m*.

scrappy ['skræpɪ] **(comp -ier, superl -iest) adj 1.** [work, speech] décousu(e) **2.** *US inf* [feisty] bagarreur (euse).

scrapyard ['skræpjɑːd] **n** parc *m* à ferraille.

scratch [skrætʃ] ■ **n 1.** [for itch] grattement *m* ▸ **the dog was having a good scratch** le chien se grattait un bon coup **2.** [wound] égratignure *f*, éraflure *f* ▸ **I've got a scratch on my hand** je me suis égratigné la main **3.** [on glass, paint] éraflure *f*
▸▸ **to be up to scratch** être à la hauteur ▸ **her work still isn't up to scratch** son travail n'est toujours pas satisfaisant ▸ **to do sthg from scratch** faire qqch à partir de rien ▸ **I learnt Italian from scratch in six months** j'ai appris l'italien en six mois en ayant commencé à zéro.
■ **vt 1.** [wound] écorcher, égratigner ▸ **she scratched her hand on the brambles** elle s'est écorché *OR* égratigné la main dans les ronces ▸ **the cat scratched my hand** le chat m'a griffé la main **2.** [mark - paint, glass] rayer, érafler ▸ **the car's hardly scratched** la voiture n'a presque rien *OR* n'a pratiquement aucune éraflure **3.** [rub] gratter ▸ **to scratch o.s.** se gratter ▸ **to scratch one's head** se gratter la tête ▸ **you've barely scratched the surface** *fig* vous avez seulement effleuré la question **4.** SPORT [cancel] annuler.
■ **vi** gratter / [person] se gratter.

scratch card **n** carte *f* à gratter.

scratchpad ['skrætʃpæd] **n** *US* bloc-notes *m*.

scratch paper *US* = ***scrap paper***.

scratchy ['skrætʃɪ] **(comp -ier, superl -iest) adj 1.** [record] qui grésille, qui craque **2.** [material] qui gratte.

scrawl [skrɔːl] ■ **n** griffonnage *m*, gribouillage *m*.
■ **vt** griffonner, gribouiller.

scrawny ['skrɔːnɪ] **(comp -ier, superl -iest) adj** [person] efflanqué(e) / [body, animal] décharné(e).

scream [skriːm] ■ **n 1.** [cry] cri *m* perçant, hurlement *m* / [of laughter] éclat *m* **2.** *inf* [funny person] **: he's a scream** il est tordant.
■ **vt** hurler.
■ **vi** [cry out] crier, hurler.

screaming ['skriːmɪŋ] **adj** [fans] qui crie, qui hurle / [tyres] qui crisse / [sirens, jets] qui hurle / [need] criant(e) ▸ **screaming headlines** grandes manchettes *fpl*.

scree [skriː] **n** éboulis *m*.

screech [skriːtʃ] ■ **n 1.** [cry] cri *m* perçant **2.** [of tyres] crissement *m*.
■ **vt** hurler.
■ **vi 1.** [cry out] pousser des cris perçants **2.** [tyres] crisser.

screen [skriːn] ■ **n 1.** [gen] écran *m* **2.** [panel] paravent *m*.
■ **vt 1.** CIN projeter, passer / TV téléviser, passer **2.** [hide] cacher, masquer **3.** [shield] protéger **4.** [candidate, employee] passer au crible, filtrer **5.** MED **: to screen sb for sthg** faire subir à qqn un test de dépistage pour qqch.
◆ ***screen off*** **vt sep** séparer par un paravent.

screen break **n** COMPUT pause *f*.

screen door **n** porte *f* avec moustiquaire.

screen dump **n** COMPUT vidage *m* d'écran.

screening ['skriːnɪŋ] **n 1.** CIN projection *f* / TV passage *m* à la télévision **2.** [for security] sélection *f*, tri *m* **3.** MED dépistage *m*.

screen memory **n** souvenir écran *m*.

screenplay ['skriːnpleɪ] **n** scénario *m*.

screen print **n** sérigraphie *f*.

screen printing **n** sérigraphie *f*.

screen process **n** sérigraphie *f*.

screen saver **n** COMPUT économiseur *m* (d'écran).

screenshot ['skriːnʃɑt] **n** copie *f* d'écran / capture *f* d'écran.

screen test **n** bout *m* d'essai.

screenwriter ['skriːnˌraɪtəʳ] **n** scénariste *mf*.

screw [skruː] ■ **n** [for fastening] vis *f*.
■ **vt 1.** [fix with screws] **: to screw sthg to sthg** visser qqch à *OR* sur qqch **2.** [twist] visser **3.** *vulg* [woman] baiser.
■ **vi** [bolt, lid] se visser.
◆ ***screw up*** **vt sep 1.** [crumple up] froisser, chiffonner **2.** [eyes] plisser / [face] tordre **3.** *v inf* [ruin] gâcher, bousiller.

screwball ['skruːbɔːl] **n** *inf* [person] cinglé *m*, -e *f*.

screwdriver ['skruːˌdraɪvəʳ] **n** [tool] tournevis *m*.

screwed-up **adj 1.** [crumpled] froissé(e), chiffonné(e) **2.** *inf* [confused] paumé(e) / [neurotic] perturbé(e), angoissé(e).

screwtop jar ['skruːtɒp-] **n** pot *m* à couvercle à pas de vis.

screwy ['skruːɪ] **adj** *inf* fou (folle), cinglé(e).

scribble ['skrɪbl] ■ **n** gribouillage *m*, griffonnage *m*.
■ **vt & vi** gribouiller, griffonner.

scribbling ['skrɪblɪŋ] **n** gribouillis *m*, gribouillage *m*.

scribe [skraɪb] **n** scribe *m*.

scrimp [skrɪmp] **vi : to scrimp and save** économiser *OR* lésiner sur tout.

scrip [skrɪp] **n 1.** FIN titre *m* provisoire **2.** [of paper] morceau *m*.

script [skrɪpt] **n 1.** [of play, film] scénario *m*, script *m* **2.** [writing system] écriture *f* **3.** [handwriting] (écriture *f*) script *m*.

scripted ['skrɪptɪd] **adj** préparé(e) à l'avance.

Scriptures ['skrɪptʃəz] **npl : the Scriptures** les (saintes) Écritures *fpl*.

scriptwriter ['skrɪpt,raɪtəʳ] **n** scénariste *mf*.

scroll [skrəʊl] ■ **n** rouleau *m*.
■ **vt** COMPUT faire défiler.
◆ ***scroll down*** **vi** COMPUT défiler vers le bas.
◆ ***scroll through*** **vt insep** COMPUT [text] parcourir.
◆ ***scroll up*** **vi** COMPUT défiler vers le haut.

scroll bar **n** COMPUT barre *f* de défilement.

scrolling ['skrəʊlɪŋ] **n** COMPUT défilement *m*.

scrooge [skru:dʒ] **n** *inf pej* grippe-sou *m*.

scrotum ['skrəʊtəm] (**pl -ta** [-tə] ***or*** **-tums**) **n** scrotum *m*.

scrounge [skraʊndʒ] *inf* ■ **vt : to scrounge money off sb** taper qqn ▸ **can I scrounge a cigarette off you?** je peux te piquer une cigarette?
■ **vi** faire le parasite ▸ **to scrounge off sb** *UK* vivre aux crochets de qqn.

scrounger ['skraʊndʒəʳ] **n** *inf* parasite *m*.

scrub [skrʌb] ■ **n 1.** [rub] **: to give sthg a scrub** nettoyer qqch à la brosse **2.** *(U)* [undergrowth] broussailles *fpl*.
■ **vt** (**pt & pp -bed, cont -bing**) [floor, clothes] laver ***or*** nettoyer à la brosse / [hands, back] frotter / [saucepan] récurer.

scrubbing brush *UK* ['skrʌbɪŋ-], ***scrub brush*** *US* **n** brosse *f* dure.

scrubland ['skrʌblænd] **n** maquis *m*, garrigue *f*.

scruff [skrʌf] **n : by the scruff of the neck** par la peau du cou.

scruffily ['skrʌfɪlɪ] **adv : scruffily dressed** dépenaillé(e), mal habillé(e).

scruffy ['skrʌfɪ] (**comp -ier, superl -iest**) **adj** mal soigné(e), débraillé(e).

scrumhalf [,skrʌm'hɑ:f] **n** demi *m* de mêlée.

scrum(mage) ['skrʌm(ɪdʒ)] **n** RUGBY mêlée *f*.

scrumptious ['skrʌmpʃəs] **adj** *inf* délicieux(euse), fameux(euse).

scrunch [skrʌntʃ] ■ **vt** écraser, faire craquer.
■ **vi** craquer, crisser.

scrunchie, ***scrunchy*** ['skrʌntʃɪ] **n** chouchou *m*.

scruples ['skru:plz] **npl** scrupules *mpl*.

scrupulous ['skru:pjʊləs] **adj** scrupuleux(euse).

scrupulously ['skru:pjʊləslɪ] **adv** scrupuleusement ▸ **scrupulously clean** d'une propreté méticuleuse ▸ **scrupulously honest** d'une honnêteté scrupuleuse.

scrutinize, *UK* ***-ise*** ['skru:tɪnaɪz] **vt** scruter, examiner attentivement.

scrutiny ['skru:tɪnɪ] **n** *(U)* examen *m* attentif.

scuba dive **vi** faire de la plongée sous-marine.

scuba diver **n** plongeur *m* sous-marin, plongeuse *f* sous-marine.

scuba diving ['sku:bə-] **n** plongée *f* sous-marine *(avec bouteilles)*.

scud [skʌd] (**pt & pp -ded, cont -ding**) **vi** *liter* [clouds] courir.

scuff [skʌf] **vt 1.** [damage] érafler **2.** [drag] **: to scuff one's feet** traîner les pieds.

scuffle ['skʌfl] ■ **n** bagarre *f*, échauffourée *f*.
■ **vi** se bagarrer, se battre.

scull [skʌl] ■ **n** aviron *m*.
■ **vi** ramer.

scullery ['skʌlərɪ] (**pl -ies**) **n** arrière-cuisine *f*.

sculpt [skʌlpt] **vt** sculpter.

sculptor ['skʌlptəʳ] **n** sculpteur *m*, -eur(e) *f* ***or*** -trice *f*.

sculptural ['skʌlptʃərəl] **adj** sculptural(e).

sculpture ['skʌlptʃəʳ] ■ **n** sculpture *f*.
■ **vt** sculpter.

scum [skʌm] **n** *(U)* **1.** [froth] écume *f*, mousse *f* **2.** *v inf pej* [person] salaud *m* **3.** *v inf pej* [people] déchets *mpl*.

scumbag ['skʌmbæg] **n** *v inf* salaud *m*, ordure *f*.

scummy ['skʌmɪ] (**comp -ier, superl -iest**) **adj 1.** [liquid] écumeux(euse) **2.** *v inf* [person] salaud.

scupper ['skʌpəʳ] **vt 1.** NAUT couler **2.** *UK fig* [plan] saboter, faire tomber à l'eau.

scurf [skɜ:f] **n** *(U)* pellicules *fpl*.

scurrilous ['skʌrələs] **adj** *fml* calomnieux(euse).

scurry ['skʌrɪ] (**pt & pp -ied**) **vi** se précipiter ▸ **to scurry away** ***or*** **off** se sauver, détaler.

scurvy ['skɜ:vɪ] **n** scorbut *m*.

scuttle ['skʌtl] ■ **n** seau *m* à charbon.
■ **vi** courir précipitamment ***or*** à pas précipités.

scythe [saɪð] ■ **n** faux *f*.
■ **vt** faucher.

SD abbr of ***South Dakota***.

SDI (abbr of ***Strategic Defense Initiative***) **n** IDS *f*.

SDLP (abbr of ***Social Democratic and Labour Party***) **n** *parti travailliste d'Irlande du Nord*.

SDP (abbr of ***Social Democratic Party***) **n** *parti social-démocrate en Grande-Bretagne*.

SE (abbr of ***south-east***) S-E.

sea [si:] ■ **n 1.** [gen] mer *f* ▸ **at sea** en mer ▸ **by sea** par mer ▸ **by the sea** au bord de la mer ▸ **out to sea** au large ▸ **to be all at sea** nager complètement **2.** *fig* [large number] multitude *f*.
■ **comp** [voyage] en mer / [animal] marin(e), de mer.
◆ ***seas*** **npl : the seas** les mers *fpl*.

sea air **n** air *m* marin ***or*** de la mer.

sea anemone **n** anémone *f* de mer.

sea bass **n** ZOOL & CULIN loup *m* de mer.

seabed ['si:bed] **n : the seabed** le fond de la mer.

seabird ['si:bɜ:d] **n** oiseau *m* marin ***or*** de mer.

seaboard ['si:bɔ:d] **n** littoral *m*, côte *f*.

sea bream **n** daurade *f*, dorade *f*.

sea breeze **n** brise *f* de mer.

seafaring ['si:,feərɪŋ] **adj** [nation] maritime ▸ **a seafaring man** un marin.

seafood ['si:fu:d] **n** *(U)* fruits *mpl* de mer.

seafront ['si:frʌnt] **n** front *m* de mer.

seagoing ['si:,gəʊɪŋ] **adj** [boat] de mer.

seagull ['si:gʌl] **n** mouette *f*.

seahorse ['si:hɔ:s] **n** hippocampe *m*.

seal [si:l] ■ **n** (pl seal *OR* -s) **1.** [animal] phoque *m* **2.** [official mark] cachet *m*, sceau *m* ▸ **seal of approval** approbation *f* ▸ **seal of quality** label *m* de qualité ▸ **to put *OR* set the seal on sthg** sceller qqch **3.** [official fastening] cachet *m* **4.** [TECH - device] joint *m* d'étanchéité / [- join] joint *m* étanche.
■ **vt 1.** [envelope] coller, fermer **2.** [document, letter] sceller, cacheter ▸ **sealed with a kiss** scellé(e) d'un baiser ▸ **her fate is sealed** *fig* son sort est réglé **3.** [block off] obturer, boucher ▸ **my lips are sealed** *fig* mes lèvres sont scellées.
◆ ***seal off*** **vt sep** [area, entrance] interdire l'accès de ▸ **the street had been sealed off** la rue avait été fermée (à la circulation).

sealable ['si:ləbl] **adj** qui peut être fermé(e) hermétiquement.

sea lane **n** couloir *m* maritime.

sealant ['si:lənt] **n** enduit *m* étanche.

sealed [si:ld] **adj** [document] scellé(e) / [envelope] cacheté(e) / [orders] scellé(e) sous pli / [jar] fermé(e) hermétiquement / [mineshaft] obturé(e), bouché(e) / [joint] étanche.

sea level **n** niveau *m* de la mer.

sealing ['si:lɪŋ] **n 1.** [hunting] chasse *f* aux phoques **2.** [of document] cachetage *m* / [of crate] plombage *m* / [of door] scellage *m* / [of shaft, mine] fermeture *f*, obturation *f*.

sealing wax **n** cire *f* à cacheter.

sea lion (pl sea lion *OR* -s) **n** otarie *f*.

sealskin ['si:lskɪn] **n** peau *f* de phoque.

seam [si:m] **n 1.** SEW couture *f* ▸ **to be bursting at the seams** *fig* être plein(e) à craquer **2.** [of coal] couche *f*, veine *f*.

seaman ['si:mən] (pl **-men** [-mən]) **n** marin *m*.

seamanship ['si:mənʃɪp] **n** habileté *f* de marin.

sea mist **n** brume *f* de mer.

seamless ['si:mlɪs] **adj 1.** SEW sans coutures **2.** *fig* [faultless] parfait(e), irréprochable.

seamstress ['semstrɪs] **n** couturière *f*.

seamy ['si:mɪ] (comp -ier, superl -iest) **adj** sordide.

séance ['seɪɒns] **n** séance *f* de spiritisme.

seaplane ['si:pleɪn] **n** hydravion *m*.

seaport ['si:pɔ:t] **n** port *m* de mer.

search [sɜ:tʃ] ■ **n** [of person, luggage, house] fouille *f* / [for lost person, thing] recherche *f*, recherches *fpl* ▸ **search for** recherche de ▸ **in search of** à la recherche de.
■ **vt** [house, area, person] fouiller / [memory, mind, drawer] fouiller dans ▸ **to search one's bag/pocket for sthg** fouiller dans son sac/sa poche pour essayer de retrouver qqch ▸ **to search a house/an area for sthg** fouiller une maison/un quartier pour essayer de retrouver qqch
▸▸ **search me!** *inf* je n'en ai pas la moindre idée!
■ **vi : to search (for sb/sthg)** chercher (qqn/qqch) / COMPUT **: to search for a file** rechercher un fichier ▸ **'searching'** 'recherche'.
◆ ***search out*** **vt sep** découvrir.

search engine **n** COMPUT moteur *m* de recherche.

searcher ['sɜ:tʃər] **n** chercheur *m*, -euse *f*.

searching ['sɜ:tʃɪŋ] **adj** [question] poussé(e), approfondi(e) / [look] pénétrant(e) / [review, examination] minutieux(euse).

searchingly ['sɜ:tʃɪŋlɪ] **adv** [look] de façon pénétrante / [examine] rigoureusement / [question] minutieusement.

searchlight ['sɜ:tʃlaɪt] **n** projecteur *m*.

search party **n** équipe *f* de secours.

search warrant **n** mandat *m* de perquisition.

searing ['sɪərɪŋ] **adj 1.** [pain] fulgurant(e) / [heat] torride **2.** *fig* [attack] virulent(e).

sea salt **n** sel *m* marin *OR* de mer.

seashell ['si:ʃel] **n** coquillage *m*.

seashore ['si:ʃɔ:r] **n : the seashore** le rivage, la plage.

seasick ['si:sɪk] **adj : to be *OR* feel seasick** avoir le mal de mer.

seasickness ['si:sɪknɪs] **n** mal *m* de mer.

seaside ['si:saɪd] **n : the seaside** le bord de la mer.

seaside resort **n** station *f* balnéaire.

season ['si:zn] ■ **n 1.** [gen] saison *f* ▸ **the start of the tourist/of the holiday season** le début de la saison touristique/des vacances ▸ **the low/high season** la basse/haute saison ▸ **in season** [food] de saison / [animal] en chaleur ▸ **out of season** [holiday] hors saison / [food] hors de saison ▸ **the hunting/fishing season** la saison de la chasse/de la pêche **2.** [of films, programmes] cycle *m* ▸ **a new season of French drama** RADIO & TV un nouveau cycle de pièces de théâtre français.
■ **vt** assaisonner, relever.

seasonable ['si:znəbl] **adj 1.** [weather] de saison **2.** [opportune] à propos, opportun(e).

seasonal ['si:zənl] **adj** saisonnier(ère).

seasonal adjustment **n** correction *f* des variations saisonnières.

seasonal affective disorder **n** troubles *mpl* de l'humeur saisonniers.

seasonally ['si:znəlɪ] **adv** de façon saisonnière ▸ **seasonally adjusted statistics** statistiques corrigées des variations saisonnières, statistiques désaisonnalisées.

seasoned ['si:znd] **adj** [traveller, campaigner] chevronné(e), expérimenté(e) / [soldier] aguerri(e).

seasoning ['si:znɪŋ] **n** assaisonnement *m*.

season ticket **n** carte *f* d'abonnement.

seat [si:t] ■ **n 1.** [gen] siège *m* / [in theatre] fauteuil *m* ▸ **take a seat!** asseyez-vous! ▸ **he kept/lost his seat** POL il a été/il n'a pas été réélu ▸ **she has a seat in Parliament** elle est député ▸ **the seat of government/of learning** le siège du gouvernement/du savoir **2.** [place to sit - in bus, train] place *f* ▸ **keep a seat for me** gardez-moi une place **3.** [of trousers] fond *m* ▸ **by the seat of one's pants** *inf* de justesse.
■ **vt 1.** [sit down] faire asseoir, placer ▸ **please be seated** veuillez vous asseoir ▸ **to seat o.s.** s'asseoir **2.** [have room for] **: the car seats five** on tient à cinq dans cette voiture ▸ **the hall seats 200** il y a 200 places assises dans cette salle.

seat belt **n** ceinture *f* de sécurité.

seated ['si:tɪd] **adj** assis(e).

-seater ['si:təʳ] **suffix : a two-seater (car)** une voiture à deux places.

seating ['si:tɪŋ] ■ **n** *(U)* [capacity] sièges *mpl*, places *fpl* (assises) ▸ **there's seating for eight round this table** on peut asseoir huit personnes autour de cette table.
■ **comp** [plan] de table ▸ **seating capacity** nombre *m* de places assises ▸ **the seating arrangements** le placement *m* **OR** la disposition *f* des gens.

SEATO ['si:təʊ] (abbr of ***Southeast Asia Treaty Organization***) **n** OTASE *f*.

sea urchin **n** oursin *m*.

seawall [ˌsi:'wɔ:l] **n** digue *f*.

seawater ['si:ˌwɔ:təʳ] **n** eau *f* de mer.

seaweed ['si:wi:d] **n** *(U)* algue *f*.

seaworthy ['si:ˌwɜ:ðɪ] **adj** en bon état de navigabilité.

sebaceous [sɪ'beɪʃəs] **adj** sébacé(e).

sec. abbr of ***second***.

SEC (abbr of ***Securities and Exchange Commission***) **n** *commission américaine des opérations de Bourse*, ≃ COB *f*.

secateurs [ˌsekə'tɜ:z] **npl** *UK* sécateur *m*.

secede [sɪ'si:d] **vi** *fml* **: to secede (from)** se séparer (de), faire sécession (de).

secession [sɪ'seʃn] **n** *fml* sécession *f*.

secluded [sɪ'klu:dɪd] **adj** retiré(e), écarté(e).

seclusion [sɪ'klu:ʒn] **n** solitude *f*, retraite *f*.

second¹ ['sekənd] ■ **n 1.** [gen] seconde *f* ▸ **wait a second!** une seconde!, (attendez) un instant! ▸ **second (gear)** seconde ▸ **I was the second to arrive** je suis arrivé deuxième **OR** le deuxième
2. *UK* UNIV ≃ licence *f* avec mention assez bien.
■ **num** deuxième, second(e) ▸ **every second person** une personne sur deux ▸ **and in the second place...** [in demonstration, argument] et en deuxième lieu... ▸ **as a goalkeeper, he's second to none** comme gardien de but, il n'a pas son pareil ▸ **he was given a second chance (in life)** on lui a accordé une seconde chance (dans la vie) ▸ **to take a second helping** se resservir ▸ **they have a second home in France** ils ont une résidence secondaire en France ▸ **his score was second only to hers** il n'y a qu'elle qui ait fait mieux que lui **OR** qui l'ait surpassé ; see also ***sixth***.
■ **vt** [proposal, motion] appuyer.
◆ ***seconds*** **npl 1.** COMM articles *mpl* de second choix
2. [of food] rabiot *m*.

second² [sɪ'kɒnd] **vt** *UK* [employee] affecter temporairement.

secondary ['sekəndrɪ] **adj** secondaire ▸ **to be secondary to** être moins important(e) que.

secondary market **n** marché *m* secondaire.

secondary modern **n** *UK* HIST ≃ collège *m*.

secondary picketing **n** *UK* *(U)* piquets *mpl* de grève de solidarité.

secondary school **n** *UK* école *f* secondaire, lycée *m*.

second best ['sekənd-] **adj** deuxième ▸ **to come off second best** se faire battre, perdre ▸ **don't settle for second best** ne choisis que ce qu'il y a de mieux.

second chamber ['sekənd-] **n** [gen] deuxième chambre *f* / [in UK] Chambre *f* des lords / [in US] Sénat *m*.

second-class ['sekənd-] **adj 1.** *pej* [citizen] de deuxième zone / [product] de second choix **2.** [ticket] de seconde **OR** deuxième classe **3.** [stamp] à tarif réduit **4.** *UK* UNIV [degree] ≃ avec mention assez bien.

second cousin ['sekənd-] **n** petit cousin *m*, petite cousine *f*.

second-degree burn ['sekənd-] **n** brûlure *f* du deuxième degré.

seconder ['sekəndəʳ] **n** *personne qui appuie une proposition*.

second floor ['sekənd-] **n** *UK* deuxième étage *m* / *US* premier étage.

second-generation ['sekənd-] **adj** [immigrant, computer] de la seconde génération.

second-guess ['sekənd-] **vt** *inf* **1.** [predict] anticiper, prévoir **2.** *esp US* [with hindsight] juger avec le recul.

second hand ['sekənd-] **n** [of clock] trotteuse *f*.

second-hand ['sekənd-] ■ **adj 1.** [goods, shop] d'occasion **2.** *fig* [information] de seconde main.
■ **adv 1.** [not new] d'occasion **2.** *fig* [indirectly] **: to hear sthg second-hand** apprendre qqch de seconde main **OR** indirectement.

second-in-command ['sekənd-] **n** commandant *m* en second.

secondly ['sekəndlɪ] **adv** deuxièmement, en second lieu.

secondment [sɪ'kɒndmənt] **n** *UK* affectation *f* temporaire.

second name ['sekənd-] **n** nom *m* de famille.

second nature ['sekənd-] **n** seconde nature *f*.

second-rate ['sekənd-] **adj** *pej* de deuxième ordre, médiocre.

second sight ['sekənd-] **n** seconde **OR** double vue *f* ▸ **to have second sight** avoir un don de double vue.

second thought ['sekənd-] **n : to have second thoughts about sthg** avoir des doutes sur qqch ▸ **on second thoughts** *UK*, **on second thought** *US* réflexion faite, tout bien réfléchi.

secrecy ['si:krəsɪ] **n** *(U)* secret *m*.

secret ['si:krɪt] ■ **adj** secret(ète) ▸ **to keep sthg secret** tenir qqch secret
▸▸ **secret ballot** vote *m* à bulletin secret.
■ **n** secret *m* ▸ **I'll tell you OR I'll let you into a secret** je vais vous dire **OR** révéler un secret ▸ **in secret** en secret.

secret agent **n** agent *m* secret.

secretarial [ˌsekrə'teərɪəl] **adj** [course, training] de secrétariat, de secrétaire ▸ **secretarial staff** secrétaires *mpl*.

secretariat [ˌsekrə'teərɪət] **n** secrétariat *m*.

secretary [*UK* 'sekrətrɪ, *US* 'sekrəˌterɪ] (pl -ies) **n 1.** [gen] secrétaire *mf* **2.** POL [minister] ministre *mf*.

secretary-general (pl **secretaries-general**) **n** secrétaire *m* général.

Secretary of State **n 1.** *UK* **: Secretary of State (for)** ministre *m* (de) **2.** *US* ≃ ministre *m* des Affaires étrangères.

secrete [sɪ'kri:t] **vt 1.** [produce] sécréter **2.** *fml* [hide] cacher.

secretion [sɪ'kri:ʃn] **n** sécrétion *f*.

secretive ['si:krətɪv] **adj** secret(ète), dissimulé(e).

secretively ['si:krətɪvlɪ] **adv** en cachette, secrètement.

secretly ['si:krɪtlɪ] **adv** secrètement.

secret police **n** police *f* secrète.

secret service **n** [in UK] ≃ Deuxième Bureau *m* / [in US] *service de protection du président, du vice-président et de leur famille.*

sect [sekt] **n** secte *f*.

sectarian [sek'teərɪən] **adj** [killing, violence] d'ordre religieux.

sectarianism [sek'teərɪənɪzm] **n** sectarisme *m*.

section ['sekʃn] ■ **n 1.** [portion - gen] section *f*, partie *f* / [- of road, pipe] tronçon *m* / [- of document, law] article *m* ▸ **the sports section** PRESS la rubrique des sports **2.** GEOM coupe *f*, section *f*.
■ **vt** sectionner.

sector ['sektəʳ] **n** secteur *m*.

secular ['sekjʊləʳ] **adj** [life] séculier(ère) / [education] laïque / [music] profane.

secularize, -ise ['sekjʊləraɪz] **vt** séculariser / [education] laïciser.

secure [sɪ'kjʊəʳ] ■ **adj 1.** [fixed - gen] fixe / [- windows, building] bien fermé(e) **2.** [safe - job, future] sûr(e) / [- valuable object] en sécurité, en lieu sûr **3.** [free of anxiety - childhood] sécurisant(e) / [- marriage] solide ▸ **to feel secure** se sentir en sécurité.
■ **vt 1.** [obtain] obtenir ▸ **to secure a majority** [gen] obtenir une majorité / POL emporter la majorité ▸ **to secure the release of sb** obtenir la libération de qqn **2.** [fasten - gen] attacher / [- door, window] bien fermer **3.** [make safe] assurer la sécurité de.

secured [sɪ'kjʊəd] **adj** FIN [debt, loan] garanti(e).

secure electronic transaction **n** COMPUT protocole *m* SET®.

securely [sɪ'kjʊəlɪ] **adv** [fixed, locked] solidement, bien.

secure server **n** COMPUT serveur *m* sécurisé.

secure unit **n** [in psychiatric hospital] quartier *m* de haute sécurité / [for young offenders] centre *m* d'éducation surveillée.

security [sɪ'kjʊərətɪ] ■ **n** (pl **-ies**) **1.** sécurité *f* ▸ **job security** sécurité de l'emploi ▸ **please call security** appelez la sécurité s'il vous plaît ▸ **there was maximum security for the President's visit** des mesures de sécurité exceptionnelles ont été prises pour la visite du président ▸ **maximum security wing** [in prison] quartier *m* de haute surveillance **2.** [guarantee] garantie *f*, caution *f* ▸ **have you anything to put up as security?** qu'est-ce que vous pouvez fournir comme garantie?
■ **comp** de sécurité.
◆ ***securities*** **npl** FIN titres *mpl*, valeurs *fpl* ▸ **government securities** titres *mpl* d'État.

security blanket **n** doudou *m*.

Security Council **n : the Security Council** le Conseil de Sécurité.

security forces **npl** forces *fpl* de sécurité.

security gate **n** [at airport] portique *m*.

security guard **n** garde *m* de sécurité.

security risk **n** *personne qui présente un risque pour la sécurité nationale ou d'une organisation.*

secy (abbr of ***secretary***) secr.

sedan [sɪ'dæn] **n** *US* berline *f*.

sedan chair **n** chaise *f* à porteurs.

sedate [sɪ'deɪt] ■ **adj** posé(e), calme.
■ **vt** donner un sédatif à.

sedation [sɪ'deɪʃn] **n** *(U)* sédation *f* ▸ **under sedation** sous calmants.

sedative ['sedətɪv] ■ **adj** sédatif(ive).
■ **n** sédatif *m*, calmant *m*.

sedentary ['sedntrɪ] **adj** sédentaire.

sediment ['sedɪmənt] **n** sédiment *m*, dépôt *m*.

sedition [sɪ'dɪʃn] **n** sédition *f*.

seditious [sɪ'dɪʃəs] **adj** séditieux(euse).

seduce [sɪ'dju:s] **vt** séduire ▸ **to seduce sb into doing sthg** amener ***OR*** entraîner qqn à faire qqch.

seduction [sɪ'dʌkʃn] **n** séduction *f*.

seductive [sɪ'dʌktɪv] **adj** séduisant(e).

seductively [sɪ'dʌktɪvlɪ] **adv** [dress] d'une manière séduisante / [smile] d'une manière enjôleuse.

see [si:] (pt **saw**, pp **seen**) ■ **vt 1.** [gen] voir ▸ **can you see me?** est-ce que tu me vois? ▸ **see you!** au revoir! ▸ **see you soon/later/tomorrow!** *etc* à bientôt/tout à l'heure/demain! *etc* ▸ **I'll see what I can do** je vais voir ce que je peux faire ▸ **see page 317** voir page 317 ▸ **there's nothing there: you're seeing things!** il n'y a rien, tu as des hallucinations! ▸ **I'll see if I can fix it** je vais voir si je peux le réparer ▸ **our car has seen better days** notre voiture a connu des jours meilleurs
2. [meet] voir ▸ **you should see a doctor** tu devrais voir ***OR*** consulter un médecin ▸ **is he seeing anyone at the moment?** [going out with] est-ce qu'il a quelqu'un en ce moment?
3. [understand, consider] voir, comprendre ▸ **I see what you mean** je vois ***OR*** comprends ce que vous voulez dire ▸ **how do you see the current situation?** que pensez-vous de la situation actuelle?
4. [accompany] **: I saw her to the door** je l'ai accompagnée ***OR*** reconduite jusqu'à la porte ▸ **I saw her onto the train** je l'ai accompagnée au train
5. [like] **: what do you see in him?** qu'est-ce que tu lui trouves?

6. [make sure] **: to see (that)...** s'assurer que...
■ **vi** voir ▸ **you see,...** voyez-vous,... ▸ **I see** je vois, je comprends ▸ **let's see, let me see** voyons, voyons voir ▸ **for all to see** au vu et au su de tous.
◆ ***seeing as, seeing that*** **conj** *inf* vu que, étant donné que.
◆ ***see about*** **vt insep** [arrange] s'occuper de.
◆ ***see off*** **vt sep 1.** [say goodbye to] accompagner (pour dire au revoir)
2. *UK* [chase away] faire partir ***OR*** fuir.
◆ ***see out*** **vt sep** [accompany to the door] reconduire ***OR*** raccompagner à la porte ▸ **can you see yourself out?** pouvez-vous trouver la sortie tout seul?
◆ ***see through*** ■ **vt insep** [scheme] voir clair dans ▸ **to see through sb** voir dans le jeu de qqn.
■ **vt sep** [deal, project] mener à terme, mener à bien ▸ **we can count on her to see the job through** on peut compter sur elle pour mener l'affaire à bien.
◆ ***see to*** **vt insep** s'occuper de, se charger de ▸ **see to it that everything's ready by 5 p.m.** veillez à ce que tout soit prêt pour 17 h.

seed [si:d] **n 1.** [of plant] graine *f* **2.** SPORT **: fifth seed** joueur classé cinquième *m*, joueuse classée cinquième *f*.
◆ ***seeds*** **npl** *fig* germes *mpl*, semences *fpl*.

seedless ['si:dlɪs] **adj** sans pépins.

seedling ['si:dlɪŋ] **n** jeune plant *m*, semis *m*.

seedy ['si:dɪ] **(comp -ier, superl -iest) adj** miteux(euse).

seeing ['si:ɪŋ] **n** [vision] vue *f*, vision *f* ▸ **seeing is believing** *prov* il faut le voir pour le croire.

seek [si:k] **(pt & pp sought) vt 1.** [gen] chercher ▸ **to seek one's fortune** chercher fortune ▸ **to seek re-election** chercher à se faire réélire / [peace, happiness] rechercher ▸ **to seek to do sthg** chercher à faire qqch ▸ **to seek revenge** chercher à se venger **2.** [advice, help] demander.
◆ ***seek out*** **vt sep** chercher.

seeker ['si:kər] **n** chercheur *m*, -euse *f* ▸ **a seeker after truth** une personne qui recherche la vérité.

seem [si:m] ■ **vi** sembler, paraître ▸ **to seem bored** avoir l'air de s'ennuyer ▸ **things aren't always what they seem** les apparences sont parfois trompeuses ▸ **to seem sad/tired** avoir l'air triste/fatigué ▸ **just do whatever seems right** fais ce que tu jugeras bon de faire ▸ **it seems like only yesterday** il me semble que c'était hier ▸ **I seem to sleep better with the window open** je crois que je dors mieux avec la fenêtre ouverte ▸ **I seem to remember...** je crois me rappeler...
■ **impers vb : it seems (that)...** il semble ***OR*** paraît que... ▸ **it seemed as though we'd known each other for years** nous avions l'impression de nous connaître depuis des années ▸ **there seems to be some mistake** on dirait qu'il y a une erreur.

seeming ['si:mɪŋ] **adj** *fml* apparent(e).

seemingly ['si:mɪŋlɪ] **adv** apparemment.

seemly ['si:mlɪ] **(comp -ier, superl -iest) adj** *dated* convenable.

seen [si:n] **pp** ➤ ***see***.

seep [si:p] **vi** suinter.

seer ['sɪər] **n** *liter* prophète *m*, prophétesse *f*.

seersucker ['sɪə,sʌkər] **n** crépon *m* de coton.

seesaw ['si:sɔ:] **n** bascule *f*.

seethe [si:ð] **vi 1.** [person] bouillir, être furieux(euse) **2.** [place] **: to be seething with** grouiller de.

seething ['si:ðɪŋ] **adj** [furious] furieux(euse).

see-through **adj** transparent(e).

segment ['segmənt] **n 1.** [section] partie *f*, section *f* **2.** [of fruit] quartier *m*.

segmentation [segmən'teɪʃən] **n** [of market, customer base] segmentation *f*.

segmented [seg'mentɪd] **adj** segmentaire.

segregate ['segrɪgeɪt] **vt** séparer.

segregated ['segrɪgeɪtɪd] **adj** POL *où la ségrégation raciale est pratiquée.*

segregation [,segrɪ'geɪʃn] **n** ségrégation *f*.

segregationist [,segrɪ'geɪʃnɪst] ■ **adj** ségrégationniste.
■ **n** ségrégationniste *mf*.

Seine [seɪn] **n : the (River) Seine** la Seine.

seismic ['saɪzmɪk] **adj** sismique.

seismograph ['saɪzməgrɑ:f] **n** sismographe *m*, séismographe *m*.

seize [si:z] **vt 1.** [grab] saisir, attraper ▸ **to seize hold of sthg** saisir ***OR*** attraper qqch **2.** [capture] s'emparer de, prendre ▸ **to seize power** s'emparer du pouvoir ▸ **the rebels have seized control of the radio station** les rebelles se sont emparés de la station de radio **3.** [arrest] arrêter **4.** *fig* [opportunity, chance] saisir, sauter sur.
◆ ***seize (up)on*** **vt insep** saisir, sauter sur.
◆ ***seize up*** **vi 1.** [body] s'ankyloser **2.** [engine, part] se gripper.

seizure ['si:ʒər] **n 1.** MED crise *f*, attaque *f* **2.** *(U)* [of town] capture *f* / [of power] prise *f*.

seldom ['seldəm] **adv** peu souvent, rarement.

select [sɪ'lekt] ■ **adj 1.** [carefully chosen] choisi(e) **2.** [exclusive] de premier ordre, d'élite.
■ **vt** sélectionner, choisir.

select committee **n** commission *f* d'enquête.

selected [sɪ'lektɪd] **adj** choisi(e).

selection [sɪ'lekʃn] **n** sélection *f*, choix *m*.

selective [sɪ'lektɪv] **adj** sélectif(ive) / [person] difficile.

selectively [sɪ'lektɪvlɪ] **adv** sélectivement, de manière sélective.

selector [sɪ'lektər] **n** [person] sélectionneur *m*, -euse *f*.

self [self] **(pl selves [selvz]) n** moi *m* ▸ **she's her old self again** elle est redevenue elle-même.

self- [self] **prefix** auto-.

self-absorbed [-əb'sɔ:bd] **adj** égocentrique.

self-addressed envelope [-ə'drest-] **n** enveloppe *f* portant ses propres nom et adresse.

self-addressed stamped envelope [-ə'drest-] **n** *US* enveloppe *f* affranchie pour la réponse.

self-adhesive **adj** autocollant(e).

self-appointed [-ə'pɔɪntɪd] **adj** *pej* **: she's the self-appointed leader** elle se pose en chef.

self-assembly **adj** *UK* qu'on monte OR assemble soi-même.

self-assertive **adj** qui sait s'affirmer.

self-assurance **n** confiance *f* en soi, assurance *f*.

self-assured **adj** sûr(e) de soi, plein(e) d'assurance.

self-aware **adj** conscient(e) de soi-même.

self-awareness **n** conscience *f* de soi.

self-catering **adj** *UK* [holiday - in house] en maison louée / [- in flat] en appartement loué.

self-centred *UK*, ***self-centered*** *US* [-'sentəd] **adj** égocentrique.

self-cleaning **adj** autonettoyant(e).

self-coloured *UK*, ***self-colored*** *US* **adj** uni(e).

self-confessed [-kən'fest] **adj** de son propre aveu.

self-confidence **n** confiance *f* en soi, assurance *f* ▸ **she is full of/she lacks self-confidence** elle a une grande/elle manque de confiance en elle.

self-confident **adj** sûr(e) de soi, plein(e) d'assurance.

self-confidently **adv** avec assurance OR aplomb.

self-congratulatory **adj** satisfait(e) de soi.

self-conscious **adj** timide, embarrassé(e).

self-consciously **adv** timidement.

self-consciousness **n** timidité *f*, gêne *f*.

self-contained [-kən'teɪnd] **adj** [flat] indépendant(e), avec entrée particulière / [person] qui se suffit à soi-même.

self-control **n** maîtrise *f* de soi.

self-controlled **adj** maître (maîtresse) de soi.

self-defeating [-dɪ'fi:tɪŋ] **adj** contraire au but recherché.

self-defence *UK*, ***self-defense*** *US* **n** autodéfense *f* ▸ **in self-defence** LAW en légitime défense / [reply] pour sa défense.

self-denial **n** abnégation *f*.

self-deprecating [-'deprɪkeɪtɪŋ] **adj : to be self-deprecating** se déprécier.

self-destruct [-dɪs'trʌkt] ■ **adj** autodestructeur(trice). ■ **vi** s'autodétruire.

self-destructive **adj** autodestructeur(trice).

self-determination **n** autodétermination *f*.

self-discipline **n** [self-control] maîtrise *f* de soi / [good behaviour] autodiscipline *f*.

self-disciplined **adj** [self-controlled] maître de soi / [well-behaved] qui fait preuve d'autodiscipline.

self-doubt **n** manque *m* de confiance en soi.

self-drive **adj** *UK* sans chauffeur.

self-educated **adj** autodidacte.

self-effacing [-ɪ'feɪsɪŋ] **adj** qui cherche à s'effacer.

self-employed [-ɪm'plɔɪd] **adj** qui travaille à son propre compte.

self-esteem **n** respect *m* de soi, estime *f* de soi.

self-evident **adj** qui va de soi, évident(e).

self-explanatory **adj** évident(e), qui ne nécessite pas d'explication.

self-expression **n** libre expression *f*.

self-focusing [-'fəʊkəsɪŋ] **adj** autofocus *(inv)*, à mise au point automatique.

self-fulfilling **adj : self-fulfilling prophecy** *prophétie défaitiste qui se réalise*.

self-governing **adj** POL autonome.

self-government **n** autonomie *f*.

self-help **n** *(U)* initiative *f* personnelle.

self-image **n** image *f* de soi-même.

self-importance **n** suffisance *f*.

self-important **adj** suffisant(e).

self-imposed [-ɪm'pəʊzd] **adj** que l'on s'impose à soi-même.

self-improvement **n** perfectionnement *m* des connaissances personnelles.

self-induced **adj** que l'on provoque soi-même.

self-indulgence **n** complaisance *f* envers soi-même, habitude *f* de ne rien se refuser.

self-indulgent **adj** *pej* [person] qui ne se refuse rien / [film, book, writer] nombriliste.

self-inflicted [-ɪn'flɪktɪd] **adj** que l'on s'inflige à soi-même, volontaire.

self-interest **n** *(U) pej* intérêt *m* personnel.

self-interested **adj** intéressé(e), qui agit par intérêt personnel.

selfish ['selfɪʃ] **adj** égoïste.

selfishness ['selfɪʃnɪs] **n** égoïsme *m*.

self-justification **n** autojustification *f*.

self-knowledge **n** connaissance *f* de soi.

selfless ['selflɪs] **adj** désintéressé(e).

selflessly ['selflɪslɪ] **adv** de façon désintéressée, avec désintéressement.

self-locking [-'lɒkɪŋ] **adj** à fermeture automatique.

self-made **adj : self-made man** self-made-man *m*.

self-medication **n** automédication *f*.

self-opinionated **adj** opiniâtre.

self-perpetuating [-pə'petʃʊeɪtɪŋ] **adj** qui se perpétue indéfiniment.

self-pity **n** apitoiement *m* sur son sort.

self-pitying **adj** qui s'apitoie sur son (propre) sort.

self-portrait **n** autoportrait *m*.

self-possessed **adj** maître (maîtresse) de soi.

self-possession **n** sang-froid *m*.

self-preservation **n** instinct *m* de conservation.

self-proclaimed [-prəˈkleɪmd] **adj** *pej* soi-disant *(inv)*, prétendu(e).

self-raising flour *UK* [-ˌreɪzɪŋ-], ***self-rising flour*** *US* **n** farine *f* avec levure incorporée.

self-regard *(U)* **n 1.** *pej* [self-interest] intérêt *m* personnel **2.** [self-respect] respect *m* de soi.

self-regulating [-ˈregjʊleɪtɪŋ] **adj** qui se réglemente soi-même.

self-reliant **adj** indépendant(e), qui ne compte que sur soi.

self-respect **n** respect *m* de soi.

self-respecting [-rɪsˈpektɪŋ] **adj** qui se respecte.

self-restraint **n** *(U)* retenue *f*, mesure *f*.

self-righteous **adj** suffisant(e).

self-righteousness **n** suffisance *f*, pharisaïsme *m fml*.

self-rising flour *US* = ***self-raising flour***.

self-rule **n** autonomie *f*.

self-sacrifice **n** abnégation *f*.

selfsame [ˈselfseɪm] **adj** exactement le même (exactement la même).

self-satisfied **adj** suffisant(e), content(e) de soi.

self-sealing [-ˈsiːlɪŋ] **adj** [envelope] autocollant(e).

self-seeking [-ˈsiːkɪŋ] **adj** égoïste.

self-service ■ **n** libre-service *m*, self-service *m*.
■ **comp** libre-service, self-service.

self-starter **n** AUT démarreur *m* automatique.

self-study ■ **n** autoformation *f*.
■ **adj** d'autoformation.

self-styled [-ˈstaɪld] **adj** *pej* soi-disant *(inv)*, prétendu(e).

self-sufficiency **n 1.** [of person - independence] indépendance *f* / [- self-assurance] suffisance *f* **2.** ECON [of nation, resources] autosuffisance *f* / POL **: (economic) self-sufficiency** autarcie *f*.

self-sufficient **adj** autosuffisant(e) ▸ **to be self-sufficient in** satisfaire à ses besoins en.

self-supporting [-səˈpɔːtɪŋ] **adj** [business, industry] financièrement indépendant(e).

self-taught **adj** autodidacte.

self-test **vi** COMPUT faire un autotest.

self-will **n** obstination *f*.

sell [sel] (pt & pp **sold**) ■ **vt 1.** [gen] vendre ▸ **to sell sthg for £100** vendre qqch 100 livres ▸ **to sell sthg to sb, to sell sb sthg** vendre qqch à qqn ▸ **the book sold 50,000 copies, 50,000 copies of the book were sold** le livre s'est vendu à 50 000 exemplaires ▸ **what really sells newspapers is scandal** ce sont les scandales qui font vraiment vendre les journaux ▸ **I'm completely sold on the idea** je suis emballé par l'idée **2.** *fig* [make acceptable] **: to sell sthg to sb, to sell sb sthg** faire accepter qqch à qqn ▸ **to sell o.s.** se faire valoir.
■ **vi 1.** [person] vendre **2.** [product] se vendre ▸ **it sells for OR at £10** il se vend 10 livres ▸ **to sell like hot cakes** se vendre comme des petits pains.
◆ ***sell off*** **vt sep** vendre, liquider.
◆ ***sell out*** ■ **vt sep : the performance is sold out** il ne reste plus de places, tous les billets ont été vendus.
■ **vi 1.** [shop] **: we've sold out** on n'en a plus **2.** [betray one's principles] être infidèle à ses principes ▸ **critics accuse her of selling out as a writer** les critiques l'accusent d'être un écrivain vendu OR sans principes.
◆ ***sell up*** **vi** *UK* vendre son affaire.

sell-by date **n** *UK* date *f* limite de vente.

seller [ˈseləʳ] **n** vendeur *m*, -euse *f*.

seller's market **n** marché *m* à la hausse.

selling [ˈselɪŋ] **n** *(U)* vente *f*.

selling point **n** avantage *m*, atout *m*, point *m* fort.

selling power **n** puissance *f* de vente.

selling price **n** prix *m* de vente.

selloff [ˈselɒf] **n** [gen] vente *f* / [of shares] dégagement *m*.

Sellotape® [ˈseləteɪp] **n** *UK* ≃ Scotch® *m*, ruban *m* adhésif.
◆ ***sellotape*** **vt** scotcher.

sell-out **n : the match was a sell-out** on a joué à guichets fermés.

seltzer [ˈseltsəʳ] **n** *US* eau *f* de seltz.

selves [selvz] **npl** ➤ ***self***.

semantic [sɪˈmæntɪk] **adj** sémantique.

semantics [sɪˈmæntɪks] **n** *(U)* sémantique *f*.

semaphore [ˈseməfɔːʳ] **n** *(U)* signaux *mpl* à bras.

semblance [ˈsembləns] **n** semblant *m*.

semen [ˈsiːmen] **n** *(U)* sperme *m*, semence *f*.

semester [sɪˈmestəʳ] **n** semestre *m*.

semi [ˈsemɪ] **n 1.** *UK inf* (abbr of ***semidetached house***) maison *f* jumelée **2.** *inf* (abbr of ***semifinal***) demi-finale *f* **3.** *US* abbr of ***semitrailer***.

semi- [ˌsemɪ] **prefix** semi-, demi-.

semiannual [ˌsemɪˈænjʊəl] *US* = ***half-yearly***.

semiautomatic [ˌsemɪˌɔːtəˈmætɪk] **adj** semi-automatique.

semicircle [ˈsemɪˌsɜːkl] **n** demi-cercle *m*.

semicircular [ˌsemɪˈsɜːkjʊləʳ] **adj** semi-circulaire, demi-circulaire.

semicolon [ˌsemɪˈkəʊlən] **n** point-virgule *m*.

semiconductor [ˌsemɪkənˈdʌktəʳ] **n** semi-conducteur *m*.

semiconscious [ˌsemɪˈkɒnʃəs] **adj** à demi conscient(e).

semidetached [ˌsemɪdɪˈtætʃt] *UK* ■ **adj** jumelé(e).
■ **n** maison *f* jumelée.

semifinal [ˌsemɪˈfaɪnl] **n** demi-finale *f*.

semifinalist [ˌsemɪ'faɪnəlɪst] **n** demi-finaliste *mf*.

seminal ['semɪnl] **adj 1.** [of semen] séminal(e) **2.** [influential] qui fait école.

seminar ['semɪnɑːʳ] **n** séminaire *m*.

seminary ['semɪnərɪ] (pl **-ies**) **n** RELIG séminaire *m*.

semiotics [ˌsemɪ'ɒtɪks] **n** *(U)* sémiotique *f*.

semiprecious ['semɪˌpreʃəs] **adj** semi-précieux(euse).

semiskilled [ˌsemɪ'skɪld] **adj** spécialisé(e).

semi-skimmed [-skɪmd] **adj** [milk] demi-écrémé.

semitrailer [ˌsemɪ'treɪləʳ] **n** *US* semi-remorque *f*.

semolina [ˌsemə'liːnə] **n** semoule *f*.

SEN (abbr of ***State Enrolled Nurse***) **n** *en Grande-Bretagne, infirmier ou infirmière diplômé(e) d'État*.

Sen. abbr of ***senator***, ***Senior***.

Senate ['senɪt] **n** POL **: the Senate** le sénat ▸ **the United States Senate** le Sénat américain.

CULTURE

Senate

Le corps législatif du gouvernement américain, le Congrès, est composé par la Chambre des représentants et par le Sénat (**Senate** ou « Chambre haute »). Ce dernier, qui compte 200 membres (deux sénateurs par État, élus pour six ans par une élection populaire directe et renouvelés par tiers tous les deux ans), a le pouvoir de destituer le président (cf. **impeachment**). Les sénateurs doivent avoir la citoyenneté américaine depuis neuf ans, résider dans l'État qu'ils représentent et être âgés d'au moins 30 ans. Le vice-président du Sénat ne prend pas part aux délibérations et ne vote qu'en cas de problème majeur : le calendrier est fixé par le leader du parti majoritaire, comportant le plus grand nombre de sénateurs.

senator ['senətəʳ] **n** sénateur *m*, -trice *f*.

send [send] (pt & pp **sent**) **vt 1.** [gen] envoyer / [letter] expédier, envoyer ▸ **to send sb sthg, to send sthg to sb** envoyer qqch à qqn ▸ **send her my love** embrasse-la pour moi ▸ **he sent (us) word that he would be delayed** il (nous) a fait savoir qu'il aurait du retard ▸ **I sent my luggage by train** j'ai fait expédier *OR* envoyer mes bagages par le train ▸ **to send sb for sthg** envoyer qqn chercher qqch ▸ **to send sb home** renvoyer qqn (chez lui) ▸ **to send sb to the doctor's/to prison** envoyer qqn chez le médecin/en prison **2.** [cause to move] **: I sent the cup flying** j'ai envoyé voler la tasse ▸ **the explosion sent glass everywhere** l'explosion a projeté des débris de verre partout ▸ **the sound sent shivers down my spine** le bruit m'a fait froid dans le dos.

◆ ***send down*** **vt sep** *UK* [send to prison] coffrer.

◆ ***send for*** **vt insep 1.** [person] appeler, faire venir **2.** [by post] commander par correspondance.

◆ ***send in*** **vt sep** [report, application] envoyer, soumettre.

◆ ***send off*** **vt sep 1.** [by post] expédier **2.** *UK* SPORT expulser.

◆ ***send off for*** **vt insep** commander par correspondance.

◆ ***send up*** **vt sep 1.** *UK inf* [imitate] parodier, ridiculiser **2.** *US* [send to prison] coffrer.

sender ['sendəʳ] **n** expéditeur *m*, -trice *f*.

send-off **n** fête *f* d'adieu.

send-up **n** *UK inf* parodie *f*.

Senegal [ˌsenɪ'gɔːl] **n** Sénégal *m* ▸ **in Senegal** au Sénégal.

Senegalese [ˌsenɪgə'liːz] ■ **adj** sénégalais(e).
■ **npl : the Senegalese** les Sénégalais *mpl*.

senile ['siːnaɪl] **adj** sénile.

senile dementia **n** démence *f* sénile.

senility [sɪ'nɪlətɪ] **n** sénilité *f*.

senior ['siːnjəʳ] ■ **adj 1.** [highest-ranking] plus haut placé(e) **2.** [higher-ranking] **: senior to sb** d'un rang plus élevé que qqn **3.** SCH [pupils, classes] grand(e) ▸ **senior year** *US* dernière année.
■ **n 1.** [older person] aîné *m*, -e *f* **2.** SCH grand *m*, -e *f*.

senior citizen **n** personne *f* âgée *OR* du troisième âge.

senior high school **n** *US* ≃ lycée *m*.

seniority [ˌsiːnɪ'ɒrətɪ] **n** [in rank] supériorité *f*, ancienneté *f*.

sensation [sen'seɪʃn] **n** sensation *f*.

sensational [sen'seɪʃənl] **adj 1.** [gen] sensationnel(elle) **2.** [pej & PRESS] à sensation.

sensationalism [sen'seɪʃnəlɪzm] **n 1.** [pej & PRESS] sensationnalisme *m* **2.** [in philosophy] sensationnisme *m* **3.** PSYCHOL sensualisme *m*.

sensationalist [sen'seɪʃnəlɪst] **adj** [pej & PRESS] à sensation.

sensationally [sen'seɪʃnəlɪ] **adv** d'une manière sensationnelle / [as intensifier] **: we found this sensationally good restaurant** *inf* on a découvert un restaurant vraiment génial.

sense [sens] ■ **n 1.** [ability, meaning] sens *m* ▸ **to make sense** [have meaning] avoir un sens ▸ **to make sense of sthg** comprendre qqch ▸ **sense of humour** sens de l'humour ▸ **sense of smell** odorat *m* ▸ **I lost all sense of time** j'ai perdu toute notion de l'heure ▸ **to have a (good) sense of direction** avoir le sens de l'orientation
2. [feeling] sentiment *m* ▸ **children need a sense of security** les enfants ont besoin de se sentir en sécurité
3. [wisdom] bon sens *m*, intelligence *f* ▸ **they didn't even have enough sense to telephone** ils n'ont même pas eu l'idée de téléphoner ▸ **there's no sense in all of us going** cela ne sert à rien *OR* c'est inutile d'y aller tous ▸ **to make sense** [be sensible] être logique ▸ **can you make (any) sense of this message?** est-ce que vous arrivez à comprendre ce message? ▸ **to see sense** entendre raison ▸ **to talk sense** parler raison ▸ **there's no sense in arguing/fighting** cela ne sert à rien de discuter/se battre

▸▸ **to come to one's senses** [be sensible again] revenir à la raison / [regain consciousness] reprendre connaissance ▸ **to take leave of one's senses** perdre la raison *OR* la tête.
■ **vt** [feel] sentir ▸ **I sensed as much** c'est bien l'impression *OR* le sentiment que j'avais.
◆ ***in a sense*** **adv** dans un sens.

senseless ['senslɪs] **adj 1.** [stupid] stupide **2.** [unconscious] sans connaissance.

senselessly ['senslɪslɪ] **adv** stupidement, de façon absurde.

sensibility [ˌsensɪ'bɪlətɪ] (pl **-ies**) **n** [physical or emotional] sensibilité *f*.
◆ ***sensibilities*** **npl** susceptibilité *f*, susceptibilités *fpl* ▸ **we must avoid offending our viewers' sensibilities** nous devons éviter de heurter la sensibilité de nos spectateurs.

sensible ['sensəbl] **adj** [reasonable] raisonnable, judicieux(euse) / [practical - clothes, shoes] pratique ▸ **it's a very sensible idea** c'est une très bonne idée ▸ **the most sensible thing to do is to phone** la meilleure chose à faire, c'est de téléphoner.

FALSE FRIENDS / FAUX AMIS

sensible

Sensible n'est pas la traduction du mot anglais *sensible.* Sensible se traduit par *sensitive.*
▸ Elle est très sensible et s'inquiète facilement / *She's very sensitive and gets easily upset*

sensibly ['sensəblɪ] **adv** raisonnablement, judicieusement.

sensitive ['sensɪtɪv] **adj 1.** [gen] **: sensitive (to)** sensible (à) ▸ **my eyes are very sensitive to bright light** j'ai les yeux très sensibles à la lumière vive ▸ **the seminar made us more sensitive to the problem** le séminaire nous a sensibilisés au problème **2.** [subject] délicat(e) **3.** [easily offended] **: sensitive (about)** susceptible (en ce qui concerne) ▸ **she's very sensitive about her height** elle n'aime pas beaucoup qu'on lui parle de sa taille.

-sensitive **suffix** sensible ▸ **heat-sensitive** sensible à la chaleur, thermosensible ▸ **price-sensitive** sensible aux fluctuations des prix ▸ **voice-sensitive** sensible à la voix.

sensitively ['sensɪtɪvlɪ] **adv** avec sensibilité.

sensitivity [ˌsensɪ'tɪvətɪ] **n** sensibilité *f*.

sensitize, ***-ise*** ['sensɪtaɪz] **vt** sensibiliser, rendre sensible.

sensor ['sensəʳ] **n** détecteur *m*.

sensory ['sensərɪ] **adj** [nerve, system] sensoriel(elle) ▸ **sensory deprivation** isolation *f* sensorielle.

sensual ['sensjʊəl] **adj** sensuel(elle).

sensuality [ˌsensjʊ'ælətɪ] **n** sensualité *f*.

sensuous ['sensjʊəs] **adj** qui affecte les sens.

sent [sent] **pt & pp** ➤ ***send***.

sentence ['sentəns] ■ **n 1.** GRAM phrase *f* **2.** LAW condamnation *f*, sentence *f*.
■ **vt : to sentence sb (to)** condamner qqn (à).

sententious [sen'tenʃəs] **adj** *fml* sentencieux(euse).

sentiment ['sentɪmənt] **n 1.** [feeling] sentiment *m* **2.** [opinion] opinion *f*, avis *m* **3.** *pej* [sentimentality] sentimentalité *f*, sensiblerie *f*.

sentimental [ˌsentɪ'mentl] **adj** sentimental(e).

sentimentalism [ˌsentɪ'mentəlɪzm] **n** sentimentalisme *m*.

sentimentality [ˌsentɪmen'tælətɪ] **n** sentimentalité *f*, sensiblerie *f*.

sentimentalize, *UK* ***-ise*** [ˌsentɪ'mentəlaɪz] ■ **vt** [to others] présenter de façon sentimentale / [to o.s.] percevoir de façon sentimentale.
■ **vi** faire du sentiment.

sentimentally [ˌsentɪ'mentəlɪ] **adv** sentimentalement, de manière sentimentale.

sentinel ['sentɪnl] **n** *liter* sentinelle *f*.

sentry ['sentrɪ] (pl **-ies**) **n** sentinelle *f*.

Seoul [səʊl] **n** Séoul.

separable ['seprəbl] **adj : separable (from)** séparable (de).

separate ■ **adj** ['seprət] **1.** [not joined] **: separate (from)** séparé(e) (de) **2.** [individual, distinct] distinct(e) ▸ **that's quite a separate matter** ça, c'est une toute autre affaire ▸ **administration and finance are in separate departments** l'administration et les finances relèvent de services différents ▸ **she likes to keep her home life separate from the office** elle tient à ce que son travail n'empiète pas sur sa vie privée.
■ **vt** ['sepəreɪt] **1.** [gen] **: to separate sb/sthg (from)** séparer qqn/qqch (de) ▸ **to separate sthg into** diviser *OR* séparer qqch en **2.** [distinguish] **: to separate sb/sthg (from)** distinguer qqn/qqch (de).
■ **vi** ['sepəreɪt] se séparer ▸ **to separate into** se diviser *OR* se séparer en.
◆ ***separates*** ['seprəts] **npl** coordonnés *mpl*.

separated ['sepəreɪtɪd] **adj** [not living together] séparé(e).

separately ['seprətlɪ] **adv** séparément.

separation [ˌsepə'reɪʃn] **n** séparation *f*.

separatism ['seprətɪzm] **n** séparatisme *m*.

separatist ['seprətɪst] **n** séparatiste *mf*.

sepia ['siːpjə] **adj** sépia *(inv)*.

Sept. (abbr of ***September***) sept.

September [sep'tembəʳ] ■ **n** septembre *m* ▸ **when are you going? - September** quand partez-vous? - en septembre ▸ **one of the hottest Septembers on record** un des mois de septembre les plus chauds qu'on ait connus ▸ **in September** en septembre ▸ **last September** en septembre dernier ▸ **this September** en septembre de cette année ▸ **next September** en septembre prochain ▸ **by September** en septembre, d'ici septembre ▸ **every September** tous les

ans en septembre ▸ **during September** pendant le mois de septembre ▸ **at the beginning of September** au début du mois de septembre, début septembre ▸ **at the end of September** à la fin du mois de septembre, fin septembre ▸ **in the middle of September** au milieu du mois de septembre, à la mi-septembre.
■ **comp** (du mois) de septembre / [election] au mois de septembre, en septembre.

CULTURE

September 11 & Ground Zero

Le 11 septembre (ou **9/11**) fait référence aux attaques terroristes d'al-Qaida perpétrées à cette date sur le territoire américain : on dénombre plus de 3 000 victimes, les Twin Towers du World Trade Center sont anéanties, le Pentagone subit de graves dommages et un quatrième avion s'écrase dans un champ du Somerset County, au sud-est de Pittsburgh, en Pennsylvanie. Après ces attentats qui ont définitivement marqué la culture et le psychisme américains, l'expression **Ground Zero** (mots du jargon militaire indiquant la zone touchée par une explosion nucléaire) est utilisée pour désigner le site où s'élevaient les tours jumelles, et qui est régulièrement visité depuis le drame par la population.

septet [sep'tet] **n** septuor *m*.

septic ['septɪk] **adj** infecté(e).

septicaemia *UK*, ***septicemia*** *US* [ˌseptɪ'si:mɪə] **n** septicémie *f*.

septic tank **n** fosse *f* septique.

sepulchre *UK* ['sepəlkər], ***sepulcher*** *US* ['sepəlkər] **n** *liter* sépulcre *m*, tombeau *m*.

sequel ['si:kwəl] **n 1.** [book, film] **: sequel (to)** suite *f* (de) **2.** [consequence] **: sequel (to)** conséquence *f* (de).

sequence ['si:kwəns] **n 1.** [series] suite *f*, succession *f* **2.** [order] ordre *m* ▸ **in sequence** par ordre **3.** [of film] séquence *f*.

sequencer ['si:kwənsər] **n** séquenceur *m*.

sequential [sɪ'kwenʃl] **adj 1.** COMPUT séquentiel(elle) **2.** *fml* [following] subséquent(e).

sequester [sɪ'kwestər], ***sequestrate*** [sɪ'kwestreɪt] **vt** séquestrer, mettre sous séquestre.

sequin ['si:kwɪn] **n** paillette *f*.

Serb = ***Serbian***.

Serbia ['sɜ:bjə] **n** Serbie *f* ▸ **in Serbia** en Serbie.

Serbian ['sɜ:bjən], ***Serb*** [sɜ:b] ■ **adj** serbe.
■ **n 1.** [person] Serbe *mf* **2.** [dialect] serbe *m*.

Serbo-Croat [ˌsɜ:bəʊ'krəʊæt], ***Serbo-Croatian*** [ˌsɜ:bəʊkrəʊ'eɪʃn] ■ **adj** serbo-croate.
■ **n** [language] serbo-croate *m*.

serenade [ˌserə'neɪd] ■ **n** sérénade *f*.
■ **vt** donner la sérénade à.

serendipity [ˌserən'dɪpətɪ] **n** *liter don de faire des découvertes (accidentelles).*

serene [sɪ'ri:n] **adj** [calm] serein(e), tranquille.

serenely [sɪ'ri:nlɪ] **adv** sereinement, avec sérénité.

serenity [sɪ'renətɪ] **n** sérénité *f*, tranquillité *f*.

serf [sɜ:f] **n** serf *m*, serve *f*.

serge [sɜ:dʒ] **n** serge *f*.

sergeant ['sɑ:dʒənt] **n 1.** MIL sergent *m*, -e *f* **2.** [in police] brigadier *m*, -ière *f*.

sergeant major **n** sergent-major *m*.

serial ['sɪərɪəl] **n** feuilleton *m*.

serial cable **n** câble *f* série.

serialization, ***-isation*** *UK* [ˌsɪərɪəlaɪ'zeɪʃn] **n** [of book] publication *f* en feuilleton / [of play, film] adaptation *f* en feuilleton.

serialize, *UK* ***-ise*** ['sɪərɪəlaɪz] **vt** [on TV] diffuser en feuilleton / [in newspaper] publier en feuilleton.

serial killer **n** tueur *m* en série.

serial killing **n : serial killings** meurtres *mpl* en série.

serially ['sɪərɪəlɪ] **adv 1.** MATHS en série **2.** PRESS [as series] en feuilleton, sous forme de feuilleton / [periodically] périodiquement, sous forme de périodique.

serial number **n** numéro *m* de série.

series ['sɪəri:z] (pl **series**) **n** série *f*.

serious ['sɪərɪəs] **adj 1.** [causing concern] [situation, problem, threat] sérieux(euse) / [illness, accident, trouble] grave ▸ **it poses a serious threat to airport security** cela constitue une menace sérieuse pour la sécurité des aéroports ▸ **his condition is described as serious** MED son état est jugé préoccupant **2.** [not joking] sérieux(euse) ▸ **I'm quite serious** je suis tout à fait sérieux, je ne plaisante absolument pas ▸ **to be serious about doing sthg** songer sérieusement à faire qqch **3.** [careful, thoughtful] sérieux(euse), sincère ▸ **don't look so serious** ne prends pas cet air sérieux ▸ **to give serious thought** *OR* **consideration to sthg** songer sérieusement à qqch **4.** [not frivolous] **: she's a serious actress** [cinema] elle fait des films sérieux / [theatre] elle joue dans des pièces sérieuses ▸ **the serious cinemagoer** le cinéphile averti.

seriously ['sɪərɪəslɪ] **adv** sérieusement / [ill] gravement / [wounded] grièvement, gravement ▸ **to take sb/sthg seriously** prendre qqn/qqch au sérieux ▸ **seriously though, what are you going to do?** sérieusement, qu'est-ce que vous allez faire? ▸ **think about it seriously before you do anything** réfléchissez-y bien avant de faire quoi que ce soit ▸ **you can't seriously expect me to believe that!** vous plaisantez, j'espère?

seriousness ['sɪərɪəsnɪs] **n 1.** [of mistake, illness] gravité *f* ▸ **in all seriousness** en toute sincérité **2.** [of person, speech] sérieux *m*.

sermon ['sɜ:mən] **n** sermon *m*.

serpent ['sɜ:pənt] **n** *liter* serpent *m*.

serrated [sɪ'reɪtɪd] **adj** en dents de scie.

serum ['sɪərəm] (pl **-s**) **n** sérum *m*.

servant ['sɜ:vənt] **n** domestique *mf*.

serve [sɜ:v] ■ **vt 1.** [work for] servir

2. [have effect] **: to serve to do sthg** servir à faire qqch ▸ **to serve a purpose** [subj: device] servir à un usage ▸ **it serves my purpose** cela fait l'affaire
3. [provide for] desservir ▸ **this recipe serves four** cette recette est prévue pour quatre personnes
4. [meal, drink, customer] servir ▸ **are you being served?** est-ce qu'on s'occupe de vous? ▸ **dinner is served** le dîner est servi ▸ **to serve sthg to sb, to serve sb sthg** servir qqch à qqn
5. LAW **: to serve sb with a summons/writ, to serve a summons/writ on sb** signifier une assignation/une citation à qqn, notifier une assignation/une citation à qqn
6. [prison sentence] purger, faire / [apprenticeship, term] faire ▸ **he has served two terms (of office) as president** il a rempli deux mandats présidentiels
7. SPORT servir
▸▸ **it serves him/you right** c'est bien fait pour lui/toi.
■ **vi** servir ▸ **Smith to serve** SPORT au service, Smith ▸ **to serve as** servir de ▸ **he served as treasurer for several years** il a exercé les fonctions de trésorier pendant plusieurs années ▸ **to serve on a committee** être membre d'un comité.
■ **n** SPORT service *m*.
◆ ***serve out, serve up*** **vt sep** [food] servir.

server ['sɜːvər] **n** COMPUT serveur *m*.

service ['sɜːvɪs] ■ **n 1.** [gen] service *m* ▸ **many people gave their services free** beaucoup de gens donnaient des prestations bénévoles ▸ **at your service** à votre service, à votre disposition ▸ **you get fast service in a supermarket** on est servi rapidement dans un supermarché ▸ **a new 24-hour banking service** un nouveau service bancaire fonctionnant 24 heures sur 24 ▸ **in/out of service** en/hors service ▸ **to be of service (to sb)** être utile (à qqn), rendre service (à qqn) **2.** [of car] révision *f* / [of machine] entretien *m* **3.** MIL service *m* ▸ **he saw active service in Korea** il a servi en Corée.
■ **vt 1.** [car] réviser / [machine] assurer l'entretien de **2.** FIN [debt] rembourser.
◆ ***services*** **npl 1.** *UK* [on motorway] aire *f* de services **2.** [armed forces] **: the services** les forces *fpl* armées **3.** [help] service *m*.

serviceable ['sɜːvɪsəbl] **adj** pratique.

service area **n** *UK* aire *f* de services.

service charge **n** service *m*.

service industry **n** industrie *f* de services ▸ **the service industries** le secteur tertiaire.

serviceman ['sɜːvɪsmən] (**pl -men** [-mən]) **n** soldat *m*, militaire *m*.

service provider **n** COMPUT fournisseur *m* d'accès.

service station **n** station-service *f*.

servicewoman ['sɜːvɪsˌwʊmən] (**pl -women** [-ˌwɪmɪn]) **n** femme *f* soldat.

servicing ['sɜːvɪsɪŋ] **n 1.** [of heating, car] entretien *m* **2.** [by transport] desserte *f*.

serviette [ˌsɜːvɪ'et] **n** *UK* serviette *f* (de table).

servile ['sɜːvaɪl] **adj** servile, obséquieux(euse).

servility [sɜː'vɪlətɪ] **n** servilité *f*.

serving ['sɜːvɪŋ] ■ **adj** [spoon, dish] de service.
■ **n** [of food] portion *f*.

sesame ['sesəmɪ] **n** sésame *m*.

sesame seed **n** graine *f* de sésame.

session ['seʃn] **n 1.** [gen] séance *f* ▸ **in session** en séance **2.** *US* [school term] trimestre *m*.

session musician **n** musicien *m*, -enne *f* de studio.

SET® (abbr of ***secure electronic transaction***) **n** COMPUT SET® *f*.

set [set] ■ **adj 1.** [fixed] fixe ▸ **there are no set rules for raising children** il n'y a pas de règles toutes faites pour l'éducation des enfants ▸ **set expression** *OR* **phrase** GRAM expression *f* figée
2. *UK* SCH [book] au programme
3. [ready] **: set (for sthg/to do sthg)** prêt(e) (à qqch/à faire qqch) ▸ **house prices are set to rise steeply** les prix de l'immobilier vont vraisemblablement monter en flèche
4. [determined] **: to be set on sthg** vouloir absolument qqch ▸ **to be set on doing sthg** être résolu(e) à faire qqch ▸ **to be dead set against sthg** s'opposer formellement à qqch
▸▸ **to be set in one's ways** tenir à ses habitudes.
■ **n 1.** [group] [of facts, conditions, characteristics] ensemble *m* / [of keys, tools, golf clubs] jeu *m* / [of stamps, books] collection *f* / [of saucepans] série *f* ▸ **they make a set** ils vont ensemble ▸ **a set of matching luggage** un ensemble de valises assorties ▸ **a full set of the encyclopedia** une encyclopédie complète ▸ **a chess set** un jeu d'échecs ▸ **a set of teeth** [natural] une dentition, une denture / [false] un dentier
2. [television, radio] poste *m*
3. CIN plateau *m* / THEAT scène *f* ▸ **set designer** CIN & TV chef décorateur *m*
4. TENNIS manche *f*, set *m*
5. [for hair] mise *f* en plis.
■ **vt** (**pt & pp set, cont -ting**) **1.** [place] placer, poser, mettre / [jewel] sertir, monter ▸ **the house is set in large grounds** la maison est située dans un grand parc ▸ **the brooch was set with pearls** la broche était sertie de perles
2. [cause to be or do] **: to set sb free** libérer qqn, mettre qqn en liberté ▸ **to set sthg in motion** mettre qqch en branle *OR* en route ▸ **to set sb's mind at rest** tranquilliser qqn ▸ **to set sthg on fire** mettre le feu à qqch ▸ **he set to work** il s'est mis au travail ▸ **his failure set him thinking** son échec lui a donné à réfléchir
3. [prepare - trap] tendre / [- table] mettre
4. [adjust] régler ▸ **I've set the alarm for six** j'ai mis le réveil à (sonner pour) six heures ▸ **how do I set the margins?** comment est-ce que je fais pour placer les marges?
5. [fix - date, deadline, target] fixer ▸ **you've set yourself a tough deadline** vous vous êtes fixé un délai très court ▸ **how are exchange rates set?** comment les taux de change sont-ils déterminés?
6. [establish - example] donner / [- trend] lancer / [- record] établir ▸ **to set the tone for** *OR* **of sthg** donner le ton de qqch
7. [homework, task] donner / [problem] poser ▸ **I set them to work tidying the garden** je les ai mis au désherbage du jardin
8. MED [bone, leg] remettre

9. [arrange] **: to set sthg to music** mettre qqch en musique ▸ **to set sb's hair** faire une mise en plis à qqn
10. [story] **: to be set in** se passer à, se dérouler à.
■ vi (pt & pp set, cont -ting) **1.** [sun] se coucher
2. [jelly] prendre / [glue, cement] durcir.
◆ ***set about*** vt insep [start] entreprendre, se mettre à ▸ **I didn't know how to set about it** je ne savais pas comment m'y prendre ▸ **to set about doing sthg** se mettre à faire qqch.
◆ ***set against*** vt sep **1.** [compare] mettre en balance ▸ **to set expenses against tax** déduire les dépenses des impôts **2.** [cause to oppose] **: to set sb against sb** monter qqn contre qqn.
◆ ***set ahead*** vt sep *US* [clock] avancer.
◆ ***set apart*** vt sep [distinguish] distinguer ▸ **her talent sets her apart from the other students** son talent la distingue des autres étudiants.
◆ ***set aside*** vt sep **1.** [save] mettre de côté ▸ **the room is set aside for meetings** la pièce est réservée aux réunions **2.** [not consider] rejeter, écarter.
◆ ***set back*** vt sep **1.** [towards the rear] **: to be set back from sthg** être en retrait de qqch
2. [delay] retarder
3. *inf* [cost] **: it set me back £300** cela m'a coûté 300 livres.
◆ ***set down*** vt sep **1.** [write down] **: to set sthg down (in writing)** coucher qqch par écrit
2. [put down] déposer.
◆ ***set in*** vi [weather, feeling] commencer, s'installer / [infection] se déclarer ▸ **panic set in** [began] la panique éclata / [lasted] la panique s'installa.
◆ ***set off*** ■ vt sep **1.** [cause] déclencher, provoquer ▸ **to set sb off laughing** faire rire qqn
2. [bomb] faire exploser / [firework] faire partir.
■ vi se mettre en route, partir.
◆ ***set on*** vt sep **: to set a dog on sb** lâcher un chien contre *OR* sur qqn.
◆ ***set out*** ■ vt sep **1.** [arrange] disposer
2. [explain] présenter, exposer.
■ vt insep [intend] **: to set out to do sthg** entreprendre *OR* tenter de faire qqch ▸ **she didn't deliberately set out to annoy you** il n'était pas dans ses intentions de vous froisser.
■ vi [on journey] se mettre en route, partir.
◆ ***set up*** ■ vt sep **1.** [organization] créer, fonder / [committee, procedure] constituer, mettre en place / [meeting] arranger, organiser ▸ **to set o.s. up** s'établir à son compte ▸ **to set up house *OR* home** s'installer ▸ **they set up house together** ils se sont mis en ménage
2. [statue, monument] dresser, ériger / [roadblock] placer, installer ▸ **to set up camp** installer *OR* dresser le camp
3. [equipment] préparer, installer ▸ **he set the chessboard up** il a disposé les pièces sur l'échiquier
4. *inf* [make appear guilty] monter un coup contre ▸ **she claims she was set up** elle prétend qu'elle est victime d'un coup monté.
■ vi [in business] s'établir ▸ **to set up on one's own** [business] s'installer à son compte / [home] prendre son propre appartement.
◆ ***set upon*** vt insep [physically or verbally] attaquer, s'en prendre à.

setback ['setbæk] n contretemps *m*, revers *m*.

set menu n menu *m* fixe.

set piece n ART & LIT morceau *m* traditionnel.

setsquare ['setskweər] n *UK* équerre *f*.

settee [se'ti:] n canapé *m*.

setter ['setər] n [dog] setter *m*.

setting ['setɪŋ] n **1.** [surroundings] décor *m*, cadre *m* **2.** [of dial, machine] réglage *m*.

settle ['setl] ■ vt **1.** [argument] régler ▸ **that's settled then** (c'est) entendu ▸ **nothing is settled yet** rien n'est encore décidé *OR* arrêté ▸ **that settles it, the party's tomorrow!** c'est décidé, la fête aura lieu demain! ▸ **the case was settled out of court** l'affaire a été réglée à l'amiable ▸ **to settle old scores** régler des comptes **2.** [bill, account] régler, payer ▸ **to settle a claim** [insurance] régler un litige **3.** [calm - nerves] calmer ▸ **to settle one's stomach** calmer les douleurs d'estomac **4.** [make comfortable] installer ▸ **to settle o.s.** s'installer.
■ vi **1.** [make one's home] s'installer, se fixer **2.** [make oneself comfortable] s'installer **3.** [dust] retomber / [sediment] se déposer ▸ **an eerie calm settled over the village** un calme inquiétant retomba sur le village ▸ **the cold settled on his chest** le rhume lui est tombé sur la poitrine **4.** [bird, insect] se poser.
◆ ***settle down*** vi **1.** [give one's attention] **: to settle down to sthg/to doing sthg** se mettre à qqch/à faire qqch **2.** [make oneself comfortable] s'installer **3.** [become respectable] se ranger ▸ **it's about time Tom got married and settled down** il est temps que Tom se marie et s'installe dans la vie **4.** [become calm] se calmer.
◆ ***settle for*** vt insep accepter, se contenter de.
◆ ***settle in*** vi s'adapter ▸ **once we're settled in, we'll invite you round** [at new house] une fois que nous serons installés, nous t'inviterons.
◆ ***settle on*** vt insep [choose] fixer son choix sur, se décider pour ▸ **they settled on a compromise** ils ont finalement choisi le compromis.
◆ ***settle up*** vi **: can we settle up?** est-ce qu'on peut faire les comptes? ▸ **to settle up (with sb)** régler (qqn).

settled ['setld] adj [weather] au beau fixe.

settlement ['setlmənt] n **1.** [agreement] accord *m* ▸ **to reach a settlement** parvenir à *OR* conclure un accord **2.** [colony] colonie *f* **3.** [payment] règlement *m* ▸ **out-of-court settlement** règlement à l'amiable.

settler ['setlər] n colon *m*.

set-to n *inf* bagarre *f*.

set-top box n boîtier *m* électronique.

set-up n *inf* **1.** [system] **: what's the set-up?** comment est-ce que c'est organisé? **2.** [trick to incriminate] coup *m* monté.

set-up costs n frais *mpl* de lancement.

set-up fee n frais *mpl* d'inscription.

seven ['sevn] num sept ; see also ***six***.

seventeen [ˌsevn'ti:n] num dix-sept ; see also ***six***.

seventeenth [ˌsevn'ti:nθ] num dix-septième ; see also ***sixth***.

seventh ['sevnθ] num septième ; see also ***sixth***.

seventh heaven n **: to be in seventh heaven** être au septième ciel.

seventieth ['sevntjəθ] **num** soixante-dixième ; see also ***sixth***.

seventy ['sevntɪ] **num** soixante-dix ; see also ***sixty***.

sever ['sevəʳ] **vt 1.** [cut through] couper **2.** *fig* [relationship, ties] rompre.

several ['sevrəl] ■ **adj** plusieurs.
■ **pron** plusieurs *mf pl*.

severance ['sevrəns] **n** *fml* [of relations] rupture *f*.

severance pay **n** indemnité *f* de licenciement.

severe [sɪ'vɪəʳ] **adj 1.** [weather] rude, rigoureux(euse) / [shock] gros (grosse), dur(e) / [pain] violent(e) / [illness, injury] grave **2.** [person, criticism] sévère.

severely [sɪ'vɪəlɪ] **adv 1.** [injured] grièvement / [damaged] sérieusement **2.** [sternly] sévèrement.

severity [sɪ'verətɪ] **n 1.** [of storm] violence *f* / [of problem, illness] gravité *f* **2.** [sternness] sévérité *f*.

sew [səʊ] (*UK* sewn, pt & pp **-ied**, *US* **sewed** *OR* sewn) **vt & vi** coudre.
◆ ***sew up*** **vt sep 1.** [join] recoudre **2.** *inf* [deal] **: it's (all) sewn up!** c'est dans la poche!

sewage ['su:ɪdʒ] **n** *(U)* eaux *fpl* d'égout, eaux usées.

sewage farm *UK*, ***sewage works*** *UK*, ***sewage plant*** *US* **n** champs *mpl* d'épandage.

sewer ['sʊəʳ] **n** égout *m*.

sewerage ['sʊərɪdʒ] **n** système *m* d'égouts.

sewing ['səʊɪŋ] **n** *(U)* **1.** [activity] couture *f* **2.** [work] ouvrage *m*.

sewing machine **n** machine *f* à coudre.

sewn [səʊn] **pp** ➤ ***sew***.

sex [seks] **n 1.** [gender] sexe *m* **2.** *(U)* [sexual intercourse] rapports *mpl* (sexuels) ▸ **to have sex with** avoir des rapports (sexuels) avec.

sex appeal **n** sex-appeal *m*.

sex change **n** changement *m* de sexe ▸ **to have a sex change** changer de sexe.

sex education **n** éducation *f* sexuelle.

sexism ['seksɪzm] **n** sexisme *m*.

sexist ['seksɪst] ■ **adj** sexiste.
■ **n** sexiste *mf*.

sex life **n** vie *f* sexuelle.

sex object **n** objet *m* sexuel.

sex offender **n** auteur *m* d'un délit sexuel.

sex shop **n** sex-shop *m*.

sex symbol **n** sex-symbol *m*.

sextet [seks'tet] **n** sextuor *m*.

sextuplet [seks'tju:plɪt] **n** sextuplé *m*, -e *f*.

sexual ['sekʃʊəl] **adj** sexuel(elle).

sexual abuse **n** *(U)* sévices *mpl* sexuels.

sexual assault **n** agression *f* sexuelle.

sexual harassment **n** harcèlement *m* sexuel.

sexual intercourse **n** *(U)* rapports *mpl* (sexuels).

sexuality [ˌsekʃʊ'ælətɪ] **n** sexualité *f*.

sexually ['sekʃʊəlɪ] **adv** sexuellement ▸ **to be sexually assaulted** être victime d'une agression sexuelle ▸ **sexually transmitted disease** maladie *f* sexuellement transmissible.

sexy ['seksɪ] (comp **-ier**, superl **-iest**) **adj** *inf* **1.** sexy *(inv)* **2.** [product] branché(e).

Seychelles [seɪ'ʃelz] **npl : the Seychelles** les Seychelles *fpl* ▸ **in the Seychelles** aux Seychelles.

SF, ***sf*** (abbr of ***science fiction***) **n** SF *f*.

SFO (abbr of ***Serious Fraud Office***) **n** *service britannique de la répression des fraudes*.

SG (abbr of ***Surgeon General***) **n** *directeur fédéral américain de la santé publique*.

SGML (abbr of ***Standard Generalized Markup Language***) **n** COMPUT SGML *m*.

Sgt (abbr of ***sergeant***) Sgt.

sh [ʃ] **excl** chut!

shabby ['ʃæbɪ] (comp **-ier**, superl **-iest**) **adj 1.** [clothes] élimé(e), râpé(e) / [furniture] minable / [person, street] miteux(euse) **2.** [behaviour] moche, méprisable.

shack [ʃæk] **n** cabane *f*, hutte *f*.

shackle ['ʃækl] **vt** enchaîner / *fig* entraver.
◆ ***shackles*** **npl** fers *mpl* / *fig* entraves *fpl*.

shade [ʃeɪd] ■ **n 1.** *(U)* [shadow] ombre *f* **2.** [lampshade] abat-jour *m inv* **3.** [colour] nuance *f*, ton *m* **4.** [of meaning, opinion] nuance *f*.
■ **vt** [from light] abriter ▸ **to shade one's eyes** s'abriter les yeux.
■ **vi : to shade into** se fondre en.
◆ ***shades*** **npl** *inf* [sunglasses] lunettes *fpl* de soleil.

shading ['ʃeɪdɪŋ] *(U)* **n** ombres *fpl*.

shadow ['ʃædəʊ] ■ **adj** *UK* POL fantôme, de l'opposition.
■ **n** ombre *f* ▸ **to be a shadow of one's former self** n'être plus que l'ombre de soi-même ▸ **there's not a** *OR* **the shadow of a doubt** il n'y a pas l'ombre d'un doute.

shadow cabinet **n** *UK* cabinet *m* fantôme.

CULTURE

Shadow Cabinet

Au Royaume-Uni, le « Cabinet fantôme » est une sorte de « contre-gouvernement » de rechange, formé à l'avance par le principal parti d'opposition en cas de chute du pouvoir en place. Il est constitué de politiciens qui occupent les mêmes fonctions et qui bénéficient des mêmes privilèges que leurs homologues du « Cabinet » réel, c'est à dire les ministres entourant le Premier ministre : il y a ainsi des ministres des Finances, de la Défense ou des Affaires étrangères « fantômes ». Au Parlement, ils occupent une aile à la Chambre des communes qui fait face aux membres du parti majoritaire au pouvoir.

shadowy ['ʃædəʊɪ] **adj 1.** [dark] ombreux(euse) **2.** [hard to see] indistinct(e) **3.** [sinister] mystérieux(euse).

shady ['ʃeɪdɪ] (comp **-ier**, superl **-iest**) **adj 1.** [garden, street] ombragé(e) / [tree] qui donne de l'ombre **2.** *inf* [dishonest] louche.

shaft [ʃɑ:ft] ■ n **1.** [vertical passage] puits *m* / [of lift] cage *f* **2.** TECH arbre *m* **3.** [of light] rayon *m* **4.** [of tool, golf club] manche *m*.
■ vt *v inf* **1.** [dupe] avoir, baiser **2.** [treat unfairly] s'en prendre à.

shag [ʃæg] ■ n **1.** [of hair, wool] toison *f* ▸ **shag (pile) carpet** moquette *f* à poils longs **2.** : **shag (tobacco)** tabac *m* (très fort) **3.** [bird] cormoran *m* huppé **4.** *vulg* [sex] : **to have a shag** baiser **5.** *US* [ballboy] ramasseur *m* de balles.
■ vt (pt & pp **-ed**) **1.** *v inf* [tire] crever ▸ **to be shagged (out)** être complètement crevé(e) *OR* HS **2.** *vulg* [have sex with] baiser **3.** *US* [fetch] aller chercher.
■ vi (pt & pp **shagged**) *vulg* [have sex] baiser.

shaggy ['ʃægɪ] (comp **-ier**, superl **-iest**) **adj** hirsute.

shaggy-dog story n histoire *f* farfelue *OR* à dormir debout.

shake [ʃeɪk] ■ vt (pt **shook**, pp **shaken**) **1.** [move vigorously - gen] secouer / [- bottle] agiter ▸ **to shake sb's hand** serrer la main de *OR* à qqn ▸ **to shake hands** se serrer la main ▸ **to shake one's head** secouer la tête / [- to say no] faire non de la tête ▸ **he shook his fist at him** il l'a menacé du poing **2.** [shock] ébranler, secouer ▸ **they were rather shaken by the news** ils ont été plutôt secoués par la nouvelle ▸ **she shook everyone with her revelations** tout le monde a été bouleversé par ses révélations.
■ vi (pt **shook**, pp **shaken**) trembler ▸ **to shake in one's shoes** avoir une peur bleue, être mort de peur.
■ n [tremble] tremblement *m* ▸ **to give sthg a shake** secouer qqch ▸ **with a shake of his head** [in refusal, resignation, sympathy] avec un hochement de tête.
◆ ***shake down*** vt sep *US inf* **1.** [rob] racketter **2.** [search] fouiller.
◆ ***shake off*** vt sep [police, pursuers] semer / [illness] se débarrasser de.

shakedown ['ʃeɪkdaʊn] n *US inf* **1.** [extortion] racket *m* **2.** [search] fouille *f*.

shaken ['ʃeɪkn] pp ➤ *shake*.

shakeout ['ʃeɪkaʊt] n *inf* FIN récession *f*.

Shakespearean [ʃeɪk'spɪərɪən] adj shakespearien(enne).

shake-up n *inf* remaniement *m*.

shakily ['ʃeɪkɪlɪ] **adv** **1.** [unsteadily - walk] d'un pas chancelant *OR* mal assuré / [- write] d'une main tremblante / [- speak] d'une voix tremblante *OR* chevrotante **2.** [uncertainly] d'une manière hésitante *OR* peu assurée ▸ **she started shakily, but then went on to win the game** au début, elle n'était pas très sûre d'elle, mais elle a fini par gagner la partie.

shaky ['ʃeɪkɪ] (comp **-ier**, superl **-iest**) **adj** [building, table] branlant(e) / [hand] tremblant(e) / [person] faible / [argument, start] incertain(e) ▸ **things got off to a shaky start** les choses ont plutôt mal commencé.

shale [ʃeɪl] n schiste *m*.

shall (*weak form* [ʃəl], *strong form* [ʃæl]) **aux vb** **1.** (*1st person sg &1st person pl*) (*to express future tense*) : **I shall be...** je serai... **2.** (*esp 1st person sg &1st person pl*) (*in questions*) : **shall we have lunch now?** tu veux qu'on déjeune maintenant? ▸ **where shall I put this?** où est-ce qu'il faut mettre ça? **3.** [will definitely] : **we shall succeed** nous réussirons **4.** (*in orders*) : **you shall tell me!** tu vas *OR* dois me le dire!

shallot [ʃə'lɒt] n échalote *f*.

shallow ['ʃæləʊ] **adj** **1.** [water, dish, hole] peu profond(e) **2.** *pej* [superficial] superficiel(elle).
◆ ***shallows*** npl bas-fond *m*.

shallowness ['ʃæləʊnɪs] n **1.** [of water, soil, dish] faible profondeur *f* **2.** [of mind, character, sentiments] manque *m* de profondeur / [of person] esprit *m* superficiel, manque *m* de profondeur / [of talk, ideas] futilité *f*.

sham [ʃæm] ■ **adj** feint(e), simulé(e).
■ n comédie *f*.
■ vi (pt & pp **-med**, cont **-ming**) faire semblant, jouer la comédie.

shambles ['ʃæmblz] n désordre *m*, pagaille *f*.

shame [ʃeɪm] ■ n **1.** (*U*) [remorse, humiliation] honte *f* ▸ **he has no sense of shame** il n'a aucune honte ▸ **have you no shame?** vous n'avez pas honte ? ▸ **to bring shame on *OR* upon sb** faire la honte de qqn ▸ **to put sb to shame** faire honte à qqn **2.** [pity] : **it's a shame (that...)** c'est dommage (que... (*+ subjunctive*)) ▸ **what a shame!** quel dommage!
■ vt faire honte à, mortifier ▸ **to shame sb into doing sthg** obliger qqn à faire qqch en lui faisant honte.

shamefaced [ˌʃeɪm'feɪst] **adj** honteux(euse), penaud(e).

shameful ['ʃeɪmfʊl] **adj** honteux(euse), scandaleux(euse).

shamefully ['ʃeɪmfʊlɪ] **adv** honteusement, indignement ▸ **she has been treated shamefully** elle a été traitée de façon honteuse ▸ **he was shamefully ignorant about the issue** son ignorance sur la question était honteuse.

shameless ['ʃeɪmlɪs] **adj** effronté(e), éhonté(e).

shamelessly ['ʃeɪmlɪslɪ] **adv** sans honte, sans vergogne, sans pudeur ▸ **to lie shamelessly** mentir effrontément ▸ **they were walking about quite shamelessly with nothing on** ils se promenaient tout nus sans la moindre gêne *OR* sans que ça ait l'air de les gêner.

shammy ['ʃæmɪ] (pl **-ies**) n : **shammy (leather)** peau *f* de chamois.

shampoo [ʃæm'pu:] ■ n (pl **-s**) shampooing *m*.
■ vt (pt & pp **-ed**, cont **-ing**) : **to shampoo sb *OR* sb's hair** faire un shampooing à qqn.

shamrock ['ʃæmrɒk] n trèfle *m*.

shandy ['ʃændɪ] (pl **-ies**) n panaché *m*.

shan't [ʃɑ:nt] = ***shall not***.

shantytown ['ʃæntɪtaʊn] n bidonville *m*.

shape [ʃeɪp] ■ n **1.** [gen] forme *f* ▸ **the room was triangular in shape** la pièce était de forme triangulaire *OR* avait la forme d'un triangle ▸ **in the shape of a T** en forme de T ▸ **she moulded the clay into shape** elle façonna l'argile ▸ **she plans to change the whole shape of the company** elle a l'intention de modifier complètement la structure de l'entreprise ▸ **to take shape** prendre forme *OR* tournure **2.** [guise] : **in the shape of** sous forme de ▸ **in any shape or form** de n'importe quelle sorte

shepherd's pie ['ʃepədz-] **n** ≃ hachis *m* Parmentier.

sherbet ['ʃɜ:bət] **n 1.** *UK* [sweet powder] poudre *f* aromatisée **2.** *US* [sorbet] sorbet *m*.

sheriff ['ʃerif] **n** *US* shérif *m*.

sherry ['ʃerɪ] (pl **-ies**) **n** xérès *m*, sherry *m*.

she's [ʃi:z] = ***she is, she has***.

Shetland ['ʃetlənd] **n : (the) Shetland (Islands)** les (îles *fpl*) Shetland *fpl* ▸ **in (the) Shetland (Islands)** dans les Shetland.

shh [ʃ] **excl** chut!

shield [ʃi:ld] ■ **n 1.** [armour] bouclier *m* **2.** *UK* [sports trophy] plaque *f*.
■ **vt : to shield sb (from)** protéger qqn (de **OR** contre).

shift [ʃɪft] ■ **n 1.** [change] changement *m*, modification *f* ▸ **(gear) shift** *US* AUT changement *m* de vitesse **2.** [period of work] poste *m* / [workers] équipe *f* ▸ **she works long shifts** elle fait de longues journées ▸ **to work shifts, to be on shifts** travailler en équipe, faire les trois-huit **3.** COMPUT [in arithmetical operation] décalage *m* / [in word processing] touche *f* de majuscule.
■ **vt 1.** [move] déplacer, changer de place ▸ **to shift the blame onto sb** rejeter la responsabilité sur qqn **2.** [change] changer, modifier ▸ **to shift gears** *US* changer de vitesse.
■ **vi 1.** [move - gen] changer de place / [- wind] tourner, changer ▸ **could you shift up a bit, please?** pourrais-tu te pousser un peu, s'il te plaît? **2.** [change] changer, se modifier **3.** *US* AUT changer de vitesse ▸ **to shift into fourth (gear)** *US* AUT passer en quatrième (vitesse).

shift key **n** touche *f* de majuscule.

shiftless ['ʃɪftlɪs] **adj** fainéant(e), paresseux(euse).

shift stick **n** *US* levier *m* de vitesse.

shift work **n** travail *m* en équipe ▸ **she does shift work** elle fait les trois-huit.

shift worker **n** *personne qui fait les trois-huit*.

shifty ['ʃɪftɪ] (comp **-ier**, superl **-iest**) **adj** *inf* sournois(e), louche.

Shiite ['ʃi:aɪt] ■ **adj** chiite.
■ **n** Chiite *mf*.

shilling ['ʃɪlɪŋ] **n** shilling *m*.

shilly-shally ['ʃɪlɪ,ʃælɪ] (pt & pp **-ied**) **vi** hésiter, être indécis(e).

shimmer ['ʃɪməʳ] ■ **n** [of sequins, jewellery, silk] chatoiement *m*, scintillement *m* / [of water] miroitement *m*.
■ **vi** [sequins, jewellery, silk] chatoyer, scintiller / [water] miroiter.

shimmering ['ʃɪmərɪŋ] **adj** [light] scintillant(e) / [jewellery, silk] chatoyant(e) / [water] miroitant(e).

shin [ʃɪn] (pt & pp **-ned**, cont **-ning**) **n** tibia *m*.
◆ ***shin up*** *UK*, ***shinny up*** *US* **vt insep** grimper à.

shinbone ['ʃɪnbəʊn] **n** tibia *m*.

shine [ʃaɪn] ■ **n** brillant *m*.
■ **vt 1.** (pt & pp **shone**) [direct] **: to shine a torch on sthg** éclairer qqch **2.** (pt & pp **shined**) [polish] faire briller, astiquer.
■ **vi** (pt & pp **shone**) briller ▸ **to shine at sthg** *fig* briller dans qqch.

shingle ['ʃɪŋgl] **n** *(U)* [on beach] galets *mpl*.
◆ ***shingles*** **n** *(U)* zona *m*.

shining ['ʃaɪnɪŋ] **adj 1.** [gleaming] brillant(e), luisant(e) **2.** [achievement] extraordinaire ▸ **to be a shining example of sthg** être un modèle de qqch.

shinny ['ʃɪnɪ] *US* ◆ ***shinny up*** **vt insep** = ***shin up***.

shiny ['ʃaɪnɪ] (comp **-ier**, superl **-iest**) **adj** brillant(e).

ship [ʃɪp] ■ **n** bateau *m* / [larger] navire *m*.
■ **vt** (pt & pp **-ped**, cont **-ping**) [goods] expédier / [troops, passengers] transporter.

shipbuilder ['ʃɪp,bɪldəʳ] **n** constructeur *m* de navires.

shipbuilding ['ʃɪp,bɪldɪŋ] **n** construction *f* navale.

ship canal **n** canal *m* maritime.

shipment ['ʃɪpmənt] **n** [cargo] cargaison *f*, chargement *m*.

shipper ['ʃɪpəʳ] **n** affréteur *m*, chargeur *m*.

shipping ['ʃɪpɪŋ] **n** *(U)* **1.** [transport] transport *m* maritime **2.** [ships] navires *mpl*.

shipping agent **n** agent *m* maritime.

shipping company **n** compagnie *f* de navigation.

shipping forecast *UK*, ***shipping news*** *US* **n** météo *f* marine.

shipping lane **n** voie *f* de navigation.

shipshape ['ʃɪpʃeɪp] **adj** bien rangé(e), en ordre.

shipwreck ['ʃɪprek] ■ **n 1.** [destruction of ship] naufrage *m* **2.** [wrecked ship] épave *f*.
■ **vt : to be shipwrecked** faire naufrage.

shipwrecked ['ʃɪprekt] **adj** naufragé(e).

shipyard ['ʃɪpjɑ:d] **n** chantier *m* naval.

shire [ʃaɪəʳ] **n** [county] comté *m*.
◆ ***Shire*** **n : the Shires** *les Comtés du centre de l'Angleterre*.

shire horse **n** *UK* cheval *m* de gros trait.

shirk [ʃɜ:k] **vt** se dérober à.

shirker ['ʃɜ:kəʳ] **n** tire-au-flanc *m inv*.

shirt [ʃɜ:t] **n** chemise *f*.

shirtsleeves ['ʃɜ:tsli:vz] **npl : to be in (one's) shirtsleeves** être en manches **OR** en bras de chemise.

shirttail ['ʃɜ:tteɪl] **n** pan *m* de chemise.

shirty ['ʃɜ:tɪ] (comp **-ier**, superl **-iest**) **adj** *UK inf* de mauvais poil, de mauvaise humeur.

shit [ʃɪt] *vulg* ■ **n 1.** [excrement] merde *f* **2.** *(U)* [nonsense] conneries *fpl* **3.** [person] salaud *m*.
■ **vi** (pt & pp **-ted OR shat**, cont **-ting**) chier.
■ **excl** merde!

shitless ['ʃɪtlɪs] **adj** *vulg* **: to be scared shitless** avoir une trouille bleue ▸ **to be bored shitless** se faire chier à mort.

shitload ['ʃɪtləʊd] **n** *vulg* **: shitloads of sthg** des tonnes de qqch.

shit-scared **adj** *vulg* **: to be shit-scared** avoir une trouille bleu.

shiver ['ʃɪvəʳ] ■ **n** frisson *m* ▸ **to give sb the shivers** *fig* donner le frisson **OR** la chair de poule à qqn.
■ **vi : to shiver (with)** trembler (de), frissonner (de).

shivery ['ʃɪvərɪ] **adj** [cold] frissonnant(e) / [frightened] frissonnant(e), tremblant(e) / [feverish] fiévreux(euse), grelottant(e) de fièvre.

shoal [ʃəʊl] **n** [of fish] banc *m*.

shock [ʃɒk] ■ **n 1.** [surprise] choc *m*, coup *m* ▸ **she got a shock when she saw me again** ça lui a fait un choc de me revoir ▸ **what a shock you gave me!** qu'est-ce que tu m'as fait peur! ▸ **the news of his death came as a terrible shock to me** la nouvelle de sa mort a été un grand choc pour moi **2.** *(U)* MED **: to be suffering from shock, to be in (a state of) shock** être en état de choc **3.** [impact] choc *m*, heurt *m* **4.** ELEC décharge *f* électrique.
■ **vt 1.** [upset] bouleverser **2.** [offend] choquer, scandaliser.

shock absorber [-əbˌzɔːbər] **n** amortisseur *m*.

shocked [ʃɒkt] **adj 1.** [upset] bouleversé(e) **2.** [offended] choqué(e), scandalisé(e).

shocker ['ʃɒkər] **n** *inf* **1.** [book] livre *m* à sensation / [film] film *m* à sensation / [news] nouvelle *f* sensationnelle / [play] pièce *f* à sensation / [story] histoire *f* sensationnelle ▸ **that's a real shocker of a story** cette histoire est vraiment choquante **2.** *hum* [atrocious person] **: you little shocker!** petit monstre!

shocking ['ʃɒkɪŋ] **adj 1.** *UK* [very bad] épouvantable, terrible **2.** [outrageous] scandaleux(euse).

shockingly ['ʃɒkɪŋlɪ] **adv 1.** [as intensifier] affreusement, atrocement ▸ **the weather has been shockingly bad lately** la météo est vraiment affreuse depuis quelque temps **2.** *UK inf* [extremely badly] très mal, lamentablement.

shockproof ['ʃɒkpruːf] **adj** antichoc *(inv)*.

shock tactics **npl** tactique *f* de choc.

shock therapy, ***shock treatment*** **n** traitement *m* par électrochocs.

shock troops **npl** troupes *fpl* de choc.

shock wave **n** onde *f* de choc.

shod [ʃɒd] ■ **pt & pp** ➤ ***shoe***.
■ **adj** chaussé(e).

shoddy ['ʃɒdɪ] **(comp -ier, superl -iest) adj** [goods, work] de mauvaise qualité / [treatment] indigne, méprisable.

shoe [ʃuː] ■ **n** chaussure *f*, soulier *m*.
■ **vt (pt & pp -ed** ***OR*** **shod, cont -ing)** [horse] ferrer.

shoebrush ['ʃuːbrʌʃ] **n** brosse *f* à chaussures.

shoe cleaner **n** produit *m* pour chaussures.

shoehorn ['ʃuːhɔːn] **n** chausse-pied *m*.

shoelace ['ʃuːleɪs] **n** lacet *m* de soulier.

shoemaker ['ʃuːˌmeɪkər] **n** [repairer] cordonnier *m* / [manufacturer] fabricant *m*, -e *f* de chaussures.

shoe polish **n** cirage *m*.

shoe repairer [-rɪˌpeərər] **n** cordonnier *m*.

shoe shop **n** magasin *m* de chaussures.

shoestring ['ʃuːstrɪŋ] ■ **adj** [budget] étroit(e).
■ **n** *fig* **: on a shoestring** à peu de frais.

shoetree ['ʃuːtriː] **n** embauchoir *m*.

shone [ʃɒn] **pt & pp** ➤ ***shine***.

shoo [ʃuː] ■ **vt** chasser.
■ **excl** ouste!

shook [ʃʊk] **pt** ➤ ***shake***.

shoot [ʃuːt] ■ **vt (pt & pp shot) 1.** [kill with gun] tuer d'un coup de feu / [wound with gun] blesser d'un coup de feu ▸ **she was shot in the arm/leg** elle a reçu une balle dans le bras/la jambe ▸ **to shoot o.s.** [kill o.s.] se tuer avec une arme à feu ▸ **to shoot o.s. in the foot** *inf* ramasser une pelle
2. *UK* [hunt] chasser
3. [fire - gun] tirer un coup de / [- bullet] tirer / [- arrow] tirer, décocher ▸ **they were shooting their rifles in the air** ils tiraient des coups de feu en l'air
4. [direct - glance, look] lancer, décocher ▸ **she shot a shy smile at him** elle lui jeta un petit sourire timide ▸ **to shoot questions at sb** bombarder qqn de questions
5. CIN tourner
6. *US* [play - pool] jouer à
7. [send] envoyer ▸ **the explosion shot debris high into the air** l'explosion a projeté des débris dans les airs.
■ **vi (pt & pp shot) 1.** [fire gun] **: to shoot on sight** tirer à vue ▸ **to shoot (at)** tirer (sur)
2. *UK* [hunt] chasser
3. [move quickly] **: to shoot in/out/past** entrer/sortir/passer en trombe, entrer/sortir/passer comme un bolide ▸ **the car shot out in front of us** [changed lanes] la voiture a déboîté tout d'un coup devant nous / [from another street] la voiture a débouché devant nous ▸ **the water shot out of the hose** l'eau a jailli du tuyau d'arrosage ▸ **debris shot into the air** des débris ont été projetés en l'air
4. CIN tourner ▸ **shoot!** moteur!, on tourne!
5. SPORT tirer, shooter.
■ **n 1.** *UK* [hunting expedition] partie *f* de chasse
2. [of plant] pousse *f*
3. CIN tournage *m*.
■ **excl** *inf* **1.** [go ahead] vas-y!
2. [damn] zut!
◆ ***shoot down*** **vt sep 1.** [aircraft] descendre, abattre
2. [person] abattre
3. *fig* [proposal] démolir / [person] descendre en flammes.
◆ ***shoot up*** **vi 1.** [child, plant] pousser vite
2. [price, inflation] monter en flèche
3. *drug sl* se shooter.

shooting ['ʃuːtɪŋ] **n 1.** [killing] meurtre *m* **2.** *(U) UK* [hunting] chasse *f*.

shooting range **n** champ *m* de tir.

shooting star **n** étoile *f* filante.

shooting stick **n** canne-siège *f*.

shoot-out **n** fusillade *f*.

shop [ʃɒp] ■ **n 1.** [store] magasin *m*, boutique *f* ▸ **to talk shop** parler métier ***OR*** boutique **2.** [workshop] atelier *m*.
■ **vi (pt & pp -ped, cont -ping)** faire ses courses ▸ **to go shopping** aller faire les courses ***OR*** commissions.
◆ ***shop around*** **vi** comparer les prix.

shopaholic [ˌʃɒpə'hɒlɪk] **n** *inf* **: he's a real shopaholic** il adore faire les boutiques.

shop assistant **n** *UK* vendeur *m*, -euse *f*.

shop floor **n : the shop floor** *fig* les ouvriers *mpl*.

shopfront ['ʃɒpfrʌnt] **n** *UK* devanture *f* (de magasin).

shopkeeper ['ʃɒpˌkiːpəʳ] **n** *esp UK* commerçant *m*, -e *f*.

shoplift ['ʃɒplɪft] **vt** voler à l'étalage.

shoplifter ['ʃɒpˌlɪftəʳ] **n** voleur *m*, -euse *f* à l'étalage.

shoplifting ['ʃɒpˌlɪftɪŋ] **n** *(U)* vol *m* à l'étalage.

shopper ['ʃɒpəʳ] **n** personne *f* qui fait ses courses.

shopping ['ʃɒpɪŋ] **n** *(U) UK* [purchases] achats *mpl*.

shopping bag **n** sac *m* à provisions.

shopping basket **n** panier *m* de course.

shopping cart *US* = ***shopping trolley***.

shopping centre *UK*, ***shopping mall*** *US*, ***shopping plaza*** *US* [-ˌplɑːzə] **n** centre *m* commercial.

shopping channel **n** TV chaîne *f* de télé-achat.

shopping list **n** liste *f* des commissions.

shopping mall, ***shopping plaza*** *US* = ***shopping centre***.

shopping trolley, ***shopping cart*** *US* **n** chariot *m*, Caddie® *m*.

shopsoiled *UK* ['ʃɒpsɔɪld], ***shopworn*** *US* ['ʃɒpwɔːn] **adj** qui a fait l'étalage, abîmé(e) (en magasin).

shop steward **n** délégué syndical *m*, déléguée syndicale *f*.

shopwalker ['ʃɒpˌwɔːkəʳ] **n** *UK* surveillant *m*, -e *f* de magasin.

shopwindow [ˌʃɒp'wɪndəʊ] **n** vitrine *f*.

shopworn *US* = ***shopsoiled***.

shore [ʃɔːʳ] **n** rivage *m*, bord *m* ▸ **on shore** à terre.
◆ ***shore up*** **vt sep** étayer, étançonner / *fig* consolider.

shore leave **n** permission *f* à terre.

shoreline ['ʃɔːlaɪn] **n** côte *f*.

shorn [ʃɔːn] ■ **pp** ➤ ***shear***.
■ **adj** tondu(e).

short [ʃɔːt] ■ **adj 1.** [not long - in time] court(e), bref (brève) / [- in space] court ▸ **she was in London for a short time** elle a passé quelque temps à Londres ▸ **the days are getting shorter** les jours raccourcissent ▸ **to have short hair** avoir les cheveux courts ▸ **to go for a short walk** faire une petite promenade ▸ **it's only a short distance from here** ce n'est pas très loin (d'ici) ▸ **short and sweet** *inf* court mais bien
2. [not tall] petit(e)
3. [curt] brusque, sec (sèche)
4. [lacking] : **time/money is short** nous manquons de temps/d'argent ▸ **we're £10 short** il nous manque 10 livres ▸ **to be short of** manquer de ▸ **I'm a bit short (of money) at the moment** je suis un peu à court (d'argent) en ce moment ▸ **to be short of breath** être essoufflé(e)
5. [abbreviated] : **to be short for** être le diminutif de ▸ **Bill is short for William** Bill est un diminutif de William.
■ **adv : to be running short of** [running out of] commencer à manquer de, commencer à être à court de ▸ **to cut sthg short** [visit, speech] écourter qqch / [discussion] couper court à qqch ▸ **to fall short of** [objective, target] ne pas atteindre / [expectations] ne pas répondre à ▸ **to stop short** s'arrêter net ▸ **to bring** *OR* **pull sb up short** arrêter qqn net.
■ **n 1.** *UK* [alcoholic drink] alcool *m* fort
2. [film] court métrage *m*.
◆ ***shorts*** **npl 1.** [gen] short *m*
2. *US* [underwear] caleçon *m*.
◆ ***for short*** **adv : he's called Bob for short** Bob est son diminutif.
◆ ***in short*** **adv** (enfin) bref.
◆ ***nothing short of*** **prep** rien moins que, pratiquement.
◆ ***short of*** **prep** [unless, without] **: short of doing sthg** à moins de faire qqch, à part faire qqch ▸ **he would do anything short of stealing** il ferait tout sauf voler.

shortage ['ʃɔːtɪdʒ] **n** manque *m*, insuffisance *f*.

short back and sides **n** *UK* coupe *f* bien dégagée.

shortbread ['ʃɔːtbred] **n** sablé *m*.

short-change **vt 1.** [subj: shopkeeper] **: to short-change sb** ne pas rendre assez à qqn **2.** *fig* [cheat] tromper, rouler.

short circuit **n** court-circuit *m*.
◆ ***short-circuit*** ■ **vt** court-circuiter.
■ **vi** se mettre en court-circuit.

shortcomings ['ʃɔːtˌkʌmɪŋz] **npl** défauts *mpl*.

shortcrust pastry ['ʃɔːtkrʌst-] **n** pâte *f* brisée.

shortcut **n 1.** [quick route] raccourci *m* **2.** [quick method] solution *f* miracle.

shorten ['ʃɔːtn] ■ **vt 1.** [holiday, time] écourter **2.** [skirt, rope] raccourcir.
■ **vi** [days] raccourcir.

shortening ['ʃɔːtnɪŋ] **n** *(U)* CULIN matière *f* grasse.

shortfall ['ʃɔːtfɔːl] **n** déficit *m*.

shorthand ['ʃɔːthænd] **n** *(U)* **1.** [writing system] sténographie *f* **2.** [abbreviation] forme *f* abrégée.

shorthanded [ˌʃɔːt'hændɪd] **adj : to be shorthanded** manquer de personnel.

shorthand typist **n** *UK dated* sténodactylo *f*.

short-haul **adj** court-courrier *(inv)*.

short list **n** liste *f* des candidats sélectionnés.
◆ ***short-list*** **vt : to be short-listed (for)** être au nombre des candidats sélectionnés (pour).

short-lived [-'lɪvd] **adj** de courte durée.

shortly ['ʃɔːtlɪ] **adv 1.** [soon] bientôt **2.** [curtly] d'une manière brusque, sèchement.

shortness ['ʃɔːtnɪs] **n 1.** [of visit] brièveté *f* **2.** [of person] petite taille *f* / [of skirt, hair] peu *m* de longueur.

short-range **adj** à courte portée.

short shrift [-'ʃrɪft] **n : to give sb short shrift** envoyer promener qqn.

shortsighted [ˌʃɔːt'saɪtɪd] **adj 1.** *UK* MED myope **2.** *fig* imprévoyant(e).

shortsightedness [ˌʃɔːt'saɪtɪdnɪs] **n 1.** *UK* MED myopie *f* **2.** *fig* myopie *f*, manque *m* de perspicacité *OR* de prévoyance.

short-sleeved **adj** à manches courtes.

short-staffed [-'stɑːft] **adj : to be short-staffed** manquer de personnel.

short-stay **adj : short-stay car park** parking *m* courte durée ▸ **short-stay patient** patient *m* hospitalisé pour une courte durée.

short story n nouvelle *f*.

short-tempered [-'tempəd] adj emporté(e), irascible.

short-term adj [effects, solution] à court terme / [problem] de courte durée.

short time n *UK* : **on short time** en chômage partiel.

short wave n *(U)* ondes *fpl* courtes.

shot [ʃɒt] ■ pt & pp ➤ ***shoot***.
■ n **1.** [gunshot] coup *m* de feu ▸ **to have** *OR* **to fire** *OR* **to take a shot at sthg** tirer sur qqch ▸ **like a shot** sans tarder, sans hésiter **2.** [marksman] tireur *m* ▸ **she's a good shot** c'est une excellente tireuse, elle tire bien **3.** SPORT [hit, kick, throw] coup *m* ▸ **good shot!** bien joué! ▸ **to call the shots** mener le jeu **4.** SPORT [heavy metal ball] : **to put the shot** lancer le poids **5.** [photograph] photo *f* / CIN plan *m* **6.** *inf* [attempt] : **to have a shot at sthg** essayer de faire qqch ▸ **give it your best shot** fais pour le mieux **7.** [injection] piqûre *f* ▸ **a shot in the arm** *fig* un coup de fouet *fig* **8.** [of alcohol] coup *m*.
■ adj *UK* [rid] : **to get shot of sthg/sb** *inf* se débarrasser de qqch/qqn.

shotgun ['ʃɒtgʌn] n fusil *m* de chasse.

shot put n [event] lancer *m* du poids / [object] poids *m*.

should [ʃʊd] aux vb **1.** [indicating duty] : **we should leave now** il faudrait partir maintenant ▸ **you should go if you're invited** tu devrais y aller si tu es invité ▸ **you shouldn't have done that!** tu n'aurais pas dû faire ça! **2.** [seeking advice, permission] : **should I go too?** est-ce que je devrais y aller aussi? **3.** [as suggestion] : **I should deny everything** moi, je nierais tout **4.** [indicating probability] : **she should be home soon** elle devrait être de retour bientôt, elle va bientôt rentrer **5.** [was or were expected] : **they should have won the match** ils auraient dû gagner le match **6.** [indicating intention, wish] : **I should like to come with you** j'aimerais bien venir avec vous ▸ **I should think so/not!** j'espère bien/bien que non! **7.** *(as conditional)* : **should you be interested, I know a good hotel there** si cela vous intéresse, je connais un bon hôtel là-bas ▸ **I'll be upstairs should you need me** je serai en haut si (jamais) vous avez besoin de moi **8.** *(in subordinate clauses)* : **we decided that you should meet him** nous avons décidé que ce serait toi qui irais le chercher **9.** [expressing uncertain opinion] : **I should think he's about 50 (years old)** je pense qu'il doit avoir dans les 50 ans.

shoulder ['ʃəʊldəʳ] ■ n **1.** [body] épaule *f* ▸ **to look over one's shoulder** se retourner ▸ **he needed a shoulder to cry on** il avait besoin de réconfort ▸ **to rub shoulders with sb** *fig* côtoyer qqn **2.** [of road] accotement *m*, bas côté *m* / *US* bande *f* d'arrêt d'urgence.
■ vt **1.** [carry] porter **2.** [responsibility] endosser.

shoulder bag n sac *m* en bandoulière.

shoulder blade n omoplate *f*.

shoulder-length adj : **shoulder-length hair** cheveux mi-longs.

shoulder strap n **1.** [on dress] bretelle *f* **2.** [on bag] bandoulière *f*.

shouldn't ['ʃʊdnt] = ***should not***.

should've ['ʃʊdəv] = ***should have***.

shout [ʃaʊt] ■ n [cry] cri *m*.
■ vt & vi crier.
◆ ***shout down*** vt sep huer, conspuer.
◆ ***shout out*** vt sep crier.

shouting ['ʃaʊtɪŋ] n *(U)* cris *mpl*.

shove [ʃʌv] ■ n : **to give sb/sthg a shove** pousser qqn/qqch.
■ vt pousser ▸ **to shove sb about** bousculer qqn ▸ **to shove clothes into a bag** fourrer des vêtements dans un sac.
◆ ***shove off*** vi **1.** [in boat] pousser au large **2.** *inf* [go away] ficher le camp, filer.

shovel ['ʃʌvl] ■ n [tool] pelle *f*.
■ vt (*UK* **-led**, cont **-ling**, *US* **-ed**, cont **-ing**) enlever à la pelle, pelleter.

show [ʃəʊ] ■ n **1.** [display] démonstration *f*, manifestation *f* ▸ **for show** pour (faire de) l'effet
2. [at theatre] spectacle *m* / [on radio, TV] émission *f* ▸ **the show must go on** *fig* & THEAT le spectacle continue
3. CIN séance *f*
4. [exhibition] exposition *f* ▸ **the agricultural/motor show** le salon de l'agriculture/de l'auto ▸ **on show** exposé(e) ▸ **flower show** floralies *fpl*.
■ vt (pt **-ed**, pp **shown** *OR* **-ed**) **1.** [gen] montrer / [profit, loss] indiquer / [respect] témoigner / [courage, mercy] faire preuve de ▸ **you have to show your pass/your ticket on the way in** il faut présenter son laissez-passer/son billet à l'entrée ▸ **he has nothing to show for all his hard work** tout son travail n'a rien donné ▸ **to show sb sthg, to show sthg to sb** montrer qqch à qqn ▸ **to show sb how to do sthg** montrer *OR* faire voir à qqn comment faire qqch ▸ **to show a preference for sthg** manifester une préférence pour qqch ▸ **it just goes to show that...** cela prouve que...
2. [escort] : **to show sb to his seat/table** conduire qqn à sa place/sa table ▸ **let me show you to your room** je vais vous montrer votre chambre
3. [film] projeter, passer / [TV programme] donner, passer.
■ vi (pt **-ed**, pp **shown** *OR* **-ed**) **1.** [indicate] indiquer, montrer
2. [be visible] se voir, être visible ▸ **their tiredness is beginning to show** ils commencent à donner des signes de fatigue
3. CIN : **what's showing tonight?** qu'est-ce qu'on joue comme film ce soir?
◆ ***show around***, ***show round*** *UK* vt sep : **to show sb around a town/a house** faire visiter une ville/une maison à qqn.
◆ ***show off*** ■ vt sep exhiber.
■ vi faire l'intéressant(e) ▸ **stop showing off!** arrête de te faire remarquer!
◆ ***show round*** vt sep *UK* = ***show around***.
◆ ***show up*** ■ vt sep **1.** [embarrass] embarrasser, faire honte à
2. [unmask] démasquer ▸ **the investigation showed him up for the coward he is** l'enquête a révélé sa lâcheté.
■ vi **1.** [stand out] se voir, ressortir
2. *inf* [arrive] s'amener, rappliquer.

showbiz ['ʃəʊbɪz] n *inf* show-biz *m*.

show business n *(U)* monde *m* du spectacle, show-business *m*.

showcase ['ʃəʊkeɪs] n *lit* & *fig* vitrine *f*.

shopkeeper ['ʃɒp,ki:pəʳ] **n** *esp UK* commerçant *m*, -e *f*.

shoplift ['ʃɒplɪft] **vt** voler à l'étalage.

shoplifter ['ʃɒp,lɪftəʳ] **n** voleur *m*, -euse *f* à l'étalage.

shoplifting ['ʃɒp,lɪftɪŋ] **n** *(U)* vol *m* à l'étalage.

shopper ['ʃɒpəʳ] **n** personne *f* qui fait ses courses.

shopping ['ʃɒpɪŋ] **n** *(U) UK* [purchases] achats *mpl*.

shopping bag **n** sac *m* à provisions.

shopping basket **n** panier *m* de course.

shopping cart *US* = ***shopping trolley***.

shopping centre *UK*, ***shopping mall*** *US*, ***shopping plaza*** *US* [-,plɑ:zə] **n** centre *m* commercial.

shopping channel **n** TV chaîne *f* de télé-achat.

shopping list **n** liste *f* des commissions.

shopping mall, ***shopping plaza*** *US* = ***shopping centre***.

shopping trolley, ***shopping cart*** *US* **n** chariot *m*, Caddie® *m*.

shopsoiled *UK* ['ʃɒpsɔɪld], ***shopworn*** *US* ['ʃɒpwɔ:n] **adj** qui a fait l'étalage, abîmé(e) (en magasin).

shop steward **n** délégué syndical *m*, déléguée syndicale *f*.

shopwalker ['ʃɒp,wɔ:kəʳ] **n** *UK* surveillant *m*, -e *f* de magasin.

shopwindow [,ʃɒp'wɪndəʊ] **n** vitrine *f*.

shopworn *US* = ***shopsoiled***.

shore [ʃɔ:ʳ] **n** rivage *m*, bord *m* ▸ **on shore** à terre.
◆ ***shore up*** **vt sep** étayer, étançonner / *fig* consolider.

shore leave **n** permission *f* à terre.

shoreline ['ʃɔ:laɪn] **n** côte *f*.

shorn [ʃɔ:n] ■ **pp** ➤ ***shear***.
■ **adj** tondu(e).

short [ʃɔ:t] ■ **adj 1.** [not long - in time] court(e), bref (brève) / [- in space] court ▸ **she was in London for a short time** elle a passé quelque temps à Londres ▸ **the days are getting shorter** les jours raccourcissent ▸ **to have short hair** avoir les cheveux courts ▸ **to go for a short walk** faire une petite promenade ▸ **it's only a short distance from here** ce n'est pas très loin (d'ici) ▸ **short and sweet** *inf* court mais bien
2. [not tall] petit(e)
3. [curt] brusque, sec (sèche)
4. [lacking] **: time/money is short** nous manquons de temps/d'argent ▸ **we're £10 short** il nous manque 10 livres ▸ **to be short of** manquer de ▸ **I'm a bit short (of money) at the moment** je suis un peu à court (d'argent) en ce moment ▸ **to be short of breath** être essoufflé(e)
5. [abbreviated] **: to be short for** être le diminutif de ▸ **Bill is short for William** Bill est un diminutif de William.
■ **adv : to be running short of** [running out of] commencer à manquer de, commencer à être à court de ▸ **to cut sthg short** [visit, speech] écourter qqch / [discussion] couper court à qqch ▸ **to fall short of** [objective, target] ne pas atteindre / [expectations] ne pas répondre à ▸ **to stop short** s'arrêter net ▸ **to bring** *OR* **pull sb up short** arrêter qqn net.
■ **n 1.** *UK* [alcoholic drink] alcool *m* fort
2. [film] court métrage *m*.
◆ ***shorts*** **npl 1.** [gen] short *m*
2. *US* [underwear] caleçon *m*.
◆ ***for short*** **adv : he's called Bob for short** Bob est son diminutif.
◆ ***in short*** **adv** (enfin) bref.
◆ ***nothing short of*** **prep** rien moins que, pratiquement.
◆ ***short of*** **prep** [unless, without] **: short of doing sthg** à moins de faire qqch, à part faire qqch ▸ **he would do anything short of stealing** il ferait tout sauf voler.

shortage ['ʃɔ:tɪdʒ] **n** manque *m*, insuffisance *f*.

short back and sides **n** *UK* coupe *f* bien dégagée.

shortbread ['ʃɔ:tbred] **n** sablé *m*.

short-change **vt 1.** [subj: shopkeeper] **: to short-change sb** ne pas rendre assez à qqn **2.** *fig* [cheat] tromper, rouler.

short circuit **n** court-circuit *m*.
◆ ***short-circuit*** ■ **vt** court-circuiter.
■ **vi** se mettre en court-circuit.

shortcomings ['ʃɔ:t,kʌmɪŋz] **npl** défauts *mpl*.

shortcrust pastry ['ʃɔ:tkrʌst-] **n** pâte *f* brisée.

shortcut **n 1.** [quick route] raccourci *m* **2.** [quick method] solution *f* miracle.

shorten ['ʃɔ:tn] ■ **vt 1.** [holiday, time] écourter **2.** [skirt, rope] raccourcir.
■ **vi** [days] raccourcir.

shortening ['ʃɔ:tnɪŋ] **n** *(U)* CULIN matière *f* grasse.

shortfall ['ʃɔ:tfɔ:l] **n** déficit *m*.

shorthand ['ʃɔ:thænd] **n** *(U)* **1.** [writing system] sténographie *f* **2.** [abbreviation] forme *f* abrégée.

shorthanded [,ʃɔ:t'hændɪd] **adj : to be shorthanded** manquer de personnel.

shorthand typist **n** *UK dated* sténodactylo *f*.

short-haul **adj** court-courrier *(inv)*.

short list **n** liste *f* des candidats sélectionnés.
◆ ***short-list*** **vt : to be short-listed (for)** être au nombre des candidats sélectionnés (pour).

short-lived [-'lɪvd] **adj** de courte durée.

shortly ['ʃɔ:tlɪ] **adv 1.** [soon] bientôt **2.** [curtly] d'une manière brusque, sèchement.

shortness ['ʃɔ:tnɪs] **n 1.** [of visit] brièveté *f* **2.** [of person] petite taille *f* / [of skirt, hair] peu *m* de longueur.

short-range **adj** à courte portée.

short shrift [-'ʃrɪft] **n : to give sb short shrift** envoyer promener qqn.

shortsighted [,ʃɔ:t'saɪtɪd] **adj 1.** *UK* MED myope **2.** *fig* imprévoyant(e).

shortsightedness [,ʃɔ:t'saɪtɪdnɪs] **n 1.** *UK* MED myopie *f* **2.** *fig* myopie *f*, manque *m* de perspicacité *OR* de prévoyance.

short-sleeved **adj** à manches courtes.

short-staffed [-'stɑ:ft] **adj : to be short-staffed** manquer de personnel.

short-stay **adj : short-stay car park** parking *m* courte durée ▸ **short-stay patient** patient *m* hospitalisé pour une courte durée.

short story n nouvelle *f*.

short-tempered [-'tempəd] adj emporté(e), irascible.

short-term adj [effects, solution] à court terme / [problem] de courte durée.

short time n *UK* : **on short time** en chômage partiel.

short wave n *(U)* ondes *fpl* courtes.

shot [ʃɒt] ■ pt & pp ➤ *shoot*.
■ n **1.** [gunshot] coup *m* de feu ▸ **to have** *OR* **to fire** *OR* **to take a shot at sthg** tirer sur qqch ▸ **like a shot** sans tarder, sans hésiter **2.** [marksman] tireur *m* ▸ **she's a good shot** c'est une excellente tireuse, elle tire bien **3.** SPORT [hit, kick, throw] coup *m* ▸ **good shot!** bien joué! ▸ **to call the shots** mener le jeu **4.** SPORT [heavy metal ball] : **to put the shot** lancer le poids **5.** [photograph] photo *f* / CIN plan *m* **6.** *inf* [attempt] : **to have a shot at sthg** essayer de faire qqch ▸ **give it your best shot** fais pour le mieux **7.** [injection] piqûre *f* ▸ **a shot in the arm** *fig* un coup de fouet *fig* **8.** [of alcohol] coup *m*.
■ adj *UK* [rid] : **to get shot of sthg/sb** *inf* se débarrasser de qqch/qqn.

shotgun ['ʃɒtgʌn] n fusil *m* de chasse.

shot put n [event] lancer *m* du poids / [object] poids *m*.

should [ʃʊd] aux vb **1.** [indicating duty] : **we should leave now** il faudrait partir maintenant ▸ **you should go if you're invited** tu devrais y aller si tu es invité ▸ **you shouldn't have done that!** tu n'aurais pas dû faire ça! **2.** [seeking advice, permission] : **should I go too?** est-ce que je devrais y aller aussi? **3.** [as suggestion] : **I should deny everything** moi, je nierais tout **4.** [indicating probability] : **she should be home soon** elle devrait être de retour bientôt, elle va bientôt rentrer **5.** [was or were expected] : **they should have won the match** ils auraient dû gagner le match **6.** [indicating intention, wish] : **I should like to come with you** j'aimerais bien venir avec vous ▸ **I should think so/not!** j'espère bien/bien que non! **7.** *(as conditional)* : **should you be interested, I know a good hotel there** si cela vous intéresse, je connais un bon hôtel là-bas ▸ **I'll be upstairs should you need me** je serai en haut si (jamais) vous avez besoin de moi **8.** *(in subordinate clauses)* : **we decided that you should meet him** nous avons décidé que ce serait toi qui irais le chercher **9.** [expressing uncertain opinion] : **I should think he's about 50 (years old)** je pense qu'il doit avoir dans les 50 ans.

shoulder ['ʃəʊldər] ■ n **1.** [body] épaule *f* ▸ **to look over one's shoulder** se retourner ▸ **he needed a shoulder to cry on** il avait besoin de réconfort ▸ **to rub shoulders with sb** *fig* côtoyer qqn **2.** [of road] accotement *m*, bas côté *m* / *US* bande *f* d'arrêt d'urgence.
■ vt **1.** [carry] porter **2.** [responsibility] endosser.

shoulder bag n sac *m* en bandoulière.

shoulder blade n omoplate *f*.

shoulder-length adj : **shoulder-length hair** cheveux mi-longs.

shoulder strap n **1.** [on dress] bretelle *f* **2.** [on bag] bandoulière *f*.

shouldn't ['ʃʊdnt] = ***should not***.

should've ['ʃʊdəv] = ***should have***.

shout [ʃaʊt] ■ n [cry] cri *m*.
■ vt & vi crier.
◆ ***shout down*** vt sep huer, conspuer.
◆ ***shout out*** vt sep crier.

shouting ['ʃaʊtɪŋ] n *(U)* cris *mpl*.

shove [ʃʌv] ■ n : **to give sb/sthg a shove** pousser qqn/qqch.
■ vt pousser ▸ **to shove sb about** bousculer qqn ▸ **to shove clothes into a bag** fourrer des vêtements dans un sac.
◆ ***shove off*** vi **1.** [in boat] pousser au large **2.** *inf* [go away] ficher le camp, filer.

shovel ['ʃʌvl] ■ n [tool] pelle *f*.
■ vt (*UK* -led, cont -ling, *US* -ed, cont -ing) enlever à la pelle, pelleter.

show [ʃəʊ] ■ n **1.** [display] démonstration *f*, manifestation *f* ▸ **for show** pour (faire de) l'effet
2. [at theatre] spectacle *m* / [on radio, TV] émission *f* ▸ **the show must go on** *fig* & THEAT le spectacle continue
3. CIN séance *f*
4. [exhibition] exposition *f* ▸ **the agricultural/motor show** le salon de l'agriculture/de l'auto ▸ **on show** exposé(e) ▸ **flower show** floralies *fpl*.
■ vt (pt -ed, pp shown *OR* -ed) **1.** [gen] montrer / [profit, loss] indiquer / [respect] témoigner / [courage, mercy] faire preuve de ▸ **you have to show your pass/your ticket on the way in** il faut présenter son laissez-passer/son billet à l'entrée ▸ **he has nothing to show for all his hard work** tout son travail n'a rien donné ▸ **to show sb sthg, to show sthg to sb** montrer qqch à qqn ▸ **to show sb how to do sthg** montrer *OR* faire voir à qqn comment faire qqch ▸ **to show a preference for sthg** manifester une préférence pour qqch ▸ **it just goes to show that...** cela prouve que...
2. [escort] : **to show sb to his seat/table** conduire qqn à sa place/sa table ▸ **let me show you to your room** je vais vous montrer votre chambre
3. [film] projeter, passer / [TV programme] donner, passer.
■ vi (pt -ed, pp shown *OR* -ed) **1.** [indicate] indiquer, montrer
2. [be visible] se voir, être visible ▸ **their tiredness is beginning to show** ils commencent à donner des signes de fatigue
3. CIN : **what's showing tonight?** qu'est-ce qu'on joue comme film ce soir?
◆ ***show around***, ***show round*** *UK* vt sep : **to show sb around a town/a house** faire visiter une ville/une maison à qqn.
◆ ***show off*** ■ vt sep exhiber.
■ vi faire l'intéressant(e) ▸ **stop showing off!** arrête de te faire remarquer!
◆ ***show round*** vt sep *UK* = ***show around***.
◆ ***show up*** ■ vt sep **1.** [embarrass] embarrasser, faire honte à
2. [unmask] démasquer ▸ **the investigation showed him up for the coward he is** l'enquête a révélé sa lâcheté.
■ vi **1.** [stand out] se voir, ressortir
2. *inf* [arrive] s'amener, rappliquer.

showbiz ['ʃəʊbɪz] n *inf* show-biz *m*.

show business n *(U)* monde *m* du spectacle, show-business *m*.

showcase ['ʃəʊkeɪs] n *lit* & *fig* vitrine *f*.

3. [health] **: to be in good/bad shape** être en bonne/mauvaise forme ▸ **the economy is in poor shape at the moment** l'économie est mal en point *OR* dans une mauvaise passe actuellement ▸ **to keep o.s.** *OR* **to stay in shape** garder la *OR* rester en forme ▸ **what sort of shape was he in?** dans quel état était-il? ▸ **to lick** *OR* **knock sb into shape** dresser qqn.
■ **vt 1.** [pastry, clay] **: to shape sthg (into)** façonner *OR* modeler qqch (en)
2. [ideas, project, character] former.
◆ ***shape up*** **vi** [person, plans] se développer, progresser / [job, events] prendre tournure *OR* forme ▸ **the new team is shaping up well** la nouvelle équipe commence à bien fonctionner.

SHAPE [ʃeɪp] (abbr of ***Supreme Headquarters Allied Powers, Europe***) **n** *quartier général des forces alliées en Europe.*

shaped [ʃeɪpt] **adj 1.** [garment] ajusté(e) / [wooden or metal object] travaillé(e) **2.** [in descriptions] **: shaped like a triangle** en forme de triangle ▸ **a rock shaped like a man's head** un rocher qui a la forme d'une tête d'homme.

-shaped ['ʃeɪpt] **suffix : egg-shaped** en forme d'œuf ▸ **L-shaped** en forme de L.

shapeless ['ʃeɪplɪs] **adj** informe.

shapelessness ['ʃeɪplɪsnɪs] **n** absence *f* de forme, aspect *m* informe.

shapely ['ʃeɪplɪ] (comp **-ier**, superl **-iest**) **adj** bien fait(e).

shard [ʃɑ:d] **n** tesson *m*.

share [ʃeəʳ] ■ **n** [portion, contribution] part *f* ▸ **to have a share in the profits** participer aux bénéfices ▸ **to have a share in a business** être l'un des associés dans une affaire ▸ **to do one's share (of the work)** faire sa part du travail.
■ **vt** partager ▸ **he shared the chocolate with his sister** il a partagé le chocolat avec sa sœur ▸ **to share the news with sb** faire part d'une nouvelle à qqn.
■ **vi : to share (in sthg)** partager (qqch).
◆ ***shares*** **npl** actions *fpl*.
◆ ***share out*** **vt sep** partager, répartir.

share capital **n** capital *m* actions.

share certificate **n** titre *m* *OR* certificat *m* d'actions.

share dealing **n** opérations *fpl* de Bourse.

share economy **n** économie *f* d'actionnariat populaire.

shareholder ['ʃeə,həʊldəʳ] **n** actionnaire *mf*.

shareholding ['ʃeə,həʊldɪŋ] **n** actionnariat *m*.

share index **n** indice *m* des valeurs boursières.

share-out **n** partage *m*, répartition *f*.

share prices **n** cours *mpl* des actions.

shareware ['ʃeəweəʳ] **n** COMPUT shareware *m*.

sharing ['ʃeərɪŋ] ■ **adj** [person] partageur(euse).
■ **n** [of money, power] partage *m*.

shark [ʃɑ:k] (pl **shark** *OR* **-s**) **n 1.** [fish] requin *m* **2.** *fig* [dishonest person] escroc *m*, pirate *m*.

sharp [ʃɑ:p] ■ **adj 1.** [knife, razor] tranchant(e), affilé(e) / [needle, pencil, teeth] pointu(e) ▸ **these scissors are sharp** ces ciseaux coupent bien ▸ **she has sharp features** elle a des traits anguleux **2.** [image, outline, contrast] net (nette) **3.** [person, mind] vif (vive) / [eyesight] perçant(e) **4.** [sudden - change, rise] brusque, soudain(e) / [- hit, tap] sec (sèche) ▸ **the car made a sharp turn** la voiture a tourné brusquement **5.** [words, order, voice] cinglant(e) ▸ **she has a sharp tongue** elle a la langue bien affilée **6.** [cry, sound] perçant(e) / [pain, cold] vif (vive) / [taste] piquant(e) **7.** MUS **: C/D sharp** do/ré dièse.
■ **adv 1.** [punctually] **: at 8 o'clock sharp** à 8 heures pile *OR* tapantes **2.** [immediately] **: sharp left/right** tout à fait à gauche/droite ▸ **look sharp (about it)!** *dated* dépêche-toi!, grouille-toi!
■ **n** MUS dièse *m*.

sharpen ['ʃɑ:pn] ■ **vt 1.** [knife, tool] aiguiser / [pencil] tailler **2.** [senses] aiguiser / [mind] affiner / [disagreement, conflict] aviver, envenimer.
■ **vi** [senses] s'aiguiser.

sharp end **n** *UK fig* **: to be at the sharp end** être en première ligne.

sharpener ['ʃɑ:pnəʳ] **n** [for pencil] taille-crayon *m* / [for knife] aiguisoir *m* (pour couteaux).

sharp-eyed [-'aɪd] **adj : she's very sharp-eyed** elle remarque tout, rien ne lui échappe.

sharply ['ʃɑ:plɪ] **adv 1.** [distinctly] nettement ▸ **this contrasts sharply with her usual behaviour** voilà qui change beaucoup de son comportement habituel **2.** [suddenly] brusquement ▸ **inflation has risen sharply since May** l'inflation est montée en flèche depuis mai **3.** [harshly] sévèrement, durement ▸ **I had to speak to her sharply about her persistent lateness** j'ai dû lui faire des observations sévères au sujet de ses retards répétés.

sharpness ['ʃɑ:pnɪs] **n 1.** [of image, outline] netteté *f* **2.** [of mind] vivacité *f* **3.** [of remarks, criticism] dureté *f*, sévérité *f*.

sharpshooter ['ʃɑ:p,ʃu:təʳ] **n** tireur *m* d'élite.

sharp-tongued [-'tʌŋd] **adj** qui a la langue acérée.

sharp-witted [-'wɪtɪd] **adj** à l'esprit vif.

shat [ʃæt] **pt & pp** ➤ ***shit***.

shatter ['ʃætəʳ] ■ **vt 1.** [window, glass] briser, fracasser **2.** [hopes, dreams] détruire.
■ **vi** se fracasser, voler en éclats.

shattered ['ʃætəd] **adj 1.** [upset] bouleversé(e) **2.** *UK inf* [very tired] flapi(e).

shattering ['ʃætərɪŋ] **adj 1.** [upsetting] bouleversant(e) **2.** *UK inf* [tiring] crevant(e), épuisant(e).

shatterproof ['ʃætəpru:f] **adj** anti-éclats.

shave [ʃeɪv] ■ **n : to have a shave** se raser ▸ **that was a close shave** *fig* on l'a échappé belle, il était moins cinq.
■ **vt 1.** [remove hair from] raser ▸ **to shave one's legs** se raser les jambes **2.** [wood] planer, raboter.
■ **vi** se raser.
◆ ***shave off*** **vt sep** [beard, hair] se raser.

shaven ['ʃeɪvn] **adj** rasé(e).

shaver ['ʃeɪvəʳ] **n** rasoir *m* électrique.

shaving ['ʃeɪvɪŋ] **n** [act] rasage *m*.
◆ ***shavings*** **npl** [of wood] copeaux *mpl* / [of metal] copeaux *mpl*, rognures *fpl* / [of paper] rognures *fpl*.

shaving brush **n** blaireau *m*.

shaving cream **n** crème *f* à raser.

shaving foam **n** mousse *f* à raser.

shaving soap **n** savon *m* à barbe.

shawl [ʃɔ:l] **n** châle *m*.

she [ʃi:] ■ **pers pron 1.** [referring to woman, girl, animal] elle ▸ **she's tall** elle est grande ▸ **SHE can't do it** elle, elle ne peut pas le faire ▸ **there she is** la voilà ▸ **if I were** OR **was she** *fml* si j'étais elle, à sa place **2.** [referring to boat, car, country] **: she's a fine ship** c'est un bateau magnifique ▸ **she can do over 120 mph** elle fait plus de 150 km à l'heure.
■ **n : it's a she** [animal] c'est une femelle / [baby] c'est une fille.
■ **comp : she-elephant** éléphant *m* femelle ▸ **she-wolf** louve *f*.

s/he (abbr of ***she/he***) il ou elle.

sheaf [ʃi:f] (pl **sheaves** [ʃi:vz]) **n 1.** [of papers, letters] liasse *f* **2.** [of corn, grain] gerbe *f*.

shear [ʃɪəʳ] (pt **-ed**, pp **-ed** OR **shorn**) **vt** [sheep] tondre.
◆ ***shears*** **npl 1.** [for garden] sécateur *m*, cisaille *f* **2.** [for dressmaking] ciseaux *mpl*.
◆ ***shear off*** ■ **vt sep** [branch] couper / [piece of metal] cisailler.
■ **vi** se détacher.

sheath [ʃi:θ] (pl **sheaths** [ʃi:ðz]) **n 1.** [for knife, cable] gaine *f* **2.** *UK dated* [condom] préservatif *m*.

sheathe [ʃi:ð] **vt 1.** [knife] engainer, rengainer **2.** [cover - gen] recouvrir / [- cable] gainer.

sheath knife **n** couteau *m* à gaine.

sheaves [ʃi:vz] **npl** ➤ ***sheaf***.

shed [ʃed] ■ **n** [small] remise *f*, cabane *f* / [larger] hangar *m*.
■ **vt** (pt & pp **shed**, cont **-ding**) **1.** [hair, skin, leaves] perdre **2.** [tears] verser, répandre ▸ **to shed blood** verser le sang **3.** [employees] se défaire de, congédier **4.** [load - subj: lorry] déverser, perdre.

she'd *(weak form* [ʃɪd], *strong form* [ʃi:d]*)* = ***she had, she would***.

sheen [ʃi:n] **n** lustre *m*, éclat *m*.

sheep [ʃi:p] (pl **sheep**) **n** mouton *m*.

sheepdog ['ʃi:pdɒg] **n** chien *m* de berger.

sheepfold ['ʃi:pfəʊld] **n** parc *m* à moutons.

sheepish ['ʃi:pɪʃ] **adj** penaud(e).

sheepishly ['ʃi:pɪʃlɪ] **adv** d'un air penaud.

sheepskin ['ʃi:pskɪn] **n** peau *f* de mouton.

sheepskin jacket **n** veste *f* en mouton.

sheepskin rug **n** (petit tapis *m* en) peau *f* de mouton.

sheer [ʃɪəʳ] **adj 1.** [absolute] pur(e) **2.** [very steep] à pic, abrupt(e) **3.** [material] fin(e).

sheet [ʃi:t] **n 1.** [for bed] drap *m* ▸ **as white as a sheet** blanc (blanche) comme un linge **2.** [of paper, glass, wood] feuille *f* / [of metal] plaque *f*.

sheet feed **n** COMPUT alimentation *f* feuille à feuille.

sheet feeder **n** COMPUT dispositif *m* d'alimentation en papier.

sheet ice **n** verglas *m*.

sheeting ['ʃi:tɪŋ] **n** *(U)* [metal] tôles *fpl* / [plastic] feuilles *fpl*.

sheet lightning **n** *(U)* éclair *m* diffus.

sheet metal **n** *(U)* tôle *f*.

sheet music **n** *(U)* partition *f*.

sheik(h) [ʃeɪk] **n** cheik *m*.

shelf [ʃelf] (pl **shelves** [ʃelvz]) **n** [for storage] rayon *m* étagère *f*.

shelf life **n** durée *f* de conservation.

shell [ʃel] ■ **n 1.** [of egg, nut, snail] coquille *f* **2.** [of tortoise crab] carapace *f* **3.** [on beach] coquillage *m* **4.** [of building car] carcasse *f* **5.** MIL obus *m*.
■ **vt 1.** [peas] écosser / [nuts, prawns] décortiquer / [eggs] enlever la coquille de, écaler **2.** MIL bombarder.
◆ ***shell out*** *inf* ■ **vt sep** débourser.
■ **vi : to shell out (for)** casquer (pour).

CONFUSABLE / PARONYME

shell

When translating **shell**, note that the French words *coquillage* and *coquille* are not interchangeable. *Coquillage* applies mostly to sea shells, whereas *coquille* refers to a shell in general as the outer layer of something.

she'll [ʃi:l] = ***she will, she shall***.

shellfire ['ʃelfaɪəʳ] **n** *(U)* tirs *mpl* d'obus.

shellfish ['ʃelfɪʃ] (pl **shellfish**) **n 1.** [creature] crustacé *m* coquillage *m* **2.** *(U)* [food] fruits *mpl* de mer.

shelling ['ʃelɪŋ] **n** MIL bombardement *m*.

shellproof ['ʃelpru:f] **adj** MIL blindé(e), à l'épreuve des obus.

shell shock **n** *(U)* psychose *f* traumatique.

shell-shocked [-ˌʃɒkt] **adj** commotionné(e) *(après une explosion)* ▸ **I'm still feeling pretty shell-shocked by it all** *fig* je suis encore sous le choc après toute cette histoire

shell suit **n** *UK survêtement en Nylon® imperméabilisé*.

shelter ['ʃeltəʳ] ■ **n** abri *m*.
■ **vt 1.** [protect] abriter, protéger **2.** [refugee, homeless person] offrir un asile à / [criminal, fugitive] cacher.
■ **vi** s'abriter, se mettre à l'abri.

sheltered ['ʃeltəd] **adj 1.** [from weather] abrité(e) **2.** [life childhood] protégé(e), sans soucis ▸ **sheltered housing** *UK* foyers-logements *mpl (pour personnes âgées ou handicapées)*.

shelve [ʃelv] ■ **vt** *fig* mettre au Frigidaire®, mettre en sommeil.
■ **vi** descendre en pente.

shelves [ʃelvz] **npl** ➤ ***shelf***.

shelving ['ʃelvɪŋ] **n** *(U)* étagères *fpl*, rayonnages *mpl*.

shenanigans [ʃɪ'nænɪgənz] **npl** *inf* [trickery] micmacs *mpl*, manigances *fpl*.

shepherd ['ʃepəd] ■ **n** berger *m*.
■ **vt** *fig* conduire.

showdown ['ʃəudaun] **n : to have a showdown with sb** s'expliquer avec qqn, mettre les choses au point avec qqn.

shower ['ʃauəʳ] ■ **n 1.** [device, act] douche *f* ▸ **to have** *UK* *OR* **take a shower** prendre une douche, se doucher **2.** [of rain] averse *f* **3.** *fig* [of questions, confetti] avalanche *f*, déluge *m* **4.** *US* [party] *fête organisée en l'honneur d'une femme qui va se marier, par exemple, et à laquelle chacun des invités offre un petit cadeau.*
■ **vt : to shower sb with** couvrir qqn de.
■ **vi** [wash] prendre une douche, se doucher.

shower cap **n** bonnet *m* de douche.

shower gel **n** gel *m* douche.

showerproof ['ʃauəpru:f] **adj** imperméable.

shower room **n** salle *f* d'eau.

showery ['ʃauərɪ] **adj** pluvieux(euse).

showily ['ʃəuɪlɪ] **adv** de façon voyante *OR* ostentatoire.

showing ['ʃəuɪŋ] **n** CIN projection *f*.

showing off **n : I've had enough of his showing off** j'en ai assez de sa vantardise.

show jumper **n** [rider] cavalier, -ère *f m (participant à des concours de saut d'obstacle)* / [horse] sauteur *m*.

show jumping [-ˌdʒʌmpɪŋ] **n** jumping *m*.

showman ['ʃəumən] (pl **-men** [-mən]) **n 1.** [at fair, circus] forain *m* **2.** *fig* [publicity-seeker] **: he's a real showman** il a le sens du spectacle.

showmanship ['ʃəumənʃɪp] **n** sens *m* du spectacle.

shown [ʃəun] **pp** ➤ ***show***.

show-off **n** *inf* m'as-tu-vu *m*, -e *f*.

show of hands **n : to have a show of hands** voter à main levée.

showpiece ['ʃəupi:s] **n** [main attraction] joyau *m*, trésor *m*.

showroom ['ʃəurum] **n** salle *f* *OR* magasin *m* d'exposition / [for cars] salle de démonstration.

showy ['ʃəuɪ] (comp **-ier**, superl **-iest**) **adj** voyant(e) / [person] prétentieux(euse).

shrank [ʃræŋk] **pt** ➤ ***shrink***.

shrapnel ['ʃræpnl] **n** *(U)* éclats *mpl* d'obus.

shred [ʃred] ■ **n 1.** [of material, paper] lambeau *m*, brin *m* **2.** *fig* [of evidence] parcelle *f* / [of truth] once *f*, grain *m*.
■ **vt** (pt & pp **-ded**, cont **-ding**) [food] râper / [paper] déchirer en lambeaux.

shredder ['ʃredəʳ] **n** [machine] destructeur *m* de documents.

shrew [ʃru:] **n** [animal] musaraigne *f*.

shrewd [ʃru:d] **adj** fin(e), astucieux(euse).

shrewdly ['ʃru:dlɪ] **adv** [act] avec perspicacité *OR* sagacité / [answer, guess] astucieusement.

shrewdness ['ʃru:dnɪs] **n** finesse *f*, perspicacité *f*.

shriek [ʃri:k] ■ **n** cri *m* perçant, hurlement *m* / [of laughter] éclat *m*.
■ **vt** hurler, crier.
■ **vi** pousser un cri perçant ▸ **to shriek with laughter** éclater de rire.

shrill [ʃrɪl] **adj** [sound, voice] aigu(ë) / [whistle] strident(e).

shrimp [ʃrɪmp] **n** crevette *f*.

shrine [ʃraɪn] **n** [place of worship] lieu *m* saint.

shrink [ʃrɪŋk] ■ **n** *inf hum* psy *mf*.
■ **vt** (pt **shrank**, pp **shrunk**) rétrécir.
■ **vi** (pt **shrank**, pp **shrunk**) **1.** [cloth, garment] rétrécir / [person] rapetisser / *fig* [income, popularity] baisser, diminuer **2.** [recoil] **: to shrink away from sthg** reculer devant qqch ▸ **to shrink from doing sthg** rechigner *OR* répugner à faire qqch.

shrinkage ['ʃrɪŋkɪdʒ] **n** rétrécissement *m* / *fig* diminution *f*, baisse *f*.

shrink-wrap **vt** emballer sous film plastique.

shrivel ['ʃrɪvl] (*UK* **-led**, cont **-ling**, *US* **-ed**, cont **-ing**) ■ **vt : to shrivel (up)** rider, flétrir.
■ **vi : to shrivel (up)** se rider, se flétrir.

shroud [ʃraud] ■ **n** [cloth] linceul *m*.
■ **vt : to be shrouded in** [darkness, fog] être enseveli(e) sous / [mystery] être enveloppé(e) de.

Shrove Tuesday ['ʃrəuv-] **n** Mardi *m* gras.

shrub [ʃrʌb] **n** arbuste *m*.

shrubbery ['ʃrʌbərɪ] **n** massif *m* d'arbustes.

shrug [ʃrʌg] ■ **n** haussement *m* d'épaules.
■ **vt** (pt & pp **-ged**, cont **-ging**) **: to shrug one's shoulders** hausser les épaules.
■ **vi** (pt & pp **-ged**, cont **-ging**) hausser les épaules.
◆ ***shrug off*** **vt sep** ignorer.

shrunk [ʃrʌŋk] **pp** ➤ ***shrink***.

shrunken ['ʃrʌŋkn] **adj** [person] ratatiné(e).

shucks [ʃʌks] **excl** *US inf dated* **1.** [it was nothing] de rien! **2.** [damn] zut!

shudder ['ʃʌdəʳ] ■ **n** frisson *m*, frémissement *m*.
■ **vi 1.** [tremble] **: to shudder (with)** frémir (de), frissonner (de) ▸ **I shudder to think** je n'ose pas y penser **2.** [shake] vibrer, trembler.

shuffle ['ʃʌfl] ■ **n 1.** [of feet] marche *f* traînante **2.** [of cards] **: to give the cards a shuffle** battre les cartes.
■ **vt 1.** [drag] **: to shuffle one's feet** traîner les pieds **2.** [cards] mélanger, battre.
■ **vi 1.** [walk] **: to shuffle in/out** entrer/sortir en traînant les pieds **2.** [fidget] remuer.

shun [ʃʌn] (pt & pp **-ned**, cont **-ning**) **vt** fuir, éviter.

shunt [ʃʌnt] **vt 1.** RAIL aiguiller **2.** *fig* [move] transférer, déplacer.

shunter ['ʃʌntəʳ] **n** RAIL [engine] locomotive *f* de manœuvre.

shush [ʃuʃ] **excl** chut!

shut [ʃʌt] ■ **adj** [closed] fermé(e).
■ **vt** (pt & pp **shut**, cont **-ting**) fermer ▸ **shut your mouth** *OR* **face !** *v inf* ta gueule!, la ferme!
■ **vi** (pt & pp **shut**, cont **-ting**) **1.** [door, window] se fermer **2.** [shop] fermer.
◆ ***shut away*** **vt sep** [valuables, papers] mettre sous clef ▸ **to shut o.s. away** s'enfermer.
◆ ***shut down*** ■ **vt sep** & **vi 1.** [close] fermer **2.** COMPUT éteindre.
■ **vi** [close] fermer.

◆ ***shut in*** **vt sep** enfermer ▸ **to shut o.s. in** s'enfermer.
◆ ***shut out*** **vt sep 1.** [noise] supprimer / [light] ne pas laisser entrer ▸ **to shut sb out** laisser qqn à la porte **2.** [feelings, thoughts] chasser.
◆ ***shut up*** *inf* ■ **vt sep** [silence] faire taire.
■ **vi** se taire.

shutdown ['ʃʌtdaʊn] **n** fermeture *f.*

shutoff ['ʃʌtɒf] **n 1.** [device] **: the automatic shutoff didn't work** le dispositif d'arrêt automatique n'a pas fonctionné **2.** [action] arrêt *m.*

shutter ['ʃʌtəʳ] **n 1.** [on window] volet *m* **2.** [in camera] obturateur *m.*

shuttered ['ʃʌtəd] **adj** [with shutters fitted] à volets / [with shutters closed] aux volets fermés.

shutter release **n** déclencheur *m* d'obturateur.

shutter speed **n** vitesse *f* d'obturation.

shuttle ['ʃʌtl] ■ **adj : shuttle service** (service *m* de) navette *f.*
■ **n** [train, bus, plane] navette *f.*
■ **vi** faire la navette.

shuttlecock ['ʃʌtlkɒk] **n** volant *m.*

shy [ʃaɪ] ■ **adj 1.** [timid] timide **2.** [wary] **: to be shy of doing sthg** avoir peur de faire qqch, hésiter à faire qqch.
■ **vi (pt & pp shied)** [horse] s'effaroucher.
◆ ***shy away from*** **vt insep : to shy away from sthg** reculer devant qqch ▸ **to shy away from doing sthg** répugner à faire qqch.

shyly ['ʃaɪlɪ] **adv** timidement.

shyness ['ʃaɪnɪs] **n** timidité *f.*

shyster ['ʃaɪstəʳ] **n** ***esp US inf*** [politician] politicien véreux *m*, politicienne véreuse *f.*

Siam [ˌsaɪ'æm] **n** Siam *m* ▸ **in Siam** au Siam.

Siamese [ˌsaɪə'mi:z] ■ **adj** siamois(e).
■ **n (pl Siamese) 1.** [person] Siamois *m*, -e *f* **2. : Siamese (cat)** chat *m* siamois.

Siamese twins **npl** [brothers] frères *mpl* siamois / [sisters] sœurs *fpl* siamoises.

SIB (abbr of ***Securities and Investment Board***) **n** *organisme britannique qui fait appliquer la réglementation concernant les investissements.*

Siberia [saɪ'bɪərɪə] **n** Sibérie *f* ▸ **in Siberia** en Sibérie.

Siberian [saɪ'bɪərɪən] ■ **adj** sibérien(enne).
■ **n** Sibérien *m*, -enne *f.*

sibling ['sɪblɪŋ] **n** [brother] frère *m* / [sister] sœur *f.*

sic [sɪk] **adv** sic.

Sicilian [sɪ'sɪljən] ■ **adj** sicilien(enne).
■ **n** [person] Sicilien *m*, -enne *f.*

Sicily ['sɪsɪlɪ] **n** Sicile *f* ▸ **in Sicily** en Sicile.

sick [sɪk] **adj 1.** [ill] malade ▸ **my secretary is off sick** ma secrétaire est en congé de maladie ▸ **they care for sick people** ils soignent les malades ▸ **to be sick with fear/worry** être malade de peur/d'inquiétude
2. [nauseous] **: to feel sick** avoir envie de vomir, avoir mal au cœur ▸ **to be sick** *UK* [vomit] vomir ▸ **to make sb sick** *fig* écœurer qqn, dégoûter qqn
3. [fed up] **: to be sick of** en avoir assez OR marre de
4. [joke, humour] macabre.

sickbay ['sɪkbeɪ] **n** infirmerie *f.*

sickbed ['sɪkbed] **n** lit *m* de malade.

sicken ['sɪkn] ■ **vt** écœurer, dégoûter.
■ **vi** *UK* **: to be sickening for sthg** couver qqch.

sickening ['sɪknɪŋ] **adj** [disgusting] écœurant(e), dégoûtant(e).

sickeningly ['sɪknɪŋlɪ] **adv : he's sickeningly pious** il est d'une piété écœurante ▸ **she's sickeningly successful** *hum* elle réussit si bien que c'en est écœurant.

sickle ['sɪkl] **n** faucille *f.*

sick leave **n** *(U)* congé *m* de maladie.

sickly ['sɪklɪ] **(comp -ier, superl -iest) adj 1.** [unhealthy] maladif(ive), souffreteux(euse) **2.** [smell, taste] écœurant(e).

sickness ['sɪknɪs] **n** *UK* **1.** [illness] maladie *f* **2.** *(U)* [nausea] nausée *f*, nausées *fpl* / [vomiting] vomissement *m*, vomissements *mpl.*

sickness benefit **n** *(U) UK* prestations *fpl* en cas de maladie.

sick pay **n** *(U)* indemnité *f* OR allocation *f* de maladie.

sickroom ['sɪkrʊm] **n** chambre *f* de malade.

side [saɪd] ■ **n 1.** [gen] côté *m* ▸ **I've got a pain in my right side** j'ai mal au côté droit ▸ **her hair is cut short at the sides** ses cheveux sont coupés court sur les côtés ▸ **write on both sides of the paper** écrivez recto verso ▸ **the right/wrong side of the cloth** l'endroit *m*/l'envers *m* du tissu ▸ **it's way on the other side of town** c'est à l'autre bout de la ville ▸ **at** OR **by my/her** *etc* **side** à mes/ses *etc* côtés ▸ **to stand to one side** se tenir sur le côté ▸ **on every side, on all sides** de tous côtés ▸ **from side to side** d'un côté à l'autre ▸ **side by side** côte à côte ▸ **the road and the river run side by side** la route longe la rivière ▸ **to put sthg to** OR **on one side** mettre qqch de côté ▸ **to take sb to one side** prendre qqn à part
2. [of table, river] bord *m* ▸ **she held on to the side of the pool** elle s'accrochait au rebord de la piscine
3. [of hill, valley] versant *m*, flanc *m*
4. [in war, debate] camp *m*, côté *m* / SPORT équipe *f*, camp / [of argument] point *m* de vue ▸ **he's told me his side of the story** il m'a donné sa version de l'affaire ▸ **to be on sb's side** être avec qqn, soutenir qqn ▸ **luck is on our side** la chance est avec nous ▸ **don't let the side down!** nous comptons sur vous! ▸ **to take sb's side** prendre le parti de qqn
5. [aspect - gen] aspect *m* / [- of character] facette *f* ▸ **she has her good side** elle a ses bons côtés ▸ **she's very good at the practical side of things** elle est excellente sur le plan pratique ▸ **to be on the safe side** pour plus de sûreté, par précaution
▸▸ **on the large/small side** plutôt grand(e)/petit(e), un peu trop grand(e)/petit(e) ▸ **to do sthg on the side** faire qqch en plus ▸ **he's on the right/wrong side of forty** il n'a pas encore/il a dépassé la quarantaine ▸ **to keep** OR **stay on the right side of sb** se faire bien voir de qqn.
■ **adj** [situated on side] latéral(e).
◆ ***side with*** **vt insep** prendre le parti de, se ranger du côté de.

sideboard ['saɪdbɔ:d] **n** [cupboard] buffet *m.*

sideboards *UK* ['saɪdbɔ:dz], ***sideburns*** *esp US* ['saɪdbɜ:nz] **npl** favoris *mpl*, rouflaquettes *fpl*.

sidecar ['saɪdkɑ:ʳ] **n** side-car *m*.

-sided ['saɪdɪd] **suffix : three/five-sided** à trois/cinq côtés ▸ **a many-sided figure** une figure polygonale ▸ **a glass-sided box** une boîte à parois de verre ▸ **elastic-sided boots** bottes avec de l'élastique sur les côtés ▸ **a steep-sided valley** une vallée encaissée.

side dish **n** accompagnement *m*, garniture *f*.

side effect **n 1.** MED effet *m* secondaire ***OR*** indésirable **2.** [unplanned result] effet *m* secondaire, répercussion *f*.

side issue **n** question *f* secondaire.

sidekick ['saɪdkɪk] **n** *inf* [friend] copain *m*, copine *f* / *pej* acolyte *mf*.

sidelight ['saɪdlaɪt] **n** *UK* AUT feu *m* de position.

sideline ['saɪdlaɪn] **n 1.** [extra business] activité *f* secondaire **2.** SPORT ligne *f* de touche ▸ **on the sideline** *fig* dans la coulisse.

sidelong ['saɪdlɒŋ] **adj & adv** de côté.

side-on **adj & adv** de côté.

side order **n** portion *f* ▸ **I'd like a side order of fries** je voudrais aussi des frites.

side plate **n** assiette *f* à pain, petite assiette.

side road **n** [not main road] route *f* secondaire / [off main road] route transversale.

sidesaddle ['saɪd,sædl] **adv : to ride sidesaddle** monter en amazone.

side salad **n** salade *f (pour accompagner un plat)*.

sideshow ['saɪdʃəʊ] **n** spectacle *m* forain.

sidestep ['saɪdstep] (**pt & pp -ped**, **cont -ping**) **vt** faire un pas de côté pour éviter ***OR*** esquiver / *fig* éviter.

side street **n** [not main street] petite rue *f* / [off main street] rue transversale.

sidetrack ['saɪdtræk] **vt : to be sidetracked** se laisser distraire.

sidewalk ['saɪdwɔ:k] **n** *US* trottoir *m*.

sidewalk café **n** *US* café *m* avec terrasse.

sideways ['saɪdweɪz] **adj & adv** de côté.

siding ['saɪdɪŋ] **n** voie *f* de garage.

sidle ['saɪdl] ◆ ***sidle up*** **vi : to sidle up to sb** se glisser vers qqn.

SIDS (abbr of ***sudden infant death syndrome***) **n** *mort subite du nourrisson*.

siege [si:dʒ] **n** siège *m*.

Sierra Leone [sɪ'erəlɪ'əʊn] **n** Sierra Leone *f* ▸ **in Sierra Leone** en Sierra Leone.

Sierra Leonean [sɪ'erəlɪ'əʊnjən] ■ **adj** de la Sierra Leone.
■ **n** habitant *m*, -e *f* de la Sierra Leone.

sieve [sɪv] ■ **n** [for flour, sand] tamis *m* / [for liquids] passoire *f* ▸ **I've got a memory like a sieve** ma mémoire est une passoire.
■ **vt** [flour] tamiser / [liquid] passer.

sift [sɪft] ■ **vt 1.** [flour, sand] tamiser **2.** *fig* [evidence] passer au crible.
■ **vi : to sift through** examiner, éplucher.

sigh [saɪ] ■ **n** soupir *m* ▸ **to heave a sigh of relief** pousser un soupir de soulagement.
■ **vi** [person] soupirer, pousser un soupir.

sighing ['saɪɪŋ] **n** *(U)* [of person] soupirs *mpl* / [of wind] murmure *m* / [of trees] bruissement *m*.

sight [saɪt] ■ **n 1.** [seeing] vue *f* ▸ **to lose/to recover one's sight** perdre/recouvrer la vue ▸ **in sight** en vue ▸ **in/out of sight** en/hors de vue ▸ **she never lets him out of her sight** elle ne le perd jamais de vue ▸ **to catch sight of** apercevoir ▸ **to know sb by sight** connaître qqn de vue ▸ **to lose sight of** perdre de vue ▸ **to shoot on sight** tirer à vue ▸ **at first sight** à première vue, au premier abord ▸ **to buy sthg sight unseen** acheter qqch sans l'avoir vu **2.** [spectacle] spectacle *m* ▸ **it was not a pretty sight** ça n'était pas beau à voir **3.** [on gun] mire *f* ▸ **to set one's sights on sthg** décider d'obtenir qqch, viser qqch ▸ **to set one's sights on doing sthg** décider de faire qqch **4.** *inf* [mess] pagaille *f* ▸ **the kitchen was a sight!** quelle pagaille dans la cuisine! **5.** *inf* [a lot] **: a sight better/worse** bien mieux/pire.
■ **vt** apercevoir.

◆ ***sights*** **npl** [of city] attractions *fpl* touristiques ▸ **I'll show you *OR* take you around the sights tomorrow** je vous ferai visiter ***OR*** voir la ville demain.

sighted ['saɪtɪd] **adj** voyant(e) ▸ **partially sighted** mal voyant.

sighting ['saɪtɪŋ] **n : there has been a sighting of the escaped criminal** on a vu le fugitif.

sightseeing ['saɪt,si:ɪŋ] **n** tourisme *m* ▸ **to go sightseeing** faire du tourisme.

sightseer ['saɪt,si:əʳ] **n** touriste *mf*.

sign [saɪn] ■ **n 1.** [gen] signe *m* ▸ **to make the sign of the cross** faire le signe de croix ▸ **no sign of** aucune trace de ▸ **there's no sign of him yet** il n'est pas encore arrivé ▸ **there's no sign of her changing her mind** rien n'indique qu'elle va changer d'avis ▸ **what sign are you?** [in astrology] de quel signe êtes-vous? **2.** [notice] enseigne *f* / AUT panneau *m*.
■ **vt** signer ▸ **to sign one's name** signer.
■ **vi 1.** [write name] signer ▸ **he signed with an X** il a signé d'une croix **2.** [use sign language] communiquer par signes.

◆ ***sign away*** **vt sep** signer la renonciation à ▸ **I felt I was signing away my freedom** j'avais l'impression qu'en signant je renonçais à ma liberté.

◆ ***sign for*** **vt insep 1.** [letter, parcel] signer à la réception de **2.** SPORT [team] signer un contrat avec.

◆ ***sign in*** **vi** signer à l'arrivée ***OR*** en arrivant.

◆ ***sign on*** **vi 1.** MIL s'engager **2.** [for course] s'inscrire **3.** *UK* [register as unemployed] s'inscrire au chômage.

◆ ***sign out*** **vi** signer à la sortie ***OR*** en sortant.

◆ ***sign up*** ■ **vt sep** [worker] embaucher / [soldier] engager.
■ **vi 1.** MIL s'engager ▸ **to sign up for the Marines** s'engager dans les marines **2.** [for course] s'inscrire ▸ **she signed up for an evening class** elle s'est inscrite à des cours du soir.

signal ['sɪgnl] ■ n signal *m* ▸ **he'll give the signal to attack** il donnera le signal de l'attaque ▸ **they are sending the government a clear signal that...** ils indiquent clairement au gouvernement que...
■ adj *fml* remarquable.
■ vt (*UK* -led, cont -ling, *US* -ed, cont -ing) **1.** [indicate] indiquer **2.** [gesture to] **: to signal sb (to do sthg)** faire signe à qqn (de faire qqch).
■ vi (*UK* -led, cont -ling, *US* -ed, cont -ing) **1.** AUT clignoter, mettre son clignotant **2.** [gesture] **: to signal to sb (to do sthg)** faire signe à qqn (de faire qqch) ▸ **she was signalling for us to stop** elle nous faisait signe de nous arrêter.

signal box *UK*, ***signal tower*** *US* n poste *m* d'aiguillage.

signalling *UK*, ***signaling*** *US* ['sɪgnəlɪŋ] ■ n **1.** AERON, AUT, NAUT & RAIL signalisation *f* **2.** [warning] avertissement *m* **3.** [of electronic message] transmission *f*.
■ comp [error, equipment] de signalisation ▸ **signalling flag** NAUT pavillon *m* de signalisation / MIL drapeau *m* de signalisation.

signally ['sɪgnəlɪ] adv *fml* remarquablement, singulièrement.

signalman ['sɪgnlmən] (pl -men [-mən]) n RAIL aiguilleur *m*.

signal tower *US* = ***signal box***.

signatory ['sɪgnətrɪ] (pl -ies) n signataire *mf*.

signature ['sɪgnətʃəʳ] n [name] signature *f*.

signature tune n *UK* indicatif *m*.

signet ring ['sɪgnɪt-] n chevalière *f*.

significance [sɪg'nɪfɪkəns] n **1.** [importance] importance *f*, portée *f* **2.** [meaning] signification *f*.

significant [sɪg'nɪfɪkənt] adj **1.** [considerable] considérable **2.** [important] important(e) **3.** [meaningful] significatif(ive).

significantly [sɪg'nɪfɪkəntlɪ] adv **1.** [considerably] considérablement, énormément **2.** [meaningfully] d'une manière significative.

signification [ˌsɪgnɪfɪ'keɪʃn] n signification *f*.

signify ['sɪgnɪfaɪ] (pt & pp -ied) vt signifier, indiquer.

signing ['saɪnɪŋ] n *UK* SPORT *footballeur etc qui a signé un contrat avec un club*.

sign language n langage *m* des signes.

signpost ['saɪnpəʊst] n poteau *m* indicateur.

signwriter ['saɪnˌraɪtəʳ] n peintre *m* en lettres.

Sikh [siːk] ■ adj sikh *(inv)*.
■ n [person] Sikh *mf*.

Sikhism ['siːkɪzm] n sikhisme *m*.

silage ['saɪlɪdʒ] n fourrage *m* ensilé.

silence ['saɪləns] ■ n silence *m*.
■ vt réduire au silence, faire taire.

silencer ['saɪlənsəʳ] n silencieux *m*.

silent ['saɪlənt] adj **1.** [person, place] silencieux(euse) ▸ **to be silent about sthg** garder le silence sur qqch **2.** CIN & LING muet(ette).

silently ['saɪləntlɪ] adv silencieusement.

silent majority n majorité *f* silencieuse.

silent partner n *US* (associé *m*) commanditaire *m*, bailleur *m* de fonds.

silhouette [ˌsɪluː'et] ■ n silhouette *f*.
■ vt **: to be silhouetted against** se profiler sur, se silhouetter sur.

silicon ['sɪlɪkən] n silicium *m*.

silicon chip n puce *f*, pastille *f* de silicium.

silicone ['sɪlɪkəʊn] n silicone *f*.

Silicon Valley n Silicon Valley *f (centre de l'industrie électronique américaine)*.

silk [sɪlk] ■ n soie *f*.
■ comp en ***OR*** de soie.

silk screen printing n sérigraphie *f*.

silkworm ['sɪlkwɜːm] n ver *m* à soie.

silky ['sɪlkɪ] (comp -ier, superl -iest) adj soyeux(euse).

sill [sɪl] n [of window] rebord *m*.

silliness ['sɪlɪnɪs] n *(U)* stupidité *f*, bêtise *f*.

silly ['sɪlɪ] (comp -ier, superl -iest) adj stupide, bête.

silo ['saɪləʊ] (pl -s) n silo *m*.

silt [sɪlt] n vase *f*, limon *m*.
◆ ***silt up*** vi s'envaser.

silver ['sɪlvəʳ] ■ adj [colour] argenté(e).
■ n *(U)* **1.** [metal] argent *m* **2.** [coins] pièces *fpl* d'argent **3.** [silverware] argenterie *f*.
■ comp en argent, d'argent.

silver foil, ***silver paper*** n *(U)* papier *m* d'argent ***OR*** d'étain.

silver medal n SPORT médaille *f* d'argent.

silver-plated [-'pleɪtɪd] adj plaqué(e) argent.

silver screen n *inf* **: the silver screen** le grand écran.

silversmith ['sɪlvəsmɪθ] n orfèvre *mf*.

silverware ['sɪlvəweəʳ] n *(U)* **1.** [dishes, spoons] argenterie *f* **2.** *US* [cutlery] couverts *mpl*.

silver wedding n noces *fpl* d'argent.

SIM (abbr of ***subscriber identity module***) n TELEC **: SIM card** carte *f* SIM.

similar ['sɪmɪləʳ] adj **: similar (to)** semblable (à), similaire (à) ▸ **they're very similar** ils se ressemblent beaucoup ▸ **other customers have had similar problems** d'autres clients ont eu des problèmes similaires ***OR*** analogues ***OR*** du même ordre.

similarity [ˌsɪmɪ'lærətɪ] (pl -ies) n **: similarity (between/to)** similitude *f* (entre/avec), ressemblance *f* (entre/avec).

similarly ['sɪmɪləlɪ] adv de la même manière, pareillement.

simile ['sɪmɪlɪ] n comparaison *f*.

simmer ['sɪməʳ] ■ vt faire cuire à feu doux, mijoter.
■ vi cuire à feu doux, mijoter.
◆ ***simmer down*** vi *inf* se calmer.

simper ['sɪmpəʳ] ■ n sourire *m* affecté.
■ vi minauder.

simpering ['sɪmpərɪŋ] adj affecté(e).

simple ['sɪmpl] **adj 1.** [gen] simple ▸ **she wore a simple black dress** elle portait une robe noire toute simple ▸ **I want a simple "yes" or "no"** répondez-moi simplement par "oui" ou par "non" ▸ **it's a simple meal to prepare** c'est un repas facile à préparer **2.** *dated* [with learning difficulties] simplet(ette), simple d'esprit.

simple interest **n** *(U)* intérêts *mpl* simples.

simple-minded [-'maɪndɪd] **adj** simplet(ette), simple d'esprit.

simple tense **n** temps *m* simple.

simpleton ['sɪmpltən] **n** *dated* niais *m*, -e *f*.

simplicity [sɪm'plɪsətɪ] **n** simplicité *f*.

simplification [ˌsɪmplɪfɪ'keɪʃn] **n** simplification *f*.

simplify ['sɪmplɪfaɪ] (**pt & pp -ied**) **vt** simplifier.

simplistic [sɪm'plɪstɪk] **adj** simpliste.

simplistically [sɪm'plɪstɪklɪ] **adv** de manière simpliste.

simply ['sɪmplɪ] **adv 1.** [gen] simplement **2.** [for emphasis] absolument ▸ **quite simply** tout simplement.

simulate ['sɪmjʊleɪt] **vt** simuler.

simulated ['sɪmjʊleɪtɪd] **adj** simulé(e).

simulation [ˌsɪmjʊ'leɪʃn] **n** simulation *f*.

simulator ['sɪmjʊleɪtəʳ] **n** simulateur *m*.

simulcast [*UK* 'sɪməlkɑ:st, *US* 'saɪməlkæst] ■ **vt** diffuser simultanément à la télévision et à la radio.
■ **adj** radiotélévisé(e).
■ **n** émission *f* radiotélévisée.

simultaneous [*UK* ˌsɪmʊl'teɪnjəs, *US* ˌsaɪməl'teɪnjəs] **adj** simultané(e).

simultaneously [*UK* ˌsɪmʊl'teɪnjəslɪ, *US* ˌsaɪməl'teɪnjəslɪ] **adv** simultanément, en même temps.

sin [sɪn] ■ **n** péché *m* ▸ **to commit a sin** pécher, commettre un péché ▸ **it would be a sin to sell it** ce serait un crime de le vendre ▸ **to live in sin** vivre en concubinage.
■ **vi** (**pt & pp -ned, cont -ning**) **: to sin (against)** pécher (contre).

sin bin **n** *inf* [in hockey and rugby] prison *f*.

since [sɪns] ■ **adv** depuis ▸ **long since** il y a longtemps ▸ **she used to be his assistant, but she's since been promoted** elle était son assistante, mais depuis elle a été promue.
■ **prep** depuis ▸ **he has been talking about it since yesterday/since before Christmas** il en parle depuis hier/depuis avant Noël.
■ **conj 1.** [in time] depuis que ▸ **I've worn glasses since I was six** je porte des lunettes depuis que j'ai six ans *OR* depuis l'âge de six ans **2.** [because] comme, puisque.

sincere [sɪn'sɪəʳ] **adj** sincère.

sincerely [sɪn'sɪəlɪ] **adv** sincèrement ▸ **Yours sincerely** [at end of letter] veuillez agréer, Monsieur/Madame, l'expression de mes sentiments les meilleurs.

sincerity [sɪn'serətɪ] **n** sincérité *f*.

sinecure ['saɪnɪˌkjʊəʳ] **n** sinécure *f*.

sinew ['sɪnju:] **n** tendon *m*.

sinewy ['sɪnju:ɪ] **adj** musclé(e).

sinful ['sɪnfʊl] **adj** [thought] mauvais(e) / [desire, act] coupable ▸ **sinful person** pécheur *m*, -eresse *f*.

sing [sɪŋ] (**pt sang, pp sung**) **vt & vi** chanter.

Singapore [ˌsɪŋə'pɔ:ʳ] **n** Singapour *m*.

Singaporean [ˌsɪŋə'pɔ:rɪən] ■ **adj** singapourien(enne).
■ **n** [person] Singapourien *m*, -enne *f*.

singe [sɪndʒ] ■ **n** légère brûlure *f*.
■ **vt** (**cont singeing**) brûler légèrement / [cloth] roussir.

singer ['sɪŋəʳ] **n** chanteur *m*, -euse *f*.

Singhalese [ˌsɪŋhə'li:z] ■ **adj** cingalais(e), ceylanais(e).
■ **n 1.** [person] Cingalais *m*, -e *f*, Ceylanais *m*, -e *f* **2.** [language] cingalais *m*.

singing ['sɪŋɪŋ] ■ **adj** [lesson, teacher] de chant.
■ **n** *(U)* chant *m*.

singing telegram **n** télégramme *m* chanté.

single ['sɪŋgl] ■ **adj 1.** [only one] seul(e), unique ▸ **the room was lit by a single lamp** la pièce était éclairée par une seule lampe ▸ **not a single one of her friends came** pas un seul de ses amis *OR* aucun de ses amis n'est venu ▸ **he gave her a single red rose** il lui a donné une rose rouge ▸ **every single** chaque ▸ **every single apple** *OR* **every single one of the apples was rotten** toutes les pommes sans exception étaient pourries **2.** [unmarried] célibataire **3.** *UK* [ticket] simple ▸ **a single ticket to Oxford** un aller (simple) pour Oxford.
■ **n 1.** *UK* [one-way ticket] billet *m* simple, aller *m* (simple) **2.** MUS (disque *m*) 45 tours *m*.
◆ ***singles*** (**pl singles**) **n** TENNIS simple *m* ▸ **the men's single champion** le champion du simple messieurs.
◆ ***single out*** **vt sep : to single sb out (for)** choisir qqn (pour) ▸ **a few candidates were singled out for special praise** quelques candidats ont eu droit à des félicitations supplémentaires.

single bed **n** lit *m* à une place.

single-breasted [-'brestɪd] **adj** [jacket] droit(e).

single-click ■ **n** clic *m*.
■ **vi : to single-click on sthg** cliquer une fois sur qqc.
■ **vi** cliquer une fois.

single cream **n** *UK* crème *f* liquide.

single currency **n** monnaie *f* unique.

single-decker (bus) [-'dekəʳ-] **n** *UK* bus *m* sans impériale.

Single European Market **n : the Single European Market** le Marché unique européen.

single file **n : in single file** en file indienne, à la file.

single-handed [-'hændɪd] **adv** tout seul (toute seule).

single-handedly [-'hændɪdlɪ] **adv 1.** [on one's own] tout seul (toute seule) **2.** [with one hand] d'une seule main.

single-minded [-'maɪndɪd] **adj** résolu(e) ▸ **to be single-minded about sthg** concentrer toute son attention sur qqch.

single-mindedly [-'maɪndɪdlɪ] **adv** avec acharnement.

single parent **n** père *m*/mère *f* célibataire.

single-parent family **n** famille *f* monoparentale.

single quotes **npl** guillemets *mpl*.

single room n chambre *f* pour une personne ***OR*** à un lit.

singles bar ['sɪŋglz] n club *m* pour célibataires.

single-sex adj SCH non mixte.

singlet ['sɪŋglɪt] n *UK* tricot *m* de peau / SPORT maillot *m*.

single ticket n *UK* billet *m* simple, aller *m* (simple).

single-user licence n COMPUT licence *f* individuelle d'utilisation.

singly ['sɪŋglɪ] adv **1.** [one at a time] séparément **2.** [alone] seul(e) **3.** [individually - packaged] individuellement ▸ **you can't buy them singly** vous ne pouvez pas les acheter à la pièce.

singsong ['sɪŋsɒŋ] ■ adj [voice] chantant(e).
■ n *UK inf* **: to have a singsong** chanter en chœur.

singular ['sɪŋgjʊlər] ■ adj singulier(ère).
■ n singulier *m*.

singularly ['sɪŋgjʊləlɪ] adv singulièrement.

Sinhalese ['sɪnəli:z] = ***Singhalese***.

sinister ['sɪnɪstər] adj sinistre.

sink [sɪŋk] ■ n [in kitchen] évier *m* / [in bathroom] lavabo *m* ▸ **double sink** évier à deux bacs.
■ vt (pt sank, pp sunk) **1.** [ship] couler ▸ **to be sunk in thought** *fig* être plongé(e) dans ses pensées ▸ **if they don't come we're sunk!** *inf* s'ils ne viennent pas, nous sommes fichus! **2.** [teeth, claws] **: to sink sthg into** enfoncer qqch dans **3.** [dig, bore - well, mine shaft] creuser, forer.
■ vi (pt sank, pp sunk) **1.** [in water - ship] couler, sombrer / [- person, object] couler ▸ **to sink like a stone** couler à pic ▸ **to sink without (a) trace** [- whereabouts unknown] disparaître sans laisser de trace / [- no longer famous] tomber dans l'oubli **2.** [ground] s'affaisser / [sun] baisser ▸ **Venice is sinking** Venise est en train de s'affaisser ▸ **the wheels sank into the mud** les roues s'enfonçaient dans la boue ▸ **his spirits sank** il a été pris de découragement ▸ **to sink into a chair** se laisser tomber dans un fauteuil ▸ **to sink to one's knees** tomber à genoux ▸ **to sink into poverty/despair** sombrer dans la misère/le désespoir ▸ **how could you sink to this?** comment as-tu pu tomber si bas? **3.** [value, amount] baisser, diminuer / [voice] faiblir ▸ **the dollar has sunk to half its former value** le dollar a perdu la moitié de sa valeur ▸ **her voice had sunk to a whisper** sa voix n'était plus qu'un murmure.
◆ ***sink in*** vi **: it hasn't sunk in yet** je n'ai pas encore réalisé.

sink board n *US* égouttoir *m*.

sinking ['sɪŋkɪŋ] n naufrage *m*.

sinking fund n fonds *m* ***OR*** caisse *f* d'amortissement.

sink school n dépotoir *m*.

sink unit n bloc-évier *m*.

sinner ['sɪnər] n pécheur *m*, -eresse *f*.

Sinn Féin [,ʃɪn'feɪn] n Sinn Féin *m*.

sinuous ['sɪnjʊəs] adj sinueux(euse).

sinus ['saɪnəs] (pl -es [-i:z]) n sinus *m inv*.

sip [sɪp] ■ n petite gorgée *f*.
■ vt (pt & pp -ped, cont -ping) siroter, boire à petits coups.

siphon ['saɪfn] ■ n siphon *m*.
■ vt **1.** [liquid] siphonner **2.** *fig* [money] canaliser.
◆ ***siphon off*** vt sep **1.** [liquid] siphonner **2.** *fig* [money] canaliser.

sir [sɜ:r] n **1.** [form of address] monsieur *m* **2.** [in titles] **: Sir Phillip Holden** sir Phillip Holden.

siren ['saɪərən] n sirène *f*.

sirloin (steak) ['sɜ:lɔɪn-] n bifteck *m* dans l'aloyau ***OR*** d'aloyau.

sisal ['saɪsl] ■ n sisal *m*.
■ adj en ***OR*** de sisal.

sissy ['sɪsɪ] (pl -ies) n *inf offens* poule *f* mouillée, dégonflé *m*, -e *f*.

sister ['sɪstər] ■ adj [organization] sœur ▸ **sister ship** navire *m* jumeau.
■ n **1.** [sibling] sœur *f* **2.** [nun] sœur *f*, religieuse *f* **3.** *UK* [senior nurse] infirmière *f* chef.

sister company n société *f* sœur.

sisterhood ['sɪstəhʊd] n RELIG communauté *f* religieuse.

sister-in-law (pl sisters-in-law) n belle-sœur *f*.

sisterly ['sɪstəlɪ] adj de sœur, fraternel(elle).

sit [sɪt] (pt & pp sat, cont -ting) ■ vt *UK* [exam] passer.
■ vi **1.** [person] s'asseoir ▸ **sit still!** tiens-toi ***OR*** reste tranquille! ▸ **to be sitting** être assis(e) ▸ **to sit on a committee** faire partie ***OR*** être membre d'un comité **2.** [court, parliament] siéger, être en séance ▸ **the council was still sitting at midnight** à minuit, le conseil siégeait toujours ***OR*** était toujours en séance **3.** [be situated] se trouver, être ▸ **the plane sat waiting on the runway** l'avion attendait sur la piste
▸▸ **to sit tight** ne pas bouger.
◆ ***sit about*** *UK*, ***sit around*** vi rester assis(e) à ne rien faire ▸ **I'm not going to sit around waiting for you** je ne vais pas passer mon temps à t'attendre.
◆ ***sit back*** vi [relax] se détendre ▸ **just sit back and close your eyes** installe-toi bien et ferme les yeux ▸ **to sit back in a chair** se caler dans un fauteuil ▸ **we can't just sit back and do nothing!** il faut que nous fassions quelque chose!
◆ ***sit down*** ■ vt sep asseoir ▸ **sit yourself down and have a drink** asseyez-vous et prenez un verre.
■ vi s'asseoir ▸ **please sit down** asseyez-vous, je vous en prie.
◆ ***sit in on*** vt insep assister à.
◆ ***sit out*** vt sep **1.** [meeting, play] rester jusqu'à la fin de **2.** [dance] **: to sit out a dance** ne pas danser.
◆ ***sit through*** vt insep rester jusqu'à la fin de.
◆ ***sit up*** vi **1.** [sit upright] se redresser, s'asseoir ▸ **the baby can sit up now** le bébé peut se tenir assis maintenant ▸ **sit up straight!** redresse-toi!, tiens-toi droit! **2.** [stay up] veiller ▸ **I'll sit up with her until the fever passes** je vais rester avec elle jusqu'à ce que sa fièvre tombe.

sitcom ['sɪtkɒm] n *inf* sitcom *f*.

sit-down ■ adj [meal] servi(e) à la table / [protest] sur le tas.
■ n *UK inf* **: to have a sit-down** (s'asseoir pour) se reposer.

site [saɪt] ■ n **1.** COMPUT site *m* **2.** [of town, building] emplacement *m* / CONSTR chantier *m*.
■ vt situer, placer.

sit-in n sit-in *m*, occupation *f* des locaux.

sitter ['sɪtəʳ] **n 1.** ART modèle *m* **2.** *inf* [babysitter] baby-sitter *mf*.

sitting ['sɪtɪŋ] **n 1.** [of meal] service *m* **2.** [of court, parliament] séance *f*.

sitting duck **n** *inf* cible *f* ***or*** proie *f* facile.

sitting room **n** salon *m*.

sitting tenant **n** *UK* locataire *mf* en possession des lieux.

situate ['sɪtjʊeɪt] **vt** situer.

situated ['sɪtjʊeɪtɪd] **adj : to be situated** être situé(e), se trouver.

situation [ˌsɪtjʊ'eɪʃn] **n 1.** [gen] situation *f* ▸ **what would you do in my situation?** qu'est-ce que tu ferais à ma place ***or*** dans ma situation? ▸ **the firm's financial situation isn't good** la situation financière de la société n'est pas bonne **2.** [job] situation *f*, emploi *m* ▸ **'situations vacant'** *UK* 'offres d'emploi'.

situation comedy **n** sitcom *f*.

sit-up **n** redressement *m* assis.

six [sɪks] ■ **num adj** six *(inv)* ▸ **she's six (years old)** elle a six ans.
■ **num pron** six *mf pl* ▸ **I want six** j'en veux six ▸ **six of us went** six d'entre nous sont allés ▸ **there were six of us** nous étions six.
■ **num n 1.** [gen] six *m inv* ▸ **two hundred and six** deux cent six ▸ **we sell them in sixes** on les vend par paquets de six **2.** [six o'clock] **: it's six** il est six heures ▸ **we arrived at six** nous sommes arrivés à six heures **3.** [six degrees] **: it's six below** il fait moins six.

six-pack **n** pack *m* de six.

six-shooter [-'ʃu:təʳ] **n** *US dated* revolver *m* à six coups.

sixteen [sɪks'ti:n] **num** seize ; see also ***six***.

sixteenth [sɪks'ti:nθ] **num** seizième ; see also ***sixth***.

sixth [sɪksθ] ■ **num adj** sixième.
■ **num adv 1.** [in race, competition] sixième, en sixième place **2.** [in list] sixièmement.
■ **num pron** sixième *mf*.
■ **n 1.** [fraction] sixième *m* **2.** [in dates] **: the sixth (of September)** le six (septembre).

sixth form **n** *UK* SCH ≃ (classe *f*) terminale *f*.

sixth form college **n** *UK établissement préparant aux A-levels*.

sixth sense **n** sixième sens *m*.

sixtieth ['sɪkstɪəθ] **num** soixantième ; see also ***sixth***.

sixty ['sɪkstɪ] (pl **-ies**) **num** soixante ; see also ***six***.
◆ ***sixties*** **npl 1.** [decade] **: the sixties** les années *fpl* soixante **2.** [in ages] **: to be in one's sixties** être sexagénaire **3.** [in temperatures] **: in the sixties** ≃ entre 15 et 20 degrés.

size [saɪz] **n** [of person, clothes, company] taille *f* / [of building] grandeur *f*, dimensions *fpl* / [of problem] ampleur *f*, taille / [of shoes] pointure *f* ▸ **the two rooms are the same size** les deux pièces sont de la même taille ***or*** ont les mêmes dimensions ▸ **what size are you?, what size do you take?** quelle taille faites-vous? ▸ **I take (a) size 40** je fais du 40 ▸ **to cut sb down to size** rabattre le caquet à qqn.
◆ ***size up*** **vt sep** [person] jauger / [situation] apprécier, peser.

-size = ***-sized***.

sizeable ['saɪzəbl] **adj** assez important(e).

-sized [-saɪzd] **suffix : medium-sized** de taille moyenne.

sizzle ['sɪzl] **vi** grésiller.

sizzling ['sɪzlɪŋ] ■ **adj 1.** [sputtering] grésillant(e) **2.** *inf* [hot] brûlant(e).
■ **adv** *inf* **: sizzling hot** brûlant(e).

SK abbr of ***Saskatchewan***.

skate [skeɪt] ■ **n 1.** [ice skate, roller skate] patin *m* **2.** (pl **skate** ***or*** **-s**) [fish] raie *f*.
■ **vi** [on ice skates] faire du patin à glace, patiner / [on roller skates] faire du patin à roulettes.
◆ ***skate over, skate around*** *UK* **vt insep** [problem] éluder, éviter.

skateboard ['skeɪtbɔ:d] **n** planche *f* à roulettes, skateboard *m*, skate *m*.

skateboarder ['skeɪtbɔ:dəʳ] **n** personne *f* qui fait du skateboard ***or*** du skate ***or*** de la planche à roulettes.

skateboarding ['skeɪtbɔ:dɪŋ] **n : to go skateboarding** faire de la planche à roulettes ***or*** du skateboard.

skater ['skeɪtəʳ] **n** [on ice] patineur *m*, -euse *f* / [on roller skates] patineur à roulettes.

skating ['skeɪtɪŋ] **n** [on ice] patinage *m* / [on roller skates] patinage à roulettes.

skating rink **n** patinoire *f*.

skein [skeɪn] **n** [of thread] écheveau *m*.

skeletal ['skelɪtl] **adj** [emaciated] squelettique.

skeleton ['skelɪtn] ■ **adj** [crew, service] squelettique, réduit(e).
■ **n** squelette *m* ▸ **to have a skeleton in the closet** ***or*** **cupboard** *UK fig* avoir un secret honteux.

skeleton key **n** passe *m*, passe-partout *m inv*.

skeleton staff **n** personnel *m* réduit.

skeptic *US* = ***sceptic***.

skeptical *US* = ***sceptical***.

skepticism *US* = ***scepticism***.

sketch [sketʃ] ■ **n 1.** [drawing] croquis *m*, esquisse *f* **2.** [description] aperçu *m*, résumé *m* **3.** [by comedian] sketch *m*.
■ **vt 1.** [draw] dessiner, faire un croquis de **2.** [describe] donner un aperçu de, décrire à grands traits.
■ **vi** dessiner.
◆ ***sketch in*** **vt sep** [details] ajouter, donner.
◆ ***sketch out*** **vt sep** esquisser, décrire à grands traits.

sketchbook ['sketʃbʊk] **n** carnet *m* à dessins.

sketchpad ['sketʃpæd] **n** bloc *m* à dessins.

sketchy ['sketʃɪ] (comp **-ier**, superl **-iest**) **adj** incomplet(ète).

skew [skju:] ■ n *UK* **: on the skew** de travers, en biais.
■ vt [distort] fausser.

skewed ['skeluːtl] adj [view, notion] partial(e).

skewer ['skjʊəʳ] ■ n brochette *f*, broche *f*.
■ vt embrocher.

skew-whiff [ˌskju:'wɪf] adj *UK inf* de guingois, de traviole.

ski [ski:] ■ n ski *m*.
■ comp de ski.
■ vi (pt & pp **skied**, cont **skiing**) skier, faire du ski.

ski boots npl chaussures *fpl* de ski.

skid [skɪd] ■ n dérapage *m* ▸ **to go into a skid** déraper.
■ vi (pt & pp **-ded**, cont **-ding**) déraper.

skid mark n trace *f* de frein OR dérapage.

skid row n *esp US inf* **: to be on skid row** être sur le pavé.

skier ['ski:əʳ] n skieur *m*, -euse *f*.

skies [skaɪz] npl ➤ *sky*.

skiing ['ski:ɪŋ] ■ n *(U)* ski *m* ▸ **to go skiing** faire du ski.
■ comp de ski.

ski instructor n moniteur *m*, -trice *f* de ski.

ski jump n [slope] tremplin *m* / [event] saut *m* à OR en skis.

skilful *UK*, ***skillful*** *US* ['skɪlfʊl] adj habile, adroit(e).

skilfully *UK*, ***skillfully*** *US* ['skɪlfʊlɪ] adv habilement, adroitement.

ski lift n remonte-pente *m*.

skill [skɪl] n **1.** *(U)* [ability] habileté *f*, adresse *f* **2.** [technique] technique *f*, art *m*.

skilled [skɪld] adj **1.** [skilful] **: skilled (in OR at doing sthg)** habile OR adroit(e) (pour faire qqch) **2.** [trained] qualifié(e).

skillet ['skɪlɪt] n *US* poêle *f* à frire.

skillful *US* = ***skilful***.

skillfully *US* = ***skilfully***.

skim [skɪm] (pt & pp **-med**, cont **-ming**) ■ vt **1.** [cream] écrémer / [soup] écumer **2.** [move above] effleurer, raser **3.** [newspaper, book] parcourir.
■ vi **: to skim through sthg** [newspaper, book] parcourir qqch.

skim(med) milk [skɪm(d)-] n lait *m* écrémé.

skimp [skɪmp] ■ vt lésiner sur.
■ vi **: to skimp on** lésiner sur.

skimpily ['skɪmpɪlɪ] adv [scantily] **: skimpily dressed** légèrement vêtu(e).

skimpy ['skɪmpɪ] (comp **-ier**, superl **-iest**) adj [meal] maigre / [clothes] étriqué(e) / [facts] insuffisant(e).

skin [skɪn] ■ n peau *f* ▸ **by the skin of one's teeth** de justesse ▸ **to jump out of one's skin** *UK* sursauter, sauter au plafond ▸ **to make sb's skin crawl** donner la chair de poule à qqn ▸ **to save OR protect one's own skin** sauver sa peau.
■ vt (pt & pp **-ned**, cont **-ning**) **1.** [dead animal] écorcher, dépouiller / [fruit] éplucher, peler **2.** [graze] **: to skin one's knee** s'érafler OR s'écorcher le genou.

skincare ['skɪnkeəʳ] n *(U)* soins *mpl* pour la peau.

skin-deep adj superficiel(elle).

skin diver n plongeur sous-marin *m*, plongeuse sous-marine *f*.

skin diving n *(U)* plongée *f* sous-marine.

skinflint ['skɪnflɪnt] n *inf* grippe-sou *m*, avare *mf*.

skin graft n greffe *f* de la peau.

skinhead ['skɪnhed] n skinhead *m*, skin *m*.

-skinned [skɪnd] suffix à la peau... ▸ **she's dark-skinned** elle a la peau foncée.

skinny ['skɪnɪ] (comp **-ier**, superl **-iest**) adj maigre.

skint [skɪnt] adj *UK inf* fauché(e), à sec.

skin test n cuti *f*, cutiréaction *f*.

skin-tight adj moulant(e), collant(e).

skip [skɪp] ■ n **1.** [jump] petit saut *m* **2.** *UK* [container] benne *f*.
■ vt (pt & pp **-ped**, cont **-ping**) [page, class, meal] sauter.
■ vi (pt & pp **-ped**, cont **-ping**) **1.** [gen] sauter, sautiller **2.** *UK* [over rope] sauter à la corde.

ski pants npl fuseau *m*.

ski pole n bâton *m* de ski.

skipper ['skɪpəʳ] n *inf* **1.** NAUT capitaine *m* **2.** *UK* SPORT capitaine *m*.

skipping ['skɪpɪŋ] n *(U) UK* saut *m* à la corde.

skipping rope n *UK* corde *f* à sauter.

ski resort n station *f* de ski.

skirmish ['skɜ:mɪʃ] ■ n escarmouche *f*.
■ vi s'engager dans une escarmouche / *fig* avoir une escarmouche.

skirt [skɜ:t] ■ n [garment] jupe *f*.
■ vt **1.** [town, obstacle] contourner **2.** [problem] éviter.
◆ ***skirt around*** vt insep **1.** [town, obstacle] contourner **2.** [problem] éviter.

skirting board ['skɜ:tɪŋ-] n *UK* plinthe *f*.

ski run n piste *f* de ski.

ski stick n bâton *m* de ski.

skit [skɪt] n sketch *m*.

skittish ['skɪtɪʃ] adj [person] frivole / [animal] ombrageux(euse).

skittle ['skɪtl] n *UK* quille *f*.
◆ ***skittles*** n *(U)* [game] quilles *fpl*.

skive [skaɪv] vi *UK inf* **: to skive (off)** s'esquiver, tirer au flanc.

skivvy ['skɪvɪ] *UK inf* ■ n (pl **-ies**) boniche *f*, bonne *f* à tout faire.
■ vi (pt & pp **-ied**) faire la boniche.

skulduggery [skʌl'dʌgərɪ] n *(U)* magouilles *fpl*.

skulk [skʌlk] vi [hide] se cacher / [prowl] rôder.

skull [skʌl] n crâne *m*.

skull and crossbones n [motif] tête *f* de mort / [flag] pavillon *m* à tête de mort.

skullcap ['skʌlkæp] n calotte *f*.

skunk [skʌŋk] n [animal] mouffette *f*.

sky [skaɪ] (pl **skies**) **n** ciel *m*.

skycap ['skaɪkæp] **n** *US* porteur *m (dans un aéroport)*.

skydiver ['skaɪˌdaɪvəʳ] **n** parachutiste *mf* qui fait de la chute libre.

skydiving ['skaɪˌdaɪvɪŋ] **n** parachutisme *m* en chute libre.

sky-high *inf* ▪ **adj** [prices] astronomique, exorbitant(e).
▪ **adv : to blow sthg sky-high** [building] faire sauter qqch / [argument, theory] démolir qqch ▸ **to go sky-high** [prices] monter en flèche.

skylark ['skaɪlɑːk] **n** alouette *f*.

skylight ['skaɪlaɪt] **n** lucarne *f*.

skyline ['skaɪlaɪn] **n** ligne *f* d'horizon.

sky marshal **n** garde *m* de sécurité *(à bord d'un avion)*.

skyscraper ['skaɪˌskreɪpəʳ] **n** gratte-ciel *m inv*.

slab [slæb] **n** [of concrete] dalle *f* / [of stone] bloc *m* / [of cake] pavé *m*.

slack [slæk] ▪ **adj 1.** [not tight] lâche **2.** [not busy] calme **3.** [person] négligent(e), pas sérieux(euse).
▪ **n** [in rope] mou *m*.
◆ ***slacks*** **npl** *dated* pantalon *m*.

slacken ['slækn] ▪ **vt** [speed, pace] ralentir / [rope] relâcher.
▪ **vi** [speed, pace] ralentir.

slag [slæg] **n** *(U)* [waste material] scories *fpl*.

slagheap ['slæghiːp] **n** terril *m*.

slain [sleɪn] **pp** ➤ ***slay***.

slalom ['slɑːləm] **n** slalom *m*.

slam [slæm] (pt & pp **-med**, cont **-ming**) ▪ **vt 1.** [shut] claquer **2.** [criticize] éreinter **3.** [place with force] **: to slam sthg on** ***OR*** **onto** jeter qqch brutalement sur, flanquer qqch sur.
▪ **vi** claquer.

slam dunk *US* ▪ **n** SPORT smash *m* au panier, slam-dunk *m*.
▪ **vt & vi** SPORT smasher.

slander ['slɑːndəʳ] ▪ **n** calomnie *f* / LAW diffamation *f*.
▪ **vt** calomnier / LAW diffamer.

slanderous ['slɑːndrəs] **adj** calomnieux(euse) / LAW diffamatoire.

slang [slæŋ] ▪ **adj** argotique.
▪ **n** *(U)* argot *m*.

slant [slɑːnt] ▪ **n 1.** [angle] inclinaison *f* ▸ **on** ***OR*** **at a slant** de biais **2.** [perspective] point *m* de vue, perspective *f*.
▪ **vt** [bias] présenter d'une manière tendancieuse.
▪ **vi** [slope] être incliné(e), pencher.

slanting ['slɑːntɪŋ] **adj** [roof] en pente.

slap [slæp] ▪ **n** claque *f*, tape *f* / [on face] gifle *f* ▸ **a slap in the face** *fig* une gifle.
▪ **vt** (pt & pp **-ped**, cont **-ping**) **1.** [person, face] gifler / [back] donner une claque ***OR*** une tape à **2.** [place with force] **: to slap sthg on** ***OR*** **onto** jeter qqch brutalement sur, flanquer qqch sur.
▪ **adv** *inf* [directly] en plein.

slapdash ['slæpdæʃ] **adj** *inf* [work] bâclé(e) / [person, attitude] négligent(e).

slapstick ['slæpstɪk] **n** *(U)* grosse farce *f*.

slap-up **adj** *UK inf* [meal] fameux(euse).

slash [slæʃ] ▪ **n 1.** [long cut] entaille *f* **2.** [oblique stroke] barre *f* oblique.
▪ **vt 1.** [cut] entailler **2.** *inf* [prices] casser / [budget, unemployment] réduire considérablement.

slasher movie ['slæʃəʳ] **n** *inf* film *m* d'horreur *inf*.

slat [slæt] **n** lame *f* / [wooden] latte *f*.

slate [sleɪt] ▪ **n** ardoise *f*.
▪ **vt** *inf* [criticize] descendre en flammes.

slatted ['slætɪd] **adj** à lames / [wooden] en lattes de bois.

slaughter ['slɔːtəʳ] ▪ **n 1.** [of animals] abattage *m* **2.** [of people] massacre *m*, carnage *m*.
▪ **vt 1.** [animals] abattre **2.** [people] massacrer.

slaughterhouse ['slɔːtəhaʊs] (pl [-haʊzɪz]) **n** abattoir *m*.

Slav [slɑːv] ▪ **adj** slave.
▪ **n** Slave *mf*.

slave [sleɪv] ▪ **n** esclave *mf* ▸ **to be a slave to sthg** *fig* être esclave de qqch.
▪ **vi** travailler comme un esclave ***OR*** un forçat ▸ **to slave over sthg** peiner sur qqch.

slaver ['sleɪvəʳ] **vi** [salivate] baver.

slavery ['sleɪvərɪ] **n** esclavage *m*.

slave trade **n : the slave trade** la traite des noirs.

Slavic ['slɑːvɪk] ▪ **adj** slave.
▪ **n** [language] slave *m* / HIST slavon *m*.

slavish ['sleɪvɪʃ] **adj** servile.

slavishly ['sleɪvɪʃlɪ] **adv** [work] comme un forçat / [copy, worship] servilement.

Slavonic [slə'vɒnɪk] = ***Slavic***.

slay [sleɪ] (pt **slew**, pp **slain**) **vt** *liter* tuer.

sleaze [sliːz] **n** [squalidness] aspect *m* miteux, caractère *m* sordide / [pornography] porno *m* / POL [corruption] corruption *f*.

sleazy ['sliːzɪ] (comp **-ier**, superl **-iest**) **adj** [disreputable] mal famé(e).

sledge *UK* [sledʒ], ***sled*** *US* [sled] **n** luge *f* / [larger] traîneau *m*.

sledgehammer ['sledʒˌhæməʳ] **n** masse *f*.

sleek [sliːk] **adj 1.** [hair, fur] lisse, luisant(e) **2.** [shape] aux lignes pures.

sleep [sliːp] ▪ **n** sommeil *m* ▸ **I only had two hours' sleep** je n'ai dormi que deux heures ▸ **you need (to get) a good night's sleep** il te faut une bonne nuit de sommeil ▸ **to go to sleep** s'endormir ▸ **my foot has gone to sleep** j'ai le pied engourdi ***OR*** endormi ▸ **to put an animal to sleep** *euph* piquer un animal.
▪ **vi** (pt & pp **slept**) **1.** [be asleep] dormir ▸ **to sleep soundly** dormir profondément ***OR*** à poings fermés **2.** [spend night] coucher ▸ **can I sleep at your place?** est-ce que je peux coucher ***OR*** dormir chez vous? ▸ **to sleep rough** *UK* coucher sur la dure.
◆ ***sleep around*** **vi** *inf pej* coucher à droite et à gauche.
◆ ***sleep in*** **vi** *UK* faire la grasse matinée.

◆ ***sleep off*** vt sep dormir pour faire passer ▸ **he's sleeping it off** *inf* il cuve son vin.
◆ ***sleep through*** vt insep **: I slept through the alarm** je n'ai pas entendu le réveil.
◆ ***sleep together*** vi coucher ensemble.
◆ ***sleep with*** vt insep coucher avec.

sleeper ['sli:pəʳ] n **1.** [person] **: to be a heavy/light sleeper** avoir le sommeil lourd/léger **2.** [RAIL - berth] couchette *f* / [- carriage] wagon-lit *m* / [- train] train-couchettes *m* **3.** *UK* [on railway track] traverse *f*.

sleepily ['sli:pılı] adv d'un air endormi.

sleepiness ['sli:pınıs] n [of person] envie *f* de dormir / [of town] torpeur *f*.

sleeping ['sli:pıŋ] adj qui dort, endormi(e).

sleeping bag n sac *m* de couchage.

sleeping car n wagon-lit *m*.

sleeping economy n économie *f* à ressources sous-exploitées.

sleeping partner n *UK* (associé *m*) commanditaire *m*, bailleur *m* de fonds.

sleeping pill n somnifère *m*.

sleeping policeman n *UK inf* ralentisseur *m*.

sleeping tablet n somnifère *m*.

sleepless ['sli:plıs] adj **: to have a sleepless night** passer une nuit blanche.

sleeplessness ['sli:plısnıs] n insomnie *f*.

sleep mode n COMPUT mode *m* veille.

sleepwalk ['sli:pwɔ:k] vi être somnambule.

sleepwalker ['sli:pˌwɔ:kəʳ] n somnambule *mf*.

sleepwalking ['sli:pˌwɔ:kıŋ] n somnambulisme *m*.

sleepy ['sli:pı] (comp -ier, superl -iest) adj **1.** [person] qui a envie de dormir **2.** [place] endormi(e).

sleet [sli:t] ■ n neige *f* fondue.
■ impers vb **: it's sleeting** il tombe de la neige fondue.

sleeve [sli:v] n **1.** [of garment] manche *f* ▸ **to have sthg up one's sleeve** *fig* avoir qqch en réserve **2.** [for record] pochette *f*.

sleeveless ['sli:vlıs] adj sans manches.

sleeve notes npl *UK texte figurant au dos des pochettes de disques*.

sleigh [sleı] n traîneau *m*.

sleight of hand [ˌslaıt-] n *(U)* **1.** [skill] habileté *f* **2.** [trick] tour *m* de passe-passe.

slender ['slendəʳ] adj **1.** [thin] mince **2.** *fig* [resources, income] modeste, maigre / [hope, chance] faible.

slept [slept] pt & pp ➤ ***sleep***.

sleuth [slu:θ] n *inf hum* limier *m*.

S level (abbr of ***Special level***) n [in UK] *examen optionnel de niveau supérieur au A level, sanctionnant la fin des études secondaires*.

slew [slu:] ■ pt ➤ ***slay***.
■ vi [car] déraper.

slice [slaıs] ■ n **1.** [thin piece] tranche *f* **2.** *fig* [of profits, glory] part *f* **3.** SPORT slice *m*.
■ vt **1.** [cut into slices] couper en tranches **2.** [cut cleanly] trancher **3.** SPORT slicer.
■ vi **: to slice through sthg** trancher qqch.

sliced bread [slaıst-] n *(U)* pain *m* en tranches.

slick [slık] ■ adj **1.** [skilful] bien mené(e), habile **2.** *pej* [superficial - talk] facile / [- person] rusé(e).
■ n nappe *f* de pétrole, marée *f* noire.

slicker ['slıkəʳ] n *US* [raincoat] ciré *m*.

slickly ['slıklı] adv [answer] habilement / [perform] brillamment ▸ **his hair shone slickly** il avait les cheveux luisants.

slide [slaıd] ■ n **1.** [in playground] toboggan *m* **2.** PHOT diapositive *f*, diapo *f* **3.** [for microscope] porte-objet *m* **4.** *UK* [for hair] barrette *f* **5.** [decline] déclin *m* / [in prices] baisse *f*.
■ vt (pt & pp **slid** [slıd]) faire glisser.
■ vi (pt & pp **slid** [slıd]) glisser ▸ **to let things slide** *fig* laisser les choses aller à vau-l'eau.

slide projector n projecteur *m* de diapositives.

slide rule n règle *f* à calcul.

slide show n diaporama *m*.

sliding door [ˌslaıdıŋ-] n porte *f* coulissante.

sliding scale [ˌslaıdıŋ-] n échelle *f* mobile.

slight [slaıt] ■ adj **1.** [minor] léger(ère) ▸ **the slightest** le moindre (la moindre) ▸ **not in the slightest** pas du tout **2.** [thin] mince.
■ n affront *m*.
■ vt offenser, faire un affront à.

slightly ['slaıtlı] adv **1.** [to small extent] légèrement **2.** [slenderly] **: slightly built** mince.

slim [slım] ■ adj (comp -mer, superl -mest) **1.** [person, object] mince **2.** [chance, possibility] faible.
■ vi (pt & pp -med, cont -ming) maigrir / *UK* [diet] suivre un régime amaigrissant.

slime [slaım] n *(U)* substance *f* visqueuse / [of snail] bave *f*.

slimline ['slımlaın] adj **1.** [butter] allégé(e) / [milk, cheese] sans matière grasse, minceur *(inv)* / [soft drink] light *(inv)* **2.** *fig* **: clothes for the new slimline you** des vêtements pour votre nouvelle silhouette allégée ▸ **the slimline version of the 1990 model** la version épurée du modèle 90.

slimmer ['slıməʳ] n *UK* personne *f* suivant un régime amaigrissant.

slimming ['slımıŋ] *UK* ■ n amaigrissement *m*.
■ adj [product] amaigrissant(e), pour maigrir.

slimness ['slımnıs] n minceur *f*.

slimy ['slaımı] (comp -ier, superl -iest) adj *lit* & *fig* visqueux(euse).

sling [slıŋ] ■ n **1.** [for arm] écharpe *f* **2.** NAUT [for loads] élingue *f*.
■ vt (pt & pp **slung**) **1.** [hammock] suspendre ▸ **to sling a bag over one's shoulder** mettre son sac en bandoulière **2.** *inf* [throw] lancer.

slingback ['slıŋbæk] n chaussure *f* à talon ouvert.

slingshot ['slıŋʃɒt] n *US* lance-pierres *m inv*.

slink [slɪŋk] (pt & pp **slunk**) **vi : to slink away** *OR* **off** s'en aller furtivement.

slip [slɪp] ■ **n 1.** [mistake] erreur *f* ▸ **a slip of the pen** *OR* **tongue** un lapsus
2. [of paper - gen] morceau *m* / [- strip] bande *f*
3. [underwear] combinaison *f*
▸▸ **to give sb the slip** *inf* fausser compagnie à qqn.
■ **vt** (pt & pp **-ped**, cont **-ping**) glisser ▸ **slip the key under the door** glissez la clé sous la porte ▸ **it slipped my mind** ça m'est sorti de la tête ▸ **to slip sthg on** enfiler qqch.
■ **vi** (pt & pp **-ped**, cont **-ping**) **1.** [slide] glisser ▸ **he slipped and fell** il glissa et tomba ▸ **the knife slipped and cut my finger** le couteau a glissé et je me suis coupé le doigt ▸ **to slip into sthg** se glisser dans qqch ▸ **the patient slipped into a coma** le patient a glissé *OR* s'est enfoncé peu à peu dans le coma ▸ **she slipped quietly into the room** elle s'est glissée discrètement dans la pièce
2. [decline] décliner ▸ **prices have slipped (by) 10%** les prix ont baissé de 10 % ▸ **to let things slip** laisser les choses aller à vau-l'eau
▸▸ **you're slipping!** tu n'es plus ce que tu étais! ▸ **to let sthg slip** laisser échapper qqch ▸ **she let (it) slip that she was selling her house** elle a laissé échapper qu'elle vendait sa maison.
◆ ***slip up*** **vi** *fig* faire une erreur.

slip-on **adj : slip-on shoes** mocassins *mpl*.
◆ ***slip-ons*** **npl** mocassins *mpl*.

slippage ['slɪpɪdʒ] **n** baisse *f*.

slipped disc *UK*, ***slipped disk*** *US* [ˌslɪpt-] **n** hernie *f* discale.

slipper ['slɪpəʳ] **n** pantoufle *f*, chausson *m*.

slippery ['slɪpərɪ] **adj** glissant(e).

slip road **n** *UK* bretelle *f*.

slipshod ['slɪpʃɒd] **adj** peu soigné(e).

slipstream ['slɪpstri:m] **n** sillage *m*.

slip-up **n** *inf* gaffe *f*.

slipway ['slɪpweɪ] **n** cale *f* de lancement.

slit [slɪt] ■ **n** [opening] fente *f* / [cut] incision *f*.
■ **vt** (pt & pp **slit**, cont **-ting**) [make opening in] faire une fente dans, fendre / [cut] inciser.

slither ['slɪðəʳ] **vi** [person] glisser / [snake] onduler.

sliver ['slɪvəʳ] **n** [of glass, wood] éclat *m* / [of meat, cheese] lamelle *f*.

slob [slɒb] **n** *inf* [in habits] saligaud *m* / [in appearance] gros lard *m*.

slobber ['slɒbəʳ] **vi** baver.

slog [slɒg] *inf* ■ **n 1.** [tiring work] corvée *f* **2.** [tiring journey] voyage *m* pénible.
■ **vi** (pt & pp **-ged**, cont **-ging**) **1.** [work] travailler comme un bœuf **2.** [move] avancer péniblement.

slogan ['sləʊgən] **n** slogan *m*.

sloop [slu:p] **n** sloop *m*.

slop [slɒp] (pt & pp **-ped**, cont **-ping**) ■ **vt** renverser.
■ **vi** déborder.

slope [sləʊp] ■ **n** pente *f* ▸ **to be on a slippery slope** *fig* être sur une pente savonneuse.
■ **vi** [land] être en pente / [handwriting, table] pencher.

sloping ['sləʊpɪŋ] **adj** [land, shelf] en pente / [handwriting] penché(e).

sloppily ['slɒpɪlɪ] **adv 1.** [work] sans soin / [dress] de façon négligée **2.** *UK inf* [sentimentally] avec sensiblerie.

sloppy ['slɒpɪ] (comp **-ier**, superl **-iest**) **adj 1.** [careless] peu soigné(e) **2.** *inf* [sentimental] sentimental(e), à l'eau de rose.

slosh [slɒʃ] ■ **vt** renverser.
■ **vi : to slosh around** [liquid] clapoter / [person] patauger.

sloshed [slɒʃt] **adj** *inf* bourré(e).

slot [slɒt] **n 1.** [opening] fente *f* **2.** [groove] rainure *f* **3.** [in schedule] créneau *m*.
◆ ***slot in*** (pt & pp **-ted in**, cont **-ting in**) ■ **vt sep** [part] insérer.
■ **vi** [part] s'emboîter.

sloth [sləʊθ] **n 1.** [animal] paresseux *m* **2.** *liter* [laziness] paresse *f*.

slot machine **n 1.** *UK* [vending machine] distributeur *m* automatique **2.** [for gambling] machine *f* à sous.

slot meter **n** *UK* compteur *m* à pièces.

slouch [slaʊtʃ] ■ **n** [posture] allure *f* avachie.
■ **vi** être avachi(e).

slough [slaʊ] ◆ ***slough off*** **vt sep 1.** [skin] **: to slough off one's skin** muer **2.** *liter* [get rid of] se débarrasser de.

Slovak ['sləʊvæk] ■ **adj** slovaque.
■ **n 1.** [person] Slovaque *mf* **2.** [language] slovaque *m*.

Slovakia [slə'vækɪə] **n** Slovaquie *f* ▸ **in Slovakia** en Slovaquie.

Slovakian [slə'vækɪən] ■ **adj** slovaque.
■ **n** Slovaque *mf*.

Slovenia [slə'vi:njə] **n** Slovénie *f* ▸ **in Slovenia** en Slovénie.

Slovenian [slə'vi:njən] ■ **adj** slovène.
■ **n** Slovène *mf*.

slovenly ['slʌvnlɪ] **adj** négligé(e).

slow [sləʊ] ■ **adj 1.** [gen] lent(e) ▸ **to make slow progress** [in work, on foot] avancer lentement ▸ **the company was slow to get off the ground** la société a été lente à démarrer **2.** [clock, watch] **: to be slow** retarder **3.** [not busy] calme ▸ **business is slow** les affaires ne marchent pas fort.
■ **adv** lentement ▸ **to go slow** [driver] aller lentement / [workers] faire la grève perlée.
■ **vt & vi** ralentir.
◆ ***slow down***, ***slow up*** **vt sep & vi** ralentir.

slow-acting **adj** à action lente.

slowcoach *UK* ['sləʊkəʊtʃ], ***slowpoke*** *US* ['sləʊpəʊk] **n** *inf* lambin *m*, -e *f*.

slowdown ['sləʊdaʊn] **n** ralentissement *m*.

slow handclap **n** applaudissements *mpl* rythmés *(pour montrer sa désapprobation)*.

slowly ['sləʊlɪ] **adv** lentement ▸ **slowly but surely** lentement mais sûrement.

slow motion **n : in slow motion** au ralenti *m*.
◆ ***slow-motion*** **adj** au ralenti.

slow-moving adj [person, car] lent(e) / [film, plot] dont l'action est lente / [market] stagnant(e) ▸ **slow-moving target** cible *f* qui bouge lentement.

slowpoke ['sləupəuk] *US* = ***slowcoach***.

SLR (abbr of ***single-lens reflex***) n reflex *m*.

sludge [slʌdʒ] n boue *f*.

slug [slʌg] ■ n **1.** [animal] limace *f* **2.** *inf* [of alcohol] rasade *f* **3.** *inf* [bullet] balle *f*.
■ vt (pt & pp **-ged**, cont **-ging**) *inf* donner un coup de poing violent à.

sluggish ['slʌgɪʃ] adj [person] apathique / [movement, growth] lent(e) / [business] calme, stagnant(e).

sluggishly ['slʌgɪʃlɪ] adv [slowly] lentement / [lethargically] mollement ▸ **the market reacted sluggishly** la bourse a réagi faiblement ▸ **the car started sluggishly** la voiture a démarré avec difficulté.

sluice [slu:s] ■ n écluse *f*.
■ vt : **to sluice sthg down** ***OR*** **out** laver qqch à grande eau.

slum [slʌm] ■ n [area] quartier *m* pauvre.
■ vt (pt & pp **-med**, cont **-ming**) : **to slum it** *inf hum* s'encanailler.

slumber ['slʌmbəʳ] *liter* ■ n sommeil *m*.
■ vi dormir paisiblement.

slumber party n *US* soirée *f* entre copines *(au cours de laquelle on regarde des films, on discute et on dort toutes ensemble)*.

slump [slʌmp] ■ n **1.** [decline] : **slump (in)** baisse *f* (de) **2.** [period of poverty] crise *f* (économique).
■ vi *lit* & *fig* s'effondrer.

slumpflation [ˌslʌmp'fleɪʃn] n ECON *forte récession accompagnée d'une inflation des prix et des salaires*.

slung [slʌŋ] pt & pp ➤ ***sling***.

slunk [slʌŋk] pt & pp ➤ ***slink***.

slur [slɜ:ʳ] ■ n **1.** [of voice] : **to speak with a slur** mal articuler **2.** [slight] : **slur (on)** atteinte *f* (à) **3.** [insult] affront *m*, insulte *f*.
■ vt (pt & pp **-red**, cont **-ring**) mal articuler.

slurp [slɜ:p] vt boire avec bruit.

slurred [slɜ:d] adj mal articulé(e).

slurry ['slʌrɪ] n AGRIC purin *m*.

slush [slʌʃ] n [snow] neige *f* fondue, sloche *f* ***Québec***.

slush fund, *US* ***slush money*** n fonds *mpl* secrets, caisse *f* noire.

slut [slʌt] n **1.** *inf* [dirty, untidy] souillon *f* **2.** *v inf* [sexually immoral] salope *f*.

sly [slaɪ] ■ adj (comp **slyer** ***OR*** **slier**, superl **slyest** ***OR*** **sliest**) **1.** [look, smile] entendu(e) **2.** [person] rusé(e), sournois(e).
■ n : **on the sly** en cachette.

slyly ['slaɪlɪ] adv **1.** [cunningly] de façon rusée, avec ruse **2.** [deceitfully] sournoisement **3.** [mischievously] avec espièglerie, de façon espiègle **4.** [secretly] discrètement.

slyness ['slaɪnɪs] n *(U)* ruse *f*.

s/m n abbr of ***sadomasochism***.

smack [smæk] ■ n **1.** [slap] claque *f* / [on face] gifle *f* **2.** [impact] claquement *m*.
■ vt **1.** [slap] donner une claque à / [face] gifler **2.** [place violently] poser violemment
▸▸ **to smack one's lips** se lécher les babines.
■ adv *inf* [directly] en plein ▸ **smack in the middle** en plein milieu.

smacking ['smækɪŋ] ■ n fessée *f* ▸ **I gave the child a good smacking** j'ai donné une bonne fessée à l'enfant.
■ adj *UK inf* : **at a smacking pace** à vive allure, à toute vitesse.

small [smɔ:l] ■ adj **1.** [gen] petit(e) ▸ **small children** les jeunes enfants **2.** [trivial] petit, insignifiant(e) **3.** COMM : **small businessmen** les petits entrepreneurs *mpl* ***OR*** patrons *mpl* ▸ **small businesses** [firms] les petites et moyennes entreprises *fpl*, les PME *fpl* / [shops] les petits commerçants *mpl*.
■ n : **the small of the back** le creux ***OR*** le bas des reins.
◆ ***smalls*** npl *UK inf dated* dessous *mpl*.

small ads [-ædz] npl *UK* petites annonces *fpl*.

small arms npl armes *fpl* (à feu) portatives.

small change n petite monnaie *f*.

small fry n menu fretin *m*.

smallholder ['smɔ:lˌhəuldəʳ] n *UK* petit cultivateur *m*, petit exploitant *m* agricole.

smallholding ['smɔ:lˌhəuldɪŋ] n *UK* petite exploitation *f* agricole.

small hours npl : **in the small hours** au petit jour ***OR*** matin.

small-minded adj [attitude, person] mesquin(e).

smallness ['smɔ:lnɪs] n [of building, person] petite taille *f* / [of amount, income] modicité *f*, petitesse *f*.

smallpox ['smɔ:lpɒks] n variole *f*, petite vérole *f*.

small print n : **the small print** les clauses *fpl* écrites en petits caractères.

small-scale adj [activity, organization] peu important(e).

small screen n : **the small screen** le petit écran.

small talk n *(U)* papotage *m*, bavardage *m*.

small-time adj de second ordre.

small-town adj provincial(e) ▸ **small-town America** l'Amérique profonde.

smarmy ['smɑ:mɪ] (comp **-ier**, superl **-iest**) adj *inf* mielleux(euse).

smart [smɑ:t] ■ adj **1.** [stylish - person, clothes, car] élégant(e) ▸ **she's a smart dresser** elle s'habille avec beaucoup de chic **2.** [clever] intelligent(e) ▸ **he's a smart lad** il n'est pas bête ▸ **it was smart of her to think of it** c'était futé de sa part d'y penser **3.** [fashionable - club, society, hotel] à la mode, in *(inv)* **4.** [quick - answer, tap] vif (vive), rapide.
■ vi **1.** [eyes, skin] brûler, piquer ▸ **my face was still smarting from the blow** le visage me cuisait encore du coup que j'avais reçu **2.** [person] être blessé(e).

smart card n carte *f* à mémoire.

smart drug n nootrope *m (médicament agissant comme un stimulant mental)*.

smarten ['smɑ:tn] ◆ ***smarten up*** **vt sep** [room] arranger ▸ **to smarten o.s. up** se faire beau (belle).

smartly ['smɑ:tlɪ] **adv 1.** [elegantly] avec beaucoup d'allure *OR* de chic, élégamment **2.** [cleverly] habilement, adroitement **3.** [briskly - move] vivement / [- act, work] rapidement, promptement **4.** [sharply - reprimand] vertement / [- reply] du tac au tac, sèchement.

smart money **n** *inf* **: all the smart money is on him to win the presidency** il est donné pour favori aux élections présidentielles.

smash [smæʃ] ■ **n 1.** [sound] fracas *m* **2.** *inf* [car crash] collision *f*, accident *m* **3.** *inf* [success] succès *m* fou **4.** SPORT smash *m*.
■ **vt 1.** [glass, plate] casser, briser **2.** *fig* [defeat] détruire.
■ **vi 1.** [glass, plate] se briser **2.** [crash] **: to smash through sthg** défoncer qqch ▸ **to smash into sthg** s'écraser contre qqch.
◆ ***smash up*** **vt sep** casser, briser / [car] bousiller.

smash-and-grab (raid) **n** *vol effectué après avoir brisé une vitrine.*

smashed [smæʃt] **adj** *inf* bourré(e).

smash hit **n** succès *m* fou.

smashing ['smæʃɪŋ] **adj** *UK inf dated* super *(inv)*.

smash-up **n** collision *f*, accident *m*.

smattering ['smætərɪŋ] **n : to have a smattering of German** savoir quelques mots d'allemand.

SME (abbr of ***small and medium-sized enterprise***) **n** PME *f*.

smear [smɪər] ■ **n 1.** [dirty mark] tache *f* **2.** MED frottis *m* **3.** [slander] diffamation *f*.
■ **vt 1.** [smudge] barbouiller, maculer **2.** [spread] **: to smear sthg onto sthg** étaler qqch sur qqch ▸ **to smear sthg with sthg** enduire qqch de qqch **3.** [slander] calomnier.

smear campaign **n** campagne *f* de diffamation.

smear test **n** *UK* frottis *m*.

smell [smel] ■ **n 1.** [odour] odeur *f* **2.** [sense of smell] odorat *m*.
■ **vt** (pt & pp **-ed** *OR* **smelt**) sentir ▸ **I can smell (something) burning** (je trouve que) ça sent le brûlé ▸ **she smelt** *OR* **she could smell alcohol on his breath** elle s'aperçut que son haleine sentait l'alcool.
■ **vi** (pt & pp **-ed** *OR* **smelt**) **1.** [flower, food] sentir ▸ **I can't smell** je ne sens rien du tout ▸ **to smell of sthg** sentir qqch ▸ **to smell good/bad** sentir bon/mauvais **2.** [smell unpleasantly] sentir (mauvais), puer ▸ **his breath smells** il a mauvaise haleine.

smelly ['smelɪ] (comp **-ier**, superl **-iest**) **adj** qui sent mauvais, qui pue.

smelt [smelt] ■ **pt & pp** ➤ ***smell***.
■ **vt** [metal] extraire par fusion / [ore] fondre.

smile [smaɪl] ■ **n** sourire *m*.
■ **vi** sourire.
■ **vt : to smile one's agreement** acquiescer d'un sourire.

smiley ['smaɪlɪ] **n** smiley *m*.

smiling ['smaɪlɪŋ] **adj** souriant(e).

smirk [smɜ:k] ■ **n** sourire *m* narquois.
■ **vi** sourire d'un air narquois.

smith [smɪθ] **n** forgeron *m*.

smithereens [ˌsmɪðə'ri:nz] **npl** *inf* **: to be smashed to smithereens** être brisé(e) en mille morceaux.

smithy ['smɪðɪ] (pl **-ies**) **n** forge *f*.

smitten ['smɪtn] **adj** *hum* **: to be smitten (with)** être fou (folle) (de).

smock [smɒk] **n** blouse *f*.

smog [smɒg] **n** smog *m*.

smoke [sməʊk] ■ **n 1.** *(U)* [from fire] fumée *f* **2.** [act of smoking] **: to have a smoke** [cigarette] fumer une cigarette / [cigar] fumer un cigare.
■ **vt & vi** fumer.

smoked [sməʊkt] **adj** [food] fumé(e).

smokeless fuel ['sməʊklɪs-] **n** *combustible qui ne produit pas de fumée.*

smokeless zone ['sməʊklɪs-] **n** *zone où la combustion de matériaux est réglementée.*

smoker ['sməʊkər] **n 1.** [person] fumeur *m*, -euse *f* **2.** RAIL compartiment *m* fumeurs.

smokescreen ['sməʊkskri:n] **n** *fig* couverture *f*.

smoke shop **n** *US* bureau *m* de tabac.

smokestack ['sməʊkstæk] **n** cheminée *f*.

smokestack industry **n** industrie *f* lourde.

smoking ['sməʊkɪŋ] **n** tabagisme *m* ▸ **'no smoking'** 'défense de fumer'.

smoking compartment *UK*, ***smoking car*** *US* **n** compartiment *m* fumeurs.

smoking gun **n** l'arme *f* du crime *fig*.

smoky ['sməʊkɪ] (comp **-ier**, superl **-iest**) **adj 1.** [room, air] enfumé(e) **2.** [taste] fumé(e).

smolder *US* = ***smoulder***.

smoldering *US* = ***smouldering***.

smooch [smu:tʃ] **vi** *inf* se bécoter.

smooth [smu:ð] ■ **adj 1.** [surface] lisse **2.** [sauce] homogène, onctueux(euse) **3.** [movement] régulier(ère) **4.** [taste] moelleux(euse) **5.** [flight, ride] confortable / [landing, take-off] en douceur **6.** *pej* [person, manner] doucereux(euse), mielleux(euse) **7.** [operation, progress] sans problèmes.
■ **vt** [hair] lisser / [clothes, tablecloth] défroisser ▸ **to smooth the way** aplanir les difficultés *OR* les obstacles.
◆ ***smooth out*** **vt sep** défroisser.
◆ ***smooth over*** **vt insep** [difficulties] aplanir / [disagreements] arranger.

smoothie ['smu:ðɪ] **n** *inf pej* **: he's a real smoothie** [in manner] il roule les mécaniques / [in speech] c'est vraiment un beau parleur.

smoothly ['smu:ðlɪ] **adv 1.** [move] sans heurt **2.** *pej* [suavely] d'un ton doucereux **3.** [without problems] sans problèmes.

smoothness ['smu:ðnɪs] **n** *(U)* **1.** [of surface] aspect *m* lisse **2.** [of mixture] onctuosité *f* **3.** [of movement] régularité *f* **4.** [of flight, ride] confort *m* **5.** *pej* [of person] caractère *m* doucereux.

smooth-talking [-ˌtəːkɪŋ] adj doucereux(euse), mielleux(euse).

smoothy ['smuːðɪ] *inf pej* = **smoothie**.

smother ['smʌðəʳ] vt **1.** [cover thickly] **: to smother sb/sthg with** couvrir qqn/qqch de **2.** [person, fire] étouffer **3.** *fig* [emotions] cacher, étouffer.

smoulder *UK*, **smolder** *US* ['sməʊldəʳ] vi *lit* & *fig* couver.

smouldering *UK*, **smoldering** *US* ['sməʊldərɪŋ] adj [fire, anger, passion] qui couve / [embers, ruins] fumant(e) / [eyes] de braise.

SMS [ˌesem'es] (abbr of ***short message system***) n sms *m*, texto *m*, mini-message *m*.

smudge [smʌdʒ] ■ n tache *f* / [of ink] bavure *f*.
■ vt [drawing, painting] maculer / [paper] faire une marque *OR* trace sur / [face] salir.

smug [smʌg] (comp **-ger**, superl **-gest**) adj suffisant(e).

smuggle ['smʌgl] vt **1.** [across frontiers] faire passer en contrebande **2.** [against rules] **: to smuggle sthg in/out** faire entrer/sortir qqch clandestinement.

smuggler ['smʌgləʳ] n contrebandier *m*, -ère *f*.

smuggling ['smʌglɪŋ] n *(U)* contrebande *f*.

smugly ['smʌglɪ] adv [say] d'un ton suffisant, avec suffisance / [look, smile] d'un air suffisant, avec suffisance.

smugness ['smʌgnɪs] n suffisance *f*.

smut [smʌt] n **1.** [dirty mark] tache *f* de suie **2.** *(U) pej* [books, talk] obscénités *fpl*.

smutty ['smʌtɪ] (comp **-ier**, superl **-iest**) adj *pej* [book, language] cochon(onne).

snack [snæk] ■ n casse-croûte *m inv*.
■ vi manger un morceau.

snack bar n snack *m*, snack-bar *m*.

snaffle ['snæfl] ■ vt **1.** *UK inf* [get] se procurer / [steal] piquer, faucher **2.** [in horseriding] mettre un bridon à.
■ n [in horseriding] **: snaffle (bit)** mors *m* brisé, bridon *m*.

snag [snæg] ■ n [problem] inconvénient *m*, écueil *m*.
■ vt (pt & pp **-ged**, cont **-ging**) accrocher.
■ vi (pt & pp **-ged**, cont **-ging**) **: to snag (on)** s'accrocher (à).

snail [sneɪl] n escargot *m*.

snail mail n *inf* COMPUT poste *f*.

snake [sneɪk] ■ n serpent *m*.
■ vi serpenter.

snap [snæp] ■ adj [decision, election] subit(e) / [judgment] irréfléchi(e) ▸ **she made a snap decision to go to Paris** elle décida tout à coup d'aller à Paris.
■ n **1.** [of branch] craquement *m* / [of fingers] claquement *m* ▸ **with a snap of his fingers** en claquant des doigts ▸ **to open/to close sthg with a snap** ouvrir/refermer qqch d'un coup sec **2.** [photograph] photo *f* **3.** *UK* [card game] ≃ bataille *f* **4.** METEOR **: a cold snap, a snap of cold weather** une vague de froid **5.** *US inf* [easy task] **: it's a snap!** c'est simple comme bonjour!
■ vt (pt & pp **-ped**, cont **-ping**) **1.** [break] casser net **2.** [move] **: to snap sthg open/shut** ouvrir/fermer qqch avec un bruit sec ▸ **to snap one's fingers** claquer des doigts **3.** [speak sharply] dire d'un ton sec.
■ vi (pt & pp **-ped**, cont **-ping**) **1.** [break] se casser net **2.** [move] **: to snap into place** s'emboîter avec un bruit sec **3.** [dog] **: to snap at** essayer de mordre **4.** [speak sharply] **: to snap (at sb)** parler (à qqn) d'un ton sec ▸ **there's no need to snap!** tu n'as pas besoin de parler sur ce ton-là! ▸▸ **to snap out of it** *inf* réagir, se secouer.
◆ ***snap up*** vt sep [bargain] sauter sur ▸ **the records were snapped up in no time** les disques sont partis *OR* se sont vendus en un rien de temps.

snap fastener n *esp US* pression *f*.

snappish ['snæpɪʃ] adj *esp US* hargneux(euse).

snappy ['snæpɪ] (comp **-ier**, superl **-iest**) adj *inf* **1.** [stylish] chic **2.** [quick] prompt(e) ▸ **make it snappy!** dépêche-toi!, et que ça saute!

snapshot ['snæpʃɒt] n photo *f*.

snare [sneəʳ] ■ n piège *m*, collet *m*.
■ vt prendre au piège, attraper.

snarl [snɑːl] ■ n grondement *m*.
■ vi gronder.

snarl-up n enchevêtrement *m* / [of traffic] embouteillage *m*.

snatch [snætʃ] ■ n [of conversation] bribe *f* / [of song] extrait *m*.
■ vt **1.** [grab] saisir **2.** *fig* [time] réussir à avoir / [opportunity] saisir ▸ **to snatch a look at sthg** regarder qqch à la dérobée.
■ vi **: to snatch at sthg** essayer de saisir qqch.

snazzy ['snæzɪ] (comp **-ier**, superl **-iest**) adj *inf* [clothes, car] beau (belle), super *(inv)* / [dresser] qui s'habille chic.

sneak [sniːk] ■ n *inf* rapporteur *m*, -euse *f*.
■ vt (*US* **snuck**) **: to sneak a look at sb/sthg** regarder qqn/qqch à la dérobée.
■ vi (*US* **snuck**) [move quietly] se glisser ▸ **to sneak up on sb** s'approcher de qqn sans faire de bruit.

sneakers ['sniːkəz] npl *esp US* tennis *mpl*, baskets *fpl*.

sneaking ['sniːkɪŋ] adj secret(ète).

sneak preview n avant-première *f*.

sneaky ['sniːkɪ] (comp **-ier**, superl **-iest**) adj *inf* sournois(e).

sneer [snɪəʳ] ■ n [smile] sourire *m* dédaigneux / [laugh] ricanement *m*.
■ vi **1.** [smile] sourire dédaigneusement **2.** [ridicule] **: to sneer at sthg** tourner qqch en ridicule.

sneering ['snɪərɪŋ] ■ adj ricaneur(euse), méprisant(e).
■ n *(U)* ricanement *m*, ricanements *mpl*.

sneeze [sniːz] ■ n éternuement *m*.
■ vi éternuer ▸ **it's not to be sneezed at!** *inf* il ne faut pas cracher dessus!

snicker ['snɪkəʳ] vi *US* ricaner.

snide [snaɪd] adj sournois(e).

sniff [snɪf] ■ n reniflement *m*.
■ vt **1.** [smell] renifler **2.** [inhale - drug] sniffer.
■ vi **1.** [to clear nose] renifler **2.** [to show disapproval] faire la grimace.
◆ ***sniff out*** vt sep **1.** [detect by sniffing] flairer **2.** *inf* [seek out] rechercher.

sniffer dog ['snɪfəʳ-] n *UK* chien *m* renifleur.

sniffle ['snɪfl] vi renifler.

snigger ['snɪgəʳ] *UK* ■ n rire *m* en dessous.
■ vi ricaner.

sniggering ['snɪgərɪŋ] *UK* ■ n *(U)* rires *mpl* en dessous / [sarcastic] ricanements *mpl*.
■ adj ricaneur(euse).

snip [snɪp] ■ n *UK inf* [bargain] bonne affaire *f*.
■ vt (pt & pp -ped, cont -ping) couper.

snipe [snaɪp] vi 1. [shoot] : **to snipe at sb/sthg** canarder qqn/qqch 2. [criticize] : **to snipe at sb** critiquer qqn sournoisement.

sniper ['snaɪpəʳ] n tireur *m* isolé.

snippet ['snɪpɪt] n fragment *m*.

snivel ['snɪvl] (*UK* -led, cont -ling, *US* -ed, cont -ing) vi geindre.

snivelling *UK*, **sniveling** *US* ['snɪvlɪŋ] ■ adj pleurnicheur(euse), larmoyant(e).
■ n *(U)* [crying] pleurnichements *mpl* ▸ **stop your snivelling!** arrête de pleurnicher comme ça!

snob [snɒb] n snob *mf*.

snobbery ['snɒbərɪ] n snobisme *m*.

snobbish ['snɒbɪʃ], **snobby** ['snɒbɪ] (comp -ier, superl -iest) adj snob *(inv)*.

snog [snɒg] (pt & pp -ged, cont -ging) *UK inf* ■ vi se rouler une pelle.
■ vt rouler une pelle à.
■ n : **to have a snog** se rouler une pelle.

snogging ['snɒgɪŋ] n *UK inf* : **there was a lot of snogging going on** ça s'embrassait dans tous les coins.

snooker ['snu:kəʳ] ■ n [game] ≃ jeu *m* de billard.
■ vt *UK inf fig* : **to be snookered** être coincé(e).

snoop [snu:p] vi *inf* fureter.

snooper ['snu:pəʳ] n *inf* fouineur *m*, -euse *f*.

snooty ['snu:tɪ] (comp -ier, superl -iest) adj *inf* prétentieux(euse).

snooze [snu:z] ■ n petit somme *m*.
■ vi faire un petit somme.

snooze button n bouton *m* de veille.

snore [snɔ:ʳ] ■ n ronflement *m*.
■ vi ronfler.

snoring ['snɔ:rɪŋ] n *(U)* ronflement *m*, ronflements *mpl*.

snorkel ['snɔ:kl] n tuba *m*.

snorkelling *UK*, **snorkeling** *US* ['snɔ:klɪŋ] n : **to go snorkelling** faire de la plongée avec un tuba.

snort [snɔ:t] ■ n [of person] grognement *m* / [of horse, bull] ébrouement *m*.
■ vi [person] grogner / [horse] s'ébrouer.
■ vt *drug sl* sniffer.

snot [snɒt] n *inf* 1. [in nose] morve *f* 2. [person] morveux *m*, -euse *f*.

snotty ['snɒtɪ] (comp -ier, superl -iest) adj *inf* 1. [snooty] prétentieux(euse) 2. [face, child] morveux(euse).

snotty-nosed adj *inf lit & fig* morveux(euse).

snout [snaʊt] n groin *m*.

snow [snəʊ] ■ n neige *f*.
■ impers vb neiger.
◆ ***snow in*** vt sep : **to be snowed in** être bloqué(e) par la neige.
◆ ***snow under*** vt sep *fig* : **to be snowed under (with)** être submergé(e) (de).

snowball ['snəʊbɔ:l] ■ n boule *f* de neige.
■ vi *fig* faire boule de neige.

snowbank ['snəʊbæŋk] n congère *f*, banc *m* de neige *Québec*.

snowbike ['snəʊbaɪk] n motoneige *f*.

snow blindness n cécité *f* des neiges.

snowboard ['snəʊˌbɔ:d] n surf *m* des neiges.

snowboarder ['snəʊˌbɔ:dəʳ] n surfeur *m*, -euse *f* (des neiges).

snowboarding ['snəʊˌbɔ:dɪŋ] n surf *m* (des neiges).

snow-boot n après-ski *m*.

snowbound ['snəʊbaʊnd] adj bloqué(e) par la neige.

snow-capped [-kæpt] adj couronné(e) de neige.

snowdrift ['snəʊdrɪft] n congère *f*.

snowdrop ['snəʊdrɒp] n perce-neige *m inv*.

snowfall ['snəʊfɔ:l] n chute *f* de neige.

snowflake ['snəʊfleɪk] n flocon *m* de neige.

snowline ['snəʊlaɪn] n limite *f* des neiges éternelles.

snowman ['snəʊmæn] (pl -men [-men]) n bonhomme *m* de neige.

snowmobile ['snəʊməbi:l] n scooter *m* des neiges, motoneige *f Québec*.

snow pea n *US* mange-tout *m inv*.

snowplough *UK*, **snowplow** *US* ['snəʊplaʊ] n chasse-neige *m inv*.

snowshoe ['snəʊʃu:] n raquette *f*.

snowstorm ['snəʊstɔ:m] n tempête *f* de neige.

snowy ['snəʊɪ] (comp -ier, superl -iest) adj neigeux(euse).

SNP (abbr of ***Scottish National Party***) n *parti nationaliste écossais*.

Snr, **snr** abbr of ***senior***.

snub [snʌb] ■ n rebuffade *f*.
■ vt (pt & pp -bed, cont -bing) snober, ignorer.

snub-nosed adj au nez retroussé.

snuck [snʌk] *US* pt & pp ➤ ***sneak***.

snuff [snʌf] n tabac *m* à priser.

snuffle ['snʌfl] vi renifler.

snuff movie n *film porno où l'acteur est tué à la fin*.

snug [snʌg] (comp -ger, superl -gest) adj 1. [person] à l'aise, confortable / [in bed] bien au chaud 2. [place] douillet(ette) 3. [close-fitting] bien ajusté(e).

snuggle ['snʌgl] vi se blottir.

snugly ['snʌglı] adv **1.** [cosily] douillettement, confortablement ▸ **soon they were settled snugly by the fire** ils se retrouvèrent bientôt réunis autour d'un bon feu **2.** [in fit] **: the skirt fits snugly** la jupe est très ajustée ▸ **the two parts fit together snugly** les deux pièces s'emboîtent parfaitement.

so [səʊ] ■ adv **1.** [to such a degree] si, tellement ▸ **so difficult (that)...** si *OR* tellement difficile que... ▸ **don't be so stupid!** ne sois pas si bête! ▸ **he's not so stupid as he looks** il n'est pas si *OR* aussi bête qu'il en a l'air ▸ **he was not so ill (that) he couldn't go out** il n'était pas malade au point de ne pas pouvoir sortir ▸ **we're so glad you could come** nous sommes si contents que vous ayez pu venir ▸ **he's so sweet/kind** il est tellement mignon/gentil ▸ **we had so much work!** nous avions tant de travail! ▸ **I've never seen so much money/many cars** je n'ai jamais vu autant d'argent/de voitures
2. [in referring back to previous statement, event etc] **: so what's the point then?** alors à quoi bon? ▸ **so you knew already?** alors tu le savais déjà? ▸ **I don't think so** je ne crois pas ▸ **I'm afraid so** je crains bien que oui ▸ **who says so?** qui dit ça? ▸ **I told you so!** je vous l'avais bien dit! ▸ **if so** si oui ▸ **is that so?** vraiment? ▸ **isn't that Jane over there? – why, so it is!** ce ne serait pas Jane là-bas? – mais si (c'est elle)! ▸ **so what have you been up to?** alors, qu'est-ce que vous devenez? ▸ **so what?** *inf* et alors?, et après? ▸ **so there!** *inf* là!, et voilà!
3. [also] aussi ▸ **so can/do/would** *etc* **I** moi aussi ▸ **she speaks French and so does her husband** elle parle français et son mari aussi ▸ **as with..., so with** il en va pour... comme pour ▸ **just as some people like family holidays, so others prefer to holiday alone** de même que certains aiment les vacances en famille, de même d'autres préfèrent passer leurs vacances tout seuls
4. [in this way] **: (like) so** comme cela *OR* ça, de cette façon ▸ **hold your arm out, so** étendez votre bras, comme cela *OR* ça ▸ **it (just) so happens that...** il se trouve (justement) que... ▸ **she likes everything (to be) just so** elle aime que tout soit parfait
5. [in expressing agreement] **: so there is** en effet, c'est vrai ▸ **so I see** c'est ce que je vois
6. [unspecified amount, limit] **: they pay us so much a week** ils nous payent tant par semaine ▸ **not so much... as** pas tant... que ▸ **it's not so much the money as the time involved** ce n'est pas tant l'argent que le temps que ça demande ▸ **or so** environ, à peu près ▸ **a year/week or so ago** il y a environ un an/une semaine.
■ **conj** alors ▸ **he said yes and so we got married** il a dit oui, alors on s'est mariés ▸ **I'm away next week so I won't be there** je suis en voyage la semaine prochaine donc *OR* par conséquent je ne serai pas là.

◆ ***so as*** conj afin de, pour ▸ **we didn't knock so as not to disturb them** nous n'avons pas frappé pour ne pas les déranger.

◆ ***so that*** conj [for the purpose that] pour que *(+ subjunctive)* ▸ **he lied so that she would go free** il a menti pour qu'elle soit relâchée ▸ **I took a taxi so that I wouldn't be late** j'ai pris un taxi pour ne pas être en retard.

SO abbr of ***standing order***.

soak [səʊk] ■ vt laisser *OR* faire tremper.
■ vi **1.** [become thoroughly wet] **: to leave sthg to soak, to let sthg soak** laisser *OR* faire tremper qqch **2.** [spread] **: to soak into sthg** tremper dans qqch ▸ **to soak through (sthg)** traverser (qqch).
◆ ***soak up*** vt sep absorber.

soaked [səʊkt] adj trempé(e) ▸ **to be soaked through** être trempé (jusqu'aux os).

soaking ['səʊkıŋ] adj trempé(e).

so-and-so n *inf* **1.** [to replace a name] **: Mr so-and-so** Monsieur Untel **2.** [annoying person] enquiquineur *m*, -euse *f*.

soap [səʊp] ■ n **1.** *(U)* [for washing] savon *m* **2.** TV soap opera *m*.
■ vt savonner.

soapbox ['səʊpbɒks] ■ n **1.** *lit* caisse *f* à savon / *fig* [for speaker] tribune *f* improvisée *OR* de fortune ▸ **get off your soapbox!** ne monte pas sur tes grands chevaux! **2.** [go-kart] chariot *m*, ≃ kart *m (sans moteur)*.
■ comp [orator] de carrefour / [oratory] de démagogue.

soap bubble n bulle *f* de savon.

soap flakes npl savon *m* en paillettes.

soap opera n soap opera *m*.

soap powder n lessive *f*.

soapsuds ['səʊpsʌdz] npl mousse *f* de savon.

soapy ['səʊpı] (comp -ier, superl -iest) adj [water] savonneux(euse) / [taste] de savon.

soar [sɔːʳ] vi **1.** [bird] planer **2.** [balloon, kite] monter **3.** [prices, temperature] monter en flèche **4.** [building, tree, mountain] s'élever, s'élancer **5.** [music, voice] monter.

soaring ['sɔːrıŋ] adj **1.** [prices, temperature] qui monte en flèche **2.** [building, tree, mountain] qui s'élève **3.** [music, voice] qui monte.

sob [sɒb] ■ n sanglot *m*.
■ vt (pt & pp -bed, cont -bing) dire en sanglotant.
■ vi (pt & pp -bed, cont -bing) sangloter.

sobbing ['sɒbıŋ] n *(U)* sanglots *mpl*.

sober ['səʊbəʳ] adj **1.** [not drunk] qui n'est pas ivre **2.** [serious] sérieux(euse) **3.** [plain - clothes, colours] sobre.
◆ ***sober up*** vi dessoûler.

sobering ['səʊbərıŋ] adj qui donne à réfléchir.

soberly ['səʊbəlı] adv [act, speak] avec sobriété *OR* modération *OR* mesure / [dress] sobrement, discrètement ▸ **he said soberly** [calmly] dit-il d'un ton posé *OR* mesuré / [solemnly] dit-il d'un ton grave.

sobriety [səʊ'braıətı] n *fml* [seriousness] sérieux *m*.

sob story n *inf pej* histoire *f* larmoyante, histoire *f* à vous fendre le cœur ▸ **he told us some sob story about his deprived childhood** il nous a parlé de son enfance malheureuse *OR* à faire pleurer dans les chaumières.

Soc. abbr of ***Society***.

so-called [-kɔːld] adj **1.** [misleadingly named] soi-disant *(inv)* **2.** [widely known as] ainsi appelé(e).

soccer ['sɒkəʳ] n football *m*.

sociable ['səʊʃəbl] adj sociable.

social ['səʊʃl] **adj** social(e) ▸ **they move in high** *OR* **the best social circles** ils évoluent dans les hautes sphères de la société.

social climber **n** *pej* arriviste *mf.*

social club **n** club *m.*

social conscience **n** conscience *f* sociale.

social democracy **n** social-démocratie *f.*

social democrat **n** social-démocrate *mf.*

social event **n** événement *m* social.

social fund **n** fonds *m* d'entraide.

socialism ['səʊʃəlɪzm] **n** socialisme *m.*

socialist ['səʊʃəlɪst] ■ **adj** socialiste.
■ **n** socialiste *mf.*

socialite ['səʊʃəlaɪt] **n** mondain *m*, -e *f.*

socialize, *UK* ***-ise*** ['səʊʃəlaɪz] **vi** fréquenter des gens ▸ **to socialize with sb** fréquenter qqn, frayer avec qqn.

socialized medicine ['səʊʃəlaɪzd-] **n** *US soins médicaux payés par les impôts.*

socializing, *UK* ***-ising*** ['səʊʃəlaɪzɪŋ] **n** fait *m* de fréquenter des gens ▸ **socializing between teachers and pupils is discouraged** les relations entre élèves et professeurs ne sont pas encouragées.

social life **n** vie *f* sociale.

socially ['səʊʃəlɪ] **adv 1.** [in society] socialement, en société **2.** [outside business] en dehors du travail.

social order **n** ordre *m* social.

social outcast **n** paria *m.*

social science **n** sciences *fpl* humaines.

social scientist **n** spécialiste *mf* des sciences humaines.

social security **n** aide *f* sociale.

social services **npl** services *mpl* sociaux.

social studies **n** *(U)* sciences *fpl* sociales.

social welfare **n** protection *f* sociale.

social work **n** *(U)* assistance *f* sociale.

social worker **n** assistant social *m*, assistante sociale *f.*

society [sə'saɪətɪ] (pl **-ies**) **n 1.** [gen] société *f* **2.** [club] association *f*, club *m.*

socioeconomic ['səʊsɪəʊˌiːkə'nɒmɪk] **adj** socio-économique.

sociolinguistics [ˌsəʊsɪəʊlɪŋ'gwɪstɪks] **n** *(U)* sociolinguistique *f.*

sociological [ˌsəʊsjə'lɒdʒɪkl] **adj** sociologique.

sociologist [ˌsəʊsɪ'ɒlədʒɪst] **n** sociologue *mf.*

sociology [ˌsəʊsɪ'ɒlədʒɪ] **n** sociologie *f.*

sock [sɒk] **n** chaussette *f* ▸ **to pull one's socks up** *UK inf fig* se secouer.

socket ['sɒkɪt] **n 1.** [for light bulb] douille *f* / [for plug] prise *f* de courant **2.** [of eye] orbite *f* / [for bone] cavité *f* articulaire.

sod [sɒd] **n 1.** [of turf] motte *f* de gazon **2.** *UK v inf* [person] con *m.*

soda ['səʊdə] **n 1.** CHEM soude *f* **2.** [soda water] eau *f* de Seltz **3.** *US* [fizzy drink] soda *m.*

soda syphon **n** siphon *m* d'eau de Seltz.

soda water **n** eau *f* de Seltz.

sodden ['sɒdn] **adj** trempé(e), détrempé(e).

sodium ['səʊdɪəm] **n** sodium *m.*

sofa ['səʊfə] **n** canapé *m.*

sofa bed **n** canapé-lit *m.*

Sofia ['səʊfjə] **n** Sofia.

soft [sɒft] **adj 1.** [not hard] doux (douce), mou (molle) ▸ **mix to a soft paste** mélanger jusqu'à obtention d'une pâte molle ▸ **soft contact lenses** lentilles *fpl* souples **2.** [smooth, not loud, not bright] doux (douce) ▸ **the cream will make your hands/the leather soft** la crème t'adoucira les mains/assouplira le cuir **3.** [without force] léger(ère) ▸ **city life has made you soft** la vie citadine t'a ramolli **4.** [caring] tendre ▸ **to be soft on sb** *inf* avoir le béguin pour qqn ▸ **to have a soft spot for sb** avoir un faible pour qqn **5.** [lenient] faible, indulgent(e) ▸ **to be soft on sb** se montrer indulgent envers qqn, faire preuve d'indulgence envers qqn ▸ **to be soft on terrorism** faire preuve de laxisme envers le terrorisme ▸ **it's the soft option** c'est la solution de facilité.

soft-boiled **adj** à la coque.

soft-core **adj** [pornography] soft *(inv).*

soft currency **n** monnaie *f* *OR* devise *f* faible.

soft drink **n** boisson *f* non alcoolisée.

soft drugs **npl** drogues *fpl* douces.

soften ['sɒfn] ■ **vt 1.** [fabric] assouplir / [substance] ramollir / [skin] adoucir **2.** [shock, blow] atténuer, adoucir **3.** [attitude] modérer, adoucir ▸ **he has softened his stance on vegetarianism** son attitude envers le végétarisme est plus modérée qu'avant.
■ **vi 1.** [substance] se ramollir **2.** [attitude, person] s'adoucir, se radoucir ▸ **to soften towards sb** se montrer plus indulgent envers qqn.
◆ ***soften up*** **vt sep** *inf* [persuade] amadouer.

softener ['sɒfnəʳ] **n** [for washing] adoucissant *m.*

softening ['sɒfnɪŋ] **n** [of substance, ground] ramollissement *m* / [of fabric, material] assouplissement *m*, adoucissement *m* / [of attitude, expression, voice] adoucissement *m* / [of colours, contrasts] atténuation *f* ▸ **there has been no softening of attitude on the part of the management** la direction n'a pas modéré son attitude
▸▸ **softening of the brain** MED ramollissement *m* cérébral.

soft focus **n** flou *m* ▸ **in soft focus** en flou.

soft furnishings **npl** *UK* tissus *mpl* d'ameublement.

softhearted [ˌsɒft'hɑːtɪd] **adj** au cœur tendre.

softly ['sɒftlɪ] **adv 1.** [gently, quietly] doucement **2.** [not brightly] faiblement **3.** [leniently] avec indulgence.

softness ['sɒftnɪs] **n 1.** [of bed, ground, substance] mollesse *f*, moelleux *m* **2.** [of skin, sound, light] douceur *f* **3.** [lenience] indulgence *f.*

soft-pedal **vi** *inf* y aller doucement.

soft sell **n** *inf* méthode *f* de vente discrète *OR* non agressive.

soft-spoken **adj** à la voix douce.

soft top **n** *inf* AUT (voiture *f*) décapotable *f.*

soft toy **n** jouet *m* en peluche.

software ['sɒftweəʳ] **n** *(U)* COMPUT logiciel *m*.

software package **n** COMPUT logiciel *m*, progiciel *m*.

softwood ['sɒftwʊd] **n** bois *m* tendre.

softy ['sɒftɪ] (pl **-ies**) **n** *inf* **1.** *pej* [weak person] mauviette *f*, poule *f* mouillée **2.** [sensitive person] **: he's a big softy** c'est un tendre.

soggy ['sɒgɪ] (comp **-ier**, superl **-iest**) **adj** trempé(e), détrempé(e).

soil [sɔɪl] ■ **n** *(U)* **1.** [earth] sol *m*, terre *f* **2.** *fig* [territory] sol *m*, territoire *m*.
■ **vt** souiller, salir.

soiled [sɔɪld] **adj** sale.

solace ['sɒləs] **n** *liter* consolation *f*, réconfort *m*.

solar ['səʊləʳ] **adj** solaire.

solarium [sə'leərɪəm] (pl **-riums** *OR* **-ria** [-rɪə]) **n** solarium *m*.

solar panel **n** panneau *m* solaire.

solar plexus [-'pleksəs] **n** plexus *m* solaire.

solar power **n** énergie *f* solaire.

solar-powered [-'paʊəd] **adj** à énergie solaire.

solar system **n** système *m* solaire.

sold [səʊld] **pt & pp** ➤ ***sell***.

solder ['səʊldəʳ] ■ **n** *(U)* soudure *f*.
■ **vt** souder.

soldering iron ['səʊldərɪŋ-] **n** fer *m* à souder.

soldier ['səʊldʒəʳ] **n** soldat *m*.
◆ ***soldier on*** **vi** persévérer.

sold-out **adj** [tickets] qui ont tous été vendus / [play, concert] qui joue à guichets fermés.

sole [səʊl] ■ **adj 1.** [only] seul(e), unique **2.** [exclusive] exclusif(ive).
■ **n 1.** [of foot] semelle *f* **2.** (pl **sole** *OR* **-s**) [fish] sole *f*.

solely ['səʊllɪ] **adv** seulement, uniquement ▸ **solely responsible** seul *OR* entièrement responsable.

solemn ['sɒləm] **adj** solennel(elle) / [person] sérieux(euse).

solemnity [sə'lemnətɪ] (pl **-ies**) **n 1.** [serious nature] sérieux *m*, gravité *f* **2.** [formality] solennité *f* ▸ **she was received with great solemnity** elle fut accueillie très solennellement **3.** *(usu pl) fml* [solemn event] solennité *f*.

solemnly ['sɒləmlɪ] **adv 1.** [speak, behave] avec solennité, sérieusement **2.** [promise, swear] solennellement.

sole trader **n** *UK* COMM entreprise *f* unipersonnelle *OR* individuelle.

solicit [sə'lɪsɪt] ■ **vt** *fml* [request] solliciter.
■ **vi** [prostitute] racoler.

soliciting [sə'lɪsɪtɪŋ] **n** [by prostitute] racolage *m*.

solicitor [sə'lɪsɪtəʳ] **n** *UK* LAW notaire *m*.

solicitous [sə'lɪsɪtəs] **adj** *fml* **1.** [caring] plein(e) de sollicitude **2.** [anxious] **: solicitous about** *OR* **for** préoccupé(e) de, soucieux(euse) de.

solid ['sɒlɪd] ■ **adj 1.** [not fluid, sturdy, reliable] solide ▸ **frozen solid** complètement gelé ▸ **he's a good solid worker** c'est un bon travailleur ▸ **we have the solid support of the electorate** nous avons le soutien massif des électeurs ▸ **to be on solid ground** *lit* être sur la terre ferme / *fig* être en terrain sûr **2.** [not hollow - tyres] plein(e) / [- wood, rock, gold] massif(ive) ▸ **they dug until they reached solid rock** ils ont creusé jusqu'à ce qu'ils atteignent la roche compacte **3.** [without interruption] **: a solid yellow line** une ligne jaune continue ▸ **two hours solid** deux heures d'affilée.
■ **n** solide *m*.

solidarity [ˌsɒlɪ'dærətɪ] **n** solidarité *f*.

solid figure **n** MATHS solide *m*.

solid fuel **n** combustible *m* solide.

solidify [sə'lɪdɪfaɪ] (pt & pp **-ied**) **vi** se solidifier.

solidly ['sɒlɪdlɪ] **adv 1.** [sturdily] solidement **2.** [completely] tout à fait, absolument **3.** [without interruption] sans s'arrêter, sans interruption.

soliloquy [sə'lɪləkwɪ] (pl **-ies**) **n** soliloque *m*.

solitaire [ˌsɒlɪ'teəʳ] **n 1.** [jewel, board game] solitaire *m* **2.** *US* [card game] réussite *f*, patience *f*.

solitary ['sɒlɪtrɪ] **adj 1.** [lonely, alone] solitaire **2.** [just one] seul(e).

solitary confinement **n** isolement *m* cellulaire.

solitude ['sɒlɪtjuːd] **n** solitude *f*.

solo ['səʊləʊ] ■ **adj** solo *(inv)*.
■ **n** (pl **-s**) solo *m*.
■ **adv** en solo.

soloist ['səʊləʊɪst] **n** soliste *mf*.

Solomon Islands ['sɒləmən-] **npl : the Solomon Islands** les îles *fpl* Salomon ▸ **in the Solomon Islands** dans les îles Salomon.

solstice ['sɒlstɪs] **n** solstice *m*.

solubility [ˌsɒljʊ'bɪlətɪ] **n** solubilité *f*.

soluble ['sɒljʊbl] **adj** soluble.

solution [sə'luːʃn] **n 1.** [to problem] **: solution (to)** solution *f* (de) **2.** [liquid] solution *f*.

solve [sɒlv] **vt** résoudre.

solvency ['sɒlvənsɪ] **n** solvabilité *f*.

solvent ['sɒlvənt] ■ **adj** FIN solvable.
■ **n** dissolvant *m*, solvant *m*.

solvent abuse **n** usage *m* de solvants.

Som. (abbr of **Somerset**) *comté anglais*.

Somali [sə'mɑːlɪ] ■ **adj** somali(e), somalien(enne).
■ **n 1.** [person] Somali *m*, -e *f*, Somalien *m*, -enne *f* **2.** [language] somali *m*.

Somalia [sə'mɑːlɪə] **n** Somalie *f* ▸ **in Somalia** en Somalie.

sombre *UK*, ***somber*** *US* ['sɒmbəʳ] **adj** sombre.

some [sʌm] ■ **adj 1.** [a certain amount, number of] **: some meat** de la viande ▸ **some money** de l'argent ▸ **some coffee** du café ▸ **some sweets** des bonbons ▸ **I met some old friends last night** j'ai rencontré de vieux amis hier soir ▸ **you must have some idea of how much it will cost** vous devez avoir une petite idée de combien ça va coûter **2.** [fairly large number or quantity of] quelque ▸ **I had some difficulty getting here** j'ai eu quelque mal à venir ici ▸ **I've**

known him for some years je le connais depuis plusieurs années *OR* pas mal d'années ▸ **we haven't seen them for some time** ça fait quelque temps qu'on ne les a pas vus

3. *(contrastive use)* [certain] **: some jobs are better paid than others** certains boulots sont mieux rémunérés que d'autres ▸ **some people like his music** il y en a qui aiment sa musique

4. [in imprecise statements] quelque, quelconque ▸ **she married some writer or other** elle a épousé un écrivain quelconque *OR* quelque écrivain ▸ **there must be some mistake** il doit y avoir erreur

5. *inf* [very good] **: that was some party!** c'était une soirée formidable!, quelle soirée!

6. *inf iro* [not very good] **: some party that was!** tu parles d'une soirée! ▸ **some help you are!** tu parles d'une aide!, beaucoup tu m'aides!

■ **pron 1.** [a certain amount] **: can I have some?** [money, milk, coffee] est-ce que je peux en prendre? ▸ **I've got too much cake: do you want some?** j'ai trop de gâteau, en voulez-vous un peu? ▸ **some of the snow had melted** une partie de la neige avait fondu ▸ **some of it is mine** une partie est à moi

2. [a certain number] quelques-uns (quelques-unes), certains (certaines) ▸ **can I have some?** [books, pens, potatoes] est-ce que je peux en prendre (quelques-uns)? ▸ **if you need pencils, take some of these/mine** si vous avez besoin de crayons à papier, prenez quelques-uns de ceux-ci/des miens ▸ **some (of them) left early** quelques-uns d'entre eux sont partis tôt ▸ **some say he lied** certains disent *OR* il y en a qui disent qu'il a menti.

■ **adv** quelque, environ ▸ **there were some 7,000 people there** il y avait quelque *OR* environ 7 000 personnes.

somebody ['sʌmbədɪ] ■ **pron** quelqu'un.
■ **n : he really thinks he's somebody** il se prend pour *OR* se croit quelqu'un.

someday ['sʌmdeɪ] **adv** un jour, un de ces jours.

somehow ['sʌmhaʊ], *US* ***someway*** ['sʌmweɪ] **adv 1.** [by some action] d'une manière ou d'une autre **2.** [for some reason] pour une raison ou pour une autre.

someone ['sʌmwʌn] **pron** quelqu'un.

someplace *US* = ***somewhere***.

somersault ['sʌməsɔ:lt] ■ **n** cabriole *f*, culbute *f*.
■ **vi** faire une cabriole *OR* culbute.

something ['sʌmθɪŋ] ■ **pron 1.** [unknown thing] quelque chose ▸ **something odd/interesting** quelque chose de bizarre/d'intéressant ▸ **something else** quelque chose d'autre, autre chose ▸ **he gave them something to eat/drink** il leur a donné à manger/boire ▸ **you can't get something for nothing** on n'a rien pour rien ▸ **there's something about him that reminds me of Gary** il y a quelque chose chez lui qui me rappelle Gary ▸ **she's something in the City/in insurance** elle travaille dans la finance/dans les assurances ▸ **or something** *inf* ou quelque chose comme ça ▸ **are you deaf or something?** tu es sourd ou quoi? **2.** [useful thing] **: (at least) that's something** c'est toujours ça, c'est déjà quelque chose ▸ **there's something in what you say** il y a du vrai dans ce que vous dites ▸▸ **to be** *OR* **have something to do with** avoir un rapport avec ▸ **that's really something!** ce n'est pas rien! ▸ **he's forty something** il a dans les quarante ans ▸ **she's something of a cook** elle est assez bonne cuisinière ▸ **I'm sure she's got something going with him** *inf* je suis sûr qu'il y a quelque chose entre elle et lui.
■ **adv : something like, something in the region of** environ, à peu près.

sometime ['sʌmtaɪm] ■ **adj** ancien(enne).
■ **adv** un de ces jours ▸ **sometime last week** la semaine dernière.

sometimes ['sʌmtaɪmz] **adv** quelquefois, parfois.

someway *US* = ***somehow***.

somewhat ['sʌmwɒt] **adv** quelque peu.

somewhere ['sʌmweəʳ], *US* ***someplace*** ['sʌmpleɪs] **adv 1.** [unknown place] quelque part ▸ **somewhere else** ailleurs ▸ **somewhere near here** près d'ici ▸ **she's somewhere around** elle est quelque part par là, elle n'est pas loin ▸ **I'm looking for somewhere to stay** je cherche un endroit où loger **2.** [used in approximations] environ, à peu près ▸ **she earns somewhere around $2,000 a month** elle gagne quelque chose comme 2 000 dollars par mois ▸▸ **to be getting somewhere** avancer, faire des progrès.

son [sʌn] **n** fils *m*.

sonar ['səʊnɑ:ʳ] **n** sonar *m*.

sonata [sə'nɑ:tə] **n** sonate *f*.

song [sɒŋ] **n** chanson *f* / [of bird] chant *m*, ramage *m* ▸ **for a song** *inf* [cheaply] pour une bouchée de pain ▸ **to make a song and dance about sthg** *UK inf* faire toute une histoire *OR* tout un plat à propos de qqch.

songbook ['sɒŋbʊk] **n** recueil *m* de chansons.

songwriter ['sɒŋ,raɪtəʳ] **n** [of lyrics] parolier *m*, -ère *f* / [of music] compositeur *m*, -trice *f* / [of lyrics and music] auteur-compositeur *m*.

sonic ['sɒnɪk] **adj** sonique.

sonic boom **n** bang *m*.

son-in-law (pl **sons-in-law**) **n** gendre *m*, beau-fils *m*.

sonnet ['sɒnɪt] **n** sonnet *m*.

sonny ['sʌnɪ] **n** *inf* fiston *m*.

son-of-a-bitch (pl **sons-of-bitches**) **n** *esp UK v inf* salaud *m*, fils *m* de pute.

sonorous ['sɒnərəs] **adj** *liter* **1.** [resonant] sonore **2.** [grandiloquent] grandiloquent(e).

soon [su:n] **adv 1.** [before long] bientôt ▸ **soon after** peu après **2.** [early] tôt ▸ **write back soon** réponds-moi vite ▸ **how soon will it be ready?** ce sera prêt quand?, dans combien de temps est-ce que ce sera prêt? ▸ **as soon as** dès que, aussitôt que
▸▸ **I'd just as soon...** je préférerais..., j'aimerais autant...

sooner ['su:nəʳ] **adv 1.** [in time] plus tôt ▸ **no sooner... than...** à peine... que... ▸ **sooner or later** tôt ou tard ▸ **the sooner the better** le plus tôt sera le mieux ▸ **no sooner said than done!** aussitôt dit, aussitôt fait! **2.** [expressing preference] **: I would sooner...** je préférerais..., j'aimerais mieux... ▸ **I'd sooner die than go through that again!** plutôt mourir que de revivre ça!

soot [sʊt] **n** suie *f*.

soothe [su:ð] **vt** calmer, apaiser.

soothing ['su:ðɪŋ] **adj 1.** [pain-relieving] lénifiant(e), lénitif(ive) **2.** [music, words] apaisant(e).

sooty ['sʊtɪ] (comp **-ier**, superl **-iest**) **adj** couvert(e) de suie.

sop [sɒp] **n** : **sop (to)** concession *f* (à).

SOP (abbr of ***standard operating procedure***) **n** *marche à suivre normale*.

sophisticated [sə'fɪstɪkeɪtɪd] **adj 1.** [stylish] raffiné(e), sophistiqué(e) **2.** [intelligent] averti(e) **3.** [complicated] sophistiqué(e), très perfectionné(e).

sophistication [səˌfɪstɪ'keɪʃn] **n 1.** [stylishness] raffinement *m*, sophistication *f* **2.** [intelligence] intelligence *f* **3.** [complexity] sophistication *f*, perfectionnement *m*.

sophomore ['sɒfəmɔːʳ] **n** *US* [in high school] étudiant *m*, -e *f* de seconde année.

soporific [ˌsɒpə'rɪfɪk] **adj** soporifique.

sopping ['sɒpɪŋ] **adj** *inf* : **sopping (wet)** tout trempé (toute trempée).

soppy ['sɒpɪ] (comp **-ier**, superl **-iest**) **adj** *inf* **1.** [sentimental - book, film] à l'eau de rose / [- person] sentimental(e) **2.** [silly] bêta(asse), bête.

soprano [sə'prɑːnəʊ] (pl **-s**) **n** [person] soprano *mf* / [voice] soprano *m*.

sorbet ['sɔːbeɪ] **n** sorbet *m*.

sorcerer ['sɔːsərəʳ] **n** sorcier *m*.

sorcery ['sɔːsərɪ] **n** sorcellerie *f*.

sordid ['sɔːdɪd] **adj** sordide.

sore [sɔːʳ] ■ **adj 1.** [painful] douloureux(euse) ▸ **to have a sore throat** avoir mal à la gorge **2.** *US* [upset] fâché(e), contrarié(e) **3.** *liter* [great] : **to be in sore need of sthg** avoir grandement besoin de qqch.
■ **n** plaie *f*.

sorely ['sɔːlɪ] **adv** *liter* [needed] grandement.

sorority [sə'rɒrətɪ] **n** *US* club *m* d'étudiantes.

sorrel ['sɒrəl] **n** oseille *f*.

sorrow ['sɒrəʊ] **n** peine *f*, chagrin *m*.

sorrowful ['sɒrəʊfʊl] **adj** *liter* triste, affligé(e).

sorrowfully ['sɒrəʊflɪ] **adv** tristement.

sorry ['sɒrɪ] ■ **adj** (comp **-ier**, superl **-iest**) **1.** [expressing apology, disappointment] désolé(e) ▸ **I'm sorry we won't be able to fetch you** je regrette que *OR* je suis désolé que nous ne puissions venir vous chercher ▸ **to be sorry about sthg** s'excuser pour qqch ▸ **to be sorry to do sthg** être désolé *OR* regretter de faire qqch ▸ **(I'm) sorry to have bothered you** (je suis) désolé de vous avoir dérangé ▸ **he said he was sorry** il a présenté ses excuses ▸ **I'm so *OR* very *OR* terribly sorry** je suis vraiment navré
2. [regretful] : **to be sorry for sthg** regretter qqch ▸ **you'll be sorry for this** tu le regretteras ▸ **I'm sorry I ever came here!** je regrette d'être venu ici!
3. [pity] : **to be *OR* to feel sorry for sb** plaindre qqn ▸ **she felt sorry for him and gave him a pound** elle eut pitié de lui et lui donna une livre ▸ **to be *OR* to feel sorry for o.s.** s'apitoyer sur soi-même *OR* sur son propre sort ▸ **he's just feeling a bit sorry for himself** il est juste un peu déprimé
4. [poor] : **in a sorry state** en piteux état, dans un triste état ▸ **they were a sorry sight after the match** ils étaient dans un triste état après le match ▸ **it's a sorry state of affairs** c'est bien triste.
■ **excl 1.** [expressing apology] pardon!, excusez-moi! ▸ **sorry, we're sold out** désolé, on n'en a plus
2. [asking for repetition] pardon?, comment?
3. [to correct oneself] non, pardon *OR* je veux dire.

sort [sɔːt] ■ **n** genre *m*, sorte *f*, espèce *f* ▸ **what sort of car have you got?** qu'est-ce que tu as comme voiture? ▸ **it's a strange sort of film** c'est un drôle de film ▸ **I think that he's some sort of specialist *OR* that he's a specialist of some sort** je crois que c'est un genre de spécialiste ▸ **I know your sort!** les gens de ton espèce, je les connais! ▸ **sort of** [rather] plutôt, quelque peu ▸ **I'm sort of glad that I missed them** je suis plutôt content de les avoir ratés ▸ **did you hit him? – well, sort of** tu l'as frappé? – en quelque sorte, oui ▸ **a sort of** une espèce *OR* sorte de ▸ **they served us champagne of a sort** ils nous ont servi une espèce de champagne ▸ **I said nothing of the sort!** je n'ai rien dit de pareil *OR* de tel!
■ **vt** trier, classer ▸ **sort the cards into two piles** répartissez les cartes en deux piles ▸ **to sort mail** trier le courrier.
◆ ***sorts*** **npl** : **of sorts** si on veut, si on peut dire ▸ **to be out of sorts** ne pas être dans son assiette, être patraque.
◆ ***sort out*** **vt sep 1.** [tidy up] ranger, classer ▸ **she needs to get her personal life sorted out** il faut qu'elle règle ses problèmes personnels **2.** [solve] résoudre ▸ **I'm trying to sort out what's been going on** j'essaie de savoir *OR* de comprendre ce qui s'est passé ▸ **things will sort themselves out in the end** les choses finiront par s'arranger ▸ **she needs time to sort herself out** il lui faut du temps pour régler ses problèmes.

sorta ['sɔːtə] *inf* = ***sort of***.

sort code **n** FIN code *m* guichet.

sortie ['sɔːtiː] **n** sortie *f*.

sorting ['sɔːtɪŋ] **n** tri *m*.

sorting office **n** centre *m* de tri.

sort-out **n** *UK inf* : **to have a sort-out** faire du rangement.

SOS (abbr of ***save our souls***) **n** SOS *m*.

so-so *inf* ■ **adj** quelconque.
■ **adv** comme ci comme ça.

soufflé ['suːfleɪ] **n** soufflé *m*.

sought [sɔːt] **pt & pp** ➤ ***seek***.

sought-after **adj** recherché(e), demandé(e).

soul [səʊl] **n 1.** [gen] âme *f* ▸ **I didn't see a soul** je n'ai pas vu âme qui vive **2.** [music] soul *m*.

soul-destroying [-dɪˌstrɔɪɪŋ] **adj** abrutissant(e).

soulful ['səʊlfʊl] **adj** [look] expressif(ive) / [song] sentimental(e).

soulless ['səʊllɪs] **adj** [job] abrutissant(e) / [place] sans âme.

soul mate **n** âme *f* sœur.

soul music **n** soul *m*.

soul-searching **n** *(U)* examen *m* de conscience.

sound [saʊnd] ■ **adj 1.** [healthy - body] sain(e), en bonne santé / [- mind] sain(e) ▸ **to be of sound mind** être sain d'esprit
2. [sturdy] solide
3. [reliable - advice] judicieux(euse), sage / [- investment] sûr(e) ▸ **we need somebody with a sound grasp of the subject** il nous faut quelqu'un ayant de solides connaissances en la matière ▸ **to show sound judgment** faire preuve de jugement.
■ **adv : to be sound asleep** dormir à poings fermés, dormir d'un sommeil profond.
■ **n** son *m* / [particular sound] bruit *m*, son *m* ▸ **don't make a sound!** surtout ne faites pas de bruit! ▸ **the speed of sound** la vitesse du son ▸ **to turn the sound up/down** monter/baisser le son OR volume ▸ **I don't like the sound of that** *fig* cela ne me dit rien qui vaille ▸ **by the sound of it...** d'après ce que j'ai compris...
■ **vt** [alarm, bell] sonner ▸ **to sound one's horn** klaxonner.
■ **vi 1.** [make a noise] sonner, retentir ▸ **it sounds hollow if you tap it** ça sonne creux lorsqu'on tape dessus ▸ **to sound like sthg** ressembler à qqch ▸ **you sound just like your brother on the phone** tu as la même voix que ton frère OR on dirait vraiment ton frère au téléphone
2. [seem] sembler, avoir l'air ▸ **the name sounded French** le nom avait l'air d'être OR sonnait français ▸ **to sound like sthg** avoir l'air de qqch, sembler être qqch ▸ **(that) sounds like a good idea** ça semble être une bonne idée ▸ **it sounds to me as though they don't want to do it** j'ai l'impression qu'ils ne veulent pas le faire.
◆ ***sound out*** **vt sep : to sound sb out (on OR about)** sonder qqn (sur).

sound barrier **n** mur *m* du son.

sound bite **n** petite phrase *f (prononcée par un homme politique etc à la radio ou à la télévision pour frapper les esprits).*

soundcard ['saʊndka:d] **n** COMPUT carte *f* son.

sound effects **npl** bruitage *m*, effets *mpl* sonores.

sound engineer **n** ingénieur *m* du son.

sounding ['saʊndɪŋ] **n** *fig* & NAUT sondage *m*.

-sounding **suffix : a foreign-sounding name** un nom à consonance étrangère.

sounding board **n 1.** THEAT abat-voix *m inv* **2.** *fig* [person] *personne sur laquelle on peut essayer une nouvelle idée.*

soundly ['saʊndlɪ] **adv 1.** [beaten] à plates coutures **2.** [sleep] profondément.

soundness ['saʊndnɪs] **n** [of argument] solidité *f*, validité *f* / [of theory, method] fiabilité *f*.

soundproof ['saʊndpru:f] **adj** insonorisé(e).

soundproofing ['saʊndpru:fɪŋ] **n** insonorisation *f*.

sound system **n** [hi-fi] chaîne *f* hifi / [PA system] sonorisation *f*.

soundtrack ['saʊndtræk] **n** bande-son *f*.

sound wave **n** onde *f* sonore.

soup [su:p] **n** soupe *f*, potage *m*.
◆ ***soup up*** **vt sep** *inf* [car] gonfler le moteur de.

souped-up [su:pt-] **adj** *inf* [engine] gonflé(e), poussé(e) / [car] au moteur gonflé OR poussé / [machine, computer program] perfectionné(e).

soup kitchen **n** soupe *f* populaire.

soup plate **n** assiette *f* creuse OR à soupe.

soup spoon **n** cuiller *f* à soupe.

sour ['saʊəʳ] ■ **adj 1.** [taste, fruit] acide, aigre **2.** [milk] aigre ▸ **to go OR turn sour** tourner à l'aigre / *fig* [relationship] mal tourner, tourner au vinaigre **3.** [ill-tempered] aigre, acerbe.
■ **vt** *fig* faire tourner au vinaigre, faire mal tourner.
■ **vi** tourner au vinaigre, mal tourner.

source [sɔ:s] **n 1.** [gen] source *f* **2.** [cause] origine *f*, cause *f*.

source language **n 1.** LING langue *f* source **2.** COMPUT langage *m* source.

source program **n** COMPUT programme *m* source.

sour cream **n** crème *f* aigre.

sour grapes **n** *(U) inf* **: what he said was just sour grapes** il a dit ça par dépit.

sourly ['saʊəlɪ] **adj** aigrement, avec aigreur.

sourness ['saʊənɪs] **n 1.** [of taste, fruit] aigreur *f*, acidité *f* **2.** [of milk, person] aigreur *f*.

south [saʊθ] ■ **n 1.** [direction] sud *m* **2.** [region] **: the south** le sud ▸ **the South of France** le Sud de la France, le Midi (de la France).
■ **adj** sud *(inv)* / [wind] du sud.
■ **adv** au sud, vers le sud ▸ **south of** au sud de.

South Africa **n** Afrique *f* du Sud ▸ **in South Africa** en Afrique du Sud ▸ **the Republic of South Africa** la République d'Afrique du Sud.

South African ■ **adj** sud-africain(e).
■ **n** [person] Sud-Africain *m*, -e *f*.

South America **n** Amérique *f* du Sud ▸ **in South America** en Amérique du Sud.

South American ■ **adj** sud-américain(e).
■ **n** [person] Sud-Américain *m*, -e *f*.

southbound ['saʊθbaʊnd] **adj** qui se dirige vers le sud / [carriageway] sud *(inv)*.

South Carolina [-ˌkærə'laɪnə] **n** Caroline *f* du Sud ▸ **in South Carolina** en Caroline du Sud.

South Dakota [-də'kəʊtə] **n** Dakota *m* du Sud ▸ **in South Dakota** dans le Dakota du Sud.

southeast [ˌsaʊθ'i:st] ■ **n 1.** [direction] sud-est *m* **2.** [region] **: the southeast** le sud-est.
■ **adj** au sud-est, du sud-est / [wind] du sud-est.
■ **adv** au sud-est, vers le sud-est ▸ **southeast of** au sud-est de.

Southeast Asia **n** Asie *f* du Sud-Est ▸ **in Southeast Asia** en Asie du Sud-Est.

southeasterly [ˌsaʊθ'i:stəlɪ] **adj** au sud-est, du sud-est / [wind] du sud-est ▸ **in a southeasterly direction** vers le sud-est.

southeastern [ˌsaʊθ'i:stən] **adj** du sud-est, au sud-est.

southerly ['sʌðəlɪ] **adj** au sud, du sud / [wind] du sud ▸ **in a southerly direction** vers le sud.

southern ['sʌðən] **adj** du sud / [France] du Midi.

Southern Africa **n** Afrique *f* australe ▸ **in Southern Africa** en Afrique australe.

southerner ['sʌðənər] **n** [gen] homme *m*, femme *f* du sud / [in continental Europe] méridional *m*, -e *f*.

southernmost ['sʌðənməʊst] **adj** le plus au sud ▸ **the southernmost town in Chile** la ville la plus au sud du Chili.

south-facing **adj** [house, wall] (exposé(e)) au sud *OR* au midi.

South Korea **n** Corée *f* du Sud ▸ **in South Korea** en Corée du Sud.

South Korean ■ **adj** sud-coréen(enne).
■ **n** Sud-Coréen *m*, -enne *f*.

South Pole **n : the South Pole** le pôle Sud.

South Vietnam **n** Sud Viêt-Nam *m* ▸ **in South Vietnam** au Sud Viêt-Nam.

South Vietnamese ■ **adj** sud-vietnamien(enne).
■ **n** Sud-Vietnamien *m*, -enne *f*.

southward ['saʊθwəd] ■ **adj** au sud, du sud.
■ **adv** = ***southwards***.

southwards ['saʊθwədz] **adv** vers le sud.

southwest [,saʊθ'west] ■ **n 1.** [direction] sud-ouest *m* **2.** [region] **: the southwest** le sud-ouest.
■ **adj** au sud-ouest, du sud-ouest / [wind] du sud-ouest.
■ **adv** au sud-ouest, vers le sud-ouest ▸ **southwest of** au sud-ouest de.

southwesterly [,saʊθ'westəlɪ] **adj** au sud-ouest, du sud-ouest / [wind] du sud-ouest ▸ **in a southwesterly direction** vers le sud-ouest.

southwestern [,saʊθ'westən] **adj** au sud-ouest, du sud-ouest.

South Yemen **n** Yémen *m* du Sud ▸ **in South Yemen** au Yémen du Sud.

souvenir [,su:və'nɪər] **n** souvenir *m*.

sou'wester [saʊ'westər] **n** [hat] suroît *m*.

sovereign ['sɒvrɪn] ■ **adj** souverain(e).
■ **n 1.** [ruler] souverain *m*, -e *f* **2.** [coin] souverain *m*.

sovereignty ['sɒvrɪntɪ] **n** souveraineté *f*.

soviet ['səʊvɪət] **n** soviet *m*.
◆ ***Soviet*** ■ **adj** soviétique.
■ **n** [person] Soviétique *mf*.

Soviet Union **n : the (former) Soviet Union** l'(ex-)Union *f* soviétique.

sow[1] [səʊ] (pt **-ed**, pp **sown** *OR* **-ed**) **vt** *lit* & *fig* semer.

sow[2] [saʊ] **n** truie *f*.

sown [səʊn] **pp** ➤ ***sow***[1].

sox [sɒks] ➤ ***bobby sox***.

soya ['sɔɪə] **n** soja *m*.

soy(a) bean ['sɔɪ(ə)-] **n** graine *f* de soja.

soy sauce [sɔɪ-] **n** sauce *f* au soja.

sozzled ['sɒzld] **adj** *UK inf* rond(e), pompette.

spa [spɑ:] **n** station *f* thermale.

spa bath **n** Jacuzzi® *m*.

space [speɪs] ■ **n 1.** [gap, roominess, outer space] espace *m* / [on form] blanc *m*, espace *m* ▸ **your books take up an awful lot of space** tes livres prennent énormément de place ▸ **he cleared a** *OR* **some space on his desk for the tray** il a fait un peu de place sur son bureau pour le plateau ▸ **please add any further details in the space provided** veuillez ajouter tout détail supplémentaire dans la case prévue à cet effet ▸ **to stare into space** regarder dans le vide **2.** [room] place *f* **3.** [of time] **: within** *OR* **in the space of ten minutes** en l'espace de dix minutes ▸ **space of time** laps *m* de temps.
■ **comp** spatial(e).
■ **vt** espacer.
◆ ***space out*** **vt sep** espacer.

space age **n : the space age** l'ère *f* spatiale.
◆ ***space-age*** **adj** de l'ère spatiale.

space bar **n** barre *f* d'espacement.

space cadet **n** *inf* taré *m*, -e *f*.

space capsule **n** capsule *f* spatiale.

spacecraft ['speɪskrɑ:ft] (pl **spacecraft**) **n** vaisseau *m* spatial.

spaceman ['speɪsmæn] (pl **-men** [-men]) **n** astronaute *m*, cosmonaute *m*.

space probe **n** sonde *f* spatiale.

space-saving **adj** qui fait gagner de la place.

spaceship ['speɪsʃɪp] **n** vaisseau *m* spatial.

space shuttle **n** navette *f* spatiale.

space station **n** station *f* orbitale *OR* spatiale.

spacesuit ['speɪssu:t] **n** combinaison *f* spatiale.

space travel **n** astronautique *f* / [science] voyages *mpl* dans l'espace.

spacewoman ['speɪs,wʊmən] (pl **-women** [-,wɪmɪn]) **n** astronaute *f*, cosmonaute *f*.

spacing ['speɪsɪŋ] **n** TYPO espacement *m*.

spacious ['speɪʃəs] **adj** spacieux(euse).

spade [speɪd] **n 1.** [tool] pelle *f* **2.** [playing card] pique *m*.
◆ ***spades*** **npl** pique *m* ▸ **the six of spades** le six de pique.

spadework ['speɪdwɜ:k] **n** *inf* gros *m* du travail.

spaghetti [spə'getɪ] **n** *(U)* spaghettis *mpl*.

Spain [speɪn] **n** Espagne *f* ▸ **in Spain** en Espagne.

spam [spæm] **n** *inf* pourriel *m*.

Spam® [spæm] **n** *pâté de jambon en conserve*.

spammer ['spæmər] **n** spammeur *m*.

spamming ['spæmɪŋ] **n** *(U)* spam *m*, arrosage *m* *offic*.

span [spæn] ■ **pt** ➤ ***spin***.
■ **n 1.** [in time] espace *m* de temps, durée *f* **2.** [range] éventail *m*, gamme *f* **3.** [of bird, plane] envergure *f* **4.** [of bridge] travée *f* / [of arch] ouverture *f*.
■ **vt** (pt & pp **-ned**, cont **-ning**) **1.** [in time] embrasser, couvrir **2.** [subj: bridge] franchir.

spandex ['spændeks] **n** *US textile proche du Lycra®*.

spangled ['spæŋgld] **adj : spangled (with)** pailleté(e) (de).

Spaniard ['spænjəd] **n** Espagnol *m*, -e *f*.

spaniel ['spænjəl] **n** épagneul *m*.

Spanish ['spænɪʃ] ■ **adj** espagnol(e).
■ **n** [language] espagnol *m*.
■ **npl : the Spanish** les Espagnols.

Spanish America n Amérique *f* hispanophone.

Spanish American ■ **adj 1.** [in US] hispanique **2.** [in Latin America] hispano-américain(e).
■ **n 1.** [in US] Hispanique *mf* **2.** [in Latin America] Hispano-Américain *m*, -e *f*.

spank [spæŋk] ■ **n** fessée *f*.
■ **vt** donner une fessée à, fesser.

spanner ['spænəʳ] **n** *UK* clé *f* à écrous.

spar [spɑːʳ] ■ **n** espar *m*.
■ **vi** (**pt & pp -red, cont -ring**) **1.** [in boxing] s'entraîner à la boxe **2.** [verbally] **: to spar (with)** se disputer (avec).

spare [speəʳ] ■ **adj 1.** [surplus] de trop ⁄ [component, clothing] de réserve, de rechange ▸ **take a spare pullover** prenez un pull de rechange ▸ **spare bed** lit *m* d'appoint
2. [available - seat, time, tickets] disponible ▸ **call in next time you have a spare moment** passez la prochaine fois que vous aurez un moment de libre ▸ **I'll have some more cake if there's any going spare** *inf* je vais reprendre du gâteau s'il en reste
3. [lean] maigre, sec, sèche *f*.
■ **n 1.** [tyre] pneu *m* de rechange ***OR*** de secours
2. [part] pièce *f* détachée ***OR*** de rechange.
■ **vt 1.** [make available - staff, money] se passer de ⁄ [- time] disposer de ▸ **spare a thought for their poor parents!** pensez un peu à leurs pauvres parents! ▸ **come and see us if you can spare the time** venez nous voir si vous avez le temps ▸ **to have an hour to spare** avoir une heure de battement ***OR*** de libre ▸ **with a minute to spare** avec une minute d'avance ▸ **do you have a few minutes to spare?** avez-vous quelques minutes de libres ***OR*** devant vous? ▸ **with £2 to spare** et il nous/lui *etc* reste encore deux livres ▸ **young people with money to spare** des jeunes qui ont de l'argent à dépenser
2. [not harm] épargner ▸ **to spare sb's feelings** ménager les sentiments de qqn ▸ **to spare sb's life** épargner la vie de qqn
3. [not use] épargner, ménager ▸ **to spare no expense** ne pas regarder à la dépense ▸ **they spared no expense on the celebrations** ils n'ont reculé devant aucune dépense pour les fêtes ▸ **we shall spare no effort to push the plan through** nous ne reculerons devant aucun effort pour faire accepter le projet
4. [save from] **: to spare sb sthg** épargner qqch à qqn, éviter qqch à qqn ▸ **I could have spared myself the bother** j'aurais pu m'épargner le dérangement.

spare part n pièce *f* détachée ***OR*** de rechange.

sparerib [speə'rɪb] **n** travers *m* de porc ▸ **barbecue spareribs** travers de porc grillés sauce barbecue.

spare room n chambre *f* d'amis.

spare time n *(U)* temps *m* libre, loisirs *mpl*.

spare tyre *UK*, ***spare tire*** *US* **n 1.** AUT pneu *m* de rechange ***OR*** de secours **2.** *hum* [fat waist] bourrelet *m* (de graisse).

spare wheel n roue *f* de secours.

sparing ['speərɪŋ] **adj : to be sparing with *OR* of sthg** être économe de qqch, ménager qqch.

sparingly ['speərɪŋlɪ] **adv** [use] avec modération ⁄ [spend] avec parcimonie.

spark [spɑːk] ■ **n** *lit & fig* étincelle *f*.
■ **vt** [interest] susciter, éveiller ⁄ [scandal] provoquer ⁄ [debate] déclencher.

sparking plug ['spɑːkɪŋ-] *UK* = ***spark plug***.

sparkle ['spɑːkl] ■ **n** *(U)* [of eyes, jewel] éclat *m* ⁄ [of stars] scintillement *m*.
■ **vi** étinceler, scintiller.

sparkler ['spɑːkləʳ] **n** [firework] cierge *m* merveilleux.

sparkling ['spɑːklɪŋ] ■ **adj 1.** [jewel, frost, glass, star] étincelant(e), scintillant(e) ⁄ [sea, lake] étincelant(e), miroitant(e) ⁄ [eyes] étincelant(e), pétillant(e) **2.** [person, conversation, wit, performance] brillant(e) **3.** [soft drink, mineral water] gazeux(euse), pétillant(e).
■ **adv : sparkling clean/white** d'une propreté/blancheur éclatante.

sparkling wine n vin *m* mousseux.

spark plug n bougie *f*.

sparring match ['spɑːrɪŋ-] **n 1.** [in boxing] combat *m* d'entraînement **2.** [argument] discussion *f* animée.

sparring partner **n 1.** [in boxing] sparring-partner *m* **2.** *fig* adversaire *m*.

sparrow ['spærəʊ] **n** moineau *m*.

sparse ['spɑːs] **adj** clairsemé(e), épars(e).

sparsely ['spɑːslɪ] **adv** [wooded, populated] peu ▸ **the room was sparsely furnished** la pièce contenait peu de meubles.

spartan ['spɑːtn] **adj** austère, de spartiate.

spasm ['spæzm] **n 1.** MED spasme *m* ⁄ [of coughing] quinte *f* **2.** [of emotion] accès *m*.

spasmodic [spæz'mɒdɪk] **adj** spasmodique.

spasmodically [spæz'mɒdɪklɪ] **adv** de façon intermittente, par à-coups.

spastic ['spæstɪk] ■ **adj** MED handicapé(e) moteur.
■ **n** MED handicapé *m*, -e *f* moteur.

spat [spæt] **pt & pp** ➤ ***spit***.

spate [speɪt] **n** [of attacks] série *f*.

spatial ['speɪʃl] **adj** spatial(e).

spatter ['spætəʳ] ■ **vt** éclabousser.
■ **vi** gicler.

spatula ['spætjʊlə] **n** spatule *f*.

spawn [spɔːn] ■ **n** *(U)* frai *m*, œufs *mpl*.
■ **vt** *fig* donner naissance à, engendrer.
■ **vi** [fish, frog] frayer.

spay [speɪ] **vt** châtrer.

SPCA (abbr of ***Society for the Prevention of Cruelty to Animals***) **n** *société américaine protectrice des animaux*, ≃ SPA *f*.

SPCC (abbr of ***Society for the Prevention of Cruelty to Children***) **n** *société américaine pour la protection de l'enfance*.

speak [spiːk] (**pt spoke, pp spoken**) ■ **vt 1.** [say] dire ▸ **to speak one's mind** dire sa pensée ***OR*** façon de penser ▸ **to speak ill of sb** dire du mal de qqn **2.** [language] parler ▸ **'English spoken'** 'ici on parle anglais'.

■ vi [general] parler ▸ **to speak to** *OR* **with sb** parler à qqn ▸ **to speak to sb about sthg** parler de qqch à qqn ▸ **to speak about sb/sthg** parler de qqn/qqch ▸ **to speak well/highly of sb** dire du bien/beaucoup de bien de qqn ▸ **speak to me!** dites(-moi) quelque chose! ▸ **nobody to speak of** pas grand-monde ▸ **nothing to speak of** pas grand-chose / [on telephone] parler ▸ **who's speaking?** [gen] qui est à l'appareil? / [switchboard] c'est de la part de qui? ▸ **Kate Smith speaking** Kate Smith à l'appareil, c'est Kate Smith ▸ **may I speak to Kate? – speaking** puis-je parler à Kate? – c'est moi

▸▸ **speak now or forever hold your peace** parlez maintenant ou gardez le silence pour toujours.

◆ ***so to speak*** adv pour ainsi dire.

◆ ***speak for*** vt insep [represent] parler pour, parler au nom de ▸ **speak for yourself!** parle pour toi! ▸ **let her speak for herself!** laisse-la s'exprimer! ▸ **it speaks for itself** cela tombe sous le sens, c'est évident ▸ **these goods are already spoken for** ces articles sont déjà réservés *OR* retenus ▸ **she's already spoken for** elle est déjà prise.

◆ ***speak out*** vi oser prendre la parole ▸ **to speak out for** parler en faveur de ▸ **to speak out against** s'élever contre, se dresser contre ▸ **she spoke out strongly against the scheme** elle a condamné le projet avec véhémence.

◆ ***speak up*** vi **1.** [support] : **to speak up for sb/sthg** parler en faveur de qqn/qqch, soutenir qqn/qqch ▸ **why didn't you speak up?** pourquoi n'avez-vous rien dit? **2.** [speak louder] parler plus fort.

-speak suffix *pej* : **computer-speak** langage *m OR* jargon *m* de l'informatique.

speaker ['spi:kər] n **1.** [person talking] personne *f* qui parle **2.** [person making speech] orateur *m* **3.** [of language] : **a German speaker** une personne qui parle allemand **4.** [loudspeaker] haut-parleur *m*.

speaker phone n téléphone *m* avec haut-parleur.

speaking ['spi:kɪŋ] ■ adv : **generally speaking** en général ▸ **politically speaking** politiquement parlant ▸ **speaking as** [in the position of] en tant que ▸ **speaking as a politician** en tant qu'homme politique ▸ **speaking of** [on the subject of] à propos de ▸ **speaking of which** justement, à ce propos.

■ n *(U)* discours *m*, parole *f*.

-speaking suffix **1.** [person] : **they're both German/Spanish-speaking** ils sont tous deux germanophones/hispanophones ▸ **a child of Polish-speaking parents** un enfant dont les parents sont de langue *OR* d'origine polonaise **2.** [country] : **French/English-speaking countries** les pays francophones/anglophones ▸ **the Arab-speaking world** le monde arabophone.

speaking clock n *UK* horloge *f* parlante.

spear [spɪər] ■ n lance *f*.

■ vt transpercer d'un coup de lance.

spearhead ['spɪəhed] ■ n fer *m* de lance.

■ vt [campaign] mener / [attack] être le fer de lance de.

spearmint ['spɪəmɪnt] ■ n **1.** [plant] menthe *f* verte / [flavour] menthe *f* **2.** [sweet] bonbon *m* à la menthe.

■ adj [flavour] de menthe / [toothpaste, chewing gum] à la menthe.

spec [spek] n *UK inf* : **on spec** à tout hasard.

special ['speʃl] ■ adj **1.** [gen] spécial(e) **2.** [needs, effort, attention] particulier(ère) ▸ **it's a special case** c'est un cas particulier *OR* à part **3.** [valued] cher (chère) ▸ **you're very special to me** je tiens beaucoup à toi.

■ n **1.** [on menu] plat *m* du jour **2.** TV émission *f* spéciale.

CULTURE

Special Relationship

Communément utilisé en Angleterre, ce terme désigne les « relations spéciales » existant entre les États-Unis et le Royaume-Uni dans les domaines de la politique et de la diplomatie. L'Angleterre devient un allié privilégié des Américains dès la Seconde Guerre mondiale et, lors de la guerre froide, cette tendance s'accentue avec la prise de position proaméricaine de Margaret Thatcher dans les années 1980, au détriment des relations engagées avec ses partenaires européens. Depuis la chute du communisme, la proximité politique qu'entretiennent les deux pays est vivement critiquée, notamment en ce qui concerne les conséquences des attentats du 11 Septembre et leur engagement respectif dans le conflit irakien.

special agent n [spy] agent *m* secret.

Special Branch n *renseignements généraux britanniques.*

special constable n *UK* auxiliaire *m* de police.

special correspondent n envoyé *m* spécial.

special delivery n *(U)* [service] exprès *m*, envoi *m* par exprès ▸ **by special delivery** en exprès.

special effects npl effets *mpl* spéciaux.

specialism ['speʃəlɪzm] n spécialisation *f* ▸ **my specialism is maths** je me spécialise dans les maths.

specialist ['speʃəlɪst] ■ adj spécialisé(e).

■ n spécialiste *mf*.

speciality *UK* [ˌspeʃɪ'ælətɪ] (pl -ies), ***specialty*** *US* ['speʃltɪ] (pl -ies) n spécialité *f*.

specialization [ˌspeʃəlaɪ'zeɪʃn] n spécialisation *f* ▸ **his specialization is computers** il est spécialisé en informatique.

specialize, *UK* ***-ise*** ['speʃəlaɪz] vi : **to specialize (in)** se spécialiser (dans).

specialized, *UK* ***-ised*** ['speʃəlaɪzd] adj spécialisé(e) ▸ **highly specialized equipment** un matériel hautement spécialisé ▸ **we need somebody with specialized knowledge** il nous faut un spécialiste.

specially ['speʃəlɪ] adv **1.** [specifically] spécialement / [on purpose] exprès **2.** [particularly] particulièrement.

special needs [- ni:dz] npl : **special needs children** enfants ayant des difficultés scolaires ▸ **special needs teacher** *enseignant spécialisé s'occupant d'enfants ayant des difficultés scolaires.*

special offer n promotion *f*.

special school n école *f* pour enfants handicapés, établissement *m* spécialisé.

specialty n *US* = ***speciality***.

species ['spi:ʃi:z] (pl **species**) n espèce *f*.

specific [spə'sɪfɪk] adj **1.** [particular] particulier(ère), précis(e) **2.** [precise] précis(e) **3.** [unique] : **specific to** propre à.
◆ ***specifics*** npl détails *mpl*.

specifically [spə'sɪfɪklɪ] adv **1.** [particularly] particulièrement, spécialement **2.** [precisely] précisément.

specification [ˌspesɪfɪ'keɪʃn] n stipulation *f*.
◆ ***specifications*** npl TECH caractéristiques *fpl* techniques, spécification *f*.

specify ['spesɪfaɪ] (pt & pp **-ied**) vt préciser, spécifier.

specimen ['spesɪmən] n **1.** [example] exemple *m*, spécimen *m* **2.** [of blood] prélèvement *m* / [of urine] échantillon *m*.

specimen copy n spécimen *m*.

specimen signature n spécimen *m* de signature.

speck [spek] n **1.** [small stain] toute petite tache *f* **2.** [of dust] grain *m*.

speckled ['spekld] adj : **speckled (with)** tacheté(e) de.

specs [speks] npl *inf* [glasses] lunettes *fpl*.

spectacle ['spektəkl] n spectacle *m*.
◆ ***spectacles*** npl [glasses] lunettes *fpl*.

spectacular [spek'tækjʊlər] ■ adj spectaculaire.
■ n pièce *f* OR revue *f* à grand spectacle.

spectacularly [spek'tækjʊləlɪ] adv [big, beautiful] spectaculairement ▸ **it went spectacularly wrong** ça s'est vraiment très mal passé.

spectate [spek'teɪt] vi regarder, être là en tant que spectateur.

spectator [spek'teɪtər] n spectateur *m*, -trice *f*.

spectator sport n sport *m* que l'on regarde en tant que spectateur.

spectre *UK*, ***specter*** *US* ['spektər] n spectre *m*.

spectrum ['spektrəm] (pl **-tra** [-trə]) n **1.** PHYS spectre *m* **2.** *fig* [variety] gamme *f*.

speculate ['spekjʊleɪt] ■ vt : **to speculate that...** émettre l'hypothèse que...
■ vi **1.** [wonder] faire des conjectures **2.** FIN spéculer.

speculation [ˌspekjʊ'leɪʃn] n **1.** [gen] spéculation *f* **2.** [conjecture] conjectures *fpl*.

speculative ['spekjʊlətɪv] adj spéculatif(ive).

speculator ['spekjʊleɪtər] n FIN spéculateur *m*, -trice *f*.

sped [sped] pt & pp ➤ ***speed***.

speech [spi:tʃ] n **1.** *(U)* [ability] parole *f* **2.** [formal talk] discours *m* ▸ **to give** OR **make a speech** faire un discours **3.** THEAT texte *m* **4.** [manner of speaking] façon *f* de parler **5.** [dialect] parler *m*.

speech day n *UK* distribution *f* des prix.

speech-impaired adj muet(ette).

speech impediment n défaut *m* d'élocution.

speechless ['spi:tʃlɪs] adj : **speechless (with)** muet(ette) (de).

speechmaking ['spi:tʃˌmeɪkɪŋ] n *(U)* discours *mpl* / *pej* beaux discours *mpl*.

speech processing n traitement *m* de la parole.

speech recognition n COMPUT reconnaissance *f* de la parole.

speech therapist n orthophoniste *mf*.

speech therapy n orthophonie *f*.

speed [spi:d] ■ n vitesse *f* / [of reply, action] vitesse, rapidité *f*.
■ vi (pt & pp **-ed** OR **sped**) **1.** [move fast] : **to speed along** aller à toute allure OR vitesse ▸ **to speed away** démarrer à toute allure **2.** AUT [go too fast] rouler trop vite, faire un excès de vitesse.
◆ ***speed up*** ■ vt sep [person] faire aller plus vite / [work, production] accélérer.
■ vi aller plus vite / [car] accélérer.

speedboat ['spi:dbəʊt] n hors-bord *m inv*.

speed bump n dos-d'âne *m inv*.

speed camera n cinémomètre *m*.

speed-dialling *UK*, ***speed-dialing*** *US* n *(U)* TELEC numérotation *f* rapide.

speedily ['spi:dɪlɪ] adv [quickly] vite, rapidement / [promptly] promptement, sans tarder / [soon] bientôt.

speeding ['spi:dɪŋ] n *(U)* excès *m* de vitesse.

speed limit n limitation *f* de vitesse.

speedo ['spi:dəʊ] (pl **-s**) n *UK inf* compteur *m* (de vitesse).

Speedos® ['spi:dəʊz] npl *US inf* caleçon *m* de bain.

speedometer [spɪ'dɒmɪtər] n compteur *m* (de vitesse).

speed trap n radar *m* de contrôle.

speedway ['spi:dweɪ] n **1.** *(U)* SPORT course *f* de motos **2.** *US* [road] voie *f* express.

speedy ['spi:dɪ] (comp **-ier**, superl **-iest**) adj rapide.

speleology [ˌspi:lɪ'ɒlədʒɪ] n spéléologie *f*.

spell [spel] ■ n **1.** [period of time] période *f* **2.** [enchantment] charme *m* / [words] formule *f* magique ▸ **to cast** OR **put a spell on sb** jeter un sort à qqn, envoûter qqn ▸ **to be under sb's spell** *lit* & *fig* être sous le charme de qqn.
■ vt (*UK* **spelt** OR **-ed**, *US* **-ed**) **1.** [word, name] écrire ▸ **they've spelt my name wrong** ils ont mal écrit mon nom **2.** *fig* [signify] signifier.
■ vi (*UK* **spelt** OR **-ed**, *US* **-ed**) épeler.
◆ ***spell out*** vt sep **1.** [read aloud] épeler **2.** [explain] : **to spell sthg out (for** OR **to sb)** expliquer qqch clairement (à qqn) ▸ **do I have to spell it out for you?** est-ce qu'il faut que je mette les points sur les i?

spellbinding ['spelˌbaɪndɪŋ] adj ensorcelant(e), envoûtant(e).

spellbound ['spelbaʊnd] adj subjugué(e).

spell-check ■ vt [text, file, document] vérifier l'orthographe de.
■ n vérification *f* orthographique.

spell-checker [-tʃekər] n correcteur *m* OR vérificateur *m* orthographique.

spelling ['spelɪŋ] n orthographe *f*.

spelling bee n *US* concours *m* d'orthographe.

spelt [spelt] *UK* pt & pp ➤ ***spell***.

spelunking [spe'lʌnkɪŋ] n *US* spéléologie *f*.

spend [spend] ■ n dépenses *fpl* ▸ **we must increase our marketing spend** nous devons augmenter le budget marketing.
■ vt (pt & pp **spent**) **1.** [pay out] **: to spend money (on)** dépenser de l'argent (pour) ▸ **I consider it money well spent** je considère que c'est un bon investissement **2.** [time, life] passer / [effort] consacrer ▸ **to spend time on sthg/on doing sthg** passer du temps sur qqch/à faire qqch ▸ **I spent a lot of time and effort on this** j'y ai consacré beaucoup de temps et d'efforts.

spender ['spendəʳ] **n : to be a big spender** être très dépensier(ère), dépenser beaucoup.

spending ['spendɪŋ] **n** *(U)* dépenses *fpl*.

spending money **n** argent *m* de poche.

spending power **n** *(U)* pouvoir *m* d'achat.

spendthrift ['spendθrɪft] **n** dépensier *m*, -ère *f*.

spent [spent] ■ **pt & pp ➤ *spend***.
■ **adj** [fuel, match, ammunition] utilisé(e) / [patience, energy] épuisé(e).

sperm [spɜːm] (pl **sperm** *OR* **-s**) **n** sperme *m*.

sperm bank **n** banque *f* de sperme.

spermicidal cream [ˌspɜːmɪ'saɪdl-] **n** crème *f* spermicide.

spermicide ['spɜːmɪsaɪd] **n** spermicide *m*.

sperm whale **n** cachalot *m*.

spew [spjuː] **vt & vi** vomir.

sphere [sfɪəʳ] **n** sphère *f*.

spherical ['sferɪkl] **adj** sphérique.

sphincter ['sfɪŋktəʳ] **n** sphincter *m*.

sphinx [sfɪŋks] (pl **-es** [-iːz]) **n** sphinx *m*.

spice [spaɪs] ■ **n 1.** CULIN épice *f* **2.** *(U)* *fig* [excitement] piment *m*.
■ **vt 1.** CULIN épicer **2.** *fig* [add excitement to] pimenter, relever.

spick-and-span [ˌspɪkən'spæn] **adj** impeccable, nickel *(inv)*.

spicy ['spaɪsɪ] (comp **-ier**, superl **-iest**) **adj 1.** CULIN épicé(e) **2.** *fig* [story] pimenté(e), piquant(e).

spider ['spaɪdəʳ] **n** araignée *f*.

spider crab **n** araignée *f* (de mer).

spider monkey **n** singe *m* araignée, atèle *m*.

spider's web, *US* ***spiderweb*** ['spaɪdəweb] **n** toile *f* d'araignée.

spidery ['spaɪdərɪ] **adj** en pattes d'araignée.

spiel [ʃpiːl] **n** *inf* baratin *m*.

spike [spaɪk] **n** [metal] pointe *f*, lance *f* / [of plant] piquant *m* / [of hair] épi *m*.
◆ ***spikes*** **npl** chaussures *fpl* à pointes.

spiked [spaɪkt] **adj** [railings] à pointes de fer / [shoes] à pointes / [tyre] clouté(e), à clous.

spiky ['spaɪkɪ] (comp **-ier**, superl **-iest**) **adj** [branch, plant] hérissé(e) de piquants / [hair] en épi.

spill [spɪl] (*UK* **spilt** *OR* **-ed**, *US* **-ed**) ■ **vt** renverser.
■ **vi 1.** [liquid] se répandre **2.** [people] **: to spill out of a building** sortir d'un bâtiment en masse.

spillage ['spɪlɪdʒ] **n** [of oil] déversement *m*.

spillover ['spɪlˌəʊvəʳ] **n 1.** [act of spilling] renversement *m* / [quantity spilt] quantité *f* renversée **2.** [excess] excédent *m* **3.** ECON retombées *fpl* (économiques).

spilt [spɪlt] *UK* **pt & pp ➤ *spill***.

spin [spɪn] ■ **n 1.** [turn] **: to give sthg a spin** faire tourner qqch **2.** AERON vrille *f* **3.** *inf* [in car] tour *m* ▸ **the car went into a spin** la voiture a fait un tête-à-queue ▸ **to be in a flat spin** être dans tous ses états **4.** SPORT effet *m* ▸ **to put spin on a ball** donner de l'effet à une balle **5.** POL **: to put the right spin on sthg** présenter qqch sous an angle favorable **6.** [in spin-dryer] essorage *m* ▸ **to give sthg a spin** essorer qqch **7.** *inf* [ride - in car] tour *m*, balade *f* ▸ **to go for a spin** faire une (petite) balade en voiture **8.** *inf* [try] **: to give sthg a spin** essayer *OR* tenter qqch.
■ **vt** (pt **span** *OR* **spun**, pp **spun**, cont **-ning**) **1.** [wheel] faire tourner ▸ **to spin a coin** jouer à pile ou face **2.** [washing] essorer **3.** [thread, wool, cloth] filer **4.** [subj: spider, silkworm] tisser **5.** SPORT [ball] donner de l'effet à **6.** [invent - tale] inventer, débiter ▸ **he spins a good yarn** il raconte bien les histoires.
■ **vi** (pt **span** *OR* **spun**, pp **spun**, cont **-ning**) tourner, tournoyer ▸ **the skater/ballerina spun on one foot** le patineur/la ballerine virevolta sur un pied ▸ **the wheels were spinning in the mud** les roues patinaient dans la boue ▸ **he suddenly spun round** il pivota sur ses talons *OR* se retourna brusquement ▸ **to spin out of control** [plane] tomber en vrille / [car] faire un tête-à-queue ▸ **my head is spinning** j'ai la tête qui tourne.
◆ ***spin out*** **vt sep** [money, story] faire durer.

CULTURE

Spin

Utilisé à la fois comme verbe et comme nom, le terme « tourner » ou « vriller » (**spin**) appartient au jargon politique (ce mot appartient à l'origine au vocabulaire sportif : au base-ball ou au billard, les joueurs font effectuer un rotation à la balle afin de modifier sa trajectoire). Il met en avant les commentaires ou les actes d'une personne, ou fait passer une information de manière biaisée afin d'influencer l'opinion publique. Il est surtout utilisé par les journalistes pour évoquer la manière dont les gouvernements présentent leurs décisions politiques : les **spin doctors**, « spécialistes du changement de direction », sont les porte-parole de la communication médiatique gouvernementale.

spina bifida [ˌspaɪnə'bɪfɪdə] **n** spina-bifida *m*.

spinach ['spɪnɪdʒ] **n** *(U)* épinards *mpl*.

spinal ['spaɪnl] **adj** [nerve, muscle] spinal(e) / [ligament, disc] vertébral(e) ▸ **a spinal injury** une blessure à la colonne vertébrale.

spinal column ['spaɪnl-] **n** colonne *f* vertébrale.

spinal cord ['spaɪnl-] **n** moelle *f* épinière.

spindle ['spɪndl] **n 1.** TECH broche *f*, axe *m* **2.** [for textiles] fuseau *m*.

spindly ['spɪndlɪ] (comp **-ier**, superl **-iest**) **adj** grêle, chétif(ive).

spin doctor **n** *pej expression désignant la personne qui au sein d'un parti politique est chargée de promouvoir l'image de celui-ci.*

spin-dry **vt** *UK* essorer.

spin-dryer **n** *UK* essoreuse *f.*

spine [spaɪn] **n 1.** ANAT colonne *f* vertébrale **2.** [of book] dos *m* **3.** [of plant, hedgehog] piquant *m.*

spine-chilling **adj** qui glace le sang.

spineless ['spaɪnlɪs] **adj** [feeble] faible, qui manque de cran.

spinner ['spɪnəʳ] **n** [of thread] fileur *m*, -euse *f.*

spinning ['spɪnɪŋ] **n** [of thread] filage *m.*

spinning top **n** toupie *f.*

spin-off **n** [by-product] dérivé *m.*

spinster ['spɪnstəʳ] **n** *dated* célibataire *f* / *pej* vieille fille *f.*

spiral ['spaɪrəl] ■ **adj** spiral(e).

■ **n** spirale *f.*

■ **vi** (*UK* **-led**, cont **-ling**, *US* **-ed**, cont **-ing**) **1.** [staircase, smoke] monter en spirale **2.** [amount, prices] monter en flèche ▸ **to spiral downwards** descendre en flèche.

spiral staircase **n** escalier *m* en colimaçon.

spire ['spaɪəʳ] **n** flèche *f.*

spirit ['spɪrɪt] ■ **n 1.** [gen] esprit *m* ▸ **that's the spirit!** voilà comment il faut réagir!, à la bonne heure! ▸ **he is with us in spirit** il est avec nous en esprit *OR* par l'esprit ▸ **she took my remarks in the wrong spirit** elle a mal pris mes remarques ▸ **the spirit of the law** l'esprit de la loi ▸ **to call up the spirits of the dead** évoquer les âmes des morts ▸ **to enter into the spirit of things** [at party] se mettre au diapason / [in work] participer de bon cœur **2.** *(U)* [determination] caractère *m*, courage *m* ▸ **his spirit was broken** il avait perdu courage.

■ **vt : to spirit sb out of a building** faire sortir qqn d'un bâtiment de façon secrète.

◆ ***spirits*** **npl 1.** [mood] humeur *f* ▸ **to be in high spirits** être gai(e) ▸ **to be in low spirits** être déprimé(e) ▸ **you must keep your spirits up** il faut garder le moral, il ne faut pas vous laisser abattre **2.** [alcohol] spiritueux *mpl.*

◆ ***spirit away*** **vt sep** [carry off secretly] faire disparaître (comme par enchantement) / [steal] escamoter, subtiliser.

spirited ['spɪrɪtɪd] **adj** fougueux(euse) / [performance] interprété(e) avec brio.

spirit level **n** niveau *m* à bulle d'air.

spiritual ['spɪrɪtʃʊəl] **adj** spirituel(elle).

spiritualism ['spɪrɪtʃʊəlɪzm] **n** spiritisme *m.*

spiritualist ['spɪrɪtʃʊəlɪst] **n** spirite *mf.*

spirituality [,spɪrɪtʃʊ'ælətɪ] **n** spiritualité *f.*

spiritually ['spɪrɪtʃʊəlɪ] **adv** spirituellement, en esprit.

spit [spɪt] ■ **n 1.** *(U)* [spittle] crachat *m* / [saliva] salive *f* **2.** [skewer] broche *f.*

■ **vi** (*UK* **spat**, cont **-ting**, *US* **spit**, cont **-ting**) cracher.

■ **impers vb** (pt & pp **spat**, cont **-ting**) *UK* **: it's spitting** il tombe quelques gouttes.

◆ ***spit out*** **vt sep** cracher ▸ **spit it out!** *inf* accouche!

spite [spaɪt] ■ **n** rancune *f* ▸ **to do sthg out of** *OR* **from spite** faire qqch par malice.

■ **vt** contrarier.

◆ ***in spite of*** **prep** en dépit de, malgré ▸ **to do sthg in spite of o.s.** faire qqch malgré soi.

spiteful ['spaɪtfʊl] **adj** malveillant(e).

spitefully ['spaɪtfʊlɪ] **adv** par dépit, par méchanceté, méchamment.

spit roast **n** rôti *m* à la broche.

◆ ***spit-roast*** **vt** faire rôtir à la broche.

spitting ['spɪtɪŋ] **n : 'no spitting'** 'défense de cracher' ▸ **he was within spitting distance of me** *inf* il était à deux pas de moi.

spitting image **n : to be the spitting image of sb** être le portrait (tout) craché de qqn.

spittle ['spɪtl] **n** *(U)* crachat *m.*

splash [splæʃ] ■ **n 1.** [sound] plouf *m* **2.** [small quantity] goutte *f* **3.** [of colour, light] tache *f.*

■ **vt 1.** [with water, mud] éclabousser ▸ **I splashed my face with cold water** *OR* **cold water onto my face** je me suis aspergé le visage d'eau froide *OR* avec de l'eau froide **2.** PRESS étaler ▸ **the story was splashed across the front page** l'affaire était étalée à la une des journaux.

■ **vi 1.** [person] **: to splash about** *OR* **around** barboter **2.** [liquid] jaillir.

◆ ***splash out*** *inf* ■ **vt sep** [money] claquer.

■ **vi : to splash out (on)** dépenser une fortune (pour).

splashdown ['splæʃdaʊn] **n** amerrissage *m.*

splashguard ['splæʃgɑːd] **n** *US* garde-boue *m inv.*

splashy ['splæʃɪ] **adj** *US inf* tape-à-l'œil.

splat [splæt] ■ **n** floc *m.*

■ **adv : to go splat** faire floc.

splatter ['splætəʳ] ■ **vt** éclabousser ▸ **splattered with mud/blood** éclaboussé de boue/sang.

■ **vi** [rain] crépiter / [mud] éclabousser.

■ **n 1.** [mark - of mud, ink] éclaboussure *f* **2.** [sound - of rain] crépitement *m.*

splay [spleɪ] ■ **vt** écarter.

■ **vi : to splay (out)** s'écarter.

spleen [spliːn] **n 1.** ANAT rate *f* **2.** *(U) fig* [anger] mauvaise humeur *f.*

splendid ['splendɪd] **adj** splendide / [work, holiday, idea] excellent(e).

splendidly ['splendɪdlɪ] **adv 1.** [marvellously] de façon splendide, splendidement **2.** [magnificently] magnifiquement.

splendour *UK*, ***splendor*** *US* ['splendəʳ] **n** splendeur *f.*

splice [splaɪs] **vt** [join - gen] coller / [- rope] épisser.

spliff [splɪf] **n** *drug sl* joint *m.*

splint [splɪnt] **n** attelle *f.*

splinter ['splɪntəʳ] ■ **n** éclat *m.*

■ **vt** [wood] fendre en éclats / [glass] briser en éclats.

■ **vi** [wood] se fendre en éclats / [glass] se briser en éclats.

splinter group **n** groupe *m* dissident.

split [splɪt] ■ **n 1.** [in wood] fente *f* **2.** [in garment - tear] déchirure *f* / [- by design] échancrure *f* **3.** POL **: split (in)**

division *f* ***OR*** scission *f* (au sein de) ▸ **there was a three-way split in the voting** les votes étaient répartis en trois groupes **4.** [difference] **: split between** écart *m* entre.
▪ **vt** (pt & pp **split**, cont **-ting**) **1.** [wood] fendre ▸ **to split sthg in two** ***OR*** **in half** casser ***OR*** fendre qqch en deux ▸ **he split his head open on the concrete** il s'est fendu le crâne sur le béton ▸ **to split the atom** PHYS fissionner l'atome ▸ **to split one's sides (laughing)** se tordre de rire **2.** [clothes] déchirer ▸ **the plastic sheet had been split right down the middle** la bâche en plastique avait été fendue en plein milieu **3.** [family & POL] diviser ▸ **the committee is split on this issue** le comité est divisé sur cette question ▸ **the vote was split down the middle** les deux camps avaient obtenu exactement le même nombre de voix **4.** [share] partager ▸ **they decided to split the work between them** ils ont décidé de se partager le travail ▸ **to split the difference** *fig* couper la poire en deux.
▪ **vi** (pt & pp **split**, cont **-ting**) **1.** [wood] se fendre / [clothes] se déchirer ▸ **the ship split in two** le navire s'est brisé (en deux) ▸ **the bag split open** le sac s'est déchiré **2.** POL se diviser / [road, path] se séparer **3.** *US inf* [leave] se casser.
◆ ***splits*** **npl : to do the splits** faire le grand écart.
◆ ***split off*** ▪ **vt sep : to split sthg off (from)** enlever ***OR*** détacher qqch (de).
▪ **vi : to split off (from)** se détacher (de).
◆ ***split up*** ▪ **vt sep : to split sthg up (into)** diviser ***OR*** séparer qqch (en) ▸ **the police split up the meeting/crowd** la police a mis fin à la réunion/dispersé la foule.
▪ **vi** [group, couple] se séparer ▸ **to split up with sb** rompre avec qqn.

split end **n** [in hair] fourche *f*.

split-level **adj** [house] à deux niveaux.

split pea **n** pois *m* cassé.

split personality **n : to have a split personality** souffrir d'un dédoublement de la personnalité.

split screen **n** écran *m* divisé.

split second **n** fraction *f* de seconde.

splitting ['splɪtɪŋ] **adj : I've got a splitting headache** j'ai un mal de tête épouvantable ***OR*** atroce.

splodge ['splɒdʒ] *UK inf* ▪ **n 1.** [splash - of paint, ink] éclaboussure *f*, tache *f* / [- of colour] tache *f* **2.** [dollop - of cream, of jam] bonne cuillerée *f*.
▪ **vt** éclabousser, barbouiller.
▪ **vi** s'étaler, faire des pâtés.

splurge [splɜːdʒ] *inf* ▪ **n 1.** [spending spree] folie *f*, folles dépenses *fpl* ▸ **I went on** ***OR*** **I had a splurge and bought a fur coat** j'ai fait une folie, je me suis acheté un manteau de fourrure **2.** [display] fla-fla *m*, tralala *m* ▸ **the book came out in a splurge of publicity** le livre est sorti avec un grand battage publicitaire ▸ **a great splurge of colour** une débauche de couleur.
▪ **vt** [spend] dépenser / [waste] dissiper ▸ **she splurged her savings on a set of encyclopedias** toutes ses économies ont été englouties par l'achat d'une encyclopédie.
◆ ***splurge out*** **vi insep** faire une folie ***OR*** des folies ▸ **to splurge out on sthg** se payer qqch.

splutter ['splʌtəʳ] ▪ **n** [of person] bafouillage *m*.
▪ **vi** [person] bredouiller, bafouiller / [engine] tousser / [fire] crépiter.

spoil [spɔɪl] (pt & pp **-ed**, *UK* **spoilt**) **vt 1.** [ruin - holiday] gâcher, gâter / [- view] gâter / [- food] gâter, abîmer **2.** [over-indulge, treat well] gâter ▸ **to spoil o.s.** s'offrir une gâterie, se faire plaisir.
◆ ***spoils*** **npl** butin *m*.

spoiled [spɔɪld] **adj** = ***spoilt***.

spoiler ['spɔɪləʳ] **n** PRESS *tactique utilisée pour s'approprier le scoop d'un journal rival.*

spoiler campaign **n** *campagne lancée par une entreprise pour minimiser l'impact d'une campagne publicitaire menée par une société concurrente.*

spoilsport ['spɔɪlspɔːt] **n** trouble-fête *mf inv*.

spoilt [spɔɪlt] ▪ *UK* **pt** & **pp** ➤ ***spoil***.
▪ **adj** [child] gâté(e).

spoke [spəʊk] ▪ **pt** ➤ ***speak***.
▪ **n** rayon *m*.

spoken ['spəʊkn] **pp** ➤ ***speak***.

spokesman ['spəʊksmən] (pl **-men** [-mən]) **n** porte-parole *m inv*.

spokesperson ['spəʊksˌpɜːsn] **n** porte-parole *mf inv*.

spokeswoman ['spəʊksˌwʊmən] (pl **-women** [-ˌwɪmɪn]) **n** porte-parole *f inv*.

sponge [spʌndʒ] ▪ **n 1.** [for cleaning, washing] éponge *f* **2.** [cake] gâteau *m* ***OR*** biscuit *m* de Savoie.
▪ **vt** (*UK* **spongeing**, *US* **sponging**) éponger.
▪ **vi** (*UK* **spongeing**, *US* **sponging**) *inf* **: to sponge off sb** taper qqn.

sponge bag **n** *UK* trousse *f* de toilette.

sponge bath **n** toilette *f* d'un malade.

sponge cake **n** gâteau *m* ***OR*** biscuit *m* de Savoie.

sponge pudding **n** *UK* pudding *m*.

sponger ['spʌndʒəʳ] **n** *inf pej* parasite *m*.

spongy ['spʌndʒɪ] (comp **-ier**, superl **-iest**) **adj** spongieux(euse).

sponsor ['spɒnsəʳ] ▪ **n** sponsor *m*.
▪ **vt 1.** [finance, for charity] sponsoriser, parrainer **2.** [support] soutenir.

sponsored walk [ˌspɒnsəd-] **n** *UK marche organisée pour recueillir des fonds.*

sponsorship ['spɒnsəʃɪp] **n** sponsoring *m*, parrainage *m*.

sponsorship deal **n** contrat *m* de sponsoring.

spontaneity [ˌspɒntə'neɪətɪ] **n** spontanéité *f*.

spontaneous [spɒn'teɪnjəs] **adj** spontané(e).

spontaneously [spɒn'teɪnjəslɪ] **adv** spontanément.

spoof [spuːf] **n : spoof (of** ***OR*** **on)** parodie *f* (de).

spook [spuːk] **vt** *inf* faire peur à.

spooky ['spuːkɪ] (comp **-ier**, superl **-iest**) **adj** *inf* qui donne la chair de poule.

spool [spuːl] ▪ **n** [gen & COMPUT] bobine *f*.
▪ **vi** faire un spooling.

spoon [spu:n] ■ **n** cuillère *f*, cuiller *f*.
■ **vt : to spoon sthg onto a plate** verser qqch dans une assiette avec une cuillère.

spoon-feed **vt** nourrir à la cuillère ▸ **to spoon-feed sb** *fig* mâcher le travail à qqn.

spoonful ['spu:nfʊl] (pl **-s** *OR* **spoonsful** ['spu:nsfʊl]) **n** cuillerée *f*.

sporadic [spə'rædɪk] **adj** sporadique.

sporadically [spə'rædɪklɪ] **adv** sporadiquement.

sport [spɔ:t] ■ **n 1.** [game] sport *m* **2.** *dated* [cheerful person] chic type *m*, chic fille *f*.
■ **vt** arborer, exhiber.
◆ ***sports*** **comp** de sport.

sporting ['spɔ:tɪŋ] **adj 1.** [relating to sport] sportif(ive) **2.** [generous, fair] chic *(inv)* ▸ **to have a sporting chance of doing sthg** avoir des chances de faire qqch.

sports car ['spɔ:ts-] **n** voiture *f* de sport.

sportscast ['spɔ:tskɑ:st] **n** *US* émission *f* sportive.

sports day **n** *UK* réunion *f* sportive scolaire.

sports jacket ['spɔ:ts-] **n** veste *f* sport.

sportsman ['spɔ:tsmən] (pl **-men** [-mən]) **n** sportif *m*.

sportsmanlike ['spɔ:tsmənlaɪk] **adj** sportif(ive).

sportsmanship ['spɔ:tsmənʃɪp] **n** sportivité *f*, esprit *m* sportif.

sports pages ['spɔ:ts-] **npl** pages *fpl* des sports.

sportsperson ['spɔ:ts,pɜ:sn] (pl **-people** [-,pi:pl]) **n** sportif *m*, sportive *f*.

sports personality ['spɔ:ts-] **n** personnalité *f* sportive.

sportswear ['spɔ:tsweəʳ] **n** *(U)* vêtements *mpl* de sport.

sportswoman ['spɔ:ts,wʊmən] (pl **-women** [-,wɪmɪn]) **n** sportive *f*.

sporty ['spɔ:tɪ] (comp **-ier**, superl **-iest**) **adj** *inf* **1.** [person] sportif(ive) **2.** [car, clothes] chic *(inv)*.

spot [spɒt] ■ **n 1.** [mark, dot] tache *f* ▸ **there isn't a spot on his reputation** sa réputation est sans tache **2.** *UK* [pimple] bouton *m* ▸ **to come out in spots** avoir une éruption de boutons **3.** [drop] goutte *f* **4.** *UK inf* [small amount] **: to have a spot of lunch** manger un morceau ▸ **to have a spot of bother** avoir quelques ennuis **5.** [place] endroit *m* ▸ **on the spot** sur place ▸ **to do sthg on the spot** faire qqch immédiatement *OR* sur-le-champ **6.** RADIO & TV numéro *m*
▸▸ **to have a soft spot for sb** avoir un faible pour qqn ▸ **to put sb on the spot** embarrasser qqn par des questions.
■ **vt** (pt & pp **-ted**, cont **-ting**) [notice] apercevoir ▸ **well spotted!** bien vu!

spot advertisement **n** spot *m* publicitaire.

spot buying **n** achats *mpl* au comptant.

spot check **n** contrôle *m* au hasard *OR* intermittent.

spotless ['spɒtlɪs] **adj** [clean] impeccable.

spotlessly ['spɒtlɪslɪ] **adv : spotlessly clean** reluisant de propreté, d'une propreté impeccable.

spotlight ['spɒtlaɪt] **n** [in theatre] projecteur *m*, spot *m* / [in home] spot *m* ▸ **to be in the spotlight** *fig* être en vedette.

spotlit [-lɪt] **adj** éclairé(e) par des projecteurs.

spot-on **adj** *UK inf* absolument exact(e) *OR* juste, dans le mille.

spot price **n** prix *m* comptant.

spotted ['spɒtɪd] **adj** [pattern, material] à pois.

spotty ['spɒtɪ] (comp **-ier**, superl **-iest**) **adj 1.** *UK* [skin] boutonneux(euse) **2.** *US* [patchy] irrégulier(ère).

spouse [spaʊs] **n** époux *m*, épouse *f*.

spout [spaʊt] ■ **n** bec *m*.
■ **vt** *pej* débiter.
■ **vi : to spout from** *OR* **out of** jaillir de.

sprain [spreɪn] ■ **n** entorse *f*.
■ **vt : to sprain one's ankle/wrist** se faire une entorse à la cheville/au poignet, se fouler la cheville/le poignet.

sprang [spræŋ] **pt** ➤ ***spring***.

sprat [spræt] **n** sprat *m*.

sprawl [sprɔ:l] ■ **n** *(U)* étendue *f*.
■ **vi 1.** [person] être affalé(e) **2.** [city] s'étaler.

sprawling ['sprɔ:lɪŋ] **adj** [city] tentaculaire.

spray [spreɪ] ■ **n 1.** *(U)* [of water] gouttelettes *fpl* / [from sea] embruns *mpl* **2.** [container] bombe *f*, pulvérisateur *m* **3.** [of flowers] gerbe *f*.
■ **vt** [product] pulvériser / [plants, crops] pulvériser de l'insecticide sur.
■ **vi : to spray over sb/sthg** asperger qqn/qqch.

spray can **n** bombe *f*.

spray-on **adj** en bombe, en aérosol ▸ **spray-on deodorant** déodorant *m* en bombe *OR* en spray.

spray paint **n** peinture *f* en bombe.

spread [spred] ■ **n 1.** [food] pâte *f* à tartiner ▸ **salmon spread** beurre *m* de saumon ▸ **chocolate spread** chocolat *m* à tartiner **2.** [of fire, disease] propagation *f* ▸ **they are trying to prevent the spread of unrest to other cities** ils essaient d'empêcher les troubles d'atteindre *OR* de gagner d'autres villes **3.** [of opinions] gamme *f* ▸ **the commission represented a broad spread of opinion** la commission représentait un large éventail d'opinions **4.** PRESS double page *f*.
■ **vt** (pt & pp **spread**) **1.** [map, rug] étaler, étendre / [fingers, arms, legs] écarter ▸ **it's time you spread your wings** il est temps que vous voliez de vos propres ailes **2.** [butter, jam] **: to spread sthg (on)** étaler qqch (sur) ▸ **he spread butter on a slice of toast** *OR* **a slice of toast with butter** il a tartiné de beurre une tranche de pain grillé **3.** [disease, rumour, germs] répandre, propager ▸ **the attack is at noon, spread the word!** l'attaque est pour midi, faites passer *OR* passez le mot! **4.** [over an area] répandre ▸ **the explosion had spread debris over a large area** l'explosion avait dispersé des débris sur une grande superficie ▸ **to spread o.s. too thinly** disperser ses efforts **5.** [in time] **: to be spread over** s'étaler sur ▸ **to spread (out) the losses over five years** répartir les pertes sur cinq ans **6.** [wealth, work] distribuer, répartir.

■ vi (pt & pp spread) **1.** [disease, rumour] se propager, se répandre ▸ **panic spread through the crowd** la panique a envahi *OR* gagné la foule ▸ **the cancer had spread through her whole body** le cancer s'était généralisé **2.** [water, cloud] s'étaler.
◆ ***spread out*** ■ vt sep **1.** [distribute] **: to be spread out** [people, houses] être dispersé(e) / [city, forest] être étendu(e) **2.** [map, rug] étaler, étendre **3.** [fingers, arms, legs] écarter.
■ vi se disperser ▸ **the search party had spread out through the woods** l'équipe de secours s'était déployée à travers les bois.

spread-eagled [-ˌi:gld] adj affalé(e).

spreadsheet ['spredʃi:t] n COMPUT tableur *m*.

spree [spri:] n **: to go on a spending *OR* shopping spree** faire des folies.

sprig [sprɪg] n brin *m*.

sprightly ['spraɪtlɪ] (comp -ier, superl -iest) adj alerte, fringant(e).

spring [sprɪŋ] ■ n **1.** [season] printemps *m* ▸ **in spring** au printemps **2.** [coil] ressort *m* **3.** [jump] saut *m*, bond *m* **4.** [water source] source *f* **5.** [resilience] élasticité *f* ▸ **the mattress has no spring left** le matelas n'a plus de ressort ▸ **he set out with a spring in his step** il est parti d'un pas alerte.
■ comp de printemps.
■ vt (pt sprang, pp sprung) **1.** [make known suddenly] **: to spring sthg on sb** annoncer qqch à qqn de but en blanc ▸ **to spring a surprise on sb** surprendre qqn **2.** [develop] **: to spring a leak** faire eau ▸ **the radiator has sprung a leak** il y a une fuite dans le radiateur **3.** *inf* [prisoner] faire sortir ▸ **the gang sprung him from prison with a helicopter** le gang l'a fait évader de prison en hélicoptère.
■ vi (pt sprang, pp sprung) **1.** [jump] sauter, bondir **2.** [move suddenly] **: to spring to one's feet** se lever d'un bond ▸ **to spring into action** passer à l'action ▸ **to spring to life** se mettre en marche ▸ **to spring shut/open** se fermer/s'ouvrir brusquement ▸ **the branch sprang back** la branche s'est redressée d'un coup ▸ **just say the first thing which springs to mind** dites simplement la première chose qui vous vient à l'esprit ▸ **where did you spring from?** *inf* d'où est-ce que tu sors? **3.** [originate] **: to spring from** provenir de ▸ **the problem springs from a misunderstanding** le problème provient *OR* vient d'un malentendu.
◆ ***spring up*** vi [problem] surgir, se présenter / [friendship] naître / [wind] se lever ▸ **new companies are springing up every day** de nouvelles entreprises apparaissent chaque jour.

springboard ['sprɪŋbɔ:d] n *lit* & *fig* tremplin *m*.

spring-clean ■ vt nettoyer de fond en comble.
■ vi faire le nettoyage de printemps.

spring-cleaning n nettoyage *m* de printemps.

spring onion n *UK* ciboule *f*.

spring roll n rouleau *m* de printemps.

spring tide n marée *f* de vive-eau.

springtime ['sprɪŋtaɪm] n **: in (the) springtime** au printemps.

springy ['sprɪŋɪ] (comp -ier, superl -iest) adj [carpet] moelleux(euse) / [mattress, rubber] élastique.

sprinkle ['sprɪŋkl] vt **: to sprinkle water over *OR* on sthg, to sprinkle sthg with water** asperger qqch d'eau ▸ **to sprinkle salt over *OR* on sthg, to sprinkle sthg with salt** saupoudrer qqch de sel.

sprinkler ['sprɪŋkləʳ] n [for water] arroseur *m*.

sprinkling ['sprɪŋklɪŋ] n [of water] quelques gouttes *fpl* / [of sand] couche *f* légère ▸ **a sprinkling of people** quelques personnes.

sprint [sprɪnt] ■ n sprint *m*.
■ vi sprinter.

sprinter ['sprɪntəʳ] n sprinter *m*.

sprite [spraɪt] n lutin *m*.

spritzer ['sprɪtsəʳ] n **: a white wine spritzer** du vin blanc additionné d'eau de Seltz.

sprocket ['sprɒkɪt] n pignon *m*.

sprout [spraʊt] ■ n **1.** [vegetable] **: (Brussels) sprouts** choux *mpl* de Bruxelles **2.** [shoot] pousse *f*.
■ vt [leaves] produire ▸ **to sprout shoots** germer.
■ vi **1.** [grow] pousser **2.** *fig* [buildings] **: to sprout (up)** surgir.

spruce [spru:s] ■ adj net (nette), pimpant(e).
■ n épicéa *m*.
◆ ***spruce up*** vt sep astiquer, briquer ▸ **to spruce o.s. up** se faire tout beau.

sprung [sprʌŋ] pp ➤ ***spring***.

spry [spraɪ] (comp -ier, superl -iest) adj vif (vive).

SPUC (abbr of ***Society for the Protection of the Unborn Child***) n *ligue contre l'avortement*.

spud [spʌd] n *inf* patate *f*.

spun [spʌn] pt & pp ➤ ***spin***.

spunk [spʌŋk] n *(U) inf* [courage] cran *m*.

spur [spɜ:ʳ] ■ n **1.** [incentive] incitation *f* **2.** [on rider's boot] éperon *m*.
■ vt (pt & pp -red, cont -ring) **1.** [encourage] **: to spur sb to do sthg** encourager *OR* inciter qqn à faire qqch **2.** [bring about] provoquer.
◆ ***on the spur of the moment*** adv sur un coup de tête, sous l'impulsion du moment.
◆ ***spur on*** vt sep encourager.

spurious ['spʊərɪəs] adj **1.** [affection, interest] feint(e) **2.** [argument, logic] faux (fausse).

spurn [spɜ:n] vt repousser.

spurt [spɜ:t] ■ n **1.** [gush] jaillissement *m* **2.** [of activity, energy] sursaut *m* **3.** [burst of speed] accélération *f* ▸ **to put on a spurt** sprinter.
■ vi **1.** [gush] **: to spurt (out of *OR* from)** jaillir (de) **2.** [run] foncer, sprinter.

sputter ['spʌtəʳ] vi [engine] tousser, bafouiller / [fire] crépiter.

spy [spaɪ] ■ n (pl spies) espion *m*.
■ vt (pt & pp spied) *inf* apercevoir.
■ vi (pt & pp spied) espionner, faire de l'espionnage ▸ **to spy on sb** espionner qqn.

spying ['spaɪɪŋ] n *(U)* espionnage *m*.

spy satellite n satellite *m* espion.

Sq.**, **sq. abbr of ***square***.

squabble ['skwɒbl] ■ **n** querelle *f*.
■ **vi : to squabble (about** *OR* **over)** se quereller (à propos de).

squad [skwɒd] **n 1.** [of police] brigade *f* **2.** MIL peloton *m* **3.** SPORT [group of players] équipe *f (parmi laquelle la sélection sera faite)*.

squad car **n** voiture *f* de police.

squadron ['skwɒdrən] **n** escadron *m*.

squadron leader **n** *UK* commandant *m*.

squalid ['skwɒlɪd] **adj** sordide, ignoble.

squall [skwɔːl] **n** [storm] bourrasque *f*.

squalor ['skwɒlər] **n** *(U)* conditions *fpl* sordides.

squander ['skwɒndər] **vt** gaspiller.

square [skweər] ■ **adj 1.** [in shape] carré(e) ▸ **one square metre** *UK* un mètre carré ▸ **three metres square** trois mètres sur trois **2.** [at right angles] à angle droit ▸ **the shelves aren't square** les étagères ne sont pas droites **3.** [even, equal] **: we're all square** [in money] nous sommes quittes ▸ **they were (all) square at two games each** SPORT ils étaient à égalité deux parties chacun **4.** *inf* [unfashionable] vieux jeu *(inv)*.
■ **n 1.** [shape & MATHS] carré *m* ▸ **a square of chocolate** un carré *OR* morceau de chocolat **2.** [in town] place *f* **3.** *inf* [unfashionable person] **: he's a square** il est vieux jeu
▸▸ **to be back to square one** se retrouver au point de départ.
■ **adv 1.** [at right angles] **: she set the box square with** *OR* **to the edge of the paper** elle a aligné la boîte sur les bords de la feuille de papier **2.** [directly] **: he hit the ball square in the middle of the racket** il frappa la balle avec le milieu de sa raquette.
■ **vt 1.** MATHS élever au carré ▸ **three squared is nine** trois au carré égale neuf **2.** [reconcile] accorder ▸ **I couldn't square the story with the image I had of him** je n'arrivais pas à faire coïncider cette histoire avec l'image que j'avais de lui **3.** SPORT **: his goal squared the match** son but a mis les équipes à égalité **4.** *inf* [arrange] arranger ▸ **can you square it with the committee?** pourriez-vous arranger cela avec le comité?
◆ ***square up*** **vi 1.** [settle up] **: to square up with sb** régler ses comptes avec qqn **2.** [for fight] **: to square up to sb** se mettre en posture de combat face à qqn ▸ **to square up to a problem** faire face à un problème.

square bracket **n** TYPO crochet *m* ▸ **in square brackets** entre crochets.

squared ['skweəd] **adj** quadrillé(e).

square dance **n** quadrille *m*.

square deal **n** arrangement *m* équitable.

squarely ['skweəlɪ] **adv 1.** [directly] carrément **2.** [honestly] honnêtement.

square meal **n** bon repas *m*.

Square Mile **n** *inf la City de Londres, dont la superficie fait environ un mile carré.*

square root **n** racine *f* carrée.

squash [skwɒʃ] ■ **n 1.** SPORT squash *m* **2.** *UK* [drink] **: orange squash** orangeade *f* **3.** [vegetable] courge *f*.
■ **vt** écraser.

squat [skwɒt] ■ **adj** (comp **-ter**, superl **-test**) courtaud(e), ramassé(e).
■ **n** [building] squat *m*.
■ **vi** (pt & pp **-ted**, cont **-ting**) **1.** [crouch] **: to squat (down)** s'accroupir **2.** [in building] squatter.

squatter ['skwɒtər] **n** squatter *m*.

squawk [skwɔːk] ■ **n** cri *m* strident *OR* perçant.
■ **vi** pousser un cri strident *OR* perçant.

squeak [skwiːk] ■ **n 1.** [of animal] petit cri *m* aigu **2.** [of door, hinge] grincement *m*.
■ **vi 1.** [mouse] pousser un petit cri aigu **2.** [door, hinge] grincer.

squeaky ['skwiːkɪ] (comp **-ier**, superl **-iest**) **adj** [voice, door] grinçant(e) / [shoes] qui craquent.

squeaky clean **adj** *inf* **1.** [hands, hair] extrêmement propre **2.** [reputation] sans tache.

squeal [skwiːl] ■ **n 1.** [of person, animal] cri *m* aigu **2.** [of brakes] grincement *m* / [of tyres] crissement *m*.
■ **vi 1.** [person, animal] pousser un cri aigu **2.** [brakes] grincer / [tyres] crisser.

squeamish ['skwiːmɪʃ] **adj** facilement dégoûté(e).

squeeze [skwiːz] ■ **n 1.** [pressure] pression *f* ▸ **he gave my hand a reassuring squeeze** il a serré ma main pour me rassurer ▸ **to put the squeeze on sb** *inf* faire pression sur qqn **2.** [amount - of liquid, paste] quelques gouttes *fpl* ▸ **a squeeze of toothpaste** un peu de dentifrice **3.** *inf* [squash] **: it was a squeeze** on était serrés comme des sardines.
■ **vt 1.** [press firmly] presser ▸ **I squeezed as hard as I could** j'ai serré aussi fort que j'ai pu **2.** [liquid, toothpaste] exprimer ▸ **a glass of freshly squeezed orange juice** une orange pressée ▸ **to squeeze the air out of** *OR* **from sthg** faire sortir l'air de qqch en appuyant dessus ▸ **to squeeze information out of sb** soutirer *OR* arracher des informations à qqn ▸ **you won't squeeze another penny out of me!** tu n'auras pas un sou de plus! **3.** [cram] **: she squeezed the ring onto her finger** elle enfila la bague avec difficulté ▸ **to squeeze sthg into sthg** entasser qqch dans qqch **4.** [constrain - profits, budget] réduire / [- taxpayer, workers] pressurer ▸ **universities are being squeezed by the cuts** les réductions (de budget) mettent les universités en difficulté.
■ **vi : to squeeze into/under** se glisser dans/sous ▸ **the lorry managed to squeeze between the posts** le camion a réussi à passer de justesse entre les poteaux.

squeezebox ['skwiːzbɒks] **n** *UK* accordéon *m*.

squeezer ['skwiːzər] **n : orange/lemon squeezer** presse-citron *m inv*.

squelch [skweltʃ] **vi : to squelch through mud** patauger dans la boue.

squib [skwɪb] **n** [firework] pétard *m* ▸ **it was a damp squib** *UK* ça a été une déception.

squid [skwɪd] (pl **squid** *OR* **-s**) **n** calmar *m*.

squidgy ['skwɪdʒɪ] (comp **-ier**, superl **-iest**) **adj** *UK inf* mou *(before vowel or silent 'h'* **mol***)* (molle), spongieux(euse).

squiffy ['skwɪfɪ] (comp -ier, superl -iest) adj *UK inf dated* pompette.

squiggle ['skwɪgl] n gribouillis *m*.

squiggly ['skwɪglɪ] adj *inf* pas droit(e), ondulé(e).

squint [skwɪnt] ■ n **: to have a squint** loucher, être atteint(e) de strabisme.
■ vi **: to squint at sthg** regarder qqch en plissant les yeux.

squire ['skwaɪəʳ] n [landowner] propriétaire *m*.

squirm [skwɜ:m] vi **1.** [wriggle] se tortiller **2.** *fig* [wince] avoir des haut-le-cœur ▸ **to squirm with embarrassment** ne plus savoir où se mettre.

squirrel [*UK* 'skwɪrəl, *US* 'skwɜ:rəl] n écureuil *m*.

squirt [skwɜ:t] ■ vt [water, oil] faire jaillir, faire gicler ▸ **to squirt sb/sthg with sthg** asperger qqn/qqch de qqch.
■ vi **: to squirt (out of)** jaillir (de), gicler (de).

squishy ['skwɪʃɪ] (comp -ier, superl -iest) adj *inf* [fruit, wax] mou *(before vowel or silent 'h'* **mol***)* (molle) / [chocolate] ramolli(e) / [ground] boueux(euse) ▸ **a squishy blob of dough** un petit tas de pâte molle.

Sr abbr of ***senior***, ***sister***.

SRC n **1.** (abbr of ***Students' Representative Council***) *comité étudiant* **2.** (abbr of ***Science Research Council***) *conseil britannique de la recherche scientifique*.

Sri Lanka [ˌsri:'læŋkə] n Sri Lanka *m* ▸ **in Sri Lanka** au Sri Lanka.

Sri Lankan [ˌsri:'læŋkn] ■ adj sri lankais(e).
■ n [person] Sri Lankais *m*, -e *f*.

SRN (abbr of ***State Registered Nurse***) n *en Grande-Bretagne, infirmier ou infirmière diplômé(e) d'État*.

SS (abbr of ***steamship***) SS.

SSA (abbr of ***Social Security Administration***) n *sécurité sociale américaine*.

ssh [ʃ] excl chut!

SSSI (abbr of ***Site of Special Scientific Interest***) n *en Grande-Bretagne, site déclaré d'intérêt scientifique*.

St **1.** (abbr of ***saint***) St, Ste **2.** abbr of ***Street***.

ST (abbr of ***Standard Time***) n *heure légale*.

stab [stæb] ■ n **1.** [with knife] coup *m* de couteau **2.** *inf* [attempt] **: to have a stab (at sthg)** essayer (qqch), tenter (qqch) **3.** [twinge] **: stab of pain** élancement *m* ▸ **stab of guilt** remords *m*.
■ vt (pt & pp -bed, cont -bing) **1.** [person] poignarder ▸ **to stab sb to death** tuer qqn d'un coup/à coups de poignard **2.** [food] piquer.
■ vi (pt & pp -bed, cont -bing) **: to stab at sthg** frapper qqch.

stabbing ['stæbɪŋ] ■ adj [pain] lancinant(e).
■ n agression *f* à coups de couteau.

stability [stə'bɪlətɪ] n stabilité *f*.

stabilize, *UK* ***-ise*** ['steɪbəlaɪz] ■ vt stabiliser.
■ vi se stabiliser.

stabilizer, *UK* ***-iser*** ['steɪbəlaɪzəʳ] n stabilisateur *m*.

stable ['steɪbl] ■ adj stable.
■ n écurie *f*.

stable lad n *UK* garçon *m* d'écurie.

staccato [stə'kɑ:təʊ] adj [note] piqué(e) / [sound, voice] saccadé(e).

stack [stæk] ■ n **1.** [pile] pile *f* **2.** *inf* [large amount] **: stacks** *OR* **a stack of** des tas de, un tas de.
■ vt **1.** [pile up] empiler **2.** [fill] **: to be stacked with** être encombré de.
◆ ***stack up*** vi *US inf* être à la hauteur.

stadium ['steɪdjəm] (pl -diums *OR* -dia [-djə]) n stade *m*.

staff [stɑ:f] ■ n [employees] personnel *m* / [of school] personnel enseignant, professeurs *mpl*.
■ vt pourvoir en personnel.

staffer ['stɑ:fəʳ] n PRESS rédacteur *m*, -trice *f*.

staffing ['stɑ:fɪŋ] n dotation *f* en personnel ▸ **staffing levels** les besoins *mpl* en personnel.

staff nurse n *UK* infirmier *m*, -ère *f*.

staff room n *UK* salle *f* des professeurs.

Staffs [stæfs] (abbr of ***Staffordshire***) *comté anglais*.

stag [stæg] (pl stag *OR* -s) n cerf *m*.

stage [steɪdʒ] ■ n **1.** [phase] étape *f*, phase *f*, stade *m* ▸ **by** *OR* **in stages** par paliers ▸ **the changes were instituted in stages** les changements ont été introduits progressivement ▸ **to do sthg stage by stage** faire qqch par étapes *OR* progressivement
2. [platform] scène *f* ▸ **stage right/left** côté jardin/cour ▸ **on stage** sur scène ▸ **to go on stage** monter sur (la) scène ▸ **to set the stage for sthg** préparer la voie à qqch
3. [acting profession] **: the stage** le théâtre.
■ vt **1.** THEAT monter, mettre en scène ▸ **it's the first time the play has been staged** c'est la première fois qu'on monte cette pièce
2. [organize] organiser ▸ **to stage a hijacking** détourner un avion ▸ **the handshake was staged for the TV cameras** la poignée de main était une mise en scène destinée aux caméras de télévision
3. [fake - accident] monter, manigancer ▸ **the murder was staged to look like a suicide** le meurtre a été maquillé en suicide.

FALSE FRIENDS / FAUX AMIS

stage

Stage n'est pas la traduction du mot anglais *stage*. Stage se traduit par *work placement*.
▸ J'ai fait un stage dans cette entreprise pendant mes études / *I did a work placement at that company while I was a student*

stagecoach ['steɪdʒkəʊtʃ] n diligence *f*.

stage designer n décorateur *m* de théâtre.

stage direction n indication *f* scénique.

stage door n entrée *f* des artistes.

stage fright n trac *m*.

stagehand ['steɪdʒhænd] n machiniste *m*.

stage-manage vt *lit* & *fig* mettre en scène.

stage manager n THEAT régisseur *m*.

stage name n nom *m* de scène.

stage set **n** THEAT décor *m*.

stagflation [stæg'fleɪʃn] **n** stagflation *f*.

stagger ['stægəʳ] ■ **vt 1.** [astound] stupéfier **2.** [working hours] échelonner / [holidays] étaler.
■ **vi** tituber.

staggering ['stægərɪŋ] **adj** stupéfiant(e).

staging ['steɪdʒɪŋ] **n** mise *f* en scène.

stagnant ['stægnənt] **adj** stagnant(e).

stagnate [stæg'neɪt] **vi** stagner.

stagnation [stæg'neɪʃn] **n** stagnation *f*.

stag night, stag party **n** [gen] soirée *f* entre hommes / [before wedding day] **: we're having** *OR* **holding a stag night for Bob** nous enterrons la vie de garçon de Bob.

staid [steɪd] **adj** guindé(e), collet monté.

stain [steɪn] ■ **n** [mark] tache *f*.
■ **vt** [discolour] tacher.

stained [steɪnd] **adj 1.** [marked] taché(e) **2.** [coloured] coloré(e).

-stained **suffix** taché ▸ **his sweat-stained shirt** sa chemise tachée de transpiration ▸ **nicotine-stained** jauni par la nicotine.

stained glass [ˌsteɪnd-] **n** *(U)* [windows] vitraux *mpl*.

stainless steel ['steɪnlɪs-] **n** acier *m* inoxydable, Inox® *m*.

stain remover [-ˌrɪmuːvəʳ] **n** détachant *m*.

stair [steəʳ] **n** marche *f*.
◆ ***stairs*** **npl** escalier *m*.

staircase ['steəkeɪs] **n** escalier *m*.

stairway ['steəweɪ] **n** escalier *m*.

stairwell ['steəwel] **n** cage *f* d'escalier.

stake [steɪk] ■ **n 1.** [share] **: to have a stake in sthg** avoir des intérêts dans qqch ▸ **we all have a stake in the education of the young** l'éducation des jeunes nous concerne tous **2.** [wooden post] poteau *m* ▸ **to die** *OR* **to be burned at the stake** mourir sur le bûcher **3.** [in gambling] enjeu *m* ▸ **to play for high stakes** jouer gros jeu ▸ **to lose one's stake** perdre sa mise.
■ **vt : to stake money (on** *OR* **upon)** jouer *OR* miser de l'argent (sur) ▸ **he had staked everything on getting the job** il avait tout misé sur l'acceptation de sa candidature ▸ **to stake one's reputation (on)** jouer *OR* risquer sa réputation (sur) ▸ **to stake a claim to sthg** revendiquer qqch.
◆ ***stakes*** **npl** enjeux *mpl* ▸ **the promotion stakes** *fig* la course à l'avancement.
◆ ***at stake*** **adv** en jeu ▸ **she has a lot at stake** elle joue gros jeu, elle risque gros.

stakeholder pension ['steɪkhəʊldəʳ] **n** *UK plan de retraite à coût réduit conçu pour les travailleurs indépendants ou à temps partiel.*

stakeout ['steɪkaʊt] **n** *esp US* surveillance *f*.

stalactite ['stæləktaɪt] **n** stalactite *f*.

stalagmite ['stæləgmaɪt] **n** stalagmite *f*.

stale [steɪl] **adj 1.** [food, water] pas frais (fraîche) / [bread] rassis(e) / [air] qui sent le renfermé **2.** [person] qui manque d'entrain.

stalemate ['steɪlmeɪt] **n 1.** [deadlock] impasse *f* **2.** CHESS pat *m*.

staleness ['steɪlnɪs] **n** [of food] manque *m* de fraîcheur.

stalk [stɔːk] ■ **n 1.** [of flower, plant] tige *f* **2.** [of leaf, fruit] queue *f*.
■ **vt** [hunt] traquer.
■ **vi : to stalk in/out** entrer/sortir d'un air hautain.

stalker ['stɔːkəʳ] **n** *criminel suivant sa victime à la trace.*

stall [stɔːl] ■ **n 1.** [in street, market] éventaire *m*, étal *m* / [at exhibition] stand *m* **2.** [in stable] stalle *f*.
■ **vt 1.** AUT caler **2.** [delay - person] faire patienter.
■ **vi 1.** AUT caler **2.** [delay] essayer de gagner du temps.
◆ ***stalls*** **npl** *UK* [in cinema, theatre] orchestre *m*.

stallholder ['stɔːlˌhəʊldəʳ] **n** *UK* marchand *m* qui possède un éventaire.

stalling ['stɔːlɪŋ] ■ **n** *(U)* atermoiements *mpl*, manœuvres *fpl* dilatoires.
■ **adj : stalling tactic** manœuvre *f* dilatoire.

stallion ['stæljən] **n** étalon *m*.

stalwart ['stɔːlwət] ■ **adj** [loyal] fidèle.
■ **n** pilier *m*.

stamen ['steɪmən] **n** étamine *f*.

stamina ['stæmɪnə] **n** *(U)* résistance *f*.

stammer ['stæməʳ] ■ **n** bégaiement *m*.
■ **vi** bégayer.

stammering ['stæmərɪŋ] **n** [through fear, excitement] bégaiement *m*, balbutiement *m* / [speech defect] bégaiement *m*.

stamp [stæmp] ■ **n 1.** [for letter] timbre *m* **2.** [tool] tampon *m* ▸ **he has an Israeli stamp in his passport** il a un tampon de la douane israélienne sur son passeport ▸ **stamp of approval** *fig* approbation *f*,, aval *m* **3.** *fig* [of authority] marque *f* ▸ **his story had the stamp of authenticity** son histoire semblait authentique **4.** [noise - of boots] bruit *m* (de bottes) / [- of audience] trépignement *m*.
■ **vt 1.** [mark by stamping] tamponner ▸ **incoming mail is stamped with the date received** le courrier qui arrive est tamponné à la date de réception ▸ **the machine stamps the time on your ticket** la machine marque *OR* poinçonne l'heure sur votre ticket **2.** [stomp] **: to stamp one's foot** taper du pied ▸ **he stamped the snow off his boots** il a tapé du pied pour enlever la neige de ses bottes **3.** [envelope, postcard] timbrer, affranchir.
■ **vi 1.** [stomp] taper du pied **2.** [tread heavily] **: he stamped up the stairs** il monta l'escalier d'un pas lourd ▸ **to stamp on sthg** marcher sur qqch.
◆ ***stamp out*** **vt sep** [fire] éteindre en piétinant / [opposition] éliminer / [corruption, crime] supprimer / [disease] éradiquer.

stamp album **n** album *m* de timbres.

stamp-collecting [-kəˌlektɪŋ] **n** philatélie *f*.

stamp collector **n** collectionneur *m*, -euse *f* de timbres, philatéliste *mf*.

stamp duty **n** *UK* droit *m* de timbre.

stamped addressed envelope ['stæmptəˌdrest-] **n** enveloppe *f* affranchie pour la réponse.

stampede [stæm'piːd] ■ **n** débandade *f*.
■ **vi** s'enfuir à la débandade.

stamp machine n distributeur *m* de timbres-poste.

stance [stæns] n *lit* & *fig* position *f*.

stand [stænd] ■ **n 1.** [stall] stand *m* / [selling newspapers] kiosque *m*
2. [frame, support - gen] support *m* / [- on bicycle, motorbike] béquille *f* / [COMM - for magazines, sunglasses] présentoir *m* ▸ **umbrella stand** porte-parapluies *m inv* ▸ **hat stand** porte-chapeaux *m inv*
3. SPORT tribune *f*
4. MIL résistance *f* ▸ **to make a stand** résister
5. [public position] position *f* ▸ **to take a stand on sthg** prendre position sur qqch
6. *US* LAW barre *f* ▸ **to take the stand** comparaître à la barre
7. [for taxis] **: (taxi) stand** station *f* de taxis.
■ **vt** (pt & pp **stood**) **1.** [place] mettre (debout), poser (debout) ▸ **to stand sthg on (its) end** faire tenir qqch debout
2. [withstand, tolerate] supporter ▸ **I can't stand it any longer!** je n'en peux plus! ▸ **I can't stand (the sight of) him!** je ne peux pas le supporter! ▸ **she's not strong enough to stand another operation** elle n'est pas assez forte pour supporter une nouvelle opération ▸ **it will stand high temperatures without cracking** cela peut résister à *OR* supporter des températures élevées sans se fissurer
3. [treat] **: to stand sb a meal/a drink** payer à déjeuner/à boire à qqn
4. LAW **: to stand trial** comparaître en jugement
5. [be likely] **: to stand to do sthg** risquer de faire qqch ▸ **they stand to make a huge profit on the deal** ils ont des chances de faire un bénéfice énorme dans cette affaire ▸ **you don't stand a chance!** vous n'avez pas la moindre chance!
■ **vi** (pt & pp **stood**) **1.** [be upright - person] être *OR* se tenir debout / [- object] se trouver / [- building] se dresser ▸ **I had to stand all the way** j'ai dû voyager debout pendant tout le trajet ▸ **don't just stand there, do something!** ne restez pas là à ne rien faire! ▸ **excuse me, you're standing on my foot** excusez-moi, vous me marchez sur le pied ▸ **stand still!** ne bouge pas!, reste tranquille! ▸ **to stand in line** *US* faire la queue ▸ **the building stands ten storeys high** l'immeuble compte dix étages
2. [stand up] se lever
3. [remain] reposer / [be left undisturbed - dough] reposer / [- tea] infuser ▸ **the machines stood idle** les machines étaient arrêtées ▸ **time stood still** le temps semblait s'être arrêté
4. [offer] tenir toujours / [decision] demeurer valable ▸ **the verdict stands unless there's an appeal** le jugement reste valable à moins que l'on ne fasse appel
5. [be in particular state] **: I'd like to know where I stand with you** j'aimerais savoir où en sont les choses entre nous ▸ **as things stand...** vu l'état actuel des choses... ▸ **unemployment/production stands at...** le nombre de chômeurs/la production est de... ▸ **he stands accused of rape** il est accusé de viol
6. [have opinion] **: where do you stand on...?** quelle est votre position sur...?
7. *UK* POL se présenter ▸ **will he stand for re-election?** va-t-il se représenter aux élections?
8. *US* [park car] se garer *(pour un court instant)* ▸ **'no standing'** 'stationnement interdit'.
◆ ***stand aside*** vi s'écarter ▸ **to stand aside in favour of sb** [gen] laisser la voie libre à qqn / POL se désister en faveur de qqn.
◆ ***stand back*** vi reculer ▸ **the painting is better if you stand back from it** le tableau est mieux si vous prenez du recul.
◆ ***stand by*** ■ **vt insep 1.** [person] soutenir
2. [statement, decision] s'en tenir à.
■ **vi 1.** [be ready - person] être *OR* se tenir prêt / [- army] être en état d'alerte ▸ **to stand by (for sthg/to do sthg)** être prêt(e) (pour qqch/pour faire qqch) ▸ **the police were standing by to disperse the crowd** la police se tenait prête à disperser la foule
2. [remain inactive] rester là.
◆ ***stand down*** vi *UK* [resign] démissionner.
◆ ***stand for*** vt insep **1.** [signify] représenter ▸ **I detest everything that they stand for!** je déteste tout ce qu'ils représentent! ▸ **the R stands for Ryan** le R signifie Ryan
2. [tolerate] supporter, tolérer ▸ **I'm not going to stand for it!** je ne le tolérerai *OR* permettrai pas!
◆ ***stand in*** vi **: to stand in for sb** remplacer qqn.
◆ ***stand out*** vi ressortir ▸ **the pink stands out against the green background** le rose ressort *OR* se détache sur le fond vert ▸ **this one book stands out from all his others** ce livre-ci surclasse tous les autres livres qu'il a écrits.
◆ ***stand up*** ■ **vt sep** *inf* [boyfriend, girlfriend] poser un lapin à.
■ **vi 1.** [rise from seat] se lever ▸ **stand up!** debout!
2. [claim, evidence] être accepté(e) ▸ **his evidence won't stand up in court** son témoignage ne sera pas valable en justice.
◆ ***stand up for*** vt insep défendre.
◆ ***stand up to*** vt insep **1.** [weather, heat] résister à
2. [person, boss] tenir tête à.

stand-alone adj COMPUT [system] autonome.

standard ['stændəd] ■ **adj 1.** [normal - gen] normal(e) / [- size] standard *(inv)* ▸ **catalytic converters are now standard features** les pots catalytiques sont désormais la norme ▸ **it was just a standard hotel room** c'était une chambre d'hôtel ordinaire **2.** [accepted] correct(e) ▸ **there's a standard procedure for reporting accidents** il y a une procédure bien établie pour signaler les accidents **3.** [basic] de base ▸ **the standard works in English poetry** les ouvrages classiques de la poésie anglaise.
■ **n 1.** [level] niveau *m* ▸ **their salaries are low by European standards** leurs salaires sont bas par rapport aux salaires européens ▸ **most of the goods are** *OR* **come up to standard** la plupart des marchandises sont de qualité satisfaisante ▸ **he sets high standards for himself** il est très exigeant avec lui-même **2.** [point of reference] critère *m* / TECH norme *f* ▸ **high safety standards** des règles de sécurité très strictes ▸ **to have high moral standards** avoir de grands principes moraux **3.** [established item] standard *m* / [tune] standard *m* ▸ **a jazz standard** un classique du jazz **4.** [flag] étendard *m*.
◆ ***standards*** npl [principles] valeurs *fpl*.

standard-bearer n *fig* porte-drapeau *m*.

standardization, *UK* ***-isation*** [ˌstændədaɪ'zeɪʃn] n **1.** [gen] standardisation *f* / [of dimensions, terms] normalisation *f* **2.** TECH [verification] étalonnage *m*.

standardize, *UK* ***-ise*** ['stændədaɪz] vt standardiser.

standard lamp n *UK* lampadaire *m*.

standard of living (pl **standards of living**) n niveau *m* de vie.

standard time n heure *f* légale.

standby ['stændbaɪ] ■ n (pl **-s**) [person] remplaçant *m*, -e *f* ▸ **on standby** prêt à intervenir.
■ comp [ticket, flight] stand-by *(inv)*.

stand-in n remplaçant *m*, -e *f*.

standing ['stændɪŋ] ■ adj [invitation, army] permanent(e) / [joke] continuel(elle) ▸ **it's a standing joke with us** c'est une vieille plaisanterie entre nous.
■ n **1.** [reputation] importance *f*, réputation *f* ▸ **people of lower/higher social standing** des gens d'une position sociale moins/plus élevée ▸ **they are a family of some standing in the community** c'est une famille qui jouit d'une certaine position dans la communauté / [ranking & SPORT] classement *m* ▸ **what's their standing in the league table?** quel est leur classement dans le championnat? **2.** [duration] : **of long standing** de longue date ▸ **we're friends of 20 years' standing** nous sommes amis depuis 20 ans.

standing charges n [on bill] frais *mpl* d'abonnement.

standing committee n comité *m* permanent.

standing order n *UK* prélèvement *m* automatique.

standing ovation n : **to give sb a standing ovation** se lever pour applaudir qqn.

standing room n *(U)* places *fpl* debout.

standoff ['stændɒf] n **1.** POL [inconclusive clash] affrontement *m* indécis / [deadlock] impasse *f* ▸ **their debate ended in a standoff** leur débat n'a rien donné **2.** *US* SPORT [tie] match *m* nul.

standoffish [ˌstænd'ɒfɪʃ] adj distant(e).

standpipe ['stændpaɪp] n colonne *f* d'alimentation.

standpoint ['stændpɔɪnt] n point *m* de vue.

standstill ['stændstɪl] n : **at a standstill** [traffic, train] à l'arrêt / [negotiations, work] paralysé(e) ▸ **to come to a standstill** [traffic, train] s'immobiliser / [negotiations, work] cesser.

stand-up adj [collar] droit(e) / [meal] (pris(e)) debout ▸ **a stand-up fight** [physical] une bagarre en règle / [verbal] une discussion violente
▸▸ **stand-up comic** *OR* **comedian** comique *mf (qui se produit seul en scène)* ▸ **stand-up counter** *OR* **diner** *US* buvette *f*.

stank [stæŋk] pt ➤ ***stink***.

stanza ['stænzə] n strophe *f*.

staple ['steɪpl] ■ adj [principal] principal(e), de base.
■ n **1.** [for paper] agrafe *f* **2.** [principal commodity] produit *m* de base.
■ vt agrafer.

staple diet n nourriture *f* de base.

staple gun n agrafeuse *f* (professionnelle).

stapler ['steɪpləʳ] n agrafeuse *f*.

star [stɑːʳ] ■ n **1.** [gen] étoile *f* ▸ **to sleep (out) under the stars** dormir *OR* coucher à la belle étoile ▸ **to have stars in one's eyes** être sur un petit nuage ▸ **his star is rising** son étoile brille chaque jour davantage ▸ **to see stars** voir trente-six chandelles
2. [celebrity] vedette *f*, star *f*
3. [asterisk] astérisque *m*.
■ comp [quality] de star ▸ **star performer** vedette *f* ▸ **to give sb star billing** mettre qqn en tête d'affiche ▸ **the hotel gives all its clients star treatment** cet hôtel offre à sa clientèle un service de première classe.
■ vt (pt & pp **-red**, cont **-ring**) CIN & THEAT avoir pour vedette ▸ **the play starred David Caffrey** la pièce avait pour vedette David Caffrey.
■ vi (pt & pp **-red**, cont **-ring**) : **to star (in)** être la vedette (de) ▸ **who starred with Redford in "The Sting"?** qui jouait avec Redford dans "l'Arnaque"?
◆ ***stars*** npl horoscope *m*.

star attraction n attraction *f* principale, clou *m*.

starboard ['stɑːbəd] ■ adj de tribord.
■ n : **to starboard** à tribord.

starch [stɑːtʃ] n amidon *m*.

starched [stɑːtʃt] adj amidonné(e).

starchy ['stɑːtʃɪ] (comp **-ier**, superl **-iest**) adj [food] féculent(e).

stardom ['stɑːdəm] n *(U)* célébrité *f*.

stare [steəʳ] ■ n regard *m* fixe.
■ vi : **to stare at sb/sthg** fixer qqn/qqch du regard.

starfish ['stɑːfɪʃ] (pl **starfish** *OR* **-es** [-iːz]) n étoile *f* de mer.

staring ['steərɪŋ] ■ adj [bystanders] curieux(euse) ▸ **with staring eyes** [fixedly] aux yeux fixes / [wide-open] aux yeux écarquillés / [blank] aux yeux vides.

stark [stɑːk] ■ adj **1.** [room, decoration] austère / [landscape] désolé(e) **2.** [reality, fact] à l'état brut / [contrast] dur(e).
■ adv : **stark naked** tout nu (toute nue), à poil.

starkly ['stɑːklɪ] adv [describe] crûment / [tell] carrément, sans ambages / [stand out] nettement.

starlight ['stɑːlaɪt] n lumière *f* des étoiles.

starling ['stɑːlɪŋ] n étourneau *m*.

starlit ['stɑːlɪt] adj [night] étoilé(e) / [countryside] illuminé(e) par les étoiles.

starry ['stɑːrɪ] (comp **-ier**, superl **-iest**) adj étoilé(e).

starry-eyed [-'aɪd] adj innocent(e).

Stars and Stripes n : **the Stars and Stripes** le drapeau des États-Unis, la bannière étoilée.

star sign n signe *m* du zodiaque.

star-studded adj avec de nombreuses vedettes.

start [stɑːt] ■ n **1.** [beginning] début *m* ▸ **to make a good/bad start** bien/mal commencer ▸ **my new boss and I didn't get off to a very good start** au début, mes rapports avec mon nouveau patron n'ont pas été des meilleurs ▸ **a second honeymoon will give us a fresh start** une deuxième lune de miel nous fera repartir d'un bon pied ▸ **I laughed from start to finish** j'ai ri du début à la fin ▸ **for a start** pour commencer, d'abord
2. [jump] sursaut *m* ▸ **she woke up with a start** elle s'est réveillée en sursaut

3. [starting place] départ *m* ▸ **to make** OR **to get an early start** [on journey] partir de bonne heure ▸ **to get a good start in life** prendre un bon départ dans la vie OR l'existence
4. [time advantage] avance *f* ▸ **he gave him 20 metres' start** OR **a 20-metre start** il lui a accordé une avance de 20 mètres.
■ **vt 1.** [begin] commencer ▸ **to start doing** OR **to do sthg** commencer à faire qqch ▸ **he started work at sixteen** il a commencé à travailler à seize ans ▸ **to get started : I got started on the dishes** je me suis mis à la vaisselle
2. [initiate, instigate - reaction, revolution, process] déclencher / [- fashion] lancer / [- rumour] faire naître ▸ **which side started the war?** quel camp a déclenché la guerre? ▸ **the fire was started by arsonists** l'incendie a été allumé par des pyromanes
3. [turn on - machine] mettre en marche / [- engine, vehicle] démarrer, mettre en marche ▸ **I couldn't get the car started** je n'ai pas réussi à faire démarrer la voiture
4. [set up - business, band] créer ▸ **to start a family** fonder un foyer.
■ **vi 1.** [begin] commencer, débuter ▸ **I didn't know where to start** je ne savais pas par quel bout commencer ▸ **she started in personnel/as an assistant** elle a débuté au service du personnel/comme assistante ▸ **to start again** OR **afresh** recommencer ▸ **starting (from) next week** à partir de la semaine prochaine ▸ **to start with** pour commencer, d'abord ▸ **I'll have the soup to start (with)** pour commencer, je prendrai du potage ▸ **houses here start at $100,000** ici, le prix des maisons démarre à 100 000 dollars
2. [function - machine] se mettre en marche / [- car] démarrer
3. [begin journey] partir ▸ **the tour starts at** OR **from the town hall** la visite part de la mairie
4. [jump] sursauter
5. *inf* [be annoying] **: don't (you) start!** ne commence pas, toi!

◆ ***start off*** ■ **vt sep** [meeting] ouvrir, commencer / [rumour] faire naître / [discussion] entamer, commencer ▸ **if you mention it, it'll only start her off again** n'en parle pas, sinon elle va recommencer.
■ **vi 1.** [begin] commencer / [begin job] débuter ▸ **it starts off with a description of the town** ça commence par une description de la ville
2. [leave on journey] partir.

◆ ***start on*** **vt insep** entamer.

◆ ***start out*** **vi 1.** [in job] débuter ▸ **he started out in business with his wife's money** il s'est lancé dans les affaires avec l'argent de sa femme
2. [leave on journey] partir.

◆ ***start up*** ■ **vt sep 1.** [business] créer / [shop] ouvrir
2. [car, engine] mettre en marche.
■ **vi 1.** [begin] commencer
2. [machine] se mettre en route / [car, engine] démarrer.

starter ['stɑːtər] **n 1.** *UK* [of meal] hors-d'œuvre *m inv* **2.** AUT démarreur *m* **3.** starter *m*.

starter motor **n** démarreur *m*.

starter pack **n** [information] *informations de base nécessaires pour commencer une activité* / [equipment] kit *m* de base.

starting block ['stɑːtɪŋ-] **n** starting-block *m*, bloc *m* de départ.

starting point ['stɑːtɪŋ-] **n** point *m* de départ.

starting price ['stɑːtɪŋ-] **n** cote *f* de départ.

starting salary ['stɑːtɪŋ-] **n** salaire *m* OR rémunération *f* de départ.

startle ['stɑːtl] **vt** faire sursauter.

startled ['stɑːtld] **adj** [person] étonné(e) / [expression, shout, glance] de surprise / [animal] effarouché(e).

startling ['stɑːtlɪŋ] **adj** surprenant(e).

start-up **n** *(U)* **1.** [launch] création *f* (d'entreprise) ▸ **start-up costs** frais *mpl* de création d'une entreprise **2.** [new company] start-up *f*, jeune pousse *f*.

starvation [stɑː'veɪʃn] **n** faim *f*.

starve [stɑːv] ■ **vt 1.** [deprive of food] affamer **2.** *fig* [deprive] **: to starve sb of sthg** priver qqn de qqch.
■ **vi 1.** [have no food] être affamé(e) ▸ **to starve to death** mourir de faim **2.** *inf* [be hungry] avoir très faim, crever OR mourir de faim.

starving ['stɑːvɪŋ] **adj** affamé(e) ▸ **think of all the starving people in the world** pense à tous ces gens qui meurent de faim dans le monde.

Star Wars **n** la Guerre des Étoiles *(nom populaire de l'Initiative de Défense Stratégique, programme militaire spatial du Président Reagan)*.

stash [stæʃ] *inf* ■ **vt 1.** [hide] planquer, cacher ▸ **he's got a lot of money stashed (away) somewhere** il a plein de fric planqué quelque part **2.** [put away] ranger.
■ **n 1.** [reserve] réserve *f* ▸ **a stash of money** un magot ▸ **the police found a big stash of guns/of cocaine** la police a découvert une importante cache d'armes/un important stock de cocaïne **2.** [hiding place] planque *f*, cachette *f* **3.** *v inf drug sl* cache *f*.
◆ ***stash away*** **vt sep** *inf* = ***stash*** *(vt)*.

state [steɪt] ■ **n** état *m* ▸ **the country is in a state of war/shock** le pays est en état de guerre/choc ▸ **chlorine in its gaseous/liquid state** le chlore à l'état gazeux/liquide ▸ **he's not in a fit state to drive** il n'est pas en état de conduire ▸ **to be in a state** être dans tous ses états ▸ **to lie in state** être exposé solennellement.
■ **comp** d'État ▸ **the carriages are used only on state occasions** les carrosses sont réservés aux cérémonies d'apparat ▸ **a state funeral** des funérailles nationales.
■ **vt 1.** [express - reason] donner / [- name and address] décliner ▸ **to state that...** déclarer que...
2. [specify] préciser ▸ **the regulations clearly state that daily checks must be made** le règlement dit OR indique clairement que des vérifications quotidiennes doivent être effectuées ▸ **to state one's case** présenter ses arguments ▸ **to state the case for the defence/the prosecution** LAW présenter le dossier de la défense/de l'accusation.
◆ ***State*** **n : the State** l'État *m*.
◆ ***States*** **npl : the States** *inf* les États-Unis *mpl*.

state-controlled **adj** étatisé(e), sous contrôle de l'État.

stated ['steɪtɪd] **adj** [amount, date] fixé(e) / [limit] prescrit(e) / [aim] déclaré(e) ▸ **it will be finished within the stated time** cela va être terminé dans les délais prescrits OR prévus ▸ **at the stated price** au prix fixé OR convenu.

State Department **n** *US* ≃ ministère *m* des Affaires étrangères.

state education **n** *UK* enseignement *m* public.

CULTURE

State Education

Ce terme désigne les deux systèmes d'écoles secondaires financées par l'État au Royaume-Uni. Les **comprehensive schools** (« établissements polyvalents »), créées en 1965 par le gouvernement travailliste, sont les plus nombreuses : elles dispensent une éducation équitable sans tenir compte des aptitudes scolaires générales. Pour les familles britanniques qui font le choix d'une éducation centrée sur des matières plus traditionnelles, les **Grammar Schools** qui existent toujours dans certaines agglomérations sont une autre possibilité. L'enfant peut y être admis à 11 ans après avoir passé un examen. 5% des élèves intègrent ces établissements.

stateless ['steɪtlɪs] **adj** apatride.

stately ['steɪtlɪ] (comp **-ier**, superl **-iest**) **adj** majestueux(euse).

stately home **n** *UK* château *m*.

statement ['steɪtmənt] **n 1.** [declaration] déclaration *f* ▸ **to put out** *OR* **to issue** *OR* **to make a statement about sthg** émettre un communiqué concernant qqch ▸ **a statement to the effect that...** une déclaration selon laquelle... **2.** LAW déposition *f* ▸ **a sworn statement** une déposition faite sous serment **3.** [from bank] relevé *m* de compte.

state of affairs **n** état *m* des choses.

state of emergency **n** état *m* d'urgence.

state of mind (pl **states of mind**) **n** humeur *f*.

state-of-the-art **adj** tout dernier (toute dernière) / [technology] de pointe.

state-owned [-'əʊnd] **adj** national(e), d'État.

state pension **n** pension *f* de l'État.

state school **n** *UK* école *f* publique.

state secret **n** secret *m* d'État.

state's evidence **n** *US* **: to turn state's evidence** témoigner contre ses complices.

stateside ['steɪtsaɪd] *US* ■ **adj** des États-Unis.
■ **adv** aux États-Unis.

statesman ['steɪtsmən] (pl **-men** [-mən]) **n** homme *m* d'État.

statesmanlike ['steɪtsmənlaɪk] **adj** [protest, reply] diplomatique / [solution] de grande envergure / [caution] pondéré(e).

statesmanship ['steɪtsmənʃɪp] **n** *(U)* habileté *f* politique.

state visit **n** POL visite *f* officielle ▸ **he's on a state visit to Japan** il est en voyage officiel au Japon.

static ['stætɪk] ■ **adj** statique.
■ **n** *(U)* parasites *mpl*.

static electricity **n** électricité *f* statique.

station ['steɪʃn] ■ **n 1.** RAIL gare *f* / [for buses, coaches] gare routière **2.** RADIO station *f* **3.** [building] poste *m* **4.** *fml* [rank] rang *m*.
■ **vt 1.** [position] placer, poster **2.** MIL poster.

stationary ['steɪʃnərɪ] **adj** immobile.

stationer ['steɪʃnə^r^] **n** papetier *m*, -ère *f* ▸ **stationer's (shop)** papeterie *f*.

stationery ['steɪʃnərɪ] **n** *(U)* [equipment] fournitures *fpl* de bureau / [paper] papier *m* à lettres.

station house **n** *US* poste *m* de police, caserne *m* de pompiers.

stationmaster ['steɪʃn,mɑːstə^r^] **n** chef *m* de gare.

station wagon **n** *US* break *m*.

statistic [stə'tɪstɪk] **n** statistique *f*.
◆ ***statistics*** **n** *(U)* [science] statistique *f*.

statistical [stə'tɪstɪkl] **adj** statistique / [expert] en statistiques / [report] de statistiques.

statistically [stə'tɪstɪklɪ] **adv** statistiquement.

statistician [,stætɪ'stɪʃn] **n** statisticien *m*, -enne *f*.

stats [stæts] *inf* = ***statistics***.

statue ['stætʃuː] **n** statue *f*.

statuesque [,stætjʊ'esk] **adj** sculptural(e).

statuette [,stætjʊ'et] **n** statuette *f*.

stature ['stætʃə^r^] **n 1.** [height, size] stature *f*, taille *f* **2.** [importance] envergure *f*.

status ['steɪtəs] **n** *(U)* **1.** [legal or social position] statut *m* **2.** [prestige] prestige *m*.

status bar **n** COMPUT barre *f* d'état.

status quo [-'kwəʊ] **n : the status quo** le statu quo.

status symbol **n** signe *m* extérieur de richesse.

statute ['stætjuːt] **n** loi *f*.

statute book **n : the statute book** ≃ le code, les textes *mpl* de loi.

statutory ['stætjʊtrɪ] **adj** statutaire.

staunch [stɔːntʃ] ■ **adj** loyal(e).
■ **vt** [flow] arrêter / [blood] étancher.

staunchly ['stɔːntʃlɪ] **adv** [loyally] loyalement, avec dévouement / [unswervingly] avec constance, fermement ▸ **their house is in a staunchly Republican area** ils habitent un quartier résolument républicain.

stave [steɪv] **n** MUS portée *f*.
◆ ***stave off*** (pt & pp **-d** *OR* **stove**) **vt sep** [disaster, defeat] éviter / [hunger] tromper.

stay [steɪ] ■ **vi 1.** [not move away] rester ▸ **to stay put** ne pas bouger
2. [as visitor - with friends] passer quelques jours / [- in town, country] séjourner ▸ **to stay in a hotel** descendre à l'hôtel ▸ **she's staying with friends** elle séjourne chez des amis ▸ **to look for a place to stay** chercher un endroit où loger
3. [continue, remain] rester, demeurer ▸ **would you like to stay for** *OR* **to dinner?** voulez-vous rester dîner? ▸ **to stay awake all night** rester éveillé toute la nuit, ne pas dormir de la nuit ▸ **let's try and stay calm** essayons de rester

calmes ▸ **personal computers are here to stay** l'ordinateur personnel est devenu indispensable ▸ **to stay away from sb** ne pas s'approcher de qqn ▸ **to stay away from a place** ne pas aller à un endroit ▸ **to stay out of sthg** ne pas se mêler de qqch
4. *Scot* [reside] habiter.
■ n [visit] séjour *m* ▸ **enjoy your stay!** bon séjour! ▸ **an overnight stay in hospital** une nuit d'hospitalisation.
◆ ***stay in*** vi rester chez soi, ne pas sortir.
◆ ***stay on*** vi rester (plus longtemps) ▸ **more pupils are staying on at school after the age of 16** de plus en plus d'élèves poursuivent leur scolarité au-delà de l'âge de 16 ans.
◆ ***stay out*** vi **1.** [from home] ne pas rentrer **2.** [strikers] rester en grève.
◆ ***stay up*** vi ne pas se coucher, veiller ▸ **to stay up late** se coucher tard.

stayer ['steɪəʳ] n *UK* [horse] stayer *m* / [person] personne *f* qui a de l'endurance.

staying power ['steɪɪŋ-] n endurance *f*.

St Bernard [*UK* -'bɜːnəd, *US* -bər'nɑːrd] n saint-bernard *m inv*.

STD n **1.** *UK* (abbr of ***subscriber trunk dialling***) *téléphone interurbain* **2.** (abbr of ***sexually transmitted disease***) MST *f*.

stead [sted] n **: to stand sb in good stead** être utile à qqn.

steadfast ['stedfɑːst] adj ferme, résolu(e) / [supporter] loyal(e).

Steadicam® ['stedɪkæm] n Steadicam® *m*.

steadily ['stedɪlɪ] adv **1.** [gradually] progressivement **2.** [regularly - breathe] régulièrement / [- move] sans arrêt **3.** [calmly] de manière imperturbable.

steady ['stedɪ] ■ adj (comp -ier, superl -iest) **1.** [gradual] progressif(ive) **2.** [regular] régulier(ère) **3.** [not shaking] ferme ▸ **to hold sthg steady** tenir qqch bien *OR* sans bouger **4.** [calm - voice] calme / [- stare] imperturbable **5.** [stable - job, relationship] stable **6.** [sensible] sérieux(euse) ▸ **inflation remains at a steady 5%** l'inflation s'est stabilisée à 5 % ▸ **steady boyfriend** petit ami *m* régulier *OR* attitré.
■ vt (pt & pp -ied) **1.** [stop from shaking] empêcher de bouger ▸ **to steady o.s.** se remettre d'aplomb **2.** [control - nerves] calmer ▸ **to steady o.s.** retrouver son calme.
■ vi (pt & pp -ied) [boat, prices, stock market] se stabiliser.

steak [steɪk] n steak *m*, bifteck *m* / [of fish] darne *f*.

steakhouse ['steɪkhaʊs] (pl [-haʊzɪz]) n grill *m*, grillroom *m*.

steal [stiːl] (pt stole, pp stolen) ■ vt voler, dérober ▸ **to steal sthg from sb** voler qqch à qqn ▸ **to steal all the credit for sthg** s'attribuer tout le mérite de qqch ▸ **to steal a look at** jeter un regard furtif à.
■ vi **1.** [take illegally] voler **2.** [move secretly] se glisser ▸ **to steal in/out** entrer/sortir à pas furtifs *OR* feutrés.

stealing ['stiːlɪŋ] n *(U)* vol *m*.

stealth [stelθ] n **: by stealth** en secret, discrètement.

Stealth bomber, ***Stealth plane*** n avion *m* furtif.

stealthily ['stelθɪlɪ] adv furtivement, subrepticement.

stealth tax n *mesure visant à augmenter les recettes du gouvernement par un moyen détourné, afin d'éviter une hausse directe et visible des impôts qui mécontenterait les citoyens.*

stealthy ['stelθɪ] (comp -ier, superl -iest) adj furtif(ive).

steam [stiːm] ■ n *(U)* vapeur *f* ▸ **to let off steam** *fig* se défouler ▸ **to run out of steam** *fig* s'essouffler.
■ comp à vapeur.
■ vt CULIN cuire à la vapeur.
■ vi **1.** [give off steam] fumer **2.** [ship] avancer.
◆ ***steam up*** ■ vt sep **1.** [mist up] embuer **2.** *fig* [make angry] **: to get steamed up (about)** s'énerver (pour).
■ vi se couvrir de buée.

steamboat ['stiːmbəʊt] n (bateau *m* à) vapeur *m*.

steamed-up [stiːmd-] adj *inf* [angry] énervé(e), dans tous ses états.

steam engine n locomotive *f* à vapeur.

steamer ['stiːməʳ] n **1.** [ship] (bateau *m* à) vapeur *m* **2.** CULIN cuiseur-vapeur *m*.

steam iron n fer *m* à vapeur.

steamroller ['stiːm,rəʊləʳ] n rouleau *m* compresseur.

steamroom ['stiːmruːm] n hammam *m*.

steam shovel n *US* bulldozer *m*.

steamy ['stiːmɪ] (comp -ier, superl -iest) adj **1.** [full of steam] embué(e) **2.** *inf* [erotic] érotique.

steel [stiːl] ■ n *(U)* acier *m*.
■ comp en acier, d'acier.
■ vt **: to steel o.s. (for)** s'armer de courage (pour).

steel industry n industrie *f* sidérurgique, sidérurgie *f*.

steel wool n paille *f* de fer.

steelworker ['stiːl,wɜːkəʳ] n sidérurgiste *mf*.

steelworks ['stiːlwɜːks] (pl **steelworks**) n aciérie *f*.

steely ['stiːlɪ] (comp -ier, superl -iest) adj **1.** [steel-coloured] acier *(inv)* **2.** [strong - person] dur(e) / [- determination, will] de fer.

steep [stiːp] adj **1.** [hill, road] raide, abrupt(e) **2.** [increase, decline] énorme **3.** *inf* [expensive] excessif(ive).

steeped [stiːpt] adj *fig* **: steeped in** imprégné(e) de.

steeple ['stiːpl] n clocher *m*, flèche *f*.

steeplechase ['stiːpltʃeɪs] n **1.** [horse race] steeplechase *m* **2.** [athletics race] steeple *m*.

steeplejack ['stiːpldʒæk] n réparateur *m* de cheminées industrielles et de clochers.

steeply ['stiːplɪ] adv **1.** [at steep angle] en pente raide **2.** [considerably] en flèche.

steer ['stɪəʳ] ■ n bœuf *m*.
■ vt **1.** [ship] gouverner / [car, aeroplane] conduire, diriger ▸ **to steer a course for** mettre le cap sur **2.** [person] diriger, guider **3.** [conversation, project] diriger ▸ **she successfully steered the company through the crisis** elle a réussi à sortir la société de la crise.
■ vi **: to steer well** [ship] gouverner bien / [car] être facile à manœuvrer ▸ **to steer clear of sb/sthg** éviter qqn/qqch.

steering ['stɪərɪŋ] n *(U)* direction *f*.

steering column n colonne *f* de direction.

steering committee n comité *m* d'organisation.

steering lock n rayon *m* de braquage.

steering wheel n volant *m*.

stellar ['stelər] adj stellaire.

stem [stem] ■ n **1.** [of plant] tige *f* **2.** [of glass] pied *m* **3.** [of pipe] tuyau *m* **4.** GRAM radical *m*.
■ vt (pt & pp **-med**, cont **-ming**) [stop] arrêter.
◆ ***stem from*** vt insep provenir de.

stem cell n MED cellule *f* souche.

stench [stentʃ] n puanteur *f*.

stencil ['stensl] ■ n pochoir *m*.
■ vt (*UK* **-led**, cont **-ling**, *US* **-ed**, cont **-ing**) faire au pochoir.

stenographer [stə'nɒgrəfər] n *US* sténographe *mf*.

stenography [stə'nɒgrəfɪ] n *US* sténographie *f*.

step [step] ■ n **1.** [pace] pas *m* ▸ **take two steps forwards/backwards** faites deux pas en avant/en arrière ▸ **I heard her step** *OR* **steps on the stairs** j'ai entendu (le bruit de) ses pas dans l'escalier ▸ **to fall into step with sb** *lit* s'aligner sur le pas de qqn / *fig* se ranger à l'avis de qqn ▸ **in/out of step with** *fig* en accord/désaccord avec ▸ **to watch one's step** faire attention où l'on marche / *fig* faire attention à ce que l'on fait
2. [action] mesure *f* ▸ **to take steps to do sthg** prendre des mesures pour faire qqch ▸ **it's a step in the right direction** c'est un pas dans la bonne direction
3. [stage] étape *f* ▸ **this promotion is a big step up for me** cette promotion est un grand pas en avant pour moi ▸ **we are still one step ahead of our competitors** nous conservons une petite avance sur nos concurrents
4. [stair] marche *f*
5. [of ladder] barreau *m*, échelon *m*
6. *US* MUS ton *m*.
■ vi (pt & pp **-ped**, cont **-ping**) **1.** [move foot] **: to step forward** avancer ▸ **to step off** *OR* **down from sthg** descendre de qqch ▸ **step inside!** entrez!
2. [tread] **: to step on/in sthg** marcher sur/dans qqch ▸ **step on it!** *inf* appuie sur le champignon!
◆ ***steps*** npl **1.** [stairs] marches *fpl*
2. *UK* [stepladder] escabeau *m*.
◆ ***step aside*** vi **1.** [move away] s'écarter
2. [leave job] démissionner.
◆ ***step back*** vi **1.** *lit* reculer
2. [pause to reflect] prendre du recul.
◆ ***step down*** vi [leave job] démissionner ▸ **he stepped down in favour of a younger person** il a cédé la place à quelqu'un de plus jeune.
◆ ***step in*** vi intervenir.
◆ ***step up*** vt sep intensifier.

step aerobics n *(U)* step *m*.

stepbrother ['step,brʌðər] n demi-frère *m*.

step-by-step ■ adv [gradually] pas à pas, petit à petit.
■ adj [point by point] **: a step-by-step guide to buying your own house** un guide détaillé pour l'achat de votre maison.

stepchild ['steptʃaɪld] (pl **-children** [-,tʃɪldrən]) n beau-fils *m*, belle-fille *f*.

stepdaughter ['step,dɔ:tər] n belle-fille *f*.

stepfather ['step,fɑ:ðər] n beau-père *m*.

stepladder ['step,lædər] n escabeau *m*.

stepmother ['step,mʌðər] n belle-mère *f*.

stepping-stone ['stepɪŋ-] n pierre *f* de gué / *fig* tremplin *m*.

stepsister ['step,sɪstər] n demi-sœur *f*.

stepson ['stepsʌn] n beau-fils *m*.

stereo ['sterɪəʊ] ■ adj stéréo *(inv)*.
■ n (pl **-s**) **1.** [appliance] chaîne *f* stéréo **2.** [sound] **: in stereo** en stéréo.

stereophonic [,sterɪə'fɒnɪk] adj stéréophonique.

stereo system n chaîne *f* stéréo.

stereotype ['sterɪətaɪp] ■ n stéréotype *m*.
■ vt stéréotyper.

stereotyped ['sterɪəʊtaɪpt] adj stéréotypé(e).

stereotypical [,sterɪəʊ'tɪpɪkl] adj stéréotypé(e).

stereotyping ['sterɪəʊ,taɪpɪŋ] n **: we want to avoid sexual stereotyping** nous voulons éviter les stéréotypes sexuels.

sterile ['steraɪl] adj stérile.

sterility [ste'rɪlətɪ] n stérilité *f*.

sterilization, *UK* ***-isation*** [,sterəlaɪ'zeɪʃn] n stérilisation *f*.

sterilize, *UK* ***-ise*** ['sterəlaɪz] vt stériliser.

sterilized, *UK* ***-ised*** ['sterəlaɪzd] adj [milk] stérilisé(e).

sterilized milk ['sterəlaɪzd-] n lait *m* stérilisé.

sterling ['stɜ:lɪŋ] ■ adj **1.** [of British money] sterling *(inv)*
2. [excellent] exceptionnel(elle).
■ n *(U)* livre *f* sterling.
■ comp [traveller's cheques] en livres sterling.

sterling area n zone *f* sterling.

sterling silver n argent *m* fin.

stern [stɜ:n] ■ adj sévère.
■ n NAUT arrière *m*.

sternly ['stɜ:nlɪ] adv sévèrement.

steroid ['stɪərɔɪd] n stéroïde *m*.

stethoscope ['steθəskəʊp] n stéthoscope *m*.

stetson ['stetsn] n chapeau *m* de cow-boy.

stevedore ['sti:vədɔ:r] n *US* docker *m*.

stew [stju:] ■ n ragoût *m*.
■ vt [meat] cuire en ragoût / [fruit] faire cuire.
■ vi **: to let sb stew** *fig* laisser mariner qqn.

steward ['stjʊəd] n **1.** [on plane, ship, train] steward *m*
2. *UK* [at demonstration, meeting] membre *m* du service d'ordre.

stewardess ['stjʊədɪs] n *dated* hôtesse *f*.

stewed [stju:d] adj **1.** CULIN **: stewed meat** ragoût *m* ▸ **we had stewed lamb for supper** au dîner, nous avons mangé un ragoût d'agneau ▸ **stewed fruit** compote *f* de fruits
2. [tea] trop infusé(e) **3.** *inf* [drunk] bourré(e), cuité(e).

stewing steak ['stju:ɪŋ-] n *(U)* *UK* bœuf *m* à braiser.

St. Ex. abbr of ***stock exchange***.

stg abbr of ***sterling***.

stick [stɪk] ■ **n** **1.** [of wood, dynamite, candy] bâton *m*
2. [walking stick] canne *f*
3. SPORT crosse *f*
▸▸ **to get the wrong end of the stick** *UK* mal comprendre ▸ **to get** *OR* **to come in for a lot of stick** *UK inf* **: the police got a lot of stick from the press** la police s'est fait éreinter *OR* démolir par la presse.
■ **vt** (pt & pp **stuck**) **1.** [push] **: to stick sthg in** *OR* **into** planter qqch dans ▸ **she stuck the revolver in his back** elle lui a enfoncé le revolver dans le dos ▸ **to stick sthg through sthg** transpercer qqch avec qqch
2. [with glue, adhesive tape] **: to stick sthg (on** *OR* **to)** coller qqch (sur) ▸ **he had posters stuck to the walls with Sellotape** il avait scotché des posters aux murs
3. *inf* [put] mettre ▸ **she stuck her head into the office/out of the window** elle a passé la tête dans le bureau/par la fenêtre ▸ **mix it all together and stick it in the oven** mélangez bien (le tout) et mettez au four
4. *UK inf* [tolerate] supporter ▸ **I can't stick him** je ne peux pas le sentir ▸ **to stick it** tenir le coup.
■ **vi** (pt & pp **stuck**) **1.** [adhere] **: to stick (to)** coller (à) ▸ **the dough stuck to my fingers** la pâte collait à mes doigts ▸ **these badges stick to any surface** ces autocollants adhèrent sur toutes les surfaces
2. [jam] se coincer ▸ **having to ask him for a loan really sticks in my throat** ça me coûte vraiment d'avoir à lui demander un prêt
3. [remain] **: to stick in sb's mind** marquer qqn
4. [extend, project] **: the antenna was sticking straight up** l'antenne se dressait toute droite ▸ **only her head was sticking out of the water** seule sa tête sortait *OR* émergeait de l'eau.

◆ ***stick around*** **vi** *inf* rester dans les parages.

◆ ***stick at*** **vt insep** [activity] persévérer dans ▸ **to stick at a job** rester dans un emploi.

◆ ***stick by*** **vt insep** [statement] s'en tenir à / [person] ne pas abandonner ▸ **don't worry, I'll always stick by you** sois tranquille, je serai toujours là pour te soutenir.

◆ ***stick out*** ■ **vt sep** **1.** [head] sortir / [hand] lever / [tongue] tirer
2. *inf* [endure] **: to stick it out** tenir le coup.
■ **vi** **1.** [protrude] dépasser ▸ **her ears stick out** elle a les oreilles décollées ▸ **my feet stuck out over the end of the bed** mes pieds dépassaient du lit
2. *inf* [be noticeable] se remarquer.

◆ ***stick out for*** **vt insep** *UK* exiger.

◆ ***stick to*** **vt insep** **1.** [follow closely] suivre
2. [principles] rester fidèle à / [decision] s'en tenir à / [promise] tenir ▸ **once I make a decision I stick to it** une fois que j'ai pris une décision, je m'y tiens *OR* je n'en démords pas ▸ **to stick to one's word** tenir (sa) parole ▸ **she's still sticking to her story** elle maintient ce qu'elle a dit ▸ **the author would be better off sticking to journalism** l'auteur ferait mieux de se cantonner au journalisme.

◆ ***stick together*** **vi** rester ensemble / *fig* se serrer les coudes.

◆ ***stick up*** ■ **vt sep** **1.** [poster, notice] afficher
2. [with gun] attaquer à main armée.
■ **vi** dépasser.

◆ ***stick up for*** **vt insep** défendre ▸ **to stick up for sb** prendre la défense *OR* le parti de qqn ▸ **stick up for yourself!** ne te laisse pas faire!

◆ ***stick with*** **vt insep** **1.** [decision, choice] s'en tenir à **2.** [follow closely] rester avec.

sticker ['stɪkəʳ] **n** [label] autocollant *m*.

stickiness ['stɪkɪnɪs] **n** [of hands, substance, surface] caractère *m* gluant *OR* poisseux.

sticking plaster ['stɪkɪŋ-] **n** *UK* sparadrap *m*.

sticking point **n** *fig* point *m* de friction.

stick insect **n** phasme *m*.

stick-in-the-mud **n** *inf* réac *mf*.

stickleback ['stɪklbæk] **n** épinoche *f*.

stickler ['stɪkləʳ] **n : to be a stickler for** être à cheval sur.

stick-on **adj** autocollant(e), adhésif(ive).

stickpin ['stɪkpɪn] **n** *US* épingle *f* de cravate.

stick shift **n** *US* levier *m* de vitesses.

stick-up **n** *inf* vol *m* à main armée.

sticky ['stɪkɪ] (comp **-ier**, superl **-iest**) **adj** **1.** [hands, sweets] poisseux(euse) / [label, tape] adhésif(ive) **2.** *inf* [awkward] délicat(e) **3.** [humid] humide.

sticky tape **n** *UK* ruban *m* adhésif.

stiff [stɪf] ■ **adj** **1.** [rod, paper, material] rigide / [shoes, brush] dur(e) / [fabric] raide **2.** [thick, difficult to stir] ferme, consistant(e) ▸ **beat the mixture until it is stiff** battez jusqu'à obtention d'une pâte consistante ▸ **beat the egg-whites until stiff** battre les blancs en neige jusqu'à ce qu'ils soient (bien) fermes **3.** [door, drawer, window] dur(e) (à ouvrir/fermer) / [joint] ankylosé(e) ▸ **I'm still stiff after playing squash the other day** j'ai encore des courbatures d'avoir joué au squash l'autre jour ▸ **to have a stiff back** avoir des courbatures dans le dos ▸ **to have a stiff neck** avoir le torticolis **4.** [formal] guindé(e) **5.** [severe - penalty] sévère / [- resistance] tenace / [- competition] serré(e) ▸ **to face stiff competition** avoir affaire à forte concurrence **6.** [difficult - task] difficile **7.** [drink] bien tassé(e) / [wind] fort(e).
■ **adv** *inf* **: to be bored stiff** s'ennuyer à mourir ▸ **to be frozen/scared stiff** mourir de froid/peur.

stiffen ['stɪfn] ■ **vt** **1.** [material] raidir / [with starch] empeser **2.** [resolve] renforcer.
■ **vi** **1.** [body] se raidir / [joints] s'ankyloser **2.** [competition, resistance] s'intensifier **3.** [wind] devenir plus fort(e), fraîchir.

stiffener ['stɪfnəʳ] **n** **1.** [starch] amidon *m* **2.** TECH raidisseur *m*.

stiffly ['stɪflɪ] **adv** **1.** [rigidly] **: stiffly starched** très empesé *OR* amidonné ▸ **he stood stiffly to attention** il se tenait raide au garde-à-vous **2.** [painfully - walk, bend] avec raideur **3.** [coldly - smile, greet] froidement, d'un air distant.

stiffness ['stɪfnɪs] **n** *(U)* **1.** [inflexibility] raideur *f*, rigidité *f* **2.** [of body, joint] ankylose *f* **3.** [formality] froideur *f*.

stifle ['staɪfl] **vt & vi** étouffer.

stifling ['staɪflɪŋ] **adj** étouffant(e).

stigma ['stɪgmə] **n** **1.** [disgrace] honte *f*, stigmate *m* **2.** BOT stigmate *m*.

stigmatize**, UK **-ise ['stɪgmətaɪz] **vt** stigmatiser.

stile [staɪl] **n** échalier *m*.

stiletto heel [stɪ'letəʊ-] **n** talon *m* aiguille.

still [stɪl] ■ **adv 1.** [up to now, up to then] encore, toujours ▶ **I've still got £5 left** il me reste encore 5 livres **2.** [even now] encore **3.** [nevertheless] tout de même **4.** *(with compar)* **: still bigger/more important** encore plus grand/plus important.
■ **adj 1.** [not moving] immobile **2.** [calm] calme, tranquille **3.** [not windy] sans vent **4.** [not fizzy - gen] non gazeux(euse) / [- mineral water] plat(e).
■ **n 1.** PHOT photo *f* **2.** [for making alcohol] alambic *m*.

stillbirth ['stɪlbɜːθ] **n** [birth] mort *f* à la naissance / [fœtus] enfant *m* mort-né, enfant *f* mort-née.

stillborn ['stɪlbɔːn] **adj** mort-né(e).

still life (pl -s) **n** nature *f* morte.

stillness ['stɪlnɪs] **n** [calmness] tranquillité *f*.

stilted ['stɪltɪd] **adj** emprunté(e), qui manque de naturel.

Stilton® ['stɪltn] **n** stilton *m*, fromage *m* de Stilton.

stilts ['stɪlts] **npl 1.** [for person] échasses *fpl* **2.** [for building] pilotis *mpl*.

stimulant ['stɪmjʊlənt] **n** stimulant *m*.

stimulate ['stɪmjʊleɪt] **vt** stimuler.

stimulating ['stɪmjʊleɪtɪŋ] **adj** stimulant(e).

stimulation [ˌstɪmjʊ'leɪʃn] **n** stimulation *f*.

stimulus ['stɪmjʊləs] (pl **-li** [-laɪ]) **n 1.** [encouragement] stimulant *m* **2.** BIOL & PSYCHOL stimulus *m*.

sting [stɪŋ] ■ **n 1.** [by bee] piqûre *f* / [of bee] dard *m* **2.** [sharp pain] brûlure *f* ▶ **to take the sting out of sthg** adoucir *OR* atténuer qqch.
■ **vt** (pt & pp **stung**) **1.** [gen] piquer **2.** [subj: criticism] blesser.
■ **vi** (pt & pp **stung**) piquer.

stinging ['stɪŋɪŋ] **adj 1.** [wound, pain] cuisant(e) / [bite, eyes] qui pique / [lash, rain] cinglant(e) **2.** [remark, joke, criticism] cinglant(e), mordant(e).

stinging nettle **n** *UK* ortie *f*.

stingray ['stɪŋreɪ] **n** pastenague *f*.

stingy ['stɪndʒɪ] (comp **-ier**, superl **-iest**) **adj** *inf* radin(e).

stink [stɪŋk] ■ **n** puanteur *f*.
■ **vi** (pt **stank** *OR* **stunk**, pp **stunk**) **1.** [smell] puer, empester **2.** *inf fig* [be worthless] ne rien valoir.

stink-bomb **n** boule *f* puante.

stinking ['stɪŋkɪŋ] *inf* ■ **adj** [cold] gros (grosse) / [weather] pourri(e) / [place] infect(e).
■ **adv : to be stinking rich** être plein(e) aux as.

stint [stɪnt] ■ **n** [period of work] part *f* de travail.
■ **vi : to stint on** lésiner sur.

stipend ['staɪpend] **n** traitement *m*, salaire *m*.

stipulate ['stɪpjʊleɪt] **vt** stipuler.

stipulation [ˌstɪpjʊ'leɪʃn] **n 1.** [statement] stipulation *f* **2.** [condition] condition *f*.

stir [stɜːʳ] ■ **n 1.** [act of stirring] **: to give sthg a stir** remuer qqch **2.** [public excitement] sensation *f*.
■ **vt** (pt & pp **-red**, cont **-ring**) **1.** [mix] remuer **2.** [move gently] agiter **3.** [move emotionally] émouvoir **4.** [move] **: to stir o.s.** se remuer.
■ **vi** (pt & pp **-red**, cont **-ring**) bouger, remuer.
◆ ***stir up*** **vt sep 1.** [dust] soulever **2.** [trouble] provoquer / [resentment, dissatisfaction] susciter / [rumour] faire naître.

stir-fry **vt** faire sauter à feu très vif.

stirring ['stɜːrɪŋ] ■ **adj** excitant(e), émouvant(e).
■ **n** [of interest, emotion] éveil *m*.

stirrup ['stɪrəp] **n** étrier *m*.

stitch [stɪtʃ] ■ **n 1.** SEW point *m* / [in knitting] maille *f* **2.** MED point *m* de suture **3.** [stomach pain] **: to have a stitch** avoir un point de côté
▶▶ **to be in stitches** être plié(e) en deux (de rire), se tenir les côtes.
■ **vt 1.** SEW coudre **2.** MED suturer.

stitching ['stɪtʃɪŋ] **n** *(U)* points *mpl*, piqûres *fpl*.

stoat [stəʊt] **n** hermine *f*.

stock [stɒk] ■ **n 1.** [supply] réserve *f* ▶ **we got in a stock of food** nous avons fait tout un stock de nourriture **2.** *(U)* COMM stock *m*, réserve *f* ▶ **in stock** en stock ▶ **out of stock** épuisé(e) ▶ **I'm afraid we're out of stock** je regrette, nous n'en avons plus en stock **3.** FIN valeurs *fpl US*, actions *fpl UK* ▶ **stocks and shares** titres *mpl* **4.** [ancestry] souche *f* **5.** CULIN bouillon *m* **6.** [livestock] cheptel *m*
▶▶ **to take stock (of)** faire le point (de).
■ **adj** classique.
■ **vt 1.** COMM vendre, avoir en stock **2.** [fill - shelves] garnir / [- lake] empoissonner.
◆ ***stock up*** **vi : to stock up (with)** faire des provisions (de).

stockade [stɒ'keɪd] **n** palissade *f*.

stockbroker ['stɒkˌbrəʊkəʳ] **n** agent *m* de change.

stockbroking ['stɒkˌbrəʊkɪŋ] **n** commerce *m* des valeurs en Bourse.

stockcar ['stɒkkɑːʳ] **n** stock-car *m*.

stock company **n** *US* société *f* anonyme par actions.

stock control **n** contrôle *m* des stocks.

stock cube **n** bouillon-cube *m*.

stock exchange **n** Bourse *f*.

stockholder ['stɒkˌhəʊldəʳ] **n** *US* actionnaire *mf*.

Stockholm ['stɒkhəʊm] **n** Stockholm.

stocking ['stɒkɪŋ] **n** [for woman] bas *m*.

stock-in-trade **n** rudiments *mpl* du métier.

stockist ['stɒkɪst] **n** *UK* dépositaire *m*, stockiste *m*.

stock market **n** Bourse *f*.

stock market boom **n** envolée *f* du marché boursier.

stock phrase **n** cliché *m*.

stockpile ['stɒkpaɪl] ■ **n** stock *m*.
■ **vt** [weapons] amasser / [food] stocker.

stockpiling ['stɒkpaɪlɪŋ] **n : to accuse sb of stockpiling** [food] accuser qqn de faire des réserves de nourriture / [weapons] accuser qqn de faire des réserves d'armes.

stockroom ['stɒkrʊm] **n** réserve *f*.

stock-still **adv** sans bouger.

stocktaking ['stɒkˌteɪkɪŋ] **n** *(U)* inventaire *m*.

stocky ['stɒkɪ] (comp **-ier**, superl **-iest**) **adj** trapu(e).

stodgy ['stɒdʒɪ] (comp **-ier**, superl **-iest**) **adj** **1.** [food] lourd(e) (à digérer) **2.** *pej* [book] indigeste.

stoic ['stəʊɪk] ■ **adj** stoïque.
■ **n** stoïque *mf*.

stoical ['stəʊɪkl] **adj** stoïque.

stoically ['stəʊɪklɪ] **adv** stoïquement, avec stoïcisme.

stoicism ['stəʊɪsɪzm] **n** stoïcisme *m*.

stoke [stəʊk] **vt** [fire] entretenir.

stole [stəʊl] ■ **pt** ➤ ***steal***.
■ **n** étole *f*.

stolen ['stəʊln] **pp** ➤ ***steal***.

stolid ['stɒlɪd] **adj** impassible.

stomach ['stʌmək] ■ **n** [organ] estomac *m* / [abdomen] ventre *m* ▸ **I can't work on an empty stomach** je ne peux pas travailler l'estomac vide ▸ **the sight was enough to turn your stomach** le spectacle avait de quoi vous soulever le cœur.
■ **vt** [tolerate] encaisser, supporter ▸ **I just can't stomach the thought of him being my boss** je ne supporte simplement pas l'idée qu'il soit mon patron.

stomachache ['stʌməkeɪk] **n : to have stomachache** *UK* OR **a stomachache** *US* avoir mal au ventre.

stomach pump **n** pompe *f* stomacale.

stomach ulcer **n** ulcère *m* de l'estomac.

stomach upset **n** embarras *m* gastrique.

stomp [stɒmp] **vi : to stomp in/out** entrer/sortir d'un pas bruyant, entrer/sortir d'un pas lourd.

stone [stəʊn] ■ **n** **1.** [rock] pierre *f* / [smaller] caillou *m* ▸ **the houses are built of stone** les maisons sont en pierre ▸ **to leave no stone unturned** remuer ciel et terre ▸ **a stone's throw from** à deux pas de **2.** *UK* [seed] noyau *m* **3.** (pl **stone** OR **-s**) *UK* [unit of measurement] = *6,348 kg*.
■ **comp** de OR en pierre.
■ **vt** [person, car] jeter des pierres sur.

Stone Age **n : the Stone Age** l'âge *m* de pierre.

stone-cold **adj** complètement froid(e) OR glacé(e).

stoned [stəʊnd] **adj** *inf* **1.** *drug sl* défoncé(e) **2.** [drunk] soûl(e), bourré(e).

stonemason ['stəʊnˌmeɪsn] **n** tailleur *m* de pierre OR pierres.

stonewall [ˌstəʊn'wɔːl] **vi** être évasif(ive).

stonewalling [ˌstəʊn'wɔːlɪŋ] **n** POL obstructionnisme *m*.

stoneware ['stəʊnweəʳ] **n** poterie *f* en grès.

stonewashed ['stəʊnwɒʃt] **adj** délavé(e).

stonework ['stəʊnwɜːk] **n** maçonnerie *f*.

stony ['stəʊnɪ] (comp **-ier**, superl **-iest**) **adj** **1.** [ground] pierreux(euse) **2.** [unfriendly] froid(e).

stony-broke **adj** *UK inf* fauché(e) (comme les blés), à sec.

stony-faced **adj** au visage impassible.

stood [stʊd] **pt & pp** ➤ ***stand***.

stooge [stuːdʒ] **n** [in comedy act] comparse *m* / *fig* pantin *m*, fantoche *m*.

stool [stuːl] **n** [seat] tabouret *m*.

stoop [stuːp] ■ **n** **1.** [bent back] **: to walk with a stoop** marcher le dos voûté **2.** *US* [of house] porche *m*.
■ **vi** **1.** [bend down] se pencher **2.** [hunch shoulders] être voûté(e) **3.** *fig* [debase oneself] **: to stoop to doing sthg** s'abaisser jusqu'à faire qqch.

stop [stɒp] ■ **n** **1.** [gen] arrêt *m* ▸ **our first stop was Brussels** nous avons fait une première halte à Bruxelles ▸ **to come to a stop** [car, train] s'arrêter / [production, growth] cesser ▸ **to put a stop to sthg** mettre un terme à qqch **2.** [full stop] point *m*.
■ **vt** (pt & pp **-ped**, cont **-ping**) **1.** [gen] arrêter / [end] mettre fin à ▸ **a woman stopped me to ask the way to the station** une femme m'a arrêté pour me demander le chemin de la gare ▸ **stop it, that hurts!** arrête, ça fait mal! ▸ **to stop doing sthg** arrêter de faire qqch ▸ **it hasn't stopped raining all day** il n'a pas arrêté de pleuvoir toute la journée ▸ **to stop work** arrêter de travailler, cesser le travail **2.** [prevent] **: to stop sb/sthg (from doing sthg)** empêcher qqn/qqch (de faire qqch)
3. *UK* [wages] retenir / [cheque] faire opposition à ▸ **the money will be stopped out of your wages** la somme sera retenue sur votre salaire
4. [block] boucher.
■ **vi** (pt & pp **-ped**, cont **-ping**) s'arrêter, cesser ▸ **my watch has stopped** ma montre s'est OR est arrêtée ▸ **does the bus stop near the church?** le bus s'arrête-t-il près de l'église? ▸ **the rain has stopped** la pluie s'est arrêtée ▸ **to stop at nothing (to do sthg)** ne reculer devant rien (pour faire qqch).
◆ ***stop off*** **vi** s'arrêter, faire halte.
◆ ***stop over*** **vi** s'arrêter un jour/quelques jours.
◆ ***stop up*** ■ **vt sep** [block] boucher.
■ **vi** *UK* veiller.

stop-and-go-policy **n** *UK* ECON politique *f* économique en dents de scie *(alternant arrêt de la croissance et mesures de relance)*, politique *f* du stop-and-go.

stopcock ['stɒpkɒk] **n** robinet *m* d'arrêt.

stopgap ['stɒpgæp] **n** bouche-trou *m*.

stoplight ['stɒplaɪt] **n** **1.** [traffic light] feu *m* rouge **2.** *UK* [brake-light] stop *m*.

stopover ['stɒpˌəʊvəʳ] **n** halte *f*.

stoppage ['stɒpɪdʒ] **n** **1.** [strike] grève *f* **2.** *UK* [deduction] retenue *f*.

stopper ['stɒpəʳ] **n** bouchon *m*.

stopping ['stɒpɪŋ] **adj** *UK* **: stopping train** train *m* omnibus.

stop press **n** nouvelles *fpl* de dernière heure.

stop sign **n** (signal *m* de) stop *m*.

stopwatch ['stɒpwɒtʃ] **n** chronomètre *m*.

storage ['stɔːrɪdʒ] **n** **1.** [of goods] entreposage *m*, emmagasinage *m* / [of household objects] rangement *m* **2.** COMPUT stockage *m*, mémorisation *f*.

storage heater **n** *UK* radiateur *m* à accumulation.

store [stɔːʳ] ■ n **1.** *esp US* [shop] magasin *m* **2.** [supply] provision *f* **3.** [place of storage] réserve *f*
⏭ **to set great store by** ***OR*** **on** accorder ***OR*** attacher beaucoup d'importance à, faire grand cas de.
■ **vt 1.** [save] mettre en réserve / [goods] entreposer, emmagasiner **2.** COMPUT stocker, mémoriser.
◆ ***in store*** **adv : who knows what the future holds in store?** qui sait ce que nous réserve l'avenir? ▸ **there's a shock in store for him** un choc l'attend.
◆ ***store up*** **vt sep** [provisions] mettre en réserve / [goods] emmagasiner / [information] mettre en mémoire, noter.

store card **n** carte *f* de crédit *(d'un grand magasin).*

store detective **n** *UK* surveillant *m*, -e *f* de magasin.

storehouse ['stɔːhaʊs] (pl [-haʊzɪz]) **n** entrepôt *m* / *fig* mine *f*.

storekeeper ['stɔːˌkiːpəʳ] **n** *US* commerçant *m*, -e *f*.

storeroom ['stɔːrʊm] **n** magasin *m*.

storey *UK* (pl **-s**), ***story*** *US* (pl **-ies**) ['stɔːrɪ] **n** étage *m*.

stork [stɔːk] **n** cigogne *f*.

storm [stɔːm] ■ **n 1.** [bad weather] orage *m* ▸ **a storm in a teacup** une tempête dans un verre d'eau **2.** *fig* [of abuse] torrent *m* / [of applause] tempête *f*.
■ **vt** MIL prendre d'assaut.
■ **vi 1.** [go angrily] **: to storm in/out** entrer/sortir comme un ouragan **2.** [speak angrily] fulminer.

storm cloud **n** nuage *m* orageux.

storming ['stɔːmɪŋ] **n** prise *f* d'assaut.

stormy ['stɔːmɪ] (comp **-ier**, superl **-iest**) **adj** *lit & fig* orageux(euse).

story ['stɔːrɪ] (pl **-ies**) **n 1.** [gen] histoire *f* ▸ **a collection of her poems and stories** un recueil de ses poèmes et nouvelles ▸ **the witness changed his story** le témoin est revenu sur sa version des faits ▸ **well, that's my story and I'm sticking to it** *hum* c'est la version officielle ▸ **or so the story goes** c'est du moins ce que l'on raconte ▸ **it's the (same) old story** c'est toujours la même histoire, c'est toujours pareil ▸ **to cut a long story short** (enfin) bref **2.** PRESS article *m* / RADIO & TV nouvelle *f* ▸ **all the papers ran** ***OR*** **carried the story** tous les journaux en ont parlé **3.** *US* = ***storey***.

storybook ['stɔːrɪbʊk] **adj** [romance] de conte de fées.

story line **n** intrigue *f*, scénario *m*.

storyteller ['stɔːrɪˌteləʳ] **n 1.** [narrator] conteur *m*, -euse *f* **2.** *euph* [liar] menteur *m*, -euse *f*.

stout [staʊt] ■ **adj 1.** [rather fat] corpulent(e) **2.** [strong] solide **3.** [resolute] ferme, résolu(e).
■ **n** *(U)* stout *m*, bière *f* brune.

stoutness ['staʊtnɪs] **n** [fatness] corpulence *f*.

stove [stəʊv] ■ **pt & pp** ➤ ***stave***.
■ **n** [for cooking] cuisinière *f* / [for heating] poêle *m*, calorifère *m* ***Québec***.

stow [stəʊ] **vt : to stow sthg (away)** ranger qqch.
◆ ***stow away*** **vi** embarquer clandestinement.

stowaway ['stəʊəweɪ] **n** passager *m* clandestin.

straddle ['strædl] **vt** enjamber / [chair] s'asseoir à califourchon sur.

strafe [strɑːf] **vt** MIL mitrailler.

straggle ['strægl] **vi 1.** [buildings] s'étendre, s'étaler / [hair] être en désordre **2.** [person] traîner, lambiner.

straggler ['stræglәʳ] **n** traînard *m*, -e *f*.

straggly ['stræglɪ] (comp **-ier**, superl **-iest**) **adj** [hair] en désordre.

straight [streɪt] ■ **adj 1.** [not bent] droit(e) / [hair] raide ▸ **keep your back straight** tiens-toi droit, redresse-toi ▸ **the picture isn't straight** le tableau n'est pas droit ***OR*** est de travers
2. [frank] franc (franche), honnête ▸ **are you being straight with me?** est-ce que tu joues franc jeu avec moi? ▸ **to give sb a straight answer** répondre franchement à qqn ▸ **to do some straight talking** parler franchement
3. [tidy] en ordre
4. [choice, exchange] simple
5. [alcoholic drink] sec (sèche), sans eau
6. *inf* [conventional] normal(e)
7. *inf* [heterosexual] hétéro *(inv)*
⏭ **let's get this straight** entendons-nous bien ▸ **to put** ***OR*** **to set the record straight** mettre les choses au clair.
■ **adv 1.** [in a straight line] droit ▸ **sit up straight!** tiens-toi droit ***OR*** redresse-toi (sur ta chaise)! ▸ **I can't think straight** je n'ai pas les idées claires
2. [directly, immediately] droit, tout de suite ▸ **straight ahead** tout droit ▸ **go straight to bed!** va tout de suite te coucher! ▸ **to come straight to the point** aller droit au fait
3. [frankly] carrément, franchement ▸ **straight up** *UK inf* [honestly] sans blague
4. [undiluted] sec, sans eau
⏭ **to go straight** [criminal] rester dans le droit chemin.
■ **n** SPORT **: the straight** la ligne droite ▸ **the final** ***OR*** **home straight** la dernière ligne droite ▸ **to keep to the straight and narrow** rester dans le droit chemin.
◆ ***straight off*** **adv** tout de suite, sur-le-champ.
◆ ***straight out*** **adv** sans mâcher ses mots.

straightaway [ˌstreɪtə'weɪ] **adv** tout de suite, immédiatement.

straighten ['streɪtn] ■ **vt 1.** [tidy - hair, dress] arranger / [- room] mettre de l'ordre dans **2.** [make straight - horizontally] rendre droit(e) / [- vertically] redresser.
■ **vi** [person] **: to straighten (up)** se redresser.
◆ ***straighten out*** **vt sep** [problem] résoudre ▸ **to straighten things out** arranger les choses.

straight face **n : to keep a straight face** garder son sérieux.

straightforward [ˌstreɪt'fɔːwәd] **adj 1.** [easy] simple **2.** [frank] honnête, franc (franche).

straightforwardly [ˌstreɪt'fɔːwәdlɪ] **adv 1.** [honestly - act, behave] avec franchise / [- answer] franchement, sans détour **2.** [without complications] simplement, sans anicroche.

straight-to-video **adj** [movie] sorti(e) directement sur cassette vidéo.

strain [streɪn] ■ **n 1.** [mental] tension *f*, stress *m* ▸ **he can't take the strain any more** il ne peut plus supporter cette situation stressante ▸ **the situation has put our family under a great deal of strain** la situation a mis notre famille à rude épreuve **2.** MED foulure *f* ▸ **back strain** tour *m* de reins **3.** TECH contrainte *f*, effort *m* ▸ **the rope snapped under the strain** la corde a rompu sous la

tension ▸ **the war is putting a great strain on the country's resources** la guerre pèse lourd sur *OR* grève sérieusement les ressources du pays **4.** [type - of plant] variété *f* / [- of virus] souche *f* **5.** [streak, touch] fond *m*, tendance *f* ▸ **there is a strain of madness in the family** il y a une prédisposition à la folie dans la famille.
■ **vt 1.** [work hard - eyes] plisser fort ▸ **to strain one's ears** tendre l'oreille ▸ **to strain every nerve** *OR* **sinew to do sthg** s'efforcer de faire qqch **2.** [MED - muscle] se froisser / [- eyes] se fatiguer ▸ **you'll strain your eyes** tu vas te fatiguer les yeux ▸ **I've strained my arm** je me suis froissé un muscle du bras ▸ **to strain one's back** se faire un tour de reins **3.** [patience] mettre à rude épreuve / [budget] grever **4.** [drain] passer **5.** TECH exercer une contrainte sur ▸ **to be strained to breaking point** être tendu au point de se rompre.
■ **vi** [try very hard] **: the dog strained at the leash** le chien tirait sur sa laisse ▸ **to strain to do sthg** faire un gros effort pour faire qqch, se donner du mal pour faire qqch.
◆ ***strains*** **npl** [of music] accords *mpl*, airs *mpl*.

strained [streɪnd] **adj 1.** [worried] contracté(e), tendu(e) **2.** [relations, relationship] tendu(e) **3.** [unnatural] forcé(e).

strainer ['streɪnəʳ] **n** passoire *f*.

strait [streɪt] **n** détroit *m*.
◆ ***straits*** **npl : in dire** *OR* **desperate straits** dans une situation désespérée.

straitened ['streɪtnd] **adj** *fml* **: in straitened circumstances** dans la gêne, dans le besoin.

straitjacket ['streɪt,dʒækɪt] **n** camisole *f* de force.

straitlaced [,streɪt'leɪst] **adj** collet monté *(inv)*.

Strait of Gibraltar **n : the Strait of Gibraltar** le détroit de Gibraltar.

Strait of Hormuz [,hɔ:'mu:ʰ] **n : the Strait of Hormuz** le détroit d'Hormuz *OR* d'Ormuz.

strand [strænd] **n 1.** [of cotton, wool] brin *m*, fil *m* / [of hair] mèche *f* **2.** [theme] fil *m*.

stranded ['strændɪd] **adj** [boat] échoué(e) / [people] abandonné(e), en rade.

strange [streɪndʒ] **adj 1.** [odd] étrange, bizarre ▸ **she has some strange ideas** elle a des idées bizarres *OR* de drôles d'idées ▸ **it's strange that he should be so late** c'est bizarre *OR* étrange qu'il ait tant de retard ▸ **strange as it may seem** aussi étrange que cela paraisse *OR* puisse paraître **2.** [unfamiliar] inconnu(e).

strangely ['streɪndʒlɪ] **adv** étrangement, bizarrement ▸ **strangely (enough)** chose curieuse.

strangeness ['streɪndʒnɪs] **n 1.** [of person, situation] étrangeté *f*, bizarrerie *f*, singularité *f* **2.** PHYS étrangeté *f*.

stranger ['streɪndʒəʳ] **n 1.** [unfamiliar person] inconnu *m*, -e *f* ▸ **to be a stranger to sthg** ne pas connaître qqch ▸ **to be no stranger to sthg** bien connaître qqch **2.** [from another place] étranger *m*, -ère *f*.

strangle ['stræŋgl] **vt** étrangler / *fig* étouffer.

stranglehold ['stræŋglhəʊld] **n 1.** [round neck] étranglement *m* **2.** *fig* [control] **: stranglehold (on)** domination *f* (de).

strangling ['stræŋglɪŋ] **n 1.** [killing] étranglement *m*, strangulation *f* / *fig* [of opposition, protest, originality] étranglement *m*, étouffement *m* **2.** [case] **: that brings to five the number of stranglings** cela porte à cinq le nombre de personnes étranglées.

strangulation [,stræŋgjʊ'leɪʃn] **n** strangulation *f*.

strap [stræp] ■ **n** [for fastening] sangle *f*, courroie *f* / [of bag] bandoulière *f* / [of rifle, dress, bra] bretelle *f* / [of watch] bracelet *m*.
■ **vt** (pt & pp **-ped**, cont **-ping**) [fasten] attacher.

strapless ['stræplɪs] **adj** sans bretelles.

strapline ['stræplaɪn] **n** signature *f*, base line *f*.

strapping ['stræpɪŋ] **adj** bien bâti(e), robuste.

strata ['strɑ:tə] **npl** ➤ ***stratum***.

Strasbourg ['stræzbɜ:g] **n** Strasbourg.

stratagem ['strætədʒəm] **n** stratagème *m*.

strategic [strə'ti:dʒɪk] **adj** stratégique.

strategically [strə'ti:dʒɪklɪ] **adv** stratégiquement, du point de vue de la stratégie.

strategist ['strætɪdʒɪst] **n** stratège *m*.

strategy ['strætɪdʒɪ] (pl **-ies**) **n** stratégie *f*.

stratified ['strætɪfaɪd] **adj 1.** GEOL stratifié(e) **2.** *fig* [society] divisé(e) en différentes couches sociales.

stratosphere ['strætə,sfɪəʳ] **n : the stratosphere** la stratosphère.

stratum ['strɑ:təm] (pl **-ta** [-tə]) **n 1.** GEOL strate *f*, couche *f* **2.** *fig* [of society] couche *f*.

straw [strɔ:] ■ **n** paille *f* ▸ **to clutch at straws** se raccrocher à n'importe quoi ▸ **the last straw** la goutte qui fait déborder le vase ▸ **that's the last straw!** ça c'est le comble!
■ **comp** de *OR* en paille.

strawberry ['strɔ:bərɪ] ■ **n** (pl **-ies**) [fruit] fraise *f*.
■ **comp** [tart, yoghurt] aux fraises / [jam] de fraises.

straw hat **n** chapeau *m* de paille.

straw poll **n** sondage *m* d'opinion.

stray [streɪ] ■ **adj 1.** [animal] errant(e), perdu(e) **2.** [bullet] perdu(e) / [example] isolé(e).
■ **n** [animal] animal *m* errant.
■ **vi 1.** [person, animal] errer, s'égarer **2.** [thoughts] vagabonder, errer.

streak [stri:k] ■ **n 1.** [line] bande *f*, marque *f* ▸ **the tears had left grubby streaks down her face** les larmes avaient laissé des traînées sales sur ses joues ▸ **to have blond streaks put in one's hair** se faire faire des mèches blondes ▸ **streak of lightning** éclair *m* **2.** [in character] côté *m* ▸ **a streak of cruelty** une propension à la cruauté **3.** [period] **: a winning/losing streak** une période *OR* série de succès/d'échecs **4.** *inf* [naked dash] **: to do a streak** *traverser un lieu public nu en courant.*
■ **vi** [move quickly] se déplacer comme un éclair.
■ **vt : the wall was streaked with paint** il y avait des traînées de peinture sur le mur ▸ **she's had her hair streaked** elle s'est fait faire des mèches.

streaked [stri:kt] **adj** [marked] **: to be streaked with** être maculé(e) de, porter des traces de.

streaky ['stri:kɪ] (comp **-ier**, superl **-iest**) **adj** [paint] qui n'est pas uniforme / [surface] couvert(e) de traces.

streaky bacon n *UK* bacon *m* assez gras.

stream [stri:m] ■ **n 1.** [small river] ruisseau *m*
2. [of liquid, light] flot *m*, jet *m* ▸ **a red hot stream of lava flowed down the mountain** une coulée de lave incandescente descendait le flanc de la montagne
3. [of people, cars] flot *m* / [of complaints, abuse] torrent *m* ▸ **we've received a steady stream of applications** nous avons reçu un flot incessant de candidatures ▸ **she unleashed a stream of insults** elle lâcha un torrent d'injures ▸ **stream of consciousness** monologue *m* intérieur
4. *UK* SCH classe *f* de niveau ▸ **we're in the top stream** nous sommes dans la section forte.
■ **vi 1.** [liquid] couler à flots, ruisseler / [light] entrer à flots ▸ **tears streamed down her face** des larmes ruisselaient sur son visage ▸ **sunlight streamed into the room** le soleil entra à flots dans la pièce
2. [people, cars] affluer ▸ **to stream in/out** entrer/sortir à flots ▸ **to stream past** passer à flots ▸ **I watched as the demonstrators streamed past** je regardai passer les flots de manifestants.
■ **vt** *UK* **1.** COMPUT transmettre en continu *(sur l'Internet)*
2. SCH répartir par niveau.

streamer ['stri:məʳ] **n** [for party] serpentin *m*.

streamline ['stri:mlaɪn] **vt 1.** [make aerodynamic] caréner, donner un profil aérodynamique à **2.** [make efficient] rationaliser.

streamlined ['stri:mlaɪnd] **adj 1.** [aerodynamic] au profil aérodynamique **2.** [efficient] rationalisé(e).

streamlining ['stri:mlaɪnɪŋ] **n 1.** AUT & AERON carénage *m* **2.** ECON & INDUST [of business, organization] rationalisation *f* / [of industry] dégraissage *m*, restructuration *f*.

street [stri:t] **n** rue *f* ▸ **it's right up his street** *inf* c'est son rayon ▸ **to be streets ahead of sb** *UK* devancer *OR* dépasser qqn de loin.

streetcar ['stri:tkɑ:ʳ] **n** *US* tramway *m*.

street-cred **n** *(U) inf* image *f* (de marque).

street lamp, street light **n** réverbère *m*.

street lighting **n** éclairage *m* des rues.

street map **n** plan *m*.

street market **n** marché *m* en plein air.

street plan **n** plan *m*.

street value **n** [of drugs] valeur *f* à la revente.

streetwise ['stri:twaɪz] **adj** *inf* averti(e), futé(e).

strength [streŋθ] **n 1.** [gen] force *f* ▸ **with all my strength** de toutes mes forces ▸ **his strength failed him** ses forces l'ont trahi *OR* abandonné ▸ **to lose strength** perdre des forces, s'affaiblir ▸ **to get one's strength back** reprendre des *OR* recouvrer ses forces ▸ **strength of character** force de caractère ▸ **strength of purpose** résolution *f* ▸ **strength of will** volonté *f* ▸ **on the strength of** [evidence] sur la foi de / [advice] en s'appuyant sur, en vertu de ▸ **he was accepted on the strength of his excellent record** il a été accepté grâce à ses excellents antécédents
2. [power, influence] puissance *f* ▸ **to go from strength to strength** connaître un succès de plus en plus éclatant, prospérer
3. [solidity, of currency] solidité *f* ▸ **the dollar has gained/fallen in strength** le dollar s'est consolidé/a chuté
4. [number] effectif *m* ▸ **in strength** en force, en grand nombre ▸ **at full strength** au (grand) complet ▸ **to be below strength** avoir un effectif insuffisant.

strengthen ['streŋθn] ■ **vt 1.** [structure, team, argument] renforcer **2.** [economy, currency, friendship] consolider **3.** [resolve, dislike] fortifier, affermir **4.** [person] enhardir.
■ **vi 1.** [sales, economy] s'améliorer **2.** [opposition] s'affermir, se renforcer **3.** [friendship] se cimenter, se consolider **4.** [currency] se raffermir.

strengthening ['streŋθənɪŋ] ■ **n 1.** [physical - of body, muscle] raffermissement *m* / [- of voice] renforcement *m* / [- of hold, grip] resserrement *m* **2.** [increase - of emotion, effect, desire] renforcement *m*, augmentation *f*, intensification *f* / [reinforcement - of character, friendship, position] renforcement *m* / [- of wind, current] renforcement *m*
3. [of structure, building] renforcement *m*, consolidation *f*
4. FIN consolidation *f*.
■ **adj** fortifiant(e), remontant(e) / MED tonifiant(e).

strenuous ['strenjʊəs] **adj** [exercise, activity] fatigant(e), dur(e) / [effort] vigoureux(euse), acharné(e).

stress [stres] ■ **n 1.** [emphasis] **: stress (on)** accent *m* (sur) ▸ **to lay stress on sthg** [fact, point, qualities] insister sur
2. [mental] stress *m*, tension *f* ▸ **to suffer from stress** être stressé ▸ **the stresses and strains of being a parent** les angoisses qu'on éprouve lorsqu'on a des enfants ▸ **to be under stress** être stressé(e) ▸ **I always work better under stress** je travaille toujours mieux quand je suis sous pression **3.** TECH **: stress (on)** contrainte *f* (sur), effort *m* (sur) ▸ **there is too much stress on the foundations** la contrainte que subissent les fondations est trop forte
4. LING accent *m*.
■ **vt 1.** [emphasize] souligner, insister sur **2.** LING accentuer.
■ **vi** *inf* stresser.
◆ ***stress out*** **vt** *inf* stresser.

stress-buster **n** *inf* éliminateur *m* de stress.

stressed [strest] **adj** [tense] stressé(e).

stressed-out **adj** *inf* stressé(e).

stressful ['stresfʊl] **adj** stressant(e).

stress management **n** gestion *f* du stress.

stretch [stretʃ] ■ **n 1.** [of land, water] étendue *f* / [of road, river] partie *f*, section *f* ▸ **a new stretch of road/motorway** un nouveau tronçon de route/d'autoroute ▸ **it's a lovely stretch of river/scenery** cette partie de la rivière/du paysage est magnifique
2. [of time] période *f* ▸ **for long stretches at a time there was nothing to do** il n'y avait rien à faire pendant de longues périodes ▸ **he did a stretch in Dartmoor** *inf* il a fait de la taule à Dartmoor
3. SPORT [exercise] étirement *m* ▸ **do a couple of stretches before breakfast** faites quelques exercices d'assouplissement avant le petit déjeuner
4. [effort] **: to be at full stretch** [factory, machine] fonctionner à plein régime / [person] se donner à fond ▸ **by no stretch of the imagination** même avec beaucoup d'imagination.
■ **vt 1.** [arms] allonger / [legs] se dégourdir / [muscles] distendre

2. [pull taut] tendre, étirer ▸ **to stretch sthg out of shape** [garment, shoes] déformer qqch
3. [overwork - person] surmener / [- resources, budget] grever ▸ **our resources are stretched to the limit** nos ressources sont exploitées OR utilisées au maximum ▸ **that's stretching it a bit (far)!** là vous exagérez!, là vous allez un peu loin! ▸ **I suppose we could stretch a point and let him stay** je suppose qu'on pourrait faire une entorse au règlement et lui permettre de rester
4. [challenge] **: to stretch sb** pousser qqn à la limite de ses capacités.
■ **vi 1.** [area] **: to stretch over** s'étendre sur ▸ **to stretch from... to** s'étendre de... à ▸ **the forest stretches as far as the eye can see** la forêt s'étend à perte de vue
2. [person, animal] s'étirer ▸ **he had to stretch to reach it** [reach out] il a dû tendre le bras pour l'atteindre / [stand on tiptoe] il a dû se mettre sur la pointe des pieds pour l'atteindre
3. [material, elastic] se tendre, s'étirer ▸ **my salary won't stretch to a new car** mon salaire ne me permet pas d'acheter une nouvelle voiture.
■ **adj** extensible.
◆ ***at a stretch*** **adv** d'affilée, sans interruption.
◆ ***stretch out*** ■ **vt sep** [arm, leg, hand] tendre ▸ **she lay stretched out in front of the television** elle était allongée par terre devant la télévision.
■ **vi** [lie down] s'étendre, s'allonger.

stretcher ['stretʃər] **n** brancard *m*, civière *f*.

stretcher party **n** équipe *f* de brancardiers.

stretchmarks ['stretʃmɑːks] **npl** vergetures *fpl*.

stretchy ['stretʃɪ] (**comp -ier, superl -iest**) **adj** extensible, élastique.

strew [struː] (**pt -ed, pp strewn** [struːn] OR **-ed**) **vt : to be strewn on** OR **over** être éparpillé(e) sur ▸ **to be strewn with** être jonché(e) de.

stricken ['strɪkn] **adj : to be stricken by** OR **with panic** être pris(e) de panique ▸ **to be stricken by an illness** souffrir OR être atteint(e) d'une maladie.

strict [strɪkt] **adj 1.** [gen] strict(e) ▸ **in the strict sense of the word** au sens strict du terme ▸ **he told me in the strictest confidence** il me l'a dit à titre strictement confidentiel ▸ **in strict secrecy** dans le plus grand secret
2. [faithful] **: she's a strict Catholic** elle observe rigoureusement la foi catholique.

strictly ['strɪktlɪ] **adv 1.** [gen] strictement ▸ **strictly speaking** à proprement parler **2.** [severely] d'une manière stricte, sévèrement.

strictness ['strɪktnɪs] **n** sévérité *f*.

stride [straɪd] ■ **n** [long step] grand pas *m*, enjambée *f* ▸▸ **to take sthg in one's stride** ne pas se laisser démonter par qqch.
■ **vi** (**pt strode, pp stridden** ['strɪdn]) marcher à grandes enjambées OR à grands pas.
◆ ***strides*** **npl** [progress] **: to make (great) strides** faire des progrès rapides.

strident ['straɪdnt] **adj 1.** [voice, sound] strident(e) **2.** [demand, attack] véhément(e), bruyant(e).

strife [straɪf] **n** *(U)* conflit *m*, lutte *f*.

strike [straɪk] ■ **n 1.** [by workers] grève *f* ▸ **to be (out) on strike** être en grève ▸ **to go on strike** faire grève, se mettre en grève
2. MIL raid *m* ▸ **to carry out air strikes against** OR **on enemy bases** lancer des raids aériens contre des bases ennemies
3. [of oil, gold] découverte *f* ▸ **it was a lucky strike** c'était un coup de chance.
■ **comp** de grève ▸ **to threaten strike action** menacer de faire OR de se mettre en grève.
■ **vt** (**pt & pp struck**) **1.** [hit - deliberately] frapper / [- accidentally] heurter ▸ **she struck him across the face** elle lui a donné une gifle ▸ **a wave struck the side of the boat** une vague a heurté le côté du bateau ▸ **to be struck by lightning** être frappé par la foudre, être foudroyé ▸ **an earthquake struck the city** un tremblement de terre a frappé la ville
2. [subj: thought] venir à l'esprit de ▸ **she strikes me as (being) very capable** elle me fait l'impression d'être très capable, elle me paraît très capable ▸ **it suddenly struck him how little had changed** il a soudain pris conscience du fait que peu de choses avaient changé ▸ **a terrible thought struck her** une idée affreuse lui vint à l'esprit
3. [impress] **: to be struck by** OR **with** être frappé(e) par ▸ **I was very struck with** *UK* OR **by** *US* **the flat** l'appartement m'a plu énormément
4. [conclude - deal, bargain] conclure ▸ **I'll strike a bargain with you** je te propose un marché
5. [light - match] frotter
6. [find] découvrir, trouver ▸ **to strike a balance (between)** trouver le juste milieu (entre) ▸ **to strike a serious/happy note** adopter un ton sérieux/gai
▸▸ **to strike a chord : does it strike a chord?** est-ce que cela te rappelle OR dit quelque chose? ▸ **to be struck blind** être frappé(e) de cécité, devenir aveugle ▸ **to be struck dumb** rester muet ▸ **to strike fear** OR **terror into sb** frapper qqn de terreur ▸ **to strike (it) lucky** avoir de la veine ▸ **to strike it rich** trouver le filon.
■ **vi** (**pt & pp struck**) **1.** [workers] faire grève
2. [hit] frapper ▸ **to strike home** [blow] porter / [missile, remark] faire mouche
3. [attack] attaquer ▸ **the murderer has struck again** l'assassin a encore frappé ▸ **we were travelling quietly along when disaster struck** nous roulions tranquillement lorsque la catastrophe s'est produite
4. [chime] sonner.
◆ ***strike back*** **vi** se venger, exercer des représailles.
◆ ***strike down*** **vt sep** terrasser.
◆ ***strike off*** **vt sep : to be struck off** être radié(e) OR rayé(e).
◆ ***strike out*** ■ **vt sep** rayer, barrer.
■ **vi** [head out] se mettre en route, partir ▸ **to strike out on one's own** [in business] se mettre à son compte.
◆ ***strike up*** ■ **vt insep 1.** [conversation] commencer, engager ▸ **to strike up a friendship (with)** se lier d'amitié (avec)
2. [music] commencer à jouer.
■ **vi** commencer à jouer.

strikebound ['straɪkbaʊnd] **adj** paralysé(e) par la grève.

strikebreaker ['straɪk,breɪkər] **n** briseur *m*, -euse *f* de grève.

strike pay n *(U)* allocation *f* de grève, allocation-gréviste *f*.

striker ['straɪkər] n **1.** [person on strike] gréviste *mf* **2.** FOOTBALL buteur *m*.

striking ['straɪkɪŋ] adj **1.** [noticeable] frappant(e), saisissant(e) **2.** [attractive] d'une beauté frappante.

striking distance n **: to be within striking distance (of)** être à deux pas (de) ▸ **to be within striking distance of doing sthg** *fig* être à deux doigts de faire qqch.

strikingly ['straɪkɪŋlɪ] adv remarquablement ▸ **a strikingly beautiful woman** une femme d'une beauté saisissante.

string [strɪŋ] ■ n **1.** *(U)* [thin rope] ficelle *f*
2. [piece of thin rope] bout *m* de ficelle ▸ **(with) no strings attached** sans conditions ▸ **to have sb on a string** *inf* mener qqn par le bout du nez ▸ **to pull strings** faire jouer le piston
3. [of beads, pearls] rang *m* ▸ **a string of islands** un chapelet d'îles ▸ **a string of fairy lights** une guirlande (électrique) ▸ **she owns a string of shops** elle est propriétaire d'une chaîne de magasins
4. [series] série *f*, suite *f*
5. [of musical instrument] corde *f*.
■ comp **: string vest** tricot *m* de peau à grosses mailles ▸ **string bag** filet *m* à provisions.
■ vt (pt & pp **strung** [strʌŋ]) **1.** [guitar, violin] monter, mettre des cordes à / [racket] corder
2. [beads, pearls] enfiler
3. [hang] suspendre ▸ **Christmas lights had been strung across the street** des décorations de Noël avaient été suspendues en travers de la rue.
◆ ***strings*** npl MUS **: the strings** les cordes *fpl*.
◆ ***string along*** (pt & pp **strung along**) vt sep *inf* [deceive] faire marcher, tromper.
◆ ***string out*** (pt & pp **strung out**) vt insep échelonner.
◆ ***string together*** (pt & pp **strung together**) vt sep *fig* aligner ▸ **she can barely string two words together in French** c'est à peine si elle peut faire une phrase en français.
◆ ***string up*** vt sep *inf* [kill by hanging] pendre.

string bean n haricot *m* vert.

stringed instrument [ˌstrɪŋd-] n instrument *m* à cordes.

stringent ['strɪndʒənt] adj strict(e), rigoureux(euse).

string quartet n quatuor *m* à cordes.

strip [strɪp] ■ n **1.** [narrow piece] bande *f* ▸ **she cut the dough/material into strips** elle coupa la pâte en lamelles/le tissu en bandes ▸ **to tear a strip off sb, to tear sb off a strip** *UK* passer un bon savon à qqn, sonner les cloches à qqn **2.** *UK* SPORT tenue *f*.
■ vt (pt & pp **-ped**, cont **-ping**) **1.** [undress] déshabiller, dévêtir ▸ **they were stripped to the waist** ils étaient torse nu, ils étaient nus jusqu'à la ceinture **2.** [remove covering] enlever ▸ **the walls need to be stripped first** [of wallpaper] il faut d'abord enlever *OR* arracher le papier peint / [of paint] il faut d'abord décaper les murs ▸ **to strip a bed** défaire un lit **3.** [take away from] **: to strip sb of sthg** dépouiller qqn de qqch ▸ **he was stripped of his rank** il a été dégradé **4.** [dismantle - engine, gun] démonter.
■ vi (pt & pp **-ped**, cont **-ping**) **1.** [undress] se déshabiller, se dévêtir **2.** [do a striptease] faire un strip-tease.
◆ ***strip off*** ■ vt sep enlever, ôter.
■ vi se déshabiller, se dévêtir.

strip cartoon n *UK* bande *f* dessinée.

strip club n boîte *f* de strip-tease.

stripe [straɪp] n **1.** [band of colour] rayure *f* **2.** [sign of rank] galon *m*.

striped [straɪpt] adj à rayures, rayé(e).

strip lighting n éclairage *m* au néon.

stripper ['strɪpər] n **1.** [performer of striptease] strip-teaseur *m*, -euse *f* **2.** [for paint] décapant *m*.

strip-search ■ n fouille *f* d'une personne dévêtue.
■ vt **: to strip-search sb** obliger qqn à se déshabiller pour le fouiller.

strip show n (spectacle *m* de) strip-tease *m*.

striptease ['strɪpti:z] n strip-tease *m*.

stripy ['straɪpɪ] (comp **-ier**, superl **-iest**) adj à rayures, rayé(e).

strive [straɪv] (pt **strove**, pp **striven** ['strɪvn]) vi **: to strive for sthg** essayer d'obtenir qqch ▸ **to strive to do sthg** s'efforcer de faire qqch.

strobe (light) ['strəʊb-] n lumière *f* stroboscopique.

strode [strəʊd] pt ➤ ***stride***.

stroke [strəʊk] ■ n **1.** MED attaque *f* cérébrale ▸ **to have a stroke** avoir une attaque **2.** [of pen, brush] trait *m* **3.** [in swimming - movement] mouvement *m* des bras / [- style] nage *f* **4.** [in rowing] coup *m* d'aviron ▸ **to be off one's stroke** ne pas être au mieux de sa forme **5.** [in golf, tennis] coup *m* **6.** [of clock] **: on the third stroke** ≃ au quatrième top ▸ **at the stroke of 12** sur le coup de minuit **7.** *UK* TYPO [oblique] barre *f* ▸ **225 stroke 62** *UK* 225 barre oblique 62 **8.** [caress] caresse *f* ▸ **she gave the cat a stroke** elle a caressé le chat **9.** [piece] **: a stroke of genius** un trait de génie ▸ **a stroke of luck** un coup de chance *OR* de veine ▸ **not to do a stroke of work** ne pas en ficher une datte *OR* rame, ne rien faire ▸ **at a stroke** d'un seul coup.
■ vt caresser.

stroll [strəʊl] ■ n petite promenade *f*, petit tour *m*.
■ vi se promener, flâner.

stroller ['strəʊlər] n *US* [for baby] poussette *f*.

strong [strɒŋ] adj **1.** [gen] fort(e) ▸ **there is a strong chance** *OR* **probability that he will win** il y a de fortes chances pour qu'il gagne ▸ **he had a strong sense of guilt** il éprouvait un fort sentiment de culpabilité ▸ **she is particularly strong in science subjects** elle est particulièrement forte dans les matières scientifiques ▸ **to bear a strong resemblance to sb** ressembler beaucoup *OR* fortement à qqn ▸ **his speech made a strong impression on them** son discours les a fortement impressionnés *OR* a eu un profond effet sur eux ▸ **strong point** point *m* fort
2. [structure, argument, friendship] solide ▸ **they have a strong case** ils ont de bons arguments ▸ **we're in a strong bargaining position** nous sommes bien placés *OR* en position de force pour négocier
3. [healthy] robuste, vigoureux(euse) ▸ **to be still going strong** [person, group] être toujours d'attaque, être solide au poste / [machine] marcher toujours bien

4. [policy, measures] énergique ▸ **he is a strong believer in discipline** il est de ceux qui croient fermement à la discipline ▸ **she is a strong supporter of the government** elle soutient le gouvernement avec ferveur
5. [intense, vivid - desire, imagination, interest] vif(vive) / [- colour] vif, fort(e) ▸ **to exert a strong influence on sb** exercer beaucoup d'influence *OR* une forte influence sur qqn
6. [in numbers] **: the crowd was 2,000 strong** il y avait une foule de 2 000 personnes
7. [team, candidate] sérieux(euse), qui a des chances de gagner ▸ **he is a strong contender for the presidency** il a de fortes chances de remporter l'élection présidentielle.

strongarm ['strɒŋɑ:m] **adj : strongarm tactics** la méthode forte.

strongbox ['strɒŋbɒks] **n** coffre-fort *m.*

stronghold ['strɒŋhəʊld] **n** *fig* bastion *m.*

strong language **n** *(U) euph* grossièretés *fpl* ▸ **to use strong language** dire des grossièretés, tenir des propos grossiers.

strongly ['strɒŋlɪ] **adv 1.** [gen] fortement ▸ **I strongly disagree with you** je ne suis pas du tout d'accord avec vous ▸ **the report was strongly critical of the hospital** le rapport était extrêmement critique à l'égard de l'hôpital ▸ **I feel very strongly about the matter** c'est un sujet *OR* une affaire qui me tient beaucoup à cœur **2.** [solidly] solidement.

strong man **n** [in circus] homme *m* fort, hercule *m.*

strong-minded [-'maɪndɪd] **adj** résolu(e).

strong room **n** chambre *f* forte.

strong-willed [-'wɪld] **adj** têtu(e), volontaire.

strop [strɒp] ■ **n** cuir *m* (à rasoir).
■ **vt (pt & pp -ped, cont -ping)** [razor] repasser sur le cuir.

stroppy ['strɒpɪ] **(comp -ier, superl -iest) adj** *UK inf* difficile.

strove [strəʊv] **pt** ➤ ***strive.***

struck [strʌk] **pt & pp** ➤ ***strike.***

structural ['strʌktʃərəl] **adj** de construction.

structuralism ['strʌktʃərəlɪzm] **n** structuralisme *m.*

structuralist ['strʌktʃərəlɪst] ■ **n** structuraliste *mf.*
■ **adj** structuraliste.

structurally ['strʌktʃərəlɪ] **adv** du point de vue de la construction.

structure ['strʌktʃər] ■ **n 1.** [organization] structure *f* **2.** [building] construction *f.*
■ **vt** structurer.

structured ['strʌktʃəd] **adj** structuré(e).

struggle ['strʌgl] ■ **n 1.** [great effort] **: struggle (for sthg/to do sthg)** lutte *f* (pour qqch/pour faire qqch) ▸ **I finally succeeded but not without a struggle** j'y suis finalement parvenu, non sans peine ▸ **it was a struggle to convince him** on a eu du mal à le convaincre **2.** [fight] bagarre *f.*
■ **vi 1.** [make great effort] **: to struggle (for)** lutter (pour) ▸ **to struggle to do sthg** s'efforcer de faire qqch **2.** [to free oneself] se débattre / [fight] se battre ▸ **she struggled with her attacker** elle a lutté contre *OR* s'est battue avec son agresseur **3.** [move with difficulty] **: to struggle to one's feet** se lever avec difficulté.
◆ ***struggle on*** **vi : to struggle on (with)** persévérer (dans).

struggling ['strʌglɪŋ] **adj** qui a du mal *OR* des difficultés.

strum [strʌm] **(pt & pp -med, cont -ming) vt** [guitar] gratter de / [tune] jouer.

strung [strʌŋ] **pt & pp** ➤ ***string.***

strung-out *v inf* **adj 1.** *drug sl* **: to be strung-out** [addicted] être accroché(e), être accro / [high] être shooté(e), planer / [suffering withdrawal symptoms] être en manque **2.** [uptight] crispé(e), tendu(e).

strut [strʌt] ■ **n 1.** CONSTR étai *m*, support *m* **2.** AERON pilier *m.*
■ **vi (pt & pp -ted, cont -ting)** se pavaner.

strychnine ['strɪkni:n] **n** strychnine *f.*

stub [stʌb] ■ **n 1.** [of cigarette] mégot *m* / [of pencil] morceau *m* **2.** [of ticket, cheque] talon *m.*
■ **vt (pt & pp -bed, cont -bing) : to stub one's toe** se cogner le doigt de pied.
◆ ***stub out*** **vt sep** écraser.

stubble ['stʌbl] **n** *(U)* **1.** [in field] chaume *m* **2.** [on chin] barbe *f* de plusieurs jours.

stubbly ['stʌblɪ] **adj (comp -ier, superl -iest) 1.** [chin, face] mal rasé(e) / [beard] de plusieurs jours / [hair] en brosse **2.** [field] couvert(e) de chaume.

stubborn ['stʌbən] **adj 1.** [person] têtu(e), obstiné(e) **2.** [stain] qui ne veut pas partir, rebelle.

stubbornly ['stʌbənlɪ] **adv** obstinément.

stubby ['stʌbɪ] **(comp -ier, superl -iest) adj** boudiné(e).

stucco ['stʌkəʊ] **n** stuc *m.*

stuck [stʌk] ■ **pt & pp** ➤ ***stick.***
■ **adj 1.** [jammed, trapped] coincé(e) ▸ **to be *OR* to get stuck in traffic** être coincé *OR* bloqué dans les embouteillages ▸ **to get stuck in the mud** s'embourber **2.** [stumped] **: to be stuck** sécher ▸ **if you get stuck go on to the next question** si tu sèches, passe à la question suivante **3.** [stranded] bloqué(e), en rade ▸ **they were *OR* they got stuck at the airport overnight** ils sont restés bloqués *OR* ils ont dû passer toute la nuit à l'aéroport **4.** *inf* [lumbered] **: as usual I got stuck with (doing) the washing-up** comme d'habitude, c'est moi qui me suis tapé la vaisselle ▸ **he was stuck with the nickname "Teddy"** le surnom de "Teddy" lui est resté.

stuck-up **adj** *inf pej* bêcheur(euse).

stud [stʌd] **n 1.** [metal decoration] clou *m* décoratif **2.** [earring] clou *m* d'oreille **3.** *UK* [on boot, shoe] clou *m* / [on sports boots] crampon *m* **4.** [of horses] haras *m* ▸ **to be put out to stud** être utilisé comme étalon.

studded ['stʌdɪd] **adj : studded (with)** parsemé(e) (de), constellé(e) (de).

student ['stju:dnt] ■ **n** étudiant *m*, -e *f.*
■ **comp** [life] estudiantin(e) / [politics] des étudiants / [disco] pour étudiants ▸ **student nurse** élève-infirmière *f.*

student card **n** carte *f* d'étudiant.

student loan **n** *prêt bancaire pour étudiants.*

students' union **n** **1.** [organization] union *f* des étudiants **2.** [building] club *m* (des étudiants).

student teacher **n** [in primary school] instituteur *m*, -trice *f* stagiaire / [in secondary school] professeur *m* stagiaire.

stud farm **n** haras *m*.

studied ['stʌdɪd] **adj** étudié(e), calculé(e).

studio ['stju:dɪəʊ] (pl **-s**) **n** studio *m* / [of artist] atelier *m*.

studio apartment **n** *US* = ***studio flat***.

studio audience **n** public *m* invité.

studio flat *UK*, ***studio apartment*** *US* **n** studio *m*.

studious ['stju:djəs] **adj** studieux(euse).

studiously ['stju:djəslɪ] **adv** studieusement.

study ['stʌdɪ] ■ **n** (pl **-ies**) **1.** [gen] étude *f* **2.** [room] bureau *m*.
■ **vt** (pt & pp **-ied**) **1.** [learn] étudier, faire des études de **2.** [examine] examiner, étudier.
■ **vi** (pt & pp **-ied**) étudier, faire ses études.

stuff [stʌf] ■ **n** *(U)* **1.** *inf* [things] choses *fpl* ▸ **he writes some good stuff** il écrit de bons trucs ▸ **they go climbing and sailing and stuff like that** ils font de l'escalade, de la voile et des trucs du même genre ▸ **and all that stuff** et tout ça ▸ **to know one's stuff** s'y connaître ▸ **that's the stuff!** c'est ça!, allez-y!
2. [substance] substance *f* ▸ **what's that sticky stuff in the sink?** qu'est-ce que c'est que ce truc gluant dans l'évier?
3. *inf* [belongings] affaires *fpl* ▸ **where's my shaving/fishing stuff?** où est mon matériel de rasage/de pêche? ▸ **clear all that stuff off the table!** enlève tout ce bazar de sur la table!
■ **vt 1.** [push] fourrer / [expressing anger, rejection] **: he told me I could stuff my report** *v inf* il m'a dit qu'il se foutait pas mal de mon rapport
2. [fill] **: to stuff sthg (with)** remplir *OR* bourrer qqch (de) ▸ **stuffed with foam** rembourré de mousse ▸ **her head is stuffed with useless information** elle a la tête farcie de renseignements inutiles
3. *inf* [with food] **: to stuff o.s. (with** *OR* **on)** se gaver (de), s'empiffrer (de)
4. CULIN farcir
5. [in taxidermy - animal, bird] empailler.
◆ ***stuff up*** **vt sep** [block] boucher.

stuffed [stʌft] **adj 1.** [filled] **: stuffed with** bourré(e) de **2.** *inf* [with food] gavé(e) **3.** CULIN farci(e) **4.** [toy] en peluche ▸ **he loves stuffed animals** il adore les peluches **5.** [preserved - animal] empaillé(e)
▸▸ **get stuffed!** *UK v inf* va te faire foutre!

stuffily ['stʌfɪlɪ] **adv** [say, reply] d'un ton désapprobateur.

stuffing ['stʌfɪŋ] **n** *(U)* **1.** [filling] bourre *f*, rembourrage *m* **2.** CULIN farce *f*.

stuffy ['stʌfɪ] (comp **-ier**, superl **-iest**) **adj 1.** [room] mal aéré(e), qui manque d'air **2.** [person, club] vieux jeu *(inv)*.

stumble ['stʌmbl] **vi** trébucher.
◆ ***stumble across***, ***stumble on*** **vt insep** tomber sur.

stumbling block ['stʌmblɪŋ-] **n** pierre *f* d'achoppement.

stump [stʌmp] ■ **n** [of tree] souche *f* / [of arm, leg] moignon *m*.
■ **vt** [subj: question, problem] dérouter, rendre perplexe.
■ **vi : to stump in/out** entrer/sortir à pas lourds.
◆ ***stumps*** **npl** CRICKET piquets *mpl*.
◆ ***stump up*** **vt insep** *UK inf* cracher, payer.

stun [stʌn] (pt & pp **-ned**, cont **-ning**) **vt 1.** [knock unconscious] étourdir, assommer **2.** [surprise] stupéfier, renverser.

stung [stʌŋ] **pt & pp** ➤ ***sting***.

stun grenade **n** grenade *f* cataplexiante.

stunk [stʌŋk] **pt & pp** ➤ ***stink***.

stunned [stʌnd] **adj 1.** [knocked out] assommé(e) **2.** *fig* abasourdi(e), stupéfait(e) ▸ **she was stunned by the news** la nouvelle l'a abasourdi.

stunner ['stʌnəʳ] **n** *inf* [woman] fille *f* superbe / [car] voiture *f* fantastique.

stunning ['stʌnɪŋ] **adj 1.** [very beautiful] ravissant(e) / [scenery] merveilleux(euse) **2.** [surprising] stupéfiant(e), renversant(e).

stunningly ['stʌnɪŋlɪ] **adv** remarquablement, incroyablement ▸ **stunningly beautiful** d'une beauté éblouissante.

stunt [stʌnt] ■ **n 1.** [for publicity] coup *m* **2.** CIN cascade *f*.
■ **vt** retarder, arrêter.

stunted ['stʌntɪd] **adj** rabougri(e).

stunt man **n** cascadeur *m*.

stunt woman **n** cascadeuse *f*.

stupefaction [ˌstju:pɪ'fækʃn] **n** stupéfaction *f*, stupeur *f*.

stupefied ['stju:pɪfaɪd] **adj** stupéfait(e).

stupefy ['stju:pɪfaɪ] (pt & pp **-ied**) **vt 1.** [tire] abrutir **2.** [surprise] stupéfier, abasourdir.

stupefying ['stju:pɪfaɪɪŋ] **adj** stupéfiant(e).

stupendous [stju:'pendəs] **adj** extraordinaire, prodigieux(euse).

stupid ['stju:pɪd] **adj 1.** [foolish] stupide, bête **2.** *inf* [annoying] fichu(e).

stupidity [stju:'pɪdətɪ] **n** *(U)* bêtise *f*, stupidité *f*.

stupidly ['stju:pɪdlɪ] **adv** stupidement.

stupor ['stju:pəʳ] **n** stupeur *f*, hébétude *f*.

sturdy ['stɜ:dɪ] (comp **-ier**, superl **-iest**) **adj** [person] robuste / [furniture, structure] solide.

sturgeon ['stɜ:dʒən] (pl **sturgeon**) **n** esturgeon *m*.

stutter ['stʌtəʳ] ■ **n** bégaiement *m*.
■ **vi** bégayer.

sty [staɪ] (pl **sties**) **n** [pigsty] porcherie *f*.

stye [staɪ] **n** orgelet *m*, compère-loriot *m*.

style [staɪl] ■ **n 1.** [characteristic manner] style *m* ▸ **I don't like his style of dressing** je n'aime pas sa façon de s'habiller ▸ **they've adopted a new management style** [approach] ils ont adopté un nouveau style de gestion ▸ **house style** TYPO [in editing] style de la maison

2. (U) [elegance] chic *m*, élégance *f* ▸ **she's got real style** elle a vraiment de l'allure OR du chic ▸ **to live in style** mener grand train, vivre dans le luxe ▸ **he likes to do things in style** il aime faire bien les choses
3. [design] genre *m*, modèle *m* ▸ **to be dressed in the latest style** être habillé à la dernière mode ▸ **all the latest styles** tous les derniers modèles.
■ **vt** [design - dress, house] créer, dessiner ▸ **to style sb's hair** coiffer qqn ▸ **styled for comfort and elegance** conçu pour le confort et l'élégance.

-style suffix dans le style de ▸ **baroque-style architecture** architecture *f* de style baroque, baroque *m*.

styling ['staılıŋ] **n** [of dress] forme *f*, ligne *f* / [of hair] coupe *f* / [of car] ligne *f* ▸ **styling gel** gel *m* coiffant.

styling mousse **n** mousse *f* coiffante.

stylish ['staılıʃ] **adj** chic *(inv)*, élégant(e).

stylishly ['staılıʃlı] **adv** [dress] avec chic, avec allure, élégamment / [live] élégamment / [write] avec style OR élégance.

stylishness ['staılıʃnıs] **n** chic *m*, élégance *f*.

stylist ['staılıst] **n** [hairdresser] coiffeur *m*, -euse *f*.

stylistic [staı'lıstık] **adj** ART, LIT & LING stylistique.

stylistically [staı'lıstıklı] **adv** d'un point de vue stylistique.

stylized, UK ***-ised*** ['staılaızd] **adj** stylisé(e).

stylus ['staıləs] (pl -es) **n** [on record player] pointe *f* de lecture, saphir *m*.

stymie ['staımı] **vt** *inf* [plan] contrarier, contrecarrer ▸ **to be stymied** [person] être coincé(e).

Styrofoam® ['staırəfəʊm] **n** polystyrène *m* expansé.

suave [swɑ:v] **adj** doucereux(euse).

sub [sʌb] **n** *inf* **1.** SPORT (abbr of ***substitute***) remplaçant *m*, -e *f* **2.** (abbr of ***submarine***) sous-marin *m* **3.** *UK* (abbr of ***subscription***) cotisation *f* **4.** *US* [sandwich] sandwich *m* (de baguette).

sub- prefix sous-, sub-.

subcommittee ['sʌbkəˌmıtı] **n** sous-comité *m*.

subconscious [ˌsʌb'kɒnʃəs] ■ **adj** inconscient(e).
■ **n : the subconscious** l'inconscient *m*.

subconsciously [ˌsʌb'kɒnʃəslı] **adv** inconsciemment.

subcontinent [ˌsʌb'kɒntınənt] **n** sous-continent *m*.

subcontract [ˌsʌbkən'trækt] **vt** sous-traiter.

subcontracting [ˌsʌbkən'træktıŋ] **adj** sous-traitant(e).

subcontractor [ˌsʌbkən'træktəʳ] **n** sous-traitant *m*.

subculture ['sʌbˌkʌltʃəʳ] **n** sous-culture *f*.

subcutaneous [ˌsʌbkju:'teınjəs] **adj** sous-cutané(e).

subdivide [ˌsʌbdı'vaıd] **vt** subdiviser.

subdivision [ˌsʌbdı'vıʒn] **n** subdivision *f*.

subdue [səb'dju:] **vt 1.** [control - rioters, enemy] soumettre, subjuguer / [- temper, anger] maîtriser, réprimer **2.** [light, colour] adoucir, atténuer.

subdued [səb'dju:d] **adj 1.** [person] abattu(e) **2.** [anger, emotion] contenu(e) **3.** [colour] doux (douce) / [light] tamisé(e).

subedit [ˌsʌb'edıt] *UK* ■ **vt** corriger, préparer pour l'impression.
■ **vi** travailler comme secrétaire de rédaction.

subeditor [ˌsʌb'edıtəʳ] **n** *UK* secrétaire *mf* de rédaction.

subentry [ˌsʌb'entrı] (pl -ies) **n** sous-entrée *f*.

subgroup ['sʌbgru:p] **n** sous-groupe *m*.

subheading ['sʌbˌhedıŋ] **n** sous-titre *m*.

subhuman [ˌsʌb'hju:mən] **adj** *pej* [crime] brutal(e), bestial(e).

subject ■ **adj** ['sʌbdʒekt] soumis(e) ▸ **to be subject to** [tax, law] être soumis à / [disease, headaches] être sujet (sujette) à ▸ **we are all subject to the rule of law** nous sommes tous soumis à la loi ▸ **the terms are subject to alteration without notice** les termes peuvent être modifiés sans préavis ▸ **subject to tax** imposable.
■ **n** ['sʌbdʒekt] **1.** [gen] sujet *m* ▸ **on the subject of** au sujet de, à propos de ▸ **don't try and change the subject** n'essaie pas de changer de conversation OR de sujet ▸ **while we're on the subject** à (ce) propos ▸ **subject: recruitment of new staff** [in letters and memos] objet: recrutement de personnel
2. SCH & UNIV matière *f* ▸ **it's not really my subject** ce n'est pas vraiment mon domaine.
■ **vt** [səb'dʒekt] **1.** [control] soumettre, assujettir
2. [force to experience] **: to subject sb to sthg** exposer OR soumettre qqn à qqch.
◆ ***subject to*** **prep** ['sʌbdʒekt] sous réserve de ▸ **subject to passing the exam** à condition de réussir l'examen.

subjection [səb'dʒekʃn] **n** sujétion *f*, soumission *f*.

subjective [səb'dʒektıv] **adj** subjectif(ive).

subjectively [səb'dʒektıvlı] **adv** subjectivement.

HOW TO ...

change the subject

Au fait, tu as des nouvelles de Jean-Pierre ? / By the way, have you heard from Jean-Pierre?

Puisqu'on parle d'argent, tu n'oublies pas que tu me dois 10 euros ? / Talking of money, you haven't forgotten that you owe me 10 euros, have you?

À propos de livres, ce n'est pas à toi que j'aurais prêté « Germinal », par hasard ? / While we're on the subject of books, it wasn't you that I lent "Germinal" to, was it?

Avant que j'oublie, ta mère a appelé / Before I forget, your mother called

Tout ça c'est très bien, mais on n'a toujours pas parlé du cadeau d'Annick / That's all well and good, but we still haven't discussed Annick's present

Et si on parlait d'autre chose ? / Let's talk about something else!

subjectivity [ˌsʌbdʒek'tɪvətɪ] **n** subjectivité *f*.

subject matter **n** *(U)* sujet *m*.

sub judice [-'dʒuːdɪsɪ] **adj** LAW en train de passer devant le tribunal.

subjugate ['sʌbdʒʊgeɪt] **vt** [people, country] conquérir, subjuguer.

subjunctive [səb'dʒʌŋktɪv] **n** GRAM **: subjunctive (mood)** (mode *m*) subjonctif *m*.

sublet [ˌsʌb'let] (pt & pp **sublet**, cont **-ting**) **vt** sous-louer.

sublimation [ˌsʌblɪ'meɪʃn] **n** sublimation *f*.

sublime [sə'blaɪm] **adj** sublime ▸ **from the sublime to the ridiculous** du sublime au ridicule ***OR*** grotesque.

sublimely [sə'blaɪmlɪ] **adv** suprêmement, souverainement.

subliminal [ˌsʌb'lɪmɪnl] **adj** subliminal(e).

submachine gun [ˌsʌbmə'ʃiːn-] **n** mitraillette *f*.

submarine [ˌsʌbmə'riːn] **n** sous-marin *m*.

submenu ['sʌbˌmenjuː] **n** COMPUT sous-menu *m*.

submerge [səb'mɜːdʒ] ■ **vt** immerger, plonger ▸ **to submerge o.s. in sthg** *fig* se plonger dans qqch.
■ **vi** s'immerger, plonger.

submerged [səb'mɜːdʒd] **adj** submergé(e) ▸ **a submerged volcano** un volcan sous-marin.

submersible [səb'mɜːsəbl] ■ **adj** submersible.
■ **n** submersible *m*.

submersion [səb'mɜːʃn] **n** **1.** [in liquid] immersion *f* / [of submarine] plongée *f* **2.** [flooding] inondation *f*.

submission [səb'mɪʃn] **n** **1.** [obedience] soumission *f* **2.** [presentation] présentation *f*, soumission *f*.

submissive [səb'mɪsɪv] **adj** soumis(e), docile.

submissively [səb'mɪsɪvlɪ] **adv** [behave, confess, accept] docilement / [yield, react] avec résignation.

submissiveness [səb'mɪsɪvnɪs] **n** soumission *f*, docilité *f*.

submit [səb'mɪt] (pt & pp **-ted**, cont **-ting**) ■ **vt** soumettre.
■ **vi : to submit (to)** se soumettre (à).

subnormal [ˌsʌb'nɔːml] **adj** arriéré(e), attardé(e).

subordinate ■ **adj** [sə'bɔːdɪnət] *fml* [less important] **: subordinate (to)** subordonné(e) (à), moins important(e) (que).
■ **n** [sə'bɔːdɪnət] subordonné *m*, -e *f*.
■ **vt** [sə'bɔːdɪneɪt] subordonner, faire passer après.

subordinate clause **n** proposition *f* subordonnée.

subordination [səˌbɔːdɪ'neɪʃn] **n** subordination *f*.

subpoena [sə'piːnə] ■ **n** LAW citation *f*, assignation *f*.
■ **vt** (pt & pp **-ed**) LAW citer ***OR*** assigner à comparaître.

sub-post office **n** *UK* petit bureau *m* de poste.

subprogram ['sʌbˌprəʊgræm] **n** COMPUT sous-programme *m*.

subroutine ['sʌbruːˌtiːn] **n** COMPUT sous-programme *m*.

subscribe [səb'skraɪb] ■ **vi** **1.** [to magazine, ISP] s'abonner, être abonné(e) **2.** [to view, belief] **: to subscribe to** être d'accord avec, approuver.
■ **vt** [money] donner.

subscriber [səb'skraɪbəʳ] **n** **1.** [to magazine, service] abonné *m*, -e *f* **2.** [to charity, campaign] souscripteur *m*, -trice *f*.

subscription [səb'skrɪpʃn] **n** **1.** [to magazine] abonnement *m* **2.** *UK* [to charity, campaign] souscription *f* **3.** *UK* [to club] cotisation *f*.

subsection ['sʌbˌsekʃn] **n** subdivision *f*, paragraphe *m*.

subsequent ['sʌbsɪkwənt] **adj** ultérieur(e), suivant(e).

subsequently ['sʌbsɪkwəntlɪ] **adv** par la suite, plus tard.

subservient [səb'sɜːvjənt] **adj** [servile] **: subservient (to)** servile (vis-à-vis de), obséquieux(euse) (envers).

subset ['sʌbset] **n** MATHS sous-ensemble *m*.

subside [səb'saɪd] **vi** **1.** [pain, anger] se calmer, s'atténuer / [noise] diminuer **2.** [CONSTR - building] s'affaisser / [- ground] se tasser.

subsidence [səb'saɪdns ***OR*** 'sʌbsɪdns] **n** [CONSTR - of building] affaissement *m* / [- of ground] tassement *m*.

subsidiarity [səbsɪdɪ'ærɪtɪ] **n** subsidiarité *f*.

subsidiary [səb'sɪdjərɪ] ■ **adj** subsidiaire.
■ **n** (pl **-ies**) **: subsidiary (company)** filiale *f*.

subsidize, *UK* ***-ise*** ['sʌbsɪdaɪz] **vt** subventionner.

subsidized industry **n** industrie *f* subventionnée.

subsidy ['sʌbsɪdɪ] (pl **-ies**) **n** subvention *f*, subside *m*.

subsist [səb'sɪst] **vi : to subsist (on)** vivre (de).

subsistence [səb'sɪstəns] **n** subsistance *f*, existence *f*.

subsistence allowance **n** *(U)* *UK* frais *mpl* de subsistance.

subsistence economy **n** économie *f* de subsistance.

subsistence farming **n** agriculture *f* d'autoconsommation.

subsistence level **n** minimum *m* vital.

substance ['sʌbstəns] **n** **1.** [gen] substance *f* **2.** [importance] importance *f*.

substance abuse **n** *fml* abus *m* de stupéfiants.

substandard [ˌsʌb'stændəd] **adj** de qualité inférieure.

substantial [səb'stænʃl] **adj** **1.** [considerable] considérable, important(e) / [meal] substantiel(elle) **2.** [solid, well-built] solide.

substantially [səb'stænʃəlɪ] **adv** **1.** [considerably] considérablement ▸ **substantially better** bien mieux ▸ **substantially bigger** beaucoup plus grand **2.** [mainly] en grande partie.

substantiate [səb'stænʃɪeɪt] **vt** *fml* prouver, établir.

substantive [sʌb'stæntɪv] **adj** *fml* [meaningful] positif(ive), constructif(ive).

substitute ['sʌbstɪtju:t] ■ **n 1.** [replacement] **: substitute (for)** [person] remplaçant *m*, -e *f* (de) / [thing] succédané *m* (de) ▸ **to be no substitute for sthg** ne pas pouvoir remplacer qqch **2.** SPORT remplaçant *m*, -e *f*.
■ **vt : to substitute A for B** substituer A à B, remplacer B par A.
■ **vi : to substitute for sb/sthg** remplacer qqn/qqch.

substitute teacher **n** *US* suppléant *m*, -e *f*.

substitution [ˌsʌbstɪ'tju:ʃn] **n** substitution *f*, remplacement *m*.

subterfuge ['sʌbtəfju:dʒ] **n** subterfuge *m*.

subterranean [ˌsʌbtə'reɪnjən] **adj** souterrain(e).

subtitle ['sʌbˌtaɪtl] **n** sous-titre *m*.

subtitled ['sʌbˌtaɪtld] **adj** sous-titré(e), avec sous-titrage.

subtitling ['sʌbˌtaɪtlɪŋ] **n** sous-titrage *m*.

subtle ['sʌtl] **adj** subtil(e).

subtlety ['sʌtltɪ] **n** subtilité *f*.

subtly ['sʌtlɪ] **adv** subtilement.

subtotal ['sʌbˌtəʊtl] **n** total *m* partiel.

subtract [səb'trækt] **vt : to subtract sthg (from)** soustraire qqch (de).

subtraction [səb'trækʃn] **n** soustraction *f*.

subtropical [ˌsʌb'trɒpɪkl] **adj** subtropical(e).

suburb ['sʌbɜ:b] **n** faubourg *m*.
◆ ***suburbs*** **npl : the suburbs** la banlieue.

suburban [sə'bɜ:bn] **adj 1.** [of suburbs] de banlieue **2.** *pej* [life] étriqué(e) / [person] à l'esprit étroit.

suburbia [sə'bɜ:bɪə] **n** *(U)* la banlieue.

subversion [səb'vɜ:ʃn] **n** subversion *f*.

subversive [səb'vɜ:sɪv] ■ **adj** subversif(ive).
■ **n** personne *f* qui agit de façon subversive.

subvert [səb'vɜ:t] **vt** subvertir, renverser.

subway ['sʌbweɪ] **n 1.** *UK* [underground walkway] passage *m* souterrain **2.** *US* [underground railway] métro *m*.

sub-zero **adj** au-dessous de zéro.

succeed [sək'si:d] ■ **vt** succéder à.
■ **vi** réussir ▸ **to succeed in doing sthg** réussir à faire qqch.

succeeding [sək'si:dɪŋ] **adj** *fml* [in future] à venir / [in past] suivant(e).

success [sək'ses] **n** succès *m*, réussite *f*.

successful [sək'sesfʊl] **adj 1.** [attempt] couronné(e) de succès ▸ **she was not successful in her application for the post** sa candidature à ce poste n'a pas été retenue ▸ **I was successful in convincing them** j'ai réussi OR je suis arrivé OR je suis parvenu à les convaincre **2.** [film, book] à succès / [person] qui a du succès ▸ **she's a successful businesswoman** elle a réussi dans les affaires.

successfully [sək'sesfʊlɪ] **adv** avec succès.

succession [sək'seʃn] **n** succession *f* ▸ **in (quick** OR **close) succession** coup sur soup.

successive [sək'sesɪv] **adj** successif(ive).

successively [sək'sesɪvlɪ] **adv** [in turn] successivement, tour à tour, l'un/l'une après l'autre.

successor [sək'sesər] **n** successeur *m*.

success story **n** réussite *f*.

succinct [sək'sɪŋkt] **adj** succinct(e).

succinctly [sək'sɪŋktlɪ] **adv** succinctement, de façon succincte.

succour *UK*, ***succor*** *US* ['sʌkər] **n** *(U) liter* secours *m*.

succulent ['sʌkjʊlənt] **adj** succulent(e).

succumb [sə'kʌm] **vi : to succumb (to)** succomber (à).

such [sʌtʃ] ■ **adj** tel (telle), pareil(eille) ▸ **such nonsense** de telles inepties ▸ **do you have such a thing as a tin-opener?** est-ce que tu aurais un ouvre-boîtes par hasard? ▸ **such money/books as I have** le peu d'argent/de livres que j'ai ▸ **such... that** tel... que.
■ **adv 1.** [for emphasis] si, tellement ▸ **it's such a horrible day!** quelle journée épouvantable! ▸ **such a lot of books** tellement de livres ▸ **such a long time** si OR tellement longtemps
2. [in comparisons] aussi.
■ **pron : and such (like)** et autres choses de ce genre ▸ **this is my car, such as it is** voilà ma voiture, pour ce qu'elle vaut ▸ **have some wine, such as there is** prenez un peu de vin, il en reste un petit fond.
◆ ***as such*** **adv** en tant que tel (telle), en soi.
◆ ***such and such*** **adj** tel et tel (telle et telle).

suchlike ['sʌtʃlaɪk] **adj** de ce genre, de la sorte.

suck [sʌk] **vt 1.** [with mouth] sucer **2.** [draw in] aspirer **3.** *fig* [involve] **: to be sucked into sthg** être impliqué(e) dans qqch.
◆ ***suck up*** **vi** *UK inf* **: to suck up (to sb)** faire de la lèche (à qqn).

sucker ['sʌkər] **n 1.** [suction pad] ventouse *f* **2.** *inf* [gullible person] poire *f*.

suckle ['sʌkl] ■ **vt** allaiter.
■ **vi** téter.

sucrose ['su:krəʊz] **n** saccharose *m*.

suction ['sʌkʃn] **n** succion *f*

suction pump **n** pompe *f* aspirante.

Sudan [su:'dɑ:n] **n** Soudan *m* ▸ **in (the) Sudan** au Soudan.

Sudanese [ˌsu:də'ni:z] ■ **adj** soudanais(e).
■ **npl : the Sudanese** les Soudanais *mpl*.

sudden ['sʌdn] **adj** soudain(e), brusque ▸ **all of a sudden** tout d'un coup, soudain.

sudden death **n** SPORT *jeu pour départager les ex aequo (le premier point perdu entraîne l'élimination immédiate).*

suddenly ['sʌdnlɪ] **adv** soudainement, tout d'un coup.

suddenness ['sʌdnnɪs] **n** soudaineté *f*.

suds [sʌdz] **npl** mousse *f* de savon.

sue [su:] **vt : to sue sb (for)** poursuivre qqn en justice (pour).

suede [sweɪd] ■ **n** daim *m*.
■ **comp** en daim.

suet ['sʊɪt] **n** graisse *f* de rognon.

Suez ['sʊɪz] **n** Suez.

Suez Canal **n : the Suez Canal** le canal de Suez.

suffer ['sʌfəʳ] ■ **vt 1.** [pain, injury] souffrir de ▸ **she suffered a lot of pain** elle a beaucoup souffert **2.** [consequences, setback, loss] subir ▸ **you'll have to suffer the consequences** vous devrez en subir les conséquences.
■ **vi** souffrir ▸ **it's the children who suffer in a marriage break-up** ce sont les enfants qui souffrent lors d'une séparation ▸ **her health is suffering under all this stress** sa santé se ressent de tout ce stress ▸ **to suffer from** MED souffrir de ▸ **to suffer from diabetes** être diabétique ▸ **they're still suffering from shock** ils sont encore sous le choc.

sufferance ['sʌfrəns] **n : on sufferance** par tolérance.

sufferer ['sʌfrəʳ] **n** MED malade *mf.*

suffering ['sʌfrɪŋ] **n** souffrance *f.*

suffice [sə'faɪs] **vi** *fml* suffire.

sufficiency [sə'fɪʃnsɪ] (pl -ies) **n** quantité *f* suffisante ▸ **the country already had a sufficiency of oil** le pays avait déjà suffisamment de pétrole *OR* du pétrole en quantité suffisante.

sufficient [sə'fɪʃnt] **adj** suffisant(e).

sufficiently [sə'fɪʃntlɪ] **adv** suffisamment.

suffix ['sʌfɪks] **n** suffixe *m.*

suffocate ['sʌfəkeɪt] **vt & vi** suffoquer.

suffocating ['sʌfəkeɪtɪŋ] **adj 1.** [heat, room] suffocant(e), étouffant(e) / [smoke, fumes] asphyxiant(e), suffocant(e) **2.** *fig* étouffant(e).

suffocation [,sʌfə'keɪʃn] **n** suffocation *f.*

suffrage ['sʌfrɪdʒ] **n** suffrage *m.*

suffragette [sʌfrə'dʒet] **n** POL suffragette *f.*

suffuse [sə'fju:z] **vt** baigner.

sugar ['ʃʊgəʳ] ■ **n** sucre *m.*
■ **vt** sucrer.

sugar beet **n** betterave *f* à sucre.

sugar bowl **n** sucrier *m.*

sugarcane ['ʃʊgəkeɪn] **n** *(U)* canne *f* à sucre.

sugar-coated [-'kəʊtɪd] **adj** dragéifié(e).

sugared ['ʃʊgəd] **adj** sucré(e).

sugar-free **adj** sans sucre.

sugar lump **n** morceau *m* de sucre.

sugar refinery **n** raffinerie *f* de sucre.

sugary ['ʃʊgərɪ] **adj 1.** [food] sucré(e) **2.** *pej* [sentimental] doucereux(euse).

suggest [sə'dʒest] **vt 1.** [propose] proposer, suggérer ▸ **I suggest (that) we do nothing for the moment** je suggère *OR* je propose que nous ne fassions rien pour l'instant ▸ **he suggested that the meeting be held next Tuesday** il a proposé de fixer la réunion à mardi prochain **2.** [imply] suggérer ▸ **just what are you suggesting?** que voulez-vous dire par là?, qu'allez-vous insinuer là?

suggestion [sə'dʒestʃn] **n 1.** [proposal] proposition *f*, suggestion *f* **2.** *(U)* [implication] suggestion *f.*

suggestive [sə'dʒestɪv] **adj** suggestif(ive) ▸ **to be suggestive of sthg** suggérer qqch.

suggestively [sə'dʒestɪvlɪ] **adv** de façon suggestive.

suicidal [sʊɪ'saɪdl] **adj** suicidaire.

suicide ['sʊɪsaɪd] **n** suicide *m* ▸ **to commit suicide** se suicider.

suicide attempt **n** tentative *f* de suicide.

suit [su:t] ■ **n 1.** [for man] costume *m*, complet *m* / [for woman] tailleur *m* **2.** [outfit] **: ski/diving suit** combinaison *f* de ski/de plongée ▸ **suit of armour** armure *f* complète **3.** [in cards] couleur *f* **4.** LAW procès *m*, action *f*
⏭ **to follow suit** *fig* faire de même.
■ **vt 1.** [subj: clothes, hairstyle] aller à **2.** [be convenient, appropriate to] convenir à ▸ **Tuesday suits me best** c'est mardi qui me convient *OR* qui m'arrange le mieux ▸ **to suit o.s.** faire comme on veut.
■ **vi** convenir, aller ▸ **will that date suit?** cette date vous convient-elle *OR* est-elle à votre convenance?

suitability [,su:tə'bɪlətɪ] **n** convenance *f* / [of candidate] aptitude *f.*

suitable ['su:təbl] **adj** qui convient, qui va.

suitably ['su:təblɪ] **adv** convenablement ▸ **suitably impressed** favorablement impressionné.

suitcase ['su:tkeɪs] **n** valise *f.*

suite [swi:t] **n 1.** [of rooms] suite *f* **2.** [of furniture] ensemble *m.*

suited ['su:tɪd] **adj 1.** [suitable] **: to be suited to/for** convenir à/pour, aller à/pour **2.** [couple] **: well suited** très bien assortis ▸ **ideally suited** faits l'un pour l'autre.

suitor ['su:təʳ] **n** *dated* soupirant *m.*

sulfate *US* = ***sulphate.***

sulfur *US* = ***sulphur.***

HOW TO ...

make a suggestion

J'aimerais faire une proposition / I'd like to make a suggestion
Et si on allait au restaurant ? / Why don't we go to a restaurant?
On va voir une exposition ? / Let's go to an exhibition.
Qu'est-ce que vous diriez d'une partie de cartes ? / How about a game of cards?
Une petite balade, ça vous dirait ? / How about going for a walk?
Tu ne veux pas qu'on aille au cinéma ? / Why don't we go to the cinema?
On pourrait peut-être lui offrir un livre / Maybe we could buy him a book
Pourquoi ne lui en parlerais-tu pas ? / Why don't you talk to him about it?
Je propose que nous en reparlions demain / I suggest we talk about this again tomorrow

sulfuric acid US = ***sulphuric acid***.

sulk [sʌlk] ■ **n** bouderie *f*.
■ **vi** bouder.

sulkily ['sʌlkɪlɪ] **adv** [act] en boudant, d'un air maussade / [answer] d'un ton maussade.

sulky ['sʌlkɪ] (comp **-ier**, superl **-iest**) **adj** boudeur(euse).

sullen ['sʌlən] **adj** maussade.

sullenly ['sʌlənlɪ] **adv** [behave] d'un air maussade ***OR*** renfrogné / [answer, say, refuse] d'un ton maussade / [agree, obey] de mauvaise grâce, à contre-cœur.

sulphate UK, ***sulfate*** US ['sʌlfeɪt] **n** sulfate *m*.

sulphur UK, ***sulfur*** US ['sʌlfəʳ] **n** soufre *m*.

sulphuric acid UK, ***sulfuric acid*** US [sʌl'fjʊərɪk-] **n** acide *m* sulfurique.

sultan ['sʌltən] **n** sultan *m*.

sultana [səl'tɑːnə] **n** UK [dried grape] raisin *m* sec.

sultry ['sʌltrɪ] (comp **-ier**, superl **-iest**) **adj** **1.** [weather] lourd(e) **2.** [sexual] sensuel(elle).

sum [sʌm] **n** **1.** [amount of money] somme *f* **2.** [calculation] calcul *m*.
◆ ***sum up*** (pt & pp **-med up**, cont **-ming up**) ■ **vt sep** [summarize] résumer.
■ **vi** récapituler.

Sumatra [sʊ'mɑːtrə] **n** Sumatra *f* ▸ **in Sumatra** à Sumatra.

Sumatran [sʊ'mɑːtrən] ■ **adj** sumatranais(e).
■ **n** Sumatranais *m*, -e *f*.

summarily ['sʌmərəlɪ] **adv** sommairement.

summarize, UK ***-ise*** ['sʌməraɪz] ■ **vt** résumer.
■ **vi** récapituler.

summary ['sʌmərɪ] ■ **adj** sommaire.
■ **n** (pl **-ies**) résumé *m*.

summation [sʌ'meɪʃn] **n** **1.** [total] addition *f* **2.** [summary] résumé *m*.

summer ['sʌməʳ] ■ **n** été *m* ▸ **in summer** en été.
■ **comp** d'été ▸ **the summer holidays** UK ***OR*** **vacation** US les grandes vacances *fpl*.

summer camp **n** US colonie *f* de vacances.

summerhouse ['sʌməhaʊs] (pl [-haʊzɪz]) **n** pavillon *m* (de verdure).

summer school **n** université *f* d'été.

summertime ['sʌmətaɪm] ■ **adj** d'été.
■ **n** été *m*.

Summer Time **n** UK heure *f* d'été.

summery ['sʌmərɪ] **adj** estival(e).

summing-up [ˌsʌmɪŋ-] (pl **summings-up** [ˌsʌmɪŋz-]) **n** LAW résumé *m*.

summit ['sʌmɪt] **n** sommet *m*.

summon ['sʌmən] **vt** **1.** [send for] appeler, convoquer **2.** LAW citer, assigner ▸ **to summon sb to appear in court** citer qqn en justice ▸ **the court summoned her as a witness** la cour l'a citée comme témoin.
◆ ***summon up*** **vt sep** rassembler.

summons ['sʌmənz] ■ **n** (pl **-es** [-iːz]) LAW assignation *f*.
■ **vt** LAW assigner.

sumo (wrestling) ['suːməʊ-] **n** sumo *m*.

sump [sʌmp] **n** UK carter *m*.

sumptuous ['sʌmptʃʊəs] **adj** somptueux(euse).

sumptuously ['sʌmptʃʊəslɪ] **adv** somptueusement.

sum total **n** somme *f* totale.

sun [sʌn] ■ **n** soleil *m* ▸ **in the sun** au soleil.
■ **vt** (pt & pp **-ned**, cont **-ning**) **: to sun o.s.** se chauffer au soleil.

Sun. (abbr of ***Sunday***) dim.

sunbathe ['sʌnbeɪð] **vi** prendre un bain de soleil.

sunbather ['sʌnbeɪðəʳ] **n** personne *f* qui prend un bain de soleil.

sunbathing ['sʌnbeɪðɪŋ] **n** *(U)* bains *mpl* de soleil.

sunbeam ['sʌnbiːm] **n** rayon *m* de soleil.

sunbed ['sʌnbed] **n** lit *m* à ultra-violets.

sun block **n** écran *m* total.

sunburn ['sʌnbɜːn] **n** *(U)* coup *m* de soleil.

sunburned ['sʌnbɜːnd], ***sunburnt*** ['sʌnbɜːnt] **adj** brûlé(e) par le soleil, qui a attrapé un coup de soleil.

sun cream **n** crème *f* solaire.

sundae ['sʌndeɪ] **n** *coupe de glace aux fruits et à la Chantilly*.

Sunday ['sʌndɪ] **n** dimanche *m* ▸ **Sunday lunch** déjeuner *m* du dimanche ***OR*** dominical ; see also ***Saturday***.

Sunday paper **n** UK *journal hebdomadaire paraissant le dimanche*.

HOW TO ...

summarize

Finalement, on peut dire qu'on s'en bien sorti / You could say that things worked out ok in the end
Après tout, ce n'est pas mon problème / After all, it isn't my problem
Tout compte fait, il est aimable / All things considered, he's quite nice
En fin de compte, je me suis bien amusé / I had a good time in the end
En gros, ça veut dire qu'ils refusent de nous aider / So basically, they are refusing to help us
En un mot, c'est non / In a word, no
Pour résumer, ils ont l'intention de porter plainte / To sum up, they intend to press charges

Sunday school **n** catéchisme *m*.

sundial ['sʌndaɪəl] **n** cadran *m* solaire.

sundown ['sʌndaʊn] **n** coucher *m* du soleil.

sun-dried **adj** séché(e) au soleil.

sundries ['sʌndrɪz] **npl** *fml* articles *mpl* divers, objets *mpl* divers.

sundry ['sʌndrɪ] **adj** *fml* divers(e) ▸ **all and sundry** tout le monde, n'importe qui.

sunflower ['sʌn,flaʊəʳ] **n** tournesol *m*.

sung [sʌŋ] **pp** ➤ ***sing***.

sunglasses ['sʌn,glɑ:sɪz] **npl** lunettes *fpl* de soleil.

sunhat ['sʌnhæt] **n** chapeau *m* de soleil.

sunk [sʌŋk] **pp** ➤ ***sink***.

sunken ['sʌŋkən] **adj 1.** [in water] coulé(e), submergé(e) **2.** [garden] en contrebas / [cheeks, eyes] creux(euse).

sunlamp ['sʌnlæmp] **n** lampe *f* à ultra-violets.

sunlight ['sʌnlaɪt] **n** lumière *f* du soleil.

sunlit ['sʌnlɪt] **adj** ensoleillé(e).

sun lotion **n** lait *m* solaire.

sunlounger ['sʌn,laʊndʒəʳ] **n** *UK* chaise *f* longue *(où l'on s'allonge pour bronzer)*.

Sunni ['sʊnɪ] (pl **-s**) **n** Sunnite *mf*.

sunny ['sʌnɪ] (comp **-ier**, superl **-iest**) **adj 1.** [day, place] ensoleillé(e) ▸ **it's sunny** il fait beau, il fait (du) soleil **2.** [cheerful] radieux(euse), heureux(euse)
▸▸| **sunny side up** *US* [egg] sur le plat.

sunrise ['sʌnraɪz] **n** lever *m* du soleil.

sunrise industry **n** industrie *f* de pointe.

sunroof ['sʌnru:f] **n** toit *m* ouvrant.

sunscreen ['sʌnskri:n] **n** écran *m* OR filtre *m* solaire.

sunset ['sʌnset] **n** coucher *m* du soleil.

sunshade ['sʌnʃeɪd] **n** parasol *m*.

sunshine ['sʌnʃaɪn] **n** lumière *f* du soleil.

sunspot ['sʌnspɒt] **n** tache *f* solaire.

sunstroke ['sʌnstrəʊk] **n** *(U)* insolation *f*.

suntan ['sʌntæn] ■ **n** bronzage *m*.
■ **comp** [lotion, cream] solaire.

suntanned ['sʌntænd] **adj** bronzé(e).

suntrap ['sʌntræp] **n** *UK* endroit très ensoleillé.

sunup ['sʌnʌp] **n** *US inf* lever *m* du soleil.

super ['su:pəʳ] **adj** *inf* génial(e), super *(inv)*.

superabundance [,su:pərə'bʌndəns] **n** surabondance *f*.

superannuated [,su:pə'rænjʊeɪtɪd] **adj 1.** [person] à la retraite, retraité(e) **2.** [object] suranné(e), désuet(ète).

superannuation ['su:pə,rænjʊ'eɪʃn] **n** *(U)* pension *f* de retraite.

superb [su:'pɜ:b] **adj** superbe.

superbly [su:'pɜ:blɪ] **adv** superbement.

Super Bowl **n** *US* **: the Super Bowl** le Super Bowl *finale du championnat des États-Unis de football américain*.

CULTURE

Super Bowl

Le dernier match de la saison de football américain a généralement lieu au début du mois de février. Il se joue entre les vainqueurs des deux conférences organisées par la Ligue nationale de football. Depuis le premier **Super Bowl**, inauguré en 1967 entre les équipes de Green Bay et de Kansas City, l'événement continue d'avoir une audience internationale considérable. Les places dans le stade atteignent des tarifs exorbitants et les annonceurs paient le prix fort pour être diffusés durant les mi-temps : en 2004, le prix moyen pour une annonce commerciale de 30 secondes vaut 2,25 millions de dollars (un site Internet est même consacré à ces publicités).

superbug ['su:pəbʌg] **n** *germe résistant aux traitements antibiotiques*.

supercilious [,su:pə'sɪlɪəs] **adj** hautain(e).

supercomputer [,su:pəkəm'pju:təʳ] **n** superordinateur *m*, supercalculateur *m*.

superficial [,su:pə'fɪʃl] **adj** superficiel(elle).

superficiality ['su:pə,fɪʃɪ'ælətɪ] **n** caractère *m* superficiel, manque *m* de profondeur.

superficially [,su:pə'fɪʃəlɪ] **adv** superficiellement.

superfluous [su:'pɜ:flʊəs] **adj** superflu(e).

Superglue® ['su:pəglu:] **n** colle *f* forte.

superhero ['su:pə,hɪərəʊ] **n** superman *m*, surhomme *m*.

superhighway ['su:pə,haɪweɪ] **n 1.** *US* autoroute *f* **2.** = ***information highway***.

superhuman [,su:pə'hju:mən] **adj** surhumain(e).

superimpose [,su:pərɪm'pəʊz] **vt : to superimpose sthg (on)** superposer qqch (à).

superintend [,su:pərɪn'tend] **vt** diriger.

superintendent [,su:pərɪn'tendənt] **n 1.** *UK* [of police] ≃ commissaire *m* **2.** [of department] directeur *m*, -trice *f*.

superior [su:'pɪərɪəʳ] ■ **adj 1.** [gen] **: superior (to)** supérieur(e) (à) **2.** [goods, craftsmanship] de qualité supérieure.
■ **n** supérieur *m*, -e *f*.

superiority [su:,pɪərɪ'ɒrətɪ] **n** supériorité *f*.

superlative [su:'pɜ:lətɪv] ■ **adj** exceptionnel(elle), sans pareil(eille).
■ **n** GRAM superlatif *m*.

superlatively [su:'pɜ:lətɪvlɪ] **adv** au plus haut degré, exceptionnellement ▸ **a superlatively good candidate** un candidat exceptionnel ▸ **she is superlatively efficient** elle est on ne peut plus efficace.

superman ['su:pəmæn] (pl **-men** [-men]) **n** [gen] surhomme *m* / *hum* superman *m*.
◆ ***Superman*** **n** [comic book hero] Superman *m*.

supermarket ['su:pəˌmɑ:kɪt] **n** supermarché *m*.

supernatural [ˌsu:pə'nætʃrəl] ■ **adj** surnaturel(elle).
■ **n** : **the supernatural** le surnaturel *m*.

superpower ['su:pəˌpaʊəʳ] **n** superpuissance *f*.

superscript ['su:pəskrɪpt] **adj** écrit(e)/imprimé(e) au-dessus de la ligne.

supersede [ˌsu:pə'si:d] **vt** remplacer.

supersonic [ˌsu:pə'sɒnɪk] **adj** supersonique.

superstar ['su:pəstɑ:ʳ] **n** superstar *f*.

superstition [ˌsu:pə'stɪʃn] **n** superstition *f*.

superstitious [ˌsu:pə'stɪʃəs] **adj** superstitieux(euse).

superstitiously [ˌsu:pə'stɪʃəslɪ] **adv** superstitieusement.

superstore ['su:pəstɔ:ʳ] **n** hypermarché *m*.

superstructure ['su:pəˌstrʌktʃəʳ] **n** superstructure *f*.

supertanker ['su:pəˌtæŋkəʳ] **n** supertanker *m*, pétrolier *m* géant.

supertax ['su:pətæks] **n** tranche *f* supérieure de l'impôt.

supervise ['su:pəvaɪz] **vt** surveiller / [work] superviser.

supervision [ˌsu:pə'vɪʒn] **n** surveillance *f* / [of work] supervision *f*.

supervisor ['su:pəvaɪzəʳ] **n** surveillant *m*, -e *f*.

supervisory ['su:pəvaɪzərɪ] **adj** de surveillance ▶ **in a supervisory role** ***OR*** **capacity** à titre de surveillant.

superwoman ['su:pəˌwʊmən] (pl **-women** [-ˌwɪmɪn]) **n** superwoman *f*.

supine ['su:paɪn] **adj** *liter* [on one's back] couché(e) ***OR*** étendu(e) sur le dos.

supper ['sʌpəʳ] **n 1.** [evening meal] dîner *m* **2.** [before bedtime] collation *f*.

supplant [sə'plɑ:nt] **vt** supplanter.

supple ['sʌpl] **adj** souple.

supplement ■ **n** ['sʌplɪmənt] supplément *m*.
■ **vt** ['sʌplɪment] compléter.

supplementary [ˌsʌplɪ'mentərɪ] **adj** supplémentaire.

supplementary benefit **n** *UK ancien nom des allocations supplémentaires accordées aux personnes ayant un faible revenu.*

supplier [sə'plaɪəʳ] **n** fournisseur *m*, -euse *f*.

supply [sə'plaɪ] ■ **n** (pl **-ies**) **1.** [store] réserve *f*, provision *f* ▶ **the nation's supply of oil** les réserves nationales de pétrole ▶ **we're getting in** ***OR*** **laying in a supply of coal** nous faisons des provisions de charbon, nous nous approvisionnons en charbon ▶ **to be in short supply** manquer ▶ **water is in short supply in the southeast** on manque d'eau dans le sud-est
2. [system] alimentation *f*
3. *(U)* ECON offre *f*.
■ **vt** (pt & pp **-ied**) **1.** [provide] : **to supply sthg (to sb)** fournir qqch (à qqn)
2. [provide to] : **to supply sb (with)** fournir qqn (en), approvisionner qqn (en) ▶ **I supplied him with the details/the information** je lui ai fourni les détails/les informations ▶ **to supply sthg with sthg** alimenter qqch en qqch ▶ **to supply electricity/water to a town** alimenter une ville en électricité/eau.
◆ ***supplies*** **npl** [food] vivres *mpl* / MIL approvisionnements *mpl* ▶ **office supplies** fournitures *fpl* de bureau.

supply teacher **n** *UK* suppléant *m*, -e *f*.

support [sə'pɔ:t] ■ **n 1.** *(U)* [physical help] appui *m* ▶ **I was holding his arm for support** je m'appuyais sur son bras **2.** *(U)* [emotional, financial help] soutien *m* ▶ **he's trying to drum up** ***OR*** **to mobilize support for his scheme** il essaie d'obtenir du soutien pour son projet ▶ **to give** ***OR*** **to lend one's support to sthg** accorder ***OR*** prêter son appui à qqch ▶ **to speak in support of a motion** appuyer une motion ▶ **they are striking in support of the miners** ils font grève par solidarité avec les mineurs ▶ **a mutual support scheme** un système d'entraide ▶ **what are your means of support?** quelles sont vos sources de revenus?
3. [object] support *m*, appui *m*
4. *(U)* COMPUT assistance *f*.
■ **vt 1.** [physically] soutenir, supporter / [weight] supporter ▶ **her legs were too weak to support her** ses jambes étaient trop faibles pour la porter
2. [emotionally] soutenir
3. [financially] subvenir aux besoins de ▶ **she has three children to support** elle a trois enfants à charge ▶ **to support o.s.** subvenir à ses propres besoins ▶ **he supports himself by teaching** il gagne sa vie en enseignant
4. [theory] être en faveur de, être partisan de / [political party, candidate] appuyer / SPORT être un supporter de ▶ **I can't support their action** je ne peux pas approuver leur action
5. [substantiate, give weight to] appuyer, confirmer ▶ **there is no evidence to support his claim** il n'y a aucune preuve pour appuyer ses dires.

support band **n** groupe *m* en première partie ▶ **who was the support band?** qui est-ce qu'il y avait en première partie?

supporter [sə'pɔ:təʳ] **n 1.** [of person, plan] partisan *m*, -e *f* **2.** SPORT supporter *m*.

support group **n** groupe *m* d'entraide.

supportive [sə'pɔ:tɪv] **adj** qui est d'un grand secours, qui soutient.

suppose [sə'pəʊz] ■ **vt** supposer ▶ **I don't suppose you could...?** [in polite requests] vous ne pourriez pas... par hasard? ▶ **you don't suppose...?** [asking opinion] vous ne pensez pas que...?
■ **vi** supposer ▶ **I suppose (so)** je suppose que oui ▶ **I suppose not** je suppose que non.
■ **conj** et si, à supposer que *(+ subjunctive)*.

supposed [sə'pəʊzd] **adj 1.** [doubtful] supposé(e) **2.** [reputed, intended] : **to be supposed to be** être censé(e) être.

supposedly [sə'pəʊzɪdlɪ] **adv** soi-disant.

supposing [sə'pəʊzɪŋ] **conj** et si, à supposer que *(+ subjunctive)*.

supposition [ˌsʌpə'zɪʃn] **n** supposition *f*.

suppository [sə'pɒzɪtrɪ] (pl **-ies**) **n** suppositoire *m*.

suppress [sə'pres] **vt 1.** [uprising] réprimer **2.** [information] supprimer ▶ **to suppress evidence** faire disparaître des preuves ▶ **to suppress the truth/a scandal** étouffer la vérité/un scandale ▸ **the government has suppressed the report** le gouvernement a interdit la parution du rapport **3.** [emotions] réprimer, étouffer.

suppression [sə'preʃn] **n 1.** [of uprising, emotions] répression *f* **2.** [of information] suppression *f*.

suppressor [sə'presəʳ] **n** ELEC dispositif *m* antiparasite.

supranational [ˌsu:prə'næʃənl] **adj** supranational(e).

supremacy [sʊ'preməsɪ] **n** suprématie *f*.

supreme [sʊ'pri:m] **adj** suprême.

Supreme Court **n** [in US] **: the Supreme Court** la Cour suprême.

supremely [sʊ'pri:mlɪ] **adv** suprêmement.

supremo [sʊ'pri:məʊ] (pl -s) **n** *UK inf* grand chef *m*.

Supt. abbr of ***superintendent***.

surcharge ['sɜ:tʃɑ:dʒ] ■ **n** [extra payment] surcharge *f* ⁄ [extra tax] surtaxe *f*.
■ **vt** surcharger.

sure [ʃʊəʳ] ■ **adj 1.** [gen] sûr(e) ▸ **insomnia is a sure sign of depression** l'insomnie est un signe incontestable de dépression ▸ **a sure grasp of the subject** *fig* des connaissances solides en la matière ▸ **to be sure of o.s.** être sûr de soi
2. [certain] **: you seem convinced, but I'm not so sure** tu sembles convaincu, mais moi j'ai des doutes ▸ **to be sure (of sthg/of doing sthg)** être sûr(e) (de qqch/de faire qqch), être certain(e) (de qqch/de faire qqch) ▸ **they're sure to get caught** ils vont sûrement se faire prendre ▸ **to make sure (that)...** s'assurer *OR* vérifier que... ; **we made sure that no one was listening** nous nous sommes assurés *OR* nous avons vérifié que personne n'écoutait ▸ **make sure you don't lose your ticket** prends garde à ne pas perdre ton billet
▸▸ **to be sure to do sthg** [remember] s'assurer de faire qqch ▸ **be sure to be on time tomorrow** il faut que vous soyez à l'heure demain ▸ **I am** *OR* **I'm sure (that)...** je suis bien certain que..., je ne doute pas que... ▸ **he'll win, I'm sure** il gagnera, j'en suis sûr ▸ **I'm not sure you're right** je ne suis pas sûr *OR* certain que vous ayez raison.
■ **adv 1.** *inf* [yes] bien sûr
2. *US* [really] vraiment.
◆ ***for sure*** **adv** sans aucun doute, sans faute ▸ **I'll give it to you tomorrow for sure** je te le donnerai demain sans faute.
◆ ***sure enough*** **adv** en effet, effectivement ▸ **she said she'd ring and sure enough she did** elle a dit qu'elle appellerait, et c'est ce qu'elle a fait.

surefire ['ʃʊəfaɪəʳ] **adj** *inf* certain(e), infaillible.

surefooted ['ʃʊəˌfʊtɪd] **adj** d'un pied sûr.

surely ['ʃʊəlɪ] **adv** sûrement.

sureness ['ʃʊənɪs] **n 1.** [certainty] certitude *f* **2.** [assurance] assurance *f* **3.** [steadiness] sûreté *f* ⁄ [accuracy] justesse *f*, précision *f*.

sure thing **excl** *US inf* d'accord!

surety ['ʃʊərətɪ] **n** *(U)* caution *f*.

surf [sɜ:f] ■ **n** ressac *m*.
■ **vt** surfer ▸ **to surf the Net** naviguer sur l'Internet.
■ **vi** surfer.

surface ['sɜ:fɪs] ■ **n** surface *f* ▸ **on the surface** *fig* à première vue, vu de l'extérieur ▸ **below** *OR* **beneath the surface** *fig* au fond ▸ **all the old tensions came** *OR* **rose to the surface when they met** *fig* toutes les vieilles discordes ont refait surface quand ils se sont revus ▸ **to scratch the surface** *fig* [of problem] effleurer le problème ⁄ [of subject] effleurer le sujet.
■ **vi 1.** [diver] remonter à la surface ⁄ [submarine] faire surface **2.** [problem, rumour] apparaître *OR* s'étaler au grand jour **3.** *inf hum* [after absence] refaire surface.

surface area **n** surface *f*, superficie *f*.

surface mail **n** courrier *m* par voie de terre/de mer.

surface-to-air **adj** sol-air *(inv)*.

surfboard ['sɜ:fbɔ:d] **n** planche *f* de surf.

surfboarding ['sɜ:fbɔ:dɪŋ] **n** surf *m*.

surfeit ['sɜ:fɪt] **n** *fml* excès *m*.

surfer ['sɜ:fəʳ] **n** surfeur *m*, -euse *f*.

surfing ['sɜ:fɪŋ] **n** surf *m*.

surge [sɜ:dʒ] ■ **n 1.** [of people, vehicles] déferlement *m* ⁄ ELEC surtension *f* **2.** [of emotion, interest] vague *f*, montée *f* ⁄ [of anger] bouffée *f* ⁄ [of sales, applications] afflux *m*.
■ **vi 1.** [people, vehicles] déferler **2.** [emotion] monter.

surgeon ['sɜ:dʒən] **n** chirurgien *m*, -ienne *f*.

surgery ['sɜ:dʒərɪ] (pl **-ies**) **n 1.** *(U)* MED [performing operations] chirurgie *f* **2.** *UK* MED [place] cabinet *m* de consultation **3.** *UK* MED & POL [consulting period] consultation *f*.

surgical ['sɜ:dʒɪkl] **adj** chirurgical(e) ▸ **surgical stocking** bas *m* orthopédique.

surgically ['sɜ:dʒɪklɪ] **adv** par intervention chirurgicale.

surgical spirit **n** *UK* alcool *m* à 90°.

Surinam [ˌsʊərɪ'næm] **n** Surinam *m*, Suriname *m* ▸ **in Surinam** au Surinam.

HOW TO ...

express supposition

Supposons qu'il ait raison et qu'elle démissionne ⁄ Supposing he's right and she does resign
En admettant qu'on commence demain, est-ce que nous tiendrons les délais ? ⁄ Assuming we start tomorrow, will we meet the deadline?
Et s'il décidait de ne plus vendre ? ⁄ What if he decided not to sell?
Et à supposer qu'il ne puisse pas être présent ? ⁄ Supposing he can't be there?
J'imagine qu'il a eu un empêchement ⁄ I guess something came up

surly ['sɜ:lɪ] (comp -**ier**, superl -**iest**) **adj** revêche, renfrogné(e).

surmise [sɜ:'maɪz] **vt** *fml* présumer.

surmount [sɜ:'maʊnt] **vt** surmonter.

surname ['sɜ:neɪm] **n** nom *m* de famille.

FALSE FRIENDS / FAUX AMIS

surname

Surnom n'est pas la traduction du mot anglais *surname*. Surnom se traduit par *nickname*.

▸ Elle s'appelle Victoire et son surnom, c'est Vic / *Her name is Victoire and her nickname is Vic*

surpass [sə'pɑ:s] **vt** *fml* dépasser.

surplus ['sɜ:pləs] ■ **adj** en surplus.
■ **n** surplus *m*.

surprise [sə'praɪz] ■ **n** surprise *f* ▸ **his resignation came as a surprise to everyone** sa démission a surpris tout le monde ▸ **to give sb a surprise** faire une surprise à qqn ▸ **to take sb by surprise** prendre qqn au dépourvu.
■ **vt** surprendre ▸ **it surprised me that they didn't give her the job** j'ai été surpris *OR* étonné qu'ils ne l'aient pas embauchée.

surprised [sə'praɪzd] **adj** surpris(e) ▸ **I wouldn't be surprised (if...)** ça ne m'étonnerait pas (que...)

surprising [sə'praɪzɪŋ] **adj** surprenant(e).

surprisingly [sə'praɪzɪŋlɪ] **adv** étonnamment.

surreal [sə'rɪəl] **adj** surréaliste.

surrealism [sə'rɪəlɪzm] **n** surréalisme *m*.

surrealist [sə'rɪəlɪst] ■ **adj** surréaliste.
■ **n** surréaliste *mf*.

surrealistic [sə,rɪəl'ɪstɪk] **adj** **1.** ART & LIT surréaliste **2.** *fig* surréel(elle), surréaliste.

surrender [sə'rendəʳ] ■ **n** reddition *f*, capitulation *f*.
■ **vt** *fml* [weapons, passport] rendre / [claim, rights] renoncer à.
■ **vi** **1.** [stop fighting] **: to surrender (to)** se rendre (à) **2.** *fig* [give in] **: to surrender (to)** se laisser aller (à), se livrer (à).

surreptitious [,sʌrəp'tɪʃəs] **adj** subreptice.

surreptitiously [,sʌrəp'tɪʃəslɪ] **adv** subrepticement, furtivement, à la dérobée.

surrogacy ['sʌrəgəsɪ] **n** maternité *f* de remplacement *OR* de substitution.

surrogate ['sʌrəgeɪt] ■ **adj** de substitution.
■ **n** substitut *m*.

surrogate mother **n** mère *f* porteuse.

surround [sə'raʊnd] ■ **n** bordure *f*.
■ **vt** entourer / [subj: police, army] cerner.

surrounding [sə'raʊndɪŋ] **adj** environnant(e).

surroundings [sə'raʊndɪŋz] **npl** environnement *m*.

surtax ['sɜ:tæks] **n** surtaxe *f*.

surveillance [sɜ:'veɪləns] **n** surveillance *f*.

survey ■ **n** ['sɜ:veɪ] **1.** [investigation] étude *f* / [of public opinion] sondage *m* **2.** [of land] levé *m* / [of building] inspection *f*.
■ **vt** [sə'veɪ] **1.** [contemplate] passer en revue **2.** [investigate] faire une étude de, enquêter sur **3.** [land] faire le levé de / [building] inspecter.

surveying [sə'veɪɪŋ] **n** [measuring - of land] arpentage *m*, levé *m* / *UK* [examination - of buildings] examen *m*.

surveyor [sə'veɪəʳ] **n** [of building] expert *m*, -e *f* / [of land] géomètre *m*.

survival [sə'vaɪvl] **n** **1.** [continuing to live] survie *f* **2.** [relic] vestige *m*.

survive [sə'vaɪv] ■ **vt** survivre à.
■ **vi** survivre.
◆ ***survive on*** **vt insep** vivre de.

surviving [sə'vaɪvɪŋ] **adj** survivant(e) ▸ **his only surviving son** son seul fils encore en vie.

survivor [sə'vaɪvəʳ] **n** survivant *m*, -e *f* / *fig* battant *m*, -e *f*.

susceptibility [sə,septə'bɪlətɪ] (pl -**ies**) **n** **1.** [predisposition - to an illness] prédisposition *f* **2.** [vulnerability] sensibilité *f* ▸ **his susceptibility to flattery** sa sensibilité à la flatterie **3.** [sensitivity] sensibilité *f*, émotivité *f* **4.** PHYS susceptibilité *f*.

susceptible [sə'septəbl] **adj : susceptible (to)** sensible (à).

sushi ['su:ʃɪ] **n** sushi *m* ▸ **sushi bar** sushi-bar *m*.

suspect ■ **adj** ['sʌspekt] suspect(e).
■ **n** ['sʌspekt] suspect *m*, -e *f*.
■ **vt** [sə'spekt] **1.** [distrust] douter de **2.** [think likely, consider guilty] soupçonner ▸ **to suspect sb of sthg** soupçonner qqn de qqch.

HOW TO ...

express surprise

Eh bien, pour une surprise c'est une surprise ! / This certainly is a surprise!.
Quelle bonne surprise ! / What a nice surprise !
Ça alors ! / Well I never!
Je n'en crois pas mes yeux ! / I can't believe my eyes!
(C'est) incroyable ! / (That's) amazing!
Alors ça, c'est la meilleure ! *inf* / I've never heard anything like it!
Tu ne devineras jamais ce qu'elle m'a dit ! / You'll never guess what she said to me!
Il faut le voir pour le croire / It has to be seen to be believed
Je n'en reviens toujours pas / I still can't get over it
Ça m'en bouche un coin ! *inf* / I'm impressed!
Ça m'a fait un de ces chocs ! *inf* / I got one hell of a shock!
Tu aurais vu sa tête ! *inf* / You should have seen his face!

suspected [sə'spektɪd] adj présumé(e) ▸ **he's undergoing tests for a suspected tumour** on est en train de lui faire des analyses pour s'assurer qu'il ne s'agit pas d'une tumeur.

suspend [sə'spend] vt **1.** [gen] suspendre **2.** [from school] renvoyer temporairement.

suspended animation [sə'spendɪd-] n hibernation *f*.

suspended sentence [sə'spendɪd-] n condamnation *f* avec sursis.

suspender belt [sə'spendər-] n *UK* porte-jarretelles *m inv*.

suspenders [sə'spendəz] npl **1.** *UK* [for stockings] jarretelles *fpl* **2.** *US* [for trousers] bretelles *fpl*.

suspense [sə'spens] n suspense *m* ▸ **to keep sb in suspense** tenir qqn en suspens.

suspension [sə'spenʃn] n **1.** [gen & AUT] suspension *f* **2.** [from school] renvoi *m* temporaire.

suspension bridge n pont *m* suspendu.

suspicion [sə'spɪʃn] n soupçon *m* ▸ **to be under suspicion** être considéré comme suspect ▸ **to have one's suspicions (about)** avoir des soupçons *OR* des doutes (sur).

suspicious [sə'spɪʃəs] adj **1.** [having suspicions] soupçonneux(euse) **2.** [causing suspicion] suspect(e), louche.

suspiciously [sə'spɪʃəslɪ] adv **1.** [with suspicious attitude] de façon soupçonneuse, avec méfiance **2.** [causing suspicion] de façon suspecte *OR* louche.

suss [sʌs] ◆ ***suss out*** vt sep *UK inf* piger, comprendre.

sustain [sə'steɪn] vt **1.** [maintain] soutenir **2.** [nourish] nourrir **3.** *fml* [suffer - damage] subir / [- injury] recevoir **4.** *fml* [weight] supporter.

sustainable [səs'teɪnəbl] adj [development, agriculture, politics] viable, durable.

sustenance ['sʌstɪnəns] n *(U) fml* nourriture *f*.

suture ['su:tʃər] n suture *f*.

svelte [svelt] adj svelte.

SW **1.** (abbr of ***short wave***) OC **2.** (abbr of ***south-west***) S-O.

swab [swɒb] n MED tampon *m*.

swagger ['swægər] ■ n air *m* de parade.
■ vi parader.

Swahili [swɑ:'hi:lɪ] ■ adj swahili(e).
■ n [language] swahili *m*.

swallow ['swɒləʊ] ■ n **1.** [bird] hirondelle *f* **2.** [of food] bouchée *f* / [of drink] gorgée *f*.
■ vt avaler / *fig* [anger, tears] ravaler.
■ vi avaler.

swam [swæm] pt ➤ ***swim***.

swamp [swɒmp] ■ n marais *m*.
■ vt **1.** [flood] submerger **2.** [overwhelm] déborder, submerger.

swan [swɒn] n cygne *m*.

swap [swɒp] ■ n [exchange] échange *m*.
■ vt (pt & pp -ped, cont -ping) **: to swap sthg (with sb/for sthg)** échanger qqch (avec qqn/contre qqch).
■ vi (pt & pp -ped, cont -ping) échanger.

swap meet n *US* foire *f* au troc.

SWAPO ['swɑ:pəʊ] (abbr of ***South West Africa People's Organization***) n SWAPO *f*.

swarm [swɔ:m] ■ n essaim *m*.
■ vi **1.** [bees] essaimer **2.** *fig* [people] grouiller ▸ **to be swarming (with)** [place] grouiller (de).

swarthy ['swɔ:ðɪ] (comp -ier, superl -iest) adj basané(e).

swashbuckling ['swɒʃˌbʌklɪŋ] adj de cape et d'épée.

swastika ['swɒstɪkə] n croix *f* gammée.

swat [swɒt] (pt & pp -ted, cont -ting) vt écraser.

swatch [swɒtʃ] n échantillon *m*.

swathe [sweɪð] ■ n [large area] étendue *f*.
■ vt *liter* emmailloter, envelopper.

swathed [sweɪðd] adj *liter* **: swathed (in)** emmailloté(e) (de), enveloppé(e) (de).

swatter ['swɒtər] n tapette *f*.

sway [sweɪ] ■ vt **1.** [cause to swing] balancer **2.** [influence] influencer.
■ vi se balancer.
■ n *fml* **: to hold sway over sb** tenir qqn sous son empire ▸ **to come under the sway of** se laisser influencer par.

Swazi ['swɑ:zɪ] n Swazi *mf*.

Swaziland ['swɑ:zɪlænd] n Swaziland *m* ▸ **in Swaziland** au Swaziland.

swear [sweər] (pt **swore**, pp **sworn**) ■ vt jurer ▸ **to swear to do sthg** jurer de faire qqch ▸ **to swear an oath** prêter serment.
■ vi jurer.
◆ ***swear by*** vt insep [have confidence in] jurer par.
◆ ***swear in*** vt sep LAW assermenter.

swearword ['sweəwɜ:d] n juron *m*, gros mot *m*.

sweat [swet] ■ n **1.** [perspiration] transpiration *f*, sueur *f* ▸ **sweat was dripping from his forehead** son front était ruisselant de sueur ▸ **to be in a cold sweat** avoir des sueurs froides **2.** *(U) inf* [hard work] corvée *f* ▸ **can you give me a hand? – no sweat!** peux-tu me donner un coup de main? – pas de problème!
■ vi **1.** [perspire] transpirer, suer ▸ **the effort made him sweat** l'effort l'a mis en sueur ▸ **she was sweating profusely** elle suait à grosses gouttes **2.** *inf* [worry] se faire du mouron ▸ **she's sweating over her homework** elle est en train de suer sur ses devoirs.
■ vt (*UK* **sweated**, *US* **sweat** *OR* **sweated**) [exude] **: to sweat blood** *fig* suer sang et eau ▸ **he sweated blood over this article** il a sué sang et eau sur cet article.

sweatband ['swetbænd] n SPORT bandeau *m* / [of hat] cuir *m* intérieur.

sweater ['swetər] n pullover *m*.

sweating ['swetɪŋ] n transpiration *f*, sudation *f*.

sweat pants n *US* pantalon *m* de jogging *OR* survêtement.

sweatshirt ['swetʃɜ:t] n sweat-shirt *m*.

sweatshop ['swetʃɒp] n ≃ atelier *m* clandestin.

sweatsuit [swɛtsju:t] n jogging *m*, survêtement *m*.

sweaty ['swetɪ] (comp **-ier**, superl **-iest**) **adj 1.** [skin, clothes] mouillé(e) de sueur **2.** [place] chaud(e) et humide / [activity] qui fait transpirer.

swede [swi:d] **n** *UK* rutabaga *m*.

Swede [swi:d] **n** Suédois *m*, -e *f*.

Sweden ['swi:dn] **n** Suède *f* ▸ **in Sweden** en Suède.

Swedish ['swi:dɪʃ] ■ **adj** suédois(e).
■ **n** [language] suédois *m*.
■ **npl : the Swedish** les Suédois *mpl*.

sweep [swi:p] ■ **n 1.** [sweeping movement] grand geste *m* **2.** [with brush] **: to give sthg a sweep** donner un coup de balai à qqch, balayer qqch **3.** [electronic] balayage *m* **4.** [chimney sweep] ramoneur *m*.
■ **vt** (**pt & pp swept**) **1.** [gen] balayer / [chimney] ramoner / [scan with eyes] parcourir des yeux ▸ **I swept the broken glass into the dustpan** j'ai poussé le verre cassé dans la pelle avec le balai ▸ **to sweep sthg under the carpet** *OR* **the rug** *fig* tirer le rideau sur qqch **2.** [move] **: to sweep sthg off sthg** enlever qqch de qqch d'un grand geste ▸ **she swept the coins off the table into her handbag** elle a fait glisser les pièces de la table dans son sac à main ▸ **to be swept out to sea** être emporté vers le large ▸ **three fishermen were swept overboard** un paquet de mer emporta trois pêcheurs ▸ **the incident swept all other thoughts from her mind** l'incident lui fit oublier tout le reste ▸ **to be swept off one's feet (by sb)** [fall in love] tomber fou amoureux (de qqn) **3.** [spread through - subj: fire, epidemic, rumour] gagner ▸ **a new craze is sweeping America** une nouvelle mode fait fureur aux États-Unis ▸ **to sweep the board** remporter tous les prix.
■ **vi** (**pt & pp swept**) **1.** [wind, fire] s'engouffrer ▸ **I watched storm clouds sweeping across the sky** je regardais des nuages orageux filer dans le ciel ▸ **the fire swept through the forest** l'incendie a ravagé la forêt **2.** [emotion] **: to sweep through sb** s'emparer de qqn **3.** [move quickly] **: to sweep along/in** avancer/entrer rapidement ▸ **he swept into/out of the room** il entra/sortit majestueusement de la pièce.
◆ ***sweep aside*** **vt sep** écarter, rejeter.
◆ ***sweep away*** **vt sep** [destroy] emporter, entraîner.
◆ ***sweep up*** ■ **vt sep** [with brush] balayer.
■ **vi** balayer.

sweeper ['swi:pə^r] **n** FOOTBALL libero *m*.

sweeping ['swi:pɪŋ] **adj 1.** [effect, change] radical(e) **2.** [statement] hâtif(ive) **3.** [curve] large.

sweepstake ['swi:psteɪk] **n** sweepstake *m*.

sweet [swi:t] ■ **adj 1.** [gen] doux (douce) / [cake, flavour, pudding] sucré(e) **2.** [kind] gentil(ille) **3.** [attractive] adorable, mignon(onne).
■ **n** *UK* **1.** [candy] bonbon *m* **2.** [dessert] dessert *m*.

sweet-and-sour **adj** aigre-doux (aigre-douce).

sweet chestnut **n** marron *m*.

sweet corn **n** maïs *m*.

sweeten ['swi:tn] **vt** sucrer.

sweetener ['swi:tnə^r] **n 1.** [substance] édulcorant *m* **2.** *inf* [bribe] pot-de-vin *m*.

sweetening ['swi:tnɪŋ] **n 1.** [substance] édulcorant *m*, édulcorants *mpl* **2.** [process - of wine] sucrage *m* / [- of water] adoucissement *m*.

sweetheart ['swi:thɑ:t] **n 1.** [term of endearment] chéri *m*, -e *f*, mon cœur *m* **2.** [boyfriend, girlfriend] petit ami *m*, petite amie *f*.

sweetly ['swi:tlɪ] **adv 1.** [pleasantly, kindly] gentiment / [cutely] d'un air mignon ▸ **she smiled at him sweetly** elle lui sourit gentiment ▸ **he was whispering sweetly in her ear** il lui chuchotait tendrement à l'oreille **2.** [smoothly] sans à-coups / [accurately] avec précision **3.** [musically] harmonieusement, mélodieusement ▸ **she sings very sweetly** elle a une voix très mélodieuse.

sweetness ['swi:tnɪs] **n 1.** [gen] douceur *f* / [of taste] goût *m* sucré, douceur **2.** [attractiveness] charme *m*.

sweet pea **n** pois *m* de senteur.

sweet potato **n** patate *f* douce.

sweet shop **n** *UK* confiserie *f*.

sweet tooth **n : to have a sweet tooth** aimer les sucreries.

swell [swel] ■ **vi** (**pt -ed, pp swollen** *OR* **-ed**) **1.** [leg, face] enfler / [lungs, balloon] se gonfler ▸ **to swell with pride** se gonfler d'orgueil **2.** [crowd, population] grossir, augmenter / [sound] grossir, s'enfler.
■ **vt** (**pt -ed, pp swollen** *OR* **-ed**) grossir, augmenter.
■ **n** [of sea] houle *f*.
■ **adj** *US inf dated* chouette, épatant(e).

swelling ['swelɪŋ] **n** enflure *f*.

sweltering ['sweltərɪŋ] **adj** étouffant(e), suffocant(e).

swept [swept] **pt & pp** ➤ ***sweep***.

swerve [swɜ:v] **vi** faire une embardée.

swift [swɪft] ■ **adj 1.** [fast] rapide **2.** [prompt] prompt(e).
■ **n** [bird] martinet *m*.

swiftly ['swɪftlɪ] **adv 1.** [quickly] rapidement, vite **2.** [promptly] promptement.

swiftness ['swɪftnɪs] **n 1.** [quickness] rapidité *f* **2.** [promptness] promptitude *f*.

swig [swɪg] *inf* ■ **vt** (**pt & pp -ged**, **cont -ging**) lamper.
■ **n** lampée *f*.

swill [swɪl] ■ **n** *(U)* [pig food] pâtée *f*.
■ **vt** *UK* [wash] laver à grande eau.

swim [swɪm] ■ **n : to have a swim** nager ▸ **to go for a swim** aller se baigner, aller nager.
■ **vi** (**pt swam, pp swum, cont -ming**) **1.** [person, fish, animal] nager **2.** [room] tourner ▸ **my head was swimming** j'avais la tête qui tournait, la tête me tournait.

swimmer ['swɪmə^r] **n** nageur *m*, -euse *f*.

swimming ['swɪmɪŋ] ■ **n** natation *f* ▸ **to go swimming** aller nager.
■ **comp** [club, competition] de natation.

swimming baths **npl** *UK* piscine *f*.

swimming cap **n** bonnet *m* de bain.

swimming costume **n** *UK* maillot *m* de bain.

swimming pool **n** piscine *f*.

swimming trunks **npl** maillot *m* ***or*** slip *m* de bain.

swimsuit ['swɪmsu:t] **n** maillot *m* de bain.

swimwear ['swɪmweəʳ] **n** *(U)* maillots *mpl* de bain.

swindle ['swɪndl] ■ **n** escroquerie *f*.
■ **vt** escroquer, rouler ▸ **to swindle sb out of sthg** escroquer qqch à qqn.

swine [swaɪn] **n** *inf* [person] salaud *m*.

swing [swɪŋ] ■ **n 1.** [child's toy] balançoire *f* ▸ **it's swings and roundabouts really** en fait, on perd d'un côté ce qu'on gagne de l'autre **2.** [change - of opinion] revirement *m* / [- of mood] changement *m*, saute *f* ▸ **the upward/downward swing of the market** FIN la fluctuation du marché vers le haut/le bas ▸ **America experienced a major swing towards conservatism** les États-Unis ont connu un important revirement vers le conservatisme **3.** [sway] balancement *m* **4.** *inf* [blow] **: to take a swing at sb** lancer ***or*** envoyer un coup de poing à qqn ▸ **he took a swing at the ball** il donna un coup pour frapper la balle
▸▸ **to be in full swing** battre son plein ▸ **to get into the swing of things** se mettre dans le bain ▸ **to go with a swing** [party] swinguer / [business] marcher très bien.
■ **vt** (pt & pp **swung**) **1.** [move back and forth] balancer ▸ **to swing one's hips** balancer les ***or*** rouler des hanches **2.** [move in a curve] faire virer ▸ **he swung a rope over a branch** il lança une corde par-dessus une branche ▸ **she swung the bat at the ball** elle essaya de frapper la balle avec sa batte **3.** *inf* [manage, pull off] **: to swing sthg** réussir ***or*** arriver à faire qqch ▸ **I think I should be able to swing it** je crois pouvoir me débrouiller.
■ **vi** (pt & pp **swung**) **1.** [move back and forth] se balancer ▸ **swinging from a cord** suspendu à une corde **2.** [turn - vehicle] virer, tourner ▸ **the lorry swung through the gate** le camion vira pour franchir le portail ▸ **to swing round** *UK* ***or*** **around** *US* [person] se retourner ▸ **to swing into action** *fig* passer à l'action **3.** [hit out] **: to swing at sb** lancer ***or*** envoyer un coup de poing à qqn ▸ **he swung at them with the hammer** il a essayé de les frapper avec le marteau **4.** [change] changer ▸ **her mood swings between depression and elation** elle passe de la dépression à l'exultation.

swing bridge **n** pont *m* tournant.

swing door *UK*, ***swinging door*** *US* **n** porte *f* battante.

swingeing ['swɪndʒɪŋ] **adj** *UK* très sévère.

swinging ['swɪŋɪŋ] **adj** *inf* **1.** [lively] animé(e), plein(e) d'entrain **2.** [uninhibited] dans le vent.

swipe [swaɪp] ■ **n : to take a swipe at** envoyer ***or*** donner un coup à.
■ **vt** *inf* [steal] faucher, piquer.
■ **vi : to swipe at** envoyer ***or*** donner un coup à.

swipe card **n** carte *f* magnétique.

swirl [swɜ:l] ■ **n** tourbillon *m*.
■ **vt** agiter, remuer.
■ **vi** tourbillonner, tournoyer.

swish [swɪʃ] ■ **n** [of tail] battement *m* / [of dress] froufrou *m*.
■ **vt** [tail] battre l'air de.
■ **vi** bruire, froufrouter.

Swiss [swɪs] ■ **adj** suisse.
■ **n** [person] Suisse *mf*.
■ **npl : the Swiss** les Suisses *mpl*.

Swiss cheese **n** emmental *m*.

swiss roll **n** *UK* gâteau *m* roulé.

switch [swɪtʃ] ■ **n 1.** [control device] interrupteur *m*, commutateur *m* / [on radio, stereo] bouton *m* **2.** [change] changement *m* **3.** *US* RAIL aiguillage *m*.
■ **vt 1.** [swap] échanger / [jobs] changer de ▸ **to switch places with sb** échanger sa place avec qqn **2.** RADIO & TV **: to switch channels/frequencies** changer de chaîne/de fréquence.
■ **vi : to switch to/from** passer à/de ▸ **can I switch to another channel?** est-ce que je peux changer de chaîne?
◆ ***switch off*** ■ **vt sep** éteindre.
■ **vi** *inf fig* décrocher.
◆ ***switch on*** **vt sep** allumer.

Switch® **n** *système de paiement non différé par carte bancaire.*

switchblade ['swɪtʃbleɪd] **n** *US* couteau *m* à cran d'arrêt.

switchboard ['swɪtʃbɔ:d] **n** standard *m*.

switchboard operator **n** standardiste *mf*.

switched-on [ˌswɪtʃt-] **adj** *inf* branché(e).

switch-hitter **n** *US* **1.** SPORT batteur *m* ambidextre **2.** *v inf* [bisexual] bi *mf*.

Switzerland ['swɪtsələnd] **n** Suisse *f* ▸ **in Switzerland** en Suisse.

swivel ['swɪvl] (*UK* **-led**, **cont -ling**, *US* **-ed**, **cont -ing**) ■ **vt** [chair] faire pivoter / [head, eyes] faire tourner.
■ **vi** [chair] pivoter / [head, eyes] tourner.

swivel chair **n** fauteuil *m* pivotant ***or*** tournant.

swollen ['swəʊln] ■ **pp** ➤ ***swell***.
■ **adj** [ankle, face] enflé(e) / [river] en crue.

swoon [swu:n] **vi** *liter* s'évanouir / *hum* se pâmer.

swoop [swu:p] ■ **n 1.** [downward flight] descente *f* en piqué ▸ **in one fell swoop** d'un seul coup **2.** [raid] descente *f*.
■ **vi 1.** [bird, plane] piquer **2.** [police, army] faire une descente.

swop [swɒp] = ***swap***.

sword [sɔ:d] **n** épée *f* ▸ **to cross swords (with sb)** croiser le fer (avec qqn).

swordfish ['sɔ:dfɪʃ] (pl **swordfish** ***or*** **-es** [-i:z]) **n** espadon *m*.

swordsman ['sɔ:dzmən] (pl **-men** [-mən]) **n** tireur *m* d'épée.

swore [swɔ:ʳ] **pt** ➤ ***swear***.

sworn [swɔːn] ■ pp ➤ ***swear***.
■ adj **1.** [committed] **: to be sworn enemies** être ennemis jurés **2.** LAW sous serment.

swot [swɒt] *UK inf* ■ n *pej* bûcheur *m*, -euse *f*.
■ vi (pt & pp **-ted**, cont **-ting**) **: to swot (for)** bûcher (pour).
◆ ***swot up*** vt sep & vi *UK inf* potasser, bûcher.

SWOT (abbr of ***strengths, weaknesses, opportunities and threats***) n forces, faiblesses, opportunités et menaces *fpl*.

SWOT analysis n analyse *f* des forces, faiblesses, opportunités et menaces.

swum [swʌm] pp ➤ ***swim***.

swung [swʌŋ] pt & pp ➤ ***swing***.

sycamore [ˈsɪkəmɔːr] n sycomore *m*.

sycophant [ˈsɪkəfænt] n flagorneur *m*, -euse *f*, lèche-bottes *mf inv*.

sycophantic [ˌsɪkəˈfæntɪk] adj [person] flatteur(euse), flagorneur(euse) / [behaviour] de flagorneur / [approval, praise] obséquieux(euse).

Sydney [ˈsɪdnɪ] n Sydney.

syllable [ˈsɪləbl] n syllabe *f*.

syllabub [ˈsɪləbʌb] n ≃ sabayon *m*.

syllabus [ˈsɪləbəs] (pl **-buses** [-bəsiːz] *OR* **-bi** [-baɪ]) n programme *m*.

symbiosis [ˌsɪmbaɪˈəʊsɪs] n *lit* & *fig* symbiose *f* ▸ **in symbiosis** en symbiose.

symbiotic [ˌsɪmbaɪˈɒtɪk] adj *lit* & *fig* symbiotique.

symbol [ˈsɪmbl] n symbole *m*.

symbolic [sɪmˈbɒlɪk] adj symbolique ▸ **to be symbolic of** être le symbole de.

symbolically [sɪmˈbɒlɪklɪ] adv symboliquement.

symbolism [ˈsɪmbəlɪzm] n symbolisme *m*.

symbolize, *UK* ***-ise*** [ˈsɪmbəlaɪz] vt symboliser.

symmetrical [sɪˈmetrɪkl] adj symétrique.

symmetrically [sɪˈmetrɪklɪ] adv symétriquement.

symmetry [ˈsɪmətrɪ] n symétrie *f*.

sympathetic [ˌsɪmpəˈθetɪk] adj **1.** [understanding] compatissant(e), compréhensif(ive) **2.** [willing to support] **: sympathetic (to)** bien disposé(e) (à l'égard de).

FALSE FRIENDS / FAUX AMIS

sympathetic

Sympathique n'est pas la traduction du mot anglais *sympathetic*. Sympathique se traduit par *nice* ou *friendly*.
▸ C'est un garçon vraiment sympathique / *He's a really nice boy*

sympathetically [ˌsɪmpəˈθetɪklɪ] adv **1.** [compassionately] avec compassion **2.** [with approval] avec bienveillance **3.** ANAT par sympathie.

sympathize, *UK* ***-ise*** [ˈsɪmpəθaɪz] vi **1.** [feel sorry] compatir ▸ **to sympathize with sb** plaindre qqn / [in grief] compatir à la douleur de qqn **2.** [understand] **: to sympathize with sthg** comprendre qqch **3.** [support] **: to sympathize with sthg** approuver qqch, soutenir qqch.

sympathizer, *UK* ***-iser*** [ˈsɪmpəθaɪzəʳ] n sympathisant *m*, -e *f*.

sympathy [ˈsɪmpəθɪ] n *(U)* **1.** [understanding] **: sympathy (for)** compassion *f* (pour), sympathie *f* (pour) **2.** [agreement] approbation *f*, sympathie *f* ▸ **to be in sympathy (with sthg)** être d'accord (avec qqch) **3.** [support] **: in sympathy (with sb)** en solidarité (avec qqn).
◆ ***sympathies*** npl **1.** [support] soutien *m*, loyauté *f* **2.** [to bereaved person] condoléances *fpl*.

symphonic [sɪmˈfɒnɪk] adj symphonique.

symphony [ˈsɪmfənɪ] (pl **-ies**) n symphonie *f*.

symphony orchestra n orchestre *m* symphonique.

symposium [sɪmˈpəʊzjəm] (pl **-siums** *OR* **-sia** [-zjə]) n symposium *m*.

symptom [ˈsɪmptəm] n symptôme *m*.

symptomatic [ˌsɪmptəˈmætɪk] adj symptomatique.

synagogue [ˈsɪnəgɒg] n synagogue *f*.

sync [sɪŋk] n *inf* **: out of sync** mal synchronisé(e) ▸ **in sync** bien synchronisé.

synchromesh gearbox [ˈsɪŋkrəʊmeʃ-] n boîte *f* de vitesses synchronisées.

HOW TO ...

express sympathy

Je suis vraiment désolé / I'm so sorry
C'est vraiment triste ! / That's so sad!
Si je peux vous aider en quoi que ce soit, surtout n'hésitez pas / You know where I am if there's anything I can do to help
Tu n'as vraiment pas de chance *ou* de bol ! *inf* / Bad luck!
Mon/Ma pauvre ! / You poor thing!
Je suis de tout cœur avec vous / My thoughts are with you
Sincères condoléances / Please accept my condolences
Ça m'a fait beaucoup de peine d'apprendre la disparition de ton père / I was so sorry to hear about the death of your father
Je vous souhaite un prompt rétablissement ! / Hope you're feeling better soon!

synchronization, *UK* ***-isation*** [ˌsɪŋkrənaɪˈzeɪʃn] **n** synchronisation *f*.

synchronize, *UK* ***-ise*** [ˈsɪŋkrənaɪz] ■ **vt** synchroniser. ■ **vi** être synchronisés(es).

synchronized swimming [ˈsɪŋkrənaɪzd-] **n** natation *f* synchronisée.

syncopated [ˈsɪŋkəpeɪtɪd] **adj** syncopé(e).

syncopation [ˌsɪŋkəˈpeɪʃn] **n** syncope *f*.

syndicate ■ **n** [ˈsɪndɪkət] syndicat *m*, consortium *m*. ■ **vt** [ˈsɪndɪkeɪt] PRESS publier dans plusieurs journaux.

syndication [sɪndɪˈkeɪʃən] **n 1.** PRESS [of article] publication *f* simultanée dans plusieurs journaux **2.** RADIO & TV syndication *f*.

syndication agency **n** PRESS agence *f* de presse.

syndrome [ˈsɪndrəʊm] **n** syndrome *m*.

synergy [ˈsɪnədʒɪ] (pl **-ies**) **n** synergie *f*.

synod [ˈsɪnəd] **n** synode *m*.

synonym [ˈsɪnənɪm] **n** : **synonym (for *OR* of)** synonyme *m* (de).

synonymous [sɪˈnɒnɪməs] **adj** : **synonymous (with)** synonyme (de).

synopsis [sɪˈnɒpsɪs] (pl **-ses** [-siːz]) **n** résumé *m* / [film] synopsis *m*.

syntax [ˈsɪntæks] **n** syntaxe *f*.

synthesis [ˈsɪnθəsɪs] (pl **-ses** [-siːz]) **n** synthèse *f*.

synthesize, *UK* ***-ise*** [ˈsɪnθəsaɪz] **vt** synthétiser / CHEM faire la synthèse de.

synthesizer, *UK* ***-iser*** [ˈsɪnθəsaɪzəʳ] **n** MUS synthétiseur *m*.

synthetic [sɪnˈθetɪk] **adj 1.** [man-made] synthétique **2.** *pej* [insincere] artificiel(elle), forcé(e).

synthetically [sɪnˈθetɪklɪ] **adv** synthétiquement.

syphilis [ˈsɪfɪlɪs] **n** syphilis *f*.

syphon [ˈsaɪfn] = ***siphon***.

Syria [ˈsɪrɪə] **n** Syrie *f* ▸ **in Syria** en Syrie.

Syrian [ˈsɪrɪən] ■ **adj** syrien(enne). ■ **n** [person] Syrien *m*, -enne *f*.

syringe [sɪˈrɪndʒ] ■ **n** seringue *f*. ■ **vt** (cont **syringeing**) [wound] seringuer / [ear] nettoyer à l'aide d'une seringue.

syrup [ˈsɪrəp] **n** *(U)* **1.** [sugar and water] sirop *m* **2.** *UK* [golden syrup] mélasse *f* raffinée.

system [ˈsɪstəm] **n 1.** [gen] système *m* ▸ **road/railway system** réseau *m* routier/de chemins de fer ▸ **transport system** réseau *m* des transports ▸ **digestive system** appareil *m* digestif **2.** [equipment - gen] installation *f* / [- electric, electronic] appareil *m* **3.** *(U)* [methodical approach] système *m*, méthode *f*
▸▸ **to get sthg out of one's system** *inf* laisser *OR* donner libre cours à qqch ▸ **to get it out of one's system** *inf* se défouler.

systematic [ˌsɪstəˈmætɪk] **adj** systématique.

systematically [ˌsɪstəˈmætɪklɪ] **adv** systématiquement.

systematize, *UK* ***-ise*** [ˈsɪstəmətaɪz] **vt** systématiser.

system disk **n** COMPUT disque *m* système.

system error **n** COMPUT erreur *f* système.

system failure **n** COMPUT panne *f* du système.

systems analysis [ˈsɪstəmz-] **n** COMPUT analyse *f* fonctionnelle.

systems analyst [ˈsɪstəmz-] **n** COMPUT analyste fonctionnel *m*, analyste fonctionnelle *f*.

systems disk [ˈsɪstəmz-] **n** COMPUT disque *m* système.

systems engineer [ˈsɪstəmz-] **n** COMPUT ingénieur *m* de système.

system software **n** *(U)* COMPUT logiciel *m* d'exploitation.

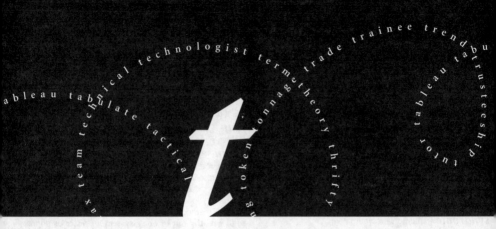

t [ti:] (pl t's ***OR*** ts), ***T*** (pl T's ***OR*** Ts) **n** [letter] t *m inv*, T *m inv*.

ta [tɑ:] **excl** *UK inf* merci!

TA (abbr of ***Territorial Army***) **n** *armée de réserve britannique*.

tab [tæb] **n 1.** [of cloth] étiquette *f* **2.** [of metal] languette *f* **3.** *US* [bill] addition *f* **4.** [on typewriter] (abbr of ***tabulator***) tabulateur *m*
⏭ **to keep tabs on sb** tenir ***OR*** avoir qqn à l'œil, surveiller qqn.

Tabasco sauce® [tə'bæskəʊ-] **n** sauce *f* Tabasco.

tabby ['tæbɪ] (pl **-ies**) **n : tabby (cat)** chat tigré *m*, chatte tigrée *f*.

tabernacle ['tæbənækl] **n** tabernacle *m*.

tab key **n** touche *f* de tabulation.

table ['teɪbl] ■ **n** table *f* ▸ **to get round the negotiating table** s'asseoir à la table des négociations ▸ **(multiplication) table** table *f* (de multiplication) ▸ **the man offered me £100 under the table** *fig* l'homme m'a offert 100 livres en dessous-de-table ▸ **to turn the tables on sb** *fig* renverser les rôles, retourner la situation.
■ **vt 1.** *UK* [propose] présenter, proposer **2.** *US* [postpone] ajourner la discussion de **3.** [schedule] prévoir, fixer ▸ **the discussion is tabled for 4 o'clock** la discussion est prévue ***OR*** a été fixée à 16 h.

tableau ['tæbləʊ] (pl **-x** [-z] ***OR*** **-s**) **n** tableau *m* vivant.

tablecloth ['teɪblklɒθ] **n** nappe *f*.

table dancer **n** danseuse *f* de bar.

table d'hôte ['tɑ:bl,dəʊt] **n : the table d'hôte** le menu à prix fixe.

table lamp **n** lampe *f*.

table licence **n** *licence autorisant la vente de boissons alcoolisées seulement aux repas*.

table linen **n** linge *m* de table.

table manners **npl : to have good/bad table manners** savoir/ne pas savoir se tenir à table.

tablemat ['teɪblmæt] **n** dessous-de-plat *m inv*.

table salt **n** sel *m* fin.

tablespoon ['teɪblspu:n] **n 1.** [spoon] cuiller *f* de service **2.** [spoonful] cuillerée *f* à soupe.

tablespoonful ['teɪbl,spu:nfʊl] **n** grande cuillerée *f*, cuillerée *f* à soupe.

tablet ['tæblɪt] **n 1.** [pill] comprimé *m*, cachet *m* **2.** [of stone] plaque *f* commémorative **3.** [of soap] savonnette *f*, pain *m* de savon.

table tennis **n** ping-pong *m*, tennis *m* de table.

tableware ['teɪblweəʳ] **n** vaisselle *f*.

table wine **n** vin *m* de table.

tabloid ['tæblɔɪd] **n : tabloid (newspaper)** tabloïd *m*, tabloïde *m* ▸ **the tabloid press** la presse populaire.

taboo [tə'bu:] ■ **adj** tabou(e).
■ **n** (pl **-s**) tabou *m*.

tabulate ['tæbjʊleɪt] **vt** présenter sous forme de tableau.

tachograph ['tækəgrɑ:f] **n** tachygraphe *m*.

tachometer [tæ'kɒmɪtəʳ] **n** tachymètre *m*.

tacit ['tæsɪt] **adj** tacite.

tacitly ['tæsɪtlɪ] **adv** tacitement.

taciturn ['tæsɪtɜ:n] **adj** taciturne.

tack [tæk] ■ **n 1.** [nail] clou *m* **2.** *US* [thumbtack] punaise *f* **3.** NAUT bord *m*, bordée *f* **4.** *fig* [course of action] tactique *f*, méthode *f* ▸ **to change tack** changer de tactique.
■ **vt 1.** [fasten with nail - gen] clouer / [- notice] punaiser **2.** SEW faufiler.
■ **vi** NAUT tirer une bordée.
◆ ***tack on*** **vt sep** *inf* ajouter, rajouter.

tackle ['tækl] ■ **n 1.** FOOTBALL tacle *m* / RUGBY plaquage *m* **2.** [equipment] équipement *m*, matériel *m* **3.** [for lifting] palan *m*, appareil *m* de levage.
■ **vt 1.** [deal with] s'attaquer à **2.** FOOTBALL tacler / RUGBY plaquer **3.** [attack] empoigner **4.** [talk to] **: to tackle sb about *OR* on sthg** parler franchement à qqn de qqch, entreprendre qqn sur qqch.

tackling ['tæklɪŋ] **n 1.** SPORT tacle *m* **2.** [of problem, job] manière *f* d'aborder.

tacky ['tækɪ] (comp **-ier**, superl **-iest**) **adj** **1.** *inf* [film, remark] d'un goût douteux / [jewellery] de pacotille **2.** [sticky] collant(e), pas encore sec (sèche).

taco ['tækəʊ] (pl **-s**) **n** *galette de maïs fourrée à la viande et au fromage.*

tact [tækt] **n** *(U)* tact *m*, délicatesse *f*.

tactful ['tæktfʊl] **adj** [remark] plein(e) de tact / [person] qui a du tact *OR* de la délicatesse.

tactfully ['tæktfʊlɪ] **adv** avec tact, avec délicatesse.

tactic ['tæktɪk] **n** tactique *f*.
◆ ***tactics*** **n** *(U)* MIL tactique *f*.

tactical ['tæktɪkl] **adj** tactique.

tactically ['tæktɪklɪ] **adv** du point de vue tactique ▸ **to vote tactically** voter utile.

tactical voter **n** POL *personne qui fait un vote utile.*

tactical voting **n** *(U)* vote *m* tactique.

tactician [tæk'tɪʃn] **n** tacticien *m*, -enne *f*.

tactile ['tæktaɪl] **adj** tactile.

tactless ['tæktlɪs] **adj** qui manque de tact *OR* délicatesse.

tactlessly ['tæktlɪslɪ] **adv** sans tact, sans délicatesse.

tad [tæd] **n** *inf* [small bit] **: a tad** un peu ▸ **the coat is a tad expensive** le manteau est un chouia trop cher.

tadpole ['tædpəʊl] **n** têtard *m*.

Tadzhikistan [tɑː,dʒɪkɪ'stɑːn] **n** Tadjikistan *m* ▸ **in Tadzhikistan** au Tadjikistan.

taffeta ['tæfɪtə] **n** *(U)* taffetas *m*.

taffy ['tæfɪ] (pl **-ies**) **n** *US* caramel *m*.

tag [tæg] ■ **n** **1.** [of cloth] marque *f* **2.** [of paper] étiquette *f* **3.** *(U)* [game] jeu *m* du chat **4.** COMPUT balise *f*.
■ **vt** (pt & pp **-ged**, cont **-ging**) marquer, étiqueter.
◆ ***tag along*** **vi** *inf* suivre.

Tagus ['teɪgəs] **n : the Tagus** le Tage.

Tahiti [tɑː'hiːtɪ] **n** Tahiti *m* ▸ **in Tahiti** à Tahiti.

Tahitian [tɑː'hiːʃn] ■ **adj** tahitien(enne).
■ **n** Tahitien *m*, -enne *f*.

tail [teɪl] ■ **n** **1.** [gen] queue *f* ▸ **with one's tail between one's legs** *fig* la queue entre les jambes **2.** [of coat] basque *f*, pan *m* / [of shirt] pan.
■ **comp** arrière.
■ **vt** *inf* [follow] filer.
◆ ***tails*** ■ **n** [side of coin] pile *f*.
■ **npl** [formal dress] queue-de-pie *f*, habit *m*.
◆ ***tail off*** **vi** **1.** [voice] s'affaiblir / [noise] diminuer **2.** [figures, sales] diminuer, baisser.

tailback ['teɪlbæk] **n** *UK* bouchon *m*.

tailcoat [,teɪl'kəʊt] **n** habit *m*, queue-de-pie *f*.

tail end **n** fin *f*.

tailfin ['teɪlfɪn] **n** dérive *f*.

tailgate ['teɪlgeɪt] **n** AUT hayon *m*.

taillight ['teɪllaɪt] **n** feu *m* arrière.

tailor ['teɪlə^r] ■ **n** tailleur *m*.
■ **vt** *fig* adapter.

tailored ['teɪləd] **adj** ajusté(e), cintré(e).

tailor-made **adj** *fig* sur mesure.

tail pipe **n** *US* tuyau *m* d'échappement.

tailplane ['teɪlpleɪn] **n** plan *m* fixe horizontal.

tailspin ['teɪlspɪn] **n** vrille *f* ▸ **to be in a tailspin** AERON vriller / *fig* être en dégringolade.

tailwind ['teɪlwɪnd] **n** vent *m* arrière.

taint [teɪnt] ■ **n** souillure *f*.
■ **vt** [reputation] souiller, entacher.

tainted ['teɪntɪd] **adj** **1.** [reputation] souillé(e), entaché(e) **2.** *US* [food] avarié(e).

Taiwan [,taɪ'wɑːn] **n** Taiwan ▸ **in Taiwan** à Taiwan.

Taiwanese [,taɪwə'niːz] ■ **adj** taiwanais(e).
■ **n** Taiwanais *m*, -e *f*.

take [teɪk] (pt **took**, pp **taken**) ■ **vt** **1.** [gen] prendre ▸ **to take a seat** prendre un siège, s'asseoir ▸ **to take control/command** prendre le contrôle/le commandement ▸ **to take an exam** passer un examen ▸ **to take a walk** se promener, faire une promenade ▸ **to take a bath/photo** prendre un bain/une photo ▸ **to take a lot of criticism** être très critiqué(e) ▸ **to take pity on sb** prendre qqn en pitié, avoir pitié de qqn ▸ **to take offence** se vexer, s'offenser ▸ **to take an interest in** s'intéresser à ▸ **he took my side in the argument** il a pris parti pour moi dans la dispute ▸ **he took the opportunity to thank them** *OR* **of thanking them** il a profité de l'occasion pour les remercier ▸ **to take sthg badly** prendre mal qqch ▸ **to take sb prisoner** faire qqn prisonnier ▸ **take Einstein (for example)** prenons (l'exemple d')Einstein ▸ **he took me for somebody else** il m'a pris pour quelqu'un d'autre
2. [lead, drive] emmener ▸ **her father takes her to school** son père l'emmène à l'école ▸ **could you take me home?** pourriez-vous me ramener *OR* me raccompagner?
3. [transport] conduire, transporter ▸ **the ambulance took him to hospital** l'ambulance l'a transporté à l'hôpital ▸ **this bus will take you to the theatre** ce bus vous conduira au théâtre
4. [carry] porter, apporter, emporter ▸ **she took her mother a cup of tea** elle a apporté une tasse de thé à sa mère ▸ **he took the map with him** il a emporté la carte
5. [derive] prendre, tirer ▸ **his article is taken directly from my book** le texte de son article est tiré directement de mon livre ▸ **a passage taken from a book** un passage extrait d'un livre
6. [accept] accepter ▸ **the owner won't take less than $100 for it** le propriétaire en veut au moins 100 dollars ▸ **I won't take "no" for an answer** pas question de refuser ▸ **take it from me, he's a crook** croyez-moi, c'est un escroc
7. [contain] contenir, avoir une capacité de
8. [tolerate] supporter ▸ **I find his constant sarcasm rather hard to take** je trouve ses sarcasmes perpétuels difficiles à supporter ▸ **we couldn't take any more** on n'en pouvait plus ▸ **she can take it** elle tiendra le coup
9. [require] demander ▸ **how long will it take?** combien de temps cela va-t-il prendre? ▸ **the flight takes three hours** le vol dure trois heures ▸ **it takes time to learn a language** il faut du temps pour apprendre une langue ▸ **it took four people to stop the brawl** ils ont dû se mettre à quatre pour arrêter la bagarre ▸ **to have what it takes to do/to be sthg** avoir les qualités nécessaires pour faire/être qqch

10. [wear] **: what size do you take?** [clothes] quelle taille faites-vous? / [shoes] vous chaussez du combien?
11. [assume] **: I take it (that)...** je suppose que..., je pense que...
12. [rent] prendre, louer
13. SCH & UNIV [exam] passer, se présenter à / [course] prendre, suivre ▸ **I took Latin and Greek at A level** ≃ j'ai pris latin et grec au bac.
■ **vi** [dye, vaccine, fire] prendre.
■ **n** CIN prise *f* de vues.
◆ ***take aback*** **vt sep** surprendre, décontenancer ▸ **to be taken aback** être décontenancé(e) *OR* surpris(e).
◆ ***take after*** **vt insep** tenir de, ressembler à.
◆ ***take apart*** **vt sep** [dismantle] démonter.
◆ ***take away*** **vt sep 1.** [remove] enlever ▸ **they took away his pension** ils lui ont retiré sa pension
2. [deduct] retrancher, soustraire ▸ **nine take away six is three** neuf moins six font trois.
◆ ***take back*** **vt sep 1.** [return] rendre, rapporter
2. [accept] reprendre ▸ **she took her husband back** elle a accepté que son mari revienne vivre avec elle
3. [statement, accusation] retirer ▸ **I take back everything I said** je retire tout ce que j'ai dit
4. [remind of the past] **: that takes me back to my childhood** ça me rappelle mon enfance.
◆ ***take down*** **vt sep 1.** [dismantle] démonter
2. [write down] prendre
3. [lower] baisser.
◆ ***take in*** **vt sep 1.** [deceive] rouler, tromper ▸ **don't be taken in by him** ne vous laissez pas rouler par lui
2. [understand] comprendre ▸ **I can't take in the fact that I've won** je n'arrive pas à croire que j'ai gagné
3. [include] englober, couvrir
4. [provide accommodation for] recueillir
5. [make smaller] reprendre.
◆ ***take off*** ■ **vt sep 1.** [remove] enlever, ôter ▸ **I tried to take her mind off her troubles** j'ai essayé de la distraire de ses ennuis ▸ **his retirement has taken ten years off him** *inf* sa retraite l'a rajeuni de dix ans
2. [have as holiday] **: to take a week/day off** prendre une semaine/un jour de congé ▸ **to take time off** prendre un congé
3. *UK* [imitate] imiter
4. [go away suddenly] **: to take o.s. off** s'en aller, partir.
■ **vi 1.** [plane] décoller
2. [go away suddenly] partir
3. [be successful] démarrer.
◆ ***take on*** ■ **vt sep 1.** [accept] accepter, prendre ▸ **to take on the responsibility for sthg** se charger de qqch ▸ **don't take on more than you can handle** ne vous surchargez pas
2. [employ] embaucher, prendre
3. [confront] s'attaquer à / [competitor] faire concurrence à / SPORT jouer contre ▸ **the unions took on the government** les syndicats se sont attaqués *OR* s'en sont pris au gouvernement.
■ **vt insep** [assume] prendre.
◆ ***take out*** **vt sep 1.** [remove - object] prendre, sortir / [- stain] ôter, enlever / [extract - tooth] arracher ▸ **to take out sb's appendix/tonsils** MED enlever l'appendice/les amygdales à qqn ▸ **to take it *OR* a lot out of sb** *inf* épuiser qqn, vider qqn
2. [delete] enlever, supprimer
3. [go out with] emmener, sortir avec
4. [subscription, insurance] prendre ▸ **to take out a mortgage** faire un emprunt-logement.
◆ ***take out on*** **vt sep : to take sthg out on sb** passer qqch sur qqn ▸ **don't take it out on me!** ne t'en prends pas à moi!
◆ ***take over*** ■ **vt sep 1.** [take control of] reprendre, prendre la direction de
2. [job] **: to take over sb's job** remplacer qqn, prendre la suite de qqn.
■ **vi 1.** [take control] prendre le pouvoir
2. [replace] prendre la relève ▸ **compact discs have taken over from records** le (disque) compact a remplacé le (disque) vinyle.
◆ ***take to*** **vt insep 1.** [person] éprouver de la sympathie pour, sympathiser avec / [activity] prendre goût à ▸ **we took to one another at once** nous avons tout de suite sympathisé
2. [begin] **: to take to drink *OR* to the bottle** se mettre à boire ▸ **to take to doing sthg** se mettre à faire qqch.
◆ ***take up*** **vt sep 1.** [begin - job] prendre ▸ **to take up singing** se mettre au chant
2. [shorten] raccourcir
3. [continue - story] reprendre, continuer
4. [discuss] **: to take an issue up with sb** aborder une question avec qqn ▸ **take it up with the boss** parlez-en au patron
5. [use up] prendre, occuper ▸ **this table takes up too much room** cette table prend trop de place *OR* est trop encombrante.
◆ ***take up on*** **vt sep 1.** [accept] **: to take sb up on an offer** accepter l'offre de qqn
2. [ask to explain] **: to take sb up on sthg** demander à qqn d'expliquer qqch.
◆ ***take upon*** **vt sep : to take it upon o.s. to do sthg** prendre sur soi de faire qqch ▸ **he took it upon himself to organize the meeting** il s'est chargé d'organiser la réunion.

CONFUSABLE / PARONYME
take
When translating to take, note that *emmener* and *emporter* are not interchangeable. *Emmener* is used with animate objects and *emporter* with inanimate objects.

takeaway *UK* ['teɪkə,weɪ], ***takeout*** *US* ['teɪkaʊt] **n 1.** [shop] restaurant *m* qui fait des plats à emporter **2.** [food] plat *m* à emporter.

take-home pay **n** salaire *m* net (après déductions).

taken ['teɪkn] ■ **pp** ➤ ***take***.
■ **adj : she was very taken with him/the idea** il/l'idée lui plaisait beaucoup.

takeoff ['teɪkɒf] **n** [of plane] décollage *m*.

takeout *US* = ***takeaway***.

takeover ['teɪk,əʊvər] **n 1.** [of company] prise *f* de contrôle, rachat *m* **2.** [of government] prise *f* de pouvoir.

takeover bid **n** offre *f* publique d'achat, OPA *f*.

taker ['teɪkər] **n** preneur *m*, -euse *f*.

takeup ['teɪkʌp] **n** [of shares] souscription *f*.

takings ['teɪkɪŋz] **npl** recette *f*.

talc [tælk], ***talcum (powder)*** ['tælkəm-] **n** talc *m*.

tale [teɪl] **n 1.** [fictional story] histoire *f*, conte *m* **2.** [anecdote] récit *m*, histoire *f*.

talent ['tælənt] **n : talent (for)** talent *m* (pour).

talented ['tæləntɪd] **adj** qui a du talent, talentueux(euse).

talent scout **n** dénicheur *m*, -euse *f* de talents.

talisman ['tælɪzmən] (pl -s) **n** talisman *m*.

talk [tɔ:k] ■ **n 1.** [conversation] discussion *f*, conversation *f* ▸ **most of the talk was about the new road** il a surtout été question de ***OR*** on a surtout parlé de la nouvelle route ▸ **he's all talk** tout ce qu'il dit, c'est du vent
2. *(U)* [gossip] bavardages *mpl*, racontars *mpl*
3. [lecture] conférence *f*, causerie *f* ▸ **to give a talk on *OR* about sthg** faire un exposé sur qqch.
■ **vi 1.** [speak] **: to talk (to sb)** parler (à qqn) ▸ **to talk about** parler de ▸ **that's no way to talk!** en voilà des façons de parler! ▸ **you can talk! *OR* look who's talking! *OR* you're a fine one to talk!** tu peux parler, toi! ▸ **to talk to o.s.** parler tout seul ▸ **talking of Lucy,...** à propos de Lucy,... ▸ **to talk big** se vanter
2. [gossip] bavarder, jaser
3. [make a speech] faire un discours, parler ▸ **to talk on *OR* about** parler de.
■ **vt** parler ▸ **to talk business/politics** parler affaires/politique ▸ **now you're talking sense** vous dites enfin des choses sensées ▸ **stop talking rubbish! *OR* nonsense!** *inf* arrête de dire des bêtises!
◆ ***talk down to*** **vt insep** parler avec condescendance à.
◆ ***talk into*** **vt sep : to talk sb into doing sthg** persuader qqn de faire qqch ▸ **she allowed herself to be talked into going** elle s'est laissé convaincre d'y aller.
◆ ***talk out of*** **vt sep : to talk sb out of doing sthg** dissuader qqn de faire qqch.
◆ ***talk over*** **vt sep** discuter de ▸ **let's talk it over** discutons-en, parlons-en.
◆ ***talk up*** **vt sep** vanter les mérites de, faire de la publicité pour.
◆ ***talks*** **npl** entretiens *mpl*, pourparlers *mpl* ▸ **official peace talks** des pourparlers officiels sur la paix.

talkative ['tɔ:kətɪv] **adj** bavard(e), loquace.

talker ['tɔ:kər] **n** causeur *m*, -euse *f*, bavard *m*, -e *f*.

talking point ['tɔ:kɪŋ-] **n** sujet *m* de conversation ***OR*** discussion.

talking-to ['tɔ:kɪŋ-] **n** *inf* savon *m*, réprimande *f* ▸ **to give sb a good talking-to** passer un bon savon à qqn.

talk show **n** TV talk-show *m*, causerie *f* télévisée.

talk time **n** *(U)* crédit *m* de communication.

tall [tɔ:l] **adj** grand(e) ▸ **how tall are you?** combien mesurez-vous? ▸ **she's 5 feet tall** elle mesure 1,50 m.

tallboy ['tɔ:lbɔɪ] **n** commode *f*.

tallness ['tɔ:lnɪs] **n** [of person] (grande) taille *f* / [of tree, building] hauteur *f*.

tall order **n : that's a tall order** c'est demander beaucoup, cela va être difficile.

tall story **n** histoire *f* à dormir debout.

tally ['tælɪ] ■ **n** (pl **-ies**) compte *m*.
■ **vi** (pt & pp **-ied**) correspondre, concorder.

talon ['tælən] **n** serre *f*, griffe *f*.

tambourine [ˌtæmbə'ri:n] **n** tambourin *m*.

tame [teɪm] ■ **adj 1.** [animal, bird] apprivoisé(e) **2.** *pej* [person] docile / [party, story, life] terne, morne.
■ **vt 1.** [animal, bird] apprivoiser **2.** [people] mater, dresser.

tamely ['teɪmlɪ] **adv** [accept, agree] docilement.

tamer ['teɪmər] **n** dompteur *m*, -euse *f*.

Tamil ['tæmɪl] ■ **adj** tamoul(e), tamil(e).
■ **n 1.** [person] Tamoul *m*, -e *f*, Tamil *m*, -e *f* **2.** [language] tamoul *m*, tamil *m*.

taming ['teɪmɪŋ] **n** [of animal] apprivoisement *m* / [of lions, tigers] domptage *m*, dressage *m*.

tamper ['tæmpər] ◆ ***tamper with*** **vt insep** [machine] toucher à / [records, file] altérer, falsifier / [lock] essayer de crocheter.

tampon ['tæmpɒn] **n** tampon *m*.

tan [tæn] ■ **adj** brun clair *(inv)*.
■ **n** bronzage *m*, hâle *m*.
■ **vi** (pt & pp **-ned**, cont **-ning**) bronzer.

tandem ['tændəm] **n** [bicycle] tandem *m* ▸ **in tandem** en tandem.

tandoori [tæn'dʊərɪ] ■ **n** tandouri *m*, tandoori *m*.
■ **comp** tandouri, tandoori.

tang [tæŋ] **n** [taste] saveur *f* forte ***OR*** piquante / [smell] odeur *f* forte ***OR*** piquante.

tangent ['tændʒənt] **n** GEOM tangente *f* ▸ **to go off at a tangent** *fig* changer de sujet, faire une digression.

tangerine [ˌtændʒə'ri:n] **n** mandarine *f*.

tangible ['tændʒəbl] **adj** tangible.

tangible assets **n** actif *m* corporel, valeurs *fpl* matérielles.

Tangier [tæn'dʒɪər] **n** Tanger.

tangle ['tæŋgl] ■ **n 1.** [mass] enchevêtrement *m*, emmêlement *m* **2.** *fig* [confusion] embrouillamini *m* ▸ **to get into a tangle** s'empêtrer, s'embrouiller.
■ **vt : to get tangled (up)** s'emmêler.
■ **vi** s'emmêler, s'enchevêtrer.
◆ ***tangle with*** **vt insep** *inf* se frotter à.

tangled ['tæŋgld] **adj** emmêlé(e) / *fig* embrouillé(e).

tango ['tæŋgəʊ] ■ **n** (pl **-es**) tango *m*.
■ **vi** danser le tango.

tangy ['tæŋɪ] (comp **-ier**, superl **-iest**) **adj** piquant(e), fort(e).

tank [tæŋk] **n 1.** [container] réservoir *m* ▸ **fish tank** aquarium *m* **2.** MIL tank *m*, char *m* (d'assaut).

tankard ['tæŋkəd] **n** chope *f*.

tanker ['tæŋkər] **n 1.** [ship - for oil] pétrolier *m* **2.** [truck] camion-citerne *m* **3.** [train] wagon-citerne *m*.

tankful ['tæŋkfʊl] **n** [of petrol] réservoir *m* plein d'essence.

tank top **n** débardeur *m*.

tanned [tænd] **adj** bronzé(e), hâlé(e).

tannin ['tænɪn] **n** tannin *m*, tanin *m*.

tanning ['tænɪŋ] **n 1.** [of skin] bronzage *m* **2.** [of hides] tannage *m* / *fig* raclée *f* ▸ **to give sb a tanning** *inf* rosser qqn.

Tannoy® ['tænɔɪ] **n** système *m* de haut-parleurs.

tantalize, *UK* ***-ise*** ['tæntəlaɪz] **vt** mettre au supplice.

tantalizing ['tæntəlaɪzɪŋ] **adj** [smell] très appétissant(e) / [possibility, thought] très tentant(e).

tantalizingly ['tæntəlaɪzɪŋlɪ] **adv** cruellement ▸ **victory was tantalizingly close** nous étions si près de la victoire que c'en était frustrant ▸ **tantalizingly slow** d'une lenteur désespérante.

tantamount ['tæntəmaʊnt] **adj : tantamount to** équivalent(e) à.

tantrum ['tæntrəm] (pl -s) **n** crise *f* de colère ▸ **to have** OR **throw a tantrum** faire OR piquer une colère.

Tanzania [,tænzə'nɪə] **n** Tanzanie *f* ▸ **in Tanzania** en Tanzanie.

Tanzanian [,tænzə'nɪən] ■ **adj** tanzanien(enne).
■ **n** Tanzanien *m*, -enne *f*.

tap [tæp] ■ **n 1.** *UK* [device] robinet *m* ▸ **on tap** [beer] en fût / *inf fig* [money, person, supply] disponible **2.** [light blow] petite tape *f*, petit coup *m* **3.** *(U)* [dancing] claquettes *fpl* ▸ **tap shoes** claquettes *fpl (chaussures)*.
■ **vt** (pt & pp **-ped**, cont **-ping**) **1.** [hit] tapoter, taper ▸ **someone tapped me on the shoulder** quelqu'un m'a tapé sur l'épaule ▸ **she was tapping her fingers on the table** elle pianotait OR tapotait sur la table **2.** [resources, energy] exploiter, utiliser ▸ **to tap sb for a loan** *inf* taper qqn **3.** [telephone, wire] mettre sur écoute.
■ **vi** (pt & pp **-ped**, cont **-ping**) taper, frapper ▸ **to tap at the door** frapper doucement à la porte.

tap dance **n** *(U)* claquettes *fpl*.

tap dancer **n** danseur *m*, -euse *f* de claquettes.

tape [teɪp] ■ **n 1.** [magnetic tape] bande *f* magnétique / [cassette] cassette *f* **2.** [strip of cloth, adhesive material] ruban *m* **3.** SPORT bande *f* d'arrivée.
■ **vt 1.** [record] enregistrer / [on video] magnétoscoper, enregistrer au magnétoscope **2.** [stick] scotcher **3.** *US* [bandage] bander.

tape deck **n** dérouleur *m* de bande magnétique.

tape drive **n** dérouleur *m* de bande (magnétique), lecteur *m* de bande (magnétique).

tape head **n** tête *f* de lecture.

tape measure **n** centimètre *m*, mètre *m*.

taper ['teɪpəʳ] ■ **n** [candle] bougie *f* fine.
■ **vi** s'effiler / [trousers] se terminer en fuseau.
◆ ***taper off*** **vi** diminuer.

tape reader **n** COMPUT lecteur *m* de bande.

tape-record [-rɪ,kɔ:d] **vt** enregistrer (au magnétophone).

tape recorder **n** magnétophone *m*.

tape recording **n** enregistrement *m* (au magnétophone).

tapered ['teɪpəd] **adj** [fingers] effilé(e), fuselé(e) / [trousers] en fuseau.

tapestry ['tæpɪstrɪ] (pl **-ies**) **n** tapisserie *f*.

tapeworm ['teɪpwɜ:m] **n** ténia *m*.

tapioca [,tæpɪ'əʊkə] **n** tapioca *m*.

tapir ['teɪpəʳ] (pl **tapir** OR **-s**) **n** tapir *m*.

tappet ['tæpɪt] **n** poussoir *m*.

tap water **n** eau *f* du robinet.

tar [tɑ:ʳ] **n** *(U)* goudron *m*.

tarantula [tə'ræntjʊlə] **n** tarentule *f*.

tardy ['tɑ:dɪ] (comp **-ier**, superl **-iest**) **adj 1.** *US* SCH en retard **2.** *fml* & *liter* [late] tardif(ive) **3.** *fml* & *liter* [slow] lent(e), nonchalant(e).

target ['tɑ:gɪt] ■ **n 1.** [of missile, bomb] objectif *m* / [for archery, shooting] cible *f* **2.** *fig* [for criticism] cible *f* **3.** *fig* [goal] objectif *m* ▸ **on target** dans les temps.
■ **vt 1.** [city, building] viser **2.** *fig* [subj: policy] s'adresser à, viser / [subj: advertising] cibler.

target audience **n** audience *f* cible.

target market **n** marché *m* cible.

tariff ['tærɪf] **n 1.** [tax] tarif *m* douanier **2.** [list] tableau *m* OR liste *f* des prix.

Tarmac® ['tɑ:mæk] **n** [material] macadam *m*.
◆ ***tarmac*** **n** AERON **: the tarmac** la piste.

tarnish ['tɑ:nɪʃ] ■ **vt** *lit* & *fig* ternir.
■ **vi** se ternir.

tarnished ['tɑ:nɪʃt] **adj** *lit* & *fig* terni(e).

tarot ['tærəʊ] **n : the tarot** le tarot, les tarots *mpl*.

tarot card **n** tarot *m*.

tarpaulin [tɑ:'pɔ:lɪn] **n** [material] toile *f* goudronnée / [sheet] bâche *f*.

tarragon ['tærəgən] **n** estragon *m*.

tart [tɑ:t] ■ **adj 1.** [bitter] acide **2.** [sarcastic] acide, acerbe.
■ **n 1.** CULIN tarte *f* **2.** *v inf* [prostitute] pute *f*, grue *f*.
◆ ***tart up*** **vt sep** *UK inf pej* [room] retaper, rénover ▸ **to tart o.s. up** se faire beau (belle).

tartan ['tɑ:tn] ■ **n** tartan *m*.
■ **comp** écossais(e).

tartar(e) sauce ['tɑ:təʳ-] **n** sauce *f* tartare.

tartness ['tɑ:tnɪs] **n** acidité *f*.

tarty ['tɑ:tɪ] (comp **-ier**, superl **-iest**) **adj** *UK v inf* vulgaire.

task [tɑ:sk] **n** tâche *f*, besogne *f*.

task force **n** MIL corps *m* expéditionnaire.

taskmaster ['tɑ:sk,mɑ:stəʳ] **n : hard taskmaster** tyran *m*.

Tasmania [tæz'meɪnjə] **n** Tasmanie *f*.

Tasmanian [tæz'meɪnjən] ■ **adj** tasmanien(enne).
■ **n** Tasmanien *m*, -enne *f*.

tassel ['tæsl] **n** pompon *m*, gland *m*.

taste [teɪst] ■ **n 1.** [gen] goût *m* ▸ **to lose one's sense of taste** perdre le goût, être atteint d'agueusie ▸ **have a taste!** goûte! ▸ **add sugar to taste** CULIN ajouter du sucre à volonté ▸ **in good/bad taste** de bon/mauvais goût ▸ **she has good taste in clothes** elle s'habille avec goût

2. *fig* [liking] : **to have expensive/simple tastes** avoir des goûts de luxe/simples ▸ **taste (for)** penchant *m* (pour), goût *m* (pour) ▸ **to develop a taste for sthg** prendre goût à qqch
3. *fig* [experience] aperçu *m* ▸ **the experience gave me a taste of life in the army** l'expérience m'a donné un aperçu de la vie militaire ▸ **a taste of things to come** un avant-goût de l'avenir ▸ **to have had a taste of sthg** avoir tâté **OR** goûté de qqch.
■ **vt 1.** [sense - food] sentir ▸ **can you taste the brandy in it?** est-ce que vous sentez le (goût du) cognac?
2. [test, try] déguster, goûter ▸ **to taste (the) wine** [in restaurant] goûter le vin / [in vineyard] déguster le vin
3. *fig* [experience] tâter de, goûter de.
■ **vi : to taste good/odd** *etc* avoir bon goût/un drôle de goût *etc* ▸ **to taste salty** avoir un goût salé ▸ **to taste of/like** avoir le goût de.

taste bud **n** papille *f* gustative.

tasteful ['teɪstfʊl] **adj** de bon goût.

tastefully ['teɪstfʊlɪ] **adv** avec goût.

tasteless ['teɪstlɪs] **adj 1.** [object, decor, remark] de mauvais goût **2.** [food] qui n'a aucun goût, fade.

tastelessly ['teɪstlɪslɪ] **adv** [decorated, dressed] sans goût.

taster ['teɪstər] **n** dégustateur *m*, -trice *f*.

tasty ['teɪstɪ] (**comp -ier, superl -iest**) **adj** [delicious] délicieux(euse), succulent(e).

tat [tæt] **n** *(U) UK inf pej* camelote *f*.

tattered ['tætəd] **adj** en lambeaux.

tatters ['tætəz] **npl : in tatters** [clothes] en lambeaux / [confidence] brisé(e) / [reputation] ruiné(e).

tattoo [tə'tu:] ■ **n** (**pl -s**) **1.** [design] tatouage *m* **2.** *UK* [military display] parade *f* **OR** défilé *m* militaire.
■ **vt** tatouer.

tattooist [tə'tu:ɪst] **n** tatoueur *m*.

tatty ['tætɪ] (**comp -ier, superl -iest**) **adj** *UK inf pej* [clothes] défraîchi(e), usé(e) / [flat, area] miteux(euse), minable.

taught [tɔ:t] **pt & pp** ➤ ***teach***.

taunt [tɔ:nt] ■ **vt** railler, se moquer de.
■ **n** raillerie *f*, moquerie *f*.

taunting ['tɔ:ntɪŋ] ■ **n** *(U)* railleries *fpl*, sarcasmes *mpl*.
■ **adj** railleur(euse), sarcastique.

Taurus ['tɔ:rəs] **n** Taureau *m* ▸ **to be (a) Taurus** être Taureau.

taut [tɔ:t] **adj** tendu(e).

tauten ['tɔ:tn] ■ **vt** tendre.
■ **vi** se tendre.

tautological [ˌtɔ:tə'lɒdʒɪkl] **adj** tautologique, pléonastique.

tautology [tɔ:'tɒlədʒɪ] **n** tautologie *f*.

tavern ['tævn] **n** taverne *f*.

tawdry ['tɔ:drɪ] (**comp -ier, superl -iest**) **adj** *pej* [jewellery] clinquant(e) / [clothes] voyant(e), criard(e).

tawny ['tɔ:nɪ] **adj** fauve.

tax [tæks] ■ **n** [on income] contributions *fpl* / ADMIN taxe *f*, impôt *m*.
■ **vt 1.** [goods] taxer ▸ **to tax one's car** *UK* acheter la vignette (automobile) **2.** [profits, business, person] imposer **3.** [strain] mettre à l'épreuve.

taxable ['tæksəbl] **adj** imposable.

taxable income **n** revenu *m* imposable, assiette *f* fiscale **OR** de l'impôt.

tax allowance **n** *UK* abattement *m* fiscal.

taxation [tæk'seɪʃn] **n** *(U)* **1.** [system] imposition *f* **2.** [amount] impôts *mpl*.

tax avoidance [-ə'vɔɪdəns] **n** évasion *f* fiscale.

tax band **n** tranche *f* d'imposition.

tax benefit **n** avantage *m* fiscal.

tax bracket **n** tranche *f* d'imposition.

tax break **n** réduction *f* d'impôt.

tax code **n** barème *m* fiscal.

tax collector **n** percepteur *m*.

tax credit **n** aide *f* fiscale, avoir *m* fiscal.

tax cut **n** baisse *f* de l'impôt.

tax-deductible [-dɪ'dʌktəbl] **adj** déductible des impôts.

tax disc **n** *UK* vignette *f*.

tax evasion **n** fraude *f* fiscale.

tax-exempt *US* = ***tax-free***.

tax exemption **n** exonération *f* d'impôt.

tax exile **n** *UK personne qui vit à l'étranger pour échapper au fisc*.

tax form **n** feuille *f* **OR** déclaration *f* d'impôts.

tax-free, *US* ***tax-exempt*** **adj** exonéré(e) (d'impôt).

tax haven **n** paradis *m* fiscal.

taxi ['tæksɪ] ■ **n** taxi *m*.
■ **vi** [plane] rouler au sol.

taxicab ['tæksɪkæb] **n** taxi *m*.

taxidermist ['tæksɪdɜ:mɪst] **n** taxidermiste *mf*.

taxi driver **n** chauffeur *m* de taxi.

taximeter ['tæksɪˌmi:tər] **n** taximètre *m*.

tax incentive **n** incitation *f* fiscale.

taxing ['tæksɪŋ] **adj** éprouvant(e).

tax inspector **n** inspecteur *m* des impôts.

taxi rank *UK*, ***taxi stand*** **n** station *f* de taxis.

taxman ['tæksmæn] (**pl -men** [-men]) **n** percepteur *m*.

taxpayer ['tæksˌpeɪər] **n** contribuable *mf*.

tax rebate **n** dégrèvement *m* d'impôts.

tax relief **n** allègement *m* **OR** dégrèvement *m* fiscal.

tax return **n** déclaration *f* d'impôts.

tax year **n** année *f* fiscale.

TB **n abbr of *tuberculosis***.

T-bone steak **n** steak *m* dans l'aloyau.

tbs., ***tbsp.*** (**abbr of *tablespoon(ful)***) cs.

TD **n 1.** (abbr of ***Treasury Department***) *ministère américain de l'Économie et des Finances* **2.** abbr of ***touchdown***.

tea [ti:] **n 1.** [drink, leaves] thé *m* **2.** *UK* [afternoon meal] goûter *m* / [evening meal] dîner *m*.

teabag ['ti:bæg] **n** sachet *m* de thé.

tea ball **n** *US* boule *f* à thé.

tea break **n** *UK pause pour prendre le thé*, ≃ pause-café *f*.

tea caddy [-ˌkædɪ] **n** boîte *f* à thé.

teacake ['ti:keɪk] **n** *UK petit pain rond avec des raisins secs.*

teach [ti:tʃ] (pt & pp **taught**) ■ **vt 1.** [instruct] apprendre ▸ **to teach sb sthg, to teach sthg to sb** apprendre qqch à qqn ▸ **she taught herself knitting/French** elle a appris à tricoter/elle a appris le français toute seule ▸ **to teach sb to do sthg** apprendre à qqn à faire qqch ▸ **to teach (sb) that...** apprendre (à qqn) que... ▸ **that taught them a lesson they won't forget** cela leur a donné une leçon dont ils se souviendront **2.** [subj: teacher] enseigner ▸ **to teach sb sthg, to teach sthg to sb** enseigner qqch à qqn ▸ **to teach school** *US* être enseignant.
■ **vi** enseigner.

teacher ['ti:tʃəʳ] **n** [in primary school] instituteur *m*, -trice *f*, maître *m*, maîtresse *f* / [in secondary school] professeur *m*.

teacher's college *US* = ***teacher training college***.

teacher's pet **n** *pej* chouchou *m*, chouchoute *f*.

teacher training college *UK*, ***teacher's college*** *US* **n** ≃ institut *m* universitaire de formation des maîtres, ≃ IUFM *m*.

teaching ['ti:tʃɪŋ] **n** enseignement *m*.

teaching aid **n** support *m* pédagogique.

teaching hospital **n** *UK* centre *m* hospitalo-universitaire, C.H.U. *m*

teaching practice **n** *(U)* stage *m* de formation.

teaching staff **npl** enseignants *mpl*.

tea cloth **n** *UK* **1.** [tablecloth] nappe *f* **2.** [tea towel] torchon *m*.

tea cosy, *US* ***tea cozy*** **n** couvre-théière *m inv*, cosy *m*.

teacup ['ti:kʌp] **n** tasse *f* à thé.

teak [ti:k] ■ **n** teck *m*.
■ **comp** en teck.

tea leaves **npl** feuilles *fpl* de thé.

team [ti:m] **n** équipe *f*.
◆ ***team up*** **vi : to team up (with sb)** faire équipe (avec qqn).

team games **npl** jeux *mpl* d'équipe.

teammate ['ti:mmeɪt] **n** co-équipier *m*, -ère *f*.

team player **n : to be a (good) team player** avoir l'esprit d'équipe.

team spirit **n** esprit *m* d'équipe.

teamster ['ti:mstəʳ] **n** *US* routier *m*, camionneur *m*.

teamwork ['ti:mwɜ:k] **n** *(U)* travail *m* d'équipe, collaboration *f*.

tea party **n** thé *m*.

teapot ['ti:pɒt] **n** théière *f*.

tear[1] [tɪəʳ] **n** larme *f* ▸ **in tears** en larmes ▸ **to burst into tears** fondre en larmes ▸ **to be bored to tears** *fig* s'ennuyer à mourir.

tear[2] [teəʳ] ■ **vt** (pt **tore**, pp **torn**) **1.** [rip] déchirer ▸ **to tear sthg open** ouvrir qqch (en le déchirant) ▸ **'tear along the dotted line'** 'détacher suivant le pointillé' ▸ **to tear sb/sthg to pieces** *fig* éreinter qqn/qqch **2.** [remove roughly] arracher ▸ **he tore the cheque from** OR **out of my hand** il m'a arraché le chèque des mains ▸ **sorry to tear you from your reading, but I need your help** *fig* je regrette de vous arracher à votre lecture, mais j'ai besoin de votre aide
▸▸ **to be torn between** être tiraillé(e) entre ▸ **I'm torn between going and staying** je suis tiraillé entre le désir de partir et celui de rester.
■ **vi** (pt **tore**, pp **torn**) **1.** [rip] se déchirer **2.** [move quickly] foncer, aller à toute allure
▸▸ **to tear loose** s'échapper.
■ **n** déchirure *f*, accroc *m*.
◆ ***tear apart*** **vt sep 1.** [rip up] déchirer, mettre en morceaux **2.** *fig* [country, company] diviser / [person] déchirer ▸ **the party was being torn apart by internal strife** le parti était déchiré OR divisé par des luttes intestines.
◆ ***tear at*** **vt insep** déchirer.
◆ ***tear away*** **vt sep : to tear o.s. away (from)** s'arracher (de OR à).
◆ ***tear down*** **vt sep** [building] démolir / [poster] arracher.
◆ ***tear off*** **vt sep** [clothes] enlever à la hâte ▸ **to tear sb off a strip** *inf*, **to tear a strip off sb** *UK inf* passer un savon à qqn, enguirlander qqn.
◆ ***tear out*** **vt sep** [page] arracher / [cheque] détacher ▸ **to tear one's hair (out)** *lit & fig* s'arracher les cheveux.
◆ ***tear up*** **vt sep** déchirer.

tearaway ['teərəˌweɪ] **n** *UK inf* casse-cou *mf inv*.

teardrop ['tɪədrɒp] **n** larme *f*.

tear duct [tɪəʳ-] **n** canal *m* lacrymal.

tearful ['tɪəfʊl] **adj 1.** [person] en larmes **2.** [event] larmoyant(e).

tearfully ['tɪəfʊlɪ] **adv** en pleurant, les larmes aux yeux.

tear gas [tɪəʳ-] **n** *(U)* gaz *m* lacrymogène.

tearing ['teərɪŋ] **adj** *inf* terrible, fou (folle).

tearjerker ['tɪəˌdʒɜ:kəʳ] **n** *hum* roman *m* OR film *m* qui fait pleurer dans les chaumières.

tearoom ['ti:rʊm] **n** salon *m* de thé.

tease [ti:z] ■ **n** taquin *m*, -e *f*.
■ **vt** [mock] **: to tease sb (about sthg)** taquiner qqn (à propos de qqch).

teaser campaign ['ti:zeʳ-] **n** campagne *f* teasing.

tea service, ***tea set*** **n** service *m* à thé.

tea shop **n** *UK* salon *m* de thé.

teasing ['ti:zɪŋ] **adj** taquin(e).

Teasmaid® ['ti:zmeɪd] **n** *UK* théière *f* automatique avec horloge incorporée.

teaspoon ['ti:spu:n] **n 1.** [utensil] petite cuillère *f*, cuillère à café **2.** [amount] cuillerée *f* à café.

teaspoonful ['ti:spu:n,fʊl] **n** cuiller *f* ***OR*** cuillère *f* à café *(mesure)*.

tea strainer **n** passoire *f*.

teat [ti:t] **n** tétine *f*.

teatime ['ti:taɪm] **n** *UK* l'heure *f* du thé.

tea towel **n** *UK* torchon *m*.

tea urn **n** fontaine *f* à thé.

techie ['tekɪ] **n** *inf* technicien *m*, -enne *f*.

technical ['teknɪkl] **adj** technique.

technical college **n** *UK* collège *m* technique.

technical drawing **n** *(U)* dessin *m* industriel.

technical foul **n** SPORT faute *f* technique.

technicality [,teknɪ'kælətɪ] (pl **-ies**) **n** **1.** [intricacy] technicité *f* **2.** [detail] détail *m* technique.

technically ['teknɪklɪ] **adv** **1.** [gen] techniquement **2.** [theoretically] en théorie.

technician [tek'nɪʃn] **n** technicien *m*, -enne *f*.

Technicolor® ['teknɪ,kʌlər] **n** *(U)* Technicolor® *m*.

technique [tek'ni:k] **n** technique *f*.

techno ['teknəʊ] **n** MUS techno *f*.

technobabble ['teknəʊ,bæbl] **n** *inf* jargon *m* technique.

technocrat ['teknəkræt] **n** technocrate *mf*.

technological [,teknə'lɒdʒɪkl] **adj** technologique.

technologist [tek'nɒlədʒɪst] **n** technologue *mf*.

technology [tek'nɒlədʒɪ] (pl **-ies**) **n** technologie *f*.

technophobe ['tɛknəfoʊb] **n** technophobe *mf*.

teddy ['tedɪ] (pl **-ies**) **n : teddy (bear)** ours *m* en peluche, nounours *m*.

tedious ['ti:djəs] **adj** ennuyeux(euse).

tedium ['ti:djəm] **n** *fml* ennui *m*.

tee [ti:] **n** GOLF tee *m*.

◆ ***tee off*** **vi** GOLF partir du tee.

teem [ti:m] **vi** **1.** [rain] pleuvoir à verse **2.** [place] **: to be teeming with** grouiller de.

teen [ti:n] **adj** *inf* [fashion] pour ados / [music, problems] d'ados.

teenage ['ti:neɪdʒ] **adj** adolescent(e).

teenager ['ti:n,eɪdʒər] **n** adolescent *m*, -e *f*.

teens [ti:nz] **npl** adolescence *f*.

teeny (weeny) [,ti:nɪ('wi:nɪ)], ***teensy (weensy)*** [,ti:nzɪ('wi:nzɪ)] **adj** *inf* minuscule, tout petit (toute petite).

tee shirt **n** tee-shirt *m*.

teeter ['ti:tər] **vi** vaciller ▸ **to teeter on the brink of** *fig* être au bord de.

teeter-totter **n** *US* bascule *f*.

teeth [ti:θ] **npl** ➤ ***tooth***.

teethe [ti:ð] **vi** [baby] percer ses dents.

teething ['ti:ðɪŋ] **n** poussée *f* dentaire, dentition *f*.

teething ring **n** anneau *m* de dentition.

teething troubles ['ti:ðɪŋ-] **npl** *fig* difficultés *fpl* initiales.

teetotal [ti:'təʊtl] **adj** qui ne boit jamais d'alcool.

teetotaller *UK*, ***teetotaler*** *US* [ti:'təʊtlər] **n** personne *f* qui ne boit jamais d'alcool.

TEFL ['tefl] (abbr of ***teaching of English as a foreign language***) **n** *enseignement de l'anglais langue étrangère*.

Teflon® ['teflɒn] ■ **n** Téflon® *m*.
■ **comp** en Téflon®.

Tehran, ***Teheran*** [,teə'rɑ:n] **n** Téhéran.

tel. (abbr of ***telephone***) tél.

Tel-Aviv [,telə'vi:v] **n : Tel-Aviv(-Jaffa)** Tel-Aviv (-Jaffa).

tele- ['telɪ] **prefix** télé-.

telebanking ['telɪ,bæŋkɪŋ] **n** *(U)* télébanque *f*.

telecast ['telɪkɑ:st] **n** émission *f* de télévision.

telecom ['telɪkɒm] **n** *(U) UK inf* télécommunications *fpl*.

telecoms ['telɪkɒmz] **npl** = ***telecom***.

telecommunications ['telɪkə,mju:nɪ'keɪʃnz] **npl** télécommunications *fpl*.

telecommuting [,telɪkə'mju:tɪŋ] **n** télétravail *m*.

teleconference ['telɪ,kɒnfərəns] **n** téléconférence *f*.

teleconferencing [,telɪ'kɒnfərənsɪng] **n** *(U)* téléconférence *f*.

telegram ['telɪgræm] **n** télégramme *m*.

telegraph ['telɪgrɑ:f] ■ **n** télégraphe *m*.
■ **vt** télégraphier.

telegraph pole *UK*, ***telegraph post*** *UK*, ***telephone pole*** *US* **n** poteau *m* télégraphique.

telemarketing ['telɪ,mɑ:kɪtɪŋ] **n** vente *f* par téléphone.

telepathic [,telɪ'pæθɪk] **adj** télépathique.

telepathy [tɪ'lepəθɪ] **n** télépathie *f*.

telephone ['telɪfəʊn] ■ **n** téléphone *m* ▸ **to be on the telephone** *UK* [connected] avoir le téléphone / [speaking] être au téléphone.
■ **vt** téléphoner à.
■ **vi** téléphoner.

telephone banking **n** FIN banque *f* au téléphone.

telephone book **n** annuaire *m*.

telephone booth **n** cabine *f* téléphonique.

telephone box **n** *UK* cabine *f* téléphonique.

telephone call **n** appel *m* téléphonique, coup *m* de téléphone.

telephone directory **n** annuaire *m*.

telephone exchange **n** central *m* téléphonique.

telephone kiosk **n** *UK* cabine *f* téléphonique.

telephone number **n** numéro *m* de téléphone.

telephone operator **n** standardiste *mf*.

telephone pole *US* = ***telegraph pole***.

telephone tapping [-'tæpɪŋ] **n** mise *f* sur écoute.

telephonist [tɪ'lefənɪst] **n** *UK* téléphoniste *mf*.

telephoto lens [,telɪ'fəʊtəʊ-] **n** téléobjectif *m*.

teleprinter ['telɪ,prɪntər], *US* ***teletypewriter*** [,telɪ'taɪp,raɪtər] **n** téléscripteur *m*.

Teleprompter® [ˌtelɪ'prɒmptəʳ] **n** téléprompteur *m*.

telesales ['telɪseɪlz] **npl** vente *f* par téléphone.

telescope ['telɪskəʊp] **n** télescope *m*.

telescopic [ˌtelɪ'skɒpɪk] **adj** télescopique.

teleshopping [ˌtelɪ'ʃɒpɪŋ] **n** téléachat *m*.

teletext ['telɪtekst] **n** télétexte *m*.

telethon ['telɪθɒn] **n** téléthon *m*.

teletypewriter *US* = ***teleprinter***.

televangelist [ˌtelɪ'vændʒəlɪst] **n** *évangéliste qui prêche à la télévision*.

televideo [telɪ'vɪdəʊ] **n** combiné *m* télémagnétoscope.

televise ['telɪvaɪz] **vt** téléviser.

television ['telɪˌvɪʒn] **n 1.** *(U)* [medium, industry] télévision *f* ▸ **on television** à la télévision **2.** [apparatus] (poste *m* de) télévision *f*, téléviseur *m*.

television campaign **n** campagne *f* télévisuelle.

television licence **n** *UK* redevance *f*.

television programme *UK*, ***television program*** *US* **n** émission *f* de télévision.

television set **n** poste *m* de télévision, téléviseur *m*.

teleworker ['telɪwɜːkəʳ] **n** télétravailleur *m*, -euse *f*.

teleworking ['telɪˌwɜːkɪŋ] **n** télétravail *m*.

telex ['teleks] ■ **n** télex *m*.
■ **vt** [message] envoyer par télex, télexer / [person] envoyer un télex à.

tell [tel] (pt & pp **told**) ■ **vt 1.** [gen] dire / [story] raconter ▸ **to tell sb (that)...** dire à qqn que... ▸ **I'm pleased to tell you you've won** j'ai le plaisir de vous informer que vous avez gagné ▸ **to tell sb sthg, to tell sthg to sb** dire qqch à qqn ▸ **can you tell me the way to the station/to Oxford?** pouvez-vous m'indiquer le chemin de la gare/la route d'Oxford? ▸ **to tell sb about sthg** dire qqch à qqn, parler à qqn de qqch ▸ **to tell sb to do sthg** dire *OR* ordonner à qqn de faire qqch ▸ **I thought I told you not to run?** je croyais t'avoir interdit *OR* défendu de courir? ▸ **I told you so!** je te l'avais bien dit!
2. [judge, recognize] savoir, voir ▸ **he can't tell the time** il ne sait pas lire l'heure ▸ **could you tell me the time?** tu peux me dire l'heure (qu'il est)? ▸ **there's no telling...** on ne peut pas savoir... ▸ **to tell right from wrong** distinguer le bien du mal.
■ **vi 1.** [speak] parler ▸ **I won't tell** je ne dirai rien à personne
2. [judge] savoir ▸ **who can tell?** qui peut savoir?, qui sait?
3. [have effect] se faire sentir ▸ **the strain is beginning to tell** la tension commence à se faire sentir.
◆ ***tell apart*** **vt sep** distinguer ▸ **I couldn't tell the twins apart** je ne pouvais pas distinguer les jumeaux l'un de l'autre.
◆ ***tell off*** **vt sep** gronder ▸ **to tell sb off for doing sthg** gronder *OR* réprimander qqn pour avoir fait qqch.

teller ['teləʳ] **n 1.** [of votes] scrutateur *m*, -trice *f* **2.** *esp US* [in bank] caissier *m*, -ère *f*.

telling ['telɪŋ] **adj** [remark] révélateur(trice).

telling-off (pl **tellings-off**) **n** réprimande *f*.

telltale ['telteɪl] ■ **adj** révélateur(trice).
■ **n** rapporteur *m*, -euse *f*, mouchard *m*, -e *f*.

telly ['telɪ] (pl **-ies**) (abbr of ***television***) **n** *UK inf* télé *f* ▸ **on telly** à la télé.

temerity [tɪ'merətɪ] **n** témérité *f*.

temp [temp] *inf* ■ **n** (abbr of ***temporary (employee)***) intérimaire *mf*.
■ **vi** *UK* travailler comme intérimaire.

temp. (abbr of ***temperature***) temp.

temper ['tempəʳ] ■ **n 1.** [angry state] **: to be in a temper** être en colère ▸ **to lose one's temper** se mettre en colère ▸ **to have a short temper** être emporté **2.** [mood] humeur *f* **3.** [temperament] tempérament *m*.
■ **vt** [moderate] tempérer.

temperament ['temprəmənt] **n** tempérament *m*.

temperamental [ˌtemprə'mentl] **adj** [volatile, unreliable] capricieux(euse).

temperamentally [ˌtemprə'mentəlɪ] **adv** de par son caractère.

temperance ['temprəns] *(U)* **n** [moderation] modération *f* / [from alcohol] tempérance *f*.

temperate ['temprət] **adj** tempéré(e).

temperature ['temprətʃəʳ] **n** température *f* ▸ **to take sb's temperature** prendre la température de qqn ▸ **to have a temperature** avoir de la température *OR* de la fièvre.

tempered ['tempəd] **adj 1.** [steel] trempé(e) **2.** [moderated] tempéré(e), modéré(e).

temper tantrum **n** crise *f* de colère ▸ **to have** *OR* **to throw a temper tantrum** piquer une colère.

tempest ['tempɪst] **n** *liter* tempête *f*.

tempestuous [tem'pestjʊəs] **adj** *liter* & *fig* orageux(euse).

tempi ['tempiː] **npl** ➤ ***tempo***.

template ['templɪt] **n** gabarit *m*.

temple ['templ] **n 1.** RELIG temple *m* **2.** ANAT tempe *f*.

templet ['templɪt] = ***template***.

tempo ['tempəʊ] (pl **-pos** *OR* **-pi** [-piː]) **n** tempo *m*.

temporal ['tempərəl] **adj 1.** [gen & GRAM] temporel(elle) **2.** [secular] temporel(elle), séculier(ière).

temporarily [ˌtempə'rerəlɪ] **adv** temporairement, provisoirement.

temporary ['tempərərɪ] **adj** temporaire, provisoire.

tempt [tempt] **vt** tenter ▸ **to tempt sb to do sthg** donner à qqn l'envie de faire qqch ▸ **to be** *OR* **feel tempted to do sthg** être tenté *OR* avoir envie de faire qqch.

temptation [temp'teɪʃn] **n** tentation *f*.

tempting ['temptɪŋ] **adj** tentant(e).

ten [ten] **num** dix ; see also ***six***.

tenable ['tenəbl] **adj 1.** [argument, position] défendable **2.** [job, post] **: tenable for** auquel on est nommé(e) pour.

tenacious [tɪ'neɪʃəs] **adj** tenace.

tenaciously [tɪ'neɪʃəslɪ] **adv** avec ténacité, obstinément.

tenacity [tɪ'næsətɪ] **n** *(U)* ténacité *f.*

tenancy ['tenənsɪ] (pl **-ies**) **n** location *f.*

tenant ['tenənt] **n** locataire *mf.*

Ten Commandments **npl : the Ten Commandments** les dix commandements *mpl.*

tend [tend] **vt 1.** [have tendency] **: to tend to do sthg** avoir tendance à faire qqch ▸ **that does tend to be the case** c'est souvent le cas ▸ **I tend to think (that)...** j'ai tendance à penser que... ▸ **his writings tend to** *OR* **towards exoticism** ses écrits tendent vers l'exotisme **2.** [look after] s'occuper de, garder ▸ **to tend to one's business/ one's guests** s'occuper de ses affaires/ses invités.

tendency ['tendənsɪ] (pl **-ies**) **n : tendency (to do sthg)** tendance *f* (à faire qqch) ▸ **a tendency towards fascism** une tendance fasciste.

tender ['tendəʳ] ■ **adj** tendre / [bruise, part of body] sensible, douloureux(euse).
■ **n** COMM soumission *f.*
■ **vt** *fml* [apology, money] offrir / [resignation] donner.

tenderize, *UK* ***-ise*** ['tendəraɪz] **vt** attendrir.

tenderly ['tendəlɪ] **adv** [caringly] tendrement.

tenderness ['tendənɪs] *(U)* **n 1.** [compassion] tendresse *f* **2.** [soreness] sensibilité *f.*

tendon ['tendən] **n** tendon *m.*

tendril ['tendrəl] **n** vrille *f.*

tenement ['tenəmənt] **n** immeuble *m.*

Tenerife [ˌtenə'ri:f] **n** Tenerife ▸ **in Tenerife** à Tenerife.

tenet ['tenɪt] **n** *fml* principe *m.*

tenner ['tenəʳ] **n** *UK inf* [amount] dix livres / [note] billet *m* de dix livres.

Tennessee [ˌtenə'si:] **n** Tennessee *m* ▸ **in Tennessee** dans le Tennessee.

tennis ['tenɪs] ■ **n** *(U)* tennis *m.*
■ **comp** de tennis.

tennis ball **n** balle *f* de tennis.

tennis court **n** court *m* de tennis.

tennis racket **n** raquette *f* de tennis.

tennis shoe **n** (chaussure *f* de) tennis *f.*

tenor ['tenəʳ] ■ **adj** [saxophone, recorder] ténor *(inv)* / [voice] de ténor.
■ **n 1.** [singer] ténor *m* **2.** *fml* [meaning] sens *m*, substance *f.*

tenpin bowling *UK* ['tenpɪn-], ***tenpins*** *US* ['tenpɪnz] **n** *(U)* bowling *m* (à dix quilles).

tense [tens] ■ **adj** tendu(e).
■ **n** temps *m.*
■ **vt** tendre.
■ **vi** se contracter.

tensed up [tenst-] **adj** contracté(e), tendu(e).

tensely ['tenslɪ] **adv** [move, react] de façon tendue / [speak] d'une voix tendue ▸ **they waited tensely for the doctor to arrive** ils ont attendu le médecin dans un état de grande tension nerveuse.

tension ['tenʃn] **n** tension *f.*

ten-spot **n** *US* billet *m* de dix dollars.

tent [tent] **n** tente *f.*

tentacle ['tentəkl] **n** tentacule *m.*

tentative ['tentətɪv] **adj 1.** [hesitant] hésitant(e) **2.** [not final] provisoire.

tentatively ['tentətɪvlɪ] **adv 1.** [hesitantly] de façon hésitante **2.** [not finally] provisoirement.

tenterhooks ['tentəhʊks] **npl : to be on tenterhooks** être sur des charbons ardents.

tenth [tenθ] **num** dixième ; see also ***sixth***.

tent peg **n** piquet *m* de tente.

tent pole **n** montant *m* *OR* mât *m* de tente.

tenuous ['tenjʊəs] **adj** ténu(e).

tenuously ['tenjʊəslɪ] **adv** de façon ténue.

tenuousness ['tenjʊəsnɪs] **n 1.** [of distinction] subtilité *f* / [of thread] ténuité *f* / [of voice] faiblesse *f* **2.** [of link, relationship] fragilité *f*, précarité *f* / [of evidence] minceur *f*, faiblesse *f* / [of argument] faiblesse *f* **3.** [of existence] précarité *f* **4.** PHYS raréfaction *f.*

tenure ['tenjəʳ] **n** *(U)* *fml* **1.** [of property] bail *m* **2.** [of job] **: to have tenure** être titulaire.

tepee ['ti:pi:] **n** tipi *m.*

tepid ['tepɪd] **adj** tiède.

tequila [tɪ'ki:lə] **n** tequila *f.*

Ter., ***Terr.*** **abbr of** ***Terrace***.

term [tɜ:m] ■ **n 1.** [word, expression] terme *m* ▸ **she told him what she thought in no uncertain terms** elle lui a dit carrément ce qu'elle pensait **2.** *UK* SCH & UNIV trimestre *m* **3.** [period of time] durée *f*, période *f* ▸ **during my term of office** [gen] pendant que j'étais en fonction / POL pendant mon mandat ▸ **a prison term** une peine de prison ▸ **in the long/short term** à long/court terme.
■ **vt** appeler.
◆ ***terms*** **npl 1.** [of contract, agreement] conditions *fpl* ▸ **under the terms of the agreement** selon les termes de l'accord ▸ **terms of payment** modalités *fpl* de paiement ▸ **not on any terms** à aucun prix, à aucune condition **2.** [basis] **: in international/real terms** en termes internationaux/réels ▸ **on equal** *OR* **the same terms** d'égal à égal ▸ **to be on good terms (with sb)** être en bons termes (avec qqn) ▸ **to be on speaking terms** s'adresser la parole, se parler ▸ **to be on speaking terms with sb** adresser la parole à qqn, parler à qqn ▸ **to come to terms with sthg** accepter qqch
▸▸ **to think in terms of doing sthg** envisager de *OR* penser faire qqch ▸ **I was thinking more in terms of a Jaguar** je pensais plutôt à une Jaguar.
◆ ***in terms of*** **prep** sur le plan de, en termes de ▸ **in terms of profits, we're doing well** pour ce qui est des bénéfices, tout va bien.

terminal ['tɜːmɪnl] ■ **adj** MED en phase terminale.
■ **n 1.** AERON, COMPUT & RAIL terminal *m* **2.** ELEC borne *f.*

terminally ['tɜːmɪnəlɪ] **adv : to be terminally ill** être en phase terminale.

terminate ['tɜːmɪneɪt] ■ **vt 1.** *fml* [end - gen] terminer, mettre fin à / [- contract] résilier **2.** [pregnancy] interrompre.
■ **vi 1.** [bus, train] s'arrêter **2.** [contract] se terminer.

termination [,tɜːmɪ'neɪʃn] **n 1.** *(U) fml* [ending - gen] conclusion *f* / [- of contract] résiliation *f* **2.** [of pregnancy] interruption *f* (volontaire) de grossesse.

termini ['tɜːmɪnaɪ] **npl** ➤ ***terminus.***

terminology [,tɜːmɪ'nɒlədʒɪ] **n** terminologie *f.*

terminus ['tɜːmɪnəs] (pl -ni [-naɪ] *OR* -nuses [-nəsiːz]) **n** terminus *m.*

termite ['tɜːmaɪt] **n** termite *m.*

termly ['tɜːmlɪ] ■ **adj** trimestriel(elle).
■ **adv** trimestriellement, par trimestre.

term paper *US* **n** SCH & UNIV dissertation *f* trimestrielle.

Terr. = ***Ter.***

terrace ['terəs] **n 1.** [patio, on hillside] terrasse *f* **2.** *UK* [of houses] rangée *f* de maisons.
◆ ***terraces*** **npl** FOOTBALL **: the terraces** les gradins *mpl.*

terraced ['terəst] **adj** [hillside] en terrasses.

terraced house **n** *UK maison attenante aux maisons voisines.*

terracotta [,terə'kɒtə] **n** terre *f* cuite.

terrain [te'reɪn] **n** terrain *m.*

terrapin ['terəpɪn] (pl **terrapin** *OR* -s) **n** tortue *f* d'eau douce.

terrestrial [tə'restrɪəl] **adj** *fml* terrestre.

terrestrial television **n** diffusion *f* hertzienne *OR* terrestre.

terrible ['terəbl] **adj** terrible / [holiday, headache, weather] affreux(euse), épouvantable ▸ **it caused terrible damage** cela a provoqué d'importants dégâts ▸ **to feel terrible** [ill] se sentir très mal / [morally] s'en vouloir beaucoup, avoir des remords.

terribly ['terəblɪ] **adv** terriblement / [sing, write, organized] affreusement mal / [injured] affreusement.

terrier ['terɪəʳ] **n** terrier *m.*

terrific [tə'rɪfɪk] **adj 1.** *inf* [wonderful] fantastique, formidable **2.** [enormous] énorme, fantastique.

terrifically [tə'rɪfɪklɪ] **adv** *inf* **1.** [extremely, enormously] extrêmement, très **2.** [very well] merveilleusement (bien).

terrified ['terɪfaɪd] **adj** terrifié(e) ▸ **to be terrified of** avoir une terreur folle *OR* peur folle de.

terrify ['terɪfaɪ] (pt & pp -ied) **vt** terrifier.

terrifying ['terɪfaɪɪŋ] **adj** terrifiant(e).

terrifyingly ['terɪfaɪɪŋlɪ] **adv** de façon terrifiante *OR* effroyable.

terrine [te'riːn] **n** terrine *f.*

territorial [,terɪ'tɔːrɪəl] **adj** territorial(e).

Territorial Army **n** *UK* **: the Territorial Army** l'armée territoriale.

territorial waters **npl** eaux *fpl* territoriales.

territory ['terətrɪ] (pl -ies) **n** territoire *m.*

terror ['terəʳ] **n** terreur *f.*

terrorism ['terərɪzm] **n** terrorisme *m.*

terrorist ['terərɪst] **n** terroriste *mf.*

terrorize*, UK* ***-ise*** ['terəraɪz] **vt** terroriser.

terror-stricken **adj** épouvanté(e).

terry(cloth) ['terɪ(klɒθ)] **n** tissu *m* éponge.

terse [tɜːs] **adj** brusque.

tersely ['tɜːslɪ] **adv** avec brusquerie.

tertiary ['tɜːʃərɪ] **adj** tertiaire.

tertiary education **n** enseignement *m* supérieur.

Terylene® ['terəliːn] **n** Térylène® *m.*

TESL ['tesl] (abbr of ***teaching of English as a second language***) **n** *enseignement de l'anglais seconde langue.*

TESSA ['tesə] (abbr of ***tax-exempt special savings account***) **n** *en Grande-Bretagne, plan d'épargne exonéré d'impôt.*

test [test] ■ **n 1.** [trial] essai *m* / [of friendship, courage] épreuve *f* ▸ **to carry out tests on sthg** effectuer des tests sur qqch ▸ **to put sb/sthg to the test** mettre qqn/qqch à l'épreuve ▸ **his courage was really put to the test** son courage fut sérieusement mis à l'épreuve *OR* éprouvé ▸ **to stand the test of time** durer, résister à l'épreuve du temps
2. [examination - of aptitude, psychological] test *m* / SCH & UNIV interrogation *f* écrite/orale / [- of driving] (examen *m* du) permis *m* de conduire
3. [MED - of blood, urine] analyse *f* / [- of eyes] examen *m* ▸ **to have a blood test** faire faire une analyse de sang ▸ **to have an eye test** se faire examiner la vue.
■ **vt 1.** [try] essayer / [determination, friendship] mettre à l'épreuve ▸ **none of our products are tested on animals** nos produits ne sont pas testés sur les animaux ▸ **to test sb's patience to the limit** mettre la patience de qqn à rude épreuve
2. SCH & UNIV faire faire une interrogation écrite/orale à ▸ **we were tested in geography** nous avons eu un contrôle de géographie ▸ **to test sb on sthg** interroger qqn sur qqch ▸ **she was tested on her knowledge of plants** on a testé *OR* vérifié ses connaissances botaniques
3. [MED - blood, urine] analyser / [- eyes, reflexes] faire un examen de ▸ **to have one's eyes tested** se faire examiner la vue.

testament ['testəmənt] **n 1.** [will] testament *m* **2.** [proof] **: testament to** témoignage *m* de.

test ban **n** interdiction *f* d'essais nucléaires.

test card **n** *UK* mire *f.*

test case **n** LAW affaire-test *f.*

test drive **n** essai *m* sur route.
◆ ***test-drive*** **vt** (pt **test-drove**, pp **test-driven**) essayer.

tester ['testəʳ] **n 1.** [person] contrôleur *m*, -euse *f* **2.** [sample] échantillon *m.*

test flight **n** vol *m* d'essai.

testicles ['testɪklz] **npl** testicules *mpl*.

testify ['testɪfaɪ] (pt & pp **-ied**) ■ **vt : to testify that...** témoigner que...
■ **vi 1.** LAW témoigner **2.** [be proof] **: to testify to sthg** témoigner de qqch.

testimonial [,testɪ'məʊnjəl] **n 1.** [character reference] recommandation *f* **2.** [tribute] témoignage *m* d'estime.

testimony [*UK* 'testɪmənɪ, *US* 'testəməʊnɪ] **n** témoignage *m*.

testing ['testɪŋ] **adj** éprouvant(e).

testing ground **n** banc *m* d'essai.

test match **n** *UK* match *m* international.

testosterone [te'stɒstərəʊn] **n** testostérone *f*.

test paper **n 1.** SCH interrogation *f* écrite **2.** CHEM papier *m* réactif.

test pattern **n** *US* mire *f*.

test pilot **n** pilote *m* d'essai.

test run **n** essai *m* ▸ **to go for a test run** faire un essai.

test tube **n** éprouvette *f*.

test-tube baby **n** bébé-éprouvette *m*.

testy ['testɪ] (comp **-ier**, superl **-iest**) **adj** [person] irritable / [remark] désobligeant(e).

tetanus ['tetənəs] **n** tétanos *m*.

tetchy ['tetʃɪ] (comp **-ier**, superl **-iest**) **adj** ombrageux(euse), qui prend ombrage facilement.

tête-à-tête [,teɪtɑː'teɪt] **n** tête-à-tête *m inv*.

tether ['teðəʳ] ■ **vt** attacher.
■ **n : to be at the end of one's tether** être au bout du rouleau.

Texan ['teksn] **n** Texan *m*, -e *f*.

Texas ['teksəs] **n** Texas *m* ▸ **in Texas** au Texas.

Tex-Mex [,teks'meks] **adj** Tex-Mex *(inv)*.

text [tekst] ■ **n 1.** [gen] texte *m* **2.** TELEC mini-message *m*.
■ **vi** TELEC envoyer un mini-message (à qn).

textbook ['tekstbʊk] **n** livre *m* ***OR*** manuel *m* scolaire.

textile ['tekstaɪl] ■ **n** textile *m*.
■ **comp** textile.
◆ ***textiles*** **npl** [industry] textile *m*.

texting ['tekstɪŋ] **n** *(U)* TELEC service *m* de mini-messages.

text message **n** TELEC mini-message *m*.

text messaging **n** *(U)* TELEC service *m* de mini-messages.

textual ['tekstjʊəl] **adj** textuel(elle), de texte ▸ **textual analysis** analyse *f* de texte ▸ **textual criticism** critique *f* littéraire d'un texte.

texture ['tekstʃəʳ] **n** texture *f* / [of paper, wood] grain *m*.

TFT (abbr of ***thin-film transistor***) **adj** TFT ▸ **TFT screen** écran *m* TFT.

TGIF *inf* (abbr of ***thank God it's Friday!***) *encore une semaine de tirée!*

TGWU (abbr of ***Transport and General Workers' Union***) **n** *le plus grand syndicat interprofessionnel britannique.*

Thai [taɪ] ■ **adj** thaïlandais(e).
■ **n 1.** [person] Thaïlandais *m*, -e *f* **2.** [language] thaï *m*.

Thailand ['taɪlænd] **n** Thaïlande *f* ▸ **in Thailand** en Thaïlande.

thalidomide [θə'lɪdəmaɪd] **n** thalidomide *f*.

Thames [temz] **n : the Thames** la Tamise.

than *(weak form* [ðən], *strong form* [ðæn]*)* **conj** que ▸ **Sarah is younger than her sister** Sarah est plus jeune que sa sœur ▸ **more than three days/50 people** plus de trois jours/50 personnes ▸ **there are more policemen than demonstrators** il y a plus de policiers que de manifestants.

thank [θæŋk] **vt** remercier ▸ **to thank sb (for)** remercier qqn (pour ***OR*** de) ▸ **you have him to thank for that** tu peux lui dire merci ▸ **you won't thank me for it** vous allez m'en vouloir ▸ **thank God *OR* goodness *OR* heavens!** Dieu merci!
◆ ***thanks*** ■ **npl** remerciements *mpl* ▸ **(many) thanks for all your help** merci (beaucoup) pour toute votre aide ▸ **received with thanks** ADMIN pour acquit.
■ **excl** merci! ▸ **thanks a lot, thanks very much** merci beaucoup, merci bien.
◆ ***thanks to*** **prep** grâce à.

thankful ['θæŋkfʊl] **adj 1.** [grateful] **: thankful (for)** reconnaissant(e) (de) **2.** [relieved] soulagé(e).

thankfully ['θæŋkfʊlɪ] **adv 1.** [with relief] avec soulagement **2.** [with gratitude] avec reconnaissance.

thankless ['θæŋklɪs] **adj** ingrat(e).

HOW TO ...

express thanks

Saying thank you
Merci beaucoup / Thank you very much
Je vous remercie / Thank you
Merci mille fois *ou* infiniment / Many thanks
Merci, c'est très gentil à vous / Thanks, that's very kind of you
Je ne sais comment vous remercier / I can't thank you enough
Je vous remercie pour votre aide / Thank you for your help
Je voulais vous remercier de m'avoir encouragé / I wanted to thank you for encouraging me

Responding to thanks
De rien / Don't mention it
Je t'en prie/Je vous en prie / You're welcome
Ce n'est rien / Don't mention it
Il n'y a pas de quoi / Not at all
Tout le plaisir est pour moi / My pleasure
Oh de rien, n'hésitez pas... / Any time!

thanksgiving ['θæŋks,gɪvɪŋ] **n** action *f* de grâce.
◆ ***Thanksgiving (Day)*** **n** *fête nationale américaine commémorant l'installation des premiers colons en Amérique.*

CULTURE
Thanksgiving

Cette fête nationale américaine importante, célébrée le quatrième jeudi du mois de novembre, commémore la première récolte faite en 1621 par les pèlerins de la colonie de Plymouth après un hiver très rude : William Bradford, le gouverneur de la colonie, officialise ce « jour de remerciement » (Thanksgiving) en organisant une grande fête qui réunit les colons et les natifs américains. Cette coutume est encore suivie par la plupart des familles américaines, qui se réunissent autour d'un dîner traditionnel (dinde farcie, purée de pommes de terre, ignames sucrés et tarte au potiron). Ce jour férié marque le début des fêtes de fin d'année et des achats de Noël.

thank you **excl : thank you (for)** merci (pour *OR* de).
◆ ***thankyou*** **n** merci *m*.

thank-you letter ['θæŋkju:-] **n** lettre *f* de remerciement.

that [ðæt] ■ **pron (pl those** [ðəʊz]**) 1.** *(demonstrative use: pl 'those')* ce, cela, ça / *(as opposed to 'this')* celui-là (celle-là) ▸ **who's that?** qui est-ce? ▸ **is that Maureen?** c'est Maureen? ▸ **is that you Susan?** c'est toi Susan? ▸ **what's that?** qu'est-ce que c'est que ça? ▸ **that's a shame** c'est dommage ▸ **I had never seen that before** je n'avais jamais vu cela *OR* ça auparavant ▸ **what did she mean by that?** qu'est-ce qu'elle voulait dire par là? ▸ **which shoes are you going to wear, these or those?** quelles chaussures vas-tu mettre, celles-ci ou celles-là? ▸ **those who** ceux (celles) qui ▸ **all those interested should contact the club secretary** tous ceux qui sont intéressés doivent contacter le secrétaire du club ▸ **it's not as hot as (all) that!** *inf* il ne fait pas si chaud que ça! ▸ **that's all we need!** il ne manquait plus que ça! ▸ **that's enough (of that)!** ça suffit!
2. *(weak form* [ðət]*, strong form* [ðæt]*)* [to introduce relative clauses - subject] qui / [- object] que / [- with prep] lequel (laquelle), lesquels (lesquelles) *(pl)* / ▸ **we came to a path that led into the woods** nous arrivâmes à un sentier qui menait dans les bois ▸ **show me the book that you bought** montre-moi le livre que tu as acheté ▸ **on the day that we left** le jour où nous sommes partis ▸ **the box that I put it in/on** le carton dans lequel/sur lequel je l'ai mis ▸ **the songs that I was thinking about** les chansons auxquelles je pensais ▸ **the woman/the film that we're talking about** la femme/le film dont nous parlons.
■ **adj** *(demonstrative: pl 'those')* ce (cette), cet *(before vowel or silent 'h')*, ces *(pl)* / *(as opposed to 'this')* ce (cette)...-là, ces...-là *(pl)* ▸ **those chocolates are delicious** ces chocolats sont délicieux ▸ **later that day** plus tard ce jour-là ▸ **I prefer that book** je préfère ce livre-là ▸ **that house over there is for sale** cette *OR* la maison là-bas est à vendre ▸ **I'll have that one** je prendrai celui-là.
■ **adv** aussi, si ▸ **it wasn't that bad/good** ce n'était pas si mal/bien que ça ▸ **there's a pile of papers on my desk that high!** il y a une pile de papiers haute comme ça sur mon bureau!
■ **conj** [ðət] que ▸ **tell him that the children aren't coming** dites-lui que les enfants ne viennent pas ▸ **he recommended that I phone you** il m'a conseillé de vous appeler.
◆ ***at that*** **adv** en plus, par surcroît.
◆ ***that is (to say)*** **adv** c'est-à-dire ▸ **I'd like to ask you something, that is, if you've got a minute** j'aimerais vous poser une question, enfin, si vous avez un instant.
◆ ***that's it*** **adv** [that's all] c'est tout ▸ **that's it, I'm leaving** ça y est, je m'en vais.
◆ ***that's that*** **adv : and that's that** un point c'est tout ▸ **well, that's that!** eh bien voilà!

thatched [θætʃt] **adj** de chaume.

Thatcherism ['θætʃərɪzm] **n** thatcherisme *m*.

that's [ðæts] = ***that is***.

thaw [θɔ:] ■ **vt** [ice] faire fondre *OR* dégeler / [frozen food] décongeler.
■ **vi 1.** [ice] dégeler, fondre / [frozen food] décongeler **2.** *fig* [people, relations] se dégeler.
■ **n** dégel *m*.

the *(weak form* [ðə]*, before vowel* [ðɪ]*, strong form* [ði:]*)* **def art 1.** [gen] le (la), l' *(+ vowel or silent 'h')*, les *(pl)* ▸ **the book** le livre ▸ **the sea** la mer ▸ **the man** l'homme ▸ **the boys/girls** les garçons/filles ▸ **the highest mountain in the world** la montagne la plus haute du monde ▸ **has the postman been?** *UK* est-ce que le facteur est passé? ▸ **the monkey is a primate** le singe est un primate ▸ **the Joneses are coming to supper** les Jones viennent dîner ▸ **you're not the John Smith, are you?** vous n'êtes pas le célèbre John Smith, si? ▸ **it's the place to go to in Paris** c'est l'endroit à la mode *OR* l'endroit chic de Paris (où il faut aller) ▸ **to play the piano** jouer du piano
2. *(with an adjective to form a noun)* **: the British** les Britanniques ▸ **the old/young** les vieux/jeunes ▸ **the impossible** l'impossible
3. [in dates] **: the twelfth of May** le douze mai ▸ **the forties** les années quarante
4. [in comparisons] **: the more... the less** plus... moins ▸ **the sooner the better** le plus tôt sera le mieux
5. [in titles] **: Alexander the Great** Alexandre le Grand ▸ **George the First** Georges Premier.

theatre *UK*, ***theater*** *US* ['θɪətəʳ] **n 1.** THEAT théâtre *m* **2.** *UK* MED salle *f* d'opération **3.** *US* [cinema] cinéma *m*.

theatregoer *UK*, ***theatergoer*** *US* ['θɪətə,gəʊəʳ] **n** habitué *m*, -e *f* du théâtre.

theatrical [θɪ'ætrɪkl] **adj** théâtral(e) / [company] de théâtre.

theft [θeft] **n** vol *m*.

their [ðeəʳ] **poss adj** leur, leurs *(pl)* ▸ **their house** leur maison ▸ **their children** leurs enfants ▸ **it wasn't their fault** ce n'était pas de leur faute à eux.

theirs [ðeəz] **poss pron** le leur (la leur), les leurs *(pl)* ▸ **that house is theirs** cette maison est la leur, cette maison est à eux/elles ▸ **it wasn't our fault, it was theirs** ce n'était pas de notre faute, c'était de la leur ▸ **a friend of theirs** un de leurs amis, un ami à eux/elles.

them *(weak form* [ðəm], *strong form* [ðem]*)* **pers pron pl** **1.** *(direct)* les ▸ **I know them** je les connais ▸ **if I were** OR **was them** si j'étais eux/elles, à leur place **2.** *(indirect)* leur ▸ **we spoke to them** nous leur avons parlé ▸ **she sent them a letter** elle leur a envoyé une lettre ▸ **I gave it to them** je le leur ai donné **3.** *(stressed, after prep, in comparisons etc)* eux (elles) ▸ **you can't expect them to do it** tu ne peux pas exiger que ce soit eux qui le fassent ▸ **with them** avec eux/elles ▸ **without them** sans eux/elles ▸ **we're not as wealthy as them** nous ne sommes pas aussi riches qu'eux/qu'elles.

thematic [θɪ'mætɪk] **adj** thématique.

theme [θi:m] **n** **1.** [topic, motif] thème *m*, sujet *m* **2.** MUS thème *m* / [signature tune] indicatif *m*.

theme park **n** parc *m* à thème.

theme pub **n** *UK* pub à thème *m*.

theme song **n** chanson *f* principale, thème *m* principal.

theme tune **n** chanson *f* principale, thème *m* principal.

themselves [ðem'selvz] **pron** **1.** *(reflexive)* se / *(after prep)* eux (elles) **2.** *(for emphasis)* eux-mêmes *mpl*, elles-mêmes *f* ▸ **they did it themselves** ils l'ont fait tout seuls.

then [ðen] **adv** **1.** [not now] alors, à cette époque ▸ **Marilyn, or Norma Jean as she was then known** Marilyn, ou Norma Jean comme elle s'appelait alors ▸ **by then** [in future] d'ici là / [in past] entre-temps ▸ **from then on** à partir de ce moment-là ▸ **since then** depuis (lors) ▸ **until then** [in future] jusque-là / [in past] jusqu'alors, jusqu'à ce moment-là
2. [next] puis, ensuite ▸ **do your homework first, then you can watch TV** fais d'abord tes devoirs, et ensuite tu pourras regarder la télé
3. [in that case] alors, dans ce cas ▸ **you were right then!** mais alors, vous aviez raison! ▸ **if x equals 10 then y...** si x égale 10 alors y... ▸ **but then again, no one can be sure** mais après tout, on ne sait jamais
4. [therefore] donc
5. [also] d'ailleurs, et puis ▸ **then there's Peter to invite** et puis il faut inviter Peter.

thence [ðens] **adv** *fml* & *liter* de là.

theologian [θɪə'ləʊdʒən] **n** théologien *m*, -ienne *f*.

theological [θɪə'lɒdʒɪkl] **adj** théologique ▸ **theological college** séminaire *m*.

theology [θɪ'ɒlədʒɪ] **n** théologie *f*.

theorem ['θɪərəm] **n** théorème *m*.

theoretical [θɪə'retɪkl] **adj** théorique.

theoretically [θɪə'retɪklɪ] **adv** théoriquement.

theorist ['θɪərɪst] **n** théoricien *m*, -enne *f*.

theorize, *UK* ***-ise*** ['θɪəraɪz] **vi** : **to theorize (about)** émettre une théorie (sur), théoriser (sur).

theory ['θɪərɪ] (pl -ies) **n** théorie *f* ▸ **in theory** en théorie.

therapeutic [,θerə'pju:tɪk] **adj** thérapeutique.

therapeutic cloning **n** clonage *m* thérapeutique.

therapist ['θerəpɪst] **n** thérapeute *mf*, psychothérapeute *mf*.

therapy ['θerəpɪ] **n** *(U)* thérapie *f*.

there [ðeəʳ] ■ **pron** **1.** [indicating existence of sthg] : **there is/are** il y a ▸ **there's someone at the door** il y a quelqu'un à la porte ▸ **there were some pieces missing** il manquait des pièces ▸ **there was no denying it** c'était indéniable ▸ **there must be some mistake** il doit y avoir erreur
2. *(with vb) fml* : **there followed an ominous silence** un silence lourd de menaces suivit.
■ **adv** **1.** [in existence, available] y, là ▸ **is anybody there?** il y a quelqu'un? ▸ **is John there, please?** [when telephoning] est-ce que John est là, s'il vous plaît?
2. [referring to place] y, là ▸ **they aren't there** ils ne sont pas là, ils n'y sont pas ▸ **who's there?** qui est là? ▸ **I'm going there next week** j'y vais la semaine prochaine ▸ **here and there** çà et là ▸ **there it is** c'est là ▸ **there he is!** le voilà! ▸ **see that woman there? that's Margot** tu vois cette femme là-bas? c'est Margot ▸ **over there** là-bas ▸ **in there** là-dedans ▸ **under there** là-dessous ▸ **it's six kilometres there and back** cela fait six kilomètres aller-retour
3. [point in conversation, particular stage] là ▸ **can I stop you there?** est-ce que je peux vous arrêter là? ▸ **we're getting there** on y arrive ▸ **we disagree there, there we disagree** nous ne sommes pas d'accord là-dessus ▸ **hello** OR **hi there!** salut! ▸ **there you go again!** ça y est, vous recommencez!
4. *inf phr* : **all/not all there** qui a/n'a plus toute sa tête.
■ **excl** : **there, I knew he'd turn up** tiens OR voilà, je savais bien qu'il s'amènerait ▸ **there now, don't cry!** allons! OR là! ne pleure pas! ▸ **there, there** allons, allons.
◆ ***there again*** **adv** après tout ▸ **but there again, no one really knows** mais après tout, personne ne sait vraiment.
◆ ***there and then***, ***then and there*** **adv** immédiatement, sur-le-champ.
◆ ***there you are*** **adv** **1.** [handing over something] voilà
2. [emphasizing that one is right] vous voyez bien ▸ **there you are, what did I tell you!** tu vois, qu'est-ce que je t'avais dit!
3. [expressing reluctant acceptance] c'est comme ça, que voulez-vous? ▸ **it wasn't the ideal solution, but there you are** OR **go** ce n'était pas l'idéal, mais enfin OR mais qu'est-ce que vous voulez.

thereabouts [ðeərə'baʊts], *US* ***thereabout*** [ðeərə'baʊt] **adv** : **or thereabouts** [nearby] par là / [approximately] environ.

thereafter [,ðeər'ɑ:ftəʳ] **adv** *fml* après cela, par la suite.

thereby [,ðeər'baɪ] **adv** *fml* ainsi, de cette façon.

therefore ['ðeəfɔ:ʳ] **adv** donc, par conséquent.

therein [,ðeər'ɪn] **adv** *fml* [inside] dedans / [in that matter] en cela.

there's [ðeəz] = ***there is***.

thereupon [,ðeərə'pɒn] **adv** *fml* sur ce, sur quoi.

thermal ['θɜ:ml] **adj** thermique / [clothes] en Thermolactyl®.

thermal reactor **n** réacteur *m* thermique.

thermal underwear **n** *(U)* sous-vêtements *mpl* en thermolactyl.

thermodynamics [,θɜ:məʊdaɪ'næmɪks] **n** *(U)* thermodynamique *f*.

thermoelectric [,θɜ:məʊɪ'lektrɪk] **adj** thermoélectrique.

thermometer [θə'mɒmɪtə^r] n thermomètre *m*.

thermonuclear [,θɜːməʊ'njuːklɪə^r] adj thermonucléaire.

thermoplastic [,θɜːməʊ'plæstɪk] ■ adj thermoplastique.

■ n thermoplastique *m*, thermoplaste *m*.

Thermos (flask)® ['θɜːməs-] n (bouteille *f*) Thermos® *m ou f*.

thermostat ['θɜːməstæt] n thermostat *m*.

thesaurus [θɪ'sɔːrəs] (pl **-es** [-iːz]) n dictionnaire *m* de synonymes.

these [ðiːz] pron pl ➤ ***this***.

thesis ['θiːsɪs] (pl **theses** ['θiːsiːz]) n thèse *f*.

they [ðeɪ] pers pron pl **1.** [people, things, animals - unstressed] ils (elles) / [- stressed] eux (elles) ▸ **they're pleased** ils sont contents (elles sont contentes) ▸ **they're pretty earrings** ce sont de jolies boucles d'oreille ▸ **they can't do it** eux (elles), ils (elles) ne peuvent pas le faire ▸ **there they are** les voilà **2.** [unspecified people] on, ils ▸ **they say it's going to snow** on dit qu'il va neiger ▸ **they're going to put up petrol prices** ils vont augmenter le prix de l'essence.

they'd [ðeɪd] = ***they had, they would***.

they'll [ðeɪl] = ***they shall, they will***.

they're [ðeə^r] = ***they are***.

they've [ðeɪv] = ***they have***.

thick [θɪk] ■ adj **1.** [gen] épais (épaisse) / [forest, hedge, fog] dense / [voice] indistinct(e) ▸ **to be 6 inches thick** avoir 15 cm d'épaisseur ▸ **the snow was thick on the ground** il y avait une épaisse couche de neige sur le sol ▸ **pubs are not very thick on the ground round here** les pubs sont plutôt rares par ici

2. *inf* [stupid] bouché(e) ▸ **he's as thick as two short planks** il est bête comme ses pieds

3. [full, covered] **: to be thick with** [dust] être couvert(e) de / [people] être plein(e) de ▸ **the shelves were thick with dust** les étagères étaient recouvertes d'une épaisse couche de poussière ▸ **thick with smoke** [from cigarettes] enfumé(e) / [from fire] plein d'une fumée épaisse ▸ **those two are as thick as thieves** ces deux-là s'entendent comme larrons en foire.

■ n **: in the thick of** au plus fort de, en plein *OR* au beau milieu de ▸ **he's really in the thick of it** [dispute, activity] il est vraiment dans le feu de l'action.

◆ ***thick and fast*** adv **: questions came thick and fast** les questions pleuvaient.

◆ ***through thick and thin*** adv envers et contre tout, quoi qu'il advienne.

thicken ['θɪkn] ■ vt épaissir.

■ vi s'épaissir.

thickener ['θɪknə^r] n [for sauce, soup] liant *m* / [for oil, paint] épaississant *m*.

thickening ['θɪknɪŋ] n épaississant *m*.

thicket ['θɪkɪt] n fourré *m*.

thickly ['θɪklɪ] adv **1.** [not thinly - spread] en couche épaisse / [- cut] en tranches épaisses **2.** [densely - wooded, populated] très **3.** [speak, say] d'une voix indistincte.

thickness ['θɪknɪs] n épaisseur *f*.

thickset [,θɪk'set] adj trapu(e).

thick-skinned [-'skɪnd] adj qui a la peau dure.

thief [θiːf] (pl **thieves**) n voleur *m*, -euse *f*.

thieve [θiːv] vt & vi voler.

thieves [θiːvz] npl ➤ ***thief***.

thieving ['θiːvɪŋ] ■ adj voleur(euse).

■ n *(U)* vol *m*.

thigh [θaɪ] n cuisse *f*.

thighbone ['θaɪbəʊn] n fémur *m*.

thimble ['θɪmbl] n dé *m* (à coudre).

thin [θɪn] ■ adj (comp **-ner**, superl **-nest**) **1.** [slice, layer, paper] mince / [cloth] léger(ère) / [person] maigre **2.** [liquid, sauce] clair(e), peu épais (peu épaisse) **3.** [sparse - crowd] épars(e) / [- vegetation, hair] clairsemé(e) ▸ **to be thin on top** [person] se dégarnir.

■ adv **: to be wearing thin** [joke] n'être plus amusant(e) ▸ **my patience is wearing thin** je suis à bout de patience.

■ vi (pt & pp **-ned**, cont **-ning**) [hair] **: to be thinning** s'éclaircir, se dégarnir.

◆ ***thin down*** vt sep [liquid, paint] délayer, diluer / [sauce] éclaircir.

thin air n **: to appear out of thin air** apparaître tout d'un coup ▸ **to disappear into thin air** disparaître complètement, se volatiliser.

thing [θɪŋ] n **1.** [gen] chose *f* ▸ **that was a silly thing to do!** ce n'était pas la chose à faire! ▸ **the (best) thing to do would be...** le mieux serait de... ▸ **for one thing** en premier lieu, pour commencer ▸ **(what) with one thing and another** au bout du compte ▸ **I must be seeing things** je dois avoir des visions ▸ **the thing is...** le problème, c'est que... ▸ **it's just one of those things** *inf* c'est comme ça, ce sont des choses qui arrivent ▸ **this is just the thing** *US inf* c'est exactement *OR* tout à fait ce qu'il faut ▸ **to have a thing about sb/sthg** *inf* [like] adorer qqn/qqch, être fou de qqn/qqch / [dislike] avoir qqn/qqch en horreur ▸ **to have a thing with sb** avoir une liaison avec qqn ▸ **it's not really my thing** ce n'est pas vraiment mon truc ▸ **to make a thing (out) of** *inf* faire tout un plat *OR* toute une histoire de ▸ **to be on to a good thing** être sur une bonne affaire ▸ **I could show him a thing or two about hang gliding** je pourrais lui apprendre une ou deux petites choses en deltaplane

2. [anything] **: I don't know a thing** je n'y connais absolument rien ▸ **she hadn't got a thing on** elle était entièrement nue ▸ **I haven't got a thing to wear** je n'ai rien à me mettre sur le dos

3. [object] chose *f*, objet *m* ▸ **what's that yellow thing on the floor?** qu'est-ce que c'est que ce truc jaune par terre? ▸ **she loves books and posters and things** elle aime les livres, les posters, ce genre de choses

4. [person] **: what a sweet little thing!** quel amour! ▸ **you poor thing!** mon pauvre!

5. *inf* [fashion] **: the thing** la mode ▸ **it's quite the thing** c'est très à la mode.

◆ ***things*** npl **1.** [clothes, possessions] affaires *fpl* ▸ **put your things away** ramassez vos affaires

2. *inf* [life, situation] **: how are things?** comment ça va? ▸ **I need time to think things over** j'ai besoin de temps pour réfléchir ▸ **it's just one of those things** ce sont des choses qui arrivent.

thingamabob ['θɪŋəmə,bɒb], ***thingamajig*** ['θɪŋəmədʒɪg], *UK* ***thingummy(jig)*** ['θɪŋəmɪ-], *UK* ***thingie***, *UK* ***thingy*** ['θɪŋɪ] **n** *inf* truc *m*, machin *m*.

think [θɪŋk] ■ **vt** (pt & pp **thought**) **1.** [believe] **: to think (that)** croire que, penser que ▸ **I thought I heard a noise** j'ai cru *OR* il m'a semblé entendre un bruit ▸ **I think so/not** je crois que oui/non, je pense que oui/non ▸ **he's a crook – I thought so *OR* I thought as much** c'est un escroc – je m'en doutais ▸ **it's expensive, don't you think?** c'est cher, tu ne trouves pas? ▸ **(just) who does he think he is?** (mais) pour qui se prend-il?
2. [have in mind] penser à ▸ **I was just thinking how ironic it all is** je pensais simplement à l'ironie de la chose ▸ **I kept thinking "why me?"** je n'arrêtais pas de me dire: pourquoi moi? ▸ **I think I'll go for a walk** je crois que je vais aller me promener
3. [imagine] s'imaginer ▸ **just think what we can do with all that money!** imaginez ce qu'on peut faire avec tout cet argent! ▸ **I can't think why you agreed to do it** je ne comprends pas *OR* je me demande bien pourquoi tu as accepté de le faire ▸ **who'd have thought it!** qui l'eût cru!
4. [remember] **: did you think to bring any money?** avez-vous pensé à apporter de l'argent?
5. [in polite requests] **: do you think you could help me?** tu pourrais m'aider?
■ **vi** (pt & pp **thought**) **1.** [use mind] réfléchir, penser ▸ **he thought for a moment** il a réfléchi un instant ▸ **to think for oneself** se faire ses propres opinions ▸ **to think aloud** penser tout haut ▸ **that's what set me thinking** c'est ce qui m'a fait réfléchir
2. [have stated opinion] **: what do you think of *OR* about his new film?** que pensez-vous de son dernier film? ▸ **to think a lot of sb/sthg** penser beaucoup de bien de qqn/qqch
▸▸ **to think on one's feet** réfléchir vite ▸ **to think better of sthg/of doing sthg** décider après tout de ne pas faire qqch ▸ **I thought better of it** je me suis ravisé ▸ **to think nothing of doing sthg** trouver tout à fait normal *OR* tout naturel de faire qqch ▸ **thank you – think nothing of it!** merci – mais je vous en prie *OR* mais c'est tout naturel! ▸ **to think twice** y réfléchir à deux fois.
■ **n** *inf* **: to have a think (about sthg)** réfléchir (à qqch).

◆ ***think about*** **vt insep : to think about sb/sthg** songer à *OR* penser à qqn/qqch ▸ **to think about doing sthg** songer à faire qqch ▸ **I'll think about it** je vais y réfléchir.

◆ ***think back*** **vi : to think back (to)** repenser (à).

◆ ***think of*** **vt insep 1.** [consider] = ***think about***
2. [remember] se rappeler ▸ **he couldn't think of the name** il ne se rappelait pas le nom, le nom ne lui venait pas ▸ **I've just thought of something, she'll be out** j'avais oublié *OR* je viens de me rappeler, elle ne sera pas là
3. [conceive] penser à, avoir l'idée de ▸ **to think of doing sthg** avoir l'idée de faire qqch ▸ **she's the one who thought of double-checking it** c'est elle qui a eu l'idée de le vérifier ▸ **what do you think of the new teacher?** comment trouvez-vous le *OR* que pensez-vous du nouveau professeur?
4. [show consideration for] penser à ▸ **I have my family to think of** il faut que je pense à ma famille.

◆ ***think out***, ***think through*** **vt sep** bien étudier, bien considérer ▸ **a well-thought-out plan** un projet bien conçu *OR* ficelé.

◆ ***think over*** **vt sep** réfléchir à ▸ **I need some time to think things over** j'ai besoin de temps pour réfléchir.

◆ ***think up*** **vt sep** imaginer.

thinker ['θɪŋkəʳ] **n** penseur *m*, -euse *f*.

thinking ['θɪŋkɪŋ] ■ **adj** qui pense, qui réfléchit.
■ **n** *(U)* opinion *f*, pensée *f* ▸ **to do some thinking** réfléchir ▸ **to my way of thinking** à mon avis.

think tank **n** comité *m* d'experts.

thinly ['θɪnlɪ] **adv 1.** [not thickly - spread] en couche mince / [- cut] en tranches minces **2.** [sparsely - wooded, populated] peu.

thinner ['θɪnəʳ] **n** diluant *m*.

thinness ['θɪnnɪs] **n** *(U)* [of slice, layer, paper] minceur *f* / [of person] maigreur *f* / [of cloth] légèreté *f*.

thin-skinned [-'skɪnd] **adj** susceptible, très sensible.

third [θɜːd] ■ **num** troisième.
■ **n** UNIV ≃ licence *f* mention passable ; see also ***sixth***.

third-class **adj** *UK* UNIV **: third-class degree** ≃ licence *f* mention passable.

third degree **n** *inf* **: to give sb the third degree** [torture] passer qqn à tabac / [interrogate] cuisiner qqn.

third-degree burns **npl** brûlures *fpl* du troisième degré.

third-generation **adj** COMPUT & TELEC de troisième génération, 3G.

thirdly ['θɜːdlɪ] **adv** troisièmement, tertio.

third party **n** tiers *m*, tierce personne *f*.

third-party insurance **n** assurance *f* de responsabilité civile.

third-rate **adj** *pej* de dernier *OR* troisième ordre.

Third World **n : the Third World** le tiers-monde.

thirst [θɜːst] **n** soif *f* ▸ **thirst for** *fig* soif de.

thirsty ['θɜːstɪ] (comp **-ier**, superl **-iest**) **adj 1.** [person] **: to be *OR* feel thirsty** avoir soif **2.** [work] qui donne soif.

thirteen [,θɜː'tiːn] **num** treize ; see also ***six***.

thirteenth [,θɜː'tiːnθ] **num** treizième ; see also ***sixth***.

thirtieth ['θɜːtɪəθ] **num** trentième ; see also ***sixth***.

thirty ['θɜːtɪ] (pl **-ies**) **num** trente ; see also ***sixty***.

thirty-something **adj** *caractéristique de certaines personnes ayant la trentaine et issues d'un milieu aisé.*

this [ðɪs] ■ **pron** (pl **these** [ðiːz]) *(demonstrative use)* ce, ceci / *(as opposed to 'that')* celui-ci (celle-ci) ▸ **this is for you** c'est pour vous ▸ **who's this?** qui est-ce? ▸ **what's this?** qu'est-ce que c'est? ▸ **this is what he told me** voici ce qu'il m'a dit ▸ **this is where I live** c'est ici que j'habite ▸ **I didn't want it to end like this** je ne voulais pas que ça finisse *OR* se termine comme ça ▸ **which sweets does she prefer, these or those?** quels bonbons préfère-t-elle, ceux-ci ou ceux-là? ▸ **this is a rose, that is a peony** ceci est une rose,

ça c'est une pivoine ▸ **this is Daphne Logan** [introducing another person] je vous présente Daphne Logan / [introducing oneself on phone] ici Daphne Logan, Daphne Logan à l'appareil ▸ **after/before this** après/avant ça ▸ **to talk about this and that** parler de choses et d'autres ▸ **to do this and that** faire toutes sortes de choses.
■ **adj 1.** *(demonstrative use)* ce (cette), cet *(before vowel or silent 'h')*, ces *(pl)* / *(as opposed to 'that')* ce (cette)...-ci, ces...-ci *(pl)* ▸ **these chocolates are delicious** ces chocolats sont délicieux ▸ **I prefer this book** je préfère ce livre-ci ▸ **I'll have this one** je prendrai celui-ci ▸ **this afternoon** cet après-midi ▸ **this morning** ce matin ▸ **this week** cette semaine ▸ **this way please** par ici s'il vous plaît
2. *inf* [a certain] un certain (une certaine).
■ **adv** aussi ▸ **it was this big** c'était aussi grand que ça ▸ **you'll need about this much** il vous en faudra à peu près comme ceci.

thistle ['θɪsl] **n** chardon *m*.

thither ['ðɪðər] ➤ ***hither***.

tho' [ðəʊ] = ***though***.

thong [θɒŋ] **n 1.** [of leather] lanière *f* **2.** *US* [flip-flop] tong *f*.

thorn [θɔ:n] **n** épine *f* ▸ **to be a thorn in sb's flesh** *OR* **side** être une source continuelle d'exaspération pour qqn.

thorny ['θɔ:nɪ] (**comp -ier, superl -iest**) **adj** *lit & fig* épineux(euse).

thorough ['θʌrə] **adj 1.** [exhaustive - search, inspection] minutieux(euse) / [- investigation, knowledge] approfondi(e) **2.** [meticulous] méticuleux(euse) **3.** [complete, utter] complet(ète), absolu(e).

thoroughbred ['θʌrəbred] **n** pur-sang *m inv*.

thoroughfare ['θʌrəfeər] **n** *fml* rue *f*, voie *f* publique.

thoroughly ['θʌrəlɪ] **adv 1.** [fully, in detail] à fond **2.** [completely, utterly] absolument, complètement.

thoroughness ['θʌrənɪs] *(U)* **n 1.** [exhaustiveness] minutie *f* **2.** [meticulousness] soin *m* méticuleux.

those [ðəʊz] **pron pl** ➤ ***that***.

though [ðəʊ] ■ **conj** bien que *(+ subjunctive)*, quoique *(+ subjunctive)*.
■ **adv** pourtant, cependant.

thought [θɔ:t] ■ **pt & pp** ➤ ***think***.
■ **n 1.** [gen] pensée *f* / [idea] idée *f*, pensée ▸ **don't give it another thought** n'y pensez plus ▸ **that's a thought!** ça, c'est une idée! ▸ **she was lost** *OR* **deep in thought** elle était absorbée par ses pensées *OR* plongée dans ses pensées ▸ **after much thought** après avoir mûrement réfléchi **2.** [intention] intention *f* ▸ **it's the thought that counts** c'est l'intention qui compte.
◆ ***thoughts*** **npl 1.** [reflections] pensées *fpl*, réflexions *fpl* ▸ **our thoughts are with you** nos pensées vous accompagnent ▸ **to collect one's thoughts** rassembler ses idées **2.** [views] opinions *fpl*, idées *fpl* ▸ **we'd like your thoughts on the matter** nous aimerions savoir ce que vous en pensez.

thoughtful ['θɔ:tfʊl] **adj 1.** [pensive] pensif(ive) **2.** [considerate - person] prévenant(e), attentionné(e) / [- remark, act] plein(e) de gentillesse.

thoughtfully ['θɔ:tfʊlɪ] **adv 1.** [considerately, kindly] avec prévenance *OR* délicatesse, gentiment **2.** [pensively] pensivement **3.** [with careful thought] d'une manière réfléchie.

thoughtfulness ['θɔ:tfʊlnɪs] *(U)* **n 1.** [pensiveness] air *m* pensif **2.** [considerateness - of person] prévenance *f* / [- of remark, act] délicatesse *f*.

thoughtless ['θɔ:tlɪs] **adj** [person] qui manque d'égards (pour les autres) / [remark, behaviour] irréfléchi(e).

thoughtlessly ['θɔ:tlɪslɪ] **adv 1.** [inconsiderately] sans aucun égard, sans aucune considération **2.** [hastily] hâtivement, sans réfléchir.

thoughtlessness ['θɔ:tlɪsnɪs] **n** *(U)* manque *m* d'égards *OR* de prévenance.

thought-provoking **adj** qui pousse à la réflexion, stimulant(e).

thousand ['θaʊznd] **num** mille ▸ **a** *OR* **one thousand** mille ▸ **thousands of** des milliers de ; see also ***six***.

thousandth ['θaʊzntθ] **num** millième ; see also ***sixth***.

thrash [θræʃ] **vt 1.** [hit] battre, rosser **2.** *inf* [defeat] écraser, battre à plates coutures.
◆ ***thrash about***, ***thrash around*** **vi** s'agiter.
◆ ***thrash out*** **vt sep** [problem] débrouiller, démêler / [idea] débattre, discuter.

thrashing ['θræʃɪŋ] **n 1.** [hitting] rossée *f*, correction *f* **2.** *inf* [defeat] défaite *f*.

thread [θred] ■ **n 1.** [gen] fil *m* **2.** [of screw] filet *m*, pas *m*.
■ **vt 1.** [needle] enfiler **2.** [move] **: to thread one's way through the crowd** se faufiler parmi la foule.

threadbare ['θredbeər] **adj** usé(e) jusqu'à la corde.

threat [θret] **n : threat (to)** menace *f* (pour).

HOW TO ...

make threats

Si vous n'arrêtez pas ce vacarme, j'appelle la police ! / If you don't stop that noise, I'll call the police!
Sortez d'ici ou j'appelle la police ! / Get out or I'll call the police!
Je te préviens, tu n'as pas intérêt à lui répéter ce que je viens de te dire / I'm warning you, you'd better not tell him what I've just said
Donne-moi ça tout de suite, sinon... / Give it to me right now, or else...
Je t'aurai prévenu... / I'm warning you...
Ma patience a des limites... / Don't try my patience....
Tu veux une claque ? *inf* / Do you want a slap?
Si jamais tu recommences... / If you ever do that again...
Arrête ou il va t'arriver des bricoles ! *inf* / Stop that or there'll be trouble!

threaten ['θretn] ■ **vt : to threaten sb (with)** menacer qqn (de) ▸ **to threaten to do sthg** menacer de faire qqch.
■ **vi** menacer.

threatening ['θretnɪŋ] **adj** menaçant(e) / [letter] de menace.

threateningly ['θretnɪŋlɪ] **adv** [behave, move] de manière menaçante, d'un air menaçant / [say] d'un ton ***OR*** sur un ton menaçant.

three [θri:] **num** trois ; see also ***six***.

three-D **adj** [film, picture] en relief.

three-day event **n** concours *m* complet d'équitation.

three-dimensional [-dɪ'menʃənl] **adj** [film, picture] en relief / [object] à trois dimensions.

threefold ['θri:fəʊld] ■ **adj** triple.
■ **adv : to increase threefold** tripler.

three-legged race [-'legɪd-] **n** course *f* à trois pieds.

three-piece **adj : three-piece suit** (costume *m*) trois pièces *m* ▸ **three-piece suite** canapé *m* et deux fauteuils assortis.

three-ply **adj** [wool] à trois fils.

three-point turn **n** *UK* demi-tour *m* en trois manœuvres.

three-quarters **npl** [fraction] trois quarts *mpl*.

threesome ['θri:səm] **n** trio *m*, groupe *m* de trois personnes.

three-star **adj** trois étoiles.

three-wheeler [-'wi:lə^r] **n** voiture *f* à trois roues.

thresh [θreʃ] **vt** battre.

threshing machine ['θreʃɪŋ-] **n** batteuse *f*.

threshold ['θreʃhəʊld] **n** seuil *m* ▸ **to be on the threshold of** *fig* être au bord ***OR*** seuil de.

threshold agreement **n** *UK* accord *m* d'indexation des salaires sur le coût de la vie.

threw [θru:] **pt** ➤ ***throw***.

thrift [θrɪft] **n 1.** *(U)* [gen] économie *f*, épargne *f* **2.** *US* [savings bank] = ***thrift institution***.

thrift institution **n** *US* caisse *f* d'épargne.

thrift shop, ***thrift store*** **n** *US magasin vendant des articles d'occasion au profit d'œuvres charitables*.

thrifty ['θrɪftɪ] (comp **-ier**, superl **-iest**) **adj** économe.

thrill [θrɪl] ■ **n 1.** [sudden feeling] frisson *m*, sensation *f* **2.** [enjoyable experience] plaisir *m*.
■ **vt** transporter, exciter.
■ **vi : to thrill to a story/the music** être transporté(e) par une histoire/la musique.

thrilled [θrɪld] **adj : thrilled (with sthg/to do sthg)** ravi(e) (de qqch/de faire qqch), enchanté(e) (de qqch/de faire qqch).

thriller ['θrɪlə^r] **n** thriller *m*.

thrilling ['θrɪlɪŋ] **adj** saisissant(e), palpitant(e).

thrive [θraɪv] (pt **-d** ***OR*** **throve**, pp **-d**) **vi** [person] bien se porter / [plant] pousser bien / [business] prospérer.

thriving ['θraɪvɪŋ] **adj** [person] bien portant(e) / [plant] qui pousse bien / [business] prospère.

throat [θrəʊt] **n** gorge *f* ▸ **to ram *OR* force sthg down sb's throat** *fig* rebattre les oreilles de qqn avec qqch ▸ **it stuck in my throat** *fig* ça m'est resté en travers de la gorge ▸ **to be at each other's throats** se disputer, se battre.

throaty ['θrəʊtɪ] (comp **-ier**, superl **-iest**) **adj** guttural(e).

throb [θrɒb] ■ **n** [of drums] battement *m* / [of pulse] pulsation *f* / [of engine] vibration *f*.
■ **vi** (pt & pp **-bed**, cont **-bing**) [heart] palpiter, battre fort / [engine] vibrer / [music] taper ▸ **my head is throbbing** j'ai des élancements dans la tête.

throbbing ['θrɒbɪŋ] **adj 1.** [rhythm] battant(e) / [drum] qui bat rythmiquement / [engine, machine] vibrant(e), vrombissant(e) **2.** [heart] battant(e), palpitant(e) **3.** [pain] lancinant(e).

throes [θrəʊz] **npl : to be in the throes of** [war, disease] être en proie à ▸ **to be in the throes of an argument** être en pleine dispute.

thrombosis [θrɒm'bəʊsɪs] (pl **-boses** [-'bəʊsi:z]) **n** thrombose *f*.

throne [θrəʊn] **n** trône *m*.

throng [θrɒŋ] ■ **n** foule *f*, multitude *f*.
■ **vt** remplir, encombrer.
■ **vi** affluer.

throttle ['θrɒtl] ■ **n** [valve] papillon *m* des gaz / [lever] commande *f* des gaz.
■ **vt** [strangle] étrangler.

through [θru:] ■ **adj 1.** [direct] direct ▸ **'no through road'** *UK*, **'not a through street'** *US* 'voie sans issue'
2. [finished] **: are you through?** tu as fini? ▸ **to be through with sthg** avoir fini qqch ▸ **she's through with him** elle en a eu assez de lui.
■ **adv 1.** [relating to place, position] **: please go through into the lounge** passez dans le salon, s'il vous plaît ▸ **to let sb through** laisser passer qqn
2. [from beginning to end] **: to read sthg through** lire qqch jusqu'au bout ▸ **to sleep through till ten** dormir jusqu'à dix heures ▸ **I left halfway through** je suis parti au milieu
3. [completely] **: to be wet through** être complètement trempé
4. *UK* TELEC **: can you put me through to Elaine/to extension 363?** pouvez-vous me passer Elaine/le poste 363?
■ **prep 1.** [relating to place, position] à travers ▸ **to travel through sthg** traverser qqch ▸ **the river flows through a deep valley** le fleuve traverse une vallée profonde ▸ **to cut through sthg** couper qqch ▸ **can you see through it?** est-ce que tu peux voir au travers? ▸ **to slip through the net** *lit* & *fig* passer à travers les mailles du filet
2. [during] pendant ▸ **she has lived through some difficult times** elle a connu ***OR*** traversé des moments difficiles ▸ **halfway through the performance** à la moitié ***OR*** au milieu de la représentation
3. [because of] à cause de ▸ **through no fault of his own, he lost his job** il a perdu son emploi sans que ce soit de sa faute
4. [by means of] par l'intermédiaire de, par l'entremise de ▸ **I sent it through the post** je l'ai envoyé par la poste ▸ **I met a lot of people through him** il m'a fait rencontrer beaucoup de gens

5. *US* [up till and including] **: Monday through Friday** du lundi au vendredi.

◆ ***through and through*** **adv** [completely] jusqu'au bout des ongles / [thoroughly] par cœur, à fond.

throughout [θru:'aʊt] ■ **prep 1.** [during] pendant, durant ▸ **throughout the meeting** pendant toute la réunion **2.** [everywhere in] partout dans.

■ **adv 1.** [all the time] tout le temps **2.** [everywhere] partout.

throughput ['θru:pʊt] **n** COMPUT débit *m*.

throve [θrəʊv] **pt** ➤ ***thrive***.

throw [θrəʊ] ■ **vt** (**pt threw, pp thrown**) **1.** [gen] jeter / [ball, javelin] lancer ▸ **could you throw me my lighter?** peux-tu me lancer mon briquet? ▸ **I threw some cold water on my face** je me suis aspergé la figure avec de l'eau froide ▸ **he threw two sixes** [in dice] il a jeté deux six ▸ **she was thrown clear** [in car accident] elle a été éjectée ▸ **to throw open** ouvrir en grand OR tout grand ▸ **to throw one's arms around sb** jeter ses bras autour de qqn ▸ **the news threw them into confusion/a panic** les nouvelles les ont plongés dans l'embarras/les ont affolés ▸ **to throw o.s. into sthg** *fig* se jeter à corps perdu dans qqch ▸ **to throw o.s. into one's work** se plonger dans son travail ▸ **to throw a pot** tourner un vase **2.** [rider] désarçonner **3.** [have suddenly - tantrum, fit] piquer **4.** *fig* [confuse] déconcerter, décontenancer ▸ **that question really threw me!** cette question m'a vraiment désarçonné!, je ne savais vraiment pas quoi répondre à cette question!

■ **n 1.** lancement *m*, jet *m* ▸ **that was a good throw!** vous avez bien visé! ▸ **his whole fortune depended on a single throw of the dice** toute sa fortune dépendait d'un seul coup de dés **2.** [cover] couverture *f*.

◆ ***throw away*** **vt sep 1.** [discard] jeter **2.** *fig* [money] gaspiller / [opportunity] perdre ▸ **you're throwing away your only chance of happiness** vous êtes en train de gâcher votre seule chance de bonheur.

◆ ***throw in*** **vt sep** [include] donner en plus OR en prime ▸ **with a special trip to Stockholm thrown in** avec en prime une excursion à Stockholm.

◆ ***throw out*** **vt sep 1.** [discard] jeter **2.** *fig* [reject] rejeter **3.** [from house] mettre à la porte / [from army, school] expulser, renvoyer.

◆ ***throw up*** ■ **vt sep** [dust, water] jeter, projeter.

■ **vi** *inf* [vomit] dégobiller, vomir.

throwaway ['θrəʊə,weɪ] **adj 1.** [disposable] jetable, à jeter **2.** [remark] désinvolte.

throwback ['θrəʊbæk] **n : throwback (to)** retour *m* (à).

throw-in **n** *UK* FOOTBALL rentrée *f* en touche, remise *f* en jeu.

thrown [θrəʊn] **pp** ➤ ***throw***.

thru [θru:] *inf US* = ***through***.

thrush [θrʌʃ] **n 1.** [bird] grive *f* **2.** MED muguet *m*.

thrust [θrʌst] ■ **n 1.** [forward movement] poussée *f* / [of knife] coup *m* **2.** [main aspect] idée *f* principale, aspect *m* principal.

■ **vt 1.** [shove] enfoncer, fourrer **2.** [jostle] **: to thrust one's way** se frayer un passage.

◆ ***thrust upon*** **vt sep : to thrust sthg upon sb** imposer qqch à qqn.

thrusting ['θrʌstɪŋ] **adj** [person] qui se met en avant.

thruway ['θru:weɪ] **n** *US* voie *f* express.

thud [θʌd] ■ **n** bruit *m* sourd.

■ **vi** (**pt & pp -ded, cont -ding**) tomber en faisant un bruit sourd.

thug [θʌg] **n** brute *f*, voyou *m*.

thumb [θʌm] ■ **n** pouce *m* ▸ **to twiddle one's thumbs** se tourner les pouces.

■ **vt** *inf* [hitch] **: to thumb a lift** faire du stop OR de l'autostop.

◆ ***thumb through*** **vt insep** feuilleter, parcourir.

thumb index **n** répertoire *m* à onglets.

thumbnail ['θʌmneɪl] ■ **adj** bref (brève), concis(e).

■ **n** ongle *m* du pouce.

thumbnail sketch **n** croquis *m* rapide.

thumbs down [,θʌmz-] **n : to get** OR **be given the thumbs down** être rejeté(e).

thumbs up [,θʌmz-] **n** [go-ahead] **: to give sb the thumbs up** donner le feu vert à qqn.

thumbtack ['θʌmtæk] **n** *US* punaise *f*.

thump [θʌmp] ■ **n 1.** [blow] grand coup *m* **2.** [thud] bruit *m* sourd.

■ **vt 1.** [hit] cogner, taper sur **2.** [place heavily] poser violemment.

■ **vi 1.** [move heavily] **: to thump in/out** entrer/sortir à pas pesants **2.** [heart] battre fort.

thumping ['θʌmpɪŋ] *UK inf* ■ **adj** [success] énorme, immense, phénoménal(e) / [difference] énorme.

■ **adv** *dated* [as intensifier] **: a thumping great meal** un repas énorme.

thunder ['θʌndəʳ] ■ **n** *(U)* **1.** METEOR tonnerre *m* **2.** *fig* [of traffic] vacarme *m* / [of applause] tonnerre *m*.

■ **vt** tonner, tonitruer.

■ **impers vb** METEOR tonner.

■ **vi** *fig* [traffic] tonner, gronder.

thunderbolt ['θʌndəbəʊlt] **n** coup *m* de foudre.

thunderclap ['θʌndəklæp] **n** coup *m* de tonnerre.

thundercloud ['θʌndəklaʊd] **n** nuage *m* orageux.

thundering ['θʌndərɪŋ] **adj** *UK inf dated* terrible, monstre.

thunderous ['θʌndərəs] **adj** [noise] assourdissant(e) ▸ **thunderous applause** un tonnerre d'applaudissements.

thunderstorm ['θʌndəstɔ:m] **n** orage *m*.

thunderstruck ['θʌndəstrʌk] **adj** *fig* stupéfait(e), sidéré(e).

thundery ['θʌndərɪ] **adj** orageux(euse).

Thur, Thurs (abbr of ***Thursday***) jeu.

Thursday ['θɜ:zdɪ] **n** jeudi *m* ; see also ***Saturday***.

thus [ðʌs] **adv** *fml* **1.** [therefore] par conséquent, donc, ainsi **2.** [in this way] ainsi, de cette façon, comme ceci.

thwart [θwɔ:t] **vt** contrecarrer, contrarier.

thyme [taɪm] **n** thym *m*.

thyroid ['θaɪrɔɪd] **n** thyroïde *f*.

tiara [tɪ'ɑ:rə] **n** [worn by woman] diadème *m*.

Tiber ['taɪbəʳ] **n : the (River) Tiber** le Tibre.

Tibet [tɪ'bet] **n** Tibet *m* ▸ **in Tibet** au Tibet.

Tibetan **[tɪ'betn]** ■ **adj** tibétain(e).
■ **n 1.** [person] Tibétain *m*, -e *f* **2.** [language] tibétain *m*.

tibia **['tɪbɪə]** (pl **-biae** [-biː] *OR* **-s**) **n** tibia *m*.

tic **[tɪk]** **n** tic *m*.

tick **[tɪk]** ■ **n 1.** *UK* [written mark] coche *f* ▸ **to put a tick beside sthg** cocher qqch **2.** [sound] tic-tac *m* **3.** [insect] tique *f*.
■ **vt** *UK* cocher.
■ **vi** faire tic-tac ▸ **what makes him tick?** *fig* je me demande comment il fonctionne.
◆ ***tick away***, ***tick by*** **vi** passer.
◆ ***tick off*** **vt sep 1.** *UK* [mark off] cocher **2.** *UK inf* [tell off] passer un savon à, enguirlander.
◆ ***tick over*** **vi** *UK* [engine, business] tourner au ralenti.

ticked **[tɪkt]** **adj** *US* en rogne.

tickertape **['tɪkəteɪp]** **n** *(U)* bande *f* de téléimprimeur.

ticket **['tɪkɪt]** **n 1.** [for access, train, plane] billet *m* / [for bus] ticket *m* / [for library] carte *f* / [label on product] étiquette *f* **2.** [for traffic offence] P.-V. *m*, papillon *m* **3.** POL liste *f* ▸ **he fought the election on a Democratic ticket** il a basé son programme électoral sur les principes du Parti démocrate.

ticket agency **n** billetterie *f*.

ticket collector **n** *UK* contrôleur *m*, -euse *f*.

ticket holder **n** personne *f* munie d'un billet.

ticket inspector **n** *UK* contrôleur *m*, -euse *f*.

ticket machine **n** distributeur *m* de billets.

ticket office **n** bureau *m* de vente des billets.

ticket tout **n** *UK* revendeur *m*, -euse *f* de billets *(sur le marché noir)*.

ticking **['tɪkɪŋ]** **n 1.** [of clock] tic-tac *m* **2.** [fabric] toile *f* (à matelas).

ticking off (pl **tickings off** ['tɪkɪŋz-]) **n** *UK inf* **: to give sb a ticking off** passer un savon à qqn, enguirlander qqn ▸ **to get a ticking off** recevoir un savon, se faire enguirlander.

tickle **['tɪkl]** ■ **vt 1.** [touch lightly] chatouiller **2.** *fig* [amuse] amuser.
■ **vi** chatouiller.

tickling **['tɪklɪŋ]** ■ **n** *(U)* [of person] chatouilles *fpl* / [of blanket] picotement *m*.
■ **adj** [throat] qui grattouille *OR* picote / [cough] d'irritation, qui gratte la gorge ▸ **you get a tickling sensation in your feet** on a une sensation de picotement dans les pieds.

ticklish **['tɪklɪʃ]** **adj 1.** [person] qui craint les chatouilles, chatouilleux(euse) **2.** *fig* [delicate] délicat(e), difficile.

tickly **['tɪklɪ]** **adj** *inf* [sensation] de chatouillis / [blanket] qui chatouille / [beard] qui pique.

tick-tack-toe **n** *US* [game] ≃ morpion *m*.

tidal **['taɪdl]** **adj** [force] de la marée / [river] à marées / [barrier] contre la marée.

tidal wave **n** raz-de-marée *m inv*.

tidbit *US* = ***titbit***.

tiddler **['tɪdlər]** **n** *UK* [fish] petit poisson *m*.

tiddly **['tɪdlɪ]** (comp **-ier**, superl **-iest**) **adj** *UK inf* **1.** [tipsy] pompette, gai(e) **2.** [tiny] minuscule.

tiddlywinks **['tɪdlɪwɪŋks]**, *US* ***tiddledywinks*** **['tɪdl(d)ɪwɪŋks]** **n** jeu *m* de puce.

tide **[taɪd]** **n 1.** [of sea] marée *f* **2.** *fig* [of opinion, fashion] courant *m*, tendance *f* / [of protest] vague *f*.
◆ ***tide over*** **vt sep** dépanner.

tidemark **['taɪdmɑːk]** **n 1.** [of sea] ligne *f* de marée haute **2.** *UK* [round bath, neck] ligne *f* de crasse.

tidily **['taɪdɪlɪ]** **adv** soigneusement, avec ordre.

tidiness **['taɪdɪnɪs]** **n** *(U)* ordre *m*.

tidings **['taɪdɪŋz]** **npl** *liter* nouvelles *fpl*.

tidy **['taɪdɪ]** ■ **adj** (comp **-ier**, superl **-iest**) **1.** [room, desk] en ordre, bien rangé(e) / [hair, dress] soigné(e) **2.** [person - in habits] ordonné(e) / [- in appearance] soigné(e) **3.** *inf* [sizeable] coquet(ette), rondelet(ette).
■ **vt** (pt & pp **-ied**) ranger, mettre de l'ordre dans.
◆ ***tidy away*** **vt sep** ranger.
◆ ***tidy up*** ■ **vt sep** ranger, mettre de l'ordre dans.
■ **vi** ranger.

tie **[taɪ]** ■ **n 1.** [necktie] cravate *f* **2.** [string, cord] cordon *m* **3.** *fig* [link] lien *m* ▸ **family ties** liens de parenté *OR* familiaux ▸ **there are strong ties between the two countries** les deux pays entretiennent d'étroites relations **4.** [in game, competition] égalité *f* de points ▸ **it was a tie for first/second place** il y avait deux premiers/seconds ex aequo ▸ **the election resulted in a tie** les candidats ont obtenu le même nombre de voix *OR* étaient à égalité des voix **5.** *US* RAIL traverse *f*.
■ **vt** (pt & pp **tied**, cont **tying**) **1.** [fasten] attacher ▸ **they tied him to a tree** il l'ont attaché *OR* ligoté à un arbre ▸ **his hands and feet were tied** ses mains et ses pieds étaient ligotés **2.** [shoelaces] nouer, attacher ▸ **to tie a knot** faire un nœud **3.** *fig* [link] **: to be tied to** être lié(e) à ▸ **the job keeps me very much tied to my desk** mon travail m'oblige à passer beaucoup de temps devant mon bureau **4.** *fig* [restricted] **: to be tied to** être cloué(e) à ▸ **they're tied to** *OR* **by the conditions of the contract** ils sont liés par les conditions du contrat.
■ **vi** (pt & pp **tied**, cont **tying**) [draw] être à égalité ▸ **they tied for third place in the competition** ils étaient troisième ex aequo au concours.
◆ ***tie down*** **vt sep** *fig* [restrict] restreindre la liberté de ▸ **she doesn't want to feel tied down** elle ne veut pas perdre sa liberté.
◆ ***tie in with*** **vt insep** concorder avec, coïncider avec ▸ **the evidence doesn't tie in with the facts** les indices dont nous disposons ne correspondent pas aux faits *OR* ne cadrent pas avec les faits ▸ **this ties in with what I said before** cela rejoint ce que j'ai dit avant.
◆ ***tie up*** **vt sep 1.** [with string, rope] attacher ▸ **the letters were tied up in bundles** les lettres étaient ficelées en liasses **2.** [shoelaces] nouer, attacher **3.** *fig* [money, resources] immobiliser ▸ **their money is all tied up in shares** leur argent est entièrement investi dans des actions **4.** [complete] conclure ▸ **there are still a few loose ends to tie up** il y a encore quelques points de détail à régler **5.** *fig* [link] **: to be tied up with** être lié(e) à.

tiebreak(er) **['taɪbreɪk(ər)]** **n 1.** TENNIS tie-break *m*, jeu *m* décisif **2.** [in game, competition] question *f* subsidiaire.

tied **[taɪd]** **adj** SPORT **: a tied match** un match nul.

tied cottage n *UK* logement *m* de fonction *(mis à la disposition d'un employé agricole etc).*

tied up adj [busy] occupé(e), pris(e).

tie-dye vt nouer et teindre.

tie-in n 1. [link] lien *m*, rapport *m* 2. [product] **: the book is a tie-in with the TV series** le livre est tiré de la série télévisée.

tiepin ['taɪpɪn] n épingle *f* de cravate.

tier [tɪəʳ] n [of seats] gradin *m* / [of cake] étage *m*.

Tierra del Fuego [tɪˌerədel'fweɪgəʊ] n Terre de Feu *f* ▸ **in Tierra del Fuego** en Terre de Feu.

tie-up n 1. [link] lien *m*, rapport *m* 2. *US* [interruption] interruption *f*, arrêt *m*.

tiff [tɪf] n bisbille *f*, petite querelle *f*.

tiger ['taɪgəʳ] n tigre *m*.

tiger cub n petit *m* du tigre.

tiger economy n *pays à l'économie très performante* ▸ **the (Asian) tiger economies** les dragons *mpl* ***OR*** les tigres *mpl* asiatiques.

tight [taɪt] ■ adj 1. [clothes, group, competition, knot] serré(e) ▸ **the dress was a tight fit** la robe était un peu juste ▸ **tight jeans** [too small] un jean trop serré / [close-fitting] un jean moulant ▸ **to be in a tight corner *OR* spot** être dans une situation difficile
2. [taut] tendu(e) ▸ **to keep (a) tight hold *OR* grasp on sthg** bien tenir qqch
3. [painful - chest] oppressé(e) / [- stomach] noué(e)
4. [schedule] serré(e), minuté(e) ▸ **it was tight but I made it in time** c'était juste, mais je suis arrivé à temps ▸ **money is a bit tight *OR* things are a bit tight at the moment** l'argent manque un peu en ce moment
5. [strict] strict(e), sévère ▸ **to run a tight ship** mener son monde à la baguette
6. [corner, bend] raide
7. *inf* [drunk] soûl(e), rond(e)
8. *inf* [miserly] radin(e), avare.
■ adv 1. [firmly, securely] bien, fort ▸ **to hold tight** tenir bien ▸ **hold tight!** tiens bon! ▸ **to shut *OR* close sthg tight** bien fermer qqch
2. [tautly] à fond ▸ **pull the thread tight** tirez ***OR*** tendez bien le fil.
◆ ***tights*** npl *UK* collant *m*, collants *mpl*.

tighten ['taɪtn] ■ vt 1. [belt, knot, screw] resserrer ▸ **to tighten one's hold *OR* grip on** resserrer sa prise sur 2. [pull tauter] tendre 3. [make stricter] renforcer.
■ vi 1. [rope] se tendre 2. [grip, hold] se resserrer.
◆ ***tighten up*** vt sep 1. [belt, screw] resserrer 2. [make stricter] renforcer.

tightfisted [ˌtaɪt'fɪstɪd] adj *pej* radin(e), pingre.

tight-fitting adj [skirt, trousers] moulant(e) / [lid] qui ferme bien.

tightknit [ˌtaɪt'nɪt] adj [family, community] uni(e).

tight-lipped [-'lɪpt] adj 1. [in anger] les lèvres serrées 2. [silent] qui ne dit rien, qui garde le silence.

tightly ['taɪtlɪ] adv 1. [closely] **: to fit tightly** être juste ▸ **to pack tightly** entasser, tasser 2. [firmly] bien, fort 3. [tautly] à fond.

tightness ['taɪtnɪs] n 1. [of clothes] étroitesse *f* 2. [in chest] oppression *f* 3. [strictness] sévérité *f*, rigueur *f*.

tightrope ['taɪtrəʊp] n corde *f* raide ▸ **to be on *OR* walking a tightrope** *fig* être sur la corde raide.

tightrope walker n funambule *mf*.

Tigré ['ti:greɪ] n Tigré *m* ▸ **in Tigré** dans le Tigré.

tigress ['taɪgrɪs] n tigresse *f*.

Tigris ['taɪgrɪs] n **: the (River) Tigris** le Tigre.

tilde ['tɪldə] n tilde *m*.

tile [taɪl] n [on roof] tuile *f* / [on floor, wall] carreau *m*.

tiled [taɪld] adj [floor, wall] carrelé(e) / [roof] couvert(e) de tuiles.

tiler ['taɪləʳ] n [of roof] couvreur *m (de toits en tuiles)* / [of floor, wall] carreleur *m*.

tiling ['taɪlɪŋ] n [of floor, wall] carrelage *m* / [of roof - action] pose *f* de tuiles / [- tiles] tuiles *fpl*.

till [tɪl] ■ prep jusqu'à ▸ **from six till ten o'clock** de six heures à dix heures.
■ conj jusqu'à ce que *(+ subjunctive)* ▸ **wait till I come back** attends que je revienne / *(after negative)* avant que *(+ subjunctive)* ▸ **it won't be ready till tomorrow** ça ne sera pas prêt avant demain.
■ n tiroir-caisse *m*.

tiller ['tɪləʳ] n NAUT barre *f*.

tilt [tɪlt] ■ n inclinaison *f*.
■ vt incliner, pencher.
■ vi s'incliner, pencher.

timber ['tɪmbəʳ] n 1. *(U)* [wood] bois *m* de charpente ***OR*** de construction 2. [beam] poutre *f*, madrier *m*.

timbered ['tɪmbəd] adj en bois.

time [taɪm] ■ n 1. [gen] temps *m* ▸ **a long time** longtemps ▸ **in a short time** dans peu de temps, sous peu ▸ **to take time** prendre du temps ▸ **these things take time** cela ne se fait pas du jour au lendemain ▸ **to be time for sthg** être l'heure de qqch ▸ **to get the time to do sthg** prendre le temps de faire qqch ▸ **it's a good time to do sthg** c'est le moment de faire qqch ▸ **to have a good time** s'amuser bien ▸ **to have a hard time doing sthg** avoir du mal à faire qqch ▸ **in good time** de bonne heure ▸ **ahead of time** en avance, avant l'heure ▸ **on time** à l'heure ▸ **to have time on one's hands *OR* time to spare** avoir du temps ▸ **it's high time (that)...** il est grand temps que... ▸ **time and a half** une fois et demie le tarif normal ▸ **to have no time for sb/sthg** ne pas supporter qqn/qqch ▸ **to make good time** [on journey] bien rouler ***OR*** marcher / [in schedule] bien avancer ▸ **she made the time to read the report** elle a pris le temps de lire le rapport ▸ **to pass the time** passer le temps ▸ **to play for time** essayer de gagner du temps ▸ **to take one's time (doing sthg)** prendre son temps (pour faire qqch) ▸ **you took your time about it!** tu en as mis du temps! ▸ **I'll finish it in my own good time** je le finirai quand bon me semblera
2. [as measured by clock] heure *f* ▸ **what time is it?, what's the time?** quelle heure est-il? ▸ **what time do you make it?** quelle heure avez-vous? ▸ **what time are we leaving?** à quelle heure partons-nous? ▸ **do you know how to tell the time?** est-ce que tu sais lire l'heure? ▸ **in a week's/year's time** dans une semaine/un an ▸ **local time** heure *f*

locale ▸ **to keep good time** être toujours à l'heure ▸ **to lose time** retarder ▸ **to pass the time of day with sb** échanger quelques mots avec qqn
3. [point in time] époque *f* ▸ **in Victorian times** à l'époque victorienne ▸ **at that time I was in Madrid** à ce moment-là j'étais *OR* j'étais alors à Madrid ▸ **an inconvenient time** un moment inopportun ▸ **by the time you get this...** le temps que tu reçoives ceci..., quand tu auras reçu ceci... ▸ **by this time next week** d'ici une semaine, dans une semaine ▸ **we'll talk about that when the time comes** nous en parlerons en temps utile ▸ **to be ahead of one's time** être en avance sur son temps ▸ **before my time** avant que j'arrive ici
4. [occasion] fois *f* ▸ **nine times out of ten the machine doesn't work** neuf fois sur dix la machine ne marche pas ▸ **many a time I've wondered...** je me suis demandé plus d'une *OR* bien des fois... ▸ **from time to time** de temps en temps, de temps à autre ▸ **time after time, time and again** à maintes reprises, maintes et maintes fois ▸ **at the best of times** même quand tout va bien ▸ **to have a good time** bien s'amuser
5. *v inf* [in prison] **: to do time** faire de la taule
6. MUS mesure *f* ▸ **in triple *OR* three-part time** à trois temps.
■ **vt 1.** [schedule] fixer, prévoir ▸ **they timed the attack for 6 o'clock** l'attaque était prévue pour 6 h
2. [race, runner] chronométrer
3. [arrival, remark] choisir le moment de.
◆ ***times*** ■ **npl** fois *fpl* ▸ **four times as much as me** quatre fois plus que moi.
■ **prep** MATHS fois.
◆ ***at a time*** **adv** d'affilée ▸ **one at a time** un par un, un seul à la fois ▸ **months at a time** des mois et des mois.
◆ ***at (any) one time*** **adv** à la fois.
◆ ***at the same time*** **adv** en même temps.
◆ ***at times*** **adv** quelquefois, parfois.
◆ ***about time*** **adv : it's about time (that)...** il est grand temps que... ▸ **about time too!** ce n'est pas trop tôt!
◆ ***for the time being*** **adv** pour le moment.
◆ ***in time*** **adv 1.** [not late] **: in time (for)** à l'heure (pour)
2. [eventually] à la fin, à la longue / [after a while] avec le temps, à la longue.

time-and-motion study **n** étude *f* de productivité *(axée sur l'efficacité des employés)*.

time bomb **n** *lit & fig* bombe *f* à retardement.

time check **n** [on radio] rappel *m* de l'heure.

time-consuming [-kən,sju:mɪŋ] **adj** qui prend beaucoup de temps.

time-critical **adj** critique en termes de temps.

timed [taɪmd] **adj** [race, test] chronométré(e) ▸ **well timed** opportun(e) ▸ **badly timed** inopportun(e).

time difference **n** décalage *m* horaire.

time-expired **adj** périmé(e), obsolète.

time frame **n** délai *m* ▸ **what's our time frame?** de combien de temps disposons-nous?

time-honoured *UK*, ***time-honored*** *US* [-,ɒnəd] **adj** consacré(e).

timekeeping ['taɪm,ki:pɪŋ] **n** ponctualité *f*.

time lag **n** décalage *m*.

time lapse **n** décalage *m* horaire.

time-lapse **adj : time-lapse photography** accéléré *m*.

timeless ['taɪmlɪs] **adj** éternel(elle).

time limit **n** délai *m*.

timely ['taɪmlɪ] (comp **-ier**, superl **-iest**) **adj** opportun(e).

time machine **n** machine *f* à voyager dans le temps.

time off **n** temps *m* libre.

time out **n 1.** SPORT temps *m* mort **2.** [break] **: to take time out to do sthg** trouver le temps de faire qqch.

timepiece ['taɪmpi:s] **n** *dated* [watch] montre *f* / [clock] horloge *f*.

timer ['taɪmə^r] **n** minuteur *m*.

time-saver **n : a dishwasher is a great time-saver** on gagne beaucoup de temps avec un lave-vaisselle.

time-saving [-'seɪvɪŋ] **adj** qui fait gagner du temps.

time scale **n** période *f* / [of project] délai *m*.

time-share **n** logement *m* en multipropriété.

time-sharing [-'ʃeərɪŋ] **n 1.** [in holiday home] multipropriété *f* **2.** COMPUT (travail *m* en) temps *m* partagé.

time sheet **n** feuille *f* de présence.

time signal **n** top *m* horaire.

time switch **n** minuterie *f*.

timetable ['taɪm,teɪbl] **n 1.** *UK* SCH emploi *m* du temps **2.** [of buses, trains] horaire *m* **3.** *UK* [schedule] calendrier *m*.

time travel **n** voyage *m* dans le temps.

timewasting ['taɪmweɪstɪŋ] **n** perte *f* de temps ▸ **the team was accused of timewasting** on a reproché à l'équipe d'avoir joué la montre.

time zone **n** fuseau *m* horaire.

timid ['tɪmɪd] **adj** timide.

timidity [tɪ'mɪdətɪ] **n** timidité *f*.

timidly ['tɪmɪdlɪ] **adv** timidement.

timing ['taɪmɪŋ] **n** *(U)* **1.** [of remark] à-propos *m inv* **2.** [scheduling] **: the timing of the election** le moment choisi pour l'élection **3.** [measuring] chronométrage *m*.

timing device **n** mouvement *m* d'horlogerie.

timpani ['tɪmpənɪ] **npl** timbales *fpl*.

tin [tɪn] ■ **n 1.** *(U)* [metal] étain *m* / [in sheets] fer-blanc *m* **2.** *UK* [can] boîte *f* de conserve **3.** *UK* [small container] boîte *f* ▸ **cake tin** [for baking] moule *m* à gâteau / [for storing] boîte *f* à gâteaux.
■ **comp** en étain, d'étain.

tin can **n** boîte *f* de conserve.

tinder ['tɪndə^r] **n** petit bois *m*.

tinfoil ['tɪnfɔɪl] **n** *(U)* papier *m* (d')aluminium.

tinge [tɪndʒ] **n 1.** [of colour] teinte *f*, nuance *f* **2.** [of feeling] nuance *f*.

tinged [tɪndʒd] **adj : tinged with** teinté(e) de.

tingle ['tɪŋgl] **vi** picoter ▸ **to tingle with** brûler de.

tingling ['tɪŋglɪŋ] **n** *(U)* picotement *m*.

tinker ['tɪŋkə^r] ■ **n** *UK* **1.** *pej* [gypsy] romanichel *m*, -elle *f* **2.** [rascal] polisson *m*, -onne *f*.
■ **vi : to tinker (with sthg)** bricoler (qqch).

tinkle ['tɪŋkl] ■ **n 1.** [sound] tintement *m* **2.** *UK inf* [phone call] **: to give sb a tinkle** passer un coup de fil à qqn.
■ **vi** [ring] tinter.

tin mine **n** mine *f* d'étain.

tinned [tɪnd] **adj** *UK* en boîte.

tinnitus [tɪ'naɪtəs] **n** acouphène *m*.

tinny ['tɪnɪ] (**comp -ier, superl -iest**) ■ **adj 1.** [sound] métallique **2.** *inf pej* [badly made] **: a tinny car** un tas de ferraille, une vraie casserole.
■ **n** *Aus* canette de bière *f inf*.

tin opener **n** *UK* ouvre-boîtes *m inv*.

tin-pot **adj** *UK inf pej* [country, dictator] de rien du tout.

tinsel ['tɪnsl] **n** *(U)* guirlandes *fpl* de Noël.

tint [tɪnt] ■ **n** teinte *f*, nuance *f* / [in hair] rinçage *m*.
■ **vt** teinter.

tinted ['tɪntɪd] **adj** [glasses, windows] teinté(e).

tiny ['taɪnɪ] (**comp -ier, superl -iest**) **adj** minuscule.

tip [tɪp] ■ **n 1.** [end] bout *m* ▸ **it's on the tip of my tongue** je l'ai sur le bout de la langue ▸ **it's just the tip of the iceberg** *fig* ce n'est que la partie émergée de l'iceberg **2.** *UK* [dump] décharge *f* / *fig* **: your room is a real tip!** *inf* quel bazar, ta chambre! **3.** [to waiter] pourboire *m* **4.** [piece of advice] tuyau *m*.
■ **vt** (**pt & pp -ped, cont -ping**) **1.** [tilt] faire basculer ▸ **to tip the scales in sb's favour** *fig* faire pencher la balance en faveur de qqn **2.** *UK* [spill] renverser **3.** [waiter] donner un pourboire à **4.** [winning horse] pronostiquer ▸ **he's tipped to be the next president** *OR* **as the next president** on pronostique qu'il sera le prochain président.
■ **vi** (**pt & pp -ped, cont -ping**) **1.** [tilt] basculer **2.** *UK* [spill] se renverser **3.** [give money to waiter] laisser un pourboire.
◆ ***tip off*** **vt sep** prévenir.
◆ ***tip over*** ■ **vt sep** renverser.
■ **vi** se renverser.

tip-off **n** tuyau *m* / [to police] dénonciation *f*.

tipped ['tɪpt] **adj** [cigarette] qui a un embout, à bout filtre.

-tipped **suffix** à bout... ▸ **steel/felt-tipped** à bout ferré/feutré ▸ **a felt-tipped pen** un crayon-feutre, un feutre.

Tipp-Ex® ['tɪpeks] *UK* ■ **n** Tipp-ex® *m*.
■ **vt** effacer avec du Tipp-Ex®.

tipple ['tɪpl] **n** *inf* **: what's your tipple?** qu'est-ce que tu aimes boire d'habitude?

tipsy ['tɪpsɪ] (**comp -ier, superl -iest**) **adj** *inf* gai(e).

tiptoe ['tɪptəʊ] ■ **n : on tiptoe** sur la pointe des pieds.
■ **vi** marcher sur la pointe des pieds.

tip-top **adj** *inf dated* excellent(e).

TIR (**abbr of** ***Transports Internationaux Routiers***) TIR.

tirade [taɪ'reɪd] **n** diatribe *f*.

Tirana, ***Tiranë*** [tɪ'rɑːnə] **n** Tirana.

tire ['taɪər] ■ **n** *US* = ***tyre***.
■ **vt** fatiguer.
■ **vi 1.** [get tired] se fatiguer **2.** [get fed up] **: to tire of** se lasser de.
◆ ***tire out*** **vt sep** épuiser.

tired ['taɪəd] **adj 1.** [sleepy] fatigué(e), las (lasse) **2.** [fed up] **: to be tired of sthg/of doing sthg** en avoir assez de qqch/de faire qqch.

tiredness ['taɪədnɪs] **n** fatigue *f*.

tireless ['taɪəlɪs] **adj** infatigable.

tirelessly ['taɪəlɪslɪ] **adv** infatigablement, inlassablement, sans ménager ses efforts.

tiresome ['taɪəsəm] **adj** ennuyeux(euse).

tiring ['taɪərɪŋ] **adj** fatigant(e).

Tirol = ***Tyrol***.

tissue ['tɪʃuː] **n 1.** [paper handkerchief] mouchoir *m* en papier **2.** *(U)* BIOL tissu *m*
▸▸ **a tissue of lies** un tissu de mensonges.

tissue paper **n** *(U)* papier *m* de soie.

tit [tɪt] **n 1.** [bird] mésange *f* **2.** *vulg* [breast] nichon *m*, néné *m*.

titbit *UK* ['tɪtbɪt], ***tidbit*** *US* ['tɪdbɪt] **n 1.** [of food] bon morceau *m* **2.** *fig* [of news] petite nouvelle *f* ▸ **a titbit of gossip** un petit potin.

tit for tat **n** un prêté pour un rendu.

titillate ['tɪtɪleɪt] ■ **vt** titiller.
■ **vi** titiller les sens.

titillation [ˌtɪtɪ'leɪʃn] **n** titillation *f*.

titivate ['tɪtɪveɪt] **vt** pomponner.

title ['taɪtl] **n** titre *m*.

titled ['taɪtld] **adj** titré(e).

title deed **n** titre *m* de propriété.

titleholder ['taɪtlˌhəʊldər] **n** SPORT tenant *m*, -e *f* du titre.

title page **n** page *f* de titre.

title role **n** rôle *m* principal.

title track **n** morceau *m* qui donne son titre à l'album.

titter ['tɪtər] **vi** rire bêtement.

tittle-tattle ['tɪtlˌtætl] **n** *(U) inf pej* ragots *mpl*, cancans *mpl*.

titular ['tɪtjʊlər] **adj** nominal(e).

T-junction **n** intersection *f* en T.

TLC **n abbr of** ***tender loving care***.

TLS (**abbr of** ***Times Literary Supplement***) **n** *édition littéraire du Times*.

TM[1] **n** (**abbr of** ***transcendental meditation***) MT *f*.

TM[2] **abbr of** ***trademark***.

TN **abbr of** ***Tennessee***.

TNT (**abbr of** ***trinitrotoluene***) **n** TNT *m*.

to *(stressed* [tuː], *unstressed before consonant* [tə], *unstressed before vowel* [tʊ]*)* ■ **prep 1.** [indicating place, direction] à ▸ **to go to Liverpool/Spain/school** aller à Liverpool/en Espagne/à l'école ▸ **let's go to town/to Susan's** allons en ville/chez Susan ▸ **to go to the butcher's** aller chez le boucher ▸ **to the left/right** à gauche/droite ▸ **our house is a mile to the south** notre maison est à un mille au sud **2.** *(to express indirect object)* à ▸ **to give sthg to sb** donner qqch à qqn ▸ **be kind to him/to animals** soyez gentil avec lui/bon envers les animaux ▸ **we were listening to the**

radio nous écoutions la radio ▸ **he refused to give an answer to my question** il refusa de répondre à ma question
3. [indicating reaction, effect] à ▸ **to my delight/surprise** à ma grande joie/surprise ▸ **it worked to our advantage** cela a tourné à notre avantage ▸ **to be to sb's liking** être au goût de qqn
4. [in stating opinion] **: to me,...** à mon avis,... ▸ **it seemed quite unnecessary to me/him** *etc* cela me/lui *etc* semblait tout à fait inutile
5. [indicating state, process] **: to drive sb to drink** pousser qqn à boire ▸ **to shoot to fame** devenir célèbre du jour au lendemain ▸ **it could lead to trouble** cela pourrait causer des ennuis ▸ **they starved to death** ils sont morts de faim
6. [as far as] à, jusqu'à ▸ **to count to 10** compter jusqu'à 10 ▸ **we work from 9 to 5** nous travaillons de 9 heures à 17 heures ▸ **from March to June** de mars (jusqu')à juin
7. [in expressions of time] moins ▸ **it's ten to three/quarter to one** il est trois heures moins dix/une heure moins le quart
8. [per] à ▸ **40 miles to the gallon** ≃ 7 litres aux cent (km) ▸ **there are 16 ounces to a pound** il y a 16 onces dans une livre
9. [accompanied by] **: a poem set to music** un poème mis en musique ▸ **we danced to the sound of guitars** on a dansé au son des guitares
10. [of, for] de ▸ **the key to the car** la clé de la voiture ▸ **a letter to my daughter** une lettre à ma fille.
■ **adv** [shut] **: push the door to** fermez la porte.
■ **with infinitive 1.** *(forming simple infinitive)* **: to walk** marcher ▸ **to laugh** rire
2. *(following another verb)* **: to begin to do sthg** commencer à faire qqch ▸ **to try to do sthg** essayer de faire qqch ▸ **to want to do sthg** vouloir faire qqch
3. *(following an adjective)* **: difficult to do** difficile à faire ▸ **ready to go** prêt à partir ▸ **I'm happy/sad to see her go** je suis content/triste de la voir partir
4. *(indicating purpose)* pour ▸ **he worked hard to pass his exam** il a travaillé dur pour réussir son examen ▸ **I did it to annoy her** je l'ai fait exprès pour l'énerver
5. *(substituting for a relative clause)* **: I have a lot to do** j'ai beaucoup à faire ▸ **he told me to leave** il m'a dit de partir
6. *(to avoid repetition of infinitive)* **: I meant to call him but I forgot to** je voulais l'appeler, mais j'ai oublié
7. [in comments] **: to be honest...** en toute franchise... ▸ **to sum up,...** en résumé,..., pour récapituler,... ▸ **to put it another way** en d'autres termes.

toad [təʊd] **n** crapaud *m.*

toad-in-the-hole **n** *UK* CULIN *plat composé de saucisses cuites au four dans une sorte de pâte à crêpes.*

toadstool ['təʊdstu:l] **n** champignon *m* vénéneux.

toady ['təʊdɪ] *pej* ■ **n** (pl **-ies**) lèche-bottes *mf inv.*
■ **vi** (pt & pp **-ied**) **: to toady (to sb)** lécher les bottes (de qqn).

to and fro **adv : to go to and fro** aller et venir ▸ **to walk to and fro** marcher de long en large.
◆ ***to-and-fro*** **adj** de va-et-vient.

toast [təʊst] ■ **n 1.** *(U)* [bread] pain *m* grillé, toast *m* **2.** [drink] toast *m* ▸ **to drink a toast to sb/sthg** lever son verre en l'honneur de qqn/à qqch.
■ **vt 1.** [bread] (faire) griller **2.** [person] porter un toast à.

toasted ['təʊstɪd] **adj : toasted sandwich** sandwich *m* grillé ▸ **toasted cheese** fromage *m* fondu.

toaster ['təʊstəʳ] **n** grille-pain *m inv.*

toast rack **n** porte-toasts *m inv.*

tobacco [tə'bækəʊ] **n** *(U)* tabac *m.*

tobacconist [tə'bækənɪst] **n** *UK* buraliste *mf* ▸ **tobacconist's (shop)** bureau *m* de tabac.

Tobago [tə'beɪgəʊ] ➤ ***Trinidad and Tobago***.

-to-be **suffix : mother-to-be** future mère *f.*

toboggan [tə'bɒgən] ■ **n** luge *f*, traîne *f* sauvage *Québec.*
■ **vi** faire de la luge, faire de la traîne sauvage *Québec*.

today [tə'deɪ] ■ **n** aujourd'hui *m.*
■ **adv** aujourd'hui.

toddle ['tɒdl] **vi** [child] marcher d'un pas hésitant.

toddler ['tɒdləʳ] **n** tout-petit *m (qui commence à marcher).*

toddy ['tɒdɪ] (pl **-ies**) **n** grog *m.*

to-die-for **adj** *inf* de rêve.

to-do (pl **-s**) **n** *inf dated* histoire *f.*

toe [təʊ] ■ **n** [of foot] orteil *m*, doigt *m* de pied / [of sock, shoe] bout *m.*
■ **vt : to toe the line** se plier.

TOEFL [tɔfl] (abbr of ***Test of English as a Foreign Language***) **n** *test d'anglais passé par les étudiants étrangers désirant faire des études dans une université américaine.*

toehold ['təʊhəʊld] **n** prise *f* ▸ **to have a toehold in a market** *fig* avoir un pied dans un marché.

toenail ['təʊneɪl] **n** ongle *m* d'orteil.

toffee ['tɒfɪ] **n** *UK* caramel *m.*

toffee apple **n** *UK* pomme *f* caramélisée.

tofu ['təʊfu:] **n** tofu *m.*

toga ['təʊgə] **n** toge *f.*

together [tə'geðəʳ] ■ **adv 1.** [gen] ensemble ▸ **they get on well together** ils s'entendent bien ▸ **she's cleverer than both of them put together** elle est plus intelligente qu'eux deux réunis ▸ **tie the two ribbons together** attachez les deux rubans l'un à l'autre **2.** [at the same time] en même temps.
■ **adj** *inf* équilibré(e).
◆ ***together with*** **prep** ainsi que.

togetherness [tə'geðənɪs] **n** *(U)* unité *f.*

toggle ['tɒgl] **n** bouton *m* de duffle-coat.

toggle switch **n** ELECTRON & COMPUT interrupteur *m* à bascule.

Togo ['təʊgəʊ] **n** Togo *m* ▸ **in Togo** au Togo.

Togolese [ˌtəʊgə'li:z] ■ **adj** togolais(e).
■ **n** Togolais *m*, -e *f.*

togs [tɒgz] **npl** *inf* fringues *fpl.*

toil [tɔɪl] *liter* ■ **n** labeur *m.*
■ **vi** travailler dur.
◆ ***toil away*** **vi : to toil away (at sthg)** travailler dur (à qqch).

toilet ['tɔɪlɪt] **n** [lavatory] toilettes *fpl*, cabinets *mpl* ▸ **to go to the toilet** aller aux toilettes *OR* aux cabinets.

toilet bag n trousse *f* de toilette.

toilet humour n humour *m* scatologique.

toilet paper n *(U)* papier *m* hygiénique.

toiletries ['tɔɪlɪtrɪz] npl articles *mpl* de toilette.

toilet roll n rouleau *m* de papier hygiénique.

toilet seat n siège *m* des cabinets *OR* W-C *OR* toilettes.

toilet soap n savonnette *f*.

toilet tissue n *(U)* papier *m* hygiénique.

toilet-trained [-ˌtreɪnd] adj propre.

toilet water n eau *f* de toilette.

to-ing and fro-ing [ˌtu:ɪŋən'frəʊɪŋ] n *(U)* allées *fpl* et venues.

token ['təʊkn] ■ adj symbolique.
■ n **1.** [voucher] bon *m* **2.** [symbol] marque *f*.
◆ ***by the same token*** adv de même.

Tokyo ['təʊkjəʊ] n Tokyo.

told [təʊld] pt & pp ➤ ***tell***.

tolerable ['tɒlərəbl] adj passable.

tolerably ['tɒlərəblɪ] adv passablement.

tolerance ['tɒlərəns] n tolérance *f*.

tolerant ['tɒlərənt] adj tolérant(e).

tolerantly ['tɒlərəntlɪ] adv avec tolérance.

tolerate ['tɒləreɪt] vt **1.** [put up with] supporter **2.** [permit] tolérer.

toleration [ˌtɒlə'reɪʃn] n *(U)* tolérance *f*.

toll [təʊl] ■ n **1.** [number] nombre *m* **2.** [fee] péage *m*
▶▶ **to take its toll** se faire sentir.
■ vt & vi sonner.

tollbooth ['təʊlbu:θ] n poste *m* de péage.

toll bridge n pont *m* à péage.

tollfree *US* ■ adj : **tollfree number** numéro *m* vert.
■ adv : **to call tollfree** appeler un numéro vert.

tollroad ['təʊlrəʊd] n route *f* à péage.

tomato [*UK* tə'mɑ:təʊ, *US* tə'meɪtəʊ] (pl -es) n tomate *f*.

tomb [tu:m] n tombe *f*.

tombola [tɒm'bəʊlə] n *esp UK* tombola *f*.

tomboy ['tɒmbɔɪ] n garçon *m* manqué.

tombstone ['tu:mstəʊn] n pierre *f* tombale.

tomcat ['tɒmkæt] n matou *m*.

tomfoolery [tɒm'fu:lərɪ] n *(U)* bêtises *fpl*.

tomorrow [tə'mɒrəʊ] ■ n demain *m*.
■ adv demain.

ton [tʌn] (pl ton *OR* -s) n **1.** *UK* [imperial] = *1016 kg* / *US* [imperial] ≃ tonne *f (= 907,2 kg)* **2.** [metric] tonne *f (= 1000 kg)*
▶▶ **to weigh a ton** *inf* peser une tonne ▶ **to come down on sb like a ton of bricks** tomber sur qqn à bras raccourcis.
◆ ***tons*** npl *inf* : **tons (of)** des tas (de), plein (de).

tonal ['təʊnl] adj tonal(e).

tone [təʊn] n **1.** [gen] ton *m* ▶ **don't (you) speak to me in that tone (of voice)!** ne me parle pas sur ce ton! **2.** [on phone] tonalité *f* / [on answering machine] bip *m* sonore ▶ **please speak after the tone** veuillez parler après le signal sonore
▶▶ **to lower the tone (of)** rabaisser le ton (de).
◆ ***tone down*** vt sep modérer.
◆ ***tone in*** vi : **to tone in (with)** s'harmoniser (avec).
◆ ***tone up*** vt sep tonifier.

tone-deaf adj qui n'a aucune oreille.

toner ['təʊnər] n **1.** [for photocopier, printer] toner *m* **2.** [cosmetic] astringent *m*, lotion *f* tonique.

Tonga ['tɒŋgə] n Tonga ▶ **in Tonga** à Tonga.

tongs [tɒŋz] npl pinces *fpl* / [for hair] fer *m* à friser.

tongue [tʌŋ] n **1.** [gen] langue *f* ▶ **to have a sharp tongue** avoir la langue bien acérée *OR* affilée ▶ **to have one's tongue in one's cheek** *inf* ne pas être sérieux ▶ **to hold one's tongue** *fig* tenir sa langue ▶ **tongues will wag** on va jaser **2.** [of shoe] languette *f*.

tongue-in-cheek adj ironique.

tongue-tied [-ˌtaɪd] adj muet(ette).

tongue twister [-ˌtwɪstər] n phrase *f* difficile à dire.

tonic ['tɒnɪk] n **1.** [tonic water] Schweppes® *m* **2.** [medicine] tonique *m* ▶ **the holiday was a real tonic** *fig* ces vacances m'ont fait beaucoup de bien.

tonic water n Schweppes® *m*.

tonight [tə'naɪt] ■ n ce soir *m* / [late] cette nuit *f*.
■ adv ce soir / [late] cette nuit.

tonnage ['tʌnɪdʒ] n tonnage *m*.

tonne [tʌn] (pl **tonne** *OR* **-s**) n tonne *f*.

tonsil ['tɒnsl] n amygdale *f*.

tonsil(l)itis [ˌtɒnsɪ'laɪtɪs] n *(U)* amygdalite *f*.

too [tu:] adv **1.** [also] aussi ▶ **I like jazz – I do too** *OR* **me too** j'aime le jazz – moi aussi ▶ **he's a professor too** [as well as sthg else] il est également professeur / [as well as sb else] lui aussi est professeur ▶ **about time too!** ce n'est pas trop tôt! **2.** [excessively] trop ▶ **she works too hard** elle travaille trop ▶ **too many people** trop de gens ▶ **it was over all too soon** ça s'était terminé bien trop tôt ▶ **I'd be only too happy to help** je serais trop heureux de vous aider ▶ **I wasn't too impressed** ça ne m'a pas impressionné outre mesure.

took [tʊk] pt ➤ ***take***.

tool [tu:l] n *lit* & *fig* outil *m* ▶ **to down tools** *UK* cesser le travail ▶ **the tools of sb's trade** les outils du métier de qqn.
◆ ***tool around*** vi *US inf* traîner.

toolbag ['tu:lbæg] n trousse *f* à outils.

tool bar n COMPUT barre *f* d'outils.

tool box n boîte *f* à outils.

tool kit n trousse *f* à outils.

toolshed ['tu:lʃed] n remise *f*, resserre *f*.

toot [tu:t] ■ n coup *m* de Klaxon®.
■ vt : **to toot one's horn** klaxonner.
■ vi klaxonner.

tooth [tu:θ] (pl teeth [ti:θ]) n dent *f* ▸ **to be long in the tooth** *UK* n'être plus tout jeune ▸ **to be fed up to the back teeth with** *UK inf* en avoir ras le bol de ▸ **to grit one's teeth** serrer les dents ▸ **to lie through one's teeth** mentir comme un arracheur de dents.

◆ ***teeth*** npl *fig* [power] **: to have no teeth** être impuissant.

toothache ['tu:θeɪk] n mal *m* OR rage *f* de dents ▸ **to have toothache** *UK*, **to have a toothache** *US* avoir mal aux dents.

toothbrush ['tu:θbrʌʃ] n brosse *f* à dents.

toothless ['tu:θlɪs] adj édenté(e).

toothpaste ['tu:θpeɪst] n (pâte *f*) dentifrice *m*.

toothpick ['tu:θpɪk] n cure-dents *m inv*.

tooth powder n poudre *f* dentifrice.

tootle ['tu:tl] vi *inf* **: to tootle off** se sauver.

top [tɒp] ■ adj **1.** [highest] du haut ▸ **the top floor** OR **storey** le dernier étage ▸ **the top button of her dress** le premier bouton de sa robe ▸ **in the top right-hand corner** dans le coin en haut à droite

2. [most important, successful - officials] important(e) / [- executives] supérieur(e) / [- pop singer] fameux(euse) / [- sportsman, sportswoman] meilleur(e) / [- in exam] premier(ère) ▸ **the top banks in the country** les grandes banques du pays

3. [maximum] maximum ▸ **at top speed** à toute vitesse ▸ **to be on top form** être en pleine forme.

■ n **1.** [highest point - of hill] sommet *m* / [- of page, pile] haut *m* / [- of tree] cime *f* / [- of list] début *m*, tête *f* ▸ **at the top of the stairs/the street** en haut de l'escalier/la rue ▸ **he searched the house from top to bottom** il a fouillé la maison de fond en comble ▸ **she filled the jar right to the top** elle a rempli le bocal à ras bord ▸ **on top** dessus ▸ **to go over the top** *UK* en faire un peu trop, exagérer ▸ **at the top of one's voice** à tue-tête ▸ **he is at the top of his form** il est au meilleur de sa forme ▸ **to blow one's top** *inf* piquer une crise, exploser

2. [lid - of bottle, tube] bouchon *m* / [- of pen] capuchon *m* / [- of jar] couvercle *m*

3. [of table, box] dessus *m*

4. [clothing] haut *m*

5. [toy] toupie *f*

6. [highest rank - in league] tête *f* / [- in scale] haut *m* / SCH premier *m*, -ère *f* ▸ **she's top of her class** elle est première de sa classe ▸ **to be top of the bill** THEAT être en tête d'affiche

7. [beginning] **: let's take it from the top** commençons par le commencement.

■ vt (pt & pp **-ped**, cont **-ping**) **1.** [be first in] être en tête de

2. [better] surpasser ▸ **to top an offer** surenchérir

3. [exceed] dépasser.

◆ ***on top of*** prep **1.** [in space] sur ▸ **suddenly the lorry was on top of him** d'un seul coup, il a réalisé que le camion lui arrivait dessus

2. [in addition to] en plus de ▸ **on top of everything else** pour couronner le tout ▸ **it's just one thing on top of another** ça n'arrête pas

3. [in control of] **: to be on top of one's work** avoir son travail bien en main

⏭ **my work is getting on top of me** je me suis laissé dépasser par mon travail ▸ **things are getting on top of me** je suis complètement dépassé.

◆ ***top up*** *UK*, ***top off*** *US* vt sep remplir ▸ **can I top up your drink** OR **top you up?** encore une goutte?

topaz ['təʊpæz] n topaze *f*.

top brass n *(U) inf* **: the top brass** les gros bonnets *mpl*.

topcoat ['tɒpkəʊt] n **1.** [item of clothing] manteau *m* **2.** [paint] dernière couche *f*.

top dog n *inf* chef *m*.

top-down adj hiérarchisé(e).

top-flight adj de premier ordre.

top floor n dernier étage *m*.

top gear n *UK* quatrième/cinquième vitesse *f*.

top hat n haut-de-forme *m*.

top-heavy adj mal équilibré(e).

topic ['tɒpɪk] n sujet *m*.

topical ['tɒpɪkl] adj d'actualité.

topknot ['tɒpnɒt] n [in hair] houppe *f*.

topless ['tɒplɪs] adj [woman] aux seins nus ▸ **topless swimsuit** monokini *m*.

top-level adj au plus haut niveau.

topmost ['tɒpməʊst] adj le plus haut (la plus haute).

top-notch adj *inf* de premier choix.

top-of-the-range adj haut de gamme *(inv)*.

topographer [tə'pɒgrəfə^r] n topographe *mf*.

topography [tə'pɒgrəfɪ] n topographie *f*.

topped [tɒpt] adj **: topped by** OR **with** recouvert(e) de.

topping ['tɒpɪŋ] n garniture *f*.

topple ['tɒpl] ■ vt renverser.

■ vi basculer.

◆ ***topple over*** vi tomber.

top-ranking [-'ræŋkɪŋ] adj [official] haut placé(e) / [player] haut classé(e).

tops [tɒps] n *inf dated* **: it's the tops!** c'est bath!

top-secret adj top secret (top secrète).

top-security adj de haute surveillance.

topsoil ['tɒpsɔɪl] n terre *f*.

topspin ['tɒpspɪn] n lift *m*.

topsy-turvy [ˌtɒpsɪ'tɜ:vɪ] ■ adj **1.** [messy] sens dessus dessous **2.** [confused] **: to be topsy-turvy** ne pas tourner rond.

■ adv [messily] sens dessus dessous.

top ten n *hit parade des dix meilleures ventes de disques pop et rock*.

top-up card n TELEC recharge *f* de téléphone mobile.

tor [tɔ:^r] n *esp UK* [hill] colline *f* rocheuse.

torch [tɔ:tʃ] n **1.** *UK* [electric] lampe *f* électrique **2.** [burning] torche *f*.

tore [tɔ:^r] pt ➤ ***tear***[2].

torment ■ **n** ['tɔ:ment] tourment *m*.
■ **vt** [tɔ:'ment] tourmenter.

tormentor [tɔ:'mentəʳ] **n** bourreau *m*.

torn [tɔ:n] **pp** ➤ ***tear***².

tornado [tɔ:'neɪdəʊ] (**pl -es** OR **-s**) **n** tornade *f*.

Toronto [tə'rɒntəʊ] **n** Toronto.

torpedo [tɔ:'pi:dəʊ] ■ **n** (**pl -es**) torpille *f*.
■ **vt** torpiller.

torpedo boat **n** torpilleur *m*.

torpor ['tɔ:pəʳ] **n** torpeur *f*.

torque [tɔ:k] **n** couple *m* (de torsion).

torrent ['tɒrənt] **n** torrent *m*.

torrential [tə'renʃl] **adj** torrentiel(elle).

torrid ['tɒrɪd] **adj** **1.** [hot] torride **2.** *fig* [passionate] ardent(e).

torso ['tɔ:səʊ] (**pl -s**) **n** torse *m*.

tortoise ['tɔ:təs] **n** tortue *f*.

tortoiseshell ['tɔ:təʃel] ■ **adj** : **tortoiseshell cat** chat *m* roux tigré.
■ **n** *(U)* [material] écaille *f*.
■ **comp** en écaille.

tortuous ['tɔ:tʃʊəs] **adj** **1.** [winding] tortueux(euse) **2.** [over-complicated] alambiqué(e).

torture ['tɔ:tʃəʳ] ■ **n** torture *f*.
■ **vt** torturer.

torturer ['tɔ:tʃərəʳ] **n** tortionnaire *mf*.

Tory ['tɔ:rɪ] *UK* ■ **adj** tory, conservateur(trice).
■ **n** (**pl -ies**) tory *mf*, conservateur *m*, -trice *f*.

toss [tɒs] ■ **vt** **1.** [throw] jeter ▸ **to toss a coin** jouer à pile ou face ▸ **to toss one's head** rejeter la tête en arrière **2.** [salad] fatiguer / [pancake] faire sauter **3.** [throw about] ballotter.
■ **vi** **1.** [with coin] jouer à pile ou face **2.** [move about] : **to toss and turn** se tourner et se retourner.
■ **n** **1.** [of coin] coup *m* de pile ou face ▸ **to win/to lose the toss** gagner/perdre à pile ou face ▸ **to argue the toss** *UK* ergoter, chicaner ▸ **I don't give a toss** *UK inf* je m'en fiche **2.** [of head] mouvement *m* brusque.
◆ ***toss up*** **vi** jouer à pile ou face.

toss-up **n** *inf* : **it was a toss-up who'd win** il était impossible de savoir qui allait gagner.

tot [tɒt] (**pt & pp -ted, cont -ting**) **n** **1.** *inf* [small child] tout-petit *m* **2.** [of drink] larme *f*, goutte *f*.
◆ ***tot up*** **vt sep** *inf* additionner.

total ['təʊtl] ■ **adj** total(e) / [disgrace, failure] complet(ète) ▸ **a total fool** un abruti fini.
■ **n** total *m* ▸ **in total** au total.
■ **vt** (*UK* **-led, cont -ling,** *US* **-ed, cont -ing**) **1.** [add up] additionner **2.** [amount to] s'élever à **3.** *US inf* [wreck] bousiller, détruire.

totalitarian [,təʊtælɪ'teərɪən] **adj** totalitaire.

totalitarianism [,təʊtælɪ'teərɪənɪzm] **n** totalitarisme *m*.

totality [təʊ'tælətɪ] **n** totalité *f*.

totally ['təʊtəlɪ] **adv** totalement ▸ **I totally agree** je suis entièrement d'accord.

tote bag [təʊt-] **n** *US* sac *m* (à provisions).

totem pole ['təʊtəm-] **n** mât *m* totémique.

toto ['təʊtəʊ] ◆ ***in toto*** **adv** *fml* entièrement, complètement.

totter ['tɒtəʳ] **vi** *lit* & *fig* chanceler.

tottering ['tɒtərɪŋ], ***tottery*** ['tɒtərɪ] **adj** chancelant(e) / [building] branlant(e) / [government] chancelant(e), déstabilisé(e) ▸ **with tottering steps** en titubant.

toucan ['tu:kən] **n** toucan *m*.

toucan crossing **n** passage *m* mixte piétons-cyclistes.

touch [tʌtʃ] ■ **n** **1.** *(U)* [sense] toucher *m* ▸ **soft to the touch** doux au toucher
2. [detail] touche *f* ▸ **to give sthg a personal touch** ajouter une note personnelle à qqch ▸ **the house needed a woman's touch** il manquait dans cette maison une présence féminine ▸ **to put the finishing touches to sthg** mettre la dernière main à qqch
3. *(U)* [skill] marque *f*, note *f*
4. [contact] : **I'll be in touch!** je te contacterai! ▸ **to keep in touch (with sb)** rester en contact (avec qqn) ▸ **she is** OR **keeps in touch with current events** elle se tient au courant de l'actualité ▸ **to get in touch with sb** entrer en contact avec qqn ▸ **he put me in touch with the director** il m'a mis en relation avec le directeur ▸ **to lose touch** [friends] se perdre de vue ▸ **to lose touch with sb** perdre qqn de vue ▸ **to be out of touch with** ne plus être au courant de
5. SPORT : **in touch** en touche
6. [small amount] : **a touch** un petit peu ▸ **he answered with a touch of bitterness** il a répondu avec une pointe d'amertume
▸▸ **it was touch and go** c'était tangent ▸ **it was touch and go whether...** il n'était pas sûr que... ▸ **he's a soft touch** [for money] on peut le taper facilement.
■ **vt** toucher ▸ **his remark touched a (raw) nerve** sa réflexion a touché un point sensible.
■ **vi** **1.** [with fingers] toucher ▸ **'do not touch!'** 'défense de toucher'
2. [be in contact] se toucher.
◆ ***a touch*** **adv** [loud, bright] un peu trop.
◆ ***touch down*** **vi** [plane] atterrir.
◆ ***touch on*** **vt insep** effleurer.

touch-and-go **adj** incertain(e).

touchdown ['tʌtʃdaʊn] **n** **1.** [of plane] atterrissage *m* **2.** [in American football] but *m*.

touché ['tu:ʃeɪ] **excl** **1.** [fencing] touché **2.** *fig* très juste.

touched [tʌtʃt] **adj** **1.** [grateful] touché(e) **2.** *inf* [slightly mad] fêlé(e).

touching ['tʌtʃɪŋ] **adj** touchant(e).

touchingly ['tʌtʃɪŋlɪ] **adv** d'une manière touchante.

touch judge **n** RUGBY juge *m* de touche.

touchline ['tʌtʃlaɪn] **n** ligne *f* de touche.

touchpaper ['tʌtʃ,peɪpəʳ] **n** papier *m* nitraté.

touch screen **n** écran *m* tactile.

touch-sensitive **adj** [screen] tactile / [key, switch] à effleurement.

touchstone ['tʌtʃstəʊn] **n** *fig* [mineral] pierre *f* de touche.

touch-tone **adj : touch-tone telephone** téléphone *m* à touches.

touch-type **vi** taper au toucher.

touchy ['tʌtʃɪ] (comp -ier, superl -iest) **adj 1.** [person] susceptible ▸ **to be touchy about sthg** ne pas aimer parler de qqch **2.** [subject, question] délicat(e).

tough [tʌf] **adj 1.** [material, vehicle, person] solide / [character, life] dur(e) ▸ **it's tough on him** c'est un coup dur pour lui **2.** [meat] dur(e) **3.** [decision, problem, task] difficile **4.** [rough - area of town] dangereux(euse) **5.** [strict] sévère ▸ **to get tough with sb** se montrer dur avec qqn ▸ **the boss takes a tough line with people who are late** le patron ne plaisante pas avec les retardataires **6.** *inf* [unfortunate] **: tough luck!** pas de veine! ▸ **that's tough!** c'est vache!, c'est dur! ▸ **that's a tough act to follow** c'est difficile de faire mieux.

toughen ['tʌfn] **vt 1.** [character] endurcir **2.** [material] renforcer.

toughened ['tʌfnd] **adj** [glass] trempé(e).

toughness ['tʌfnɪs] *(U)* **n 1.** [resilience] dureté *f* **2.** [of material] solidité *f* **3.** [of decision, problem, task] difficulté *f* **4.** [strictness] sévérité *f*.

toupee ['tu:peɪ] **n** postiche *m*.

tour [tʊəʳ] ■ **n 1.** [journey] voyage *m* / [by pop group] tournée *f* **2.** [of town, museum] visite *f*, tour *m*.
■ **vt** visiter.
■ **vi : to tour round a country** *UK* visiter un pays.

tourer *UK* ['tʊərəʳ], ***touring car*** *US* **n** voiture *f* de tourisme.

touring ['tʊərɪŋ] ■ **adj** [show, theatre group] en tournée / [exhibition] ambulant(e).
■ **n** tourisme *m* ▸ **to go touring** faire du tourisme.

tourism ['tʊərɪzm] **n** tourisme *m*.

tourist ['tʊərɪst] **n** touriste *mf*.

tourist class **n** classe *f* touriste.

tourist (information) office **n** office *m* de tourisme.

touristy ['tʊərɪstɪ] **adj** *pej* touristique.

tournament ['tɔ:nəmənt] **n** tournoi *m*.

tourniquet ['tʊənɪkeɪ] **n** tourniquet *m*.

tour operator **n** voyagiste *m*.

tousle ['taʊzl] **vt** ébouriffer.

tout [taʊt] ■ **n** revendeur *m* de billets.
■ **vt** [tickets] revendre / [goods] vendre.
■ **vi : to tout for trade** racoler les clients.

tow [təʊ] ■ **n : to give sb a tow** remorquer qqn ▸ **'on tow'** *UK* 'véhicule en remorque' ▸ **with sb in tow** à la suite de qqn.
■ **vt** remorquer.

towards [tə'wɔ:dz], *US* ***toward*** [tə'wɔ:d] **prep 1.** [gen] vers / [movement] vers, en direction de ▸ **we headed towards Chicago** nous avons pris la direction de Chicago ▸ **the negotiations are a first step towards peace** *fig* les négociations sont un premier pas sur le chemin de la paix **2.** [in attitude] envers ▸ **she's very hostile towards me** elle est très hostile à mon égard **3.** [for the purpose of] pour ▸ **the money is going towards a new car** l'argent contribuera à l'achat d'une nouvelle voiture.

CONFUSABLE / PARONYME
towards

When translating **towards**, note that *vers* and *envers* are not interchangeable. *Vers* means in the direction of, while *envers* indicates an attitude.

towaway zone ['təʊəweɪ-] **n** *US zone de stationnement interdit sous peine de mise à la fourrière.*

towbar ['təʊbɑ:] **n** barre *f* de remorquage.

towel ['taʊəl] **n** serviette *f* / [tea towel] torchon *m*.

towelling *UK*, ***toweling*** *US* ['taʊəlɪŋ] ■ **n** *(U)* tissu *m* éponge.
■ **comp** en tissu éponge.

towel rail **n** porte-serviettes *m inv*.

tower ['taʊəʳ] ■ **n** tour *f* ▸ **a tower of strength** un appui solide.
■ **vi** s'élever ▸ **to tower over sb/sthg** dominer qqn/qqch.

tower block **n** *UK* tour *f*.

towering ['taʊərɪŋ] **adj** imposant(e).

town [taʊn] **n** ville *f* ▸ **to go out on the town** faire la tournée des grands ducs ▸ **to go to town on sthg** *fig* ne pas lésiner sur qqch.

town centre **n** *UK* centre-ville *m*.

town clerk **n** ≃ secrétaire *mf* de mairie.

town council **n** *UK* conseil *m* municipal.

town hall **n** *UK* mairie *f*.

town house **n** [fashionable house] hôtel *m* particulier.

town plan **n** *UK* plan *m* de ville.

town planner **n** *UK* urbaniste *mf*.

town planning **n** *UK* urbanisme *m*.

townsfolk ['taʊnzfəʊk], ***townspeople*** ['taʊnzˌpi:pl] **npl** citadins *mpl*.

township ['taʊnʃɪp] **n 1.** [in South Africa] township *f* **2.** [in US] ≃ canton *m*.

towpath ['təʊpɑ:θ] (pl [-pɑ:ðz]) **n** chemin *m* de halage.

towrope ['təʊrəʊp] **n** câble *m* de remorquage.

tow truck **n** *US* dépanneuse *f*.

toxic ['tɒksɪk] **adj** toxique.

toxicity [tɒk'sɪsətɪ] **n** toxicité *f*.

toxic shock syndrome **n** syndrome *m* du choc toxique.

toxin ['tɒksɪn] **n** toxine *f*.

toy [tɔɪ] **n** jouet *m*.
◆ ***toy with*** **vt insep 1.** [idea] caresser **2.** [coin] jouer avec ▸ **to toy with one's food** manger du bout des dents.

toy boy **n** *inf jeune amant d'une femme plus âgée* étalon *m*.

toy shop **n** magasin *m* de jouets.

trace [treɪs] ■ n trace *f* ▸ **traces of cocaine were found in his blood** l'analyse de son sang a révélé des traces de cocaïne ▸ **we've lost all trace of her** nous ignorons ce qu'elle est devenue ▸ **without trace** sans laisser de traces.
■ vt 1. [relatives, criminal] retrouver / [development, progress] suivre / [history, life] retracer ▸ **she traced him as far as New York** elle a suivi sa piste jusqu'à New York ▸ **the film traces the rise to power of a gangland boss** ce film relate l'ascension d'un chef de gang 2. [on paper] tracer.

traceable ['treɪsəbl] adj [object] retrouvable, qui peut être retrouvé.

trace element n oligo-élément *m*.

tracer bullet ['treɪsər-] n balle *f* traçante.

tracing ['treɪsɪŋ] n [copy] calque *m*.

tracing paper ['treɪsɪŋ-] n *(U)* papier-calque *m*.

track [træk] ■ n 1. [path] chemin *m* ▸ **off the beaten track** hors des sentiers battus 2. SPORT piste *f* ▸ **motor-racing track** *UK* autodrome *m* ▸ **track and field** athlétisme *m* 3. RAIL voie *f* ferrée 4. [of animal, person] trace *f* ▸ **to hide** *OR* **cover one's tracks** brouiller les pistes ▸ **the terrorists had covered their tracks well** les terroristes n'avaient pas laissé de traces ▸ **to stop dead in one's tracks** s'arrêter net 5. [on record, tape] piste *f*
▸▸ **to keep track of sb** rester en contact avec qqn ▸ **to keep track of** [events] suivre ▸ **we like to keep track of current affairs** nous aimons nous tenir au courant de l'actualité ▸ **to lose track of sb** perdre contact avec qqn ▸ **to lose track of** [events] ne plus suivre ▸ **he lost track of what he was saying** il a perdu le fil de ce qu'il disait ▸ **to lose track of time** perdre la notion du temps ▸ **to be on the right track** être sur la bonne voie ▸ **to be on the wrong track** être sur la mauvaise piste ▸ **to make tracks** *inf* mettre les voiles.
■ vt 1. [follow] suivre la trace de 2. *US* [tread] **: don't track mud into the house!** ne traîne pas de boue dans la maison!
■ vi [camera] faire un travelling.
◆ ***track down*** vt sep [criminal, animal] dépister / [object, address] retrouver.

track and field n *US* athlétisme *m*.

trackball ['trækbɔːl] n COMPUT boule *f* de commande.

tracker ['trækər] n 1. [person - gen] poursuivant *m*, -e *f* / [- in hunting] traqueur *m*, -euse *f* 2. [device] appareil *m* de poursuite.

tracker dog ['trækər-] n chien *m* policier.

tracker fund n FIN fonds *m* indiciel *OR* à gestion indicielle.

track event n épreuve *f* sur piste.

tracking ['trækɪŋ] ■ n 1. poursuite *f* / [of missile] repérage *m* 2. *US* SCH *répartition des élèves en sections selon leurs aptitudes*.
■ comp [radar, satellite] de poursuite.

tracking station ['trækɪŋ-] n station *f* d'observation.

track record n palmarès *m*.

track shoes npl chaussures *fpl* à pointes.

tracksuit ['træksuːt] n survêtement *m*.

tract [trækt] n 1. [pamphlet] tract *m* 2. [of land, forest] étendue *f* 3. MED appareil *m*, système *m*.

traction ['trækʃn] n *(U)* 1. PHYS traction *f* 2. MED extension *f* ▸ **in traction** en extension.

traction engine n locomobile *f*.

tractor ['træktər] n tracteur *m*.

tractor-trailer n *US* semi-remorque *m*.

trade [treɪd] ■ n 1. *(U)* [commerce] commerce *m* ▸ **domestic/foreign trade** commerce intérieur/extérieur ▸ **trade is brisk** les affaires vont bien ▸ **to do a good** *OR* **roaring trade** faire des affaires en or
2. [illicit dealings] trafic *m* ▸ **the drug trade** le trafic de drogue
3. [job] métier *m* ▸ **by trade** de son état ▸ **to be in the trade** être du métier.
■ vt [exchange] **: to trade sthg (for)** échanger qqch (contre).
■ vi 1. COMM faire du commerce ▸ **to trade (with sb)** commercer (avec qqn) ▸ **he trades in clothing** il est négociant en confection, il est dans la confection ▸ **to trade at a loss** vendre à perte
2. *US* [shop] **: to trade at** *OR* **with** faire ses courses à *OR* chez.
◆ ***trade in*** vt sep [exchange] échanger, faire reprendre.

trade agreement n accord *m* commercial.

trade association n association *f* professionnelle.

trade barrier n barrière *f* douanière.

trade deficit n déficit *m* commercial.

Trade Descriptions Act n *loi britannique contre la publicité mensongère*.

trade discount n remise *f* confraternelle *OR* à la profession.

trade fair n exposition *f* commerciale.

trade gap n déficit *m* commercial.

trade-in n reprise *f*.

trademark ['treɪdmɑːk] n 1. COMM marque *f* de fabrique 2. *fig* [characteristic] marque *f*.

trade name n nom *m* de marque.

trade-off n compromis *m*.

trade price n prix *m* de gros.

trader ['treɪdər] n marchand *m*, -e *f*, commerçant *m*, -e *f*.

trade route n route *f* commerciale.

trade secret n secret *m* de fabrication.

tradesman ['treɪdzmən] (pl **-men** [-mən]) n commerçant *m*.

tradespeople ['treɪdzˌpiːpl] npl commerçants *mpl*.

trade(s) union n *UK* syndicat *m*.

Trades Union Congress n *UK* **: the Trades Union Congress** la Confédération des syndicats britanniques.

trade(s) unionist [-'juːnjənɪst] n *UK* syndicaliste *mf*.

trade unionism n syndicalisme *m*.

trade wind n alizé *m*.

trading ['treɪdɪŋ] n *(U)* commerce *m*.

trading estate n *UK* zone *f* industrielle.

trading floor n FIN corbeille *f*.

trading hours n heures *fpl* d'ouverture.

trading stamp **n** timbre-prime *m*.

trading standards officer **n** *UK* fonctionnaire *m* du service de la répression des fraudes.

tradition [trə'dɪʃn] **n** tradition *f*.

traditional [trə'dɪʃənl] **adj** traditionnel(elle).

traditionalist [trə'dɪʃnəlɪst] ■ **n** traditionaliste *mf*.
■ **adj** traditionaliste.

traditionally [trə'dɪʃnəlɪ] **adv** traditionnellement.

traffic ['træfɪk] ■ **n** *(U)* **1.** [vehicles] circulation *f* ▸ **there is a great deal of traffic on the roads** les routes sont encombrées ▸ **road closed to heavy traffic** route interdite aux poids lourds **2.** [illegal trade] **: traffic (in)** trafic *m* (de).
■ **vi** (pt & pp **-ked**, cont **-king**) **: to traffic in** faire le trafic de.

traffic circle **n** *US* rond-point *m*.

traffic island **n** refuge *m*.

traffic jam **n** embouteillage *m*.

trafficker ['træfɪkə^r] **n : trafficker (in)** trafiquant *m*, -e *f* (de).

traffic lights **npl** feux *mpl* de signalisation.

traffic offence *UK*, ***traffic violation*** *US* **n** infraction *f* au code de la route.

traffic police **n** [speeding, safety] police *f* de la route / [point duty] police *f* de la circulation.

traffic policeman **n** agent *m* de police / [on point duty] agent *m* de la circulation.

traffic sign **n** panneau *m* de signalisation.

traffic violation *US* = ***traffic offence***.

traffic warden **n** *UK* contractuel *m*, -elle *f*.

tragedy ['trædʒədɪ] (pl **-ies**) **n** tragédie *f*.

tragic ['trædʒɪk] **adj** tragique.

tragically ['trædʒɪklɪ] **adv** tragiquement, de façon tragique.

tragicomic [ˌtrædʒɪ'kɒmɪk] **adj** tragi-comique.

trail [treɪl] ■ **n 1.** [path] sentier *m* ▸ **to blaze a trail** *fig* faire œuvre de pionnier **2.** [trace] piste *f* ▸ **on the trail of** sur la piste de.
■ **vt 1.** [drag] traîner **2.** [follow] suivre.
■ **vi 1.** [drag, move slowly] traîner **2.** SPORT [lose] **: to be trailing** être mené(e).
◆ ***trail away***, ***trail off*** **vi** s'estomper.

trailblazer ['treɪlˌbleɪzə^r] **n** *fig* pionnier *m*, -ère *f*.

trailblazing ['treɪlˌbleɪzɪŋ] **adj** de pionnier.

trailer ['treɪlə^r] **n 1.** [vehicle - for luggage] remorque *f* / [- for living in] caravane *f* **2.** CIN bande-annonce *f*.

trailer park **n** *US terrain aménagé pour les camping-cars.*

train [treɪn] ■ **n 1.** RAIL train *m* ▸ **to transport goods by train** transporter des marchandises par voie ferrée *OR* rail **2.** [of dress] traîne *f*.
■ **vt 1.** [teach] **: to train sb to do sthg** apprendre à qqn à faire qqch **2.** [for job] former ▸ **to train sb as/in** former qqn comme/dans ▸ **to train sb up** former *OR* préparer qqn ▸ **the dogs have been trained to detect explosives** les chiens ont été dressés pour détecter les explosifs **3.** SPORT **: to train sb (for)** entraîner qqn (pour) **4.** [plant] faire grimper **5.** [gun, camera] braquer ▸ **he trained his gun on us** il a braqué son arme sur nous.
■ **vi 1.** [for job] **: to train (as)** recevoir *OR* faire une formation (de) ▸ **she's training as a teacher** elle suit une formation pédagogique **2.** SPORT **: to train (for)** s'entraîner (pour).

trained [treɪnd] **adj** formé(e).

trainee [treɪ'ni:] ■ **adj** stagiaire, apprenti(e).
■ **n** stagiaire *mf*.

trainer ['treɪnə^r] **n 1.** [of animals] dresseur *m*, -euse *f* **2.** SPORT entraîneur *m*.
◆ ***trainers*** **npl** *UK* chaussures *fpl* de sport.

training ['treɪnɪŋ] **n** *(U)* **1.** [for job] **: training (in)** formation *f* (de) **2.** SPORT entraînement *m*.

training camp **n** camp *m* d'entraînement / MIL base *f* école.

training college **n** *UK* école *f* professionnelle.

training course **n** cours *m OR* stage *m* de formation.

training shoes **npl** *UK* chaussures *fpl* de sport.

train of thought **n : my/his train of thought** le fil de mes/ses pensées.

train set **n** train *m* électrique.

train-spotter [-spɒtə^r] **n** *UK* **1.** passionné *m*, -e *f* de trains **2.** *inf* [nerd] crétin *m*, -e *f*.

train station **n** *US* gare *f*.

traipse [treɪps] **vi** traîner.

trait [treɪt] **n** trait *m*.

traitor ['treɪtə^r] **n** traître *m*.

trajectory [trə'dʒektərɪ] (pl **-ies**) **n** trajectoire *f*.

tram [træm], ***tramcar*** ['træmkɑ:^r] **n** *UK* tram *m*, tramway *m*.

tramlines ['træmlaɪnz] **npl** *UK* **1.** [for trams] voies *fpl* de tram **2.** TENNIS lignes *fpl* de côté.

tramp [træmp] ■ **n 1.** [homeless person] clochard *m*, -e *f* **2.** *US inf* [woman] traînée *f*.
■ **vt** [countryside] parcourir, battre ▸ **to tramp the streets** battre le pavé.
■ **vi** marcher d'un pas lourd.

trample ['træmpl] ■ **vt** piétiner.
■ **vi : to trample on sthg** piétiner qqch ▸ **to trample on sb** *fig* bafouer qqn.

trampoline ['træmpəli:n] **n** trampoline *m*.

trance [trɑ:ns] **n** transe *f* ▸ **in a trance** en transe.

tranche [trænʃ] **n** [of loan, payment, shares] tranche *f*.

trannie, ***tranny*** ['trænɪ] (pl **-ies**) **n** *UK inf* [transistor radio] transistor *m*.

tranquil ['træŋkwɪl] **adj** tranquille.

tranquillity *UK*, ***tranquility*** *US* [træŋ'kwɪlətɪ] **n** tranquillité *f*.

tranquillize, *UK* ***-ise***, *US* ***tranquilize*** ['træŋkwɪlaɪz] **vt** mettre sous tranquillisants *OR* calmants.

tranquillizer *UK*, ***tranquilizer*** *US* ['træŋkwɪlaɪzə^r] **n** tranquillisant *m*, calmant *m*.

transact [træn'zækt] **vt** traiter, régler.

transaction [træn'zækʃn] **n** transaction *f*.

transatlantic [ˌtrænzət'læntɪk] **adj** [flight, crossing] transatlantique / [politics] d'outre-Atlantique.

transceiver [træn'siːvəʳ] **n** émetteur-récepteur *m*.

transcend [træn'send] **vt** transcender.

transcendental [ˌtrænsen'dentl] **adj** transcendantal(e).

transcendental meditation [ˌtrænsen'dentl-] **n** méditation *f* transcendantale.

transcribe [træn'skraɪb] **vt** transcrire.

transcript ['trænskrɪpt] **n** transcription *f*.

transcription [træn'skrɪpʃn] **n** transcription *f*.

transept ['trænsept] **n** transept *m*.

transfer ■ **n** ['trænsfɜːʳ] **1.** [gen] transfert *m* / [of power] passation *f* / [of money] virement *m* ▸ **transfer of ownership from sb to sb** transfert *m* OR translation *f* de propriété de qqn à qqn ▸ **transfer of power** passation *f* de pouvoir **2.** *UK* [design] décalcomanie *f* **3.** *US* [ticket] *ticket permettant de changer de train ou de bus sans payer de supplément*.
■ **vt** [træns'fɜːʳ] (pt & pp **-red**, cont **-ring**) **1.** [gen] transférer / [power, control] faire passer / [money] virer **2.** [employee] transférer, muter **3.** TELEC **: I'd like to transfer the charges** *UK* je voudrais téléphoner en PCV ▸ **I'm transferring you now** [operator] je vous mets en communication.
■ **vi** [træns'fɜːʳ] (pt & pp **-red**, cont **-ring**) être transféré.

transferable [træns'fɜːrəbl] **adj** transférable, transmissible ▸ **not transferable** [ticket] non cessible.

transference ['trænsfərəns] **n** [of power] passation *f*.

transfer fee **n** *UK* SPORT prix *m* d'un transfert.

transfer list **n** *UK* liste *f* des joueurs transférables.

transfigure [træns'fɪgəʳ] **vt** transfigurer.

transfix [træns'fɪks] **vt : to be transfixed with fear** être paralysé(e) par la peur.

transform [træns'fɔːm] **vt : to transform sb/sthg (into)** transformer qqn/qqch (en).

transformation [ˌtrænsfə'meɪʃn] **n** transformation *f*.

transformer [træns'fɔːməʳ] **n** ELEC transformateur *m*.

transfusion [træns'fjuːʒn] **n** transfusion *f*.

transgenic [trænz'dʒenɪk] **adj** transgénique.

transgress [træns'gres] *fml* ■ **vt** transgresser.
■ **vi** pécher.

transgression [træns'greʃn] **n** *fml* **1.** [fault] faute *f* **2.** *(U)* [doing wrong] transgression *f*.

transience ['trænzɪəns] **n** caractère *m* éphémère OR transitoire.

transient ['trænzɪənt] ■ **adj** passager(ère).
■ **n** *US* [person] voyageur *m*, -euse *f* en transit.

transistor [træn'zɪstəʳ] **n** transistor *m*.

transistor radio **n** transistor *m*.

transit ['trænsɪt] **n : in transit** en transit.

transit camp **n** camp *m* volant.

transition [træn'zɪʃn] **n** transition *f* ▸ **in transition** en transition.

transitional [træn'zɪʃənl] **adj** de transition.

transitive ['trænzɪtɪv] **adj** GRAM transitif(ive).

transit lounge **n** salle *f* de transit.

transitory ['trænzɪtrɪ] **adj** transitoire.

translate [træns'leɪt] ■ **vt** traduire.
■ **vi** [person] traduire / [expression, word] se traduire.

translation [træns'leɪʃn] **n** traduction *f*.

translator [træns'leɪtəʳ] **n** traducteur *m*, -trice *f*.

translucent [trænz'luːsnt] **adj** translucide.

transmission [trænz'mɪʃn] **n 1.** [gen] transmission *f* **2.** RADIO & TV [programme] émission *f* **3.** *US* AUT boîte *f* de vitesses.

transmit [trænz'mɪt] (pt & pp **-ted**, cont **-ting**) **vt** transmettre.

transmitter [trænz'mɪtəʳ] **n** émetteur *m*.

transparency [trans'pærənsɪ] (pl **-ies**) **n 1.** PHOT diapositive *f* / [for overhead projector] transparent *m* **2.** *(U)* [quality] transparence *f*.

transparent [træns'pærənt] **adj** transparent(e).

transpire [træn'spaɪəʳ] *fml* ■ **vt : it transpires that...** on a appris que...
■ **vi** [happen] se passer, arriver.

transplant ■ **n** ['trænsplɑːnt] MED greffe *f*, transplantation *f*.
■ **vt** [træns'plɑːnt] **1.** MED greffer, transplanter **2.** [seedlings] repiquer **3.** [move] transplanter.

transplantation [ˌtrænsplɑːn'teɪʃn] **n 1.** BOT [of seedling] repiquage *m* / [of plant] transplantation *f* **2.** *fig* [of people] transplantation *f*.

transport ■ **n** ['trænspɔːt] transport *m*.
■ **vt** [træn'spɔːt] transporter.

transportable [træn'spɔːtəbl] **adj** transportable.

transportation [ˌtrænspɔː'teɪʃn] **n** *esp US* transport *m*.

transport cafe **n** *UK* restaurant *m* de routiers, routier *m*.

transporter [træn'spɔːtəʳ] **n** [for cars] transporteur *m* de voitures.

transpose [træns'pəuz] **vt** transposer.

transsexual [træns'sekʃuəl] **n** transsexuel(elle).

transvestism [trænz'vestɪzm] **n** travestisme *m*, transvestisme *m*.

transvestite [trænz'vestaɪt] **n** travesti *m*, -e *f*.

trap [træp] ■ **n** piège *m*.
■ **vt** (pt & pp **-ped**, cont **-ping**) prendre au piège ▸ **to be trapped** être coincé ▸ **to be trapped in a relationship** être piégé dans une relation.

trapdoor [ˌtræp'dɔːʳ] **n** trappe *f*.

trapeze [trə'piːz] **n** trapèze *m*.

trapper ['træpəʳ] **n** trappeur *m*, -euse *f*.

trappings ['træpɪŋz] **npl** signes *mpl* extérieurs.

trash [træʃ] **n** *(U)* **1.** *US* [refuse] ordures *fpl* **2.** *inf pej* [poor-quality thing] camelote *f*.

trashcan ['træʃkæn] **n** *US* poubelle *f*.

trash collector **n** *US* éboueur *m*, éboueuse *f*.

trashy ['træʃɪ] (comp **-ier**, superl **-iest**) **adj** *inf* qui ne vaut rien, nul (nulle).

trauma ['trɔ:mə] **n** MED trauma *m* / *fig* traumatisme *m*.

traumatic [trɔ:'mætɪk] **adj** traumatisant(e).

traumatize, *UK* ***-ise*** ['trɔ:mətaɪz] **vt** traumatiser.

travel ['trævl] ■ **n** *(U)* voyage *m*, voyages *mpl*.
■ **vt** (*UK* **-led**, cont **-ling**, *US* **-ed**, cont **-ing**) parcourir ▸ **I travelled 50 miles to get here** j'ai fait 80 km pour venir ici.
■ **vi** (*UK* **-led**, cont **-ling**, *US* **-ed**, cont **-ing**) **1.** [make journey] voyager ▸ **she's travelling (about** *OR* **around) somewhere in Asia** elle est en voyage quelque part en Asie **2.** [move - current, signal] aller, passer / [- news] se répandre, circuler ▸ **news travels fast** les nouvelles vont vite.
◆ ***travels*** **npl** voyages *mpl*.

travel agency **n** agence *f* de voyages.

travel agent **n** agent *m* de voyages ▸ **to/at the travel agent's** à l'agence *f* de voyages.

travelator ['trævəleɪtəʳ] = ***travolator***.

travel brochure **n** dépliant *m* touristique.

Travelcard ['trævlkɑ:d] **n** carte *f* d'abonnement *(pour les transports en commun à Londres)*.

traveler *US* = ***traveller*** etc .

travel insurance **n** *(U)* **: to take out travel insurance** prendre une assurance-voyage.

travelled *UK*, ***traveled*** *US* ['trævld] **adj 1.** [person] qui a beaucoup voyagé **2.** [road, route] **: much travelled** très fréquenté(e).

traveller *UK*, ***traveler*** *US* ['trævləʳ] **n 1.** [person on journey] voyageur *m*, -euse *f* **2.** [sales representative] représentant *m* **3.** = ***New Age travel(l)er***.

traveller's cheque *UK*, ***traveler's check*** *US* **n** chèque *m* de voyage.

travelling *UK*, ***traveling*** *US* ['trævlɪŋ] **adj 1.** [theatre, circus] ambulant(e) **2.** [clock, bag] de voyage / [allowance] de déplacement ▸ **travelling time** durée *f* du voyage.

travelling expenses *UK*, ***traveling expenses*** *US* **npl** frais *mpl* de déplacement.

travelling salesman *UK*, ***traveling salesman*** *US* **n** représentant *m*.

travelogue, *US* ***travelog*** ['trævəlɒg] **n 1.** [talk] compte-rendu *m* *OR* récit *m* de voyage **2.** [film] documentaire *m*.

travelsick ['trævəlsɪk] **adj : to be travelsick** avoir le mal de la route/de l'air/de mer.

travel sickness **n** mal *m* de la route/de l'air/de mer.

traverse ['trævəs *OR* ˌtrə'vɜ:s] **vt** *fml* traverser.

travesty ['trævəstɪ] (pl **-ies**) **n** parodie *f*.

travolator ['trævəleɪtəʳ] **n** tapis *m* *OR* trottoir *m* roulant.

trawl [trɔ:l] ■ **n** [fishing net] chalut *m*.
■ **vt** [area of sea] pêcher au chalut dans.
■ **vi : to trawl for cod/mackerel** pêcher la morue/le hareng au chalut.

trawler ['trɔ:ləʳ] **n** chalutier *m*.

tray [treɪ] **n** plateau *m*.

treacherous ['tretʃərəs] **adj** traître (traîtresse).

treachery ['tretʃərɪ] **n** traîtrise *f*.

treacle ['tri:kl] **n** *UK* mélasse *f*.

tread [tred] ■ **n 1.** [on tyre] bande *f* de roulement / [of shoe] semelle *f* ▸ **there's no tread left** [on tyre] le pneu est lisse **2.** [way of walking] pas *m* / [sound] bruit *m* de pas.
■ **vt** (pt **trod**, pp **trodden**) [crush] **: to tread grapes** fouler du raisin ▸ **to tread sthg underfoot** fouler qqch aux pieds, piétiner qqch ▸ **to tread sthg into** écraser qqch dans ▸ **to tread water** nager sur place.
■ **vi** (pt **trod**, pp **trodden**) **: to tread (on)** marcher (sur) ▸ **to tread carefully** *fig* y aller doucement.

treadle ['tredl] **n** pédale *f*.

treadmill ['tredmɪl] **n 1.** [wheel] trépigneuse *f* **2.** *fig* [dull routine] routine *f*, train-train *m*.

treas. (abbr of ***treasurer***) trés.

treason ['tri:zn] **n** trahison *f*.

treasure ['treʒəʳ] ■ **n** trésor *m*.
■ **vt** [object] garder précieusement / [memory] chérir.

treasure hunt **n** chasse *f* au trésor.

treasurer ['treʒərəʳ] **n** trésorier *m*, -ère *f*.

treasure trove **n** LAW trésor *m* *objets de valeur trouvés et que personne n'a réclamés*.

treasury ['treʒərɪ] (pl **-ies**) **n** [room] trésorerie *f*.
◆ ***Treasury*** **n : the Treasury** le ministère des Finances.

treasury bill **n** bon *m* du Trésor.

treat [tri:t] ■ **vt 1.** [gen] traiter ▸ **to treat sb like a child** traiter qqn en enfant ▸ **to treat sthg as a joke** prendre qqch à la rigolade **2.** [on special occasion] **: to treat sb to sthg** offrir *OR* payer qqch à qqn ▸ **to treat o.s. to sthg** s'offrir qqch, se payer qqch.
■ **n 1.** [gift] cadeau *m* ▸ **to give sb a treat** faire plaisir à qqn ▸ **this is my treat** [pay for meal, drink] c'est moi qui régale **2.** [delight] plaisir *m*.

treatise ['tri:tɪz] **n : treatise (on)** traité *m* (de).

treatment ['tri:tmənt] **n** traitement *m*.

treaty ['tri:tɪ] (pl **-ies**) **n** traité *m*.

treble ['trebl] ■ **adj 1.** [MUS - voice] de soprano / [- recorder] aigu (aiguë) **2.** [triple] triple.
■ **n** [on stereo control] aigu *m* / [boy singer] soprano *m*.
■ **vt** & **vi** tripler.

treble clef **n** clef *f* de sol.

tree [tri:] **n 1.** [gen] arbre *m* ▸ **to be barking up the wrong tree** *fig* se tromper d'adresse **2.** COMPUT arbre *m*, arborescence *f*.

treehouse ['tri:haʊs] (pl [-haʊzɪz]) **n** *cabane construite dans un arbre*.

tree-hugger **n** *inf hum* & *pej* écolo *mf*.

tree-lined **adj** bordé(e) d'arbres.

tree surgeon **n** arboriculteur *m*, -trice *f*.

treetop ['tri:tɒp] **n** cime *f*.

tree trunk **n** tronc *m* d'arbre.

trek [trek] ■ **n** randonnée *f*.
■ **vi** (pt & pp **-ked**, cont **-king**) faire une randonnée / *fig* se traîner.

trellis ['trelɪs] **n** treillis *m*.

tremble ['trembl] **vi** trembler.

trembling ['tremblɪŋ] ■ **adj 1.** [body - with cold] frissonnant(e), grelottant(e) / [- in fear, excitement] frémissant(e), tremblant(e) / [hands] tremblant(e) **2.** [voice - with emotion] vibrant(e) / [- with fear] tremblant(e) / [- because of old age] chevrotant(e) ▸ **with a trembling voice** [- speaker] d'une ***OR*** la voix tremblante / [- singer] d'une ***OR*** la voix chevrotante.
■ **n** [from cold] tremblement *m*, frissonnement *m* / [from fear] tremblement *m*, frémissement *m*.

tremendous [trɪ'mendəs] **adj 1.** [size, success, difference] énorme / [noise] terrible **2.** *inf* [really good] formidable.

tremendously [trɪ'mendəslɪ] **adv** [exciting, expensive, big] extrêmement / [loud] terriblement.

tremor ['tremər] **n** tremblement *m*.

tremulous ['tremjʊləs] **adj** *liter* [voice] tremblant(e) / [smile] timide.

trench [trentʃ] **n** tranchée *f*.

trenchant ['trentʃənt] **adj** mordant(e), incisif(ive).

trench coat **n** trench-coat *m*.

trench warfare **n** *(U)* guerre *f* de tranchées.

trend [trend] **n** [tendency] tendance *f*.

trendily ['trendɪlɪ] **adv** *inf* [dress] branché *(adv)*.

trendsetter ['trend,setər] **n** personne *f* qui lance une mode.

trendy [trendɪ] *inf* ■ **adj** (comp -ier, superl -iest) branché(e), à la mode.
■ **n** (pl -ies) personne *f* branchée.

trepidation [,trepɪ'deɪʃn] **n** *fml* **: in *OR* with trepidation** avec inquiétude.

trespass ['trespəs] **vi** [on land] entrer sans permission ▸ **'no trespassing'** 'défense d'entrer'.

trespasser ['trespəsər] **n** intrus *m*, -e *f* ▸ **'trespassers will be prosecuted'** 'défense d'entrer sous peine de poursuites'.

trestle ['tresl] **n** tréteau *m*.

trestle table **n** table *f* à tréteaux.

triage ['tri:ɑ:ʒ] **n** MED triage *m (des malades, des blessés)*.

trial ['traɪəl] **n 1.** LAW procès *m* ▸ **to be on trial (for)** passer en justice (pour) ▸ **to bring sb to trial** faire passer ***OR*** traduire qqn en justice ▸ **his case comes up for trial in September** son affaire passe en jugement en septembre **2.** [test, experiment] essai *m* ▸ **to give sthg a trial** mettre qqch à l'essai, essayer qqch ▸ **on trial** à l'essai ▸ **by trial and error** en tâtonnant **3.** [unpleasant experience] épreuve *f* ▸ **trials and tribulations** tribulations *fpl*.

trial basis **n : on a trial basis** à l'essai.

trial period **n** période *f* d'essai.

trial run **n** essai *m*.

trial-size(d) **adj** [pack, box] d'essai.

triangle ['traɪæŋgl] **n 1.** [gen] triangle *m* **2.** *US* [set square] équerre *f*.

triangular [traɪ'æŋgjʊlər] **adj** triangulaire.

triathlon [traɪ'æθlɒn] (pl -s) **n** triathlon *m*.

tribal ['traɪbl] **adj** tribal(e).

tribalism ['traɪbəlɪzm] **n** tribalisme *m*.

tribe [traɪb] **n** tribu *f*.

tribulation [,trɪbjʊ'leɪʃn] **n** ➤ ***trial***.

tribunal [traɪ'bju:nl] **n** tribunal *m*.

tribune ['trɪbju:n] **n** HIST tribun *m*.

tributary ['trɪbjʊtrɪ] (pl **-ies**) **n** affluent *m*.

tribute ['trɪbju:t] **n** tribut *m*, hommage *m* ▸ **to pay tribute to** payer tribut à, rendre hommage à ▸ **to be a tribute to sthg** témoigner de qqch.

trice [traɪs] **n : in a trice** en un clin d'œil.

triceps ['traɪseps] (pl **triceps *OR*** -es [-i:z]) **n** triceps *m*.

trick [trɪk] ■ **n 1.** [to deceive] tour *m*, farce *f* ▸ **to play a trick on sb** jouer un tour à qqn ▸ **a trick of the light** un effet d'optique **2.** [to entertain] tour *m* ▸ **what a dirty *OR* mean *OR* nasty trick to play!** quel sale tour! **3.** [knack] truc *m* ▸ **that will do the trick** *inf* ça fera l'affaire **4.** [in card games] pli *m*, levée *f*.
■ **comp** [knife, moustache] truqué(e), faux (fausse) ▸ **trick photography** truquage *m* photographique.
■ **vt** attraper, rouler ▸ **you've been tricked!** vous vous êtes fait rouler! ▸ **to trick sb into doing sthg** amener qqn à faire qqch (par la ruse) ▸ **she was tricked out of her inheritance** on lui a escroqué son héritage.

trickery ['trɪkərɪ] **n** *(U)* ruse *f*.

trickle ['trɪkl] ■ **n** [of liquid] filet *m* ▸ **a trickle of people/letters** quelques personnes/lettres.
■ **vi** [liquid] dégouliner ▸ **to trickle in/out** [people] entrer/sortir par petits groupes.

trickle-down **adj : trickle-down economics** *théorie selon laquelle le bien-être des riches finit par profiter aux classes sociales défavorisées.*

trick or treat **n** une gâterie ou une farce *(phrase rituelle des enfants déguisés qui font la quête le soir de Halloween).*

trick question **n** question-piège *f*.

trickster ['trɪkstər] **n** [swindler] filou *m*, escroc *m*.

tricky ['trɪkɪ] (comp -ier, superl -iest) **adj** [difficult] difficile.

tricycle ['traɪsɪkl] **n** tricycle *m*.

trident ['traɪdnt] **n** trident *m*.

tried [traɪd] ■ **pt** & **pp** ➤ ***try***.
■ **adj : tried and tested** [method, system] qui a fait ses preuves.

trier ['traɪər] **n : to be a trier** être persévérant(e).

trifle ['traɪfl] **n 1.** *UK* CULIN ≃ diplomate *m* **2.** [unimportant thing] bagatelle *f*.
◆ ***a trifle*** **adv** un peu, un tantinet.
◆ ***trifle with*** **vt insep** badiner avec / [sb's affections] se jouer de.

trifling ['traɪflɪŋ] **adj** insignifiant(e).

trigger ['trɪgər] ■ **n** [on gun] détente *f*, gâchette *f*.
■ **vt** déclencher, provoquer.
◆ ***trigger off*** **vt sep** déclencher, provoquer.

trigger-happy **adj** *inf* [individual] qui a la gâchette facile / [country] prêt à déclencher la guerre pour un rien, belliqueux(euse).

trigonometry [ˌtrɪgəˈnɒmətrɪ] **n** trigonométrie *f.*

trilby [ˈtrɪlbɪ] (pl **-ies**) **n** *UK* feutre *m.*

trilingual [traɪˈlɪŋgwəl] **adj** trilingue.

trill [trɪl] ■ **n** trille *m.*
■ **vi** triller.

trillions [ˈtrɪljənz] **npl** *inf* **: trillions (of)** tout un tas (de), plein (de).

trilogy [ˈtrɪlədʒɪ] (pl **-ies**) **n** trilogie *f.*

trim [trɪm] ■ **adj** (comp **-mer**, superl **-mest**) **1.** [neat and tidy] net (nette) **2.** [slim] svelte.
■ **n 1.** [of hair] coupe *f* **2.** [on clothes] garniture *f* / [inside car] garniture intérieure.
■ **vt** (pt & pp **-med**, cont **-ming**) **1.** [cut - gen] couper / [- hedge] tailler **2.** [decorate] **: to trim sthg (with)** garnir *OR* orner qqch (de).
◆ ***trim away, trim off*** **vt sep** couper.

trimester [traɪˈmestəʳ] **n 1.** *US* trimestre *m* **2.** [gen] trois mois *mpl.*

trimmed [trimd] **adj : trimmed with** [clothes] orné(e) de.

trimming [ˈtrɪmɪŋ] **n 1.** [on clothing] parement *m* **2.** CULIN garniture *f.*

Trinidad and Tobago [ˈtrɪnɪdæd-] **n** Trinité-et-Tobago *f* ▸ **in Trinidad and Tobago** à Trinité-et-Tobago.

Trinidadian [ˌtrɪnɪˈdædɪən] ■ **adj** trinidadien(enne).
■ **n** Trinidadien *m*, -enne *f.*

Trinity [ˈtrɪnətɪ] **n** RELIG **: the Trinity** la Trinité.

trinket [ˈtrɪŋkɪt] **n** bibelot *m.*

trio [ˈtriːəʊ] (pl **-s**) **n** trio *m.*

trip [trɪp] ■ **n 1.** [journey] voyage *m* ▸ **I had to make three trips into town** j'ai dû aller trois fois en ville *OR* faire trois voyages en ville **2.** *drug sl* trip *m.*
■ **vt** (pt & pp **-ped**, cont **-ping**) [make stumble] faire un croche-pied à.
■ **vi** (pt & pp **-ped**, cont **-ping**) [stumble] **: to trip (over)** trébucher (sur) ▸ **she tripped over the wire** elle s'est pris le pied dans le fil.
◆ ***trip up*** ■ **vt sep 1.** [make stumble] faire un croche-pied à **2.** [catch out] prendre en défaut.
■ **vi insep 1.** [fall] trébucher **2.** [make a mistake] gaffer, faire une gaffe.

tripartite [ˌtraɪˈpɑːtaɪt] **adj** triparti(e), tripartite.

tripe [traɪp] **n** *(U)* **1.** CULIN tripe *f* **2.** *inf* [nonsense] bêtises *fpl*, idioties *fpl.*

triple [ˈtrɪpl] ■ **adj** triple.
■ **vt** & **vi** tripler.

triple jump **n : the triple jump** le triple saut.

triplets [ˈtrɪplɪts] **npl** triplés *mpl*, triplées *fpl.*

triplicate [ˈtrɪplɪkət] ■ **adj** en trois exemplaires.
■ **n : in triplicate** en trois exemplaires.

tripod [ˈtraɪpɒd] **n** trépied *m.*

Tripoli [ˈtrɪpəlɪ] **n** Tripoli.

tripper [ˈtrɪpəʳ] **n** *UK* excursionniste *mf.*

trip switch **n** interrupteur *m.*

tripwire [ˈtrɪpwaɪəʳ] **n** fil *m* de détente.

trite [traɪt] **adj** *pej* banal(e).

triumph [ˈtraɪəmf] ■ **n** triomphe *m.*
■ **vi : to triumph (over)** triompher (de).

triumphal [traɪˈʌmfl] **adj** triomphal(e).

triumphalist [traɪˈʌmfəlɪst] **adj** triomphaliste.

triumphant [traɪˈʌmfənt] **adj** [exultant] triomphant(e).

triumphantly [trɪˈʌmfəntlɪ] **adv** de façon triomphante, triomphalement.

triumvirate [traɪˈʌmvɪrət] **n** HIST triumvirat *m.*

trivet [ˈtrɪvɪt] **n 1.** [over fire] trépied *m* **2.** [to protect table] dessous-de-plat *m inv.*

trivia [ˈtrɪvɪə] **n** *(U)* [trifles] vétilles *fpl*, riens *mpl.*

trivial [ˈtrɪvɪəl] **adj** insignifiant(e).

triviality [ˌtrɪvɪˈælətɪ] (pl **-ies**) **n** banalité *f.*

trivialize, *UK* ***-ise*** [ˈtrɪvɪəlaɪz] **vt** banaliser.

trod [trɒd] **pt** ➤ ***tread.***

trodden [ˈtrɒdn] **pp** ➤ ***tread.***

Trojan [ˈtrəʊdʒən] ■ **adj** troyen(enne).
■ **n** Troyen *m*, -enne *f* ▸ **to work like a Trojan** travailler comme un nègre *OR* une bête de somme.

troll [trəʊl] **n** troll *m.*

trolley [ˈtrɒlɪ] (pl **-s**) **n 1.** *UK* [for shopping, luggage] chariot *m*, caddie® *m* **2.** *UK* [for food, drinks] chariot *m*, table *f* roulante **3.** *US* [tram] tramway *m*, tram *m.*

trolleybus [ˈtrɒlɪbʌs] **n** trolleybus *m.*

trolley case **n** *UK* valise *f* à roulettes.

trollop [ˈtrɒləp] **n** *dated* & *pej* [prostitute] putain *f* / [slut] souillon *f.*

trombone [trɒmˈbəʊn] **n** MUS trombone *m.*

troop [truːp] ■ **n** bande *f*, troupe *f.*
■ **vi : to troop in/out/off** entrer/sortir/partir en groupe.
◆ ***troops*** **npl** troupes *fpl.*

troop carrier **n** [ship] transport *m* de troupes / [plane] avion *m* de transport militaire.

trooper [ˈtruːpəʳ] **n 1.** MIL soldat *m* **2.** *US* [policeman] policier *m (appartenant à la police d'un État).*

troopship [ˈtruːpʃɪp] **n** transport *m.*

trophy [ˈtrəʊfɪ] (pl **-ies**) **n** trophée *m.*

tropical [ˈtrɒpɪkl] **adj** tropical(e).

Tropic of Cancer [ˈtrɒpɪk-] **n : the Tropic of Cancer** le tropique du Cancer.

Tropic of Capricorn [ˈtrɒpɪk-] **n : the Tropic of Capricorn** le tropique du Capricorne.

tropics [ˈtrɒpɪks] **npl : the tropics** les tropiques *mpl.*

trot [trɒt] ■ **n** [of horse] trot *m.*
■ **vi** (pt & pp **-ted**, cont **-ting**) trotter.
◆ ***on the trot*** **adv** *inf* de suite, d'affilée.
◆ ***trot out*** **vt sep** *pej* débiter.

Trotskyism [ˈtrɒtskɪɪzm] **n** trotskisme *m.*

trotter [ˈtrɒtəʳ] **n** [pig's foot] pied *m* de porc.

trouble ['trʌbl] ■ n *(U)* **1.** [difficulty] problème *m*, difficulté *f* ▸ **to be in trouble** avoir des ennuis ▸ **I've never been in trouble with the police** je n'ai jamais eu d'ennuis *OR* d'histoires avec la police ▸ **to get into trouble** s'attirer des ennuis ▸ **he got his friends into trouble** il a causé des ennuis à ses amis ▸ **the baby hardly gives me any trouble** le bébé ne me donne pratiquement aucun mal ▸ **to have trouble doing sthg** avoir du mal *OR* des difficultés à faire qqch ▸ **to be in/to get into trouble** [climber, swimmer, business] être/se trouver en difficulté ▸ **the trouble (with sb/sthg) is...** l'ennui (avec qqn/qqch), c'est que...
2. [bother] peine *f*, mal *m* ▸ **to take the trouble to do sthg** se donner la peine de faire qqch ▸ **you shouldn't have gone to all this trouble** il ne fallait pas vous donner tout ce mal *OR* tant de peine ▸ **it's no trouble!** ça ne me dérange pas! ▸ **it's not worth the trouble, it's more trouble than it's worth** cela n'en vaut pas la peine, le jeu n'en vaut pas la chandelle ▸ **to be asking for trouble** chercher les ennuis
3. [pain, illness] mal *m*, ennui *m* ▸ **I have kidney/back trouble** j'ai des ennuis rénaux/des problèmes de dos
4. [fighting] bagarre *f* / POL troubles *mpl*, conflits *mpl* ▸ **the trouble began when the police arrived** l'agitation a commencé quand la police est arrivée.
■ **vt 1.** [worry, upset] peiner, troubler ▸ **what troubles me is that we've had no news** ce qui m'inquiète, c'est que nous n'avons pas eu de nouvelles
2. [bother] déranger ▸ **I won't trouble you with the details just now** je vous ferai grâce des *OR* épargnerai les détails pour l'instant ▸ **can I trouble you to open the window?** est-ce que je peux vous demander d'ouvrir la fenêtre?
3. [give pain to] faire mal à ▸ **his back is troubling him** il a des problèmes de dos.
◆ ***troubles*** **npl 1.** [worries] ennuis *mpl*
2. POL troubles *mpl*, conflits *mpl*.

troubled ['trʌbld] **adj 1.** [worried] inquiet(ète) **2.** [disturbed - period] de troubles, agité(e) / [- country] qui connaît une période de troubles.

trouble-free adj sans problèmes.

troublemaker ['trʌbl,meɪkər] **n** fauteur *m*, -trice *f* de troubles.

troubleshoot ['trʌbl,ʃu:t] **vi 1.** [overseer, envoy] régler un problème **2.** [mechanic] localiser une panne.

troubleshooter ['trʌbl,ʃu:tər] **n** expert *m*, spécialiste *mf*.

troublesome ['trʌblsəm] **adj** [job] pénible / [cold] gênant(e) / [back, knee] qui fait souffrir.

trouble spot **n** point *m* chaud.

trough [trɒf] **n 1.** [for animals - with water] abreuvoir *m* / [- with food] auge *f* **2.** [low point - of wave] creux *m* / *fig* point *m* bas **3.** METEOR dépression *f*.

trounce [traʊns] **vt** *inf* écraser.

troupe [tru:p] **n** troupe *f*.

trouser press ['traʊzər-] **n** presse *f* à pantalons.

trousers ['traʊzəz] **npl** pantalon *m*.

trouser suit ['traʊzər-] **n** *UK* tailleur-pantalon *m*.

trousseau ['tru:səʊ] (pl -x [-z] *OR* -s) **n** trousseau *m*.

trout [traʊt] (pl **trout** *OR* -s) **n** truite *f*.

trove [trəʊv] ➤ ***treasure trove***.

trowel ['traʊəl] **n** [for gardening] déplantoir *m* / [for cement, plaster] truelle *f*.

truancy ['tru:ənsɪ] **n** absentéisme *m*.

truant ['tru:ənt] **n** [child] élève *mf* absentéiste ▸ **to play truant** *UK* faire l'école buissonnière.

truce [tru:s] **n** trêve *f*.

truck [trʌk] ■ **n 1.** *esp US* [lorry] camion *m* **2.** RAIL wagon *m* à plate-forme.
■ **vt** *US* transporter par camion.

truck driver **n** *esp US* routier *m*.

trucker ['trʌkər] **n** *US* routier *m*, -ière *f*.

truck farm **n** *US* jardin *m* maraîcher.

trucking ['trʌkɪŋ] **n** *US* camionnage *m*.

truckload ['trʌkləʊd] **n 1.** *esp US* [lorryload] cargaison *f (d'un camion)* ▸ **a truckload of soldiers** un camion de soldats ▸ **medical aid arrived by the truckload** l'aide médicale arriva par camions entiers **2.** *US inf fig* **: a truckload of** un tas de.

truck stop **n** *US* relais *m* routier.

truculent ['trʌkjʊlənt] **adj** agressif(ive).

trudge [trʌdʒ] ■ **n** marche *f* pénible.
■ **vi** marcher péniblement.

true ['tru:] ■ **adj 1.** [factual] vrai(e) ▸ **can it be true?** est-ce possible? ▸ **to come true** se réaliser **2.** [genuine] vrai(e), authentique ▸ **she was a true democrat** c'était une démocrate dans l'âme ▸ **true love** le grand amour **3.** [exact] exact(e) ▸ **he's not a genius in the true sense of the word** ce n'est pas un génie au vrai sens du terme **4.** [faithful] fidèle, loyal(e) ▸ **she was true to her word** elle a tenu parole ▸ **the painting is very true to life** le tableau est très ressemblant ▸ **true to form, he arrived half an hour late** fidèle à son habitude *OR* comme à son habitude, il est arrivé avec une demi-heure de retard **5.** TECH droit(e) / [wheel] dans l'axe.
■ **adv** [aim, shoot, sing] juste ▸ **it doesn't ring true** cela sonne faux.

true-life **adj** vrai(e), vécu(e).

truffle ['trʌfl] **n** truffe *f*.

truism ['tru:ɪzm] **n** truisme *m*.

truly ['tru:lɪ] **adv 1.** [gen] vraiment **2.** [sincerely] vraiment, sincèrement
▸▸ **yours truly** [at end of letter] je vous prie de croire à l'expression de mes sentiments distingués.

trump [trʌmp] ■ **n** atout *m*.
■ **vt** couper.

trump card **n** *fig* atout *m*.

trumped-up ['trʌmpt-] **adj** *pej* inventé(e) de toutes pièces.

trumpet ['trʌmpɪt] ■ **n** trompette *f*.
■ **vi** [elephant] barrir.

trumpeter ['trʌmpɪtər] **n** trompettiste *mf*.

truncate [trʌŋ'keɪt] **vt** tronquer.

truncated [trʌŋ'keɪtɪd] **adj** tronqué(e).

truncheon ['trʌntʃən] **n** *UK* matraque *f*.

trundle ['trʌndl] ■ **vt** [cart, wheelbarrow] pousser lentement.
■ **vi** aller lentement.

trunk [trʌŋk] **n 1.** [of tree, person] tronc *m* **2.** [of elephant] trompe *f* **3.** [box] malle *f* **4.** *US* [of car] coffre *m*.
◆ ***trunks*** **npl** maillot *m* de bain.

trunk call **n** *UK* communication *f* interurbaine.

trunk road **n** *UK* (route *f*) nationale *f*.

truss [trʌs] **n 1.** MED bandage *m* herniaire **2.** CONSTR ferme *f*.

trust [trʌst] ■ **vt 1.** [have confidence in] avoir confiance en, se fier à ▸ **to trust sb to do sthg** compter sur qqn pour faire qqch ▸ **trust Mark to put his foot in it!** *hum* pour mettre les pieds dans le plat, on peut faire confiance à Mark! ▸ **trust you!** cela ne m'étonne pas de toi!
2. [entrust] **: to trust sb with sthg** confier qqch à qqn
3. *fml* [hope] **: I trust not** j'espère que non ▸ **to trust (that)...** espérer que...
■ **vi 1.** [believe] **: to trust in God** croire en Dieu
2. [have confidence] **: to trust to luck** s'en remettre à la chance.
■ **n 1.** *(U)* [faith] **: trust (in sb/sthg)** confiance *f* (en qqn/dans qqch) ▸ **to take sthg on trust** accepter qqch les yeux fermés ▸ **you can't take everything he says on trust** on ne peut pas croire sur parole tout ce qu'il dit ▸ **to put** *OR* **place one's trust in sb** faire confiance à qqn
2. *(U)* [responsibility] responsabilité *f* ▸ **a position of trust** un poste de confiance
3. FIN **: to set up a trust for sb** instituer un fidéicommis pour qqn ▸ **in trust** en dépôt
4. COMM trust *m*.

trust company **n** société *f* fiduciaire.

trusted ['trʌstɪd] **adj** [person] de confiance / [method] qui a fait ses preuves.

trusted third party **n** COMPUT [for Internet transactions] tierce partie *f* de confiance.

trustee [trʌs'ti:] **n** FIN & LAW fidéicommissaire *mf* / [of institution] administrateur *m*, -trice *f*.

trusteeship [ˌtrʌs'ti:ʃɪp] **n** FIN & LAW fidéicommis *m* / [of institution] fonction *f* d'administrateur.

trust fund **n** fonds *m* en fidéicommis.

trust hospital **n** *hôpital britannique ayant opté pour l'autogestion mais qui reçoit toujours son budget de l'État.*

trusting ['trʌstɪŋ] **adj** confiant(e).

trustingly ['trʌstɪŋlɪ] **adv** en toute confiance.

trustworthiness ['trʌstˌwɜ:ðɪnɪs] **n 1.** [reliability - of person] loyauté *f*, sérieux *m* / [- of information, source] fiabilité *f* **2.** [accuracy - of report, figures] fiabilité *f*, justesse *f* **3.** [honesty] honnêteté *f*.

trustworthy ['trʌstˌwɜ:ðɪ] **adj** digne de confiance.

trusty ['trʌstɪ] (comp **-ier**, superl **-iest**) **adj** *hum* fidèle.

truth [tru:θ] **n** vérité *f* ▸ **there's some truth in what he says** il y a du vrai dans ce qu'il dit ▸ **to tell the truth** dire la vérité ▸ **in (all) truth** à dire vrai, en vérité.

truth drug **n** sérum *m* de vérité.

truthful ['tru:θfʊl] **adj** [person, reply] honnête / [story] véridique.

truthfully ['tru:θfʊlɪ] **adv** [answer, speak] honnêtement, sans mentir / [sincerely] sincèrement, vraiment.

truthfulness ['tru:θfʊlnɪs] **n** [of person] honnêteté *f* / [of portrait] fidélité *f* / [of story, statement] véracité *f*.

try [traɪ] ■ **vt** (pt & pp **-ied**) **1.** [attempt, test] essayer / [food, drink] goûter ▸ **to try to do sthg** essayer de faire qqch ▸ **to try one's best** *OR* **hardest** faire de son mieux ▸ **he tried his best to explain** il a essayé d'expliquer de son mieux ▸ **try it, you'll like it** essayez *OR* goûtez-y donc, vous aimerez
2. LAW juger ▸ **he was tried for murder** il a été jugé pour meurtre
3. [put to the test] éprouver, mettre à l'épreuve ▸ **the method has been tried and tested** la méthode a fait ses preuves ▸ **to try one's luck (at sthg)** tenter sa chance (à qqch) ▸ **it's enough to try the patience of a saint** même un ange n'aurait pas la patience.
■ **vi** (pt & pp **-ied**) essayer ▸ **to try and do sthg** essayer de faire qqch ▸ **to try for sthg** essayer d'obtenir qqch.
■ **n** (pl **-ies**) **1.** [attempt] essai *m*, tentative *f* ▸ **to have a try at sthg** essayer de faire qqch ▸ **to give sthg a try** essayer qqch ▸ **it's worth a try** cela vaut la peine d'essayer
2. RUGBY essai *m*.
◆ ***try on*** **vt sep** [clothes] essayer ▸ **try it on for size** essayez-le pour voir la taille
▸▸ **to try it on with sb** *UK inf* essayer de voir jusqu'où on peut pousser qqn.
◆ ***try out*** **vt sep** essayer.

trying ['traɪɪŋ] **adj** pénible, éprouvant(e).

try-out **n** *inf* essai *m*.

tsar [zɑ:ʳ] **n** tsar *m*.

T-shirt **n** tee-shirt *m*.

tsp. (abbr of ***teaspoon***) cc.

T-square **n** té *m*.

TT abbr of ***teetotal***.

TTP (abbr of ***trusted third party***) **n** COMPUT [for Internet transactions] TPC *f (tierce partie de confiance)*.

Tuareg ['twɑ:reg] **n** [person] Touareg *m*, -ègue *f*.

tub [tʌb] **n 1.** [of ice cream - large] boîte *f* / [- small] petit pot *m* / [of margarine] barquette *f* **2.** [bath] baignoire *f*.

tuba ['tju:bə] **n** tuba *m*.

tubby ['tʌbɪ] (comp **-ier**, superl **-iest**) **adj** *inf* rondouillard(e), boulot(otte).

tube [tju:b] **n 1.** [cylinder, container] tube *m* **2.** ANAT **: bronchial tubes** bronches *fpl* **3.** *UK* [underground train] métro *m* ▸ **the tube** [system] le métro ▸ **by tube** en métro.

tubeless ['tju:blɪs] **adj** [tyre] sans chambre à air.

tuber ['tju:bəʳ] **n** tubercule *m*.

tubercular [tju:'bɜ:kjʊləʳ] **adj** tuberculeux(euse).

tuberculosis [tju:ˌbɜ:kjʊ'ləʊsɪs] **n** tuberculose *f*.

tube station **n** *UK* station *f* de métro.

tubing ['tju:bɪŋ] **n** *(U)* tubes *mpl*, tuyaux *mpl*.

tubular ['tju:bjʊləʳ] **adj** tubulaire.

TUC **n** *UK* abbr of ***Trades Union Congress***.

tuck [tʌk] ■ **n** SEW rempli *m*.
■ **vt** [place neatly] ranger.
◆ ***tuck away*** **vt sep** [store] mettre de côté ***OR*** en lieu sûr ▸ **to be tucked away** [village, house] être caché(e) ***OR*** blotti(e).
◆ ***tuck in*** ■ **vt 1.** [child, patient] border **2.** [clothes] rentrer.
■ **vi** *inf* boulotter ▸ **tuck in!** allez-y, mangez!
◆ ***tuck up*** **vt sep** [child, patient] border.

tuck shop **n** *UK* [at school] *petite boutique qui vend des bonbons et des gâteaux.*

Tudor ['tju:dəʳ] **adj 1.** HIST des Tudors **2.** ARCHIT Tudor *(inv).*

Tue., ***Tues.*** (abbr of ***Tuesday***) mar.

Tuesday ['tju:zdeɪ] **n** mardi *m* ; see also ***Saturday***.

tuft [tʌft] **n** touffe *f*.

tug [tʌg] ■ **n 1.** [pull] **: to give sthg a tug** tirer sur qqch **2.** [boat] remorqueur *m*.
■ **vt** (pt & pp **-ged**, cont **-ging**) tirer.
■ **vi** (pt & pp **-ged**, cont **-ging**) **: to tug (at)** tirer (sur).

tugboat ['tʌgbəʊt] **n** remorqueur *m*.

tug-of-love **n** *UK inf conflit entre des parents pour obtenir la garde des enfants.*

tug-of-war **n** lutte *f* de traction à la corde / *fig* lutte acharnée.

tuition [tju:'ɪʃn] **n** *(U)* cours *mpl*.

tulip ['tju:lɪp] **n** tulipe *f*.

tulle [tju:l] **n** tulle *m*.

tumble ['tʌmbl] ■ **vi 1.** [person] tomber, faire une chute / [water] tomber en cascades **2.** *fig* [prices] tomber, chuter.
■ **n** chute *f*, culbute *f*.
◆ ***tumble to*** **vt insep** *UK inf* piger.

tumbledown ['tʌmbldaʊn] **adj** délabré(e), qui tombe en ruines.

tumble-dry **vt** faire sécher en machine.

tumble-dryer [-ˌdraɪəʳ] **n** sèche-linge *m inv*.

tumbler ['tʌmbləʳ] **n** [glass] verre *m* (droit).

tumescent [ˌtju:'mesnt] **adj** tumescent(e).

tummy ['tʌmɪ] (pl **-ies**) **n** *inf* ventre *m*.

tumour *UK*, ***tumor*** *US* ['tju:məʳ] **n** tumeur *f*.

tumult ['tju:mʌlt] **n** tumulte *m*.

tumultuous ['tju:mʌltjʊəs] **adj** tumultueux(euse) / [applause] frénétique.

tuna [*UK* 'tju:nə, *US* 'tu:nə] (pl **tuna** ***OR*** -s) **n** thon *m*.

tundra ['tʌndrə] **n** toundra *f*.

tune [tju:n] ■ **n 1.** [song, melody] air *m* **2.** [harmony] **: in tune** [instrument] accordé(e), juste / [play, sing] juste ▸ **out of tune** [instrument] mal accordé(e) / [play, sing] faux ▸ **to the tune of** *fig* d'un montant de ▸ **to be in/out of tune (with)** *fig* être en accord/désaccord (avec) ▸ **to change one's tune** *inf* changer de ton.
■ **vt 1.** MUS accorder **2.** RADIO & TV régler **3.** [engine] régler.
■ **vi** RADIO & TV **: to tune to a channel** se mettre sur une chaîne.
◆ ***tune in*** **vi** RADIO & TV être à l'écoute ▸ **to tune in to** se mettre sur.
◆ ***tune up*** **vi** MUS accorder son instrument.

tuned-in [tju:nd-] **adj** *inf* branché(e).

tuneful ['tju:nfʊl] **adj** mélodieux(euse).

tunefully ['tju:nfʊlɪ] **adv** mélodieusement.

tuneless ['tju:nlɪs] **adj** discordant(e).

tunelessly ['tju:nlɪslɪ] **adv** [with no tune] de manière peu mélodieuse / [out of tune] faux *(adv).*

tuner ['tju:nəʳ] **n 1.** RADIO & TV syntoniseur *m*, tuner *m* **2.** MUS [person] accordeur *m*.

tuner amplifier **n** ampli-tuner *m*.

tungsten ['tʌŋstən] ■ **n** tungstène *m*.
■ **comp** au tungstène.

tunic ['tju:nɪk] **n** tunique *f*.

tuning ['tju:nɪŋ] **n 1.** MUS accord *m* **2.** RADIO & TV réglage *m* **3.** AUT réglage *m*, mise *f* au point.

tuning fork ['tju:nɪŋ-] **n** diapason *m*.

Tunis ['tju:nɪs] **n** Tunis.

Tunisia [tju:'nɪzɪə] **n** Tunisie *f* ▸ **in Tunisia** en Tunisie.

Tunisian [tju:'nɪzɪən] ■ **adj** tunisien(enne).
■ **n** [person] Tunisien *m*, -enne *f*.

tunnel ['tʌnl] ■ **n** tunnel *m*.
■ **vi** (*UK* **-led**, cont **-ling**, *US* **-ed**, cont **-ing**) faire ***OR*** creuser un tunnel.

tunnel vision **n** rétrécissement *m* du champ visuel / *fig* & *pej* vues *fpl* étroites.

tunny ['tʌnɪ] (pl **tunny** ***OR*** **-ies**) **n** thon *m*.

tuppence ['tʌpəns] **n** *UK dated* deux pence *mpl*.

Tupperware® ['tʌpəweəʳ] ■ **n** Tupperware® *m*.
■ **comp** en Tupperware®.

turban ['tɜ:bən] **n** turban *m*.

turbid ['tɜ:bɪd] **adj** trouble.

turbine ['tɜ:baɪn] **n** turbine *f*.

turbo ['tɜ:bəʊ] (pl **-s**) **n** turbo *m*.

turbocharged ['tɜ:bəʊtʃɑ:dʒd] **adj** turbo *(inv).*

turbodiesel [ˌtɜ:bəʊ'di:zl] **n** turbodiesel *m*.

turbojet [ˌtɜ:bəʊ'dʒet] **n** [engine] turboréacteur *m* / [plane] avion *m* à turboréacteur.

turboprop [ˌtɜ:bəʊ'prɒp] **n** [engine] turbopropulseur *m* / [plane] avion *m* à turbopropulseur.

turbot ['tɜ:bət] (pl **turbot** ***OR*** -s) **n** turbot *m*.

turbulence ['tɜ:bjʊləns] **n** *(U)* **1.** [in air, water] turbulence *f* **2.** *fig* [unrest] agitation *f*.

turbulent ['tɜ:bjʊlənt] **adj 1.** [air, water] agité(e) **2.** *fig* [disorderly] tumultueux(euse), agité(e).

turd [tɜ:d] **n** *v inf* **1.** [excrement] merde *f* **2.** *pej* [person] con *m*, salaud *m*.

tureen [tə'ri:n] **n** soupière *f*.

turf [tɜ:f] ■ **n** (pl -s, *UK* **turves** [tɜ:vz]) **1.** [grass surface] gazon *m* **2.** *US inf* [of gang] territoire *m* réservé **3.** [clod] motte *f* de gazon.
■ **vt** gazonner.
◆ ***turf out*** **vt sep** *UK inf* [person] virer / [old clothes] balancer, bazarder.

turf accountant **n** *UK* bookmaker *m*.

turgid ['tɜ:dʒɪd] **adj** *fml* [style, writing] pompeux(euse), ampoulé(e).

Turk [tɜ:k] **n** Turc *m*, Turque *f*.

Turkestan, ***Turkistan*** [ˌtɜ:kɪ'stɑ:n] **n** Turkistan *m* ▸ **in Turkestan** au Turkistan.

turkey ['tɜ:kɪ] (pl -s) **n** dinde *f*.

Turkey ['tɜ:kɪ] **n** Turquie *f* ▸ **in Turkey** en Turquie.

Turkish ['tɜ:kɪʃ] ■ **adj** turc (turque).
■ **n** [language] turc *m*.
■ **npl : the Turkish** les Turcs *mpl*.

Turkish bath **n** bain *m* turc.

Turkish delight **n** loukoum *m*.

Turkmenian [ˌtɜ:k'menɪən] **adj** turkmène.

Turkmenistan [ˌtɜ:kmenɪ'stɑ:n] **n** Turkménistan *m*.

turmeric ['tɜ:mərɪk] **n** curcuma *m*.

turmoil ['tɜ:mɔɪl] **n** agitation *f*, trouble *m*.

turn ['tɜ:n] ■ **n 1.** [in road] virage *m*, tournant *m* / [in river] méandre *m* ▸ **'no right turn'** 'défense de tourner à droite' ▸ **at every turn** *fig* à tout instant, à tout bout de champ
2. [revolution, twist] tour *m*
3. [change] tournure *f*, tour *m* ▸ **it was an unexpected turn of events** les événements ont pris une tournure imprévue ▸ **things took a turn for the worse/better** les choses se sont aggravées/améliorées
4. [in game] tour *m* ▸ **it's my turn** c'est (à) mon tour ▸ **in turn** tour à tour, chacun (à) son tour ▸ **I told Sarah and she in turn told Paul** je l'ai dit à Sarah qui, à son tour, l'a dit à Paul ▸ **to take (it in) turns to do sthg** *UK* faire qqch à tour de rôle
5. [end - of year, century] fin *f*
6. *UK* [performance] numéro *m*
7. *UK* MED crise *f*, attaque *f*
8. [tendency, style] **: to have an optimistic turn of mind** être optimiste de nature *OR* d'un naturel optimiste ▸ **turn of phrase** tournure *f* *OR* tour *m* de phrase
▸▸ **to do sb a good turn** rendre (un) service à qqn ▸ **done to a turn** *UK inf* CULIN **: the chicken was done to a turn** le poulet était cuit à point.
■ **vt 1.** [gen] tourner / [omelette, steak] retourner ▸ **turn the knob to the right** tournez le bouton vers la droite ▸ **to turn sthg inside out** retourner qqch ▸ **to turn one's thoughts/attention to sthg** tourner ses pensées/son attention vers qqch ▸ **she turned the conversation to sport** elle a orienté la conversation vers le sport ▸ **the very thought of food turns my stomach** l'idée même de manger me soulève le cœur ▸ **to turn a cartwheel** faire la roue
2. [change] **: to turn sthg into** changer qqch en ▸ **they're turning the book into a film** ils adaptent le livre pour l'écran
3. [become] **: to turn red** rougir ▸ **his hair is turning grey** ses cheveux grisonnent ▸ **the demonstration turned nasty** la manifestation a mal tourné ▸ **to turn professional** passer *OR* devenir professionnel ▸ **I had just turned twenty** je venais d'avoir vingt ans ▸ **it has only just turned four o'clock** il est quatre heures passées de quelques secondes
4. [ankle] tordre.
■ **vi 1.** [gen] tourner / [person] se tourner, se retourner ▸ **they turned towards me** ils se sont tournés vers moi *OR* de mon côté ▸ **the crane turned (through) 180º** la grue a pivoté de 180 ° ▸ **the car turned into our street** la voiture a tourné dans notre rue ▸ **I don't know where *OR* which way to turn** *fig* je ne sais plus quoi faire
2. [in book] **: to turn to a page** se reporter *OR* aller à une page
3. [for consolation] **: to turn to sb/sthg** se tourner vers qqn/qqch ▸ **I don't know who to turn to** je ne sais pas à qui m'adresser *OR* qui aller trouver
4. [change] **: the weather has turned** le temps a changé ▸ **to turn into** se changer en, se transformer en ▸ **their love turned to hate** leur amour se changea en haine *OR* fit place à la haine.

◆ ***turn against*** **vt insep** se retourner contre.

◆ ***turn around*** **vt sep** = ***turn round***.

◆ ***turn away*** ■ **vt sep** [refuse entry to] refuser.
■ **vi** se détourner.

◆ ***turn back*** ■ **vt sep** [sheets] replier / [person, vehicle] refouler.
■ **vi** rebrousser chemin ▸ **my mind is made up, there is no turning back** ma décision est prise, je n'y reviendrai pas.

◆ ***turn down*** **vt sep 1.** [reject] rejeter, refuser ▸ **she turned me down flat** *inf* elle m'a envoyé balader
2. [radio, volume, gas] baisser.

◆ ***turn in*** **vi** *inf* [go to bed] se pieuter.

◆ ***turn off*** ■ **vt insep** [road, path] quitter.
■ **vt sep** [radio, TV, engine, gas] éteindre / [tap] fermer.
■ **vi** [leave path, road] tourner ▸ **we turned off at junction 5** nous avons pris la sortie d'autoroute 5.

◆ ***turn on*** ■ **vt sep 1.** [radio, TV, engine, gas] allumer / [tap] ouvrir ▸ **to turn the light on** allumer la lumière
2. *inf* [excite sexually] exciter.
■ **vt insep** [attack] attaquer ▸ **his colleagues turned on him** ses collègues s'en sont pris à lui.

◆ ***turn out*** ■ **vt sep 1.** [light, gas fire] éteindre
2. [produce] produire ▸ **he turns out a book a year** il écrit un livre par an
3. [eject - person] mettre dehors ▸ **he turned his daughter out of the house** il a mis sa fille à la porte *OR* a chassé sa fille de la maison
4. [empty - pocket, bag] retourner, vider ▸ **turn the cake out onto a plate** démoulez le gâteau sur une assiette.
■ **vt insep : to turn out to be** s'avérer ▸ **it turned out to be a success** en fin de compte, cela a été une réussite ▸ **it turns out that...** il s'avère *OR* se trouve que...
■ **vi 1.** [end up] finir ▸ **the story turned out happily** l'histoire s'est bien terminée *OR* a bien fini
2. [arrive - person] venir.

◆ ***turn over*** ■ **vt sep 1.** [playing card, stone] retourner / [page] tourner ▸ **to turn over a new leaf** s'acheter une conduite

2. [consider] retourner dans sa tête ▸ **I was turning the idea over in my mind** je tournais et retournais *OR* ruminais l'idée dans ma tête
3. [hand over] rendre, remettre ▸ **to turn sb over to the authorities** livrer qqn aux autorités.
■ **vi 1.** [roll over] se retourner
2. *UK* TV changer de chaîne.
◆ ***turn round*** *UK*, ***turn around*** *US* ■ **vt sep 1.** [reverse] retourner
2. [wheel, words] tourner
3. [change nature of] **: to turn a company round** COMM faire prospérer une entreprise qui périclitait, sauver une entreprise de la faillite.
■ **vi** [person] se retourner.
◆ ***turn up*** ■ **vt sep 1.** [TV, radio] mettre plus fort / [gas] monter
2. [find, unearth] découvrir ▸ **her research turned up some interesting new facts** sa recherche a révélé de nouveaux détails intéressants.
■ **vi 1.** [arrive - person] se pointer
2. [be found - person, object] être retrouvé / [- opportunity] se présenter ▸ **her bag turned up eventually** elle a fini par retrouver son sac ▸ **I'll take the first job that turns up** je prendrai le premier poste qui se présentera.

turnabout ['tɜ:nəbaʊt] **n** [of situation] revirement *m* / [of policy] changement *m*.

turnaround *US* = ***turnround***.

turncoat ['tɜ:nkəʊt] **n** *pej* renégat *m*.

turned-on **adj** *inf* **1.** [up-to-date] branché(e), câblé(e) **2.** [aroused] excité(e) ▸ **to get turned-on** s'exciter.

turning ['tɜ:nɪŋ] **n** *UK* [off road] route *f* latérale ▸ **take the first turning on the left** prenez la première à gauche.

turning circle **n** rayon *m* de braquage.

turning point **n** tournant *m*, moment *m* décisif.

turnip ['tɜ:nɪp] **n** navet *m*.

turn-off **n 1.** [road] sortie *f* (de route), route *f* transversale, embranchement *m* **2.** *inf* [loss of interest] **: it's a real turn-off** [gen] c'est vraiment à vous dégoûter / [sexual] ça vous coupe vraiment l'envie.

turn-on **n** *inf* **: he finds leather a turn-on** il trouve le cuir excitant, le cuir l'excite.

turnout ['tɜ:naʊt] **n** [at election] taux *m* de participation / [at meeting] assistance *f*.

turnover ['tɜ:n,əʊvəʳ] **n** *(U)* **1.** [of personnel] renouvellement *m* **2.** FIN chiffre *m* d'affaires.

turnpike ['tɜ:npaɪk] **n** *US* autoroute *f* à péage.

turnround *UK* ['tɜ:nraʊnd], ***turnaround*** *US* ['tɜ:nəraʊnd] **n 1.** COMM **: turnround (time)** délai *m* **2.** [change] retournement *m*.

turn signal lever **n** *US* (manette *f* de) clignotant *m*.

turnstile ['tɜ:nstaɪl] **n** tourniquet *m*.

turntable ['tɜ:n,teɪbl] **n** platine *f*.

turn-up **n** *UK* [on trousers] revers *m inv* ▸ **a turn-up for the books** *inf* une sacrée surprise.

turpentine ['tɜ:pəntaɪn] **n** térébenthine *f*.

turps [tɜ:ps] **n** *UK inf* térébenthine *f*.

turquoise ['tɜ:kwɔɪz] ■ **adj** turquoise *(inv)*.
■ **n 1.** [mineral, gem] turquoise *f* **2.** [colour] turquoise *m*.

turret ['tʌrɪt] **n** tourelle *f*.

turtle ['tɜ:tl] (pl **turtle** *OR* **-s**) **n** tortue *f* de mer.

turtledove ['tɜ:tldʌv] **n** tourterelle *f*.

turtleneck ['tɜ:tlnek] **n** [garment] pull *m* à col montant / [neck] col *m* montant.

turves [tɜ:vz] *UK* **npl** ➤ ***turf***.

tusk [tʌsk] **n** défense *f*.

tussle ['tʌsl] ■ **n** lutte *f*.
■ **vi** se battre ▸ **to tussle over sthg** se disputer qqch.

tut [tʌt] **excl** mais non!, allons donc!

tutor ['tju:təʳ] ■ **n 1.** [private] professeur *m* particulier **2.** *UK* UNIV directeur *m*, -trice *f* d'études.
■ **vt : to tutor sb (in sthg)** donner à qqn des cours particuliers (de qqch).

tutorial [tju:'tɔ:rɪəl] ■ **adj** [group, class] de travaux dirigés.
■ **n** travaux *mpl* dirigés.

tutu ['tu:tu:] **n** tutu *m*.

tux ['tʌks] **n** *UK inf* smoking *m*.

tuxedo [tʌk'si:dəʊ] (pl **-s**) **n** *UK* smoking *m*.

TV (abbr of ***television***) ■ **n 1.** *(U)* [medium, industry] télé *f* ▸ **on TV** à la télé **2.** [apparatus] (poste *m* de) télé *f*.
■ **comp** de télé.

TV dinner **n** repas *m* surgelé *(sur un plateau)*.

TV movie **n** téléfilm *m*.

twaddle ['twɒdl] **n** *(U) inf* bêtises *fpl*, fadaises *fpl*.

twang [twæŋ] ■ **n 1.** [sound] bruit *m* de pincement **2.** [accent] nasillement *m*.
■ **vt** [guitar] pincer.
■ **vi** [wire, string] vibrer.

tweak [twi:k] **vt** *inf* [ear] tirer / [nose] tordre.

twee [twi:] **adj** *UK pej* mièvre.

tweed [twi:d] ■ **n** tweed *m*.
■ **comp** de *OR* en tweed.

tweenage ['twi:neɪdʒ] **adj** *inf* préadolescence *f*.

tweenager ['twi:neɪdʒəʳ] **n** *inf* préadolescent *m*, -e *f*.

tweet [twi:t] **vi** gazouiller.

tweezers ['twi:zəz] **npl** pince *f* à épiler.

twelfth [twelfθ] **num** douzième ; see also ***sixth***.

Twelfth Night **n** la fête des Rois.

twelve [twelv] **num** douze ; see also ***six***.

twentieth ['twentɪəθ] **num** vingtième ; see also ***sixth***.

twenty ['twentɪ] (pl **-ies**) **num** vingt ; see also ***six***.

twenty-twenty vision **n** vision *f* de dix dixièmes à chaque œil.

twerp [twɜ:p] **n** *inf* crétin *m*, -e *f*, andouille *f*.

twice [twaɪs] **adv** deux fois ▸ **twice a day** deux fois par jour ▸ **he earns twice as much as me** il gagne deux fois plus que moi ▸ **twice as big** deux fois plus grand ▸ **twice my size/age** le double de ma taille/mon âge.

twiddle ['twɪdl] ■ **vt** jouer avec.
■ **vi : to twiddle with sthg** jouer avec qqch.

twig [twɪg] **n** brindille *f*, petite branche *f*.

twilight ['twaɪlaɪt] **n** crépuscule *m*.

twill [twɪl] **n** sergé *m*.

twin [twɪn] ■ **adj** jumeau (jumelle) / *UK* [town] jumelé(e) ▸ **twin beds** lits *mpl* jumeaux.
■ **n** jumeau *m*, jumelle *f*.

twin-bedded [-'bedɪd] **adj** à deux lits.

twin beds **npl** lits *m* jumeaux.

twin carburettor **n** *UK* carburateur *m* double-corps.

twine [twaɪn] ■ **n** *(U)* ficelle *f*.
■ **vt : to twine sthg round** *UK* ***or*** **around** *US* **sthg** enrouler qqch autour de qqch.

twin-engined [-'endʒɪnd] **adj** bimoteur.

twinge [twɪndʒ] **n** [of pain] élancement *m* ▸ **a twinge of guilt** un remords.

twinkie ['twɪŋkɪ] **n** *US* [cake] *petit gâteau fourré à la crème*.

twinkle ['twɪŋkl] ■ **n** [of stars, lights] scintillement *m* / [in eyes] pétillement *m*.
■ **vi** [star, lights] scintiller / [eyes] briller, pétiller.

twinkling ['twɪŋklɪŋ] ■ **adj 1.** [star, gem, sea] scintillant(e), brillant(e) **2.** [eyes] pétillant(e), brillant(e) **3.** *fig* [feet] agile.
■ **n** *(U)* **1.** [of star, light, gem] scintillement *m* **2.** [in eyes] pétillement *m* ▸ **in the twinkling of an eye** en un clin d'œil.

twin room **n** chambre *f* à deux lits.

twin set **n** *UK* twin-set *m*.

twin town **n** *UK* ville *f* jumelée.

twin tub **n** machine *f* à double tambour.

twirl [twɜ:l] ■ **vt** faire tourner.
■ **vi** tournoyer.

twist [twɪst] ■ **n 1.** [in road] zigzag *m*, tournant *m* / [in river] méandre *m*, coude *m* / [in rope] entortillement *m* ▸ **to get (o.s.) into a twist about sthg** [get angry] s'énerver au sujet de qqch / [get upset] se mettre dans tous ses états **2.** [turn] **: to give the lid a twist** [to open] dévisser le couvercle / [to close] visser le couvercle **3.** *fig* [in plot] rebondissement *m* ▸ **the book gives a new twist to the old story** le livre donne une nouvelle tournure ***or*** un tour nouveau à cette vieille histoire ▸ **it's difficult to follow the twists and turns of his argument** il est difficile de suivre les méandres de son argumentation.
■ **vt 1.** [wind, curl] entortiller ▸ **the seat-belt got twisted** la ceinture (de sécurité) s'est entortillée **2.** [contort] tordre ▸ **the railings were twisted out of shape** les grilles étaient toutes tordues ▸ **her face was twisted with pain** *fig* ses traits étaient tordus par la douleur, la douleur lui tordait le visage **3.** [turn] tourner / [lid - to open] dévisser / [- to close] visser ▸ **if you twist his arm, he'll agree to go** si tu insistes un peu, il voudra bien y aller **4.** [sprain] **: to twist one's ankle** se tordre ***or*** se fouler la cheville **5.** [words, meaning] déformer.
■ **vi 1.** [river, path] zigzaguer **2.** [be contorted] se tordre **3.** [turn] **: to twist round** *UK* ***or*** **around** *US* se retourner.

twisted ['twɪstɪd] **adj** *pej* tordu(e).

twister ['twɪstər] **n** *US* tornade *f*.

twisty ['twɪstɪ] (comp **-ier**, superl **-iest**) **adj** *inf* sinueux(euse), en zigzag.

twit [twɪt] **n** *UK inf* crétin *m*, -e *f*.

twitch [twɪtʃ] ■ **n** tic *m*.
■ **vt** [rope] tirer d'un coup sec / [ears - subj: animal] remuer.
■ **vi** [muscle, eye, face] se contracter.

twitchy ['twɪtʃɪ] **adj** [person] agité(e), nerveux(euse).

twitter ['twɪtər] **vi 1.** [bird] gazouiller **2.** *pej* [person] jacasser.

two [tu:] **num** deux ▸ **in two** en deux ; see also ***six***.

two-bit **adj** *pej* de pacotille.

two-dimensional **adj** à deux dimensions / *pej* superficiel(elle), simpliste.

two-door **adj** [car] à deux portes.

twofaced [ˌtu:'feɪst] **adj** *pej* fourbe.

twofold ['tu:fəʊld] ■ **adj** double.
■ **adv** doublement ▸ **to increase twofold** doubler.

two-handed [-'hændɪd] **adj** à deux poignées.

two-hander **n** CIN & THEAT film *m* à deux personnages.

two-piece **adj : two-piece swimsuit** deux-pièces *m inv* ▸ **two-piece suit** [for man] costume *m* (deux-pièces).

two-ply **adj** [yarn] à deux fils / [wood] à deux épaisseurs.

two-seater **n** [car] voiture *f* à deux places / [plane] biplace *m*.

twosome ['tu:səm] **n** *inf* couple *m*.

two-stroke ■ **adj** à deux temps.
■ **n** deux-temps *m inv*.

two-time **vt** *inf* tromper.

two-tone **adj** de deux tons.

two-way **adj** [traffic, trade] dans les deux sens ▸ **two-way radio** poste *m* émetteur-récepteur.

two-way street **n** rue *f* à circulation dans les deux sens.

two-wheeler **n** [motorbike] deux-roues *m* / [bicycle] bicyclette *f*, deux-roues *m*.

TX abbr of ***Texas***.

tycoon [taɪ'ku:n] **n** magnat *m*.

type [taɪp] ■ **n 1.** [sort, kind] genre *m*, sorte *f* / [model] modèle *m* / [in classification] type *m* **2.** [person] **: he's not the marrying type** il n'est pas du genre à se marier ▸ **he's/she's not my type** *inf* lui/elle, ce n'est pas mon genre ***or*** type **3.** *(U)* TYPO caractères *mpl*.
■ **vt** [letter, reply] taper (à la machine) ▸ **to type data into a computer** introduire des données dans un ordinateur.
■ **vi** taper (à la machine).
◆ ***type up*** **vt sep** taper.

-type **suffix** du type, genre.

typecast ['taɪpkɑ:st] (pt & pp **typecast**) **vt : to be typecast** être cantonné aux mêmes rôles ▸ **to be typecast as** être cantonné dans le rôle de.

typeface ['taɪpfeɪs] **n** TYPO œil *m* de caractère.

typescript ['taɪpskrɪpt] **n** texte *m* dactylographié.

typeset ['taɪpset] (pt & pp **typeset**, cont **-ting**) **vt** composer.

typesetter ['taɪp,setəʳ] **n** [worker] compositeur *m*, -trice *f* / [machine] linotype *f*.

typesetting ['taɪp,setɪŋ] **n** TYPO composition *f*.

typewriter ['taɪp,raɪtəʳ] **n** machine *f* à écrire.

typewritten ['taɪp,rɪtn] **adj** dactylographié(e), tapé(e) à la machine.

typhoid (fever) ['taɪfɔɪd-] **n** typhoïde *f*.

typhoon [taɪ'fu:n] **n** typhon *m*.

typhus ['taɪfəs] **n** typhus *m*.

typical ['tɪpɪkl] **adj : typical (of)** typique (de), caractéristique (de) ▸ **that's typical (of him/her)!** c'est bien de lui/d'elle!

typically ['tɪpɪklɪ] **adv** typiquement.

typify ['tɪpɪfaɪ] (pt & pp **-ied**) **vt 1.** [characterize] être caractéristique de **2.** [represent] représenter.

typing ['taɪpɪŋ] **n** dactylo *f*, dactylographie *f*.

typing error **n** faute *f* de frappe.

typing pool **n** bureau *m* OR pool *m* des dactylos.

typist ['taɪpɪst] **n** dactylo *mf*, dactylographe *mf*.

typo ['taɪpəʊ] **n** *inf* coquille *f*.

typographic(al) error [,taɪpə'græfɪk(l)-] **n** faute *f* typographique.

typography [taɪ'pɒgrəfɪ] **n** typographie *f*.

tyrannical [tɪ'rænɪkl] **adj** tyrannique.

tyranny ['tɪrənɪ] **n** tyrannie *f*.

tyrant ['taɪrənt] **n** tyran *m*.

tyre UK, ***tire*** US ['taɪəʳ] **n** pneu *m*.

tyre pressure UK, ***tire pressure*** US **n** pression *f* (de gonflage).

Tyrol, ***Tirol*** ['tɪrɒl] **n** Tyrol *m*.

Tyrolean [tɪrə'li:ən], ***Tyrolese*** [,tɪrə'li:z] ■ **adj** tyrolien(enne).

■ **n** Tyrolien *m*, -enne *f*.

Tyrrhenian Sea [tɪ'ri:nɪən-] **n : the Tyrrhenian Sea** la mer Tyrrhénienne.

tzar [zɑ:ʳ] = ***tsar***.

u [juː] (pl **u's** *OR* **us**), ***U***[1] (pl U's *OR* Us) **n** [letter] u *m inv*, U *m inv*.

U[2] (abbr of ***universal***) *en Grande-Bretagne, désigne un film tous publics*.

UAW (abbr of ***United Automobile Workers***) **n** *syndicat américain de l'industrie automobile*.

UB40 (abbr of ***unemployment benefit form 40***) **n** *en Grande-Bretagne, carte de pointage pour bénéficier de l'allocation de chômage*.

U-bend **n** siphon *m*.

ubiquitous [juːˈbɪkwɪtəs] **adj** omniprésent(e).

UCAS [ˈjuːkas] (abbr of ***Universities and Colleges Admissions Service***) **n** *organisme gérant les inscriptions dans les universités au Royaume-Uni*.

UCATT [juːkæt] (abbr of ***Union of Construction, Allied Trades and Technicians***) **n** *syndicat britannique des employés du bâtiment*.

UCCA [ˈʌkə] (abbr of ***Universities Central Council on Admissions***) **n** *ancien organisme centralisant les demandes d'inscription dans les universités britanniques, maintenant remplacé par l' UCAS*.

UCL (abbr of ***University College, London***) **n** *université londonienne*.

UCW (abbr of ***The Union of Communication Workers***) **n** *syndicat britannique des communications*.

UDA (abbr of ***Ulster Defence Association***) **n** *ancienne organisation paramilitaire protestante en Irlande du Nord*.

UDC (abbr of ***Urban District Council***) **n** *conseil d'une communauté urbaine*.

udder [ˈʌdəʳ] **n** mamelle *f*.

UDI (abbr of ***unilateral declaration of independence***) **n** *déclaration unilatérale d'indépendance*.

UDR (abbr of ***Ulster Defence Regiment***) **n** *régiment de réservistes en Irlande du Nord*.

UEFA [juːˈeɪfə] (abbr of ***Union of European Football Associations***) **n** UEFA *f*.

UFC (abbr of ***Universities Funding Council***) **n** *organisme répartissant les crédits entre les universités en Grande-Bretagne*.

UFO (abbr of ***unidentified flying object***) **n** OVNI *m*, ovni *m*.

Uganda [juːˈgændə] **n** Ouganda *m* ▸ **in Uganda** en Ouganda.

Ugandan [juːˈgændən] ■ **adj** ougandais(e).
■ **n** [person] Ougandais *m*, -e *f*.

ugh [ʌg] **excl** pouah!, beurk!

ugliness [ˈʌglɪnɪs] *(U)* **n** **1.** [unattractiveness] laideur *f* **2.** *fig* [unpleasantness] caractère *m* pénible *OR* désagréable.

ugly [ˈʌglɪ] (comp **-ier**, superl **-iest**) **adj** **1.** [unattractive] laid(e) **2.** *fig* [unpleasant] pénible, désagréable.

UHF (abbr of ***ultra-high frequency***) **n** UHF.

uh-huh [ʌˈhʌ] **excl** *inf* **: uh-huh!** [as conversation filler] ah ah! / [in assent] oui oui!, OK!

UHT (abbr of ***ultra-heat treated***) UHT.

UK (abbr of ***United Kingdom***) **n** Royaume-Uni *m*, R.U. *m*

Ukraine [juːˈkreɪn] **n : the Ukraine** l'Ukraine *f* ▸ **in the Ukraine** en Ukraine.

Ukrainian [juːˈkreɪnjən] ■ **adj** ukrainien(enne).
■ **n** **1.** [person] Ukrainien *m*, -enne *f* **2.** [language] ukrainien *m*.

ukulele [ˌjuːkəˈleɪlɪ] **n** guitare *f* hawaïenne, ukulélé *m*.

Ulan Bator [uˈlɑːnˈbɑːtɔ] **n** Oulan-Bator.

ulcer [ˈʌlsəʳ] **n** ulcère *m*.

ulcerated [ˈʌlsəreɪtɪd] **adj** ulcéré(e).

Ulster [ˈʌlstəʳ] **n** Ulster *m* ▸ **in Ulster** dans l'Ulster.

Ulsterman [ˈʌlstəmən] (pl **-men** [-mən]) **n** habitant *m* *OR* natif *m* de l'Ulster.

Ulster Unionist Party **n** *parti politique essentiellement protestant favorable au maintien de l'Ulster au sein du Royaume-Uni*.

ulterior [ʌlˈtɪərɪəʳ] **adj : ulterior motive** arrière-pensée *f*.

ultimata [ˌʌltɪˈmeɪtə] **npl** ➤ ***ultimatum***.

ultimate [ˈʌltɪmət] ■ **adj** **1.** [final] final(e), ultime **2.** [most powerful] ultime, suprême.
■ **n : the ultimate in** le fin du fin dans.

ultimately [ˈʌltɪmətlɪ] **adv** [finally] finalement.

ultimatum [ˌʌltɪˈmeɪtəm] (pl **-tums** *OR* **-ta** [-tə]) **n** ultimatum *m*.

ultra- [ˈʌltrə] **prefix** ultra-.

ultramarine [ˌʌltrəməˈriːn] **adj** (bleu) outremer *(inv)*.

ultrasonic [ˌʌltrəˈsɒnɪk] **adj** ultrasonique.

ultrasound [ˈʌltrəsaʊnd] **n** *(U)* ultrasons *mpl*.

ultraviolet [ˌʌltrəˈvaɪələt] **adj** ultra-violet(ette).

um [ʌm] **excl** heu!

umbilical cord [ʌmˈbɪlɪkl-] **n** cordon *m* ombilical.

umbrage [ˈʌmbrɪdʒ] **n : to take umbrage (at)** prendre ombrage (de).

umbrella [ʌmˈbrelə] ■ **n** [portable] parapluie *m* / [fixed] parasol *m*.
■ **adj** [organization] qui en regroupe plusieurs autres.

umbrella fund **n** fonds *m* de consolidation.

UMIST [ˈjuːmɪst] (abbr of ***University of Manchester Institute of Science and Technology***) **n** *institut de science et de technologie de l'université de Manchester.*

umpire [ˈʌmpaɪəʳ] ■ **n** arbitre *m*.
■ **vt** arbitrer.
■ **vi** être l'arbitre.

umpteen [ˌʌmpˈtiːn] **num adj** *inf* je ne sais combien de.

umpteenth [ˌʌmpˈtiːnθ] **num adj** *inf* énième.

UMW (abbr of ***United Mineworkers of America***) **n** *syndicat américain de mineurs.*

UN (abbr of ***United Nations***) **n : the UN** l'ONU *f*, l'Onu *f*.

unabashed [ˌʌnəˈbæʃt] **adj** nullement décontenancé(e).

unabated [ˌʌnəˈbeɪtɪd] **adj : the rain continued unabated** la pluie continua de tomber sans répit.

unable [ʌnˈeɪbl] **adj : to be unable to do sthg** ne pas pouvoir faire qqch, être incapable de faire qqch.

unabridged [ˌʌnəˈbrɪdʒd] **adj** intégral(e).

unacceptable [ˌʌnəkˈseptəbl] **adj** inacceptable.

unacceptably [ˌʌnəkˈseptəblɪ] **adv** [noisy, rude] à un point inacceptable *OR* inadmissible.

unaccompanied [ˌʌnəˈkʌmpənɪd] **adj 1.** [child] non accompagné(e) / [luggage] sans surveillance **2.** [song] a cappella, sans accompagnement.

unaccountable [ˌʌnəˈkaʊntəbl] **adj 1.** [inexplicable] inexplicable **2.** [not responsible] **: to be unaccountable for sthg** ne pas être responsable de qqch ▸ **to be unaccountable to sb** ne pas être responsable envers *OR* devant qqn.

unaccountably [ˌʌnəˈkaʊntəblɪ] **adv** [inexplicably] de façon inexplicable, inexplicablement.

unaccounted [ˌʌnəˈkaʊntɪd] **adj : to be unaccounted for** manquer.

unaccustomed [ˌʌnəˈkʌstəmd] **adj 1.** [unused] **: to be unaccustomed to sthg/to doing sthg** ne pas être habitué(e) à qqch/à faire qqch **2.** [not usual] inaccoutumé(e), inhabituel(elle).

unacknowledged [ˌʌnəkˈnɒlɪdʒd] **adj 1.** [unrecognized - truth, fact] non reconnu(e) / [- qualities, discovery] non reconnu(e), méconnu(e) **2.** [ignored - letter] resté(e) sans réponse.

unacquainted [ˌʌnəˈkweɪntɪd] **adj : to be unacquainted with sb/sthg** ne pas connaître qqn/qqch.

unadulterated [ˌʌnəˈdʌltəreɪtɪd] **adj 1.** [unspoilt - wine] non frelaté(e) / [- food] naturel(elle) **2.** [absolute - joy] sans mélange / [- nonsense, truth] pur et simple (pure et simple).

unadventurous [ˌʌnədˈventʃərəs] **adj** qui manque d'audace.

unadvisable [ˌʌnədˈvaɪzəbl] **adj** imprudent(e), à déconseiller ▸ **it is unadvisable for her to travel** les voyages lui sont déconseillés, il vaut mieux qu'elle évite de voyager.

unaffected [ˌʌnəˈfektɪd] **adj 1.** [unchanged] **: unaffected (by)** non affecté(e) (par) **2.** [natural] naturel(elle).

unafraid [ˌʌnəˈfreɪd] **adj** sans crainte, sans peur.

unaided [ˌʌnˈeɪdɪd] **adj** sans aide.

unambiguous [ˌʌnæmˈbɪgjʊəs] **adj** non équivoque.

unambitious [ˌʌnæmˈbɪʃəs] **adj** sans ambition, peu ambitieux(euse).

un-American [ˈʌn-] **adj** anti-américain(e).

unanimity [ˌjuːnəˈnɪmətɪ] **n** unanimité *f*.

unanimous [juːˈnænɪməs] **adj** unanime.

unanimously [juːˈnænɪməslɪ] **adv** à l'unanimité.

unannounced [ˌʌnəˈnaʊnst] **adj** sans tambour ni trompette.

unanswered [ˌʌnˈɑːnsəd] **adj** qui reste sans réponse.

unappealing [ˌʌnəˈpiːlɪŋ] **adj** peu attirant(e).

unappetizing, *UK* ***-ising*** [ˌʌnˈæpɪtaɪzɪŋ] **adj** peu appétissant(e).

unappreciated [ˌʌnəˈpriːʃɪeɪtɪd] **adj** peu apprécié(e).

unappreciative [ˌʌnəˈpriːʃɪətɪv] **adj : unappreciative (of)** indifférent(e) (à).

unapproachable [ˌʌnəˈprəʊtʃəbl] **adj** inabordable, d'un abord difficile.

unarguably [ʌnˈɑːgjʊəblɪ] **adv** incontestablement.

unarmed [ˌʌnˈɑːmd] **adj** non armé(e).

unarmed combat **n** combat *m* sans armes.

unashamed [ˌʌnəˈʃeɪmd] **adj** [luxury] insolent(e) / [liar, lie] effronté(e), éhonté(e).

unashamedly [ˌʌnəˈʃeɪmɪdlɪ] **adv** [brazenly] sans honte, sans scrupule / [openly] sans honte, sans se cacher ▸ **she lied quite unashamedly** elle mentait absolument sans vergogne, c'était une menteuse tout à fait éhontée ▸ **he is unashamedly greedy** il est d'une gourmandise éhontée.

unassailable [ˌʌnəˈseɪləbl] **adj** [fort, city] imprenable, inébranlable / [certainty, belief] inébranlable / [reputation] inattaquable / [argument, reason] inattaquable, irréfutable.

unassisted [ˌʌnəˈsɪstɪd] **adj** sans aide.

unassuming [ˌʌnəˈsjuːmɪŋ] **adj** modeste, effacé(e).

unattached [ˌʌnəˈtætʃt] **adj 1.** [not fastened, linked] **: unattached (to)** indépendant(e) (de) **2.** [without partner] libre, sans attaches.

unattainable [ˌʌnəˈteɪnəbl] **adj** inaccessible.

unattended [ˌʌnəˈtendɪd] **adj** [luggage, shop] sans surveillance / [child] seul(e).

unattractive [ˌʌnəˈtræktɪv] **adj 1.** [not beautiful] peu attrayant(e), peu séduisant(e) **2.** [not pleasant] déplaisant(e).

unauthorized, *UK* ***-ised*** [ˌʌnˈɔːθəraɪzd] **adj** non autorisé(e).

unauthorized access **n** COMPUT accès *m* non autorisé.

unavailable [ˌʌnəˈveɪləbl] **adj** qui n'est pas disponible, indisponible.

unavoidable [ˌʌnəˈvɔɪdəbl] **adj** inévitable.

unavoidable costs **npl** coûts *mpl* induits.

unavoidably [ˌʌnəˈvɔɪdəblɪ] **adj** inévitablement ▸ **to be unavoidably detained** être retardé pour des raisons indépendantes de sa volonté.

unaware [ˌʌnəˈweəʳ] **adj** ignorant(e), inconscient(e) ▸ **to be unaware of sthg** ne pas avoir conscience de qqch, ignorer qqch.

unawares [ˌʌnəˈweəz] **adv : to catch** ***OR*** **take sb unawares** prendre qqn au dépourvu.

unbalanced [ˌʌnˈbælənst] **adj 1.** [biased] tendancieux(euse), partial(e) **2.** [deranged] déséquilibré(e).

unbearable [ʌnˈbeərəbl] **adj** insupportable.

unbearably [ʌnˈbeərəblɪ] **adv** insupportablement ▸ **it's unbearably hot** il fait une chaleur insupportable.

unbeatable [ˌʌnˈbiːtəbl] **adj** imbattable.

unbeaten [ˌʌnˈbiːtn] **adj** [fighter, team] invaincu(e) / [record, price] non battu(e).

unbecoming [ˌʌnbɪˈkʌmɪŋ] **adj** [unattractive] peu seyant(e).

unbeknown(st) [ˌʌnbɪˈnəʊn(st)] **adv : unbeknownst to** à l'insu de.

unbelievable [ˌʌnbɪˈliːvəbl] **adj** incroyable.

unbelievably [ˌʌnbɪˈliːvəblɪ] **adv** incroyablement ▸ **to be unbelievably stupid** être d'une bêtise incroyable.

unbend [ˌʌnˈbend] (pt & pp **unbent**) **vi** [relax] se détendre.

unbending [ˌʌnˈbendɪŋ] **adj** inflexible, intransigeant(e).

unbent [ˌʌnˈbent] **pt & pp** ➤ ***unbend***.

unbia(s)sed [ˌʌnˈbaɪəst] **adj** impartial(e).

unblemished [ˌʌnˈblemɪʃt] **adj** *fig* sans tache.

unblock [ˌʌnˈblɒk] **vt** déboucher.

unbolt [ˌʌnˈbəʊlt] **vt** déverrouiller.

unborn [ˌʌnˈbɔːn] **adj** [child] qui n'est pas encore né(e).

unbreakable [ˌʌnˈbreɪkəbl] **adj** incassable.

unbridled [ˌʌnˈbraɪdld] **adj** effréné(e), débridé(e).

unbroken [ˌʌnˈbrəʊkn] **adj 1.** [line] continu(e) / [surface, expanse] continu(e), ininterrompu(e) / [sleep, tradition, peace] ininterrompu(e) **2.** [crockery, eggs] intact(e), non cassé(e) / [fastening, seal] intact(e), non brisé(e) / [record] non battu(e) **3.** *fig* [promise] tenu(e), non rompu(e) ▸ **despite all her troubles, her spirit remains unbroken** malgré tous ses ennuis, elle garde le moral ***OR*** elle ne se laisse pas abattre **4.** [voice] qui n'a pas (encore) mué **5.** [horse] indompté(e).

unbuckle [ˌʌnˈbʌkl] **vt** déboucler.

unbutton [ˌʌnˈbʌtn] **vt** déboutonner.

uncalled-for [ˌʌnˈkɔːld-] **adj** [remark] déplacé(e) / [criticism] injustifié(e).

uncannily [ʌnˈkænɪlɪ] **adv** [accurate, familiar] étrangement / [quiet] mystérieusement, étrangement.

uncanny [ʌnˈkænɪ] (comp **-ier**, superl **-iest**) **adj** étrange, mystérieux(euse) / [resemblance] troublant(e).

uncared-for [ˌʌnˈkeəd-] **adj** délaissé(e), négligé(e).

uncaring [ˌʌnˈkeərɪŋ] **adj** qui ne se soucie pas des autres.

unceasing [ˌʌnˈsiːsɪŋ] **adj** *fml* incessant(e), continuel (elle).

uncensored [ˌʌnˈsensəd] **adj** non censuré(e).

unceremonious [ˈʌnˌserɪˈməʊnjəs] **adj** brusque.

unceremoniously [ˈʌnˌserɪˈməʊnjəslɪ] **adj** brusquement.

uncertain [ʌnˈsɜːtn] **adj** incertain(e) ▸ **in no uncertain terms** sans mâcher ses mots.

uncertainly [ʌnˈsɜːtnlɪ] **adv** avec hésitation, d'une manière hésitante.

uncertainty [ʌnˈsɜːtntɪ] (pl **-ies**) **n** incertitude *f*, doute *m* ▸ **to be in a state of uncertainty** être dans le doute ▸ **I am in some uncertainty as to whether I should tell him** je ne sais pas trop ***OR*** je ne suis pas trop sûre si je dois le lui dire ou non.

unchain [ˌʌnˈtʃeɪn] **vt** désenchaîner.

unchallenged [ˌʌnˈtʃælɪndʒd] **adj** incontesté(e), indiscuté(e).

unchanged [ˌʌnˈtʃeɪndʒd] **adj** inchangé(e).

unchanging [ˌʌnˈtʃeɪndʒɪŋ] **adj** invariable, immuable.

uncharacteristic [ˈʌnˌkærəktəˈrɪstɪk] **adj** inhabituel(elle).

uncharacteristically [ˈʌnˌkærəktəˈrɪstɪklɪ] **adv** d'une façon peu caractéristique.

uncharitable [ˌʌnˈtʃærɪtəbl] **adj** peu charitable.

HOW TO ...

express uncertainty

Ce n'est pas si sûr / It's not at all sure
Rien n'est encore sûr / Nothing has been decided yet
Rien n'est moins sûr / It's not at all sure
Nous n'avons encore aucune certitude / We still don't know anything for certain
Je doute qu'il réussisse / I doubt that he'll succeed
Ça m'étonnerait que ça marche / I'd be surprised if it worked
J'hésite encore à y aller / I still don't know whether to go or not
Il se peut qu'elle vous rappelle / She may call you

uncharted [ˌʌnˈtʃɑːtɪd] **adj** [land, sea] qui n'est pas sur la carte ▸ **uncharted territory** *fig* domaine inexploré.

unchecked [ˌʌnˈtʃekt] **adj** non maîtrisé(e), sans frein.

uncivilized**, UK **-ised [ˌʌnˈsɪvɪlaɪzd] **adj** non civilisé(e), barbare.

unclassified [ˌʌnˈklæsɪfaɪd] **adj** [documents] non classé(e) / [information] non secret(ète).

uncle [ˈʌŋkl] **n** oncle *m*.

unclean [ˌʌnˈkliːn] **adj 1.** [dirty] sale **2.** RELIG impur(e).

unclear [ˌʌnˈklɪəʳ] **adj 1.** [message, meaning, motive] qui n'est pas clair(e) **2.** [uncertain - person, future] incertain(e).

Uncle Sam l'Oncle Sam *(personnage représentant les États-Unis dans la propagande pour l'armée).*

unclothed [ˌʌnˈkləʊðd] **adj** nu(e), sans vêtements.

uncluttered [ˌʌnˈklʌtəd] **adj** [room] dépouillé(e), simple / [style of writing] sobre / [design] dépouillé(e) / [mind, thinking] clair(e), net(nette).

uncomfortable [ˌʌnˈkʌmftəbl] **adj 1.** [shoes, chair, clothes] inconfortable / *fig* [fact, truth] désagréable **2.** [person - physically] qui n'est pas à l'aise / [- ill at ease] mal à l'aise.

uncomfortably [ˌʌnˈkʌmftəblɪ] **adv 1.** [in physical discomfort] inconfortablement **2.** *fig* [uneasily] avec gêne.

uncommitted [ˌʌnkəˈmɪtɪd] **adj** non engagé(e).

uncommon [ʌnˈkɒmən] **adj 1.** [rare] rare **2.** *fml* [extreme] extraordinaire.

uncommonly [ʌnˈkɒmənlɪ] **adv** *fml* extraordinairement.

uncommunicative [ˌʌnkəˈmjuːnɪkətɪv] **adj** peu expansif(ive), peu communicatif(ive).

uncomplaining [ˌʌnkəmˈpleɪnɪŋ] **adj** qui ne se plaint pas.

uncomplicated [ˌʌnˈkɒmplɪkeɪtɪd] **adj** simple, peu compliqué(e).

uncomprehending [ˈʌnˌkɒmprɪˈhendɪŋ] **adj** qui ne comprend pas.

uncomprehendingly [ˈʌnˌkɒmprɪˈhendɪŋlɪ] **adv** sans comprendre.

uncompromising [ˌʌnˈkɒmprəmaɪzɪŋ] **adj** intransigeant(e).

uncompromisingly [ˌʌnˈkɒmprəmaɪzɪŋlɪ] **adv** sans concession, de manière intransigeante.

unconcerned [ˌʌnkənˈsɜːnd] **adj** [not anxious] qui ne s'inquiète pas.

unconditional [ˌʌnkənˈdɪʃənl] **adj** inconditionnel (elle).

unconditionally [ˌʌnkənˈdɪʃnəlɪ] **adv** [accept, surrender] inconditionnellement, sans condition.

unconfirmed [ˌʌnkənˈfɜːmd] **adj** non confirmé(e).

uncongenial [ˌʌnkənˈdʒiːnjəl] **adj** *fml* peu agréable.

unconnected [ˌʌnkəˈnektɪd] **adj** [facts, events] sans rapport.

unconquered [ˌʌnˈkɒŋkəd] **adj** qui n'a pas été conquis(e).

unconscious [ʌnˈkɒnʃəs] ■ **adj 1.** [having lost consciousness] sans connaissance **2.** *fig* [unaware] **: to be unconscious of** ne pas avoir conscience de, ne pas se rendre compte de **3.** [unnoticed - desires, feelings] inconscient(e).
■ **n** PSYCHOL inconscient *m*.

unconsciously [ʌnˈkɒnʃəslɪ] **adv** inconsciemment.

unconsciousness [ʌnˈkɒnʃəsnɪs] **n** *(U)* **1.** MED [coma] perte *f* de connaissance / [fainting] évanouissement *m* **2.** [lack of awareness] inconscience *f*.

unconstitutional [ˈʌnˌkɒnstɪˈtjuːʃənl] **adj** inconstitutionnel(elle), anticonstitutionnel(elle).

uncontested [ˌʌnkənˈtestɪd] **adj** incontesté(e) / [election] sans opposition.

uncontrollable [ˌʌnkənˈtrəʊləbl] **adj 1.** [unrestrainable - emotion, urge] irrépressible, irrésistible / [- increase, epidemic] qui ne peut être enrayé(e) **2.** [unmanageable - person] impossible, difficile.

uncontrollably [ˌʌnkənˈtrəʊləblɪ] **adv 1.** [helplessly] irrésistiblement ▸ **he was laughing uncontrollably** il avait le fou rire ▸ **I shook uncontrollably** je tremblais sans pouvoir m'arrêter **2.** [out of control] **: the boat rocked uncontrollably** on n'arrivait pas à maîtriser le tangage du bateau **3.** [fall, increase] irrésistiblement.

uncontrolled [ˌʌnkənˈtrəʊld] **adj** [emotion, urge] non contenu(e) / [increase] effréné(e) / [inflation, epidemic] galopant(e).

uncontroversial [ˈʌnˌkɒntrəˈvɜːʃl] **adj** qui ne prête pas à controverse, incontestable.

unconventional [ˌʌnkənˈvenʃənl] **adj** peu conventionnel(elle), original(e).

unconventionally [ˌʌnkənˈvenʃnəlɪ] **adv** [live, think] d'une manière originale ***OR*** peu conventionnelle / [dress] d'une manière originale.

unconvinced [ˌʌnkənˈvɪnst] **adj** qui n'est pas convaincu(e), sceptique.

unconvincing [ˌʌnkənˈvɪnsɪŋ] **adj** peu convaincant(e).

unconvincingly [ˌʌnkənˈvɪnsɪŋlɪ] **adv** [argue, lie] d'un ton ***OR*** d'une manière peu convaincante, peu vraisemblablement.

uncooked [ˌʌnˈkʊkt] **adj** non cuit(e), cru(e).

uncool [ˌʌnˈkuːl] **adj** *inf* pas cool.

uncooperative [ˌʌnkəʊˈɒpərətɪv] **adj** peu coopératif(ive).

uncork [ˌʌnˈkɔːk] **vt** déboucher.

uncorroborated [ˌʌnkəˈrɒbəreɪtɪd] **adj** non corroboré(e).

uncountable [ˌʌnˈkaʊntəbl] **adj 1.** [numberless] incalculable, innombrable **2.** GRAM non dénombrable.

uncouth [ʌnˈkuːθ] **adj** grossier(ère).

uncover [ʌnˈkʌvəʳ] **vt** découvrir.

uncritical [ˌʌnˈkrɪtɪkl] **adj** [naïve] dépourvu(e) d'esprit critique, non critique / [unquestioning] inconditionnel(elle).

uncultured [ˌʌnˈkʌltʃəd] **adj** [manners, person] inculte / [accent, speech] qui manque de raffinement.

uncurl [ˌʌnˈkɜːl] **vi** [hair] se défriser, se déboucler / [wire, snake] se dérouler.

uncut [ˌʌn'kʌt] **adj 1.** [film] intégral(e), sans coupures **2.** [jewel] brut(e), non taillé(e).

undamaged [ˌʌn'dæmɪdʒd] **adj** non endommagé(e), intact(e).

undaunted [ˌʌn'dɔːntɪd] **adj** non découragé(e).

undecided [ˌʌndɪ'saɪdɪd] **adj** [person] indécis(e), irrésolu(e) / [issue] indécis(e).

undefeated [ˌʌndɪ'fiːtɪd] **adj** invaincu(e).

undemanding [ˌʌndɪ'mɑːndɪŋ] **adj** [task] peu astreignant(e), peu exigeant(e) / [person] peu exigeant(e).

undemocratic ['ʌnˌdeməʊ'krætɪk] **adj** antidémocratique, peu démocratique.

undemonstrative [ˌʌndɪ'mɒnstrətɪv] **adj** peu expansif(ive), peu démonstratif(ive).

undeniable [ˌʌndɪ'naɪəbl] **adj** indéniable, incontestable.

undeniably [ˌʌndɪ'naɪəblɪ] **adv** [true] incontestablement, indiscutablement.

under ['ʌndər] ■ **prep 1.** [gen] sous ▸ **I can't see anything under it** je ne vois rien (en-)dessous ▸ **he wore a white shirt under his jacket** il portait une chemise blanche sous sa veste ▸ **it can only be seen under a microscope** on ne peut le voir qu'au microscope
2. [less than] moins de ▸ **children under five** les enfants de moins de cinq ans ▸ **everything is under £5** tout est à moins de 5 livres
3. [subject to - effect, influence] sous ▸ **under duress/threat** sous la contrainte/la menace ▸ **under sedation/treatment** MED sous calmants/traitement ▸ **under the circumstances** dans ces circonstances, étant donné les circonstances ▸ **to be under an obligation to sb** être redevable à qqn, avoir une dette de reconnaissance envers qqn ▸ **to be under the impression that...** avoir l'impression que... ▸ **she has two assistants under her** elle a deux assistants sous ses ordres
4. [undergoing] **: under consideration** à l'étude, à l'examen ▸ **under discussion** en discussion ▸ **under review** qui doit être révisé
5. [according to] selon, conformément à ▸ **under the new law, all this will change** avec la nouvelle loi, tout ceci va changer ▸ **under (the terms of) his will/the agreement** selon (les termes de) son testament/l'accord
6. [in classification] **: she writes under the name of Heidi Croft** elle écrit sous le nom de Heidi Croft.
■ **adv 1.** [underneath] dessous / [underwater] sous l'eau ▸ **to go under** [company] couler, faire faillite
2. [less] au-dessous ▸ **items at £20 and under** des articles à 20 livres et au-dessous ▸ **you have to be 16 or under to enter** il faut avoir 16 ans ou moins pour se présenter.

under- **prefix** sous-.

underachiever [ˌʌndərə'tʃiːvər] **n** *personne dont les résultats ne correspondent pas à ses possibilités.*

underage [ʌndər'eɪdʒ] **adj** mineur(e) ▸ **underage drinking** consommation *f* d'alcool par les mineurs ▸ **underage sex** rapports *mpl* sexuels entre des mineurs.

underarm ['ʌndərɑːm] ■ **adj** [deodorant] pour les aisselles.
■ **adv** [throw, bowl] par en-dessous.

underbrush ['ʌndəbrʌʃ] **n** *(U) US* sous-bois *m inv.*

undercarriage ['ʌndəˌkærɪdʒ] **n** train *m* d'atterrissage.

undercharge [ˌʌndə'tʃɑːdʒ] **vt** faire payer insuffisamment à.

underclothes ['ʌndəkləʊðz] **npl** sous-vêtements *mpl.*

undercoat ['ʌndəkəʊt] **n** [of paint] couche *f* de fond.

undercook [ˌʌndə'kʊk] **vt** ne pas assez cuire.

undercover ['ʌndəˌkʌvər] ■ **adj** secret(ète).
■ **adv** clandestinement.

undercurrent ['ʌndəˌkʌrənt] **n** *fig* [tendency] courant *m* sous-jacent.

undercut [ˌʌndə'kʌt] (pt & pp **undercut**, cont **-ting**) **vt** [in price] vendre moins cher que.

underdeveloped [ˌʌndədɪ'veləpt] **adj** [country] sous-développé(e) / [person] qui n'est pas complètement développé(e) ***OR*** formé(e).

underdog ['ʌndədɒg] **n : the underdog** l'opprimé *m* / SPORT celui (celle) que l'on donne perdant(e).

underdone [ˌʌndə'dʌn] **adj** [food] pas assez cuit(e) / [steak] saignant(e).

underemployment [ˌʌndərɪm'plɔɪmənt] **n** sous-emploi *m.*

underestimate ■ **n** [ʌndər'estɪmət] sous-estimation *f.*
■ **vt** [ˌʌndər'estɪmeɪt] sous-estimer.

underestimation ['ʌndərˌestɪ'meɪʃn] **n** sous-estimation *f.*

underexposed [ˌʌndərɪk'spəʊzd] **adj** PHOT sous-exposé(e).

underfinanced [ˌʌndə'faɪnænst] **adj** insuffisamment financé(e).

underfoot [ˌʌndə'fʊt] **adv** sous les pieds ▸ **to trample sthg underfoot** fouler qqch aux pieds ▸ **the ground underfoot** le sol.

undergo [ˌʌndə'gəʊ] (pt **-went**, pp **-gone** [-'gɒn]) **vt** subir / [pain, difficulties] éprouver.

undergraduate [ˌʌndə'grædjʊət] ■ **adj** [course, studies] pour étudiants de licence.
■ **n** étudiant *m*, -e *f* qui prépare la licence.

underground ■ **adj** ['ʌndəgraʊnd] **1.** [below the ground] souterrain(e) **2.** *fig* [secret] clandestin(e).
■ **adv** [ˌʌndə'graʊnd] **: to go/be forced underground** entrer dans la clandestinité.
■ **n** ['ʌndəgraʊnd] **1.** *UK* [subway] métro *m* **2.** [activist movement] résistance *f.*

underground economy **n** économie *f* souterraine ***OR*** immergée.

undergrowth ['ʌndəgrəʊθ] **n** *(U)* sous-bois *m inv.*

underhand [ˌʌndə'hænd] **adj** sournois(e), en dessous.

underinsured [ˌʌndərɪn'ʃʊəd] **adj** sous-assuré(e).

underlay ['ʌndəleɪ] **n** [for carpet] thibaude *f.*

underlie [ˌʌndə'laɪ] (pt **underlay** [ˌʌndə'leɪ], pp **underlain** [ˌʌndə'leɪn]) **vt** sous-tendre, être à la base de.

underline [ˌʌndə'laɪn] **vt** souligner.

underlying [ˌʌndə'laɪɪŋ] **adj** sous-jacent(e).

undermanned [ˌʌndəˈmænd] **adj** à court de personnel *OR* de main d'œuvre.

undermentioned [ˌʌndəˈmenʃnd] **adj** *fml* (cité(e)) ci-dessous.

undermine [ˌʌndəˈmaɪn] **vt** *fig* [weaken] saper, ébranler.

underneath [ˌʌndəˈni:θ] ■ **prep 1.** [beneath] sous, au-dessous de **2.** [in movements] sous.
■ **adv 1.** [beneath] en dessous, dessous **2.** *fig* [fundamentally] au fond.
■ **adj** *inf* d'en dessous.
■ **n** [underside] **: the underneath** le dessous.

undernourished [ˌʌndəˈnʌrɪʃt] **adj** sous-alimenté(e).

underpaid ■ **pt & pp** [ˌʌndəˈpeɪd] ➤ ***underpay***.
■ **adj** [ˈʌndəpeɪd] sous-payé(e).

underpants [ˈʌndəpænts] **npl** slip *m*.

underpass [ˈʌndəpɑ:s] **n** [for cars] passage *m* inférieur / [for pedestrians] passage *m* souterrain.

underpay [ˌʌndəˈpeɪ] (**pt & pp -paid**) **vt** sous-payer.

underperform [ˌʌndəpəˈfɔ:m] **vi** rester en deçà de ses possibilités.

underpin [ˌʌndəˈpɪn] (**pt & pp -ned, cont -ning**) **vt** étayer.

underplay [ˌʌndəˈpleɪ] **vt** réduire l'importance de, minimiser.

underprice [ˌʌndəˈpraɪs] **vt** mettre un prix trop bas à.

underprivileged [ˌʌndəˈprɪvɪlɪdʒd] **adj** défavorisé(e), déshérité(e).

underproduction [ˌʌndəprəˈdʌkʃn] **n** sous-production *f*.

underrated [ˌʌndəˈreɪtɪd] **adj** sous-estimé(e).

underscore [ˌʌndəˈskɔ:ʳ] **vt** *lit & fig* souligner.

undersea [ˈʌndəsi:] **adj** sous-marin(e).

undersecretary [ˌʌndəˈsekrətərɪ] (**pl -ies**) **n** sous-secrétaire *m*.

undersell [ˌʌndəˈsel] (**pt & pp -sold**) **vt** COMM vendre moins cher que ▸ **to undersell o.s.** *fig* ne pas se mettre assez en valeur.

undershirt [ˈʌndəʃɜ:t] **n** *US* maillot *m* de corps.

underside [ˈʌndəsaɪd] **n : the underside** le dessous.

undersigned [ˈʌndəsaɪnd] **n** *fml* **: I, the undersigned** je soussigné(e).

undersize(d) [ˌʌndəˈsaɪz(d)] **adj** trop petit(e).

underskirt [ˈʌndəskɜ:t] **n** jupon *m*.

undersold [ˌʌndəˈsəʊld] **pt & pp** ➤ ***undersell***.

understaffed [ˌʌndəˈstɑ:ft] **adj** à court de personnel.

understand [ˌʌndəˈstænd] (**pt & pp -stood**) ■ **vt 1.** [gen] comprendre ▸ **is that understood?** est-ce compris? ▸ **I understand your need to be independent** je comprends bien que vous ayez besoin d'être indépendant ▸ **to make o.s. understood** se faire comprendre **2.** *fml* [be informed] **: I understand (that)...** je crois comprendre que..., il paraît que... ▸ **I understand you need a loan** j'ai cru comprendre que *OR* si j'ai bien compris, vous avez besoin d'un prêt ▸ **they are understood to have fled the country** il paraît qu'ils ont fui le pays **3.** [interpret] entendre ▸ **what do you understand by "soon"?** qu'est-ce que vous entendez par "bientôt" ? ▸ **the object of the sentence is understood** GRAM l'objet de la phrase est sous-entendu.
■ **vi** comprendre ▸ **if you do that once more you're out, understand?** faites ça encore une fois et vous êtes viré, compris?

understandable [ˌʌndəˈstændəbl] **adj** compréhensible.

understandably [ˌʌndəˈstændəblɪ] **adv 1.** [speak] de façon compréhensible **2.** [naturally] naturellement.

understanding [ˌʌndəˈstændɪŋ] ■ **n 1.** [knowledge, sympathy] compréhension *f* ▸ **it was my understanding that...** j'avais compris que... ▸ **they have little understanding of what the decision involves** ils ne comprennent pas très bien ce que la décision entraînera ▸ **he showed great understanding** il a fait preuve de beaucoup de compréhension **2.** [agreement] accord *m*, arrangement *m* ▸ **to come to an understanding (over)** s'entendre (sur) ▸ **on the understanding that...** à condition que... *(+ subjunctive)*.
■ **adj** [sympathetic] compréhensif(ive).

understandingly [ˌʌndəˈstændɪŋlɪ] **adv** avec compréhension, avec bienveillance.

understate [ˌʌndəˈsteɪt] **vt** réduire l'importance de, minimiser.

understated [ˌʌndəˈsteɪtɪd] **adj** discret (ète).

understatement [ˌʌndəˈsteɪtmənt] **n 1.** [inadequate statement] affirmation *f* en dessous de la vérité **2.** *(U)* [quality of understating] euphémisme *m*.

understood [ˌʌndəˈstʊd] **pt & pp** ➤ ***understand***.

HOW TO ...

say you have or haven't understood

Saying you have understood

Ah oui, je comprends maintenant / Oh yes, now I understand
Ça y est, j'ai compris maintenant / Now I get it
Oui, je vois où vous voulez en venir / Yes, I see what you're getting at
Oui oui, d'accord / Yes, OK
Ah d'accord... ! / Oh, I see...!

Saying you haven't understood

Excusez-moi, mais je ne suis pas sûr d'avoir bien compris / Sorry, but I'm not sure that I've understood correctly
Attendez, là je ne vous suis plus ! / Hold on, you've lost me there!
Je suis un peu perdu là... / I'm a little confused...
Désolé, mais je ne comprends toujours pas / Sorry, but I still don't understand

understudy ['ʌndəˌstʌdɪ] (pl **-ies**) **n** doublure *f*.

undertake [ˌʌndə'teɪk] (pt **-took**, pp **-taken** [-'teɪkn]) **vt 1.** [take on - gen] entreprendre / [- responsibility] assumer **2.** [promise] **: to undertake to do sthg** promettre de faire qqch, s'engager à faire qqch.

undertaker ['ʌndəˌteɪkəʳ] **n** entrepreneur *m* des pompes funèbres.

undertaking [ˌʌndə'teɪkɪŋ] **n 1.** [task] entreprise *f* **2.** [promise] promesse *f*.

undertone ['ʌndətəʊn] **n 1.** [quiet voice] voix *f* basse **2.** [vague feeling] courant *m*.

undertook [ˌʌndə'tʊk] **pt** ➤ ***undertake***.

undertow ['ʌndətəʊ] **n** courant *m* sous-marin.

undervalue [ˌʌndə'væljuː] **vt** [house, antique] sous-évaluer / [person] sous-estimer, mésestimer.

underwater [ˌʌndə'wɔːtəʳ] ■ **adj** sous-marin(e).
■ **adv** sous l'eau.

underwear ['ʌndəweəʳ] **n** *(U)* sous-vêtements *mpl*.

underweight [ˌʌndə'weɪt] **adj** qui ne pèse pas assez, qui est trop maigre.

underwent [ˌʌndə'went] **pt** ➤ ***undergo***.

underworld ['ʌndəˌwɜːld] **n** [criminal society] **: the underworld** le milieu, la pègre.

underwrite ['ʌndəraɪt] (pt **-wrote**, pp **-written**) **vt 1.** FIN garantir **2.** [in insurance] garantir, assurer contre.

underwriter ['ʌndəˌraɪtəʳ] **n** assureur *m*.

underwritten ['ʌndəˌrɪtn] **pp** ➤ ***underwrite***.

underwrote ['ʌndərəʊt] **pt** ➤ ***underwrite***.

undeserved [ˌʌndɪ'zɜːvd] **adj** immérité(e).

undeservedly [ˌʌndɪ'zɜːvɪdlɪ] **adv** injustement, indûment.

undeserving [ˌʌndɪ'zɜːvɪŋ] **adj** [person] peu méritant(e) / [cause] peu méritoire ▸ **he is quite undeserving of such praise** il est parfaitement indigne de ***OR*** il ne mérite pas du tout de telles louanges.

undesirable [ˌʌndɪ'zaɪərəbl] **adj** indésirable.

undeveloped [ˌʌndɪ'veləpt] **adj** [land] non exploité(e), inexploité(e).

undid [ˌʌn'dɪd] **pt** ➤ ***undo***.

undies ['ʌndɪz] **npl** *inf* dessous *mpl*, lingerie *f*.

undignified [ʌn'dɪgnɪfaɪd] **adj** peu digne, qui manque de dignité.

undiluted [ˌʌndaɪ'ljuːtɪd] **adj 1.** [quality, emotion] sans mélange **2.** [liquid] non dilué(e).

undiplomatic [ˌʌndɪplə'mætɪk] **adj** peu diplomate.

undischarged [ˌʌndɪs'tʃɑːdʒd] **adj** [debt] non acquitté(e), non liquidé(e) ▸ **undischarged bankrupt** [person] failli *m* non réhabilité.

undisciplined [ʌn'dɪsɪplɪnd] **adj** indiscipliné(e).

undiscovered [ˌʌndɪ'skʌvəd] **adj** non découvert(e).

undiscriminating [ˌʌndɪs'krɪmɪneɪtɪŋ] **adj** qui manque de discernement.

undisguised [ˌʌndɪs'gaɪzd] **adj** non déguisé(e), non dissimulé(e).

undisputed [ˌʌndɪ'spjuːtɪd] **adj** incontesté(e).

undistinguished [ˌʌndɪ'stɪŋgwɪʃt] **adj** médiocre, quelconque.

undivided [ˌʌndɪ'vaɪdɪd] **adj** indivisé(e), entier(ère).

undo [ˌʌn'duː] (pt **-did**, pp **-done**) **vt 1.** [unfasten] défaire **2.** [nullify] annuler, détruire.

undoing [ˌʌn'duːɪŋ] **n** *(U) fml* perte *f*, ruine *f*.

undone [ˌʌn'dʌn] ■ **pp** ➤ ***undo***.
■ **adj 1.** [unfastened] défait(e) **2.** [task] non accompli(e).

undoubted [ʌn'daʊtɪd] **adj** indubitable, certain(e).

undoubtedly [ʌn'daʊtɪdlɪ] **adv** sans aucun doute.

undreamed-of [ʌn'driːmdɒv], ***undreamt-of*** [ʌn'dremtɒv] **adj** inimaginable.

undress [ˌʌn'dres] ■ **vt** déshabiller.
■ **vi** se déshabiller.

undressed [ˌʌn'drest] **adj** déshabillé(e) ▸ **to get undressed** se déshabiller.

undrinkable [ˌʌn'drɪŋkəbl] **adj** [unfit to drink] non potable / [disgusting] imbuvable.

undue [ˌʌn'djuː] **adj** *fml* excessif(ive).

undulate ['ʌndjʊleɪt] **vi** onduler.

undulating ['ʌndjʊleɪtɪŋ] **adj** [curves, hills] onduleux(euse).

unduly [ˌʌn'djuːlɪ] **adv** *fml* trop, excessivement.

undying [ʌn'daɪɪŋ] **adj** *liter* éternel(elle).

unearned income [ˌʌnɜːnd-] **n** *(U)* rentes *fpl*.

unearth [ˌʌn'ɜːθ] **vt 1.** [dig up] déterrer **2.** *fig* [discover] découvrir, dénicher.

unearthly [ʌn'ɜːθlɪ] **adj 1.** [ghostly] mystérieux(euse) **2.** *inf* [uncivilized - time of day] indu(e), impossible.

unease [ʌn'iːz] **n** *(U)* malaise *m*.

uneasily [ʌn'iːzɪlɪ] **adv 1.** [anxiously - wait, watch] anxieusement, avec inquiétude / [- sleep] d'un sommeil agité **2.** [with embarrassment] avec gêne, mal à l'aise.

uneasy [ʌn'iːzɪ] (comp **-ier**, superl **-iest**) **adj** [person, feeling] mal à l'aise, gêné(e) / [peace] troublé(e), incertain(e) / [silence] gêné(e).

uneatable [ˌʌn'iːtəbl] **adj** [not fit to eat] non comestible / [disgusting] immangeable.

uneaten [ˌʌn'iːtn] **adj** non mangé(e).

uneconomic ['ʌnˌiːkə'nɒmɪk] **adj** peu économique, peu rentable.

uneconomical ['ʌnˌiːkə'nɒmɪkl] **adj** [wasteful] peu rentable.

uneducated [ˌʌn'edjʊkeɪtɪd] **adj** [person] sans instruction.

unelectable [ˌʌnɪ'lektəbl] **adj** [person] inéligible / [party] incapable de remporter des élections.

unemotional [ˌʌnɪ'məʊʃənl] **adj** qui ne montre ***OR*** trahit aucune émotion.

unemployable [ˌʌnɪm'plɔɪəbl] **adj** inapte au travail.

unemployed [ˌʌnɪm'plɔɪd] ■ **adj** au chômage, sans travail.
■ **npl : the unemployed** les chômeurs *mpl*.

unemployment [ˌʌnɪm'plɔɪmənt] **n** chômage *m*.

unemployment benefit UK, ***unemployment compensation*** US **n** allocation *f* de chômage.

unending [ʌn'endɪŋ] **adj** sans fin, interminable.

unenthusiastic [ʌnɪnˌθjuːzɪ'æstɪk] **adj** peu enthousiaste.

unenthusiastically [ˌʌnɪnθjuːzɪ'æstɪklɪ] **adv** [say] sans enthousiasme / [welcome] tièdement.

unenviable [ˌʌn'envɪəbl] **adj** peu enviable.

unequal [ˌʌn'iːkwəl] **adj 1.** [different] inégal(e) **2.** [unfair] injuste.

unequalled UK, ***unequaled*** US [ˌʌn'iːkwəld] **adj** inégalé(e).

unequivocal [ˌʌnɪ'kwɪvəkl] **adj** sans équivoque.

unequivocally [ˌʌnɪ'kwɪvəklɪ] **adv** sans équivoque, clairement.

unerring [ˌʌn'ɜːrɪŋ] **adj** sûr(e), infaillible.

UNESCO [juː'neskəʊ] (abbr of ***United Nations Educational, Scientific and Cultural Organization***) **n** UNESCO *f*, Unesco *f*.

unethical [ʌn'eθɪkl] **adj** immoral(e).

uneven [ˌʌn'iːvn] **adj 1.** [not flat - surface] inégal(e) / [- ground] accidenté(e) **2.** [inconsistent] inégal(e) **3.** [unfair] injuste.

unevenly [ˌʌn'iːvnlɪ] **adv 1.** [divide, spread] inégalement ▸ **the contestants are unevenly matched** les adversaires ne sont pas de force égale **2.** [cut, draw] irrégulièrement.

uneventful [ˌʌnɪ'ventfʊl] **adj** sans incidents.

unexceptional [ˌʌnɪk'sepʃənl] **adj** qui n'a rien d'exceptionnel.

unexpected [ˌʌnɪk'spektɪd] **adj** inattendu(e), imprévu(e).

unexpectedly [ˌʌnɪk'spektɪdlɪ] **adv** subitement, d'une manière imprévue.

unexplained [ˌʌnɪk'spleɪnd] **adj** inexpliqué(e).

unexploded [ˌʌnɪk'spləʊdɪd] **adj** [bomb] non explosé(e), non éclaté(e).

unexpurgated [ˌʌn'ekspəgeɪtɪd] **adj** non expurgé(e), intégral(e).

unfailing [ʌn'feɪlɪŋ] **adj** qui ne se dément pas, constant(e).

unfailingly [ʌn'feɪlɪŋlɪ] **adv** inlassablement, toujours.

unfair [ˌʌn'feəʳ] **adj** injuste.

unfair dismissal **n** licenciement *m* injuste ***OR*** abusif.

unfairly [ˌʌn'feəlɪ] **adv** [treat] inéquitablement, injustement / [compete] déloyalement ▸ **to be unfairly dismissed** INDUST être victime d'un licenciement abusif.

unfairness [ˌʌn'feənɪs] **n** injustice *f*.

unfaithful [ˌʌn'feɪθfʊl] **adj** infidèle.

unfaithfully [ˌʌn'feɪθfʊlɪ] **adv** infidèlement.

unfamiliar [ˌʌnfə'mɪljəʳ] **adj 1.** [not well-known] peu familier(ère), peu connu(e) **2.** [not acquainted] **: to be unfamiliar with sb/sthg** mal connaître qqn/qqch, ne pas connaître qqn/qqch.

unfashionable [ˌʌn'fæʃnəbl] **adj** démodé(e), passé(e) de mode / [person] qui n'est plus à la mode.

unfasten [ˌʌn'fɑːsn] **vt** défaire.

unfavourable UK, ***unfavorable*** US [ˌʌn'feɪvrəbl] **adj** défavorable.

unfavourably UK, ***unfavorably*** US [ˌʌn'feɪvrəblɪ] **adv** défavorablement.

unfazed [ʌn'feɪzd] **adj** *inf* imperturbable, impassible.

unfeeling [ʌn'fiːlɪŋ] **adj** impitoyable, insensible.

unfinished [ˌʌn'fɪnɪʃt] **adj** inachevé(e).

unfit [ˌʌn'fɪt] **adj 1.** [not in good health] qui n'est pas en forme **2.** [not suitable] **: unfit (for)** impropre (à) / [person] inapte (à).

unflagging [ˌʌn'flægɪŋ] **adj** inlassable, infatigable.

unflappable [ˌʌn'flæpəbl] **adj** *esp UK* imperturbable, flegmatique.

unflattering [ˌʌn'flætərɪŋ] **adj** peu flatteur(euse).

unflinching [ʌn'flɪntʃɪŋ] **adj** inébranlable.

unfold [ʌn'fəʊld] ■ **vt 1.** [map, newspaper] déplier **2.** [explain - plan, proposal] exposer.
■ **vi** [become clear] se dérouler.

unforeseeable [ˌʌnfɔː'siːəbl] **adj** imprévisible.

unforeseen [ˌʌnfɔː'siːn] **adj** imprévu(e).

unforgettable [ˌʌnfə'getəbl] **adj** inoubliable.

unforgivable [ˌʌnfə'gɪvəbl] **adj** impardonnable.

unforgivably [ˌʌnfə'gɪvəblɪ] **adv** impardonnablement.

unforgiving [ˌʌnfə'gɪvɪŋ] **adj** implacable, impitoyable, sans merci.

unformatted [ˌʌn'fɔːmætɪd] **adj** COMPUT non formaté(e).

unforthcoming [ʌnˌfɔːθ'kʌmɪŋ] **adj : he was very unforthcoming about the date of the elections** il s'est montré très discret sur la date des élections.

unfortunate [ʌn'fɔːtʃnət] **adj 1.** [unlucky] malheureux(euse), malchanceux(euse) **2.** [regrettable] regrettable, fâcheux(euse).

unfortunately [ʌn'fɔːtʃnətlɪ] **adv** malheureusement.

unfounded [ˌʌn'faʊndɪd] **adj** sans fondement, dénué(e) de tout fondement.

unfriendly [ˌʌn'frendlɪ] (**comp -ier, superl -iest**) **adj** hostile, malveillant(e).

unfulfilled [ˌʌnfʊl'fɪld] **adj 1.** [ambition, potential, prophecy] non réalisé(e), inaccompli(e) / [promise] non tenu(e) **2.** [person, life] insatisfait(e), frustré(e).

unfurl [ˌʌn'fɜːl] **vt** déployer.

unfurnished [ˌʌn'fɜːnɪʃt] **adj** non meublé(e).

ungainly [ʌn'geɪnlɪ] **adj** gauche.

ungenerous [ˌʌn'dʒenərəs] **adj 1.** [mean - person] peu généreux(euse) / [- amount] mesquin(e) **2.** [unkind] peu charitable, mesquin(e).

ungodly [ˌʌn'gɒdlɪ] **adj 1.** [irreligious] impie, irréligieux(euse) **2.** *inf* [unreasonable] indu(e), impossible.

ungracious [ˌʌn'greɪʃəs] **adj** désagréable.

ungrammatical [ˌʌngrəˈmætɪkl] **adj** agrammatical(e), non grammatical(e).

ungrateful [ʌnˈgreɪtfʊl] **adj** ingrat(e), peu reconnaissant(e).

ungratefully [ʌnˈgreɪtfʊlɪ] **adv** de manière ingrate, avec ingratitude.

ungratefulness [ʌnˈgreɪtfʊlnɪs] **n** ingratitude *f*.

unguarded [ˌʌnˈgɑːdɪd] **adj 1.** [house, camp] sans surveillance **2.** [careless] **: in an unguarded moment** dans un moment d'inattention.

unhappily [ʌnˈhæpɪlɪ] **adv 1.** [sadly] tristement **2.** [unfortunately] malheureusement.

unhappiness [ʌnˈhæpɪnɪs] **n** *(U)* tristesse *f*, chagrin *m*.

unhappy [ʌnˈhæpɪ] (comp **-ier**, superl **-iest**) **adj 1.** [sad] triste, malheureux(euse) **2.** [uneasy] **: to be unhappy (with *OR* about)** être inquiet(ète) (au sujet de) **3.** [unfortunate] malheureux(euse), regrettable.

unharmed [ˌʌnˈhɑːmd] **adj** indemne, sain et sauf (saine et sauve).

UNHCR (abbr of ***United Nations High Commission for Refugees***) **n** HCR *m*.

unhealthily [ʌnˈhelθɪlɪ] **adv** d'une manière malsaine.

unhealthy [ʌnˈhelθɪ] (comp **-ier**, superl **-iest**) **adj 1.** [person, skin] maladif(ive) / [conditions, place] insalubre, malsain(e) / [habit] malsain **2.** *fig* [undesirable] malsain(e).

unheard [ˌʌnˈhɜːd] **adj : her warning went unheard** on n'a pas tenu compte de son avertissement.

unheard-of [ʌnˈhɜːdɒv] **adj 1.** [unknown] inconnu(e) **2.** [unprecedented] sans précédent, inouï(e).

unheeded [ˌʌnˈhiːdɪd] **adj : his advice went unheeded** on n'a pas suivi *OR* écouté ses conseils.

unhelpful [ˌʌnˈhelpfʊl] **adj 1.** [person, attitude] peu serviable, peu obligeant(e) **2.** [advice, book] qui n'aide en rien, peu utile.

unhesitating [ʌnˈhezɪteɪtɪŋ] **adj** [reply] immédiat(e), spontané(e) / [belief] résolu(e), ferme / [person] résolu(e), qui n'hésite pas.

unhindered [ʌnˈhɪndəd] **adj** sans obstacles, sans encombre.

unhinged [ˌʌnˈhɪndʒd] **adj** déséquilibré(e).

unhook [ˌʌnˈhʊk] **vt 1.** [dress, bra] dégrafer **2.** [coat, picture, trailer] décrocher.

unhurt [ˌʌnˈhɜːt] **adj** indemne, sain et sauf (saine et sauve).

unhygienic [ˌʌnhaɪˈdʒiːnɪk] **adj** non hygiénique.

UNICEF [ˈjuːnɪˌsef] (abbr of ***United Nations International Children's Emergency Fund***) **n** UNICEF *m*, Unicef *m*.

unicorn [ˈjuːnɪkɔːn] **n** licorne *f*.

unicycle [ˈjuːnɪsaɪkl] **n** monocyle *m*.

unidentified [ˌʌnaɪˈdentɪfaɪd-] **adj** non identifié(e).

unidentified flying object **n** objet *m* volant non identifié.

unification [ˌjuːnɪfɪˈkeɪʃn] **n** unification *f*.

uniform [ˈjuːnɪfɔːm] ■ **adj** [rate, colour] uniforme / [size] même.

■ **n** uniforme *m*.

uniformity [ˌjuːnɪˈfɔːmətɪ] **n** uniformité *f*.

uniformly [ˈjuːnɪfɔːmlɪ] **adv** uniformément.

unify [ˈjuːnɪfaɪ] (pt & pp **-ied**) **vt** unifier.

unifying [ˈjuːnɪfaɪɪŋ] **adj** qui unifie, unificateur(trice).

unilateral [ˌjuːnɪˈlætərəl] **adj** unilatéral(e).

unilateral disarmament **n** désarmement *m* unilatéral.

unilaterally [ˌjuːnɪˈlætərəlɪ] **adv 1.** [act, decide] unilatéralement **2.** MED **: to be paralysed unilaterally** être paralysé d'un seul côté, être hémiplégique.

unimaginable [ˌʌnɪˈmædʒɪnəbl] **adj** inimaginable, inconcevable.

unimaginably [ˌʌnɪˈmædʒɪnəblɪ] **adv** incroyablement, invraisemblablement.

unimaginative [ˌʌnɪˈmædʒɪnətɪv] **adj** qui manque d'imagination, peu imaginatif(ive).

unimpaired [ˌʌnɪmˈpeəd] **adj** intact(e).

unimpeded [ˌʌnɪmˈpiːdɪd] **adj** sans entrave.

unimportant [ˌʌnɪmˈpɔːtənt] **adj** sans importance, peu important(e).

unimpressed [ˌʌnɪmˈprest] **adj** qui n'est pas impressionné(e).

uninformed [ˌʌnɪnˈfɔːmd] **adj** [person] non informé(e) / [opinion] mal informé(e) / [reader] non averti(e) ▸ **to make an uninformed guess** deviner au hasard.

uninhabitable [ˌʌnɪnˈhæbɪtəbl] **adj** inhabitable.

uninhabited [ˌʌnɪnˈhæbɪtɪd] **adj** inhabité(e).

uninhibited [ˌʌnɪnˈhɪbɪtɪd] **adj** sans inhibitions, qui n'a pas d'inhibitions.

uninitiated [ˌʌnɪˈnɪʃɪeɪtɪd] **npl : the uninitiated** les non-initiés, les profanes.

uninjured [ˌʌnˈɪndʒəd] **adj** qui n'est pas blessé(e), indemne.

uninspiring [ˌʌnɪnˈspaɪrɪŋ] **adj** qui n'a rien d'inspirant.

uninstall [ˌʌnɪnˈstɔːl] **vt** désinstaller.

unintelligent [ˌʌnɪnˈtelɪdʒənt] **adj** inintelligent(e).

unintentional [ˌʌnɪnˈtenʃənl] **adj** involontaire, non intentionnel(elle).

uninterested [ˌʌnˈɪntrəstɪd] **adj** indifférent(e).

uninterrupted [ˈʌnˌɪntəˈrʌptɪd] **adj** ininterrompu(e), continu(e).

uninvited [ˌʌnɪnˈvaɪtɪd] **adj** qui n'a pas été invité(e).

union [ˈjuːnjən] ■ **n 1.** [trade union] syndicat *m* **2.** [alliance] union *f*.

■ **comp** syndical(e).

union bashing **n** *UK inf* antisyndicalisme *m*.

unionism [ˈjuːnjənɪzm] **n 1.** INDUST syndicalisme *m* **2.** POL unionisme *m*.

unionist [ˈjuːnjənɪst] ■ **adj** INDUST syndicaliste.

■ **n 1.** INDUST syndicaliste *mf* **2.** POL unioniste *mf* / [in American Civil War] nordiste *mf*.

unionize, *UK* **-ise** ['ju:njənaɪz] **vt** syndiquer.

Union Jack **n** *UK* **: the Union Jack** l'Union Jack *m*, le drapeau britannique.

union shop **n** *US* atelier *m* d'ouvriers syndiqués.

unique [ju:'ni:k] **adj 1.** [exceptional] unique, exceptionnel(elle) **2.** [exclusive] **: unique to** propre à **3.** [very special] unique.

uniquely [ju:'ni:klɪ] **adv 1.** [exclusively] uniquement **2.** [exceptionally] exceptionnellement.

unique selling point, ***unique selling proposition*** **n** proposition *f* unique de vente.

unisex ['ju:nɪseks] **adj** unisexe.

unison ['ju:nɪzn] **n** unisson *m* ▸ **in unison** à l'unisson / [say] en chœur, en même temps.

UNISON ['ju:nɪzn] **n** *"super-syndicat" britannique des services publics.*

unit ['ju:nɪt] **n 1.** [gen] unité *f* **2.** [machine part] élément *m*, bloc *m* **3.** [of furniture] élément *m* ▸ **storage unit** meuble *m* de rangement **4.** [department] service *m* **5.** [chapter] chapitre *m*.

unit cost **n** prix *m* de revient unitaire.

unite [ju:'naɪt] ■ **vt** unifier.
■ **vi** s'unir.

united [ju:'naɪtɪd] **adj 1.** [in harmony] uni(e) ▸ **to be united in sthg** être uni dans qqch **2.** [unified] unifié(e).

United Arab Emirates **npl : the United Arab Emirates** les Émirats *mpl* arabes unis.

united front **n : to present a united front** montrer un front uni.

United Kingdom **n : the United Kingdom** le Royaume-Uni.

CULTURE

United Kingdom

Le Royaume-Uni est composé de l'Angleterre, du pays de Galles, de l'Écosse et de l'Irlande du Nord, mais géographiquement le terme « Grande-Bretagne » désigne l'Angleterre, le pays de Galles et l'Écosse. Les îles britanniques comprennent la Grande-Bretagne, l'Irlande du Nord et la République d'Irlande (Eire), ainsi que les îles environnantes (îles de Man, Hébrides, Orchades, Shetland, Scilly et Anglo-normandes).

United Nations **n : the United Nations** les Nations *fpl* Unies.

United States **n : the United States (of America)** les États-Unis *mpl* (d'Amérique) ▸ **in the United States** aux États-Unis.

unit price **n** prix *m* unitaire.

unit trust **n** *UK* société *f* d'investissement à capital variable.

unity ['ju:nətɪ] **n** *(U)* unité *f*.

Univ. abbr of ***University***.

universal [,ju:nɪ'vɜ:sl] **adj** universel(elle).

universal joint **n** joint *m* universel OR de cardan.

universally [,ju:nɪ'vɜ:səlɪ] **adv** universellement ▸ **a universally held opinion** une opinion qui prévaut partout ▸ **he is universally liked/admired** tout le monde l'aime bien/l'admire.

universe ['ju:nɪvɜ:s] **n** univers *m*.

university [,ju:nɪ'vɜ:sətɪ] ■ **n** (pl **-ies**) université *f*.
■ **comp** universitaire / [lecturer] d'université ▸ **university student** étudiant *m*, -e *f* à l'université.

unjust [,ʌn'dʒʌst] **adj** injuste.

unjustifiable [ʌn'dʒʌstɪfaɪəbl] **adj** injustifiable.

unjustifiably [ʌn'dʒʌstɪfaɪəblɪ] **adv** sans justification.

unjustified [ʌn'dʒʌstɪfaɪd] **adj** injustifié(e).

unjustly [,ʌn'dʒʌstlɪ] **adv** injustement, à tort.

unkempt [,ʌn'kempt] **adj** [clothes, person] négligé(e), débraillé(e) / [hair] mal peigné(e).

unkind [ʌn'kaɪnd] **adj 1.** [uncharitable] méchant(e), pas gentil(ille) **2.** *fig* [weather, climate] rude, rigoureux(euse).

unkindly [ʌn'kaɪndlɪ] **adv** méchamment.

unknowingly [,ʌn'nəʊɪŋlɪ] **adv** à mon/son *etc* insu, sans m'en/s'en *etc* apercevoir.

unknown [,ʌn'nəʊn] ■ **adj** inconnu(e).
■ **n** [person] inconnu *m*, -e *f* ▸ **the unknown** l'inconnu *m*.

unlace [,ʌn'leɪs] **vt** défaire, délacer.

unladen [,ʌn'leɪdn] **adj** sans charge ▸ **unladen weight** poids *m* à vide.

unlawful [,ʌn'lɔ:fʊl] **adj** illégal(e).

unlawfully [,ʌn'lɔ:fʊlɪ] **adv** illicitement, illégalement.

unleaded [,ʌn'ledɪd] ■ **adj** sans plomb.
■ **n** essence *f* sans plomb.

unleash [,ʌn'li:ʃ] **vt** *liter* déchaîner.

unleavened [,ʌn'levnd] **adj** sans levain, azyme.

unless [ən'les] **conj** à moins que *(+ subjunctive)* ▸ **unless I'm mistaken** à moins que je (ne) me trompe ▸ **unless otherwise informed** sauf avis contraire.

unlicensed [,ʌn'laɪsənst] **adj** [person] qui ne détient pas de licence / [activity] non autorisé(e), illicite / [vehicle] sans vignette / [restaurant, premises] qui ne détient pas de licence de débit de boissons.

unlike [,ʌn'laɪk] **prep 1.** [different from] différent(e) de **2.** [in contrast to] contrairement à, à la différence de **3.** [not typical of] **: it's unlike you to complain** cela ne te ressemble pas de te plaindre.

unlikely [ʌn'laɪklɪ] **adj 1.** [event, result] peu probable, improbable / [story] invraisemblable ▸ **in the unlikely event of my winning** au cas improbable où je gagnerais **2.** [bizarre - clothes] invraisemblable ▸ **he seems an unlikely choice** il semble un choix peu judicieux.

unlimited [ʌn'lɪmɪtɪd] **adj** illimité(e).

unlisted [ʌn'lɪstɪd] **adj** *US* [phone number] qui est sur la liste rouge.

unlit [,ʌn'lɪt] **adj 1.** [lamp, fire, cigarette] non allumé(e) **2.** [street, building] non éclairé(e).

unload [,ʌn'ləʊd] **vt** décharger ▸ **to unload sthg on** OR **onto sb** *fig* se décharger de qqch sur qqn.

unlock [ˌʌn'lɒk] **vt** ouvrir.

unloved [ˌʌn'lʌvd] **adj** qui n'est pas aimé(e) ▸ **to feel unloved** ne pas se sentir aimé.

unluckily [ʌn'lʌkɪlɪ] **adv** malheureusement.

unlucky [ʌn'lʌkɪ] (comp **-ier**, superl **-iest**) **adj 1.** [unfortunate - person] malchanceux(euse), qui n'a pas de chance / [- experience, choice] malheureux(euse) **2.** [object, number] qui porte malheur.

unmanageable [ʌn'mænɪdʒəbl] **adj** [vehicle, parcel] peu maniable / [hair] difficiles à coiffer.

unmanly [ˌʌn'mænlɪ] (comp **-ier**, superl **-iest**) **adj** qui n'est pas viril.

unmanned [ˌʌn'mænd] **adj** sans équipage.

unmarked [ˌʌn'mɑːkt] **adj 1.** [uninjured - body, face] sans marque **2.** [unidentified - box, suitcase] sans marque d'identification / [- police car] banalisé(e).

unmarried [ˌʌn'mærɪd] **adj** célibataire, qui n'est pas marié(e).

unmask [ˌʌn'mɑːsk] **vt** démasquer / [truth, hypocrisy] dévoiler.

unmatched [ˌʌn'mætʃt] **adj** sans pareil(eille).

unmentionable [ʌn'menʃnəbl] **adj** [subject] dont il ne faut pas parler / [word] qu'il ne faut pas dire.

unmetered [ʌn'miːtəd] **adj** illimité(e).

unmistakable [ˌʌnmɪ'steɪkəbl] **adj** facilement reconnaissable.

unmistakably [ˌʌnmɪ'steɪkəblɪ] **adv 1.** [undeniably] indéniablement, sans erreur possible **2.** [visibly] visiblement, manifestement.

unmitigated [ʌn'mɪtɪgeɪtɪd] **adj** [disaster] total(e) / [evil] non mitigé(e).

unmoved [ˌʌn'muːvd] **adj : unmoved (by)** indifférent(e) (à).

unnamed [ˌʌn'neɪmd] **adj** [person] anonyme / [object] sans dénomination.

unnatural [ʌn'nætʃrəl] **adj 1.** [unusual] anormal(e), qui n'est pas naturel(elle) **2.** [affected] peu naturel(elle) / [smile] forcé(e).

unnaturally [ʌn'nætʃrəlɪ] **adv** [behave, laugh, walk] bizarrement, de façon peu naturelle.

unnecessarily [*UK* ʌn'nesəsərɪlɪ, *US* ˌʌnnesə'serəlɪ] **adv** sans nécessité ***or*** raison.

unnecessary [ʌn'nesəsərɪ] **adj** [remark, expense, delay] inutile ▸ **it's unnecessary to do sthg** ce n'est pas la peine de faire qqch.

unnerving [ˌʌn'nɜːvɪŋ] **adj** troublant(e).

unnoticed [ˌʌn'nəʊtɪst] **adj** inaperçu(e).

UNO (abbr of ***United Nations Organization***) **n** ONU *m*, Onu *m*.

unobserved [ˌʌnəb'zɜːvd] **adj** inaperçu(e).

unobtainable [ˌʌnəb'teɪnəbl] **adj** impossible à obtenir.

unobtrusive [ˌʌnəb'truːsɪv] **adj** [person] effacé(e) / [object] discret(ète) / [building] que l'on remarque à peine.

unoccupied [ˌʌn'ɒkjʊpaɪd] **adj** [house] inhabité(e) / [seat] libre.

unofficial [ˌʌnə'fɪʃl] **adj** non officiel(elle).

unofficially [ˌʌnə'fɪʃəlɪ] **adv** [informally] officieusement / [in private] en privé.

unopened [ˌʌn'əʊpənd] **adj** non ouvert(e), qui n'a pas été ouvert(e).

unorthodox [ˌʌn'ɔːθədɒks] **adj** peu orthodoxe.

unpack [ˌʌn'pæk] ■ **vt** [suitcase] défaire / [box] vider / [clothes] déballer.
■ **vi** défaire ses bagages.

unpaid [ˌʌn'peɪd] **adj 1.** [person] bénévole / [work] sans rémunération, bénévole **2.** [rent] non acquitté(e) / [bill] impayé(e).

unpalatable [ʌn'pælətəbl] **adj** d'un goût désagréable / *fig* dur(e) à avaler.

unparalleled [ʌn'pærəleld] **adj** [success, crisis] sans précédent / [beauty] sans égal.

unpatriotic ['ʌnˌpætrɪ'ɒtɪk] **adj** [person] peu patriote / [act] antipatriotique.

UN peacekeeping forces **n** les casques *mpl* bleus.

unpick [ˌʌn'pɪk] **vt** découdre.

unpin [ˌʌn'pɪn] (pt & pp **-ned**, cont **-ning**) **vt** [sewing, hair] retirer les épingles de.

unplanned [ˌʌn'plænd] **adj** imprévu(e) / [pregnancy] accidentel(elle).

unpleasant [ʌn'pleznt] **adj** désagréable.

unpleasantly [ʌn'plezntlɪ] **adv** désagréablement, de façon déplaisante.

unpleasantness [ʌn'plezntnɪs] **n** caractère *m* désagréable.

unplug [ʌn'plʌg] (pt & pp **-ged**, cont **-ging**) **vt** débrancher.

unpolished [ˌʌn'pɒlɪʃt] **adj 1.** [not shined - floor] non poli(e) / [- furniture, shoes] non ciré(e) **2.** [not accomplished] peu raffiné(e).

unpolluted [ˌʌnpə'luːtɪd] **adj** non pollué(e).

unpopular [ˌʌn'pɒpjʊləʳ] **adj** impopulaire.

unpopularity ['ʌnˌpɒpjʊ'lærətɪ] **n** impopularité *f*.

unprecedented [ʌn'presɪdəntɪd] **adj** sans précédent.

unpredictable [ˌʌnprɪ'dɪktəbl] **adj** imprévisible.

unpredictably [ˌʌnprɪ'dɪktəblɪ] **adv** de façon imprévisible.

unprejudiced [ˌʌn'predʒʊdɪst] **adj** sans préjugés.

unprepared [ˌʌnprɪ'peəd] **adj** non préparé(e) ▸ **to be unprepared for sthg** ne pas s'attendre à qqch.

unprepossessing ['ʌnˌpriːpə'zesɪŋ] **adj** peu avenant(e).

unpretentious [ˌʌnprɪ'tenʃəs] **adj** sans prétention.

unprincipled [ʌn'prɪnsəpld] **adj** sans scrupules.

unprintable [ˌʌn'prɪntəbl] **adj** *fig* qu'on ne peut pas répéter, grossier(ère).

unproductive [ˌʌnprə'dʌktɪv] **adj** improductif(ive).

unprofessional [ˌʌnprəˈfeʃənl] **adj** [person, work] peu professionnel(elle) / [attitude] contraire à l'éthique de la profession.

unprofitable [ˌʌnˈprɒfɪtəbl] **adj** peu rentable.

UNPROFOR [ˈʌnprəfɔː] (abbr of ***United Nations Protection Force***) **n** FORPRONU *f.*

unprompted [ˌʌnˈprɒmptɪd] **adj** spontané(e).

unpronounceable [ˌʌnprəˈnaʊnsəbl] **adj** imprononçable.

unprotected [ˌʌnprəˈtektɪd] **adj** sans protection.

unprovoked [ˌʌnprəˈvəʊkt] **adj** sans provocation.

unpublished [ˌʌnˈpʌblɪʃt] **adj** inédit(e).

unpunished [ˌʌnˈpʌnɪʃt] **adj : to go unpunished** rester impuni(e).

unputdownable [ˌʌnpʊtˈdaʊnəbl] **adj** *UK inf* [book, novel] passionnant(e), dont on a du mal à s'arracher.

unqualified [ˌʌnˈkwɒlɪfaɪd] **adj 1.** [person] non qualifié(e) / [teacher, doctor] non diplômé(e) **2.** [success] formidable / [support] inconditionnel(elle).

unquestionable [ʌnˈkwestʃənəbl] **adj** [fact] incontestable / [honesty] certain(e).

unquestionably [ʌnˈkwestʃənəblɪ] **adv** indéniablement, incontestablement.

unquestioning [ʌnˈkwestʃənɪŋ] **adj** aveugle, absolu(e).

unravel [ʌnˈrævl] (*UK* **-led**, cont **-ling**, *US* **-ed**, cont **-ing**) **vt 1.** [undo - knitting] défaire / [- fabric] effiler / [- threads] démêler **2.** *fig* [solve] éclaircir.

unreadable [ˌʌnˈriːdəbl] **adj** illisible.

unreal [ˌʌnˈrɪəl] **adj** [strange] irréel(elle).

unrealistic [ˌʌnrɪəˈlɪstɪk] **adj** irréaliste.

unrealistically [ˌʌnrɪəˈlɪstɪklɪ] **adv : his hopes were unrealistically high** ses espoirs étaient trop grands pour être réalistes.

unreasonable [ʌnˈriːznəbl] **adj** qui n'est pas raisonnable, déraisonnable.

unreasonably [ʌnˈriːznəblɪ] **adv** déraisonnablement.

unrecognizable [ˌʌnˈrekəgnaɪzəbl] **adj** méconnaissable.

unrecognized [ˌʌnˈrekəgnaɪzd] **adj 1.** [person] non reconnu(e) **2.** [achievement, talent] méconnu(e).

unrecorded [ˌʌnrɪˈkɔːdɪd] **adj** non enregistré(e).

unrefined [ˌʌnrɪˈfaɪnd] **adj 1.** [not processed] non raffiné(e), brut(e) **2.** [vulgar] peu raffiné(e).

unrehearsed [ˌʌnrɪˈhɜːst] **adj** [performance] sans répétition / [speech, response] improvisé(e).

unrelated [ˌʌnrɪˈleɪtɪd] **adj : to be unrelated (to)** n'avoir aucun rapport (avec).

unrelenting [ˌʌnrɪˈlentɪŋ] **adj** implacable.

unreliability [ˈʌnrɪˌlaɪəˈbɪlətɪ] **n 1.** [of person] manque *m* de sérieux **2.** [of method, machine] manque *m* de fiabilité.

unreliable [ˌʌnrɪˈlaɪəbl] **adj** [machine, method] peu fiable / [person] sur qui on ne peut pas compter.

unrelieved [ˌʌnrɪˈliːvd] **adj** [pain, gloom] constant(e).

unremarkable [ˌʌnrɪˈmɑːkəbl] **adj** quelconque.

unremitting [ˌʌnrɪˈmɪtɪŋ] **adj** inlassable.

unrepeatable [ˌʌnrɪˈpiːtəbl] **adj** [comment] qu'on ne peut pas répéter.

unrepentant [ˌʌnrɪˈpentənt] **adj** impénitent(e).

unrepresentative [ˌʌnreprɪˈzentətɪv] **adj : unrepresentative (of)** peu représentatif(ive) (de).

unrequited [ˌʌnrɪˈkwaɪtɪd] **adj** non partagé(e).

unreserved [ˌʌnrɪˈzɜːvd] **adj 1.** [support, admiration] sans réserve **2.** [seat] non réservé(e).

unreservedly [ˌʌnrɪˈzɜːvɪdlɪ] **adv 1.** [without qualification] sans réserve, entièrement **2.** [frankly] sans réserve, franchement.

unresolved [ˌʌnrɪˈzɒlvd] **adj** non résolu(e).

unresponsive [ˌʌnrɪˈspɒnsɪv] **adj : to be unresponsive to** ne pas réagir à.

unrest [ˌʌnˈrest] **n** *(U)* troubles *mpl.*

unrestrained [ˌʌnrɪˈstreɪnd] **adj** effréné(e).

unrestricted [ˌʌnrɪˈstrɪktɪd] **adj** sans restriction, illimité(e).

unrewarding [ˌʌnrɪˈwɔːdɪŋ] **adj** ingrat(e).

unripe [ˌʌnˈraɪp] **adj** qui n'est pas mûr(e).

unrivalled *UK*, ***unrivaled*** *US* [ʌnˈraɪvld] **adj** sans égal(e).

unroll [ˌʌnˈrəʊl] **vt** dérouler.

unruffled [ˌʌnˈrʌfld] **adj** [person] imperturbable.

unruly [ʌnˈruːlɪ] (comp **-ier**, superl **-iest**) **adj** [crowd, child] turbulent(e) ▸ **unruly hair** les cheveux indisciplinés.

unsafe [ˌʌnˈseɪf] **adj 1.** [dangerous] dangereux(euse) **2.** [in danger] **: to feel unsafe** ne pas se sentir en sécurité.

unsaid [ˌʌnˈsed] **adj : to leave sthg unsaid** passer qqch sous silence.

unsaleable, *US* ***unsalable*** [ˌʌnˈseɪləbl] **adj** invendable.

unsatisfactory [ˈʌnˌsætɪsˈfæktərɪ] **adj** qui laisse à désirer, peu satisfaisant(e).

unsatisfied [ˌʌnˈsætɪsfaɪd] **adj 1.** [person - unhappy] insatisfait(e), mécontent(e) / [- unconvinced] non convaincu(e) **2.** [desire] insatisfait(e), inassouvi(e).

unsatisfying [ˌʌnˈsætɪsfaɪɪŋ] **adj 1.** [activity, task] peu gratifiant(e), ingrat(e) **2.** [unconvincing] peu convaincant(e) **3.** [meal - insufficient] insuffisant(e), peu nourrissant(e) / [- disappointing] décevant(e).

unsavoury *UK*, ***unsavory*** *US* [ˌʌnˈseɪvərɪ] **adj** [person] peu recommandable / [district] mal famé(e).

unscathed [ˌʌnˈskeɪðd] **adj** indemne.

unscheduled [*UK* ˌʌnˈʃedjuːld, *US* ˌʌnˈskedʒʊld] **adj** non prévu(e).

unscientific [ˈʌnˌsaɪənˈtɪfɪk] **adj** peu scientifique.

unscrew [ˌʌnˈskruː] **vt** dévisser.

unscripted [ˌʌnˈskrɪptɪd] **adj** improvisé(e).

unscrupulous [ʌnˈskruːpjʊləs] **adj** sans scrupules.

unscrupulously [ʌnˈskruːpjʊləslɪ] **adv** sans scrupules, peu scrupuleusement.

unseat [ˌʌn'siːt] **vt** **1.** [rider] désarçonner **2.** *fig* [MP] faire perdre son siège à / [leader] faire perdre sa position à.

unsecured loan [ˌʌn'sɪ'kjʊəd-] **n** prêt *m* non-garanti.

unseeded [ˌʌn'siːdɪd] **adj** qui n'est pas classé(e) en tête de série.

unseemly [ʌn'siːmlɪ] (comp **-ier**, superl **-iest**) **adj** inconvenant(e).

unseen [ˌʌn'siːn] **adj** [not observed] inaperçu(e).

unselfish [ˌʌn'selfɪʃ] **adj** désintéressé(e).

unselfishly [ˌʌn'selfɪʃlɪ] **adv** de manière désintéressée.

unsettle [ˌʌn'setl] **vt** perturber.

unsettled [ˌʌn'setld] **adj** **1.** [person] perturbé(e), troublé(e) **2.** [weather] variable, incertain(e) **3.** [argument] qui n'a pas été résolu(e) / [situation] incertain(e).

unsettling [ˌʌn'setlɪŋ] **adj** inquiétant(e).

unshak(e)able [ʌn'ʃeɪkəbl] **adj** inébranlable.

unshaven [ˌʌn'ʃeɪvn] **adj** non rasé(e).

unsheathe [ˌʌn'ʃiːð] **vt** dégainer.

unsightly [ʌn'saɪtlɪ] **adj** laid(e).

unskilled [ˌʌn'skɪld] **adj** non qualifié(e).

unsociable [ʌn'səʊʃəbl] **adj** sauvage.

unsocial [ˌʌn'səʊʃl] **adj : to work unsocial hours** *UK* travailler en dehors des heures normales.

unsold [ˌʌn'səʊld] **adj** invendu(e).

unsolicited [ˌʌnsə'lɪsɪtɪd] **adj** non sollicité(e).

unsolved [ˌʌn'sɒlvd] **adj** non résolu(e).

unsophisticated [ˌʌnsə'fɪstɪkeɪtɪd] **adj** simple.

unsound [ˌʌn'saʊnd] **adj** **1.** [theory] mal fondé(e) / [decision] peu judicieux(euse) **2.** [building, structure] en mauvais état.

unspeakable [ʌn'spiːkəbl] **adj** indescriptible.

unspeakably [ʌn'spiːkəblɪ] **adv** indescriptiblement.

unspecified [ˌʌn'spesɪfaɪd] **adj** non spécifié(e).

unspoiled [ˌʌn'spɔɪld], ***unspoilt*** [ˌʌn'spɔɪlt] **adj** intact(e) / [countryside] qui n'a pas été défiguré(e).

unspoken [ˌʌn'spəʊkən] **adj** [thought, wish] inexprimé(e) / [agreement] tacite.

unsporting [ˌʌn'spɔːtɪŋ] **adj** qui n'est pas fair-play.

unstable [ˌʌn'steɪbl] **adj** instable.

unstated [ˌʌn'steɪtɪd] **adj** non déclaré(e).

unsteadily [ˌʌn'stedɪlɪ] **adv** [walk] d'un pas chancelant **OR** incertain, en titubant / [speak] d'une voix mal assurée / [hold, write] d'une main tremblante.

unsteady [ˌʌn'stedɪ] (comp **-ier**, superl **-iest**) **adj** [hand] tremblant(e) / [table, ladder] instable.

unstinting [ˌʌn'stɪntɪŋ] **adj** [praise, support] sans réserve / [person] généreux(euse), prodigue.

unstoppable [ˌʌn'stɒpəbl] **adj** qu'on ne peut pas arrêter.

unstrap [ˌʌn'stræp] (pt & pp **-ped**, cont **-ping**) **vt** défaire les attaches de.

unstructured [ˌʌn'strʌktʃəd] **adj** non structuré(e).

unstuck [ˌʌn'stʌk] **adj : to come unstuck** [notice, stamp, label] se décoller / *fig* [plan, system] s'effondrer / *fig* [person] essuyer un échec.

unsubscribe [ˌʌnsəb'skraɪb] **vi : to unsubscribe (from)** se désinscrire (de).

unsubstantiated [ˌʌnsəb'stænʃɪeɪtɪd] **adj** sans fondement.

unsuccessful [ˌʌnsək'sesfʊl] **adj** [attempt] vain(e) / [meeting] infructueux(euse) / [candidate] refusé(e).

unsuccessfully [ˌʌnsək'sesfʊlɪ] **adv** en vain, sans succès.

unsuitable [ˌʌn'suːtəbl] **adj** qui ne convient pas / [clothes] peu approprié(e) ▸ **to be unsuitable for** ne pas convenir à.

unsuitably [ˌʌn'suːtəblɪ] **adv** [behave] de façon inconvenante / [dress] d'une manière inadéquate.

unsuited [ˌʌn'suːtɪd] **adj** **1.** [not appropriate] **: to be unsuited to/for** ne pas convenir à/pour **2.** [not compatible] **: to be unsuited (to each other)** ne pas aller ensemble.

unsung [ˌʌn'sʌŋ] **adj** [hero] méconnu(e).

unsure [ˌʌn'ʃɔːʳ] **adj** **1.** [not certain] **: to be unsure (about/of)** ne pas être sûr(e) (de) **2.** [not confident] **: to be unsure (of o.s.)** ne pas être sûr(e) de soi.

unsurpassed [ˌʌnsə'pɑːst] **adj** non surpassé(e).

unsurprisingly [ˌʌnsə'praɪzɪŋlɪ] **adv** bien entendu, évidemment.

unsuspecting [ˌʌnsə'spektɪŋ] **adj** qui ne se doute de rien.

unsuspectingly [ˌʌnsə'spektɪŋlɪ] **adv** sans se douter de rien, sans se méfier.

unsweetened [ˌʌn'swiːtnd] **adj** non sucré(e).

unswerving [ʌn'swɜːvɪŋ] **adj** [loyalty, determination] inébranlable.

unsympathetic ['ʌnˌsɪmpə'θetɪk] **adj** [unfeeling] indifférent(e).

unsympathetically ['ʌnˌsɪmpə'θetɪklɪ] **adv** [speak, behave] sans montrer la moindre sympathie.

untamed [ˌʌn'teɪmd] **adj** [animal] sauvage / *fig* [person] farouche.

untangle [ˌʌn'tæŋgl] **vt** [string, hair] démêler.

untapped [ˌʌn'tæpt] **adj** inexploité(e).

untaxed [ˌʌn'tækst] **adj** non imposé(e).

untenable [ˌʌn'tenəbl] **adj** indéfendable.

unthinkable [ʌn'θɪŋkəbl] **adj** impensable.

unthinkingly [ʌn'θɪŋkɪŋlɪ] **adv** sans réfléchir.

untidy [ʌn'taɪdɪ] (comp **-ier**, superl **-iest**) **adj** [room, desk] en désordre / [work, handwriting] brouillon *(inv)* / [person, appearance] négligé(e).

untie [ˌʌn'taɪ] (cont **untying**) **vt** [knot, parcel, shoelaces] défaire / [prisoner] détacher.

until [ən'tɪl] ■ **prep 1.** [gen] jusqu'à ◗ **until now** jusqu'ici ◗ **until then** jusque-là **2.** *(after negative)* avant ◗ **not until tomorrow** pas avant demain ◗ **we weren't told the news until four o'clock** on ne nous a appris la nouvelle qu'à quatre heures.
■ **conj 1.** [gen] jusqu'à ce que *(+ subjunctive)* ◗ **I laughed until I cried** j'ai ri aux larmes **2.** *(after negative)* avant que *(+ subjunctive)* ◗ **don't sign until you've checked everything** ne signe rien avant d'avoir tout vérifié.

untimely [ʌn'taɪmlɪ] **adj** [death] prématuré(e) ⁄ [arrival] intempestif(ive) ⁄ [remark] mal à propos ⁄ [moment] mal choisi(e).

untiring [ʌn'taɪərɪŋ] **adj** infatigable.

untitled [ˌʌn'taɪtld] **adj** [painting] sans titre ⁄ [person] non titré(e).

untold [ˌʌn'təʊld] **adj** [amount, wealth] incalculable ⁄ [suffering, joy] indescriptible.

untouchable [ˌʌn'tʌtʃəbl] ■ **adj** intouchable.
■ **n** [in India] intouchable *mf* ⁄ *fig* paria *m*.

untouched [ˌʌn'tʌtʃt] **adj 1.** [unharmed - person] indemne ⁄ [- thing] intact(e) **2.** [uneaten - meal] auquel on n'a pas touché.

untoward [ˌʌntə'wɔːd] **adj** malencontreux(euse).

untrained [ˌʌn'treɪnd] **adj 1.** [person, worker] sans formation **2.** [voice] non travaillé(e) ⁄ [mind] non formé(e).

untrammelled *UK*, ***untrammeled*** *US* [ʌn'træməld] **adj** *fml* libre.

untranslatable [ˌʌntræns'leɪtəbl] **adj** intraduisible.

untreated [ˌʌn'triːtɪd] **adj 1.** MED non soigné(e) **2.** [sewage, chemical] non traité(e).

untried [ˌʌn'traɪd] **adj** [method] qui n'a pas été mis(e) à l'épreuve ⁄ [product] qui n'a pas été essayé(e).

untroubled [ˌʌn'trʌbld] **adj** [undisturbed] **: to be untroubled by sthg** rester impassible devant qqch.

untrue [ˌʌn'truː] **adj 1.** [not accurate] faux (fausse), qui n'est pas vrai(e) **2.** [unfaithful] **: to be untrue to sb** être infidèle à qqn.

untrustworthy [ˌʌn'trʌstˌwɜːðɪ] **adj** [person] qui n'est pas digne de confiance.

untruth [ˌʌn'truːθ] **n** mensonge *m*.

untruthful [ˌʌn'truːθfʊl] **adj** [person] menteur(euse) ⁄ [statement] mensonger(ère).

untutored [ˌʌn'tjuːtəd] **adj** [person] peu instruit(e).

unusable [ˌʌn'juːzəbl] **adj** inutilisable.

unused **adj 1.** [ˌʌn'juːzd] [clothes] neuf (neuve) ⁄ [machine] qui n'a jamais servi ⁄ [land] qui n'est pas exploité **2.** [ʌn'juːst] [unaccustomed] **: to be unused to sthg/to doing sthg** ne pas avoir l'habitude de qqch/de faire qqch.

unusual [ʌn'juːʒl] **adj** rare, inhabituel(elle).

unusually [ʌn'juːʒəlɪ] **adv** exceptionnellement.

unvarnished [ʌn'vɑːnɪʃt] **adj** *fig* [truth] tout nu (toute nue) ⁄ [account] sans embellissement.

unveil [ˌʌn'veɪl] **vt** *lit* & *fig* dévoiler.

unwaged [ˌʌn'weɪdʒd] **adj** *UK* non salarié(e).

unwanted [ˌʌn'wɒntɪd] **adj** [object] dont on ne se sert pas ⁄ [child] non désiré(e) ◗ **to feel unwanted** se sentir mal-aimé(e).

unwarranted [ʌn'wɒrəntɪd] **adj** injustifié(e).

unwavering [ʌn'weɪvərɪŋ] **adj** [determination] inébranlable.

unwelcome [ʌn'welkəm] **adj** [news, situation] fâcheux(euse) ⁄ [visitor] importun(e) ◗ **to make sb feel unwelcome** faire sentir à qqn qu'il dérange.

unwell [ˌʌn'wel] **adj : to be/feel unwell** ne pas être/se sentir bien.

unwholesome [ˌʌn'həʊlsəm] **adj** malsain(e).

unwieldy [ʌn'wiːldɪ] (**comp -ier, superl -iest**) **adj 1.** [cumbersome] peu maniable **2.** *fig* [system] lourd(e) ⁄ [method] trop complexe.

unwilling [ˌʌn'wɪlɪŋ] **adj : to be unwilling to do sthg** ne pas vouloir faire qqch ◗ **to be an unwilling helper** aider à contrecœur.

unwillingly [ʌn'wɪlɪŋlɪ] **adv** à contrecœur, contre son gré.

unwind [ˌʌn'waɪnd] (**pt & pp -wound**) ■ **vt** dérouler.
■ **vi** *fig* [person] se détendre.

unwise [ˌʌn'waɪz] **adj** imprudent(e), peu sage.

unwisely [ˌʌn'waɪzlɪ] **adv** imprudemment.

unwitting [ʌn'wɪtɪŋ] **adj** *fml* involontaire.

unwittingly [ʌn'wɪtɪŋlɪ] **adv** *fml* involontairement.

unworkable [ˌʌn'wɜːkəbl] **adj** impraticable.

unworldly [ˌʌn'wɜːldlɪ] **adj** détaché(e) de ce monde.

unworthy [ʌn'wɜːðɪ] (**comp -ier, superl -iest**) **adj** [undeserving] **: unworthy (of)** indigne (de).

unwound [ˌʌn'waʊnd] **pt & pp** ➤ ***unwind***.

unwrap [ˌʌn'ræp] (**pt & pp -ped, cont -ping**) **vt** défaire.

unwritten law [ˌʌnrɪtn-] **n** droit *m* coutumier.

unyielding [ʌn'jiːldɪŋ] **adj** inflexible.

unzip [ˌʌn'zɪp] (**pt & pp -ped, cont -ping**) **vt 1.** ouvrir la fermeture éclair de **2.** COMPUT [file] dézipper, décompresser.

up [ʌp] ■ **adv 1.** [towards or in a higher position] en haut ◗ **he's on his way up** il monte ◗ **they had coffee sent up** ils ont fait monter du café ◗ **she's up in her bedroom** elle est en haut dans sa chambre ◗ **we walked up to the top** on est montés jusqu'en haut ◗ **a house up in the mountains** une maison à la montagne ◗ **pick it up!** ramasse-le! ◗ **the sun came up** le soleil s'est levé ◗ **up there** là-haut ◗ **she wears her hair up** elle porte ses cheveux relevés ◗ **up in the air** en l'air
2. [into an upright position] **: to stand up** se lever ◗ **to sit up** s'asseoir (bien droit) ◗ **up you get!** allez, lève-toi! ◗ **'fragile – this way up'** 'fragile – haut'
3. [northwards] **: I'm coming up to York next week** je viens à York la semaine prochaine ◗ **up north** dans le nord
4. [along a road, river] **: their house is a little further up** leur maison est un peu plus loin
5. [close up, towards] **: to come up to sb** s'approcher de qqn ◗ **up close** de près

6. [to a higher level or degree] **: prices are going up** les prix augmentent ▸ **the temperature soared up into the thirties** la température est montée au-dessus de trente degrés ▸ **speak up** parlez plus fort
7. [indicating completion] **: drink up!** finissez vos verres! ▸ **eat up your greens** mange tes légumes.
■ **prep 1.** [towards or in a higher position] en haut de ▸ **up a hill/mountain** en haut d'une colline/d'une montagne ▸ **up a ladder** sur une échelle ▸ **I went up the stairs** j'ai monté l'escalier ▸ **further up the wall** plus haut sur le mur
2. [at far end of] **: they live up the road from us** ils habitent un peu plus haut *OR* loin que nous (dans la même rue) ▸ **her flat is just up the corridor** son appartement est juste au bout du couloir
3. [against current of river] **: up the river** en amont ▸ **to sail up the Amazon** remonter l'Amazone en bateau.
■ **adj 1.** [in a raised position] levé(e) ▸ **her hood was up so I couldn't see her face** sa capuche était relevée, si bien que je ne voyais pas sa figure
2. [out of bed] levé(e) ▸ **I was up at six today** je me suis levé à six heures aujourd'hui ▸ **she was up late last night** elle s'est couchée *OR* elle a veillé tard hier soir ▸ **so you're up and about again?** [after illness] alors tu n'es plus alité?
3. [at an end] **: the five weeks are up next Monday** les cinq semaines finissent *OR* se terminent lundi prochain ▸ **time's up** c'est l'heure
4. *UK* [under repair] **: 'road up'** 'attention travaux'
5. *inf* [wrong] **: is something up?** il y a quelque chose qui ne va pas? ▸ **what's up?** qu'est-ce qui ne va pas?, qu'est-ce qu'il y a?
■ **n : ups and downs** hauts et bas *mpl*.
■ **vt** (pt & pp **-ped**, cont **-ping**) *inf* [price, cost] augmenter.
◆ ***up against*** **prep : we came up against a lot of opposition** nous nous sommes heurtés à une forte opposition ▸ **to be up against it** avoir beaucoup de mal (à s'en sortir).
◆ ***up and down*** ■ **adv : to jump up and down** sauter ▸ **to walk up and down** faire les cent pas ▸ **she looked us up and down** elle nous a regardé de haut en bas.
■ **prep : she's up and down the stairs all day** elle n'arrête pas de monter et descendre l'escalier toute la journée ▸ **she looked up and down the ranks of soldiers** elle passa les troupes en revue ▸ **we walked up and down the avenue** nous avons arpenté l'avenue.
◆ ***up to*** **prep 1.** [as far as] jusqu'à
2. [indicating level] jusqu'à ▸ **it could take up to six weeks** cela peut prendre jusqu'à six semaines ▸ **it's not up to standard** ce n'est pas de la qualité voulue, ceci n'a pas le niveau requis
3. [well or able enough for] **: to be up to doing sthg** [able to] être capable de faire qqch / [well enough for] être en état de faire qqch ▸ **I'm not up to going back to work** je ne suis pas encore en état de reprendre le travail ▸ **my French isn't up to much** mon français ne vaut pas grand-chose *OR* n'est pas fameux
4. *inf* [secretly doing something] **: what are you up to?** qu'est-ce que tu fabriques? ▸ **they're up to something** ils mijotent quelque chose, ils préparent un coup
5. [indicating responsibility] **: it's not up to me to decide** ce n'est pas moi qui décide, il ne m'appartient pas de décider ▸ **it's up to you** c'est à vous de voir.
◆ ***up until*** **prep** jusqu'à.

up-and-coming **adj** à l'avenir prometteur.

up-and-up **n : to be on the up-and-up** *UK* [improving] aller de mieux en mieux / *US* [honest] honnête.

upbeat ['ʌpbiːt] **adj** optimiste.

upbraid [ʌp'breɪd] **vt : to upbraid sb (for sthg/for doing sthg)** réprimander qqn (pour qqch/pour avoir fait qqch).

upbringing ['ʌpˌbrɪŋɪŋ] **n** éducation *f*.

update [ˌʌp'deɪt] **vt** mettre à jour.

upend [ʌp'end] **vt 1.** *lit* [object] mettre debout / [person] mettre la tête en bas **2.** *fig* [upset] bouleverser.

upfront [ˌʌp'frʌnt] ■ **adj : upfront (about)** franc (franche) (au sujet de).
■ **adv** [in advance] d'avance.

upgradable [ʌp'greɪdəbl] **adj** COMPUT extensible.

upgrade [ˌʌp'greɪd] ■ **n 1.** [of hardware, system] augmentation *f* de puissance **2.** [of software] mise *f* à jour, actualisation *f*.
■ **vt** [facilities, software] améliorer / [hardware, system] optimiser / [employee] promouvoir / [pay] augmenter.

upheaval [ʌp'hiːvl] **n** bouleversement *m*.

upheld [ʌp'held] **pt & pp** ➤ ***uphold***.

uphill [ˌʌp'hɪl] ■ **adj 1.** [slope, path] qui monte **2.** *fig* [task] ardu(e).
■ **adv : to go uphill** monter.

uphold [ʌp'həʊld] (pt & pp **-held**) **vt** [law] maintenir / [decision, system] soutenir.

upholster [ʌp'həʊlstəʳ] **vt** rembourrer.

upholstery [ʌp'həʊlstərɪ] **n** rembourrage *m* / [of car] garniture *f* intérieure.

upkeep ['ʌpkiːp] **n** entretien *m*.

upland ['ʌplənd] **adj** des hautes terres.
◆ ***uplands*** **npl** hautes terres *fpl*.

uplift [ʌp'lɪft] **vt** élever / [person] élever l'âme de.

uplifting [ʌp'lɪftɪŋ] **adj** édifiant(e).

uplighter ['ʌplaɪtəʳ] **n** *applique qui diffuse une lumière dirigée vers le haut.*

upload ['ʌpləʊd] ■ **n** COMPUT téléchargement *m (vers le serveur)*.
■ **vt & vi** COMPUT télécharger *(vers le serveur)*.

up-market **adj** haut de gamme *(inv)*.

upon [ə'pɒn] **prep** *fml* sur ▸ **upon our arrival in Rome** à notre arrivée à Rome ▸ **upon hearing the news...** à ces nouvelles... ▸ **we receive thousands upon thousands of offers each year** nous recevons plusieurs milliers de propositions chaque année ▸ **summer/the weekend is upon us** l'été/le week-end approche.

upper ['ʌpəʳ] ■ **adj** supérieur(e).
■ **n** [of shoe] empeigne *f*.

upper case **n** TYPO haut *m* de casse.
◆ ***upper-case*** **adj : an upper-case letter** une majuscule.

upper class **n : the upper class** la haute société.
◆ ***upper-class*** **adj** [accent, person] aristocratique.

uppercut ['ʌpəkʌt] **n** uppercut *m*.

upper hand **n : to have the upper hand** avoir le dessus ▸ **to gain** *OR* **get the upper hand** prendre le dessus.

uppermost ['ʌpəməʊst] **adj** le plus haut (la plus haute) ▸ **it was uppermost in his mind** c'était sa préoccupation majeure.

upper sixth **n** *UK* SCH (classe *f*) terminale *f*.

Upper Volta [-'vɒltə] **n** Haute-Volta *f* ▸ **in Upper Volta** en Haute-Volta.

uppity ['ʌpətɪ] **adj** *inf* prétentieux(euse).

upright ■ **adj 1.** [ˌʌp'raɪt] [person] droit(e) / [structure] vertical(e) / [chair] à dossier droit ▸ **upright freezer** congélateur *m* armoire ▸ **upright vacuum cleaner** aspirateur *m* balai **2.** ['ʌpraɪt] *fig* [honest] droit(e).
■ **adv** [ˌʌp'raɪt] [stand, sit] droit.
■ **n** ['ʌpraɪt] montant *m*.

upright piano **n** piano *m* droit.

uprising ['ʌpˌraɪzɪŋ] **n** soulèvement *m*.

uproar ['ʌprɔːʳ] **n 1.** *(U)* [commotion] tumulte *m* **2.** [protest] protestations *fpl*.

uproarious [ʌp'rɔːrɪəs] **adj 1.** [noisy] tumultueux(euse) **2.** [amusing] tordant(e).

uproot [ʌp'ruːt] **vt** *lit* & *fig* déraciner.

upscale ['ʌpskeɪl] **adj** *US* haut de gamme.

upset [ʌp'set] ■ **adj 1.** [distressed] peiné(e), triste / [offended] vexé(e) **2.** MED **: to have an upset stomach** avoir l'estomac dérangé.
■ **n : to have a stomach upset** avoir l'estomac dérangé.
■ **vt** (pt & pp **upset**, cont **-ting**) **1.** [distress] faire de la peine à **2.** [plan, operation] déranger **3.** [overturn] renverser.

upsetting [ʌp'setɪŋ] **adj** [distressing] bouleversant(e).

upshot ['ʌpʃɒt] **n** résultat *m*.

upside ['ʌpsaɪd] **n** [of situation] avantage *m*.

upside down [ˌʌpsaɪd-] ■ **adj** à l'envers.
■ **adv** à l'envers ▸ **to turn sthg upside down** *fig* mettre qqch sens dessus dessous.

upstage [ˌʌp'steɪdʒ] **vt** éclipser.

upstairs [ˌʌp'steəz] ■ **adj** d'en haut, du dessus.
■ **adv** en haut.
■ **n** étage *m*.

upstanding [ˌʌp'stændɪŋ] **adj** droit(e).

upstart ['ʌpstɑːt] **n** parvenu *m*, -e *f*.

upstate [ˌʌp'steɪt] *US* ■ **adj : upstate New York** la partie nord de l'État de New York.
■ **adv** dans/vers le nord de l'État.

upstream [ˌʌp'striːm] ■ **adj** d'amont ▸ **to be upstream (from)** être en amont (de).
■ **adv** vers l'amont / [swim] contre le courant.

upsurge ['ʌpsɜːdʒ] **n : upsurge (of/in)** recrudescence *f* (de).

upswing ['ʌpswɪŋ] **n : upswing (in)** [popularity] remontée *f* (de) ▸ **an upswing in economic activity** une reprise de l'activité économique.

uptake ['ʌpteɪk] **n : to be quick on the uptake** saisir vite ▸ **to be slow on the uptake** être lent(e) à comprendre.

uptight [ʌp'taɪt] **adj** *inf* tendu(e).

uptime ['ʌptaɪm] **n** COMPUT temps *m* de bon fonctionnement.

up-to-date **adj 1.** [modern] moderne **2.** [most recent - news] tout dernier (toute dernière) **3.** [informed] **: to keep up-to-date with** se tenir au courant de.

up-to-the-minute **adj** de dernière minute.

uptown [ˌʌp'taʊn] *US* ■ **adj** [area] résidentiel(elle).
■ **adv** dans/vers les quartiers résidentiels.

upturn ['ʌptɜːn] **n : upturn (in)** reprise *f* (de).

upturned [ʌp'tɜːnd] **adj** [car, cup] renversé(e) / [nose] retroussé(e).

upward ['ʌpwəd] ■ **adj** [movement] ascendant(e) / [look, rise] vers le haut.
■ **adv** *US* = ***upwards***.

upward-compatible **adj** COMPUT compatible vers le haut.

upwardly-mobile ['ʌpwədlɪ-] **adj** ECON susceptible de promotion sociale.

upward mobility **n** ECON mobilité *f* sociale.

upwards ['ʌpwədz] **adv** vers le haut.
◆ ***upwards of*** **prep** plus de.

upwind [ˌʌp'wɪnd] **adj : to be upwind of sthg** être dans le vent ***or*** au vent par rapport à qqch.

URA (abbr of ***Urban Renewal Administration***) **n** *administration américaine des rénovations urbaines*.

Urals ['jʊərəlz] **npl : the Urals** l'Oural *m* ▸ **in the Urals** dans l'Oural.

uranium [jʊ'reɪnjəm] **n** uranium *m*.

Uranus ['jʊərənəs] **n** [planet] Uranus *f*.

urban ['ɜːbən] **adj** urbain(e).

urbane [ɜː'beɪn] **adj** courtois(e).

urbanize, *UK* ***-ise*** ['ɜːbənaɪz] **vt** urbaniser.

urban renewal **n** réaménagement *m* des zones urbaines.

urchin ['ɜːtʃɪn] **n** *dated* gamin *m*, -e *f*.

Urdu ['ʊəduː] **n** ourdou *m*.

urge [ɜːdʒ] ■ **n** forte envie *f* ▸ **to have an urge to do sthg** avoir une forte envie de faire qqch.
■ **vt 1.** [try to persuade] **: to urge sb to do sthg** pousser qqn à faire qqch, presser qqn de faire qqch **2.** [advocate] conseiller.

urgency ['ɜːdʒənsɪ] **n** *(U)* urgence *f*.

urgent ['ɜːdʒənt] **adj** [letter, case, request] urgent(e) / [plea, voice, need] pressant(e).

urgently ['ɜːdʒəntlɪ] **adv** d'urgence / [appeal] d'une manière pressante.

urinal [ˌjʊə'raɪnl] **n** urinoir *m*.

urinary ['jʊərɪnərɪ] **adj** urinaire.

urinate ['jʊərɪneɪt] **vi** uriner.

urine ['jʊərɪn] **n** urine *f*.

URL (abbr of ***uniform resource locator***) **n** COMPUT URL *m (adresse électronique)*.

urn [ɜːn] **n 1.** [for ashes] urne *f* **2.** [for tea] **: tea urn** fontaine *f* à thé.

Uruguay ['jʊərəgwaɪ] **n** Uruguay *m* ▸ **in Uruguay** en Uruguay.

Uruguayan [ˌjʊərə'gwaɪən] ■ adj uruguayen(enne).
■ n Uruguayen *m*, -enne *f*.

us [ʌs] pers pron nous ▸ **can you see/hear us?** vous nous voyez/entendez? ▸ **it's us** c'est nous ▸ **you can't expect us to do it** vous ne pouvez pas exiger que ce soit nous qui le fassions ▸ **she gave it to us** elle nous l'a donné ▸ **with/without us** avec/sans nous ▸ **they are more wealthy than us** ils sont plus riches que nous ▸ **some of us** quelques-uns d'entre nous.

US n abbr of ***United States***.

CULTURE

US Open

En 1881, cet événement sportif américain, considéré comme un divertissement, est un tournoi de tennis exclusivement réservé aux hommes. De nouvelles formes de tournois apparaissent ensuite, qui seront officialisées en 1968 : le simple dames, les doubles et les doubles mixtes. C'est le début de l'histoire de l'**Open**, l'un des événements du tennis les plus important : les matchs se disputent au **West Side Tennis Club** de Forest Hills, dans le quartier du Queens à New York. Aujourd'hui, ils ont lieu à **Flushing Meadows**, toujours dans le Queens.

USA n **1.** abbr of ***United States of America*** **2.** (abbr of ***United States Army***) *armée de terre américaine*.

usable ['ju:zəbl] adj utilisable.

USAF (abbr of ***United States Air Force***) n *armée de l'air américaine*.

usage ['ju:zɪdʒ] n **1.** LING usage *m* **2.** *(U)* [handling, treatment] traitement *m*.

USB (abbr of ***universal serial bus***) n COMPUT USB *m*.

USCG (abbr of ***United States Coast Guard***) n *service de surveillance côtière américain*.

USDA (abbr of ***United States Department of Agriculture***) n *ministère américain de l'Agriculture*.

USDAW ['ʌzdɔ:] (abbr of ***Union of Shop, Distributive and Allied Workers***) n *syndicat britannique des personnels de la distribution*.

USDI (abbr of ***United States Department of the Interior***) n *ministère américain de l'Intérieur*.

use ■ n [ju:s] **1.** [act of using] utilisation *f*, emploi *m* ▸ **to be in use** être utilisé ▸ **to be out of use** être hors d'usage ▸ **to wear out with use** s'user ▸ **to make use of sthg** utiliser qqch ▸ **'directions for use'** 'mode d'emploi' ▸ **'for your personal use'** pour votre usage personnel ▸ **'for external/internal use only'** MED 'à usage externe/interne' ▸ **'for use in case of emergency'** 'à utiliser en cas d'urgence'
2. [ability to use] usage *m* ▸ **to let sb have the use of sthg** prêter qqch à qqn ▸ **she lost the use of her legs** elle a perdu l'usage de ses jambes
3. [usefulness] **: to be of use** être utile ▸ **he's not much use as a secretary** il n'est pas brillant comme secrétaire ▸ **it's no use** ça ne sert à rien ▸ **what's the use (of doing sthg)?** à quoi bon (faire qqch)?
4. [practical application] usage *m*, emploi *m* ▸ **we found a use for the old fridge** nous avons trouvé un emploi pour le vieux frigo.
■ aux vb [ju:s] **: I used to live in London** avant j'habitais à Londres ▸ **he didn't use to be so fat** il n'était pas si gros avant ▸ **there used to be a tree here** (autrefois) il y avait un arbre ici.
■ vt [ju:z] **1.** [gen] utiliser, se servir de, employer ▸ **these are the notebooks he used** ce sont les cahiers qu'il a utilisés ▸ **we use this room as an office** nous nous servons de cette pièce comme bureau, cette pièce nous sert de bureau ▸ **the car's using a lot of oil** la voiture consomme beaucoup d'huile
2. *pej* [exploit] se servir de.
◆ ***use up*** vt sep [supply] épuiser / [food] finir / [money] dépenser ▸ **she used up the leftovers to make soup** elle a utilisé les restes pour faire un potage.

use-by date n date *f* limite de consommation.

used adj **1.** [ju:zd] [handkerchief, towel] sale **2.** [ju:zd] [car] d'occasion **3.** [ju:st] [accustomed] **: to be used to sthg/to doing sthg** avoir l'habitude de qqch/de faire qqch ▸ **to get used to sthg** s'habituer à qqch.

useful ['ju:sfʊl] adj utile ▸ **she's a useful person to know** c'est une femme qu'il est bon de connaître ▸ **make yourself useful and help me tidy up** rends-toi utile et aide-moi à ranger ▸ **to come in useful** être utile.

usefully ['ju:sfʊlɪ] adv utilement ▸ **you could usefully devote a further year's study to the subject** tu pourrais consacrer avec profit une année d'étude supplémentaire au sujet.

usefulness ['ju:sfʊlnɪs] n *(U)* utilité *f*.

useless ['ju:slɪs] adj **1.** [gen] inutile **2.** *inf* [person] incompétent(e), nul (nulle).

uselessly ['ju:slɪslɪ] adv inutilement.

uselessness ['ju:slɪsnɪs] n *(U)* inutilité *f*.

Usenet® ['ju:znet] n Usenet® *m*, forum *m* électronique.

user ['ju:zəʳ] n [of product, machine] utilisateur *m*, -trice *f* / [of service] usager *m*.

user-friendly adj convivial(e), facile à utiliser.

user-interface n *fig* & COMPUT interface *f* utilisateur.

user name n COMPUT nom *m* de l'utilisateur.

USES (abbr of ***United States Employment Service***) n *services américains de l'emploi*.

usher ['ʌʃəʳ] ■ n placeur *m*.
■ vt **: to usher sb in/out** faire entrer/sortir qqn.

usherette [ˌʌʃə'ret] n ouvreuse *f*.

USIA (abbr of ***United States Information Agency***) n *agence américaine de renseignements*.

USM n **1.** (abbr of ***United States Mail***) ≃ la Poste **2.** (abbr of ***United States Mint***) ≃ la Monnaie.

USN (abbr of ***United States Navy***) n *marine de guerre américaine*.

USP (abbr of ***unique selling point*** OR ***proposition***) n proposition *f* unique de vente.

USPHS (abbr of ***United States Public Health Service***) n *aux États-Unis, Direction des affaires sanitaires et sociales.*

USS (abbr of ***United States Ship***) *expression précédant le nom d'un bâtiment de la marine américaine.*

USSR (abbr of ***Union of Soviet Socialist Republics***) **n : the (former) USSR** l'(ex-)URSS *f* ▸ **in the USSR** en URSS.

usu. abbr of ***usually***.

usual [ˈjuːʒəl] adj habituel(elle) ▸ **let's meet at the usual time** retrouvons-nous à l'heure habituelle *OR* à la même heure que d'habitude ▸ **she's her usual self again** elle est redevenue elle-même ▸ **as usual** comme d'habitude ▸ **life goes on as usual** la vie continue.

usually [ˈjuːʒəlɪ] adv d'habitude, d'ordinaire.

usurp [juːˈzɜːp] vt usurper.

usury [ˈjuːʒʊrɪ] n *(U)* usure *f*.

UT abbr of ***Utah***.

Utah [ˈjuːtɑː] n Utah *m* ▸ **in Utah** dans l'Utah.

utensil [juːˈtensl] n ustensile *m*.

uterus [ˈjuːtərəs] (pl **-ri** [-raɪ] *OR* **-ruses** [-rəsiːz]) n utérus *m*.

utilitarian [ˌjuːtɪlɪˈteərɪən] adj utilitaire.

utilitarianism [ˌjuːtɪlɪˈteərɪənɪzm] n utilitarisme *m*.

utility [juːˈtɪlətɪ] (pl **-ies**) n **1.** *(U)* [usefulness] utilité *f* **2.** [public service] service *m* public **3.** COMPUT utilitaire *m*.

utility room n buanderie *f*.

utilization [ˌjuːtɪlaɪˈzeɪʃn] n utilisation *f*.

utilize, *UK* ***-ise*** [ˈjuːtəlaɪz] vt utiliser / [resources] exploiter, utiliser.

utmost [ˈʌtməʊst] ■ adj le plus grand (la plus grande) ▸ **with the utmost respect,...** avec tout le respect que je vous dois,...
■ **n : the utmost in comfort** ce qui se fait de mieux en matière de confort ▸ **to do one's utmost** faire tout son possible, faire l'impossible ▸ **to the utmost** au plus haut point.

utopia [juːˈtəʊpjə] n utopie *f*.

utopian, ***Utopian*** [juːˈtəʊpjən] ■ adj utopique.
■ n utopiste *mf*.

utter [ˈʌtəʳ] ■ adj total(e), complet(ète).
■ vt prononcer / [cry] pousser.

utterly [ˈʌtəlɪ] adv complètement.

U-turn n demi-tour *m* / *fig* revirement *m*.

UV (abbr of ***ultra-violet***) UV.

UV-A, ***UVA*** (abbr of ***ultra-violet-A***) UVA.

UV-B, ***UVB*** (abbr of ***ultra-violet-B***) UVB.

UWIST [ˈjuːwɪst] (abbr of ***University of Wales Institute of Science and Technology***) n *institut de science et de technologie de l'université du pays de Galles.*

Uzbek [ˈʊzbek] ■ adj ouzbek.
■ n **1.** [person] Ouzbek *mf* **2.** [language] ouzbek *m*.

Uzbekistan [ʊzˌbekɪˈstɑːn] n Ouzbékistan *m* ▸ **in Uzbekistan** en Ouzbékistan.

V

v[1] [viː] (pl v's *OR* vs), ***V*** (pl V's *OR* Vs) **n** [letter] v *m inv*, V *m inv*.

v[2] **1.** (abbr of ***verse***) v. **2.** [cross-reference] (abbr of ***vide***) v. **3.** abbr of ***versus*** **4.** (abbr of ***volt***) v.

VA abbr of ***Virginia***.

vac (abbr of ***vacation***) **n** *UK inf* vacances *fpl*.

vacancy ['veɪkənsɪ] (pl **-ies**) **n 1.** [job] poste *m* vacant **2.** [room available] chambre *f* à louer ▸ **'vacancies'** 'chambres à louer' ▸ **'no vacancies'** 'complet'.

vacant ['veɪkənt] **adj 1.** [room] inoccupé(e) / [chair, toilet] libre ▸ **the room becomes vacant tomorrow** la chambre sera libérée *OR* disponible demain **2.** [job, post] vacant(e) **3.** [look, expression] distrait(e) ▸ **I asked a question and she just looked vacant** j'ai posé une question et elle a eu l'air de ne pas comprendre.

vacant lot **n** terrain *m* inoccupé / *US* terrain *m* vague / [for sale] terrain *m* à vendre.

vacantly ['veɪkəntlɪ] **adv** d'un air distrait.

vacate [və'keɪt] **vt** quitter.

vacation [və'keɪʃn] **n** *US* vacances *fpl*.

vacationer [və'keɪʃənə^r] **n** *US* vacancier *m*, -ère *f*.

vacation resort **n** *US* camp *m* de vacances.

vaccinate ['væksɪneɪt] **vt** vacciner.

vaccination [ˌvæksɪ'neɪʃn] **n** vaccination *f*.

vaccine [*UK* 'væksiːn, *US* væk'siːn] **n** vaccin *m*.

vacillate ['væsəleɪt] **vi** hésiter.

vacuous ['vækjʊəs] **adj** *fml* [eyes, look] vide, sans expression / [remark] sot(sotte), niais(e) / [film, novel] idiot(e), dénué(e) de tout intérêt / [life] vide de sens.

vacuum ['vækjʊəm] ■ **n 1.** *fig* & TECH vide *m* **2.** [cleaner] aspirateur *m*.
■ **vt** [room] passer l'aspirateur dans / [carpet] passer à l'aspirateur.

vacuum cleaner **n** aspirateur *m*.

vacuum flask **n** *UK* (bouteille *f*) Thermos® *f*.

vacuum-packed **adj** emballé(e) sous vide.

vacuum pump **n** pompe *f* à vide.

vagabond ['vægəbɒnd] **n** *liter* vagabond *m*, -e *f*.

vagaries ['veɪgərɪz] **npl** caprices *mpl*.

vagina [və'dʒaɪnə] **n** vagin *m*.

vaginal [və'dʒaɪnl] **adj** vaginal(e) ▸ **vaginal discharge** pertes *fpl* blanches ▸ **vaginal smear** frottis *m* vaginal.

vagrancy ['veɪgrənsɪ] **n** vagabondage *m*.

vagrant ['veɪgrənt] **n** vagabond *m*, -e *f*.

vague [veɪg] **adj 1.** [gen] vague, imprécis(e) **2.** [absent-minded] distrait(e).

vaguely ['veɪglɪ] **adv** vaguement.

vagueness ['veɪgnɪs] **n 1.** [imprecision - of instructions, statement] imprécision *f*, manque *m* de clarté **2.** [of memory] imprécision *f*, manque *m* de précision / [of feeling] vague *m*, caractère *m* vague *OR* indistinct **3.** [of shape] flou *m*, caractère *m* indistinct **4.** [absent-mindedness] distraction *f*.

vain [veɪn] **adj 1.** [futile, worthless] vain(e) **2.** *pej* [conceited] vaniteux(euse).
◆ ***in vain*** **adv** en vain, vainement.

vainly ['veɪnlɪ] **adv 1.** [in vain] en vain, vainement **2.** [conceitedly] avec vanité.

valance ['væləns] **n 1.** [on bed] tour *m* de lit **2.** *US* [over window] cantonnière *f*.

vale [veɪl] **n** *liter* val *m*.

valedictory [ˌvælɪ'dɪktərɪ] **adj** *fml* d'adieu.

valentine card ['væləntaɪn-] **n** carte *f* de la Saint-Valentin.

Valentine's Day ['væləntaɪnz-] **n : (St) Valentine's Day** la Saint-Valentin.

valet ['væleɪ *OR* 'vælɪt] **n** valet *m* de chambre.

valet parking **n : 'valet parking'** 'voiturier'.

valet service **n 1.** [for clothes] service *m* pressing **2.** [for cars] nettoyage *m* complet.

Valetta, ***Valleta*** [və'letə] **n** la Valette.

valiant ['væljənt] **adj** vaillant(e).

valiantly ['væljəntlɪ] **adv** vaillamment, courageusement.

valid ['vælɪd] **adj 1.** [reasonable] valable **2.** [legally usable] valide.

validate ['vælɪdeɪt] **vt** valider.

validation [ˌvælɪ'deɪʃn] n **1.** [of argument, claim] confirmation *f*, preuve *f* **2.** [of document] validation *f*.

validity [və'lɪdətɪ] n validité *f*.

Valium® ['vælɪəm] n Valium® *m*.

Valletta = ***Valetta***.

valley ['vælɪ] (pl -s) n vallée *f*.

valour *UK*, ***valor*** *US* ['vælər] n *(U) fml* & *liter* bravoure *f*.

valuable ['væljʊəbl] adj **1.** [advice, time, information] précieux(euse) **2.** [object, jewel] de valeur.
◆ ***valuables*** npl objets *mpl* de valeur.

valuation [ˌvæljʊ'eɪʃn] n **1.** *(U)* [pricing] estimation *f*, expertise *f* **2.** [estimated price] valeur *f* estimée **3.** [opinion] opinion *f*.

value ['vælju:] ■ n valeur *f* ▸ **this necklace is of great value** ce collier vaut cher ▸ **he had nothing of value to add** il n'avait rien d'important *OR* de valable à ajouter ▸ **to be good value** être d'un bon rapport qualité-prix ▸ **property is going up/down in value** l'immobilier prend/perd de la valeur ▸ **to get value for money** en avoir pour son argent ▸ **to place a high value on sthg** accorder beaucoup de valeur à qqch ▸ **to put a value on sthg** évaluer *OR* estimer qqch ▸ **to take sb/sthg at face value** prendre qqn/qqch au pied de la lettre.
■ vt **1.** [estimate price of] expertiser ▸ **they valued the house at £50,000** ils ont estimé *OR* évalué la maison à 50 000 livres **2.** [cherish] apprécier ▸ **we greatly value your help** nous apprécions beaucoup *OR* nous vous sommes très reconnaissants de votre aide ▸ **does he value your opinion?** votre opinion lui importe-t-elle?
◆ ***values*** npl [morals] valeurs *fpl*.

value-added tax [-ædɪd-] n taxe *f* sur la valeur ajoutée.

valued ['vælju:d] adj précieux(euse).

value judg(e)ment n jugement *m* de valeur.

valuer ['væljʊər] n expert *m*.

valve [vælv] n [on tyre] valve *f* / TECH soupape *f*.

vamoose [və'mu:s] vi *inf* s'éclipser.

vampire ['væmpaɪər] n vampire *m*.

van [væn] n **1.** AUT camionnette *f* **2.** *UK* RAIL fourgon *m*.

V and A (abbr of ***Victoria and Albert Museum***) n *grand musée londonien des arts décoratifs*.

vandal ['vændl] n vandale *mf*.

vandalism ['vændəlɪzm] n vandalisme *m*.

vandalize, *UK* ***-ise*** ['vændəlaɪz] vt saccager.

vanguard ['vængɑ:d] n avant-garde *f* ▸ **in the vanguard of** à l'avant-garde de.

vanilla [və'nɪlə] ■ n vanille *f*.
■ comp [ice cream, yoghurt] à la vanille.

vanish ['vænɪʃ] vi disparaître.

vanishing point ['vænɪʃɪŋ-] n point *m* de fuite.

vanity ['vænətɪ] n **1.** *(U) pej* vanité *f* **2.** *US* [furniture] coiffeuse *f*.

vanity publishing n publication *f* à compte d'auteur.

vanity unit n *élément de salle de bains avec lavabo encastré*.

vanquish ['væŋkwɪʃ] vt *liter* vaincre.

vantagepoint ['vɑ:ntɪdʒˌpɔɪnt] n [for view] bon endroit *m* / *fig* position *f* avantageuse.

vaporizer ['veɪpəraɪzər] n **1.** [gen] vaporisateur *m* / [for perfume, spray] atomiseur *m*, pulvérisateur *m* **2.** MED [inhaler] inhalateur *m* / [for throat] pulvérisateur *m*.

vapour *UK*, ***vapor*** *US* ['veɪpər] n *(U)* vapeur *f* / [condensation] buée *f*.

vapour trail *UK*, ***vapor trail*** *US* n traînée *f* de vapeur.

variable ['veərɪəbl] ■ adj variable / [mood] changeant(e).
■ n variable *f*.

variable costs n coûts *mpl* *OR* frais *mpl* variables.

variance ['veərɪəns] n *fml* : **at variance (with)** en désaccord (avec).

variant ['veərɪənt] ■ adj différent(e).
■ n variante *f*.

variation [ˌveərɪ'eɪʃn] n : **variation (in)** variation *f* (de).

varicose veins ['værɪkəʊs-] npl varices *fpl*.

varied ['veərɪd] adj varié(e).

variegated ['veərɪgeɪtɪd] adj **1.** [gen] bigarré(e) **2.** BOT panaché(e).

variety [və'raɪətɪ] (pl -ies) n **1.** [gen] variété *f* ▸ **there isn't much variety in the menu** le menu n'est pas très varié *OR* n'offre pas un grand choix ▸ **there is a wide variety of colours/styles to choose from** il y a un grand choix de couleurs/styles ▸ **in a variety of ways** de diverses manières **2.** [type] variété *f*, sorte *f* ▸ **different varieties of cheese** différentes sortes de fromage, fromages variés.

variety show n spectacle *m* de variétés.

various ['veərɪəs] adj **1.** [several] plusieurs **2.** [different] divers.

varnish ['vɑ:nɪʃ] ■ n vernis *m*.
■ vt vernir.

varnished ['vɑ:nɪʃt] adj verni(e).

vary ['veərɪ] (pt & pp -ied) ■ vt varier.
■ vi : **to vary (in/with)** varier (en/selon), changer (en/selon).

varying ['veərɪɪŋ] adj qui varie, variable.

vascular ['væskjʊlər] adj vasculaire.

vase [*UK* vɑ:z, *US* veɪz] n vase *m*.

vasectomy [və'sektəmɪ] (pl -ies) n vasectomie *f*.

Vaseline® ['væsəli:n] n vaseline *f*.

vast [vɑ:st] adj vaste, immense.

vastly ['vɑ:stlɪ] adv extrêmement, infiniment.

vastness ['vɑ:stnɪs] n immensité *f*.

vat [væt] n cuve *f*.

VAT [væt *OR* vi:eɪ'ti:] (abbr of ***value-added tax***) n TVA *f*.

Vatican ['vætɪkən] n : **the Vatican** le Vatican.

Vatican City n l'État *m* de la cité du Vatican, le Vatican ▸ **in Vatican City** au Vatican.

vault [vɔ:lt] ■ **n 1.** [in bank] chambre *f* forte **2.** [roof] voûte *f* **3.** [jump] saut *m* **4.** [in church] caveau *m*.
■ **vt** sauter.
■ **vi : to vault over sthg** sauter (par-dessus) qqch.

vaulted ['vɔ:ltɪd] **adj** voûté(e).

vaulting horse ['vɔ:ltɪŋ-] **n** cheval-d'arçons *m inv*.

vaunted ['vɔ:ntɪd] **adj** *fml* **: much vaunted** tant vanté(e).

VC **n 1.** (abbr of ***vice-chairman***) vice-président *m* **2.** (abbr of ***Victoria Cross***) *la plus haute distinction militaire britannique*.

VCR (abbr of ***video cassette recorder***) **n** magnétoscope *m*.

VD (abbr of ***venereal disease***) **n** *(U)* MST *f*.

VDU (abbr of ***visual display unit***) **n** moniteur *m*.

veal [vi:l] **n** *(U)* veau *m*.

veer [vɪə^r] **vi** virer ▸ **to veer off course** [car] quitter sa route / [boat, plane, wind-surfer] quitter sa trajectoire ▸ **her mood veers between euphoria and black depression** *fig* son humeur oscille entre l'euphorie et un profond abattement ***or*** va de l'euphorie à un profond abattement.

veg [vedʒ] **n** *inf* **1.** (abbr of ***vegetable***) légume *m* **2.** *(U)* (abbr of ***vegetables***) légumes *mpl*.

vegan ['vi:gən] ■ **adj** végétalien(enne).
■ **n** végétalien *m*, -enne *f*.

vegeburger ['vedʒəˌbɜ:gə^r] **n** hamburger *m* végétarien.

vegetable ['vedʒtəbl] ■ **n** légume *m*.
■ **adj** [matter, protein] végétal(e) / [soup, casserole] de ***or*** aux légumes.

vegetable garden **n** jardin *m* potager.

vegetable knife **n** couteau *m* à légumes.

vegetable oil **n** huile *f* végétale.

vegetarian [ˌvedʒɪ'teərɪən] ■ **adj** végétarien(enne).
■ **n** végétarien *m*, -enne *f*.

vegetarianism [ˌvedʒɪ'teərɪənɪzm] **n** végétarisme *m*.

vegetate ['vedʒɪteɪt] **vi** *pej* végéter.

vegetation [ˌvedʒɪ'teɪʃn] **n** *(U)* végétation *f*.

veggie ['vedʒɪ] (abbr of ***vegetarian***) *UK inf* ■ **adj** végétarien(enne).
■ **n** végétarien *m*, -enne *f*.

vehement ['vi:ɪmənt] **adj** véhément(e).

vehemently ['vi:ɪməntlɪ] **adv** avec véhémence.

vehicle ['vi:ɪkl] **n** *lit* & *fig* véhicule *m*.

vehicular [vɪ'hɪkjʊlə^r] **adj** *fml* [transport] de véhicules ▸ **vehicular traffic** circulation *f*.

veil [veɪl] **n** *lit* & *fig* voile *m*.

veiled [veɪld] **adj** [threat, reference] voilé(e).

vein [veɪn] **n 1.** ANAT veine *f* **2.** [of leaf] nervure *f* **3.** [of mineral] filon *m* **4.** [mood] **: in the same vein** dans le même style.

Velcro® ['velkrəʊ] **n** Velcro® *m*.

vellum ['veləm] **n** vélin *m*.

velocity [vɪ'lɒsətɪ] (pl **-ies**) **n** vélocité *f*.

velour [və'lʊə^r] **n** velours *m*.

velvet ['velvɪt] ■ **n** velours *m*.
■ **comp** de ***or*** en velours.

vend [vend] **vt** *fml* & LAW vendre.

vendetta [ven'detə] **n** vendetta *f*.

vending machine ['vendɪŋ-] **n** distributeur *m* automatique.

vendor ['vendə^r] **n 1.** *fml* [salesperson] marchand *m*, -e *f* **2.** LAW vendeur *m*, -eresse *f*.

veneer [və'nɪə^r] **n** placage *m* / *fig* apparence *f*.

venerable ['venərəbl] **adj** vénérable.

venerate ['venəreɪt] **vt** vénérer.

veneration [ˌvenə'reɪʃn] **n** vénération *f*.

venereal disease [vɪ'nɪərɪəl-] **n** maladie *f* vénérienne.

Venetian [vɪ'ni:ʃn] ■ **adj** vénitien(enne).
■ **n** Vénitien *m*, -enne *f*.

venetian blind [vɪˌni:ʃn-] **n** store *m* vénitien.

Venezuela [ˌvenɪz'weɪlə] **n** Venezuela *m* ▸ **in Venezuela** au Venezuela.

Venezuelan [ˌvenɪz'weɪlən] ■ **adj** vénézuélien(enne).
■ **n** Vénézuélien *m*, -enne *f*.

vengeance ['vendʒəns] **n** vengeance *f* ▸ **it began raining with a vengeance** il a commencé à pleuvoir très fort ▸ **she's back with a vengeance** elle fait un retour en force.

vengeful ['vendʒfʊl] **adj** vengeur(eresse).

Venice ['venɪs] **n** Venise.

venison ['venɪzn] **n** venaison *f*.

venom ['venəm] **n** *lit* & *fig* venin *m*.

venomous ['venəməs] **adj** *lit* & *fig* venimeux(euse).

vent [vent] ■ **n** [pipe] tuyau *m* / [opening] orifice *m* ▸ **to give vent to** donner libre cours à.
■ **vt** [anger, feelings] donner libre cours à ▸ **to vent sthg on sb** décharger qqch sur qqn.

ventilate ['ventɪleɪt] **vt** ventiler.

ventilation [ˌventɪ'leɪʃn] **n** ventilation *f*.

ventilator ['ventɪleɪtə^r] **n** ventilateur *m*.

Ventimiglia [ventɪ'mɪljə] **n** Vintimille.

ventriloquist [ven'trɪləkwɪst] **n** ventriloque *mf*.

venture ['ventʃə^r] ■ **n** entreprise *f* ▸ **a business venture** une entreprise commerciale, un coup d'essai commercial.
■ **vt** risquer ▸ **she didn't dare venture an opinion on the subject** elle n'a pas osé exprimer sa pensée à ce sujet ▸ **to venture to do sthg** se permettre de faire qqch.
■ **vi** s'aventurer ▸ **to venture into politics** se lancer dans la politique ▸ **I wouldn't venture out of doors in this weather** je ne me risquerais pas à sortir par ce temps.

venture capital **n** capital-risque *m*.

venture capitalist **n** spécialiste *mf* de la prise de risques.

venturesome ['ventʃəsəm] **adj 1.** [person] téméraire **2.** [action] risqué(e).

venue ['venju:] **n** lieu *m*.

Venus ['vi:nəs] **n** [planet] Vénus *f*.

veracity [və'ræsətɪ] **n** véracité *f*.

veranda(h) [və'rændə] **n** véranda *f*.

verb [vɜ:b] **n** verbe *m*.

verbal ['vɜ:bl] **adj** verbal(e).

verbally ['vɜ:bəlɪ] **adv** verbalement.

verbatim [vɜ:'beɪtɪm] **adj & adv** mot pour mot.

verbose [vɜ:'bəʊs] **adj** verbeux(euse).

verdict ['vɜ:dɪkt] **n 1.** LAW verdict *m* **2.** [opinion] **: verdict (on)** avis *m* (sur).

verge [vɜ:dʒ] **n 1.** [of lawn] bordure *f* / *UK* [of road] bas-côté *m*, accotement *m* **2.** [brink] **: the country has been brought to the verge of civil war** le pays a été amené au seuil de la guerre civile ▸ **on the verge of sthg** au bord de qqch ▸ **on the verge of doing sthg** sur le point de faire qqch.

◆ ***verge (up)on*** **vt insep** friser, approcher de ▸ **his feeling was one of panic verging on hysteria** il ressentait une sorte de panique proche de l'hystérie *OR* qui frôlait l'hystérie.

verger ['vɜ:dʒəʳ] **n** bedeau *m*.

verifiable ['verɪfaɪəbl] **adj** vérifiable.

verification [ˌverɪfɪ'keɪʃn] **n** vérification *f*.

verify ['verɪfaɪ] **(pt & pp -ied) vt** vérifier.

veritable ['verɪtəbl] **adj** *hum & fml* véritable.

vermilion [və'mɪljən] ■ **adj** vermillon *(inv)*.
■ **n** vermillon *m*.

vermin ['vɜ:mɪn] **npl** vermine *f*.

Vermont [vɜ:'mɒnt] **n** Vermont *m* ▸ **in Vermont** dans le Vermont.

vermouth ['vɜ:məθ] **n** vermouth *m*.

vernacular [və'nækjʊləʳ] ■ **adj** vernaculaire.
■ **n** dialecte *m*.

verruca [və'ru:kə] **(pl -cas** *OR* **-cae [-kaɪ]) n** verrue *f* plantaire.

versa ➤ ***vice versa***.

versatile ['vɜ:sətaɪl] **adj** [person, player] aux talents multiples / [machine, tool, food] souple d'emploi.

versatility [ˌvɜ:sə'tɪlətɪ] **n** [of person] variété *f* de talents / [of machine, tool] souplesse *f* d'emploi.

verse [vɜ:s] **n 1.** *(U)* [poetry] vers *mpl* **2.** [stanza] strophe *f* **3.** [in Bible] verset *m*.

versed [vɜ:st] **adj : to be well versed in sthg** être versé(e) dans qqch.

version ['vɜ:ʃn] **n** version *f*.

versus ['vɜ:səs] **prep 1.** SPORT contre **2.** [as opposed to] par opposition à.

vertebra ['vɜ:tɪbrə] **(pl -brae [-bri:]) n** vertèbre *f*.

vertebrate ['vɜ:tɪbreɪt] **n** vertébré *m*.

vertical ['vɜ:tɪkl] **adj** vertical(e).

vertical integration **n** FIN intégration *f* verticale.

vertically ['vɜ:tɪklɪ] **adv** verticalement.

vertigo ['vɜ:tɪgəʊ] **n** *(U)* vertige *m* ▸ **to suffer from vertigo** avoir le vertige.

verve [vɜ:v] **n** verve *f*.

very ['verɪ] ■ **adv 1.** [as intensifier] très ▸ **be very careful** faites très *OR* bien attention ▸ **very few/little** très peu ▸ **very much** beaucoup ▸ **I very much hope to be able to come** j'espère bien que je pourrai venir ▸ **at the very least** tout au moins ▸ **I very nearly fell** j'ai bien failli tomber ▸ **very last/first** tout dernier/premier ▸ **the very same day** le jour même ▸ **of one's very own** bien à soi **2.** [as euphemism] **: not very** pas très.
■ **adj : the very room/book** la pièce/le livre même ▸ **the very man/thing I've been looking for** juste l'homme/la chose que je cherchais ▸ **at the very end** [of street, row] tout au bout / [of story, month] tout à la fin ▸ **at that very moment** juste à ce moment-là ▸ **the very idea!** quelle idée!

◆ ***very well*** **adv** très bien ▸ **I can't very well tell him...** je ne peux tout de même pas lui dire que...

vespers ['vespəz] **n** *(U)* vêpres *fpl*.

vessel ['vesl] **n** *fml* **1.** [boat] vaisseau *m* **2.** [container] récipient *m*.

vest [vest] **n 1.** *UK* [undershirt] maillot *m* de corps **2.** *US* [waistcoat] gilet *m*.

vested interest ['vestɪd-] **n : vested interest (in)** intérêt *m* particulier (à).

vestibule ['vestɪbju:l] **n 1.** *fml* [entrance hall] vestibule *m* **2.** *US* [on train] sas *m*.

vestige ['vestɪdʒ] **n** vestige *m*.

vestry ['vestrɪ] **(pl -ies) n** sacristie *f*.

Vesuvius [vɪ'su:vjəs] **n** le Vésuve.

vet [vet] ■ **n 1.** *UK* (abbr of ***veterinary surgeon***) vétérinaire *mf* **2.** *US* (abbr of ***veteran***) ancien combattant *m*, vétéran *mf*.
■ **vt (pt & pp -ted, cont -ting)** *UK* [candidates] examiner avec soin.

veteran ['vetrən] ■ **adj** [experienced] chevronné(e).
■ **n 1.** MIL ancien combattant *m*, vétéran *mf* **2.** [experienced person] vétéran *m*.

veteran car **n** *UK* voiture *f* d'époque *(construite avant 1905)*.

Veteran's Day **n** *aux États-Unis, fête nationale en l'honneur des anciens combattants (le 11 novembre)*.

veterinarian [ˌvetərɪ'neərɪən] **n** *US* vétérinaire *mf*.

veterinary science ['vetərɪnrɪ-] **n** science *f* vétérinaire.

veterinary surgeon ['vetərɪnrɪ-] **n** *UK fml* vétérinaire *mf*.

veto ['vi:təʊ] ■ **n (pl -es)** veto *m*.
■ **vt (pt & pp -ed, cont -ing)** opposer son veto à.

vetting ['vetɪŋ] **n** *(U) UK* [of candidates] examen *m* minutieux.

vex [veks] **vt** contrarier.

vexed question [ˌvekst-] **n** question *f* controversée.

VFD (abbr of ***voluntary fire department***) **n** *pompiers bénévoles aux États-Unis*.

vg (abbr of ***very good***) tb.

VGA (abbr of ***video graphics array/adapter***) **n** COMPUT VGA *m*.

vgc (abbr of ***very good condition***) TBE, tbe.

VHF (abbr of ***very high frequency***) VHF.

VHS (abbr of ***video home system***) **n** VHS *m*.

VI abbr of ***Virgin Islands***.

via ['vaɪə] **prep 1.** [travelling through] via, par **2.** [by means of] au moyen de.

viability [ˌvaɪə'bɪlətɪ] **n** viabilité *f*.

viable ['vaɪəbl] **adj** viable.

viaduct ['vaɪədʌkt] **n** viaduc *m*.

vibes [vaɪbz] **npl** *inf* (abbr of ***vibrations***) atmosphère *f*, ambiance *f* ▸ **they give off really good/bad vibes** avec eux le courant passe vraiment bien/ne passe vraiment pas ▸ **I get really bad vibes from her** je la sens vraiment mal.

vibrant ['vaɪbrənt] **adj** vibrant(e).

vibrate [vaɪ'breɪt] **vi** vibrer.

vibration [vaɪ'breɪʃn] **n** vibration *f*.

vicar ['vɪkəʳ] **n** [in Church of England] pasteur *m*.

vicarage ['vɪkərɪdʒ] **n** presbytère *m*.

vicarious [vɪ'keərɪəs] **adj : to take a vicarious pleasure in sthg** retirer du plaisir indirectement de qqch.

vicariously [vɪ'keərɪəslɪ] **adv 1.** [experience] indirectement ▸ **she lived vicariously through her reading** elle vivait par procuration à travers ses lectures **2.** [authorize] par délégation, par procuration.

vice [vaɪs] **n 1.** [immorality, fault] vice *m* **2.** [tool] étau *m*.

vice- [vaɪs] **prefix** vice-.

vice-admiral **n** vice-amiral *m*.

vice-chairman **n** vice-président *m*, -e *f*.

vice-chancellor **n** *UK* UNIV président *m*, -e *f*.

vice-president **n** vice-président *m*, -e *f*.

vice-principal **n** SCH directeur *m* adjoint, directrice *f* adjointe.

vice squad **n** brigade *f* des mœurs.

vice versa [ˌvaɪsɪ'vɜːsə] **adv** vice versa.

vicinity [vɪ'sɪnətɪ] **n : in the vicinity (of)** aux alentours (de), dans les environs (de).

vicious ['vɪʃəs] **adj** violent(e), brutal(e).

vicious circle **n** cercle *m* vicieux.

viciously ['vɪʃəslɪ] **adv** [attack, beat] brutalement, violemment / [criticize] avec malveillance, méchamment.

viciousness ['vɪʃəsnɪs] **n** violence *f*, brutalité *f*.

vicissitudes [vɪ'sɪsɪtjuːdz] **npl** *fml* vicissitudes *fpl*.

victim ['vɪktɪm] **n** victime *f* ▸ **a fund for victims of cancer** des fonds pour les cancéreux ***OR*** les malades du cancer ▸ **to fall victim to sthg** devenir la victime de qqch.

victimization [ˌvɪktɪmaɪ'zeɪʃn] **n** [for beliefs, race, differences] fait *m* de prendre pour victime / [reprisals] représailles *fpl* ▸ **there must be no further victimization of workers** il ne doit pas y avoir d'autres représailles contre les ouvriers.

victimize, *UK* ***-ise*** ['vɪktɪmaɪz] **vt** faire une victime de.

victor ['vɪktəʳ] **n** vainqueur *m*.

Victoria Cross [vɪk'tɔːrɪə-] **n** Croix *f* de Victoria.

Victoria Falls [vɪk'tɔːrɪə-] **npl** les chutes *fpl* Victoria.

Victorian [vɪk'tɔːrɪən] **adj** victorien(enne).

Victoriana [ˌvɪktɔːrɪ'ɑːnə] **n** *(U)* objets *mpl* de l'époque victorienne.

victorious [vɪk'tɔːrɪəs] **adj** victorieux(euse).

victory ['vɪktərɪ] (pl **-ies**) **n : victory (over)** victoire *f* (sur).

video ['vɪdɪəʊ] ■ **n** (pl **-s**) **1.** [medium, recording] vidéo *f* **2.** *UK* [machine] magnétoscope *m* **3.** [cassette] vidéocassette *f*.

■ **comp** vidéo *(inv)*.

■ **vt** (pt & pp **-ed**, cont **-ing**) **1.** [using video recorder] enregistrer sur magnétoscope **2.** [using camera] faire une vidéo de, filmer.

video camera **n** caméra *f* vidéo.

video cassette **n** vidéocassette *f*.

video clip **n** clip *m*, vidéoclip *m*, clip *m* vidéo.

videoconference ['vɪdɪəʊ'kɒnfərəns] **n** vidéoconférence *f*.

video conferencing **n** vidéoconférence *f*.

video diary **n** journal *m* vidéo.

videodisc *UK*, ***videodisk*** *US* ['vɪdɪəʊdɪsk] **n** vidéodisque *m*.

video game **n** jeu *m* vidéo.

video machine **n** magnétoscope *m*.

video-on-demand **n** *service de location de vidéos par câble.*

videophone ['vɪdɪəʊfəʊn] **n** vidéophone *m*, visiophone *m*.

videorecorder ['vɪdɪəʊrɪˌkɔːdəʳ] **n** magnétoscope *m*.

video recording **n** enregistrement *m* vidéo.

video shop *UK*, ***video store*** *US* **n** vidéoclub *m*.

videotape ['vɪdɪəʊteɪp] **n 1.** [cassette] vidéocassette *f* **2.** *(U)* [ribbon] bande *f* vidéo.

vie [vaɪ] (pt & pp **vied**, cont **vying**) **vi : to vie for sthg** lutter pour qqch ▸ **to vie with sb (for sthg/to do sthg)** rivaliser avec qqn (pour qqch/pour faire qqch).

Vienna [vɪ'enə] **n** Vienne.

Viennese [ˌvɪə'niːz] ■ **adj** viennois(e).

■ **n** Viennois *m*, -e *f*.

Vietnam [*UK* ˌvjet'næm, *US* ˌvjet'nɑːm] **n** Viêt-nam *m* ▸ **in Vietnam** au Viêt-nam.

Vietnamese [ˌvjetnə'miːz] ■ **adj** vietnamien(enne).

■ **n** [language] vietnamien *m*.

■ **npl : the Vietnamese** les Vietnamiens.

view [vjuː] ■ **n 1.** [opinion] opinion *f*, avis *m* ▸ **that's the official view** c'est le point de vue officiel ▸ **view on sthg** opinion sur qqch ▸ **in my view** à mon avis ▸ **to take the view that...** être d'avis que...

2. [scene, sight] vue *f* ▸ **an aerial view of New York** une vue aérienne de New York ▸ **a room with a view** une chambre avec vue ▸ **you get a better view from here** on voit mieux d'ici ▸ **to come into view** apparaître ▸ **to hide sthg from view** [accidentally] cacher qqch de la vue / [deliberately] cacher qqch aux regards

3. [perspective, outlook] **: in view** en vue ▸ **with this end in view** avec *OR* dans cette intention ▸ **he has *OR* takes a gloomy view of life** il a une vue pessimiste de la vie.
■ **vt 1.** [consider] considérer ▸ **how do you view this matter?** quel est votre avis sur cette affaire?
2. [look at, examine - gen] examiner / [- house] visiter ▸ **viewed from above/from afar** vu d'en haut/de loin.
◆ ***in view of*** **prep** vu, étant donné ▸ **in view of this** ceci étant.
◆ ***with a view to*** **conj** dans l'intention de, avec l'idée de ▸ **they bought the house with a view to their retirement** ils ont acheté la maison en pensant à leur retraite.

viewdata ['vju:ˌdeɪtə] **n** vidéotex *m*.

viewer ['vju:əʳ] **n 1.** TV téléspectateur *m*, -trice *f* **2.** [for slides] visionneuse *f*.

viewfinder ['vju:ˌfaɪndəʳ] **n** viseur *m*.

viewing ['vju:ɪŋ] ■ **n** *(U)* **1.** TV programme *m*, programmes *mpl*, émissions *fpl* ▸ **late-night viewing on BBC 2** émissions de fin de soirée sur BBC 2 ▸ **his latest film makes exciting viewing** son dernier film est un spectacle passionnant **2.** [of showhouse, exhibition] visite *f* **3.** ASTRON observation *f*.
■ **comp 1.** TV [time, patterns] d'écoute ▸ **a young viewing audience** de jeunes téléspectateurs ▸ **viewing figures** taux *m* *OR* indice *m* d'écoute ▸ **at peak viewing hours** aux heures de grande écoute **2.** ASTRON & METEOR [conditions] d'observation.

viewpoint ['vju:pɔɪnt] **n** point *m* de vue.

vigil ['vɪdʒɪl] **n** veille *f* / RELIG vigile *f*.

vigilance ['vɪdʒɪləns] **n** vigilance *f*.

vigilant ['vɪdʒɪlənt] **adj** vigilant(e).

vigilante [ˌvɪdʒɪ'læntɪ] **n** membre *m* d'un groupe d'autodéfense.

vigor *US* = ***vigour***.

vigorous ['vɪgərəs] **adj** vigoureux(euse).

vigorously ['vɪgərəslɪ] **adv** vigoureusement, énergiquement.

vigour *UK*, ***vigor*** *US* ['vɪgəʳ] **n** vigueur *f*.

Viking ['vaɪkɪŋ] ■ **adj** viking *(inv)*.
■ **n** Viking *mf*.

vile [vaɪl] **adj** [mood] massacrant(e), exécrable / [person, act] vil(e), ignoble / [food] infect(e), exécrable.

vilify ['vɪlɪfaɪ] (pt & pp -ied) **vt** calomnier.

villa ['vɪlə] **n** villa *f* / [bungalow] pavillon *m*.

village ['vɪlɪdʒ] **n** village *m*.

villager ['vɪlɪdʒəʳ] **n** villageois *m*, -e *f*.

villain ['vɪlən] **n 1.** [of film, book] méchant *m*, -e *f* / [of play] traître *m* **2.** [criminal] bandit *m*.

Vilnius ['vɪlnɪəs] **n** Vilnious.

VIN (abbr of ***vehicle identification number***) **n** *numéro d'immatriculation*.

vinaigrette [ˌvɪnɪ'gret] **n** vinaigrette *f*.

vindicate ['vɪndɪkeɪt] **vt** justifier.

vindication [ˌvɪndɪ'keɪʃn] **n** justification *f*.

vindictive [vɪn'dɪktɪv] **adj** vindicatif(ive).

vindictively [vɪn'dɪktɪvlɪ] **adv** vindicativement.

vine [vaɪn] **n** vigne *f*.

vinegar ['vɪnɪgəʳ] **n** vinaigre *m*.

vine leaf **n** feuille *f* de vigne.

vineyard ['vɪnjəd] **n** vignoble *m*.

vintage ['vɪntɪdʒ] ■ **adj 1.** [wine] de grand cru **2.** [classic] typique.
■ **n** année *f*, millésime *m*.

vintage car **n** *UK* voiture *f* d'époque *(construite entre 1919 et 1930)*.

vintage wine **n** vin *m* de grand cru.

vintner ['vɪntnəʳ] **n** négociant *m* en vins.

vinyl ['vaɪnɪl] ■ **n** vinyle *m*.
■ **comp** de *OR* en vinyle.

viola [vɪ'əʊlə] **n** alto *m*.

violate ['vaɪəleɪt] **vt** violer.

violation [ˌvaɪə'leɪʃn] **n** violation *f*.

violence ['vaɪələns] **n** violence *f*.

violent ['vaɪələnt] **adj 1.** [gen] violent(e) **2.** [colour] criard(e).

violently ['vaɪələntlɪ] **adv** violemment / [die] de mort violente.

violet ['vaɪələt] ■ **adj** violet(ette).
■ **n 1.** [flower] violette *f* **2.** [colour] violet *m*.

violin [ˌvaɪə'lɪn] **n** violon *m*.

violinist [ˌvaɪə'lɪnɪst] **n** violoniste *mf*.

VIP (abbr of ***very important person***) **n** VIP *mf*.

viper ['vaɪpəʳ] **n** vipère *f*.

viral ['vaɪrəl] **adj** viral(e).

virgin ['vɜ:dʒɪn] ■ **adj** *liter* [land, forest, soil] vierge.
■ **n** [woman] vierge *f* / [man] garçon *m*/homme *m* vierge.

virginal ['vɜ:dʒɪnl] ■ **n** MUS **: virginals** virginal *m*.
■ **adj** virginal(e).

Virginia [və'dʒɪnjə] **n** Virginie *f* ▸ **in Virginia** en Virginie.

Virgin Islands **n : the Virgin Islands** les îles *fpl* Vierges ▸ **in the Virgin Islands** dans les îles Vierges.

virginity [və'dʒɪnətɪ] **n** virginité *f*.

Virgo ['vɜ:gəʊ] (pl -s) **n** Vierge *f* ▸ **to be (a) Virgo** être Vierge.

virile ['vɪraɪl] **adj** viril(e).

virility [vɪ'rɪlətɪ] **n** virilité *f*.

virtual ['vɜ:tʃʊəl] **adj** virtuel(elle) ▸ **it's a virtual certainty** c'est quasiment *OR* pratiquement certain.

virtually ['vɜ:tʃʊəlɪ] **adv** virtuellement, pratiquement.

virtual memory **n** COMPUT mémoire *f* virtuelle.

virtual reality **n** réalité *f* virtuelle.

virtue ['vɜ:tju:] **n 1.** [good quality] vertu *f* **2.** [benefit] **: virtue (in doing sthg)** mérite *m* (à faire qqch).
◆ ***by virtue of*** **prep** *fml* en vertu de.

virtuosity [ˌvɜːtjʊ'ɒsɪtɪ] **n** virtuosité *f.*

virtuoso [ˌvɜːtjʊ'əʊzəʊ] (pl **-sos** OR **-si** [-siː]) **n** virtuose *mf.*

virtuous ['vɜːtʃʊəs] **adj** vertueux(euse).

virulent ['vɪrʊlənt] **adj** virulent(e).

virus ['vaɪrəs] **n** COMPUT & MED virus *m.*

virus check **n** COMPUT détection *f* de virus.

virus-free **adj** COMPUT dépourvu(e) de virus.

visa ['viːzə] **n** visa *m.*

vis-à-vis [ˌviːzɑː'viː] **prep** *fml* par rapport à.

visceral ['vɪsərəl] **adj** viscéral(e).

viscose ['vɪskəʊs] **n** viscose *f.*

viscosity [vɪ'skɒsətɪ] **n** viscosité *f.*

viscount ['vaɪkaʊnt] **n** vicomte *m.*

viscous ['vɪskəs] **adj** visqueux(euse).

vise [vaɪs] **n** *US* étau *m.*

visibility [ˌvɪzɪ'bɪlətɪ] **n** visibilité *f.*

visible ['vɪzəbl] **adj** visible.

visible earnings **n** gains *mpl* visibles.

visibly ['vɪzəblɪ] **adv** visiblement.

vision ['vɪʒn] **n 1.** *(U)* [ability to see] vue *f* **2.** [foresight, dream] vision *f* **3.** *(U)* TV image *f.*

visionary ['vɪʒənrɪ] ■ **adj** visionnaire.
■ **n** (pl **-ies**) visionnaire *mf.*

visit ['vɪzɪt] ■ **n** visite *f* ▸ **on a visit** en visite ▸ **visit of a website** visite d'un site.
■ **vt** [person] rendre visite à / [place] visiter.
◆ ***visit with*** **vt insep** *US* **1.** [go and see] aller voir **2.** [chat to] parler avec.

visiting ['vɪzɪtɪŋ] **adj** [circus, performers] de passage / [lecturer] invité(e) / [birds] de passage, migrateur(euse) ▸ **the visiting team** SPORT les visiteurs.

visiting card ['vɪzɪtɪŋ-] **n** *UK* carte *f* de visite.

visiting hours ['vɪzɪtɪŋ-] **npl** heures *fpl* de visite.

visiting time = ***visiting hours***.

visitor ['vɪzɪtəʳ] **n** [to person] invité *m*, -e *f* / [to place] visiteur *m*, -euse *f* / [to hotel] client *m*, -e *f.*

visitors' book **n** *UK* livre *m* d'or / [in hotel] registre *m.*

visitor's passport **n** *UK* passeport *m* temporaire.

visor ['vaɪzəʳ] **n** visière *f.*

vista ['vɪstə] **n** [view] vue *f.*

VISTA ['vɪstə] (abbr of ***Volunteers in Service to America***) **n** *programme américain d'aide aux personnes les plus défavorisées.*

visual ['vɪʒʊəl] **adj** visuel(elle).

visual aids **npl** supports *mpl* visuels.

visual arts **npl** arts *mpl* plastiques.

visual display unit **n** écran *m* de visualisation.

visualize, *UK* ***-ise*** ['vɪʒʊəlaɪz] **vt** se représenter, s'imaginer.

visually ['vɪʒʊəlɪ] **adv** visuellement ▸ **visually handicapped** *UK*, **visually impaired** *US* malvoyant(e).

vital ['vaɪtl] **adj 1.** [essential] essentiel(elle) **2.** [full of life] plein(e) d'entrain.

vitality [vaɪ'tælətɪ] **n** vitalité *f.*

vitally ['vaɪtəlɪ] **adv** absolument.

vital statistics **npl** *inf* [of woman] mensurations *fpl.*

vitamin [*UK* 'vɪtəmɪn, *US* 'vaɪtəmɪn] **n** vitamine *f.*

vitriolic [ˌvɪtrɪ'ɒlɪk] **adj** au vitriol.

viva ['vaɪvə] *UK* = ***viva voce***.

vivacious [vɪ'veɪʃəs] **adj** enjoué(e).

vivacity [vɪ'væsətɪ] **n** vivacité *f.*

viva voce [ˌvaɪvə'vəʊsɪ] **n** *UK* examen *m* oral.

vivid ['vɪvɪd] **adj 1.** [bright] vif (vive) **2.** [clear - description] vivant(e) / [- memory] net (nette), précis(e).

vividly ['vɪvɪdlɪ] **adv** [describe] d'une manière vivante / [remember] clairement.

vivisection [ˌvɪvɪ'sekʃn] **n** vivisection *f.*

vixen ['vɪksn] **n** [fox] renarde *f.*

viz [vɪz] (abbr of ***vide licet***) c.-à-d.

VLF (abbr of ***very low frequency***) **n** *très basse fréquence.*

V-neck **n** [neck] décolleté *m* en V / [sweater] pull *m* à décolleté en V.

VOA (abbr of ***Voice of America***) **n** *station radiophonique américaine à destination de l'étranger.*

vocab ['vəʊkæb] **n** *inf* abbr of ***vocabulary***.

vocabulary [və'kæbjʊlərɪ] (pl **-ies**) **n** vocabulaire *m.*

vocal ['vəʊkl] **adj 1.** [outspoken] qui se fait entendre **2.** [of the voice] vocal(e).
◆ ***vocals*** **npl** chant *m.*

vocal cords **npl** cordes *fpl* vocales.

vocalist ['vəʊkəlɪst] **n** chanteur *m*, -euse *f (dans un groupe).*

vocation [vəʊ'keɪʃn] **n** vocation *f.*

vocational [vəʊ'keɪʃənl] **adj** professionnel(elle).

vociferous [və'sɪfərəs] **adj** bruyant(e).

vociferously [və'sɪfərəslɪ] **adv** bruyamment, en vociférant.

VOD (abbr of ***video-on-demand***) **n** vidéo *f* à la demande, VOD *f.*

vodka ['vɒdkə] **n** vodka *f.*

vogue [vəʊg] ■ **adj** en vogue, à la mode.
■ **n** vogue *f*, mode *f* ▸ **in vogue** en vogue, à la mode.

voice [vɔɪs] ■ **n 1.** [gen] voix *f* ▸ **to raise/lower one's voice** élever/baisser la voix ▸ **to keep one's voice down** parler bas **2.** [influence] **: to have a voice in** avoir son mot à dire dans.
■ **vt** [opinion, emotion] exprimer.

voice box **n** larynx *m.*

voice mail n COMPUT messagerie *f* vocale ▸ **to send/receive voice mail** envoyer/recevoir un message sur une boîte vocale.

voice-over n voix *f* off.

voice recognition n COMPUT reconnaissance *f* de la parole.

void [vɔɪd] ■ adj **1.** [invalid] nul (nulle) ; ➤ ***null*** **2.** *fml* [empty] : **void of** dépourvu(e) de, dénué(e) de.
■ n vide *m*.
■ vt annuler.

voile [vɔɪl] n *(U)* voile *m*.

vol. (abbr of ***volume***) vol.

volatile [*UK* ˈvɒlətaɪl, *US* ˈvɒlətl] adj [situation] explosif(ive) / [person] lunatique, versatile / [market] instable.

vol-au-vent [ˈvɒləʊvɑ̃] n vol-au-vent *m inv*.

volcanic [vɒlˈkænɪk] adj volcanique.

volcano [vɒlˈkeɪnəʊ] (pl **-es** *OR* **-s**) n volcan *m*.

vole [vəʊl] n campagnol *m*.

Volga [ˈvɒlgə] n : **the (River)Volga** la Volga.

volition [vəˈlɪʃn] n *fml* : **of one's own volition** de son propre gré.

volley [ˈvɒlɪ] ■ n (pl -s) **1.** [of gunfire] salve *f* **2.** *fig* [of questions, curses] torrent *m* / [of blows] volée *f*, pluie *f* **3.** SPORT volée *f*.
■ vt frapper à la volée, reprendre de volée.

volleyball [ˈvɒlɪbɔːl] n volley-ball *m*.

volt [vəʊlt] n volt *m*.

Volta [ˈvɒltə] n Volta *f*.

voltage [ˈvəʊltɪdʒ] n voltage *m*, tension *f*.

voluble [ˈvɒljʊbl] adj volubile, loquace.

volume [ˈvɒljuːm] n **1.** [gen] volume *m* **2.** [of work, letters] quantité *f* / [of traffic] densité *f*.

volume control n réglage *m* du volume.

volume mailing n multipostage *m*, publipostage *m* groupé.

volume of sales n volume *m* de ventes, chiffre *m* d'affaires.

voluminous [vəˈluːmɪnəs] adj *fml* **1.** [garment] immense **2.** [container] volumineux(euse).

voluntarily [*UK* ˈvɒləntrɪlɪ, *US* ˌvɒlənˈterəlɪ] adv volontairement.

voluntary [ˈvɒləntrɪ] adj **1.** [not obligatory] volontaire **2.** [unpaid] bénévole.

voluntary liquidation n liquidation *f* volontaire.

voluntary redundancy n *UK* départ *m* volontaire.

voluntary work n travail *m* bénévole, bénévolat *m*.

volunteer [ˌvɒlənˈtɪəʳ] ■ n **1.** [gen & MIL] volontaire *mf* **2.** [unpaid worker] bénévole *mf*.
■ vt **1.** [offer] : **to volunteer to do sthg** se proposer *OR* se porter volontaire pour faire qqch **2.** [information, advice] donner spontanément.
■ vi **1.** [offer one's services] : **to volunteer (for)** se porter volontaire (pour), proposer ses services (pour) **2.** MIL s'engager comme volontaire.

voluptuous [vəˈlʌptʃʊəs] adj voluptueux(euse).

vomit [ˈvɒmɪt] ■ n vomi *m*.
■ vi vomir.

vomiting [ˈvɒmɪtɪŋ] n *(U)* vomissements *mpl*.

voracious [vəˈreɪʃəs] adj vorace.

voraciously [vəˈreɪʃəslɪ] adv [consume, eat] voracement, avec voracité / [read] avec voracité, avidement.

vortex [ˈvɔːteks] (pl **-texes** [-teksiːz] *OR* **-tices** [-tɪsiːz]) n vortex *m* / *fig* [of events] tourbillon *m*.

vote [vəʊt] ■ n **1.** [individual decision] : **vote (for/against)** vote *m* (pour/contre), voix *f* (pour/contre) ▸ **the candidate got 15,000 votes** le candidat a recueilli 15 000 voix ▸ **to count the votes** [gen] compter les votes *OR* les voix / POL dépouiller le scrutin
2. [ballot] vote *m* ▸ **to have a vote on sthg** voter sur qqch, mettre qqch au vote ▸ **to put sthg to the vote** procéder à un vote sur qqch
3. [right to vote] droit *m* de vote.
■ vt **1.** [declare] élire
2. [choose] : **to vote Labour/Republican** voter travailliste/républicain ▸ **to vote to do sthg** voter *OR* se prononcer pour faire qqch ▸ **they voted to return to work** ils ont voté le retour au travail.
■ vi : **France is voting this weekend** la France va aux urnes ce week-end ▸ **to vote (for/against)** voter (pour/contre) ▸ **let's vote on it!** mettons cela aux voix!
◆ ***vote in*** vt sep [person, government] élire / [new law] voter, adopter.
◆ ***vote out*** vt sep évincer par un vote.

vote of confidence (pl **votes of confidence**) n vote *m* de confiance.

vote of no confidence (pl **votes of no confidence**) n motion *f* de censure.

vote of thanks (pl **votes of thanks**) n discours *m* de remerciement.

voter [ˈvəʊtəʳ] n électeur *m*, -trice *f*.

voting [ˈvəʊtɪŋ] n scrutin *m*.

voting booth n isoloir *m*.

vouch [vaʊtʃ] ◆ ***vouch for*** vt insep répondre de, se porter garant de.

voucher [ˈvaʊtʃəʳ] n bon *m*, coupon *m*.

vow [vaʊ] ■ n vœu *m*, serment *m*.
■ vt : **to vow to do sthg** jurer de faire qqch ▸ **to vow (that)...** jurer que...

vowel [ˈvaʊəl] n voyelle *f*.

vox pop [ˌvɒksˈpɒp] n *UK inf émission de radio ou de TV avec intervention du public*.

voyage [ˈvɔɪɪdʒ] n voyage *m* en mer / [in space] vol *m*.

voyeur [vwɑːˈjɜːʳ] n voyeur *m*, -euse *f*.

voyeurism [vwɑːˈjɜːrɪzm] n voyeurisme *m*.

VP n abbr of ***vice-president***.

vs abbr of ***versus***.

V-shaped **adj** en (forme de) V.

V-sign **n : to give the V-sign** [for victory, approval] faire le V de la victoire ▸ **to give sb the V-sign** *UK* [as insult] ≃ faire un bras d'honneur à qqn.

VSO (abbr of ***Voluntary Service Overseas***) **n** *organisation britannique envoyant des travailleurs bénévoles dans des pays en voie de développement pour contribuer à leur développement technique.*

VSOP (abbr of ***very special old pale***) *appellation réservée à certains cognacs et armagnacs.*

VT abbr of ***Vermont***.

VTOL ['vi:tɒl] (abbr of ***vertical takeoff and landing***) **n** ADAV *m*.

VTR (abbr of ***video tape recorder***) **n** magnétoscope *m*.

vulgar ['vʌlgəʳ] **adj 1.** [in bad taste] vulgaire **2.** [offensive] grossier(ère).

vulgarity [vʌl'gærətɪ] *(U)* **n 1.** [poor taste] vulgarité *f* **2.** [offensiveness] grossièreté *f*.

vulnerability [ˌvʌlnərə'bɪlətɪ] **n** vulnérabilité *f*.

vulnerable ['vʌlnərəbl] **adj** vulnérable ▸ **vulnerable to** [attack] exposé(e) à / [colds] sensible à.

vulture ['vʌltʃəʳ] **n** *lit* & *fig* vautour *m*.

vulva ['vʌlvə] (pl -s OR **vulvae** [-vi:]) **n** vulve *f*.

W

w ['dʌblju:] (pl w's *OR* ws), ***W¹*** (pl W's *OR* Ws) **n** [letter] w *m inv*, W *m inv*.

W² **1.** (abbr of ***west***) O, W **2.** (abbr of ***watt***) w.

WA abbr of ***Washington***.

wacky ['wækɪ] (comp **-ier**, superl **-iest**) **adj** *inf* farfelu(e).

wad [wɒd] **n 1.** [of cotton wool, paper] tampon *m* **2.** [of banknotes, documents] liasse *f* **3.** [of tobacco] chique *f* / [of chewing-gum] boulette *f*.

wadding ['wɒdɪŋ] **n** rembourrage *m*, capitonnage *m*.

waddle ['wɒdl] **vi** se dandiner.

wade [weɪd] **vi** patauger.
◆ ***wade through*** **vt insep** *fig* se taper.

wadge [wɒdʒ] **n** *UK inf* morceau *m* / [of papers] tas *m*.

wading pool ['weɪdɪŋ-] **n** *US* pataugeoire *f*.

wafer ['weɪfəʳ] **n** [thin biscuit] gaufrette *f*.

wafer-thin **adj** mince comme du papier à cigarette *OR* une pelure d'oignon.

waffle ['wɒfl] ■ **n 1.** CULIN gaufre *f* **2.** *UK inf* [vague talk] verbiage *m*.
■ **vi** parler pour ne rien dire.

waft [wɑ:ft *OR* wɒft] **vi** flotter.

wag [wæg] (pt & pp **-ged**, cont **-ging**) ■ **vt** remuer, agiter.
■ **vi** [tail] remuer.

wage [weɪdʒ] ■ **n** salaire *m*, paie *f*, paye *f*.
■ **vt : to wage war against** faire la guerre à.
◆ ***wages*** **npl** salaire *m*.

wage claim **n** revendication *f* salariale.

wage differential **n** écart *m* des salaires.

wage earner [-ˌɜ:nəʳ] **n** salarié *m*, -e *f*.

wage freeze **n** blocage *m* des salaires.

wage packet **n** *UK* **1.** [envelope] enveloppe *f* de paye **2.** *fig* [pay] paie *f*, paye *f*.

wager ['weɪdʒəʳ] **n** pari *m*.

wage rise **n** *UK* augmentation *f* de salaire.

waggish ['wægɪʃ] **adj** *inf* facétieux(euse), plaisant(e).

waggle ['wægl] *inf* ■ **vt** agiter, remuer / [ears] remuer.
■ **vi** remuer.

waggon ['wægən] *UK* = ***wagon***.

wagon ['wægən] **n 1.** [horse-drawn] chariot *m*, charrette *f* **2.** *UK* RAIL wagon *m*.

waif [weif] **n** enfant abandonné *m*, enfant abandonnée *f*.

wail [weɪl] ■ **n** gémissement *m*.
■ **vi** gémir.

wailing ['weɪlɪŋ] **n** *(U)* gémissements *mpl*, plaintes *fpl*.

waist [weɪst] **n** taille *f*.

waistband ['weɪstbænd] **n** ceinture *f*.

waistcoat ['weɪskəʊt] **n** *esp UK* gilet *m*.

-waisted ['weɪstɪd] **suffix : a low/high-waisted dress** une robe à taille basse/haute.

waistline ['weɪstlaɪn] **n** taille *f*.

wait [weɪt] ■ **n** attente *f* ▸ **to have a long wait** attendre longtemps ▸ **to lie in wait for** être à l'affût de, guetter.
■ **vi** attendre ▸ **I can't wait to see you** je brûle d'impatience de te voir ▸ **(just) you wait!** tu ne perds rien pour attendre! ▸ **wait and see!** tu vas bien voir! ▸ **wait a minute** *OR* **second** *OR* **moment!** [interrupting person] minute (papillon)! / [interrupting oneself] attends voir! ▸ **wait until I've finished** attendez que j'aie fini ▸ **to keep sb waiting** faire attendre qqn ▸ **'keys cut while you wait'** 'clés minute'.
■ **vt 1.** *US inf* [delay] retarder ▸ **don't wait dinner for me** ne m'attendez pas pour vous mettre à table **2.** *US* [serve at] **: to wait tables** servir à table, faire le service.
◆ ***wait about*** *UK*, ***wait around*** **vi** attendre / [waste time] perdre son temps à attendre.
◆ ***wait for*** **vt insep** attendre ▸ **to wait for sb to do sthg** attendre que qqn fasse qqch ▸ **wait for it!** *UK hum* tiens-toi bien!
◆ ***wait on*** **vt insep** [serve food to] servir.
◆ ***wait up*** **vi 1.** veiller, ne pas se coucher **2.** *US inf* [wait] **: hey, wait up!** attendez-moi!

waiter ['weɪtəʳ] **n** garçon *m*, serveur *m*.

waiting game ['weɪtɪŋ-] **n** politique *f* d'attente.

waiting list ['weɪtɪŋ-] **n** liste *f* d'attente.

waiting room ['weɪtɪŋ-] **n** salle *f* d'attente.

waitress ['weɪtrɪs] **n** serveuse *f*.

wait state **n** COMPUT état *m* d'attente.

waive [weɪv] vt [fee] renoncer à / [rule] prévoir une dérogation à.

waiver ['weɪvəʳ] n LAW dérogation *f*.

wake [weɪk] ■ n [of ship] sillage *m* ▸ **in one's wake** *fig* dans son sillage ▸ **in the wake of** *fig* à la suite de.
■ vt (pt **woke** *OR* **-d**, pp **woken** *OR* **-d**) réveiller.
■ vi (pt **woke** *OR* **-d**, pp **woken** *OR* **-d**) se réveiller.
◆ ***wake up*** ■ vt sep réveiller.
■ vi 1. [wake] se réveiller 2. *fig* [become aware] **: to wake up (to sthg)** prendre conscience (de qqch), se sensibiliser (à qqch).

waken ['weɪkən] *fml* ■ vt réveiller.
■ vi se réveiller.

waking ['weɪkɪŋ] ■ adj [hours] de veille ▸ **she spends her waking hours reading** elle passe tout son temps à lire ▸ **a waking dream** une rêverie, une rêvasserie.
■ n [state] (état *m* de) veille *f*.

Wales [weɪlz] n pays *m* de Galles ▸ **in Wales** au pays de Galles.

walk [wɔ:k] ■ n 1. [way of walking] démarche *f*, façon *f* de marcher 2. [journey - for pleasure] promenade *f* / [- long distance] marche *f* ▸ **it's a long walk** c'est loin à pied ▸ **to go for a walk** aller se promener, aller faire une promenade ▸ **I took my mother for a walk** j'ai emmené ma mère en promenade *OR* faire un tour ▸ **did you take the dog for a walk?** as-tu promené *OR* sorti le chien? 3. [route] promenade *f* ▸ **a coastal walk** un chemin côtier.
■ vt 1. [accompany - person] accompagner / [- dog] promener ▸ **may I walk you home?** puis-je vous raccompagner? 2. [distance] faire à pied ▸ **you can walk it in 10 minutes** il faut 10 minutes (pour y aller) à pied ▸ **to walk the streets** [homeless] être sur le pavé / [in search] arpenter la ville / [prostitute] faire le trottoir.
■ vi 1. [gen] marcher ▸ **did you walk all the way?** avez-vous fait tout le chemin à pied? ▸ **to walk on one's hands** marcher sur les mains, faire l'arbre fourchu 2. [for pleasure] se promener ▸ **I'm walking on air!** je suis aux anges!
◆ ***walk away with*** vt insep *inf fig* gagner *OR* remporter haut la main ▸ **she walked away with all the credit** c'est elle qui a reçu tous les honneurs.
◆ ***walk in on*** vt insep [interrupt] déranger / [in embarrassing situation] prendre en flagrant délit ▸ **we walked in on her as she was getting dressed** nous sommes entrés sans prévenir pendant qu'elle s'habillait.
◆ ***walk off*** vt sep [headache, cramp] faire une promenade pour se débarrasser de.
◆ ***walk off with*** vt insep *inf* 1. [steal] faucher 2. [win easily] gagner *OR* remporter haut la main.
◆ ***walk out*** vi 1. [leave suddenly] partir 2. [go on strike] se mettre en grève, faire grève.
◆ ***walk out on*** vt insep quitter.

walkabout ['wɔ:kə,baʊt] n *UK* [by president] bain *m* de foule.

walker ['wɔ:kəʳ] n [for pleasure] promeneur *m*, -euse *f* / [long-distance] marcheur *m*, -euse *f*.

walkie-talkie [,wɔ:kɪ'tɔ:kɪ] n talkie-walkie *m*.

walk-in adj 1. [cupboard] assez grand(e) pour qu'on puisse y entrer 2. *US* [easy] facile.

walking ['wɔ:kɪŋ] n *(U)* marche *f* (à pied), promenade *f*.

walking shoes npl chaussures *fpl* de marche.

walking stick n canne *f*.

Walkman® ['wɔ:kmən] n baladeur *m*, Walkman® *m*.

walk of life (pl **walks of life**) n milieu *m*.

walk-on adj [part, role] de figurant(e).

walkout ['wɔ:kaʊt] n [strike] grève *f*, débrayage *m*.

walkover ['wɔ:k,əʊvəʳ] n victoire *f* facile.

walkway ['wɔ:kweɪ] n passage *m* / [between buildings] passerelle *f*.

wall [wɔ:l] n 1. [of room, building] mur *m* / [of rock, cave] paroi *f* ▸ **to come up against a brick wall** se heurter à un mur ▸ **to drive sb up the wall** *inf* rendre qqn fou, taper sur le système de qqn 2. ANAT paroi *f*.

wallchart ['wɔ:ltʃɑ:t] n planche *f* murale.

wall cupboard n placard *m* mural.

walled [wɔ:ld] adj fortifié(e).

wallet ['wɒlɪt] n portefeuille *m*.

wallflower ['wɔ:l,flaʊəʳ] n 1. [plant] giroflée *f* 2. *inf fig* [person] **: to be a wallflower** faire tapisserie.

wall hanging n tenture *f*.

Walloon [wɒ'lu:n] ■ adj wallon(onne).
■ n 1. [person] Wallon *m*, -onne *f* 2. [language] wallon *m*.

wallop ['wɒləp] *inf* ■ n gros coup *m*.
■ vt [person] flanquer un coup à / [ball] taper fort dans.

wallow ['wɒləʊ] vi 1. [in liquid] se vautrer 2. [in emotion] **: to wallow in** se complaire dans.

wall painting n peinture *f* murale.

wallpaper ['wɔ:l,peɪpəʳ] ■ n [for wall, computer screen] papier *m* peint.
■ vt tapisser.

Wall Street n Wall Street *m (quartier financier de New York)*.

wall-to-wall adj **: wall-to-wall carpet** moquette *f*.

wally ['wɒlɪ] (pl **-ies**) n *UK inf* idiot *m*, -e *f*, andouille *f*.

walnut ['wɔ:lnʌt] n 1. [nut] noix *f* 2. [tree, wood] noyer *m*.

walrus ['wɔ:lrəs] (pl **walrus** *OR* **-es** [-i:z]) n morse *m*.

waltz [wɔ:ls] ■ n valse *f*.
■ vi 1. [dance] valser, danser la valse 2. *inf* [walk confidently] marcher d'un air dégagé *OR* de façon désinvolte.

wan [wɒn] (comp **-ner**, superl **-nest**) adj pâle, blême.

WAN [wæn] n abbr of ***wide area network***.

wand [wɒnd] n baguette *f*.

wander ['wɒndəʳ] vi 1. [person] errer ▸ **don't wander off the path** ne vous écartez pas du chemin 2. [mind] divaguer / [thoughts] vagabonder ▸ **he wandered off the topic** il s'est écarté du sujet ▸ **her attention began to wander** elle commença à être de moins en moins attentive.

wanderer ['wɒndərəʳ] n vagabond *m*, -e *f*.

wandering ['wɒndərɪŋ] adj ambulant(e).

wanderlust ['wɒndəlʌst] n bougeotte *f*, envie *f* de voyager.

wane [weɪn] ■ **n : on the wane** en déclin / [power, interest] faiblissant(e).
■ **vi 1.** [influence, interest] diminuer, faiblir **2.** [moon] décroître.

wangle ['wæŋgl] **vt** *inf* se débrouiller pour obtenir.

wank [wæŋk] *UK vulg* ■ **vi** se branler.
■ **n** branlette *f* ▸ **to have a wank** se faire une branlette.

wanker ['wæŋkəʳ] **n** *UK vulg* branleur *m*.

wanna ['wɒnə] *esp US* = ***want a, want to***.

wannabe ['wɒnə,bi:] **n** *inf se dit de quelqu'un qui veut être ce qu'il ne peut pas être* ▸ **a Britney Spears wannabe** un clone de Britney Spears.

want [wɒnt] ■ **n 1.** [need] besoin *m*
2. [lack] manque *m* ▸ **for want of** faute de, par manque de ▸ **I'll take this novel for want of anything better** faute de mieux je vais prendre ce roman ▸ **if we failed, it wasn't for want of trying** nous avons échoué mais ce n'est pas faute d'avoir essayé
3. [deprivation] pauvreté *f*, besoin *m* ▸ **to be in want** être dans le besoin *OR* dans la misère.
■ **vt 1.** [wish, desire] vouloir ▸ **to want sthg badly** avoir très envie de qqch ▸ **to want to do sthg** vouloir faire qqch ▸ **she doesn't want to** elle n'en a pas envie ▸ **to want sb to do sthg** vouloir que qqn fasse qqch ▸ **I want you to wait here** je veux que tu attendes ici ▸ **someone wants you** *OR* **you're wanted on the phone** quelqu'un vous demande au téléphone
2. [desire sexually] désirer, avoir envie de
3. *inf* [need] avoir besoin de ▸ **do you have everything you want?** avez-vous tout ce qu'il vous faut? ▸ **you want to be more careful** tu devrais être plus prudent ▸ **there are still a couple of things that want doing** il y a encore quelques petites choses à faire *OR* qu'il faut faire.

want ad **n** *US inf* petite annonce *f*.

wanted ['wɒntɪd] **adj : to be wanted (by the police)** être recherché(e) (par la police).

wanting ['wɒntɪŋ] **adj : to be wanting in** manquer de ▸ **to be found wanting** ne pas être à la hauteur ▸ **not to be found wanting** être à la hauteur.

wanton ['wɒntən] **adj** [destruction, neglect] gratuit(e).

WAP [wæp] (abbr of ***wireless application protocol***) **n** TELEC WAP *m* ▸ **WAP phone** téléphone *m* WAP.

war [wɔ:ʳ] ■ **n** guerre *f* ▸ **to go to war** entrer *OR* se mettre en guerre ▸ **to have been in the wars** *UK* être dans un sale état.
■ **vi** (pt & pp **-red**, cont **-ring**) se battre.

War., Warks. (abbr of **Warwickshire**) *comté anglais*.

warble ['wɔ:bl] **vi** [bird] gazouiller.

war crime **n** crime *m* de guerre.

war criminal **n** criminel *m*, -elle *f* de guerre.

war cry **n** cri *m* de guerre.

ward [wɔ:d] **n 1.** [in hospital] salle *f* **2.** *UK* POL circonscription *f* électorale **3.** LAW pupille *mf*.
◆ ***ward off*** **vt insep** [danger] écarter / [disease, blow] éviter / [evil spirits] éloigner.

war dance **n** danse *f* guerrière.

warden ['wɔ:dn] **n 1.** [of park] gardien *m*, -enne *f* **2.** *UK* [of youth hostel, hall of residence] directeur *m*, -trice *f* **3.** *US* [of prison] directeur *m*, -trice *f*.

warder ['wɔ:dəʳ] **n** *UK* [in prison] gardien *m*, -enne *f*.

ward of court **n** pupille *mf* sous tutelle judiciaire.

wardrobe ['wɔ:drəʊb] **n** garde-robe *f*.

wardrobe mistress **n** *UK* costumière *f*.

warehouse ['weəhaʊs] (pl [-haʊzɪz]) **n** entrepôt *m*, magasin *m*.

wares [weəz] **npl** marchandises *fpl*.

warfare ['wɔ:feəʳ] **n** *(U)* guerre *f*.

war game **n 1.** [military exercise] manœuvres *fpl* militaires **2.** [game of strategy] jeu *m* de stratégie militaire.

warhead ['wɔ:hed] **n** ogive *f*, tête *f*.

warily ['weərəlɪ] **adv** avec précaution *OR* circonspection.

warlike ['wɔ:laɪk] **adj** belliqueux(euse).

warm [wɔ:m] ■ **adj 1.** [gen] chaud(e) ▸ **are you warm enough?** tu as assez chaud? ▸ **it's warm today** il fait chaud aujourd'hui **2.** [friendly] chaleureux(euse).
■ **vt** chauffer.
◆ ***warm over*** **vt sep** *US lit & fig* resservir.
◆ ***warm to*** **vt insep** [person] se prendre de sympathie pour / [idea, place] se mettre à aimer.
◆ ***warm up*** ■ **vt sep** réchauffer.
■ **vi 1.** [person, room] se réchauffer **2.** [machine, engine] chauffer **3.** SPORT s'échauffer.

warm-blooded [-'blʌdɪd] **adj** à sang chaud.

war memorial **n** monument *m* aux morts.

warm front **n** METEOR front *m* chaud.

warm-hearted [-'hɑ:tɪd] **adj** chaleureux(euse), affectueux(euse).

warmly ['wɔ:mlɪ] **adv 1.** [in warm clothes] **: to dress warmly** s'habiller chaudement **2.** [in a friendly way] chaleureusement.

warmness ['wɔ:mnɪs] **n** chaleur *f*.

warmonger ['wɔ:,mʌŋgəʳ] **n** belliciste *mf*.

warmongering ['wɔ:,mʌŋgərɪŋ] ■ **n** *(U)* [activities] activités *fpl* bellicistes / [attitude] bellicisme *m* / [propaganda] propagande *f* belliciste.
■ **adj** belliciste.

warmth [wɔ:mθ] **n** chaleur *f*.

warm-up **n** SPORT échauffement *m*.

warn [wɔ:n] ■ **vt** avertir, prévenir ▸ **to warn sb of sthg** avertir qqn de qqch ▸ **to warn sb not to do sthg** conseiller à qqn de ne pas faire qqch, déconseiller à qqn de faire qqch.
■ **vi : to warn of sthg** annoncer un risque de qqch.

warning ['wɔ:nɪŋ] ■ **adj** d'avertissement.
■ **n** avertissement *m* ▸ **thanks for the warning** merci de m'avoir prévenu *OR* m'avoir averti ▸ **he left without any warning** il est parti sans prévenir ▸ **they gave us advance warning of the meeting** ils nous ont prévenus de la réunion.

warning light **n** voyant *m*, avertisseur *m* lumineux.

warning triangle **n** *UK* triangle *m* de signalisation.

warp [wɔːp] ■ vt 1. [wood] gauchir, voiler 2. [personality] fausser, pervertir.
■ vi [wood] gauchir, se voiler.
■ n [of cloth] chaîne *f*.

warpath ['wɔːpɑːθ] n : **to be on the warpath** *fig* être sur le sentier de la guerre.

warped [wɔːpt] adj 1. [wood] gauchi(e) 2. [personality, idea] perverti(e).

warrant ['wɒrənt] ■ n LAW mandat *m*.
■ vt 1. [justify] justifier 2. [guarantee] garantir.

warrant officer n adjudant *m*, -e *f*.

warranty ['wɒrəntɪ] (pl -ies) n garantie *f*.

warren ['wɒrən] n terrier *m*.

warring ['wɔːrɪŋ] adj en guerre.

warrior ['wɒrɪə^r] n guerrier *m*, -ère *f*.

Warsaw ['wɔːsɔː] n Varsovie ▸ **the Warsaw Pact** le pacte de Varsovie.

warship ['wɔːʃɪp] n navire *m* de guerre.

wart [wɔːt] n verrue *f*.

wart hog n phacochère *m*.

wartime ['wɔːtaɪm] ■ adj de guerre.
■ n : **in wartime** en temps de guerre.

war-torn adj déchiré(e) par la guerre.

war widow n veuve *f* de guerre.

wary ['weərɪ] (comp -ier, superl -iest) adj prudent(e), circonspect(e) ▸ **to be wary of** se méfier de ▸ **to be wary of doing sthg** hésiter à faire qqch.

was *(weak form* [wəz], *strong form* [wɒz]*)* pt ➤ ***be***.

wash [wɒʃ] ■ n 1. [act] lavage *m* ▸ **to have a wash** *UK* se laver ▸ **to give sthg a wash** laver qqch ▸ **this floor needs a good wash** ce plancher a bien besoin d'être lavé *OR* nettoyé
2. [clothes] lessive *f* ▸ **your shirt is in the wash** [laundry basket] ta chemise est au (linge) sale / [machine] ta chemise est à la lessive ▸ **the stain came out in the wash** la tache est partie au lavage
3. [from boat] remous *m*.
■ vt 1. [clean] laver ▸ **to wash one's hands** se laver les mains ▸ **she washed her hair** elle s'est lavé la tête *OR* les cheveux ▸ **to wash the dishes** faire *OR* laver la vaisselle ▸ **to wash clothes** faire la lessive
2. [carry] : **the waves washed the oil/body onto the beach** les vagues ont rejeté le pétrole/corps sur la plage ▸ **the crew was washed overboard** l'équipage a été emporté par une vague.
■ vi se laver.
◆ ***wash away*** vt sep emporter.
◆ ***wash down*** vt sep 1. [food] arroser
2. [clean] laver à grande eau.
◆ ***wash out*** vt sep 1. [stain, dye] faire partir, enlever
2. [container] laver.
◆ ***wash up*** ■ vt sep 1. *UK* [dishes] : **to wash the dishes up** faire *OR* laver la vaisselle
2. [subj: sea, river] rejeter ▸ **several dolphins were washed up on shore** plusieurs dauphins se sont échoués sur la côte.
■ vi 1. *UK* [wash dishes] faire *OR* laver la vaisselle
2. *US* [wash oneself] se laver.

washable ['wɒʃəbl] adj lavable.

wash-and-wear adj qui ne nécessite aucun repassage.

washbag ['wɒʃˌbæg] n trousse *f* de toilette.

washbasin *UK* ['wɒʃˌbeɪsn], ***washbowl*** *US* ['wɒʃbəʊl] n lavabo *m*.

washcloth ['wɒʃˌklɒθ] n *US* gant *m* de toilette.

washed-out [ˌwɒʃt-] adj 1. [pale] délavé(e) 2. [exhausted] lessivé(e).

washed-up [ˌwɒʃt-] adj *inf* [person] fini(e) / [project] fichu(e).

washer ['wɒʃə^r] n 1. TECH rondelle *f* 2. [washing machine] machine *f* à laver.

washer-dryer n machine *f* à laver séchante.

washing ['wɒʃɪŋ] n *(U)* 1. [action] lessive *f* 2. [clothes] linge *m*, lessive *f*.

washing line n corde *f* à linge.

washing machine n machine *f* à laver.

washing powder n *UK* lessive *f*, détergent *m*.

Washington ['wɒʃɪŋtən] n 1. [state] : **Washington State** l'État *m* de Washington 2. [city] : **Washington D.C.** Washington.

washing-up n *UK* vaisselle *f*.

washing-up liquid n *UK* liquide *m* pour la vaisselle.

washout ['wɒʃaʊt] n *inf* fiasco *m*.

washroom ['wɒʃrʊm] n *US* toilettes *fpl*.

wasn't [wɒznt] = ***was not***.

wasp [wɒsp] n guêpe *f*.

Wasp, ***WASP*** [wɒsp] (abbr of ***White Anglo-Saxon Protestant***) n *inf personne de race blanche, d'origine anglo-saxonne et protestante*.

CULTURE

Wasp

Le terme **White Anglo-Saxon Protestants** (« protestants anglo-saxons blancs ») désigne généralement les membres privilégiés de la classe dominante américaine : on utilise des mots tels que **Waspy**, **Waspish**, **Waspdom** ou **Waspishness** pour dénoncer un manque de diversité culturelle ou une trop grande prédominance de la race blanche. Après son élection et l'incroyable popularité dont il a bénéficié, le président J.F. Kennedy, de confession catholique, est la première figure politique à avoir ébranlé cette classe politique élitiste.

waspish ['wɒspɪʃ] adj revêche, grincheux(euse).

wastage ['weɪstɪdʒ] n gaspillage *m*.

waste [weɪst] ■ adj [material] de rebut / [fuel] perdu(e) / [area of land] en friche.
■ n 1. [misuse] gaspillage *m* ▸ **it's a waste of money** [extravagance] c'est du gaspillage / [bad investment] c'est de l'argent perdu ▸ **to go to waste** [gen] être gaspillé / [food] se perdre / [work] ne servir à rien ▸ **I'm not going to let the opportunity go to waste** je ne vais pas laisser passer

l'occasion ▸ **a waste of time** une perte de temps ▸ **to lay waste to sthg, to lay sthg waste** ravager *OR* dévaster qqch **2.** *(U)* [refuse] déchets *mpl*, ordures *fpl*.
■ vt [money, food, energy] gaspiller / [time, opportunity] perdre ▸ **don't waste your breath trying to convince them** ne perds pas ton temps à essayer de les convaincre.
◆ ***wastes*** **npl** *liter* étendues *fpl* désertes.

wastebasket *US* = ***wastepaper basket***.

waste bin **n** *UK* [in kitchen] poubelle *f*, boîte *f* à ordures / [for paper] corbeille *f* (à papier).

wasted ['weɪstɪd] **adj 1.** [material, money] gaspillé(e) / [energy, opportunity, time] perdu(e) / [attempt, effort] inutile, vain(e) / [food] inutilisé(e) ▸ **a wasted journey** un voyage raté **2.** [figure, person] décharné(e) / [limb - emaciated] décharné(e) / [- enfeebled] atrophié(e).

waste disposal unit **n** broyeur *m* d'ordures.

wasteful ['weɪstfʊl] **adj** [person] gaspilleur(euse) / [activity] peu économique.

waste ground **n** *(U)* *UK* terrain *m* vague.

wasteland ['weɪst,lænd] **n** [in country] terre *f* à l'abandon / *UK* [in city] terrain *m* vague.

waste paper **n** papier *m* de rebut.

wastepaper basket, ***wastepaper bin*** *UK* [,weɪst'peɪpər-], *US* ***wastebasket*** ['weɪst,bɑːskɪt] **n** corbeille *f* à papier.

waste pipe **n** (tuyau *m* de) vidange *f*.

waste product **n** INDUST déchet *m* de production *OR* de fabrication / [physiological] déchet *m* *(de l'organisme)*.

watch [wɒtʃ] ■ **n 1.** [timepiece] montre *f*
2. [act of watching] **: to keep watch** faire le guet, monter la garde ▸ **to keep watch by sb's bed** veiller au chevet de qqn ▸ **to keep watch on sb/sthg** surveiller qqn/qqch ▸ **the police kept a close watch on the suspect** la police a surveillé le suspect de près
3. [guard] garde *f* / NAUT [shift] quart *m*.
■ **vt 1.** [look at] regarder ▸ **they watch a lot of television** ils regardent beaucoup la télévision ▸ **watch how I do it** regardez *OR* observez comment je fais
2. [spy on, guard] surveiller
3. [be careful about] faire attention à ▸ **watch where you're going!** regardez devant vous! ▸ **watch your language!** surveille ton langage! ▸ **watch it!** *inf* attention! ▸ **watch your step** *lit* & *fig* faites attention *OR* regardez où vous mettez les pieds.
■ **vi** regarder.
◆ ***watch out*** **vi** faire attention, prendre garde.
◆ ***watch over*** **vt insep** veiller sur ▸ **God will watch over you** Dieu vous protégera.

watchdog ['wɒtʃdɒg] **n 1.** [dog] chien *m* de garde **2.** *fig* [organization] organisation *f* de contrôle.

watchful ['wɒtʃfʊl] **adj** vigilant(e).

watchmaker ['wɒtʃ,meɪkər] **n** horloger *m*, -ère *f*.

watchman ['wɒtʃmən] (pl **-men** [-mən]) **n** gardien *m*.

watchword ['wɒtʃwɜːd] **n** mot *m* d'ordre.

water ['wɔːtər] ■ **n 1.** [liquid] eau *f* ▸ **to pour** *OR* **throw cold water on sthg** *fig* se montrer négatif à l'égard de qqch ▸ **to tread water** flotter ▸ **that's all water under the bridge** tout ça, c'est du passé ▸ **you're in hot water now** *inf* tu vas avoir de gros ennuis, tu es dans de beaux draps ▸ **I'm trying to keep my head above water** *inf* j'essaye de me maintenir à flot *OR* de faire face **2.** [urine] **: to pass water** uriner.
■ **vt** arroser.
■ **vi 1.** [eyes] pleurer, larmoyer **2.** [mouth] **: my mouth was watering** j'en avais l'eau à la bouche ▸ **it made my mouth water** cela m'a fait venir l'eau à la bouche.
◆ ***waters*** **npl** [sea] eaux *fpl* ▸ **in Japanese waters** dans les eaux (territoriales) japonaises.
◆ ***water down*** **vt sep 1.** [dilute] diluer / [alcohol] couper d'eau **2.** *pej* [plan, demand] atténuer, modérer / [play, novel] édulcorer.

water bed **n** lit *m* d'eau.

water bird **n** oiseau *m* aquatique.

water birth **n** accouchement *m* sous l'eau.

water biscuit **n** cracker *m*, craquelin *m*.

waterborne ['wɔːtəbɔːn] **adj** [disease] d'origine hydrique.

water bottle **n** gourde *f*, bidon *m* (à eau).

water buffalo **n** karbau *m*, kérabau *m*.

water cannon **n** canon *m* à eau.

water chestnut **n** châtaigne *f* d'eau.

water closet **n** *dated* toilettes *fpl*, waters *mpl*.

watercolour *UK*, ***watercolor*** *US* ['wɔːtə,kʌlər] **n 1.** [picture] aquarelle *f* **2.** [paint] peinture *f* à l'eau, couleur *f* pour aquarelle.

water-cooled [-,kuːld] **adj** à refroidissement par eau.

water cooler **n** distributeur *m* d'eau fraîche.

watercourse ['wɔːtəkɔːs] **n** cours *m* d'eau.

watercress ['wɔːtəkres] **n** cresson *m*.

watered-down [,wɔːtəd-] **adj** *pej* modéré(e), atténué(e) / [version] édulcoré(e).

waterfall ['wɔːtəfɔːl] **n** chute *f* d'eau, cascade *f*.

water feature **n** fontaine *f* d'intérieur.

waterfront ['wɔːtəfrʌnt] **n** quais *mpl*.

water heater **n** chauffe-eau *m inv*.

waterhole ['wɔːtəhəʊl] **n** mare *f*, point *m* d'eau.

watering can ['wɔːtərɪŋ-] **n** arrosoir *m*.

watering hole **n** [for animals] point *m* d'eau / *inf hum* [pub] ≃ bistrot *m*, ≃ bar *m*.

water jump **n** brook *m*.

water level **n** niveau *m* de l'eau.

water lily **n** nénuphar *m*.

waterline ['wɔːtəlaɪn] **n** NAUT ligne *f* de flottaison.

waterlogged ['wɔːtəlɒgd] **adj 1.** [land] détrempé(e) **2.** [vessel] plein(e) d'eau.

water main **n** conduite *f* principale d'eau.

watermark ['wɔːtəmɑːk] **n 1.** [in paper] filigrane *m* **2.** [showing water level] laisse *f*.

watermelon ['wɔːtə,melən] **n** pastèque *f*.

water meter **n** compteur *m* d'eau.

water pipe **n** conduite *f* d'eau.

water pistol **n** pistolet *m* à eau.

water polo n water-polo *m*.

water power n énergie *f* hydraulique, houille *f* blanche.

waterproof ['wɔ:təpru:f] ■ **adj** imperméable.
■ **n** *UK* imperméable *m*.
■ **vt** imperméabiliser.

water rates **npl** *UK* taxe *f* sur l'eau.

water-resistant **adj** qui résiste à l'eau.

watershed ['wɔ:təʃed] **n** **1.** *fig* [turning point] tournant *m*, moment *m* critique **2.** TV **: the Watershed** *l'heure après laquelle l'émission de programmes destinés aux adultes est autorisée.*

waterside ['wɔ:təsaɪd] ■ **adj** au bord de l'eau.
■ **n : the waterside** le bord de l'eau.

water skiing **n** ski *m* nautique.

water softener **n** adoucisseur *m* d'eau.

water-soluble **adj** soluble dans l'eau.

waterspout ['wɔ:təspaʊt] **n** trombe *f*.

water supply **n** alimentation *f* en eau, approvisionnement *m* d'eau.

water table **n** niveau *m* hydrostatique.

water tank **n** réservoir *m* d'eau, citerne *f*.

watertight ['wɔ:tətaɪt] **adj** **1.** [waterproof] étanche **2.** *fig* [excuse, contract] parfait(e) / [argument] irréfutable / [plan] infaillible.

water tower **n** château *m* d'eau.

waterway ['wɔ:təweɪ] **n** voie *f* navigable.

waterworks ['wɔ:təwɜ:ks] (**pl waterworks**) **n** [building] installation *f* hydraulique, usine *f* de distribution d'eau.

watery ['wɔ:tərɪ] **adj** **1.** [food, drink] trop dilué(e) / [tea, coffee] pas assez fort(e) **2.** [pale] pâle.

watt [wɒt] **n** watt *m*.

wattage ['wɒtɪdʒ] **n** puissance *f* **OR** consommation *f* en watts.

wave [weɪv] ■ **n** **1.** [of hand] geste *m*, signe *m* **2.** [of water, emotion, nausea] vague *f* **3.** [of light, sound] onde *f* / [of heat] bouffée *f* **4.** [in hair] cran *m*, ondulation *f*.
■ **vt** **1.** [arm, handkerchief] agiter / [flag, stick] brandir **2.** [signal to] **: he waved the car on** il a fait signe à la voiture d'avancer.
■ **vi** **1.** [with hand] faire signe de la main ▸ **to wave at OR to sb** faire signe à qqn, saluer qqn de la main **2.** [flags, trees] flotter.
◆ ***wave aside*** **vt sep** *fig* [dismiss] écarter, rejeter.
◆ ***wave down*** **vt sep : to wave down a vehicle** faire signe à un véhicule de s'arrêter.

wave band **n** bande *f* de fréquences, gamme *f* d'ondes.

wavelength ['weɪvleŋθ] **n** longueur *f* d'ondes ▸ **to be on the same wavelength** *fig* être sur la même longueur d'ondes.

wave power **n** énergie *f* des vagues.

waver ['weɪvəʳ] **vi** **1.** [falter] vaciller, chanceler **2.** [hesitate] hésiter, vaciller **3.** [fluctuate] fluctuer, varier.

wavy ['weɪvɪ] (**comp -ier, superl -iest**) **adj** [hair] ondulé(e) / [line] onduleux(euse).

wax [wæks] ■ **n** *(U)* **1.** [in candles, polish] cire *f* / [for skis] fart *m* **2.** [in ears] cérumen *m*.
■ **vt** cirer / [skis] farter.
■ **vi** **1.** *dated & hum* [become] devenir ▸ **to wax and wane** connaître des hauts et des bas **2.** [moon] croître.

waxen ['wæksən] **adj** cireux(euse).

wax paper **n** *US* papier *m* sulfurisé.

waxworks ['wæksw3:ks] (**pl waxworks**) **n** [museum] musée *m* de cire.

way [weɪ] ■ **n** **1.** [means, method] façon *f* ▸ **there are several ways to go OR of going about it** il y a plusieurs façons OR moyens de s'y prendre ▸ **she has her own way of cooking fish** elle a sa façon à elle de cuisiner le poisson ▸ **ways and means** moyens *mpl* ▸ **to get OR have one's way** obtenir ce qu'on veut ▸ **she expects to have everything her own way** elle s'attend à ce qu'on lui fasse ses quatre volontés ▸ **it doesn't matter to them one way or another** ça leur est égal
2. [manner, style] façon *f*, manière *f* ▸ **in their own (small) way they fight racism** à leur façon OR dans la limite de leurs moyens, ils luttent contre le racisme ▸ **in the same way** de la même manière OR façon ▸ **this/that way** comme ça, de cette façon ▸ **in a way** d'une certaine manière, en quelque sorte ▸ **it's important in many ways** c'est important à bien des égards ▸ **in a big/small way** à un haut/moindre degré ▸ **I am in no way responsible** je ne suis absolument pas OR aucunement responsable ▸ **try to see it my way** mettez-vous à ma place ▸ **to her way of thinking** à son avis ▸ **she got into/out of the way of getting up early** elle a pris/perdu l'habitude de se lever tôt ▸ **to be in a bad way** être en mauvais état
3. [skill] **: to have a way with** savoir comment s'y prendre avec ▸ **to have a way of doing sthg** avoir le chic pour faire qqch
4. [route, path] chemin *m* ▸ **what's the shortest OR quickest way to town?** quel est le chemin le plus court pour aller en ville? ▸ **way in** entrée *f* ▸ **way out** sortie *f* ▸ **their decision left her no way out** leur décision l'a mise dans une impasse ▸ **to be out of one's way** [place] ne pas être sur sa route ▸ **on the OR one's way** sur le OR son chemin ▸ **across OR over the way** juste en face ▸ **to be under way** [ship] faire route / *fig* [meeting] être en cours ▸ **to get under way** [ship] se mettre en route / *fig* [meeting] démarrer ▸ **'give way'** *UK* AUT 'vous n'avez pas la priorité' ▸ **to be in the way** gêner ▸ **I can't see, the cat is in the way** je ne vois pas, le chat me gêne ▸ **to be out of the way** [finished] être fini / [not blocking] ne pas gêner ▸ **her social life got in the way of her studies** *fig* ses sorties l'empêchaient d'étudier ▸ **to go out of one's way to do sthg** se donner du mal pour faire qqch ▸ **to keep out of sb's way** éviter qqn ▸ **keep out of the way!** restez à l'écart! ▸ **to make one's way** aller ▸ **to make one's way towards** se diriger vers ▸ **to make way for** faire place à ▸ **to stand in sb's way** *fig* [subj: obstacle] gêner qqn / [subj: person] s'opposer à la volonté de qqn ▸ **to work one's way** progresser ▸ **I worked my way through college** j'ai travaillé pour payer mes études
5. [direction] **: get in, I'm going your way** montez, je vais dans la même direction que vous ▸ **to go/look/come this way** aller/regarder/venir par ici ▸ **the right/wrong way round** [in sequence] dans le bon/mauvais ordre ▸ **she had her hat on the wrong way round** elle avait mis son

chapeau à l'envers ▸ **the right/wrong way up** dans le bon/mauvais sens ▸ **he didn't know which way to look** [embarrassed] il ne savait plus où se mettre ▸ **everything's going my way** *inf* tout marche comme je veux en ce moment **6.** [distance] **: all the way** tout le trajet / *fig* [support] jusqu'au bout ▸ **most of the way** presque tout le trajet OR chemin ▸ **a long way** loin ▸ **it's a long way to Berlin** Berlin est loin ▸ **we've come a long way** [from far away] nous venons de loin / [made progress] nous avons fait du chemin ▸ **to go a long way towards doing sthg** *fig* contribuer largement à faire qqch

▸▸ **to give way** [under weight, pressure] céder ▸ **no way!** pas question!

■ adv *inf* [a lot] largement ▸ **way better** bien mieux ▸ **she's way ahead of her class** elle est très en avance sur sa classe.

◆ ***ways*** npl [customs, habits] coutumes *fpl*.

◆ ***by the way*** adv au fait.

◆ ***by way of*** prep **1.** [via] par

2. [as a sort of] en guise de ▸ **by way of illustration** à titre d'exemple.

◆ ***in the way of*** prep comme.

-way suffix **: one-way street** rue *f* à sens unique ▸ **a four-way discussion** une discussion à quatre participants ▸ **there was a three-way split of the profits** les bénéfices ont été divisés en trois.

waylay [ˌweɪ'leɪ] (pt & pp **-laid** [-'leɪd]) vt arrêter (au passage).

way of life n façon *f* de vivre.

way-out adj *inf* excentrique.

wayside ['weɪsaɪd] n [roadside] bord *m* (de la route) ▸ **to fall by the wayside** *fig* tomber à l'eau.

wayward ['weɪwəd] adj qui n'en fait qu'à sa tête / [behaviour] capricieux(euse).

WC (abbr of ***water closet***) n W.-C. *mpl*

WCC (abbr of ***World Council of Churches***) n *assemblée mondiale des Églises*.

we [wi:] pers pron nous ▸ **we can't do it** nous, nous ne pouvons pas le faire ▸ **as we say in France** comme on dit en France ▸ **we British** nous autres Britanniques.

weak [wi:k] adj **1.** [gen] faible ▸ **geography is my weak subject** je suis faible en géographie ▸ **to become** OR **to get** OR **to grow weak** OR **weaker** s'affaiblir ▸ **we were weak with** OR **from hunger** nous étions affaiblis par la faim ▸ **I went weak at the knees** mes jambes se sont dérobées sous moi, j'avais les jambes en coton ▸ **in a weak moment** dans un moment de faiblesse **2.** [delicate] fragile **3.** [unconvincing] peu convaincant(e) **4.** [drink] léger(ère).

weaken ['wi:kn] ■ vt **1.** [undermine] affaiblir **2.** [reduce] diminuer **3.** [physically - person] affaiblir / [- structure] fragiliser.

■ vi faiblir.

weak-kneed [-ni:d] adj *inf pej* lâche.

weakling ['wi:klɪŋ] n *pej* mauviette *f*.

weakly ['wi:klɪ] adv faiblement.

weak-minded [-'maɪndɪd] adj [weak-willed] faible de caractère.

weakness ['wi:knɪs] n **1.** *(U)* [physical - of person] faiblesse *f* / [- of structure] fragilité *f* **2.** [liking] **: to have a weakness for sthg** avoir un faible pour qqch **3.** [imperfect point] point *m* faible, faiblesse *f*.

weal [wi:l] n marque *f*.

wealth [welθ] n **1.** *(U)* [riches] richesse *f* **2.** [abundance] **: a wealth of** une profusion de.

wealth tax n *UK* impôt *m* sur la fortune.

wealthy ['welθɪ] (comp **-ier**, superl **-iest**) adj riche.

wean [wi:n] vt **1.** [baby, lamb] sevrer **2.** [discourage] **: to wean sb from** OR **off sthg** [interest, habit] faire perdre qqch à qqn / [drugs, alcohol] détourner qqn de qqch.

weapon ['wepən] n arme *f*.

weaponize ['wepənaɪz] vt militariser.

weaponry ['wepənrɪ] n *(U)* armement *m*.

weapons-grade adj militaire.

wear [weəʳ] ■ n *(U)* **1.** [type of clothes] tenue *f* ▸ **for everyday wear** pour porter tous les jours ▸ **women's wear** vêtements *mpl* pour femmes

2. [damage] usure *f* ▸ **wear and tear** usure

3. [use] **: these shoes have had a lot of wear** ces chaussures ont fait beaucoup d'usage ▸ **to get a lot of wear from** OR **out of sthg** faire durer qqch ▸ **to be the worse for wear** être fatigué / [drunk] être mûr.

■ vt (pt **wore**, pp **worn**) **1.** [clothes, hair] porter ▸ **what shall I wear?** qu'est-ce que je vais mettre? ▸ **do you always wear make-up?** tu te maquilles tous les jours? ▸ **she wears her hair in a bun** elle porte un chignon

2. [damage] user ▸ **her shoes were worn thin** ses chaussures étaient complètement usées ▸ **to wear holes in sthg** trouer OR percer peu à peu qqch.

■ vi (pt **wore**, pp **worn**) **1.** [deteriorate] s'user ▸ **the stone had worn smooth** la pierre était polie par le temps

2. [last] **: to wear well** durer longtemps, faire de l'usage ▸ **this coat has worn well** ce manteau a bien servi ▸ **to wear badly** ne pas durer longtemps

▸▸ **to wear thin** [excuse] ne plus marcher ▸ **her patience was wearing thin** *fig* elle était presque à bout de patience.

◆ ***wear away*** ■ vt sep [rock, wood] user / [grass] abîmer.

■ vi [rock, wood] s'user / [grass] s'abîmer.

◆ ***wear down*** ■ vt sep **1.** [material] user

2. [person, resistance] épuiser.

■ vi s'user ▸ **the heels have worn down** les talons sont usés.

◆ ***wear off*** vi disparaître ▸ **the novelty soon wore off** l'attrait de la nouveauté a vite passé.

◆ ***wear on*** vi [time] passer lentement / [evening, afternoon] se traîner / [discussion] traîner en longueur.

◆ ***wear out*** ■ vt sep **1.** [shoes, clothes] user

2. [person] épuiser.

■ vi s'user ▸ **this material will never wear out** ce tissu est inusable.

wearable ['weərəbl] adj mettable.

wearily ['wɪərɪlɪ] adv péniblement ▸ **to sigh wearily** pousser un soupir de lassitude.

weariness ['wɪərɪnɪs] n lassitude *f*.

wearing ['weərɪŋ] adj [exhausting] épuisant(e).

weary ['wɪərɪ] (comp **-ier**, superl **-iest**) **adj 1.** [exhausted] las (lasse) / [sigh] de lassitude **2.** [fed up] **: to be weary of sthg/of doing sthg** être las de qqch/de faire qqch.

weasel ['wɪ:zl] **n** belette *f*.

weather ['weðəʳ] ■ **n** temps *m* ▸ **what's the weather like?** quel temps fait-il? ▸ **good weather** beau temps ▸ **weather permitting** si le temps le permet ▸ **to make heavy weather of it** se compliquer la tâche ▸ **to be under the weather** être patraque.
■ **vt** [crisis, problem] surmonter ▸ **will he weather the storm?** va-t-il se tirer d'affaire *OR* tenir le coup?
■ **vi** [rock] s'éroder / [wood] s'user.

weather-beaten [-ˌbi:tn] **adj 1.** [face, skin] tanné(e) **2.** [building, stone] abîmé(e) par les intempéries.

weathercock ['weðəkɒk] **n** girouette *f*.

weathered ['weðəd] **adj** [stone] érodé(e) / [building, wood] qui a souffert des intempéries.

weather forecast **n** météo *f*, prévisions *fpl* météorologiques.

weatherman ['weðəmæn] (pl **-men** [-men]) **n** météorologue *m*.

weather map **n** carte *f* météorologique.

weatherproof ['weðəpru:f] **adj** [clothing] imperméable / [building] à l'épreuve des intempéries.

weather report **n** bulletin *m* météorologique.

weather ship **n** navire *m* météo.

weather station **n** station *f OR* observatoire *m* météorologique.

weather vane [-veɪn] **n** girouette *f*.

weave [wi:v] ■ **n** tissage *m*.
■ **vt** (pt **wove**, pp **woven**) **1.** [using loom] tisser **2.** [move] **: to weave one's way** se faufiler.
■ **vi** (pt **wove**, pp **woven**) [move] se faufiler.

weaver ['wi:vəʳ] **n** tisserand *m*, -e *f*.

web, Web [web] **n 1.** [cobweb] toile *f* (d'araignée) **2.** COMPUT **: the web** le Web, la Toile **3.** *fig* [of lies] tissu *m*.

webbed [webd] **adj** palmé(e).

webbing ['webɪŋ] **n** *(U)* sangles *fpl*.

web browser **n** navigateur *m*.

webcam ['webkæm] **n** webcam *f*.

webcast ['webkæst] ■ **n** webcast *m*.
■ **vt** diffuser sur l'Internet.

webcasting ['webkæstɪŋ] **n** webcasting *m*.

web designer **n** concepteur *m* de site Web.

web-footed [-'fʊtɪd] **adj** aux pieds palmés.

web hosting **n** hébergement *m* de sites Web.

weblog ['weblɒg] **n** weblog *m*.

webmaster ['webˌmɑstəʳ] **n** webmaster *m*, webmestre *m*.

web page, Web page **n** page *f* Web.

website, Web site ['websaɪt] **n** site *m* Internet *OR* Web.

web space **n** espace *m* Web.

webzine ['webzi:n] **n** webzine *m*.

wed [wed] (pt & pp **wed** *OR* **-ded**) *liter* ■ **vt** épouser.
■ **vi** se marier.

Wed. (abbr of ***Wednesday***) mer.

we'd [wi:d] = ***we had, we would***.

wedded ['wedɪd] **adj** [life, bliss] conjugal / [committed] **: wedded to** dévoué(e) à.

wedding ['wedɪŋ] **n** mariage *m*.

wedding anniversary **n** anniversaire *m* de mariage.

wedding band = ***wedding ring***.

wedding cake **n** pièce *f* montée.

wedding day **n** jour *m* du mariage ▸ **on their wedding day** le jour de leur mariage.

wedding dress **n** robe *f* de mariée.

wedding reception **n** réception *f* de mariage.

wedding ring **n** alliance *f*.

wedge [wedʒ] ■ **n 1.** [for steadying] cale *f* **2.** [for splitting] coin *m* ▸ **to drive a wedge between** *fig* semer la discorde entre ▸ **the thin end of the wedge** *fig* le commencement de la fin **3.** [of cake, cheese] morceau *m*.
■ **vt** caler.

wedlock ['wedlɒk] **n** *(U) liter* mariage *m*.

Wednesday ['wenzdɪ] **n** mercredi *m* ; see also ***Saturday***.

wee [wi:] ■ **adj** *Scot* petit(e).
■ **n** *UK inf* pipi *m*.
■ **vi** *UK inf* faire pipi.

weed [wi:d] ■ **n 1.** [plant] mauvaise herbe *f* **2.** *UK inf* [feeble person] mauviette *f*.
■ **vt** désherber.
◆ ***weed out*** **vt sep** éliminer.

weeding ['wi:dɪŋ] **n** désherbage *m*.

weedkiller ['wi:dˌkɪləʳ] **n** désherbant *m*.

weedy ['wi:dɪ] (comp **-ier**, superl **-iest**) **adj** *UK inf* [feeble] qui agit comme une mauviette.

week [wi:k] **n** semaine *f* ▸ **in one week, in one week's time** dans huit jours, d'ici une semaine ▸ **Saturday week** *UK*, **a week on Saturday** *UK*, **a week from Saturday** *US* samedi en huit ▸ **week in week out** semaine après semaine.

weekday ['wi:kdeɪ] **n** jour *m* de semaine.

weekend [ˌwi:k'end] **n** week-end *m*, fin *m* de semaine ▸ **on** *OR* **at the weekend** le week-end.

weekend bag **n** sac *m* de voyage.

weekly ['wi:klɪ] ■ **adj** hebdomadaire.
■ **adv** chaque semaine.
■ **n** hebdomadaire *m*.

weeknight ['wi:kˌnaɪt] **n** soir *m* de la semaine ▸ **I can't go out on weeknights** je ne peux pas sortir le soir en semaine.

weeny ['wi:nɪ] **adj** *UK inf* tout petit (toute petite).

weep [wi:p] ■ **n : to have a weep** pleurer.
■ **vt** & **vi** (pt & pp **wept**) pleurer.

weeping ['wi:pɪŋ] ■ **adj** [person] qui pleure / [walls, wound] suintant(e).
■ **n** *(U)* larmes *fpl*, pleurs *mpl*.

weeping willow [ˌwi:pɪŋ-] n saule *m* pleureur.

weepy ['wi:pɪ] (comp -ier, superl -iest) adj [person] pleurnicheur(euse) / [film] sentimental(e).

weewee n & vi = ***wee***.

weft [weft] n trame *f*.

weigh [weɪ] vt 1. [gen] peser 2. NAUT : **to weigh anchor** lever l'ancre.

◆ ***weigh down*** vt sep 1. [physically] : **to be weighed down with sthg** plier sous le poids de qqch 2. [mentally] : **to be weighed down by** *OR* **with sthg** être accablé par qqch.

◆ ***weigh (up)on*** vt insep peser à.

◆ ***weigh out*** vt sep peser.

◆ ***weigh up*** vt sep 1. *UK* [consider carefully] examiner ▶ **to weigh up the pros and cons** peser le pour et le contre 2. [size up] juger, évaluer.

weighbridge ['weɪbrɪdʒ] n *UK* pont-bascule *m*.

weighing machine ['weɪɪŋ-] n balance *f*.

weight [weɪt] ■ n *lit* & *fig* poids *m* ▶ **to put on** *OR* **gain weight** prendre du poids, grossir ▶ **to lose weight** perdre du poids, maigrir ▶ **a set of weights** une série de poids ▶ **to lift weights** soulever des poids *OR* des haltères ▶ **she's watching her weight** elle fait attention à sa ligne ▶ **to pull one's weight** faire sa part du travail, participer à la tâche ▶ **to take the weight off one's feet** se reposer, s'asseoir ▶ **that's a weight off my mind** je suis vraiment soulagé ▶ **to throw one's weight about** faire l'important ▶ **to carry weight** avoir du poids ▶ **she's worth her weight in gold** elle vaut son pesant d'or.

■ vt : **to weight sthg (down)** [hold in place] maintenir qqch avec un poids / [make heavier] alourdir qqch.

weighted ['weɪtɪd] adj : **to be weighted in favour of/against** être favorable/défavorable à.

weighting ['weɪtɪŋ] n indemnité *f*.

weightlessness ['weɪtlɪsnɪs] n apesanteur *f*.

weightlifter ['weɪtˌlɪftəʳ] n haltérophile *m*.

weightlifting ['weɪtˌlɪftɪŋ] n haltérophilie *f*.

weight training n musculation *f*.

weightwatcher ['weɪtˌwɒtʃəʳ] n [person - on diet] personne *f* qui suit un régime / [- figure-conscious] personne *f* qui surveille son poids.

weighty ['weɪtɪ] (comp -ier, superl -iest) adj [serious] important(e), de poids.

weir [wɪəʳ] n *UK* barrage *m*.

weird [wɪəd] adj bizarre.

weirdo ['wɪədəʊ] (pl -s) n *inf* drôle de type *m*.

welcome ['welkəm] ■ adj 1. [guest, help] bienvenu(e) ▶ **to make sb welcome** faire bon accueil à qqn ▶ **this cheque is most welcome** ce chèque arrive opportunément *OR* tombe bien ▶ **that's a welcome sight!** c'est un spectacle à réjouir le cœur! 2. [free] : **you're welcome to...** n'hésitez pas à... ▶ **you're welcome to join us** n'hésitez pas à vous joindre à nous ▶ **she's welcome to him!** je ne le lui envie pas! 3. [in reply to thanks] : **you're welcome** il n'y a pas de quoi, de rien.

■ n accueil *m* ▶ **they gave him a warm welcome** ils lui ont fait bon accueil ▶ **she said a few words of welcome** elle a prononcé quelques mots de bienvenue ▶ **to overstay** *OR* **to outstay one's welcome** abuser de l'hospitalité de ses hôtes.

■ vt 1. [receive] accueillir ▶ **we welcomed him with open arms** nous l'avons accueilli à bras ouverts 2. [approve of] se réjouir de ▶ **he welcomed the news** il s'est réjoui de la nouvelle, il a accueilli la nouvelle avec joie ▶ **I welcomed the opportunity to speak to her** j'étais content d'avoir l'occasion de lui parler.

■ excl bienvenue! ▶ **welcome back** *OR* **home!** content de vous revoir!

welcoming ['welkəmɪŋ] adj accueillant(e).

weld [weld] ■ n soudure *f*.

■ vt souder.

welder [weldəʳ] n soudeur *m*, -euse *f*.

welding ['weldɪŋ] n soudage *m* / [of groups] union *f*.

welfare ['welfeəʳ] ■ adj social(e).

■ n 1. [well-being] bien-être *m* 2. *US* [income support] assistance *f* publique.

welfare state n État-providence *m*.

well [wel] ■ adj (comp better, superl best) bien ▶ **I'm very well, thanks** je vais très bien, merci ▶ **all is well** tout va bien ▶ **(all) well and good** très bien ▶ **it's all very well pretending you don't care, but...** c'est bien beau de dire que ça t'est égal, mais... ▶ **just as well** aussi bien ▶ **to get well** se remettre, aller mieux ▶ **'get well soon'** [on card] 'bon rétablissement' ▶ **you're looking** *OR* **you look well** vous avez l'air en forme.

■ adv bien ▶ **she speaks French very well** elle parle très bien (le) français ▶ **the team was well beaten** l'équipe a été battue à plates coutures ▶ **everyone speaks well of you** tout le monde dit du bien de vous ▶ **to go well** aller bien ▶ **to do well** s'en sortir ▶ **well done!** bravo! ▶ **well and truly** bel et bien ▶ **it's well worth the money** ça vaut largement la dépense ▶ **I can well believe it** je le crois facilement *OR* sans peine ▶ **to be well in with sb** *inf* être bien avec qqn ▶ **you're well out of it** *inf* c'est mieux comme ça pour toi ▶ **to be well up on sthg** s'y connaître en qqch ▶ **she's well over forty** elle a bien plus de quarante ans ▶ **let me know well in advance** prévenez-moi longtemps à l'avance.

■ n [for water, oil] puits *m*.

■ excl 1. [in hesitation] heu!, eh bien! ▶ **well, as I was saying...** donc, je disais que..., je disais donc que... ▶ **well, obviously I'd like to come but...** disons que, bien sûr, j'aimerais venir mais...

2. [to correct oneself] bon!, enfin! ▶ **I've known her for ages, well at least three years** ça fait des années que je la connais, enfin au moins trois ans

3. [to express resignation] : **oh well!** eh bien! ▶ **(oh) well, that's life** bon enfin, c'est la vie

4. [in surprise] tiens! ▶ **well, look who's here!** ça alors, regardez qui est là!

◆ ***as well*** adv 1. [in addition] aussi, également

2. [with same result] : **I/you** *etc* **may** *OR* **might as well (do sthg)** je/tu *etc* ferais aussi bien (de faire qqch).

◆ ***as well as*** conj en plus de, aussi bien que.

◆ ***well up*** vi : **tears welled up in her eyes** les larmes lui montaient aux yeux.

we'll [wi:l] = ***we shall***, ***we will***.

well-adjusted adj bien dans sa peau.

well-advised [-əd'vaɪzd] **adj** sage ▸ **you would be well-advised to do sthg** tu ferais bien de faire qqch.

well-appointed [-ə'pɔɪntɪd] **adj** bien équipé(e).

well-attended [-ə'tendɪd] **adj : the meeting was well-attended** il y avait beaucoup de monde à la réunion.

well-balanced **adj** (bien) équilibré(e).

well-behaved [-bɪ'heɪvd] **adj** sage.

wellbeing [ˌwel'bi:ɪŋ] **n** bien-être *m*.

well-bred [-'bred] **adj** bien élevé(e).

well-brought-up **adj** bien élevé(e).

well-built **adj** bien bâti(e).

well-chosen **adj** bien choisi(e).

well-deserved [-dɪ'zɜ:vd] **adj** bien mérité(e).

well-disposed **adj : to be well-disposed to** *OR* **towards sb** être bien disposé(e) envers qqn ▸ **to be well-disposed towards sthg** être favorable à qqch.

well-done **adj** CULIN bien cuit(e).

well-dressed [-'drest] **adj** bien habillé(e).

well-earned [-ɜ:nd] **adj** bien mérité(e).

well-educated **adj** cultivé(e), instruit(e).

well-established **adj** bien établi(e).

well-fed **adj** bien nourri(e).

well-groomed [-'gru:md] **adj** soigné(e).

wellhead ['welhed] **n** source *f*.

well-heeled [-'hi:ld] **adj** *inf* nanti(e).

wellies ['welɪz] *inf* **npl** *UK* = ***wellington boots***.

well-informed **adj : to be well-informed (about/on)** être bien informé(e) (sur).

Wellington ['welɪŋtən] **n** Wellington.

wellington boots ['welɪŋtən-], ***wellingtons*** ['welɪŋtənz] **npl** *UK* bottes *fpl* de caoutchouc.

well-intentioned [-ɪn'tenʃnd] **adj** bien intentionné(e).

well-kept **adj 1.** [building, garden] bien tenu(e) **2.** [secret] bien gardé(e).

well-known **adj** bien connu(e).

well-made **adj** bien fait(e).

well-mannered [-'mænəd] **adj** bien élevé(e).

well-meaning **adj** bien intentionné(e).

well-meant **adj** [action, remark] bien intentionné(e).

well-nigh [-naɪ] **adv** presque, pratiquement.

well-off **adj 1.** [rich] riche **2.** [well-provided] **: to be well-off for sthg** être bien pourvu(e) en qqch ▸ **he doesn't know when he is well-off** *inf* il ne connaît pas son bonheur.

well-paid **adj** bien payé(e).

well-preserved **adj** *fig* bien conservé(e).

well-proportioned [-prə'pɔ:ʃnd] **adj** bien proportionné(e).

well-read [-'red] **adj** cultivé(e).

well-rounded [-'raʊndɪd] **adj** [education, background] complet(ète).

well-spoken **adj** qui parle bien.

well-thought-of **adj** qui a une bonne réputation.

well-thought-out **adj** bien conçu(e).

well-timed [-'taɪmd] **adj** bien calculé(e), qui vient à point nommé.

well-to-do **adj** riche.

well-versed **adj : to be well-versed in sthg** bien connaître qqch.

wellwisher ['welˌwɪʃər] **n** admirateur *m*, -trice *f*.

well-woman clinic **n** *UK* centre *m* de santé pour femmes.

Welsh [welʃ] ■ **adj** gallois(e).
■ **n** [language] gallois *m*.
■ **npl : the Welsh** les Gallois *mpl*.

Welsh Assembly **n** Assemblée *f* galloise *OR* du pays de Galles.

Welshman ['welʃmən] (**pl -men** [-mən]) **n** Gallois *m*.

Welsh rarebit [-'reəbɪt] **n** toast *m* au fromage chaud.

Welshwoman ['welʃˌwʊmən] (**pl -women** [-ˌwɪmɪn]) **n** Galloise *f*.

welter ['weltər] **n** [of ideas, emotions] confusion *f*.

welterweight ['weltəweɪt] **n** poids *m* welter.

wend [wend] **vt** *liter* **: to wend one's way homewards** [set off] se mettre en route pour rentrer à la maison / [be on one's way] être sur le chemin de la maison.

wendy house ['wendɪ-] **n** *UK* maison *f* en modèle réduit *(pour jouer)*.

went [went] **pt** ➤ ***go***.

wept [wept] **pt & pp** ➤ ***weep***.

were [wɜ:r] ➤ ***be***.

we're [wɪər] = ***we are***.

weren't [wɜ:nt] = ***were not***.

werewolf ['wɪəwʊlf] (**pl -wolves** [-wʊlvz]) **n** loup-garou *m*.

west [west] ■ **n 1.** [direction] ouest *m* **2.** [region] **: the west** l'ouest *m*.
■ **adj** ouest *(inv)* / [wind] d'ouest.
■ **adv** de l'ouest, vers l'ouest ▸ **west of** à l'ouest de.
◆ ***West*** **n** POL **: the West** l'Occident *m*.

West Africa **n** Afrique *f* occidentale.

West African ■ **n** habitant *m*, -e *f* de l'Afrique occidentale.
■ **adj** [languages, states] de l'Afrique occidentale, ouest-africain(e).

West Bank **n : the West Bank** la Cisjordanie ▸ **on the West Bank** en Cisjordanie.

westbound ['westbaʊnd] **adj** en direction de l'ouest.

West Country **n** *UK* **: the West Country** le sud-ouest de l'Angleterre.

West End **n** *UK* **: the West End** le West-End *(quartier des grands magasins et des théâtres, à Londres)*.

westerly ['westəlɪ] **adj** à l'ouest / [wind] de l'ouest ▸ **in a westerly direction** vers l'ouest.

western ['westən] ■ **adj 1.** [gen] de l'ouest **2.** POL occidental(e).
■ **n** [book, film] western *m*.

Westerner ['westənər] **n 1.** POL Occidental *m*, -e *f* **2.** [inhabitant of west of country] personne *f* de l'ouest.

westernization [,westənaɪ'zeɪʃn] **n** occidentalisation *f*.

westernize, *UK* **-ise** ['westənaɪz] **vt** occidentaliser.

westernmost ['westənməʊst] **adj** le plus à l'ouest.

Western Samoa **n** Samoa *fpl* occidentales ▸ **in Western Samoa** dans les Samoa occidentales.

West German ■ **adj** ouest-allemand(e).
■ **n** Allemand *m*, -e *f* de l'Ouest.

West Germany **n : (former) West Germany** (ex-)Allemagne *f* de l'Ouest ▸ **in West Germany** en Allemagne de l'Ouest.

West Indian ■ **adj** antillais(e).
■ **n** Antillais *m*, -e *f*.

West Indies [-'ɪndi:z] **npl : the West Indies** les Antilles *fpl* ▸ **in the West Indies** aux Antilles.

Westminster ['westmɪnstər] **n** *quartier de Londres où se situe le Parlement britannique*.

West Virginia **n** Virginie-Occidentale *f* ▸ **in West Virginia** en Virginie-Occidentale.

westward ['westwəd] **adj & adv** vers l'ouest.

westwards ['westwədz] **adv** vers l'ouest.

wet [wet] (cont **-ting**) ■ **adj** (comp **-ter**, superl **-test**) **1.** [damp, soaked] mouillé(e) ▸ **to get wet** se faire mouiller ▸ **to be wet through** [person] être trempé jusqu'aux os *OR* complètement trempé **2.** [rainy] pluvieux(euse) ▸ **in wet weather** par temps de pluie, quand il pleut **3.** [not dry - paint, cement] frais (fraîche) **4.** *UK inf pej* [weak, feeble] ramolli(e) ▸ **don't be so wet!** tu es une vraie lavette!
■ **n** *UK inf* POL modéré *m*, -e *f*.
■ **vt** (pt & pp **wet** *OR* **-ted**) mouiller ▸ **to wet the bed** faire pipi au lit ▸ **to wet o.s.** [child] mouiller sa culotte / *inf* [be terrified] pisser dans son froc.

wet blanket **n** *inf pej* rabat-joie *m inv*.

wet dream **n** éjaculation *f OR* pollution *f* nocturne.

wet-look **adj** brillant(e).

wetness ['wetnɪs] **n 1.** [dampness] humidité *f* **2.** *UK inf pej* [feebleness] faiblesse *f*.

wet nurse **n** nourrice *f*.

wet rot **n** pourriture *f* humide.

wet suit **n** combinaison *f* de plongée.

WEU (abbr of ***Western European Union***) **n** UEO *f*.

we've [wi:v] = ***we have***.

whack [wæk] *inf* ■ **n 1.** *UK* [share] part *f* **2.** [hit] grand coup *m*.
■ **vt** donner un grand coup à, frapper fort.

whacked [wækt] **adj** *UK inf* [exhausted] crevé(e).

whacky ['wækɪ] **adj** = ***wacky***.

whale [weɪl] **n** baleine *f* ▸ **to have a whale of a time** *inf* drôlement bien s'amuser.

whaling ['weɪlɪŋ] **n** pêche *f* à la baleine.

wham [wæm] **excl** *inf* vlan!

wharf [wɔ:f] (pl **-s** *OR* **wharves** [wɔ:vz]) **n** quai *m*.

what [wɒt] ■ **adj 1.** *(in direct, indirect questions)* quel (quelle), quels (quelles) *(pl)* ▸ **what day is it?** quel jour sommes-nous? ▸ **what colour is it?** c'est de quelle couleur? ▸ **he asked me what colour it was** il m'a demandé de quelle couleur c'était
2. [as many as, as much as] **: I gave her what money I had** je lui ai donné le peu d'argent que j'avais
3. *(in exclamations)* quel (quelle), quels (quelles) *(pl)* ▸ **what a surprise!** quelle surprise! ▸ **what a pity!** comme c'est *OR* quel dommage! ▸ **what lovely children you have!** quels charmants enfants vous avez! ▸ **what an idiot I am!** ce que je peux être bête!
■ **pron 1.** [interrogative - subject] qu'est-ce qui / [- object] qu'est-ce que, que / [- after prep] quoi ▸ **what's that?** qu'est-ce que c'est que ça? ▸ **what are they doing?** qu'est-ce qu'ils font?, que font-ils? ▸ **what's the Spanish for "light"?** comment dit-on "lumière" en espagnol? ▸ **what is going on?** qu'est-ce qui se passe? ▸ **what's the matter?, what is it?** qu'est-ce qu'il y a? ▸ **what's new?** quoi de neuf? ▸ **what are they talking about?** de quoi parlent-ils? ▸ **what about another drink/going out for a meal?** et si on prenait un autre verre/allait manger au restaurant? ▸ **what about the rest of us?** et nous alors? ▸ **what if...?** et si...? ▸ **Mum? – what? – can I go out?** Maman? – quoi? – est-ce que je peux sortir?
2. [relative - subject] ce qui / [- object] ce que ▸ **I saw what happened/fell** j'ai vu ce qui s'était passé/était tombé ▸ **you can't have what you want** tu ne peux pas avoir ce que tu veux ▸ **what you need is a hot bath** ce qu'il vous faut, c'est un bon bain chaud.
■ **excl** [expressing disbelief] comment!, quoi! ▸ **what, another new dress?** quoi, encore une nouvelle robe?

whatever [wɒt'evər] ■ **adj** quel (quelle) que soit ▸ **I'll take whatever fruit you have** je prendrai ce que vous avez comme fruits ▸ **for whatever reason, he changed his mind** pour une raison quelconque, il a changé d'avis ▸ **any book whatever** n'importe quel livre ▸ **no chance whatever** pas la moindre chance ▸ **nothing whatever** rien du tout.
■ **pron 1.** quoi que *(+ subjunctive)* ▸ **I'll do whatever I can** je ferai tout ce que je peux ▸ **whatever it costs, I want that house** je veux cette maison à tout prix ▸ **whatever can this be?** qu'est-ce que cela peut-il bien être? ▸ **whatever that may mean** quoi que cela puisse bien vouloir dire ▸ **or whatever** ou n'importe quoi d'autre **2.** [indicating lack of interest] **: shall I take the red or the green? – whatever** *inf* je prends le rouge ou le vert? – n'importe.

whatnot ['wɒtnɒt] **n** *inf* **1.** [thing] machin *m* **2.** [other things] **: and whatnot** et d'autres bricoles.

whatsoever [,wɒtsəʊ'evər] **adj : I had no interest whatsoever** je n'éprouvais pas le moindre intérêt ▸ **nothing whatsoever** rien du tout.

wheat [wi:t] **n** blé *m*.

wheat germ **n** germe *m* de blé.

wheatmeal ['wi:tmi:l] **n** farine *f* de blé.

wheedle ['wi:dl] **vt : to wheedle sb into doing sthg** enjôler qqn pour qu'il fasse qqch ▸ **to wheedle sthg out of sb** enjôler qqn pour obtenir qqch.

wheel [wi:l] ■ **n** **1.** [gen] roue *f* **2.** [steering wheel] volant *m.*
■ **vt** pousser.
■ **vi : to wheel (round)** *UK* ***OR*** **around** *US* se retourner brusquement.

wheelbarrow ['wi:lˌbærəʊ] **n** brouette *f.*

wheelbase ['wi:lbeɪs] **n** empattement *m.*

wheelchair ['wi:lˌtʃeəʳ] **n** fauteuil *m* roulant.

wheelclamp ['wi:lˌklæmp] ■ **n** sabot *m* de Denver.
■ **vt : my car was wheelclamped** on a mis un sabot à ma voiture.

-wheeled **suffix** à roues ▸ **four-wheeled** à quatre roues.

wheeler-dealer ['wi:ləʳ-] **n** *pej* combinard *m.*

wheelie bin ['wi:lɪ-] **n** poubelle *f (avec des roues).*

wheeling and dealing ['wi:lɪŋ-] **n** *(U) pej* combines *fpl.*

wheeze [wi:z] ■ **n** [sound] respiration *f* sifflante.
■ **vi** respirer avec un bruit sifflant.

wheezy ['wi:zɪ] (**comp -ier, superl -iest**) **adj** [person] poussif(ive) / [cough] sifflant(e) / [voice, chest] d'asthmatique.

whelk [welk] **n** bulot *m*, buccin *m.*

when [wen] ■ **adv** *(in direct, indirect questions)* quand ▸ **when does the plane arrive?** quand ***OR*** à quelle heure arrive l'avion? ▸ **he asked me when I would be in London** il m'a demandé quand je serais à Londres ▸ **when is the best time to call?** quel est le meilleur moment pour appeler?
■ **conj** **1.** [referring to time] quand, lorsque ▸ **he came to see me when I was abroad** il est venu me voir quand j'étais à l'étranger ▸ **will you still love me when I'm old?** m'aimeras-tu encore quand je serai vieux? ▸ **I had just walked in the door when the phone rang** je venais juste d'arriver quand le téléphone a sonné ▸ **one day when I was on my own** un jour que ***OR*** où j'étais tout seul ▸ **do you remember when we met?** te souviens-tu du jour où nous nous sommes connus? ▸ **on the day when it happened** le jour où cela s'est passé ▸ **when completed, the factory will employ 100 workers** une fois terminée, l'usine emploiera 100 personnes **2.** [whereas, considering that] alors que.

whenever [wen'evəʳ] ■ **conj** quand / [each time that] chaque fois que ▸ **I go to visit her whenever I can** je vais la voir dès que je peux.
■ **adv** n'importe quand ▸ **let's assume he started work in April or whenever** *inf* supposons qu'il ait commencé à travailler en avril ou quelque chose comme ça.

where [weəʳ] ■ **adv** *(in direct, indirect questions)* où ▸ **where do you live?** où habitez-vous? ▸ **do you know where he lives?** est-ce que vous savez où il habite? ▸ **where are you from?** d'où êtes-vous? ▸ **where do you stand on this issue?** quelle est votre position sur cette question?
■ **conj** **1.** [referring to place, situation] où ▸ **this is where...** c'est là que... ▸ **it rains a lot where we live** il pleut beaucoup là où nous habitons ▸ **he showed me where the students live** il m'a montré l'endroit où habitent les étudiants ▸ **that's where she's mistaken** c'est là qu'elle se trompe ▸ **the judge is uncompromising where drugs are concerned** le juge est intraitable lorsqu'il ***OR*** quand il s'agit de drogue ▸ **where possible** là où ***OR*** quand c'est possible **2.** [whereas] alors que ▸ **where others see a horrid brat, I see a shy little boy** là où les autres voient un affreux moutard, je vois un petit garçon timide.

whereabouts ■ **adv** [ˌweərə'baʊts] où.
■ **npl** ['weərəbaʊts] **: their whereabouts are still unknown** on ne sait toujours pas où ils se trouvent.

whereas [weər'æz] **conj** alors que.

whereby [weə'baɪ] **conj** *fml* par lequel (laquelle), au moyen duquel (de laquelle).

wheresoever [ˌweəsəʊ'evəʳ] **conj** = *wherever.*

whereupon [ˌweərə'pɒn] **conj** *fml* après quoi, sur quoi.

wherever [weər'evəʳ] ■ **conj** où que *(+ subjunctive).*
■ **adv** **1.** [no matter where] n'importe où **2.** [where] où donc ▸ **wherever did you hear that?** mais où donc as-tu entendu dire cela?

wherewithal ['weəwɪðɔ:l] **n** *fml* **: to have the wherewithal to do sthg** avoir les moyens de faire qqch.

whet [wet] (**pt & pp -ted, cont -ting**) **vt : to whet sb's appetite for sthg** donner à qqn envie de qqch.

whether ['weðəʳ] **conj** **1.** [indicating choice, doubt] si **2.** [no matter if] **: whether I want to or not** que je le veuille ou non.

whew [hwju:] **excl** ouf!

whey [weɪ] **n** petit-lait *m.*

which [wɪtʃ] ■ **adj** **1.** *(in direct, indirect questions)* quel (quelle), quels (quelles) *(pl)* ▸ **which house is yours?** quelle maison est la tienne? ▸ **which one?** lequel (laquelle) ? ▸ **which way should we go?** par où devrions-nous aller?
2. [to refer back to sthg] **: in which case** auquel cas.
■ **pron** **1.** *(in direct, indirect questions)* lequel (laquelle), lesquels (lesquelles) *(pl)* ▸ **which do you prefer?** lequel préférez-vous? ▸ **show me which you prefer** montrez-moi celui que vous préférez ▸ **I can't decide which to have** je ne sais vraiment pas lequel prendre ▸ **which is the freshest?** quel est le plus frais? ▸ **which of you saw the accident?** qui de vous a vu l'accident? ▸ **which is which?** lequel est-ce?
2. [in relative clauses - subject] qui / [- object] que / [- after prep] lequel (laquelle), lesquels (lesquelles) *(pl)* ▸ **take the slice which is nearer to you** prends la tranche qui est le plus près de toi ▸ **the television which we bought** le téléviseur que nous avons acheté ▸ **the settee on which I am sitting** le canapé sur lequel je suis assis ▸ **the film of which you spoke** le film dont vous avez parlé
3. [referring back] [subject] ce qui / [object] ce que ▸ **why did you say you were ill, which nobody believed?** pourquoi as-tu dit que tu étais malade, ce que personne n'a cru? ▸ **then they arrived, after which things got better** puis ils sont arrivés, après quoi tout est allé mieux.

whichever [wɪtʃ'evəʳ] ■ **adj** **1.** [indicating choice or preference] **: grants will be given to whichever students most need them** des bourses seront accordées à ceux des étudiants qui en ont le plus besoin ▸ **choose whichever colour you prefer** choisissez la couleur que vous préférez, n'importe laquelle **2.** [no matter what] quel (quelle) que soit ▸ **whichever job you take, it will mean a lot of travelling** quel que soit le poste que vous preniez, vous serez obligé de beaucoup voyager.

■ pron 1. [the one that] celui qui *m*, celle qui *f*, ceux qui *mpl*, celles qui *fpl* ▸ **will whichever of you arrives first turn on the heating?** celui d'entre vous qui arrivera le premier pourra-t-il allumer le chauffage? **2.** [no matter which one] n'importe lequel (laquelle) ▸ **whichever of the routes you choose, allow about two hours** quel que soit le chemin que vous choisissiez, comptez environ deux heures.

whiff [wɪf] n **1.** [of perfume, smoke] bouffée *f* / [of food] odeur *f* **2.** *fig* [sign] signe *m*.

while [waɪl] ■ n moment *m* ▸ **let's stay here for a while** restons ici un moment ▸ **we've been waiting for a while** nous attendons depuis un moment ▸ **for a long while** longtemps ▸ **after a while** après quelque temps ▸ **to be worth one's while** valoir la peine.
■ conj **1.** [during the time that] pendant que **2.** [as long as] tant que **3.** [whereas] alors que.
◆ ***while away*** vt sep passer.

whilst [waɪlst] conj *US* = ***while***.

whim [wɪm] n lubie *f*.

whimper ['wɪmpəʳ] ■ n gémissement *m*.
■ vt & vi gémir.

whimsical ['wɪmzɪkl] adj saugrenu(e).

whine [waɪn] ■ n gémissement *m*, longue plainte *f*.
■ vi **1.** [make sound] gémir **2.** [complain] : **to whine (about)** se plaindre (de).

whinge [wɪndʒ] (cont **whingeing**) vi *UK* : **to whinge (about)** se plaindre (de).

whingeing ['wɪndʒɪŋ] *UK inf* ■ n *(U)* gémissement *m* / *pej* pleurnicherie *f*, plainte *f*.
■ adj [person] pleurnicheur(euse) / [voice] plaintif(ive).

whip [wɪp] ■ n **1.** [for hitting] fouet *m* **2.** POL chef *m* de file *(d'un groupe parlementaire)*.
■ vt (pt & pp **-ped**, cont **-ping**) **1.** [gen] fouetter ▸ **the cold wind whipped her face** le vent glacial lui fouettait le visage ▸ **whip the egg whites** battez les blancs en neige ▸ **his speech whipped them all into a frenzy** *fig* son discours les a tous rendus frénétiques ▸ **I'll soon whip the team into shape** *fig* j'aurai bientôt fait de mettre l'équipe en forme **2.** [take quickly] **: to whip sthg out** sortir qqch brusquement ▸ **to whip sthg off** ôter OR enlever qqch brusquement **3.** *inf* [defeat] vaincre, battre **4.** *UK inf* [steal] faucher, piquer.
◆ ***whip up*** vt sep [provoke] stimuler, attiser.

whiplash injury ['wɪplæʃ-] n coup *m* du lapin.

whipped cream [wɪpt-] n crème *f* fouettée.

whippet ['wɪpɪt] n whippet *m*.

whipping ['wɪpɪŋ] n [as punishment - child] correction *f* / [- prisoner] coups *mpl* de fouet.

whip-round n *UK inf* : **to have a whip-round** faire une collecte.

whirl [wɜːl] ■ n *lit* & *fig* tourbillon *m* ▸ **I/my mind was in a whirl** tout tourbillonnait en moi/dans ma tête ▸▸ **let's give it a whirl** *inf* tentons le coup.
■ vt : **to whirl sb/sthg round** *UK*, OR **around** *US* [spin round] faire tourbillonner qqn/qqch.
■ vi tourbillonner / *fig* [head, mind] tourner.

whirlpool ['wɜːlpuːl] n tourbillon *m*.

whirlpool bath n = ***spa bath***.

whirlwind ['wɜːlwɪnd] ■ adj *fig* éclair *(inv)*.
■ n tornade *f*.

whirr [wɜːʳ] ■ n [of engine] ronronnement *m*.
■ vi [engine] ronronner.

whisk [wɪsk] ■ n CULIN fouet *m*, batteur *m* (à œufs).
■ vt **1.** [move quickly] emmener OR emporter rapidement **2.** CULIN battre.

whisker ['wɪskəʳ] n moustache *f*.
◆ ***whiskers*** npl favoris *mpl*.

whisky *UK* (pl **-ies**), ***whiskey*** *US* (*Ir* **-s**) ['wɪskɪ] n whisky *m*.

whisper ['wɪspəʳ] ■ n murmure *m* ▸ **to speak in a whisper** parler tout bas OR à voix basse ▸ **not a whisper of this to anyone!** *fig* n'en soufflez mot à personne!
■ vt murmurer, chuchoter ▸ **to whisper sthg to sb** chuchoter qqch à qqn ▸ **I whispered the answer to her** je lui ai soufflé la réponse ▸ **to whisper sweet nothings to sb** susurrer des mots doux à l'oreille de qqn.
■ vi chuchoter ▸ **to whisper to sb** parler OR chuchoter à l'oreille de qqn.

whispering ['wɪspərɪŋ] n chuchotement *m*.

whispering campaign n campagne *f* de diffamation.

whist [wɪst] n whist *m*.

whistle ['wɪsl] ■ n **1.** [sound] sifflement *m* **2.** [device] sifflet *m*.
■ vt & vi siffler.

whistle-blower n *inf personne qui vend la mèche*.

whistle-stop tour n : **to make a whistle-stop tour of** [subj: politician] faire une tournée éclair dans.

whit [wɪt] n brin *m*.

Whit [wɪt] n *UK* Pentecôte *f*.

white [waɪt] ■ adj **1.** [in colour] blanc (blanche) ▸ **to go** OR **turn white** [hair] blanchir / [face] pâlir **2.** *US* [coffee, tea] au lait.
■ n **1.** [colour, of egg, eye] blanc *m* **2.** [person] Blanc *m*, Blanche *f*.
◆ ***whites*** npl **1.** SPORT tenue *f* blanche **2.** [washing] linge *m* blanc.

white blood cell n globule *m* blanc.

whiteboard ['waɪtbɔːd] n tableau *m* blanc.

whitecaps n *US* = ***white horses***.

white Christmas n Noël *m* blanc.

white-collar adj de bureau.

white elephant n *fig* objet *m* coûteux et inutile.

white fish n *UK poissons à chair blanche*.

white goods npl **1.** [linen] articles *mpl* de blanc **2.** [household machines] électroménager *m*.

white-haired [-'heəd] adj aux cheveux blancs.

Whitehall ['waɪthɔːl] n *rue de Londres, centre administratif du gouvernement britannique*.

white heat n *fig* & PHYS chaleur *f* incandescente ▸ **in the white heat of passion** au plus fort de la passion ▸ **anti-war feelings have reached white heat** les sentiments d'hostilité par rapport à la guerre ont atteint un paroxysme.

white horses npl *UK* [of waves] moutons *mpl*.

white-hot adj chauffé(e) à blanc.

White House n : **the White House** la Maison-Blanche.

CULTURE

White House

La « Maison-Blanche », à Washington, est la résidence privée du président américain et de ses proches. C'est le plus vieux bâtiment public de la capitale : la première pierre est posée en 1792 et le premier président John Adams s'installe dans les locaux en 1800. L'appellation « Maison-Blanche » est officialisée par le président Theodore Roosevelt, qui la fait graver en en-tête sur son papier à lettres. Le bâtiment est incendié par les troupes britanniques en 1814, puis entièrement repeint en blanc. Ce terme désigne de manière plus générale la présidence et l'Administration américaines.

white knight n chevalier *m* blanc.

white-knuckle adj : **white-knuckle ride** tour *m* de manège terrifiant.

white lie n pieux mensonge *m*.

white light n lumière *f* blanche.

white magic n magie *f* blanche.

white meat n viande *f* blanche.

whiten ['waɪtn] vt & vi blanchir.

whitener ['waɪtnəʳ] n agent *m* blanchissant.

whiteness ['waɪtnɪs] n blancheur *f*.

white noise n son *m* blanc.

whiteout ['waɪtaʊt] n jour *m* blanc.

white paper n POL livre *m* blanc.

white sauce n sauce *f* blanche.

White Sea n : **the White Sea** la mer Blanche.

white spirit n *UK* white-spirit *m*.

white-tie adj [dinner] en habit.

white trash n *pej* pauvres blancs *mpl*.

whitewash ['waɪtwɒʃ] ■ n **1.** *(U)* [paint] chaux *f* **2.** *pej* [cover-up] : **a government whitewash** une combine du gouvernement pour étouffer l'affaire.
■ vt **1.** [paint] blanchir à la chaux **2.** *pej* [cover up] blanchir.

whitewater rafting ['waɪt,wɔ:təʳ-] n raft *m*, rafting *m*.

white wedding n mariage *m* en blanc.

white wine n vin *m* blanc.

whiting ['waɪtɪŋ] (pl **whiting** *OR* **-s**) n merlan *m*.

Whit Monday [wɪt-] n le lundi *m* de Pentecôte.

Whitsun ['wɪtsn] n Pentecôte *f*.

whittle ['wɪtl] vt [reduce] : **to whittle sthg away** *OR* **down** réduire qqch.

whiz, whizz [wɪz] ■ n *inf* : **to be a whiz at sthg** être un as de qqch.
■ vi (pt & pp **-zed**, cont **-zing**) [go fast] aller à toute allure.

whiz(z) kid n *inf* petit prodige *m*.

who [hu:] pron **1.** *(in direct, indirect questions)* qui ▸ **who are you?** qui êtes-vous? ▸ **I didn't know who she was** je ne savais pas qui c'était **2.** *(in relative clauses)* qui ▸ **he's the doctor who treated me** c'est le médecin qui m'a soigné ▸ **I don't know the person who came to see you** je ne connais pas la personne qui est venue vous voir.

WHO (abbr of ***World Health Organization***) n OMS *f*.

who'd [hu:d] = ***who had, who would***.

whodu(n)nit [,hu:'dʌnɪt] n *inf* polar *m*.

whoever [hu:'evəʳ] pron **1.** [any person who] quiconque ▸ **whoever wants it can have it** celui qui le veut peut le prendre **2.** [the person who] celui qui *m*, celle qui *f*, ceux qui *mpl*, celles qui *fpl* ▸ **whoever answered the phone had a nice voice** la personne qui a répondu au téléphone avait une voix agréable **3.** [indicating surprise, astonishment] qui donc ▸ **whoever can that be?** qui cela peut-il bien être? **4.** [no matter who] qui que *(+ subjunctive)* ▸ **come out, whoever you are!** montrez-vous, qui que vous soyez! ▸ **whoever wins** qui que ce soit qui gagne.

whole [həʊl] ■ adj **1.** [entire, complete] entier(ère) ▸ **it took me a whole day to paint the kitchen** j'ai mis une journée entière *OR* toute une journée pour peindre la cuisine ▸ **there are two whole months still to go** il reste deux mois entiers ▸ **she won the whole lot** elle a gagné le tout **2.** [for emphasis] : **a whole lot of questions** toute une série de questions ▸ **a whole lot bigger** bien plus gros ▸ **a whole new idea** une idée tout à fait nouvelle
3. CULIN [milk] entier(ère) / [grain] complet(ète).
■ adv : **to swallow sthg whole** avaler qqch en entier.
■ n **1.** [all] : **the whole of the school** toute l'école ▸ **the whole of the summer** tout l'été
2. [unit, complete thing] tout *m*.
◆ ***as a whole*** adv dans son ensemble ▸ **considered as a whole, the festival was a remarkable success** dans son ensemble, le festival a été un vrai succès ▸ **is it true of America as a whole?** est-ce vrai pour toute l'Amérique *OR* l'Amérique en général?
◆ ***on the whole*** adv dans l'ensemble.

wholefood ['həʊlfu:d] n *UK* aliments *mpl* complets.

wholehearted [,həʊl'hɑ:tɪd] adj [unreserved] sans réserve ▸ **she gave them her wholehearted support** elle leur a donné un soutien sans réserve *OR* sans faille ▸ **he is a wholehearted supporter of our cause** [devoted] il est dévoué corps et âme à notre cause.

whole-hearted [-'hɑ:tɪd] adj sans réserve, total(e).

wholeheartedly [,həʊl'hɑ:tɪdlɪ] adv [unreservedly] de tout cœur ▸ **I agree wholeheartedly** j'accepte de tout (mon) cœur ▸ **he flung himself wholeheartedly into his new job** il s'est jeté corps et âme dans son nouveau travail.

wholemeal ['həʊlmi:l] *UK*, ***whole wheat*** *US* adj complet(ète).

wholemeal bread n *(U) UK* pain *m* complet.

whole note n *US* ronde *f*.

wholesale ['həʊlseɪl] ■ adj **1.** [buying, selling] en gros / [price] de gros **2.** *pej* [excessive] en masse.
■ adv **1.** [in bulk] en gros **2.** *pej* [excessively] en masse.

wholesaler ['həʊl,seɪləʳ] n marchand *m* de gros, grossiste *mf*.

wholesome ['həʊlsəm] adj sain(e).

whole wheat *US* = ***wholemeal***.

who'll [hu:l] = ***who will***.

wholly ['həʊlɪ] adv totalement.

whom [hu:m] pron *fml* **1.** *(in direct, indirect questions)* qui ▸ **whom did you phone?** qui avez-vous appelé au téléphone? ▸ **for/of/to whom** pour/de/à qui **2.** *(in relative clauses)* que ▸ **the girl whom he married** la jeune fille qu'il a épousée ▸ **the man of whom you speak** l'homme dont vous parlez ▸ **the man to whom you were speaking** l'homme à qui vous parliez.

whoop [wu:p] ■ n cri *m*.
■ vi pousser des cris (de joie/de triomphe).

whoopee [wʊ'pi:] excl youpi!

whooping cough ['hu:pɪŋ-] n coqueluche *f*.

whoops [wʊps] excl oups!

whoosh [wʊʃ] *inf* ■ n [of water, air] jet *m*.
■ vi [water] jaillir.

whop [wɒp] vt *inf* battre à plates coutures.

whopper ['wɒpəʳ] n *inf* **1.** [something big] **: it's a real whopper** c'est absolument énorme **2.** [lie] mensonge *m* énorme.

whopping ['wɒpɪŋ] *inf* ■ adj énorme.
■ adv **: a whopping great lorry/lie** un camion/mensonge absolument énorme.

whore [hɔ:ʳ] n *offens* putain *f*.

who're ['hu:əʳ] = ***who are***.

whose [hu:z] ■ pron *(in direct, indirect questions)* à qui ▸ **whose is this?** à qui est ceci?
■ adj **1.** à qui ▸ **whose car is that?** à qui est cette voiture? ▸ **whose son is he?** de qui est-il le fils? **2.** *(in relative clauses)* dont ▸ **that's the boy whose father's an MP** c'est le garçon dont le père est député ▸ **the girl whose mother you phoned yesterday** la fille à la mère de qui *OR* de laquelle tu as téléphoné hier.

whosoever [ˌhu:səʊ'evəʳ] pron *dated* quiconque.

who's who [hu:z-] n [book] Bottin® *m* mondain.

who've [hu:v] = ***who have***.

why [waɪ] ■ adv *(in direct questions)* pourquoi ▸ **why did you lie to me?** pourquoi m'as-tu menti? ▸ **why don't you all come?** pourquoi ne pas tous venir?, pourquoi est-ce que vous ne viendriez pas tous? ▸ **why not?** pourquoi pas?
■ conj pourquoi ▸ **I don't know why he said that** je ne sais pas pourquoi il a dit cela.
■ pron **: there are several reasons why he left** il est parti pour plusieurs raisons, les raisons pour lesquelles il est parti sont nombreuses ▸ **I don't know the reason why** je ne sais pas pourquoi.
■ excl tiens!
◆ ***why ever*** adv pourquoi donc.

WI[1] n abbr of ***Women's Institute***.

WI[2] **1.** abbr of ***West Indies*** **2.** abbr of ***Wisconsin***.

wick [wɪk] n [of candle, lighter] mèche *f*
▸▸ **to get on sb's wick** *UK inf* taper sur les nerfs de qqn.

wicked ['wɪkɪd] adj **1.** [evil] mauvais(e) **2.** [mischievous, devilish] malicieux(euse) **3.** *inf* [very good] génial(e), super *(inv)*.

wickedly ['wɪkɪdlɪ] adv **1.** [with evil intent] méchamment, avec méchanceté **2.** [mischievously] malicieusement.

wickedness ['wɪkɪdnɪs] n **1.** RELIG [sin, evil] iniquité *f*, vilenie *f* / [cruelty - of action, crime] méchanceté *f* / [- of thought] méchanceté *f*, vilenie *f* **2.** [mischievousness - of look, sense of humour, smile] caractère *m* malicieux *OR* espiègle, malice *f*.

wicker ['wɪkəʳ] adj en osier.

wickerwork ['wɪkəwɜ:k] ■ n vannerie *f*.
■ comp en osier.

wicket ['wɪkɪt] n **1.** CRICKET [stumps, dismissal] guichet *m* **2.** CRICKET [pitch] terrain *m* entre les guichets.

wicket keeper n CRICKET gardien *m* de guichet.

wide [waɪd] ■ adj **1.** [gen] large ▸ **how wide is the room?** quelle est la largeur de la pièce? ▸ **to be six metres wide** faire six mètres de large *OR* de largeur ▸ **we need to see the problem in a wider context** il faut que nous envisagions le problème dans un contexte plus général ▸ **there are wider issues at stake here** des problèmes plus vastes sont ici en jeu
2. [gap, difference] grand(e) ▸ **the gap between rich and poor remains wide** l'écart (existant) entre les riches et les pauvres demeure considérable
3. [experience, knowledge, issue] vaste ▸ **she has wide experience in this area** elle a une longue *OR* grande expérience dans ce domaine ▸ **he has a wide knowledge of music** il a de vastes connaissances *OR* des connaissances approfondies en musique ▸ **a wide range of products** COMM une gamme importante de produits ▸ **a wide variety of colours** un grand choix de couleurs
4. [eyes] écarquillé(e) ▸ **his eyes were wide with terror** ses yeux étaient agrandis par l'épouvante
5. [off-target] qui passe à côté ▸ **to be wide of the mark** *UK lit* rater *OR* être passé loin de la cible / *fig* être loin de la vérité *OR* du compte.
■ adv **1.** [broadly] largement ▸ **open wide!** ouvrez grand! ▸ **place your feet wide apart** écartez bien les pieds
2. [off-target] **: the shot went wide** le coup est passé loin du but *OR* à côté.

-wide suffix **: state-wide** à travers tout l'État, dans l'ensemble de l'État ▸ **world-wide** à travers le monde (entier).

wide-angle lens n PHOT objectif *m* grand angle.

wide area network n réseau *m* étendu.

wide-awake adj tout à fait réveillé(e).

wide boy n *UK inf pej* escroc *m*.

wide-eyed [-'aɪd] adj **1.** [surprised, frightened] aux yeux écarquillés **2.** [innocent] aux yeux grands ouverts.

widely ['waɪdlɪ] adv **1.** [smile, vary] largement **2.** [extensively] beaucoup ▸ **to be widely read** avoir beaucoup lu ▸ **it is widely believed that...** beaucoup pensent que..., nombreux sont ceux qui pensent que... ▸ **widely known** largement *OR* bien connu, largement *OR* bien connue.

widen ['waɪdn] ■ vt **1.** [make broader] élargir **2.** [gap, difference] agrandir, élargir.
■ vi **1.** [become broader] s'élargir **2.** [gap, difference] s'agrandir, s'élargir **3.** [eyes] s'agrandir.

wide open adj grand ouvert (grande ouverte) ▸ **the wide open spaces** les grands espaces.

wide-ranging [-'reɪndʒɪŋ] **adj** varié(e) / [consequences] de grande envergure.

wide screen **n** TV & CIN écran *m* 16/9.

wide-screen **adj** [television, film, format] 16/9.

widespread ['waɪdspred] **adj** très répandu(e).

widow ['wɪdəʊ] **n** veuve *f*.

widowed ['wɪdəʊd] **adj** veuf (veuve).

widower ['wɪdəʊəʳ] **n** veuf *m*.

width [wɪdθ] **n** largeur *f* ▸ **in width** de large.

widthways ['wɪdθweɪz] **adv** en largeur.

wield [wi:ld] **vt** **1.** [weapon] manier **2.** [power] exercer.

wife [waɪf] (pl **wives** [waɪvz]) **n** femme *f*, épouse *f*.

wig [wɪg] **n** perruque *f*.

wiggle ['wɪgl] *inf* ■ **n** **1.** [movement] tortillement *m* **2.** [wavy line] ondulation *f*.
■ **vt** remuer.
■ **vi** se tortiller.

wiggly ['wɪglɪ] (comp **-ier**, superl **-iest**) **adj** *inf* [line] ondulé(e).

wigwam ['wɪgwæm] **n** wigwam *m*.

wild [waɪld] ■ **adj** **1.** [animal, attack, scenery, flower] sauvage ▸ **wild strawberries** fraises *fpl* des bois **2.** [weather, sea] déchaîné(e) ▸ **it was a wild night** ce fut une nuit de tempête **3.** [laughter, hope, plan] fou (folle) ▸ **the crowd went wild** la foule s'est déchaînée ▸ **to run wild** être déchaîné ▸ **the book's success was beyond his wildest dreams** le succès de son livre dépassait ses rêves les plus fous **4.** [eyes] de fou (de folle) / [hair] en bataille ▸ **to be wild with grief/happiness/jealousy** être fou de douleur/joie/jalousie ▸ **a wild-looking young man** un jeune homme à l'air farouche **5.** [random] fantaisiste ▸ **I made a wild guess** j'ai dit ça au hasard ▸ **to take a wild swing at sthg** lancer le poing au hasard pour atteindre qqch **6.** *inf* [very enthusiastic] **: the speaker received wild applause** l'orateur reçut des applaudissements frénétiques ▸ **to be wild about** être dingue de.
■ **n : in the wild** dans la nature.
◆ ***wilds*** **npl : the wilds of** le fin fond de ▸ **to live in the wilds** habiter en pleine nature.

wild card **n** COMPUT caractère *m* joker.

wildcat ['waɪldkæt] **n** [animal] chat *m* sauvage.

wildcat strike **n** grève *f* sauvage.

wildebeest ['wɪldɪbi:st] (pl **wildebeest** *OR* **-s**) **n** gnou *m*.

wilderness ['wɪldənɪs] **n** étendue *f* sauvage ▸ **to be in the wilderness** *fig* faire une traversée du désert.

wildfire ['waɪld,faɪəʳ] **n : to spread like wildfire** se répandre comme une traînée de poudre.

wild flower **n** fleur *f* sauvage.

wild-goose chase **n** *inf* **: it turned out to be a wild-goose chase** ça s'est révélé être totalement inutile.

wildlife ['waɪldlaɪf] **n** *(U)* faune *f* et flore *f*.

wildlife park **n** réserve *f* naturelle.

wildly ['waɪldlɪ] **adv** **1.** [enthusiastically, fanatically] frénétiquement **2.** [guess, suggest] au hasard / [shoot] dans tous les sens **3.** [very - different, impractical] tout à fait **4.** [menacingly] farouchement.

wild rice **n** riz *m* sauvage.

wild West **n** *inf* **: the wild West** le Far West.

wiles [waɪlz] **npl** artifices *mpl*.

wilful UK, ***willful*** US ['wɪlfʊl] **adj** **1.** [determined] obstiné(e) **2.** [deliberate] délibéré(e).

wilfully UK, ***willfully*** US ['wɪlfʊlɪ] **adv** **1.** [deliberately] délibérément **2.** [obstinately] obstinément, avec entêtement.

will[1] [wɪl] ■ **n** **1.** [mental] volonté *f* ▸ **against one's will** contre son gré ▸ **at will** à volonté ▸ **a battle of wills** une lutte d'influences ▸ **she no longer has the will to live** elle n'a plus envie de vivre **2.** [document] testament *m* ▸ **last will and testament** dernières volontés *fpl*.
■ **vt : to will sthg to happen** prier de toutes ses forces pour que qqch se passe ▸ **to will sb to do sthg** concentrer toute sa volonté sur qqn pour qu'il fasse qqch ▸ **she willed herself to keep walking** elle s'est forcée à poursuivre sa marche ▸ **I could feel the crowd willing me on** je sentais que la foule me soutenait.

will[2] [wɪl] **modal vb** **1.** *(to express future tense)* **: I will see you next week** je te verrai la semaine prochaine ▸ **when will you have finished it?** quand est-ce que vous l'aurez fini? ▸ **I'll be arriving at six** j'arriverai à six heures ▸ **will you be here next week? yes I will/no I won't** est-ce que tu seras là la semaine prochaine? oui/non ▸ **do you think she'll marry him? – I'm sure she will/won't** est-ce que tu crois qu'elle va se marier avec lui? – je suis sûr que oui/non ▸ **when they come home the children will be sleeping** quand ils rentreront, les enfants dormiront *OR* seront endormis
2. [indicating willingness] **: will you have some more tea?** voulez-vous encore du thé? ▸ **I'll carry your suitcase** je vais porter votre valise ▸ **I won't do it** je refuse de le faire, je ne veux pas le faire ▸ **I won't go – oh yes you will!** je n'irai pas – oh (que) si! ▸ **will you marry me? – yes, I will/no, I won't** veux-tu m'épouser? – oui/non
3. [in commands, requests] **: you will leave this house at once** tu vas quitter cette maison tout de suite ▸ **close that window, will you?** ferme cette fenêtre, veux-tu? ▸ **will you be quiet!** veux-tu te taire!, tu vas te taire! ▸ **you won't forget, will you?** tu n'oublieras pas, n'est-ce pas? ▸ **won't you join us for lunch?** vous déjeunerez bien avec nous?
4. [indicating possibility, what usually happens] **: the hall will hold up to 1000 people** la salle peut abriter jusqu'à 1000 personnes ▸ **this will stop any draughts** ceci supprimera tous les courants d'air ▸ **pensions will be paid monthly** les pensions sont payées tous les mois ▸ **the machine will wash up to 5 kilos of laundry** la machine peut laver jusqu'à 5 kilos de linge ▸ **the car won't start** la voiture ne veut pas démarrer
5. [expressing an assumption] **: that'll be your father** cela doit être ton père ▸ **she'll be grown up by now** elle doit être grande maintenant
6. [indicating irritation] **: well, if you will leave your toys everywhere...** que veux-tu, si tu t'obstines à laisser traîner tes jouets partout... ▸ **she will keep phoning me** elle n'arrête pas de me téléphoner ▸ **she will have the last word** il faut toujours qu'elle ait le dernier mot.

willful US = ***wilful***.

willing ['wɪlɪŋ] **adj** **1.** [prepared] **: if you're willing** si vous voulez bien ▸ **to be willing to do sthg** être disposé(e) *OR* prêt(e) à faire qqch **2.** [eager] enthousiaste.

willingly ['wɪlɪŋlɪ] **adv** volontiers.

willingness ['wɪlɪŋnɪs] **n** **1.** [preparedness] **: willingness to do sthg** bonne volonté *f* à faire qqch **2.** [keenness] enthousiasme *m*.

willow (tree) ['wɪləʊ-] **n** saule *m*.

willowy ['wɪləʊɪ] **adj** svelte.

willpower ['wɪl,paʊəʳ] **n** volonté *f*.

willy ['wɪlɪ] (pl **-ies**) **n** *UK inf* zizi *m*.

willy-nilly [,wɪlɪ'nɪlɪ] **adv** **1.** [at random] n'importe comment **2.** [wanting to or not] bon gré mal gré.

wilt [wɪlt] **vi** [plant] se faner / *fig* [person] dépérir.

Wilts [wɪlts] (abbr of ***Wiltshire***) *comté anglais*.

wily ['waɪlɪ] (comp **-ier**, superl **-iest**) **adj** rusé(e).

Wimbledon ['wɪmbəldn] **n** *tournois annuel de tennis à Londres*.

CULTURE

Wimbledon

C'est l'un des plus importants tournois mondiaux de tennis, qui a lieu chaque année durant quinze jours, à partir de la dernière semaine de juin, sur les courts en herbe du All England Club à Wimbledon, au sud de Londres. Cet événement fait partie des quatre tournois du grand chelem. Si en 1877 il n'attirait qu'une centaine de spectateurs, ils sont aujourd'hui plus de 500 000, avec en plus une énorme couverture médiatique mondiale. Cette manifestation sportive génère, en plus de la pression commerciale, d'énormes enjeux financiers et des investissements importants, comme la construction d'un court avec un toit modulable permettant de jouer sous la pluie.

wimp [wɪmp] **n** *inf pej* mauviette *f*.

WIMP (abbr of ***window, icon, mouse, pull-down menu***) **n** WIMP *m*.

win [wɪn] ■ **n** victoire *f*.
■ **vt** (pt & pp **won**, cont **-ning**) **1.** [game, prize, competition] gagner ▸ **she won a gold medal in the Olympics** elle a obtenu une médaille d'or aux jeux Olympiques ▸ **we have won a great victory** nous avons remporté une grande victoire **2.** [support, approval] obtenir / [love, friendship] gagner.
■ **vi** gagner ▸ **they're winning three nil** ils gagnent trois à zéro ▸ **you/I** *etc* **can't win** il n'y a rien à faire.
◆ ***win over, win round*** *UK* **vt sep** convaincre, gagner à sa cause ▸ **he has won several of his former opponents over to his ideas** il a rallié plusieurs de ses anciens adversaires à ses idées.

wince [wɪns] ■ **vi : to wince (at/with)** [with body] tressaillir (à/de) / [with face] grimacer (à/de).
■ **n** tressaillement *m*.

winch [wɪntʃ] ■ **n** treuil *m*.
■ **vt** hisser à l'aide d'un treuil.

Winchester disk ['wɪntʃestəʳ-] **n** disque *m* (dur) Winchester.

wind[1] [wɪnd] ■ **n** **1.** METEOR vent *m* ▸ **the wind is changing** le vent tourne ▸ **to run like the wind** courir comme le vent **2.** [breath] souffle *m* ▸ **he had the wind knocked out of him** SPORT on lui a coupé le souffle, on l'a mis hors d'haleine ▸ **to get one's second wind** reprendre haleine *OR* son souffle **3.** *(U)* [in stomach] gaz *mpl* ▸ **to break wind** *euph* lâcher un vent **4.** [in orchestra] **: the wind** les instruments *mpl* à vent
▸▸ **to get wind of sthg** *inf* avoir vent de qqch ▸ **to put the wind up sb** *inf* flanquer la frousse à qqn ▸ **there's something in the wind** il se prépare quelque chose ▸ **to take the wind out of sb's sails** couper l'herbe sous le pied à qqn.
■ **vt** **1.** [knock breath out of] couper le souffle à ▸ **don't worry, I'm only winded** ne t'inquiète pas, j'ai la respiration coupée, c'est tout **2.** *UK* [baby] faire faire son rot à.

wind[2] [waɪnd] (pt & pp **wound**) ■ **vt** **1.** [string, thread] enrouler ▸ **I wound a scarf round my neck** j'ai enroulé une écharpe autour de mon cou ▸ **to wind sb round** *OR* **around one's little finger** mener qqn par le bout du nez **2.** [clock] remonter
▸▸ **to wind its way** [river, road] serpenter.
■ **vi** [river, road] serpenter ▸ **the river winds through the valley** le fleuve décrit des méandres dans la vallée *OR* traverse la vallée en serpentant.
◆ ***wind back*** **vt sep** [tape] rembobiner.
◆ ***wind down*** ■ **vt sep** **1.** *UK* [car window] baisser **2.** [business] cesser graduellement.
■ **vi** **1.** [clock] ralentir **2.** [relax] se détendre.
◆ ***wind forward*** **vt sep** [tape] embobiner.
◆ ***wind up*** ■ **vt sep** **1.** [finish - meeting] clôturer / [- business] liquider **2.** *UK* [clock, car window] remonter ▸ **to be wound up (about sthg)** *inf fig* être à cran (à cause de qqch) **3.** *UK inf* [deliberately annoy] faire marcher **4.** *inf* [end up] **: to wind up doing sthg** finir par faire qqch.
■ **vi** *inf* [end up] finir ▸ **he wound up in jail** il a fini *OR* s'est retrouvé en prison.

windbreak ['wɪndbreɪk] **n** pare-vent *m inv*.

windcheater *UK* ['wɪnd,tʃiːtəʳ], ***windbreaker*** *US* ['wɪnd,breɪkəʳ] **n** coupe-vent *m inv*.

windchill factor ['wɪndtʃɪl-] **n** *facteur d'abaissement de la température provoqué par le vent*.

winded ['wɪndɪd] **adj** essoufflé(e).

windfall ['wɪndfɔːl] **n** **1.** [fruit] fruit *m* que le vent a fait tomber **2.** [unexpected gift] aubaine *f*.

windfall profits, windfall revenues **npl** profits *mpl* inattendus *OR* exceptionnels.

windfall tax **n** impôt *m* sur les gains exceptionnels.

windfarm ['wɪndfɑːm] **n** champ *m* d'éoliennes.

winding ['waɪndɪŋ] **adj** sinueux(euse).

wind instrument [wɪnd-] **n** instrument *m* à vent.

windmill ['wɪndmɪl] **n** moulin *m* à vent.

window ['wɪndəʊ] **n** **1.** [gen & COMPUT] fenêtre *f* **2.** [pane of glass, in car] vitre *f* **3.** [of shop] vitrine *f*.

window box **n** jardinière *f*.

window cleaner **n** laveur *m*, -euse *f* de vitres.

window dressing **n** *(U)* **1.** [in shop] étalage *m* **2.** *fig* [non-essentials] façade *f*.

window envelope **n** enveloppe *f* à fenêtre.

window frame **n** châssis *m* de fenêtre.

window ledge **n** rebord *m* de fenêtre.

windowpane **n** vitre *f*.

window seat **n** [in room] banquette *f* sous la fenêtre / [in train, plane] place *f* côté fenêtre.

window shade **n** *US* store *m*.

window-shopping **n** lèche-vitrines *m inv* ▸ **to go window-shopping** (aller) faire du lèche-vitrines.

windowsill ['wɪndəʊsɪl] **n** [outside] rebord *m* de fenêtre / [inside] appui *m* de fenêtre.

windpipe ['wɪndpaɪp] **n** trachée *f*.

wind power [wɪnd-] **n** énergie *f* du vent *OR* éolienne.

windscreen *UK* ['wɪndskri:n], ***windshield*** *US* ['wɪndʃi:ld] **n** pare-brise *m inv*.

windscreen washer **n** *UK* lave-glace *m*.

windscreen wiper [-ˌwaɪpəʳ] **n** *UK* essuie-glace *m*.

windshield *US* = ***windscreen***.

windsock ['wɪndsɒk] **n** manche *f* à air.

windsurf ['wɪndsɜ:f] **vi** faire de la planche à voile.

windsurfer ['wɪndˌsɜ:fəʳ] **n** **1.** [person] véliplanchiste *mf* **2.** [board] planche *f* à voile.

windsurfing ['wɪndˌsɜ:fɪŋ] **n : to go windsurfing** faire de la planche à voile.

windswept ['wɪndswept] **adj** **1.** [scenery] balayé(e) par les vents **2.** [person] échevelé(e) / [hair] ébouriffé(e).

wind tunnel [wɪnd-] **n** soufflerie *f*, tunnel *m* aérodynamique.

wind turbine **n** éolienne *f*.

wind-up [waɪnd-] ■ **adj** [mechanism] **: a wind-up toy/watch** un jouet/une montre à remontoir.
■ **n** *UK inf* **: is this a wind-up?** est-ce qu'on veut me faire marcher?

Windward Islands ['wɪndwəd-] **n : the Windward Islands** les îles *fpl* du Vent.

windy ['wɪndɪ] (comp **-ier**, superl **-iest**) **adj** venteux(euse) ▸ **it's windy** il fait *OR* il y a du vent.

wine [waɪn] **n** vin *m*.

wine bar **n** *UK* bar *m* à vin.

wine bottle **n** bouteille *f* à vin.

wine box **n** Cubitainer® *m*.

wine cellar **n** cave *f* (à vin).

wineglass ['waɪnglɑ:s] **n** verre *m* à vin.

winegrower ['waɪnˌgrəʊəʳ] **n** viticulteur *m*, -trice *f*, vigneron *m*, -onne *f*.

wine list **n** carte *f* des vins.

wine merchant **n** *UK* marchand *m*, -e *f* de vins.

winepress ['waɪnpres] **n** pressoir *m*.

wine rack **n** casier *m* à vin.

wine tasting [-ˌteɪstɪŋ] **n** dégustation *f* (de vins).

wine vinegar **n** vinaigre *m* de vin.

wine waiter **n** sommelier *m*.

wing [wɪŋ] **n** aile *f*.
◆ ***wings*** **npl** **1.** THEAT **: the wings** les coulisses *fpl* **2.** [pilot's badge] galons *mpl*.

wing commander **n** *UK* lieutenant-colonel *m*.

winger ['wɪŋəʳ] **n** SPORT ailier *m*.

wing forward **n** [in rugby] ailier *m*.

wing mirror **n** rétroviseur *m* extérieur.

wing nut **n** vis *f* à ailettes.

wingspan ['wɪŋspæn] **n** envergure *f*.

wink [wɪŋk] ■ **n** clin *m* d'œil ▸ **to have forty winks** *inf* faire un petit roupillon ▸ **not to sleep a wink, not to get a wink of sleep** *inf* ne pas fermer l'œil.
■ **vi** **1.** [with eyes] **: to wink (at sb)** faire un clin d'œil (à qqn) **2.** *liter* [lights] clignoter.

winkle ['wɪŋkl] **n** bigorneau *m*.
◆ ***winkle out*** **vt sep** extirper ▸ **to winkle sthg out of sb** arracher qqch à qqn.

Winnebago® [ˌwɪnɪ'beɪgəʊ] **n** camping-car *m*, autocaravane *f offic*.

winner ['wɪnəʳ] **n** [person] gagnant *m*, -e *f*.

winning ['wɪnɪŋ] **adj** **1.** [victorious, successful] gagnant(e) **2.** [pleasing] charmeur(euse).
◆ ***winnings*** **npl** gains *mpl*.

winning post **n** poteau *m* d'arrivée.

Winnipeg ['wɪnɪˌpeg] **n** Winnipeg.

wino ['waɪnəʊ] (pl **-s**) **n** *inf* ivrogne *mf*.

winsome ['wɪnsəm] **adj** *liter* séduisant(e).

winter ['wɪntəʳ] ■ **n** hiver *m* ▸ **in winter** en hiver.
■ **comp** d'hiver.

winter sports **npl** sports *mpl* d'hiver.

wintertime ['wɪntətaɪm] **n** *(U)* hiver *m* ▸ **in wintertime** en hiver.

wint(e)ry ['wɪntrɪ] **adj** d'hiver.

wipe [waɪp] ■ **n** **1.** [action of wiping] **: to give sthg a wipe** essuyer qqch, donner un coup de torchon à qqch **2.** [cloth] lingette *f*.
■ **vt** essuyer.
◆ ***wipe away*** **vt sep** [tears] essuyer.
◆ ***wipe out*** **vt sep** **1.** [erase] effacer **2.** [eradicate] anéantir.
◆ ***wipe up*** **vt sep** & **vi** essuyer.

wiper ['waɪpəʳ] **n** [windscreen wiper] essuie-glace *m*.

wire ['waɪəʳ] ■ **n** **1.** *(U)* [metal] fil *m* de fer **2.** [cable] fil *m* **3.** *esp US* [telegram] télégramme *m*.
■ **comp** en fil de fer.
■ **vt** **1.** [fasten, connect] **: to wire sthg to sthg** relier qqch à qqch avec du fil de fer **2.** [ELEC - plug] installer / [- house] faire l'installation électrique de **3.** *esp US* [send telegram to] télégraphier à.

wire brush **n** brosse *f* métallique.

wire cutters **npl** cisaille *f*.

wired ['waɪəd] **adj** **1.** ELEC [to an alarm] relié(e) à un système d'alarme **2.** [wiretapped] mis(e) sur écoute **3.** [bra] à tiges métalliques **4.** *inf* [psyched-up] surexcité(e).

wirefree ['waɪəfriː] **adj** sans fil.

wireless ['waɪəlɪs] **n** *dated* T.S.F. *f*

wire netting **n** *(U)* grillage *m*.

wiretap ['waɪətæp] (pt & pp **-ped**, cont **-ping**) ■ **vt** mettre sur écoute.
■ **vi** mettre un téléphone sur écoute.
■ **n** : **they put a wiretap on his phone** ils ont mis son téléphone sur écoute.

wire-tapping [-ˌtæpɪŋ] **n** *(U)* écoute *f* téléphonique.

wire wool **n** *UK* paille *f* de fer.

wiring ['waɪərɪŋ] **n** *(U)* installation *f* électrique.

wiry ['waɪərɪ] (comp **-ier**, superl **-iest**) **adj** **1.** [hair] crépu(e) **2.** [body, man] noueux(euse).

Wisconsin [wɪs'kɒnsɪn] **n** Wisconsin *m* ▸ **in Wisconsin** dans le Wisconsin.

wisdom ['wɪzdəm] **n** sagesse *f*.

wisdom tooth **n** dent *f* de sagesse.

wise [waɪz] **adj** sage ▸ **to get wise to sthg** *inf* piger qqch ▸ **to be no wiser, to be none the wiser** ne pas en savoir plus (pour autant), ne pas être plus avancé.
◆ ***wise up*** **vi** *esp US* piger.

-wise **suffix** **1.** [in the direction of] dans le sens de ▸ **length-wise** dans le sens de la longueur **2.** [in the manner of] à la manière de, comme ▸ **he edged crab-wise up to the bar** il s'approcha du bar en marchant de côté comme un crabe **3.** *inf* [as regards] côté ▸ **money-wise the job leaves a lot to be desired** le poste laisse beaucoup à désirer côté argent.

wisecrack ['waɪzkræk] **n** *pej* vanne *f*.

wise guy **n** *inf* malin *m*.

wisely ['waɪzlɪ] **adv** sagement, avec sagesse.

wish [wɪʃ] ■ **n** **1.** [desire] souhait *m*, désir *m* ▸ **wish for sthg/to do sthg** désir de qqch/de faire qqch ▸ **she had no great wish to travel** elle n'avait pas très envie de voyager ▸ **it was his last wish** c'était sa dernière volonté ▸ **she went against my wishes** elle a agi contre ma volonté ▸ **wish list** desiderata *mpl*
2. [magic request] vœu *m* ▸ **he got his wish, his wish came true** son vœu s'est réalisé.
■ **vt** **1.** [want] : **to wish to do sthg** souhaiter faire qqch ▸ **I wish (that) he'd come** j'aimerais bien qu'il vienne ▸ **I wish I'd never come!** je n'aurais jamais dû venir ▸ **I wish I could** si seulement je pouvais ▸ **I wish you'd be more careful** j'aimerais que vous fassiez plus attention ▸ **to wish sb dead** souhaiter la mort de qqn ▸ **I don't wish to appear rude, but...** *fml* je ne voudrais pas paraître grossier mais...
2. [expressing hope] : **to wish sb sthg** souhaiter qqch à qqn ▸ **I wish you (good) luck** je vous souhaite bonne chance.
■ **vi** [by magic] : **to wish for sthg** souhaiter qqch ▸ **what more could a man/woman wish for?** que peut-on souhaiter de plus? ▸ **to wish upon a star** *liter* faire un vœu en regardant une étoile.
◆ ***wishes*** **npl** : **best wishes** meilleurs vœux ▸ **(with) best wishes** [at end of letter] bien amicalement ▸ **best wishes on your graduation (day)** toutes mes/nos félicitations à l'occasion de l'obtention de votre diplôme.
◆ ***wish on*** **vt sep** : **to wish sthg on sb** souhaiter qqch à qqn ▸ **I wouldn't wish this headache on anyone** je ne souhaite à personne d'avoir un mal de tête pareil.

wishbone ['wɪʃbəʊn] **n** bréchet *m*.

wishful thinking [ˌwɪʃful-] **n** : **that's just wishful thinking** c'est prendre mes/ses *etc* désirs pour des réalités.

wishy-washy ['wɪʃɪˌwɒʃɪ] **adj** *inf pej* [person] sans personnalité / [ideas] vague.

wisp [wɪsp] **n** **1.** [tuft] mèche *f* **2.** [small cloud] mince filet *m* OR volute *f*.

wispy ['wɪspɪ] (comp **-ier**, superl **-iest**) **adj** [hair] fin(e).

wistful ['wɪstfʊl] **adj** nostalgique.

wistfully ['wɪstfʊlɪ] **adv** d'un air triste et rêveur.

wit [wɪt] **n** **1.** [humour] esprit *m* **2.** [funny person] homme *m* d'esprit, femme *f* d'esprit **3.** [intelligence] : **to have the wit to do sthg** avoir l'intelligence de faire qqch.
◆ ***wits*** **npl** : **to have** OR **keep one's wits about one** être attentif(ive) OR sur ses gardes ▸ **to be scared out of one's wits** *inf* avoir une peur bleue ▸ **to be at one's wits' end** ne plus savoir que faire.

witch [wɪtʃ] **n** sorcière *f*.

witchcraft ['wɪtʃkrɑːft] **n** sorcellerie *f*.

witchdoctor ['wɪtʃˌdɒktəʳ] **n** sorcier *m*.

witch-hazel **n** hamamélis *m*.

witch-hunt **n** *pej* chasse *f* aux sorcières.

with [wɪð] **prep** **1.** [in company of] avec ▸ **I play tennis with his wife** je joue au tennis avec sa femme ▸ **I have no one to go with** je n'ai personne avec qui aller ▸ **we stayed with them for a week** nous avons passé une semaine chez eux ▸ **you can leave it with me** je m'en occupe, laissez-moi faire ▸ **duck with orange sauce** canard *m* à l'orange / [an employee of] : **she's with the UN** elle travaille à l'ONU
2. [indicating opposition] avec ▸ **to argue with sb** discuter avec qqn ▸ **the war with Germany** la guerre avec OR contre l'Allemagne
3. [indicating means, manner, feelings] avec ▸ **I washed it with detergent** je l'ai lavé avec un détergent ▸ **the room was hung with balloons** la pièce était ornée de ballons

HOW TO ...
express wishes

J'espère qu'il n'y aura pas trop de monde / I hope it won't be too busy
J'aimerais tellement qu'ils viennent avec nous ! / I'd love them to come with us!
Ça serait vraiment bien qu'il accepte de rester / It'd be great if he agreed to stay
Si seulement tu avais été plus discret ! / If only you'd been a bit more discreet!
Je donnerais n'importe quoi pour être en vacances / I'd give anything to be on holiday
Pourvu qu'elle dise oui ! / I just hope she says yes!

▸ **covered/furnished/lined with** couvert/meublé/doublé de ▸ **"All right", she said with a smile** "Très bien", dit-elle en souriant *OR* avec un sourire ▸ **his eyes filled with tears** ses yeux se remplirent de larmes ▸ **she was trembling with fright** elle tremblait de peur ▸ **with care** avec soin ▸ **he knocked the guard out with one blow** il assomma le gardien d'un (seul) coup
4. [having] avec ▸ **a man with a beard** un homme avec une barbe, un barbu ▸ **the man with the moustache** l'homme à la moustache ▸ **which boy? – the one with the torn jacket** quel garçon? – celui qui a la veste déchirée ▸ **a city with many churches** une ville qui a de nombreuses églises ▸ **the computer comes with a printer** l'ordinateur est vendu avec une imprimante
5. [regarding] **: he's very mean with money** il est très près de ses sous, il est très avare ▸ **what will you do with the house?** qu'est-ce que tu vas faire de la maison? ▸ **the trouble with her is that...** l'ennui avec elle *OR* ce qu'il y a avec elle c'est que... ▸ **it's an obsession with her** c'est une manie chez elle
6. [indicating simultaneity] **: I can't do it with you watching me** je ne peux pas le faire quand *OR* pendant que tu me regardes
7. [because of] **: with the weather as it is, we've decided to stay at home** vu le temps qu'il fait *OR* étant donné le temps, nous avons décidé de rester à la maison ▸ **with my luck, I'll probably lose** avec ma chance habituelle, je suis sûr de perdre ▸ **sick** *OR* **ill with malaria** atteint du paludisme
▸▸ **I'm with you** [I understand] je vous suis / [I'm on your side] je suis des vôtres / [I agree] je suis d'accord avec vous.

withdraw [wɪð'drɔː] (pt **-drew**, pp **-drawn**) ■ **vt 1.** *fml* [remove] **: to withdraw sthg (from)** enlever qqch (de) ▸ **the car has been withdrawn (from sale)** la voiture a été retirée de la vente **2.** [money, troops, remark] retirer.
■ **vi 1.** *fml* [leave] **: to withdraw (from)** se retirer (de) **2.** MIL se replier ▸ **to withdraw from** évacuer ▸ **to withdraw to safety** se mettre à l'abri **3.** [quit, give up] **: to withdraw (from)** se retirer (de) ▸ **she has decided to withdraw from politics** elle a décidé de se retirer de la politique.

withdrawal [wɪð'drɔːəl] **n 1.** [gen] **: withdrawal (from)** retrait *m* (de) **2.** MIL repli *m* **3.** MED manque *m*.

withdrawal symptoms **npl** crise *f* de manque.

withdrawn [wɪð'drɔːn] ■ **pp** ➤ ***withdraw***.
■ **adj** [shy, quiet] renfermé(e).

withdrew [wɪð'druː] **pt** ➤ ***withdraw***.

wither ['wɪðəʳ] ■ **vt** flétrir.
■ **vi 1.** [dry up] se flétrir **2.** [weaken] mourir.

withered ['wɪðəd] **adj** flétri(e).

withering ['wɪðərɪŋ] **adj** [look] foudroyant(e).

withhold [wɪð'həʊld] (pt & pp **-held** [-'held]) **vt** [services] refuser / [information] cacher / [salary] retenir.

within [wɪ'ðɪn] ■ **prep 1.** [inside] à l'intérieur de, dans ▸ **within her** en elle, à l'intérieur d'elle-même ▸ **the man's role within the family is changing** le rôle de l'homme au sein de la famille est en train de changer **2.** [budget, comprehension] dans les limites de / [limits] dans ▸ **within the framework of the agreement** dans le cadre de l'accord **3.** [less than - distance] à moins de / [- time] d'ici, en moins de ▸ **within the week** avant la fin de la semaine ▸ **accurate to within 0.1 of a millimetre** précis au dixième de millimètre près.
■ **adv** à l'intérieur ▸ **from within** de l'intérieur.

with it **adj** *inf* **1.** [alert] réveillé(e) ▸ **get with it!** réveille-toi!, secoue-toi! **2.** *dated* [fashionable] dans le vent.

without [wɪð'aʊt] ■ **prep** sans ▸ **without a coat** sans manteau ▸ **I left without seeing him** je suis parti sans l'avoir vu ▸ **I left without him seeing me** je suis parti sans qu'il m'ait vu ▸ **he took it without so much as a thank you** il l'a pris sans même dire merci ▸ **to go without sthg** se passer de qqch.
■ **adv : to go** *OR* **do without** s'en passer.

withstand [wɪð'stænd] (pt & pp **-stood** [-'stʊd]) **vt** résister à.

witless ['wɪtlɪs] **adj** sot (sotte), stupide.

witness ['wɪtnɪs] ■ **n 1.** [gen] témoin *mf* ▸ **to call sb as (a) witness** citer qqn comme témoin ▸ **witness for the prosecution/defence** témoin à charge/décharge ▸ **to be witness to sthg** être témoin de qqch **2.** [testimony] **: to bear witness to sthg** témoigner de qqch.
■ **vt 1.** [accident, crime] être témoin de **2.** *fig* [changes, rise in birth rate] assister à **3.** [countersign] contresigner.

witness box *UK*, ***witness stand*** *US* **n** barre *f* des témoins.

witter ['wɪtəʳ] **vi** *UK inf pej* radoter, parler pour ne rien dire.

witticism ['wɪtɪsɪzm] **n** mot *m* d'esprit.

witty ['wɪtɪ] (comp **-ier**, superl **-iest**) **adj** plein(e) d'esprit, spirituel(elle).

wives [waɪvz] **npl** ➤ ***wife***.

wizard ['wɪzəd] **n** magicien *m* / *fig* as *m*, champion *m*, -onne *f*.

wizened ['wɪznd] **adj** ratatiné(e).

wk (abbr of ***week***) sem.

Wm. (abbr of ***William***) *Guillaume*.

WO **n** abbr of ***warrant officer***.

wobble ['wɒbl] **vi** [hand, wings] trembler / [chair, table] branler.

wobbly ['wɒblɪ] (comp **-ier**, superl **-iest**) **adj** *inf* [jelly] tremblant(e) / [table] branlant(e).

woe [wəʊ] **n** *liter* malheur *m*.

woeful ['wəʊfʊl] **adj 1.** [sad - person, look, news, situation] malheureux(euse), très triste / [- scene, tale] affligeant(e), très triste **2.** [very poor] lamentable, épouvantable, consternant(e).

woefully ['wəʊfʊlɪ] **adv 1.** [sadly - look, smile] très tristement **2.** [badly - perform, behave] lamentablement ▸ **our funds are woefully inadequate** nous manquons cruellement de fonds.

wok [wɒk] **n** wok *m*.

woke [wəʊk] **pt** ➤ ***wake***.

woken ['wəʊkn] **pp** ➤ ***wake***.

wolf [wʊlf] (pl **wolves** ['wʊlvz]) **n** [animal] loup *m*.
◆ ***wolf down*** **vt sep** *inf* engloutir.

wolf whistle **n** sifflement *m* admiratif *(à l'adresse d'une femme).*

wolves ['wʊlvz] **npl** ➤ ***wolf.***

woman ['wʊmən] (pl **women**) ■ **n** femme *f.*

■ **comp : woman doctor** femme *f* médecin ▸ **woman footballer** footballeuse *f* ▸ **woman taxi driver** femme *f* chauffeur de taxi ▸ **woman teacher** professeur *m* femme.

womanhood ['wʊmənhʊd] **n** *(U)* **1.** [adult life] **: to reach womanhood** devenir une femme **2.** [women] femmes *fpl.*

womanize, *UK* ***-ise*** ['wʊmənaɪz] **vi** *pej* courir les femmes.

womanizer ['wʊmənaɪzər] **n** coureur *m* de jupons.

womanly ['wʊmənlɪ] **adj** féminin(e).

womb [wu:m] **n** utérus *m.*

wombat ['wɒmbæt] **n** wombat *m.*

women ['wɪmɪn] **npl** ➤ ***woman.***

women's group **n** groupe *m* féministe.

Women's Institute **n** *UK* **: the Women's Institute** l'association locale des femmes.

women's lib **n** libération *f* de la femme.

women's liberation **n** libération *f* de la femme.

Women's Movement **n** mouvement *m* féministe.

women's refuge **n** centre *m* d'accueil pour les femmes.

won [wʌn] **pt & pp** ➤ ***win.***

wonder ['wʌndər] ■ **n 1.** *(U)* [amazement] étonnement *m* ▸ **the children were filled with wonder** les enfants étaient émerveillés **2.** [cause for surprise] **: it's a wonder (that)...** c'est un miracle que... ▸ **no wonder!** ce n'est pas étonnant!, cela vous étonne? ▸ **it's no** *OR* **little** *OR* **small wonder (that)...** il n'est pas étonnant que... ▸ **no wonder they refused** ce n'est pas étonnant qu'ils aient refusé **3.** [amazing thing, person] merveille *f* ▸ **the seven wonders of the world** les sept merveilles du monde ▸ **to work** *OR* **do wonders** faire des merveilles.

■ **vt 1.** [speculate] **: I wonder where she's gone** je me demande où elle est allée ▸ **to wonder (if** *OR* **whether)** se demander (si) **2.** [in polite requests] **: I wonder whether you would mind shutting the window?** est-ce que cela ne vous ennuierait pas de fermer la fenêtre? ▸ **I wonder if you could help me** pourriez-vous m'aider s'il vous plaît?

■ **vi 1.** [speculate] se demander ▸ **it makes you wonder** cela donne à penser *OR* réfléchir ▸ **to wonder about sthg** s'interroger sur qqch **2.** *liter* [be amazed] **: to wonder at sthg** s'étonner de qqch ▸ **I don't wonder** cela ne m'étonne pas.

wonderful ['wʌndəfʊl] **adj** merveilleux(euse).

wonderfully ['wʌndəfʊlɪ] **adv 1.** [very well] merveilleusement, à merveille **2.** [for emphasis] extrêmement.

wonderland ['wʌndəlænd] **n** pays *m* merveilleux.

wondrous ['wʌndrəs] *liter* ■ **adj** merveilleux(euse).

■ **adv** = ***wondrously.***

wondrously ['wʌndrəslɪ] **adv** *liter* merveilleusement.

wonky ['wɒŋkɪ] (comp **-ier**, superl **-iest**) **adj** *UK inf* bancal(e).

wont [wəʊnt] ■ **adj : to be wont to do sthg** avoir l'habitude de faire qqch.

■ **n** *dated & liter* **: as is one's wont** comme à son habitude *OR* à l'accoutumée.

won't [wəʊnt] = ***will not.***

woo [wu:] **vt 1.** *liter* [court] courtiser **2.** [try to win over] chercher à rallier (à soi *OR* à sa cause).

wood [wʊd] ■ **n** bois *m* ▸ **touch** *UK OR* **knock on** *US* **wood!** touchons du bois! ▸ **you can't see the wood for the trees** *UK* ce sont les arbres qui cachent la forêt.

■ **comp** en bois.

◆ ***woods*** **npl** bois *mpl.*

woodchip ['wʊdtʃɪp] **n** [composite wood] aggloméré *m.*

wooded ['wʊdɪd] **adj** boisé(e).

wooden ['wʊdn] **adj 1.** [of wood] en bois **2.** *pej* [actor] gauche.

wooden spoon **n** cuillère *f* de bois ▸ **to win** *OR* **get the wooden spoon** *UK fig* être classé dernier.

woodland ['wʊdlənd] **n** région *f* boisée.

woodlouse ['wʊdlaʊs] (pl **-lice** [-laɪs]) **n** cloporte *m.*

woodpecker ['wʊd,pekər] **n** pivert *m.*

wood pigeon **n** ramier *m.*

woodshed ['wʊdʃed] **n** bûcher *m.*

woodwind ['wʊdwɪnd] **n : the woodwind** les bois *mpl.*

woodwork ['wʊdwɜ:k] **n** menuiserie *f.*

woodworm ['wʊdwɜ:m] **n** ver *m* du bois ▸ **to have woodworm** être piqué par les vers.

woof [wʊf] ■ **n** aboiement *m.*

■ **excl** ouah!

wool [wʊl] **n** laine *f* ▸ **to pull the wool over sb's eyes** *inf* rouler qqn (dans la farine).

woollen *UK*, ***woolen*** *US* ['wʊlən] **adj** en laine, de laine.

◆ ***woollens*** **npl** lainages *mpl.*

woolly, *US* ***wooly*** ['wʊlɪ] ■ **adj** (comp **-ier**, superl **-iest**) **1.** [woollen] en laine, de laine **2.** *inf* [idea, thinking] confus(e).

■ **n** *inf* lainage *m.*

woolly-headed [-'hedɪd] **adj** *inf pej* confus(e).

woozy ['wu:zɪ] (comp **-ier**, superl **-iest**) **adj** *inf* sonné(e).

Worcester sauce ['wʊstər-] **n** *(U) sauce épicée à base de soja et de vinaigre.*

Worcs (abbr of **Worcestershire**) *ancien comté anglais.*

word [wɜ:d] ■ **n 1.** LING mot *m* ▸ **in your own words** dans vos mots à vous ▸ **too stupid for words** vraiment trop bête ▸ **he didn't say a word** il n'a rien dit, il n'a pas dit un mot ▸ **with these words they left** sur ces mots *OR* là-dessus, ils sont partis ▸ **word for word** [repeat, copy] mot pour mot / [translate] mot à mot ▸ **in other words** en d'autres mots *OR* termes ▸ **not in so many words** pas exactement ▸ **in a word** en un mot ▸ **by word of mouth** de bouche à oreille ▸ **lazy isn't the word for it!** paresseux, c'est peu dire! ▸ **from the word go** dès le départ ▸ **to put in a (good) word for sb** glisser un mot en faveur de qqn ▸ **just say the word** vous n'avez qu'un mot à dire ▸ **to have a word (with sb)** parler (à qqn) ▸ **to have words with sb** *inf* avoir des

mots avec qqn ▸ **to have the last word** avoir le dernier mot ▸ **she doesn't mince her words** elle ne mâche pas ses mots ▸ **to weigh one's words** peser ses mots ▸ **I couldn't get a word in edgeways** je n'ai pas réussi à placer un seul mot ▸ **he took the words out of my mouth** il a dit exactement ce que j'allais dire
2. [talk] mot *m*, mots *mpl*, parole *f*, paroles *fpl* ▸ **to have a word with sb about sthg** toucher un mot OR deux mots à qqn au sujet de qqch ▸ **can I have a word with you about the meeting?** est-ce que je peux vous dire deux mots à propos de la réunion?
3. *(U)* [news] nouvelles *fpl* ▸ **he sent word to say he had arrived safely** il a envoyé un mot pour dire qu'il était bien arrivé
4. [promise] parole *f* ▸ **to give sb one's word** donner sa parole à qqn ▸ **to break one's word** manquer à sa parole ▸ **to be as good as one's word, to be true to one's word** tenir (sa) parole ▸ **we'll have to take your word for it** nous sommes bien obligés de vous croire.
■ **vt** [letter, reply] rédiger ▸ **we sent a strongly worded protest** nous avons envoyé une lettre de protestation bien sentie.

word-for-word **adj** [repetition, imitation] mot pour mot / [translation] littéral(e).

word game **n** jeu *m* de lettres.

wording ['wɜ:dɪŋ] **n** *(U)* termes *mpl*.

word-of-mouth **adj** [account] oral(e), verbal(e).

word-perfect **adj : he had his lines word-perfect** il connaissait ses répliques au mot près.

wordplay ['wɜ:dpleɪ] **n** *(U)* jeux *mpl* de mots.

word processing **n** *(U)* COMPUT traitement *m* de texte.

word processor [-ˌprəʊsesər] **n** COMPUT machine *f* à traitement de texte.

wordwrap ['wɜ:dræp] **n** COMPUT retour *m* à la ligne automatique.

wordy ['wɜ:dɪ] (comp **-ier**, superl **-iest**) **adj** *pej* verbeux(euse).

wore [wɔ:r] **pt** ➤ ***wear***.

work [wɜ:k] ■ **n 1.** *(U)* [employment] travail *m*, emploi *m* ▸ **to be in work** avoir un emploi ▸ **out of work** sans emploi, au chômage ▸ **at work** au travail ▸ **to take time off work** prendre des congés ▸ **he's a friend from work** c'est un collègue
2. [activity, tasks] travail *m* ▸ **she put a lot of work into that book** elle a beaucoup travaillé sur ce livre ▸ **to start work, to set to work** se mettre au travail ▸ **to take work home** prendre du travail à la maison ▸ **to have one's work cut out doing sthg** OR **to do sthg** avoir du mal OR de la peine à faire qqch ▸ **to make short** OR **light work of sthg** expédier qqch
3. ART & LIT œuvre *f* ▸ **works of fiction** des ouvrages de fiction
▸▸ **he's a nasty piece of work** *UK inf* c'est un salaud.
■ **vt 1.** [person, staff] faire travailler ▸ **I worked my way through college** j'ai travaillé pour payer mes études à l'université ▸ **to work o.s. to death** se tuer à la tâche
2. [achieve, accomplish] **: the story worked its magic on the public** l'histoire a enchanté le public ▸ **to work wonders** faire merveille
3. [machine] faire marcher ▸ **this switch works the furnace** ce bouton actionne OR commande la chaudière
4. [wood, metal, land] travailler
5. [cause to become] **: to work o.s. into a rage** se mettre en rage
6. [make] **: to work one's way through a crowd** se frayer un chemin à travers une foule ▸ **to work one's way along** avancer petit à petit ▸ **he worked his way to the top** il est parvenu au sommet à la force du poignet.
■ **vi 1.** [do a job] travailler ▸ **he works as a teacher** il a un poste d'enseignant ▸ **to work on sthg** travailler à qqch
2. [function] fonctionner, marcher ▸ **the lift never works** l'ascenseur est toujours en panne ▸ **a pump worked by hand** une pompe actionnée à la main
3. [succeed] marcher ▸ **your idea just won't work** ton idée ne peut pas marcher
4. [have effect] **: to work against sb** jouer contre qqn ▸ **to work against sthg** aller à l'encontre de qqch
5. [become] **: to work loose** se desserrer ▸ **to work free** se libérer.
◆ ***works*** ■ **n** [factory] usine *f* ▸ **a printing works** une imprimerie.
■ **npl 1.** [mechanism] mécanisme *m*
2. [digging, building] travaux *mpl*
3. *inf* [everything] **: the works** tout le tralala.
◆ ***work off*** **vt sep** [anger] passer.
◆ ***work on*** **vt insep 1.** [pay attention to] travailler à
2. [take as basis] se baser sur.
◆ ***work out*** ■ **vt sep 1.** [plan, schedule] mettre au point ▸ **she had it all worked out** elle avait tout planifié
2. [total, answer] trouver
3. [figure out] arriver à comprendre ▸ **I can't work her out** je n'arrive pas à la comprendre.
■ **vi 1.** [figure, total] **: to work out at** *UK* OR **to** *US* se monter à ▸ **that works out at three hours a week** ça fait trois heures par semaine
2. [turn out] se dérouler
3. [be successful] (bien) marcher ▸ **it didn't work out between them** les choses ont plutôt mal tourné entre eux
4. [train, exercise] s'entraîner.
◆ ***work up*** **vt sep 1.** [excite] **: he works himself up** OR **gets himself worked up over nothing** il s'énerve pour rien ▸ **to work o.s. up into a rage** se mettre en rage
2. [generate] **: to work up an appetite** s'ouvrir l'appétit ▸ **to work up enthusiasm** s'enthousiasmer ▸ **to work up courage** trouver du courage.

workable ['wɜ:kəbl] **adj** [plan] réalisable / [system] fonctionnel(elle).

workaday ['wɜ:kədeɪ] **adj** *pej* ordinaire, commun(e).

workaholic [ˌwɜ:kə'hɒlɪk] **n** bourreau *m* de travail.

workbasket ['wɜ:kˌbɑ:skɪt] **n** corbeille *f* à ouvrage.

workbench ['wɜ:kbentʃ] **n** établi *m*.

workbook ['wɜ:kbʊk] **n** cahier *m* d'exercices.

workday ['wɜ:kdeɪ] **n 1.** [day's work] journée *f* de travail
2. [not weekend] jour *m* ouvrable.

worked up [ˌwɜ:kt-] **adj** dans tous ses états.

worker ['wɜ:kər] **n** travailleur *m*, -euse *f*, ouvrier *m*, -ère *f* ▸ **to be a hard/fast worker** travailler dur/vite ▸ **to be a good worker** bien travailler.

work ethic **n** *exaltation des valeurs liées au travail.*

work experience **n : the course includes two months' work experience** le programme comprend un stage en entreprise de deux mois.

workforce ['wɜ:kfɔ:s] **n** main *f* d'œuvre.

workhouse ['wɜ:khaʊs] **n 1.** *UK* [poorhouse] hospice *m* **2.** *US* [prison] maison *f* de correction.

working ['wɜ:kɪŋ] **adj 1.** [in operation] qui marche **2.** [having employment] qui travaille **3.** [conditions, clothes, hours] de travail.
◆ ***workings*** **npl** [of system, machine] mécanisme *m* ▸ **I'll never understand the workings of his mind** *fig* je ne comprendrai jamais ce qui se passe dans sa tête.

CULTURE

Working Hours

Au Royaume-Uni, le temps de travail réglementaire varie entre 35 et 38 heures, sauf dans les hôpitaux, l'hôtellerie et la restauration, où il peut atteindre 60 heures. La plupart des Anglais travaillent bien plus, sans compensation financière, ou bénéficient du **flexitime** (« horaires flexibles »), les employés choisissant alors librement leurs heures de travail. Ils ont de 4 à 5 semaines de congés annuels, mais ils ne partent généralement que 15 jours d'affilée. De nouvelles initiatives européennes accordent un congé sans solde aux personnes voulant s'occuper de leurs enfants ou de proches malades ou âgés. Les Américains travaillent souvent plus de 40 heures et leurs congés varient généralement entre une et quatre semaines, ou parfois plus en fonction de leur ancienneté dans l'entreprise.

working capital **n** *(U)* **1.** [assets minus liabilities] fonds *mpl* de roulement **2.** [available money] capital *m* d'exploitation.

working class **n : the working class** la classe ouvrière.
◆ ***working-class*** **adj** ouvrier(ère).

working day **n** *UK* = ***workday***.

working group **n** *UK* groupe *m* de travail.

working knowledge **n** connaissance *f* pratique.

working lunch **n** déjeuner *m* de travail.

working majority **n** majorité *f* suffisante.

working man **n** ouvrier *m*.

working model **n** modèle *m* opérationnel.

working order **n : in working order** en état de marche.

working party **n** *UK* groupe *m* de travail.

working title **n** titre *m* provisoire.

working week **n** *UK* semaine *f* de travail.

work-in-progress **n** travail *m* en cours.

workload ['wɜ:kləʊd] **n** quantité *f* de travail.

workman ['wɜ:kmən] (**pl -men** [-mən]) **n** ouvrier *m*.

workmanlike ['wɜ:kmənlaɪk] **adj 1.** [efficient - approach, person] professionnel(elle) **2.** [well made - artefact] bien fait(e), soigné(e) ▸ **he wrote a workmanlike report** il a fait un compte rendu très sérieux **3.** [serious - attempt, effort] sérieux(euse).

workmanship ['wɜ:kmənʃɪp] **n** *(U)* travail *m*.

workmate ['wɜ:kmeɪt] **n** camarade *mf* **OR** collègue *mf* de travail.

work of art **n** *lit & fig* œuvre *f* d'art.

workout ['wɜ:kaʊt] **n** séance *f* d'entraînement.

work permit [-,pɜ:mɪt] **n** permis *m* de travail.

workplace ['wɜ:kpleɪs] **n** lieu *m* de travail.

workroom ['wɜ:krʊm] **n** salle *f* de travail.

works council **n** *UK* comité *m* d'entreprise.

work sheet **n** COMPUT feuille *f* de travail.

workshop ['wɜ:kʃɒp] **n** atelier *m*.

workshy ['wɜ:kʃaɪ] **adj** *UK* fainéant(e).

workspace ['wɜ:kspeɪs] **n** COMPUT bureau *m*.

workstation ['wɜ:k,steɪʃn] **n** COMPUT poste *m* de travail.

work surface **n** plan *m* de travail.

worktable ['wɜ:k,teɪbl] **n** table *f* de travail.

worktop ['wɜ:ktɒp] **n** *UK* plan *m* de travail.

work-to-rule **n** *UK* grève *f* du zèle.

workweek **n** *US* = ***working week***.

world [wɜ:ld] ■ **n** [gen] monde *m* ▸ **to see the world** voir du pays, courir le monde ▸ **the developing world** les pays *mpl* en voie de développement ▸ **to bring a child into the world** mettre un enfant au monde ▸ **we live in different worlds** nous ne vivons pas sur la même planète ▸ **he lives in a world of his own** il vit dans un monde à lui ▸ **to be worlds apart** [in lifestyle] avoir des styles de vie complètement différents / [in opinions] avoir des opinions complètement différentes ▸ **what/where in the world...?** que/où diable...? ▸ **the world over** dans le monde entier ▸ **the animal/plant world** le règne animal/végétal
▸▸ **to be dead to the world** dormir profondément ▸ **to get the best of both worlds** gagner sur tous les plans ▸ **to think the world of sb** admirer qqn énormément, ne jurer que par qqn ▸ **to do sb the** *UK* **OR a world of good** faire un bien fou à qqn, faire énormément de bien à qqn ▸ **I wouldn't hurt her for the world** je ne lui ferais de mal pour rien au monde ▸ **a world of difference** une énorme différence.
■ **comp** [power] mondial(e) / [language] universel(elle) / [tour] du monde.

World Bank **n : the World Bank** la Banque mondiale.

world-class **adj** de niveau international.

World Cup ■ **n : the World Cup** la Coupe du monde.
■ **comp** de Coupe du monde.

world economy **n** conjoncture *f* économique mondiale.

world-famous **adj** de renommée mondiale ▸ **to become world-famous** acquérir une renommée mondiale.

worldly ['wɜ:ldlɪ] **adj** de ce monde, matériel(elle) ▸ **worldly goods** *liter* biens *mpl*.

worldly-wise **adj** qui a l'expérience du monde.

world music **n** world music *f*.

world power n puissance *f* mondiale.

World Series n *US* : **the World Series** *le championnat américain de baseball*.

CULTURE

World Series

Inaugurées en 1903, les **World Series** désignent le champion de base-ball aux USA après une série de rencontres entre le vainqueur de chaque conférence, la **National League** et l'**American League**. Longtemps considéré comme « le passe-temps de l'Amérique », le base-ball est de nos jours l'une des manifestations sportives les plus appréciées aux États-Unis. La tradition veut que ce soit le président qui donne le coup d'envoi en étant le premier lanceur.

World Trade Organization n Organisation *f* mondiale du commerce.

world view n *vue métaphysique du monde*.

world war n guerre *f* mondiale ▸ **World War I, the First World War** la Première Guerre mondiale ▸ **World War II, the Second World War** la Seconde Guerre mondiale.

World War I n la Première Guerre mondiale.

World War II n la Deuxième Guerre mondiale.

world-weary adj [person] las (lasse) du monde / [cynicism, sigh] blasé(e).

worldwide ['wɜːldwaɪd] ■ adj mondial(e).
■ adv dans le monde entier.

World Wide Web n : **the World Wide Web** le World Wide Web.

worm [wɜːm] ■ n [animal] ver *m*.
■ vt : **to worm one's way** [move] avancer à plat ventre *OR* en rampant ▸ **to worm one's way into sb's affections** gagner insidieusement l'affection de qqn.
◆ ***worms*** npl [parasites] vers *mpl*.
◆ ***worm out*** vt sep : **to worm sthg out of sb** soutirer qqch à qqn.

WORM (abbr of ***write once read many times***) COMPUT WORM.

worn [wɔːn] ■ pp ➤ ***wear***.
■ adj **1.** [threadbare] usé(e) **2.** [tired] las (lasse).

worn-out adj **1.** [old, threadbare] usé(e) **2.** [tired] épuisé(e).

worried ['wʌrɪd] adj soucieux(euse), inquiet(ète) ▸ **you really had me worried** vous m'avez fait faire bien du souci ▸ **to be worried (about)** se faire du souci (à propos de) ▸ **to be worried sick** se faire un sang d'encre.

worriedly ['wʌrɪdlɪ] adv [say] avec un air inquiet.

worrier ['wʌrɪəʳ] n anxieux *m*, -euse *f*.

worry ['wʌrɪ] ■ n (pl -ies) **1.** [feeling] souci *m* ▸ **her sons are a constant worry to her** ses fils lui causent constamment des soucis *OR* du souci ▸ **he was sick with worry about her** il se rongeait les sangs pour elle *OR* à son sujet **2.** [problem] souci *m*, ennui *m*.
■ vt (pt & pp -ied) inquiéter, tracasser ▸ **you really worried me** je me suis vraiment inquiété à cause de toi ▸ **he was worried by her sudden disappearance** il était inquiet de sa disparition subite.
■ vi s'inquiéter ▸ **to worry about** se faire du souci au sujet de ▸ **there's nothing to worry about** il n'y a pas lieu de s'inquiéter ▸ **don't worry!, not to worry!** ne vous en faites pas!

worrying ['wʌrɪɪŋ] adj inquiétant(e).

worryingly ['wʌrɪɪŋlɪ] adv : **the project is worryingly late** le projet a pris un retard inquiétant.

worse [wɜːs] ■ adj **1.** [not as good] pire ▸ **the news is even worse than we expected** les nouvelles sont encore plus mauvaises que nous ne pensions ▸ **things are worse than you imagine** les choses vont plus mal que vous l'imaginez ▸ **to get worse** [situation] empirer ▸ **to get worse and worse** aller de mal en pis ▸ **and, to make matters worse, he swore at the policeman** et pour tout arranger, il a insulté le policier
2. [more ill] : **he's worse today** il va plus mal aujourd'hui ▸ **her headache got worse** son mal de tête s'est aggravé ▸ **he's apparently none the worse for his drinking session last night** il n'a pas l'air de se ressentir de sa beuverie d'hier soir.
■ adv plus mal ▸ **he behaved worse than ever** il ne s'est jamais aussi mal conduit ▸ **they're even worse off** c'est encore pire pour eux ▸ **worse off** [financially] plus pauvre.
■ n pire *m* ▸ **there's worse to come, worse is to come** [in situation] le pire est à venir / [in story] il y a pire encore ▸ **for the worse** pour le pire ▸ **a change for the worse** une détérioration ▸ **to take a turn for the worse** [health, situation] se détériorer, se dégrader.

worsen ['wɜːsn] vt & vi empirer.

worsening ['wɜːsnɪŋ] adj qui va en empirant.

worship ['wɜːʃɪp] ■ vt (*US* -ed, cont -ing, *UK* -ped, cont -ping) adorer.
■ n **1.** *(U)* RELIG culte *m* **2.** [adoration] adoration *f*.
◆ ***Worship*** n : **Your/Her/His Worship** Votre/Son Honneur *m*.

worshipper *UK*, ***worshiper*** *US* ['wɜːʃɪpəʳ] n **1.** RELIG fidèle *mf* **2.** [admirer] adorateur *m*, -trice *f*.

worst [wɜːst] ■ adj : **the worst** le pire (la pire), le plus mauvais (la plus mauvaise) ▸ **his worst enemy** son pire ennemi ▸ **the fighting was worst near the border** les combats les plus violents se sont déroulés près de la frontière ▸ **and, worst of all, I lost my keys** et le pire de tout, c'est que j'ai perdu mes clés.
■ adv le plus mal ▸ **the worst affected area** la zone la plus touchée.
■ n : **the worst** le pire ▸ **things** *OR* **matters were at their worst** les affaires étaient au plus mal, les choses ne pouvaient pas aller plus mal ▸ **to get the worst of it** [in fight] avoir le dessous ▸ **if the worst comes to the worst** au pire.
◆ ***at (the) worst*** adv au pire.

worst-case adj : **the worst-case scenario** le scénario catastrophe.

worsted ['wʊstɪd] n laine *f* peignée.

worth [wɜːθ] ■ prep **1.** [in value] **: to be worth sthg** valoir qqch ▸ **to be worth £40,000** valoir 40 000 livres ▸ **how much is it worth?** combien cela vaut-il? ▸ **their friendship is worth a lot to her** leur amitié a beaucoup de prix pour elle **2.** [deserving of] **: it's worth a visit** cela vaut une visite ▸ **it's/she is worth it** cela/elle en vaut la peine ▸ **it wasn't worth the effort** cela ne valait pas la peine de faire un tel effort, ça n'en valait pas la peine ▸ **to be worth doing sthg** valoir la peine de faire qqch ▸ **is the film worth seeing?** est-ce que le film vaut la peine d'être vu? ▸ **it would be worth your while to check** *OR* **checking** vous auriez intérêt à vérifier.

■ n valeur *f* ▸ **a week's/£20 worth of groceries** pour une semaine/20 livres d'épicerie.

worthless ['wɜːθlɪs] adj **1.** [object] sans valeur, qui ne vaut rien **2.** [person] qui n'est bon à rien.

worthlessness ['wɜːθlɪsnɪs] n **1.** [of goods, land] absence *f* totale de valeur **2.** [of attempt] inutilité *f* / [of advice, suggestion] inutilité *f* **3.** [of person] nullité *f*.

worthwhile [ˌwɜːθ'waɪl] adj [job, visit] qui en vaut la peine / [charity] louable.

worthy ['wɜːðɪ] (comp -ier, superl -iest) adj **1.** [deserving of respect] digne **2.** [deserving] **: to be worthy of sthg** mériter qqch **3.** *pej* [good but unexciting] méritant(e).

would [wʊd] modal vb **1.** *(in reported speech)* **: she said she would come** elle a dit qu'elle viendrait
2. [indicating likelihood] **: what would you do?** que ferais-tu? ▸ **what would you have done?** qu'aurais-tu fait? ▸ **they wouldn't have come if they'd known** ils ne seraient pas venus s'ils avaient su ▸ **I would be most grateful** je vous en serais très reconnaissant
3. [indicating willingness] **: she wouldn't go** elle ne voulait pas y aller ▸ **the car wouldn't start** la voiture ne voulait pas démarrer ▸ **he would do anything for her** il ferait n'importe quoi pour elle
4. *(in polite questions)* **: would you like a drink?** voulez-vous *OR* voudriez-vous à boire? ▸ **would you mind closing the window?** cela vous ennuierait de fermer la fenêtre? ▸ **would you like to see her?** aimeriez-vous *OR* voudriez-vous la voir?
5. [indicating inevitability] **: he would say that** j'étais sûr qu'il allait dire ça, ça ne m'étonne pas de lui ▸ **he would!** c'est bien de lui!
6. [giving advice] **: I would report it if I were you** si j'étais vous je préviendrais les autorités
7. [expressing opinions] **: I would prefer** je préférerais ▸ **I would rather have gone alone** j'aurais mieux aimé y aller seul ▸ **I would imagine it's warmer than here** j'imagine qu'il fait plus chaud qu'ici ▸ **I would have thought (that)...** j'aurais pensé que...
8. [indicating habit] **: he would smoke a cigar after dinner** il fumait un cigare après le dîner ▸ **she would often complain about the neighbours** elle se plaignait souvent des voisins.

would-be adj prétendu(e).

wouldn't ['wʊdnt] = ***would not***.

would've ['wʊdəv] = ***would have***.

wound[1] [wuːnd] ■ n blessure *f* ▸ **to lick one's wounds** *fig* panser ses plaies.
■ vt blesser.

wound[2] [waʊnd] pt & pp ➤ ***wind***[2].

wounded ['wuːndɪd] ■ adj blessé(e).
■ npl **: the wounded** les blessés *mpl*.

wounding ['wuːndɪŋ] adj blessant(e).

wound-up [waʊnd-] adj **1.** [clock] remonté(e) / [car window] remonté(e), fermé(e) **2.** *inf* [tense - person] crispé(e), très tendu(e).

wove [wəʊv] pt ➤ ***weave***.

woven ['wəʊvn] pp ➤ ***weave***.

wow [waʊ] excl *inf* oh là là!

WP ■ n (abbr of ***word processing, word processor***) TTX *m*.
■ (abbr of ***weather permitting***) *si le temps le permet*.

WPC (abbr of ***woman police constable***) n *UK femme agent de police* ▸ **WPC Roberts** l'agent Roberts.

wpm (abbr of ***words per minute***) mots/min.

WRAC [ræk] (abbr of ***Women's Royal Army Corps***) n *section féminine de l'armée de terre britannique*.

WRAF [ræf] (abbr of ***Women's Royal Air Force***) n *section féminine de l'armée de l'air britannique*.

wrangle ['ræŋgl] ■ n dispute *f*.
■ vi **: to wrangle (with sb over sthg)** se disputer (avec qqn à propos de qqch).

wrap [ræp] ■ vt (pt & pp -ped, cont -ping) **1.** [cover in paper, cloth] **: to wrap sthg (in)** envelopper *OR* emballer qqch (dans) ▸ **to wrap sthg around** *OR* **round** *UK* **sthg** enrouler qqch autour de qqch **2.** [encircle] **: to wrap one's hands around** *OR* **round** *UK* **sthg** entourer qqch de ses mains ▸ **to wrap one's fingers around** *OR* **round** *UK* **sthg** entourer qqch de ses doigts ▸ **to wrap one's arms around** *OR* **round** *UK* **sb** enlacer qqn.
■ n [garment] châle *m*.
◆ ***wrap up*** ■ vt sep **1.** [cover in paper or cloth] envelopper, emballer **2.** *inf* [complete] conclure, régler.
■ vi [put warm clothes on] **: wrap up well** *OR* **warmly!** couvrez-vous bien!

wraparound ['ræpəˌraʊnd] ■ adj [skirt] portefeuille *(inv)* ▸ **wraparound sunglasses** lunettes *fpl* de soleil panoramiques ▸ **wraparound rear window** AUT lunette *f* arrière panoramique.
■ n **1.** [skirt] jupe *f* portefeuille **2.** COMPUT mise à la ligne *f* automatique des mots.
◆ ***wraparounds*** npl [sunglasses] lunettes *fpl* de soleil panoramiques.

wrapped up [ræpt-] adj *inf* **: to be wrapped up in sthg** être absorbé(e) par qqch ▸ **to be wrapped up in sb** ne penser qu'à qqn.

wrapper ['ræpər] n papier *m* / *UK* [of book] jaquette *f*, couverture *f*.

wrapping ['ræpɪŋ] n emballage *m*.

wrapping paper n *(U)* papier *m* d'emballage.

wrath [rɒθ] n *(U) liter* courroux *m*.

wreak [riːk] vt [destruction, havoc] entraîner.

wreath [riːθ] n couronne *f*.

wreathe [riːð] vt *liter* couronner.

wreck [rek] ■ **n 1.** [car, plane, ship] épave *f* **2.** *inf* [person] loque *f* ▸ **I feel a wreck** je me sens épuisé ▸ **I look a wreck** j'ai l'air d'une véritable loque.
■ **vt 1.** [destroy] détruire **2.** NAUT provoquer le naufrage de ▸ **to be wrecked** s'échouer **3.** [spoil - holiday] gâcher / [- health, hopes, plan] ruiner.

wreckage ['rekɪdʒ] **n** *(U)* débris *mpl.*

wrecker ['rekəʳ] **n** *US* [vehicle] dépanneuse *f.*

wren [ren] **n** roitelet *m.*

wrench [rentʃ] ■ **n 1.** [tool] clef *f* anglaise **2.** [injury] entorse *f* **3.** [emotional] déchirement *m.*
■ **vt 1.** [pull violently] tirer violemment ▸ **to wrench sthg off** arracher qqch **2.** [arm, leg, knee] se tordre.

wrest [rest] **vt** *liter* **: to wrest sthg from sb** arracher violemment qqch à qqn.

wrestle ['resl] ■ **vt** lutter.
■ **vi 1.** [fight] **: to wrestle (with sb)** lutter (contre qqn) **2.** *fig* [struggle] **: to wrestle with sthg** se débattre *OR* lutter contre qqch.

wrestler ['resləʳ] **n** lutteur *m*, -euse *f.*

wrestling ['reslɪŋ] **n** lutte *f.*

wretch [retʃ] **n** pauvre diable *m.*

wretched ['retʃɪd] **adj 1.** [miserable] misérable **2.** *inf* [damned] fichu(e), maudit(e).

wriggle ['rɪgl] ■ **vt** remuer, tortiller.
■ **vi** remuer, se tortiller.
◆ ***wriggle out of*** **vt insep : to wriggle out of sthg** se tirer de qqch ▸ **to wriggle out of doing sthg** éviter de faire qqch.

wring [rɪŋ] **(pt & pp wrung) vt 1.** [washing] essorer, tordre **2.** [hands, neck] tordre.
◆ ***wring out*** **vt sep** essorer, tordre.

wringing ['rɪŋɪŋ] **adj : wringing (wet)** [person] trempé(e) / [clothes] mouillé(e), à tordre.

wrinkle ['rɪŋkl] ■ **n 1.** [on skin] ride *f* **2.** [in cloth] pli *m.*
■ **vt** plisser.
■ **vi** se plisser, faire des plis.

wrinkled ['rɪŋkld], ***wrinkly*** ['rɪŋklɪ] **adj 1.** [skin] ridé(e) **2.** [cloth] froissé(e).

wrist [rɪst] **n** poignet *m.*

wristband ['rɪstbænd] **n** [of watch] bracelet *m.*

wristwatch ['rɪstwɒtʃ] **n** montre-bracelet *f.*

writ [rɪt] **n** acte *m* judiciaire.

write [raɪt] **(pt wrote, pp written)** ■ **vt 1.** [gen & COMPUT] écrire ▸ **to write sb a letter** écrire une lettre à qqn ▸ **he wrote her a postcard** il lui a envoyé une carte postale ▸ **perplexity was written all over his face** *fig* la perplexité se lisait sur son visage
2. *US* [person] écrire à
3. [cheque, prescription, will] faire.
■ **vi** [gen & COMPUT] écrire ▸ **to write to sb** *UK* écrire à qqn ▸ **she wrote and told me about it** elle m'a écrit pour me le raconter ▸ **at the time of writing** au moment où j'écris ▸ **she writes for 'The Independent'** elle écrit dans 'The Independent' ▸ **he writes on** *OR* **about archeology** il écrit sur l'archéologie.
◆ ***write back*** ■ **vt sep : to write a letter back** répondre par une lettre.
■ **vi** répondre ▸ **he wrote back rejecting their offer** il a renvoyé une lettre refusant leur offre.
◆ ***write down*** **vt sep 1.** écrire, noter
2. FIN & COMM [in price] réduire le prix de.
◆ ***write in*** **vi** écrire ▸ **hundreds wrote in to complain** des centaines de personnes ont écrit pour se plaindre.
◆ ***write into*** **vt sep : to write a clause into a contract** insérer une clause dans un contrat.
◆ ***write off*** ■ **vt sep 1.** [project] considérer comme fichu ▸ **the plan had to be written off** le projet a dû être abandonné ▸ **three months' hard work was simply written off** on a perdu trois mois de travail acharné
2. [debt, investment] passer aux profits et pertes
3. [person] considérer comme fini ▸ **he was written off as a failure** on a considéré qu'il n'y avait rien de bon à en tirer
4. *UK inf* [vehicle] bousiller ▸ **she wrote off her new car** *UK* elle a complètement démoli sa voiture neuve.
■ **vi** écrire pour demander des renseignements ▸ **to write off to sb** écrire à qqn ▸ **to write off for sthg** écrire pour demander qqch.
◆ ***write up*** **vt sep** [notes] mettre au propre ▸ **he wrote up his ideas in a report** il a consigné ses idées dans un rapport.

write-down **n** FIN dépréciation *f.*

write-off **n** *inf* [vehicle] **: to be a write-off** *UK* être complètement démoli(e).

write-protect **vt** COMPUT protéger en écriture.

write-protected **adj** COMPUT [disk] protégé(e) (en écriture).

writer ['raɪtəʳ] **n 1.** [as profession] écrivain *m*, -e *f* **2.** [of letter, article, story] auteur *m*, -(e) *f.*

writer's block **n** angoisse *f* de la page blanche.

write-up **n** *inf* critique *f.*

writhe [raɪð] **vi** se tordre.

writing ['raɪtɪŋ] **n** *(U)* **1.** [handwriting, activity] écriture *f* ▸ **in writing** par écrit **2.** [something written] écrit *m.*
◆ ***writings*** **npl** écrits *mpl.*

writing case **n** *UK* nécessaire *m* de correspondance.

writing desk **n** secrétaire *m.*

writing paper **n** *(U)* papier *m* à lettres.

written ['rɪtn] ■ **pp** ➤ ***write.***
■ **adj** écrit(e).

WRNS (abbr of ***Women's Royal Naval Service***) **n** *section féminine de la marine de guerre britannique.*

wrong [rɒŋ] ■ **adj 1.** [not normal, not satisfactory] qui ne va pas ▸ **is something wrong?** y a-t-il quelque chose qui ne va pas? ▸ **what's wrong?** qu'est-ce qui ne va pas? ▸ **there's something wrong with the switch** l'interrupteur ne marche pas bien ▸ **something is wrong** *OR* **there's something wrong with my elbow** j'ai quelque chose au coude

▸ **there's nothing wrong with her decision/reasoning** sa décision/son raisonnement est parfaitement valable ▸ **there's nothing wrong with you** vous êtes en parfaite santé ▸ **there wasn't much wrong with the car** la voiture n'avait pas grand-chose
2. [not suitable] qui ne convient pas ▸ **you've got the wrong attitude** vous n'avez pas l'attitude qu'il faut *OR* la bonne attitude ▸ **it was the wrong thing to do/say** ce n'était pas la chose à faire/dire ▸ **he got hold of the wrong end of the stick** il a tout compris de travers ▸ **they got off on the wrong foot** ils se sont mal entendus au départ
3. [not correct - answer, address] faux (fausse), mauvais(e) / [- decision] mauvais(e) ▸ **to be wrong** [person] avoir tort ▸ **to be wrong about sb** se tromper sur le compte de qqn ▸ **to be wrong to do sthg** avoir tort de faire qqch ▸ **to take the wrong road/train** se tromper de route/de train ▸ **the clock/my watch is wrong** le réveil/ma montre n'est pas à l'heure ▸ **the biscuit went down the wrong way** j'ai avalé le gâteau de travers
4. [morally bad] **: cheating is wrong** c'est mal de tricher ▸ **it's wrong that anyone should have to live in poverty** il est injuste que des gens soient obligés de vivre dans la misère ▸ **it's wrong to...** c'est mal de...
■ **adv** [incorrectly] mal ▸ **to get sthg wrong** se tromper à propos de qqch ▸ **you've got her all wrong** vous vous trompez complètement sur son compte ▸ **to go wrong** [make a mistake] se tromper, faire une erreur / [stop functioning] se détraquer ▸ **something has gone wrong with the TV** la télé est tombée en panne ▸ **don't get me wrong** *inf* comprenez-moi bien.
■ **n** mal *m* ▸ **to be in the wrong** être dans son tort.
■ **vt** faire du tort à ▸ **she felt deeply wronged** elle se sentait gravement lésée.

wrongdoer [ˌrɒŋ'duːəʳ] **n 1.** [delinquent] malfaiteur *m*, délinquant *m*, -e *f* **2.** [sinner] pécheur *m*, -eresse *f*.

wrongdoing [ˌrɒŋ'duːɪŋ] **n** mal *m*, méfait *m*.

wrong-foot *UK* **vt 1.** SPORT prendre à contre-pied **2.** *fig* [surprise] prendre par surprise *OR* au dépourvu.

wrongful ['rɒŋfʊl] **adj** [unfair] injuste / [arrest, dismissal] injustifié(e).

wrongfully ['rɒŋfʊlɪ] **adv** à tort.

wrongly ['rɒŋlɪ] **adv 1.** [unsuitably] mal **2.** [mistakenly] à tort.

wrong number **n** faux numéro *m*.

wrote [rəʊt] **pt** ➤ ***write***.

wrought iron [rɔːt-] **n** fer *m* forgé.

wrung [rʌŋ] **pt & pp** ➤ ***wring***.

WRVS (abbr of ***Women's Royal Voluntary Service***) **n** *association de femmes au service des déshérités.*

wry [raɪ] **adj 1.** [amused - smile, look] amusé(e) / [- humour] ironique **2.** [displeased] désabusé(e).

wt. (abbr of ***weight***) pds.

WTO (abbr of ***World Trade Organization***) **n** OMC *f*.

WV abbr of ***West Virginia***.

WW abbr of ***world war***.

WWW (abbr of ***World Wide Web***) **n** WWW *m*.

WY abbr of ***Wyoming***.

Wyoming [waɪ'əʊmɪŋ] **n** Wyoming *m* ▸ **in Wyoming** dans le Wyoming.

WYSIWYG ['wɪzɪwɪg] (abbr of ***what you see is what you get***) WYSIWYG, tel écran, tel écrit.

x [eks] (pl x's *OR* xs), ***X*** (pl X's *OR* Xs) **n 1.** [letter] x *m inv*, X *m inv* **2.** [unknown thing] x *m inv* **3.** [to mark place] croix *f* **4.** [at end of letter] **: XXX** grosses bises.

x-axis **n** axe *m* des x, abscisse *f*.

X certificate **n** *UK signalait (jusqu'en 1982) un film interdit aux moins de 18 ans.*

X chromosome **n** chromosome *m* X.

xenophobia [,zenə'fəʊbjə] **n** xénophobie *f*.

xenophobic [,zenə'fəʊbɪk] **adj** xénophobe.

Xerox® ['zɪərɒks] ■ **n 1.** [machine] photocopieuse *f* **2.** [copy] photocopie *f*.
■ **vt** photocopier.

XL (abbr of ***extra-large***) **n** XL *m*.

Xmas ['eksməs] ■ **n** Noël *m*.
■ **comp** de Noël.

XML [,eksem'el] (abbr of ***Extensible Markup Language***) **n** COMPUT XML *m*.

X-rated [-reɪtɪd] **adj** *dated* [film] interdit(e) aux mineurs *OR* aux moins de 18 ans.

X-ray ■ **n 1.** [ray] rayon *m* X **2.** [picture] radiographie *f*, radio *f*.
■ **vt** radiographier.

xylophone ['zaɪləfəʊn] **n** xylophone *m*.

Y

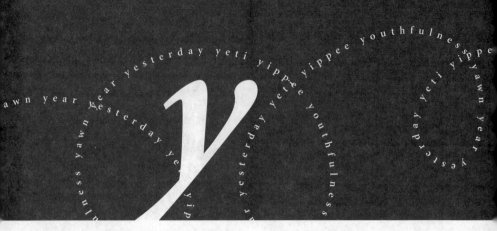

y [waɪ] (pl y's *OR* ys), ***Y*** (pl Y's *OR* Ys) **n** **1.** [letter] y *m inv*, Y *m inv* **2.** MATHS y *m inv*.

yacht [jɒt] **n** yacht *m*.

yachting ['jɒtɪŋ] **n** yachting *m*.

yachtsman ['jɒtsmən] (pl **-men** [-mən]) **n** yachtman *m*.

yachtswoman ['jɒtsˌwʊmən] (pl **-women** [-ˌwɪmɪn]) **n** yachtwoman *f*.

yahoo [jɑː'huː] **n** rustre *m*.

yak [jæk] **n** yack *m*.

Yale lock® [jeɪl-] **n** serrure *f* à barillet.

yam [jæm] **n** igname *f*.

Yangtze ['jæŋtsɪ] **n : the Yangtze** le Yang-tseu-kiang, le Yangzi Jiang *m*.

yank [jæŋk] **vt** tirer d'un coup sec.

Yank [jæŋk] **n** *UK inf* Amerloque *mf (terme péjoratif désignant un Américain)*.

Yankee ['jæŋkɪ] **n** **1.** *UK inf* [American] Amerloque *mf (terme péjoratif désignant un Américain)* **2.** *US* [citizen] Yankee *mf*.

CULTURE

Yankee

Pour les Américains, ce terme désigne un compatriote originaire du nord du pays : durant la Guerre civile, les soldats des États fédérés du Sud utilisaient le mot **yankee** ou **yanks** pour parler des soldats de l'Union. Pour les autres, en particulier les Anglais, c'était davantage une expression péjorative pour qualifier les Américains. Durant la guerre révolutionnaire, les troupes britanniques chantaient **Yankee Doodle** pour se moquer de leurs ennemis (cette chanson est cependant devenue le chant de ralliement des troupes américaines), et pendant la Première et la Seconde Guerre mondiale, les Américains notamment les GI, ont gardé leur surnom de Yankees.

yap [jæp] (pt & pp **-ped**, cont **-ping**) **vi** **1.** [dog] japper **2.** *pej* [person] jacasser.

yard [jɑːd] **n** **1.** [unit of measurement] yard *m (= 91,44 cm)* **2.** [walled area] cour *f* **3.** [area of work] chantier *m* **4.** *US* [attached to house] jardin *m*.

yardstick ['jɑːdstɪk] **n** mesure *f*.

yarn [jɑːn] **n** **1.** [thread] fil *m* **2.** *inf* [story] histoire *f* ▸ **to spin sb a yarn** raconter une histoire à qqn.

yashmak ['jæʃmæk] **n** litham *m*.

yawn [jɔːn] ■ **n** **1.** [when tired] bâillement *m* ▸ **to give a yawn** bâiller **2.** *UK inf* [boring event] **: it was a real yawn** c'était vraiment ennuyeux.

■ **vi** **1.** [when tired] bâiller **2.** [gape] s'ouvrir, béer.

y-axis **n** axe *m* des y *OR* des ordonnées.

Y chromosome **n** chromosome *m* Y.

yd abbr of ***yard***.

yeah [jeə] **adv** *inf* ouais.

year [jɪəʳ] **n** **1.** [calendar year] année *f* ▸ **in the year 1607** en (l'an) 1607 **2.** [period of 12 months] année *f*, an *m* ▸ **to be 21 years old** avoir 21 ans ▸ **all (the) year round** toute l'année ▸ **year in year out** année après année ▸ **he earns over £40,000 a year** il gagne plus de 40 000 livres par an **3.** [financial year] année *f* ▸ **the year 2002-03** l'exercice 2002-03.

◆ ***years*** **npl** [long time] années *fpl* ▸ **I haven't seen her for years** je ne l'ai pas vue depuis des années ▸ **for years and years** pendant des années.

CONFUSABLE / PARONYME

year

When translating year, note that the French words *an* and *année* are not interchangeable. *An* is used when specifying the number of years and *année* is used when the emphasis is on duration.

yearbook ['jɪəbʊk] **n** annuaire *m*, almanach *m*.

year-end ■ **adj** *UK* de fin d'année ▸ **a year-end report** un rapport annuel.

■ **n : at the year-end** à la fin de l'année, en fin d'année.

year-end accounts **n** compte *m* de résultats.

year-end profits **n** bénéfices *mpl* de fin d'exercice.

yearling **['jɪəlɪŋ]** **n** yearling *m.*

yearly **['jɪəlɪ]** ■ **adj** annuel(elle).
■ **adv** **1.** [once a year] annuellement **2.** [every year] chaque année ▸ **twice yearly** deux fois par an.

yearn [jɜːn] **vi : to yearn for sthg/to do sthg** aspirer à qqch/à faire qqch.

yearning ['jɜːnɪŋ] **n : yearning (for sb/sthg)** désir *m* ardent (pour qqn/de qqch).

year-on-year ■ **adj** [growth, decline] d'une année à l'autre.
■ **adv** [grow, decline] d'une année à l'autre.

year-round **adj** [activity] qui dure toute l'année, sur toute l'année / [facility] qui fonctionne toute l'année.

yeast [jiːst] **n** levure *f.*

yell [jel] ■ **n** hurlement *m.*
■ **vi** & **vt** hurler.

yellow ['jeləʊ] ■ **adj** **1.** [colour] jaune **2.** [cowardly] lâche.
■ **n** jaune *m.*
■ **vi** jaunir.

yellow card **n** FOOTBALL carton *m* jaune.

yellow fever **n** fièvre *f* jaune.

yellow lines **n** bandes *fpl* jaunes.

yellowness ['jeləʊnɪs] **n** *(U)* couleur *f* jaune.

Yellow Pages® **n : the Yellow Pages** les pages *fpl* jaunes.

Yellow River **n : the Yellow River** le fleuve Jaune.

Yellow Sea **n : the Yellow Sea** la mer Jaune.

yelp [jelp] ■ **n** jappement *m.*
■ **vi** japper.

Yemen ['jemən] **n** Yémen *m* ▸ **in Yemen** au Yémen.

Yemeni ['jemənɪ] ■ **adj** yéménite.
■ **n** Yéménite *mf.*

yen [jen] **n** **1.** (pl **yen**) [Japanese currency] yen *m* **2.** (pl **-s**) [longing] **: to have a yen for sthg/to do sthg** avoir une forte envie de qqch/de faire qqch.

yeoman of the guard ['jəʊmən-] (pl **yeomen of the guard** ['jəʊmən-]) **n** *UK* hallebardier *m* de la garde royale.

yep [jep] **adv** *inf* ouais.

yer [jɜː] **adj** *inf* [e-mail] votre, ton (tates).

yes [jes] ■ **adv** **1.** [gen] oui ▸ **yes, please** oui, s'il te/vous plaît **2.** [expressing disagreement] si **3.** [indeed] en effet, vraiment ▸ **she was rash, yes, terribly rash** elle a été imprudente, vraiment très imprudente.
■ **n** oui *m inv* ▸ **to count the yeses** compter les oui OR les votes pour.

yes-man **n** *pej* béni-oui-oui *m inv.*

yesterday ['jestədɪ] ■ **n** hier *m* ▸ **the day before yesterday** avant-hier.
■ **adv** hier.

yet [jet] ■ **adv** **1.** [gen] encore ▸ **not yet** pas encore ▸ **she isn't here yet** elle n'est pas encore là ▸ **yet again** encore une fois ▸ **as yet** jusqu'ici ▸ **I have yet to meet her** je ne l'ai pas encore rencontrée ▸ **they won't be here for another hour yet** ils ne seront pas là avant une heure ▸ **yet faster** encore plus vite ▸ **yet another bomb** encore une bombe **2.** déjà ▸ **have they finished yet?** est-ce qu'ils ont déjà fini? ▸ **is he here yet?** est-il déjà là?
■ **conj** et cependant, mais ▸ **he was firm yet kind** il était sévère mais juste ▸ **they had no income yet they still had to pay taxes** ils n'avaient pas de revenus et pourtant ils devaient payer des impôts.

yeti ['jetɪ] **n** yéti *m.*

yew [juː] **n** if *m.*

Y-fronts **npl** *UK* slip *m.*

YHA (abbr of ***Youth Hostels Association***) **n** *association britannique des auberges de jeunesse.*

Yiddish ['jɪdɪʃ] ■ **adj** yiddish *(inv).*
■ **n** [language] yiddish *m.*

yield [jiːld] ■ **n** rendement *m* ▸ **high-yield crops** récoltes à rendement élevé ▸ **an 8% yield on investments** des investissements qui rapportent 8 %.
■ **vt** **1.** [produce] produire ▸ **the investment bond will yield 11%** le bon d'épargne rapportera 11 % **2.** [give up] céder / *fig* & MIL **: to yield ground** céder du terrain.
■ **vi** **1.** [gen] **: to yield (to)** céder (à) **2.** *US* AUT [give way] **: 'yield'** 'cédez le passage'.

yippee [*UK* jɪ'piː, *US* 'jɪpɪ] **excl** hourra!

Y2K (abbr of ***the year 2000***) **n** **1.** [year] l'an 2000 **2.** COMPUT le bogue de l'an 2000.

YMCA (abbr of ***Young Men's Christian Association***) **n** *union chrétienne de jeunes gens (proposant notamment des services d'hébergement).*

yo [jəʊ] **excl** *inf* salut!

yob(bo) ['jɒb(əʊ)] **n** *UK inf* voyou *m*, loubard *m.*

yodel ['jəʊdl] (*UK* **-led**, cont **-ling**, *US* **-ed**, cont **-ing**) **vi** iodler, jodler.

yoga ['jəʊgə] **n** yoga *m.*

yoghourt, ***yoghurt***, ***yogurt*** [*UK* 'jɒgət, *US* 'jəʊgərt] **n** yaourt *m.*

yoke [jəʊk] **n** *lit* & *fig* joug *m.*

yokel ['jəʊkl] **n** *pej* péquenaud *m*, -e *f.*

yolk [jəʊk] **n** jaune *m* (d'œuf).

yonder ['jɒndəʳ] **adv** *liter* là-bas.

Yorks. [jɔːks] (abbr of ***Yorkshire***) *comté anglais.*

Yorkshire pudding ['jɔːkʃəʳ-] **n** *pâte à choux cuite qui accompagne le rosbif.*

Yorkshire terrier ['jɔːkʃəʳ-] **n** Yorkshire-terrier *m.*

you [juː] **pers pron** **1.** [subject - sg] tu / [- polite form, pl] vous ▸ **you're a good cook** tu es/vous êtes bonne cuisinière ▸ **are you French?** tu es/vous êtes français? ▸ **you French** vous autres Français ▸ **you idiot!** espèce d'idiot! ▸ **you and yours** vous et les vôtres/toi et les tiens ▸ **if I were** OR **was you** si j'étais toi/vous, à ta/votre place ▸ **there you are** [- you've appeared] te/vous voilà / [- have this] voilà, tiens/tenez ▸ **that jacket really isn't you** cette veste n'est pas vraiment ton/votre style
2. [object - unstressed, sg] te / [- polite form, pl] vous ▸ **I can see you** je te/vous vois ▸ **I gave it to you** je te/vous l'ai donné

3. [object - stressed, sg] toi / [- polite form, pl] vous ▸ **I don't expect you to do it** je n'exige pas que ce soit toi qui le fasses/vous qui le fassiez
4. [after prep, in comparisons *etc* - sg] toi / [- polite form, pl] vous ▸ **we shall go without you** nous irons sans toi/vous ▸ **I'm shorter than you** je suis plus petit que toi/vous ▸ **between you and me** entre nous
5. [anyone, one] on ▸ **you have to be careful** on doit faire attention ▸ **you never know** on ne sait jamais ▸ **you take the first on the left** prenez la première à gauche ▸ **exercise is good for you** l'exercice est bon pour la santé.

you'd [ju:d] = ***you had, you would***.

you-know-what n *inf euph* **: does he know about the you-know-what?** est-ce qu'il est au courant du... tu vois de quoi je veux parler ***OR*** ce que je veux dire?

you-know-who n *inf euph* qui tu sais, qui vous savez.

you'll [ju:l] = ***you will***.

young [jʌŋ] ■ **adj** jeune ▸ **families with young children** les familles qui ont des enfants en bas âge ▸ **my younger brother** mon frère cadet, mon petit frère ▸ **he's young for his age** il est jeune pour son âge, il ne fait pas son âge.
■ **npl 1.** [young people] **: the young** les jeunes *mpl* **2.** [baby animals] les petits *mpl*.

younger ['jʌŋgəʳ] **adj** plus jeune.

youngish ['jʌŋɪʃ] **adj** assez jeune.

young man **n** jeune homme *m*.

youngster ['jʌŋstəʳ] **n** jeune *m*.

young woman **n** jeune femme *f*.

your [jɔ:ʳ] **poss adj 1.** *(referring to one person)* ton (ta), tes *(pl)* / *(polite form, pl)* votre, vos *(pl)* ▸ **your dog** ton/votre chien ▸ **your house** ta/votre maison ▸ **your children** tes/vos enfants ▸ **what's your name?** comment t'appelles-tu/vous appelez-vous? ▸ **it wasn't your fault** ce n'était pas de ta faute à toi/de votre faute à vous ▸ **I think you've broken your finger** je crois que vous vous êtes cassé le doigt **2.** *(impersonal, one's)* son (sa), ses *(pl)* ▸ **your attitude changes as you get older** on change sa manière de voir en vieillissant ▸ **it's good for your teeth/hair** c'est bon pour les dents/les cheveux ▸ **your average Englishman** l'Anglais moyen.

you're [jɔ:ʳ] = ***you are***.

yours [jɔ:z] **poss pron** *(referring to one person)* le tien (la tienne), les tiens (les tiennes) *(pl)* / *(polite form, pl)* le vôtre (la vôtre), les vôtres *(pl)* ▸ **that desk is yours** ce bureau est à toi/à vous, ce bureau est le tien/le vôtre ▸ **it wasn't her fault, it was yours** ce n'était pas de sa faute, c'était de ta faute à toi/de votre faute à vous ▸ **a friend of yours** un ami à toi/vous, un de tes/vos amis.
◆ ***Yours*** **adv** [in letter] ➤ ***faithfully***, ***sincerely*** *etc*.

yourself [jɔ:'self] (pl **-selves** [-'selvz]) **pron 1.** [reflexive - sg] te / [- polite form, pl] vous / [after preposition - sg] toi / [- polite form, pl] vous **2.** [for emphasis - sg] toi-même / [- polite form] vous-même / [- pl] vous-mêmes ▸ **did you do it yourself?** tu l'as/vous l'avez fait tout seul?

yours truly **pron** *inf* bibi, mézigue.

youth [ju:θ] **n 1.** *(U)* [period, quality] jeunesse *f* **2.** [young man] jeune homme *m* **3.** *(U)* [young people] jeunesse *f*, jeunes *mpl*.

youth club **n** centre *m* de jeunes.

youth custody **n** *UK* détention *f* de mineurs, éducation *f* surveillée.

youthful ['ju:θfʊl] **adj 1.** [eager, innocent] de jeunesse, juvénile **2.** [young] jeune.

youthfulness ['ju:θfʊlnɪs] **n** jeunesse *f*.

youth hostel **n** auberge *f* de jeunesse.

youth hostelling [-'hɒstəlɪŋ] **n** *UK* **: to go youth hostelling** voyager en dormant dans des auberges de jeunesse.

you've [ju:v] = ***you have***.

yowl [jaʊl] ■ **n** [of dog, person] hurlement *m* / [of cat] miaulement *m*.
■ **vi** [dog, person] hurler / [cat] miauler.

yo-yo ['jəʊjəʊ] **n** yo-yo *m*.

yr abbr of ***year***.

yrs (abbr of ***yours***) **pron** [e-mail] votre.

YTS (abbr of ***Youth Training Scheme***) **n** *programme gouvernemental britannique d'insertion des jeunes dans la vie professionnelle*.

Yucatan [ˌjʌkə'tɑ:n] **n** Yucatán *m*.

yuck [jʌk] **excl** *inf* berk!

yucky ['jʌkɪ] (comp **-ier**, superl **-iest**) **adj** *inf* dégueulasse.

Yugoslav = ***Yugoslavian***.

Yugoslavia [ˌju:gə'slɑ:vɪə] **n** Yougoslavie *f* ▸ **in Yugoslavia** en Yougoslavie ▸ **the former Yugoslavia** l'ex-Yougoslavie.

Yugoslavian [ˌju:gə'slɑ:vɪən], ***Yugoslav*** [ˌju:gə'slɑ:v] ■ **adj** yougoslave.
■ **n** Yougoslave *mf*.

yule log [ju:l-] **n 1.** [piece of wood] bûche *f* **2.** [cake] bûche *f* de Noël.

yuletide ['ju:ltaɪd] **n** *(U) liter* époque *f* de Noël.

yummy ['jʌmɪ] (comp **-ier**, superl **-iest**) **adj** *inf* délicieux(euse).

yuppie, ***yuppy*** (pl **-ies**) ['jʌpɪ] **n** *inf* yuppie *mf*.

YWCA (abbr of ***Young Women's Christian Association***) **n** *union chrétienne de jeunes filles (proposant notamment des services d'hébergement)*.

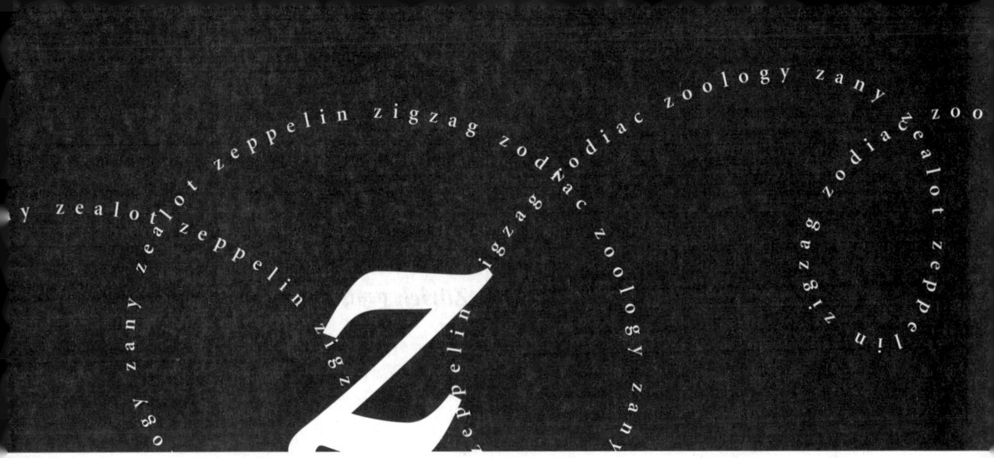

z [*UK* zed, *US* zi:] (pl z's *OR* zs), *US* ***Z*** (pl Z's *OR* Zs) **n** [letter] z *m inv*, Z *m inv*.

Zagreb ['zɑ:greb] **n** Zagreb.

Zaïre [zɑ:'ɪəʳ] **n** Zaïre *m* ▸ **in Zaïre** au Zaïre.

Zaïrese [zɑ:'ɪəri:z] ■ **adj** zaïrois(e).
■ **n** Zaïrois *m*, -e *f*.

Zambesi, ***Zambezi*** [zæm'bi:zɪ] **n : the Zambesi** le Zambèze.

Zambia ['zæmbɪə] **n** Zambie *f* ▸ **in Zambia** en Zambie.

Zambian ['zæmbɪən] ■ **adj** zambien(enne).
■ **n** Zambien *m*, -enne *f*.

zany ['zeɪnɪ] (comp **-ier**, superl **-iest**) **adj** *inf* dingue.

Zanzibar [ˌzænzɪ'bɑ:] **n** Zanzibar *m*.

zap [zæp] (pt & pp **-ped**, cont **-ping**) ■ **vt** [kill] descendre, tuer.
■ **vi 1.** *inf* **: to zap (off) somewhere** foncer quelque part **2.** TV zapper.

zeal [zi:l] **n** zèle *m*.

zealot ['zelət] **n** *fml* fanatique *mf*.

zealous ['zeləs] **adj** zélé(e).

zealously ['zeləslɪ] **adv** avec zèle *OR* ardeur.

zebra [*UK* 'zebrə, *US* 'zi:brə] (pl **zebra** *OR* **-s**) **n** zèbre *m*.

zebra crossing **n** *UK* passage *m* pour piétons.

Zen (Buddhism) [zen-] **n** bouddhisme *m* zen.

zenith [*UK* 'zenɪθ, *US* 'zi:nəθ] **n** *lit* & *fig* zénith *m*.

zeppelin ['zepəlɪn] **n** zeppelin *m*.

zero [*UK* 'zɪərəʊ, *US* 'zi:rəʊ] ■ **adj** zéro, aucun(e) ▸ **zero gravity** apesanteur *f*.
■ **n** (pl **zero** *OR* **-es**) zéro *m* ▸ **40 below zero** 40 degrés au-dessous de zéro, moins 40.
◆ ***zero in on*** **vt insep 1.** [subj: weapon] se diriger droit sur **2.** [subj: person] s'attaquer (d'entrée de jeu) à.

zero growth **n** croissance *f* zéro.

zero hour **n** heure *f* H.

zero-rated [-ˌreɪtɪd] **adj** *UK* exempt(e) de TVA.

zero-rating **n** franchise *f* de TVA, taux *m* zero.

zest [zest] **n** *(U)* **1.** [excitement] piquant *m* **2.** [eagerness] entrain *m* **3.** [of orange, lemon] zeste *m*.

zigzag ['zɪgzæg] ■ **n** zigzag *m*.
■ **vi** (pt & pp **-ged**, cont **-ging**) zigzaguer.

zilch [zɪltʃ] **n** *US inf* zéro *m*, que dalle.

Zimbabwe [zɪm'bɑ:bwɪ] **n** Zimbabwe *m* ▸ **in Zimbabwe** au Zimbabwe.

Zimbabwean [zɪm'bɑ:bwɪən] ■ **adj** zimbabwéen(enne).
■ **n** Zimbabwéen *m*, -enne *f*.

Zimmer frame® ['zɪməʳ-] **n** déambulateur *m*.

zinc [zɪŋk] **n** zinc *m*.

Zionism ['zaɪənɪzm] **n** sionisme *m*.

Zionist ['zaɪənɪst] ■ **adj** sioniste.
■ **n** Sioniste *mf*.

zip [zɪp] ■ **n** *UK* [fastener] fermeture *f* Éclair®.
■ **vi 1.** [with zip fastener] **: to zip open/shut** s'ouvrir/se fermer à l'aide d'une fermeture Éclair® *OR* à glissière **2.** *inf* [verb of movement] **: to zip past** passer comme une flèche.
■ **vt 1.** [with zip fastener] **: to zip sthg open/shut** fermer/ouvrir la fermeture Éclair® *OR* à glissière de qqch **2.** COMPUT zipper.
◆ ***zip up*** **vt sep** (pt & pp **-ped**, cont **-ping**) [jacket] remonter la fermeture Éclair® de / [bag] fermer la fermeture Éclair® de.

zip code **n** *US* code *m* postal.

Zip disk® **n** COMPUT disque *m* zip.

Zip drive® **n** COMPUT lecteur *m* de zips.

zip fastener **n** *UK* = ***zip***.

zipper ['zɪpəʳ] **n** *US* = ***zip***.

zip-up **adj** [bag, coat] à fermeture Éclair®, zippé(e).

zit [zɪt] **n** *esp US inf* bouton *m*.

zither ['zɪðəʳ] **n** cithare *f*.

zodiac ['zəʊdɪæk] **n : the zodiac** le zodiaque ▸ **sign of the zodiac** signe *m* du zodiaque.

zombie **['zɒmbɪ] n** *fig* & *pej* zombi *m*.

zone **[zəʊn] n** zone *f*.

zoo **[zu:] n** zoo *m*.

zoological **[ˌzəʊə'lɒdʒɪkl] adj** zoologique.

zoologist **[zəʊ'ɒlədʒɪst] n** zoologiste *mf*.

zoology **[zəʊ'ɒlədʒɪ] n** zoologie *f*.

zoom **[zu:m] ■ vi** *inf* **1.** [move quickly] aller en trombe **2.** [rise rapidly] monter en flèche.
■ n PHOT zoom *m*.
◆ *zoom in* **vi** CIN **: to zoom in (on)** faire un zoom (sur).
◆ *zoom off* **vi** *inf* partir en trombe.

zoom lens **n** zoom *m*.

zucchini **[zu:'ki:nɪ] (pl zucchini) n** *US* courgette *f*.

Zulu **['zu:lu:] ■ adj** zoulou(e).
■ n 1. [person] Zoulou *m*, -e *f* **2.** [language] zoulou *m*.

Zürich **['zjʊərɪk] n** Zurich.

Conjugaisons

English irregular Verbs

Conjugaisons

	1 avoir	2 être	3 chanter
present indicative	j'ai tu as il, elle a nous avons vous avez ils, elles ont	je suis tu es il, elle est nous sommes vous êtes ils, elles sont	je chante tu chantes il, elle chante nous chantons vous chantez ils, elles chantent
imperfect	il, elle avait	il, elle était	il, elle chantait
past historic	il, elle eut ils, elles eurent	il, elle fut ils, elles furent	il, elle chanta ils, elles chantèrent
future	j'aurai il, elle aura	je serai il, elle sera	je chanterai il, elle chantera
present conditional	j'aurais il, elle aurait	je serais il, elle serait	je chanterais il, elle chanterait
present subjunctive	que j'aie qu'il, elle ait que nous ayons qu'ils, elles aient	que je sois qu'il, elle soit que nous soyons qu'ils, elles soient	que je chante qu'il, elle chante que nous chantions qu'ils, elles chantent
imperfect subjunctive	qu'il, elle eût qu'ils, elles eussent	qu'il, elle fût qu'ils, elles fussent	qu'il, elle chantât qu'ils, elles chantassent
imperative	aie ayons ayez	sois soyons soyez	chante chantons chantez
present participle	ayant	étant	chantant
past participle	eu, eue	été	chanté, e

	4 baisser	5 pleurer	6 jouer
present indicative	je baisse tu baisses il, elle baisse nous baissons vous baissez ils, elles baissent	je pleure tu pleures il, elle pleure nous pleurons vous pleurez ils, elles pleurent	je joue tu joues il, elle joue nous jouons vous jouez ils, elles jouent
imperfect	il, elle baissait	il, elle pleurait	il, elle jouait
past historic	il, elle baissa ils, elles baissèrent	il, elle pleura ils, elles pleurèrent	il, elle joua ils, elles jouèrent
future	je baisserai il, elle baissera	je pleurerai il, elle pleurera	je jouerai il, elle jouera
present conditional	je baisserais il, elle baisserait	je pleurerais il, elle pleurerait	je jouerais il, elle jouerait
present subjunctive	que je baisse qu'il, elle baisse que nous baissions qu'ils, elles baissent	que je pleure qu'il, elle pleure que nous pleurions qu'ils, elles pleurent	que je joue qu'il, elle joue que nous jouions qu'ils, elles jouent
imperfect subjunctive	qu'il, elle baissât qu'ils, elles baissassent	qu'il, elle pleurât qu'ils, elles pleurassent	qu'il, elle jouât qu'ils, elles jouassent
imperative	baisse baissons baissez	pleure pleurons pleurez	joue jouons jouez
present participle	baissant	pleurant	jouant
past participle	baissé, e	pleuré, e	joué, e

	7 saluer	8 arguer	9 copier
present indicative	je salue tu salues il, elle salue nous saluons vous saluez ils, elles saluent	j'argue, arguë tu argues, arguës il, elle argue, arguë nous arguons vous arguez ils, elles arguent, arguënt	je copie tu copies il, elle copie nous copions vous copiez ils, elles copient
imperfect	il, elle saluait	il, elle arguait	il, elle copiait
past historic	il, elle salua ils, elles saluèrent	il, elle argua ils, elles arguèrent	il, elle copia ils, elles copièrent
future	je saluerai il, elle saluera	j'arguerai, arguërai il, elle arguera, arguëra	je copierai il, elle copiera
present conditional	je saluerais il, elle saluerait	j'arguerais, arguërais il, elle arguerait, arguërait	je copierais il, elle copierait
present subjunctive	que je salue qu'il, elle salue que nous saluions qu'ils, elles saluent	que j'argue, arguë qu'il, elle argue, arguë que nous arguions qu'ils, elles arguent, arguënt	que je copie qu'il, elle copie que nous copiions qu'ils, elles copient
imperfect subjunctive	qu'il, elle saluât qu'ils, elles saluassent	qu'il, elle arguât qu'ils, elles arguassent	qu'il, elle copiât qu'ils, elles copiassent
imperative	salue saluons saluez	argue, arguë arguons arguez	copie copions copiez
present participle	saluant	arguant	copiant
past participle	salué, e	argué, e	copié, e

	10 prier *	11 payer **	12 grasseyer
present indicative	je prie tu pries il, elle prie nous prions vous priez ils, elles prient	je paie, paye tu paies, payes il, elle paie, paye nous payons vous payez ils, elles paient, payent	je grasseye tu grasseyes il, elle grasseye nous grasseyons vous grasseyez ils, elles grasseyent
imperfect	il, elle priait	il, elle payait	il, elle grasseyait
past historic	il, elle pria ils, elles prièrent	il, elle paya ils, elles payèrent	il, elle grasseya ils, elles grasseyèrent
future	je prierai il, elle priera	je paierai, payerai il, elle paiera, payera	je grasseyerai il, elle grasseyera
present conditional	je prierais il, elle prierait	je paierais, payerais il, elle paierait, payerait	je grasseyerais il, elle grasseyerait
present subjunctive	que je prie qu'il, elle prie que nous priions qu'ils, elles prient	que je paie, paye qu'il, elle paie, paye que nous payions qu'ils, elles paient, payent	que je grasseye qu'il, elle grasseye que nous grasseyions qu'ils, elles grasseyent
imperfect subjunctive	qu'il, elle priât qu'ils, elles priassent	qu'il, elle payât qu'ils, elles payassent	qu'il, elle grasseyât qu'ils, elles grasseyassent
imperative	prie prions priez	paie, paye payons payez	grasseye grasseyons grasseyez
present participle	priant	payant	grasseyant
past participle	prié, e	payé, e	grasseyé, e

***** Note the presence of two i's in the 1st and 2nd person plural of the imperfect indicative and the present subjunctive: nous *priions, vous priiez.*

****** Verbs in **-ayer** such as *payer* can either keep the **y** in all their forms or replace the **y** by **i** before mute **e** (in the endings : **-e, -es, -ent, -erai**). The pronunciation is different depending on which form is chosen: *je paye* [pɛj] or *je paie* [pɛ]. In the 1st and 2nd person plural of the imperfect indicative and the present subjunctive, there is an **i** after the **y**.

	13 ployer	14 essuyer	15 créer
present indicative	je ploie tu ploies il, elle ploie nous ployons vous ployez ils, elles ploient	j'essuie tu essuies il, elle essuie nous essuyons vous essuyez ils, elles essuient	je crée tu crées il, elle crée nous créons vous créez ils, elles créent
imperfect	il, elle ployait	il, elle essuyait	il, elle créait
past historic	il, elle ploya ils, elles ployèrent	il, elle essuya ils, elles essuyèrent	il, elle créa ils, elles créèrent
future	je ploierai il, elle ploiera	j'essuierai il, elle essuiera	je créerai il, elle créera
present conditional	je ploierais il, elle ploierait	j'essuierais il, elle essuierait	je créerais il, elle créerait
present subjunctive	que je ploie qu'il, elle ploie que nous ployions qu'ils, elles ploient	que j'essuie qu'il, elle essuie que nous essuyions qu'ils, elles essuient	que je crée qu'il, elle crée que nous créions qu'ils, elles créent
imperfect subjunctive	qu'il, elle ployât qu'ils, elles ployassent	qu'il, elle essuyât qu'ils, elles essuyassent	qu'il, elle créât qu'ils, elles créassent
imperative	ploie ployons ployez	essuie essuyons essuyez	crée créons créez
present participle	ployant	essuyant	créant
past participle	ployé, e	essuyé, e	créé, e

	16 avancer *	17 manger **	18 céder
present indicative	j'avance tu avances il, elle avance nous avançons vous avancez ils, elles avancent	je mange tu manges il, elle mange nous mangeons vous mangez ils, elles mangent	je cède tu cèdes il, elle cède nous cédons vous cédez ils, elles cèdent
imperfect	il, elle avançait	il, elle mangeait	il, elle cédait
past historic	il, elle avança ils, elles avancèrent	il, elle mangea ils, elles mangèrent	il, elle céda ils, elles cédèrent
future	j'avancerai il, elle avancera	je mangerai il, elle mangera	je céderai, cèderai il, elle cédera, cèdera
present conditional	j'avancerais il, elle avancerait	je mangerais il, elle mangerait	je céderais, cèderais il, elle céderait, cèderait
present subjunctive	que j'avance qu'il, elle avance que nous avancions qu'ils, elles avancent	que je mange qu'il, elle mange que nous mangions qu'ils, elles mangent	que je cède qu'il, elle cède que nous cédions qu'ils, elles cèdent
imperfect subjunctive	qu'il, elle avançât qu'ils, elles avançassent	qu'il, elle mangeât qu'ils, elles mangeassent	qu'il, elle cédât qu'ils, elles cédassent
imperative	avance avançons avancez	mange mangeons mangez	cède cédons cédez
present participle	avançant	mangeant	cédant
past participle	avancé, e	mangé, e	cédé, e

***** *Annoncer, commencer, déplacer, effacer, lancer* and *placer* are conjugated in the same way as *avancer.* Note that verbs in **–cer** change **c** to **ç** in front of the vowels **a** and **o**: *il avança, nous avançons,* etc.
****** Note that verbs in **–ger**, such as *juger* and *manger,* retain an **e** after the **g** in front of the vowels **a** and **o**: *je mangeais, nous mangeons,* etc.

	19 semer	20 rapiécer	21 acquiescer
present indicative	je sème tu sèmes il, elle sème nous semons vous semez ils, elles sèment	je rapièce tu rapièces il, elle rapièce nous rapiéçons vous rapiécez ils, elles rapiècent	j'acquiesce tu acquiesces il, elle acquiesce nous acquiesçons vous acquiescez ils, elles acquiescent
imperfect	il, elle semait	il, elle rapiéçait	il, elle acquiesçait
past historic	il, elle sema ils, elles semèrent	il, elle rapiéça ils, elles rapiécèrent	il, elle acquiesça ils, elles acquiescèrent
future	je sèmerai il, elle sèmera	je rapiécerai, rapiècerai il, elle rapiécera, rapiècera	j'acquiescerai il, elle acquiescera
present conditional	je sèmerais il, elle sèmerait	je rapiécerais, rapiècerais il, elle rapiécerait, rapiècerait	j'acquiescerais il, elle acquiescerait
present subjunctive	que je sème qu'il, elle sème que nous semions qu'ils, elles sèment	que je rapièce qu'il, elle rapièce que nous rapiécions qu'ils, elles rapiècent	que j'acquiesce qu'il, elle acquiesce que nous acquiescions qu'ils, elles acquiescent
imperfect subjunctive	qu'il, elle semât qu'ils, elles semassent	qu'il, elle rapiéçât qu'ils, elles rapiéçassent	qu'il, elle acquiesçât qu'ils, elles acquiesçassent
imperative	sème semons semez	rapièce rapiéçons rapiécez	acquiesce acquiesçons acquiescez
present participle	semant	rapiéçant	acquiesçant
past participle	semé, e	rapiécé, e	acquiescé

	22 siéger *	23 déneiger	24 appeler**
present indicative	je siège tu sièges il, elle siège nous siégeons vous siégez ils, elles siègent	je déneige tu déneiges il, elle déneige nous déneigeons vous déneigez ils, elles déneigent	j'appelle tu appelles il, elle appelle nous appelons vous appelez ils, elles appellent
imperfect	il, elle siégeait	il, elle déneigeait	il, elle appelait
past historic	il, elle siégea ils, elles siégèrent	il, elle déneigea ils, elles déneigèrent	il, elle appela ils, elles appelèrent
future	je siégerai, siègerai il, elle siégera, siègera	je déneigerai il, elle déneigera	j'appellerai il, elle appellera
present conditional	je siégerais, siègerais il, elle siégerait, siègerait	je déneigerais il, elle déneigerait	j'appellerais il, elle appellerait
present subjunctive	que je siège qu'il, elle siège que nous siégions qu'ils, elles siègent	que je déneige qu'il, elle déneige que nous déneigions qu'ils, elles déneigent	que j'appelle qu'il, elle appelle que nous appelions qu'ils, elles appellent
imperfect subjunctive	qu'il, elle siégeât qu'ils, elles siégeassent	qu'il, elle déneigeât qu'ils, elles déneigeassent	qu'il, elle appelât qu'ils, elles appelassent
imperative	siège siégeons siégez	déneige déneigeons déneigez	appelle appelons appelez
present participle	siégeant	déneigeant	appelant
past participle	siégé	déneigé, e	appelé, e

* *Assiéger* conjugates in the same way as *siéger,* but the past participle is variable: *assiégé, assiégée.*
** Most verbs ending in **–eler** behave like *appeler* and double the final –l before mute –**e**: *j'appelle, tu appelleras,* etc.

	25 peler	26 interpeller	27 jeter *
present indicative	je pèle tu pèles il, elle pèle nous pelons vous pelez ils, elles pèlent	j'interpelle tu interpelles il, elle interpelle nous interpellons vous interpellez ils, elles interpellent	je jette tu jettes il, elle jette nous jetons vous jetez ils, elles jettent
imperfect	il, elle pelait	il, elle interpellait	il, elle jetait
past historic	il, elle pela ils, elles pelèrent	il, elle interpella ils, elles interpellèrent	il, elle jeta ils, elles jetèrent
future	je pèlerai il, elle pèlera	j'interpellerai il, elle interpellera	je jetterai il, elle jettera
present conditional	je pèlerais il, elle pèlerait	j'interpellerais il, elle interpellerait	je jetterais il, elle jetterait
present subjunctive	que je pèle qu'il, elle pèle que nous pelions qu'ils, elles pèlent	que j'interpelle qu'il, elle interpelle que nous interpellions qu'ils, elles interpellent	que je jette qu'il, elle jette que nous jetions qu'ils, elles jettent
imperfect subjunctive	qu'il, elle pelât qu'ils, elles pelassent	qu'il, elle interpellât qu'ils, elles interpellassent	qu'il, elle jetât qu'ils, elles jetassent
imperative	pèle pelons pelez	interpelle interpellons interpellez	jette jetons jetez
present participle	pelant	interpellant	jetant
past participle	pelé, e	interpellé, e	jeté, e

* Most verbs ending in **–eter** behave like *jeter* and double the final **–t** before a mute **–e**: *je jette, tu jetteras,* etc.

	28 acheter	29 dépecer	30 envoyer
present indicative	j'achète tu achètes il, elle achète nous achetons vous achetez ils, elles achètent	je dépèce tu dépèces il, elle dépèce nous dépeçons vous dépecez ils, elles dépècent	j'envoie tu envoies il, elle envoie nous envoyons vous envoyez ils, elles envoient
imperfect	il, elle achetait	il, elle dépeçait	il, elle envoyait
past historic	il, elle acheta ils, elles achetèrent	il, elle dépeça ils, elles dépecèrent	il, elle envoya ils, elles envoyèrent
future	j'achèterai il, elle achètera	je dépècerai il, elle dépècera	j'enverrai il, elle enverra
present conditional	j'achèterais il, elle achèterait	je dépècerais il, elle dépècerait	j'enverrais il, elle enverrait
present subjunctive	que j'achète qu'il, elle achète que nous achetions qu'ils, elles achètent	que je dépèce qu'il, elle dépèce que nous dépecions qu'ils, elles dépècent	que j'envoie qu'il, elle envoie que nous envoyions qu'ils, elles envoient
imperfect subjunctive	qu'il, elle achetât qu'ils, elles achetassent	qu'il, elle dépeçât qu'ils, elles dépeçassent	qu'il, elle envoyât qu'ils, elles envoyassent
imperative	achète achetons achetez	dépèce dépeçons dépecez	envoie envoyons envoyez
present participle	achetant	depeçant	envoyant
past participle	acheté, e	dépecé, e	envoyé, e

	31 aller *	32 finir	33 haïr
present indicative	je vais tu vas il, elle va nous allons vous allez ils, elles vont	je finis tu finis il, elle finit nous finissons vous finissez ils, elles finissent	je hais tu hais il, elle hait nous haïssons vous haïssez ils, elles haïssent
imperfect	il, elle allait	il, elle finissait	il, elle haïssait
past historic	il, elle alla ils, elles allèrent	il, elle finit ils, elles finirent	il, elle haït ils, elles haïrent
future	j'irai il, elle ira	je finirai il, elle finira	je haïrai il, elle haïra
present conditional	j'irais il, elle irait	je finirais il, elle finirait	je haïrais il, elle haïrait
present subjunctive	que j'aille qu'il, elle aille que nous allions qu'ils, elles aillent	que je finisse qu'il, elle finisse que nous finissions qu'ils, elles finissent	que je haïsse qu'il, elle haïsse que nous haïssions qu'ils, elles haïssent
imperfect subjunctive	qu'il, elle allât qu'ils, elles allassent	qu'il, elle finît qu'ils, elles finissent	qu'il, elle haït qu'ils, elles haïssent
imperative	va allons allez	finis finissons finissez	hais haïssons haïssez
present participle	allant	finissant	haïssant
past participle	allé, e	fini, e	haï, e

* *Aller* is conjugated with *être* in compound tenses. The imperative of *aller* is *vas* when it is followed by y: *vas-y*. *S'en aller* in the imperative gives: *va-t'en, allons-nous-en, allez-vous-en*.
In compound tenses, *aller* can be replaced by *être* and conjugated with *avoir*: *je suis allé* or *j'ai été*.

	34 ouvrir	35 fuir	36 dormir *
present indicative	j'ouvre tu ouvres il, elle ouvre nous ouvrons vous ouvrez ils, elles ouvrent	je fuis tu fuis il, elle fuit nous fuyons vous fuyez ils, elles fuient	je dors tu dors il, elle dort nous dormons vous dormez ils, elles dorment
imperfect	il, elle ouvrait	il, elle fuyait	il, elle dormait
past historic	il, elle ouvrit ils, elles ouvrirent	il, elle fuit ils, elles fuirent	il, elle dormit ils, elles dormirent
future	j'ouvrirai il, elle ouvrira	je fuirai il, elle fuira	je dormirai il, elle dormira
present conditional	j'ouvrirais il, elle ouvrirait	je fuirais il, elle fuirait	je dormirais il, elle dormirait
present subjunctive	que j'ouvre qu'il, elle ouvre que nous ouvrions qu'ils, elles ouvrent	que je fuie qu'il, elle fuie que nous fuyions qu'ils, elles fuient	que je dorme qu'il, elle dorme que nous dormions qu'ils, elles dorment
imperfect subjunctive	qu'il, elle ouvrît qu'ils, elles ouvrissent	qu'il, elle fuît qu'ils, elles fuissent	qu'il, elle dormît qu'ils, elles dormissent
imperative	ouvre ouvrons ouvrez	fuis fuyons fuyez	dors dormons dormez
present participle	ouvrant	fuyant	dormant
past participle	ouvert, e	fui, e	dormi

* *Endormir* conjugates in the same way as *dormir,* but the past participle is variable: *endormi, endormie*.

	37 mentir *	38 servir	39 acquérir
present indicative	je mens tu mens il, elle ment nous mentons vous mentez ils, elles mentent	je sers tu sers il, elle sert nous servons vous servez ils, elles servent	j'acquiers tu acquiers il, elle acquiert nous acquérons vous acquérez ils, elles acquièrent
imperfect	il, elle mentait	il, elle servait	il, elle acquérait
past historic	il, elle mentit ils, elles mentirent	il, elle servit ils, elles servirent	il, elle acquit ils, elles acquirent
future	je mentirai il, elle mentira	je servirai il, elle servira	j'acquerrai il, elle acquerra
present conditional	je mentirais il, elle mentirait	je servirais il, elle servirait	j'acquerrais il, elle acquerrait
present subjunctive	que je mente qu'il, elle mente que nous mentions qu'ils, elles mentent	que je serve qu'il, elle serve que nous servions qu'ils, elles servent	que j'acquière qu'il, elle acquière que nous acquérions qu'ils, elles acquièrent
imperfect subjunctive	qu'il, elle mentît qu'ils, elles mentissent	qu'il, elle servît qu'ils, elles servissent	qu'il, elle acquît qu'ils, elles acquissent
imperative	mens mentons mentez	sers servons servez	acquiers acquérons acquérez
present participle	mentant	servant	acquérant
past participle	menti	servi, e	acquis, e

* *Démentir* conjugates in the same way as *mentir,* but the past participle is variable: *démenti, démentie.*

	40 venir	41 cueillir	42 mourir
present indicative	je viens tu viens il, elle vient nous venons vous venez ils, elles viennent	je cueille tu cueilles il, elle cueille nous cueillons vous cueillez ils, elles cueillent	je meurs tu meurs il, elle meurt nous mourons vous mourez ils, elles meurent
imperfect	il, elle venait	il, elle cueillait	il, elle mourait
past historic	il, elle vint ils, elles vinrent	il, elle cueillit ils, elles cueillirent	il, elle mourut ils, elles moururent
future	je viendrai il, elle viendra	je cueillerai il, elle cueillera	je mourrai il, elle mourra
present conditional	je viendrais il, elle viendrait	je cueillerais il, elle cueillerait	je mourrais il, elle mourrait
present subjunctive	que je vienne qu'il, elle vienne que nous venions qu'ils, elles viennent	que je cueille qu'il, elle cueille que nous cueillions qu'ils, elles cueillent	que je meure qu'il, elle meure que nous mourions qu'ils, elles meurent
imperfect subjunctive	qu'il, elle vînt qu'ils, elles vinssent	qu'il, elle cueillît qu'ils, elles cueillissent	qu'il, elle mourût qu'ils, elles mourussent
imperative	viens venons venez	cueille cueillons cueillez	meurs mourons mourez
present participle	venant	cueillant	mourant
past participle	venu, e	cueilli, e	mort, e

	43 partir	44 revêtir	45 courir
present indicative	je pars tu pars il, elle part nous partons vous partez ils, elles partent	je revêts tu revêts il, elle revêt nous revêtons vous revêtez ils, elles revêtent	je cours tu cours il, elle court nous courons vous courez ils, elles courent
imperfect	il, elle partait	il, elle revêtait	il, elle courait
past historic	il, elle partit ils, elles partirent	il, elle revêtit ils, elles revêtirent	il, elle courut ils, elles coururent
future	je partirai il, elle partira	je revêtirai il, elle revêtira	je courrai il, elle courra
present conditional	je partirais il, elle partirait	je revêtirais il, elle revêtirait	je courrais il, elle courrait
present subjunctive	que je parte qu'il, elle parte que nous partions qu'ils, elles partent	que je revête qu'il, elle revête que nous revêtions qu'ils, elles revêtent	que je coure qu'il, elle coure que nous courions qu'ils, elles courent
imperfect subjunctive	qu'il, elle partît qu'ils, elles partissent	qu'il, elle revêtît qu'ils, elles revêtissent	qu'il, elle courût qu'ils, elles courussent
imperative	pars partons partez	revêts revêtons revêtez	cours courons courez
present participle	partant	revêtant	courant
past participle	parti, e	revêtu, e	couru, e

	46 faillir *	47 défaillir	48 bouillir
present indicative	je faillis, faux tu faillis, faux il, elle faillit, faut nous faillissons, faillons vous faillissez, faillez ils, elles faillissent, faillent	je défaille tu défailles il, elle défaille nous défaillons vous défaillez ils, elles défaillent	je bous tu bous il, elle bout nous bouillons vous bouillez ils, elles bouillent
imperfect	il, elle faillissait, faillait	il, elle défaillait	il, elle bouillait
past historic	il, elle faillit ils, elles faillirent	il, elle défaillit ils, elles défaillirent	il, elle bouillit ils, elles bouillirent
future	je faillirai, faudrai il, elle faillira, faudra	je défaillirai, défaillerai il, elle défaillira, défaillera	je bouillirai il, elle bouillira
present conditional	je faillirais, faudrais il, elle faillirait, faudrait	je défaillirais, défaillerais il, elle défaillirait, défaillerait	je bouillirais il, elle bouillirait
present subjunctive	que je faillisse, faille qu'il, elle faillisse, faille que nous faillissions, faillions qu'ils, elles faillissent, faillent	que je défaille qu'il, elle défaille que nous défaillions qu'ils, elles défaillent	que je bouille qu'il, elle bouille que nous bouillions qu'ils, elles bouillent
imperfect subjunctive	qu'il, elle faillît qu'ils, elles faillissent	qu'il, elle défaillît qu'ils, elles défaillissent	qu'il, elle bouillît qu'ils, elles bouillissent
imperative	faillis, faux faillissons, faillons faillissez, faillez	défaille défaillons défaillez	bous bouillons bouillez
present participle	faillissant, faillant	défaillant	bouillant
past participle	failli	défailli	bouilli, e

* The most often used conjugation for *faillir* is that which follows the same pattern as *finir*. *Faillir* is rarely used in its conjugated forms.

	49 gésir *	50 saillir	51 ouïr **
present indicative	je gis tu gis il, elle gît nous gisons vous gisez ils, elles gisent	– – il, elle saille – – ils, elles saillent	j'ouïs, ois tu ouïs, ois il, elle ouït, oit nous ouïssons, oyons vous ouïssez, oyez ils, elles ouïssent, oient
imperfect	il, elle gisait	il, elle saillait	il, elle ouïssait, oyait
past historic	–	il, elle saillit ils, elles saillirent	il, elle ouït ils, elles ouïrent
future	–	– il, elle saillera	j'ouïrai, orrais il, elle ouïra, orra
present conditional	–	– il, elle saillerait	j'ouïrais il, elle ouïrait, orrait
present subjunctive	–	– qu'il, elle saille – qu'ils, elles saillent	que j'ouïsse, oie qu'il, elle ouïsse, oie que nous ouïssions, oyions qu'ils, elles ouïssent, oient
imperfect subjunctive	–	qu'il, elle saillît qu'ils, elles saillissent	qu'il, elle ouït qu'ils, elles ouïssent
imperative	–	–	ouïs, ois ouïssons, oyons ouïssez, oyez
present participle	gisant	saillant	oyant
past participle	–	sailli, e	ouï, e

* *Gésir* is defective in other tenses and modes.
** *Ouïr* is only used in the present infinitive, past participle *ouï(e)* and in compound tenses.

	52 recevoir *	53 devoir	54 mouvoir
present indicative	je reçois tu reçois il, elle reçoit nous recevons vous recevez ils, elles reçoivent	je dois tu dois il, elle doit nous devons vous devez ils, elles doivent	je meus tu meus il, elle meut nous mouvons vous mouvez ils, elles meuvent
imperfect	il, elle recevait	il, elle devait	il, elle mouvait
past historic	il, elle reçut ils, elles reçurent	il, elle dut ils, elles durent	il, elle mut ils, elles murent
future	je recevrai il, elle recevra	je devrai il, elle devra	je mouvrai il, elle mouvra
present conditional	je recevrais il, elle recevrait	je devrais il, elle devrait	je mouvrais il, elle mouvrait
present subjunctive	que je reçoive qu'il, elle reçoive que nous recevions qu'ils, elles reçoivent	que je doive qu'il, elle doive que nous devions qu'ils, elles doivent	que je meuve qu'il, elle meuve que nous mouvions qu'ils, elles meuvent
imperfect subjunctive	qu'il, elle reçût qu'ils, elles reçussent	qu'il, elle dût qu'ils, elles dussent	qu'il, elle mût qu'ils, elles mussent
imperative	reçois recevons recevez	dois devons devez	meus mouvons mouvez
present participle	recevant	devant	mouvant
past participle	reçu, e	dû, due, dus, dues	mû, mue, mus, mues

* Note that **c** changes to **ç** before **o** or **u**: *je reçois, j'ai reçu,* etc.

	55 émouvoir	56 promouvoir *	57 vouloir
present indicative	j'émeus tu émeus il, elle émeut nous émouvons vous émouvez ils, elles émeuvent	je promeus tu promeus il, elle promeut nous promouvons vous promouvez ils, elles promeuvent	je veux tu veux il, elle veut nous voulons vous voulez ils, elles veulent
imperfect	il, elle émouvait	il, elle promouvait	il, elle voulait
past historic	il, elle émut ils, elles émurent	il, elle promut ils, elles promurent	il, elle voulut ils, elles voulurent
future	j'émouvrai il, elle émouvra	je promouvrai il, elle promouvra	je voudrai il, elle voudra
present conditional	j'émouvrais il, elle émouvrait	je promouvrais il, elle promouvrait	je voudrais il, elle voudrait
present subjunctive	que j'émeuve qu'il, elle émeuve que nous émeuvions qu'ils, elles émeuvent	que je promeuve qu'il, elle promeuve que nous promouvions qu'ils, elles promeuvent	que je veuille qu'il, elle veuille que nous voulions qu'ils, elles veuillent
imperfect subjunctive	qu'il, elle émût qu'ils, elles émussent	qu'il, elle promût qu'ils, elles promussent	qu'il, elle voulût qu'ils, elles voulussent
imperative	émeus émouvons émouvez	promeus promouvons promouvez	veux, veuille voulons, veuillons voulez, veuillez
present participle	émouvant	promouvant	voulant
past participle	ému, e	promu, e	voulu, e

***** Conjugated forms of this verb are rare.

	58 pouvoir *	59 savoir	60 valoir
present indicative	je peux, puis tu peux il peut nous pouvons vous pouvez ils, elles peuvent	je sais tu sais il, elle sait nous savons vous savez ils, elles savent	je vaux tu vaux il, elle vaut nous valons vous valez ils, elles valent
imperfect	il, elle pouvait	il, elle savait	il, elle valait
past historic	il, elle put ils, elles purent	il, elle sut ils, elles surent	il, elle valut ils, elles valurent
future	je pourrai il, elle pourra	je saurai il, elle saura	je vaudrai il, elle vaudra
present conditional	je pourrais il, elle pourrait	je saurais il, elle saurait	je vaudrais il, elle vaudrait
present subjunctive	que je puisse qu'il, elle puisse que nous puissions qu'ils, elles puissent	que je sache qu'il, elle sache que nous sachions qu'ils, elles sachent	que je vaille qu'il, elle vaille que nous valions qu'ils, elles vaillent
imperfect subjunctive	qu'il, elle pût qu'ils, elles pussent	qu'il, elle sût qu'ils, elles sussent	qu'il, elle valût qu'ils, elles valussent
imperative	–	sache sachons sachez	vaux valons valez
present participle	pouvant	sachant	valant
past participle	pu	su, e	valu, e

***** *Pouvoir* has no imperative. The 1st person singular interrogative, 'can I?', is *puis-je ?* (and not *peux-je ?*).

	61 prévaloir	62 voir	63 prévoir
present indicative	je prévaux tu prévaux il, elle prévaut nous prévalons vous prévalez ils, elles prévalent	je vois tu vois il, elle voit nous voyons vous voyez ils, elles voient	je prévois tu prévois il, elle prévoit nous prévoyons vous prévoyez ils, elles prévoient
imperfect	il, elle prévalait	il, elle voyait	il, elle prévoyait
past historic	il, elle prévalut ils, elles prévalurent	il, elle vit ils, elles virent	il, elle prévit ils, elles prévirent
future	je prévaudrai il, elle prévaudra	je verrai il, elle verra	je prévoirai il, elle prévoira
present conditional	je prévaudrais il, elle prévaudrait	je verrais il, elle verrait	je prévoirais il, elle prévoirait
present subjunctive	que je prévale qu'il, elle prévale que nous prévalions qu'ils, elles prévalent	que je voie qu'il, elle voie que nous voyions qu'ils, elles voient	que je prévoie qu'il, elle prévoie que nous prévoyions qu'ils, elles prévoient
imperfect subjunctive	qu'il, elle prévalût qu'ils, elles prévalussent	qu'il, elle vît qu'ils, elles vissent	qu'il, elle prévît qu'ils, elles prévissent
imperative	prévaux prévalons prévalez	vois voyons voyez	prévois prévoyons prévoyez
present participle	prévalant	voyant	prévoyant
past participle	prévalu, e	vu, e	prévu, e

	64 pourvoir	65 asseoir *	66 surseoir
present indicative	je pourvois tu pourvois il, elle pourvoit nous pourvoyons vous pourvoyez ils, elles pourvoient	j'assieds, j'assois tu assieds, assois il, elle assied, assoit nous asseyons, assoyons vous asseyez, assoyez ils, elles asseyent, assoient	je sursois tu sursois il, elle sursoit nous sursoyons vous sursoyez ils, elles sursoient
imperfect	il, elle pourvoyait	il, elle asseyait, assoyait	il, elle sursoyait
past historic	il, elle pourvut ils, elles pourvurent	il, elle assit ils, elles assirent	il, elle sursit ils, elles sursirent
future	je pourvoirai il, elle pourvoira	j'assiérai, j'assoirai il, elle assiéra, assoira	je surseoirai il, elle surseoira
present conditional	je pourvoirais il, elle pourvoirait	j'assiérais, j'assoirais il, elle assiérait, assoirait	je surseoirais il, elle surseoirait
present subjunctive	que je pourvoie qu'il, elle pourvoie que nous pourvoyions qu'ils, elles pourvoient	que j'asseye, j'assoie qu'il, elle asseye, assoie que nous asseyions, assoyions qu'ils, elles asseyent, assoient	que je sursoie qu'il, elle sursoie que nous sursoyions qu'ils, elles sursoient
imperfect subjunctive	qu'il, elle pourvût qu'ils, elles pourvussent	qu'il, elle assît qu'ils, elles assissent	qu'il, elle sursît qu'ils, elles sursissent
imperative	pourvois pourvoyons pourvoyez	assieds, assois asseyons, assoyons asseyez, assoyez	sursois sursoyons sursoyez
present participle	pourvoyant	asseyant, assoyant	sursoyant
past participle	pourvu, e	assis, e	sursis

***** Forms with **oi** are often written **eoi**: je m'asseois, il, elle asseoira, que tu asseoies, ils, elles asseoiraient.

	67 seoir	**68 pleuvoir ***	**69 falloir**
present indicative	– – il, elle sied – – ils, elles siéent	– – il pleut – – –	– – il faut – – –
imperfect	il, elle seyait	il pleuvait	il fallait
past historic	–	il plut –	il fallut –
future	– il, elle siéra	– il pleuvra	– il faudra
present conditional	– il, elle siérait	– il pleuvrait	– il faudrait
present subjunctive	– qu'il, elle siée – qu'ils, elles siéent	– qu'il pleuve – –	– qu'il faille – –
imperfect subjunctive	–	qu'il plût –	qu'il fallût –
imperative	–	–	–
present participle	seyant	pleuvant	–
past participle	–	plu	fallu

* *Pleuvoir* is an impersonal verb. It has no imperative. *Pleuvoir* can be used in the plural in the figurative sense: *les injures pleuvent, pleuvaient,* etc.

	70 échoir	**71 déchoir**	**72 choir**
present indicative	– – il, elle échoit – – ils, elles échoient	je déchois tu déchois il, elle déchoit nous déchoyons vous déchoyez ils, elles déchoient	je chois tu chois il, elle choit – – ils, elles choient
imperfect	il, elle échoyait	–	–
past historic	il, elle échut ils, elles échurent	il, elle déchut ils, elles déchurent	il, elle chut ils, elles churent
future	– il, elle échoira, écherra	je déchoirai il, elle déchoira	je choirai, cherrai il, elle choira, cherra
present conditional	– il, elle échoirait, écherrait	je déchoirais il, elle déchoirait	je choirais, cherrais il, elle choirait, cherrait
present subjunctive	– qu'il, elle échoie – qu'ils, elles échoient	que je déchoie qu'il, elle déchoie que nous déchoyions qu'ils, elles déchoient	–
imperfect subjunctive	qu'il, elle échût qu'ils, elles échussent	qu'il, elle déchût qu'ils, elles déchussent	qu'il, elle chût –
imperative	–	–	–
present participle	échéant	–	–
past participle	échu, e	déchu, e	chu, e

	73 vendre	74 répandre	75 répondre
present indicative	je vends tu vends il, elle vend nous vendons vous vendez ils, elles vendent	je répands tu répands il, elle répand nous répandons vous répandez ils, elles répandent	je réponds tu réponds il, elle répond nous répondons vous répondez ils, elles répondent
imperfect	il, elle vendait	il, elle répandait	il, elle répondait
past historic	il, elle vendit ils, elles vendirent	il, elle répandit ils, elles répandirent	il, elle répondit ils, elles répondirent
future	je vendrai il, elle vendra	je répandrai il, elle répandra	je répondrai il, elle répondra
present conditional	je vendrais il, elle vendrait	je répandrais il, elle répandrait	je répondrais il, elle répondrait
present subjunctive	que je vende qu'il, elle vende que nous vendions qu'ils, elles vendent	que je répande qu'il, elle répande que nous répandions qu'ils, elles répandent	que je réponde qu'il, elle réponde que nous répondions qu'ils, elles répondent
imperfect subjunctive	qu'il, elle vendît qu'ils, elles vendissent	qu'il, elle répandît qu'ils, elles répandissent	qu'il, elle répondît qu'ils, elles répondissent
imperative	vends vendons vendez	répands répandons répandez	réponds répondons répondez
present participle	vendant	répandant	répondant
past participle	vendu, e	répandu, e	répondu, e

	76 mordre	77 perdre	78 rompre
present indicative	je mords tu mords il, elle mord nous mordons vous mordez ils, elles mordent	je perds tu perds il, elle perd nous perdons vous perdez ils, elles perdent	je romps tu romps il, elle rompt nous rompons vous rompez ils, elles rompent
imperfect	il, elle mordait	il, elle perdait	il, elle rompait
past historic	il, elle mordit ils, elles mordirent	il, elle perdit ils, elles perdirent	il, elle rompit ils, elles rompirent
future	je mordrai il, elle mordra	je perdrai il, elle perdra	je romprai il, elle rompra
present conditional	je mordrais il, elle mordrait	je perdrais il, elle perdrait	je romprais il, elle romprait
present subjunctive	que je morde qu'il, elle morde que nous mordions qu'ils, elles mordent	que je perde qu'il, elle perde que nous perdions qu'ils, elles perdent	que je rompe qu'il, elle rompe que nous rompions qu'ils, elles rompent
imperfect subjunctive	qu'il, elle mordît qu'ils, elles mordissent	qu'il, elle perdît qu'ils, elles perdissent	qu'il, elle rompît qu'ils, elles rompissent
imperative	mords mordons mordez	perds perdons perdez	romps rompons rompez
present participle	mordant	perdant	rompant
past participle	mordu, e	perdu, e	rompu, e

	79 prendre	80 craindre	81 peindre
present indicative	je prends tu prends il, elle prend nous prenons vous prenez ils, elles prennent	je crains tu crains il, elle craint nous craignons vous craignez ils, elles craignent	je peins tu peins il, elle peint nous peignons vous peignez ils, elles peignent
imperfect	il, elle prenait	il, elle craignait	il, elle peignait
past historic	il, elle prit ils, elles prirent	il, elle craignit ils, elles craignirent	il, elle peignit ils, elles peignirent
future	je prendrai il, elle prendra	je craindrai il, elle craindra	je peindrai il, elle peindra
present conditional	je prendrais il, elle prendrait	je craindrais il, elle craindrait	je peindrais il, elle peindrait
present subjunctive	que je prenne qu'il, elle prenne que nous prenions qu'ils, elles prennent	que je craigne qu'il, elle craigne que nous craignions qu'ils, elles craignent	que je peigne qu'il, elle peigne que nous peignions qu'ils, elles peignent
imperfect subjunctive	qu'il, elle prît qu'ils, elles prissent	qu'il, elle craignît qu'ils, elles craignissent	qu'il, elle peignît qu'ils, elles peignissent
imperative	prends prenons prenez	crains craignons craignez	peins peignons peignez
present participle	prenant	craignant	peignant
past participle	pris, e	craint, e	peint, e

	82 joindre	83 battre	84 mettre
present indicative	je joins tu joins il, elle joint nous joignons vous joignez ils, elles joignent	je bats tu bats il, elle bat nous battons vous battez ils, elles battent	je mets tu mets il, elle met nous mettons vous mettez ils, elles mettent
imperfect	il, elle joignait	il, elle battait	il, elle mettait
past historic	il, elle joignit ils, elles joignirent	il, elle battit ils, elles battirent	il, elle mit ils, elles mirent
future	je joindrai il, elle joindra	je battrai il, elle battra	je mettrai il, elle mettra
present conditional	je joindrais il, elle joindrait	je battrais il, elle battrait	je mettrais il, elle mettrait
present subjunctive	que je joigne qu'il, elle joigne que nous joignions qu'ils, elles joignent	que je batte qu'il, elle batte que nous battions qu'ils, elles battent	que je mette qu'il, elle mette que nous mettions qu'ils, elles mettent
imperfect subjunctive	qu'il, elle joignît qu'ils, elles joignissent	qu'il, elle battît qu'ils, elles battissent	qu'il, elle mît qu'ils, elles missent
imperative	joins joignons joignez	bats battons battez	mets mettons mettez
present participle	joignant	battant	mettant
past participle	joint, e	battu, e	mis, e

	85 moudre	86 coudre	87 absoudre *
present indicative	je mouds tu mouds il, elle moud nous moulons vous moulez ils, elles moulent	je couds tu couds il, elle coud nous cousons vous cousez ils, elles cousent	j'absous tu absous il, elle absout nous absolvons vous absolvez ils, elles absolvent
imperfect	il, elle moulait	il, elle cousait	il, elle absolvait
past historic	il, elle moulut ils, elles moulurent	il, elle cousit ils, elles cousirent	il, elle absolut ils, elles absolurent
future	je moudrai il, elle moudra	je coudrai il, elle coudra	j'absoudrai il, elle absoudra
present conditional	je moudrais il, elle moudrait	je coudrais il, elle coudrait	j'absoudrais il, elle absoudrait
present subjunctive	que je moule qu'il, elle moule que nous moulions qu'ils, elles moulent	que je couse qu'il, elle couse que nous cousions qu'ils, elles cousent	que j'absolve qu'il, elle absolve que nous absolvions qu'ils, elles absolvent
imperfect subjunctive	qu'il, elle moulût qu'ils, elles moulussent	qu'il, elle cousît qu'ils, elles cousissent	qu'il, elle absolût qu'ils, elles absolussent
imperative	mouds moulons moulez	couds cousons cousez	absous absolvons absolvez
present participle	moulant	cousant	absolvant
past participle	moulu, e	cousu, e	absous, oute

* The past historic and the imperfect subjunctive are rare.

	88 résoudre	89 suivre	90 vivre *
present indicative	je résous tu résous il, elle résout nous résolvons vous résolvez ils, elles résolvent	je suis tu suis il, elle suit nous suivons vous suivez ils, elles suivent	je vis tu vis il, elle vit nous vivons vous vivez ils, elles vivent
imperfect	il, elle résolvait	il, elle suivait	il, elle vivait
past historic	il, elle résolut ils, elles résolurent	il, elle suivit ils, elles suivirent	il, elle vécut ils, elles vécurent
future	je résoudrai il, elle résoudra	je suivrai il, elle suivra	je vivrai il, elle vivra
present conditional	je résoudrais il, elle résoudrait	je suivrais il, elle suivrait	je vivrais il, elle vivrait
present subjunctive	que je résolve qu'il, elle résolve que nous résolvions qu'ils, elles résolvent	que je suive qu'il, elle suive que nous suivions qu'ils, elles suivent	que je vive qu'il, elle vive que nous vivions qu'ils, elles vivent
imperfect subjunctive	qu'il, elle résolût qu'ils, elles résolussent	qu'il, elle suivît qu'ils, elles suivissent	qu'il, elle vécût qu'ils, elles vécussent
imperative	résous résolvons résolvez	suis suivons suivez	vis vivons vivez
present participle	résolvant	suivant	vivant
past participle	résolu, e	suivi, e	vécu, e

* *Survivre* conjugates in the same way as *vivre,* but the past participle *(survécu)* is invariable.

	91 paraître *	92 naître	93 croître
present indicative	je parais tu parais il, elle paraît nous paraissons vous paraissez ils, elles paraissent	je nais tu nais il, elle naît nous naissons vous naissez ils, elles naissent	je croîs tu croîs il, elle croît nous croissons vous croissez ils, elles croissent
imperfect	il, elle paraissait	il, elle naissait	il, elle croissait
past historic	il, elle parut ils, elles parurent	il, elle naquit ils, elles naquirent	il, elle crût ils, elles crûrent
future	je paraîtrai il, elle paraîtra	je naîtrai il, elle naîtra	je croîtrai il, elle croîtra
present conditional	je paraîtrais il, elle paraîtrait	je naîtrais il, elle naîtrait	je croîtrais il, elle croîtrait
present subjunctive	que je paraisse qu'il, elle paraisse que nous paraissions qu'ils, elles paraissent	que je naisse qu'il, elle naisse que nous naissions qu'ils, elles naissent	que je croisse qu'il, elle croisse que nous croissions qu'ils, elles croissent
imperfect subjunctive	qu'il, elle parût qu'ils, elles parussent	qu'il, elle naquît qu'ils, elles naquissent	qu'il, elle crût qu'ils, elles crûssent
imperative	parais paraissons paraissez	nais naissons naissez	croîs croissons croissez
present participle	paraissant	naissant	croissant
past participle	paru, e	né, e	crû, crue, crus, crues

***** Note the circumflex **î** when **i** comes before **t** in verbs ending in **–aître**.

	94 accroître	95 rire *	96 conclure **
present indicative	j'accrois tu accrois il, elle accroît nous accroissons vous accroissez ils, elles accroissent	je ris tu ris il, elle rit nous rions vous riez ils, elles rient	je conclus tu conclus il, elle conclut nous concluons vous concluez ils, elles concluent
imperfect	il, elle accroissait	il, elle riait	il, elle concluait
past historic	il, elle accrut ils, elles accrurent	il, elle rit ils, elles rirent	il, elle conclut ils, elles conclurent
future	j'accroîtrai il, elle accroîtra	je rirai il, elle rira	je conclurai il, elle conclura
present conditional	j'accroîtrais il, elle accroîtrait	je rirais il, elle rirait	je conclurais il, elle conclurait
present subjunctive	que j'accroisse qu'il, elle accroisse que nous accroissions qu'ils, elles accroissent	que je rie qu'il, elle rie que nous riions qu'ils, elles rient	que je conclue qu'il, elle conclue que nous concluions qu'ils, elles concluent
imperfect subjunctive	qu'il, elle accrût qu'ils, elles accrussent	qu'il, elle rît qu'ils, elles rissent	qu'il, elle conclût qu'ils, elles conclussent
imperative	accrois accroissons accroissez	ris rions riez	conclus concluons concluez
present participle	accroissant	riant	concluant
past participle	accru, e	ri	conclu, e

***** *Rire* takes two **i**'s in the 1st and 2nd person plural of the imperfect indicative and the present subjunctive: *(que) nous riions, (que) vous riiez.*

****** *Inclure* and *occlure* conjugate in the same way as *conclure,* but their past participles are *inclus, incluse, occlus, occluse.*

	97 nuire *	98 conduire	99 écrire
present indicative	je nuis tu nuis il, elle nuit nous nuisons vous nuisez ils, elles nuisent	je conduis tu conduis il, elle conduit nous conduisons vous conduisez ils, elles conduisent	j'écris tu écris il, elle écrit nous écrivons vous écrivez ils, elles écrivent
imperfect	il, elle nuisait	il, elle conduisait	il, elle écrivait
past historic	il, elle nuisit ils, elles nuisirent	il, elle conduisit ils, elles conduisirent	il, elle écrivit ils, elles écrivirent
future	je nuirai il, elle nuira	je conduirai il, elle conduira	j'écrirai il, elle écrira
present conditional	je nuirais il, elle nuirait	je conduirais il, elle conduirait	j'écrirais il, elle écrirait
present subjunctive	que je nuise qu'il, elle nuise que nous nuisions qu'ils, elles nuisent	que je conduise qu'il, elle conduise que nous conduisions qu'ils, elles conduisent	que j'écrive qu'il, elle écrive que nous écrivions qu'ils, elles écrivent
imperfect subjunctive	qu'il, elle nuisît qu'ils, elles nuisissent	qu'il, elle conduisît qu'ils, elles conduisissent	qu'il, elle écrivît qu'ils, elles écrivissent
imperative	nuis nuisons nuisez	conduis conduisons conduisez	écris écrivons écrivez
present participle	nuisant	conduisant	écrivant
past participle	nui	conduit, e	écrit, e

* *Luire* and *reluire* have an alternative past historic form: *je luis, je reluis,* etc.

	100 suffire	101 confire *	102 dire
present indicative	je suffis tu suffis il, elle suffit nous suffisons vous suffisez ils, elles suffisent	je confis tu confis il, elle confit nous confisons vous confisez ils, elles confisent	je dis tu dis il, elle dit nous disons vous dites ils, elles disent
imperfect	il, elle suffisait	il, elle confisait	il, elle disait
past historic	il, elle suffit ils, elles suffirent	il, elle confit ils, elles confirent	il, elle dit ils, elles dirent
future	je suffirai il, elle suffira	je confirai il, elle confira	je dirai il, elle dira
present conditional	je suffirais il, elle suffirait	je confirais il, elle confirait	je dirais il, elle dirait
present subjunctive	que je suffise qu'il, elle suffise que nous suffisions qu'ils, elles suffisent	que je confise qu'il, elle confise que nous confisions qu'ils, elles confisent	que je dise qu'il, elle dise que nous disions qu'ils, elles disent
imperfect subjunctive	qu'il, elle suffît qu'ils, elles suffissent	qu'il, elle confît qu'ils, elles confissent	qu'il, elle dît qu'ils, elles dissent
imperative	suffis suffisons suffisez	confis confisons confisez	dis disons dites
present participle	suffisant	confisant	disant
past participle	suffi	confit, e	dit, e

* *Circoncire* conjugates in the same way as *confire,* but its past participle is *circoncis, circoncise.*

	103 contredire	104 maudire	105 bruire *
present indicative	je contredis tu contredis il, elle contredit nous contredisons vous contredisez ils, elles contredisent	je maudis tu maudis il, elle maudit nous maudissons vous maudissez ils, elles maudissent	je bruis tu bruis il, elle bruit – – –
imperfect	il, elle contredisait	il, elle maudissait	il, elle bruyait
past historic	il, elle contredit ils, elles contredirent	il, elle maudit ils, elles maudirent	–
future	je contredirai il, elle contredira	je maudirai il, elle maudira	je bruirai il, elle bruira
present conditional	je contredirais il, elle contredirait	je maudirais il, elle maudirait	je bruirais il, elle bruirait
present subjunctive	que je contredise qu'il, elle contredise que nous contredisions qu'ils, elles contredisent	que je maudisse qu'il, elle maudisse que nous maudissions qu'ils, elles maudissent	–
imperfect subjunctive	qu'il, elle contredît qu'ils, elles contredissent	qu'il, elle maudît qu'ils, elles maudissent	–
imperative	contredis contredisons contredisez	maudis maudissons maudissez	–
present participle	contredisant	maudissant	–
past participle	contredit, e	maudit, e	bruit

***** Traditionally *bruire* is only used in the present indicative, imperfect (*je bruyais, tu bruyais,* etc), future and conditional; *bruisser* (conjugation 3) is used more and more to replace *bruire,* especially in all the defective forms.

	106 lire	107 croire	108 boire
present indicative	je lis tu lis il, elle lit nous lisons vous lisez ils, elles lisent	je crois tu crois il, elle croit nous croyons vous croyez ils, elles croient	je bois tu bois il, elle boit nous buvons vous buvez ils, elles boivent
imperfect	il, elle lisait	il, elle croyait	il, elle buvait
past historic	il, elle lut ils, elles lurent	il, elle crut ils, elles crurent	il, elle but ils, elles burent
future	je lirai il, elle lira	je croirai il, elle croira	je boirai il, elle boira
present conditional	je lirais il, elle lirait	je croirais il, elle croirait	je boirais il, elle boirait
present subjunctive	que je lise qu'il, elle lise que nous lisions qu'ils, elles lisent	que je croie qu'il, elle croie que nous croyions qu'ils, elles croient	que je boive qu'il, elle boive que nous buvions qu'ils, elles boivent
imperfect subjunctive	qu'il, elle lût qu'ils, elles lussent	qu'il, elle crût qu'ils, elles crussent	qu'il, elle bût qu'ils, elles bussent
imperative	lis lisons lisez	crois croyons croyez	bois buvons buvez
present participle	lisant	croyant	buvant
past participle	lu, e	cru, e	bu, e

	109 faire	110 plaire	111 taire
present indicative	je fais tu fais il, elle fait nous faisons vous faites ils, elles font	je plais tu plais il, elle plaît nous plaisons vous plaisez ils, elles plaisent	je tais tu tais il, elle tait nous taisons vous taisez ils, elles taisent
imperfect	il, elle faisait	il, elle plaisait	il, elle taisait
past historic	il, elle fit ils, elles firent	il, elle plut ils, elles plurent	il, elle tut ils, elles turent
future	je ferai il, elle fera	je plairai il, elle plaira	je tairai il, elle taira
present conditional	je ferais il, elle ferait	je plairais il, elle plairait	je tairais il, elle tairait
present subjunctive	que je fasse qu'il, elle fasse que nous fassions qu'ils, elles fassent	que je plaise qu'il, elle plaise que nous plaisions qu'ils, elles plaisent	que je taise qu'il, elle taise que nous taisions qu'ils, elles taisent
imperfect subjunctive	qu'il, elle fît qu'ils, elles fissent	qu'il, elle plût qu'ils, elles plussent	qu'il, elle tût qu'ils, elles tussent
imperative	fais faisons faites	plais plaisons plaisez	tais taisons taisez
present participle	faisant	plaisant	taisant
past participle	fait, e	plu	tu, e

	112 extraire	113 clore	114 vaincre *
present indicative	j'extrais tu extrais il, elle extrait nous extrayons vous extrayez ils, elles extraient	je clos tu clos il, elle clôt nous closons vous closez ils, elles closent	je vaincs tu vaincs il, elle vainc nous vainquons vous vainquez ils, elles vainquent
imperfect	il, elle extrayait	–	il, elle vainquait
past historic	–	–	il, elle vainquit ils, elles vainquirent
future	j'extrairai il, elle extraira	je clorai il, elle clora	je vaincrai il, elle vaincra
present conditional	j'extrairais il, elle extrairait	je clorais il, elle clorait	je vaincrais il, elle vaincrait
present subjunctive	que j'extraie qu'il, elle extraie que nous extrayions qu'ils, elles extraient	que je close qu'il, elle close que nous closions qu'ils, elles closent	que je vainque qu'il, elle vainque que nous vainquions qu'ils, elles vainquent
imperfect subjunctive	–	–	qu'il, elle vainquît qu'ils, elles vainquissent
imperative	extrais extrayons extrayez	clos – –	vaincs vainquons vainquez
present participle	extrayant	closant	vainquant
past participle	extrait, e	clos, e	vaincu, e

***** The only irregularity of the verb *vaincre* is that it does not take a **t** at the end of the 3rd person singular of the present indicative. Note that **c** becomes **qu** in front of all vowels except **u**.

	115 frire	116 foutre
present indicative	je fris tu fris il, elle frit – – –	je fous tu fous il, elle fout nous foutons vous foutez ils, elles foutent
imperfect	–	il, elle foutait
past historic	–	–
future	je frirai il, elle frira	je foutrai il, elle foutra
present conditional	je frirais il, elle frirait	je foutrais il, elle foutrait
present subjunctive	–	que je foute qu'il, elle foute que nous foutions qu'ils, elles foutent
imperfect subjunctive	–	–
imperative	fris – –	fous foutons foutez
present participle	–	foutant
past participle	frit, e	foutu, e

English irregular verbs

infinitif	prétérit	participe passé
arise	arose	arisen
awake	awoke	awoken
be	was, were	been
bear	bore	borne
beat	beat	beaten
become	became	become
befall	befell	befallen
begin	began	begun
behold	beheld	beheld
bend	bent	bent
beseech	besought	besought
beset	beset	beset
bet	bet, betted	bet, betted
bid	bid, bade	bid, bidden
bind	bound	bound
bite	bit	bitten
bleed	bled	bled
blow	blew	blown
break	broke	broken
breed	bred	bred
bring	brought	brought
build	built	built
burn	burnt, burned	burnt, burned
burst	burst	burst
buy	bought	bought
can	could	—
cast	cast	cast
catch	caught	caught
choose	chose	chosen
cling	clung	clung
come	came	come
cost	cost	cost
creep	crept	crept
cut	cut	cut
deal	dealt	dealt
dig	dug	dug
do	did	done
draw	drew	drawn
dream	dreamed, dreamt	dreamed, dreamt
drink	drank	drunk
drive	drove	driven
dwell	dwelt, dwelled	dwelt, dwelled
eat	ate	eaten
fall	fell	fallen
feed	fed	fed
feel	felt	felt
fight	fought	fought
find	found	found
flee	fled	fled
fling	flung	flung
fly	flew	flown
forbear	forbore	forborne
forbid	forbade	forbidden
forecast	forecast	forecast
forego	forewent	foregone
foresee	foresaw	foreseen
foretell	foretold	foretold
forget	forgot	forgotten
forgive	forgave	forgiven
forsake	forsook	forsaken
freeze	froze	frozen
get	got	got (*Am* gotten)

infinitif	prétérit	participe passé
give	gave	given
go	went	gone
grind	ground	ground
grow	grew	grown
hang	hung, hanged	hung, hanged
have	had	had
hear	heard	heard
hide	hid	hidden
hit	hit	hit
hold	held	held
hurt	hurt	hurt
keep	kept	kept
kneel	knelt, kneeled	knelt, kneeled
know	knew	known
lay	laid	laid
lead	led	led
lean	leant, leaned	leant, leaned
leap	leapt, leaped	leapt, leaped
learn	learnt, learned	learnt, learned
leave	left	left
lend	lent	lent
let	let	let
lie	lay	lain
light	lit, lighted	lit, lighted
lose	lost	lost
make	made	made
may	might	—
mean	meant	meant
meet	met	met
mistake	mistook	mistaken
mow	mowed	mown, mowed
pay	paid	paid
put	put	put
quit	quit, quitted	quit, quitted
read	read	read
rend	rent	rent
rid	rid	rid
ride	rode	ridden
ring	rang	rung
rise	rose	risen
run	ran	run
saw	sawed	sawn
say	said	said
see	saw	seen
seek	sought	sought
sell	sold	sold
send	sent	sent
set	set	set
shake	shook	shaken
shall	should	—
shear	sheared	shorn, sheared
shed	shed	shed
shine	shone	shone
shoot	shot	shot
show	showed	shown
shrink	shrank	shrunk
shut	shut	shut
sing	sang	sung
sink	sank	sunk
sit	sat	sat
slay	slew	slain
sleep	slept	slept

infinitif	prétérit	participe passé
slide	slid	slid
sling	slung	slung
slink	slunk	slunk
slit	slit	slit
smell	smelt, smelled	smelt, smelled
sow	sowed	sown, sowed
speak	spoke	spoken
speed	sped, speeded	sped, speeded
spell	spelt, spelled	spelt, spelled
spend	spent	spent
spill	spilt, spilled	spilt, spilled
spin	spun	spun
spit	spat	spat
split	split	split
spoil	spoiled, spoilt	spoiled, spoilt
spread	spread	spread
spring	sprang	sprung
stand	stood	stood
steal	stole	stolen
stick	stuck	stuck
sting	stung	stung
stink	stank	stunk
stride	strode	stridden
strike	struck	struck, stricken
strive	strove	striven
swear	swore	sworn
sweep	swept	swept
swell	swelled	swollen, swelled
swim	swam	swum
swing	swung	swung
take	took	taken
teach	taught	taught
tear	tore	torn
tell	told	told
think	thought	thought
throw	threw	thrown
thrust	thrust	thrust
tread	trod	trodden
upset	upset	upset
wake	woke	woken
waylay	waylaid	waylaid
wear	wore	worn
weave	wove, weaved	woven, weaved
wed	wedded	wedded
weep	wept	wept
wet	wetted, wet	wetted, wet
will	would	—
win	won	won
wind	wound	wound
withdraw	withdrew	withdrawn
withhold	withheld	withheld
withstand	withstood	withstood
wring	wrung	wrung
write	wrote	written

Imprimé en Italie par «La Tipografica Varese S.p.A.» Varese

Abbreviations used in this dictionary

abbreviation	abbr / abr	abréviation
adjective	adj	adjectif
administration, administrative	ADMIN	administration
adverb	adv	adverbe
aeronautics, aviation	AERON / AÉRON	aéronautique
agriculture, farming	AGR(IC)	agriculture
anatomy	ANAT	anatomie
archaeology	ARCHAEOL / ARCHÉOL	archéologie
architecture	ARCHIT	architecture
slang	arg	argot
article	art	article
astrology	ASTROL	astrologie
astronomy	ASTRON	astronomie
Australian English	Austr	anglais australien
automobile, cars	AUT(OM)	automobile
auxiliary	aux	auxiliaire
biology	BIOL	biologie
botany	BOT	botanique
Canadian English	Can	anglais canadien
chemistry	CHEM / CHIM	chimie
cinema, film-making	CIN(EMA)	cinéma
commerce, business	COMM	commerce
compound	comp	nom anglais utilisé en apposition
comparative	compar	comparatif
computers, computer science	COMPUT	informatique
conjunction	conj	conjonction
construction	CONSTR	construction
continuous	cont	progressif
sewing	COUT	couture
culinary, cooking	CULIN	cuisine, art culinaire
definite	def / déf	défini
demonstrative	dem / dém	démonstratif
juridical, legal	DR	juridique
economics	ECON / ÉCON	économie
electricity	ELEC / ÉLECTR	électricité
electronics	ELECTRON / ÉLECTRON	électronique
especially	esp	particulièrement
euphemism	euph / euphém	euphémisme
exclamation	excl	interjection
feminine	f	féminin
informal	fam	familier
figurative	fig	figuré
finance, financial	FIN	finances
formal	fml	soutenu
generally, in most cases	gen / gén	généralement
geography, geographical	GEOG / GÉOGR	géographie
geology, geological	GEOL / GÉOL	géologie
geometry	GEOM / GÉOM	géométrie
grammar	GRAM(M)	grammaire
history	HIST	histoire
humorous	hum	humoristique
impersonal	impers	impersonnel
indefinite	indef / indéf	indéfini
industry	INDUST	industrie
informal	inf	familier
infinitive	infin	infinitif
computers, computer science	INFORM	informatique
offensive	injur	injurieux
inseparable	insep	non séparable
exclamation	interj	interjection
interrogative	interr	interrogatif
invariable	inv	invariable
Irish English	Ir	anglais irlandais
ironic	iro / iron	ironique
linguistics	LING	linguistique
literal	lit / litt	littéral
literature	LIT / LITTÉR	littérature
literary	liter / littéraire	littéraire
phrase(s)	loc	locution(s)
masculine	m	masculin
mathematics	MATH(S)	mathématiques
medicine	MED / MÉD	médecine